Matt Jesson

C000194109

REEDS OKI NAUTICAL ALMANAC 2005

Editors Neville Featherstone, Peter Lambie

Free updates are available at www.reedsalmanac.co.uk

Published by Adlard Coles Nautical 2004

First published 1980. This edition published 2004

IMPORTANT NOTE

The information, charts, maps and diagrams in this Almanac should not be relied on for navigational purposes as this Almanac is intended as an aid to navigation only. The information contained within should be used in conjunction with official hydrographic data. Whilst every care has been taken in its compilation, this Almanac may contain inaccuracies and is no substitute for the relevant official hydrographic charts and data, which should always be consulted in advance of, and whilst, navigating in the area.

The publishers, editors and their agents accept no responsibility for any errors or omissions, or for any accidents or mishaps which may arise from its use.

Before using any waypoint or coordinate listed in this Almanac it must first be plotted on an appropriate official hydrographic chart to check its usefulness, accuracy and appropriateness for the prevailing weather and tidal conditions.

The decision to use and rely on any of the data in this Almanac is entirely at the discretion of, and is the sole responsibility of, the Captain of the vessel employing it.

Production manager
Chris Stevens

Cartography
Chris Stevens, Jamie Russell

Cover photograph
Oki Challenge yacht, courtesy of Mark Lloyd

Adlard Coles Nautical
37 Soho Square
London, W1D 3QZ
Tel: +44 (0)207 758 0200
Fax: +44 (0)207 758 0222/0333
Email: info@reedsalmanac.co.uk
www.reedsalmanac.co.uk

ISBN 0 7136 7060 6 - Reeds Oki Nautical Almanac 2005

ISBN 0 7136 7062 2 - Reeds Oki Looseleaf Almanac 2005

ISBN 0 7136 7175 0 - Reeds Oki Looseleaf Update Pack 2005

A CIP catalogue record for this book is available from the British Library. Printed in the UK

Oki Systems (UK) Ltd
550 Dundee Road
Slough, Berks, SL1 4LE
Tel: +44 (0)1753 819819
Fax: +44 (0)1753 819899
www.oki.co.uk
www.okieuropeanchallenge.com

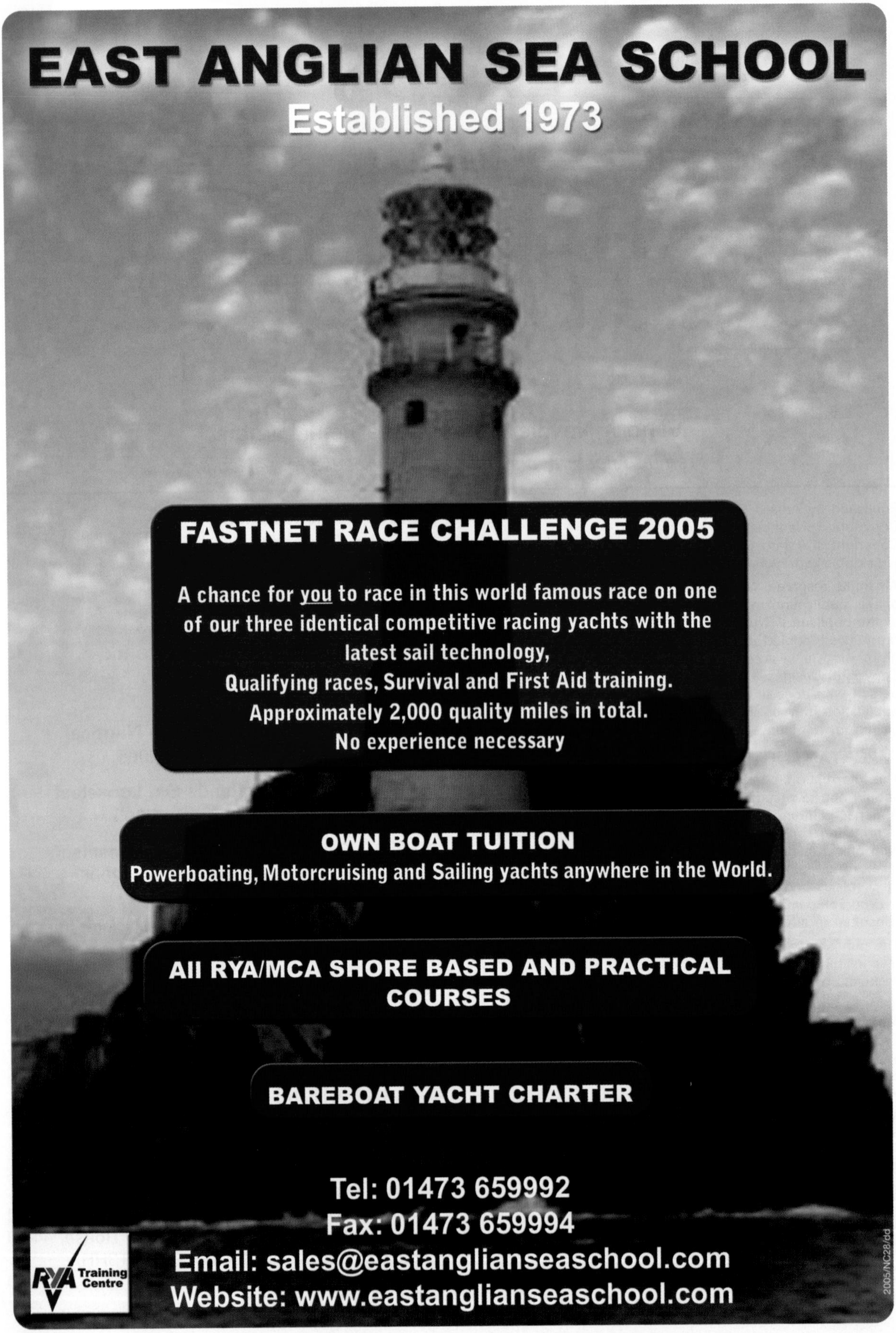
EAST ANGLIAN SEA SCHOOL
Established 1973
FASTNET RACE CHALLENGE 2005
A chance for you to race in this world famous race on one of our three identical competitive racing yachts with the latest sail technology,
Qualifying races, Survival and First Aid training.
Approximately 2,000 quality miles in total.
No experience necessary
OWN BOAT TUITION
Powerboating, Motorcruising and Sailing yachts anywhere in the World.
All RYA/MCA SHORE BASED AND PRACTICAL COURSES
BAREBOAT YACHT CHARTER
Tel: 01473 659992
Fax: 01473 659994
Email: sales@eastanglianseaschool.com
Website: www.eastanglianseaschool.com
RYA Training Centre
2005/NC28/dd

Contents

ADMIRALTY
LEISURE
Plan your dream with charts you can trust
Caribbean Leisure Folios
• 4 new Admiralty A2 size Folios covering Virgin, Leeward & Windward Islands - £39.50 per folio
• Convenient size for small chart tables & airline baggage
• Navigate more confidently with the familiar format of standard Admiralty charts
• WGS 84 positions can be plotted directly - metric soundings
Available from Admiralty Chart Agents & retailers and all good chandlers. For more details and How to Buy information visit www.admiraltyleisure.co.uk or call UKHO helpdesk 01823 723366
2005/NC26/e

CC MARINE
INNOVATORS OF MARINE TAPE TECHNOLOGY
The producers of 'Rubbaweld', the original self amalgamating marine tape also manufacture a complete range of specialised products for every yachtsman's needs.
Rubbaweld
Self amalgamating marine tape
Ripstop
Spinnaker/sail repair tape
Aquabond
Rapid epoxy putty
Kevlar
Sail repair tape
Maintape
Heavy duty sail repair tape
Hatchseal
Marine neoprene adhesive strip
Riggers tape
Adhesive backed
Rubbaweld
Mast boot
Mylar
Crystal clear sail repair tape
PVC tape
Flame retardant BS3924
Velcro
Hook & loop
Reflexite FD 1403
Solas/DTI approved
Marine repair tape
Strong adhesive waterproof cloth
CC Marine Services Ltd, Waldegraves Industrial Park,
West Mersea, Colchester, Essex CO5 8SE
Telephone: 01206 381801 Fax: 01206 381820
Available from all good chandlers
2005/NC5/je

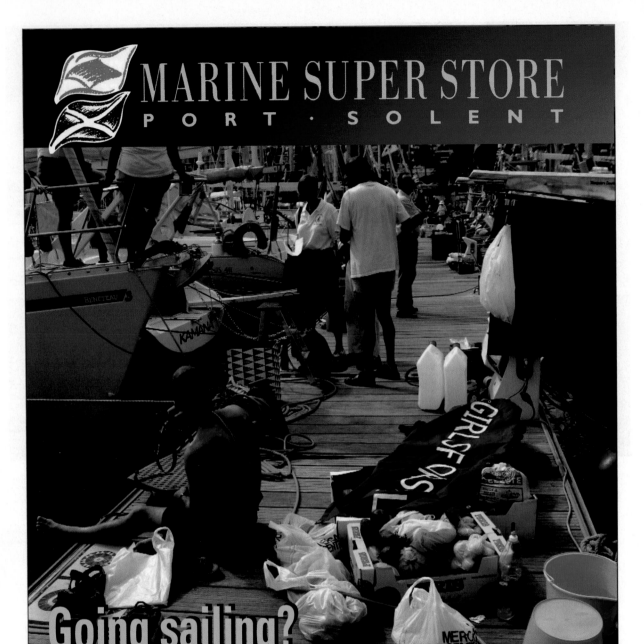

ROYAL NAVY
RESERVES
Fancy a change of scenery?
Maybe the
Royal Naval Reserve
is for you...
visit the website at
royalnavy.mod.uk/rnr
08456 07 55 55
The MOD has introduced a policy of routine notification of reserve service to civilian employers. You will be required to provide full details of your employer on joining the reserve forces and you will then be expected to inform them of your reserve liability. Recruits are normally aged between 16 and 40 (45 for ex-RN), male or female and physically fit. Nationality - you must be a British, Irish or Commonwealth citizen to join the RNR. A number of career paths however, are only available to British Citizens. Certain posts may also require CRB disclsoure clearance.
Type 23 Frigate off Umm Qasr during Operation TELIC - Photographer - LA(Phot) Angie Pearce (Crown copyright)

Ramsgate Marina
Look at what we can offer You!
Have you considered a permanent mooring at the Royal Harbour Marina, Ramsgate?
• Kent's premier marina offering safe mooring 365 days a year with superb facilities
• Sheltered mooring with 24 hour security, CCTV and foot patrols. Electricity, fuel and water.
• 40 tonne boat hoist at competitive prices.
• Full repair facilities ashore and afloat.
• Undercover workshop available.
• Good road access.
• Please visit our website for our current fees and charges.
2005/NC4/e
Contact us on
01843 572100
or e-mail us on
ramsgatemarina@thanet.gov.uk
H-6
THANET
DISTRICT COUNCIL
www.ramsgatemarina.co.uk

BEAUFORT SCALE SEA STATES

In enclosed waters or near land with an offshore wind, wave heights will be less but possibly steeper – particularly with wind against tide. Wave height for a given wind strength depends upon the distance it has travelled and the length of time for which the wind has been blowing.

Photography
© **Crown** – Force 0, 11
© **G.J.Simpson** – Force 1, 2, 7
© **I.G. MacNeil** – Force 3, 4, 5, 6
© **W.A.E. Smith** – Force 8
© **J.P. Laycock** – Force 9
© **G. Allen** – Force 10
© **J.F.Thomson** – Force 12

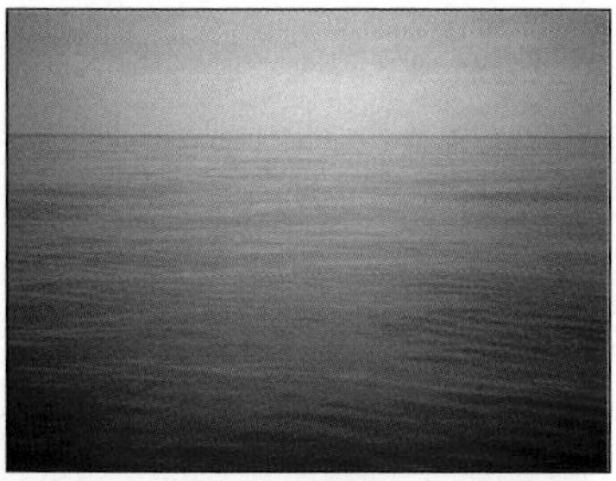

Force 0 0-1 Kts Calm Wave Ht 0m

Force 1 1-3 Kts Light Air
Wave Ht 0m

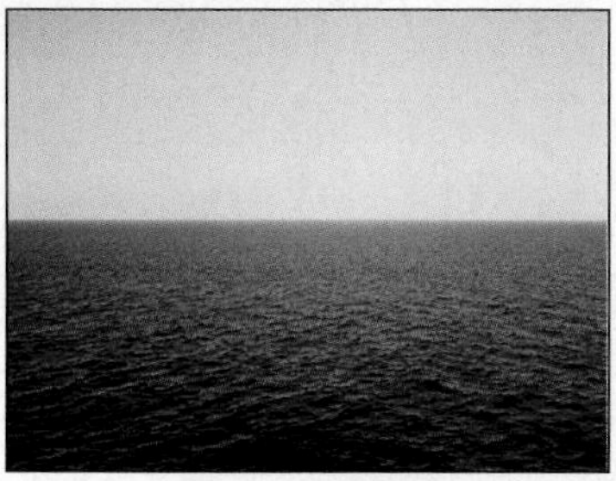

Force 2 4-6 Kts Light Breeze
Wave Ht 0.1m

Force 3 7-10 Kts Gentle Breeze
Wave Ht 0.4m

Force 4 11-16 Kts Moderate Breeze
Wave Ht 1m

Force 5 17-21 Kts Fresh Breeze
Wave Ht 2m

Force 6 22-27 Kts Strong Breeze
Wave Ht 3m

Force 7 28-33 Kts Near Gale
Wave Ht 4m

Force 8 34-40 Kts Gale
Wave Ht 5.5m

Force 9 41-47 Kts Severe Gale
Wave Ht 7m

Force 10 48-55 Kts Storm
Wave Ht 9m

Force 11 56-63 Kts Violent Storm
Wave Ht 11m

Force 12 64 plus Kts Hurricane
Wave Ht 14m

WAYPOINT 1
MARINE ELECTRONICS LTD
Main Agents for:
Raymarine, Simrad, Silva, Mcmurdo, Lowrance, Icom, Garmin, Mastervolt, CMap, Navionics and many more.
We can supply and install Marine PC/ Software, Radar and Navigational Aids, Instruments and Autopilots, Fishfinders, Communications and Safety Equipment, Audio - Visual and more.
Your first port of call for Marine Electronics
Ocean Building,
Queen Anne's Battery,
Plymouth, Devon, PL4 0LP
Tel 01752 661913 Fax 01752 661931
enquiries@waypoint-1.co.uk
Shop on-line at
www.waypoint-1.co.uk
2005/NC32/dd

INSURANCE GUIDE

Yacht Insurance

Nothing is ever certain at sea and, however careful a skipper may be, a boat is always at risk of being seriously damaged, even becoming a total loss or causing damage to third parties.

Owners should insure their boat for her full value, not necessarily the same as the purchase price. Any appreciable discrepancy between price paid and proposed insured value should however be explained to the insurer and agreed with them as, in the event of a claim, they may repudiate on the grounds of mis-disclosure of material facts. A reasonable basis for the insured value is that in normal market conditions how much would you have to pay for a boat that is the same and of similar age and condition? In any case you should read the proposal form carefully, and answer the various questions accurately and truthfully. Remember that answers to questions such as where is the boat normally kept? What fuel is used? etc, if altered, become a material fact. Otherwise insurers may subsequently be entitled to avoid liability in the event of a claim.

A policy normally covers the boat for a certain period in commission each year. If you need to extend the period, be sure to tell the company beforehand. Similarly cover is arranged for a certain cruising area. Make certain that the agreed limits are kept to, or make special arrangements when necessary.

The policy contains a number of warranties and conditions, either implied or expressed. These can be identified by reading the various sections carefully, and usually include the following important points:

1. If any loss or damage occurs the owner must take all steps necessary to minimise further loss, and the underwriters will contribute to charges properly incurred in taking such steps.
2. Charter or hire of the boat is not covered, except by special arrangement.
3. If an incident may give rise to a claim, prompt notice must be given to the underwriters.
4. The amount payable for a claim may be reduced for fair wear and tear of sails, rigging etc.
5. Theft of equipment is only covered where forcible entry or removal can be shown. Outboards must be locked to the boat. Check that there is no exclusion for outboard falling overboard.
6. Sails which are split by the wind are not generally insured, unless caused by the yacht being stranded or in collision. Also excluded is damage to sails while racing, unless caused by the boat being stranded, sunk, on fire or in collision.
7. Damage to or loss of an engine or other mechanical or electrical items is only covered if caused by the yacht being flooded, sunk, stranded, burned or in collision; or by theft of the entire boat; or by theft following forcible entry; or by malicious acts.
8. Personal effects can be included, if specially arranged.
9. Boats with a maximum designed speed of 17 knots or more are subject to 'Speedboat Clauses' which specify certain conditions and generally attract higher premiums.
10. Cover for at least £1,000,000 Third Party Liability is recommended. Normally somebody using the boat with the consent of the owner is covered, but this should be confirmed.
11. When in transit or trailing by road, a boat may be covered for accidental loss or damage, but the policy excludes all third party liabilities or offences against the road traffic legislation.
12. If no claim is made under the policy, most insurers will grant a no-claim bonus.
13. In the case of yachts over 15 years old, most underwriters require a recent survey on first insurance and after a change of ownership, followed by periodic surveys thereafter.
14. A Marine policy is not assignable. The moment the ownership changes the old policy is dead and should be cancelled.

Marine Insurance policies contain 'conditions' which usually includes that the owner must keep the boat and its equipment in seaworthy condition and in a proper state of repair.

Some insurers argue that single handed sailing infers under manning and therefore the boat is not seaworthy. Failure to disclose on the proposal that the yacht is habitually sailed single or short-handed may be held as failure to disclose material facts, so tell your insurer and get it agreed.

Marine insurance is a specialised business. Either deal with a broker or intermediary who is experienced in yacht insurance or get proposal forms from several established firms who advertise in the yachting press; it will be apparent that some insurers give wider cover than others. Return those forms which best seem to meet your needs, and then compare the quotations. However, firms with the lowest premiums are not necessarily the best at settling claims. Useful information is given in RYA booklet G9 *The Yachtsman's Lawyer* and *Marine Law for Boat Owners* by Edmund Whelan.

CHARTERS GUIDE

DARTMOUTH YACHT CHARTERS

Tel/Fax: 01803 883718
Email: sue@dartmouthyachtcharters.co.uk

Bareboat and Skippered Yacht Charters from Dartmouth in S.W. England.
European charters available from
Greece, Croatia, S. Brittany, Canaries and Cyprus

RYA approved Sail training from Competent Crew to Yachtmaster
Practical and Theory courses available.
Website: www.dartmouthyachtcharters.co.uk
www.devonandwestyachtschool.co.uk
www.dartmarinenav.co.uk

2005/CG1/je

FOUR SEASONS YACHT CHARTER LTD

BAREBOAT & SKIPPERED CHARTERS

First 40.7's, Jeanneau 43, First 435

Tel: 02392 511789
www.fourseasonscharter.co.uk
Email: info@fourseasonscharter.co.uk

2004/CG4/cd

Personally Tailored Yacht Charters

Yacht Charter Specialists offering quality yachts at competitive prices operating from Portsmouth Harbour. "Camper and Nicholson's Marina"

PT YACHT CHARTERS
PERSONALLY TAILORED

Yacht Charter

- *Skippered Charter*
- *Bareboat*
- *Corporate Hospitality*
- *Channel Cruises*
- *Newly qualified day skippers*
- *Holidays and Charter a berth*

Yacht Charter Management

THE FLEET

- *Offering 100 % Charter income return*
- *This is growing each year with new yachts coming online frequently*
- *Looking after your yacht as it should be and making the cost of yachting affordable*
- *Offering yachts from 32ft - 52ft there is plenty to choose from.*
- *Don't hesitate to contact us for more details or please view our website.*

Web: www.pt-yachtcharters.com
Email: info@pt-yachtcharters.com
Office: 023 92 521 585
Mobile: 07876 203535

2005/CG2/e

Patriot Charters and Sail School MILFORD MARINA, PEMBROKESHIRE SA73 3AF

Sail in glorious Pembrokeshire

Tel: 01437 741202

All RYA Practical Sailing Courses
Beginners Welcome
Adventure cruises to Ireland or Scillies.
Skippered Charter a Swan 43.

RYA Training Centre

E-mail: **sail@patriotcharters.co.uk**
or see our website at:
www.patriotcharters.co.uk

2004/CG5/a

TEMPLECRAFT

Yacht Charters

for bareboat and flotilla sailing in the Ionians

ATOL 2149 · ABSC Association of Bonded Sailing Companies · ABTOT 5040 · Bonded tour operators

Call NOW 01273 812333 Fax 01273 813952
Templecraft Yacht Charters, Middleham, Ringmer, Lewes BN8 5EY
www.templecraft.com Email: tc@templecraft.com

2004/CG3/e

SETSAIL HOLIDAYS

ATOL 4203 PROTECTED · ABTOT 5190 · YCA BONDED · British Marine Federation

GREECE · TURKEY · CROATIA · MAJORCA

LEARN TO SAIL IN TURKEY COURSES

Flotilla & Bareboat Charter

- ***One & two week sailing holidays***
- ***Flights from Gatwick & Manchester***

Call **01787 310445** Fax 01787 378078 Website www.setsail.co.uk email boats@setsail.co.uk

2004/CG6/d

Yacht Charter

Chartering has become very big business in recent years. On one side of the coin a yachtsman can help to pay some of his running costs or the instalments on his marine mortgage by chartering his boat. On the other side, chartering allows a person who does not own a boat, for whatever reason, to get afloat and enjoy a holiday not necessarily in home waters but perhaps in more reliably sunny climes. In either case it is important to have a proper written agreement which covers every conceivable eventuality.

Many people prefer to charter a yacht for two or three weeks a year, rather than face the continuing responsibility and costs of looking after a boat throughout the year. There are plenty of charter boats on offer around the UK, with some of them in delightful areas such as the west coasts of Scotland and Ireland. Chartering in home waters is naturally cheaper, because travel costs are much reduced. Also, if required, it is feasible to change crews during the charter. Since air fares are now cheaper in real terms, it may make good economic sense to sail in established areas like the Mediterranean or Caribbean (including the British Virgin Islands, the Bahamas and Florida), where the weather is likely to be reliable. One of the attractions of chartering is to explore different places and these now extend as far afield as the Indian and Pacific Oceans, including the Great Barrier Reef in Australia.

All charter yachts are fitted with radiotelephones, allowing them to keep in touch with base, and invaluable should any problem arise with the boat. The company should have a service, which in a few hours can reach any yacht which has trouble with gear or engine, for example. With the larger companies the spares back-up is usually very impressive, with makes and types of equipment rationalised amongst their fleet, which may number 50 boats or more. Apply early, so as to take up any cheap fares on offer. Also remember that a three week holiday is more economical per week than a fortnight's holiday, both in terms of travel costs and particularly since a few charter companies make reductions for the third week of a charter.

Most companies will arrange for provisioning the boat in advance, to a scale agreed by the charterers. It is often wise to take advantage of such a scheme, since there may be no convenient shops on arrival. 'Split provisioning' provides enough food if three or four main meals are taken ashore each week. The inventory is normally very comprehensive and the firm should provide a detailed list. Although items such as snorkel gear are included binoculars are usually not provided. It may be advisable to take your own pilot guide to the area concerned. The firm will almost certainly give a 'chart briefing' ashore, in which will be described the better anchorages and shore facilities, where to get items such as ice,etc.

Flotilla sailing is a good opportunity for less experienced sailors to start cruising, with advice from the flotilla 'leader' always readily available. The boats will be fitted with VHF radiotelephones, so that help is readily on call. Most flotilla operations are in relatively small yachts, sleeping four or six persons, and often ideal for a family holiday. The leader knows the area, the best anchorages, the more attractive harbours, and the places ashore where food and drink are good and cheap. He can also help, where necessary, with language problems, Customs formalities and the like.

Whatever company or private owner you charter from, find out as much as possible about the firm or individual concerned, preferably from people who have had first-hand experience of the boats or boat. Carefully check the equipment provided against a comprehensive list. Pay particular regard to navigational items and to safety equipment. What is the age of the boat, and is she the best type for your purpose? Does the accommodation really match your requirements? Look closely at insurance to see what excess is included, and check the third party cover, which should be for at least £1,000,000. What sort of service is provided in the event of some problem developing with the boat during the charter period (probably none, if you are chartering from a private individual). If the boat becomes unusable, what refund will be offered?

A proper form of written agreement is essential, covering such items as: the date, time and place to take over and hand back the boat; booking deposit; balance of the charter money (payable before the charter starts); arrangements for cancellation; a security deposit for loss or damage (returnable on completion of the charter); any insurance excess which the charterer may have to bear; cruising limits, where applicable; payment for items such as fuel, harbour dues, food, laundry etc; what penalty may be imposed for late return of the boat; and, if crew are carried, who pays for their food.

The Yacht Charter Association (YCA), which is a part of the BMIF, oversees the business. It exists to raise standards and protect the customer. UK charter companies which belong to the YCA, agree to abide by the YCA's standards and requirements in respect of service, operations and maintenance.

Further information from the Secretary, Yacht Charter Association Ltd, Deacon's Boatyard, Bursledon Bridge, Southampton, Hants SO31 8AZ. Tel: 023 8040 7075; Fax: 023 8040 7076; e-mail charter@yca.co.uk Website www.yca.co.uk.

Extract from the *Reeds Yachtsman's Handbook*

BROKERS GUIDE

Yacht Brokers

Yacht brokers provide an important service and if you are buying a boat of any size, it is highly advisable to deal through one. They can advise on the suitability of a boat for your particular purpose, and can then track down those most likely to meet your needs. They can help to arrange both the slipping and the survey of the selected boat (very useful if you happen to live elsewhere), a marine mortgage if required and with insurance. They can check details such as the inventory of the boat, and ensure that the documentation is properly completed so that title is fully transferred. Most brokers (frequently members of the ABYA) operate under a *Code of Practice for the Sale of Used Boats,* copies of which are obtainable from the BMIF or RYA.

A standard form of agreement is used, setting out the following terms: The agreed purchase price; 10% is paid when the agreement is signed, allowing the purchaser to have the yacht lifted out and surveyed at his own expense; the survey should normally be completed within 14 days, although this can be longer, by agreement. Within a stated period from completion of survey, if any material defects have been found, the purchaser may either reject the yacht (giving notice of the defects discovered), or ask the seller either to make good such shortcomings or reduce the price. The form also details the obligations of the two parties, default by the purchaser, the transfer of risk, and arbitration procedure in a dispute. A broker is legally liable to divulge any known defects to a purchaser when acting in a sale. If the sale proceeds, the agreement states that the yacht is considered to have been accepted by the buyer and the balance of the agreed price is due if:

a. a period of 14 days elapses, and no survey has been made; or

b. after an agreed time after the survey the purchaser has not acted; or

c. the seller remedies any specified defects to the satisfaction of the surveyor; or

d. an agreed reduction in price is made.

The buyer should also be aware that if the seller is a private individual (ie he or she is not selling the boat in the course of trade or business), and if that fact is known to the buyer, there is no question of any warranty on the sale of a second-hand boat because the buyer is quite at liberty to inspect the craft and to satisfy himself as to her condition – either personally or by employing a surveyor. Unquestionably a survey should always be made, except perhaps in the case of a very small and cheap boat where the buyer has enough knowledge and experience to detect any serious faults.

Buying yachts can be a complex business, particularly when the boat, the seller and the buyer are all miles apart. Two brokers are often involved, and access must be provided by the yard or marina where the boat is lying. Consequently the Code of Practice provides for a fair split of the total commission between those involved. The seller of the boat pays an agreed commission based on the selling price. For guidance the normal rates (plus VAT) are: 8% of the price for vessels in the UK; 10% for vessels on inland waters. 10% also applies if the vessel, owner or buyer are abroad.

SELLING THROUGH A YACHT BROKER

Selling a yacht through a yacht broker may be a useful and appropriate course of action for a number of people. It eliminates most of the work and problems involved with a private sale, and because a broker has access to a wide market it may enable a higher price to be obtained or a quicker sale to be achieved.

When instructing a broker to sell a boat, the owner will be asked to complete a form which requires full particulars of the boat and of her material condition. It is important that these are accurately stated. You must also agree with the broker at the outset whether or not he is to be the sole agent.

A broker acts as a go-between for buyers and sellers of yachts all over the world. If a broker is appointed as sole agent he will pass full details of the boat to other selected brokers, who will usually receive half of the eventual commission if they produce a sale. These central listing facilities allow the interchange of information about all the boats for sale between all the various participating brokerage firms, so that the net is spread as wide as possible.

Very importantly, a broker is able to advise on the correct price at which a boat should be offered – a price that is likely to attract response, but which will be fair to the seller. It is in the broker's interest to obtain the best price, as his commission is based on it.

Any advertising copy or materials produced by the broker must be accurate because he is liable under the Trade Descriptions Act. He will advertise the boat and handle all enquiries and inspections. When a potential buyer appears the broker will prepare a Sale Agreement on a standard form of contract. If the sale proceeds after survey, he can advise the owner regarding any defects that may have been found to negotiate a fair price. Finally the broker prepares the Bill of Sale, and ensures that title is not transferred until the purchase money has been received.

Extract from the *Reeds Yachtsman's Handbook*

SURVEYORS GUIDE

RICHARD AYERS

YACHT SURVEYOR & CONSULTANT

INSURANCE ASSESSMENT
NEW CONSTRUCTION, INSURANCE & REFIT
M.R.I.N. COMPANION R.I.N.A. RYA/DTP YACHT MASTER

5A CHURCH STREET, MODBURY, DEVON PL21 0QW
TELEPHONE: 01548 830496 MOBILE: 07831 118056
FAX: 01548 830917

2005/SG3/a

Lee Battrick

Marine Surveyor

Sweet Briar, Rue du Trachy, Millbrook, St. Helier, Jersey JE2 3JN

Tel/Fax: 01534 611143 Mobile: 07797 742510

30 Years of Experience in the Marine Industry with excellent contacts in the Channel Islands.

- Surveys for condition, reinsurance surveys, valuations, constancy.
- Damage surveys on behalf of insurers, 24 hour availability in the event of incidents.
- Prompt service, reports generally within 3 days.
- Able to travel easily to other Channels Islands and France.

YDSA Tonnage meaurements. YDSA (MCA) Level 2 Nominated Surveyor. Bureau Veritas Nominated Surveyor. Member International Association of Marine Investigators (IAMI). Member, Society of Naval Architects and Marine Engineers (SNAME)

2005/SG4/je

DAVID M. CANNELL & ASSOCIATES

NAVAL ARCHITECTS - CONSULTANTS - SURVEYORS

Design of power and Sailing Vessels, Yachts and Commercial
Surveys - GRP, Steel, Aluminium & Wood,
Newbuild and Refit Surveys
Expert Witness for Litigation
MCA Codes of Practice Surveys
Preparation of Specifications and Contracts
Technical Analysis.

Members YDSA, RINA, BAE

River House, Quay Street, Wivenhoe, Essex C07 9DD, U.K
Tel: +44 (0)1206 823 337 Fax: +44 (0)1206 825 939
email: enquires@dmcmarine.com www.dcmarine.com

2005/SG5/e

MARTIN EVANS

AMYDSA

Yacht & Small Craft Surveyor

All materials, traditional and modern

YDSA

- Pre-purchase and Insurance surveys and valuations
- Damage assessment and Repair supervision
- General Consultancy (e.g. osmosis checks, in-water corrosion tests)
- Tonnage Measurement for Part 1 British Registration
- MCA Compliance inspections

ASSOCIATE MEMBER OF YACHT DESIGNERS & SURVEYORS ASSOCIATION

For friendly advice, contact:

Tel/Fax: 01255 677883 Mobile: 07887 724055 E-mail: shipshape@ntlworld.com
Pilot's Cottage, Quay Lane, Kirby-le-Soken, Essex CO13 0DS

2005/SG7/j

W.A. MacGregor

A.R.I.N.A., F. Inst. Diag. Eng

Y.D.S.A

Marine Surveyors
Felixstowe, Suffolk IP11 3SJ

Tel: 01394 676034 Fax: 01394 675515
Mobile: 07860 361279

Yacht & Small Craft, all materials
MCA Coding and Marine Consultancy

2005/SG2/j

2005/SG6/je

Superyacht Surveys

Yacht & Motor Yacht Surveys
Technical & Legal Consultant
MCA Compliance

Tony McGrail

228 Stony Lane,
Burton, Christchurch,
Dorset BH23 7LB

Superyacht Surveys

Tel: 01202 480545
Mobile: 07711 329314
mcgrailtony@yahoo.co.uk
www.tonymcgrail.com

BOATCARE YACHT SURVEYS

Surveys of Sailing and Motor Yachts and Marine Consultancy.

For a full range of professional services, pre-purchase survey, insurance survey, free advice or for a competitive quotation contact Simon May

2005/SG8/je

Hamble/Solent/National and International

Tel/Fax: 02380 454498 Mob: 07939 208840

survey@boatcareyachtsurveys.co.uk
www.boatcareyachtsurveys.co.uk

Navigate this way

Surveying & Specialist Marine Services - by professionals

- Tonnage measurement ✓
- Condition & insurance surveys ✓
- Boat registration ✓
- Supervision of repairs ✓
- Supervision of new build ✓
- Boat valuations ✓
- MCA code compliance certification ✓

Y.D.S.A

If you need a boat survey or other specialist marine service, head in our direction. YDSA members are professionals with a track record of experience and competence. Please contact the Yacht Designers & Surveyors Association on tel: 01730 710425, email info@ybdsa.co.uk or visit our website www.ybdsa.co.uk for more information ... we're ready to assist.

2005/SG1/e

Yacht Surveyors

The idea of getting a boat surveyed usually arises when you are thinking about buying a boat or you've had a collision or a serious grounding. Alternatively your insurers might have asked for one or you are trying to get Part I British Registry. Perhaps even you have become involved in a dispute and need an expert witness. For whatever your reason, it is essential to select a surveyor with the proper qualifications who has been personally recommended by someone experienced that you trust.

There are several different types of survey available and which you select will depend on what you need. The best known is the Full Condition Survey which will tell you the condition of the boat you are considering buying. Certainly it would be very foolish to buy a second-hand boat without having a proper survey done, with the boat out of the water. It is also often approriate to have your boat surveyed before selling her, so that you can discover and rectify any problems before the buyer discovers them and demands an overgenerous discount to cover them.

The purpose of a full survey is to determine the condition of the entire yacht: hull, machinery, gear and all the equipment relating to her operation. A competent surveyor should report on every aspect of the boat's structure, depending on the materials concerned. He should comment on whether the condition of the various items is attributable to fair wear and tear, or whether other factors such as poor design, inferior materials, bad workmanship or lack of maintenance are involved. His examination should include all items such as fastenings, chain plates, shafting, steering gear and rudder fittings.

The surveyor will not usually provide an engine survey, and the engine itself may need to be surveyed separately as this is the province of the marine engineer. However the surveyor should certainly be able to assess its general condition. If you have any concerns about the engines, ask the surveyor or broker to help you find a local marine engineer. Similarly surveyors are not usually insured to go up the mast and tell you about the masthead fittings. There are modern rigging testing techniques and equipment which will give you information about this. Again, you should ask for a specialist report if you are concerned, or if this is of particular importance to you.

A hull condition survey is just that and is clearly more limited in scope. As well as full and hull condition surveys, surveyors assess accident damage for insurance purposes, and oversee repairs or modifications.

Insurers need surveys for accident reports and for when you insure your boat. These are two different types of survey - the accident report may need to be very detailed, giving insurers the information they need to assess the level of damage and whether it is repairable, etc. If, for instance, the accident was due to fire, they will want to know how the fire started. A Full Condition Survey will often be requested before an insurance policy is provided.

For Part I Registration a tonnage measurement is a much quicker survey and does not relate to the condition of the boat. It is simply a measurement and verification of the boat.

In cases where a dispute arises, some of our more senior members are experienced in providing expert witness reports for the Court, and others can act as arbitrators to settle technical disputes. Some surveyors specialise in particular types of boat, such as steel inland-waterways boats, or old wooden boats.

The surveyor will ask you for information on the boat before he agrees to do the survey for you. Be clear what it is that you are asking for so that you get what you intended. Instruct the surveyor in writing; the details are important as they will form the basis of a contract with him.

To get a proper survey you need a proper surveyor, and sadly a small minority of surveyors lack the knowledge and experience required. Members of the Yacht Designers and Surveyors Association (YDSA), have to pass exams, satisfy a probationary period and hold Professional Indemnity insurance.

For names of member surveyors near the boat's location, contact the YDSA, Wheel House, Petersfield Rd, Whitehill, Bordon, Hants, GU35 9BU. Tel 01420 473862; Fax 01420 488328.

Three other organisations, dealing partly with yachts and commercial vessels, are:

The International Institute of Marine Surveyors, Stone Lane, Gosport, Hants PO12 1SS. Tel 023 9258 8000; Fax 023 9258 8002. iims@compuserve.com www.iims.org.uk

The Society of Consulting Marine Engineers and Ships Surveyors, c/o 202 Lambeth Rd, London SE1 7LQ; Tel 020 7261 0869; Fax 020 7261 0871. scms@btinternet.com

The Institute of Marine Engineers, 80 Coleman Street, London EC2R 5BJ. Tel 020 7382 2600; Fax 020 7382 2670.

Extract from the *Reeds Yachtsman's Handbook*

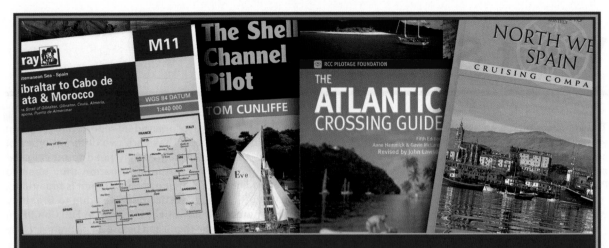

NAVIGATION LIGHTS

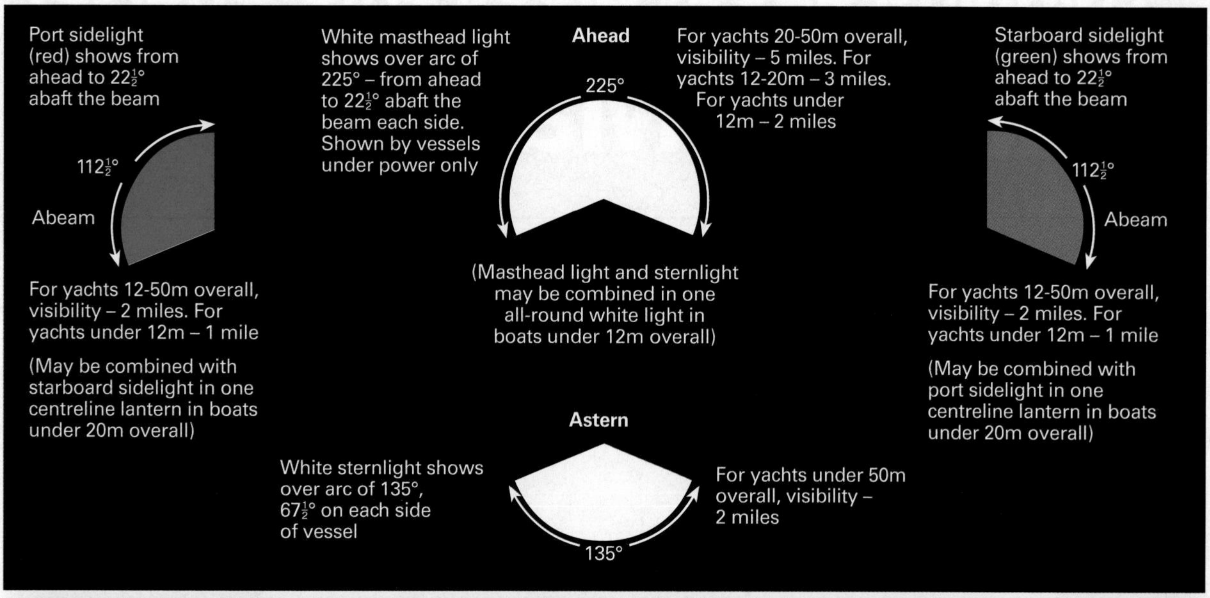
Port sidelight (red) shows from ahead to 22½° abaft the beam
112½°
Abeam
For yachts 12-50m overall, visibility – 2 miles. For yachts under 12m – 1 mile
(May be combined with starboard sidelight in one centreline lantern in boats under 20m overall)
White masthead light shows over arc of 225° – from ahead to 22½° abaft the beam each side. Shown by vessels under power only
Ahead
225°
For yachts 20-50m overall, visibility – 5 miles. For yachts 12-20m – 3 miles. For yachts under 12m – 2 miles
(Masthead light and sternlight may be combined in one all-round white light in boats under 12m overall)
Starboard sidelight (green) shows from ahead to 22½° abaft the beam
112½°
Abeam
For yachts 12-50m overall, visibility – 2 miles. For yachts under 12m – 1 mile
(May be combined with port sidelight in one centreline lantern in boats under 20m overall)
Astern
White sternlight shows over arc of 135°, 67½° on each side of vessel
135°
For yachts under 50m overall, visibility – 2 miles

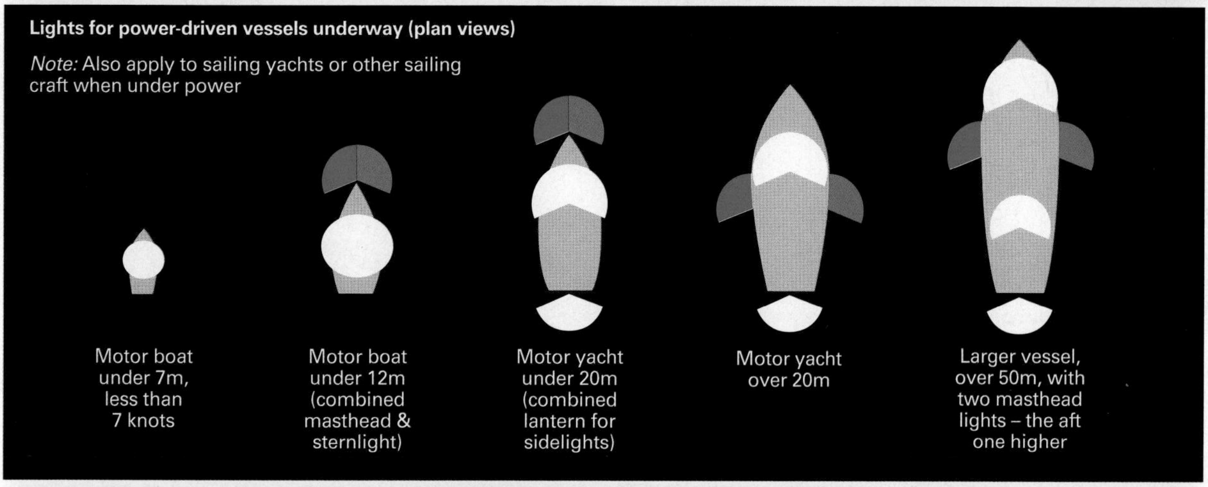
Lights for power-driven vessels underway (plan views)
Note: Also apply to sailing yachts or other sailing craft when under power
Motor boat under 7m, less than 7 knots
Motor boat under 12m (combined masthead & sternlight)
Motor yacht under 20m (combined lantern for sidelights)
Motor yacht over 20m
Larger vessel, over 50m, with two masthead lights – the aft one higher

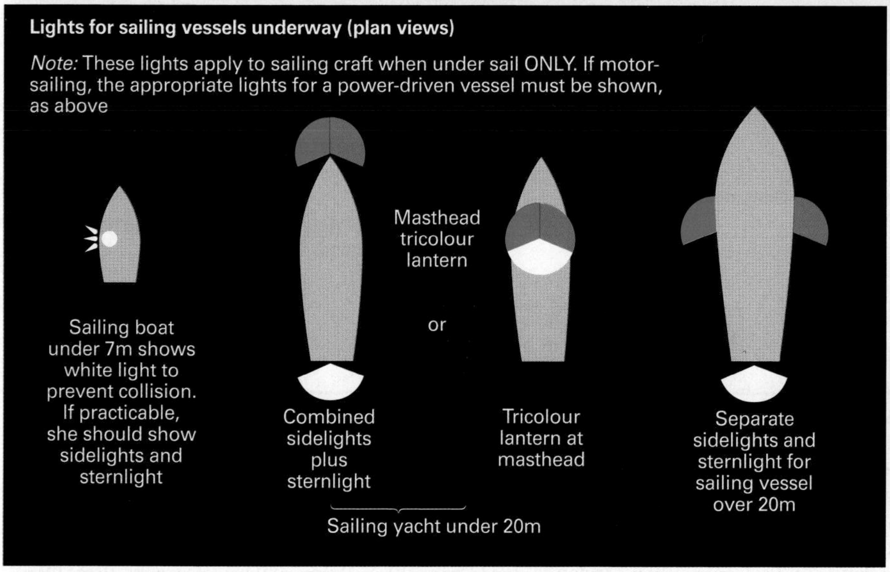
Lights for sailing vessels underway (plan views)
Note: These lights apply to sailing craft when under sail ONLY. If motor-sailing, the appropriate lights for a power-driven vessel must be shown, as above
Sailing boat under 7m shows white light to prevent collision. If practicable, she should show sidelights and sternlight
Masthead tricolour lantern
or
Combined sidelights plus sternlight
Tricolour lantern at masthead
Sailing yacht under 20m
Separate sidelights and sternlight for sailing vessel over 20m

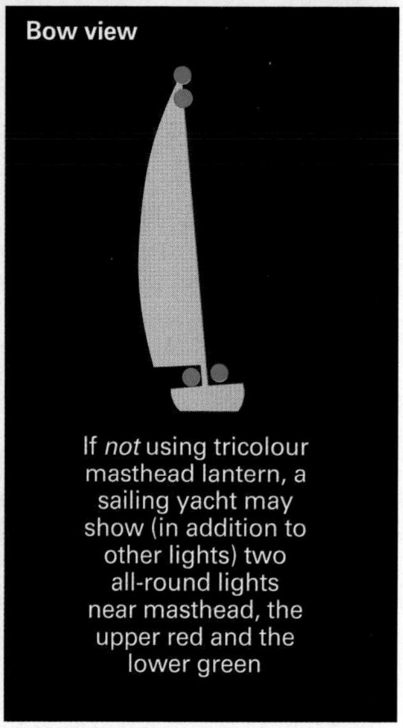
Bow view
If not using tricolour masthead lantern, a sailing yacht may show (in addition to other lights) two all-round lights near masthead, the upper red and the lower green

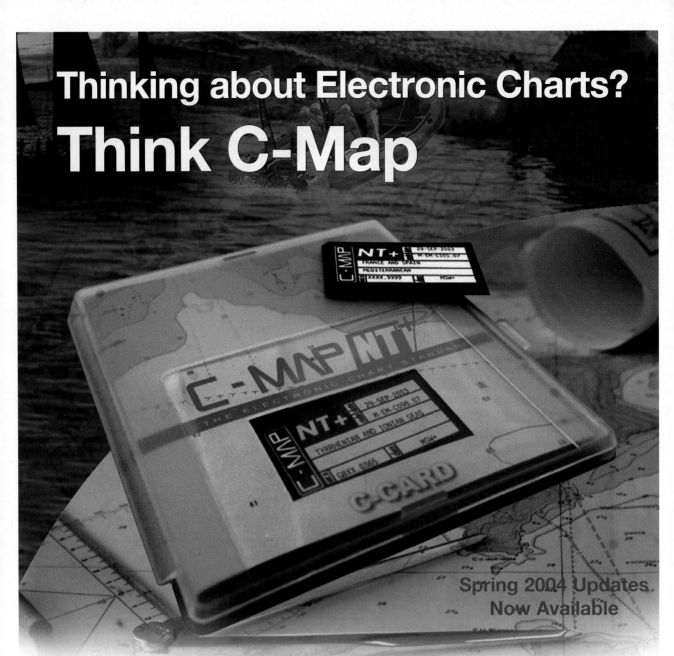

PRINCIPAL NAVIGATION LIGHTS AND SHAPES

(Note: All vessels seen from starboard side)

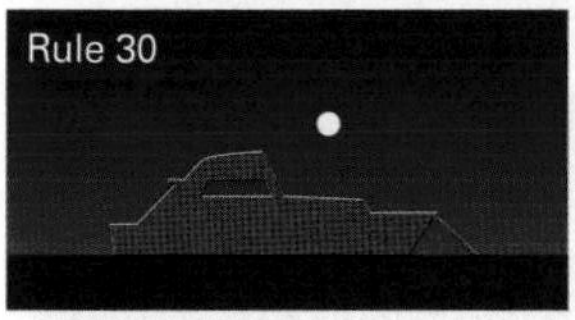
Rule 30

Vessel at anchor

All-round white light; if over 50m, a second light aft and lower

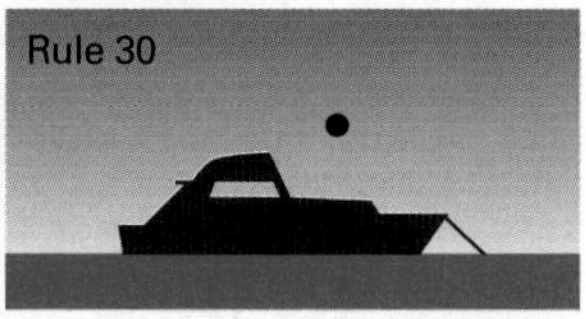
Rule 30

Black ball forward

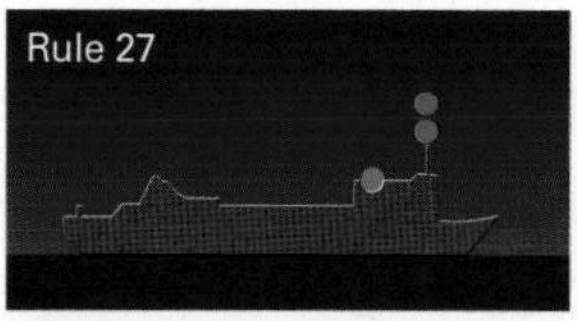
Rule 27

Not under command

Two all-round red lights, plus sidelights and sternlight when making way

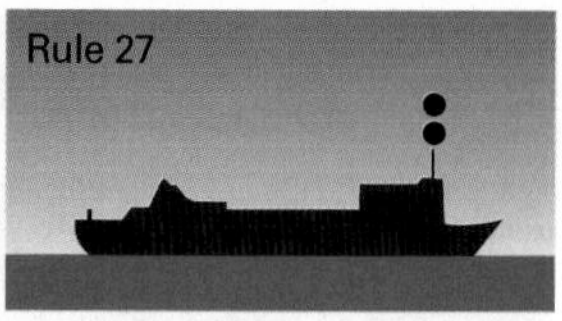
Rule 27

Two black balls vertically

Rule 25

Motor sailing

Cone point down, forward

Rule 27

Divers down

Letter 'A' International Code

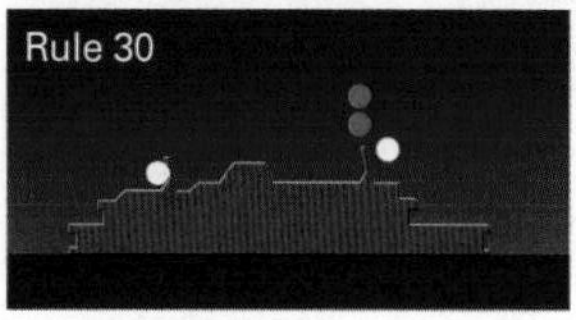
Rule 30

Vessel aground

Anchor light(s), plus two all-round red lights in a vertical line

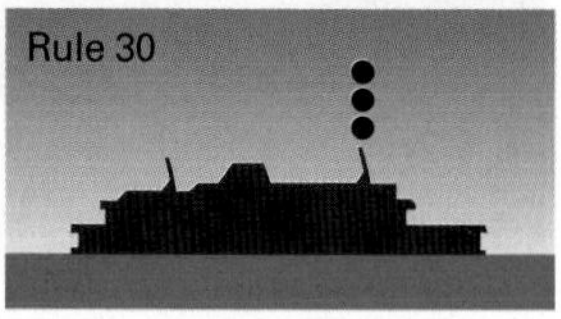
Rule 30

Three black balls in a vertical line

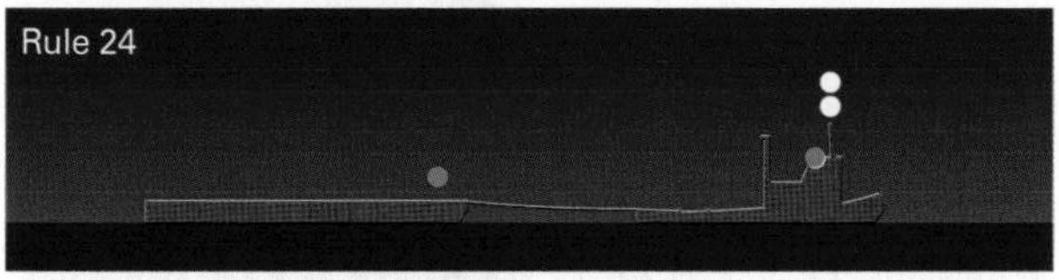
Rule 24

Vessels being towed and towing

Vessel towed shows sidelights (forward) and sternlight

Tug shows two masthead lights, sidelights, sternlight, yellow towing light

Rule 24

Towing by day – Length of tow more than 200m

Towing vessel and tow display diamond shapes. By night, the towing vessel shows three masthead lights instead of two as for shorter tows

---

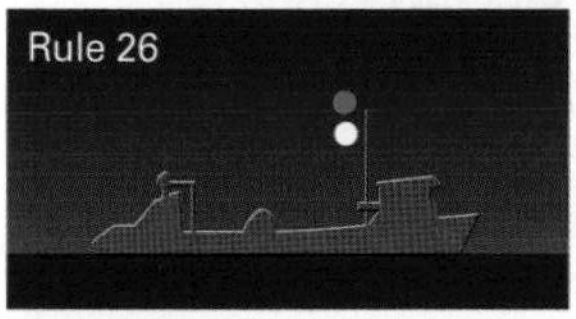
Rule 26

Vessel fishing

All-round red light over all-round white, plus sidelights and sternlight when making way

Rule 26

Fishing/Trawling

A shape consisting of two cones point to point in a vertical line one above the other

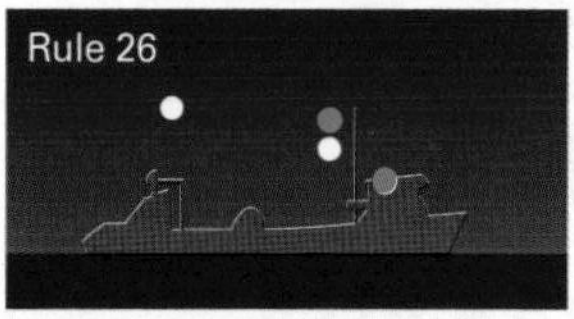
Rule 26

Vessel trawling

All-round green light over all-round white, plus sidelights and sternlight when making way

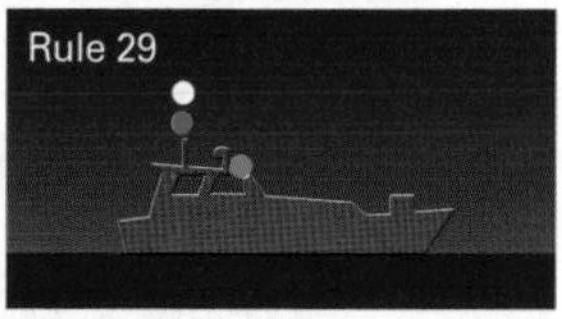
Rule 29

Pilot boat

All-round white light over all-round red, plus sidelights and sternlight when underway, or anchor light

---

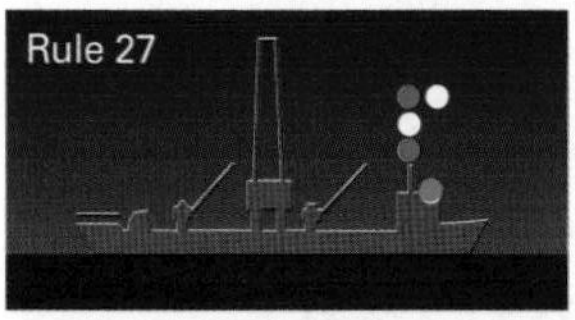
Rule 27

Vessel restricted in her ability to manoeuvre

All-round red, white, red lights vertically, plus normal steaming lights when making way

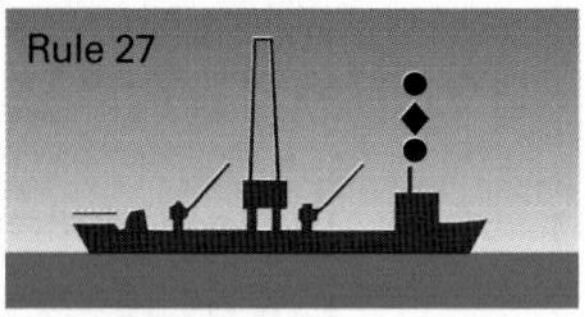
Rule 27

Three shapes in a vertical line ball, diamond, ball

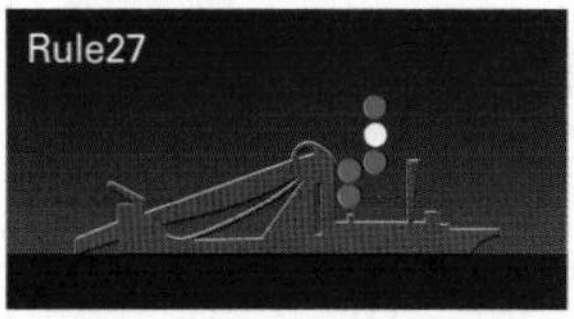
Rule27

Dredger

As left, plus two all-round red lights (or two balls) on foul side, and two all-round green (or two diamonds) on clear side

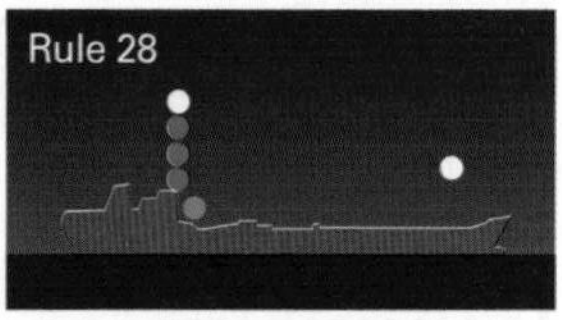
Rule 28

Constrained by draught

Three all-round red lights in a vertical line, plus normal steaming lights. By day – a cylinder

LONDON'S CHANDLERY BY THE THAMES

for all your boating needs

screws	varnish	lighting
engines	boatlocks	lifejackets
spares	paddles	anchors
paints	pumps	chains
ropes	flags	fenders
service	books	vhf
horns	nuts	

2005/NC31/je

CHAS NEWENS MARINE

THE BOAT HOUSE, EMBANKMENT, PUTNEY, LONDON, SW15 1LB

sales@chastheboat.com

Ⓣ0208 788 4587 Ⓕ0208 780 2339

W F PRICE & CO Ltd

ADMIRALTY CHART AGENTS
& NAUTICAL BOOKSELLERS

ESTABLISHED 1838

WAPPING WHARF, BRISTOL BS1 6UD

TEL: BRISTOL 0117 929 2229 - FAX 0117 930 4403

E-MAIL: sales@wfprice.com www.wfprice.com

2005/NC30/d

docklands

Dublin City Moorings

Custom House Quay, Docklands, Dublin 1

the only mooring in the Centre of Dublin City

Beside the Custom House and IFSC.
Electricity/water. Showers/toilets. 24 hour security.
Swipe card access.
Telephone +353 1 8183300 Fax: +353 1 8183399

Email: info@dublindocklands.ie Website: http://www.dublindocklands.ie

2005/NC11/me

MAIL ORDER HOTLINE
Telephone:
(02380) 632725

INTERNET
www.shamrock.co.uk
E-MAIL
sales@shamrock.co.uk

Shamrock Chandlery

Shamrock Quay, William Street, Northam, Southampton SO14 5QL

OPEN 7 DAYS A WEEK
COME RAIN OR SHINE

2005/NC1/j

NOTICE TO MARINERS

Safety is Paramount at sea.
We stock a full range of Ocean Safety Equipment

OCEAN SAFETY — Pains Wessex SAFETY SYSTEMS — XM YACHTING

- Flares
- Lifejackets
- Horseshoes
- Fire Extinguishers
- Life Raft Hire
- Fire Blankets

EUROCARD MasterCard VISA AMERICAN EXPRESS

All Major Credit Cards & Cheques accepted. UK Mainland – £5 carriage Europe – posted at cost.

Visit our chandlery website and check our prices.

OVERSEAS CUSTOMERS
We will quote delivery charges on all non UK mainland orders.
All orders will be despatched within 24 hours.

B. COOKE & SON LTD

'KINGSTON OBSERVATORY'
56/59 MARKET PLACE
HULL, HU1 1RH

ESTABLISHED 1863 - 142 YEARS OF SERVICE TO NAVIGATION

INTERNATIONAL ADMIRALTY CHART AGENTS

Worldwide stock of Admiralty Charts and Publications
Admiralty Raster (ARCS) Chart Service Navigator and Skipper - programmes to suit your Individual Requirements
Full Chart Correction and Customised Service for Tracings and Notices to Mariners
All Nautical Publications Stocked - Visitors Welcome

MANUFACTURE OF MAGNETIC COMPASSES AND BINNACLES

For All Classes of Vessel
Azimuth Mirrors, Pelorus, Sextants, Clinometers, Clocks and Barometers.
Supply and Service Electronic Repeaters, Off Course Alarms, Auto Pilots, Latest GPs etc.
All Engine Room Requirements.
Parallel Rulers and Dividers, Chartroom Instruments.
MCA Certified Compass Adjusters available 24 hours a day

MARINE PROGRAMMES FOR IBM PC & COMPATIBLE COMPUTERS

Voyage Planner, PC Stability, Draft & Trim, PC Sightmaster, PC Oilsurvey, Container Ship Stability, MArine Surveyor's Compilation, Showtide++ and PC Draft Survey
LAtest Psion Computers, Accessories & Software

All Enquiries Welcome, no matter how small

Tel: 01482 223454 / 224412

Fax: 01482 219793 Telex: 597636
E-mail: bcs@cooke.karoo.co.uk
Web: www.bcookeandsonsltd.co.uk

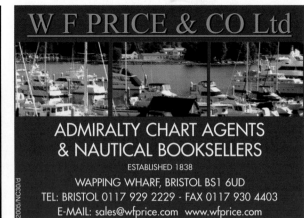

2005/NC3/a

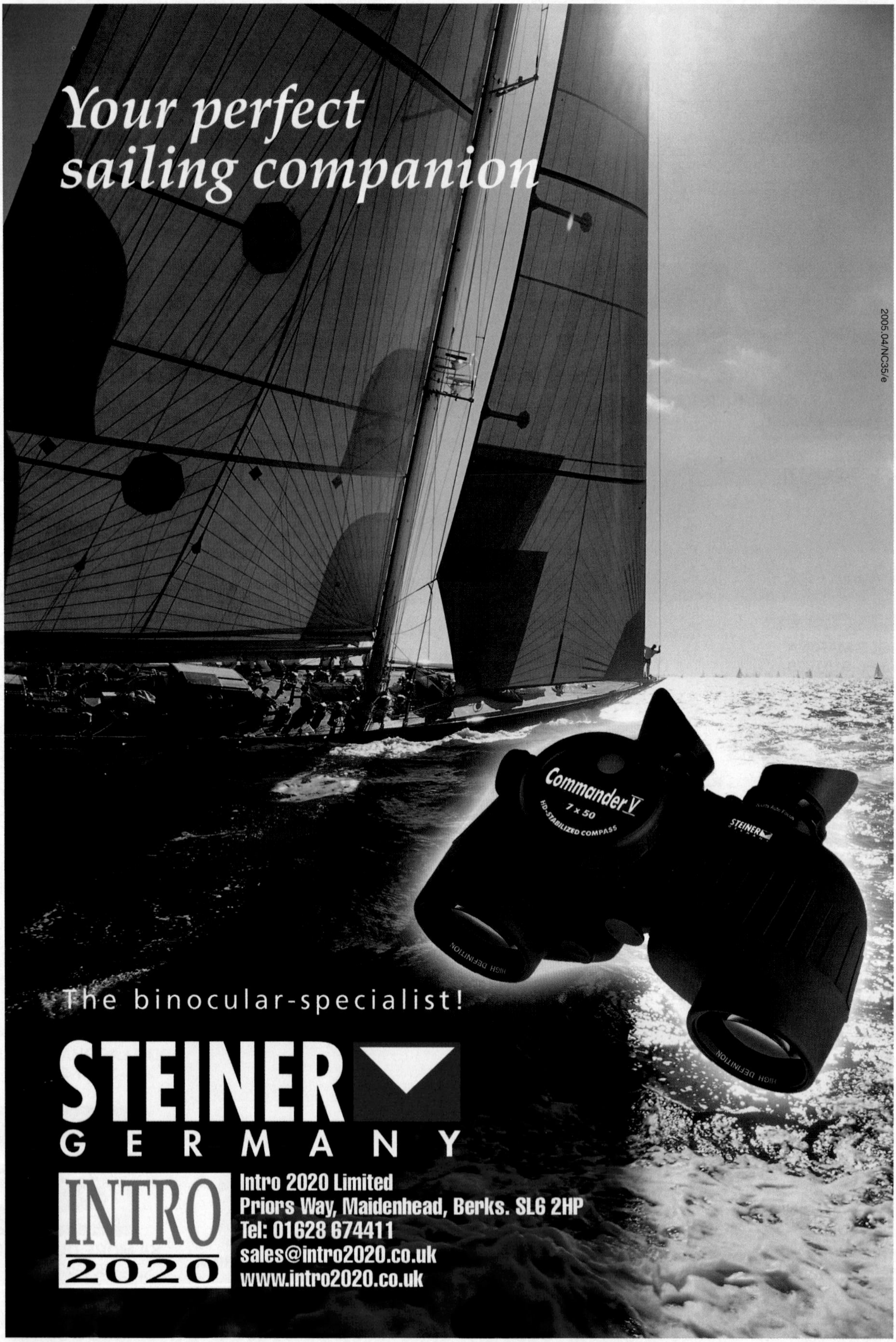
Your perfect sailing companion
Commander V
7 x 50
HD-STABILIZED COMPASS
STEINER
HIGH DEFINITION
The binocular-specialist!
STEINER
GERMANY
INTRO 2020
Intro 2020 Limited
Priors Way, Maidenhead, Berks. SL6 2HP
Tel: 01628 674411
sales@intro2020.co.uk
www.intro2020.co.uk
2005.04/NC35/e

IF YOU WANT TO GET MORE FROM YOUR OFFICE PRINTING...

ASK OKI

If you want to get more from your office printer, Oki has the answer. We have a close understanding of the needs of small and medium sized businesses and have a range of products that make printing high-quality documents fast and affordable

Every business knows that the quality of its printed communications can significantly enhance its relationships with customers. Whether you're printing letters, invoices, labels, brochures, banners or business cards, what you produce sends out clear messages about your business and what it stands for.

At Oki we believe that high-quality office printing isn't just for big business. We know that small and medium sized businesses have a real need to produce professional-looking materials in-house - without the expense and lack of flexibility involved in sending the job to the local print shop. And they want the freedom to use either black and white or colour without worrying about their budgets.

That's why we've produced a guide to office printing called "The printer, it's not just for letters" - to help businesses like yours choose the right office printer for your needs and then draw the maximum benefit from it.

And it's why we focus on making our products - from colour and black-and-white printers to fax machines and multifunction devices - affordable and easy to use.

Our colour print solutions (C Series digital LED printers) are changing the workplace. We've designed them to be make the job of print management easier and they answer a real commercial need, to make every piece of business communication work harder for you.

And if it's a monochrome printer you need, we have a wide range of models too (B Series digital printers) from compact desktop, to fully featured high-speed workgroup units.

But meeting our customers' needs involves much more than just delivering the technology. We also offer a comprehensive package of consultancy to help businesses to get more from their hardware investment. Delivered through our network of resellers and distributors and a dedicated Oki technical support team, our consultancy provides advice and guidance on all aspects of the document lifecycle - document creation & content; document management & security; document finishing; and document distribution & archiving.

And Oki has demonstrated a strong commitment to product development throughout its 120-year history. We're continually striving to allow customers to get extra benefits from our products. But this isn't at the expense of the environment - we also promote the recycling of all the components used in our main printing and fax products.

We also work closely with industry bodies such as Intellect and AIIM to develop and support best practice guidelines for document management in the business community. Oki is also one of the founding member of The Imaging Consumables Coalition of Europe (ICCE). An organisation formed to protect consumers and the distribution chain from 'counterfeit' products.

Now is the time to review the way you communicate. To find out more about how Oki's range of print solutions could help your business, call 0800 9176015 or visit our website at **www.oki.co.uk**. The site also has details of Oki representatives in your area.

OKI EUROPEAN CHALLENGE 2005

EXCEED YOUR EXPECTATIONS

Oki, the business printed communications company, is proud to sponsor Europe's first truly democratic yacht race, the Oki European Challenge 2005.

A brand new initiative in the world of sailing, the Oki European Challenge is designed to bring ordinary Europeans into the sport, capturing the imagination of the European public and encouraging the support of European business.

The race will kick off in the summer of 2005 and will see a fleet (10 - 15 boats) of evenly matched Beneteau First 47.7 yachts race around Europe in 12 separate legs, calling at 13 ports in 11 different countries. The race will stop in each port for five days and will take approximately 15 weeks to complete. The Oki European Challenge will start in Poland and visit Germany, Denmark, Sweden, Holland, the UK, France, Portugal, Spain, and Italy, before finishing in Monaco.

Anticipation of the race is already building in Oki's European markets following the Promotional Tour of the race route which took place between June and September 2004. The Promotional Tour saw a number of the Beneteau yachts visit all the markets in advance and provided the opportunity for those keen to get involved to meet the event organisers in their own countries - all part of the race's core ethos to make the event as attractive and accessible as possible.

WHY GET INVOLVED?

- What sets this race apart is its European nature and the diversity of people and companies who will be involved. What unites them all is a desire to grow - physically, emotionally or professionally.

- This is a business focused race. The race structure and the benefits have been specifically designed to help build European business. Over 100 businesses will become involved in the race, benefiting from profile building and networking opportunities.

- Competition is the life blood of the race and every leg will be strongly contested - the overall winners receiving the Oki European Challenge Trophy in Monte Carlo.

- But the race is also about collaboration. Fair play and sportsmanship is central to the event ethos and crew collaboration will be central to their success. Sharing information and experience, networking and open and honest work practices will all become the hallmarks of the Oki European Challenge's business relationships.

- And for those looking for an exciting and challenging sabbatical, the realistic three month timescale of the race is the typical duration of a short-term break from a demanding career. With crew applications accepted from all nationalities and from people from all walks of life, the Oki European Challenge promises a unique and life changing experience.

HOW TO GET INVOLVED

CREW

A great race becomes so on account of the people involved - the individuals who inspire the race, the people and companies who help make it happen and the participants whose spirit and determination bring the event to life.
This is the first time such an event has been run in Europe, over such a short time frame and with such a truly open selection process. It has been deliberately designed to make sailing more accessible to more people, offering complete beginners the chance to participate in a major international sporting event as well as an exciting adventure.
Due to popular demand since the launch of the Oki European Challenge the additional option of taking part in either the northern or southern legs of the event at a reduced cost has been introduced by the organisers.
Each yacht's crew will be made up of one professionally qualified skipper and nine crew members. Crew members need no previous sailing experience and can be complete beginners as training will be provided.

Anyone who is aged between 18 and 70 at the start of the race and is medically fit to sail can apply online at:
WWW.OKIEUROPEANCHALLENGE.COM

OKI

YACHT PARTNER
Each individual yacht will have a Yacht Partner who will benefit from high profile exposure during the race. Yacht Partners will be able to name and brand their yacht, benefiting from exposure in media coverage, on the website and be provided with links to their website from the official race website. They will become automatic members of the.....

.....BUSINESS FORUM
This is an alternative tier of sponsorship to becoming a Yacht Partner. The Business Forum is a specially created group of businesses which will bring senior level representatives of companies together to exchange and share information. Business Forum members will benefit from networking events and access to contact details for all other members, branding on a yacht and the opportunity to use the fleet for corporate hospitality or day sails.

OFFICIAL SUPPLIERS
The race will also appoint official suppliers such as the official technical clothing, which will be supplied by Henri-Lloyd. Other opportunities exist for companies that provide relevant services.

RACE CHARITY
Save the Children has been appointed as the official charity for the Oki European Challenge and all monies raised from activities related to the event will be donated to the Charity. Save the Children is the UK's largest independent international children's charity. It has been fighting for children's rights for over 80 years to deliver immediate and lasting improvements to children's lives worldwide.

OKI'S INVOLVEMENT
In the last year, Oki's sales in Western Europe jumped threefold taking it from being the region's sixth largest colour printer manufacturer by market share to being the second biggest. Although in the past Oki had managed its brand at a local market level, now it saw the opportunity to capitalize on this rapid rate of growth by consolidating its European branding.

"We spent the last two years looking at our brand profile throughout Europe where we're represented in 60 different countries," explains Chris Gill, Managing Director, Oki Systems (UK) Ltd. "We had clear criteria for what we wanted from any new European marketing initiative; to unify Oki's European business both internally and from a customer facing perspective and also to build a strong and positive reputation within the European business audience, raising the profile of the brand and generating high visibility."

Sports sponsorship was a clear option, and sailing, which is becoming increasingly popular in Europe with over 30 million Europeans participating in the sport, emerged as a strong contender. Oki approached the sponsorship from a purely business perspective, only taking the title sponsorship of the Oki European Challenge because it was able to tailor the event to fulfill its fundamental criteria. The European business focus of the race was very attractive to Oki and the adaptability of the race structure even allowed Oki to alter the race route to take in it's key European markets.

Once Oki had decided sponsorship was the best way to cultivate its corporate image, its plans were put into action at a pace seldom seen in the sponsorship industry.

"We are incredibly excited about this race" says Andrew Montgomery, Managing Director, Oki Europe. "We are delighted to be working in partnership with so many businesses and believe that the Oki European Challenge 2005 will enable us to become a major European business brand. With both the EU and the appeal of sailing growing, now is the perfect time to invest in this hugely exciting sport."

"We are delighted that Oki has truly embraced the world of sailing" says Michael Kay, Race Organiser.

Further information on the race can be found at
WWW.OKIEUROPEANCHALLENGE.COM

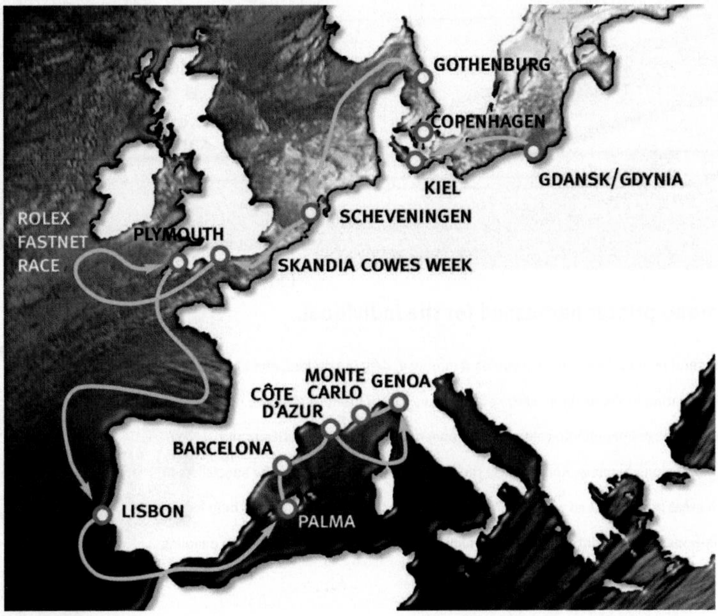
GOTHENBURG
COPENHAGEN
KIEL
GDANSK/GDYNIA
SCHEVENINGEN
ROLEX
FASTNET
RACE
PLYMOUTH
SKANDIA COWES WEEK
MONTE
CARLO
GENOA
CÔTE
D'AZUR
BARCELONA
LISBON
PALMA

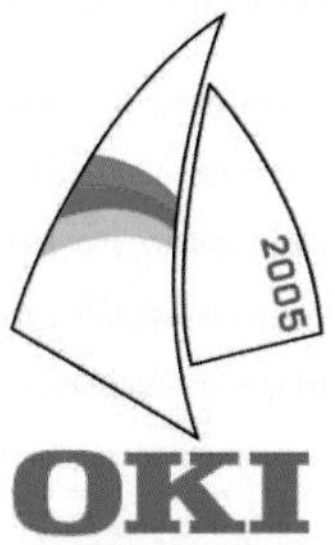
2005
OKI
EUROPEAN CHALLENGE

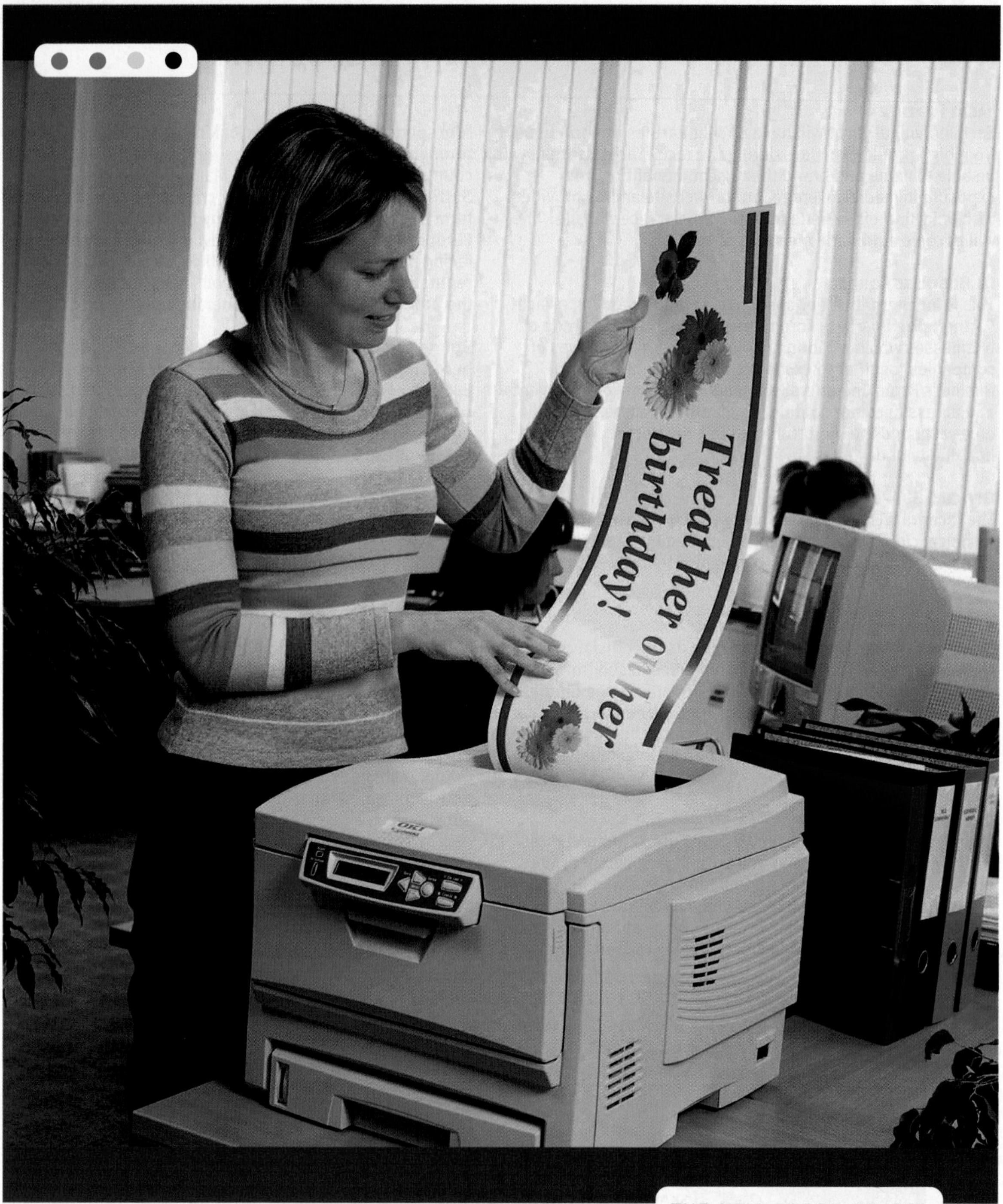
Treat her on her
birthday!

Introduction

Contents

0.0 EDITORIAL

The family of almanacs published by Nautical Data Ltd was acquired by Adlard Coles Nautical in December 2003. Adlard Coles plan to continue and improve the high quality and reliability of the series and to make it even more relevant to a wider range of boaters. To this end, we welcome readers' feedback and opinions. (See section 0.4.)

For the first time we welcome Oki Systems (UK) Ltd as title sponsors for the Almanac series. Oki are specialists in developing, manufacturing and marketing business printing solutions and related support services to business consumers, and they already have a link with sailing through their sponsorship of the Oki European Challenge – the first truly democratic European yacht race. We are delighted to have Oki on board.

For the 2005 edition Peter Lambie has taken over as Co-Editor, bringing with him a wealth of experience in command of Trinity House vessels, High Speed and Ro-Ro ferries, as well as cruising his own boat extensively in UK and European waters. We welcome him to the team.

The 2005 Almanac has been extensively improved and upgraded with the addition of many new chartlets, recommended small craft routes, slipway information, clearer tidal data, many thousands of updates to buoyage and lights, as well as improvements in layout and presentation. We hope these will enable you to gain full enjoyment of your time on the water.

One GPS-related matter deserves a mention: EGNOS (European Geostationary Navigation Overlay Service) due to be operational in June 2004, is a regional improvement to GPS, on a par with the American (WAAS) and Japanese (MSAS) equivalents. Net result: accuracy to within 5 metres. Visit www.esa.int for the latest info.

0.1 A FAMILY OF ALMANACS

0.1.1 The Reeds Oki Nautical Almanac
This Almanac (RONA) contains in one volume all the nautical information needed to navigate the waters around the British Isles and from North Denmark to Gibraltar.

Updates are posted on the website (www.reedsalmanac.co.uk) from Jan-June and an update Supplement is issued in April; see 0.5.2

0.1.2 Reeds Oki Looseleaf Nautical Almanac is a looseleaf version of RONA, with annual update packs. Supplied in a stout binder, information can be added/ removed to suit individual tastes.

0.1.3 Three wire-bound Almanacs in a concise, yet detailed format, provide regional coverage:

Reeds Oki Channel Almanac covers the Isles of Scilly to Dover and Calais to L'Aberwrac'h.

Reeds Oki Western Almanac covers the Western UK and the coasts of Ireland.

Reeds Oki Eastern Almanac covers the Eastern UK and the coast from Kiel Canal to Gravelines.

0.1.4 Reeds PBO Small Craft Almanac is compiled and published by Adlard Coles Nautical in association with *Practical Boat Owner* magazine. It contains all the tidal and navigational information needed to take a boat from Denmark, around the British Isles and down to Gibraltar.

0.2 OTHER REEDS TITLES

Related to the family of Reeds Oki Almanacs and published under the Reeds brand are:

- *Reeds Astro Navigation Tables 2005*. Concise, light and able to lie flat on the chart table, this annual publication contains all the information an ocean-going sailor needs in order to navigate by the sun, moon, planets and stars.

- *Reeds Yacht Buyer's Guide* is a brand new publication providing a complete reference to new and second-hand yachts in the 20-40ft size range. It is ideal for prospective buyers, and will appear in the latter part of 2004.
- Finally, all seafarers will find the *Reeds Skipper's Handbook* an invaluable pocket-sized aide memoire for all those easily forgotten navigational matters which need to be refreshed quickly. Now in its fourth edition, it is the perfect on-board ready reckoner.

Visit www.adlardcoles.com for further details.

0.3 USING THE ALMANAC

0.3.1 Numbering system

The nine chapters are divided into numbered sections, prefaced by the number of the chapter. Thus the sections in Chapter 7, for example, are numbered 7.1, 7.2 etc.

Within each section the key paragraphs are numbered. Thus in section 7.2 (say) the main paragraphs are numbered 7.2.1, 7.2.2, 7.2.3, etc.

Diagrams carry the chapter number and a figure in brackets, ie: Fig. 7 (1), Fig. 7 (2), Fig. 7 (3), etc.

Tables carry the chapter number and a figure in brackets, thus: Table 3 (1), Table 3 (2), etc.

Chapter 9 is divided into 25 geographic areas, each containing harbour, coastal and tidal information.

0.3.2 Contents and Index

The main paragraph headings and page numbers of each section are listed on the contents page at the start of each chapter and geographic area. A full index is at the back of the bound Almanac.

0.3.3 Acknowledgments

The Editors thank the many individuals and official bodies who have kindly provided essential information and advice in the preparation of this Almanac. They include the UK Hydrographic Office, Trinity House, Northern Lighthouse Board, Irish Lights, HM Nautical Almanac Office, HM Stationery Office, HM Customs & Excise, Meteorological Office, British Telecom, BBC and IBA, Maritime and Coastguard Agency, Royal National Lifeboat Institution, Koninklijke Nederlandse Redding Maatschappij (KNRM), Deutsche Gesellschaft zur Rettung Schiffbrüchiger (DgzRS), Port of London Authority, Associated British Ports, countless Harbour Masters and our many individual port agents. Surgeon Cdr H L Proctor RD RNR and Miss F J Proctor RGN BNSt have kindly provided the excellent First Aid section in Chapter 7.

Chartlets, tidal stream diagrams and tidal curves are reproduced from Admiralty Charts and Publications by permission of the UK Hydrographic Office (Licence No HO313/961001/01) and the Controller of HMSO.

Information from the Admiralty List of Lights, Admiralty Sailing Directions, Admiralty Tide Tables, and the Admiralty List of Radio Signals is also reproduced with the permission of the UK Hydrographic Office and the Controller of HMSO.

Acknowledgment is also made to the UK Hydrographic Office for supplying UK and foreign tidal predictions; and to the following foreign authorities for permission to use the tidal predictions stated:

Royal Danish Administration of Navigation and Hydrography, Farvandsvæsnet: Esbjerg.

Bundesamt für Seeschifffahrt und Hydrographie: Helgoland, Wilhelmshaven & Cuxhaven. (Authorisation number BSH 8095.02/99-Z1102.)

Rijkswaterstaat, The Netherlands: Vlissingen and Hoek van Holland.

French Hydrographic and Oceanographic Service (SHOM): Dunkerque, Dieppe, Le Havre, Cherbourg, St Malo, Brest, Pointe de Grave tidal predictions and Brest tidal coefficients. Published under authorisiation no. 81/2004. This copy has not been checked by SHOM.

Marinho Instituto Hidrográfico, Portugal: Lisboa, Authorisation No 3/2004.

The tidal stream diagrams in 9.1.5, and the tidal stream arrows in 9.12.3 & 9.13.3, are printed by kind permission of, respectively, the Royal Cruising Club and the Irish Cruising Club.

Extracts from the following are published by permission of the Controller of HM Stationery Office: *International Code of Signals, 1969*; *Meteorological Office Weather Services for Shipping*.

Phases of the Moon, Eclipse notes and Sun/Moon rising and setting times are derived from the current edition of the Nautical Almanac, and are included by permission of HM Nautical Almanac Office and the Council for the Central Laboratory of the Research Councils.

DISCLAIMER: No National Hydrographic Office has verified the information in this product and none accepts liability for the accuracy of reproduction or any modifications made thereafter. No National Hydrographic Office warrants that this product satisfies national or international regulations regarding the use of the appropriate products for navigation.

Chartlets are only intended for reference and should not be used for navigation. Always consult fully updated navigational charts for the latest information.

0.4 HELP IMPROVE THE ALMANACS

0.4.1 Suggestions for improvements

The Editors always appreciate suggestions for improving the content or layout. Ideas based on experience and practical use afloat are especially valuable. It is not always feasible to implement every suggestion received, but all will be carefully considered; even minor ideas are welcome.

Please write your comments on the Update card, or send them by letter, fax or email direct to:

The Editor, Reeds Oki Nautical Almanac, Adlard Coles Nautical, 37 Soho Square, London W1D 3QZ. Tel: 020 7758 0200 Fax: 020 7758 0222/0333 email: info@reedsalmanac.co.uk.

0.4.2 Notifying errors

Although great care has been taken in compiling the Almanac from countless sources, a few errors may still occur. Please tell the Editors of any such instances.

0.5 CORRECTIONS

0.5.1 Sources of corrections

It is most important that charts and navigational publications – such as this Almanac – are kept up to date. Corrections to Admiralty charts and publications are issued weekly in *Admiralty Notices to Mariners*, obtainable from Admiralty Chart Agents; or they can be viewed at Customs Houses or Mercantile Marine Offices; or downloaded from www.ukho.gov.uk.

This Almanac is corrected to Notices to Mariners, Weekly edition No. 24/2004 dated 10 June 2004.

0.5.2 Updates

Free monthly updates are posted on the website from Jan to June. To register for these FREE, simply complete the online registration form at: www.reedsalmanac.co.uk

Alternatively a printed Update, published in April 2005, containing corrections up to 31 March 2005, can be obtained by returning the enclosed Update card, together with a cheque for £2 for postage and packing (or by sending an A4 sized envelope stamped for 150gms) to:

Adlard Coles Nautical, 37 Soho Square, London W1D 3QZ.

Users are advised to incorporate the corrections as soon as possible, and certainly before using the Almanac for planning or at sea. Data in the Almanac is volatile.

0.5.3 Record of corrections

Tick the box when the relevant corrections have been made. Week 24/2004 is when official corrections were last inserted in the 2005 Almanac.

2004 Weekly Notices to Mariners

25	☐	**32**	☐	**39**	☐	**46**	☐
26	☐	**33**	☐	**40**	☐	**47**	☐
27	☐	**34**	☐	**41**	☐	**48**	☐
28	☐	**35**	☐	**42**	☐	**49**	☐
29	☐	**36**	☐	**43**	☐	**50**	☐
30	☐	**37**	☐	**44**	☐	**51**	☐
31	☐	**38**	☐	**45**	☐	**52**	☐

2005 Weekly Notices to Mariners

1	☐	**14**	☐	**27**	☐	**40**	☐
2	☐	**15**	☐	**28**	☐	**41**	☐
3	☐	**16**	☐	**29**	☐	**42**	☐
4	☐	**17**	☐	**30**	☐	**43**	☐
5	☐	**18**	☐	**31**	☐	**44**	☐
6	☐	**19**	☐	**32**	☐	**45**	☐
7	☐	**20**	☐	**33**	☐	**46**	☐
8	☐	**21**	☐	**34**	☐	**47**	☐
9	☐	**22**	☐	**35**	☐	**48**	☐
10	☐	**23**	☐	**36**	☐	**49**	☐
11	☐	**24**	☐	**37**	☐	**50**	☐
12	☐	**25**	☐	**38**	☐	**51**	☐
13	☐	**26**	☐	**39**	☐	**52**	☐

The logo of the CHART AND NAUTICAL INSTRUMENT TRADE ASSOCIATION, founded in 1918. With the full support of the Hydrographer of the Navy and leading manufacturers of nautical instruments, members of the Association are able to place their experience and service at the disposal of the shipping industry and all navigators

CHART SUPPLY AND CORRECTION SERVICES

The CNITA counts among its members many of the leading Admiralty Chart Agents who can supply your requirements from a single chart or publication to a world-wide outfit and special folio requirements from comprehensive stocks in all the major ports. Carefully trained chart correctors are available to examine and correct all Admiralty charts.

THE CNITA TRACING SERVICE

Although tracings have been in use by the Royal Navy and Admiralty Chart Agents for many years, it was the Chart Committee of the Chart and Nautical Instrument Trade Association that successfully negotiated with the Hydrographer of the Navy for them to become available to the merchant navigator and private user.

The CNITA tracing overlay correction service is available from all Admiralty Chart Agents who are members of the Association, and is now supplied to more than 5,000 vessels each week. Each tracing wallet contains the weekly "Notices to Mariners" and tracings printed with the relevant details of the area surrounding the correction, making the correction of each chart a simpler operation. All that the user has to do is match the tracing to the chart, pierce through the small circle showing the exact position of the correction and, in conjunction with the "Notices to Mariners", transfer the information onto the chart. Navigating Officers welcome the tracings system for its accuracy and speed. Onboard chart correction time can be cut by 80% and Masters can now rest assured that their charts are kept continually up to date. Reasonably priced, these tracings are economical and an invaluable contribution to safety at sea.

COMPASS ADJUSTING AND NAUTICAL INSTRUMENTS

CNITA Members who provide Compass Adjusting services use Compass Adjusters having professional qualifications recognised in the locality in which they operate. The relevant qualification for the United Kingdom is the Certificate of Competency as Compass Adjuster, the examination for which is conducted by the Maritime and Coastguard Agency with the assistance of the CNITA in assessing the evidence of practical adjusting skills submitted by the Candidate. CNITA Members can provide Compass Adjusters, who are available day and night to "swing" ships, in most major ports and elsewhere by arrangement.

Members of the CNITA, many with life long experience in this field, can advise you when buying all your nautical instruments. Most suppliers provide an instrument repair service combining traditional craftsmanship with modern methods to ensure that instruments are serviced and tested to a high standard.

ARE YOU COMPLYING WITH THE LATEST INTERNATIONAL REGULATIONS?

Chart and Nautical Instrument Trade Association members established in most U.K. ports and overseas are able to advise you. For full details of the Association, its activities and its services to the Navigator, write to:- The Secretaries, CHART AND NAUTICAL INSTRUMENT TRADE ASSOCIATION, Dalmore House, 310 St. Vincent Street, Glasgow G2 5QR, United Kingdom, Email: cnita@biggartbaillie.co.uk, Web: www.cnita.com

PORTS WHERE SHIPS' COMPASSES ARE ADJUSTED AND BRITISH ADMIRALTY CHARTS ARE AVAILABLE

HanseNautic, Herrengraben 31, 20459, HAMBURG, Tel: 00 49 40 3748110, Fax: 00 49 40 366400

Brown, Son & Ferguson Ltd, 4-10 Darnley Street, GLASGOW, G41 2SD, Tel: 0141-429 1234, Fax: 0141-420 1694

Carmichael & Clarke Co Ltd, 1202 Unicorn Trade Centre, 131 Des Voeux Road, Central, HONG KONG Tel: 00 852 2581 2678, Fax: 00 852 2582 2722, Email: carmi@hkstar.com

B Cooke & Son Ltd*, Kingston Observatory, 58/59 Market Place, HULL HU1 1RH Tel: 01482 224412/223454, Fax: 01482 219793

D.P.M. Singapore Pte Ltd, 1 Maritime Square #13-03, World Trade Centre, SINGAPORE 099253 Tel: 00 65 2704060, Fax: 00 65 2763858, Email: dpmspore@mbox3.singnet.com.sg

DPM (UK) Ltd, Port of Liverpool Building, 2nd Floor, Pier Head, LIVERPOOL, L3 1BY Tel: 0151 236 2776 Fax: 0151 236 4577, Email: iaca@dpm.co.uk

George Falconer (Nautical) Ltd, 1/Floor, Hong Kong Jewellery Bldg, 178-180 Queen's Road, Central, HONG KONG Tel: 00 852 28542882 Fax: 00 852 28158056

J Garraio & Co Lda, Avenida 24 De Julho, 2-1 D.1200 LISBON, PORTUGAL Tel: 00 3511 3473081, Fax: 00 3511 3428950

Thomas Gunn Navigation Services Ltd*, Anchor House, 62 Regents Quay, ABERDEEN AB11 5AR Tel: 01224 595045, Fax: 01224 584702, Email: tgns@globalnet.co.uk, www.thomasgunn.globalnet.co.uk

Kelvin Hughes Charts & Maritime Supplies*, New North Road, Hainault, ILFORD, Essex IG6 2UR Tel: 0208 500 1020 Fax: 0208 559 8535

Captain L N Jordanov, 13-A Han Omurtag Str., P.O.B. 14, VARNA 9001, BULGARIA Tel: 00 359 52 242018 Fax: 00 359 52 242018

John Lilley & Gillie Ltd* Clive Street NORTH SHEILDS, Tyne & Wear NE29 6LF Tel: 0191 257 2217, Fax: 0191-257 1521, Email: sales@lilleyandgillie.co.uk

"Magnetico" D.A. Dedegikas 100 Colocotroni Str. PIRAEUS 185 35, GREECE Tel: 00 30 1 4178976, Fax: 00 30 1 4178206

Marine Instruments* The Wheelhouse, Upton Slip, FALMOUTH, Cornwall TR11 3DQ Tel: 01326 312414, Fax: 01326 211414, Email: info@marineinstruments.co.uk

Maritime Services, 3440 Bridgeway Street, VANCOUVER, BC V5K 1B6, CANADA Tel: 00 1 604 294444, Fax: 00 1 604 2945879

Bogerd-Martin NV, Oude Leeuwenrui 37, ANTWERP 2000, BELGIUM Tel: 00 32 3 2134170, Fax: 00 32 3 2326167 Email: sales@martin.be

Maryland Nautical Sales, Inc, 1400 E. Clement Street, BALTIMORE, Maryland 21230, USA, Tel: 00 1 410 752 4268, Fax: 00 1 410 685 5068, Email: sales@mdnautical.com, www.mdnautical.com

Motion Smith 78 Shenton Way #01-03, SINGAPORE 079120 Tel: 00 65 2205098 Fax: 00 65 2254902

Nautisk Forlag A/S, Dronningensgate 8B, PO Box 68 Sentrum, N-0101 OSLO, NORWAY Tel: 00 47 2200 1281, Fax: 00 47 2200 1280, Email: sales@nautisk.com, http: www.nautisk.com

Captain Stephan Nedelchev Soc. Co. Cerro Largo 920, MONTEVIDEO, URUGUAY Tel: 00 5982 9167988 Fax: 00 5982 9167990

W F Price & Co Ltd Wapping Wharf, BRISTOL BS1 6UD Tel: 0117 9292229, Fax: 0117 9304403

Riviera-Charts Galerie du Port, 26-30 Rue Lacan, 06600 ANTIBES, France Tel: 00 33 493 344566, Fax: 00 33 493 344336, Email admiralty@riviera.fr, www.riviera-charts.com

Seath Instruments (1992) Ltd* Unit 30, Colville Rd Works, Colville Road, LOWESTOFT, Suffolk NR33 9QS Tel: 01502 573811, Fax: 01502 514173

Small Craft Deliveries Ltd Navigation House, 4 Wilford Bridge Road, MELTON, Woodbridge IP12 1RJ Tel: 01394 382600, Fax: 01394 387672, Telex: 51 317210, Email: sales@scd-charts.co.uk

A M Smith (Marine) Ltd 33 Epping Way, Chingford, LONDON E4 7PB Tel: 0208-529 6988 Fax: 0208-524 4498

Chien Hong Inteligence Inc. Company Ltd, 198-1 Ta Tong 1st Road, Kaohsiung 800, TAIWAN, R.O.C. Tel: 00 86 7 2217367, Fax: 00 86 7 2818180, Email: taisengt@ms22.hinet.net

The Tyneside Shop 5 John Ross House, 22 Victoria Embankment, DURBAN 4001, SOUTH AFRICA Tel: 00 27 31 3377005, Fax: 00 27 31 3328139, Email: tyneside@global.co.za

Todd Chart Agency Ltd Navigation House, 85 High Street, BANGOR, Northern Ireland BT20 5BD Tel: 028 9146 6640, Fax: 028 9147 1070, Email: admiralty@toddchart.co.uk, www.toddchart.com

G Undery & Son* PO Box 235 - Unit 31, The New Harbours, GIBRALTAR Tel: 00 350 40402 (B), 00 350 73107, Fax: 00 350 46489

Vanos S.A. 90 Dim. Moutsopoulou Str., 184 41 PIRAEUS, GREECE Tel: 00 30 1 4829911, Fax: 00 30 1 4812313/4817607

Iver C Weilbach & Co A/S, 35 Toldbodgade, Postbox 1560, DK-1253, COPENHAGEN K, DENMARK Tel: 00 45 33 135927, Fax: 00 45 33 935927

Those marked * have U.K. Maritime, & Coastguard Agency certificated, Compass Adjusters

2005/NM2/ed

Chapter 1

Reference data

C1

Contents

1.1 ABBREVIATIONS & SYMBOLS

The following abbreviations & symbols feature in Reeds Almanacs and in some Admiralty charts and publications. See also Chapter 5, page 106. The quaintly named Chart 5011 (it is a booklet) is the ultimate authority on Symbols & Abbreviations.

AB	Alongside berth
ABP	Associated British Ports
AC,	Shore power (electrical)
AC, ACA	Admiralty Chart, AC Agent
Aff Mar	Affaires Maritimes
aka	Also known as
ALL	Admiralty List of Lights
ALRS	Admiralty List of Radio Signals
Al	Alternating light
AM	Amplitude Modulation
ANWB	Dutch Tourist Association of Road & Waterway Users
ARCC	Aeronautical Rescue Co-ordination Centre
ATM	Automatic telling machine, cashpoint
ATT	Admiralty Tide Tables
ATT	Atterisage (landfall/SWM) buoy
Auto	Météo Répondeur Automatique
B.	Bay, Black
Bar,	Licensed bar
BH	Boat Hoist (tons)
bk	Broken
Bkwtr	Breakwater
BMS	Bulletin Météorologique Spécial (Strong wind/Gale warning)
Bn, bcn(s)	Beacon, beacon(s)
BSH	German Hydrographic Office/chart(s)
BST	British Summer Time
Bu	Blue
BWB	British Waterways Board
By(s)	Buoy, buoys
BY,	Boatyard
C.	Cape, Cabo, Cap
C	Crane (tons)
c	Coarse (sand)
ca	Cable (length 185m)
Cas	Castle
CD	Chart datum
CEVNI	Code Européen de Voies de la Navigation Intérieure (inland system)
cf	Compare (cross-reference)
CG	Coastguard
CH,	Chandlery
chan.	Channel (navigational)
Ch	Channel (VHF)
Ch, ✠	Church
Chy	Chimney
Col	Column, pillar, obelisk
Corr	Correction
CROSS	Centre Régional Opérationnel de Surveillance et Sauvetage (= MRCC)
CRS	Coast Radio Station
Cup	Cupola
Cy	Clay
D	Diesel fuel (by hose)
Dec	Declination
dest	Destroyed
DG	De-gaussing (range)
DGPS	Differential GPS
Dia	Diaphone (fog signal)
Dir Lt	Directional light
discont	Discontinued
DLR	Dockland Light Railway
dm	Decimetre(s)
Dn(s)	Dolphin(s)
DR	Dead Reckoning
DSC	Digital Selective Calling
DST	Daylight Saving Time
DW	Deep Water (route)
DYC	Dutch Yacht Chart(s)
DZ	Danger Zone (buoy)

E	East
EC	Early closing
ECM	East cardinal mark (buoy/beacon)
ECM	Éditions Cartographiques Maritimes
ED	Existence doubtful, European Datum
El	Electrical repairs
Elev	Elevation
Ent.	Entrance
EP	Estimated position
ETA	Estimated Time of Arrival
ETD	Estimated Time of Departure
F	Fixed light
f	Fine (eg sand)
F&A	Fore and aft, (berth/mooring)
Fcst	Forecast
FFL	Fixed and Flashing light
Fl	Flashing light
FM	Frequency Modulation
Fog Det lt	Fog Detector light
Freq, Fx	Frequency
FS	Flagstaff, Flagpole
ft	Foot, feet
Ft	Fort
FV	Fishing vessel
FW, t	Fresh water supply
G	Gravel, Green
Gas	Calor Gas
Gaz	Camping Gaz
GC	Great-circle
GDOP	Geometrical Dilution of Precision
GHA	Greenwich Hour Angle
GMDSS	Global Maritime Distress and Safety System
grt	Gross Registered Tonnage
Gy	Grey
H, Hrs, h	Hour(s)
H–, H+	Minutes before/after the hour
H24	Continuous
HAT	Highest Astronomical Tide
HF	High Frequency
HFP	High Focal Plane buoy
HIE	Highlands & Islands Enterprise
HJ	Day Service only, Sunrise to Sunset
HM	Harbour Master
HMC	HM Customs
HMSO	Her Majesty's Stationery Office
HN	Night Service only, Sunset to Sunrise
HO	Office hours, Hydrographic Office
(hor)	Horizontally disposed
HT	High Tension (overhead electricity line)
HW	High Water
HX	No fixed hrs
IALA	International Association of Lighthouse Authorities
iaw	In accordance with
IDM	Isolated Danger Mark (buoy/beacon)
IHO	International Hydrographic Organisation
IMO	International Maritime Organisation
INMARSAT	International Maritime Satellite Organisation
intens	Intensified
IPTS	International Port Traffic Signals
IQ	Interrupted quick flashing light
IRPCS	International Regulations for the Prevention of Collision at Sea
Is, I	Island, islet
ISAF	International Sailing Federation
Iso	Isophase light
ITU	International Telecommunications Union
ITZ	Inshore Traffic Zone (TSS)
IUQ	Interrupted ultra quick flashing light
IVQ	Interrupted very quick flashing light
kn	knot(s)
Kos	Kosangas
kW	Kilowatts
L	Lake, Loch, Lough, Landing place
Lat	Latitude
LAT	Lowest Astronomical Tide
Lanby, q	Large Automatic Navigational buoy
LB, °	Lifeboat, inshore lifeboat
Ldg	Leading (light)
L Fl	Long flash
LH	Left hand
LNTM	Local Notice To Mariners
LOA	Length overall
Long	Longitude
LPG	Liquefied Petroleum Gas
LT	Local time
Lt(s), ☆ ⋆	Light(s)
Lt F, q	Light float
Lt V, ⛴	Light vessel
M	Moorings, Sea mile(s), Mud
m	Metre(s)
Mag	Magnetic, magnitude (of Star)
MCA	Maritime and Coastguard Agency
ME	Marine engineering repairs
Météo	Météorologie/Weather
MHWN	Mean High Water Neaps
MHWS	Mean High Water Springs
MHz	Megahertz
ML	Mean Level (tidal)
MLWN	Mean Low Water Neaps
MLWS	Mean Low Water Springs
MMSI	Maritime Mobile Service Identity
Mo	Morse
Mon	Monument, Monday
MRCC	Maritime Rescue Co-ordination Centre
MRSC	Maritime Rescue Sub-Centre
MSI	Marine Safety Information

N	North
NB	Nota Bene, Notice Board
NCI	National Coastwatch Institution
NCM	North Cardinal Mark (buoy/beacon)
NGS	Naval Gunfire Support (buoy)
NM	Notice(s) to Mariners
np	Neap tides
NP	Naval Publication (plus number)
NRT	Net registered tonnage
NT	NationalTrust (land/property)
Obscd	Obscured
Obstn	Obstruction
Oc	Occulting light
ODAS	Ocean Data Acquisition System
Or	Orange
OT	Other times
P	Petrol supply (by hose), Pebbles
(P)	Preliminary (NM)
PA	Position approximate
PC	Portuguese chart
PD	Position doubtful
PHM	Port-hand Mark (buoy/beacon)
PLA	Port of London Authority
PO, Y	Post Office
Prog	Prognosis (weather charts)
prom	Prominent
Pt(e).	Point(e)
Pta	Punta (point)
Q	Quick flashing light
QHM	Queen's Harbour Master
R	Red, Restaurant, River, Rock
Racon	RadarTransponder Beacon
Ramark	Radar Beacon
RCC	Rescue Co-ordination Centre
RG	Emergency RDF Station
RH	Right hand
Rk, Rky	Rock, Rocky
RNLI	Royal National Lifeboat Institution
Ro-Ro	Roll-on Roll-off (ferry terminal)
R/T	Radiotelephony
Ru	Ruins
S	South, Sand
S, St, Ste	Saint(s)
SAR	Search and Rescue
SBM	Single buoy mooring
SC	Sailing Club, Spanish chart
SCM	South Cardinal Mark (buoy/beacon)
SD	Sailing Directions, Semi-Diameter
SD	Sounding of doubtful depth
sf	Stiff
Sh	Shells, Shoal
SHM	Starboard-hand Mark (buoy/beacon), Simplified Harmonic Method (tides)
SHOM	French Hydrographic Office/Chart
Si	Silt
SIGNI	Signalisation de Navigation Intérieure (Dutch inland buoyage system)
SM	Sailmaker
X	Shipwright (esp wooden hulls)
SMS	Short Message Service (mobile text)
SNSM	Société Nationale de Sauvetage en Mer (French lifeboat service)
so	Soft (eg mud)
SOLAS	Safety of Life at Sea (IMO Convention)
Sp	Spire
sp	Spring tides
SPM	Special Mark (buoy/beacon)
SR	Sunrise
SS	Sunset, Signal Station
SSB	Single Sideband (Radio)
St	Stones
Stbd	Starboard
subm	Submerged
SWM	SafeWater Mark (buoy/beacon)
sy	Sticky (eg mud)
(T), (Temp)	Temporary
tbc	To be confirmed
tbn	To be notified
TD	Temp Discontinued (fog signal)
TE	Temp Extinguished (light)
tfn	Till further notice (cf ufn)
Tr, twr	Tower
TSS	Traffic Separation Scheme
£	In transit with, ie ldg marks/lts
ufn	Until further notice
uncov	Uncovers
UQ	Ultra Quick flashing light
UT	UniversalTime
Var	Variation (magnetic)
Vel	Velocity
(vert)	Vertically disposed
Vi	Violet
vis	Visibility, visible
VLCC	Very large crude carrier
VNF	Voie Navigable de France (canals)
VQ	Very Quick flashing light
VTS	Vessel Traffic Service
W	West, White
WCM	West Cardinal Mark (buoy/beacon)
Wd	Weed
wef	With effect from
WGS	World Geodetic System (GPS datum)
WIP	Work in progress
Wk, ⊥ ⊕	Wreck
WMO	World Meteorological Organisation
WPT, K	Waypoint
Wx	Weather
Y	Yellow, Amber, Orange
YC, B	Yacht Club

1.2 LANGUAGE GLOSSARIES

English	German	French	Spanish	Dutch
ASHORE				
Ashore	An Land	A terre	A tierra	Aan land
Airport	Flughafen	Aéroport	Aeropuerto	Vliegveld
Bank	Bank	Banque	Banco	Bank
Boathoist	Bootskran	Travelift	Travelift	Botenlift
Boatyard	Bootswerft	Chantier naval	Astilleros	Jachtwerf
Bureau de change	Wechselstelle	Bureau de change	Cambio	Geldwisselkantoor
Bus	Bus	Autobus	Autobús	Bus
Chandlery	Yachtausrüster	Shipchandler	Efectos navales	Scheepswinkel
Chemist	Apotheke	Pharmacie	Farmacia	Apotheek
Dentist	Zahnarzt	Dentiste	Dentista	Tandarts
Doctor	Arzt	Médecin	Médico	Dokter
Engineer	Motorenservice	Mécanicien	Mecánico	Monteur
Ferry	Fähre	Ferry/transbordeur	Ferry	Veer/Pont
Garage	Autowerkstatt	Station service	Garage	Garage
Harbour	Hafen	Port	Puerto	Haven
Hospital	Krankenhaus	Hôpital	Hospital	Ziekenhuis
Mast crane	Mastenkran	Grue	Grúa	Mastenkraan
Post office	Postamt	Bureau de poste/PTT	Correos	Postkantoor
Railway station	Bahnhof	Gare de chemin de fer	Estación de ferrocanil	Station
Sailmaker	Segelmacher	Voilier	Velero	Zeilmaker
Shops	Geschäfte	Boutiques	Tiendas	Winkels
Slip	Slip	Cale	Varadero	Helling
Supermarket	Supermarkt	Supermarché	Supermercado	Supermarkt
Taxi	Taxi	Taxi	Taxis	Taxi
Village	Ort	Village	Pueblo	Dorp
Yacht club	Yachtclub	Club nautique	Club náutico	Jachtclub
ENGINE AND MACHINERY				
Air filter	Luftfilter	Filtre à air	Filtro a aire	Luchtfilter
Battery	Batterie	Batterie/accumulateur	Baterías	Accu
Bilge pump	Bilgepumpe	Pompe de cale	Bomba de achique	Bilgepomp
Carburettor	Vergaser	Carburateur	Carburador	Carburateur
Charging	Laden	Charger	Cargador	Opladen
Compression	Kompression	Compression	Compresión	Compressie
Cooling water	Kühlwasser	Eau de refroidissement	Agua refrigerado	Koelwater
Diesel	Diesel	Gazole	Gas-oil	Dieselolie
Diesel engine	Dieselmotor	Moteur diésel	Motor a gas-oil	Dieselmotor
Dynamo	Lichtmaschine	Alternateur	Alternador	Dynamo
Electrical wiring	Elektrik	Réseau électrique	Circuito eléctrico	Elektrische bedrading
Engine mount	Motorenfundament	Support moteur	Bancada del motor	Motorsteun
Engine oil	Maschinenöl	Huile de moteur	Aceite motor	Motorolie
Exhaust pipe	Auspuff	Tuyau d'échappement	Tubos de escape	Uitlaat
Fuel filter	Kraftstoffilter	Filtre de fuel	Filtro de combustible	Brandstoffilter
Fuel tank	Tank, Kraftstofftank	Réservoir à fuel	Tanque de Combustible	Brandstof tank
Fuse	Sicherung	Fusible	Fusible	Zekering
Gearbox	Getriebe	Transmission	Transmisión	Keerkoppeling
Generator	Generator	Groupe électrogène	Generador	Generator
Grease	Fett	Graisse	Grasa	Vet
Head gasket	Zylinderkopfdichtung	Joint de culasse	Junta de culata	Koppakking
Holding tank	Schmutzwassertank	Réservoir à eaux usées	Tanque aguas negras	Vuilwatertank
Inboard engine	Einbaumotor	Moteur in-bord	Motor intraborda	Binnenboordmotor
Injectors	Einspritzdüsen	Injecteurs	Inyectores	Injectoren
Main engine	Hauptmaschine	Moteur principal	Motor	Hoofdmotor
Outboard engine	Außenborder	Moteur hors-bord	Motor fuera borda	Buitenboordmotor
Petrol	Benzin	Essence	Gasolina	Benzine
Petrol engine	Benzinmotor	Moteur à essence	Motor a gasolina	Benzinemotor
Propeller	Propeller	Hélice	Hélice	Schroef
Propeller bracket	Propeller-Halterung	Chaise	Arbotante	Schroefsteun

English	German	French	Spanish	Dutch
Regulator	Regler	Régulateur de charge	Regulador	Regulateur
Shaft	Welle	Arbre d'hélice	Eje	As
Spark plug	Zündkerze	Bougie	Bujia	Bougie
Starter	Starter	Démarreur	Arranque	Startmotor
Stern gland	Stopfbuchse	Presse étoupe	Bocina	Schroefasdoorvoer
Throttle	Gas	Accélérateur	Acelerador	Gashendel
Water tank	Wassertank	Réservoir à eau	Tanque de agua	Watertank
Water pump	Wasserpumpe	Pompe à eau	Bomba de agua	Waterpomp

GENERAL YACHTING TERMS

One	Ein	Un	Uno	Een
Two	Zwei	Deux	Duo	Twee
Three	Drei	Trois	Tres	Drie
Four	Vier	Quatre	Cuatro	Vier
Five	Fünf	Cinq	Cinco	Vijf
Six	Sechs	Six	Seis	Zes
Seven	Sieben	Sept	Siete	Zeven
Eight	Acht	Huit	Ocho	Acht
Nine	Neun	Neuf	Nueve	Negen
Ten	Zehn	Dix	Diez	Tien
Aft	Achtern, achteraus	En arriere	Atrás	Achter; achteruit
Ahead	Voraus	Par l'avant	Avante	Vooruit
Anchor	Anker	Ancre	Ancia	Anker
Anchor chain	Ankerkette	Chaîne d'ancre	Cadena	Ankerketting
Anchor warp	Ankerleine	Orin	Cabo	Ankerlijn
Anchor winch	Ankerwinsch	Guindeau	Molinete	Ankerlier
Astern	achtern	Par L'arrière	Hacia atrás	Achteruit, slaan
Babystay	Babystag	Babystay	Babystay	Baby stag
Backstay	Achterstag	Pataras	Estay de popa	Achterstag
Beating	Kreuzen	Louvoyer	Ciñendo a rabier	Kruisen
Bilge	Bilge	Galbord	Sentina	Bilge
Bilge keel	Kimmkiel	Bi-quilles	Quillas de balance	Kimkiel
Block	Block	Poulie	Motón	Blok
Boat	Boot	Bateau	Barco	Boot
Boom	Baum	Bôme	Botavara	Giek
Bow	Bug	Etrave	Proa	Boeg
Bridgedeck	Brückendeck	Bridgedeck	Bridgedeck	Brugdek
Cabin	Kajüte	Cabine	Cabina	Kajuit
Cap shrouds	Oberwanten	Gal haubans	Obenques altos	Hoofdwanten
Centreboard	Schwert	Dérive	Orza	Midzwaard
Cockpit	Cockpit	Cockpit	Bañera	Cockpit
Companionway	Niedergang	Descente	Entrada cámera	Opgang
Cruising chute	Cruising chute	Spi asymétrique	MPS	Halfwinder
Cutter stay	Kutterstag	Etai intermédiaire	Estay de tringqueta	Kotterstag
Deck	Deck	Pont	Cubierta	Dek
Dinghy	Jolle	Annexe	Chinchorro	Bijboot
Fender	Fender	Défense	Defensa	Stootwil
Ferry	Fähre	Ferry	Ferry	Veerboot
Fin keel	Kurzkiel	Quille courte	Quilla de aleta	Finkieler
Foresail	Vorsegel	Voile avant/foc	Foque	Kluiver
Forestay	Vorstag	Etai	Estay	Voorstag
Genoa	Genua	Génois	Génova	Genua
Halyard	Fall	Drisse	Driza	Val
Hull	Rumpf	Coque	Carena	Romp
Inflatable	Schlauchboot	Gonflable	Bote Hinchable	Opblaasbare boot
Jumper	Jumpstag	Guignol	Violín	Diamanstag
Keel	Kiel	Quille	Quilla	Kiel
Long keel	Langkiel	Quille longue	Quilla corrida	Langkieler
Lower shrouds	Unterwanten	Bas haubans	Obenques bajos	Onderwanten
Mainsail	Großsegel	Grand' voile	Mayor	Grootzeil
Mast	Mast	Mât	Mast	Mast

English	German	French	Spanish	Dutch
Mizzen	Besan	Artimon	Mesana	Bezaan
Motoring	Motoren	Naviguer au moteur	Navegar a motor	Op de motor
Navigate	Navigieren	Naviguer	Navegar	Navigeren
Port	Backbord	Bâbord	Babor	Bakboord
Pulpit	Bugkorb	Balcon avant	Púlpito	Preekstoel
Pushpit	Heckkorb	Balcon arrière	Balcón de popa	Hekrailing
Railing	Reling	Rambarde	Guardamencebos	Railing
Reaching	Raumschodts	Au portant	Viento a través	Ruime wind
Rigging	Rigg	Gréement	Jarcia	Tuigage
Rope	Tauwerk	Cordage	Cabo	Touw
Rudder	Ruder	Safran/gouvernail	Pala deTimón	Roer
Running	Vorm Wind	Vent arrière	Viento a favor	Voor de wind
Running backstay	Backstag	Bastaque	Burde volanto	Bakstag
Sail batten	Segellatte	Latte	Sables	Zeillat
Sailing	Segeln	Naviguer à la voile	Navegar a velas	Zeilen
Shackle	Schäkel	Manille	Grillete	Sluiting
Sheet	Schoot	Ecoute	Escota	Schoot
Ship	Schiff	Navire	Buque	Schip
Shrouds	Wanten	Haubans	Obenques	Wanten
Spinnaker	Spinnaker	Spi	Spi	Spinnaker
Spinnaker boom	Spinnakerbaum	Tangon de spi	Tangon	Spinnaker boom
Spreader	Oberwantspreiz	Barre de Flèche	encapilladura	Zaling
Stanchion	Seerelingsstütze	Chandelier	Candelero	Scepter
Starboard	Steuerbord	Tribord	Estribor	Stuurboord
Staysail	Stagsegel	Trinquette	Trinquete	Stagzeil
Steamer	Dampfer	Vapeur	Buque de vapor	Stoomschip
Stern	Heck	Arrière	Popa	Spiegel
Storm jib	Sturmfock	Tourmentin	Tormentin	Stormfok
Storm trysail	Trysegel	Voile de cape	Vela de capa	Trysail
Superstructure	Aufbau	Superstructure	Superestructura	Opbouw
Tender	Beiboot	Annexe	Anexo (bote)	Bijboot
Tiller	Pinne	Barre franche	Caña	Helmstok
Toe rail	Fußleiste	Rail de fargue	Regala	Voetrail
Topsides	Rumpfseiten	Oeuvres mortes	Obra muerta	Vrijboord
Underwater hull	Unterwasserschiff	Oeuvres vives	Obra viva	Onderwaterschip
Upwind	Am Wind	Au vent	Vienta en contra	Aan de wind
Wheel	Rad	Barre à roue	Rueda	Stuurwiel
Winch	Winsch	Winch	Winche	Lier
Working jib	Arbeitsfock	Foc de route	Foque	Werkfok
Yacht	Yacht	Yacht	Yate	Jacht

NAVIGATION

Abeam	Querab	Par le travers	Por el través	Dwarsscheeps
Ahead	Voraus	Par l'avant	Avante	Voor
Astern	Achteraus	Par l'arrière	Atrás	Achter
Bearing	Peilung	Relèvement	Maración	Peiling
Buoy	Tonne	Bouée	Boya	Boei/ton
Binoculars	Fernglas	Jumelles	Prismáticos	Verrekijker
Channel	Kanal	Chenal	Canal	Kanaal/geul
Chart	Seekarte	Carte	Carta náutica	Zeekaart
Compass	Kompass	Compas	Compás	Kompas
Compass course	Kompass Kurs	Cap du compas	Rumbo de aguja	Kompaskoers
Current	Strömung	Courant	Coriente	Stroom
Dead reckoning	Koppelnavigation	Estime	Estimación	Gegist bestek
Degree	Grad	Degré	Grado	Graad
Deviation	Deviation	Déviation	Desvio	Deviatie
Distance	Entfernung	Distance	Distancia	Afstand, verheid
Downstream	Flußabwärts	En aval	Río abajo	Stroomafwaarts
East	Ost	Est	Este	Oost
Ebb	Ebbe	Jusant	Marea menguante	Eb
Echosounder	Echolot	Sondeur	Sonda	Dieptemeter

English	German	French	Spanish	Dutch
Estimated position	Gegißte Position	Point estimé	Posición estimado	Gegiste positie
Fathom	Faden	Une brasse	Braza	Vadem
Feet	Fuß	Pieds	Pie	Voet
Flood	Flut	Flot	Flujo de marea	Vloed
GPS	GPS	GPS	GPS	GPS
Handbearing compass	Handpeilkompass	Compas de relèvement	Compás de marcaciones	Handpeil kompas
Harbour guide	Hafenhandbuch	Guide du port	Guia del Puerto	Havengids
High water	Hochwasser	Pleine mer	Altamer	Hoog water
Latitude	Geographische Breite		Latitude	Latitud Breedte
Leading lights	Feuer in Linie	Alignement	Luz de enfilación	Geleidelichten
Leeway	Abdrift	Dérive	Hacia sotavento	Drift
Lighthouse	Leuchtturm	Phare	Faro	Vuurtoren
List of lights	LeuchtfeuerVerzeichnis	Liste des feux	Listude de Luces	Lichtenlijst
Log	Logge	Loch	Corredera	Log
Longitude	Geographische Länge	Longitude	Longitud	Lengte
Low water	Niedrigwasser	Basse mer	Bajamar	Laagwater
Metre	Meter	Mètre	Metro	Meter
Minute	Minute	Minute	Minuto	Minuut
Nautical almanac	Nautischer Almanach	Almanach nautique	Almanaque náutico	Nautische almanak
Nautical mile	Seemeile	Mille nautique	Milla marina	Zeemijl
Neap tide	Nipptide	Morte-eau	Marea muerta	Doodtij
North	Nord	Nord	Norte	Noord
Pilot	Lotse	Pilote	Práctico	Loods/Gids
Pilotage book	Handbuch	Instructions nautiques	Derrotero	Vaarwijzer
RDF	Funkpeiler	Radio gonio	Radio-gonió	Radiorichtingzoeker
Radar	Radar	Radar	Radar	Radar
Radio receiver	Radio, Empfänger	Récepteur radio	Receptor de radio	Radioontvanger
Radio transmitter	Sender	Emetteur radio	Radio-transmisor	Radiozender
River outlet	Flußmündung	Embouchure	Embocadura	Riviermond
South	Süd	Sud	Sud, Sur	Zuid
Spring tide	Spring tide	Vive-eau	Marea viva	Springtij/springvloed
Tide	Tide, Gezeit	Marée	Marea	Getijde
Tide tables	Tidenkalender	Annuaire des marées	Anuario de mareas	Getijdetafel
True course	Wahrer Kurs	Cap vrai	Rumbo	Ware Koers
Upstream	Flußaufwärts	En amont	Río arriba	Stroomopwaarts
VHF	UKW	VHF	VHF	Marifoon
Variation	Variation	Déclinaison magnétique		Variación Variatie
Waypoint	Wegpunkt	Point de rapport	Waypoint	Waypoint/Route punt
West	West	Ouest	Oeste	West
OFFICIALDOM				
Certificate of registry	Schiffszertifikat	Acte de francisation	Documentos de matrícuia	Zeebrief
Check in	Einklarieren	Enregistrement	Registrar	Check-in
Customs	Zoll	Douanes	Aduana	Douane
Declare	Verzollen	Déclarer	Declarar	Aangeven
Harbour master	Hafenmeister	Capitaine du port	Capitán del puerto	Haven Kantor
Insurance	Versicherung	Assurance	Seguro	Verzekering
Insurance certificate	Versicherungspolice	Certificat d'assurance	Certificado deseguro	Verzekeringsbewijs
Passport	Paß	Passeport	Pasaporte	Paspoort
Police	Polizei	Police	Policía	Politie
Pratique	Verkehrserlaubnis	Pratique	Prático	Verlof tot ontscheping
Register	Register	Liste de passagers	Lista de tripulantes/rol	Register
Ship's log	Logbuch	Livre de bord	Cuaderno de bitácora	Logboek
Ship's papers	Schiffspapiere	Papiers de bateau	Documentos del barco	Scheepspapieren
Surveyor	Gutachter	Expert maritime	Inspector	Opzichter, expert
SAFETY/DISTRESS				
Assistance	Hilfeleistung	Assistance	Asistencia	Assistentie
Bandage	Verband	Pansement	Vendas	Verband
Burns	Verbrennung	Brûlures	Quemadura	Brandwonden
Capsize	Kentern	Sancir, chavirer	Volcó	Omslaan
Coastguard	Küstenwache	Garde de côte	Guarda costas	Kustwacht

English	German	French	Spanish	Dutch
Dismasted	Mastbruch	Démâté	Desarbolar	Mastbreuk
Distress	Seenot	Détresse	Pena	Nood
Distress flares	Signalraketen	Fusées de détresse	Bengalas	Noodvuurwerk
Doctor	Doktor	Médecin	Médico	Dokter/Arts
EPIRB	EPIRB	Balise de détresse	Baliza	EPIRB
Emergency	Notfall	Urgence	Emergencias	Noodgeval
Exhaustion	Erschöpfung	Epuisement	Agotamiento	Uitputting
Fever	Fieber	Fièvre	Fiebre	Koorts
Fire extinguisher	Feuerlöscher	Extincteur	Extintor	Brandblusser
First aid	Erste Hilfe	Premier secours	Primeros auxillos	Eerste hulp
Fracture	Fraktur	Cassure	Fractura	Breuk
Grounded	Aufgelaufen	Echoué	Encallado	Vastgelopen
Harness	Lifebelt	Harnais	Arnés de seguridad	Harnas
Headache	Kopfschmerz	Mal à la tête	Dolor de cabeza	Hoofdpijn
Heart attack	Herzanfall	Crise cardiaque	Ataque corazón	Hartaanval
Helicopter	Hubschrauber	Hélicoptère	Helicóptero	Helikopter
Hospital	Krankenhaus	Hôpital	Hospital	Ziekenhuis
Illness	Krankheit, Übelkeit	Maladie	Enfermo	Ziekte
Injury	Verletzung	Blessure	Lesión	Verwonding
Jackstay	Strecktau	Contre-étai	Violín	Veiligheidstag
Lifeboat	Rettungsboot	Canot de sauvetage	Lancha de salvamento	Reddingsboot
Liferaft	Rettungsinsel	Radeau de sauvetage	Balsa salvavidas	Reddingsvlot
Lifejacket	Schwimmweste	Gilet de sauvetage	Chaleco salvavidas	Reddingsvest
Man overboard	Mann über Bord	Homme à la mer	Hombre al agua	Man over boord
Pulse	Puls	Pouls	Pulso	Hartslag
Rest	Ruhen	Repos	Reposo	Rust
Seacock	Seeventil	Vanne	Grifos de fondo	Afsluiter
Seasickness	Seekrankheit	Mal de mer	Mareo	Zeeziekte
Seaworthy	Seetüchtig	Marin	Marinero	Zeewaardig
Shock	Schock	Choc	Choque	Shock
Sinking	Sinken	En train de couler	Hundiendo	Zinken
Sleep	Schlaf	Sommeil	Sueño	Slaap
Tow line	Schleppleine	Filin de remorque	Cabo	Sleeplijn
Unconscious	Bewußtlos	Inconscient	Inconsciente	Buiten bewustzijn
Wound	Wunde	Blessure	Herida	Wond
HARBOURS				
Anchoring	Ankern	Mouiller l'ancre	Fondear	Ankeren
Breakwater	Außenmole	Brise-lame	Escolera	Pier
Cable	Kabel	Encablure	Cadena	Kabel
Catwalk	Schlengel	Passerelle	Pasarela	Loopplank
Commercial port	Handelshafen	Port de commerce	Puerto comercial	Commerciele haven
Customs office	Zollamt	Bureau de douane	Aduanas	Douanekantoor
Depth	Wassertiefe	Profondeur	Profundidad	Diepte
Dries	Trockenfallend	Estran	Descubierto	Droogvallend
Drying port	Trockenfallender Hafen	Port d'échouage	Puerto secarse	Droogvallende haven
Ferry terminal	Fährterminal	Gare maritime	Terminal marítmo	Veersteiger
Firing range	Schießgebiet	Zone de tir	Zona de tiro	Schietoefeningen
Fishing harbour	Fischereihafen	Port de pêche	Puerto de pesca	Vissershaven
Foul ground	unreiner Grund	Fond malsain	Fondo sucio	Slechte grond
Visitors' berths	Gastliegeplätze	Place visiteurs	Amarradero visitantes	Gastenplaatsen
Harbour entrance	Hafeneinfahrt	Entrée du port	Entradas	Haveningang
Harbourmaster's office	Hafenmeisterei	Capitainerie	Capitania	Havenkantoor
Hazard	Hindernis	Danger	Peligro	Gevaar
Height	Höhe	Hauteur	Alturas	Hoogte
Jetty	Steg	Jetée	Malecón	Steiger
Landing place	Anlegeplatz	Point d'accostage	Embarcadero	Plaats om aan land te gaan
Lock	Schleuse	Ecluse	Esclusa	Sluis
Marina	Marina	Marina	Marina	Marina
Mooring	Anlegen	Mouillage	Fondeadero	Meerplaats
Permitted	Erlaubt	Autorisé	Permitido	Toegestaan

English	German	French	Spanish	Dutch
Pier	Pier, Mole	Appontement/quai	Muelle	Pier
Prohibited	Verboten	Interdit	Prohibido	Verboden
Prohibited area	Sperrgebiet	Zone interdite	Zona de prohibida	Verboden gebied
Swell	Schwell	Houle	Mar de fondo	Deining
Swing bridge	Drehbrücke	Pont tournant	Puente giratorio	Draaibrug
Underwater	Unterwasser	Sous-marin	Debajo del agua	Onderwater
Wreck	Wrack	Epave	Naufrago	Wrak
Yacht club	Yachtclub	Club nautique	Club náutico	Jachtclub
Yacht harbour	Yachthafen	Port de plaisance	Puerto deportive	Jachthaven
WEATHER				
Air mass	Luftmasse	Masse d'air	Massa de aire	Luchtmassa
Anticyclone	Antizyklonisch/hoch	Anticyclone	Anticiclón	Hogedrukgebied
Area	Gebiet	Zone	Zona	Gebied
Backing wind	RückdrehenderWind	Vent revenant	Rolar el viento	Krimpende wind
Barometer	Barometer	Baromètre	Barómetro	Barometer
Breeze	Brise	Brise	Brisa	Bries
Calm	Flaute	Calme	Calma	Kalmte
Centre	Zentrum	Centre	Centro	Centrum
Clouds	Wolken	Nuages	Nube	Wolken
Cold	Kalt	Froid	Frio	Koud
Cold front	Kaltfront	Front froid	Frente frio	Koufront
Cyclonic	Zyklonisch	Cyclonique	Ciclonica	Cycloonachtig
Decrease	Abnahme	Affaiblissement	Disminución	Afnemen
Deep	Tief	Profond	Profundo	Diep
Deepening	Vertiefend	Se Creusant	Ahondamiento	Verdiepend
Depression	Sturmtief	Dépression	Depresión	Depressie
Direction	Richtung	Direction	Direción	Richting
Dispersing	Auflösend	Se dispersant	Disipación	Oplossend
Disturbance	Störung	Perturbation	Perturbación	Storing
Drizzle	Niesel	Bruine	Lioviena	Motregen
East	Ost	Est	Este	Oost
Extending	Ausdehnung	S'étendant	Extension	Uitstrekkend
Extensive	Ausgedehnt	Etendu	General	Uitgebreid
Falling	Fallend	Descendant	Bajando	Dalend
Filling	Auffüllend	Se comblant	Relleno	Vullend
Fog	Nebel	Brouillard	Niebla	Nevel
Fog bank	Nebelbank	Banc de brume	Banco de niebla	Mistbank
Forecast	Vorhersage	Prévision	Previsión	Vooruitzicht
Frequent	Häufig	Fréquent	Frecuenta	Veelvuldig
Fresh	Frisch	Frais	Fresco	Fris
Front	Front	Front	Frente	Front
Gale	Sturm	Coup de vent	Temporal	Storm
Gale warning	Sturmwarnung	Avis de coup de vent	Aviso de temporal	Stormwaarschuwing
Good	Gut	Bon	Bueno	Goed
Gradient	Druckunterschied	Gradient	Gradiente	Gradient
Gust, squall	Bö	Rafale	Ráfaga	Windvlaag/bui
Hail	Hagel	Grêle	Granizo	Hagel
Haze	Diesig	Brume	Calina	Nevel
Heavy	Schwer	Abondant	Abunante	Zwaar
High	Hoch	Anticyclone	Alta presión	Hoog
Increasing	Zunehmend	Augmentant	Aumentar	Toenemend
Isobar	Isobar	Isobare	Isobara	Isobaar
Isolated	Vereinzelt	Isolé	Aislado	Verspreid
Lightning	Blitze	Eclair de foudre	Relampago	Bliksem
Local	Örtlich	Local	Local	Plaatselijk
Low	Tief	Dépression	Baja presión	Laag
Mist	Dunst	Brume légere	Nablina	Nevel
Moderate	Mäßig	Modéré	Moderado	Matig
Moderating	Abnehmend	Se modérant	Medianente	Matigend
Moving	Bewegend	Se déplacant	Movimiento	Bewegend

English	German	French	Spanish	Dutch
North	Nord	Nord	Septentrional	Noorden
Occluded	Okklusion	Occlus	Okklusie	Occlusie
Poor	Schlecht	Mauvais	Mal	Slecht
Precipitation	Niederschlag	Précipitation	Precipitación	Neerslag
Pressure	Druck	Pression	Presión	Druk
Rain	Regen	Pluie	lluvia	Regen
Ridge	Hochdruckbrücke	Dorsale	Cresta	Rug
Rising	Ansteigend	Montant	Subiendo	Stijgend
Rough	Rauh	Agitée	Bravo o alborotado	Ruw
Sea	See	Mer	Mar	Zee
Seaway	Seegang	Haute mer	Alta mar	Zeegang
Scattered	Vereinzelt	Sporadiques	Difuso	Verspreid
Shower	Schauer	Averse	Aguacero	Bui
Slight	Leicht	Legère	Leicht	Licht
Slow	Langsam	Lent	Lent	Langzaam
Snow	Schnee	Neige	Nieve	Sneeuw
South	Süd	Sud	Sur	Zuiden
Storm	Sturm	Tempête	Temporal	Storm
Sun	Sonne	Soleil	Sol	Zon
Swell	Schwell	Houle	Mar de fondo	Deining
Thunder	Donner	Tonnerre	Tormenta	Donder
Thunderstorm	Gewitter	Orage	Tronada	Onweer
Trough	Trog, Tiefausläufer	Thalweg	Seno	Trog
Variable	Umlaufend	Variable	Variable	Veranderlijk
Veering	Rechtdrehend	Tournant a l' (Ouest/Est)	Dextrogiro	Ruimende wind
Warm front	Warmfront	Front chaud	Frente calido	Warmtefront
Weather	Wetter	Temps	Tiempo	Weer
Wind	Wind	Vent	Viento	Wind
Weather report	Wetterbericht	Bulletin Météo	Previsión meteorologica	Weerbericht

PORTUGUESE GLOSSARY

NAVIGATION	NAVEGACIÓN
Alternating (Al)	luz alternada
Anchorage	fundeadouro
Basin	doca, bacia
Bar	barra
Bay	baía
Beacon (Bn)	baliza
Bell	sino
Black (B)	preto
Breakwater, mole	quebra-mar, molhe
Bridge	ponte
Buoy	bóia
Can (PHM)	cilíndrica
Chart Datum (CD)	zero hidrográfico
Cone, conical (SHM)	cónica
Conspicuous (conspic)	conspicuo
East (E)	este
Fixed (F)	luz fixa
Flashing	luz relâmpagos
Flood/ebb stream	corrente enchente/vasante
Green (G)	verde
High Water (HW)	preia mar (PM)
Height, headroom, clearance	altura
Island	ilha
Isolated danger (IDM)	perigo isolado
Knot (kn)	nó
Landfall (SWM)	aterragem
Leading light	farol de enfiamento
Leading line, transit	enfiamento
Lighthouse	farol
Lightship	barco-farol
Low Water (LW)	baixa mar (BM)
Mussel beds/rafts	viveiros
Neaps (np)	águas mortas
North (N)	norte
Obscured	obscurecido
Occulting (Oc)	ocultações
Point, headland	ponta
Port (side)	bombordo
Quick flashing (Q)	relâmpagos rápidos
Range	amplitude de maré
Rate/set (tide)	força/direcção
Red, (R)	vermelho
River	rio
Rock	rocha
Reef	recife
Sandhill, dunes	dunas de areia
Shoal	baixo
Slack water, stand	águas paradas
South (S)	sul
Special mark (SPM)	marca especiá
Springs (sp)	águas vivas
Starboard	estibordo
Strait(s)	estreito
Stripe/band	faixas verticais/horizontais

Tide tables	Tabela de marés
Tidal stream atlas	Atlas de marés
Topmark	alvo
West (W)	oeste
Whistle	apito
White (W)	branco
Wreck	naufrágio
Yellow (Y)	amarelo

FACILITIES	FACILIDADOS
Beam	boca
Boat hoist (BH)	portico elevador
Boatyard (BY)	estaleiro
Chandlery (CH)	aprestos
Coastguard (CG)	policia marítima
Crane (C)	guindaste
Customs (n)	alfândega
Diesel (D)	gasóleo
Draught	calado
Dredged	dragado
Engineer (ME)	engenheiro
Fresh water (FW)	aguada
Harbour Master	capitanía
Insurance certificate	certificado de seguro
Jetty	molhe
Length overall (LOA)	comprimento
Lifeboat (LB)	barco salva-vidas
Lock	eclusa
Methylated spirits	alcool metílico
Mooring buoy	bólia de atracação
Petrol (P)	gasolina
Paraffin	petróleo
Registration number	número do registo
Slipway (slip)	rampa
Sailmaker (SM)	veleir
Yacht harbour, marina	doca de recreio

METEOROLOGY	METEOROLOGIA
High (anticyclone)	anticiclone
Breakers	arrebentação
Calm (F0)	calma
Choppy	mareta
Cloudy	nublado
Drizzle	chuvisco
Front, warm/cold	frente, quente/fria
Fog	nevoeiro
Fresh breeze (F5)	vento frêsco
Gale (F8)	vento muito forte
Gentle breeze (F3)	vento bonançoso
Gust	rajada
Hail	saraiva
Haze	cerração
Light airs (F1)	aragem
Light breeze (F2)	vento fraco
Low (depression)	depressão
Mist	neblina
Moderate breeze (F4)	vento moderado
Near gale (F7)	vento forte
Overfalls (tide race)	bailadeiras
Pressure, rise/fall	pressão, subida/descida
Rain	chuva
Ridge (high)	crista
Rough sea	mar bravo
Severe gale (F9)	vento tempestuoso
Short/steep (sea state)	mar cavado
Shower	aguaceiro
Squall	borrasca
Slight sea	mar chão
Storm (F10)	temporal
Strong breeze (F6)	vento muito frêsco
Swell	ondulação
Thunderstorm	trovoada
Trough	linha de baixa pressão
Visibility, poor; good	fraca, má; bôa

FIRST AID	PRIMEIROS SOCORROS
Antibiotic	antibiótico
Bandage	ligadura
Bleeding	sangrar
Burn	queimadura
Chemist	farmácia
Dehydration	desidratação
Dentist	dentista
Drown, to	afogar-se
Fever	febre
Heart attack	ataque de coração
Pain	dôr
Painkiller	analgésico
Poisoning	envenenamento
Shock	choque
Splint	colocar em talas
Sticking plaster	adesivo
Stomach upset	cólicas
Stretcher	maca
Sunburn	queimadura des
Swelling	inchação
Toothache	dôr dos dentes
Unconscious	sem sentidos

ASHORE	A TERRA
Bakery	padaria, pastelaria
Beach	praia
Bus station	estação de camionetas
Butcher shop	açougue
Ironmonger	ferreiroa
Launderette	lavanderia
Market	mercad
Post Office	correio (CTT)
Railway station	estação de comboios
Stamps	sellos

1.3 USEFUL ADDRESSES, WEB SITES AND/OR E-MAIL ADDRESSES

Adlard Coles Nautical (Imprint of A & C Black)
37 Soho Square, London W1D 3QZ. ☎ 0207 775 0200. ℻ 0207 775 0222. adlardcoles@acblack.com

Amateur Yacht Research Society
BCM AYRS, London WC1N 3XX. ☎/℻ 01727 862268 ayrs@fishwick.demon.co.uk

Association of Brokers and Yacht Agents
(also YBDSA), Wheel House, Petersfield Road, Whitehill, Bordon, Hants GU35 7BU. ☎ 01420 473862. ℻ 01420 488328.

BBC Radio
Broadcasting House, London W1A 1AA. ☎ 020 7580 4468. www.bbc.co.uk

British Marine Industries Federation (BMIF)
Boating Industry House, Mead Lake Place, Thorpe Lea Road, Egham, Surrey TW20 8HE. ☎ 01784 473377. ℻ 01784 439678. www.bmif.co.uk

British Sub-Aqua Club
Telford's Quay, Ellesmere Port, South Wirral, Cheshire L65 4FY. ☎ 0151 350 6200. ℻ 0151 350 6215. www.@bsac.com postmaster@bsac.com

British Waterways
Willow Grange, Church Road, Watford, Herts WD1 3QX. ☎ 01923 226422. ℻ 01923 226081. www.british waterways.co.uk

British Waterways (Caledonian Canal)
Seaport Marina, Canal Office, Muirtown Wharf, Inverness IV3 5LS. ☎ 01463 233140. ℻ 01463 710942

British Waterways (Crinan Canal)
Pier Square, Canal Office, Ardrishaig, Lochgilphead, Argyll PA30 8DZ. ☎ 01546 603210. ℻ 01546 603941.

British Waterways (Scotland)
Regional Office, Canal House, Applecross Street, Glasgow G4 9SP. ☎ 0141 332 6936. ℻ 0141 331 1688.

Coastguard, HM. See Maritime & Coastguard Agency.

Clyde Cruising Club
Suite 101, The Pentagon Centre, 36 Washington Street, Glasgow G3 8AZ. ☎ 0141 221 2774. ℻ 0141 221 2775. hazel@clydecruising.demon.co.uk www.clyde.org

Cowes Combined Clubs
Secretary, 18 Bath Rd, Cowes, Isle of Wight PO31 7QN. ☎ 01983 295744. ℻ 01983 295329. ccc@cowesweek.co.uk

Cruising Association (CA)
CA House, 1 Northey St, Limehouse Basin, London E14 8BT. ☎ 020 7537 2828. ℻ 020 7537 2266 www.cruising.org.uk office @cruising.org.uk

HM Customs and Excise
Ground Floor, New King's Beam House, 22 Upper Ground, London SE1 9PJ London N3 2JY. ☎ 020 7865 5804. ℻ 020 7865 5910. www.hmce.gov.uk

Cutty Sark Trust
2 Greenwich Church Street, London SE10 9BG. ☎ 020 8858 2698; ℻ 020 8858 6976. www.cuttysark.org.uk info@cuttysark.org.uk

Flag Institute, The
44 Middleton Road, Acomb, York YO24 3AS. ☎ 01904 339985. michael.faul@virgin.net

Guernsey Tourist Board
PO Box 23, North Esplanade, St Peter Port, Guernsey, Channel Isles GY1 3AN. ☎ 01481 726611. ℻ 01481 721246. www.guernseytourism.gov.gg

Hydrographic Office
Admiralty Way, Taunton, Somerset TA1 2DN. ☎ 01823 337900. ℻ 01823 284077. www.hydro.gov.uk

Imray Laurie Norie & Wilson Ltd
Wych House, The Broadway, St Ives, Cambs PE27 5BT. ☎ 01480 462114. ℻ 01480 496109. www.imray.com ilnw@imray.com

Inland Waterways Association
PO Box 114, Rickmansworth, Herts WD3 1ZY. ☎ 01923 711114. ℻ 01923 897000. iwa@waterways.org.uk www.waterways.org.uk

Institute of Marine Engineers
80 Coleman St, London EC2R 5BJ. ☎ 020 7382 2600; ℻ 020 7382 2670.

International Institute of Marine Surveyors
Stone Lane, Gosport, Hants PO12 1SS. ☎ 023 9258 8000; ℻ 023 9258 8002.

International Maritime Organisation (IMO)
4 Albert Embankment, London SE1 7SR. ☎ 020 7735 7611. ℻ 020 7587 3210. www.imo.org info@imo.org

International Maritime Satellite Org. (Inmarsat)
99 City Rd, London EC1Y 1AX. ☎ 020 7728 1000. ℻ 020 7728 1044. www.inmarsat.com

Jersey Tourist Office
Liberation Square, St Helier, Jersey JE1 1BB, Channel Isles. ☎ 01534 500700. ℻ 01534 500808. www.jersey.com

Junior Offshore Group
28 Nodes Road, Cowes, Isle of Wight PO31 8AB. ☎/℻ 01983 291192. www.jog.org.uk

Kelvin Hughes Ltd
Mail Order Dept., Kilgraston House, Southampton St, Southampton SO15 2ED. ☎ 023 8063 4911. ℻ 023 8033 0014. southampton@kelvinhighes.co.uk www.bookharbour.com
Head Office: New North Road, Hainault, Ilford, Essex IG6 2UR. ☎ 0208 502 6887. ℻ 0208 500 0837.

Little Ship Club
Bell Wharf Lane, Upper Thames St, London EC4R 3TB. ☎ 020 7236 7729. ℻ 020 7236 9100. www.little-ship-club.co.uk

Lloyd's
One Lime Street, London EC3M 7HA. ☎ 020 7327 5408; ℻ 020 7327 6827. www.lloyds.com lloyds-salvage@lloyds.com

Lloyd's Register
(Passenger Ship and Special Service Craft Group), 71 Fenchurch St, London EC3M 4BS. ☎ 020 7423 2325; 📠 020 7423 2016. psg-general@lr.org www.lr.org

Marine Accident Investigation Branch (MAIB)
First Floor, Carlton House, Carlton Place, Southampton SO15 2DZ. ☎ 023 8039 5500. 📠 023 8023 2459. maib@dft.gsi.gov.uk www.dft.gov.uk

Maritime and Coastguard Agency (MCA)
Spring Place, 105 Commercial Rd, Southampton SO15 1EG. ☎ 023 8032 9100; Info 0870 6006 505. 📠 023 8032 9105. www.mcga.gov.uk infoline@mcga.gov.uk

Maritime Trust
2 Greenwich Church Street, London SE10 9BG. ☎ 020 8858 2698. 📠 020 8858 6976. www.cuttysark.org.uk info@cuttysark.org.uk

Medway Yachting Association
c/o Medway Yacht Club, Lower Upnor, Rochester, Kent ME2 4XB. ☎ 01634 7188899.

Meteorological Office
FitzRoy Road, Exeter EX1 3PB. Customer service centre ☎ 0845 300 0300. 📠 0845 300 1300. www.met-office.gov.uk enquiries@metoffice.com

Motor Boat and Yachting
King's Reach Tower, Stamford St, London SE1 9LS. ☎ 020 7261 5333. 📠 020 7261 5419 www.mby.com

National Coastwatch Institution (NCI)
4a Trafalgar Sq, Fowey PL23 1AZ. ☎ 0870 787 2147; 📠 0870 164 1893. info@nci.org.uk www.nci.org.uk

Nautical Data Limited
The Book Barn, Westbourne, Hants PO10 8RS. ☎ 01243 389352. 📠 01243 379136. www.nauticaldata.com editorial@nauticaldata.com

National Federation of Sea Schools
Purlins, 159 Woodlands Rd, Woodlands, Southampton SO40 7GL. ☎/📠 023 8029 3822. kay@nfss.co.uk www.nfss.co.uk

National Import Reliefs Unit
Custom House, Killyhevlin Industrial Estate, Enniskillen, BT74 4EJ. e 028 6632 2298. (028 6632 4018.

Nautical Institute
202 Lambeth Road, London SE1 7LQ. ☎ 020 7928 1351; 📠 020 7401 2817. sec@nautinst.org pubs@nautinst.org www.nautinst.org

Northern Lighthouse Board
84 George St, Edinburgh EH2 3DA. ☎ 0131 226 7051. 📠 0131 220 2093. www.nlb.org.uk enquiries@nlb.org.uk

Oki Systems (UK) Ltd
550 Dundee Rd, Slough, SL1 4LE. ☎ 0800 917 6015.

Port of London Authority (PLA)
Baker's Hall, Hart Lane, London EC3R 6RB. ☎ 020 7743 7900. 📠 020 7743 7999. portoflondon.co.uk (London River House, Gravesend ☎ 01474 562200).

Practical Boat Owner
Westover House, West Quay Road, Poole, Dorset BH15 1JG. ☎ 01202 440820. 📠 01202 440860. www.pbo.co.uk pbo@ipcmedia.com

Radio Licensing Centre
www.radiolicencecentre. co.uk
Ships Licences, PO Box 1495, Bristol BS99 3QS. ☎ 0870 243 4433.
Amateur Radio and CB Licences, PO Box 885, Bristol BS99 5LG. ☎ 0117 925 8333.

Registry of Shipping and Seamen (RSS)
MCA Cardiff, Anchor Court, Ocean Way, Cardiff CF24 5JW; or RSS, PO Box 420, Cardiff CF24 5XR. ☎ 029 2044 8800; 📠 029 2044 8820. www.mcga.org.uk rss@mcga.gov.uk Part I Registration ☎ 029 2044 8841 to 8845. Part III, SSR, ☎ 029 2044 8856/7.

Royal Cruising Club (RCC)
At the Royal Thames Yacht Club (see below).

Royal Institute of Naval Architects
10 Upper Belgrade St, London SW1X 8BQ. ☎ 020 7235 4622; 📠 020 7259 5912. hq@rina.org.uk www.rina.org.uk

Royal Institute of Navigation (RIN)
Royal Geographical Society, 1 Kensington Gore, London SW7 2AT. ☎ 020 7591 3130. 📠 020 7591 3131. www.rin.org.uk rindir@atlas.co.uk

Royal National Lifeboat Institution (RNLI)
West Quay Road, Poole, Dorset BH15 1HZ. ☎ 01202 663000. 📠 01202 663167. info@rnli.org www.lifeboats.org.uk

Royal Naval Sailing Association (RNSA).
10 Haslar Marina, Haslar Rd, Gosport, Hants PO12 1NU. ☎ 023 9252 1100. 📠 023 9252 1122. rnsa@compuserve.com www.rnsa.co.uk

Royal Ocean Racing Club (RORC)
20 St James's Place, London SW1A 1NN. ☎ 020 7493 2248. 📠 020 7493 5252. www.rorc.org rorc@stjames.demon.co.uk
RORC Rating Office, Seahorse Building, Bath Road, Lymington, Hants SO41 9SE. ☎ 01590 677030; 📠 01590 679478.

Royal Thames Yacht Club (RTYC)
60 Knightsbridge, London SW1X 7LF. ☎ 020 7235 2121. 📠 020 7235 9470. www.royalthames.com club@royalthames.com

Royal Yachting Association (RYA)
RYA House, Ensign Way, Hamble, Hants SO31 4YA. ☎ 023 8062 7400 or 0845 345 0400. 📠 023 8062 9924 or 0845 345 0329. www.rya.org.uk admin@rya.org.uk

Royal Yachting Association (Scotland)
Caledonia House, South Gyle, Edinburgh EH12 9DQ. ☎ 0131 317 7388. 📠 0131 317 8566. helen@ryascotland.freeserve.co.uk

Small Ships Register
See Registry of Shipping and Seamen.
Society of Consulting Marine Engineers and Ships Surveyors, c/o 202 Lambeth Rd, London SE1 7LQ; ☎ 020 7261 0869; ℻ 020 7261 0871. scms@btinternet.com
Solent Cruising and Racing Association
18 Bath Road, Cowes, Isle of Wight PO31 7QN. ☎ 01983 295744. ℻ 01983 295329. www.scra.org.uk
Sport England (aka English Sports Council)
3rd floor, Victoria House, Bloomsbury Sq, London WC1B 4SE. ☎ 0845 8508 508; ℻ 020 7383 5740. info@english.sports.gov.uk www.sportengland.org
Stationery Office, The
St Crispin's House, Duke St, Norwich NR3 1PD. ☎ 0870 600 5522; ℻ 0870 600 5533. www.the-stationery-office.co.uk esupport@theso.co.uk Shop at: clicktso.com
Trinity House, Corporation of
Tower Hill, London EC3N 4DH. ☎ 020 7481 6900 ℻ 0117 7480 7662. www.trinityhouse.co.uk hcooper@admin.thls.org
Yacht Charter Association Ltd
Deacon's Boatyard, Bursledon Bridge, Southampton, Hants SO31 8AZ. ☎ 023 8040 7075; ℻ 023 8040 7076. charter@yca.co.uk www.yca.co.uk
Yacht Designers and Surveyors Association
(also Association of Brokers & Yacht Agents), The Glass Works, Penns Rd, Petersfield, Hants GU32 2EW. info@ybdsa.co.uk www.ybdsa.co.uk ☎ 01730 710425. ℻ 01730 710423.
Yacht Harbour Association
Evegate Park Barn, Smeeth, Ashford, Kent TN25 6SX. ☎ 01303 814434. ℻ 01303 814364. sueheale@tyha.freeserve.co.uk
Yachting Monthly
King's Reach Tower, Stamford St, London SE1 9LS. www.yachtingmonthly. com ☎ 020 7261 6040. ℻ 020 7261 7555. yachting_monthly@ipcmedia.com
Yachting World
King's Reach Tower, Stamford St, London SE1 9LS. ☎ 020 7261 6800. ℻ 020 7261 6818. www.yachting-world.com yachting-world@ipcmedia.com

BELGIUM
British Embassy
85 Aarlenstraat, 1040 Brussels. ☎ +32 2 2876 211. ℻ +32 2 287 62 70 (Consular).
Dienst der Kust Havens-Hydrografie
Administratief Centrum, Vrijhavenstraat 3, B-8400 Oostende. ☎ +32 3 222 0811. ℻ +32 3 231 2062.
Royal Meteorological Institute of Belgium
Ringlaan 3, B-31180 Brussels. ☎ +32 2 373 0508. ℻ +32 2 373 0528. rmiinfo@oma.be
Belgian Tourist Information Centre
Grasmarkt 63, B-1000 Brussels. ☎ +32 2 504 0390. ℻ +32 2 504 0270. www.visitbelgium.com
Royal Belgian Sailing Club
Zeebrugge ☎ +32 50 544 903.
Royal Yacht Club van Belgie
Antwerpen ☎ +32 3 219 2784.

DENMARK
British Embassy
Kastelsvej 36-40, DK-2100 København Ø. ☎ +45 35 44 52 42. ℻ +45 35 44 52 53 (Consular). info@britishembassy.dk
Danish Hydrographic Office
Kort-og Matrikelstyrelsen, Rentemestervej 8, DK-2400 København. ☎ +45 35 87 50 50. ℻ +45 35 87 50 57. kms@kms.dk
Danmarks Meteorologiske Institut (DMI)
Lyngbyvej 100, DK-2100 København Ø. ☎ +45 39 15 75 00. ℻ +45 39 27 10 80. www.dmi.dk
Dansk Sejlunion
(Danish sailing association) Stadion 20, 2605 Brøndby. ☎ +45 43 26 26 26. ℻ +45 43 26 21 91.
DMU Danske Fritidssejlere
(Motorboats) Tjørnelund 32, 2635 Ishøj. ☎ +45 43 53 66 67.
Søfartsstyrelsen
(Safety for yachts) Søsportens Sikkerhedsråd Vermundsgade 38C, DK-2100 København Ø. ☎ +45 39 27 15 15. ℻ +45 39 17 44 01

FRANCE
British Embassy
35 rue du Faubourg St Honoré, 75383 Paris, Cedex 08, ☎ +33 1 44 51 31 00. ℻ +33 1 44 51 31 27 (Consular).
Comité d'Etudes et des Services des Assureurs Maritimes (CESAM). (Insurance companies' surveyors group) 20 rue Vivienne, 75082 Paris. ☎ +33 1 42 96 12 13. ℻ +33 1 42 96 34 59.
CROSS Gris Nez
62179 Audinghen. ☎ +33 3 21 87 21 87. ℻ +33 3 21 87 78 55. grisnezmrcc@hotmail.com
CROSS Jobourg
Route d'Auderville, 50440 Jobourg. ☎ +33 2 33 52 72 13. ℻ +33 2 33 52 71 72. jobourg.mrcc@wanadoo.fr
CROSS Corsen
Pte de Corsen, 29810 Plouarzel. ☎ +33 2 98 89 3131. ℻ +33 2 98 89 65 75. cross-corsen@equipement.gouv.fr
CROSSA Étel
Av. Bougo, Chateau de la Garenne, 56410 Etel. ☎ +33 2 97 55 35 35. ℻ +33 2 97 55 49 34. cross-etel@equipement.gouv.fr
Douanes - Bureau d'Information
(Customs Info Office) 23 bis, rue de l'Université, 75700 Paris. ☎ +33 1 44 74 47 03. ℻ +33 1 44 74 49 37.
Service Hydrographique et Océanographique de la Marine (SHOM = French Hydrographer)
13 rue du Chatellier, BP 30316, 29603 Brest Cedex. ☎ +33 2 98 03 09 17. ℻ +33 2 98 47 11 42. www.shom.fr

Météo-France
1 Quai Branly, 75340 Paris Cedex 07. www.meteo.fr marine@meteo.fr ☎ +33 1 45 56 74 36. ℻ +33 1 45 56 71 70.

Société Nationale de Sauvetage en Mer (SNSM)
(Lifeboat Society) 9 rue de Chaillot, 75116 Paris. ☎ +33 1 56 89 30 00. ℻ +33 1 56 89 30 01.

Yacht Club de France
41 avenue Foch, 75116 Paris. ☎ +33 1 47 04 10 00. ℻ +33 1 47 04 10 01.

GERMANY

British Embassy
Wilhelmstrasse 70, 10117 Berlin. ☎ 00 49 30 20 45 7-0. ℻ 00 49 30 20 45 75 79. info@britischebotschaft.de

Bundesamt für Seeschiffahrt und Hydrographie (BSH). (German HO) Bernhard-Nocht-Str 78, 20359 Hamburg. ☎ +49 40 3190-0. ℻ +49 40 3190 50 00. www.bsh.de

Deutscher Segler-Verbrand
(Yachting association) Gründgensstr 18, 22309 Hamburg. ☎ 00 49 40 632 0090. ℻ 00 49 40 6320 0928. www.dsv.org

Deutscher Wetterdienst (DWD)
(Met office) Frankfurter Str 135, 63067 Offenbach. ☎ +49 69 80 620. ℻ +49 69 8062 4484. www.dwd.de seeschifffahrt@dwd.de

Deutscher Gesellschaft zur Rettung Schiffbrüchiger
(DGzRS = Rescue service). PO Box 10 63 40, 28063 Bremen. ☎ +49 421 53707-0. ℻ +49 421 53707-690. www.dgzrs.de info@dgzrs.de

Seefunk - DP07 (Coast radio company)
Estedeich 84, D-21129 Hamburg. ☎ +49 40 2385 5782. ℻ +49 40 7413 4242. info@dp07.com www.dp07.com

National Tourist Board
Beethovenstrasse 69, D-60325 Frankfurt/Main. ☎ +49 0 6997 4640. ℻ +49 0 6975 1903. info@d-z-t.com www.germany-tourism.de

IRELAND, REPUBLIC OF

Irish Coastguard (IRCG)
Department of Commmunications, Marine & Natural Resources, Leeson Lane, Dublin 2.
☎ +353 1 619 9349. ℻ +353 1 676 2666.

Irish Cruising Club
See Imray entry. www.irishcruisingclub.com publications@irishcruisingclub

Irish Lights, Commissioners of
16 Lower Pembroke St, Dublin 2. ☎ +353 1 662 4525; ℻ +353 1 661 8094. www.cil.ie cil@aol.iol.ie

Irish Met Service (Met Eireann)
HQ, Glasnevin Hill, Dublin 9. ☎ +353 1 806 4200; ℻ +353 1 806 4247. www.met.ie met.eireann@met.ie

Irish Sailing Association
3 Park Rd, Dun Laoghaire, Co Dublin. ☎ +353 1 280 0239. ℻ +353 1 280 7558. www.sailing.ie

Irish Tourist Board
150 New Bond St, London W1S 2AQ. ☎ 0171 518 0800. ℻ 0171 493 9065. www.ireland.travel.ie

NETHERLANDS

British Embassy
Lange Voorhout 10, 2514 ED Den Haag.
☎ +31 70 427 0427. ℻ +31 70 427 0345

ANWB Hoofdkantoor
PO Box 93200, 2509 BA Den Haag.
☎ +31 70 314 7147. ℻ +31 70 314 6966.

Dienst der Hydrografie
Koninklijke Marine, Badhuisweg 167, PO Box 90704, 2597 JN Den Haag. ☎ +31 70 316 2801. ℻ +31 70 316 2843. info@hydro.nl www.hydro.nl

Koninklijke Nederlands Meteorologisch Instituut
Postbus 210, Wilhelminalaan 10, 3730 AE De Bilt. ☎ +30 220 6911. ℻ +30 221 0407. www.knmi.nl

Stichting Classificatie Waterrecreatiebedrijven
(Classification of Marinas etc) PO Box 93345, 2509 AH Den Haag. ☎ +31 70 328 3807.

Koninklijke Nederlands Watersport Verbond
(Dutch sailing association)
PO Box 85393, 3508 AJ Utrecht.
☎ +31 30 656 6550. ℻ +31 30 656 4783.

Koninklijke Nederlandse Motorboot Club
(Royal Dutch motorboat club) Zoorstede 7, 3431 HK Nieuwegein. ☎ 00 31 30 603 9935. ℻ 00 31 30 605 3834.

PORTUGAL

British Embassy
Rua de São Bernardo 33, 1249-082 Lisboa.
☎ +351 21 3924 000. ℻ +351 21 3914 185.
chancery@lisbon.mail.fco.gov.uk

Hydrographic Office
Instituto Hidrografico, Rua das Trinas 49, 1296 Lisboa. ☎ +351 21 3914 000. ℻ +351 21 3914 199. mail@hidrografico.pt

Instituto de Meteorologia
Rua C ao Aeroporto, 1749-077 Lisboa. ☎ +351 21 848 3961. ℻ +351 21 840 2370.www.meteo.pt

SPAIN

British Embassy
Calle de Fernando el Santo 16, 28010 Madrid.
☎ +34 91 700 82 00. ℻ +34 91 700 83 09.

Hydrographic Office
Instituto Hidrografico de la Marina, Plaza de San Severiano No 3, 11007 CADIZ. ☎ +34 956 599 414. ℻ +34 956 275 358. ihmesp@retemail.es

Instituto Nacional de Meteorologa
C/Leonardo Prieto Castro, 8 (Ciudad Universitaria), 28071 Madrid. ☎ +34 91 581 9810. ℻ +34 91 581 9811. www.inm.es infomet@inm.es

Spanish Tourist Office (UK)
22-23 Manchester Square, London W1U 3PX; e 020 7486 8077, (020 7186 8034. londres@tourspain.es www.tourspain.uk

1.4 ADMIRALTY LEISURE CHARTS

Formerly 'Small Craft' charts; folded. Price £13.50

Chart	Title	Scale
Area 1		
26	Harbours on S coast of Devon	Various
28	Salcombe	1:12,500
30	Plymouth Sound	1:12,500
32	Falmouth Harbour	Various
34	Isles of Scilly	1:25,000
147	Helford River	Various
154	Appr's to Falmouth	1:35,000
442	Lizard to Berry head	1:150,000
777	Land's End to Falmouth	1:75,000
871	R. Tamar, Lynher & Tavy	Various
883	Scilly, St Mary's & principal off-islands	1:12,500
1148	Isles of Scilly to Land's End	1:75,000
1267	Falmouth to Plymouth	1:75,000
1613	Eddystone to Brixham	1:75,000
1634	Salcombe to Brixham	1:25,000
2172	Hbrs/Anchs: S coast of England	Various
2253	Dartmouth	Various
2454	Start Pt to Needles	1:150,000
2565	St Agnes Hd to Dodman Pt	1:150,000
2610	Portland Bill to Anvil Pt	1:40,000
2615	Portland Bill to Needles	1:75,000
2655	English Chan, W entrance	1:325,000
2656	English Chan, Central	1:325,000
2675	English Channel	1:500,000
3315	Berry Hd to Portland Bill	1:75,000
Area 2		
2021	Hbrs/Anchs, W Solent	Various
2022	Hbrs/Anchs, E Solent	Various
2035	W appr's to Solent	1:25,000
2036	Solent & Southampton Water	1:25,000
2037	E appr's to Solent	1:25,000
2041	Southampton	1:10,000
2045	Outer appr's to Solent	1:75,000
2175	Poole Bay	1:20,000
2450	Anvil Pt to Beachy Hd	1:150,000
2611	Poole Harbour & appr's	1:12,500
2631	Portsmouth Harbour	1:7,500
2793	Cowes Hbr and R Medina	Various
3418	Langstone & Chichester Hbrs	1:20,000
Area 3		
323	Dover Strait, East	1:75,000
536	Beachy Hd to Dungeness	1:75,000
1406	Dover and Calais to Orford Ness and Scheveningen	1:250,000
1652	Selsey Bill to Beachy Hd	1:75,000
1828	Dover to N Foreland	1:37,000
1892	Dover Strait, West	1:75,500
2449	Dover Strait to Westerschelde	1:150,000
2451	Beachy Hd to S Foreland and Fécamp to Cap Gris-Nez	1:150,000
Area 4		
1183	Thames Estuary	1:100,000
1185	Thames, Sea Reach	1:25,000
1408	Harwich and Rotterdam to Cromer and Terschelling	1:300,000
1536	Appr's to Great Yarmouth & Lowestoft	1:40,000
1543	Winterton Ness to Orford Ness	1:75,000
1607	Thames Estuary, South	1:50,000
1834	R Medway, Garrison Pt to Folly Pt	1:12,500
1975	Thames Estuary, North	1:50,000
2052	Orford Ness to the Naze	1:50,000
2482	R Medway and The Swale	Various
2484	Thames, Canvey to London Bridge	Various
2693	Appr's to R. Stour, Orwell & Deben	1:25,000
2695	Plans on E coast of England	Various
3741	R Colne and Blackwater	Various
3750	R Crouch and Roach	1:12,500
Area 5		
106	Cromer to Smith's Knoll	1:75,000
107	Appr's to R Humber	1:75,000
108	Approaches to The Wash	1:75,000
121	Flamborough Hd to Withernsea	1:75,000
129	Whitby to Flamborough Hd	1:75,000
134	R Tees to Scarborough	1:75,000
152	R Tyne to R Tees	1:75,000
156	Farne Is to R Tyne	1:75,000
160	St Abb's Hd to Farne Is	1:75,000
Area 6		
175	Fife Ness to St Abb's Hd	1:75,000
190	Montrose to Fife Ness	1:75,000
210	Newburgh to Montrose	1:75,000
213	Fraserburgh to Newburgh	1:75,000
Area 7		
222	Buckie to Fraserburgh	1:75,000
223	Dunrobin Pt to Buckie	1:75,000
Area 8		
2169	Appr's to Firth of Lorne	1:75,000
2171	Sound of Mull	1:75,000
2326	Loch Crinan to Firth of Lorne	1:25,000
2390	Sound of Mull	1:25,000
2635	Scotland, West coast	1:500,000
Area 9		
1866	Ports in Firth of Clyde	1:7,500
1867	Clyde, Hunterston Chan & Rothesay Snd	1:12,500
1906	Kyles of Bute	Various
1907	Firth of Clyde	1:25,000
1994	Approaches to R Clyde	Various
2000	Gareloch	1:12,500
2126	Appr's to Firth of Clyde	1:75,000
2131	Firth of Clyde and Loch Fyne	1:75,000
2220	Firth of Clyde, Plada to Inchmarnock	1:36,000
2491	Ardrossan to Largs	1:25,000
2724	North Channel to Firth of Lorne	1:200,000
Area 10		
1464	Menai Strait	Various
1826	Irish Sea, East	1:200,000
1970	Caernarfon Bay	1:75,000
1977	Holyhead to Great Ormes Hd	1:75,000
1978	Great Ormes Hd to Liverpool	1:75,000
Area 11		
1076	Linney Hd to Oxwich Pt	Various
1121	Irish Sea, St George's to N Chans	1:500,000
1123	W appr's to St George's and Bristol Chans	1:500,000
1149	Pendeen to Trevose Hd	1:75,000
1152	Bristol Chan, Nash Pt to Sand Pt	1:50,000
1156	Trevose Hd to Hartland Pt	1:75,000
1160	Plans on Somerset & Devon coast	1:20,000
1161	Swansea Bay	1:25,000
1164	Hartland Pt to Ilfracombe, inc Lundy	1:75,000
1165	Bristol Chan, Worms Hd to Watchet	1:75,000
1166	R Severn, Avonmouth to Sharpness	1:25,000
1176	Severn Estuary, to Avonmouth	Various
1178	Appr's to Bristol Channel	1:200,000
1179	Bristol Channel	1:150,000
1182	Appr's to Barry and Cardiff	Various
1410	St George's Channel	1:200,000
1478	St Govan's Hd to St David's Hd	1:75,000
1971	Cardigan Bay, North	1:75,000
1973	Cardigan Bay, South	1:75,000
2878	Appr's to Milford Haven	1:25,000
Area 12		
1411	Irish Sea, West	1:200,000
1468	Arklow to The Skerries	1:100,000
1777	Cork, lower hbr and appr's	1:12,500
1787	Carnsore Pt to Wicklow	1:100,000
1840	Bantry Bay	1:30,000
2046	Waterford Harbour	1:25,000
2049	Old Hd of Kinsale to Tuskar Rk	1:150,000
2092	Toe Hd to Old Hd of Kinsale	1:50,000
2129	Long Island to Castlehaven	1:30,000
2156	Strangford Lough	1:37,500

2424	Kenmare River to Cork Harbour	1:150,000
2495	Kenmare River	1:60,000
2552	Dunmanus Bay	Various
Area 13		
44	Nose of Howth to Ballyquintin Pt	1:100,000
1753	Belfast Lough	1:37,500
2199	North Channel, North	1:75,000
Area 17		
1106	Appr's to Cherbourg	1:50,000
1349	Ports in Normandy	Various
2135	Pte de Barfleur to Pte de la Percée	1:60,000
2136	Pte de la Percée to Ouistreham	1:60,000
2146	Appr's to Le Havre	1:60,000
2613	Cherbourg to Fécamp	1:150,000
Area 18		
3659	Cap Fréhel to Îles Chausey	1:50,000
3674	L'Ost-Pic to Cap Fréhel	1:50,000
Area 19		
60	Alderney and The Casquets	1:25,000
807	Guernsey and Herm	Various
808	East Guernsey, Herm and Sark	Various
1137	Appr's to St Helier	1:25,000
2669	Channel Is and adjacent French coast	1:150,000
3653	Guernsey to Alderney & French coast	1:50,000
3654	Guernsey, Herm and Sark	1:50,000
3655	Jersey and adjacent French coast	1:50,000
Area 20		
2668	Île Vierge to Roches Douvres	1:150,000
2694	Le Four to Goulet de Brest	1:50,000
3668	Le Four to Anse de Kernic	1:50,000
3669	Anse de Kernic to Les Sept Îles	1:50,000
3670	Les Sept Îles to L'Ost-Pic	1:50,000
3674	L'Ost-Pic to Cap Fréhel, plus Le Légué	1:50,000

1.4.1 ADMIRALTY LEISURE FOLIOS

Formerly 'Small Craft' Folios. A2 size sheets. £37.50 per folio.

Chart	Title	Scale
SC 5600	**The Solent and approaches**	
1	Outer approaches to The Solent	1:150,000
2	Isle of Wight, S coast	1:75,000
2B	Lymington River	Various
3	Needles Channel	1:25,000
3B	Beaulieu and Newtown Rivers	Various
4	Yarmouth to Beaulieu River	1:25,000
4B	River Hamble	1:5,000
5	River Hamble (and Hythe) to Cowes	1:25,000
5B	River Test	1:10,000
6	River Itchen & Ashlett Creek	1:10,000
6B	Entrance to Portsmouth Harbour	1:7,500
7	Spithead	1:25,000
7B	Approaches to Fareham Lake	1:7,500
8	Approaches to Port Solent	1:7,500
8B	Langstone Harbour	1:20,000
9	Appr's to Langstone & Chichester Hbrs	1:25,000
9B	Harbours and Creeks in the The Solent	Various
10	E approaches to The Solent	1:25,000
11	Chichester Harbour	1:20,000
12	Cowes Harbour & River Medina	Various
SC 5601	**E Devon and Dorset, Exmouth to Christchurch**	
1	Start Point to The Needles	1:325,000
2	Teignmouth to Lyme Regis	1:75,000
3	Lyme Regis Hbr to Portland Bill, inc W Bay	1:75,000
4	Portland Bill to St Alban's Head	1:75,000
5	St Alban's Head to The Needles	1:75,000
6	River Exe, Topsham, Exeter	1:16,000
7	Weymouth and Portland Harbours	1:20,000
8	Swanage and Studland Bays	1:12,500
9	Poole Harbour, East	1:12,500
10	Poole Harbour, West	1:12,500
11	Plans on the Dorset Coast	Various
12	Christchurch Harbour & River Stour	1:7,500
SC 5602	**The West Country, Falmouth to Teignmouth**	
1	The West Country and approaches	1:325,000
2	Falmouth to Fowey, inc Mevagissey plan	1:75,000
3	Fowey to Plymouth, inc Polperro, Looe	1:75,000
4	Plymouth to Salcombe	1:75,000
5	Salcombe to Teignmouth, inc 3 plans	1:75,000
6	Falmouth to Truro	1:16,000
7	Fowey Harbour and to Lostwithiel	1:6,250
8	Plymouth Sound, appr's and R Yealm	1:25,000
9	Rivers Tamar, Lynher & Tavy	1:25,000
10	Salcombe Harbour and to Kingsbridge	1:15,000
11	Dartmouth Harbour and Dittisham	1:8,000
12	River Dart to Totnes	1:8,000
SC 5603	**Falmouth to Padstow, inc Isles of Scilly**	
1	Falmouth to Padstow	1:250,000
2	Falmouth to Penzance, inc 2 plans	1:75,000
3	Penzance to St Ives, inc 2 plans	1:75,000
4	Pendeen to Penhale Pt, inc St Ives	1:75,000
5	Newquay to Padstow, inc 3 plans	1:75,000
6	Hbrs/xages, Lizard to Falmouth	Various
7	Penzance & Bay, Mousehole, Newlyn	1:12,500
8	Isles of Scilly, Southern part	1:25,000
9	Isles of Scilly, Northern part	1:25,000
10	St Mary's Pool to St Agnes	1:12,500
11	St Mary's Pool to Tresco	1:12,500
12	St Martin's and the Eastern Isles	1:12,500
SC 5604	**The Channel Islands**	
1	Channel Is and approaches	1:500,000
2	Alderney to Jersey, and adjacent France	1:150,000
3	Appr's to Lézardrieux and Paimpol	1:150,000
4	Jersey to St Malo	1:150,000
5	Alderney	1:25,000
6	Guernsey, Herm and Sark	1:60,000
7	The Little Russel	1:25,000
8	Sark and approaches to Gorey	1:25,000
9	Jersey	1:60,000
10	Approaches to St Helier	1:25,000
11	Approaches to Guernsey	1:150,000
SC 5605	**Chichester to Ramsgate, inc Dover Strait**	
1	W and N appr's to Dover Strait – planning	1:500,000
2	Dover to Calais & Calais	1:150,000
3	Chichester to Worthing	1:75,000
4	Worthing to Newhaven, inc Shoreham	1:75,000
5	Newhaven to Hastings, inc Sovereign Hbr	1:75,000
6	Hastings to Dungeness, inc Rye plan	1:75,000
7	Dungeness to S Foreland	1:75,000
8	Dover to Deal, inc Ramsgate plan	1:37,500
9	Deal to Ramsgate	1:37,500
10	Gravelines to Nieuwpoort, inc 2 plans	1:100,000
11	N'haven, L'hampton, Brighton, Folkestone	1:6,250
12	Dover and Shoreham	1:6,250
SC 5606	**Thames Estuary, Ramsgate to Canvey Island**	
1	Southern N Sea and Dover Strait	1:250,000
2	Southern Thames Estuary	1:100,000
3	Dover Strait to Gull Stream	1:75,000
4	Gull Stream to Princes Channel	1:50,000
5	Princes Channel to Medway appr chan	1:50,000
6	Whitaker Channel to West Swin	1:50,000
7	Havengore bridge to Southend-on-sea	1:25,000
8	Southend-on-sea to Canvey Island	1:25,000
9	Medway Approach Channel	1:25,000
10	R Medway and West Swale, inc Ferry Reach	1:25,000
11	R Medway to Chatham Reach	1:25,000
12	The Swale and upper R Medway	1:25,000
SC 5607	**Thames Estuary, Essex and Suffolk coast**	
1	Orford Ness to Oostende	1:250,000
2	Foulness Point to Landguard Point	1:100,000
3	Outer apprs to R Blackwater	1:50,000
4	Southern apprs to Harwich	1:50,000
5	Harwich to Orford Ness	1:50,000
6	Apprs to Harwich & Woodbridge Haven	1:25,000
7	River Stour & Orwell, Ipswich	1:25,000
8	Rivers Ore and Alde, inc Orford Haven	1:25,000
9	W Mersea and Brightlingsea	1:25,000
10	R Blackwater to Maldon, inc 3 plans	1:25,000
11	R Colne, W Mersea and Brightlingsea	1:25,000
12	Rivers Crouch and Roach	1:25,000
13	Upper River Crouch, plan of Burnham-o-C	1:25,000
14	Walton Backwaters	1:12,500

1.5 CONVERSION TABLES

1.5.1 Conversion factors

To convert	Multiply by	To convert	Multiply by
Area			
sq in to sq mm	645·16	sq mm to sq in	0·00155
sq ft to sq m	0·0929	sq m to sq ft	10·76
Length (See 1.4.2 for Feet to metres, and vv)			
in to mm	25·40	mm to in	0·0394
yds to m	0·914	m to yds	1·094
fathoms to m	1·8288	m to fathoms	0·5468
nautical miles (M) to kilometres	1·852	kilometres to nautical miles	0·539957
nautical miles to statute miles	1·1515	statute miles to nautical miles	0·8684
(1 cable equals 0·1 M, approx 185m)			
Velocity (See Ch 5 for knots to m/sec)			
ft/sec to m/sec	0·3048	m/sec to ft/sec	3·281
ft/sec to miles/hr	0·682	miles/hr to ft/sec	1·467
ft/min to m/sec	0·0051	m/sec to ft/min	196·8
knots to miles/hr	1·1515	miles/hr to knots	0·868
knots to km/hr	1·852	km/hr to knots	0·54
Mass			
lb to kg	0·4536	kg to lb	2·205
tons to tonnes (1000 kg)	1·016	tonnes to tons (2240 lb)	0·9842
Pressure (See Ch 5 for °C to °F)			
inches of mercury to millibars	33·86	millibars to inches of mercury	0·0295
lb/sq in to kg/sq cm	0·0703	kg/sq cm to lb/sq in	14·22
lb/sq in to atmospheres	0·068	atmospheres to lb/sq in	14·7
Volume			
cu ft to galls	6·25	galls to cu ft	0·16
cu ft to litres	28·33	litres to cu ft	0·035
Capacity			
pints to litres	0·568	litres to pints	1·76
galls to litres	4·546	litres to galls	0·22
Imp galls to US galls	1·2	US galls to Imp galls	0·833

1.5.2 Feet to metres, metres to feet

Explanation: The central columns of figures in blue type can be referred to the left to convert metres into feet, or to the right to convert feet into metres, e.g. five lines down: 5 metres = 16·40 feet, or 5 feet = 1·52 metres. Alternatively multiply feet by 0·3048 for metres, or multiply metres by 3·2808 for feet.

Feet		Metres	Feet		Metres	Feet		Metres	Feet		Metres
3·28	1	0·30	45·93	14	4·27	88·58	27	8·23	131·23	40	12·19
6·56	2	0·61	49·21	15	4·57	91·86	28	8·53	134·51	41	12·50
9·84	3	0·91	52·49	16	4·88	95·14	29	8·84	137·80	42	12·80
13·12	4	1·22	55·77	17	5·18	98·43	30	9·14	141·08	43	13·11
16·40	5	1·52	59·06	18	5·49	101·71	31	9·45	144·36	44	13·41
19·69	6	1·83	62·34	19	5·79	104·99	32	9·75	147·64	45	13·72
22·97	7	2·13	65·62	20	6·10	108·27	33	10·06	150·92	46	14·02
26·25	8	2·44	68·90	21	6·40	111·55	34	10·36	154·20	47	14·33
29·53	9	2·74	72·18	22	6·71	114·83	35	10·67	157·48	48	14·63
32·81	10	3·05	75·46	23	7·01	118·11	36	10·97	160·76	49	14·94
36·09	11	3·35	78·74	24	7·32	121·39	37	11·28	164·04	50	15·24
39·37	12	3·66	82·02	25	7·62	124·67	38	11·58			
42·65	13	3·96	85·30	26	7·92	127·95	39	11·89			

1.6 CALENDAR, 2005

1.6.1 UK PUBLIC HOLIDAYS 2005. All dates are subject to confirmation

ENGLAND & WALES: Jan 1, Mar 25, Mar 28, May 2, May 30 Aug 29, Dec 25, Dec 26

NORTHERN IRELAND: Jan 1, Mar 17, Mar 25, Mar 28, May 2, May 30, Jul 12, Aug 29, Dec 25, Dec 26

SCOTLAND: Jan 1, Jan 2, Jan 3, Jan 4, Mar 25, May 2, May 30, Aug 1, Dec 25, Dec 26

1.6.2 PHASES OF THE MOON 2005 (All times UT)

New Moon ●				First Quarter ◐				Full Moon ○				Last Quarter ◑			
	d	h	m		d	h	m		d	h	m		d	h	m
Jan	10	12	03	Jan	17	06	57	Jan	25	10	32	Jan	03	17	46
Feb	08	22	28	Feb	16	00	16	Feb	24	04	54	Feb	02	07	27
Mar	10	09	10	Mar	17	19	19	Mar	25	20	58	Mar	03	17	36
Apr	08	20	32	Apr	16	14	37	Apr	24	10	06	Apr	02	00	50
May	08	08	45	May	16	08	56	May	23	20	18	May	01	06	24
-	-	-	-	-	-	-	-	-	-	-	-	May	30	11	47
Jun	06	21	55	Jun	15	01	22	Jun	22	04	14	Jun	28	18	23
Jul	06	12	02	Jul	14	15	20	Jul	21	11	00	Jul	28	03	19
Aug	05	03	05	Aug	13	02	38	Aug	19	17	53	Aug	26	15	18
Sep	03	18	45	Sep	11	11	37	Sep	18	02	01	Sep	25	06	41
Oct	03	10	28	Oct	10	19	01	Oct	17	12	14	Oct	25	01	17
Nov	02	01	24	Nov	09	01	57	Nov	16	00	57	Nov	23	22	11
Dec	01	15	01	Dec	08	09	36	Dec	15	16	15	Dec	23	19	36
Dec	31	03	12	-	-	-	-	-	-	-	-	-	-	-	-

1.6.3 ECLIPSE NOTES 2005

1. A partial eclipse of the Sun on 3 October will be visible from Europe, including the British Isles.
2. No eclipses of the Moon will be visible from Europe, or the British Isles, during 2005.

1.6.4 STANDARD TIMES (Corrected to June 2004)

a. Standard Time is the time legally kept in a country during all but the summer months. It is sometimes known as Zone Time, a reference to the 24 Time Zones, each with a width of 15° Longitude, into which the world is divided. Zone 0 is centred on the Greenwich Meridian and is where Universal Time (UT) is kept. (UT has replaced GMT in common parlance, although for most practical purposes the two are identical).

b. **Countries whose Standard Time is UT**
Standard time is UT in Great Britain, The Channel Islands, Northern Ireland, The Irish Republic, Iceland, Faeroes, Portugal and Morocco.

c. **Countries whose Standard Time differs from UT**
Standard Time is one hour ahead of UT in Denmark, Germany, Netherlands, Belgium, France, Spain and Gibraltar.

In these countries 1 hour should therefore be added to UT to give Standard Time, or subtracted from Standard Time to give UT.

d. **Daylight Saving Time** (DST, or BST in the UK) is kept during the summer months in most European, and many other, countries. DST is one hour ahead of Standard Time. In EU countries DST is kept from the last Sunday in March until the Saturday before the last Sunday in October (but in Denmark DST ends on the last Sunday in October). Thus in 2005 DST is kept from 0100 UT Mar 27 until 0100 UT October 29.

e. **Tide Tables.** Note that Zone Time is quoted at the top left corner of each page of tidal predictions. For countries in (c) above, the Zone Time is known as –0100; this means that 1 hour must be subtracted from the printed tide times to give UT. This sometimes causes confusion, but remember that the times with a yellow background are in the country's Standard Time. In the summer (no yellow background) 1 hour must therefore be added to the printed time in order to obtain DST. See also Chapter 8, 8.1.2.

Chapter 2

Regulations

Contents

2.1 CRUISING FORMALITIES

2.1.1 Documentation

Before your annual cruise check that Yacht and Personal documents are in-date. It saves time, especially abroad, if these documents are readily available for inspection in transparent folders.

a. Yacht documents

Registration certificate (2.1.2). Marine insurance valid for the intended cruising area, including third-party cover (2.1.3). Proof of VAT status (2.5.1). Ship's radio licence (5.2.3). Ship's Log, itinerary and a crew list.

b. Personal documents

Valid passports and Forms E.111. Certificate of Competence, e.g. ICC or Yachtmaster (2.1.4). Radio Operator's certificate of competence, Pts 1 & 2 (5.4.3).

c. Health regulations

Comply with health regulations (e.g. report any infectious disease); check if vaccination certificates may be needed.

d. Customs regulations

Conform to HM Customs regulations (2.2) and any foreign customs regulations in countries visited (2.3). All countries are sensitive to the importation (including carriage on board) of illegal quantities of alcohol and tobacco, but drugs are their principal target (2.2.9).

2.1.2 Registration

The Merchant Shipping Act 1995 and related Merchant Shipping (Registration of Ships) Regulations govern the registration of British ships in the UK.

The Register of British Ships is in 4 parts, covering:

Part I Merchant ships and pleasure vessels.
Part II Fishing vessels.
Part III Small ships (Small Ships Register).
Part IV Bareboat charter ships.

a. Registration under Part I is a relatively complex and expensive business (£115), since a yacht has to be surveyed and follows the same procedure as a large merchant vessel. It costs £46 to renew for 5 years. The certificate establishes the ship's nationality and tonnage. Details of registered ownership and mortgages can be obtained from the RSS at Cardiff.

b. Part III, usually called *The Small Ships Register (SSR)*, is for ships whose owners only want a simple registration, sufficient for most purposes. A small ship is deemed to be < 24 metres LOA. SSR satisfies the law that a British yacht proceeding abroad must be registered, and it also meets the registration requirement for a privileged ensign, but it registers neither 'Title' nor mortgages. The cost is £10 for a five-year period, and measurement is a simple matter of taking the LOA of the boat.

Details and application forms are available via www.mcga.gov.uk or rss@mcga.gov.uk or contact: Registry of Shipping and Seamen (RSS), Anchor Court, Ocean Way, Cardiff CF24 5JW.
☎ 029 2044 8800; 📠 029 2044 8820.

2.1.3 Insurance

Any cruising boat should be protected by adequate insurance against possible loss or damage. The value for which a boat is insured should be the replacement cost of the boat and all equipment. Note the various warranties which are implied or expressed in the policy. It is also essential to insure against third-party risks, and cover for at least £1,500,000 is now normal. Policies invariably nominate the period in commission and cruising area; the latter must be adjusted, if cruising beyond the usual Brest to R. Elbe limits. Owners have a duty to disclose all relevant facts; failure to do so may invalidate a policy.

2.1.4 International Certificate of Competence

An International Certificate of Competence (ICC) (Pleasure Craft), valid for 5 years, is required in most European countries, especially those whose inland waterways are to be cruised. It can be endorsed for power or sail, inland or coastal waters, or all four. An endorsement for inland waterways requires a short, written test on CEVNI (Inland ColRegs) to be passed.

If evidence of Competence (eg Day Skipper or above) is not held, a practical test will be required before the ICC is issued. Apply to the RYA ☎ 0845 345 0370 or www.rya.org.uk.

2.2 HM CUSTOMS

2.2.1 The European Union (EU)

EU yachtsmen can move freely within the EU, provided that all taxes due, such as Customs duty, VAT, or any other Customs charges, have been paid in one of the EU countries. But most nations still carry out random checks on yachts to stop illegal goods, especially drugs, from entering their country. You may also be asked to provide evidence that the VAT, or equivalent, has been paid on your vessel so it is useful to carry on board suitable documentary evidence.

EU and EEA countries are: Austria, Belgium, Denmark, Finland, France, Germany, Greece, Holland, Iceland, Italy, Luxembourg, Norway, Portugal (including the Azores and Madeira), Republic of Ireland, Spain (including the Balearic Islands, but not the Canary Islands), Sweden, and the UK (including Gibraltar, but not the Isle of Man and the Channel Islands).

The Channel Islands and the Canary Islands do not operate a VAT system under EU rules, and are therefore treated as outside the EU single market.

2.2.2 Customs Notice No 8 (Dec 2002)

This Notice *'Sailing your pleasure craft to/from the UK'* is the UK's interpretation of what the law says about pleasure craft and compliance with customs and excise requirements, as summarised below. This Notice and further information may be obtained from the National Advice Service, ☎ 0845 010 9000, which is open 0800–2000 Mon-Fri. Or, for further information, visit HM Customs' web site at: **www.hmce.gov.uk**

Yachtsmen are warned that a boat may be searched at any time. Penalties are severe for non-declaration of prohibited or restricted goods, and the carriage and non-declaration of prohibited drugs and firearms. If goods are smuggled the vessel itself may be seized and the persons concerned liable to a heavy fine and/or prison sentence following prosecution. It is a good idea to have a copy of Notice No 8 aboard.

2.2.3 Duty-free stores

Duty-free stores may be allowed on vessels going south of Brest or north of the north bank of the Eider (Denmark), by prior application to a Customs office, and subject to certain conditions. Duty-free stores cannot be taken to the Republic of Ireland or the Channel Islands. Contact the National Advice Service for details of how to embark stores, or re-ship previously landed surplus duty-free stores, and of the conditions to be satisfied. Stores being shipped under bond, or on which repayment of Customs charges is being claimed, are normally placed under a Customs seal on board. These goods must not be used in UK waters without paying customs charges, and you will be liable to pay if you interrupt or abandon the voyage. For more info read Notice 69A *Duty free ship's stores.*

2.2.4 Notice of departure

a. To another EU country: No report is needed, unless requested by a Customs Officer.

b. To a country which is outside the EU:

You must notify HM Customs on Part 1 of Form C1331 of your departure. Copies of this form are available from most yacht clubs and marinas, Customs Offices, the National Advice Service or from the Customs and Excise Website. The completed form will need to be returned to Customs before you expect to leave the UK by handing it to a Customs Officer, placing it in a Customs post box or taking or posting it to a Customs office. Form C1331 is valid for up to 48hours from the stated time of departure. Retain Part 2 on board for use on your return. If your voyage is abandoned, Part 2 should be delivered to the same location to which the original form was sent, marked 'voyage abandoned'.

Failure to give notice of departure may result in delay and inconvenience on return and possible prosecution.

2.2.5 Arrival from an EU country

If arriving directly from another EU country there is no need to fly flag 'Q', complete any paperwork, or contact Customs. You must, however, contact the Customs 'Yachtline' on 0845 723 1110 if you have goods to declare, or have non-EU nationals on board. You must also declare any animals or birds; any prohibited or restricted goods such as controlled drugs, firearms, or radio transmitters not approved for use in UK; counterfeit goods; any duty-free stores; or the boat itself if duty and VAT are owed on it. Further details of which goods are classified as prohibited or restricted are given in Notice No 1.

If you bring back large quantities of alcohol or tobacco, a Customs Officer may ask you about the purposes for which you hold the goods. The officer will take all the factors of the situation into account, including your explanation. If the Officer is satisfied the goods are being imported into the UK for a commercial purpose, the goods, **along with any vessel used to transport them,** will be liable to seizure and may not be returned.

2.2.6 Arrival from a non-EU country

If arriving directly from a country outside the EU (including the Channel Islands), yachts are subject to

Customs control. As soon as UK Territorial Waters are entered, ie the 12-mile limit, complete Part 2 of Form C1331 and fly the flag 'Q' where it can easily be seen until formalities are complete.

On arrival, you must telephone the Customs 'Yachtline' on 0845 723 1110 and you will need to inform them if any of the following apply: VAT has not been paid on the vessel; you have goods in excess of your allowances which are detailed in Notice 1; you have duty-free stores on board; you have prohibited or restricted goods; someone on board has a notifiable illness; someone on board needs immigration clearance; or repairs or modifications (other than running repairs) have been carried out since the vessel left the EU. You must also declare to the Customs officer if you have any goods, which you intend to leave in the UK when you depart.

You will need to comply with any further instructions that the Customs officer gives you. Failure to comply will make you liable to a penalty. You must not land any persons or goods or transfer them to another vessel until a Customs officer says you may.

Usually the 'Yachtline' officer will ask you to complete sections (i) and (iii) and the declaration box on Form C1331. If you already had a Form C1331 Part 2 on board when you left the UK, you should fill in section (iii) amending details of persons on board if necessary and sign and date the form again.

2.2.7 Immigration

In most yachting centres the Customs Officer also acts as the Immigration Officer. Anyone aboard who is not an EU national must get an Immigration Officer's permission to enter the UK from any country other than the Isle of Man, the Channel Islands, or Eire. The skipper is responsible for ensuring that this is done.

2.2.8 Customs telephone numbers

The National Yachtline (☎ 0845 723 1110) must only be used by yachtsmen wishing to discharge their obligation to clear customs on return to the UK from a non-EU country (2.3.6). Use the National Advice Service (☎ 0845 010 9000) for all other customs queries and requests for forms and notices.

2.2.9 Drug smuggling

The prevention of drug smuggling is a key role for HM Customs. Public support is very important. If you see a suspicious incident or know of suspicious activity, telephone 0800 595000. This is a 24 hours, free and confidential Action line. There may be a reward.

2.3 FOREIGN CUSTOMS

Other EU countries should apply the regulations outlined in 2.2.1 to 2.2.6 above, and any Customs formalities are likely to be minimal. Before departure, skippers are recommended to check the procedures in force in their destination country.

2.3.1 The Schengen Treaty

In 1985 France, Germany, Luxembourg, Netherlands and Belgium signed a Convention which abolished internal border controls and established a single external border, around what is sometimes called 'Schengen-land'. Today all 17 EU members, except the UK and Eire, are signatories to Schengen and the decisions taken since 1985 are now part of EU law.

Those travelling from the UK to a Schengen country, or vice versa, are crossing the external border and may be subject to additional checks. Thus, Belgium and the Netherlands require a vessel to report on arrival even if coming from another EU country. The RYA can provide national forms which are simply a crew list (DoB, place of birth, passport No, nationality) and brief itinerary (last/next ports, dates etc).

In practice these forms are not always requested, but if you have them aboard you may avoid fines which can legally be imposed for not observing Schengen/ EU law. On arrival check with the HM whether any Customs or Immigration forms require filling in. The HM may well shrug and raise an eyebrow.

2.4. VAT AND THE SINGLE MARKET

2.4.1 General

An EU resident can move a yacht between member states without restriction, providing VAT has been paid. Documentary evidence supporting a vessel's VAT status should be carried at all times.

If in doubt as to what evidence you need to provide to establish the VAT status of your vessel, you should contact the relevant authorities in the Member State you intend to visit, or their Embassy in the UK. Further information is contained in Customs leaflet *UK guide for Yachts,* which is available on the Customs website; also see Notice 8, section 6.

2.4.2 Temporary importation (TI)

A vessel can be temporarily imported for private use within the EU by a non-EU resident under Temporary Importation relief provided the vessel is registered outside the EU or owned by a person established outside the EU. An application for authorisation should be made in the Member State where the vessel first enters the EU.

In the UK an application in duplicate should be submitted to Customs on Form C108 together with a notice of arrival [Form C1331 Part 2 (iii)].

The vessel can remain in the EU for a maximum of 18 months. If a longer period is required a written application explaining why must be made to customs. For UK-issued authorisation apply to the National Import Reliefs Unit (address para 1.5).

Temporary Importation relief for vessels may only be used by EU residents in the limited circumstance that are summarised in Notice 8 Section 5. Full details

C2

of the relief are given in Notice 308. The application form and Notices are available on the Customs website or from the National Advice Service.

2.5 INTERNATIONAL REGULATIONS FOR PREVENTING COLLISIONS AT SEA

2.5.1 Introduction

The 1972 International Regulations for Preventing Collisions at Sea (IRPCS), also referred to as Colregs or Rule of the Road, are discussed below in notes – only to help understand some rules of special interest to yachtsmen. They should be read – not in isolation, but in conjunction with the complete IRPCS which are given in full in *The Reeds Yachtsman's Handbook*, together with diagrams and explanatory notes; also in RYA booklet G2.

However, because the exact wording of the IRPCS is important, Rules 10 (TSS) and 12 to 19 (Conduct of vessels in sight of one another; and in restricted visibility) are quoted verbatim in italics. This does not imply that Chapter 2 should be consulted in the heat of the moment, since every yachtsman must have a sound working knowledge of the Rules – but an aide-memoire is sometimes handy.

2.5.2 Part A: General

Rule 2 (Responsibility). The rules must be interpreted in a seamanlike way if collisions are to be avoided. No vessel has a 'right of way' over another regardless of special circumstances – eg other vessels underway or at anchor, shallow water, poor visibility, TSS, fishing fleets etc – or the handling characteristics of the vessels concerned in the prevailing conditions. Sometimes vessels may need to depart from the rules to avoid immediate danger (Rule 2b).

Rule 3 (Definitions). A sailing vessel is so defined when she is under sail only. When under power she must show the lights for a power-driven vessel, and when under sail and power a cone, point-down, forward (Rule 25). A "Wing-in-Ground" (effect) craft, is *'a multimodal craft which, in its main operational mode, flies in close proximity to the surface by utilising surface-effect action'* (Rules 3 (m) and 18).

2.5.3 Part B: Steering and Sailing Rules
Section I – In any visibility

Rule 5 (Look-out). This vital rule requires a good look-out to be kept at all times, using eyes, ears, radar and VHF, particularly at night or in poor visibility.

Rule 6 (Safe speed). Visibility, traffic density (including concentrations of fishing or other vessels), depth of water, the state of wind, sea and current, proximity of navigational dangers, and the manoeuvrability of the boat, especially her stopping distance and turning ability in the prevailing conditions – all dictate what is a safe speed. Excessive speed gives less time to assess the situation and take avoiding action, and produces a worse collision if such action fails.

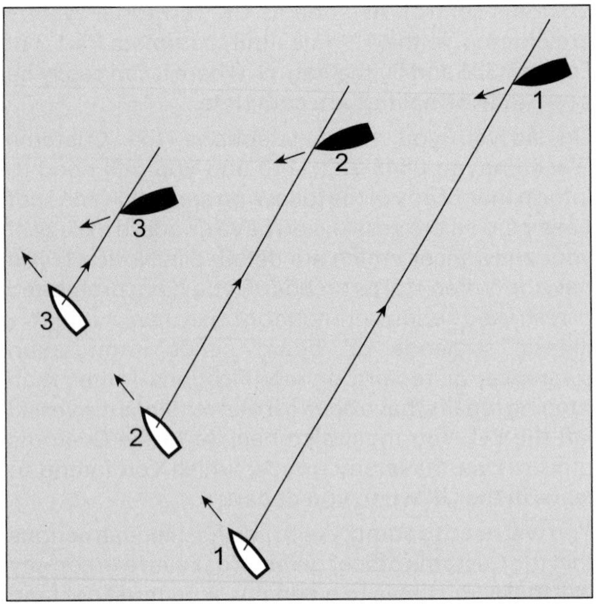

1
2
3
3
2
1

Fig. 2(1) Rule 7. The bearing of black from white is steady. Before position 2 white should have altered to starboard by at least 45° to pass under black's stern.

Rule 7 (Risk of collision). If there is any doubt, assume that there is a risk. A yacht should take a series of compass bearings on a closing ship – see Fig. 2 (1). Unless the bearings change appreciably, a risk of collision exists. Radar, properly used, offers early warning of risk of collision, but assumptions should not be made based on scanty, especially radar, information.

Rule 8 (Action to avoid collision). Such action must be positive, seamanlike and taken early. Large alterations of course and/or speed are more obvious to the other skipper, especially at night or on radar. Slow down, stop (or even go astern under power). While avoiding one vessel, watch out for others.

In complying with Rules 7 and 8, a skipper or crew should ask themselves the following three questions and take action if so required. (This is not in the IRPCS, but it concentrates the mind.)

1. Is there a risk of collision?
2. If there is, am I the give-way vessel?
3. If I am, what action must I take?

Rule 9 (Narrow channels). Keep to starboard, as near the outer limit of the channel or fairway as is safe and practical whether under power or sail. A vessel under 20m LOA or a sailing yacht shall not impede larger vessels confined to a channel. A vessel shall not cross a narrow channel if such crossing would impede a vessel which can only safely navigate within the channel; and shall avoid anchoring in such channels.

Rule 10 (TSS). TSS are essential to the safety of larger vessels and, whilst inconvenient for yachtsmen, must

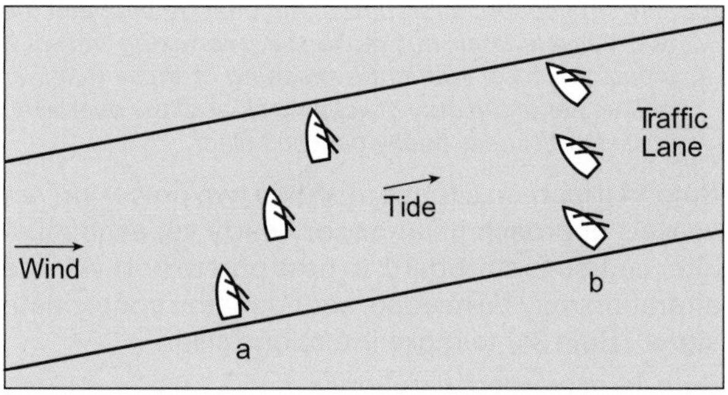
Traffic Lane
Tide
Wind
b
a

Fig. 2(2) Rule 10c. A yacht crossing a TSS lane must head at right angles to the lane axis, as in (a), regardless of the course made good as a result of wind or tidal streams. Yacht (b) is not heading at right angles and is therefore on an incorrect course.

be avoided where possible, or accepted as another element of passage planning. TSS are shown on most charts and in Chapter 9 of this Almanac.

All vessels, including yachts, must conform to TSS. However, when two vessels meet or converge in a TSS with a risk of collision, Rule 10 does not modify any other provisions of the IRPCS. Note well that craft <20m LOA, and any sailing yacht, shall not impede a power vessel using a traffic lane (10j). Rather than using the TSS lanes, it is better to use inshore traffic zones (ITZ) – usually the most sensible action for a yacht. If, unusually, obliged to join or leave a lane, do so at its extremity; if joining or leaving at the side, do so at as shallow an angle as possible. Follow the general direction of traffic in the correct lane.

Rule 10 is worded as follows:

(a) This Rule applies to traffic separation schemes adopted by the Organization (IMO) and does not relieve any vessel of her obligation under any other Rule.

(b) A vessel using a traffic separation scheme shall:

(i) proceed in the appropriate traffic lane in the general direction of traffic flow for that lane;

(ii) so far as practicable keep clear of a traffic separation line or separation zone;

(iii) normally join or leave a traffic lane at the termination of the lane, but when joining or leaving from either side shall do so at as small an angle to the general direction of traffic flow as practicable.

(c) A vessel shall so far as practicable avoid crossing traffic lanes, but if obliged to do so shall cross on a heading as nearly as practicable at right angles to the general direction of traffic flow.

(d) (i) A vessel shall not use an inshore traffic zone when she can safely use the appropriate traffic lane within the adjacent traffic separation scheme. However, vessels of less than 20 metres in length, sailing vessels and vessels engaged in fishing may use the inshore traffic zone.

(ii) Notwithstanding sub-paragraph (d) (i) a vessel may use an inshore traffic zone when en route to or from a port, offshore installation or structure, pilot station or any other place situated within the traffic zone, or to avoid immediate danger.

(e) A vessel other than a crossing vessel or a vessel joining or leaving a lane shall not normally enter a separation zone or cross a separation line except:

(i) in cases of emergency to avoid immediate danger;

(ii) to engage in fishing within a separation zone.

(f) A vessel navigating in areas near the terminations of traffic separation schemes shall do so with particular caution.

(g) A vessel shall so far as practicable avoid anchoring in a traffic separation scheme or in areas near its terminations.

(h) A vessel not using a traffic separation scheme shall avoid it by as wide a margin as is practicable.

(i) A vessel engaged in fishing shall not impede the passage of any vessel following a traffic lane.

(j) A vessel of less than 20 metres in length or a sailing vessel shall not impede the safe passage of a power-driven vessel following a traffic lane.

(k) A vessel restricted in her ability to manoeuvre when engaged in an operation for the maintenance of safety of navigation in a traffic separation scheme is exempted from complying with this Rule to the extent necessary to carry out the operation.

(l) A vessel restricted in her ability to manoeuvre when engaged in an operation for the laying, servicing or picking up of a submarine cable, within a traffic separation scheme, is exempted from complying with this Rule to the extent necessary to carry out the operation.

2.5.4 Section II – Vessels in sight of one another

Rule 12 (Sailing vessels).

When two yachts under sail are at risk of collision, (a) (i) and (ii) below are clear. (a) (iii) deals with the situation where doubt arises as to which tack a windward yacht is on. Rule 12 does not apply if either yacht is motor sailing.

Fig. 2 (3) illustrates the practical application of the rules in the three cases mentioned above.

Two other practical situations might cause doubt about the application of Rule 12:

i. For the purpose of this rule the windward side is deemed to be the side opposite to that on which the mainsail is carried. But when running downwind under spinnaker alone, windward would be the side on which the spinnaker boom is set (normally opposite to the mainsail).

ii. When hove-to. This would depend on the most likely position of the mainsail if it were set.

Rule 12 is worded as follows:

(a) When two sailing vessels are approaching one another, so as to involve risk of collision, one of them shall keep out of the way of the other as follows:

(i) when each has the wind on a different side, the vessel which has the wind on the port side shall keep out of the way of the other;

(ii) when both have the wind on the same side, the vessel which is to windward shall keep out of the way of the vessel which is to leeward;

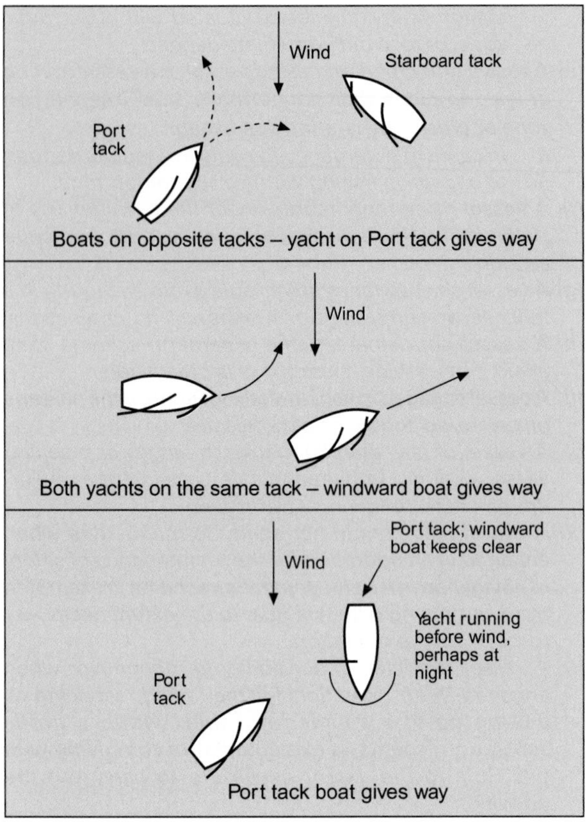
Wind
Starboard tack
Port
tack
Boats on opposite tacks – yacht on Port tack gives way
Wind
Both yachts on the same tack – windward boat gives way
Wind
Port tack; windward
boat keeps clear
Yacht running
before wind,
perhaps at
night
Port
tack
Port tack boat gives way

Fig. 2(3) Rule 12. A port tack yacht keeps clear. If both yachts are on the same tack the windward boat keeps clear. If in doubt, port tack always keep clear.

(iii) if a vessel with the wind on the port side sees a vessel to windward and cannot determine with certainty whether the other vessel has the wind on the port or on the starboard side, she shall keep out of the way of the other.

(b) For the purposes of this Rule the windward side shall be deemed to be the side opposite to that on which the mainsail is carried or, in the case of a square-rigged vessel, the side opposite to that on which the largest fore-and-aft sail is carried.

Rule 13 (Overtaking). An overtaking vessel, whether power or sail, shall keep clear of the vessel being overtaken. Overtaking means overhauling the other vessel from a direction more than 22½° abaft her beam.

Rule 13 is worded as follows:

(a) Notwithstanding anything contained in the Rules of Part B, Sections I & II any vessel overtaking any other shall keep out of the way of the vessel being overtaken.

(b) A vessel shall be deemed to be overtaking when coming up with another vessel from a direction more than 22½° abaft her beam, that is, in such a position with reference to the vessel she is overtaking, that at night she would be able to see only the sternlight of that vessel but neither of her sidelights.

(c) When a vessel is in any doubt as to whether she is overtaking another, she shall assume that this is the case and act accordingly.

(d) Any subsequent alteration of the bearing between the two vessels shall not make the overtaking vessel a crossing vessel within the meaning of these Rules or relieve her of the duty of keeping clear of the overtaken vessel until she is finally past and clear.

Rule 14 (Head-on situation). When two power-driven vessels approach head-on, or nearly so, each must alter course to starboard, to pass port to port. A large alteration may be needed, sounding the appropriate signal (Rule 34) to make intentions clear.

Rule 14 is worded as follows:

(a) When two power-driven vessels are meeting on reciprocal or nearly reciprocal courses so as to involve risk of collision each shall alter her course to starboard so that each shall pass on the port side of the other.

(b) Such a situation shall be deemed to exist when a vessel sees the other ahead or nearly ahead and by night she could see the masthead lights of the other in a line or nearly in a line and/or both sidelights and by day she observes the corresponding aspect of the other vessel.

(c) When a vessel is in any doubt as to whether such a situation exists she shall assume that it does exist and act accordingly.

Rule 15 (Crossing situation). When two power-driven vessels are crossing with a risk of collision, the one with the other on her own starboard side must keep clear; if possible, avoid crossing ahead of the other. The give-way vessel should normally alter to starboard to pass astern of the other. Exceptionally, an alteration to port may be justified (eg, shoal water to starboard), in which case a large alteration may be needed to avoid crossing ahead of the other.

Rule 15 is worded as follows:

When two power-driven vessels are crossing so as to involve risk of collision, the vessel which has the other on her own starboard side shall keep out of the way and shall, if the circumstances of the case admit, avoid crossing ahead of the other vessel.

Rule 16 (Action by give-way vessel).
The wording is clear. "*Early and substantial ... well clear*" are the key words:

Every vessel which is directed to keep out of the way of another vessel shall, so far as possible, take early and substantial action to keep well clear.

Rule 17 (Action by stand-on vessel). This rule describes a deteriorating sequence of events and the actions that a stand-on vessel shall take if it appears that the give-way vessel is failing to keep clear.

First, the stand-on vessel may manoeuvre to avoid collision (17a. ii). In taking such action, a power-driven vessel shall, if possible, not alter course to port for a vessel on her own port side (17c). [Normally she would alter substantially to starboard, to minimise the risk of both vessels turning towards each other].

Second, when the stand-on vessel finds herself so close that collision cannot be avoided by the action of the give-way vessel alone, the stand-on vessel *shall* take such action (17b), as will best aid to avoid collision. This is likely to be drastic, eg Full astern and/or helm hard over.

Rule 17 is worded as follows:

(a) (i) Where one of two vessels is to keep out of the way the other shall keep her course and speed.

(ii) The latter vessel may however take action to avoid collision by her manoeuvre alone, as soon as it becomes apparent to her that the vessel required to keep out of the way is not taking appropriate action in compliance with these Rules.

(b) When, from any cause, the vessel required to keep her course and speed finds herself so close that collision cannot be avoided by the action of the give way vessel alone, she shall take such action as will best aid to avoid collision.

(c) A power-driven vessel which takes action in a crossing situation in accordance with sub-paragraph (a) (ii) of this Rule to avoid collision with another power-driven vessel shall, if the circumstances of the case admit, not alter course to port for a vessel on her own port side.

(d) This Rule does not relieve the give-way vessel of her obligation to keep out of the way.

Rule 18 (Responsibilities between vessels). This rule lays down priorities according to manoeuvrability. The hierarchy is clear & logical; (b) applies to yachts. New para (f) includes WIG craft, defined in Rule 3 (m). It flies on an air-cushion created by its own very fast forward speed; it is more an aircraft than a vessel.

Rule 18 is worded as follows:

Except where Rules 9, 10 and 13 otherwise require:

(a) A power-driven vessel underway shall keep out of the way of:

(i) a vessel not under command;

(ii) a vessel restricted in her ability to manoeuvre;

(iii) a vessel engaged in fishing;

(iv) a sailing vessel.

(b) A sailing vessel underway shall keep out of the way of:

(i) a vessel not under command;

(ii) a vessel restricted in her ability to manoeuvre;

(iii) a vessel engaged in fishing.

(c) A vessel engaged in fishing when underway shall, so far as possible, keep out of the way of:

(i) a vessel not under command;

(ii) a vessel restricted in her ability to manoeuvre.

(d) (i) Any vessel other than a vessel not under command or a vessel restricted in her ability to manoeuvre shall, if the circumstances of the case admit, avoid impeding the safe passage of a vessel constrained by her draught, exhibiting the signals in Rule 28.

(ii) A vessel constrained by her draught shall navigate with particular caution having full regard to her special condition.

(e) A seaplane on the water shall, in general, keep well clear of all vessels and avoid impeding their navigation. In circumstances, however, where risk of collision exists, she shall comply with the Rules of this Part.

(f) (i) A WIG craft shall, when taking off, landing and in flight near the surface, keep well clear of all other vessels and avoid impeding their navigation;

(ii) A WIG craft operating on the water surface shall comply with the Rules of this Part as a power-driven vessel.

2.5.5 Section III – Vessels in restricted visibility

C2

Rule 19 (Restricted visibility). In or near an area of poor visibility vessels must proceed at a safe speed (b). If a fog signal is heard forward of the beam, slow down but maintain steerage way (e).

If a vessel is detected by radar alone (d), decide whether a close quarters situation is developing and/or a collision risk exists. If the latter, take early action to avoid collision. The negative wording of (d) (i) and (ii) can be translated more positively as: Alter course to starboard to avoid a vessel on your port side or off the starboard bow, unless you are overtaking the other vessel. Alter course to port to avoid a vessel off your starboard quarter. Do not alter course towards a vessel abeam or abaft the beam.

Safety dictates that you: sound the appropriate fog signal, keep a good lookout, have an efficient radar reflector, or better still a radar which you are competent to use, and keep clear of shipping lanes. In thick fog it is best to anchor in shallow water; not easy if you have just cleared a shipping lane in mid-Channel.

Rule 19 is worded as follows:

(a) This Rule applies to vessels not in sight of one another when navigating in or near an area of restricted visibility.

(b) Every vessel shall proceed at a safe speed adapted to the prevailing circumstances and conditions of restricted visibility. A power-driven vessel shall have her engines ready for immediate manoeuvre.

(c) Every vessel shall have due regard to the prevailing circumstances and conditions of restricted visibility when complying with the Rules of Section 1 of this Part.

(d) A vessel which detects by radar alone the presence of another vessel shall determine if a close-quarters situation is developing and/or risk of collision exists. If so, she shall take avoiding action in ample time, provided that when such action consists of an alteration of course, so far as possible the following shall be avoided:

(i) an alteration of course to port for a vessel forward of the beam, other than for a vessel being overtaken;

(ii) an alteration of course towards a vessel abeam or abaft the beam.

(e) Except where it has been determined that a risk of collision does not exist, every vessel which hears apparently forward of her beam the fog signal of another vessel, or which cannot avoid a close-quarters situation with another vessel forward of her beam, shall reduce her speed to the minimum at which she can be kept on her course. She shall if necessary take all her way off and in any event navigate with extreme caution until danger of collision is over.

2.5.6 Part C: Lights and shapes

Rule 20 (Application). The required lights must be shown from sunset to sunrise, and by day in restricted visibility. The required shapes must be shown by day.

Rule 21 (Definitions).The types of navigation lights are defined, and illustrated on the next two pages.

Rule 23 (Power driven vessels underway). (c) requires a WIG craft, when taking off, landing and in flight near the surface, to show a high-intensity all-round Fl R light (see also Rules 3 and 18). (d) (i) A power-driven vessel <12m LOA may combine her masthead light and sternlight into one all-round Ⓦ light.

Rule 25 (Sailing vessels underway). In a sailing yacht <20m LOA, the sidelights and sternlight may be combined in one tricolour lamp at the masthead (25b). This gives excellent visibility for the lights, and maximum brightness for minimum battery drain. A tricolour light should not be switched on at the same time as the normal sidelights and sternlight, and must never be used when under power.

A yacht, even with sails set, which is also being driven by engine must show the lights of a power-driven vessel, and by day, a cone, point-down, forward. A sailing vessel under way may, in addition to her normal sidelights and sternlight, show near the masthead two all-round lights, Ⓡ over Ⓖ (25c). These lights must not be shown at the same time as the tricolour light described above.

Rule 27 (Vessels not under command, or restricted in their ability to manoeuvre). The lights & shapes required by this rule do not apply to vessels <12m LOA; but fly flag 'A' if engaged in diving operations.

Rule 30 (Anchored or grounded vessels). Yachts at anchor, like other vessels, <u>shall</u> show an anchor light or ball. This requirement has safety and insurance implications, assists other mariners and is often enforced abroad. Rules 30e and 30f grant two minor exemptions for yachts <7m LOA and <12m LOA.

2.5.7 Part D: Sound and Light signals

Rule 32 (Definitions).

•	A short blast of foghorn (about 1 second).
—	A prolonged blast (four to six seconds).

Rule 33 (Equipment for sound signals).
Vessels >12m LOA must have a foghorn and a bell. A boat <12m LOA may carry other means of making an efficient sound signal. Efficiency should be judged against its audibility within the enclosed bridge of a large ship, with conflicting background noises.

Rule 34 (Manoeuvring and warning signals).
Power-driven vessels in sight of each other:

The following sound signals may be supplemented by light flashes:

•	I am altering course to starboard.
• •	I am altering course to port.
• • •	I am operating astern propulsion.
• • • • •	I do not understand your intentions/actions or I doubt if sufficient action is being taken to avoid collision.

In a narrow channel:

— — •	I intend to overtake on your starboard side.
— — • •	I intend to overtake you on your port side.
— • — •	I agree with your overtaking signal.
—	Warning by vessel nearing a bend where other vessels may not be visible.

Rule 35 (Sound signals in restricted visibility).

—	Power-driven vessel making way.
— —	Power-driven vessel underway, but stopped and not making way.
— • •	Vessel not under command; restricted in her ability to manoeuvre; constrained by her draught; or engaged in fishing, towing or pushing; **or a sailing vessel**.
— • • •	Vessel being towed, or if more than one vessel is towed, the last vessel in the tow.
• • • •	Pilot vessel engaged on pilotage duties.

The maximum interval between sound signals for vessels under way in restricted visibility is two minutes, but more frequently if other craft are near. For flag and sound signals which have a special meaning under IRPCS, see the asterisked items in the first colour illustration of Chapter 5.

Bell rung rapidly for about 5 seconds, every minute.

=	Vessel at anchor.

Gong rung rapidly for about 5 seconds after the above signal, every minute; the bell being sounded in the fore part of the vessel and the gong aft

=	Vessel of 100m or more in length at anchor.
• — •	Vessel at anchor (optional extra sound signal).

Bell rung rapidly for about 5 seconds, with three separate and distinct strokes of the bell before and after the rapid ringing

=	Vessel aground.

2.5.8 Annexes I to IV

Annexes I and III give technical details of lights, shapes and sound signals. Annex II gives additional lights which may be shown by fishing vessels working close together. Annex IV, introduced by Rule 37, details the signals which may be used in distress or when in need of assistance. These are illustrated in Fig. 7(1).

PLATE 1 NAVIGATION LIGHTS

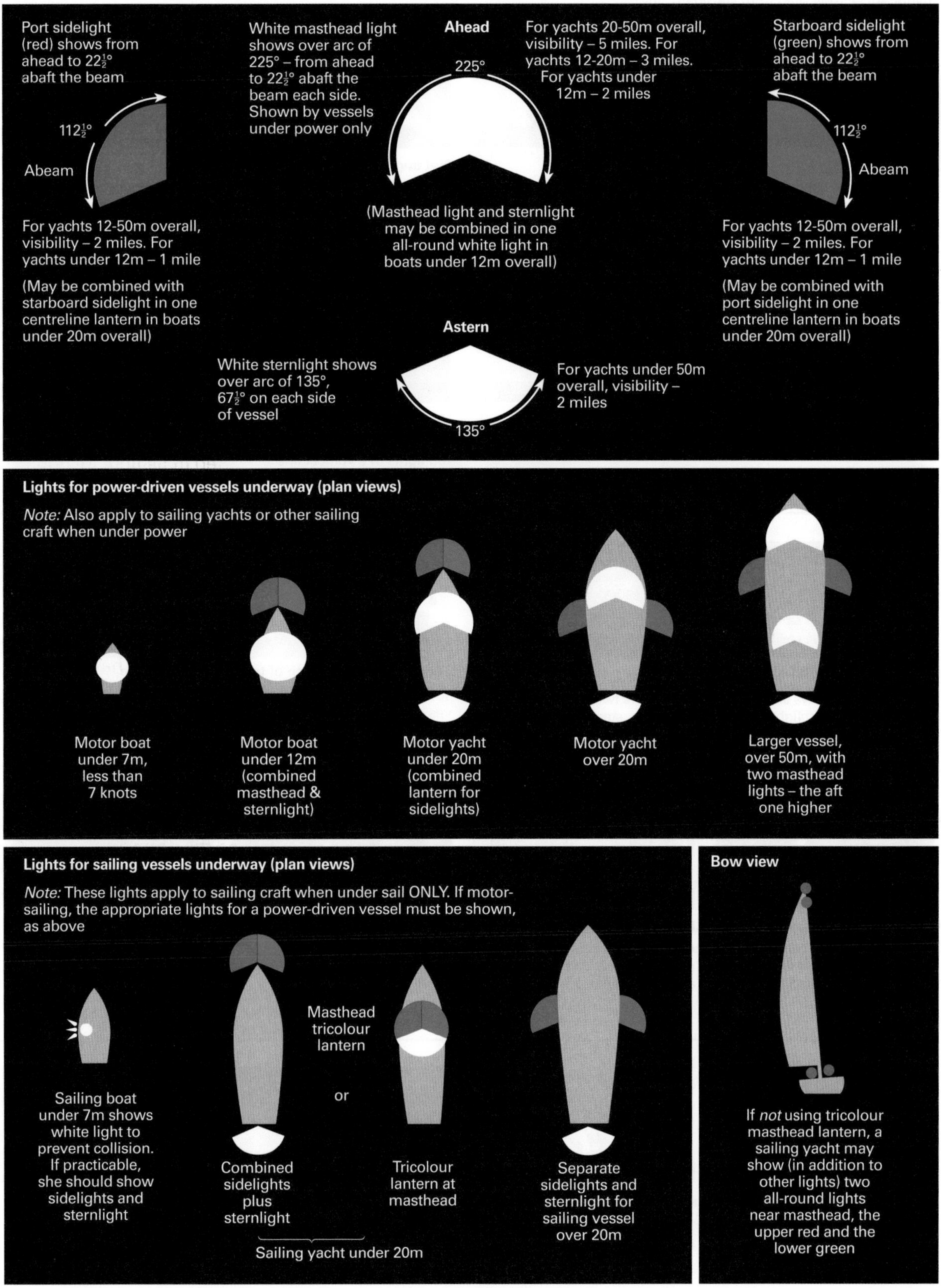
Port sidelight (red) shows from ahead to 22½° abaft the beam
112½°
Abeam
For yachts 12-50m overall, visibility – 2 miles. For yachts under 12m – 1 mile
(May be combined with starboard sidelight in one centreline lantern in boats under 20m overall)
White masthead light shows over arc of 225° – from ahead to 22½° abaft the beam each side. Shown by vessels under power only
Ahead
225°
For yachts 20-50m overall, visibility – 5 miles. For yachts 12-20m – 3 miles. For yachts under 12m – 2 miles
(Masthead light and sternlight may be combined in one all-round white light in boats under 12m overall)
Starboard sidelight (green) shows from ahead to 22½° abaft the beam
112½°
Abeam
For yachts 12-50m overall, visibility – 2 miles. For yachts under 12m – 1 mile
(May be combined with port sidelight in one centreline lantern in boats under 20m overall)
Astern
White sternlight shows over arc of 135°, 67½° on each side of vessel
135°
For yachts under 50m overall, visibility – 2 miles
Lights for power-driven vessels underway (plan views)
Note: Also apply to sailing yachts or other sailing craft when under power
Motor boat under 7m, less than 7 knots
Motor boat under 12m (combined masthead & sternlight)
Motor yacht under 20m (combined lantern for sidelights)
Motor yacht over 20m
Larger vessel, over 50m, with two masthead lights – the aft one higher
Lights for sailing vessels underway (plan views)
Note: These lights apply to sailing craft when under sail ONLY. If motor-sailing, the appropriate lights for a power-driven vessel must be shown, as above
Sailing boat under 7m shows white light to prevent collision. If practicable, she should show sidelights and sternlight
Masthead tricolour lantern
or
Combined sidelights plus sternlight
Tricolour lantern at masthead
Sailing yacht under 20m
Separate sidelights and sternlight for sailing vessel over 20m
Bow view
If not using tricolour masthead lantern, a sailing yacht may show (in addition to other lights) two all-round lights near masthead, the upper red and the lower green

PLATE 2 PRINCIPAL NAVIGATION LIGHTS AND SHAPES

(Note: All vessels seen from starboard side)

Rule 30

Vessel at anchor

All-round white light; if over 50m, a second light aft and lower

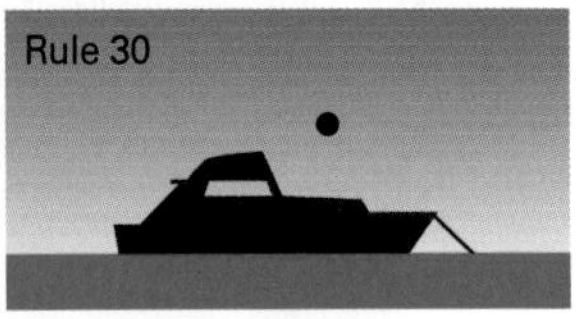
Rule 30

Black ball forward

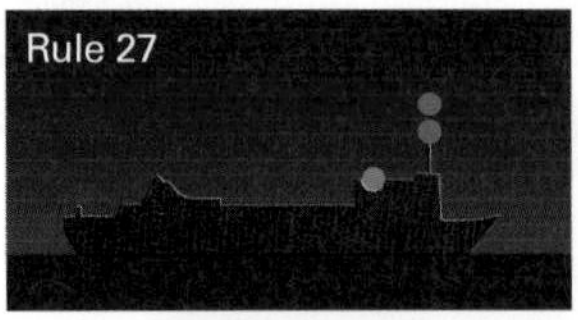
Rule 27

Not under command

Two all-round red lights, plus sidelights and sternlight when making way

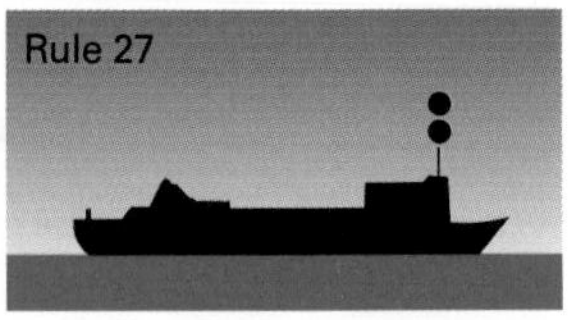
Rule 27

Two black balls vertically

Rule 25

Motor sailing

Cone point down, forward

Rule 27

Divers down

Letter 'A' International Code

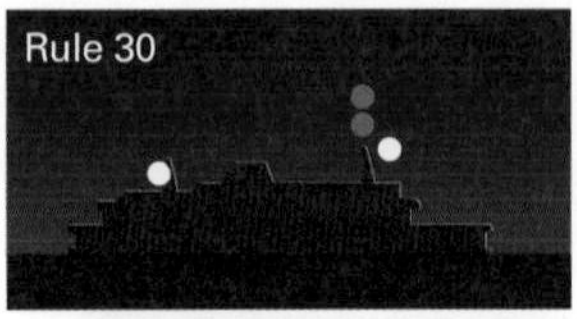
Rule 30

Vessel aground

Anchor light(s), plus two all-round red lights in a vertical line

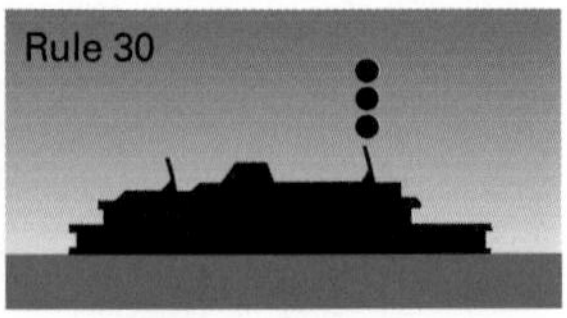
Rule 30

Three black balls in a vertical line

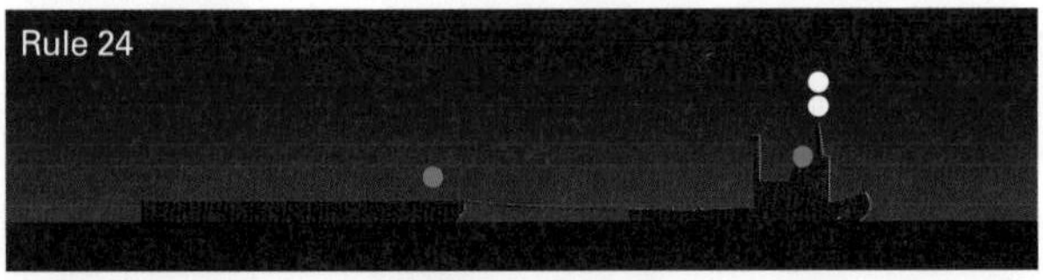
Rule 24

Vessels being towed and towing

Vessel towed shows sidelights (forward) and sternlight

Tug shows two masthead lights, sidelights, sternlight, yellow towing light

Rule 24

Towing by day – Length of tow more than 200m

Towing vessel and tow display diamond shapes. By night, the towing vessel shows three masthead lights instead of two as for shorter tows

---

Rule 26

Vessel fishing

All-round red light over all-round white, plus sidelights and sternlight when making way

Rule 26

Fishing/Trawling

A shape consisting of two cones point to point in a vertical line one above the other

Rule 26

Vessel trawling

All-round green light over all-round white, plus sidelights and sternlight when making way

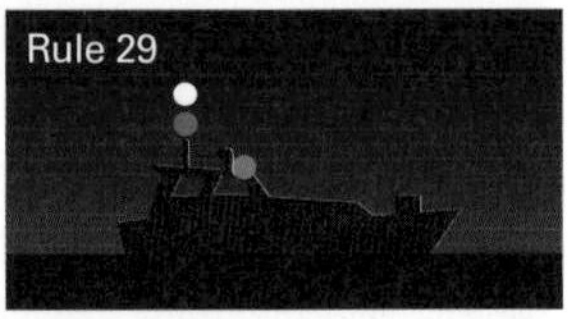
Rule 29

Pilot boat

All-round white light over all-round red, plus sidelights and sternlight when underway, or anchor light

---

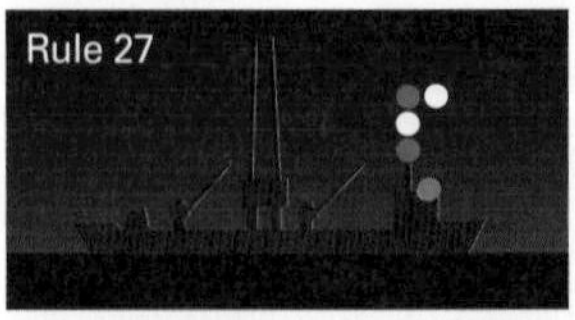
Rule 27

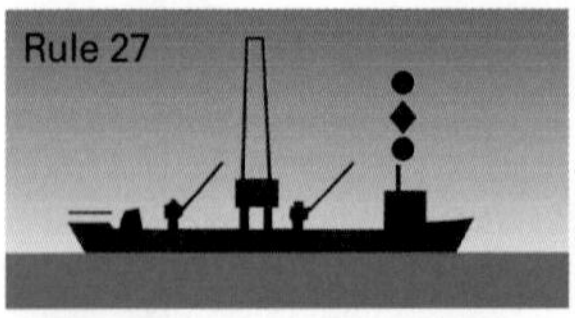
Rule 27

Vessel restricted in her ability to manoeuvre

All-round red, white, red lights vertically, plus normal steaming lights when making way

Three shapes in a vertical line ball, diamond, ball

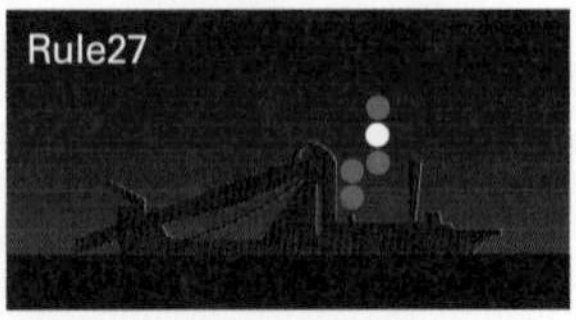
Rule27

Dredger

As left, plus two all-round red lights (or two balls) on foul side, and two all-round green (or two diamonds) on clear side

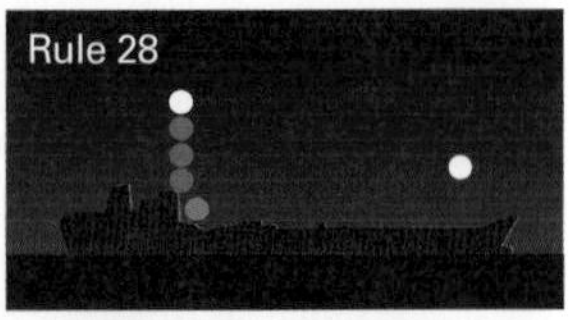
Rule 28

Constrained by draught

Three all-round red lights in a vertical line, plus normal steaming lights. By day – a cylinder

Chapter 3

Coastal Navigation

Contents

3.1 DEFINITIONS AND TERMS

3.1.1 General

The information given here covers a few of the more important aspects of basic coastal navigation in simplified form, together with useful tables.

The Reeds Yachtsman's Handbook provides a more extensive reference on coastal navigation covering all aspects of pilotage.

3.1.2 Position

Position on the Earth's surface can be expressed in two ways. By Latitude and Longitude, or by a bearing and distance from a known position.

The latitude of a place is its angular distance measured in degrees (°), minutes (') and decimals of a minute from 0° to 90° north or south of the equator.

The longitude of a place is measured in degrees (°), minutes ('), and decimals of a minute from 0° to 180° east or west from the Greenwich meridian.

3.1.3 Direction

Direction is measured clockwise from north in a three-figure group, i.e. 000° to 359°. Thus east is written as 090°, and west 270°.

Direction may be referenced to three different norths namely:

(1) **True North** as measured from the Geographic North Pole.

(2) **Magnetic North** as measured from the Magnetic North Pole, which does not coincide with the Geographic Pole.

(3) **Compass North** as measured from the north-seeking end of the compass needle.

Bearings and tracks as given on charts, or quoted in publications, are normally True bearings.

Wind direction is normally given in points of the compass clockwise from a cardinal or quadrantal point rather than in degrees, i.e. N, NNE, NE by N, etc. There are 32 points of the compass, with each point equal to 11¼°.

Tidal streams are always expressed in the direction towards which they are running.

3.1.4 Compass variation and deviation

The magnetic compass is the most vital navigational instrument in a cruising boat. It is affected by: **variation** (the angular difference between True and Magnetic North), which alters from place to place, and year to year, and is shown on the chart, normally at the compass rose; and by **deviation** (the angular difference between Magnetic and Compass North which is caused by the boat's own magnetic field. Deviation varies according to the boat's heading. Following a compass swing and adjustment of the compass, any residual deviation is shown, for different headings on a deviation card. With a properly adjusted compass, deviation should not be more than about 2° on any heading – in which case it can often be ignored except on long passages.

When converting a True course or a True bearing to Magnetic: add westerly (+) variation or deviation and subtract easterly (–).

When converting a Magnetic course or bearing to True: subtract westerly (–) variation or deviation, and add easterly (+).

3.1.5 Distance

Distance at sea is measured in nautical miles (M). A nautical mile is defined as the length of one minute of latitude. The length of a nautical mile varies with latitude and measures 6,108 feet at the Pole and 6,046 feet at the Equator. The International nautical mile is taken as being 6,076 feet or 1,852 metres.

Short distances are measured in cables. A cable is one tenth of a nautical mile, which for practical purposes approximates to 200 yards or 600 feet in length and is always used for navigational purposes irrespective of the latitude.

Distances must always be measured from the latitude scale of a chart, and not the longitude scale because the length of one minute of longitude on the earth varies from being roughly equal to a minute of latitude at the Equator, to zero length at the Pole. The longitude scale is therefore of no value as a measure of distance.

3.1.6 Speed

Speed at sea is measured in knots. A knot is one nautical mile per hour. The relationship between speed, time and distance is expressed in the formula:

$$\text{Speed} = \frac{\text{Distance (miles)}}{\text{Sailing time (hours)}}$$

or: $\text{Distance} = \text{Speed x sailing time}$

or: $\text{Sailing time} = \frac{\text{Distance}}{\text{Speed}}$

A time, speed and distance table is given in Table 3 (4).

A log measures distance run through the water and most logs today also incorporate a speed indicator. Course and speed made good over the ground can be obtained from position-fixing devices such as GPS.

3.1.7 Depth

Depths and heights are given in metres (m). Depths of water are measured by echo sounder (or lead line). Note whether the sounder indicates depth below the water level, the transducer, or the base of the keel.

Chart Datum (CD) is the level below which the tide never, or very rarely, falls. Charted depths and drying heights shown on charts are always referenced to CD. The height of tide is the height of the sea surface above Chart Datum at any instant. Heights of lights, structures or land which never covers are given above MHWS. Tidal height calculations are in Chapter 8.

3.2 IALA BUOYAGE

IALA Buoyage System (Region A)
International buoyage is harmonised into a single system (region A includes all of Europe).

(1) **Lateral Marks**: are used in conjunction with a direction of buoyage, shown by a special arrow on the chart. Around the British Isles the general direction is from SW to NE in open waters, but from seaward when approaching a harbour, river or estuary. Where port or starboard lateral marks do not rely on can or conical buoy shapes for identification, they carry, where practicable, the appropriate topmarks. Any numbering or lettering follows the direction of buoyage, evens to port and odds to starboard.
In Region A, port-hand marks are coloured red, and port-hand buoys are can or spar shaped. Any topmark fitted is a single red can. Any light fitted is red, any rhythm. Starboard-hand marks are coloured green, and starboard-hand buoys are conical or spar shaped. Any topmark fitted is a single green cone, point up. Any light fitted is green, any rhythm. In exceptional cases starboard-hand marks may be coloured black.

R R

Port Hand marks
Light: red
Rhythm: any

Navigable channel

Direction of buoyage

G G

Starboard Hand marks
Light: green
Rhythm: any

(2) **Cardinal marks**: are named after the quadrant in which the mark is placed, in relation to the danger or point indicated. The four quadrants (north, east, south and west) are bounded by the True bearings NW-NE, NE-SE, SE-SW and SW-NW, taken from the point of interest. The name of a cardinal mark indicates that it should be passed on the named side. For example, a NCM (situated in the quadrant between NW and NE from the point of interest) should be passed on its north side; an ECM on its East side, and so on.
A cardinal mark may indicate the safe side on which to pass a danger, or that the deepest water is on the named side of the mark, or it may draw attention to a feature in a channel such as a bend, junction or fork, or the end of a shoal.
Their lights are white, and are either VQ or Q. VQ lights flash at a rate of 80 to 159 flashes per minute, usually either 100 or 120, and Q flash at a rate of between 50 to 79 flashes per minute. A long flash is one of not less than two seconds duration.

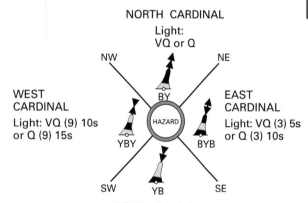

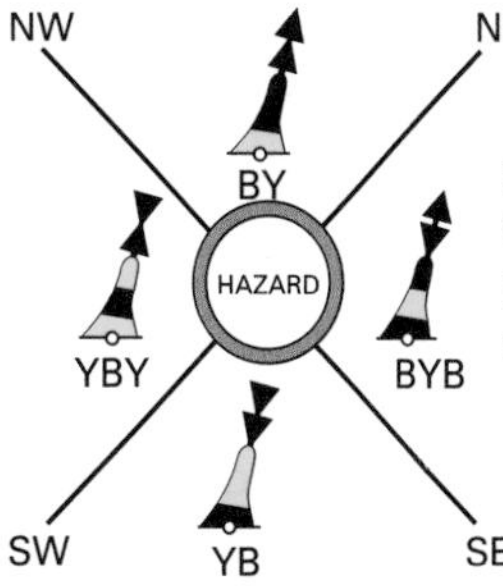
NORTH CARDINAL
Light:
VQ or Q
NW
NE
BY
WEST
CARDINAL
Light: VQ (9) 10s
or Q (9) 15s
HAZARD
EAST
CARDINAL
Light: VQ (3) 5s
or Q (3) 10s
YBY
BYB
SW
YB
SE
SOUTH CARDINAL
Light: VQ (6) + L Fl 10s or Q (6) + L Fl 15s

BRB BRB

(3) **Isolated danger marks**: are placed on or above an isolated danger such as a rock or a wreck which has navigable water all around it. Any light is white, flashing twice.

RW RW

(4) **Safe water marks:** indicate that there is navigable water all round the mark, and are used for mid-channel or landfall marks. Buoys are spherical, pillar with spherical topmark, or spar shaped, and are coloured with red and white vertical stripes. Any topmark fitted is a single red sphere. When lit, any light is white – either occulting, isophase, or Morse code (A), or showing a single long-flash every 10 seconds.

Y Y Y Y

(5) **Special marks**: do not primarily assist navigation, but indicate a special area or feature (e.g. spoil grounds, exercise areas, water-ski areas, cable or pipeline marks, outfalls, Ocean Data Acquisition Systems (ODAS), or traffic separation marks where conventional channel marks may cause confusion). Special marks are yellow, and any shape not conflicting with lateral or safe water marks. If can, spherical or conical are used they indicate the side on which to pass. Any topmark fitted is a yellow X. Any light fitted is yellow, and may have any rhythm not used for white lights.

New dangers (which may be natural obstructions such as a sandbank, or a wreck) are marked in accordance with the rules above, and lit accordingly. For a very grave danger one of the marks may be duplicated.

C3

3.2 IALA BUOYAGE contd

Preferred Channels

At a division, the preferred channel may be shown by lateral marks with red or green bands: Preferred Channel indicated by light (if any)-

to starboard:

a Port lateral mark with green band Flashing red (2 + 1)

to port:

a Starboard lateral mark with red band Flashing green (2 + 1)

RGR RGR

Preferred channel to Starboard

Navigable channel

Direction of buoyage

GRG GRG

Preferred channel to Port

3.3 LIGHTS

3.3.1 Light characteristics

The abbreviations for, and characteristics of, marine lights are shown in Fig. 3.(3) opposite, or in **Admiralty Chart 5011** (an A4 booklet).

3.3.2 Light sectors, arcs of visibility

The limits of light sectors and arcs of visibility, and the alignment of directional and leading lights, are always given as seen from seaward by an observer aboard ship looking towards the light. All bearings are given in True, starting from 000°, and going clockwise to 359°. For example, the sector of a white light listed as W090°-180° would be seen over an arc of 90° by any vessel between due West and due North of that light.

Coloured sector lights are often used to guide vessels up narrow channels or warn of a dangerous area. The navigable portion of a channel may be covered by a white pencil beam, flanked by red and green sectors. If you stray to port you see red; if to starboard you see green.

Example (1): Ouistreham main light is a simple sectored light, listed as Oc WR 4s 37m **W17M**, R13M, vis W151°-115°, R115°-151°. This is depicted in Fig. 3 (1).

Bold type indicates a light with a nominal range of >15M which is 37 metres above the level of MHWS, occulting every 4s and has white and red sectors.

The red sector of the light has a nominal range of 13M; it is visible over an arc of 36°, i.e. between 115° (WNW of the light) and 151° (NW of the light). The white sector of the light is visible from 151° clockwise right round to 115°, an angular coverage of 324°; the white sector has a nominal range of **17M**.

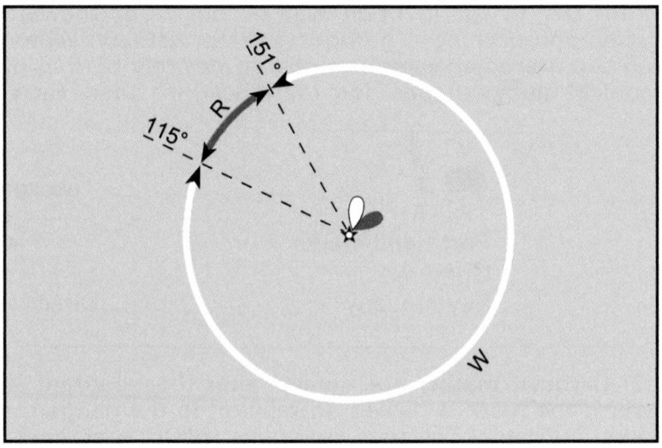
151°
R
115°
W

Fig. 3(1)

Example (2): A slightly more complex sectored light is shown below in Fig 3 (2). It is listed as:
Q WRG 9m 10M, vis: G015°-058°(43°), W058°-065°(7°), R065°-103°(38°), G103°-143·5°(40·5°), W143·5°-146·5°(3°), R146·5°-015° (228·5°).

It is a quick flashing light, with an elevation of 9 metres above MHWS, and a nominal range of 10M. It has white, red and green sectors – in fact two sectors of each colour. After plotting these sectors, it will be seen that there are two sets of WRG directional sectors, such that in each case a narrow white sector is flanked by a red sector to port and a green sector to starboard. These sectors provide the guidance described in paragraph 2 of the text of 3.3.2.

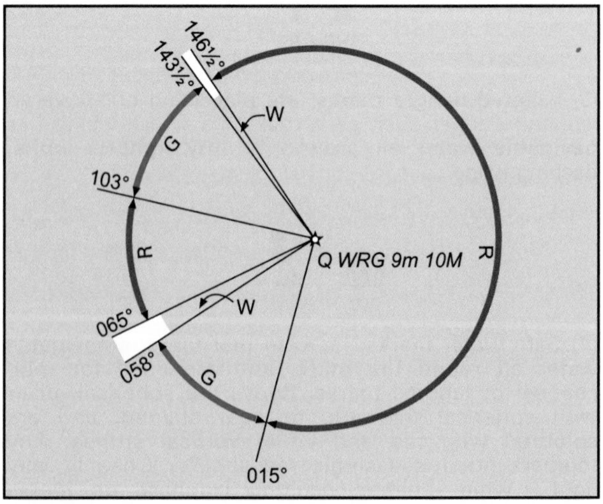
146½°
143½°
W
G
103°
R
Q WRG 9m 10M
R
W
065°
058°
G
015°

Fig. 3 (2)

Fig. 3 (3) Light characteristics

CLASS OF LIGHT		International abbreviations	National abbreviations	Illustration Period shown I——————I
FIXED		F		
OCCULTING *(total duration of light longer than dark)*				
Single-occulting		Oc	Occ	
Group-occulting	eg	Oc(2)	Gp Occ(2)	
Composite group-occulting	eg	Oc(2+3)	Gp Occ(2+3)	
ISOPHASE *(light and dark equal)*		Iso		
FLASHING *(total duration of light shorter than dark)*				
Single-flashing	Fl			
Long-flashing *(flash 2s or longer)*		L Fl		
Group-flashingeg	Fl(3)	Gp Fl(3)		
Composite group-flashing	eg	Fl(2+1)	Gp Fl(2+1)	
QUICK *(50 to 79, usually either 50 or 60, flashes per minute)*				
Continuous quick		Q	Qk Fl	
Group quick	eg	Q(3)	Qk Fl(3)	
Interrupted quick		IQ	Int Qk Fl	
VERY QUICK *(80 to 159, usually either 100 or 120, flashes per minute)*				
Continuous very quick		VQ	V Qk Fl	
Group very quick	eg	VQ(3)	V Qk Fl(3)	
Interrupted very quick		IVQ	Int V Qk Fl	
ULTRA QUICK *(160 or more, usually 240 to 300, flashes per minute)*				
Continuous ultra quick		UQ		
Interrupted ultra quick		IUQ		
MORSE CODE	eg	Mo(K)		
FIXED AND FLASHING		F Fl		
ALTERNATING	eg	Al. WR	Alt. WR	

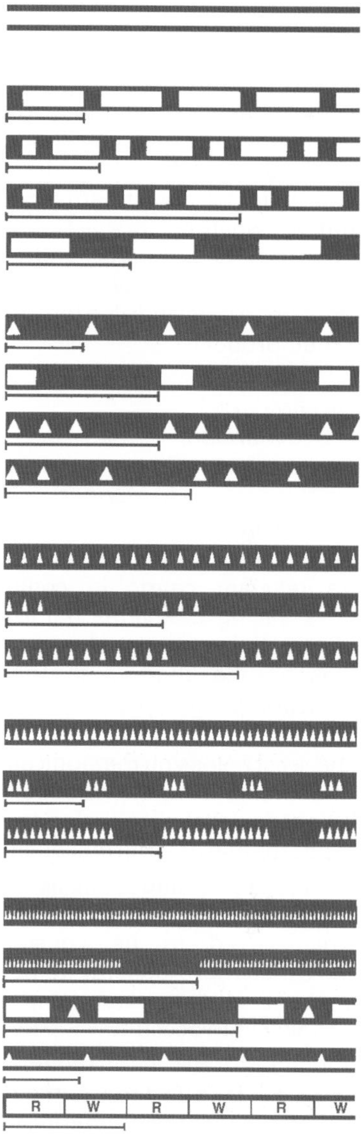

R
W
R
W
R
W

COLOUR	International abbreviations	NOMINAL RANGE in miles		International abbreviations
White	W *(may be omitted)*	Light with single range	eg	15M
Red	R	Light with two different ranges	eg	15/10M
Green	G	Light with three or more ranges	eg	15-7M
Blue	Bu			
Violet	Vi	**PERIOD** is given in seconds	eg	90s
Yellow	Y	**DISPOSITION** horizontally disposed		(hor)
Orange	Y	vertically disposed	(vert)	
Amber	Y	**ELEVATION** is given in metres (m) or feet (ft) above MHWS		

C3

3.4 PASSAGE PLANNING

3.4.1 General

Regulation 34 of the Safety of Life at Sea (SOLAS) convention (Chapter V) legally requires voyage planning on all vessels that go to sea. Mariners are expected to make a careful assessment of any proposed voyage taking into account all dangers of navigation, tidal predictions and other relevant factors including crew competence.

Any passage, however short, must be pre-planned. Even in very familiar waters you should at the very least know the state of the tide (springs/neaps; HW/LW times and heights), tidal streams and have studied an up-to-date weather forecast. The necessary chart(s) should be aboard and visiting the Hydrographic Office (UK) Websites will assist in getting them up to date and also locate your nearest agent for their products:

General
www.hydro.gov.uk
For Notices to Mariners
www.ukho.gov.uk/notices_to_mariners.html
For Searchable Notices to Mariners
www.nmwebsearch.com

When you have decided where you intend going, study the relevant charts in conjunction with yachtsman's sailing directions (Pilots) or cruising guides. Much of the navigational work such as laying-off courses on the chart, measuring distances, selecting waypoints and tidal calculations can be done in advance.

Using a check list helps you methodically prepare for the trip, thus minimising the risk of careless errors and omissions (see below). Finally, prepare a check list of those items that need further detailed planning.

3.4.2 Passage planning check list

The following is a suggested list of navigational items which need to be considered before departure. Other more general items such as the boat, crew and feeding arrangements may also need to be taken into account.

- Note the times of HW at the reference port(s).
- Tidal streams tend to form gates to a yacht on passage so you need to know the critical points of any tidal gates which affect your passage together with the times of favourable and adverse tides.
- Insert the dates and times of HW applicable on each page of the tidal stream atlas.
- Note the critical heights and times of any tides which may affect the departure, crossing bars, or destination harbours.
- Note potential dangers en route: clearing lines, distances off dangers, Traffic Separation Schemes, busy shipping lanes, etc.
- Consider visual and radio aids to be used.
- Prepare a detailed pilotage plan for entry to any unfamiliar harbour, final destination or refuge port.
- Consider the entry criteria for alternative harbours which might be required during the planned passage.
- Ensure that charts covering the intended route and alternative harbours that might be used are up to date and on board together with a copy of the current Almanac, Yachtsman's Handbook, and correcting Supplement, or the relevant lists of lights, radio and communication aids, and pilotage information.

Having completed all the necessary planning the weather is a major factor which is likely to have considerable impact and may well cause you to alter your original plans.

3.5 NAVIGATION TABLES

3.5.1 Tables – Explanations

Brief explanations are given below, where necessary, on the use of the tables on the next 6 pages.

Table 3 (1) – Distance of horizon

Enter with height of eye (in metres), and extract distance of horizon (miles). The actual distance may be affected by abnormal refraction

Table 3 (2) – Lights – rising or dipping distance

Enter with height of eye and height of light to extract the range of a light when rising or dipping above/below the horizon.

Table 3 (3) – Distance off by Vertical Sextant Angle

Enter with the height of the object (in metres) and read across the page until the required sextant angle (corrected for index error) is met. Extract the distance of the object (miles) at the head of the column. Caution is needed when the base of the object (e.g. a lighthouse) is below the horizon. For precise ranges the distance that sea level is below MHWS must be added to the height of the object (above MHWS) before entering the table.

Table 3 (4) – Distance for a given speed and time

Enter with time (in decimals of an hour, or in minutes) and speed (in knots) to determine distance run (in M).

Table 3 (5) – True bearing of Sun at sunrise and sunset

A compass can be checked against the amplitude of the Sun when rising or setting. You only need to know the approx latitude and the Sun's declination. Enter with the approximate latitude and declination (obtained from Table 3 (6)). The tabulated figure is the True bearing, measured from north if declination is north or from south if declination is south, towards the east if rising or towards the west if setting. Having extracted the True bearing, apply variation before comparing with the compass to determine deviation on course steered. The bearing of the Sun should be taken when its lower limb is a little over half a diameter above the horizon.

Table 3 (6) – Sun's declination

Enter with the appropriate date band and read across to the centre column. Extract declination (bold type) noting whether it is North or South.

TABLE 3 (1) Distance of horizon for various heights of eye

Height of eye (metres)	Height of eye (feet)	Horizon distance (M)	Height of eye (metres)	Height of eye (feet)	Horizon distance (M)	Height of eye (metres)	Height of eye (feet)	Horizon distance (M)
1	3·3	2·1	21	68·9	9·5	41	134·5	13·3
2	6·6	2·9	22	72·2	9·8	42	137·8	13·5
3	9·8	3·6	23	75·5	10·0	43	141·1	13·7
4	13·1	4·1	24	78·7	10·2	44	144·4	13·8
5	16·4	4·7	25	82·0	10·4	45	147·6	14·0
6	19·7	5·1	26	85·3	10·6	46	150·9	14·1
7	23·0	5·5	27	88·6	10·8	47	154·2	14·3
8	26·2	5·9	28	91·9	11·0	48	157·5	14·4
9	29·6	6·2	29	95·1	11·2	49	160·8	14·6
10	32·8	6·6	30	98·4	11·4	50	164·0	14·7
11	36·1	6·9	31	101·7	11·6	51	167·3	14·9
12	39·4	7·2	32	105·0	11·8	52	170·6	15·0
13	42·7	7·5	33	108·3	12·0	53	173·9	15·2
14	45·9	7·8	34	111·6	12·1	54	177·2	15·3
15	49·2	8·1	35	114·8	12·3	55	180·4	15·4
16	52·5	8·3	36	118·1	12·5	56	183·7	15·6
17	55·8	8·6	37	121·4	12·7	57	187·0	15·7
18	59·1	8·8	38	124·7	12·8	58	190·3	15·9
19	62·3	9·1	39	128·0	13·0	59	193·6	16·0
20	65·6	9·3	40	131·2	13·2	60	196·9	16·1

TABLE 3 (2) Lights – distance off when rising or dipping (M)

Height of light		Height of eye									
		metres	1	2	3	4	5	6	7	8	9	10
metres	feet	feet	3	7	10	13	16	20	23	26	30	33
10	33		8·7	9·5	10·2	10·8	11·3	11·7	12·1	12·5	12·8	13·2
12	39		9·3	10·1	10·8	11·4	11·9	12·3	12·7	13·1	13·4	13·8
14	46		9·9	10·7	11·4	12·0	12·5	12·9	13·3	13·7	14·0	14·4
16	53		10·4	11·2	11·9	12·5	13·0	13·4	13·8	14·2	14·5	14·9
18	59		10·9	11·7	12·4	13·0	13·5	13·9	14·3	14·7	15·0	15·4
20	66		11·4	12·2	12·9	13·5	14·0	14·4	14·8	15·2	15·5	15·9
22	72		11·9	12·7	13·4	14·0	14·5	14·9	15·3	15·7	16·0	16·4
24	79		12·3	13·1	13·8	14·4	14·9	15·3	15·7	16·1	16·4	17·0
26	85		12·7	13·5	14·2	14·8	15·3	15·7	16·1	16·5	16·8	17·2
28	92		13·1	13·9	14·6	15·2	15·7	16·1	16·5	16·9	17·2	17·6
30	98		13·5	14·3	15·0	15·6	16·1	16·5	16·9	17·3	17·6	18·0
32	105		13·9	14·7	15·4	16·0	16·5	16·9	17·3	17·7	18·0	18·4
34	112		14·2	15·0	15·7	16·3	16·8	17·2	17·6	18·0	18·3	18·7
36	118		14·6	15·4	16·1	16·7	17·2	17·6	18·0	18·4	18·7	19·1
38	125		14·9	15·7	16·4	17·0	17·5	17·9	18·3	18·7	19·0	19·4
40	131		15·3	16·1	16·8	17·4	17·9	18·3	18·7	19·1	19·4	19·8
42	138		15·6	16·4	17·1	17·7	18·2	18·6	19·0	19·4	19·7	20·1
44	144		15·9	16·7	17·4	18·0	18·5	18·9	19·3	19·7	20·0	20·4
46	151		16·2	17·0	17·7	18·3	18·8	19·2	19·6	20·0	20·3	20·7
48	157		16·5	17·3	18·0	18·6	19·1	19·5	19·9	20·3	20·6	21·0
50	164		16·8	17·6	18·3	18·9	19·4	19·8	20·2	20·6	20·9	21·3
55	180		17·5	18·3	19·0	19·6	20·1	20·5	20·9	21·3	21·6	22·0
60	197		18·2	19·0	19·7	20·3	20·8	21·2	21·6	22·0	22·3	22·7
65	213		18·9	19·7	20·4	21·0	21·5	21·9	22·3	22·7	23·0	23·4
70	230		19·5	20·3	21·0	21·6	22·1	22·5	22·9	23·2	23·6	24·0
75	246		20·1	20·9	21·6	22·2	22·7	23·1	23·5	23·9	24·2	24·6
80	262		20·7	21·5	22·2	22·8	23·3	23·7	24·1	24·5	24·8	25·2
85	279		21·3	22·1	22·8	23·4	23·9	24·3	24·7	25·1	25·4	25·8
90	295		21·8	22·6	23·3	23·9	24·4	24·8	25·2	25·6	25·9	26·3
95	312		22·4	23·2	23·9	24·5	25·0	25·4	25·8	26·2	26·5	26·9
metres	feet	metres	1	2	3	4	5	6	7	8	9	10
Height of light		feet	3	7	10	13	16	20	23	26	30	33
		Height of eye										

TABLE 3 (3) Distance off by Vertical Sextant Angle

Height of object ft	m	Distance of object (nautical miles) 0·1	0·2	0·3	0·4	0·5	0·6	0·7	0·8	0·9	1·0	1·1	1·2	1·3	1·4	1·5	1·6
		° ′	° ′	° ′	° ′	° ′	° ′	° ′	° ′	° ′	° ′	° ′	° ′	° ′	° ′	° ′	° ′
33	**10**	3 05	1 33	1 02	0 46	0 37	0 31	0 27	0 23	0 21	0 19	0 17	0 15	0 14	0 13	0 12	0 12
39	**12**	3 42	1 51	1 14	0 56	0 45	0 37	0 32	0 28	0 25	0 22	0 20	0 19	0 17	0 16	0 15	0 14
46	**14**	4 19	2 10	1 27	1 05	0 52	0 43	0 37	0 32	0 29	0 26	0 24	0 22	0 20	0 19	0 17	0 16
53	**16**	4 56	2 28	1 39	1 14	0 59	0 49	0 42	0 37	0 33	0 30	0 27	0 25	0 23	0 21	0 20	0 19
59	**18**	5 33	2 47	1 51	1 24	1 07	0 56	0 48	0 42	0 37	0 33	0 30	0 28	0 26	0 24	0 22	0 21
66	**20**	6 10	3 05	2 04	1 33	1 14	1 02	0 53	0 46	0 41	0 37	0 34	0 31	0 29	0 27	0 25	0 23
72	**22**	6 46	3 24	2 16	1 42	1 22	1 08	0 58	0 51	0 45	0 41	0 37	0 34	0 31	0 29	0 27	0 26
79	**24**	7 23	3 42	2 28	1 51	1 29	1 14	1 04	0 56	0 49	0 45	0 40	0 37	0 34	0 32	0 30	0 28
85	**26**	7 59	4 01	2 41	2 01	1 36	1 20	1 09	1 00	0 54	0 48	0 44	0 40	0 37	0 34	0 32	0 30
92	**28**	8 36	4 19	2 53	2 10	1 44	1 27	1 14	1 05	0 58	0 52	0 47	0 43	0 40	0 37	0 35	0 32
98	**30**	9 12	4 38	3 05	2 19	1 51	1 33	1 20	1 10	1 02	0 56	0 51	0 46	0 43	0 40	0 37	0 35
105	**32**	9 48	4 56	3 18	2 28	1 58	1 39	1 25	1 14	1 06	0 59	0 54	0 49	0 46	0 42	0 40	0 37
112	**34**	10 24	5 15	3 30	2 38	2 06	1 45	1 30	1 19	1 10	1 03	0 57	0 53	0 49	0 45	0 42	0 39
118	**36**	11 00	5 33	3 42	2 47	2 14	1 51	1 35	1 24	1 14	1 07	1 01	0 56	0 51	0 48	0 45	0 42
125	**38**	11 36	5 41	3 55	2 56	2 21	1 58	1 41	1 28	1 18	1 11	1 04	0 59	0 54	0 50	0 47	0 44
131	**40**	12 11	6 10	4 07	3 05	2 28	2 04	1 46	1 33	1 22	1 14	1 07	1 02	0 57	0 53	0 49	0 46
138	**42**	12 47	6 28	4 19	3 15	2 36	2 10	1 51	1 37	1 27	1 18	1 11	1 05	1 00	0 56	0 52	0 49
144	**44**	13 22	6 46	4 32	3 24	2 43	2 16	1 57	1 42	1 31	1 22	1 14	1 08	1 03	0 58	0 54	0 51
151	**46**	13 57	7 05	4 44	3 33	2 51	2 22	2 02	1 47	1 35	1 25	1 18	1 11	1 06	1 01	0 57	0 53
157	**48**	14 32	7 23	4 56	3 42	2 58	2 28	2 07	1 51	1 39	1 29	1 21	1 14	1 09	1 04	0 59	0 56
164	**50**	15 07	7 41	5 09	3 52	3 05	2 35	2 13	1 56	1 43	1 33	1 24	1 17	1 11	1 06	1 02	0 58
171	**52**	15 41	7 59	5 21	4 01	3 13	2 41	2 18	2 01	1 47	1 36	1 28	1 20	1 14	1 09	1 04	1 00
177	**54**	16 15	8 18	5 33	4 10	3 20	2 47	2 23	2 05	1 51	1 40	1 31	1 23	1 17	1 12	1 07	1 03
184	**56**	16 49	8 36	5 45	4 19	3 28	2 53	2 28	2 10	1 55	1 44	1 34	1 27	1 20	1 14	1 09	1 05
190	**58**	17 23	8 54	5 58	4 29	3 35	2 59	2 34	2 15	2 00	1 48	1 38	1 30	1 23	1 17	1 12	1 07
197	**60**	17 57	9 12	6 10	4 38	3 42	3 05	2 39	2 19	2 04	1 51	1 41	1 33	1 26	1 20	1 14	1 10
203	**62**	18 31	9 30	6 22	4 47	3 50	3 12	2 44	2 24	2 08	1 55	1 45	1 36	1 29	1 22	1 17	1 12
210	**64**	19 04	9 48	6 34	4 56	3 57	3 18	2 50	2 28	2 12	1 59	1 48	1 39	1 31	1 25	1 19	1 14
217	**66**	19 37	10 06	6 46	5 05	4 05	3 24	2 53	2 33	2 16	2 02	1 51	1 42	1 34	1 27	1 22	1 17
223	**68**	20 10	10 24	6 59	5 15	4 12	3 30	3 00	2 38	2 20	2 06	1 55	1 45	1 37	1 30	1 24	1 19
230	**70**	20 42	10 42	7 11	5 24	4 19	3 36	3 05	2 42	2 24	2 09	1 58	1 48	1 40	1 33	1 27	1 21
236	**72**	21 15	11 00	7 23	5 33	4 27	3 42	3 11	2 47	2 48	2 14	2 01	1 51	1 43	1 35	1 29	1 24
246	**75**	22 03	11 27	7 41	5 47	4 38	3 52	3 19	2 54	2 35	2 19	2 07	1 56	1 47	1 39	1 33	1 27
256	**78**	22 50	11 54	7 59	6 01	4 49	4 01	3 27	3 01	2 41	2 24	2 12	2 01	1 51	1 43	1 36	1 30
266	**81**	23 37	12 20	8 18	6 14	5 00	4 10	3 35	3 08	2 47	2 30	2 17	2 05	1 56	1 47	1 40	1 34
276	**84**	24 24	12 47	8 36	6 28	5 11	4 19	3 42	3 15	2 53	2 36	2 22	2 10	2 00	1 51	1 44	1 37
289	**88**	25 25	13 22	9 00	6 46	5 26	4 32	3 53	3 24	3 01	2 43	2 28	2 16	2 06	1 57	1 49	1 42
302	**92**	26 25	13 57	9 24	7 05	5 40	4 44	4 04	3 33	3 10	2 51	2 35	2 22	2 11	2 02	1 54	1 47
315	**96**	27 24	14 32	9 48	7 23	5 55	4 56	4 14	3 42	3 18	2 58	2 42	2 28	2 17	2 07	1 59	1 51
328	**100**	28 22	15 07	10 12	7 41	6 10	5 09	4 25	3 52	3 26	3 05	2 49	2 35	2 23	2 13	2 04	1 56
341	**104**	29 19	15 41	10 36	7 59	6 24	5 21	4 35	4 01	3 34	3 13	2 55	2 41	2 28	2 18	2 09	2 01
358	**109**	30 29	16 24	11 06	8 22	6 43	5 36	4 48	4 12	3 44	3 22	3 04	2 48	2 36	2 24	2 15	2 06
374	**114**	31 37	17 06	11 36	8 45	7 01	5 51	5 02	4 24	3 55	3 31	3 12	2 56	2 43	2 31	2 21	2 12
394	**120**	32 56	17 57	12 11	9 12	7 23	6 10	5 17	4 38	4 07	3 42	3 22	3 05	2 51	2 39	2 28	2 19
427	**130**	35 04	19 20	13 10	9 57	8 00	6 40	5 44	5 01	4 28	4 01	3 39	3 21	3 05	2 52	2 41	2 31
459	**140**	37 05	20 42	14 09	10 42	8 36	7 11	6 10	5 24	4 48	4 19	3 56	3 36	3 20	3 05	2 53	2 42
492	**150**	39 00	22 03	15 07	11 27	9 12	7 41	6 36	5 47	5 09	4 38	4 13	3 52	3 34	3 19	3 05	2 54
574	**175**		25 17	17 29	13 17	10 42	8 57	7 41	6 44	6 00	5 24	4 55	4 30	4 09	3 52	3 36	3 23
656	**200**		28 22	19 48	15 07	12 11	10 12	8 46	7 41	6 51	6 10	5 36	5 09	4 45	4 25	4 07	3 52
738	**225**			22 03	16 54	13 39	11 27	9 51	8 38	7 41	6 56	6 18	5 47	5 20	4 58	4 38	4 21
820	**250**			24 14	18 39	15 07	12 41	10 55	9 35	8 32	7 41	7 00	6 25	5 56	5 30	5 09	4 49
902	**275**			26 20	20 22	16 32	13 54	11 59	10 31	9 22	8 27	7 41	7 03	6 31	6 03	5 39	5 18
984	**300**				22 03	17 57	15 07	13 02	11 27	10 12	9 12	8 23	7 41	7 06	6 36	6 10	5 47
1148	**350**					20 42	17 29	15 07	13 17	11 51	10 42	9 45	8 57	8 16	7 41	7 11	6 44
1312	**400**						19 48	17 09	15 07	13 30	12 11	11 07	10 12	9 26	8 46	8 12	7 41
ft	m	0·1	0·2	0·3	0·4	0·5	0·6	0·7	0·8	0·9	1·0	1·1	1·2	1·3	1·4	1·5	1·6

Height of object — Distance of object (nautical miles)

TABLE 3 (3) Distance off by Vertical Sextant Angle (continued)

Height of object ft	m	1·8	2·0	2·2	2·4	2·6	2·8	3·0	3·2	3·4	3·6	3·8	4·0	4·2	4·4	4·6	5·0
		° ′	° ′	° ′	° ′	° ′	° ′	° ′	° ′	° ′	° ′	° ′	° ′	° ′	° ′	° ′	° ′
33	**10**	0 10															
39	**12**	0 12	0 11	0 10	0 10												
46	**14**	0 14	0 13	0 12	0 11	0 10											
53	**16**	0 16	0 15	0 13	0 12	0 11	0 11	0 10									
59	**18**	0 19	0 17	0 15	0 14	0 13	0 12	0 11	0 10	0 10							
66	**20**	0 21	0 19	0 17	0 15	0 14	0 13	0 12	0 12	0 11	0 10	0 10					
72	**22**	0 23	0 20	0 19	0 17	0 16	0 15	0 14	0 13	0 12	0 11	0 11	0 10				
79	**24**	0 25	0 22	0 20	0 19	0 17	0 16	0 15	0 14	0 13	0 12	0 12	0 11	0 11	0 10		
85	**26**	0 27	0 24	0 22	0 20	0 19	0 17	0 16	0 15	0 14	0 13	0 13	0 12	0 11	0 11	0 10	
92	**28**	0 29	0 26	0 24	0 22	0 20	0 19	0 17	0 16	0 15	0 14	0 14	0 13	0 12	0 12	0 11	0 10
98	**30**	0 31	0 28	0 25	0 23	0 21	0 20	0 19	0 17	0 16	0 15	0 15	0 14	0 13	0 13	0 12	0 11
105	**32**	0 33	0 30	0 27	0 25	0 23	0 21	0 20	0 19	0 17	0 16	0 16	0 15	0 14	0 13	0 13	0 12
112	**34**	0 35	0 31	0 29	0 26	0 24	0 23	0 21	0 20	0 19	0 17	0 17	0 16	0 15	0 14	0 14	0 13
118	**36**	0 37	0 33	0 30	0 28	0 26	0 24	0 22	0 21	0 20	0 19	0 18	0 17	0 16	0 15	0 14	0 13
125	**38**	0 39	0 35	0 32	0 29	0 27	0 25	0 24	0 22	0 21	0 20	0 19	0 18	0 17	0 16	0 15	0 14
131	**40**	0 41	0 37	0 34	0 31	0 29	0 27	0 25	0 23	0 22	0 21	0 20	0 19	0 18	0 17	0 16	0 15
138	**42**	0 43	0 40	0 35	0 32	0 30	0 28	0 26	0 24	0 23	0 22	0 21	0 19	0 19	0 18	0 17	0 16
144	**44**	0 45	0 41	0 37	0 34	0 31	0 29	0 27	0 25	0 24	0 23	0 22	0 20	0 19	0 19	0 18	0 16
151	**46**	0 47	0 43	0 39	0 36	0 33	0 30	0 28	0 27	0 25	0 24	0 22	0 21	0 20	0 19	0 19	0 17
157	**48**	0 49	0 45	0 40	0 37	0 34	0 32	0 30	0 28	0 26	0 25	0 23	0 22	0 21	0 20	0 19	0 18
164	**50**	0 52	0 46	0 42	0 39	0 36	0 33	0 31	0 29	0 27	0 26	0 24	0 23	0 22	0 21	0 20	0 19
171	**52**	0 54	0 48	0 44	0 40	0 37	0 34	0 32	0 30	0 28	0 27	0 25	0 24	0 23	0 22	0 21	0 19
177	**54**	0 56	0 50	0 46	0 42	0 39	0 36	0 33	0 31	0 29	0 28	0 26	0 25	0 24	0 23	0 22	0 20
184	**56**	0 58	0 52	0 47	0 43	0 40	0 37	0 35	0 32	0 31	0 29	0 27	0 26	0 25	0 24	0 23	0 21
190	**58**	1 00	0 54	0 49	0 45	0 41	0 38	0 36	0 34	0 32	0 30	0 28	0 27	0 26	0 24	0 23	0 21
197	**60**	1 02	0 56	0 51	0 46	0 43	0 40	0 37	0 35	0 33	0 31	0 29	0 28	0 26	0 25	0 24	0 22
203	**62**	1 04	0 58	0 52	0 48	0 44	0 41	0 38	0 36	0 34	0 32	0 30	0 29	0 27	0 26	0 25	0 23
210	**64**	1 06	0 59	0 54	0 49	0 46	0 42	0 40	0 37	0 35	0 33	0 31	0 30	0 28	0 27	0 26	0 24
217	**66**	1 08	1 01	0 56	0 51	0 47	0 44	0 41	0 38	0 36	0 34	0 32	0 31	0 29	0 28	0 27	0 25
223	**68**	1 10	1 03	0 57	0 53	0 49	0 45	0 42	0 39	0 37	0 35	0 33	0 32	0 30	0 29	0 27	0 25
230	**70**	1 12	1 05	0 59	0 54	0 50	0 46	0 43	0 41	0 38	0 36	0 34	0 32	0 31	0 29	0 28	0 26
236	**72**	1 14	1 07	1 01	0 56	0 51	0 48	0 45	0 42	0 39	0 37	0 35	0 33	0 32	0 30	0 29	0 27
246	**75**	1 17	1 10	1 03	0 58	0 54	0 50	0 46	0 44	0 41	0 39	0 37	0 35	0 33	0 32	0 30	0 28
256	**78**	1 20	1 12	1 06	1 00	0 56	0 52	0 48	0 45	0 43	0 40	0 38	0 36	0 34	0 33	0 31	0 29
266	**81**	1 23	1 15	1 08	1 03	0 58	0 54	0 50	0 47	0 44	0 42	0 40	0 38	0 36	0 34	0 33	0 30
276	**84**	1 27	1 18	1 11	1 05	1 00	0 56	0 52	0 49	0 46	0 43	0 41	0 39	0 37	0 35	0 34	0 31
289	**88**	1 31	1 22	1 14	1 08	1 03	0 58	0 54	0 51	0 48	0 45	0 43	0 41	0 39	0 37	0 36	0 33
302	**92**	1 35	1 25	1 18	1 11	1 06	1 01	0 57	0 53	0 50	0 47	0 45	0 43	0 41	0 39	0 37	0 34
315	**96**	1 39	1 29	1 21	1 14	1 09	1 04	0 59	0 56	0 52	0 49	0 47	0 45	0 42	0 41	0 39	0 36
328	**100**	1 43	1 33	1 24	1 17	1 11	1 06	1 02	0 58	0 55	0 52	0 49	0 46	0 44	0 42	0 40	0 37
341	**104**	1 47	1 36	1 28	1 20	1 14	1 09	1 04	1 00	0 57	0 54	0 51	0 48	0 46	0 44	0 42	0 39
358	**109**	1 52	1 41	1 32	1 24	1 18	1 12	1 07	1 03	1 00	0 56	0 53	0 51	0 48	0 46	0 44	0 40
374	**114**	1 58	1 46	1 36	1 28	1 21	1 16	1 11	1 06	1 02	0 59	0 56	0 53	0 50	0 48	0 46	0 42
394	**120**	2 04	1 51	1 41	1 33	1 26	1 20	1 14	1 10	1 06	1 02	0 59	0 56	0 53	0 51	0 48	0 45
427	**130**	2 14	2 01	1 50	1 41	1 33	1 26	1 20	1 15	1 11	1 07	1 03	1 00	0 57	0 55	0 52	0 48
459	**140**	2 24	2 10	1 58	1 48	1 40	1 33	1 27	1 21	1 16	1 12	1 08	1 05	1 02	0 59	0 56	0 52
492	**150**	2 35	2 19	2 07	1 56	1 47	1 39	1 33	1 27	1 22	1 17	1 13	1 10	1 06	1 03	1 01	0 56
574	**175**	3 00	2 42	2 28	2 15	2 05	1 56	1 48	1 41	1 36	1 30	1 25	1 21	1 17	1 14	1 11	1 05
656	**200**	3 26	3 05	2 49	2 35	2 23	2 13	2 04	1 56	1 49	1 43	1 38	1 33	1 28	1 24	1 21	1 14
738	**225**	3 52	3 29	3 10	2 54	2 41	2 29	2 19	2 10	2 03	1 56	1 50	1 44	1 39	1 35	1 31	1 24
820	**250**	4 17	3 52	3 31	3 13	2 58	2 46	2 35	2 25	2 16	2 09	2 02	1 56	1 50	1 45	1 41	1 33
902	**275**	4 43	4 15	3 52	3 32	3 16	3 02	2 50	2 39	2 30	2 22	2 14	2 08	2 01	1 56	1 51	1 42
984	**300**	5 09	4 38	4 13	3 52	3 34	3 19	3 05	2 54	2 44	2 35	2 26	2 19	2 13	2 07	2 01	1 51
1148	**350**	6 00	5 24	4 55	4 30	4 09	3 52	3 36	3 23	3 11	3 00	2 51	2 42	2 35	2 28	2 21	2 10
1312	**400**	6 51	6 10	5 36	5 09	4 45	4 25	4 07	3 52	3 38	3 26	3 15	3 05	2 57	2 49	2 41	2 28
ft	**m**	**1·8**	**2·0**	**2·2**	**2·4**	**2·6**	**2·8**	**3·0**	**3·2**	**3·4**	**3·6**	**3·8**	**4·0**	**4·2**	**4·4**	**4·6**	**5·0**
Height of object		**Distance of object (nautical miles)**															

Table 3 (4) Distance for a given speed and time

Time: Decimal of hr	Time: Mins	Speed in knots: 2·5	3·0	3·5	4·0	4·5	5·0	5·5	6·0	6·5	7·0	7·5	8·0	8·5	9·0	9·5	10·0	Time: Mins	Time: Decimal of hr
·0167	**1**				0·1	0·1	0·1	0·1	0·1	0·1	0·1	0·1	0·1	0·1	0·2	0·2	0·2	**1**	·0167
·0333	**2**	0·1	0·1	0·1	0·1	0·1	0·2	0·2	0·2	0·2	0·2	0·2	0·3	0·3	0·3	0·3	0·3	**2**	·0333
·0500	**3**	0·1	0·1	0·2	0·2	0·2	0·2	0·3	0·3	0·3	0·3	0·4	0·4	0·4	0·4	0·5	0·5	**3**	·0500
·0667	**4**	0·1	0·2	0·2	0·3	0·3	0·3	0·4	0·4	0·4	0·5	0·5	0·5	0·6	0·6	0·6	0·7	**4**	·0667
·0833	**5**	0·2	0·2	0·3	0·3	0·4	0·4	0·5	0·5	0·5	0·6	0·6	0·7	0·7	0·7	0·8	0·8	**5**	·0833
·1000	**6**	0·2	0·3	0·3	0·4	0·4	0·5	0·5	0·6	0·6	0·7	0·7	0·8	0·8	0·9	0·9	1·0	**6**	·1000
·1167	**7**	0·3	0·4	0·4	0·5	0·5	0·6	0·6	0·7	0·8	0·8	0·9	0·9	1·0	1·1	1·1	1·2	**7**	·1167
·1333	**8**	0·3	0·4	0·5	0·5	0·6	0·7	0·7	0·8	0·9	0·9	1·0	1·1	1·1	1·2	1·3	1·3	**8**	·1333
·1500	**9**	0·4	0·4	0·5	0·6	0·7	0·7	0·8	0·9	1·0	1·0	1·1	1·2	1·3	1·3	1·4	1·5	**9**	·1500
·1667	**10**	0·4	0·5	0·6	0·7	0·8	0·8	0·9	1·0	1·1	1·2	1·3	1·3	1·4	1·5	1·6	1·7	**10**	·1667
·1833	**11**	0·5	0·5	0·6	0·7	0·8	0·9	1·0	1·1	1·2	1·3	1·4	1·5	1·6	1·6	1·7	1·8	**11**	·1833
·2000	**12**	0·5	0·6	0·7	0·8	0·9	1·0	1·1	1·2	1·3	1·4	1·5	1·6	1·7	1·8	1·9	2·0	**12**	·2000
·2167	**13**	0·5	0·6	0·8	0·9	1·0	1·1	1·2	1·3	1·4	1·5	1·6	1·7	1·8	2·0	2·0	2·2	**13**	·2167
·2333	**14**	0·6	0·7	0·8	0·9	1·0	1·2	1·3	1·4	1·5	1·6	1·7	1·9	2·0	2·1	2·2	2·3	**14**	·2333
·2500	**15**	0·6	0·7	0·9	1·0	1·1	1·2	1·4	1·5	1·6	1·8	1·9	2·0	2·1	2·2	2·4	2·5	**15**	·2500
·2667	**16**	0·7	0·8	0·9	1·1	1·2	1·3	1·5	1·6	1·7	1·9	2·0	2·1	2·3	2·4	2·5	2·7	**16**	·2667
·2833	**17**	0·7	0·8	1·0	1·1	1·3	1·4	1·6	1·7	1·8	2·0	2·1	2·3	2·4	2·5	2·7	2·8	**17**	·2833
·3000	**18**	0·7	0·9	1·0	1·2	1·3	1·5	1·6	1·8	1·9	2·1	2·2	2·4	2·5	2·7	2·8	3·0	**18**	·3000
·3167	**19**	0·8	1·0	1·1	1·3	1·4	1·6	1·7	1·9	2·1	2·1	2·4	2·5	2·7	2·9	3·0	3·2	**19**	·3167
·3333	**20**	0·8	1·0	1·2	1·3	1·5	1·7	1·8	2·0	2·2	2·3	2·5	2·7	2·8	3·0	3·2	3·3	**20**	·3333
·3500	**21**	0·9	1·0	1·2	1·4	1·6	1·7	1·9	2·1	2·3	2·4	2·6	2·8	3·0	3·1	3·3	3·5	**21**	·3500
·3667	**22**	0·9	1·1	1·3	1·5	1·7	1·8	2·1	2·2	2·4	2·6	2·8	2·9	3·1	3·3	3·5	3·7	**22**	·3667
·3833	**23**	1·0	1·1	1·3	1·5	1·7	1·9	2·1	2·3	2·5	2·7	2·9	3·1	3·3	3·4	3·6	3·8	**23**	·3833
·4000	**24**	1·0	1·2	1·4	1·6	1·8	2·0	2·2	2·4	2·6	2·8	3·0	3·2	3·4	3·6	3·8	4·0	**24**	·4000
·4167	**25**	1·0	1·3	1·5	1·7	1·9	2·1	2·3	2·5	2·7	2·9	3·1	3·3	3·5	3·8	4·0	4·2	**25**	·4167
·4333	**26**	1·1	1·3	1·5	1·7	1·9	2·2	2·4	2·6	2·8	3·0	3·2	3·5	3·7	3·9	4·1	4·3	**26**	·4333
·4500	**27**	1·1	1·3	1·6	1·8	2·0	2·2	2·5	2·7	2·9	3·1	3·4	3·6	3·8	4·0	4·3	4·5	**27**	·4500
·4667	**28**	1·2	1·4	1·6	1·9	2·1	2·3	2·6	2·8	3·0	3·3	3·5	3·7	4·0	4·2	4·4	4·7	**28**	·4667
·4833	**29**	1·2	1·5	1·7	1·9	2·2	2·4	2·7	2·9	3·1	3·4	3·6	3·9	4·1	4·3	4·6	4·8	**29**	·4833
·5000	**30**	1·2	1·5	1·7	2·0	2·2	2·5	2·7	3·0	3·2	3·5	3·7	4·0	4·2	4·5	4·7	5·0	**30**	·5000
·5167	**31**	1·3	1·6	1·8	2·1	2·3	2·6	2·8	3·1	3·4	3·6	3·9	4·1	4·4	4·7	4·9	5·2	**31**	·5167
·5333	**32**	1·3	1·6	1·9	2·1	2·4	2·7	2·9	3·2	3·5	3·7	4·0	4·3	4·5	4·8	5·1	5·3	**32**	·5333
·5500	**33**	1·4	1·6	1·9	2·2	2·5	2·7	3·0	3·3	3·6	3·8	4·1	4·4	4·7	4·9	5·2	5·5	**33**	·5500
·5667	**34**	1·4	1·7	2·0	2·3	2·6	2·8	3·1	3·4	3·7	4·0	4·3	4·5	4·8	5·1	5·4	5·7	**34**	·5667
·5833	**35**	1·5	1·7	2·0	2·3	2·6	2·9	3·2	3·5	3·8	4·1	4·4	4·7	5·0	5·2	5·5	5·8	**35**	·5833
·6000	**36**	1·5	1·8	2·1	2·4	2·7	3·0	3·3	3·6	3·9	4·2	4·5	4·8	5·1	5·4	5·7	6·0	**36**	·6000
·6117	**37**	1·6	1·8	2·1	2·4	2·8	3·1	3·4	3·7	4·0	4·3	4·6	4·9	5·2	5·5	5·8	6·1	**37**	·6117
·6333	**38**	1·6	1·9	2·2	2·5	2·8	3·2	3·5	3·8	4·1	4·4	4·7	5·1	5·4	5·7	6·0	6·3	**38**	·6333
·6500	**39**	1·6	1·9	2·3	2·6	2·9	3·2	3·6	3·9	4·2	4·5	4·9	5·2	5·5	5·8	6·2	6·5	**39**	·6500
·6667	**40**	1·7	2·0	2·3	2·7	3·0	3·3	3·7	4·0	4·3	4·7	5·0	5·3	5·7	6·0	6·3	6·7	**40**	·6667
·6833	**41**	1·7	2·0	2·4	2·7	3·1	3·4	3·8	4·1	4·4	4·8	5·1	5·5	5·8	6·1	6·5	6·8	**41**	·6833
·7000	**42**	1·7	2·1	2·4	2·8	3·1	3·5	3·8	4·2	4·5	4·9	5·2	5·6	5·9	6·3	6·6	7·0	**42**	·7000
·7167	**43**	1·8	2·2	2·5	2·9	3·2	3·6	3·9	4·3	4·7	5·0	5·4	5·7	6·1	6·5	6·8	7·2	**43**	·7167
·7333	**44**	1·8	2·2	2·6	2·9	3·3	3·7	4·0	4·4	4·8	5·1	5·5	5·9	6·2	6·6	7·0	7·3	**44**	·7333
·7500	**45**	1·9	2·2	2·6	3·0	3·4	3·7	4·1	4·5	4·9	5·2	5·6	6·0	6·4	6·7	7·1	7·5	**45**	·7500
·7667	**46**	1·9	2·3	2·7	3·1	3·5	3·8	4·2	4·6	5·0	5·4	5·8	6·1	6·5	6·9	7·3	7·7	**46**	·7667
·7833	**47**	2·0	2·3	2·7	3·1	3·5	3·9	4·3	4·7	5·1	5·5	5·9	6·3	6·7	7·0	7·4	7·8	**47**	·7833
·8000	**48**	2·0	2·4	2·8	3·2	3·6	4·0	4·4	4·8	5·2	5·6	6·0	6·4	6·8	7·2	7·6	8·0	**48**	·8000
·8167	**49**	2·0	2·5	2·9	3·3	3·7	4·1	4·5	4·9	5·3	5·7	6·1	6·5	6·9	7·4	7·8	8·2	**49**	·8167
·8333	**50**	2·1	2·5	2·9	3·3	3·7	4·2	4·6	5·0	5·4	5·8	6·2	6·7	7·1	7·5	7·9	8·3	**50**	·8333
·8500	**51**	2·1	2·5	3·0	3·4	3·8	4·2	4·7	5·1	5·5	5·9	6·4	6·8	7·2	7·6	8·1	8·5	**51**	·8500
·8667	**52**	2·2	2·6	3·0	3·5	3·9	4·3	4·8	5·2	5·6	6·1	6·5	6·9	7·4	7·8	8·2	8·7	**52**	·8667
·8833	**53**	2·2	2·6	3·1	3·5	4·0	4·4	4·9	5·3	5·7	6·2	6·6	7·1	7·5	7·9	8·4	8·8	**53**	·8833
·9000	**54**	2·2	2·7	3·1	3·6	4·0	4·5	4·9	5·4	5·8	6·3	6·7	7·2	7·6	8·1	8·5	9·0	**54**	·9000
·9167	**55**	2·3	2·8	3·2	3·7	4·1	4·6	5·0	5·5	6·0	6·4	6·9	7·3	7·8	8·3	8·7	9·2	**55**	·9167
·9333	**56**	2·3	2·8	3·3	3·7	4·2	4·7	5·1	5·6	6·1	6·5	7·0	7·5	7·9	8·4	8·9	9·3	**56**	·9333
·9500	**57**	2·4	2·8	3·3	3·8	4·3	4·7	5·2	5·7	6·2	6·6	7·1	7·6	8·1	8·5	9·0	9·5	**57**	·9500
·9667	**58**	2·4	2·9	3·4	3·9	4·4	4·8	5·3	5·8	6·3	6·8	7·3	7·7	8·2	8·7	9·2	9·7	**58**	·9667
·9833	**59**	2·5	2·9	3·4	3·9	4·4	4·9	5·4	5·9	6·4	6·9	7·4	7·9	8·4	8·8	9·3	9·8	**59**	·9833
1·0000	**60**	2·5	3·0	3·5	4·0	4·5	5·0	5·5	6·0	6·5	7·0	7·5	8·0	8·5	9·0	9·5	10·0	**60**	1·0000
Decimal of hr	Mins	2·5	3·0	3·5	4·0	4·5	5·0	5·5	6·0	6·5	7·0	7·5	8·0	8·5	9·0	9·5	10·0	Mins	Decimal of hr
Time		Speed in knots																Time	

Table 3 (4) Distance for a given speed and time (continued)

Time: Decimal of hr	Time: Mins	10·5	11·0	11·5	12·0	12·5	13·0	13·5	14·0	14·5	15·0	15·5	16·0	17·0	18·0	19·0	20·0	Time: Mins	Time: Decimal of hr
		Speed in knots																	
·0167	**1**	0·2	0·2	0·2	0·2	0·2	0·2	0·2	0·2	0·2	0·3	0·3	0·3	0·3	0·3	0·3	0·3	**1**	·0167
·0333	**2**	0·3	0·4	0·4	0·4	0·4	0·4	0·4	0·5	0·5	0·5	0·5	0·5	0·6	0·6	0·6	0·7	**2**	·0333
·0500	**3**	0·5	0·5	0·6	0·6	0·6	0·6	0·7	0·7	0·7	0·7	0·8	0·8	0·8	0·8	0·9	1·0	**3**	·0500
·0667	4	0·7	0·7	0·8	0·8	0·8	0·9	0·9	0·9	1·0	1·0	1·0	1·1	1·1	1·2	1·3	1·3	**4**	·0667
·0833	**5**	0·9	0·9	1·0	1·0	1·0	1·1	1·1	1·2	1·2	1·2	1·3	1·3	1·4	1·5	1·6	1·7	**5**	·0833
·1000	**6**	1·0	1·1	1·1	1·2	1·2	1·3	1·3	1·4	1·4	1·5	1·5	1·6	1·7	1·8	1·9	2·0	**6**	·1000
·1167	**7**	1·2	1·3	1·3	1·4	1·5	1·5	1·6	1·6	1·7	1·8	1·8	1·9	2·0	2·1	2·2	2·3	**7**	·1167
·1333	**8**	1·4	1·5	1·5	1·6	1·7	1·7	1·8	1·9	1·9	2·0	2·1	2·1	2·3	2·4	2·5	2·7	**8**	·1333
·1500	**9**	1·6	1·6	1·7	1·8	1·9	1·9	2·0	2·1	2·1	2·2	2·3	2·4	2·5	2·7	2·8	3·0	**9**	·1500
·1667	**10**	1·8	1·8	1·9	2·0	2·1	2·2	2·3	2·3	2·4	2·5	2·6	2·7	2·8	3·0	3·2	3·3	**10**	·1667
·1833	**11**	1·9	2·0	2·1	2·2	2·3	2·4	2·5	2·6	2·7	2·7	2·8	2·9	3·1	3·3	3·5	3·7	**11**	·1833
·2000	**12**	2·1	2·2	2·3	2·4	2·5	2·6	2·7	2·8	2·9	3·0	3·1	3·2	3·4	3·6	3·8	4·0	**12**	·2000
·2167	**13**	2·3	2·4	2·5	2·6	2·7	2·8	2·9	3·0	3·1	3·2	3·3	3·5	3·7	3·9	4·1	4·3	**13**	·2167
·2333	**14**	2·4	2·6	2·7	2·8	2·9	3·0	3·1	3·3	3·4	3·5	3·6	3·7	4·0	4·2	4·4	4·7	**14**	·2333
·2500	**15**	2·6	2·7	2·9	3·0	3·1	3·2	3·4	3·5	3·6	3·7	3·9	4·0	4·2	4·5	4·7	5·0	**15**	·2500
·2667	**16**	2·8	2·9	3·1	3·2	3·3	3·5	3·6	3·7	3·9	4·0	4·1	4·3	4·5	4·8	5·1	5·3	**16**	·2667
·2833	**17**	3·0	3·1	3·3	3·4	3·5	3·7	3·8	4·0	4·1	4·2	4·4	4·5	4·8	5·1	5·4	5·7	**17**	·2833
·3000	**18**	3·1	3·3	3·4	3·6	3·7	3·9	4·0	4·2	4·3	4·5	4·6	4·8	5·1	5·4	5·7	6·0	**18**	·3000
·3167	**19**	3·3	3·5	3·6	3·8	4·0	4·1	4·3	4·4	4·6	4·8	4·9	5·1	5·4	5·7	6·0	6·3	**19**	·3167
·3333	**20**	3·5	3·7	3·8	4·0	4·2	4·3	4·5	4·7	4·8	5·0	5·2	5·3	5·7	6·0	6·3	6·7	**20**	·3333
·3500	**21**	3·7	3·8	4·0	4·2	4·4	4·5	4·7	4·9	5·1	5·2	5·4	5·6	5·9	6·3	6·6	7·0	**21**	·3500
·3667	**22**	3·9	4·0	4·2	4·4	4·6	4·8	5·0	5·1	5·3	5·5	5·7	5·9	6·2	6·6	7·0	7·3	**22**	·3667
·3833	**23**	4·0	4·2	4·4	4·6	4·8	5·0	5·2	5·4	5·6	5·7	5·9	6·1	6·5	6·9	7·3	7·7	**23**	·3833
·4000	**24**	4·2	4·4	4·6	4·8	5·0	5·2	5·4	5·6	5·8	6·0	6·2	6·4	6·8	7·2	7·6	8·0	**24**	·4000
·4167	**25**	4·4	4·6	4·8	5·0	5·2	5·4	5·6	5·8	6·0	6·3	6·5	6·7	7·1	7·5	7·9	8·3	**25**	·4167
·4333	**26**	4·5	4·8	5·0	5·2	5·4	5·6	5·8	6·1	6·3	6·5	6·7	6·9	7·4	7·8	8·2	8·7	**26**	·4333
·4500	**27**	4·7	4·9	5·2	5·4	5·6	5·8	6·1	6·3	6·5	6·7	7·0	7·2	7·6	8·1	8·5	9·0	**27**	·4500
·4667	**28**	4·9	5·1	5·4	5·6	5·8	6·1	6·3	6·5	6·8	7·0	7·2	7·5	7·9	8·4	8·9	9·3	**28**	·4667
·4833	**29**	5·1	5·3	5·6	5·8	6·0	6·3	6·5	6·8	7·0	7·2	7·5	7·7	8·2	8·7	9·2	9·7	**29**	·4833
·5000	**30**	5·2	5·5	5·7	6·0	6·2	6·5	6·7	7·0	7·2	7·5	7·7	8·0	8·5	9·0	9·5	10·0	**30**	·5000
·5167	**31**	5·4	5·7	5·9	6·2	6·5	6·7	7·0	7·2	7·5	7·8	8·0	8·3	8·8	9·3	9·8	10·3	**31**	·5167
·5333	**32**	5·6	5·9	6·1	6·4	6·7	6·9	7·2	7·5	7·7	8·0	8·3	8·5	9·1	9·6	10·1	10·7	**32**	·5333
·5500	**33**	5·8	6·0	6·3	6·6	6·9	7·1	7·4	7·7	8·0	8·2	8·5	8·8	9·3	9·9	10·4	11·0	**33**	·5500
·5667	**34**	6·0	6·2	6·5	6·8	7·1	7·4	7·7	7·9	8·2	8·5	8·8	9·1	9·6	10·2	10·8	11·3	**34**	·5667
·5833	**35**	6·1	6·4	6·7	7·0	7·3	7·6	7·9	8·2	8·5	8·7	9·0	9·3	9·9	10·5	11·1	11·7	**35**	·5833
·6000	**36**	6·3	6·6	6·9	7·2	7·5	7·8	8·1	8·4	8·7	9·0	9·3	9·6	10·2	10·8	11·4	12·0	**36**	·6000
·6117	**37**	6·4	6·7	7·0	7·3	7·6	8·0	8·3	8·6	8·9	9·2	9·5	9·8	10·4	11·0	11·6	12·2	**37**	·6117
·6333	**38**	6·6	7·0	7·3	7·6	7·9	8·2	8·5	8·9	9·2	9·5	9·8	10·1	10·8	11·4	12·0	12·7	**38**	·6333
·6500	**39**	6·8	7·1	7·5	7·8	8·1	8·4	8·8	9·1	9·4	9·7	10·1	10·4	11·0	11·7	12·3	13·0	**39**	·6500
·6667	**40**	7·0	7·3	7·7	8·0	8·3	8·7	9·0	9·3	9·7	10·0	10·3	10·7	11·3	12·0	12·7	13·3	**40**	·6667
·6833	**41**	7·2	7·5	7·9	8·2	8·5	8·9	9·2	9·6	9·9	10·2	10·6	10·9	11·6	12·3	13·0	13·7	**41**	·6833
·7000	**42**	7·3	7·7	8·0	8·4	8·7	9·1	9·4	9·8	10·1	10·5	10·8	11·2	11·9	12·6	13·3	14·0	**42**	·7000
·7167	**43**	7·5	7·9	8·2	8·6	9·0	9·3	9·7	10·0	10·4	10·8	11·1	11·5	12·2	12·9	13·6	14·3	**43**	·7167
·7333	**44**	7·7	8·1	8·4	8·8	9·2	9·5	10·0	10·3	10·6	11·0	11·4	11·7	12·5	13·2	13·9	14·7	**44**	·7333
·7500	**45**	7·9	8·2	8·6	9·0	9·4	9·7	10·1	10·5	10·9	11·2	11·6	12·0	12·7	13·5	14·2	15·0	**45**	·7500
·7667	**46**	8·1	8·4	8·8	9·2	9·6	10·0	10·4	10·7	11·1	11·5	11·9	12·3	13·0	13·8	14·6	15·3	**46**	·7667
·7833	**47**	8·2	8·6	9·0	9·4	9·8	10·2	10·6	11·0	11·4	11·7	12·1	12·5	13·3	14·1	14·9	15·7	**47**	·7833
·8000	**48**	8·4	8·8	9·2	9·6	10·0	10·4	10·8	11·2	11·6	12·0	12·4	12·8	13·6	14·4	15·2	16·0	**48**	·8000
·8167	**49**	8·6	9·0	9·4	9·8	10·2	10·6	11·0	11·4	11·8	12·2	12·7	13·1	13·9	14·7	15·5	16·3	**49**	·8167
·8333	**50**	8·7	9·2	9·6	10·0	10·4	10·8	11·2	11·7	12·1	12·5	12·9	13·3	14·2	15·0	15·8	16·7	**50**	·8333
·8500	**51**	8·9	9·3	9·8	10·2	10·6	11·0	11·5	11·9	12·3	12·7	13·2	13·6	14·4	15·3	16·1	17·0	**51**	·8500
·8667	**52**	9·1	9·5	10·0	10·4	10·8	11·3	11·7	12·1	12·6	13·0	13·4	13·9	14·7	15·6	16·5	17·3	**52**	·8667
·8833	**53**	9·3	9·7	10·2	10·6	11·0	11·5	11·9	12·4	12·8	13·2	13·7	14·1	15·0	15·9	16·8	17·7	**53**	·8833
·9000	**54**	9·4	9·9	10·3	10·8	11·2	11·7	12·1	12·6	13·0	13·5	13·9	14·4	15·3	16·2	17·1	18·0	**54**	·9000
·9167	**55**	9·6	10·1	10·5	11·0	11·5	11·9	12·4	12·8	13·3	13·8	14·2	14·7	15·6	16·5	17·4	18·3	**55**	·9167
·9333	**56**	9·8	10·3	10·7	11·2	11·7	12·1	12·6	13·1	13·5	14·0	14·5	14·9	15·9	16·8	17·7	18·7	**56**	·9333
·9500	**57**	10·0	10·4	10·9	11·4	11·9	12·3	12·8	13·3	13·8	14·2	14·7	15·2	16·1	17·1	18·0	19·0	**57**	·9500
·9667	**58**	10·2	10·6	11·1	11·6	12·1	12·6	13·1	13·5	14·0	14·5	15·0	15·5	16·4	17·4	18·4	19·3	**58**	·9667
·9833	**59**	10·3	10·8	11·3	11·8	12·3	12·8	13·3	13·8	14·3	14·7	15·2	15·7	16·7	17·7	18·7	19·7	**59**	·9833
1·0000	**60**	10·5	11·0	11·5	12·0	12·5	13·0	13·5	14·0	14·5	15·0	15·5	16·0	17·0	18·0	19·0	20·0	**60**	1·0000
Decimal of hr	Mins	10·5	11·0	11·5	12·0	12·5	13·0	13·5	14·0	14·5	15·0	15·5	16·0	17·0	18·0	19·0	20·0	Mins	Decimal of hr
Time		Speed in knots																Time	

C3

TABLE 3 (5) True bearing of Sun at sunrise and sunset

LAT	DECLINATION 0°	1°	2°	3°	4°	5°	6°	7°	8°	9°	10°	11°	LAT
	°	°	°	°	°	°	°	°	°	°	°	°	
30°	90	88·8	87·7	86·5	85·4	84·2	83·1	81·9	80·7	79·6	78·4	77·3	30°
31°	90	88·8	87·7	86·5	85·3	84·2	83·0	81·9	80·6	79·5	78·3	77·1	31°
32°	90	88·8	87·6	86·5	85·3	84·1	82·9	81·7	80·5	79·4	78·2	77·0	32°
33°	90	88·8	87·6	86·4	85·2	84·0	82·8	81·6	80·4	79·2	78·0	76·8	33°
34°	90	88·8	87·6	86·4	85·2	84·0	82·7	81·5	80·3	79·1	77·9	76·7	34°
35°	90	88·8	87·5	86·3	85·1	83·9	82·7	81·4	80·2	79·0	77·8	76·5	35°
36°	90	88·8	87·5	86·3	85·0	83·8	82·6	81·3	80·1	78·8	77·6	76·3	36°
37°	90	88·7	87·5	86·2	85·0	83·7	82·5	81·2	80·0	78·7	77·4	76·2	37°
38°	90	88·7	87·5	86·2	84·9	83·6	82·4	81·1	79·8	78·5	77·3	76·0	38°
39°	90	88·7	87·4	86·1	84·8	83·6	82·3	81·0	79·7	78·4	77·1	75·8	39°
40°	90	88·7	87·4	86·1	84·8	83·5	82·1	80·8	79·5	78·2	76·9	75·6	40°
41°	90	88·7	87·3	86·0	84·7	83·4	82·0	80·7	79·4	78·0	76·7	75·3	41°
42°	90	88·6	87·3	86·0	84·6	83·3	81·9	80·6	79·2	77·8	76·5	75·1	42°
43°	90	88·6	87·3	85·9	84·5	83·1	81·8	80·4	79·0	77·6	76·3	74·9	43°
44°	90	88·6	87·2	85·8	84·4	83·0	81·6	80·2	78·8	77·4	76·0	74·6	44°
45°	90	88·6	87·2	85·7	84·3	82·9	81·5	80·1	78·6	77·2	75·8	74·3	45°
46°	90	88·6	87·1	85·7	84·2	82·8	81·3	79·9	78·4	77·0	75·5	74·0	46°
47°	90	88·5	87·1	85·6	84·1	82·6	81·2	79·7	78·2	76·7	75·2	73·7	47°
48°	90	88·5	87·0	85·5	84·0	82·5	81·0	79·5	78·0	76·5	75·0	73·4	48°
49°	90	88·5	86·9	85·4	83·9	82·4	80·8	79·3	77·7	76·2	74·6	73·1	49°
50°	90	88·4	86·9	85·3	83·8	82·2	80·6	79·1	77·5	75·9	74·3	72·7	50°
51°	90	88·4	86·8	85·2	83·6	82·0	80·4	78·8	77·2	75·6	74·0	72·4	51°
52°	90	88·4	86·7	85·1	83·5	81·9	80·2	78·6	76·9	75·3	73·6	71·9	52°
53°	90	88·3	86·7	85·0	83·3	81·7	80·0	78·3	76·6	74·9	73·2	71·5	53°
54°	90	88·3	86·6	84·9	83·2	81·5	79·8	78·0	76·3	74·6	72·8	71·1	54°
55°	90	88·2	86·5	84·8	83·0	81·3	79·5	77·7	76·0	74·2	72·4	70·6	55°
56°	90	88·2	86·4	84·6	82·8	81·0	79·2	77·4	75·6	73·8	71·9	70·0	56°
57°	90	88·2	86·3	84·5	82·6	80·8	78·9	77·0	75·2	73·3	71·4	69·5	57°
58°	90	88·1	86·2	84·3	82·4	80·5	78·6	76·7	74·8	72·8	70·9	68·9	58°
59°	90	88·1	86·1	84·2	82·2	80·3	78·3	76·3	74·3	72·3	70·3	68·3	59°
60°	90	88·0	86·0	84·0	82·0	80·0	77·9	75·9	73·8	71·8	69·7	67·6	60°

LAT	DECLINATION 12°	13°	14°	15°	16°	17°	18°	19°	20°	21°	22°	23°	LAT
	°	°	°	°	°	°	°	°	°	°	°	°	
30°	76·1	74·9	73·8	72·6	71·4	70·3	69·1	67·9	66·7	65·5	64·4	63·2	30°
31°	76·0	74·8	73·6	72·4	71·2	70·0	68·9	67·7	66·5	65·3	64·1	62·9	31°
32°	75·8	74·6	73·4	72·2	71·0	69·8	68·6	67·4	66·2	65·0	63·8	62·6	32°
33°	75·6	74·4	73·2	72·1	70·8	69·6	68·4	67·1	65·9	64·7	63·5	62·2	33°
34°	75·5	74·2	73·0	71·8	70·6	69·3	68·1	66·9	65·6	64·4	63·1	61·9	34°
35°	75·3	74·1	72·8	71·6	70·3	69·1	67·8	66·6	65·3	64·1	62·8	61·5	35°
36°	75·1	73·8	72·6	71·3	70·1	68·8	67·5	66·3	65·0	63·7	62·4	61·1	36°
37°	74·9	73·6	72·4	71·1	69·8	68·5	67·2	65·9	64·6	63·3	62·0	60·7	37°
38°	74·7	73·4	72·0	70·8	69·5	68·2	66·9	65·6	64·3	62·9	61·6	60·3	38°
39°	74·5	73·2	71·9	70·5	69·2	67·9	66·6	65·2	63·9	62·5	61·2	59·8	39°
40°	74·2	72·9	71·6	70·2	68·9	67·6	66·2	64·8	63·5	62·1	60·7	59·3	40°
41°	74·0	72·7	71·3	69·9	68·6	67·2	65·8	64·4	63·0	61·6	60·2	58·8	41°
42°	73·7	72·4	71·0	69·6	68·2	66·8	65·4	64·0	62·6	61·2	59·7	58·3	42°
43°	73·5	72·1	70·7	69·3	67·9	66·4	65·0	63·6	62·1	60·7	59·2	57·7	43°
44°	73·2	71·8	70·3	68·9	67·5	66·0	64·6	63·1	61·6	60·1	58·6	57·1	44°
45°	72·9	71·4	70·0	68·5	67·0	65·6	64·1	62·6	61·1	59·5	58·0	56·4	45°
46°	72·6	71·1	69·6	68·1	66·6	65·1	63·6	62·0	60·5	58·9	57·4	55·8	46°
47°	72·2	70·7	69·2	67·7	66·2	64·6	63·1	61·5	59·9	58·3	56·7	55·0	47°
48°	71·9	70·3	68·8	67·2	65·7	64·1	62·5	60·9	59·3	57·6	55·9	54·3	48°
49°	71·5	69·9	68·4	66·8	65·1	63·5	61·9	60·2	58·6	56·9	55·2	53·4	49°
50°	71·1	69·5	67·9	66·2	64·6	62·9	61·3	59·6	57·8	56·1	54·3	52·6	50°
51°	70·7	69·1	67·4	65·7	64·0	62·3	60·6	58·8	57·1	55·3	53·5	51·6	51°
52°	70·3	68·6	66·9	65·1	63·4	61·6	59·9	58·1	56·3	54·4	52·5	50·6	52°
53°	69·8	68·1	66·3	64·5	62·7	60·9	59·1	57·3	55·4	53·5	51·5	49·5	53°
54°	69·3	67·5	65·7	63·9	62·0	60·2	58·3	56·4	54·4	52·4	50·4	48·3	54°
55°	68·7	66·9	65·1	63·2	61·3	59·4	57·4	55·4	53·4	51·3	49·2	47·1	55°
56°	68·2	66·3	64·4	62·4	60·5	58·5	56·5	54·4	52·3	50·1	47·9	45·7	56°
57°	67·6	65·6	63·6	61·6	59·6	57·5	55·4	53·3	51·1	48·9	46·5	44·2	57°
58°	66·9	64·9	62·8	60·8	58·7	56·5	54·3	52·1	49·8	47·4	45·0	42·5	58°
59°	66·2	64·1	62·0	59·8	57·6	55·4	53·1	50·8	48·4	45·9	43·3	40·7	59°
60°	65·4	63·3	61·1	58·8	56·5	54·2	51·8	49·4	46·8	44·2	41·5	38·6	60°

Table 3 (6) Sun's declination for 2005

South		Declination	North	
Dec 6 – Jan 5		23°	Jan 5 – Jun4	
Jan 06 - Jan 11	Nov 29 - Dec 05	22°	May 28 - Jun 03	Jul 07 - Jul 14
Jan 12 - Jan 17	Nov 23 - Nov 28	21°	May 22 - May 27	Jul 15 - Jul 19
Jan 18 - Jan 21	Nov 19 - Nov 22	20°	May 17 - May 21	Jul 20 - Jul 24
Jan 22 - Jan 25	Nov 15 - Nov 18	19°	May 13 - May 16	Jul 25 - Jul 29
Jan 26 - Jan 29	Nov 11 - Nov 14	18°	May 09 - May 12	Jul 30 - Aug 02
Jan 30 - Feb 02	Nov 07 - Nov 10	17°	May 05 - May 08	Aug 03 - Aug 05
Feb 03 - Feb 05	Nov 04 - Nov 06	16°	May 02 - May 04	Aug 06 - Aug 09
Feb 06 - Feb 08	Nov 01 - Nov 03	15°	Apr 29 - May 01	Aug 10 - Aug 12
Feb 09 - Feb 11	Oct 29 - Oct 31	14°	Apr 26 - Apr 28	Aug 13 - Aug 15
Feb 12 - Feb 14	Oct 26 - Oct 28	13°	Apr 23 - Apr 25	Aug 16 - Aug 18
Feb 15 - Feb 17	Oct 23 - Oct 25	12°	Apr 20 - Apr 22	Aug 19 - Aug 21
Feb 18 - Feb 20	Oct 20 - Oct 22	11°	Apr 17 - Apr 19	Aug 22 - Aug 24
Feb 21 - Feb 23	Oct 17 - Oct 19	10°	Apr 14 - Apr 16	Aug 25 - Aug 27
Feb 24 - Feb 25	Oct 15 - Oct 16	9°	Apr 11 - Apr 13	Aug 28 - Aug 30
Feb 26 - Feb 28	Oct 12 - Oct 14	8°	Apr 08 - Apr 10	Aug 31 - Sep 02
Mar 01 - Mar 02	Oct 09 - Oct 11	7°	Apr 06 - Apr 07	Sep 03 - Sep 04
Mar 03 - Mar 05	Oct 07 - Oct 08	6°	Apr 03 - Apr 05	Sep 05 - Sep 07
Mar 06 - Mar 08	Oct 04 - Oct 06	5°	Apr 01 - Apr 02	Sep 08 - Sep 10
Mar 09 - Mar 10	Oct 01 - Oct 03	4°	Mar 29 - Mar 31	Sep 11 - Sep 12
Mar 11 - Mar 13	Sep 29 - Sep 30	3°	Mar 26 - Mar 28	Sep 13 - Sep 15
Mar 14 - Mar 15	Sep 26 - Sep 28	2°	Mar 24 - Mar 25	Sep 16 - Sep 18
Mar 16 - Mar 18	Sep 24 - Sep 25	1°	Mar 21 - Mar 23	Sep 19 - Sep 20
Mar 19 - Mar 20	Sep 21 - Sep 23	0°	Mar 19 - Mar 20	Sep 21 - Sep 23

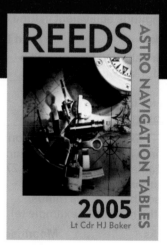

3.6 SUN AND MOON TABLES – RISING, SETTING AND TWILIGHTS

3.6.1 Rising and Setting Phenomena

The tables of Sunrise, Sunset and Twilights, Moonrise and Moonset enable the degree of darkness around twilight and throughout the night to be estimated.

3.6.2 Contents of Tables 3(7), 3(8) and 3(9)

Table 3 (7) provides Local Mean Times (LMT) for every third day of the year, of morning Nautical Twilight, Sunrise, Sunset and evening Civil Twilight for latitude 50°N and latitude variations (*v*). Use the left-hand sign in the tabular entry for *v* for Sunrise, and the right-hand sign for Sunset. The latitude corrections in Table 3 (8) for Sunrise, Sunset and Twilights, enable the LMT for latitudes in the range 30°N to 60°N to be found.

Table 3 (9) gives times of Moonrise and Moonset for each day for latitude 50°N and latitude variations (v). The latitude correction table enables the LMT for latitudes in the range 30°N to 60°N to be found.

The tabular values are for the Greenwich Meridian, and are approximately the LMT of the corresponding phenomena for the other meridians. Expressing the longitude in time, the UT is obtained from:

$$\mathrm{UT} = \mathrm{LMT} \ {}^{+\text{west}}_{-\text{east}} \ \text{longitude}$$

For Moonrise and Moonset a further small correction of one minute for every seven degrees of longitude is also required, which is added to the LMT if west, subtracted if east.

At Sunrise and Sunset the upper limb of the Sun is on the horizon at sea level. The Sun's zenith distance is 96° for Civil Twilight and 102° for Nautical Twilight. At Civil Twilight the brightest stars are visible and the horizon is clearly defined. At Nautical Twilight the horizon is not visible.

At Moonrise and Moonset the Moon's upper limb is on the horizon at sea level.

3.6.3 Example (a): The Sun – rising, setting and twilights

Find the UT of the beginning of morning Nautical Twilight, Sunrise, Sunset and the end of evening Civil Twilight on 10 March 2004 for latitude 49°10'N longitude 08°03'W.

From table 3(7), for 10 March, *v* = – 10 for the beginning of Nautical Twilight, *v* = + 8 for Sunrise; *v* = – 8 for Sunset and v = 0 for the end of Civil Twilight. From table 3 (8) the latitude corrections for Nautical Twilight, Sunrise, Sunset and Civil Twilight are + 1 mins, – 1 mins, + 1 mins and 0 mins respectively. Note that for Sunset, the sign of the correction has to be reversed because v is minus.

Convert longitude from degrees and minutes of arc to whole minutes of time, by multiplying the degrees of longitude by 4 and adding a further correction of 0 mins, 1 min, 2 mins, 3 mins or 4 mins when the minutes of longitude are in the range 0' to 7', 8' to 22', 23' to 37', 38' to 52' or 53' to 59', respectively.

The longitude equivalent in time of 08°03'W is + (8 x 4 + 1) = + 33 mins.

Remarks	Naut Twilight		Sunrise		Sunset		Civil Twilight	
Tabular value, 10 Mar	05h	14m	06h	24m	17h	57m	18h	30m
Corr'n for latitude		+ 1m		– 1m		+ 1m		0m
LMT	05h	15m	06h	23m	17h	58m	18h	30m
Corr'n for longitude	+ 0h	33m	+ 0h	33m	+ 0h	33m	+ 0h	33m
UT of phenomenon	05h	48m	06h	56m	18h	31m	19h	3m

3.6.4 Example (b): The Moon – rising and setting

Find the UT of Moonrise and Moonset on 13 June 2004 for latitude 39°22'N, longitude 10°42'W.

From Table 3(9) for 13 June, *v*=–27 for Moonrise and *v*=+36 for Moonset. The latitude correction for Moonrise and Moonset is + 16 mins and – 22 mins, respectively. Note the reversal of the sign of the correction for Moonset, because *v* is minus.

Using the method in example (a), the longitude equivalent in time of 10°42'W is + 44mins.

Remarks	Moonrise		Moonset	
Tabular value, 13 June	01h	35m	15h	57m
Corr'n for latitude		+ 16m		– 22m
LMT	01h	51m	15h	35m
Corr'n for longitude		+ 44m		+ 44m
UT of phenomenon	02h	35m	16h	19m

These times can be increased by +1min to allow for the effect of longitude on the LMT of the phenomenon. See text at end of Table 3 (9) for the instructions.

TABLE 3 (7) 2005 – SUNRISE, SUNSET and TWILIGHTS

Date	Naut Twi	*v*	Sun–rise	*v*	Sun–set	Civil Twi	*v*	Date	Naut Twi	*v*	Sun–rise	*v*	Sun–set	Civil Twi	*v*
	h m		h m		h m	h m			h m		h m		h m	h m	
Jan 1	06 39	+39	07 59	+63	–16 09	16 47	–51	Jul 3	02 09	–114	03 56	–67	+20 12	20 56	+ 83
4	06 39	38	07 58	62	16 12	16 50	50	6	02 12	112	03 59	66	20 10	20 54	82
7	06 39	37	07 57	60	16 16	16 54	49	9	02 17	109	04 01	65	20 09	20 52	80
10	06 38	36	07 56	59	16 20	16 57	47	12	02 21	106	04 04	63	20 06	20 49	78
13	06 36	35	07 54	57	16 24	17 01	46	15	02 26	103	04 07	62	20 04	20 46	76
16	06 35	+33	07 52	+55	–6 28	17 05	–44	18	02 32	–100	04 11	–60	+20 01	20 42	+74
19	06 33	32	07 49	53	16 33	17 09	42	21	02 38	96	04 15	58	19 57	20 38	72
22	06 30	30	07 46	51	16 38	17 14	40	24	02 43	93	04 18	56	19 54	20 34	69
25	06 28	28	07 43	49	16 43	17 18	38	27	02 49	89	04 22	54	19 50	20 29	66
28	06 25	26	07 39	47	16 48	17 23	36	30	02 55	85	04 26	51	19 45	20 24	64
31	06 21	+24	07 35	+44	–16 53	17 28	–34	Aug 2	03 02	–81	04 31	–49	+19 41	20 19	+61
Feb 3	06 17	22	07 31	41	16 58	17 32	32	5	03 08	77	04 35	46	19 36	20 14	58
6	06 13	19	07 26	39	17 03	17 37	29	8	03 14	73	04 39	44	19 31	20 08	55
9	06 09	17	07 21	36	17 08	17 42	27	11	03 20	69	04 44	41	19 26	20 02	52
12	06 04	15	07 16	33	17 13	17 47	24	14	03 26	66	04 48	39	19 20	19 56	49
15	05 59	+12	07 11	+31	–17 18	17 52	–21	17	03 32	–62	04 53	–36	+19 14	19 50	+46
18	05 54	9	07 05	28	17 24	17 57	19	20	03 38	58	04 57	33	19 09	19 44	43
21	05 49	7	06 59	25	17 29	18 02	16	23	03 43	54	05 01	30	19 03	19 37	40
24	05 43	4	06 53	22	17 34	18 07	13	26	03 49	51	05 06	28	18 56	19 31	37
27	05 38	+1	06 47	19	17 39	18 11	10	29	03 55	47	05 10	25	18 50	19 24	34
Mar 2	05 32	–2	06 41	+16	–17 44	18 16	–8	Sep 1	04 00	–44	05 15	–22	+18 44	19 17	+31
5	05 25	4	06 35	13	17 49	18 21	5	4	04 05	40	05 19	19	18 38	19 11	28
8	05 19	7	06 29	11	17 54	18 26	–2	7	04 11	37	05 24	16	18 31	19 04	25
11	05 13	10	06 22	8	17 59	18 31	+1	10	04 16	34	05 28	13	18 25	18 57	22
14	05 06	13	06 16	5	18 03	18 36	4	13	04 21	30	05 33	11	18 18	18 51	19
17	04 59	–16	06 09	+2	–18 08	18 40	+7	16	04 26	–27	05 37	–8	+18 11	18 44	+16
20	04 53	20	06 03	–1	+18 13	18 45	10	19	04 31	24	05 42	5	18 05	18 37	13
23	04 46	23	05 56	4	18 18	18 50	13	22	04 36	21	05 46	–2	+17 58	18 30	10
26	04 39	26	05 50	7	18 22	18 55	16	25	04 41	18	05 51	+1	–17 51	18 24	7
29	04 32	29	05 43	10	18 27	19 00	19	28	04 45	15	05 55	4	17 45	18 17	4
Apr 1	04 25	–33	05 37	–13	+18 32	19 05	+22	Oct 1	04 50	–12	06 00	+7	–17 38	18 11	+1
4	04 18	36	05 30	16	18 37	19 10	25	4	04 55	9	06 05	10	17 32	18 04	–2
7	04 10	39	05 24	18	18 41	19 15	28	7	05 00	6	06 09	12	17 25	17 58	5
10	04 03	43	05 18	21	18 46	19 20	31	10	05 04	–3	06 14	15	17 19	17 51	7
13	03 56	46	05 11	24	18 51	19 25	34	13	05 09	0	06 19	18	17 13	17 45	10
16	03 49	–50	05 05	–27	+18 55	19 30	+37	16	05 13	+3	06 23	+21	–17 07	17 39	–13
19	03 41	54	04 59	30	19 00	19 35	40	19	05 18	6	06 28	24	17 01	17 34	16
22	03 34	57	04 53	33	19 05	19 40	44	22	05 22	8	06 33	27	16 55	17 28	18
25	03 27	61	04 47	35	19 09	19 45	47	25	05 27	11	06 38	29	16 49	17 23	21
28	03 20	65	04 42	38	19 14	19 50	50	28	05 32	13	06 43	32	16 44	17 17	24
May 1	03 13	–69	04 36	–41	+19 19	19 56	+53	31	05 36	+16	06 48	+35	–16 39	17 12	–26
4	03 06	72	04 31	43	19 23	20 01	56	Nov 3	05 40	18	06 53	38	16 33	17 08	29
7	02 59	76	04 26	46	19 28	20 06	59	6	05 45	21	06 58	40	16 29	17 03	31
10	02 53	80	04 21	49	19 32	20 11	62	9	05 49	23	07 03	43	16 24	16 59	33
13	02 46	84	04 17	51	19 37	20 16	65	12	05 54	25	07 08	45	16 20	16 55	36
16	02 40	–88	04 13	–53	+19 41	20 21	+67	15	05 58	+27	07 13	+48	–16 16	16 51	–38
19	02 34	92	04 09	56	19 45	20 25	70	18	06 02	29	07 18	50	16 12	16 48	40
22	02 29	96	04 05	58	19 49	20 30	73	21	06 06	31	07 22	52	16 09	16 45	42
25	02 23	99	04 02	60	19 53	20 34	75	24	06 10	33	07 27	54	16 06	16 43	44
28	02 18	103	03 59	61	19 56	20 38	77	27	06 14	34	07 31	56	16 04	16 41	45
31	02 14	–106	03 57	–63	+19 59	20 42	+79	30	06 17	+35	07 35	+58	–16 02	16 39	–47
Jun 3	02 10	109	03 54	64	20 02	20 46	81	Dec 3	06 21	37	07 39	60	16 00	16 38	48
6	02 07	112	03 53	66	20 05	20 49	82	6	06 24	38	07 43	61	15 59	16 37	49
9	02 04	114	03 51	67	20 07	20 51	84	9	06 27	39	07 46	62	15 58	16 36	50
12	02 02	116	03 51	68	20 09	20 54	85	12	06 30	39	07 49	63	15 58	16 36	51
15	02 01	–117	03 50	–68	+20 11	20 56	+85	15	06 32	+40	07 52	+64	–15 58	16 37	–52
18	02 00	118	03 50	69	20 12	20 57	86	18	06 34	40	07 54	64	15 59	16 38	52
21	02 00	118	03 51	69	20 13	20 58	86	21	06 36	40	07 56	64	16 00	16 39	52
24	02 01	118	03 51	69	20 13	20 58	86	24	06 37	40	07 57	64	16 02	16 41	52
27	02 03	117	03 53	68	20 13	20 58	85	27	06 38	40	07 58	64	16 04	16 43	52
30	02 05	–116	03 54	–68	+20 13	20 57	+84	30	06 39	+40	07 59	+63	–16 07	16 45	–51
Jul 3	02 09	–114	03 56	–67	+20 12	20 56	+83	Jan 2	06 39	+39	07 59	+62	–16 10	16 48	–50

TABLE 3 (8) 2005 – SUNRISE, SUNSET and TWILIGHTS

Corrections to Sunrise and Sunset

N. Lat	30°	35°	40°	45°	50°	52°	54°	56°	58°	60°
v	m	m	m	m	m	m	m	m	m	m
0	0	0	0	0	0	0	0	0	0	0
2	–2	–2	–1	–1	0	0	+1	+1	+2	+2
4	4	3	2	1	0	+1	1	2	3	4
6	6	5	4	2	0	1	2	3	4	6
8	8	6	5	3	0	1	2	4	6	7
10	–10	–8	–6	–3	0	+1	+3	+5	+7	+9
12	12	10	7	4	0	2	4	6	8	11
14	14	11	8	4	0	2	4	7	10	13
16	16	13	9	5	0	2	5	8	11	15
18	18	14	10	6	0	3	6	9	12	16
20	–20	–16	–12	–6	0	+3	+6	+10	+14	+18
22	22	18	13	7	0	3	7	11	15	20
24	24	19	14	8	0	4	7	12	16	22
26	26	21	15	8	0	4	8	13	18	24
28	28	22	16	9	0	4	9	14	19	26
30	–30	–24	–17	–10	0	+4	+9	+15	+21	+28
32	32	26	19	10	0	5	10	16	22	30
34	34	27	20	11	0	5	11	17	24	32
36	36	29	21	11	0	5	11	18	25	34
38	38	31	22	12	0	6	12	19	27	36
40	–40	–32	–23	–13	0	+6	+13	+20	+28	+38
42	42	34	24	13	0	6	13	21	30	40
44	44	35	26	14	0	7	14	22	31	42
46	46	37	27	15	0	7	15	23	33	44
48	48	39	28	15	0	7	15	24	35	47
50	–50	–40	–29	–16	0	+8	+16	+26	+36	+49
52	52	42	30	17	0	8	17	27	38	51
54	54	44	32	17	0	8	17	28	40	54
56	56	45	33	18	0	9	18	29	42	56
58	58	47	34	19	0	9	19	30	43	59
60	–60	–49	–35	–19	0	+9	+20	+32	+45	+62
62	62	50	36	20	0	10	20	33	47	64
64	64	52	38	21	0	10	21	34	49	67
66	66	53	39	22	0	10	22	36	51	70
68	68	55	40	22	0	11	23	37	54	74
70	–70	–57	–41	–23	0	+11	+24	+38	+56	+77

If *v* is negative reverse the sign of the correction

Corrections to Nautical Twilight

N. Lat	30°	35°	40°	45°	50°	52°	54°	56°	58°	60°
v	m	m	m	m	m	m	m	m	m	m
+40	–40	–31	–22	–12	0	+5	+11	+17	+24	+31
30	30	23	16	9	0	4	8	12	17	22
20	20	15	10	5	0	2	5	7	10	13
+10	–10	–7	–5	–2	0	+1	+2	+3	+3	+4
0	0	+1	+1	+1	0	–1	–1	–2	–3	–4
–10	+10	+9	+7	+4	0	–2	–4	–7	–10	–13
20	20	17	13	7	0	3	7	12	17	23
30	30	25	18	10	0	5	11	17	24	33
40	40	33	24	14	0	7	14	23	33	44
50	50	41	30	17	0	–8	18	29	42	57
–60	+60	+49	+37	+21	0	–10	–22	–36	–52	–73
70	70	58	43	24	0	12	27	44	65	95
80	80	66	49	28	0	15	32	54	83	–136
90	90	75	56	32	0	17	39	67	–116	TAN
100	100	83	63	37	0	20	47	–88	TAN	TAN
–110	+110	+92	+70	+42	0	–24	–59	TAN	TAN	TAN
–120	+120	+101	+78	+47	0	–29	–81	TAN	TAN	TAN

Corrections to Civil Twilight

N. Lat	30°	35°	40°	45°	50°	52°	54°	56°	58°	60°
v	m	m	m	m	m	m	m	m	m	m
–50	+50	+40	+28	+15	0	–7	–15	–24	–33	–44
40	40	32	23	12	0	6	12	18	26	34
30	30	24	17	9	0	4	8	13	19	25
20	20	16	11	6	0	3	5	8	12	15
–10	+10	+8	+5	+3	0	–1	–2	–4	–5	–7
0	0	0	0	0	0	0	+1	+1	+2	+2
+10	–10	–8	–6	–4	0	+2	4	6	8	11
20	20	16	12	7	0	3	7	11	15	20
30	30	24	18	10	0	5	10	16	22	30
40	40	33	24	13	0	6	13	21	30	41
+50	–50	–41	–30	–17	0	+8	+17	+27	+39	+52
60	60	49	36	20	0	10	21	33	48	66
70	70	57	42	24	0	12	25	41	60	84
80	80	66	49	27	0	14	30	49	74	110
83	83	68	50	29	0	14	32	52	80	121
+86	–86	–71	–52	–30	0	+15	+33	+56	+86	+137

The times on the previous page are the local mean times (LMT) of morning nautical twilight, sunrise, sunset and evening civil twilight for latitude 50°N, together with their variations *v*. The variations are the differences in minutes of time between the time of the phenomenon for latitudes 50°N and 30°N. The sign on the left-handside of v (between sunrise and sunset) applies to sunrise, and the sign on the right-hand side applies to sunset. The LMT of the phenomenon for latitudes between 30°N and 60°N is found by applying the corrections in the tables above to the tabulated times as follows:

Sunrise and sunset: To determine the LMT of sunrise or sunset, take out the tabulated time and *v* corresponding to the required date. Using *v* and latitude as arguments in the table of "Corrections to Sunrise and Sunset", extract the correction. This table is for positive *v*. If *v* is minus, reverse the sign of the correction. Apply the correction to the tabulated time.

Nautical twilight: To determine the LMT of morning nautical twilight, follow the same method as for sunrise and sunset, but use the table of "Corrections to Nautical Twilight". This table includes both positive and negative values of *v*. The entry TAN stands for Twilight All Night, because the Sun does not reach an altitude of –12°.

Civil twilight: To determine the LMT of evening civil twilight follow the same method as for nautical twilight, but use the table of "Corrections to Civil Twilight". This table includes both positive and negative values of *v*.

Convert LMT to UT by adding the longitude in time if west (+), or subtracting if east (–).

Examples of the use of these tables are given in 3.6.3

TABLE 3 (9) **2005 – MOONRISE and MOONSET**

	JANUARY				MARCH				MAY				JULY			
Day	Rise	v	Set	v	Rise	v	Set	v	Rise	v	Set	v	Rise	v	Set	v
	h m		h m		h m		h m		h m		h m		h m		h m	
1	22 13	–17	11 09	+23	24 10	+57	08 31	–45	02 16	+67	10 39	–63	00 24	–40	15 41	+51
2	23 25	–1	11 22	+8	00 10	57	08 52	61	02 40	50	12 06	44	00 43	56	16 57	67
3	24 39	+15	11 34	–7	01 33	73	09 21	77	02 58	33	13 30	26	01 06	70	18 10	80
4	00 39	15	11 48	22	02 53	86	10 02	88	03 13	+15	14 51	–8	01 38	82 1	9 16	88
5	01 56	32	12 04	38	04 05	91	11 01	91	03 27	–1	16 10	+10	02 19	89	20 12	89
6	03 19	+50	12 24	–56	05 00	+86	12 18	–84	03 40	–17	17 29	+27	03 13	–89	20 54	+84
7	04 46	68	12 53	72	05 40	73	13 46	68	03 55	34	18 48	45	04 16	81	21 26	73
8	06 13	83	13 34	85	06 08	55	15 17	49	04 12	50	20 07	61	05 25	70	21 50	60
9	07 32	90	14 35	90	06 29	37	16 46	30	04 34	66	21 24	76	06 36	55	22 08	45
10	08 33	86	15 54	83	06 46	19	18 12	–11	05 03	79	22 34	86	07 46	40	22 22	31
11	09 17	+72	17 25	–68	07 01	+1	19 35	+8	05 41	–88	23 34	+90	08 56	–25	22 35	+16
12	09 46	54	18 58	48	07 15	–15	20 56	25	06 31	90	24 21	87	10 05	–10	22 47	+2
13	10 08	36	20 26	29	07 30	32	22 16	43	07 31	85	00 21	87	11 15	+6	22 58	–13
14	10 24	19	21 49	–11	07 47	48	23 35	60	08 39	74	00 56	77	12 27	22	23 11	28
15	10 39	+2	23 08	+6	08 08	64	24 50	74	09 50	60	01 22	64	13 43	39	23 27	44
16	10 52	–14	24 25	+23	08 35	–77	00 50	+74	11 01	–45	01 41	+50	15 04	+56	23 48	–61
17	11 06	29	00 25	23	09 11	87	02 00	85	12 13	30	01 57	35	16 29	73	24 17	77
18	11 22	45	01 40	39	09 58	90	03 01	90	13 24	–14	02 10	21	17 52	87	00 17	77
19	11 42	59	02 54	55	10 55	86	03 49	88	14 37	+2	02 22	+6	19 06	92	01 01	89
20	12 06	73	04 07	69	12 02	77	04 26	79	15 52	19	02 34	–10	20 03	85	02 04	91
21	12 39	–83	05 16	+81	13 12	–63	04 53	+67	17 11	+36	02 48	–26	20 43	+70	03 26	–82
22	13 22	88	06 18	88	14 25	48	05 14	53	18 35	54	03 04	42	21 10	52	04 59	65
23	14 16	87	07 10	87	15 38	32	05 31	38	20 02	72	03 25	60	21 31	33	06 33	45
24	15 20	79	07 50	81	16 50	–16	05 44	23	21 28	86	03 55	76	21 47	+15	08 03	25
25	16 29	67	08 20	70	18 04	0	05 57	+8	22 42	92	04 38	88	22 01	–2	09 29	–6
26	17 41	–52	08 43	+56	19 19	+17	06 09	–8	23 38	+86	05 39	–91	22 15	–19	10 51	+12
27	18 53	37	09 01	42	20 36	34	06 22	24	24 18	72	06 57	83	22 30	36	12 11	29
28	20 04	21	09 16	27	21 57	52	06 37	40	00 18	72	08 24	68	22 48	52	13 30	46
29	21 15	–6	09 29	+13	23 21	69	06 57	57	00 45	55	09 53	49	23 10	67	14 47	63
30	22 27	+10	09 41	–2	24 43	84	07 23	73	01 05	37	11 18	31	23 38	80	16 02	77
31	23 42	+27	09 54	–17	00 43	+84	08 00	–86	01 21	+20	12 40	–13	24 17	–88	17 11	+87

	FEBRUARY				APRIL				JUNE				AUGUST			
1	25 00	+44	10 08	–33	01 58	+92	08 53	–92	01 35	+4	13 58	+5	00 17	–88	18 09	+90
2	01 00	44	10 26	49	02 57	89	10 03	88	01 48	–13	15 16	22	01 06	90	18 55	86
3	02 23	61	10 49	66	03 41	78	11 25	75	02 02	29	16 33	39	02 07	85	19 30	77
4	03 47	78	11 23	81	04 12	62	12 53	57	02 18	45	17 51	55	03 14	74	19 55	64
5	05 08	89	12 12	90	04 34	44	14 21	38	02 38	60	19 08	71	04 25	60	20 14	50
6	06 16	+90	13 21	–89	04 51	+27	15 46	–19	03 04	–74	20 20	+83	05 37	–45	20 30	+35
7	07 07	80	14 47	77	05 06	+9	17 08	–1	03 38	85	21 24	89	06 47	29	20 43	21
8	07 43	64	16 19	59	05 20	–7	18 29	+17	04 24	90	22 16	88	07 56	–14	20 54	+6
9	08 08	46	17 52	39	05 34	24	19 50	35	05 20	87	22 55	81	09 05	+1	21 06	–9
10	08 27	27	19 20	20	05 50	41	21 10	52	06 26	78	23 24	69	10 16	17	21 18	24
11	08 42	+10	20 43	–1	06 09	–57	22 28	+68	07 36	–65	23 45	+55	11 29	+33	21 32	–39
12	08 57	–7	22 04	+16	06 33	72	23 43	81	08 47	51	24 02	41	12 46	50	21 50	55
13	09 11	23	23 22	33	07 05	84	24 49	89	09 58	35	00 02	41	14 07	67	22 14	71
14	09 26	39	24 39	50	07 48	90	00 49	89	11 08	20	00 16	26	15 29	82	22 50	85
15	09 44	55	00 39	50	08 42	89	01 43	90	12 18	–4	00 28	+12	16 46	91	23 42	92
16	10 07	–69	01 54	+65	09 46	–81	02 25	+84	13 30	+12	00 40	–3	17 50	+90	24 53	–89
17	10 37	81	03 06	78	10 55	69	02 56	73	14 46	28	00 53	19	18 36	79	00 53	89
18	11 17	88	04 12	87	12 07	55	03 19	59	16 06	46	01 07	35	19 09	62	02 21	75
19	12 07	89	05 07	89	13 19	39	03 36	44	17 31	64	01 25	52	19 32	42	03 56	56
20	13 08	83	05 51	84	14 32	23	03 51	29	18 58	80	01 50	69	19 50	24	05 29	35
21	14 17	–71	06 24	+74	15 44	–7	04 04	+14	20 20	+90	02 26	–83	20 06	+5	06 59	–15
22	15 28	57	06 49	61	16 59	+9	04 16	–1	21 26	90	03 19	91	20 20	–12	08 26	+4
23	16 41	42	07 08	47	18 16	27	04 29	17	22 14	78	04 32	88	20 35	29	09 49	22
24	17 53	26	07 23	32	19 37	45	04 43	33	22 46	62	06 00	75	20 51	46	11 11	40
25	19 05	10	07 37	17	21 02	63	05 01	50	23 09	43	07 32	56	21 12	62	12 32	58
26	20 18	+6	07 49	+2	22 28	+79	05 25	–67	23 27	+25	09 01	–37	21 38	–76	13 50	+73
27	21 32	+22	08 01	–13	23 48	90	05 58	82	23 42	+8	10 26	–18	22 14	87	15 03	85
28	22 49	+39	08 15	–29	24 54	91	06 47	91	23 55	–8	11 47	0	23 00	91	16 05	91
29					00 54	91	07 53	90	24 09	24	13 06	+17	23 58	88	16 55	89
30					01 42	+82	09 13	–79	00 09	–24	14 23	+34	25 04	78	17 33	81
31													01 04	–78	18 01	+69

C3

TABLE 3 (9) *continued* 2005 – MOONRISE and MOONSET

Day	SEPTEMBER Rise	v	Set	v	NOVEMBER Rise	v	Set	v
	h m		h m		h m		h m	
1	19 52	– 10	07 54	+ 3	18 47	– 88	11 44	+ 88
1	02 14	-65	18 21	+55	06 06	+34	16 08	-40
2	03 26	50	18 38	40	07 26	51	16 27	56
3	04 37	34	18 51	25	08 48	68	16 51	72
4	05 47	19	19 03	+10	10 09	83	17 27	86
5	06 56	-3	19 14	-4	11 24	92	18 17	93
6	08 07	+12	19 26	-19	12 25	+91	19 25	-89
7	09 20	29	19 39	35	13 09	80	20 46	77
8	10 35	45	19 55	51	13 40	65	22 13	60
9	11 54	62	20 17	67	14 03	47	23 40	41
10	13 15	78	20 47	81	14 21	29	25 04	22
11	14 32	+90	21 30	-91	14 35	+12	01 04	-22
12	15 39	93	22 32	92	14 49	-5	02 27	-4
13	16 30	85	23 51	83	15 03	22	03 49	+15
14	17 07	70	25 21	66	15 19	39	05 12	33
15	17 33	52	01 21	66	15 38	56	06 35	51
16	17 53	+33	02 54	-46	16 04	-72	07 58	+68
17	18 09	+15	04 25	26	16 38	84	09 16	82
18	18 24	-3	05 53	-6	17 23	91	10 26	90
19	18 38	21	07 19	+13	18 21	89	11 21	90
20	18 54	38	08 44	32	19 28	80	12 03	83
21	19 13	-56	10 08	+50	20 39	-67	12 33	+71
22	19 38	71	11 30	67	21 51	52	12 54	57
23	20 10	84	12 47	81	23 02	37	13 11	42
24	20 52	91	13 56	90	24 11	21	13 25	27
25	21 47	90	14 52	91	00 11	21	13 37	+13
26	22 51	-83	15 34	+85	01 21	-6	13 48	-2
27	24 01	70	16 05	74	02 31	+10	14 00	17
28	00 01	70	16 28	60	03 44	26	14 13	32
29	01 12	56	16 45	45	05 02	43	14 30	49
30	02 24	40	16 59	30	06 23	61	14 51	65
	OCTOBER				DECEMBER			
1	03 34	-24	17 11	+16	07 47	+77	15 23	-81
2	04 44	-9	17 23	+1	09 07	89	16 08	91
3	05 55	+7	17 34	-14	10 15	92	17 11	91
4	07 08	23	17 47	30	11 07	84	18 31	81
5	08 24	40	18 02	46	11 43	70	19 59	65
6	09 43	+57	18 22	-62	12 08	+52	21 27	-46
7	11 04	74	18 49	77	12 27	34	22 53	27
8	12 22	87	19 28	89	12 42	+17	24 15	9
9	13 32	93	20 23	93	12 56	0	00 15	-9
10	14 28	89	21 34	87	13 10	-17	01 36	+9
11	15 08	+77	22 59	-73	13 25	-33	02 56	+27
12	15 36	60	24 28	54	13 42	50	04 17	45
13	15 57	41	00 28	54	14 05	66	05 38	62
14	16 14	23	01 56	35	14 35	80	06 57	77
15	16 29	+5	03 23	-15	15 15	89	08 10	87
16	16 43	-12	04 48	+4	16 09	-90	09 11	+91
17	16 58	30	06 13	22	17 13	84	09 58	86
18	17 15	47	07 38	41	18 23	72	10 32	75
19	17 37	64	09 02	59	19 35	58	10 57	62
20	18 06	79	10 24	75	20 46	42	11 15	47
21	18 44	-89	11 38	+87	21 56	-27	11 30	+33
22	19 35	91	12 41	92	23 05	-12	11 42	18
23	20 36	86	13 30	88	24 13	+4	11 54	+4
24	21 45	76	14 06	78	00 13	4	12 05	-11
25	22 56	61	14 31	65	01 24	19	12 17	26
26	24 08	-46	14 51	+51	02 37	+36	12 32	-41
27	00 08	46	15 06	36	03 55	53	12 51	58
28	01 18	31	15 19	22	05 18	70	13 17	74
29	02 29	-15	15 30	+7	06 40	84	13 55	87
30	03 39	+1	15 42	-8	07 56	92	14 51	92
31	04 51	+17	15 54	-24	08 56	+89	16 05	-87

Corrections to Moonrise and Moonset

N Lat	30°	35°	40°	45°	50°	52°	54°	56°	58°	60°
v	m	m	m	m	m	m	m	m	m	m
0	0	0	0	0	0	0	0	0	0	0
2	–2	–2	–1	–1	0	0	+1	+1	+1	+2
4	4	3	2	1	0	+1	1	2	3	4
6	6	5	3	2	0	1	2	3	4	5
8	8	6	5	3	0	1	2	4	5	7
10	–10	–8	–6	–3	0	+1	+3	+5	+7	+9
12	12	10	7	4	0	2	4	6	8	11
14	14	11	8	4	0	2	4	7	9	12
16	16	13	9	5	0	2	5	8	11	14
18	18	14	10	6	0	3	5	9	12	16
20	–20	–16	–12	–6	0	+3	+6	+10	+14	+18
22	22	18	13	7	0	3	7	11	15	20
24	24	19	14	8	0	3	7	12	16	22
26	26	21	15	8	0	4	8	13	18	23
28	28	22	16	9	0	4	9	14	19	25
30	–30	–24	–17	–9	0	+4	+9	+15	+21	+27
32	32	26	18	10	0	5	10	16	22	29
34	34	27	20	11	0	5	10	17	23	31
36	36	29	21	11	0	5	11	18	25	33
38	38	31	22	12	0	6	12	19	26	35
40	–40	–32	–23	–13	0	+6	+12	+20	+28	+37
42	42	34	24	13	0	6	13	21	30	39
44	44	35	26	14	0	7	14	22	31	42
46	46	37	27	15	0	7	15	23	33	44
48	48	39	28	15	0	7	15	24	34	46
50	–50	–40	–29	–16	0	+8	+16	+25	+36	+48
52	52	42	30	17	0	8	17	26	38	51
54	54	44	32	17	0	8	17	28	39	53
56	56	45	33	18	0	9	18	29	41	56
58	58	47	34	19	0	9	19	30	43	58
60	–60	–48	–35	–19	0	+9	+20	+31	+45	+61
62	62	50	36	20	0	10	20	33	47	64
64	64	52	38	21	0	10	21	34	49	67
66	66	53	39	22	0	10	22	35	51	70
68	68	55	40	22	0	11	23	37	53	73
70	–70	–57	–41	–23	0	+11	+24	+38	+55	+76
72	72	58	43	24	0	11	24	40	58	80
74	74	60	44	24	0	12	25	41	60	83
76	76	62	45	25	0	12	26	43	62	87
78	78	63	46	26	0	13	27	44	65	91
80	–80	–65	–48	–27	0	+13	+28	+46	+68	+96
82	82	67	49	27	0	13	29	48	70	101
84	84	68	50	28	0	14	30	49	73	106
86	86	70	51	29	0	14	31	51	77	112
88	88	72	53	30	0	15	32	53	80	119
90	–90	–73	–54	–30	0	+15	+33	+55	+84	+127

If *v* is minus reverse the sign of the correction

The daily times of moonrise and moonset given above are the local mean times (LMT) of the phenomena for latitude 50°N, together with their variations *v*. The variations are the differences in minutes between the time of the phenomenon for latitudes 50N° and 30°N. The LMT of the phenomenon for latitudes between 30°N and 60°N is found as follows:

Take out the tabulated time and v corresponding to the required date. Using *v* and latitude as arguments in the table above of "Corrections to Moonrise and Moonset", extract the correction. This table is for positive *v*. If *v* is minus, reverse the sign of the correction. Apply the correction to the tabulated time.

Add a small extra correction of 1m for every 7° of longitude if west. Subtract if east.

Convert LMT to UT by adding the longitude in time if west, or subtracting if east.

Examples of the use of these tables are given in 3.6.4

Chapter 4

Radio Navigational Aids

Contents

4.1 INTRODUCTION

4.1.1 Types of systems

Two fixing systems are presently available. Satellite navigation is provided by the Global Positioning System (GPS), and a hyperbolic area navigation system by Loran-C. Each aid has its own merits for particular applications and coverage.

The choice of aids largely depends on the boat use, the owner's requirements and interests, and the waters sailed. Depending on the receiver used, GPS provides global fixes with an accuracy of better than 50m in any weather. Loran-C provides fixes within coverage areas but with less accuracy.

4.2 SATELLITE SYSTEMS

4.2.1 Global Positioning System (GPS)

GPS provides highly accurate, worldwide, continuous three-dimensional position fixing (latitude, longitude and altitude), together with velocity and time data in all weather conditions.

The GPS constellation, shown in Fig. 4(1), consists of 24 operational satellites configured in six orbital planes with an inclination of 55° to the Equator. Three further satellites operate as active spares, giving 27 satellites in use. The satellites circle the earth in approximately 12 hour orbits at a height of about 10,900M.

GPS provides two levels of service. These are:

(1) Standard Positioning Service (SPS)

(2) Precise Positioning Service (PPS)

SPS is available to all civil users at no cost. PPS is reserved strictly for military purposes.

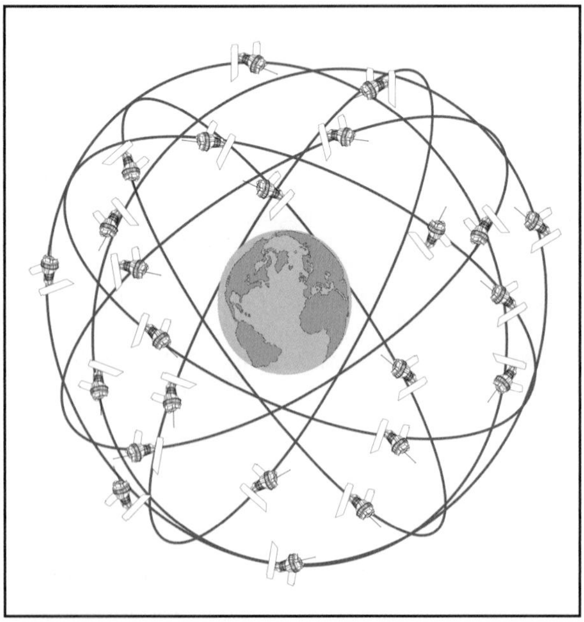

Fig. 4 (1) The GPS constellation consists of 27 satellites (24 operational plus 3 active spares). Satellite spacing is such that at least four are in view from anywhere on earth.

The principle on which GPS works is the accurate measurement of the range, or distance, from the receiver to a number of satellites transmitting accurately timed signals together with information on their accurate position in space. In very simplistic terms each satellite transmits a PPS and SPS code saying 'this is my position and this is the time'.

By accurately knowing the times of transmission and reception of the signal you can establish the transit time. Multiply the transit time by the speed of light (161,829 nautical miles per second) to get the range to the satellite. If similar measurements are made on three satellites, three intersecting range circles, each centred on the satellite's position at the time of transmission, are obtained. If no other errors are present, the intersection of the three range circles represents the yacht's position.

Selective Availability (SA) was turned off on 01 May 2000 and resulted in improved accuracy becoming available. GPS basic system errors are relatively small. For SPS they are about 19-20m. Any remaining system errors are due to signal propagation delays in the ionosphere and atmosphere. To eliminate such errors a dual-frequency receiver is required plus a second civil satellite frequency. The latter will not become available until 2005.

With SA switched off, accuracy will to some extent depend on the quality of the receiver coupled with improved technology on the latest satellites. A 12-channel receiver is likely to be more accurate than an 8 Channel. 20 metres accuracy is likely to be normal, but up to 10 metres may be achievable with a quality receiver.

GPS receivers vary from single-channel to multi-channel. Better quality fixing is obtained by tracking more than the minimum three satellites required to produce a two-dimensional fix (i.e. latitude and longitude). A receiver having a minimum of six dedicated channels is the most suitable for use on a yacht. The more channels available the better.

In conventional coastal navigation it is generally recommended to avoid using any visual position lines where the angle of cut is less than 30°. The accuracy of GPS fixes equally depends on the angle of cut of its position lines, but this is more difficult to appreciate because the geometry of the satellites is constantly changing. The receiver, rather than the navigator, selects those satellites which offer the best fix geometry.

4.2.2 Dilution of precision

The efficiency of the satellite geometry is indicated by the Dilution of Precision (DOP) factor which is computed from the angular separation between various satellites. The greater the separation the better the fix geometry is, and the lower the DOP value.

Performance is most likely to be degraded when there are less than 5 satellites visible, or when DOP is greater than 5. Since high DOP is caused by poor satellite geometry, these events usually coincide.

The potential inaccuracy of a 2D GPS fix resulting from poor geometry is expressed by a factor called the Horizontal Dilution of Precision (HDOP). The accuracy of a GPS fix varies with the capability of the user's receiver and receiver-to-satellite geometry. Receivers are programmed to select satellites which give the lowest HDOP value. Should the HDOP value exceed a certain figure, usually 4 or 5, then receivers give a warning, or cease computing fixes until satellite geometry improves.

4.2.3 Horizontal chart datum

GPS fixes are referenced to the World Geodetic System 84 (WGS 84) datum. This means that satellite fixes cannot be directly plotted on many Admiralty charts, which are still referenced to a local datum. Corrections need to be applied to achieve the full benefit of GPS accuracy.

Virtually all Admiralty charts of the UK are now issued in the WGS 84 datum. Charts of N Europe are almost invariably to WGS 84. Further south many charts are still referred to ED 50 but this situation is changing steadily. However, the datum is always published on the chart.

The HO are finishing the conversion of all 331 UK charts from OSGB 36 to the WGS 84/ETRS 89 datum with completion due during 2004. Charts always state the datum used in a note 'Satellite-Derived Positions' printed under the main title. This shows the amount of correction required between satellite and chart positions.

The approximate difference between WGS 84, OSGB 36 and ED 50 horizontal chart datums in the Dover Strait are shown in Fig.4 (2). The amount of the error will vary at each location but can be substantial in some parts of the world such as the Pacific.

Good receivers allow users a choice of many chart

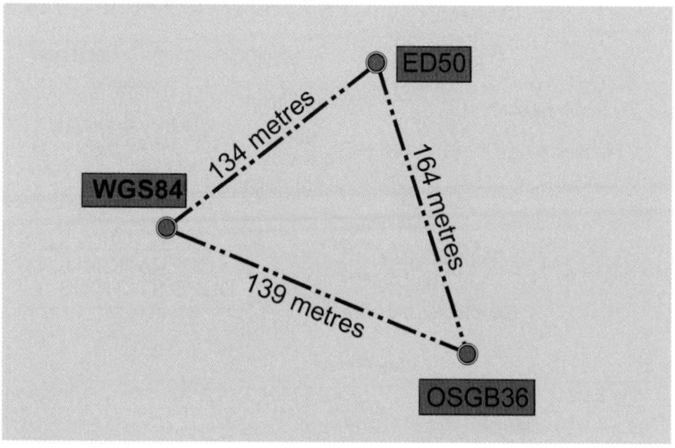
ED50
WGS84
OSGB36
134 metres
164 metres
139 metres

Fig. 4 (2) Chart datum differences in the Dover Strait

datums. Ensure that the chart datum set on the receiver is the same as the datum stated on the chart.

There are two ways of handling chart datums:

1. Set the receiver to WGS 84 and manually apply the datum shifts given on the chart before plotting position.

2. Alternatively, set the receiver datum to the same datum as the chart in use. In practical terms, this means that a yacht leaving the UK on WGS 84 charts **must** change to ED 50 before using ED 50 charts of the continental coast.

Whilst the change over to all WGS 84 is underway, it is essential to check the datum of your chart. Do not assume that an adjacent chart will be the same datum. Extreme caution is required and procedure (1) above may be the best course of action.

4.2.4 Differential GPS

Differential GPS (dGPS) is a method of locally improving the basic accuracy of GPS. With the increased accuracy of basic GPS provided by EGNOS, it is unlikely that dGPS will appeal to the average yachtsman, but it is suitable for high accuracy work.

The basic principle of dGPS is that a reference station compares observed GPS satellite pseudo-ranges with calculated pseudo-ranges, for all satellites in view, derived by knowing the reference station position very precisely. Observed differences in pseudo-ranges are then re-transmitted by the reference station to the users' GPS receiver via a data-link, (see p.88 for details of European stations). A set capable of receiving selected marine radio beacons, and equipped with a demodulator for the dGPS messages is required and is interfaced to the GPS receiver. It will automatically apply the transmitted corrections to the navigational data. Once the errors at a particular time and place are established, differential corrections can be applied to achieve an accuracy of better than ± 10m.

4.2.5 EGNOS

The European Geostationary Navigation Overlay System (EGNOS) should be fully operational by mid 2004. It covers a large area of Europe and the Atlantic. By correcting GPS signals it improves accuracy down to 2m. It indicates the degree of certainty within an area enclosed by a circle with the spot at the centre. This shows your position and how much it could be in error.

The majority of new GPS receivers available are EGNOS enabled. Existing users should check that their receiver is likewise so as to obtain the improved accuracy and benefits of this system.

4.2.6 GPS integrity monitoring

Urgent information on GPS is given in HMCG navigation warning broadcasts on VHF or MF, and by any Navtex station under message category J.

Information is also obtainable from the US Coast Guard GPS Information Centre (GPSIC) on ☎ 00 1 703 313 5907 which gives a prerecorded daily status message. GPSIC duty personnel can be contacted on ☎: 00 1 703 313 5900 (📠: 00 1 703 313 5931/5932).

4.2.6 Differential GPS Stations

Note: Tx= Transmitting Station number which is included in Type 7 messages
R= Reference Station(s) number which is included in the header of Type 1 or Type 9 messages

UNITED KINGDOM

Butt of Lewis Lt 58°30'·94N 06°15'·65W
295·50 kHz 200M Tx 444/R 686

Flamborough Head Lt 54°06'·98N 00°04'·96W
290·50kHz 150M Tx 447/R 684

Girdle Ness Lt 57°08'·34N 02°02'·91W
297·00kHz 150M Tx 446/R 685

Lizard Lt 49°57'·61N 05°12'·13W
306·00 kHz 150M Tx 441/R 681

Nash Point Lt 51°24'·06N 03°33'·13W
309·50 kHz 100M Tx 449/R 689

North Foreland 51°22'·52N 01°26'·85E
299·50 kHz 100M Tx 448/R 683

Point Lynas Lt 53°24'·98N 04°17'·35W
297·50 kHz 150M Tx 442/R 688

S. Catherine's Point Lt 50°34'·54N 01°17'·87W
307·50 kHz 100M Tx 440/R 682

Stirling 56°04'·3N 04°03'·6W
285·50kHz 200M Tx 443/R 693

Sumburgh 59°51'·25N 01°16'·49W
291·50 kHz 200M Tx 445/R 687

Wormleighton 52°11'·8N 01°21'·9W
291·00 kHz 170M Tx 439/R 691

IRELAND

Tory Island Lt 55°16'·36N 08°14'·97W
288·50 kHz 200M Tx 435/R 670

Loop Head Lt 52°33'·68N 09°55'·96W
293·00 kHz 150M Tx 432/R 665

Mizen Head 51°27'·00N 09°49'·24W
284·00 kHz 150M Tx 430/R 660

DENMARK

Blåvandshuk Lt 55°33'·52N 08°05'·07E
290·00 kHz 150M Tx 452/R 705 706

Skagen W Lt 57°44'·98N 10°35'·78E
296·00 kHz 100M Tx 453/R 710 711

GERMANY

Helgoland 54°11'·00N 07°53'·00E
298·50kHz 70M Tx 492/R 822 823

NETHERLANDS

Vlieland Lt 53°27'·02N 05°37'·60E
294·00kHz 120M Tx 428/R 655 656

Hoek van Holland 51°58'·90N 04°06'·83E
312·50kHz 120M Tx 425/R 650 651

BELGIUM

Oostende 51°14'·36N 02°55'·94E
312·00kHz 38M Tx 420/R 640 641

FRANCE

Cap Ferret Lt 44°38'·77N 01°14'·84W
310·00kHz 97M Tx 336/R 466

La Hague 49°34'·00N 01°46'·00W
299·00kHz 97M R 460

Pont de Buis 48°18'·00N 04°05'·00W
308·50kHz 110M R 462

Pen Men, Île de Groix 47°38'·97N 03°30'·36W
309·00kHz 100M R 463

Les Sables d'Olonne 46°31'·00N 01°48'·00W
307·00kHz 110M R 464

SPAIN (North and North-West Coast)

Punta Estaca de Bares Lt 43°47'·17N 07°41'·07W
293·00kHz 100M Tx 352/R 505 506

Cabo Finisterre Lt 42°53'·00N 09°16'·23W
289·00kHz 100M Tx 354/R 507 508

PORTUGAL

Cabo Carvoeiro 39°22'·00N 09°24'·00W
311·50kHz 100M Tx 340/R 480 481

Sagres 37°40'·00N 08°57'·00W
305·50kHz 100M Tx 341/R 482 483

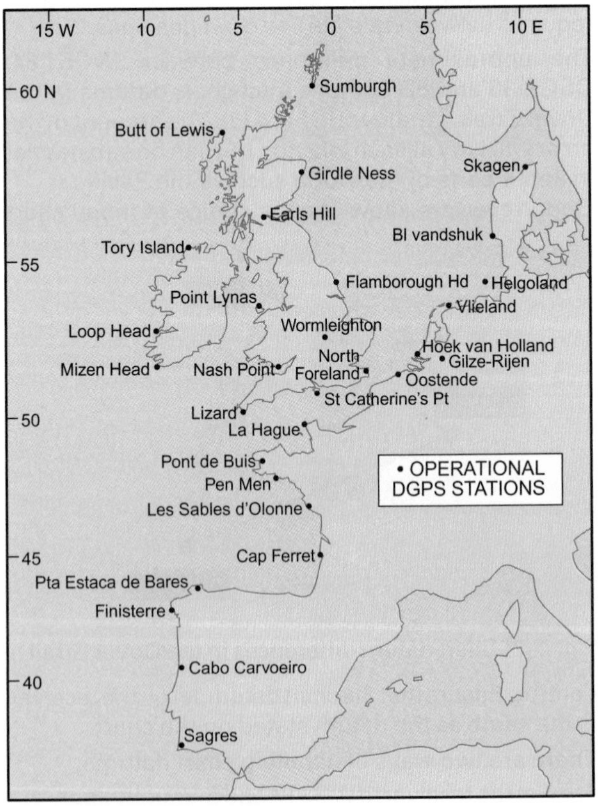
15 W
10
5
0
5
10 E
60 N
55
50
45
40
Sumburgh
Butt of Lewis
Girdle Ness
Skagen
Earls Hill
Bl vandshuk
Tory Island
Flamborough Hd
Helgoland
Point Lynas
Vlieland
Wormleighton
Loop Head
Hoek van Holland
North Foreland
Gilze-Rijen
Mizen Head
Nash Point
Oostende
St Catherine's Pt
Lizard
La Hague
Pont de Buis
Pen Men
Les Sables d'Olonne
• OPERATIONAL DGPS STATIONS
Cap Ferret
Pta Estaca de Bares
Finisterre
Cabo Carvoeiro
Sagres

Fig. 4 (3) DGPS Station locations

4.3 HYPERBOLIC SYSTEMS

4.3.1 Loran-C

Loran-C is a long-range hyperbolic system suitable for navigation within the coverage area. It provides continuous fixing and the groundwave can be received at ranges of 800-1200M. Loran-C pulses also propagate as skywaves which may be received at much greater range, but with much less accuracy.

Four Loran-C chains form the **North-West European Loran C system (NELS)** and provide extensive coverage over North-West Europe, and the British Isles. See Fig. 4 (4).

The basic principle on which Loran-C works is the accurate measurement of the time difference in the arrival of pulse signals transmitted from a Master and Secondary station. Loran Chains consist of three to five transmitters and operate in sequenced pairs. The time difference obtained from each pair of transmitters determines an exclusive hyperbolic curve of constant time difference and the intersection of two or more curves produces the fix.

Loran-C radio wave propagation is affected by the path over which the signal travels. Several factors can affect overall system accuracy such as the type of terrain over which the radio waves pass, range from transmitters, system geometry, weather, electronic noise, angle of cut of position lines and gradient, and synchronisation errors between transmitters.

Signals which pass over open seawater do so at a known predictable velocity which approaches the speed of light. If the signal path passes over hills, mountains, forests etc it slows down and is far less predictable. Its path is therefore deflected from its seawater path. Variations between the velocity of propagation over sea water and over different land masses are know as the *Additional Secondary Factor, or ASF*. Corrections may be applied to compensate for this variation. A programme for mapping ASF in Northern Europe is underway.

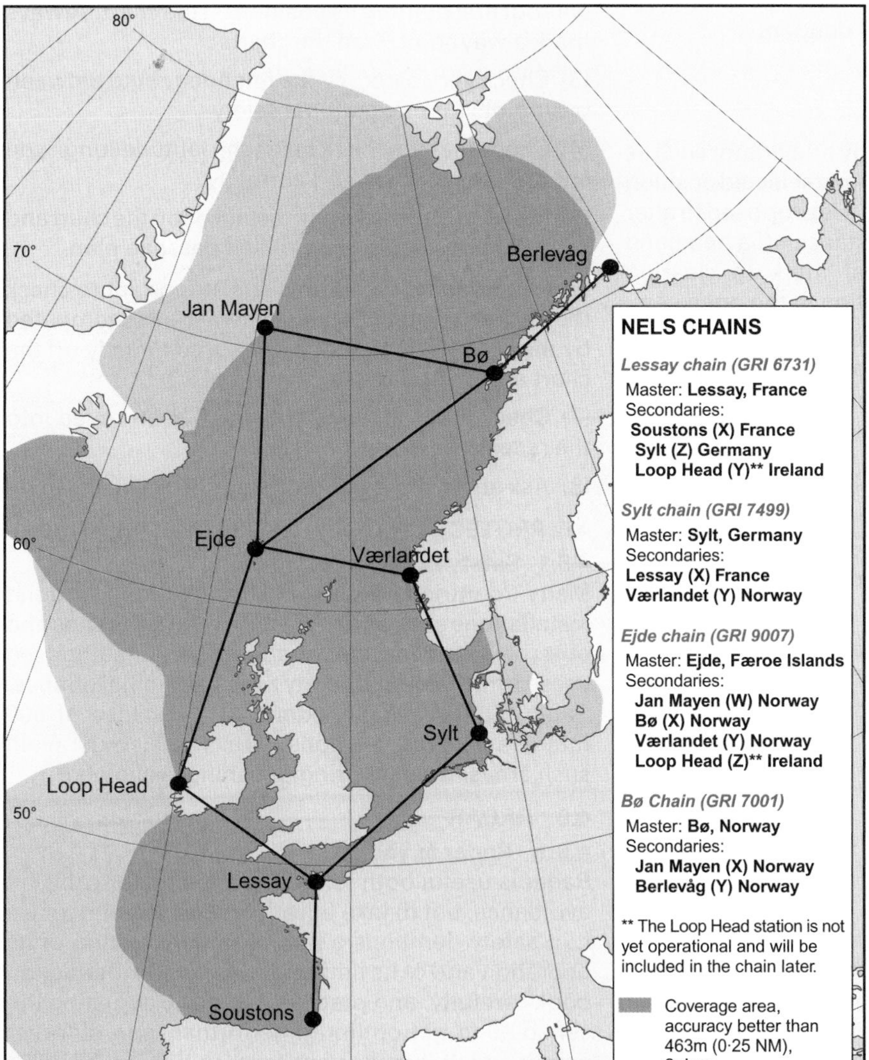
80°
70°
60°
50°
40°
10°
0°
10°
Jan Mayen
Berlevåg
Bø
Ejde
Værlandet
Sylt
Loop Head
Lessay
Soustons
NELS CHAINS
Lessay chain (GRI 6731)
Master: Lessay, France
Secondaries:
Soustons (X) France
Sylt (Z) Germany
Loop Head (Y)** Ireland
Sylt chain (GRI 7499)
Master: Sylt, Germany
Secondaries:
Lessay (X) France
Værlandet (Y) Norway
Ejde chain (GRI 9007)
Master: Ejde, Færoe Islands
Secondaries:
Jan Mayen (W) Norway
Bø (X) Norway
Værlandet (Y) Norway
Loop Head (Z)** Ireland
Bø Chain (GRI 7001)
Master: Bø, Norway
Secondaries:
Jan Mayen (X) Norway
Berlevåg (Y) Norway
** The Loop Head station is not yet operational and will be included in the chain later.
Coverage area, accuracy better than 463m (0·25 NM), 2 drms
Coverage contours of the complete NELS

Fig. 4 (4) – NW European Loran-C chains (NELS)

Using the groundwave, Loran-C absolute accuracy varies from about 185 metres or better to 463 metres (0·1 to 0·25M) depending on position and range from transmitters within the coverage area.

4.3.2 Navigational displays

Modern GPS or Loran-C receivers present navigators with continuous read-out of position but also very useful navigational information such as course and speed made good, along and across track error, distance and time to go to the next waypoint, etc. Many receivers can simultaneously display position, course and speed made good. Probably the most useful of these displays, especially with GPS, is the course and speed made good facility where the continuous read-out can be directly compared to the required track.

The same data, if compared with course and speed through the water, can also be used to quickly calculate tidal set and drift.

Electronic systems are only aids to navigation and are subject to fixed and variable errors, or on rare occasions even total failure. It is therefore essential to log the yacht's position, course and speed from the receiver display and to plot your position on the chart at regular intervals. This enables you to quickly work up a DR/EP in the event of equipment failure. In any case, it is always sound practice to maintain a DR plot, or to at least to plot your position by any other available means. This will provide a separate check that the boat is on track and clearing all dangers.

4.4 WAYPOINTS

4.4.1 Waypoint navigation

A waypoint is any point chosen by a navigator such as a departure point or destination, any selected position along the intended route where it is proposed to alter course, a point at a selected distance off a headland lighthouse, buoy, navigational mark (a clearing Waypoint), or any chosen position in the open sea.

Always study the chart first and plot the position of any planned waypoint before loading the coordinates into electronic equipment. This ensures that any projected route will not take you across shallows, into danger, or even across land. Never load a published waypoint without first plotting its position on the chart. It helps to tag either a number or a name onto each waypoint. A waypoint listing may be assembled in any order required to form a route or sailing plan.

Many waypoints are given in Chapter 9. For individual harbours those shown under NAVIGATION are safe positions from which to approach a harbour. Those below the harbour name and after the county (or foreign equivalent) locate the harbour entrance and provide a good final waypoint.

Various waypoints are given in section 3 or 4 of each Area in the lists of 'Lights, Buoys, and Waypoints'. They are shown underlined.

Latitude and longitude are normally stated to one-hundredth of a minute, taken from a large-scale chart. A chart using a different datum or based on a different survey may give a slightly different position. Charts may also contain small errors, just like the read-out from an electronic instrument.

As all the Admiralty charts of the UK are now issued in WGS 84 Datum it is vitally important that you know which datum is being used both for the chart and also which datum is set on the GPS receiver.

4.4.3 Loading waypoints

The greatest care needs to be taken when loading waypoint coordinates into electronic equipment. Always check that you have taken the position off the chart correctly. Any error in the entry of latitude/longitude coordinates into the receiver will result in a navigational error if undetected. It is particularly important to understand the format required to enter data into the receiver.

Following the precautions listed below will help prevent errors being made when loading waypoints:

(1) Check the datum used on the navigational chart and ensure the navigation receiver is set to the same datum (or apply appropriate shifts if required)

(2) A published waypoint should never be used without first plotting its position on the chart. Always mark a waypoint ⊕ on the chart.

(3) Check very carefully the intended route between waypoints for navigational safety.

(4) Check that you have taken the latitude/longitude coordinates off the chart correctly.

(5) Measure the tracks and distances on the chart and record the results in a simplified passage plan.

(6) After loading waypoints it is important to check the track and distances between waypoints computed by the receiver with those measured directly off the chart and shown in the passage plan.

(7) Check that the waypoints have been keyed into the receiver memory correctly.

(8) Ask another crew member to check it if possible.

4.5 PROTECTION OF OFFSHORE INSTALLATIONS

4.5.1 Safety Zones

Many Countries now establish safety zones around installations such as gas and oil exploration sites and other devices. Most have made entry by unauthorised vessels into declared safety zones a criminal offence. Safety Zones usually extend to a distance of 500 metres around installations and all vessels must avoid such areas. No anchoring or fishing is allowed.

4.6 RADAR

4.6.1 Radar in yachts

Radar is useful both for navigation and for collision avoidance, but to take full advantage of it and to use it in safety demands a proper understanding of its operation and of its limitations. Read the instruction book carefully, and practise using and adjusting the set so as to get optimum performance in different conditions. It is important to learn how to interpret what is seen on the display.

Radar, which is short for Radio Direction And Range, makes use of super high frequency radio waves transmitted in very short concentrated pulses. Each pulse lasts less than a microsecond and the number of such pulses transmitted per second normally lies between 800 and 3000. The duration or length of a single pulse is called pulse length. The number of pulses transmitted per second defines the pulse repetition rate (PRR). The returned pulses are displayed on a screen.

Radar beams do not discriminate so well in bearing as they do in range, so an accurate fix is sometimes best obtained by a radar range and a visual bearing of the same object.

The effective range of radar is approximately line of sight, but this can be decreased or increased by abnormal conditions. Most yacht radars therefore have a maximum range of about 16 to 24M. Radar will not detect a low-lying coastline which is over the radar horizon.

4.6.2 Radar for collision avoidance

Yacht radars usually have a head up display, i.e. with the ships head at the top of the screen and your own boat at the centre of the display, apparently stationary. More modern radars can be interfaced to an electronic compass so as to provide a North-up display, i.e. North shown conventionally at the top of the display.

If a vessel is moving in the same direction and at the same speed, it is stationary relative to your own boat, and its echo should be sharp and well defined.

If an echo is on a steady bearing, and the range is decreasing, there is risk of collision. To determine the proper action to take it is necessary to plot an approaching echo three or four times, in order to determine its actual course and speed, and how close it will actually approach.

4.6.3 Radar as a navigation aid

Radar can be a very useful aid to navigation when used properly, but one needs to be aware of its limitations. Radar cannot see behind other objects, or round corners; it may not pick up small objects, or differentiate between two targets that are close together. Objects with sharp features such as buildings give a better reflection than those with curved or sloping surfaces. High or rocky cliffs make a good target, but chalk cliffs give a poor response, especially when dry. Low coastlines should be approached with extreme caution as the first thing to show on radar may be hills some distance inland.

4.7 RACONS (RADAR BEACONS)

4.7.1 Description

A Racon is a transponder beacon which, when triggered by a transmission from a vessel's radar, sends back a distinctive signal which appears on the vessel's radar display. Almost all Racons are fitted to major light-vessels, lighthouses and buoys. They are shown on charts by a magenta circle and the word Racon.

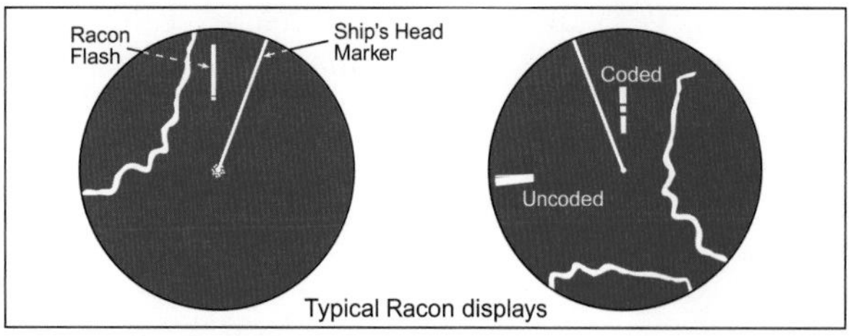
Racon
Flash
Ship's Head
Marker
Coded
Uncoded
Typical Racon displays

Fig. 4 (5) – Radar beacon responses

In most cases the Racon flash on the radar display is a line extending radially outward from a point slightly beyond the actual position of the Racon, due to the slight delay in the response of the Racon apparatus. Thus the distance to the spot of the Racon flash is a little more than the vessels real distance from the Racon. Some Racons give a flash composed of a Morse identification signal, often with a tail to it, the length of the tail depending on the number of Morse characters, see Fig 4 (5).

The typical maximum range of a Racon is 10M, but may be as much as 25M. In practice, picking up a Racon at greater ranges depends on the power and elevation of both the Racon and the boat's radar. With abnormal radio propagation, a spurious Racon flash may be seen at much greater distances than the beacon's normal range, appearing at any random position along the correct bearing on the display. Only rely on a Racon flash if it appears to be consistent, and the boat is believed to be within its quoted range. At short range a Racon sometimes causes unwanted interference on the radar display, and this may be reduced by adjusting the rain clutter control on the radar receiver.

4.7.2 Racon details

Details of the racons within the area covered by this almanac are in the Lights, Buoys and Waypoints sections [9.(Area No).4] in chapter 9. They appear after the characteristics of their host light.

Details given are:

a. The Morse identification signal.

b. Approximate range in nautical miles (M).

c. The angular sector if it differs from 360°, within which theRacon signal can be received.

Most Racons respond throughout 360°.

The majority of Racons sweep the frequency range of marine 3cm (X-band) radar emissions. The older type of Racon (swept frequency) take 30 to 90 seconds to sweep the band.

The newer type of Racon (frequency agile) responds immediately to both 3cm and 10cm (S-band) emissions. In order that the Racon response should not obscure wanted echoes, the agile response is switched 'on' and 'off' at a predetermined rate to suit the installation.

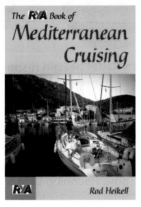

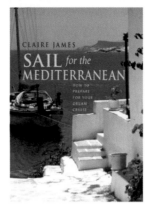

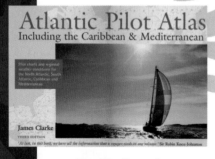

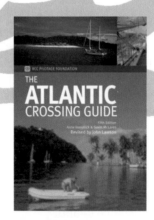

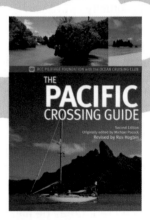

Chapter 5

Communications

Contents

5.1 INTRODUCTION

Communications are largely a means to an end, so this chapter concentrates on the various methods by which yachtsmen can communicate. Coast Radio Stations, Vessel Traffic Services and other routine situations are also covered in this chapter.

But where the subject matter being received or sent is more important than the means, it is dealt with under those subjects – to which cross references are given below. For example Distress signals are best dealt with in Chapter 7 Safety.

5.2 CROSS REFERENCES

5.2.1. Navigational warnings

These are covered in Chapter 3.

5.2.2. Weather information

See Chapter 6 for all forms of weather broadcasts and meteorological warnings. Navtex provides both navigational, meteorological warnings and other Marine Safety Information (MSI), but is most often used by yachtsmen for obtaining weather bulletins; details are therefore in Chapter 6.

5.2.3 Navtex

Navtex as the MSI component of GMDSS is also referred to in Chapter 7.

5.2.4 Visual Distress and emergency signals

Details of Distress signals, visual signals between shore and ships in distress, signals used by SAR aircraft, and directing signals used by aircraft are given in Chapter 7.

5.2.5 Distress, Urgency & Safety traffic by R/T

There are agreed international procedures for passing R/T messages concerning vessels in Distress and SAR operations – or for lesser emergencies and medical assistance or situations where Urgency or Safety messages are appropriate. These are fully described in Chapter 7, together with the Global Maritime Distress and Safety System (GMDSS).

5.2.6 Port Operations

VHF channels for Port Operations are specified in Chapter 9 under individual harbours and marinas.

5.2.7 Port Traffic signals

International Port Traffic signals (IPTS) are shown in 9.0.4. On the Continent they are now widely used – but obsolescent national signals may sometimes be seen in a few minor ports.

5.3 THE INTERNATIONAL CODE OF SIGNALS

5.3.1 Description

Marine communication is based on the International Code of Signals (1987 edition) published by IMO, which provides for safety of navigation and of persons, especially where there are language problems. The present Code came into force in 1969 and is available in nine languages: English, French, Italian, German, Japanese, Spanish, Norwegian, Russian and Greek. Ships, aircraft and shore stations can communicate with each other in these languages without knowing a foreign tongue, provided they have a copy of the appropriate Code. The English language edition is published by HMSO.

5.3.2 Using the International Code

The Code can be used to convey information by: voice, using R/T or loud-hailer; the Morse code by flashing light and sound signals; alphabetical flags and numeral pendants; or by hand flags.

Signals consist of: single-letter signals which are urgent or much used; two-letter signals in the General Section; and three-letter signals starting with the letter 'M' in the Medical Section.

The diagram opposite shows the Code flags for letters and numerals, the phonetic alphabet and figures, the Morse code for letters and numerals, and the meanings of important or common single-letter signals.

Yachtsmen may also see or hear the following important two-letters signals :

RY You should proceed at slow speed when passing me (or vessels making signals)

NC I am in distress and require immediate assistance

YG You appear to be contravening the rules of a Traffic Separation Scheme

NE2 You should proceed with great caution; submarines are exercising in this area

5.4 RADIO COMMUNICATIONS

5.4.1 Radio Telephony (R/T)

Most small craft communicate using a VHF radio telephone. VHF gives a range of 30-40M depending on the aerial heights involved.

Medium Frequency (MF) gives much greater ranges (typically 100-300M), but must be Single Sideband (SSB). Double sideband (DSB) transmissions are prohibited except for emergency transmissions on 2182 kHz, the international MF Distress frequency.

High Frequency (HF) radio, which is more powerful and gives a much longer range than MF, is needed for ocean passages. The alternative to HF radio is satellite communications (see 5.6).

5.4.2 Regulations

The regulations for using R/T communications are in the ***Handbook for Marine Radio Communication*** (Lloyds of London Press). They are lengthy and form part of the syllabus and examination.

Some of the more important stipulations are: operators must not divulge the contents of messages

PLATE 3 INTERNATIONAL CODE OF SIGNALS, CODE FLAGS, PHONETIC ALPHABET, MORSE SYMBOLS AND SINGLE-LETTER SIGNALS

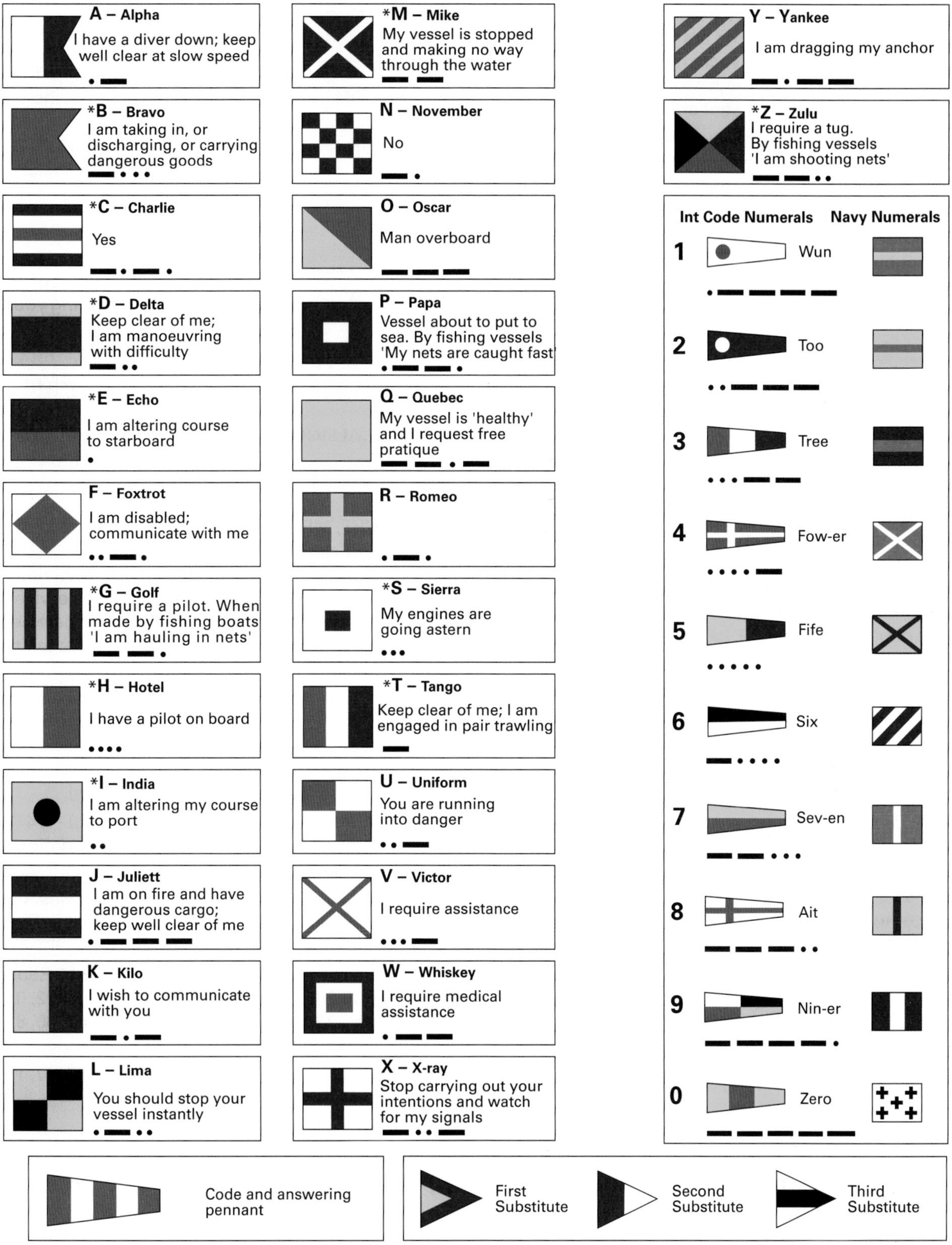
A – Alpha
I have a diver down; keep well clear at slow speed
• —
*B – Bravo
I am taking in, or discharging, or carrying dangerous goods
— • • •
*C – Charlie
Yes
— • — •
*D – Delta
Keep clear of me; I am manoeuvring with difficulty
— • •
*E – Echo
I am altering course to starboard
•
F – Foxtrot
I am disabled; communicate with me
• • — •
*G – Golf
I require a pilot. When made by fishing boats 'I am hauling in nets'
— — •
*H – Hotel
I have a pilot on board
• • • •
*I – India
I am altering my course to port
• •
J – Juliett
I am on fire and have dangerous cargo; keep well clear of me
• — — —
K – Kilo
I wish to communicate with you
— • —
L – Lima
You should stop your vessel instantly
• — • •
*M – Mike
My vessel is stopped and making no way through the water
— —
N – November
No
— •
O – Oscar
Man overboard
— — —
P – Papa
Vessel about to put to sea. By fishing vessels 'My nets are caught fast'
• — — •
Q – Quebec
My vessel is 'healthy' and I request free pratique
— — • —
R – Romeo
• — •
*S – Sierra
My engines are going astern
• • •
*T – Tango
Keep clear of me; I am engaged in pair trawling
—
U – Uniform
You are running into danger
• • —
V – Victor
I require assistance
• • • —
W – Whiskey
I require medical assistance
• — —
X – X-ray
Stop carrying out your intentions and watch for my signals
— • • —
Y – Yankee
I am dragging my anchor
— • — —
*Z – Zulu
I require a tug. By fishing vessels 'I am shooting nets'
— — • •
Int Code Numerals
Navy Numerals
1 Wun • — — — —
2 Too • • — — —
3 Tree • • • — —
4 Fow-er • • • • —
5 Fife • • • • •
6 Six — • • • •
7 Sev-en — — • • •
8 Ait — — — • •
9 Nin-er — — — — •
0 Zero — — — — —
Code and answering pennant
First Substitute
Second Substitute
Third Substitute

Signals marked * when made by sound may only be used in compliance with the Collision regulations Rules 34 and 35

C5

heard; distress calls have priority; coast radio stations, or Coastguard rescue centres, as appropriate control communications in their respective areas. Check that the channel is free before transmitting; unnecessary or superfluous messages are prohibited, as is bad language; in harbour a yacht may not use inter-ship channels except for safety; a radio log must be used to record all messages sent and received.

Communications between MRCC/SCs and second parties are taped, as are intercepted communications with a third party. The following statement is included at the request of the MCA:

"Radio & phone calls to/from CG Centres are recorded for public safety, prevention/detection of crime and to maintain the operational standards of HM CG".

5.4.3 Radio Licences

a. The **vessel** requires a Ship Radio Licence for any VHF, UHF, MF, HF, satellite or EPIRB equipment on board. It is issued by: The Radio Licensing Centre, PO Box 1495, Bristol, BS99 3QS. ☎ 0870 243 4433. 📠 0117 975 8911. This allows the use of international maritime channels, Ch M for communications between yachts, marinas and clubs, and M2 for race control.

b. The **person** in charge of a set requires a Certificate of Competence (Pt 1) and Authority to Operate (Pt 2). For most yachtsmen this will be the Short Range Certificate (SRC), incorporating GMDSS procedures. The RYA is responsible for the conduct of an examination, for which the syllabus is detailed in RYA booklet G26. The former Restricted Certificate of Competence (VHF only) is no longer being issued, but remains valid for VHF-only radios.

c. Citizen's Band (CB) and Amateur (Ham) Radio can be useful means of communication for other than safety matters, but only supplement proper maritime radio on VHF, MF or HF. CB and Amateur Radio licences are issued by: The Radio Licensing Centre, PO Box 885, Bristol, BS99 5LG. ☎ 0117 925 8333.

5.4.4 RT procedures

Communications between a ship and a Coast radio station are controlled by the latter, except for Distress, Urgency or Safety messages. Between two ships, the ship called chooses a working channel.

Before making a call, decide exactly what you wish to say; writing the message down may help. Speak slowly and distinctly. Names or important words can be repeated or spelt phonetically; see 5.4.5 for the use and meanings of common prowords.

Give your position as Lat/Long or the yacht's bearing and distance from a charted object, eg "My position 225° Isle of May 4M" means you are 4M SW of the Isle of May. Use the 360° True bearing notation and the 24 hours clock, specifying UT, LT, etc.

5.4.5 Prowords

The following prowords should be used to simplify and expedite communications:

ACKNOWLEDGE	Have you received and understood?
CONFIRM	My version is ... is that correct?
CORRECTION	An error has been made; the correct version is ...
I SAY AGAIN	I repeat ... (eg important words).
I SPELL	What follows is spelt phonetically.
OUT	End of work.
OVER	I have completed this part of my message, and am inviting you to reply.
RECEIVED	Receipt acknowledged.
SAY AGAIN	Repeat your message (or part indicated).
STATION CALLING	Used when a station is unsure of the identity of the station which is calling.

5.5 VHF, MF and HF RADIO

5.5.1 VHF radio

VHF is used by most vessels, coast radio stations, ports, coastguard centres and other rescue services. Its range is slightly better than the line of sight between the transmitting and receiving aerials. It pays to fit a good aerial, as high as possible.

VHF sets may be Simplex, i.e. transmit and receive on the same frequency, so that only one person can talk at a time; Semi-Duplex, i.e. transmit and receive on different frequencies; or Duplex, i.e. simultaneous semi-duplex, so that conversation is normal.

Marine VHF frequencies are in the band 156·00–174·00 MHz. Frequencies are known by their international channel number (Ch), as shown below:

Channels are grouped for three main purposes, but some can be used for more than one purpose. They are shown in their preferred order of usage:

(1) ***Public correspondence:*** (via Coast Radio Stations). Ch 26, 27, 25, 24, 23, 28, 04, 01, 03, 02, 07, 05, 84, 87, 86, 83, 85, 88, 61, 64, 65, 62, 66, 63, 60, 82, 78, 81. All channels can be used for duplex.

(2) ***Inter-ship:*** Ch 06, 08, 10, 13, 09, 72, 73, 69, 77, 15, 17. These are all simplex channels.

(3) ***Port Operations:***

Simplex: Ch 12, 14, 11, 13, 09, 68, 71, 74, 69, 73, 17, 15.

Duplex: Ch 20, 22, 18, 19, 21, 05, 07, 02, 03, 01, 04, 78, 82, 79, 81, 80, 60, 63, 66, 62, 65, 64, 61, 84.

The following channels have one specific purpose:

Ch 0 (156·00 MHz): SAR ops, not available to yachts.

Ch 13 (156·650 MHz): bridge-to-bridge communications relating to safety of navigation; a possible channel for calling a merchant ship if no contact on Ch 16.

Ch 16 (156·80 MHz): Distress, Safety and calling. Ch 16 will be monitored by ships, Coastguard rescue centres (and, in some areas, any remaining Coast radio stations) for Distress and Safety until at least 2005, in parallel with DSC Ch 70. Yachts should monitor Ch 16. After an initial call, the stations concerned **must** switch to a working channel, except for Safety matters.

Ch 10 (156·500 MHz), **23** (161·750 MHz), **84** (161·825 MHz) and **86** (161·925 MHz): by HMCG for MSI broadcasts.

Ch 67 (156·375 MHz): by all UK Coastguard centres as the Small Craft Safety Channel, accessed via Ch 16.

Ch 70 (156·525 MHz): exclusively for digital selective calling for Distress and Safety purposes.

Ch 80 (157·025 MHz): the primary working channel between yachts and UK marinas.

Ch M (157·85 MHz): the secondary working channel.

Ch M2 (161·425 MHz): for race control, with Ch M as stand-by. YCs may apply to use Ch M2.

5.5.2 MF radio

MF radiotelephones operate in the 1605-4200 kHz wavebands. Unlike VHF and HF, MF transmissions tend to follow the curve of the earth, which makes them suitable for direction-finding equipment. For this reason, and because of their good range, the marine Distress radiotelephone frequency is in the MF band (2182 kHz).

5.5.3 HF radio

HF radiotelephones use frequencies in the 4, 8, 12, 16 and 22 MHz bands (short wave) that are chosen to suit propagation conditions. HF is more expensive than MF and requires more power, but can provide worldwide coverage – but a good installation and correct operation are essential for satisfactory results.

Whereas MF transmissions follow the curve of the earth, HF waves travel upwards and bounce off the ionosphere back to earth. Reception is better at night when the ionosphere is denser. The directional properties of HF transmissions are poor, so there is no HF Distress frequency.

5.6 SATELLITE COMMUNICATIONS

5.6.1 Inmarsat

The International Maritime Satellite Organisation (Inmarsat) provides satellite communication (Satcom) worldwide via satellites in geostationary orbits above the equator over the Atlantic, Pacific and Indian Oceans. Satcom is more reliable and gives better reception than HF SSB radio. The satellites are the link between Coast Earth Stations (CES) ashore, operated by organisations such as BT, and the ship-board terminals called Ship Earth Stations (SES).

For a shore-ship call, a CES connects the land-based communication network with the satellite system. The message originated on land is transmitted to a ship by one of the satellites. Conversely a ship-shore call is received, via the satellite, by the CES, which transmits it onwards over land-based networks.

Onboard ship (SES) there are several standards of terminal:

Standard 'A' terminals, with a big antenna only suitable for larger vessels, have direct dialling telephone, Telex, data and fax facilities.

Standard 'C' transmit/receive data or text (but not voice). Both 'A' and 'C' offer speedy connection to HM Coastguard's MRCC at Falmouth for Distress, Safety, etc.

More recently, Inmarsat 'B' was launched as an improved successor to Inmarsat 'A', while Standard 'M' now makes satellite telephone, fax and data services available to a wider range of yachts, using smaller and less expensive equipment.

5.7 COAST RADIO STATIONS (CRS)

5.7.1 Introduction

In recent years many European nations have closed, or plan to, their coast radio stations. There are now no CRS in the UK, France, Netherlands and Belgium. All CRS remain operational in Ireland, Denmark, Spain and Portugal. In Germany a commercial company, Schiffsmeldedienst (SMD), provides a limited public correspondence service, ie link calls.

Details of national CRS are given below in 5.9.

5.7.2 Functions

CRS control communications and provide link calls to connect vessels at sea into the shore telephone network, operating on nominated VHF channels and MF or HF frequencies; see 5.8.

At scheduled times CRS also transmit traffic lists (messages awaiting ships at sea), navigational warnings (Chapter 3), weather bulletins and gale warnings as required (Chapter 6). Do not use a designated broadcast channel at about the time of a scheduled broadcast.

They may also deal with Distress and Urgency calls on Ch 16.

The Coastguard, or foreign equivalents, do not handle commercial link calls. Their task is to monitor Distress, Urgency and Safety calls on Ch 70 DSC, Ch 16, or MF DSC 2187·5 kHz – and to organise SAR operations.

5.7.3 Track Reports

A Track Report (TR) may be passed to a CRS or Coastguard centre, as appropriate, stating a yacht's point of departure, destination, ETA and number of people onboard. This is an obvious safety measure, especially in remote regions, should a yacht become overdue. On arrival be sure to inform the local CRS or CG and ask that your TR be cancelled with the original CRS/CG.

5.8 LINK CALLS

5.8.1 Making a VHF link call

a. Within range (up to 40M), listen for a 'clear' channel, ie no transmissions. A busy channel will have either carrier noise, speech or the engaged signal (a series of pips).

b. Call the CRS on a working channel related to the position of the yacht. Calls should state the calling channel and last at least 6 seconds in order to activate the CRS's ship-call latch equipment.

For example:

Bilbao Radio, this is Yacht Seabird, Seabird, Golf Oscar Romeo India Four, Channel 27, Over.

A four-tone signal or pips indicate a temporary delay, but you will be answered when an operator is free.

c. When the call is accepted you will hear pips, indicating that the channel has been engaged. Wait for the operator to speak. If no response, do not change channel since you may lose your turn.

If the pips are not heard, the station's transmitter has not been activated or may be out of range. Try another station or call again when closer.

d. The operator will request: Vessel's call sign (phonetics) and name, accounting code (see 5.8.2), type of message (e.g. telegram, telephone call) and the telephone number required (and in the case of a personal call the name of the person called).

5.8.2 Paying for a link call

Calls are accounted for worldwide by quoting an 'Accounting Authority Indicator Code' (AAIC). This must previously have been arranged with an ITU-recognised authority such as Cable and Wireless, who use GB 02 as the AAIC. All CRS have the complete ITU listing of ship stations and their AAIC.

5.8.3 MF link calls

Calls should be initiated on 2182 kHz or the nominated working frequency. The Coast station will allocate a working channel, and cue you into the system.

5.8.4 Autolink RT

Autolink RT gives direct dialling from ship to shore into national and international telephone networks without going through a CRS operator. It functions through an on-board unit which is easily connected to the radio, and which does not interfere with normal manual operation. It is not common on yachts.

This service on VHF, MF and HF gives quicker access, cheaper calls, call scrambling on some units where privacy is required, and simplified accounting. Last number redial and a ten-number memory store are available.

Do not use Autolink for Distress, Urgency and Safety (including medical) calls, but use the normal manual procedure on VHF Ch 16 or 2182 kHz.

5.9 CRS BY COUNTRIES

5.9.1 Channel Islands

St Peter Port and Jersey CRS are operated by the States of Guernsey and Jersey respectively. They handle link calls as well as Distress and Urgency situations.

St Peter Port Radio

VHF **20**, 62 (link calls only), 16, 67 (On request Ch 16 for yacht safety messages). MF 1764 kHz.
DSC Ch 70: **MMSI** 002320064.

Traffic lists: Vessels for which traffic is held are called individually Ch 16.

Jersey Radio

VHF **82,** 25 (link calls only), 16, 67 (Small craft Distress and Safety working; pre-call on 16). MF 1659 kHz.
DSC Ch 70: **MMSI** 002320060;

Weather messages, navigational warnings and traffic lists are broadcast on Ch 25, 82 and 1659 kHz at 0645*, 0745*, 0845*, 1245, 1845 and 2245 UT.
*1 hour earlier when DST is in force.

5.9.2 Republic of Ireland

The main CRS at Malin Head, Dublin and Valentia are co-located with Coastguard centres. Remote CRS sites, as listed below, provide full coastal coverage in the three regions (NW,SE and SW Ireland).

Traffic Lists are broadcast at the times given below. Navigational warnings are broadcast at times given in Chapter 3. See Chapter 6 for times and details of gale warnings and weather bulletins. Broadcasts are made on a working channel/frequency after pre-warning on Ch 16 and 2182 kHz. Ch 67 is only used for Safety messages.

Link calls from ship-shore are available on both VHF and MF. Call CRS on a working VHF channel, only using Ch 16 if in difficulty or emergency.

For shore-to-ship telephone calls, ships should listen to Traffic Lists and pass their intended voyage or position to Malin Head Radio, Dublin Radio or Valentia Radio, as appropriate. Update voyage details by TR.

CRS in NW and SE Ireland

These stations, as shown below and opposite, routinely broadcast Traffic lists at every odd H +03 (except 0303 and 0703) from 0103 to 2303 UT on the VHF channels listed.

NW Ireland (clockwise from the west)

Clifden Radio	VHF 26
Belmullet Radio	VHF 83
Donegal Bay Radio	VHF 02
Glen Head Radio	VHF 24
MALIN HEAD RADIO	VHF 23 . MF 1677 kHz

SE Ireland

Carlingford Radio	VHF 04
DUBLIN RADIO	VHF 83 (No MF)
Wicklow Head Radio	VHF 02
Rosslare Radio	VHF 23
Mine Head Radio	VHF 83

CRS in SW Ireland

CRS, as shown below, broadcast Traffic lists routinely at every odd H+33 UT, except 0133 and 0533, on VHF channels listed. The broadcast Channel is in bold where more than one is shown. The broadcast channel is in bold where more than one is shown.

SW Ireland

Cork Radio	VHF 26
Bantry Radio	VHF 23.
Mizen Radio	VHF 04.
VALENTIA RADIO	VHF 24. MF 1752 kHz
Shannon Radio	VHF 28
Galway Radio	VHF 04

Fig. 5 (1) Irish Coast Radio Stations

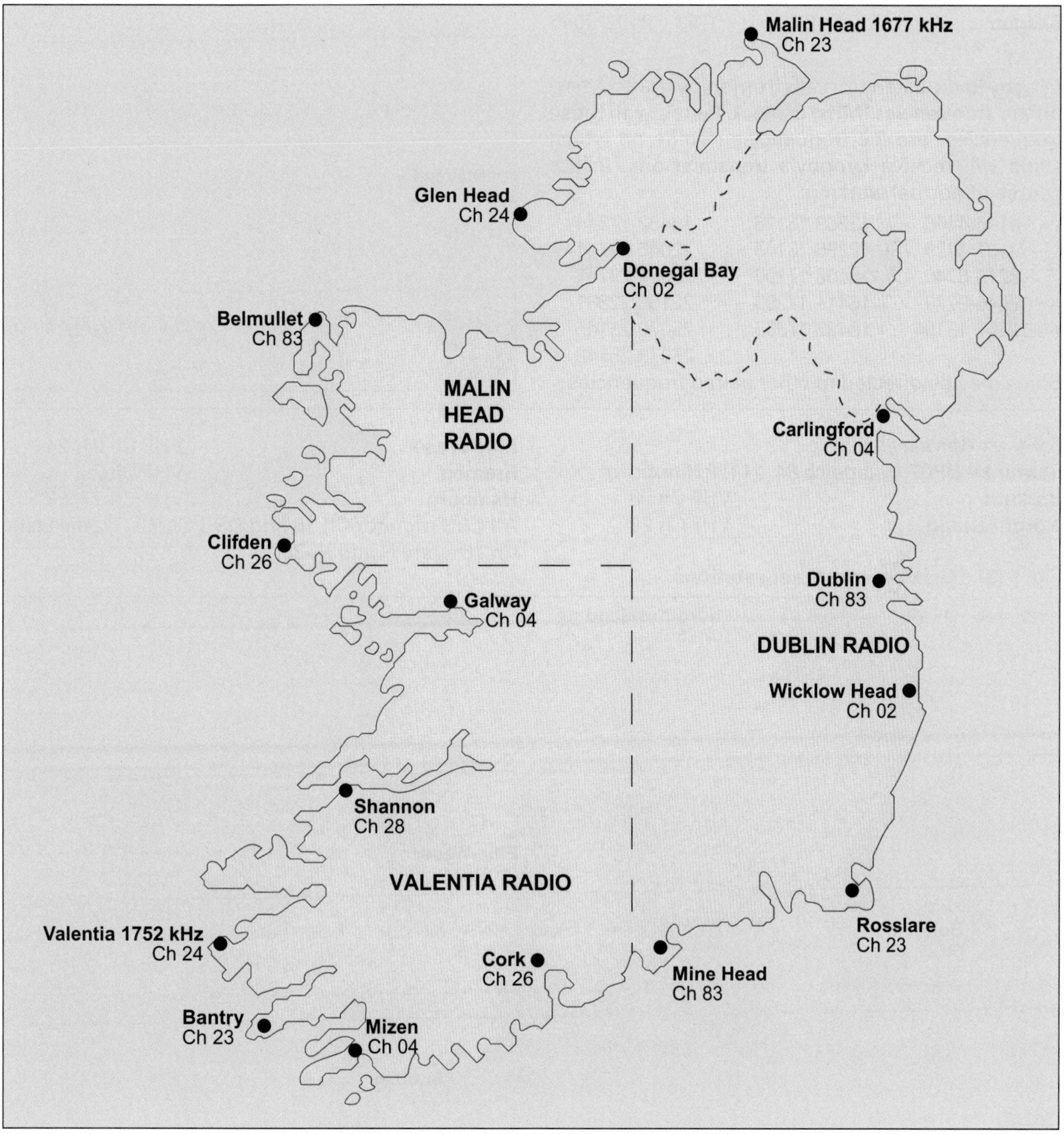
Malin Head 1677 kHz
Ch 23
Glen Head
Ch 24
Donegal Bay
Ch 02
Belmullet
Ch 83
MALIN HEAD RADIO
Carlingford
Ch 04
Clifden
Ch 26
Galway
Ch 04
Dublin
Ch 83
DUBLIN RADIO
Wicklow Head
Ch 02
Shannon
Ch 28
VALENTIA RADIO
Rosslare
Ch 23
Valentia 1752 kHz
Ch 24
Cork
Ch 26
Mine Head
Ch 83
Bantry
Ch 23
Mizen
Ch 04

C5

5.9.3 Denmark

All Danish VHF/MF CRS are remotely controlled by **Lyngby Radio** and use the callsign **Lyngby Radio**. The stations listed below monitor Ch 16 and DSC Ch 70, H24. Call on working frequencies, to keep Ch 16 clear. MF stations do not monitor 2182 kHz.

Traffic lists are broadcast on all VHF channels every odd H+05.

VHF and MF CRS	VHF Ch	Tx	Rx
Lyngby 55°50'N 11°25'E	**07**, 85	**1704**	2045
Blåvand	23	**1734**	2045, 2078
Bovbjerg	02	**1734**	2045, 2078
Hanstholm	01		
Hirtshals	66		
Skagen	04	**1758**	2102, 2045

HF RT

Lyngby Radio listens for calls from ships transmitting on the frequencies (MHz) in black. Paired with these frequencies are the frequencies in blue on which ships will receive Lyngby's transmissions, in the course of normal working:

4116	4408	12269	13116	16462	17344
4137	4429	12296	13143	22045	22741
8216	8740	16408	17290	22051	22747
8246	8770	16411	17293	22105	22801
12257	13104	16423	17305	25070	26145
				25073	26148

Ships may be directed to other paired frequencies.

Fig. 5 (2) Danish coast radio stations

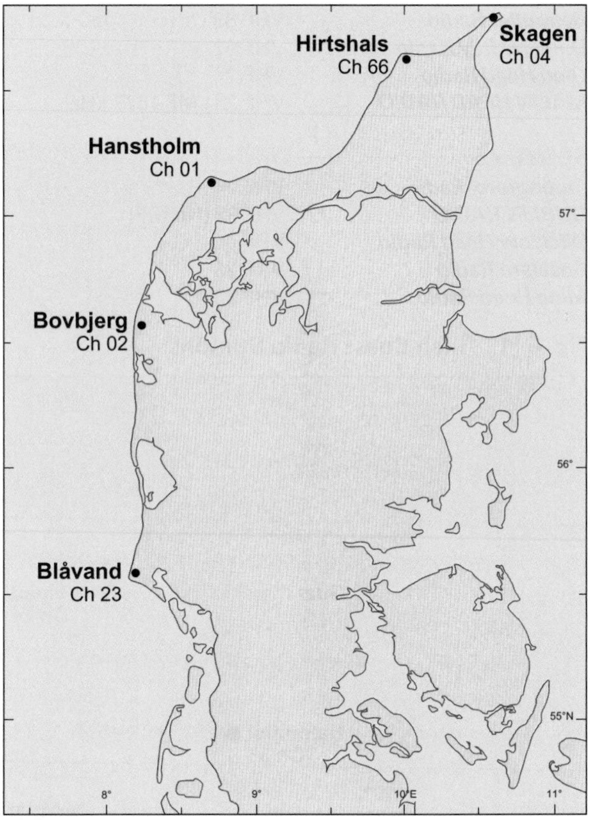
Skagen
Ch 04
Hirtshals
Ch 66
Hanstholm
Ch 01
Bovbjerg
Ch 02
Blåvand
Ch 23
57°
56°
55°N
8°
9°
10°E
11°

5.9.4 Germany

Seefunk – DP07, Estedeich 84, 21129 Hamburg

Borkum	VHF Ch 28
Nordfriesland	VHF Ch 26
Elbe Weser	VHF Ch 01, 24
Bremen	VHF Ch 25
Hamburg	VHF Ch 27, 83

All CRS monitor Ch 16 and DSC Ch 70. Traffic Lists: Ch 16 every H and H+30.

Fig. 5 (3) German coast radio stations

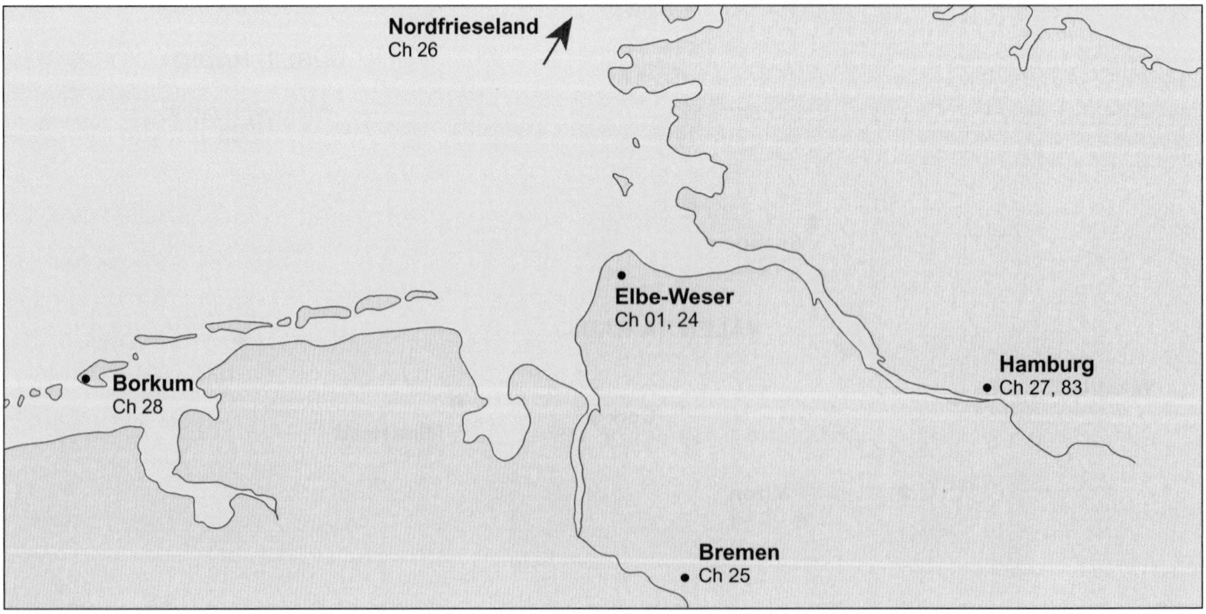
Nordfrieseland
Ch 26
Elbe-Weser
Ch 01, 24
Hamburg
Ch 27, 83
Borkum
Ch 28
Bremen
Ch 25

5.9.5 Belgium

OOSTENDE RADIO ☎ +32 59 702438.
DSC Ch 70 and 2187·5 kHz (H24). MMSI 002050480. MF 2761, 3629 kHz. VHF Ch 27, 85.Traffic Lists: 2761 kHz every even H+20.

Middelkerke Ch 27, 85.
De Panne (French border) Ch **78**, 85
Zeebrugge Ch 27, 63

Antwerpen Radio, VHF 07, **24**, 27. Traffic lists: Ch 24 every H+05. DSC Ch 70; MMSI 002050485.

Fig. 5 (4) Spanish and Portuguese CRS

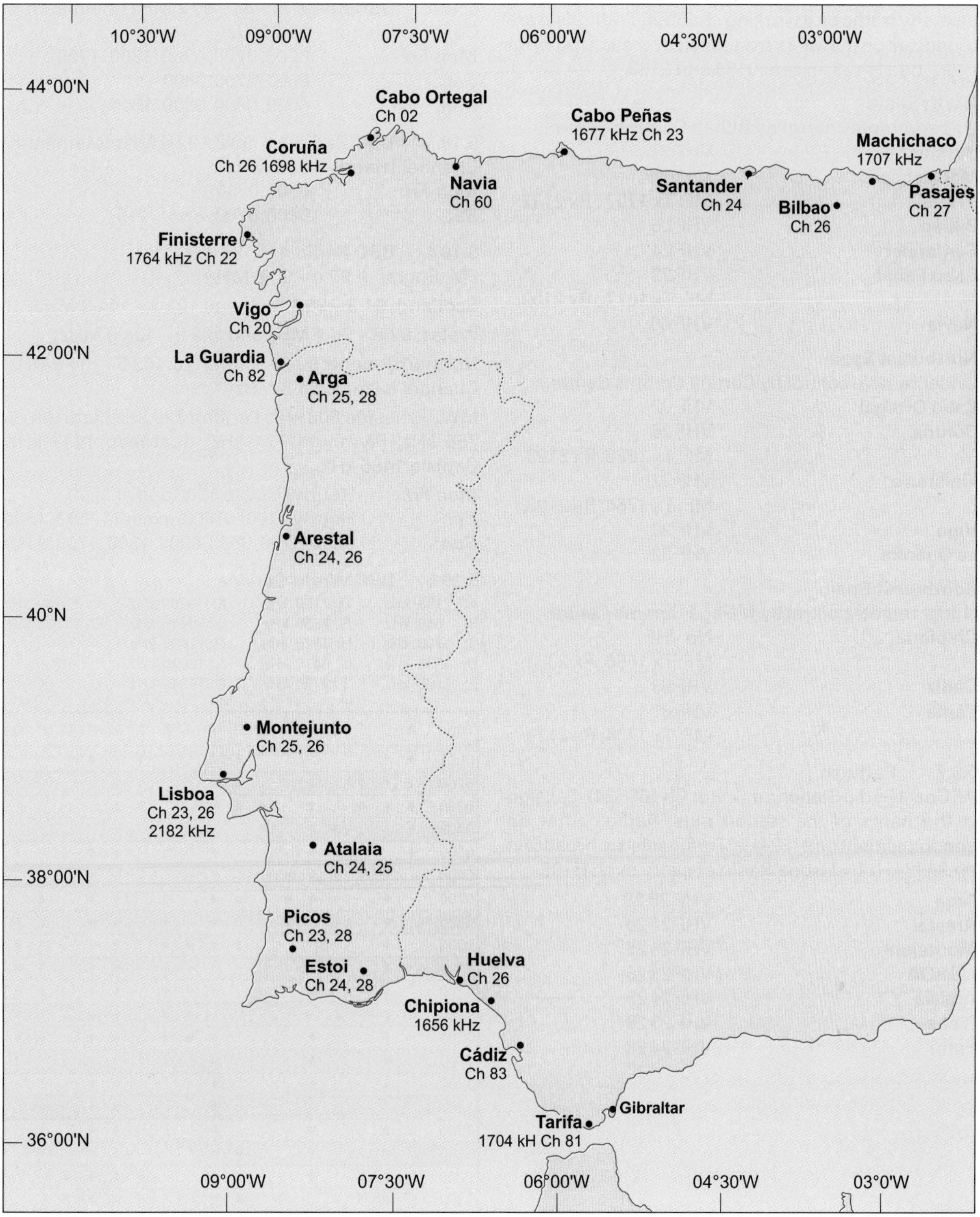
10°30'W
09°00'W
07°30'W
06°00'W
04°30'W
03°00'W
44°00'N
42°00'N
40°N
38°00'N
36°00'N
Cabo Ortegal
Ch 02
Cabo Peñas
1677 kHz Ch 23
Machichaco
1707 kHz
Coruña
Ch 26 1698 kHz
Navia
Ch 60
Santander
Ch 24
Bilbao
Ch 26
Pasajes
Ch 27
Finisterre
1764 kHz Ch 22
Vigo
Ch 20
La Guardia
Ch 82
Arga
Ch 25, 28
Arestal
Ch 24, 26
Montejunto
Ch 25, 26
Lisboa
Ch 23, 26
2182 kHz
Atalaia
Ch 24, 25
Picos
Ch 23, 28
Estoi
Ch 24, 28
Huelva
Ch 26
Chipiona
1656 kHz
Cádiz
Ch 83
Gibraltar
Tarifa
1704 kH Ch 81
09°00'W
07°30'W
06°00'W
04°30'W
03°0'W

5.9.6 Spain

In N and NW Spain CRS do **not** keep continuous watch on Ch 16, so call on a working channel. In SW Spain call initially on Ch 16; you will be switched to a working channel. All callsigns are the name of the remote station, plus 'Radio'.

Traffic lists are not broadcast on VHF, but CRS will pass any traffic on a working channel. Traffic lists are broadcast on the MF Tx frequencies for each region at every odd H +33, except 0133 and 2133.

North Spain

Under remote control by Bilbao Comms Centre:

Pasajes	VHF 27
Machichaco	No VHF
	MF: Tx 1707 ; Rx 2132.
Bilbao	VHF 26
Santander	VHF 24
Cabo Peñas	VHF 23
	MF: Tx 1677 ; Rx 2102.
Navia	VHF 60

Northwest Spain

Under remote control by Coruña Comms Centre:

Cabo Ortegal	VHF 02
Coruña	VHF 26
	MF: Tx 1698; Rx 2123.
Finisterre	VHF 22
	MF: Tx 1764; Rx 2108.
Vigo	VHF 20
La Guardia	VHF 82

Southwest Spain

Under remote control by Malaga Comms Centre:

Chipiona	No VHF
	MF: Tx 1656; Rx 2081.
Cádiz	VHF 83
Tarifa	VHF 81
	MF: Tx 1704; Rx 2129.

5.9.7 Portugal

All Coast Radio Stations monitor Ch 16 (H24). Callsign is the name of the station plus 'Radio'. After an announcement on 2182 kHz, Traffic lists are broadcast on 2693 kHz by Lisboa Radio at every even H+05.

Arga	VHF 25 28
Arestal	VHF 24 26
Montejunto	VHF 25 26
LISBOA	VHF 23 26
Atalaia	VHF 24 25
Picos	VHF 23 28
Estoi	VHF 24 28

5.10 RADIO TIME SIGNALS

5.10.1 BBC Radio 1 97·6 – 99·8 MHz (Mainland)

Channel Islands 97·1 MHz
1053 kHz, 1089 kHz

Mon-Fri: 0700, 0800
Sat: 1300 ***Sun:*** Nil

5.10.2 BBC Radio 2 88 – 90·2 MHz (Mainland)

Channel Islands 89·6 MHz
Mon-Fri: 0000, 0700, 0800, 1300, 1700
Sat: 0000, 0700, 0800
Sun: 0000, 0800, 0900, 1900

5.10.3 BBC Radio 3 90·2 – 92·4 MHz (Mainland)

Channel Islands 91·1 MHz
Mon-Fri: 0700, 0800
Sat: 0600, 0700 ***Sun:*** Nil

5.10.4 BBC Radio 4 198 kHz LW

FM. England: 92·4 – 94·6 MHz;

Scotland: 91·3 – 96·1 MHz and 103·5 – 104·9 MHz;

Wales: 92·8 – 96·1 MHz and 103·5 – 104·9 MHz;

Northern Ireland: 93·2 – 96·0 MHz & 103·5 – 104·6 MHz; Channel Islands: 94·8 MHz.

MW. Tyneside 603 kHz; London 720 kHz; Redruth 756 kHz; Plymouth 774 kHz; Aberdeen 1449 kHz; Carlisle 1485 kHz.

Mon-Fri: Hourly 0600 to 1900 and at 2200
Sat: Hourly 0700 to 1600, except 1200 & 1500
Sun: 0600, 0700, 0800, 0900, 1300, 1700, 2100

5.10.5 BBC World Service

A: 198 kHz	F: 7150 kHz	K: 9760 kHz	P: 17640 kHz
B: 648 kHz	G: 7230 kHz	L: 9915 kHz	Q: 17705 kHz
C: 1296 kHz	H: 7325 kHz	M: 12095 kHz	
D: 3955 kHz	I: 9410 kHz	N: 15070 kHz	
E: 6195 kHz	J: 9750 kHz	O: 15340 kHz	

Time	A	B	C	D	E	F	G	H	I	J	K	L	M	N	O	P	Q
0000	♦	♦						♦				♦	♦	♦			
0200	♦	♦	♦		♦			♦	♦			♦	♦				
0300	♦	♦	♦		♦		♦	♦	♦			♦	♦				
0400	♦			♦	♦		♦		♦				♦				
0500	♦			♦	♦				♦				♦	♦			
0600		♦	♦	♦	♦	♦			♦				♦	♦			
0700		♦			♦	♦		♦	♦		♦		♦	♦		♦	
0800		♦				♦		♦	♦		♦		♦	♦		♦	♦
0900		♦						♦	♦	♦	♦		♦	♦		♦	♦
1100		♦							♦	♦	♦		♦	♦		♦	♦
1200		♦							♦	♦	♦		♦	♦		♦	♦
1300		♦							♦	♦	♦		♦	♦		♦	♦
1500		♦			♦				♦	♦	♦		♦	♦		♦	♦
1600		♦			♦				♦		♦		♦	♦			♦
1700		♦			♦				♦				♦	♦			
1800					♦				♦				♦	♦			
1900		♦			♦				♦				♦	♦			
2000		♦			♦			♦	♦				♦	♦			
2200		♦	♦		♦			♦	♦			♦	♦	♦	♦		
2300		♦	♦					♦	♦			♦	♦	♦	♦		

5.10.6 Worldwide time signals

Rugby, UK (MSF) continuously broadcasts UT (GMT) signals on a carrier frequency of 60 kHz. The signal carries adequate field strength throughout the UK and can be received widely in north and west Europe. The National Physical Laboratory, Teddington offers a helpline on +44 (0)208 943 6493.

Fort Collins, Colorado (WWV) and Kekaha, Hawaii (WWVH) broadcast UT signals continuously on frequencies 2·5, 5, 10, 15 and 20 (not Kekaha) MHz.

The station is identified by a voice announcement in English every thirty minutes, approximately on the hour and half-hour. The hour is signalled by a 1500 Hz tone and minutes and seconds by 1200 Hz tones.

Semi-silent periods with no audio tone or special announcements occur from H+43 to 51 at WWV, and H+08 to 19 at WWVH.

Additional information is also broadcast as follows: At H+08 and H+09 WWV broadcasts Atlantic weather in two parts and Eastern N. Pacific weather at H+10. WWVH broadcasts storm information for the Pacific from H+48 to 51.

5.11 VESSEL TRAFFIC SERVICES (VTS)

VTS primarily assist commercial shipping and depend on careful use of communications. Yachts can derive some benefit from them by:

a. Being aware of what commercial ships are doing;
b. Thereby being better able to avoid them; and
c. Making use of radar assistance if the need arises.

A VTS both formalises, and is shorthand for, services which have existed for many years. These include: Position reporting; procedural control of traffic (not to be confused with TSS, although the two may exist in close proximity to one another); radar surveillance; compulsory monitoring of VHF channels for: traffic, weather, navigational and tidal information; pilotage advice, instructions and berthing details.

Yachts should monitor VTS radio channels for any constraints on their movements. It is rarely necessary (and often undesirable) for yachts to transmit on a busy VTS channel; indeed many marine authorities discourage this. In Dutch and German waters the letter of the law is often more rigidly enforced than elsewhere; violations may incur on-the-spot fines.

VTS usually exist in areas of high traffic density with complex routeing and/or navigational constraints, eg shoal water, narrow channels and tight bends. These conditions are stressful and demanding even for the professional mariner. Yachts should therefore keep out of the way, eg just outside buoyed channels.

VTS diagrams are given in the relevant geographic area of Chapter 9, with detailed notes in the port text.

5.12 FLAG ETIQUETTE

Historically flags were used to pass messages at sea. Although this is now mostly done by radio, flags are still used to express identity – by national ensigns, club burgees, etc. Here is brief guidance on their use.

5.12.1 Ensign

A yacht's ensign is the national maritime flag corresponding to the nationality of her owner. Thus a British yacht should wear the Red Ensign, unless she qualifies for a special ensign (see 5.12.2). It goes without saying that the national ensign should be kept clean and in good repair. At sea the ensign must be worn when meeting other vessels, when entering or leaving foreign ports, or when approaching forts, Signal and CG stations, etc. Increasingly it has become the practice to leave the ensign (and burgee) flying at all times in foreign waters – even at night in harbour, assuming that the boat is not unattended. In British harbours it is customary for the ensign to be hoisted at 0800 (0900 between 1 November and 14 February) or as soon after that time as people come on board; and lowered at sunset (or 2100 LT if earlier) or before that time if the crew is leaving the boat.

The ensign should normally be worn at the stern, but if this is not possible the nearest position should be used, e.g. at the peak in a gaff-rigged boat, at the mizzen masthead in a ketch or yawl, or about two-thirds up the leech of the mainsail. In harbour or at anchor the proper position is at the stern.

The ensign should not be worn when racing (after the five minute gun). It should be hoisted on finishing or when retiring.

5.12.2 Special ensigns

Members of certain clubs may apply for permission to wear a special ensign (e.g. Blue Ensign, defaced Blue Ensign, or defaced Red Ensign). For this purpose the yacht must either be a registered ship under Part I of the Merchant Shipping Act 1995 and of at least 2 tons gross tonnage, or be registered under the Merchant Shipping Act 1983 (Small Ships Register) and of at least 7 metres overall length. The owner or owners must be British subjects, and the yacht must not be used for any professional, business or commercial purpose. Full details can be obtained from the Secretaries of the clubs concerned.

A special ensign must only be worn when the owner is on board or ashore in the vicinity, and only when the yacht is flying the burgee (or a Flag Officer's flag) of the club concerned. The permit must be carried on board. When the yacht is sold, or the owner ceases to be a member of the club, the permit must be returned to the Secretary of the club.

5.12.3 Burgee

A burgee shows that a yacht is in the charge of a member of the club indicated, and does not necessarily indicate ownership. It should be flown at the masthead.

Should this be impossible due to wind sensors, radio antenna, etc. the burgee may be flown at the starboard spreader, but this should be avoided unless absolutely necessary. A yacht should not fly more than one burgee. A burgee is not flown when a yacht is racing. If the yacht is on loan, or is chartered, it is correct to use the burgee of the skipper or charterer – not that of the absent owner. Normal practice has been to lower the burgee at night, at the same time as the ensign, but nowadays many owners leave the burgee flying if they are on board or ashore in the vicinity.

5.12.4 Flag Officer's flag

Clubs authorise their Flag Officers to fly special swallow-tailed flags, with the same design as the club burgee and in place of it. The flags of a vice-commodore and a rear-commodore carry one and two balls respectively. A Flag Officer's flag is flown day and night while he is on board, or ashore nearby. A Flag Officer should fly his flag with the Red Ensign (or special ensign, where authorised) in preference to the burgee of some other club.

5.12.5 Choice of burgee

An owner who is not a Flag Officer, and who belongs to more than one club, should normally fly the burgee (and if authorised the special ensign) of the senior club in the harbour where the yacht is lying. An exception may be if another club is staging a regatta or similar function.

5.12.6 Courtesy ensign

It is customary when abroad to fly a small maritime ensign of the country concerned at the starboard spreader. A courtesy ensign must not be worn below any other flag on the same halyard. Thus a club burgee, if usually flown at the starboard spreader, must be shifted to the port spreader when abroad, permitting the courtesy ensign to be close up at the starboard spreader. The correct courtesy flag for a foreign yacht in British waters is the Red Ensign. British yachts do not fly a courtesy flag in the Channel Islands since these are part of the British Isles.

5.12.7 House flag

An owner may fly his personal flag when he is on board in harbour, provided it does not conflict with the design of some existing flag. A house flag is normally rectangular, and is flown at the crosstrees in a sloop or cutter, at the mizzen masthead in a ketch or yawl, or at the foremast head in a schooner.

5.12.8 Salutes

Yachts should salute all Royal Yachts, and all warships of whatever nationality. A salute is made by dipping the ensign (only). The vessel saluted responds by dipping her ensign, and then re-hoisting it, whereupon the vessel saluting re-hoists hers. It is customary for a Flag Officer to be saluted (not more than once a day) by a yacht flying the burgee of that club.

5.12.9 Dressing ship

Dressing overall (as opposed to dressing with masthead flags) is normally only done in harbour and marks national festivals. The international code flags and pennants (see Plate 3) are flown in the following order from stem to masthead(s) to stern:
E, Q, p 3, G, p 8, Z, p 4, W, p 6, P, p 1, I, Code, T, Y, B, X, 1st Sub, H, 3rd Sub, D, F, 2nd Sub, U, A, O, M, R, p 2, J, p 0, N, p 9, K, p 7, V, p 5, L, C, S. (Total = 40).

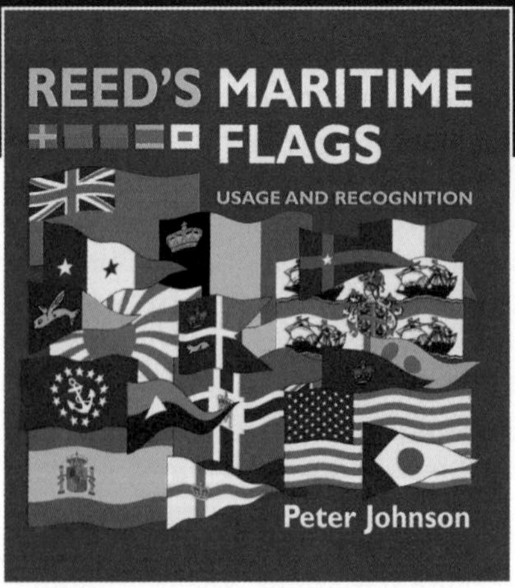
REED'S MARITIME FLAGS
USAGE AND RECOGNITION
Peter Johnson

PLATE 4 ENSIGNS AND FLAGS

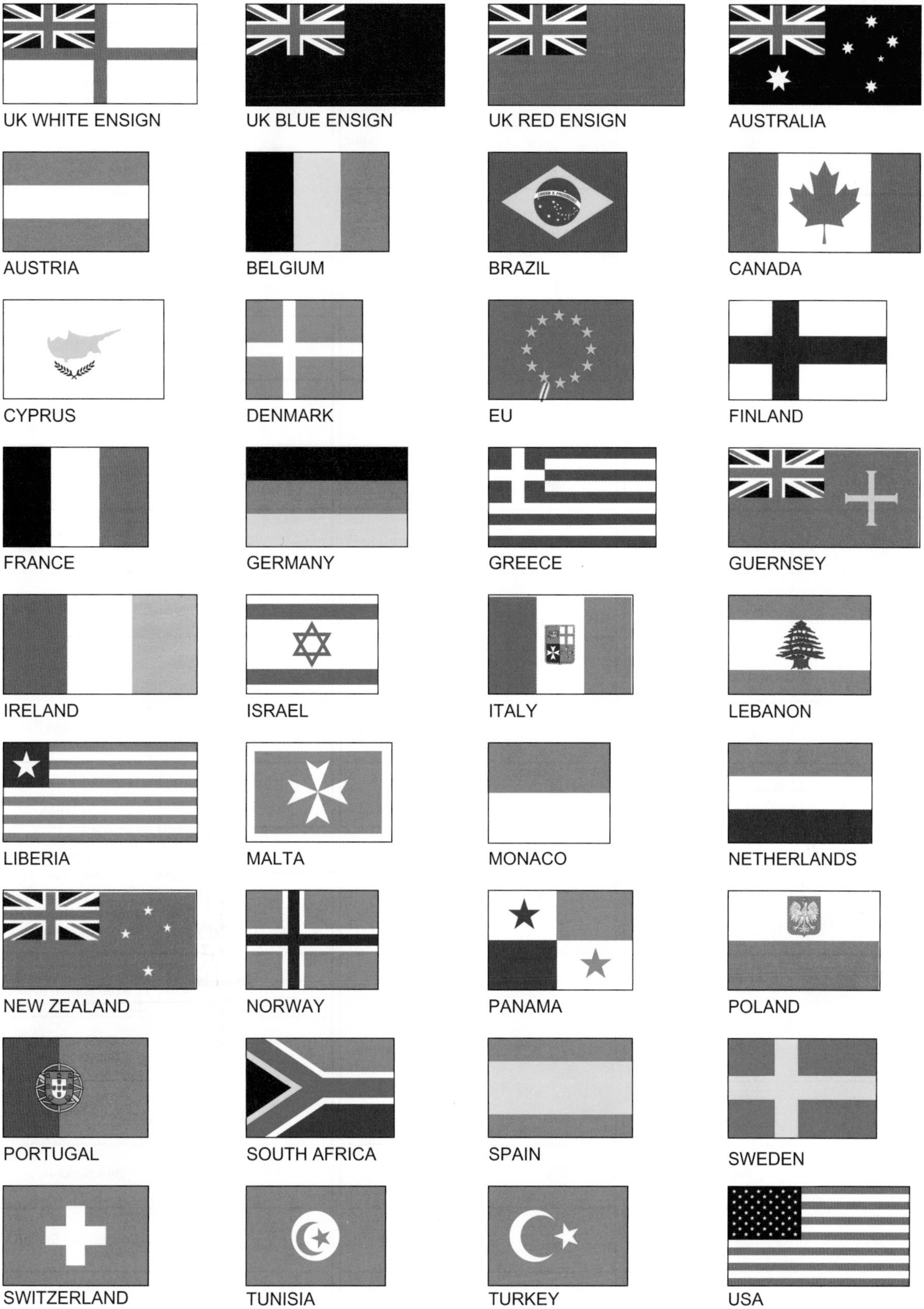
UK WHITE ENSIGN
UK BLUE ENSIGN
UK RED ENSIGN
AUSTRALIA
AUSTRIA
BELGIUM
BRAZIL
CANADA
CYPRUS
DENMARK
EU
FINLAND
FRANCE
GERMANY
GREECE
GUERNSEY
IRELAND
ISRAEL
ITALY
LEBANON
LIBERIA
MALTA
MONACO
NETHERLANDS
NEW ZEALAND
NORWAY
PANAMA
POLAND
PORTUGAL
SOUTH AFRICA
SPAIN
SWEDEN
SWITZERLAND
TUNISIA
TURKEY
USA

PLATE 5 ADMIRALTY SYMBOLS

Symbol	Meaning
Pyl 28 Pyl	Power transmission line with pylons and safe overhead clearance
20	Vertical clearance above High Water
	Harbourmaster's Office
	Custom office
	Hospital
	Post office
	Yacht harbour, Marina
	Radio reporting point
	Example of a fixed (a) and floating (b) mark
	Mooring buoy
	Wreck showing any part at level of chart datum
	Lighted port hand beacon
(1₆) (2₇) 3₇	Rock which covers and uncovers, height above chart datum
	Rock awash at level of chart datum
	Visitors' Berth
	Fuel Station (Petrol, Diesel)
	Public Slipway
	Water Tap
	Public landing, steps, ladder

Symbol	Meaning
	Church
	Radio mast, television mast
	Monument (including column, pillar, obelisk, statue)
	Chimney
	Flare stack (on land)
	Tanks
	Recommended anchorage
	Rescue station, lifeboat station, rocket station
	Fishing harbour
	Fishing prohibited
	Withy - starboard hand
	Withy - port hand
	Floodlit
	Marsh
	Kelp
	Crane
	Inn and Restaurant
WC	Public Toilets
P	Public Car Park
	Laundrette
	Yacht Club, Sailing Club

Symbol	Meaning
2 0 2 5 10 20	Drying contour LW line, Chart Datum Below 5m blue ribbon or differing blue tints may be shown
	Anchoring prohibited
	Marine Farm
	Wreck, depth unknown, danger to navigation
	Wreck, depth unknown, no danger to navigation
4₆ Wk	Wreck, depth obtained by sounding
4₆ Wk	Wreck, swept by wire to the depth shown
	Submarine cable
	Buried pipeline
	Overfalls, tide rips and races
	Limit of safety zone around offshore installation
	Light
	Dangerous underwater rock of unknown depth
20 (12₂) (5₇) (2₈)	Dangerous underwater rock of known depth
	Caravan Site Camping Site
	Public Telephone
	Bird Sanctuary
CG	Coastguard Station
	Woods in general

Chapter 6

Weather

Contents

C6

6.1. MEASUREMENTS

6.1.1 Beaufort wind scale and sea states

Force	Wind speed (knots)	(km/h)	(m/sec)	Description	Deep sea criteria	Probable mean (max) wave ht(m)
0	<1	0–2	0–0·5	Calm	Like a mirror	–
1	1–3	2–6	0·3–1·5	Light air	Ripples like scales are formed	0·1 (0·1)
2	4–6	7–11	1·6–3·3	Light breeze	Small wavelets, still short but more pronounced, not breaking	0·1 (0·3)
3	7–10	13–19	3·4–5·4	Gentle breeze	Large wavelets, crests begin to break; a few white horses	0·6 (1)
4	11–16	20–30	5·5–7·9	Moderate breeze	Small waves growing longer; fairly frequent white horses	1 (1·5)
5	17–21	31–39	8·0–10·7	Fresh breeze	Moderate waves, taking more pronounced form; many white horses, perhaps some spray	2 (2·5)
6	22–27	41–50	10·8–13·8	Strong breeze	Large waves forming; white foam crests more extensive; probably some spray	3 (4)
7	28–33	52–61	13·9–17·1	Near gale	Sea heaps up; white foam from breaking waves begins to blow in streaks	4 (5·5)
8	34–40	63–74	17·2–20·7	Gale	Moderately high waves of greater length; edge of crests break into spindrift; foam blown in well-marked streaks	5·5 (7·5)
9	41–47	76–87	20·8–24·4	Strong gale	High waves with tumbling crests; dense streaks of foam; spray may affect visibility	7 (10)
10	48–55	89–102	24·5–28·4	Storm	Very high waves with long overhanging crests; dense streams of foam make surface of sea white. Heavy tumbling sea; visibility affected	9 (12·5)
11	56–63	104–117	28·5–32·6	Violent storm	Exceptionally high waves; sea completely covered with long white patches of foam; edges of wave crests blown into froth. Visibility affected	11·5 (16)
12	64 plus	118 plus	32·7 plus	Hurricane	Air filled with foam and spray; sea completely white with driving spray; visibility very seriously affected	14 (—)

Notes: (1) The actual force exerted on a sail is proportional to the square of the windspeed. Thus a wind of Force 6 (say 25 knots) has more than three times the 'weight' of of a wind of Force 4 (say 14 knots) – which is why even a small increase in windspeed, or gusts, have a significant effect on a sailing yacht.

(2) The probable mean wave heights, maximum in brackets, are a guide to what may be expected in the open sea, away from land.

Swell:

(a) Length (m) of swell waves		(b) Height (m) of swell waves	
Short	0-100	Low	0-2
Average	100-200	Moderate	2-4
Long	over 200	Heavy	over 4

6.1.2 Beaufort wind scale and sea states

PLATE 6
BEAUFORT SCALE AND SEA STATES

Wave height for a given wind strength depends upon the distance travelled (fetch) and the length of time for which the wind has been blowing; see table opposite. In enclosed waters or near land with an offshore wind, wave heights will be less but possibly steeper – particularly with wind against tide.

Photography
© **Crown** – Force 0, 11
© **G.J.Simpson** – Force 1, 2, 7
© **I.G. MacNeil** – Force 3, 4, 5, 6
© **W.A.E. Smith** – Force 8
© **J.P. Laycock** – Force 9
© **G. Allen** – Force 10
© **J.F.Thomson** – Force 12

Force 0 0-1 Kts Calm Wave Ht 0m

Force 1 1-3 Kts Light Air
Wave Ht 0.1m

Force 2 4-6 Kts Light Breeze
Wave Ht 0.2m

Force 3 7-10 Kts Gentle Breeze
Wave Ht 0.6m

Force 4 11-16 Kts Moderate Breeze
Wave Ht 1m

Force 5 17-21 Kts Fresh Breeze
Wave Ht 2m

Force 6 22-27 Kts Strong Breeze
Wave Ht 3m

Force 7 28-33 Kts Near Gale
Wave Ht 4m

Force 8 34-40 Kts Gale
Wave Ht 5.5m

Force 9 41-47 Kts Severe Gale
Wave Ht 7m

Force 10 48-55 Kts Storm
Wave Ht 9m

Force 11 56-63 Kts Violent Storm
Wave Ht 11.5m

Force 12 64 plus Kts Hurricane
Wave Ht 14m

6.1.3 Barometer and temperature conversion scales

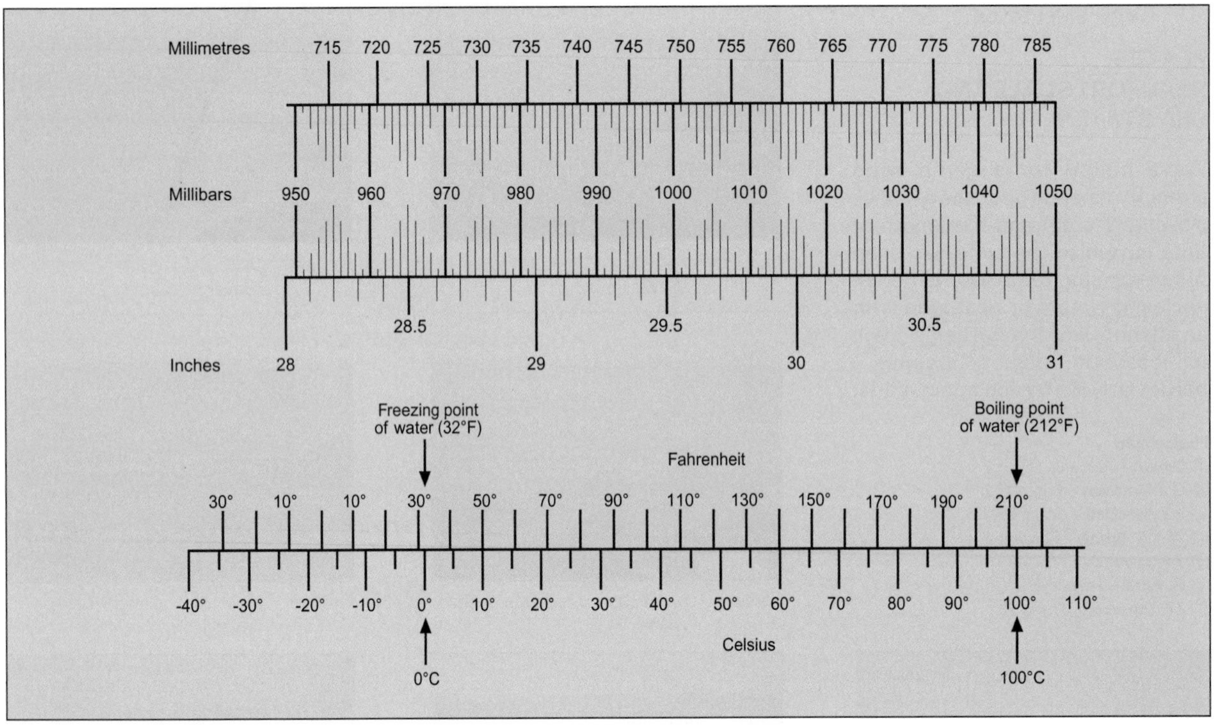
Millimetres
715 720 725 730 735 740 745 750 755 760 765 770 775 780 785
Millibars
950 960 970 980 990 1000 1010 1020 1030 1040 1050
28.5 29.5 30.5
Inches
28 29 30 31
Freezing point of water (32°F)
Boiling point of water (212°F)
Fahrenheit
30° 10° 10° 30° 50° 70° 90° 110° 130° 150° 170° 190° 210°
-40° -30° -20° -10° 0° 10° 20° 30° 40° 50° 60° 70° 80° 90° 100° 110°
Celsius
0°C
100°C

6.1.4 Terms used in weather bulletins

a. Speed of movement of pressure systems

Slowly:	< 15 knots
Steadily:	15 to 25 knots
Rather quickly:	25 to 35 knots
Rapidly:	35 to 45 knots
Very rapidly:	> 45 knots

b. Visibility

Good:	> 5 miles
Moderate:	2 – 5 miles
Poor:	1000 metres – 2 miles
Fog:	Less than 1000 metres

c. Barometric pressure changes (tendency)

Rising or falling slowly: Pressure change of 0·1 to 1·5 millibars in the preceding 3 hours.

Rising or falling: Pressure change of 1·6 to 3·5 millibars in the preceding 3 hours.

Rising or falling quickly: Pressure change of 3·6 to 6 millibars in the preceding 3 hours.

Rising or falling very rapidly: Pressure change of more than 6 millibars in the preceding 3 hours.

Now rising (or falling): Pressure has been falling (rising) or steady in the preceding 3 hours, but at the time of observation was definitely rising (falling).

d. Gale warnings

A **Gale** warning means that winds of at least force 8 (34-40 knots) or gusts reaching 43-51 knots are expected somewhere within the area, but not necessarily over the whole area. **Severe Gale** means winds of at least force 9 (41-47 knots) or gusts reaching 52-60 knots. **Storm** means winds of force 10 (48-55 knots) or gusts of 61-68 knots. **Violent Storm** means winds of force 11 (56-63 kn) or gusts of 69 kn or more; and **Hurricane Force** means winds of force 12 (64 knots or more).

Gale warnings remain in force until amended or cancelled ('gales now ceased'). If a gale persists for more than 24 hours the warning is re-issued.

e. Timing of gale warnings

Imminent	Within 6 hrs of time of issue
Soon	6 – 12 hrs from time of issue
Later	More than 12 hrs from time of issue

f. Strong wind warnings

Issued, if possible 6 hrs in advance, when winds F6 or more are expected up to 5M offshore; valid for 12 hrs.

g. Wind

Wind direction: Indicates the direction from which the wind is blowing.

Winds becoming cyclonic: Indicates that there will be considerable changes in wind direction across the path of a depression within the forecast area.

Veering: A clockwise change in the wind direction, eg SW to W.

Backing: An anti-clockwise change in the wind direction, eg W to SW.

SOURCES OF WEATHER INFORMATION

Around the UK and along the coasts of NW and W Europe there is no shortage of weather information, both forecast and actual. From this any competent yachtsman should be able to compare his own analysis with that issued by professional forecasters.

The sources of this information are national Met Offices whose forecasts are disseminated by the following means: Broadcasts by national and local radio stations, Coastguard centres and Coast radio stations; Navtex; telephone recordings, fax messages, mobile text messages (SMS) and the Internet.

The Met Office has moved from Bracknell to:

FitzRoy Road, Exeter, Devon EX1 3PB. Tel 0845 300 0300; Fax 0845 300 1300. enquiries@metoffice.com www.met-office.gov.uk

At the BBC a useful information tel is 0870 010 0222.

6.2 RADIO BROADCASTING

6.2.1 BBC Radio 4 Shipping forecast

BBC Radio 4 broadcasts shipping forecasts at:

0048 LT[1]	LW, MW, FM
0536 LT[1]	LW, MW, FM
1201 LT	LW only
1754 LT	LW, FM (Sat/Sun)

[1] Includes weather reports from coastal stations

Frequencies:

LW		198 kHz
MW	**Tyneside:**	603 kHz
	London and N Ireland:	720 kHz
	Redruth:	756 kHz
	Plymouth & Enniskillen:	774 kHz
	Aberdeen:	1449 kHz
	Carlisle:	1485 kHz
FM	**England:**	92·4 – 94·6 MHz
	Scotland:	91·3 – 96·1 MHz
		103·5 – 104·9 MHz
	Wales:	92·8 – 96·1 MHz &
		103·5 – 104·9 MHz
	N Ireland	93·2 – 96·0 MHz
		103·5 – 104·6 MHz
	Channel Islands:	94·8 MHz

6.2.2 Contents of the Shipping forecast

The forecast contains:

A summary of gale warnings in force at time of issue; a general synopsis of weather systems and their expected development over the next 24 hours; and a forecast of wind direction/force, weather and visibility in each sea area for the next 24 hours.

Gale warnings are also broadcast at the earliest juncture in Radio 4 programmes after receipt, as well as after the next news bulletin. Sea area **Trafalgar** is only included in the 0048 forecast.

Shipping forecasts cover large sea areas, and rarely include the detailed variations that may occur near land. The Inshore waters forecast (see 6.2.3) can be more helpful to yachtsmen on coastal passages.

Weather reports from coastal stations follow the 0048 and 0535 forecasts. They include wind direction and force, present weather, visibility, and sea-level pressure and tendency, if available. The stations are shown overleaf in 6.2.5 and in Fig 6 (1).

6.2.3 BBC Radio 4 Inshore waters forecast,

A forecast for inshore waters (up to 12M offshore) around the UK and N Ireland, valid until 1800, is broadcast after the 0048 and 0535 coastal station reports. It includes a general synopsis, forecasts of wind direction and force, visibility and weather for stretches of inshore waters. These are defined by well-known places and headlands: from Duncansby Head clockwise via Berwick-upon-Tweed, Whitby, North Foreland, St Catherine's Pt, Land's End, Colwyn Bay, Mull of Kintyre (inc L. Foyle to Carlingford Lough), Cape Wrath, Orkney and Shetland; see Fig 6 (7).

Strong Wind Warnings are issued by the Met Office whenever winds of Force 6 or more are expected over coastal waters up to 5M offshore.

Reports of actual weather at the stations below are broadcast only after the 0048 inshore waters forecast: Boulmer, *Bridlington*, Sheerness, St Catherine's Point*, *Scilly**, Milford Haven, Aberporth, Valley, Liverpool (Crosby), *Ronaldsway*, Larne, Machrihanish*, Greenock, *Stornoway*, *Lerwick*, Wick*, Aberdeen and Leuchars. These stations are shown in Fig 6 (1). * automatic station. Stations in italics also feature in the 0048 and 0536 shipping forecasts.

6.2.4 BBC general (land) forecasts

Land area forecasts may include an outlook period up to 48 hours beyond the shipping forecast, more details of frontal systems and weather along the coasts. The most comprehensive land area forecasts are broadcast by BBC Radio 4 on the frequencies in 6.2.1.

Land area forecasts – Wind strength

Wind descriptions used in land forecasts, with their Beaufort scale equivalents, are:

Calm:	0	Fresh:	5
Light:	1–3	Strong:	6 – 7
Moderate:	4	Gale:	8

Land area forecasts – Visibility

The following definitions apply to land forecasts:

Mist:	Visibility between 2000m and 1000m
Fog:	Visibility less than 1000m
Dense fog:	Less than 50m

C6

6.2.5 UK Shipping forecast areas

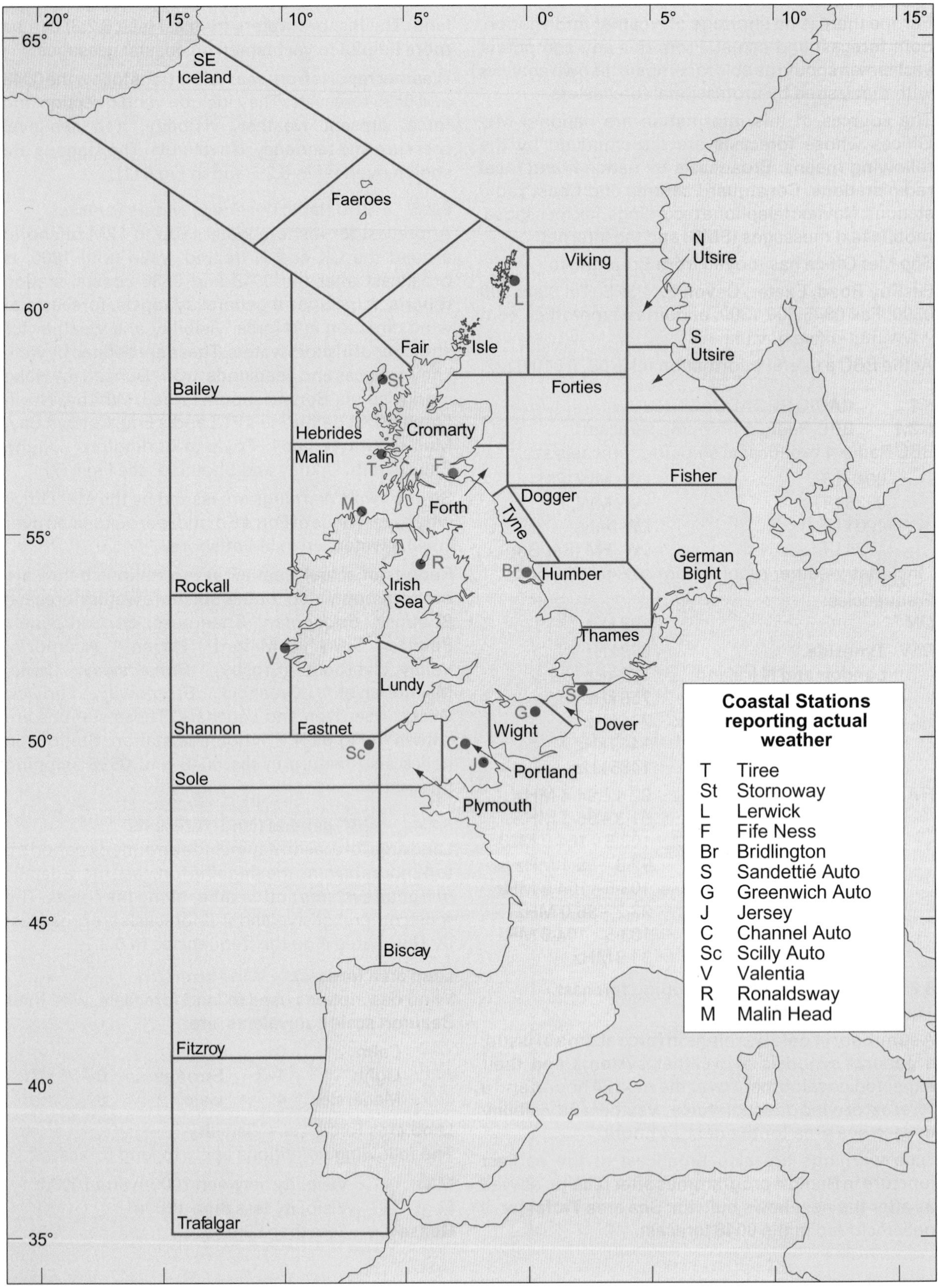

20°
15°
10°
5°
0°
5°
10°
15°
65°
60°
55°
50°
45°
40°
35°
SE Iceland
Faeroes
N Utsire
Viking
L
Fair
Isle
S Utsire
St
Bailey
Forties
Hebrides
Cromarty
Malin
T
F
Fisher
M
Forth
Dogger
Tyne
R
Br
Humber
German Bight
Rockall
Irish Sea
Thames
V
Lundy
S
G
Dover
Shannon
Fastnet
Wight
Sc
C
J
Portland
Sole
Plymouth
Biscay
Fitzroy
Trafalgar
Coastal Stations reporting actual weather
T Tiree
St Stornoway
L Lerwick
F Fife Ness
Br Bridlington
S Sandettié Auto
G Greenwich Auto
J Jersey
C Channel Auto
Sc Scilly Auto
V Valentia
R Ronaldsway
M Malin Head

6.2.6 Shipping Forecast Record

Shipping Forecast Record

Time/Day/Date ....

GENERAL SYNOPSIS at .... UT/BST

System	Present position	Movement	Forecast position	at

Gales	SEA AREA FORECAST	Wind (At first)	Wind (Later)	Weather	Visibility
	VIKING				
	NORTH UTSIRE				
	SOUTH UTSIRE				
	FORTIES				
	CROMARTY				
	FORTH				
	TYNE				
	DOGGER				
	FISHER				
	GERMAN BIGHT				
	HUMBER				
	THAMES				
	DOVER				
	WIGHT				
	PORTLAND				
	PLYMOUTH				
	BISCAY				
	FITZROY				
	TRAFALGAR (0048)				
	SOLE				
	LUNDY				
	FASTNET				
	IRISH SEA				
	SHANNON				
	ROCKALL				
	MALIN				
	HEBRIDES				
	BAILEY				
	FAIR ISLE				
	FAEROES				
	S E ICELAND				

COASTAL REPORTS at .... UT BST	Wind Direction	Wind Force	Weather	Visibility	Pressure	Change
Tiree (T)						
Stornoway (St)						
Lerwick (L)						
Fife Ness (F)						
Bridlington (Br)						
Sandettie auto (S)						

COASTAL REPORTS	Wind Direction	Wind Force	Weather	Visibility	Pressure	Change
Greenwich auto (G)						
Jersey (J)						
Channel auto (C)						
Scilly auto (Sc)						
Valentia (V)						
Ronaldsway (R)						
Malin Head (M)						

6.2.7 Geostrophic scales

When interpreting a synoptic chart it often helps to be able to estimate the Beaufort wind Force; similarly the speed in knots at which warm and cold or occluded fronts are moving – hence when a warm front or a post-cold front clearance may arrive.

3 geostrophic scales are needed: one for wind speed, another for the movement of warm fronts and a third for cold and occluded fronts (which are assumed to move at the same speed). The scales to the right are calibrated for isobars at 2 millibar intervals and are reasonably accurate between Latitudes 40° and 60°N.

Set your dividers between adjacent isobars, then read off from the left (high) end of the scale the wind Force or frontal speed. Or make a perspex scale and place it at 90° across the isobars.

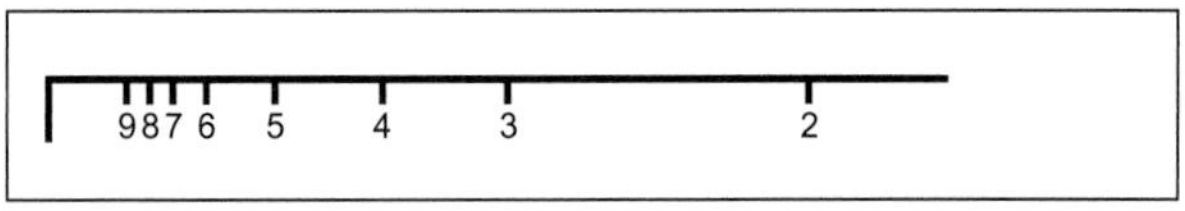
9876
5
4
3
2

Wind in Beaufort Force

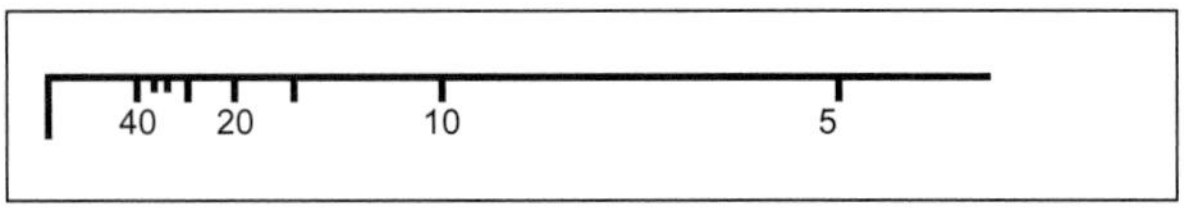
40
20
10
5

Warm front movement in knots

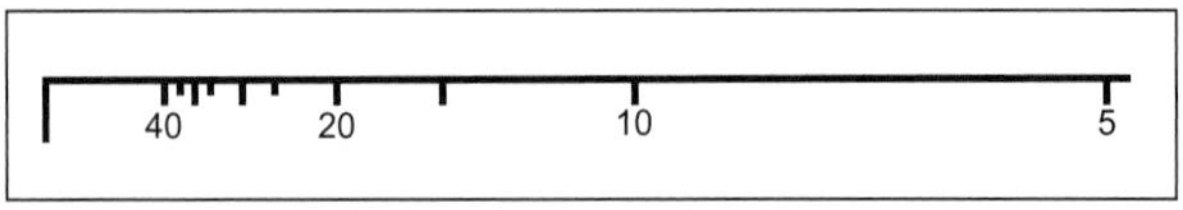
40
20
10
5

Cold front or Occlusion movement in knots

6.2.8 UK Local radio stations

Some local radio stations (both BBC and commercial) broadcast marine weather forecasts and small craft warnings. The scope and quality of these forecasts vary considerably. Broadcast times, which frequently change, are Local; call the ☎ for the latest schedule. Land forecasts cover large areas but, unlike marine forecasts, rarely give wind direction and speed.

Gale warnings and Strong wind warnings (F6+ expected within the next 12 hrs, up to 5M offshore) are usually broadcast at the first programme break or after the first news bulletin following receipt.

For Channel Islands, see 6.12.

BBC RADIO CORNWALL
95·2, 96·0, 103·9 MHz. 630, 657 kHz. ☎ 01872 275436
M-F 0605, 0645, 0715, 0815, 1035, 1225, 1730.
Sat 0608, 0645, 0720, 0820, 1310.
Sun 0820, 0845, 0920, 1310.

BBC RADIO DEVON
94·8, 95·8, 103·4 MHz. 801, 855, 990, 1458 kHz. ☎ 01752 260323
M-F 0533, 0633, 0833, 1330, 1733.
Sat 0605, 0833, 1309 (1307 on *Sun*).

BBC RADIO SOLENT
96·1, 103·8 MHz. 999, 1359 kHz (W Dorset). ☎ 02380 331311
M-Fri 0645, 0845; Hrly 0530-1130, 1325-1525, 1630-1830.
Sat Hrly 0630-1130 (except 0730); 1310, 1757, 2305.
Sun Hrly 0630-1130; 1505 (week's outlook).

BBC RADIO KENT
96·7, 97·6, 104·2 MHz. 774, 1602 kHz. ☎ 01892 670000
M-F 0630, 0730, 0830, 1230, 1730, 1830.
Sat 0730, 0830, 1305. *Sun* 0830, 0930, 1305.

BBC ESSEX
95·3, 103·5 MHz. 729, 765, 1530 kHz. ☎ 01245 616000
M-F 0744, 0844; HWs at 1744, 1844.
Sat 0743, 0843, 1206, 1306.
Sun 0743, 0843. Five days forecast at 0725, 1140, 1756.

BBC RADIO SUFFOLK
95·5, 95·9, 103·9, 104·6 MHz. ☎ 01473 250000
M-F 0617, 0717, 0817, 1305, 1805.
S-S 0705, 0805, 1305.

BBC RADIO HUMBERSIDE
95·9 MHz. 1485 kHz. ☎ 01482 323232
M-F 0632, 0732, 0832, 1230, 1630, 1730, 1830.
Sat 0630, 0730, 0830; Hrly 0600-1400 & 1800-2200.
Sun 0832, 0915 (long range forecast), 1310

BBC RADIO CLEVELAND
95·0 MHz. ☎ 01642 225211
M-F 0645, 0745, 0845, 1645.
Sat 0745, 0845, 0945. *Sun* 0745, 0845.

BBC RADIO NEWCASTLE
95·4, 96·0, 103·7, 104·4 MHz. 1458 kHz. ☎ 0191 232 4141
M-F 0510, 0555, 0655, 0755, 0855, 1155, 1255, 1655, 1755.
S-S 0755, 0855, 0955 and 1155 (Sat only).

BBC RADIO SCOTLAND
92·7 - 94·3 MHz. 810 kHz.
M-F 0604, 0658, 0758, then H+00 (0900-1200, 1400-1600), then 1658, 1758, 2157, 2357.
S-Sun 0658, *0700, then H+00 (0900-1300), then 1758, *1825, 2158. *Detailed forecast, synopsis, outlook at these times on Saturday. OT: brief forecast.

NEVIS RADIO (Lochaber)
96·6, 97·0, 102·3, 102·4 MHz
M-Sun 0710, 0730, 0810, 0830, 091,0 0930, then every H+06 (1000-2359).

RADIO FOYLE
93·1 MHz. 792 kHz. ☎ 02871 378600
M-Sun Every H+00 (0900-1200), 1230, 1400, 1500, 1600, 1730

BBC RADIO CUMBRIA
95·6, 96·1, 104·1 MHz. 756, 837, 1458 kHz. ☎ 01228 592444
M-F & Sat/Sun Marine forecasts are issued on the hour (0500-2359) along with the Farmers & Fells forecasts.

BBC RADIO MERSEYSIDE
95·8 MHz. 1485 kHz. ☎ 0151 708 5500
M-F 0705, 0805, 1208, 1310, 1605, 1716, 1746. *Sat* 0742

BBC RADIO WALES
BBC Radio Wales broadcasts a general forecast and synopsis in English on 657 (NE Wales), 882 (All Wales) & 1125 (Mid Wales) kHz, at the times below:
M-Fri 0658, 0758, 0903, 1259, 1734
Sat 0903, 1259, 1759
Sun 0859, 1259, 1759
A brief summary and forecast may be broadcast after the news on the hour. Gale warnings are broadcast on receipt. [BBC Radio Cymru broadcasts only in Welsh, on FM].

Fig. 6 (1) Stations reporting actual weather via BBC Radio 4, telephone recordings or SMS

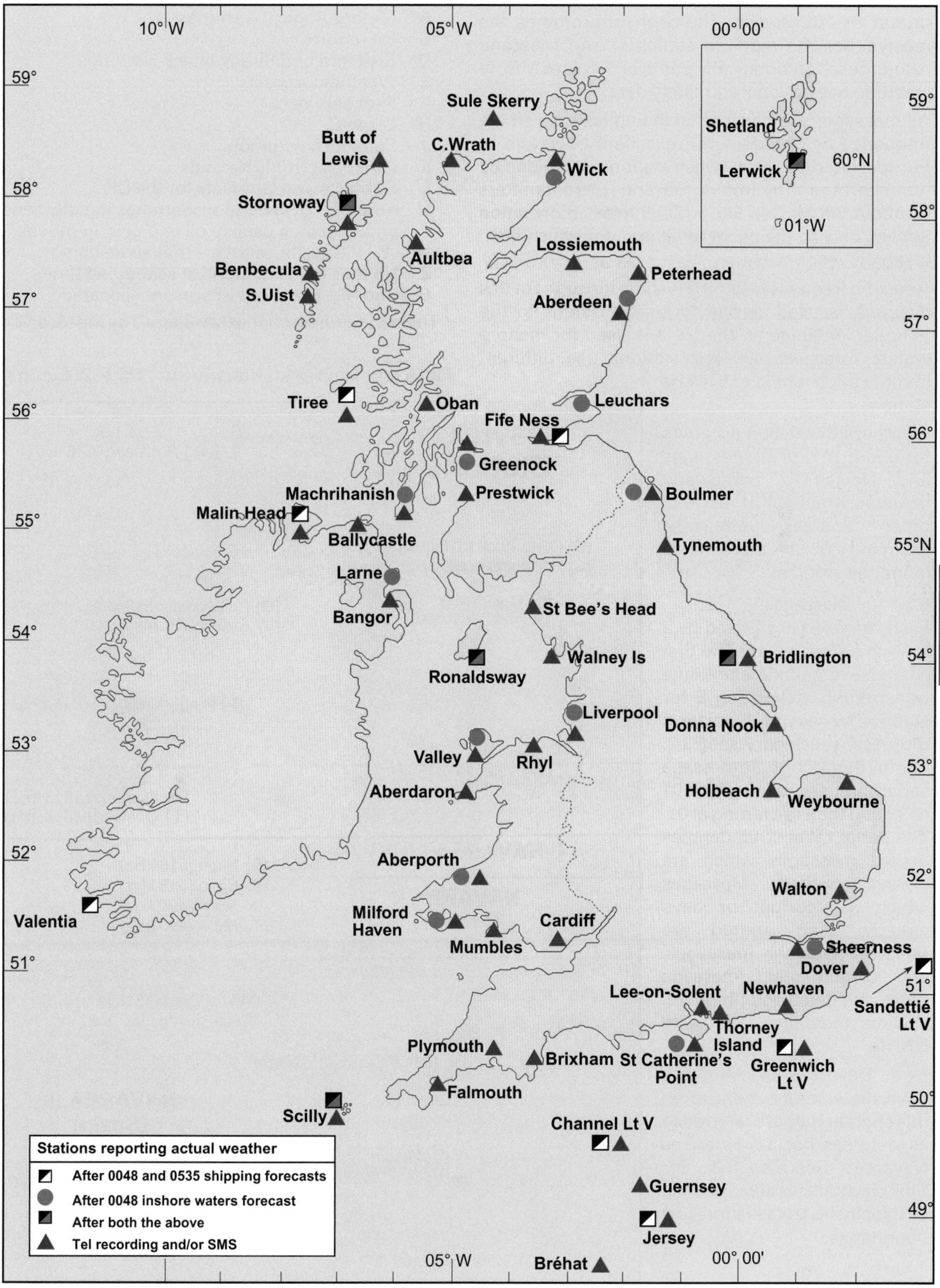
10° W
05° W
00° 00'
59°
58°
57°
56°
55°
54°
53°
52°
51°
55°N
50°
49°
Shetland
Lerwick
60°N
01°W
Sule Skerry
Butt of Lewis
C.Wrath
Wick
Stornoway
Aultbea
Lossiemouth
Peterhead
Benbecula
S.Uist
Aberdeen
Tiree
Oban
Leuchars
Fife Ness
Greenock
Machrihanish
Prestwick
Boulmer
Malin Head
Ballycastle
Tynemouth
Larne
Bangor
St Bee's Head
Ronaldsway
Walney Is
Bridlington
Liverpool
Donna Nook
Valley
Rhyl
Aberdaron
Holbeach
Weybourne
Aberporth
Walton
Valentia
Milford Haven
Cardiff
Mumbles
Sheerness
Dover
Sandettié Lt V
Lee-on-Solent
Newhaven
Thorney Island
Plymouth
Brixham
St Catherine's Point
Greenwich Lt V
Falmouth
Scilly
Channel Lt V
Guernsey
Jersey
Bréhat
Stations reporting actual weather
After 0048 and 0535 shipping forecasts
After 0048 inshore waters forecast
After both the above
Tel recording and/or SMS

6.3 NAVTEX

Navtex uses a dedicated aerial, receiver and integral printer or LCD screen. The user programmes the receiver for the required station(s) and message categories. It automatically prints or displays MSI, ie weather, navigational and safety data.

All messages are transmitted in English on a single frequency of 518 kHz, with excellent coverage of Europe. Interference between stations is avoided by time sharing and by limiting the range of transmitters to about 300M. See Fig 6 (2). Navtex information applies only to the geographic area for which each station is responsible.

A second frequency, 490 kHz (in blue throughout this chapter), is used abroad for transmissions in the national language; in the UK it is used for inshore waters forecasts. 490 kHz stations use different identification letters to 518 kHz stations.

Weather information accounts for about 75% of all messages and Navtex is particularly valuable when out of range of other sources, otherwise occupied or if there is a language problem.

6.3.1 Messages

Each message is prefixed by a four-character group. The first character is the code letter of the transmitting station (eg **E** for Niton). The second character is the message category, see 6.3.2. The third and fourth are message serial numbers, running from 01 to 99 and then re-starting at 01. The serial number 00 denotes urgent messages which are always printed. Messages which are corrupt or have already been printed are rejected. Weather messages, and certain other message types, are dated and timed. All Navtex messages end with NNNN.

Note: Navareas and Metareas have the same boundaries; in this chapter they are referred to as Metareas, but in chapter 3 as Navareas. See also 6.2.5 for Shipping forecast areas and Fig. 6 (3) for Inshore waters forecast boundaries.

6.3.2 Message categories

A* Navigational warnings
B* Meteorological warnings
C Ice reports
D* SAR info and Piracy attack warnings
E Weather forecasts
F Pilot service
H Loran-C
J Satellite navigation
K Other electronic Navaids
L Subfacts and Gunfacts for the UK
V Amplifying navigation warnings initially sent under A; plus weekly oil and gas rig moves.
W – **Y** Special service – trial allocation
Z No messages on hand at scheduled time
G, I and **M** – **U** are not at present allocated

* These categories cannot be rejected by the receiver.

Fig. 6 (2) Navtex stations/areas – UK & W Europe

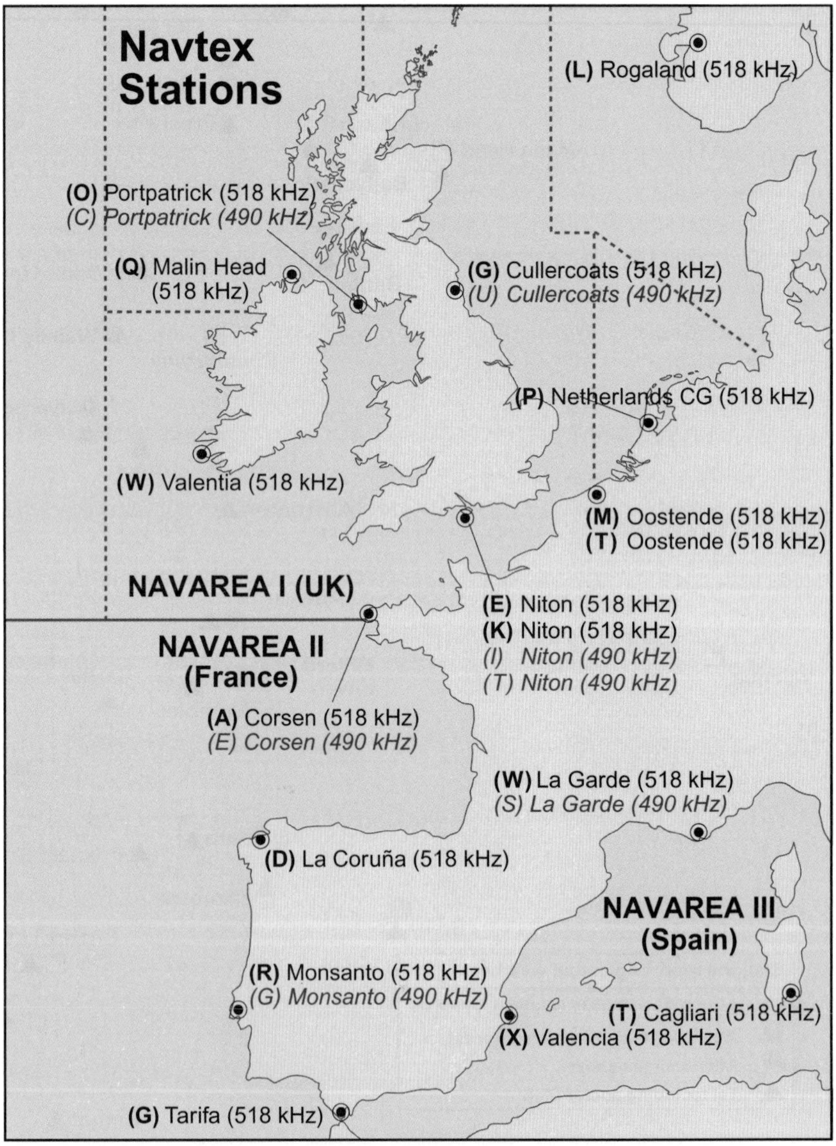
Navtex Stations
(L) Rogaland (518 kHz)
(O) Portpatrick (518 kHz)
(C) Portpatrick (490 kHz)
(Q) Malin Head (518 kHz)
(G) Cullercoats (518 kHz)
(U) Cullercoats (490 kHz)
(P) Netherlands CG (518 kHz)
(W) Valentia (518 kHz)
(M) Oostende (518 kHz)
(T) Oostende (518 kHz)
NAVAREA I (UK)
(E) Niton (518 kHz)
(K) Niton (518 kHz)
(I) Niton (490 kHz)
(T) Niton (490 kHz)
NAVAREA II (France)
(A) Corsen (518 kHz)
(E) Corsen (490 kHz)
(W) La Garde (518 kHz)
(S) La Garde (490 kHz)
(D) La Coruña (518 kHz)
NAVAREA III (Spain)
(R) Monsanto (518 kHz)
(G) Monsanto (490 kHz)
(T) Cagliari (518 kHz)
(X) Valencia (518 kHz)
(G) Tarifa (518 kHz)

6.3.3 UK 518 kHz stations

The times (UT) of weather messages are in bold; the times of an extended outlook (a further 2 or 3 days beyond the shipping forecast period) are in italics. The Sea Areas covered follow the sequence on page 113.

G –	**Cullercoats**	*0100*	0500	**0900**	1300	1700	**2100**
	Fair Isle clockwise to Thames, excluding N & S Utsire, Fisher and German Bight.						
O –	**Portpatrick**	*0220*	**0620**	1020	1420	**1820**	2220
	Lundy clockwise to SE Iceland.						
E –	**Niton**	*0040*	0440	**0840**	1240	1640	**2040**
	Thames clockwise to Fastnet, excluding Trafalgar.						

6.3.4 UK 490 kHz stations

These provide forecasts for the Inshore waters (12M offshore) of the UK, including Shetland, plus a national 3 day outlook for inshore waters. Times are UT.

U –	**Cullercoats**	Cape Wrath to North Foreland	0720		1920	
C –	**Portpatrick**	St David's Head to Cape Wrath		0820		2020
I –	**Niton**	The Wash to Colwyn Bay	0520		1720	

6.3.5 Navtex coverage abroad

Selected Navtex stations in Metareas I to III, with their identity codes and transmission times are listed below. Times of weather messages are shown in **bold**. Gale warnings are usually transmitted 4 hourly.

METAREA I (Co-ordinator – UK)		**Transmission times (UT)**					
K –	**Niton** (Note 1)	0140	0540	0940	1340	1740	2140
T –	**Niton** (Note 2)	0310	**0710**	1110	1510	**1910**	2310
W –	**Valentia**, Eire (Note 3)	0340	**0740**	**1140**	1540	**1940**	**2340**
Q –	**Malin Head**, Eire (Note 3)	0240	**0640**	**1040**	1440	**1840**	**2240**
P –	**Netherlands CG**, Den Helder	**0230**	0630	1030	**1430**	1830	2230
M –	**Oostende**, Belgium (Note 4)	0200	0600	1000	1400	1800	2200
T –	**Oostende**, Belgium (Note 5)	0310	**0710**	1110	1510	**1910**	2310
L –	**Rogaland**, Norway	**0150**	0550	0950	**1350**	1750	2150

Note 1 In English, no weather; only Nav warnings for the French coast from Cap Gris Nez to Île de Bréhat.
2 In French, weather info (and Nav warnings) for sea areas Humber to Ouessant (Plymouth).
3 See 6.7b and Fig. 6(4) for the Atlantic areas covered at 1040, 2240 by 'Q' and at 1140, 2340 by 'W'.
4 No weather information, only Nav warnings for NavArea Juliett.
5 Forecasts and strong wind warnings for Thames and Dover, plus nav info for the Belgian coast.

METAREA II (Co-ordinator – France)							
A –	**Corsen**, Le Stiff, France	**0000**	0400	0800	**1200**	1600	2000
E –	**Corsen**, Le Stiff, France (In French)	0040	0440	**0840**	1240	1640	**2040**
D –	**Coruña**, Spain	0030	0430	**0830**	1230	1630	**2030**
R –	**Monsanto**, Portugal	**0250**	**0650**	**1050**	**1450**	**1850**	**2250**
G –	**Monsanto**, Portugal (In Portuguese)	**0100**	**0500**	**0900**	**1300**	**1700**	**2100**
F –	**Horta**, Açores, Portugal	**0050**	**0450**	**0850**	**1250**	**1650**	**2050**
J –	**Horta**, Açores, Portugal (In Portuguese)	**0130**	**0530**	**0930**	**1330**	**1730**	**2130**
G –	**Tarifa**, Spain (English & Spanish)	0100	0500	**0900**	1300	1700	**2100**
I –	**Las Palmas**, Islas Canarias, Spain	0120	0520	**0920**	**1320**	**1720**	2120
METAREA III (Co-ordinator – Spain)							
X –	**Valencia**, Spain (English & Spanish)	0350	**0750**	1150	1550	**1950**	2350
W –	**La Garde**, (Toulon), France	0340	0740	**1140**	1540	1940	**2340**
S –	**La Garde**, (Toulon), France (In French)	0300	**0700**	1100	1500	**1900**	2300

Fig. 6 (3) Inshore waters forecasts – Area boundaries used by the Coastguard

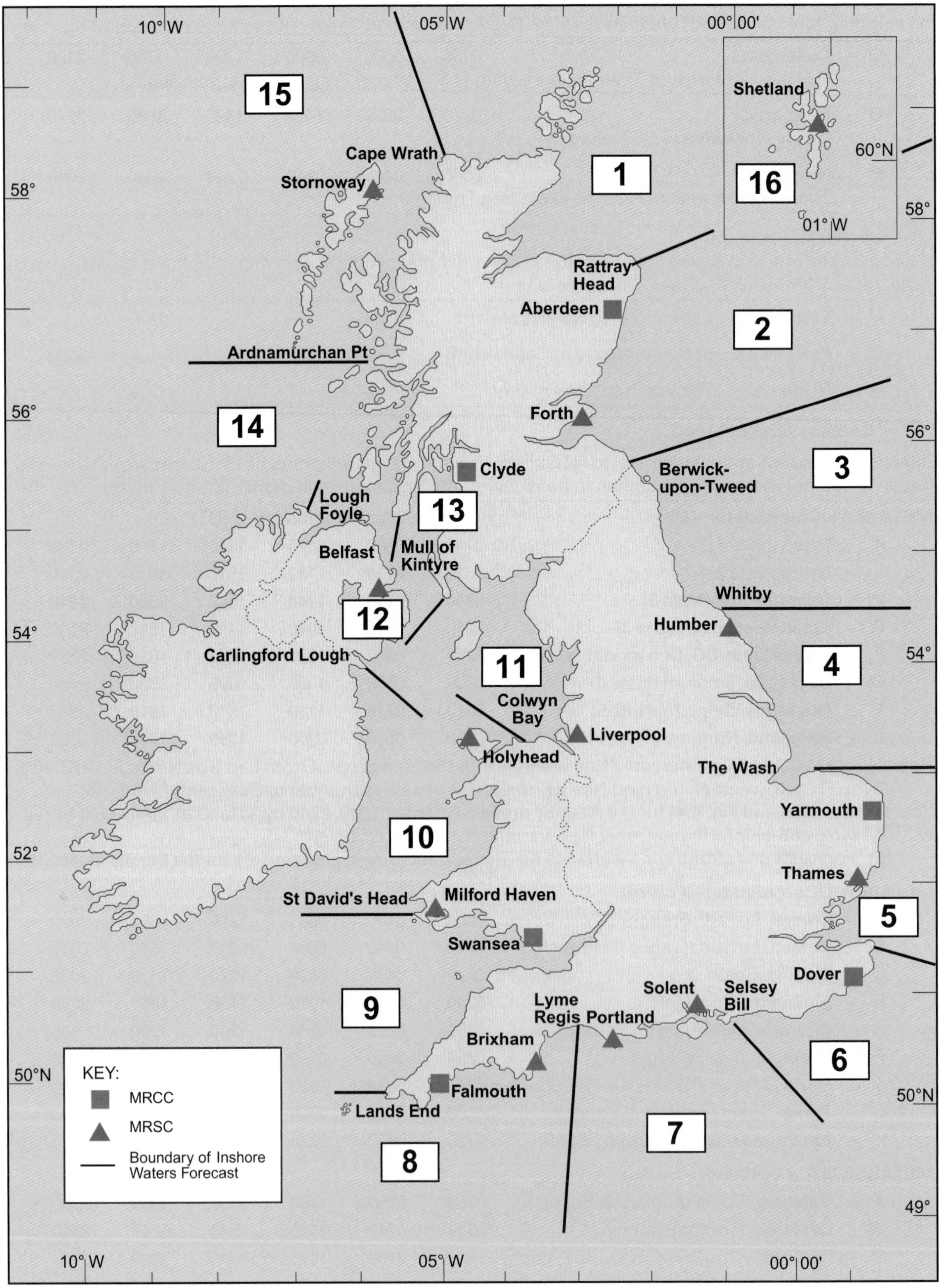

10° W
05° W
00° 00'
15
Cape Wrath
Stornoway
1
Shetland
16
60°N
01° W
58°
Rattray Head
Aberdeen
2
Ardnamurchan Pt
56°
14
Forth
Clyde
Berwick-upon-Tweed
3
Lough Foyle
13
Belfast
Mull of Kintyre
Whitby
Humber
12
54°
Carlingford Lough
11
4
Colwyn Bay
Liverpool
Holyhead
The Wash
Yarmouth
10
52°
Thames
St David's Head
Milford Haven
5
Swansea
Dover
9
Solent
Selsey Bill
Lyme Regis
Portland
Brixham
6
50°N
Falmouth
Lands End
7
8
49°
KEY:
MRCC
MRSC
Boundary of Inshore Waters Forecast

6.4 BROADCASTS BY HM COASTGUARD

6.4.1 Shipping and Inshore waters forecasts

Coastguard Centres routinely broadcast the Shipping forecast for their adjacent sea areas, twice daily at the times given below in italics.

Forecasts for local Inshore waters are broadcast every 4 hours as given below. Fig. 6(3) shows the boundaries and defining features of the 16 areas used by the CG for inshore waters forecasts. In the forecast these areas are referred to by defining places/headlands.

VHF Channels 10, 23, 73, 84 and 86 are used for all such broadcasts, after an announcement on Ch 16 of which VHF Channel to select. See also 6.4.3 below.

The following MF frequencies are also used, after an announcement on 2182 kHz: **Falmouth** 2226 kHz; **Solent** 1641 kHz; **Yarmouth** 1869 kHz; **Humber** 2226 kHz; **Aberdeen** 2226 kHz; **Shetland** 1770 kHz; **Stornoway** 1743 kHz; **Clyde** 1883 kHz; **Holyhead** 1880 kHz; and **Milford Haven** 1767 kHz.

Gale or strong wind warnings, weather messages and shipping forecasts are broadcast after initial announcements on VHF Ch 16 and 2182 kHz.

6.4.2 Actual weather

On request, CG Centres may report the actual weather in their vicinity. The CG stress that they are not qualified Met observers and such reports may be no more than a look out of the widow or originate from passing ships and yachts.

BROADCASTS OF SHIPPING AND INSHORE WATERS FORECASTS BY THE COASTGUARD

Coastguard.	Shipping forecast areas	Inshore waters forecast areas	Broadcast times UT					
South Coast								
Falmouth	Plymouth, Lundy, Fastnet, Sole, FitzRoy	8 & 9	0140	0540	*0940*	1340	1740	*2140*
Brixham	Plymouth, Portland	8	0050	0450	*0850*	1250	1650	*2050*
Portland	Plymouth, Portland, Wight	7 & 8	0220	0620	*1020*	1420	1820	*2220*
Solent	Portland, Wight	6 & 7	0040	0440	*0840*	1240	1640	*2040*
Dover	Thames, Dover, Wight	5, 6 & 7	0105	0505	*0905*	1305	1707	*2105*
East Coast								
Thames	Thames, Dover	5	0010	0410	*0810*	1210	1610	*2010*
Yarmouth	Humber, Thames	5	0040	0440	*0840*	1240	1640	*2040*
Humber	Humber, Tyne, Dogger, German Bight	3 & 4	0340	*0740*	1140	1540	*1940*	2340
Forth	Forth, Tyne, Dogger, Forties	2	0205	0605	*1005*	1405	1805	*2205*
Aberdeen	Fair I, Cromarty, Forth, Forties	1 & 2	0320	*0720*	1120	1520	*1920*	2320
Shetland	Faeroes, Fair I, Viking	1 & 16	0105	0505	*0905*	1305	1705	*2105*
West Coast								
Stornoway	Fair I, Faeroes, Bailey, Hebrides, Malin, Rockall	15	0110	0510	*0910*	1310	1710	*2110*
Clyde	Bailey, Hebrides, Rockall, Malin	13, 14 & 15	0020	0420	*0820*	1220	1620	*2020*
Belfast	Irish Sea, Malin	12	0305	*0705*	1105	1505	*1905*	2305
Liverpool	Irish Sea, Malin	11	0210	0610	*1010*	1410	1810	*2210*
Holyhead	Irish Sea	10	0235	*0635*	1035	1435	*1835*	2235
Milford Haven	Lundy, Irish Sea, Fastnet	9 & 10	0335	*0735*	1135	1535	*1935*	2335
Swansea	Lundy, Irish Sea, Fastnet	9	0005	0405	*0805*	1205	1605	*2005*

6.4.3 CG transmitters and VHF channels

The VHF channels/positions of remote transmitters used for the broadcasts in 6.4.1 are listed below. Thus a relevant channel can be pre-selected and/or verified by prior announcement on Ch 16.

FALMOUTH MRCC		
Trevose Head	86	50°33′N 05°02′W
St Mary's	23	49°56′N 06°18′W
Lizard	86	49°58′N 05°12′W
Falmouth	23	50°09′N 05°06′W
Brixham MRSC		
Fowey	86	50°20′N 04°38′W
Rame Head	10	50°19′N 04°13′W
Salcombe	84	50°15′N 03°45′W
East Prawle	73	50°13′N 03°42′W
Dartmouth	23	50°21′N 03°35′W
Berry Head	86	50°24′N 03°29′W
Teignmouth	10	50°34′N 03°32′W
Beer Head	84	50°41′N 03°05′W
Portland MRSC		
Beer Head	86	50°41′N 03°05′W
Bincleaves (Weymouth)	73	50°36′N 02°27′W
Grove Pt (Portland Bill)	10	50°33′N 02°25′W
Hengistbury Head	73	50°43′N 01°46′W
Solent MRSC		
Needles	86	50°39′N 01°35′W
Boniface (Ventnor, IoW)	23	50°36′N 01°12′W
Newhaven	86	50°47′N 00°03′E
DOVER MRCC (See Chapter 7 for CNIS broadcasts)		
Fairlight (Hastings)	23	50°52′N 00°39′E
Langdon Battery (Dover)	86	51°08′N 01°21′E
North Foreland	86	51°23′N 01°27′E

Thames MRSC		
Shoeburyness	23	51°31′N 00°47′E
Bradwell (R Blackwater)	86	51°44′N 00°53′E
Walton-on-the-Naze	73	51°51′N 01°17′E
Bawdsey (R Deben)	84	52°00′N 01°25′E
YARMOUTH MRCC		
Lowestoft	86	52°29′N 01°46′E
Yarmouth	84	52°36′N 01°43′E
Trimingham (Cromer)	23	52°54′N 01°21′E
Langham (Blakeney)	86	52°57′N 00°58′E
Guy's Head (Wisbech)	84	52°48′N 00°13′E
Skegness	23	53°09′N 00°21′E
Humber MRSC		
Easington (Spurn Hd)	84	53°39′N 00°06′E
Flamborough Head	23	54°07′N 00°05′W
Whitby	84	54°29′N 00°36′W
Hartlepool	23	54°42′N 01°10′W
Cullercoats (Blyth)	84	55°04′N 01°28′W
Newton	23	55°31′N 01°37′W
Forth MRSC		
St Abbs/Cross Law	86	55°54′N 02°12′W
Craigkelly (Burntisland)	86	56°04′N 03°14′W
Fife Ness	23	56°17′N 02°35′W
Tay Law (Dundee)	86	56°28′N 02°59′W
Inverbervie	23	56°51′N 02°16′W
ABERDEEN MRCC		
Greg Ness (Aberdeen)	86	57°08′N 02°03′W
Peterhead	86	57°31′N 01°46′W
Windyheads Hill	23	57°39′N 02°14′W
Banff	23	57°38′N 02°31′W
Foyers (Loch Ness)	86	57°14′N 04°31′W
Rosemarkie (Cromarty)	86	57°38′N 04°05′W
Thrumster (Wick)	84	58°24′N 03°07′W
Noss Head (Wick)	84	58°29′N 03°03′W
Dunnet Head (Thurso)	84	58°40′N 03°22′W
Ben Tongue	23	58°30′N 04°24′W
Durness (Loch Eriboll)	23	58°34′N 04°44′W
Shetland MRSC		
Wideford Hill (Kirkwall)	23	58°59′N 03°01′W
Fitful Head (Sumburgh)	10	59°54′N 01°23′W
Shetland MRSC	84	60°10′N 01°08′W
Collafirth (Sullom Voe)	73	60°32′N 01°23′W
Saxa Vord (Unst)	23	60°42′N 00°51′W
Stornoway MRSC		
Butt of Lewis	10	58°28′N 06°14′W
Portnaguran (Stornoway)	84	58°15′N 06°10′W
Forsneval (W Lewis)	73	58°13′N 07°00′W
Melvaig (L. Ewe)	67	57°50′N 05°47′W
Rodel (S Harris)	10	57°45′N 06°57′W
Clettreval (N Uist)	73	57°37′N 07°26′W
Skriag (Portree, Skye)	67	57°23′N 06°15′W
Drumfearn (SE Skye)	84	57°12′N 05°48′W
Barra	10	57°01′N 07°30′W
Arisaig (S of Mallaig)	73	56°55′N 06°50′W
CLYDE MRCC		
Glengorm (N Mull)	23	56°38′N 06°08′W
Tiree	73	56°31′N 06°57′W
Torosay (E Mull)	10	56°27′N 05°43′W
Clyde MRCC	23	55°58′N 04°48′W
South Knapdale (L Fyne)	23	55°55′N 05°28′W
Kilchiaran (W Islay)	84	55°46′N 06°27′W
Lawhill (Ardrossan)	86	55°42′N 04°50′W
Ru Stafnish (Kintyre)	10	55°22′N 05°32′W
Belfast MRSC		
Navar (Lower L. Erne)	73	54°28′N 07°54′W
Limvady (L. Foyle)	84	55°06′N 06°53′W
West Torr (Fair Head)	73	55°12′N 06°06′W
Black Mountain (Belfast)	86	54°35′N 06°01′W
Orlock Point (Bangor)	84	54°40′N 05°35′W
Slievemartin (Rostrevor)	73	54°06′N 06°10′W
Liverpool MRSC		
Caldbeck (Carlisle)	10	54°46′N 03°07′W
Snaefell (Isle of Man)	86	54°16′N 04°28′W
Langthwaite (Lancaster)	73	54°02′N 02°46′W
Moel-y-Parc (Anglesey)	23	53°13′N 04°28′W
Holyhead MRSC		
Great Ormes Head	84	53°20′N 03°51′W
Holyhead MRSC	10	53°19′N 04°38′W
Mynydd Rhiw	73	52°50′N 04°38′W
Milford Haven MRSC		
Blaenplwyf (Aberystwyth)	84	52°22′N 04°06′W
Dinas Hd (Fishguard)	86	52°00′N 04°54′W
St Ann's Head	84	51°40′N 05°11′W
Tenby (Monkstone)	86	51°42′N 04°41′W
SWANSEA MRCC		
Mumbles	84	51°34′N 03°59′W
St. Hillary (Barry)	86	51°27′N 03°25′W
Severn Bridges	84	51°36′N 02°38′W
Combe Martin	86	51°12′N 04°03′W
Hartland Point	84	51°01′N 04°31′W

6.5 FORECASTERS

Met Office forecasters offer a H24 telephone briefing from the UK or abroad on the general synopsis, weather windows and outlook, plus questions & answers; ☎ + 44 (0) 8700 767 888, £17·00 flat rate by credit card. For a Fax forecast, 📠 + 44 (0) 8700 767 888, £3 by credit card.

Call a forecaster in Gibraltar ☎ + 44 (0) 8700 767 818 for a briefing (5-10 mins on average) on weather in the Med or Canaries. Pay £15·00 flat rate by credit card.

6.6 HF RADIO FACSIMILE BROADCASTS

Fax machines able to receive pictorial images such as weathercharts are useful aboard yachts and in marina offices. Isobaric charts (actual and forecast), sea and swell charts, satellite cloud images, sea temperature charts and wind charts are all of direct interest to the blue water yachtsman. For details of foreign stations see the *Admiralty List of Radio Signals, Vol 3.*

6.6.1 Northwood, London: HF Radio-Fax

Frequencies (H24): 2618·5, 4610, 8040,11086·5 kHz. Area: Eastern N Atlantic and western Med. This service, provided by the RN Fleet Met Centre, may be withdrawn without notice for military reasons.

Schedule of selected broadcasts (UT)

0000 72h surface prognosis
0100 72h surface prognosis
0200 72h surface prognosis
0236 Schedule
0300 Surface analysis
0348 Gale summary
0400 Surface analysis
0500 Surface analysis
0524 24h surface prognosis
0600 Gale summary
0700 Gale summary
0748 24h significant wind areas
0800 24h surface prognosis
0812 48 h significant wind areas
0824 72h significant wind areas
0836 96h significant wind areas
0848 48h surface prognosis
0900 Surface analysis
0912 72h surface prognosis
0924 24h sea swell
1000 24h surface prognosis
1100 Surface analysis
1124 96h surface prognosis
1136 120h surface prognosis
1148 Gale summary
1200 Surface analysis
1300 24h surface prognosis
1324 24h Poor visibility
1400 72h surface prognosis
1424 Schedule
1500 Surface analysis
1536 Ocean frontal positions (Thurs)
1548 Gale summary
1600 48h surface prognosis
1700 48h surface prognosis
1736 24h surface prognosis
1800 Surface analysis
1900 Gale summary
1912 24h sea swell
2000 48h surface prognosis
2012 72h surface prognosis
2024 96h surface prognosis
2036 120h surface prognosis
2100 Surface analysis
2112 24h significant wind areas
2124 48h significant wind areas
2136 72h significant wind areas
2148 96h significant wind areas
2200 24h surface prognosis
2300 Surface analysis

6.7 HIGH SEAS BULLETINS

In the N Atlantic part of Metarea 1, which extends out to 35°W [see Fig. 6(4) below], weather information is available from:

a. SafetyNET which is a part of GMDSS providing MSI to vessels in A3 Sea Areas. Goonhilly Coast Earth Station (CES) transmits Met information via the **AOR-E** and **AOR-W** Inmarsat-C satellites at 0930 & 2130 UT. (See also Fig 6(5) for MetArea II SafetyNET areas).

b. Navtex stations at Malin Head (Q) and Valentia (W) covering the E Northern and E Central sections, and sea areas Sole, Shannon, Rockall and Bailey.

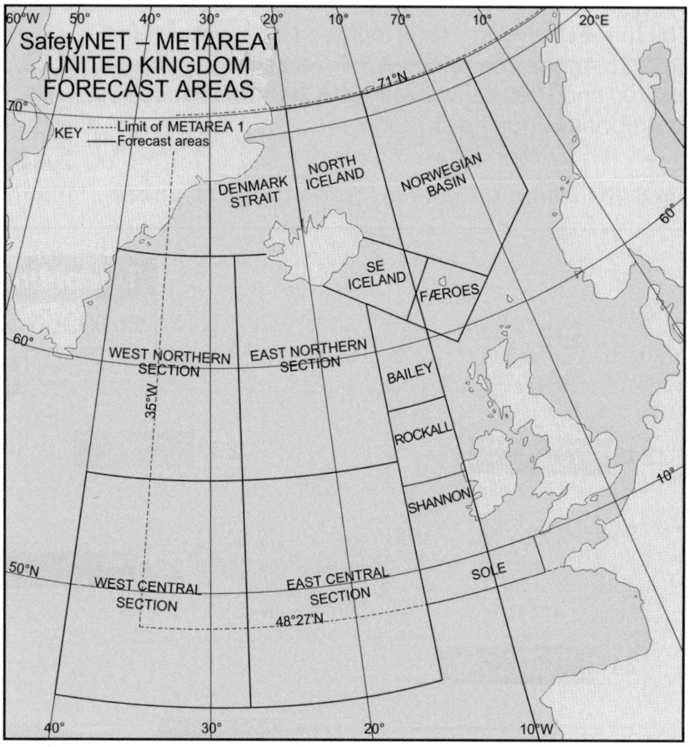
SafetyNET – METAREA I
UNITED KINGDOM
FORECAST AREAS
KEY
Limit of METAREA 1
Forecast areas
DENMARK STRAIT
NORTH ICELAND
NORWEGIAN BASIN
SE ICELAND
FÆROES
WEST NORTHERN SECTION
EAST NORTHERN SECTION
BAILEY
ROCKALL
SHANNON
SOLE
WEST CENTRAL SECTION
EAST CENTRAL SECTION
35°W
48°27'N
71°N
70°
60°
50°N
60°W
50°
40°
30°
20°
10°
0°
10°
20°E
10°W

Fig. 6 (4) Metarea I – SafetyNET forecast areas

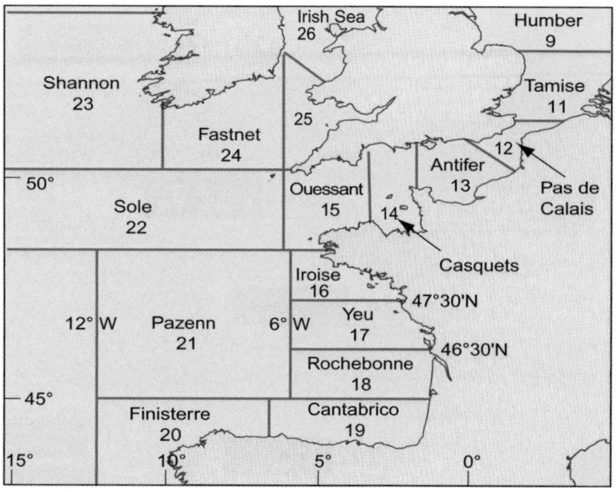
Irish Sea
26
Humber
9
Shannon
23
Tamise
11
Fastnet
24
25
12
Antifer
13
Pas de Calais
50°
Sole
22
Ouessant
15
14
Casquets
Iroise
16
47°30'N
12°W
Pazenn
21
6°W
Yeu
17
46°30'N
Rochebonne
18
45°
Finisterre
20
Cantabrico
19
15°
10°
5°
0°

Fig. 6 (5) Metarea II – SafetyNET forecast areas

6.8 WEATHER BY TELEPHONE

Marinecall offers 3 types of recorded forecasts as shown below in 6.8.1, 6.8.2 and 6.8.3.

6.8.1 5-day forecasts for Inshore waters

For any of 16 UK inshore areas, call **09066 526 + the Area number** shown in green on Fig. 6(6). For a National inshore waters forecast for 3 to 5 days dial the suffix 234. 09066 calls cost 60p/min from a landline. Calls from mobiles may be subject to network charges.

Forecasts cover the waters out to 12M offshore for up to 5 days and include: General situation, strong wind or gale warnings in force, wind, weather, visibility, sea state, max air temp and meansea temp.

The initial 2 day forecast is followed by a forecast for days 3 & 4 and outlook for day 5. Forecasts are updated at 0700 and 1900 daily. Area 250 (Channel Islands) is additionally updated at 1300.

The local inshore forecast for Shetland is only available from Shetland CG on ☎ 01595 692976.

6.8.2 Current weather

Current weather, updated hourly, gives summaries for next 6 hours at over 200 locations around the UK. Dial 09066 526 + any number shown in green on Fig. 6(6) – then select Option 2.

6.8.3 Forecasts for Offshore planning

For 2 to 5-day planning forecasts for offshore areas, updated 0800 daily, call **09066 526** + the number shown in red on Fig. 6(6), ie: **251** English Channel; **252** Southern North Sea; **253** Irish Sea; **254** Biscay; **255** NW Scotland; **256** Northern North Sea.

6.8.4 Contacting Marinecall

For further information contact: Marinecall Customer Services, iTouch (UK) Ltd, Avalon House, 57-63 Scrutton House, London EC2A 4PF. ☎ 0871 200 3985; 📠 0870 600 4229. www.marinecall.co.uk marinecall@itouch.co.uk

Fig 6 (6) Inshore & Offshore forecasts by Telephone

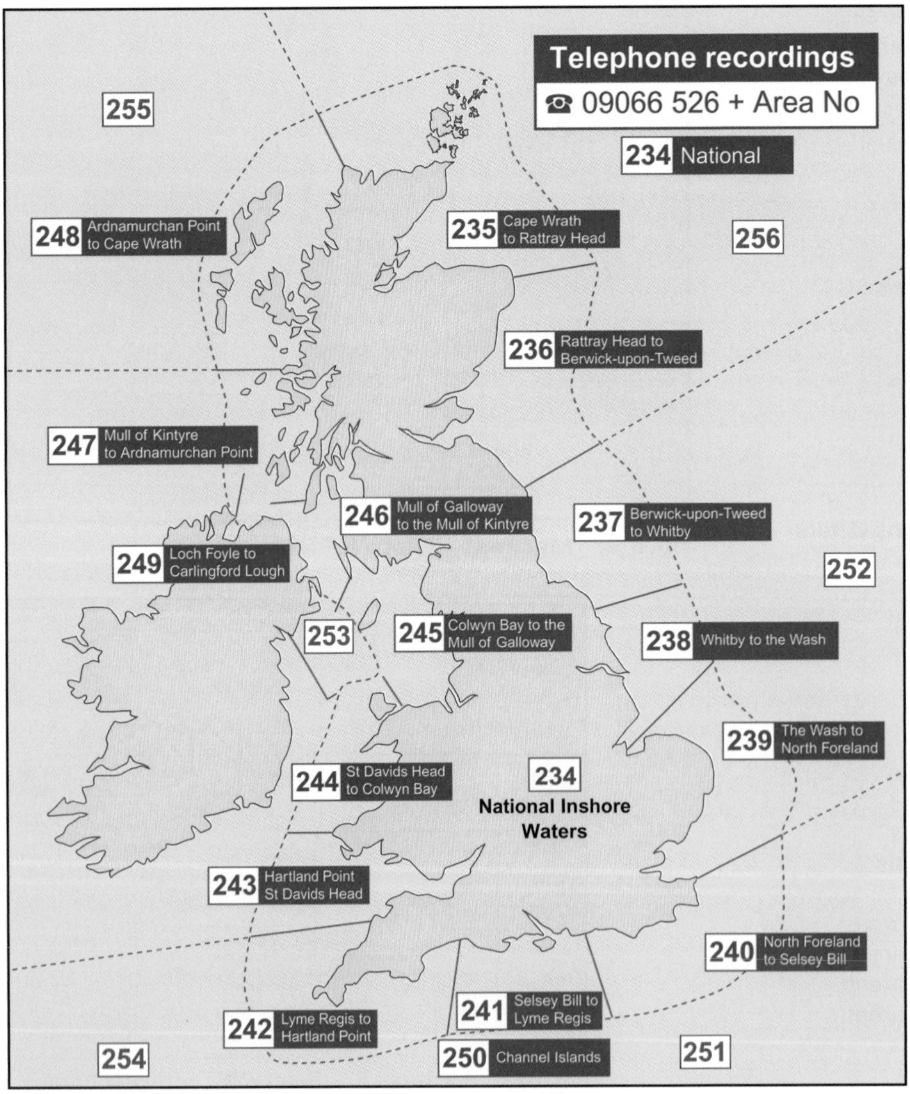
Telephone recordings
☎ 09066 526 + Area No
234 National
255
256
248 Ardnamurchan Point to Cape Wrath
235 Cape Wrath to Rattray Head
236 Rattray Head to Berwick-upon-Tweed
247 Mull of Kintyre to Ardnamurchan Point
246 Mull of Galloway to the Mull of Kintyre
237 Berwick-upon-Tweed to Whitby
252
249 Loch Foyle to Carlingford Lough
253
245 Colwyn Bay to the Mull of Galloway
238 Whitby to the Wash
239 The Wash to North Foreland
244 St Davids Head to Colwyn Bay
234
National Inshore Waters
243 Hartland Point St Davids Head
240 North Foreland to Selsey Bill
241 Selsey Bill to Lyme Regis
242 Lyme Regis to Hartland Point
254
250 Channel Islands
251

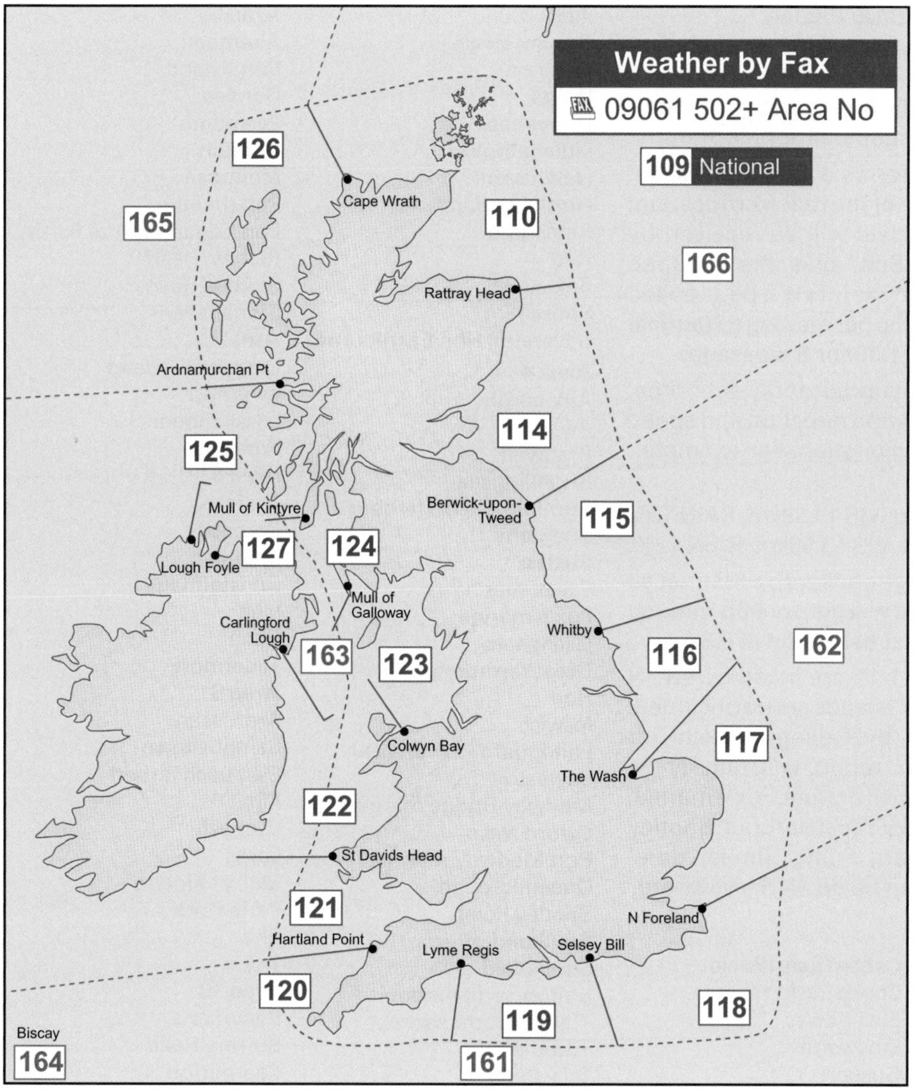
Weather by Fax
09061 502+ Area No
109 National
126
165
Cape Wrath
110
166
Rattray Head
Ardnamurchan Pt
114
125
Berwick-upon-Tweed
115
Mull of Kintyre
127
124
Lough Foyle
Mull of Galloway
Carlingford Lough
Whitby
162
163
123
116
Colwyn Bay
117
The Wash
122
St Davids Head
121
N Foreland
Hartland Point
Lyme Regis
Selsey Bill
120
118
119
Biscay
164
161

Fig. 6 (7) Inshore and Offshore forecast areas and their Fax suffixes

6.9 WEATHER BY FAX

6.9.1 Inshore waters forecasts

These forecasts for up to 48 hrs, plus 2 synoptic charts, are obtained by dialling 09061 502 + the Area No shown in green on Fig. 6 (7). For a National inshore 3-5 day forecast the suffix is 109.

The forecasts include the general situation; gale and strong wind warnings in force; max air temp; sea temp; wind speed/direction; probability and strength of gusts; weather; visibility; sea state; surf; tidal data.

Two levels of service are available:

Standard, at £1/min, which gives a 48 hrs forecast and synoptic chart for today and tomorrow.

Premium at £1.50/min includes the above, plus a tabulated hourly forecast over the next 6 hrs for 4 key places in the Area.

The Fax numbers above and in Fig. 6(7) are for the Premium service.

6.9.2 Offshore forecasts

For 2–5 day forecasts and 48/72/96/120 hour synoptic charts for the offshore Areas shown in red on Fig. 6 (7) dial 09061 502 + Number of the area required.

The forecasts include wind, weather, visibility and sea states, but are briefer than those in 6.9.1. Day 5 is covered by an Outlook.

Two levels of service are available: Standard, at £1/min, which gives a planning forecast and four synoptic charts for days 2-5.

Premium at £1.50/min includes the above, plus four diagrams of significant wave height contours in the Area. The Fax numbers above and in Fig. 6(7) are for the Premium service.

6.9.3 Marinecall FaxDirect

This offers discounted rates to regular users of the Premium services. For example over 6 months, 1 Fax/week costs £68.15 inc VAT; 3 faxes/week £188; and 7 faxes/week £405.38.

6.10 WEATHER BY MOBILE 'PHONE

6.10.1 Short Message Service (SMS, or texting)

'Marinecall Mobile' using SMS provides:
The current weather, plus the forecast for 6 hrs later, at any one of 170 coastal locations, all updated hourly.

To obtain this info, which forms a single message, type **Nautical** plus the name of the required location; then send it to 83141; the data will be received by return. Or type **Nautical Sub**, plus the required location, send it to 83141 and the info will be supplied daily by 0900. The charge is 25p per message; **Nautical Sub**(scribers) are billed at £1.50 for 6 messages.

These reports/forecasts contain: Location, date, time; max temperature °C; mean wind direction and speed (kt); vis in km; % risk of precipitation. For example:

Exmouth: 1/4/05
10am: 11c, WD 250d, WS 12kt, VIS 17.59km, RAIN 10%
4pm: 12c, WD 290d, WS 14kt, VIS 13.50km, RAIN 12%.

For convenience the message ends with a Marinecall Tel No; by pressing 'Dial' you will get, for 60p/minute, the 2-5 day recorded forecast described at 6.8.1.

Coastal locations in Areas 1-11 are listed below; N Ireland, Eire and the Channel Islands are not included. Readers will find that simply by dialling 'Ipswich', for example, a single weather report will quickly be obtained that is valid for Ipswich marina, Fox's marina, Woolverstone marina, Suffolk Yacht Harbour, Shotley Point marina and Landguard Point. Similar time-saving Collective Names can be applied elsewhere.

Area 1
Anvil Point
Brixham
Dart marina
Darthaven
Exmouth
Falmouth
Fowey
Helford River
Lizard Point
Longships
Lyme Regis
Mayflower marina
Newton Ferrers, R Yealm
Penzance
Plymouth Yacht Haven
Portland Bill
Queen Anne's Battery
Salcombe
Start Point
Sutton Harbour
Torquay
Weymouth

Area 2
Bembridge Harbour
Birdham Pool
Buckler's Hard
Chichester
Christchurch
Cobbs Quay (Poole)
Cowes Yacht Haven
East Cowes
Emsworth
Gosport
Hamble Point
Haslar
Hythe
Island Harbour, R Medina
Lymington marina, Berthon
Lymington Yacht Haven
Mercury Yacht harbour
Swanwick marina
Needles Fairway
Northney marina
Ocean Village
Poole Town Quay
Port Hamble
Port Solent
Ryde
Salterns
Shamrock Quay
Southsea
Sparkes Yacht harbour
St Catherines Point
Town Quay (Southampton)
Wootton Creek
Yarmouth, Isle of Wight

Area 3
Beachy Head
Brighton
Dover
Dungeness
Littlehampton
Newhaven
North Foreland
Ramsgate
Rye
Selsey Bill
Shoreham
Sovereign Hbr, Eastbourne

Area 4
Aldeburgh
Allington
Bradwell
Brightlingsea
Burnham Yacht Harbour
Chatham
Cuxton
Essex marina
Fox's marina
Gillingham
Great Yarmouth
Hoo
Ipswich
Landguard Pt (Harwich)
Lowestoft
Medway Bridge marina
Orford Ness
Port Medway marina
Queenborough
Shotley Point
Southend-on-sea
Southwold
Suffolk Yacht harbour
Tidemill Yacht harbour
Titchmarsh
Tollesbury
Whitstable
Woolverstone

Area 5
Amble
Berwick
Blyth
Boston
Bridlington
Cromer
Flamborough Head
Grimsby
Hartlepool
Holy Island
Hull
King's Lynn
Royal Quays marina, R Tyne
Spurn Head
St Peter's marina, R Tyne
Sunderland
Wells-next-the-Sea
Whitby

Area 6
Aberdeen
Burntisland
Dundee
Eyemouth
Granton
Montrose
Peterhead
Port Edgar (Firth of Forth)
Rattray Head
St Abbs Head
Stonehaven

Area 7
Duncansby Head
Inverness
Lossiemouth
Whitehills

Area 8
Ardfern
Corpach
Craobh
Dunstaffnage
Iona
Oban
Tobermory

Area 9
Ardrossan
Campbeltown
East Loch Tarbert
Kip
Lamlash
Largs
Mull of Kintyre
Portpatrick
Rhu
Troon

Area 10
Beaumaris
Burrow Head
Caernarfon
Conwy
Glasson Dock
Holyhead
Kirkcudbright
Liverpool
Maryport
Port Dinorwic
Preston
Whitehaven
Wyre Dock (Fleetwood)

Area 11
Abersoch
Aberystwyth
Bardsey Island
Bristol Floating Hbr
Milford Dock (Haven)
Neyland (Milford Haven)
Padstow
Penarth (Cardiff)
Portishead
Pwllheli
South Bishop (Lt ho)
Swansea

6.11 OTHER WEATHER SOURCES

6.11.1 Internet

The UK Met Office site at **www.metoffice.com** has extensive weather information, including 2 day and 3 – 5 day inshore forecasts, 2 –5 day planning data, shipping forecasts, gale warnings, coastal reports, surface pressure charts and satellite images.

A pre-paid 'ticket' system (£10 for 20 tickets) pays for services used (MetWEB). To open a credit card account call ☎ 0845 300 0300 [+44 (0) 1344 855680 from abroad] or e-mail **sales@metoffice.com**

Foreign Met Offices are a further mine of information and their websites, e-mail and postal addresses are listed in Chapter 1, 1.3.

6.11.2 Press

Some national and regional papers include a synoptic chart which, in the absence of any other chart, can help to interpret the shipping forecast – unless the paper is already out of date when you buy it.

6.11.3 Television

Most TV forecasts show a synoptic chart and satellite pictures – a useful guide to the weather situation. In some remote areas abroad a TV forecast in a bar, cafe or even shop window may be the best or only source of weather information.

In the UK Ceefax (BBC) gives the weather index on page 400, weather warnings on p.405 and inshore waters forecasts on p.409. Teletext (ITN) has general forecasts on page 151, shipping forecasts on page 157 and inshore waters forecasts on page 158. Antiope is the equivalent French system.

6.11.4 Volmet

Volmet is a specialised aviation meteorological service which provides continuous reports of actual weather and/or forecasts for certain civil and military airports. These reports are in a semi-coded format containing aeronautical terms and abbreviations. They are therefore of little practical use to the vast majority of yachtsmen.

Volmet transmits on HF SSB and the Aeronautical VHF band which is not available to yachtsmen on a typical marine VHF radio. Civilian and military HF frequencies are mentioned below for the benefit of those with suitable equipment and a knowledge of QNH, QFE, RVR, CAVOK and the like:

Shannon Volmet broadcasts on: 3413 kHz (HN), 5505 and 8957 kHz (H24) and 13264 kHz (HJ).

The RAF Volmet broadcasts on: 5450 kHz (H24) and 11253 kHz (H24).

For further information on civilian Volmet contact the Civil Aviation Authority. For military Volmet contact No 1 AIDU, RAF Northolt, West End Road, Ruislip, Middlesex HA4 6NG.

C6

6.12 CHANNEL ISLANDS

6.12.1 Jersey Meteorological Department

Call ☎ 0900 665 0022 for the Channel Islands recorded shipping forecast. For Guernsey only, this service is available on ☎ 069 69 88 00. It is chargeable; more detailed information on request ☎ +44 (0) 1534 745550. The forecast includes a general situation, 24hr forecast for wind, weather, visibility, sea state, swell, sea temperature, plus 2 & 4 day outlooks and St Helier tide times/heights. The area is between 50°N, 03°W and the French coast from Cap de la Hague to Ile de Brehat.

6.12.2 Weather information by radio

Jersey Radio 1659 kHz and Ch 25 82
Storm warnings on receipt and at 0307, 0907, 1507 and 2107 UT. Near-gale warnings, synopsis, 24h forecast and outlook for next 24 hrs (Channel Islands south of 50°N and east of 03°W), plus reports from stations are broadcast at 0645[1], 0745[1], 0845[1] LT & 1245, 1845 and 2245 UT. [1] 1 hr earlier when DST in force.

BBC Radio Jersey 1026 kHz and 88·8 MHz
Storm warnings on receipt. Wind info for local waters: Mon-Fri 0725, 0825, 1325, 1725 LT; Sat/Sun 0825. Shipping forecast for local waters: Mon-Fri @ H+00 (0600-1900, after the news) and 0625 & 1825 LT; Sat/Sun @ H+00 (0700-1300, after the news) and 0725 LT.

BBC Radio Guernsey 93·2 MHz, 1116 kHz
Weather bulletins for the waters around Guernsey, Herm and Sark are broadcast Mon-Fri at 0630, 0730 and 0830 LT; Sat/Sun at 0730 and 0830 LT. They contain forecast, synopsis, coastal forecast, storm warnings and wind strength. In the summer coastal reports are included from: Jersey, Guernsey, Alderney, Cap de la Hague, Cherbourg, Dinard, Portland and Chan Lt V.

NATIONAL WEATHER INFORMATION ABROAD

6.13 IRELAND

6.13.1 Irish Coast Radio Stations

Weather bulletins for the Irish Sea and up to 30M off the Irish coast are broadcast on VHF at 0103, 0403, 0703, 1003, 1303, 1603, 1903 & 2203UT after an announcement on Ch 16. Broadcasts are given 1 hour earlier when DST is in force. Bulletins include gale warnings, synopsis and a 24-hour forecast. Stations and VHF Ch, anti-clockwise from Malin Head, are:

MALIN HEAD	23	**Mizen**	04
Glen Head	24	**Bantry**	23
Donegal Bay	02	**Cork**	26
Belmullet	83	**Mine Head**	83
Clifden	26	**Rosslare**	23
Galway	04	**Wicklow Head**	02
Shannon	28	**DUBLIN**	83
VALENTIA	24	**Carlingford**	04

Gale warnings are broadcast on these VHF channels on receipt and at 0033, 0633, 1233 and 1833UT, after an announcement on Ch 16.

Valentia Radio broadcasts forecasts for sea areas Shannon and Fastnet on 1752 kHz at 0833 & 2033 UT, and on request. It also broadcasts gale warnings on 1752 kHz on receipt and at 0303, 0903, 1503 and 2103 (UT) after an announcement on 2182 kHz.

6.13.2 Radio Telefís Éireann (RTE) Radio 1

RTE Radio 1 on 567, 729kHz and FM (88·2-95·2MHz) broadcasts at 0602, 1255, 1655 and 2355LT daily a situation, forecast and coastal reports for Irish coastal waters and the Irish Sea. The forecast includes: wind, weather, vis, swell and outlook for a further 24 hrs.

Coastal reports contain wind, weather, vis, plus pressure (hPa) and tendency, which is described as:

Steady	=	0 - 0·4 hPA
Rising/falling slowly	=	0·5 -1·9
Rising/falling	=	2·0 -3·4
Rising/falling rapidly	=	3·5 -5·9
Rising/falling very rapidly	=	> 6·0.

Amongst the main transmitters and FM freq's are:

East Coast Radio: Kippure 89·1 MHz.
At: Every H+06 (0700-1800 LT) after the news bulletin. Broadcasts a general forecast, storm warnings and wind strength for area Dublin Bay to Arklow Head.

South East Radio: Mount Leinster 89·6 MHz.
At: 0712 LT (Mon-Fri) and every H+30 (0700-1800 LT) H24 after commercial break. Broadcasts a detailed general forecast and synopsis for coastal waters, including storm warnings if adverse weather is forecast.

WLR FM: Faha Ring 95·1 & Carrickferrish 97·5 MHz. At every H+03 and 1315 1815 LT broadcasts a general forecast, gale warnings, wind strength for area from Youghal to Kilmore Quay. Tidal information included from Jun-Sep.

Radio Kerry: Main transmitters: Mullaghanish 90·0 MHz, Three Rock 88·5, Kippure 89·1, Mount Leinster 89·6, Maghera 88·8, Truskmore 88·2, Holywell Hill 89·2 and Clermont Cairn 95·2.

Broadcasts include a general forecast, synopsis, gale warnings and wind strength for the coastal area from Cork to Shannon.

6.13.3 Storm warnings

Gale warnings are broadcast by: RTE Radio 1 on 567, 729 kHz and FM (88·2-95·2MHz) with hourly news bulletins.

Fig. 6 (9) shows the Provinces, headlands, sea areas and CRS which are referred to in weather bulletins. Forecasts for coastal waters cover areas within 30M of the shore. The Irish Sea covers the open waters of the area shown.

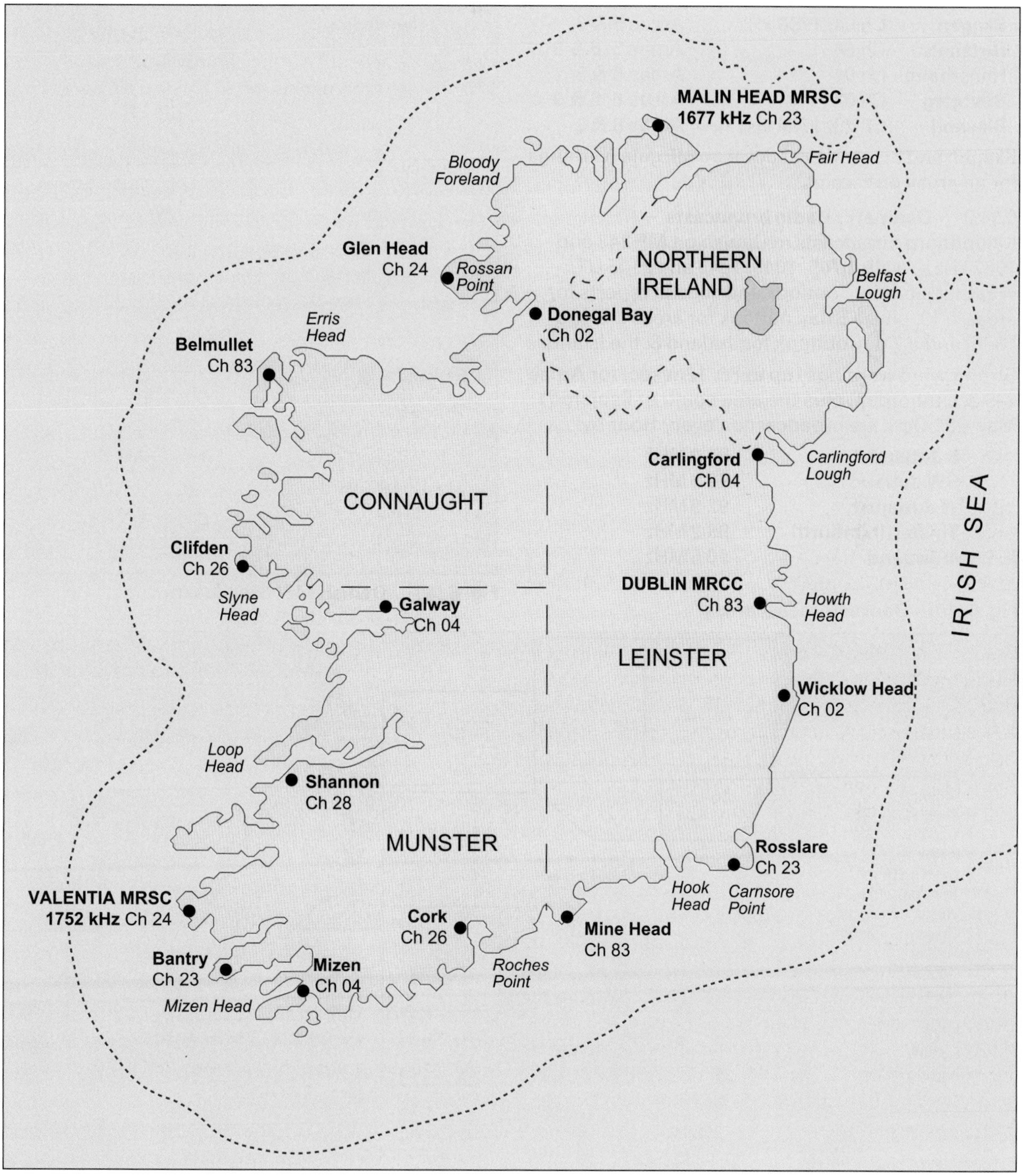

MALIN HEAD MRSC
1677 kHz Ch 23
Fair Head
Bloody Foreland
Glen Head
Ch 24
Rossan Point
NORTHERN IRELAND
Belfast Lough
Donegal Bay
Ch 02
Erris Head
Belmullet
Ch 83
Carlingford
Ch 04
Carlingford Lough
CONNAUGHT
IRISH SEA
Clifden
Ch 26
DUBLIN MRCC
Ch 83
Howth Head
Slyne Head
Galway
Ch 04
LEINSTER
Wicklow Head
Ch 02
Loop Head
Shannon
Ch 28
MUNSTER
Rosslare
Ch 23
Hook Head
Carnsore Point
VALENTIA MRSC
1752 kHz Ch 24
Cork
Ch 26
Mine Head
Ch 83
Bantry
Ch 23
Mizen
Ch 04
Roches Point
Mizen Head

6.13.4 Telephone and Fax

The latest Sea area forecast and gale warnings can be obtained through Weatherdial ☎ 1550 123 855. The same information, plus isobaric, swell and wave charts are available by Fax on ☎ 1570 131 838 (H24).

Central Forecast Office, Dublin (H24)	(01) 424655
Dublin Airport Met	(01) 379900 ext 4531
Cork Airport Met (0900–2000)	(021) 965974
Shannon Airport Met (H24)	(061) 61333

6.14 DENMARK

6.14.1 Gale warnings & forecasts are broadcast on receipt, or on request, in Danish/English by remote CRS (below), all using callsign *Lyngby Radio:*

Skagen	Ch 04, 1758 kHz	Areas 5 & 6
Hirtshals	Ch 66	Areas 5, 6 & 8
Hanstholm	Ch 01	Areas 6 & 8
Bovbjerg	Ch 02	Areas 6, 8 & 9
Blåvand	Ch 23, 1734 kHz	Areas 8 & 9

Skagen and Blåvand broadcast on MF gale warnings for all areas on receipt.

6.14.2 Danmarks Radio broadcasts

Kalundborg broadcasts in Danish on MF 243 and 1062 kHz at 0445, 0745, 1045, 1645 and 2145 UT: Weather situation, outlook and coastal reports for areas 1-19, plus a 5 day outlook for areas 2-9 and 13-15 and a 7 day outlook for Jutland & the Islands.

Strong wind warnings (up to F6, 12m/sec) for Areas 2–5 & Limfjorden, plus the area south of Esbjerg (1 May – 31 Oct), are broadcast on every Hour by:

S Jutland	97·2 MHz
SW Jutland	92·3 MHz
W Jutland	92·9 MHz
Thisted (Limfjord)	99·2 MHz
N Jutland	96·6 MHz

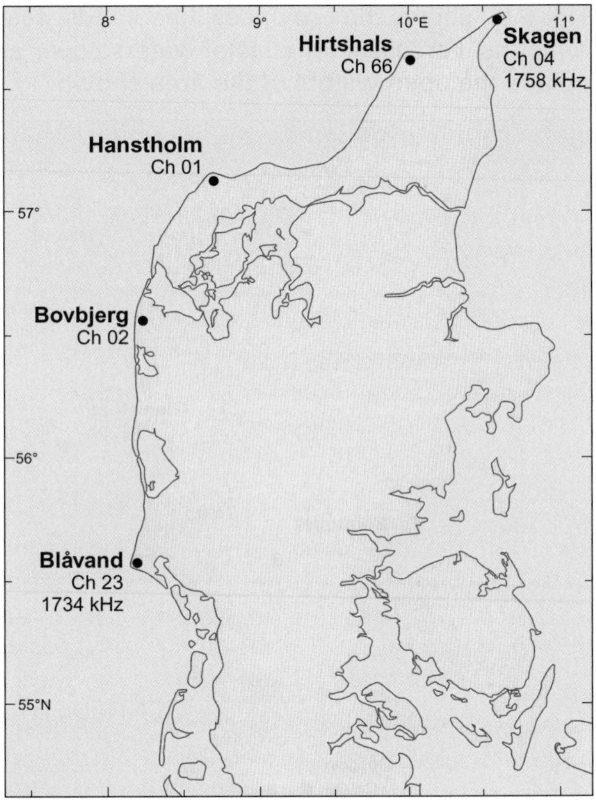
8°
9°
10°E
11°
Hirtshals
Ch 66
Skagen
Ch 04
1758 kHz
Hanstholm
Ch 01
57°
Bovbjerg
Ch 02
56°
Blåvand
Ch 23
1734 kHz
55°N

Fig. 6 (11) Danish MSI broadcasts

Fig. 6 (10) Danish forecast areas

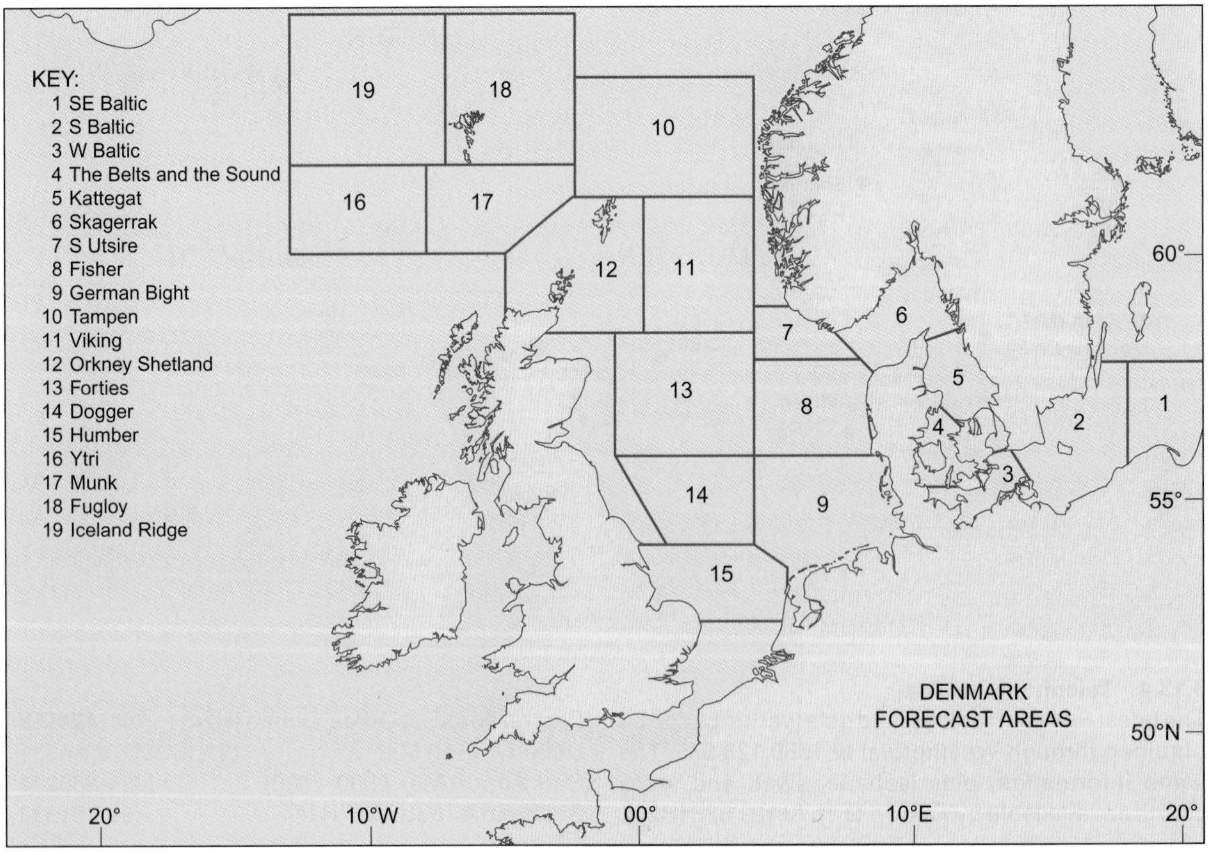
KEY:
1 SE Baltic
2 S Baltic
3 W Baltic
4 The Belts and the Sound
5 Kattegat
6 Skagerrak
7 S Utsire
8 Fisher
9 German Bight
10 Tampen
11 Viking
12 Orkney Shetland
13 Forties
14 Dogger
15 Humber
16 Ytri
17 Munk
18 Fugloy
19 Iceland Ridge
19
18
10
16
17
12
11
6
7
5
13
8
4
2
1
3
14
9
15
60°
55°
50°N
DENMARK
FORECAST AREAS
20°
10°W
00°
10°E
20°

6.15 GERMANY

6.15.1 Deutsche Wetterdienst (DWD)

The German weather service provides weather info through a databank which is updated twice daily; more often for weather reports and text forecasts. German Weather Service, Frankfurter Str 135, 63067 Offenbach. ☎ + 49 (0) 69 8062-0. Fax + 49 (0) 69 8062 4484. www.dwd.de seeschifffahrt@dwd.de.

SEEWIS (Marine weather information system) allows data to be accessed by telephone/modem and fed into an onboard computer.

6.15.2 Traffic Centres

Traffic Centres broadcast local storm warnings, weather messages, visibility and ice reports (when appropriate) in German. (E) = in **English** and German.

Traffic Centre	VHF Ch	Every
German Bight Traffic (E)	80	H+00
Ems Traffic	15, 18, 20, 21	H+50
Jade Traffic	20, 63	H+10
Bremerhaven Weser	02, 04, 05, 07, 21, 22, 82	H+20
Bremen Weser Traffic	19, 78, 81	H+30
Hunte Traffic	63	H+30
Cuxhaven Elbe Traffic (E)	71 (outer Elbe)	H+35
Brunsbüttel Elbe Traffic (E)	68 (lower Elbe)	H+05
Kiel Kanal II (E-bound)	02	H+15 & H+45
KielKanal III (W-bound)	03	H+20 & H+50

6.15.3 CRS – Seefunk (DPO7)

Seefunk CRS broadcast gale and strong wind warnings, synopsis, 12h forecast, outlook for a further 12h and coastal reports, in German, for areas B10-B12 and N9-N11 at 0745Ⓐ, **0945**, 1245, **1645** and **1945**Ⓐ UT. Ⓐonly in summer.

Hamburg (Control centre)	Ch 83
Borkum	Ch 28
Bremen	Ch 25
Elber-Weser	Ch 24
Nordfriesland	Ch 26

A 4-5 day outlook for the North and Baltic Seas is broadcast at the times above in bold.

6.15.4 Radio broadcasting

North German Radio (NDR)

a. NDR 1 Welle Nord (FM)

A synopsis, 12hrs forecast and 24 hrs outlook are broadcast in German at 0730 UT (1 May – 30 Sept) for Helgoland, Elbe and North Frisian coast by: **Helgoland** 88·9 MHz; **Hamburg** 89·5 & 90·3 MHz; **Flensburg** 89·6 MHz; **Heide** 90·5 MHz; **Sylt** 90·9 MHz; **Kiel** 91·3 MHz.

b. NDR 4 Hamburg (MW)

A synopsis, 12hrs forecast and outlook for a further 12 hrs are broadcast in German at 0005, 0830 and 2200 UT on 702 (Flensburg) & 972 (Hamburg) kHz for areas B10-B14 and N9-N12; plus North Sea station reports.

Radio Bremen (MW and FM)

A 12hrs wind forecast for Areas B11 and N10 is broadcast in German on receipt by: **Bremerhaven** 936 kHz; 89·3, 92·1, 95·4 & 100·8 MHz; and **Bremen** 88·3, 93·8, 96·7 & 101·2 MHz.

6.15.5 HF Radio

Offenbach (Main) broadcasts in **English** on 4583, 7646 and 10100·8 kHz at 0305,0535 , 0835, 1135, 1435, 1735 and 2035 UT: Weather reports for the North and Baltic Seas. At 0355,1530 UT: Medium term weather reports for the North Sea and 5 day prognosis for areas N1-12, A5, A6 and IJsselmeer.

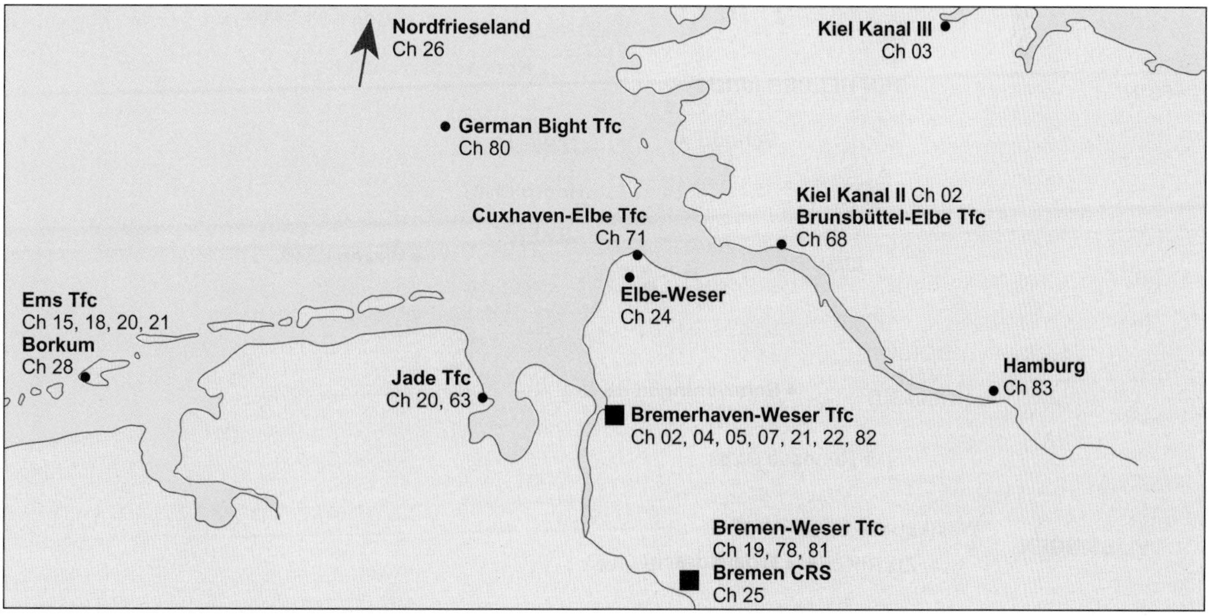
Nordfrieseland
Ch 26
Kiel Kanal III
Ch 03
German Bight Tfc
Ch 80
Kiel Kanal II Ch 02
Brunsbüttel-Elbe Tfc
Ch 68
Cuxhaven-Elbe Tfc
Ch 71
Elbe-Weser
Ch 24
Ems Tfc
Ch 15, 18, 20, 21
Borkum
Ch 28
Jade Tfc
Ch 20, 63
Hamburg
Ch 83
Bremerhaven-Weser Tfc
Ch 02, 04, 05, 07, 21, 22, 82
Bremen-Weser Tfc
Ch 19, 78, 81
Bremen CRS
Ch 25

Fig. 6 (12) German MSI broadcasts

6.15.6 Telephone forecasts

For forecast and outlook (1 April – 30 Sept) call 0190 1160 (only within Germany) plus two digits for the following areas:

45 North Frisian Islands and Helgoland
46 R Elbe to Hamburg
47 Weser Estuary and Jade Bay
48 East Frisian Islands and Ems Estuary
53 For inland pleasure craft
54 Denmark
55 Netherlands, IJsselmeer, Schelde, Maas

For year-round weather synopsis, forecast and outlook, call 0190 1169 plus two digits as follows:

20 General information
21 North Sea and Baltic
22 German Bight and SW North Sea
31 Reports for North Sea and Baltic
59 Current wind strength for North Sea coasts

For the latest wind and storm warnings for individual areas of the North Sea coasts, call +49 40 3196 628 (H24). If no warning is in force, a wind forecast for the German Bight is given.

6.16 NETHERLANDS

6.16.1 Netherlands Coastguard

a. VHF weather broadcasts

Forecasts for Dutch coastal waters up to 30M offshore (including IJsselmeer) are transmitted in **English** and Dutch at 0805, 1305, 1905, 2305 LT on the VHF channels shown below, without prior announcement on Ch 16. Gale warnings are broadcast on receipt and at 0333, 0733, 1133, 1533, 1933 and 2333 UT.

Westkapelle	Ch 23	**Hoorn**	Ch 83
Woensdrecht	Ch 83	**Wezep**	Ch 23
Renesse	Ch 83	**Kornwerderzand**	Ch 23
Scheveningen	Ch 23	**West Terschelling**	Ch 83
Schoorl	Ch 83	**Schiermonnikoog**	Ch 23
Den Helder	Ch 23	**Appingedam**	Ch 83

Goeree CG station broadcasts a weather forecast forecast in Dutch, Ch 25 @ H +30 (H24).

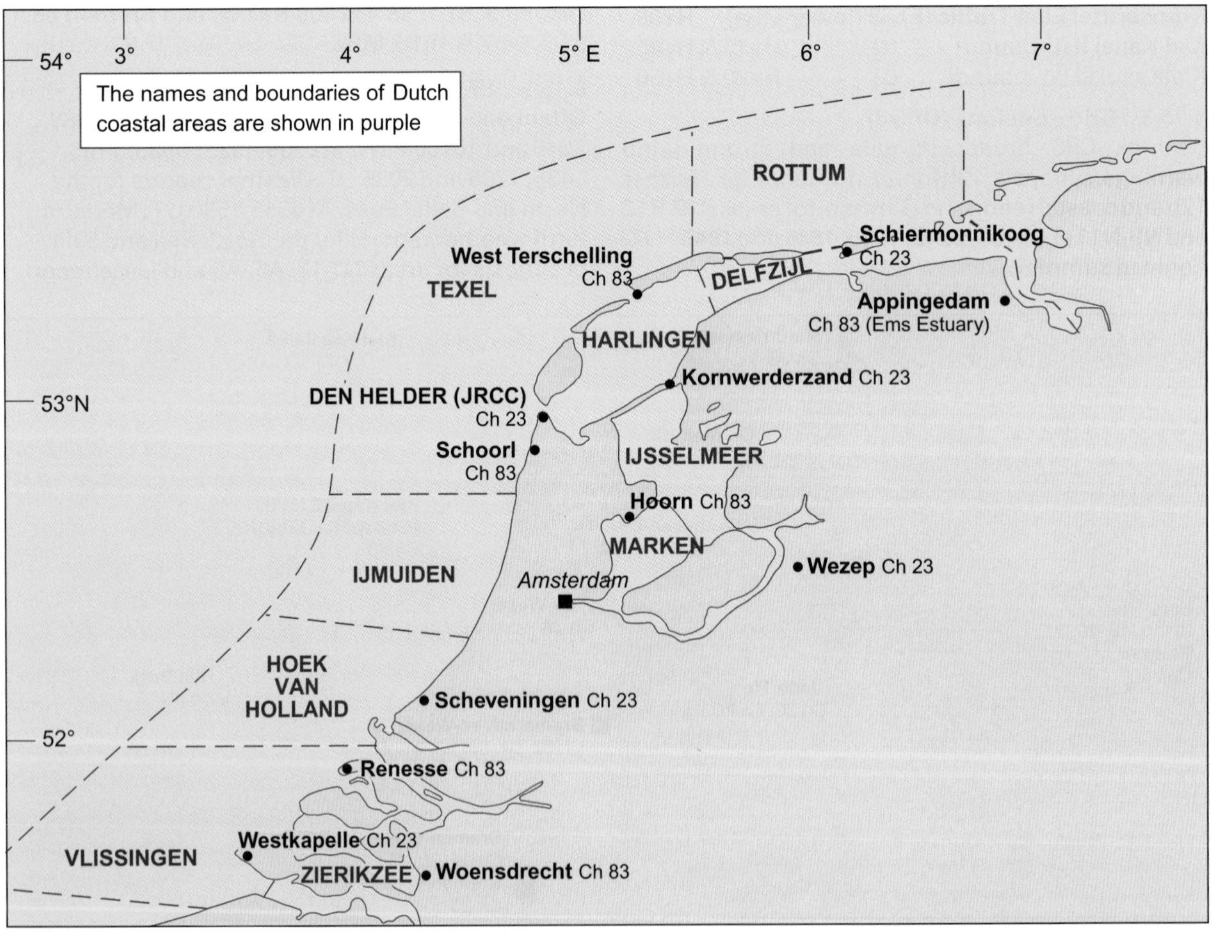
54°
3°
4°
5° E
6°
7°
53°N
52°
The names and boundaries of Dutch coastal areas are shown in purple
ROTTUM
Schiermonnikoog
Ch 23
West Terschelling
Ch 83
TEXEL
DELFZIJL
Appingedam
Ch 83 (Ems Estuary)
HARLINGEN
Kornwerderzand Ch 23
DEN HELDER (JRCC)
Ch 23
Schoorl
Ch 83
IJSSELMEER
Hoorn Ch 83
MARKEN
Wezep Ch 23
IJMUIDEN
Amsterdam
HOEK VAN HOLLAND
Scheveningen Ch 23
Renesse Ch 83
Westkapelle Ch 23
VLISSINGEN
ZIERIKZEE
Woensdrecht Ch 83

Fig. 6 (13) Netherlands MSI broadcasts

a. **MF weather broadcasts**
Forecasts for areas Dover, Thames, Humber, German Bight, Dogger, Fisher, Forties and Viking is broadcast in **English** at 0940 & 2140 UT on 3673 kHz. Gale warnings for these areas are broadcast in **English** on receipt and at 0333, 0733, 1133, 1533, 1933 and 2333 UT.

6.16.2 Radio Noord-Holland (FM)
Coastal forecasts, gale warnings and wind strength are broadcast in Dutch, Mon-Fri at 0730, 0838, 1005, 1230 and 1705LT; Sat/Sun 1005, by:

Wieringermeer 93.9 MHz and **Haarlem** 97.6 MHz.

6.17 BELGIUM

6.17.1 Coast Radio Stations

Oostende Radio broadcasts strong wind warnings and a forecast valid for sea areas Thames and Dover in **English** and Dutch on VHF Ch 27 and 2761 kHz at 0820 and 1720 UT. Strong wind warnings arealso broadcast on receipt and at the end of the next two silent periods.

Antwerpen Radio broadcasts on VHF Ch 24 in **English** and Dutch for the Schelde estuary: Gale warnings on receipt, at the end of the next two silent periods and every odd H+05. Also strong wind warnings (F6+) on receipt and at every H+03 and H+48.

6.18 FRANCE

The French Met Office (Météo-France) issues a free annual booklet 'Le Guide Marine' which summarises the various means by which weather forecasts and warnings are broadcast or otherwise disseminated. It can often be obtained from marina offices, on the internet (www.meteo.fr) or from Météo-France, Direction de la Production, Service de prévision marine, 42 ave Gaspard-Coriolis, 31057 Toulouse-Cedex; tel 05.61.07.80.80.

6.18.1 CROSS VHF broadcasts

CROSS routinely broadcasts Weather bulletins in French, after an announcement on Ch 16. These contain: a repeat of any Gale warnings in force, general situation, a 24 hrs forecast (actual weather, wind, sea state and visibility) and further weather trends for coastal waters. VHF working channels, coastal areas covered to 20M offshore, remote stations and times (local) are shown below. In the English Channel broadcasts can be given in English, on request Ch 16. Gale warnings feature in Special Met Bulletins (*Bulletins Météorologique Spéciaux* or BMS). They are routinely broadcast in French and **English** by all stations at H+03 and at other times as shown below.

CROSS GRIS-NEZ

Ch 79 Belgian border to Baie de la Somme

Dunkerque	0720, 1603, 1920
St Frieux	0710, 1545, 1910
Ailly	0703, 1533, 1903

CROSS JOBOURG

Ch 80 Baie de la Somme to Cap de la Hague

Antifer	0803, 1633, 2003
Port-en-Bessin	0745, 1615, 1945
Jobourg	0733, 1603, 1933

Cap de la Hague to Pointe de Penmarc'h

Jobourg	0715, 1545, 1915
Granville	0703, 1533, 1903

Gale warnings for areas 13-14 in **English** on receipt, on request and at H+20 and H+50. Coastal BMS in French on receipt and at H+03. 'Jobourg Traffic' (VTS) broadcasts traffic info and BMS in French and **English** on Ch 80 at H+20 and H+50.

CROSS CORSEN

Ch 79 Cap de la Hague to Pointe de Penmarc'h
(Times in **bold** = 1 May to 30 Sep only).

Cap Fréhel	0545, 0803, **1203**, 1633, 2003
Bodic	0533, 0745, **1145**, 1615, 1945
Ile de Batz	0515, 0733, **1133**, 1603, 1933
Le Stiff	0503, 0715, **1115**, 1545, 1915
Pte du Raz	0445, 0703, **1103**, 1533, 1903

Gale warnings for areas 14-16 in French & **English** on receipt and at every H+03.

CROSS ÉTEL

Ch 80 Pte de Penmarc'h to l'Anse de l'Aiguillon
(46° 15'N 01°10'W)

Penmarc'h	0703, 1533, 1903
Ile de Groix	0715, 1545, 1915
Belle Ile	0733, 1603, 1933
St Nazaire	0745, 1615, 1945
Ile d'Yeu	0803, 1633, 2003
Les Sables d'Olonne	0815, 1645, 2015

Gale warnings for areas 16-17 in French & **English** on receipt and at every H+03.

Ch 79 L'Anse de l'Aiguillon to Spanish border

Chassiron	0703, 1533, 1903
Soulac	0715, 1545, 1915
Cap Ferret	0733, 1603, 1933
Contis	0745, 1615, 1945
Biarritz	0803, 1633, 2003

Gale warnings for areas 17-19 in French & **English** on receipt and at every H+03.

6.18.2 CROSS MF broadcasts

CROSS **Gris Nez** and **Corsen** broadcast routine weather bulletins and gale warnings on 1650 kHz and 2677kHz in French at the times below. A prior announcement on 2182 kHz states the working frequency to be used. Gale warnings are broadcast on receipt, at every H+03 and at the times below.

CROSS	Routine bulletins	Areas
Gris Nez	0833, 2033 LT	10-13
Corsen	0815, 2015 LT	13-29

C6

Fig. 6 (14) Weather broadcasts by CROSS on VHF

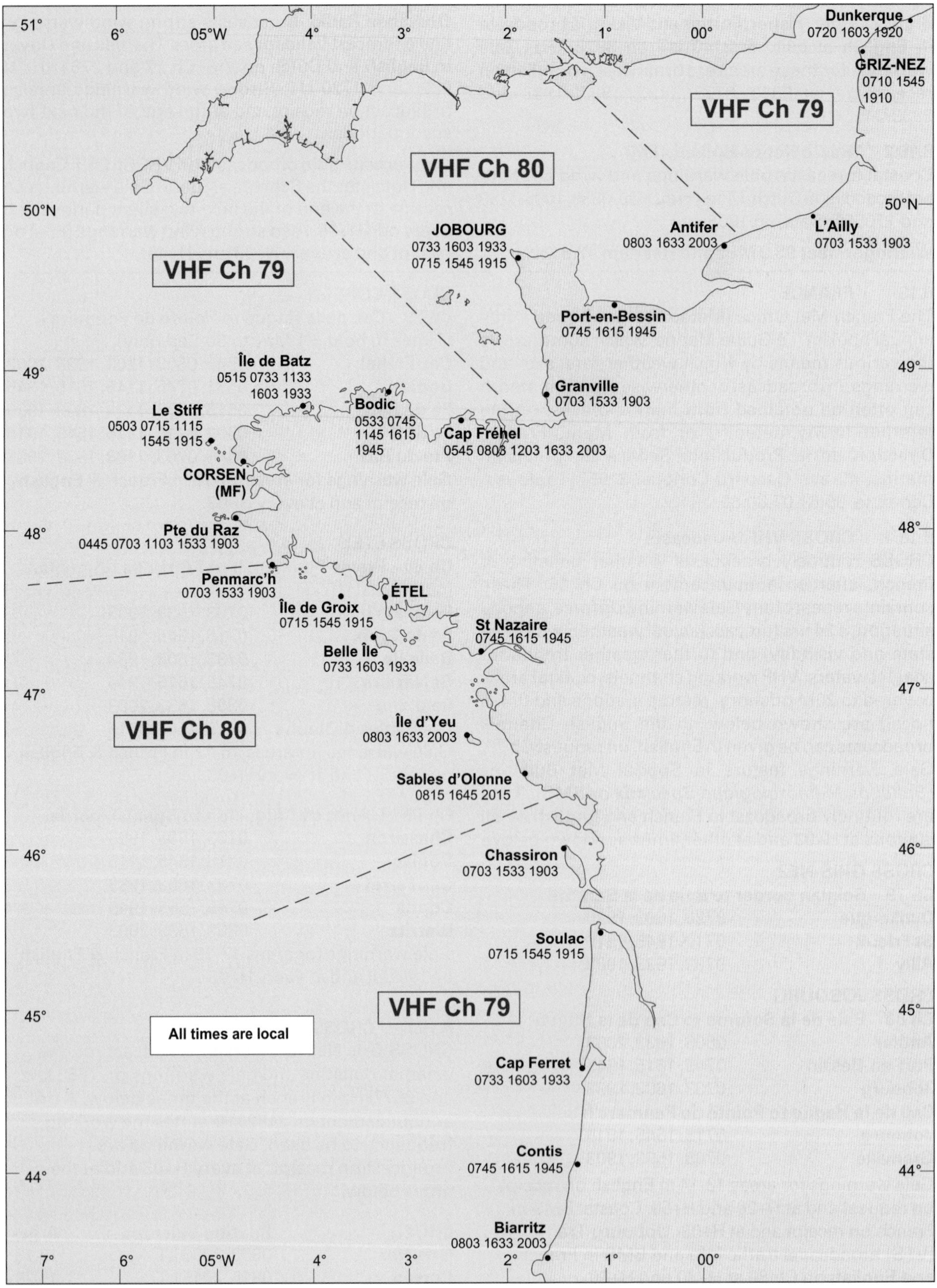
51°
6°
05°W
4°
3°
2°
1°
00°
Dunkerque
0720 1603 1920
GRIZ-NEZ
0710 1545
1910
VHF Ch 79
VHF Ch 80
50°N
Antifer
0803 1633 2003
L'Ailly
0703 1533 1903
JOBOURG
0733 1603 1933
0715 1545 1915
VHF Ch 79
Port-en-Bessin
0745 1615 1945
49°
Île de Batz
0515 0733 1133
1603 1933
Granville
0703 1533 1903
Le Stiff
0503 0715 1115
1545 1915
Bodic
0533 0745
1145 1615
1945
Cap Fréhel
0545 0803 1203 1633 2003
CORSEN
(MF)
48°
Pte du Raz
0445 0703 1103 1533 1903
Penmarc'h
0703 1533 1903
ÉTEL
Île de Groix
0715 1545 1915
St Nazaire
0745 1615 1945
Belle Île
0733 1603 1933
47°
VHF Ch 80
Île d'Yeu
0803 1633 2003
Sables d'Olonne
0815 1645 2015
46°
Chassiron
0703 1533 1903
Soulac
0715 1545 1915
45°
VHF Ch 79
All times are local
Cap Ferret
0733 1603 1933
44°
Contis
0745 1615 1945
Biarritz
0803 1633 2003
7°

6.18.3 Radio broadcasting

France Inter (LW) 162 kHz (1852m)

For all areas: storm warnings, synopsis, 24h fcst and outlook, broadcast in French for Areas 1 to 29 at 2003 LT daily. Stations which broadcast on MW at 0640 LT include **Paris** 864 kHz, **Brest** 1404 kHz, **Bordeaux** 1206 kHz, **Bayonne** 1494 kHz and **Toulouse** 945 kHz.

RADIO FRANCE INTERNATIONALE (RFI)

RFI broadcasts weather messages in French on HF at 1130 UT daily. Frequencies and reception areas are: 6175 kHz North Sea, English Channel, Bay of Biscay. 15300, 15515, 17570 and 21645 kHz the North Atlantic, E of 50°W. Engineering bulletins indicating frequency changes are transmitted between H+53 and H+00.

Radio Bleue (MW)

Essentially a music programme, but with forecasts in French at 0655 LT covering:

English Channel & North Sea:	**Paris**	864 kHz
	Lille	1377 kHz
English Channel & E Atlantic:	**Rennes**	711 kHz
	Brest	1404 kHz
Bay of Biscay & E Atlantic:	**Bordeaux**	1206 kHz
	Bayonne	1494 kHz

Local radio (FM)

Radio France Cherbourg 100·7 MHz

Coastal forecast, storm warnings, visibility, wind strength, tidal information, small craft warnings, in French, for the Cherbourg peninsula, broadcast 0829 LT by:

St Vaast-la-Hougue	85·0 MHz
Cherbourg	100·7 MHz
Cap de la Hague	99·8 MHz
Carteret	99·9 MHz

6.184 Forecasts by fax and/or telephone

a. The BQR (Bulletin Quotidien des Renseignements) is a very informative daily bulletin by fax, displayed in most Capitaineries and YC's.

b. For each French port, under TELEPHONE, Météo is the ☎ of a local Met Office.

c. Auto gives the ☎ for recorded inshore and Coastal forecasts; dial 08·36·68·08·dd (dd is the Département No, shown under each port). To select the inshore (rivage) or Coastal (Côte; out to 20M offshore) bulletin, say "STOP" as your choice is spoken. Inshore bulletins contain 5 day forecasts, local tides, signals, sea temperature, surf conditions, etc. strong wind/gale warnings, general synopsis, 24hrs forecast and outlook.

d. For Offshore bulletins (zones du large) for Channel and North Sea, Atlantic or Mediterranean, dial ☎ 08·36·68·08·08. To select desired offshore area say "STOP" as it is named. Offshore bulletins contain strong wind/gale warnings, the general synopsis and forecast, and the 5 day outlook.

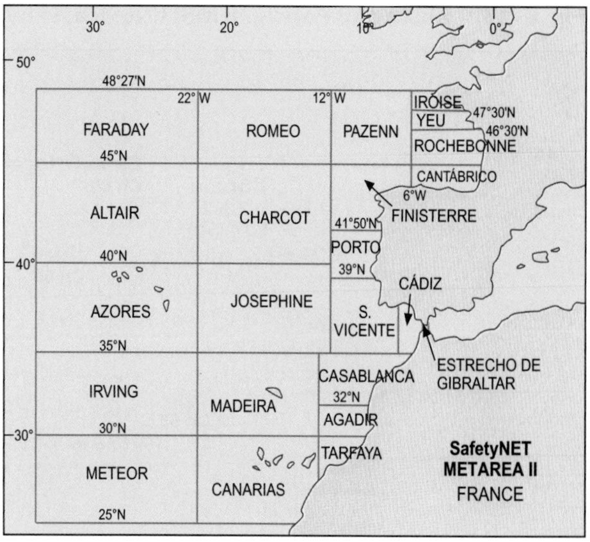

30°
20°
10°
0°
50°
48°27'N
22°W
12°W
FARADAY
ROMEO
PAZENN
IROISE
YEU
47°30'N
46°30'N
ROCHEBONNE
45°N
CANTÁBRICO
6°W
ALTAIR
CHARCOT
41°50'N
FINISTERRE
PORTO
40°
40°N
39°N
CÁDIZ
AZORES
JOSEPHINE
S. VICENTE
35°N
ESTRECHO DE GIBRALTAR
CASABLANCA
32°N
IRVING
MADEIRA
AGADIR
30°
30°N
TARFAYA
SafetyNET
METAREA II
FRANCE
METEOR
CANARIAS
25°N

Fig. 6 (15) French forecast areas

6.19 NORTH AND NORTH WEST SPAIN

6.19.1 Coast Radio Stations

VHF weather warnings and 48h coastal forecasts are broadcast in Spanish at 0840, 1240 & 2010 (UT) by: **Pasajes** Ch 27; **Bilbao** Ch 26; **Santander** Ch 24; **Cabo Peñas** Ch 26; **Navia** Ch 60; **Cabo Ortegal** Ch 02; **La Coruña** Ch 26; **Finisterre** Ch 22; **Vigo** Ch 65; and **La Guardia** Ch 21 .

MF gale warnings, synopsis and 24h/48h forecasts for Atlantic areas are broadcast at 0703 1303 1903 (UT) by: **Machichaco** 1707 kHz; **Cabo Peñas** 1677 kHz; **La Coruña** 1698 kHz; and **Finisterre** 1764 kHz.

6.19.2 Recorded telephone forecasts

For a telephone weather recording in Spanish, call:

☎ 906 365 372 for Cantábrico and Galicia coasts.

☎ 906 365 374 for High Seas bulletins; Fig. 6(17). This service is only available within Spain or for Autolink-equipped vessels.

6.19.3 Coastguard MRCC/MRSC

Gale warnings and coastal forecastsare broadcast in Spanish and English on receipt and as listed below:

Bilbao MRCC	Ch 10	4 hourly from 0033
Santander MRSC	Ch 74	4 hourly from 0245
Gijón MRCC	Ch 10	2 hourly (0215-2215)
Coruña MRSC	Ch 10	4 hourly from 0005
Finisterre MRCC	Ch 11	4 hourly from 0233
Vigo MRSC	Ch 10	4 hourly from 0015

Note: **Bilbao** also broadcasts High Seas gale warnings and forecasts 4 hourly from 0233.

6.19.3 Radio Nacional de España (MW)

Broadcasts storm warnings, synopsis and 12h or 18h forecasts for Cantábrico and Galicia at 1100, 1400, 1800 & 2200 LT in Spanish. Stations/frequencies are:

San Sebastián	774 kHz	**Oviedo**	729 kHz
Bilbao	639 kHz	**La Coruña**	639 kHz
Santander	855 kHz		

Fig. 6 (16) Spain and Portugal: MSI broadcasts by CRS and MRCCs/MRSCs (All times UT)

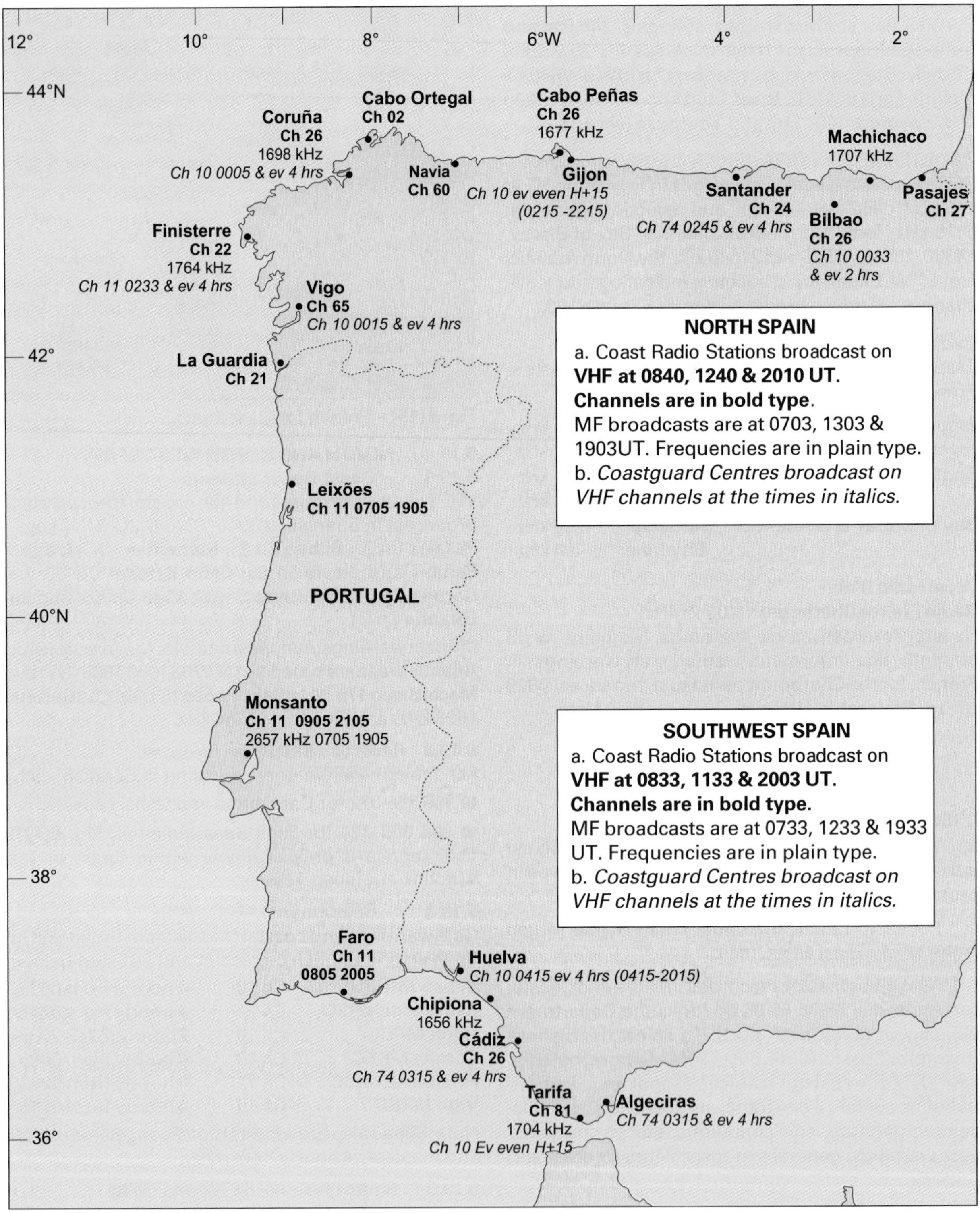
12°
10°
8°
6°W
4°
2°
44°N
42°
40°N
38°
36°
Cabo Ortegal
Ch 02
Coruña
Ch 26
1698 kHz
Ch 10 0005 & ev 4 hrs
Cabo Peñas
Ch 26
1677 kHz
Navia
Ch 60
Gijon
Ch 10 ev even H+15
(0215 -2215)
Machichaco
1707 kHz
Santander
Ch 24
Ch 74 0245 & ev 4 hrs
Pasajes
Ch 27
Bilbao
Ch 26
Ch 10 0033
& ev 2 hrs
Finisterre
Ch 22
1764 kHz
Ch 11 0233 & ev 4 hrs
Vigo
Ch 65
Ch 10 0015 & ev 4 hrs
La Guardia
Ch 21
NORTH SPAIN
a. Coast Radio Stations broadcast on
VHF at 0840, 1240 & 2010 UT.
Channels are in bold type.
MF broadcasts are at 0703, 1303 &
1903UT. Frequencies are in plain type.
b. Coastguard Centres broadcast on
VHF channels at the times in italics.
Leixões
Ch 11 0705 1905
PORTUGAL
Monsanto
Ch 11 0905 2105
2657 kHz 0705 1905
SOUTHWEST SPAIN
a. Coast Radio Stations broadcast on
VHF at 0833, 1133 & 2003 UT.
Channels are in bold type.
MF broadcasts are at 0733, 1233 & 1933
UT. Frequencies are in plain type.
b. Coastguard Centres broadcast on
VHF channels at the times in italics.
Faro
Ch 11
0805 2005
Huelva
Ch 10 0415 ev 4 hrs (0415-2015)
Chipiona
1656 kHz
Cádiz
Ch 26
Ch 74 0315 & ev 4 hrs
Tarifa
Ch 81
1704 kHz
Ch 10 Ev even H+15
Algeciras
Ch 74 0315 & ev 4 hrs

Fig. 6 (17) Spanish forecast areas

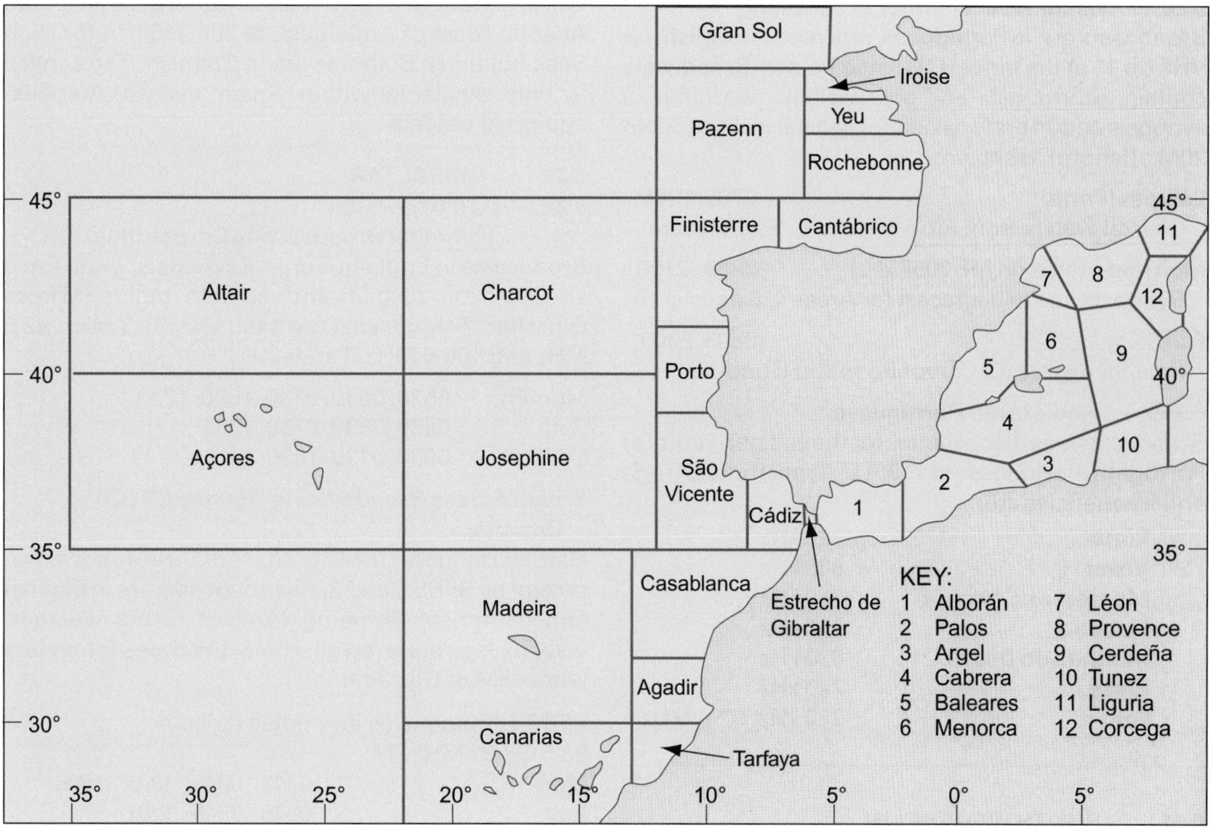
Gran Sol
Iroise
Yeu
Pazenn
Rochebonne
45°
Finisterre
Cantábrico
45°
11
7
8
12
Altair
Charcot
6
9
40°
Porto
5
40°
4
Açores
Josephine
10
São Vicente
3
2
Cádiz
1
35°
35°
Casablanca
Estrecho de Gibraltar
Madeira
KEY:
1 Alborán
2 Palos
3 Argel
4 Cabrera
5 Baleares
6 Menorca
7 Léon
8 Provence
9 Cerdeña
10 Tunez
11 Liguria
12 Corcega
Agadir
30°
Canarias
Tarfaya
35°
30°
25°
20°
15°
10°
5°
0°
5°

Fig. 6 (18) Portuguese forecast areas

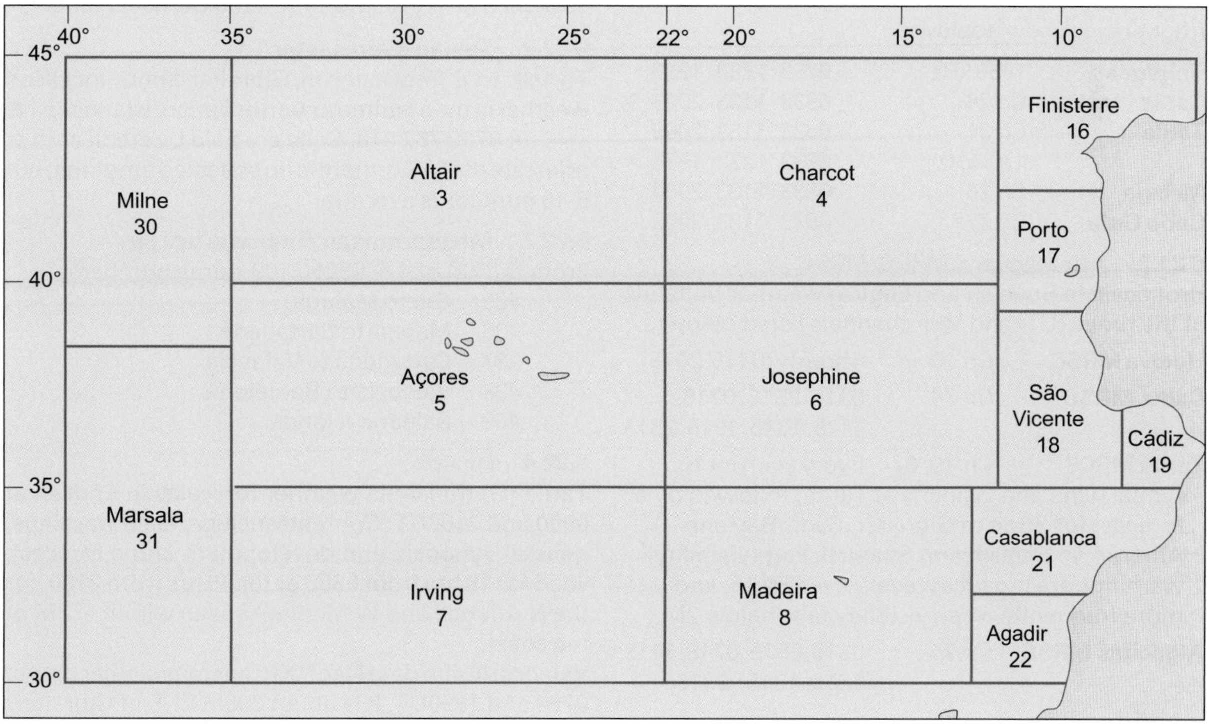
40°
35°
30°
25°
22°
20°
15°
10°
45°
Finisterre 16
Milne 30
Altair 3
Charcot 4
Porto 17
40°
Açores 5
Josephine 6
São Vicente 18
Cádiz 19
35°
Casablanca 21
Marsala 31
Irving 7
Madeira 8
Agadir 22
30°

6.20 PORTUGAL

6.20.1 Radionaval weather broadcasts

Broadcasts are in Portuguese, repeated in **English**, on VHF Ch 11 at the times (UT) listed below. Broadcasts contain: Storm, gale and poor visibility warnings; a synopsis and 24 hrs forecasts for coastal waters (out to 20M offshore) as shown:

Leixões (Porto) 0705, 1905
Coastal waters from Rio Minho to C. São Vicente.

Monsanto (also on MF 2657 kHz) 0905, 2105
Synopsis and 24h forecast for Areas 4, 6 and 16-19.

Faro 0805, 2005
Coastal waters, C. Carvoeiro to Rio Guadiana.

6.20.2 Radiofusão Portuguesa

Broadcasts weather bulletins for the coastal waters of Portugal in Portuguese at 1100 UT. Transmitters (N-S) and frequencies are:

Porto	720 kHz
Viseu	666 kHz
Montemor (Coimbra)	630 kHz
Lisboa 1	666 kHz
Miranda do Douro	630 kHz
Elvas	720 kHz
Faro	720 kHz, 97·6 MHz

6.21 SOUTH WEST SPAIN

6.21.1 Coast radio stations

The following CRS broadcast gale warnings, synopsis and 48h forecasts for Atlantic and Mediterranean areas, in Spanish, at the times (UT) and on the VHF or MF frequencies shown below:

Chipiona	1656 kHz	0733	1233	1933
Cadiz	Ch 26	0833	1133	2003
Tarifa	Ch 81	0833	1133	2003
	1704kHz	0733	1233	1933
Malaga	Ch 26	0833	1133	2003
Cabo Gata	Ch 27	0833	1133	2003

6.21.2 Coastguard MRCC/MRSC

Broadcast in Spanish and **English** weather bulletins at the times (UT) and VHF channels listed below:

Huelva MRSC Ch 10 4 hourly (0415-2015)

Cadiz MRSC Ch 74 0315, 0515, 0715, 1115, 1515, 1915, 2315

Tarifa MRCC Ch 10, 67 Every even H+15.
Actual wind and visibility at Tarifa, followed by a forecast for Strait of Gibraltar, Cádiz Bay and Alborán, in **English** and Spanish. Fog (visibility) warnings are broadcast every even H+15, and more frequently when visibility falls below 2M.

Algeciras MRSC Ch 74 0315, 0515, 0715, 1115 1515, 1915, 2315

6.21.3 Recorded telephone forecasts

Call ☎ 906 365 373 for a coastal waters bulletin for the Atlantic coast of Andalucia. ☎ 906 365 374 for High Seas bulletins. Bulletins are in Spanish. The service is only available within Spain and to Autolink-equipped vessels.

6.22 GIBRALTAR

6.22.1 Radio Gibraltar

(Gibraltar Broadcasting Corporation)

Broadcasts in English: General synopsis, wind force and direction, visibility and sea state, radius 5M from Gibraltar. Frequencies are 1458 kHz, 91·3 MHz, 92·6 MHz and 100·5 MHz. Times (UT):

Mon-Fri:	0530, 0630, 0730, 1030, 1230
Sat:	0530, 0630, 0730, 1030
Sun:	0630, 0730, 1030

British Forces Broadcasting Service (BFBS) Gibraltar

Gale warnings for the Gibraltar area are broadcast on receipt by BFBS 1 and 2. All broadcasts are in English and comprise: Shipping forecast, wind, weather, visbility, sea state, swell, HW & LW times for waters within 5M of Gibraltar.

BFBS 1 frequencies and times (Local):
93·5, 97·8* MHz FM.

Mon-Fri:	0745	0845	1005	1605
Sat:	0845	0945	1202	
Sun:	0845	0945	1202	1602

* This frequency is reported to have greater range.

BFBS 2 frequencies and time:
89·4, 99·5 MHz FM. Mon-Fri: 1200 **UK Local time**

6.22.2 Talk to a forecaster

To talk to a forecaster in Gibraltar about localised weather in the Mediterranean or Canary Islands call ☎ + 44 (0) 8700 767 818. Calls are paid by credit card at a flat rate of £15·00; there is no specified time limit, but 5-10 minutes is average.

6.22.3 Mediterranean forecasts by Fax

From the UK dial 📠 09060 100 + area numbers:

435	Gib to Malaga
436	Malaga to Cartagena
437	Cartagena to Valencia
438	Valencia to Barcelona
439	Balearic Islands

6.22.4 Navtex

Tarifa [G] transmits weather forecasts in English at 0900 and 2100UT. Contents include: Gale warnings, general synopsis and development and a forecast, valid for 18 hrs from 0900 or for 36 hrs from 2100, for the N Atlantic and W Mediterranean within 450M of the coast.
Valencia (Cabo de la Nao) [X] transmits similar data at 0750 and 1950UT. It is about 300M ENE of Gibraltar.

Chapter 7

Safety

Contents

C7

7.1 SAFETY EQUIPMENT

7.1.1 Learning about safety

Every year an unknown number of people take to the water for the first time. All have some idea of what they will find out there, but invariably they discover that the reality is very different to what they imagined. Challenges are found to be far harder but pleasures may be even sweeter. If you rely solely on learning by your own experience you will sooner or later find yourself in a situation that you really do not want to be in. The secret is to learn from other people's experience as well - read as much as you can and think things through on dry land. If you are new to sailing, pick a crew with some experience.

To survive at sea you have to be able to rise to the challenges of wind and tide. To do this you need knowledge and experience.

The skipper is responsible for the safety of the boat and all on board. He/she must ensure that:

(1) The boat is suitable in design and in construction for her intended purpose.

(2) The boat is maintained in good condition.

(3) The crew is competent and sufficiently strong.

(4) The necessary safety and emergency equipment is carried, is in good condition, and the crew know how to use it.

A crew briefing on safety is a vital element of survival. It should be done *before* casting off and should consist of:

- showing where the instructions for sending a MAYDAY are kept - see 7.4
- showing where the Life-saving Signal information is kept - see fig 7 (1)
- showing where flares, fire extinguishers, lifejackets, lifelines, liferaft, First Aid Box, bilge pump are located
- familiarisation with the handling of sheets and halyards and using the engine.
- familiarisation with deploying the anchor

In the UK, the RNLI, MCA, RYA, BMF and other key marine organisations have formed the Safety on the Sea Group, and implement accident prevention campaigns. A full range of products, services and booklets are available from these organisations and agencies, many free of charge, that help the mariner to prepare for sea.

The RNLI provides a range of free sea safety services to any sea user:-

- Free onboard face-to-face advice about relevant safety equipment
- Free demonstrations of emergency equipment and distress procedures (flares, man overboard recovery etc)

The RYA provides training and cruising advice for leisure sailors, ☎ 08453 450400 for more information.

The MCA provide the Voluntary Safety Identification Scheme – a free boat registration service – see 7.10.3.

7.1.2 Safety equipment – legal requirements

All boats regardless of size are now required by the IMO to carry certain safety equipment such as compass, corrected charts and radar reflector *if practicable*. Racing yachts must comply with these requirements as well as club regulations.

7.1.3 Recommended Safety equipment for seagoing yachts 5·5 – 13·7m LOA.

The minimum equipment which should be carried for (a) coastal and (b) offshore cruising is listed in Table 7.1 on page 170. The RNLI provide a free onboard service called SEA Check (Safety Equipment Advisory Check) which is based on the RYA's recommended equipment list. This free service is designed to provide impartial advice to all. ☎ 0800 328 0600.

7.2 DEFINITIONS OF EMERGENCY

7.2.1 Distress

Distress is the most serious degree of emergency. It applies to any situation where a boat or person is threatened by grave and imminent danger and requires immediate assistance. The RT prefix associated with a Distress message is MAYDAY – see 6.4. A Distress call has priority over all other transmissions.

7.2.2 Urgency

Urgency is a lesser degree of emergency concerning the safety of a boat or person. Examples include, a vessel disabled but not sinking; medical problems (see also 7.5.2). The RT prefix associated with an Urgency message is PAN PAN – see 7.5.1.

7.2.3 Safety

Safety is the least serious degree of emergency, usually associated with a warning of hazardous navigational or meteorological circumstances. The RT prefix associated with a Safety message is SÉCURITÉ – see 7.5.3.

7.3 DISTRESS SIGNALS

7.3.1 Authority

Distress signals must only be made with the authority of the skipper, and only if the boat or a person is in grave and imminent danger, and help is urgently required; or on behalf of another vessel in distress, which for some reason is unable to make a Distress signal. When the problem is resolved, the Distress call must be cancelled by the co-ordinating station using the prowords SEELONCE FEENEE - see 7.4.4/6.

7.3.2 Mobile telephones

Using a mobile telephone to call the Coastguard on 999 (or 112) is not a substitute for radio communication on VHF Ch 16 or 2182 kHz when a vessel is in a distress or other emergency situation. They should be used as a last resort eg in the event of VHF failure. They have limited coverage and are not monitored, unlike Ch 16, which continues to be monitored by HM CG. A mobile telephone call cannot be heard by vessels nearby which might be able to help. Other vessels can only be called by mobile telephone if so fitted and the number is known. On-scene SAR communications may be hampered.

7.3.3 Visual and audible distress signals

A full list of the recognised distress signals is given in Annex IV of the IRPCS. The following are those most appropriate to yachts and small craft, together with notes on their use.

(a) Continuous sounding of any fog signalling apparatus.

In order to avoid confusion, this is best done by a succession of letters SOS in Morse (••• ——— •••).

(b) An SOS signal made by any method.

For a yacht the most likely methods are by sound signal or flashing light, as in (a) above.

(c) The International Code signal 'NC'.

This can be made by international code flag hoist. See Chapter 5, Plate 3.

(d) A square flag with a ball, or anything resembling a ball, above or below it.

This is not too difficult to contrive from any square flag, and a round fender or anchor ball.

(e) A rocket parachute flare or a hand-held flare showing a red light.

Fig 7(1) shows how flares are used to attract attention together with methods of communicating with SAR teams once help has arrived. It is mandatory to carry this information on all boats going to sea and it should be kept in a place which is known to all members of the crew.

A red flare is the most effective distress signal at night. Flares serve two purposes: first to raise the alarm, and then to pinpoint the boat's position. Within about three miles from land a hand flare will do both. At greater distances a red parachute rocket (which projects a suspended flare to a height of more than 1,000ft, or 300m, and which burns for more than 40 seconds) is needed to raise the alarm, but hand flares are useful to indicate the boat's position.

Hold hand flares firmly, downwind of yourself. Rockets turn into wind; fire them vertically in normal conditions, or aim about 15° downwind in strong winds. Do not aim them into wind, or they will not gain altitude. If there is low cloud, fire rockets at 45° downwind, so that the flare burns under the cloud.

Note: White flares are not distress signals, but are used to indicate your presence to another vessel on a collision course; or to acknowledge the sighting of a red flare. An outfit of at least four is suggested for boats which make night passages. When using them, shield your eyes to protect night vision.

(f) An orange-coloured smoke signal.

By day orange smoke signals are more effective than flares, although the smoke disperses quickly in a strong wind.

(g) Slow and repeated raising/lowering of arms outstretched to each side.

The arms should be raised and lowered together, above and below the horizontal.

7.4 MAYDAY CALLS

7.4.1. Sending a MAYDAY call

This should normally be transmitted on VHF DSC Ch 70 or MF DSC 2187·5 kHz or on VHF Ch 16 but any frequency may be used if help may thereby be obtained more quickly.

Distress, Urgency and Safety messages from vessels at sea are free of charge. A distress call has priority over all other transmissions. If heard, cease all transmissions that may interfere with the distress call or messages, and listen on the frequency concerned.

Train your crew, as necessary, so that everybody can send a distress message. It is very helpful to display the MAYDAY message format close to the radio. Before making the call, first:

- Check main battery switch ON
- Switch radio ON, and select HIGH power (25 watts)
- Select VHF Ch 16 (or 2182 kHz for MF)
- Press and hold down the transmit button, and say slowly and distinctly:
- **MAYDAY MAYDAY MAYDAY**
- **THIS IS** .... (name of boat, spoken three times)
- **MAYDAY** ...... (name of boat spoken once)
- **MY POSITION IS** .... (latitude and longitude, or true bearing and distance from a known point)
- Nature of distress ..... (sinking, on fire, etc.)
- Aid required .... (immediate assistance)
- Number of persons on board ....
- Any other important, helpful information (eg if the yacht is drifting, whether distress rockets are being fired)
- **OVER.**

On completion of the distress message, release the transmit button and listen. The yacht's position is of vital importance, and should be repeated if time allows.

Vessels fitted with GMDSS equipment should make a DSC distress alert on VHF Ch 70, or MF 2187·5 kHz before sending a distress message on RT. (see 7.6.5).

7.4.2 MAYDAY acknowledgement

In coastal waters an immediate acknowledgment should be expected, as follows:

> **MAYDAY** .... (name of station sending the distress message, spoken three times)
>
> **THIS IS** .... (name of station acknowledging, spoken three times)
>
> **RECEIVED MAYDAY.**

If an acknowledgment is not received, check the set and repeat the distress call.

If you hear a distress message, write down the details, and if you can help you should acknowledge accordingly, but only after giving an opportunity for the nearest coastguard station or some larger vessel to do so.

7.4.3 MAYDAY relay

If you hear a distress message from a vessel, and it is not acknowledged, you should pass on the message as follows:

> **MAYDAY RELAY** .... (spoken three times)
>
> **THIS IS** .... (name of vessel re-transmitting the distress message, spoken three times), followed by the intercepted message.

7.4.4 Control of MAYDAY traffic

A MAYDAY call imposes general radio silence, until the vessel concerned or some other authority (e.g. the nearest Coastguard) cancels the distress. If necessary the station controlling distress traffic may impose radio silence as follows:

> **SEELONCE MAYDAY**, followed by its name or other identification, on the distress frequency.
>
> If some other station nearby believes it necessary to do likewise, it may transmit:
>
> **SEELONCE DISTRESS**, followed by its name or other identification.

7.4.5 Relaxing radio silence

When appropriate the station controlling distress traffic may relax radio silence so that normal working is resumed with caution on the distress frequency, with subsequent communications from the casualty prefixed by the Urgency signal (below).

When complete radio silence is no longer necessary on a frequency being used for distress traffic, the controlling station may relax radio silence as follows, indicating that restricted working may be resumed:

> **MAYDAY**
>
> **ALL STATIONS** (spoken three times)
>
> **THIS IS** .... (name or callsign)
>
> The time ....
>
> The name of the vessel in distress ....
>
> **PRUDONCE**

If distress working continues on other frequencies these will be identified. For example, PRUDONCE on 2182 kHz, but SEELONCE on VHF Ch 16.

7.4.6 Cancelling radio silence

When all distress traffic has ceased, normal working is authorised as follows:

> **MAYDAY**
>
> **ALL STATIONS** (spoken three times)
>
> **THIS IS** .... (name or callsign)
>
> The time ....
>
> The name of the vessel in distress
>
> **SEELONCE FEENEE.**

7.5 URGENCY AND SAFETY

7.5.1 Pan-Pan – Urgency signal

The R/T Urgency signal, consisting of the words PAN-PAN spoken three times, indicates that a vessel, or station, has a very urgent message concerning the safety of a ship or person.

Messages prefixed by PAN PAN take priority over all traffic except distress, and are sent on VHF Ch 16 or on 2182 kHz. The Urgency signal is appropriate when someone is lost overboard or urgent medical advice or attention is needed. It should be cancelled when the urgency is over.

Here is an example of an Urgency call and message from the yacht Seabird, disabled off the Needles.

> **PAN-PAN, PAN-PAN, PAN-PAN**
>
> **ALL STATIONS** (spoken three times)
>
> **THIS IS THE YACHT SEABIRD, SEABIRD, SEABIRD**
>
> Two nine zero degrees two miles from Needles lighthouse
> Dismasted and propeller fouled
>
> Anchor dragging and drifting east north east towards Shingles Bank
>
> Require urgent tow
>
> **OVER.**

If the message itself is long or is a medical call, or communications traffic is heavy, it should be passed on a working frequency after an initial call on Ch 16 or 2182 kHz. Where necessary this should be indicated at the end of the initial call.

If you hear an Urgency call you should respond in the same way as for a Distress call.

If help is needed, but the boat is in no immediate danger, the proper signal is 'V' (Victor) International Code, meaning 'I require assistance'. This can be sent as a flag signal, or by light or sound in Morse code (•••—) (See Chapter 5, Plate 3).

7.5.2 Medical help by RT

Medical advice and assistance can be obtained through any UK HM Coastguard MRCC/MRSC. The initial call should be made on VHF DSC Ch 70, VHF RT Ch 16, or MF DSC 2187·5 kHz. In an emergency the proword **PAN PAN** can be used with a call on Ch 16.

The caller will be directed to a working frequency and while a doctor is being summoned to the telephone, the Coastguard will ask a number of questions relating to the patients name, age, sex, condition/symptons and details of the vessel including position, next port of call, ETA and nearest harbour if required to divert.

HM Coastguard will be directed by the instructions of the doctor as to the course of action to be taken in relation to treatment/evacuation of the casualty.

The International Code signal 'W' (Whiskey •——), means 'I require medical assistance' and can be made by a number of means; (See Chapter 5, Plate 3).

7.5.3 Sécurité – Safety signal

This consists of the word **SÉCURITÉ** (pronounced SAY-CURE-E-TAY) spoken three times, and indicates that the station is about to transmit an important navigational or meteorological warning. Such messages usually originate from a Coastguard Radio Station or a Coast Radio Station, and are transmitted on a working frequency after an announcement on the distress frequency.

Safety messages are usually addressed to 'All stations', and are often transmitted at the end of the first available silence period. An example of a "Securite" message would be:

> **SAYCUREETAY**. . . . . . (spoken three times)
>
> **THIS IS** . . . . . . (spoken three times)
>
> **ALL STATIONS** . . . . . . (spoken three times)
>
> followed by Coastguard Radio Station (or Coast Radio Station) identification, instructions to move to another channel, etc., and the message.

7.6 GMDSS

7.6.1 Introduction

The Global Maritime Distress and Safety System (GMDSS) is an improved maritime distress and safety communications system adopted by the International Maritime Organisation (IMO).

GMDSS was first introduced in Feb 1992 and became fully operational on 1 Feb 1999. The speed with which the various elements of GMDSS have been put in place varies from sea area to sea area according to national policies.

The Coastguard will cease its dedicated headset VHF Distress Watch on 31 Jan 2005. It is important to note that ceasing the dedicated distress watches does not dispense with the capability to monitor the VHF Distress Channel 16 and 2182 kHz since these will still be needed to talk to a distressed vessel after the GMDSS DSC electronic alert. These frequencies will also be required to maintain communications with other ships assisting in the distress situation. Therefore, after 31 January 2005 HM Coastguard will keep a loudspeaker watch on the VHF Distress Channel and currently do so on 2182 kHz.

Recommended reading:

ALRS, Vol 5. (UK Hydrographic Office).
GMDSS for small craft. (Clemmetsen/Fernhurst).
VHF DSC Handbook. (Fletcher/Reed's Publications).

7.6.2 Objective

The objective of GMDSS is to alert SAR authorities ashore and ships in the vicinity to a distress incident by means of a combination of satellite and terrestrial communication, and navigation systems. As a result a coordinated SAR operation can be mounted rapidly and reliably anywhere in the world. GMDSS also provides urgency and safety communications, and promulgates Marine Safety Information (MSI); see 7.6.9.

Regardless of the sea areas in which they operate, vessels complying with GMDSS must be able to perform certain functions:

- transmit ship-to-shore distress alerts by two independent means;
- transmit ship-to-ship distress alerts;
- transmit and receive safety information, e.g. navigation and weather warnings;
- transmit signals for locating incidents;
- receive shore-to-ship distress alerts;
- receive ship-to-ship distress alerts;
- transmit and receive communications for SAR co-ordination.

GMDSS regulations apply to all ships over 300 tons engaged in international voyages, but they affect all seagoing craft. Although not obligatory for yachts, some features of GMDSS are already of interest and, as equipment becomes more affordable, yachtsmen may decide to fit GMDSS voluntarily. This will become an increasing necessity as the present system for sending and receiving distress calls is run down.

7.6.3 Distress alerting

GMDSS requires participating ships to be able to send distress alerts by two out of three independent means. These are:

1 Digital selective calling (DSC) using VHF Ch 70, MF 2187·5 kHz, or HF distress and alerting frequencies in the 4, 6, 8,12 and 16 MHz bands.

2 EPIRBs (406 MHz/121·5MHz; float-free or manually operated) using the Cospas/Sarsat satellite system; or the Inmarsat system in the 1·6 GHz band. Both types transmit distress messages which include the position and identification of the vessel in distress. See 7.7 for further details of EPIRBs.

3 Inmarsat, via ship terminals.

7.6.4 Communications

GMDSS uses both terrestrial and satellite-based communications. Terrestrial communications, ie VHF, MF and HF, are employed in Digital Selective Calling (see below). Satellite communications come in the form of INMARSAT and Cospas/Sarsat.

7.6.5 Digital Selective Calling

DSC is a fundamental part of GMDSS. It is so called because information is sent by a burst of digital code; selective because it is addressed to another DSC radio-telephone.

Under GMDSS, every vessel and relevant shore station has a 9-digit identification number, known as an MMSI (Maritime Mobile Service Identity) that is used for identification in all DSC messages.

DSC is used to transmit distress alerts from ships, and to receive distress acknowledgments from ships or shore stations. DSC can also be used for relay purposes and for Urgency, Safety and routine calling and answering.

In practice, a DSC distress call sent on VHF might work roughly as follows:

Yachtsman presses the distress button; the set automatically switches to Ch 70 and transmits a coded distress message before reverting to Ch I6.

Any ship will reply directly by voice on Ch 16. But a CRS would send a distress acknowledgment on Ch 70 (automatically turning off the distress transmission), before replying on Ch 16. If a distress acknowledgment is not received from a CRS, the call will automatically be repeated about every four minutes.

7.6.6 Inmarsat

Inmarsat (International Maritime Satellite system), through four geostationary satellites positioned over each of the four ocean areas, provides near-global communications except in the polar regions above about Latitudes 70°N and 70°S.

Additionally, 1·6 GHz satellite L-band EPIRBs, provide global distress alerting through Inmarsat satellites operating through Inmarsat. This is referred to as Inmarsat 'E' which provides an alternative alerting system to 406 MHz EPIRBs which utilise the Cospas/Sarsat satellite system. Inmarsat 'E' EPIRBs can also be equipped with an optional 121·5 MHz locator beacon for homing purposes and/or optional Search and Rescue Radar Transponder (SART).

7.6.7 Transmitting Distress Alerts

A Distress call using DSC is known as a Distress Alert. It is transmitted on Ch 70 and is automatically repeated five times. Whenever possible, a DSC Distress Alert should always include the last known position and time in UT. Position information is normally entered automatically from an interfaced GPS, but can be entered manually if required. The nature of the distress can also be selected from the receiver menu. The vessels identity (MMSI number) is automatically included. Subsequent communication will be carried out on a notified channel, normally Ch 16.

Understand and follow the procedures for your VHF/DSC equipment. The Distress Alert is transmitted as follows:

(a) Tune the transmitter to the DSC Distress channel (VHF Ch 70 or MF 2187·5 kHz).

(b) If time permits, key in or select on the DSC equipment the nature of the distress; the vessel's last known position and time and the type of distress communication subsequently required (RT).

(c) Hold down the SOS button for 5 seconds and the alert will be transmitted.

Once a DSC Distress acknowledgement has been received, or after waiting for about 15 seconds, the vessel in distress should immediately transmit the Distress Message by voice on Ch 16. (see 7.4).

In the event of inadvertently transmitting a Distress alert it is important to cancel the false Distress Alert immediately by making an all stations call and cancelling the false alert sent at (date and time).

7.6.8 Cospas/Sarsat

The US/Russian Cospas/Sarsat satellites complement the various other Satcom systems. They not only detect an emergency signal transmitted by an EPIRB, but also locate it to a high degree of accuracy.

There are four Cospas/Sarsat satellites operating in low polar orbits. In addition to these, there are six Geolut experimental ground receiving stations and four Geosar geostationary satellites capable of receiving alerts from 406 MHz beacons. Geosar satellites have the capability to provide almost immediate distress alerts using existing 406 MHz beacons, although currently without providing distress location because there is no Doppler shift on the uplink frequency. However, this is not a problem if the EPIRB is provided with an inbuilt GPS receiver to provide location directly.

Currently, IMO is planning to terminate 121·5 MHz alerting services sometime after the year 2009. All Cospas/Sarsat satellites launched up to 2006 will be equipped with 121·5 MHz alerting systems.

7.6.9 Sea Areas

For the purposes of GMDSS, the world's sea area are divided into four categories in each of which ships must carry certain types of radio equipment. The UK has declared its coastal waters to be an A1 area, but intends to continue guarding VHF Channel 16 until 01 Feb 2005. VHF DSC is fully operational at all UK Coastguard Co-ordination Centres.

France has declared the English Channel to be an A1 area. As most UK yachtsmen will operate in an A1 area, a VHF radio and a Navtex receiver will initially meet GMDSS requirements. As suitable VHF DSC sets become available (and affordable) it will make sense to re-equip with DSC equipment.

The types of areas are:

A1	an area within RT coverage of at least one VHF Coast or Coastguard radio station in which continuous alerting via DSC is available. Range: roughly 40 miles from the CRS/CG.
A2	an area, excluding sea area A1, within RT coverage of at least one MF CRS/CG in which continuous DSC alerting is available. Range: roughly 100-150 miles from the CRS/CG.
A3	an area, excluding sea areas A1 and A2, within coverage of an Inmarsat satellite between 70°N and 70°S in which continuous alerting is available.
A4	an area outside sea areas A1, A2 and A3. In practice this means the polar regions.

7.6.10 Maritime Safety Information (MSI)

MSI refers to the vital meteorological, navigational and SAR messages which, traditionally, have been broadcast to vessels at sea by CRSs in Morse and by RT on VHF and MF.

GMDSS broadcasts MSI in English by two independent but complementary means, Navtex and SafetyNet:

Navtex on MF (518 kHz and 490 kHz) covers coastal/offshore waters out to about 300 miles from transmitters. SafetyNet uses the Inmarsat satellites to cover beyond MF range. The Enhanced Group Call (EGC) service is a part of SafetyNet which enables MSI to be sent selectively by Inmarsat-C satellites to groups of users in any of the 4 oceans.

MSI is prepared/coordinated by the nations which control the 16 Navareas used for Nav and Met warnings; see 4.7. The UK controls Navarea I, which covers the Atlantic between 48°27'N and 71°N, out to 35°W.

7.7 EPIRBs

7.7.1 Types and installation

There are two types of approved Emergency Position Indicating Radio Beacons (EPIRB), those transmitting on the emergency frequencies of 121·5 MHz (civilian aeronautical distress) or 406 MHz, or on both.

A third type transmits on 243·0 MHz (military aeronautical distress). 121·5 MHz and 243·0 MHz are monitored by Air Traffic Control and many aircraft; survivors should switch on an EPIRB without delay.

Dependent on type, they must be installed in a proper location so they can float free and automatically activate if the yacht sinks. Many EPIRBs have lanyards intended to secure the EPIRB to a life raft or person in the water and lanyards must not be used for securing the EPIRB to the yacht. This would clearly prevent a float-free type from activating and the EPIRB would be lost with the yacht should it sink.

7.7.2 Operation

All three frequencies can be picked up by the Cospas/Sarsat (C-S) system which uses four near-polar orbital satellites to detect and localise the signals. The processed positions are passed automatically to a Mission Control Centre (MCC) for assessment of any SAR action required; the UK MCC is co-located with ARCC Kinloss.

C-S location accuracy is normally better than 5 km on 406 MHz and better than 20 km on 121·5 and 243·0 MHz. Dedicated SAR aircraft can home on 121·5 MHz and 243·0 MHz, but not on 406 MHz. Typically a helicopter at 1,000 feet can receive homing signals from about 30M range whilst a fixed-wing aircraft at higher altitudes is capable of homing from about 60M.

Airliners flying on commercial air routes often receive and relay information on alerts on 121·5 MHz EPIRBs at up to 200M range. Best results will invariably be obtained from those 406 MHz EPIRBs which also transmit a 121·5 MHz signal for homing purposes.

7.7.3 Registration and false alerts

406 MHz EPIRBs transmit data which contains a unique code which identifies the individual beacon. It is now a mandatory requirement to register details of any 406 MHz or 1·6 GHz EPIRBs fitted to a UK vessel with the appropriate authority

Any changes regarding an EPIRB which is already registered must also be notified to that authority. It is an offence by the Owner and/or the Operator if either of the the above requirements are not carried out.

Registrations should be sent to: The EPIRB Register, HM Coastguard, Southern Region, Pendennis Point, Castle Drive, Falmouth TR11 4WZ, Cornwall.,
☎ +44 (0) 1326 211569 📠 +44 (0) 1326 319264.

False alerts caused by inadvertent or incorrect use of EPIRBs puts a significant burden on SAR resources. The likelihood of a false alert coinciding with a genuine distress situation is real; in consequence SAR forces could be delayed in responding to a genuine distress – with tragic results.

If an EPIRB is activated, whether accidentally or intentionally, make every reasonable effort to advise the SAR authorities as soon as possible.

7.7.4 SART

A SART (SAR transponder) is not an EPIRB; it is more akin to a small portable Racon (section 4.7). When interrogated by a search radar a SART responds with a series of easily identifiable blips visible on the radar screen. It is often carried in life rafts to assist searching ships and aircraft in finding survivors; it should be mounted at least 1m above sea level. It operates on 9GHz and has a range of about 5M from a ship's radar, and up to 40M from an aircraft.

For maximum range, a mounting as high as possible should be chosen. A SART lying flat on the floor of a liferaft will give a range of about 1·8M; when standing upright on the floor, about 2·5M and floating in the water about 2·0M.

Warning Note: A SART will only respond to an X-Band (3cm) radar and will not be seen on a S-Band (10cm) radar.

7.8 SEARCH AND RESCUE (SAR) – UK

7.8.1 Introduction

Around the United Kingdom, the lead authority is HM Coastguard, which initiates and co-ordinates all civil maritime SAR. To assist; the RNLI provide lifeboats; the Ministry of Defence provide declared fixed wing aircraft and helicopters, together with other aircraft and ships which may be available. HM Coastguard also provides SAR helicopters, and Emergency Towing Vessels at selected sites, and Rescue Teams to assist with coastal searches and other coastal incidents, including cliff and mud rescue.

The ARCC at Kinloss also mans the UK Cospas/Sarsat Mission Control Centre (MCC) which receives satellite data from emergency distress beacons on 121·5 MHz, 243·0 MHz and 406 MHz (7.6.4).

7.8.2 Raising the alarm

If an incident afloat is seen from shore, dial 999 and ask for the Coastguard. You will be asked to report on the incident, and possibly to stay near the telephone for further communications. If at sea you receive a distress signal and you are in a position to give assistance, you are obliged to do so with all speed, unless, or until, you are specifically released.

When alerted the Coastguard summons the most appropriate help, i.e. they may direct vessels in the vicinity of the distress; request the launch of an RNLI lifeboat; scramble a military or Coastguard SAR helicopter; other vessels may be alerted through Coastguard Coordination Centres, Coast Radio Stations abroad, or by satellite communications.

7.8.3 Royal National Lifeboat Institution (RNLI)
The RNLI is a registered charity which saves life at sea. It provides, on call, a 24-hour lifeboat service up to 50M out from the coasts of the UK and Irish Republic. There are 230 lifeboat stations, at which are stationed 320 all-weather and inshore lifeboats ranging from 4·9 to 17·0m in length. There are 131 lifeboats in the reserve fleet. All new lifeboats are capable of at least 25 knots.

When launched on service, lifeboats over 10m keep watch on VHF and MF DSC (Digital Selective Calling) as well as a listening watch on Ch 16. They can also use alternative frequencies to contact other vessels, SAR aircraft, HM Coastguard or Coast radio stations or other SAR agencies. All lifeboats are fitted with VHF and show a quick-flashing blue light when on operational service.

In addition to providing the lifeboat service, the RNLI is also busy promoting water safety. Accordingly, the RNLI provides a FREE comprehensive water safety service to members and the general public including safety advice, safety publications and demonstrations. The RNLI's aim is to save lives and prevent accidents by helping people be prepared through water safety awareness. For more details of how the RNLI can help you to be safer at sea, call the RNLI on 0800 328 0600, email seasafety@rnli.org.uk or visit www.rnli org.uk.
To support the RNLI by becoming a member, contact: RNLI, West Quay Road, Poole, Dorset BH15 1HZ.
Tel 01202 663000. Fax 01202 663167.

7.9 HM Coastguard

7.9.1 Organisation

HM Coastguard combined with the Marine Safety Agency in April 1998 to form the Maritime and Coastguard Agency (MCA) www.mcagency.org.uk. The locations of HM Coastguard Coordination Centres are shown in Table 7(1) and Fig. 7(2).

HM Coastguard initiates and co-ordinates civil maritime SAR around the UK and over a large part of the eastern Atlantic. Its domain is divided into three Maritime Search and Rescue Regions (SRRs), with Maritime Rescue Co-ordination Centres (MRCCs) at Falmouth, Dover, Great Yarmouth, Aberdeen, the Clyde and Swansea.

Each SRR is divided into districts, each under a Maritime Rescue Sub-Centre (MRSC). Their boundaries are stated in Table 7 (1) and shown on the maps at the start of Areas 1–11 in Chapter 9. The telephone number of the nearest MRCC/MRSC (or other national equivalent) is shown for each harbour.

Within each of the eighteen districts thus formed there is an organisation of Auxiliary Coastguard Rescue Teams, grouped within sectors under the management of regular Coastguard Officers.

There are about 560 regular Coastguard Officers. More than 3,100 Auxiliary Coastguards are on call for emergencies. The Coastguard is also responsible for persons in distress or missing on the coastline and has search, cliff rescue and mud rescue capabilities (at selected locations).

7.9.2 Functions

HM Coastguard is responsible for:

(1) Maintaining an electronic radio watch on VHF DSC Channel 70 around the whole of the UK coastline, effectively, within sight of land, 0-30M offshore. The UK has been declared fully operational for GMDSS Sea Area A1.

(2) Maintaining a continuous listening radio watch on 156·8 MHz the VHF Distress, Urgency, Safety and calling frequency (VHF Ch 16) to a range of at least 30M offshore.

(3) Maintaining and electronic radio watch on MF DSC on 2187·5 kHz at selected stations, effectively, within 30M - 150M offshore.

Note: The MCA have no plans to designate any shore based station for HF DSC. An agreement with Denmark, allows Lyngby radio to forward any HF DSC alert messages to the UK, via MRCC Yarmouth.

(4) Broadcasting MSI to set schedules on VHF and MF RT, including Negative Tidal Surge Warnings, Subfacts and Gunfacts, ice warnings (when appropriate) and interruption to electronic navigational aids.

For Distress, Urgency and Safety calls covering UK waters, all rescue centres keep watch on VHF DSC Ch 70, VHF RT Channel 16, and, at selected stations, on MF DSC 2187·5 kHz.

VHF Channels 10, 23, 67, 73, 84 and 86 are working channels; Ch 67 is the Small Craft Safety channel, accessed via Channel 16. Details of VHF or MF working frequencies will be given after an initial announcement on VHF Ch 16.

Coastguard MRCC/MRSC's are also responsible for responding to PAN PAN calls and providing telephone link calls to a doctor for medical advice. Initial call should be made on MF or VHF DSC, Ch 16, or 2182 kHz. The caller will be advised of an appropriate working channel/frequency.

NOTE: HM Coastguard does not provide a commercial telephone link call service.

Radio and telephone traffic to and from Coastguard Co-ordination Centres is recorded for the purposes of public safety, preventing and detecting crime.

The Radiotelephone call sign of an MRCC or MRSC is its geographical name, followed by 'Coastguard' e.g, SOLENT COASTGUARD.

In the Dover Strait the Channel Navigation Information Service (CNIS) provides a 24 hrs radar watch and a radio safety service for all shipping. See Table 7(1).

All Coastguard Coordination Centres provide Maritime Safety Information broadcasts at four hourly intervals. Information will include WZ Navigational Warnings, Gale Warnings, Local Inshore Forecasts, Tidal Surge Warnings, and local navigation warnings. Each coordination centre follows a separate broadcast schedule. Skippers/Owners should listen to these scheduled broadcasts and avoid requesting individual forecasts.

Gale warnings and WZ Navigation Warnings are broadcast on receipt then at 4 hourly intervals in accordance with the MSI Broadcast Schedule. A brochure HM Coastguard Broadcast Times for Maritime Safety Information – MCA/064 is available from MCA HQ, Southampton.

7.10 MARITIME SEARCH AND RESCUE REGIONS

7.10.1 Search and Rescue Regions

One of the most important aspects of GMDSS is the establishment of a Global Search and Rescue Plan.

The IMO and ICAO, the two agencies of the United Nations devoted to maritime and aeronautical safety are both working towards this aim.

As party to SOLAS, and the IMO/ICAO conventions a State is obliged to provide certain maritime or aeronautical SAR coordination and services.

A Search and Rescue Region (SRR) is an area of defined dimensions associated with a Rescue Coordination Centre within which SAR services are provided. The purpose of having an SRR is to clearly define who has primary responsibility for coordinating responses to distress situations in every area of the world and to enable rapid distribution of the distress alerts to the appropriate RCC.

The delimitation of an SRR is not related to, and shall not prejudice, the delimitation of any boundary between States. Such areas are established to ensure that primary responsibility for coordinating SAR services for that geographical area is assumed by some state.

In practice, SAR services may not necessarily be provided by their designated state. In such cases, SAR facilities are likely to be provided by the nearest country having the most appropriate SAR assets. Few SRRs world-wide have the agreement of all neighbouring states, but those in the British Isles and NW Europe have. By far the majority of SSRs have either been unilaterally declared, and are operated by the responsible state, according to a tacit acceptance by neighbouring states, or are awaiting formal approval between neighbouring states.

7.10.2 Emergency VHF DF

A number of HM Coastguard MRCC/MRSCs can provide VHF DF bearings to yachts in distress. The stations operate direction finding antenna around the coast of UK from which the bearings of vessels within range, and transmitting on VHF, can be determined.

On request from a vessel in distress the Coastguard station will transmit from the direction-finding site the bearing of the vessel from the direction finding antenna.

This service is only available for emergency use. Call on VHF Ch 16. Bearings will be passed on Ch 16 or 67 by the CG Centre as the yacht's true bearing from the DF site. Direction finding sites are shown on Admiralty charts and on the Area maps in this almanac by the ◉RG symbol.

In the Channel Is a yacht in distress should transmit on Ch 16 or Ch 67 for Guernsey or Ch 82 for Jersey.

France operates a similar VHF Direction Finding Service which is remotely controlled by CROSS, a signal station or a Naval lookout station. CROSS stations keep watch on Ch 16, 11 and 67. Signal stations and Lookout stations keep watch on Ch 16

7.10.3 MCA Voluntary Safety Identification Scheme

This free scheme provides useful information about your boat and its equipment which will assist the Coastguard toward a successful SAR operation. Complete a Form CG66, obtainable from the local Coastguard station, harbour master or marina or www.mcagency.org.uk. The completed cards should be returned to your nearest Coastguard Coordination Centre where they will be logged into a data file. Tell the Coastguard if the ownership, name of the craft, or any address given on Form CG66 changes. A tear-off section can be given to a friend or relative so that they know which Coastguard station to contact if they are concerned for the boat's safety. A CG66 is kept for two years. If it is not renewed within that time, the old CG66 data will be removed from the CG records.

It is not the function of HM Coastguard to maintain watch for boats on passage, but they will record information by phone before departure or from intermediate ports, or while on passage by visual signals or VHF Ch 67 (the Small Craft Safety Channel).

When using Ch 67 for safety messages, skippers should give the name of the MRCC/MRSC holding the boat's CG66. In these circumstances the Coastguard must be told of any change to the planned movements of the boat, and it is important that they are informed of the boat's safe arrival at her ultimate destination – so as to avoid needless overdue action being taken.

7.10.4 National Coastwatch Institution (NCI)

The NCI, is a charity dedicated to the safety of all who use UK Coastal Waters. Formed in 1994, it functions by re-introducing Visual Watch Stations around the UK coast, usually by re-opening the now abandoned Coastguard lookouts. Huge stretches of coastline are solely reliant on the volunteer NCI watchkeepers to provide the vitally important visual watch link with HM Coastguard, the RNLI and other SAR services. Many life-threatening incidents occur and many lives saved as a direct result of an NCI Watchkeeper.

VHF Ch16 is monitored to detect weak distress transmissions and all passing small boat traffic is logged to assist in the search for any craft reported missing. A further service provided to the maritime community lies in the NCI Stations informing local tourist offices and radio stations of actual weather conditions, and being available during daylight hours to provide a similar service to any yachtsman who telephones the station for information of conditions outside the shelter of the harbour. 24 Stations are operational, and others will be added as funds permit.

In poor visibility some stations keep a radar watch to 20M offshore. They are able to report the actual local weather on request, see below for ☎.

Most NCI stations can warn a yacht by light signal of an apparently dangerous course, eg 'U' ••— = You are standing into danger.

The following NCI stations were operating in 2003:

Stepper Point (Padstow)	07810 898041
Boscastle (North Cornwall)	01840 250965
St Ives	01736 799398
Cape Cornwall (Land's End) Ⓡ	01736 787890
Gwennap Head (Land's End) Ⓡ	01736 871351
Penzance	01736 367063
Bass Point (Lizard) Ⓡ	01326 290212
Portscatho (Falmouth East)	01872 580180
Charlestown	01726 817068
Polruan (Fowey)	01726 870291
Rame Head (Plymouth)	01752 823706
Prawle Point Ⓡ	01548 511259
Exmouth	01395 222492
Portland Bill Ⓡ	01305 860178
St Alban's Head Ⓡ	01929 439220
Peverill Pt, Swanage Ⓡ	01929 422596
Folkestone	01303 227132
Herne Bay	01227 743208
Holehaven	01268 696971
Southend	01702 299330
Felixstowe	01394 670808
Gorleston (Great Yarmouth)	01493 440384
Mundesley (Norfolk) Ⓡ	01263 722399
Hartlepool Ⓡ	01429 274931

Ⓡ = Radar equipped.

For further information contact:
NCI Head Office,
4a Trafalgar Square, Fowey, Cornwall PL23 1AZ.
☎/📠 0870 787 2147
e-mail: nci@springfresh.co.uk
web: http://www.nci.org.uk

7.11 SIGNALS USED IN DISTRESS SITUATIONS

7.11.1 Visual signals, shore to ships

If no radio link is possible, the following may be used to a vessel in distress or stranded off the UK coast. These are shown in Fig. 7(1) and this information must be carried aboard in an accessible place. The crews attention should be drawn to this before departure.

(a) Acknowledgment of distress signal.
By day: Orange smoke signal, or combined light and sound signal consisting of three signals fired at about one-minute intervals.
By night: White star rocket consisting of three single signals at about one-minute intervals.

(b) Landing signals for small boats.
Vertical motion of a white flag or arms (white light or flare by night), or signalling K (—•—) by light or sound = This is the best place to land.
Direction may be given by placing a steady white light or flare at a lower level.

Horizontal motion of a white flag or arms extended horizontally (white light or flare by night), or signalling S (•••) = Landing here is highly dangerous.

In addition, a better landing place may be signalled by carrying a white flag (flare or light), or by firing a white star signal in the direction indicated; or by signalling R (•—•) if a better landing is to the right of the direction of approach, or L (•—••) if it is to the left.

(c) Signals for shore life-saving apparatus.

Vertical motion of a white flag or the arms (or of a white light or flare) = Affirmative; or specifically, Rocket line is held; Tail block is made fast; Hawser is made fast; Man is in breeches buoy; or Haul away.

Horizontal motion of a white flag or the arms (or of a white light or flare) = Negative; or specifically, Slack away or Avast (stop) hauling.

NB: Rocket rescue equipment is no longer used by HM CG. Some larger vessels carry a line-throwing appliance requiring on-shore liaison before use.

(d) Warning signal.

International Code signal U (••—) or NF = You are running into danger. A white flare, white star rocket, or explosive signal may be used to draw attention to the above signals.

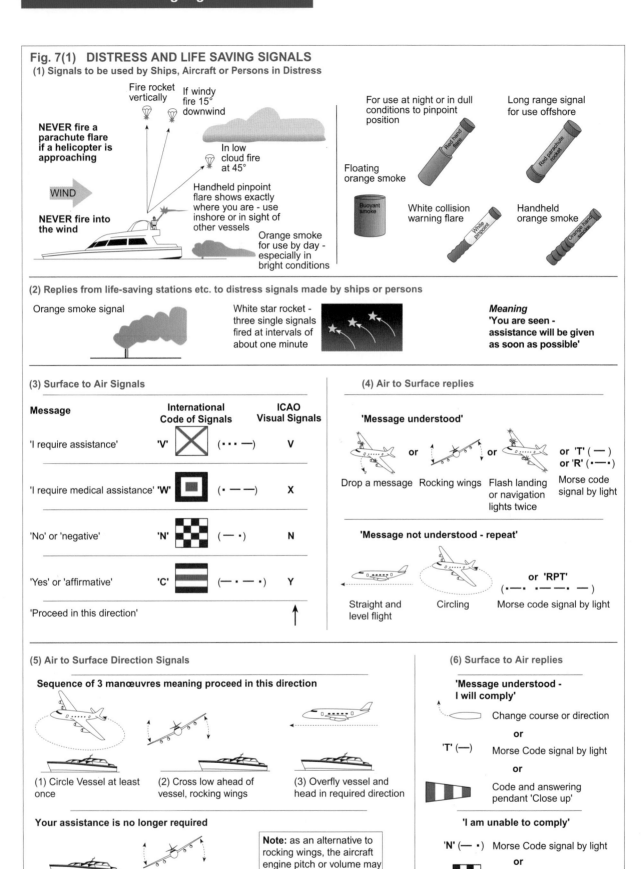

Fig. 7(1) DISTRESS AND LIFE SAVING SIGNALS

(1) Signals to be used by Ships, Aircraft or Persons in Distress

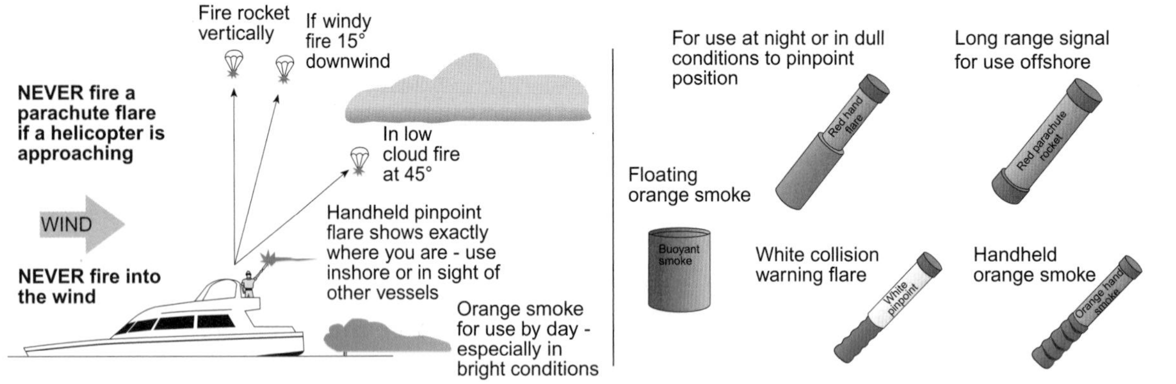
Fire rocket vertically
If windy fire 15° downwind
NEVER fire a parachute flare if a helicopter is approaching
In low cloud fire at 45°
WIND
Handheld pinpoint flare shows exactly where you are - use inshore or in sight of other vessels
NEVER fire into the wind
Orange smoke for use by day - especially in bright conditions
For use at night or in dull conditions to pinpoint position
Long range signal for use offshore
Red hand flare
Red parachute rocket
Floating orange smoke
Buoyant smoke
White collision warning flare
White pinpoint
Handheld orange smoke
Orange hand smoke

(2) Replies from life-saving stations etc. to distress signals made by ships or persons

Orange smoke signal

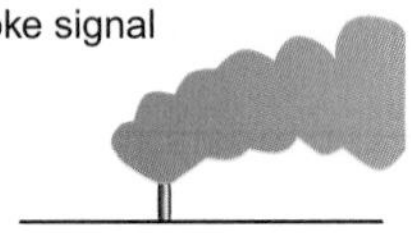

White star rocket - three single signals fired at intervals of about one minute

Meaning
'You are seen - assistance will be given as soon as possible'

(3) Surface to Air Signals

Message	International Code of Signals		ICAO Visual Signals
'I require assistance'	'V'	(· · · —)	V
'I require medical assistance'	'W'	(· — —)	X
'No' or 'negative'	'N'	(— ·)	N
'Yes' or 'affirmative'	'C'	(— · — ·)	Y
'Proceed in this direction'			↑

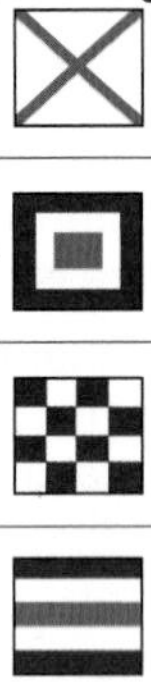

(4) Air to Surface replies

'Message understood'

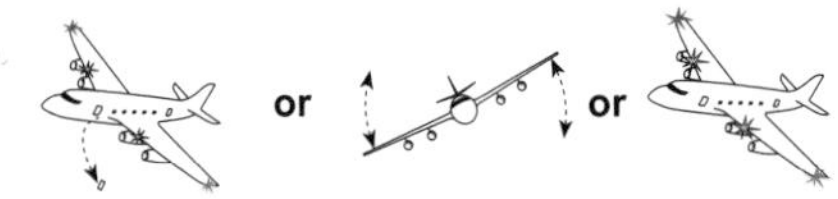
or
or

Drop a message or Rocking wings or Flash landing or navigation lights twice or **'T'** (—) or **'R'** (· — ·) Morse code signal by light

'Message not understood - repeat'

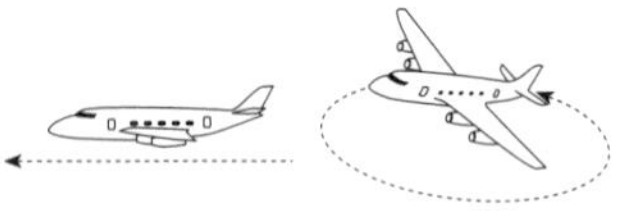

Straight and level flight

Circling

or 'RPT' (· — · · — — · —) Morse code signal by light

(5) Air to Surface Direction Signals

Sequence of 3 manœuvres meaning proceed in this direction

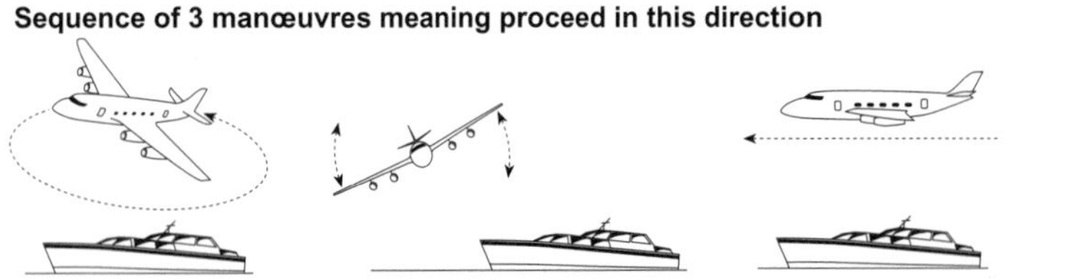

(1) Circle Vessel at least once

(2) Cross low ahead of vessel, rocking wings

(3) Overfly vessel and head in required direction

Your assistance is no longer required

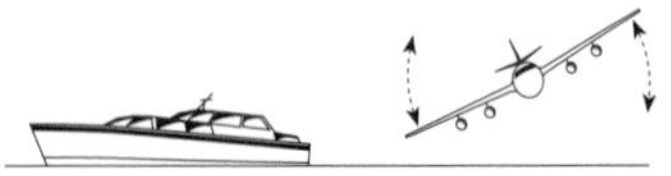

Cross low astern of vessel rocking wings

Note: as an alternative to rocking wings, the aircraft engine pitch or volume may be varied

(6) Surface to Air replies

'Message understood - I will comply'

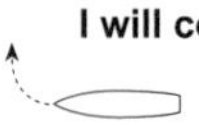

Change course or direction

or

'T' (—) Morse Code signal by light

or

Code and answering pendant 'Close up'

'I am unable to comply'

'N' (— ·) Morse Code signal by light

or

International flag 'N'

DISTRESS AND LIFE SAVING SIGNALS (continued)

(7) Landing signals for the guidance of small boats with crews or persons in distress. By night white lights or flares are used instead of white flags.

		Other signals	*Meaning*
	**Vertical** motion of a white flag) or of the arms	International Code letter **'K'** (— • —) by light or sound	**'This is the best place to land'** (An indication of direction may be given by a steady white light or flare at a lower level)
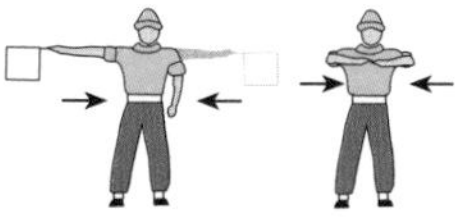	**Horizontal** motion of a white flag or of the arms extended horizontally	International Code letter **'S'** (• • •) by light or sound	**'Landing here is highly dangerous'**
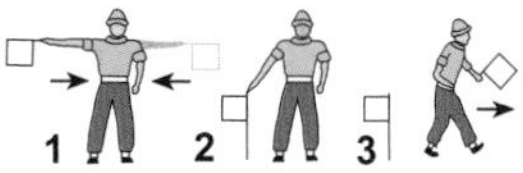	**Horizontal** motion of a white flag followed by **2**. placing the white flag in the ground and **3**. by carrying another white flag in the direction to be indicated.	**1**. Signalling the code letter **'S'** (• • •), followed by the code letter **'R'** (• — •) if the better landing place is more to the right in the direction of the approach, or **2**, by the code letter **'L'** (• — • •) if the better landing place is more to the left in the direction of approach	**'Landing here is highly dangerous. A more favourable location for landing is in the direction indicated'**

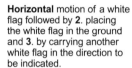

---

(8) Signals to be made in connection with the use of shore apparatus for life-saving

Signal	*Meaning*	Signal	*Meaning*
Vertical motion of a white flag (or white light or flare by night) or of the arms 	**In general:** 'affirmative' Specifically: 'rocket line is held - tail block is made fast - hawser is made fast - man is in the breeches buoy - haul away'	**Horizontal** motion of a white flag (or white light or flare by night) or of the arms 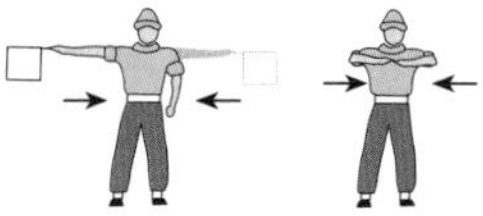	**In general:** negative. Specifically : slack away - stop hauling

---

(9) Signals to be used to warn a ship which is standing into danger

International Code flag **'U'**

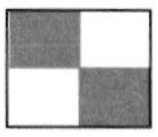

or **'NF'**

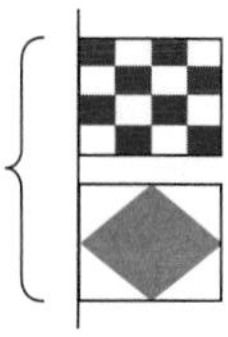

International Code signal **'U'** by light or sound • • —

---

(10) Signals used by Sub-Aqua divers

'I am OK'

'I need assistance'

C7

7.11.2 Signals used by SAR aircraft

A searching aircraft normally flies at about 3,000–5,000ft, or below cloud, firing a green Very light every five or ten minutes and at each turning point.

On seeing a green flare, a yacht in distress should take the following action:

(1) Wait for the green flare to die out.

(2) Fire one red flare.

(3) Fire another red flare after about 20 seconds. (This allows the aircraft to line up on the bearing.)

(4) Fire a third red flare when the aircraft is overhead, or if it appears to be going badly off course.

Other signals are shown in the fig 7 (1).

7.11.3 Directing signals by aircraft

(1) Fig 7 (1) (5/6) shows how a vessel is directed towards a ship or aircraft in distress, how to communicate that assistance by the vessel is no longer required and how a vessel may reply.

7.12 HELICOPTER RESCUE

7.12.1 Capability

SAR helicopters in the UK are based at Culdrose, Portland, Lee-on-Solent, Wattisham, Leconfield, Boulmer, Lossiemouth, Sumburgh, Stornoway, Prestwick, Valley and Chivenor.

Sea King SAR helicopters can operate to a range of 300 miles and can rescue up to 18 survivors. The Sea King's automatic hover control system permits rescues at night and in fog.

7.12.2 Communications

SAR helicopters are generally fitted with VHF, FM and AM, UHF and HF SSB RT and can communicate with lifeboats, etc., on VHF FM. Communications between ship and helicopter should normally be on VHF Ch 16 or 67; 2182 kHz SSB may also be available. If contact is difficult, communication can often be achieved through a Nimrod aircraft if on scene, or through a lifeboat or HM Coastguard.

When the helicopter is sighted by a boat in distress, a flare (fired away from, not at, the helicopter), an orange smoke signal, dye marker or an Aldis lamp (not pointed directly at the helicopter) will assist recognition – very important if other vessels are in the vicinity. Cockpit dodgers with the boat's name or sail number are useful aids to identification.

7.12.3 On the yacht

Survivors from a yacht with a mast may need to be picked up from a dinghy or life raft streamed at least 100ft (30m) away. In a small yacht with no dinghy, survivors (wearing life jackets) may need to be picked up from the water, at the end of a long warp. It is very important that no survivor boards a life raft or jumps into the sea until instructed to do so by the helicopter (either by VHF Ch 16 or 67) or by the winchman (by word of mouth). Sails should be lowered and lashed and it is helpful if the drift of the boat is reduced by a sea anchor.

If a crewman descends from the helicopter, he will take charge. Obey his instructions quickly. Never secure the winch wire to the yacht, and beware that it may carry a lethal static charge if it is not dipped (earthed) in the sea before handling.

7.12.4 Double lift

Survivors may be lifted by double lift in a strop, accompanied by the crewman in a canvas seat. Or it may be necessary, with no crewman, for a survivor to position himself in the strop. Put your head and shoulders through the strop so that the padded part is in the small of the back and the toggle is in front of the face. Pull the toggle down, as close to the chest as possible. When ready, give a thumbs-up sign with an extended arm, and place both arms close down by the side of the body (resist the temptation to hang on to the strop). On reaching the helicopter, do exactly as instructed by the crew. Injured persons can be lifted strapped into a special stretcher carried in the helicopter.

7.12.5 Hi-line

In some circumstances a 'Hi-line technique' may be used. This is a rope tail, attached to the helicopter winch wire by a weak link, and weighted at its lower end. When it is lowered to the yacht do not make it fast, but coil it down carefully. The helicopter pays out the winch wire and then moves to one side of the yacht and descends, while the yacht takes in the slack (keeping it outboard and clear of all obstructions) until the winch hook and strop are on board.

One of the helicopter crew may be lowered with the strop. When ready to lift, the helicopter ascends and takes in the wire. Pay out the tail, keeping enough weight on it to keep it taut until the end is reached, then cast it off well clear of the yacht. But if a further lift is to be made the tail should be retained on board (not made fast) to facilitate recovery of the strop for the next lift.

When alighting from a helicopter, beware of the tail rotor which can be difficult to see. Obey all instructions given by the helicopter crew.

7.13 ABANDON SHIP

Do not abandon a yacht until she is definitely sinking. A yacht is easier to find than a liferaft and provides better shelter. While she is still afloat use her resources (such as R/T, for distress calls) and put extra equipment in the liferaft or lash into the dinghy (which should also be taken, if possible). Make all preparations.

Before entering the liferaft, and cutting it adrift:

(a) Send a MAYDAY call, saying that yacht is being

abandoned, with position and number of people on board.

(b) Dress warmly with sweaters, etc, under oilskins, and life jacket on top. Take extra clothes.

(c) Fill any available containers with fresh water to about ¾ full, so that they will float.

(d) Collect additional food, tins and tin-opener.

(e) Collect navigational gear, EPIRB, SART, handheld VHF, torch, extra flares, bucket, length of line, First-aid kit, knife, fenders etc. Some of items (c) – (e) should already be in a survival bag, essential when a yacht is abandoned in a hurry.

Launch the liferaft on the lee side of the yacht, having first checked the painter is secured to a strongpoint. The painter may be up to 10m long; after about 3-4m give a sharp tug to activate the CO_2 bottle. If the liferaft inflates upside down, try to right it from the yacht. Keep the liferaft close alongside and try to board it without getting into the water.

Once in the liferaft, plan for the worst, i.e., a long period before rescue. Protection, Location, Water, Food are your priorities – in that order. Always believe that you will survive.

(a) Keep the inside of the raft as dry as possible. Huddle together for warmth. Close the openings as necessary, but keep a good lookout for shipping and aircraft.

(b) Stream the drogue if necessary for stability, or so as to stay near the original position.

(c) Take anti-seasick pills.

(d) Ration fresh water to ½litre per person per day; none in the first 24 hours. Do not drink sea water or urine. Collect rain water.

(e) Use flares sparingly, on the skipper's orders.

7.14 HAZARDS

7.14.1 Submarines

Fishing vessels and occasionally yachts have been snagged or hit by submarines operating just below the surface. The best advice available to yachtsmen is:

(a) Listen to Subfacts (7.14.2).

(b) Avoid charted submarine exercise areas.

(c) Keep clear of any vessel flying the Code Flags 'NE2' meaning that submarines are in the vicinity.

(d) Run your engine or generator even when under sail.

(e) Operate your echo sounder.

(f) At night show deck-level navigation lights, ie on pulpit and stern.

The risk is greatest in the English Channel, the Irish Sea, the Firth of Clyde, North Channel, off W Scotland and especially at night. Submarine exercise areas are shown by name/number in 9.1.16, 9.2.31, 9.8.22 and 9.9.19.

7.14.2 Subfacts

These are broadcast warnings of planned or known submarine activity. Subfacts (South Coast) give details relevant to the English Channel; see 9.1.16 & 9.2.31. They are broadcast by **Falmouth MRCC** after an initial announcement on VHF Ch 16 at 0140 UT and every 4 hours thereafter, and by **Brixham MRSC** at 0050 and every 4 hours thereafter.

Subfacts (Clyde) give details relevant to the W coast of Scotland (see 9.8.22 and 9.9.19). They are broadcast by **Stornoway MRCC** after an initial announcement on VHF Ch 16 at 0110 UT and every 4 hours thereafter, by **Clyde MRCC** on VHF Ch 16 at 0020 UT and every 4 hours thereafter, and by **Belfast MRSC** after an initial announcement on VHF Ch 16 at 0305 UT and every 4 hours thereafter.

7.14.3 Gunfacts

Gunfacts are warnings of intended naval firing practice broadcast to mariners. They do not restrict the passage of any vessel. The onus for safety lies with the naval unit concerned. The broadcasts include:

(a) Time (LT) and approximate location of firings, with a declared safe distance in M.

(b) Whether illuminants are to be fired.

Gunfacts include underwater explosions, gunnery and missile firings. For underwater explosions only broadcasts will be made on Ch 16 at 1 hr, 30 mins, and immediately prior to detonation.

Gunfacts (S Coast) are issued by FOST, Plymouth for English Channel exercise areas (9.1.16 and 9.2.31). Gunfacts are broadcast by Falmouth MRCC after an initial announcement on VHF Ch 16 at 0140 UT and every 4 hours thereafter, and by Brixham MRSC after an initial announcement on VHF Ch 16 at 0050 and every 4 hours thereafter.

Gunfacts (Ship) are issued by a nominated warship and cover activity in all UK areas except the English Channel. Broadcasts are made daily at 0800 and 1400 LT on Ch 06 or 67 after an announcement on Ch 16. Subfacts and Gunfacts are also transmitted on NAVTEX.

7.15 NAVIGATIONAL WARNINGS

7.15.1 General

The world is divided into 16 sea areas (Navareas I to XVI). Each Navarea has a Co-ordinating country responsible for issuing Long-range nav warnings. These are transmitted in English and other languages at scheduled times by RT, radiotelex and fax. Warnings cover navigational aids, wrecks, dangers of all kinds, SAR operations, cable laying, naval exercises, etc.

Coastal and Local warnings may also be issued. Coastal warnings, up to 100 or 200 miles offshore, are broadcast in English and their national language by Coast radio stations. Local warnings are issued by harbour authorities in the national language.

7.15.2 United Kingdom

The UK is the Area Co-ordinator for Navarea I. Long-range Navigational warnings are broadcast by Coastguard Centres after an initial announcement on Ch 16 and by Navtex every 4 hours and by SafetyNet once a day. (Navarea I warnings are not broadcast by RT). They are also published in weekly *Notices to Mariners,* together with a list of warnings still in force.

WZ (Coastal) warnings are broadcast by Coastguard Coordination Centres every four hours. An initial announcement will be made on Ch 16 indicating which working channel (10, 23, 73, 84 or 86) the broadcast will be made on at the times indicated in 4.10.1 for the Sea Regions lettered A to N in Fig. 4 (1). Coastal Warnings are also transmitted on Navtex. Important warnings are broadcast on VHF Ch 16 and/or 2182 kHz at any time required.

Vessels which encounter dangers to navigation should notify other craft and the nearest Coastguard coordination centre, prefacing the message by the Safety signal (see 7.2.3).

7.15.3 Denmark

Navigational warnings are broadcast by Lyngby Radio on MF 1704 kHz, 1734 kHz, 1738 kHz, or 2586 kHz, and on various VHF channels (see Fig. 7 (4)) on receipt and at scheduled times, after an initial announcement on MF 2182 kHz or VHF Ch 16 kHz.

7.15.4 Germany

Navigational warnings *(Nautische Warnnachricht)* for the North Sea coast are contained in IJmuiden Navtex (P) transmissions. Dangers to navigation should be reported to *Seewarn Cuxhaven.*

7.15.5 Netherlands

Navigational warnings are broadcast by Netherlands Coastguard (IJmuiden) on MF 3673 kHz, VHF Ch 23 and /or Ch 83, on receipt and at scheduled times, after an initial announcement on MF DSC 2187·5 kHz, VHF DSC Ch 70 or VHF Ch 16, and on Navtex (P).

7.15.6 Belgium

Navigational warnings are broadcast by Oostende Radio on MF 2761 kHz and VHF Ch 27 on receipt and at scheduled times after an initial announcement on MF DSC 2187·5 kHz, VHF DSC Ch 70 or VHF Ch 16, and on Navtex.

Navigational warnings for the Schelde are broadcast by Antwerpen on Ch 24 on receipt and every H+03 and H+48.

7.15.7 France

See 7.20 for details of French MSI navigational warning broadcasts.

7.15.8 Spain and Portugal

Navigational warnings are broadcast by Spanish and Portuguese Coast Radio Stations and MRCCs/MRSCs on MF 2182 kHz or VHF Ch 16 before being broadcast on the scheduled frequency or Channel number.

Fig. 7 (2) UK Coastguard centres

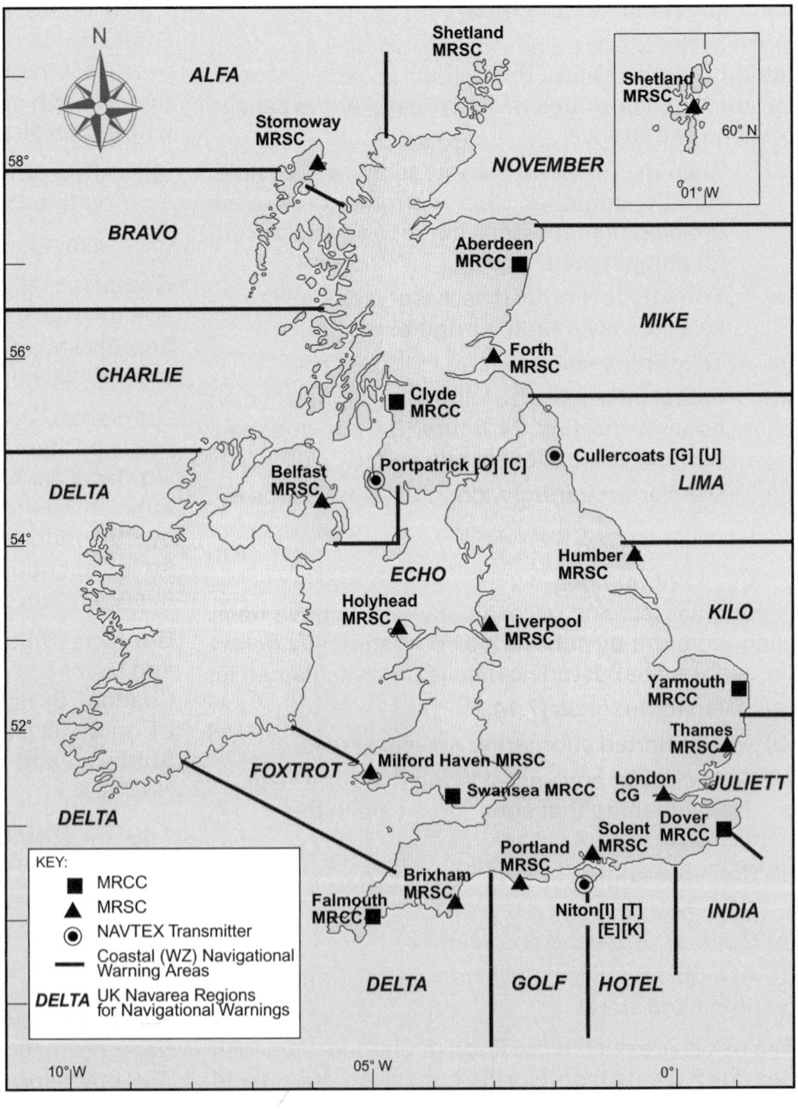
N
ALFA
BRAVO
CHARLIE
DELTA
ECHO
FOXTROT
GOLF
HOTEL
INDIA
JULIETT
KILO
LIMA
MIKE
NOVEMBER
Shetland MRSC
Stornoway MRSC
Aberdeen MRCC
Forth MRSC
Clyde MRCC
Portpatrick [O] [C]
Cullercoats [G] [U]
Belfast MRSC
Humber MRSC
Holyhead MRSC
Liverpool MRSC
Yarmouth MRCC
Thames MRSC
Milford Haven MRSC
Swansea MRCC
London CG
Dover MRCC
Solent MRSC
Portland MRSC
Brixham MRSC
Falmouth MRCC
Niton[I] [T] [E][K]
60° N
01° W
58°
56°
54°
52°
10° W
05° W
0°
KEY:
MRCC
MRSC
NAVTEX Transmitter
Coastal (WZ) Navigational Warning Areas
DELTA UK Navarea Regions for Navigational Warnings

TABLE 7 (1) HM Coastguard MRCCs and MRSCs

All Centres have operational A1 DSC VHF CH 70. All A2 DSC stations are operational, as indicated by 2187·5 kHz. WZ (Coastal) Navigation Warnings, Gale Warnings and Inshore Forecasts are as follows:

Stations additionally broadcasting Gunfacts and Subfacts are indicated by *.

FALMOUTH COASTGUARD (MRCC)
50°09'N 05°03'W. DSC MMSI 002320014 (2187·5 kHz)
Pendennis Point, Castle Drive, Falmouth TR11 4WZ.
☎ 01326 317575. Fax 01326 318342.
Area from Marsland Mouth to Dodman Point.
On VHF Ch 16*, MF 2226 kHz Navigation Warnings at: 0140 0540 0940 1340 1740 and 2140 UT.

BRIXHAM COASTGUARD (MRSC)
50°24'N 03°31'W. DSC MMSI 002320013
King's Quay, Brixham TQ5 9TW.
☎ 01803 882704. Fax 01803 882780.
Area from Dodman Point to Topsham.
On VHF Ch 16* Navigation Warnings at: 0050 0450 0850 1250 1650 2050 UT

PORTLAND COASTGUARD (MRSC)
50°36'N 02°27'W. DSC MMSI 002320012
Custom House Quay, Weymouth DT4 8BE.
☎ 01305 760439. Fax 01305 760452.
Area from Topsham to Chewton Bunney.
On VHF Ch 16 Navigation Warnings at: 0220 0620 1020 1420 1820 and 2220 UT

SOLENT COASTGUARD (MRSC)
50°48'N 01°12'W. DSC MMSI 002320011
44A Marine Parade West, Lee-on-Solent, Gosport PO13 9NR.
☎ 02392 552100. Fax 02392 551763.
Area from Chewton Bunney to Beachy Head.
Call Ch 67 (H24) for safety traffic.
On VHF Ch 16, MF 1641 kHz Navigation Warnings at: 0040 0440 0840 1240 1640 and 2040 UT

DOVER COASTGUARD (MRCC)
50°08'N 01°20'E. DSC MMSI 002320010
Langdon Battery, Swingate, Dover CT15 5NA.
☎ 01304 210008. Fax 01304 202137.
Area from Beachy Head to Reculver Towers.
On VHF Ch 16, Navigation Warnings at: 0105 0505 0905 1305 1705 and 2105 UT
Operates Channel Navigation Information Service (CNIS) which broadcasts nav and tfc info on Ch 11 every H+40 (and at H+55 in bad vis).

LONDON COASTGUARD
51°30'N 00°05'E. DSC MMSI 002320063
Thames Barrier Navigation Centre, Unit 28, 34 Bowater Road, Woolwich, London SE18 5TF.
☎ 0208 312 7380. Fax 0208 312 7679.
Area River Thames from Shell Haven Point (North Bank) and Egypt (South Bank) to Teddington.
NOTE: Does not broadcast MSI. Call on VHF Ch 16 *London Coastguard.*

THAMES COASTGUARD (MRSC)
51°51'N 01°17'E. DSC MMSI 002320009
East Terrace, Walton-on-the-Naze CO14 8PY.
☎ 01255 675518. Fax 01255 675249.
Area from Reculver Towers to Southwold.
On VHF Ch 16 Navigation Warnings at: 0010 0410 0810 1210 1610 and 2010 UT

YARMOUTH COASTGUARD (MRCC)
52°37'N 01°43'E. DSC MMSI 002320008
Haven Bridge House, Great Yarmouth NR30 1HZ.
☎ 01493 851338. Fax 01493 852307.
Area from Southwold to Haile Sand Fort.
On VHF Ch 16, MF 1869 kHz Navigation Warnings at: 0040 0440 0840 1240 1640 and 2040 UT

HUMBER COASTGUARD (MRSC)
54°06'N 00°11'W. DSC MMSI 002320007 (2187·5 kHz)
Lime Kiln Lane, Bridlington, N Humberside YO15 2LX.
☎ 01262 672317. Fax 01262 606915.
Area from Haile Sand Fort to the Scottish border.
On VHF Ch 16, MF 2226 kHz Navigation Warnings at: 0340 0740 1140 1540 1940 and 2340 UT

FORTH COASTGUARD (MRSC)
56°17'N 02°35'W. DSC MMSI 002320005
Fifeness, Crail, Fife KY10 3XN.
☎ 01333 450666. Fax 01333 450725.
Area from English border to Doonies Point.
On VHF Ch 16 Navigation Warnings at: 0205 0605 1005 1405 1805 and 2205 UT

ABERDEEN COASTGUARD (MRCC)
57°08'N 02°05'W. DSC MMSI 002320004 (2187·5 kHz)
Marine House, Blaikies Quay, Aberdeen AB11 5PB.
☎ 01224 592334. Fax 01224 575920.
Area from Doonies Pt to C. Wrath, incl Pentland Firth.
On VHF Ch 16, On MF 2226 kHz Navigation Warnings at: 0320 0720 1120 1520 1920 and 2320 UT

SHETLAND COASTGUARD (MRSC)
60°09'N 01°08'W. DSC MMSI 002320001(2187·5 kHz)
The Knab, Knab Rd, Lerwick ZE1 0AX.
☎ 01595 692976. Fax 01595 694810.
Area from Covers Shetland, Orkney and Fair Isle.
On VHF Ch 16, MF 1770 kHz Navigation Warnings at: 0105 0505 0905 1305 1705 2105 UT

STORNOWAY COASTGUARD (MRSC)
58°12'N 06°22'W. DSC MMSI 002320024 (2187·5 kHz)
Battery Point, Stornoway, Isle of Lewis HS1 2RT.
☎ 01851 702013. Fax 01851 704387.
Area from Cape Wrath to Ardnamurchan Point.
Mainland, Narra to Butt of Lewis, Western Is and St Kilda.
On VHF Ch 16, MF 1743 kHz Navigation Warnings at: 0110 0510 0910 1310 1710 2110 UT

CLYDE COASTGUARD (MRCC)
55°58′N 04°48′W. DSC MMSI 002320022 (2187·5 kHz)
Navy Buildings, Eldon St, Greenock PA16 7QY.
☎ 01475 729988. 📠 01475 786955.
Area from Ardnamurchan Point to Mull of Galloway.
On VHF Ch 16*, MF 1883 kHz Navigation Warnings, Strong wind warnings and gale warnings at: 0020 0420 0820 1220 1620 2020 UT

BELFAST COASTGUARD (MRSC)
54°40′N 05°40′W. DSC MMSI 002320021
Bregenz House, Quay St, Bangor, Co Down BT20 5ED.
☎ 02891 463933. 📠 02891 465886.
Area covers Northern Ireland.
On VHF Ch 16* Navigation Warnings at: 0305 0705 1105 1505 1905 and 2305 UT

LIVERPOOL COASTGUARD (MRSC)
53°30′N 03°03′W. DSC MMSI 002320019
Hall Road West, Crosby, Liverpool L23 8SY
☎ 0151 9313341 📠 0151 9313347
Area from Mull of Galloway to Queensferry.
On VHF Ch 16 Navigation Warnings at 0210 0610 1010 1410 1810 and 2210 UT

HOLYHEAD COASTGUARD (MRSC)
53°19′N 04°38′W. DSC MMSI 002320018 (2187·5 kHz)
Holyhead, Anglesey, Gwynedd LL65 1ET
☎ 01407 762051 📠 01407 764373
Area from Queensferry to Friog
On VHF Ch 16 Navigation Warnings at: 0235 0635 1035 1435 1835 and 2235 UT

MILFORD HAVEN COASTGUARD (MRSC)
51°41′N 05°10′W. DSC MMSI 002320017 (2187·5 kHz)
Gorsewood Drive, Hakin, Milford Haven, Pembs SA73 2HB.
☎ 01646 690909. 📠 01646 692176.
Area from Friog to River Towy.
On VHF Ch 16, MF 1767 kHz Navigation Warnings at: 0335 0735 1135 1535 1935 and 2335 UT

SWANSEA COASTGUARD (MRCC)
51°34′N 03°58′W. DSC MMSI 002320016
Tutt Head, Mumbles, Swansea SA3 4EX.
☎ 01792 366534. 📠 01792 369005.
Area from River Towy to Marsland Mouth.
On VHF Ch 16 Navigation Warnings at: 0005 0405 0805 1205 1605 and 2005 UT

CHANNEL ISLANDS

ST PETER PORT RADIO (CRS)
49°27'·00N 02°32'00W. DSC MMSI 002320064
☎: 01481 720672. 📠: 01534 714177
Area covers the Channel Islands Northern area; Alderney Radio keeps watch Ch 16 HJ.
On VHF Ch 20, MF 1764 kHz Navigation Warnings at: 0133 0533 0933 1333 1733 and 2133 UT

JERSEY RADIO (CRS)
49°10'·85N 02°14'30W. DSC MMSI 002320060
☎: 01534 741121. 📠: 01534 499089
Area covers the Channel Islands Southern area.
On VHF Ch 25 82, MF 1658 kHz Navigation Warnings at: 0645 0433 0745 0845 1245 1633 1845 2033 2245 UT

7.16 IRISH COAST GUARD

The Irish Coast Guard is part of the Department of Marine, Leeson Lane, Dublin 2. ☎ (01) 6620922; 📠 (01) 662 0795.

The Coast Guard co-ordinates all SAR operations around the coast of Ireland through Dublin MRCC, Malin Head MRSC and Valentia MRSC. It liaises with UK and France during any rescue operation within 100M of the Irish coast.

The MRCC/MRSCs are co-located with the Coast radio stations of the same name and manned by the same staff. All stations maintain H24 listening watch on VHF Ch 16. If ashore dial 999 and ask for Marine Rescue in an emergency.

Details of the MRCC/MRSCs are as follows:

DUBLIN (MRCC)

53°20'N 06°15W. DSC MMSI 002500300 (+2187·5 kHz).
☎ +353 1 662 0922/3; 📠 +353 1 662 0795.
Covers Carlingford Lough to Youghal.

VALENTIA (MRSC)

51°56'N 10°21'W. DSC MMSI 002500200 (+2187·5 kHz).
☎ +353 669 476 109; 📠 +353 669 476 289.
Covers Youghal to Slyne Head.

MALIN HEAD (MRSC)

55°22'N 07°20W. DSC MMSI 002500100 (+2187·5 kHz).
☎ +353 77 70103; 📠 +353 77 70221.
Covers Slyne Head to Lough Foyle.

7.16.1 SAR RESOURCES

The Irish Coast Guard provides some 50 units around the coast and is on call 24 hours a day. Some of these units have a specialist cliff climbing capability.

A helicopter, based at Shannon, can respond within 15 to 45 minutes and operate to a radius of 200M. It is equipped with infrared search equipment and can uplift 14 survivors. In addition helicopters (based at Finner Camp in Donegal and at Baldonnel, Dublin) can operate to 150 miles by day and 70 miles at night.

Other military and civilian aircraft and vessels, together with the Garda and lighthouse service can be called upon.

The RNLI maintains four stations around the coast and some 26 lifeboats. Additionally, six individually community-run inshore rescue boats are available.

7.15.2 COAST AND CLIFF RESCUE SERVICES

This comprises about 50 stations manned by volunteers, who are trained in first aid and equipped with inflatables, breeches buoys, cliff ladders etc. Their ☎ numbers (the Leader's residence) are given, where appropriate, under each port.

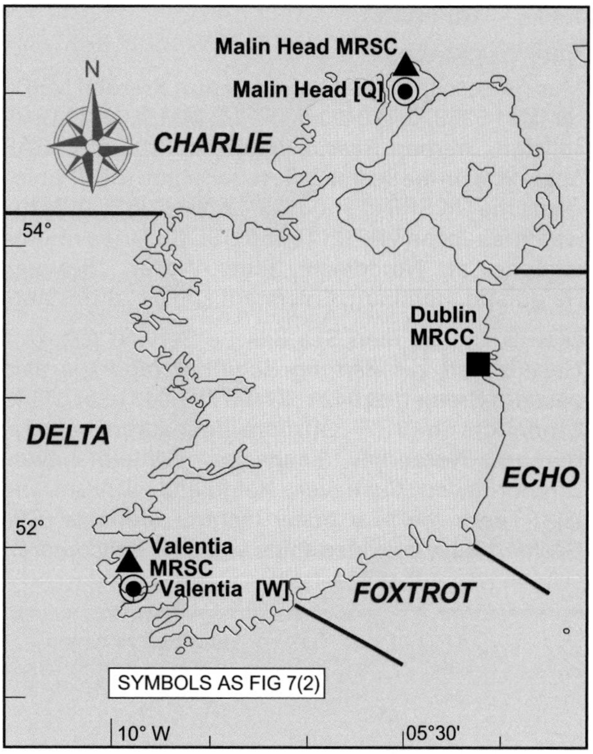

Malin Head MRSC
N
Malin Head [Q]
CHARLIE
54°
Dublin
MRCC
DELTA
ECHO
52°
Valentia
MRSC
Valentia [W]
FOXTROT
SYMBOLS AS FIG 7(2)
10° W
05°30'

Fig. 7 (3) Irish Coastguard centres

7.17 DANISH COAST GUARD

The Danish Coast Guard is controlled remotely from Lyngby through Blavand and Skagen CRS.

Lyngby is an operational Coast DSC station working via Blavand and Skagen on VHF Ch 70 MMSI 002191000.

There are at least 12 lifeboats stationed at the major harbours along this west facing coast.

MSI Navigational Warnings are broadcast on VHF from Lyngby at 0133 0533 0933 1333 1733 2133 on channels shown.

MF broadcasts are transmitted on 1758KHz from Skajen and 1734KHz from Blavand.

Firing Practice areas exist at:

Tranum and Blokhus ☎ 98235088 or call *Tranum* on VHF Ch 16.

Nymindegab ☎ 75289355 or call *Nymindegab* on VHF Ch 16.

Oksbøl ☎ 76541213 or call *Oksbøl* on VHF Ch 16; (Lyngby Radio broadcast firing warnings at 0705 1705).

Rømø E ☎ 74755219 or call *Fly Rømø* on VHF Ch 16; Rømø W ☎ 74541340.

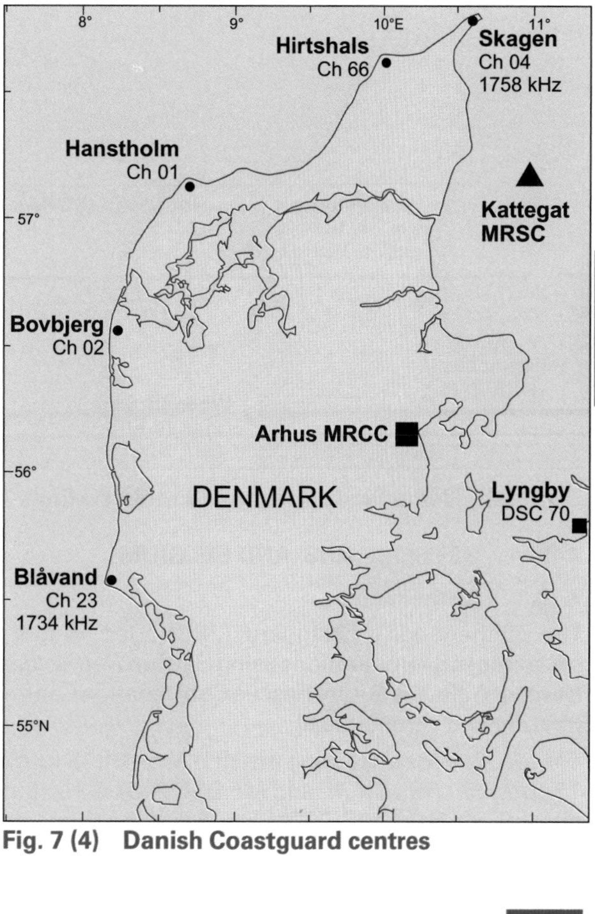

8°
9°
10°E
11°
Hirtshals
Ch 66
Skagen
Ch 04
1758 kHz
Hanstholm
Ch 01
57°
Kattegat
MRSC
Bovbjerg
Ch 02
Arhus MRCC
56°
DENMARK
Lyngby
DSC 70
Blåvand
Ch 23
1734 kHz
55°N

Fig. 7 (4) Danish Coastguard centres

7.18 GERMANY

SAFETY SERVICES

Marine Rescue Co-ordination Centre Bremen MRCC (☎ 0421 536870; 📠 0421 5368714; MMSI 002111240) callsign *Bremen Rescue Radio,* coordinates SAR operations in the Search & Rescue Region (SRR) which abuts the UK SRR at about 55°12'N 03°30'E. A 24 hrs watch is kept on VHF Ch 16 and DSC Ch 70 via remote stations at Norddeich, Elbe Weser, Bremen, Helgoland, Hamburg, Eiderstedt and Nordfriesland.

DGzRS, the German Sea Rescue Service *(Deutsch Gesellschaft zur Rettung Schiffbrüchiger)* is also based at Bremen (☎ 0421 537 0777; 📠 0421 537 0714). It monitors Ch 16 H24. Offshore lifeboats are based at Borkum, Norderney, Langeoog, Wilhelmshaven, Bremer-haven, Cuxhaven, Helgoland, Amrum and List. There are also many inshore lifeboats. The German Navy provides ships and SAR helicopters.

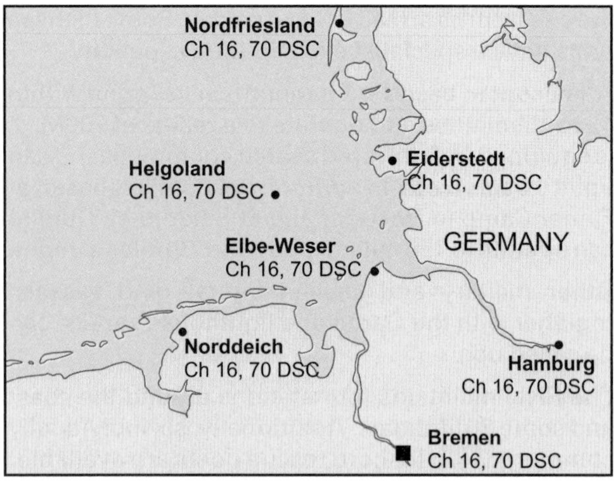
Nordfriesland
Ch 16, 70 DSC
Helgoland
Ch 16, 70 DSC
Eiderstedt
Ch 16, 70 DSC
GERMANY
Elbe-Weser
Ch 16, 70 DSC
Norddeich
Ch 16, 70 DSC
Hamburg
Ch 16, 70 DSC
Bremen
Ch 16, 70 DSC

Fig. 7 (5) German Coastguard radio stations

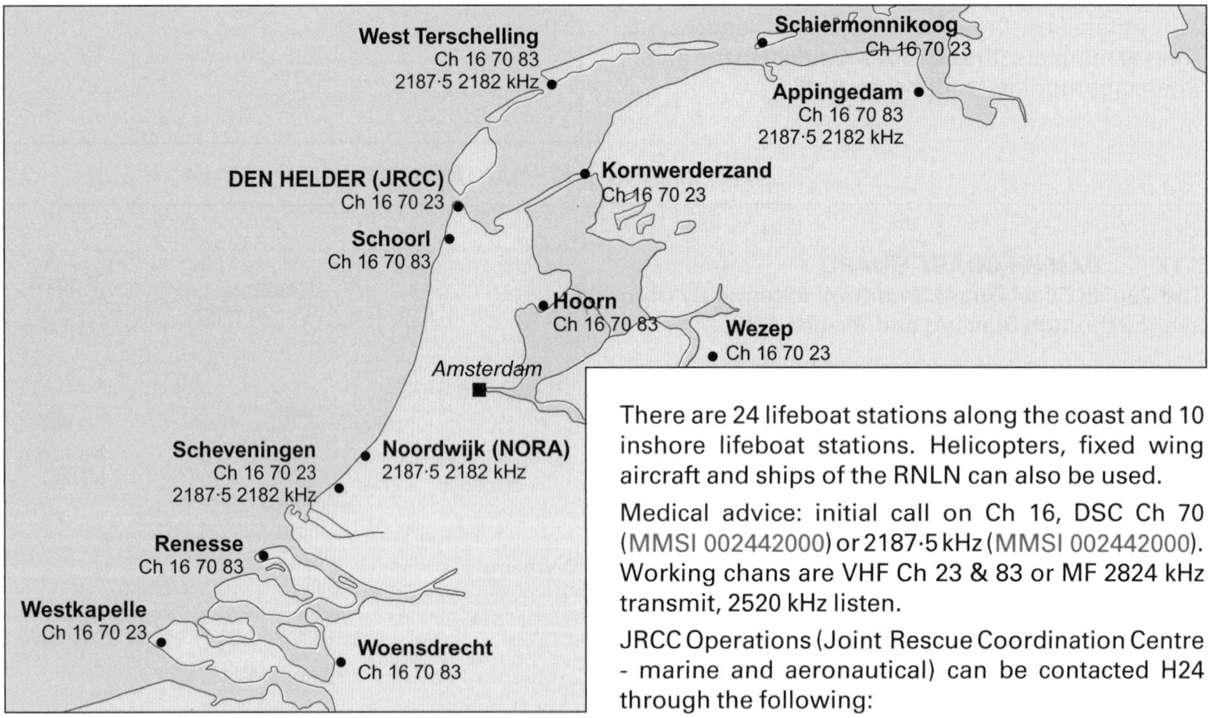
West Terschelling
Ch 16 70 83
2187·5 2182 kHz
Schiermonnikoog
Ch 16 70 23
Appingedam
Ch 16 70 83
2187·5 2182 kHz
DEN HELDER (JRCC)
Ch 16 70 23
Kornwerderzand
Ch 16 70 23
Schoorl
Ch 16 70 83
Hoorn
Ch 16 70 83
Wezep
Ch 16 70 23
Amsterdam
Scheveningen
Ch 16 70 23
2187·5 2182 kHz
Noordwijk (NORA)
2187·5 2182 kHz
Renesse
Ch 16 70 83
Westkapelle
Ch 16 70 23
Woensdrecht
Ch 16 70 83

Fig. 7 (6) Netherlands Coastguard radio stations

7.19 NETHERLANDS AND BELGIUM

7.19.1 Netherlands

The Netherlands Coastguard (JRCC Den Helder) coordinates SAR operations using callsign *Den Helder Rescue.* A JRCC is a Joint Rescue Coordination Centre (marine and aeronautical).

The JRCC keeps a listening watch H24 on Ch 16 (until 1 Feb 2005), DSC Ch 70, and MF DSC 2187·5kHz (but not on 2182kHz); MMSI 002442000. Working channels are VHF 67 & 73.

There are 24 lifeboat stations along the coast and 10 inshore lifeboat stations. Helicopters, fixed wing aircraft and ships of the RNLN can also be used.

Medical advice: initial call on Ch 16, DSC Ch 70 (MMSI 002442000) or 2187·5 kHz (MMSI 002442000). Working chans are VHF Ch 23 & 83 or MF 2824 kHz transmit, 2520 kHz listen.

JRCC Operations (Joint Rescue Coordination Centre - marine and aeronautical) can be contacted H24 through the following:

For emergency:
☎ + 31 (0) 900 0111. 📠 + 31 (0) 223 658358;

Operational telephone number:
☎ + 31 (0) 223 542300

or HO for Admin/info
☎+ 31 (0) 255 546546. 📠+31 223 658300.

Inmarsat 'C': 424477710

NAVIGATIONAL WARNINGS

Navigational warnings (*Nautische Warnnachricht)* for the North Sea coast are contained in IJmuiden Navtex (P) transmissions. Dangers to navigation should be reported to Seewarn Cuxhaven.

7.19.2 Belgium

SAR GENERAL

The Belgian Pilotage Service coordinates SAR operations from Oostende MRCC. The MRCC is connected by telephone to the Oostende Coast Radio Station (OST) which maintains listening watch H24 on Ch 16, 2182kHz and DSC Ch 70 and 2187·5kHz. MMSI 002050480. ☎ 059 706565; 📠 059 701339. Antwerpen CRS, remotely controlled by Oostende CRS, has MMSI 002050485. DSC Ch 70.

Telephone and Fax numbers are:

MRCC Oostende ☎ +32(0) 59 701000;
📠 +32(0) 59 703605.

MRSC Nieuwpoort ☎ +32(0) 58 230000;
📠 +32(0) 58 231575.

MRSC Zeebrugge ☎ +32(0) 50 550801.
📠 +32(0) 50 547400.

RCC Brussels (Point of contact for Cospas/Sarsat):
☎ +32(0) 2 226 8856 (Mon-Fri 0600-1500 UT).

Offshore and inshore lifeboats are based at Nieuwpoort, Oostende and Zeebrugge.

The Belgian Air Force provides helicopters from Koksijde near the French border. The Belgian Navy also cooperates in SAR operations.

Navigational warnings are broadcast by Oostende Radio on receipt and at scheduled times on 2761 kHz and VHF Ch 27. Also by Oostende Navtex (M) at: 0200, 0600, 1000, 1400, 1800, 2200 UT for the SW part of the North Sea.

7.20 FRANCE – CROSS

Four Centres Régionaux Opérationnels de Surveillance et de Sauvetage (CROSS) cover the Channel and Atlantic coasts; see Fig. 7 (5). CROSS is an MRCC. CROSS provides a permanent, H24, all weather operational presence along the French coast and liaises with foreign CGs. CROSS' main functions include:

(1) Co-ordinating Search and Rescue.
(2) Navigational surveillance.
(3) Broadcasting navigational warnings.
(4) Broadcasting weather information.
(5) Anti-pollution control.
(6) Marine and fishery surveillance.

Fig. 7 (7) CROSS centres

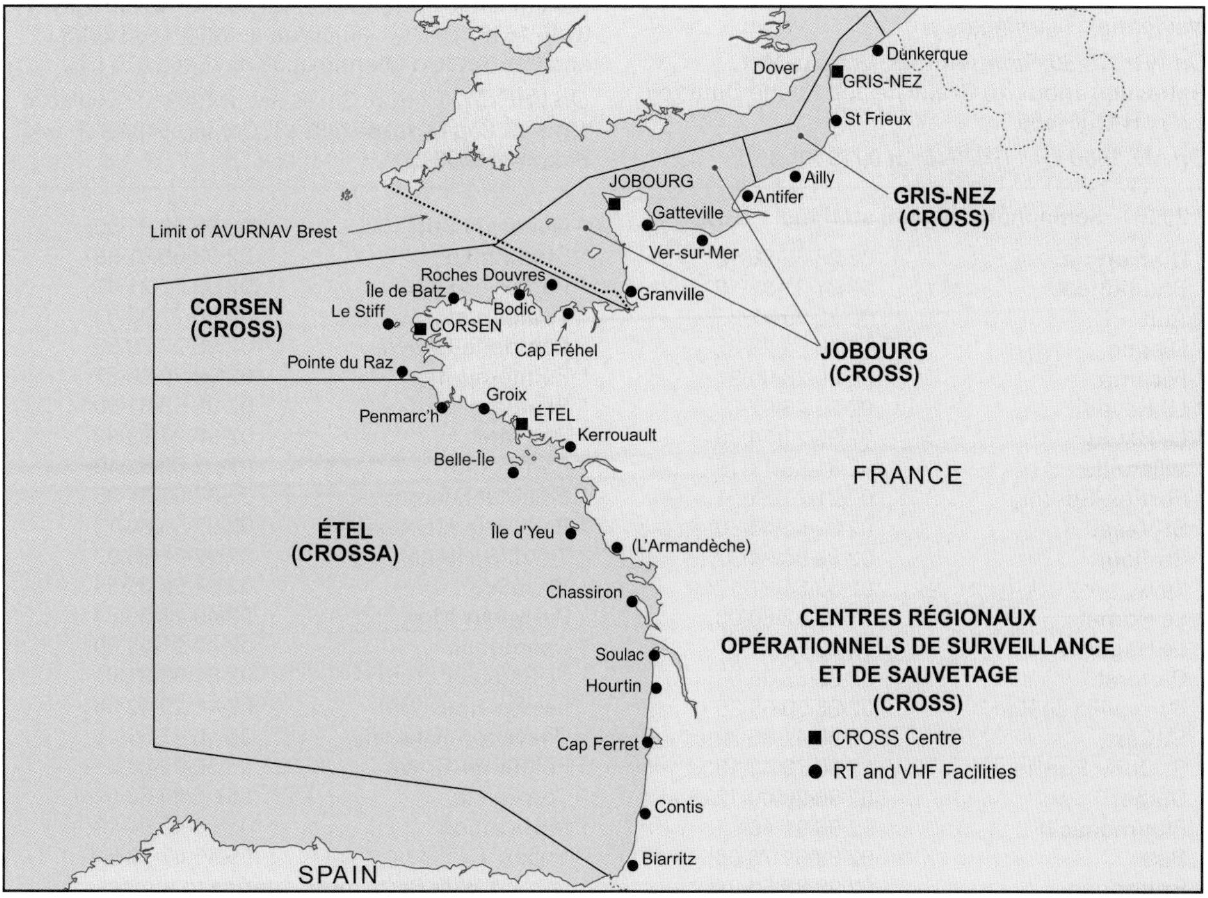
Dover
Dunkerque
GRIS-NEZ
St Frieux
Ailly
Antifer
GRIS-NEZ
(CROSS)
JOBOURG
Gatteville
Ver-sur-Mer
Limit of AVURNAV Brest
Roches Douvres
Île de Batz
Bodic
Granville
CORSEN
(CROSS)
Le Stiff
CORSEN
Cap Fréhel
JOBOURG
(CROSS)
Pointe du Raz
Groix
Penmarc'h
ÉTEL
Kerrouault
Belle-Île
FRANCE
ÉTEL
(CROSSA)
Île d'Yeu
(L'Armandèche)
Chassiron
CENTRES RÉGIONAUX
OPÉRATIONNELS DE SURVEILLANCE
ET DE SAUVETAGE
(CROSS)
Soulac
Hourtin
CROSS Centre
Cap Ferret
RT and VHF Facilities
Contis
Biarritz
SPAIN

All centres keep watch on VHF Ch 16 and Ch 70 (DSC), and broadcast gale warnings and weather forecasts and local navigational warnings; see Chapter 6.

CROSSA Étel specialises in providing medical advice and responds to alerts from Cospas/Sarsat satellites.

CROSS can be contacted by R/T, by ☎, through Coast radio stations, via the National Gendarmerie or Affaires Maritimes, or via a Semaphore station. Call *Semaphore* stations on Ch 16 (working Ch 10) or by ☎ as listed later in this section.

In addition to their safety and SAR functions, CROSS stations using, for example, the call sign *Corsen Traffic* monitor Traffic Separation Schemes in the Dover Strait, off Casquets and off Ouessant. They also broadcast navigational warnings and weather forecasts. See Chapter 6 for times and VHF channels.

7.20.1 CROSS stations

All stations co-ordinate SAR on VHF Ch 15 67 68 73.
DSC Ch 70. All stations have Emergency ☎ 1616.

CROSS Gris-Nez
50°52'N 01°35'E MMSI 002275100
☎ 03·21·87·21·87 📠 03·21·87·78·55
Belgian Border to Cap d'Antifer
DSC Ch 70 MF 2187·5 kHz

Navigation Warnings

On VHF Ch 79: From: Dunkerque, Gris-Nez, Saint-Frieux, and L'Ailly every H+10

On MF 1650 kHz: Gris-Nez at 0833 2033 UT

CROSS Jobourg
49°41'N 01°54'W MMSI 002275200
☎ 02·33·52·72·13 📠 02·33·52·71·72
Cap de la Hague to Mont St Michel

Navigation Warnings

On VHF Ch 80: From: Antifer, Ver-sur-Mer, Gatteville, Jobourg, Granville and Roche Douvres every H+20/H+50.

On MF 1650 kHz: Gris-Nez at 0915 2115 LT

CROSS Corsen
48°24'N 04°47'W MMSI 002275300
☎ 02·98·89·31·31 📠 02·98·89·65·75
Mont St Michel to Pointe de Penmarc'h

Navigation Warnings

On MF 2677 kHz: From CROSS Corsen at 0735 1935 LT

CROSS Étel
47°39'N 03°12'W MMSI 002275000
☎ 02·97·55·35·35 📠 02·97·55·49·34
Pointe de Penmarc'h to the Spanish Border

Navigation Warnings

On VHF Ch 80: From: Penmarc'h 0703 1533 1903 LT, Ile de Groix at 0715 1545 1915 LT.
Belle-Ile at 0733 1603 1933 LT, Saint-Nazaire at 0745 1615 1945 LT, Ile d'Yeu at 0803 1633 2003 LT, and Les Sable d'Olonne at 0815 1645 2015 LT.

On VHF Ch 79 From: Chassiron at 1903 LT, Soulac at 1915 LT, Cap Ferrat at 1933 LT, Contis at 1945 LT, and Biarritz at 2003 LT.

7.20.2 Semaphore (Signal) stations

* Dunkerque	03·28·66·86·18
Boulogne	03·21·31·32·10
Ault	03·22·60·47·33
Dieppe	02·35·84·23·82
* Fécamp	02·35·28·00·91
* La Hève	02·35·46·07·81
* Le Havre	02·35·21·74·39
Villerville	02·31·88·11·13
* Port-en-Bessin	02·31·21·81·51
St-Vaast	02·33·54·44·50
* Barfleur	02·33·54·04·37
Lévy	02·33·54·31·17
* Le Homet	02·33·92·60·08
La Hague	02·33·52·71·07
Carteret	02·33·53·85·08
Barneville Le Roc	02·33·50·05·85
St-Cast	02·96·41·85·30
* St Quay-Portrieux	02·96.70.42.18
Bréhat	02·96·20·00·12
* Ploumanac'h	02·96·91·46·51
Batz	02·98·61·76·06
* Brignogan	02·98·83·50·84
* Ouessant Stiff	02·98·48·81·50
* St-Mathieu	02·98·89·01·59
* Portzic (Ch 08)	02·98·22·21·47
Toulinguet	02·98·27·90·02
Cap-de-la-Chèvre	02·98·27·09·55
* Pointe-du-Raz	02·98·70·66·57
* Penmarc'h	02·98·58·61·00
Beg Meil	02·98·94·98·92
* Port-Louis	02·97·82·52·10
Étel Mât Fenoux	02·97·55·35·35
Beg Melen (Groix)	02·97·86·80·13
Talut (Belle-Île)	02·97·31·85·07
St-Julien	02·97·50·09·35
Piriac-sur-Mer	02·40·23·59·87
* Chemoulin	02·40·91·99·00
St-Sauveur (Yeu)	02·51·58·31·01
Les Baleines (Ré)	05·46·29·42·06
Chassiron (Oléron)	05·46·47·85·43
* Pointe-de-Grave	05·56·09·60·03
Cap Ferret	05·56·60·60·03
Messanges	05·58·48·94·10
* Socoa	05·59·47·18·54

* H24. Remainder sunrise to sunset.

7.20.3 EMERGENCY VHF DF SERVICE

A yacht in emergency can call CROSS on VHF Ch 16, 11 or 67 to obtain a bearing. This will be passed as the true bearing of the yacht *from* the DF station. The Semaphore stations listed in 7.19.2 are also equipped with VHF DF. They keep watch on Ch 16 and other continuously scanned frequencies, which include Ch 1-29, 36, 39, 48, 50, 52, 55, 56 and 60-88.

7.19.4 MEDICAL

The Service d'Aide Médicale Urgente (SAMU) can be contacted via CROSS. CROSS Étel specialises in providing medical advice. It can be contacted via:

AREA 17	
Lille	03·20·54·22·22
Le Havre	02·35·47·15·15
Caen	02·31·44·88·88
AREA 18	
Saint Brieuc	02·96·94·28·95
AREA 20	
Brest	02·98·46·11·33
AREA 21	
Vannes	02·97·54·22·11
Nantes	02·40·08·37·77
AREA 22	
La Rochelle	05·46·27·32·15
Bordeaux	05·56·96·70·70
Bayonne	05·59·63·33·33

7.19.5 Semaphore stations

These stations keep a visual, radar and radio watch (VHF Ch 16) around the coast. They show visual gale warning signals, will repeat forecasts and offer local weather reports. They relay emergency calls to CROSS and are equipped with VHF DF; see 7.20.2.

7.19.6 Lifeboats

The lifeboat service Société National de Sauvetage en Mer (SNSM) comes under CROSS, but ashore it is best to contact local lifeboat stations direct; Telephone numbers are given in Chapter 9 for each port under SNSM. A hefty charge may be levied if a SNSM lifeboat attends a vessel not in distress.

7.19.7 Navigation warnings

Long-range warnings are broadcast by Inmarsat SafetyNet for Navarea II, which includes the west coast of France. The north coast lies in Navarea I.

Avurnavs (AVis URgents aux NAVigateurs) are regional Coastal and Local warnings issued by two regional authorities:

(1) **Brest** – for the west coast of France and the western Channel to Mont St Michel; and

(2) **Cherbourg** – for the eastern Channel from Mont St Michel to the Belgian frontier.

Avurnavs are broadcast by Niton and Brest on Navtex, and on MF by Jobourg and CROSS Gris Nez; urgent ones on receipt and after next silence period, and at scheduled times. Warnings are prefixed by 'Sécurité Avurnav', followed by the name of the station.

Local warnings for coastal waters are broadcast in French and **English** by CROSS as follows:

CROSS	*VHF Ch*	*Times (local)*
Dunkerque	79	H+10
CROSS Gris Nez	79	H+10
	1650 kHz	0833 2033 LT
Saint Frieux	79	H+10
L'Ailly	79	H+10
CROSS Jobourg	80	H+20 & H+50
	1650 kHz	0915 2115 LT
Granville	80	H+20
Roche Douvre	80	H+20 & H+50
CROSS Corsen	79	H+10 & H+40
	2677 kHz	0735 1935 LT
Bodic	79	H+10 & H+40
Ile de Batz	79	H+10 & H+40
Le Stiff	79	H+10 & H+40
Pointe du Raz	79	H+10 & H+40
CROSS Étel	80	On receipt

7.21 SPAIN AND PORTUGAL

7.21.1 Spain and Portugal – MRCC/MRSC

MRCCs and MRSCs are primarily responsible for handling Distress, Safety and Urgency communications. Madrid MRCC coordinates SAR on the N , and NW coasts of Spain through six MRCC/MRSCs. All stations monitor VHF Ch 16 and 2182 kHz H24 and VHF DSC Ch 70 (H24).

In Portugal, the Portuguese Navy coordinates SAR in two regions, Lisboa and Santa Maria (Azores).

In SW Spain and the Gibraltar Strait MRCC Tarifa coordinates SAR.

Digital Selective Calling (DSC) is operational as shown below. MRCC/MRSCs also broadcast weather as shown in Chapter 6. MRCC/MRSCs do not handle commercial link calls.

Search and Rescue operations and the prevention of pollution in Spain is undertaken by the National Society for Maritime Rescue and Safety (Salvamento y Seguridad – SASEMA).

A shipping forecast is broadcast, in Spanish, every two hours from Salvamento Marítimao's regional centres and copies of this can usually be obtained from most yacht clubs.

NORTH AND NORTH-WEST SPAIN

Bilbao MRCC MMSI 002240996	43°21'N 03°02'W ☎ 94 483 9286; 📠 94 483 9161	Ch 10: Nav warnings every 4 hours from 0233 UT DSC Ch 70, 2187·5 kHz
Santander MRSC MMSI 002241009	43°28'N 03°43'W ☎ 942 213 030; 📠 942 213 638	Ch 11: Nav warnings every 4 hours from 0045 UT DSC Ch 70 2187·5 kHz
Gijón MRCC MMSI 002240997	43°37'N 05°42'W ☎ 985 326 050; 📠 985 320 908	Ch 10 Nav warnings every H+15 DSC Ch 70, 2187·5 kHz
Coruña MRSC MMSI 002241022	43°22'N 08°23'W ☎ 981 209 548; 📠 981 209 518 Call: *Coruña Traffic*	Ch 13, 16, 67, Ch 13: Nav warnings every 4 hours from 0205 UT DSC Ch 70, 2187·5 kHz
Finisterre MRCC MMSI 002240993 Call: *Finisterre Traffic*	42°42'N 08°59'W ☎ 981 767 320; 📠 981 767 740 DSC Ch 70, 2187·5 kHz	Ch 11 16 2182 kHz. Ch 11: Nav warnings every 4 hours from 0033 UT
Vigo MRSC MMSI 002240998	42°10'N 08°41'W ☎ 986 297 403; 📠 986 290 455	Ch 11 16 2182 kHz. DSC Ch 70, 2187·5 kHz Ch 10: Nav warnings every 4 hours from 0215 UT

PORTUGAL

Lisboa MRCC 38°41'N 09°19'W
Ch 23 25 26 27 28 MF 2182 2578 2693 kHz
MMSI 002630100
☎ 351 21 419 0098
📠 351 21 419 9900
DSC Ch 70; 2187·5 kHz
VHF Services controlled from Lisboa:

Arga	Ch 25 28 83
Arestal	Ch 24 26 85
Montejunto	Ch 23 27 87
Atalaia	Ch 24 26 85
Picos	Ch 23 27 85
Estoi	Ch 24 28 86

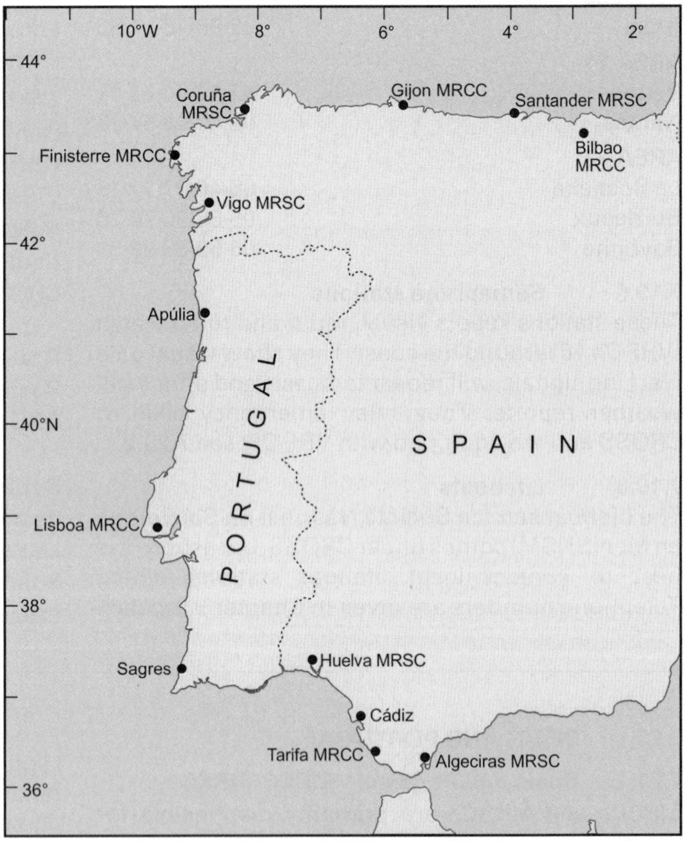
10°W
8°
6°
4°
2°
44°
42°
40°N
38°
36°
Coruña MRSC
Gijon MRCC
Santander MRSC
Bilbao MRCC
Finisterre MRCC
Vigo MRSC
Apúlia
PORTUGAL
SPAIN
Lisboa MRCC
Sagres
Huelva MRSC
Cádiz
Tarifa MRCC
Algeciras MRSC

Fig. 7 (8) Spanish & Portuguese Coastguard radio stations

SOUTH WEST SPAIN

Tarifa MRCC MMSI 002240994	36°01'N 05°35'W ☎ 956 681 452; 📠 956 680 606	Ch 16 10 74, 2182 kHz (all H24); Call: *Tarifa Traffic* Ch 10 74: Nav warnings every even H+15 and on receipt DSC Ch 70, 2187·5 kHz (H24)
Algeciras MRSC MMSI 002241001	36°08'N 05°26'W ☎ 956 585 404; 📠 956 585 402	Ch 15 16 74 DSC Ch 70 Nav warnings on request

7.22 MEDICAL ADVICE BY R/T

Medical advice can be obtained almost anywhere in European waters (and elsewhere) by making an all-stations 'PAN-PAN' call or a DSC Urgency Alert to the Coastguard, or to a Coast Radio Station (CRS) in those countries where CRS are still in being. You will be connected to a suitable medical authority – usually a doctor or the nearest hospital.

The Urgency signal 'PAN PAN' is always advised, especially abroad because it is internationally understood and cuts through most language problems. **Urgent help needed** is shown in bold type against the more serious medical problems in the preceding pages and this implies a Pan-Pan call. You should also recognise that as a layman you are not qualified to judge how serious the casualty's condition is – so get the best possible advice and/or help as quickly as possible.

Be prepared to give a detailed summary of the patient's symptoms, eg pulse rate, breathing rate, temperature, skin colour, conscious state (with reference to pupil size, responses to verbal command and to firm pinching; see 7.22.15), site and description of any pain, site and type of injury, amount of blood lost.

If medical help is needed by way of a doctor coming aboard, or if a serious casualty has to be off-lifted, the arrangements will be made by the Coastguard. For what it's worth, the message is passed free of charge.

If the situation is truly not urgent, then either it can wait until you get into harbour or at least you can forewarn the port authority so that a doctor or para-medics can meet you on arrival. Such a call could be made in adequate time on the harbour's working channel.

7.22.1 FIRST AID AFLOAT

The objectives of First Aid at sea are:

a. to preserve life;
b. to prevent further damage;
c. to relieve pain and distress; and
d. to deliver a live casualty ashore.

With any casualty be calm, reassuring and methodical and try to examine the whole casualty if time and circumstances permit.

7.22.2 EMERGENCY RESUSCITATION – ABC

The immediate procedure for any collapsed or apparently unconscious person is:

Assess whether or not the casualty is conscious. Carefully shake his shoulders and ask loudly 'What's happened?' or 'Are you allright?' or give a command such as 'Open your eyes'. An unconscious casualty will not respond.

A Airway.

Remove any visible obstruction from his mouth (leave well-fitting dentures in place). Listen at mouth for breathing. Tilt head backwards, using head tilt and chin lift to maintain clear airway – Fig. 7(9).

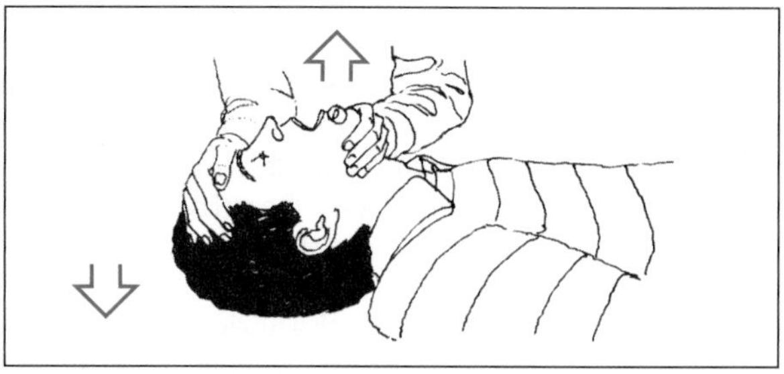

Fig. 7(9) Ensuring clear airway: head tilt and chin lift.

Place in recovery position if breathing – Fig. 7(10).

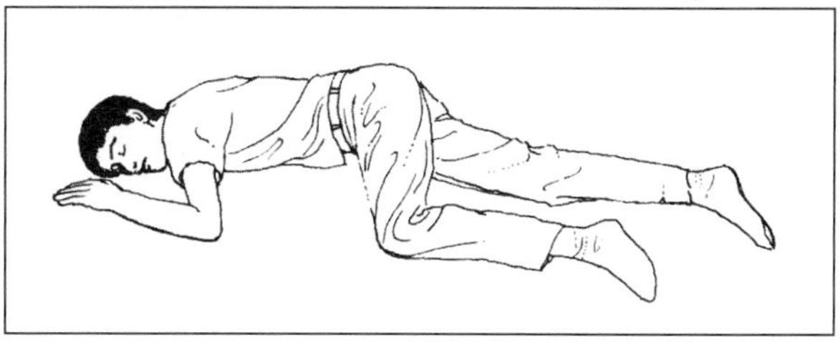

Fig. 7(10) Recovery position.

B Breathing.

If not breathing and airway clear, start mouth to mouth ventilation, Fig. 7(11).

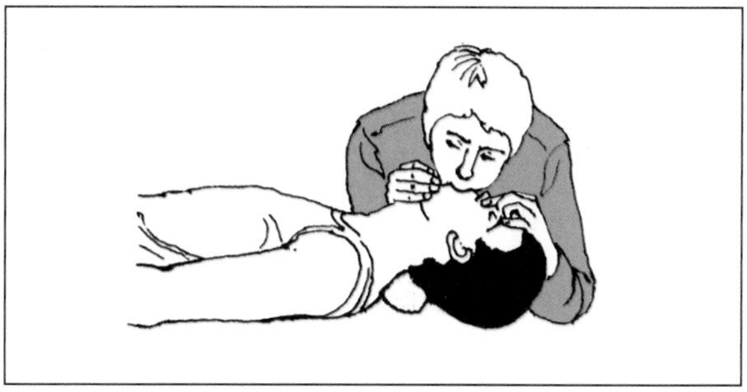

Fig. 7(11) Mouth to mouth ventilation.

Keeping the airway open, check whether the casualty is breathing normally by **looking** for chest movement, **listening** at the mouth for breath sounds and **feeling** for breath on your cheek. Look, listen and feel for 10 seconds before deciding that breathing is absent. If the casualty is not breathing and airway is clear, start mouth to mouth resuscitation by giving **2 rescue breaths**. Kneel beside casualty, maintain head tilt and chin lift, pinch nostrils. Take a deep breath and blow two full breaths into patient's mouth. Watch for rise and fall of chest.

C Circulation.

Once you have given **2 rescue breaths**, assess the casualty for signs of circulation by looking, listening and feeling for normal breathing, coughing or movement or improvement in colour. Check for signs of circulation for no more than 10 seconds. If there are no signs of a circulation or you are at all unsure, assume that the heart has stopped. This is called **Cardiac Arrest.** The casualty will be unconscious and may appear very pale, grey or bluish in colour. An artificial circulation will have to be provided by chest compression. If the circulation stops, the breathing will stop also; casualties with cardiac arrest will need both resue breathing and chest compression; a combination known as CardioPulmonary Resuscitation (**CPR**). Start external chest compression. Lay casualty on hard, flat surface. Kneel beside casualty; with the index and middle fingers of your lower hand, locate one of the casualty's lower ribs on the side nearest to you.

Slide your finger tips along the rib to the point at which it meets the breastbone. Place your middle finger at this point and the index finger beside it on the breastbone.

Place the heel of your other hand on the breastbone; slide it down to meet your index finger. This is the point at which you will apply pressure.

Place the heel of your first hand on top of the other hand and interlock your fingers.

Depress breastbone 40 - 50mm (1½ - 2in) then release, Fig. 7(12).

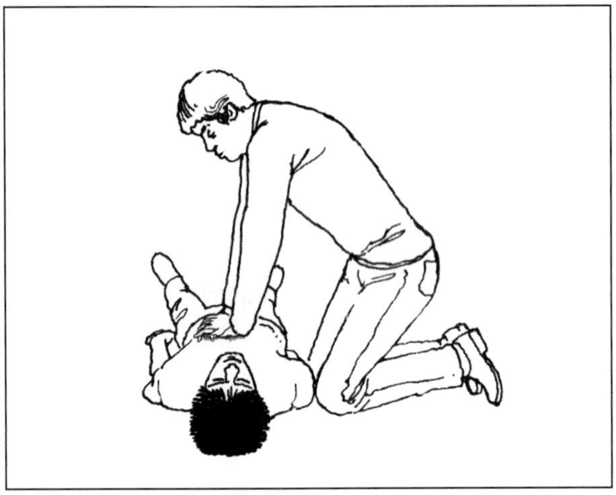

Fig. 7(12) Chest compression: body/hand position

With either one or two operators give 15 chest compressions and continue cycles of 2 breaths to 15 compressions, see fig 7(13) and fig 7(14). Use a compression rate of 100 per minute. Chest compression must always be combined with rescue breathing so after every 15 compressions, give 2 effective rescue breaths. Do not stop.

Action plan for the resuscitation of adults

Casualty is unconscious but is breathing normally:

1 turn casualty into the recovery position
2 urgent help needed
3 check for continued breathing

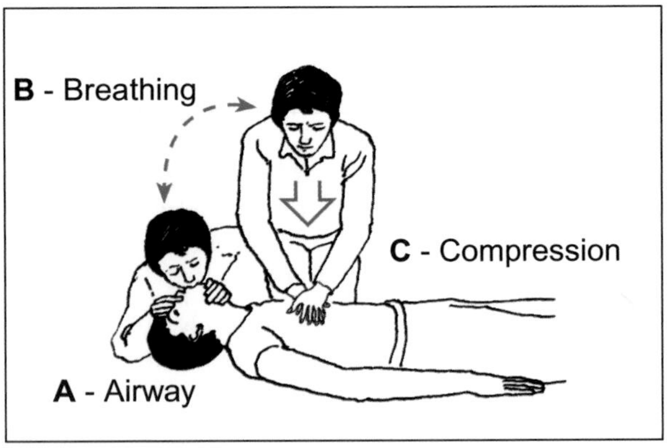
B - Breathing
C - Compression
A - Airway

Fig. 7(13) One operator

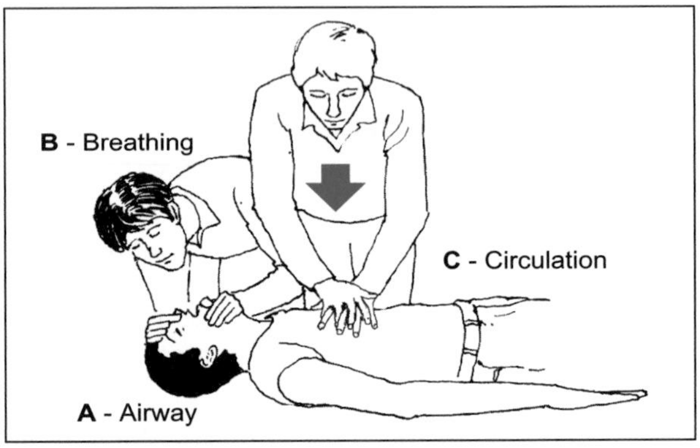
B - Breathing
C - Circulation
A - Airway

Fig. 7(14) Two operators.

Casualty is unconscious and not breathing:

1 urgent help needed
2 Give 2 effective rescue breaths
3 check for signs of circulation

If no sign of a circulation, give 15 chest compressions and continue in cycle of 2 breaths to 15 compressions.

If breathing restarts place casualty in the recovery position.

Children

Blow into both mouth and nose if necessary but resuscitate at same rate as adult but for external chest compression use one hand or just fingers for a baby. In the case of a baby give up to 5 initial rescue breaths. Use a faster breathing rate (one inflation every three seconds), and smaller breaths. For external chest compression use gentle compression with one hand only, or just fingers for a baby; use a compression rate, of up to 100 per minute, one breath every 5 compressions.

It is unlikely that the casualty's pulse will return spontaneously without other more advanced techniques (especially defibrillation) so do not waste time by stopping **CPR** to check the circulation. Only stop and re-check if the casualty shows signs of life (movement or breathing). Otherwise, carry on until either the emergency services arrive, another rescuer can take over, or you are too exhausted to keep going. Exception: hypothermia victim (see 7.22.3).

Problems during resuscitation

Drowning and hypothermia

These casualties may exhibit all the signs of apparent death, yet may still recover totally. Abandon resuscitation reluctantly and only after thorough and repeated attempts have been made to warm the victim.

7.22.3 DROWNING

The resuscitation of an apparently drowned person may be complicated by two factors:

1 A sudden illness (eg a stroke) or an accident (eg a blow to the head) may have precipitated the fall into the water.

2 The time spent in the water may have produced marked hypothermia. The water around the UK is rarely warmer than 15°C (60°F).

During resue and after resuscititation try to keep head low so that vomit is not inhaled and water drains from the mouth.

Management

a. **A Airway**. Clear airway: seaweed, dentures etc.

b. **B Breathing**. If not breathing start mouth to mouth ventilation as soon as possible and in the water if practicable. See 7.22.2.

c. **C Circulation**. If pulse absent, start chest compression as soon as aboard. See 7.22.2.

d. If stomach bulging, turn on to side to empty water, or he may vomit large quantities of water which could be inhaled.

e. Prevent cooling. Remove wet clothes; wrap in blankets to warm.

f. Continue resuscitation until victim revives or death is certain. Hypothermia may mimic death. Do not abandon resuscitation until person has been warmed or signs of death persist despite attempts at warming:

g. Once revived, put in recovery position, Fig. 7(9).

h. Any person rescued from drowning may collapse in the next 24 hours as the lungs react to inhaled water. **Urgent help needed**.

7.22.4 HYPOTHERMIA

Lowered body temperature will follow immersion in sea or prolonged exposure on deck.

Symptoms include: unreasonable behaviour followed by apathy and confusion; unsteady gait, stumbling, slurring of speech; pale, cold skin; slow, weak pulse; slow breathing; shivering. Leads to collapse, unconsciousness and ultimately death.

Management

a. *A Airway* control; put in recovery position.

b. *B Breathing*. If not breathing, start mouth to mouth ventilation.

c. *C Circulation*. Be prepared to use chest compressions.

d. Remove wet clothing. Avoid wind chill. Dry and wrap in blankets or sleeping bag plus warm hat and cover, if available, in foil survival bag. Urgent help needed.

e. Give hot sweet drinks if conscious.

f. Do not give alcohol, or rub the skin, or place very hot objects against skin.

7.22.5 BLOCKAGE OF AIRWAY AND CHOKING

If blockage by some object (e.g. a peanut) is suspected, turn the casualty on his side and give up to five sharp back slaps with the flat of the hand between the shoulder blades. Check mouth and remove any obstruction.

If unsuccessful, wrap both your arms around the victim's waist from behind, and give five sharp upwards thrusts with both fists into the abdomen above the navel but below the ribs so as to initiate coughing. Clear object from mouth.

In unconscious adult administer abdominal thrusts with the victim lying on his back. Attempt mouth to mouth breathing. Do not give up. Infants and small children should just be given five forceful blows on the back before proceeding to chest thrusts which are performed in the same way as chest compressions but should be sharper and performed at a slower rate with each thrust trying to relieve the obstruction. Continue if no relief, with the sequence of 5 rescue breaths, 5 back blows and 5 chest thrusts.

7.22.6 SHOCK

Shock can result from almost any accident or medical emergency and, depending upon the cause, may range in severity from a simple faint to near death. Shock occurs when the delivery of oxygen to the tissues is impaired because of inadequate or inefficient circulation of the blood. Possible causes include:

a. Loss of blood – internal or external bleeding.

b. Loss of fluid – diarrhoea, peritonitis, burns.

c. Heart failure – heart attack.

d. Lung failure – drowning.

e. Brain failure – stroke, head injury.

f. Illness – diabetes.

Signs and symptoms

Thirst, apathy, nausea, restlessness. Pale, cold, clammy skin, sweating. Rapid, weak pulse. Rapid, shallow breathing. Dull, sunken eyes, bluish lips, lead to collapse.

Management

a. ABC – airway, breathing, circulation (see 7.22.2).

b. Control bleeding, if present.

c. Lie flat; elevate legs to 20°.

Exceptions:

i Bleeding from mouth – use recovery position.

ii Unconscious – use recovery position.

iii Chest injury – sitting may be preferred.

d. Splint any fractures; avoid movement.

e. Avoid chilling, keep warm.

f. Relieve pain – give pain killers.
Exceptions:
i Head injury with impaired consciousness.
ii Cases with severe breathing difficulty.

g. Reassure the casualty.

h. Do not let the casualty eat, drink, smoke or move unnecessarily. If he complains of thirst, moisten the lips with a little water.

Exception: fluids may be life saving in cases of dehydration (e.g. diarrhoea, vomiting, severe burns). Give half a cup of water at 15 minute intervals. Add a pinch of salt and a little sugar. Never give alcohol. Avoid in severe abdominal pain or internal injury.

Never attempt to give fluids by mouth to an unconscious person.

Collapse and signs of shock after an accident when external blood loss is absent or slight must suggest internal bleeding. Clues may be few. The casualty may cough or vomit blood, or pass blood in urine or from bowel. He may complain of worsening pain in abdomen or chest. **Urgent help needed**.

Medical illnesses, such as diabetes, severe infections or heart disease, may produce shock without giving many clues as to the cause. **Urgent help needed**.

Acquaint yourself with any medical problems of crew before a long passage. There should be a record on board of any medication being taken by any member of the crew, including the skipper (see 7.22.22).

7.22.7 BLEEDING – OPEN WOUND

Bleeding is often very dramatic, but is virtually always controllable.

Management

a. Apply firm continuous direct pressure; bandage on a large pad. If bleeding continues, bandage more pads on top of initial pads; then press directly over wound for at least 10 minutes (blood takes this time to clot).

b. Elevate if wound is on a limb.

c. Do NOT apply a tourniquet. This practice is out of date due to the danger of losing a limb.

7.22.8 BLEEDING – INTERNAL (CLOSED INJURY)

Follows fractured bones, crush injuries, or rupture of organs such as the liver or spleen. Shock may appear rapidly. **Urgent help needed**.

7.22.9 NOSE BLEED

Lean forwards and pinch the soft part of the nose firmly for at least 10 minutes to allow the blood to clot. Do not blow nose or try to remove clot.

If bleeding continues repeat the pressure for longer than 10 minutes. If still bleeding after 30 minutes insert as much 50mm (2in) gauze bandage (moistened with water) as you can, using forceps to feed the bandage into the nose. **Urgent help needed**.

7.22.10 CUTS AND WOUNDS

Often dramatic but only potentially serious if nerves, tendons or blood vessels are severed.

a. Clean thoroughly with antiseptic. Remove dirt or other foreign bodies in the wound.

b. Small clean cuts can be closed using Steristrips Skin must be dry. Use as many Steristrips as necessary to keep the skin edges together. Leave for five days at least.

c. Larger deep cuts may require special suture techniques; apply a dressing and seek help. Do not try amateur surgery at sea.

d. Ragged lacerations or very dirty wounds. Do not attempt to close these; dead tissues may have to be trimmed away to prevent infection. Clean as well as possible, sprinkle antibiotic powder in wound and apply a dressing. *Seek help.*

If in doubt a wound is best left open and lightly covered to keep it clean and dry.

Fingers and toes

Blood may collect under the nail following an injury. Release the blood by piercing the nail with a red hot needle or paper clip. It will not hurt!

7.22.11 FRACTURES AND DISLOCATIONS – GENERAL

Fracture = a broken bone. Dislocation = a displaced joint. Both result from major trauma and will produce pain (which is worse on attempted movement), localised swelling, abnormal shape, and a grating feeling on movement (when a fracture is present). Blood vessels or nerves around the fracture or dislocation may also be damaged resulting in a cold, pale, or numb limb below the site of the injury. Fractures of large bones such as the femur (upper leg) will result in major internal bleeding and may cause shock. When complications occur **urgent help is needed**.

Early application of a splint and elevation of the injured limb where possible will reduce pain and minimise complications. Treat for shock and pain.

7.22.12 SPECIFIC FRACTURES AND DISLOCATIONS

Skull. See head injury (7.22.15).

Nose. Control bleeding by pinching (7.22.9).

Cheek. Caused by a direct blow. Rarely serious but requires specialist care.

Jaw. Beware of associated brain or spine injury. Remove blood and teeth fragments; leave loose teeth in place; protect broken teeth (see 7.22.23c). Ensure airway is clear. Commence regular antiseptic mouth washes and antibiotics. Support jaw with bandage over top of head. Give only fluids by mouth.

Neck. May result from a direct blow, a fall or a whiplash type injury. If conscious, casualty may complain of pain, tingling, numbness or weakness in limbs below the injury. *Mishandling may damage the spinal cord, resulting in paralysis or death.* Avoid movement and support head. Immobilise by wrapping a folded towel around the neck. If movement is necessary then lift the victim as one rigid piece, never allowing the neck to bend. **Urgent help needed.**

Spine. Fracture of the spine may occur below the neck but the results may be similar and mishandling of the victim may greatly worsen the damage. Avoid movement if possible. Lift the casualty without allowing the spine to sag. **Urgent help needed.**

Ribs. See chest injury (7.22.16). Often very painful. Strapping is not advised.

Upper Limb

a. Collar bone (clavicle). Support arm in sling, Fig. 7(14).

b. Dislocated shoulder. If this has happened before, the casualty may reduce the dislocation himself; otherwise do not attempt reduction in case a fracture exists.

c. Upper arm (humerus). Support the arm with a collar and cuff as demonstrated below inside the shirt i.e. tie a clove hitch around the wrist, loop the ends behind the neck, Fig. 7(15).

d. Forearm and wrist. Splint (e.g. with battens or pieces of wood). Do not bandage tightly. Elevate or support in a sling.

e. Fingers. Elevate hand and, unless badly crushed, leave unbandaged; keep moving. If very wobbly, bandage to adjacent finger.

Lower Limb

a. Thigh. Shock may be considerable. Splint by strapping to other leg with padding between the legs. Gently straighten the casualty's lower leg. If necessary apply traction at the ankle to help straighten the leg. Do not bandage too tightly.

b. Knee. Twisting injuries or falls damage the ligaments and cartilages of the knee. Very painful and swollen. Treat as for fracture.

c. Lower leg. Pad very well. Splint using oar, broom handle or similar pieces of wood.

d. Ankle. Fracture or severe sprain may be indistinguishable. Immobilise in neutral position with foot at right angles. Elevate the limb.

To be really effective a splint must be rigid and extend to the joints above and below the fracture. This is not always possible. The splint must be very well padded.

If the limb beyond the bandage or splint becomes swollen or discoloured, the bandage must be loosened to improve circulation. If you improvise a splint it is essential not to enclose the whole limb and risk cutting off the circulation (see reference to non-use of tourniquet 7.22.7c).

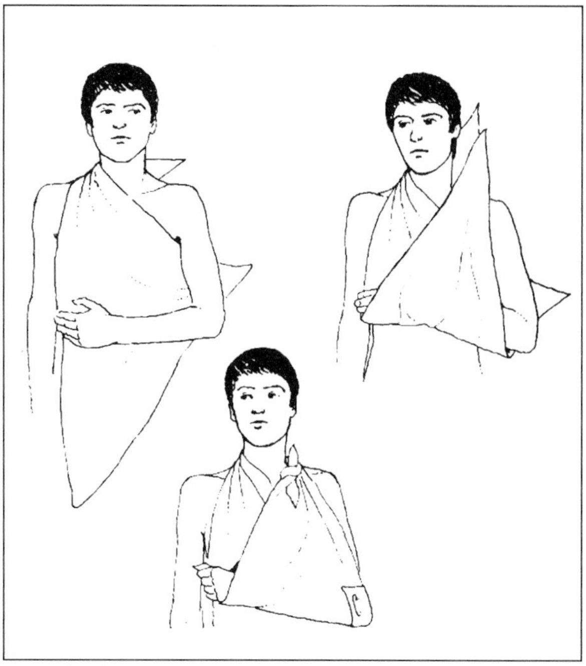

Fig. 7(15) Sling

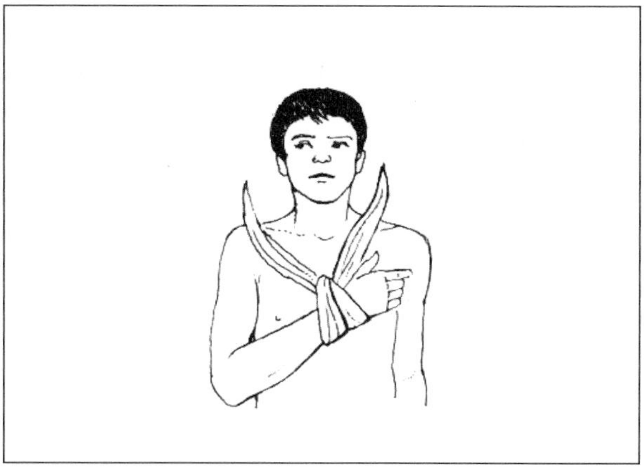

Fig. 7(16) Collar and cuff

As a general rule, if a fracture is suspected then seek advice. (see 7.22.11).

7.22.13 COMPOUND FRACTURES

If a deep wound overlies the fracture, or the bone ends are visible, do not try to close the wound or replace the bone ends. Clean thoroughly with antiseptic and cover with sterile dressing. *Seek help.* Commence antibiotics if help delayed.

7.22.14 STRAINS AND SPRAINS

Torn ligaments, pulled muscles and other injuries. Rest the injured part; elevate if possible; apply ice packs (wrapped in a towel) if possible at sea; administer pain-killers. If in doubt, treat as a fracture and immobilise.

C7

7.22.15 HEAD INJURY

A blow to the head, with or without fracture, may result in immediate unconsciousness or more delayed effects.

Management

a. Immediate unconsciousness, but quick recovery with slight drowsiness or headache. Prescribe rest and watch carefully.

b. Immediate unconsciousness, no sign of recovery. Put in recovery position (beware of associated spine injury). Check airway. Observe the following and record every 10 minutes: pulse rate, breathing rate, pupil size (both sides), responses to verbal command, response to firm pinching. **Urgent help needed**.

c. Delayed deterioration (either not unconscious immediately, or apparently recovering then worsening). Increasing drowsiness, change in mental state and eventually unconsciousness. Treat as (b) above. **Urgent help needed**.

Scalp wounds may bleed profusely. Control with very firm pressure; cut away hair, and close using Steristrips if no fracture beneath. *If in doubt seek help.* Avoid giving drugs after head injury.

7.22.16 CHEST INJURY

May result in fractured ribs. These are very painful, and breathing may be uncomfortable and shallow. The fractured ribs may puncture the lung, or if a number of ribs are each broken in two places (e.g. after crush injury) then this flail segment of the chest may seriously impair breathing.

Management

a. Airway, breathing, circulation (see 7.22.2).

b. Casualty may be more comfortable sitting up.

c. Plug any hole with a pad if air is sucking in and out.

d. Support any unstable chest segment with your hand.

e. For fractured ribs prescribe rest and strong pain-killers if necessary. Very painful.

Avoid tight strapping lest it restricts breathing even further. **Urgent help needed** for any case with impaired breathing.

7.22.17 EYE PROBLEMS

All eye injuries or illnesses are potentially serious. Never put old or previously opened ointment or drops into an eye; serious infection could result.

a. Foreign object. Flush the eye with clean water, pull the bottom lid out to inspect, remove object with a clean tissue. For objects under upper eyelid, ask casualty to grasp lashes and pull the upper lid over the lower lid. Blinking under water may also remove the object. After removal of object, instil sterile antibiotic ointment inside pulled out lower lid. Cover with pad.

b. Corrosive fluid. Flush continuously with water for 15 minutes. Give pain-killers and chloramphenicol ointment; cover with pad. *Seek help as soon as possible.*

c. Infection (conjunctivitis). A sticky, weeping eye with yellow discharge. Chloramphenicol ointment four times per day.

7.22.18 BURNS AND SCALDS

a. Move the victim into fresh air to avoid inhaling smoke.

b. ABC – Airway, Breathing, Circulation.

c. Stop further injury: dip the whole of the burnt part into cold water for 10 - 15 minutes. Seawater is excellent but may be very painful.

d. Remove only loose clothing. Do not pull off clothing stuck to the skin.

e. Cover with sterile dressing. If skin broken or blistered, use sterile paraffin gauze beneath the dressing. Separate burnt fingers with paraffin gauze. Never use adhesive dressings.

f. Do not prick blisters or apply ointments.

g. Elevate burnt limb and immobilise.

h. Give strong pain-killers.

i. Treat for shock: give frequent and copious drinks of water.

j. Commence antibiotics for major burns.

k. If burns extensive or deep, **urgent help needed**.

Sunburn may be very severe. Treat as for any other burn. If skin unbroken apply calamine lotion; give pain-killers. For prevention use only filter preparations with high protection factor.

7.22.19 FROSTBITE

Usually affects toes, fingers, ears or nose. The affected part may be very painful, numb, stiff and discoloured. Warm gently (e.g. on someone else's back). Immersion in water less than 43°C (110°F) is satisfactory; higher temperatures will cause more damage. Do not rub the affected part with anything.

7.22.20 POISONING

Poison may reach the body when swallowed, inhaled or injected through the skin (e.g. bites and stings).

General management

a. ABC: Airway, Breathing, Circulation.

b. Recovery position if unconscious.

c. *Seek help.*

Swallowed poison

The poison container may have instructions or suggest antidote(s). For corrosive or petroleum products (e.g. acids, alkalis, bleach, detergent, petrol) *do not induce* vomiting. Administer copious fluids (eg milk).

For other substances (e.g. pills, medicines) do not induce vomiting – it is often ineffective and may cause further harm to the casualty. If collapsed or unconscious, **urgent help needed**.

Inhaled poison

Poison may be inhaled from sources such as carbon monoxide or other exhaust fumes, bottled gas which has leaked into bilge, or fire extinguisher gas. Carbon monoxide inhalation produces cherry red lips and skin. Move into fresh air immediately. If breathing absent, commence resuscitation. **Urgent help needed**.

Bites and stings

Injected poison from bites and stings usually only causes local swelling and discomfort, but some individuals may react severely. For insect stings, resuscitate if collapse occurs; otherwise give rest, pain-killers, antihistamines (e.g. chlorpheniramine). In warmer water, sea snakes and various sea stingers can inject extremely deadly poison: prevent drowning, resuscitate if necessary; if sting caused by jelly fish or Portuguese Man O'War etc, pour vinegar onto sting to reduce further poison release.

If the victim becomes weak and breathless, lightly compress the limb above the wound with a rolled up roller bandage to delay spread of poison; do not apply a tourniquet. Commence resuscitation. **Urgent help needed**.

Many large cities maintain a 24-hour poison information centre. Use the radio for advice.

7.22.21 SEASICKNESS

Basically an inner ear disturbance caused by motion. Fear, anxiety, fatigue and boredom aggravate the condition. May manifest itself as lethargy, dizziness or headache as well as nausea and vomiting.

Avoid strong food tastes, and too much alcohol. Take small amounts of fluid and food (e.g. biscuits) frequently if you feel ill. Avoid fatigue; adequate sleep will often relieve the sick feeling. Keep warm. Stay on deck, and concentrate on some task if possible. Ensure that sick crew on deck are secured by lifeline. Turn in if all else fails. Vomiting may cause serious loss of fluid.

No one remedy is suitable for every person. Try the various preparations until you find one that is effective with minimal side effects; most tend to cause a dry mouth and some tiredness. Available tablets include: Avomine (promethazine) and Stugeron (cinnarizine). Take the first tablet some hours before sailing, and then regularly for as long as necessary. Take a tablet just before going to sleep if possible. Various preparations can be applied behind the ear or worn as a wrist band.

7.22.22 SUDDEN ILLNESS

Acquaint yourself with any medical problems of the crew (and skipper!) before a long passage. Ask medical advice on likely symptoms and treatment; unless forewarned, diagnosis may otherwise be very difficult once at sea.

a. Abdominal pain (minor).

i Upper abdomen, intermittent, burning, no tenderness, otherwise well. May follow large alcohol intake. Eased by milk or antacid. Bland meals. No alcohol.

ii More generalised, cramping or colicky pain, no tenderness, may have diarrhoea or vomiting. May be gastroenteritis or food poisoning. Take oral fluid with a pinch of salt added. Avoid dehydration. Seek advice.

b. Abdominal pain (major). Severe abdominal pain, usually constant and generalised. Abdomen may be rigid or very tender to touch, fever may be present, rapid pulse rate, generally unwell, nausea and vomiting. Make the casualty comfortable, give pain relief (injection if possible). Give nothing to eat or drink. **Urgent help needed**.

c. Allergies. Mild cases may just have a rash which responds to calamine lotion and antihistamine tablets. Severe cases may collapse with breathing difficulty and require emergency ABC resuscitation. Seek advice.

d. Constipation. Common at sea. Prevent by eating fruit, vegetables, bran and if necessasry, anti-constipation medication (e.g. senna preparations).

e. Convulsions. Casualty may be a known epileptic. Insert twisted cloth between teeth to protect tongue. Prevent injury. Recovery position; protect airway (he may still look very blue). After fit, allow him to sleep. **Urgent help needed**.

f. Diabetes. A diabetic may become unconscious if his blood sugar is too high or too low. For hyperglycaemia (too much sugar) insulin is needed. Hypoglycaemia (too little sugar) may be caused by too much insulin, unusual stress or exercise, or too little food. In either case, if rousable, first give sweets, sugar, soft drinks. If recovery not rapid, **urgent help needed**.

g. Diarrhoea. Can become serious, especially in young children if much fluid is lost. Stop food, give plenty of fluid. Water is sufficient in most cases, or alternatively, add salt (1 teaspoonful/litre) and sugar (4-5 teaspoonful/litre) to water. Lomotil or Imodium tablets very effective in adults.

h. Fever. May be associated with anything from common cold, appendicitis, heat stroke to an infected toe. Except for major abdominal problems, prescribe copious fluids, paracetamol or aspirin (not in the case of children) and antibiotics if infection is present. Seek advice.

j. Heart attack. Severe central chest pain; may spread to shoulders, neck or arms. Sweating, then bluish lips, then collapse. Breathing and heart may stop. Give one aspirin tablet 300mg.

i Early symptoms; rest, reassure. **Urgent help needed.**

ii If unconscious: recovery position; observe breathing and pulse.

iii If breathing stops or pulse absent, commence mouth to mouth ventilation and chest compression immediately and do not stop. See 7.22.1

k. Heat stroke. Cool casualty by spraying with cold water or wrap the casualty in a cold wet sheet until their temperature falls to 38°C, under the tongue; encourage drinking (one teaspoon of salt per pint of water). If casualty stops sweating, has a rapid pounding pulse and is becoming unconscious, **seek help urgently.**

l. Stroke. Sudden unconsciousness, paralysis or weakness on one side of body, slurring of speech. Recovery position, air way control. **Urgent help needed.**

7.22.23 TOOTHACHE

Dental pain seems worse at sea, and prevention is better than cure. For a long voyage consider carrying a dental mirror, tongue spatula, pen torch, cotton wool rolls, tweezers, zinc oxide powder and oil of cloves (or a ready-mixed temporary filling, e.g. Coltisol). Dentanurse is an emergency treatment pack which enables an amateur to make basic temporary repairs, eg replacing crowns, lost fillings. It contains zinc oxide and Eugenol.

Management

a. Throbbing toothache, made worse by hot or cold or when bitten on. If an obvious cavity is present, clean out and apply zinc oxide paste (made by incorporating as much zinc oxide powder as possible into three drops of oil of cloves, to form a thick putty). Take paracetamol.

b. Dull toothache, tender to bite on; gum swollen or red with possible discharge. Treat as above but also take an antibiotic.

c. Broken tooth or filling. Cover exposed surfaces with zinc oxide paste. Teeth which have been knocked out should be placed in a clean container with milk or moist gauze and taken to a dentist at the first opportunity for reimplantation.

d. Bleeding gums. Clean teeth more thoroughly. If accompanied by foul odour and metallic taste, use regular hot salt water rinses and antibiotics.

e. Pain round wisdom tooth. Toothbrush to clean area; use hot salt water rinses; take antibiotics and painkillers.

f. Mouth ulcers. Hot salt water rinses.

7..22.24 FISH HOOKS

Push the hook round until the point and barb appear. Cut off the point and barb and withdraw the hook. Dress the holes and give an antibiotic.

7.22.25 CHILDREN

Children may become ill with alarming rapidity. Ear and throat infections are especially common. Children are also more susceptible to effects of dehydration, so if ill encourage to drink copious fluids. Reduce drug dosage to a proportion of adult dose based on weight. [Average adult 70kg (155lb)]. Seek advice.

7.22.26 DRUGS

Paracetamol 500mg tablets	painkiller	1–2 tablets every 4 hours
Dihydrocodeine 30mg tablets	strong painkiller	1–2 tablets every 4 hours
Chlorpheniramine 4mg tablets	antihistamine	1 tablet every 8 hours
Aludrox	indigestion	1–2 before meals
Loperamide 2mg capsules	diarrhoea	Take 2 capsules initially followed by 1 after each loose stool, up to a maximum of 8 per day
Senokot tablets	constipation	2–4 tablets daily
Tetracycline 250mg	antibiotic	1 capsule 4 times daily
Amoxycillin 250mg	antibiotic	250–500mg every 8 hours (beware penicillin allergy)
Erythromycin 250mg	antibiotic	For penicillin-allergic adult 4 tablets daily
Cinnarizine 15mg	seasickness tablets	2 before voyage then 1 every 8 hours

7.22.27 INJECTIONS

A doctor's prescription is required for injections. Stringent regulations apply to injectable painkiller drugs, which are probably only warranted for long passages. It is safest to inject into the muscle on the outer part of the mid-thigh. Clean the area, then plunge the needle swiftly an inch or so through the skin, pull back on the plunger to ensure that a blood vessel has not been entered, then slowly complete the injection.

7.22.28 NORMAL PHYSIOLOGICAL MEASUREMENTS

a.	Pulse rate.	Adults 60–80/minute. Children up to 100/minute.
b.	Breathing.	12–15/minute.
c.	Temperature.	36·7°C (98·4°F)

7.22.29 SUGGESTIONS FOR A FIRST AID KIT

A made-up Offshore First Aid Kit can be bought for about £65. Your doctor or chemist may suggest alternatives. Prescriptions are needed for most of the drugs listed in 7.22.26. Out of date drugs are potentially dangerous – destroy them. Special preparations are available for children. Stow the following suggested items in a readily accessible, clearly marked waterproof container:

Triangular bandage x 2 (doubles as bandage or sling)
Crepe bandage 75mm x 2

Gauze bandage 50mm x 2

Elastoplast 75mm x 1

Band Aids (or similar) various shapes and sizes

Wound dressing bpc, 1 large, 1 medium

Sterile non-adhesive dressing (Melolin) x 5

Paraffin gauze sterile dressings x 5 packs

Steristrips x 5 packs

Cotton wool

Scissors and forceps, good stainless steel

Safety pins

Thermometer

Disposable gloves

Antiseptic solution (e.g. Savlon)

Sunscreen with high protection factor

Antibiotic powder or spray

Tinaderm powder (athlete's foot)

Calamine lotion (bites, stings and sunburn)

Insect repellent (DEET, diethyltoluamide)

Individual choice of anti-seasick tablets

Chloramphenicol eye ointment

Additional items for extended cruising

Do not forget vaccinations – a course may need to start as much as 6 months before departure.

Syringes 2ml x 2 (if carrying injections)

Dental kit – see 7.22.23

Moisture cream (for cracked hand and lips)

7.22.30 FORM E111

For cruising in European waters it is sensible to carry Form E111, *Certificate of entitlement to benefits in kind during a stay in a member state.* Form E111 is actually contained within a very informative 52 page booklet *Health advice for travellers,* aka T6; this is obtainable from a Post Office where the E111 must be completed and stamped. It is useful to have several photocopies of the Form E111 as the foreign doctor or pharmacist may need to retain a copy.

E111 allows yachtsmen to obtain medical treatment on a reciprocal basis, although it will not cover the full charge. Details of how to claim in the 18 member countries of the EEA (the 15 EC members plus Iceland, Liechtenstein and Norway) are given in the T6 booklet. A further 40+ countries world-wide have reciprocal health care agreements with the UK. But many others, including USA, Latin America, Canada, India, the Far East and Africa, do not; if cruising these areas private health insurance may be advisable.

Yachtsmen cruising abroad may naturally be concerned about the possibility of being given infected blood. Under normal circumstances it is not possible to carry blood or plasma in a yacht. If a blood transfusion is essential, try to ensure that the blood used has been screened against HIV and Hepatitis B.

If you are cruising to distant destinations you may wish to take additional sterile needles and syringes, for example if you or a crewman are diabetic. Seek advice from your doctor or local hospital before leaving. Syringes and needles are attractive to intravenous drug abusers so should be locked away securely.

7.22.31 FIRST AID TRAINING

Most of us would benefit from and probably welcome regular attendance at a refresher training course, perhaps every other year. This enables us to keep abreast of the latest methods, treatments and medical opinion – and to remind ourselves of techniques which happily we are not often called upon to utilise. Such courses are run by the First Aid specialists at the St John Ambulance; at bodies like the RYA, Cruising Association and by yacht clubs as part of their winter training schedules.

7.22.32 FIRST AID BOOKS

The following books give detailed advice and at least one should be on board (the crew should be advised as to its location):

First Aid Manual of St John Ambulance, St Andrew's Ambulance Association and the British Red Cross (Dorling Kindersley, 8th edition 1997, £11.99). Clear and authoritative text, profusely illustrated in colour. A quick reference guide is included on Emergency First Aid.

Resuscitation Council (UK) Resuscitation for the Citizen - Sixth edition.

The Ship's Captain Medical Guide (TSO, 22nd edition, £33.00). Official handbook for merchant ships.

First Aid at Sea by D Justins & C Berry (Adlard Coles, 3rd edition 1993, £9.99). Easy reference guide.

The First Aid Companion by Dr R Haworth (Fernhurst)

First Aid Afloat by Dr R Haworth (Fernhurst)

Advanced First Aid afloat by Dr Peter Eastman

Your Offshore Doctor by Dr Michael Beilan (Adlard Coles).

TABLE 7.1: Based on these risk levels, the following is a precis of the main items of safety equipment recommended to be carried. Note: A bullet • recommends that the item be carried, but the number, method or contents is left to the skipper.

		CATEGORY			
		A	B	C	D
1.	**Means of propulsion** (Sailing yachts only)				
1.2	A trysail, or deep reef to reduce the mainsail luff to 60% of full hoist, and a storm jib	•	•	•	
1.3	For engine starting, a battery isolated from all other electrical systems, or hand cranking	•	•	•	
2.	**Number of anchors**, with appropriate lengths/diameter of warp & chain or chain only	2+	2	2	1
3.	**Bailing and bilge pumping**				
3.2	Buckets of 9-14 ltrs capacity with lanyard and strongly secured handle	2	2	2	
3.3	Manual bilge pumps, operable with all hatches closed	2	2	1	
3.4	Softwood bungs attached adjacent to all through-hull fittings, able to be closed	•	•	•	•
4.	**Detection equipment**				
4.1	Radar reflector properly mounted and as big as is reasonable	•	•	•	
4.2	Fixed nav lights, iaw IRPCS; 4.3 Foghorn; 4.4 Powerful torch	•	•	•	
	Motoring cone (sail only); anchor ball and light	•	•	•	•
5.	**Pyrotechnics (in date)**				
5.1	Hand-held red flares	6	4	4	2
5.2	Buoyant orange smoke signals	2	2		
5.3	Red parachute rockets	1	2	4	2
5.4	Hand-held orange smoke signals			2	2
5.5	Hand-held white flares	4	4	4	
6.	**Fire fighting equipment**				
6.1	Fire blanket (BS EN 1869) for all yachts with cooking equipment	•	•	•	•
6.2	For yachts with a galley or carrying engine fuel: multi-purpose extinguishers of minimum fire rating 5A/34B to BS EN 3	3	2	1	1
6.3	Additionally, for yachts with both a galley and carrying engine fuel: multi-purpose extinguishers of minimum fire rating 5A/34B to BS EN 3	1	1	1	1
6.4	Additionally, for yachts with engines over 25hp, a fixed automatic or semi-automatic fire fighting system to discharge into the engine space	•	•	•	•
7.	**Personal safety equipment for each crew member** (see 13.3.6, .7 and .8)				
7.1	Warm clothing, oilskins, seaboots and hat	•	•	•	•
7.3	Lifejacket (BS EN 396) 150 Newtons	1	1	1	
7.4	Lifejacket light	1	1		
7.5	Spray face cover; 7.7 Immersion suit, per crew member	1			
7.6	Safety harness, per crew member (for yachts with enclosed wheelhouse, one harness for 50% of the crew)	1	1	1	
7.8	Jackstays and cockpit clip-on strong points	•	•	•	•
8.	**Liferaft**				
8.1	Inflatable dinghy, designed or adapted for saving life, sufficient for all on board		1	1	
8.2	Liferaft, designed solely for saving life, sufficient for all on board	1			
8.3	Emergency grab-bag (see text for contents)	1	1	1	
9.	**Man overboard recovery equipment**				
9.1	Horseshoe life-belts fitted with drogue and self-igniting light	2	2	1	
9.2	Buoyant sling on floating line – may replace 1 horseshoe lifebelt if 2 are carried	1	1		
9.3	Buoyant heaving line, at least 30m long, with quoit	1	1	1	
9.4	Boarding ladder capable of rapid and secure attachment	1	1	1	
9.5	Dan buoy with a large flag	1	1		
10.	**Radio**				
10.1	Radio receiver able to receive forecasts on 198kHz and local radio station forecasts	1	1	1	1
10.2	VHF Marine band radio telephone	1	1	1	1
10.3	Digital Selective Calling controller to class D (MPT 1279)	1	1		
10.4	Marine band HF/SSB radio; 10.5 406 MHz EPIRB registered in the vessel's name	1			
10.6	Navtex; 10.8 Emergency VHF radio aerial; 10.9 Waterproof hand-held VHF radio	1	1		
10.7	Radar transponder (SART)	1			
11.	**Navigational equipment**				
11.2	Charts, tide tables and navigational publications of the cruising area and adjacent areas	•	•	•	
11.3	Steering compass, able to be illuminated and a hand-bearing compass	1	1	1	1
11.5	Drawing instruments; 11.6 Barometer; 11.7 Echosounder & lead-line; 11.9 Watch or clock	1	1	1	
11.8	Radio nav system, Loran C and/or GPS	1	1		
11.10	Distance measuring log; 11.11 Binoculars	1	1	1	
11.12	Sextant, the Nautical Almanac (TSO) and sight reduction tables	1			
12.	**First aid kit and manual** (see 7.22.1)	1	1	1	
13.	**General equipment**				
13.1	Emergency tiller (all wheel-steered vessels)	1	1	1	1
13.2	Towing warp; 13.10 Bosun's chair (sit harness BS EN 813 1997)	1	1	1	
13.3	Warps and fenders; 13.6 Repair tools; 13.7 Spares, engine, electrics, shackles and twine	•	•	•	•
13.4	Waterproof torch	3	2	2	1
13.5	Rigid or inflatable tender	•	•	•	
13.8	Emergency fresh water, separate from main tanks; 13.9 Emergency repair materials	•	•		

Chapter 8

Tides

Contents

8.1 GENERAL

8.1.1 Introduction

This chapter is a reminder of how to use the tidal data contained in Chapter 9, where the daily times and heights of High Water (HW) and Low Water (LW) are given for Standard Ports; plus time and height differences for Secondary Ports. Tidal predictions are for average meteorological conditions. In abnormal weather the times and heights of HW and LW may vary considerably; see 8.8.

The Admiralty Tide Tables (ATT) are the source for all tidal predictions in this almanac. ATT for the world are published in four volumes as follows:

NP 201 UK & Ireland (including Channel ports from Hook of Holland to Brest);

NP 202 Europe (excluding UK, Ireland and Channel ports), Mediterranean and the Atlantic;

NP 203 Indian Ocean and South China Sea; and

NP 204 Pacific Ocean.

8.1.2 Times

Standard Port predictions are given in the Standard, or Zone, Time indicated at the top left-hand corner of each page, i.e. in UT (Zone 0) for the UK, Channel Islands, Eire and Portugal. In Denmark, Germany, Netherlands, Belgium,France and Spain Standard Time is UT +1 (Zone –1). To convert Zone –1 times to UT, subtract 1 hour.

When DST (BST in UK) is in force during the summer months (no pale yellow tinting), one hour must be added to the predicted times to obtain DST (= LT).

Under each Secondary Port listed in Chapter 9 are its Zone Time, and the time differences required to calculate the times of HW and LW at the Secondary Port in the Zone Time of that Port. If DST is required, then one hour is added *after* the Secondary Port time difference has been applied – not before.

8.1.3. Spanish secondary Ports referenced to Lisboa

In Areas 23 and 25, several Spanish ports use Lisboa as Standard Port. Time differences for these ports, when applied to the printed times of HW and LW for Lisboa (UT), automatically give HW and LW times in the Zone Time for Spain (ie UT–1). No corrections are required, except for DST, when applicable.

8.2 DEFINITIONS

Definitions [see below and Fig. 8 (1)] are amplified in the *Reeds Yachtsman's Handbook*.

8.2.1 Chart datum

Chart datum (CD) is the reference level above which heights of tide are predicted, and below which charted depths are measured. Hence the actual depth of water is the charted depth (at that place) plus the height of tide (at that time).

8.2.2 Lowest Astonomical Tide (LAT)

LAT is the lowest sea level predicted under average meteorological conditions. It is used as the CD for most British ports. Charted depths on Admiralty charts of the UK are based on LAT as CD, but where tidal predictions and charted depths are not referenced to the same datum (eg LAT), errors can occur resulting in an over-estimation of depth by as much as 0·5m.

8.2.3 Ordnance Datum (Newlyn) [OD(N)]

OD(N) is the plane to which all features on UK land maps are referred. It approximates to MSL at Newlyn, Cornwall. The difference between CD and OD(N) is quoted in this Almanac at the foot of each page of tidal predictions. Abroad differences between CD and the national land levelling plane are similarly quoted.

8.2.4 Charted depth

Charted depth is the distance of the sea bed below CD; sometimes erroneously referred to as a sounding (which is the depth below sea level). Values in metres and decimetres (0·1m) are printed all over charts.

8.2.5 Drying height

Drying height is the height above CD of the top of any feature at times covered by water. The figures are underlined on the chart, in metres and decimetres on metric charts. The depth of water is the height of tide (at the time) minus the drying height. If the result is negative, then that feature is above water level.

8.2.6 Heights of lights, bridges, etc

Heights of lights, bridges, overhead cables etc are measured above the level of MHWS; see 8.5. On French charts such heights are measured above MSL.

8.2.7 Height of tide

The height of the tide is the vertical distance of sea level above (or very occasionally below) CD. Predicted heights are given in metres and decimetres.

8.2.8 Rise/Fall of tide

The Rise of the tide is the amount the tide has risen since the earlier Low Water. The Fall of a tide is the amount the tide has fallen since the last High Water.

8.2.9 Duration

Duration is the time between LW and the next HW, normally slightly more than six hours. It can be used to calculate the approximate time of LW when only the time of HW is known.

8.2.10 Interval

The interval is a period of time quoted in hours and minutes before (–) or after (+) HW. Intervals are printed in hourly increments (–6hrs to +6hrs) along the bottom of each tidal curve diagram in Chapter 9.

8.2.11 Spring tides

Springs occur roughly every 16 days, near to Full and New Moon, when the tide-raising forces of Sun and Moon are at a maximum.

Fig. 8(1) Tidal definitions shown pictorially

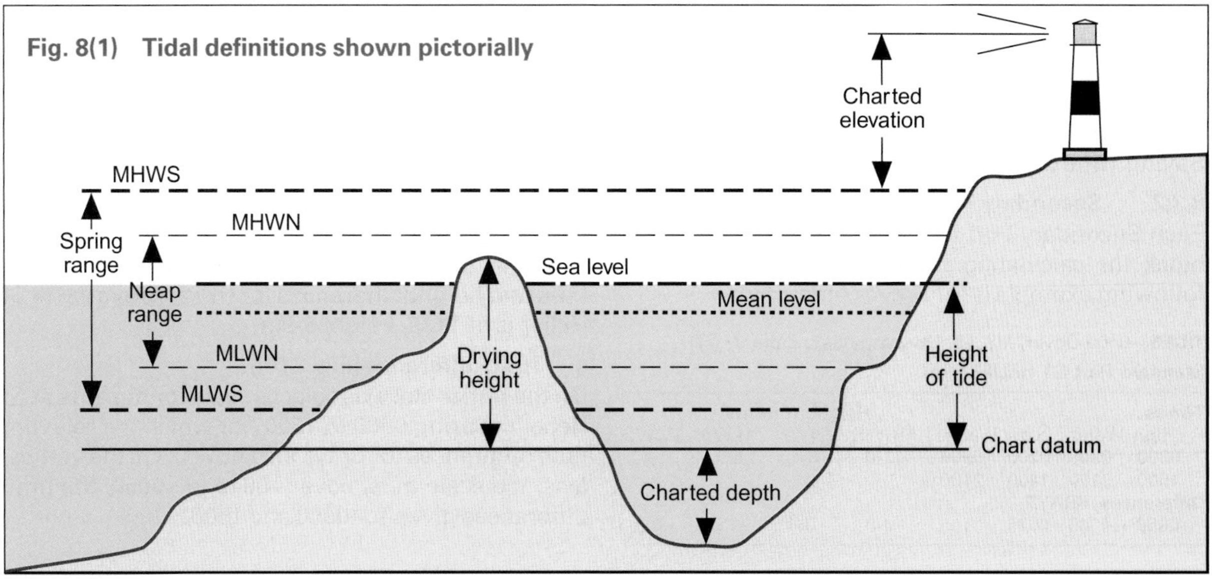
Charted elevation
MHWS
MHWN
Spring range
Neap range
Sea level
Mean level
MLWN
MLWS
Drying height
Height of tide
Chart datum
Charted depth

8.2.12 Neap tides
Neaps occur roughly every 16 days, near the Moon's first and last quarters, when the tide-raising forces of Sun and Moon are at a minimum.

8.2.13 Mean High Water and Low Water Springs/Neaps
Mean High Water Springs (MHWS) and Mean High Water Neaps (MHWN) are the averages of predicted HW heights of Spring or Neap tides over a period of 18·6 years. Similarly, Mean Low Water Springs (MLWS) and Neaps (MLWN) are the averages of LW heights for Spring and Neap tides respectively.

8.2.14 Mean Level
Mean Level (ML) is the average of the heights of MHWS, MHWN, MLWS and MLWN.

8.2.15 Range
The range of a tide is the difference between the heights of successive HWs and LWs. Spring range is the difference between MHWS and MLWS, and Neap range is the difference between MHWN and MLWN.

8.2.16 Tidal Coefficients
In France the size (range) of a tide is quantified by Tidal Coefficients. These are listed for each day of the year and explained in 9.20.26.

8.2.17 Standard Port
A port whose tidal characteristics are suitable as a reference for other ports along the adjacent coasts. Predictions for 46 Standard Ports are in Chapter 9.

8.2.18 Secondary Port
A port with similar tidal characteristics to those of its Standard port. Secondary port time and height differences are applied to Standard port predictions. 'Secondary' does not imply lesser importance.

8.3 CALCULATING TIMES AND HEIGHTS OF HIGH AND LOW WATER

8.3.1 Standard Ports
Standard Ports, for which daily predictions are given in Chapter 9, are listed below by their Areas:

1 Falmouth, Devonport, Dartmouth.
2 Portland, Poole, Southampton, Portsmouth.
3 Shoreham, Dover.
4 Sheerness, London Bridge, Burnham-on-Crouch*, Walton-on-the-Naze, Lowestoft.
5 Immingham, Tyne (North Shields).
6 Leith, Aberdeen.
7 Lerwick.
8 Ullapool, Oban.
9 Greenock.
10 Liverpool, Holyhead.
11 Milford Haven, Avonmouth.
12 Dublin, Cobh.
13 Belfast, Galway.
14 Esbjerg.
15 Helgoland, Cuxhaven and Wilhelmshaven.
16 Hook of Holland, Vlissingen.
17 Dieppe, Le Havre, Cherbourg.
18 St Malo.
19 St Peter Port, St Helier.
20 Brest.†
21 Nil.
22 Pointe de Grave.
23 Nil.
24 Lisboa.
25 Gibraltar.

* Daily predictions given, although not an Admiralty Standard Port.

† Brest tidal coefficients are at 9.20.26.

Predicted times and heights of HW and LW are tabulated for each Standard Port in Chapter 9 (as listed above). Importantly, these are only predictions and take no account of the effects of wind and barometric pressure (see 8.8). See 8.1.2 for Daylight Saving Time (DST).

8.3.2 Secondary Ports – times of HW and LW

Each Secondary Port listed in Chapter 9 has a data block for calculating times of HW and LW. The following example is for Braye (Alderney):

TIDES –0400 Dover; ML 3·5; Duration 0545; Zone 0 (UT)
Standard Port ST HELIER (⟶)

Times				**Height (metres)**			
High Water		Low Water		MHWS	MHWN	MLWN	MLWS
0300	0900	0200	0900	11·0	8·1	4·0	1·4
1500	2100	1400	2100				
Differences BRAYE							
+0050	+0040	+0025	+0105	–4·8	–3·4	–1·5	–0·5

Here –0400 Dover indicates that, on average, HW Braye occurs 4 hours 00 minutes before HW Dover (the times of HW Dover, in UT, can be found on the bookmark). Duration 0545 indicates that LW Braye occurs 5 hours and 45 minutes before its HW. This is a very rough and ready method. The arrow after the Standard Port name merely points to where the tide tables are in the book.

The usual and more accurate method uses Standard Port times and Secondary Port time differences as in the block. Thus when HW at St Helier occurs at 0300 and 1500, the difference is + 0050, and HW at Braye then occurs at 0350 and 1550. When HW at St Helier occurs at 0900 and 2100, the difference is + 0040, and HW at Braye occurs at 0940 and 2140.

If, as is usually the case, HW St Helier occurs at some other time, then the difference for Braye must be found by interpolation: by eye, by the graphical method, or by calculator. Thus, by eye, when HW St Helier occurs at 1200 (midway between 0900 and 1500), the difference is + 0045 (midway between +0040 and +0050), and HW Braye occurs at 1245. The same method is used for calculating the times of LW.

The times thus obtained are in the Zone Time of the Secondary Port.

8.3.3 Secondary Ports – heights of HW and LW

The Secondary Port data block also contains height Differences which are applied to the heights of HW and LW at the Standard Port. Thus when the height of HW at St Helier is 11·0m (MHWS), the difference is – 4·8m, so the height of HW Braye is 6·2m (MHWS). When the height of HW St Helier is 8·1m (MHWN), the difference is – 3·4m, and the height of HW at Braye is 4·7m (MHWN).

If, as is likely, the height of tide at the Standard Port differs from the Mean Spring or Neap level, then the height difference also must be interpolated: by eye, by graph or by calculator. Thus, by eye, if the height of HW St Helier is 9·55m (midway between MHWS and MHWN), the difference is – 4·1m, and the height of HW Braye is 5·45m (9·55–4·1m).

8.3.4 Graphical method for interpolating time and height differences

Any suitable squared paper can be used, having chosen convenient scales; see Figs. 8(2) and 8(3). For example, using the data for Braye in 8.3.2, find the time and height differences for HW at Braye if HW St Helier is at 1126, height 8·9m.

a. Time difference [Fig. 8 (2)]

On the horizontal axis select a scale for the time at St Helier covering 0900 to 1500 (for which the relevant time differences for Braye are known). On the vertical axis, the scale must cover +0040 to +0050, the time differences given for 0900 and 1500.

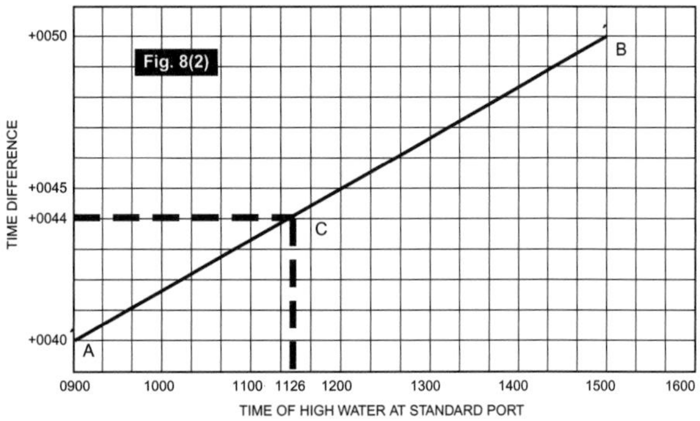
Fig. 8(2)
+0050
+0045
+0044
+0040
TIME DIFFERENCE
A
B
C
0900
1000
1100
1126
1200
1300
1400
1500
1600
TIME OF HIGH WATER AT STANDARD PORT

Plot point A, the time difference (+0040) for HW St Helier at 0900; and point B, the time difference (+0050) for HW St Helier at 1500. Join AB. Enter the graph at time 1126 (HW St Helier); intersect AB at C then go horizontally to read +0044 on the vertical axis. On that morning HW Braye is 44 minutes after HW St Helier, ie 1210.

b. Height difference [Fig. 8 (3)]

In Fig. 8 (3), the horizontal axis covers the height of HW at St Helier (i.e. 8·1 to 11·0m) and the vertical axis shows the relevant height differences (– 3·4 to – 4·8m).

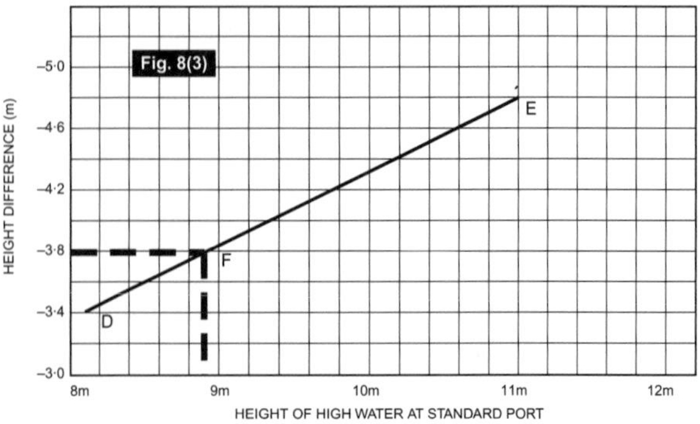
Fig. 8(3)
-5·0
-4·6
-4·2
-3·8
-3·4
-3·0
HEIGHT DIFFERENCE (m)
D
E
F
8m
9m
10m
11m
12m
HEIGHT OF HIGH WATER AT STANDARD PORT

Plot point D, the height difference (– 3·4m) at Neaps when the height of HW St Helier is 8·1m; and E, the height difference (– 4·8m) at Springs when the height of HW St Helier is 11·0m. Join DE. Enter the graph at 8·9m (the height of HW St Helier that morning) and mark F where that height meets DE. From F follow the horizontal line to read off the corresponding height difference: – 3·8m. So that morning the height of HW Braye is 5·1m.

8.4 CALCULATING INTERMEDIATE TIMES AND HEIGHTS OF TIDE

(1) On the Leith tidal curve diagram, Fig. 8 (4), plot the heights of HW and LW before and after the required time; join them by a sloping line.

(2) Enter the HW time and other times as necessary in the boxes below the curves.

(3) From the required time, go vertically to the curves. The Spring curve is red, and the Neap curve (where it differs) is blue. Interpolate between the curves by comparing the actual range, in this example 4·4m, with the Mean Ranges printed beside the curves. Never extrapolate. In this example the Spring curve applies.

(4) Go horizontally to the sloping line plotted in (1), thence vertically to the height scale, to extract 4·2m.

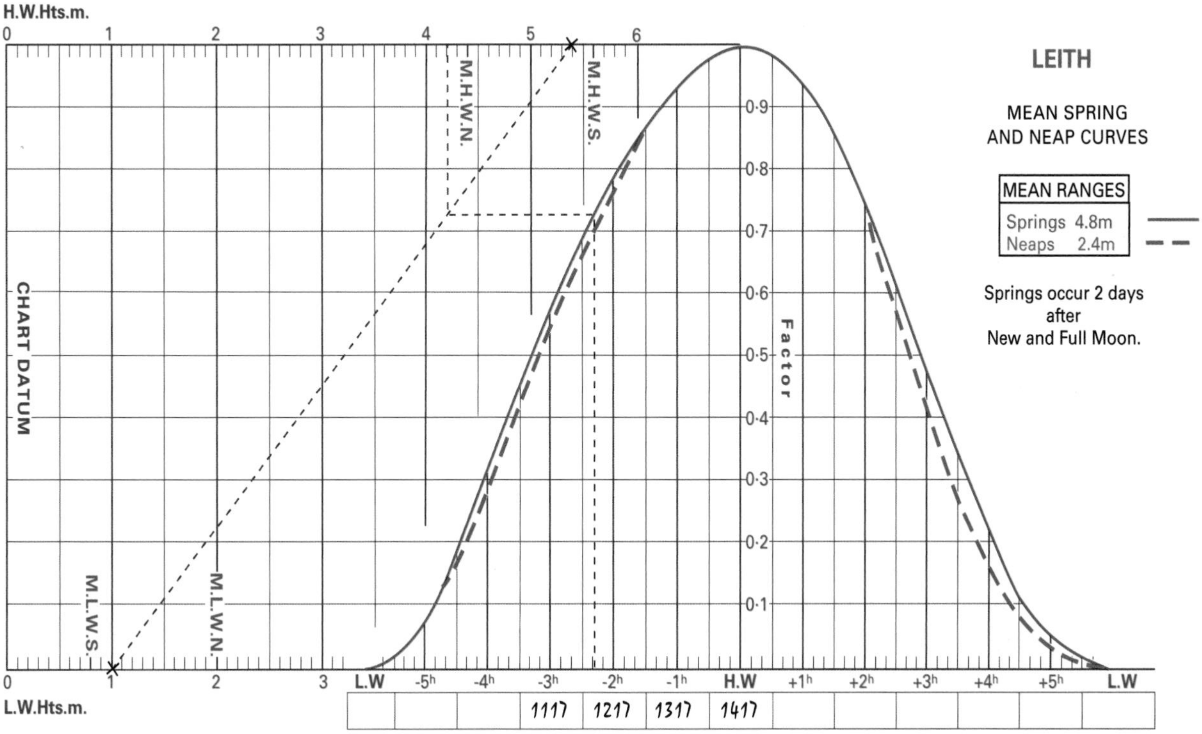

H.W.Hts.m.
0 1 2 3 4 5 6
M.H.W.N.
M.H.W.S.
LEITH
MEAN SPRING AND NEAP CURVES
MEAN RANGES
Springs 4.8m
Neaps 2.4m
Springs occur 2 days after New and Full Moon.
CHART DATUM
Factor
0·9
0·8
0·7
0·6
0·5
0·4
0·3
0·2
0·1
M.L.W.S.
M.L.W.N.
0 1 2 3
L.W.Hts.m.
L.W -5h -4h -3h -2h -1h H.W +1h +2h +3h +4h +5h L.W
1117 1217 1317 1417

Fig. 8(4)

8.4.1 Standard Ports

Intermediate heights and times are best calculated from the Mean Spring and Neap Curves for Standard Ports in Chapter 9. Examples below are for Leith, on a day when the predictions are:

	UT	Ht (m)
22	0202	5·3
	0752	1·0
	1417	5·4
Tu	2025	0·5

Example 1: Find the height of tide at Leith at 1200.

Example 2: Find the time in the afternoon when the height of tide has fallen to 3·7m.

(1) On Fig. 8 (5) overleaf, plot the heights of HW and LW above and below the required height of tide; join them by a sloping line.

(2) Enter the HW time and others to cover the required timescale, in the boxes below the curves.

(3) From the required height, drop vertically to the sloping line and thence horizontally to the curves. Interpolate between them as in Example 1; do not extrapolate. In this example the actual range is 4·9m, so the Spring curve applies.

(4) Drop vertically to the time scale, and read off the time required, 1637.

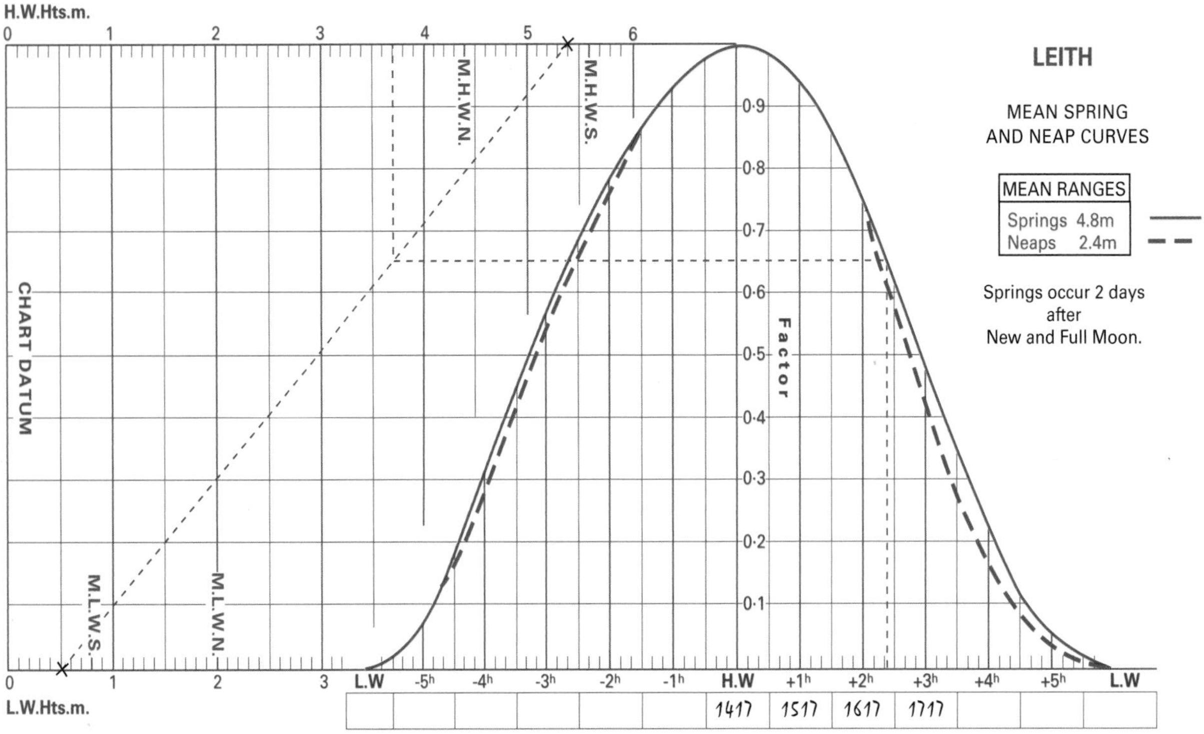
H.W.Hts.m.
0 1 2 3 4 5 6
M.H.W.N.
M.H.W.S.
LEITH
MEAN SPRING AND NEAP CURVES
MEAN RANGES
Springs 4.8m
Neaps 2.4m
Springs occur 2 days after New and Full Moon.
CHART DATUM
Factor
0·9 0·8 0·7 0·6 0·5 0·4 0·3 0·2 0·1
M.L.W.S.
M.L.W.N.
0 1 2 3
L.W.Hts.m.
L.W -5h -4h -3h -2h -1h H.W +1h +2h +3h +4h +5h L.W
1417 1517 1617 1717

Fig. 8(5)

8.4.2 Secondary Ports

On coasts where there is little change of shape between tidal curves for adjacent Standard Ports, and where the duration of rise or fall at the Secondary Port is like that of the appropriate Standard Port (i.e. where HW and LW time differences are nearly the same), intermediate times and heights may be calculated from the tidal curves for the Standard Port in a similar manner to 8.4.1. The curves are entered with the times and heights of HW and LW at the Secondary Port, calculated as in 8.3.2 and 8.3.3.

Interpolate by eye between the curves, using the range at the Standard Port as argument. Do not extrapolate. Use the Spring curve for ranges greater than Springs, and the Neap curve for ranges less than Neaps. With a large change in duration between Springs and Neaps the results may have a slight error, greater near LW.

For places from Bournemouth to Selsey Bill (where the tide is complex) special curves are given in 9.2.12.

8.4.3 The use of factors

Factors are an alternative to the tidal curve method of tidal prediction, and remain popular with those raised on this method. By definition a factor of 1 = HW, and 0 = LW. Tidal curve diagrams show the factor of the range attained at times before and after HW. So the factor represents the percentage of the mean range (for the day in question) which has been reached at any particular time. Simple equations used are:

$$\text{Range} \times \text{Factor} = \text{Rise}$$

or

$$\text{Factor} = \text{Rise} \div \text{Range}$$

In determining or using the factor it may be necessary to interpolate between the Spring and Neap curves as described in 8.4.2.

Factors are particularly useful when calculating hourly predicted heights for ports with special tidal problems (9.2.12).

8.4.4 The 'Twelfths' rule

The 'Twelfths' rule is a way of estimating by mental arithmetic the approximate height of the tide between HW and LW. The rule assumes that the duration of rise or fall is six hours, the tidal curve is symmetrical and approximately a sine curve. Thus the rule does not work in areas such as the Solent where the above conditions do not apply.

From one LW to the next HW, and vice versa, the tide rises or falls by:

1/12th of its range in the 1st hour
2/12ths of its range in the 2nd hour
3/12ths of its range in the 3rd hour
3/12ths of its range in the 4th hour
2/12ths of its range in the 5th hour
1/12th of its range in the 6th hour

8.4.5 Co-Tidal and Co-Range charts

These charts are used to obtain a tidal prediction (time and height) for some offshore position, as distinct from port or coastal locations which are covered by tide tables. Admiralty charts for the following areas off NW Europe are:

5057 Dungeness to Hoek van Holland;
5058 British Isles and adjacent waters; and
5059 Southern North Sea.

They depict Co-Range and Co-Tidal lines, as defined below, with detailed instructions for use.

A Co-Range line joins points of equal 'Mean Spring (or Neap) Range' which are quite simply 'the difference in level between MHWS and MLWS (or MHWN and MLWN)'.

A Co-Tidal line joins points of equal 'Mean HW (or LW) Time Interval' which is defined as 'the mean time interval between the passage of the Moon over the Prime (Greenwich) Meridian and the time of the next HW (or LW) at the place concerned'.

To find times and heights of tide at an offshore location, say in the Thames Estuary, needs some preplanning, especially if intending to navigate through a shallow gat. The 'Tidal Stream Atlas for the Thames Estuary' (NP 249) also contains Co-Tidal and Co-Range charts. These are more clearly arranged and described than charts 5057 – 5059, but prior study is still worthwhile. The calculations require predictions for Sheerness, Walton-on-the-Naze or Margate, depending on where you are.

8.5 CALCULATING CLEARANCES BELOW OVERHEAD OBJECTS

To calculate whether a boat can pass underneath bridges, power cables or other overhead objects, it often helps to draw a diagram. The height of such objects, as given on the chart, is measured above MHWS, so the actual clearance will usually be more than the figure given. Fig. 8 (6) shows how the dimensions relate to CD.

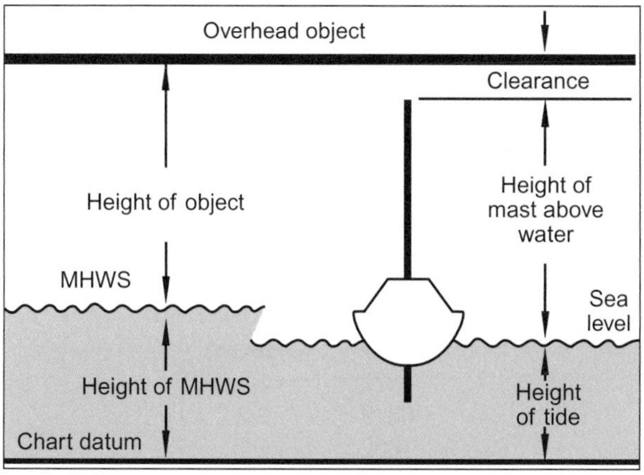
Overhead object
Clearance
Height of object
Height of mast above water
MHWS
Sea level
Height of MHWS
Height of tide
Chart datum

Fig. 8 (6) Calculating masthead clearance

Having sorted out the various dimensions, insert them in the following simple formula, carefully observing the conventions for brackets:

Clearance = (Height of object above MHWS + height of MHWS) minus (height of tide at the time + height of the masthead above water level).

8.6 TIDAL PREDICTION BY COMPUTER

Tidal prediction by computer or calculator is simple, accurate and fast – therefore arguably better than by traditional means. But much depends on whether you like and trust computers – especially at sea. The UKHO offers three tidal prediction programmes.

8.6.1 EasyTide

EasyTide is a free, on-line tidal prediction service for the leisure sailor. It provides tidal predictions for the current day, plus the next 6 consecutive days. Times and heights of HW and LW for the required port are presented in both tabular and graphical formats. Over 6,000 standard and secondary ports are available worldwide. To open EasyTide visit www.ukho.gov.uk/easytide. It's as easy as that.

8.6.2 DP 560 SHM for Windows

SHM, the Simplified Harmonic Method of tidal prediction, is a simple Windows-based programme supplied on CD-ROM. [DP = Digital Product]. It is safe, accurate, fast and user-friendly. It costs £30 + VAT and is everlasting, ie it has no date limit; nor is there any limit to the number of ports which can be stored.

The user inputs Harmonic Constants which can be found either in Part III of Admiralty Tide Tables (NP201-204; £20 per volume) or in Tidal Harmonic Constants for European waters (NP 160; £8.60). ATT are of course updated annually, NP 160 approx every 5 years; so it is important to use the latest version.

Predictions are then displayed as a printable graph of height against time for a period of up to 24 hours and up to 7 consecutive days.

8.6.3 TotalTide

TotalTide (DP 550) is claimed to be the world's most comprehensive tidal prediction system. It is aimed primarily at commercial shipping and satisfies the UK Safety of Navigation Regulations 2002, ie it replaces paper tide tables. It may be of interest to owners of world-girdling mega-yachts and ample resources.

It gives fast and accurate tidal predictions for 7,000+ ports and tidal stream data for 3,000+ locations worldwide. The single CD contains a free calculation programme, and, if desired, all 7 geographic 'area data sets' (ADS). World-wide coverage costs £490 + VAT, but each ADS can be bought for £70 + VAT, with the calculation programme included free of charge.

Access is through a permit system. Annual updates are available, and are essential to satisfy safety regulations, although TotalTide will continue to run without them but with diminishing accuracy.

Coverage of the ADS is as follows:

1. Europe, Med and northern waters 2. S Atlantic and Indian Ocean 3. Indian Ocean (north) and Red Sea to Singapore 4. Singapore to Japan 5. Australia to Indonesia 6. Pacific Ocean, inc New Zealand; and 7. North America (east coast) and Caribbean.

TotalTide displays 7 days of times and heights of HW and LW in both tabular and graphical formats. Other useful facilities include: a display of heights at specified times and time intervals; a continuous plot of height against time; indications of periods of daylight and twilight, moon phases, springs/neaps; the option to insert the yacht's draft; calculations of under-keel and overhead clearances.

TotalTide will run on any of the following versions of Microsoft Windows: 98 (retail build); 98 SE; Millenium; NT v.4 SP4; 2000; ME or XP. Internet Explorer v.4.01 or later is also required. A free demonstration is available on www.ukho.gov.uk. This site also contains a witty and interesting plain man's guide to the history and practice of predicting tides – recommended.

8.6.4 Commercial software

Various commercial firms sell tidal prediction software for use on computers or calculators. Such software is mostly based on NP 159 and can often predict many years ahead. But it remains essential to instal annual updates.

8.7 TIDAL STREAMS

8.7.1 General

Tidal streams are the horizontal movement of water caused by the vertical rise and fall of the tide. They normally change direction about every six hours. They are quite different from ocean currents, such as the Gulf Stream, which run for long periods in the same direction. The direction, or set, of a tidal stream is always expressed as that toward which it is running.

The speed, or rate, of tidal streams is important to yachtsmen because it is often about 2 knots, much more in some areas and at Springs. In a few places rates reach 6-8 knots; 16 knots has been recorded in the Pentland Firth.

8.7.2 Tidal stream Atlases

Admiralty Tidal Stream Atlases, as listed below, show the rate and set of tidal streams in the more important areas around the UK and NW Europe.

The set of the streams is shown by arrows which are graded in weight and, where possible, in length to indicate the rate of the tidal stream. Thus ⟶ indicates a weak stream and ⟶ indicates a strong stream. The figures against the arrows give the mean Neap and Spring rates in tenths of a knot: thus 19,34 indicates a mean Neap rate of 1·9 knots and a mean Spring rate of 3·4 knots. The comma between 19 and 34 indicates approximately where the observations were taken. Tidal atlases rarely show the details of inshore eddies, due to limitations of scale.

Tidal stream chartlets in this Almanac, are derived from the following Admiralty tidal stream atlases.

NP	Ed'n	Year	Title
209	4th	1986	Orkney and Shetland Islands
218	5th	1995	North coast of Ireland, West coast of Scotland
219	2nd	1991	Portsmouth Hbr and approaches
220	2nd	1991	Rosyth Hbr and approaches
221	2nd	1991	Plymouth Hbr and approaches
222	1st	1992	Firth of Clyde and approaches
233	3rd	1995	Dover Strait
249	2nd	1985	Thames Estuary, with co-tidal charts
250	4th	1992	English Channel
251	3rd	1976	North Sea, S part
252	3rd	1975	North Sea, NW part
253	1st	1978	North Sea, E part
254	1st	2003	Falmouth to Teignmouth
255	1st	2003	Falmouth to Padstow, inc Scilly
256	4th	1992	Irish Sea and Bristol Channel
257	3rd	1973	Approaches to Portland
263	1st	2003	Lyme Bay
264	5th	1993	The Channel Islands and adjacent coasts of France
265	1st	1978	France, west coast
337	4th	1993	Solent and adjacent waters

Lettered diamonds ◊ on many medium scale charts refer to tables on the chart giving for that position: the set and Spring and Neap rates at hourly intervals before and after HW at a convenient Standard Port.

Useful tidal stream information is also provided in Admiralty Pilots, including times of slack water, when the tide turns, overfalls and/or race conditions. Along open coasts the turn of the tidal stream does not necessarily occur at HW and LW; it often occurs at about half tide. The tidal stream usually turns earlier inshore than offshore. In large bays the tide often sets towards the coast.

8.7.3 Calculating tidal stream rates

Using Fig. 8(7) the rate of a tidal stream at intermediate times can be predicted, assuming that it varies as a function of the range of tide at Dover.

Example: Calculate the rate of the tidal stream off the northern tip of Skye at 0420 UT on a day when the heights of tide at Dover are:

UT	Ht (m)
0328	1·4
0819	6·3
1602	1·1
2054	6·4

Fig. 8(7) Graph for Calculating tidal stream rates

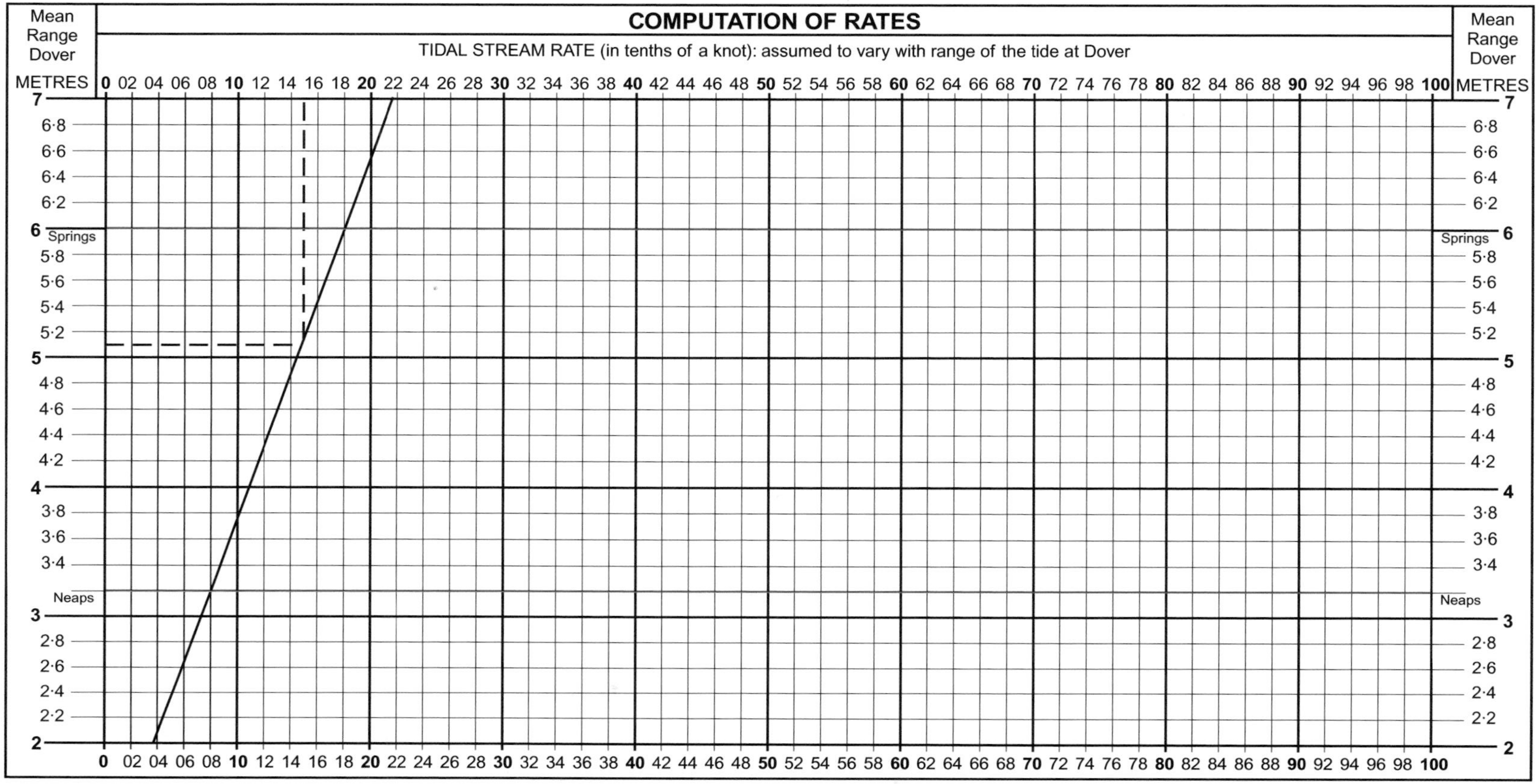

COMPUTATION OF RATES
TIDAL STREAM RATE (in tenths of a knot): assumed to vary with range of the tide at Dover
Mean Range Dover
METRES
0 02 04 06 08 10 12 14 16 18 20 22 24 26 28 30 32 34 36 38 40 42 44 46 48 50 52 54 56 58 60 62 64 66 68 70 72 74 76 78 80 82 84 86 88 90 92 94 96 98 100
7 6·8 6·6 6·4 6·2 6 5·8 5·6 5·4 5·2 5 4·8 4·6 4·4 4·2 4 3·8 3·6 3·4 3 2·8 2·6 2·4 2·2 2
Springs
Neaps

The mean Range at Dover is therefore:

$$\frac{(4{\cdot}9 + 5{\cdot}2 + 5{\cdot}3)}{3} = 5{\cdot}1\text{m}$$

The relevant chartlet, in Chapter 9 or in NP 218 *(N Ireland and W Scotland tidal stream atlas)*, is that for '4 hours before HW Dover' which gives mean Neap and Spring rates of 0·8 and 1·8 kn respectively.

On Fig. 8 (7), from the Rates scale mark 08 on the horizontal Neaps line; likewise 18 on the Springs line. Join these two marks with a straight line. From the range 5·1 on the vertical scale, 'Mean Range Dover', go horizontally to cut the straight line just drawn. From this point go vertically to the Rates scale, top or bottom, and read off the predicted rate: 15 or 1·5 knots in this example. Preserve Fig. 8 (7) for future use with a perspex sheet, clear Fablon or tracing paper.

8.7.4 Tidal streams in rivers

Tidal streams in rivers are influenced by the local topography of the river bed as well as by the phases of the Moon. At or near Springs, in a river which is obstructed, for example, by sandbanks at the entrance, the time of HW gets later going up the river; the time of LW also gets later, but more rapidly so the duration of the flood becomes shorter, and duration of ebb becomes longer. At the entrance the flood stream starts at an interval after LW which increases with the degree of obstruction of the channel; this interval between local LW and the start of the flood increases with the distance up river. The ebb begins soon after local HW along the length of the river. Hence the duration of flood is less than that of the ebb and the difference increases with distance up river.

The flood stream is normally stronger than the ebb, and runs harder during the first half of the rise of tide.

At Neaps the flood and ebb both start soon after local LW and HW respectively, and their durations and rates are roughly equal.

8.8 METEOROLOGICAL EFFECTS

Any deviations from average values of wind and pressure cause corresponding differences between the predicted and actual tide. Prolonged strong winds and unusually high/low barometric pressure significantly affect tidal heights. Early or late times of HW or LW are principally caused by the wind. The effects of wind or pressure individually may not be great. For example a 34mb deviation in barometric pressure (which is rare) will, after some time, cause a change in level of only 0·3m.

But the combined effect, which is more likely, may be much greater. At Portsmouth, for example, strong east winds coupled with high pressure, may reduce predicted levels by up to 1 metre and delay the times of HW and LW by up to 1 hour. Strong westerlies and low pressure may do the opposite in similar degree.

8.8.1 Wind

Wind raises the sea level on a lee shore and lowers it on a windward, but there are wide variations due to topography. Thus, the effects on the south coast of the UK may be very different from those off the east coast. Winds below Force 5 have little practical effect. Strong on/offshore winds may also alter the predicted times of High or Low Water by up to one hour.

Strong winds blowing parallel to a coast tend to set up long waves, which travel along the coast. Sea level is raised at the crest of these waves (positive surge) and lowered in the troughs (negative surge). A storm surge is an unusually severe positive surge. Under exceptional conditions this can raise the height of HW by a metre or more; a negative surge can lower the height of LW by the same amount – clearly more serious for yachtsmen and other mariners.

Large bights or estuaries, eg the southern North Sea and the Thames estuary, are prone to such surges.

8.8.2 Barometric pressure

Sea levels are lowered by high pressure and raised by low, but usually over a period of time and a wide area.

Higher than average atmospheric pressure is of more practical concern because the water level will be lower than predicted. Mean sea level pressures are quoted in Admiralty Pilots: 1017mb, for example, along the UK south coast in July; 1014mb in January. 1013mb at Wick in July; 1007mb in January.

Severe conditions giving rise to a storm surge as described in 8.8.1 are likely to be caused by a deep depression, where the low barometric pressure tends to raise the sea level still more.

Intense minor depressions, line squalls or other abrupt changes in the weather can cause wave oscillations, a phenomenon known as a seiche. The wave period can vary from a few minutes up to two hours, with heights up to a metre – usually less, rarely more. Certain harbours, eg Wick and Fishguard, due to their shape or size, are particularly prone to *seiches* especially in winter.

8.8.3 Storm Warning Services

The Meteorological Office operates a Storm Tide Warning Service to warn of possible coastal flooding caused by abnormal meteorological conditions.

A Negative Storm Surge Warning Service warns of abnormally low tidal levels in the Dover Strait, Thames Estuary and Southern North Sea, caused by Negative surges. Warnings are issued 6-12 hrs ahead of when tidal levels at Dover, Sheerness or Lowestoft are forecast to be 1 metre or more below predicted levels.

Such warnings are broadcast on Navtex, by the Channel Navigation Information Service and by the relevant Coastguard Centres on the VHF and MF frequencies normally used for navigation warnings. This service only operates September to April.

Chapter 9

Harbours, Coasts and Tides

Contents

9.0.1 Map of Areas

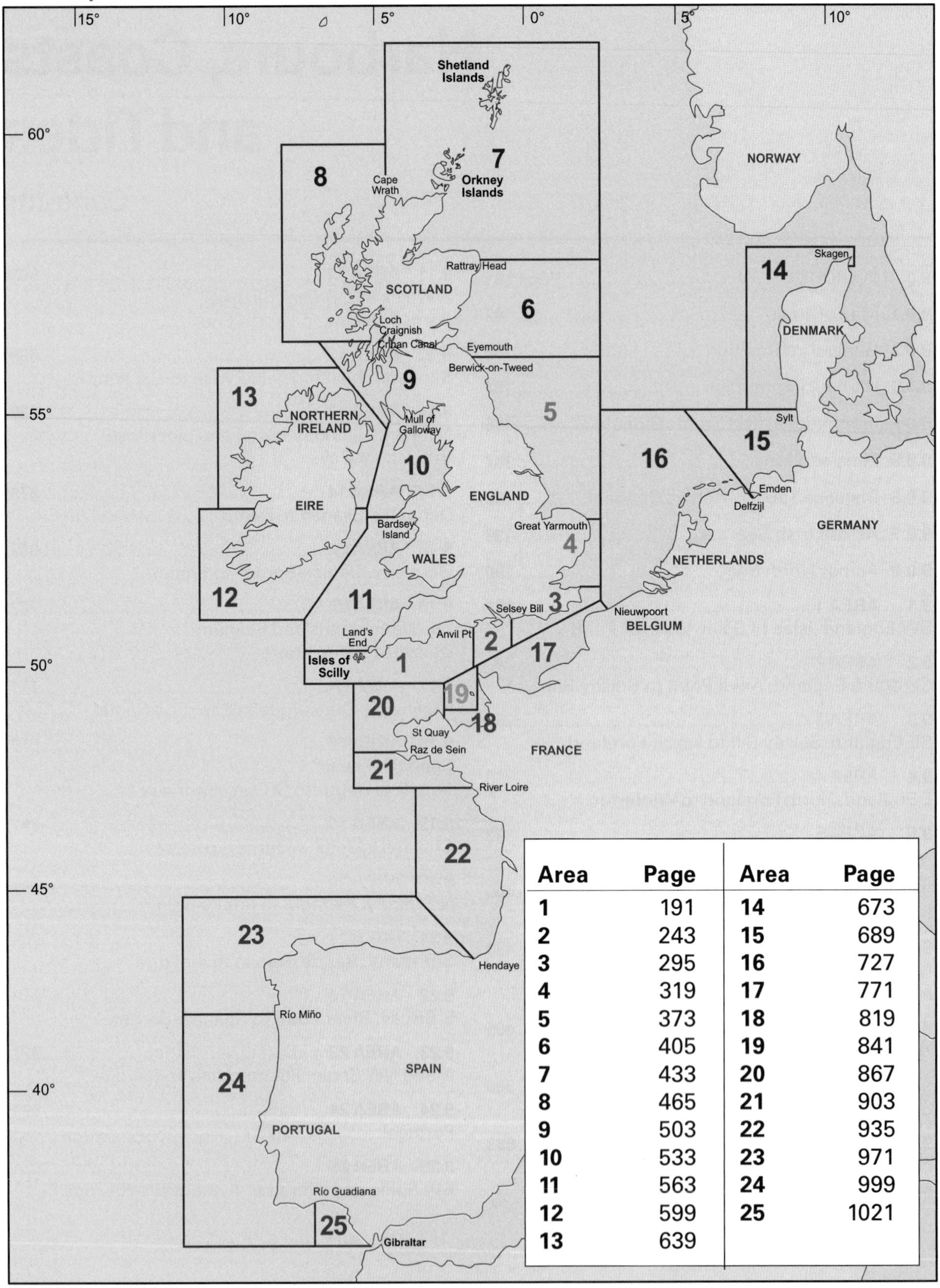
15°
10°
5°
0°
5°
10°
60°
55°
50°
45°
40°
Shetland Islands
7
Orkney Islands
8
Cape Wrath
NORWAY
Rattray Head
14
Skagen
SCOTLAND
6
DENMARK
Loch Craignish
Crinan Canal
Eyemouth
Berwick-on-Tweed
9
13
NORTHERN IRELAND
5
Mull of Galloway
Sylt
10
16
15
ENGLAND
Emden
Delfzijl
EIRE
GERMANY
Great Yarmouth
Bardsey Island
4
WALES
NETHERLANDS
12
11
3
Selsey Bill
Nieuwpoort
BELGIUM
Land's End
Anvil Pt
2
17
Isles of Scilly
1
19
20
18
St Quay
Raz de Sein
FRANCE
21
River Loire
22
23
Hendaye
Río Miño
SPAIN
24
PORTUGAL
Río Guadiana
25
Gibraltar

Area	Page	Area	Page
1	191	14	673
2	243	15	689
3	295	16	727
4	319	17	771
5	373	18	819
6	405	19	841
7	433	20	867
8	465	21	903
9	503	22	935
10	533	23	971
11	563	24	999
12	599	25	1021
13	639		

9.0.2 General information

Harbour, coastal and tidal information is given for each of the 25 Areas shown on the map at 9.0.1, with detailed text and chartlets of 428 harbours and notes on 465 lesser harbours and anchorages. The information provided enables a skipper to assess whether he can get into a harbour (tidal height, depth, wind direction etc), and whether he wants to enter the harbour (shelter, facilities available, cost of berthing etc). Abbreviations and symbols are in Introduction. Language glossaries are 1.4.

Each Area is arranged as follows:

Index of the harbours covered in that area.

A map of the area showing: the positions of the harbours covered; principal lights; location of Emergency RDF Stations; location of CG Centres with their boundaries; the amount of Magnetic Variation at various locations; a table of distances in nautical miles by the most direct route, avoiding dangers, between selected places in that area and in adjacent areas (see also Tables of distances across the English Channel, Irish and North Seas in this Introduction).

Tidal stream chartlets for the area, based on Admiralty tidal stream atlases (by kind permission of the Hydrographer of the Navy and the Controller, HM Stationery Office), showing the rates and directions of tidal streams for each hour referenced to HW Dover and to HW at the relevant Standard Port. For how to use tidal stream charts see 8.7.2.

A list of principal coastal lights, fog signals and useful waypoints in the area. More powerful lights (range 15M or more) are in **bold** type ☆; light-vessels and Lanbys are in *CAPITAL ITALICS*; fog signals are in *italics*. Racons are in ***bold italics***; Latitude and longitude are shown for a selection of lights and marks, some of which are underlined as useful waypoints. Some are on land or on a hazard and are included for navigating a chosen distance off the waypoint. Unless otherwise stated, lights are white. Elevations are in metres (m) above MHWS, and nominal ranges in nautical miles (M). Where appropriate, a brief description is given of the lighthouse or tower. Arcs of visibility, sector limits, and alignment of leading lights etc are true bearings as seen from seaward measured in a clockwise direction. Where a longitude is given (e.g. 04°12'·05W) W stands for West; W also means white but it is always obvious which is the correct word.

Passage information briefly calls attention in note form to some of the principal features of the coast, recommended routes, offlying dangers, tide races, better anchorages etc.

Special notes in certain Areas give information specific to that country or Area.

9.0.3 HARBOUR information

a. Below the **harbour name**, the County or Unitary Council (or equivalent abroad) is given, followed by the lat/long of the harbour entrance, or equivalent. This lat/long may be used as a final waypoint after the approach WPT ⊕ given under Navigation. NB: A published waypoint should never be used without first plotting its position on the chart.

b. A **harbour rating** is given after the lat/long. It grades a port for ease of access, facilities available and its attractiveness as a place. Although inevitably subjective, it offers a useful shorthand as to what a yachtsman may expect to find. The rating, shown below the port name as 3 symbols is based on the following criteria:

Ease of access (☸):

☸☸☸ This port can be entered in *gales from most directions and at all states of tide, by day or night.*

☸☸ Accessible in *strong winds* from most quarters; *possible tidal or pilotage constraints.*

☸ Only accessible in *calm, settled* conditions by day with *no swell; there may be a bar and difficult pilotage.*

Facilities available (👍):

👍👍👍 *Most facilities* for yacht and crew.

👍👍 *All domestic facilities,* but probably only a boatyard.

👍 *Usual domestic needs*; possibly some basic marine facilities.

Attractiveness (✿):

✿✿✿ An attractive place; visit, if necessary *going a little out of your way* to do so.

✿✿ Normal for this part of the coast; *if convenient* visit the port concerned.

✿ Visit only if alternatives are unavailable. *Expect to be disappointed* and subject to inconvenience.

This rating system, modified for harbours in this Almanac, was originated by the late Robin Brandon and used in successive editions of his *South Biscay Pilot,* published by Adlard Coles Nautical.

c. **Chart numbers** for Admiralty (AC), Imray Laurie Norie & Wilson (Imray), Stanfords (Stan) or foreign charts are listed, smallest scale first. The *numbers* of Admiralty Small Craft or Leisure Craft editions and folios are shown in *italics*. The Ordnance Survey (OS. 1:50,000) Map numbers are given for UK and Eire.

d. **Chartlets** are based on British Admiralty, French, Dutch, German, Danish, Spanish and Portuguese charts (as acknowledged in the Introduction).

Please note that these chartlets are not designed or intended for pilotage or navigation, although every effort has been made to ensure that they accurately portray the harbour concerned. The publishers and editors disclaim any responsibility for resultant accidents or damage if they are so used. The largest scale official chart, properly corrected, should always be used.

Due to limitations of scale, chartlets do not always cover the whole area referred to in the text nor do they always contain the approach waypoint ⊕. Not every depth, mark or feature can be shown. Depths and drying heights are shown in metres below/above Chart Datum; elevations (m) are above MHWS. Drying areas and the 5m depth contour are shown as follows.

- Dries
- <5m
- >5m

e. **Tidal predictions** are all provided by the UK Hydrographic Office, with permissions from the Danish, German, Dutch, French and Portuguese Hydrographic Offices.

For each Standard Port daily predictions of times and heights of HW/LW are given. Zone times are given, but times are not adjusted for Daylight Saving Time (better known in UK as British Summer Time); corrections for DST only apply to the non-shaded areas in the tables. In UK, Eire and Portugal times are in UT.

At the foot of each page of tidal predictions is given the height difference between Chart Datum at the port in question and Ordnance Datum (Newlyn), for UK ports. For foreign ports the height difference is referenced to the relevant national land survey datum. This enables tidal levels along a stretch of coast to be referred to a common horizontal plane. Further notes are contained in the Admiralty Tide Tables where the height differences are also tabulated.

Time and height differences for Secondary Ports are referenced to the most suitable (not always the nearest) Standard Port. The average time difference between local HW and HW Dover is given, so that the UT (±15 minutes) of local HW can be quickly found. Times of HW Dover are in 9.3.13 and, for quick reference, on a bookmark which also lists Range together with a visual indication of the state of the tide (Springs or Neaps). Duration (quoted for most ports), if deducted from time of HW, gives the approx time of the previous LW.

Mean Level (ML) is also quoted. Given ML and the height of HW, the range and therefore height of LW can also be calculated; see also Chapter 8.

Tidal Coefficients for Brest are listed and explained under Brest and are applicable to all French ports on the Channel and Atlantic coasts. They indicate not only whether Springs or Neaps apply, but also quantify the size of a tide without resort to calculating range. They can be used to specify access hours to tidally-limited harbours.

f. **Tidal curves** are given for Standard Ports and those other ports for which full predictions are shown. Use the appropriate (np/sp) curve for tidal calculations (ie finding the height of tide at a given time, or the time for a given height). See Chapter 8 for tidal calculations.

HW–3 means 3 hrs before local HW; HW +2 means 2 hrs after. Secondary curves are given in 9.2.11 for ports between Swanage and Selsey Bill where special tidal conditions exist.

g. **Shelter** assesses the degree of shelter and advises on access, berths (for charges see under Facilities), moorings and anchorages. Access times, if quoted, are approx figures relative to mean HW. They are purely a guide for a nominal 1·5m draft, plus safety clearance, and take no account of hull form, springs/neaps, flood/ebb, swell or nature of the bottom. Their purpose is to alert a skipper to possible tidal problems. Times of lock and bridge openings etc are local (LT), unless otherwise stated.

h. **Navigation** gives the lat/long of a waypoint (⊕) suitable for starting the approach, with its bearing/distance to the hbr ent or next significant feature; some ⊕s may be off the harbour chartlet. **NB: A published waypoint should never be used without first plotting its position on the chart.** Approach chans, buoyage, speed limits and hazards are also described.

Wrecks around the UK which are of historic or archaeological interest are protected under the Protection of Wrecks Act 1973. About 40 sites, as detailed in Annual Notice to Mariners No 16 and depicted on the larger scale Admiralty charts, are listed in this almanac under the nearest harbour or in Passage Information. Unauthorised interference, including anchoring and diving on such sites, may lead to a substantial fine.

j. **Lights and Marks** includes as much detail as space permits; some data may also be shown on the chartlet and/or in Coastal lights, fog signals and waypoints for that Area. Traffic signals for individual harbours are shown in each area: German (9.15.6), Dutch, Belgian (9.16.6)French (9.17.6). International Port Traffic Signals are shown in 9.0.4.

k. **R/T** (Radio Telephone) quotes VHF Channels related to each port, marina or VTS. If not obvious, the callsign of a station is shown in *italics*. Frequencies are indicated by their International Maritime Services Channel (Ch) designator. UK Marina Channels are

80 and M or M1, formerly 37. M2 is allocated to some YCs for race control. MF frequencies, if shown, are in kHz. Initial contact should be made on the working Ch, rather than on Ch 16. Where known, preferred channels are shown in bold type, thus **14**. If there is a choice of calling channel, always say which channel you are using; eg, *'Dover Port Control, this is NONSUCH, NONSUCH on Channel 74, over'*. This avoids confusion if the station being called is working more than one channel.

Where local times are stated, the letters LT are added. H24 means continuous watch. Times of scheduled broadcasts are shown (for example) as H +20, ie 20 minutes past the hour.

l. **Telephone** is followed by the dialling code in brackets, which is not repeated for individual ☎ numbers. But it may be repeated or augmented under **Facilities** if different or additional codes also apply. Eg, Portsmouth and Gosport numbers are both on (023 92) as listed; but Fareham's different code (01329) is quoted separately.

In the UK the ☎s of the relevant Coastguard MRCC/MRSC are given under each port, but in an emergency dial 999 and ask for the Coastguard.

Information on making international calls from/to the UK is given in Special Notes together with ☎s for marine emergencies abroad. EU countries use ☎ 112 for emergency calls to Fire, Police, Ambulance, as well as their national emergency ☎s.

m. **Facilities** available at the harbour, marinas and yacht clubs are listed first, followed by an abbreviated summary of those marine services provided commercially (for abbreviations see the Introduction and the bookmark). See also the Marina and Waypoint Guide which is provided free with the Almanac for commercial listings. Note: Facilities at Yacht Clubs are usually available to crews who arrive by sea and belong to a recognised club.

Town facilities are also listed, including Post Office (✉), Bank (Ⓑ), Railway Station (⇌), or airport (✈). Abroad, the nearest port with a UK ferry link is given (see also 9.0.5).

n. **The overnight cost of a visitors alongside berth** (AB) The price quoted is per metre LOA (unless otherwise stated) during high season (usually June to Sept), at the previous year's rates. Harbour dues, if applicable, and VAT are included. In the UK the cost of mains electricity is usually extra. The cost of pile moorings, 🅥s or ⚓ where these are the norm, may be given, if no AB is provided. The number of Ⓥ berths is from marina info. and estimates how many permanent berth-holders are expected to be away at any one time. To avoid disappointment contact the marina well in advance.

FACILITIES FOR DISABLED PEOPLE

RYA Sailability is an organisation operating in the UK under the auspices of the RYA to open up sailing and its related facilities to disabled sailors.

Facilities include car parking; ramps for wheel chair access to buildings and pontoons; purpose-built toilets and showers; and at Largs (Ayrshire) a special pontoon and sailing championships. Facilities for those with sight or hearing disabilities are not widely available. Symbols used in the text of Chapter 9 are self explanatory: ♿, ⊕ and ⊘, ⊘.

ENVIRONMENTAL GUIDANCE

The following notes are pure common sense:

a. In principle never ditch rubbish at sea.

b. Keep it onboard and dispose of it ashore in harbour refuse bins (which are provided almost everywhere) or take it home if there are none. The 🗑 symbol is used in this almanac to indicate that waste bins are provided where you might not think they are.

c. Readily degradable foodstuffs may be ditched at sea when more than 3M offshore (12M in the English Channel and North Sea).

d. Foodstuffs which are not readily degradable, eg skins and peelings, should not be ditched at sea.

e. Other rubbish, eg packaging of plastic, glass, metal, paper and cardboard; fabrics; ropelines and netting, should *never* be ditched at sea.

f. Sewage. Use shoreside toilets if you do not have a holding tank. In this case only use the onboard heads when well offshore.

g. Do not discharge any foul water into a marina, anchorage or moorings area and keep washing up water to a minimum.

h. If you do not have a holding tank you should fit one as soon as possible. These are already compulsory in some countries and even the UK will eventually introduce this legislation. Pump-out facilities (⛽) are shown on chartlets and in the text where they are known to exist. If there are none, do not pump out your tanks until you are at least 3M offshore.

j. Oils and oily waste are particularly harmful to the water, fish and wildlife. Take old engine oil ashore to a recognised disposal point. Do not allow an automatic bilge pump to pump oily bilge water overboard.

k. Toxic waste, eg some antifoulings, cleaning chemicals, old batteries, should be disposed of ashore at a proper facility.

l. Row ashore whenever possible - less pollution than an outboard and good exercise.

m. Wild birds, plants, fish and marine animals are usually abundant along coastlines. Respect protected sites; keep away from nesting sites and breeding colonies. Minimise noise, wash and disturbance.

n. Go ashore at recognised landing places. Do not anchor or dry out where important and vulnerable seabed species exist, eg soft corals, eel grass.

No	Lights		Main message
1		Flashing	Serious emergency – all vessels to stop or divert according to instructions
2		Fixed or Slow Occulting	Vessels shall not proceed (*Note:* Some ports may use an exemption signal, as in 2a below)
3			Vessels may proceed. One-way traffic
4			Vessels may proceed. Two-way traffic
5			A vessel may proceed only when she has received specific orders to do so. (*Note:* Some ports may use an exemption signal, as in 5a below)
			Exemption signals and messages
2a	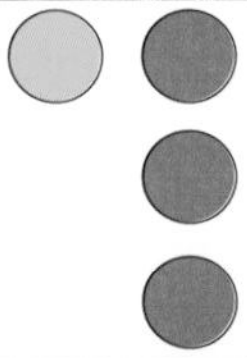	Fixed or Slow Occulting	Vessels shall not proceed, except that vessels which navigate outside the main channel need not comply with the main message
5a	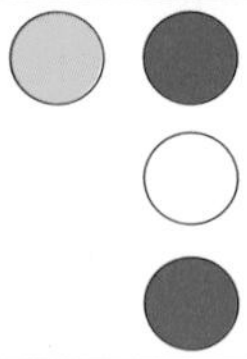		A vessel may proceed when she has received specific orders to do so, except that vessels which navigate outside the main channel need not comply with the main message
			Auxiliary signals and messages
	White and/or yellow lights, displayed to the right of the main lights		Local meanings, as promulgated in local port orders

9.0.4 INTERNATIONAL PORT TRAFFIC SIGNALS

The international system is gradually being introduced, but its general adoption is likely to take many years.

(a) The main movement message given by a port traffic signal always comprises three lights, disposed vertically. No additional light shall be added to the column carrying the main message. (The fact that the main message always consists of three vertical lights allows the mariner to recognise it as a traffic signal, and not lights of navigational significance.) The signals may also be used to control traffic at locks and bridges.

(b) Red lights indicate 'Do not proceed'.

(c) Green lights indicate 'Proceed, subject to the conditions stipulated'. Note that, to avoid confusion, red and green lights are never displayed together.

(d) Some signals may be omni-directional – i.e. exhibited to all vessels simultaneously: others must be directional, and be shown either to vessels entering or to vessels leaving harbour.

(e) The 'Serious Emergency' signal must be flashing, at least 60 flashes per minute. All other signals must be either fixed or slow occulting (the latter useful when background glare is a problem). A mixture of fixed and occulting lights must not be used.

(f) Signal No 5 is based on the assumption that another means of communication such as VHF radio, signal lamp, loud-hailer, or auxiliary signal will be used to inform a vessel that she may specifically proceed.

(g) A single yellow light, displayed to the left of the column carrying main messages Nos 2 or 5, at the level of the upper light, may be used to indicate that 'Vessels which can safely navigate outside the main channel need not comply with the main message'. This signal, as shown at Nos 2a and 5a, is of obvious significance to yachtsmen.

(h) Signals which are auxiliary to the main message may be devised by local authorities. Such auxiliary signals should employ only white and/or yellow lights, and should be displayed to the right of the column carrying the main message. Ports with complex entrances and much traffic may need many auxiliary signals, which will have to be documented. Smaller harbours with less traffic may only need one or two of the basic signals, such as Nos 2 and 4.

9.0.5 FERRIES AROUND UK AND TO/FROM THE CONTINENT

This Table is a condensed version of many detailed schedules. It is intended to show broadly what is available and to help when cruise plans and/or crew movements are subject to change at short notice.

NOTES: 1. **Hours** = approx duration of day crossing. 2. **Frequency** = number of one-way sailings per day in summer. Specific day(s) of the week may be shown, if non-daily. 3. ☎ **Bookings** may be via a centralised number applicable to all routes.

From	To	Hours	Frequency	Company	☎ Bookings
A.	CROSS CHANNEL (France, Belgium; and to Spain)				
Plymouth (Mar-Nov)	Santander	18	2 wkly	Brittany Ferries	0870 5360360
Plymouth	Roscoff	6	1-3	Brittany Ferries	0870 5360360
Poole	Cherbourg	4¼	1-2	Brittany Ferries	0870 5360360
Poole	Cherbourg	2¼ (HSS)	1 (Seasonal)	Brittany Ferries	0870 5360360
Portsmouth	St Malo	9	1	Brittany Ferries	0870 5360360
Portsmouth	Ouistreham (Caen)	6	3	Brittany Ferries	0870 5360360
Portsmouth	Le Havre	5½	3	P&O Ferries	0870 5202020
Portsmouth	Bilbao	35	Sat,Tu	P&O Ferries	0870 5202020
Portsmouth	Cherbourg	4¾	2-3	P&O Ferries	0870 5202020
Portsmouth	Cherbourg	2¾ (Cat)	2-3 (Seasonal)	P&O Ferries	0870 5202020
Portsmouth	Caen	3½ (Cat)	1-2 (Seasonal)	P&O Ferries	0870 5202020
Newhaven	Dieppe	2 (Cat)	2-3 (Seasonal)	Hoverspeed	0870 2408070
Newhaven	Dieppe	4/5½	3	Transmanche	0800 91712010
Dover	Calais	1 (Cat)	14	Hoverspeed	0870 5240241
Dover	Calais	1¼-1½	19	Sea France	0870 5711711
Dover	Calais	1¼	35	P&O Ferries	0870 5202020
Dover	Dunkerque	2	10(W/day) 8(W/end)	Norfolkline	0870 8701020
B.	NORTH SEA				
Harwich	Hook of Holland	6¼	1	Stena Line	0870 5707070
Harwich	Hook of Holland	3¾ (HSS)	2	Stena Line	0870 5707070
Harwich	Cuxhaven	18	Alternate days.	DFDS Seaways	0870 5333000
Harwich	Esbjerg	17	3 wkly	DFDS Seaways	0870 5333000
Hull	Rotterdam	10	1	P&O Ferries	0870 5202020
Hull	Zeebrugge	12½	1	P&O Ferries	0870 5202020
Newcastle	Amsterdam	15	1	DFDS Seaways	0870 5333000
Newcastle	Gothenburg	26	F,M	DFDS Seaways	0870 5333000
Newcastle	Kristiensand	18	F,M	DFDS Seaways	0870 5333000
Newcastle	Stavanger/Bergen	19/26	W, F, Sun	Fjord Line	0191 2961313
C.	SCOTLAND				
Aberdeen	Lerwick/Kirkwall	various	Tu,Th,Sat,Sun	NorthLink Ferries	0845 6000449
Lerwick	Bergen	10-11	M	Smyril Line	01595 690845
Lerwick	Norway,Faroe, Iceland & Denmark		Various	Smyril Line	01595 690845
Rosyth	Zeebrugge	17½	1	Superfast Ferries	0870 2340870
Scrabster	Stromness	1½	3	NorthLink Ferries	0845 6000449
Ullapool	Stornoway	2¾	2-3	Caledonian MacBrayne	08705 650000

Caledonian MacBrayne run ferries to 23 West Scottish islands and many mainland ports; see 9.8.23 for details, inc other companies.

From	To	Hours	Frequency	Company	☎ Bookings
D.	IRISH SEA (and Eire-France)				
Cork	Roscoff	14	Sat	Brittany Ferries	021 4277801
Cork	Swansea	10	1 (not Tu)	Swansea/Cork Ferries	01792 456116
Rosslare	Cherbourg	18	Alternate days.	Irish Ferries	016 383333
Rosslare	Roscoff	16	Alternate days.	Irish Ferries	016 383333
Rosslare	Pembroke Dock	3¾	2	Irish Ferries	0870 5171717
Rosslare	Fishguard	3½/1¾ (Cat)	2/4	Stena Line	0870 5707070
Dun Laoghaire	Holyhead	3¾/1¾ (HSS)	2/4	Stena Line	0870 5707070
Dublin	Holyhead	3¼/1¾ (FF)	2/3	Irish Ferries	0870 5171717
Belfast	Stranraer	3¼/1¾ (HSS)	7	Stena Line	0870 5707070
Belfast	Liverpool	8	1-2 Tues/Sat	Norse Ferries	0870 6004321
Larne	Cairnryan	1¾/1 (HSS)	6/2 (Seasonal)	P&O Irish Sea Ferries	0870 2424666
Douglas, IOM*	Heysham	3¾	2	IOM Steam Packet Co.	01624 661661
Douglas, IOM	Liverpool	3½/2½ (Cat)	2	IOM Steam Packet Co.	01624 661661

*Also less frequent sailings from Douglas to Belfast (4¾), Dublin (4¾), Fleetwood (3¼) and Ardrossan (8).

From	To	Hours	Frequency	Company	☎ Bookings
E.	CHANNEL ISLANDS				
Guernsey/Jersey	Portsmouth	13/9	1 (not Su)	Condor Ferries	01305 761551
Jersey	Poole	3¾ (Cat)	2	Condor Ferries	01305 761551
Jersey	Weymouth	3¾ (Cat)	2	Condor Ferries	01305 761551
Guernsey	Poole	2½ (Cat)	2	Condor Ferries	01305 761551
Guernsey	Weymouth	2 (Cat)	2	Condor Ferries	01305 761551
Jersey†	St Malo	1¼ (Cat)	2	Condor Ferries	01305 761551
Guernsey	St Malo	1¾ (Cat)	1-2	Condor Ferries	01305 761551

†Also Jersey (St Helier) to Guernsey, Sark, Granville; and Jersey (Gorey) to Portbail and Carteret.

9.0.6 Distances (M) across the English Channel

England / France/CI	Longships	Falmouth	Fowey	Plymouth bkwtr	Salcombe	Dartmouth	Torbay	Exmouth	Weymouth	Poole Hbr Ent	Needles Lt Ho	Nab Tower	Littlehampton	Shoreham	Brighton	Newhaven	Eastbourne	Rye	Folkestone	Dover
Le Conquet	112	112	123	125	125	137	144	155	172	188	194	212	230	240	245	249	261	278	295	301
L'Aberwrac'h	102	97	106	107	105	117	124	135	153	168	174	192	211	219	224	228	239	257	275	280
Roscoff	110	97	101	97	91	100	107	117	130	144	149	165	184	193	197	200	211	229	246	252
Trébeurden	120	105	106	102	94	102	109	120	129	142	147	164	181	190	194	197	208	226	244	249
Tréguier	132	112	110	101	94	98	102	112	116	128	132	147	162	170	174	177	188	206	224	229
Lézardrieux	142	121	118	107	94	100	105	114	115	126	130	140	157	165	169	172	184	201	219	224
St Quay-Portrieux	159	137	135	124	111	115	121	129	127	135	135	146	162	171	174	178	189	207	225	230
St Malo	172	149	146	133	118	120	124	132	125	130	130	143	157	166	170	173	184	202	220	225
St Helier	155	130	123	108	93	95	100	108	99	104	104	115	132	140	144	147	158	176	194	199
St Peter Port	139	113	104	89	73	70	75	81	71	79	83	97	112	120	124	127	135	156	174	179
Braye (Alderney)	146	116	106	89	72	69	71	75	54	60	62	73	91	100	103	106	114	136	153	159
Cherbourg	168	138	125	107	92	87	88	93	66	64	63	68	81	90	92	96	102	122	140	145
St Vaast-la-Hougue	194	164	150	132	116	111	112	116	83	76	72	71	80	87	88	90	96	115	132	138
Ouistreham	229	198	185	167	151	146	147	147	117	107	100	86	91	92	91	90	92	106	125	130
Deauville	236	205	192	174	158	153	154	154	122	111	104	88	89	88	87	85	87	101	120	125
Le Havre	231	200	187	169	153	148	148	148	118	105	97	82	82	83	82	79	80	94	115	120
Fécamp	242	212	197	179	163	157	157	157	120	105	96	75	71	68	65	62	62	72	90	95
Dieppe	268	237	222	204	188	180	180	180	142	125	117	91	80	75	70	64	63	60	70	75
Boulogne	290	258	242	224	208	198	195	191	153	135	127	97	81	71	66	59	47	33	28	25
Calais	305	272	257	239	223	213	210	209	168	150	141	111	96	86	81	74	62	43	26	22

NOTES

1. This Table applies to Areas 1 – 3 and 17 – 20, each of which also contains its own internal Distance Table. Approximate distances in nautical miles are by the most direct route, while avoiding dangers and allowing for Traffic Separation Schemes.
2. For ports within the Solent, add the appropriate distances given in 9.2.6 to those shown above under either Needles light house or Nab Tower.

9.0.7 Distances (M) across the Irish Sea

Ireland \ Scotland England Wales	Port Ellen (Islay)	Campbeltown	Troon	Portpatrick	Mull of Galloway	Kirkcudbright	Maryport	Fleetwood	Pt of Ayre (IOM)	Port St Mary (IOM)	Liverpool	Holyhead	Pwllheli	Fishguard	Milford Haven	Swansea	Avonmouth	Ilfracombe	Padstow	Longships
Tory Island	75	107	132	119	134	170	185	215	156	171	238	207	260	279	307	360	406	355	372	399
Malin Head	45	76	101	88	103	139	154	184	125	140	207	176	229	248	276	329	375	324	341	368
Lough Foyle	38	61	86	73	88	124	139	169	110	125	192	161	214	233	261	314	360	309	326	353
Portrush	31	50	76	64	80	116	131	161	102	117	184	153	206	225	253	306	352	301	318	345
Carnlough	42	35	57	32	45	81	96	126	67	78	149	115	168	187	215	268	314	363	280	307
Larne	51	39	58	24	37	72	88	118	58	70	141	106	159	178	206	259	305	254	271	298
Carrickfergus	64	48	65	26	34	69	85	115	55	66	138	101	154	173	201	254	300	249	266	293
Bangor	63	48	64	22	30	65	81	111	51	62	134	97	150	169	197	250	296	245	262	289
Strangford Lough	89	72	84	36	30	63	76	97	41	37	107	69	121	141	167	219	265	214	231	258
Carlingford Lough	117	100	112	64	60	90	103	112	70	51	118	67	111	124	149	202	248	197	214	241
Dun Laoghaire	153	136	148	100	93	119	126	120	93	69	119	56	82	94	109	162	208	157	174	201
Wicklow	170	153	165	117	108	133	140	127	108	83	123	56	67	71	90	143	189	138	155	182
Arklow	182	165	177	129	120	144	149	133	117	93	131	64	71	65	79	132	179	128	144	167
Rosslare	215	202	208	161	154	179	180	164	152	125	156	90	83	55	58	109	157	110	119	137
Tuskar Rock	216	203	209	162	155	179	182	165	152	126	152	91	82	48	51	105	150	103	112	130
Dunmore East	250	237	243	196	189	213	216	199	186	160	189	127	116	79	76	130	177	124	127	136
Youghal	281	268	274	227	220	244	247	230	217	191	220	158	147	110	103	156	200	148	139	138
Crosshaven	300	287	293	246	239	263	266	249	236	210	239	177	166	131	118	170	216	163	151	144
Baltimore	346	333	339	292	285	309	312	295	282	256	285	223	212	172	160	209	254	198	178	161
Fastnet Rock	354	341	347	300	293	317	320	303	290	264	293	231	220	181	169	216	260	207	185	170

NOTES

This Table applies to Areas 9 – 13, each of which also contains its own internal Distance Table. Approximate distances in nautical miles are by the most direct route, whilst avoiding dangers and Traffic Separation Schemes.

9.0.8 Distances (M) across the North Sea

UK \ Norway to France	Bergen	Stavanger	Lindesnes	Skagen	Esjberg	Sylt (List)	Brunsbüttel	Helgoland	Bremerhaven	Willhelmshaven	Delfzijl	Den Helder	IJmuiden	Scheveningen	Roompotsluis	Vlissingen	Zeebrugge	Oostende	Nieuwpoort	Dunkerque
Lerwick	210	226	288	403	428	442	517	470	510	500	493	486	497	505	551	550	552	555	562	588
Kirkwall	278	275	323	438	439	452	516	467	507	497	481	460	473	481	515	514	516	519	526	545
Wick	292	283	323	437	428	440	498	449	489	479	458	433	444	451	485	484	486	489	496	514
Inverness	356	339	381	485	461	462	529	479	519	509	487	460	471	478	513	512	514	517	524	542
Fraserburgh	288	266	296	410	383	384	451	404	444	434	412	385	396	403	430	429	431	434	441	456
Aberdeen	308	279	298	411	371	378	433	382	432	412	386	353	363	369	401	400	402	405	412	426
Dundee	362	329	339	451	394	401	448	396	436	426	395	352	359	364	390	389	385	388	395	412
Port Edgar	391	355	362	472	409	413	457	405	445	435	401	355	361	366	391	390	386	389	396	413
Berwick-on-Tweed	374	325	320	431	356	361	408	355	395	385	355	310	315	320	342	341	337	340	347	364
Hartlepool	409	353	340	440	340	331	367	312	352	342	302	241	243	247	266	265	261	264	271	288
Grimsby	463	395	362	452	324	318	342	291	332	325	288	187	182	185	199	198	190	191	201	198
Kings Lynn	485	416	379	466	330	333	343	292	344	336	283	184	183	183	197	195	187	188	198	195
Lowestoft	508	431	380	453	308	300	295	262	284	271	218	118	104	98	95	99	87	87	89	106
Harwich	540	461	410	483	330	331	320	287	309	296	243	147	126	114	94	100	84	77	80	80
Brightlingsea	558	479	428	501	348	349	338	305	327	314	261	165	144	105	108	106	92	88	86	87
Burnham-on-Crouch	567	488	437	510	357	358	347	314	336	323	270	174	151	112	109	115	99	92	93	95
London Bridge	620	543	490	560	400	408	395	361	382	374	320	222	199	149	153	149	134	125	126	114
Sheerness	580	503	450	520	360	367	353	319	340	334	280	180	157	109	113	109	94	85	86	74
Ramsgate	575	498	446	516	368	346	339	305	323	315	262	161	144	121	89	85	77	65	58	42
Dover	588	511	459	529	378	359	352	328	336	328	275	174	155	132	101	92	79	65	58	44

NOTES

This Table applies to Areas 3 – 7 and 14 – 17, each of which also contains its own internal Distance Table. Approximate distances in nautical miles are by the most direct route, while avoiding dangers and allowing for Traffic Separation Schemes.

1

Area 1

South-West England
Isles of Scilly to Anvil Point

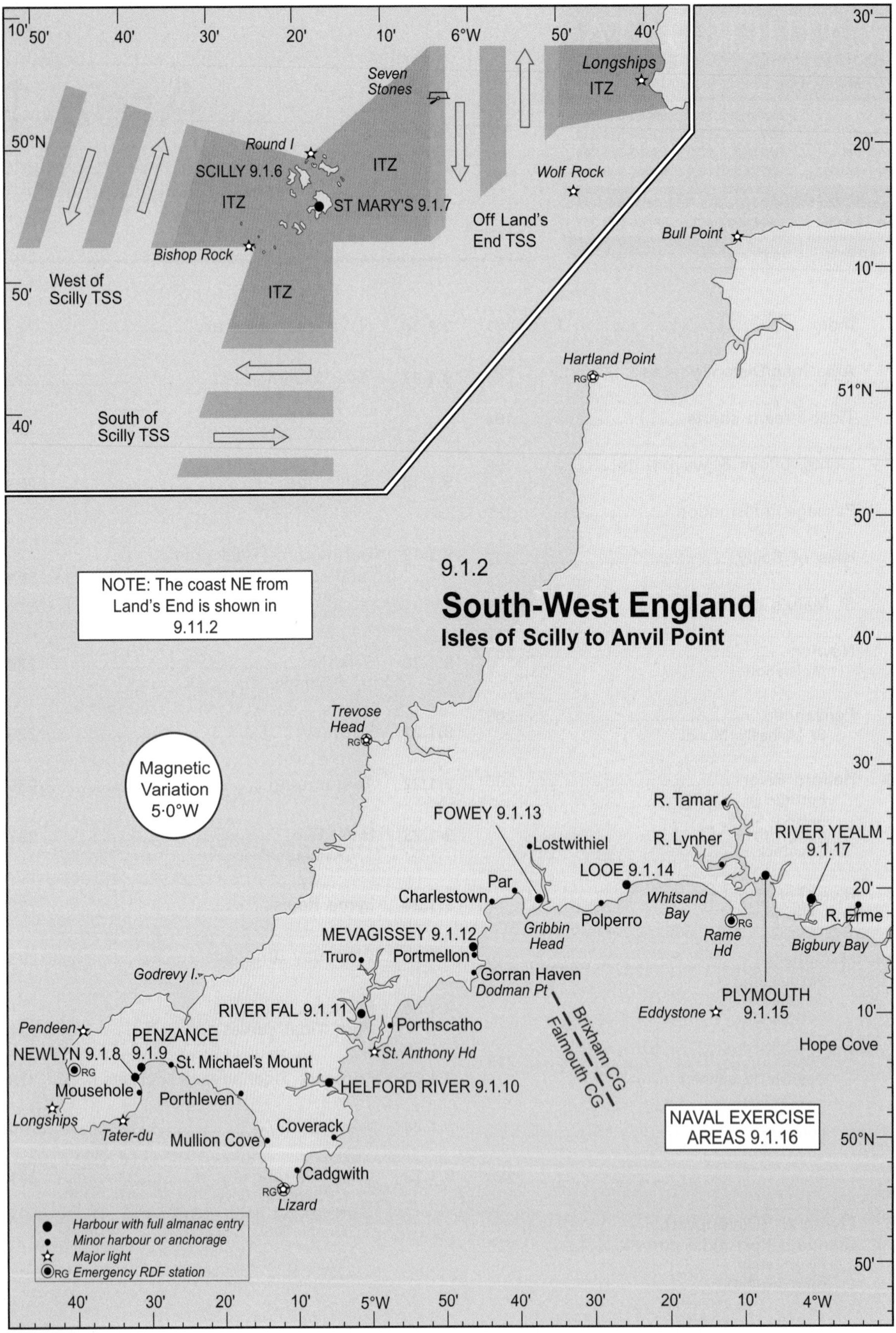
9.1.2
South-West England
Isles of Scilly to Anvil Point
NOTE: The coast NE from Land's End is shown in 9.11.2
Magnetic Variation 5·0°W
Seven Stones
Longships
ITZ
Round I
SCILLY 9.1.6
ITZ
ITZ
ST MARY'S 9.1.7
Wolf Rock
Off Land's End TSS
Bishop Rock
ITZ
West of Scilly TSS
South of Scilly TSS
Bull Point
Hartland Point
Trevose Head
R. Tamar
FOWEY 9.1.13
Lostwithiel
R. Lynher
RIVER YEALM 9.1.17
LOOE 9.1.14
Par
Charlestown
Whitsand Bay
R. Erme
Gribbin Head
Polperro
Rame Hd
Bigbury Bay
MEVAGISSEY 9.1.12
Truro
Portmellon
Gorran Haven
Dodman Pt
Godrevy I.
Brixham CG
Falmouth CG
PLYMOUTH 9.1.15
Eddystone
RIVER FAL 9.1.11
Porthscatho
Hope Cove
Pendeen
PENZANCE 9.1.9
NEWLYN 9.1.8
St. Michael's Mount
St. Anthony Hd
HELFORD RIVER 9.1.10
Mousehole
Porthleven
Longships
Tater-du
Mullion Cove
Coverack
NAVAL EXERCISE AREAS 9.1.16
Cadgwith
Lizard
Harbour with full almanac entry
Minor harbour or anchorage
Major light
RG Emergency RDF station
10' 50' 40' 30' 20' 10' 6°W 50' 40'
50°N
50'
40'
30'
20'
10'
51°N
50'
40'
30'
20'
10'
50°N
50'
40' 30' 20' 10' 5°W 50' 40' 30' 20' 10' 4°W

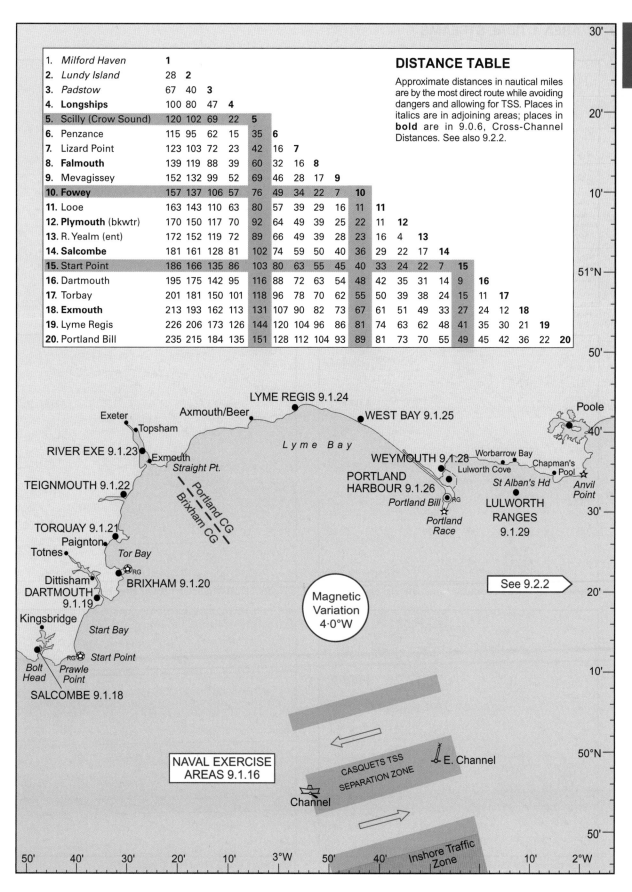

DISTANCE TABLE

Approximate distances in nautical miles are by the most direct route while avoiding dangers and allowing for TSS. Places in italics are in adjoining areas; places in **bold** are in 9.0.6, Cross-Channel Distances. See also 9.2.2.

1. *Milford Haven*	**1**																			
2. *Lundy Island*	28	**2**																		
3. *Padstow*	67	40	**3**																	
4. **Longships**	100	80	47	**4**																
5. Scilly (Crow Sound)	120	102	69	22	**5**															
6. Penzance	115	95	62	15	35	**6**														
7. Lizard Point	123	103	72	23	42	16	**7**													
8. **Falmouth**	139	119	88	39	60	32	16	**8**												
9. Mevagissey	152	132	99	52	69	46	28	17	**9**											
10. **Fowey**	157	137	106	57	76	49	34	22	7	**10**										
11. Looe	163	143	110	63	80	57	39	29	16	11	**11**									
12. **Plymouth** (bkwtr)	170	150	117	70	92	64	49	39	25	22	11	**12**								
13. R. Yealm (ent)	172	152	119	72	89	66	49	39	28	23	16	4	**13**							
14. **Salcombe**	181	161	128	81	102	74	59	50	40	36	29	22	17	**14**						
15. Start Point	186	166	135	86	103	80	63	55	45	40	33	24	22	7	**15**					
16. Dartmouth	195	175	142	95	116	88	72	63	54	48	42	35	31	14	9	**16**				
17. Torbay	201	181	150	101	118	96	78	70	62	55	50	39	38	24	15	11	**17**			
18. **Exmouth**	213	193	162	113	131	107	90	82	73	67	61	51	49	33	27	24	12	**18**		
19. Lyme Regis	226	206	173	126	144	120	104	96	86	81	74	63	62	48	41	35	30	21	**19**	
20. Portland Bill	235	215	184	135	151	128	112	104	93	89	81	73	70	55	49	45	42	36	22	**20**

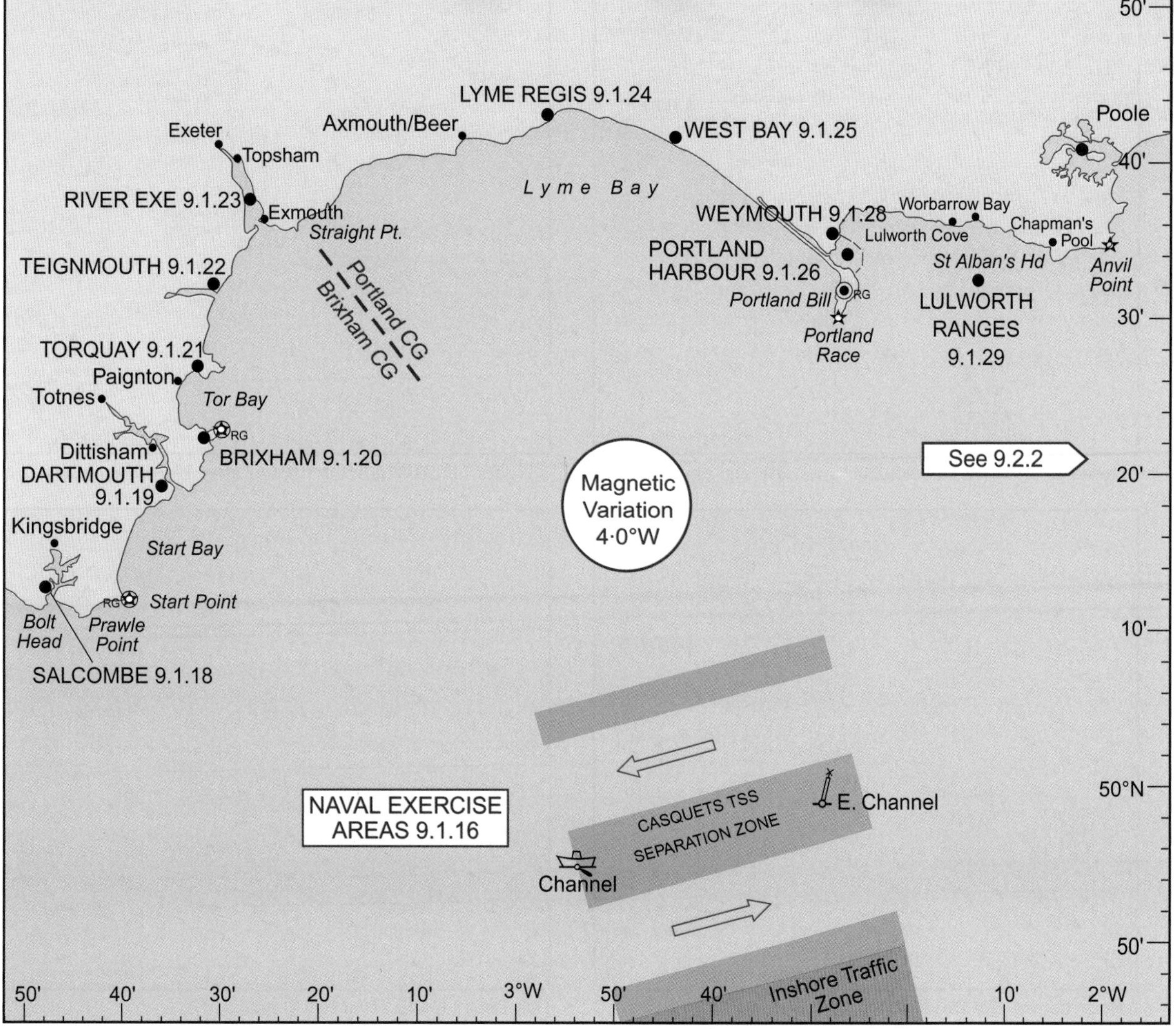
LYME REGIS 9.1.24
Exeter
Axmouth/Beer
WEST BAY 9.1.25
Poole
Topsham
Lyme Bay
RIVER EXE 9.1.23
Exmouth
Straight Pt.
WEYMOUTH 9.1.28
Worbarrow Bay
Chapman's Pool
Lulworth Cove
TEIGNMOUTH 9.1.22
Portland CG
Brixham CG
PORTLAND HARBOUR 9.1.26
St Alban's Hd
Anvil Point
Portland Bill
LULWORTH RANGES 9.1.29
Portland Race
TORQUAY 9.1.21
Paignton
Totnes
Tor Bay
Dittisham
BRIXHAM 9.1.20
DARTMOUTH 9.1.19
See 9.2.2
Magnetic Variation 4·0°W
Kingsbridge
Start Bay
Start Point
Bolt Head
Prawle Point
SALCOMBE 9.1.18
NAVAL EXERCISE AREAS 9.1.16
CASQUETS TSS SEPARATION ZONE
E. Channel
Channel
Inshore Traffic Zone
30'
20'
10'
51°N
50'
40'
30'
20'
10'
50°N
50'
40'
30'
20'
10'
3°W
2°W
RG

9.1.3 AREA 1 TIDAL STREAMS

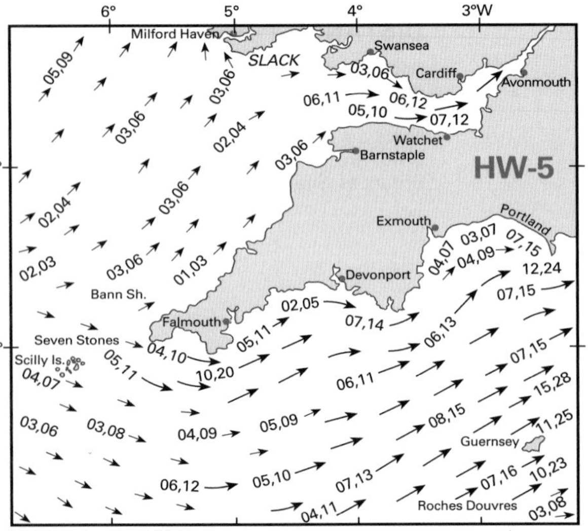
6°
5°
4°
3°W
51°
50°
Milford Haven
SLACK
Swansea
Cardiff
Avonmouth
Watchet
Barnstaple
HW-5
Exmouth
Portland
Devonport
Bann Sh.
Falmouth
Seven Stones
Scilly Is.
Guernsey
Roches Douvres

5 Hours before HW Dover (0040 after HW Devonport)

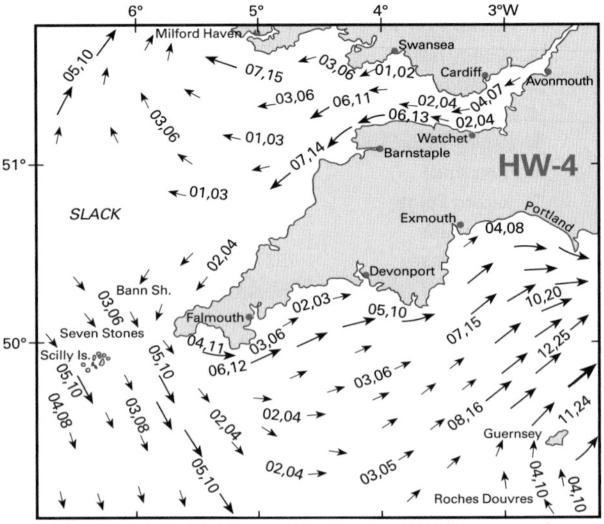
6°
5°
4°
3°W
51°
50°
Milford Haven
Swansea
Cardiff
Avonmouth
Watchet
Barnstaple
HW-4
SLACK
Exmouth
Portland
Devonport
Bann Sh.
Falmouth
Seven Stones
Scilly Is.
Guernsey
Roches Douvres

4 Hours before HW Dover (0140 after HW Devonport)

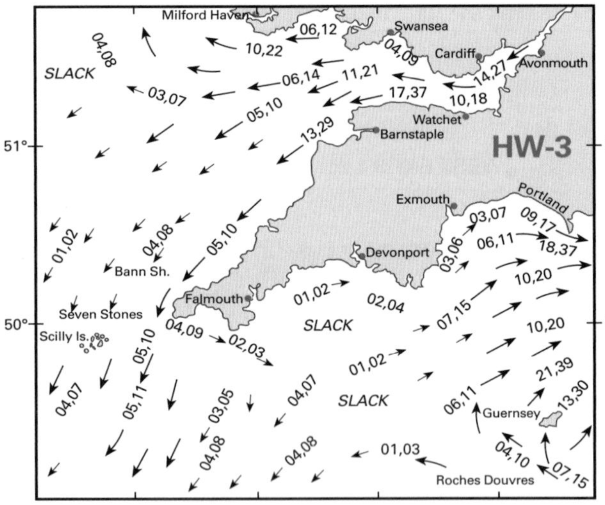
51°
50°
Milford Haven
Swansea
Cardiff
Avonmouth
SLACK
Watchet
Barnstaple
HW-3
Exmouth
Portland
Devonport
Bann Sh.
Falmouth
Seven Stones
Scilly Is.
SLACK
SLACK
Guernsey
Roches Douvres

3 Hours before HW Dover (0240 after HW Devonport)

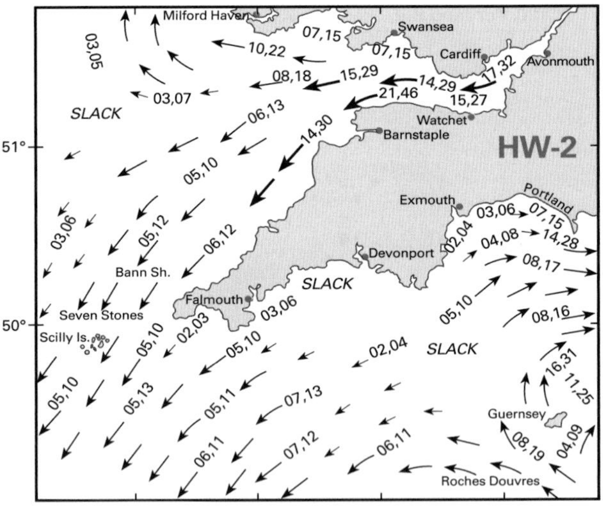
51°
50°
Milford Haven
Swansea
Cardiff
Avonmouth
SLACK
Watchet
Barnstaple
HW-2
Exmouth
Portland
Devonport
Bann Sh.
SLACK
Falmouth
Seven Stones
Scilly Is.
SLACK
Guernsey
Roches Douvres

2 Hours before HW Dover (0340 after HW Devonport)

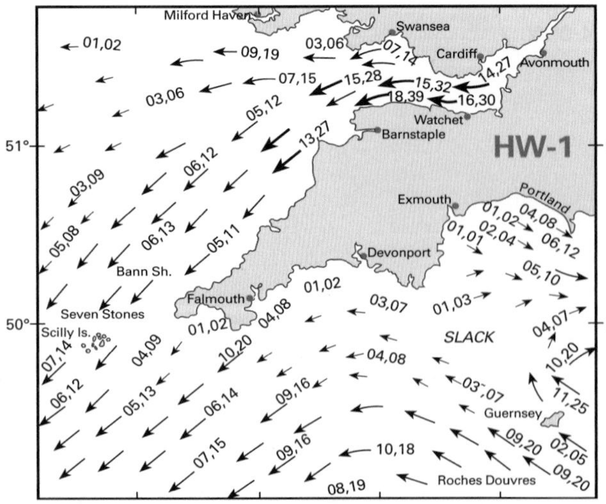
51°
50°
Milford Haven
Swansea
Cardiff
Avonmouth
Watchet
Barnstaple
HW-1
Exmouth
Portland
Devonport
Bann Sh.
Falmouth
Seven Stones
Scilly Is.
SLACK
Guernsey
Roches Douvres

1 Hour before HW Dover (0440 after HW Devonport)

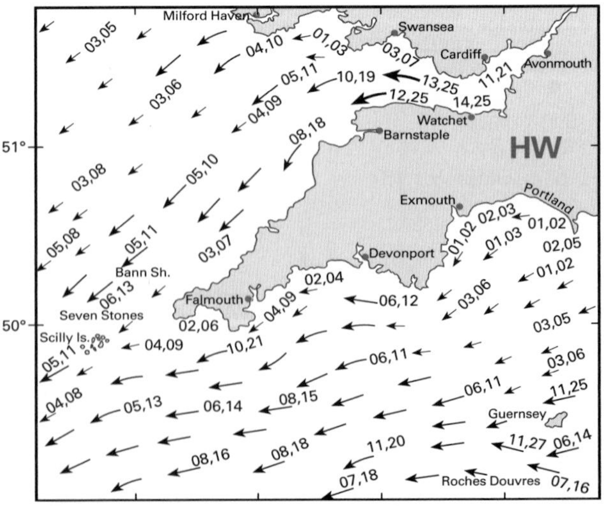
51°
50°
Milford Haven
Swansea
Cardiff
Avonmouth
Watchet
Barnstaple
HW
Exmouth
Portland
Devonport
Bann Sh.
Falmouth
Seven Stones
Scilly Is.
Guernsey
Roches Douvres

HW Dover (0540 after HW Devonport)

Eastward 9.2.3 Portland 9.1.27 Isle of Wight 9.2.22 Northward 9.11.3 Southward 9.20.3 Channel Is 9.19.3

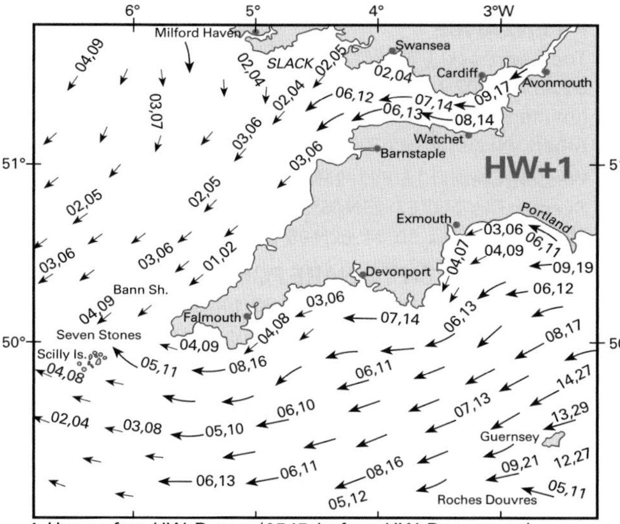
6°
5°
4°
3°W
51°
50°
HW+1
Milford Haven
Swansea
Cardiff
Avonmouth
Watchet
Barnstaple
Exmouth
Portland
Devonport
Falmouth
Bann Sh.
Seven Stones
Scilly Is.
Guernsey
Roches Douvres
SLACK
04,09
03,07
02,04
02,05
02,04
06,12
07,14
09,17
06,13
08,14
03,06
03,06
02,05
02,05
03,06
03,06
01,02
04,09
04,09
04,08
05,11
08,16
03,06
07,14
06,13
03,06
06,11
04,07
04,09
09,19
06,12
08,17
04,08
02,04
03,08
05,10
06,10
06,11
07,13
14,27
13,29
06,13
06,11
08,16
09,21
12,27
05,12
05,11

1 Hour after HW Dover (0545 before HW Devonport)

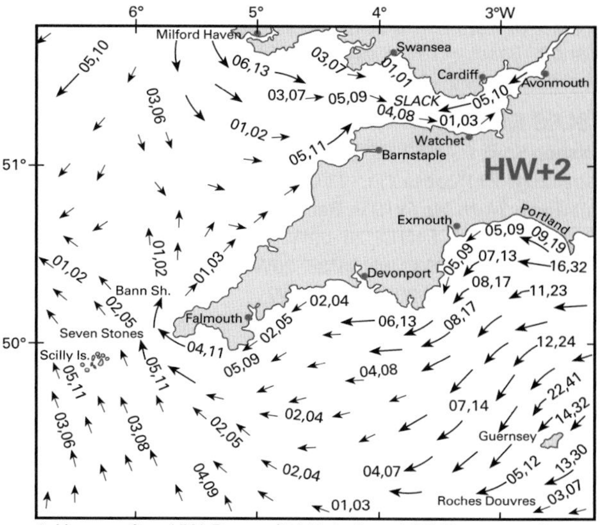
6°
5°
4°
3°W
51°
50°
HW+2
Milford Haven
Swansea
Cardiff
Avonmouth
Watchet
Barnstaple
Exmouth
Portland
Devonport
Falmouth
Bann Sh.
Seven Stones
Scilly Is.
Guernsey
Roches Douvres
SLACK
05,10
06,13
03,07
01,01
03,07
05,09
05,10
04,08
01,03
03,06
01,02
05,11
05,09
09,19
07,13
16,32
08,17
11,23
01,02
01,02
01,03
02,05
02,04
06,13
08,17
04,11
05,09
12,24
04,08
22,41
05,11
05,11
02,04
07,14
14,32
03,06
03,08
02,05
02,04
04,07
05,12
13,30
04,09
01,03
03,07

2 Hours after HW Dover (0445 before HW Devonport)

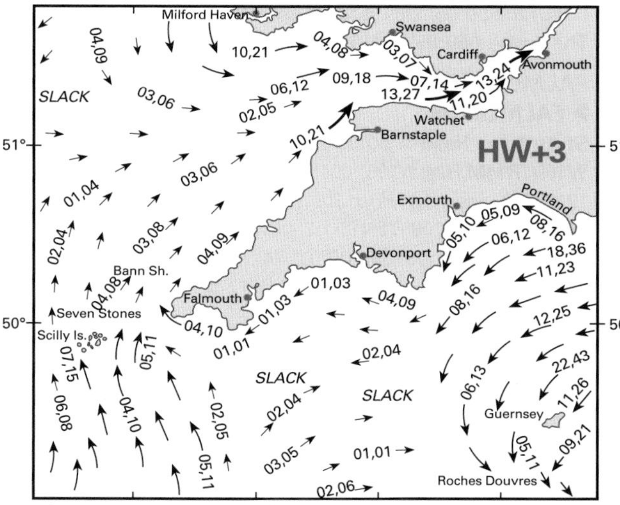
51°
50°
HW+3
Milford Haven
Swansea
Cardiff
Avonmouth
Watchet
Barnstaple
Exmouth
Portland
Devonport
Falmouth
Bann Sh.
Seven Stones
Scilly Is.
Guernsey
Roches Douvres
SLACK
SLACK
SLACK
04,09
10,21
04,08
03,07
03,06
06,12
09,18
07,14
13,24
13,27
11,20
02,05
10,21
03,06
01,04
03,08
04,09
05,10
05,09
06,12
08,16
18,36
02,04
04,08
01,03
01,03
11,23
04,10
04,09
08,16
12,25
01,01
02,04
07,15
05,11
06,13
22,43
06,08
04,10
02,05
02,04
11,26
05,11
03,05
01,01
05,11
09,21
02,06

3 Hours after HW Dover (0345 before HW Devonport)

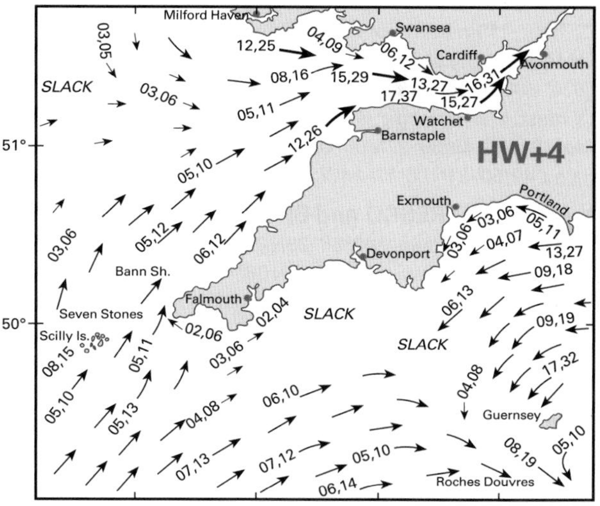
51°
50°
HW+4
Milford Haven
Swansea
Cardiff
Avonmouth
Watchet
Barnstaple
Exmouth
Portland
Devonport
Falmouth
Bann Sh.
Seven Stones
Scilly Is.
Guernsey
Roches Douvres
SLACK
SLACK
SLACK
03,05
12,25
04,09
06,12
03,06
08,16
15,29
13,27
16,31
17,37
15,27
05,11
12,26
05,10
03,06
03,06
05,11
04,07
13,27
05,12
06,12
09,18
02,06
02,04
06,13
08,15
05,11
03,06
09,19
05,10
05,13
04,08
06,10
04,08
17,32
07,13
07,12
05,10
08,19
05,10
06,14

4 Hours after HW Dover (0245 before HW Devonport)

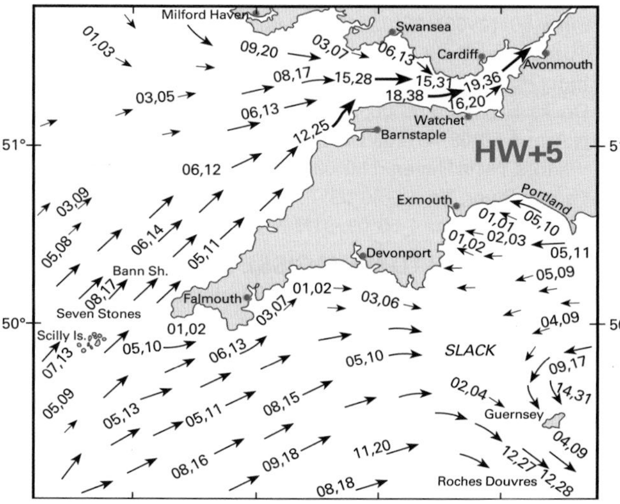
51°
50°
HW+5
Milford Haven
Swansea
Cardiff
Avonmouth
Watchet
Barnstaple
Exmouth
Portland
Devonport
Falmouth
Bann Sh.
Seven Stones
Scilly Is.
Guernsey
Roches Douvres
SLACK
01,03
09,20
03,07
06,13
08,17
15,28
15,31
19,36
03,05
18,38
16,20
06,13
12,25
06,12
03,09
05,08
06,14
05,11
01,01
05,10
01,02
02,03
05,11
05,09
08,17
01,02
03,06
03,07
01,02
04,09
05,10
06,13
05,10
09,17
07,13
05,09
05,13
05,11
08,15
02,04
14,31
08,16
09,18
11,20
12,27
04,09
08,18
12,28

5 Hours after HW Dover (0145 before HW Devonport)

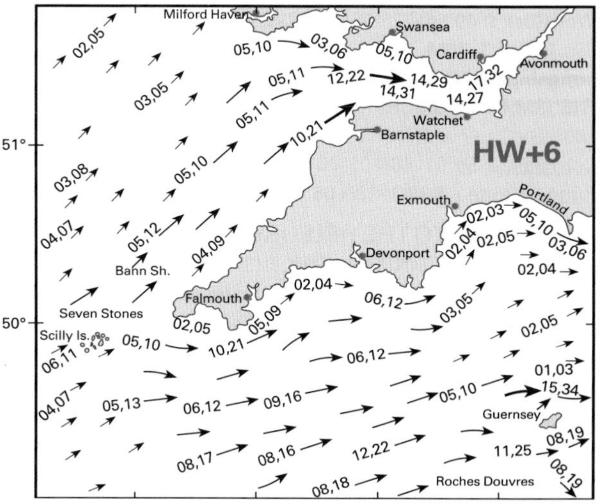
51°
50°
HW+6
Milford Haven
Swansea
Cardiff
Avonmouth
Watchet
Barnstaple
Exmouth
Portland
Devonport
Falmouth
Bann Sh.
Seven Stones
Scilly Is.
Guernsey
Roches Douvres
02,05
05,10
03,06
05,10
05,11
12,22
14,29
17,32
03,05
14,31
14,27
05,11
10,21
05,10
03,08
04,07
05,12
04,09
02,03
05,10
02,04
02,05
03,06
02,04
02,04
06,12
03,05
02,05
05,09
05,10
10,21
06,12
06,11
01,03
15,34
04,07
05,13
06,12
09,16
05,10
08,19
08,17
08,16
12,22
11,25
08,19
08,18

6 Hours after HW Dover (0045 before HW Devonport)

PLOT WAYPOINTS ON YOUR CHART BEFORE USING THEM

9.1.4 LIGHTS, BUOYS AND WAYPOINTS

Blue print = light with a nominal range of 15M or more. CAPITALS = place or feature. *CAPITAL ITALICS* = light-vessel, light float or Lanby. *Italics* = Fog signal. ***Bold italics*** = Racon. Useful waypoints are underlined. Abbreviations are in Chapter 1.

ISLES OF SCILLY TO LAND'S END

Bishop Rock ☆ 49°52'·37N 06°26'·74W, Fl (2) 15s 44m **24M**; part obsc 204°-211°, obsc 211°-233°, 236°-259°; Gy ○ twr with helo platform; *Horn Mo (N) 90s*; ***Racon T, 18M, 254°-215°.***
Gunner 49°53'·64N 06°25'·09W.
Round Rock 49°53'·10N 06°25'·20W.
Old Wreck 49°54'·26N 06°22'·81W.
St Agnes, Old light house, conspic; 49°53'·55N 06°20'·74W.

▶ ST MARY'S

Peninnis Hd ☆ 49°54'·28N 06°18'·22W, Fl 20s 36m **17M**; 231°-117° but part obsc 048°-083° within 5M; W ○ twr on B frame, B cupola.
Spanish Ledge 49°53'·94N 06°18'·86W, Q (3) 10s; *Bell.*
Bartholomew Ledges 49°54'·37N 06°19'·89W, QR 12m.
N Bartholomew 49°54'·49N 06°19'·99W, Fl R 5s.
Bacon Ledge 49°55'·22N 06°19'·27W, Fl R 5s.
Ldg lts 097·3°. Front, 49°55'·12N 06°18'·52W, Iso RW (vert) 2s; Or △. Rear, 110m from front, Oc WR (vert) 10s; Or X on W bcn.
St Mary's Pool pier ☆ 49°55'·11N 06°19'·00W, Fl WRG 2s 5m 4M; R070°-100°, W100°-130°, G130°-070°.
TV mast, 119m conspic; R lts; 49°55'·95N 06°18'·32W.
Crow Rock 49°56'·27N 06°18'·50W, Fl (2) 10s.
Hats 49°56'·21N 06°17'·14W.

▶ AROUND TRESCO and BRYHER

Tresco Flats, Hulman 49°56'·29N 06°20'·31W, Fl G 4s.
Tresco Abbey, conspic, 49°56'·87N 06°19'·77W.
Spencers Ledge 49°54'·78N 06°22'·06W, Q (6) + L Fl 15s.
Steeple Rock 49°55'·46N 06°24'·24W, Q (9) 15s.
Round Island ☆ 49°58'·74N 06°19'·40W, Fl 10s 55m **18M**, shown during periods of reduced vis only; 021°-288°; W ○ twr; *Horn (4) 60s*; ***Racon M, 10M.***
St Martin's daymark, RW bcn; 49°57'·99N 06°15'·98W.

▶ SCILLY TO LAND'S END

Seven Stones 50°03'·62N 06°04'·34W, Fl (3) 30s 12m **25M**; H24; R hull; *Horn (3) 60s*; ***Racon O, 15M.***
Wolf Rock ☆ 49°56'·72N 05°48'·57W, Fl 15s 34m **16M**; H24; *Horn 30s*; ***Racon T, 10M.***
Longships ☆ 50°04'·01N 05°44'·81W, Iso WR 10s 35m **W16M, R15**/13M; R189°-208°, R (unintens) 208°-307°, R307°-327°, W327°-189°; Gy ○ twr with helicopter platform; *Horn 10s.*
Carn Base 50°01'·48N 05°46'·18W, Q (9) 15s.
Runnel Stone 50°01'·19N 05°40'·36W, Q (6) + L Fl 15s; *Whis.*

LAND'S END TO THE HELFORD RIVER

Tater-du ☆ 50°03'·14N 05°34'·68W, Fl (3) 15s 34m **20M**; 241°-074°; W ○ twr. Also FR 31m 13M, 060°-074° over Runnel stone and in places 074°-077° within 4M; *Horn (2) 30s.*

▶ MOUSEHOLE

N pier ☆ 50°04'·98N 05°32'·27W, 2 FG (vert) 8m 4M; replaced by FR when hbr closed; Gy mast.
Low Lee 50°05'·56N 05°31'·38W, Q (3) 10s.

▶ NEWLYN

S Pier ☆ 50°06'·19N 05°32'·57W, Fl 5s 10m 9M; W ○ twr; 253°-336°.
N Pier ☆ 50°06'·19N 05°32'·62W, FWG 4m 2M; G238°-248°, W over hbr. Mary Williams pier ☆ 50°06'·18N 05°32'·74W, 2 FR 8m 2M.

▶ PENZANCE

The Gear (rock) 50°06'·62N 05°31'·62W, Fl (2) 10s.
S Pier ☆ 50°07'·07N 05°31'·68W, Fl WR 5s 11m **W17M**, R12M; R (unintens) 159°-224°, R224°-268°, W268°-344·5°, R344·5°-shore.
Albert (N) pier ☆ 50°07'·09N 05°31'·80W, 2 FG (vert) 11m 2M.
Western Cressar 50°07'·24N 05°31'·13W.
Ryeman Rks 50°07'·25N 05°30'·33W.
Mountamopus 50°04'·62N 05°26'·27W, Q (6) + L Fl 15s.

▶ PORTHLEVEN TO NARE POINT

S Pier ☆ 50°04'·91N 05°19'·09W, FG 10m 4M; G col, lts shown when hbr is open. A 2nd FG 10m 4M inside the hbr aligns 046° with the pierhead ☆.
Lizard ☆ 49°57'·61N 05°12'·13W, Fl 3s 70m **26M**; H24; 250°-120°, partly visible 235°-250°; W 8-sided twr; *Horn 30s.*
Manacle 50°02'·81N 05°01'·92W, Q (3) 10s; *Bell.*
Helston 50°04'·96N 05°00'·82W, Fl Y 2·5s.

▶ HELFORD RIVER

August Rock 50°06'·11N 05°04'·93W, (PA); (seasonal).
Car Croc 50°05'·26N 05°05'·43W, (PA).
The Voose 50°05'·81N 05°06'·96W.

FALMOUTH TO PLYMOUTH

▶ FALMOUTH

St Anthony Head ☆ 50°08'·47N 05°00'·96W, Iso WR 15s 22m, **W16M, R14M,** H24; W295°-004°, R004°-022° over Manacles, W022°-172°; W 8-sided twr; *Horn 30s.*
Black Rock 50°08'·72N 05°02'·00W.
Black Rock 50°08'·68N 05°01'·74W, Q (3) 10s.
Castle 50°08'·99N 05°01'·62W, Fl G 2·5s.
St Mawes 50°09'·09N 05°01'·42W.
The Governor 50°09'·15N 05°02'·40W, VQ (3) 5s.
West Narrows 50°09'·38N 05°02'·07W, Fl (2) R 10s.
East Narrows 50°09'·43N 05°01'·90W, Fl (2) G 10s.
The Vilt 50°09'·99N 05°02'·28W, Fl (4) G 15s.
Northbank 50°10'·36N 05°02'·13W, Fl R 4s.
St Just 50°10'·42N 05°01'·72W, QR.
Messack 50°11'·31N 05°02'·22W, Fl G 15s.
Carick 50°11'·59N 05°02'·74W, Fl (2) G 10s.
Pill 50°12'·05N 05°02'·40W, Fl (3) G 15s.
Turnerware Bar 50°12'·40N 05°02'·15W, Fl G 5s.

Inner Harbour

Docks, E bkwtr ☆ 50°09'·34N 05°02'·96W, 2 FR (vert) 2m.
N Arm ☆ 50°09'·41N 05°03'·20W, Q 19m 3M.
Visitors Yacht Haven ☆ 50°09'·27N 05°03'·91W, 2 FR (vert).
Penryn River, No. 1 50°09'·77N 05°04'·34W, QR.
Falmouth marina 50°09'·91N 05°04'·99W, VQ (3) 5s.

▶ FALMOUTH TO MEVAGISSEY

Naval gunnery targets (D006A) off Dodman Point:
'A' 50°08'·53N 04°46'·38W, Fl Y 10s.
'B' 50°10'·32N 04°45'·00W, Fl Y 5s.
'C' 50°10'·42N 04°47'·51W, Fl Y 2s.
Gwineas 50°14'·49N 04°45'·39W, Q (3) 10s; *Bell.*

▶ MEVAGISSEY

Victoria Pier ☆ 50°16'·15N 04°46'·93W, Fl (2) 10s 9m 12M; *Dia 30s.*
Puckey's Ground (Diffuser) 50°19'·50N 04°43'·08W.

Royal Fowey YC 50°18'·45N 04°43'·02W (PA, April-Oct).
Cannis Rock 50°18'·37N 04°39'·95W, Q (6) + L Fl 15s; *Bell.*
Gribbin Hd, R/W banded twr 26m high, 50°19'·02N 04°40'·39W.

▶ FOWEY

Fowey ☆ 50°19'·62N 04°38'·84W, L Fl WR 5s 28m W11M, R9M; R284°-295°, W295°-028°, R028°-054°; W 8-sided twr, R lantern.
St Catherine's Pt ☆ 50°19'·69N 04°38'·66W, Fl R 2·5s 15m 2M; 150°-295°.
Lamp Rock ☆ 50°19'·70N 04°38'·38W, Fl G 5s 7m 2M; 088°-205°.
Whitehouse Pt ☆ 50°19'·98N 04°38'·24W, Iso WRG 3s 11m W11M, R/G8M; G017°-022°, W022°-032°, R032°-037°; R col.
New Quay Cellars, ☆ 50°20'·48N 04°37'·88W, Iso G 2s 5m2M.

▶ POLPERRO

Udder Rock 50°18'·93N 04°33'·85W, VQ (6) + L Fl 10s; *Bell.*
Tidal basin, W pier ☆ 50°19'·86N 04°30·96W, F 4m 4M; FR when hbr closed in bad weather.
Spy House Pt ☆ 50°19'·81N 04°30'·70W, Iso WR 6s 30m 7M; W288°-060°, R060°-288°.

▶ LOOE, EDDYSTONE and WHITSAND BAY

Ranneys 50°19'·86N 04°26'·37W, Q (6) + L Fl 15s.
Mid Main 50°20'·55N 04°26'·94W, Q (3) 10s 2M.
Banjo Pier ☆ 50°21'·05N 04°27'·06W, Oc WR 3s 8m **W15M,** R12M; R207°-267°, W267°-313°, R313°-332°.
White Rock, ☆ 50°21'·03N 04°27'·09W, Fl R 3s 5m 2M.
Nailzee Pt, 50°21'·01N 04°27'·08W, *Siren (2) 30s; fishing.*

Eddystone ☆ 50°10'·85N 04°15'·94W, Fl (2) 10s 41m **17M.** Same twr, Iso R 10s 28m 8M; 110·5°-130·5° over Hand Deeps; Gy twr, helicopter platform; *Horn 30s;* **Racon T, 10M.**
Hand Deeps 50°12'·69N 04°21'·11W, Q (9) 15s.

Artificial reef (ex-HMS Scylla) 50°19'·54N 04°15'·37W, Fl R 5s.

PLYMOUTH

▶ PLYMOUTH SOUND, WESTERN CHANNEL

Rame Head, S end 50°18'·67N 04°13'·37W, (unlit).
Draystone 50°18'·85N 04°11'·07W, Fl (2) R 5s.
Open Sea magnetic Range (OSR) South 50°18'·86N 04°10'·11W, Fl Y 2s. OSR North 50°19'·00N 04°09'·93W, Fl Y 2s.
Knap 50°19'·56N 04°10'·02W, Fl G 5s.
Plymouth bkwtr W ☆ 50°20'·07N 04°09'·53W, Fl WR 10s 19m W12M, R9M; W262°-208°, R208°-262°; W ○ twr. Same twr, Iso 4s 12m 10M; 033°-037°; *Horn 15s.*
Maker ☆ 50°20'·51N 04°10'·87W, Fl (2) WRG 10s 29m, W11M, R/G6M; G270°-330°, W330°-004°, R004°-050°; W twr, R stripe.
Queens Ground 50°20'·29N 04°10'·08W, Fl (2) R 10s.
New Ground 50°20'·47N 04°09'·44W, Fl R 2s.
The Bridge Channel.
No 1, QG 4m; 50°21'·03N 04°09'·53W. No 2, QR 4m. No 3, Fl (3) G 10s 4m. No 4, Fl (4) R 10s 4m; 50°21'·08N 04°09'·63W.
Bridge, Fl (2) Bu 5s 5m 3M; 140°-210°; 325m SW of No 4 bcn.

▶ PLYMOUTH SOUND, EASTERN CHANNEL

Wembury Pt ☆ 50°19'·01N 04°06'·63W, Oc Y 10s 45m; occas.
Shag Stone 50°19'·07N 04°07'·60W, unlit bcn.
West Tinker 50°19'·25N 04°08'·65W, VQ (9) 10s.
East Tinker 50°19'·20N 04°08'·31W, Q (3) 10s.
Whidbey 50°19'·53N 04°07'·27W, Oc (2) WRG 10s 29m, W8M, R/G6M, H24; 000°-G-137·5°-W-139·5°-R-159°; Or and W col.
Bkwtr E 50°20'·01N 04°08'·25W, L Fl WR 10s 9m W8M, R6M; R190°-353°, W353°-001°, R001°-018°, W018°-190°.

Staddon Pt 50°20'·17N 04°07'·54W, Oc WRG 10s 15m W8M, R/G5M; H24. 348°-G-038°-W-050°-R-090°; W structure, R bands.
West Staddon 50°20'·17N 04°07'·84W, Q (9) 15s 6m 3M.
Bovisand Pier 50°20'·24N 04°07·72W, 2 FG (vert) 17m 3M.
Duke Rk 50°20'·32N 04°08'·23W, VQ (9) 10s.
Withyhedge Dir ☆ 070° (for W Chan). 50°20'·75N 04°07'·44W, WRG 13m W13M, R/G5M; H24; FG060°-065°, Al WG 065°-069° (W phase increasing with brg), F W 069°-071°, Al WR071°-075° (R phase increasing with brg), F R075°-080°; W ▽, orange stripe on col. Same col, Fl (2) Bu 5s; 120°-160°.

▶ JUNCTION OF EASTERN & WESTERN CHANNELS

Ldg lts 349°. Front, Mallard Shoal 50°21'·60N 04°08'·33W, Q WRG 5m W10M, R/G3M; W △, Or bands; G233°-043°, R043°-067°, G067°-087°, W087°-099°, R099°-108° ldg sector. Rear, 396m from front, Hoe Oc G 1·3s 11m 3M, 310°-040°; W ▽, Or bands.
Melampus 50°21'·15N 04°08'·73W, Fl R 4s.
S Mallard 50°21'·51N 04°08'·30W, VQ (6) + L Fl 10s.
W Mallard 50°21'·57N 04°08'·36W, QG.
Mount Batten bkwtr ☆ 50°21'·56N 04°08'·13W, 2 FG (vert) 7m 4M.
S Winter 50°21'·40N 04°08'·55W, Q (6) + L Fl 15s.
NE Winter 50°21'·54N 04°08'·50W, QR.
NW Winter 50°21'·55N 04°08'·70W, VQ (9) 10s.

▶ QAB, SUTTON HARBOUR and PYH

QAB (Queen Anne's Battery) ldg lts ☆ 048·5°. Front, 50°21'·84N 04°07'·84W, FR, Or/W bcn. Rear, Dir Oc WRG 7.5s 14m 3M; G038°-047·2°, W047·2°-049·7°, R049·7°-060·5°.
QAB bkwtr knuckle ☆ 50°21'·85N 04°08'·02W, Oc G 8s 5m 2M.
Fishers Nose ☆ 50°21'·80N 04°08'·02W, Fl (3) R 10s 6m 4M.
Sutton Hbr, lock 50°21'·98N 04°07'·96W; IPTS.
PYH (Plymouth Yacht Haven), outer bkwtr, E end 50°21'·59N 04°07'·15W, 2 FG (vert).

▶ DRAKE CHANNEL and THE NARROWS

Asia 50°21'·47N 04°08'·85W, Fl (2) R 5s.
Millbay Pier ☆ 50°21'·75N 04°09'·17W, QG 10m 2M.
St Nicholas 50°21'·55N 04°09'·20W, QR.
N Drakes Is 50°21'·52N 04°09'·38W, Fl R 4s.
E Vanguard 50°21'·47N 04°10'·70W, QG.
W Vanguard 50°21'49N 04°09'·98W, Fl G 3s.
Devils Point 50°21'·59N 04°10'·05W, QG 5m 3M; Fl 5s in fog.
Battery 50°21'·52N 04°10'·21W, Fl R 2s.
Mount Wise, Dir ☆ 343°. 50°21'·96N 04°10'·33W, WRG 7m, W13M, R/G5M; H24. FG331°-338, Al WG 338°-342° W phase increasing with brg, F W342°-344°, Al WR344°-348° R phase increasing with bearing, F R348°-351°. In fog, F, 341·5°-344·5°.
Ocean Court, 50°21'·85N 04°10'·11W, Dir Q WRG 15m, W11M, R/G3M; G010°-080°, W080°-090°, R090°-100°.
Mayflower marina, outer bkwtr, E end, 2 FR (vert).

PLYMOUTH TO START POINT

▶ RIVER YEALM

The Sand Bar 50°18'·59N 04°04'·12W, Fl R 5s (Apr-Oct).
East Sand Bar 50°18'·60N 04°04'·06W, (Apr-Oct).
Naval Gunfire Support (NGS) buoys, 5.4M SW of Bolt Tail:
NGS West 50°11'·13N 04°00'·86W, Fl Y 5s.
NGS East 50°11'·23N 03°59'·06W, Fl Y 10s.

▶ SALCOMBE

Racing marks (Apr-Sep) in The Range (seaward of the Bar):
Starehole 50°12'·53N 03°46'·87W. Gara 50°12'·83N 03°45'·27W.

PLOT WAYPOINTS ON YOUR CHART BEFORE USING THEM

Gammon 50°12'·03N 03°45'·57W. Prawle 50°12'·13N 03°43'·87W.
Sandhill Point Dir ☆ 000°. 50°13'·77N 03°46'·67W, Fl WRG 2s 27m W10M, R/G7M; G182·5°-357·5°, W357·5°-002·5°; R002·5°-182·5°; R/W ◇ on W mast. Pound Stone, 230m S, R/W in line 000°.
Bass Rk 50°13'·48N 03°46'·71W, QR.
Wolf Rk 50°13'·53N 03°46'·58W, QG.
Blackstone Rk 50°13'·61N 03°46'·51W, Q (2) G 8s 4m 2M.
Ldg lts 042·5°. Front 50°14'·53N 03°45'·31W, Q 5m 8M. Rear, 180m from front, Q 45m 8M.
Off Fort Charles (ruins): Old Harry 50°13'·69N 03°46'·59W; & Castle 50°13'·73N 03°46'·52W.
Short stay/landing pontoon ☆ 50°14'·25N 03°45'·95W, 2 FR (vert).
Start Pt ☆ 50°13'·33N 03°38'·54W, Fl (3) 10s 62m **25M**; 184°-068°. Same twr: FR 55m 12M ; 210°-255° over Skerries Bank; *Horn 60s.*
Skerries Bank 50°16'·31N 03°33'·76W; *Bell.*

START POINT TO PORTLAND BILL

▶ DARTMOUTH

Royal Dart YC racing marks (Apr-Oct) outside the harbour:
RDYC 1 50°18'·83N 03°35'·32W.
RDYC 2 50°18'·71N 03°33'·37W.
RDYC 3 50°20'·10N 03°31'·49W.
Day, 167m, 50°20'·53N 03°32'·55W; 9 ca E of Dartmouth Cas.
Kingswear Dir ☆ 328°. 50°20'·81N 03°34'·10W, Iso WRG 3s 9m 8M; G318°-325°, W325°-331°, R331°-340°; W ○ twr.
Dir ☆ 104·5°. 50°20'·65N 03°33'·80W, 5m 9M; 102°-107°.
Mewstone 50°19'·92N 03°31'·89W, VQ (6) + L Fl 10s.
West Rock 50°19'·86N 03°32'·47W, Q (6) + L Fl 15s.
Homestone 50°19'·60N 03°33'·56W, QR.
Castle Ledge 50°19'·99N 03°33'·12W, Fl G 5s.
Checkstone 50°20'·45N 03°33'·81W, Fl (2) R 5s.
Bayards Cove Dir ☆ 293°. 50°20'·85N 03°34'·64W, Fl WRG 2s 5m 6M; G280°-289°, W289°-297°, R297°-shore.
Kingswear marina 'A' ☆ 50°21'·00N 03°34'·39W, 2 FG (vert).
Darthaven marina, S end ☆ 50°21'·45N 03°34'·58W, 2 FG (vert).
Dart marina, centre ☆ 50°21'·51N 03°34'·60W, 2 FR (vert).
Anchor Stone 50°22'·78N 03°35'·30W, Fl (2) R 5s 1M.

▶ BRIXHAM

Berry Head ☆ 50°23'·97N 03°29'·01W, Fl (2) 15s 58m 14M; 100°-023°; W twr. R lts on radio mast 5·7M NW.
Victoria bkwtr ☆ 50°24'·33N 03°30'·78W, Oc R 15s 9m 6M; W twr.
Fairway Dir ☆ 159°. 50°23'·83N 03°30'·57W, Iso WRG 5s 4m 6M; G145°-157°, W157°-161°, R161°-173°.
No. 1 50°24'·30N 03°30'·89W, Fl G.
No. 2 50°24'·32N 03°30'·83W, Fl R.
No. 3 50°24'·11N 03°30'·77W, L Fl G.
No. 4 50°24'·13N 03°30'·72W, L Fl R.
Marina ent ☆ 50°23'·96N 03°30'·60W, two Fl R 5s (vert) 4m 2M.
S side ☆ 50°23'·91N 03°30'·57W, 2 FR (vert) 4m; events pontoon.
FV basin ☆s: 2 FG (vert); Q; and QG 6m 3M, elbow of New pier.

▶ PAIGNTON

Black Rock outfall 50°25'·95N 03°33'·15W, Q (3) 10s 5m 3M.
E Quay ☆ 50°25'·96N 03°33'·35W, QR 7m 3M.

▶ TORQUAY

50°27'·42N 03°31'·80W, QG (May-Sep); 85m off Haldon Pier.
Haldon Pier (E) ☆ 50°27'·43N 03°31'·73W, QG 9m 6M.
Princess Pier (W) ☆ 50°27'·46N 03°31'·73W, QR 9m 6M.
Marina pontoons, SE ends ☆ 2 FR (vert). S pier, 2 FG (vert).

▶ TEIGNMOUTH

Outfall 50°31'·95N 03°27'·78W, Fl Y 5s; 288°/1·3M to hbr ent.
Two ☆ FR 10/11m 3/6M, 370m SW of Teignmouth Pierhead, should be ignored for normal navigational purposes. Ditto any small non-standard buoys near the Bar, for use by pilots.
Trng wall, middle 50°32'·33N 03°29'·93W, Oc R 6s 4m 3M.
The Point 50°32'·42N 03°30'·05W, Oc G 6s 3M & FG (vert).
50°32'·50N 03°30'·11W, Fl R 2s.
50°32'·53N 03°30'·00W, (PA) Fl G 2s.
Detached ⓥ pontoon, 50°32'·61N 03°29'·95W (PA), unlit.
50°32'·63N 03°30'·03W, Fl R 2s.
Bathing pontoon ☆ 50°32'·80N 03°29'·20W, Fl Y 10s (Jun-Sep).

▶ RIVER EXE and EXMOUTH

E Exe 50°36'·00N 03°22'·38W, Q (3) 10s.
No. 1 50°36'·20N 03°22'·83W, QG.
No. 2 50°36'·10N 03°22'·90W.
No. 4 50°36'·19N 03°23'·36W.
No. 3 50°36'·29N 03°23'·40W, Fl G 2s.
No. 6 50°36'·32N 03°23'·59W, VQ R.
No. 7 50°36'·38N 03°23'·90W, QG.
No. 8 50°36'·38N 03°24'·11W, QR.
Ldg lts 305°. Front, 50°36'·99N 03°25'·34W, Iso 2s 6m 7M. Rear, 57m from front, Q 12m 7M.
No. 10 50°36'·73N 03°24'·77W, Fl R 3s.
No. 12 Warren Pt 50°36'·91N 03°25'·40W.
Exmouth Quay, ☆ 50°36'·99N 03°25'·46W, 2 FG (vert) 7m 3M.
Straight Pt ☆ 50°36'·49N 03°21'·76W, Fl R 10s 34m 7M; 246°-071°.
Outfall 50°36'·25N 03°21'·50W, Fl Y 5s.
DZN 50°36'·82N 03°19'·30W, Fl Y 3s.
DZS 50°36'·12N 03°19'·42W, Fl Y 5s.

▶ SIDMOUTH and AXMOUTH

Sidmouth ☆ 50°40'·49'N 03°14'·45W, Fl R 5s 5m 2M.
Axmouth jetty ☆ 50°42'·12N 03°03'·31W, Fl G 4s 7m 2M.

▶ LYME REGIS

Outfall Q (6) + L Fl 15s; 50°43'·17N 02°55'·66W.
Ldg lts 296°. Front, Victoria Pier ☆ 50°43'·19N 02°56'·17W, Oc WR 8s 6m, W9M, R7M; R296°-116°, W116°-296°; Bu col. Rear, 240m from front, FG 8m 9M.

▶ WEST BAY (BRIDPORT)

Outfall Y 50°41'·96N 02°46'·38W, Fl Y 5s.
W pier ☆ 50°42'·56N 02°45'·85W, FR 3m 2M (occas).
E pier ☆ 50°42'·56N 02°45'·83W, FG 3m 2M (occas).
W pier root ☆ 50°42'·64N 02°45'·84W, Iso R 2s 9m 5M.
Chesil Beach outfall 50°33'·99N 02°28'·91W, Fl Y 10s.

PORTLAND BILL TO ANVIL POINT

Portland Bill lt ho ☆ 50°30'·85N 02°27'·38W, Fl (4) 20s 43m **25M**. 221°-244°, gradu changes from 1 Fl to 4 Fl; 244°-117°, shows 4 Fl; 117°-141°, gradu changes from 4 Fl to 1 Fl; W ○ twr; *Dia 30s*. Same twr, FR 19m 13M; 271°-291° over The Shambles. W obelisk, 18m, is close S on the tip of the Bill.
W Shambles 50°29'·78N 02°24'·40W, Q (9) 15s; *Bell.*
E Shambles 50°30'·78N 02°20'·08W, Q (3) 10s; *Bell.*
Noise Range, centred on 50°33'·80N 02°24'·28W; four SPM buoys: S pair Fl Y 3s; N pair Fl Y 5s.

▶ PORTLAND HARBOUR

Outer Breakwater D Head (S end) ☆ 50°34'·18N 02°25'·23W, Oc R 30s 12m 5M. S Ship Channel is permanently closed.

Outer Breakwater (N end) ☆ 50°35'·11N 02°24'·87W, QR 14m 5M; vis 013°-268°. E Ship Chan is used by commercial ships.
NE Bkwtr (A Hd) ☆ 50°35'·16N 02°25'·07W, Fl 10s 22m **20M**.
NE Bkwtr (B Hd) ☆ 50°35'·65N 02°25'·88W, Oc R 15s 11m 5M.
N Arm (C Hd) ☆ 50°35'·78N 02°25'·96W, Oc G 10s 11m 5M.
Wellworthy ☆ 50°35'·29N 02°27'·77W, Fl (4) 10s 3m 5M; W bn.
New Channel ☆ 50°34'·90N 02°27'·69W, L Fl 10s 3m 5M; W bn.
Ferrybridge ldg lts 288°: Front QG; rear Iso G 4s.

Portland Port, NW (or Q) pier head, ☆ 50°34'·38N 02°26'·28W, Fl R 5s 5m 5M.
NW Pier, elbow, ☆ 50°34'·35N 02°26'·42W, Fl R 2s 6m 2M.

▶WEYMOUTH

DG Range ⚓,Fl Y 2s, 50°36'·36N 02°26'·22W; plus 2 unlit ⚓s.
Ldg lts 239·6°: both FR 5/7m 7M; Front 50°36'·46N 02°26'·87W, R ♦ on W post; rear 17m from front, R ♦ on W mast.

N Pier hd ☆ 50°36'·59N 02°26'·63W, 2 FG (vert) 9m 6M.
S Pier hd ☆ 50°36'·57N 02°26'·49W, Q 10m 9M; tfc sigs 190m SW. Lifting bridge, tfc sigs (3FR or 3FG vert) 1000m W.
4 BY ⚓s, FlY 2·5s, within 1 cable of 50°35'·16N 02°21'·41W.

▶ LULWORTH COVE TO ANVIL POINT

Lulworth Cove ent, E point 50°37'·00N 02°14'·78W.
When firing in progress: Bindon Hill ☆ 50°37'·33N 02°13'·65W and St Alban's Hd ☆ 50°34'·75N 02°03'·40W, both Iso R 2s.
Atomic Outfall ⚓ 50°35'·03N 02°11'·64W, Fl Y 5s.

Naval target buoys on St Alban's Ledge:
DZ 'A' ⚓, Fl Y 2s, 50°33'·35N 02°06'·53W.
DZ 'B' ⚓, Fl Y 10s, 50°32'·11N 02°05'·92W.
DZ 'C' ⚓, Fl Y 5s, 50°32'·77N 02°04'·56W.
Anvil Pt ☆ 50°35'·51N 01°57'·60W, Fl 10s 45m **19M**; vis 237°-076° (H24); W ○ twr and dwelling.

9.1.5 PASSAGE INFORMATION

Current Pilots and guides include: The *Channel Cruising Companion* (Nautical Data Ltd/Featherstone & Aslett); *West Country Cruising Companion* (Nautical Data Ltd/Fishwick) and Admiralty *Channel Pilot* (NP 27). See 9.0.6 for distances across the Channel, and 9.3.5 for cross-Channel passages. Admiralty Leisure Folio SC5603 covers Scilly to Falmouth (and Padstow), SC5602 Falmouth to Teignmouth and SC5601 Exmouth to Christchurch. Each contains 12 A2 size charts in a clear plastic wallet and costs £37.50 (2004). Three new Admiralty Tidal stream atlases were published in 2003/2004: NP 255 Padstow to Falmouth including the Isles of Scilly; NP 254 Falmouth to Teignmouth; and NP 263 Lyme Bay.

NORTH CORNWALL (charts *1149, 1156*) For the coast of North Cornwall see 9.11.5. For St Ives to Padstow see 9.11.26. Certain information is repeated below for continuity and convenience.

The approaches to the Bristol Chan along N coast of Cornwall are very exposed, with little shelter in bad weather. From Land's End to St Ives the coast is rugged with high cliffs. Padstow is a refuge, except in strong NW winds. In these waters yachts need to be sturdy and well equipped, since if bad weather develops no shelter may be at hand. Streams are moderate W of Lundy, but strong around the island, and much stronger towards the Bristol Channel proper.

ISLES OF SCILLY (9.1.6 and charts *34, 883*) There are 50 islands, extending 21-31M WSW of Land's End, with many rky outcrops and offlying dangers. Although they are all well charted, care is needed particularly in poor vis. See 9.1.6 and 9.1.7 for details of this rewarding and compact cruising ground.

Several approach transits are shown on chart 34, and these should be followed, because the tidal streams around the islands are difficult to predict with accuracy. They run harder off points and over rks, where overfalls may occur. Yachts must expect to lie to their anchors. No one anchorage gives shelter from all winds and swell, so be ready to move at short notice.

Conspic landmarks are Bishop Rk lt ho, Round Island lt ho, the disused lt ho on St Agnes, the daymark at the E end of St Martin's, Penninis lt ho at the S end of St Mary's, and the TV mast and CG sig stn (at the old telegraph tower) both in the NW corner of St Mary's and visible from almost anywhere in Scilly.

ISLES OF SCILLY TO LAND'S END (chart *1148*) The Seven Stones (rks) lie 7M NE of the Isles of Scilly and 15M W of Land's End; many of them dry, with ledges in between. They are marked by lt F (fog sig) on E side. Wolf Rk (lt, fog sig) is 8M SW of Land's End, and is steep-to. The N/S lanes of Land's End TSS are roughly defined by the Longitude of Seven Stones to the west and of Wolf Rk to the east; both have Racons. The ITZ, W of Longships, is 3M wide; see 9.1.2.

▶*Between Scilly and Land's End (chart 1148) streams are rotatory, clockwise. Relative to HW Dover (sp rates about 1kn), they set W from HWD; N from HW + 2; NE from HW + 4; E from HW –6; SSE from HW – 4; and SW from HW – 2.*

For the 5-6hrs passage to Scilly leave the Runnel Stone at HWD–2; a fair W-going tide lasts for only 3hrs, with cross tides setting SW then NW to N. Consider arriving at dawn. For the return passage tidal streams are a little less critical.◀

LAND'S END (charts *1148, 1149, 777* and *2345*). The Land's End peninsula (30M Penzance to St Ives) is often a dangerous lee shore and always a critical tidal gate. There are many inshore and offlying rks and no ports of refuge. The main features are:

Gwennap Head, with the Runnel Stone (buoyed) 1M to the S; Land's End and Longships reef 1M to the W; Cape Cornwall and The Brisons; Pendeen Head and The Wra. Further to the E the coast of N Cornwall is described in 9.11.5.

The Runnel Stone (0·5m) lies 7ca S of Gwennap Hd, with rks and uncharted wrecks closer inshore. These dangers are in the R sectors of Longships and Tater-du lts. Passage between the Runnel Stone and Gwennap is not advised even in calm weather and at HW. From Gwennap Hd to Land's End, 2M NW, rks extend up to 1½ca offshore, and depths are irregular to seaward causing a bad sea in strong W winds over a W-going tide.

4 cables S of Land's End Armed Knight, a jagged 27m high rock, overlooks Longships. This is an extensive and very dangerous reef made up of Carn Bras, on which the lt ho stands, and other rky islets. About 5ca to the E and NE are Kettle's Bottom 5m and Shark's Fin 3·4m, both isolated and very dangerous drying rks. The ½M wide passage between Land's End and Kettle's Bottom is safe in calm, settled weather, but never at night. To clear Kettle's Bottom and Shark's Fin, keep the Brisons High summit just open W of Low summit brg 001°. ▶*Local streams exceed 4kn at Sp and are unpredictable.*◀ In adverse weather navigate in the ITZ, well W of Longships.

Whitesand Bay (chart 2345) is 1M NNE of Land's End. After rounding Cowloe Rks and its drying offliers, Little Bo 3·4m and Bo Cowloe 6m, the transit 150° of two bns on the cliffs E of Sennen Cove leads to a fair weather ⚓ in about 2m on the S side of the bay, only safe in offshore winds. Sennen Ch tr (110m) is conspic, almost on this transit.

Cape Cornwall (conspic ruined chy) is about 3M further N. It overlooks The Brisons, two rky islets (27 and 22m, High and Low summits) about 5ca to SW. There is no safe passage inside The Brisons. The Vyneck is a rk drying 1·8m 3ca NW of Cape Cornwall.

3M to NNE is Pendeen Hd (lt ho) and the Wra (or Three Stone Oar), drying rks, close N. Between C Cornwall and Pendeen overfalls and a race extend up to 1½M offshore; avoid except in calm weather and at slack water. Midway between Cape Cornwall and Pendeen a conspic TV mast is 1M inland.

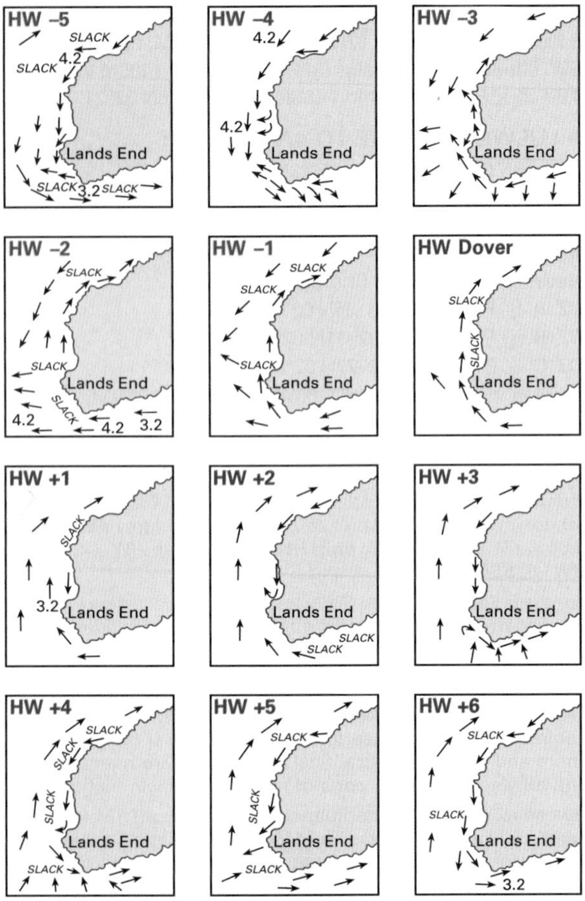
HW –5
SLACK
SLACK 4.2
Lands End
SLACK 3.2 SLACK
HW –4
4.2
4.2
Lands End
HW –3
Lands End
HW –2
SLACK
SLACK
Lands End
SLACK
4.2
4.2 3.2
HW –1
SLACK
SLACK
SLACK
Lands End
HW Dover
SLACK
SLACK
Lands End
HW +1
SLACK
3.2
Lands End
HW +2
Lands End
SLACK
SLACK
HW +3
Lands End
HW +4
SLACK
SLACK
SLACK
Lands End
SLACK
HW +5
SLACK
SLACK
Lands End
SLACK
HW +6
SLACK
SLACK
Lands End
3.2

The Editors thank most warmly the Royal Cruising Club Pilotage Foundation for their kind permission to use material written by Hugh Davies and first published in Yachting Monthly magazine. This includes the unique tidal stream chartlets above which are of major assistance in rounding Land's End.

▶***Tidal Strategy*** *Streams run hard round Land's End, setting N/S and E/W past it. It is truly a tidal gate, and one which favours a N-bound passage – with careful timing nearly $9\frac{1}{2}$ hrs of fair tide can be carried, from HWD –3 to HWD +5. Stay close inshore to use currents running counter to the tidal streams. The chartlets referenced to HW Dover, illustrate tidal streams and inshore currents.*

Example N-bound: At HWD+1 the N-going flood starts off Gwennap and does not turn NE along the N Cornish coast until HWD+3, but as early as HWD–3 an inshore current is beginning to run N'ly. So, N-bound, use this by arriving off Runnel Stone at HWD–2 and then keep within $\frac{1}{4}$M of the shore. If abeam Brisons at HWD, the tide and current should serve for the next 6 or 7 hrs to make good St Ives, or even Newquay and Padstow.

Example S-bound: If S-bound from St Ives to Newlyn, aim to reach the Runnel Stone by HWD+5, ie with 2 hrs of E-going tide in hand for the remaining 9M to Newlyn. This would entail leaving St Ives 5 hrs earlier, at HWD, to make the 20M passage; buck a foul tide for the first 3 hrs but use an inshore S-going current, keeping as close inshore as prudent, but having to move offshore to clear the Wra and the Brisons. This timing would suit passage from S Wales and Bristol Chan, going inshore of Longships if the weather suits.

From Ireland, ie Cork or further W, the inshore passage would not benefit. But plan to be off the Runnel Stone at HWD+5 if bound for Newlyn; or at HWD+3 if bound for Helford/Falmouth, with the W-going stream slackening and 5 hrs of fair tide to cover the remaining 20M past the Lizard.◀

GWENNAP HEAD TO LIZARD POINT (chart *777*) Close E of Gwennap there is no anch off Porth Curno, due to cables. Approaching Mount's Bay, the Bucks (3·3m) are 2ca ESE of Tater-du lt ho. Gull Rk (24m) is 9ca NE of Tater-du, close off the E point of Lamorna Cove. Little Heaver (dries) is 100m SW of Gull Rk, and Kemyel Rk (dries) is $1\frac{3}{4}$ca ENE. Mousehole (9.1.8) is a small drying hbr, sheltered from W and N, but exposed to E or S winds, when ent may be shut. Approach from SW side of St Clement's Is. In W winds there is good anch off the hbr.

Low Lee, a dangerous rk (1·1m) marked by ECM lt buoy, is 4ca NE of Penlee Pt. Carn Base (rock 1·8m) lies 3ca NNW of Low Lee. Newlyn (9.1.8) is the only hbr in Mount's B safe to appr in strong onshore winds, but only near HW. From here to Penzance (9.1.9) beware unmarked Dog Rk (1·1m) and The Gear (1·9m, IDM lt bcn).

From Penzance to St Michael's Mount the head of the Bay is shoal, drying 4ca off in places. Dangers include Cressar Rks, Long Rk, Hogus Rks, and Outer Penzeath Rk. Venton chy on with pierheads of St Michael's Mount hbr at 084° leads S of these dangers. This tiny hbr dries 2·1m, but is well sheltered, with anch about 1ca W of ent, see 9.1.9.

Two dangerous rks, Guthen Rk and Maltman Rk (0·9m), lie 2ca W and S of St Michael's Mount. 1M SE is The Greeb (7m), with rks between it and shore. The Bears (dry) lie $1\frac{3}{4}$ca E of The Greeb. The Stone (dries) is 5ca S of Cudden Pt, while offshore is Mountamopus shoal marked by a SCM lt buoy. Welloe Rk (0·8m) lies 5ca SW of Trewavas Hd.

Porthleven is a small tidal hbr, entered between Great and Little Trigg Rks and pier on S side. Dry out alongside in inner hbr, closed in bad weather when appr is dangerous. In fair weather there is good anch off Porth Mellin, about $1\frac{1}{2}$ca NE of Mullion Is; Porth Mellin hbr (dries) is for temp use only. 2·5M W of Lizard Pt is The Boa, a rky shoal on which sea breaks in SW gales.

Lizard Point (lt, fog sig) is a bold, steep headland (chart 2345). From W to E, the outer rks, all drying, are Mulvin, ($2\frac{1}{2}$ca SW of Lizard Pt), Taylor's Rk (2ca SSW); Clidgas Rks (5ca SW of lt ho), Men Hyr Rk (4·1m) and the Dales or Stags (5ca SSW), and Enoch Rk (3ca S). A dangerous race extends 2-3M S when stream is strong in either direction, worst in W'ly winds against W-going tide. There may be a race SE of the Lizard. ▶*Keep at least 3M to seaward if going outside the race where slack water occurs at about HW Devonport –3 and +3. Closer inshore the stream turns E at HW Devonport –5, and W at HW +2, rates up to 3kn at sp. An inshore passage is shorter, but is never free of rough water.*◀ Either side of local LW ($\frac{1}{2}$hr before LW Devonport = HW Dover) the drying rks above will be visible, but beware Vrogue, a dangerous sunken rk (1·8m), 1M E of the Lizard lt ho, and Craggan Rks (1·5m) 1M N of Vrogue Rk. If awaiting slack water, there are, from W to E, ⚓s at Kynance Cove, Housel Cove (NE of the lt ho and below conspic hotel), Church Cove, Cadgwith and Coverack.

LIZARD POINT TO GRIBBIN HEAD (chart *1267*) N of Black Head rks extend at least 1ca offshore; a rk drying 1·6m lies off Chynhalls Pt. Coverack gives good anch in W winds, see 9.1.10. From Dolor Pt to E of Lowland Pt are drying rks $2\frac{1}{2}$ca offshore. The Manacles (dry), $7\frac{1}{2}$ca E and SE of Manacle Pt, are marked by ECM lt buoy and are in R sector of St Anthony Hd lt. ▶*Off the Manacles the stream runs NE from HW Devonport – 0345, and SW from HW+ 0200, sp rates 1·25kn.*◀ From E of the Manacles there are no offshore dangers on courses NNW to Helford River ent (9.1.10) or N to River Fal (9.1.11).

3M NNE from St Anthony Hd, Porthscatho offers safe anch in W'lies (9.1.12). Gull Rk (38m high) lies 6ca E of Nare Hd, at W side of Veryan B. The Whelps (dry 4·6m) are 5ca SW of Gull Rk. There is a passage between Gull Rk and the shore. In Veryan B beware Lath Rk (2·1m) 1M SE of Portloe.

On E side of Veryan B, Dodman Pt is a 110m rounded shoulder, with a conspic stone cross. Depths are irregular for 1M S, with heavy overfalls in strong winds over sp tide, when it is best to pass 2M off. 3 SPM lt buoys (targets) lie 2·3 to 4·8M SSE of Dodman Pt. For details of naval gunnery practice between Dodman Pt and Gribbin Head, see 9.1.13.

Gorran Haven, a sandy cove with L-shaped pier which dries at sp, is a good anch in offshore winds. 2·1M NE of Dodman Pt, and 1M ENE of Gorran Haven, is Gwineas Rk (8m high) and Yaw Rk (0·9m), marked by ECM lt buoy. Passage inside Gwineas Rk is possible, but not advised in strong onshore winds or poor vis. Portmellon and Mevagissey B, (9.1.12) are good anchs in offshore winds. For Charlestown and Par, see 9.1.13.

GRIBBIN HEAD TO START POINT (charts *1267, 1613*) Gribbin Hd has a conspic daymark, a □ tr 25m high with R & W bands. In bad weather the sea breaks on rocks round Head. Cannis Rk (4·3m) is 2½ca SE, marked by SCM lt buoy. 3M E of Fowey (9.1.13) is Udder Rk (0·6m) marked by a SCM lt buoy, 5ca offshore in E part of Lantivet Bay. Larrick Rk (4·3m) is 1½ca off Nealand Pt.

Polperro hbr dries, but the inlet gives good anch in offshore winds, see 9.1.13. Beware E Polca Rk roughly in mid-chan. E of Polperro shoals lie 2½ca off Downend Point. The chan between Hannafore Pt and Looe Island nearly dries. The Ranneys (dry) are rks extending 2½ca E and SE of the Island, see 9.1.14. S of Looe Island there are overfalls in bad weather. A buoyed artificial reef (ex-HMS Scylla) lies 1·4M NW of Rame Hd.

Eddystone rks (chart 1613) lie 8M S of Rame Hd. Shoals extend 3ca E. Close NW of the lt ho is the stump of the old lt ho. The sea can break on Hand Deeps, sunken rks 3·4M NW of Eddystone, marked by a WCM light buoy.

Rame Hd, on W side of ent to Plymouth Sound (9.1.15), is conspic cone-shaped, with small chapel on top; rks extend about 1ca off and wind-over-tide overfalls may be met 1·5M to seaward. Approaching Plymouth from the W, clear Rame Hd and Penlee Point by about 8ca, then steer NNE for W end of the Breakwater. At the SE ent to Plymouth Sound, Great Mewstone (59m) is a conspic rky islet 4ca off Wembury Pt. Approaching from the E keep at least 1M offshore until clear of the drying Mewstone Ledge, 2½ca SW of Great Mewstone. The Slimers, which dry, lie 2ca E of Mewstone. E and W Ebb Rks (awash) lie 2½ca off Gara Pt (chart 30). Wembury Bay gives access to R. Yealm (9.1.17).

See 9.1.16 for naval exercise areas from the Isles of Scilly to Start Point. These areas are used by submarines and warships, especially near Plymouth. Yachts should try to stay clear.

Between Gara Pt and Stoke Pt, 2·5M to E, dangers extend about 4ca offshore in places. In Bigbury Bay beware Wells Rk and other dangers 5ca S of Erme Hd. From Bolt Tail to Bolt Hd keep 5ca offshore to clear Greystone Ledge, sunken rks near Ham Stone (11m), and Gregory Rks 5ca SE of Ham Stone. The Little Mew Stone and Mew Stone lie below dramatic Bolt Head. Keep approx 7½ca SE of the Mewstones before turning N for Salcombe (9.1.18).

START POINT TO STRAIGHT POINT (charts *1613, 3315*) Start Pt (lt, horn) is 3M ENE of Prawle Pt; it is a long headland with conspic radio masts, distinctive cock's comb spine and W lt ho near end. Black Stone rk is visible (6m high) 2½ca SSE of the lt ho, with Cherrick Rks (1m) a cable further S; other drying rks lie closer inshore. The stream runs 4kn at sp, causing a race extending 1½M to the E and 1M to the S. In fair weather the overfalls can be avoided by passing close to seaward of rks; there is no clear-cut inshore passage as such. ▶*In bad weather keep at least 2M off. 1M off Start the stream sets SW from HW Devonport +4 to HW–3, and NE from HW–2 to HW+3; thus slack water is about HW–2½ and HW +3½. Inshore it turns 30 minutes earlier.*◀

Skerries Bank, on which sea breaks in bad weather, is 6ca NNE of Start Point (chart 1634). It has least depth of 2·1m at the S end, only 9ca NE of Start Pt. In offshore winds there is good anch in 3m 1ca off Hallsands (1M NW of Start). Between Dartmouth (9.1.19) and Brixham (9.1.20) rks extend 5ca offshore.

Berry Head (lt) is a bold, flat-topped headland (55m), giving a good radar return. ▶*Here the stream turns N at HW Devonport – 0105, and S at HW+ 0440, sp rates 1·5kn.*◀ In Torbay (chart 26) the more obvious dangers are steep-to, but beware the Sunker 100m SW of Ore Stone, and Morris Rogue 5ca W of Thatcher Rk.

There are good anchs in Babbacombe B and in Anstey's cove in W winds; beware the Three Brothers (drying rks), S side of Anstey's cove. From Long Quarry Pt for 4M N to Teignmouth (9.1.22) there are no offlying dangers. ▶*Off Teignmouth the NNE-going stream begins at HW Devonport – 0135, and the SSW-going at HW+ 0510. In the ent the flood begins at HW Devonport – 0535, and the ebb at HW +0040. The stream runs hard off Ferry Pt; the ent is dangerous in onshore winds.*◀

Between Teignmouth and Dawlish rks extend 1ca offshore. Beware Dawlish Rk (2·1m) about 5ca off N end of town. Warren Sands and Pole Sands lie W of ent to the River Exe (9.1.23), and are liable to shift. Along the Exmouth side of the chan, towards Orcomb Pt and Straight Pt (lt), drying rks and shoals extend up to 2½ca offshore. There is a firing range at Straight Point with danger area extending 1·5M east, marked by two DZ lt buoys.

LYME BAY (chart 3315). Lyme Bay stretches 50M ENE from Start Pt to Portland Bill. ▶*Tides are weak, rarely more than 0·75kn. From west to east the tidal curve becomes progressively more distorted, especially on the rising tide. The rise is relatively fast for the 1st hr after LW; then slackens noticeably for the next 1½ hrs, before resuming the rapid rate of rise. There is often a stand at HW, not very noticeable at Start Point but lasting about 1½ hrs at Lyme Regis.*◀

Between Torbay and Portland there is no hbr accessible in onshore winds, and yachtsmen must take care not to be caught on a lee shore. There are no dangers offshore. In offshore winds there is a good anch NE of Beer Hd, the western-most chalk cliff in England. 3·5M E of Lyme Regis (9.1.24) is Golden Cap (186m and conspic). High Ground and Pollock are rks 7ca offshore, 2M and 3M ESE of Golden Cap.

From 6M E of Bridport (9.1.25), Chesil Beach runs SE for about 8M to the N end of the Portland peninsula. From a distance The Isle of Portland does indeed look like an island, with its distinctive wedge-shaped profile sloping down from 144m at the N to the Bill at the S tip. Although mostly steep-to, an 18m high, white obelisk on the tip of the Bill warns of a rocky ledge extending about 50m S of the Bill. If the topmost window on the lighthouse appear above the top of the obelisk, you are clear of the outermost rock, but still very close inshore.

If heading up-Channel from Start Point, Dartmouth or Torbay time your departure to pass Portland Bill with a fair tide at all costs, especially at springs. If late, there is temp'y anchorage close inshore at Chesil Cove, abeam the highest part of Portland.

Continued overleaf

THE PORTLAND RACE (chart *2255*) South of the Bill lies Portland Race in which severe and very dangerous sea states occur. Even in settled weather it should be carefully avoided by small craft, although at neaps it may be barely perceptible.

The Race occurs at the confluence of two strong S-going tidal streams which run down each side of Portland for almost 10 hours out of 12 at springs. These streams meet the main E-W stream of the Channel, producing large eddies on either side of Portland and a highly confused sea state with heavy overfalls in the Race. The irregular contours of the sea-bed, which shoals abruptly from depths of over 100m some 2M south of the Bill to as little as 9m on Portland Ledge 1M further N, greatly contribute to the violence of the Race. Portland Ledge strongly deflects the flow of water upwards, so that on the flood the Race lies SE of the Bill and vice versa on the ebb. Conditions deteriorate with wind-against-tide, especially at springs; in an E'ly gale against the flood stream the Race may spread eastward to The Shambles bank. The Race normally extends about 2M S of the Bill, but further S in bad weather.

►*The Tidal Stream chartlets at 9.1.27 show the approx hourly positions of the Race. They are referenced to HW Plymouth (Devonport), to accord with the Admiralty Tidal Stream Atlas NP257 Approaches to Portland. They are also sub-referenced to HW Portland and Dover for those leaving Weymouth or for those on passage S of the Bill. The smaller scale chartlets at 9.2.3 show the main English Channel streams referenced to HW at Dover and Portsmouth.*◄

Small craft may avoid the Race either by passing clear to seaward of it, between 3 and 5M S of the Bill; or by using the inshore passage if conditions suit. This passage is a stretch of relatively smooth water between 1ca and 3ca off the Bill (depending on wind), which should not however be used at night under power due to lobster pots. ►*Timing is important to catch "slackish" water around the Bill, i.e:*

Westbound: from HW Plymouth + 5 to HW – 5
(HW Dover – 1 to HW + 2, or HW Portland + 4 to HW – 6).
Eastbound: from HW Plymouth – 2 to HW + 2
(HW Dover + 5 to HW – 4, or HW Portland – 3 to HW + 1).

From either direction, close Portland at least 2M N of the Bill to utilise the S-going stream; once round the Bill, the N-going stream will set a yacht away from the Race area.◄

PORTLAND BILL TO ANVIL POINT (chart *2610*) The Shambles bank is about 3M E of Portland Bill, and should be avoided at all times. In bad weather the sea breaks heavily on it. It is marked by buoys on its E and W ends. E of Weymouth are rky ledges extending 3ca offshore as far as Lulworth Cove, which provides a reasonable anch in fine, settled weather and offshore winds; as do Worbarrow Bay and Chapman's Pool (9.1.29).

A firing range extends 5M offshore between Lulworth and St Alban's Hd. Yachts should avoid the range when it is in use or pass through the area as quickly as possible; see 9.1.29. Beware Kimmeridge Ledges, which extend over 5ca seaward.

St Alban's Head (107m and conspic) is steep-to and has a dangerous race off it which may extend 3M seaward. The race lies to the E on the flood and to the W on the ebb; the latter is the more dangerous. A narrow passage, at most 5ca wide and very close inshore, avoids the worst of the overfalls; do not expect to get away with dry decks. ►*There is an eddy on W side of St Alban's Head, where the stream runs almost continuously SE. 1M S of St Alban's Head the ESE stream begins at HW Portsmouth + 0520, and the WNW stream at HW –0030, with sp rates of 4·75kn.*◄

The cliffy coastline between St Alban's Hd and Anvil Pt (lt) is steep-to quite close inshore. Measured mile beacons stand either side of Anvil Pt lt ho; the track is 083.5°.

9.1.6 ISLES OF SCILLY

The Isles of Scilly are made up of 48 islands and numerous rocky outcrops, covering an area approx 10M by 7M and lying 21 – 31M WSW of Land's End. Only six islands are inhabited: St Mary's, St Martin's, Tresco, Bryher, St Agnes and Gugh. The islands belong to the Duchy of Cornwall. Arrangements for visiting uninhabited islands are given in a booklet *Duchy of Cornwall - Information for visiting craft* obtainable from HM, Hugh Town Hbr, St Mary's. There is a LB and CG Sector Base at St Mary's. **Historic Wrecks** (see 9.0.3h) are at 49°52'·2N 06°26'·5W Tearing Ledge, 2ca SE of Bishop Rk Lt; and at 49°54'·30N 06°19'·89W, Bartholomew Ledges, 5ca N of Gugh.

CHARTS AC 1148 (Scilly to Lands End), *34, 883* (both essential); Imray C7; Stanfords 2, 13; OS 203

TIDES Standard Port is Devonport. Differences for St Mary's are given in 9.1.7. Tidal heights, times, and streams are irregular. See overleaf for 12 hourly tidal stream chartlets and AC 34 for 5 tidal stream diamonds, all referred to HW Plymouth.

SHELTER The Isles of Scilly are exposed to Atlantic swell and wind. Weather can be unpredictable and fast-changing. It is not a place for inexperienced navigators or poorly equipped yachts. Normal yacht ⚓s may drag on fine sand, even with plenty of scope, but holding is mostly good. That said, the islands are attractive, interesting and rewarding. The following are some of the many ⚓s, anti-clockwise:

HUGH TOWN HBR (St Mary's). See 9.1.7.

PORTH CRESSA (St Mary's, S of Hugh Town). Beware of dangers on each side of ent and submarine cables. Good ⚓ (2m) in W/NW'lies, but exposed to swell from SE to SW.

WATERMILL COVE (NE corner of St Mary's). Excellent shelter in winds S to NW. ⚓ in approx 5m.

TEAN SOUND (St Martin's, W end). Needs careful pilotage, but attractive ⚓ in better weather. More suitable for shoal draught boats which can ⚓ or take the ground out of main tidal stream in chan. **St Martin's Hotel** ☎ 422092, D, FW, 7 Ⓜs £10 inc showers, 🛒, R, Bar. Several other ⚓s can be used in settled weather.

ST HELEN'S POOL (S of St Helen's Is). Ent via St Helen's Gap to ⚓ in 1·5m - 7m. Secure, but may be swell near HW; see chartlet.

OLD GRIMSBY (NE side of Tresco). Green Porth & Raven's Porth, divided by a quay, form the Old Grimsby Hbr; both dry 2·3m. Beware cable in Green Porth. ⚓s 1½ca NE of quay in 2·5m; access more difficult than New Grimsby. Well sheltered in SW'lies but open to swell if wind veers N of W. Facilities: 6 Ⓜs (R cans) £10, L (quay), hotel, slip.

NEW GRIMSBY (between Tresco and Bryher; see chartlet). Appr (line E) through New Grimsby Sound, or with adequate rise of tide across Tresco Flats. Good shelter except in NW'lies. Popular ⚓ between Hangman Is and the quay in 1·5 - 4·5m. Beware cables. 22 Ⓜs £10 via Tresco Estate ☎ 22849, 📠 22807; VHF Ch 08 for R, Bar, FW, 🛒, ✉. Ferry to St Mary's.

THE COVE (St Agnes/Gugh). Well sheltered from W and N winds, except when the sand bar between the islands covers near HWS with a strong NW wind. Beware cables.

PORTH CONGER (St Agnes/Gugh). On the N side of the sandbar, sheltered in winds from E through S to W. May be uncomfortable when the bar is covered. Facilities: L (two quays), ferry to St Mary's; in Middle Town (¾M), St Agnes, 🛒, ✉, R, Bar.

NAVIGATION For TSS to the E, S and W, see 9.1.2. If unable to identify approach ldg lines/marks, then it is best to lie off. Many chans between islands have dangerous shallows, often with rky ledges. Some of the commoner ldg lines, as on chartlet, include:

Line A: *North Carn of Mincarlo ≠ W extremity of Great Minalto 307·1°.* This is the usual ent to St Mary's Road, via St Mary's Sound. From the E or SE avoid Gilstone Rk (dries 4m) 3ca E of Peninnis Hd. Spanish Ledges, off Gugh, are marked by an ECM buoy; thence past Woolpack SCM bn, Bartholomew Ledges lt bcn and N Bartholomew PHM buoy Fl R 5s to ent St Mary's Rd on 040·5° (see Line B).

Line B: *St Martin's daymark ≠ the summit of Creeb 040·5°.* This clears Woodcock Ledge which breaks in bad weather.

Line C: *Summit of Castle Bryher ≠ gap between the summits of Great Smith 350·5°.* This passes through Smith Sound, between the drying rocks off St Agnes and Annet.

Line D: *Summit of Great Ganilly just open north of Bant's Carn 059°*. From the SW enter Broad Sound between Bishop Rk lt ho and Flemming's Ledge, 7ca to the N; pass between Round Rk NCM and Gunner SCM buoys to Old Wreck NCM By; beware Jeffrey Rk, close to port. Ldg marks are more than 7M off and at first not easy to see. Smith Sound, 350° between St Agnes and Annet may also be used.

Line E: *St Agnes Old lt ho ≠ Carn Irish 099·7°*. From WNW, this line goes close N of Crim Rocks and the Gunners.

Line F: *St Agnes Old lt ho ≠ Tins Walbert bcn 127°*. The NW Passage is about 7ca wide with good ldg marks, but beware cross tide. A WCM lt buoy marks Steeple Rk (0·1m). Intercept Line D for St Mary's Road.

Line G: *Star Castle Hotel ≠ W side of Hangman Is 157°*. From the N, leads into New Grimsby Sound between Bryher and Tresco. Crossing Tresco Flats need adequate rise of tide (plan for max drying ht of 1·7m) and moderate vis.

Line H: *Summit of Samson Hill ≠ the NE extremity of Innisidgen 284·5°*. From the E or NE: Crow Sound can be rough in strong E or S winds, but, with sufficient rise of tide, is not difficult. From the NE pass close to Menawethan and Biggal Rk, avoiding Trinity Rk and the Ridge, which break in bad weather. Hats SCM buoy marks a shoal with an old boiler, (0·6m) on it. Maintain 284·5° between Bar Pt and Crow Bar (0·7m), passing N of Crow Rk IDM lt bn (for best water), then turn SSW for St Mary's.

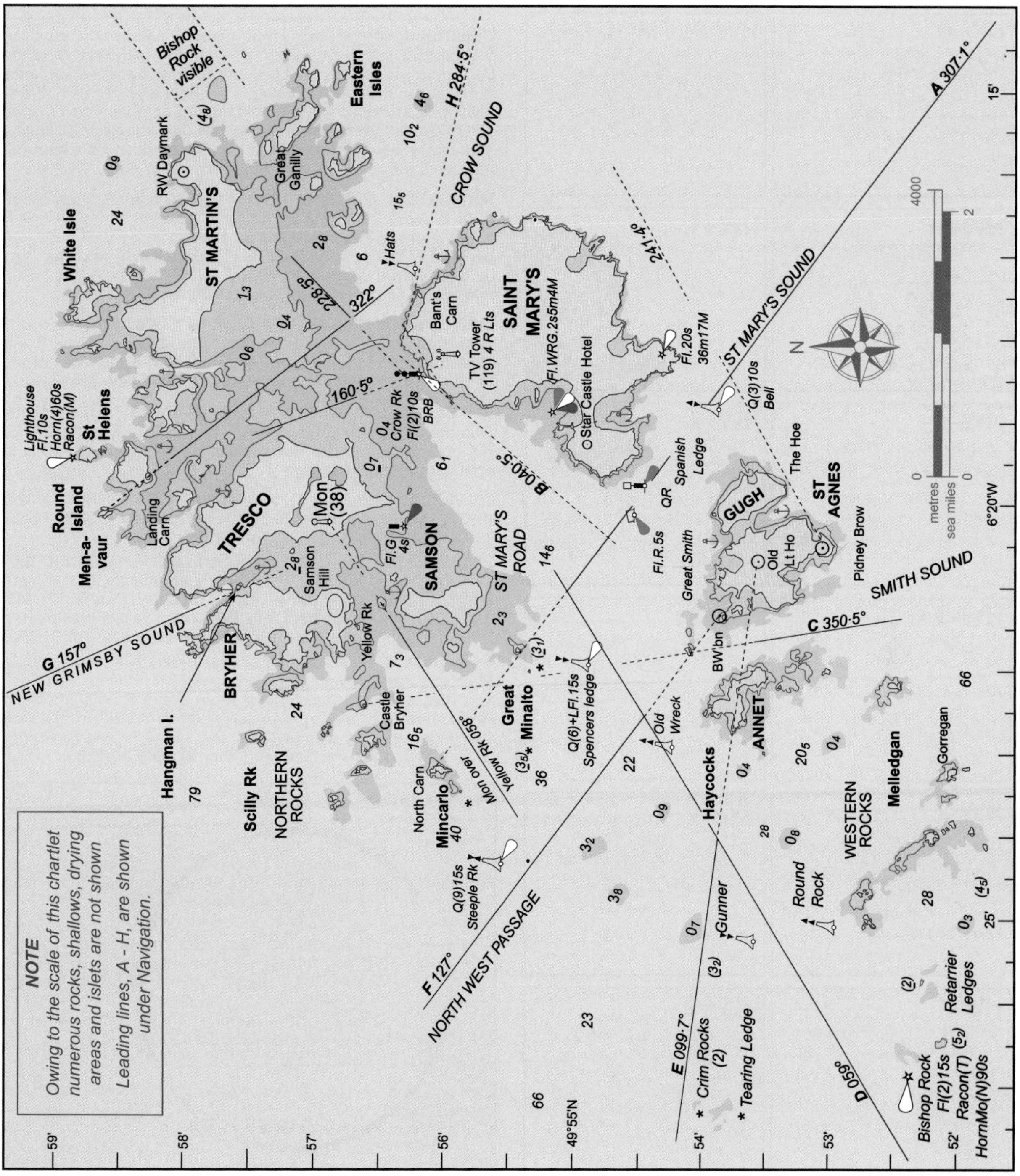
NOTE
Owing to the scale of this chartlet numerous rocks, shallows, drying areas and islets are not shown
Leading lines, A - H, are shown under Navigation.
Bishop Rock visible
Eastern Isles
H 284·5°
CROW SOUND
ST MARTIN'S
RW Daymark
Great Ganilly
White Isle
Hats
SAINT MARY'S
Bant's Carn
TV Tower (119) 4 R Lts
Fl.WRG.2s5m4M
Star Castle Hotel
Fl.20s 36m17M
241·4°
228·5°
322°
160·5°
Lighthouse Fl.10s Horn(4)60s Racon(M)
St Helens
Round Island
Men-a-vaur
TRESCO
Landing Carn
Crow Rk Fl(2)10s BRB
Mon (38)
Samson Hill
SAMSON
Fl.G 4s
ST MARY'S ROAD
B 040·5°
ST MARY'S SOUND
Q(3)10s Bell
A 307·1°
Spanish Ledge
QR
Fl.R.5s
Great Smith
GUGH
The Hoe
ST AGNES
Old Lt Ho
Pidney Brow
SMITH SOUND
C 350·5°
BW bn
G 157°
NEW GRIMSBY SOUND
BRYHER
Hangman I.
Yellow Rk
Castle Bryher
Yellow Rk 058° Mon over
Great Minalto
Q(6)+LFl.15s Spencers ledge
Old Wreck
ANNET
Scilly Rk
NORTHERN ROCKS
North Carn
Mincarlo
Haycocks
WESTERN ROCKS
Melledgan
Gorregan
Q(9)15s Steeple Rk
Round Rock
Gunner
NORTH WEST PASSAGE
F 127°
E 099·7°
Crim Rocks
Tearing Ledge
D 059°
Bishop Rock Fl(2)15s Racon(T) HornMo(N)90s
Retarrier Ledges
metres
sea miles
49°55'N
6°20'W

LIGHTS AND MARKS See 9.1.4 for lts, including Seven Stones lt float, Wolf Rock lt ho and Longships lt ho. A working knowledge of the following daymarks and conspic features will greatly aid pilotage (from NE to SW):
St Martin's E end: Conical bcn twr (56m) with RW bands.
Round Is: roughly conical shaped, with W lt ho 19/55m high.
Tresco: Abbey & FS, best seen from S. Cromwell's Castle and Hangman Is from the NW.
Bryher: Watch Hill, stone bn (43m); rounded Samson Hill.
St Mary's: TV & radio masts at N end, all with R lts, are visible from anywhere in Scilly. Crow Rk IDM bn, 11m on rk drying 4·6m, at N.
St Agnes: Old lt ho, ○ W tr, visible from all directions.
Bishop Rk lt ho: Grey ○ tr, 44m; helo pad above lamp.

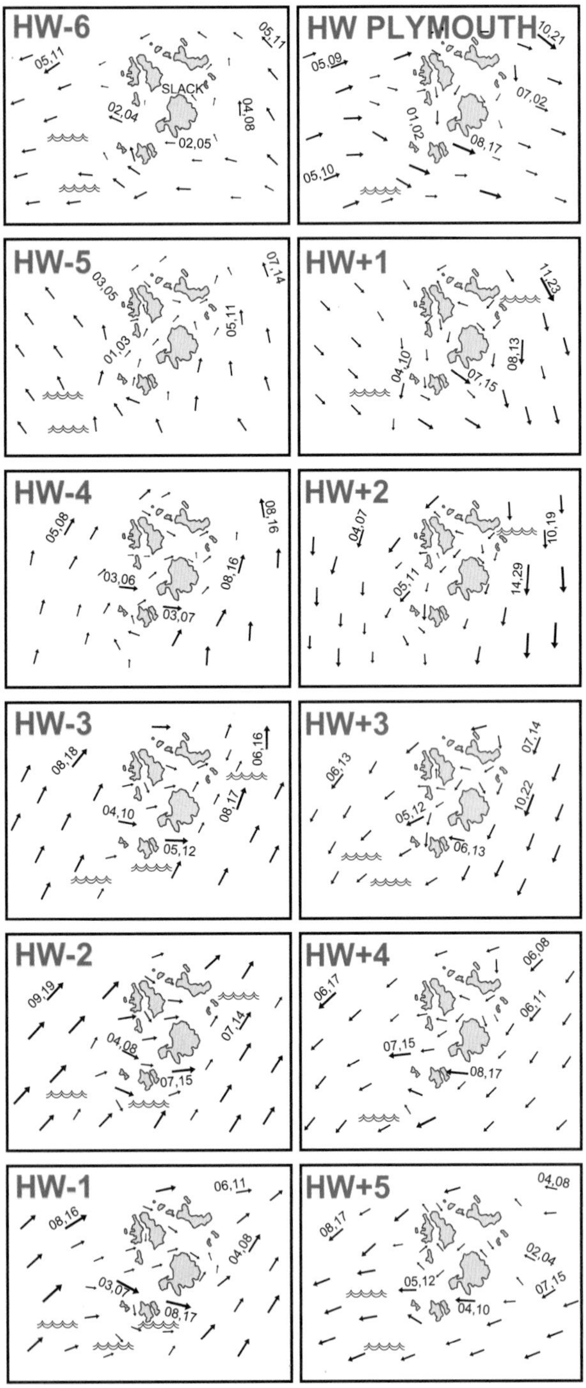
HW-6
SLACK
HW PLYMOUTH
HW-5
HW+1
HW-4
HW+2
HW-3
HW+3
HW-2
HW+4
HW-1
HW+5

9.1.7 ST MARY'S

Isles of Scilly **49°55'·14N 06°18'·71W**

CHARTS AC *34, 883*; Imray C7; Stanfords 2; OS 203

TIDES –0630 Dover; ML 3·2; Duration 0600; Zone 0 (UT)

Standard Port PLYMOUTH (⟶)

Times				**Height (metres)**			
High Water		Low Water		MHWS	MHWN	MLWN	MLWS
0000	0600	0000	0600	5·4	4·3	2·1	0·8
1200	1800	1200	1800				
Differences ST MARY'S							
–0035	–0100	–0040	–0025	+0·2	–0·1	–0·2	–0·1

SHELTER Good in St Mary's Pool where 38 Y 🅐s lie in 5 trots close E of the LB ⌂ in 1·5-2·1m. No ⚓ S of a line from the pier hd to the LB slip; to seaward of the LB ⌂; off the pier hd where the ferry turns, and in the apprs. Holding in the Pool is poor and in W/NW gales it is notorious for yachts dragging ⚓, when Porth Cressa (9.1.6) is safer. Hbr speed limit 3kn. NB: do not impede *Scillonian III* the ferry which arrives about 1200 and sails at 1630 Mon-Fri; Sat times vary with month. Also cargo ship thrice weekly.

NAVIGATION WPT 49°53'·96N 06°18'·83W (abm Spanish Ledge ECM lt buoy) 307°/1·2M via St Mary's Sound to transit line B (040°). The 097·3° transit leads S of Bacon Ledge (0·3m) marked by PHM lt buoy. A charted 151° transit leads into the Pool between Bacon Ledge and the Cow & Calf (drying 0·6 and 1·8m). Pilotage is compulsory for yachts >30m LOA.

LIGHTS AND MARKS See chartlet and 9.1.4. 097·3° ldg marks: W bcns; front, orange △; rear, orange x; lts as chartlet. The R and G sectors of the Pierhd lt are not on the expected sides of the W sector. Buzza Hill twr and power stn chy (48m) are conspic.

R/T *St Mary's Hbr* VHF Ch 14 16 (0800-1700LT). Pilot Ch 69 16. *Falmouth CG* gives radio cover Ch 16, 23 of Scilly and the TSS/ITZ off Land's End. Do not hesitate to call Falmouth CG if in emergency/gales/dragging ⚓.

TELEPHONE (Dial code 01720) HM ☎/📠 422768; MRCC (01326) 317575; Marinecall 09066 526242; Ⓗ 422392; Dr 422628; Police 08705 777444; Pilot 422066; Tourist Info 422536.

FACILITIES D & FW at pier outer berth 0930-1100 & 1630-1800 Mon-Fri; OT see HM for FW (nil or limited quantity in summer). D ☎ Sibleys 422431; P (cans) via HM; Gas, Gaz, Slip, ⚒, CH, ME, SM, El. Hbr Office will hold mail for visiting yachts if addressed c/o HM, Hugh Town, TR21 0HU. **Hbr 🅐 dues:** £10 <18m LOA.

Hugh Town EC Wed; essential shops, R, Bar, ACA, 🏪, ✉, Ⓑ, ⊡. **Mainland access**: Ferry dep Penzance 0915 Mon-Fri (not Sun) and 1630 St Mary's (Sat varies); about 2¾hrs crossing, booking ☎ 0345-105555 (see also 9.0.4). Helicopter (☎ 422646) to Penzance (⇄) and fixed wing ✈ to St Just (Land's End), Exeter, Newquay, Bristol, Plymouth and Southampton, ☎ 0345 105555.

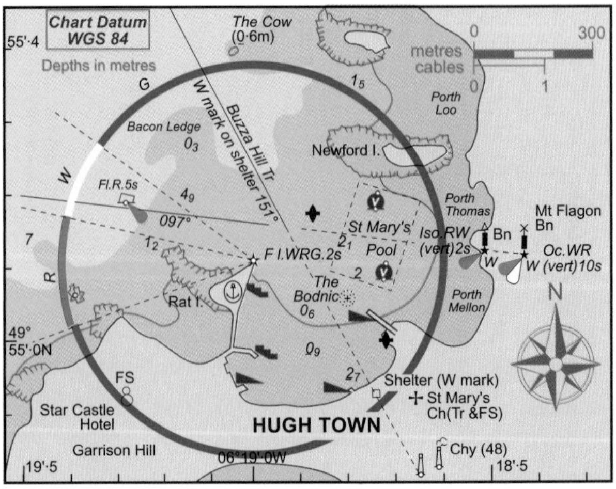
Chart Datum WGS 84
Depths in metres
55'·4
The Cow (0·6m)
metres
cables
Porth Loo
Bacon Ledge
Buzza Hill Tr
W mark on shelter 151°
Newford I.
Fl.R.5s
097°
Porth Thomas
Mt Flagon Bn
St Mary's Pool
Iso RW (vert)2s
Bn
Oc.WR W (vert)10s
F I.WRG.2s
The Bodnic
Rat I.
Porth Mellon
49° 55'·0N
FS
Shelter (W mark)
St Mary's Ch(Tr &FS)
Star Castle Hotel
HUGH TOWN
Garrison Hill
Chy (48)
06°19'·0W
19'·5
18'·5

9.1.8 NEWLYN

Cornwall **50°06'·19N 05°32'.58W**

CHARTS AC 777, 2345; Imray C7, 2400.10; Stanfords 2; OS 203

TIDES –0635 Dover; ML 3·2; Duration 0555; Zone 0 (UT)

Standard Port PLYMOUTH (⟶)

Times				Height (metres)			
High Water		Low Water		MHWS	MHWN	MLWN	MLWS
0000	0600	0000	0600	5·4	4·3	2·1	0·8
1200	1800	1200	1800				
Differences NEWLYN							
–0040	–0110	–0035	–0025	+0·1	0·0	–0·2	0·0

SHELTER Good, except in SE winds when heavy swell enters hbr; access at all tides. FVs have priority. Yachts berth on SW side of Mary Williams Pier, usually rafted on a FV. No visitor moorings, no ⚓ in hbr. Good ⚓ in Gwavas Lake in offshore winds.

NAVIGATION WPT 50°06'·19N 05°31'·80W, 270°/0·5M to S pier. From NE, beware The Gear and Dog Rk 3½ca NE of hbr ent; from S, avoid Low Lee (1·1m) ECM buoy Q(3)10s and Carn Base (1·8m).

LIGHTS AND MARKS See chartlet and 9.1.4. S pier hd, W tr, R base and cupola; Fl 5s, same as Penzance pierhead, 033°/1M. N pierhd, G sector (238°-248°) clears The Gear; W sector over hbr.

R/T Call: *Newlyn Hbr* VHF Ch 09 **12** 16 (Mon-Fri 0800-1700, Sat 0800-1200LT).

TELEPHONE (Dial code 01736) HM 362523, outside office hrs 361017, Customs 332709; MRCC, Marinecall, Police, Ⓗ, Dr: as for Penzance.

FACILITIES Mary Williams Pier £1.17 (every 3rd night free). **Services:** Slip, D (cans), FW, C (6 ton), ME, ⚒, SM, Gas, El, Ⓔ, CH. **Town** EC Wed; launderette, supermarket, R, Bar, ✉, Ⓑ (a.m only), bus to Penzance for ⇌, ✈. Facilities for yachts may be improved in the future.

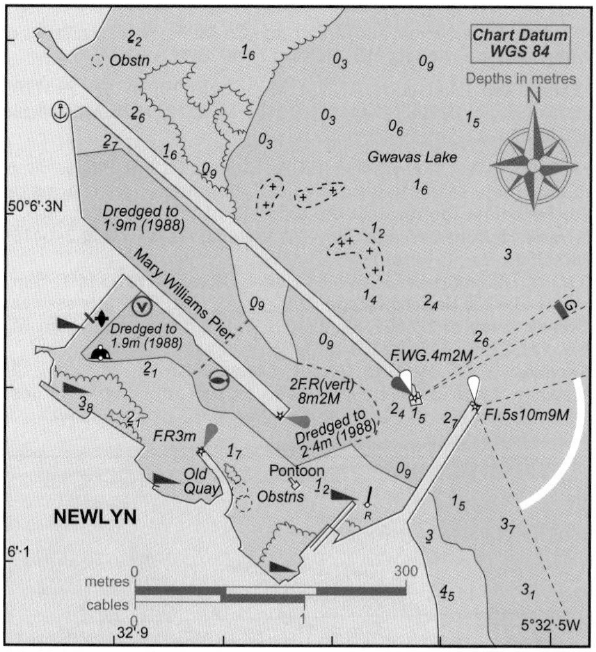
Chart Datum WGS 84
Depths in metres
N
Obstn
Gwavas Lake
50°6'·3N
Dredged to 1·9m (1988)
Mary Williams Pier
Dredged to 1.9m (1988)
F.WG.4m2M
2F.R(vert) 8m2M
Dredged to 2·4m (1988)
Fl.5s10m9M
F.R3m
Old Quay
Pontoon
Obstns
NEWLYN
6'·1
metres
cables
300
32'·9
5°32'·5W

ADJACENT HARBOUR

MOUSEHOLE, Cornwall, **50°04'·97N 05°32'·26W.** AC 2345. HW +0550 on Dover; Tides as Newlyn; ML 3·2m; Duration 0600. Shelter good except in NE and S or SE winds; protected by St Clements Is from E'lies. Best appr from S, midway between St Clements Is and bkwtr. Ent 11m wide; hbr dries approx 2·4m, access HW±3. Ent is closed with timber baulks from Nov-Apl. N pier lt, see 9.1.4; 2 FR (vert) = hbr closed. HM ☎ (01736) 731511. Per night £10, multi hull £12. Facilities limited: FW, supermarket, Slip. Buses to Penzance.

9.1.9 PENZANCE

Cornwall **50°07'·09N 05°31'·68W**

CHARTS AC 777, 2345; Imray C7, 2400.10; Stanfords 2; OS 203

TIDES –0635 Dover; ML 3·2; Duration 0550; Zone 0 (UT)

Standard Port PLYMOUTH (⟶)

Times				Height (metres)			
High Water		Low Water		MHWS	MHWN	MLWN	MLWS
0000	0600	0000	0600	5·4	4·3	2·1	0·8
1200	1800	1200	1800				
Differences PENZANCE are the same as for Newlyn (9.1.8)							
PORTHLEVEN							
–0045	–0105	–0030	–0025	0·0	–0·1	–0·2	0·0
LIZARD POINT							
–0045	–0100	–0030	–0030	–0·2	–0·2	–0·3	–0·2

SHELTER Excellent in the wet dock (gates open HW –2 to +1); hard stbd after the gate to raft up, or as directed. 12 waiting buoys are laid S of S pier lt ho. ⚓/dry out close N of Wet Dock or ⚓ E of hbr, but Mounts Bay is an unsafe ⚓ in S or SE winds, which, if strong, also render the hbr ent dangerous. Hbr speed limit 5kn.

NAVIGATION WPT 50°06'·77N 05°31'·06W, 306°/0·5M to S pier hd. Beware Gear Rk, IDM bcn Fl(2) 10s, 0·4M S. Western Cressar (4ca NE of ent) and Ryeman Rks are marked by unlit SCM bns.

LIGHTS AND MARKS Hbr lts often hard to see against shore lts. There are no ldg lts/marks. Dock ent sigs (R/G), are shown from FS at N side of Dock gate, but may not be given for yachts. 3FG (vert) by night = Dock gates open; 3FR = gates shut.

R/T VHF Ch 09 **12** 16 (HW –2 to HW +1, and office hrs).

TELEPHONE (Dial code 01736) HM 366113, in emergency 07779 264335, Customs 366114; MRCC (01326) 317575; Marinecall 09066 526242; Police 08705 777444; Dr 363866; Ⓗ 362382.

FACILITIES Wet Dock (50 Ⓥ), £1.28 (every 3rd night free), M, D by hose, C (3 ton), showers £1; **S Pier** D, FW; **Penzance SC** ☎ 364989, Bar, L, FW, R; **Services:** Slip (dry dock), ME, El, CH, SM, ⚒, Gas, Gaz. **Town** EC Wed (winter only); P cans, launderette, supermarket, R, Bar, ✉, Ⓑ, ⇌, ✈. There are long-term plans to improve yacht facilities.

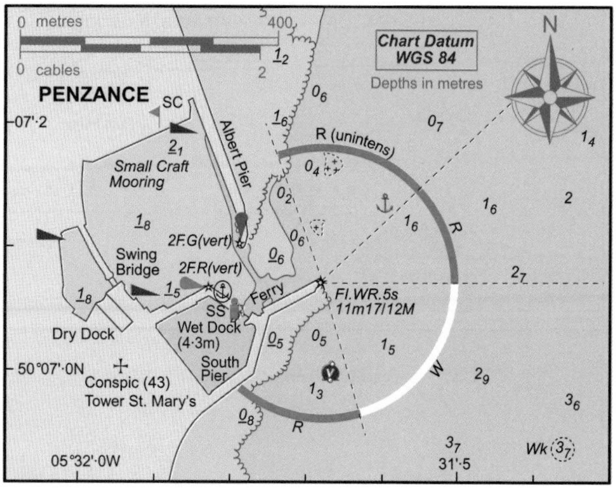
0 metres 400
0 cables 2
Chart Datum WGS 84
Depths in metres
N
PENZANCE
SC
07'·2
Albert Pier
R (unintens)
Small Craft Mooring
2F.G(vert)
Swing Bridge
2F.R(vert)
Ferry
Fl.WR.5s 11m17/12M
Dry Dock
Wet Dock (4·3m)
South Pier
SS
50°07'·0N
Conspic (43) Tower St. Mary's
R
W
Wk
05°32'·0W
31'·5

ADJACENT HARBOUR

ST MICHAEL'S MOUNT, Cornwall, **50°07'·17N 05°28'·67W.** AC 2345, 777. HW +0550 on Dover; Tides as Penzance; ML 3·2m; Duration 0550. Shelter good from N to SE, but only in fair wx. Hbr dries 2·1; approx 3·3m at MHWS and 1·4m at MHWN. Beware: Hogus Rks (5·5) 250m NW of hbr; Outer Penzeath Rk (0·4) 5ca W of hbr; and Maltman Rk (0·9) 1ca SSW of the Mount. There are no lts. Dry out against W pier or ⚓ W of the hbr in 2-3m on sand, space for 6 boats. HM ☎ 710265 (HO). **Facilities**: FW, R, café. Marazion, 3ca to N: R, Bar, supermarket, ✉, EC Wed; Mounts Bay SC.

ADJACENT HARBOURS ON THE LIZARD PENINSULA

PORTHLEVEN, Cornwall, **50°04´·92N 05°19´·13W**. AC *777,* 2345. HW –0635 on Dover; ML 3·1m; Duration 0545. See 9.1.9. Hbr dries 2m above the old LB ho but has approx 2·3m in centre of ent; access HW±3. It is very exposed to W and SW. Beware rks round pier hd and Deazle Rks to W. Lt on S pier, FG 10m 4M, = hbr open. Inside hbr FG, 033°-067°, shown as required by vessels entering. Visitors berth on the quay 2m, E side of inner hbr. HM ☎ (01326) 574270. Facilities: **Inner Hbr** AB £8, FW, L, ME, P & D(cans). **Village** EC Wed; ✉, ⓓ, R, Ⓑ, 🛒, Bar.

MULLION COVE, Cornwall, **50°00´·90N, 05°15´·54W**. AC *777,* 2345. Lizard HW –0630 on Dover, –0050 and –0·2m on HW Devonport; ML 3·0m; Duration 0545. Porth Mellin hbr dries about 2·4m and is open to W'lies. ⚓ in Mullion Cove is safer especially in lee of Mullion Island where there is approx 3·5m, but local knowledge advised. NT owns the island and the hbr. Due to lack of space, visiting boats may only stay in hbr briefly to load/ unload. No lts. There is a slip on E side of hbr. HM ☎ (01326) 240222. Only facilities at Mullion village (1M) EC Wed; Bar, 🛒.

Historic Wrecks (see 9.0.3h) are located at:
50°03'·44N 05°17'·16W (*St Anthony*), 2M SE of Porthleven.
50°02'·37N 05°16'·46W (*Schiedam*), 1·5M N of Mullion Is.
49°58'·54N 05°14'·51W, Rill Cove, 1·4M NW of Lizard Pt.
49°57'·49N 05°12'·98W, (*Royal Anne*) The Stags, Lizard Pt.

CADGWITH, Cornwall, **49°59´·22N 05°10´·68W**. AC *154,* 2345. HW –0625 on Dover; –0030 on Devonport; –0·2m on Devonport; ML 3·0m. See Differences Lizard Pt under 9.1.9. Hbr dries; it is divided by The Todden, a rky outcrop. Beware the extension of this, rks called The Mare; also beware Boa Rk to ESE which cover at quarter tide. ⚓ off The Mare in about 2–3m, but not recommended in on-shore winds. There are no lts. Many local FVs operate from here and are hauled up on the shingle beach. Facilities: ✉, Bar, R, V (1M at Ruan Minor).

COVERACK, Cornwall, **50°01´·44N 05°05´·66W**. AC *154,* 147. HW –0620 on Dover; ML 3·0m; Duration 0550. See 9.1.10. The tiny hbr dries and is full of small FVs. It has 3·3m at MHWS and 2·2m at MHWN. In good weather and off-shore winds it is better to ⚓ outside. From the S beware the Guthens, off Chynhalls Pt; from the N, Davas and other rks off Lowland Pt, and to the NE Manacle Rks (ECM lt buoy). There are no lts. HM ☎ (01326) 280545. Facilities: EC Tues; FW (hotel) D, P (cans) from garage (2M uphill), 🛒, ✉.

9.1.10 HELFORD RIVER

Cornwall **50°05'·79N 05·06'·06W** (Ent)

CHARTS AC *154,* 147, *5602*; Imray C6, 2400.11; Stanfords 2, 23; OS 204

TIDES –0615 Dover; ML 3·0; Duration 0550; Zone 0 (UT)

Reference Port PLYMOUTH (⟶)

Times				Height (metres)			
High Water		Low Water		MHWS	MHWN	MLWN	MLWS
0000	0600	0000	0600	5·4	4·3	2·1	0·8
1200	1800	1200	1800				
Differences HELFORD RIVER (Ent)							
–0030	–0035	–0015	–0010	–0·2	–0·2	–0·3	–0·2
COVERACK							
–0030	–0050	–0020	–0015	–0·2	–0·2	–0·3	–0·2

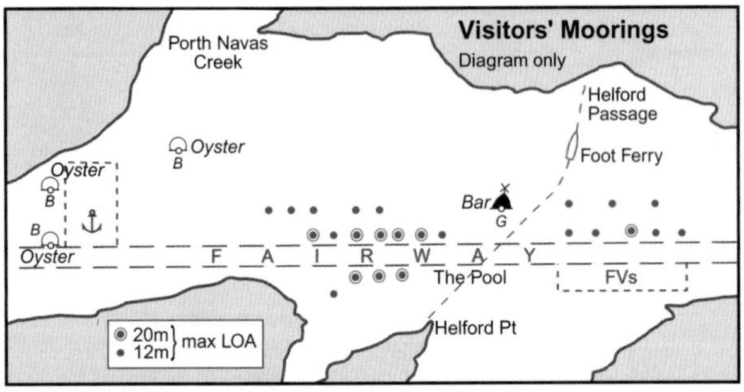
Visitors' Moorings
Diagram only
Porth Navas Creek
Helford Passage
Oyster B
Oyster B
B
Oyster
Foot Ferry
Bar
G
F A I R W A Y
The Pool
FVs
Helford Pt
20m
12m
max LOA

SHELTER Excellent, except in E'lies. Moorings Officer administers Ⓥs which are G can buoys marked 'Visitors' or have G pick-up buoys; see diagram. ⚓ only where marked on diagram/chartlet; yachts >15m LOA in Durgan Bay. No ⚓ in the river and creeks W of Porth Navas Creek due to oyster beds (local bye-law).

NAVIGATION WPT 50°05´·86N 05°04´·84W, 270°/1·9M to The Pool. From N beware August Rock marked by unlit SHM buoy. From SE keep well off Nare Pt and Dennis Hd. Speed limit 6kn in river. Chan up to Gweek is buoyed.

LIGHTS AND MARKS Marks as chartlet, all unlit. The Voose, a rky reef E of Bosahan Pt, is marked by NCM buoy. The Bar SHM buoy (partly obsc'd by moorings) marks a drying mud bank.

R/T Moorings Officer and Water taxi Ch M. Ferry also acts as a water taxi, on request HO. Helford River SC Ch **80** M.

TELEPHONE (Dial code 01326) Moorings Officer ☎ 250770/ 250749; Police 08705 777444; Ⓗ 572151; MRCC 317575; Marinecall 09066 526242.

FACILITIES Ⓥs £1.00-£1.42/m (LOAs <10m to >12m). Please ditch rubbish only at the Helford River SC, the Shipwright's Arms or the Ferryboat Inn; protect the wild life of this beautiful river.
N bank: Helford Passage Slip, FW, V; **Porth Navas YC** ☎ 340419/ 340065 R, Bar, C (3 ton), M, ⛽, FW.
S bank: Gillan Creek CH, FW, M. **Helford River SC** ☎ 231460, Slip, FW, R, Bar, ⓓ; **Helford village** P&D (cans), Gas, Gaz, bus service.
Gweek Quay ☎ 221657, 📠 221685, info@gweek-quay.com M, FW, CH, El, ⚒, ME, C (100 ton), BH.
Services: ✉ @ Helford, Gweek, Mawnan-Smith, Mawgan; Ⓑ Mawnan-Smith (Jan-Sep, Mon, Wed, Fri a.m only. Oct-May Tues, Fri a.m); ⇌ (bus to Falmouth); ✈ (Penzance or Newquay).

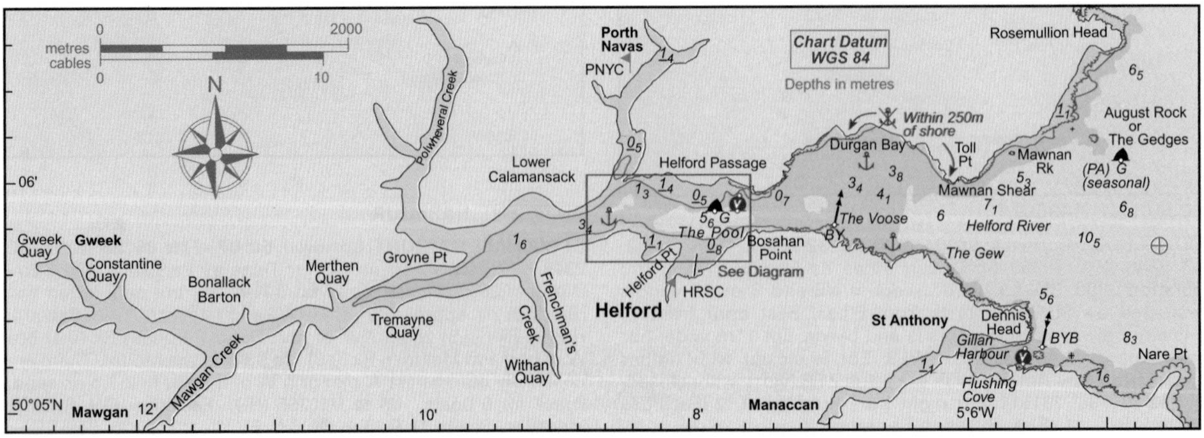
metres 0 2000
cables 0 10
N
Chart Datum WGS 84
Depths in metres
Porth Navas
PNYC
Rosemullion Head
Polwheveral Creek
Lower Calamansack
Helford Passage
Within 250m of shore
Durgan Bay
Toll Pt
Mawnan Rk
August Rock or The Gedges
(PA) G (seasonal)
Mawnan Shear
The Voose
Helford River
The Pool
Bosahan Point
See Diagram
The Gew
Gweek Quay
Gweek
Constantine Quay
Bonallack Barton
Merthen Quay
Groyne Pt
Helford Pt
HRSC
Helford
Frenchman's Creek
Tremayne Quay
Mawgan Creek
Withan Quay
St Anthony
Dennis Head
Gillan Harbour
BYB
Nare Pt
Flushing Cove
Mawgan
Manaccan
06'
50°05'N
12'
10'
8'
5°6'W

TIME ZONE (UT)
For Summer Time add ONE hour in **non-shaded areas**

ENGLAND – FALMOUTH

LAT 50°09′N LONG 5°03′W

TIMES AND HEIGHTS OF HIGH AND LOW WATERS

SPRING & NEAP TIDES
Dates in red are SPRINGS
Dates in blue are NEAPS

YEAR **2005**

JANUARY

Day	Time	m	Time	m	Time	m	Time	m
1 SA	0224	1.6	0820	4.8	1450	1.6	2046	4.5
2 SU	0259	1.7	0859	4.7	1528	1.7	2127	4.4
3 M	0340	1.8	0942	4.6	1614	1.8	◑ 2216	4.3
4 TU	0432	1.9	1035	4.5	1715	1.9	2316	4.3
5 W	0543	2.0	1140	4.5	1832	1.9		
6 TH	0023	4.4	0706	2.0	1252	4.5	1946	1.8
7 F	0136	4.5	0820	1.8	1405	4.6	2053	1.6
8 SA	0244	4.7	0927	1.5	1514	4.8	2157	1.4
9 SU	0347	5.0	1029	1.3	1616	5.0	2256	1.2
10 M	0442	5.3	1126	1.0	1711	5.2	● 2350	1.0
11 TU	0533	5.5	1220	0.7	1805	5.3		
12 W	0042	0.8	0626	5.6	1310	0.6	1859	5.3
13 TH	0130	0.7	0717	5.6	1358	0.6	1949	5.2
14 F	0215	0.8	0805	5.6	1442	0.7	2036	5.1
15 SA	0257	0.9	0851	5.4	1524	0.9	2120	4.9
16 SU	0337	1.2	0933	5.1	1604	1.2	2201	4.7
17 M	0418	1.5	1015	4.8	1646	1.5	◐ 2245	4.5
18 TU	0503	1.7	1104	4.5	1735	1.8	2342	4.3
19 W	0600	2.0	1208	4.3	1837	2.1		
20 TH	0049	4.2	0713	2.2	1320	4.2	1951	2.1
21 F	0155	4.3	0834	2.1	1426	4.3	2105	2.0
22 SA	0254	4.5	0942	1.9	1522	4.4	2203	1.8
23 SU	0344	4.7	1034	1.6	1609	4.6	2250	1.5
24 M	0427	4.9	1117	1.5	1650	4.8	2330	1.5
25 TU	0505	5.1	1156	1.3	1727	4.9	○	
26 W	0007	1.3	0543	5.1	1232	1.2	1806	4.9
27 TH	0041	1.3	0621	5.2	1304	1.2	1844	4.9
28 F	0113	1.2	0659	5.1	1335	1.2	1920	4.8
29 SA	0142	1.3	0732	5.1	1403	1.2	1952	4.8
30 SU	0210	1.3	0803	5.0	1432	1.3	2022	4.7
31 M	0239	1.4	0833	4.9	1502	1.4	2053	4.6

FEBRUARY

Day	Time	m	Time	m	Time	m	Time	m
1 TU	0313	1.5	0906	4.8	1537	1.5	2131	4.5
2 W	0353	1.6	0951	4.6	1623	1.7	◑ 2225	4.4
3 TH	0448	1.9	1055	4.4	1728	1.9	2339	4.3
4 F	0613	2.0	1216	4.3	1904	2.0		
5 SA	0103	4.3	0753	1.9	1346	4.4	2034	1.8
6 SU	0226	4.6	0915	1.6	1506	4.6	2147	1.5
7 M	0335	4.9	1022	1.3	1610	4.9	2249	1.2
8 TU	0433	5.3	1119	0.8	1704	5.1	● 2342	0.8
9 W	0523	5.5	1211	0.5	1755	5.3		
10 TH	0031	0.6	0614	5.7	1258	0.3	1844	5.4
11 F	0116	0.4	0701	5.7	1342	0.3	1929	5.3
12 SA	0158	0.4	0746	5.6	1422	0.4	2010	5.3
13 SU	0235	0.6	0825	5.4	1458	0.6	2046	5.1
14 M	0309	0.9	0859	5.2	1530	1.0	2114	4.8
15 TU	0342	1.3	0928	4.8	1602	1.5	2142	4.6
16 W	0417	1.6	0959	4.5	1639	1.8	◐ 2219	4.3
17 TH	0501	2.0	1046	4.1	1730	2.2	2322	4.1
18 F	0609	2.3	1217	3.9	1846	2.4		
19 SA	0108	4.0	0745	2.4	1356	3.9	2027	2.3
20 SU	0225	4.2	0925	2.1	1501	4.2	2145	2.0
21 M	0321	4.5	1019	1.7	1552	4.5	2234	1.6
22 TU	0407	4.8	1101	1.4	1634	4.7	2314	1.4
23 W	0447	5.0	1139	1.2	1711	4.9	2351	1.2
24 TH	0525	5.1	1214	1.0	1749	5.0	○	
25 F	0025	1.0	0603	5.2	1246	0.9	1826	5.0
26 SA	0055	1.0	0639	5.2	1315	0.9	1859	5.0
27 SU	0124	0.9	0712	5.2	1343	0.9	1928	5.0
28 M	0151	1.0	0740	5.1	1410	1.0	1955	4.9

MARCH

Day	Time	m	Time	m	Time	m	Time	m
1 TU	0218	1.1	0808	5.0	1438	1.1	2023	4.8
2 W	0250	1.2	0839	4.8	1510	1.4	2058	4.6
3 TH	0327	1.5	0924	4.5	1551	1.6	◑ 2151	4.4
4 F	0419	1.8	1029	4.3	1652	2.0	2309	4.2
5 SA	0546	2.1	1159	4.1	1843	2.2		
6 SU	0047	4.2	0746	2.0	1345	4.2	2029	1.9
7 M	0220	4.5	0912	1.5	1506	4.5	2142	1.5
8 TU	0327	4.9	1015	1.1	1603	4.9	2238	1.0
9 W	0420	5.3	1107	0.6	1652	5.2	2328	0.7
10 TH	0507	5.5	1154	0.3	1737	5.3	●	
11 F	0013	0.4	0553	5.6	1238	0.2	1821	5.4
12 SA	0055	0.3	0637	5.6	1318	0.2	1901	5.4
13 SU	0133	0.3	0717	5.5	1355	0.3	1935	5.3
14 M	0208	0.5	0751	5.3	1427	0.7	2004	5.1
15 TU	0238	0.9	0819	5.0	1455	1.1	2027	4.9
16 W	0307	1.3	0843	4.7	1523	1.5	2052	4.6
17 TH	0337	1.6	0912	4.4	1553	1.8	◐ 2128	4.4
18 F	0414	2.0	0954	4.0	1637	2.2	2221	4.1
19 SA	0521	2.4	1106	3.8	1759	2.5	2357	3.9
20 SU	0659	2.5	1329	3.8	1941	2.4		
21 M	0155	4.1	0858	2.1	1437	4.1	2115	2.0
22 TU	0253	4.4	0950	1.7	1526	4.4	2204	1.6
23 W	0340	4.7	1031	1.4	1608	4.7	2244	1.4
24 TH	0421	5.0	1108	1.1	1646	4.9	2321	1.1
25 F	0500	5.1	1143	0.9	1722	5.0	○ 2356	0.9
26 SA	0536	5.2	1217	0.8	1758	5.1		
27 SU	0029	0.8	0613	5.2	1249	0.7	1831	5.1
28 M	0100	0.7	0646	5.2	1319	0.7	1902	5.1
29 TU	0130	0.8	0718	5.1	1348	0.9	1930	5.1
30 W	0200	0.9	0750	5.0	1418	1.1	2002	4.9
31 TH	0233	1.2	0827	4.8	1452	1.4	2042	4.7

APRIL

Day	Time	m	Time	m	Time	m	Time	m
1 F	0314	1.5	0914	4.5	1536	1.7	2138	4.5
2 SA	0410	1.8	1022	4.2	1643	2.1	◑ 2256	4.2
3 SU	0547	2.1	1201	4.0	1844	2.2		
4 M	0043	4.3	0745	1.9	1347	4.2	2022	1.8
5 TU	0212	4.6	0900	1.5	1456	4.6	2126	1.4
6 W	0312	5.0	0956	1.0	1548	4.9	2219	1.0
7 TH	0401	5.3	1045	0.6	1632	5.2	2305	0.6
8 F	0445	5.5	1130	0.4	1712	5.3	● 2348	0.4
9 SA	0527	5.5	1211	0.3	1751	5.4		
10 SU	0028	0.4	0607	5.5	1250	0.4	1827	5.3
11 M	0105	0.5	0644	5.3	1324	0.6	1858	5.2
12 TU	0138	0.7	0715	5.1	1355	0.9	1922	5.1
13 W	0208	1.0	0740	4.9	1422	1.2	1947	4.9
14 TH	0236	1.3	0807	4.6	1448	1.5	2016	4.7
15 F	0304	1.6	0839	4.3	1515	1.9	2054	4.4
16 SA	0339	2.0	0925	4.0	1556	2.2	◐ 2146	4.2
17 SU	0444	2.3	1031	3.8	1722	2.5	2303	4.0
18 M	0619	2.4	1244	3.8	1856	2.4		
19 TU	0106	4.1	0752	2.1	1358	4.1	2018	2.1
20 W	0213	4.4	0856	1.7	1448	4.4	2114	1.7
21 TH	0301	4.6	0943	1.4	1532	4.6	2200	1.4
22 F	0345	4.9	1025	1.1	1612	4.9	2242	1.1
23 SA	0426	5.0	1105	0.9	1650	5.0	2321	0.9
24 SU	0506	5.1	1143	0.8	1726	5.1	○ 2359	0.8
25 M	0544	5.2	1220	0.7	1802	5.2		
26 TU	0036	0.7	0623	5.2	1256	0.8	1838	5.2
27 W	0112	0.8	0701	5.1	1331	0.9	1914	5.2
28 TH	0149	0.9	0740	5.0	1407	1.1	1953	5.0
29 F	0229	1.2	0825	4.7	1448	1.4	2038	4.8
30 SA	0316	1.5	0919	4.5	1538	1.7	2135	4.6

Chart Datum: 2·91 metres below Ordnance Datum (Newlyn)

TIME ZONE (UT)
For Summer Time add ONE hour in **non-shaded areas**

ENGLAND – FALMOUTH

LAT 50°09′N LONG 5°03′W

TIMES AND HEIGHTS OF HIGH AND LOW WATERS

SPRING & NEAP TIDES
Dates in red are SPRINGS
Dates in blue are NEAPS

YEAR **2005**

MAY

Date	Day	Time	m	Time	m	Time	m	Time	m
1	SU	0419	1.7	1027	4.2	1651	2.0	◑ 2252	4.4
2	M	0551	1.9	1204	4.2	1834	2.0		
3	TU	0032	4.4	0725	1.7	1328	4.3	1957	1.7
4	W	0148	4.7	0833	1.4	1429	4.6	2058	1.4
5	TH	0245	4.9	0928	1.1	1519	4.9	2150	1.1
6	F	0335	5.1	1017	0.8	1603	5.1	2237	0.8
7	SA	0420	5.2	1101	0.7	1643	5.2	2320	0.7
8	SU	0500	5.3	1143	0.6	1720	5.2	●	
9	M	0000	0.7	0537	5.2	1221	0.7	1753	5.2
10	TU	0037	0.8	0613	5.1	1254	0.9	1823	5.2
11	W	0111	1.0	0643	4.9	1325	1.1	1849	5.1
12	TH	0141	1.2	0712	4.8	1354	1.4	1919	4.9
13	F	0211	1.5	0744	4.6	1423	1.6	1953	4.8
14	SA	0242	1.6	0821	4.3	1454	1.9	2033	4.5
15	SU	0320	1.9	0908	4.1	1536	2.1	2124	4.3
16	M	0417	2.1	1010	4.0	1645	2.3	◐ 2228	4.2
17	TU	0535	2.2	1134	3.9	1808	2.3	2351	4.2
18	W	0650	2.0	1258	4.1	1919	2.1		
19	TH	0111	4.3	0753	1.7	1355	4.3	2018	1.8
20	F	0209	4.5	0847	1.5	1444	4.5	2110	1.5
21	SA	0259	4.7	0937	1.3	1530	4.8	2159	1.3
22	SU	0348	4.9	1024	1.1	1614	5.0	2246	1.1
23	M	0434	5.0	1110	0.9	1656	5.1	○ 2332	0.9
24	TU	0518	5.1	1155	0.9	1737	5.2		
25	W	0016	0.8	0603	5.1	1239	0.9	1821	5.3
26	TH	0101	0.8	0650	5.1	1322	1.0	1905	5.3
27	F	0146	0.9	0738	5.0	1407	1.1	1952	5.2
28	SA	0233	1.0	0830	4.8	1454	1.3	2041	5.0
29	SU	0324	1.3	0925	4.6	1546	1.5	2137	4.8
30	M	0423	1.5	1029	4.5	1649	1.7	◑ 2245	4.7
31	TU	0534	1.5	1145	4.4	1804	1.8		

JUNE

Date	Day	Time	m	Time	m	Time	m	Time	m
1	W	0004	4.6	0648	1.5	1253	4.4	1917	1.7
2	TH	0113	4.6	0754	1.5	1352	4.6	2020	1.5
3	F	0212	4.7	0852	1.3	1444	4.7	2116	1.4
4	SA	0304	4.8	0944	1.2	1531	4.9	2207	1.2
5	SU	0352	4.9	1032	1.1	1614	5.0	2253	1.1
6	M	0434	4.9	1115	1.1	1652	5.1	● 2335	1.1
7	TU	0511	4.9	1154	1.1	1725	5.1		
8	W	0014	1.1	0547	4.9	1230	1.2	1757	5.1
9	TH	0050	1.2	0622	4.8	1303	1.3	1829	5.0
10	F	0123	1.3	0655	4.7	1335	1.5	1904	4.9
11	SA	0156	1.5	0732	4.5	1407	1.5	1940	4.8
12	SU	0229	1.5	0813	4.4	1441	1.7	2022	4.7
13	M	0305	1.7	0858	4.3	1518	1.9	2106	4.5
14	TU	0349	1.8	0946	4.2	1605	2.0	2155	4.4
15	W	0444	1.9	1042	4.1	1708	2.1	◐ 2254	4.4
16	TH	0550	1.9	1147	4.2	1819	2.0	2358	4.4
17	F	0655	1.8	1249	4.3	1924	1.8		
18	SA	0104	4.5	0755	1.6	1348	4.4	2023	1.6
19	SU	0208	4.6	0853	1.5	1445	4.6	2121	1.5
20	M	0309	4.7	0949	1.3	1540	4.9	2217	1.3
21	TU	0405	4.9	1044	1.2	1632	5.1	2311	1.0
22	W	0459	5.0	1137	1.0	1720	5.2	○	
23	TH	0003	0.9	0552	5.1	1228	0.9	1809	5.4
24	F	0055	0.7	0645	5.1	1318	0.9	1901	5.4
25	SA	0145	0.7	0738	5.1	1406	0.9	1951	5.4
26	SU	0234	0.8	0830	5.0	1453	1.0	2040	5.3
27	M	0322	0.9	0921	4.9	1540	1.2	2131	5.1
28	TU	0410	1.1	1013	4.7	1629	1.4	◑ 2224	4.9
29	W	0503	1.4	1109	4.6	1724	1.5	2325	4.7
30	TH	0601	1.5	1209	4.4	1827	1.7		

JULY

Date	Day	Time	m	Time	m	Time	m	Time	m
1	F	0029	4.5	0705	1.6	1308	4.4	1934	1.8
2	SA	0133	4.4	0810	1.7	1406	4.5	2039	1.7
3	SU	0231	4.5	0911	1.6	1459	4.6	2139	1.6
4	M	0324	4.5	1005	1.5	1547	4.8	2231	1.5
5	TU	0411	4.6	1053	1.5	1629	4.9	2317	1.4
6	W	0452	4.7	1135	1.4	1706	5.0	● 2358	1.3
7	TH	0529	4.8	1214	1.3	1741	5.0		
8	F	0037	1.3	0607	4.8	1250	1.3	1818	5.0
9	SA	0112	1.3	0645	4.7	1323	1.4	1854	5.0
10	SU	0144	1.4	0724	4.6	1354	1.5	1931	4.9
11	M	0215	1.4	0802	4.6	1424	1.5	2008	4.8
12	TU	0245	1.5	0839	4.5	1454	1.6	2043	4.7
13	W	0317	1.5	0917	4.4	1527	1.7	2121	4.6
14	TH	0354	1.6	0956	4.3	1609	1.8	◐ 2204	4.5
15	F	0441	1.7	1046	4.3	1706	1.9	2300	4.4
16	SA	0548	1.8	1149	4.3	1825	1.9		
17	SU	0008	4.4	0705	1.8	1300	4.3	1943	1.8
18	M	0125	4.4	0818	1.7	1411	4.5	2053	1.6
19	TU	0241	4.6	0925	1.5	1516	4.8	2158	1.4
20	W	0349	4.8	1028	1.3	1615	5.1	2259	1.1
21	TH	0447	5.0	1126	1.0	1708	5.3	○ 2355	0.8
22	F	0542	5.1	1220	0.8	1759	5.5		
23	SA	0048	0.5	0636	5.2	1310	0.6	1851	5.6
24	SU	0137	0.4	0728	5.3	1357	0.6	1940	5.6
25	M	0222	0.4	0816	5.2	1440	0.7	2027	5.5
26	TU	0305	0.6	0900	5.1	1520	0.9	2110	5.3
27	W	0345	0.9	0942	4.9	1600	1.2	2151	5.0
28	TH	0425	1.3	1024	4.6	1642	1.5	◑ 2235	4.6
29	F	0510	1.6	1114	4.4	1733	1.8	2334	4.3
30	SA	0605	1.9	1219	4.2	1841	2.1		
31	SU	0050	4.1	0718	2.1	1330	4.2	2004	2.1

AUGUST

Date	Day	Time	m	Time	m	Time	m	Time	m
1	M	0203	4.1	0841	2.0	1433	4.4	2121	1.9
2	TU	0303	4.3	0948	1.8	1526	4.6	2218	1.7
3	W	0354	4.5	1039	1.6	1610	4.8	2305	1.5
4	TH	0437	4.6	1122	1.4	1649	5.0	2346	1.3
5	F	0514	4.8	1201	1.3	1726	5.1	●	
6	SA	0023	1.2	0552	4.8	1236	1.2	1803	5.1
7	SU	0057	1.1	0630	4.8	1307	1.2	1840	5.1
8	M	0126	1.2	0707	4.8	1335	1.2	1915	5.0
9	TU	0153	1.2	0740	4.8	1401	1.3	1947	5.0
10	W	0218	1.3	0810	4.7	1426	1.4	2015	4.9
11	TH	0244	1.4	0839	4.6	1454	1.5	2043	4.7
12	F	0314	1.5	0912	4.5	1528	1.6	2121	4.6
13	SA	0352	1.6	0957	4.4	1615	1.8	◐ 2216	4.4
14	SU	0447	1.9	1103	4.2	1729	2.1	2333	4.2
15	M	0620	2.1	1225	4.3	1918	2.0		
16	TU	0103	4.2	0759	1.9	1353	4.5	2041	1.7
17	W	0233	4.5	0915	1.6	1506	4.8	2151	1.4
18	TH	0342	4.8	1020	1.3	1604	5.2	2250	0.9
19	F	0438	5.0	1116	0.9	1655	5.5	○ 2344	0.6
20	SA	0528	5.3	1206	0.6	1744	5.7		
21	SU	0033	0.3	0618	5.4	1254	0.4	1833	5.7
22	M	0119	0.2	0706	5.4	1337	0.4	1919	5.7
23	TU	0200	0.3	0749	5.4	1416	0.5	2001	5.5
24	W	0238	0.5	0828	5.2	1452	0.8	2038	5.3
25	TH	0313	0.9	0902	5.0	1526	1.1	2110	4.9
26	F	0346	1.3	0932	4.7	1601	1.5	◑ 2141	4.6
27	SA	0421	1.7	1006	4.4	1644	2.0	2221	4.2
28	SU	0509	2.2	1101	4.1	1749	2.3	2350	3.9
29	M	0624	2.4	1255	4.0	1933	2.4		
30	TU	0142	3.9	0823	2.4	1411	4.2	2112	2.1
31	W	0246	4.1	0935	2.0	1507	4.5	2204	1.7

Chart Datum: 2·91 metres below Ordnance Datum (Newlyn)

TIME ZONE (UT)
For Summer Time add ONE hour in **non-shaded areas**

ENGLAND – FALMOUTH

LAT 50°09′N LONG 5°03′W

TIMES AND HEIGHTS OF HIGH AND LOW WATERS

SPRING & NEAP TIDES
Dates in red are SPRINGS
Dates in blue are NEAPS

YEAR **2005**

SEPTEMBER

Day	Time	m	Day	Time	m
1 TH	0337 1022 1552 2247	4.4 1.6 4.8 1.5	16 F	0335 1009 1551 2236	4.9 1.2 5.3 0.8
2 F	0418 1103 1630 2325	4.7 1.4 5.0 1.2	17 SA	0424 1059 1639 2325	5.2 0.8 5.6 0.4
3 SA ●	0455 1139 1707	4.9 1.2 5.2	18 SU ○	0509 1146 1723	5.4 0.5 5.7
4 SU	0000 0530 1213 1742	1.1 5.0 1.1 5.2	19 M	0010 0553 1230 1807	0.3 5.5 0.4 5.8
5 M	0031 0606 1242 1818	1.0 5.0 1.0 5.2	20 TU	0053 0636 1311 1850	0.2 5.5 0.4 5.7
6 TU	0059 0640 1309 1850	1.0 5.0 1.1 5.2	21 W	0132 0715 1347 1928	0.4 5.4 0.6 5.5
7 W	0124 0711 1333 1919	1.0 5.0 1.1 5.1	22 TH	0206 0749 1421 2000	0.7 5.3 0.9 5.2
8 TH	0149 0738 1358 1945	1.1 4.9 1.2 5.0	23 F	0238 0816 1452 2027	1.1 5.0 1.3 4.8
9 F	0214 0804 1426 2013	1.3 4.8 1.4 4.8	24 SA	0307 0840 1524 2054	1.5 4.7 1.7 4.5
10 SA	0243 0837 1500 2052	1.5 4.6 1.5 4.6	25 SU	0338 0913 1602 ◑ 2133	1.9 4.5 2.1 4.1
11 SU	0319 0925 1545 ◐ 2152	1.7 4.4 1.9 4.3	26 M	0421 1004 1706 2239	2.4 4.2 2.5 3.8
12 M	0412 1035 1700 2316	2.1 4.3 2.2 4.1	27 TU	0540 1149 1857	2.7 4.0 2.6
13 TU	0556 1207 1911	2.3 4.2 2.2	28 W	0118 0756 1344 2049	3.8 2.6 4.2 2.2
14 W	0103 0755 1347 2038	4.2 2.1 4.5 1.7	29 TH	0223 0908 1440 2136	4.1 2.1 4.5 1.8
15 TH	0235 0910 1458 2142	4.5 1.6 4.9 1.3	30 F	0312 0952 1524 2215	4.5 1.7 4.8 1.5

OCTOBER

Day	Time	m	Day	Time	m
1 SA	0352 1031 1603 2251	4.8 1.5 5.0 1.2	16 SU	0403 1036 1617 2300	5.3 0.8 5.6 0.5
2 SU	0429 1106 1640 2325	5.0 1.2 5.2 1.0	17 M	0445 1121 1700 ○ 2343	5.4 0.6 5.7 0.5
3 M	0504 1139 1715 ● 2356	5.1 1.1 5.3 0.9	18 TU	0525 1203 1741	5.5 0.5 5.6
4 TU	0537 1211 1750	5.2 1.0 5.3	19 W	0024 0604 1243 1820	0.5 5.5 0.6 5.5
5 W	0026 0610 1240 1823	0.9 5.2 1.0 5.2	20 TH	0101 0639 1318 1854	0.7 5.4 0.8 5.3
6 TH	0055 0641 1308 1852	1.0 5.2 1.0 5.2	21 F	0134 0709 1351 1924	1.0 5.3 1.1 5.0
7 F	0122 0710 1336 1922	1.1 5.1 1.2 5.0	22 SA	0204 0734 1422 1950	1.3 5.1 1.5 4.7
8 SA	0150 0740 1407 1957	1.3 5.0 1.4 4.8	23 SU	0233 0803 1453 2021	1.6 4.8 1.8 4.4
9 SU	0222 0819 1444 2043	1.5 4.8 1.6 4.6	24 M	0303 0840 1531 2105	2.0 4.6 2.2 4.1
10 M	0301 0911 1534 ◐ 2146	1.8 4.6 1.9 4.3	25 TU	0344 0931 1630 ◑ 2209	2.4 4.3 2.5 3.9
11 TU	0359 1022 1701 2312	2.2 4.4 2.3 4.1	26 W	0500 1045 1804	2.7 4.1 2.6
12 W	0557 1158 1908	2.4 4.3 2.1	27 TH	0030 0642 1254 1951	3.9 2.6 4.2 2.3
13 TH	0109 0748 1338 2026	4.2 2.1 4.6 1.6	28 F	0144 0813 1358 2046	4.1 2.3 4.4 1.9
14 F	0225 0855 1442 2124	4.6 1.6 5.0 1.2	29 SA	0233 0904 1445 2128	4.4 1.9 4.7 1.6
15 SA	0317 0948 1532 2214	5.0 1.2 5.4 0.8	30 SU	0315 0946 1527 2206	4.7 1.5 5.0 1.4
			31 M	0355 1025 1607 2244	5.0 1.4 5.1 1.2

NOVEMBER

Day	Time	m	Day	Time	m
1 TU	0432 1102 1645 2320	5.1 1.2 5.2 1.0	16 W	0459 1137 1715 ○ 2356	5.4 0.9 5.4 0.9
2 W	0507 1138 1721 ● 2355	5.2 1.1 5.3 1.0	17 TH	0534 1217 1753	5.4 0.9 5.3
3 TH	0542 1214 1758	5.3 1.0 5.2	18 F	0034 0608 1254 1827	1.0 5.3 1.1 5.1
4 F	0030 0617 1248 1834	1.0 5.3 1.0 5.2	19 SA	0107 0639 1328 1858	1.2 5.2 1.3 4.9
5 SA	0103 0651 1323 1912	1.1 5.2 1.2 5.0	20 SU	0139 0709 1400 1928	1.5 5.1 1.5 4.7
6 SU	0138 0729 1401 1954	1.3 5.1 1.4 4.8	21 M	0209 0741 1434 2004	1.7 4.9 1.8 4.5
7 M	0216 0813 1446 2046	1.5 5.0 1.5 4.6	22 TU	0242 0822 1511 2050	2.0 4.7 2.0 4.3
8 TU	0303 0908 1543 2147	1.8 4.8 1.9 4.4	23 W	0322 0911 1601 ◑ 2147	2.2 4.5 2.3 4.1
9 W	0407 1015 1705 ◐ 2311	2.1 4.6 2.0 4.3	24 TH	0419 1012 1710 2304	2.4 4.3 2.4 4.0
10 TH	0546 1145 1845	2.2 4.5 1.9	25 F	0539 1130 1828	2.5 4.3 2.3
11 F	0047 0719 1311 1958	4.4 2.0 4.7 1.6	26 SA	0032 0656 1250 1934	4.1 2.3 4.4 2.0
12 SA	0156 0825 1414 2055	4.6 1.6 5.0 1.3	27 SU	0135 0759 1350 2028	4.3 2.1 4.6 1.8
13 SU	0249 0920 1506 2146	4.9 1.4 5.2 1.1	28 M	0225 0852 1442 2116	4.6 1.8 4.7 1.5
14 M	0337 1009 1553 2233	5.2 1.1 5.3 0.9	29 TU	0312 0940 1529 2202	4.8 1.5 4.9 1.4
15 TU	0419 1055 1637 2316	5.3 0.9 5.4 0.8	30 W	0357 1026 1614 2246	5.0 1.4 5.0 1.2

DECEMBER

Day	Time	m	Day	Time	m
1 TH	0439 1110 1658 ● 2330	5.1 1.2 5.1 1.1	16 F	0513 1159 1733	5.2 1.2 5.0
2 F	0518 1153 1741	5.3 1.1 5.2	17 SA	0014 0548 1238 1809	1.3 5.2 1.3 4.9
3 SA	0012 0600 1237 1825	1.1 5.3 1.0 5.2	18 SU	0050 0622 1314 1843	1.4 5.2 1.4 4.8
4 SU	0055 0643 1321 1910	1.2 5.3 1.1 5.1	19 M	0124 0655 1348 1919	1.5 5.1 1.5 4.7
5 M	0138 0728 1406 1959	1.3 5.3 1.2 4.9	20 TU	0156 0732 1421 1957	1.6 5.0 1.6 4.6
6 TU	0223 0817 1455 2051	1.4 5.2 1.4 4.8	21 W	0229 0812 1455 2039	1.7 4.8 1.7 4.4
7 W	0312 0908 1548 2147	1.5 5.0 1.5 4.6	22 TH	0302 0855 1531 2124	1.9 4.7 1.9 4.3
8 TH	0408 1008 1650 ◐ 2254	1.7 4.9 1.6 4.5	23 F	0340 0940 1615 ◑ 2214	2.0 4.5 2.0 4.2
9 F	0516 1117 1804	1.9 4.7 1.7	24 SA	0430 1031 1713 2313	2.2 4.4 2.1 4.2
10 SA	0007 0633 1231 1915	4.5 1.9 4.7 1.7	25 SU	0537 1133 1821	2.2 4.4 2.1
11 SU	0114 0744 1337 2019	4.6 1.8 4.8 1.5	26 M	0018 0651 1239 1927	4.2 2.2 4.4 2.0
12 M	0213 0846 1435 2115	4.7 1.6 4.9 1.5	27 TU	0122 0757 1346 2028	4.4 2.0 4.5 1.8
13 TU	0306 0942 1527 2206	4.9 1.5 5.0 1.4	28 W	0224 0858 1448 2125	4.6 1.8 4.6 1.6
14 W	0354 1032 1614 2253	5.0 1.3 5.0 1.3	29 TH	0321 0955 1547 2220	4.8 1.5 4.8 1.4
15 TH	0436 1117 1656 ○ 2335	5.2 1.2 5.0 1.2	30 F	0414 1050 1640 2312	5.0 1.3 5.0 1.2
			31 SA ●	0502 1141 1728	5.2 1.1 5.1

Chart Datum: 2·91 metres below Ordnance Datum (Newlyn)

9.1.11 RIVER FAL

Cornwall **50°08′·61N 05°01′·48W** (Ent)

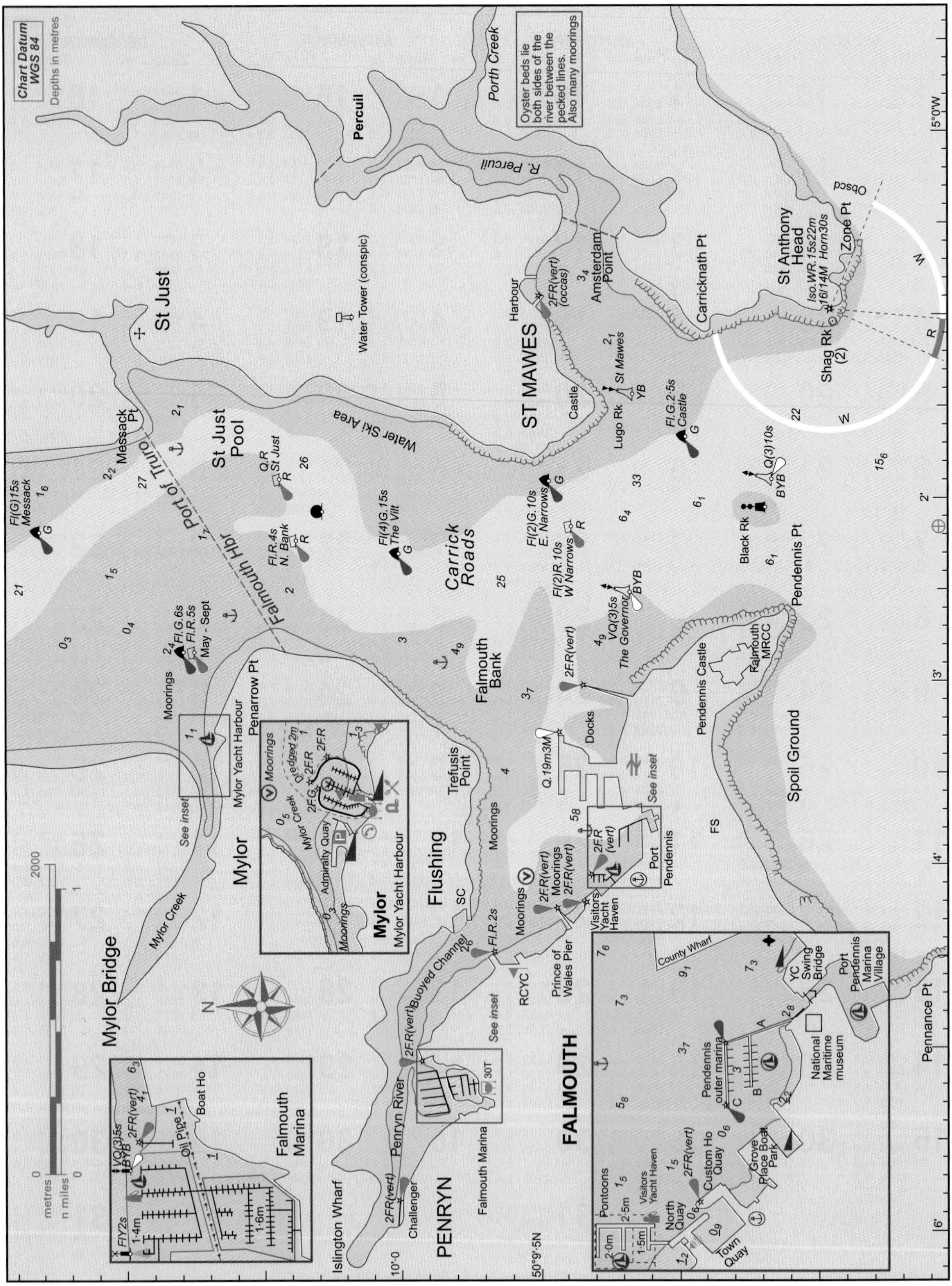
Chart Datum WGS 84
Depths in metres
Oyster beds lie both sides of the river between the pecked lines. Also many moorings
Percuil
Porth Creek
R. Percuil
St Just
St Just Pool
Water Tower (conspic)
Water Ski Area
Messack Pt
Port of Truro
Falmouth Hbr
ST MAWES
Harbour
Amsterdam Point
Castle
Lugo Rk
Carricknath Pt
St Anthony Head
Iso.WR.15s22m 16/14M Horn30s
Zone Pt
Shag Rk (2)
Obscd
Carrick Roads
Falmouth Bank
Black Rk
Pendennis Pt
Pendennis Castle
Falmouth MRCC
Spoil Ground
Docks
Port Pendennis
Visitors Yacht Haven
Prince of Wales Pier
RCYC
FALMOUTH
Mylor
Mylor Yacht Harbour
Penarrow Pt
Mylor Creek
Mylor Bridge
Flushing
Trefusis Point
Buoyed Channel
Penryn River
PENRYN
Islington Wharf
Falmouth Marina
Challenger
Moorings
See inset
National Maritime museum
Pendennis outer marina
Custom Ho Quay
North Quay
Town Quay
Grove Place Boat Park
County Wharf
Swing Bridge
Port Pendennis Marina Village
Pennance Pt
Boat Ho
Oil Pipe
Admiralty Quay

CHARTS AC *154, 32,* 18, *5602;* Imray C6, Y58; Stan 2, 23, L16; OS 204.

TIDES –0610 Dover; ML 3·0; Duration 0550; Zone 0 (UT). Daily predictions (⟵) and tidal curve (⟶). HW Truro, sp & nps, is approx HW Falmouth –0022 and –2·0m; Truro dries at LW.

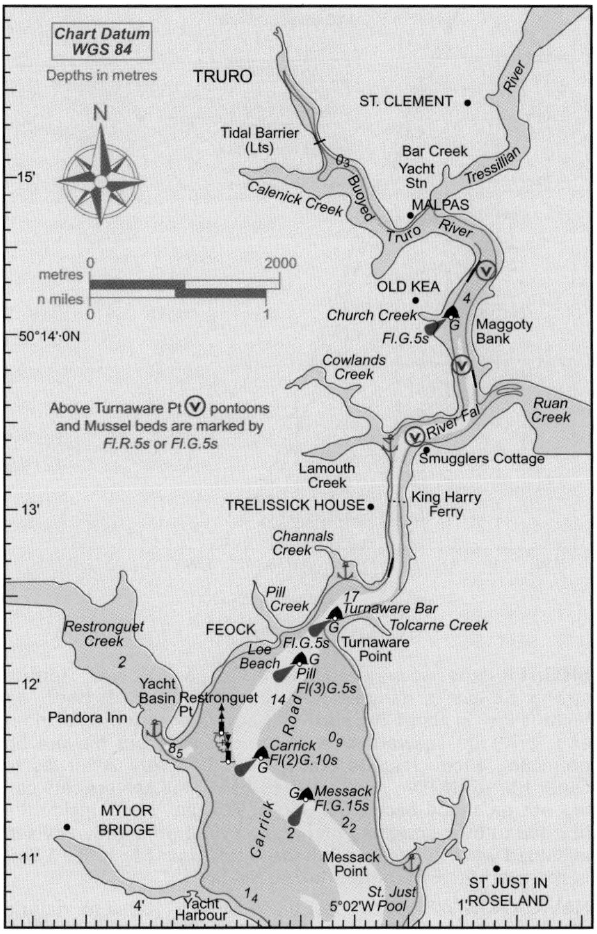
Chart Datum
WGS 84
Depths in metres
TRURO
ST. CLEMENT
N
Tidal Barrier (Lts)
Bar Creek Yacht Stn
Tressillian
River
Calenick Creek
Buoyed
MALPAS
Truro River
metres 0 2000
n miles 0 1
OLD KEA
Church Creek
Maggoty Bank
Fl.G.5s
Cowlands Creek
Above Turnaware Pt Ⓥ pontoons and Mussel beds are marked by Fl.R.5s or Fl.G.5s
Ruan Creek
River Fal
Smugglers Cottage
Lamouth Creek
King Harry Ferry
TRELISSICK HOUSE
Channals Creek
Pill Creek
Turnaware Bar
Tolcarne Creek
Restronguet Creek
FEOCK
Fl.G.5s
Turnaware Point
Loe Beach
Pill Fl(3)G.5s
Yacht Basin
Restronguet Pt
Pandora Inn
Carrick Fl(2)G.10s
Carrick Road
Messack Fl.G.15s
MYLOR BRIDGE
Messack Point
St. Just Pool
ST JUST IN ROSELAND
Yacht Harbour
5°02'W
–15'
–50°14'·0N
–13'
–12'
–11'

SHELTER Excellent. There are many Ⓥ berths, see below; also 18 clearly marked G ⓥs, on SW side of the fairway, owned by Falmouth Hbr Commissioners or the Royal Cornwall YC.

Visitors Yacht Haven, pontoons (100 AB) linked to North Quay are dredged 2 - 2.5m; max draft 2m.

Port Pendennis Marina, access HW±3 via lock with tfc lts. Outer marina (45 + 20 Ⓥ) in about 3m has H24 access.

Falmouth Marina, 6ca beyond RCYC up the Penryn R, is accessible at all times min depth 2m. On near appr pass within 20m of outside pontoon, 2FR (vert), and leave ECM lt bn (hard to see), close to stbd to keep in narrow ent chan. Unlit PHM and SHM buoys, close NE of ECM bn, mark the Penryn R; speed limit 8kn.

Mylor Yacht Hbr, on the W bank of Carrick Road, is well sheltered from W'lies but uncomfortable in strong E'lies. It is dredged inside to 2m below CD but not in the appr chan.

Restronguet Creek, further up the W bank has good ⚓ in pool (12·4m max depth), but most of the creek dries.

St Mawes Hbr, on E bank, offers excellent shelter except from SW winds, when ⚓ above Amsterdam Pt. 9 G ⓥs (contact SC). Good ⚓ off St Just, but uncomfortable in strong W/SW'lies.

Up **River Fal** and **Truro River** are Ⓥ pontoons: E of Channals Creek, N of Ruan Creek and in Mopus Reach. Good ⚓s in Tolcarne Creek, Channals Creek, Tolverne, Ruan Creek, Church Creek, Mopus Reach & Malpas (Bar Creek Yacht Stn ¼M up Tresillian R has ⓥs). **Truro**, drying AB by HM's office and N of Tesco 🛒; showers. 5kn speed limit in upper reaches and creeks.

NAVIGATION WPT 50°08'·00N 05°02'·00W, 015°/7ca to Black Rock ECM lt buoy. Ent is 1M wide and deep. Access in any weather or tide although fresh on-shore winds over an ebb tide make it a bit rough. The only hazard is Black Rk, (2·1m) almost in the middle of the ent; pass either side, but at night the E chan is advised keeping E of the ECM lt buoy. Outside the buoyed chans large areas are quite shallow; care is needed below half tide.

Falmouth is a deep water port, taking ships up to 90,000 tons; appropriate facilities are available. Take care not to impede shipping or ⚓ in prohib areas. Beware oyster beds, especially in Penryn and Percuil Rivers.

Mylor Creek dries or is shoal, <1m, but Mylor Pool has many moorings in up to 2·4m, and some pontoon berths. A PHM and SHM buoy mark the ent to the fairway. **Restronguet Creek** has a 12m deep pool at its ent, but dries above Pandora Inn. Beware Carick Carlys Rk 0·8m, 3ca E of ent, marked by a NCM & SCM post.

River Fal proper flows into the N end of Carrick Roads at Turnaware Pt; beware strong tides and rips. There are ⚓s off the various creeks. 8ca NW of Malpas a flood barrage, lit by 2 FR/FG (vert), is usually open; 3 Fl R lts show when it is closed. Truro dries to soft mud, but access HW±2½.

St Mawes Hbr In appr keep S of the SCM buoy marking Lugo Rk, 0·6m, which is always covered. The river dries above Percuil.

LIGHTS AND MARKS See chartlet and 9.1.4. St Anthony Hd lt (H24), R sector covers the Manacles Rks.

R/T Call: *Falmouth Hbr Radio*, VHF Ch **12** 14 16 (Mon-Fri 0800-1700LT); Hbr launch *Killigrew* Ch 12. Customs launch *Curlew* Ch 12 16. Port Pendennis Marina, Royal Cornwall YC, Falmouth Marina and Mylor Yacht Hbr: Ch **80**, M (H24). Visitors Yacht Haven Ch 12 16. Malpas Marine and St Mawes SC: Ch M (HO). Falmouth CG Ch 16, 23, 67 provides radio coverage of the TSS/ITZ off Land's End; see 9.1.2. Water taxi Ch 16 06.

TELEPHONE (Dial code Falmouth 01326; Truro 01872) HM Falmouth 312285/314379, ℻ 211352; HM Penryn 373352; HM St Mawes 270553; HM Truro 224231; MRCC 317575; Marinecall 09066 526242; Weather 42534; Police 08705 777444; Dr 434800; Ⓗ Truro 274242.

FACILITIES FALMOUTH **Port Pendennis Marina** ☎ 311113, ℻ 313344, www.portpendennis.com, £2.00, access H24 to outer pontoons (45 + 20 Ⓥ); ⓥs, YC (R, ⊡, CH, tennis court); Inner marina access HW±3. National Maritime Museum.

Visitors Yacht Haven (100) ☎ 312285 (Apr-Sept inc), ℻ 211352, Access H24, max draft 2m. P&D ☎ 07815 955263, Ch 12, early am to evening; ⊡. AB £1.79, Visitors' ⚓, £0.59, up to 200m east of Yacht Haven in 2-5m. as £1.14, 350m N..

Falmouth Marina (280+20 Ⓥ), ☎ 316620, ℻ 313939, £2.00 inc free AC for 1st 2 nights; CH, 🛒, D, ME, El, ⚒, ⊡, BH (30 ton), C (20 ton), Gas, Gaz, SM, Bar, R, ♿; access H24. A pipe-line/sill drying 1·8m bisects the marina E/W.

Services: Slip, BH (60 ton), C (48 ton), ME, ⚒, El, M, SM, Gaz, CH, ACA, FW. Fuel Barge, D only, as chartlet, Ch 16.

Town 🛒, R, Bar, ✉, Ⓑ, ⇌, ✈ (Plymouth or Newquay).

PENRYN/FLUSHING (01326) **Challenger Marine** ☎ 377222, ℻ 377800; M, FW, El, P & D (cans, 500m), Slip, ME, C (12 ton), ⚒, SM, ACA, BY, CH. (45 AB (drying), 240 moorings 2m) £1.33.

MYLOR (01326) **Mylor Yacht Hbr** (140 AB +40 Ⓥ + 240M, 2m) £2.00 ☎ 372121, ℻ 372120, Access HW±1, D, P, Slip, BH (35 ton), CH, Gas, Gaz, ⚒, ME, El, Ⓔ, C (4 ton), 🛒, R, Bar, ⊡. (enlarged 2002)

RESTRONGUET (01326) **Yacht Basin** ☎ 373613, Slip, M, ⚒, Ⓔ, CH, Gas, Gaz; **Pandora Inn** ☎ 372678, 🛒, R, Bar, pontoon dries 1·9m.

ST MAWES (01326) 270553 **Inner Hbr** FW, Slip. **Services:** M, ⓥs (contact SC), BY, ME, ⚒, El, SM, Gas.

MALPAS/TRURO (01872) **Bar Creek Yacht Stn** ☎ 273919, M; **Malpas Marine** ☎ 271260, M, CH, ME, El, ⚒, access H24 except LWS±1.

Truro ☎ 272130, AB or Ⓥ pontoon or ⓥ = £6, £2.75 for ⚓, access HW ±2½ via tidal barrage gates. **City** 🛒, R, Bar, ✉, Ⓑ, ⇌, CH, Gas.

YACHT CLUBS Port of Falmouth Sailing Ass'n ☎ 211555; Royal Cornwall YC (RCYC) ☎ 311105/312126 (Sec'y), M, Slip, FW, R, Bar; Falmouth Town SC ☎ 377061; Falmouth Watersports Ass'n ☎ 211223; Flushing SC ☎ 374043; Mylor YC ☎ 374391, Bar; Restronguet SC ☎ 374536; St Mawes SC ☎ 270686.

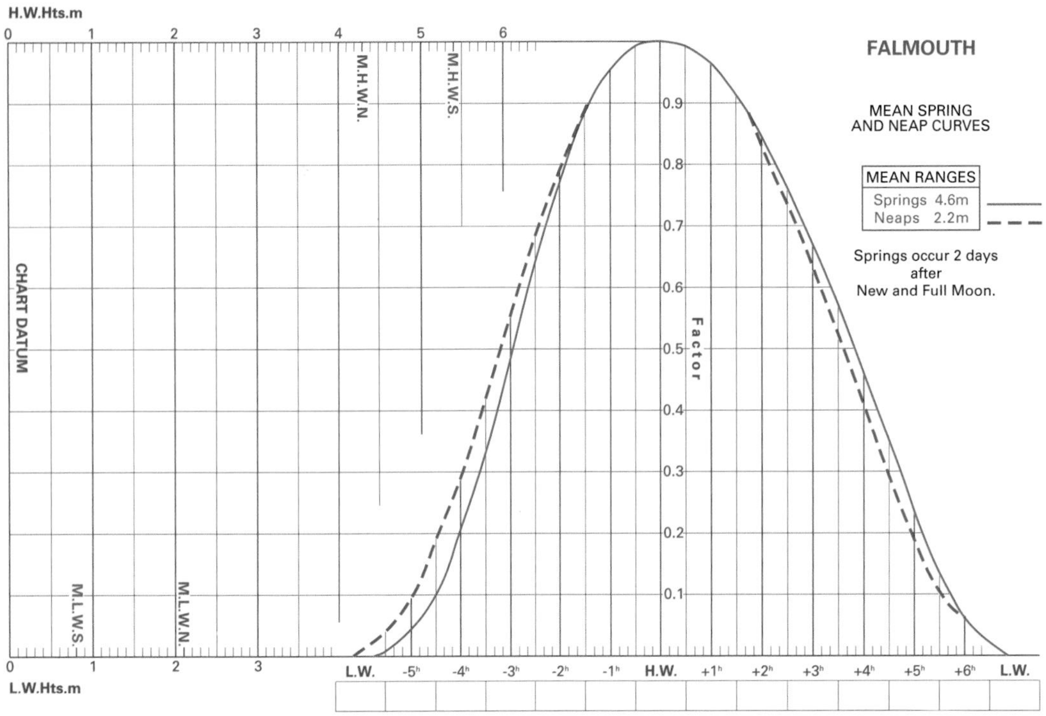
H.W.Hts.m
FALMOUTH
MEAN SPRING AND NEAP CURVES
MEAN RANGES
Springs 4.6m
Neaps 2.2m
Springs occur 2 days after New and Full Moon.
M.H.W.N.
M.H.W.S.
CHART DATUM
Factor
M.L.W.S.
M.L.W.N.
L.W.Hts.m
L.W.
H.W.
L.W.

OTHER HARBOURS AND ANCHORAGES BETWEEN ST ANTHONY HEAD AND MEVAGISSEY

PORTSCATHO, Cornwall, **50°10′·84N 04°58′·32W**. AC 1267, *154*. HW –0600 on Dover, HW –0025 and –0·2m on Devonport; ML 3·0m; Duration 0550. Small drying hbr, but in settled weather and off-shore winds ⚓ outside moorings in good holding. No lts. HM ☎ (01872) 580616. Facilities: 🛒, FW, R, Bar, Slip, P & D (cans), Ⓑ 1000-1230 Mon, Wed, Fri, ✉.

GORRAN HAVEN, Cornwall, **50°14′·49N 04°47′·16W**. AC *1267*, 148. HW –0600 on Dover, HW –0010 and –0·1m on Devonport. Shelter good with flat sand beach for drying out in off-shore wind; good ⚓ 100 to 500m E of harbour. Not suitable ⚓ when wind is in E. Beware Gwineas Rk and Yaw Rk marked by ECM lt buoy. Beware pot markers on appr. Fin keelers without legs should not ⚓ closer than 300m from hbr wall where depth is 1·8m at MLWS. Facilities: 🛒, Bar, R.

PORTMELLON, Cornwall, **50°15′·74N 04°46′·98W**. AC*1267*, 148. HW –0600 on Dover, HW –0010 and –0·1m on Devonport; ML 3·1m; Duration 0600. Shelter good but only suitable as a temp ⚓ in settled weather and off-shore winds. There are no lts. Facilities: Bar (serves food in summer).

9.1.12 MEVAGISSEY

Cornwall **50°16′·16N 04°46′·93W** ⚙⚙⚓⚓✿✿✿

CHARTS AC *1267*, 148, 147, *5602*; Imray C6, 2400.9; Stanfords 2, 23; OS 204

TIDES –0600 Dover; ML 3·1; Duration 0600; Zone 0 (UT)

Standard Port PLYMOUTH (⟶)

Times				Height (metres)			
High Water		Low Water		MHWS	MHWN	MLWN	MLWS
0000	0600	0000	0600	5·5	4·4	2·2	0·8
1200	1800	1200	1800				
Differences MEVAGISSEY							
–0015	–0020	–0010	–0005	–0·1	–0·1	–0·2	–0·1

SHELTER Exposed only to E'lies; if >F3 go to Fowey. Appr in strong SE'lies is dangerous. Access all tides. ⚡ berth on Victoria Pier in about 2m, clear of D hose/pleasure trips at inner end. 2 AB on seaward side of Victoria Pier, but beware lip projecting 71cm, fendered in season. Two fore & aft ⚡s in Outer hbr off N Pier, on request to HM. Bilge keelers/cats can dry out on sandy beach, SE side of W Quay. No ⚓ inside the hbr due to over-crowding and many FVs. ⚓ off is only advised in settled weather with no E in the wind. Inner hbr (dries 1·5m) is reserved for FVs, unless taking on FW.

NAVIGATION WPT 50°16′·16N 04°45′·98W, 270°/6ca to Victoria pier head. Beware rky ledges off N Quay. Speed limit 3kn.

LIGHTS AND MARKS As chartlet and 9.1.4. S Pier lt ho is conspic.

R/T HM Ch 16 14 (Summer 0900-2100. Winter 0900-1700); call on 16 for berth.

TELEPHONE (Dial code 01726) HM 843305, (home 842496); MRSC (01803) 882704; Marinecall 09066 526242; Police 08705 777444; Dr 843701.

FACILITIES **Outer Hbr** AB (S Quay) £10 all LOAs, M, FW, D; **Inner Hbr** Slip, FW, C (1 ton). **Services:** BY, ⚒ (wood), CH, ♿. **Village** EC Thurs; 🛒, R, ▣, Gas, Bar, Ice, ✉, Ⓑ (Jun-Sep 1000-1430, Oct-Jun 1000-1300), ⇌ (bus to St Austell), ✈ Newquay.

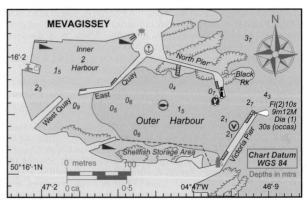

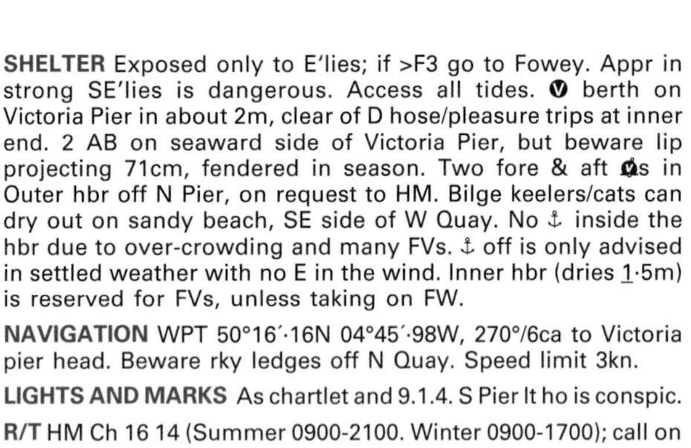
MEVAGISSEY
Inner Harbour
North Pier
Black Rk
Quay
East
West Quay
Outer Harbour
Victoria Pier
Shellfish Storage Area
Fl(2)10s 9m12M Dia (1) 30s (occas)
Chart Datum WGS 84
Depths in mtrs
0 metres 100
0 ca 0.5
16'·2
50°16'·1N
47'·2
04°47'W
46'·9
N

GUNNERY RANGE OFF DODMAN PT AND GRIBBIN HEAD

Naval gunnery practice takes place to seaward of Dodman Pt and Gribbin Hd, under the control of Flag Officer Sea Training (FOST), HMS Drake, Plymouth PL2 2BG. For info ☎ (01752) 557550 (H24) or call *FOST OPS* on VHF Ch 74, which is monitored by all warships in the areas S of Plymouth.

Firing is by day only, approx 1-2 times per week, in a 2 hrs block, although actual firing only lasts about 15 mins. Planned firings are broadcast in Gunfacts (see 7.14.3) and Navtex. Advance details are also printed in local newspapers and are available from HMs at Fowey, Looe, Polperro and Mevagissey. Firings are not planned for 2 weeks at Christmas and 4 weeks in August.

The range is in danger areas D.006A and D.007A & B (see 9.1.16). Warships, between 2·5 and 9M SSE of Gribbin Hd, fire WSW at 3 SPM target buoys, Fl Y, which lie from 2·7 to 4·7M SSE of Dodman Pt. The RN will ensure that safety requirements can be met; if not possible, ie due to vessels in the range area, then firing will not take place. A helicopter conducts range safety surveillance. A range safety boat will advise other craft of firings and may suggest a slight course alteration to clear the area. Yachts are legally entitled to transit through the range area.

MINOR HARBOURS BETWEEN MEVAGISSEY AND FOWEY

CHARLESTOWN, Cornwall, **50°19′·84N 04°45′·35W.** AC *1267* 148, 31. HW –0555 on Dover, –0010 on Devonport; HW –0·1m on Devonport; ML 3·1m; Duration 0605. HM ☎ 01726 70241, 📠 61839, VHF Ch 12 16. Once a china clay port, it now runs square riggers for filming. Enter the inner hbr via entry gate as arranged with HM on Ch 14 or ☎ (01726) 67526, but only in W'lies. Ent dries and should only be attempted by day and in off-shore winds with calm weather. Hbr is closed in SE winds. Waiting buoys 2ca S of hbr. Bkwtrs 2FG & 2FR(vert) 5m 1M. Ent sig: ● (night) = hbr shut. VHF Ch14 16 (HW –2, only when vessel expected). Facilities: www.square-sail.com, EC Thurs; AB, FW, P & D (cans or pre-arranged tanker), R, Bar, V at ⊠, ME, SM.

PAR, Cornwall, **50°20′·61N 04°42′·06W.** AC *1267* 148, 31. HW –0555 on Dover; ML 3·1m; Duration 0605. See 9.1.13. A china clay port, only in emergency for yachts; dries 1·2m. 4 chys are conspic 2½ca W of ent. Beware Killyvarder Rk (dries 2·4m) 3ca SE of ent, marked by unlit SHM bn. Only attempt ent by day, in calm weather with off-shore winds. Ent sigs: R shape (day) or ● lt (night) = port closed or vessel leaving. VHF Ch 12 16 (by day, HW –2 to HW +1). HM ☎ (01726) 817337. Facilities: EC Thurs; Bar, FW.

9.1.13 FOWEY

Cornwall **50°19′·65N 04°38′·54W**

CHARTS AC *1267*, 148, 31, *5602*; Imray C6, 2400.7/8; Stanfords 2, 23; OS 204

TIDES –0540 Dover; ML 2·9; Duration 0605; Zone 0 (UT

Standard Port PLYMOUTH (⟶) 163-165)

Times				**Height (metres)**			
High Water		Low Water		MHWS	MHWN	MLWN	MLWS
0000	0600	0000	0600	5·5	4·4	2·2	0·8
1200	1800	1200	1800				
Differences FOWEY							
–0010	–0015	–0010	–0005	–0·1	–0·1	–0·2	–0·2
LOSTWITHIEL							
+0005	–0010	Dries		–4·1	–4·1	Dries	
PAR							
–0010	–0015	–0010	–0005	–0·4	–0·4	–0·4	–0·2

SHELTER Good, but exposed to winds from S to SW. Gales from these directions can cause heavy swell in the lower hbr and confused seas, especially on the ebb. Entry at any tide in any conditions. Fowey is a busy commercial clay port. Speed limit 6kn. All Ⓥs are marked 'FHC VISITORS'. Overnight fees on Ⓥ/ pontoon: average £1.20/m, but £1.44/m in Mixtow Pill. Reductions for 3 days or 1 week.

Craft should berth/moor as directed by Hbr Patrol. Ⓥ pontoons are in situ May-Oct. **Pont Pill**, on the E side, offers double-berth fore and aft Ⓥs and AB in 2m on a 36m floating pontoon; there is also a refuse barge and RNSA members' buoy. Opposite Albert Quay, on the E side of the chan there is a trot of single swinging Ⓥs and another 36m pontoon. At **Albert Quay** the 'T' shaped landing pontoon is for short stay (2 hrs), plus FW. A second short stay (2 hrs) landing pontoon is 250m up-river, at Berrills BY; also at Polruan. A Ⓥ pontoon (double-sided) is off the E bank, midway between Bodinnick and Mixtow Pill. At **Mixtow Pill** (5ca upriver) is a quieter 135m, shore-linked pontoon in 2·2m, Ⓥ on S side. Landing place and boat storage ashore. A Ⓥ is 30m N of Wiseman's Pt.

NAVIGATION WPT 50°19′·33N 04°38′·80W, 027°/7ca through hbr ent to Whitehouse Pt Dir lt in W sector. Appr in W sector of Fowey lt ho. 3M E of ent beware Udder Rk marked by SCM lt buoy. From SW beware Cannis Rk (4ca SE of

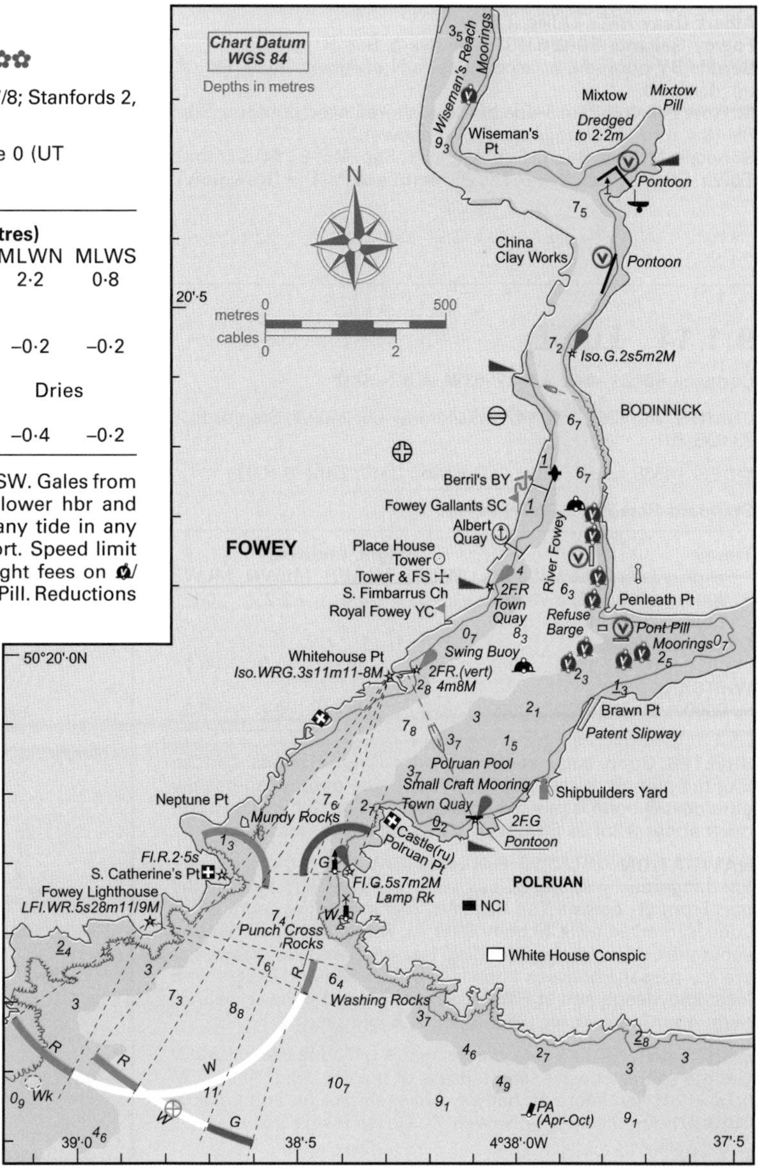

Chart Datum
WGS 84
Depths in metres
Wiseman's Reach
Moorings
Mixtow
Mixtow Pill
Dredged to 2·2m
Wiseman's Pt
Pontoon
N
China Clay Works
Pontoon
20'·5
metres
cables
0
500
0
2
Iso.G.2s5m2M
BODINNICK
Berril's BY
Fowey Gallants SC
Albert Quay
FOWEY
Place House Tower
Tower & FS
S. Fimbarrus Ch
Royal Fowey YC
River Fowey
Penleath Pt
Town Quay
Refuse Barge
Pont Pill
Moorings
Swing Buoy
50°20'·0N
Whitehouse Pt
Iso.WRG.3s11m11-8M
2FR.(vert)
4m8M
Brawn Pt
Patent Slipway
Polruan Pool
Small Craft Moorings
Shipbuilders Yard
Neptune Pt
Mundy Rocks
Town Quay
2F.G
Pontoon
Castle(ru)
Polruan Pt
Fl.R.2·5s
S. Catherine's Pt
Fowey Lighthouse
LFl.WR.5s28m11/9M
Fl.G.5s7m2M
Lamp Rk
POLRUAN
NCI
Punch Cross Rocks
White House Conspic
Washing Rocks
Wk
R
W
G
PA
(Apr-Oct)
39'·0
38'·5
4°38'·0W
37'·5

FOWEY *continued*

Gribbin Hd) marked by SCM lt buoy. Entering hbr, keep well clear of Punch Cross Rks to stbd. Give way to the Bodinnick-Caffa-Mill ferry. Unmarked chan is navigable up to Golant, but moorings restrict ⚓ space. Lerryn (1·6M) and Lostwithiel (3M) (18m power cables and 5.3m rail bridge) are accessible on the tide by shoal draft.

LIGHTS AND MARKS See chartlet and 9.1.4. An unlit RW tr 33m on Gribbin Hd (1·3M WSW of hbr ent) is conspic from all sea directions, as is a white house 3ca E of hbr ent. Fowey lt ho is conspic. The W sector (022°-032°) of Whitehouse Pt dir lt leads safely through the 200m wide hbr ent. At the ent Lamp Rk lt and St Catherine's Point lt are both lamp boxes, only visible from within the hbr.

R/T Call *Fowey Hbr Radio* Ch **12** 16 (HO). Hbr Patrol (0900-2000LT) Ch 12. Water taxi Ch 06. Pilots & Tugs Ch 09, 12.

TELEPHONE (Dial code 01726) HM 832471, 📠 833738; MRSC (01803) 882704; NCI 870291 @ Polruan; Marinecall 09066 526242; Police (0990) 777444; Ⓗ 832241; Dr 832451.

FACILITIES From seaward: **Polruan Quay** Pontoon, Slip, L, FW, C (3 ton), D: Note this is the only fuel available by hose at Fowey/ Polruan. **Royal Fowey YC** ☎ 832245, FW, R, Bar, Showers.
Albert Quay HM's Office, L, FW.
Fowey Gallants SC ☎ 832335, Showers, Bar, R.
Berrills BY pontoon, ♿ access, 250m N of Albert Quay, FW, ⛽, oil disposal.
Mixtow Pill, Ⓥ AB on S side of 135m, shore-linked pontoon; Slip, BH (8.4 ton) by arrangement, FW, showers.
Services: M, Gas, Gaz, CH, ACA, Ⓔ, BY, Slip, ME, El, ⚒, C (7 ton).
Town EC Wed/Sat; R, Bar, ✉, Ⓑ, ⇌ (bus to Par), ✈ (Newquay).

MINOR HARBOUR BETWEEN FOWEY AND LOOE

POLPERRO, Cornwall, **50°19′·78N 04°30′·79W**. AC *1267,* 148. HW –0554 on Dover; HW –0007 and –0·2m on Devonport; ML 3·1m; Duration 0610. Shelter good, but hbr dries about 2m; 3·3m at MHWS and 2·5m at MHWN. The ent is 9·8m wide (closed by gate in bad weather, but the inner basin remains tidal). Berth on E side of ent or pick up one of 4 seasonal buoys outside ent. Beware The Ranney to W of ent, and the rks to E. Lights: see chartlet and 9.1.4. Spy House Pt shows W to seaward (288°-060°) with R sectors inshore. A FW lt on the W pier hd shows FR (black ball by day) when gate to inner Basin is shut. Measured distance bns, 1M and 2·2M to ENE, show Dir FW (occas). HM on Fish Quay, ☎ (01503) 272809 or 07968 374118; AB £1.25; FW on quays. EC Sat, R, Bar, ✉.

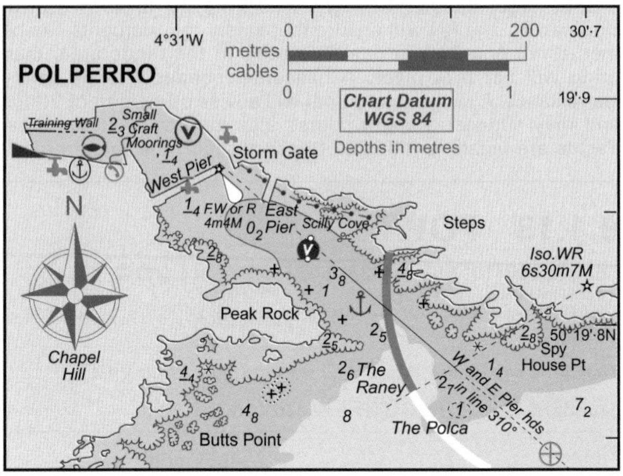
POLPERRO
4°31'W
30'·7
19'·9
metres
cables
0
200
1
Chart Datum
WGS 84
Depths in metres
Training Wall
Small Craft Moorings
West Pier
Storm Gate
F.W or R 4m4M
East Pier
Scilly Cove
Steps
Peak Rock
Chapel Hill
Iso.WR 6s30m7M
50°19'·8N
Spy House Pt
The Raney
The Polca
W and E Pier hds in line 310°
Butts Point
N

9.1.14 LOOE

Cornwall **50°21′·04N 04°27′·03W**

CHARTS AC *1267,* 148, 147, *5602*; Imray C6, 2400.7; Stanfords 2, 23; OS 201

TIDES –0538 Dover; ML 3·0; Duration 0610; Zone 0 (UT)

Standard Port PLYMOUTH (⟶)

Times				Height (metres)			
High Water		Low Water		MHWS	MHWN	MLWN	MLWS
0000	0600	0000	0600	5·5	4·4	2·2	0·8
1200	1800	1200	1800				
Differences LOOE							
–0010	–0010	–0005	–0005	–0·1	–0·2	–0·2	–0·2
WHITSAND BAY							
0000	0000	0000	0000	0·0	+0·1	–0·1	+0·2

SHELTER Good, but uncomfortable in strong SE winds. ⚓ in 2m E of the pier hd; access approx HW ±1½. The outer chan has rky outcrops. Ⓥ berth is marked on shelter, W side of hbr. The berth dries about 3·3m to firm, level sand; rafting is possible.

NAVIGATION WPT 50°20′·68N 04°25′·60W, 290°/1·0M to hbr ent. Ent dangerous in strong SE'lies, when seas break heavily on the bar. From W, beware The Ranneys, reef extending 500m SE of Looe Is, marked by SCM buoy Q (6) + L Fl 15s. 3ca NE of hbr ent, avoid the Limmicks, rks extending 1½ca offshore. Do not attempt the rky passage between Looe Is and the mainland except with local knowledge and at HW. At sp, ebb tide runs up to 5kn. At night appr in W sector (267°-313°) of Banjo pier hd lt.

LIGHTS AND MARKS See chartlet and 9.1.4. Looe Island (aka St George's Is) is conspic (45m), 8ca S of the ent. Mid Main ECM lt bn is off Hannafore Pt, halfway between pier hd and Looe Is. Siren (2) 30s (fishing) at Nailzee Pt. No lts inside hbr.

R/T VHF Ch 16 (occas).

TELEPHONE (Dial code 01503) HM 262839; CG 262138; MRSC (01803) 882704; Marinecall 09066 526242; Police 08705 777444; Dr 263195.

FACILITIES W Looe Quay AB £1.08, Slip, P & D (cans), FW, ME, El; **E Looe Quay** For FVs, but access HW ±3 for D, Slip; **Looe SC** ☎ 262559, L, R, Bar. **Services:** ⚒ (Wood), Ⓔ, ⚒, Gas. **Town** P, FW, 🛒, R, Bar, ♿, ⊡, ✉, Ⓑ, ⇌, ✈ (Plymouth).

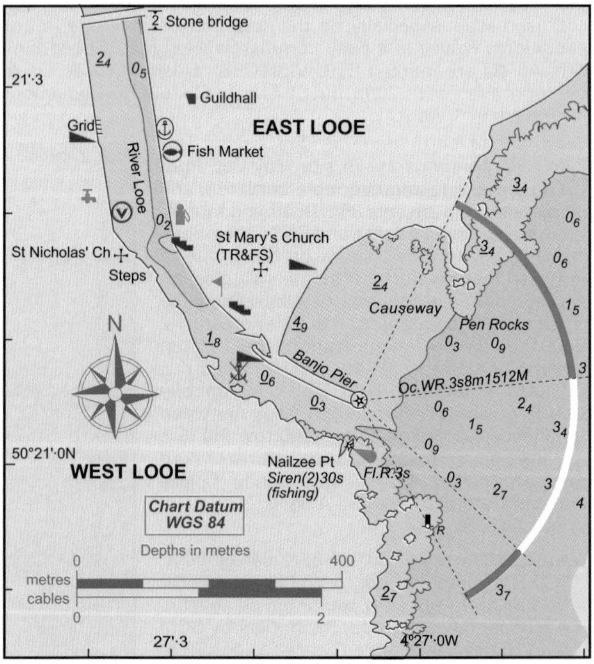
Stone bridge
21'·3
Guildhall
EAST LOOE
Grid
River Looe
Fish Market
St Mary's Church (TR&FS)
St Nicholas' Ch
Steps
Causeway
Pen Rocks
Banjo Pier
Oc.WR.3s8m15M
N
50°21'·0N
WEST LOOE
Nailzee Pt
Siren(2)30s (fishing)
Fl.R.3s
Chart Datum
WGS 84
Depths in metres
metres
cables
0
400
2
27'·3
4°27'·0W

TIME ZONE (UT)
For Summer Time add ONE hour in **non-shaded areas**

ENGLAND – PLYMOUTH

LAT 50°22′N LONG 4°11′W

TIMES AND HEIGHTS OF HIGH AND LOW WATERS

SPRING & NEAP TIDES
Dates in red are **SPRINGS**
Dates in blue are **NEAPS**

YEAR **2005**

JANUARY

Day	Time	m	Time	m	Time	m	Time	m
1 SA	0234	1.7	0850	4.9	1500	1.7	2115	4.6
2 SU	0309	1.8	0928	4.8	1538	1.8	2155	4.5
3 M	0350	1.9	1010	4.7	1624	1.9	◑ 2243	4.4
4 TU	0442	2.0	1102	4.6	1725	2.0	2342	4.4
5 W	0553	2.1	1205	4.6	1842	2.0		
6 TH	0050	4.5	0716	2.1	1319	4.6	1956	1.9
7 F	0204	4.6	0830	1.9	1434	4.7	2103	1.7
8 SA	0315	4.8	0937	1.6	1546	4.9	2207	1.4
9 SU	0419	5.1	1039	1.3	1649	5.1	2306	1.2
10 M	0516	5.4	1136	1.0	1746	5.3	●	
11 TU	0000	1.0	0608	5.6	1230	0.7	1839	5.4
12 W	0052	0.8	0659	5.7	1320	0.6	1931	5.4
13 TH	0140	0.7	0749	5.7	1408	0.6	2020	5.3
14 F	0225	0.8	0836	5.7	1452	0.7	2106	5.2
15 SA	0307	0.9	0920	5.5	1534	0.9	2148	5.0
16 SU	0347	1.2	1001	5.2	1614	1.2	2229	4.8
17 M	0428	1.5	1042	4.9	1656	1.6	◐ 2312	4.6
18 TU	0513	1.8	1130	4.6	1745	1.9		
19 W	0007	4.4	0610	2.1	1234	4.4	1847	2.2
20 TH	0116	4.3	0723	2.3	1348	4.3	2001	2.2
21 F	0224	4.4	0844	2.2	1456	4.4	2115	2.1
22 SA	0325	4.6	0952	2.0	1554	4.5	2213	1.9
23 SU	0416	4.8	1044	1.7	1642	4.7	2300	1.6
24 M	0500	5.0	1127	1.5	1724	4.9	2340	1.5
25 TU	0539	5.2	1206	1.3	1802	5.0	○	
26 W	0017	1.3	0617	5.2	1242	1.2	1840	5.0
27 TH	0051	1.3	0654	5.3	1314	1.2	1917	5.0
28 F	0123	1.2	0731	5.2	1345	1.2	1952	4.9
29 SA	0152	1.3	0804	5.2	1413	1.2	2023	4.9
30 SU	0220	1.3	0834	5.1	1442	1.3	2052	4.8
31 M	0249	1.4	0903	5.0	1512	1.4	2122	4.7

FEBRUARY

Day	Time	m	Time	m	Time	m	Time	m
1 TU	0323	1.5	0935	4.9	1547	1.6	2159	4.6
2 W	0403	1.7	1019	4.7	1633	1.8	◑ 2252	4.5
3 TH	0458	2.0	1121	4.5	1738	2.0		
4 F	0004	4.4	0623	2.1	1242	4.4	1914	2.1
5 SA	0131	4.4	0803	2.0	1414	4.5	2044	1.9
6 SU	0256	4.7	0925	1.7	1537	4.7	2157	1.6
7 M	0407	5.0	1032	1.3	1643	5.0	2259	1.2
8 TU	0506	5.4	1129	0.8	1738	5.2	● 2352	0.8
9 W	0558	5.6	1221	0.5	1829	5.4		
10 TH	0041	0.6	0647	5.8	1308	0.3	1917	5.5
11 F	0126	0.4	0733	5.8	1352	0.3	2001	5.4
12 SA	0208	0.4	0817	5.7	1432	0.4	2041	5.4
13 SU	0245	0.6	0855	5.5	1508	0.6	2115	5.2
14 M	0319	0.9	0928	5.3	1540	1.0	2143	4.9
15 TU	0352	1.3	0956	4.9	1612	1.5	2210	4.7
16 W	0427	1.7	1027	4.6	1649	1.9	◐ 2246	4.4
17 TH	0511	2.1	1113	4.2	1740	2.3	2347	4.2
18 F	0619	2.4	1243	4.0	1856	2.5		
19 SA	0136	4.1	0755	2.5	1425	4.0	2037	2.4
20 SU	0255	4.3	0935	2.2	1532	4.3	2155	2.1
21 M	0353	4.6	1029	1.8	1624	4.6	2244	1.7
22 TU	0440	4.9	1111	1.4	1707	4.8	2324	1.4
23 W	0521	5.1	1149	1.2	1746	5.0		
24 TH	0001	1.2	0600	5.2	1224	1.0	○ 1823	5.1
25 F	0035	1.0	0637	5.3	1256	0.9	1859	5.1
26 SA	0105	1.0	0712	5.3	1325	0.9	1931	5.1
27 SU	0134	0.9	0744	5.3	1353	0.9	2000	5.1
28 M	0201	1.0	0812	5.2	1420	1.0	2026	5.0

MARCH

Day	Time	m	Time	m	Time	m	Time	m
1 TU	0228	1.1	0839	5.1	1448	1.1	2053	4.9
2 W	0300	1.2	0909	4.9	1520	1.4	2127	4.7
3 TH	0337	1.5	0952	4.6	1601	1.7	◑ 2219	4.5
4 F	0429	1.9	1056	4.4	1702	2.1	2335	4.3
5 SA	0556	2.2	1225	4.2	1853	2.3		
6 SU	0114	4.3	0756	2.1	1413	4.3	2039	2.0
7 M	0250	4.6	0922	1.6	1537	4.6	2152	1.5
8 TU	0359	5.0	1025	1.1	1636	5.0	2248	1.0
9 W	0453	5.4	1117	0.6	1726	5.3	2338	0.7
10 TH	0541	5.6	1204	0.3	1812	5.4	●	
11 F	0023	0.4	0627	5.7	1248	0.2	1854	5.5
12 SA	0105	0.3	0710	5.7	1328	0.2	1933	5.5
13 SU	0143	0.3	0749	5.6	1405	0.3	2007	5.4
14 M	0218	0.5	0822	5.4	1437	0.7	2035	5.2
15 TU	0248	0.9	0849	5.1	1505	1.1	2057	5.0
16 W	0317	1.3	0913	4.8	1533	1.5	2121	4.7
17 TH	0347	1.7	0941	4.5	1603	1.9	◐ 2156	4.5
18 F	0424	2.1	1022	4.1	1647	2.3	2248	4.2
19 SA	0531	2.5	1132	3.9	1809	2.6		
20 SU	0023	4.0	0709	2.6	1357	3.9	1951	2.5
21 M	0224	4.2	0908	2.2	1507	4.2	2125	2.1
22 TU	0324	4.5	1000	1.8	1558	4.5	2214	1.7
23 W	0412	4.8	1041	1.4	1641	4.8	2254	1.4
24 TH	0454	5.1	1118	1.1	1720	5.0	2331	1.1
25 F	0534	5.2	1153	0.9	1757	5.1	○	
26 SA	0006	0.9	0611	5.3	1227	0.8	1832	5.2
27 SU	0039	0.8	0646	5.3	1259	0.7	1904	5.2
28 M	0110	0.7	0719	5.3	1329	0.7	1934	5.2
29 TU	0140	0.8	0750	5.2	1358	0.9	2002	5.2
30 W	0210	0.9	0821	5.1	1428	1.1	2033	5.0
31 TH	0243	1.2	0857	4.9	1502	1.4	2112	4.8

APRIL

Day	Time	m	Time	m	Time	m	Time	m
1 F	0324	1.5	0943	4.6	1546	1.8	2206	4.6
2 SA	0420	1.9	1049	4.3	1653	2.2	◑ 2322	4.3
3 SU	0557	2.2	1227	4.1	1854	2.3		
4 M	0110	4.4	0755	2.0	1416	4.3	2032	1.9
5 TU	0241	4.7	0910	1.5	1527	4.7	2136	1.4
6 W	0343	5.1	1006	1.0	1620	5.0	2229	1.0
7 TH	0434	5.4	1055	0.6	1705	5.3	2315	0.6
8 F	0519	5.6	1140	0.4	1747	5.4	● 2358	0.4
9 SA	0602	5.6	1221	0.3	1825	5.5		
10 SU	0038	0.4	0641	5.6	1300	0.4	1900	5.4
11 M	0115	0.5	0717	5.4	1334	0.6	1930	5.3
12 TU	0148	0.7	0747	5.2	1405	0.9	1954	5.2
13 W	0218	1.0	0812	5.0	1432	1.2	2018	5.0
14 TH	0246	1.3	0838	4.7	1458	1.6	2046	4.8
15 F	0314	1.7	0909	4.4	1525	2.0	2123	4.5
16 SA	0349	2.1	0953	4.1	1606	2.3	◐ 2214	4.3
17 SU	0454	2.4	1058	3.9	1732	2.6	2329	4.1
18 M	0629	2.5	1311	3.9	1906	2.5		
19 TU	0134	4.2	0802	2.2	1427	4.2	2028	2.2
20 W	0242	4.5	0906	1.8	1519	4.5	2124	1.8
21 TH	0332	4.7	0953	1.4	1604	4.7	2210	1.4
22 F	0417	5.0	1035	1.1	1645	5.0	2252	1.1
23 SA	0459	5.1	1115	0.9	1724	5.1	2331	0.9
24 SU	0540	5.2	1153	0.8	1801	5.2	○	
25 M	0009	0.8	0618	5.3	1230	0.7	1836	5.3
26 TU	0046	0.7	0656	5.3	1306	0.8	1911	5.3
27 W	0122	0.8	0733	5.2	1341	0.9	1946	5.3
28 TH	0159	0.9	0812	5.1	1417	1.1	2024	5.1
29 F	0239	1.2	0855	4.8	1458	1.4	2108	4.9
30 SA	0326	1.5	0947	4.6	1548	1.8	2203	4.7

Chart Datum: 3·22 metres below Ordnance Datum (Newlyn)

TIME ZONE (UT)
For Summer Time add ONE hour in **non-shaded areas**

ENGLAND – PLYMOUTH

LAT 50°22′N LONG 4°11′W

TIMES AND HEIGHTS OF HIGH AND LOW WATERS

SPRING & NEAP TIDES
Dates in red are **SPRINGS**
Dates in blue are **NEAPS**

YEAR **2005**

MAY

Day		Time	m	Time	m	Time	m	Time	m
1	SU	0429	1.8	1054	4.3	1701	2.1	◑ 2318	4.5
2	M	0601	2.0	1230	4.3	1844	2.1		
3	TU	0059	4.5	0735	1.8	1356	4.4	2007	1.8
4	W	0217	4.8	0843	1.4	1459	4.7	2108	1.4
5	TH	0316	5.0	0938	1.1	1551	5.0	2200	1.1
6	F	0407	5.2	1027	0.8	1636	5.2	2247	0.8
7	SA	0453	5.3	1111	0.7	1717	5.3	2330	0.7
8	SU	0534	5.4	1153	0.6	1755	5.3	●	
9	M	0010	0.7	0612	5.3	1231	0.7	1827	5.3
10	TU	0047	0.8	0646	5.2	1304	0.9	1856	5.3
11	W	0121	1.0	0716	5.0	1335	1.1	1922	5.2
12	TH	0151	1.2	0744	4.9	1404	1.4	1951	5.0
13	F	0221	1.5	0815	4.7	1433	1.7	2024	4.9
14	SA	0252	1.7	0851	4.4	1504	2.0	2103	4.6
15	SU	0330	2.0	0937	4.2	1546	2.2	2152	4.4
16	M	0427	2.2	1037	4.1	1655	2.4	◐ 2255	4.3
17	TU	0545	2.3	1159	4.0	1818	2.4		
18	W	0017	4.3	0700	2.1	1325	4.2	1929	2.2
19	TH	0139	4.4	0803	1.8	1424	4.4	2028	1.9
20	F	0238	4.6	0857	1.5	1515	4.6	2120	1.6
21	SA	0330	4.8	0947	1.3	1602	4.9	2209	1.3
22	SU	0420	5.0	1034	1.1	1647	5.1	2256	1.1
23	M	0507	5.1	1120	0.9	1730	5.2	○ 2342	0.9
24	TU	0553	5.2	1205	0.9	1812	5.3		
25	W	0026	0.8	0637	5.2	1249	0.9	1854	5.4
26	TH	0111	0.8	0723	5.2	1332	1.0	1937	5.4
27	F	0156	0.9	0810	5.1	1417	1.1	2023	5.3
28	SA	0243	1.0	0900	4.9	1504	1.3	2111	5.1
29	SU	0334	1.3	0953	4.7	1556	1.6	2205	4.9
30	M	0433	1.5	1056	4.6	1659	1.8	◑ 2312	4.8
31	TU	0544	1.6	1210	4.5	1814	1.9		

JUNE

Day		Time	m	Time	m	Time	m	Time	m
1	W	0030	4.7	0658	1.6	1320	4.5	1927	1.8
2	TH	0141	4.7	0804	1.5	1421	4.7	2030	1.6
3	F	0241	4.8	0902	1.3	1515	4.8	2126	1.4
4	SA	0335	4.9	0954	1.2	1603	5.0	2217	1.2
5	SU	0424	5.0	1042	1.1	1647	5.1	2303	1.1
6	M	0507	5.0	1125	1.1	1726	5.2	● 2345	1.1
7	TU	0546	5.0	1204	1.1	1800	5.2		
8	W	0024	1.1	0621	5.0	1240	1.2	1831	5.2
9	TH	0100	1.2	0655	4.9	1313	1.3	1902	5.1
10	F	0133	1.3	0728	4.8	1345	1.5	1936	5.0
11	SA	0206	1.5	0804	4.6	1417	1.6	2012	4.9
12	SU	0239	1.6	0844	4.5	1451	1.8	2052	4.8
13	M	0315	1.8	0927	4.4	1528	2.0	2135	4.6
14	TU	0359	1.9	1014	4.3	1615	2.1	2223	4.5
15	W	0454	2.0	1109	4.2	1718	2.2	◐ 2320	4.5
16	TH	0600	2.0	1212	4.3	1829	2.1		
17	F	0024	4.5	0705	1.9	1316	4.4	1934	1.9
18	SA	0132	4.6	0805	1.7	1417	4.5	2033	1.7
19	SU	0237	4.7	0903	1.5	1516	4.7	2131	1.5
20	M	0340	4.8	0959	1.3	1612	5.0	2227	1.3
21	TU	0438	5.0	1054	1.2	1705	5.2	2321	1.0
22	W	0533	5.1	1147	1.0	1755	5.3	○	
23	TH	0013	0.9	0626	5.2	1238	0.9	1843	5.5
24	F	0105	0.7	0718	5.2	1328	0.9	1933	5.5
25	SA	0155	0.7	0810	5.2	1416	0.9	2022	5.5
26	SU	0244	0.8	0900	5.1	1503	1.0	2110	5.4
27	M	0332	0.9	0949	5.0	1550	1.2	2159	5.2
28	TU	0420	1.1	1040	4.8	1639	1.4	◑ 2251	5.0
29	W	0513	1.4	1135	4.7	1734	1.6	2350	4.8
30	TH	0611	1.6	1235	4.5	1837	1.8		

JULY

Day		Time	m	Time	m	Time	m	Time	m
1	F	0056	4.6	0715	1.7	1336	4.5	1944	1.9
2	SA	0201	4.5	0820	1.8	1435	4.6	2049	1.8
3	SU	0301	4.6	0921	1.7	1530	4.7	2149	1.7
4	M	0356	4.6	1015	1.6	1619	4.9	2241	1.5
5	TU	0444	4.7	1103	1.5	1702	5.0	2327	1.4
6	W	0526	4.8	1145	1.4	1740	5.1	●	
7	TH	0008	1.3	0604	4.9	1224	1.3	1815	5.1
8	F	0047	1.3	0641	4.9	1300	1.3	1851	5.1
9	SA	0122	1.3	0718	4.8	1333	1.4	1927	5.1
10	SU	0154	1.4	0756	4.7	1404	1.5	2003	5.0
11	M	0225	1.4	0833	4.7	1434	1.6	2039	4.9
12	TU	0255	1.5	0909	4.6	1504	1.7	2113	4.8
13	W	0327	1.6	0945	4.5	1537	1.8	2149	4.7
14	TH	0404	1.7	1024	4.4	1619	1.9	◐ 2231	4.6
15	F	0451	1.8	1113	4.4	1716	2.0	2326	4.5
16	SA	0558	1.9	1214	4.4	1835	2.0		
17	SU	0034	4.5	0715	1.9	1327	4.4	1953	1.9
18	M	0153	4.5	0828	1.8	1440	4.6	2103	1.7
19	TU	0311	4.7	0935	1.5	1548	4.9	2208	1.4
20	W	0421	4.9	1038	1.3	1648	5.2	2309	1.1
21	TH	0521	5.1	1136	1.0	1742	5.4	○	
22	F	0005	0.8	0616	5.2	1230	0.8	1833	5.6
23	SA	0058	0.5	0709	5.3	1320	0.6	1924	5.7
24	SU	0147	0.4	0800	5.4	1407	0.6	2012	5.7
25	M	0232	0.4	0846	5.3	1450	0.7	2057	5.6
26	TU	0315	0.6	0929	5.2	1530	0.9	2139	5.4
27	W	0355	0.9	1010	5.0	1610	1.2	2219	5.1
28	TH	0435	1.3	1051	4.7	1652	1.5	◑ 2302	4.7
29	F	0520	1.7	1140	4.5	1743	1.9	2359	4.4
30	SA	0615	2.0	1246	4.3	1851	2.2		
31	SU	0117	4.2	0728	2.2	1358	4.3	2014	2.2

AUGUST

Day		Time	m	Time	m	Time	m	Time	m
1	M	0232	4.2	0851	2.1	1503	4.5	2131	2.0
2	TU	0334	4.4	0958	1.9	1558	4.7	2228	1.8
3	W	0426	4.6	1049	1.7	1643	4.9	2315	1.5
4	TH	0510	4.7	1132	1.4	1723	5.1	2356	1.3
5	F	0549	4.9	1211	1.3	1801	5.2	●	
6	SA	0033	1.2	0626	4.9	1246	1.2	1837	5.2
7	SU	0107	1.1	0703	4.9	1317	1.2	1913	5.2
8	M	0136	1.2	0739	4.9	1345	1.2	1947	5.1
9	TU	0203	1.2	0812	4.9	1411	1.3	2018	5.1
10	W	0228	1.3	0841	4.8	1436	1.4	2045	5.0
11	TH	0254	1.4	0909	4.7	1504	1.5	2113	4.8
12	F	0324	1.5	0941	4.6	1538	1.7	2149	4.7
13	SA	0402	1.7	1025	4.5	1625	1.9	◐ 2243	4.5
14	SU	0457	2.0	1129	4.3	1739	2.2	2358	4.3
15	M	0630	2.2	1252	4.4	1928	2.1		
16	TU	0131	4.3	0809	2.0	1422	4.6	2051	1.8
17	W	0303	4.6	0925	1.7	1537	4.9	2201	1.4
18	TH	0414	4.9	1030	1.3	1637	5.3	2300	0.9
19	F	0511	5.1	1126	0.9	1729	5.6	○ 2354	0.6
20	SA	0603	5.4	1216	0.6	1818	5.8		
21	SU	0043	0.3	0651	5.5	1304	0.4	1906	5.8
22	M	0129	0.2	0738	5.5	1347	0.4	1951	5.8
23	TU	0210	0.3	0820	5.5	1426	0.5	2032	5.6
24	W	0248	0.5	0858	5.3	1502	0.8	2108	5.4
25	TH	0323	0.9	0931	5.1	1536	1.1	2139	5.0
26	F	0356	1.3	1000	4.8	1611	1.6	◑ 2209	4.7
27	SA	0431	1.8	1033	4.5	1654	2.1	2248	4.3
28	SU	0519	2.3	1127	4.2	1759	2.4		
29	M	0016	4.0	0634	2.5	1322	4.1	1943	2.5
30	TU	0210	4.0	0833	2.5	1440	4.3	2122	2.2
31	W	0317	4.2	0945	2.1	1538	4.6	2214	1.8

Chart Datum: 3·22 metres below Ordnance Datum (Newlyn)

TIME ZONE (UT)
For Summer Time add ONE hour in **non-shaded areas**

ENGLAND – PLYMOUTH

LAT 50°22′N LONG 4°11′W

TIMES AND HEIGHTS OF HIGH AND LOW WATERS

SPRING & NEAP TIDES
Dates in red are SPRINGS
Dates in blue are NEAPS

YEAR **2005**

SEPTEMBER

Date	Day	Time	m	Time	m	Time	m	Time	m
1	TH	0409	4.5	1032	1.7	1624	4.9	2257	1.5
2	F	0451	4.8	1113	1.4	1703	5.1	2335	1.2
3	SA	0529	5.0	1149	1.2	1741	5.3	●	
4	SU	0010	1.1	0605	5.1	1223	1.1	1816	5.3
5	M	0041	1.0	0640	5.1	1252	1.0	1851	5.3
6	TU	0109	1.0	0713	5.1	1319	1.1	1923	5.3
7	W	0134	1.0	0743	5.1	1343	1.1	1951	5.2
8	TH	0159	1.1	0810	5.0	1408	1.2	2016	5.1
9	F	0224	1.3	0835	4.9	1436	1.4	2044	4.9
10	SA	0253	1.5	0907	4.7	1510	1.6	2121	4.7
11	SU	0329	1.8	0953	4.5	1555	2.0	◐ 2220	4.4
12	M	0422	2.2	1102	4.4	1710	2.3	2342	4.2
13	TU	0606	2.4	1233	4.3	1921	2.3		
14	W	0131	4.3	0805	2.2	1416	4.6	2048	1.8
15	TH	0305	4.6	0920	1.7	1529	5.0	2152	1.3
16	F	0407	5.0	1019	1.2	1623	5.4	2246	0.8
17	SA	0457	5.3	1109	0.8	1712	5.7	2335	0.4
18	SU	0543	5.5	1156	0.5	1758	5.8	○	
19	M	0020	0.3	0627	5.6	1240	0.4	1841	5.9
20	TU	0103	0.2	0709	5.6	1321	0.4	1923	5.8
21	W	0142	0.4	0747	5.5	1357	0.6	2000	5.6
22	TH	0216	0.7	0820	5.4	1431	0.9	2031	5.3
23	F	0248	1.1	0846	5.1	1502	1.3	2057	4.9
24	SA	0317	1.5	0910	4.8	1534	1.8	2123	4.6
25	SU	0348	2.0	0942	4.6	1612	2.2	◑ 2201	4.2
26	M	0431	2.5	1031	4.3	1716	2.6	2306	3.9
27	TU	0550	2.8	1214	4.1	1907	2.7		
28	W	0146	3.9	0806	2.7	1412	4.3	2059	2.3
29	TH	0253	4.2	0918	2.2	1510	4.6	2146	1.9
30	F	0343	4.6	1002	1.8	1556	4.9	2225	1.5

OCTOBER

Date	Day	Time	m	Time	m	Time	m	Time	m
1	SA	0424	4.9	1041	1.5	1636	5.1	2301	1.2
2	SU	0502	5.1	1116	1.2	1713	5.3	2335	1.0
3	M	0538	5.2	1149	1.1	1750	5.4	●	
4	TU	0006	0.9	0612	5.3	1221	1.0	1824	5.4
5	W	0036	0.9	0644	5.3	1250	1.0	1856	5.3
6	TH	0105	1.0	0714	5.3	1318	1.0	1925	5.3
7	F	0132	1.1	0742	5.2	1346	1.2	1954	5.1
8	SA	0200	1.3	0812	5.1	1417	1.4	2028	4.9
9	SU	0232	1.5	0849	4.9	1454	1.7	2113	4.7
10	M	0311	1.9	0940	4.7	1544	2.0	◐ 2214	4.4
11	TU	0409	2.3	1049	4.5	1711	2.4	2338	4.2
12	W	0607	2.5	1224	4.4	1918	2.2		
13	TH	0137	4.3	0758	2.2	1406	4.7	2036	1.7
14	F	0255	4.7	0905	1.7	1512	5.1	2134	1.2
15	SA	0349	5.1	0958	1.2	1604	5.5	2224	0.8
16	SU	0436	5.4	1046	0.8	1650	5.7	2310	0.5
17	M	0519	5.5	1131	0.6	1734	5.8	○ 2353	0.5
18	TU	0600	5.6	1213	0.5	1815	5.7		
19	W	0034	0.5	0638	5.6	1253	0.6	1853	5.6
20	TH	0111	0.7	0712	5.5	1328	0.8	1927	5.4
21	F	0144	1.0	0741	5.4	1401	1.1	1956	5.1
22	SA	0214	1.3	0806	5.2	1432	1.5	2021	4.8
23	SU	0243	1.7	0834	4.9	1503	1.9	2051	4.5
24	M	0313	2.1	0910	4.7	1541	2.3	2134	4.2
25	TU	0354	2.5	0959	4.4	1640	2.6	◑ 2236	4.0
26	W	0510	2.8	1112	4.2	1814	2.7		
27	TH	0057	4.0	0652	2.7	1321	4.3	2001	2.4
28	F	0212	4.2	0823	2.4	1427	4.5	2056	2.0
29	SA	0303	4.5	0914	2.0	1516	4.8	2138	1.7
30	SU	0347	4.8	0956	1.6	1559	5.1	2216	1.4
31	M	0427	5.1	1035	1.4	1640	5.2	2254	1.2

NOVEMBER

Date	Day	Time	m	Time	m	Time	m	Time	m
1	TU	0505	5.2	1112	1.2	1719	5.3	2330	1.0
2	W	0541	5.3	1148	1.1	1756	5.4	●	
3	TH	0005	1.0	0616	5.4	1224	1.0	1832	5.3
4	F	0040	1.0	0650	5.4	1258	1.0	1907	5.3
5	SA	0113	1.1	0724	5.3	1333	1.2	1944	5.1
6	SU	0148	1.3	0801	5.2	1411	1.4	2025	4.9
7	M	0226	1.6	0844	5.1	1456	1.6	2115	4.7
8	TU	0313	1.9	0937	4.9	1553	2.0	2215	4.5
9	W	0417	2.2	1042	4.7	1715	2.1	◐ 2337	4.4
10	TH	0556	2.3	1210	4.6	1855	2.0		
11	F	0114	4.5	0729	2.1	1339	4.8	2008	1.7
12	SA	0225	4.7	0835	1.7	1443	5.1	2105	1.3
13	SU	0320	5.0	0930	1.4	1537	5.3	2156	1.1
14	M	0409	5.3	1019	1.1	1625	5.4	2243	0.9
15	TU	0452	5.4	1105	0.9	1710	5.5	2326	0.8
16	W	0533	5.5	1147	0.9	1750	5.5	○	
17	TH	0006	0.9	0609	5.5	1227	0.9	1827	5.4
18	F	0044	1.0	0642	5.4	1304	1.1	1900	5.2
19	SA	0117	1.2	0712	5.3	1338	1.3	1930	5.0
20	SU	0149	1.5	0741	5.2	1410	1.6	2000	4.8
21	M	0219	1.8	0813	5.0	1444	1.9	2035	4.6
22	TU	0252	2.1	0852	4.8	1521	2.1	2119	4.4
23	W	0332	2.3	0940	4.6	1611	2.4	◑ 2215	4.2
24	TH	0429	2.5	1039	4.4	1720	2.5	2330	4.1
25	F	0549	2.6	1155	4.4	1838	2.4		
26	SA	0059	4.2	0706	2.4	1317	4.5	1944	2.1
27	SU	0203	4.4	0809	2.2	1419	4.7	2038	1.9
28	M	0255	4.7	0902	1.9	1512	4.8	2126	1.6
29	TU	0343	4.9	0950	1.6	1601	5.0	2212	1.4
30	W	0429	5.1	1036	1.4	1647	5.1	2256	1.2

DECEMBER

Date	Day	Time	m	Time	m	Time	m	Time	m
1	TH	0512	5.2	1120	1.2	1732	5.2	● 2340	1.1
2	F	0553	5.4	1203	1.1	1815	5.3		
3	SA	0022	1.1	0634	5.4	1247	1.0	1858	5.3
4	SU	0105	1.2	0716	5.4	1331	1.1	1942	5.2
5	M	0148	1.3	0800	5.4	1416	1.2	2030	5.0
6	TU	0233	1.4	0847	5.3	1505	1.4	2120	4.9
7	W	0322	1.6	0937	5.1	1558	1.6	2215	4.7
8	TH	0418	1.8	1035	5.0	1700	1.7	◐ 2320	4.6
9	F	0526	2.0	1143	4.8	1814	1.8		
10	SA	0033	4.6	0643	2.0	1258	4.8	1925	1.8
11	SU	0142	4.7	0754	1.9	1405	4.9	2029	1.6
12	M	0242	4.8	0856	1.7	1505	5.0	2125	1.5
13	TU	0337	5.0	0952	1.5	1559	5.1	2216	1.4
14	W	0426	5.1	1042	1.3	1647	5.1	2303	1.3
15	TH	0509	5.3	1127	1.2	1730	5.1	○ 2345	1.2
16	F	0548	5.3	1209	1.2	1808	5.1		
17	SA	0024	1.3	0622	5.3	1248	1.3	1843	5.0
18	SU	0100	1.4	0655	5.3	1324	1.4	1916	4.9
19	M	0134	1.5	0728	5.2	1358	1.5	1951	4.8
20	TU	0206	1.7	0804	5.1	1431	1.7	2028	4.7
21	W	0239	1.8	0843	4.9	1505	1.8	2109	4.5
22	TH	0312	2.0	0924	4.8	1541	2.0	2152	4.4
23	F	0350	2.1	1008	4.6	1625	2.1	◑ 2241	4.3
24	SA	0440	2.3	1058	4.5	1723	2.2	2339	4.3
25	SU	0547	2.3	1158	4.5	1831	2.2		
26	M	0044	4.3	0701	2.3	1306	4.5	1937	2.1
27	TU	0150	4.5	0807	2.1	1414	4.6	2038	1.9
28	W	0254	4.7	0908	1.9	1519	4.7	2135	1.7
29	TH	0353	4.9	1005	1.6	1619	4.9	2230	1.4
30	F	0447	5.1	1100	1.3	1713	5.1	2322	1.2
31	SA	0536	5.3	1151	1.1	1803	5.2	●	

Chart Datum: 3·22 metres below Ordnance Datum (Newlyn)

9.1.15 PLYMOUTH

Devon **50°20'·04N 04°10'·07W** (W Chan) ❁❁❁◊◊◊✿✿✿
50°20'·04N 04°08'·07W (E Chan)

CHARTS AC *1267, 1613, 5602*, 1900, *30*, 1902, 1901, 1967, *871*; Imray C14, C6; Stanfords 2, 22, L13; OS 201

TIDES –0540 Dover; ML 3·3; Duration 0610; Zone 0 (UT)
Standard Port PLYMOUTH (⟵)

Times				**Height (metres)**			
High Water		Low Water		MHWS	MHWN	MLWN	MLWS
0000	0600	0000	0600	5·5	4·4	2·2	0·8
1200	1800	1200	1800				
Differences BOVISAND PIER							
0000	–0020	0000	–0010	–0·2	–0·1	0·0	+0·1
TURNCHAPEL (Cattewater)							
0000	0000	+0010	–0015	0·0	+0·1	+0·2	+0·1
JUPITER POINT (R. Lynher)							
+0010	+0005	0000	–0005	0·0	0·0	+0·1	0·0
ST GERMANS (R. Lynher)							
0000	0000	+0020	+0020	–0·3	–0·1	0·0	+0·2
SALTASH (R. Tamar)							
0000	+0010	0000	–0005	+0·1	+0·1	+0·1	+0·1
LOPWELL (R. Tavy)							
No data		Dries	Dries	–2·6	–2·7	Dries	Dries
CARGREEN (R. Tamar)							
0000	+0010	+0020	+0020	0·0	0·0	–0·1	0·0
COTEHELE QUAY (R. Tamar)							
0000	+0020	+0045	+0045	–0·9	–0·9	–0·8	–0·4

NOTE: Winds from SE to W increase the flood and retard the ebb; vice versa in winds from the NW to E.

SHELTER Good to excellent at 4 major and some minor marinas, several anchorages around the Sound and up the Rivers Lynher

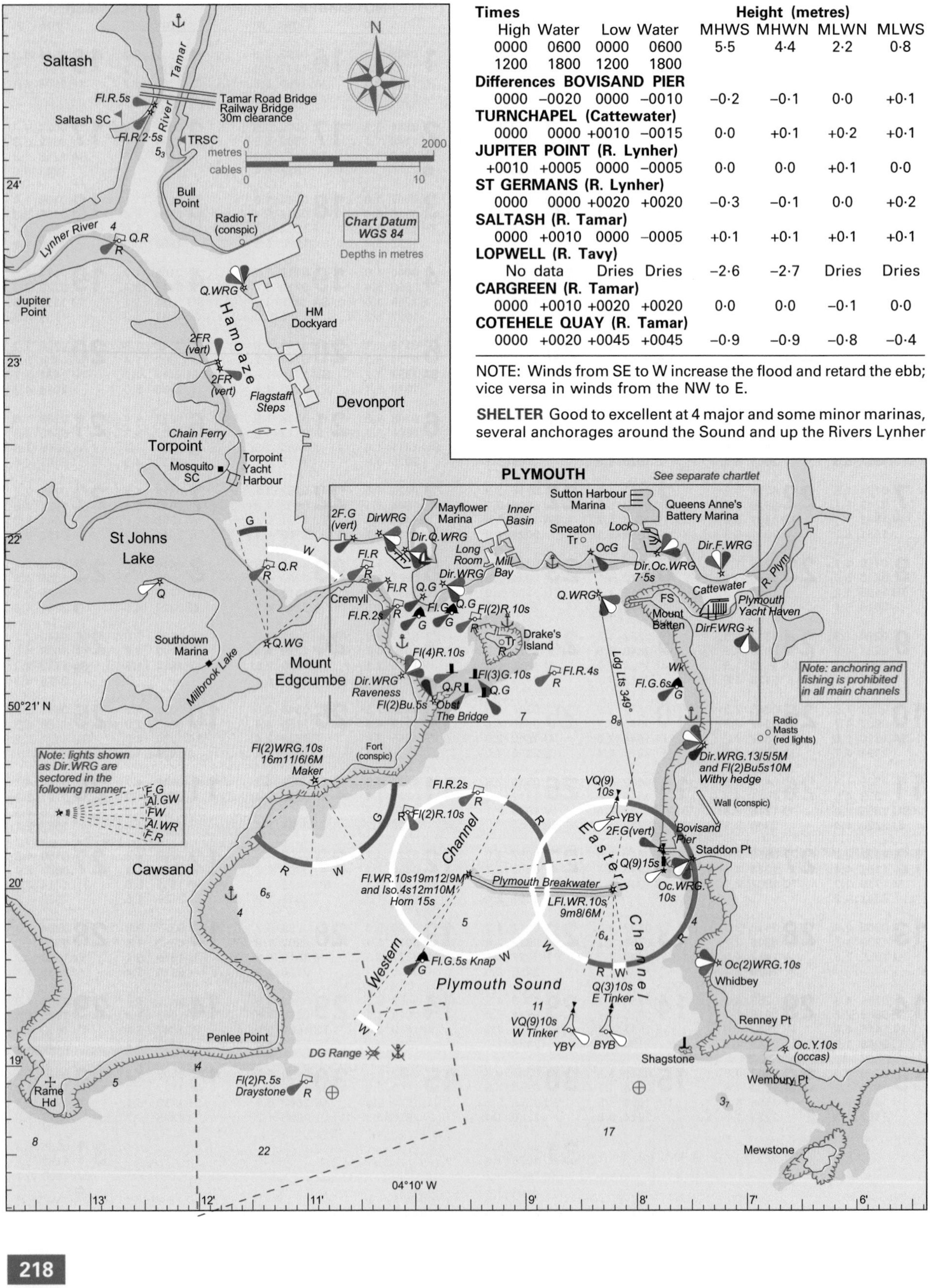
Saltash
River Tamar
Tamar Road Bridge
Railway Bridge
30m clearance
Saltash SC
TRSC
Bull Point
Radio Tr (conspic)
Chart Datum WGS 84
Depths in metres
Lynher River
Jupiter Point
Hamoaze
HM Dockyard
Devonport
Flagstaff Steps
Chain Ferry
Torpoint
Mosquito SC
Torpoint Yacht Harbour
St Johns Lake
Southdown Marina
Millbrook Lake
Mount Edgcumbe
Cremyll
PLYMOUTH
See separate chartlet
Sutton Harbour Marina
Queens Anne's Battery Marina
Mayflower Marina
Inner Basin
Smeaton Tr
Long Room
Mill Bay
Drake's Island
Cattewater
Mount Batten
Plymouth Yacht Haven
R. Plym
Note: anchoring and fishing is prohibited in all main channels
Radio Masts (red lights)
Dir.WRG.13/5/5M and Fl(2)Bu5s10M Withy hedge
Wall (conspic)
Bovisand Pier
Staddon Pt
Note: lights shown as Dir.WRG are sectored in the following manner:
F.G
Al.GW
FW
Al.WR
F.R
Fl(2)WRG.10s 16m11/6/6M Maker
Fort (conspic)
Raveness
The Bridge
Cawsand
Fl.WR.10s19m12/9M and Iso.4s12m10M Horn 15s
Plymouth Breakwater
LFl.WR.10s 9m8/6M
Eastern Channel
Western Channel
Fl.G.5s Knap
Plymouth Sound
Q(3)10s E Tinker
VQ(9)10s W Tinker
Oc(2)WRG.10s
Whidbey
Renney Pt
Oc.Y.10s (occas)
Shagstone
Wembury Pt
Mewstone
Penlee Point
DG Range
Fl(2)R.5s Draystone
Rame Hd
Ldg Lts 349°
04°10' W
50°21' N

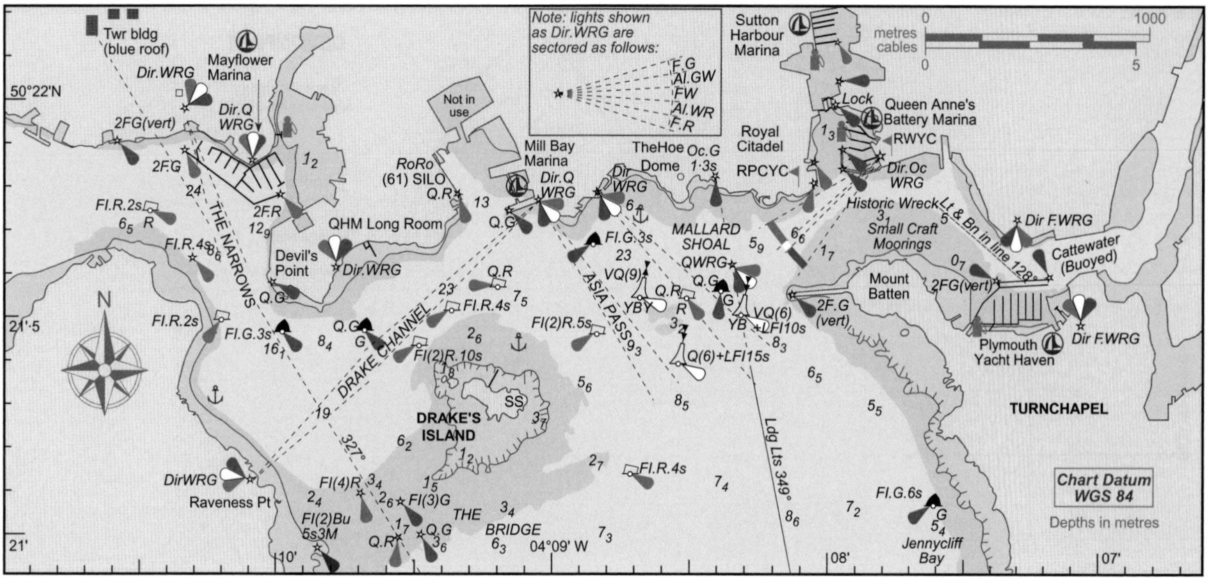
Twr bldg
(blue roof)
Dir.WRG
Mayflower
Marina
50°22'N
2FG(vert)
Dir.Q
WRG
2F.G
24
1₂
Fl.R.2s
6₅ R
2F.R
12₉
QHM Long Room
Fl.R.4s
8₆
THE NARROWS
Devil's
Point
Dir.WRG
Q.G
21'.5
Fl.R.2s
Fl.G.3s
16₁
8₄
Q.G
G
N
Not in
use
RoRo
(61) SILO
Q.R
13
Q.G
Mill Bay
Marina
Dir.Q
WRG
Note: lights shown
as Dir.WRG are
sectored as follows:
F.G
Al.GW
FW
Al.WR
F.R
TheHoe
Dir
Dome
Oc.G
1·3s
WRG
Royal
Citadel
RPCYC
Sutton
Harbour
Marina
metres
cables
0
1000
5
Lock
Queen Anne's
Battery Marina
RWYC
1₃
Dir.Oc
WRG
Historic Wreck
3₁
Small Craft
Moorings
Ldg Lt & Bn in line 128°
Dir F.WRG
Cattewater
(Buoyed)
MALLARD
SHOAL
5₉
6₆
1₇
0₇
Mount
Batten
2FG(vert)
2F.G
(vert)
Fl.G.3s
23
QWRG
Q.G
VQ(9)
Q.R
YBY
R
G
VQ(6)
YB
+LFl10s
3₇
Q(6)+LFl15s
8₃
ASIA PASS
9₃
Q.R
Fl.R.4s
7₅
2₃
DRAKE CHANNEL
Fl(2)R.5s
2₆
Fl(2)R.10s
1₈
5₆
SS
DRAKE'S
ISLAND
3₇
6₂
1₉
327°
6₅
8₅
5₅
Plymouth
Yacht Haven
Dir F.WRG
TURNCHAPEL
Ldg Lts 349°
DirWRG
Raveness Pt
Fl(4)R
3₄
1₅
2₄
2₆
Fl(3)G
Fl(2)Bu
5s3M
Q.R
1₇
Q.G
3₆
THE
BRIDGE
6₃
3₄
7₃
04°09' W
2₇
Fl.R.4s
7₄
8₆
7₂
Fl.G.6s
G
5₄
Jennycliff
Bay
Chart Datum
WGS 84
Depths in metres
21'
10'
08'
07'

and Tamar. Marinas to E and W of the city centre, as well as in the Cattewater, off Torpoint and in Millbrook Lake are itemised under Facilities. Around the Sound there are ⚓s, sheltered according to the wind, in Cawsand Bay, Barn Pool (below Mt Edgcumbe), N of Drake's Island, below The Hoe and in Jennycliff Bay. Also good shelter W of Cremyll and off the Hamoaze in the R Lynher and in the R Tamar/Tavy above Saltash (see overleaf).

Plymouth is a Naval Base, a ferry port (Mill Bay*), commercial port (Cattewater*) and FV hbr (Sutton Harbour). The whole hbr is under the jurisdiction of the QHM, but asterisked areas are controlled by ABP and Cattewater Commissioners.

NAVIGATION From the west: WPT 50°18'·81N 04°10'·90W (abeam Draystone PHM buoy), 035°/1·5M to W Bkwtr lt. From the east: WPT 50°18'·81N 04°08'·00W, 000°/1·2M to abeam E Bkwtr lt. The Sound can be entered via the W (main) or E Chans which are well lit/buoyed, but in strong W'lies the E Chan can be a hazardous lee shore for yachts. It is vital to keep well clear of the unlit Shag Stone. There are 3·2m patches NE of E Tinker ECM lt buoy. Yachts need not keep to the deep water chans; they must give way to the Torpoint chain ferries at 50°22'·50N 04°11'·30W.

The Bridge (short cut between Drake's Is and Mt Edgcumbe) is marked by 2 PHM and 2 SHM bns, lights as chartlet. Both PHM bns have tide gauges calibrated to show height of tide above CD; least charted depth is 1·3m. The LH (blue roof) of 3 conspic high-rise blocks leads 327° through The Bridge.

Speed limits: 10kn* N of The Breakwater; 8kn in Cattewater (where vessels <20m LOA keep clear of vessels >20m LOA); 4kn N of Fisher's Nose and 5kn in Sutton Hbr.
*Vessels <15m LOA are exempt from the 10kn limit when more than 400m from the shore and in the access lane for water/jet skiers defined by lines from Fisher's Nose to the W end of Mount Batten Bkwtr; and from Royal Plymouth Corinthian YC to W Mallard buoy. Here the speed limit is under review as of 2/2004.

Historic Wrecks (see 9.0.3h) are at: 50°21'·73N 04°07'·70W (N of Mt Batten), 50°19'·00N 04°11'·64W and 50°18'·61N 04°12'·05W.

LIGHTS AND MARKS Principal daymarks: conical Rame Head to the W; Great Mew Stone & Staddon Heights to the E; The Breakwater; on The Hoe: Smeaton Tower (R/W bands) & the Naval War Memorial; at Mill Bay the 61m Silo; and, overlooking The Narrows and Mayflower marina, Ocean Court (a white bldg).

See chartlets and 9.1.4 for the many lts; some hard to see against shore lts. Dir WRG lts defining the main chans are shown H24** from: Whidbey (138·5°), Staddon Pt (044°), Withyhedge (070°), W Hoe bn (315°), Western King (271°), Mill Bay** (048·5°), Ravenness (225°), Mount Wise (343°), and Ocean Court** (085°). ** Not H24

Notes: In fog W lts may, on request to Port Control, be shown from: Mallard (front ldg lt) Fl 5s; West Hoe bn F; Eastern King Fl 5s; Ravenness Fl (2) 15s; Mount Wise F; Ocean Court Fl 5s. Major lts in The Sound show QY if mains power fails. N of The Bkwtr, four large mooring buoys (C, D, E & F) have Fl Y lts.

R/T *Longroom Port Control* Ch **14** (H24). Monitor 14 underway. Mayflower & QAB marinas, Plymouth Yacht Haven and Torpoint Yacht Hbr: Ch **80** M. *Sutton Lock,* for opening and marina, Ch **12** (H24). *Cattewater Hbr* Ch 14 (Mon-Fri, 0900-1700LT). *Mill Bay Docks* Ch 12 14 (only during ferry ops).

TELEPHONE (Dial code 01752) QHM 836952; DQHM 836485; Flagstaff Port Control (RN dockyard) 552413; Longroom Port Control (Millbay) 836528, ℻ 836401; Cattewater HM 665934; ABP at Mill Bay 662191; MRSC (01803) 882704; Marinecall 09066 526242; Police 0990 777444; Dr 663138; Ⓗ 668080.

FACILITIES **Marinas** (W to E)
Torpoint Yacht Hbr (60+20 Ⓥ) ☎/℻ 813658, £1.56, access H24, dredged 2m. BY, C, ME, El, ⚒, Diver, SM. Fuel barge ☎ 07803 029237 0830-1600, all week except Wed.
Southdown marina (35 inc Ⓥ) ☎/℻ 823084, £1.17, access HW±4; AB on pontoon (2m) or on drying quay; D, C (5ton).
Mayflower marina (300+50 Ⓥ) ☎ 556633, ℻ 606896; £2.30 (inc AC), £3/hr short stay, 6 hrs max; P, D, ME, El, ⚒, C (2 ton), BH (25 ton), CH, Slip, Gas, Gaz, LPG, Divers, SM, BY, YC, 🛒, R, Bar, ▣.
Mill Bay Village marina ☎ 226785, ℻ 226785, VHF Ch M. NO VISITORS. Ent lts = Oc R 4s & Oc G 4s, not on chartlet.
Queen Anne's Battery (QAB) marina (240+60 Ⓥ) ☎ 671142, ℻ 266297, £2.70, P, D, ME, El, ⚒, FW, BH (20 ton), C (50 ton), CH, Gas, Gaz, ▣, SM, Slip, 🛒, Bar, YC.
Sutton Hbr marina (310) ☎ 204186, ℻ 223521, £2.37, P, D, El, ME, ⚒, CH, C, BH (25 ton), Slip. Call *Sutton Lock* Ch 12 to enter lock (flood protection scheme), which retains CD +3m in the marina; when >3m above CD, free-flow in force. IPTS: signals 1, 2 & 3. Lock operates H24, free; secure to floating pontoons both sides.
Plymouth Yacht Haven (450 inc Ⓥ) ☎ 404231, 07721 498422 (1900-0800), ℻ 484177, £2.20 inc AC, dredged 2·25m, D (H24), CH, ME, El, Gas, mobile C (12 ton), BH (65 ton), 🛒, ▣, ♿, Bar, R. Water taxi: daily 0700-2300, 5 mins to Barbican, Ch M or ☎. Also a ferry ½ hrly from Mount Batten pier to the Barbican.

YACHT CLUBS **Royal Western YC of England** ☎ 660077, M, Bar, R; **Royal Plymouth Corinthian YC** ☎ 664327, VHF Ch M, M, R, Bar, Slip; **Plym YC** ☎ 404991; **RNSA** ☎ 557679; **Mayflower SC** ☎ 492566; **Torpoint Mosquito SC** ☎ 812508, R, Bar visitors welcome; **Saltash SC** ☎ 845988.
Services All facilities available. **City** all facilities, ⇌, ✈.

NAVAL ACTIVITY Info on Naval activities may be obtained from Naval Ops, ☎ 501182 (H24); Devonport Ops Room ☎ 563777 Ext 2182/3; or www.qhmplymouth.org.uk. Naval vessels have right of way in the main and DW channels; obey MOD Police orders.

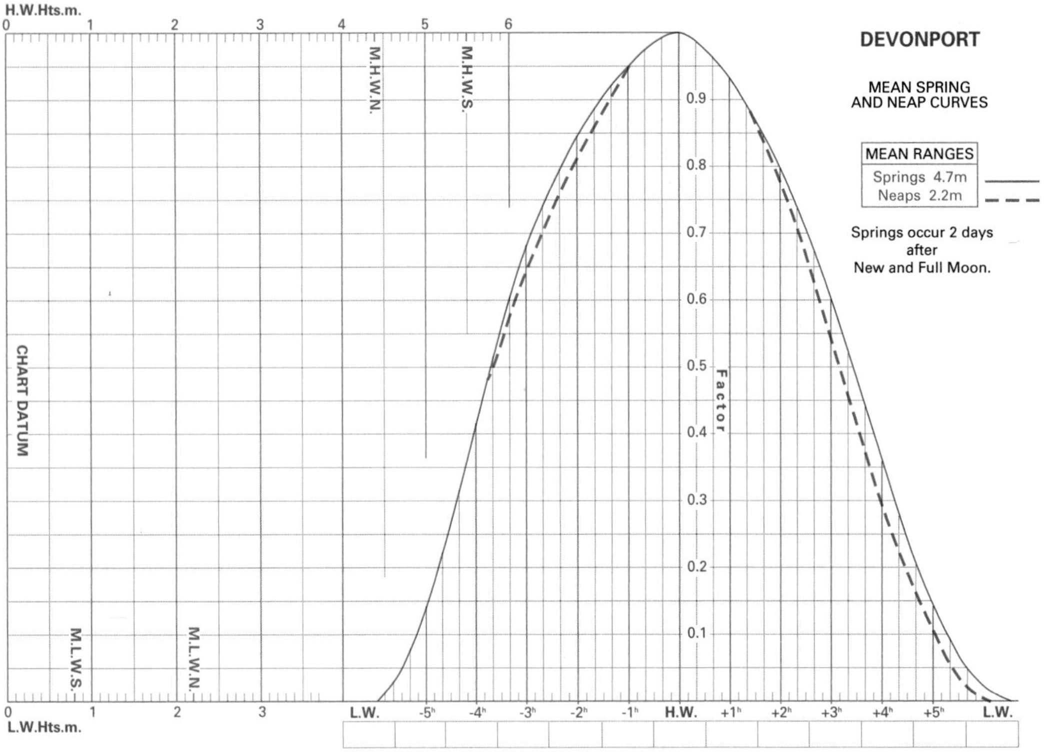
DEVONPORT
MEAN SPRING AND NEAP CURVES
MEAN RANGES
Springs 4.7m
Neaps 2.2m
Springs occur 2 days after New and Full Moon.
H.W.Hts.m.
M.H.W.N.
M.H.W.S.
CHART DATUM
M.L.W.S.
M.L.W.N.
L.W.Hts.m.
Factor
0.9
0.8
0.7
0.6
0.5
0.4
0.3
0.2
0.1
L.W.
-5h
-4h
-3h
-2h
-1h
H.W.
+1h
+2h
+3h
+4h
+5h
L.W.

Submarine operations: do not pass within 200m or cross astern within 800m of any submarine under way. Submarines may secure to a buoy close N of the Breakwater; they will show a Fl Y anti-collision lt. For Subfacts in the W English Chan see 9.1.16. **Diving**: Keep clear of Bovisand Pier, the Breakwater Fort and Ravenness Pt when diving signals (Flag A) are displayed. Flag N flown from pier indicates steps temporarily occupied.

TRAFFIC SIGNALS Traffic is controlled H24 by the following combinations of 3 lts WRG (vert), Fl or Oc, shown from Drake's Island and at Flagstaff Port Control Station in the Dockyard. These signals and any hoisted by HM Ships apply to the waters off the dockyard port and 125m either side of the deep water chan out to the W Ent. The Cattewater, Mill Bay Docks and Sutton Hbr are excluded. Except for the first, the meanings differ from IPTS.

Signal	Meaning
Unlit	No restrictions, unless passed on VHF
●●● All Fl	Serious Emergency All traffic suspended
●●● All Oc	Outgoing traffic only may proceed along the recommended track. Crossing traffic to seek approval from Port Control*
●●● All Oc	Incoming traffic only may proceed along the recommended track. Crossing traffic to seek approval from Port Control*
●● Ⓦ All Oc	Vessels may proceed in either direction, but shall give a wide berth to HM Ships using the recommended track

*Call Port Control Ch 13 or 14, but craft <20m LOA may proceed in the contrary direction, with care, not impeding the passage of vessels for which the signal is intended. 'Recommended track' is the charted pecked line used by deep draught ships.

Wind Strength Warning Flags and Lights Wind flags (R & W vert stripes) are flown at QAB and Mayflower marinas and at The Camber (HO only) to warn of excessive winds as follows:
1 wind flag (1 Oc Ⓦ lt) = Force 5 - 7 (17-27kn).
2 wind flags (2 Oc Ⓦ lts, vert) = > Force 7 (>27kn).
Note: These flags are supplemented by Oc Ⓦ lt(s) shown from Drake's Island, HJ when no traffic light signal is in force.

RIVER LYNHER (or ST GERMANS) AC 871. This river flows into The Hamoaze about 0·8M SSW of the Tamar Bridge. It is navigable on the tide for some 4M inland.

The chan, entered at Lynher PHM lt buoy, is marked by 2 more lt buoys in the first mile to Sandacre Pt and carries 2-5m up to Ince Castle. Thereafter it carries less than 1m or dries, except at Dandy Hole, a pool with 3-5m. Here the navigable chan bends NW and dries completely; it is marked by small R and G posts.

There are ⚓s, amid local moorings: off Sand Acre Bay (N bank, beware foul ground); in 2·5-5m at the ent to Forder Lake (N bank opposite Jupiter Pt); SE of Ince Pt and Castle in about 3m; and at Dandy Hole. The pontoons at Jupiter Pt are for naval use only. Caution: underwater cables/gaspipe, as charted. St Germans Quay is private, but temp AB, M may be pre-arranged with Quay SC ☎ (01503) 250370. Facilities: 🛒, Bar, ✉ (½M).

RIVER TAMAR (and TAVY) AC 871. The drying R Tavy flows into the Tamar 1¼M above the bridges, but power lines (9·5m) and a bridge (7·6m) at its mouth, restrict access to un-masted craft up to Bere Ferrers or the weir at Lopwell.

The R Tamar is navigable on the tide for 10M to Morwhellam or a further 2M to Gunnislake weir. Cargreen village on the W bank is 0·7M beyond the Tavy, with many local moorings and ⚓ in 2·5-5m. Weirquay on E bank has a SC, BY, M and fuel; just downstream overhead cables have 16m clearance. Upstream the river S-bends, narrows and partly dries, passes Cotehele Quay and then turns 90° stbd to Calstock; possible AB, M, or ⚓ above the viaduct in 2m. Above Halton Quay depths vary from 0·1m to > 2·5m.

Facilities: **Tamar River SC** ☎ 362741. **Jubilee Green** (W bank, close N of Tamar Bridge) has pontoon in about 3m for max LOA 10m. **Weir Quay SC** ☎ (01822) 840960, M, CH, ME; **Calstock BY** ☎ (01822) 832502, access HW ±3, M, ME, SH, C (8 ton), BH (10 ton). Facilities: P, D, 🛒, Bar, Ⓑ (Mon a.m.), ⇌.

9.1.16 NAVAL EXERCISE AREAS (SUBFACTS & GUNFACTS)

Submarines and warships use the areas below and others eastwards to Nab Tr (see 9.2.27). Areas where submarines are planned to operate during all or part of the ensuing 24 hrs are broadcast daily by the Coastguard as shown below. Subfacts and Gunfacts are mentioned on Navtex by Niton at 0440 and 1640 UT daily. Further information may be obtained from Naval Ops, Plymouth ☎ (01752) 557550, 📠 (01752) 557774.

See 7.14.1 for general advice on submarine activity which also occurs in other sea areas. Submarines on the surface and at periscope depth will maintain constant listening watch on VHF Ch 16. The former will comply strictly with IRPCS; the latter will not close to within 1500 yds of a FV without express permission from the FV.

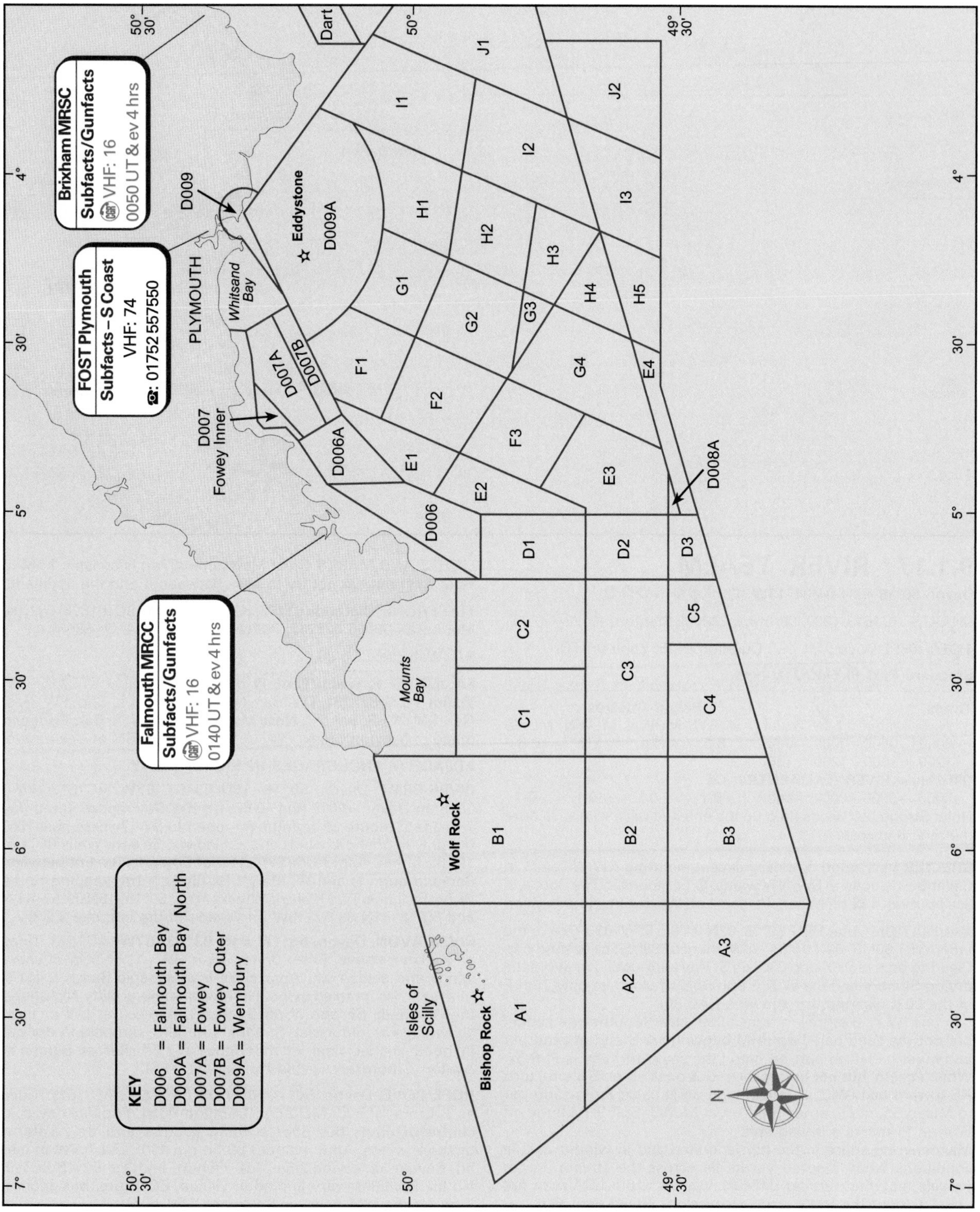
Brixham MRSC
Subfacts/Gunfacts
VHF: 16
0050 UT & ev 4 hrs
FOST Plymouth
Subfacts – S Coast
VHF: 74
☎: 01752 557550
Falmouth MRCC
Subfacts/Gunfacts
VHF: 16
0140 UT & ev 4 hrs
KEY
D006 = Falmouth Bay
D006A = Falmouth Bay North
D007A = Fowey
D007B = Fowey Outer
D009A = Wembury
PLYMOUTH
Whitsand Bay
Eddystone
D009
D009A
D007 Fowey Inner
D007A
D007B
D006A
D006
D008A
Dart
Mounts Bay
Wolf Rock
Isles of Scilly
Bishop Rock
A1
A2
A3
B1
B2
B3
C1
C2
C3
C4
C5
D1
D2
D3
E1
E2
E3
E4
F1
F2
F3
G1
G2
G3
G4
H1
H2
H3
H4
H5
I1
I2
I3
J1
J2
N
50° 30'
50°
49° 30'
4°
30'
5°
6°
7°

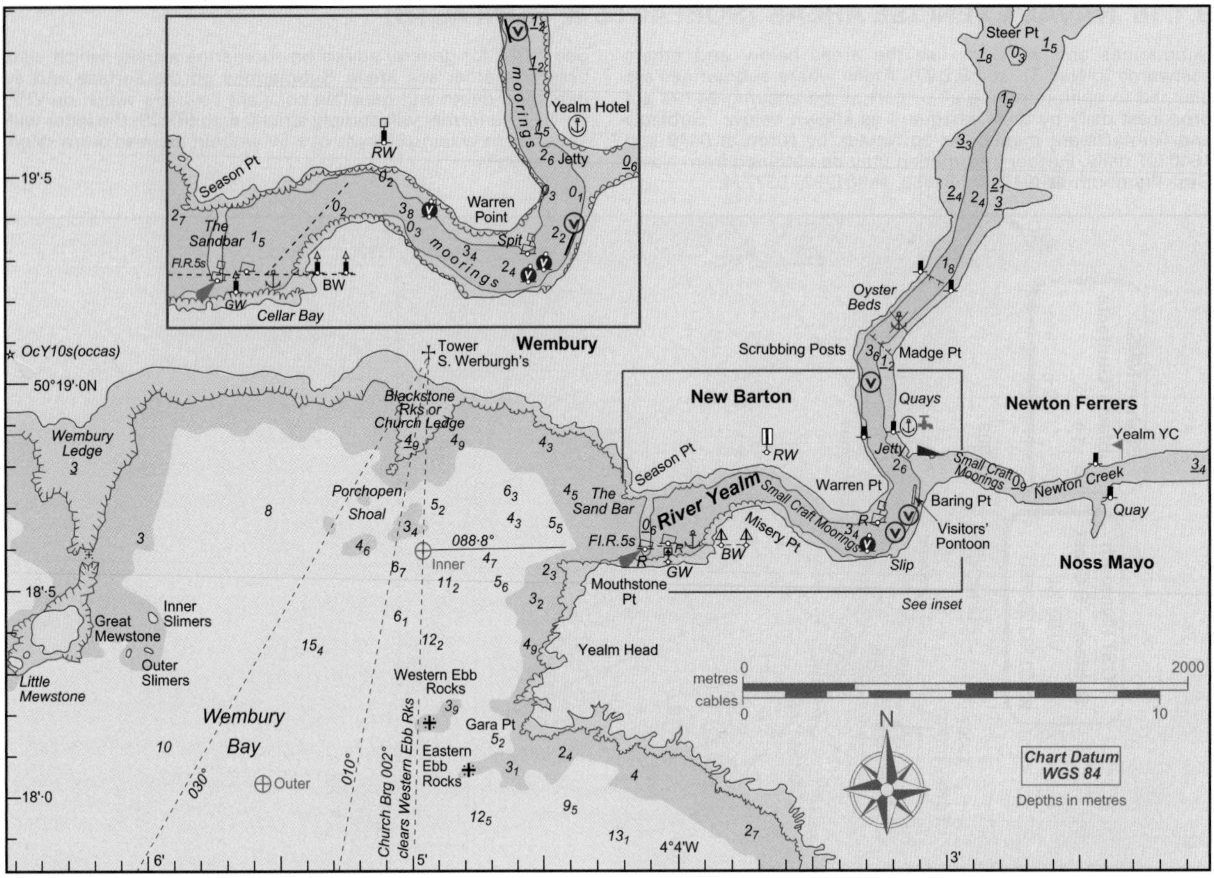
Steer Pt
Yealm Hotel
mooring
Jetty
RW
Season Pt
Warren Point
The Sandbar
Spit
moorings
Fl.R.5s
BW
GW
Cellar Bay
OcY10s(occas)
50°19'·0N
19'·5
18'·5
18'·0
Tower S. Werburgh's
Wembury
Scrubbing Posts
Madge Pt
Oyster Beds
New Barton
Quays
Newton Ferrers
Yealm YC
Wembury Ledge
Blackstone Rks or Church Ledge
Porchopen Shoal
The Sand Bar
River Yealm
Small Craft Moorings
Warren Pt
Baring Pt
Newton Creek
Quay
Visitors' Pontoon
Misery Pt
Fl.R.5s
088·8°
Inner
Mouthstone Pt
Slip
Noss Mayo
See inset
Great Mewstone
Inner Slimers
Outer Slimers
Little Mewstone
Yealm Head
Western Ebb Rocks
Gara Pt
Eastern Ebb Rocks
Wembury Bay
Outer
030°
010°
Church Brg 002° clears Western Ebb Rks
metres
cables
Chart Datum WGS 84
Depths in metres
4°4'W
6'
5'
3'

9.1.17 RIVER YEALM

Devon **50°18'·58N 04°04'·13W** (Ent) ❁❁◊◊✿✿✿

CHARTS AC *1613*, 1900, *30*; Imray 2400.6; Stanfords 2, 22; OS 201

TIDES 0522 Dover; ML 3·2; Duration 0615; Zone 0 (UT)

Standard Port PLYMOUTH (⟵)

Times				Height (metres)			
High Water		Low Water		MHWS	MHWN	MLWN	MLWS
0000	0600	0000	0600	5·5	4·4	2·2	0·8
1200	1800	1200	1800				
Differences RIVER YEALM ENTRANCE							
+0006	+0006	+0002	+0002	–0·1	–0·1	–0·1	–0·1

Note: Strong SW winds hold up the ebb and raise levels, as does the river if in spate.

SHELTER Very good. Ent easy except in strong SW/W'lies. ⚓ in Cellar Bay is open to SW-NW winds. Ⓥ pontoons in The Pool and 3ca up-river. 1 Ⓥ off Misery Pt and 2 off Warren Pt. No ⚓ in river.

NAVIGATION Outer WPT 50°18'·03N 04°05'·55W, 033°/7ca to the Inner WPT 50°18'·59N 04°04'·98W; thence 089°/5·5ca to sand bar. Clearing brgs of 010° and 030° on St Werburgh's ch twr avoid the drying Slimers and the W & E Ebb Rocks (which lie only 75m E of the 002° clearing brg shown on AC 30).

Ldg bns (W △, B stripe) in transit 089° clear Mouthstone Ledge, but **not** the sand bar. Two PHM buoys mark S end of sand bar and **must** be left to port on entry; the seaward buoy is Fl R 5s. When abeam, **but not before**, bcn (G ▲ on W □) on S shore, turn NE toward bcn (W □, R stripe) high on N bank. From sand bar to Misery Pt, river carries only 1m at MLWS. Spit PHM buoy off Warren Pt marks a drying spit.

Manoeuvring space in the hbr is limited and in wind-over-tide conditions when moored yachts lie across the stream, larger vessels may find turning difficult. Vessels >18m LOA may not enter without the HM's prior permission. Speed limit 6kn.

LIGHTS AND MARKS Great Mewstone (57m) is conspic 1·5M to W of river ent; do not try to pass between it and the mainland.

TELEPHONE (Dial code 01752) HM 872533; MRSC (01803) 882704; Marinecall 09066 526242; Police (0990) 777444; Dr 880392.

R/T Water taxi Ch 08.

FACILITIES R Yealm/Pool: Ⓥ pontoon, Ⓥ or ⚓ = £1.27, L, FW; **Yealm YC** ☎ 872291, FW, Bar; **Newton Ferrers** L, Slip, FW, Gas, Gaz, SM, 🛒, R, Bar, ✉; **Noss Mayo** L, Slip, FW, R, Bar; **Bridgend** (head of Newton Creek) FW, ⛽; Nearest fuel 3M at Yealmpton.

ADJACENT ANCHORAGES IN BIGBURY BAY

RIVER ERME, Devon, **50°18'·15N 03°57'·67W**. AC *1613*. HW –0525 on Dover; +0015 and –0·6m on HW Devonport. Temp day ⚓ in 3m at mouth of drying river, open to SW. Access near HW, but only in offshore winds and settled wx. Beware Wells Rk (1m) 1M SE of ent. Appr from SW, clear of Edwards Rk. Ent between Battisborough Is and W. Mary's Rk (dries 1·1m) keeping to the W. No facilities. Two Historic Wrecks are at 50°18'·15N 03°57'·41W and 50°18'·41N 03°57'·19W on W side of the ent; see 9.0.3h.

RIVER AVON, Devon, **50°16'·64N 03°53'·67W**. AC *1613*. Tides as R Erme, above. Enter drying river HW –1, only in offshore winds and settled wx. Appr close E of conspic Burgh Is (⚓) & Murray's Rks, marked by bn. Narrow chan hugs cliffy NW shore, then S-bends SE and N off Bantham. A recce at LW or local knowledge would assist. Streams run hard, but able to dry out in good shelter clear of moorings. 🛒, ✉, Bar at Bantham. Aveton Gifford accessible by dinghy, 2·5M.

HOPE COVE, Devon, **50°14'·65N 03°51'·78W**. AC *1613*. Tides as R Erme, above; ML 2·6m; Duration 0615. Popular day ⚓ in centre of cove, but poor holding ground and only safe in offshore winds. Appr with old LB ho brg 110° and ⚓ SW of pier hd. Beware rk, drying 2·5m, ½ca offshore and 3ca E of Bolt Tail. No lts. Facilities: very limited in village, EC Thurs; but good at Kingsbridge (6M bus), or Salcombe (4M bus).

9.1.18 SALCOMBE

Devon **50°14'·03N 03°46'·03W** ❀❀◊◊◊✿✿✿

CHARTS AC *1613, 1634, 28, 5602*; Imray C6, 2400.1 & .5; Stanfords 2, 12, 22, L14; OS 202

TIDES –0523 Dover; ML 3·1; Duration 0615; Zone 0 (UT)

Standard Port PLYMOUTH (⟵)

Times				Height (metres)			
High Water		Low Water		MHWS	MHWN	MLWN	MLWS
0100	0600	0100	0600	5·5	4·4	2·2	0·8
1300	1800	1300	1800				
Differences SALCOMBE							
0000	+0010	+0005	–0005	–0·2	–0·3	–0·1	–0·1
START POINT							
+0015	+0015	+0005	+0010	–0·1	–0·2	+0·1	+0·2

SHELTER Perfectly protected hbr but entrance exposed to S winds which can cause an uncomfortable swell in the ⚓ off the town. The spring flood reaches 2.5knLimited ⚓ on SE side between ferry and fuel barge, and on Middle Ground. Not all the 21 deep water ◆s are clearly marked or easy to find; call HM's launch Ch 14 for assistance. Good shelter at Ⓥ pontoon in The Bag. Short stay pontoon (½ hour max, 0700-1900, for FW/stores) by HM's office has 2m.

NAVIGATION WPT 50°12'·43N 03°46'·67W, 000°/1·3M to Sandhill Pt lt. The bar (least depth 1·0m) can be dangerous at sp ebb tides with strong on-shore winds/swell. Access HW±4½, but at springs this window applies only if swell height does not exceed 1m. The Bar is not as dangerous as rumour may have it, except in the above conditions; if in doubt, call HM Ch 14 before approaching. Rickham Rk, E of the Bar, has 3·1m depth. The estuary is 4M long and has 8 drying creeks off it. Speed limit 8kn; radar checks in force. A Historic Wreck (50°12'·70N 03°44'·33W) is at Moor Sand, 1M WNW of Prawle Pt; see 9.0.3h.

LIGHTS AND MARKS Lts as chartlet and 9.1.4. Outer 000° ldg marks: front, Poundstone R/W bn on with rear, Sandhill Pt R/W bn; close N of which a conspic gabled house is more easily seen. At night stay in the W sector (357·5°-002·5°) of Sandhill Pt Dir lt 000°. Beware Bass Rk (0·8m) close W of ldg line marked by PHM lt buoy; and Wolf Rk (0·6m), marked by SHM lt buoy, close E of ldg line. After passing Wolf Rk, leave Black Stone Rk (5m), G/W lt bcn, well to stbd and pick up inner ldg lts 042·5°, making good the hbr Wpt (under Title), which is abeam the first ◆.

R/T Ch 14 *Salcombe Hbr* or *Launch* (May to mid-Sep: daily 0600 -2100 (2200 Jul, Aug); rest of year: Mon-Fri 0900-1600). *Harbour taxi* Ch 12. ICC HQ, call *Egremont* Ch M. *Fuel Barge* Ch 06.

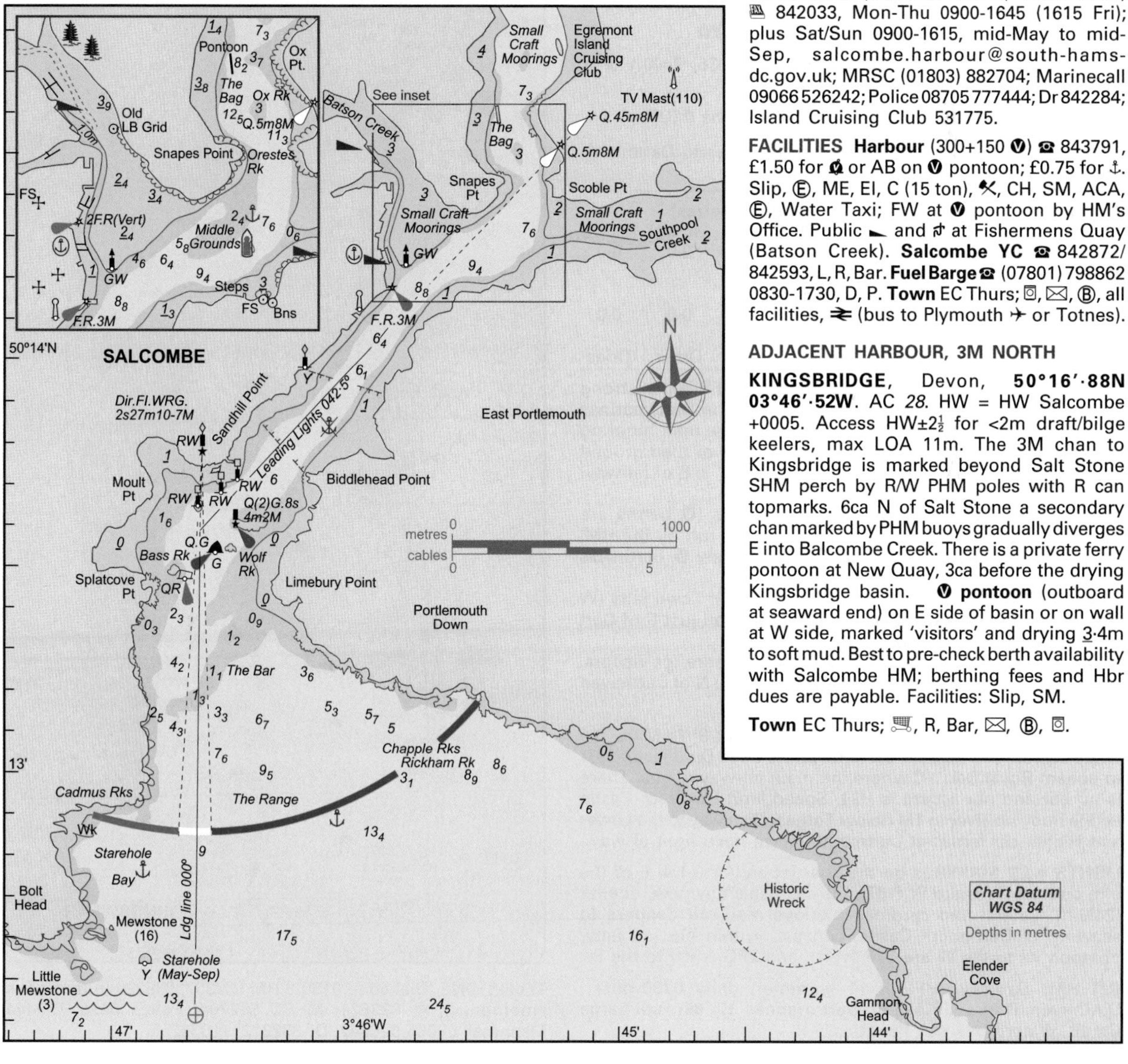

SALCOMBE
50°14'N
13'
See inset
Batson Creek
Small Craft Moorings
Egremont Island Cruising Club
TV Mast(110)
Q.45m8M
Q.5m8M
The Bag
Snapes Pt
Scoble Pt
Southpool Creek
GW
F.R.3M
Sandhill Point
Dir.Fl.WRG. 2s27m10-7M
Leading Lights 042·5°
East Portlemouth
Moult Pt
Biddlehead Point
Q(2)G.8s 4m2M
Bass Rk
Wolf Rk
Q.G
QR
Splatcove Pt
Limebury Point
Portlemouth Down
metres 0 1000
cables 0 5
The Bar
Chapple Rks
Rickham Rk
Cadmus Rks
The Range
Wk
Starehole Bay
Bolt Head
Mewstone (16)
Ldg line 000°
Starehole Y (May-Sep)
Little Mewstone (3)
Historic Wreck
Chart Datum WGS 84
Depths in metres
Elender Cove
Gammon Head
47'
3°46'W
45'
44'
Pontoon
Ox Pt.
Ox Rk
Old LB Grid
Snapes Point
Orestes Rk
FS
2F.R(Vert)
Middle Grounds
Steps
Bns

TELEPHONE (Dial code 01548) HM 843791, 📠 842033, Mon-Thu 0900-1645 (1615 Fri); plus Sat/Sun 0900-1615, mid-May to mid-Sep, salcombe.harbour@south-hams-dc.gov.uk; MRSC (01803) 882704; Marinecall 09066 526242; Police 08705 777444; Dr 842284; Island Cruising Club 531775.

FACILITIES **Harbour** (300+150 Ⓥ) ☎ 843791, £1.50 for ⚓ or AB on Ⓥ pontoon; £0.75 for ⚓. Slip, Ⓔ, ME, El, C (15 ton), ⚒, CH, SM, ACA, Ⓔ, Water Taxi; FW at Ⓥ pontoon by HM's Office. Public ⊿ and ⛲ at Fishermens Quay (Batson Creek). **Salcombe YC** ☎ 842872/ 842593, L, R, Bar. **Fuel Barge** ☎ (07801) 798862 0830-1730, D, P. **Town** EC Thurs; ⓐ, ✉, Ⓑ, all facilities, ⇌ (bus to Plymouth ✈ or Totnes).

ADJACENT HARBOUR, 3M NORTH

KINGSBRIDGE, Devon, **50°16'·88N 03°46'·52W**. AC *28*. HW = HW Salcombe +0005. Access HW±2½ for <2m draft/bilge keelers, max LOA 11m. The 3M chan to Kingsbridge is marked beyond Salt Stone SHM perch by R/W PHM poles with R can topmarks. 6ca N of Salt Stone a secondary chan marked by PHM buoys gradually diverges E into Balcombe Creek. There is a private ferry pontoon at New Quay, 3ca before the drying Kingsbridge basin. Ⓥ **pontoon** (outboard at seaward end) on E side of basin or on wall at W side, marked 'visitors' and drying 3·4m to soft mud. Best to pre-check berth availability with Salcombe HM; berthing fees and Hbr dues are payable. Facilities: Slip, SM.

Town EC Thurs; 🛒, R, Bar, ✉, Ⓑ, ⓐ.

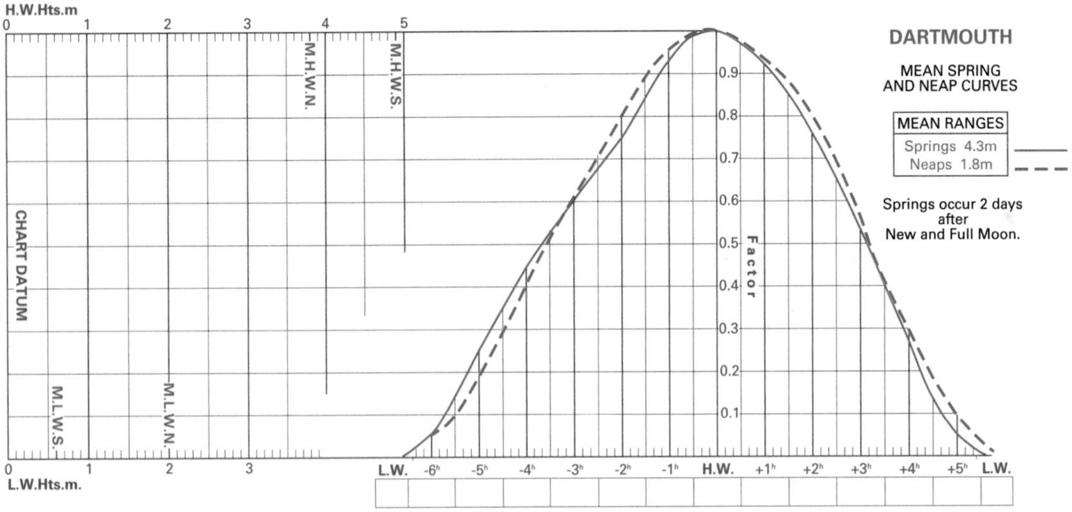
H.W.Hts.m
0 1 2 3 4 5
M.H.W.N.
M.H.W.S.
CHART DATUM
M.L.W.S.
M.L.W.N.
Factor
0.9
0.8
0.7
0.6
0.5
0.4
0.3
0.2
0.1
0 1 2 3
L.W.Hts.m.
L.W. -6h -5h -4h -3h -2h -1h H.W. +1h +2h +3h +4h +5h L.W.
DARTMOUTH
MEAN SPRING AND NEAP CURVES
MEAN RANGES
Springs 4.3m
Neaps 1.8m
Springs occur 2 days after New and Full Moon.

9.1.19 DARTMOUTH

Devon **50°20'·66N 03°33'·96W** ❁❁❁◊◊◊✿✿✿

CHARTS AC *1613, 1634, 5602, 2253*; Imray C5, 2400.1 & 4; Stanfords 2, 12, 22, L15; OS 202

TIDES –0510 Dover; ML 2·8; Duration 0630; Zone 0 (UT)

DARTMOUTH (⟶) The differences below refer to Dartmouth predictions, not to Plymouth.

Times				Height (metres)			
High Water		Low Water		MHWS	MHWN	MLWN	MLWS
0100	0600	0100	0600	4·9	3·8	2·0	0·6
1300	1800	1300	1800				
Differences GREENWAY QUAY (DITTISHAM)							
+0015	+0020	+0025	+0010	0·0	0·0	0·0	0·0
TOTNES							
+0015	+0015	+0115	+0035	–1·4	–1·5	Dries	Dries

SHELTER Excellent inside hbr, but ent can be difficult in strong SE to SW winds. Darthaven, Dart and Noss-on-Dart marinas offer Ⓥ berths. In mid-stream there are 6 large unlit mooring buoys for commercial vessels/FVs; do not ⚓ over their ground chains, as shown on AC 2253. Only space to ⚓ is E of fairway, from abeam Nos 3 to 5 buoys.

Elsewhere in the hbr the extensive pontoons (Ⓥ berths are marked by blue flags) and mooring trots are run by the HM, who should be called by VHF/☎. The most likely Ⓥ berths/Ⓥs (blue with black 'V') from S to N are:

W bank: pontoon off Dartmouth YC (May-Sep); Town jetty (W side only) near Boat Camber; N end of pontoon just S of Dart marina (26'/8m max LOA).

E of fairway: The 2 pontoons N of Fuel barge are for visitors. NB: Visitors may berth on six pontoons (KP-KU) N of Darthaven marina by arrangement with HM.

NAVIGATION WPT 50°19'·53N 03°32'·83W, 328°/1·5M in the white sector of Kingswear Dir lt. Bayard's Cove Dir lt leads 293° to abeam Royal Dart YC where the main fairway opens. There is no bar and hbr access is H24. Speed limit 6kn from Castle Ledge buoy up-river to 1M below Totnes. Give way to the Lower and Higher car ferries at Dartmouth which have right of way.

LIGHTS AND MARKS as on the chartlet and/or 9.1.4. E of the ent, on Inner Froward Pt (167m) is a conspic daymark, obelisk (24·5m). Lateral and cardinal lt buoys mark all dangers to seaward of Dartmouth Castle, conspic. Within hbr, all jetty/pontoon lts to the W are 2FR (vert); and 2FG (vert) to the E.

R/T HM: *Dartnav* VHF Ch 11 (summer, daily 0730-dusk). Darthaven, Dart and Noss-on-Dart marinas, Ch **80**. Fuel barge Ch 06. Water taxis, see Facilities.

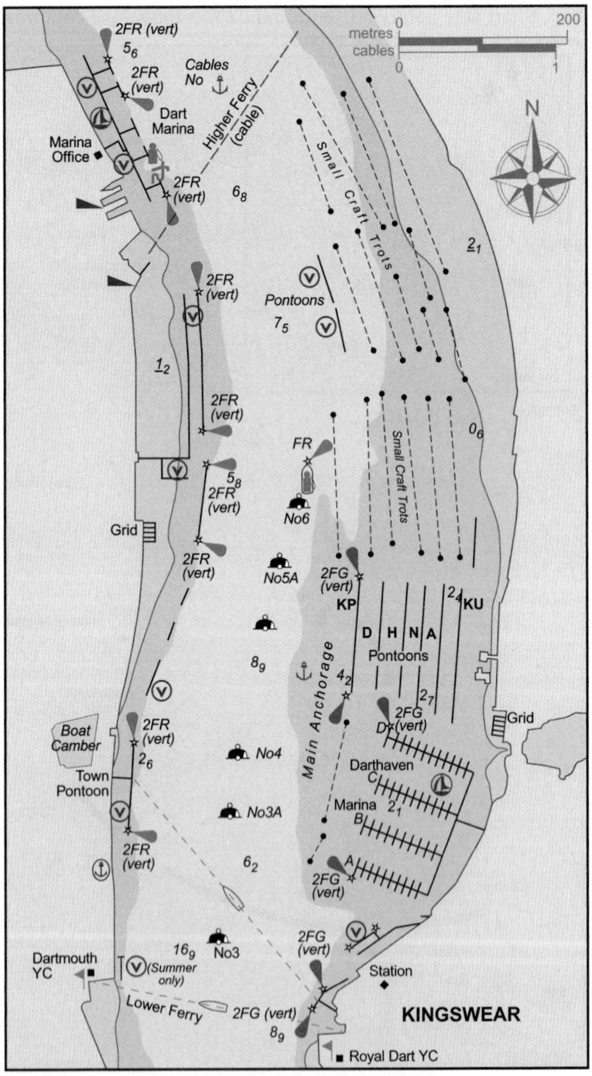
metres 0 200
cables 0 1
N
2FR (vert)
Cables No
2FR (vert)
Dart Marina
Marina Office
Higher Ferry (cable)
Small Craft Trots
2FR (vert)
2FR (vert)
Pontoons
2FR (vert)
FR
No6
Grid
2FR (vert)
2FR (vert)
No5A
2FG (vert)
KP
KU
D H N A
Pontoons
Main Anchorage
2FG (vert)
Grid
Boat Camber
2FR (vert)
No4
Town Pontoon
Darthaven Marina
No3A
2FR (vert)
2FG (vert)
No3
2FG (vert)
Dartmouth YC
(Summer only)
Station
Lower Ferry
2FG (vert)
KINGSWEAR
Royal Dart YC

TELEPHONE (Dial code 01803) HM 832337, 835220 (out of hours emergency), ⊠ 833631; MRSC 882704; Police 0990 777444; Marinecall 09066 526242; Dr 832212; Ⓗ 832255.

FACILITIES Dart Harbour & Navigation Authority (DHNA), hm@dartharbour.org.uk www.dartharbour.org.uk ☎ 832337, 🖷 833631; (450+90 Ⓥ) £0.50 to £1.00/m (buoys to pontoons), FW, Slip. Total charges = berth/marina fee, inc £0.50 Hbr dues & VAT.

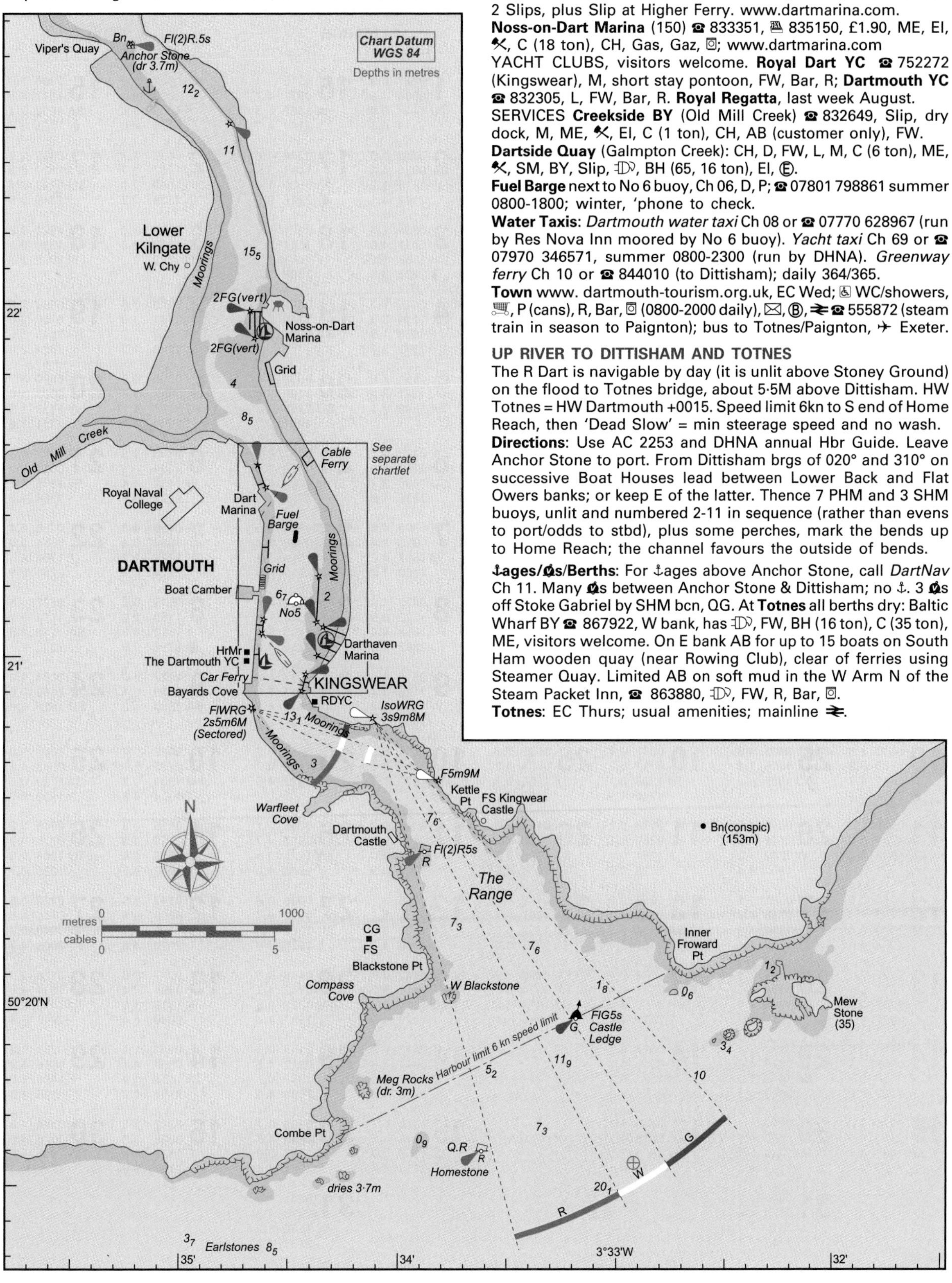
Chart Datum WGS 84
Depths in metres
Viper's Quay
Bn
Fl(2)R.5s
Anchor Stone (dr 3.7m)
12₂
11
Lower Kilngate
W. Chy
Moorings
15₅
2FG(vert)
Noss-on-Dart Marina
2FG(vert)
Grid
4
8₅
22'
Old Mill Creek
Cable Ferry
See separate chartlet
Royal Naval College
Dart Marina
Fuel Barge
DARTMOUTH
Grid
Moorings
Boat Camber
6₇
No5
2
Darthaven Marina
HrMr
The Dartmouth YC
21'
Car Ferry
KINGSWEAR
Bayards Cove
RDYC
FlWRG 2s5m6M (Sectored)
13₁
Moorings
IsoWRG 3s9m8M
Moorings
3
F5m9M
Kettle Pt
FS Kingwear Castle
N
Warfleet Cove
Dartmouth Castle
7₆
Fl(2)R5s
R
Bn(conspic) (153m)
The Range
metres 0 1000
cables 0 5
7₃
CG
FS
Blackstone Pt
7₆
Inner Froward Pt
1₂
Compass Cove
W Blackstone
1₈
0₆
Mew Stone (35)
50°20'N
Harbour limit 6 kn speed limit
FlG5s Castle Ledge
G
3₄
11₉
Meg Rocks (dr. 3m)
5₂
10
7₃
Combe Pt
0₉
Q.R
R
Homestone
G
W
dries 3·7m
20₁
R
3₇
Earlstones 8₅
35'
34'
3°33'W
32'

Darthaven Marina (230+12 Ⓥ) ☎ 752545, 🖷 752722, £2.00, ME, El, Gas, Gaz, ⊡, ⚒, CH, Bar, R, BH (35 ton), Ⓔ; www.darthaven.co.uk

Dart Marina (110, inc up to 30 Ⓥs) ☎ 833351, 🖷 832307, £2.70, D, ⛽ at fuel berth, ME, El, ⚒, C (9 ton), Gas, Gaz, CH, Bar, R, ⊡, 2 Slips, plus Slip at Higher Ferry. www.dartmarina.com.

Noss-on-Dart Marina (150) ☎ 833351, 🖷 835150, £1.90, ME, El, ⚒, C (18 ton), CH, Gas, Gaz, ⊡; www.dartmarina.com

YACHT CLUBS, visitors welcome. **Royal Dart YC** ☎ 752272 (Kingswear), M, short stay pontoon, FW, Bar, R; **Dartmouth YC** ☎ 832305, L, FW, Bar, R. **Royal Regatta**, last week August.

SERVICES **Creekside BY** (Old Mill Creek) ☎ 832649, Slip, dry dock, M, ME, ⚒, El, C (1 ton), CH, AB (customer only), FW.

Dartside Quay (Galmpton Creek): CH, D, FW, L, M, C (6 ton), ME, ⚒, SM, BY, Slip, ⌶, BH (65, 16 ton), El, Ⓔ.

Fuel Barge next to No 6 buoy, Ch 06, D, P; ☎ 07801 798861 summer 0800-1800; winter, 'phone to check.

Water Taxis: *Dartmouth water taxi* Ch 08 or ☎ 07770 628967 (run by Res Nova Inn moored by No 6 buoy). *Yacht taxi* Ch 69 or ☎ 07970 346571, summer 0800-2300 (run by DHNA). *Greenway ferry* Ch 10 or ☎ 844010 (to Dittisham); daily 364/365.

Town www. dartmouth-tourism.org.uk, EC Wed; ♿ WC/showers, 🛒, P (cans), R, Bar, ⊡ (0800-2000 daily), ✉, Ⓑ, ⇌ ☎ 555872 (steam train in season to Paignton); bus to Totnes/Paignton, ✈ Exeter.

UP RIVER TO DITTISHAM AND TOTNES

The R Dart is navigable by day (it is unlit above Stoney Ground) on the flood to Totnes bridge, about 5·5M above Dittisham. HW Totnes = HW Dartmouth +0015. Speed limit 6kn to S end of Home Reach, then 'Dead Slow' = min steerage speed and no wash.

Directions: Use AC 2253 and DHNA annual Hbr Guide. Leave Anchor Stone to port. From Dittisham brgs of 020° and 310° on successive Boat Houses lead between Lower Back and Flat Owers banks; or keep E of the latter. Thence 7 PHM and 3 SHM buoys, unlit and numbered 2-11 in sequence (rather than evens to port/odds to stbd), plus some perches, mark the bends up to Home Reach; the channel favours the outside of bends.

⚓ages/Ⓥs/Berths: For ⚓ages above Anchor Stone, call *DartNav* Ch 11. Many Ⓥs between Anchor Stone & Dittisham; no ⚓. 3 Ⓥs off Stoke Gabriel by SHM bcn, QG. At **Totnes** all berths dry: Baltic Wharf BY ☎ 867922, W bank, has ⌶, FW, BH (16 ton), C (35 ton), ME, visitors welcome. On E bank AB for up to 15 boats on South Ham wooden quay (near Rowing Club), clear of ferries using Steamer Quay. Limited AB on soft mud in the W Arm N of the Steam Packet Inn, ☎ 863880, ⌶, FW, R, Bar, ⊡.

Totnes: EC Thurs; usual amenities; mainline ⇌.

TIME ZONE (UT)
For Summer Time add ONE hour in **non-shaded areas**

ENGLAND – DARTMOUTH

LAT 50°21′N LONG 3°34′W

TIMES AND HEIGHTS OF HIGH AND LOW WATERS

SPRING & NEAP TIDES
Dates in red are SPRINGS
Dates in blue are NEAPS

YEAR **2005**

JANUARY

Day	Time	m	Day	Time	m
1 SA	0232 0911 1458 2135	1.5 4.3 1.5 4.0	16 SU	0344 1020 1611 2248	1.0 4.6 1.0 4.2
2 SU	0307 0948 1535 2214	1.6 4.2 1.6 3.9	17 M	0425 1100 1652 ◐ 2330	1.3 4.3 1.4 4.0
3 M	0347 1029 1621 ◑ 2301	1.7 4.1 1.7 3.8	18 TU	0509 1147 1740	1.6 4.0 1.7
4 TU	0438 1120 1721 2359	1.8 4.0 1.8 3.8	19 W	0023 0605 1249 1843	3.8 1.9 3.8 2.0
5 W	0548 1221 1838	1.9 4.0 1.8	20 TH	0132 0719 1405 1957	3.7 2.1 3.7 2.0
6 TH	0105 0712 1335 1952	3.9 1.9 4.0 1.7	21 F	0242 0841 1515 2112	3.8 2.0 3.8 1.9
7 F	0221 0827 1452 2100	4.0 1.7 4.1 1.5	22 SA	0345 0950 1615 2211	4.0 1.8 3.9 1.7
8 SA	0335 0935 1607 2205	4.2 1.4 4.3 1.2	23 SU	0438 1043 1704 2259	4.2 1.5 4.1 1.4
9 SU	0441 1038 1712 2305	4.5 1.1 4.5 1.0	24 M	0523 1126 1748 2339	4.4 1.3 4.3 1.3
10 M	0540 1135 1811 ● 2359	4.8 0.8 4.7 0.8	25 TU	0603 1205 1827 ○	4.6 1.1 4.4
11 TU	0633 1230 1903	5.0 0.5 4.8	26 W	0016 0642 1242 1904	1.1 4.6 1.0 4.4
12 W	0052 0723 1320 1954	0.6 5.1 0.4 4.8	27 TH	0051 0718 1314 1940	1.1 4.7 1.0 4.4
13 TH	0139 0811 1407 2042	0.5 5.1 0.4 4.7	28 F	0123 0754 1344 2014	1.0 4.6 1.0 4.3
14 F	0224 0857 1450 2127	0.6 5.1 0.5 4.6	29 SA	0151 0826 1412 2045	1.1 4.6 1.0 4.3
15 SA	0305 0940 1531 2207	0.7 4.9 0.7 4.4	30 SU	0219 0855 1440 2113	1.1 4.5 1.1 4.2
			31 M	0247 0924 1510 2142	1.2 4.4 1.2 4.1

FEBRUARY

Day	Time	m	Day	Time	m
1 TU	0321 0955 1544 2218	1.3 4.3 1.4 4.0	16 W	0424 1046 1645 ◐ 2304	1.5 4.0 1.7 3.8
2 W	0400 1038 1629 ◑ 2310	1.5 4.1 1.6 3.9	17 TH	0507 1131 1735	1.9 3.6 2.1
3 TH	0454 1138 1733	1.8 3.9 1.8	18 F	0003 0614 1258 1852	3.6 2.2 3.4 2.3
4 F	0020 0618 1257 1910	3.8 1.9 3.8 1.9	19 SA	0152 0751 1443 2034	3.5 2.3 3.4 2.2
5 SA	0147 0759 1431 2041	3.8 1.8 3.9 1.7	20 SU	0314 0933 1552 2153	3.7 2.0 3.7 1.9
6 SU	0315 0922 1557 2155	4.1 1.5 4.1 1.4	21 M	0414 1027 1646 2243	4.0 1.6 4.0 1.5
7 M	0428 1031 1705 2258	4.4 1.1 4.4 1.0	22 TU	0502 1110 1730 2323	4.3 1.2 4.2 1.2
8 TU	0529 1128 1802 ● 2351	4.8 0.6 4.6 0.6	23 W	0545 1148 1811	4.5 1.0 4.4
9 W	0623 1220 1854	5.0 0.3 4.8	24 TH	0000 0625 1223 ○ 1848	1.0 4.6 0.8 4.5
10 TH	0041 0711 1308 1940	0.4 5.2 0.1 4.9	25 F	0035 0701 1256 1923	0.8 4.7 0.7 4.5
11 F	0126 0756 1351 2023	0.2 5.2 0.1 4.8	26 SA	0105 0736 1325 1954	0.8 4.7 0.7 4.5
12 SA	0207 0839 1430 2102	0.2 5.1 0.2 4.8	27 SU	0133 0807 1352 2022	0.7 4.7 0.7 4.5
13 SU	0243 0916 1506 2135	0.4 4.9 0.4 4.6	28 M	0200 0834 1419 2048	0.8 4.6 0.8 4.4
14 M	0317 0948 1537 2203	0.7 4.7 0.8 4.3			
15 TU	0349 1015 1609 2229	1.1 4.3 1.3 4.1			

MARCH

Day	Time	m	Day	Time	m
1 TU	0227 0900 1446 2114	0.9 4.5 0.9 4.3	16 W	0315 0934 1530 2141	1.1 4.2 1.3 4.1
2 W	0258 0930 1518 2147	1.0 4.3 1.2 4.1	17 TH	0344 1001 1600 ◐ 2215	1.5 3.9 1.7 3.9
3 TH	0334 1011 1558 ◑ 2238	1.3 4.0 1.5 3.9	18 F	0421 1041 1643 2306	1.9 3.5 2.1 3.6
4 F	0426 1114 1658 2352	1.7 3.8 1.9 3.7	19 SA	0526 1149 1804	2.3 3.3 2.4
5 SA	0551 1241 1849	2.0 3.6 2.1	20 SU	0039 0705 1414 1947	3.4 2.4 3.3 2.3
6 SU	0129 0752 1430 2036	3.7 1.9 3.7 1.8	21 M	0242 0905 1526 2122	3.6 2.0 3.6 1.9
7 M	0309 0919 1557 2150	4.0 1.4 4.0 1.3	22 TU	0344 0958 1619 2212	3.9 1.6 3.9 1.5
8 TU	0420 1023 1658 2247	4.4 0.9 4.4 0.8	23 W	0433 1040 1703 2253	4.2 1.2 4.2 1.2
9 W	0516 1116 1750 2337	4.8 0.4 4.7 0.5	24 TH	0517 1117 1744 2330	4.5 0.9 4.4 0.9
10 TH	0605 1203 1837 ●	5.0 0.1 4.8	25 F	0558 1152 1822 ○	4.6 0.7 4.5
11 F	0022 0652 1248 1918	0.2 5.1 0.0 4.9	26 SA	0005 0636 1226 1856	0.7 4.7 0.6 4.6
12 SA	0105 0734 1328 1956	0.1 5.1 0.0 4.9	27 SU	0039 0710 1259 1928	0.6 4.7 0.5 4.6
13 SU	0142 0811 1404 2029	0.1 5.0 0.1 4.8	28 M	0110 0742 1329 1957	0.5 4.7 0.5 4.6
14 M	0217 0844 1435 2056	0.3 4.8 0.5 4.6	29 TU	0139 0812 1357 2024	0.6 4.6 0.7 4.6
15 TU	0246 0910 1503 2118	0.7 4.5 0.9 4.4	30 W	0209 0843 1427 2054	0.7 4.5 0.9 4.4
			31 TH	0241 0918 1500 2133	1.0 4.3 1.2 4.2

APRIL

Day	Time	m	Day	Time	m
1 F	0322 1003 1543 2225	1.3 4.0 1.6 4.0	16 SA	0346 1012 1603 ◐ 2233	1.9 3.5 2.1 3.7
2 SA	0417 1107 1649 ◑ 2339	1.7 3.7 2.0 3.7	17 SU	0450 1116 1727 2346	2.2 3.3 2.4 3.5
3 SU	0552 1243 1850	2.0 3.5 2.1	18 M	0624 1326 1902	2.3 3.3 2.3
4 M	0125 0751 1434 2029	3.8 1.8 3.7 1.7	19 TU	0150 0758 1445 2024	3.6 2.0 3.6 2.0
5 TU	0259 0907 1547 2134	4.1 1.3 4.1 1.2	20 W	0300 0903 1539 2121	3.9 1.6 3.9 1.6
6 W	0403 1004 1642 2227	4.5 0.8 4.4 0.8	21 TH	0352 0951 1625 2208	4.1 1.2 4.1 1.2
7 TH	0456 1054 1728 2314	4.8 0.4 4.7 0.4	22 F	0439 1034 1708 2251	4.4 0.9 4.4 0.9
8 F	0543 1139 1812 ● 2357	5.0 0.2 4.8 0.2	23 SA	0522 1114 1748 2330	4.5 0.7 4.5 0.7
9 SA	0627 1220 1850	5.0 0.1 4.9	24 SU	0604 1152 1826 ○	4.6 0.6 4.6
10 SU	0038 0705 1300 1924	0.2 5.0 0.2 4.8	25 M	0008 0643 1230 1900	0.6 4.7 0.5 4.7
11 M	0115 0740 1333 1953	0.3 4.8 0.4 4.7	26 TU	0046 0720 1306 1935	0.5 4.7 0.6 4.7
12 TU	0147 0809 1404 2016	0.5 4.6 0.7 4.6	27 W	0122 0756 1340 2008	0.6 4.6 0.7 4.7
13 W	0217 0834 1430 2040	0.8 4.4 1.0 4.4	28 TH	0158 0834 1416 2046	0.7 4.5 0.9 4.5
14 TH	0244 0859 1456 2107	1.1 4.1 1.4 4.2	29 F	0237 0916 1456 2129	1.0 4.2 1.2 4.3
15 F	0312 0930 1523 2143	1.5 3.8 1.8 3.9	30 SA	0324 1006 1545 2222	1.3 4.0 1.6 4.1

Chart Datum: 2·62 metres below Ordnance Datum (Newlyn)

TIME ZONE (UT)
For Summer Time add ONE hour in **non-shaded areas**

ENGLAND – DARTMOUTH

LAT 50°21′N LONG 3°34′W

TIMES AND HEIGHTS OF HIGH AND LOW WATERS

SPRING & NEAP TIDES
Dates in red are SPRINGS
Dates in blue are NEAPS

YEAR **2005**

MAY

Date	Day	Time	m	Time	m	Time	m	Time	m	Moon
1	SU	0426	1.6	1112	3.7	1657	1.9	2335	3.9	◑
2	M	0556	1.8	1245	3.7	1840	1.9			
3	TU	0114	3.9	0731	1.6	1413	3.8	2003	1.6	
4	W	0235	4.2	0840	1.2	1518	4.1	2105	1.2	
5	TH	0336	4.4	0936	0.9	1612	4.4	2158	0.9	
6	F	0428	4.6	1025	0.6	1658	4.6	2246	0.6	
7	SA	0516	4.7	1110	0.5	1741	4.7	2329	0.5	
8	SU	0558	4.8	1152	0.4	1820	4.7			●
9	M	0009	0.5	0637	4.7	1231	0.5	1852	4.7	
10	TU	0047	0.6	0710	4.6	1304	0.7	1920	4.7	
11	W	0121	0.8	0739	4.4	1334	0.9	1945	4.6	
12	TH	0150	1.0	0807	4.3	1403	1.2	2013	4.4	
13	F	0220	1.3	0837	4.1	1431	1.5	2046	4.3	
14	SA	0250	1.5	0912	3.8	1502	1.8	2124	4.0	
15	SU	0327	1.8	0957	3.6	1543	2.0	2211	3.8	
16	M	0424	2.0	1055	3.5	1651	2.2	2313	3.7	◐
17	TU	0540	2.1	1215	3.4	1813	2.2			
18	W	0033	3.7	0656	1.9	1341	3.6	1925	2.0	
19	TH	0155	3.8	0759	1.6	1442	3.8	2024	1.7	
20	F	0256	4.0	0854	1.3	1535	4.0	2117	1.4	
21	SA	0350	4.2	0945	1.1	1623	4.3	2207	1.1	
22	SU	0442	4.4	1033	0.9	1710	4.5	2255	0.9	
23	M	0530	4.5	1119	0.7	1754	4.6	2341	0.7	○
24	TU	0618	4.6	1204	0.7	1837	4.7			
25	W	0025	0.6	0701	4.6	1249	0.7	1918	4.8	
26	TH	0111	0.6	0746	4.6	1331	0.8	2000	4.8	
27	F	0155	0.7	0832	4.5	1416	0.9	2045	4.7	
28	SA	0241	0.8	0921	4.3	1502	1.1	2132	4.5	
29	SU	0331	1.1	1012	4.1	1553	1.4	2224	4.3	
30	M	0429	1.3	1114	4.0	1655	1.6	2330	4.2	◑
31	TU	0539	1.4	1226	3.9	1809	1.7			

JUNE

Date	Day	Time	m	Time	m	Time	m	Time	m	Moon
1	W	0045	4.1	0654	1.4	1336	3.9	1923	1.6	
2	TH	0157	4.1	0800	1.3	1439	4.1	2027	1.4	
3	F	0259	4.2	0859	1.1	1535	4.2	2123	1.2	
4	SA	0355	4.3	0952	1.0	1624	4.4	2215	1.0	
5	SU	0446	4.4	1041	0.9	1710	4.5	2302	0.9	
6	M	0530	4.4	1124	0.9	1750	4.6	2344	0.9	●
7	TU	0611	4.4	1203	0.9	1825	4.6			
8	W	0023	0.9	0646	4.4	1240	1.0	1855	4.6	
9	TH	0100	1.0	0719	4.3	1313	1.1	1926	4.5	
10	F	0132	1.1	0751	4.2	1344	1.3	1959	4.4	
11	SA	0205	1.3	0826	4.0	1416	1.4	2034	4.3	
12	SU	0237	1.4	0905	3.9	1449	1.6	2113	4.2	
13	M	0313	1.6	0947	3.8	1526	1.8	2155	4.0	
14	TU	0356	1.7	1033	3.7	1612	1.9	2242	3.9	
15	W	0450	1.8	1127	3.6	1714	2.0	2337	3.9	◐
16	TH	0555	1.8	1228	3.7	1824	1.9			
17	F	0040	3.9	0701	1.7	1332	3.8	1930	1.7	
18	SA	0148	4.0	0801	1.5	1435	3.9	2030	1.5	
19	SU	0255	4.1	0900	1.3	1536	4.1	2129	1.3	
20	M	0400	4.2	0957	1.1	1633	4.4	2225	1.1	
21	TU	0500	4.4	1053	1.0	1728	4.6	2320	0.8	
22	W	0557	4.5	1146	0.8	1820	4.7			○
23	TH	0012	0.7	0651	4.6	1238	0.7	1907	4.9	
24	F	0105	0.5	0741	4.6	1328	0.7	1956	4.9	
25	SA	0154	0.5	0832	4.6	1415	0.7	2044	4.9	
26	SU	0242	0.6	0921	4.5	1501	0.8	2131	4.8	
27	M	0329	0.7	1008	4.4	1547	1.0	2218	4.6	
28	TU	0417	0.9	1058	4.2	1635	1.2	2309	4.4	◑
29	W	0509	1.2	1152	4.1	1729	1.4			
30	TH	0006	4.2	0606	1.4	1250	3.9	1833	1.6	

JULY

Date	Day	Time	m	Time	m	Time	m	Time	m	Moon
1	F	0111	4.0	0711	1.5	1352	3.9	1940	1.7	
2	SA	0218	3.9	0816	1.6	1453	4.0	2046	1.6	
3	SU	0320	4.0	0918	1.5	1550	4.1	2147	1.5	
4	M	0417	4.0	1013	1.4	1641	4.3	2240	1.3	
5	TU	0506	4.1	1102	1.3	1725	4.4	2326	1.2	
6	W	0550	4.2	1144	1.2	1804	4.5			●
7	TH	0007	1.1	0629	4.3	1223	1.1	1840	4.5	
8	F	0047	1.1	0705	4.3	1300	1.1	1915	4.5	
9	SA	0122	1.1	0741	4.2	1332	1.2	1950	4.5	
10	SU	0153	1.2	0818	4.1	1403	1.3	2025	4.4	
11	M	0224	1.2	0854	4.1	1432	1.4	2100	4.3	
12	TU	0253	1.3	0930	4.0	1502	1.5	2134	4.2	
13	W	0325	1.4	1004	3.9	1534	1.6	2208	4.1	
14	TH	0401	1.5	1043	3.8	1616	1.7	2249	4.0	◐
15	F	0447	1.6	1131	3.8	1712	1.8	2343	3.9	
16	SA	0553	1.7	1230	3.8	1831	1.8			
17	SU	0049	3.9	0711	1.7	1343	3.8	1949	1.7	
18	M	0210	3.9	0824	1.6	1458	4.0	2100	1.5	
19	TU	0330	4.1	0933	1.3	1609	4.3	2206	1.2	
20	W	0443	4.3	1037	1.1	1711	4.6	2308	0.9	
21	TH	0545	4.5	1135	0.8	1806	4.8			○
22	F	0004	0.6	0641	4.6	1230	0.6	1857	5.0	
23	SA	0058	0.3	0733	4.7	1320	0.4	1947	5.1	
24	SU	0146	0.2	0822	4.8	1406	0.4	2034	5.1	
25	M	0230	0.2	0907	4.7	1448	0.5	2118	5.0	
26	TU	0313	0.4	0949	4.6	1527	0.7	2159	4.8	
27	W	0352	0.7	1029	4.4	1607	1.0	2238	4.5	
28	TH	0431	1.1	1109	4.1	1648	1.3	2320	4.1	◑
29	F	0516	1.5	1157	3.9	1738	1.7			
30	SA	0015	3.8	0610	1.8	1301	3.7	1847	2.0	
31	SU	0133	3.6	0724	2.0	1415	3.7	2010	2.0	

AUGUST

Date	Day	Time	m	Time	m	Time	m	Time	m	Moon
1	M	0250	3.6	0848	1.9	1522	3.9	2129	1.8	
2	TU	0354	3.8	0956	1.7	1619	4.1	2226	1.6	
3	W	0448	4.0	1048	1.5	1705	4.3	2314	1.3	
4	TH	0533	4.1	1131	1.2	1747	4.5	2355	1.1	
5	F	0614	4.3	1210	1.1	1826	4.6			●
6	SA	0033	1.0	0651	4.3	1246	1.0	1901	4.6	
7	SU	0107	0.9	0727	4.3	1317	1.0	1937	4.6	
8	M	0135	1.0	0802	4.3	1344	1.0	2009	4.5	
9	TU	0202	1.0	0834	4.3	1410	1.1	2040	4.5	
10	W	0227	1.1	0902	4.2	1434	1.2	2106	4.4	
11	TH	0252	1.2	0930	4.1	1502	1.3	2134	4.2	
12	F	0322	1.3	1001	4.0	1535	1.5	2208	4.1	
13	SA	0359	1.5	1044	3.9	1622	1.7	2301	3.9	◐
14	SU	0453	1.8	1146	3.7	1734	2.0			
15	M	0014	3.7	0626	2.0	1307	3.8	1924	1.9	
16	TU	0147	3.7	0805	1.8	1440	4.0	2048	1.6	
17	W	0322	4.0	0922	1.5	1557	4.3	2159	1.2	
18	TH	0435	4.3	1029	1.1	1659	4.7	2259	0.7	
19	F	0534	4.5	1125	0.7	1753	5.0	2353	0.4	○
20	SA	0628	4.8	1215	0.4	1843	5.2			
21	SU	0043	0.1	0715	4.9	1304	0.2	1930	5.2	
22	M	0129	0.0	0801	4.9	1346	0.2	2013	5.2	
23	TU	0209	0.1	0842	4.9	1425	0.3	2053	5.0	
24	W	0246	0.3	0919	4.7	1500	0.6	2129	4.8	
25	TH	0321	0.7	0951	4.5	1533	0.9	2159	4.4	
26	F	0353	1.1	1019	4.2	1608	1.4	2228	4.1	◑
27	SA	0427	1.6	1051	3.9	1650	1.9	2306	3.7	
28	SU	0515	2.1	1144	3.6	1754	2.2			
29	M	0032	3.4	0630	2.3	1338	3.5	1939	2.3	
30	TU	0227	3.4	0830	2.3	1458	3.7	2119	2.0	
31	W	0337	3.6	0943	1.9	1558	4.0	2212	1.6	

Chart Datum: 2·62 metres below Ordnance Datum (Newlyn)

TIME ZONE (UT)
For Summer Time add ONE hour in **non-shaded areas**

ENGLAND – DARTMOUTH

LAT 50°21′N LONG 3°34′W

TIMES AND HEIGHTS OF HIGH AND LOW WATERS

SPRING & NEAP TIDES
Dates in red are SPRINGS
Dates in blue are NEAPS

YEAR **2005**

SEPTEMBER

Date	Day	Time	m	Time	m	Time	m	Time	m	Moon
1	TH	0430	3.9	1031	1.5	1646	4.3	2256	1.3	
2	F	0514	4.2	1112	1.2	1726	4.5	2334	1.0	
3	SA	0553	4.4	1148	1.0	1805	4.7			●
4	SU	0009	0.9	0630	4.5	1222	0.9	1841	4.7	
5	M	0041	0.8	0704	4.5	1252	0.8	1915	4.7	
6	TU	0109	0.8	0737	4.5	1319	0.9	1946	4.7	
7	W	0133	0.8	0806	4.5	1342	0.9	2013	4.6	
8	TH	0158	0.9	0832	4.4	1407	1.0	2038	4.5	
9	F	0223	1.1	0856	4.3	1434	1.2	2105	4.3	
10	SA	0251	1.3	0928	4.1	1508	1.4	2141	4.1	
11	SU	0327	1.6	1012	3.9	1552	1.8	2239	3.8	◐
12	M	0419	2.0	1120	3.8	1706	2.1	2359	3.6	
13	TU	0601	2.2	1248	3.7	1917	2.1			
14	W	0147	3.7	0801	2.0	1434	4.0	2045	1.6	
15	TH	0324	4.0	0917	1.5	1549	4.4	2150	1.1	
16	F	0428	4.4	1017	1.0	1645	4.8	2245	0.6	
17	SA	0520	4.7	1108	0.6	1735	5.1	2334	0.2	
18	SU	0607	4.9	1155	0.3	1823	5.2			○
19	M	0019	0.1	0652	5.0	1240	0.2	1905	5.3	
20	TU	0103	0.0	0733	5.0	1321	0.2	1946	5.2	
21	W	0141	0.2	0809	4.9	1356	0.4	2022	5.0	
22	TH	0215	0.5	0842	4.8	1429	0.7	2052	4.7	
23	F	0246	0.9	0907	4.5	1500	1.1	2118	4.3	
24	SA	0315	1.3	0931	4.2	1531	1.6	2143	4.0	
25	SU	0345	1.8	1002	4.0	1609	2.0	2220	3.6	◑
26	M	0427	2.3	1049	3.7	1712	2.4	2324	3.3	
27	TU	0545	2.6	1230	3.5	1903	2.5			
28	W	0203	3.3	0802	2.5	1429	3.7	2056	2.1	
29	TH	0312	3.6	0915	2.0	1529	4.0	2144	1.7	
30	F	0403	4.0	1000	1.6	1617	4.3	2223	1.3	

OCTOBER

Date	Day	Time	m	Time	m	Time	m	Time	m	Moon
1	SA	0446	4.3	1040	1.3	1658	4.5	2300	1.0	
2	SU	0525	4.5	1115	1.0	1736	4.7	2334	0.8	
3	M	0602	4.6	1148	0.9	1815	4.8			●
4	TU	0005	0.7	0637	4.7	1220	0.8	1849	4.8	
5	W	0036	0.7	0708	4.7	1250	0.8	1920	4.7	
6	TH	0105	0.8	0738	4.7	1318	0.8	1948	4.7	
7	F	0131	0.9	0805	4.6	1345	1.0	2016	4.5	
8	SA	0159	1.1	0834	4.5	1416	1.2	2050	4.3	
9	SU	0230	1.3	0910	4.3	1452	1.5	2134	4.1	
10	M	0309	1.7	1000	4.1	1541	1.8	2233	3.8	◐
11	TU	0406	2.1	1107	3.9	1707	2.2	2355	3.6	
12	W	0602	2.3	1240	3.8	1914	2.0			
13	TH	0153	3.7	0754	2.0	1423	4.1	2033	1.5	
14	F	0314	4.1	0902	1.5	1531	4.5	2132	1.0	
15	SA	0410	4.5	0956	1.0	1625	4.9	2222	0.6	
16	SU	0458	4.8	1045	0.6	1713	5.1	2309	0.3	
17	M	0543	4.9	1130	0.4	1758	5.2	2352	0.3	○
18	TU	0625	5.0	1212	0.3	1840	5.1			
19	W	0034	0.3	0702	5.0	1253	0.4	1917	5.0	
20	TH	0111	0.5	0736	4.9	1328	0.6	1950	4.8	
21	F	0143	0.8	0804	4.8	1400	0.9	2018	4.5	
22	SA	0213	1.1	0828	4.6	1430	1.3	2043	4.2	
23	SU	0241	1.5	0855	4.3	1501	1.7	2112	3.9	
24	M	0311	1.9	0931	4.1	1538	2.1	2154	3.6	
25	TU	0351	2.3	1018	3.8	1636	2.4	2254	3.4	◑
26	W	0506	2.6	1130	3.6	1809	2.5			
27	TH	0112	3.4	0648	2.5	1337	3.7	1957	2.2	
28	F	0229	3.6	0819	2.2	1445	3.9	2053	1.8	
29	SA	0322	3.9	0911	1.8	1536	4.2	2136	1.5	
30	SU	0408	4.2	0954	1.4	1620	4.5	2214	1.2	
31	M	0449	4.5	1034	1.2	1702	4.6	2253	1.0	

NOVEMBER

Date	Day	Time	m	Time	m	Time	m	Time	m	Moon
1	TU	0528	4.6	1111	1.0	1743	4.7	2329	0.8	
2	W	0605	4.7	1147	0.9	1821	4.8			●
3	TH	0004	0.8	0641	4.8	1223	0.8	1856	4.7	
4	F	0040	0.8	0714	4.8	1258	0.8	1931	4.7	
5	SA	0113	0.9	0747	4.7	1332	1.0	2007	4.5	
6	SU	0147	1.1	0823	4.6	1410	1.2	2047	4.3	
7	M	0225	1.4	0905	4.5	1454	1.4	2135	4.1	
8	TU	0311	1.7	0957	4.3	1550	1.8	2234	3.9	
9	W	0414	2.0	1100	4.1	1711	1.9	2354	3.8	◐
10	TH	0551	2.1	1226	4.0	1851	1.8			
11	F	0129	3.9	0725	1.9	1355	4.2	2004	1.5	
12	SA	0243	4.1	0832	1.5	1501	4.5	2102	1.1	
13	SU	0340	4.4	0928	1.2	1557	4.7	2154	0.9	
14	M	0430	4.7	1017	0.9	1647	4.8	2242	0.7	
15	TU	0515	4.8	1104	0.7	1733	4.9	2325	0.6	
16	W	0557	4.9	1146	0.7	1815	4.9			○
17	TH	0005	0.7	0634	4.9	1226	0.7	1852	4.8	
18	F	0044	0.8	0706	4.8	1304	0.9	1924	4.6	
19	SA	0117	1.0	0736	4.7	1337	1.1	1953	4.4	
20	SU	0148	1.3	0804	4.6	1409	1.4	2022	4.2	
21	M	0218	1.6	0835	4.4	1442	1.7	2056	4.0	
22	TU	0250	1.9	0913	4.2	1519	1.9	2139	3.8	
23	W	0329	2.1	1000	4.0	1608	2.2	2234	3.6	◑
24	TH	0426	2.3	1057	3.8	1716	2.3	2347	3.5	
25	F	0544	2.4	1211	3.8	1834	2.2			
26	SA	0114	3.6	0702	2.2	1333	3.9	1940	1.9	
27	SU	0220	3.8	0805	2.0	1437	4.1	2035	1.7	
28	M	0314	4.1	0859	1.7	1531	4.2	2123	1.4	
29	TU	0403	4.3	0948	1.4	1622	4.4	2210	1.2	
30	W	0451	4.5	1035	1.2	1710	4.5	2255	1.0	

DECEMBER

Date	Day	Time	m	Time	m	Time	m	Time	m	Moon
1	TH	0535	4.6	1119	1.0	1756	4.6	2339	0.9	●
2	F	0618	4.8	1202	0.9	1840	4.7			
3	SA	0021	0.9	0658	4.8	1247	0.8	1922	4.7	
4	SU	0105	1.0	0739	4.8	1330	0.9	2005	4.6	
5	M	0147	1.1	0822	4.8	1415	1.0	2051	4.4	
6	TU	0231	1.2	0908	4.7	1503	1.2	2140	4.3	
7	W	0320	1.4	0957	4.5	1555	1.4	2234	4.1	
8	TH	0415	1.6	1053	4.4	1656	1.5	2337	4.0	◐
9	F	0522	1.8	1200	4.2	1809	1.6			
10	SA	0048	4.0	0639	1.8	1313	4.2	1921	1.6	
11	SU	0158	4.1	0750	1.7	1422	4.3	2025	1.4	
12	M	0300	4.2	0853	1.5	1524	4.4	2122	1.3	
13	TU	0357	4.4	0950	1.3	1620	4.5	2214	1.2	
14	W	0448	4.5	1041	1.1	1710	4.5	2302	1.1	
15	TH	0532	4.7	1126	1.0	1754	4.5	2344	1.0	○
16	F	0613	4.7	1208	1.0	1833	4.5			
17	SA	0023	1.1	0647	4.7	1248	1.1	1907	4.4	
18	SU	0100	1.2	0719	4.7	1324	1.2	1939	4.3	
19	M	0133	1.3	0751	4.6	1357	1.3	2013	4.2	
20	TU	0205	1.5	0826	4.5	1429	1.5	2050	4.1	
21	W	0237	1.6	0904	4.3	1503	1.6	2130	3.9	
22	TH	0310	1.8	0944	4.2	1538	1.8	2211	3.8	
23	F	0347	1.9	1027	4.0	1622	1.9	2259	3.7	◑
24	SA	0436	2.1	1116	3.9	1719	2.0	2356	3.7	
25	SU	0542	2.1	1214	3.9	1827	2.0			
26	M	0059	3.7	0657	2.1	1321	3.9	1933	1.9	
27	TU	0207	3.9	0803	1.9	1431	4.0	2035	1.7	
28	W	0313	4.1	0905	1.7	1539	4.1	2133	1.5	
29	TH	0414	4.3	1003	1.4	1641	4.3	2229	1.2	
30	F	0510	4.5	1059	1.1	1736	4.5	2321	1.0	
31	SA	0600	4.7	1150	0.9	1828	4.6			●

Chart Datum: 2·62 metres below Ordnance Datum (Newlyn)

9.1.20 BRIXHAM

Devon 50°24'·31N 03°30'·85W
❁❁❁◊◊◊✿✿

CHARTS AC *3315, 1613, 1634, 5602, 26*; Imray C5, 2400.3; Stan 2, 12, 22; OS 202

TIDES –0505 Dover; ML 2·9; Duration 0635; Zone 0 (UT). Standard Port **PLYMOUTH** (⟵). Use Differences for **TORQUAY** below.

SHELTER Very good in marina; good at YC pontoon in SW corner of hbr, but outer hbr is dangerous in strong NW'lies. White Ⓥs to E of main fairway. Inner hbr dries. W of hbr are ⚓s in Fishcombe Cove and Elberry Cove (beware water skiers).

NAVIGATION WPT 50°24'·70N 03°31'·09W, (3ca off chartlet), 159°/0·4M to hbr ent in W sector of Dir lt. No dangers; easy access. Inshore around Torbay controlled areas (May-Sep, mainly for swimmers) are marked by unlit Y SPM buoys; boats may enter with caution, speed limit 5kn.

LIGHTS AND MARKS Berry Hd, a conspic headland and good radar return, is 1·25M ESE of ent. Dir lt at SE end of hbr leads 159° into the fairway, which is marked by two pairs of lateral lt buoys. See chartlet and 9.1.4 for lt details.

R/T Marina: Ch 80. YC and Water Taxi: *Shuttle* Ch M. HM Ch 14, 16 (May-Sept 0800-1800LT; Oct-Apr 0900-1700, Mon-Fri). Brixham CG: Ch 16, 10, 67, 73.

TELEPHONE (Dial code 01803) Marina ☎ 882929 📠 882737; HM 853321; Pilot 882214; MRSC 882704; Marinecall 09066 526242; Police 08705 777444; Dr 855897; ⊞ 882153.

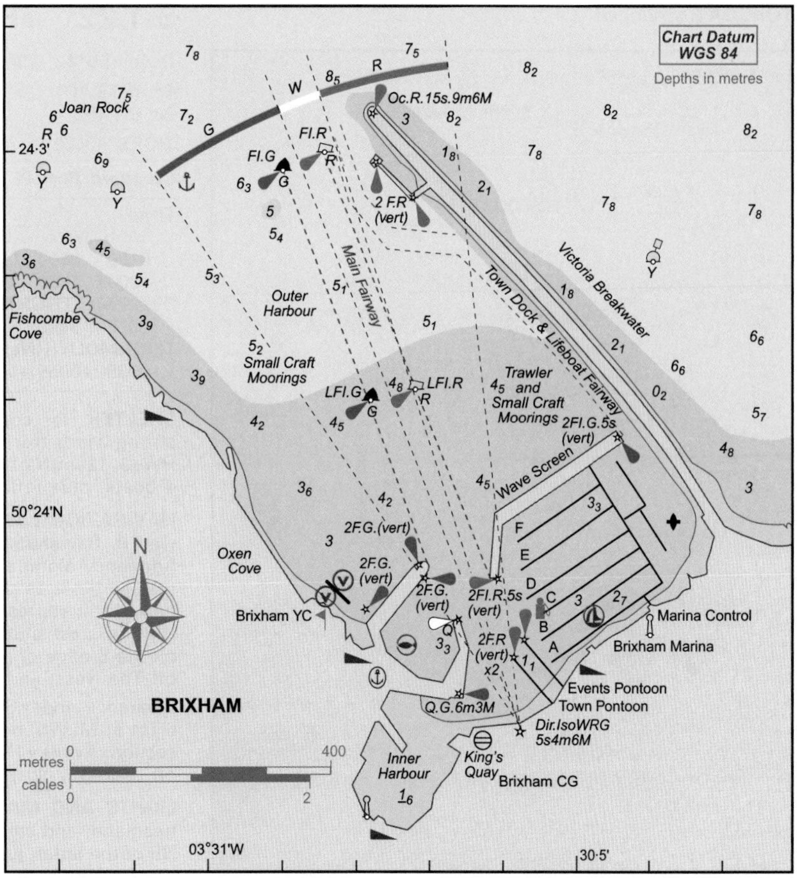
Chart Datum WGS 84
Depths in metres
Joan Rock
Oc.R.15s.9m6M
Fl.R
Fl.G
2 F.R (vert)
Victoria Breakwater
Town Dock & Lifeboat Fairway
Main Fairway
Outer Harbour
Fishcombe Cove
Small Craft Moorings
LFl.G
LFl.R
Trawler and Small Craft Moorings
2Fl.G.5s (vert)
Wave Screen
50°24'N
2F.G.(vert)
Oxen Cove
Brixham YC
2F.G. (vert)
2Fl.R.5s (vert)
2F.R (vert) x2
Marina Control
Brixham Marina
Events Pontoon
Town Pontoon
Q.G.6m3M
Dir.IsoWRG 5s4m6M
BRIXHAM
Inner Harbour
King's Quay
Brixham CG
metres
cables
03°31'W
30·5'

FACILITIES Marina (480 inc Ⓥ) torquaymarina@mdlmarinas.co.uk www.marinas.co.uk £2.70>10m, £1.95 <10m, access H24, D (0900-1800, Apr-Sep inc), ⊡. **Hbr Office** (New Fish Quay) Slip, M, L, FW, C (2 ton), D. **Brixham YC** ☎ 853332, Ⓥ pontoon, M, L, Slip, FW, R, Bar. **Services:** CH, ACA, ME, P (cans), El, Ⓔ.
Town R, Bar, ⊡, ✉, Ⓑ, bus to Paignton ⇌, ✈ (Exeter).

MINOR HARBOUR 2·3M NW OF BRIXHAM

PAIGNTON, Devon, **50°25'·96N 03°33'·36W**. AC *1613, 26*. HW –0500 on Dover, +0035 on Devonport; HW –0·6m on Devonport; ML 2·9m; Duration 0640. Hbr dries 1·3m and is only suitable for max LOA 8·2m. E winds cause a heavy swell in hbr. Drying rks extend 180m E from E pier to Black Rk, ECM tr; Lts as in 9.1.4. HM (summer only) ☎ (01803) 557812. **Paignton SC** ☎ 525817; Facilities: M, ME, ⚒, Gas, CH, ACA.

9.1.21 TORQUAY

Devon **50°27'·45N 03°31'·73W** ❁❁❁◊◊◊✿✿

CHARTS AC *3315, 1613, 5602, 26*; Imray C5, 2400.1 & .3; Stanfords 2, 12, 22; OS 202

TIDES –0500 Dover; ML 2·9; Duration 0640; Zone 0 (UT)

Standard Port PLYMOUTH (⟵)

Times				Height (metres)			
High Water		Low Water		MHWS	MHWN	MLWN	MLWS
0100	0600	0100	0600	5·5	4·4	2·2	0·8
1300	1800	1300	1800				
Differences TORQUAY							
+0025	+0045	+0010	0000	–0·6	–0·7	–0·2	–0·1

Note: There is often a stand of about 1 hour at HW

SHELTER Good, but some swell in hbr with strong SE winds. Visitors berth in the marina, on Haldon Pier pontoon and on a pontoon in the Old Hbr, N side of S Pier in 2m. At the ent to the Old (inner) Hbr a wall with sill/flapgate (11·6m wide) retains 1·0m–2·8m. Above it a footbridge with lifting centre section opens on request VHF Ch 14 when the flapgate is in use, approx HW –3½ to +3, 0700-2300 Apr-Sep. Do not pass under the bridge when it is lowered. No ⚓ in hbr. ⚓s at Hope Cove, Anstey's Cove & Babbacombe Bay, NW of Hope's Nose, are sheltered in W'lies.

NAVIGATION WPT 50°27'·03N 03°31'·57W, 339°/0·40M to SHM buoy close off Haldon pier; keep a good lookout, semi-blind ent. Access at all tides, but in strong SE winds backwash may make the narrow ent difficult. Speed limit 5 knots in the hbr.

Inshore around Torbay controlled areas (May-Sep, mainly for swimmers) are marked by unlit Y SPM buoys; boats may enter with caution, speed limit 5 knots.

LIGHTS AND MARKS Ore Stone (32m rk) is conspic off Hope's Nose, 2.3M E of hbr ent. Many conspic white bldgs, but none unique. No ldg marks/lts. Lts, as on chartlet, may be hard to see against town lts. IPTS sigs 2 & 4 control ent/exit at Old Hbr.

R/T Marina Ch **80** (H24), M. *Torquay Hbr* Ch **14** 16 (May-Sep 0800-1800LT; Oct-Apr 0900-1700, M-F). *Torquay Fuel* Ch M.

TELEPHONE (Dial code 01803) HM 292429/07774 432288; MRSC 882704; Police 08705 777444; Marinecall 09066 526242; Dr 212429; ⊞ 614567.

FACILITIES Marina (440 + 60 Ⓥ, £2.70) ☎ 200210, 📠 200225, ME, Gas, Gaz, ♿, ⊡, SM, Ⓔ, El, ⚒, CH, ACA, www.marinas.co.uk.

Old (inner) Hbr AB, FW; **S Pier** AB, FW, C (6 ton), P, D & LPG at fuel pontoon on S side: Torquay Fuel ☎ 294509 & VHF Ch M (Apr-Sept, 0830-1900 Mon-Sat, 1000-1900 Sun).

Haldon Pier AB, FW; **Royal Torbay YC** ☎ 292006, R, Bar.

Town 🛒, R, ⊡, Bar, ✉, Ⓑ, ⇌, ✈ (Exeter or Plymouth).

TORQUAY *continued*

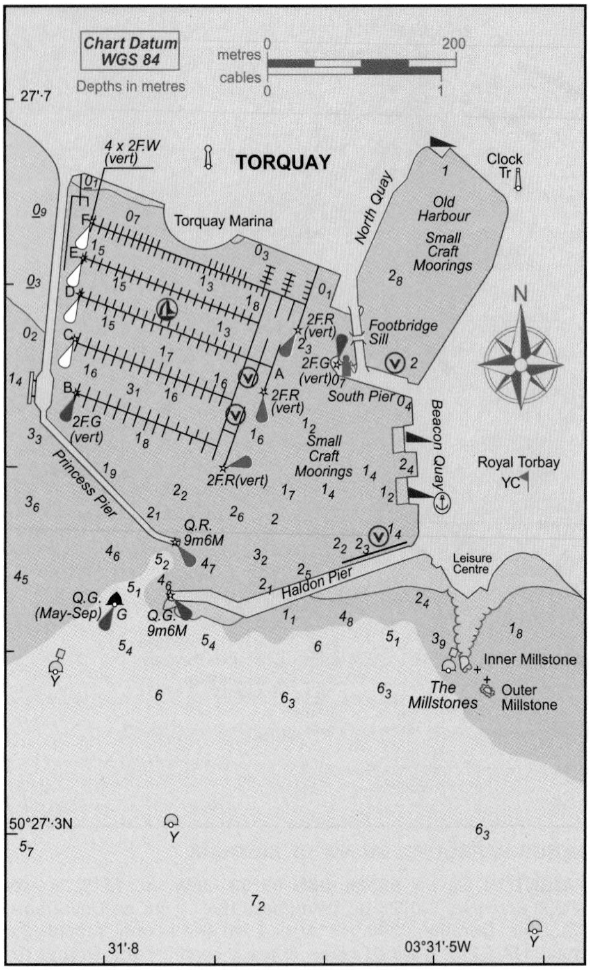
Chart Datum WGS 84
Depths in metres
metres
cables
TORQUAY
Torquay Marina
Old Harbour
Small Craft Moorings
North Quay
Clock Tr
Footbridge Sill
South Pier
Beacon Quay
Royal Torbay YC
Princess Pier
Haldon Pier
Leisure Centre
Inner Millstone
The Millstones
Outer Millstone
4 x 2F.W (vert)
2F.R (vert)
2F.G (vert)
2F.R(vert)
Q.R. 9m6M
Q.G. (May-Sep)
Q.G. 9m6M
27'·7
50°27'·3N
31'·8
03°31'·5W

9.1.22 TEIGNMOUTH

Devon **50°32'·39N 03°30'·07W** (Abeam The Point) ❁❁◊◊✿✿

CHARTS AC *3315, 5602, 26*; Imray C5, 2400.1 & .3; Stanfords 2, 12, 22; OS 192

TIDES –0450 Dover; ML 2·7; Duration 0625; Zone 0 (UTC)

Standard Port PLYMOUTH (⟵)

Times				Height (metres)			
High Water		Low Water		MHWS	MHWN	MLWN	MLWS
0100	0600	0100	0600	5·5	4·4	2·2	0·8
1300	1800	1300	1800				
Differences TEIGNMOUTH (Approaches)							
+0025	+0040	0000	0000	–0·7	–0·8	–0·3	–0·2
TEIGNMOUTH (New Quay)							
+0025	+0055	+0040	+0005	–0·8	–0·8	–0·2	+0·1

SHELTER Hbr completely sheltered, but entry difficult with strong winds from NE to S when surf forms on the bar. Access HW±3. 120m N of SHM lt buoy, Fl G 2s, is a 20m Ⓥ pontoon for 4 boats, plus rafting in suitable weather. Speed limit is 8kn.

NAVIGATION WPT 50°32'·35N 03°29'·14W, 270°/5ca to training wall lt. Bar shifts very frequently and is dredged with equal frequency along an E-W axis. The bar/channel as depicted on the chartlet is as shown on the latest edition of AC 26, but is not necessarily representative. Appr chan is not buoyed so contact HM for latest situation. Small nondescript buoys, laid by Pilots on the S edge of appr chan, cannot be relied upon. Beware rks off The Ness; and variable extent of The Salty flats.

Clearance under Shaldon bridge is 2·9m at MHWS and approx 6·7m at MLWS; near its N end there is a 9m wide drawbridge section. Avoid a Historic wreck site (50°32'·95N 03°29'·24W; just off chartlet), close inshore ENE of Ch twr (see 9.0.3h).

LIGHTS AND MARKS The Ness, a 50m high red sandstone headland, and church tower are both conspic from afar. Close NE of the latter, just off N edge of chartlet, Teign Corinthian YC bldg (cream colour) is also conspic. A Y can buoy, Fl Y 5s, at 50°31'·97N 03°27'·77W marks the seaward end of outfall, 103° The Ness 1·29M. The two FR (NNE of The Point) are not ldg lts and should be ignored. N of The Point, two F Bu lts on quay align 022°, but are not official ldg lts.

R/T VHF Ch 12 16 (Mon-Fri: 0800-1700; Sat 0900-1200 LT).

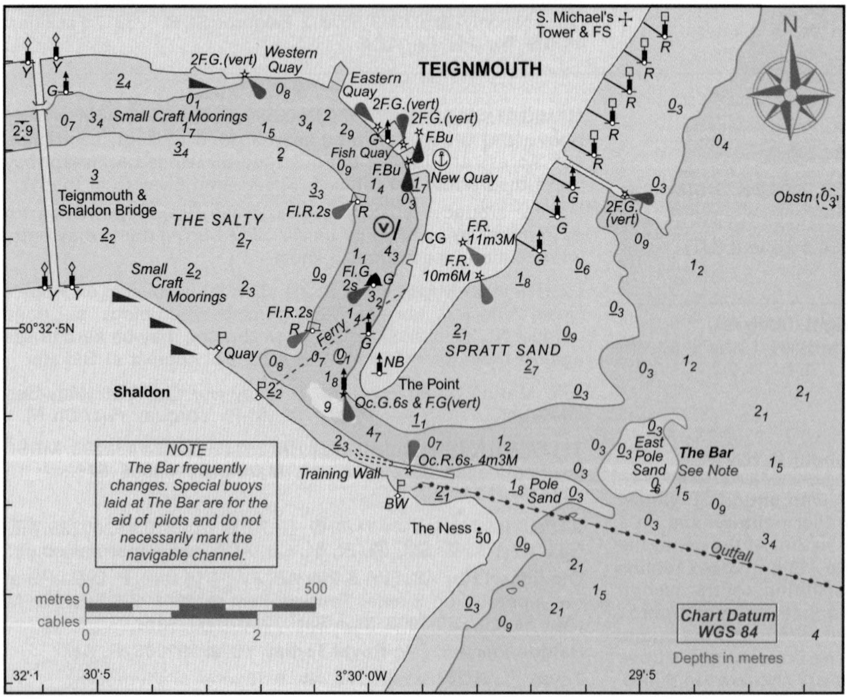
TEIGNMOUTH
S. Michael's Tower & FS
Western Quay
Eastern Quay
Small Craft Moorings
Fish Quay
New Quay
Teignmouth & Shaldon Bridge
THE SALTY
Small Craft Moorings
Shaldon
Quay
Ferry
The Point
SPRATT SAND
East Pole Sand
The Bar See Note
Pole Sand
Training Wall
The Ness
Outfall
Obstn
2F.G.(vert)
F.Bu
Fl.R.2s
Fl.G 2s
CG
F.R. 11m3M
F.R. 10m6M
Oc.G.6s & F.G(vert)
Oc.R.6s. 4m3M
NOTE
The Bar frequently changes. Special buoys laid at The Bar are for the aid of pilots and do not necessarily mark the navigable channel.
metres
cables
Chart Datum WGS 84
Depths in metres
50°32'·5N
32'·1
30'·5
3°30'·0W
29'·5

TELEPHONE (Dial code 01626) HM 773165, 📠 775162; MRSC (01803) 882704; Marinecall 09066 526242; Police 08705 777444; Dr 774355; Ⓗ 772161.

FACILITIES Ⓥ pontoon £1.00/m. **East Quay Polly Steps** Slip (up to 10m); **Teign Corinthian YC** ☎ 772734, Ⓥ £8.00, M, Bar;

Services: ME, CH, El, Slip, BY, ⚒, C (8 ton), Gas, Gaz, FW, CH, Ⓔ.

Town EC Thurs; P & D (cans, 1M), L, FW, 🛒, R, ⊡, Bar, ✉, Ⓑ, ⇌, ✈ (Exeter).

9.1.23 RIVER EXE

Devon **50°36'·94N 03°25'·40W** (Abeam Exmouth) ❁❁❁◊◊◊✿✿

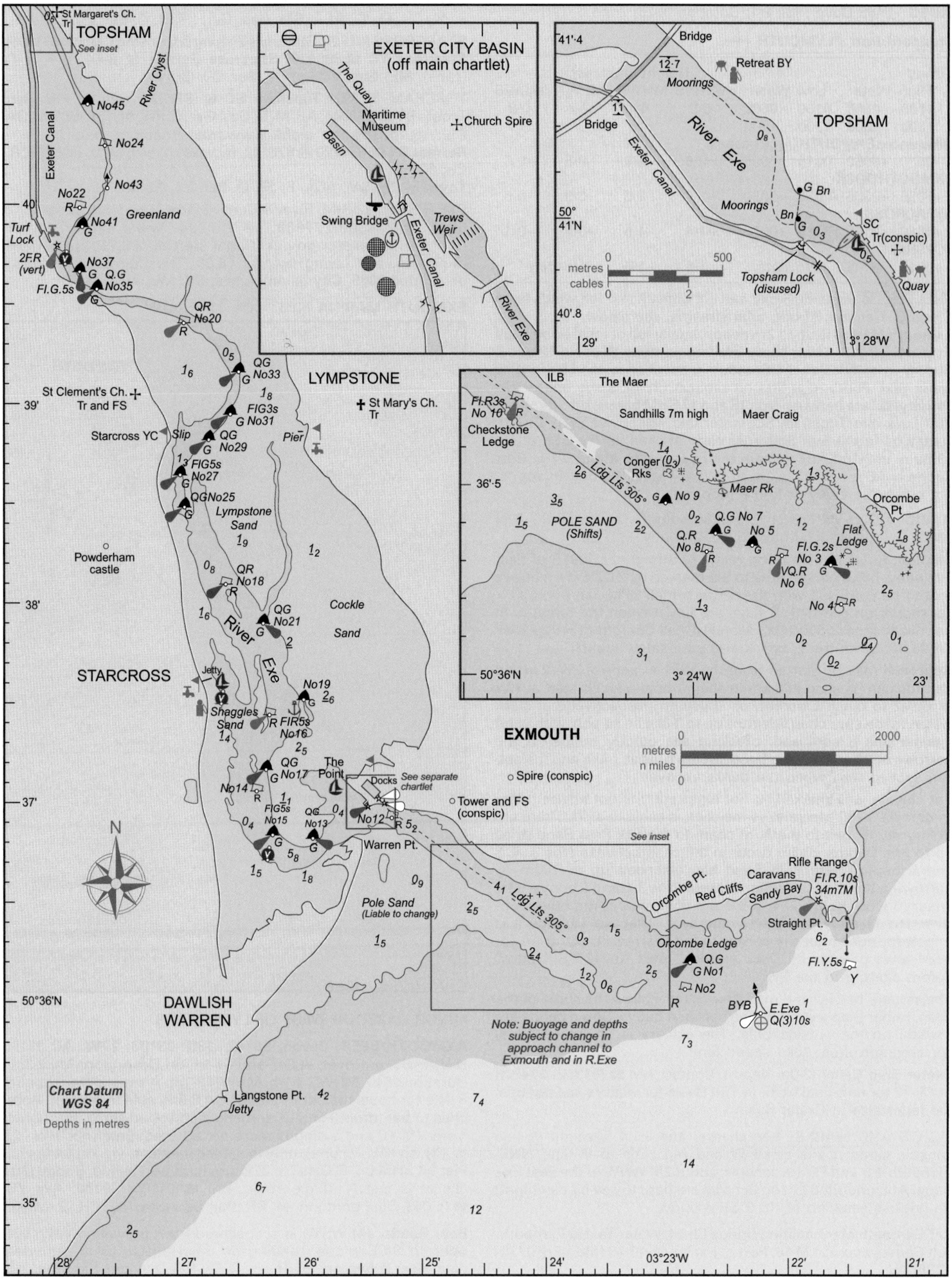
St Margaret's Ch. Tr
TOPSHAM
See inset
River Clyst
Exeter Canal
No45
No24
No43
No22
Greenland
Turf Lock
No41
2F.R (vert)
No37
Q.G
No35
Fl.G.5s
QR
No20
QG
No33
St Clement's Ch. Tr and FS
FlG3s
No31
Starcross YC
Slip
QG
No29
FlG5s
No27
QGNo25
Lympstone Sand
Powderham castle
QR
No18
River Exe
QG
No21
Cockle Sand
LYMPSTONE
St Mary's Ch. Tr
Pier
STARCROSS
Jetty
No19
Shaggles Sand
FlR5s
No16
QG
No17
No14
FlG5s
No15
QG
No13
No12
The Point
Docks
See separate chartlet
Warren Pt.
Pole Sand (Liable to change)
Ldg Lts 305°
EXMOUTH
Spire (conspic)
Tower and FS (conspic)
See inset
Orcombe Pt.
Red Cliffs
Caravans
Sandy Bay
Rifle Range
Fl.R.10s 34m7M
Straight Pt.
Orcombe Ledge
Q.G
No1
No2
BYB
E.Exe
Q(3)10s
Fl.Y.5s
Y
DAWLISH WARREN
Note: Buoyage and depths subject to change in approach channel to Exmouth and in R.Exe
Langstone Pt.
Jetty
Chart Datum WGS 84
Depths in metres
metres
n miles
EXETER CITY BASIN (off main chartlet)
The Quay
Maritime Museum
Church Spire
Basin
Swing Bridge
Exeter Canal
Trews Weir
River Exe
Bridge
Retreat BY
Moorings
TOPSHAM
River Exe
Exeter Canal
G Bn
Bn
SC
Tr(conspic)
Topsham Lock (disused)
Quay
metres
cables
ILB
The Maer
Fl.R3s No 10
Checkstone Ledge
Sandhills 7m high
Maer Craig
Conger Rks
Maer Rk
Ldg Lts 305°
No 9
Q.G No 7
No 5
POLE SAND (Shifts)
Q.R No 8
Fl.G.2s No 3
VQ.R No 6
No 4
Orcombe Pt
Flat Ledge
50°36'N
3° 24'W
50°36'N
03°23'W

RIVER EXE *continued*

CHARTS AC *3315, 5601,* 2290; Imray C5, 2400.1 &.2; Stanfords 2, 12, 22; OS 192

TIDES −0445 Dover; ML 2·1; Duration 0625; Zone 0 (UT)

Standard Port PLYMOUTH (⟵)

Times				Height (metres)			
High Water		Low Water		MHWS	MHWN	MLWN	MLWS
0100	0600	0100	0600	5·5	4·4	2·2	0·8
1300	1800	1300	1800				
Differences EXMOUTH (Approaches)							
+0030	+0050	+0015	+0005	−0·9	−1·0	−0·5	−0·3
EXMOUTH DOCK							
+0035	+0055	+0050	+0020	−1·5	−1·6	−0·9	−0·6
STARCROSS							
+0040	+0110	+0055	+0025	−1·4	−1·5	−0·8	−0·1
TOPSHAM							
+0045	+0105	No data		−1·5	−1·6	No data	

SHELTER Good inside R Exe, but ent difficult in fresh winds from E and S. Caution: strong tidal streams, see below.
Exmouth Marina is up to 2m deep, usually full of local boats. Call Exmouth HM Ch 14 for berth. Waiting pontoon W of No 12 buoy. Strong cross tides at ent. Pontoon in ent chan is used by ferries/water taxi. Footbridge lifts on request Ch 14; stays open HN.
Estuary. Ⓥs are between Nos 15 and 17 SHM buoys, off Starcross, Turf Lock and Topsham SC; water taxi will advise (VHF Ch M). ⚓ may be found E of Starcross clear of chan, ie 1ca SSE of No 19 buoy in 2·1m. At **Topsham** the river carries about 0·4m. Best option is AB (pontoon in 1m at LW) at Trouts BY; or ⚓ in appr's, dry out at the Quay or find a mooring.

NAVIGATION WPT East Exe ECM buoy Q (3)10s, 50°36'·00N 03°22'·37W, 294°/0·71M to No 3 SHM buoy, Fl G 2s.

Caution: Royal Marine firing range at Straight Pt, just E of East Exe buoy, has a danger area to SE, marked by 2 DZ SPM lt buoys (not to be confused with the sewer outfall SPM can buoy, Fl Y 5s, shown on chartlet). R flags are flown when the range is in use (likely times 0800-1600, Mon-Fri); call *Straight Pt Range* VHF Ch 08 16. From the E, check also with safety launch.

Approach may be started from the WPT at approx LW+2 when hazards can be seen and some shelter obtained. Or start at HW −1 or −2 to reach Exmouth or Topsham (respectively) at slack water. In the appr chan tide runs up to 3·3kn on sp ebb; with wind against tide a confused, breaking sea quickly builds. In the narrows off Warren Pt the flood stream runs at 3-4kn and the ebb can exceed 4½kn when the banks uncover.

Ent chan is well marked/lit, but night entry is not advised. Up-to-date AC 2290 essential as the chan is liable to shift. There are drying rky ledges to the N of chan; to the SW Pole Sand dries up to 3m. Depths <0·3m occur in the chan between Nos 3, 4, 5 and 6 buoys. Here Pole Sand has extended up to 100m N, narrowing the chan to <100m between Nos 3, 6 and 5 buoys; best water to stbd. Buoys 2, 4, 5 & 9 are unlit, plus some others up-river. No 11 buoy has been withdrawn. After No 10 buoy it is important not to cut the corner round Warren Pt; stand on for 0·5M toward Exmouth Dock and well past No 12 PHM buoy, before altering to the SW.

The estuary bed is sand/mud, free of rks. Follow the curve of the chan, rather than a straight line between buoys. Some bends are marked on the outside only. The estuary is an international conservation area. 10kn speed limit.

Exeter Ship Canal (3·0m depth). Contact HM ☎ (01392) 274306 or Ch 12 for non-tidal berth in Turf Basin for visitors and lay-ups; the latter also in Exeter Basin.

LIGHTS AND MARKS See chartlet and 9.1.4. Straight Pt has conspic caravan site close W and red cliffs to W and NNE. Exmouth ✠ tr and FS are conspic, about 2M WNW of the East Exe buoy. At Exmouth 305° ldg bcns/lts are hard to see by day/night; do not use seaward of No 9 SHM buoy.

R/T Exmouth Marina/lifting bridge Ch 14; Water Taxi at Exmouth, call *Conveyance* Ch M 16. Port of Exeter Ch 12 16 (Mon-Fri: 0730-1730LT).

TELEPHONE (Dial code 01395) MRSC (01803) 882704; Marinecall 09066 526242; Police 08705 777444; Dr 273001; Ⓗ 279684.

FACILITIES EXMOUTH (01395) **Marina,** ☎ 269314, £12.00 for Ⓥ; D, waiting pontoon. **Exe SC** ☎ 264607, M (check if vacant). **Town** P, ⚒, CH, El, Ⓔ, ACA, SM, Gas, Gaz, 🛒, R, 🗊, Bar, ✉, Ⓑ, ⇌.

STARCROSS (01626) **Starcross Fishing & Cruising Club** ☎ 891996; **Starcross YC** ☎ 890470; **Starcross Garage** ☎ 890225, P & D (cans), ME, Gas. **Village** 🛒, Bar, ✉, Ⓑ, ⇌.

TOPSHAM (01392) **Topsham SC** ☎ 877524, Slip, L, FW, Bar; **Trouts BY** ☎ 873044, AB, M, D, Gas, Gaz, C, FW, ⚒, CH. <9.1m LOA £12; >9.1m £14 per night. www.troutsboatyard.co.uk
Retreat BY ☎ 874720 📠 876182, (access HW±2), M, D, FW, ME, C, CH, ⚒.
Town P, CH, SM, ACA, R, 🛒, 🗊, Bar, ✉, Ⓑ, ⇌.

EXETER (01392) HM, River & Canal Office, Haven Rd, Exeter EX2 8DU, ☎ 274306/277888, 📠 250234. www.exeter.gov.uk river.canal@exeter.gov.uk Canal berths, £8.75 for 2 days minimum, and laying up. Ⓥs £6.00. The City Basin is being developed 2005. **City** all amenities; CH, ME, ACA, ⇌, ✈.

EXMOUTH MARINA 50°37'·00N 03°25'·37W

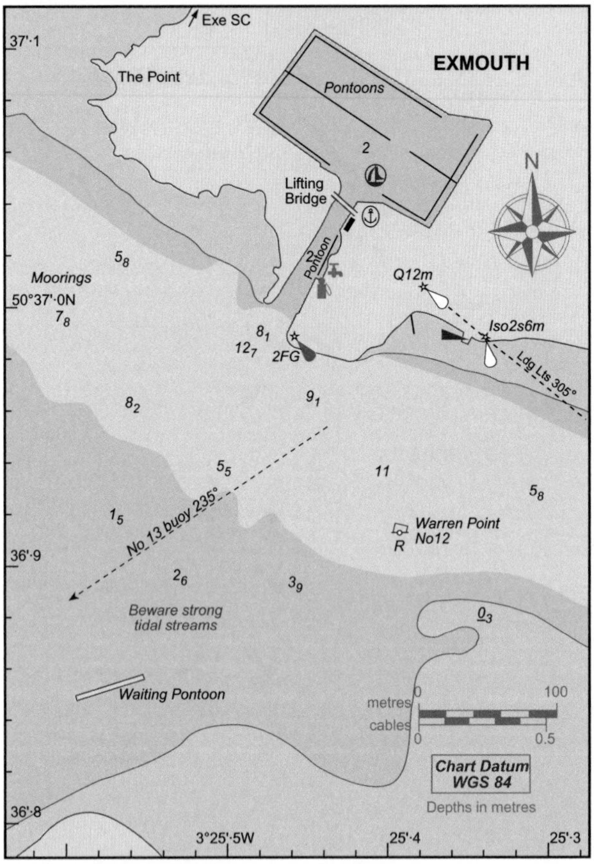
Exe SC
37'·1
The Point
EXMOUTH
Pontoons
Lifting Bridge
N
Moorings
50°37'·0N
Pontoon
Q12m
Iso2s6m
2FG
Ldg Lts 305°
No 13 buoy 235°
Warren Point No12
R
36'·9
Beware strong tidal streams
Waiting Pontoon
metres
cables
0
100
0.5
Chart Datum WGS 84
Depths in metres
36'·8
3°25'·5W
25'·4
25'·3

MINOR HARBOUR WEST OF LYME REGIS

AXMOUTH/BEER, Devon, **50°42'·13N 03°03'·27W**. AC 3315. HW −0455 on Dover, +0045 and −1·1m on Devonport; ML 2·3m; Duration 0640. MHWS 4·1m, MHWN 3·1m. A small drying hbr on R Axe for boats max draft 1·2m, LOA 8·5m, able to dry out. Appr chan to bar (dries 0·5m), is unmarked and often shifts. Prior brief from HM/YC and a dinghy recce are advised. Enter nps HW −2½ to +1½; sp HW −2½ or −½; only in settled weather, via 7m wide ent. Pier hd SHM bn, Fl G 4s 7m 2M; turn hard port inside. Bridge (2m cl'nce) is just N of moorings. HM ☎ (01297) 22180; **Axe YC** ☎ 20043, Slip, pontoon, M, BH, Bar; **Services:** ME, CH, D (cans).

Beer Roads, 1M WSW, is ⚓ sheltered from prevailing W'ly, but open to S/SE winds. Landing on open beach, as in centuries past. **Beer & Seaton:** EC Thurs; R, 🛒, P & D (cans), Bar, Gas, ✉.

9.1.24 LYME REGIS

Dorset **50°43'·20N 02°56'·19W**

CHARTS AC *3315, 5601*; Imray C5; Stanfords 2, 12, 22; OS 193

TIDES –0455 Dover; ML 2·4; Duration 0700; Zone 0 (UT)

Standard Port PLYMOUTH (⟵)

Times				**Height (metres)**			
High Water		Low Water		MHWS	MHWN	MLWN	MLWS
0100	0600	0100	0600	5·5	4·4	2·2	0·8
1300	1800	1300	1800				
Differences LYME REGIS							
+0040	+0100	+0005	–0005	–1·2	–1·3	–0·5	–0·2

NOTE: Rise is relatively fast for the 1st hour after LW, but slackens for the next 1½ hrs, after which the rapid rate is resumed. There is often a stand of about 1½ hours at HW.

SHELTER Good in the hbr (dries up to 2.1m), but in strong E/SE winds swell enters and it may be best to dry inside the North Wall. A stone pier, The Cobb, protects the W and S sides of the hbr; a rocky extension to E end of this pier covers at half tide and is marked by unlit PHM bcn. Access about HW±2½. Max LOA 9m in hbr. Dry out on clean, hard sand against Victoria Pier (0.3 – 1.3m) or in settled weather ⚓ as shown. 8 R cylindrical Ⓥs lie in 1·5-2m. Beware numerous fishing floats and moorings.

NAVIGATION WPT 50°43'·03N 02°55'·69W, 296°/0·35M to front ldg lt; best to be just inside W sector until hbr ent opens.

LIGHTS AND MARKS Ldg lts 296°, as chartlet; rear ldg lt hard to see against town lts. R flag on Victoria Pier = Gale warning in force.

R/T Call *Lyme Regis Hbr Radio* Ch 16; work Ch 14.

TELEPHONE (Dial code 01297) HM ☎/℻ 442137, Mobile 07870 240645; MRSC (01305) 760439; Marinecall 09066 526241; Police (01305) 768970; Dr 445777.

FACILITIES Harbour (The Cobb) AB £8.00 (4.0-6.9m), £12.00 (>7m), Ⓥs £5, Slip, M, FW, P & D (cans), (mobile); **Lyme Regis SC** ☎ 442800, FW, ♿, R, Bar; **Lyme Regis Power Boat Club** ☎ 443788, R, Bar; **Services:** ME, ✕, El, Ⓔ, CH, ACA (Axminster, 5M). **Town** EC Thurs; 🛒, R, Bar, Gas, Gaz, ✉, Ⓑ, ⓓ, bus to Axminster ⇌, ✈ (Exeter).

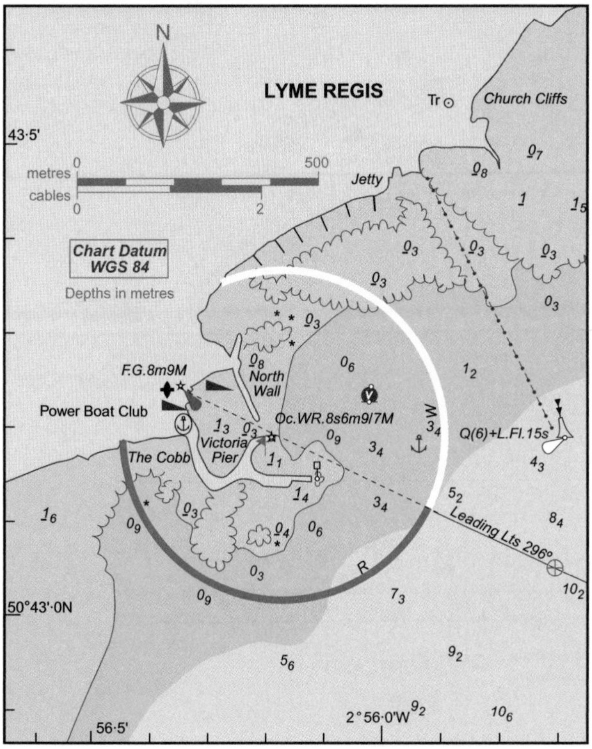
LYME REGIS
N
Church Cliffs
Tr
Jetty
Chart Datum WGS 84
Depths in metres
metres
cables
500
F.G.8m9M
Power Boat Club
North Wall
Victoria Pier
The Cobb
Oc.WR.8s6m9/7M
Q(6)+L.Fl.15s
Leading Lts 296°
43·5'
50°43'·0N
56·5'
2°56'·0W

9.1.25 WEST BAY (BRIDPORT)

Dorset **50°42'·55N 02°45'·86W**

CHARTS AC *3315, 5601*; Imray C5; Stanfords 2, 12, 22; OS 193

TIDES –0500 Dover; ML 2·3; Duration 0650; Zone 0 (UT)

Standard Port PLYMOUTH (⟵)

Times				**Height (metres)**			
High Water		Low Water		MHWS	MHWN	MLWN	MLWS
0100	0600	0100	0600	5·5	4·4	2·2	0·8
1300	1800	1300	1800				
Differences BRIDPORT (West Bay)							
+0025	+0040	0000	0000	–1·4	–1·4	–0·6	–0·2
CHESIL BEACH							
+0040	+0055	–0005	+0010	–1·6	–1·5	–0·5	0·0
CHESIL COVE							
+0035	+0050	–0010	+0005	–1·5	–1·6	–0·5	–0·2

NOTE: Rise is relatively fast for first hr after LW; it then slackens for the next 1½ hrs, after which the rapid rise is resumed. There is often a stand of about 1½ hrs at HW.

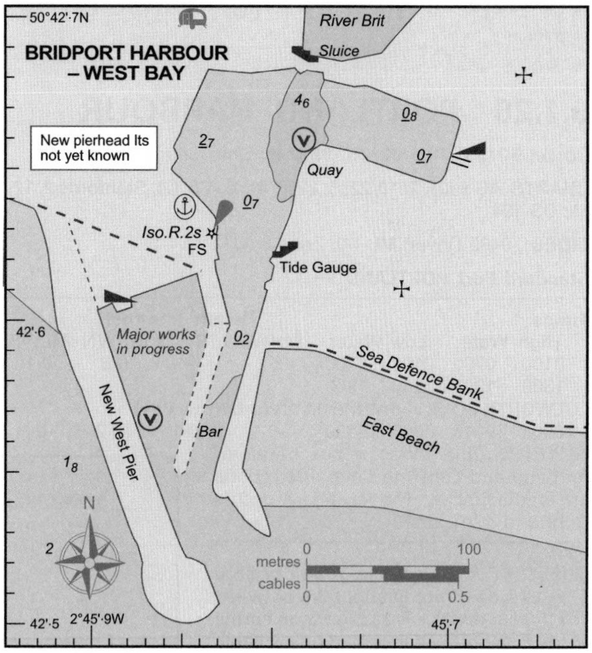
BRIDPORT HARBOUR – WEST BAY
50°42'·7N
River Brit
Sluice
New pierhead lts not yet known
Quay
Iso.R.2s
FS
Tide Gauge
Major works in progress
New West Pier
Bar
Sea Defence Bank
East Beach
N
metres
cables
100
0.5
42'·6
42'·5
2°45'·9W
45'·7

SHELTER Access and shelter should be much improved in on-shore winds. By Nov 2004 (at the earliest) a new 230m long W pier is due to be completed with a Ⓥ pontoon alongside. Most (pecked outline) of the old W pier will have been demolished and the E pier slightly lengthened; access may be temporarily restricted. Call HM Ch 11 for an update and a berth. The inner hbr dries apart from a pool and former coaster berth scoured 2·1m by sluice water, but it is very crowded with FVs and local boats.

NAVIGATION WPT 50°41'·58N 02°46'·09W, 011°/0·75M to ent. No offshore dangers. SPM buoy, Fl Y 5s, marks sewer outfall 5ca SSW of ent.

LIGHTS AND MARKS ☆ 2 F Y 8m 5M, approx 50°42'·50N 02°45'·90W marks WIP (temp'y Dec 2003). Entry sig: B ● = hbr closed.

R/T Call: *Bridport Radio* VHF Ch 11 16.

TELEPHONE (Dial code 01308) HM ☎ ℻ 423222, Mobile 07870 240644; MRSC (01305) 760439; Marinecall 09066 526241; Police (01305) 768970; Dr 421109.

FACILITIES Hbr AB £8.00 (<7m LOA), £12.00 (>7m), M, FW, Slip, P & D (cans), ⓓ, ✕, ME, 🛒, R. **Town** CH, 🛒, R, Bar, ✉, Ⓑ, ⇌ (bus to Axminster), ✈ (Exeter). Bridport town is 1½M N of the hbr.

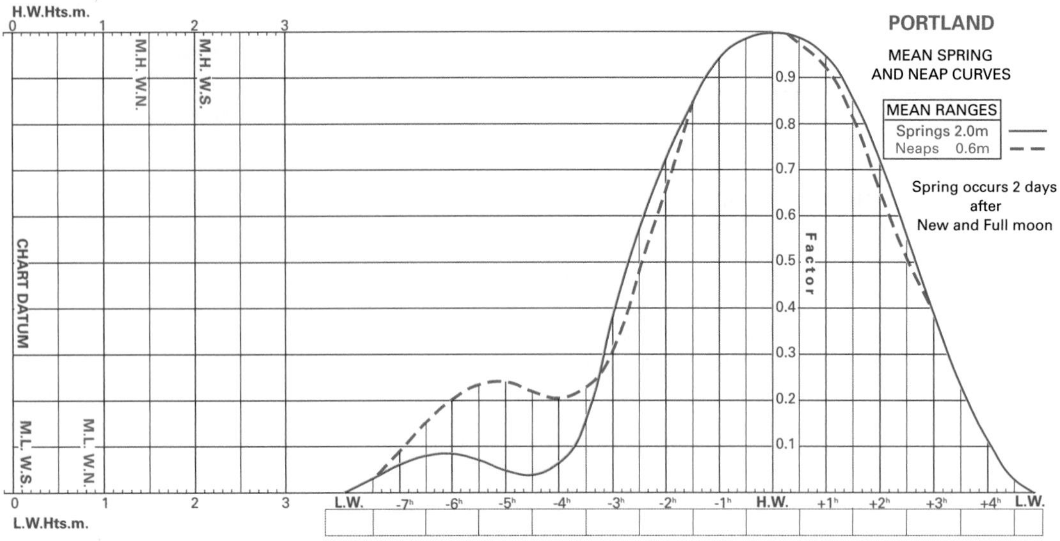
H.W.Hts.m.
PORTLAND
MEAN SPRING AND NEAP CURVES
MEAN RANGES
Springs 2.0m
Neaps 0.6m
Spring occurs 2 days after New and Full moon
M.H.W.N.
M.H.W.S.
CHART DATUM
M.L.W.S.
M.L.W.N.
Factor
L.W.Hts.m.
L.W.
H.W.

9.1.26 PORTLAND HARBOUR

Dorset **50°35'·78N 02°25'·95W** (N Ship Chan) ❀❀❀◊◊✿

CHARTS AC *5601, 2610,* 2255, 2268; Imray C5, C4; Stanfords 2, 12, 15; OS 194

TIDES –0430 Dover; ML 1·0; Zone 0 (UT)

Standard Port PORTLAND (⟶)

Times				**Height (metres)**			
High Water		Low Water		MHWS	MHWN	MLWN	MLWS
0100	0700	0100	0700	2·1	1·4	0·8	0·1
1300	1900	1300	1900				
LULWORTH COVE and MUPE BAY (Worbarrow Bay)							
+0005	+0015	–0005	0000	+0·1	+0·1	+0·2	+0·1

NOTE: Double LWs occur between Portland and Lulworth Cove. Predictions are for the first LW. The second LW occurs from 3 to 4 hrs later.

SHELTER Poor, due to lack of wind breaks. ⚓ on W side of hbr in about 3m between ☆ Fl (4) 10s and ☆ L Fl 10s. Pontoon berths at the Sailing Academy may be available for 1 or 2 night stays. Further E a marina is planned. East Fleet is only suitable for small, unmasted craft.

NAVIGATION WPT 50°35'·97N 02°25'·24W, 240°/0·5M to N Ship Chan, (preferred for yachts). E Ship Chan is for commercial vessels. The S Chan is permanently closed. Speed limit 6kn in the depicted areas and within 150m of any bkwtr or hbr premises. Vessels <10m may exceed 12kn in the undepicted areas. Beware: rky reef extending 1ca NE of Castle Cove SC; shoals E of Small Mouth; and fast ferry cats ex-Weymouth. Portland Race is very dangerous (see 9.1.5 and 9.1.27 for timing and tidal chartlets); avoid the Shambles.

LIGHTS & MARKS A Hd lt ho is conspic. 4 noise range buoys Fl.Y are 7ca SE of D Head; 3 degaussing buoys (1 lit) are 400m SE of Weymouth S Pier hd. Portland Bill lt ho Fl (4) 20s; W twr, R band. See 9.1.4 for varying number of flashes in different arcs. FR lt, same tr, shows over the Shambles. Other lights as chartlet.

R/T *Portland Hbr Radio* Ch 14, 20, 28, 71, **74**. Monitor Ch 74 for commercial movements. Clearance for yachts to enter/exit hbr is not required; yachts should use the N Ship Channel.

TELEPHONE (Dial code 01305) Port Control 824044, Fax 824055; ⓗ 824055; MRSC 760439; Marinecall 09066 526241; Police 768970; Dr (GP) 820422; ⓗ (Emergency) 820341.

FACILITIES Portland Port www.portland-port.co.uk. Hbr dues apply to yachts: £3.60 daily for 6 – 9.15m LOA, but are not often collected for visitors. **Castle Cove SC** ☎ 783708, M, L, FW; **Services:** Slip, M, L, FW, ME, ⚒, C, CH, El (mobile workshop). **Weymouth & Portland Sailing Academy** (hosts National/ International racing) ☎ 860101, Fax 820099; www.wpsa.org.uk **Town** ✉, Ⓑ, Bar, R, ⇌ (bus to Weymouth), ✈ (Bournemouth).

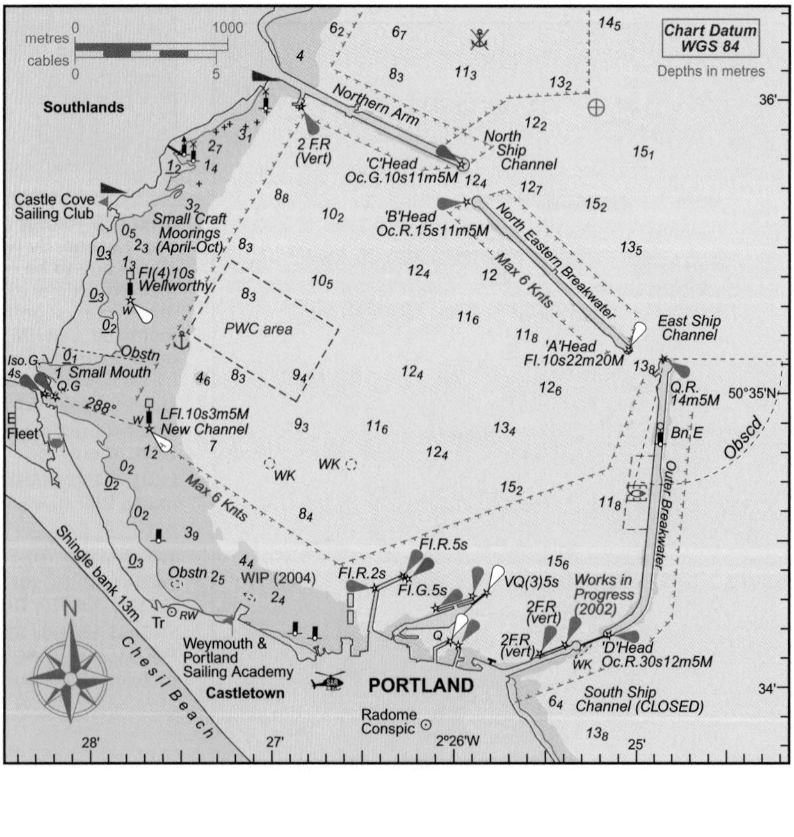
Chart Datum WGS 84
Depths in metres
metres
cables
Southlands
Castle Cove Sailing Club
Small Craft Moorings (April-Oct)
Fl(4)10s Wellworthy
PWC area
Obstn
1 Small Mouth
Iso.G. 4s
Q.G
288°
LFl.10s3m5M New Channel
Fleet
Max 6 Knts
Shingle bank 13m
Chesil Beach
Northern Arm
2 F.R (Vert)
'C'Head Oc.G.10s11m5M
North Ship Channel
'B'Head Oc.R.15s11m5M
North Eastern Breakwater
Max 6 Knts
'A'Head Fl.10s22m20M
East Ship Channel
Q.R. 14m5M
Bn E
Obscd
Outer Breakwater
Fl.R.5s
Fl.R.2s
Fl.G.5s
VQ(3)5s
Works in Progress (2002)
2F.R (vert)
'D'Head Oc.R.30s12m5M
WIP (2004)
Obstn
Weymouth & Portland Sailing Academy
Castletown
PORTLAND
Radome Conspic
South Ship Channel (CLOSED)
50°35'N
36'
34'
28'
27'
2°26'W
25'

TIME ZONE (UT)
For Summer Time add ONE hour in **non-shaded areas**

ENGLAND – PORTLAND

LAT 50°34′N LONG 2°26′W

TIMES AND HEIGHTS OF HIGH AND LOW WATERS

SPRING & NEAP TIDES
Dates in red are SPRINGS
Dates in blue are NEAPS

YEAR **2005**

JANUARY

Date	Day	Time	m	Time	m	Time	m	Time	m
1	SA	0222	0.5	0925	1.7	1447	0.5	2156	1.5
2	SU	0253	0.6	0957	1.6	1523	0.5	2233	1.4
3	M	0331	0.6	1037	1.6	1610	0.5	◑ 2322	1.4
4	TU	0425	0.7	1129	1.5	1714	0.6		
5	W	0029	1.4	0540	0.7	1240	1.5	1828	0.6
6	TH	0153	1.4	0703	0.7	1406	1.5	1941	0.5
7	F	0314	1.6	0818	0.7	1530	1.6	2049	0.5
8	SA	0421	1.7	0926	0.6	1642	1.7	2152	0.4
9	SU	0520	1.9	1027	0.5	1747	1.8	2249	0.3
10	M	0616	2.1	1122	0.3	1846	1.9	● 2343	0.3
11	TU	0709	2.2	1214	0.2	1940	2.0		
12	W	0032	0.2	0758	2.3	1304	0.2	2029	2.1
13	TH	0119	0.2	0845	2.3	1351	0.2	2114	2.0
14	F	0204	0.2	0929	2.2	1436	0.2	2156	1.9
15	SA	0246	0.3	1009	2.1	1521	0.3	2234	1.8
16	SU	0328	0.4	1047	1.9	1606	0.4	2311	1.6
17	M	0411	0.5	1124	1.7	1654	0.5	◐ 2350	1.5
18	TU	0459	0.7	1204	1.5	1746	0.6		
19	W	0038	1.4	0600	0.8	1255	1.4	1846	0.7
20	TH	0143	1.4	0716	0.8	1405	1.3	1952	0.7
21	F	0304	1.4	0839	0.8	1530	1.3	2057	0.7
22	SA	0409	1.5	0944	0.7	1636	1.4	2152	0.6
23	SU	0501	1.7	1033	0.6	1729	1.5	2241	0.5
24	M	0547	1.8	1116	0.5	1818	1.6	2325	0.4
25	TU	0630	1.9	1157	0.4	1902	1.7	○	
26	W	0006	0.4	0710	2.0	1236	0.3	1942	1.8
27	TH	0045	0.3	0749	2.0	1311	0.3	2019	1.8
28	F	0120	0.3	0824	2.0	1342	0.2	2051	1.8
29	SA	0150	0.3	0856	1.9	1408	0.2	2120	1.7
30	SU	0217	0.3	0924	1.8	1434	0.3	2145	1.6
31	M	0243	0.3	0951	1.7	1503	0.3	2211	1.5

FEBRUARY

Date	Day	Time	m	Time	m	Time	m	Time	m
1	TU	0313	0.4	1020	1.6	1538	0.3	2244	1.5
2	W	0350	0.5	1057	1.5	1624	0.4	◑ 2331	1.4
3	TH	0444	0.6	1150	1.4	1730	0.5		
4	F	0040	1.4	0606	0.7	1309	1.4	1859	0.6
5	SA	0219	1.4	0751	0.7	1455	1.4	2033	0.6
6	SU	0355	1.6	0923	0.6	1633	1.5	2149	0.5
7	M	0508	1.8	1029	0.4	1746	1.7	2248	0.3
8	TU	0609	2.0	1122	0.3	1845	1.9	● 2339	0.2
9	W	0703	2.2	1210	0.1	1935	2.1		
10	TH	0025	0.1	0750	2.4	1255	0.0	2019	2.1
11	F	0108	0.0	0833	2.4	1337	-0.1	2058	2.1
12	SA	0148	0.0	0911	2.3	1417	0.0	2133	2.0
13	SU	0225	0.1	0945	2.1	1454	0.1	2203	1.9
14	M	0300	0.2	1015	1.9	1530	0.2	2230	1.7
15	TU	0333	0.4	1042	1.7	1604	0.4	2257	1.5
16	W	0406	0.5	1111	1.5	1638	0.6	◐ 2331	1.4
17	TH	0447	0.7	1150	1.3	1724	0.7		
18	F	0021	1.3	0610	0.8	1252	1.2	1852	0.8
19	SA	0140	1.3	0817	0.8	1440	1.2	2028	0.8
20	SU	0329	1.4	0936	0.7	1624	1.3	2134	0.7
21	M	0439	1.6	1020	0.6	1721	1.4	2223	0.5
22	TU	0531	1.7	1059	0.4	1809	1.6	2306	0.4
23	W	0617	1.9	1137	0.3	1852	1.8	2347	0.3
24	TH	0659	2.0	1214	0.2	1931	1.9	○	
25	F	0025	0.2	0737	2.1	1249	0.1	2006	1.9
26	SA	0100	0.1	0812	2.1	1319	0.1	2037	1.9
27	SU	0131	0.1	0843	2.0	1348	0.1	2104	1.8
28	M	0159	0.1	0910	1.9	1415	0.1	2126	1.8

MARCH

Date	Day	Time	m	Time	m	Time	m	Time	m
1	TU	0225	0.2	0935	1.8	1442	0.2	2149	1.7
2	W	0252	0.2	1002	1.6	1511	0.3	2218	1.6
3	TH	0324	0.4	1035	1.5	1549	0.4	◑ 2257	1.5
4	F	0410	0.5	1124	1.4	1647	0.6		
5	SA	0001	1.4	0537	0.7	1245	1.3	1842	0.7
6	SU	0145	1.4	0756	0.7	1450	1.3	2035	0.7
7	M	0342	1.5	0928	0.6	1637	1.5	2147	0.5
8	TU	0500	1.8	1025	0.3	1742	1.8	2240	0.3
9	W	0558	2.1	1112	0.1	1833	2.0	2326	0.1
10	TH	0648	2.3	1155	0.0	1918	2.1	●	
11	F	0008	0.0	0731	2.4	1236	-0.1	1958	2.2
12	SA	0048	-0.1	0811	2.4	1315	-0.2	2033	2.2
13	SU	0125	-0.1	0846	2.3	1351	-0.1	2104	2.1
14	M	0200	0.0	0916	2.1	1424	0.0	2130	1.9
15	TU	0231	0.1	0941	1.9	1453	0.2	2151	1.7
16	W	0259	0.3	1004	1.6	1517	0.4	2213	1.6
17	TH	0324	0.5	1029	1.4	1532	0.5	◐ 2240	1.4
18	F	0350	0.6	1102	1.2	1553	0.7	2321	1.3
19	SA	0445	0.8	1204	1.1	1651	0.8		
20	SU	0038	1.3	0757	0.8	1408	1.1	1957	0.8
21	M	0235	1.3	0916	0.7	1614	1.3	2108	0.7
22	TU	0409	1.5	0955	0.5	1703	1.5	2156	0.5
23	W	0503	1.7	1031	0.4	1746	1.7	2239	0.4
24	TH	0550	1.9	1107	0.2	1827	1.8	2319	0.2
25	F	0634	2.0	1143	0.1	1905	1.9	○ 2356	0.1
26	SA	0713	2.1	1217	0.0	1941	2.0		
27	SU	0031	0.0	0749	2.1	1250	0.0	2012	2.0
28	M	0104	0.0	0821	2.1	1321	0.0	2040	2.0
29	TU	0135	0.1	0850	2.0	1351	0.1	2104	1.9
30	W	0204	0.1	0916	1.8	1421	0.2	2129	1.8
31	TH	0234	0.2	0946	1.7	1452	0.3	2159	1.6

APRIL

Date	Day	Time	m	Time	m	Time	m	Time	m
1	F	0311	0.4	1024	1.5	1531	0.5	2241	1.5
2	SA	0404	0.6	1119	1.4	1640	0.7	◑ 2349	1.4
3	SU	0552	0.7	1250	1.3	1849	0.8		
4	M	0141	1.4	0802	0.7	1503	1.4	2029	0.7
5	TU	0330	1.6	0916	0.5	1625	1.6	2132	0.5
6	W	0439	1.8	1007	0.3	1721	1.8	2221	0.3
7	TH	0534	2.0	1050	0.1	1809	2.0	2304	0.2
8	F	0623	2.2	1131	0.0	1851	2.1	● 2345	0.1
9	SA	0706	2.3	1210	-0.1	1930	2.2		
10	SU	0023	0.0	0744	2.3	1248	-0.1	2004	2.2
11	M	0100	0.0	0818	2.2	1322	0.0	2033	2.1
12	TU	0133	0.1	0846	2.0	1353	0.1	2056	1.9
13	W	0204	0.2	0909	1.8	1420	0.3	2116	1.8
14	TH	0231	0.3	0932	1.6	1438	0.4	2136	1.6
15	F	0254	0.5	0957	1.4	1451	0.6	2159	1.5
16	SA	0321	0.6	1029	1.2	1515	0.7	◐ 2233	1.4
17	SU	0414	0.8	1134	1.1	1609	0.9	2345	1.3
18	M	0705	0.8	1334	1.1	1916	0.9		
19	TU	0138	1.3	0828	0.7	1534	1.3	2031	0.8
20	W	0316	1.5	0914	0.5	1624	1.5	2121	0.6
21	TH	0419	1.6	0952	0.4	1708	1.7	2204	0.4
22	F	0511	1.8	1029	0.2	1750	1.8	2244	0.3
23	SA	0557	2.0	1105	0.1	1830	2.0	2322	0.2
24	SU	0641	2.0	1141	0.0	1908	2.1	○ 2358	0.1
25	M	0721	2.1	1217	0.0	1943	2.1		
26	TU	0034	0.1	0756	2.1	1253	0.1	2015	2.1
27	W	0110	0.1	0830	2.0	1329	0.1	2045	2.0
28	TH	0146	0.2	0903	1.8	1406	0.3	2117	1.9
29	F	0226	0.3	0940	1.7	1447	0.4	2154	1.7
30	SA	0314	0.4	1026	1.5	1539	0.6	2244	1.6

Chart Datum: 0·93 metres below Ordnance Datum (Newlyn)

TIME ZONE (UT)
For Summer Time add ONE hour in **non-shaded areas**

ENGLAND – PORTLAND

LAT 50°34′N LONG 2°26′W

TIMES AND HEIGHTS OF HIGH AND LOW WATERS

SPRING & NEAP TIDES
Dates in red are SPRINGS
Dates in blue are NEAPS

YEAR **2005**

MAY

Date	Day	Time	m	Time	m	Time	m	Time	m
1	SU	0421	0.6	1131	1.4	1657	0.7	◑ 2358	1.5
2	M	0559	0.7	1310	1.4	1839	0.8		
3	TU	0140	1.5	0740	0.6	1446	1.5	2005	0.7
4	W	0304	1.7	0847	0.4	1554	1.7	2105	0.6
5	TH	0408	1.8	0937	0.3	1648	1.8	2154	0.4
6	F	0502	1.9	1021	0.2	1735	2.0	2237	0.3
7	SA	0552	2.0	1102	0.1	1819	2.1	2318	0.2
8	SU	0636	2.1	1142	0.1	1858	2.1	● 2357	0.2
9	M	0716	2.1	1219	0.1	1933	2.1		
10	TU	0034	0.2	0749	2.0	1255	0.2	2002	2.0
11	W	0111	0.2	0818	1.8	1328	0.3	2026	1.9
12	TH	0144	0.3	0844	1.7	1356	0.4	2048	1.8
13	F	0214	0.4	0910	1.5	1417	0.5	2112	1.7
14	SA	0240	0.5	0939	1.4	1436	0.6	2136	1.6
15	SU	0310	0.6	1016	1.3	1505	0.7	2210	1.5
16	M	0358	0.7	1115	1.2	1602	0.8	◐ 2307	1.4
17	TU	0535	0.7	1248	1.2	1805	0.9		
18	W	0040	1.4	0718	0.7	1422	1.3	1938	0.8
19	TH	0215	1.4	0816	0.6	1528	1.5	2035	0.7
20	F	0326	1.6	0901	0.4	1620	1.6	2121	0.5
21	SA	0425	1.7	0943	0.3	1707	1.8	2204	0.4
22	SU	0518	1.8	1024	0.2	1753	2.0	2246	0.3
23	M	0607	1.9	1106	0.2	1836	2.1	○ 2328	0.2
24	TU	0653	2.0	1148	0.1	1917	2.1		
25	W	0010	0.2	0736	2.0	1232	0.2	1957	2.1
26	TH	0053	0.2	0819	2.0	1316	0.2	2037	2.1
27	F	0138	0.2	0901	1.9	1401	0.3	2118	2.0
28	SA	0227	0.3	0947	1.8	1450	0.5	2204	1.9
29	SU	0321	0.4	1040	1.7	1546	0.6	2258	1.7
30	M	0424	0.5	1143	1.6	1651	0.7	◑	
31	TU	0003	1.7	0538	0.5	1257	1.5	1806	0.7

JUNE

Date	Day	Time	m	Time	m	Time	m	Time	m
1	W	0117	1.6	0657	0.5	1409	1.6	1922	0.7
2	TH	0227	1.7	0804	0.5	1513	1.6	2027	0.6
3	F	0330	1.7	0859	0.4	1609	1.7	2121	0.6
4	SA	0427	1.7	0948	0.4	1700	1.8	2208	0.5
5	SU	0519	1.8	1032	0.3	1746	1.9	2252	0.4
6	M	0607	1.8	1114	0.3	1828	2.0	● 2335	0.4
7	TU	0649	1.8	1155	0.3	1905	2.0		
8	W	0015	0.4	0726	1.8	1234	0.3	1937	2.0
9	TH	0055	0.4	0759	1.7	1311	0.4	2006	1.9
10	F	0132	0.4	0829	1.7	1344	0.5	2034	1.8
11	SA	0206	0.4	0900	1.6	1413	0.5	2102	1.7
12	SU	0235	0.5	0933	1.5	1438	0.6	2131	1.6
13	M	0303	0.5	1010	1.4	1507	0.7	2203	1.5
14	TU	0338	0.6	1054	1.3	1549	0.7	2245	1.5
15	W	0428	0.6	1154	1.3	1651	0.8	◐ 2344	1.4
16	TH	0536	0.6	1309	1.3	1812	0.8		
17	F	0103	1.4	0650	0.6	1424	1.4	1927	0.7
18	SA	0225	1.5	0755	0.5	1529	1.5	2029	0.6
19	SU	0337	1.6	0853	0.4	1626	1.7	2124	0.5
20	M	0440	1.7	0947	0.3	1719	1.9	2216	0.4
21	TU	0538	1.8	1040	0.3	1810	2.0	2307	0.3
22	W	0634	1.9	1131	0.2	1900	2.1	○ 2358	0.3
23	TH	0727	2.0	1222	0.2	1949	2.2		
24	F	0047	0.2	0817	2.0	1311	0.2	2036	2.2
25	SA	0137	0.2	0905	2.0	1400	0.3	2123	2.1
26	SU	0227	0.2	0953	1.9	1448	0.3	2209	2.0
27	M	0317	0.3	1039	1.8	1536	0.4	2255	1.9
28	TU	0410	0.3	1128	1.7	1628	0.5	◑ 2344	1.8
29	W	0506	0.4	1220	1.6	1724	0.6		
30	TH	0036	1.7	0606	0.5	1318	1.5	1827	0.7

JULY

Date	Day	Time	m	Time	m	Time	m	Time	m
1	F	0137	1.6	0711	0.5	1423	1.5	1937	0.7
2	SA	0244	1.5	0816	0.6	1528	1.6	2045	0.7
3	SU	0350	1.5	0915	0.6	1627	1.6	2144	0.7
4	M	0450	1.5	1007	0.5	1718	1.7	2235	0.6
5	TU	0543	1.6	1054	0.5	1804	1.8	2320	0.5
6	W	0630	1.7	1137	0.4	1845	1.9	●	
7	TH	0002	0.4	0712	1.7	1219	0.4	1922	1.9
8	F	0043	0.4	0750	1.7	1258	0.4	1956	1.9
9	SA	0121	0.4	0824	1.7	1335	0.4	2028	1.9
10	SU	0156	0.3	0856	1.7	1407	0.4	2059	1.8
11	M	0224	0.4	0927	1.6	1433	0.4	2128	1.7
12	TU	0248	0.4	0957	1.5	1457	0.5	2156	1.6
13	W	0315	0.4	1028	1.5	1526	0.5	2226	1.5
14	TH	0349	0.4	1104	1.4	1606	0.6	◐ 2304	1.5
15	F	0436	0.5	1154	1.4	1702	0.6	2356	1.4
16	SA	0539	0.5	1304	1.4	1817	0.7		
17	SU	0109	1.4	0654	0.6	1431	1.4	1938	0.7
18	M	0244	1.4	0813	0.5	1549	1.6	2056	0.6
19	TU	0410	1.6	0927	0.5	1655	1.8	2203	0.5
20	W	0522	1.7	1030	0.4	1755	2.0	2302	0.4
21	TH	0626	1.9	1126	0.3	1851	2.1	○ 2355	0.2
22	F	0723	2.0	1217	0.2	1943	2.3		
23	SA	0044	0.1	0813	2.1	1305	0.1	2031	2.3
24	SU	0131	0.1	0859	2.1	1350	0.1	2114	2.3
25	M	0217	0.1	0940	2.1	1433	0.2	2155	2.2
26	TU	0301	0.1	1019	1.9	1515	0.3	2233	2.0
27	W	0344	0.2	1056	1.8	1557	0.4	2310	1.8
28	TH	0429	0.4	1134	1.6	1642	0.5	◑ 2348	1.6
29	F	0518	0.5	1217	1.5	1735	0.7		
30	SA	0032	1.4	0615	0.6	1316	1.4	1845	0.8
31	SU	0138	1.3	0728	0.7	1443	1.4	2018	0.8

AUGUST

Date	Day	Time	m	Time	m	Time	m	Time	m
1	M	0317	1.3	0850	0.7	1600	1.5	2136	0.8
2	TU	0433	1.4	0950	0.7	1658	1.6	2225	0.7
3	W	0530	1.5	1037	0.6	1747	1.8	2306	0.6
4	TH	0619	1.6	1119	0.5	1830	1.9	2346	0.4
5	F	0701	1.7	1200	0.4	1909	2.0	●	
6	SA	0024	0.3	0739	1.8	1239	0.3	1945	2.0
7	SU	0102	0.3	0812	1.8	1316	0.3	2018	2.0
8	M	0135	0.2	0843	1.8	1348	0.2	2048	2.0
9	TU	0203	0.2	0911	1.8	1414	0.3	2116	1.9
10	W	0226	0.2	0936	1.7	1437	0.3	2140	1.7
11	TH	0249	0.3	0959	1.6	1500	0.4	2204	1.6
12	F	0316	0.3	1026	1.5	1529	0.5	2233	1.5
13	SA	0352	0.4	1104	1.4	1612	0.6	◐ 2314	1.4
14	SU	0445	0.5	1202	1.4	1724	0.7		
15	M	0020	1.3	0610	0.7	1332	1.4	1911	0.8
16	TU	0204	1.3	0759	0.7	1522	1.5	2054	0.7
17	W	0400	1.5	0926	0.6	1642	1.8	2204	0.5
18	TH	0519	1.7	1027	0.4	1746	2.0	2258	0.3
19	F	0620	1.9	1119	0.2	1841	2.2	○ 2346	0.1
20	SA	0712	2.1	1205	0.1	1930	2.4		
21	SU	0031	0.0	0758	2.2	1249	0.0	2014	2.5
22	M	0115	-0.1	0838	2.2	1331	0.0	2054	2.4
23	TU	0156	-0.1	0915	2.2	1410	0.0	2130	2.3
24	W	0235	0.0	0948	2.0	1447	0.2	2202	2.0
25	TH	0312	0.2	1018	1.8	1523	0.3	2232	1.8
26	F	0348	0.4	1046	1.6	1600	0.5	◑ 2300	1.5
27	SA	0425	0.6	1119	1.5	1645	0.7	2335	1.3
28	SU	0511	0.8	1205	1.4	1802	0.9		
29	M	0032	1.2	0638	0.9	1329	1.3	2020	0.9
30	TU	0315	1.2	0831	0.9	1544	1.4	2133	0.8
31	W	0431	1.3	0932	0.8	1641	1.6	2210	0.7

Chart Datum: 0·93 metres below Ordnance Datum (Newlyn)

TIME ZONE (UT)
For Summer Time add ONE hour in **non-shaded areas**

ENGLAND – PORTLAND

LAT 50°34′N LONG 2°26′W

TIMES AND HEIGHTS OF HIGH AND LOW WATERS

SPRING & NEAP TIDES
Dates in red are SPRINGS
Dates in blue are NEAPS

YEAR **2005**

SEPTEMBER

Day	Time	m	Day	Time	m
1 TH	0519 1015 1726 2244	1.5 0.6 1.8 0.5	16 F	0512 1016 1729 2244	1.8 0.4 2.1 0.2
2 F	0600 1054 1807 2320	1.7 0.5 1.9 0.4	17 SA	0604 1102 1820 2328	2.0 0.2 2.3 0.1
3 SA	0639 1134 1846 ● 2357	1.8 0.3 2.0 0.2	18 SU	0650 1145 1906 ○	2.2 0.1 2.4
4 SU	0715 1212 1922	1.9 0.2 2.1	19 M	0009 0732 1227 1948	-0.1 2.3 0.0 2.5
5 M	0032 0748 1248 1956	0.2 2.0 0.2 2.1	20 TU	0050 0810 1306 2026	-0.1 2.3 0.0 2.4
6 TU	0105 0819 1320 2026	0.1 2.0 0.2 2.0	21 W	0128 0843 1342 2059	-0.1 2.2 0.1 2.2
7 W	0133 0845 1347 2053	0.1 1.9 0.2 1.9	22 TH	0203 0913 1417 2128	0.1 2.1 0.2 2.0
8 TH	0157 0908 1410 2117	0.2 1.8 0.3 1.8	23 F	0235 0937 1449 2152	0.3 1.9 0.4 1.7
9 F	0220 0929 1433 2140	0.3 1.7 0.4 1.7	24 SA	0303 0959 1520 2216	0.5 1.7 0.6 1.5
10 SA	0245 0955 1459 2209	0.4 1.6 0.5 1.5	25 SU	0323 1025 1556 ◑ 2246	0.7 1.5 0.8 1.3
11 SU	0314 1029 1537 ◐ 2249	0.5 1.5 0.6 1.4	26 M	0337 1104 1728 2345	0.8 1.4 0.9 1.1
12 M	0400 1125 1656	0.6 1.4 0.8	27 TU	0420 1219 2020	1.0 1.3 0.9
13 TU	0000 0552 1301 1921	1.3 0.8 1.4 0.8	28 W	0337 0758 1514 2110	1.2 1.0 1.4 0.8
14 W	0207 0807 1510 2058	1.3 0.8 1.6 0.7	29 TH	0420 0902 1609 2139	1.4 0.8 1.6 0.6
15 TH	0406 0923 1630 2156	1.5 0.6 1.8 0.5	30 F	0454 0944 1650 2211	1.5 0.7 1.8 0.5

OCTOBER

Day	Time	m	Day	Time	m
1 SA	0529 1023 1731 2246	1.7 0.5 1.9 0.3	16 SU	0537 1039 1751 2301	2.1 0.3 2.2 0.1
2 SU	0605 1102 1811 2322	1.9 0.4 2.0 0.2	17 M	0620 1121 1837 ○ 2342	2.2 0.2 2.3 0.0
3 M	0641 1139 1849 ● 2356	2.0 0.2 2.1 0.1	18 TU	0701 1200 1918	2.3 0.1 2.3
4 TU	0716 1214 1925	2.1 0.2 2.1	19 W	0020 0737 1238 1955	0.0 2.3 0.1 2.2
5 W	0028 0747 1246 1958	0.1 2.1 0.2 2.1	20 TH	0057 0810 1314 2027	0.1 2.2 0.2 2.1
6 TH	0058 0815 1315 2026	0.2 2.1 0.2 2.0	21 F	0130 0836 1348 2053	0.2 2.1 0.3 1.9
7 F	0126 0839 1342 2052	0.2 2.0 0.3 1.9	22 SA	0159 0858 1420 2116	0.4 1.9 0.5 1.6
8 SA	0152 0903 1409 2119	0.3 1.9 0.4 1.7	23 SU	0222 0917 1450 2140	0.6 1.7 0.7 1.4
9 SU	0219 0931 1441 2152	0.4 1.7 0.5 1.6	24 M	0235 0939 1523 2210	0.7 1.6 0.8 1.3
10 M	0250 1008 1528 ◐ 2241	0.6 1.6 0.7 1.4	25 TU	0248 1011 1651 ◑ 2311	0.9 1.5 0.9 1.2
11 TU	0341 1109 1718	0.8 1.5 0.8	26 W	0319 1119 1900	1.0 1.4 0.9
12 W	0005 0607 1256 1928	1.3 0.9 1.5 0.8	27 TH	0303 0703 1318 2012	1.2 1.0 1.4 0.8
13 TH	0232 0801 1457 2043	1.4 0.8 1.6 0.6	28 F	0341 0818 1504 2053	1.4 0.9 1.5 0.6
14 F	0356 0906 1607 2135	1.6 0.7 1.9 0.4	29 SA	0413 0906 1559 2130	1.6 0.7 1.7 0.5
15 SA	0450 0955 1702 2219	1.9 0.5 2.1 0.2	30 SU	0447 0947 1645 2206	1.8 0.6 1.8 0.4
			31 M	0524 1026 1730 2241	1.9 0.4 2.0 0.3

NOVEMBER

Day	Time	m	Day	Time	m
1 TU	0603 1102 1812 2316	2.1 0.3 2.0 0.2	16 W	0629 1134 1849 ○ 2351	2.2 0.3 2.1 0.2
2 W	0640 1137 1852 ● 2350	2.1 0.3 2.1 0.2	17 TH	0707 1213 1927	2.2 0.3 2.0
3 TH	0715 1211 1929	2.2 0.3 2.1	18 F	0028 0739 1252 1959	0.3 2.1 0.4 1.9
4 F	0024 0747 1246 2002	0.2 2.1 0.3 2.0	19 SA	0103 0806 1328 2027	0.4 2.1 0.4 1.8
5 SA	0058 0817 1320 2034	0.3 2.1 0.4 1.9	20 SU	0134 0829 1403 2053	0.5 1.9 0.5 1.6
6 SU	0133 0847 1357 2109	0.4 2.0 0.5 1.7	21 M	0200 0853 1436 2121	0.6 1.8 0.6 1.5
7 M	0210 0921 1443 2151	0.5 1.8 0.6 1.6	22 TU	0220 0918 1510 2156	0.7 1.7 0.7 1.3
8 TU	0255 1006 1549 2250	0.7 1.7 0.7 1.5	23 W	0242 0949 1601 ◑ 2249	0.8 1.6 0.8 1.3
9 W	0407 1112 1725 ◐	0.9 1.6 0.8	24 TH	0325 1040 1741	0.9 1.5 0.8
10 TH	0022 0555 1254 1901	1.4 0.9 1.6 0.7	25 F	0016 0527 1207 1900	1.2 1.0 1.4 0.8
11 F	0211 0730 1428 2010	1.5 0.9 1.7 0.6	26 SA	0158 0717 1344 1955	1.3 0.9 1.5 0.7
12 SA	0323 0836 1534 2103	1.7 0.7 1.8 0.4	27 SU	0307 0817 1459 2039	1.5 0.8 1.6 0.5
13 SU	0416 0927 1630 2149	1.9 0.6 2.0 0.3	28 M	0357 0904 1558 2118	1.7 0.7 1.7 0.4
14 M	0504 1012 1720 2232	2.0 0.5 2.1 0.2	29 TU	0442 0945 1650 2157	1.8 0.6 1.8 0.3
15 TU	0548 1054 1806 2312	2.1 0.4 2.1 0.2	30 W	0525 1024 1738 2237	2.0 0.5 1.9 0.3

DECEMBER

Day	Time	m	Day	Time	m
1 TH	0608 1104 1824 ● 2319	2.1 0.4 2.0 0.3	16 F	0642 1158 1908	2.0 0.5 1.8
2 F	0649 1145 1908	2.2 0.4 2.0	17 SA	0010 0717 1239 1944	0.4 2.1 0.4 1.8
3 SA	0001 0728 1228 1950	0.3 2.2 0.4 2.0	18 SU	0049 0748 1318 2016	0.4 2.0 0.4 1.7
4 SU	0044 0807 1312 2032	0.3 2.1 0.4 1.9	19 M	0124 0817 1355 2046	0.5 2.0 0.5 1.6
5 M	0129 0847 1359 2115	0.4 2.1 0.4 1.8	20 TU	0156 0846 1429 2117	0.5 1.9 0.5 1.6
6 TU	0215 0930 1452 2203	0.5 2.0 0.5 1.7	21 W	0223 0916 1457 2151	0.6 1.8 0.6 1.5
7 W	0307 1019 1552 2300	0.6 1.9 0.6 1.6	22 TH	0247 0947 1525 2229	0.7 1.6 0.6 1.4
8 TH	0407 1119 1702 ◐	0.7 1.8 0.6	23 F	0318 1022 1604 ◑ 2318	0.7 1.5 0.6 1.3
9 F	0008 0519 1230 1815	1.6 0.8 1.7 0.6	24 SA	0406 1112 1702	0.8 1.5 0.7
10 SA	0124 0637 1344 1923	1.6 0.8 1.7 0.6	25 SU	0026 0520 1222 1814	1.3 0.8 1.4 0.6
11 SU	0235 0750 1453 2022	1.6 0.8 1.7 0.5	26 M	0146 0648 1347 1923	1.4 0.8 1.4 0.6
12 M	0336 0851 1554 2115	1.7 0.7 1.8 0.5	27 TU	0259 0800 1505 2022	1.5 0.7 1.5 0.5
13 TU	0430 0944 1649 2203	1.8 0.6 1.8 0.4	28 W	0359 0859 1612 2117	1.7 0.6 1.6 0.5
14 W	0518 1031 1740 2248	1.9 0.6 1.8 0.4	29 TH	0453 0952 1711 2210	1.8 0.6 1.7 0.4
15 TH	0602 1116 1826 ○ 2330	2.0 0.5 1.8 0.4	30 F	0543 1044 1806 2302	2.0 0.5 1.8 0.3
			31 SA	0633 1133 1859 ● 2353	2.1 0.4 1.9 0.3

Chart Datum: 0·93 metres below Ordnance Datum (Newlyn)

PORTLAND TIDAL STREAMS 9.1.27

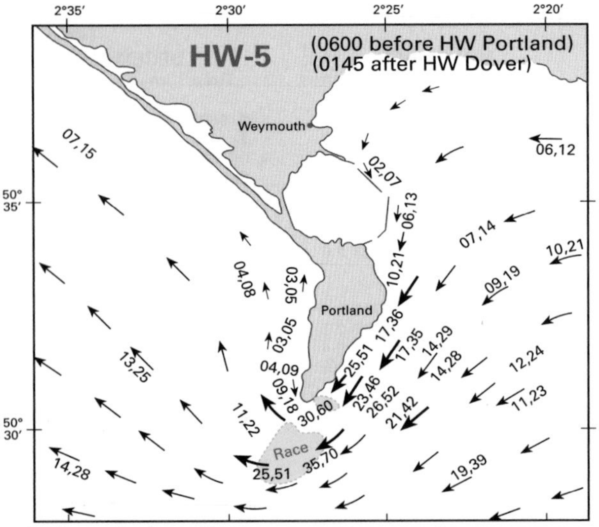
2°35′
2°30′
2°25′
2°20′
50° 35′
50° 30′
HW-5
(0600 before HW Portland)
(0145 after HW Dover)
Weymouth
Portland
Race
07,15
06,12
02,07
06,13
07,14
10,21
10,21
04,08
03,05
09,19
17,36
03,05
13,25
25,51
17,35
14,29
04,09
14,28
12,24
09,18
23,46
30,60
26,52
11,23
11,22
21,42
35,70
25,51
14,28
19,39

5 Hours before HW Plymouth (Devonport)

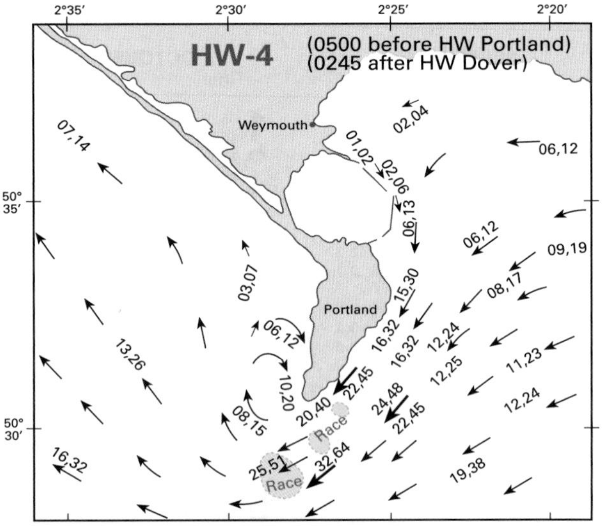
2°35′
2°30′
2°25′
2°20′
50° 35′
50° 30′
HW-4
(0500 before HW Portland)
(0245 after HW Dover)
Weymouth
Portland
Race
07,14
02,04
01,02
02,06
06,12
06,13
06,12
09,19
03,07
15,30
08,17
13,26
06,12
16,32
12,24
16,32
11,23
10,20
22,45
12,25
20,40
24,48
12,24
08,15
22,45
16,32
25,51
32,64
19,38

4 Hours before HW Plymouth (Devonport)

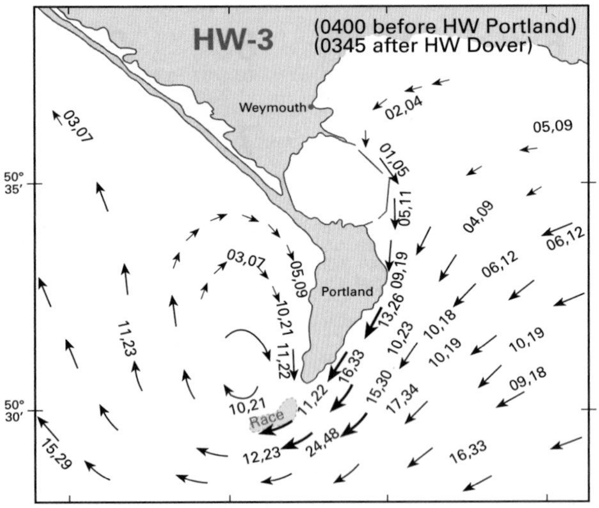
50° 35′
50° 30′
HW-3
(0400 before HW Portland)
(0345 after HW Dover)
Weymouth
Portland
Race
03,07
02,04
05,09
01,05
05,11
04,09
06,12
03,07
05,09
09,19
06,12
13,26
10,21
10,18
11,23
10,23
10,19
11,22
10,19
16,33
09,18
15,30
10,21
11,22
17,34
15,29
12,23
24,48
16,33

3 Hours before HW Plymouth (Devonport)

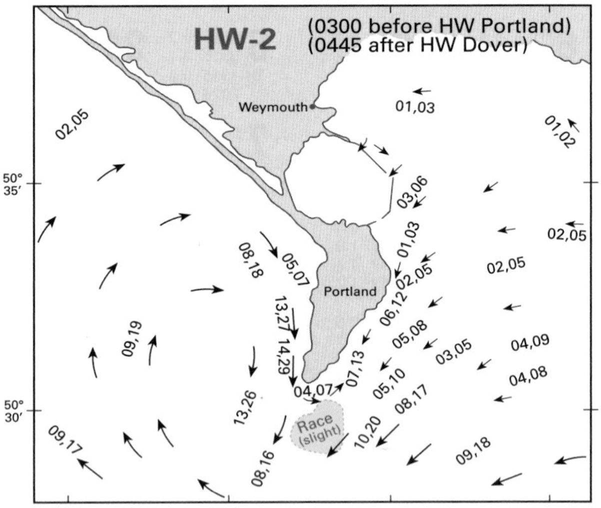
50° 35′
50° 30′
HW-2
(0300 before HW Portland)
(0445 after HW Dover)
Weymouth
Portland
Race (slight)
02,05
01,03
01,02
03,06
01,03
02,05
08,18
05,07
02,05
13,27
06,12
09,19
05,08
14,29
03,05
04,09
07,13
04,08
04,07
05,10
13,26
08,17
09,17
10,20
09,18
08,16

2 Hours before HW Plymouth (Devonport)

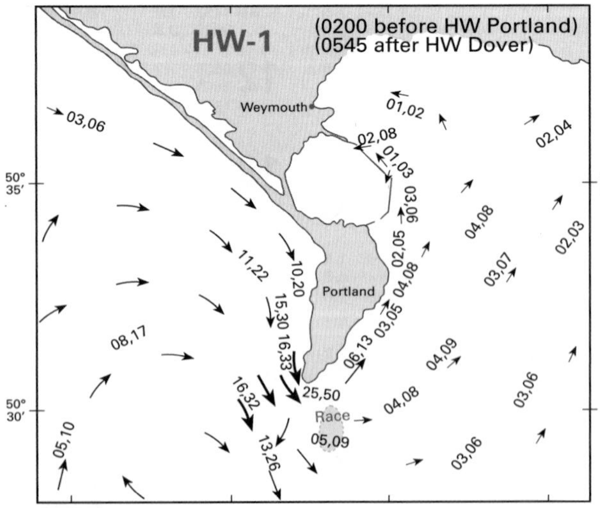
50° 35′
50° 30′
HW-1
(0200 before HW Portland)
(0545 after HW Dover)
Weymouth
Portland
Race
03,06
01,02
02,08
02,04
01,03
03,06
04,08
02,05
02,03
11,22
10,20
04,08
03,07
15,30
16,33
03,05
08,17
06,13
04,09
16,32
25,50
04,08
03,06
05,10
05,09
13,26
03,06

1 Hour before HW Plymouth (Devonport)

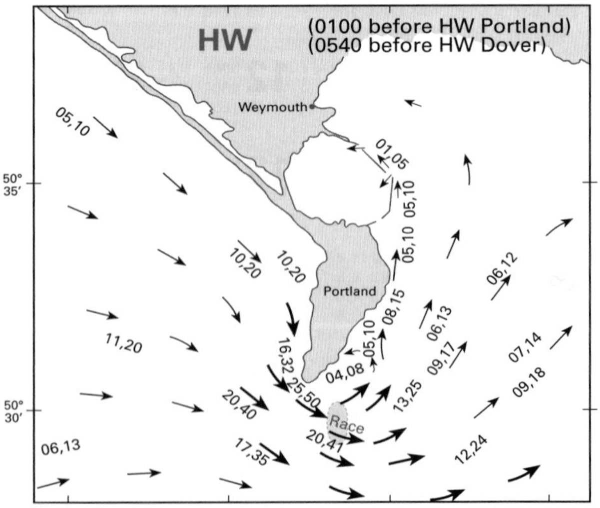
50° 35′
50° 30′
HW
(0100 before HW Portland)
(0540 before HW Dover)
Weymouth
Portland
Race
05,10
01,05
05,10
05,10
10,20
10,20
06,12
08,15
11,20
05,10
06,13
16,32
09,17
07,14
04,08
25,50
13,25
20,40
09,18
06,13
20,41
17,35
12,24

HW Plymouth (Devonport)

General Area 1: 9.1.3 and 9.2.3

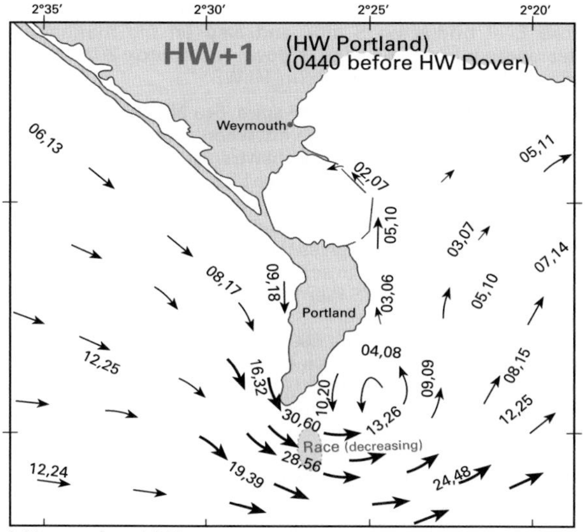
2°35′
2°30′
2°25′
2°20′
HW+1
(HW Portland)
(0440 before HW Dover)
Weymouth
Portland
50° 35′
50° 30′
06,13
02,07
05,11
05,10
03,07
07,14
08,17
09,18
03,06
05,10
12,25
04,08
09,09
08,15
16,32
10,20
13,26
12,25
30,60
Race (decreasing)
28,56
19,39
24,48
12,24

I Hour after HW Plymouth (Devonport)

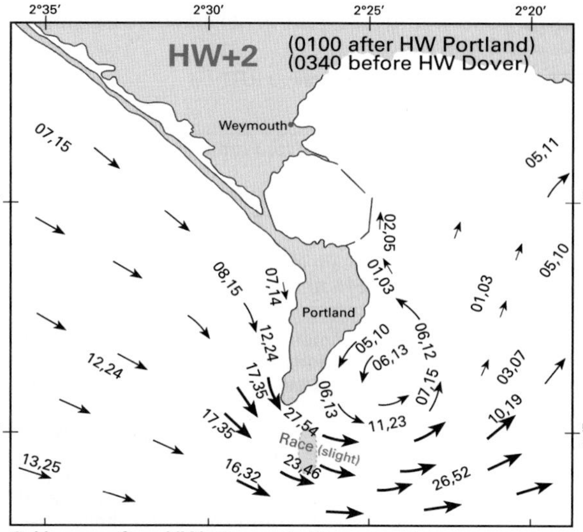
2°35′
2°30′
2°25′
2°20′
HW+2
(0100 after HW Portland)
(0340 before HW Dover)
Weymouth
Portland
50° 35′
50° 30′
07,15
05,11
02,05
05,10
08,15
07,14
01,03
01,03
12,24
05,10
06,12
06,13
03,07
12,24
17,35
06,13
07,15
10,19
17,35
27,54
11,23
Race (slight)
13,25
16,32
23,46
26,52

2 Hours after HW Plymouth (Devonport)

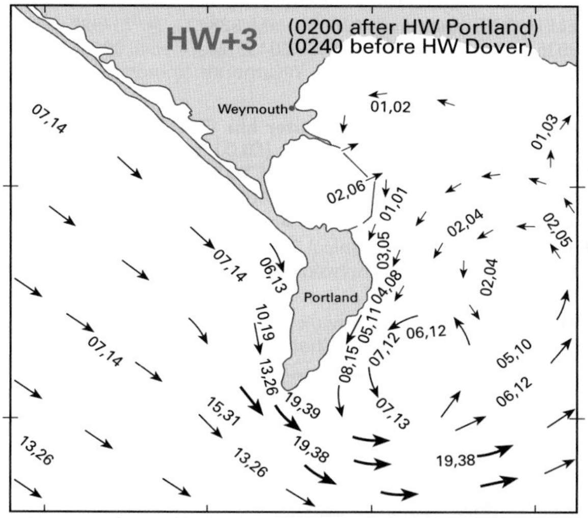
2°35′
2°30′
2°25′
2°20′
HW+3
(0200 after HW Portland)
(0240 before HW Dover)
Weymouth
Portland
50° 35′
50° 30′
07,14
01,02
01,03
02,06
01,01
02,05
03,05
02,04
07,14
06,13
04,08
02,04
10,19
05,11
06,12
08,15
07,12
05,10
07,14
13,26
06,12
19,39
15,31
07,13
19,38
13,26
13,26
19,38

3 Hours after HW Plymouth (Devonport)

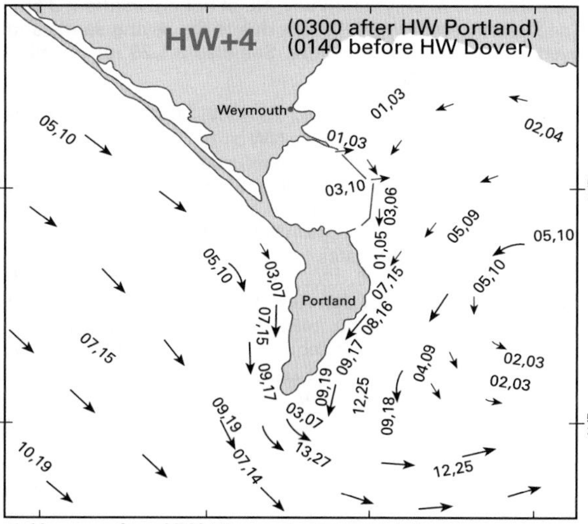
2°35′
2°30′
2°25′
2°20′
HW+4
(0300 after HW Portland)
(0140 before HW Dover)
Weymouth
Portland
50° 35′
50° 30′
01,03
05,10
01,03
02,04
03,10
03,06
05,09
05,10
05,10
03,07
01,05
07,15
05,10
07,15
08,16
07,15
09,17
02,03
09,17
04,09
02,03
09,19
12,25
09,19
09,18
03,07
10,19
07,14
13,27
12,25

4 Hours after HW Plymouth (Devonport)

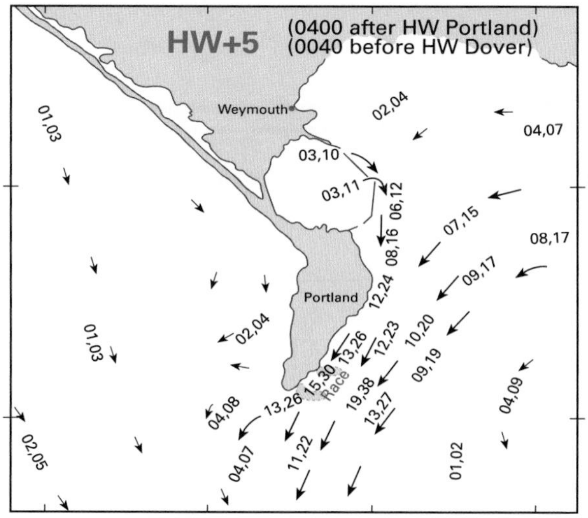
2°35′
2°30′
2°25′
2°20′
HW+5
(0400 after HW Portland)
(0040 before HW Dover)
Weymouth
Portland
50° 35′
50° 30′
01,03
02,04
04,07
03,10
03,11
06,12
07,15
08,16
08,17
09,17
12,24
02,04
13,26
12,23
10,20
01,03
15,30
Race
19,38
09,19
04,09
04,08
13,26
13,27
02,05
04,07
11,22
01,02

5 Hours after HW Plymouth (Devonport)

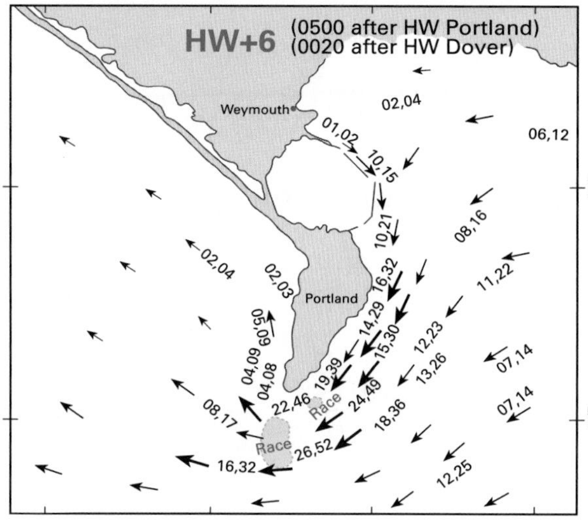
2°35′
2°30′
2°25′
2°20′
HW+6
(0500 after HW Portland)
(0020 after HW Dover)
Weymouth
Portland
50° 35′
50° 30′
02,04
01,02
06,12
10,15
08,16
10,21
02,04
02,03
16,32
11,22
05,09
14,29
04,09
15,30
12,23
04,08
19,39
13,26
07,14
22,46
Race
24,49
08,17
18,36
07,14
Race
26,52
16,32
12,25

6 Hours after HW Plymouth (Devonport)

9.1.28 WEYMOUTH

Dorset **50°36'·57N 02°26'·58W** ❀❀❀◊◊◊✿✿✿

CHARTS AC *5601, 2610,* 2255, 2268, *2172*; Imray C5, C4; Stanfords 2, 12, 15; OS 194

TIDES –0438 Dover; ML 1·1; Zone 0 (UT)

Standard Port PORTLAND (⟵)

Predictions for Weymouth are as for Portland. Mean ranges are small: 0·6m at np and 2·0m at sp.
NOTE: Double LWs occur between Portland and Lulworth Cove; predictions are for first LW. A LW stand lasts about 4 hrs at sp and 1 hr at nps.
Due to an eddy, the tidal stream in Weymouth Roads is W-going at all times except HW –0510 to HW –0310.

SHELTER Good, but swell enters outer hbr and The Cove in strong E winds. Berthing options from seaward:
In The Cove on Ⓥ pontoons S side if <10m or N side if >10m (Custom House Quay) off RDYC; fender boards are available elsewhere. In season rafting-up is the rule. (The quays between The Cove and the lifting bridge are reserved for FVs).
The municipal pontoons just W of the lifting bridge (see chartlet) are for residents only; no visitors. N of these Weymouth Marina, dredged 2·5m, has 290 berths in complete shelter; best to pre-call Ch 80 for a berth.
It is feasible to ⚓ in Weymouth Bay, NE of hbr ent in about 3·5m, but necessarily some way offshore due to the drying sands and buoyed watersport areas inshore. See also 9.1.26 for possible ⚓ in Portland Harbour.

NAVIGATION WPT 50°36'·69N 02°26'·23W, 240°/2ca to abeam S pierhd. The hbr ent lies deep in the NW corner of Weymouth Bay; in some conditions it could be confused with the N ent to Portland Hbr. Hbr speed limit is 'Dead Slow'. Comply with IPTS. High Speed Ferries operate in the area. NOTE: If heading E, check Lulworth firing programme; see opposite and the Supplement for current dates.
The bridge lifts 0800, 1000, 1200, 1400, 1600, 1800 & 2000 mid-Apr to mid-Sep; **plus 2100 Jun-Aug**. Mid-Sep to mid-Apr bridge only lifts at 0800, 1000, 1200, 1400, 1600, 1800. All times local. 1 hr's notice by telephone is required for all lifts in the winter.
Five mins before lift times, craft should be visible to the bridge, and listening VHF Ch 12 for any broadcasts; outbound vessels usually have priority. 3FR or 3FG (vert) on both sides of the bridge are tfc lts, not navigational lts. Waiting pontoons are close E of bridge on S side and also on the marina side. Clearances when the bridge is down are approx 2·7m MHWS, 3·8m MHWN, 4·6m MLWN, 5·2m MLWS.

LIGHTS AND MARKS Conspic ✠ spire, 6ca NNW of hbr ent, is a useful daymark to help find the ent when approaching from the E or from SE past the Portland bkwtrs. Note: On the E side of Portland Hbr (see 9.1.26), approx 7ca ESE of 'D' Head lt, are 4 SPM lt buoys (marking a Noise range).
Lts: see chartlet and 9.1.4. Portland 'A' Head lt ho is a conspic W tr 1·7M SE of hbr ent; it gives the best initial guidance at night. Pierhead lts may be hard to see against shore lts. Caution: About 500m SE of Weymouth S Pier there are 3 SPM buoys (one Fl Y 2s) marking DG Range.
Ldg lts 240°, 2 FR (H24), are 500m inside the pierhds; daymarks (same position) are R open ◊s on W poles; they are not visible until the hbr ent is opened.
IPTS must be obeyed. They are shown from a RW mast near the root of the S pier. There is one additional signal:
2 ● over 1 ● = Ent and dep prohib (ent obstructed).
If no sigs are shown, you are clear to enter or leave with caution.

R/T *Weymouth Harbour* VHF Ch 12 (0800-2000 in summer and when vessel due); *Weymouth Town Bridge* also on 12 (at opening times). *Weymouth Marina* Ch 80. Ch 60 for diesel.

TELEPHONE (Dial code 01305) HM 838423, 📠 767927; Bridge 789357; Marina 767576; MRSC 760439; Marinecall 09066 526241; Police 768970; Dr 774466; 🄷 Weymouth (minor injuries only) 760022, Dorchester 251150.

FACILITIES (From seaward) **Outer hbr** (The Cove and Custom House Quay): AB £1.80 inc shwrs (£6.00 for <4 hrs); **Weymouth SC** ☎ 785481, M, Bar. **Royal Dorset YC** ☎ 786258, M, Bar.
Marina ☎ 767576, 📠 767575; (290 inc Ⓥ) £2.50 inc shwrs (£6 for <4 hrs <12m). **Services:** CH, ⚒, Gaz, Rigger, Slip, ME, Ⓔ, El, CH.
Fuel. VHF Ch 60. D, Mechanical Services (outer hbr or by bowser) ☎ mob 07831 263524. Quayside Fuel (by bowser) ☎ mob 07747 182181 or 07977 337620.
Town www.weymouth.gov.uk, ⓟ, 🛒, R, Bar, ✉, Ⓑ, ⇌, ✈ (Bournemouth), Ferries to Channel Is, St Malo.

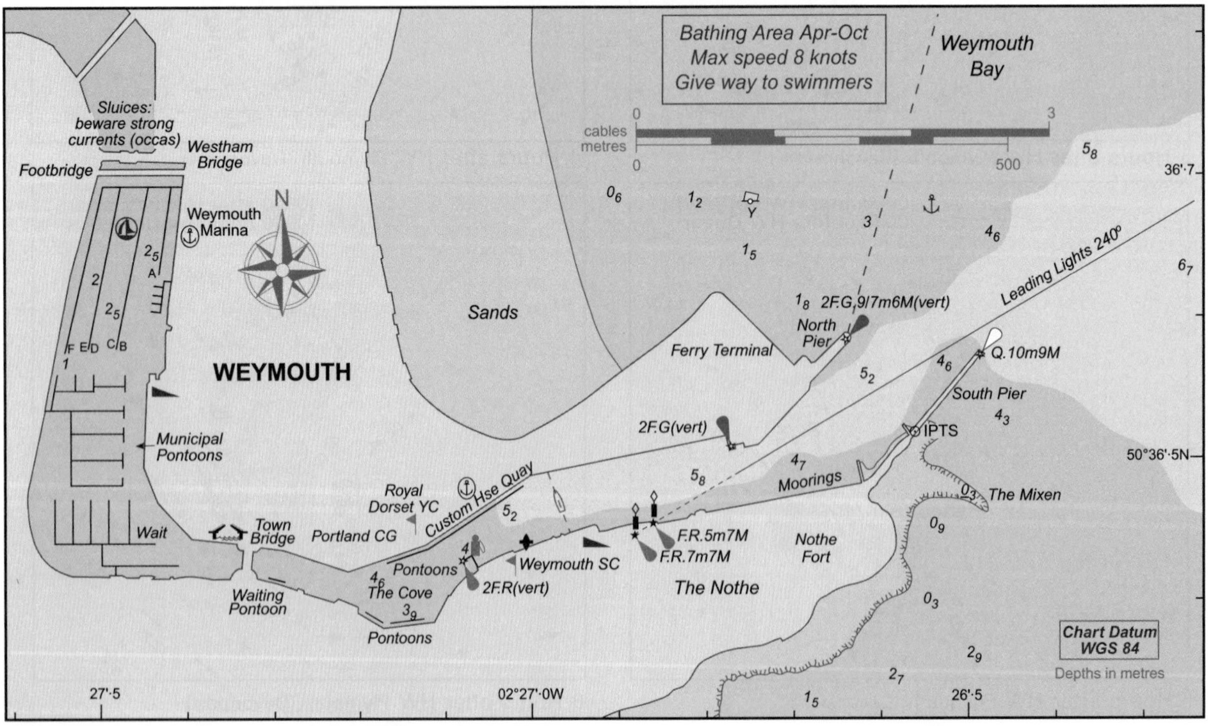
Bathing Area Apr-Oct
Max speed 8 knots
Give way to swimmers
Weymouth Bay
cables
metres
Sluices: beware strong currents (occas)
Westham Bridge
Footbridge
Weymouth Marina
WEYMOUTH
Sands
Municipal Pontoons
Ferry Terminal
North Pier
2F.G,9/7m6M(vert)
Leading Lights 240°
Q.10m9M
South Pier
IPTS
2F.G(vert)
Moorings
The Mixen
Royal Dorset YC
Custom Hse Quay
Wait
Town Bridge
Portland CG
Pontoons
The Cove
Waiting Pontoon
2F.R(vert)
Weymouth SC
F.R.5m7M
F.R.7m7M
The Nothe
Nothe Fort
Chart Datum WGS 84
Depths in metres
36'·7
50°36'·5N
27'·5
02°27'·0W
26'·5

9.1.29 LULWORTH FIRING RANGES

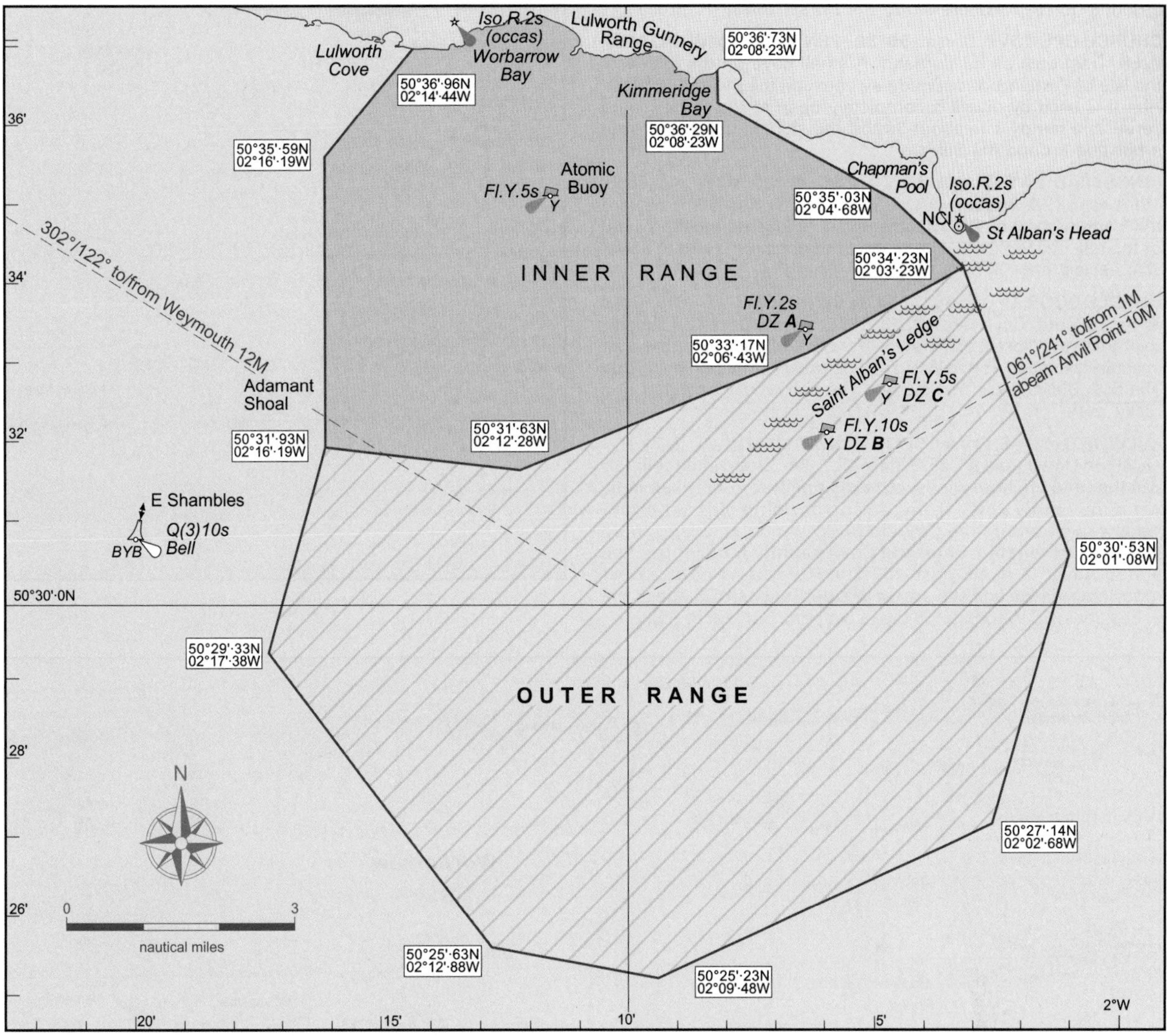
Iso.R.2s
(occas)
Lulworth Gunnery Range
Worbarrow Bay
Lulworth Cove
50°36'·96N 02°14'·44W
50°36'·73N 02°08'·23W
Kimmeridge Bay
50°36'·29N 02°08'·23W
50°35'·59N 02°16'·19W
Atomic Buoy
Fl.Y.5s
Y
Chapman's Pool
Iso.R.2s
(occas)
NCI
St Alban's Head
50°35'·03N 02°04'·68W
50°34'·23N 02°03'·23W
302°/122° to/from Weymouth 12M
INNER RANGE
Fl.Y.2s
DZ A
50°33'·17N 02°06'·43W
Saint Alban's Ledge
Fl.Y.5s
DZ C
Fl.Y.10s
DZ B
061°/241° to/from 1M abeam Anvil Point 10M
Adamant Shoal
50°31'·93N 02°16'·19W
50°31'·63N 02°12'·28W
E Shambles
Q(3)10s
Bell
BYB
50°30'·53N 02°01'·08W
50°30'·0N
50°29'·33N 02°17'·38W
OUTER RANGE
36'
34'
32'
28'
26'
N
0
3
nautical miles
50°27'·14N 02°02'·68W
50°25'·63N 02°12'·88W
50°25'·23N 02°09'·48W
20'
15'
10'
5'
2°W

Lulworth Firing Ranges comprise an inner (D026) and an outer (D026B) sea danger area; the former is more likely to impact on yachts, so to speak. See chartlet above and AC 2610.

The inner area, shaded pink, extends 5·5M offshore. It runs from just E of Lulworth Cove coastwise to Kimmeridge Bay, thence seaward clockwise and back to just E of Lulworth. The Lat/Longs of boundary corners are shown.

The outer area extends 12M offshore and adjoins the seaward boundary of the inner as shown. It is rarely used.

Information: Firing times and recorded range activity are available H24 primarily from Ansafone ☎ (01929) 404819; or secondly, during office hours from Range Control ☎ (01929) 400907, 📠 404912. Times can also be obtained from Range Control and Range Safety Boats (Ch 08), Portland CG (Ch 16), the St Alban's Head National Coastwatch station ☎ (01929) 439220; and from local HMs, marinas, YCs and newspapers. Firing times are broadcast daily by Radio Solent (1359kHz, 999kHz or 96·1MHz FM) Mon-Fri at 0533, 0645, 0845, 1745LT and Sat-Sun at 0633, 0745LT. Annual firing weekends and No Firing periods are given in the Almanac Supplement and at www.reedsalmanac.co.uk.

Naval firing: Warships may use the inner and outer areas, firing eastward from Adamant Shoal (50°33'N 02°19'W) at the 3 DZ target buoys, (up to 3M SW of St Alban's Head) which should be avoided by at least 1M. Warships fly red flags and other vessels/helicopters may patrol the area.

Army firing takes place on the inner range most weekdays from 0930-1700 (1230 on Fri), often on Tues and Thurs nights for 3-4 hrs and for up to six weekends per year. There is NO firing in Aug and on Public Holidays. When firing is in progress red flags (at night Iso R 2s) are flown from St Alban's Head and Bindon Hill. However some red flags are flown whether or not firing is taking place; these mark the boundary of the range's land area.

Regulations: When the ranges are active the Range Safety boats will intercept yachts in the range and request them (Ch 08) to clear the range as quickly as possible.

However all the land danger area and the inner sea danger area are subject to *The Lulworth Ranges Byelaws 1978 operative from 10 Nov 1978 - Statutory Instruments 1978 No 1663.* A key passage states: *The Byelaws shall not apply to any vessel in the ordinary course of navigation, not being used for fishing, in the Sea Area and remaining in the Sea Area no longer than is reasonably necessary to pass through the Sea Area.*

Yachts should therefore make every reasonable effort to keep clear when firing is in progress. If on passage between Weymouth and Anvil Point, a track via 50°30'N 02°10'W just clips the SW corner of the inner range, avoids St Alban's Race and is only 3·3M longer than a direct track.

The Range Safety boats, which are capable of 30kn, are based in Portland Harbour. Their Y mooring buoys in Lulworth Cove and Chapman's Pool were taken out of service Spring 2004.

ANCHORAGES BETWEEN PORTLAND BILL AND ANVIL PT

Essential to read *Inshore along the Dorset Coast* (P. Bruce).

CHURCH OPE COVE, Dorset, **50°32´·26N 02°25´·64W**. AC 2255, 2268. Tidal data as for Portland. A small cove on the E side of the Isle of Portland, about midway between the Bill and Portland Hbr. It is used by divers & completely open to the E, but could serve as a tempy ⚓ in about 3m off the shingle beach, to await a fair tide around the Bill.

RINGSTEAD BAY, Dorset, **50°37´·83N 02°20´·48W**. AC 2610. Tides as for Weymouth, 4M to WSW. Tempy ⚓ in 3-5m toward the E end of the bay. Ringstead Ledges, drying, define the W end of the bay. Rks on the E side restrict the effective width to about 3ca; easiest appr is from SE.

DURDLE DOOR, Dorset, **50°37´·27N 02°16´·58W**. AC 2610. Tides as for Lulworth Cove (see 9.1.26), 1M E. Durdle Door is a conspic rock archway. Close E of it Man o' War Cove offers ⚓ for shoal draft in settled weather. To the W, ⚓ may be found, with caution, inside The Bull, Blind Cow, The Cow and The Calf which form part of a rocky reef.

LULWORTH COVE, Dorset, **50°37´·00N 02°14´·82W.** AC *2172*. HW –0449 on Dover, see 9.1.26. Tides; ML 1·2m. Good shelter in fair weather and offshore winds, but ocasionally a squally katabatic wind may blow down from the surrounding cliffs at night. Heavy swell enters the Cove in S/SW winds; if strong the ⚓ becomes untenable. Enter the Cove slightly E of centre. 8kn speed limit. ⚓ in NE part in 2·5m. Holding is poor. Local moorings, village and slip are on W side; Tyneham village to the E. Facilities: EC Wed/Sat; FW tap in car park, Bar, ✉, R, Slip.

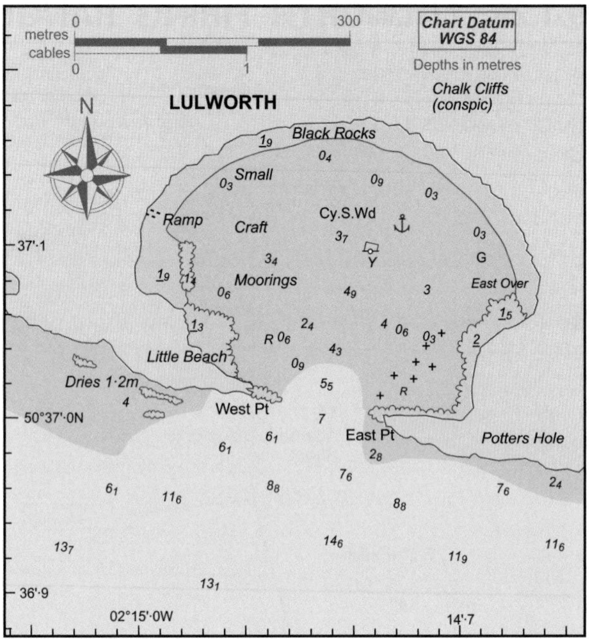
Chart Datum WGS 84
Depths in metres
metres
cables
LULWORTH
Chalk Cliffs (conspic)
Black Rocks
Small Craft Moorings
Ramp
Cy.S.Wd
East Over
Little Beach
Dries 1·2m
West Pt
East Pt
Potters Hole
37'·1
50°37'·0N
36'·9
02°15'·0W
14'·7

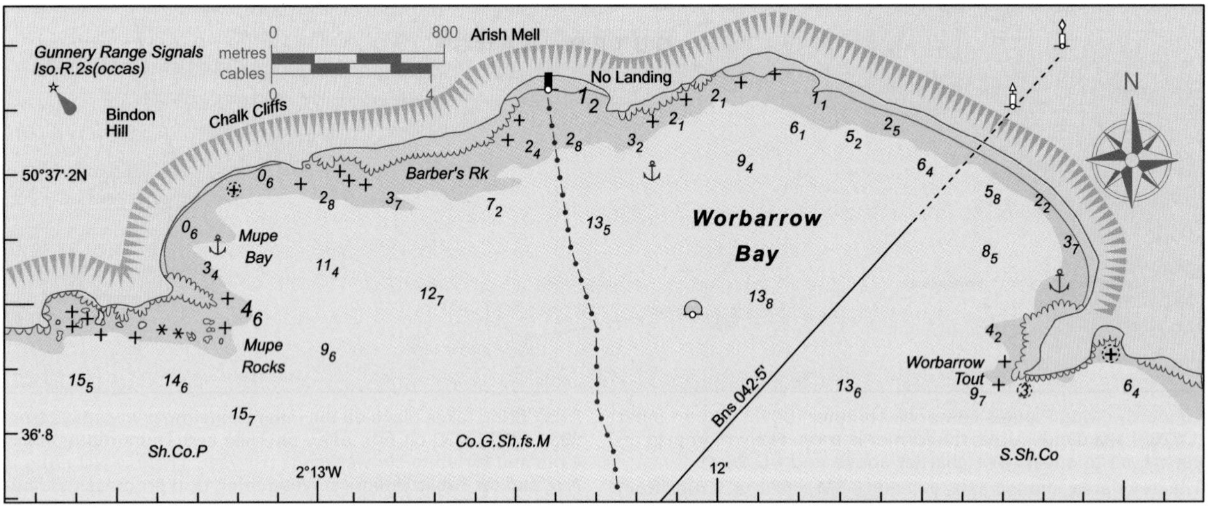
Gunnery Range Signals Iso.R.2s(occas)
metres
cables
Arish Mell
No Landing
Bindon Hill
Chalk Cliffs
Barber's Rk
50°37'·2N
Mupe Bay
Mupe Rocks
Worbarrow Bay
Worbarrow Tout
Bns 042.5°
36'·8
Sh.Co.P
Co.G.Sh.fs.M
S.Sh.Co
2°13'W
12'

WORBARROW BAY, Dorset, **50°37'·03N 02°12'·08W.** AC *2172*. Tides as Lulworth Cove/Mupe Bay, see 9.1.26. Worbarrow is a 1½M wide bay, close E of Lulworth Cove. It is easily identified from seaward by the V-shaped gap in the hills at Arish Mell, centre of bay just E of Bindon Hill. Bindon Hill also has a white chalk scar due to cliff falls. Caution: Mupe Rks at W end and other rks 1ca off NW side. ⚓s in about 3m sheltered from W or E winds at appropriate end. The bay lies within Lulworth Ranges (see overleaf); landing prohib at Arish Mell. No lights/facilities.

CHAPMAN'S POOL, Dorset, **50°35'·53N 02°03'·93W.** AC *2172*. Tidal data: interpolate between Mupe Bay (9.1.26) and Swanage (9.2.6). Chapman's Pool, like Brandy Bay and Kimmeridge Bay, is picturesque and comfortable when the wind is off-shore. ⚓ in depths of about 3m in centre of bay to avoid tidal swirl). From here to St Alban's Hd the stream runs SSE almost continuously due to a back eddy. No lts. Facilities: at Worth Matravers (1.5M walk) village shop and 'Square & Compass' pub, ☎ 01929 439229.

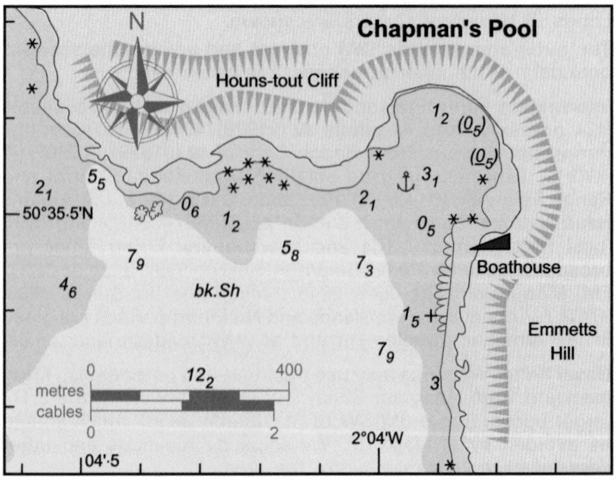
Chapman's Pool
Houns-tout Cliff
50°35·5'N
bk.Sh
Boathouse
Emmetts Hill
metres
cables
2°04'W
04'·5

WEATHER DATA

WEATHER FORECASTS BY FAX & TELEPHONE

Coastal/Inshore	2-day by Fax	5-day by Phone
South West	09061 502 120	09066 526 242
Mid Channel	09061 502 119	09066 526 241
Channel East	09061 502 118	09066 526 240
National (3-5 day)	09061 502 109	09066 526 234
Offshore	**2-5 day by Fax**	**2-5 day by Phone**
English Channel	09061 502 161	09066 526 251

09066 CALLS COST 60P PER MIN. 09061 CALLS COST £1.50 PER MIN.

Area 2

2

Central Southern England
Portland Bill to Selsey Bill

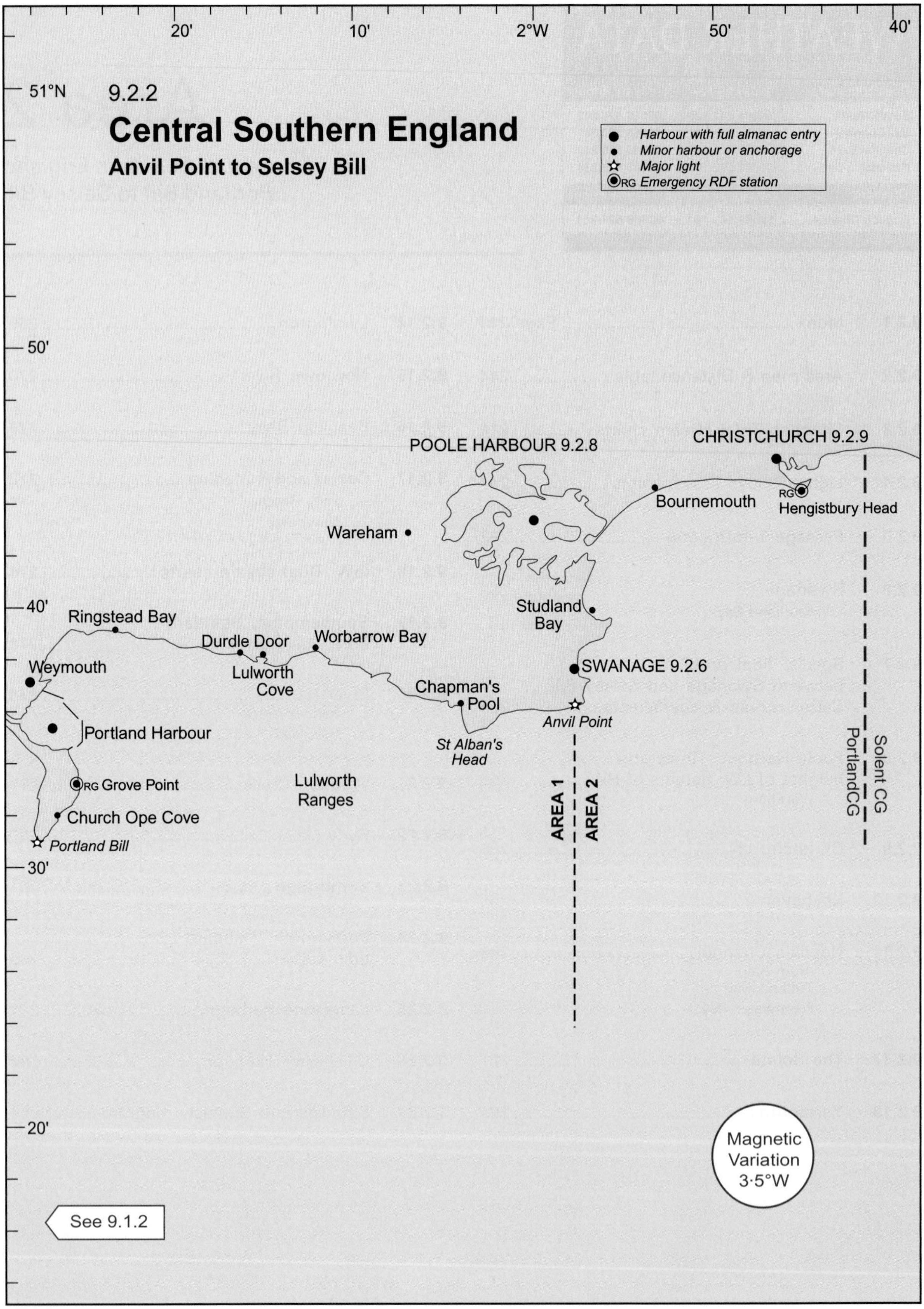
20'
10'
2°W
50'
40'
51°N
9.2.2
Central Southern England
Anvil Point to Selsey Bill
Harbour with full almanac entry
Minor harbour or anchorage
Major light
RG Emergency RDF station
50'
POOLE HARBOUR 9.2.8
CHRISTCHURCH 9.2.9
Bournemouth
RG
Hengistbury Head
Wareham
40'
Ringstead Bay
Studland
Bay
Durdle Door
Worbarrow Bay
Weymouth
Lulworth
Cove
SWANAGE 9.2.6
Chapman's
Pool
Anvil Point
Portland Harbour
St Alban's
Head
Solent CG
PortlandCG
RG Grove Point
Lulworth
Ranges
AREA 1
AREA 2
Church Ope Cove
Portland Bill
30'
20'
Magnetic
Variation
3·5°W
See 9.1.2

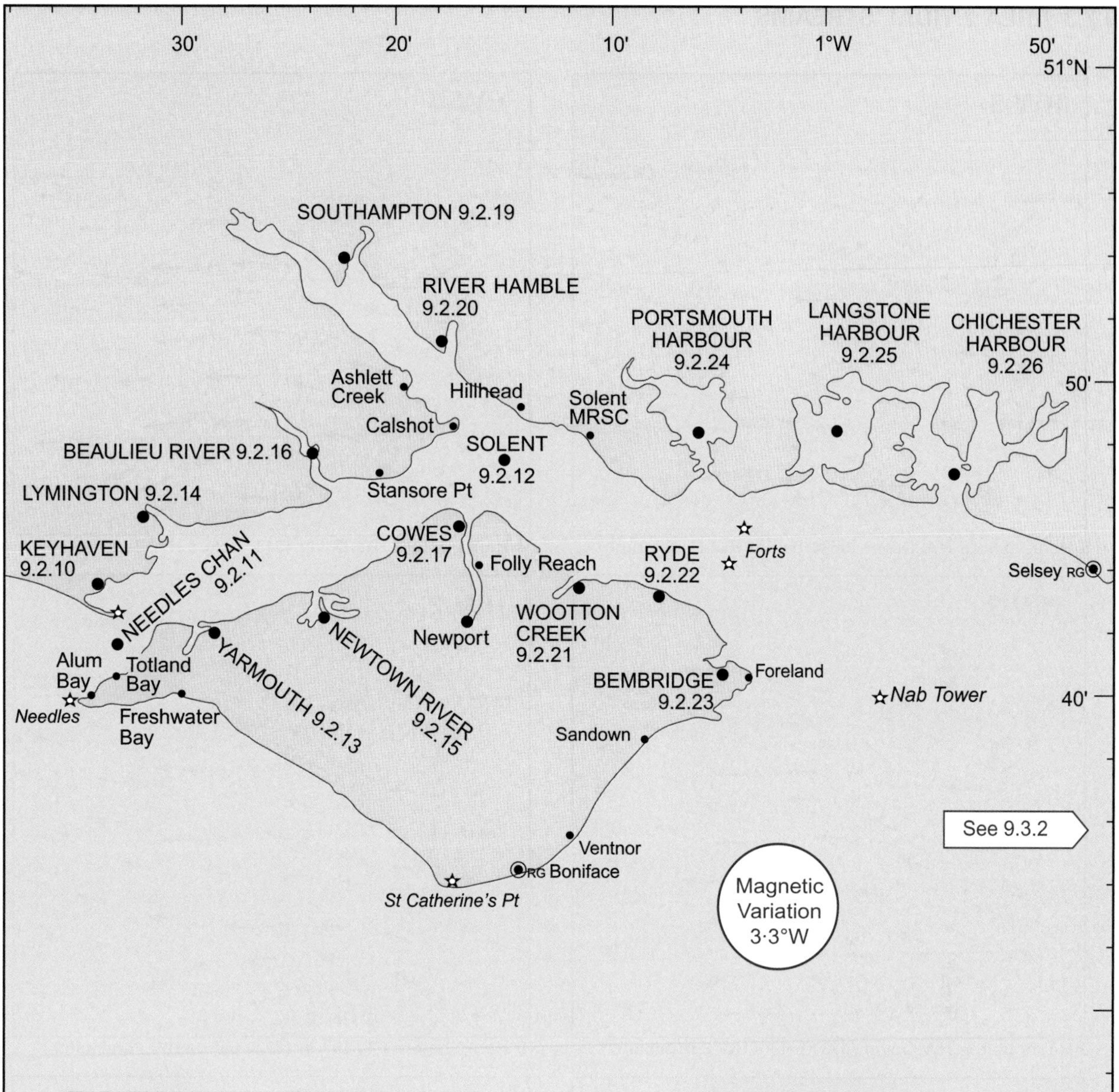
30'
20'
10'
1°W
50'
51°N
50'
40'
SOUTHAMPTON 9.2.19
RIVER HAMBLE 9.2.20
PORTSMOUTH HARBOUR 9.2.24
LANGSTONE HARBOUR 9.2.25
CHICHESTER HARBOUR 9.2.26
Ashlett Creek
Hillhead
Solent MRSC
Calshot
SOLENT 9.2.12
BEAULIEU RIVER 9.2.16
Stansore Pt
LYMINGTON 9.2.14
COWES 9.2.17
Folly Reach
KEYHAVEN 9.2.10
NEEDLES CHAN 9.2.11
RYDE 9.2.22
Forts
Selsey RG
WOOTTON CREEK 9.2.21
Newport
NEWTOWN RIVER 9.2.15
YARMOUTH 9.2.13
Alum Bay
Totland Bay
Needles
Freshwater Bay
BEMBRIDGE 9.2.23
Foreland
Nab Tower
Sandown
Ventnor
RG Boniface
St Catherine's Pt
See 9.3.2
Magnetic Variation 3·3°W

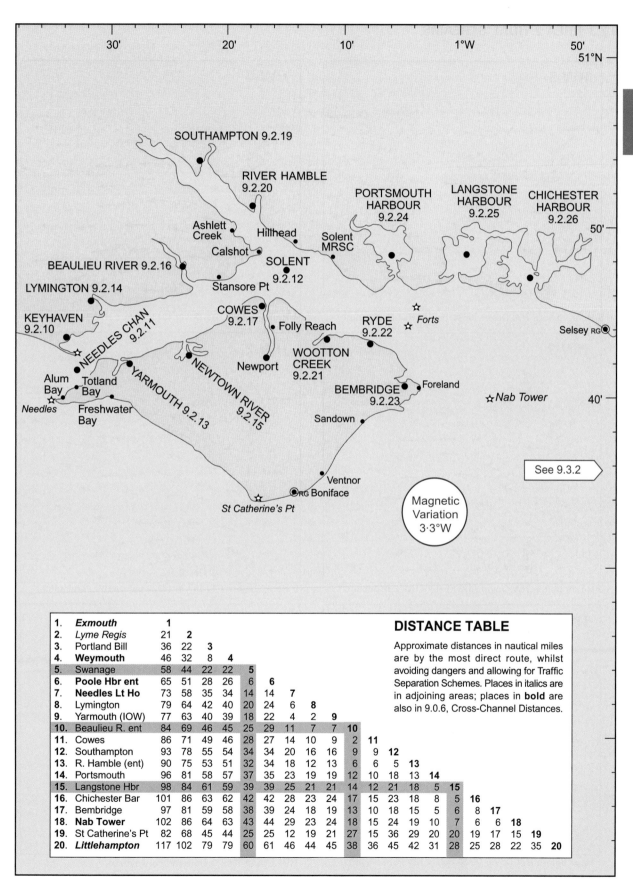

DISTANCE TABLE

Approximate distances in nautical miles are by the most direct route, whilst avoiding dangers and allowing for Traffic Separation Schemes. Places in italics are in adjoining areas; places in **bold** are also in 9.0.6, Cross-Channel Distances.

1. ***Exmouth***	**1**																			
2. *Lyme Regis*	21	**2**																		
3. Portland Bill	36	22	**3**																	
4. **Weymouth**	46	32	8	**4**																
5. Swanage	58	44	22	22	**5**															
6. **Poole Hbr ent**	65	51	28	26	6	**6**														
7. **Needles Lt Ho**	73	58	35	34	14	14	**7**													
8. Lymington	79	64	42	40	20	24	6	**8**												
9. Yarmouth (IOW)	77	63	40	39	18	22	4	2	**9**											
10. Beaulieu R. ent	84	69	46	45	25	29	11	7	7	**10**										
11. Cowes	86	71	49	46	28	27	14	10	9	2	**11**									
12. Southampton	93	78	55	54	34	34	20	16	16	9	9	**12**								
13. R. Hamble (ent)	90	75	53	51	32	34	18	12	13	6	6	5	**13**							
14. Portsmouth	96	81	58	57	37	35	23	19	19	12	10	18	13	**14**						
15. Langstone Hbr	98	84	61	59	39	39	25	21	21	14	12	21	18	5	**15**					
16. Chichester Bar	101	86	63	62	42	42	28	23	24	17	15	23	18	8	5	**16**				
17. Bembridge	97	81	59	58	38	39	24	18	19	13	10	18	15	5	6	8	**17**			
18. **Nab Tower**	102	86	64	63	43	44	29	23	24	18	15	24	19	10	7	6	6	**18**		
19. St Catherine's Pt	82	68	45	44	25	25	12	19	21	27	15	36	29	20	20	19	17	15	**19**	
20. ***Littlehampton***	117	102	79	79	60	61	46	44	45	38	36	45	42	31	28	25	28	22	35	**20**

9.2.3 AREA 2 TIDAL STREAMS

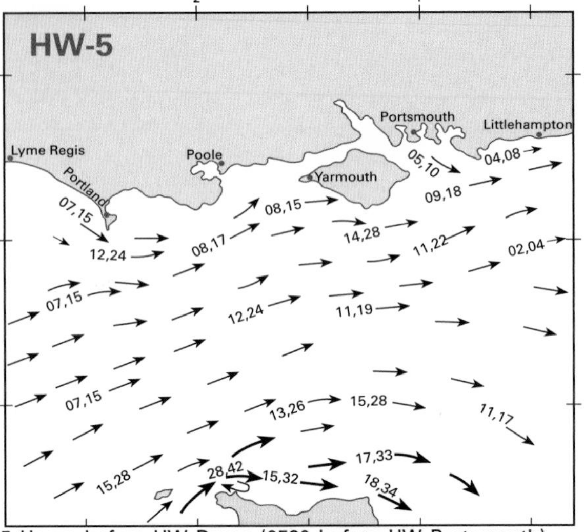

HW-5
Lyme Regis
Portland
Poole
Yarmouth
Portsmouth
Littlehampton
05,10
04,08
09,18
08,15
07,15
12,24
08,17
14,28
11,22
02,04
07,15
12,24
11,19
07,15
13,26
15,28
11,17
15,28
28,42
15,32
17,33
18,34

5 Hours before HW Dover (0530 before HW Portsmouth)

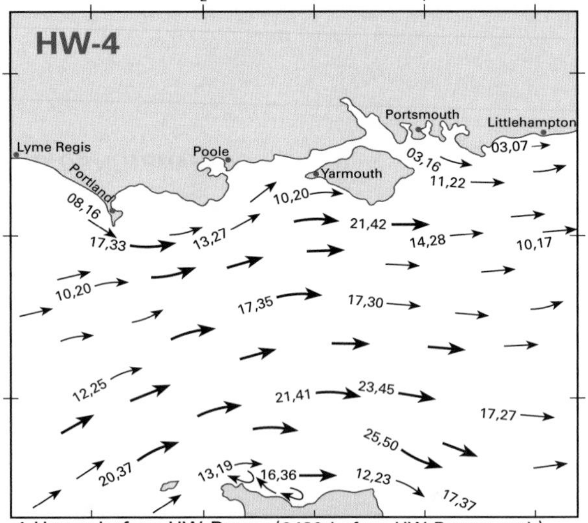

HW-4
Lyme Regis
Portland
Poole
Yarmouth
Portsmouth
Littlehampton
03,16
03,07
11,22
10,20
08,16
17,33
13,27
21,42
14,28
10,17
10,20
17,35
17,30
12,25
21,41
23,45
17,27
20,37
13,19
16,36
12,23
25,50
17,37

4 Hours before HW Dover (0430 before HW Portsmouth)

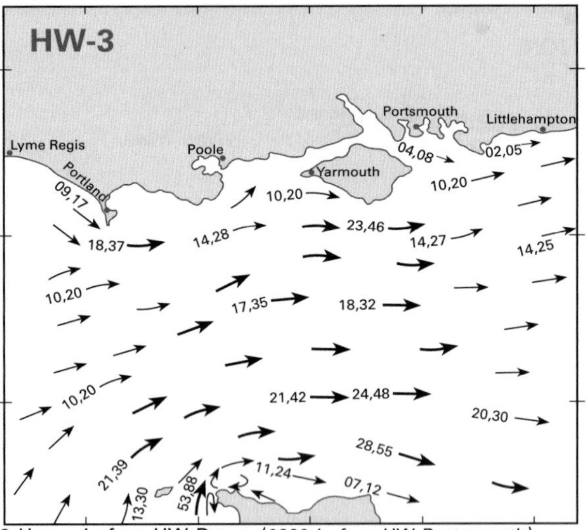

HW-3
Lyme Regis
Portland
Poole
Yarmouth
Portsmouth
Littlehampton
04,08
02,05
10,20
10,20
09,17
18,37
14,28
23,46
14,27
14,25
10,20
17,35
18,32
10,20
21,42
24,48
20,30
28,55
21,39
13,30
53,88
11,24
07,12

3 Hours before HW Dover (0330 before HW Portsmouth)

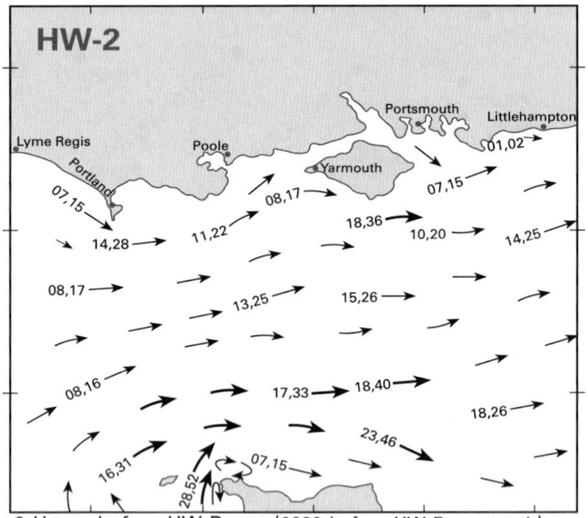

HW-2
Lyme Regis
Portland
Poole
Yarmouth
Portsmouth
Littlehampton
01,02
07,15
08,17
07,15
14,28
11,22
18,36
10,20
14,25
08,17
13,25
15,26
08,16
17,33
18,40
18,26
23,46
16,31
28,52
07,15

2 Hours before HW Dover (0230 before HW Portsmouth)

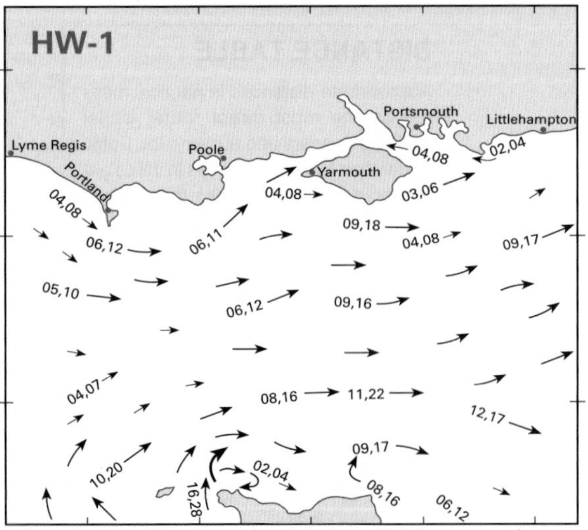

HW-1
Lyme Regis
Portland
Poole
Yarmouth
Portsmouth
Littlehampton
04,08
02,04
04,08
04,08
03,06
09,18
06,12
06,11
04,08
09,17
05,10
06,12
09,16
04,07
08,16
11,22
12,17
10,20
09,17
16,28
02,04
08,16
06,12

1 Hour before HW Dover (0130 before HW Portsmouth)

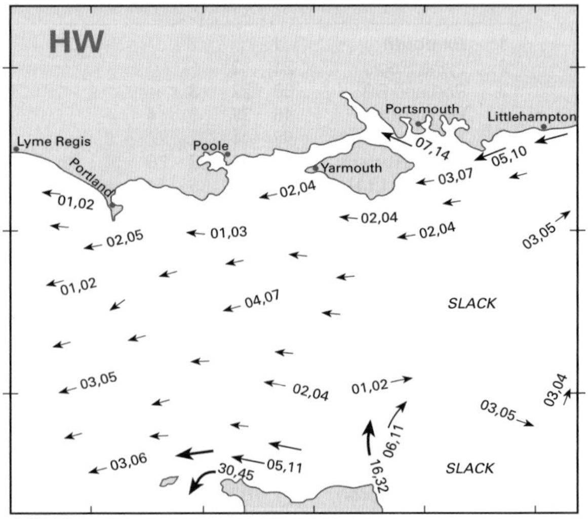

HW
Lyme Regis
Portland
Poole
Yarmouth
Portsmouth
Littlehampton
07,14
05,10
03,07
01,02
02,04
02,04
02,05
01,03
02,04
03,05
01,02
04,07
SLACK
03,05
02,04
01,02
03,04
03,05
06,11
03,06
30,45
05,11
16,32
SLACK

HW Dover (0030 before HW Portsmouth)

Westward 9.1.3 Portland 9.2.8 Isle of Wight 9.2.24 Eastward 9.3.3 Southward 9.18.3 Channel Is 9.19.3

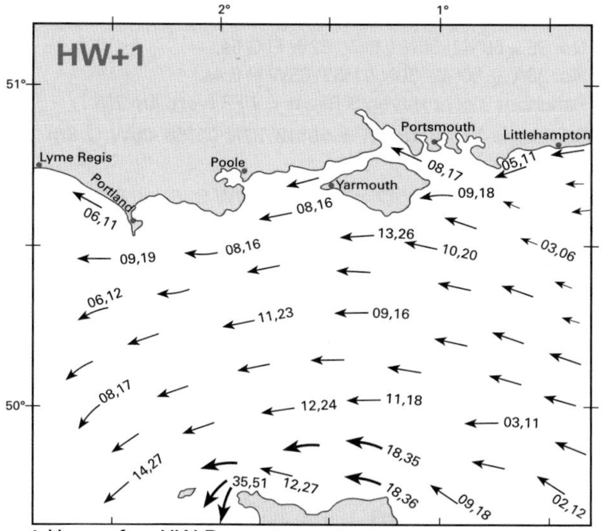
HW+1
2°
1°
51°
50°
Portsmouth
Littlehampton
Lyme Regis
Poole
Portland
Yarmouth
08,17
05,11
09,18
06,11
08,16
13,26
03,06
09,19
08,16
10,20
06,12
11,23
09,16
08,17
12,24
11,18
03,11
14,27
18,35
35,51
12,27
18,36
09,18
02,12
1 Hour after HW Dover (0030 after HW Portsmouth)

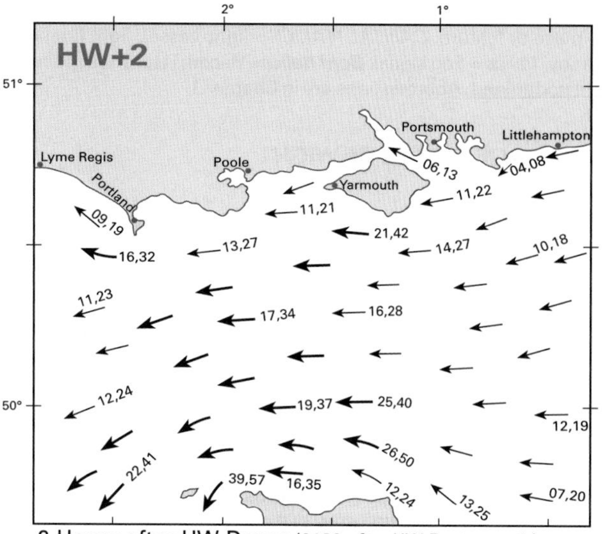
HW+2
2°
1°
51°
50°
Portsmouth
Littlehampton
Lyme Regis
Poole
Portland
Yarmouth
06,13
04,08
11,22
11,21
09,19
21,42
16,32
13,27
14,27
10,18
11,23
17,34
16,28
12,24
19,37
25,40
12,19
22,41
26,50
39,57
16,35
12,24
13,25
07,20
2 Hours after HW Dover (0130 after HW Portsmouth)

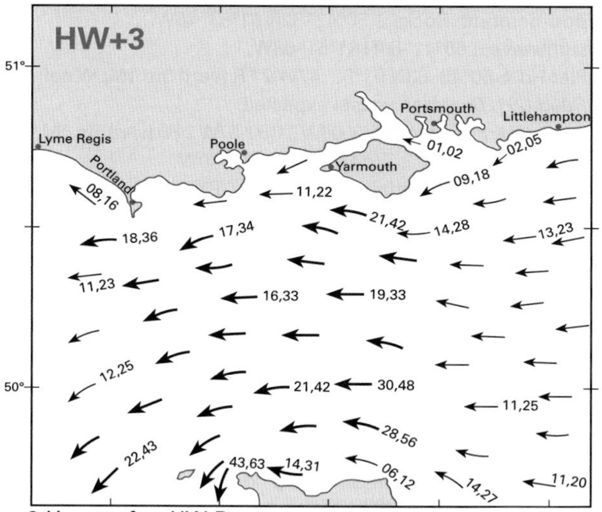
HW+3
51°
50°
Portsmouth
Littlehampton
Lyme Regis
Poole
Portland
Yarmouth
01,02
02,05
09,18
08,16
11,22
21,42
14,28
18,36
17,34
13,23
11,23
16,33
19,33
12,25
21,42
30,48
11,25
28,56
22,43
43,63
14,31
06,12
14,27
11,20
3 Hours after HW Dover (0230 after HW Portsmouth)

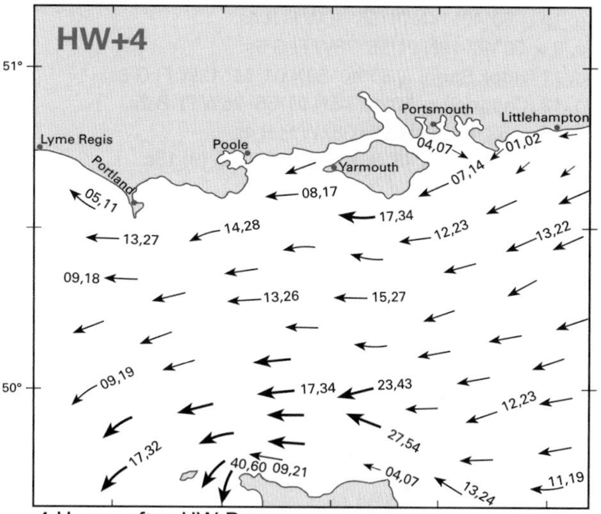
HW+4
51°
50°
Portsmouth
Littlehampton
Lyme Regis
Poole
Portland
Yarmouth
04,07
01,02
07,14
05,11
08,17
17,34
13,27
14,28
12,23
13,22
09,18
13,26
15,27
09,19
17,34
23,43
12,23
27,54
17,32
40,60
09,21
04,07
13,24
11,19
4 Hours after HW Dover (0330 after HW Portsmouth)

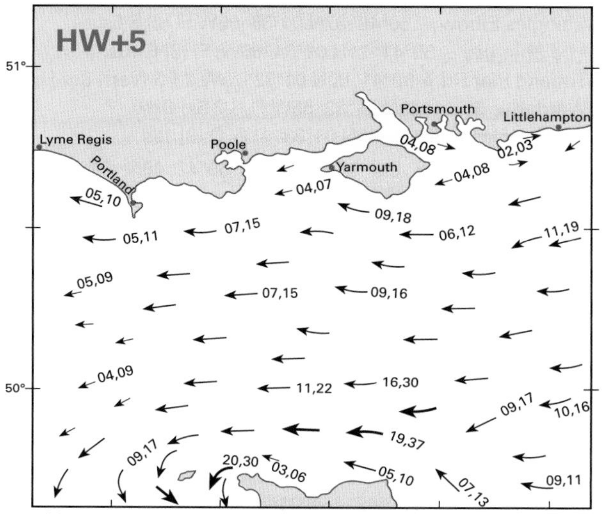
HW+5
51°
50°
Portsmouth
Littlehampton
Lyme Regis
Poole
Portland
Yarmouth
04,08
02,03
04,08
04,07
05,10
09,18
05,11
07,15
06,12
11,19
05,09
07,15
09,16
04,09
11,22
16,30
09,17
10,16
19,37
09,17
20,30
03,06
05,10
07,13
09,11
5 Hours after HW Dover (0430 after HW Portsmouth)

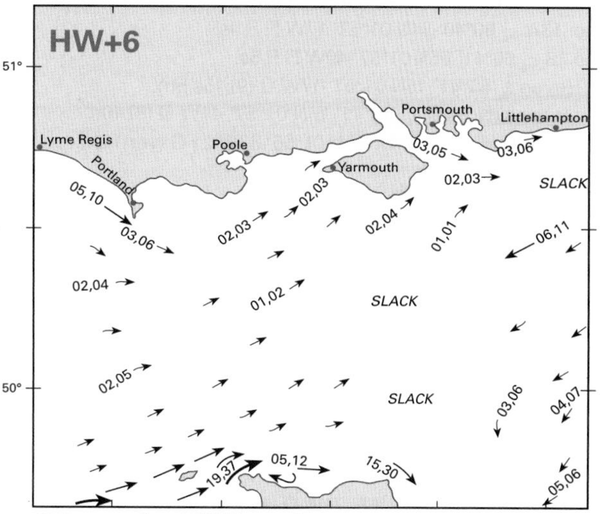
HW+6
51°
50°
Portsmouth
Littlehampton
Lyme Regis
Poole
Portland
Yarmouth
03,05
03,06
02,03
SLACK
05,10
02,03
03,06
02,03
02,04
01,01
06,11
02,04
01,02
SLACK
02,05
SLACK
03,06
04,07
19,37
05,12
15,30
05,06
6 Hours after HW Dover (0530 after HW Portsmouth)

2

PLOT WAYPOINTS ON YOUR CHART BEFORE USING THEM

9.2.4 LIGHTS, BUOYS AND WAYPOINTS

Blue print = light with a nominal range of 15M or more. CAPITALS = place or feature. *CAPITAL ITALICS* = light-vessel, light float or Lanby. *Italics* = Fog signal. ***Bold italics*** = Racon. Useful waypoints are underlined. Abbreviations are in Chapter 1.

SWANAGE TO ISLE OF WIGHT

▶ SWANAGE

Pier Hd 50°36'·56N 01°56'·95W 2 FR (vert) 6m 3M.
Peveril Ledge 50°36'·41N 01°56'·10W QR.

▶ POOLE

Poole Bar (No. 1) 50°39·32N 01°55'·16W QG; *Bell.*
(Historic wreck) 50°39'·70N 01°54'·86W Fl Y 5s.

▶ SWASH CHANNEL

South Hook 50°39'·70N 01°55'·20W.
No. 2 50°39'·22N 01°55'·24W Fl R 2s.
No. 3 50°39'·76N 01°55'·49W Fl G 3s.
No. 4 50°39'·72N 01°55'·60W Fl R 2s.
Training Bank 50°39'·84N 01°55'·92W 2 FR (vert).
No. 10 50°40'·14N 01°55'·90W Fl R 4s.
No. 9 50°40'·19N 01°55'·78W Fl G 5s.
No. 11 (Hook Sand) 50°40'·50N 01°56'·13W Fl G 3s.
No. 12 (Channel) 50°40'·45N 01°56'·26W Fl R 2s.
No. 14 50°40'·82N 01°56'·82W Fl R 4s.
No. 13 Swash 50°48'·88N 01°56'·70W Q (9) 15s.
Haven Ferry landing, 2 FG (vert) 3m.
South Haven Pt, 50°40'·81N 01°57'·00W 2 FR (vert) 5m.

▶ EAST LOOE CHANNEL

Groyne, S end 50°40'·95N 01°56'·86W Fl G 3s.
Groyne 50°40'·95N 01°56'·73W 2 FG (vert).
Groyne 50°40'·99N 01°56'·59W 2 FG (vert).
North Hook 50°41'·01N 01°56'·44W Fl (2) R 5s.
East Looe 50°41'·34N 01°55'·94W QR.
East Hook 50°40'·58W 01°55'·23W.

South Deep. Marked by lit and unlit Bns from ent South of Brownsea Castle to Furzey Is.

▶ BROWNSEA ROADS

No. 18A 50°40'·94N 01°57'·17W Fl R 4s.
No.18 50°41'·06N 01°57'·40W Fl R 5s.
N Haven 50°41'·15N 01°57'·17W Q (9) 15s 5m.
Brownsea (No. 42) 50°41'·16N 01°57'·41W Q (3) 10s.
RMYC Pier Hds 50°41'·35N 01°56'·83W 2 FG (vert) 2M.

▶ MIDDLE SHIP CHANNEL

No. 20 50°41'·38N 01°57'·10W Q (6) + L Fl 15s; *Bell.*
No. 44 50°41'·43N 01°57'·25W Fl R 4s
Marked by PHM and SHM Lt Bys.
No. 43 50°41'·68N 01°57'·02W Fl G 3s.
Aunt Betty (No. 50) 50°41'·96N 01°57'·39W Q (3)10s.
Diver (No. 51) 50°42'·28N 01°58'·34W Q (9) 15s.

▶ NORTH CHANNEL

The chan to Salterns Marina, Parkstone and Poole Quay is well marked by and .

Bullpit 50°41'·72N 01°56'·71W Q (9) 15s 7m 4M.
No. 31 50°42'·17N 01°57'·07W Fl G 5s.
Salterns Marina Outer Bkwtr Hd 50°42'·23N 01°57'·10W 2 FR (vert) 2M; Tfc sigs.
Inner Bkwtr Hd 2 FG (vert) 3M.
No. 35 50°42'·35N 01°57'·62W Fl G 5s.
No. 38A 50°42'·30N 01°57'·63W Fl R 4s.
Parkstone Yacht Haven S Bkwtr 2 FR (vert) 4m 2M.
Parkstone YC platform 50°42'·37N 01°58'·08W Q 8m 1M; hut on dolphin.
Stakes No. 55 50°42'·43N 01°59'·01W Q (6) + L Fl 15s.
Little Chan, Oyster Bank 50°42'·63N 01°59'·11W QG.

▶ WAREHAM CHANNEL

Wareham Chan initially marked by and , and then by stakes.

No. 71 Hutchins 50°42'·20N 02°00'·56W Fl G 5s.
No. 72 50°42'·15N 02°00'·60W Fl R 5s.
No. 82 50°42'·09N 02°03'·22W Fl R 5s.
No. 84 50°41'·95N 02°03'·64W QR.
Wareham R Bn 50°41'·61N 02°04'·58W Fl R 4s.

▶ BOURNEMOUTH

Branksome Chine Outfall 50°42'·24N 01°54'·31W.
Bournemouth Rocks 50°42'·32N 01°53'·40W.
Lightwave 50°41'·50N 01°51'·68W.
Pier Hd 50°42'·83N 01°52'·47W 2 FR (vert) 9m 1M; W col; *Reed (2)120s* when vessel expected.
Boscombe Pier Hd 50°43'·08W 01°50'·57W 2 FR (vert) 7m 1M.
Boscombe Outfall 50°42'·89N 01°50'·40W.
Portman Rayine Outfall 50°42'·92N 01°49'·11W.
Hengistbury Head, groyne 50°42'·66N 01°44'·94W.
Christchurch Ledge 50°41'·53N 01°41'·69W (Apr-Oct).

WESTERN APPROACHES TO THE SOLENT

▶ NEEDLES CHANNEL

Needles Fairway 50°38'·24N 01°38'·98W L Fl 10s; *Whis.*
SW Shingles 50°39'·35N 01°37'·47W Fl R 2·5s.
Bridge 50°39'·63N 01°36'·88W VQ (9) 10s; ***Racon (T) 10M.***

Needles ☆ 50°39'·73N 01°35'·50W Oc (2) WRG 20s 24m W17M, R14M, R13M G14M; ○ Twr, R band and lantern; vis: Rshore-300°, W300°-083°; R (unintens) 083°-212°, W212°-217°, G217°-224°. *Horn (2) 30s;* H24.

Shingles Elbow 50°40'·37N 01°36'·05W Fl (2) R 5s.
Mid Shingles 50°41'·21N 01°34'·66W; Fl (3) R 10s.
Totland Pier Hd 50°41'·00N 01°32'·75W 2 FG (vert) 6m 2M.
Warden 50°41'·48N 01°33'·55W Fl G 2·5s; *Bell.*
NE Shingles 50°41'·96N 01°33'·41W Q (3) 10s.

Hurst Point Ldg Lts 042°. Front 50°42'·48N 01°33'·03W FL (4) WR 15s 23m W13M, R11M; W ○ Twr; vis: W(unintens) 080°-104°, W234°-244°, R244°-250°, W250°-053°.

Same Twr, Iso WRG 4s 19m W21M, R18M, G17M; vis: G038·8°-040·8°, W040·8°-041·8°, R041·8°-043·8°; By day W7M, R5M, G5M.

▶ NORTH CHANNEL

North Head 50°42'·69N 01°35'·52W Fl (3) G 10s.

THE WEST SOLENT

Sconce 50°42'·53N 01°31'·43W Q; *Bell.*
Victoria Pier Hd 50°42'·45N 01°31'·16W 2 FG (vert) 4M.
Black Rock 50°42'·58N 01°30'·64W Fl G 5s.

▶ YARMOUTH

East Fairway 50°42'·64N 01°29'·88W Fl R 2s.

Yarmouth Road 50°42'·53N 01°30'·17W Fl Y 4s.

Pier Head, centre, 50°42'·51N 01°29'·97W 2 FR (vert) 2M; G col. High intensity FW (occas).

Ldg Lts 187·6° Front 50°42'·36N 01°30'·06 W FG 5m 2M, Rear, 63m from front, FG 9m 2M; both W ◊.

Yarmouth 2 50°42'·89N 01°29'·49W Fl Y 2·5s; (Apr-Oct).

Yarmouth 4 50°42'·88N 01°28'·50W Fl Y 2·5s; (Apr-Oct).

▶ LYMINGTON

Jack in the Basket 50°44'·27N 01°30'·57W Fl R 2s 9m.

Ldg Lts 319·5°. Front, 50°45'·19N 01°31'·65W FR 12m 8M; vis: 309·5°-329·5°. Rear, 363m from front, FR 17m 8M.

Cross Boom No. 2 50°44'·36N 01°30'·58W Fl R 2s 4m 3M; R □ on pile.

No. 1 50°44'·41N 01°30'·48W Fl G 2s 2m 3M; G △ on pile.

Lymington Yacht Haven Ldg Lts 244°. Front 50°45'·09N 01°31'·53W FY 4m; R △. Rear, 22m from front, FY 6m; R ▽.

▶ SOLENT MARKS

Berthon 50°44'·20N 01°29'·22W Fl 4s; (Mar-Dec).

Durn's Pt posts, S end 50°45'·40N 01°27'·06W QR; dolphin.

Hamstead Ledge 50°43'·87N 01°26'18W Fl (2) G 5s.

Newtown River 50°43'·75N 01°24'·91W Fl R 4s.

W Lepe 50°45'·24N 01°24'·09W Fl R 5s.

Salt Mead 50°44'·51N 01°23'·04W Fl (3) G 10s.

Gurnard Ledge 50°45'·51N 01°20'·59W Fl (4) G 15s.

E Lepe 50°46'·11N 01°20'·91W Fl (2) R 5s; *Bell*.

Lepe Spit 50°46'·78N 01°20'·64W Q (6) + L Fl 15s.

Gurnard 50°46'·22N 01°18'·84W Q.

▶ BEAULIEU RIVER

Millenium Dir lt 334°. 50°47'·12N 01°21'·90W Oc Q WRG 4s 13m W4M, R3M, G3M; vis: G321°-331°, W331°-337°, R337°-347°.

Beaulieu Spit, E end 50°46'·85N 01°21'·76W Fl R 5s 3M; R dolphin; vis: 277°-037°.

No. 1 50°46'·91N 01°21'·70W.

No 2 50°46'·92N 01°21'·78W.

Ent Chan Bn Nos. 5 , 9 , 19 , and 21 , all Fl G 4s;
Bn Nos 12 and 20 , both Fl R 4s.

Bucklers Hard Marina 50°48'·04N 01°25'·37W. 2 FR (vert).

CENTRAL SOLENT AND SOUTHAMPTON WATER

▶ SOLENT MARKS

Lepe Spit 50°46'·78N 01°20'·64W Q (6) + L Fl 15s.

NE Gurnard 50°47'·06N 01°19'·42W Fl (3) R 10s.

W Bramble 50°47'·20N 01°18'·65W VQ (9) 10s; *Bell*; ***Racon (T) 3M***.

Thorn Knoll 50°47'·50N 01°18'·44W Fl G 5s.

Bourne Gap 50°47'·83N 01°18'·34W Fl R 3s.

West Knoll 50°47'·43N 01°17'·84W. Fl Y 2·5s

North Thorn 50°47'·91N 01°17'·84W QG.

Stanswood Outfall 50°48'·26N 01°18'·82W Iso R 10s 6m 5M; 4 FR Lts; *Horn (1) 20s*.

▶ CALSHOT REACH

East Knoll 50°47'·96N 01°16'·83W.

CALSHOT SPIT 50°48'·35N 01°17'·64W Fl 5s 12m 11M; R hull, Lt Twr amidships; *Horn (2) 60s*.

Calshot 50°48'·44N 01°17'·03W VQ; *Bell*.

Castle Point 50°48'·71N 01°17'·67W IQ R 10s.

Reach 50°49'·05N 01°17'·65W Fl (3) G 10s.

Black Jack 50°49'·13N 01°18'·09W Fl (2) R 4s.

Hook 50°49'·52N 01°18'·30W QG; *Horn (1) 15s*.

Coronation 50°49'·55N 01°17'·62W Fl Y 5s.

Fawley Chan No. 2 50°49'·49N 01°18'·84W Fl R 3s.

Bald Head 50°49'·90N 01°18'·25W.

▶ RIVER HAMBLE

Hamble Pt 50°50'·15N 01°18'·66W Q (6) + L Fl 15s.

No. 1 50°50'·34N 01°18'·65W QG 2m 2M.

No. 2 50°50'·39N 01°18'·77W Q (3) 10s 2m 2M.

No. 3 50°50'·45N 01°18'·65W Fl G 4s 2m 2M.

No. 4 50°50'·49N 01°18'·83W Fl R 4s 2m 2M.

No. 6 50°50'·63N 01°18'·83W QR 2m 2M.

Hamble Common Dir lt 351·7°, 50°51'·00N 01°18'·84W Oc (2) WRG 12s 5m W4M; R4M; G4M; vis: G348·7°-350·7°, W350·7°-352·7°, R352·7°-354·7°.

Pile 50°51'·01N 01°18'·44W Fl (2+1) R 10s 2M.

Sailing Club Dir lt 028·9° 50°51'·10N 01°18'·34W Iso WRG 6s 5m W4M, R4M, G4M: vis: G025·9°-027·9°, W027·9°-029·9°, R029·9°-031·9°.

Hamble Pt Quay 50°51'·02N 01°18'·56W 2 FR.

RSYC offshore pontoon 50°51'·50N 01°18'·70W Fl R 4s.

▶ SOUTHAMPTON WATER

Esso Marine terminal, SE end 50°50'·06N 01°19'·42W 2 FR (vert) 9m 10M.

BP Hamble Jetty 50°50'·92N 01°19'·42W 2 FG (vert) 5/3m 2M (on each side of the 4 dolphins).

Greenland 50°51'·11N 01°20'·38W IQ G 10s.

Cadland 50°51'·02N 01°20'·54W Fl R 3s.

After Barn 50°51'·53N 01°20'·82W.

Deans Lake 50°51'·40N 01°21'·59W.

Lains Lake 50°51'·59N 01°21'·65W Fl (2) R 4s.

Hound 50°51'·68N 01°21'·52W Fl (3) G 10s.

Netley 50°52'·03N 01°21'·81W Fl G 3s.

Deans Elbow 50°52'·16N 01°22'·76W Oc R 4s.

NW Netley 50°52'·31N 01°22'·73W Fl G 7s.

Moorhead 50°52'·55N 01°22'·90W.

Weston Shelf 50°52'·71N 01°23'·26W Fl (3) G 15s.

▶ ASHLETT CREEK

Ashlett No. 2 50°49'·97N 01°19'·62W.

Ashlett No. 4 50°49'·93N 01°19'·76W.

▶ HYTHE

Hythe Pier Hd 50°52'·49N 01°23'·61W 2 FR (vert) 12m 5M.

Hythe Marina Ent 50°52'·63N 01°23'·88W Q (3) 10s.

Hythe Pile 50°52'·62N 01°23'·867W Fl (2) R 5s.

Hythe Lock ent 50°52'·55N 01°23'·98W FG.

Hythe Lock ent 50°52'·54N 01°23'·96W FR; SS Tfc.

Hythe Knock 50°52'·83N 01°23'·81W Fl R 3s.

▶ SOUTHAMPTON/RIVER ITCHEN

Swinging Ground No. 1 50°53'·00N 01°23'·44W Oc G 4s.

E side. No. 1 50°53'·15N 01°23'·40W QG.

No. 2 50°53'·29N 01°23'·38W Fl G 5s 2M.

No. 3 50°53'·48N 01°23'·28W Fl G 7s.

No. 4 50°53'·62N 01°23'·16W QG 4m 2M.

PLOT WAYPOINTS ON YOUR CHART BEFORE USING THEM

Ocean Village Marina 50°53'·70N 01°23'·36W 2 FR (vert).

Itchen Bridge. FW on bridge span each side marks main chan. 2 FG (vert) 2M each side on E pier. 2 FR (vert) 2M each side on W pier.

Crosshouse 50°54'·04N 01°23'·20W Oc R 5s 5m 2M.
Chapel 50°54'·14N 01°23'·22W Fl G 3s 5m 3M.
Shamrock Quay SW end 50°54'·49N 01°22'·93W 2 FR (vert) 4m, and NE end 2 FR (vert) 4m.
No. 5 50°54'·50N 01°22'·76W Fl G 3s.
No. 6 50°54'·58N 01°22'·63W Fl R 3s.
No. 7 50°54'·60N 01°22'·49W Fl (2) G 5s.
No. 9 50°54'·73N 01°22'·48W Fl (4) G 10s.
Kemps Marina Jetty Hd 50°54'·82N 01°22'·66W 2 FG (vert) 5m 1M.

▶ SOUTHAMPTON/RIVERTEST

Queen Elizabeth II Terminal, S end 50°53'·00N 01°23'·71W 4 FG (vert) 16m 3M.
Gymp 50°53'·17N 01°24'·30W QR.
Lower Foul Gnd 50°53'·26N 01°24'·55W Fl (2) R 10s.
Town Quay Ldg Lts 329°, both FY 12/22m 3/2M (occas).
Town Quay 50°53'·55N 01°24'·33W 2 FG (vert) & FY (occas).
Town Quay Marina Ent 50°53'·64N 01°24'·24W 2 FG (vert).
Gymp Elbow 50°53'·50N 01°24'·68W Oc R 4s.
Upper Foul Gnd 50°53'·53N 01°24'·89W Fl (2) R 10s.
Pier Hd 50°53'·67N 01°24'·66W QG.
Dibden Bay 50°53'·70N 01°24'·92W Q.
Swinging Gnd No. 2 50°53'·82N 01°25'·12W Fl (2) R 10s.
Cracknore 50°53'·94N 01°25'·20W Oc R 8s.
Marchwood 50°53'·98N 01°25'·57W Fl Y 2·5s.
Swinging Gnd No. 6 50°54'·22N 01°26'·14W Fl R 3s.
Millbrook 50°54'·12N 01°26'·82W QR.
Bury 50°54'·14N 01°27'·12W Fl R 5s.
Eling 50°54'·47N 01°27'·85W Q (3) 10s.

THE EAST SOLENT

▶ NORTH CHANNEL/HILLHEAD

Calshot 50°48'·44N 01°17'·03W VQ; *Bell (1) 30s.*
Hillhead 50°48'·07N 01°16'·00W Fl R 2·5s.
Hillhead 50°49'·06N 01°14'·78W; Or Bn.
E Bramble 50°47'·23N 01°13'·64W VQ (3) 5s.

▶ COWES

West Knoll 50°47'·43N 01°17'·84W. Fl Y 2·5s.
Spanker (seasonal) 50°47'·11N 01°18'·08W FlY 4s.
South Bramble 50°46'·98N 01°17'·72W Fl G 2·5s.
Prince Consort 50°46'·42N 01°17'·55W VQ.
Prince Consort Shoal 50°46'·29N 01°17'·71W Fl (4) Y 10s.
No. 1 50°46'·07N 01°18'·03W Fl G 3s.
No. 2 50°46'·07N 01°17'·87W QR.
Trinity House 50°46'·14N 01°17'·23W Fl Y 5s.
E Bkwtr Hd 50°45'·88N 01°17'·52W Fl R 3s 3M.
No. 4 50°45'·85N 01°17'·72W Fl (3) R 5s.

Cowes Yachthaven, North end 50°45'·72N 01°17'·69W 2 FG (vert) 6m.
No. 6 50°45'·66N 01°17'·56W Fl (2) R 5s.
E Cowes Marina N end 50°45'·11N 01°17'·51W 2 FR (vert).

▶ EASTERN SOLENT MARKS

West Ryde Middle 50°46'·48N 01°15'·79W Q (9) 15s.
Norris 50°45'·97N 01°15'·51W Fl (3) R 10s.
North Ryde Middle 50°46'·61N 01°14'·31W Fl (4) R 20s.
South Ryde Middle 50°46'·13N 01°14'·16W Fl G 5s.
Peel Bank 50°45'·49N 01°13'·35W Fl (2) R 5s.
Peel Wreck 50°44'·90N 01°13'·41W.
SE Ryde Middle 50°45'·93N 01°12'·10W VQ (6)+L Fl 10s.
NE Ryde Middle 50°46'·21N 01°11'·88W Fl (2) R 10s.

▶ WOOTTON

Wootton Beacon 50°44'·53N 01°12'·13W Q 1M; (NB).

Dir lt 50°44'·03N 01°12'·86W Oc WRG 10s vis: G220·8°-224·3°, W224°-225·8°, R225·8°-230·8°.

No. 1 50°44'·40N 01°12'·34W Fl (2) G 5s.
No. 2 50°44'·25N 01°12'·47W Fl R 5s.
No. 3 50°44'·28N 01°12'·52W Fl G 3s.

▶ EASTERN SOLENT MARKS

Mother Bank 50°45'·49N 01°11'·21W Fl R 3s.
Browndown 50°46'·57N 01°10'·95W Fl G 15s.
Ft Gilkicker 50°46'·43N 01°08'·47W Oc G 10s 7M.

▶ RYDE

Ryde Pier, 50°44'·34N 01°09'·72W NW corner, N and E corner marked by 2 FR (vert). In fog FY from N corner, vis: 045°-165°, 200°-320°.

Leisure Hbr E side 50°43'·99N 01°09'·29W 2 FR (vert) 7m 1M. FY 6m shown when depth of water in Hbr greater than 1m; 2 FY 6m when depth exceeds 1·5m, and 2 FY when depth of water greater than 1·5m.

Hbr W side 50°43'·97N 01°09'·33W Fl G 3s 7m 1M.

▶ EASTERN SOLENT MARKS

N Sturbridge 50°45'·33N 01°08'·23W VQ.
SW Mining Gnd 50°44'·66N 01°08'·04W.
NE Mining Gnd 50°44'·74N 01°06'·39W Fl Y 10s.

▶ PORTSMOUTH APPROACHES

Horse Sand Ft 50°45'·01N 01°04'·34W Iso G 2s 21m 8M.
Saddle 50°45'·20N 01°04'·98W VQ (3) G 10s.
Horse Sand 50°45'·53N 01°05'·27W Fl G 2·5s.
Outer Spit 50°45'·58N 01°05'·50W Q (6) + L Fl 15s.
Mary Rose 50°45'·80N 01°06'·20W Fl Y 5s.
Boyne 50°46'·15N 01°05'·26W Fl G 5s.
Spit Refuge 50°46'·15N 01°05'·46W Fl R 5s.
Spit Sand Fort 50°46'·24N 01°05'·94W Fl R 5s 18m 7M.
Castle (NB) 50°46'·45N 01°05'·38W Fl (2) G 6s.

Southsea Castle N corner 50°46'·69N 01°05'·33W Iso 2s 16m 11M, W stone Twr, B band; vis: 337°-071°.

Southsea Castle Dir lt 001·5° 50°46'·69N 01°05'·33W WRG 11m W13M, R5M, G5M; same structure; vis: FG 351·5°-357·5°, Al WG 357·5°-000° (W phase incr with brg), FW 000°-003°, AlWR 003°-005·5° (R phase incr with brg), FR 005·5°-011·5°.

Ridge 50°46'·44N 01°05'·65W Fl (2) R 6s.
No. 1 Bar (NB) 50°46'·77N 01°05'·81W Fl (3) G 10s.
No. 2 50°46'·69N 01°05'·97W Fl (3) R 10s.
No. 3 50°47'·08N 01°06'·24W QG.
No. 4 50°47'·01N 01°06'·36W QR.
Victoria Pile 50°47'·35N 01°06'·49W Oc G 15s 1M.

▶ PORTSMOUTH HARBOUR

Fort Blockhouse 50°47'·37N 01°06'·74W Dir lt 320°; WRG 6m W13M, R5M, G5M; vis: Oc G 310°-316°, Al WG 316°-318·5° (W phase incr with brg), Oc 318·5°-321·5°, Al WR 321·5°-324° (R phase incr with brg), Oc R 324°-330°. 2 FR (vert) 20m E.

Haslar Marina NE end 50°47'·56N 01°06'·92W QG.

The Point 50°47'·57N 01°06'·57W QG 2M.
Ballast 50°47'·62N 01°06'·84W Fl R 2·5s.
Gosport Marina SE end 50°47'·79N 01°06'·96W 2 FR (vert).
Hbr Ent Dir lt (NB) (Fuel Jetty) 50°47'·85N 01°06'·98W WRG 2m 1M; vis: Iso G 2s 322·5°-330°, Al WG 330°-332·5°, Iso 2s 332·5°-335° (main chan), Al WR 335°-337·5°, Iso R 2s 337·5°-345° (Small Boat Chan) H24.
Port Solent Lock ent 50°50'·61N 01°06'·37W Fl (4) G 10s.

EASTERN APPROACHES TO THE SOLENT

Outer Nab 1 50°38'·18N 00°56'·88W VQ (9) 10s.
Outer Nab 2 50°38'·43N 00°57'·70W VQ (3) 5s.
Nab Tower ☆ 50°40'·08N 00°57'·15W Fl 10s 27m **16M**, *Horn (2) 30s*; ***Racon (T) 10M.***
N 2 50°41'·03N 00°56'·74W Fl Y 2·5s. 6M
N 1 50°41'·26N 00°56'·52W Fl Y 5s.
N 4 50°41'·50N 00°57'·02W Fl Y 2·5s.
N 3 50°41'·63N 00°56'·74W Fl Y 5s.
N 5 50°41'·99N 00°56'·97W Fl Y 5s.
N 7 50°42'·35N 00°57'·20W Fl Y 5s.
New Grounds 50°41'·84N 00°58'·49W VQ (3) 5s.
Nab End 50°42'·63N 00°59'·49W Fl R 5s; *Whis.*
Dean Tail 50°42'·99N 00°59'·17W Fl G 5s.
Dean Tail S 50°43'·04N 00°59'·57W Q (6) + L Fl 10s.
Dean Tail N 50°43'·13N 00°59'·57W Q.
Horse Tail 50°43'·23N 01°00'·23W Fl (2) G 10s.
Nab East 50°42'·86N 01°00'·80W Fl (2) R 10s.
Dean Elbow 50°43'·69N 01°01'·88W Fl (3) G 15s.
St Helens 50°43'·36N 01°02'·41W Fl (3) R 15s.
Horse Elbow 50°44'·26N 01°03'·88W QG.
Horse Elbow Wreck 50°44'·43N 01°03'·43W.
Warner 50°43'·87N 01°03'·99W QR; *Whis.*
No Man's Land Ft 50°44'·40N 01°05'·70W Iso R 2s 21m 8M.

▶ BEMBRIDGE

St Helen's Fort ☆ (IOW) 50°42'·30N 01°05'·05W Fl (3) 10s 16m 8M; large ○ stone structure.
Bembridge Tide Gauge 50°42'·46N 01°05'·02W Fl Y 2s 1M.

SOUTH EAST COAST OF THE ISLE OF WIGHT

St Catherine's Point ☆ 50°34'·54N 01°17'·87W Fl 5s 41m **27M**; vis: 257°-117°; FR 35m **17M** (same Twr) vis: 099°-116°.
Ventnor Haven W Bwtr 50°35'·50N 01°12'·30W 2 FR (vert) 3M
Sandown Pier Hd 50°39'·05N 01°09'·18W 2 FR (vert) 7m 2M.
W Princessa 50°40'·16N 01°03'·65W Q (9) 15s.
Bembridge Ledge 50°41'·15N 01°02'·81W Q (3) 10s.

▶ LANGSTONE AND APPROACHES

Eastney Pt Fraser Trials Range 50°47'·19N 01°02'·22W FR, Oc (2) Y 10s, and FY Lts (occas) when firing taking place.
Winner 50°45'·10N 01°00'·10W.
Roway Wk 50°46'·11N 01°02'·28W Fl (2) 5s.
Langstone Fairway 50°46'·32N 01°01'·36W L Fl 10s.
Eastney Pt Outfall 50°47'·23N 01°01'·68W QR 2m 2M.
Eastney landing stage 50°47'·79N 01°01'·78W Fl R 20s.
East Milton 50°48'·14N 01°01'·71W Fl (4) R 10s.
NW Sinah 50°48'·14N 01°01'·58W Fl G 5s.
S Lake 50°49'·49N 00°59'·88W Fl G 3s 3m 2M.
Binness 50°49'·63N 00°59'·95W Fl R 3s 3m 2M.

▶ CHICHESTER ENTRANCE

West Pole 50°45'·71N 00°56'·50W Fl WR 5s W7M, R5M; vis: W321°-081°. R081°-321°.
Chichester Bar 50°45'·92N 00°56'·46W Fl (2) R 10s 14m 2M; Tide gauge.
Eastoke 50°46'·66N 00°56'·16W QR 2m 3M.
West Winner 50°46'·88N 00°55'·98W QG; Tide gauge.

▶ EMSWORTH CHANNEL

Fishery 50°47'·40N 00°56'·00W Q (6) + L Fl 15s.
NW Pilsey 50°47'·50N 00°56'·20W Fl G 5s.
Verner 50°48'·20N 00°56'·63W Fl R 10s.
Marker Pt 50°48'·91N 00°56'·72W Fl (2) G 10s 8m.
Emsworth 50°49'·66N 00°56'·76W Q (6) + L Fl 15s; tide gauge.
Fishermans 50°50'·14N 00°56'·42W Fl (3) R 10s.
Echo 50°50'·55N 00°56'·19W Fl (3) G 10s.
NE Hayling 50°49'·64N 00°56'·85W Fl (2) R 10s 8m.
Sweare Deep 50°49'·99N 00°57'·47W Fl (3) R 10s.
Northney 50°50'·11N 00°57'·79W Fl (4) R 10s, tide gauge.

▶ CHICHESTER CHANNEL

NW Winner 50°47'·19N 00°55'·92W Fl G 10s.
N Winner 50°47'·31N 00°55'·83W Fl (2) G 10s.
Mid Winner 50°47'·38N 00°55'·69W Fl (3) G 10s.
Stocker 50°47'·45N 00°55'·43W Fl (3) R 10s.
East Head Spit 50°47'·40N 00°54'·90W Fl (4) G 10s.
Sandhead 50°47'·49N 00°54'·59W Fl (4) R 10s.
NE Sandhead 57°47'·56N 00°54'·39W Fl R 10s.
Camber 50°47'·87N 00°54'·06W Q (6) + L Fl 15s.
Chalkdock 50°48'·49N 00°53'·30W Fl (2) G 10s.
Fairway 50°48'·63N 00°52'·37W Fl (3) G 10s.
Itchenor Jetty 50°48'·48N 00°51'·97W 2 FG (vert); tide gauge.
Birdham 50°48'·34N 00°50'·26W Fl (4) G 10s; depth gauge.
Chichester Marina (CM) 50°48'·44N 00°49'·98W Fl G 5s 6m; tide gauge.

List below any other waypoints that you use regularly

Description	Latitude	Longitude	Description	Latitude	Longitude

9.2.5 PASSAGE INFORMATION

Reference books include: Admiralty *Channel Pilot*; *Channel Cruising Companion* (Nautical Data Ltd/Featherstone & Aslett); and *Solent Cruising Companion* (Nautical Data Ltd/ Aslett). See 9.0.6 for distances across the Channel, and 9.3.5 and 9.18.5 for notes on cross-Channel passages. Admiralty Small Craft Folio 5601 covers Portland to the Needles, contains 10 A2 size charts in a clear plastic wallet and costs £37.00 (2003). Encapsulated Solent and Chichester Hbr Racing Charts (Nautical Data Ltd).

SWANAGE TO CHRISTCHURCH BAY (chart *2615*) ▶*There is deep water quite close inshore between St Alban's Hd and Anvil Pt (lt). 1M NE of Durlston Hd, Peveril Ledge runs 2½ca seaward, causing quite a bad race which extends nearly 1M eastwards, particularly on W-going stream against a SW wind. Proceeding towards the excellent shelter of Poole Harbour (9.2.12), overfalls may be met off Ballard Pt and Old Harry on the W-going stream.*◀ Studland Bay (9.2.10 and chart 2172) is a good anch especially in NW to S winds. Anch about 4ca WNW of Handfast Pt. Avoid foul areas on chart.

Poole Bay offers good sailing in waters sheltered from W and N winds, with no dangers to worry the average yacht. ▶ *Tidal streams are weak N of a line between Handfast Pt and Hengistbury Hd and within Christchurch Bay.* ◀ Hengistbury Hd is a dark headland, S of Christchurch hbr (9.2.13), with a groyne extending 1ca S and Beerpan Rks a further 100m E of groyne. Beware lobster pots in this area. Christchurch Ledge extends 2·75M SE from Hengistbury Hd. ▶ *The tide runs hard over the ledge at sp, and there may be overfalls.* ◀

WESTERN APPROACHES TO SOLENT (charts *2219, 2050*) The Needles (see 9.2.15) are distinctive rks at the W end of the Isle of Wight. The adjacent chalk cliffs of High Down are conspic from afar, but the lt ho may not be seen by day until relatively close. Goose Rk, dries, is about 50m WNW of the lt ho, 100-150m WSW of which is a drying wreck. When rounding the Needles an offing of 1½ca will clear these. The NW side of Needles Chan is defined by the Shingles bank, parts of which dry and on which the sea breaks violently in the least swell. The SE side of the bank is fairly steep-to, the NW side shelves more gradually. ▶ *On the ebb the stream sets very strongly (3·4kn) WSW across the Shingles.*◀ The Needles Channel is well lit and buoyed and in fair weather presents no significant problems. But even a SW F4 over the ebb will cause breaking seas near Bridge and SW Shingles buoys.

In bad weather broken water and overfalls extend along The Bridge, a reef which runs 8ca W of the lt ho with extremity marked by WCM lt buoy. ▶ *S to W gales against the ebb raise very dangerous breaking seas in the Needles Chan, here only 250m wide. The sea state can be at its worst shortly after LW when the flood has just begun. There is then no wind-over-tide situation, but a substantial swell is raised as a result of the recently turned stream.*◀ In such conditions use the E route to the Solent, S of the IOW and via Nab Tower; or find shelter at Poole or Studland.

In strong winds the North Channel, N of the Shingles, is preferable to the Needles Channel. The two join S of Hurst Pt, where overfalls and tide rips may be met. Beware The Trap, a shoal spit 150m SE of Hurst Castle.

In E winds Alum B, close NE of the Needles, is an attractive daytime anch with its coloured cliffs, but beware Long Rk (dries) in middle of B, and Five Fingers Rk 1½ca SW of Hatherwood Pt on N side. Totland Bay is good anch in settled weather, but avoid Warden Ledge.

THE SOLENT (charts *2040, 394*) Within the Solent there are few dangers in mid-chan. The most significant is Bramble bank (dries) between Cowes and Calshot. The main shipping chan (buoyed) passes S and W of the Brambles, but yachts can use the North Chan to the NE of the Brambles at any state of tide. ▶ *Tidal streams are strong at sp, but principally follow the direction of the main chan.* ◀ A Precautionary Area between Cowes and Calshot provides priority and safety for large commercial shippings; see 9.2.16.

Several inshore spits, banks, rocks and ledges, which a yachtsman should know, include: Pennington and Lymington Spits on the N shore; Black Rk 4ca W of entrance to Yarmouth (9.2.17); Hamstead Ledge 8ca W of entrance to Newtown River (9.2.19) and Saltmead Ledge 1·5M to E; Gurnard Ledge 1·5M W of Cowes; Lepe, Middle and Beaulieu Spit, S and W of the ent to Beaulieu R. (9.2.20); the shoals off Stone Pt, marked by Lepe Spit SCM buoy and where a bn marks cable area; Shrape Mud, which extends N from the breakwater of Cowes hbr (9.2.21) and along to Old Castle Pt; the shoals and isolated rks which fringe the island shore from Old Castle Pt to Ryde (9.2.26), including either side of the ent to Wootton Creek (9.2.25); and Calshot Spit which extends almost to the lt F which marks the turn of chan into Southampton Water.

Southampton Water is a busy commercial waterway with large tankers, containerships, lesser craft and high speed ferries. Yachts should monitor VHF Ch 12 to ascertain shipping movements. Between the Esso jetty off Fawley and the BP jetty on the E side the channel is narrow for large vessels; yachts can easily stay clear by seeking shoal water. N of this area there is adequate water for yachts close outboard of the main buoyed channel; the banks are of gently shelving soft mud, apart from foul ground between Hythe and Marchwood. Unlit marks and large mooring buoys may however be hard to see against the many shore lights. Except in strong N'lies, Southampton Water and the R Test and Itchen provide sheltered sailing. The River Hamble is convenient, but somewhat crowded.

Depending on the wind direction, there are many good anchs: For example, in W winds there is anch on E side of Hurst, as close inshore as depth permits, NE of Hurst lt. In S winds, or in good weather, anch W of Yarmouth hbr ent, as near shore as possible, but reasonably close to town, see 9.2.17. In winds between W and N there is good anch in Stanswood Bay, about 1M NE of Stansore Pt. Just N of Calshot Spit there is shelter from SW and W. Osborne Bay, 2M E of Cowes, is sheltered from winds between S and W; in E winds Gurnard Bay, to the W of Cowes, is preferable. In N winds anch in Stokes Bay. At E end of IOW there is good anch off Bembridge in winds from S, SW or W; but clear out if wind goes into E.

There are also places which a shoal-draught boat can explore at the top of the tide, such as Ashlett Creek (9.2.24) between Fawley and Calshot, Eling up the R Test, and the upper reaches of the R Medina (9.2.21).

ISLE OF WIGHT – SOUTH COAST (chart *2045*) From the Needles eastward to Freshwater Bay the cliffs can be approached to within 1ca, but beyond the E end of chalk cliffs there are ledges off Brook and Atherfield which require at least 5ca offing. ▶ *The E-going stream sets towards these dangers. 4M SSW of the Needles the stream turns E x N at HW Portsmouth + 0530, and W at HW – 0030, sp rate 2kn.*

St Catherine's lt ho (lt, RC) is conspic. It is safe to pass 2ca off, but a race occurs off the Point and can be very dangerous at or near sp with a strong opposing wind; particularly SE of the Pt on a W-going stream in a W gale, when St Catherine's should be given a berth of at least 2M. 1·25M SE of the Pt the stream turns E x N at HW Portsmouth + 0520, and W x S at HW – 0055, sp rate 3·75kn. ◀

Rocks extend about 2½ca either side of Dunnose where a race occurs. ▶ *In Sandown Bay anch off Shanklin or Sandown where the streams are weak inshore. Off the centre of the Bay they turn NE x E at HW Portsmouth + 0500, and SW x W at HW – 0100, sp rates 2 kn.* ◀ The Yarborough Monument is conspic above Culver Cliff. Whitecliff Bay provides an anch in winds between W and N. From here to Foreland (Bembridge Pt) the coast is fringed by a ledge of rks (dry) extending up to 3ca offshore, and it is advisable to keep to seaward (E) of Bembridge Ledge ECM lt buoy.

EASTERN APPROACHES TO SOLENT (charts *2050, 2045*) 4·5M E of Foreland is Nab Tr (lt, fog sig), a conspic steel and concrete structure (28m), marking Nab Shoal for larger vessels and of no direct significance to yachtsmen. NW of Nab Tr, the E approach to the Solent via Spithead, presents few problems and is far safer in SW/W gales than the Needles Channel.

The main chan is well buoyed and easy to follow, but there is plenty of water for the normal yacht to the S of it when approaching No Man's Land Fort and Horse Sand Fort, . A submerged barrier lies N of the latter, but the barrier to SW of the former is reported demolished and therefore yachts may pass SW of No Man's Land Fort with caution; a racing mark is planned to mark a possible passage. Ryde Sand dries extensively and is a trap for the unwary; so too is Hamilton Bank on the W side of the chan to Portsmouth (9.2.28).

Nab Tr is also a most useful landmark when approaching the E end of Isle of Wight, or when making for the hbrs of Langstone (9.2.29) or Chichester (9.2.30). Both these hbrs, with offlying sands, are on a dangerous lee shore in strong S'ly winds. East and West Winner flank the ent to Langstone Hbr. Similarly, E and W Pole Sands, drying 1m, lie either side of the ent chan from Chichester Bar bn. SE from Chichester Bar the whole of Bracklesham Bay is shallow, with a pronounced inshore set at certain states of the tide; keep at least 2M offshore. Further along a low-lying coast is Selsey Bill with extensive offshore rocks and shoals. Pass these to seaward of the Owers SCM lt buoy, or via the Looe Chan (see 9.3.5) in suitable conditions. Boulder SHM lt buoy is at the W ent to this chan, about 6M SE of Chichester Bar bn. Medmery Bank, 3·7m, is 1M WNW of Boulder.

9.2.6 SWANAGE

Dorset **50°36'·81N 01°57'·05W**

CHARTS AC *5601, 2172, 2610, 2175*; Imray C4; Stanfords 7,12, 15; OS 195

TIDES HW Sp–0235 & +0125, Np–0515 & +0120 on Dover; ML 1·5

Standard Port POOLE HARBOUR (⟶)

Times				Height (metres)			
High Water		Low Water		MHWS	MHWN	MLWN	MLWS
—	—	0500	1100	2·2	1·7	1·2	0·6
—	—	1700	2300				
Differences SWANAGE							
—	—	–0045	–0055	–0·2	–0·1	0·0	–0·1

NOTE: From Swanage to Christchurch double HWs occur except at nps. HW differences refer to the higher HW when there are two and are approximate.

SHELTER Good ⚓ in winds from SW to N, but bad in E/SE winds >F4 due to swell which may persist for 6 hrs after a blow. >F6 holding gets very difficult; Poole is nearest refuge. AB is feasible on S side of pier (open Apr-Oct) subject to wind and sea state; pleasure 'steamers' use the N side.

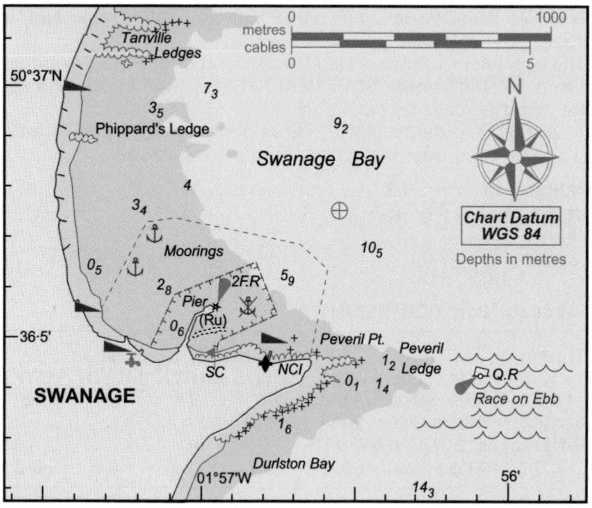
metres
cables
0
1000
5
Tanville Ledges
50°37'N
N
Phippard's Ledge
Swanage Bay
Chart Datum WGS 84
Depths in metres
Moorings
2F.R
Pier
(Ru)
36·5'
Peveril Pt.
Peveril Ledge
Q.R
Race on Ebb
SC
NCI
SWANAGE
Durlston Bay
01°57'W
56'

NAVIGATION WPT 50°36'·73N 01°56'·58W, 054°/234° from/to pier hd, 0·30M. Coming from S beware Peveril Ledge and its Race which can be vicious with a SW wind against the main ebb. It is best to keep 1M seaward of Durlston Head and Peveril Point. On the W side of Swanage Bay, keep clear of Tanville and Phippards Ledges, approx 300m offshore. To the S of the pier are the ruins of an old pier.

LIGHTS AND MARKS The 2 FR (vert) on the pier is difficult to see due to confusing street lts. Peveril Ledge PHM buoy is lit Q.R but may also be hard to pick out at night due to Anvil Pt lt; keep 0·5M clear of it to the E.

R/T None.

TELEPHONE (Dial code 01929) Pier 427058, mob 0780 1616216; MRSC (01305) 760439; Marinecall 09066 526241; Police (01202) 855544; Dr 422231; ⊞ 422202.

FACILITIES **Pier**, L*, FW, AB* £1, £3 for <3hrs; after 2100 gain access to pier from ashore via **Swanage SC** ☎ 422987, Slip, L, FW, Bar, ♿; **Boat Park** (Peveril Pt), Slip, FW, L; **Services:** Diving. **Town** P & D (cans, 1½M), FW, 🛒, R, Bar, ✉, Ⓑ, ⇌ (bus connection to Wareham), ✈ (Hurn).

ADJACENT ANCHORAGE

STUDLAND BAY, Dorset, **50°38'·73N 01°55'·90W**. AC*2172*, 2175. Tides approx as for Swanage (9.2.11). Shelter is good except in N/E winds. Beware Redend Rocks off S shore. Best ⚓ in about 3m, 3ca NW of The Yards (3 odd projections on the chalk cliffs near Handfast Pt). **Village**: EC Thurs; FW, ⛽, 🛒, R, Bar, ✉, hotel, P&D (cans), No marine facilities. A Historic Wreck (see 9.0.3h) is at 50°39'·70N 01°54'·87W, 4·5ca NNE of Poole Bar Buoy.

9.2.7 SPECIAL TIDAL CURVES FROM BOURNEMOUTH TO SELSEY

Due to the complex tidal variations between Bournemouth and Selsey Bill, applying the usual secondary port time & height differences gives only approximate predictions. More accurate values are obtained by using the individual curves discussed below. **Individual curves**, as shown on the following two pages, are given for each port to cater for the rapidly changing tidal characteristics and distorted tidal curves in this area. Because their low water (LW) points are more sharply defined than high water (HW), *the times on these curves are referenced to LW*, but in all other respects they are used as described in Chapter 7.

Critical curve. Since the curves at hbrs from Bournemouth to Yarmouth, IOW differ considerably in shape and duration between Springs and Neaps, the tide cannot adequately be defined by only Sp and Np curves. A third, "critical", curve is therefore shown for that Portsmouth range (as indicated in the lower right of the graph) at which the heights of the two HWs are equal for the port concerned. Interpolation should be between this critical curve and either the Sp or Np curve, as appropriate.

Note that whilst the critical curve extends throughout the tidal cycle, the spring and neap curves stop at the higher HW. Thus, for example, at 7hrs after LW Lymington, with a Portsmouth range of 3·8m (near Sp), the factor should be referenced to the next LW; whereas if the Portsmouth range had been 2·0m (near Np), it should be referenced to the previous LW.

The procedure is shown step-by-step in the following example using the **Differences BOURNEMOUTH** and the special curves for Bournemouth below.

Example: Find the height of tide at Bournemouth at 0220 on a day when the tidal predictions for Portsmouth are:

November

18	0110	4·6
	0613	1·1
SA	1318	4·6
	1833	1·0

Standard Port PORTSMOUTH

Times				**Height (metres)**			
High Water		Low Water		MHWS	MHWN	MLWN	MLWS
0000	0600	0500	1100	4·7	3·8	1·9	0·8
1200	1800	1700	2300				
Differences BOURNEMOUTH							
−0240	+0055	−0050	−0030	−2·7	−2·2	−0·8	−0·3

(a) Complete the upper part of the tidal prediction form (next Col), the contents of boxes 8*, 9* and 10* are obtained by interpolation.

(b) On the left of the Bournemouth tidal curve diagram, plot the Secondary Port HW and LW heights [1·9m and 0·7m from (a) above], and join these points with a sloping line.

(c) The time required (0220) is 3hr 7min before the time of LW at the Secondary Port, so from this point draw a line vertically up towards the curves.

(d) It is necessary to interpolate for the day's range at Portsmouth (3·5m), which is about mid-way between the spring curve (3·9m) and the critical curve (2·8m). (This incidentally gives a point level with a factor of 0·84).

STANDARD PORT Portsmouth TIME/~~HEIGHT~~ REQUIRED 0220

SECONDARY PORT Bournemouth DATE 18 Nov TIME ZONE 0 (GMT)

	TIME		HEIGHT		
STANDARD PORT	HW	LW	HW	LW	RANGE
	1	2 0613	3 4.6	4 1.1	5 3.5
Seasonal change	Standard Port		6	6	
DIFFERENCES	7*	8* -0046	9* -2.7	10* -0.4	
Seasonal change	Standard Port		11	11	
SECONDARY PORT	12	13 0527	14 1.9	15 0.7	
Duration	16				

STANDARD PORT .... TIME/HEIGHT REQUIRED ....

SECONDARY PORT .... DATE .... TIME ZONE ....

	TIME		HEIGHT		
STANDARD PORT	HW	LW	HW	LW	RANGE
	1	2	3	4	5
Seasonal change	Standard Port		6	6	
DIFFERENCES	7*	8*	9*	10*	
Seasonal change	Standard Port		11	11	
SECONDARY PORT	12	13	14	15	
Duration	16				

(e) From this point draw a horizontal line to intersect the sloping line constructed in (b) above.

(f) From the intersection of the horizontal line and the sloping line, proceed vertically to the height scale at the top, and read off the height of tide at 0220 = 1·7m.

Note: From Bournemouth to Christchurch double HWs occur, except at nps. HW height differences, as given for each secondary port, always apply to the higher HW (that which reaches a factor of 1·0 on the curves). This higher HW should be used to obtain the range at the Secondary Port. HW time differences, which are not needed for this example, also refer to the higher HW.

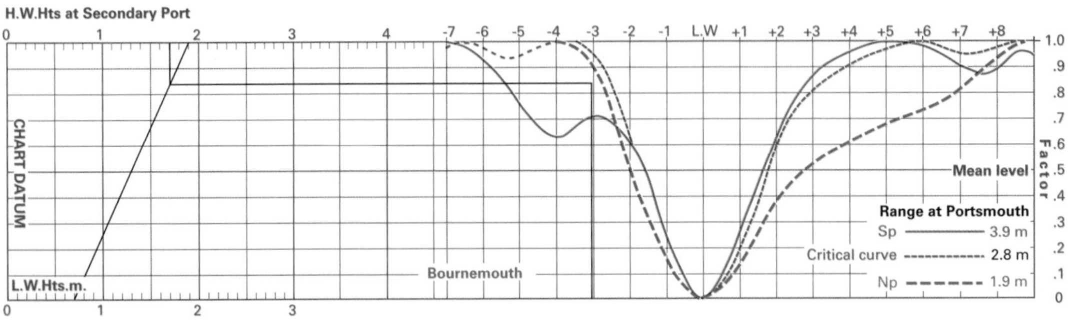

H.W.Hts at Secondary Port
0 1 2 3 4
-7 -6 -5 -4 -3 -2 -1 L.W +1 +2 +3 +4 +5 +6 +7 +8
1.0 .9 .8 .7 .6 .5 .4 .3 .2 .1 0
Factor
CHART DATUM
L.W.Hts.m.
Bournemouth
Mean level
Range at Portsmouth
Sp 3.9 m
Critical curve 2.8 m
Np 1.9 m

TIDAL CURVES: BOURNEMOUTH TO SELSEY BILL Individual tidal curves for places between Swanage and Selsey Bill are given below; their use is explained above. In this area the times of LW are much more sharply defined than the times of HW; the curves are therefore drawn with their times related to LW instead of HW. Apart from referencing the times to LW, the procedure for obtaining intermediate times and heights of tide is the same as for normal Secondary Ports (see 8.4.2). For places between Bournemouth and Yarmouth IOW a third curve is shown, for the range at Portsmouth at which the two HWs are equal at the port concerned; for interpolation between these curves see the previous page.

Note 1.* Due to the constriction of the R Medina, Newport requires special treatment since the hbr dries 1·4m. The calculation should be made using the LW time and height differences for Cowes, and the HW height differences for Newport. Any calculated heights which fall below 1·4m should be treated as 1·4m.

Note 2.*** Wareham and Tuckton LWs do not fall below 0·7m except under very low river flow conditions.

The Table (Intermediate heights of tide: Swanage to Nab Tower) at the end of this section offers a less accurate but quicker method of finding intermediate heights of tide for certain places between Swanage and Nab Tower. It is reproduced from earlier Admiralty Tide Tables.

Note 1. The green tinted area represents the period when the tide stands or in which a second HW may occur.
2. The upper of the three HW and LW height figures given is for mean spring tides, the middle for average tides and the lower for mean neap tides.

To use this table, determine whether the time required is nearer to HW or LW at Portsmouth; work out the interval (between time required and the nearest HW or LW at Portsmouth). Extract the height of the relevant predicted HW or LW. By interpolation between the heights of HW (left hand column) or LW (right hand column), read off the height of tide under the appropriate column (hours before/after HW or hours before/after LW).

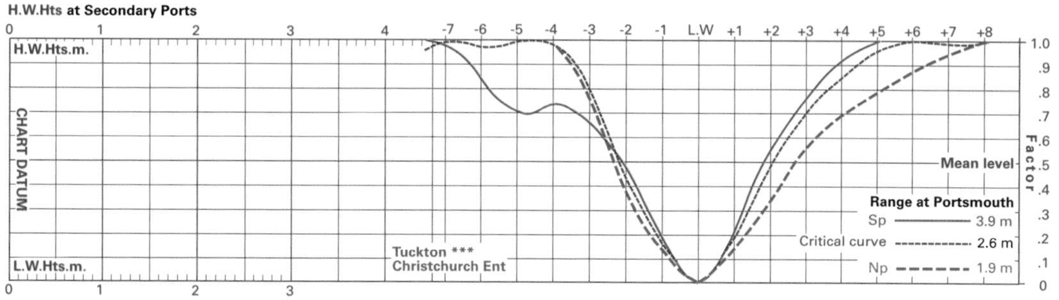
H.W.Hts at Secondary Ports
H.W.Hts.m.
CHART DATUM
L.W.Hts.m.
-7 -6 -5 -4 -3 -2 -1 L.W +1 +2 +3 +4 +5 +6 +7 +8
Factor
Mean level
Range at Portsmouth
Sp 3.9 m
Critical curve 2.6 m
Np 1.9 m
Tuckton ***
Christchurch Ent

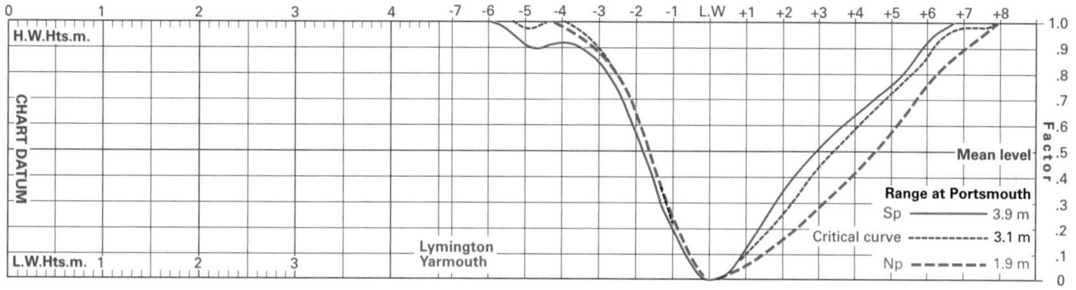
H.W.Hts.m.
CHART DATUM
L.W.Hts.m.
-7 -6 -5 -4 -3 -2 -1 L.W +1 +2 +3 +4 +5 +6 +7 +8
Factor
Mean level
Range at Portsmouth
Sp 3.9 m
Critical curve 3.1 m
Np 1.9 m
Lymington
Yarmouth

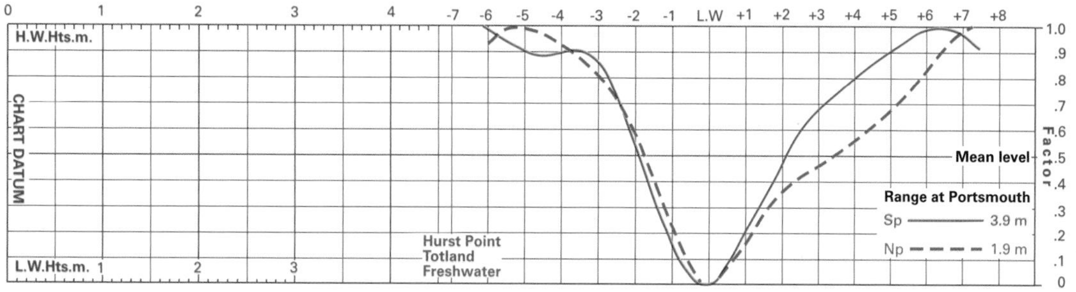
H.W.Hts.m.
CHART DATUM
L.W.Hts.m.
-7 -6 -5 -4 -3 -2 -1 L.W +1 +2 +3 +4 +5 +6 +7 +8
Factor
Mean level
Range at Portsmouth
Sp 3.9 m
Np 1.9 m
Hurst Point
Totland
Freshwater

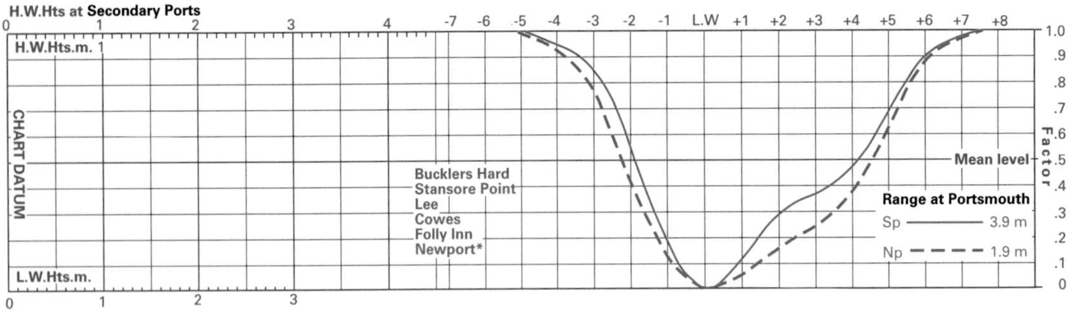
H.W.Hts at Secondary Ports
H.W.Hts.m.
CHART DATUM
L.W.Hts.m.
Bucklers Hard
Stansore Point
Lee
Cowes
Folly Inn
Newport*
L.W
Mean level
Factor
Range at Portsmouth
Sp 3.9 m
Np 1.9 m

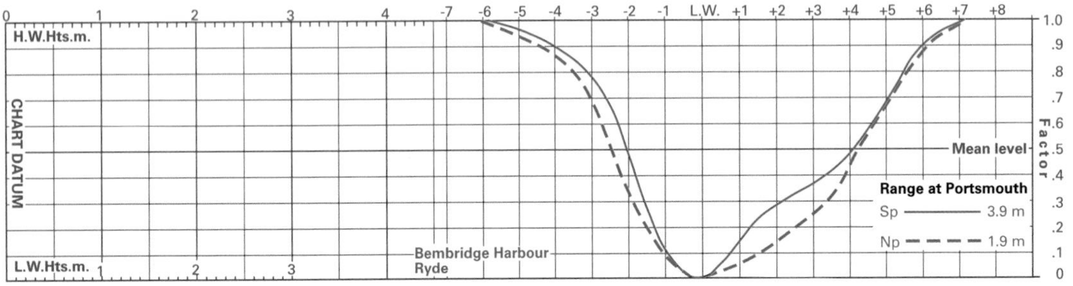
H.W.Hts.m.
CHART DATUM
L.W.Hts.m.
Bembridge Harbour
Ryde
L.W.
Mean level
Factor
Range at Portsmouth
Sp 3.9 m
Np 1.9 m

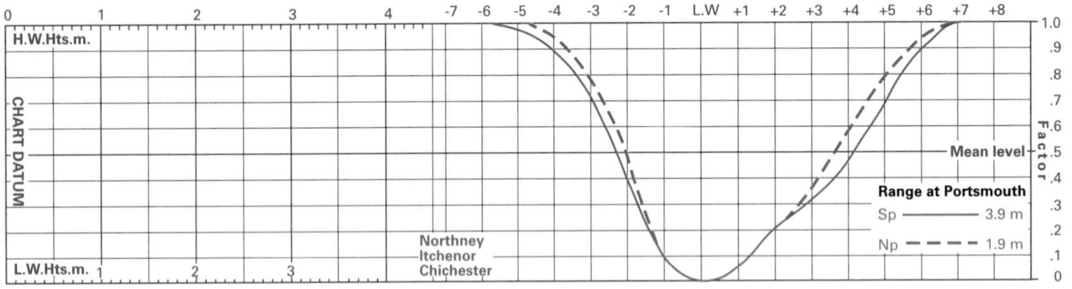
H.W.Hts.m.
CHART DATUM
L.W.Hts.m.
Northney
Itchenor
Chichester
L.W
Mean level
Factor
Range at Portsmouth
Sp 3.9 m
Np 1.9 m

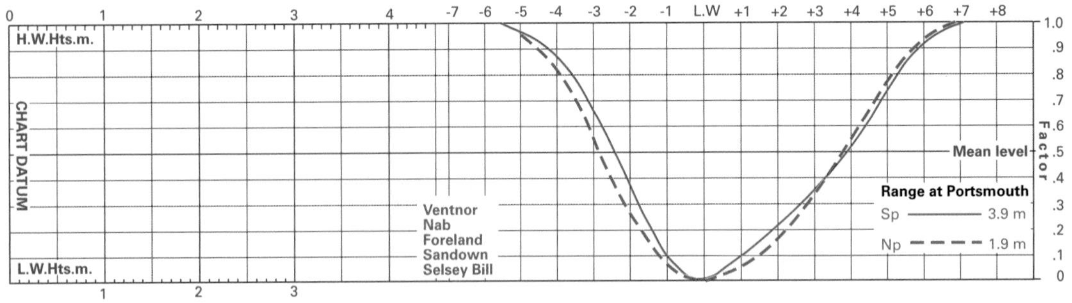
H.W.Hts.m.
CHART DATUM
L.W.Hts.m.
Ventnor
Nab
Foreland
Sandown
Selsey Bill
L.W
Mean level
Factor
Range at Portsmouth
Sp 3.9 m
Np 1.9 m

HEIGHTS OF TIDE AT POOLE (TOWN QUAY)

The four curves below are an alternative to those shown earlier in this section. They derive from Reeds Nautical Almanac where they found favour, but their accuracy (as with many things tidal) should be treated as approximate. They enable a speedy estimate to be made of the Height of Tide at hourly intervals after the time of the preceding LW at Poole (Town Quay). The curves are drawn for LW heights of 0·3, 0·6 (MLWS), 0·9 and 1·2 metres (MLWN) above Chart Datum. The small range of tide (neaps 0·4m; springs 1·5m) is immediately apparent, as are the HW stand at neaps and the double HWs at springs.

Note: All references are to LW because at Poole (and at other ports between Swanage and Selsey) the times and heights of LW are more sharply defined than those of HW. HW times & heights are complicated by a stand of tide at HW at neaps and by double HWs at springs. The times of 1st and 2nd HWs cannot therefore be readily predicted with any accuracy.

Procedure:

1. Extract time and height of the preceding LW from the Poole tidal predictions (⟶).
2. Using the tidal curve graph whose LW height is closest to the predicted height of LW, enter at the time required, ie corresponding to the appropriate number of hours after last LW.
3. Extract the estimated height of tide (above CD).

3a. For a more exact estimate, repeat the process using the next nearest curve, then interpolate.

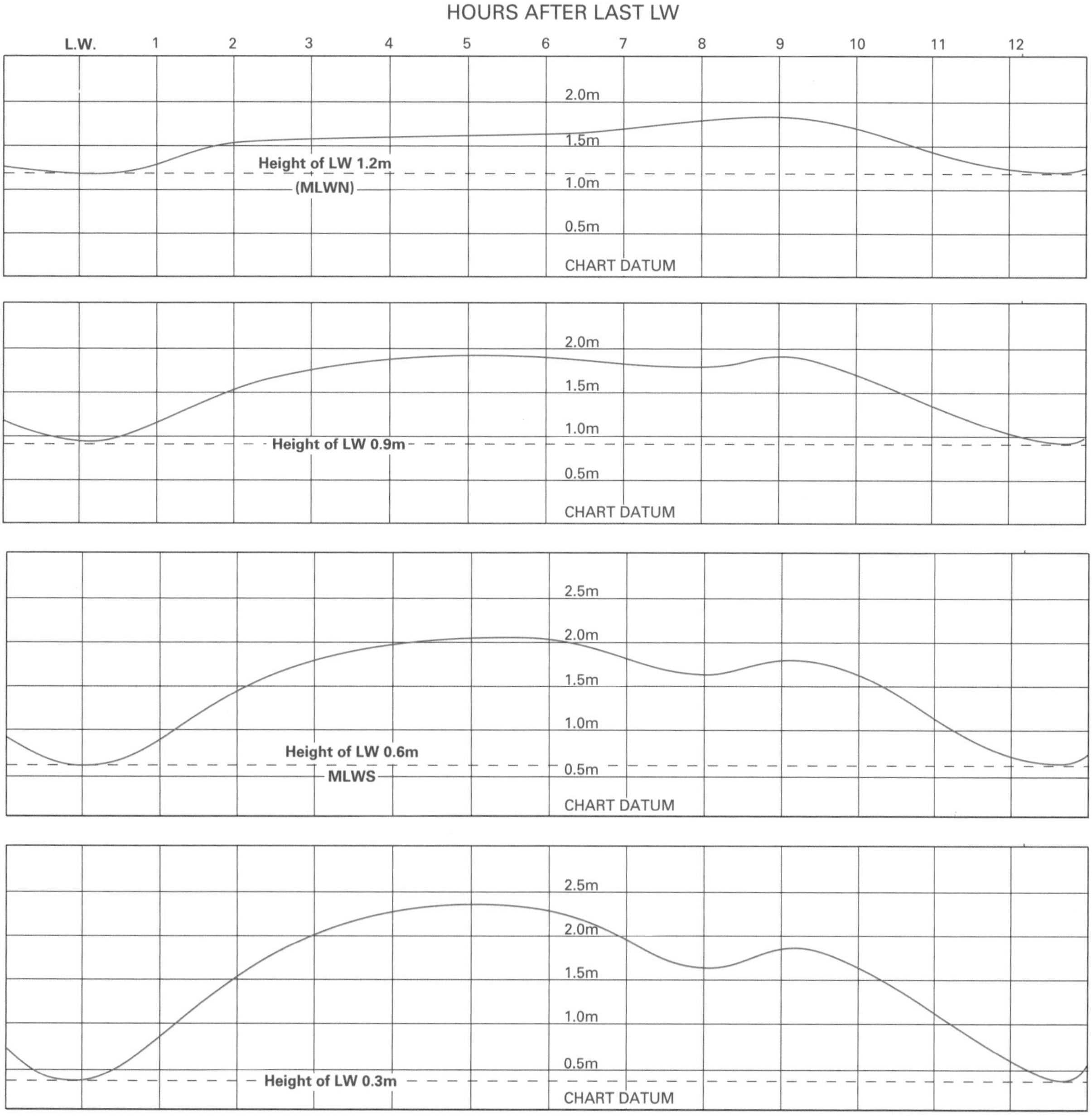
HOURS AFTER LAST LW
L.W.
1
2
3
4
5
6
7
8
9
10
11
12
2.0m
1.5m
Height of LW 1.2m
(MLWN)
1.0m
0.5m
CHART DATUM
2.0m
1.5m
1.0m
Height of LW 0.9m
0.5m
CHART DATUM
2.5m
2.0m
1.5m
1.0m
Height of LW 0.6m
MLWS
0.5m
CHART DATUM
2.5m
2.0m
1.5m
1.0m
0.5m
Height of LW 0.3m
CHART DATUM

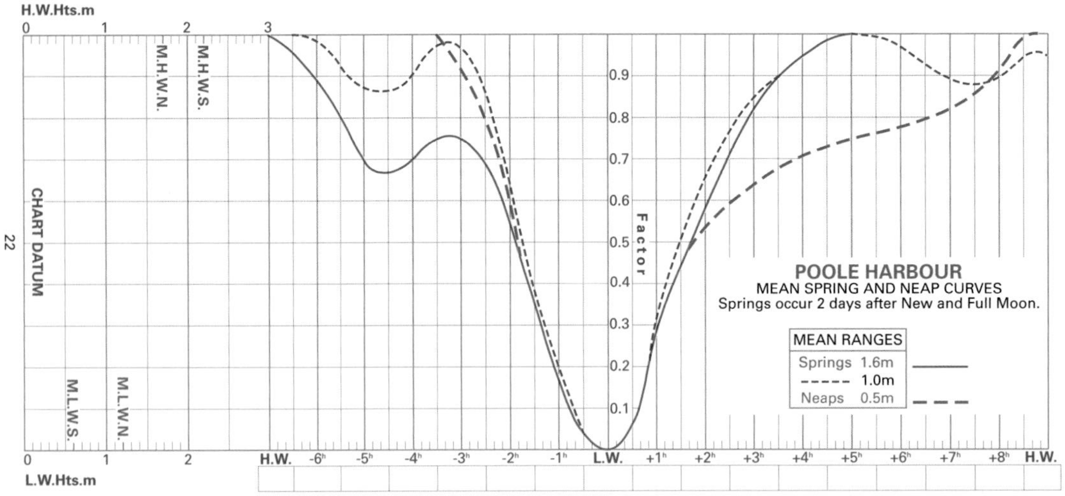
H.W.Hts.m
M.H.W.N.
M.H.W.S.
CHART DATUM
M.L.W.S.
M.L.W.N.
L.W.Hts.m
Factor
0.9
0.8
0.7
0.6
0.5
0.4
0.3
0.2
0.1
H.W. -6h -5h -4h -3h -2h -1h L.W. +1h +2h +3h +4h +5h +6h +7h +8h H.W.
POOLE HARBOUR
MEAN SPRING AND NEAP CURVES
Springs occur 2 days after New and Full Moon.
MEAN RANGES
Springs 1.6m
1.0m
Neaps 0.5m

9.2.8 POOLE HARBOUR

Dorset **50°40'·93N 01°56'·96W** (Ent) ❁❁❁◊◊◊✿✿✿

CHARTS AC *5601, 2175, 2611*; Imray C4, Y23; Stanfords 7, 12, 15; OS 195

TIDES Town Quay ML 1·6; Zone 0 (UT)

Daily predictions of the times and hts of LW (but only the hts of HW) are (⟶) for the Standard Port of **POOLE HARBOUR** (near the Ro-Ro terminal); sp and neap curves are above. (The tidal curves (⟵) simplify intermediate calculations.) Secondary Port differences are given below.

Standard Port POOLE HARBOUR (⟶)

Times				Height (metres)			
High Water		Low Water		MHWS	MHWN	MLWN	MLWS
–	–	0500	1100	2·2	1·7	1·2	0·6
–	–	1700	2300				
Differences POOLE HARBOUR ENTRANCE							
–	–	–0025	–0010	0·0	0·0	0·0	0·0
POTTERY PIER							
–	–	+0010	+0010	–0·2	0·0	+0·1	+0·2
CLEAVEL POINT							
–	–	–0005	–0005	–0·1	–0·2	0·0	–0·1
WAREHAM (River Frome)							
–	–	+0130	+0045	0·0	0·0	0·0	+0·3

Double HWs occur, except at nps. The ht of the 2nd HW is always about 1·8m; only the ht of the 1st HW varies from sp to nps. The tide is above Mean Level (1·6m) from about LW+2 to next LW–2. Strong and continuous winds from E to SW may raise sea levels by as much as 0·2m; W to NE winds may lower levels by 0·1m. Barometric pressure effects are as much as 0.3m, see Chapter 8.

SHELTER An excellent hbr with narrow ent; access in all conditions except very strong E/SE winds. Yachts can berth at Dolphin Boat Haven or Poole Quay and, on request, in marinas listed under Facilities. ⚓s wherever sheltered from the wind and clear of chans, moorings and shellfish beds; especially in South Deep, off W end of Brownsea Is and off Shipstal Point, all within a Quiet Area (see chartlet and speed limits).

NAVIGATION WPT Poole Bar (No 1 SHM) Buoy, QG, 50°39'·32N 01°55'·16W, 328° to Haven Hotel, 1·95M. In strong SE-S winds the Bar is dangerous especially on the ebb. In Studland Bay and close to training bank beware lobster pots. From Poole Bar to Shell Bay a recreational **Boat Chan**, suitable for craft < 3m draught, parallels the W side of the Swash Channel, close to the E of the Training Bank.

East Looe Chan (buoyed) is liable to shift and may have less water than charted; only 1m was reported 1ca ENE of East Looe PHM buoy. 5 groynes to the N are marked by SHM bns, the two most W'ly are lit, 2 FG (vert).

Within the hbr the two chans (Middle Ship and North) up to Poole Quay are clearly marked by lateral buoys, lit, with cardinal buoys at divisions. Outside the chans there are extensive shoal or drying areas. High Speed Ferries operate in the area.

Middle Ship Chan is dredged 6·0m for ferries to/from the Hamworthy terminal; it is mostly only 80m wide. Leisure craft should keep out of Middle Ship Chan, by using a **Boat Chan** which parallels S of the dredged chan between the PHM buoys and, further outboard, stakes with PHM topmarks marking the edge of the bank. Depth is 2·0m in this chan, but 1·5m closer to the stakes. Caution: When large ferries pass, a temporary, but significant reduction in depth may be remedied by closing the PHM buoys.

North Channel, the other option remains usable for yachts/leisure craft; best water is on the outside of chan bends.

Lulworth gunnery range (see 9.2.9). Yachtsmen cruising to the W should pre-check for activity, as shown in the HM's office and in the Supplements to this Almanac.

Regulations **A 6 knots** speed limit applies from Stakes SCM buoy, past Poole Quay and Poole Bridge up to Cobbs Quay in Holes Bay. It also applies within the S half of the hbr which is designated as a Quiet Area (see chartlet). A 4kn speed limit applies within the Dolphin Boat Haven.

A 10 knots speed limit applies to the rest of the hbr, from the seaward app chans (defined by an arc of radius 1400m centred on S Haven Pt, 50°40'·81N 01°56'·99W) westward to the junction of R Frome with R Trent at 02°04'·60W. Max speeding fine £1000.

Exemptions. The 10kn speed limit does not apply:

a. From 1 Oct to 31 Mar to vessels in the North, Middle Ship and Wareham Chans only.

b. to water-skiers within the water-ski area between Gold Pt and No 82 PHM buoy (Wareham Chan; see chartlet). Permits must be obtained from the HM.

c. to users of Personal Water Craft (PWC) operating in a designated area N of Brownsea Island. Note: PWCs must not enter the Quiet Area in the S of the hbr, nor linger in the hbr ent. Permits must be obtained from the HM.

Sandbanks Chain Ferry shows a B ● above the leading Control cabin when it is about to leave the slipway and to indicate the direction of travel. A Fl W lt (strobe rotating) is exhibited automatically above the leading Control cabin when the ferry starts moving. In fog it sounds 1 long and 2 short blasts every 2 mins. When stationary at night it shows a FW lt; in fog it rings a bell for 5 sec every minute. Although it does not enjoy right of way, it is sense not to impede it.

LIGHTS AND MARKS See chartlet and 9.2.4 for main buoys, beacons and lts.

Poole Bridge traffic lights, shown from bridge tr:

● = Do not approach bridge;

Fl● = Bridge lifting, proceed with caution; ● = Proceed.

Bridge lifts routinely for small craft at: Mon-Fri 0930, 1030, 1230, 1430, 1630, 1830, 2130; Sat, Sun & Bank hols = as Mon-Fri, plus 0730; at 2345 daily bridge will also lift if any vessels are waiting. Each lift only permits one cycle of traffic in each direction. Pleasure craft may pass when the bridge lifts on request for a

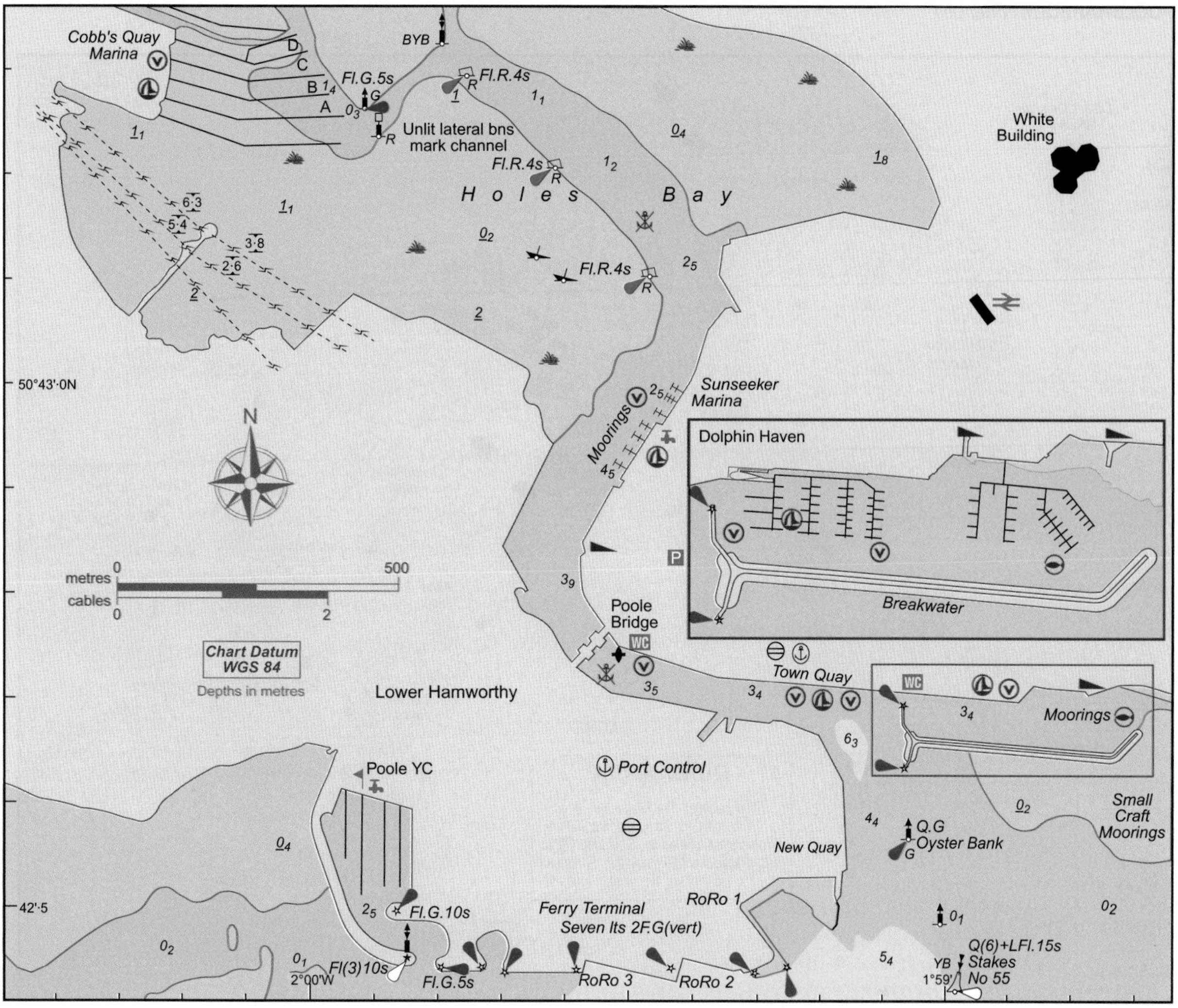
Cobb's Quay Marina
BYB
D
C
B 1_4
A 0_3
Fl.G.5s
G
Fl.R.4s
R
1
1_1
Unlit lateral bns mark channel
Fl.R.4s
R
0_4
1_2
1_8
White Building
Holes Bay
1_1
6·3
5·4
3·8
2·6
2
0_2
Fl.R.4s
R
2_5
2
50°43'·0N
N
Sunseeker Marina
2_5
Moorings
4_5
Dolphin Haven
Breakwater
metres 0 500
cables 0 2
3_9
Poole Bridge
Chart Datum WGS 84
Depths in metres
Lower Hamworthy
3_5
Town Quay
3_4
3_4
Moorings
6_3
Poole YC
Port Control
0_4
0_2
Small Craft Moorings
4_4
Q.G
Oyster Bank
G
New Quay
42'·5
2_5
Fl.G.10s
Ferry Terminal
Seven lts 2F.G(vert)
RoRo 1
0_1
0_2
0_2
0_1
Fl(3)10s
2°00'W
Fl.G.5s
RoRo 3
RoRo 2
5_4
Q(6)+LFl.15s
YB
Stakes
1°59'
No 55

commercial vessel; monitor Ch 14. Bridge will not usually lift during weekday road traffic Rush Hours 0730-0930 and 1630-1830.

R/T Call: *Poole Hbr Control* VHF Ch 14 16 (H24). Dolphin Boat Haven Ch 80; Salterns Marina Ch M 80; Parkstone Haven Ch M; Poole YC Haven, call *Pike* Ch M; Dorset Yacht Co Ch 37, M1; Poole Bridge, call *PB* Ch 14. Cobbs Quay, call *CQ Base* Ch 80.

TELEPHONE (Dial code 01202) HM 440233, 📠 440231, Hr Control 440230; Dolphin Boat Haven 649488; Bridge 674115; MRSC (01305) 760439; Met (02392) 228844; Marinecall 09066 526241; Police 552099; Ⓗ 665511.

FACILITIES The following are some of the many facilities:

Marinas (from seaward)
Salterns Marina (300, few Ⓥ) ☎ 709971, 📠 700398, ≤10m £30, max draft 2·5m, P & D (H24), ME, El, Ⓔ, ⚒, CH, Gas, Gaz, C (5 ton), BH (45 T), Bar, R, ⊡. Appr from No 31 SHM buoy Fl G5s.
Parkstone Haven, (Parkstone YC ☎ 743610), some Ⓥ berths, £16; dredged 2m. Access from North Chan near No 35 SHM buoy, Fl G 5s. Appr chan, dredged 2·5m, is marked by SHM buoy (Fl G 3s), 2 PHM and 3 SHM unlit buoys. Ldg daymarks 006°, both Y ◊s; ldg lts, front Iso Y 4s, rear FY. 2 FG and 2FR (vert) on bkwtr hds.
Poole Quay-Dolphin Boat Haven (100 Ⓥ) ☎/📠 649488, max draft 3.0m, £2.58, (£1.70 Town Quay, limited space), Haven Office open 0700-2200 Apr-Sep.
Dorset Yacht Co (56 AB +Ⓥ if space; 90M and ⛽) ☎ 674531, 📠 677518, £3.20 and £1.30, C (5 ton), BH (50 ton), Club bar/food; ent marked by 2FR (vert) and two 2FG (vert). Water taxi, weekends 1/4 to 1/10.

Beyond Poole Bridge:
Sunseeker International Marina (50) ☎ 685335, ⚒, D, BH (30 ton), C (36 ton), FW, ME, El, CH, 🛒, R, Bar.
Cobbs Quay Marina (850, some visitors) ☎ 674299, 📠 665217, £2.70, Slip, P, D, Gas, LPG, ⊡, SM, ME, El, Ⓔ, ⚒, C (10 ton), CH, R, Bar.
Public Landing Places: On Poole Quay. **Fuel** Poole Bay Fuel barge (May-Sep 0900-1800; moored near Aunt Betty buoy, No 50) P, D, Gas, Gaz, 🛒, Off licence. **Corrals** (S side of Poole Quay adjacent bridge) D; **Salterns marina** D. **Yacht Clubs: Royal Motor YC** ☎ 707227, M, Bar, R; **Poole Bay YC; Parkstone YC** ☎ 743610 (Parkstone Haven); **Poole YC** ☎ 672687. **Services** A complete range of marine services is available; consult marina/HM for exact locations. **Town** EC Wed; ✉, Ⓑ, ⇌, ✈. Ferries to Cherbourg, St Malo (seasonal) and Channel Islands (seasonal).

WAREHAM, Dorset, **50°41´·03N 02°06´·56W**. AC *2611*. HW –0030 (Np), +0320 (Sp) on Dover (see 9.2.11 & .12). Shelter very good. Access approx HW±2, via narrow and winding chan and R Frome, but well marked by lit buoys and posts lit to N of Giggers Is; keep to the outside of all bends. Passage is unlit beyond 2°04'·60W. There is a water-ski area between this buoy and Gold Pt on the N side of the Arne peninsula. Beware prohib ⚓s (salmon holes) marked on the chart. Max draft 1·2m to Wareham Quay. 4kn speed limit in river.
Facilities: **Ridge Wharf Yacht Centre** (180+6 visitors) (½M upstream of R Frome ent) ☎ (01929) 552650, £15.50, Access HW±2 approx AB, M, FW, P, D, ME, El, Gas, BH (18 ton), Slip, ⚒, CH; **Redclyffe YC** ☎ 551227 (½M below bridge); **Wareham Quay** AB, FW, R. **Town** EC Wed, P & D (cans), 🛒, Gas, R, Bar, ✉, Ⓑ, ⇌.

POOLE HARBOUR *continued*

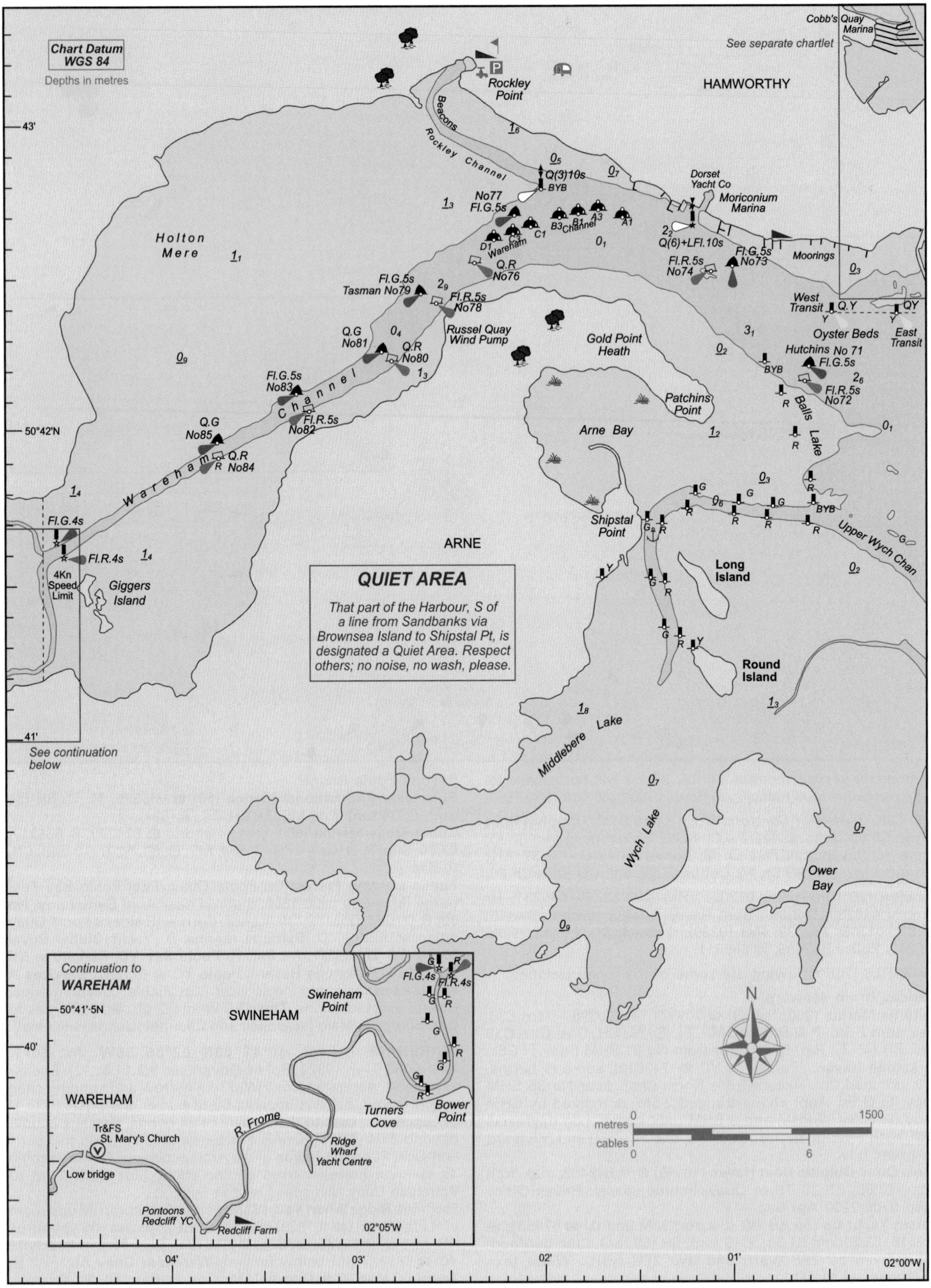
Chart Datum WGS 84
Depths in metres
Rockley Point
HAMWORTHY
Cobb's Quay Marina
See separate chartlet
Beacons
Rockley Channel
Q(3)10s BYB
Dorset Yacht Co
Moriconium Marina
No77 Fl.G.5s
Wareham Channel
Holton Mere
Q(6)+LFl.10s
Fl.G.5s No73
Moorings
Fl.R.5s No74
Q.R No76
Fl.G.5s Tasman No79
Fl.R.5s No78
West Transit
Q.Y
QY
East Transit
Oyster Beds
Russel Quay Wind Pump
Gold Point Heath
Hutchins No 71 Fl.G.5s
Fl.R.5s No72
Q.G No81
Q.R No80
Fl.G.5s No83
Fl.R.5s No82
Patchins Point
Arne Bay
Balls Lake
50°42'N
Q.G No85
Q.R No84
Shipstal Point
Upper Wych Chan
ARNE
Fl.G.4s
Fl.R.4s
4Kn Speed Limit
Giggers Island
Long Island
QUIET AREA
That part of the Harbour, S of a line from Sandbanks via Brownsea Island to Shipstal Pt, is designated a Quiet Area. Respect others; no noise, no wash, please.
Round Island
Middlebere Lake
See continuation below
Wych Lake
Ower Bay
Continuation to WAREHAM
50°41'·5N
SWINEHAM
Swineham Point
WAREHAM
Tr&FS St. Mary's Church
Low bridge
R. Frome
Ridge Wharf Yacht Centre
Turners Cove
Bower Point
Pontoons Redcliff YC
Redcliff Farm
02°05'W
metres 0 1500
cables 0 6
43'
41'
40'
04'
03'
02'
01'
02°00'W

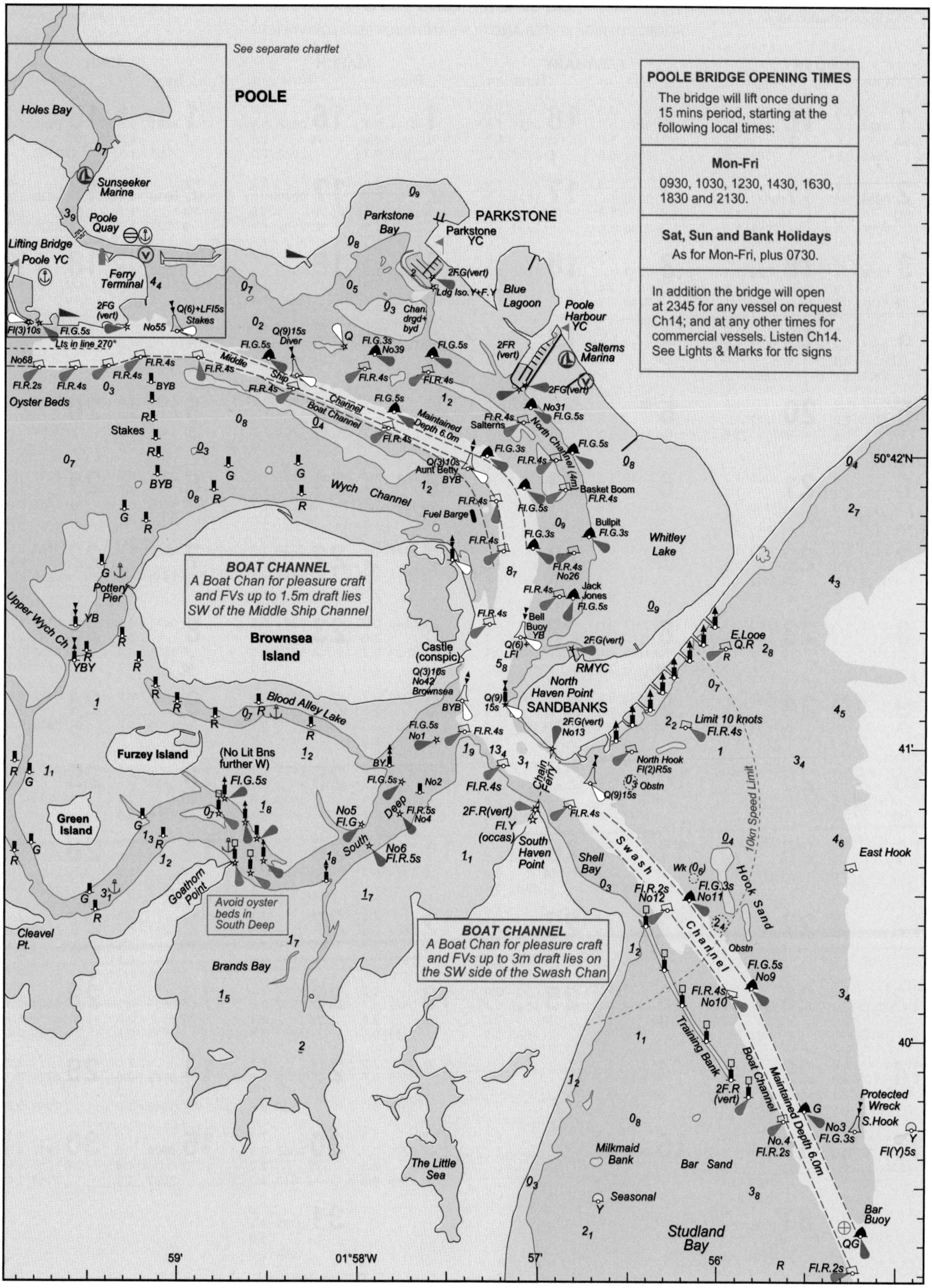
See separate chartlet
POOLE
Holes Bay
Sunseeker Marina
Poole Quay
Lifting Bridge
Poole YC
Ferry Terminal
2FG (vert)
Q(6)+LFl5s
Stakes
No55
Fl(3)10s
Fl.G.5s
Lts in line 270°
POOLE BRIDGE OPENING TIMES
The bridge will lift once during a 15 mins period, starting at the following local times:
Mon-Fri
0930, 1030, 1230, 1430, 1630, 1830 and 2130.
Sat, Sun and Bank Holidays
As for Mon-Fri, plus 0730.
In addition the bridge will open at 2345 for any vessel on request Ch14; and at any other times for commercial vessels. Listen Ch14. See Lights & Marks for tfc signs
Parkstone Bay
PARKSTONE
Parkstone YC
2F.G(vert)
Ldg Iso.Y+F.Y
Blue Lagoon
Poole Harbour YC
Salterns Marina
Chan. drgd+ byd
Q(9)15s Diver
Q
Fl.G.3s No39
Fl.G.5s
2FR (vert)
No68
Fl.R.4s
Fl.R.2s
Oyster Beds
BYB
Stakes
Middle Ship Channel
Boat Channel
Maintained Depth 6.0m
Salterns
North Channel (4m)
No31
2FG(vert)
Fl.G.3s
Q(3)10s Aunt Betty
Wych Channel
Fuel Barge
Basket Boom
Bullpit
Whitley Lake
No26
Jack Jones
Bell Buoy
Q(6)+ LFl
BOAT CHANNEL
A Boat Chan for pleasure craft and FVs up to 1.5m draft lies SW of the Middle Ship Channel
Pottery Pier
Upper Wych Ch
YB
YBY
Brownsea Island
Castle (conspic)
Q(3)10s No42 Brownsea
Q(9) 15s
North Haven Point
SANDBANKS
RMYC
2F.G(vert) No13
E.Looe Q.R
Blood Alley Lake
Furzey Island
(No Lit Bns further W)
Fl.G.5s No1
Fl.G.5s
No2
Limit 10 knots
North Hook Fl(2)R5s
Obstn
Q(9)15s
Chain Ferry
10kn Speed Limit
Green Island
No5 Fl.G
South Deep
Fl.R.5s No4
2F.R(vert)
Fl.Y (occas)
South Haven Point
Shell Bay
Swash Channel
Hook Sand
East Hook
Goathorn Point
Avoid oyster beds in South Deep
No6 Fl.R.5s
Wk
No11
No12
Cleavel Pt.
Brands Bay
BOAT CHANNEL
A Boat Chan for pleasure craft and FVs up to 3m draft lies on the SW side of the Swash Chan
Fl.G.5s No9
Fl.R.4s No10
Training Bank
Boat Channel
Maintained Depth 6.0m
2F.R (vert)
Protected Wreck
S.Hook
Fl(Y)5s
No3 Fl.G.3s
No.4 Fl.R.2s
The Little Sea
Milkmaid Bank
Bar Sand
Seasonal
Studland Bay
Bar Buoy
QG
Fl.R.2s
50°42'N
41'
40'
59'
01°58'W
57'
56'

Note - HW times are not shown because they cannot be predicted with reasonable accuracy. Approximate times can be gained using LW times and the Tidal Curves at the start of this section.

TIME ZONE (UT)
For Summer Time add ONE hour in **non-shaded areas**

ENGLAND – POOLE HARBOUR

LAT 50°42′N LONG 1°59′W

HEIGHTS OF HIGH WATER AND TIMES AND HEIGHTS OF LOW WATERS

SPRING & NEAP TIDES
Dates in red are **SPRINGS**
Dates in blue are **NEAPS**

YEAR **2005**

JANUARY

Date	Day	Time	m	Time	m	Time	m	Time	m
1	SA		2.0	0728	1.0		1.9	1948	0.9
2	SU		1.9	0809	1.1		1.9	2030	1.0
3	M		1.9	0858	1.2		1.8	◑ 2121	1.0
4	TU		1.9	0956	1.2		1.8	2221	1.1
5	W		1.9	1103	1.2		1.8	2329	1.1
6	TH		1.9	1215	1.2		1.8		
7	F	0040	1.0		2.0	1324	1.0		1.9
8	SA	0148	1.0		2.1	1426	0.9		2.0
9	SU	0248	0.9		2.2	1523	0.7		2.1
10	M	0344	0.8		2.3	1617	0.6	●	2.3
11	TU	0437	0.7		2.3	1708	0.6		
12	W		2.3	0528	0.7		2.3	1757	0.5
13	TH		2.3	0617	0.7		2.3	1845	0.5
14	F		2.3	0705	0.7		2.1	1931	0.6
15	SA		2.2	0753	0.7		2.1	2017	0.7
16	SU		2.1	0841	0.8		2.0	2103	0.8
17	M		2.0	0932	1.0		1.9	◐ 2152	0.9
18	TU		1.9	1029	1.1		1.8	2248	1.1
19	W		1.8	1135	1.2		1.6	2356	1.2
20	TH		1.8	1247	1.2		1.6		
21	F	0108	1.2		1.8	1350	1.2		1.7
22	SA	0209	1.2		1.9	1442	1.0		1.8
23	SU	0300	1.1		1.9	1527	0.9		1.9
24	M	0343	1.0		2.0	1607	0.9		2.0
25	TU	0422	0.9		2.0	1644	0.8	○	2.0
26	W	0459	0.8		2.0	1720	0.7		
27	TH		2.0	0533	0.8		2.0	1753	0.7
28	F		2.0	0605	0.8		2.0	1823	0.7
29	SA		2.0	0635	0.8		2.0	1852	0.7
30	SU		2.0	0706	0.8		2.0	1924	0.7
31	M		2.0	0740	0.9		1.9	2000	0.8

FEBRUARY

Date	Day	Time	m	Time	m	Time	m	Time	m
1	TU		2.0	0821	0.9		1.9	2042	0.9
2	W		1.9	0910	1.0		1.8	◑ 2136	1.0
3	TH		1.9	1013	1.2		1.8	2246	1.2
4	F		1.8	1137	1.2		1.7		
5	SA	0014	1.2		1.8	1309	1.1		1.8
6	SU	0140	1.1		1.9	1422	0.9		2.0
7	M	0247	0.9		2.1	1521	0.7		2.1
8	TU	0343	0.8		2.2	1613	0.6	●	2.2
9	W	0433	0.6		2.3	1701	0.4		
10	TH		2.3	0520	0.6		2.3	1746	0.4
11	F		2.3	0604	0.5		2.3	1829	0.4
12	SA		2.3	0647	0.5		2.2	1909	0.4
13	SU		2.3	0727	0.6		2.1	1946	0.6
14	M		2.1	0805	0.7		2.0	2023	0.8
15	TU		2.0	0845	0.9		1.9	2103	0.9
16	W		1.9	0931	1.0		1.7	◐ 2152	1.2
17	TH		1.8	1034	1.2		1.6	2304	1.3
18	F		1.6	1202	1.3		1.5		
19	SA	0036	1.4		1.6	1324	1.3		1.6
20	SU	0152	1.3		1.7	1423	1.1		1.8
21	M	0246	1.1		1.8	1508	1.0		1.9
22	TU	0328	1.0		1.9	1547	0.8		2.0
23	W	0405	0.8		2.0	1624	0.7		2.0
24	TH	0441	0.8		2.0	1659	0.7	○	2.1
25	F	0514	0.7		2.0	1732	0.6		
26	SA		2.1	0544	0.7		2.0	1801	0.6
27	SU		2.1	0612	0.7		2.0	1829	0.6
28	M		2.1	0642	0.7		2.0	1859	0.7

MARCH

Date	Day	Time	m	Time	m	Time	m	Time	m
1	TU		2.1	0714	0.7		2.0	1933	0.7
2	W		2.0	0752	0.8		1.9	2014	0.9
3	TH		1.9	0838	0.9		1.8	◑ 2106	1.0
4	F		1.8	0941	1.1		1.7	2222	1.2
5	SA		1.7	1119	1.2		1.7		
6	SU	0011	1.3		1.7	1307	1.1		1.8
7	M	0142	1.1		1.9	1419	0.9		2.0
8	TU	0245	0.9		2.0	1513	0.7		2.1
9	W	0336	0.7		2.1	1601	0.5		2.3
10	TH	0422	0.6		2.2	1645	0.4	●	2.3
11	F	0504	0.4		2.3	1726	0.4		
12	SA		2.3	0544	0.4		2.3	1805	0.4
13	SU		2.3	0622	0.4		2.2	1840	0.4
14	M		2.3	0656	0.6		2.1	1913	0.6
15	TU		2.1	0729	0.7		2.0	1945	0.8
16	W		2.0	0802	0.8		1.9	2020	1.0
17	TH		1.9	0840	1.0		1.8	◐ 2105	1.2
18	F		1.7	0935	1.2		1.6	2219	1.4
19	SA		1.5	1115	1.4		1.5		
20	SU	0007	1.4		1.5	1253	1.3		1.6
21	M	0131	1.3		1.6	1356	1.2		1.8
22	TU	0224	1.2		1.8	1440	1.0		1.9
23	W	0304	0.9		1.9	1519	0.8		2.0
24	TH	0340	0.8		1.9	1555	0.7		2.0
25	F	0414	0.7		2.0	1630	0.6	○	2.1
26	SA	0446	0.6		2.0	1702	0.6		
27	SU		2.1	0516	0.6		2.1	1733	0.6
28	M		2.1	0547	0.6		2.1	1803	0.6
29	TU		2.1	0618	0.6		2.1	1836	0.6
30	W		2.1	0653	0.6		2.0	1913	0.7
31	TH		2.0	0732	0.7		2.0	1956	0.9

APRIL

Date	Day	Time	m	Time	m	Time	m	Time	m
1	F		1.9	0821	0.9		1.8	2054	1.1
2	SA		1.8	0930	1.1		1.7	◑ 2221	1.2
3	SU		1.6	1117	1.2		1.7		
4	M	0010	1.2		1.7	1257	1.0		1.8
5	TU	0133	1.0		1.8	1403	0.9		2.0
6	W	0231	0.8		2.0	1455	0.7		2.1
7	TH	0318	0.7		2.1	1539	0.5		2.3
8	F	0401	0.5		2.2	1621	0.4	●	2.3
9	SA	0441	0.4		2.2	1700	0.4		
10	SU		2.3	0519	0.4		2.2	1736	0.4
11	M		2.3	0554	0.5		2.2	1809	0.6
12	TU		2.2	0627	0.6		2.1	1841	0.7
13	W		2.1	0657	0.7		2.0	1913	0.8
14	TH		2.0	0729	0.8		1.9	1948	1.0
15	F		1.9	0806	1.0		1.8	2033	1.2
16	SA		1.7	0856	1.2		1.6	◐ 2142	1.4
17	SU		1.6	1025	1.3		1.6	2326	1.4
18	M		1.5	1206	1.3		1.6		
19	TU	0050	1.3		1.6	1314	1.2		1.8
20	W	0145	1.2		1.7	1401	1.0		1.9
21	TH	0227	1.0		1.8	1441	0.8		2.0
22	F	0303	0.8		1.9	1517	0.7		2.0
23	SA	0338	0.7		2.0	1553	0.7		2.1
24	SU	0412	0.6		2.0	1628	0.6	○	2.1
25	M	0446	0.6		2.1	1703	0.6		
26	TU		2.2	0521	0.6		2.1	1739	0.6
27	W		2.2	0559	0.6		2.1	1819	0.7
28	TH		2.1	0640	0.6		2.1	1902	0.8
29	F		2.0	0726	0.7		2.0	1953	0.9
30	SA		1.9	0822	0.9		1.9	2058	1.0

Chart Datum: 1·40 metres below Ordnance Datum (Newlyn)

Note - HW times are not shown because they cannot be predicted with reasonable accuracy. Approximate times can be gained using LW times and the Tidal Curves at the start of this section.

TIME ZONE (UT)
For Summer Time add ONE hour in **non-shaded areas**

ENGLAND – POOLE HARBOUR

LAT 50°42′N LONG 1°59′W

HEIGHTS OF HIGH WATER AND TIMES AND HEIGHTS OF LOW WATERS

SPRING & NEAP TIDES
Dates in red are SPRINGS
Dates in blue are NEAPS

YEAR **2005**

MAY

Date	Day	Time m
1	SU	1.8; 0936 1.0; 1.8; ◑ 2221 1.2
2	M	1.7; 1106 1.0; 1.8; 2350 1.1
3	TU	1.8; 1230 1.0; 1.9
4	W	0105 1.0; 1.9; 1334 0.8; 2.0
5	TH	0203 0.8; 2.0; 1426 0.7; 2.1
6	F	0251 0.7; 2.0; 1510 0.6; 2.2
7	SA	0334 0.6; 2.1; 1552 0.6; 2.2
8	SU	0415 0.6; 2.1; 1631 0.6; ● 2.2
9	M	0453 0.6; 2.1; 1708 0.6
10	TU	2.2; 0528 0.6; 2.1; 1742 0.7
11	W	2.1; 0602 0.7; 2.1; 1816 0.8
12	TH	2.1; 0634 0.8; 2.0; 1850 0.9
13	F	2.0; 0707 0.9; 1.9; 1926 1.0
14	SA	1.9; 0744 1.0; 1.8; 2010 1.2
15	SU	1.8; 0831 1.1; 1.8; 2107 1.3
16	M	1.6; 0936 1.2; 1.7; ◐ 2225 1.4
17	TU	1.6; 1058 1.3; 1.7; 2346 1.3
18	W	1.6; 1210 1.2; 1.8
19	TH	0048 1.2; 1.6; 1305 1.0; 1.9
20	F	0136 1.0; 1.8; 1350 0.9; 2.0
21	SA	0217 0.9; 1.9; 1432 0.8; 2.0
22	SU	0257 0.8; 2.0; 1512 0.7; 2.1
23	M	0337 0.7; 2.1; 1554 0.7; ○ 2.1
24	TU	0418 0.6; 2.1; 1637 0.7; 2.2
25	W	0502 0.6; 2.1; 1722 0.7
26	TH	2.2; 0547 0.6; 2.2; 1809 0.7
27	F	2.1; 0636 0.6; 2.1; 1900 0.7
28	SA	2.1; 0728 0.7; 2.1; 1955 0.8
29	SU	2.0; 0826 0.8; 2.0; 2056 0.9
30	M	1.9; 0930 0.9; 2.0; ◑ 2204 1.0
31	TU	1.8; 1039 0.9; 1.9; 2316 1.0

JUNE

Date	Day	Time m
1	W	1.8; 1149 0.9; 2.0
2	TH	0026 1.0; 1.8; 1254 0.9; 2.0
3	F	0127 0.9; 1.9; 1350 0.8; 2.0
4	SA	0219 0.8; 1.9; 1438 0.8; 2.1
5	SU	0306 0.8; 2.0; 1523 0.8; 2.1
6	M	0349 0.7; 2.0; 1605 0.8; ● 2.1
7	TU	0429 0.7; 2.0; 1644 0.8; 2.1
8	W	0507 0.7; 2.0; 1721 0.8
9	TH	2.1; 0543 0.7; 2.0; 1757 0.8
10	F	2.0; 0617 0.8; 2.0; 1833 0.9
11	SA	2.0; 0651 0.9; 2.0; 1909 1.0
12	SU	1.9; 0727 0.9; 1.9; 1948 1.1
13	M	1.8; 0806 1.0; 1.9; 2032 1.2
14	TU	1.8; 0852 1.0; 1.8; 2125 1.2
15	W	1.7; 0947 1.1; 1.8; ◐ 2225 1.2
16	TH	1.7; 1049 1.1; 1.8; 2330 1.2
17	F	1.7; 1152 1.1; 1.9
18	SA	0032 1.1; 1.8; 1252 1.0; 1.9
19	SU	0128 1.0; 1.9; 1347 0.9; 2.0
20	M	0220 0.9; 2.0; 1439 0.8; 2.1
21	TU	0310 0.7; 2.0; 1531 0.8; 2.1
22	W	0401 0.7; 2.1; 1622 0.7; ○ 2.2
23	TH	0451 0.6; 2.2; 1714 0.7
24	F	2.2; 0542 0.6; 2.2; 1805 0.7
25	SA	2.2; 0633 0.6; 2.2; 1856 0.7
26	SU	2.1; 0724 0.6; 2.2; 1948 0.7
27	M	2.1; 0816 0.6; 2.1; 2042 0.8
28	TU	2.0; 0910 0.7; 2.1; ◑ 2138 0.9
29	W	1.9; 1006 0.8; 2.0; 2238 0.9
30	TH	1.8; 1105 0.9; 1.9; 2342 1.0

JULY

Date	Day	Time m
1	F	1.8; 1208 1.0; 1.9
2	SA	0048 1.0; 1.8; 1312 1.0; 1.9
3	SU	0149 1.0; 1.8; 1409 1.0; 1.9
4	M	0242 0.9; 1.9; 1500 1.0; 2.0
5	TU	0328 0.9; 1.9; 1545 0.9; 2.0
6	W	0411 0.8; 2.0; 1626 0.9; ● 2.0
7	TH	0450 0.8; 2.0; 1705 0.9; 2.0
8	F	0527 0.8; 2.0; 1742 0.9
9	SA	2.0; 0602 0.8; 2.0; 1817 0.9
10	SU	2.0; 0634 0.8; 2.0; 1850 0.9
11	M	1.9; 0706 0.8; 2.0; 1923 0.9
12	TU	1.9; 0738 0.9; 1.9; 1958 1.0
13	W	1.9; 0814 0.9; 1.9; 2039 1.0
14	TH	1.8; 0857 1.0; 1.9; ◐ 2127 1.1
15	F	1.8; 0949 1.0; 1.8; 2226 1.2
16	SA	1.8; 1052 1.1; 1.8; 2336 1.2
17	SU	1.8; 1204 1.1; 1.9
18	M	0050 1.0; 1.8; 1318 1.0; 1.9
19	TU	0159 0.9; 1.9; 1423 0.9; 2.0
20	W	0258 0.8; 2.0; 1521 0.8; 2.1
21	TH	0353 0.7; 2.1; 1615 0.7; ○ 2.2
22	F	0445 0.6; 2.3; 1707 0.6
23	SA	2.2; 0535 0.4; 2.3; 1756 0.6
24	SU	2.2; 0623 0.4; 2.3; 1844 0.6
25	M	2.2; 0710 0.4; 2.3; 1931 0.6
26	TU	2.1; 0755 0.6; 2.2; 2017 0.7
27	W	2.0; 0840 0.7; 2.1; 2105 0.8
28	TH	1.9; 0927 0.8; 2.0; ◑ 2157 0.9
29	F	1.8; 1020 1.0; 1.9; 2258 1.1
30	SA	1.7; 1124 1.2; 1.8
31	SU	0010 1.2; 1.6; 1239 1.2; 1.8

AUGUST

Date	Day	Time m
1	M	0124 1.2; 1.7; 1348 1.2; 1.8
2	TU	0224 1.0; 1.8; 1444 1.1; 1.9
3	W	0312 0.9; 1.9; 1530 1.0; 1.9
4	TH	0353 0.8; 2.0; 1611 0.9; 2.0
5	F	0432 0.8; 2.0; 1648 0.8; ● 2.0
6	SA	0508 0.7; 2.0; 1724 0.8
7	SU	2.0; 0541 0.7; 2.0; 1756 0.8
8	M	2.0; 0612 0.7; 2.0; 1826 0.8
9	TU	2.0; 0640 0.7; 2.0; 1854 0.8
10	W	2.0; 0708 0.8; 2.0; 1925 0.8
11	TH	1.9; 0739 0.8; 2.0; 2001 0.9
12	F	1.9; 0817 0.9; 1.9; 2044 1.0
13	SA	1.8; 0905 1.0; 1.9; ◐ 2140 1.1
14	SU	1.8; 1009 1.2; 1.8; 2257 1.2
15	M	1.7; 1137 1.3; 1.8
16	TU	0034 1.2; 1.8; 1310 1.2; 1.9
17	W	0154 1.0; 1.9; 1420 1.0; 2.0
18	TH	0254 0.8; 2.1; 1517 0.8; 2.1
19	F	0346 0.6; 2.2; 1608 0.7; ○ 2.2
20	SA	0435 0.4; 2.3; 1655 0.6; 2.3
21	SU	0521 0.4; 2.4; 1741 0.5
22	M	2.3; 0604 0.4; 2.4; 1824 0.5
23	TU	2.3; 0646 0.4; 2.3; 1905 0.6
24	W	2.2; 0726 0.6; 2.2; 1946 0.7
25	TH	2.1; 0804 0.7; 2.1; 2026 0.8
26	F	1.9; 0845 0.9; 2.0; ◑ 2111 1.0
27	SA	1.8; 0934 1.1; 1.8; 2211 1.2
28	SU	1.6; 1043 1.3; 1.6; 2335 1.3
29	M	1.6; 1214 1.4; 1.6
30	TU	0104 1.3; 1.7; 1334 1.3; 1.7
31	W	0208 1.2; 1.8; 1430 1.2; 1.9

Chart Datum: 1·40 metres below Ordnance Datum (Newlyn)

Note - HW times are not shown because they cannot be predicted with reasonable accuracy. Approximate times can be gained using LW times and the Tidal Curves at the start of this section.

TIME ZONE (UT)
For Summer Time add ONE hour in **non-shaded areas**

ENGLAND – POOLE HARBOUR

LAT 50°42′N LONG 1°59′W

HEIGHTS OF HIGH WATER AND TIMES AND HEIGHTS OF LOW WATERS

SPRING & NEAP TIDES
Dates in red are SPRINGS
Dates in blue are NEAPS

YEAR **2005**

SEPTEMBER

Date	Day	Time	m	Time	m	Time	m	Time	m
1	TH	0254	1.0		1.9	1513	1.0		1.9
2	F	0332	0.8		2.0	1550	0.9		2.0
3	SA ●	0408	0.7		2.1	1625	0.8		2.0
4	SU	0443	0.7		2.1	1659	0.7		2.0
5	M	0516	0.6		2.1	1730	0.7		
6	TU		2.0	0544	0.6		2.1	1757	0.7
7	W		2.0	0611	0.7		2.1	1824	0.7
8	TH		2.0	0638	0.7		2.1	1854	0.8
9	F		2.0	0708	0.8		2.0	1928	0.9
10	SA		1.9	0745	0.9		1.9	2010	1.0
11	SU ◐		1.9	0832	1.1		1.8	2107	1.2
12	M		1.7	0943	1.3		1.8	2238	1.3
13	TU		1.6	1134	1.4		1.7		
14	W	0033	1.2		1.8	1310	1.2		1.9
15	TH	0150	1.0		2.0	1415	1.0		2.0
16	F	0245	0.8		2.1	1506	0.8		2.1
17	SA	0332	0.6		2.3	1552	0.6		2.3
18	SU ○	0416	0.4		2.4	1636	0.5		2.3
19	M	0459	0.4		2.4	1718	0.4		
20	TU		2.3	0538	0.4		2.4	1757	0.4
21	W		2.3	0616	0.4		2.3	1835	0.6
22	TH		2.2	0652	0.6		2.2	1911	0.7
23	F		2.1	0727	0.8		2.1	1947	0.8
24	SA		2.0	0804	1.0		1.9	2028	1.0
25	SU ◑		1.8	0852	1.2		1.8	2124	1.3
26	M		1.6	1007	1.4		1.6	2258	1.4
27	TU		1.6	1150	1.5		1.6		
28	W	0037	1.4		1.7	1313	1.4		1.7
29	TH	0143	1.2		1.9	1407	1.2		1.8
30	F	0226	1.0		2.0	1446	1.0		1.9

OCTOBER

Date	Day	Time	m	Time	m	Time	m	Time	m
1	SA	0303	0.9		2.0	1521	0.9		2.0
2	SU	0338	0.7		2.1	1555	0.8		2.0
3	M ●	0411	0.7		2.1	1627	0.7		2.1
4	TU	0443	0.7		2.1	1658	0.7		2.1
5	W	0513	0.7		2.1	1726	0.7		
6	TH		2.1	0541	0.7		2.1	1755	0.7
7	F		2.1	0610	0.7		2.1	1828	0.8
8	SA		2.1	0644	0.8		2.0	1905	0.8
9	SU		2.0	0725	1.0		2.0	1951	1.0
10	M ◐		1.9	0818	1.2		1.8	2054	1.2
11	TU		1.8	0941	1.3		1.7	2235	1.3
12	W		1.7	1131	1.3		1.7		
13	TH	0020	1.2		1.9	1257	1.2		1.9
14	F	0131	1.0		2.0	1357	0.9		2.0
15	SA	0224	0.8		2.2	1445	0.8		2.1
16	SU	0309	0.6		2.3	1529	0.6		2.3
17	M ○	0351	0.5		2.4	1611	0.6		2.3
18	TU	0432	0.4		2.4	1651	0.5		2.3
19	W	0510	0.5		2.3	1730	0.6		
20	TH		2.3	0546	0.6		2.3	1805	0.6
21	F		2.2	0621	0.7		2.2	1840	0.8
22	SA		2.1	0656	0.9		2.0	1915	0.9
23	SU		2.0	0733	1.0		1.9	1955	1.1
24	M		1.8	0821	1.3		1.8	2047	1.3
25	TU ◑		1.7	0932	1.4		1.6	2211	1.4
26	W		1.6	1111	1.5		1.6	2348	1.4
27	TH		1.7	1233	1.4		1.6		
28	F	0058	1.3		1.8	1328	1.3		1.8
29	SA	0145	1.1		1.9	1409	1.1		1.9
30	SU	0224	0.9		2.0	1445	0.9		2.0
31	M	0300	0.8		2.1	1519	0.8		2.0

NOVEMBER

Date	Day	Time	m	Time	m	Time	m	Time	m
1	TU	0334	0.8		2.1	1552	0.8		2.1
2	W ●	0407	0.7		2.1	1624	0.7		2.1
3	TH	0440	0.7		2.2	1658	0.7		
4	F		2.2	0514	0.7		2.2	1733	0.7
5	SA		2.2	0551	0.8		2.1	1812	0.7
6	SU		2.1	0632	0.9		2.1	1856	0.8
7	M		2.0	0721	1.0		2.0	1949	0.9
8	TU		1.9	0822	1.2		1.9	2057	1.1
9	W ◐		1.9	0942	1.2		1.8	2222	1.2
10	TH		1.9	1110	1.2		1.8	2347	1.1
11	F		1.9	1227	1.1		1.9		
12	SA	0058	0.9		2.1	1328	0.9		2.0
13	SU	0153	0.8		2.2	1418	0.8		2.1
14	M	0240	0.7		2.3	1504	0.7		2.2
15	TU	0324	0.7		2.3	1547	0.7		2.2
16	W ○	0405	0.7		2.3	1628	0.6		2.2
17	TH	0444	0.7		2.3	1706	0.7		
18	F		2.2	0521	0.7		2.2	1743	0.7
19	SA		2.1	0557	0.8		2.1	1818	0.8
20	SU		2.1	0634	0.9		2.0	1854	0.9
21	M		2.0	0712	1.1		1.9	1933	1.0
22	TU		1.9	0757	1.3		1.8	2019	1.2
23	W ◑		1.8	0853	1.4		1.7	2118	1.3
24	TH		1.8	1008	1.4		1.6	2234	1.3
25	F		1.8	1127	1.4		1.6	2347	1.3
26	SA		1.8	1231	1.3		1.7		
27	SU	0046	1.2		1.9	1319	1.2		1.8
28	M	0133	1.1		2.0	1401	1.0		1.9
29	TU	0215	1.0		2.1	1439	0.9		2.0
30	W	0254	0.9		2.1	1517	0.8		2.1

DECEMBER

Date	Day	Time	m	Time	m	Time	m	Time	m
1	TH ●	0333	0.8		2.2	1557	0.7		2.1
2	F	0414	0.8		2.2	1638	0.7		2.2
3	SA	0456	0.8		2.2	1722	0.7		
4	SU		2.2	0541	0.8		2.2	1808	0.7
5	M		2.2	0630	0.8		2.1	1858	0.7
6	TU		2.1	0722	0.9		2.0	1952	0.8
7	W		2.1	0821	1.0		2.0	2051	0.9
8	TH ◐		2.0	0926	1.0		1.9	2156	0.9
9	F		2.0	1036	1.1		1.9	2305	1.0
10	SA		2.0	1147	1.0		1.9		
11	SU	0013	1.0		2.0	1252	1.0		1.9
12	M	0115	0.9		2.1	1350	0.9		2.0
13	TU	0210	0.9		2.1	1440	0.9		2.0
14	W	0259	0.9		2.1	1527	0.8		2.1
15	TH ○	0343	0.8		2.2	1610	0.8		2.1
16	F	0425	0.8		2.1	1651	0.8		2.1
17	SA	0504	0.8		2.1	1729	0.8		
18	SU		2.1	0542	0.9		2.1	1804	0.8
19	M		2.1	0618	0.9		2.0	1840	0.9
20	TU		2.0	0655	1.0		1.9	1915	0.9
21	W		2.0	0732	1.1		1.9	1951	1.0
22	TH		1.9	0813	1.2		1.8	2032	1.1
23	F ◑		1.9	0900	1.3		1.7	2120	1.2
24	SA		1.8	0957	1.3		1.7	2217	1.2
25	SU		1.8	1102	1.3		1.7	2321	1.2
26	M		1.8	1209	1.3		1.7		
27	TU	0027	1.2		1.9	1310	1.2		1.8
28	W	0127	1.1		2.0	1403	1.0		1.9
29	TH	0220	1.0		2.1	1452	0.9		2.0
30	F	0310	0.9		2.1	1541	0.8		2.1
31	SA ●	0400	0.8		2.2	1629	0.7		2.2

Chart Datum: 1·40 metres below Ordnance Datum (Newlyn)

9.2.9 CHRISTCHURCH

Dorset **50°43'·53N 01°44'·33W** ❁❁◊◊✿✿✿

CHARTS AC *5601, 2172, 2035*; Imray C4; Stanfords 7, 12, 24; OS 195

TIDES HW Sp –0210, Np, –0140 Dover; ML 1·2; Zone 0 (UT)

Standard Port PORTSMOUTH (⟶)

Times				Height (metres)			
High Water		Low Water		MHWS	MHWN	MLWN	MLWS
0000	0600	0500	1100	4·7	3·8	1·9	0·8
1200	1800	1700	2300				
Differences BOURNEMOUTH							
–0240	+0055	–0050	–0030	–2·7	–2·2	–0·8	–0·3
CHRISTCHURCH (Entrance)							
–0230	+0030	–0035	–0035	–2·9	–2·4	–1·2	–0·2
CHRISTCHURCH (Quay)							
–0210	+0100	+0105	+0055	–2·9	–2·4	–1·0	0·0
CHRISTCHURCH (Tuckton bridge)							
–0205	+0110	+0110	+0105	–3·0	–2·5	–1·0	+0·1

NOTE: Double HWs occur, except near nps; predictions are for the higher HW. Near nps there is a stand; predictions are for mid-stand. Tidal levels are for inside the bar. Outside the bar the tide is about 0·6m lower at sp. Floods (or drought) in the Rivers Avon and Stour cause considerable variations from predicted hts. See 9.2.11.

SHELTER Good in lee of Hengistbury Hd, elsewhere exposed to SW winds. R Stour, navigable at HW up to Tuckton, and the R Avon up to the first bridge, give good shelter in all winds. Most ⚓s in the hbr dry. No ⚓ in chan. No berthing at ferry jetty by Mudeford sandbank. Hbr speed limit 4kn. Fishing licence obligatory.

NAVIGATION WPT 50°43'·53N 01°43'·58W, 270° to NE end of Mudeford Quay 0·5M. The bar/chan is liable to shift. The ent is difficult on the ebb which reaches 4-5kn in 'The Run'. Recommended ent/dep at HW/stand. Chan inside hbr is narrow and mostly shallow (approx 0·3m) soft mud; mean ranges are 1·2m sp and 0·7m nps. Beware groynes S of Hengistbury Hd, Beerpan and Yarranton Rks.

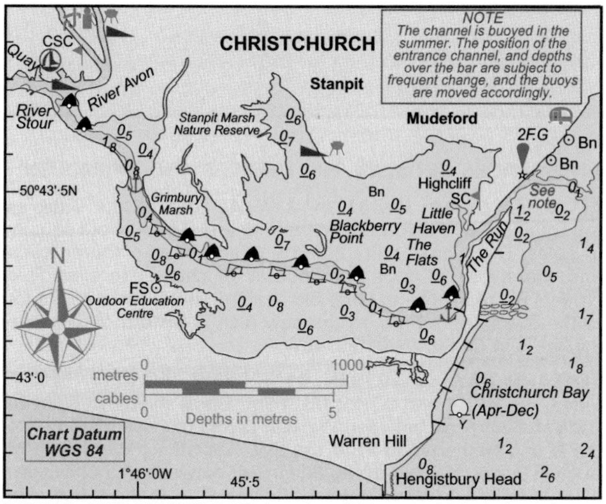
CHRISTCHURCH
NOTE
The channel is buoyed in the summer. The position of the entrance channel, and depths over the bar are subject to frequent change, and the buoys are moved accordingly.
CSC
Quay
River Avon
River Stour
Stanpit
Stanpit Marsh Nature Reserve
Mudeford
2F.G
Bn
Highcliff SC
See note
Little Haven
Blackberry Point
The Flats
The Run
Grimbury Marsh
FS
Oudoor Education Centre
50°43'·5N
43'·0
metres
cables
Depths in metres
Chart Datum WGS 84
Warren Hill
Christchurch Bay
(Apr-Dec)
Hengistbury Head
1°46'·0W
45'·5

LIGHTS AND MARKS 2 FG (vert) at NE end of Mudeford Quay. Unlit chan buoys in hbr and apps are locally laid Apr-Oct inc; info from ☎ 483250.

R/T None.

TELEPHONE (Dial code 01202) HM 495061, 📠 482200; MRSC (01305) 760439; Marinecall 09066 526241; Police 855544; Ⓗ 303626; Casualty 704167.

FACILITIES **Elkins BY** ☎ 483141, AB £16; **Rossiter Yachts** ☎ 483250, AB £16; **Christchurch SC (CSC)** ☎ 483150, limited AB £9.50, monohulls only, max LOA 9m.
Services: M*, L*, D, P (cans), FW, El, ⚒, CH, ACA, Gas, C (10 ton), Slip. **Town** ✉, Ⓑ, ⇌, ✈ (Bournemouth).

9.2.10 KEYHAVEN

Hampshire **50°42'·85N 01·33'·26W** ❁❁◊◊✿✿✿

CHARTS AC *5600, 2021, 2035*; Imray C4, C3; Stanfords 7, 11, 12, 24, 25; OS 196

TIDES –0020, +0105 Dover; ML 2·0; Zone 0 (UT)

Standard Port PORTSMOUTH (⟶)

Times				Height (metres)			
High Water		Low Water		MHWS	MHWN	MLWN	MLWS
0000	0600	0500	1100	4·7	3·8	1·9	0·8
1200	1800	1700	2300				
Differences HURST POINT							
–0115	–0005	–0030	–0025	–2·0	–1·5	–0·5	–0·1
TOTLAND BAY							
–0130	–0045	–0035	–0045	–2·2	–1·7	–0·4	–0·1
FRESHWATER BAY							
–0210	+0025	–0040	–0020	–2·1	–1·5	–0·4	0·0

NOTE: Double HWs occur at or near sp; predictions are then for the 1st HW. Off springs there is a stand of about 2 hrs; predictions are then for mid-stand. See 9.2.11.

SHELTER Good, but the river gets extremely congested. Access HW ±4½. Ent difficult on ebb. All moorings and ⚓s are exposed to winds across the marshland. The 'U' bend carries 2-2.5m but Keyhaven and Mount Lakes all but dry.

NAVIGATION WPT 50°42'·73N 01°32'·58W, 295° to chan ent, 0·40M. Ent should not be attempted in strong E winds. Bar is constantly changing. Leave chan SHM buoys well to stbd. Beware lobster pots. Approaching from the W, beware The Shingles bank over which seas break and which partly dries. At Hurst Narrows give 'The Trap' a wide berth.

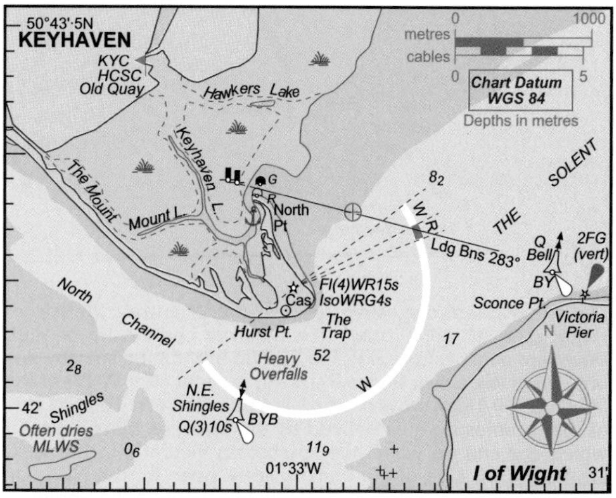
50°43'·5N
KEYHAVEN
KYC
HCSC
Old Quay
Hawkers Lake
Keyhaven L.
The Mount
Mount L.
North Pt
metres
cables
Chart Datum WGS 84
Depths in metres
THE SOLENT
W.R.
Ldg Bns 283°
Fl(4)WR15s
IsoWRG4s
Cas
Hurst Pt.
The Trap
Heavy Overfalls
North Channel
N.E. Shingles
Q(3)10s
BYB
Shingles
Often dries
MLWS
Q Bell
2FG (vert)
BY
Sconce Pt.
Victoria Pier
I of Wight
01°33'W
31'

LIGHTS AND MARKS When E of Hurst Point lt, two ldg bns ('X' topmarks) lead 283° to ent of buoyed chan; the R & G ent buoys marked with dayglo reflective tape are the more visible. See 9.2.4 and chartlet above for sectors of light at Hurst Point. The sectors of Hurst Pt Iso WRG 4s have been deliberately omitted from the above chartlet for clarity.

R/T None.

TELEPHONE (Dial code 01590) R. Warden ☎/📠 645695; MRSC (01705) 552100; Marinecall 09066 526241; Police 08450 454545; Dr 643022; Ⓗ 677011.

FACILITIES **Quay** Slip, L; **Keyhaven YC** ☎ 642165, C, M, L (on beach), FW, Bar; **New Forest District Council** ☎ (01703) 285000, Slip, M; **Milford-on-Sea** P, D, FW, CH, 🛒, R, Bar; **Hurst Castle SC** M, L, FW;
Services: Slip, ME, El, ⚒, C (9 ton), CH.
Village EC (Milford-on-Sea) Wed; R, Bar, CH, 🛒, ✉ and Ⓑ (Milford-on-Sea), ⇌ (bus to New Milton), ✈ (Hurn).

9.2.11 NEEDLES CHANNEL

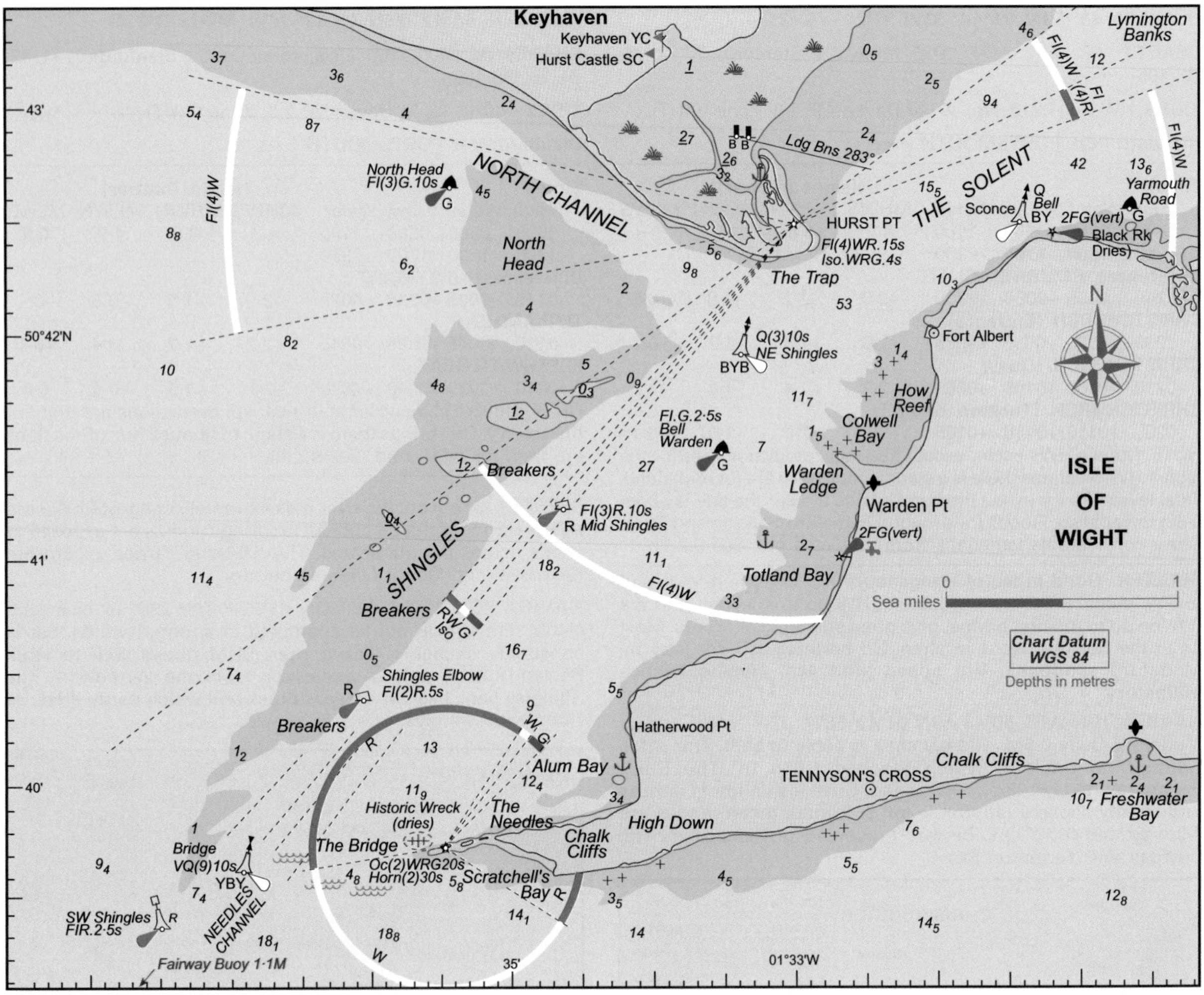
Keyhaven
Keyhaven YC
Hurst Castle SC
Lymington Banks
Fl(4)W
Fl(4)R
Ldg Bns 283°
North Head
Fl(3)G.10s
G
NORTH CHANNEL
North Head
HURST PT
Fl(4)WR.15s
Iso.WRG.4s
The Trap
THE SOLENT
Sconce
Q
Bell
BY
2FG(vert)
Yarmouth Road
Black Rk
Dries
Fort Albert
Q(3)10s
NE Shingles
BYB
How Reef
Colwell Bay
Fl.G.2·5s
Bell
Warden
Warden Ledge
Warden Pt
2FG(vert)
ISLE
OF
WIGHT
Breakers
Fl(3)R.10s
R Mid Shingles
SHINGLES
Totland Bay
Sea miles
Chart Datum
WGS 84
Depths in metres
Breakers
RWG
Iso
Shingles Elbow
Fl(2)R.5s
Breakers
Hatherwood Pt
W
G
R
Alum Bay
Historic Wreck
(dries)
The Needles
TENNYSON'S CROSS
Chalk Cliffs
Freshwater Bay
High Down
Chalk Cliffs
The Bridge
Bridge
VQ(9)10s
YBY
Oc(2)WRG20s
Horn(2)30s
Scratchell's Bay
SW Shingles
Fl.R.2·5s
NEEDLES CHANNEL
Fairway Buoy 1·1M
43'
50°42'N
41'
40'
35'
01°33'W

The Needles are distinctive rocks at the W end of the Isle of Wight (see AC *5600,* 2035*)*. The adjacent chalk cliffs of High Down are conspic from afar; the light ho may not be seen by day until relatively close. Goose Rk, dries, is about 50m WNW of the light ho, 100-150m WSW of which is a drying wreck. The NW side of the Needles Chan is defined by the Shingles bank, parts of which dry and on which the sea breaks violently in the least swell. The SE side of the bank is fairly steep-to, the NW side shelves more gently. Dredgers frequently work on the Shingles. On the ebb the stream sets very strongly (3-4kn) WSW across the Shingles. The Needles Chan is well lit/buoyed and in fair weather presents no significant problems. But even a SW Force 4 against the ebb will raise breaking seas near Bridge and SW Shingles buoys.

In bad weather broken water and overfalls extend along The Bridge, a reef which runs 8ca W of the lt ho with its W extremity marked by Bridge WCM lt buoy. S to W gales against the ebb raise very dangerous breaking seas in the Needles Chan, here only 250m wide. The sea state can be at its worst shortly after LW when the flood has just begun. There is then no wind-over-tide situation, but a substantial swell is raised as a result of the recently turned stream. In such conditions use the E route to the Solent, S of the IOW and via Nab Tower; or find shelter at Poole or Studland.

In strong winds the North Channel, N of the Shingles, is preferable to the Needles Channel. The two join S of Hurst Point where overfalls and tide rips may be met. Beware The Trap, a shoal spit extending 150m SE of Hurst Castle.

ANCHORAGES BETWEEN THE NEEDLES AND YARMOUTH

ALUM BAY, 50°40'·10N 01°34'·33W. *AC 2021, 5600.4*. Tides as for Totland Bay. Very good shelter in E and S winds, but squally in gales. Distinctive white cliffs to S and multi-coloured cliffs and chairlift to E. Appr from due W of chairlift to clear Five Fingers Rk, to the N and Long Rk, a reef drying 0·9m at its E end, to the S. ⚓ in about 4m off the new pier. A Historic Wreck (see 9.0.3h) is at 50°39'·7N 01°35'·45W.

TOTLAND BAY, 50°40'·98N 01°32'·86W. *AC 2219, 5600.4.* Tides, see 9.2.14 and 9.2.11; ML 1·9m. Good shelter in E'lies in wide shelving bay between Warden Ledge (rks 4ca offshore) to the N and Hatherwood Pt to the SW. Appr W of Warden SHM buoy Fl G 2·5s to ⚓ out of the tide in 2m between pier (2FG vert) and old LB house; good holding. Colwell Bay, to the N between Warden Pt and Fort Albert, is generally rky and shallow.

ANCHORAGE EAST OF THE NEEDLES, SOUTH IOW

FRESHWATER BAY, 50°40'·07N 01°30'·61W. AC *2021, 5600.4.* Tides see 9.2.14 and 9.2.11; ML 1·6m. Good shelter from the N, open to the S. The bay is 3·2M E of Needles lt ho and 1·2M E of Tennyson's Cross. Conspic marks:on W side Redoubt Fort; a hotel on N side; Stag and Mermaid Rks to the E. The bay is shallow, with rky drying ledges ¾ca either side and a rk (0·1m) almost in the centre. Best to ⚓ in about 2m just outside. 🛒, R, Bar, ✉.

9.2.12 THE SOLENT

Charts AC 2045, 2036, *5600* (10 A2 size charts £37.00).

Reference *Solent Cruising Companion* Aslett/Nautical Data Ltd; *Solent Hazards* Peter Bruce; *Solent Year Book* SCRA; ***Yachtsman's Guide*** ABP Southampton; www.solentports.co.uk

Vessel Traffic Service (VTS) Southampton VTS operates on VHF Ch **12** 14, and advises shipping in the Solent between the Needles and Nab Tower including Southampton Water. Portsmouth Hbr and its approaches N of a line from Gilkicker Pt to Outer Spit buoy are controlled on Ch **11** by QHM Portsmouth.

The VTS monitors and co-ordinates the safe passage of commercial ships which must report at designated points. It includes compulsory pilotage, a radar service on request, berthing instructions and tug assistance.

By listening on VHF Ch 12 Southampton, or Ch 11 for QHM Portsmouth, pleasure craft are able, particularly at night or in poor visibility to be forewarned of ship movements and thus plan accordingly. Following an initial call on Ch 12, VTS makes broadcasts on Ch 14 to indicate the movements of commercial vessels over 150m LOA within the next hour. These broadcasts will be made on or shortly after each hour and will also include details of when the Moving Prohibited Zone (see below) will be implemented together with tidal information and weather conditions at the Dock Head Southampton.

Pleasure Craft and Commercial Shipping ***Consideration must be given to the restricted field of vision from large ships at close quarters, their limited ability to manoeuvre at slow speeds and their minimal under keel clearance in restricted waters. Smaller shipping keeping clear of these vessels will be encountered outside of the channel. Maintain a proper lookout, especially astern. When crossing the Main fairway, do so at 90° to it. Southampton Hbr byelaw 2003/10 refers.***

A **Precautionary Area** covers a critical part of the Solent where large vessels make tight turns. The area (see chartlet) covers the Approach to, and the Thorn Chan. It is marked by Prince Consort NCM, Gurnard NCM, NE Gurnard PHM, Bourne Gap PHM, Calshot Spit lt Float, Castle Pt PHM, Black Jack PHM, Reach SHM, Calshot NCM, N Thorn SHM, Thorn Knoll SHM, W Bramble WCM and S Bramble SHM.

This area is used by many pleasure craft and has to be negotiated by large ships bound to/from Southampton normally via the E Solent. Inbound ships pass Prince Consort NCM turning to the WSW toward Gurnard NCM, before starting their critical stbd turn into the Thorn Chan. They turn to port around Calshot to clear the area into Southampton Water.

To minimise the risk of collision with small craft, any large vessel >150m LOA, when in the Precautionary Area is enclosed by a **Moving Prohibited Zone** (MPZ) which extends 1000m ahead of the vessel and 100m on either beam. ***Small craft <20m LOA must remain outside this MPZ, using seamanlike anticipation of likely turns.***

A large vessel, displaying a B cylinder by day or 3 all-round ● lts (vert) by night, will normally be preceded by a Hbr patrol launch showing a flashing blue light and using working Ch 12 (callsign *SP*).

The VTS will identify large ships and approx timings of MPZ as part of the hourly broadcasts (see above). All pleasure craft in the vicinity are strongly advised to monitor Ch 12 in order to create a mental picture. Be particularly alert when in, or approaching, the triangle defined by E.Lepe, Hook and W. Ryde Middle buoys.

VHF Radio Telephone Since Ch 16 is a DISTRESS, SAFETY and CALLING Ch, if another calling Ch is available, use it in preference to Ch 16; otherwise, use Ch 16 as briefly as possible to make contact before changing to a working Ch. Note also that initial contact with Solent CG should be on Ch 67, not Ch 16 (see below). For ship-to-ship messages the recognised VHF channels include 06, 08, 72 and 77.

Yachts in the Solent should listen on Ch 12 and on Ch 11 for Portsmouth. Other Ch's are listed under each port entry.

Local Signals Outward bound vessels will as required use the appropriate sound signals to indicate their intention to alter course to Port when exiting the Solent to the East.

Southampton patrol launches have HARBOUR MASTER painted on their cabin sides. At night a fixed blue all-round light is shown above the white masthead light. A flashing blue light may also be shown when patrolling large vessels.

Solent Coastguard The Maritime Rescue Sub Centre (MRSC) at Lee-on-Solent ☎ (02392) 552100 coordinates all SAR activities in Solent District, which is bounded by a line from Highcliffe south to mid-channel; E to the Greenwich Lt V; thence N to Beachy Head. It is the busiest CG District in the UK, because of the huge concentration of pleasure craft within its bounds.

It is manned H24, year round by at least 3 CG Officers who can call on the RNLI, Solent Safety rescue boats and the CG Rescue helicopter based at Lee. Sector and Auxiliary CGs are based on the IOW, Calshot, Eastney, Hayling, Littlehampton, Shoreham, Newhaven and elsewhere. Solent CG keeps watch on VHF Ch 67 and 16. Uniquely, the initial call to *Solent Coastguard* should be made on (working) Ch 67, since Ch 16 is often very busy. Ch 67 is also busy and is only for essential traffic. Correct R/T procedure must be maintained.

Weather message are broadcast by Solent CG after an announcement on Ch 16. See Chapter 6 for schedule.

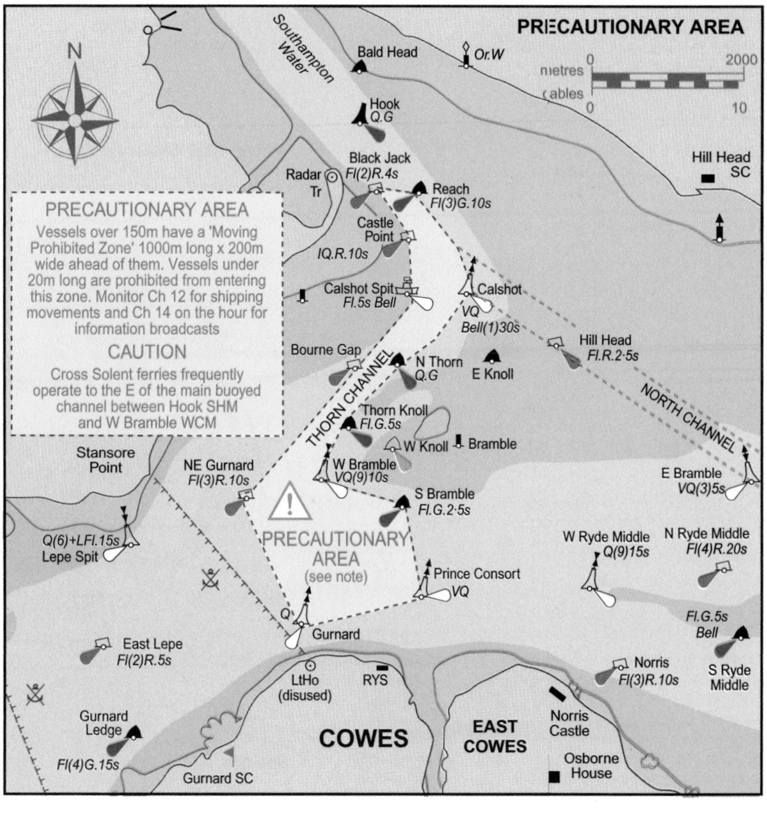
PRECAUTIONARY AREA
metres 0 2000
cables 0 10
N
Southampton Water
Bald Head
Or.W
Hook Q.G
Black Jack Fl(2)R.4s
Radar Tr
Reach Fl(3)G.10s
Hill Head SC
PRECAUTIONARY AREA
Vessels over 150m have a 'Moving Prohibited Zone' 1000m long x 200m wide ahead of them. Vessels under 20m long are prohibited from entering this zone. Monitor Ch 12 for shipping movements and Ch 14 on the hour for information broadcasts
CAUTION
Cross Solent ferries frequently operate to the E of the main buoyed channel between Hook SHM and W Bramble WCM
Castle Point
IQ.R.10s
Calshot Spit Fl.5s Bell
Calshot VQ Bell(1)30s
Hill Head Fl.R.2·5s
Bourne Gap
N Thorn Q.G
E Knoll
THORN CHANNEL
NORTH CHANNEL
Thorn Knoll Fl.G.5s
W Knoll
Bramble
Stansore Point
NE Gurnard Fl(3)R.10s
W Bramble VQ(9)10s
E Bramble VQ(3)5s
S Bramble Fl.G.2·5s
Q(6)+LFl.15s Lepe Spit
PRECAUTIONARY AREA (see note)
W Ryde Middle Q(9)15s
N Ryde Middle Fl(4)R.20s
Prince Consort VQ
Gurnard
Fl.G.5s Bell
East Lepe Fl(2)R.5s
LtHo (disused)
RYS
Norris Fl(3)R.10s
S Ryde Middle
Gurnard Ledge Fl(4)G.15s
COWES
EAST COWES
Norris Castle
Osborne House
Gurnard SC

9.2.13 YARMOUTH

Isle of Wight **50°42'·42N 01°30'·05W**

CHARTS AC *2037, 2021, 5600*; Imray C15, C3; Stanfords 25, 24, 115; OS 196

TIDES Sp –0050, +0150, Np +0020 Dover; ML 2·0; Zone 0 (UT)

Standard Port PORTSMOUTH (⟶)

Times				Height (metres)			
High Water		Low Water		MHWS	MHWN	MLWN	MLWS
0000	0600	0500	1100	4·7	3·8	1·9	0·8
1200	1800	1700	2300				
Differences YARMOUTH							
–0105	+0005	–0025	–0030	–1·7	–1·2	–0·3	0·0

NOTE: Double HWs occur at or near sp; at other times there is a stand lasting about two hrs. Predictions refer to the first HW when there are two; otherwise to the middle of the stand. See 9.2.11.

SHELTER Good from all directions of wind and sea, but swell enters if wind strong from N/NE. Hbr dredged 2m from ent to bridge; access H24. Moor fore-and-aft on piles, on the Town Quay, or on pontoon. Boats over 15m LOA, 4m beam or 2·4m draft should give notice of arrival. Berthing on S Quay is normally only for fuel, C, FW, or to load people/cargo. Hbr gets very full in season and may be closed to visitors. 38 Or ⓥs outside hbr (see chartlet) and ⚓ further to the N or S.

NAVIGATION WPT 50°42'·58N 01°30'·01W, 188° to abeam car ferry terminal, 2ca. Dangers on appr are Black Rock (SHM buoy Fl G 5s) and shoal water to the N of the E/W bkwtr. Beware ferries and their wash even when berthed alongside. Caution: strong ebb in the ent at sp. Speed limit 4kn in hbr and 6kn in approaches. ⚓ prohib in hbr and beyond R Yar road bridge. This swing bridge (R and G Traffic lts) opens for 10 mins for access to the moorings and BYs up-river at Saltern Quay: (May-Sept) 0800, 0900, 1000, 1200, 1400, 1600, 1730, 1830, 2000LT; and on request (Oct-May). The river is navigable by dinghy at HW almost up to Freshwater. A **Historic Wreck** (see 9.0.3h) is at 50°42'·55N 01°29'·67W, 2ca ExN from end of pier; marked by Y SPM buoy.

LIGHTS AND MARKS Ldg bns (2 W ◊ on B/W masts) and ldg lts (FG 5/9m 2M), on quay, 188°. When hbr is closed to visitors (eg when full in summer or at week-ends) R flags are flown at the dolphin and inner E pier, (illuminated). In fog a high intensity ○ lt is shown from the pier hd and from the inner E pier.

R/T HM VHF Ch 68. Water Taxi Ch 15.

TELEPHONE (Dial code 01983 = code for whole of IOW) HM 760321, 📠 761192; MRSC (023 92) 552100; Marinecall 0898 500457; Police 08450 454545; Dr 760434.

FACILITIES **Hbr** £10.50 (Tue–Thu) £12.50 other days (30ft) (£4.50-£5.50 < 4hrs) on piles, Town Quay, pontoon or ⓥ; Slip, P, D, L, ME, Gaz, FW, C (5 ton), Ice;
Yarmouth SC ☎ 760270, Bar, L;
Royal Solent YC ☎ 760256, Bar, R, L, Slip;
Services Note: BY in SW corner but most marine services/BYs are located near Salterns Quay, 500m up-river above the bridge, or ½M by road. BY, Slip, ME, El, CH, Gas, Gaz, LPG, SM, C, Divers.
Town EC Wed; R, Bar, ✉, Ⓑ (May-Sept 1000-1445, Sept-May a.m. only), ⇌ (Lymington), ✈ (Bournemouth/Southampton).

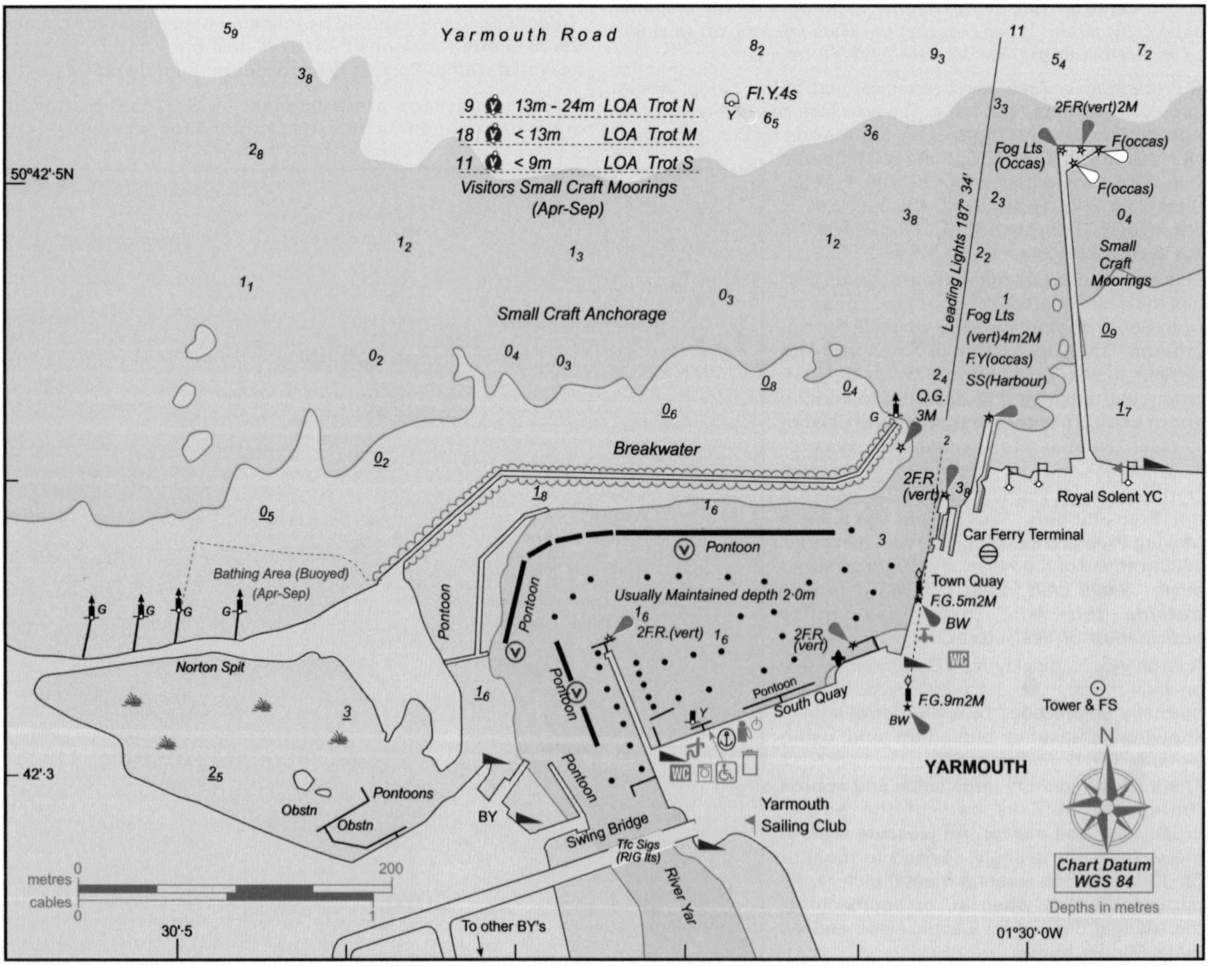
Yarmouth Road
9 13m - 24m LOA Trot N
18 < 13m LOA Trot M
11 < 9m LOA Trot S
Visitors Small Craft Moorings (Apr-Sep)
Fl.Y.4s
Y
50°42'·5N
2F.R(vert)2M
Fog Lts (Occas)
F(occas)
Small Craft Moorings
Leading Lights 187° 34'
Small Craft Anchorage
Fog Lts (vert)4m2M F.Y(occas) SS(Harbour)
Q.G. 3M
G
Breakwater
2F.R (vert)
Royal Solent YC
Car Ferry Terminal
Pontoon
Town Quay
F.G.5m2M
BW
Bathing Area (Buoyed) (Apr-Sep)
Usually Maintained depth 2·0m
2F.R.(vert)
Norton Spit
Pontoon
South Quay
F.G.9m2M
Tower & FS
42'·3
Pontoons
Obstn
BY
YARMOUTH
Yarmouth Sailing Club
Swing Bridge
Tfc Sigs (R/G lts)
River Yar
metres 0 200
cables 0 1
30'·5
To other BY's
01°30'·0W
Chart Datum WGS 84
Depths in metres
N

9.2.14 LYMINGTON

Hampshire **50°45'·13N 01·31'·40W** ❁❁❁♁♁♁✿✿✿

CHARTS AC *5600, 2035, 2021*; Imray C3, C15; Stanfords 11, 25; OS 196

TIDES Sp –0040, +0100, Np +0020 Dover; ML 2·0; Zone 0 (UT)

Standard Port PORTSMOUTH (⟶)

Times				Height (metres)			
High Water		Low Water		MHWS	MHWN	MLWN	MLWS
0000	0600	0500	1100	4·7	3·8	1·9	0·8
1200	1800	1700	2300				
Differences LYMINGTON							
–0110	+0005	–0020	–0020	–1·7	–1·2	–0·5	–0·1

NOTE: Double HWs occur at or near sp and on other occasions there is a stand lasting about 2hrs. Predictions refer to the first HW when there are two. At other times they refer to the middle of the stand. See 9.2.11.

R/T Marinas VHF Ch **80** M (office hrs).

TELEPHONE (Dial code 01590) HM 672014, 📠 671823; MRSC (023 92) 552100; Marinecall 09066 526241; Police 08450 454545; Dr 672953; Ⓗ 677011.

FACILITIES Marinas:
Lymington Yacht Haven (475+100 visitors), 2m depth, all tides access, ☎ 677071, 📠 678186, £2.59, P, D, ⛽, BY, ME, El, ✂, C (25 ton), BH (50 ton), CH, Gas, Gaz, LPG, ▣, ♿ ⚓ (mobile) ;
Lymington Marina (300+100 visitors), ☎ 673312, 📠 676353, £2.77, Slip, P, D, ME, El, ✂, CH, BH (45 ton), C, (80 ton), Gas, Gaz, ▣, ♿;
Town Quay AB £1.50 for 9m, M, FW, WC's, Slip (see HM); **Bath Road** public pontoon, FW, WC's, ♿, Ⓔ, SM.
Clubs: Royal Lymington YC ☎ 672677, R, Bar, ♿; **Lymington Town SC** ☎ 674514, AB, R, Bar.
Services: M, FW, ME, El, ✂, C (16 ton), CH, Ⓔ, SM, ACA.
Town every facility including ✉, Ⓑ, ⇌, ✈ (Bournemouth or Southampton).

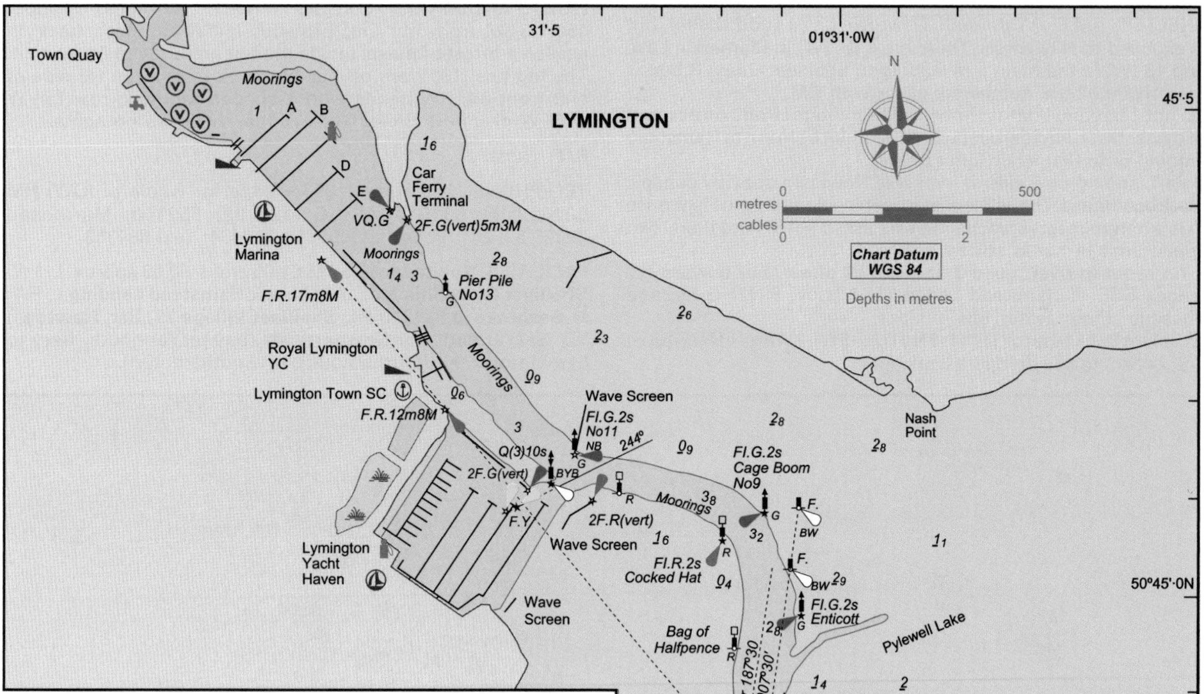
31'·5
01°31'·0W
Town Quay
Moorings
LYMINGTON
Car Ferry Terminal
VQ.G
2F.G(vert)5m3M
Lymington Marina
F.R.17m8M
Pier Pile No13
Royal Lymington YC
Lymington Town SC
F.R.12m8M
Q(3)10s
2F.G(vert)
BYB
Wave Screen
Fl.G.2s No11 NB
244°
2F.R(vert)
Lymington Yacht Haven
Fl.R.2s Cocked Hat
Bag of Halfpence
Fl.G.2s Cage Boom No9
Fl.G.2s Enticott
Pylewell Lake
Nash Point
Chart Datum WGS 84
Depths in metres
metres
cables
45'·5
50°45'·0N

Dir 187°30'
Dir 007°30'
Pylewell Boom
Fl.G.2s
Awash at High Water Springs
Fl.R.2s Seymor's Post
Fl.G.2s Tar Barrel
319°30'
Fl.G.2s No7
No 5
No 6
Fl.R.2s No 4
Fl.G.2s No 3
Fl.G.2s No1
YC Starting Platform
Fl.R.2s4m3M Cross Boom

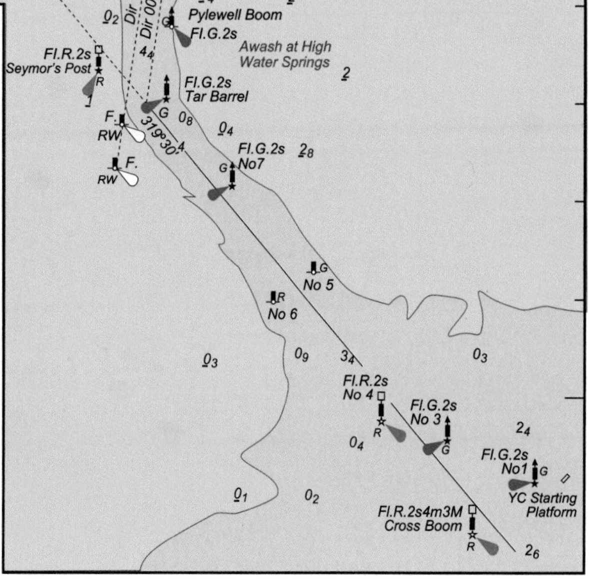

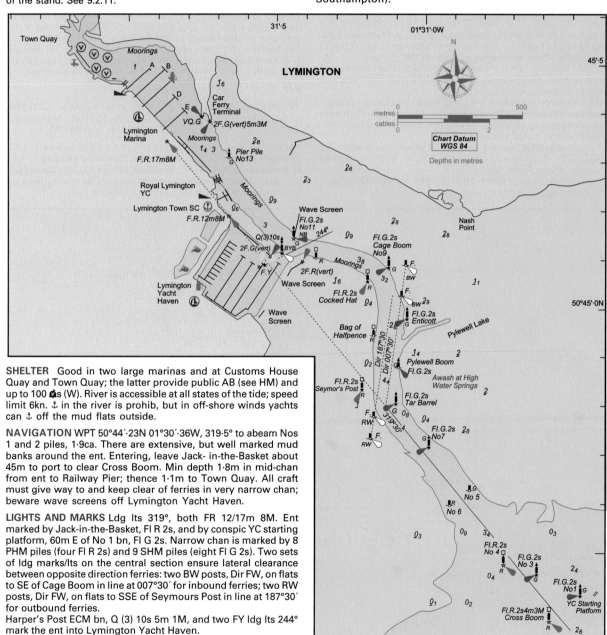

SHELTER Good in two large marinas and at Customs House Quay and Town Quay; the latter provide public AB (see HM) and up to 100 ⚓s (W). River is accessible at all states of the tide; speed limit 6kn. ⚓ in the river is prohib, but in off-shore winds yachts can ⚓ off the mud flats outside.

NAVIGATION WPT 50°44'·23N 01°30'·36W, 319·5° to abeam Nos 1 and 2 piles, 1·9ca. There are extensive, but well marked mud banks around the ent. Entering, leave Jack- in-the-Basket about 45m to port to clear Cross Boom. Min depth 1·8m in mid-chan from ent to Railway Pier; thence 1·1m to Town Quay. All craft must give way to and keep clear of ferries in very narrow chan; beware wave screens off Lymington Yacht Haven.

LIGHTS AND MARKS Ldg lts 319°, both FR 12/17m 8M. Ent marked by Jack-in-the-Basket, Fl R 2s, and by conspic YC starting platform, 60m E of No 1 bn, Fl G 2s. Narrow chan is marked by 8 PHM piles (four Fl R 2s) and 9 SHM piles (eight Fl G 2s). Two sets of ldg marks/lts on the central section ensure lateral clearance between opposite direction ferries: two BW posts, Dir FW, on flats to SE of Cage Boom in line at 007°30′ for inbound ferries; two RW posts, Dir FW, on flats to SSE of Seymours Post in line at 187°30′ for outbound ferries.
Harper's Post ECM bn, Q (3) 10s 5m 1M, and two FY ldg lts 244° mark the ent into Lymington Yacht Haven.

9.2.15 NEWTOWN RIVER

Isle of Wight **50°43′·45N 01°24′·66W**

CHARTS AC *5600, 2035, 2036, 2021*; Imray C3, C15; Stanfords 11, 24, 25; OS 196

TIDES Sp –0108, Np +0058, Dover; ML 2·3; Zone 0 (UT)

Standard Port PORTSMOUTH (⟶)

Times				**Height (metres)**			
High Water		Low Water		MHWS	MHWN	MLWN	MLWS
0000	0600	0500	1100	4·7	3·8	1·9	0·8
1200	1800	1700	2300				
Differences SOLENT BANK (Data approximate)							
–0100	0000	–0015	–0020	–1·3	–1·0	–0·3	–0·1

NOTE: Double HWs occur at or near springs; at other times there is a stand which lasts about 2hrs. Predictions refer to the first HW when there are two. At other times they refer to the middle of the stand. See 9.2.11.

SHELTER 3½M E of Yarmouth, Newtown gives good shelter, but is exposed to N'ly winds. There are 6 Øs (W) in Clamerkin Lake and 18 (W) in the main arm leading to Shalfleet Quay, R buoys are private all are numbered; check with HM.

Do not ⚓ beyond boards showing "Anchorage Limit" on account of oyster beds. Fin keel boats can stay afloat from ent to Hamstead landing or to Clamerkin Limit Boards.

Public landing on E side of river N of Newtown quay by conspic black boathouse. The whole eastern peninsula ending in Fishhouse Pt is a nature reserve; yachtsmen are asked not to land there. 5kn speed limit in hbr is strictly enforced.

If no room in river, good ⚓ in 3-5m W of ent, but beware rky ledges SSE of Hamstead Ledge SHM buoy, Fl (2) G 5s, and possible under water obstructions.

At Solent Bank (approx 50°44′·5N 01°25′·5W), 1M NW of Newtown ent, expect to see dredgers working.

NAVIGATION WPT 50°43′·83N 01°25′·18W, 130° to ldg bn, 0·46M. From W, make good Hamstead Ledge SHM buoy, thence E to pick up ldg marks. From E, keep N of Newtown gravel banks where W/SW winds over a sp ebb can raise steep breaking seas; leave PHM Fl.R4s bar buoy to port. Best ent is from about HW –4, on the flood but while the mud flats are still visible. Ent lies between two shingle spits and can be rough in N winds especially near HW. There is only about 0·9m over the bar.

Inside the ent many perches mark the mud banks. Near junction to Causeway Lake depth is only 0·9m and beyond this water quickly shoals.

At ent to Clamerkin Lake (1·2 -1·8m) keep to SE to avoid gravel spit off W shore, marked by two PHM perches; the rest of chan is marked by occas perches. Beware many oyster beds in Western Haven and Clamerkin Lake.

There is a rifle range at top of Clamerkin Lake and in Spur Lake; R flags flown during firing. High voltage power line across Clamerkin at 50°42′·81N 01°22′·66W has clearance of only 9m and no shore markings.

LIGHTS AND MARKS Conspic TV mast (152m) bearing about 150° (3·3M from hbr ent) provides initial approach track. In season a forest of masts inside the hbr are likely to be evident. The ldg bns, 130°, are off Fishhouse Pt in mud on NE side of ent: front bn, RW bands with Y-shaped topmark; rear bn, W with W disc in B circle. Once inside, there are no lights.

R/T None.

TELEPHONE (Dial code 01983 = code for whole of IOW) HM 531622; Fax 531914; MRSC (023 92) 552100; Marinecall 09066 526241; Police 528000; Dr 760434; Taxi 884353.

FACILITIES **Newtown Quay** M £1.05 and ⚓ £0.55 approx, L, FW; **Shalfleet Quay** Slip, M, L, AB; **Lower Hamstead Landing** L, FW; **R. Seabroke** ☎ 531213, ⚒; **Shalfleet Village** 🛒, Bar. **Newtown** ✉, Ⓑ (Yarmouth or Newport), ⇌ (bus to Yarmouth, ferry to Lymington), ✈ (Bournemouth or Southampton).

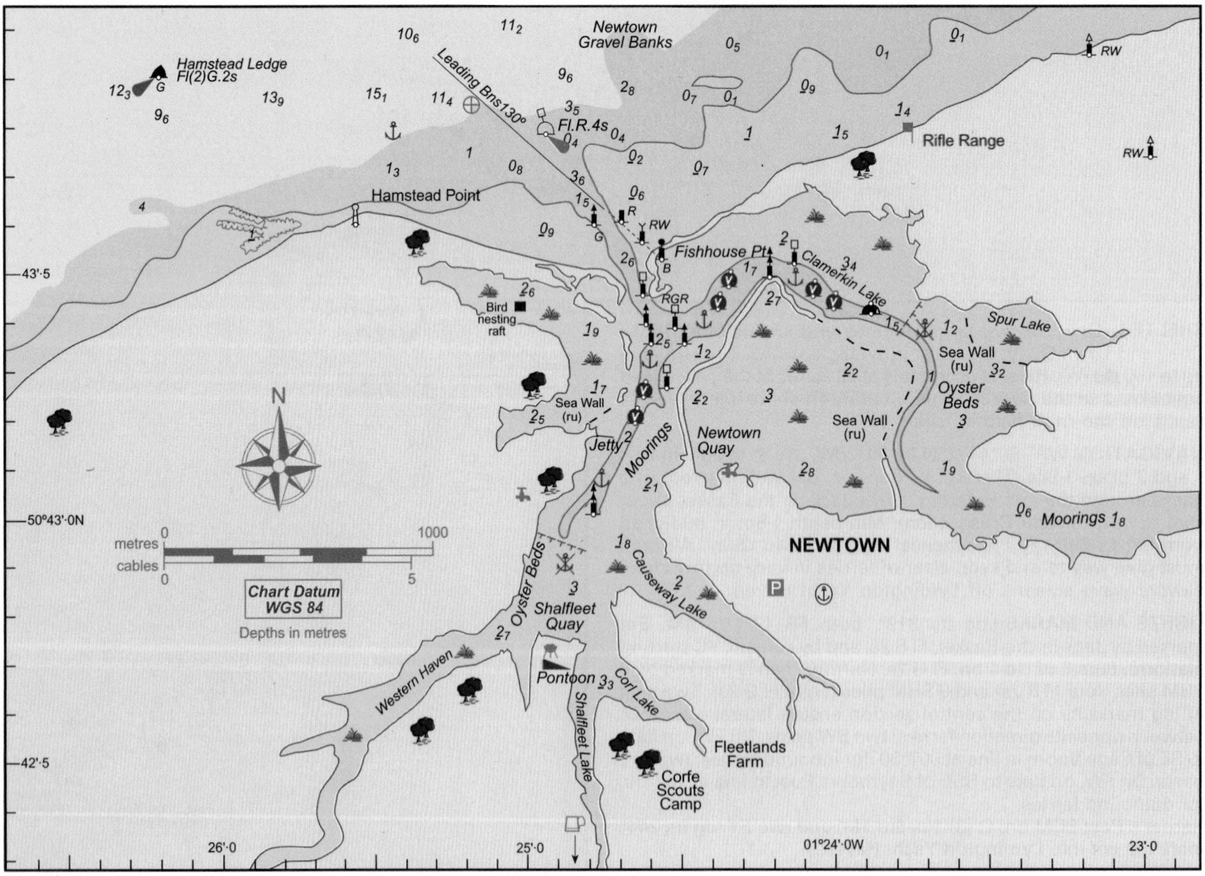

Newtown Gravel Banks
Hamstead Ledge Fl(2)G.2s
Leading Bns 130°
Fl.R.4s
Rifle Range
RW
Hamstead Point
Fishhouse Pt
Clamerkin Lake
Spur Lake
Bird nesting raft
Sea Wall (ru)
Oyster Beds
Jetty
Moorings
Newtown Quay
43′·5
50°43′·0N
42′·5
metres 0 1000
cables 0 5
Chart Datum WGS 84
Depths in metres
NEWTOWN
Moorings
Causeway Lake
Shalfleet Quay
Western Haven
Pontoon
Corf Lake
Shalfleet Lake
Fleetlands Farm
Corfe Scouts Camp
26′·0
25′·0
01°24′·0W
23′·0

9.2.16 BEAULIEU RIVER

Hampshire **50°46'·89N 01°21'·72W** (Ent) ❀❀◊◊◊✿✿✿

CHARTS AC *5600, 2036, 2035, 2021*; Imray C3, C15; Stanfords 11, 24, 25; OS 196

TIDES –0100 and +0140 Dover; ML 2·4; Zone 0 (UT)

Standard Port PORTSMOUTH (⟶)

Times				**Height (metres)**			
High Water		Low Water		MHWS	MHWN	MLWN	MLWS
0000	0600	0500	1100	4·7	3·8	1·9	0·8
1200	1800	1700	2300				
BUCKLER'S HARD							
–0040	–0010	+0010	–0010	–1·0	–0·8	–0·2	–0·3
STANSORE POINT							
–0050	–0010	–0005	–0010	–0·8	–0·5	–0·3	–0·1

NOTE: Double HWs occur at or near springs; the 2nd HW is approx 1¾ hrs after the 1st. On other occasions there is a stand which lasts about two hrs. The predictions refer to the first HW when there are two, or to the middle of the stand. See 9.2.11.

SHELTER Very good in all winds. ⚓ possible in reach between Lepe Ho and Beaulieu River SC, but preferable to proceed to Buckler's Hard Yacht Hbr (AB and Ⓥ pile moorings).
Many of the landing stages/slips shown on the chartlet (and AC 2021) are privately owned and not to be used. The uppermost reaches of the river are best explored first by dinghy due to the lack of channel markers and the short duration of the HW stand. Alongside drying berths at Palace House just below weir. **Rabies:** Craft with animals from abroad are prohibited in the river.

NAVIGATION WPT 50°46'·53N 01°21'·33W, 324° to abeam Beaulieu Spit dolphin (Fl R 5s), 4ca. Ent dangerous LW±2. There are patches drying 0·3m approx 100m S of Beaulieu Spit. 1ca further SSE, close W of the ldg line, are shoal depths 0·1m. At night keep in W sector of Lepe lt till No4 SHbn. Lepe Spit SCM buoy, Q (6) + L Fl 15s, is 7ca E of Beaulieu Spit dolphin at 50°46'.78N 01°20'·63W.
The swatchway off Beaulieu River SC is closed. A speed limit of 5kn applies to the whole river.

LIGHTS AND MARKS Ldg marks at ent 324° must be aligned exactly due to shoal water either side of ldg line. The front is No 2 bn, R with Or dayglow topmark, △ shape above □; the rear is Lepe Ho. Beaulieu Spit, R dolphin with W band, Fl R 5s 3M vis 277°-037°; ra refl, should be left approx 40m to port. Lepe bn Oc WRG 4s. The old CG cottages and Boat House are conspic, approx 320m E of Lepe Ho.

The river is clearly marked by R and G bns and perches. SHM bns 5, 9, 19 and 21 are all Fl G 4s; PHM bns 8,12 and 20 are Fl R 4s. Marina pontoons A, C and E have 2FR (vert).

R/T None.

TELEPHONE (Dial code 01590) HM 616200, 📠 616211; MRSC (023 92) 552100; Marinecall 09066 526241; Police 08450 454545; Dr 612451 or (023 80) 845955; Ⓗ 77011.

FACILITIES Buckler's Hard Yacht Hbr £2.80 (110+20 Ⓥ), £11 <3hrs, or £1.25 on piles, ☎ 616200, 📠 616211, email river@beaulieu.co.uk, P, D, FW, ME, El, ⚒, C (1 ton), BH (26 ton), SM, Gas, Gaz, CH, R, Bar.
Village V (☎ 616293), R, Bar, ✉ (Beaulieu), cashpoint, ⇌ (bus to Brockenhurst), ✈ (Bournemouth or Soton).

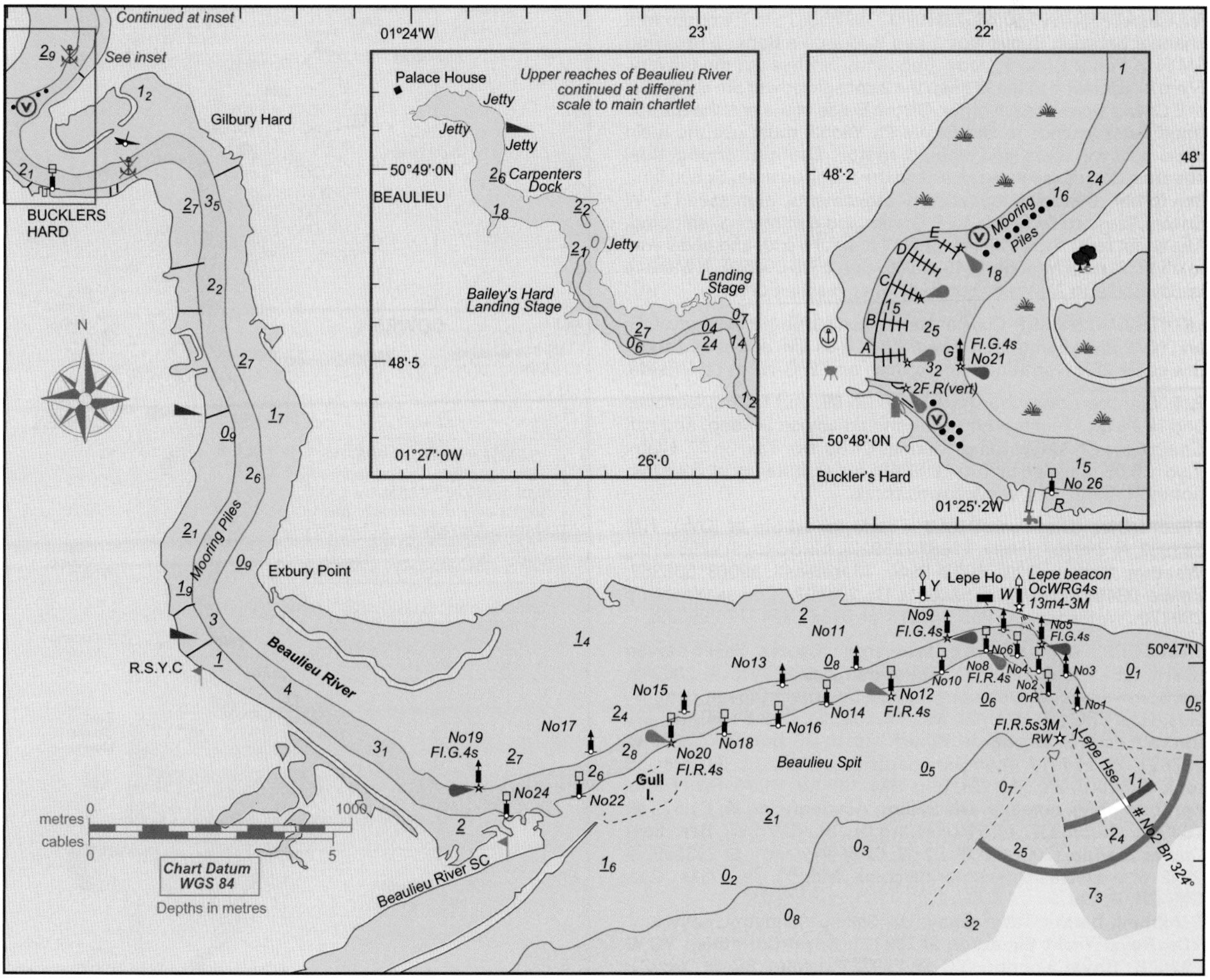
Continued at inset
See inset
Gilbury Hard
BUCKLERS HARD
N
Palace House
Upper reaches of Beaulieu River continued at different scale to main chartlet
Jetty
50°49'·0N
BEAULIEU
Carpenters Dock
Bailey's Hard Landing Stage
Landing Stage
48'·5
01°27'·0W
26'·0
01°24'W
23'
22'
48'·2
Mooring Piles
Fl.G.4s
No21
2F.R(vert)
50°48'·0N
Buckler's Hard
No 26
01°25'·2W
48'
Mooring Piles
Exbury Point
R.S.Y.C
Beaulieu River
Lepe Ho
Lepe beacon OcWRG4s 13m4-3M
50°47'N
Fl.G.4s
Fl.R.4s
No19
No17
No15
No13
No11
No9
No24
No22
No20
No18
No16
No14
No12
No10
No8
No6
No5
No4
No3
No2
No1
Gull I.
Beaulieu Spit
Fl.R.5s3M RW
Lepe Hse
No2 Bn 324°
metres
cables
1000
Chart Datum WGS 84
Depths in metres
Beaulieu River SC

9.2.17 COWES/RIVER MEDINA

Isle of Wight 50°45'·89N 01°17'·80W ❁❁❁◊◊◊✿✿✿

CHARTS AC *5600, 2035, 2036, 2793*; Imray C3, C15; Stanfords 11, 24, 25; OS 196

TIDES +0029 Dover; ML 2·7; Zone 0 (UT)

Standard Port PORTSMOUTH (⟶)

Times				Height (metres)			
High Water		Low Water		MHWS	MHWN	MLWN	MLWS
0000	0600	0500	1100	4·7	3·8	1·9	0·8
1200	1800	1700	2300				
Differences COWES							
−0015	+0015	0000	−0020	−0·5	−0·3	−0·1	0·0
FOLLY INN							
−0015	+0015	0000	−0020	−0·6	−0·4	−0·1	+0·2
NEWPORT							
No data		No data		−0·6	−0·4	+0·1	+0·8

NOTE: Double HWs occur at or near sp. On other occasions a stand occurs lasting up to 2hrs; times given represent the middle of the stand. See 9.2.11, especially for Newport.

SHELTER Good at Cowes Yacht Haven and above the chain ferry, but outer hbr exposed to N and NE winds. ⚓ prohib in hbr. Visitors may pick up/secure to any mooring/piles/pontoon so labelled, ie: 9 large Ⓥs off The Green and off The Parade; Thetis Pontoon (short stay/overnight only, dredged 2·0m); pontoons S of the chain ferry (W Cowes); 'E' Pontoon off E Cowes SC. See opposite for pontoons in Folly Reach; Island Harbour marina on E bank beyond Folly Inn and in Newport (dries). Good ⚓ in Osborne Bay, 2M E, sheltered from SE to W; no landing.

NAVIGATION WPT 50°46'·23N 01°17'·99W, 347°/167° from/to mid channel between Buoys Nos 1 and 2. Bramble Bank, 1·1m, lying 1M N of Prince Consort buoy, frequently catches out the unwary. From N, to clear it to the W keep the 2 conspic power stn chimneys at E Cowes open of each other. On the E side of the ent, the Shrape (mud flats) extends to Old Castle Pt. Yachts must use the main chan near W shore and should motor. Caution: strong tidal streams; do not sail through or ⚓ in the mooring area. Speed limit 6kn in hbr. Beware frequent ferry movements, high-speed to W Cowes, large ro-ro ferries to E Cowes and commercial shipping. The chain ferry shows all round Fl W lt at fore-end, and gives way to all tfc; it runs Mon-Sat: 0435-0005, Sun 0635-0005LT. R Medina is navigable to Newport, but the upper reaches dry.

LIGHTS AND MARKS Chan ent is marked by No 1 SHM buoy, QG, and No 2 PHM buoy, QR. E bkwtr hd Fl R 3s 3M. Jetties and some dns show 2FR (vert) on E side of hbr, and 2FG (vert) on W side.

R/T Monitor *Cowes Hbr Radio* VHF Ch **69**; and for hbr launches and HM's Ⓥs. Yachts >30m LOA should advise arr/dep, and call *Chain Ferry* Ch 69 if passing. Marinas Ch 80. *Hbr Taxi* Ch 77. *Water Taxi* Ch 06. Casualties: (Ch 16/67/69) for ambulance at Fountain pontoon. Web site www.cowes.co.uk.

TELEPHONE (Dial code 01983 = code for whole of IOW) HM 293952, 📠 299357, (Folly 07887 725922); MRSC (023) 9255 2100; Weather Centre (023) 8022 8844; Marinecall 09068 505357; Police 08450 454545; Ⓗ 524081; Dr 294902; Cowes Yachting 280770; Water taxis 07050 344818 or 07831 331717/299033.

FACILITIES **Marinas** (from seaward) : **Cowes Yacht Haven** (CYH), (35+ 200 Ⓥ, £2.00, £2.65@w/end),s ☎ 299975, 📠 200332, www.cowesyachthaven.com, info@cowesyachthaven.com, ♿, Gas, Gaz, LPG (all H24), El, ME, ⚒, SM, Ⓔ, C (2·5 ton), BH (35 ton), R, Ice, ▣. **Shepards Wharf** (up to 75 berths, £1.80) ☎ 297821, 📠 294814, mail@shepards.co.uk,ME, El, Ⓔ, BH (18 ton), C (6 ton), BY, SM, CH, Slip. **HM**: 100 AB, £1.20; FW (Thetis pontoon only), some ♿. **UK Sailing Academy** (10 Ⓥ, £1.52), ☎ 294941, 📠 295938, info@uksa.org.uk, ♿, ⛽, FW, Bar. **East Cowes Marina,** (200+100 Ⓥ, £2.00, £2.50@w/end), ☎ 293983, 📠 299276, www.eastcowesmarina.co.uk, ME, ⚒, 🛒, Gas, Gaz, SM, CH, R, Bar.

Scrubbing berths: Town Quay, UK Sailing Academy, Folly Inn.

YCs: Royal Yacht Squadron ☎ 292191; **Royal Corinthian YC** ☎ 292608; **Royal London YC** ☎ 299727; **Island SC** ☎ 296621;

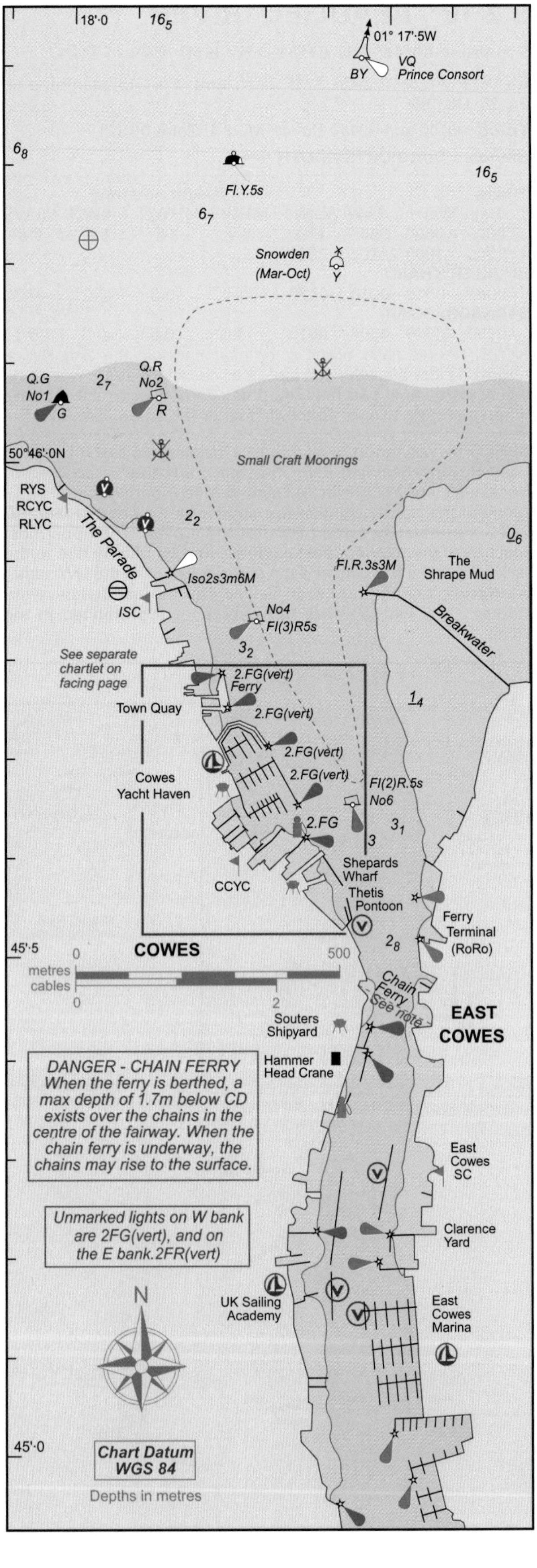
18'·0
01° 17'·5W
VQ
Prince Consort
BY
Fl.Y.5s
Snowden
(Mar-Oct)
Q.G
No1
Q.R
No2
50°46'·0N
Small Craft Moorings
RYS
RCYC
RLYC
The Parade
Iso2s3m6M
ISC
No4
Fl(3)R5s
Fl.R.3s3M
The Shrape Mud
Breakwater
See separate chartlet on facing page
2.FG(vert)
Ferry
Town Quay
2.FG(vert)
2.FG(vert)
2.FG(vert)
Cowes Yacht Haven
Fl(2)R.5s
No6
2.FG
CCYC
Shepards Wharf
Thetis Pontoon
Ferry Terminal (RoRo)
45'·5
COWES
metres
cables
500
Chain Ferry See note
EAST COWES
Souters Shipyard
Hammer Head Crane
DANGER - CHAIN FERRY
When the ferry is berthed, a max depth of 1.7m below CD exists over the chains in the centre of the fairway. When the chain ferry is underway, the chains may rise to the surface.
East Cowes SC
Unmarked lights on W bank are 2FG(vert), and on the E bank.2FR(vert)
Clarence Yard
N
UK Sailing Academy
East Cowes Marina
45'·0
Chart Datum WGS 84
Depths in metres

Royal Ocean Racing Club ☎ 295144 (manned only in Cowes Week); **Cowes Corinthian YC** ☎ 296333; **East Cowes SC** see www.eastcowessc.co.uk; **Cowes Combined Clubs** ☎ 295744, 📠 295329, ccc@cowesweek.co.uk. Cowes Week is normally 1st full week in Aug.
Ferries: Red Funnel ☎ (023) 8033 4010, 📠 8063 9438, post@redfunnel. co.uk, www.redfunnel.co.uk, all to Soton: Car/pax from E Cowes; foot pax from W Cowes; **Chain Ferry** ☎ 293041.
Services: All marine services are available. See *Port Handbook & Directory* for details (free from HM, hbr launches, marinas and Cowes Yachting). **FW** from marinas, Old Town Quay, Whitegates public pontoon, Thetis pontoon and Folly Inn pontoon. **Fuel:** CYH, LPG only, H24; Lallows BY (P & D); MST pontoon off Souters BY (P & D).
Town www.cowes.co.uk, Bar, ⊡, Slip, ✉, Ⓑ, Gas, Gaz Ⓔ, CH, R, 🛒, El.

RIVER MEDINA, FOLLY REACH TO NEWPORT

FOLLY REACH, 50°44'·03N 01°16'·99W. Above Medham ECM bn, VQ (3) 5s, there are depths of 1m to S Folly bn, QG. There are Ⓥ pontoons along W bank, S of residents' ones. HM ☎ 07974 864627 and Ch 69 *Folly Launch*. **Folly Inn** ♿, ☎ 297171, AB (pontoon) £1.50, M*, Slip, scrubbing berth.
Island Harbour Marina (5ca S of Folly Inn), (100 + 80 Ⓥ), £2.17; 2.0m), ☎ 822999, 📠 526020, www.island-harbour.co.uk, ♿, BH (25 ton), Gas, Gaz, ⊡, ME, CH, BY, Slip, Bar, R. VHF Ch 80 *Island Harbour Control*. Excellent shelter; appr via marked, dredged chan with waiting pontoon to stbd, withies to port. Access HW ±2½ to lock 0900–1730 (tfc lts). *Ryde* paddle steamer is conspic.

NEWPORT, 50°42´·21N 01°17´·43W. Tides see 9.2.11 and 9.2.21. Above Island Hbr marina the 1·2M long chan to Newport dries, but from HW Portsmouth –1½ to HW +2 it carries 2m or more. S from Folly Inn, the hbr authority is IoW Council. Speed limit 6kn up to Seaclose, S of Newport Rowing Club (NRC); thence 4kn to Newport. The chan, which is buoyed and partially lit, favours the W bank; night appr not recommended. Power lines have 33m clearance. Ldg marks/lts are 192°, W ◊ bns 7/11m, on the E bank, both lit 2FR (hor). Newport, Ⓥs' pontoons on the E/SE sides of the basin have 1·4m HW ±2. Bilge keelers lie alongside pontoons on soft mud; fin keelers against quay wall on firm, level bottom. Fender boards can be supplied.
Newport Yacht Hbr (50 Ⓥs, £1.20), ♿, HM ☎ 525994, 📠 823545, VHF Ch 69 (HO or as arranged), ⛽, FW, BY, C (10 ton), R; Classic Boat Centre.
Town P & D (cans), El, ⚒, Slip, Gaz, Gas, Ⓑ, Bar, Dr, Ⓗ, ✉, ⊡, R, 🛒.

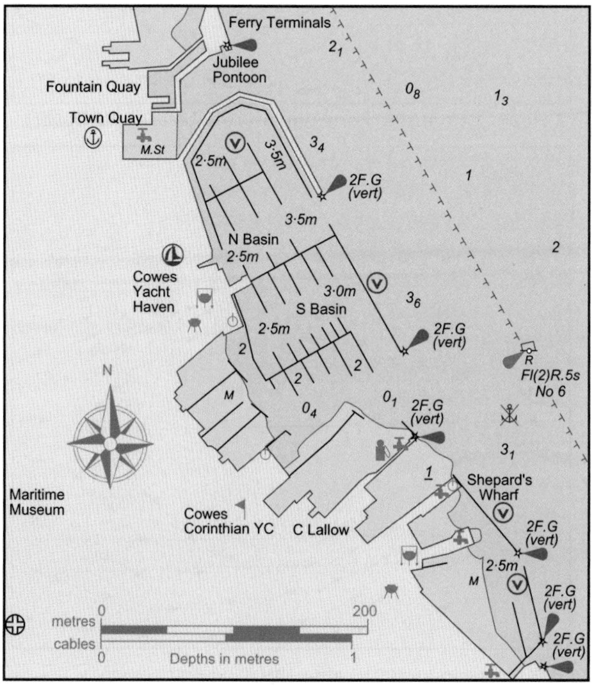
Ferry Terminals
Jubilee Pontoon
Fountain Quay
Town Quay
M.St
N Basin
S Basin
Cowes Yacht Haven
2F.G (vert)
Fl(2)R.5s No 6
Shepard's Wharf
Maritime Museum
Cowes Corinthian YC
C Lallow
metres
cables
Depths in metres

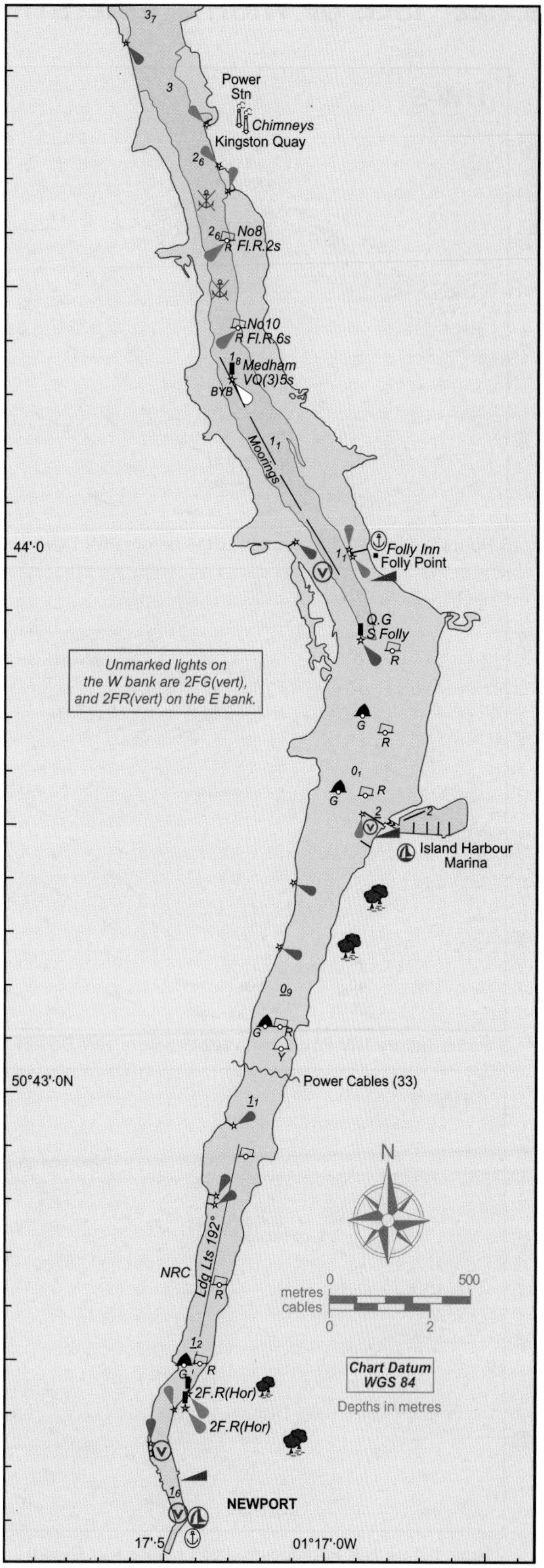
Power Stn
Chimneys
Kingston Quay
No8 Fl.R.2s
No10 Fl.R.6s
Medham VQ(3)5s
BYB
Moorings
44'·0
Folly Inn
Folly Point
Q.G
S Folly
Unmarked lights on the W bank are 2FG(vert), and 2FR(vert) on the E bank.
Island Harbour Marina
50°43'·0N
Power Cables (33)
NRC
Ldg Lts 192°
2F.R(Hor)
NEWPORT
17'·5
01°17'·0W
metres
cables
Chart Datum WGS 84
Depths in metres

9.2.22 ISLE OF WIGHT TIDAL STREAMS

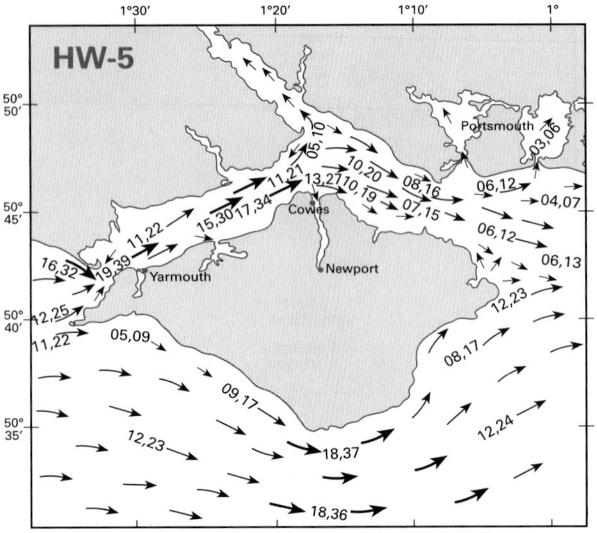
1°30′
1°20′
1°10′
1°
HW-5
50° 50′
50° 45′
50° 40′
50° 35′
Portsmouth
Cowes
Newport
Yarmouth
05,10
03,06
10,20
08,16
06,12
04,07
11,21
13,21
10,19
07,15
15,30
17,34
11,22
19,39
16,32
06,12
06,13
12,25
11,22
05,09
12,23
08,17
09,17
12,24
12,23
18,37
18,36

5 Hours before HW Portsmouth (0445 before HW Dover)

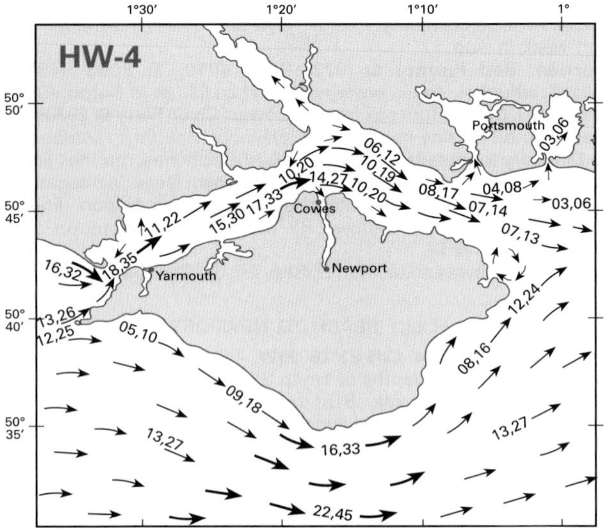
1°30′
1°20′
1°10′
1°
HW-4
50° 50′
50° 45′
50° 40′
50° 35′
Portsmouth
Cowes
Newport
Yarmouth
03,06
06,12
10,19
10,20
14,21
10,20
08,17
04,08
07,14
03,06
15,30
17,33
11,22
18,35
16,32
07,13
13,26
12,25
05,10
12,24
08,16
09,18
13,27
16,33
13,27
22,45

4 Hours before HW Portsmouth (0345 before HW Dover)

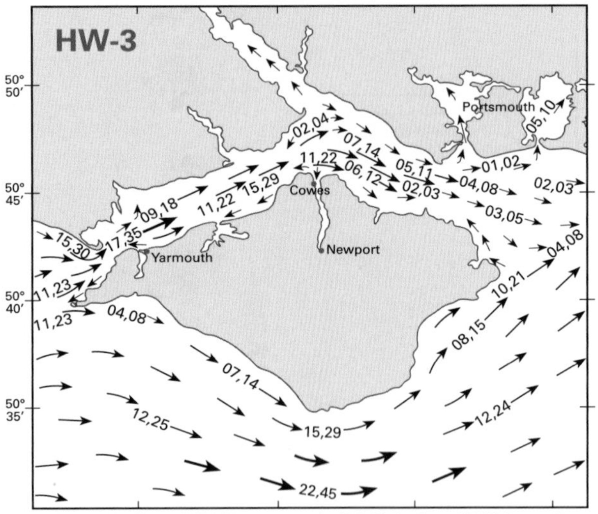
HW-3
50° 50′
50° 45′
50° 40′
50° 35′
Portsmouth
Cowes
Newport
Yarmouth
05,10
02,04
07,14
11,22
06,12
05,11
01,02
02,03
04,08
02,03
15,29
11,22
09,18
17,35
15,30
03,05
04,08
11,23
11,23
04,08
10,21
08,15
07,14
12,25
15,29
12,24
22,45

3 Hours before HW Portsmouth (0245 before HW Dover)

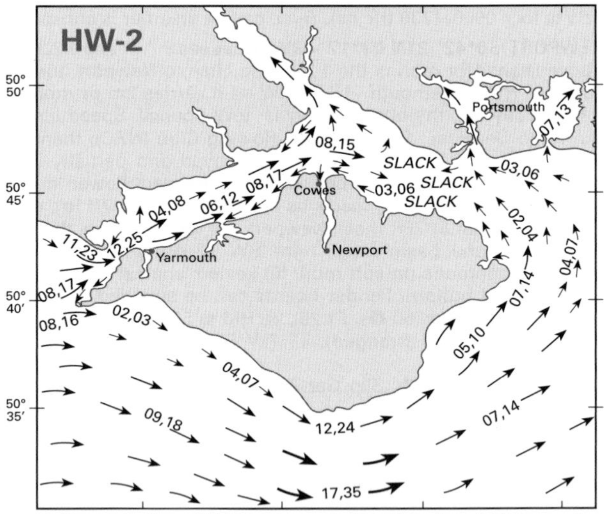
HW-2
50° 50′
50° 45′
50° 40′
50° 35′
Portsmouth
Cowes
Newport
Yarmouth
07,13
08,15
SLACK
03,06
08,17
06,12
04,08
03,06
SLACK
SLACK
12,25
11,23
02,04
04,07
08,17
08,16
02,03
07,14
05,10
04,07
09,18
12,24
07,14
17,35

2 Hours before HW Portsmouth (0145 before HW Dover)

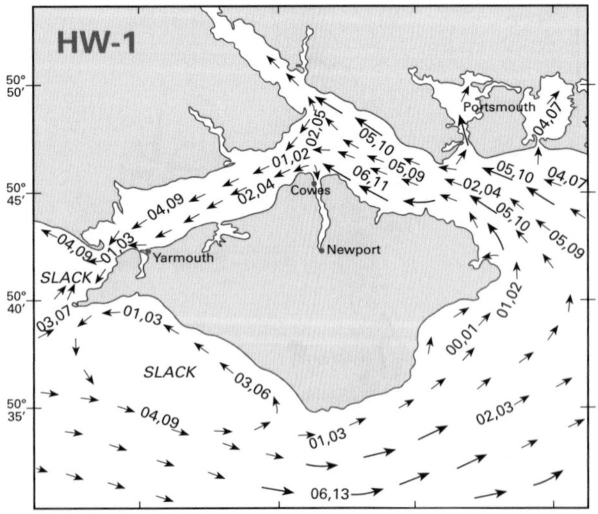
HW-1
50° 50′
50° 45′
50° 40′
50° 35′
Portsmouth
Cowes
Newport
Yarmouth
04,07
02,05
05,10
05,09
01,02
06,11
05,10
04,07
02,04
02,04
04,09
05,10
05,09
04,09
01,03
SLACK
03,07
01,03
01,02
00,01
SLACK
03,06
04,09
01,03
02,03
06,13

1 Hour before HW Portsmouth (0045 before HW Dover)

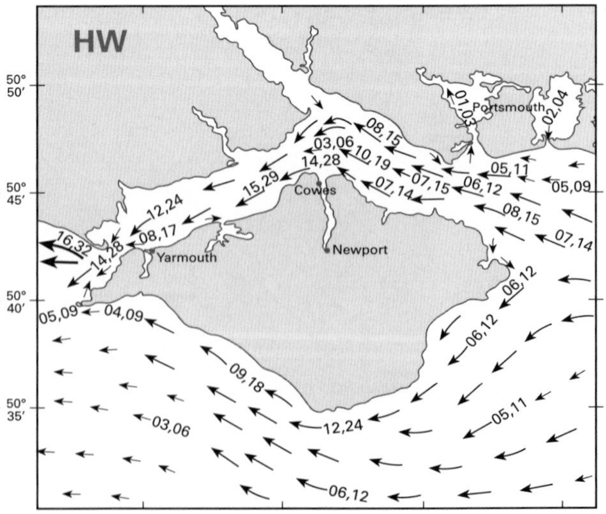
HW
50° 50′
50° 45′
50° 40′
50° 35′
Portsmouth
Cowes
Newport
Yarmouth
01,03
02,04
08,15
03,06
10,19
14,28
07,15
06,12
05,11
05,09
15,29
07,14
12,24
08,15
08,17
07,14
16,32
14,28
06,12
05,09
04,09
06,12
09,18
05,11
03,06
12,24
06,12

HW Portsmouth (0015 after HW Dover)

General Area 2: 9.2.3

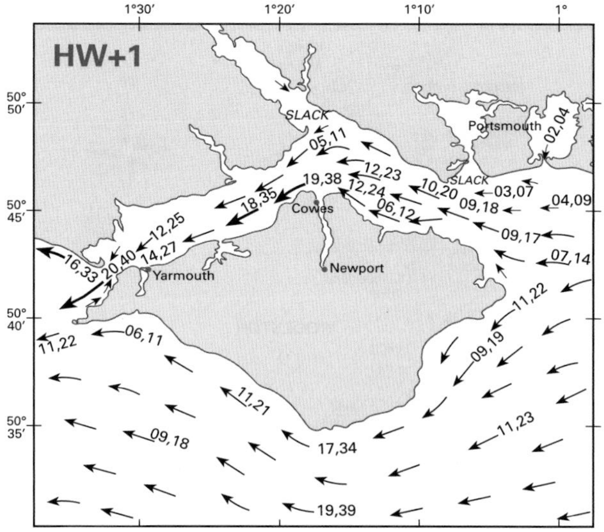
HW+1
1°30'
1°20'
1°10'
1°
50° 50'
50° 45'
50° 40'
50° 35'
SLACK
05,11
12,23
SLACK
19,38
12,24
10,20
03,07
18,35
06,12
09,18
04,09
12,25
09,17
14,27
20,40
07,14
16,33
Portsmouth
02,04
Cowes
Yarmouth
Newport
11,22
11,22
06,11
09,19
11,21
09,18
11,23
17,34
19,39

1 Hour after HW Portsmouth (0115 after HW Dover)

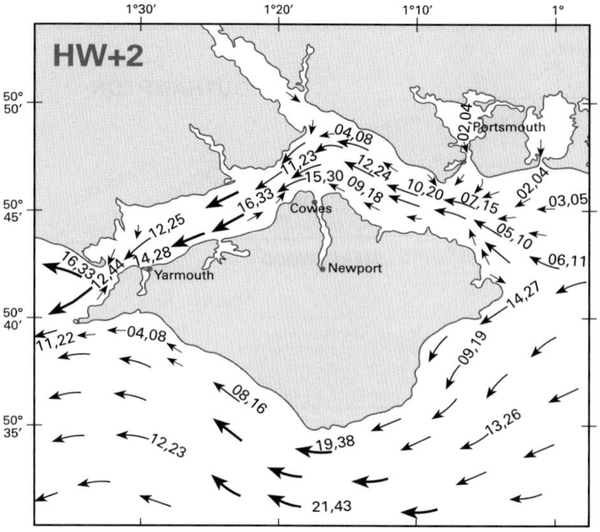
HW+2
1°30'
1°20'
1°10'
1°
50° 50'
50° 45'
50° 40'
50° 35'
04,08
11,23
12,24
15,30
09,18
10,20
07,15
02,04
03,05
02,04
16,33
05,10
12,25
06,11
14,28
12,44
16,33
Portsmouth
Cowes
Yarmouth
Newport
14,27
11,22
04,08
09,19
08,16
13,26
12,23
19,38
21,43

2 Hours after HW Portsmouth (0215 after HW Dover)

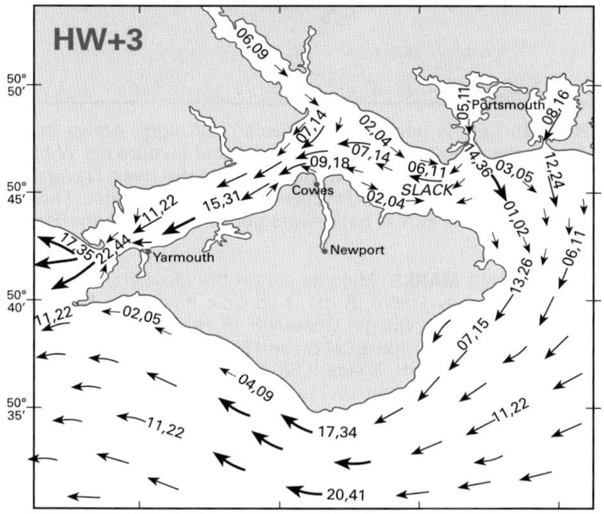
HW+3
1°30'
1°20'
1°10'
1°
50° 50'
50° 45'
50° 40'
50° 35'
06,09
05,11
08,16
07,14
02,04
07,14
14,36
12,24
09,18
06,11
03,05
15,31
SLACK
11,22
02,04
01,02
06,11
17,35
22,44
Portsmouth
Cowes
Yarmouth
Newport
13,26
11,22
02,05
07,15
04,09
11,22
11,22
17,34
20,41

3 Hours after HW Portsmouth (0315 after HW Dover)

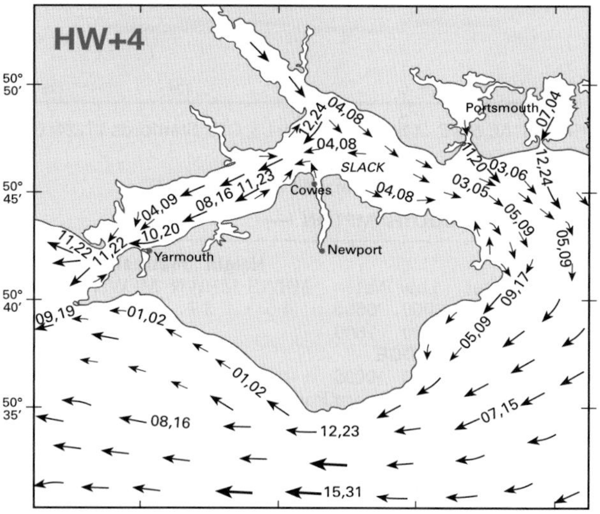
HW+4
1°30'
1°20'
1°10'
1°
50° 50'
50° 45'
50° 40'
50° 35'
12,24
04,08
07,04
04,08
11,20
03,06
SLACK
12,24
11,23
03,05
08,16
04,08
04,09
05,09
10,20
05,09
11,22
11,22
09,17
Portsmouth
Cowes
Yarmouth
Newport
09,19
01,02
05,09
01,02
07,15
08,16
12,23
15,31

4 Hours after HW Portsmouth (0415 after HW Dover)

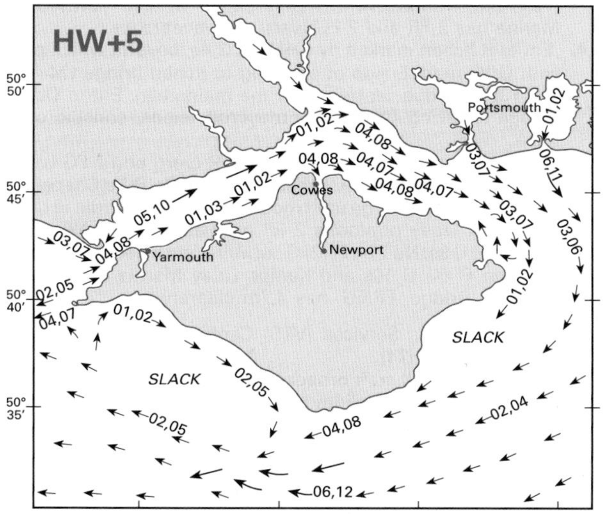
HW+5
1°30'
1°20'
1°10'
1°
50° 50'
50° 45'
50° 40'
50° 35'
01,02
01,02
04,08
03,07
04,08
04,07
06,11
01,02
04,08
04,07
05,10
01,03
03,07
03,07
04,08
03,06
02,05
01,02
04,07
01,02
Portsmouth
Cowes
Yarmouth
Newport
SLACK
SLACK
02,05
02,05
04,08
02,04
06,12

5 Hours after HW Portsmouth (0515 after HW Dover)

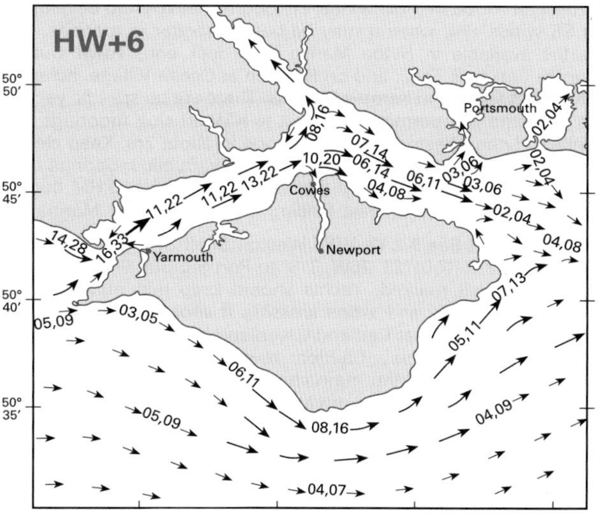
HW+6
1°30'
1°20'
1°10'
1°
50° 50'
50° 45'
50° 40'
50° 35'
08,16
02,04
07,14
10,20
06,14
06,11
03,06
02,04
03,06
11,22
11,22
13,22
04,08
02,04
14,28
16,33
04,08
Portsmouth
Cowes
Yarmouth
Newport
07,13
05,09
03,05
05,11
06,11
05,09
08,16
04,09
04,07

6 Hours after HW Portsmouth (0615 after HW Dover)

9.2.19 SOUTHAMPTON

Hampshire **50°52′·93N 01°23′·49W** ❁❁❁◊◊◊✿✿

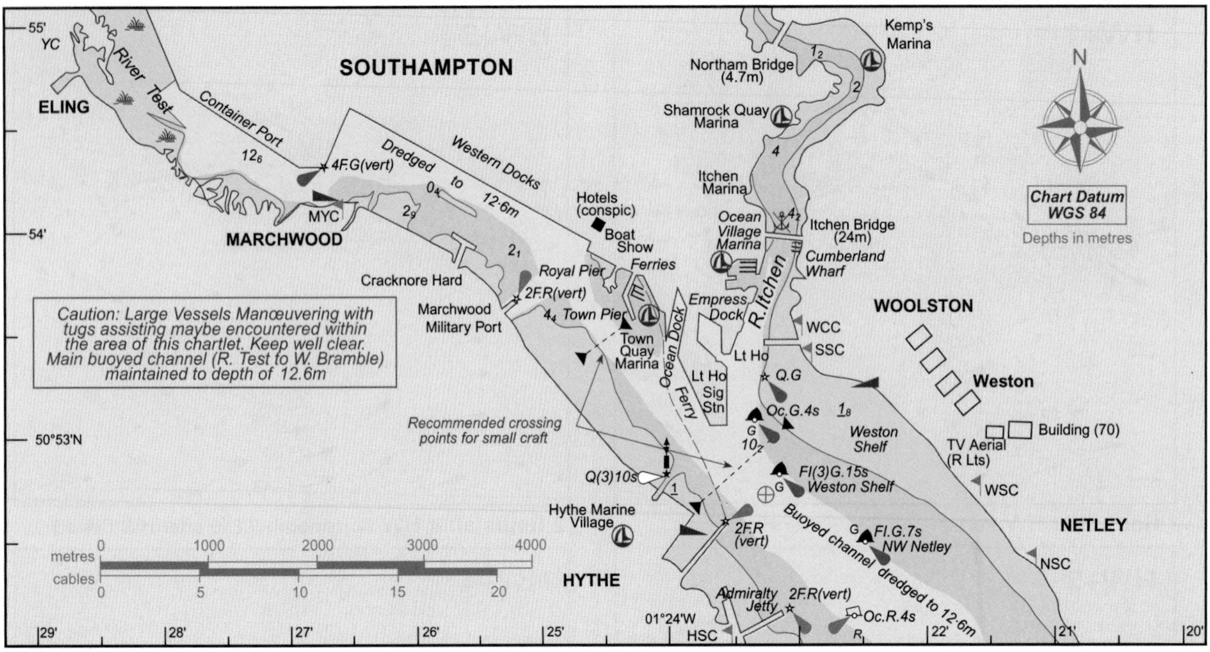
SOUTHAMPTON
ELING
YC
River Test
Container Port
12₆
4F.G(vert)
Dredged to 12·6m
Western Docks
MYC
MARCHWOOD
Cracknore Hard
Marchwood Military Port
Hotels (conspic)
Boat Show
Royal Pier
Ferries
2F.R(vert)
4₄ Town Pier
Town Quay Marina
Ocean Dock
Ferry
Caution: Large Vessels Manœuvering with tugs assisting maybe encountered within the area of this chartlet. Keep well clear. Main buoyed channel (R. Test to W. Bramble) maintained to depth of 12.6m
Recommended crossing points for small craft
Q(3)10s
Hythe Marine Village
HYTHE
Admiralty Jetty
2F.R(vert)
2F.R (vert)
Oc.R.4s
Buoyed channel dredged to 12·6m
Northam Bridge (4.7m)
Kemp's Marina
Shamrock Quay Marina
Itchen Marina
Ocean Village Marina
Itchen Bridge (24m)
Cumberland Wharf
Empress Dock
R. Itchen
Lt Ho
Lt Ho Sig Stn
WCC
SSC
WOOLSTON
Weston
Q.G
Oc.G.4s
Weston Shelf
Fl(3)G.15s Weston Shelf
Fl.G.7s NW Netley
Building (70)
TV Aerial (R Lts)
WSC
NETLEY
NSC
HSC
Chart Datum WGS 84
Depths in metres
N
metres 0 1000 2000 3000 4000
cables 0 5 10 15 20
55'
54'
50°53'N
29' 28' 27' 26' 25' 01°24'W 22' 21' 20'

CHARTS AC *5600, 2036, 2041*; Imray C3, C15; Stanfords 11, 24; OS 196

TIDES HW (1st) –0001 Dover; ML 2·9; Zone 0 (UT)

Standard Port SOUTHAMPTON (⟶)

Times				Height (metres)			
High Water		Low Water		MHWS	MHWN	MLWN	MLWS
0400	1100	0000	0600	4·5	3·7	1·8	0·5
1600	2300	1200	1800				
Differences REDBRIDGE							
–0020	+0005	0000	–0005	–0·1	–0·1	–0·1	–0·1

Southampton is a Standard Port and tidal predictions for each day of the year are given above. At sp there are two separate HWs about two hrs apart; at nps there is a long stand. Predictions are for the first HW when there are two, otherwise for the middle of the stand. See 9.2.11. NE gales and a high barometer may lower sea level by 0·6m.

SHELTER Good in most winds, although a heavy chop develops in SE winds >F4, when it may be best to shelter in marinas. ⓥ berths available in Hythe Marina (with lock ent), Town Quay marina (ent to R Test), and on R Itchen at Ocean Village, Itchen, Shamrock Quay and Kemp's Marinas. There are no specific yacht ⚓s but temp ⚓ is permitted (subject to HM) off club moorings at Netley, Hythe, Weston and Marchwood in about 2m. Keep clear of main or secondary chans and Hythe Pier. Public moorings for larger yachts opposite Royal Pier near Gymp Elbow PHM buoy in 4m (contact HM); nearest landing is at Town Quay Marina.

NAVIGATION See 9.2.12. WPT Weston Shelf SHM buoy, Fl (3) G 15s, 50°52′·71N 01°23′·26W, 318° to Port Sig Stn, 0·40M. Main chans are well marked. Yachts should keep just outside the buoyed lit fairway and ***when crossing it should do so at 90°***, abeam Fawley chy, at Cadland/Greenland buoys, abeam Hythe and abeam Town Quay. Caution: several large unlit buoys off Hythe, both sides of the main chan, and elsewhere.

It is essential to keep clear of very large tankers operating from Fawley and commercial shipping from Southampton. See 9.2.16, Precautionary Area between Cowes and Calshot. Frequent Hi.Speed & Ro-Ro ferries operate through the area.

R Test There is foul ground at Marchwood and Royal Pier; extensive container port beyond. Eling Chan dries.

R Itchen Care is necessary, particularly at night. Above Itchen Bridge the chan bends sharply to port and favours the W bank. There are unlit moorings in the centre of the river. Navigation above Northam Bridge (4·7m clearance) is not advisable. There is a speed limit of 6kn in both rivers above the line Hythe Pier to Weston Shelf.

LIGHTS AND MARKS Main lts are on the chartlet and in 9.2.4. Fawley chimney (198m, R lts) is conspic day/night. Note also:

1. Hythe Marina Village, close NW of Hythe Pier: appr chan marked by Q (3) 10s, ECM bn and Fl (2) R 5s PHM bn. Lock ent, N side 2 FG (vert); S side 2 FR (vert).
2. Southampton Water divides at Dock Head which is easily identified by conspic silos and a high lattice mast showing traffic sigs which are mandatory for commercial vessels, but may be disregarded by yachts outside the main chans. Beware large ships manoeuvering off Dock Head, and craft leaving Rivers Itchen and Test.
3. Dock Hd, W side (Queen Elizabeth II Terminal, S end) 4 FG (vert) 3M; framework tr; marks ent to R Test. Town Quay Marina has 2 FR and 2 FG (vert) on wavebreaks.
4. Ent to R Itchen marked by SHM Oc G 4s, beyond which piles with G lts mark E side of chan ldg to Itchen bridge (24·4m); a FW lt at bridge centre marks the main chan. Ent to Ocean Village is facing Vosper Thorneycroft sheds, conspic on E bank.
5. Above Itchen Bridge, marked by 2 FR (vert) and 2 FG (vert), the principal marks are: Crosshouse bn Oc R 5s;Chapel bn Fl G 3s. **Caution:** 8 large unlit mooring buoys in middle of river. Shamrock Quay pontoons 2 FR (vert)at SW and NE ends; No 5 bn Fl G 3s; No 7 bn Fl (2) G 5s; Millstone Pt jetty 2 FR (vert); No 9 bn Fl (4) G 10s and Kemps Quay Marina 2 FG (vert). Northam Bridge, FR/FG, has 4·7m clearance.

R/T Vessel Traffic Services (VTS) Centre. Call: *Southampton VTS* Ch **12** 14 16 (H24).

Traffic info for small craft broadcast on Ch 12 on the hour 0600-2200 Fri-Sun and Bank Holiday Mons from Easter to last weekend in Oct. From 1 June to 30 Sept broadcasts are every day at the same times.

Southampton Hbr Patrol Call: *Southampton Patrol* VHF Ch **12** 16, 01-28, 60-88 (H24). Marinas VHF Ch **80** M.

Fuel barges in R Itchen, call *Wyefuel* Ch 08.

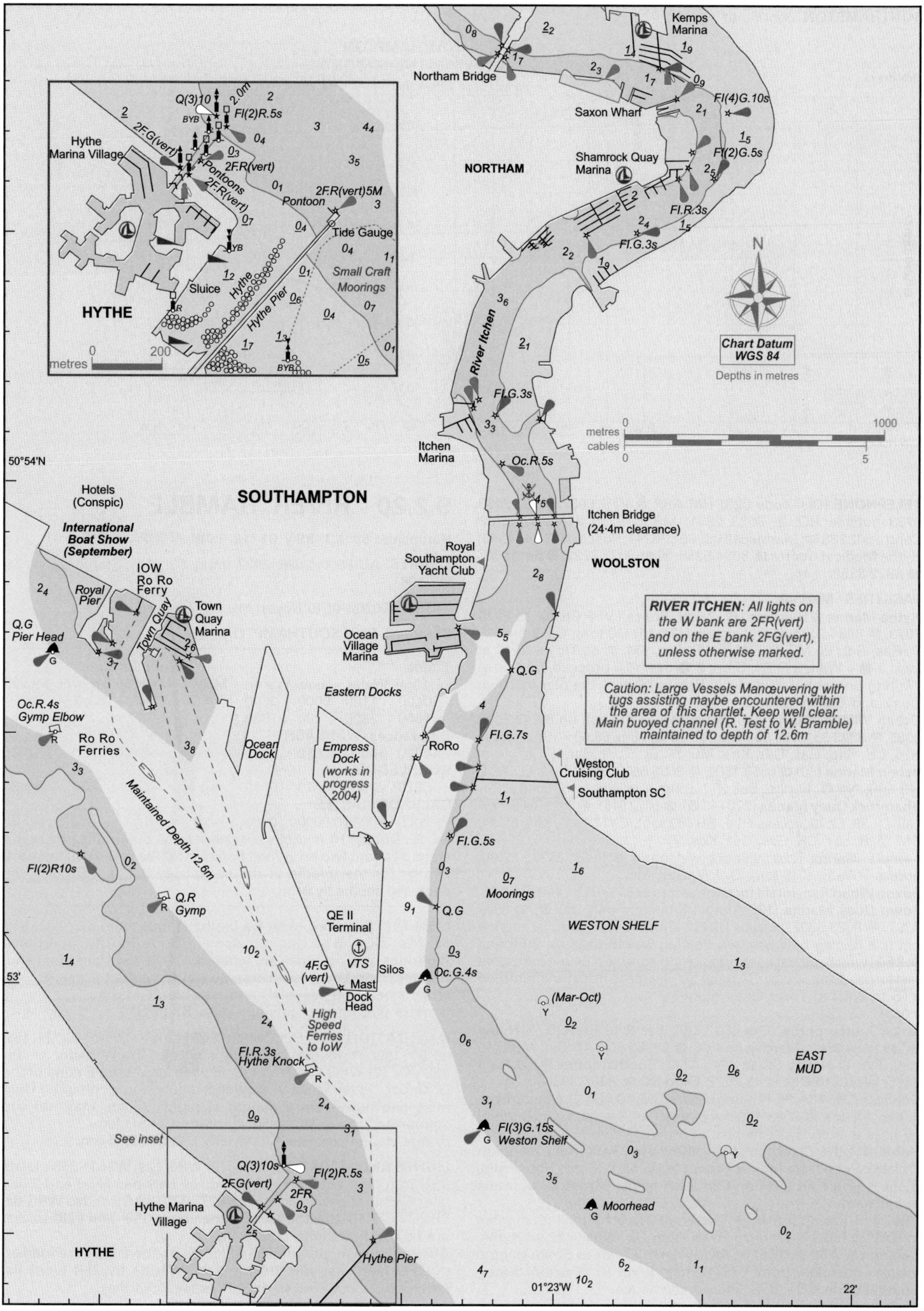
Kemps Marina
Northam Bridge
Saxon Wharf
Fl(4)G.10s
Fl(2)G.5s
Shamrock Quay Marina
NORTHAM
Fl.R.3s
Fl.G.3s
N
Chart Datum WGS 84
Depths in metres
River Itchen
Fl.G.3s
metres
cables
0
1000
0
5
Itchen Marina
Oc.R.5s
50°54'N
Hotels (Conspic)
SOUTHAMPTON
Itchen Bridge (24·4m clearance)
International Boat Show (September)
Royal Southampton Yacht Club
WOOLSTON
IOW Ro Ro Ferry
Royal Pier
Town Quay Marina
Town Quay
Q.G Pier Head
RIVER ITCHEN: All lights on the W bank are 2FR(vert) and on the E bank 2FG(vert), unless otherwise marked.
Ocean Village Marina
Q.G
Eastern Docks
Caution: Large Vessels Manœuvering with tugs assisting maybe encountered within the area of this chartlet. Keep well clear. Main buoyed channel (R. Test to W. Bramble) maintained to depth of 12.6m
Oc.R.4s Gymp Elbow
Ro Ro Ferries
Ocean Dock
Empress Dock (works in progress 2004)
RoRo
Fl.G.7s
Weston Cruising Club
Southampton SC
Maintained Depth 12.6m
Fl.G.5s
Fl(2)R10s
Moorings
Q.R Gymp
Q.G
WESTON SHELF
QE II Terminal
VTS
Silos
4F.G (vert)
Mast Dock Head
Oc.G.4s
53'
(Mar-Oct)
High Speed Ferries to IoW
EAST MUD
Fl.R.3s Hythe Knock
Fl(3)G.15s Weston Shelf
See inset
Q(3)10s
Fl(2)R.5s
2FG(vert)
2FR
Hythe Marina Village
Moorhead
HYTHE
Hythe Pier
01°23'W
22'
Q(3)10
2.0m
Fl(2)R.5s
Hythe Marina Village
2FG(vert)
Pontoons
2FR(vert)
2F.R(vert)5M
Pontoon
Tide Gauge
Small Craft Moorings
Sluice
Hythe
Hythe Pier
HYTHE
metres
0
200

SOUTHAMPTON *continued*

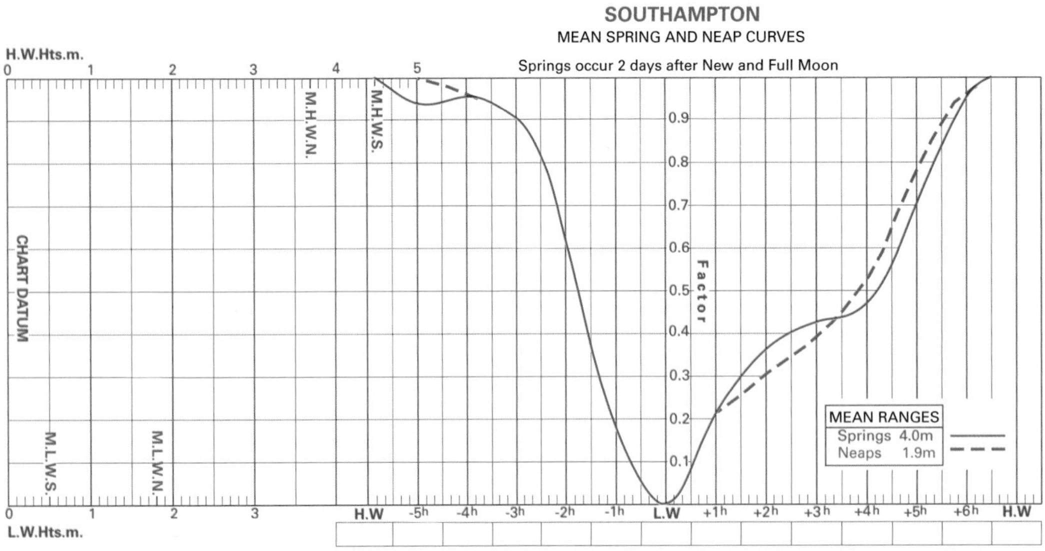
SOUTHAMPTON
MEAN SPRING AND NEAP CURVES
Springs occur 2 days after New and Full Moon
H.W.Hts.m.
0
1
2
3
4
5
M.H.W.N.
M.H.W.S.
CHART DATUM
M.L.W.S.
M.L.W.N.
L.W.Hts.m.
Factor
0.9
0.8
0.7
0.6
0.5
0.4
0.3
0.2
0.1
MEAN RANGES
Springs 4.0m
Neaps 1.9m
H.W
-5h
-4h
-3h
-2h
-1h
L.W
+1h
+2h
+3h
+4h
+5h
+6h
H.W

TELEPHONE (Dial code 023) HM ABP & VTS 8033 0022, 8033 9733 outside HO; 📠 8023 2991; MRSC 9255 2100; Weather Centre 8022 8844; Marinecall 09066 526241; Police 08450 454545; Hythe Medical Centre ☎ 8084 5955; Ⓗ ☎ 8077 7222, R Soton YC ☎ 8022 3352.

FACILITIES Marinas:

Hythe Marina (210+some Ⓥ; 2·5m). Pre-call VHF Ch 80. ☎ 8020 7073, 📠 8084 2424, £2.70, access H24; BH (30 ton), C (12 ton), P, D, Gas, Gaz, El, ME, ⚒, CH, 🛒, R, Bar, SM, ⚓, ♿. Tfc lts (vert) at lock: 3 ● = Wait; 3 Fl R = Stop; 2 ● over ○ = proceed, free-flow. Waiting pontoon outside lock. Ferries from Hythe pier to Town Quay and Ocean Village.

Ocean Village Marina (450; Ⓥ welcome). Pre-call Ch 80, ☎ 8022 9385, 📠 8023 3515, £2.60 <15m, £3.25 15-18m, £3.60 > 18m, access H24, CH, Slip, Gas, Gaz, Kos, ME, ⚒, ▣, 🛒, R, Bar, ♿;

Itchen Marina (50) ☎ 8063 1500, 📠 8033 5606; VHF Ch 12. D, BY, C (40 ton); No Ⓥ berths, but will assist a vessel in difficulty.

Shamrock Quay Marina (220+40 Ⓥ). ☎ 8022 9461, 📠 8021 3808. Pre-call Ch 80. £2.70, access H24, BH (63 ton), C (12 ton), ME, El, ⚒, SM, ▣, R, Bar, CH, Gas, Gaz, Kos, V;

Kemp's Marina (220; visitors welcome) ☎ 8063 2323, £2.50, access HW±3½, C (5 ton), D, FW, Gas, ME;

Saxon Wharf Repair/refit for large yachts ☎ 8033 9490, 📠 8021 3808;

Town Quay Marina (133 Annual B/holders only, no Ⓥ) ☎ 8023 4397, 📠 8023 5302, access H24 (2·6m); CH, ▣, R, Bar, ♿; marina ent is a dogleg between two floating wavebreaks (☆ 2 FR and ☆ 2 FG) which appear continuous from seaward. Beware adjacent fast ferries. Craft >20m LOA must get clearance from Southampton VTS to ent/dep Town Quay marina.

YACHT CLUBS

Royal Southampton YC ☎ 8022 3352, Bar, R, M, FW, L, ▣, ♿; **Hythe SC** ☎ 8084 6563; **Marchwood YC** ☎ 02380 666141, Bar, M, C (10 ton), FW, L; **Netley SC** ☎ 8045 4272; **Southampton SC** ☎ 8044 6575; **Weston SC** ☎ 8045 2527; **Eling SC** ☎ 8086 3987.

Services CH, ACA, ⚒, Rigging, Spars, SM, ME, El, Ⓔ. Note: D from Itchen Marine ☎ 8063 1500 above Itchen Bridge, nearest petrol by hose is from Hythe marina.

Hards at Hythe, Cracknore, Eling, Mayflower Park (Test), Northam (Itchen). Public landings at Cross House hard, Cross House slip, Block House hard (Itchen), Carnation public hard & Cowporters public hard.

City 🛒, R, Bar, Ⓑ, ✉, ⇌, ✈, Car ferry/Fast cat for foot passengers to IOW, ☎ 8033 3042; ferry Town Quay, ☎ 8084 0722, to Hythe.

Reference ABP publish a *Yachtsman's Guide to Southampton Water* obtainable from VTS Centre, Berth 37, Eastern Docks, Southampton SO1 1GG. Please send s.a.e.

9.2.20 RIVER HAMBLE

Hampshire **50°50'·99N 01°18'·50W** ✲✲✲◊◊◊✿✿

CHARTS AC *5600, 2036, 2022*; Imray C3, C15; Stanfords 11, 24; OS 196

TIDES +0020, –0010 Dover; ML 2·9; Zone 0 (UT)

Standard Port SOUTHAMPTON (⟶)

Times				**Height (metres)**			
High Water		Low Water		MHWS	MHWN	MLWN	MLWS
0400	1100	0000	0600	4·5	3·7	1·8	0·5
1600	2300	1200	1800				
Differences WARSASH							
+0020	+0010	+0010	0000	0·0	+0·1	+0·1	+0·3
BURSLEDON							
+0020	+0020	+0010	+0010	+0·1	+0·1	+0·2	+0·2
CALSHOT CASTLE							
0000	+0025	0000	0000	0·0	0·0	+0·2	+0·3

NOTE: Double HWs occur at or near sp; at other times there is a stand of about two hrs. Predictions are for the first HW if there are two or for the middle of the stand. See 9.2.11. NE gales can decrease depths by 0·6m.

SHELTER Excellent, with Ⓥs berths at four main marinas, and at YCs, SCs, BYs and on some Hbr Authority pontoons. Pontoons at all marinas are lettered A, B et seq from the S end. Crableck and Universal Yards do not have Ⓥs berths. In mid-stream between Warsash and Hamble Pt Marina is a clearly marked Ⓥ pontoon, between piles B1 to B10.

NAVIGATION WPT Hamble Pt SCM buoy, Q (6) + L Fl 15s, 50°50'·15N 01°18'·66W, is in the centre of the W sector of Dir 352°, Oc (2) WRG 12s; Nos 1, 3, 5, piles are on the E edge of the G sector. River is very crowded; anchoring prohibited. Unlit piles and buoys are a danger at night. Yachts may not use spinnakers above Warsash Maritime Centre jetty.
Bridge clearances: Road 4·0m; Rly 6·0m; M27 4·3m.

LIGHTS AND MARKS Dir ☆, Oc (2) WRG 12s, W351°-353°, leads 352° into river ent. and when midway between No 5 and 7 bns alter 028° in the white sector, W027°-029°, of Dir ☆, Iso WRG 6s. Piles Nos 1-10 (to either side of the above 352° and 028° tracks) are lit and fitted with radar refl.
Above Warsash, pontoons and jetties on the E side are marked by 2FG (vert) lts, and those on the W side by 2FR (vert) lts. Lateral piles are Fl G 4s or Fl R 4s (see chartlet).

RIVER HAMBLE *continued*

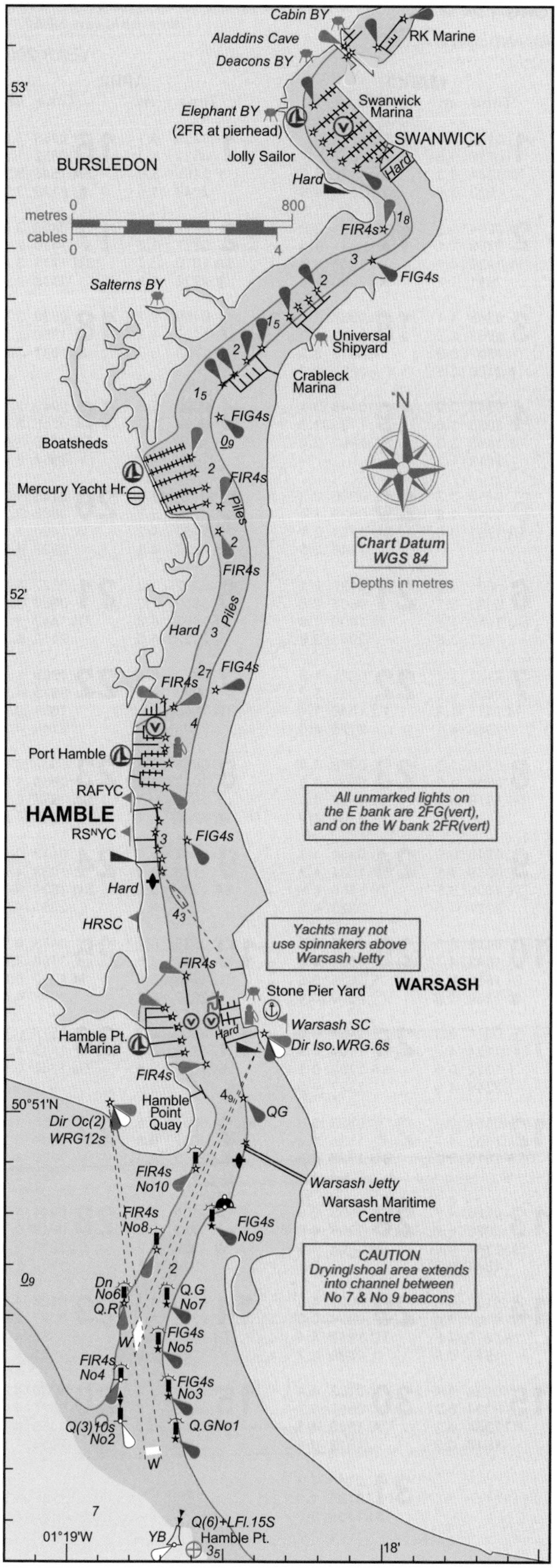
Cabin BY
Aladdins Cave
Deacons BY
RK Marine
Elephant BY
(2FR at pierhead)
Swanwick Marina
SWANWICK
BURSLEDON
Jolly Sailor
Hard
metres
cables
0
800
0
4
FlR4s
FlG4s
Salterns BY
Universal Shipyard
Crableck Marina
N
Boatsheds
Mercury Yacht Hr
Piles
Chart Datum WGS 84
Depths in metres
Port Hamble
RAFYC
HAMBLE
RS^N YC
All unmarked lights on the E bank are 2FG(vert), and on the W bank 2FR(vert)
HRSC
Yachts may not use spinnakers above Warsash Jetty
Stone Pier Yard
WARSASH
Warsash SC
Dir Iso.WRG.6s
Hamble Pt. Marina
Hamble Point Quay
QG
Dir Oc(2) WRG12s
FlR4s No10
Warsash Jetty
Warsash Maritime Centre
FlR4s No8
FlG4s No9
CAUTION
Drying/shoal area extends into channel between No 7 & No 9 beacons
Dn No6 Q.R
Q.G No7
FlG4s No5
FlR4s No4
FlG4s No3
Q(3)10s No2
Q.G No1
W
Q(6)+LFl.15S
YB
Hamble Pt.
01°19'W
18'
53'
52'
50°51'N

R/T Commercial and all vessels over 20m call: *Hamble Radio* Ch **68** (Apr-Sep: daily 0600-2200. Oct-Mar: daily 0700-1830). Marinas Ch **80** M. Water Taxi 02380 454512, Ch 77. See also 9.2.23 for VTS and info broadcasts.

TELEPHONE

HM ☎ 01489 576387, HM patrol mob's 07718 146380/81/99, 📠 580718; MRSC 023 9255 2100; Marinecall 09066 526241; Police 08450 454545; Seastart 0800 885500.

FACILITIES **Marinas** (from seaward):

Hamble Pt Marina (220) ☎ 02380 452464, 📠 456440; pre-call Ch 80. Access H24; £2.70, CH, BH (65 ton), C (7 ton), Ⓔ, El, Gas, Gaz, ME, ⚒, 🛒, YC, Bar;

Stone Pier Yard (56) ☎ 01489 583813, 📠 579860. Access H24; £2.00, FW, ⛽, C (20 ton), CH, LPG, D, Gas, Gaz, ME, ⚒.

Port Hamble Marina (310+ Ⓥ) ☎ 02380 452741, 📠 455206; pre-call Ch 80. Access H24; £2.70, ▣, Bar, BH (60 ton), C (7 ton), CH, D, P, Ⓔ, Gas, Gaz, ME, ⚒, El, SM, Slip;

Mercury Yacht Hbr (346+ Ⓥ) ☎ 02380 455994, 📠 457369; pre-call Ch 80. Access H24; £2.70, Bar, BH (20 ton), El, Slip, CH, D, Ⓔ, Gas, Gaz, ME, P, ⚒, SM, 🛒, ▣;

Universal Marina ☎ 01489 574272, BY 01489 570053; BH (30 ton), CH, ME.

Swanwick Marina (380+ Ⓥ) ☎ 01489 885000 (after 1700, 01489 885262), 📠 885509, £2.40, £6.50 <4hrs, BH (60 ton), C (12 ton), CH, D, Ⓔ, Gas, Gaz, ⊖, ▣, ME, P, ✉, ⚒, SM, 🛒, (Access H24).

The Hbr Authority jetty in front of the conspic B/W HM's Office at Warsash has limited AB, also Ⓥ pontoons in mid-stream (both £1.50 for 24hrs), ⚓, showers and toilets on shore. A public jetty is on the W bank near the Bugle carpark.

YACHT CLUBS

Hamble River SC ☎ 02380 452070; **RAFYC** ☎ 02380 452208, Bar, R, L; **Royal Southern YC** ☎ 02380 450300; **Warsash SC** ☎ 01489 583575.

SERVICES

A very wide range of marine services is available; consult marina/HM for locations. CH, Ⓔ, BY, AB, C (12 ton), FW, Gas, Gaz, M, ME, R, ⚒, Slip, SM; Riggers, BH (25 ton), ACA, Divers. **Piper Marine Services** ☎ 02380 454563, (or call *Piper Fuel* Ch M), D, P.

Hards. At Warsash, Hamble and Swanwick.

Slips at Warsash, Hamble, Bursledon & Lower Swanwick.

Maintenance piles at Warsash by HM's slipway; on W bank upriver of public jetty near Bugle; by slip opposite Swanwick marina.

✉ (Hamble, Bursledon, Warsash and Lower Swanwick); (Hamble, Bursledon, Sarisbury Green, Swanwick, Warsash); ⇄ (Hamble and Bursledon); ✈ (Southampton).

Hamble River Guide available from HM.

ADJACENT HARBOURS

ASHLETT CREEK, Hants, **50°50'·01N 01°19'·49W**. AC *5600.8, 2022, 1905.* Tides approx as Calshot Castle (opposite). Small drying (2·1m) inlet across from R Hamble; best for shoal-draft vessels. Appr at HW close to Esso Marine Terminal. Unlit chan, marked by 3 PHM buoys, 1 SHM buoy and 2 PHM bns, has four 90° bends. Ldg bns are hard to find; local knowledge desirable. Berth at drying quay. Facilities: AB, M, FW, Slip, Hard, Pub. **Esso SC**.

HILL HEAD, Hants, **50°49'·08N 01°14'·54W**. AC *5600.8, 2022, 1905.* HW +0030 on Dover; see 9.2.28 LEE-ON-SOLENT diffs. Short term ⚓ for small craft at mouth of R Meon. Bar dries ¼M offshore. Ent dries 1·2m at MLWS. Appr on 030° towards Hill Head SC ho (W, conspic); Small hbr to W inside ent (very narrow due to silting)where yachts can lie in soft mud alongside wall. Facilities: **Hill Head SC** ☎ (01329) 664843. **Hill Head village** EC Thurs; ✉, CH, 🛒, P & D (cans).

Note - Double HWs occur at Southampton. The predictions are for the first HW.

TIME ZONE (UT)
For Summer Time add ONE hour in **non-shaded areas**

ENGLAND –SOUTHAMPTON

LAT 50°54′N LONG 1°24′W

TIMES AND HEIGHTS OF HIGH AND LOW WATERS

SPRING & NEAP TIDES
Dates in red are SPRINGS
Dates in blue are NEAPS

YEAR **2005**

JANUARY

Date	Day	Time	m	Time	m	Time	m	Time	m
1	SA	0150	4.2	0734	1.5	1402	4.1	1950	1.4
2	SU	0231	4.1	0814	1.6	1443	4.0	2032	1.5
3	M	0317	4.0	0902	1.7	1531	3.9	◑ 2123	1.6
4	TU	0411	3.9	1001	1.8	1630	3.8	2226	1.7
5	W	0514	3.9	1109	1.8	1738	3.8	2338	1.7
6	TH	0622	4.0	1221	1.7	1851	3.9		
7	F	0049	1.6	0727	4.2	1329	1.5	1958	4.1
8	SA	0155	1.4	0828	4.3	1432	1.2	2059	4.3
9	SU	0255	1.2	0924	4.5	1529	0.9	2154	4.5
10	M	0351	1.0	1016	4.7	1623	0.7	● 2246	4.6
11	TU	0444	0.8	1106	4.7	1714	0.5	2336	4.7
12	W	0535	0.7	1155	4.8	1803	0.4		
13	TH	0025	4.7	0623	0.7	1243	4.7	1849	0.4
14	F	0114	4.6	0711	0.7	1331	4.6	1934	0.6
15	SA	0202	4.5	0757	0.9	1418	4.4	2019	0.8
16	SU	0250	4.4	0844	1.1	1506	4.2	2104	1.1
17	M	0341	4.2	0933	1.4	1558	4.0	◐ 2153	1.4
18	TU	0435	4.0	1029	1.6	1656	3.8	2252	1.7
19	W	0537	3.8	1135	1.8	1806	3.6		
20	TH	0001	1.8	0646	3.8	1247	1.8	1923	3.7
21	F	0112	1.9	0754	3.9	1352	1.7	2031	3.8
22	SA	0214	1.8	0851	4.0	1446	1.5	2123	3.9
23	SU	0304	1.6	0937	4.1	1531	1.3	2205	4.1
24	M	0348	1.4	1016	4.2	1612	1.1	2242	4.2
25	TU	0428	1.2	1051	4.3	1649	0.9	○ 2315	4.3
26	W	0505	1.1	1124	4.3	1725	0.8	2346	4.3
27	TH	0540	1.0	1156	4.3	1758	0.8		
28	F	0018	4.3	0612	1.0	1229	4.3	1827	0.8
29	SA	0051	4.3	0641	1.0	1302	4.3	1856	0.9
30	SU	0124	4.3	0711	1.1	1335	4.2	1926	1.0
31	M	0159	4.2	0744	1.2	1410	4.1	2000	1.1

FEBRUARY

Date	Day	Time	m	Time	m	Time	m	Time	m
1	TU	0237	4.1	0823	1.3	1450	4.0	2041	1.3
2	W	0321	4.0	0911	1.5	1540	3.9	◑ 2134	1.6
3	TH	0418	3.9	1013	1.7	1646	3.8	2245	1.8
4	F	0532	3.9	1136	1.8	1811	3.7		
5	SA	0015	1.8	0655	3.9	1306	1.6	1938	3.9
6	SU	0140	1.6	0812	4.1	1422	1.3	2050	4.1
7	M	0249	1.3	0916	4.3	1524	1.0	2149	4.4
8	TU	0347	1.0	1009	4.6	1618	0.6	● 2240	4.6
9	W	0439	0.7	1058	4.7	1707	0.3	2326	4.7
10	TH	0527	0.4	1143	4.8	1752	0.2		
11	F	0011	4.8	0611	0.4	1227	4.8	1833	0.1
12	SA	0053	4.7	0653	0.4	1308	4.7	1912	0.3
13	SU	0134	4.6	0731	0.6	1348	4.5	1949	0.5
14	M	0214	4.4	0809	0.8	1429	4.3	2024	0.9
15	TU	0255	4.2	0847	1.2	1511	4.0	2102	1.3
16	W	0338	3.9	0930	1.6	1600	3.7	◐ 2150	1.7
17	TH	0432	3.7	1031	1.9	1707	3.5	2303	2.1
18	F	0548	3.5	1200	2.1	1846	3.4		
19	SA	0041	2.2	0723	3.6	1328	2.0	2014	3.6
20	SU	0200	2.0	0834	3.7	1430	1.7	2111	3.8
21	M	0252	1.7	0922	4.0	1515	1.4	2151	4.1
22	TU	0334	1.4	1000	4.1	1554	1.1	2225	4.2
23	W	0412	1.1	1033	4.3	1630	0.8	2255	4.3
24	TH	0447	0.9	1103	4.3	1705	0.7	○ 2323	4.4
25	F	0520	0.8	1133	4.4	1737	0.6	2353	4.4
26	SA	0551	0.7	1203	4.4	1806	0.6		
27	SU	0023	4.4	0619	0.7	1235	4.4	1833	0.6
28	M	0055	4.4	0647	0.7	1307	4.4	1901	0.7

MARCH

Date	Day	Time	m	Time	m	Time	m	Time	m
1	TU	0128	4.3	0718	0.9	1341	4.3	1933	0.9
2	W	0204	4.2	0753	1.1	1420	4.1	2011	1.2
3	TH	0245	4.1	0838	1.3	1507	3.9	◑ 2100	1.5
4	F	0340	3.9	0938	1.6	1615	3.7	2213	1.8
5	SA	0458	3.7	1110	1.8	1751	3.6		
6	SU	0001	1.9	0638	3.7	1258	1.7	1932	3.8
7	M	0137	1.7	0805	4.0	1417	1.3	2046	4.1
8	TU	0246	1.3	0908	4.2	1516	0.9	2140	4.4
9	W	0340	0.9	0959	4.5	1606	0.5	2227	4.6
10	TH	0428	0.5	1043	4.7	1651	0.2	● 2309	4.8
11	F	0511	0.3	1124	4.7	1732	0.0	2348	4.8
12	SA	0551	0.2	1203	4.7	1810	0.1		
13	SU	0026	4.7	0628	0.2	1241	4.6	1845	0.2
14	M	0103	4.6	0702	0.4	1318	4.5	1916	0.5
15	TU	0138	4.4	0734	0.7	1354	4.2	1946	0.9
16	W	0213	4.2	0805	1.1	1432	4.0	2018	1.4
17	TH	0251	3.9	0841	1.5	1516	3.7	◐ 2059	1.8
18	F	0337	3.6	0932	1.9	1618	3.5	2207	2.2
19	SA	0448	3.4	1104	2.2	1802	3.4		
20	SU	0008	2.3	0639	3.4	1254	2.1	1946	3.5
21	M	0137	2.1	0804	3.6	1400	1.8	2043	3.8
22	TU	0229	1.8	0855	3.8	1446	1.4	2122	4.0
23	W	0308	1.4	0932	4.0	1524	1.1	2154	4.2
24	TH	0344	1.1	1004	4.2	1600	0.8	2223	4.3
25	F	0418	0.8	1034	4.3	1635	0.6	○ 2252	4.4
26	SA	0451	0.6	1104	4.4	1708	0.5	2322	4.5
27	SU	0523	0.5	1135	4.4	1739	0.5	2354	4.5
28	M	0553	0.5	1208	4.5	1808	0.5		
29	TU	0027	4.5	0624	0.6	1243	4.4	1839	0.7
30	W	0102	4.4	0657	0.7	1320	4.3	1913	0.9
31	TH	0140	4.3	0735	1.0	1402	4.2	1954	1.2

APRIL

Date	Day	Time	m	Time	m	Time	m	Time	m
1	F	0225	4.1	0822	1.3	1455	3.9	2048	1.6
2	SA	0324	3.9	0927	1.6	1610	3.7	◑ 2210	1.9
3	SU	0450	3.7	1107	1.8	1753	3.7		
4	M	0002	1.9	0634	3.7	1249	1.6	1928	3.9
5	TU	0130	1.6	0755	3.9	1401	1.2	2033	4.2
6	W	0232	1.2	0853	4.2	1456	0.8	2122	4.5
7	TH	0322	0.8	0940	4.4	1543	0.5	2205	4.6
8	F	0406	0.5	1022	4.6	1625	0.3	● 2245	4.7
9	SA	0447	0.3	1100	4.6	1705	0.2	2322	4.7
10	SU	0525	0.2	1137	4.6	1741	0.2	2357	4.6
11	M	0600	0.3	1213	4.5	1815	0.4		
12	TU	0031	4.5	0632	0.5	1249	4.4	1845	0.7
13	W	0105	4.3	0702	0.8	1325	4.2	1914	1.1
14	TH	0139	4.1	0731	1.1	1402	4.0	1946	1.5
15	F	0215	3.9	0806	1.5	1446	3.7	2026	1.9
16	SA	0259	3.6	0852	1.8	1545	3.5	◐ 2129	2.2
17	SU	0403	3.4	1010	2.1	1713	3.5	2319	2.3
18	M	0539	3.4	1156	2.1	1851	3.6		
19	TU	0049	2.2	0710	3.5	1310	1.8	1954	3.8
20	W	0145	1.8	0808	3.7	1400	1.5	2037	4.0
21	TH	0227	1.5	0850	3.9	1442	1.2	2112	4.2
22	F	0305	1.1	0925	4.1	1521	0.9	2144	4.3
23	SA	0342	0.8	0959	4.3	1558	0.7	2217	4.5
24	SU	0417	0.6	1033	4.4	1634	0.6	○ 2251	4.5
25	M	0453	0.5	1108	4.5	1710	0.5	2326	4.6
26	TU	0528	0.5	1145	4.5	1745	0.6		
27	W	0004	4.6	0604	0.5	1226	4.5	1822	0.7
28	TH	0044	4.5	0643	0.7	1309	4.4	1903	1.0
29	F	0128	4.3	0727	1.0	1358	4.2	1951	1.3
30	SA	0220	4.1	0821	1.3	1459	4.0	2054	1.6

Chart Datum: 2·74 metres below Ordnance Datum (Newlyn)

Note - Double HWs occur at Southampton. The predictions are for the first HW.

TIME ZONE (UT)
For Summer Time add ONE hour in **non-shaded areas**

ENGLAND –SOUTHAMPTON

LAT 50°54′N LONG 1°24′W

TIMES AND HEIGHTS OF HIGH AND LOW WATERS

SPRING & NEAP TIDES
Dates in red are SPRINGS Dates in blue are NEAPS

YEAR **2005**

MAY

Day	Time	m	Day	Time	m
1	0326	3.9	16	0332	3.6
	0932	1.5		0928	1.9
	SU 1619	3.8		M 1626	3.6
	◑ 2219	1.8		◐ 2221	2.2
2	0452	3.7	17	0443	3.5
	1102	1.6		1048	1.9
	M 1751	3.9		TU 1741	3.7
	2352	1.7		2342	2.1
3	0622	3.8	18	0600	3.5
	1226	1.5		1203	1.8
	TU 1909	4.0		W 1848	3.8
4	0106	1.5	19	0045	1.8
	0733	4.0		0706	3.7
	W 1332	1.2		TH 1302	1.6
	2008	4.3		1940	4.0
5	0205	1.2	20	0135	1.5
	0829	4.2		0758	3.9
	TH 1425	0.9		F 1351	1.3
	2056	4.4		2024	4.2
6	0254	0.9	21	0219	1.2
	0915	4.3		0842	4.1
	F 1512	0.7		SA 1436	1.1
	2139	4.5		2104	4.3
7	0338	0.7	22	0302	1.0
	0957	4.4		0923	4.2
	SA 1554	0.6		SU 1519	0.9
	2217	4.5		2144	4.5
8	0418	0.5	23	0343	0.8
	1036	4.4		1004	4.4
	SU 1634	0.5		M 1602	0.8
	● 2254	4.5		○ 2224	4.6
9	0457	0.5	24	0426	0.6
	1113	4.4		1046	4.5
	M 1712	0.6		TU 1645	0.7
	2329	4.4		2305	4.6
10	0532	0.6	25	0508	0.6
	1149	4.3		1130	4.5
	TU 1747	0.8		W 1728	0.7
				2349	4.6
11	0003	4.4	26	0552	0.6
	0604	0.7		1216	4.5
	W 1225	4.2		TH 1813	0.8
	1819	1.0			
12	0038	4.2	27	0035	4.5
	0636	0.9		0638	0.7
	TH 1303	4.1		F 1306	4.4
	1851	1.3		1902	1.0
13	0114	4.1	28	0126	4.3
	0707	1.2		0728	0.9
	F 1342	4.0		SA 1402	4.3
	1925	1.6		1956	1.2
14	0152	3.9	29	0223	4.2
	0742	1.4		0824	1.1
	SA 1426	3.9		SU 1504	4.1
	2007	1.8		2059	1.5
15	0236	3.7	30	0327	4.0
	0827	1.7		0929	1.3
	SU 1520	3.7		M 1615	4.0
	2103	2.1		◑ 2211	1.6
			31	0440	3.9
				1041	1.4
				TU 1729	4.0
				2324	1.6

JUNE

Day	Time	m	Day	Time	m
1	0554	3.9	16	0456	3.6
	1151	1.4		1052	1.7
	W 1837	4.1		TH 1740	3.8
				2336	1.8
2	0031	1.4	17	0601	3.7
	0700	4.0		1157	1.7
	TH 1254	1.3		F 1840	3.9
	1935	4.2			
3	0130	1.3	18	0037	1.7
	0758	4.0		0704	3.8
	F 1349	1.2		SA 1258	1.5
	2026	4.3		1936	4.1
4	0221	1.1	19	0133	1.4
	0848	4.1		0801	4.0
	SA 1439	1.1		SU 1354	1.3
	2111	4.3		2027	4.3
5	0307	1.0	20	0226	1.2
	0933	4.2		0853	4.1
	SU 1524	1.0		M 1447	1.2
	2152	4.3		2116	4.4
6	0350	0.9	21	0317	0.9
	1015	4.2		0943	4.3
	M 1607	1.0		TU 1538	1.0
	● 2231	4.3		2204	4.5
7	0431	0.8	22	0407	0.8
	1054	4.2		1032	4.4
	TU 1647	1.0		W 1629	0.9
	2307	4.3		○ 2252	4.6
8	0509	0.8	23	0457	0.6
	1132	4.2		1122	4.5
	W 1725	1.1		TH 1720	0.8
	2343	4.2		2341	4.6
9	0545	0.9	24	0547	0.6
	1209	4.2		1212	4.5
	TH 1802	1.2		F 1810	0.8
10	0019	4.2	25	0031	4.6
	0618	1.0		0636	0.6
	F 1247	4.1		SA 1304	4.5
	1837	1.3		1901	0.9
11	0057	4.1	26	0123	4.5
	0651	1.1		0726	0.7
	SA 1326	4.1		SU 1358	4.4
	1912	1.5		1953	1.0
12	0135	4.0	27	0216	4.3
	0726	1.3		0818	0.8
	SU 1407	4.0		M 1454	4.3
	1950	1.7		2048	1.2
13	0216	3.9	28	0312	4.2
	0805	1.5		0911	1.0
	M 1452	3.9		TU 1552	4.2
	2035	1.8		◑ 2145	1.3
14	0302	3.8	29	0411	4.0
	0851	1.6		1008	1.2
	TU 1542	3.8		W 1652	4.1
	2129	1.9		2245	1.4
15	0355	3.7	30	0514	3.9
	0947	1.7		1108	1.4
	W 1639	3.8		TH 1755	4.1
	◐ 2231	1.9		2348	1.5

JULY

Day	Time	m	Day	Time	m
1	0619	3.8	16	0500	3.7
	1211	1.5		1055	1.7
	F 1857	4.0		SA 1743	3.9
				2341	1.8
2	0051	1.5	17	0612	3.7
	0724	3.8		1209	1.7
	SA 1313	1.5		SU 1852	4.0
	1955	4.0			
3	0150	1.5	18	0053	1.6
	0824	3.9		0725	3.9
	SU 1410	1.5		M 1322	1.6
	2048	4.1		1958	4.1
4	0243	1.3	19	0201	1.4
	0917	4.0		0832	4.0
	M 1502	1.4		TU 1427	1.4
	2135	4.1		2058	4.3
5	0330	1.2	20	0303	1.1
	1003	4.0		0931	4.3
	TU 1548	1.3		W 1527	1.2
	2216	4.2		2153	4.5
6	0413	1.1	21	0359	0.8
	1044	4.1		1024	4.4
	W 1632	1.3		TH 1623	0.9
	● 2254	4.2		○ 2244	4.6
7	0453	1.0	22	0452	0.6
	1121	4.2		1115	4.6
	TH 1712	1.2		F 1715	0.7
	2330	4.2		2333	4.7
8	0531	1.0	23	0542	0.4
	1156	4.2		1204	4.7
	F 1750	1.2		SA 1805	0.6
9	0005	4.2	24	0021	4.7
	0605	1.0		0629	0.3
	SA 1232	4.2		SU 1253	4.7
	1824	1.2		1852	0.6
10	0040	4.2	25	0109	4.6
	0638	1.0		0715	0.4
	SU 1306	4.2		M 1341	4.6
	1857	1.3		1938	0.7
11	0115	4.1	26	0156	4.5
	0709	1.1		0759	0.5
	M 1342	4.1		TU 1428	4.5
	1929	1.4		2024	0.9
12	0151	4.0	27	0243	4.3
	0741	1.2		0843	0.8
	TU 1419	4.1		W 1517	4.3
	2004	1.5		2110	1.1
13	0228	3.9	28	0333	4.1
	0816	1.3		0929	1.1
	W 1459	4.0		TH 1608	4.1
	2043	1.6		◑ 2201	1.4
14	0310	3.9	29	0428	3.9
	0859	1.5		1021	1.5
	TH 1544	3.9		F 1706	3.9
	◐ 2131	1.7		2301	1.7
15	0359	3.8	30	0533	3.7
	0951	1.6		1126	1.8
	F 1639	3.9		SA 1814	3.8
	2231	1.8			
			31	0014	1.8
				0652	3.6
				SU 1242	1.9
				1928	3.8

AUGUST

Day	Time	m	Day	Time	m
1	0128	1.8	16	0029	1.8
	0809	3.7		0704	3.8
	M 1354	1.9		TU 1306	1.8
	2033	3.9		1941	4.0
2	0230	1.6	17	0152	1.6
	0909	3.9		0822	4.0
	TU 1451	1.7		W 1421	1.5
	2125	4.0		2049	4.2
3	0319	1.4	18	0257	1.2
	0956	4.0		0924	4.3
	W 1538	1.5		TH 1523	1.2
	2207	4.1		2144	4.5
4	0401	1.2	19	0353	0.8
	1034	4.1		1016	4.5
	TH 1620	1.3		F 1617	0.8
	2242	4.2		○ 2233	4.7
5	0439	1.0	20	0443	0.4
	1108	4.2		1103	4.7
	F 1658	1.1		SA 1706	0.6
	● 2315	4.3		2319	4.8
6	0515	0.9	21	0530	0.2
	1139	4.3		1148	4.8
	SA 1734	1.0		SU 1752	0.4
	2346	4.3			
7	0549	0.8	22	0003	4.8
	1209	4.3		0613	0.1
	SU 1806	1.0		M 1232	4.8
				1834	0.4
8	0017	4.3	23	0046	4.8
	0619	0.8		0653	0.2
	M 1240	4.3		TU 1314	4.7
	1835	1.0		1915	0.5
9	0049	4.2	24	0128	4.6
	0646	0.9		0732	0.4
	TU 1311	4.2		W 1356	4.6
	1903	1.1		1953	0.8
10	0121	4.2	25	0210	4.4
	0713	1.0		0809	0.8
	W 1344	4.2		TH 1437	4.3
	1931	1.2		2032	1.1
11	0153	4.1	26	0253	4.1
	0743	1.2		0847	1.2
	TH 1418	4.1		F 1522	4.1
	2004	1.4		◑ 2115	1.5
12	0229	4.0	27	0342	3.8
	0818	1.4		0933	1.7
	F 1457	4.0		SA 1615	3.8
	2045	1.5		2212	1.9
13	0312	3.9	28	0448	3.6
	0903	1.6		1040	2.1
	SA 1546	3.9		SU 1729	3.6
	◐ 2139	1.8		2337	2.1
14	0411	3.8	29	0626	3.5
	1005	1.8		1220	2.2
	SU 1653	3.8		M 1906	3.6
	2255	1.9			
15	0532	3.7	30	0112	2.1
	1132	2.0		0759	3.6
	M 1818	3.8		TU 1346	2.1
				2020	3.8
			31	0218	1.8
				0858	3.9
				W 1442	1.9
				2111	4.0

Chart Datum: 2·74 metres below Ordnance Datum (Newlyn)

Note - Double HWs occur at Southampton. The predictions are for the first HW.

TIME ZONE (UT)
For Summer Time add ONE hour in **non-shaded areas**

ENGLAND –SOUTHAMPTON

LAT 50°54′N LONG 1°24′W

TIMES AND HEIGHTS OF HIGH AND LOW WATERS

SPRING & NEAP TIDES
Dates in red are SPRINGS
Dates in blue are NEAPS

YEAR **2005**

SEPTEMBER

Date	Day	Time	m	Time	m	Time	m	Time	m
1	TH	0303	1.5	0940	4.1	1524	1.6	2149	4.2
2	F	0341	1.2	1014	4.2	1600	1.3	2222	4.3
3	SA	0417	1.0	1044	4.3	1635	1.1	● 2251	4.3
4	SU	0451	0.8	1111	4.4	1709	0.9	2319	4.4
5	M	0524	0.7	1139	4.4	1740	0.8	2348	4.4
6	TU	0553	0.7	1208	4.4	1808	0.9		
7	W	0018	4.4	0619	0.8	1238	4.4	1833	0.9
8	TH	0049	4.3	0644	0.9	1310	4.3	1900	1.1
9	F	0122	4.3	0713	1.1	1343	4.3	1932	1.2
10	SA	0157	4.2	0747	1.3	1421	4.1	2012	1.5
11	SU	0240	4.0	0832	1.6	1511	4.0	◐ 2107	1.8
12	M	0342	3.8	0937	2.0	1623	3.8	2231	2.0
13	TU	0514	3.7	1120	2.1	1803	3.8		
14	W	0022	1.9	0658	3.8	1305	1.9	1934	4.0
15	TH	0146	1.6	0816	4.1	1417	1.5	2040	4.3
16	F	0247	1.1	0912	4.4	1513	1.1	2131	4.6
17	SA	0338	0.7	1000	4.7	1602	0.7	2216	4.7
18	SU	0425	0.3	1043	4.8	1647	0.4	○ 2258	4.8
19	M	0508	0.2	1124	4.9	1730	0.3	2339	4.8
20	TU	0548	0.1	1204	4.9	1809	0.3		
21	W	0018	4.8	0625	0.3	1243	4.7	1846	0.5
22	TH	0058	4.6	0700	0.6	1321	4.5	1920	0.8
23	F	0136	4.4	0734	1.0	1359	4.3	1954	1.2
24	SA	0217	4.1	0808	1.4	1439	4.0	2032	1.6
25	SU	0304	3.8	0850	1.9	1528	3.7	◑ 2124	2.0
26	M	0409	3.6	0959	2.3	1643	3.5	2255	2.3
27	TU	0554	3.5	1156	2.4	1832	3.5		
28	W	0042	2.2	0733	3.7	1325	2.2	1953	3.7
29	TH	0148	1.9	0830	3.9	1416	1.9	2042	4.0
30	F	0232	1.6	0909	4.2	1455	1.6	2119	4.1

OCTOBER

Date	Day	Time	m	Time	m	Time	m	Time	m
1	SA	0309	1.3	0941	4.3	1530	1.3	2150	4.3
2	SU	0344	1.0	1010	4.4	1604	1.0	2219	4.4
3	M	0418	0.8	1037	4.5	1636	0.9	● 2248	4.4
4	TU	0451	0.7	1105	4.5	1708	0.8	2317	4.5
5	W	0521	0.7	1135	4.5	1737	0.8	2349	4.5
6	TH	0550	0.8	1207	4.5	1806	0.8		
7	F	0022	4.5	0618	0.9	1241	4.5	1836	1.0
8	SA	0058	4.4	0650	1.1	1318	4.4	1911	1.2
9	SU	0138	4.2	0729	1.4	1400	4.2	1955	1.5
10	M	0227	4.0	0819	1.7	1455	4.0	◐ 2056	1.8
11	TU	0337	3.8	0934	2.0	1616	3.8	2229	2.0
12	W	0516	3.8	1124	2.1	1758	3.8		
13	TH	0014	1.8	0652	4.0	1256	1.8	1922	4.0
14	F	0129	1.5	0801	4.3	1400	1.4	2022	4.3
15	SA	0226	1.1	0853	4.6	1452	1.0	2111	4.6
16	SU	0314	0.7	0937	4.8	1539	0.7	2154	4.7
17	M	0358	0.4	1018	4.9	1622	0.5	○ 2234	4.8
18	TU	0440	0.3	1057	4.9	1702	0.4	2313	4.7
19	W	0519	0.4	1135	4.8	1740	0.5	2351	4.7
20	TH	0555	0.6	1212	4.7	1816	0.7		
21	F	0029	4.5	0629	0.8	1249	4.5	1849	0.9
22	SA	0108	4.3	0702	1.2	1325	4.3	1921	1.3
23	SU	0149	4.1	0736	1.6	1405	4.0	1958	1.6
24	M	0235	3.9	0819	2.0	1452	3.8	2046	2.0
25	TU	0337	3.7	0924	2.3	1558	3.6	◑ 2204	2.2
26	W	0505	3.6	1109	2.4	1732	3.5	2345	2.2
27	TH	0638	3.7	1236	2.3	1859	3.7		
28	F	0056	2.0	0739	3.9	1331	2.0	1955	3.9
29	SA	0146	1.7	0823	4.2	1413	1.7	2037	4.1
30	SU	0226	1.4	0858	4.3	1450	1.4	2111	4.2
31	M	0304	1.1	0930	4.4	1526	1.1	2144	4.4

NOVEMBER

Date	Day	Time	m	Time	m	Time	m	Time	m
1	TU	0340	0.9	1001	4.5	1600	0.9	2216	4.5
2	W	0415	0.8	1033	4.6	1635	0.8	● 2250	4.5
3	TH	0450	0.8	1107	4.6	1709	0.8	2325	4.6
4	F	0524	0.9	1143	4.6	1744	0.8		
5	SA	0003	4.5	0559	1.0	1222	4.5	1821	1.0
6	SU	0045	4.4	0638	1.2	1304	4.4	1903	1.2
7	M	0131	4.3	0724	1.4	1353	4.2	1953	1.4
8	TU	0228	4.1	0822	1.7	1454	4.0	2058	1.7
9	W	0342	4.0	0940	1.9	1614	3.9	◐ 2223	1.8
10	TH	0510	4.0	1112	1.9	1742	3.9	2350	1.7
11	F	0631	4.1	1230	1.7	1857	4.1		
12	SA	0058	1.4	0734	4.3	1332	1.4	1956	4.3
13	SU	0155	1.1	0826	4.5	1424	1.1	2046	4.4
14	M	0243	0.9	0911	4.7	1510	0.9	2130	4.5
15	TU	0328	0.7	0952	4.7	1554	0.7	2211	4.6
16	W	0410	0.7	1031	4.7	1635	0.7	○ 2251	4.6
17	TH	0450	0.7	1109	4.6	1714	0.7	2330	4.5
18	F	0528	0.9	1146	4.5	1750	0.9		
19	SA	0008	4.4	0604	1.1	1224	4.4	1824	1.0
20	SU	0048	4.3	0639	1.3	1301	4.2	1858	1.3
21	M	0129	4.2	0715	1.6	1341	4.1	1934	1.5
22	TU	0213	4.0	0757	1.9	1426	3.9	2017	1.8
23	W	0306	3.9	0851	2.1	1520	3.7	◑ 2114	2.0
24	TH	0409	3.8	1004	2.3	1627	3.6	2230	2.1
25	F	0521	3.8	1124	2.2	1742	3.6	2345	2.0
26	SA	0629	3.9	1228	2.0	1850	3.8		
27	SU	0046	1.8	0724	4.0	1320	1.8	1944	3.9
28	M	0136	1.6	0809	4.2	1404	1.5	2029	4.1
29	TU	0220	1.4	0849	4.4	1446	1.3	2109	4.3
30	W	0302	1.2	0928	4.5	1527	1.1	2149	4.4

DECEMBER

Date	Day	Time	m	Time	m	Time	m	Time	m
1	TH	0343	1.0	1006	4.6	1607	0.9	● 2228	4.5
2	F	0424	0.9	1046	4.7	1648	0.8	2310	4.6
3	SA	0506	0.9	1128	4.7	1730	0.8	2353	4.6
4	SU	0549	1.0	1212	4.6	1815	0.9		
5	M	0040	4.5	0635	1.1	1259	4.5	1901	1.0
6	TU	0131	4.4	0725	1.3	1352	4.3	1954	1.2
7	W	0229	4.3	0823	1.5	1451	4.2	2054	1.3
8	TH	0333	4.2	0929	1.6	1557	4.1	◐ 2201	1.4
9	F	0444	4.1	1041	1.6	1709	4.0	2311	1.5
10	SA	0554	4.1	1151	1.6	1819	4.0		
11	SU	0018	1.4	0658	4.2	1255	1.5	1923	4.1
12	M	0118	1.3	0755	4.3	1352	1.3	2019	4.2
13	TU	0212	1.2	0845	4.4	1443	1.2	2109	4.3
14	W	0301	1.1	0931	4.5	1530	1.0	2155	4.3
15	TH	0346	1.1	1013	4.5	1614	1.0	○ 2237	4.3
16	F	0429	1.1	1052	4.4	1654	0.9	2316	4.3
17	SA	0510	1.1	1130	4.4	1733	0.9	2355	4.3
18	SU	0548	1.2	1207	4.3	1808	1.0		
19	M	0033	4.3	0624	1.3	1245	4.3	1842	1.1
20	TU	0112	4.2	0700	1.4	1322	4.2	1916	1.3
21	W	0151	4.1	0737	1.6	1402	4.0	1952	1.4
22	TH	0233	4.0	0817	1.8	1444	3.9	2032	1.6
23	F	0319	3.9	0905	1.9	1532	3.8	◑ 2122	1.8
24	SA	0412	3.9	1002	2.0	1628	3.7	2223	1.9
25	SU	0512	3.8	1108	2.0	1734	3.7	2332	1.9
26	M	0616	3.9	1215	1.9	1842	3.7		
27	TU	0038	1.8	0716	4.0	1315	1.7	1944	3.9
28	W	0137	1.6	0811	4.2	1410	1.5	2038	4.1
29	TH	0230	1.4	0900	4.4	1500	1.2	2128	4.3
30	F	0320	1.2	0947	4.5	1549	1.0	2214	4.4
31	SA	0408	1.0	1033	4.6	1637	0.8	● 2301	4.6

Chart Datum: 2·74 metres below Ordnance Datum (Newlyn)

9.2.21 WOOTTON CREEK

Isle of Wight **50°44′·09N 01°12′·77W**

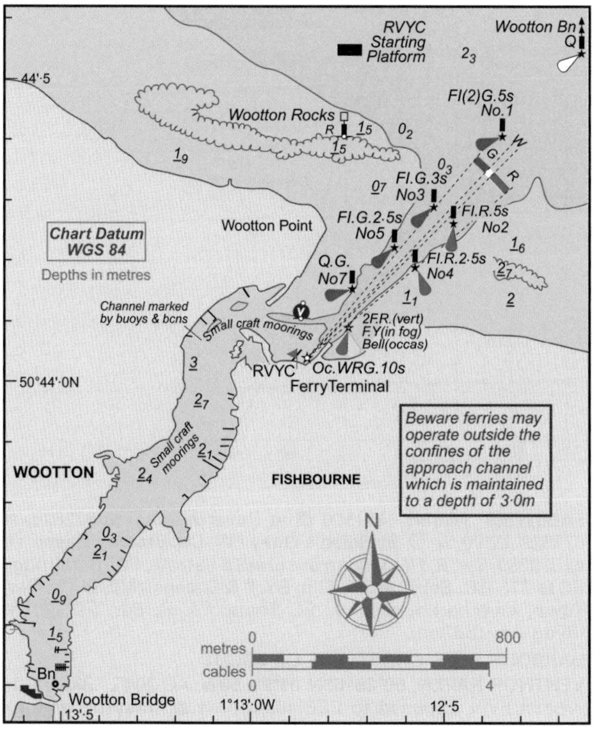
RVYC Starting Platform
Wootton Bn Q
44'·5
Fl(2)G.5s No.1
Wootton Rocks
R
Fl.G.3s No3
Fl.R.5s No2
Chart Datum WGS 84
Depths in metres
Wootton Point
Fl.G.2·5s No5
Q.G. No7
Fl.R.2·5s No4
Channel marked by buoys & bcns
Small craft moorings
2FR.(vert) F.Y(in fog) Bell(occas)
RVYC
Oc.WRG.10s
Ferry Terminal
50°44'·0N
Beware ferries may operate outside the confines of the approach channel which is maintained to a depth of 3·0m
WOOTTON
Small craft moorings
FISHBOURNE
N
metres 0 800
cables 0 4
Bn
Wootton Bridge
13'·5
1°13'·0W
12'·5

CHARTS AC *5600, 394, 2022*; Imray C3, C15; Stanfords 11, 24, 25; OS 196

TIDES +0023 Dover; ML 2·8; Zone 0 (UT). Use RYDE differences 9.2.26; see also 9.2.11.

SHELTER Good except in stormy N or E winds. Above the ferry, the creek dries. Moor to RVYC pontoons (dry); No ⚓ in the fairway. Speed limit 5kn.

NAVIGATION WPT Wootton NCM Bn, Q, 50°44′·53N 01°12′·13W, 044°/224° from/to ferry slip, 0·64M. Beware large ferries which may operate outside the confines of the approach channel when proceeding to and from Fishbourne Ferry Terminal. When under sail, beating in against the ebb is difficult.

LIGHTS AND MARKS Ent to creek due S of SE Ryde Middle SCM and 1·75M W of Ryde Pier. Visitors from/to the W should round the starting platform and No 1 bn. The chan is marked by four SHM bns and two PHMs, all lit. Keep in W sector of Dir lt, Oc WRG 10s, G221°-224°, W224°-225½°, R225½°-230½°. By ferry terminal, turn onto ldg marks on W shore △ ▽, which form a ◊ when in transit 270°.

R/T None.

TELEPHONE (Dial code 01983) Royal Victoria YC 882325; MRSC (023 92) 552100; Fairway Association 883097; Marinecall 09066 526241; Police 08450 454545; Dr 562955.

FACILITIES **Royal Victoria YC** ☎ 882325, Slip, AB £1.00/m (min £5.00), FW, R, ♿, Bar; **Village** EC = Thurs, Wootton Bridge = Wed; ✉ (Wootton Bridge, Ryde), Ⓑ (Ryde), ⇌ (ferry to Portsmouth), ✈ (Southampton).

9.2.22 RYDE

Isle of Wight **50°43′·98N 01°09′·31W**

CHARTS AC *5600, 2045,* 2036; Imray C3, C15; Stanfords 11, 24; OS 196

TIDES +0022 Dover; ML 2·8m; Zone 0 (UT). See also 9.2.11.

Standard Port PORTSMOUTH (⟶)

Times				Height (metres)			
High Water		Low Water		MHWS	MHWN	MLWN	MLWS
0000	0600	0500	1100	4·7	3·8	1·9	0·8
1200	1800	1700	2300				
Differences RYDE							
–0010	+0010	–0005	–0010	–0·2	–0·1	0·0	+0·1

SHELTER Small hbr 300m E of Ryde Pier; dries approx 2·3m. Access for shoal draft approx HW–2½ to +2. Berth on E'ly of three pontoons; long and fin keel yachts should dry out against the bkwtr.

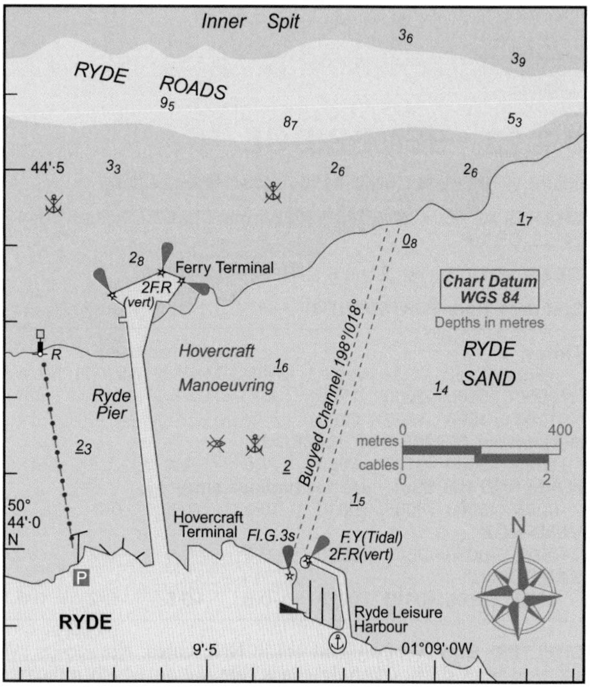
Inner Spit
RYDE ROADS
44'·5
Ferry Terminal
2F.R (vert)
Chart Datum WGS 84
Depths in metres
R
Hovercraft Manoeuvring
Buoyed Channel 198°/018°
RYDE SAND
Ryde Pier
metres 0 400
cables 0 2
50° 44'·0 N
Hovercraft Terminal
Fl.G.3s
F.Y(Tidal) 2F.R(vert)
N
RYDE
Ryde Leisure Harbour
9'·5
01°09'·0W

NAVIGATION WPT 50°44′·35N 01°09′·24W, No 1 SHM buoy, 198° to hbr ent, 6ca. From the E, best to stay North of No Man's Land Fort and SW Mining Ground Y buoy to clear Ryde Sands. Drying channel 197° across Ryde Sands (1·5m - 1·7m) is marked by 3 SHM and 3 PHM unlit buoys. Beware hovercraft manoeuvering between Ryde pier and marina; and High Speed Ferries from/to pierhead.

LIGHTS AND MARKS Ryde Ch spire (Holy Trinity) brg 200° gives initial appr. Hbr ent lts are 2 FR and Fl G 3s 7m 1M. Ryde pier is lit by 3 sets of 2FR (vert) and a FY fog lt.

R/T *Ryde Harbour* VHF Ch 80.

TELEPHONE (Dial code 01983) HM ☎/📠 613879, mob 07970 009899; MRSC (023 92) 552100; Marinecall 09066 526241; Police 08450 454545; Ⓗ 524081.

FACILITIES **Marina** (100+70 Ⓥ) ☎/📠 613879, rydeharbour@amserve.net, www.rydeharbour.com £1.20, Slip, ⓘ, ♿, ✉. **Services:** P & D (cans) from garage, Gas, 🛒, R, Bar, contact HM before arrival. **Town** all domestic facilities nearby. Hovercraft from slip next to hbr to Southsea. Fast cat (passenger) from Ryde Pier to Portsmouth for mainland ⇌; ✈ Southampton.

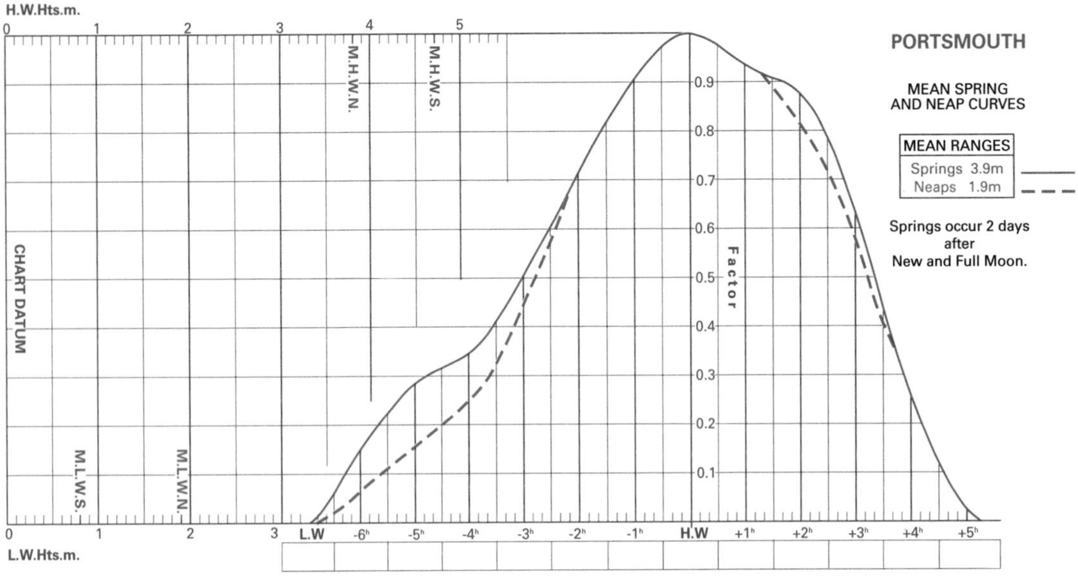
H.W.Hts.m.
0 1 2 3 4 5
M.H.W.N.
M.H.W.S.
PORTSMOUTH
MEAN SPRING AND NEAP CURVES
MEAN RANGES
Springs 3.9m
Neaps 1.9m
Springs occur 2 days after New and Full Moon.
CHART DATUM
Factor
0.9
0.8
0.7
0.6
0.5
0.4
0.3
0.2
0.1
M.L.W.S.
M.L.W.N.
L.W.Hts.m.
L.W -6h -5h -4h -3h -2h -1h H.W +1h +2h +3h +4h +5h

9.2.23 BEMBRIDGE

Isle of Wight **50°41'·62N 01°06'·40W** ❀❀◊◊◊✿✿

CHARTS AC *5600, 2045, 2037, 2022*; Imray C15, C3, C9; Stanfords 10, 24, 25; OS 196

TIDES +0020 Dover; Zone 0 (UT). See 9.2.11

Standard Port PORTSMOUTH (⟶)

Times				Height (metres)			
High Water		Low Water		MHWS	MHWN	MLWN	MLWS
0000	0600	0500	1100	4·7	3·8	1·9	0·8
1200	1800	1700	2300				
Differences BEMBRIDGE HARBOUR							
+0020	0000	+0100	+0020	–1·5	–1·4	–1·3	–1·0
FORELAND (LB Slip) – use for harbour entry							
–0005	0000	+0005	+0010	+0·1	+0·1	0·0	+0·1
VENTNOR							
–0025	–0030	–0025	–0030	–0·8	–0·6	–0·2	+0·2
SANDOWN							
0000	+0005	+0010	+0025	–0·6	–0·5	–0·2	0·0

SHELTER Good, but difficult ent in NNE gales. No access LW ±2½ for 1·5m draft; carefully check tide gauge which indicates depth over the bar. Speed limit 6kn. Ⓥ berths on pontoons at Duver Marina or Fisherman's Wharf; drying out facility on sand to port just inside hbr ent (⚓ F&A). No ⚓ in chan and hbr, but Priory Bay is sheltered ⚓ in winds from S to WNW (dries inshore but ½M off gives 1·5m).

NAVIGATION WPT tide gauge, Fl Y 2s, 50°42'·46N 01°05'·02W, approx 2ca E of ent to well-buoyed, but unlit chan. The bar, between Nos 6 and 10 buoys, almost dries. Avoid the gravel banks between St Helen's Fort, Nodes Pt and N to Seaview, by keeping to ent times above.

LIGHTS AND MARKS St Helens Fort Fl (3) 10s 16m 8M; ⚓ within 1ca radius of Fort. Conspic W seamark on shore where chan turns S. Beware many unlit Y racing marks off Bembridge and Seaview (Mar-Oct).

R/T Call *Bembridge Marina* VHF Ch **80**; *Hbr Launch* Ch M.

TELEPHONE (Dial code 01983) HM 872828 📠 872922; MRSC (023 92) 552100; Marinecall 09066 526241; Police 08450 454545; Dr 872614.

FACILITIES **Marina** (40+100 Ⓥ at Duver Marina) ☎ 872828, 📠 872922, £2.00, ♿, 🅆; **St Helen's Quay** FW, CH; **Brading Haven YC** ☎ 872289, Bar, R, FW; **Drying out area** £6 flat rate, FW. **Bembridge SC** ☎ 872686; **Services:** M, Slip, BY, P & D (cans), ME, El, ⚒, Gas. **Town** www.harbours.co.uk, EC Thurs; 🛒, R, Bar, ✉, Ⓑ, ⇌ (Ryde), ✈ (So'ton).

HARBOUR ON S COAST ISLE OF WIGHT

VENTNOR HAVEN, 50°35'·53N 01°21'·50W. AC 2045. Bkwtrs to protect FV's. Exposed to ESE'lies. Some ⚓ (may be drying), ☎ 07976 009260 for availability; **Services:** ⚒ on quay, P & D (cans). **Town** All domestic facilities, some up a steep hill.

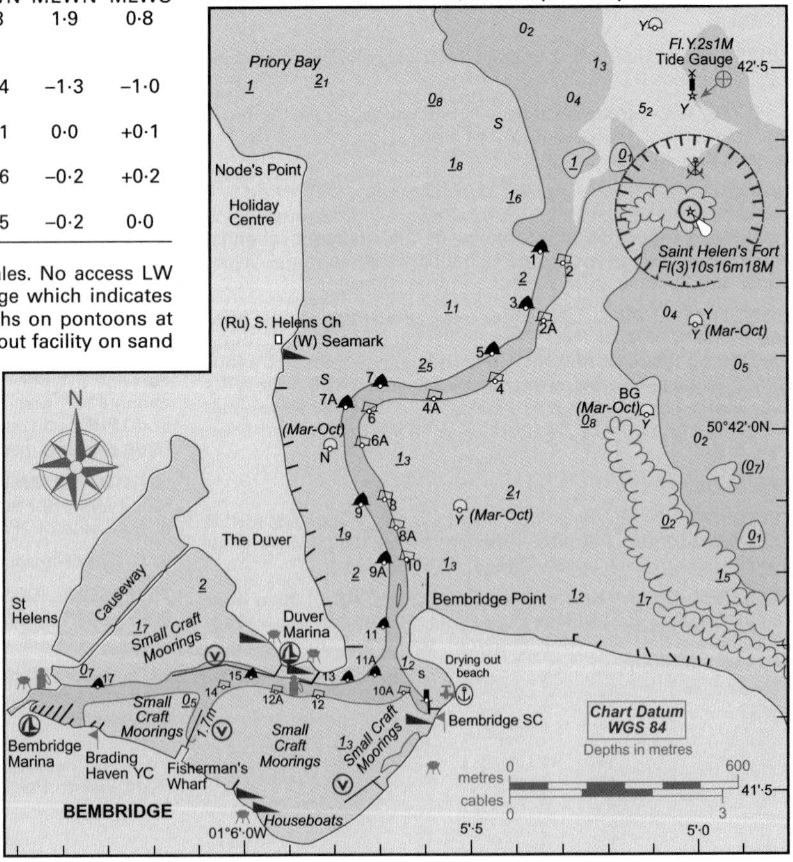
Priory Bay
Node's Point
Holiday Centre
Fl.Y.2s1M
Tide Gauge
42'·5
Saint Helen's Fort
Fl(3)10s16m18M
Y (Mar-Oct)
(Ru) S. Helens Ch
(W) Seamark
BG (Mar-Oct)
50°42'·0N
(Mar-Oct)
Y (Mar-Oct)
The Duver
Bembridge Point
St Helens
Causeway
Small Craft Moorings
Duver Marina
Drying out beach
Bembridge SC
Chart Datum WGS 84
Depths in metres
Small Craft Moorings
Small Craft Moorings
Small Craft Moorings
Bembridge Marina
Brading Haven YC
Fisherman's Wharf
BEMBRIDGE
Houseboats
01°6'·0W
metres
cables
0
600
0
3
41'·5
5'·5
5'·0

TIME ZONE (UT)
For Summer Time add ONE hour in **non-shaded areas**

ENGLAND – PORTSMOUTH

LAT 50°48′N LONG 1°07′W

TIMES AND HEIGHTS OF HIGH AND LOW WATERS

SPRING & NEAP TIDES
Dates in red are **SPRINGS**
Dates in blue are **NEAPS**

YEAR **2005**

JANUARY

Date	Day	Time	m	Time	m	Time	m	Time	m
1	SA	0224	4.3	0743	1.6	1427	4.1	2003	1.4
2	SU	0305	4.2	0824	1.7	1508	4.1	2045	1.5
3	M	0350	4.2	0913	1.8	1556	4.0	◑ 2136	1.6
4	TU	0443	4.1	1011	1.9	1652	3.9	2236	1.7
5	W	0544	4.1	1118	1.9	1800	3.9	2344	1.7
6	TH	0653	4.2	1230	1.8	1917	4.0		
7	F	0055	1.6	0759	4.3	1339	1.6	2028	4.2
8	SA	0203	1.5	0859	4.5	1441	1.3	2132	4.4
9	SU	0303	1.3	0955	4.7	1538	1.0	2229	4.6
10	M	0359	1.1	1047	4.8	1632	0.8	● 2324	4.8
11	TU	0452	1.0	1138	4.8	1723	0.7		
12	W	0016	4.8	0543	0.9	1229	4.8	1812	0.6
13	TH	0107	4.9	0632	0.9	1319	4.8	1900	0.6
14	F	0157	4.8	0720	0.9	1408	4.6	1946	0.7
15	SA	0245	4.7	0808	1.0	1456	4.5	2032	0.9
16	SU	0332	4.6	0856	1.2	1543	4.3	2118	1.1
17	M	0419	4.4	0947	1.5	1632	4.1	◐ 2207	1.4
18	TU	0509	4.2	1044	1.7	1725	3.9	2303	1.7
19	W	0606	4.0	1150	1.9	1831	3.7		
20	TH	0011	1.9	0712	3.9	1302	1.9	1949	3.7
21	F	0123	1.9	0819	4.0	1405	1.8	2058	3.8
22	SA	0224	1.8	0916	4.1	1457	1.6	2152	4.0
23	SU	0315	1.7	1002	4.2	1542	1.4	2235	4.2
24	M	0358	1.5	1041	4.3	1622	1.3	2312	4.3
25	TU	0437	1.3	1117	4.4	1659	1.1	○ 2346	4.4
26	W	0514	1.2	1151	4.4	1735	1.0		
27	TH	0020	4.4	0548	1.2	1226	4.4	1808	1.0
28	F	0054	4.4	0620	1.2	1300	4.4	1838	1.0
29	SA	0127	4.4	0650	1.2	1333	4.3	1907	1.0
30	SU	0200	4.4	0721	1.2	1407	4.3	1939	1.0
31	M	0234	4.4	0755	1.3	1442	4.2	2015	1.1

FEBRUARY

Date	Day	Time	m	Time	m	Time	m	Time	m
1	TU	0312	4.3	0836	1.4	1523	4.1	2057	1.3
2	W	0355	4.2	0925	1.6	1612	4.0	◑ 2151	1.6
3	TH	0451	4.1	1028	1.8	1718	3.9	2301	1.8
4	F	0605	4.0	1152	1.8	1844	3.8		
5	SA	0029	1.8	0729	4.0	1324	1.7	2012	4.0
6	SU	0155	1.7	0843	4.2	1437	1.4	2124	4.3
7	M	0302	1.4	0945	4.5	1536	1.0	2224	4.5
8	TU	0358	1.1	1039	4.7	1628	0.7	● 2317	4.7
9	W	0448	0.8	1130	4.8	1716	0.5		
10	TH	0006	4.9	0535	0.7	1219	4.8	1801	0.4
11	F	0052	4.9	0619	0.6	1305	4.8	1844	0.4
12	SA	0136	4.9	0702	0.6	1348	4.7	1924	0.5
13	SU	0217	4.8	0742	0.8	1429	4.5	2001	0.8
14	M	0255	4.6	0820	1.0	1509	4.3	2038	1.1
15	TU	0333	4.4	0900	1.3	1549	4.1	2118	1.4
16	W	0412	4.1	0946	1.6	1633	3.8	◐ 2207	1.8
17	TH	0459	3.9	1049	1.9	1732	3.6	2319	2.1
18	F	0607	3.7	1217	2.1	1904	3.5		
19	SA	0051	2.2	0741	3.7	1339	2.0	2039	3.7
20	SU	0207	2.0	0856	3.8	1438	1.7	2137	4.0
21	M	0301	1.7	0946	4.0	1523	1.5	2219	4.2
22	TU	0343	1.5	1026	4.2	1602	1.2	2255	4.3
23	W	0420	1.2	1101	4.3	1639	1.0	2328	4.4
24	TH	0456	1.1	1135	4.3	1714	0.9	○ 2359	4.5
25	F	0529	0.9	1207	4.4	1747	0.8		
26	SA	0030	4.5	0559	0.9	1240	4.4	1816	0.8
27	SU	0102	4.5	0627	0.9	1313	4.4	1844	0.8
28	M	0133	4.5	0657	0.9	1346	4.4	1914	0.9

MARCH

Date	Day	Time	m	Time	m	Time	m	Time	m
1	TU	0205	4.5	0729	1.0	1420	4.4	1948	1.0
2	W	0240	4.4	0807	1.1	1459	4.2	2029	1.3
3	TH	0321	4.2	0853	1.4	1548	4.0	◑ 2121	1.6
4	F	0415	4.0	0956	1.7	1656	3.8	2237	1.9
5	SA	0533	3.8	1134	1.9	1830	3.8		
6	SU	0026	2.0	0710	3.8	1322	1.7	2008	3.9
7	M	0157	1.7	0835	4.1	1434	1.4	2120	4.3
8	TU	0300	1.3	0937	4.4	1528	1.0	2215	4.6
9	W	0351	1.0	1029	4.6	1616	0.6	2303	4.8
10	TH	0437	0.7	1116	4.7	1700	0.4	● 2347	4.9
11	F	0519	0.5	1201	4.8	1741	0.4		
12	SA	0028	4.9	0559	0.4	1243	4.8	1820	0.4
13	SU	0107	4.9	0637	0.5	1322	4.7	1855	0.5
14	M	0143	4.8	0711	0.7	1400	4.6	1928	0.8
15	TU	0217	4.6	0744	0.9	1436	4.4	2000	1.1
16	W	0249	4.4	0817	1.2	1512	4.1	2035	1.5
17	TH	0324	4.1	0855	1.6	1555	3.9	◐ 2120	1.9
18	F	0408	3.8	0950	1.9	1651	3.6	2234	2.2
19	SA	0511	3.5	1130	2.2	1820	3.5		
20	SU	0022	2.3	0654	3.5	1308	2.1	2013	3.7
21	M	0146	2.1	0831	3.7	1411	1.8	2111	4.0
22	TU	0239	1.8	0922	3.9	1455	1.5	2152	4.2
23	W	0319	1.4	1001	4.1	1534	1.2	2226	4.3
24	TH	0355	1.1	1035	4.2	1610	0.9	2258	4.4
25	F	0429	0.9	1108	4.3	1645	0.8	○ 2329	4.5
26	SA	0501	0.8	1142	4.4	1717	0.7		
27	SU	0001	4.5	0531	0.7	1216	4.5	1748	0.7
28	M	0033	4.6	0602	0.7	1250	4.5	1818	0.7
29	TU	0106	4.6	0633	0.7	1326	4.5	1851	0.8
30	W	0140	4.5	0708	0.8	1403	4.4	1928	1.0
31	TH	0217	4.4	0747	1.0	1446	4.3	2011	1.3

APRIL

Date	Day	Time	m	Time	m	Time	m	Time	m
1	F	0300	4.2	0836	1.4	1540	4.0	2109	1.7
2	SA	0358	3.9	0945	1.7	1652	3.8	◑ 2236	1.9
3	SU	0520	3.7	1132	1.8	1830	3.8		
4	M	0025	1.9	0701	3.8	1312	1.6	2001	4.0
5	TU	0148	1.6	0824	4.0	1418	1.3	2105	4.4
6	W	0246	1.2	0922	4.3	1510	0.9	2156	4.6
7	TH	0333	0.9	1011	4.5	1554	0.6	2241	4.8
8	F	0416	0.6	1056	4.7	1636	0.5	● 2322	4.9
9	SA	0456	0.5	1138	4.7	1715	0.5		
10	SU	0001	4.9	0534	0.5	1218	4.7	1751	0.5
11	M	0037	4.8	0609	0.6	1255	4.7	1824	0.7
12	TU	0110	4.7	0642	0.7	1331	4.5	1856	0.9
13	W	0142	4.5	0712	0.9	1406	4.4	1928	1.2
14	TH	0214	4.3	0744	1.2	1443	4.2	2003	1.5
15	F	0248	4.1	0821	1.6	1526	3.9	2048	1.9
16	SA	0331	3.8	0911	1.9	1621	3.7	◐ 2157	2.2
17	SU	0430	3.6	1040	2.1	1739	3.6	2341	2.3
18	M	0556	3.4	1221	2.1	1919	3.7		
19	TU	0105	2.1	0736	3.6	1329	1.8	2024	3.9
20	W	0200	1.8	0836	3.8	1416	1.5	2107	4.1
21	TH	0242	1.5	0918	4.0	1456	1.2	2144	4.3
22	F	0318	1.2	0956	4.2	1532	1.0	2219	4.4
23	SA	0353	1.0	1033	4.3	1608	0.9	2254	4.5
24	SU	0427	0.8	1111	4.4	1643	0.8	○ 2329	4.6
25	M	0501	0.7	1150	4.5	1718	0.7		
26	TU	0006	4.7	0536	0.7	1230	4.6	1754	0.8
27	W	0043	4.7	0614	0.7	1310	4.6	1834	0.9
28	TH	0122	4.6	0655	0.8	1354	4.5	1917	1.1
29	F	0205	4.4	0741	1.0	1443	4.1	2008	1.3
30	SA	0254	4.2	0837	1.3	1543	4.1	2113	1.6

Chart Datum: 2·73 metres below Ordnance Datum (Newlyn)

TIME ZONE (UT)
For Summer Time add ONE hour in **non-shaded areas**

ENGLAND – PORTSMOUTH

LAT 50°48′N LONG 1°07′W

TIMES AND HEIGHTS OF HIGH AND LOW WATERS

SPRING & NEAP TIDES
Dates in red are **SPRINGS**
Dates in blue are **NEAPS**

YEAR **2005**

MAY

Date	Day	Time	m	Time	m	Time	m	Time	m
1	SU	0357	4.0	0951	1.5	1656	4.0	◑ 2236	1.8
2	M	0516	3.8	1121	1.6	1823	4.0		
3	TU	0005	1.7	0646	3.9	1245	1.5	1939	4.2
4	W	0120	1.5	0800	4.1	1349	1.2	2039	4.4
5	TH	0218	1.2	0857	4.3	1441	1.0	2129	4.6
6	F	0306	1.0	0946	4.4	1525	0.8	2214	4.7
7	SA	0349	0.8	1031	4.5	1607	0.7	2255	4.7
8	SU	0430	0.7	1114	4.6	1646	0.7	● 2333	4.7
9	M	0508	0.7	1153	4.6	1723	0.8		
10	TU	0008	4.7	0543	0.8	1231	4.5	1757	0.9
11	W	0041	4.6	0617	0.9	1307	4.5	1831	1.1
12	TH	0113	4.5	0649	1.1	1343	4.4	1905	1.3
13	F	0147	4.3	0722	1.3	1421	4.2	1941	1.6
14	SA	0223	4.1	0759	1.5	1504	4.0	2025	1.8
15	SU	0305	3.9	0846	1.7	1555	3.9	2122	2.1
16	M	0358	3.7	0951	1.9	1658	3.8	◐ 2240	2.2
17	TU	0505	3.6	1113	2.0	1809	3.8		
18	W	0001	2.1	0620	3.6	1225	1.8	1916	3.9
19	TH	0103	1.9	0729	3.7	1320	1.6	2009	4.1
20	F	0151	1.6	0824	3.9	1405	1.4	2055	4.3
21	SA	0232	1.3	0911	4.1	1447	1.2	2137	4.4
22	SU	0312	1.1	0956	4.3	1527	1.0	2219	4.5
23	M	0352	0.9	1042	4.5	1609	0.9	○ 2301	4.6
24	TU	0433	0.8	1127	4.6	1652	0.9	2343	4.7
25	W	0517	0.7	1213	4.6	1737	0.9		
26	TH	0027	4.7	0602	0.7	1301	4.7	1824	0.9
27	F	0113	4.6	0651	0.8	1351	4.6	1915	1.0
28	SA	0201	4.5	0743	0.9	1445	4.5	2010	1.2
29	SU	0255	4.3	0841	1.1	1545	4.4	2111	1.4
30	M	0356	4.1	0945	1.3	1650	4.3	◑ 2219	1.5
31	TU	0505	4.0	1054	1.4	1759	4.2	2331	1.5

JUNE

Date	Day	Time	m	Time	m	Time	m	Time	m
1	W	0618	4.0	1204	1.4	1905	4.3		
2	TH	0041	1.5	0726	4.0	1309	1.3	2004	4.4
3	F	0142	1.3	0826	4.1	1405	1.2	2057	4.4
4	SA	0234	1.2	0919	4.2	1453	1.1	2145	4.5
5	SU	0321	1.1	1008	4.3	1538	1.1	2228	4.5
6	M	0404	1.0	1052	4.4	1620	1.1	● 2307	4.5
7	TU	0444	1.0	1133	4.4	1659	1.1	2343	4.5
8	W	0522	1.0	1211	4.4	1736	1.2		
9	TH	0017	4.5	0558	1.0	1247	4.4	1812	1.2
10	F	0051	4.4	0632	1.1	1324	4.3	1848	1.4
11	SA	0126	4.3	0706	1.3	1402	4.3	1924	1.5
12	SU	0203	4.1	0742	1.4	1443	4.2	2003	1.7
13	M	0243	4.0	0821	1.5	1527	4.1	2047	1.8
14	TU	0328	3.9	0907	1.6	1616	4.0	2140	1.9
15	W	0419	3.8	1002	1.7	1710	4.0	◐ 2240	1.9
16	TH	0518	3.8	1104	1.7	1809	4.0	2345	1.9
17	F	0623	3.8	1207	1.7	1910	4.1		
18	SA	0047	1.7	0729	3.9	1307	1.6	2006	4.2
19	SU	0143	1.5	0830	4.1	1402	1.4	2059	4.4
20	M	0235	1.3	0926	4.3	1454	1.2	2149	4.5
21	TU	0325	1.0	1020	4.4	1546	1.1	2238	4.6
22	W	0416	0.9	1112	4.6	1637	1.0	○ 2327	4.7
23	TH	0506	0.7	1203	4.7	1729	0.9		
24	F	0016	4.7	0557	0.7	1255	4.7	1820	0.9
25	SA	0106	4.7	0648	0.7	1347	4.7	1911	0.9
26	SU	0157	4.6	0739	0.7	1440	4.7	2003	1.0
27	M	0250	4.5	0831	0.8	1534	4.6	2057	1.1
28	TU	0345	4.3	0925	1.0	1628	4.5	◑ 2153	1.3
29	W	0441	4.2	1021	1.2	1724	4.3	2253	1.4
30	TH	0540	4.0	1120	1.4	1823	4.2	2357	1.5

JULY

Date	Day	Time	m	Time	m	Time	m	Time	m
1	F	0645	3.9	1223	1.5	1924	4.2		
2	SA	0103	1.5	0752	3.9	1327	1.6	2023	4.2
3	SU	0204	1.5	0854	4.0	1424	1.5	2118	4.2
4	M	0257	1.4	0949	4.1	1515	1.5	2205	4.3
5	TU	0343	1.3	1037	4.2	1600	1.4	2247	4.3
6	W	0426	1.2	1118	4.3	1641	1.3	● 2324	4.4
7	TH	0505	1.1	1156	4.4	1720	1.3	2358	4.4
8	F	0542	1.1	1231	4.4	1757	1.3		
9	SA	0032	4.3	0617	1.1	1306	4.4	1832	1.3
10	SU	0108	4.3	0649	1.1	1342	4.3	1905	1.3
11	M	0143	4.2	0721	1.2	1418	4.3	1938	1.4
12	TU	0219	4.1	0753	1.3	1455	4.2	2013	1.5
13	W	0257	4.1	0829	1.4	1533	4.2	2054	1.6
14	TH	0338	4.0	0912	1.5	1616	4.1	◐ 2142	1.7
15	F	0427	3.9	1004	1.6	1707	4.0	2241	1.8
16	SA	0528	3.9	1107	1.7	1811	4.0	2351	1.8
17	SU	0642	3.9	1219	1.7	1922	4.1		
18	M	0105	1.6	0759	4.0	1333	1.6	2029	4.2
19	TU	0214	1.4	0907	4.2	1438	1.4	2129	4.4
20	W	0313	1.1	1007	4.4	1536	1.2	2223	4.6
21	TH	0408	0.9	1102	4.6	1630	1.0	○ 2315	4.7
22	F	0500	0.7	1155	4.8	1722	0.8		
23	SA	0006	4.7	0550	0.5	1246	4.9	1811	0.7
24	SU	0056	4.7	0638	0.5	1335	4.9	1859	0.7
25	M	0145	4.7	0725	0.5	1423	4.8	1946	0.8
26	TU	0233	4.6	0810	0.7	1509	4.7	2032	0.9
27	W	0320	4.4	0855	0.9	1554	4.5	2120	1.1
28	TH	0407	4.2	0942	1.2	1640	4.3	◑ 2212	1.4
29	F	0458	4.0	1035	1.5	1732	4.1	2313	1.7
30	SA	0559	3.8	1139	1.8	1836	3.9		
31	SU	0025	1.8	0718	3.7	1254	1.9	1950	3.9

AUGUST

Date	Day	Time	m	Time	m	Time	m	Time	m
1	M	0139	1.8	0837	3.8	1403	1.9	2057	4.0
2	TU	0239	1.6	0938	4.0	1459	1.7	2150	4.1
3	W	0327	1.4	1025	4.2	1545	1.5	2232	4.2
4	TH	0408	1.2	1105	4.3	1626	1.4	2308	4.3
5	F	0447	1.1	1140	4.4	1703	1.2	● 2341	4.3
6	SA	0523	1.0	1213	4.4	1739	1.1		
7	SU	0014	4.3	0556	0.9	1245	4.4	1811	1.1
8	M	0047	4.3	0627	0.9	1317	4.4	1841	1.1
9	TU	0120	4.3	0655	1.0	1349	4.4	1909	1.2
10	W	0152	4.3	0723	1.1	1420	4.4	1940	1.2
11	TH	0225	4.2	0754	1.2	1453	4.3	2016	1.4
12	F	0302	4.1	0832	1.4	1530	4.2	2059	1.5
13	SA	0347	4.0	0920	1.6	1618	4.1	◐ 2155	1.7
14	SU	0447	3.9	1024	1.9	1723	4.0	2312	1.9
15	M	0609	3.8	1152	2.0	1848	3.9		
16	TU	0049	1.8	0742	3.9	1325	1.9	2011	4.1
17	W	0209	1.5	0858	4.2	1435	1.6	2117	4.4
18	TH	0309	1.1	0959	4.5	1532	1.2	2212	4.6
19	F	0401	0.8	1052	4.7	1623	0.9	○ 2303	4.7
20	SA	0450	0.5	1141	4.9	1710	0.7	2351	4.8
21	SU	0536	0.4	1227	5.0	1756	0.6		
22	M	0037	4.8	0619	0.4	1312	5.0	1839	0.6
23	TU	0123	4.8	0701	0.5	1355	4.9	1920	0.7
24	W	0205	4.7	0741	0.7	1435	4.7	2001	0.9
25	TH	0247	4.5	0819	1.0	1514	4.5	2041	1.2
26	F	0329	4.2	0900	1.3	1553	4.3	◑ 2126	1.5
27	SA	0415	3.9	0949	1.7	1639	4.0	2226	1.9
28	SU	0514	3.7	1058	2.1	1742	3.7	2350	2.1
29	M	0649	3.6	1229	2.2	1923	3.7		
30	TU	0119	2.0	0827	3.8	1349	2.1	2044	3.8
31	W	0223	1.8	0925	4.0	1445	1.8	2136	4.1

Chart Datum: 2·73 metres below Ordnance Datum (Newlyn)

TIME ZONE (UT)
For Summer Time add ONE hour in **non-shaded areas**

ENGLAND – PORTSMOUTH

LAT 50°48′N LONG 1°07′W

TIMES AND HEIGHTS OF HIGH AND LOW WATERS

SPRING & NEAP TIDES
Dates in red are SPRINGS
Dates in blue are NEAPS

YEAR **2005**

SEPTEMBER

Day	Time	m	Day	Time	m
1 TH	0309	1.5	16 F	0300	1.1
	1009	4.2		0946	4.6
	1528	1.6		1521	1.1
	2215	4.2		2159	4.6
2 F	0347	1.2	17 SA	0347	0.7
	1045	4.4		1034	4.8
	1605	1.3		1607	0.8
	2249	4.3		2246	4.8
3 SA	0423	1.0	18 SU	0431	0.5
	1117	4.5		1119	5.0
	1640	1.1		1651	0.6
	● 2320	4.4		○ 2330	4.9
4 SU	0458	0.9	19 M	0514	0.4
	1147	4.5		1202	5.0
	1714	1.0		1733	0.5
	2350	4.4			
5 M	0531	0.8	20 TU	0014	4.9
	1216	4.5		0553	0.4
	1745	1.0		1243	5.0
				1812	0.5
6 TU	0021	4.4	21 W	0056	4.8
	0559	0.8		0631	0.5
	1247	4.5		1322	4.9
	1812	1.0		1850	0.7
7 W	0053	4.4	22 TH	0135	4.7
	0626	0.9		0707	0.8
	1316	4.5		1358	4.7
	1839	1.0		1926	0.9
8 TH	0124	4.4	23 F	0214	4.5
	0653	1.0		0742	1.1
	1346	4.5		1433	4.5
	1909	1.1		2002	1.2
9 F	0157	4.4	24 SA	0253	4.3
	0723	1.1		0819	1.5
	1418	4.4		1510	4.2
	1943	1.3		2043	1.6
10 SA	0233	4.2	25 SU	0337	4.0
	0800	1.4		0907	1.9
	1455	4.2		1553	3.9
	2025	1.5		◑ 2139	2.0
11 SU	0318	4.1	26 M	0436	3.7
	0847	1.7		1022	2.3
	1543	4.0		1655	3.6
	◐ 2122	1.8		2313	2.2
12 M	0422	3.8	27 TU	0616	3.6
	0958	2.0		1205	2.4
	1653	3.9		1850	3.6
	2253	2.0			
13 TU	0554	3.7	28 W	0052	2.2
	1149	2.2		0805	3.8
	1829	3.8		1328	2.2
				2023	3.8
14 W	0048	1.9	29 TH	0158	1.9
	0737	3.9		0900	4.1
	1325	1.9		1422	1.9
	2002	4.1		2112	4.0
15 TH	0205	1.5	30 F	0241	1.6
	0851	4.3		0939	4.3
	1430	1.5		1501	1.6
	2107	4.4		2148	4.2

OCTOBER

Day	Time	m	Day	Time	m
1 SA	0318	1.3	16 SU	0324	0.8
	1013	4.4		1010	4.9
	1536	1.3		1544	0.8
	2220	4.3		2224	4.8
2 SU	0353	1.0	17 M	0406	0.6
	1043	4.5		1053	5.0
	1610	1.1		1626	0.7
	2250	4.4		○ 2307	4.9
3 M	0426	0.9	18 TU	0447	0.5
	1113	4.6		1134	5.0
	1642	1.0		1706	0.6
	● 2321	4.5		2349	4.9
4 TU	0458	0.9	19 W	0525	0.6
	1143	4.6		1213	4.9
	1713	0.9		1745	0.7
	2353	4.5			
5 W	0528	0.9	20 TH	0029	4.8
	1213	4.6		0601	0.8
	1741	0.9		1250	4.8
				1820	0.8
6 TH	0025	4.6	21 F	0108	4.7
	0556	0.9		0636	1.0
	1245	4.6		1324	4.7
	1810	1.0		1855	1.1
7 F	0100	4.6	22 SA	0145	4.5
	0625	1.0		0711	1.3
	1317	4.5		1358	4.4
	1843	1.1		1930	1.3
8 SA	0135	4.5	23 SU	0224	4.3
	0659	1.2		0748	1.6
	1352	4.4		1434	4.2
	1920	1.2		2010	1.7
9 SU	0215	4.3	24 M	0308	4.0
	0740	1.5		0836	2.0
	1432	4.3		1517	3.9
	2006	1.5		2102	2.0
10 M	0305	4.1	25 TU	0405	3.8
	0833	1.8		0947	2.3
	1525	4.0		1616	3.7
	◐ 2109	1.8		◑ 2226	2.2
11 TU	0416	3.9	26 W	0528	3.7
	0956	2.1		1126	2.4
	1641	3.8		1743	3.6
	2250	2.0			
12 W	0550	3.8	27 TH	0003	2.2
	1146	2.1		0712	3.8
	1819	3.8		1248	2.2
				1930	3.7
13 TH	0035	1.8	28 F	0113	2.0
	0727	4.1		0813	4.0
	1312	1.8		1343	2.0
	1948	4.1		2026	3.9
14 F	0146	1.5	29 SA	0200	1.7
	0833	4.4		0854	4.2
	1412	1.4		1424	1.7
	2049	4.4		2105	4.1
15 SA	0239	1.1	30 SU	0239	1.4
	0924	4.7		0929	4.4
	1500	1.1		1500	1.4
	2139	4.6		2140	4.3
			31 M	0315	1.2
				1002	4.5
				1534	1.2
				2214	4.4

NOVEMBER

Day	Time	m	Day	Time	m
1 TU	0349	1.1	16 W	0420	0.9
	1035	4.6		1107	4.9
	1607	1.1		1643	0.8
	2249	4.5		○ 2328	4.7
2 W	0422	1.0	17 TH	0459	0.9
	1109	4.6		1146	4.8
	1639	1.0		1721	0.9
	● 2326	4.6			
3 TH	0455	1.0	18 F	0008	4.7
	1143	4.7		0536	1.0
	1713	0.9		1222	4.7
				1758	1.0
4 F	0003	4.7	19 SA	0046	4.6
	0529	1.0		0612	1.2
	1220	4.7		1257	4.6
	1748	0.9		1833	1.2
5 SA	0042	4.7	20 SU	0123	4.5
	0606	1.1		0649	1.4
	1257	4.6		1331	4.4
	1827	1.0		1909	1.4
6 SU	0123	4.6	21 M	0202	4.3
	0647	1.3		0727	1.7
	1337	4.5		1408	4.2
	1911	1.2		1948	1.6
7 M	0210	4.4	22 TU	0246	4.1
	0736	1.5		0812	2.0
	1423	4.3		1450	4.0
	2004	1.4		2034	1.8
8 TU	0306	4.2	23 W	0336	4.0
	0837	1.8		0908	2.2
	1522	4.1		1541	3.8
	2112	1.7		◑ 2133	2.0
9 W	0417	4.1	24 TH	0438	3.9
	0957	1.9		1023	2.3
	1635	4.0		1644	3.7
	◐ 2237	1.8		2249	2.1
10 TH	0541	4.1	25 F	0549	3.9
	1125	1.9		1142	2.3
	1802	4.0		1758	3.7
11 F	0002	1.7	26 SA	0002	2.0
	0701	4.2		0657	4.0
	1242	1.7		1246	2.1
	1921	4.1		1909	3.8
12 SA	0113	1.4	27 SU	0101	1.9
	0804	4.5		0751	4.1
	1343	1.4		1334	1.9
	2022	4.3		2006	3.9
13 SU	0208	1.2	28 M	0148	1.7
	0856	4.7		0837	4.3
	1433	1.2		1416	1.6
	2114	4.5		2054	4.1
14 M	0255	1.0	29 TU	0230	1.5
	0943	4.8		0919	4.5
	1519	1.0		1454	1.4
	2201	4.7		2138	4.3
15 TU	0339	0.9	30 W	0309	1.3
	1027	4.9		0959	4.6
	1602	0.9		1532	1.2
	2246	4.7		2221	4.5

DECEMBER

Day	Time	m	Day	Time	m
1 TH	0348	1.2	16 F	0440	1.2
	1039	4.7		1125	4.6
	1612	1.0		1706	1.1
	● 2304	4.6		2353	4.5
2 F	0429	1.1	17 SA	0519	1.2
	1120	4.7		1201	4.6
	1653	0.9		1744	1.1
	2347	4.7			
3 SA	0511	1.1	18 SU	0031	4.5
	1201	4.7		0557	1.3
	1737	0.9		1237	4.5
				1819	1.2
4 SU	0032	4.7	19 M	0108	4.5
	0556	1.1		0633	1.4
	1245	4.7		1312	4.4
	1823	0.9		1855	1.3
5 M	0120	4.7	20 TU	0145	4.4
	0645	1.2		0710	1.6
	1331	4.6		1348	4.2
	1913	1.0		1930	1.4
6 TU	0211	4.6	21 W	0224	4.3
	0737	1.3		0747	1.7
	1422	4.4		1427	4.1
	2007	1.2		2006	1.5
7 W	0307	4.5	22 TH	0306	4.2
	0836	1.5		0828	1.9
	1519	4.3		1508	4.0
	2106	1.3		2047	1.7
8 TH	0410	4.4	23 F	0352	4.1
	0941	1.6		0915	2.0
	1623	4.1		1555	3.8
	◐ 2211	1.4		◑ 2135	1.8
9 F	0517	4.3	24 SA	0443	4.0
	1051	1.7		1012	2.1
	1732	4.1		1648	3.8
	2320	1.5		2232	1.9
10 SA	0625	4.3	25 SU	0542	4.0
	1202	1.6		1117	2.1
	1844	4.1		1752	3.8
				2336	1.9
11 SU	0028	1.5	26 M	0644	4.0
	0728	4.4		1224	2.0
	1307	1.5		1902	3.8
	1949	4.2			
12 M	0130	1.4	27 TU	0042	1.8
	0825	4.5		0745	4.2
	1405	1.4		1325	1.8
	2048	4.3		2008	4.0
13 TU	0225	1.3	28 W	0142	1.7
	0916	4.6		0839	4.3
	1455	1.3		1418	1.6
	2141	4.4		2106	4.2
14 W	0314	1.3	29 TH	0235	1.5
	1003	4.6		0930	4.5
	1542	1.2		1507	1.3
	2230	4.5		2159	4.4
15 TH	0358	1.2	30 F	0325	1.3
	1046	4.7		1017	4.6
	1625	1.1		1556	1.1
	○ 2313	4.5		2249	4.6
			31 SA	0415	1.2
				1104	4.7
				1644	0.9
				● 2338	4.7

Chart Datum: 2·73 metres below Ordnance Datum (Newlyn)

9.2.24 PORTSMOUTH

Hampshire **50°47'·38N 01°06'·67W** (Entrance) ❀❀❀◊◊◊✿✿

CHARTS AC *5600, 2045, 2037,* 2625, *2631,* 2629, 2628; Imray C9, C3, C15; Stanfords 11, 10; OS 197

TIDES +0029 Dover; ML 2·8; Zone 0 (UT)

Standard Port PORTSMOUTH (⟵)

Times				Height (metres)			
High Water		Low Water		MHWS	MHWN	MLWN	MLWS
0500	1000	0000	0600	4·7	3·8	1·9	0·8
1700	2200	1200	1800				
Differences LEE-ON-THE-SOLENT							
−0005	+0005	−0015	−0010	−0·2	−0·1	+0·1	+0·2

See also 9.2.11. Strong winds from NE to SE, coupled with a high barometer, may lower levels by 1m and delay times of HW and LW by 1hr; the opposite may occur in strong W'lies with low pressure.

SHELTER Excellent. This very large hbr affords shelter in some area for any wind. There are two marinas on the Gosport side, three at Fareham and one at the N end of Portchester Lake, plus several yacht pontoons/jetties and many moorings (see Facilities).
Good shelter in The Camber, but this is a busy little commercial dock and often full; beware the Isle of Wight car ferry docking near the ent.
Portsmouth is a major naval base and Dockyard Port; all vessels come under the QHM's authority. If > 20m LOA, ask QHM's permission (VHF Ch 11) to enter, leave or move in hbr, especially in fog. Fishing and ⚓ in chans are prohib.

NAVIGATION WPT No 4 Bar buoy, QR, 50°47'·01N 01°06'·36W, 330° to hbr ent (W side), 4½ca. Beware very strong tides in hbr ent, commercial shipping and ferries, Gosport ferry and HM Ships. High Speed Ferries operate within the area.

Approaches: From the W, yachts can use the Swashway Chan (to NW of Spit Sand Fort) which carries about 2m; keep War Memorial and RH edge of block of flats on at 049°. The Inner Swashway Chan (Round Tr on 029°) carries only 0·1m; local knowledge required. Approaching inshore from E, the submerged barrier, which extends from Southsea to Horse Sand Fort, should only be crossed via the unlit Inshore Boat passage (0·9m) 1ca off the beach, marked by R & G piles; or via the Main Passage (min depth 1·2m) 7ca further S, marked by G pile and dolphin, QR.

Small Boat Channel (QHM Portsmouth LNTM 06/2004 refers) It is mandatory for yachts/craft < 20m LOA to use this chan. when entering or leaving the hbr. It runs parallel to and outboard of the W edge of the main dredged chan., from abeam No 4 Bar buoy, QR (off Clarence Pier) to Ballast buoy, Fl R 2·5s, and extends about 50m off Fort Blockhouse. A depth gauge is on pile BC4. Yachts may not enter on the E side of the main channel, and may only cross the main chan N of Ballast or S of No 4 Bar buoys. Yachts may enter/exit the Small Boat Chan. anywhere on its W.side. They must motor (if fitted) between the No 4 Bar - Ballast buoys and when crossing to/from Gunwharf Qy/Camber (approval from QHM VHF **11** req'd). Beware, winds at the ent may be fickle or gusty and tides run hard. The Small Boat Chan may be used even if the main chan is closed.
At night the Small Boat Chan is covered by the Oc R sector (324°-330°) of the Dir WRG lt on Fort Blockhouse (W side of hbr ent), until close to the hbr ent. Thereafter the Iso R 2s sector (337·5°-345°) of the Dir WRG lt 2m 1M (dolphin E of Gosport Marina) leads 341° through the ent and close abeam Ballast Bank PHM buoy, Fl R 2·5s.

Speed limit is 10kn within hbr and within 1000 yds of the shore in any part of the Dockyard Port; speed = speed through the water. Outside the hbr ent, the Dockyard Port limits embrace the Solent from Hillhead and Old Castle Pt (close NE of Cowes) eastward to Eastney and Shanklin (IOW), thence almost out to Nab Tr (see AC 394 & 2050).

Exclusion Zones: Do not approach within 50m of any Naval Vessel or Establishment or within 500m of any Naval vessel underway (by day: 2 diamond shapes vert, by night: 2 Fl R vert). Escort vessels (Fl Bu lts) are armed and will assume you have hostile intentions if you are within 500m and fail to respond.

Historic Wrecks (see 9.0.3h) are at: 50°45'·8N 01°06'·2W (site of *Mary Rose*), marked by SPM buoys; 5ca SSW of Spit Sand Ft. *Invincible* lies at 50°44'·34N 01°02'·23W, 117° Horse Sand Fort 1·45M, marked by SPM buoy.

Navigational Piles should not be approached too closely as many are on steep-to mud; those lit in Portchester lake may be difficult to locate due to background lighting.

LIGHTS AND MARKS From E of the IOW, Nab Tower, Fl 10s 27m 16M, is conspic about 10M SE of the hbr ent. In the inner appr's there are 3 conspic forts: Horse Sand Fort, Iso G 2s; No Man's Land Fort, Iso R 2s, and Spit Sand Fort, Fl R 5s.
Ldg marks/lts: St Jude's ✠ spire and Southsea Castle lt ho in transit 003° lead between Outer Spit SCM buoy, Q (6) + L Fl 15s, and Horse Sand SHM buoy, Fl G 2·5s. At night keep in the W sector (000°-003°) between the Al WG and Al WR sectors of the Dir lt (H24) on Southsea Castle, which also shows a lt Iso 2s 16m 11M, vis 337°-071° (94°).

FIRING RANGE **Tipner Rifle Range** as shown on chartlet. The danger area extends 2,500m from firing range. When firing is in progress, R flag or ● lt on Tipner Range FS indicates yachts should clear the range danger area or transit it as quickly as possible.

R/T Yachts should monitor Ch **11** (H24) for traffic/nav info. For the Camber call *Portsmouth Hbr Radio* (Commercial Port) Ch 11 14 (H24).
Haslar Marina and *Port Solent* Ch **80** M (H24). *Gosport Marina* call Ch **80** M (HO). Fareham Marine Ch M (summer 0900-1730). Wicor Marina Ch 80 (0900-1730, Mon-Sat). Gunwharf Quay Ch 80. **Naval activities** to the S/SE of Portsmouth and IOW may be advised by Solent CG Ch 67 or ☎ 9255 2100; or Naval Ops ☎ 9272 2008. Naval vessels use Ch 13. The positions and times of naval firings and underwater explosions are broadcast daily at 0800 and 1400LT Ch 06; preceded by a Securité call on Ch 16. Warnings of underwater explosions will also be broadcast on Ch 16 at 1 hour, at 30 mins and just before the detonation.

TELEPHONE Dial codes: Portsmouth/Gosport 023; Fareham 01329. QHM 9272 3124; DQHM 9272 3794/℻ 9272 2831; Hbr Control (H24) 9272 3694; Commercial Docks 9229 7395; Camber Berthing Offices ☎ 9229 7395 Ext 310; MRSC 9255 2100; Marinecall 09066 526241; Weather Centre 8022 8844; Police 08450 454545; Dr Fareham Health Centre (01329) 282911; Ⓗ 9282 2331.

FACILITIES
Marinas (from seaward)
Haslar Marina, ☎ 9260 1201, ℻ 9260 2201, £2.50, (550+ 50 ⓥ); Access H24; ⓥ at L pontoon, near conspic former lt ship, Bar & R (☎ 9252 5200); Gas, Gaz, CH, ME, Ⓔ, ▣, Slip (upstream of Haslar bridge). RNSA berths at S end.
Gosport Marina (520, ⓥ space varies) ☎ 9252 4811, ℻ 9258 9541, www.cnmarinas.com, £2.50, P, D, ME, EI, ⚒, BH (180, 10 ton), CH, ⛟, Gas, Gaz, SM, ▣. Note: There are RNSA pontoons at the N end of Cold Hbr, inside the Fuel Jetty.
Royal Clarence Marina ☎ 9252 3810, ℻ 9252 3980, www.royalclarencemarina.co.uk (130), ⓥ space varies £18/ yacht (winter £12) Access H24.
Town centres
Gosport: ✉, Ⓑ, SM, ACA; ⇌ (Portsmouth), ✈ (Southampton).
City of Portsmouth (3M); ✉, Ⓑ, CH, P, D, ACA, EI, Ⓔ, ME, ⚒, BY, SM, Slip, C. ⇌, Ferries to Caen (Ouistreham), Cherbourg, Le Havre, Caen, St Malo, Bilbao, Santander (winter) and IoW (see 9.0.4); ✈ (Southampton).
Gunwharf Quays ☎ 9283 6732, ℻ 9283 6738, www.gunwharf-quays.com, FW, ⛽, ⓥ £3.00 (winter £2.00), short stay £8, booking advisable. Craft <20m bound for Gunwharf must enter hbr through the Small Boat Chan and only cross the Main Chan N of Ballast Buoy after obtaining permission from QHM on VHF Ch 11. Return by same route and again only with permission from QHM.
Water Taxis from Haslar Jetty, Gunwharf and HMS Warrior.
For Traffic Signals, Fog Routine, Fareham and Port Solent Marina details, see over.

PORTSMOUTH *continued*

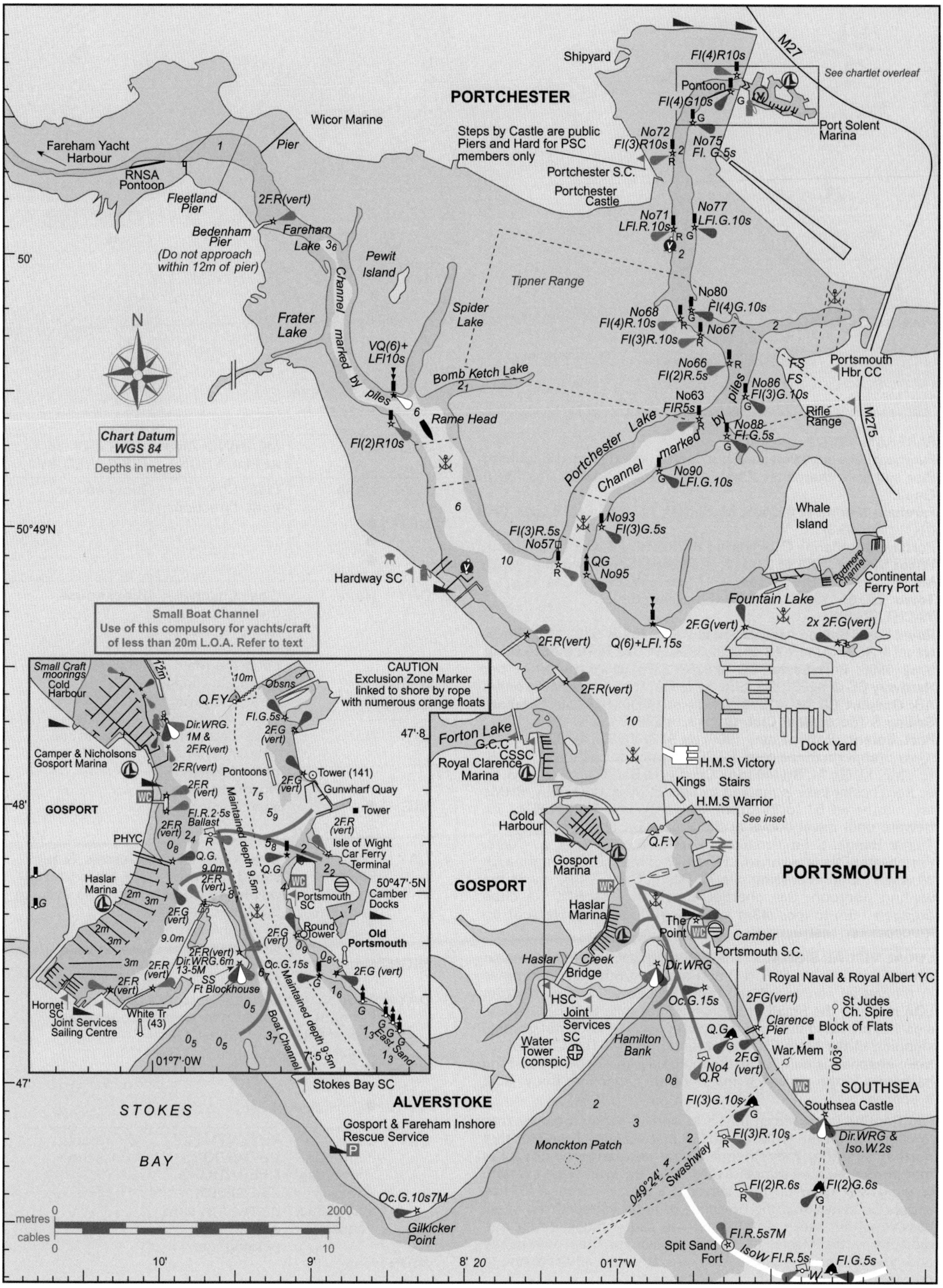
PORTCHESTER
Shipyard
Fl(4)R10s
Pontoon
Fl(4)G10s
See chartlet overleaf
M27
Port Solent Marina
Wicor Marine
Fareham Yacht Harbour
RNSA Pontoon
Pier
Fleetland Pier
2F.R(vert)
Bedenham Pier
(Do not approach within 12m of pier)
Fareham Lake
Steps by Castle are public Piers and Hard for PSC members only
Portchester S.C.
Portchester Castle
No72 Fl(3)R10s
No75 Fl. G.5s
No71 LFl.R.10s
No77 LFl.G.10s
Pewit Island
Tipner Range
Channel marked by piles
Frater Lake
Spider Lake
No80 Fl(4)G.10s
No68 Fl(4)R.10s
No67 Fl(3)R.10s
VQ(6)+ LFl10s
Bomb Ketch Lake
No66 Fl(2)R.5s
Portsmouth Hbr CC
No86 Fl(3)G.10s
No63 FlR5s
Rifle Range
M275
Rame Head
Fl(2)R10s
No88 Fl.G.5s
Portchester Lake Channel marked by piles
Chart Datum WGS 84
Depths in metres
No90 LFl.G.10s
Whale Island
No93 Fl(3)G.5s
Fl(3)R.5s No57
QG No95
Hardway SC
Continental Ferry Port
Rudmore Channel
Fountain Lake
Small Boat Channel
Use of this compulsory for yachts/craft of less than 20m L.O.A. Refer to text
2F.G(vert)
2x 2F.G(vert)
2F.R(vert)
Q(6)+LFl.15s
2F.R(vert)
Dock Yard
Forton Lake
G.C.C
CSSC
Royal Clarence Marina
H.M.S Victory
Kings Stairs
H.M.S Warrior
See inset
Cold Harbour
Q.F.Y
Gosport Marina
GOSPORT
PORTSMOUTH
Haslar Marina
The Point
Camber
Portsmouth S.C.
Haslar Creek Bridge
Dir.WRG
Royal Naval & Royal Albert YC
HSC
Oc.G.15s
2FG(vert)
Joint Services SC
St Judes Ch. Spire
Clarence Pier
Block of Flats
Water Tower (conspic)
Hamilton Bank
Q.G
No4 Q.R
2F.G (vert)
War Mem
003°
SOUTHSEA
Fl(3)G.10s
Southsea Castle
Dir.WRG & Iso.W.2s
Fl(3)R.10s
Swashway
049°24'
Monckton Patch
Fl(2)R.6s
Fl(2)G.6s
Spit Sand Fort
Fl.R.5s7M
IsoW
Fl.R.5s
Fl.G.5s
Stokes Bay SC
ALVERSTOKE
STOKES BAY
Gosport & Fareham Inshore Rescue Service
Oc.G.10s7M
Gilkicker Point
Small Craft moorings Cold Harbour
12m
10m
Obsns
CAUTION
Exclusion Zone Marker linked to shore by rope with numerous orange floats
Q.F.Y
Fl.G.5s
2F.G (vert)
Dir.WRG. 1M & 2F.R(vert)
Camper & Nicholsons Gosport Marina
2F.R(vert)
Pontoons
Tower (141)
Gunwharf Quay
Tower
47'·8
GOSPORT
Fl.R.2·5s
Ballast
Maintained depth 9.5m
Isle of Wight Car Ferry Terminal
PHYC
Q.G.
Haslar Marina
9.0m
50°47'·5N
Camber Docks
Portsmouth SC
Round Tower
Old Portsmouth
9.0m
2F.R(vert)
Dir.WRG.6m 13-5M
SS Ft Blockhouse
Oc.G.15s
2F.G (vert)
Hornet SC
Joint Services Sailing Centre
White Tr (43)
Boat Channel
East Sand
01°7'·0W
50'
50°49'N
48'
47'
metres 0 2000
cables 0 10
10'
9'
8'
01°7'W

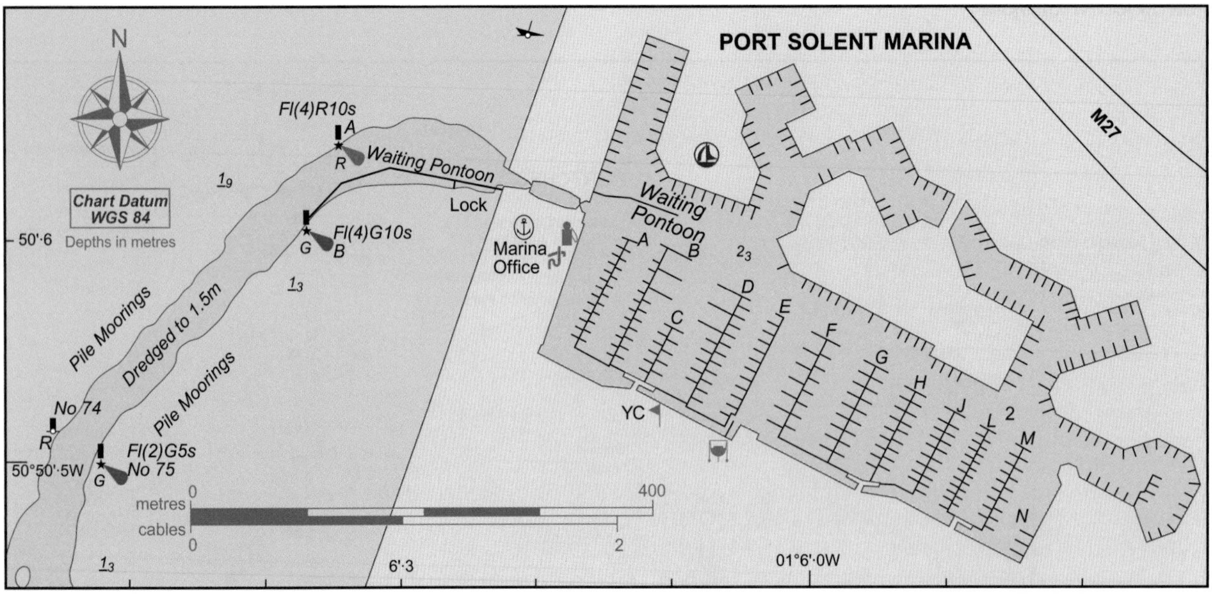
PORT SOLENT MARINA
M27
N
Chart Datum WGS 84
50'·6 Depths in metres
Fl(4)R10s
A
R
Waiting Pontoon
Lock
Fl(4)G10s
G B
Marina Office
Waiting Pontoon
A B
C D E F G H J L 2 M N
Pile Moorings
Dredged to 1.5m
Pile Moorings
No 74
R
Fl(2)G5s
No 75
50°50'·5W
G
YC
0 400
metres
cables
0 2
6'·3
01°6'·0W

FAREHAM (01329)
Fareham Lake is well marked, but only partially lit up to Bedenham Pier and unlit thereafter. Chan dries 0·9m in final 5ca to Town Quay.
Fareham Marine ☎ 822445, M, Slip, D, FW, ME, El, 🛒, Bar, CH; (Access HW±3);
Portsmouth Marine Engineering ☎ 232854, AB, Ⓥ £10, C (7 ton).
Wicor Marine (200) ☎ 237112, ℻ 825660, Scrubbing slip, M, D, ME, ⚒, CH, ⚓, BH (10 ton), C (7 ton), FW, El, Ⓔ, Gas, Gaz.
Town: ✉, Ⓑ, 🛒, Bar, ⇌, ✈ (Southampton).
YACHT CLUBS
Royal Naval Sailing Association ☎ 9252 1100, ℻ 9252 1122; **Royal Naval & Royal Albert YC** ☎ 9282 5924, M, Bar; **Portsmouth SC** ☎ 9282 0596; **Portchester SC** ☎ 9237 6375, ⚓ (close No71 bn; **Hardway SC** ☎ 9258 1875, Slip, M, L, FW, C (mast stepping only), AB; **Gosport CC** ☎ (01329) 47014 or (0860) 966390; **Fareham Sailing & Motor Boat Club** ☎ (01329) 280738.
Port Solent, Portchester, (900) ☎ 9221 0765, ℻ 9232 4241, www.premiermarinas.com, £2.25, £5/yacht for <4hrs, P, D, FW, ⚓, ME, El, Ⓔ, ⚒, BH (40 ton), CH, 🛒, R, Bar, Gas, Gaz, LPG, ▣, ♿. Portchester Lake is marked by lit/unlit piles; unusually, PHMs are numbered 57 to 74 (from seaward), and SHMs 95 to 75. Beware unlit naval buoys at the S end. Do not delay crossing Tipner Range, S limit marked by piles 63/87 and N by 70/78. Portchester Castle is conspic 5ca SSW of marina. Call marina Ch 80 when inbound passing pile 78. Pile B, Fl (4) G 10s, marks the waiting pontoon. See chartlet above. Access H24 via chan dredged 1·5m to lock (43m x 9·1m); enter on 3 ● (vert) or on loudspeaker instructions.

LOCAL VISUAL SIGNALS The traffic signals, tabled in the next column, are shown at Fort Blockhouse Sig Stn and sometimes in the vessel concerned and must be obeyed. But craft <20m LOA may use the Small Boat Chan H24 despite the displayed tfc sigs 1-3, provided they proceed with caution and do not impede shipping in the Main Channel. Monitor Ch 11. The Channel (or main channel) is defined as the main navigable channels of the harbour and the approach channel from Outer Spit buoy; Rule 9 applies.

Fog Routine is broadcast on Ch 11 and 13, when it comes into force, ie when the QHM considers that visibility is so low that normal shipping movements would be dangerous. Yachts may continue at the skipper's discretion, but with great caution, keeping well clear of the main and approach channels. They should be aware that the presence of radar echoes from small vessels within the main channel can cause much doubt and difficulty to the Master of a large vessel. For their own safety and that of major vessels they are strongly advised not to proceed. Monitor VHF Ch 11 at all times.

SIGNAL	MEANING AND APPLICATION	HOISTED/ DISPLAYED BY
1. DAY None. NIGHT ● ● ●	Clear Channel – both directions.	Blockhouse.
2. DAY None. NIGHT ○ ●	Clear Channel – only outgoing traffic allowed. No vessel shall enter the main or approach channel from seaward.	Blockhouse.
3. DAY None. NIGHT ● ○	Clear Channel – only incoming traffic allowed. No other vessel shall leave the harbour.	Blockhouse.
4. DAY Code Pennant above Pennant Zero. NIGHT None	Clear Channel – signal flown by privileged vessel. Such vessels are to be given a clear passage.	Vessels & tugs in whose favour signal is in force
5. DAY Code Pennant above flag Alpha. NIGHT ● ○ ●	Diving – vessel conducting diving.	By vessel concerned.
6. DAY Code Pennant above flag Romeo above flag Yankee. NIGHT None	POTENTIALLY HAZARDOUS OPERATIONS. You should proceed at slow speed when passing me.	By vessel concerned.

9.2.25 LANGSTONE HARBOUR

Hampshire **50°47'·23N 01°01'·54W** (Ent)

CHARTS AC *5600, 2045, 3418*; Imray C3, Y33; Stanfords 11, 10; OS 196, 197

TIDES +0022 Dover; Zone 0 (UT)

Standard Port PORTSMOUTH (⟵)

Times				**Height (metres)**			
High Water		Low Water		MHWS	MHWN	MLWN	MLWS
0500	1000	0000	0600	4·7	3·8	1·9	0·8
1700	2200	1200	1800				
Differences LANGSTONE							
0000	0000	+0010	+0010	+0·1	+0·1	0·0	0·0
NAB TOWER							
+0015	0000	+0015	+0015	–0·2	0·0	+0·2	0·0

SHELTER Very good in marina (2·4m) to W inside ent, access HW±3 over tidal flap 1·6m CD; waiting pontoon. Ent is 7m wide. 6 Y Ⓐs at W side of hbr ent, 6 more on E side; max LOA 9m. Or ⚓ out of the fairway in Russell's Lake or Langstone Chan (water ski area); or see HM (E side of ent). Hbr speed limit 10kn, or 5kn in Southsea Marina channel.

NAVIGATION WPT 50°46'·31N 01°01'·36W, Langstone Fairway SWM beacon, L Fl 10s, 168°/348° from/to QR lt at ent, 0·94M. Bar has about 1·2m. Ent chan lies between East and West Winner drying banks, which afford some protection. Appr is easy in most weather, best from HW –3 to +1, but avoid entry against the ebb, esp at sp and in strong onshore winds. In strong S/SE winds do not attempt entry.

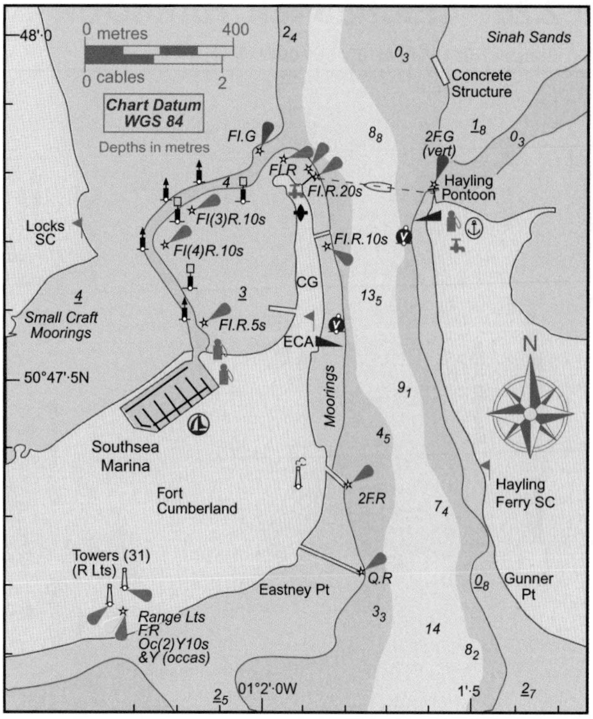
metres 400
cables 2
Chart Datum WGS 84
Depths in metres
Sinah Sands
Concrete Structure
Hayling Pontoon
Locks SC
Small Craft Moorings
Southsea Marina
Fort Cumberland
Moorings
Hayling Ferry SC
Towers (31) (R Lts)
Eastney Pt
Gunner Pt
Range Lts F.R Oc(2)Y10s &Y (occas)
Fl.G
Fl.R
Fl.R.20s
Fl(3)R.10s
Fl(4)R.10s
Fl.R.10s
Fl.R.5s
2F.G (vert)
2F.R
Q.R
CG
ECA
48'·0
50°47'·5N
01°2'·0W
1'·5

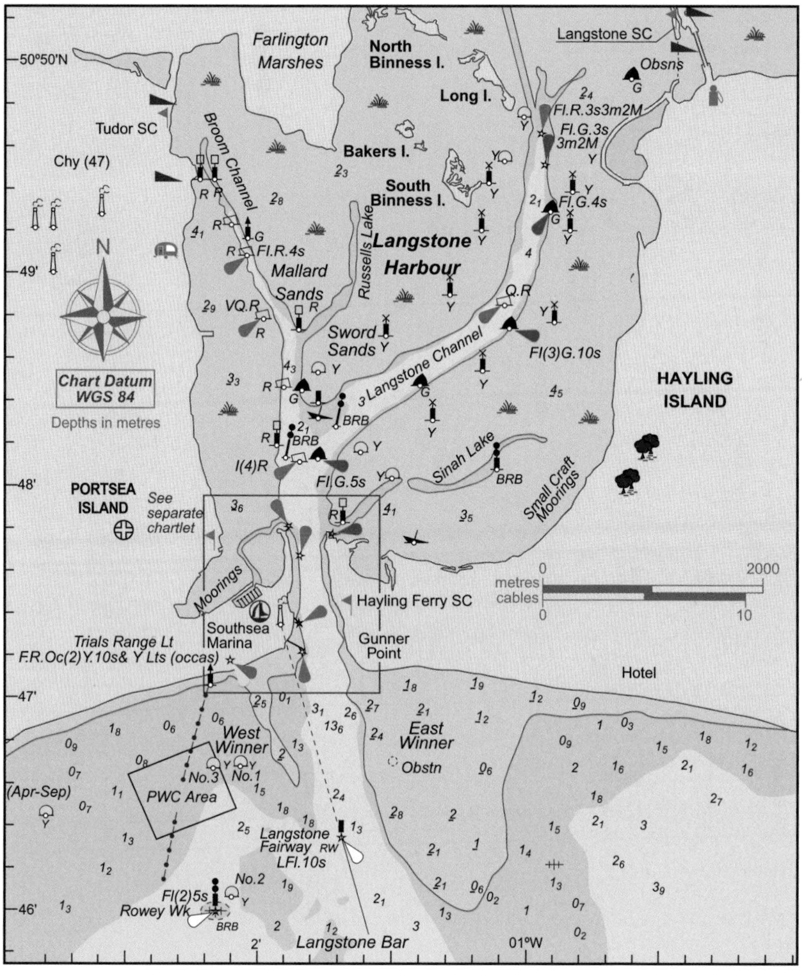
Farlington Marshes
North Binness I.
Langstone SC
Obsns
Long I.
Tudor SC
Chy (47)
Broom Channel
Bakers I.
South Binness I.
Langstone Harbour
Russells Lake
Mallard Sands
Sword Sands
Langstone Channel
Sinah Lake
Small Craft Moorings
HAYLING ISLAND
PORTSEA ISLAND
See separate chartlet
Chart Datum WGS 84
Depths in metres
Moorings
Southsea Marina
Hayling Ferry SC
Gunner Point
Hotel
Trials Range Lt F.R.Oc(2)Y.10s& Y Lts (occas)
West Winner
East Winner
Obstn
PWC Area
(Apr-Sep)
No.3
No.1
No.2
Langstone Fairway RW LFl.10s
Fl(2)5s Rowey Wk
Langstone Bar
Fl.R.3s3m2M
Fl.G.3s 3m2M
Fl.G.4s
Fl.R.4s
VQ.R
Q.R
Fl(3)G.10s
I(4)R
Fl.G.5s
BRB
metres 2000
cables 10
50°50'N
49'
48'
47'
46'
2'
01°W

LIGHTS AND MARKS Ldg marks (concrete dolphins), or Fairway beacon in line with conspic chy, leads 344° just clear of East Winner. The ent itself deepens and favours the W side. The narrow appr chan to Southsea Marina is marked by 5 SHM piles, only the first of which is lit, Fl G. There are 9 PHM piles; see chartlet for details. The lock has R/G ent sigs, as it is too narrow for 2 boats to pass.

R/T Harbour VHF Ch 12 16 (Summer 0830-1700 daily. Winter: Mon-Fri 0830-1700; Sat-Sun 0830-1300). Marina Ch **80** M.

TELEPHONE Dial code 023 HM 9246 3419, 📠 9246 7144; MRSC 9255 2100; Marinecall 09066 526241; Police 0845 0454545; Dr 9246 5721.

FACILITIES Southsea Marina (300) ☎ 9282 2719, 📠 9282 2220, www.premiermarinas.com, £1.50, £5/yacht on waiting pontoon, Access HW±3, D, SH, BH (20 ton), C (6 ton), Gaz, 🛒, Bar, R;
Hayling Pontoon (E side of ent), AB, Ⓐ £8.90, P, D, FW, L, Slip; **Langstone SC** ☎ 9248 4577, Slip, M, L, FW, Bar;
Eastney Cruising Ass'n (ECA) ☎ 9273 4103, 6 Ⓐs; **Hayling Ferry SC; Locks SC** ☎ 9282 9833; **Tudor SC** (Hilsea) ☎ 9266 2002, Slip, M, FW, Bar.
Towns: EC Havant Wed; ✉ (Eastney, Hayling), Ⓑ (Havant, Hayling, Emsworth), ⇌ (bus to Havant), ✈ (Southampton).

9.2.26 CHICHESTER HARBOUR

W. Sussex **50°46'·86N 00°56'·06W** ❁❁◊◊◊✿✿✿

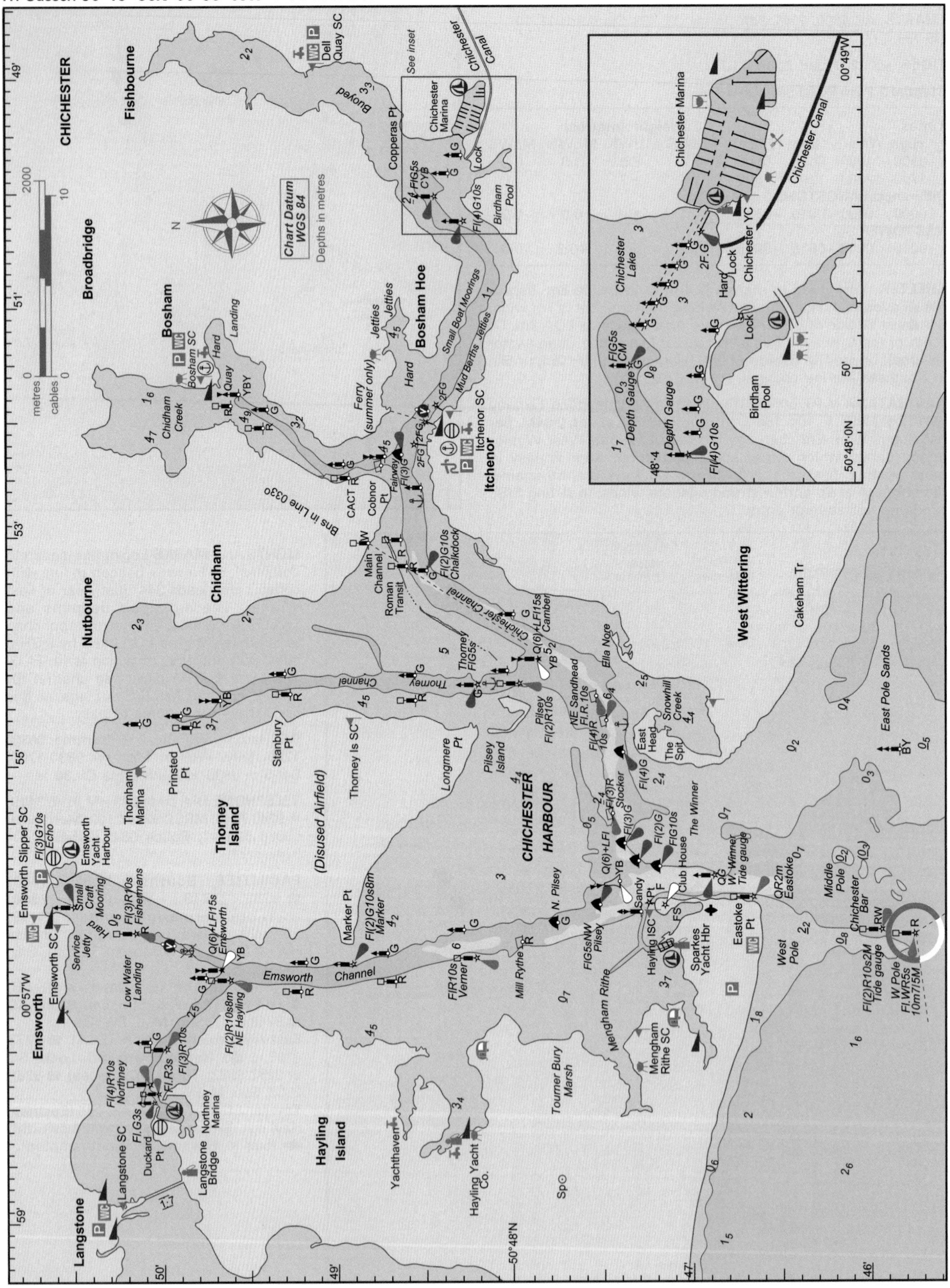
CHICHESTER
Fishbourne
Broadbridge
Bosham
Chidham
Nutbourne
Emsworth
Langstone
Thorney Island
(Disused Airfield)
Hayling Island
Itchenor
Bosham Hoe
West Wittering
CHICHESTER HARBOUR
Chichester Marina
Chichester Canal
Birdham Pool
Chart Datum WGS 84
Depths in metres
Emsworth Channel
Thorney Channel
Chichester Channel
Pilsey Island
East Pole Sands
Cakeham Tr
Tourner Bury Marsh
Sparkes Yacht Hbr
Mengham Rithe SC
Northney Marina
Langstone Bridge
Emsworth Yacht Harbour
Thornham Marina
Dell Quay SC
Itchenor SC
Bosham SC
Chichester YC
Hayling Yacht Co.
Yachthaven
Emsworth Slipper SC
Emsworth SC
Langstone SC
Bns in Line 033°
See inset

CHARTS AC *5600, 2045, 3418*; Imray C9, C3, Y33; Stanfords 11, 10; OS 197

TIDES +0027 Dover; ML 2·8; Zone 0 (UT); see curves on 9·2·13

Standard Port PORTSMOUTH (⟵)

Times				Height (metres)			
High Water		Low Water		MHWS	MHWN	MLWN	MLWS
0500	1000	0000	0600	4·7	3·8	1·9	0·8
1700	2200	1200	1800				
Differences CHICHESTER HARBOUR ENTRANCE							
−0010	+0005	+0015	+0020	+0·2	+0·2	0·0	+0·1
NORTHNEY							
+0010	+0015	+0015	+0025	+0·2	0·0	−0·2	−0·3
ITCHENOR							
−0005	+0005	+0005	+0025	+0·1	0·0	−0·2	−0·2
BOSHAM							
0000	+0010	No data		+0·2	+0·1	No data	
DELL QUAY							
+0005	+0015	No data		+0·2	+0·1	No data	
SELSEY BILL							
−0005	−0005	+0035	+0035	+0·6	+0·6	0·0	0·0

SHELTER Excellent in all five main chans, ie: Emsworth, Thorney, Chichester, Bosham, Itchenor Reach and Fishbourne. There are six yacht hbrs and marinas (see FACILITIES); also about 50 🅥s at Emsworth and Itchenor. ⚓s in Thorney Chan off Pilsey Is; off E Head (uncomfortable in NE winds); and in Chichester Chan off Chalkdock Pt. Hbr speed limit of 8kn; max fine £1000.

NAVIGATION WPT 50°45'·32N 00°56'·64W, 013° to West Pole Bn, 0·4M. Best entry is HW −3 to +1, to avoid confused seas on the ebb, esp in onshore winds >F 5. Do not attempt entry in S'ly gales. Bar is dredged 1·5m, but after gales depths may vary ±0·75m. Leave West Pole Bn (tide gauge) close to port; the chan N'ward is effectively only about 200m wide.

APPROACHES: **From the W**, the astern transit 255° of No Man's Land Fort and Ryde ✠ spire (hard to see) leads to the West Pole Bn. Closer in, transit 064° of Target NCM Bn with Cakeham Tr leads 4ca S of West Pole Bn; thence alter 013° as Eastoke Pt opens to E of West Pole Bn. West Pole PHM bn, Fl WR 5s, must be rounded to clear W Pole Spit, dries 0·2m.

From the E/SE, via Looe Chan, keep W for 2M, then alter NW to pick up an astern brg 184° of Nab Tr, toward the West Pole Bn, so as to clear the shoals of Bracklesham Bay. Note: An Historic Wreck (Hazardous) lies at 50°45'·13N 00°51'·56W, brg 105°/3·2M from Bar Bn; see 9.0.3h.

ENTRANCE: Pass between Eastoke bn QR and W Winner bn QG (tide gauge) leaving Eastoke bn 50m to port, to avoid a drying spit. Three SHM lt buoys mark the edge of The Winner shoal, dries, to stbd of the ent. Near Fishery SCM buoy, Q (6) + L Fl 15s, depths may change and buoys are moved accordingly. Here the chan divides: N toward Emsworth and ENE toward Chichester. Stocker's Sand, dries 2·4m, is marked by 3 PHM lt buoys. East Head SHM, Fl (4) G 10s, marks start of anchorage.

EMSWORTH CHANNEL: Chan is straight, broad, deep and well marked/lit in the 2·5M reach to Emsworth SCM bn, Q (6) + L Fl 15s, where Sweare Deep forks NW to Northney. An unlit ECM bn marks chan to Sparkes Yacht Hbr.

THORNEY CHANNEL: Strangers should go up at half-flood. Ent is at Camber SCM bn, Q (6) + L Fl 15s; pass between Pilsey and Thorney Lt bns, thereafter chan is marked by perches. Above Stanbury Pt chan splits, Prinsted Chan to port (full of moorings) and Nutbourne Chan to stbd; both dry at N ends. There is plenty of room to ⚓ in Thorney Chan, well protected from E and SE winds.

CHICHESTER CHANNEL runs up to Itchenor Reach and Bosham Chan. From NE Sandhead PHM by, Fl R 10s, transit 033° of Roman Transit bn on with Main Chan bn and distant clump of trees leads to Chalkdock Bn, Fl (2) G 10s. A measured half mile is marked by Y perches on the stbd side of Chichester ch running S of Chalkdock. Here alter 082° to Fairway buoy, Fl (3) G 10s; At Deep End SCM bn turn N into Bosham Chan, or ESE into Itchenor Reach, for Birdham Pool and Chichester Marina. ⚓ prohib in Itchenor Reach and Bosham Chan.

LIGHTS AND MARKS Bar Bn, R wooden bn, Fl (2) R 10s 14m 2M; tide gauge. 2ca S at 50°45'·71N 00°56'·48W is West Pole PHM bn, Fl WR 5s 10m 7/5M, vis W321°-081°, R081°-321°.

The E side of the ent chan is marked by W Winner SHM pile, QG, with tide gauge; and by 3 SHM buoys: NW Winner Fl G 10s; N Winner Fl (2) G10s; Mid Winner Fl (3) G 10s. All chans within the hbr are well marked by day. Emsworth & Thorney Chans are partly lit; Bosham Chan is unlit. Itchenor Reach is unlit except for Birdham Pool and CYB entrance bns.

R/T *Chichester Hbr Radio* VHF Ch **14** 16 (Apr-Sep: 0830-1700; Sat 0900-1300) or Chichester Hbr Patrol (w/e's Apr-Sep). Emsworth Yacht Hbr and Northney Marina Ch **80** M. Chichester Marina Ch 80.

TELEPHONE (Dial code 01243, except Hayling Island 023) Chichester Hbr Office 512301, 🖷513026, harbourmaster @conservancy.co.uk, www.conservancy.co.uk (incl current weather at bar); MRSC (023 92) 552100; Marinecall 09066 526241; Police 0845 0454545; Ⓗ 787970.

FACILITIES

HAYLING ISLAND (023) **Sparkes Yacht Hbr** (150 + 30 Ⓥ) ☎ 9246 3572, mob 07770 365610, 🖷 9246 5741, £2.40, access all tides via chan dredged 2m; pontoons have 1·6m. ME, El, P, D, M, Gas, Gaz, LPG, ⊡, ⚒, C (25 ton), CH. From close N of Sandy Pt, appr on transit 277° of 2 x bns; thence alter S, past 3 PHM bns to marina.

Northney Marina (228+27 Ⓥ) ☎ (023) 9246 6321, 🖷 (023) 9246 1467; pre-call Ch 80. Access all tides via chan 1m; £2.70,£6 <4hrs, D, LPG, El, ⚒, CH, ME, BH (35 ton), Bar, R; **Services:** Slip, BH (8 ton), P. EC Wed.

EMSWORTH CHANNEL **Emsworth Yacht Hbr** (200+20 Ⓥ) ☎ 377727, 🖷 373432, £2.00; access HW±2 over 2·4m sill which maintains 1·5m inside, Slip, Gas, ME, El, ⚒, P, D, BH (60 ton), C (20 ton). **Service jetty** (E of Emsworth SC) 50m long, ☆ 2FR (vert); access HW±4. Free for <2 hrs stay, FW. **Slips** at South St, Kings St, and Slipper Mill; contact the Warden ☎ 376422. Ferry £1 to moorings Ch 14 *Emsworth Mobile*. **Services:** ME, ⚒, CH, El, ACA; Emsworth EC Wed.

THORNEY CHANNEL **Thornham Marina** (77+6 Ⓥ), ☎ 375335, 🖷 371522, £1.25, appr via drying chan, P & D (cans), FW, ⚒, ME, C (10 ton), BH (12 ton), Slip, R, Bar. **Services:** CH, BY.

CHICHESTER CHANNEL/ITCHENOR REACH

Hard available at all stages of the tide. There are berths for approx 40 yachts at Itchenor on both buoys and pontoons. £5.00 per night. **Services:** Slip, P & D (cans), ⚒, FW, M, El, Ⓔ, ME, showers in hbr office, ♁. Ferry/Water taxi VHF Ch 08, ☎ 07970 378350 to Bosham and Birdham.

BOSHAM CHANNEL For moorings (200+) contact the Quaymaster ☎ 573336. ⚓ prohib in chan which mostly dries, access HW±2.

Bosham Quay Hard, L, FW, AB; **Services:** SM. EC Wed.

CHICHESTER LAKE **Birdham Pool:** (230+10 Ⓥ) ☎ 512310, 🖷 513163, £2.10, enter chan at Birdham SHM bn, Fl (4) G 10s, with depth gauge; access HW ±3 via lock. **Services:** Slip, P, D, El, Ⓔ, ⚒, CH, Gas, ME, SM, C (3 ton).

Chichester Marina: (1000+50 Ⓥ) ☎ 512731, 🖷 513472, £1.95, £0.90 for <4hrs. Enter chan at CM SHM pile, Fl G 5s, with depth gauge; 6kn speed limit. The well marked chan dries 0·5m restricted access LW ±1½ springs; a waiting pontoon is outside the lock.

Traffic sigs:

Q ● (S of tr) = <1m water in chan.

Q ○ (top of tr) = both gates open (free flow).

Lock sigs: ● = Wait; ● = Enter.

Call lock-keeper on Ch 80, ☎ 512731, 24H year round to book exit except during free-flow.

Services: Slip, P, D, ME, El, ⚒, Gas, Gaz, LPG, CH, BY, BH (65 ton), 🛒, R, Bar, ⊡, ACA, SM, ♿.

FISHBOURNE CHANNEL **Dell Quay:** Possible drying berth against the Quay, apply to Hbr Office, public slip. **Services:** ⚒, Slip, BH, M, L.

YACHT CLUBS

Bosham SC ☎ 572341; **Chichester YC** ☎ 512918, R, Bar, ⊡; **Chichester Cruiser and Racing Club** ☎ 371731; **Dell Quay SC** ☎ 785080; **Emsworth SC** ☎ 373065; **Emsworth Slipper SC** ☎ 372523; **Hayling Island SC** ☎ (023) 9246 3768; **Itchenor SC** ☎ 512400; **Mengham Rithe SC** ☎ (023) 9246 3337; **Thorney Island SC; W Wittering SC.**

Cobnor Activities Centre Trust (at Cobnor Pt) gets many young people, inc disabled ♿, afloat. ☎ 01243 572791.

9.2.27 NAVAL EXERCISE AREAS (SUBFACTS & GUNFACTS)

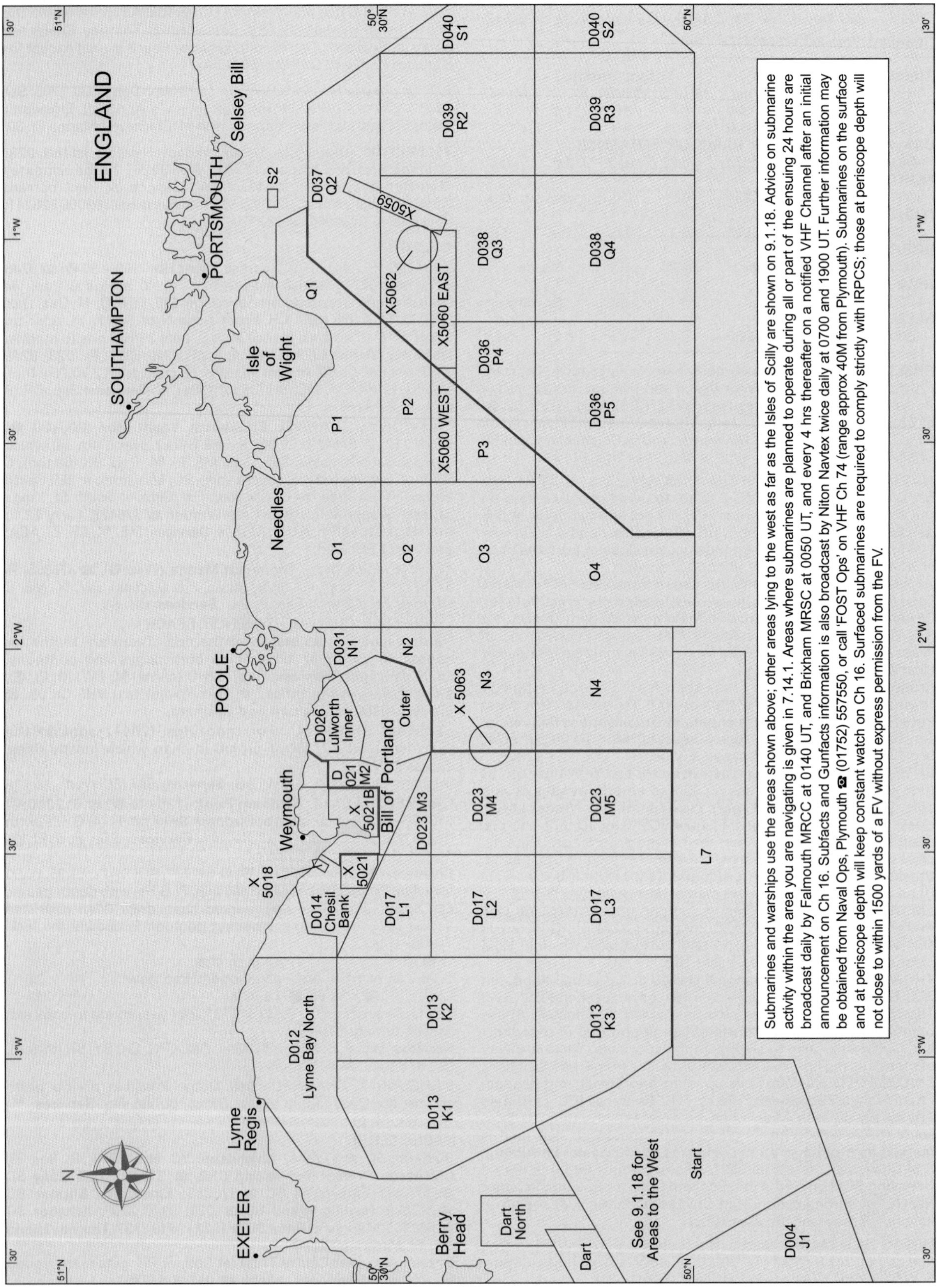
ENGLAND
SOUTHAMPTON
PORTSMOUTH
Selsey Bill
Isle of Wight
Needles
POOLE
Weymouth
Bill of Portland
Lyme Regis
EXETER
Berry Head
Start
Dart
Dart North
See 9.1.18 for Areas to the West
D004 J1
D013 K1
D013 K2
D013 K3
D012 Lyme Bay North
D014 Chesil Bank
X 5018
X 5021
X 5021B
D 021 M2
D026 Lulworth Inner
Outer
D031 N1
N2
N3
N4
X 5063
D017 L1
D017 L2
D017 L3
L7
D023 M3
D023 M4
D023 M5
O1
O2
O3
O4
P1
P2
P3
X5060 WEST
X5060 EAST
X5062
X5059
D036 P4
D036 P5
Q1
D037 Q2
D038 Q3
D038 Q4
S2
D039 R2
D039 R3
D040 S1
D040 S2
51°N
50° 30'N
50°N
3°W
2°W
1°W
30'

Submarines and warships use the areas shown above; other areas lying to the west as far as the Isles of Scilly are shown on 9.1.18. Advice on submarine activity within the area you are navigating is given in 7.14.1. Areas where submarines are planned to operate during all or part of the ensuing 24 hours are broadcast daily by Falmouth MRCC at 0140 UT, and Brixham MRSC at 0050 UT, and every 4 hrs thereafter on a notified VHF Channel after an initial announcement on Ch 16. Subfacts and Gunfacts information is also broadcast by Niton Navtex twice daily at 0700 and 1900 UT. Further information may be obtained from Naval Ops, Plymouth ☎ (01752) 557550, or call 'FOST Ops' on VHF Ch 74 (range approx 40M from Plymouth). Submarines on the surface and at periscope depth will keep constant watch on Ch 16. Surfaced submarines are required to comply strictly with IRPCS; those at periscope depth will not close to within 1500 yards of a FV without express permission from the FV.

Area 3

South-East England
Selsey Bill to North Foreland

3

9.3.2

South-East England

Selsey Bill to North Foreland

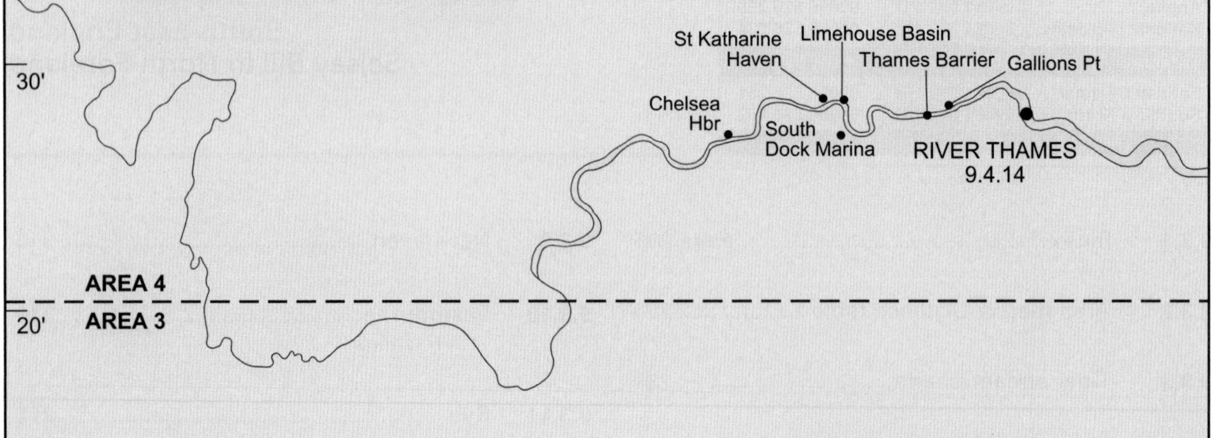

30'
St Katharine Haven
Limehouse Basin
Thames Barrier
Gallions Pt
Chelsea Hbr
South Dock Marina
RIVER THAMES
9.4.14
AREA 4
AREA 3
20'
10'
51°N

		1	2	3	4	5	6	7	8	9	10	11	12	13	14	15	16	17	18
1.	*Portland Bill Lt*	**1**																	
2.	*Nab Tower*	60	**2**																
3.	Boulder Lt Buoy	65	5	**3**															
4.	Owers Lt Buoy	69	11	8	**4**														
5.	**Littlehampton**	78	19	13	12	**5**													
6.	**Shoreham**	90	32	24	21	13	**6**												
7.	**Brighton**	93	35	28	24	17	5	**7**											
8.	**Newhaven**	97	40	34	29	24	12	7	**8**										
9.	Beachy Head Lt	104	46	41	36	30	20	14	8	**9**									
10.	Eastbourne	111	51	45	40	34	24	19	12	7	**10**								
11.	**Rye**	129	72	67	62	56	46	41	34	25	23	**11**							
12.	Dungeness Lt	134	76	71	66	60	50	44	38	30	26	9	**12**						
13.	**Folkestone**	152	92	84	81	76	65	60	53	43	40	23	13	**13**					
14.	Dover	157	97	89	86	81	70	65	58	48	45	28	18	5	**14**				
15.	Ramsgate	172	112	104	101	96	85	80	73	63	60	43	33	20	15	**15**			
16.	N Foreland Lt	175	115	107	104	99	88	83	76	66	63	46	36	23	18	3	**16**		
17.	*Sheerness*	206	146	139	135	132	119	114	107	97	96	79	67	54	49	34	31	**17**	
18.	*London Bridge*	248	188	184	177	177	161	156	149	139	141	124	109	96	91	76	73	45	**18**

DISTANCE TABLE

Approximate distances in nautical miles are by the most direct route, whilst avoiding dangers and allowing for Traffic Separation Schemes. Places in italics are in adjoining areas; places in **bold** are in 9.0.6, Cross-Channel Distances; places underlined are in 9.0.8, Distances across the North Sea.

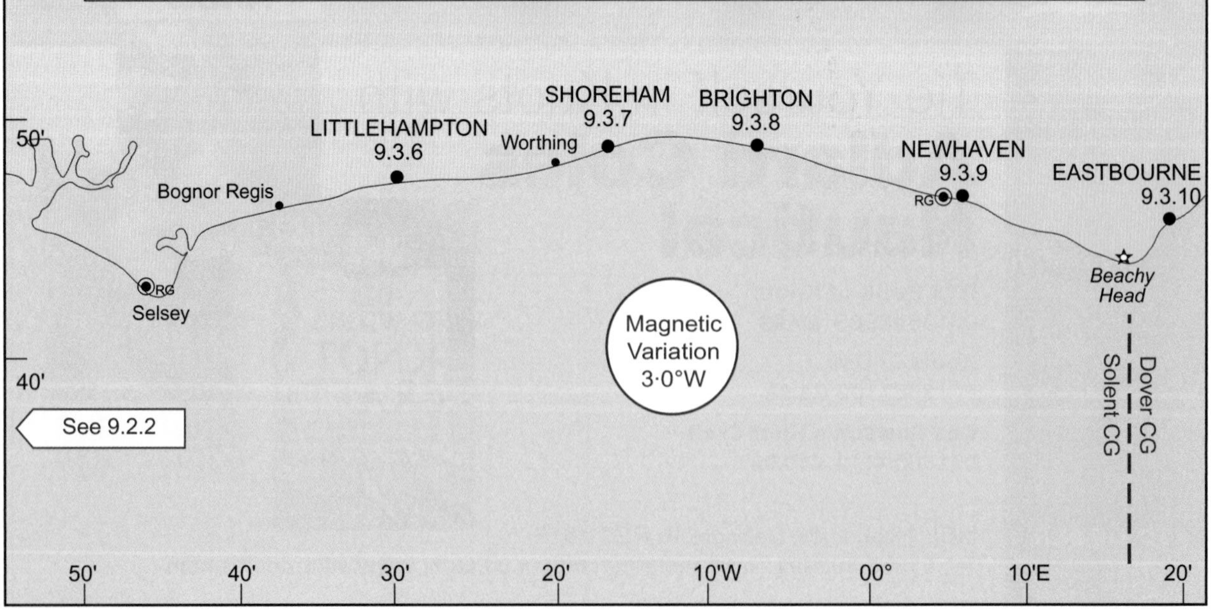

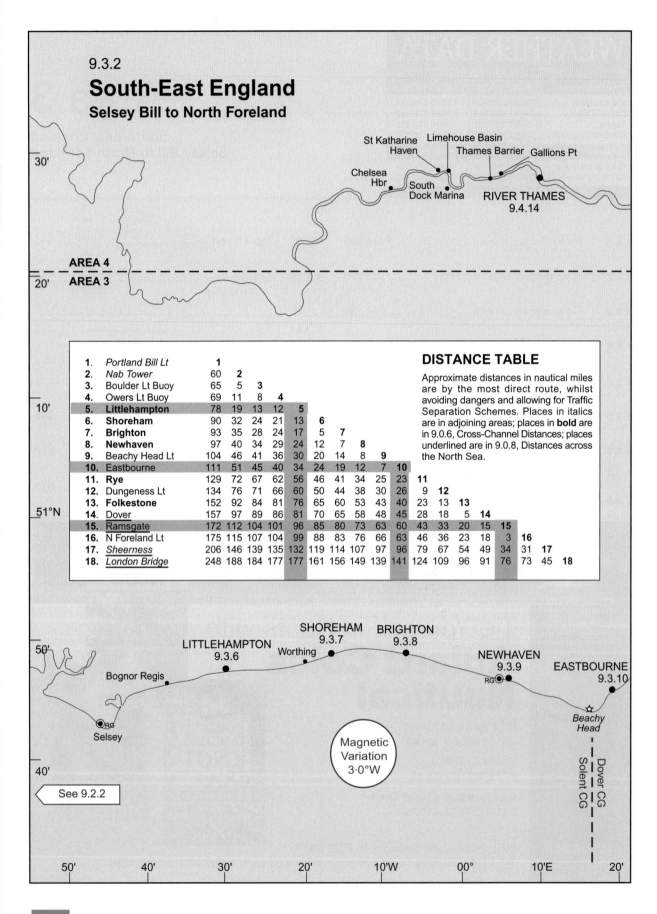

50'
SHOREHAM
9.3.7
BRIGHTON
9.3.8
LITTLEHAMPTON
9.3.6
Worthing
NEWHAVEN
9.3.9
EASTBOURNE
9.3.10
Bognor Regis
RG
Selsey
Beachy Head
Magnetic Variation 3·0°W
Solent CG
Dover CG
40'
See 9.2.2
50'
40'
30'
20'
10'W
00°
10'E
20'

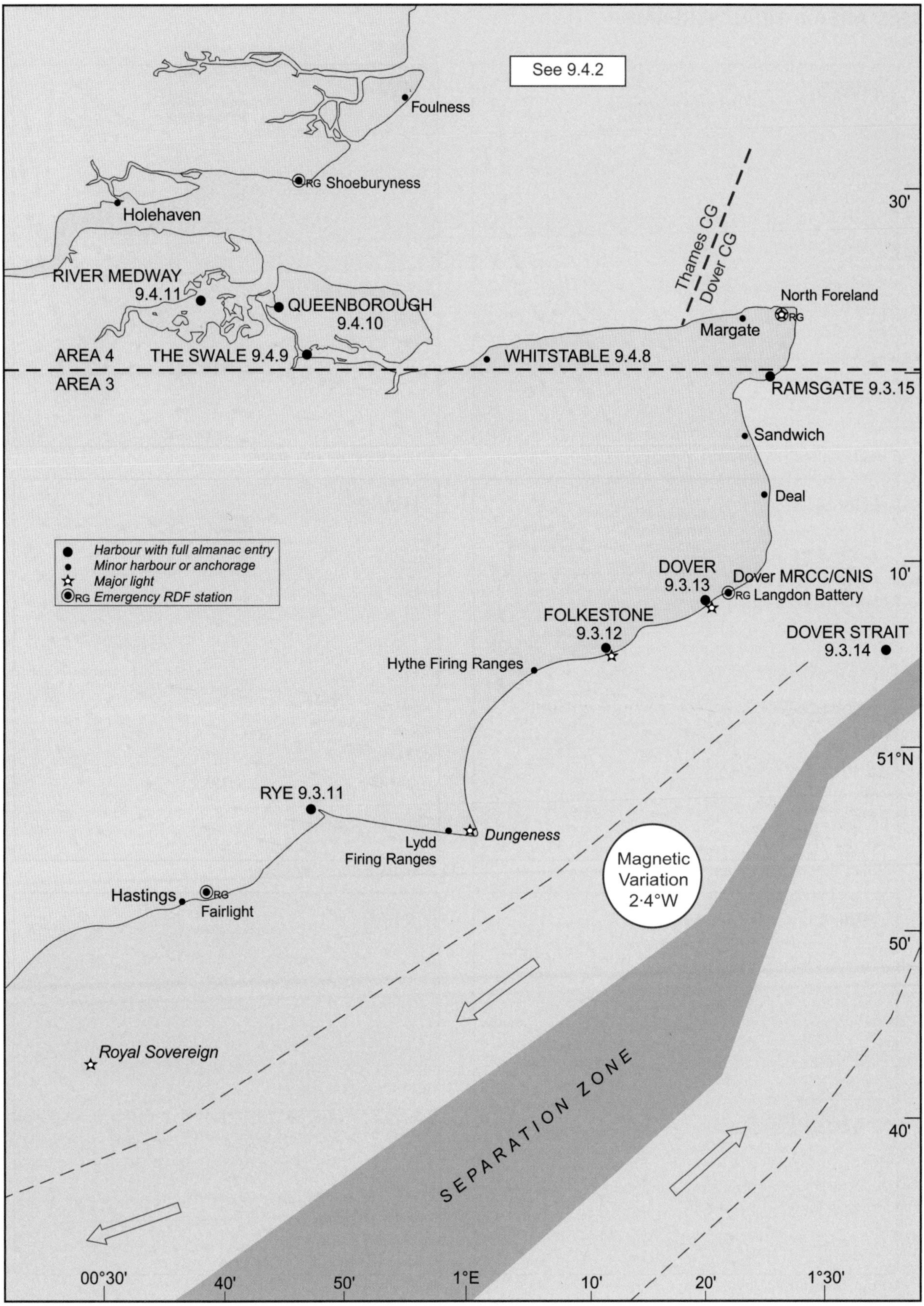
See 9.4.2
Foulness
Shoeburyness
Holehaven
Thames CG
Dover CG
RIVER MEDWAY
9.4.11
QUEENBOROUGH
9.4.10
North Foreland
Margate
AREA 4
THE SWALE 9.4.9
WHITSTABLE 9.4.8
AREA 3
RAMSGATE 9.3.15
Sandwich
Deal
Harbour with full almanac entry
Minor harbour or anchorage
Major light
RG Emergency RDF station
DOVER
9.3.13
Dover MRCC/CNIS
RG Langdon Battery
FOLKESTONE
9.3.12
DOVER STRAIT
9.3.14
Hythe Firing Ranges
RYE 9.3.11
Dungeness
Lydd
Firing Ranges
Magnetic
Variation
2·4°W
Hastings
RG
Fairlight
Royal Sovereign
SEPARATION ZONE
30'
10'
51°N
50'
40'
00°30'
40'
50'
1°E
10'
20'
1°30'

9.3.3 AREA 3 TIDAL STREAMS

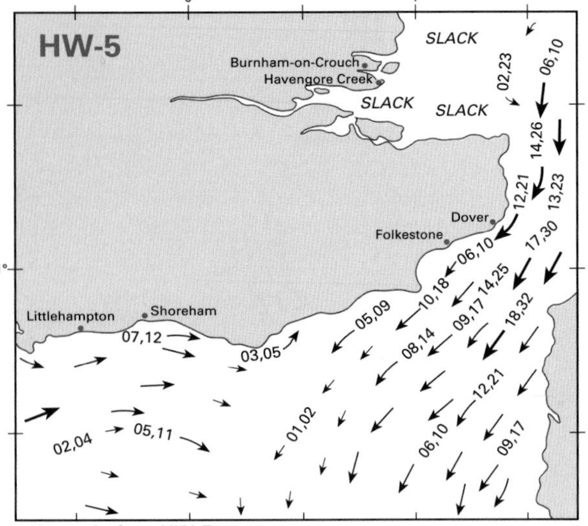
HW-5
0°
1°
51°
Burnham-on-Crouch
Havengore Creek
SLACK
SLACK
SLACK
02,23
06,10
14,26
13,23
12,21
Dover
Folkestone
06,10
17,30
10,18
14,25
09,17
18,32
05,09
08,14
Littlehampton
Shoreham
07,12
03,05
12,21
01,02
06,10
09,17
02,04
05,11
5 Hours before HW Dover

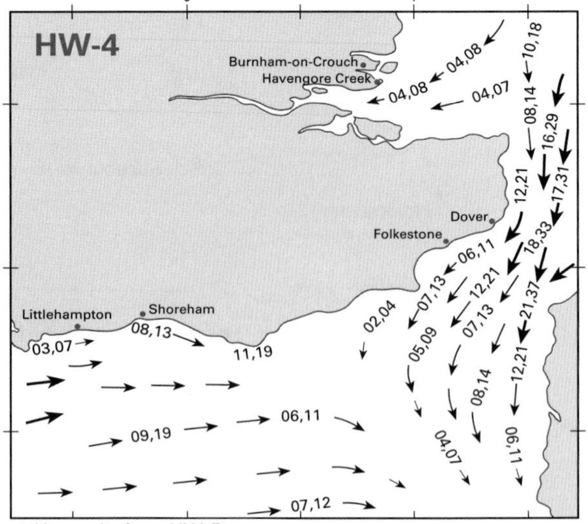
HW-4
0°
1°
51°
Burnham-on-Crouch
Havengore Creek
04,08
04,08
04,07
10,18
08,14
16,29
17,31
12,21
Dover
Folkestone
18,33
06,11
12,21
07,13
07,13
21,37
02,04
05,09
Littlehampton
Shoreham
08,13
03,07
11,19
08,14
12,21
09,19
06,11
04,07
06,11
07,12
4 Hours before HW Dover

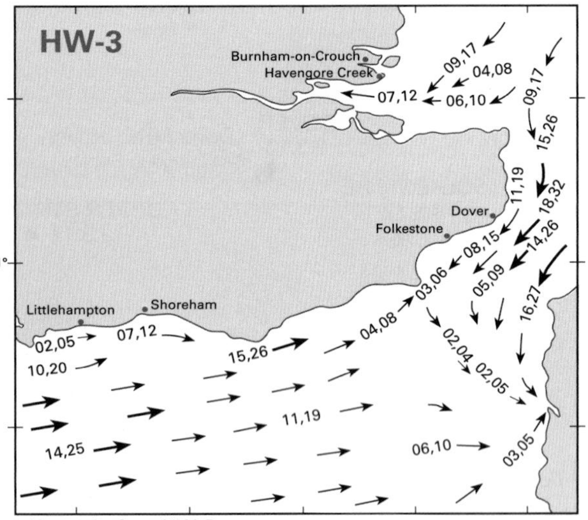
HW-3
51°
Burnham-on-Crouch
Havengore Creek
09,17
04,08
07,12
06,10
09,17
15,26
11,19
18,32
Dover
Folkestone
08,15
14,26
03,06
05,09
16,27
Littlehampton
Shoreham
02,05
07,12
10,20
15,26
04,08
02,04
02,05
11,19
14,25
06,10
03,05
3 Hours before HW Dover

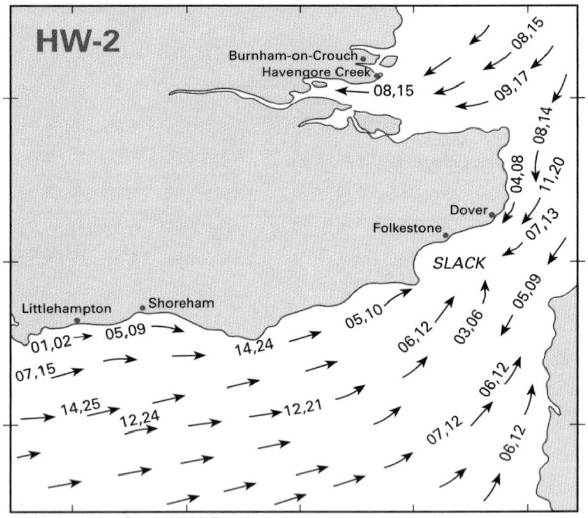
HW-2
51°
Burnham-on-Crouch
Havengore Creek
08,15
08,15
09,17
08,14
04,08
11,20
Dover
Folkestone
07,13
SLACK
Littlehampton
Shoreham
01,02
05,09
05,10
05,09
14,24
06,12
03,06
07,15
14,25
12,24
12,21
06,12
07,12
06,12
2 Hours before HW Dover

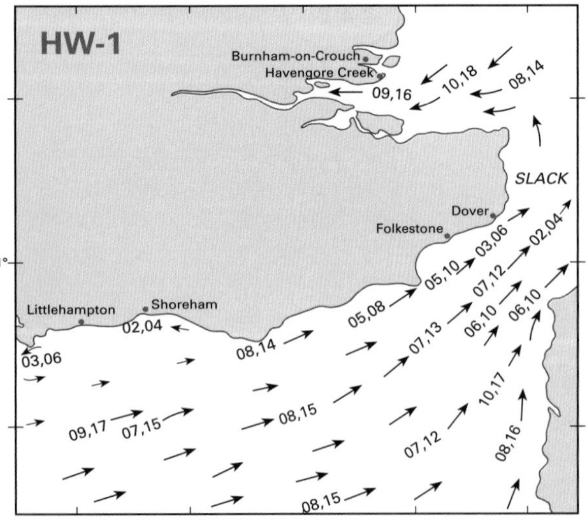
HW-1
51°
Burnham-on-Crouch
Havengore Creek
09,16
10,18
08,14
SLACK
Dover
Folkestone
03,06
02,04
05,10
07,12
Littlehampton
Shoreham
02,04
05,08
06,10
06,10
03,06
08,14
07,13
09,17
07,15
08,15
10,17
07,12
08,16
08,15
1 Hour before HW Dover

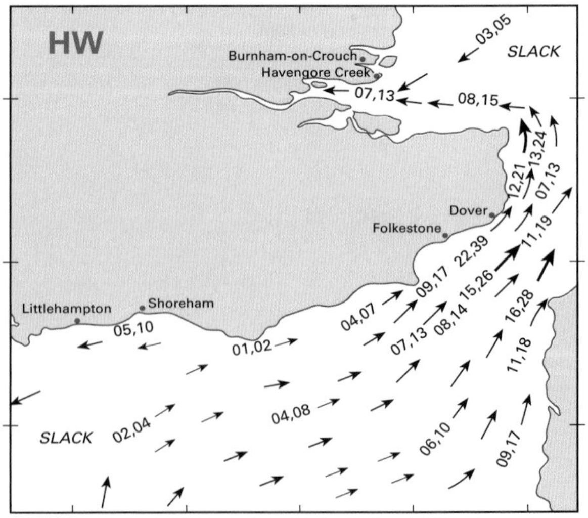
HW
51°
Burnham-on-Crouch
Havengore Creek
03,05
SLACK
07,13
08,15
13,24
12,21
07,13
Dover
Folkestone
11,19
22,39
09,17
15,26
Littlehampton
Shoreham
05,10
04,07
01,02
07,13
08,14
16,28
11,18
SLACK
02,04
04,08
06,10
09,17
HW Dover

Westward 9.2.3 Southward 9.17.3 Northward 9.4.3 Thames Estuary 9.4.8 Eastward 9.16.3

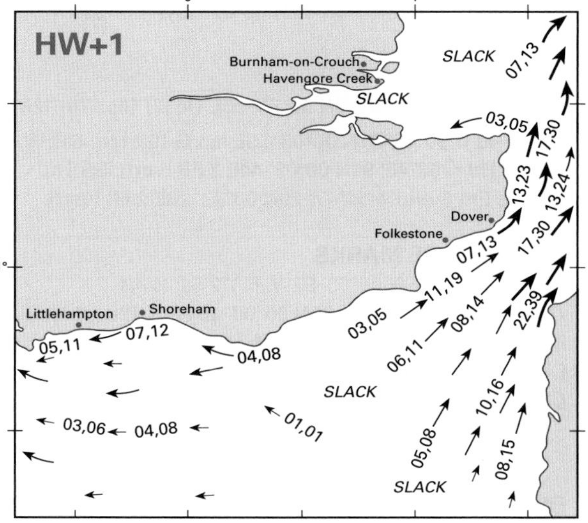
HW+1
Burnham-on-Crouch
Havengore Creek
SLACK
SLACK
07,13
03,05
17,30
13,23
13,24
Dover
Folkestone
07,13
17,30
11,19
22,39
08,14
03,05
06,11
Littlehampton
Shoreham
05,11
07,12
04,08
SLACK
10,16
05,08
03,06
04,08
01,01
08,15
SLACK

1 Hour after HW Dover

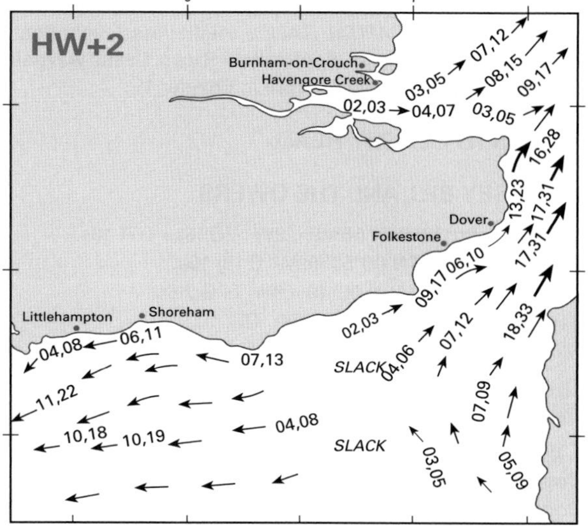
HW+2
Burnham-on-Crouch
Havengore Creek
07,12
03,05
08,15
09,17
02,03
04,07
03,05
16,28
13,23
Dover
Folkestone
17,31
17,31
06,10
09,17
18,33
02,03
07,12
04,06
Littlehampton
Shoreham
04,08
06,11
07,13
SLACK
11,22
07,09
10,18
10,19
04,08
SLACK
03,05
05,09

2 Hours after HW Dover

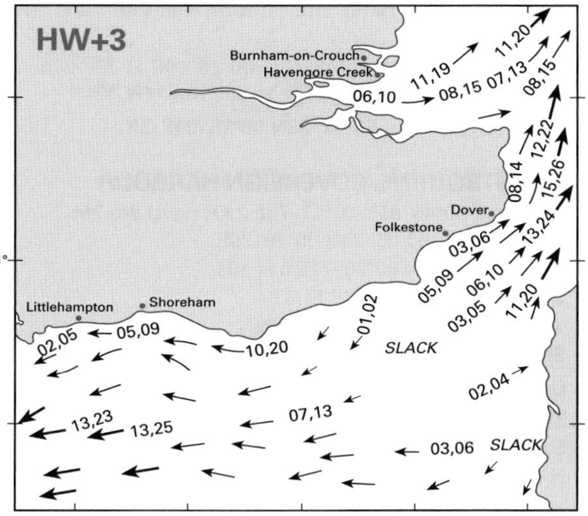
HW+3
Burnham-on-Crouch
Havengore Creek
11,19
11,20
06,10
08,15
07,13
08,15
12,22
08,14
15,26
Dover
Folkestone
03,06
13,24
05,09
06,10
03,05
11,20
01,02
Littlehampton
Shoreham
02,05
05,09
10,20
SLACK
02,04
13,23
13,25
07,13
03,06
SLACK

3 Hours after HW Dover

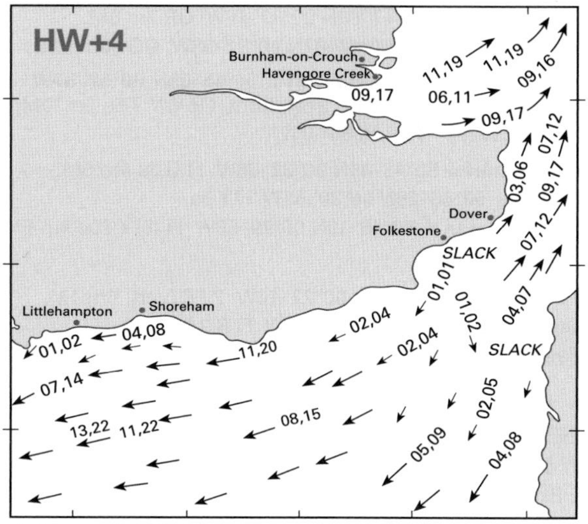
HW+4
Burnham-on-Crouch
Havengore Creek
11,19
11,19
09,17
06,11
09,16
09,17
07,12
03,06
09,17
Dover
Folkestone
07,12
SLACK
01,01
01,02
04,07
SLACK
Littlehampton
Shoreham
02,04
01,02
04,08
11,20
02,04
07,14
02,05
13,22
11,22
08,15
05,09
04,08

4 Hours after HW Dover

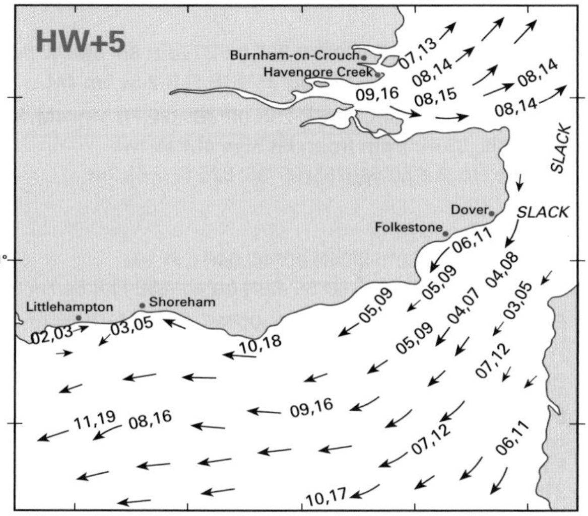
HW+5
Burnham-on-Crouch
Havengore Creek
07,13
08,14
08,14
09,16
08,15
08,14
SLACK
Dover
SLACK
Folkestone
06,11
05,09
04,08
05,09
04,07
03,05
Littlehampton
Shoreham
02,03
03,05
10,18
05,09
07,12
11,19
08,16
09,16
07,12
06,11
10,17

5 Hours after HW Dover

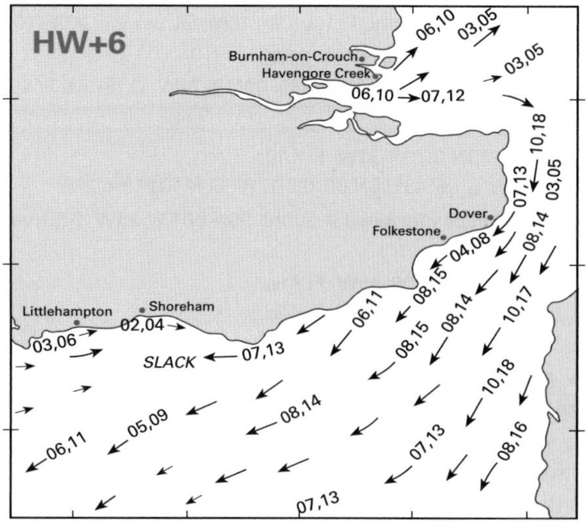
HW+6
Burnham-on-Crouch
Havengore Creek
06,10
03,05
03,05
06,10
07,12
10,18
07,13
03,05
Dover
Folkestone
04,08
08,14
08,15
06,11
08,14
10,17
Littlehampton
Shoreham
02,04
03,06
SLACK
07,13
08,15
10,18
05,09
08,14
06,11
07,13
08,16
07,13

6 Hours after HW Dover

PLOT WAYPOINTS ON YOUR CHART BEFORE USING THEM

9.3.4 LIGHTS, BUOYS AND WAYPOINTS

Blue print = light with a nominal range of 15M or more. CAPITALS = place or feature. *CAPITAL ITALICS* = light-vessel, light float or Lanby. *Italics* = Fog signal. ***Bold italics*** = Racon. Useful waypoints are underlined. Abbreviations are in Chapter 1.

OWERS TO BEACHY HEAD

▶ SELSEY BILL AND THE OWERS

S Pullar 50°38'·84N 00°49'·29W VQ (6) + L Fl 10s.
Pullar 50°40'·47N 00°50'·09W Q (9) 15s.
Boulder 50°41'·56N 00°49'·09W Fl G 2·5s.
Street 50°41'·69N 00°48'·89W QR.
Mixon 50°42'·35N 00°46'·21W Fl R 5s.

Owers 50°38'·63N 00°41'·19W Q (6) + L Fl 15s; *Whis*; ***Racon (O) 10M***.

E Borough Hd 50°41'·54N 00°39'·09W Q (3) 10s *Bell*.
Bognor Regis Outfall 50°45'·22N 00°41'·66W.
Bognor Regis Pier Hd 50°46'·73N 00°40'·54W 2 FR (vert).

▶ LITTLEHAMPTON

West Pier Hd 50°47'·88N 00°32'·46W QR 7m 6M.
Training Wall Hd 50°47'·87N 00°32'·38W QG 10m 2M.

Ldg Lts 346°. Front, E Pier Hd 50°48'·09N 00°32'·51W FG 6m 7M; B col. Rear, 64m from front, Oc WY 7·5s 9m10M; W twr; vis: W290°-356°, Y356°-042°.

UMA Wharf 50°48'·45N 00°32'·68W Fl G 3s 4m 5M.
Outfall 50°46'·26N 00°30'·55W Fl Y 5s.
Littlehampton 50°46'·19N 00°29'·56W Fl (5) Y 20s 9m 5M.

▶ WORTHING

Pier Head 50°48'·42N 00°22'·16W 2 FR (vert) 6m 1M.
Outfall 50°48'·38N 00°20'·34W Fl R 2·5s 3m.
Beecham 50°48'·46N 00°19'·50W Fl (2) R 10s.

▶ SHOREHAM

Express 50°47'·28N 00°17'·09W Fl Y 5s; (Apr-Oct).
W Bkwtr Head 50°49'·49N 00°14'·89W Fl R 5s 7m 7M.
E Bkwtr Head 50°49'·54N 00°14'·80W Fl G 5s 8M; *Siren 120s*.

Ldg Lts 355°. Middle Pier Front, 50°49'·75N 00°14'·88W Oc 5s 8m 10M; W watch-house, R base; tidal Lts, tfc sigs; *Horn 20s*. Rear, 192m from front, Fl 10s 13m 15M; Gy twr vis: 283°-103°.

Outfall 50°49'·47N 00°14'·39W.
Shoreham Outfall 50°47'·88N 00°13'·72W Q (6) + L Fl 15s.

▶ BRIGHTON

50°47'·83N 00°11'·31W Fl Y 10s.
West Pier 50°49'·05N 00°09'·17W Fl R 10s 13m 2M.

Marine Palace Pier Head 50°48'·90N 00°08'·25W 2 FR(vert) 10m 2M.

50°47'·67N 00°08'·45W Fl Y 6s.
50°46'·62N 00°07'·08W Fl Y 3s.
50°46'·64N 00°04'·83W Fl Y 2s.

▶ BRIGHTON MARINA

Black Rk Ledge 50°48'·07N 00°06'·46W Fl Y 4s.

W Bkwtr Hd 50°48'·50N 00°06'·38W QR 10m 7M; W ○ structure, R bands; *Horn (2) 30s*.

E Bkwtr Hd 50°48'·47N 00°06'·37W QG 8m 7M and Fl (4) WR 20s 16m W10M, R8M; W pillar, G bands; vis: R260°-295°, W295°-100°.

50°48'·58N 00°06'·37W Fl G 3s.
50°48'·60N 00°06'·45W Fl R 3s.
Saltdean Outfall 50°46'·72N 00°02'·13W Fl Y 5s.

▶ NEWHAVEN

Bkwtr Head 50°46'·56N 00°03'·50E Oc (2) 10s 17m 12M.
E Pier Hd 50°46'·81N 00°03'·59E Iso G 10s 12m 6M; W twr.
W Pier Hd 50°46'·91N 00°03'·44E 2 FR (vert); SS Tfc.
Marina Ent S end 50°47'·20N 00°03'·26E 2 FR (vert).

▶ OFFSHORE MARKS

CS 1 50°33'·69N 00°03'·92W Fl Y 2·5s; *Whis*.
GREENWICH 50°24'·54N 00°00'·10 Fl 5s 12m 15M; Riding light FW; R hull; ***Racon (M) 10M***; *Horn 30s*.
CS 2 50°39'·14N 00°32'·60E Fl Y 5s.
CS 3 50°52'·04N 01°02'·18E Fl Y 10s; *Bell*.

BEACHY HEAD TO DUNGENESS

Beachy Head ☆ 50°44'·03N 00°14'·49E Fl (2) 20s 31m **20M**; W round twr, R band and lantern; vis: 248°-101°; (H24); *Horn 30s*.

Royal Sovereign ☆ 50°43'·45N 00°26'·09E Fl 20s 28m 12M; W ○ twr, R band on W cabin on col; *Horn (2) 30s*.

Royal Sovereign 50°44'·23N 00°25'·84E QR.

▶ EASTBOURNE/SOVEREIGN HARBOUR

Pier Hd 50°45'·95N 00°17'·73E 2 FR (vert) 8m 2M.
Langney Pt 50°46'·74N 00°19'·90E.
SH 50°47'·40N 00°20'·71E L Fl 10s.
50°47'·38N 00°20'·33E Fl G 5s.
50°47'·36N 00°20'·21E Fl G 3s.
Sovereign Hr Marina 50°47'·24N 00°19'·83E Fl (3) 15s 12m 7M.

Dir lt 258° 50°47'·28N 00°19'·71E Fl WRG 5s 4m 1M; vis: G252·5°-256·5°, W256·5°-259·5°, R259·5°-262·5°.

S Bkwtr Hd 50°47'·30N 00°20'·03E Fl (4) R 12s 3m 6M.
N Bkwtr Hd 50°47'·35N 00°19'·95E Fl G 5s 3m 6M.

St Leonard's Outfall 50°49'·31N 00°31'·95E Fl Y 5s.

▶ HASTINGS

Pier Hd 50°51'·06N 00°34'·36E 2 FR (vert) 8m 5M; W hut.
W Bkwtr Hd 50°51'·19N 00°35'·61E Fl R 2·5s 5m 4M.

Ldg Lts 356·3°. Front, 50°51'·29N 00°35'·38E FR 14m 4M. Rear, West Hill, 357m from front, FR 55m 4M; W twr.
Groyne No. 3 50°51'·28N 00°35'·82E Fl G 5s 2m.

▶ RYE

Rye Fairway 50°54'·04N 00°48'·04E L Fl 10s.
W Groyne Hd No. 2 50°55'·58N 00°46'·55E Fl R 5s 7m 6M.

E Arm Hd No. 1 50°55'·73N 00°46'·46E Q (9) 15s 7m 5M; G △; *Horn 7s*.

Dungeness Outfall 50°54'·45N 00°58'·21E Q (6) + L Fl 15s.

Dungeness ☆ 50°54'·81N 00°58'·56E Fl 10s 40m **21M**; B ○ twr, W bands and lantern, floodlit; Part obsc 078°-shore; (H24). F RG 37m 10M (same twr); vis: R057°-073°, G073°-078°, R196°-216°; *Horn (3) 60s*.

FR Lts shown between 2·4M and 5·2M WNW when firing taking place. QR on radio mast 1·2M NW.

DUNGENESS TO NORTH FORELAND

▶ OFFSHORE MARKS

Bullock Bank 50°46'·94N 01°07'·60E VQ; *Whis.*
Ridens SE 50°43'·47N 01°18'·87E VQ (3) 5s.
Colbart SW 50°48'·86N 01°16'·30E VQ (6) + L Fl 10s; *Whis.*
South Varne 50°55'·64N 01°17'·30E Q (6) + L Fl 15s; *Whis.*
Mid Varne 50°58'·94N 01°19'·88E VQ(9)10s.
East Varne 50°58'·22N 01°20'·90E VQ(3)5s.
Colbart N 50°57'·45N 01°23'·29E VQ.

VARNE 51°01'·29N 01°23'·90E Fl R 20s12m **19M**; ***Racon (T) 10M***; *Horn 30s.*

CS 4 51°08'·62N 01°33'·92E Fl (4)Y 15s; *Whis.*
CS 5 51°23'·03N 01°49'·89E Fl Y 2.5s.
MPC 51°06'·12N 01°38'·20E Fl Y 2·5s; ***Racon (O) 10M.***

▶ FOLKESTONE

Hythe Flats Outfall 51°02'·52N 01°05'·32E Fl Y 5s.

Breakwater Head ☆ 51°04'·56N 01°11'·69E Fl (2) 10s 14m **22M**; *Dia (4) 60s.* In fog Fl 2s; vis: 246°-306°, intens 271·5°-280·5°.

Outer Hbr E Pier Hd ☆ 51°04'·76N 01°11'·38E QG 16m 1M.
Shakespeare Cliff W end ☆ 51°06'·08N 01°16'·01E Fl R 5s.
Shakespeare Cliff E end ☆ 51°06'·31N 01°16'·85E Fl R 5s.

▶ DOVER

Admiralty Pier Extension Head ☆ 51°06'·69N 01°19'·66E Fl 7·5s 21m **20M**; W twr; vis: 096°-090°, obsc in The Downs by S Foreland inshore of 226°; *Horn 10s;* Int Port Tfc sigs.

S Bkwtr W Hd ☆ 51°06'·78N 01°19'·80E Oc R 30s 21m **18M**; W twr.

Dunkirk Jetty Head ☆ 51°06'·88N 01°18'·98E QR 7m.
Dolphin Jetty Head 51°07'·05N 01°18'·71E QG 3m 2M.
Crosswall Quay (Ent to Dover Marina) ☆ 51°07'·08N 01°18'·65E F WR: vis: R283°-323°, W324°-333°; H24.

Knuckle ☆ 51°07'·04N 01°20'·49E Fl (4) WR 10s 15m **W15M**, R13M; W twr; vis: R059°-239°, W239°-059°.

N Head ☆ 51°07'·20N 01°20'·61E Fl R 2·5s 11m 5M.

Eastern Arm Hd ☆ 51°07'·31N 01°20'·59E Fl G 5s 12m 5M; *Horn (2) 30s*; Int port tfc sigs.

S GOODWIN 51°07'·97N 01°28'·49E Fl (2) 20s 12m **15M**; R hull; *Horn (2) 60s.*

SW Goodwin 51°08'·50N 01°28'·88E Q (6) + L Fl 15s.
S Goodwin 51°10'·60N 01°32'·26E Fl (4) R 15s.
SE Goodwin 51°12'·99N 01°34'·45E Fl (3) R 10s.

E GOODWIN 51°13'·26N 01°36'·37E Fl 15s 12m **23M**; R hull with lt twr amidships; ***Racon (T) 10M***; *Horn 30s.*

E Goodwin 51°15'·67N 01°35'·69E Q (3) 10s.
NE Goodwin 51°20'·31N 01°34'·16E Q (3) 10s; ***Racon (M) 10M.***

▶ DEAL

Pier Hd ☆ 51°13'·42N 01°24'·54E 2 FR (vert) 7m 5M.
Sandown Outfall 51°14'·49N 01°24'·45E Fl R 2·5s; Ra refl.

▶ THE DOWNS

Deal Bank 51°12'·92N 01°25'·57E; QR.

Goodwin Fork 51°14'·33N 01°26'·86E Q (6) + L Fl 15s; *Bell.*

Downs 51°14'·50N 01°26'·22E Fl (2) R 5s; *Bell.*

▶ GULL STREAM

W Goodwin 51°15'·61N 01°27'·38E Fl G 5s.
S Brake 51°15'·77N 01°26'·82E Fl (3) R 10s.
NW Goodwin 51°16'·57N 01°28'·57E Q (9) 15s; *Bell.*
Brake 51°16'·98N 01°28'·19E Fl (4) R 15s; *Bell.*
N Goodwin 51°17'·91N 01°30'·20E Fl G 2·5s.
Gull Stream 51°18'·26N 01°29'·69E QR.
Gull 51°19'·57N 01°31'·30E VQ (3) 5s.
Goodwin Knoll 51°19'·57N 01°32'·20E Fl (2) G 5s.

▶ RAMSGATE CHANNEL

B2 51°18'·07N 01°24'·00E.
W Quern 51°18'·98N 01°25'·39E Q (9) 15s.

▶ RIVER STOUR/SANDWICH

Channel marked by small lateral buoys/beacons which are moved to meet changes in channel.

▶ RAMSGATE

RA 51°19'·60N 01°30'·13E Q(6) + L Fl 15s.
E Brake 51°19'·47N 01°29'·20E Fl R 5s.
No. 1 51°19'·56N 01°27'·29E QG.
No. 2 51°19'·46N 01°27'·28E Fl (4) R 10s.
No. 3 51°19'·56N 01°26'·61E Fl G 2·5s.
No. 4 51°19'·46N 01°26'·60E QR.
N Quern 51°19'·41N 01°26'·11E Q.
No. 5 51°19'·56N 01°25'·91E Q (6) + L Fl 15s.
No. 6 51°19'·46N 01°25'·91E Fl (2) R 5s.
South Bkwtr Hd 51°19'·46N 01°25'·41E VQ R 10m 5M.
N Bkwtr Hd 51°19'·56N 01°25'·47E QG 10m 5M.

Western Marine terminal Dir lt 270° , 51°19'·51N 01°24'·85E Oc WRG 10s 10m 5M; B △, Or stripe; vis: G259°-269°, W269°-271°, R271°-281°. Rear 493m from front Oc 5s 17m 5M; B ▽, Or stripe; vis: 263°-278°.

▶ BROADSTAIRS

Broadstairs Knoll 51°20'·88N 01°29'·48E Fl R 2·5s.
Pier SE End ☆ 51°21'·50N 01°26'·74E 2 FR (vert) 7m 4M.
Elbow 51°23'·23N 01°31'·59E Q.

North Foreland ☆ 51°22'·49N 01°26'·70E Fl (5) WR 20s 57m **W19M**, **R16M**, **R15M**; W 8-sided twr; vis: Wshore-150°, R(**16M**)150°-181°, R(**15M**) 181°-200°, W200°-011°; H24.

▶ OFFSHORE MARKS

F1 51°11'·21N 01°44'·91E Fl (4)Y 15s.
South Falls 51°13'·84N 01°43'·93E Q (6) + L Fl 15s; *Bell.*
Mid Falls 51°18'·63N 01°46'·99E Fl (3) R 10s; *Bell.*
Inter Bank 51°16'·47N 01°52'·23E Fl Y 5s; *Bell;* ***Racon (M)10M.***
F2 51°20'·41N 01°56'·19E Fl (4)Y 15s; *Bell.*

NOTES

9.3.5 PASSAGE INFORMATION

Reference books include: Admiralty *Channel Pilot*; *Channel Cruising Companion* (Nautical Data Ltd/Featherstone/Aslett). See 9.0.6 for cross-Channel distances. An Admiralty Small Craft Folio SC 5605, 12 A2 charts, price £37.50 (2004) covers Chichester to Ramsgate and the Dover Strait.

THE EASTERN CHANNEL This area embraces the greatest concentration of commercial shipping in the world. *In such waters the greatest danger to any yacht is a collision with a larger vessel, especially in poor visibility.* Even for coastal cruising it is essential to know about the TSS and ITZ; eg, note that the SW-bound TSS lane from the Dover Strait passes only 3.5M off Dungeness. Radar surveillance of the Dover Strait (9.3.14) is maintained at all times by the Channel Navigation Information Service (CNIS).Additional to the many large ships passing through the traffic lanes, there are fast ferries, ro-ro ferries, and hovercraft crossing between English and Continental ports; warships and submarines on exercises; fishing vessels operating both inshore and offshore; many other yachts; and static dangers such as lobster pots and fishing nets which are concentrated in certain places.

► *In this area the weather has a big effect on tidal streams, and on the range of tides. The rates of tidal streams vary with the locality, and are greatest in the narrower parts of the Channel and off major headlands. In the Dover Strait sp rates can reach 4kn, but elsewhere in open water they seldom exceed 2kn.* ◄ Also N winds, which give smooth water and pleasant sailing off the shores of England, can cause rough seas on the French coast; and vice versa. With strong S'lies the English coast between Isle of Wight and Dover is very exposed, and shelter is hard to find. The Dover Strait has a funnelling effect and in strong winds can become very rough.

SELSEY BILL AND THE OWERS (chart *1652*) Selsey Bill is a low headland, off which lie the Owers, groups of rks and shoals extending 3M to the S, and 5M to the SE. Just W and SW of the Bill, The Streets (awash) extend 1·25M seaward. 1·25M SSW of the Bill are The Grounds (or Malt Owers) and The Dries (dry). 1M E of The Dries, and about 1·25M S of the lifeboat house on E side of Selsey Bill is The Mixon a group of rks marked by bn at E end.

Immediately S of the above dangers is the Looe Chan, which runs E/W about 7½ca S of Mixon bn. It is marked by buoys at W end, where it is narrowest between Brake (or Cross) Ledge on N side and Boulder Bank to the S. In daylight, good visibility and moderate weather, the Looe Chan is an easy and useful short cut. ► *The E-going stream begins at HW Portsmouth + 0430, and the W-going at HW Portsmouth – 0135, sp rates 2·5 kn.* ◄ Beware lobster pots in this area.

In poor visibility or in bad weather (and always in darkness) keep S of the Owers SCM lt buoy, 7M SE of Selsey Bill, marking SE end of Owers. ► *Over much of the Owers there is less than 3m, and large parts virtually dry; so a combination of tidal stream and strong wind produces heavy breaking seas and overfalls over a large area.* ◄

OWERS TO BEACHY HEAD (chart *1652*) The coast from Selsey Bill to Brighton is low, faced by a shingle beach, and with few offlying dangers, Bognor Rks (dry in places) extend 1·75M E from a point 1M W of the pier, and Bognor Spit extends E and S from the end of them. Middleton ledge are rks running 8ca offshore, about 1·5M E of Bognor pier, with depths of less than 1m. Shelley Rks lie 5ca S of Middleton ledge, with depths of less than 1m.

Winter Knoll, about 2·5M SSW of Littlehampton (9.3.6) has depths of 2·1m. Kingston Rks, depth 2m, lie about 3·25M ESE of Littlehampton. An unlit outfall bn is 3ca off Goring-on-sea (2M W of Worthing pier). Grass Banks, an extensive shoal with 2m depth at W end, lie about 1M S of Worthing pier. Elbow shoal, with depth of 3·1m, lies E of Grass Banks.

Off Shoreham (9.3.7) Church Rks, with depth of 0·3m, lie 1·5M W of the hbr ent and 2½ca offshore. Jenny Rks, with depth 0·9m, are 1·25M E of the ent, 3ca offshore.

At Brighton (9.3.8) the S Downs form the coastline, and high chalk cliffs are conspic from here to Beachy Head. There are no dangers more than 3ca offshore, until Birling Gap, where a rky ledge begins, on which is built Beachy Head lt ho (fog sig). Head Ledge (dries) extends about 4ca S. ► *2M S of Beachy Hd the W-going stream begins at HW Dover + 0030, and the E-going at HW Dover – 0520, sp rates 2·25kn. In bad weather there are overfalls off the Head, which should then be given a berth of 2M.* ◄

BEACHY HEAD TO DUNGENESS (chart *536*) Royal Sovereign lt tr (fog sig) is 7·4M E of Beachy Head. The extensive Royal Sovereign shoals lie from 3M NW of the tr to 1·5M N of it, and have a minimum depth of 3·5m. ► *There are strong eddies over the shoals at sp, and the sea breaks on them in bad weather.* ◄

On the direct course from Royal Sovereign lt tr to clear Dungeness there are no dangers. Along the coast in Pevensey B and Rye B there are drying rky ledges or shoals extending 5ca offshore in places. These include Boulder Bank near Wish tr, S of Eastbourne (9.3.10); Oyster Reef off Cooden; Bexhill Reef off Bexhill-on-Sea; Bopeep Rks off St Leonards; and the shoals at the mouth of R Rother, at entrance to Rye (9.3.11). There are also banks 2-3M offshore, on which the sea builds in bad weather. Avoid the firing range danger area between Rye and Dungeness (lt, fog sig, RC). The nuclear power station is conspic at SE extremity of the low-lying spit. The Pt is steep-to on SE side. Good anch close NE of Dungeness.

DUNGENESS TO NORTH FORELAND (charts *1892, 1828*) From Dungeness to Folkestone (9.3.12) the coast forms a bay. Beware Roar bank, depth 2·7m, E of New Romney: otherwise there are no offlying dangers, apart from Hythe firing range. Good anch off Sandgate in offshore winds. ► *Off Folkestone the E-going stream starts at HW Dover – 0155, sp rate 2kn; the W-going at HW Dover + 0320, sp rate 1·5kn.* ◄

Passing Dover (9.3.13) and S Foreland keep 1M offshore. Do not pass too close to Dover, because ferries/jetfoils leave at speed, and there can be considerable backwash and lumpy seas off the breakwaters. 8M S of Dover in the TSS is the Varne, a shoal 7M long with least depth 3·3m and heavy seas in bad weather, marked by Lanby and 3 buoys. ► *Between S and N Foreland the N-going stream begins at about HW Dover – 0150, and the S-going at about HW Dover + 0415.* ◄

The Goodwin Sands are drying, shifting shoals, extending about 10M from S to N, and 5M from W to E at their widest part. The E side is relatively steep-to; large areas dry up to 2·7m. The sands are well marked by lt Fs and buoys. Kellett Gut is an unmarked chan about 5ca wide, running SW/NE through the middle of the sands, but it is not regularly surveyed and is liable to change. The Gull Stream (buoyed) leads from The Downs, inside Goodwin Sands and outside Brake Sands to the S of Ramsgate (9.3.15). The Ramsgate chan leads inside the Brake Sands and Cross Ledge.

LYDD Firing Ranges off Lydd, centred on 50°54′N 00°53′E: a Sea Danger Area extends 3M offshore and stretches E from Rye Fairway buoy to a N/S line approx 1·5M W of Dungeness lt ho. When firing takes places, about 300 days p.a. 0830–1630LT (often to 2300), R flags/R lts are displayed ashore and a Range Safety Craft may be on station. Call Lydd Ranges Ch 06 13 16 72 **73** or ☎ 01303 225518/225519 📠 225638 or 225467 for 24H pre-recorded message. Radar fixes may also be obtained by VHF. Vessels may legally transit through the Sea Danger Area, but should not enter or remain in it for other purposes. If possible vessels should transit S of Stephenson Shoal.

HYTHE Firing Ranges (centred on 51°02′N 01°03′E) have a Sea Danger Area extending 2M offshore, from Hythe to Dymchurch (approx 5M and 8M WSW of Folkestone hbr). Vessels may legally transit through the Sea Danger Area, but should not enter or remain in it for other purposes. When firing takes place, about 300 days p.a. 0830–1630LT (often to 2300), R flags/R lts are displayed ashore and a Range Safety Craft may be on station. Radar fixes may also be obtained by VHF. Call *Hythe Ranges* Ch 06 13 16 **73** or ☎ 01303 225879, 📠 225924 or 225861 for 24H pre-recorded message

CROSS-CHANNEL PASSAGES This section applies broadly to any crossing, ranging from the short (4-5hrs) Dover Strait route, through the much used, medium length Solent-Cherbourg route (13hrs; see 9.17.5), to the longer passages (20+hrs) from SW England to North Brittany. Distances are tabulated at 9.0.6. Whatever the length of passage, thorough planning is the key to a safe and efficient crossing. Maximum experience of crossing the Channel as crew/navigator is also invaluable, before the psychological hurdle of first skippering a boat across.

A **Planning check-list** must oblige a skipper/navigator to:

a. Study the meteorological situation several days before departure, so that windows of opportunity, eg high pressure, may be predicted and bad weather avoided.

b. Consider the forecast wind direction and likely shifts, so that the probability of obtaining a good slant can be improved. Prevailing winds are SW/W, except in the spring when NE/ E winds are equally likely. The advantages of getting well to windward cannot be over-emphasised. If heading for St Malo from Brighton, for example, it might pay to make westing along the coast (working the tides to advantage) so as to depart from St Catherine's Point, the Needles, Anvil Point or even Portland Bill when crossing towards Barfleur, Cherbourg, Cap de la Hague or Alderney.

c. Choose the route, departure points and landfalls so that time on passage and out of sight of identifiable marks is minimised. This can much reduce anxiety and fatigue (which may soon become apparent in a family crew). The risk of navigational errors, particularly those due to leeway and tidal streams, is also reduced. It is sound practice to take back bearings on the departure mark.

d. Take account of tidal constraints at the point of departure and destination; and en route tidal gates, eg Hurst Narrows.

e. ▶ *Work out the hourly direction and rate of tidal streams expected during (and after) the crossing; so as to lay off the total drift angle required to make good the desired track. Only rarely do 6 hours of E-going tide cancel out 6 hours of W-going (or vice versa); streams off the French coast are usually stronger. Try to arrive up-tide of destination. Note the times and areas of races and overfalls and keep well clear.* ◀

f. Consider actions to be taken in poor visibility/fog when the range at which marks may be seen is much reduced (and risk of collision with other vessels equally increased). Fog is unlikely in summer (except in certain notorious areas, eg off Ushant) and visibility is often greater than 6M. A landfall at night or dawn/dusk is frequently easier due to the additional range provided by lights.

g. Observe the legal requirement to head at 90° across any TSS; consider motoring to expedite such crossing.

h. Make use of additional navigational info such as soundings, for example when crossing the distinctive contours of the Hurd Deep; the rising or dipping ranges of major lights; fixing on clearly identifiable radar targets, if so equipped; and the sighting of TSS buoys and light floats. Note: The charted 2M exclusion circle around EC2 buoy applies only to IMO-Convention vessels, ie not yachts.

j. Keep a harbour of refuge in mind if caught out by fog, gales or gear failure. For example, if unable to make Cherbourg in a strong SSW'ly and E-going tide, it may be better to bear away and run for St Vaast in the lee of the peninsular. Or heave to and stay at sea.

k. Finally, even if using electronic navigation, write up the ship's log and maintain a DR plot. This is both a safeguard, and a source of pride (when proven accurate); it also ensures the highest degree of navigational awareness.

Routes from ports within Area 3 Passages from Brighton, Newhaven or Eastbourne to Dieppe or adjacent French ports are relatively short and direct. The route crosses the Dover Strait TSS whose SW-bound lane lies only 7M S of Beachy Head. A departure from close W of CS2 buoy will satisfy the 90° crossing rule and minimise the time spent in the TSS. During the 19M crossing of the TSS, it is worth listening to the VHF broadcasts of navigational and traffic information made by CNIS. These include details of vessels which appear to be contravening Rule 10.

Dover to Calais or Boulogne is only about 25M (see 9.3.14) but the route crosses the congested Dover Strait TSS. Study the tidal streams. Keep a very sharp lookout for ships in the traffic lanes and ferries crossing them. Do not attempt to cross in fog or poor visibility.

3

9.3.6 LITTLEHAMPTON

W. Sussex **50°47′·87N 00°32′·43W**

CHARTS AC *5605, 1652, 1991*; Imray C12, C9; Stanfords 9; OS 197

TIDES +0015 Dover; ML 2·8; Zone 0 (UT)

Standard Port SHOREHAM (⟶)

Times				**Height (metres)**			
High Water		Low Water		MHWS	MHWN	MLWN	MLWS
0500	1000	0000	0600	6·3	4·8	1·9	0·6
1700	2200	1200	1800				
Differences LITTLEHAMPTON (ENT)							
+0010	0000	−0005	−0010	−0·4	−0·4	−0·2	−0·2
LITTLEHAMPTON (UMA WHARF)							
+0015	+0005	0000	+0045	−0·7	−0·7	−0·3	+0·2
ARUNDEL							
No data	+0120	No data		−3·1	−2·8	No data	
PAGHAM							
+0015	0000	−0015	−0025	−0·7	−0·5	−0·1	−0·1
BOGNOR REGIS							
+0010	−0005	−0005	−0020	−0·6	−0·5	−0·2	−0·1

NOTE: Tidal hts in hbr are affected by flow down R Arun. Tide seldom falls lower than 0·9m above CD.

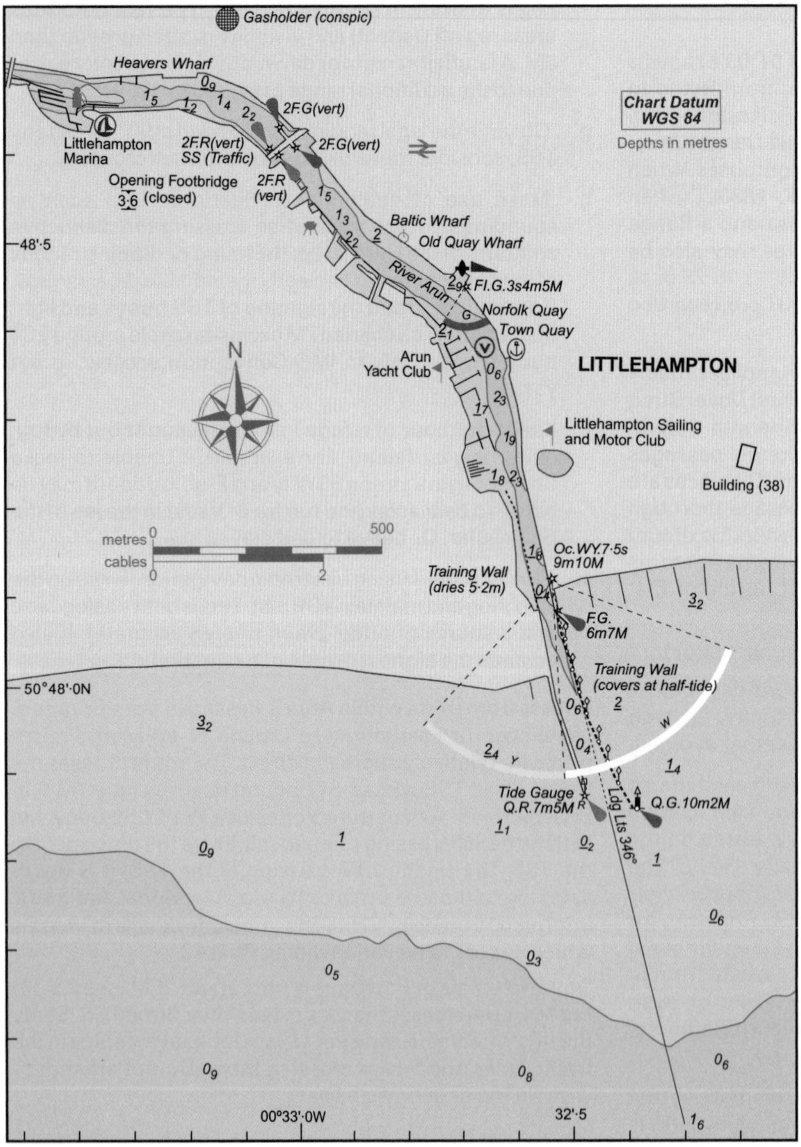
Gasholder (conspic)
Heavers Wharf
Littlehampton Marina
2F.R(vert) SS (Traffic)
2F.G(vert)
2F.G(vert)
Opening Footbridge 3·6 (closed)
2F.R (vert)
Chart Datum WGS 84
Depths in metres
Baltic Wharf
Old Quay Wharf
48'·5
River Arun
Fl.G.3s4m5M
Norfolk Quay
Town Quay
Arun Yacht Club
LITTLEHAMPTON
N
Littlehampton Sailing and Motor Club
Building (38)
metres 0 500
cables 0 2
Oc.WY.7·5s 9m10M
Training Wall (dries 5·2m)
F.G. 6m7M
50°48'·0N
Training Wall (covers at half-tide)
W
Y
Tide Gauge Q.R.7m5M
Q.G.10m2M
Ldg Lts 346°
00°33'·0W
32'·5

SHELTER Good. Ent dangerous in strong SE winds which cause swell up the hbr. The bar (0·7 to 1·0m) is rough in SW'lies. Visitors berth initially at Town Quay where marked and contact HM.

NAVIGATION WPT 50°47′·53N 00°32′·30W, 346° to front ldg lt, 0·60M. Bar ½M offshore. Hbr accessible from HW–3 to HW+2½ for approx 1·5m draft. The ebb runs so fast (4 – 6 kn) at sp that yachts may have difficulty entering. From HW–1 to HW+4 a strong W-going tidal stream sets across the ent; keep to E side. Speed limit 6½kn.

On E side of ent chan a training wall which covers at half-tide is marked by 7 poles and lit bn at S end. The W pier is a long, prominent structure of wood piles; beware shoal ground within its arm. A tide gauge on end shows height of tide above CD. To obtain depth on the bar subtract 0·6m from indicated depth. **River Arun.** A retractable footbridge (3·6m clearance MHWS; 9·4m above CD) 3ca above Town Quay gives access for masted craft to Littlehampton marina. It is opened by request to HM before 1630 previous day. The River Arun is navigable on the tide by small, unmasted craft for 24M via Ford, Arundel and beyond; consult HM.

LIGHTS AND MARKS High-rise bldg (38m) is conspic 0·4M NNE of hbr ent. A pile with small platform and ☆, Fl Y (5) 20s 5M, is 2·5M SE of hbr ent at 50°46'·1N 00°29'·5W.

Ldg lts 346°: Front FG on B column; Rear, lt ho Oc WY 7·5s at root of E bkwtr, W 290°-356°, Y 356°-042°. The Fl G 3s lt at Norfolk Wharf leads craft upstream, once inside hbr ent.

When Pilot boat with P1 at the bow displays the Pilot flag 'H' (WR vert halves) or ○ over ● lts, all boats keep clear of ent; large ship moving.

Footbridge sigs, from high mast to port: Fl G lt = open; Fl R = closed.

Bridge's retractable centre section (22m wide) has 2 FR (vert) to port and 2 FG (vert) to stbd at both upstream and downstream ends.

R/T HM VHF Ch 71 16 (0900-1700LT); Pilots Ch 71 16 when vessel due. Bridge Ch 71. Marinas Ch **80** M (office hrs).

TELEPHONE (Dial code 01903)
HM 721215, 📠 739472,
duty officer mob 07775 743078 e-mail harbour@littlehampton.org.uk; MRSC (01705) 552100; Marinecall 09066 526240; Police 08456 070999; Dr 714113.

FACILITIES **Town Quay**, AB £15 <8m, £16 >8m, ⛽, FW, ⊡, C (5 ton), ME, ✕; **Services**: BY, M, ✕ (Wood), ACA. Showers/toilets in Hbr.Office.

Littlehampton Sailing & Motor Club ☎ 715859, M, FW, Bar;

Arun YC (90+10 visitors), £10.00, ☎ 714533, (dries; access HW±3), M, ⛽, FW, Bar, Slip, R, Showers, ♿;

Littlehampton Marina (120 + some Ⓥ), £2.00, ☎ 713553, 📠 732264, Slip, BH (12 ton), P, D, 🛒, R, Bar, ✕, ME, ♿;

Ship and Anchor Marina, about 2M up-river at Ford, (50+, some visitors) ☎ (01243) 551262, (access HW±4), Slip, FW, ME, ✕, CH, 🛒, R, Bar.

Town EC Wed; P, D, 🛒, R, Bar, ✉, Ⓑ, ⇌, ✈ (Shoreham).

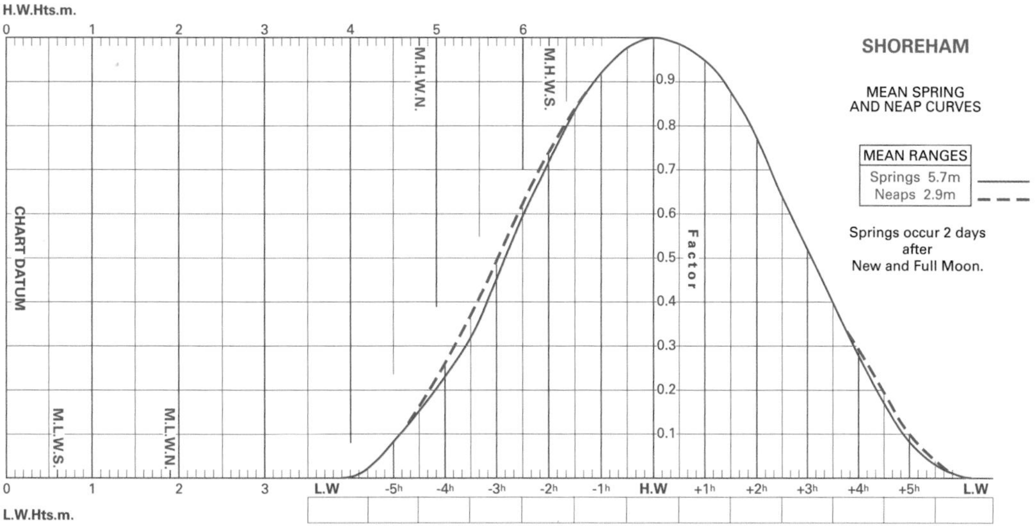
H.W.Hts.m.
L.W.Hts.m.
CHART DATUM
M.H.W.N.
M.H.W.S.
M.L.W.S.
M.L.W.N.
Factor
L.W
H.W
SHOREHAM
MEAN SPRING
AND NEAP CURVES
MEAN RANGES
Springs 5.7m
Neaps 2.9m
Springs occur 2 days
after
New and Full Moon.

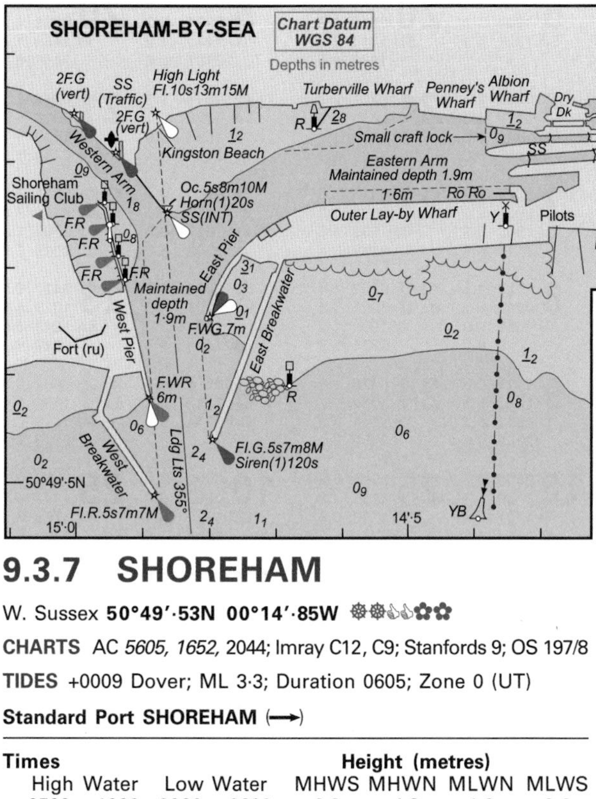
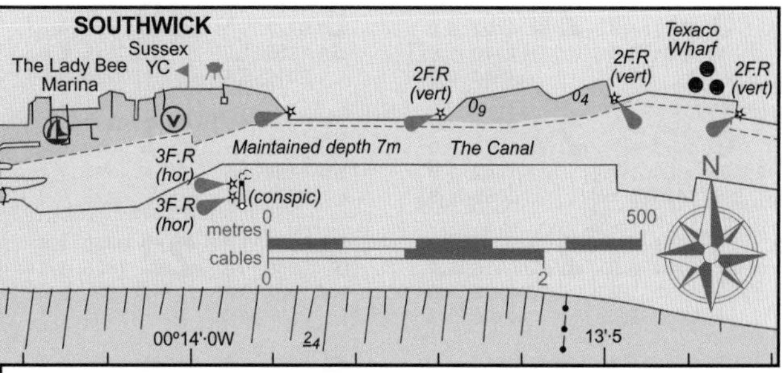
SHOREHAM-BY-SEA
Chart Datum
WGS 84
Depths in metres
SOUTHWICK
Sussex
YC
The Lady Bee
Marina
Texaco
Wharf
High Light
Fl.10s13m15M
Turberville Wharf
Penney's
Wharf
Albion
Wharf
Dry
Dk
Small craft lock
Kingston Beach
Eastern Arm
Maintained depth 1.9m
Ro Ro
Outer Lay-by Wharf
Pilots
Maintained depth 7m
The Canal
3F.R
(hor)
(conspic)
metres
cables
Shoreham
Sailing Club
Western Arm
Oc.5s8m10M
Horn(1)20s
SS(INT)
SS
(Traffic)
East Pier
Maintained
depth
1·9m
F.WG.7m
East Breakwater
West Pier
Fort (ru)
F.WR
6m
Ldg Lts 355°
Fl.G.5s7m8M
Siren(1)120s
West
Breakwater
Fl.R.5s7m7M
50°49'·5N
15'·0
14'·5
00°14'·0W
13'·5
YB

9.3.7 SHOREHAM

W. Sussex **50°49'·53N 00°14'·85W** ❀❀◊◊✿✿

CHARTS AC *5605, 1652,* 2044; Imray C12, C9; Stanfords 9; OS 197/8

TIDES +0009 Dover; ML 3·3; Duration 0605; Zone 0 (UT)

Standard Port SHOREHAM (⟶)

Times				**Height (metres)**			
High Water		Low Water		MHWS	MHWN	MLWN	MLWS
0500	1000	0000	0600	6·3	4·8	1·9	0·6
1700	2200	1200	1800				
Differences WORTHING							
+0010	0000	−0005	−0010	−0·1	−0·2	0·0	0·0

SHELTER Excellent, once through the lock and into The Canal. The shallow water (dredged 1·9m) at the ent can be very rough in strong on-shore winds and dangerous in onshore gales. Lady Bee and Aldrington (E end of The Canal) marinas, least depth 2m, both welcome visitors. They are managed by the Hbr Authority. Note: major works may be in progress at Lady Bee Marina; check situation before visiting. Visitors are advised not to use the drying Western Arm if possible. Hbr speed limit = 4kn.

NAVIGATION WPT 50°49'·23N 00°14'·81W, 355° to front ldg lt, 0·52M. From E, beware Jenny Rks (0·9m) and from the W, Church Rks (0·3m). The Eastern Arm leads to Prince George Lock, the N'ly of two locks, which opens H24 @ H+30 for arrivals and H for departures; also, if not busy, at other times on request VHF Ch 14. Lock ent is 6m wide, pontoon inside on S wall; sill is 0·26m below CD, denying access only at about LWS±1. Lock will advise exact depth on Ch 14. Waiting space on S side of central lead-in pier. Commercial ships use Prince Philip lock; yachts to keep clear. A Ro-Ro ramp and terminal are on S side of lock.

LIGHTS AND MARKS Radio mast is conspic 170m N of High lt. A SCM buoy, Q(6) + L Fl 15s, marking outfall diffusers, bears 157°/1·8M from hbr ent. Chimney as shown 100m high, silver with blk top. 3F.R(hor) at top and 3F.R(hor) half way up. SYC yacht race signal mast on Shoreham Beach 00°16'·06W.
Ldg lts 355°: front Oc 5s 8m 10M; rear High lt, Fl 10s 13m 15M.
Traffic Sigs IPTS (Sigs 2 and 5, Oc) are shown from Middle Pier.
Note : ○ Fl lt exempts small craft.
Oc R 3s (from LB ho, directed at E or W Arms) = No exit.
Lock Sigs (Comply strictly to avoid turbulence):
3 ● (vert) = do not approach lock.
● ○ ● (vert) = clear to approach lock.

R/T Call *Shoreham Hbr Radio* VHF Ch **14** 16 (H24) HM and lock. Lock will advise Lady Bee marina of arrivals, 0830-1800 M-Sat; 1000-1400 Sun.

TELEPHONE (Dial code 01273) HM 592613, 📠 592492; Locks 592366; MRSC (023 92) 552100; Marinecall 09066 526240; Police 08456 070999; Ⓗ 455622; Dr 461101.

FACILITIES **Lady Bee Marina** (110+10 Ⓥ) ☎ 593801 (0900-1700), mob 07802 848915, 📠 870349, (best to pre-book), £16.50/yacht inc lock fee 1st night, then £12. Access as lock times, AB, P & D (cans), CH, ME, El, ⚒, SM, R, 🛒, Slip.
Sussex YC ☎/📠 464868, welcomes visitors, but has only one AB in The Canal, so prior notice advised; also a drying ½ tide pontoon in the Western Arm (limited Ⓥ), R, Bar, ♿.
Services: P & D also on N side of W Arm HW±3; ACA.
Town EC Wed; ⓪, ✉, Ⓑ, ⇌, ✈.

TIME ZONE (UT)
For Summer Time add ONE hour in **non-shaded areas**

ENGLAND – SHOREHAM

LAT 50°50′N LONG 0°15′W

TIMES AND HEIGHTS OF HIGH AND LOW WATERS

SPRING & NEAP TIDES
Dates in red are SPRINGS
Dates in blue are NEAPS

YEAR **2005**

JANUARY

Date	Time	m	Time	m	Time	m	Time	m
1 SA	0211	5.6	0824	1.5	1420	5.4	2043	1.5
2 SU	0249	5.5	0904	1.7	1501	5.3	2124	1.6
3 M	0333	5.3	0952	1.8	1550	5.1	◑ 2213	1.7
4 TU	0427	5.2	1050	1.8	1650	5.0	2313	1.8
5 W	0533	5.2	1157	1.8	1804	5.0		
6 TH	0023	1.8	0647	5.2	1309	1.7	1920	5.1
7 F	0136	1.7	0754	5.5	1415	1.5	2027	5.4
8 SA	0242	1.5	0855	5.8	1516	1.2	2127	5.7
9 SU	0341	1.2	0951	6.0	1611	0.9	2224	6.0
10 M	0435	1.0	1044	6.2	1703	0.7	● 2319	6.2
11 TU	0527	0.8	1136	6.4	1754	0.6		
12 W	0011	6.4	0617	0.7	1228	6.4	1844	0.5
13 TH	0102	6.5	0706	0.7	1318	6.4	1933	0.5
14 F	0151	6.4	0756	0.8	1406	6.2	2021	0.6
15 SA	0237	6.3	0845	0.9	1453	6.0	2109	0.8
16 SU	0323	6.1	0934	1.2	1540	5.7	2157	1.1
17 M	0409	5.7	1025	1.4	1629	5.3	◐ 2248	1.4
18 TU	0459	5.4	1122	1.7	1725	5.0	2346	1.8
19 W	0557	5.1	1229	1.9	1829	4.8		
20 TH	0057	2.0	0702	5.0	1340	1.9	1944	4.8
21 F	0208	2.0	0814	5.0	1442	1.8	2056	4.9
22 SA	0307	1.8	0916	5.2	1535	1.6	2150	5.2
23 SU	0356	1.6	1003	5.4	1619	1.4	2234	5.5
24 M	0438	1.4	1043	5.6	1659	1.2	2312	5.7
25 TU	0516	1.3	1119	5.7	1735	1.1	○ 2347	5.8
26 W	0551	1.2	1152	5.8	1810	1.0		
27 TH	0019	5.9	0625	1.1	1223	5.8	1844	1.0
28 F	0049	5.9	0657	1.1	1253	5.8	1915	1.0
29 SA	0117	5.9	0728	1.1	1324	5.8	1944	1.0
30 SU	0147	5.9	0757	1.2	1357	5.8	2013	1.1
31 M	0220	5.8	0830	1.2	1432	5.7	2048	1.2

FEBRUARY

Date	Time	m	Time	m	Time	m	Time	m
1 TU	0258	5.7	0910	1.4	1513	5.5	2130	1.4
2 W	0342	5.5	1000	1.6	1604	5.2	◑ 2223	1.6
3 TH	0439	5.2	1104	1.8	1710	5.0	2334	1.9
4 F	0557	5.0	1228	1.9	1843	4.9		
5 SA	0106	1.9	0727	5.1	1355	1.7	2010	5.1
6 SU	0230	1.7	0842	5.4	1506	1.3	2121	5.5
7 M	0335	1.3	0945	5.8	1604	0.9	2221	5.9
8 TU	0429	1.0	1040	6.1	1655	0.6	● 2315	6.3
9 W	0519	0.7	1131	6.4	1744	0.4		
10 TH	0004	6.5	0606	0.5	1220	6.5	1830	0.3
11 F	0050	6.7	0651	0.5	1305	6.5	1915	0.3
12 SA	0132	6.6	0735	0.5	1347	6.4	1957	0.4
13 SU	0212	6.5	0817	0.7	1426	6.2	2037	0.7
14 M	0249	6.2	0857	0.9	1503	5.8	2115	1.0
15 TU	0326	5.8	0936	1.3	1544	5.4	2154	1.4
16 W	0407	5.4	1020	1.7	1632	5.0	◐ 2241	1.8
17 TH	0500	4.9	1117	2.0	1736	4.6	2349	2.2
18 F	0609	4.6	1251	2.2	1855	4.4		
19 SA	0135	2.3	0730	4.6	1418	2.1	2031	4.6
20 SU	0247	2.1	0855	4.8	1515	1.8	2135	5.0
21 M	0339	1.7	0948	5.2	1600	1.4	2218	5.4
22 TU	0420	1.4	1028	5.5	1638	1.2	2254	5.7
23 W	0456	1.2	1102	5.7	1714	1.0	2327	5.9
24 TH	0530	1.0	1133	5.9	1748	0.9	○ 2357	6.0
25 F	0603	0.9	1202	6.0	1821	0.8		
26 SA	0024	6.1	0634	0.9	1232	6.0	1851	0.8
27 SU	0052	6.1	0703	0.9	1302	6.0	1918	0.8
28 M	0121	6.1	0731	0.9	1333	6.0	1946	0.8

MARCH

Date	Time	m	Time	m	Time	m	Time	m
1 TU	0153	6.0	0802	0.9	1407	5.9	2019	1.0
2 W	0228	5.9	0840	1.1	1446	5.7	2100	1.2
3 TH	0310	5.6	0927	1.4	1534	5.3	◑ 2153	1.6
4 F	0404	5.2	1031	1.7	1640	4.9	2308	2.0
5 SA	0526	4.8	1204	2.0	1829	4.7		
6 SU	0056	2.1	0715	4.8	1348	1.8	2007	5.0
7 M	0227	1.7	0839	5.2	1500	1.3	2120	5.5
8 TU	0329	1.3	0942	5.7	1555	0.9	2215	6.0
9 W	0419	0.8	1033	6.1	1642	0.5	2303	6.4
10 TH	0505	0.5	1120	6.4	1727	0.3	● 2347	6.6
11 F	0548	0.4	1204	6.5	1809	0.2		
12 SA	0028	6.7	0630	0.3	1245	6.5	1849	0.3
13 SU	0107	6.6	0709	0.4	1323	6.4	1927	0.4
14 M	0141	6.4	0745	0.6	1357	6.2	2001	0.7
15 TU	0213	6.1	0819	0.9	1429	5.8	2035	1.0
16 W	0243	5.7	0853	1.2	1503	5.4	2110	1.4
17 TH	0316	5.3	0931	1.6	1547	5.0	◐ 2154	1.9
18 F	0402	4.8	1023	2.0	1652	4.5	2256	2.3
19 SA	0521	4.4	1140	2.3	1815	4.3		
20 SU	0048	2.5	0648	4.3	1344	2.2	1952	4.5
21 M	0221	2.2	0825	4.6	1447	1.9	2107	4.9
22 TU	0313	1.8	0922	5.0	1532	1.5	2149	5.4
23 W	0353	1.4	1001	5.4	1609	1.2	2224	5.7
24 TH	0428	1.1	1034	5.7	1644	1.0	2256	5.9
25 F	0502	0.9	1105	5.9	1718	0.8	○ 2326	6.1
26 SA	0535	0.8	1135	6.0	1751	0.7	2355	6.2
27 SU	0607	0.7	1207	6.1	1822	0.7		
28 M	0025	6.2	0637	0.7	1239	6.2	1851	0.7
29 TU	0056	6.2	0708	0.7	1312	6.1	1923	0.7
30 W	0130	6.1	0742	0.8	1348	6.0	2000	0.9
31 TH	0207	5.9	0822	1.0	1429	5.7	2044	1.2

APRIL

Date	Time	m	Time	m	Time	m	Time	m
1 F	0250	5.5	0912	1.4	1520	5.3	2142	1.7
2 SA	0348	5.0	1021	1.7	1638	4.8	◑ 2306	2.0
3 SU	0524	4.7	1200	1.9	1828	4.7		
4 M	0056	2.0	0710	4.8	1340	1.7	2002	5.1
5 TU	0218	1.6	0831	5.2	1446	1.2	2107	5.6
6 W	0314	1.1	0929	5.7	1537	0.8	2158	6.1
7 TH	0401	0.7	1017	6.1	1622	0.5	2242	6.4
8 F	0444	0.5	1101	6.3	1704	0.4	● 2324	6.6
9 SA	0525	0.4	1142	6.4	1744	0.4		
10 SU	0002	6.6	0603	0.4	1221	6.4	1821	0.5
11 M	0038	6.5	0640	0.5	1256	6.2	1856	0.6
12 TU	0110	6.2	0714	0.7	1329	6.0	1930	0.8
13 W	0139	6.0	0746	0.9	1400	5.8	2003	1.1
14 TH	0207	5.6	0820	1.2	1433	5.4	2039	1.5
15 F	0239	5.2	0859	1.5	1515	5.0	2122	1.9
16 SA	0322	4.8	0948	1.9	1618	4.6	◐ 2223	2.2
17 SU	0437	4.4	1058	2.2	1737	4.5	2348	2.4
18 M	0606	4.3	1238	2.2	1857	4.6		
19 TU	0135	2.2	0726	4.5	1401	2.0	2011	4.9
20 W	0232	1.9	0831	4.9	1450	1.6	2101	5.3
21 TH	0314	1.5	0916	5.2	1530	1.3	2140	5.6
22 F	0351	1.2	0953	5.6	1607	1.0	2215	5.9
23 SA	0427	0.9	1029	5.8	1643	0.9	2249	6.1
24 SU	0502	0.8	1105	6.0	1718	0.8	○ 2323	6.2
25 M	0537	0.7	1141	6.1	1753	0.7	2358	6.3
26 TU	0613	0.6	1218	6.2	1830	0.7		
27 W	0035	6.2	0650	0.6	1257	6.1	1909	0.8
28 TH	0113	6.1	0731	0.8	1338	6.0	1952	1.0
29 F	0156	5.8	0818	1.0	1426	5.7	2043	1.3
30 SA	0246	5.5	0914	1.3	1527	5.3	2147	1.6

Chart Datum: 3·27 metres below Ordnance Datum (Newlyn)

3

TIME ZONE (UT)
For Summer Time add ONE hour in **non-shaded areas**

ENGLAND – SHOREHAM

LAT 50°50′N LONG 0°15′W

TIMES AND HEIGHTS OF HIGH AND LOW WATERS

SPRING & NEAP TIDES
Dates in red are **SPRINGS**
Dates in blue are **NEAPS**

YEAR **2005**

MAY

Date	Day	Time	m	Time	m	Time	m	Time	m
1	SU	0354	5.1	1025	1.6	1648	5.0	◑ 2310	1.8
2	M	0525	4.8	1155	1.7	1819	5.0		
3	TU	0042	1.8	0655	4.9	1319	1.5	1940	5.3
4	W	0155	1.4	0808	5.3	1421	1.2	2041	5.7
5	TH	0250	1.1	0904	5.6	1511	0.9	2131	6.0
6	F	0336	0.8	0952	5.9	1555	0.7	2215	6.2
7	SA	0419	0.6	1036	6.1	1637	0.6	2256	6.3
8	SU	0459	0.6	1117	6.1	1717	0.7	● 2334	6.3
9	M	0538	0.6	1156	6.1	1755	0.7		
10	TU	0009	6.1	0614	0.7	1231	6.0	1831	0.9
11	W	0041	6.0	0649	0.8	1305	5.9	1905	1.0
12	TH	0112	5.8	0722	1.0	1339	5.7	1940	1.2
13	F	0142	5.5	0758	1.2	1414	5.4	2017	1.5
14	SA	0216	5.2	0837	1.5	1455	5.2	2102	1.8
15	SU	0259	4.9	0925	1.7	1548	4.9	2156	2.0
16	M	0400	4.6	1024	2.0	1656	4.7	◐ 2304	2.2
17	TU	0519	4.5	1135	2.0	1804	4.7		
18	W	0021	2.1	0630	4.5	1251	1.9	1907	4.9
19	TH	0131	1.9	0731	4.8	1353	1.7	2002	5.2
20	F	0223	1.6	0824	5.1	1441	1.4	2049	5.5
21	SA	0307	1.3	0910	5.4	1524	1.2	2132	5.8
22	SU	0348	1.0	0953	5.7	1605	1.0	2213	6.0
23	M	0428	0.8	1036	5.9	1647	0.9	○ 2254	6.2
24	TU	0510	0.7	1119	6.1	1730	0.8	2336	6.2
25	W	0554	0.6	1203	6.1	1815	0.8		
26	TH	0020	6.2	0639	0.6	1250	6.1	1901	0.8
27	F	0106	6.1	0727	0.7	1339	6.0	1951	1.0
28	SA	0156	5.9	0819	0.9	1433	5.8	2046	1.2
29	SU	0252	5.6	0916	1.1	1534	5.6	2148	1.4
30	M	0357	5.3	1022	1.3	1641	5.4	◑ 2259	1.5
31	TU	0509	5.1	1134	1.4	1753	5.4		

JUNE

Date	Day	Time	m	Time	m	Time	m	Time	m
1	W	0013	1.5	0624	5.1	1245	1.4	1903	5.4
2	TH	0120	1.4	0733	5.2	1346	1.3	2005	5.6
3	F	0217	1.2	0832	5.4	1439	1.2	2059	5.7
4	SA	0307	1.1	0924	5.6	1528	1.1	2146	5.8
5	SU	0353	1.0	1011	5.7	1612	1.0	2229	5.9
6	M	0435	0.9	1053	5.8	1655	1.0	● 2308	5.9
7	TU	0516	0.9	1133	5.8	1734	1.0	2344	5.8
8	W	0554	0.9	1210	5.8	1812	1.1		
9	TH	0019	5.8	0630	1.0	1247	5.8	1848	1.2
10	F	0052	5.6	0706	1.1	1322	5.7	1923	1.3
11	SA	0125	5.5	0742	1.2	1358	5.5	2001	1.4
12	SU	0200	5.3	0820	1.4	1434	5.4	2042	1.6
13	M	0238	5.1	0902	1.5	1515	5.2	2128	1.8
14	TU	0323	4.9	0949	1.7	1604	5.1	2220	1.9
15	W	0419	4.8	1043	1.8	1702	5.0	◐ 2320	1.9
16	TH	0526	4.7	1142	1.8	1805	5.0		
17	F	0022	1.8	0632	4.8	1246	1.8	1905	5.1
18	SA	0124	1.7	0733	5.0	1346	1.6	2001	5.4
19	SU	0220	1.4	0829	5.3	1442	1.4	2054	5.6
20	M	0312	1.2	0922	5.6	1534	1.2	2144	5.9
21	TU	0402	0.9	1013	5.8	1625	1.0	2233	6.1
22	W	0451	0.8	1104	6.0	1715	0.9	○ 2322	6.2
23	TH	0541	0.6	1156	6.2	1805	0.8		
24	F	0012	6.2	0631	0.6	1248	6.2	1855	0.8
25	SA	0104	6.2	0722	0.6	1340	6.2	1947	0.8
26	SU	0155	6.1	0814	0.7	1432	6.1	2040	0.9
27	M	0248	5.9	0908	0.8	1524	6.0	2136	1.1
28	TU	0343	5.7	1004	1.0	1618	5.8	◑ 2235	1.2
29	W	0440	5.4	1102	1.2	1714	5.6	2336	1.4
30	TH	0541	5.2	1203	1.4	1814	5.4		

JULY

Date	Day	Time	m	Time	m	Time	m	Time	m
1	F	0040	1.5	0646	5.1	1307	1.5	1918	5.3
2	SA	0142	1.5	0754	5.1	1407	1.5	2022	5.3
3	SU	0239	1.4	0856	5.2	1503	1.5	2118	5.4
4	M	0331	1.3	0949	5.3	1553	1.4	2206	5.5
5	TU	0417	1.2	1036	5.5	1638	1.3	2249	5.6
6	W	0459	1.1	1117	5.6	1719	1.2	● 2327	5.7
7	TH	0539	1.1	1155	5.7	1757	1.2		
8	F	0002	5.7	0615	1.1	1231	5.8	1833	1.2
9	SA	0036	5.6	0650	1.1	1305	5.7	1908	1.2
10	SU	0108	5.6	0725	1.1	1337	5.7	1942	1.3
11	M	0139	5.5	0759	1.2	1407	5.6	2017	1.4
12	TU	0212	5.4	0833	1.3	1439	5.5	2053	1.5
13	W	0248	5.3	0909	1.4	1516	5.4	2134	1.6
14	TH	0330	5.2	0950	1.5	1601	5.3	◐ 2222	1.7
15	F	0421	5.0	1041	1.7	1656	5.1	2321	1.8
16	SA	0524	4.9	1144	1.8	1804	5.1		
17	SU	0030	1.8	0642	4.9	1258	1.8	1918	5.2
18	M	0142	1.6	0757	5.1	1411	1.7	2025	5.4
19	TU	0248	1.4	0901	5.4	1516	1.4	2125	5.7
20	W	0346	1.1	1001	5.8	1612	1.1	2221	6.0
21	TH	0440	0.8	1056	6.1	1705	0.9	○ 2314	6.2
22	F	0531	0.6	1150	6.3	1756	0.7		
23	SA	0006	6.3	0620	0.5	1241	6.5	1845	0.6
24	SU	0057	6.4	0710	0.4	1330	6.5	1934	0.6
25	M	0145	6.3	0758	0.5	1416	6.5	2023	0.7
26	TU	0231	6.2	0846	0.6	1500	6.3	2111	0.8
27	W	0317	5.9	0933	0.8	1545	6.0	2200	1.1
28	TH	0404	5.6	1022	1.2	1631	5.6	◑ 2253	1.4
29	F	0455	5.2	1116	1.5	1724	5.3	2354	1.7
30	SA	0556	4.9	1223	1.9	1827	5.0		
31	SU	0107	1.9	0710	4.7	1338	2.0	1943	4.9

AUGUST

Date	Day	Time	m	Time	m	Time	m	Time	m
1	M	0217	1.8	0833	4.8	1444	1.9	2057	5.0
2	TU	0315	1.6	0936	5.1	1538	1.7	2152	5.3
3	W	0402	1.4	1023	5.4	1623	1.5	2236	5.5
4	TH	0444	1.2	1104	5.6	1703	1.3	2313	5.7
5	F	0521	1.1	1139	5.8	1739	1.2	● 2346	5.7
6	SA	0556	1.0	1213	5.9	1814	1.1		
7	SU	0017	5.8	0630	1.0	1243	5.9	1846	1.1
8	M	0046	5.8	0703	1.0	1310	5.9	1918	1.1
9	TU	0114	5.7	0732	1.0	1336	5.9	1947	1.2
10	W	0143	5.7	0759	1.1	1405	5.8	2016	1.2
11	TH	0215	5.6	0829	1.2	1438	5.7	2050	1.3
12	F	0252	5.5	0906	1.4	1518	5.5	2133	1.5
13	SA	0337	5.2	0954	1.6	1607	5.2	◐ 2230	1.8
14	SU	0435	4.9	1058	1.9	1715	5.0	2348	1.9
15	M	0604	4.8	1225	2.0	1850	4.9		
16	TU	0119	1.8	0740	4.9	1358	1.9	2012	5.2
17	W	0238	1.5	0854	5.3	1509	1.5	2118	5.6
18	TH	0339	1.1	0955	5.8	1605	1.1	2215	6.0
19	F	0430	0.7	1049	6.2	1654	0.8	○ 2306	6.3
20	SA	0518	0.5	1139	6.5	1742	0.5	2355	6.5
21	SU	0604	0.3	1225	6.7	1828	0.4		
22	M	0041	6.6	0649	0.3	1310	6.7	1912	0.4
23	TU	0125	6.5	0733	0.4	1351	6.6	1956	0.6
24	W	0206	6.3	0815	0.6	1429	6.4	2037	0.8
25	TH	0245	6.0	0855	0.9	1507	6.0	2118	1.1
26	F	0325	5.6	0936	1.3	1548	5.6	◑ 2202	1.6
27	SA	0413	5.1	1023	1.8	1638	5.1	2258	2.0
28	SU	0515	4.7	1128	2.2	1744	4.7		
29	M	0027	2.2	0632	4.5	1313	2.3	1907	4.6
30	TU	0157	2.1	0818	4.6	1428	2.2	2044	4.8
31	W	0258	1.8	0923	5.1	1522	1.8	2139	5.2

Chart Datum: 3·27 metres below Ordnance Datum (Newlyn)

TIME ZONE (UT)
For Summer Time add ONE hour in **non-shaded areas**

ENGLAND – SHOREHAM

LAT 50°50′N LONG 0°15′W

TIMES AND HEIGHTS OF HIGH AND LOW WATERS

SPRING & NEAP TIDES
Dates in red are SPRINGS
Dates in blue are NEAPS

YEAR **2005**

SEPTEMBER

Date	Day	Time	m	Time	m	Time	m	Time	m
1	TH	0344	1.5	1007	5.5	1604	1.5	2220	5.5
2	F	0423	1.2	1043	5.8	1641	1.3	2254	5.7
3	SA	0458	1.0	1116	5.9	1715	1.1	● 2324	5.9
4	SU	0531	0.9	1146	6.0	1748	1.0	2351	5.9
5	M	0604	0.9	1213	6.1	1820	1.0		
6	TU	0018	6.0	0634	0.9	1238	6.1	1849	1.0
7	W	0046	6.0	0701	0.9	1305	6.0	1915	1.0
8	TH	0115	6.0	0726	1.0	1333	6.0	1943	1.1
9	F	0146	5.9	0757	1.1	1406	5.9	2017	1.2
10	SA	0221	5.7	0835	1.4	1444	5.6	2100	1.5
11	SU	0304	5.3	0923	1.7	1532	5.2	◐ 2159	1.8
12	M	0404	4.9	1033	2.1	1645	4.8	2325	2.1
13	TU	0552	4.7	1214	2.2	1841	4.8		
14	W	0112	2.0	0735	4.9	1356	1.9	2007	5.1
15	TH	0233	1.5	0850	5.5	1502	1.4	2113	5.7
16	F	0328	1.0	0947	6.0	1553	1.0	2205	6.1
17	SA	0415	0.6	1035	6.4	1638	0.6	2252	6.5
18	SU	0459	0.4	1119	6.7	1722	0.4	○ 2337	6.6
19	M	0542	0.3	1202	6.8	1804	0.4		
20	TU	0019	6.6	0623	0.3	1243	6.8	1845	0.4
21	W	0100	6.5	0703	0.5	1320	6.6	1924	0.6
22	TH	0137	6.3	0741	0.7	1355	6.3	2001	0.9
23	F	0212	6.0	0817	1.1	1428	5.9	2037	1.2
24	SA	0249	5.6	0854	1.5	1505	5.4	2117	1.7
25	SU	0335	5.1	0939	1.9	1554	4.9	◑ 2209	2.1
26	M	0439	4.7	1042	2.4	1707	4.5	2328	2.4
27	TU	0559	4.4	1238	2.6	1833	4.4		
28	W	0128	2.3	0747	4.6	1404	2.3	2020	4.7
29	TH	0231	2.0	0855	5.1	1457	1.9	2114	5.1
30	F	0317	1.6	0937	5.5	1537	1.5	2151	5.5

OCTOBER

Date	Day	Time	m	Time	m	Time	m	Time	m
1	SA	0354	1.3	1011	5.8	1612	1.2	2223	5.8
2	SU	0428	1.1	1042	6.0	1645	1.1	2252	5.9
3	M	0501	0.9	1111	6.1	1718	1.0	● 2320	6.0
4	TU	0533	0.9	1138	6.2	1750	0.9	2349	6.1
5	W	0604	0.9	1205	6.2	1819	0.9		
6	TH	0019	6.1	0631	0.9	1235	6.2	1847	0.9
7	F	0050	6.1	0700	1.0	1307	6.1	1919	1.0
8	SA	0123	6.0	0735	1.2	1341	5.9	1957	1.2
9	SU	0201	5.7	0817	1.4	1421	5.6	2044	1.5
10	M	0248	5.3	0911	1.8	1514	5.1	◐ 2148	1.9
11	TU	0358	4.9	1028	2.1	1642	4.8	2318	2.1
12	W	0552	4.8	1213	2.2	1835	4.8		
13	TH	0104	1.9	0726	5.1	1345	1.8	1957	5.2
14	F	0216	1.5	0835	5.6	1445	1.3	2058	5.7
15	SA	0309	1.0	0927	6.1	1533	0.9	2147	6.2
16	SU	0354	0.7	1012	6.5	1616	0.6	2232	6.4
17	M	0436	0.5	1055	6.7	1658	0.5	○ 2314	6.6
18	TU	0517	0.5	1135	6.7	1739	0.5	2355	6.5
19	W	0557	0.5	1213	6.6	1818	0.6		
20	TH	0033	6.4	0634	0.7	1249	6.4	1854	0.8
21	F	0109	6.2	0710	0.9	1322	6.1	1930	1.0
22	SA	0144	5.9	0746	1.2	1354	5.8	2005	1.3
23	SU	0221	5.6	0824	1.6	1429	5.3	2045	1.7
24	M	0306	5.2	0909	2.0	1516	4.9	2136	2.1
25	TU	0408	4.8	1009	2.4	1630	4.5	◑ 2244	2.4
26	W	0523	4.6	1135	2.5	1752	4.4		
27	TH	0027	2.4	0643	4.7	1320	2.4	1916	4.6
28	F	0147	2.1	0800	5.0	1417	2.0	2023	5.0
29	SA	0236	1.8	0849	5.4	1459	1.6	2105	5.3
30	SU	0316	1.5	0926	5.7	1536	1.3	2140	5.6
31	M	0352	1.2	0959	5.9	1611	1.1	2213	5.9

NOVEMBER

Date	Day	Time	m	Time	m	Time	m	Time	m
1	TU	0427	1.1	1031	6.1	1645	1.0	2247	6.0
2	W	0500	1.0	1103	6.2	1719	0.9	● 2321	6.1
3	TH	0534	1.0	1136	6.2	1753	0.9	2356	6.2
4	F	0607	1.0	1211	6.2	1828	0.9		
5	SA	0032	6.1	0644	1.0	1248	6.1	1906	1.0
6	SU	0111	6.0	0725	1.2	1328	5.9	1950	1.2
7	M	0156	5.8	0813	1.5	1415	5.6	2042	1.5
8	TU	0251	5.4	0913	1.7	1517	5.2	2148	1.7
9	W	0408	5.1	1029	2.0	1645	5.0	◐ 2311	1.9
10	TH	0540	5.1	1159	2.0	1816	5.0		
11	F	0038	1.7	0701	5.3	1318	1.7	1931	5.3
12	SA	0147	1.4	0806	5.7	1418	1.3	2031	5.7
13	SU	0241	1.1	0859	6.1	1507	1.0	2122	6.0
14	M	0328	0.9	0945	6.3	1552	0.8	2208	6.2
15	TU	0411	0.8	1028	6.4	1634	0.7	2251	6.3
16	W	0453	0.8	1108	6.4	1715	0.7	○ 2331	6.3
17	TH	0533	0.8	1146	6.3	1755	0.8		
18	F	0010	6.2	0611	1.0	1222	6.2	1832	0.9
19	SA	0047	6.1	0648	1.1	1256	5.9	1908	1.1
20	SU	0123	5.9	0725	1.4	1330	5.7	1944	1.3
21	M	0201	5.6	0803	1.6	1406	5.4	2024	1.6
22	TU	0244	5.3	0847	1.9	1450	5.0	2111	1.9
23	W	0335	5.0	0940	2.1	1548	4.7	◑ 2207	2.1
24	TH	0439	4.9	1045	2.3	1701	4.6	2315	2.2
25	F	0545	4.8	1159	2.3	1811	4.6		
26	SA	0029	2.2	0648	5.0	1312	2.1	1913	4.8
27	SU	0135	2.0	0745	5.2	1407	1.8	2007	5.1
28	M	0226	1.7	0832	5.5	1451	1.5	2053	5.4
29	TU	0310	1.5	0914	5.8	1532	1.3	2135	5.7
30	W	0350	1.3	0954	6.0	1612	1.1	2216	5.9

DECEMBER

Date	Day	Time	m	Time	m	Time	m	Time	m
1	TH	0430	1.2	1033	6.1	1652	1.0	● 2257	6.1
2	F	0510	1.1	1113	6.2	1733	0.9	2339	6.2
3	SA	0552	1.0	1155	6.2	1816	0.9		
4	SU	0023	6.2	0635	1.0	1239	6.2	1901	0.9
5	M	0110	6.1	0722	1.1	1326	6.0	1950	1.0
6	TU	0200	5.9	0814	1.3	1418	5.8	2043	1.2
7	W	0256	5.8	0912	1.4	1518	5.5	2143	1.4
8	TH	0401	5.6	1018	1.6	1627	5.3	◐ 2251	1.5
9	F	0511	5.5	1130	1.6	1740	5.2		
10	SA	0001	1.5	0621	5.5	1240	1.6	1852	5.3
11	SU	0108	1.5	0727	5.6	1343	1.4	1957	5.4
12	M	0208	1.4	0826	5.7	1438	1.3	2054	5.6
13	TU	0301	1.3	0917	5.9	1528	1.1	2145	5.7
14	W	0350	1.2	1004	6.0	1615	1.0	2231	5.9
15	TH	0435	1.1	1046	6.0	1658	1.0	○ 2314	5.9
16	F	0517	1.1	1126	6.0	1739	1.0	2354	6.0
17	SA	0557	1.2	1203	5.9	1817	1.0		
18	SU	0031	5.9	0633	1.2	1239	5.8	1853	1.1
19	M	0108	5.8	0710	1.3	1313	5.7	1929	1.2
20	TU	0145	5.7	0746	1.5	1348	5.5	2007	1.4
21	W	0220	5.5	0825	1.6	1424	5.3	2046	1.6
22	TH	0258	5.4	0909	1.8	1504	5.1	2130	1.7
23	F	0340	5.2	0957	2.0	1552	4.9	◑ 2219	1.9
24	SA	0432	5.0	1053	2.1	1653	4.8	2315	2.0
25	SU	0536	5.0	1154	2.1	1804	4.8		
26	M	0018	2.0	0641	5.0	1259	2.0	1910	4.9
27	TU	0123	2.0	0740	5.2	1400	1.8	2009	5.1
28	W	0224	1.8	0834	5.5	1455	1.5	2103	5.4
29	TH	0317	1.5	0924	5.8	1545	1.2	2153	5.7
30	F	0407	1.3	1012	6.0	1633	1.0	2242	6.0
31	SA	0454	1.1	1059	6.2	1720	0.8	● 2331	6.2

Chart Datum: 3·27 metres below Ordnance Datum (Newlyn)

9.3.8 BRIGHTON

E. Sussex **50°48′·53N 00°06′·38W**

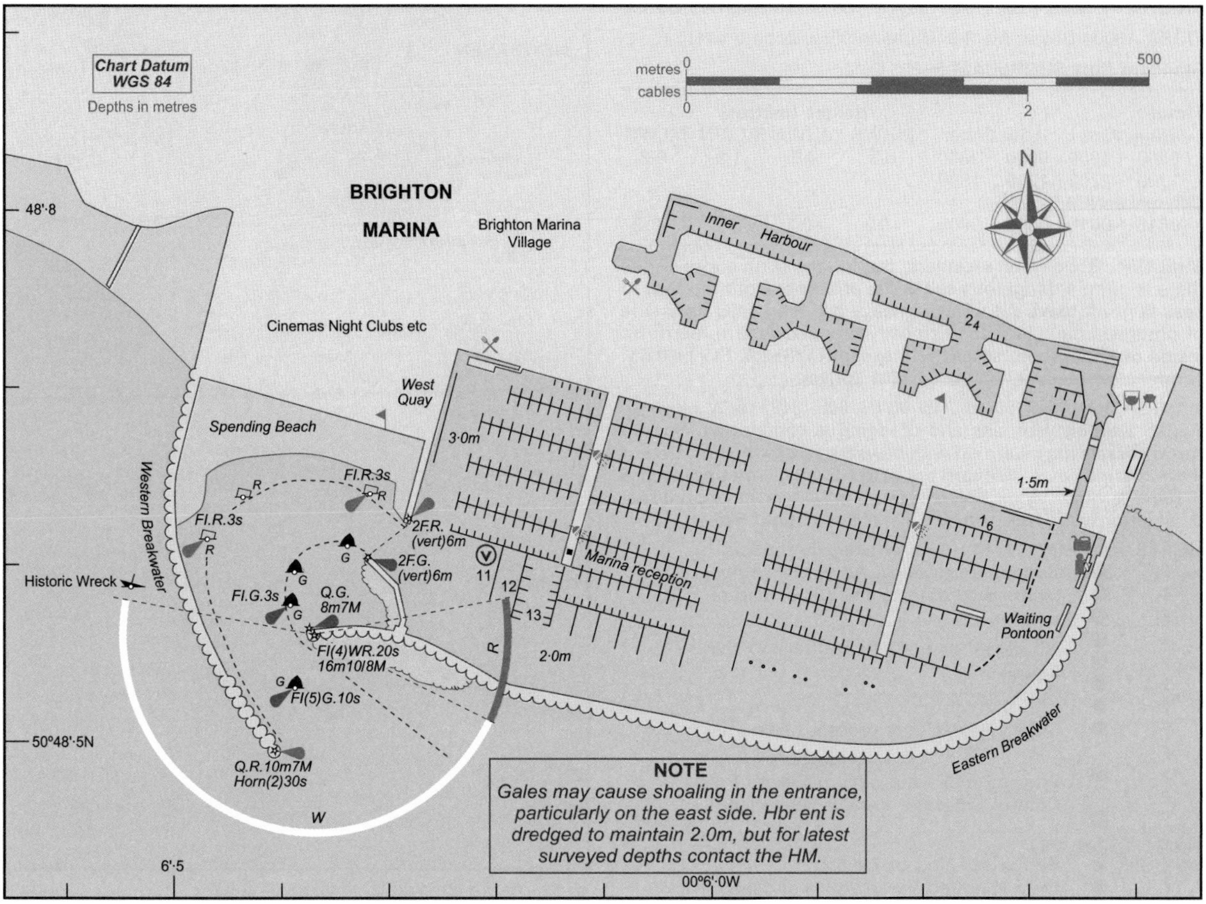
Chart Datum
WGS 84
Depths in metres
metres 0
500
cables 0
2
N
BRIGHTON
MARINA
Brighton Marina
Village
Inner Harbour
Cinemas Night Clubs etc
West
Quay
Spending Beach
Western Breakwater
Fl.R.3s
R
Fl.R.3s
2F.R.
(vert)6m
2F.G.
(vert)6m
Historic Wreck
Fl.G.3s
G
Q.G.
8m7M
Fl(4)WR.20s
16m10/8M
Fl(5)G.10s
Q.R.10m7M
Horn(2)30s
W
R
3·0m
2·0m
Marina reception
11
12
13
1·5m
16
24
Waiting
Pontoon
Eastern Breakwater
NOTE
Gales may cause shoaling in the entrance, particularly on the east side. Hbr ent is dredged to maintain 2.0m, but for latest surveyed depths contact the HM.
48′·8
50°48′·5N
6′·5
00°6′·0W

CHARTS AC *5605, 1652, 1991*; Imray C12, C31, C9; Stanfords 9; OS 198

TIDES +0004 Dover; ML 3·5; Duration 0605; Zone 0 (UT)

Standard Port SHOREHAM (⟵)

Times				**Height (metres)**			
High Water		Low Water		MHWS	MHWN	MLWN	MLWS
0500	1000	0000	0600	6·3	4·8	1·9	0·6
1700	2200	1200	1800				
Differences BRIGHTON							
0000	–0005	0000	0000	+0·3	+0·2	+0·1	0·0

SHELTER Good in the marina under all conditions, but in strong S'ly winds confused seas can make the final appr very rough. Speed limit 5kn.

NAVIGATION WPT 50°48′·23N 00°06′·39W, 000° to W bkwtr lt, 0·26M. Ent chan dredged 2·0m, but after gales shoaling occurs especially on E side; craft drawing >1·5m should keep to the W side of chan until past the second SHM buoy. In heavy weather, best appr is from SSE to avoid worst of the backlash from bkwtrs; beware shallow water E of ent in R sector of lt Fl (4) WR 20s.W-going stream starts at Brighton HW–1½ and E-going at HW+4½. Inshore the sp rate reaches approx 1·5kn. A Historic Wreck (see 9.0.3h) is at 50°48′·6N 00°06′·49W, immediately W of the marina's W bkwtr.

LIGHTS AND MARKS The marina is at the E end of the town, where white cliffs extend eastward. Daymark: conspic white hospital block, brg 334° leads to ent. Six Y spar lt buoys used as racing buoys:

1. 50°48′·06N 00°06′·41W
2. 50°47′·61N 00°08′·43W
3. 50°46′·61N 00°07′·00W
4. 50°47′·00N 00°15′·33W
5. 50°48′·40N 00°19′·40W
6. 50°46′·63N 00°04′·76W

A sewer outfall can buoy, Fl Y 5s is 1·1M off the coast. Navigational lts may be hard to see against shore glare: E bkwtr Fl (4) WR 20s (intens) 16m 10/8M; vis R260°-295°, W295°-100°. E bkwtr hd QG 8m 7M. W bkwtr hd, tr R/W bands, QR 10m 7M; Horn (2) 30s. Inner Hbr lock controlled by normal R/G lts, 0800-1800LT.

R/T Call: *Brighton Control* VHF Ch **M** 80 16 (H24).

TELEPHONE (Dial code 01273) HM 819919, Fax 675082; MRSC (023 92) 552100; Marinecall 09066 526240; Police 08456 070999; Ⓗ 696955; Dr 686863.

FACILITIES **Marina** (1300+200 visitors) ☎ 819919, Fax 675082, brighton@premiermarinas.com, www.premiermarinas.com, £2.10, £6 for < 4 hrs, Gas, Gaz, ⊡, R, Bar, BY, BH (60 ton), C (35 ton), ⚓, ♿; Inner Hbr has least depth of 2·4m. Fuel pontoon (P, D, LPG, Gas): H24.
Brighton Marina YC ☎ 818711, Bar, R.
Services El, Ⓔ, ME, ⚒, CH, ACA, Divers, Riggers, 🛒, Superstore.
Hbr Guides available from Hbr Office or by post.
Bus service from marina; timetable info ☎ 674881. Electric railway runs from marina to Palace Pier, Mar-Oct. **Town** V, R, Bar, ✉, Ⓑ, ⇌, ✈ (Shoreham).

9.3.9 NEWHAVEN

E. Sussex **50°46'·84N 00°03'·53E** ❂❂❂◊◊◊✿✿

CHARTS AC *5605, 1652,* 2154; Imray C31, C9, C12; Stanfords 9; OS 198

TIDES +0004 Dover; ML 3·6; Duration 0550; Zone 0 (UT)

Standard Port SHOREHAM (⟵)

Times				Height (metres)			
High Water		Low Water		MHWS	MHWN	MLWN	MLWS
0500	1000	0000	0600	6·3	4·8	1·9	0·6
1700	2200	1200	1800				
Differences NEWHAVEN							
–0015	–0010	0000	0000	+0·2	+0·1	–0·1	–0·2

SHELTER Good in all weathers, but in strong on-shore winds there is often a dangerous sea at the ent. Appr from the SW, to pass 50m off bkwtr hd to avoid heavy breaking seas on E side of dredged chan. At marina (mostly dredged to 2m), berth on inside of Ⓥ pontoon, access H24 except LWS±2½. Sw br 0.4M N opens on request. Lewes lies 7M upriver.

NAVIGATION WPT 50°46'·24N 00°03'·60E, 348° to W bkwtr lt, 0·32M. Caution: Hbr silts and dredging is continuous. Ferries/cargo vessels may warp off with hawsers across the hbr. Do not leave marina when 3FR(vert) are lit at NE ent. Do not proceed S of RoRo terminal when 3FR(vert) are lit at NW corner of pontoon. Beware ferries; check on VHF Ch 12. Speed limit 5kn.

LIGHTS AND MARKS Lt Ho on W bkwtr is conspic.

Fl F Fl	● ● ●	Serious emergency. All vessels stop or divert according to instructions from Port Control
F F F	● ● ●	No vessel to proceed contrary to this signal
F F F	● ● ○	Small vessels may proceed. Two way traffic
F F F	● ○ ●	Proceed only when instructed by Port Control. All other vessels keep clear

Swing bridge sigs:

Iso G 2s	●	Bridge opening or closing.
F	●	Only N-bound vessels may proceed.
F	●	Only S-bound vessels may proceed.

R/T Port VHF Ch 12 16 (H24). Swing bridge opening Ch 12. Marina Ch **80** M (0800-1700).

TELEPHONE (Dial code 01273) HM 612868 (H24), 📠 612878; Hbr Sig Stn 517922; MRSC (023 92) 552100; Marinecall 09066 526240; Police 08456 070999; Dr 515076; Ⓗ 609411 (Casualty 696955).

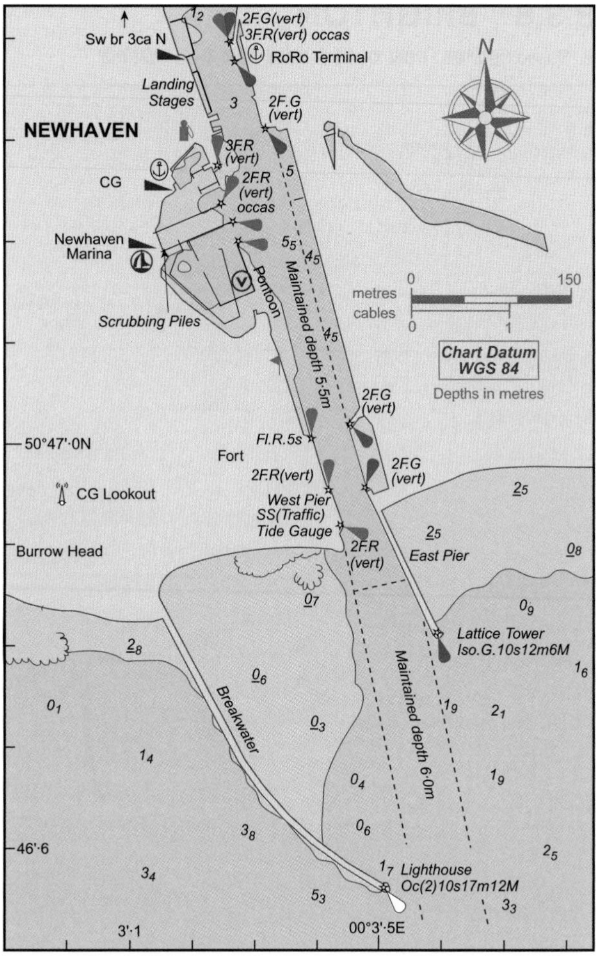
Sw br 3ca N
2F.G(vert)
3F.R(vert) occas
RoRo Terminal
N
Landing Stages
2F.G (vert)
NEWHAVEN
3F.R (vert)
CG
2F.R (vert) occas
Newhaven Marina
Pontoon
Maintained depth 5·5m
metres
cables
0
150
1
Scrubbing Piles
Chart Datum WGS 84
Depths in metres
2F.G (vert)
50°47'·0N
Fl.R.5s
Fort
2F.R(vert)
2F.G (vert)
CG Lookout
West Pier SS(Traffic) Tide Gauge
Burrow Head
2F.R (vert)
East Pier
Lattice Tower Iso.G.10s12m6M
Breakwater
Maintained depth 6·0m
46'·6
Lighthouse Oc(2)10s17m12M
3'·1
00°3'·5E

FACILITIES Marina (300+20 Ⓥ) ☎ 513881, 📠 510493, £1.60, D (1ca N of marina ent), ME, El, ⚒, BH (18 ton), C (10 ton), CH, Gas, Gaz, Slip, 🛒, R, Bar, 🗇, ♿; **Newhaven & Seaford SC** ☎ (01323) 890077, M, FW. **Town** EC Wed; ACA, SM, P, Ⓔ, 🛒, R, Bar, ✉, Ⓑ, ⇌, ✈ (Shoreham), ferries to Dieppe.

9.3.10 EASTBOURNE

E. Sussex **50°47'·34N 00°19'·90E** ❂❂◊◊◊✿✿

CHARTS AC *536, 5605*; Imray C31, C12, C8; Stanfords 9; OS 199

TIDES –0005 Dover; ML 3·8; Duration 0540; Zone 0 (UT)

Standard Port SHOREHAM (⟵)

Times				Height (metres)			
High Water		Low Water		MHWS	MHWN	MLWN	MLWS
0500	1000	0000	0600	6·3	4·8	1·9	0·6
1700	2200	1200	1800				
Differences EASTBOURNE							
–0010	–0005	+0015	+0020	+1·1	+0·6	+0·2	+0·1

SHELTER Good, but appr is exposed to and can be unsafe in NE/SE winds above F5. In F5 or 6, time arrival for HW±1½. Access via buoyed chan and twin locks into inner basin (4m). The channel is prone to shoaling after gales and is dredged regularly. If uncertain of up-to-date situation, contact HM before entry.

NAVIGATION WPT 50°47'·37N 00°20'·81E, SWM buoy 'SH', L Fl 10s, 259° to hbr ent, 0·45M. There are shoals to the NE in Pevensey Bay and from 2·5M SE toward Royal Sovereign lt (tide rips). From Beachy Hd, keep 0·75M offshore to clear Holywell Bank.

LIGHTS AND MARKS Beachy Hd lt, Fl (2) 20s, is 4·7M SW; Royal Sovereign lt, Fl 20s, is 5·5M to SE. Martello tr No 66 at root of S bkwtr has high intens Xenon lt, Fl (3) 15s 12m 7M, vis H24. From E, by day R roofs are conspic. Dir lt, Fl WRG 5s 4m1M, W256·5°-259·5°, leads 258° through appr channel. A wreck on N side is marked by 2 SHM buoys, Fl G 5s and Fl G 3s. N and S bkwtr hds,

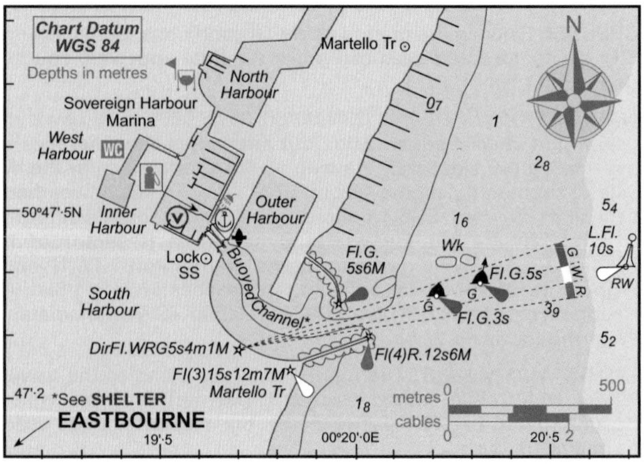
Chart Datum WGS 84
Depths in metres
Martello Tr
N
North Harbour
Sovereign Harbour Marina
West Harbour
50°47'·5N
Inner Harbour
Outer Harbour
Lock SS
Buoyed Channel*
Fl.G. 5s6M
Wk
Fl.G.5s
L.Fl. 10s
RW
South Harbour
Fl.G.3s
DirFl.WRG5s4m1M
Fl(4)R.12s6M
Fl(3)15s12m7M
Martello Tr
47'·2
*See SHELTER
EASTBOURNE
metres
cables
500
19'·5
00°20'·0E
20'·5

EASTBOURNE *continued*
both painted white, are Fl G 5s 3m 6M and Fl (4) R 12s 3m 6M. Eastbourne pier, 2 FR, is 2M S of hbr ent; an unlit PHM buoy is approx 5ca S. 5kn speed limit in chan and hbr.

R/T Monitor *Sovereign Harbour* VHF Ch **17**, 15 (H24) for nav info and locks/berthing. IPTS (Sigs 2, 3 & 5) for each lock indicate lock availability; gates close every H and H+30. Pontoons inside the lock.

TELEPHONE (Dial code 01323) HM 470099, 🖷 470077; MRSC (01304) 210008; Marinecall 09066 526240; Police 08456 070999; Dr 720555; Ⓗ 417400.

FACILITIES **Sovereign Marina** (Up to 800 and 300 in tidal hbr), ☎ 470099, 🖷 470077, £2.19, D, P, LPG (H24), BH (50 tons), Gas, Gaz, ME, ⚒, CH, ⛴, ▣, ♿, YC, Bar. R. including **Retail Park** with S/ market and all domestic facilities. **Town** (2½M) all needs, ⇌, ✈ (Gatwick).

ADJACENT ANCHORAGE

HASTINGS, E Sussex, **50°50′·88N 00°35′·50E**. AC *536*. Tides, see 9.3.11; ML 3·8m; Duration 0530. Strictly a settled weather ⚓ or emergency shelter; landing places on pier. The stone bkwtr is in disrepair and serves only to protect FVs. Beware dangerous wreck 3ca SE of pier head. Ldg lts 356°, both FR 14/55m 4M: front on W metal column; rear 357m from front, on 5-sided W tr on West Hill. Pier hd 2 FR (vert) 8m 5M from white hut; W bkwtr hd Fl R 2·5s 5m 4M; Fl G 5s 2m, 30m from head of No3 Groyne (E bkwtr). A Historic Wreck (*Amsterdam*; see 9.0.3h) is about 2M W of pier, close inshore at 50°50′·7N 00°31′·65E. Facilities: EC Wed. ACA (St Leonard's). Few marine services, but all shore needs at Hastings and St Leonard's. YC ☎ (01424) 420656.

3

9.3.11 RYE

E. Sussex **50°55′·60N 00°46′·58E** ❁❁◊◊✿✿✿

CHARTS AC *5605, 536, 1991*; Imray C31, C12, C8; Stanfords 9; OS 189

TIDES ML 2·0; Zone 0 (UT); Duration 3·25hrs sp, 5hrs nps

Standard Port DOVER (⟶)

Times				Height (metres)			
High Water		Low Water		MHWS	MHWN	MLWN	MLWS
0000	0600	0100	0700	6·8	5·3	2·1	0·8
1200	1800	1300	1900				
Differences RYE (approaches)							
+0005	–0010	No data		+1·0	+0·7	No data	
RYE HARBOUR							
+0005	–0010	Dries		–1·4	–1·7	Dries	
HASTINGS							
0000	–0010	–0030	–0030	+0·8	+0·5	+0·1	–0·1

SHELTER Very good in R Rother which dries completely to soft mud. Rye Bay is exposed to prevailing SW'lies with little shelter, when there is good ⚓ in lee of Dungeness (6M to E). In N'lies ⚓ 5ca N of the Rye Fairway buoy.
Rye Hbr is a small village, ¾M inside ent on W bank, used by commercial shipping. Berth initially on Admiralty Jetty (E bank) and see HM for AB or M. No ⚓. Max speed 6kn.
Rye Town (a Cinque Port) is 2M up river. Enter via Rock Channel for Ⓥ AB along NE side of Strand Quay.

NAVIGATION WPT Rye Fairway SWM By, L Fl 10s, 50°54′·04N 00°48′·02E, 330° to W Arm tripod lt, 1·81M. Bar dries 2·75m about 2ca offshore and needs care when wind >F6 from SE to SW. Enter HW –2 to HW +2. Beware: Bar and shoals E and W of ent with ground swell or surf; narrow ent (42m) and chan (30m); flood runs 4·5kn (max HW –2 to HW –1).
Depth of water over the bar can be judged by day from horizontal timbers at base of West Arm tripod structure (approx 2ca N of the bar) these are set at 1·5, 3 and 4·5m above CD.

For information on Lydd and Hythe Firing Ranges see 9.3.5.

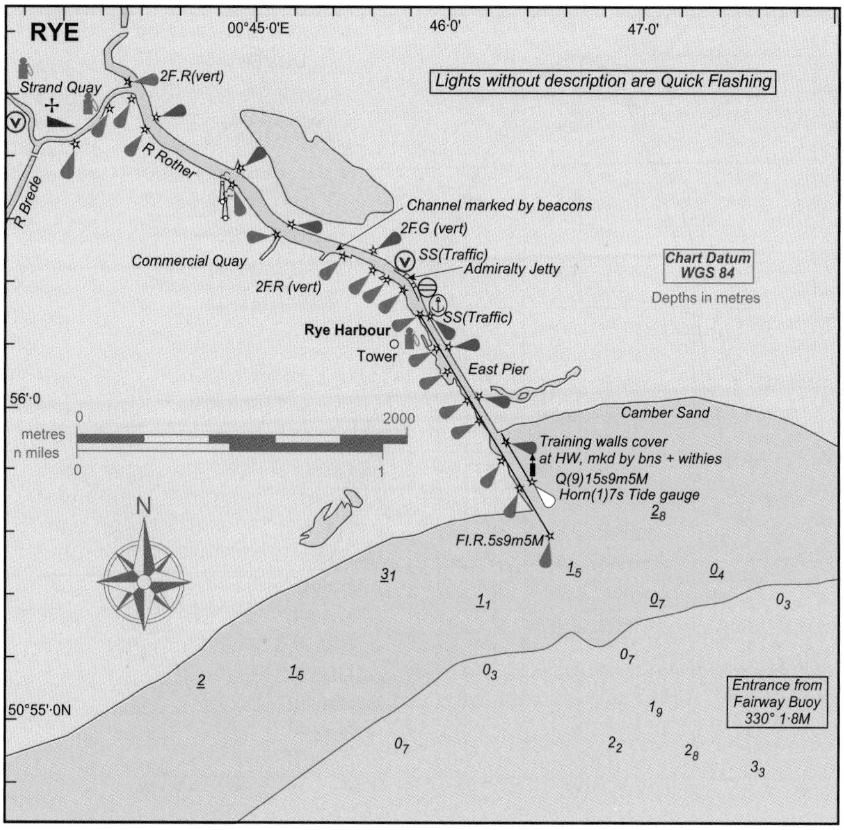
RYE
00°45·0'E
46·0'
47·0'
Lights without description are Quick Flashing
Strand Quay
2F.R(vert)
R Rother
R Brede
Channel marked by beacons
2F.G (vert)
SS(Traffic)
Admiralty Jetty
Commercial Quay
2F.R (vert)
SS(Traffic)
Chart Datum WGS 84
Depths in metres
Rye Harbour
Tower
East Pier
56'·0
metres
n miles
0
2000
0
1
Camber Sand
Training walls cover at HW, mkd by bns + withies
Q(9)15s9m5M
Horn(1)7s Tide gauge
N
Fl.R.5s9m5M
Entrance from Fairway Buoy 330° 1·8M
50°55'·0N

LIGHTS AND MARKS W Arm lt Fl R 5s 7m 6M, wooden tripod, radar reflector. E Arm hd, Q (9) 15s 7m 5M; Horn 7s, G △. On E Pier a floodlit 'Welcome to Rye' sign is considered helpful. Rock Chan ent marked by a QR and QG lt buoy.
IPTS (Sigs 2 & 5 only) are shown to seaward (3M) from HM's office and up-river (1M) from HM's office.

R/T VHF Ch 14 (0900-1700LT, HW±2 or when vessel due). To avoid cargo ships monitor Ch 14 before arr/dep.

TELEPHONE (Dial code 01797) HM 225225, 🖷 227429; MRCC (01304) 210008; Marinecall 09066 526240; Police 08456 6070999; Dr 222031; Ⓗ 222109.

FACILITIES (from seaward) **Admiralty Jetty** Slip, M, L, FW;
Rye Hbr ME, El, BY, ⚒, CH, C (15 ton), C (3 ton), Slip (26 ton), Ⓔ, ACA; **Rye Hbr SC** (Sec'y) ☎ 223376. **Rye Town, Strand Quay** AB approx £5.40/yacht, wood fendering posts against solid wall with numbered ladders. M, P & D (50m, cans), FW, ⛽, Showers, ♿; **Town** EC Tues; ✉, Ⓑ, 🛒, ⇌, ✈ (Lydd). Note: A Historic Wreck (*Anne*; see 9.0.3h) is about 4M WSW of Rye, close inshore at 50°53′·42N 00°41′·91E.

9.3.12 FOLKESTONE

Kent **51°04'·59N 01°11'·67E**

CHARTS AC *5605, 1892, 1991*; Imray C12, C8; Stanfords 20, 9; OS 179

TIDES –0010 Dover; ML 3·9; Duration 0500; Zone 0 (UT)
Standard Port DOVER (⟶)

Times				Height (metres)			
High Water		Low Water		MHWS	MHWN	MLWN	MLWS
0000	0600	0100	0700	6·8	5·3	2·1	0·8
1200	1800	1300	1900				
Differences FOLKESTONE							
–0020	–0005	–0010	–0010	+0·4	+0·4	0·0	–0·1
DUNGENESS							
–0010	–0015	–0020	–0010	+1·0	+0·6	+0·4	+0·1

SHELTER Good except in strong E-S winds when seas break at the hbr ent. Inner Hbr, dries 1·7m, has many FVs and local shoal draft boats. Visitors contact FY&MBC for F&A mooring if vacant; access approx HW±2. Berth on S Quay; fender board needed. Depth gauge on hd of E Pier. Ferries have ceased to use the hbr; no plans for development.

NAVIGATION WPT 51°04'·33N 01°11'·89E, 330° to bkwtr hd lt, 0·26M. Beware drying Mole Hd Rks and Copt Rks to stbd of the ent; from/to the NE, keep well clear of the latter due to extended sewer outfall pipe. For Hythe and Lydd Firing Ranges see 9.3.5.

LIGHTS AND MARKS Hotel block is conspic at W end of Inner Hbr. Ldg lts 295° at old ferry terminal, FR and FG (occas).

R/T Call *Folkestone Port Control* Ch 15, 16.

TELEPHONE (Dial code 01303) HM 715354 (H24), 715392; MRCC (01304) 210008; Marinecall 09066 526240; Police 850055.

FACILITIES **Inner S Quay** £10 for AB or ⚓, Slip (free), FW; **Folkestone Y & MB Club** ☎ 251574, D, FW, L, Slip, M, Bar, ♿.
Town EC Wed (larger shops open all day); P & D (cans, 100 yds), R, Bar, ✉, Ⓑ, ⇌, ✈ (Lydd).

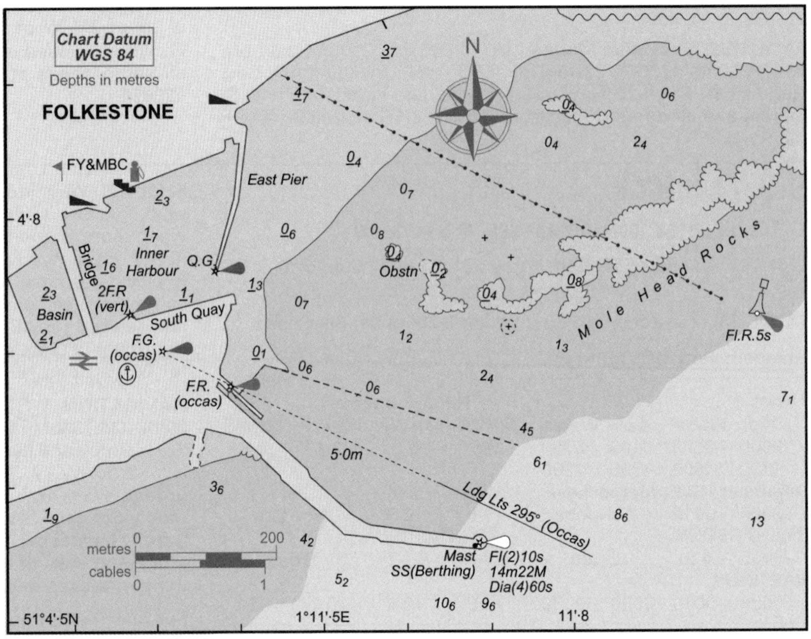
Chart Datum WGS 84
Depths in metres
FOLKESTONE
FY&MBC
East Pier
Inner Harbour
Bridge
Basin
South Quay
2F.R (vert)
Q.G.
F.G. (occas)
F.R. (occas)
Obstn
Mole Head Rocks
Fl.R.5s
Ldg Lts 295° (Occas)
Mast
SS(Berthing)
Fl(2)10s 14m22M
Dia(4)60s
5·0m
metres 0 200
cables 0 1
51°4'·5N
1°11'·5E
11'·8

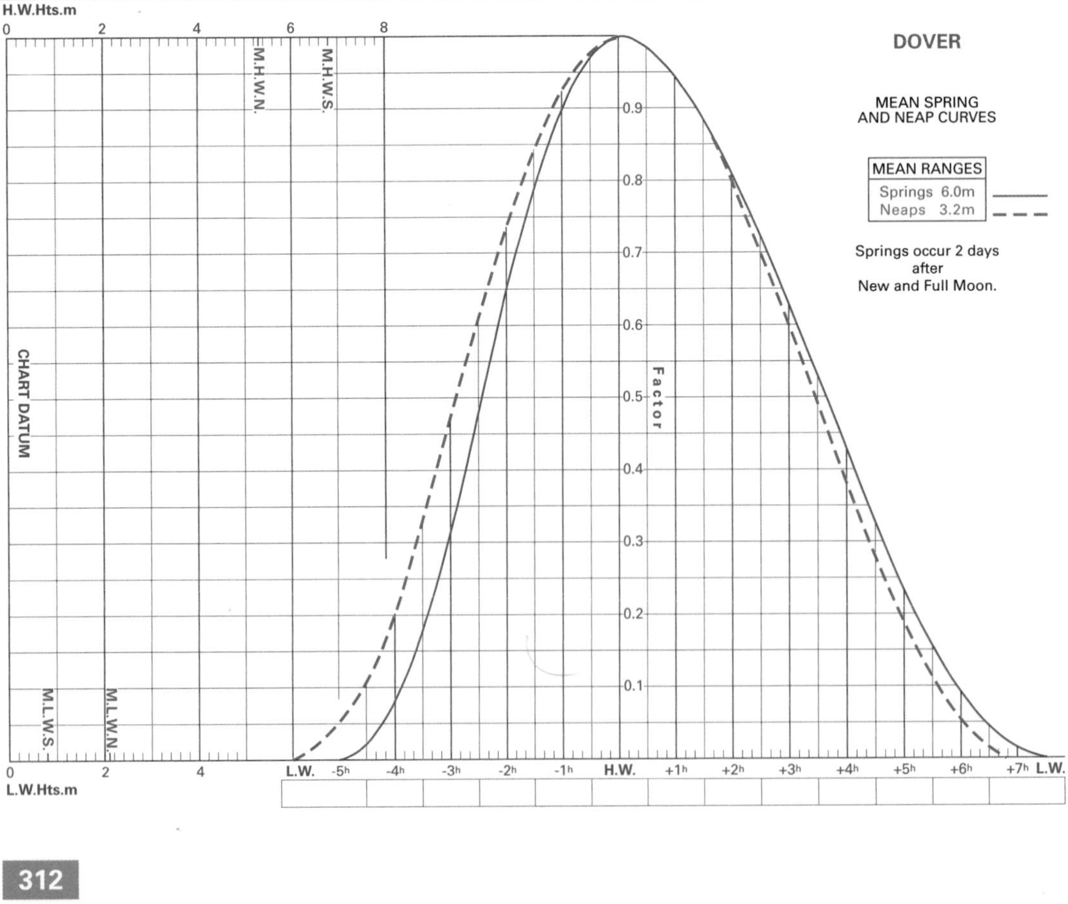
H.W.Hts.m
M.H.W.N.
M.H.W.S.
CHART DATUM
M.L.W.S.
M.L.W.N.
L.W.Hts.m
Factor
L.W. -5h -4h -3h -2h -1h H.W. +1h +2h +3h +4h +5h +6h +7h L.W.
DOVER
MEAN SPRING AND NEAP CURVES
MEAN RANGES
Springs 6.0m
Neaps 3.2m
Springs occur 2 days after New and Full Moon.

9.3.13 DOVER

Kent **51°06'·74N 01°19'·73E** (W ent) ❀❀❀◊◊◊✿✿
51°07'·25N 01°20'·61E (E ent)

CHARTS AC *5605, 1892, 1828, 1698*; Imray C30, C12, C8, 2100 series; Stanfords 9, 20; OS 179

TIDES 0000 Dover; ML 3·7; Duration 0505; Zone 0 (UT)

Standard Port DOVER (⟶)

Times				Height (metres)			
High Water		Low Water		MHWS	MHWN	MLWN	MLWS
0000	0600	0100	0700	6·8	5·3	2·1	0·8
1200	1800	1300	1900				
Differences DEAL							
+0010	+0020	+0010	+0005	−0·6	−0·3	0·0	0·0

SHELTER Very good in marina, 3 options: a. Tidal hbr, E of waiting pontoon (1·5m), access H24. 3 pontoons in 2·5m. b. Granville Dock, access via gate approx HW±4, 120 AB. c. Wellington Dock. Dock gates, and swing bridge, open HW ±2 nps and approx HW–1½ to HW+2½ sp, depending on range; 147 AB. In the Outer Hbr ⚓ is tenable in offshore winds, but exposed to winds from NE through S to SW; in gales a heavy sea builds up. Small craft may not be left unattended at ⚓ in Outer Hbr. High Speed Ferries operating.

NAVIGATION WPT from SW, 51°06'·18N 01°19'·67E, 000° to Admiralty Pier lt ho, 0·5M. WPT from NE, 51°07'·30N 01°21'·41E, 090°/270° from/to S end Eastern Arm, 0·5M. Beware lumpy seas/overfalls outside the bkwtrs and the frequent ferries and catamarans using both ents. Strong tides across ents and high walls make ent under sail slow and difficult; use of engine very strongly recommended. Inside the W ent do not pass between NCM buoy, Q, (marking wreck) and the S bkwtr.

Specific permission to ent/leave the hbr via E or W ent must first be obtained from Port Control on VHF Ch 74. Comply with any VHF instructions from Port Control or hbr patrol launch. Clearance for small/slow craft is not normally given until within 200m of ent; advise if you have no engine. Ⓥ are welcomed and usually escorted by hbr launch to the marina.

If no VHF, Stay clear of entrance, attract attention of Port Control (E arm) with five short lamp flashes. Hbr launch will escort you in. Do not use W entrance.

Q ○ lt from Port Control tr or patrol launch = keep clear of ent you are approaching. Beware catamarans on rounding Prince of Wales pier.

Marina sigs: In the final appr, especially near LW, stay in deep water as defined by the W sector (324°-333°) of the F WR lt, 2 unlit SHM poles and a G conical buoy. IPTS are shown, plus a small Fl ● lt 5 min before bridge is swung.

Note: A Historic Wreck (see 9.0.3h) is adjacent to the Eastern Arm bkwtr at 51°07'·6N 01°20'·7E (see chartlet). There are 4 more Historic Wrecks on the Goodwin Sands.

3

LIGHTS AND MARKS Lts as on chartlet & 9.3.4. Port Control tr (conspic) is at S end of E Arm and shows IPTS (for ferries only) for the E ent on panels; for W ent, IPTS are on panels near Admiralty Pier sig stn.

R/T Call: *Dover Port Control* VHF Ch **74** 12 16. Hbr launch Ch 74. *Dover Marina* Ch 80, only within tidal hbr/marina. Chan Nav Info Service (CNIS) broadcasts tfc/ nav/wx/tidal info Ch 11 at H+40; also, if vis < 2M, at H+55. *Dover Coastguard* Ch **69** 16 80, gives TSS surveillance.

TELEPHONE (Dial code 01304) HM 240400 ext 4520, 📠 225144, Duty HM mob 07836 262713; Port Control 240400 ext 5530, Marina 241663, pr.doverport.co.uk; MRCC 210008; Marinecall 09066 526240; Police 240055; Ⓗ 201624.

FACILITIES Marina (373 inc Ⓥ) ☎ 241663, 📠 242549, £1.95 tidal hbr, £1.70 Granville Dock, £1.40 Wellington Dock. www.doverport.co.uk; **Services:** C, Slip, D, LPG, Gas, Gaz, ⊡, BH (50 ton), ME, El, ⚒, SM, CH, ACA, Ⓔ (H24). **Royal Cinque Ports YC** ☎ 206262, L, M, C, FW, Bar; **White Cliffs M & YC** ☎ 211666, www.wcmyc.co.uk; **Town**: www.doverport.co.uk, P (cans), 🛒, R, Bar, ✉, Ⓑ, ⇌, ✈ (Manston). Ferries to Dunkerque, Calais and Boulogne.

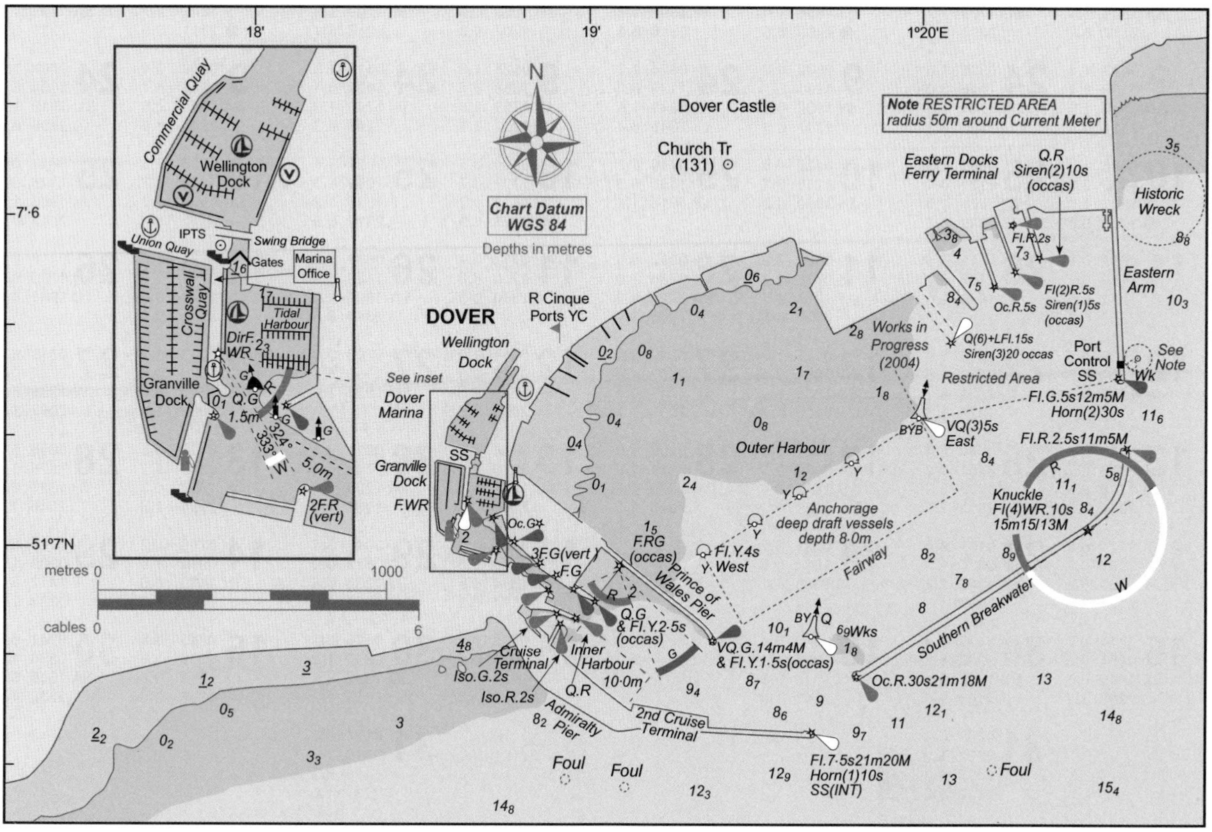
18'
19'
1°20'E
7'·6
51°7'N
Dover Castle
Church Tr (131)
Note RESTRICTED AREA radius 50m around Current Meter
Chart Datum WGS 84
Depths in metres
Eastern Docks Ferry Terminal
Q.R Siren(2)10s (occas)
Historic Wreck
Eastern Arm
Works in Progress (2004)
Q(6)+LFl.15s Siren(3)20 occas
Port Control SS
See Note
Restricted Area
Fl.G.5s12m5M Horn(2)30s
VQ(3)5s East
Fl.R.2.5s11m5M
Outer Harbour
Anchorage deep draft vessels depth 8·0m
Fairway
Knuckle Fl(4)WR.10s 15m15/13M
Southern Breakwater
Oc.R.30s21m18M
Fl.7·5s21m20M Horn(1)10s SS(INT)
Foul
DOVER
Wellington Dock
R Cinque Ports YC
See inset
Dover Marina
Granville Dock
F.WR
Oc.G
3F.G(vert)
F.G
Q.G & Fl.Y.2·5s (occas)
F.RG (occas)
Fl.Y.4s West
Prince of Wales Pier
VQ.G.14m4M & Fl.Y.1·5s(occas)
Cruise Terminal
Inner Harbour
Iso.G.2s
Iso.R.2s
Q.R
Admiralty Pier
2nd Cruise Terminal
metres 0 1000
cables 0 6
Commercial Quay
Wellington Dock
IPTS
Union Quay
Swing Bridge
Gates
Marina Office
Crosswall Quay
Tidal Harbour
Dir F. WR
Granville Dock
Q.G 1.5m
324° 333° W
2F.R (vert)

TIME ZONE (UT)
For Summer Time add ONE hour in **non-shaded areas**

ENGLAND – DOVER

LAT 51°07′N LONG 1°19′E

TIMES AND HEIGHTS OF HIGH AND LOW WATERS

SPRING & NEAP TIDES
Dates in red are SPRINGS
Dates in blue are NEAPS

YEAR **2005**

JANUARY

Date	Day	Time	m	Time	m	Time	m	Time	m
1	SA	0158	6.1	0917	1.6	1414	5.8	2128	1.8
2	SU	0235	6.0	0957	1.7	1454	5.7	2209	1.9
3	M	0320	5.9	1041	1.8	1544	5.6	◑ 2255	2.0
4	TU	0415	5.8	1133	1.9	1647	5.5	2353	2.1
5	W	0523	5.7	1238	1.9	1806	5.5		
6	TH	0107	2.2	0635	5.7	1351	1.9	1918	5.6
7	F	0225	2.0	0742	5.9	1501	1.7	2020	5.8
8	SA	0334	1.8	0843	6.1	1606	1.4	2117	6.1
9	SU	0437	1.4	0939	6.4	1708	1.2	2211	6.4
10	M	0536	1.2	1035	6.6	1807	1.0	● 2303	6.6
11	TU	0632	0.9	1128	6.7	1903	0.9	2352	6.7
12	W	0728	0.8	1219	6.7	1956	0.9		
13	TH	0040	6.8	0820	0.7	1308	6.6	2044	0.9
14	F	0127	6.8	0909	0.7	1357	6.5	2127	1.0
15	SA	0214	6.7	0954	0.8	1445	6.3	2208	1.2
16	SU	0302	6.5	1037	1.0	1535	6.0	2248	1.4
17	M	0351	6.2	1120	1.3	1628	5.7	◐ 2332	1.7
18	TU	0445	5.9	1207	1.7	1728	5.4		
19	W	0024	2.0	0547	5.6	1303	2.0	1836	5.3
20	TH	0127	2.2	0659	5.4	1406	2.1	1947	5.3
21	F	0236	2.2	0812	5.5	1512	2.1	2051	5.5
22	SA	0344	2.1	0915	5.6	1613	1.9	2143	5.7
23	SU	0440	1.8	1006	5.8	1703	1.7	2227	6.0
24	M	0526	1.6	1046	6.0	1744	1.6	2305	6.2
25	TU	0605	1.4	1121	6.1	1821	1.5	○ 2339	6.3
26	W	0641	1.3	1153	6.1	1856	1.4		
27	TH	0010	6.4	0716	1.3	1224	6.2	1929	1.4
28	F	0040	6.4	0751	1.2	1253	6.2	2003	1.3
29	SA	0107	6.4	0826	1.2	1318	6.2	2037	1.3
30	SU	0135	6.4	0900	1.2	1346	6.2	2109	1.4
31	M	0207	6.4	0933	1.3	1421	6.2	2142	1.5

FEBRUARY

Date	Day	Time	m	Time	m	Time	m	Time	m
1	TU	0245	6.3	1008	1.4	1503	6.0	2220	1.7
2	W	0331	6.1	1051	1.7	1554	5.8	◑ 2308	1.9
3	TH	0429	5.8	1147	1.9	1703	5.4		
4	F	0015	2.2	0549	5.6	1306	2.1	1843	5.3
5	SA	0147	2.2	0722	5.6	1434	2.0	2009	5.5
6	SU	0311	1.9	0840	5.8	1551	1.7	2116	5.9
7	M	0424	1.5	0945	6.1	1702	1.3	2213	6.2
8	TU	0531	1.1	1041	6.5	1806	1.0	● 2303	6.6
9	W	0632	0.8	1131	6.7	1902	0.8	2347	6.8
10	TH	0726	0.5	1215	6.7	1950	0.6		
11	F	0029	7.0	0812	0.4	1256	6.7	2030	0.6
12	SA	0111	7.0	0854	0.4	1335	6.6	2106	0.7
13	SU	0151	6.9	0930	0.6	1414	6.4	2139	0.9
14	M	0231	6.7	1004	0.9	1455	6.2	2210	1.2
15	TU	0313	6.3	1037	1.3	1540	5.8	2242	1.6
16	W	0359	5.9	1113	1.7	1634	5.4	◐ 2323	2.0
17	TH	0456	5.5	1203	2.2	1742	5.1		
18	F	0027	2.4	0609	5.1	1316	2.4	1902	5.0
19	SA	0153	2.5	0737	5.1	1433	2.4	2024	5.2
20	SU	0311	2.3	0901	5.3	1543	2.1	2126	5.5
21	M	0415	1.9	0954	5.6	1641	1.8	2210	5.9
22	TU	0506	1.6	1031	5.9	1727	1.6	2245	6.1
23	W	0547	1.4	1101	6.1	1806	1.4	2316	6.3
24	TH	0624	1.2	1130	6.2	1841	1.3	○ 2345	6.4
25	F	0700	1.1	1159	6.3	1914	1.2		
26	SA	0013	6.5	0734	1.0	1226	6.3	1945	1.1
27	SU	0040	6.6	0807	1.0	1252	6.4	2016	1.1
28	M	0108	6.6	0837	1.0	1320	6.5	2046	1.1

MARCH

Date	Day	Time	m	Time	m	Time	m	Time	m
1	TU	0140	6.6	0907	1.1	1353	6.4	2117	1.2
2	W	0216	6.5	0940	1.3	1434	6.2	2153	1.5
3	TH	0300	6.2	1021	1.6	1523	5.9	◑ 2240	1.8
4	F	0356	5.8	1115	2.0	1630	5.4	2347	2.2
5	SA	0526	5.3	1239	2.3	1834	5.1		
6	SU	0128	2.3	0722	5.3	1422	2.1	2006	5.4
7	M	0300	2.0	0844	5.7	1545	1.8	2113	5.8
8	TU	0419	1.5	0947	6.1	1659	1.3	2207	6.3
9	W	0528	1.0	1038	6.5	1759	0.9	2252	6.7
10	TH	0624	0.6	1122	6.7	1848	0.7	● 2333	6.9
11	F	0712	0.4	1200	6.8	1930	0.5		
12	SA	0011	7.0	0753	0.3	1235	6.8	2005	0.5
13	SU	0048	7.0	0828	0.4	1309	6.7	2036	0.7
14	M	0125	6.9	0859	0.6	1344	6.5	2104	0.9
15	TU	0200	6.7	0926	0.9	1421	6.3	2130	1.2
16	W	0236	6.3	0952	1.3	1500	5.9	2156	1.6
17	TH	0317	5.9	1019	1.8	1550	5.5	◐ 2230	2.0
18	F	0413	5.4	1059	2.3	1658	5.1	2324	2.4
19	SA	0530	5.0	1221	2.6	1820	4.9		
20	SU	0112	2.6	0659	4.9	1400	2.6	1948	5.0
21	M	0239	2.4	0835	5.1	1513	2.3	2057	5.4
22	TU	0344	2.0	0927	5.5	1612	1.9	2140	5.8
23	W	0436	1.6	1000	5.8	1700	1.6	2213	6.1
24	TH	0519	1.3	1029	6.1	1740	1.3	2243	6.3
25	F	0557	1.1	1059	6.3	1815	1.2	○ 2312	6.5
26	SA	0634	1.0	1128	6.4	1849	1.1	2341	6.6
27	SU	0709	0.9	1156	6.5	1921	1.0		
28	M	0011	6.7	0742	0.9	1225	6.6	1953	1.0
29	TU	0042	6.7	0813	0.9	1256	6.6	2024	1.0
30	W	0116	6.7	0844	1.0	1332	6.5	2057	1.2
31	TH	0154	6.5	0919	1.3	1415	6.2	2137	1.5

APRIL

Date	Day	Time	m	Time	m	Time	m	Time	m
1	F	0241	6.1	1002	1.7	1508	5.8	2227	1.8
2	SA	0345	5.6	1101	2.1	1632	5.3	◑ 2340	2.2
3	SU	0538	5.2	1235	2.3	1828	5.2		
4	M	0124	2.2	0721	5.3	1416	2.1	1954	5.5
5	TU	0254	1.8	0839	5.7	1537	1.7	2059	5.9
6	W	0410	1.3	0936	6.1	1644	1.2	2149	6.4
7	TH	0513	0.9	1022	6.4	1738	0.9	2232	6.7
8	F	0604	0.6	1101	6.6	1823	0.7	● 2311	6.9
9	SA	0648	0.4	1136	6.7	1901	0.6	2348	6.9
10	SU	0726	0.5	1209	6.7	1935	0.7		
11	M	0024	6.9	0757	0.6	1243	6.6	2004	0.8
12	TU	0059	6.7	0825	0.8	1317	6.5	2030	1.0
13	W	0132	6.5	0848	1.1	1352	6.3	2054	1.3
14	TH	0206	6.2	0910	1.5	1430	6.0	2120	1.6
15	F	0245	5.8	0938	1.8	1516	5.6	2156	2.0
16	SA	0341	5.3	1018	2.2	1621	5.2	◐ 2247	2.4
17	SU	0458	5.0	1122	2.6	1738	5.0		
18	M	0025	2.6	0618	4.9	1319	2.6	1857	5.1
19	TU	0157	2.4	0739	5.1	1434	2.3	2006	5.4
20	W	0300	2.0	0836	5.4	1530	1.9	2053	5.7
21	TH	0352	1.6	0915	5.8	1618	1.6	2129	6.0
22	F	0438	1.3	0949	6.0	1701	1.4	2202	6.3
23	SA	0521	1.1	1021	6.3	1741	1.2	2235	6.5
24	SU	0602	1.0	1054	6.4	1819	1.1	○ 2308	6.6
25	M	0641	0.9	1126	6.5	1856	1.0	2342	6.7
26	TU	0718	0.8	1200	6.6	1931	0.9		
27	W	0018	6.7	0752	0.9	1238	6.6	2007	1.0
28	TH	0058	6.6	0828	1.1	1320	6.5	2046	1.2
29	F	0144	6.4	0909	1.3	1411	6.2	2132	1.5
30	SA	0241	6.0	0958	1.7	1516	5.8	2230	1.8

Chart Datum: 3·67 metres below Ordnance Datum (Newlyn)

TIME ZONE (UT)
For Summer Time add ONE hour in **non-shaded areas**

ENGLAND – DOVER

LAT 51°07′N LONG 1°19′E

TIMES AND HEIGHTS OF HIGH AND LOW WATERS

SPRING & NEAP TIDES
Dates in red are SPRINGS Dates in blue are NEAPS

YEAR **2005**

MAY

Day	Time	m	Day	Time	m
1	0402	5.6	16	0424	5.1
	1104	2.0		1051	2.4
SU	1640	5.5	M	1651	5.2
◑	2349	2.0	◐	2338	2.3
2	0539	5.4	17	0534	5.0
	1236	2.1		1216	2.5
M	1809	5.4	TU	1759	5.2
3	0118	1.9	18	0103	2.2
	0707	5.5		0642	5.1
TU	1400	1.9	W	1338	2.3
	1929	5.6		1903	5.4
4	0236	1.6	19	0208	2.0
	0818	5.8		0739	5.4
W	1511	1.6	TH	1438	2.0
	2032	6.0		1956	5.6
5	0345	1.2	20	0302	1.7
	0912	6.1		0825	5.7
TH	1612	1.3	F	1531	1.8
	2122	6.3		2039	5.9
6	0445	0.9	21	0353	1.4
	0956	6.3		0905	6.0
F	1705	1.1	SA	1619	1.5
	2206	6.5		2118	6.2
7	0536	0.8	22	0442	1.2
	1034	6.4		0943	6.2
SA	1751	0.9	SU	1706	1.3
	2246	6.6		2157	6.4
8	0619	0.7	23	0530	1.0
	1110	6.5		1021	6.4
SU	1830	0.9	M	1751	1.1
●	2324	6.7	○	2238	6.6
9	0655	0.8	24	0615	0.9
	1144	6.5		1101	6.5
M	1904	0.9	TU	1834	1.0
				2319	6.7
10	0000	6.6	25	0658	0.9
	0725	1.0		1143	6.6
TU	1220	6.5	W	1916	1.0
	1934	1.0			
11	0036	6.5	26	0004	6.6
	0752	1.1		0740	1.0
W	1256	6.4	TH	1229	6.6
	2001	1.2		1959	1.0
12	0111	6.3	27	0052	6.5
	0815	1.4		0824	1.1
TH	1332	6.2	F	1320	6.5
	2027	1.4		2047	1.1
13	0146	6.0	28	0147	6.3
	0840	1.6		0912	1.3
F	1410	6.0	SA	1416	6.3
	2058	1.6		2140	1.3
14	0225	5.7	29	0251	6.0
	0913	1.8		1007	1.5
SA	1452	5.7	SU	1519	6.1
	2137	1.9		2241	1.5
15	0317	5.4	30	0404	5.8
	0955	2.1		1111	1.7
SU	1546	5.4	M	1625	5.9
	2227	2.1	◑	2348	1.6
			31	0521	5.6
				1220	1.8
			TU	1736	5.8

JUNE

Day	Time	m	Day	Time	m
1	0057	1.5	16	0002	2.0
	0636	5.6		0538	5.3
W	1328	1.8	TH	1227	2.2
	1850	5.8		1754	5.5
2	0203	1.4	17	0108	1.9
	0743	5.7		0640	5.4
TH	1430	1.6	F	1337	2.1
	1955	5.9		1855	5.6
3	0307	1.3	18	0211	1.8
	0838	5.9		0735	5.6
F	1531	1.5	SA	1441	1.9
	2050	6.1		1950	5.8
4	0408	1.2	19	0310	1.6
	0925	6.0		0824	5.8
SA	1628	1.4	SU	1539	1.7
	2138	6.2		2040	6.1
5	0502	1.2	20	0407	1.4
	1006	6.1		0911	6.1
SU	1717	1.3	M	1635	1.4
	2222	6.3		2129	6.3
6	0547	1.2	21	0502	1.2
	1046	6.2		0959	6.3
M	1759	1.2	TU	1728	1.2
●	2303	6.3		2218	6.5
7	0624	1.2	22	0555	1.1
	1124	6.3		1047	6.4
TU	1836	1.2	W	1818	1.0
	2342	6.3	○	2309	6.6
8	0657	1.3	23	0647	1.0
	1202	6.3		1137	6.6
W	1910	1.3	TH	1909	0.9
9	0019	6.2	24	0000	6.6
	0725	1.4		0738	1.0
TH	1240	6.3	F	1227	6.6
	1940	1.3		2001	0.9
10	0056	6.1	25	0054	6.5
	0753	1.5		0829	1.0
F	1316	6.2	SA	1319	6.6
	2011	1.4		2054	0.9
11	0131	5.9	26	0149	6.4
	0824	1.6		0920	1.1
SA	1352	6.1	SU	1411	6.5
	2046	1.6		2146	0.9
12	0208	5.8	27	0246	6.2
	0859	1.7		1009	1.2
SU	1427	5.9	M	1504	6.4
	2124	1.7		2237	1.0
13	0248	5.6	28	0345	6.0
	0939	1.9		1057	1.3
M	1507	5.7	TU	1559	6.2
	2209	1.8	◑	2329	1.2
14	0336	5.4	29	0445	5.8
	1025	2.0		1148	1.5
TU	1555	5.6	W	1657	6.0
	2300	1.9			
15	0434	5.3	30	0022	1.4
	1119	2.2		0548	5.7
W	1652	5.5	TH	1244	1.7
◐				1800	5.8

JULY

Day	Time	m	Day	Time	m
1	0120	1.5	16	0004	1.9
	0654	5.5		0523	5.4
F	1344	1.8	SA	1229	2.2
	1909	5.7		1757	5.6
2	0220	1.7	17	0116	2.0
	0757	5.6		0644	5.4
SA	1447	1.8	SU	1350	2.1
	2015	5.8		1910	5.7
3	0324	1.7	18	0232	1.9
	0853	5.7		0754	5.6
SU	1550	1.8	M	1506	1.9
	2113	5.8		2016	5.9
4	0425	1.6	19	0340	1.6
	0943	5.8		0855	5.9
M	1647	1.6	TU	1611	1.6
	2205	6.0		2118	6.1
5	0516	1.6	20	0443	1.4
	1028	6.0		0952	6.2
TU	1734	1.5	W	1712	1.3
	2249	6.1		2215	6.4
6	0558	1.5	21	0544	1.2
	1109	6.2		1044	6.4
W	1815	1.4	TH	1810	1.0
●	2329	6.1	○	2309	6.5
7	0634	1.5	22	0642	1.0
	1147	6.3		1134	6.7
TH	1852	1.4	F	1907	0.8
8	0006	6.1	23	0001	6.6
	0707	1.5		0737	0.9
F	1224	6.3	SA	1222	6.8
	1925	1.4		2001	0.6
9	0041	6.1	24	0050	6.7
	0739	1.5		0827	0.8
SA	1258	6.3	SU	1308	6.9
	1959	1.4		2050	0.5
10	0113	6.0	25	0137	6.6
	0811	1.5		0911	0.8
SU	1329	6.2	M	1354	6.8
	2034	1.4		2135	0.6
11	0143	5.9	26	0224	6.5
	0845	1.6		0950	0.9
M	1358	6.1	TU	1440	6.7
	2109	1.4		2216	0.7
12	0212	5.8	27	0311	6.2
	0920	1.6		1029	1.1
TU	1428	6.1	W	1527	6.5
	2146	1.5		2257	1.0
13	0244	5.8	28	0401	6.0
	0957	1.7		1109	1.4
W	1505	6.0	TH	1617	6.2
	2225	1.6	◑	2341	1.4
14	0324	5.7	29	0456	5.6
	1037	1.9		1156	1.8
TH	1551	5.8	F	1714	5.8
◐	2309	1.8			
15	0416	5.5	30	0032	1.8
	1125	2.0		0600	5.4
F	1648	5.7	SA	1256	2.1
				1821	5.5
			31	0136	2.1
				0714	5.3
			SU	1406	2.2
				1942	5.4

AUGUST

Day	Time	m	Day	Time	m
1	0245	2.1	16	0204	2.2
	0827	5.4		0743	5.4
M	1519	2.1	TU	1443	2.1
	2058	5.5		2013	5.7
2	0355	2.0	17	0324	1.9
	0927	5.6		0852	5.8
TU	1624	1.9	W	1557	1.7
	2156	5.7		2120	6.0
3	0454	1.8	18	0433	1.5
	1014	5.9		0949	6.2
W	1717	1.6	TH	1702	1.3
	2240	5.9		2217	6.4
4	0540	1.6	19	0537	1.2
	1054	6.2		1039	6.6
TH	1800	1.4	F	1804	0.9
	2316	6.1	○	2307	6.6
5	0619	1.5	20	0635	0.9
	1130	6.3		1124	6.9
F	1837	1.3	SA	1900	0.6
●	2348	6.1		2352	6.8
6	0652	1.5	21	0726	0.7
	1203	6.4		1207	7.0
SA	1910	1.3	SU	1949	0.4
7	0019	6.2	22	0034	6.8
	0723	1.4		0809	0.6
SU	1234	6.4	M	1249	7.1
	1942	1.2		2032	0.4
8	0047	6.1	23	0114	6.8
	0754	1.4		0846	0.7
M	1301	6.4	TU	1329	7.0
	2015	1.2		2110	0.5
9	0112	6.1	24	0153	6.6
	0825	1.4		0920	0.8
TU	1326	6.4	W	1411	6.9
	2047	1.2		2144	0.7
10	0136	6.1	25	0234	6.4
	0856	1.4		0952	1.1
W	1353	6.3	TH	1453	6.6
	2118	1.3		2218	1.2
11	0204	6.1	26	0320	6.0
	0927	1.5		1026	1.5
TH	1426	6.3	F	1539	6.1
	2150	1.5	◑	2255	1.6
12	0240	6.0	27	0412	5.6
	1001	1.7		1106	2.0
F	1507	6.1	SA	1634	5.7
	2227	1.7		2343	2.1
13	0325	5.8	28	0517	5.3
	1042	1.9		1205	2.4
SA	1558	5.8	SU	1743	5.3
◐	2315	2.0			
14	0426	5.5	29	0054	2.5
	1139	2.2		0635	5.1
SU	1710	5.5	M	1332	2.6
				1912	5.1
15	0025	2.2	30	0216	2.5
	0605	5.2		0804	5.2
M	1308	2.4	TU	1457	2.4
	1849	5.4		2050	5.3
			31	0334	2.3
				0912	5.6
			W	1608	2.0
				2146	5.7

Chart Datum: 3·67 metres below Ordnance Datum (Newlyn)

TIME ZONE (UT)
For Summer Time add ONE hour in **non-shaded areas**

ENGLAND – DOVER

LAT 51°07′N LONG 1°19′E

TIMES AND HEIGHTS OF HIGH AND LOW WATERS

SPRING & NEAP TIDES
Dates in red are SPRINGS
Dates in blue are NEAPS

YEAR **2005**

SEPTEMBER

Date	Day	Time	m	Time	m	Time	m	Time	m
1	TH	0436	1.9	0957	6.0	1701	1.6	2225	5.9
2	F	0523	1.7	1034	6.2	1742	1.4	2255	6.1
3	SA	0600	1.5	1105	6.4	1816	1.3	● 2322	6.3
4	SU	0631	1.4	1135	6.5	1847	1.2	2349	6.3
5	M	0700	1.3	1202	6.5	1918	1.1		
6	TU	0015	6.3	0728	1.3	1228	6.5	1949	1.1
7	W	0039	6.3	0758	1.3	1253	6.5	2019	1.2
8	TH	0102	6.4	0828	1.3	1320	6.5	2047	1.2
9	F	0131	6.4	0857	1.4	1352	6.5	2118	1.4
10	SA	0207	6.3	0931	1.6	1432	6.2	2154	1.7
11	SU	0252	5.9	1012	1.9	1522	5.8	◐ 2242	2.1
12	M	0352	5.4	1110	2.3	1645	5.3	2354	2.4
13	TU	0600	5.1	1246	2.5	1851	5.3		
14	W	0150	2.4	0736	5.4	1431	2.2	2013	5.6
15	TH	0316	2.0	0844	5.8	1548	1.7	2117	6.1
16	F	0425	1.5	0938	6.3	1654	1.2	2209	6.5
17	SA	0525	1.1	1024	6.7	1751	0.8	2254	6.8
18	SU	0617	0.8	1106	7.0	1842	0.5	○ 2333	6.9
19	M	0702	0.7	1145	7.2	1926	0.4		
20	TU	0009	6.9	0740	0.6	1224	7.2	2004	0.4
21	W	0045	6.8	0814	0.7	1302	7.1	2037	0.6
22	TH	0122	6.7	0845	0.9	1340	6.8	2108	1.0
23	F	0201	6.4	0914	1.2	1420	6.5	2136	1.4
24	SA	0244	6.1	0943	1.6	1504	6.0	2206	1.9
25	SU	0336	5.6	1017	2.1	1601	5.5	◑ 2244	2.4
26	M	0441	5.3	1110	2.5	1713	5.1		
27	TU	0005	2.8	0559	5.0	1259	2.7	1841	5.0
28	W	0149	2.8	0731	5.2	1432	2.5	2028	5.2
29	TH	0308	2.4	0843	5.6	1541	2.1	2119	5.6
30	F	0407	2.0	0928	5.9	1630	1.7	2153	5.9

OCTOBER

Date	Day	Time	m	Time	m	Time	m	Time	m
1	SA	0452	1.7	1001	6.2	1709	1.4	2220	6.2
2	SU	0529	1.5	1031	6.4	1743	1.2	2246	6.3
3	M	0600	1.3	1058	6.5	1815	1.1	● 2313	6.4
4	TU	0630	1.3	1126	6.6	1848	1.1	2340	6.5
5	W	0700	1.2	1153	6.6	1920	1.1		
6	TH	0005	6.5	0731	1.2	1221	6.6	1950	1.1
7	F	0033	6.6	0802	1.3	1251	6.6	2020	1.3
8	SA	0106	6.5	0834	1.4	1327	6.5	2053	1.5
9	SU	0145	6.3	0910	1.6	1409	6.2	2133	1.8
10	M	0234	5.9	0956	2.0	1507	5.7	◐ 2224	2.2
11	TU	0347	5.4	1100	2.3	1704	5.3	2344	2.5
12	W	0554	5.2	1244	2.4	1846	5.4		
13	TH	0141	2.4	0719	5.5	1421	2.0	2002	5.7
14	F	0303	1.9	0825	6.0	1534	1.5	2102	6.2
15	SA	0407	1.5	0917	6.4	1636	1.1	2150	6.5
16	SU	0502	1.1	1001	6.8	1730	0.7	2231	6.7
17	M	0550	0.9	1042	7.0	1816	0.6	○ 2308	6.8
18	TU	0631	0.8	1121	7.1	1857	0.6	2343	6.9
19	W	0708	0.8	1158	7.0	1933	0.7		
20	TH	0018	6.8	0741	0.9	1235	6.9	2003	0.9
21	F	0055	6.6	0812	1.1	1312	6.7	2031	1.3
22	SA	0133	6.4	0840	1.4	1351	6.3	2056	1.6
23	SU	0215	6.1	0908	1.7	1435	5.9	2124	2.0
24	M	0305	5.7	0943	2.1	1533	5.4	2202	2.4
25	TU	0408	5.4	1033	2.5	1644	5.1	◑ 2302	2.8
26	W	0520	5.1	1211	2.7	1802	5.0		
27	TH	0103	2.8	0639	5.2	1346	2.5	1928	5.2
28	F	0223	2.5	0752	5.5	1451	2.1	2027	5.5
29	SA	0321	2.2	0841	5.8	1540	1.8	2105	5.8
30	SU	0407	1.8	0916	6.1	1623	1.5	2136	6.1
31	M	0446	1.6	0947	6.3	1702	1.3	2206	6.3

NOVEMBER

Date	Day	Time	m	Time	m	Time	m	Time	m
1	TU	0523	1.4	1017	6.5	1740	1.2	2236	6.4
2	W	0558	1.3	1048	6.6	1817	1.1	● 2306	6.5
3	TH	0633	1.2	1121	6.7	1853	1.1	2337	6.6
4	F	0708	1.2	1154	6.7	1927	1.2		
5	SA	0012	6.6	0743	1.3	1232	6.6	2001	1.3
6	SU	0052	6.5	0820	1.4	1314	6.4	2039	1.5
7	M	0138	6.3	0903	1.6	1406	6.1	2125	1.8
8	TU	0237	5.9	0955	1.9	1520	5.7	2222	2.1
9	W	0400	5.6	1106	2.1	1702	5.5	◐ 2346	2.3
10	TH	0531	5.5	1236	2.1	1827	5.5		
11	F	0119	2.2	0650	5.7	1357	1.8	1938	5.8
12	SA	0233	1.9	0755	6.0	1506	1.4	2036	6.1
13	SU	0335	1.5	0849	6.4	1607	1.1	2124	6.3
14	M	0430	1.3	0935	6.6	1701	0.9	2205	6.5
15	TU	0519	1.1	1017	6.8	1748	0.9	2243	6.6
16	W	0602	1.0	1057	6.8	1828	0.9	○ 2319	6.6
17	TH	0640	1.0	1136	6.7	1903	1.0	2357	6.6
18	F	0714	1.1	1214	6.6	1933	1.2		
19	SA	0035	6.5	0746	1.3	1252	6.4	2001	1.5
20	SU	0114	6.4	0816	1.5	1331	6.1	2027	1.7
21	M	0155	6.2	0847	1.7	1414	5.8	2058	2.0
22	TU	0239	5.9	0924	2.0	1505	5.5	2138	2.3
23	W	0331	5.6	1011	2.2	1607	5.2	◑ 2229	2.5
24	TH	0432	5.4	1116	2.4	1714	5.1	2342	2.6
25	F	0539	5.3	1237	2.4	1823	5.1		
26	SA	0111	2.6	0644	5.4	1346	2.2	1922	5.3
27	SU	0218	2.3	0739	5.6	1442	1.9	2010	5.6
28	M	0312	2.1	0823	5.9	1533	1.7	2050	5.9
29	TU	0401	1.8	0901	6.1	1621	1.4	2126	6.1
30	W	0446	1.6	0939	6.3	1707	1.3	2203	6.3

DECEMBER

Date	Day	Time	m	Time	m	Time	m	Time	m
1	TH	0530	1.4	1017	6.5	1751	1.2	● 2240	6.5
2	F	0611	1.2	1057	6.6	1832	1.1	2320	6.6
3	SA	0652	1.2	1139	6.6	1913	1.2		
4	SU	0003	6.6	0734	1.2	1225	6.5	1954	1.3
5	M	0050	6.6	0818	1.2	1315	6.4	2039	1.4
6	TU	0142	6.4	0908	1.4	1412	6.1	2130	1.6
7	W	0241	6.2	1004	1.5	1521	5.9	2228	1.8
8	TH	0346	6.0	1107	1.6	1637	5.7	◐ 2333	1.9
9	F	0455	5.9	1213	1.7	1752	5.7		
10	SA	0041	1.9	0607	5.9	1320	1.6	1900	5.7
11	SU	0148	1.9	0715	5.9	1424	1.5	2000	5.8
12	M	0251	1.7	0815	6.1	1529	1.4	2053	6.0
13	TU	0353	1.6	0908	6.2	1629	1.3	2140	6.1
14	W	0449	1.4	0956	6.3	1720	1.3	2223	6.3
15	TH	0536	1.3	1040	6.4	1803	1.3	○ 2303	6.4
16	F	0618	1.3	1122	6.4	1839	1.3	2343	6.4
17	SA	0655	1.3	1201	6.3	1912	1.4		
18	SU	0021	6.4	0729	1.4	1239	6.2	1942	1.5
19	M	0100	6.4	0802	1.5	1316	6.1	2012	1.7
20	TU	0136	6.2	0835	1.6	1354	5.9	2044	1.8
21	W	0212	6.1	0911	1.7	1432	5.7	2121	1.9
22	TH	0248	5.9	0951	1.8	1514	5.5	2203	2.1
23	F	0329	5.7	1036	2.0	1604	5.3	◑ 2250	2.2
24	SA	0420	5.5	1129	2.1	1707	5.2	2347	2.4
25	SU	0523	5.4	1233	2.1	1814	5.2		
26	M	0058	2.4	0629	5.4	1341	2.1	1914	5.4
27	TU	0212	2.3	0728	5.6	1445	1.9	2006	5.6
28	W	0316	2.0	0821	5.9	1544	1.7	2054	5.9
29	TH	0414	1.7	0910	6.1	1640	1.4	2140	6.1
30	F	0506	1.4	0959	6.4	1731	1.2	2227	6.4
31	SA	0555	1.2	1047	6.5	1820	1.1	● 2314	6.6

Chart Datum: 3·67 metres below Ordnance Datum (Newlyn)

9.3.14 DOVER STRAIT

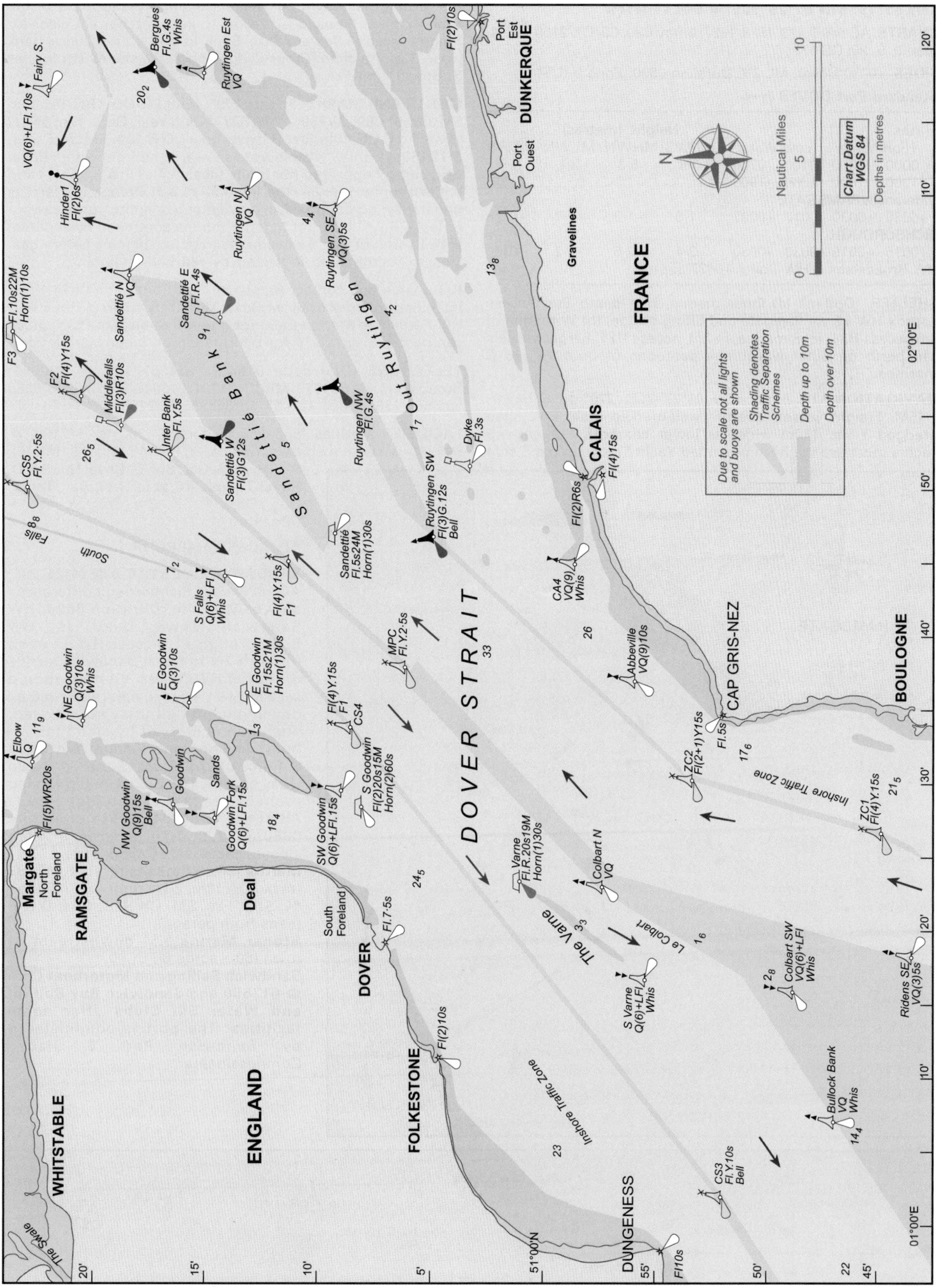
DOVER STRAIT
ENGLAND
FRANCE
WHITSTABLE
RAMSGATE
Margate
North Foreland
Deal
South Foreland
DOVER
FOLKESTONE
DUNGENESS
DUNKERQUE
Port Est
Port Ouest
Gravelines
CALAIS
CAP GRIS-NEZ
BOULOGNE
The Swale
Goodwin Sands
Sandettié Bank
Out Ruytingen
The Varne
Le Colbart
Inshore Traffic Zone
Falls
South Falls
Elbow Q
NE Goodwin Q(3)10s Whis
E Goodwin Q(3)10s
E Goodwin Fl.15s21M Horn(1)30s
NW Goodwin Q(9)15s Bell
Goodwin Fork Q(6)+LFl.15s
SW Goodwin Q(6)+LFl.15s
S Goodwin Fl(2)20s15M Horn(2)60s
Fl(4)Y.15s F1 CS4
MPC Fl.Y.2·5s
S Falls Q(6)+LFl Whis
Fl(4)Y.15s F1
Sandettié Fl.5s24M Horn(1)30s
Ruytingen SW Fl(3)G.12s Bell
Dyke Fl.3s
Inter Bank Fl.Y.5s
Sandettié W Fl(3)G12s
Middlefalls Fl(3)R10s
F2 Fl(4)Y15s
F3 Fl.10s22M Horn(1)10s
CS5 Fl.Y.2·5s
Sandettié N VQ
Sandettié E Fl.R.4s
Ruytingen NW Fl.G.4s
Ruytingen N VQ
Ruytingen SE VQ(3)5s
Hinder1 Fl(2)6s
VQ(6)+LFl.10s Fairy S.
Bergues Fl.G.4s Whis
Ruytingen Est VQ
Fl(2)10s
Fl(2)R6s
Fl(4)15s
CA4 VQ(9) Whis
Abbeville VQ(9)10s
Fl.5s
ZC2 Fl(2+1)Y15s
ZC1 Fl(4)Y.15s
Varne Fl.R.20s19M Horn(1)30s
Colbart N VQ
S Varne Q(6)+LFl Whis
Colbart SW VQ(6)+LFl Whis
Ridens SE VQ(3)5s
Bullock Bank VQ Whis
CS3 Fl.Y.10s Bell
Fl(5)WR20s
Fl.7·5s
Fl(2)10s
Fl10s
Due to scale not all lights and buoys are shown
Shading denotes Traffic Separation Schemes
Depth up to 10m
Depth over 10m
Nautical Miles
0
5
10
N
Chart Datum WGS 84
Depths in metres
01°00'E
10'
20'
30'
40'
50'
02°00'E
51°00'N
55'
50'
45'
5'
10'
15'
20'

9.3.15 RAMSGATE

Kent **51°19′·51N 01°25′·50E** ❁❁❁◊◊◊✿✿✿

CHARTS AC *5605, 323, 1828,* 1827; Imray C30, C8, C1, 2100 series; Stan 9, 5, 20; OS 179

TIDES +0030 Dover; ML 2·7; Duration 0530; Zone 0 (UT)

Standard Port DOVER (⟵)

Times				Height (metres)			
High Water		Low Water		MHWS	MHWN	MLWN	MLWS
0000	0600	0100	0700	6·8	5·3	2·1	0·8
1200	1800	1300	1900				
Differences RAMSGATE							
+0030	+0030	+0017	+0007	−1·6	−1·3	−0·7	−0·2
RICHBOROUGH							
+0015	+0015	+0030	+0030	−3·4	−2·6	−1·7	−0·7

HW Broadstairs = HW Dover +0037 approx.

SHELTER Options (a) inner marina, min depth 3m. Access approx HW ±2 via flap gate and lifting bridge, (b) W marina in 3m access H24, (c) E marina, in 2m, access H24. Larger vessels can berth on outer wavebreak pontoons of both W and E marinas.

NAVIGATION WPT 51°19′·43N 01°27′·70E, 270° to S bkwtr, 1·45M. Freight vessels use the well-marked main E-W chan dredged 7·5m, 110m wide; as lower chartlet). For ent/dep yachts must use the Recommended Yacht Track on the S side of the main buoyed chan. Ent/dep under power, or advise Port Control if unable to motor. Ent/dep Royal Hbr directly; cross the turning basin without delay. Holding area to the S of the S bkwtr must be used by yachts to keep the hbr ent clear for freight vessels. Beware Dike Bank to the N and Quern Bank close S of the chan. Cross Ledge and Brake shoals are further S. Speed limit 5kn.

LIGHTS AND MARKS Ldg lts 270°: front Dir Oc WRG 10s 10m 5M, G259°-269°, W269°-271°, R271°-281°; rear, Oc 5s 17m 5M. N bkwtr hd = QG 10m 5M; S bkwtr hd = VQ R 10m 5M. At E Pier, **IPTS** (Sigs 2 and 3) visible from seaward and from within Royal Hbr, control appr into hbr limits (abeam Nos 1 & 2 buoys) and ent/exit to/from Royal Hbr. In addition a Fl Orange lt = ferry is under way; no other vessel may enter Hbr limits from seaward or leave Royal Hbr. Ent to inner marina controlled by separate IPTS to stbd of ent. Siren sounded approx 10 mins before gate closes; non-opening indicated by red ball or light.

R/T Listen and contact *Ramsgate Port Control* on Ch14 when intending to enter or leave Royal Hbr. Only when in Royal Hbr call *Ramsgate Marina* Ch80 for a berth. Ramsgate Dock Office can be called on Ch14 for information on Inner Marina Lock.

TELEPHONE (Dial code 01843) HM 572100, 📠 590941; Broadstairs HM 861879; MRCC (01304) 210008; Marinecall 09068 500 455/456; Police 222053; Dr 852853; Ⓗ 225544.

FACILITIES Marinas (500+300 visitors) £1.70, ☎ 572100, 📠 590941, www. ramsgatemarina.co.uk, BH (40 ton), Ⓔ, ME, El, ⚒, CH, ACA, Gaz, SM, ▣; **Royal Hbr** P & D. **Royal Temple YC** ☎ 591766, Bar. **Town**; Gas, Gaz, 🛒, R, Bar, ✉, Ⓑ, ⇌, ✈ (Manston).

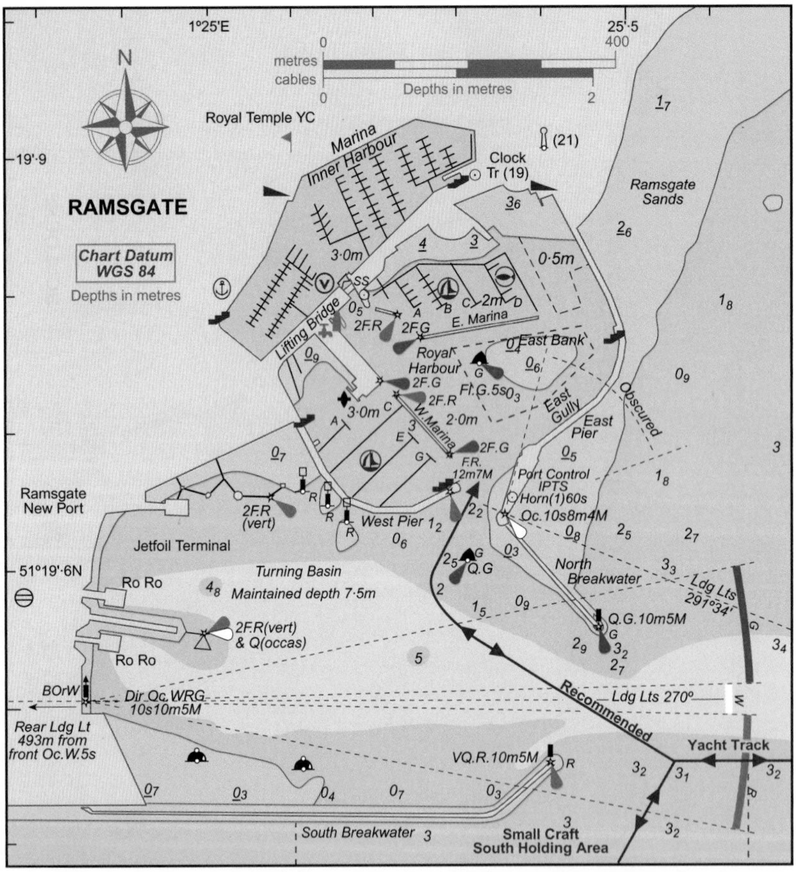

1°25′E
25′·5
metres
cables
0
400
2
Depths in metres
N
Royal Temple YC
Marina
Inner Harbour
Clock Tr (19)
(21)
RAMSGATE
Chart Datum WGS 84
Depths in metres
Ramsgate Sands
3·0m
0·5m
Lifting Bridge
2F.R
2F.G
E. Marina
Royal Harbour
East Bank
Fl.G.5s
East Gully
W. Marina
East Pier
Obscured
3·0m
2·0m
2F.G
F.R. 12m7M
Port Control IPTS
Horn(1)60s
Oc.10s8m4M
Ramsgate New Port
2F.R (vert)
West Pier
Jetfoil Terminal
51°19′·6N
Ro Ro
Turning Basin
Maintained depth 7·5m
North Breakwater
Ldg Lts 291°34′
Q.G
Q.G.10m5M
2F.R(vert) & Q(occas)
Ro Ro
BOrW
Dir.Oc.WRG 10s10m5M
Rear Ldg Lt 493m from front Oc.W.5s
Recommended
Ldg Lts 270°
Yacht Track
VQ.R.10m5M
South Breakwater
Small Craft South Holding Area
19′·9

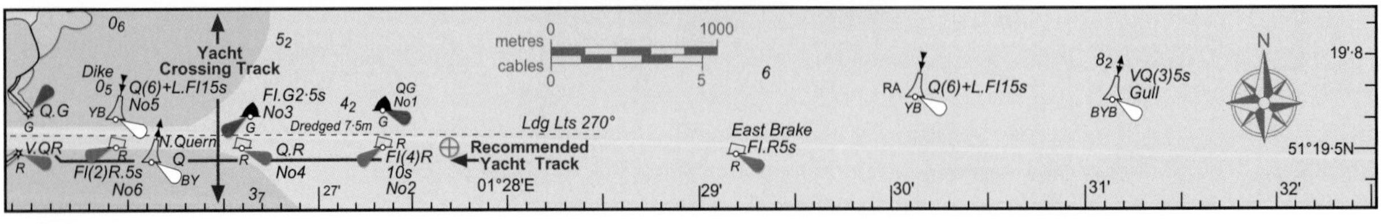

Yacht Crossing Track
Dike
Q(6)+L.Fl15s
No5
Q.G
Fl.G2·5s
No3
QG
No1
Dredged 7·5m
Ldg Lts 270°
metres
cables
0
1000
5
N.Quern
VQR
Fl(2)R.5s
No6
Q.R
No4
Fl(4)R 10s
No2
Recommended Yacht Track
01°28′E
East Brake
Fl.R5s
Q(6)+L.Fl15s
VQ(3)5s
Gull
N
19′·8
51°19·5N
27′
29′
30′
31′
32′

ADJACENT HARBOUR

SANDWICH, Kent, **51°16′·83N 01°21′·20E.** AC 1827 *1828*. Richborough differences above; ML 1·4m; Duration 0520. HW Sandwich Town quay is HW Richborough +1. Access HW ±1 at sp for draft 2m to reach Sandwich; arrive off ent at HW Dover. Visitors should seek local knowledge before arriving by day; night ent definitely not advised. The chan is marked by small lateral buoys and beacons. Visitors' berths on S bank of the River Stour at Town Quay ☎ (01304) 612162. Limited turning room before the swing bridge (opens 1H notice ☎ 01304 620644 or Mobile 0860 378792, 1·7m clearance when closed. Facilities: EC Wed; Slip;
Marina (50 + some visitors) ☎ 613783 (max LOA 18m, 2·1m draft), BH (15 ton), ⚒, Slip, FW, SM, CH, ME, Gas; D & P (cans from garage);
Stonar Marina ½M downstream of town (50 + some Ⓥ) £1.00.
Sandwich Sailing and Motorboat Club ☎ 617650 and **Sandwich Bay Sailing and Water Ski Clubs** offer some facilities. The port is administered by Sandwich Port & Haven Commissioners.

Area 4

East England
North Foreland to Great Yarmouth

9.4.2

East England

North Foreland to Great Yarmouth

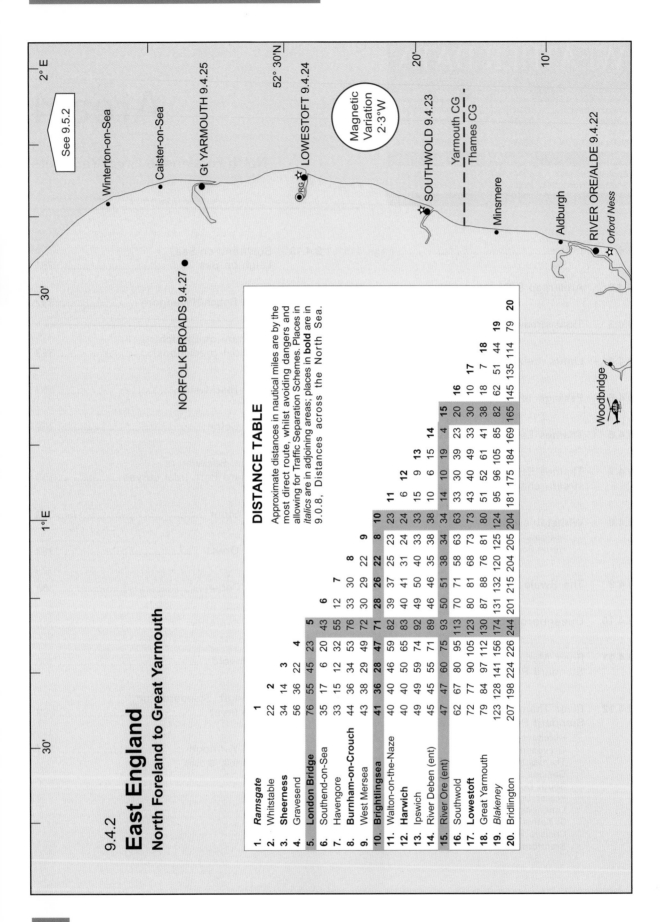

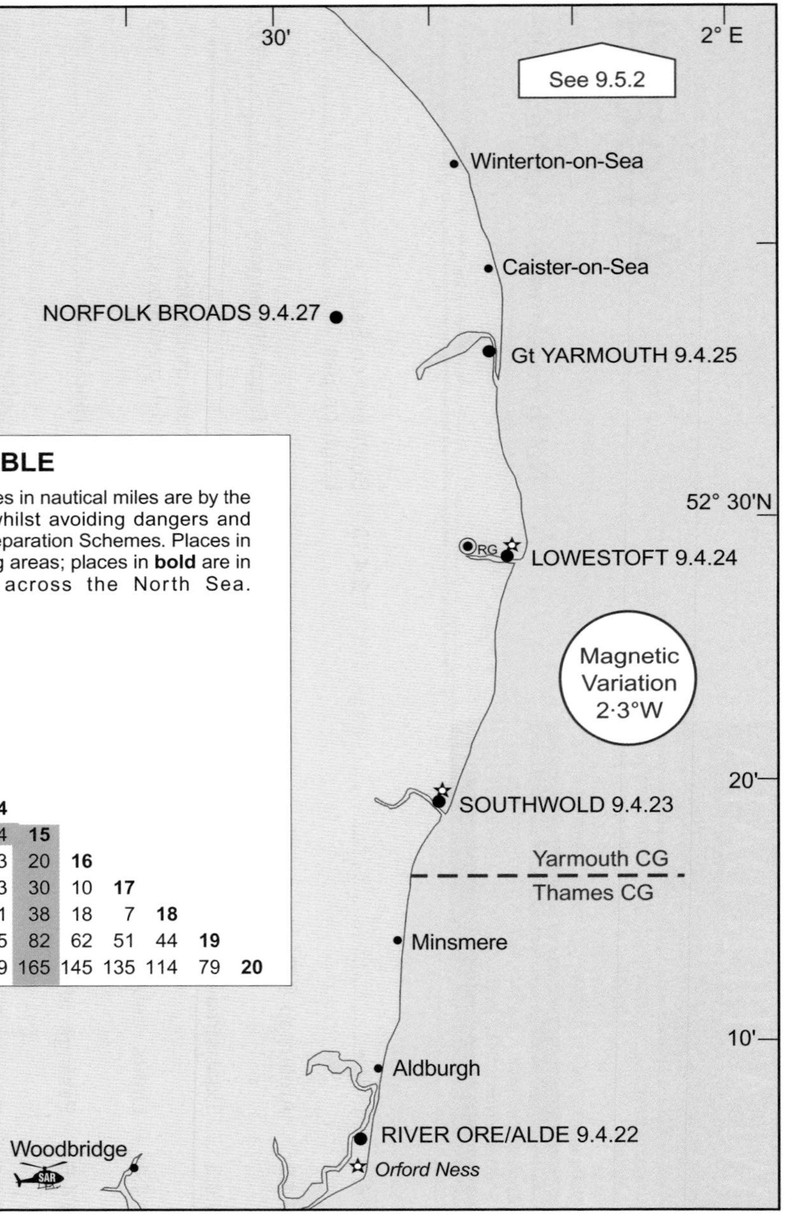
30'
1° E
30'
2° E
See 9.5.2
Winterton-on-Sea
Caister-on-Sea
NORFOLK BROADS 9.4.27
Gt YARMOUTH 9.4.25
52° 30'N
RG
LOWESTOFT 9.4.24
Magnetic Variation 2·3°W
20'
SOUTHWOLD 9.4.23
Yarmouth CG
Thames CG
Minsmere
10'
Aldburgh
RIVER ORE/ALDE 9.4.22
Orford Ness
Woodbridge
SAR

DISTANCE TABLE

Approximate distances in nautical miles are by the most direct route, whilst avoiding dangers and allowing for Traffic Separation Schemes. Places in *italics* are in adjoining areas; places in **bold** are in 9.0.8, Distances across the North Sea.

1.	***Ramsgate***	**1**																		
2.	Whitstable	22	**2**																	
3.	**Sheerness**	34	14	**3**																
4.	Gravesend	56	36	22	**4**															
5.	**London Bridge**	76	55	45	23	**5**														
6.	Southend-on-Sea	35	17	6	20	43	**6**													
7.	Havengore	33	15	12	32	55	12	**7**												
8.	**Burnham-on-Crouch**	44	36	34	53	76	33	30	**8**											
9.	West Mersea	43	38	29	49	72	30	29	22	**9**										
10.	**Brightlingsea**	**41**	**36**	**28**	**47**	**71**	**28**	**26**	**22**	**8**	**10**									
11.	Walton-on-the-Naze	40	40	46	59	82	39	37	25	23	23	**11**								
12.	**Harwich**	40	40	50	65	83	40	41	31	24	24	6	**12**							
13.	Ipswich	49	49	59	74	92	49	50	40	33	33	15	9	**13**						
14.	River Deben (ent)	45	45	55	71	89	46	46	35	38	38	10	6	15	**14**					
15.	River Ore (ent)	47	47	60	75	93	50	51	38	34	34	14	10	19	4	**15**				
16.	Southwold	62	67	80	95	113	70	71	58	63	63	33	30	39	23	20	**16**			
17.	**Lowestoft**	72	77	90	105	123	80	81	68	73	73	43	40	49	33	30	10	**17**		
18.	Great Yarmouth	79	84	97	112	130	87	88	76	81	80	51	52	61	41	38	18	7	**18**	
19.	*Blakeney*	123	128	141	156	174	131	132	120	125	124	95	96	105	85	82	62	51	44	**19**
20.	Bridlington	207	198	224	226	244	201	215	204	205	204	181	175	184	169	165	145	135	114	79	**20**

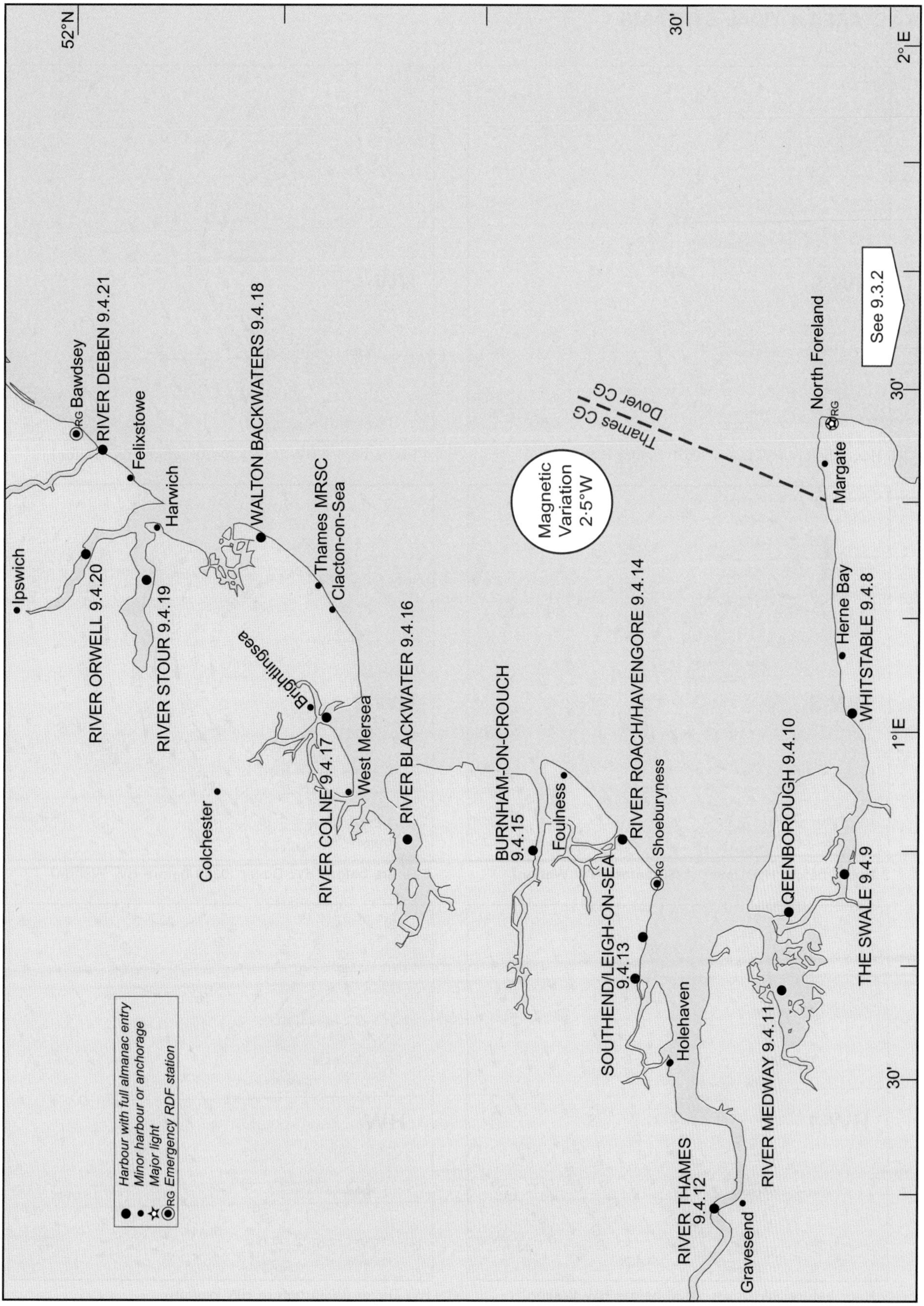
52°N
30'
2° E
30'
1°E
30'
Ipswich
RIVER ORWELL 9.4.20
RIVER STOUR 9.4.19
RG Bawdsey
RIVER DEBEN 9.4.21
Felixstowe
Harwich
WALTON BACKWATERS 9.4.18
Thames MRSC
Clacton-on-Sea
Brightlingsea
Colchester
RIVER COLNE 9.4.17
West Mersea
RIVER BLACKWATER 9.4.16
BURNHAM-ON-CROUCH
9.4.15
Foulness
RIVER ROACH/HAVENGORE 9.4.14
RG Shoeburyness
SOUTHEND/LEIGH-ON-SEA
9.4.13
Holehaven
RIVER THAMES
9.4.12
Gravesend
RIVER MEDWAY 9.4.11
QEENBOROUGH 9.4.10
THE SWALE 9.4.9
WHITSTABLE 9.4.8
Herne Bay
Margate
North Foreland
RG
Magnetic
Variation
2·5°W
Thames CG
Dover CG
See 9.3.2
Harbour with full almanac entry
Minor harbour or anchorage
Major light
RG Emergency RDF station

9.4.3 AREA 4 TIDAL STREAMS

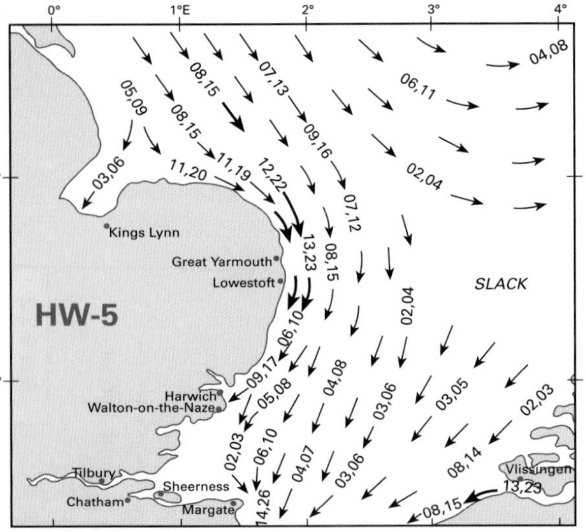
0°
1°E
2°
3°
4°
53°
52°
Kings Lynn
Great Yarmouth
Lowestoft
Harwich
Walton-on-the-Naze
Tilbury
Sheerness
Chatham
Margate
Vlissingen
HW-5
SLACK

5 Hours before HW Dover (0530 before HW Walton)

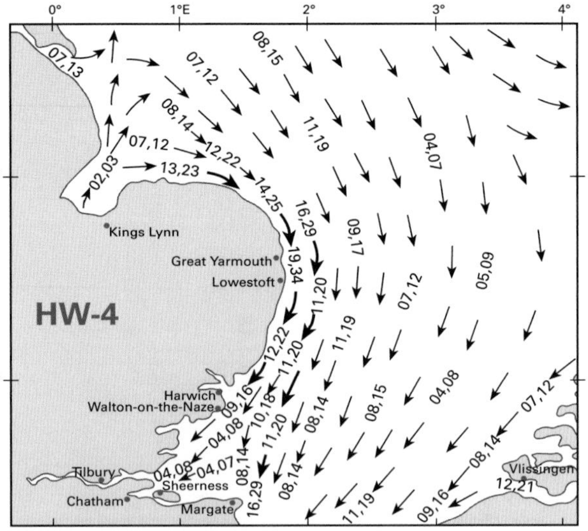
0°
1°E
2°
3°
4°
53°
52°
Kings Lynn
Great Yarmouth
Lowestoft
Harwich
Walton-on-the-Naze
Tilbury
Sheerness
Chatham
Margate
Vlissingen
HW-4

4 Hours before HW Dover (0430 before HW Walton)

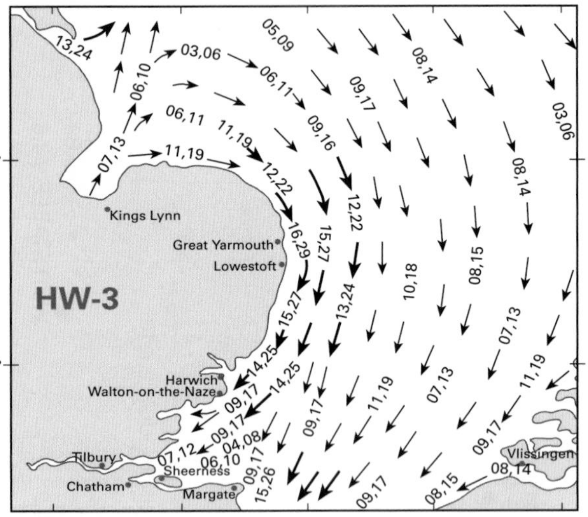
53°
52°
Kings Lynn
Great Yarmouth
Lowestoft
Harwich
Walton-on-the-Naze
Tilbury
Sheerness
Chatham
Margate
Vlissingen
HW-3

3 Hours before HW Dover (0330 before HW Walton)

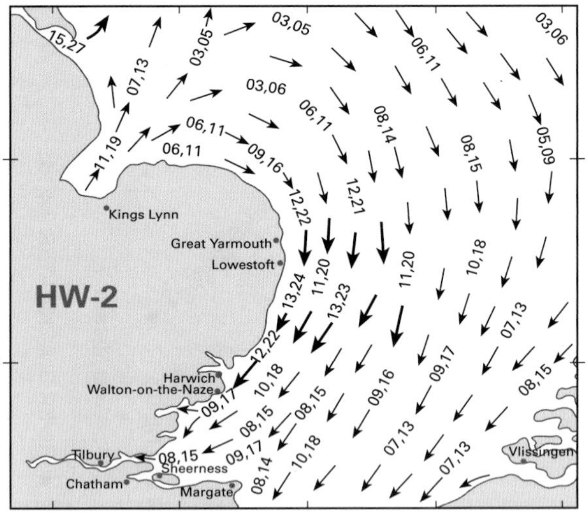
53°
52°
Kings Lynn
Great Yarmouth
Lowestoft
Harwich
Walton-on-the-Naze
Tilbury
Sheerness
Chatham
Margate
Vlissingen
HW-2

2 Hours before HW Dover (0230 before HW Walton)

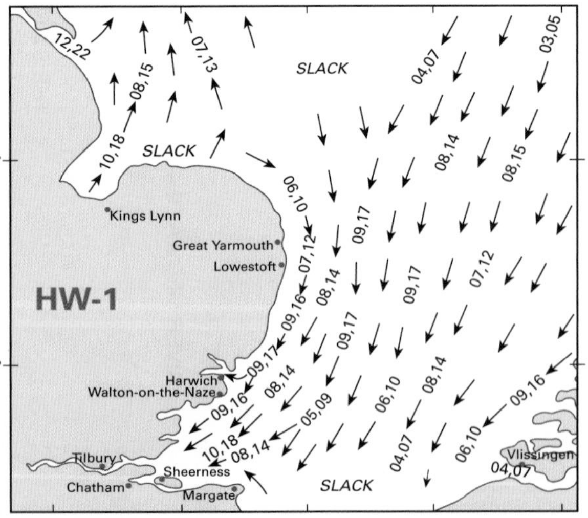
53°
52°
Kings Lynn
Great Yarmouth
Lowestoft
Harwich
Walton-on-the-Naze
Tilbury
Sheerness
Chatham
Margate
Vlissingen
HW-1
SLACK
SLACK
SLACK

1 Hour before HW Dover (0130 before HW Walton)

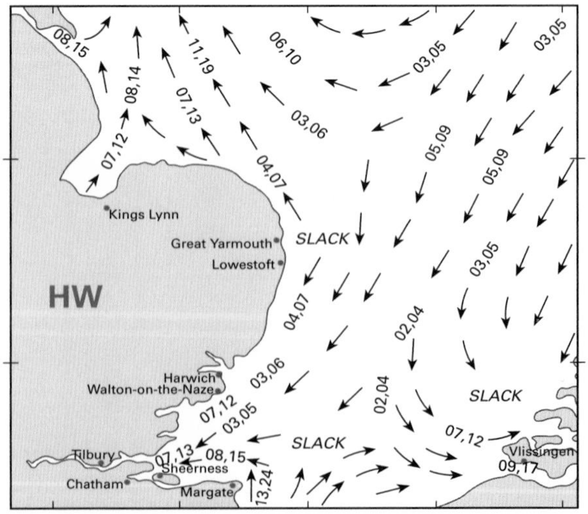
53°
52°
Kings Lynn
Great Yarmouth
Lowestoft
Harwich
Walton-on-the-Naze
Tilbury
Sheerness
Chatham
Margate
Vlissingen
HW
SLACK
SLACK
SLACK

HW Dover (0030 before HW Walton)

Southward 9.3.3 Thames Estuary 9.4.7 Northward 9.5.3 Eastward 9.16.3

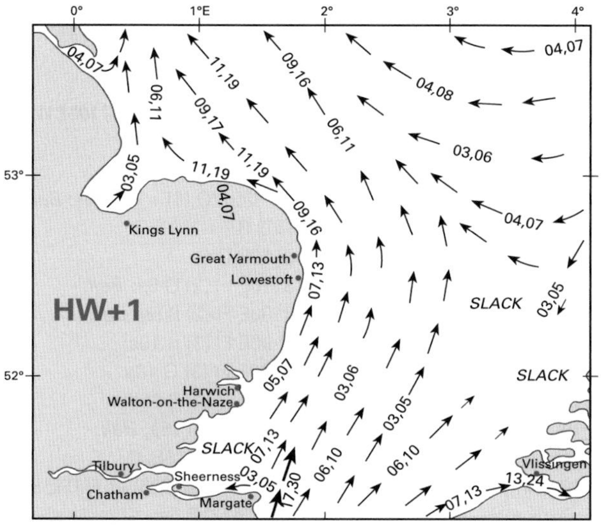
HW+1
0°
1°E
2°
3°
4°
53°
52°
Kings Lynn
Great Yarmouth
Lowestoft
Harwich
Walton-on-the-Naze
Tilbury
Sheerness
Chatham
Margate
Vlissingen
SLACK

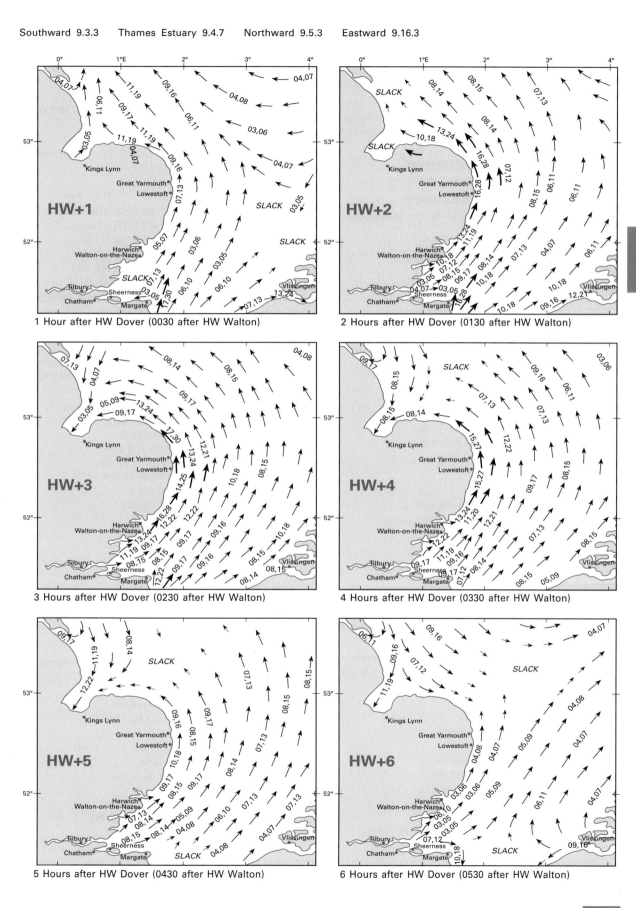

1 Hour after HW Dover (0030 after HW Walton)

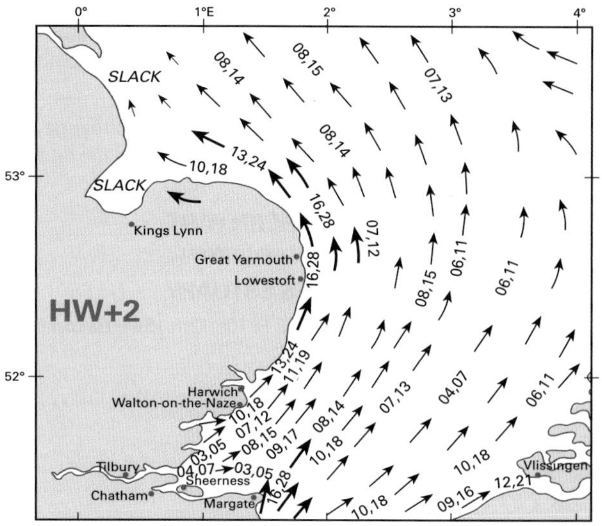
HW+2
0°
1°E
2°
3°
4°
53°
52°
Kings Lynn
Great Yarmouth
Lowestoft
Harwich
Walton-on-the-Naze
Tilbury
Sheerness
Chatham
Margate
Vlissingen
SLACK

2 Hours after HW Dover (0130 after HW Walton)

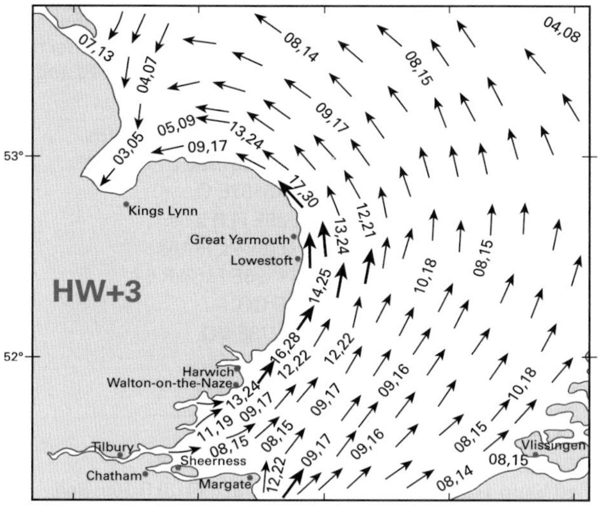
HW+3
53°
52°
Kings Lynn
Great Yarmouth
Lowestoft
Harwich
Walton-on-the-Naze
Tilbury
Sheerness
Chatham
Margate
Vlissingen

3 Hours after HW Dover (0230 after HW Walton)

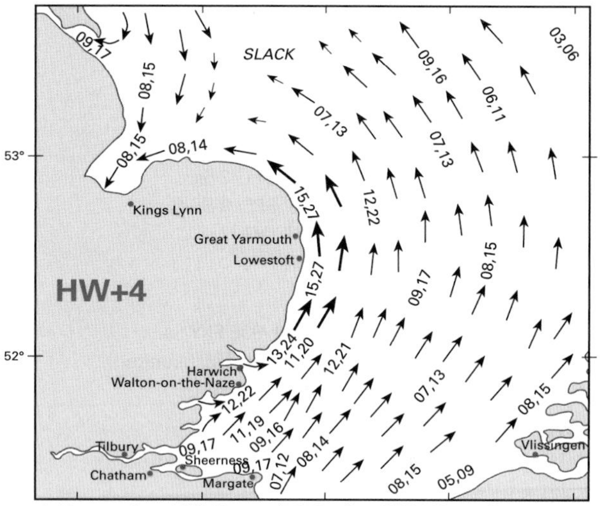
HW+4
53°
52°
Kings Lynn
Great Yarmouth
Lowestoft
Harwich
Walton-on-the-Naze
Tilbury
Sheerness
Chatham
Margate
Vlissingen
SLACK

4 Hours after HW Dover (0330 after HW Walton)

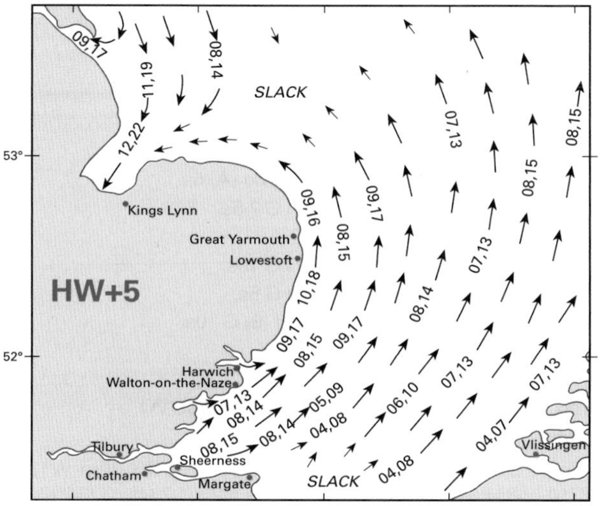
HW+5
53°
52°
Kings Lynn
Great Yarmouth
Lowestoft
Harwich
Walton-on-the-Naze
Tilbury
Sheerness
Chatham
Margate
Vlissingen
SLACK

5 Hours after HW Dover (0430 after HW Walton)

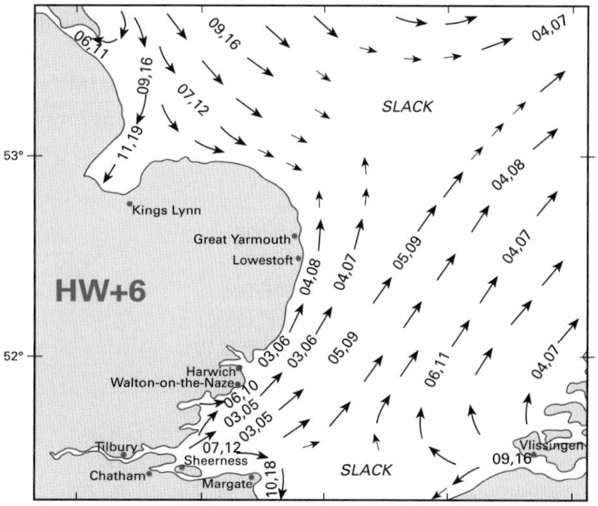
HW+6
53°
52°
Kings Lynn
Great Yarmouth
Lowestoft
Harwich
Walton-on-the-Naze
Tilbury
Sheerness
Chatham
Margate
Vlissingen
SLACK

6 Hours after HW Dover (0530 after HW Walton)

PLOT WAYPOINTS ON YOUR CHART BEFORE USING THEM

9.4.4 LIGHTS, BUOYS AND WAYPOINTS

Blue print = light with a nominal range of 15M or more. CAPITALS = place or feature. *CAPITAL ITALICS* = light-vessel, light float or Lanby. *Italics* = Fog signal. ***Bold italics*** = Racon. Useful waypoints are underlined. Abbreviations are in Chapter 1.

IMPORTANT NOTE. Changes are regularly made to buoyage in the Thames Estuary. Check Notices to Mariners for the latest information.

THAMES ESTUARY – SOUTHERN PART
(Direction of buoyage generally East to West)

▶ APPROACHES TO THAMES ESTUARY

Foxtrot 3 ⊏ 51°23'·85N 02°00'·51E Fl 10s 12m 15M; ***Racon (T) 10M***; *Horn 10s.*

Falls Hd ↕ 51°28'·23N 01°49'·89E Q.
Drill Stone ↕ 51°25'·88N 01°42'·89E Q (3) 10s *Bell.*
NE Spit ↕ 51°27'·93N 01°29'·89E VQ (3) 5s.
East Margate ⌿ 51°27'·03N 01°26'·40E Fl R 2·5s.
Elbow ↕ 51°23'·23N 01°31'·59E Q.
Foreness Pt Outfall ⌿ 51°24'·61N 01°26'·02E Fl R 5s.
Longnose ⌿ 51°24'·15N 01°26'·08E.
Longnose Spit ↕ 51°23'·92N 01°25'·75E.

▶ MARGATE
Stone Pier Hd ⌿ 51°23'·45N 01°22'·69E FR 18m 4M.

▶ GORE CHANNEL
SE Margate ↕ 51°24'·05N 01°20'·40E Q (3) 10s.
S Margate ▲ 51°23'·83N 01°16'·65E Fl G 2·5s.
Plum Pudding ⌂ 51°22'·97N 01°15'·62E; R Buoy.
Hook Spit ▲ 51°24'·08N 01°12'·26E QG.
E Last ⌿ 51°24'·06N 01°11'·84E QR.

▶ HERNE BAY
Beltinge Bay Bn ↕ 51°22'·73N 01°08'·63E Fl Y 5s.
Pier Hd ⌿ 51°22'·91N 01°06'·89E Q 18m 4M, (isolated).
N Pier Hd ⌿ 51°22'·43N 01°07'·27E 2 FR (vert).

▶ WHITSTABLE
Whitstable Street ↕ 51°23'·85N 01°01'·59E Q.
Oyster ⌿ 51°22'·14N 01°01'·16E Fl (2) R 10s.
NE Arm ⌿ 51°21'·84N 01°01'·58E F 15m 8M; W mast; also FR 10m 5M (same structure) shown when ent/dep prohib.
W Quay Dn ⌿ 51°21'·85N 01°01'·46E Fl WRG 5s 2m W5M, R3M, G3M; vis: W118°-156°, G156°-178°, R178°-201°.
E Quay, N End ⌿ 51°21'·86N 01°01'·51E 2 FR (vert) 4m 1M.
S Quay ⌿ Dir lt122°. 51°21'·76N 01°01·70E Dir Oc WRG 5s 7m: vis: G 117·5°-120·5°, W120·5°-123·5°, R 3s 123·5°-126·5°.

▶ THE SWALE
Columbine ▲ 51°24'·26N 01°01'·35E.
Columbine Spit ▲ 51°23'·86N 01°00'·03E.
Ham Gat ▲ 51°23'·08N 00°58'·32E.
Pollard Spit ⌿ 51°22'·98N 00° 58'·57E QR.
Sand End ▲ 51°21'·43N 00°55'·90E Fl G 5s.
Horse Sand ▲ 51°20'·86N 00°54'·41E Fl G 10s.
Faversham Spit ↕ 51°20'·77N 00°54'·19E.
Fowley Spit ↕ 51°21'·50N 00°51'·47E Q (3) 10s.
Queenborough Hard S1 ⌿ 51°24'·99N 00°44'·18E Fl R 3s.
Queenborough Pt (S) ⌿ 51°25'·34N 00°44'·03E Fl R 4s.
Queenborough Pt (N) ⌿ 51°25'·45N 00°44'·00E QR 3m 2M.
Queenborough Spit ↕ 51°25'·81N 00°43'·93E Q (3) 10s.

▶ QUEENS CHANNEL/FOUR FATHOMS CHANNEL
E Margate ⌿ 51°27'·03N 01°26'·40E Fl R 2·5s.
Spaniard ↕ 51°26'·23N 01°04'·00E Q (3) 10s.
Spile ▲ 51°26'·43N 00°55'·70E Fl G 2·5s.

▶ PRINCES CHANNEL
Outer Tongue ↕ 51°30'·73N 01°26'·40E L Fl 10s; ***Racon (T) 10M***; *Whis.*
Tongue Sand E ↕ 51°29'·48N 01°22'·21E VQ (3) 5s.
Tongue Sand N ↕ 51°29'·68N 01°22'·03E Q.
Outer Princes ↕ 51°28'·97N 01°20'·62E VQ (6) + L Fl 10s; *Bell.*
Princes ⌿ 51°28'·74N 01°18'·26E VQ R.
Princes No.1 ▲ 51°29'·20N 01°16'·02E Q G
Princes No.3 ▲ 51°29'·33N 01°13'·10E Fl (2) G 5s; *Bell.*
Princes No.2 ⌿ 51°28'·81N 01°13'·08E Fl (2) R 5s; *Bell.*
Princes No.4 ⌿ 51°28'·83N 01°09'·90E Fl (3) R 10s.
Princes No.5 ▲ 51°29'·50N 01°09'·90E Fl (3) G 10s.
Princes No.6 ⌿ 51°29'·18N 01°06'·58E Fl (4) R 15s.
Princes No.7 ↕ 51°29'·58N 01°07'·11E Q (9) 15s; *Bell.*
Shivering Sand Twr N ↕ 51°30'·01N 01°04'·76E. Q.
Shivering Sand Twr S ↕ 51°29'·78N 01°04'·83E Q (6) + L Fl 15s; *Bell.*
E Redsand ⌿ 51°29'·41N 01°04'·05E Fl (2) R 5s.

▶ FOULGER'S GAT/KNOB CHANNEL
Note: The N Edinburgh Channel has silted and is no longer buoyed. Fisherman's Gat is the commercial ship channel but Foulger's Gat is now marked at either end with SWMs and is suitable for leisure craft - see below*.

Long Sand Inner* ⌿ 51°38'·77N 01°26'·00E Mo 'A' 15s.
Long Sand Outer* ⌿ 51°35'·87N 01°26'·58E L Fl 10s.
Shingles Patch ↕ 51°33'·01N 01°15'·37E Q.
N Shingles ⌿ 51°32'·79N 01°14'·25E Fl R 2·5s.
Tizard ↕ 51°32'·93N 01°12'·90E Q (6) + L Fl 15s.
Mid Shingles ⌿ 51°31'·96N 01°11'·98E Fl (2) R 5s.
NE Knob ▲ 51°32'·03N 01°10'·00E QG.
NW Shingles ↕ 51°31'·26N 01°09'·73E VQ.
SE Knob ▲ 51°30'·89N 01°06'·41E Fl G 5s.
Knob ↕ 51°30'·69N 01°04'·28E Iso 5s; *Bell.*

▶ OAZE DEEP
Oaze Deep ▲ 51°30'·03N 01°00'·70E Fl (2) G 5s.
Red Sand Trs N ⌿ 51°28'·73N 00°59'·32E Fl (3) R 10s; *Bell.*
N Oaze ⌿ 51°30'·03N 00°57'·65E QR.
SW Oaze ↕ 51°29'·06N 00°56'·93E Q (6) + L Fl 15s.
W Oaze ↕ 51°29'·06N 00°55'·43E Q (9) 15s.
Cant ⊥ 51°27'·77N 00°53'·36E (unlit).
East Cant ⌿ 51°28'·53N 00°55'·60E QR.
Mid Cant ↕ 51°26'·88N 00°49'·80E Q.

▶ MEDWAY, SHEERNESS
Medway ↕ 51°28'·83N 00°52'·81E Mo (A) 6s.
No. 1 ▲ 51°28'·55N 00°50'·50E Fl G 2·5s.
No. 2 ↕ 51°28'·33N 00°50'·52E Q.
No. 7 ▲ 51°27'·91N 00°47'·52E Fl G 10s.
No. 9 ▲ 51°27'·74N 00°46'·61E Fl G 5s.
No. 11 ▲ 51°27'·51N 00°45'·80E Fl (3) G 10s.
Grain Edge ▲ 51°27'·61N 00°45'·46E.
W Cant ⌿ 51°27'·20N 00°45'·48E QR.
Jacobs Bank Obstn ↕ 51°26'·97N 00°45'·18E VQ.
Grain Hard ▲ 51°26'·98N 00°44'·17E Fl G 5s.

Isle of Grain ☆ 51°26'·70N 00°43'·38E Q WRG 20m W13M, R7M, G8M; R & W ◇ on R twr; vis R220°-234°, G234°-241°, W241°-013°.

N. Kent 51°26'·14N 00°43'·46E QG.
S. Kent 51°25'·99N 00°43'·64E QR.
Queenborough Spit 51°25'·81N 00°43'·93E Q (3) 10s.
Victoria 51°25'·96N 00°42'·96E Fl (3) G 10s.
Z1 51°25'·78N 00°41'·61E Fl (2) 10s.
Z2 51°25'·64N 00°41'·64E Q.
Stangate Spit 51°25'·41N 00°41'·55E VQ (3) 5s.
Stoke No. 13 51°25'·76N 00°39'·81E Fl G 5s.
East Bulwark 51°25'·36N 00°39'·24E Fl (3) G 15s.
No. 15 51°24'·75N 00°38'·43E Fl G 10s.
Bishop No. 16 51°24'·71N 00°38'·78E Fl (2) R 10s.
No. 22 51°24'·51N 00°36'·08E Fl R 5s.
Darnett No. 23 51°24'·59N 00°35'·62E IQ G.
Darnett Ness No. 6 51°24'·45N 01°35'·73E QR 12m 3M.
Folly No. 25 51°24'·09N 00°35'·24E Fl (3) G 10s.
Gillingham Reach No. 27 51°23'·91N 00°34'·71E Fl G 10s.

RIVERTHAMES

▶ SEA REACH, NORE AND YANTLET

No. 1 51°29'·45N 00°52'·57E Fl Y 2·5s; ***Racon (T) 10M.***
No. 2 51°29'·40N 00°49'·75E Iso 5s.
No. 3 51°29'·33N 00°46'·54E L Fl 10s.
No. 4 51°29'·61N 00°44'·18E Fl Y 2·5s.
No. 5 51°29'·95N 00°41'·44E Iso 5s.
No. 6 51°30'·03N 00°39'·83E Iso 2s.
No. 7 51°30'·10N 00°37'·04E Fl Y 2·5s; ***Racon (T) 10M.***
Nore Swatch 51°28'·28N 00°45'·55E Fl (4) R 15s.
Mid Swatch 51°28'·68N 00°44'·16E Fl G 5s.
W Nore Sand 51°29'·41N 00°40'·85E Fl (3) R 10s.
East Blyth 51°29'·72N 00°37'·80E Fl (2) R 10s.
West Leigh Middle 51°30'·48N 00°38'·82E QG.
Chapman 51°30'·43N 00°36'·93E Fl (3) G 10s; *Bell.*
Scars Elbow 51°30'·33N 00°34'·57E Fl G 2·5s.
Mid Blyth 51°30'·08N 00°32'·38E Q.
Mucking No. 1 51°29'·85N 00°28'·44E QG; *Bell.*
Mucking No. 3 51°29'·34N 00°27'·68E Fl G 2·5s.
Mucking No. 7 51°28'·03N 00°26'·77E Fl G 5s.
Higham 51°27'·40N 00°26'·84E Fl (2) R 5s.
Ovens 51°27'·49N 00°26'·35E QG; *Bell.*
Tilbury 51°27'·16N 00°25'·49E Q (6) + L Fl 15s.
Diver 51°27'·08N 00°24'·56E L Fl G 10s.

▶ LEIGH-ON-SEA/SOUTHEND-ON-SEA

Leigh 51°31'·07N 00°42'·56E.

Southend Pier E End 51°30'·87N 00°43'·40E 2 FG (vert) 7m; *Horn Mo (N) 30s, Bell (1) 5s (reserve).*

Pier W Head 51°30·89N 00°43'·28E 2 FG (vert) 13m 8M.
West Shoebury 51°30'·23N 00°45'·73E Fl G 2·5s.
SE Leigh 51°29'·42N 00°47'·07E Q (6) + L Fl 15s.
Shoebury 51°30'·29N 00°49'·26E Fl (3) G 10s 5m 5M.
Inner Shoebury 51°30'·99N 00°49'·16E Fl Y 2·5s.
S Shoebury 51°30'·43N 00°52'·39E Fl G 5s.

▶ CANVEY ISLAND/HOLEHAVEN

Jetty Hd E end 51°30'·39N 00°34'·13E 2 FG (vert); *Bell 10s.*
W end 51°30'·39N 00°34'·05E 2 FG (vert) 13m 8M.

Shornmead 51°26'·92N 00°26'·24E Fl (2) WR 10s 12m 11/7M, W11M, W7M, R11M; vis W070°-084°, R(Intens)084°-089°, W(Intens)089°-094°, W094°-250°.

▶ GRAVESEND

Northfleet Upper 51°26'·93N 00°20'·06E Oc WRG 10s 30m **W16M**, R12M, G12M; vis: R126°-149°, W149°-159°, G159°-268°, W268°-279°. Tanker Warning Light also shown (occas) Iso 6s 30m 6M.

Broadness 51°28'·02N 00°18'·60E Oc R 5s 12m 12M.

QEII Bridge Centre 51°27'·88N 00°15'·52E Iso 10s 55m.

Crayford Ness 51°28'·94N 00°12'·71E Fl 5s 19m 14M and F 17m 3M.

Cross Ness 51°30'·78N 00°07'·71E Fl 5s 11m 8M.

▶ THAMES TIDAL BARRIER

Span B (51°29'·73N 00°02'·23E) is used for small craft/yachts Eastbound and Span G (51°29'·91N 00°02'·21E) is used for small craft/yachts Westbound. Spans B, C, D, E, F & G are navigable. Spans C to F are for larger vessels. All spans display a F GR. A **Green** ⟶ indicates span open for navigation. A **Red X** indicates span closed to navigation. In low visibility F lights are shown either side of those spans which are displaying a **Green** ⟶.

4

▶ SOUTH DOCK MARINA

Marina Ent 51°29'·65N 00°01'·97W.

▶ LIMEHOUSE BASIN MARINA/REGENT'S CANAL

Limehouse Basin Marina Lock ent 51°30'·56N 00°02'·26W.

▶ ST KATHARINE YACHT HAVEN

St Katherine Haven Ent 51°30'·36N 00°04'·35W.

▶ CHELSEA HARBOUR MARINA

Chelsea Harbour Ent 51°28'·48N 00°10'·81W.

THAMES ESTUARY – NORTHERN PART

▶ KENTISH KNOCK

Kentish Knock 51°38'·53N 01°40·39E Q (3) 10s; *Whis.*
S Knock 51°34'·13N 01°34'·29E Q (6) + L Fl 15s; *Bell.*

▶ KNOCK JOHN CHANNEL

No. 7 51°32'·03N 01°06'·40E Fl (4) G 15s.
No. 5 51°32'·78N 01°08'·58E Fl (3) G 10s.
No. 4 51°32'·63N 01°08'·72E L Fl R 10s.
No. 2 51°33'·11N 01°09'·85E Fl (3) R 10s.
No. 3 51°33'·23N 01°09'·70E Q (6) + L Fl 15s.
No. 1 51°33'·75N 01°10'·72E Fl G 5s.
Knock John 51°33'·61N 01°11'·37E Fl (2) R 5s.

▶ BLACK DEEP

No. 12 51°33'·83N 01°13'·50E Fl (4) R 15s.
No. 11 51°34'·33N 01°13'·40E Fl (3) G 10s.
No. 10 51°34'·74N 01°15'·60E Fl (3) R 10s.
No. 9 51°35'·13N 01°15'·09E Q (6) + L Fl 15s.
No. 8 51°36'·36N 01°20'·43E Q (9) 15s.
No. 7 51°37'·08N 01°17'·69E QG.
No. 6 51°38'·53N 01°24'·41E Fl R 2·5s.
No. 5 51°39'·53N 01°23'·00E VQ (3) 5s; *Bell.*
No. 4 51°41'·42N 01°28'·49E Fl (2) R 5s.
Long Sand Beacon 51°41'·47N 01°29'·46E.
No. 3 51°41'·98N 01°25'·97E Fl (3) G 15s.
No. 1 51°44'·03N 01°28'·09E Fl G 5s.
No. 2 51°45'·63N 01°32'·20E Fl (4) R 15s.
Sunk Head Tower 51°46'·63N 01°30'·51E Q; *Whis.*
Black Deep 51°47'·10N 01°34'·68E QR.
Trinity 51°49'·03N 01°36'·39E Q (6) + L Fl 15s; *Whis.*
Long Sand Head 51°47'·90N 01°39'·42E VQ; *Bell.*

PLOT WAYPOINTS ON YOUR CHART BEFORE USING THEM

▶ FISHERMANS GAT
Outer Fisherman 51°33'·89N 01°25'·01E Q (3) 10s.
Fisherman No. 1 51°34'·53N 01°23'·57E Fl G 2·5s.
Fisherman No. 2 51°34'·35N 01°23'·01E Fl R 2·5s.
Fisherman No. 3 51°34'·72N 01°22'·94E Fl G 5s.
Fisherman No. 4 51°35'·25N 01°21'·35E Fl (2) R 5s.
Fisherman No. 5 51°35'·52N 01°21'·75E Fl (2) G 5s.
Inner Fisherman 51°36'·07N 01°19'·87E Q R.

▶ BARROW DEEP
SW Barrow 51°32'·29N 01°00'·31E Q(6) + L Fl 15s; *Bell.*
Barrow No. 14 51°31'·83N 01°00'·43E Fl R 2·5s.
Barrow No. 13 51°32'·82N 01°03'·07E Fl (2) G 5s.
Barrow No. 12 51°32'·77N 01°04'·13E Fl (2) R 5s.
Barrow No.11 51°34'·08N 01°06'·70E Fl (3) G 10s.
Barrow No. 9 51°35'·34N 01°10'·30E VQ (3) 5s.
Barrow No. 8 51°35'·03N 01°11'·40E Fl (2) R 5s.
Barrow No. 6 51°37'·30N 01°14'·69E Fl (4) R 15s.
Barrow No. 5 51°40'·03N 01°16'·20E Fl G 10s.
Barrow No. 4 51°39'·88N 01°17'·48E VQ (9) 10s.
Barrow No. 3 51°42'·02N 01°20'·24E Q (3) 10s; ***Racon (M)10M.***
Barrow No. 2 51°41'·98N 01°22'·89E Fl (2) R 5s.

▶ WEST SWIN AND MIDDLE DEEP
Blacktail (W) 51°31'·46N 00°55'·19E Iso G 10s 10m 6M.
Blacktail Spit 51°31'·47N 00°56'·74E Fl (3) G 10s.
Blacktail (E) 51°31'·79N 00°56'·46E Iso G 5s 10m 6M.
Maplin 51°34'·03N 01°02'·30E Q (3) 10s; *Bell.*
W Swin 51°33'·40N 01°01'·97E QR.
Maplin Edge 51°35'·33N 01°03'·64E.
Maplin Bank 51°35'·50N 01°04'·70E Fl (3) R 10s.

▶ EAST SWIN (KING'S) CHANNEL
NE Maplin 51°37'·43N 01°04'·90E Fl G 5s; *Bell.*
W Hook Middle 51°39'·18N 01°07'·97E.
S Whitaker 51°40'·23N 01°09'·05E Fl (2) G 10s.
N Middle 51°41'·03N 01°11'·88E.
W Sunk 51°44'·33N 01°25'·80E Q (9) 15s.
Gunfleet Spit 51°45'·33N 01°21'·70E Q (6) + L Fl 15s; *Bell.*
Gunfleet Old Lt Ho 51°46'·09N 01°20'·39E.

WHITAKER CHANNEL AND RIVER CROUCH
Whitaker 51°41'·43N 01°10'·51E Q (3) 10s; *Bell.*
Whitaker No. 6 51°40'·69N 01°08'·06E Q.
Swin Spitway 51°41'·95N 01°08'·35E Iso 10s; *Bell.*
Whitaker 51°39'·64N 01°06'·16E.
North Swallow 51°40'·54N 01°03'·54E
Swallow Tail 51°40'·47N 01°04'·70E.
Ridge 51°40'·13N 01°04'·87E Fl R 10s.
Foulness 51°39'·85N 01°03'·81E Fl (2) R 10s.
Sunken Buxey 51°39'·54N 01°00'·59E Q.
Buxey No. 1 51°39'·18N 01°01'·01E VQ (6) + L Fl 10s.
Buxey No. 2 51°38'·98N 01°00'·15E Q.
Outer Crouch 51°38'·38N 00°58'·48E Q (6) + L Fl 15s.
Crouch 51°37'·62N 00°56'·38E Fl R 10s.
Inner Crouch 51°37'·22N 00°55'·14E L Fl 10s.

▶ RIVER ROACH/HAVENGORE
Branklet By 51°36'·97N 00°52'·14E.

▶ BURNHAM-ON-CROUCH
Horse Shoal 51°37'·10N 00°51'·52E Q.
Fairway No. 1 51°37'·10N 00°51'·00E QG.
Fairway No. 3 51°37'·18N 00°49'·90E QG.
Fairway No. 5 51°37'·19N 00°49'·57E QG.
Fairway No. 9 51°37'·36N 00°48'·77E QG.
Fairway No. 2 51°37'·31N 00°48'·70E QR.
Fairway No. 11 51°37'·43N 00°48'·30E QG.
Burnham Yacht Hbr 51°37'·50N 00°48'·24E Fl Y 5s.

▶ RAY SAND CHANNEL
Buxey 51°41'·16N 01°01'·29E (unlit).

▶ GOLDMER GAT/WALLET
NE Gunfleet 51°49'·93N 01°27'·79E Q (3) 10s.
Wallet No. 2 51°48'·88N 01°22'·99E Fl R 5s.
Wallet No. 4 51°46'·53N 01°17'·23E Fl (4) R 10s.
Walton Pier Hd 51°50'·60N 01°16'·80E 2 FG (vert) 5m 2M.
Wallet Spitway 51°42'·86N 01°07'·30E L Fl 10s; *Bell.*
Knoll 51°43'·88N 01°05'·07E Q.
Eagle 51°44'·13N 01°03'·82E QG.
N Eagle 51°44'·71N 01°04'·32E Q.
NW Knoll 51°44'·35N 01°02'·17E Fl (2) R 5s.
Colne Bar 51°44'·61N 01°02'·57E Fl (2) G 5s.
Bench Head 51°44'·69N 01°01'·10E Fl (3) G 10s.

▶ RIVER BLACKWATER
The Nass 51°45'·83N 00°54'·83E VQ (3) 5s 6m 2M.
Thirslet 51°43'·73N 00°50'·39E Fl (3) G 10s.
No. 1 51°43'·44N 00°48'·02E.
Small 51°43'·22N 00°47'·47E Fl (2) R 3s.
No. 2 51°42'·81N 00°46'·47E Fl R 3s.
Osea Island Pier Hd 51°43'·10N 00°46'·48E 2 FG (vert).
No. 3 51°42'·91N 00°46'·05E Fl (2) G 6s.
Southey Creek No. 4 51°43'·06N 00°45'·20E.
N Double No. 7 51°43'·24N 00°44'·75E Fl G 3s.
S Double No. 6 51°43'·16N 00°44'·74E.
No. 8 51°43'·93N 00°43'·24E Fl (2) R 3s.

▶ RIVER COLNE/BRIGHTLINGSEA
Inner Bench Head No. 2 51°45'·96N 01°01'·74E Fl (2) R 5s.
Colne Pt No. 1 51°46'·01N 01°01'·92E Fl G 3s.
No. 8 51°46'·97N 01°00'·98E QR.
No. 9 51°47'·36N 01°01'·07E Fl G 3s.
No. 13 51°47'·74N 01°00'·76E Fl G.
Brightlingsea Spit 51°48'·08N 01°00'·70E Q (6) + L Fl 15s.
Brightlingsea 51°48'·22N 01°01'·08E Fl (3) G 5s.
Brightlingsea 51°48'·26N 01°01'·04E Fl R 5s.

Ldg lts 041°. Front, 51°48'·39N 01°01'·20E FR 7m 4M; W□, R stripe on post; vis: 020°-080°. Rear, 50m from front, FR 10m 4M; W□, R stripe on post. FR lts are shown on 7 masts between 1·5M and 3M NW when firing occurs.

Hardway Hd 51°48'·26N 01°01'·40E 2 FR (vert) 2m.
Batemans twr 51°48'·34N 01°00'·65E FY 12m.
No. 24 51°50'·16N 00°58'·83E Fl R.
Rowhedge Wharf 51°51'·23N 00°57'·10E FY 11m.

▶ CLACTON-ON-SEA
Berthing arm 51°47'·04N 01°09'·42E 2 FG (vert) 5m 4M; *Reed (2) 120s* (occas).

▶ WALTON BACKWATERS
Naze Tower 51°51'·87N 01°17'·29E.
Pye End 51°55'·03N 01°17'·90E L Fl 10s.
Orwell YC No. 2 51°54'·62N 01°16'·80E.
Crab Knoll No. 3 51°54'·40N 01°16'·41E Fl (2) G 10s.

Heather J No. 5 51°54'·28N 01°16'·23E.
High Hill No. 4 51°54'·05N 01°15'·96E Fl R 10s.
No. 7 51°53'·83N 01°15'·62E Fl G 10s.
No. 6 51°53'·78N 01°15'·66E.
Pickard No. 8 51°53'·63N 01°15'·55E.
Island Point 51°53'·36N 01°15'·36E Q.
Frank Bloom 51°53'·27N 01°15'·49E.
Colin Bloom 51°53'·33N 01°15'·42E.
Exchem 51°53'·18N 01°14'·91E.
Baines No. 10 51°53'·38N 01°15'·40E.
No. 12 51°53'·26N 01°15'·51E.
East Coast Sails 51°53'·21N 01°15'·54E Fl G 5s.
Stone Pt 51°53'·07N 01°15'·65E.
Ingle 51°52'·91N 01°15'·77E Fl G 5s.

HARWICH APPROACHES

(Direction of buoyage North to South)

▶ MEDUSA CHANNEL

Medusa 51°51'·23N 01°20'·35E Fl G 5s.
Stone Banks 51°53'·19N 01°19'·23E FlR 5s.
Pennyhole 51°53'·55N 01°18'·00E (Mar-Sep).

▶ CORK SAND /ROUGH SHOALS

S Cork 51°51'·33N 01°24'·09E Q (6) + L Fl 15s.
Armada Racing Mark 51°52'·83N 01°22'·19E (Mar-Sep).
Cork Ledge Racing Mark 51°54'·50N 01°23'·40E (Mar-Sep).
Roughs Tower SE 51°53'·64N 01°28'·94E Q (3) 10s.
Roughs Tower NW 51°53'·80N 01°28'·76E Q (9) 15s.
Cork Sand 51°55'·51N 01°25'·42E Fl (3) R 10s.

▶ HARWICH CHANNEL

SUNK 51°51'·03N 01°34'·89E Fl (2) 20s 12m **16M**; R hull with lt twr; ***Racon (T)***; *Horn (2) 60*s.

S Threshold 51°52'·20N 01°33'·14E Fl (4) Y 10s.
S Shipwash 2 By(s) 51°52'·71N 01°33'·97E Q (6) + L Fl 15s.
Outer Tidal Bn 51°52'·85N 01°32'·34E Mo (U) 15s 2m 3M.
E Fort Massac 51°53'·36N 01°32'·79E VQ (3) 5s.
W Fort Massac 51°53'·36N 01°32'·49E VQ (9) 10s.
Walker 51°53'·79N 01°33'·90E QR.
N Threshold 51°54'·49N 01°33'·47E Fl Y 5s.
SW Shipwash 51°54'·75N 01°34'·21E Q (9)15s.
Haven 51°55'·76N 01°35'·56E Mo (A) 5s.
W Shipwash 51°57'·13N 01°35'·89E Fl (2) R 10s.
NW Shipwash 51°58'·98N 01°37'·01E Fl R 5s.
Harwich App (HA) 51°56'·75N 01°30'·66E Iso 5s.
Cross 51°56'·23N 01°30'·48E Fl (3) Y 10s.
Harwich Chan No. 1 51°56'·13N 01°27'·06E Fl Y 2·5s; ***Racon (T)10M***.
Harwich Chan No. 3 51°56'·04N 01°25'·54E Fl (3) Y 10s.
Harwich Chan No. 5 51°55'·96N 01°24'·01E Fl (5) Y 10s.
Harwich Chan No. 7 51°55'·87N 01°22'·49E Fl (3) Y 10s.
S Bawdsey 51°57'·23N 01°30'·22E Q (6) + L Fl 15s; *Whis*.
Washington 51°56'·52N 01°26'·60E QG.
Felixstowe Ledge 51°56'·30N 01°23'·72E Fl (3) G 10s.
Wadgate Ledge 51°56'·16N 01°21'·99E Fl (4) G 15s.
Cobbolds Pt 51°57'·64N 01°22'·16E (Apr-Oct).
Platters 51°55'·64N 01°20'·97E; Q (6) + L Fl 15s.
Rolling Ground 51°55'·55N 01°19'·75E QG.
Beach End 51°55'·62N 01°19'·21E Fl (2) G 5s.
NW Beach 51°55'·89N 01°18'·88E Fl (3) G 10s; *Bell*.
Fort 51°56'·20N 01°18'·88E Fl (4) G 15s.
Cork Sand Yacht Bn 51°55'·21N 01°25'·20E VQ 2M.
Rough 51°55'·19N 01°31'·00E VQ.
Pitching Ground 51°55'·43N 01°21'·05E Fl (4) R 15s.
Inner Ridge 51°55'·38N 01°20'·20E QR.
Deane 51°55'·36N 01°19'·28E L Fl R 6s.
Landguard 51°55'·45N 01°18'·84E Q.
NW Beach 51°55'·89N 01°18'·88E Fl (3) G 10s; *Bell*.
Cliff Foot 51°55'·71N 01°18'·54E Fl R 5s.
S Shelf 51°56'·19N 01°18'·47E Fl (2) R 5s.
N Shelf 51°56'·68N 01°18'·59E QR.
Harwich Shelf 51°56'·84N 01°18'·07E Q (3) 10s (Apr-Oct).
Grisle 51°56'·88N 01°18'·33E Fl R 2·5s.

4

RIVERS STOUR AND ORWELL

▶ RIVER STOUR/HARWICH

Shotley Spit 51°57'·21N 01°17'·69E Q (6) + L Fl 15s.
Shotley Marina Lock E side Dir lt 339·5° 51°57'·46N 01°16'·60E 3m 1M (uses Moiré pattern); Or structure.
Shotley Marina Ent E side 51°57'·26N 01°16'·72E Fl (4) G 15s.
Shotley Marina 51°57'·26N 01°16'·74E VQ (3) 5s.
Shotley Ganges Pier East Head ☆ 51°57'·21N 01°16'·23E 2 FG (vert) 4m 1M; G post.
Guard 51°57'·07N 01°17'·86E Fl R 5s; *Bell*.
Ganges 51°57'·10N 01°17'·03E Fl G 5s.
Bristol 51°57'·05N 01°16'·22E Fl (2) G 5s.
Bathside 51°56'·93N 01°15'·89E Fl (2) R 5s
Parkeston 51°57'·09N 01°15'·34E Fl (3) G 10s.
Ramsey 51°57'·03N 01°14'·17E L Fl G 10s.
Erwarton Ness 51°57'·11N 01°13'·24E Q (6) + L Fl 15s 4M.
Holbrook 51°57'·22N 01°10'·36E VQ (6) + L Fl 10s 4M.

▶ RIVER ORWELL/IPSWICH

College 51°57'·54N 01°17'·33E Fl (2) R 10s.
Pepys 51°57'·74N 01°16'·90E Fl (4) R 15s.
Fagbury 51°57'·96N 01°16'·81E Fl G 2·5s.
Orwell 51°58'·17N 01°16'·54E Q R.
No. 1 51°58'·28N 01°16'·65E Fl G 5s.
Trimley 51°59'·06N 01°16'·66E Fl G 2·5s.
Stratton 51°59'·42N 01°16'·38E Fl G 5s.
Suffolk Yacht Harbour. Ldg lts 51°59'·73N 01°16'·09E. Front Iso Y 1M, Rear Oc Y 4s 1M.
Woolverstone Marina ☆ 52°00'·48N 01°11'·58E 2 FR (vert).
Orwell Bridge ☆ 52°01'·63N 01°09'·83E FY 39m 3M at centre; 2 FR (vert) on Pier 9 and 2 FG (vert) on Pier 10.
No. 12 (off Fox's Marina) 52°02'·11N 01°09'·33E Fl R 5s.
Ipswich Lock SS (Tfc) 52°02'·81N 01°09'·65E.
Neptune Marina 52°03'·13N 01°09'·67E.

HARWICH TO ORFORDNESS

▶ FELIXSTOWE/R. DEBEN/WOODBRIDGE HAVEN

Felixstowe Town Pier Hd ☆ 51°57'·39N 01°20'·92E 2 FG (vert) 7m.
Woodbridge Haven 51°58'·55N 01°24'·25E Mo(A)15s.
Martello Spit 51°58'·56N 01°23'·24E.
Deben 51°59'·30N 01°23'·53E.
Horse Sand 51°59'·85N 01°23'·27E.
Felixtowe Ferry, E side ☆ 51°59'·42N 01°23'·62E 2 FG (vert).
W side ☆ 51°59'·37N 01°23'·47E 2 FR (vert).

PLOT WAYPOINTS ON YOUR CHART BEFORE USING THEM

▶ RIVER ORE/RIVER ALDE
Orford Haven ⚲ 52°01'·85N 01°28'·28E L Fl 10s; *Bell.*
Oxley ⌂ 52°02'·08N 01°27'·87E (Apr-Oct).
Weir ▲ 52°02'·10N 01°27'·64W (Apr-Oct).
Dovey's Point ⌀ 52°03'·81N 01°29'·85W.

▶ OFFSHORE MARKS
S Galloper ⌀ 51°43'·98N 01°56'·39E Q (6) L Fl 15s; *Racon (T)10M*; *Whis.*

N Galloper ⌀ 51°50'·03N 01°59'·39E Q.
S Inner Gabbard ⌀ 51°51'·23N 01°52'·29E Q (6) + L Fl 15s.
N Inner Gabbard ⌀ 51°59'·13N 01°55'·99E Q.

Outer Gabbard ⌀ 51°57'·83N 02°04'·19E Q (3) 10s; *Racon (O)10M*; *Whis.*

NHR-SE ▲51°45'·39N 02°39'·89E Fl G 5s.
NHR-S ⚲ 51°51'·35N 02°28'·71E Fl Y 10s; *Bell.*

▶ SHIPWASH/BAWDSEY BANK
E Shipwash ⌀ 51°57'·08N 01°37'·89E VQ (3) 5s.
NW Shipwash ⌂ 51°58'·98N 01°37'·01E Fl R 5s.
N Shipwash ⌀52°01'·73N 01°38'·27E Q 7M; *Racon (M) 10M*; *Bell.*
S Bawdsey ⌀ 51°57'·23N 01°30'·22E Q (6) + L Fl 15s; *Whis.*
Mid Bawdsey ▲ 51°58'·88N 01°33'·59E Fl (3) G 10s.
NE Bawdsey ▲ 52°01'·73N 01°36'·09E Fl G 10s.

▶ CUTLER/WHITING BANKS
Cutler ▲ 51°58'·51N 01°27'·48E QG.
SW Whiting ⌀ 52°00'·96N 01°30'·69E Q (6) + L Fl 10s.
Whiting Hook ⌂ 52°02'·98N 01°31'·82E.
NE Whiting ⌀ 52°03'·61N 01°33'·32E Q (3) 10s.

ORFORDNESS TO WINTERTON
(Direction of buoyage is South to North)
Orford Ness ☆ 52°05'·03N 01°34'·46E Fl 5s 28m **20M**; W ○ twr, R bands. F WRG 14m **W17M**, R13M, **G15M** (same twr). vis: R shore-210°, R038°-047°, G047°-shore; *Racon (T) 18M*.

FR 13m 12M vis: 026°-038° over Whiting Bank.
Aldeburgh Ridge ⌂ 52°06'·72N 01°36'·95E QR.

Sizewell Cooling Water intake and outfall ☆ 52°12'·91N 01°37'·97E each Fl R 5s 5m 3M.

▶ SOUTHWOLD
Southwold ☆ 52°19'·63N 01°40'·89E Fl (4) WR 20s 37m **W16M**, **R12M**, R14M; vis R (intens) 204°-215°, W215°-001°.
S Pier Head ☆ 52°18'·79N 01°40'·49E QR 4m 2M.
N Pier Head ☆ 52°18'·80N 01°40'·53E Fl G 1·5s 4m 4M.

▶ LOWESTOFT AND APPROACHES VIA STANFORD CHANNEL
E Barnard ⌀ 52°25'·14N 01°46'·38E Q (3) 10s.
Newcome Sand ⌀ 52°26'·28N 01°46'·97E QR.
S Holm ⌀ 52°27'·05N 01°47'·15E VQ (6) + L Fl 10s.
Stanford ⌂ 52°27'·35N 01°46'·67E Fl R 2·5s.
SW Holm ▲ 52°27'·87N 01°46'·99E Fl (2) G 5s.
Claremont Pier ☆ 52°27'·89N 01°44'·87E Oc WR 8s 5m W8M, R6M; vis: W223·8°-229·8°, R229·8°-223·8°.
Outer Hbr S Pier Hd ☆ 52°28'·29N 01°45'·36E ☆ Oc R 5s 12m 6M; *Horn (4) 60s*; Tfc sigs.
N Pier Hd ☆ 52°28'·32N 01°45'·39E Oc G 5s 12m 8M.
N Newcome ⌂ 52°28'·39N 01°46'·37E Fl (4) R 15s.
Lowestoft ☆ 52°29'·22N 01°45'·35E Fl 15s 37m **23M**; W twr; part obscd 347°-shore.

▶ LOWESTOFT NORTH ROAD AND CORTON ROAD
Lowestoft Ness SE ⌀ 52°28'·84N 01°46'·25E Q (6) + L Fl 15s.
Lowestoft Ness N ⌀ 52°28'·89N 01°46'·23E VQ (3) 5s; *Bell.*
W Holm ▲ 52°29'·80N 01°47'·09E Fl (3) G 10s.
NW Holm ▲ 52°31'·93N 01°46'·70E Fl (4) G 15s.

▶ GREAT YARMOUTH APPROACHES VIA HOLM CHANNEL
E Newcome ⌂ 52°28'·51N 01°49'·21E Fl (2) R 5s.
Corton ⌀ 52°31'·13N 01°51'·39E Q (3) 10s; *Whis.*
E. Holm ⌂ 52°30'·64N 01°49'·72E Fl (3) R 10s.
S Corton ⌀ 52°32'·47N 01°49'·36E Q (6) + L Fl 15s; *Bell.*
NE Holm ⌂ 52°32'·30N 01°48'·20E Fl R 2·5s.
Holm ▲ 52°33'·53N 01°47'·96E Fl G 2·5s.
White Swan ⌂ 52°33'·40N 01°44'·29E.
Holm Sand ⌀ 52°33'·36N 01°46'·85E Q.

▶ GREAT YARMOUTH/GORLESTON
W Corton ⌀ 52°34'·59N 01°46'·62E Q (9) 15s.

Ldg lts 264°. Front, 52°34'·33N 01°43'·97E Oc 3s 6m 10M. Rear, Brush Oc 6s 7m 10M, also FR 20m 6M; R ○ twr.

Gorleston South Pier Hd ☆ 52°34'·33N 01°44'·28E Fl R 3s 11m 11M; vis: 235°-340°; *Horn (3) 60s.*

N Pier Hd ☆ 52°34'·38N 01°44'·38E QG 8m 6M; vis: 176°-078°.

Haven Bridge ☆ 52°36'·40N 01°43'·38E marked by pairs of 2 FR (vert) and 2 FG (vert) showing up and down stream.

List below any other waypoints that you use regularly					
Description	Latitude	Longitude	Description	Latitude	Longitude

9.4.5 PASSAGE INFORMATION

Reference books include: *East Coast Rivers* - new edition 2004(Nautical Data Ltd/Harber) from the Swale to Lowestoft. The Admiralty NP 28 *Dover Strait Pilot* and NP54 *North Sea (West) Pilot*. The Admiralty Small Craft Folio 5606 covers The Thames Estuary (southern) and 5607 the Thames Estuary (northern). 5606 contains 12 and 5607 14 A2 size charts in a clear plastic wallet and cost £37.50/folio (2004).

THE THAMES ESTUARY (chart *1183, 1975*) To appreciate the geography of the Thames Estuary there is a well-known analogy between its major sandbanks and the fingers and thumb of the left hand, outstretched palm-down: With the thumb lying E over Margate Sand, the index finger covers Long Sand; the middle finger represents Sunk Sand and the third finger delineates West and East Barrow; the little finger points NE along Buxey and Gunfleet Sands.

The intervening channels are often intricate, but the main ones, in sequence from south to north, are:

a. between the Kent coast and thumb – Four Fathoms, Horse, Gore and South Chans; sometimes known as the overland route due to relatively shallow water.

b. between thumb and index finger – Queens and Princes Chans leading seaward to Knock Deep.

c. between index and middle fingers – Knob Chan leading to Knock Deep via the Edinburgh Chans across Long Sand and the Shingles. Knock John Chan and Black Deep, the main shipping channels which are restricted to vessels drawing more than 6m.

d. between middle and third fingers – Barrow Deep.

e. between third and little fingers – W and E Swin, Middle Deep and Whitaker Chan leading seaward to King's Chan.

f. between little finger and the Essex coast – The Wallet and Goldmer Gat.

The sandbanks shift constantly in the Thames Estuary. Up-to-date charts showing the latest buoyage changes are essential, but it is unwise to put too much faith in charted depths over the banks; a reliable echosounder is vital. The main chans carry much commercial shipping and are well buoyed and lit, but this is not so in lesser chans and swatchways which are convenient for yachtsmen, particularly when crossing the estuary from N to S, or vice versa. Unlit, unmarked minor chans should be used with great caution, which could indeed be the hallmark of all passage-making in the Thames Estuary. Good visibility is needed to pick out buoys/marks, and to avoid shipping.

CROSSING THE THAMES ESTUARY (See 9.4.6) ▶ *Study the tides carefully and understand them, so as to work the streams to best advantage and to ensure sufficient depth at the times and places where you expect to be, or might be later (see 9.4.3 and 9.4.7). In principle it is best to make most of the crossing on a rising tide, ie departing N Foreland or the vicinity of the Whitaker buoy at around LW. The stream runs 3kn at sp in places, mostly along the chans but sometimes across the intervening banks. With wind against tide a short, steep sea is raised, particularly in E or NE winds.* ◀

Making N from N Foreland to Orford Ness or beyond (or vice versa) it may be preferable to keep to seaward of the main banks, via Kentish Knock and Long Sand Head buoys, thence to N Shipwash lt buoy 14M further N.

Bound NW from N Foreland it is approximately 26M to the Rivers Crouch, Blackwater or Colne. A safe route is through either the Princes Channel or Fisherman's Gat, thence S of the Tizard, Knob and West Barrow banks to the West Swin, before turning NE into Middle Deep and the East Swin. This is just one of many routes which could be followed, depending on wind direction, tidal conditions and confidence in electronic aids in the absence of marks.

A similar, well-used route in reverse, ie to the SE, lies via the Wallet Spitway, to the Whitaker lt buoy, through Barrow Swatchway to SW Sunk bn; thence via the N Edinburgh Chan, toward the E Margate lt buoy keeping E of Tongue Sand tr. Beware shoal waters off Barrow and Sunk Sands.

Port Control London can give navigational help to yachts on VHF Ch 12; Thames CG at Walton-on-the-Naze can also assist. The Thames Navigation Service has radar coverage between the Naze and Margate, eastward to near the Dutch coast.

4

NORTH FORELAND TO LONDON BRIDGE N Foreland has a conspic lt ho, (chart 1828), with buoys offshore. ▶ *From HW Dover –0120 to +0045 the stream runs N from The Downs and W into Thames Estuary. From HWD + 0045 to + 0440 the N-going stream from The Downs meets the E-going stream from Thames Estuary, which in strong winds causes a bad sea. From HWD –0450 to –0120 the streams turn W into Thames Estuary and S towards The Downs. If bound for London, round N Foreland against the late ebb in order to carry a fair tide from Sheerness onward.* ◀

For vessels drawing less than 2m the most direct route from North Foreland to the Thames and Medway is via South Chan, Gore Chan, Horse Chan, Kentish Flats, Four Fathom Chan and Cant; but it is not well marked particularly over the Kentish Flats. An alternative, deeper route is East of Margate Sand and the Tongue, to set course through Princes Channel to Oaze Deep; larger vessels proceed via the North Edinburgh Channel. ▶ *W-going streams begin at approx HW Sheerness –0600 and E-going at HW Sheerness +0030.* ◀

Margate or Whitstable (9.4.8) afford little shelter for yachts. The Swale (9.4.9) provides an interesting inside route S of the Isle of Sheppey with access to Sheerness and the R Medway (9.4.11). If sailing from N Foreland to the Thames, Queenborough (9.4.10) offers the first easily accessible, all-tide, deep-water shelter. The Medway Chan is the main appr to Sheerness from the Warp and the Medway Fairway buoy.

To clear tanker berths yachts should navigate as follows:

Inward from north - keep close to starboard hand buoys, at West Leigh Middle cross to the south side of the Yanlet Channel, making sure the fairway is clear, make for the E Blyth buoy before turning onto the inward track, remember outward vessels will pass close to the port hand buoys. The Mid Blyth, West Blyth and Lower Hope buoys can be safely passed to the south. Cross to the correct side in Lower Hope Reach as rapidly as possible, when it is safe to do so.

Outward to north - as above in reverse, but crossing to the north between Sea Reach Nos 4 & 5 buoys.

Inward from south - keep well clear of the Sea Reach Channel to the south, crossing to the north side in the Lower Hope as described above.

SHOEBURYNESS TO RIVER COLNE (charts *1185, 1975*) Maplin and Foulness Sands extend nearly 6M NE from Foulness Pt, the extremity being marked by Whitaker bn. On N side of Whitaker chan leading to R. Crouch (9.4.15) and R. Roach (9.4.14) lies Buxey Sand, inshore of which is the Ray Sand chan (dries), a convenient short cut between R. Crouch and R. Blackwater with sufficient rise of tide.

To seaward of Buxey Sand and the Spitway, Gunfleet Sand extends 10M NE, marked by buoys and dries in places. ► *A conspic disused lt tr stands on SE side of Gunfleet Sand, about 6M SSE of the Naze tr, and here the SW-going (flood) stream begins about HW Sheerness + 0600, and the NE-going stream at about HW Sheerness – 0030, sp rates 2kn.* ◄

The Rivers Blackwater (9.4.16) and Colne (9.4.17) share a common estuary which is approached from the NE via NE Gunfleet lt buoy; thence along Goldmer Gat and the Wallet towards Knoll and Eagle lt buoys. For the Colne turn NNW via Colne Bar buoy towards Inner Bench Hd buoy keeping in mid-chan. For R. Blackwater, head WNW for NW Knoll and Bench Hd buoys. From the S or SE, make for the Whitaker ECM buoy, thence through the Spitway, via Swin Spitway and Wallet Spitway buoys to reach Knoll buoy and deeper water.

RIVER COLNE TO HARWICH (chart *1975*, 1593) 4M SW of the Naze tr at Hollands Haven a conspic radar tr (67m, unlit) is an excellent daymark. From the S, approach Walton and Harwich via the Medusa chan about 1M E of Naze tr. At N end of this chan, 1M off Dovercourt, Pye End buoy marks chan SSW to Walton Backwaters (9.4.18). Harwich and Landguard Point are close to the N. Making Harwich from the SE beware the drying Cork Sand, which lies N/S.

Sunk lt Float (Fog sig), 11M E of The Naze, marks the outer apprs to Harwich (9.4.19), an extensive and well sheltered hbr accessible at all times (chart *2693*). The Harwich DW channel begins 1·5M NNW of Sunk lt Float and runs N between Rough and Shipwash shoals, then W past the Cork Sand PHM lt buoy. Constantly used by commercial shipping, approach should be via the Recommended Track for yachts.

Approaching from NE and 2M off the ent to R. Deben (9.4.21), beware Cutler shoal, with least depth of 1·2m, marked by SHM buoy on E side; Wadgate Ledge and the Platters are about 1·5M ENE of Landguard Point. ► *S of Landguard Point the W-going (flood) stream begins at HW Harwich + 0600, and the E-going stream at HW Harwich, sp rates about 1·5kn. Note: HW Harwich is never more than 7 mins after HW Walton; LW times are about 10 mins earlier.* ◄

HARWICH TO ORFORD NESS (chart *2052*) Shipwash shoal, buoyed and with a drying patch, runs NNE from 9M E of Felixstowe to 4M SSE of Orford Ness. Inshore of this is Shipway Chan, then Bawdsey Bank, buoyed with depths of 2m, on which the sea breaks in E'ly swell. The Sledway Chan lies between Bawdsey Bank and Whiting Bank (buoyed) which is close SW of Orford Ness, and has depths less than 1m. Hollesley Chan, about 1M wide, runs inshore W and N of this bank. In the SW part of Hollesley B is the ent to Orford Haven and the R Ore/Alde (9.4.22).

► *There are overfalls S of Orford Ness on both the ebb and flood streams. 2M E of Orford Ness the SW-going stream begins at HW Harwich +0605, sp rate 2·5kn; the NE-going stream begins at HW Harwich –0010, sp rate 3kn.* ◄

Note: The direction of local buoyage becomes S to N off Orford Ness (52°05'N).

ORFORD NESS TO GREAT YARMOUTH (chart 1543) N of Orford Ness seas break on Aldeburgh Ridge (1.3m), but the coast is clear of offlying dangers past Aldeburgh and Southwold (9.4.23), as far as Benacre Ness, 5M S of Lowestoft. Sizewell power stn is a conspic 3 bldg 1·5M N of Thorpe Ness. Keep 1·5M offshore to avoid fishing floats.

► *Lowestoft (9.4.25) is best approached from both S and E by the buoyed/lit Stanford chan, passing E of Newcome Sand and SW of Holm Sand; beware possible strong set across hbr ent.* ◄ From the N, approach through Cockle Gatway, Caister Road, Yarmouth Road, passing Great Yarmouth; then proceed S through Gorleston, Corton and Lowestoft North Roads (buoyed). ► *1M E of hbr ent, the S-going stream begins at HW Dover –0600, and the N-going at HW Dover, sp rates 2·6kn.* ◄ A large Offshore Wind Farm complex is under construction on the Middle Scroby (2004).

In the approaches to Great Yarmouth (9.4.25) from seaward the banks are continually changing; use the buoyed chans which, from N and S, are those described in the preceding paragraph. But from the E the shortest approach is via Corton ECM lt buoy and the Holm Channel leading into Gorleston Road. ► *The sea often breaks on North Scroby, Middle Scroby and Caister Shoal (all of which dry), and there are heavy tide rips over parts of Corton and South Scroby Sands, Middle and South Cross Sands, and Winterton Overfalls.* ◄

► *1M NE of ent to Gt Yarmouth the S-going stream begins at HW Dover –0600, and the N-going at HW Dover – 0015, sp rates 2·3kn. Breydon Water (tidal) affects streams in the Haven; after heavy rain the out-going stream at Brush Quay may exceed 5kn.* ◄ For Norfolk Broads, see 9.4.25. About 12M NE of Great Yarmouth lie Newarp Banks, on which the sea breaks in bad weather.

CROSSING FROM THAMES ESTUARY TO BELGIUM OR THE NETHERLANDS (charts 1610, 1872, 3371, *1406*, 1408) Important factors in choosing a route include the need to head at 90° across the various TSSs; to avoid areas where traffic converges; to make full use of available ITZs and to keep well clear of offshore oil/gas activities (see 9.5.5). It is best to avoid the areas westward of W Hinder lt, around Nord Hinder lt buoy and the Maas routes W of the Hook of Holland. For Distances across N Sea, see 9.0.8 and for further notes on North Sea crossings, see 9.16.5.

From Rivers Crouch, Blackwater, Colne or from Harwich take departure from Long Sand Hd lt buoy to S Galloper lt buoy, thence to W Hinder lt (see 9.16.5), crossing the TSS at right angles near Garden City lt buoy. ► *Care must be taken throughout with tidal streams, which may be setting across the yacht's track.* ◄ The area is relatively shallow, and in bad weather seas are steep and short.

For ports between Hook of Holland and Texel it may be best to diverge to the NE so as to cross the several Deep Water (DW) routes, and their extensions, as quickly as possible, to the N of Nord Hinder lt buoy and the Maas TSS. If bound for ports NE of Texel keep well S of the TX1 lt buoy and then inshore of the Off Texel-Vlieland-Terschelling-German Bight TSS, which is well buoyed on its S side.

9.4.6 THAMES ESTUARY

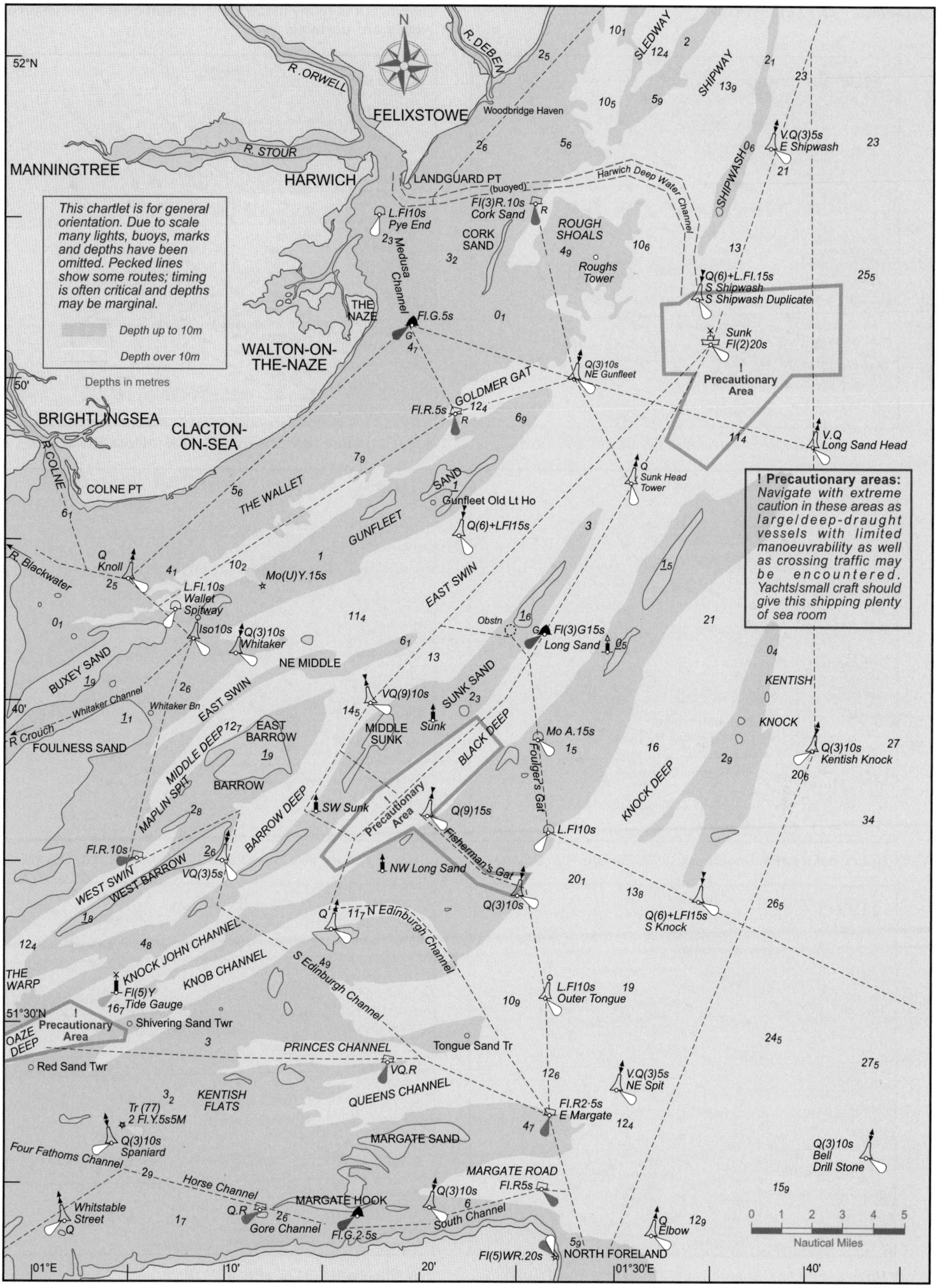
N
52°N
R. ORWELL
R. DEBEN
FELIXSTOWE
Woodbridge Haven
R. STOUR
MANNINGTREE
HARWICH
LANDGUARD PT
(buoyed)
Harwich Deep Water Channel
SLEDWAY
SHIPWAY
SHIPWASH
V.Q(3)5s
E Shipwash
This chartlet is for general orientation. Due to scale many lights, buoys, marks and depths have been omitted. Pecked lines show some routes; timing is often critical and depths may be marginal.
Depth up to 10m
Depth over 10m
Depths in metres
L.Fl10s
Pye End
Fl(3)R.10s
Cork Sand
CORK SAND
ROUGH SHOALS
Roughs Tower
Medusa Channel
THE NAZE
Fl.G.5s
Q(6)+L.Fl.15s
S Shipwash
S Shipwash Duplicate
Sunk
Fl(2)20s
WALTON-ON-THE-NAZE
Q(3)10s
NE Gunfleet
Precautionary Area
GOLDMER GAT
Fl.R.5s
50'
BRIGHTLINGSEA
CLACTON-ON-SEA
R COLNE
COLNE PT
THE WALLET
V.Q
Long Sand Head
Q
Sunk Head Tower
SAND
Gunfleet Old Lt Ho
GUNFLEET
Q(6)+LFl15s
! Precautionary areas:
Navigate with extreme caution in these areas as large/deep-draught vessels with limited manoeuvrability as well as crossing traffic may be encountered. Yachts/small craft should give this shipping plenty of sea room
R. Blackwater
Q
Knoll
Mo(U)Y.15s
L.Fl.10s
Wallet Spitway
EAST SWIN
Iso10s
Q(3)10s
Whitaker
Obstn
Fl(3)G15s
Long Sand
NE MIDDLE
BUXEY SAND
Whitaker Channel
Whitaker Bn
EAST SWIN
VQ(9)10s
SUNK SAND
KENTISH
KNOCK
40'
R Crouch
FOULNESS SAND
MIDDLE DEEP
EAST BARROW
MIDDLE SUNK
Sunk
BLACK DEEP
Mo A.15s
Q(3)10s
Kentish Knock
MAPLIN SPIT
BARROW
Fouliger's Gat
KNOCK DEEP
BARROW DEEP
SW Sunk
Precautionary Area
Q(9)15s
L.Fl10s
Fl.R.10s
Fisherman's Gat
WEST SWIN
WEST BARROW
VQ(3)5s
NW Long Sand
Q(3)10s
Q(6)+LFl15s
S Knock
Q
N Edinburgh Channel
THE WARP
KNOCK JOHN CHANNEL
KNOB CHANNEL
S Edinburgh Channel
Fl(5)Y
Tide Gauge
L.Fl10s
Outer Tongue
51°30'N
OAZE DEEP
Precautionary Area
Shivering Sand Twr
PRINCES CHANNEL
Tongue Sand Tr
Red Sand Twr
VQ.R
V.Q(3)5s
NE Spit
KENTISH FLATS
Tr (77)
2 Fl.Y.5s5M
QUEENS CHANNEL
Fl.R2·5s
E Margate
Q(3)10s
Spaniard
MARGATE SAND
Q(3)10s
Bell
Drill Stone
Four Fathoms Channel
Horse Channel
MARGATE ROAD
Whitstable Street
Q
MARGATE HOOK
Q(3)10s
Fl.R5s
Q.R
Gore Channel
South Channel
Fl.G.2·5s
Q
Elbow
Fl(5)WR.20s
NORTH FORELAND
0 1 2 3 4 5
Nautical Miles
01°E
10'
20'
01°30'E
40'

9.4.7 THAMES ESTUARY TIDAL STREAMS

Due to very strong rates of tidal streams in some areas, eddies may occur. Where possible, some indication of these is shown, but in many areas there is insufficient information or eddies are unstable.

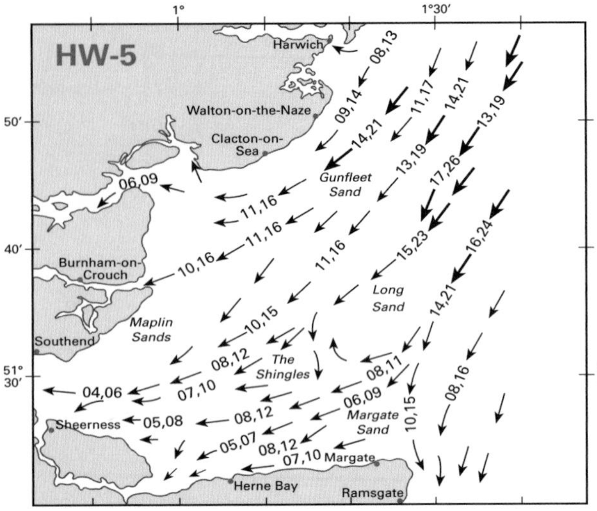
HW-5
Harwich
Walton-on-the-Naze
Clacton-on-Sea
Gunfleet Sand
Burnham-on-Crouch
Long Sand
Maplin Sands
Southend
The Shingles
Sheerness
Margate Sand
Margate
Herne Bay
Ramsgate

5 Hours before HW Sheerness (0335 before HW Dover)

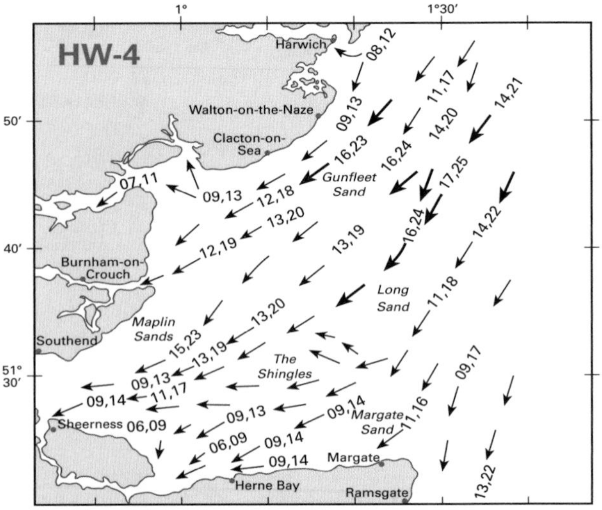
HW-4
Harwich
Walton-on-the-Naze
Clacton-on-Sea
Gunfleet Sand
Burnham-on-Crouch
Long Sand
Maplin Sands
Southend
The Shingles
Sheerness
Margate Sand
Margate
Herne Bay
Ramsgate

4 Hours before HW Sheerness (0235 before HW Dover)

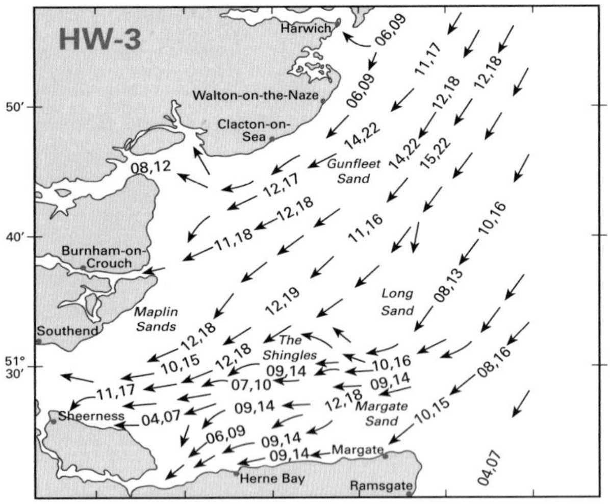
HW-3
Harwich
Walton-on-the-Naze
Clacton-on-Sea
Gunfleet Sand
Burnham-on-Crouch
Long Sand
Maplin Sands
Southend
The Shingles
Sheerness
Margate Sand
Margate
Herne Bay
Ramsgate

3 Hours before HW Sheerness (0135 before HW Dover)

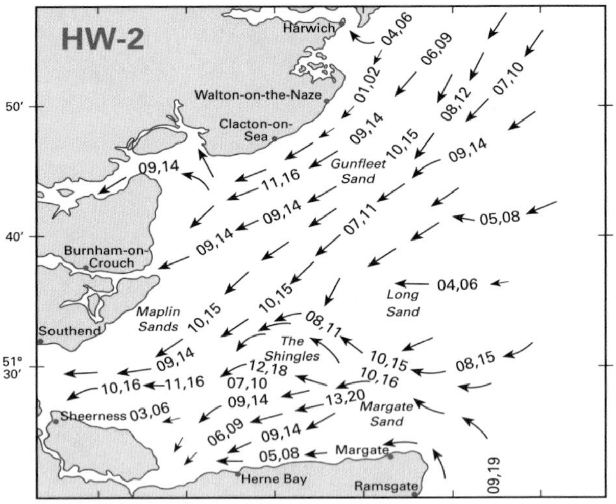
HW-2
Harwich
Walton-on-the-Naze
Clacton-on-Sea
Gunfleet Sand
Burnham-on-Crouch
Long Sand
Maplin Sands
Southend
The Shingles
Sheerness
Margate Sand
Margate
Herne Bay
Ramsgate

2 Hours before HW Sheerness (0035 before HW Dover)

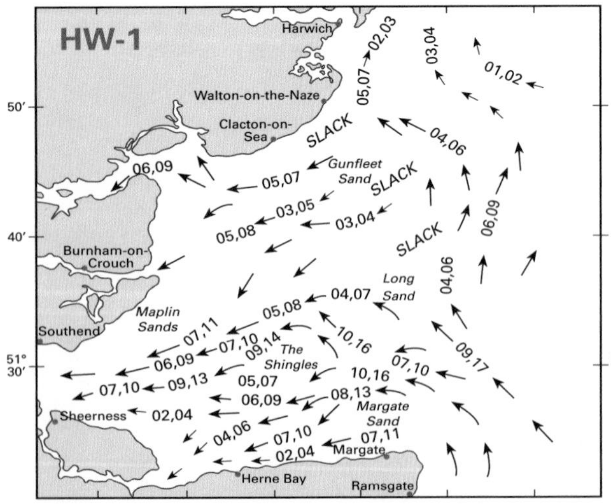
HW-1
Harwich
Walton-on-the-Naze
Clacton-on-Sea
SLACK
Gunfleet Sand
SLACK
SLACK
Burnham-on-Crouch
Long Sand
Maplin Sands
Southend
The Shingles
Sheerness
Margate Sand
Margate
Herne Bay
Ramsgate

1 Hour before HW Sheerness (0025 before HW Dover)

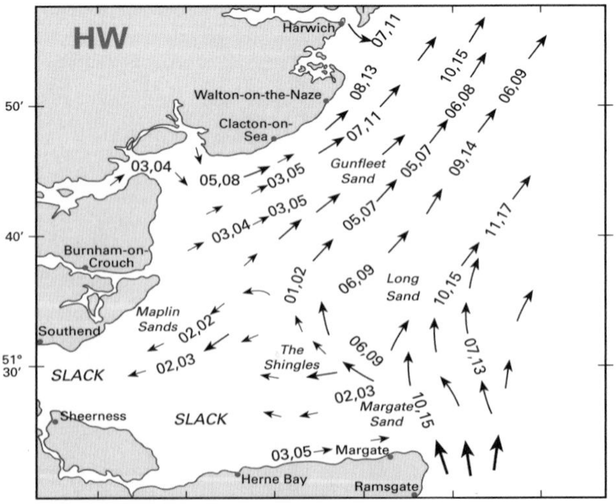
HW
Harwich
Walton-on-the-Naze
Clacton-on-Sea
Gunfleet Sand
Burnham-on-Crouch
Long Sand
Maplin Sands
Southend
SLACK
The Shingles
Sheerness
SLACK
Margate Sand
Margate
Herne Bay
Ramsgate

HW Sheerness (0125 after HW Dover)

Due to very strong rates of tidal streams in some areas, eddies may occur. Where possible, some indication of these is shown, but in many areas there is insufficient information or eddies are unstable.

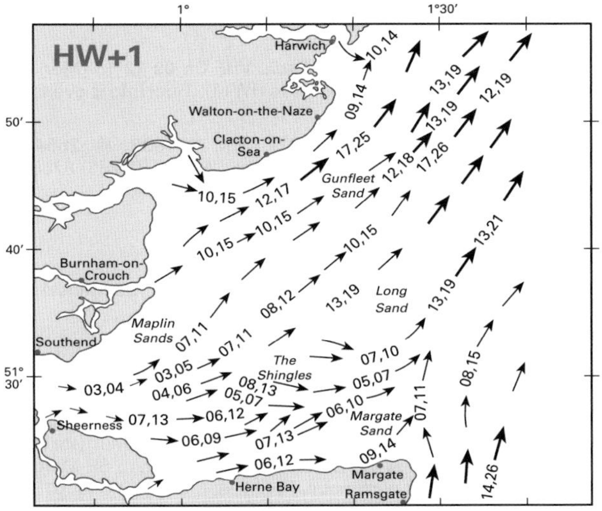
HW+1
Harwich
Walton-on-the-Naze
Clacton-on-Sea
Gunfleet Sand
Burnham-on-Crouch
Long Sand
Maplin Sands
Southend
The Shingles
Sheerness
Margate Sand
Margate
Herne Bay
Ramsgate

1 Hour after HW Sheerness (0225 after HW Dover)

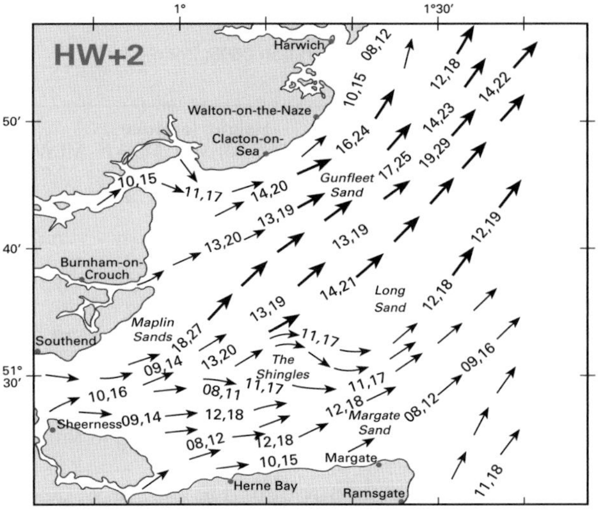
HW+2
Harwich
Walton-on-the-Naze
Clacton-on-Sea
Gunfleet Sand
Burnham-on-Crouch
Long Sand
Maplin Sands
Southend
The Shingles
Sheerness
Margate Sand
Margate
Herne Bay
Ramsgate

2 Hours after HW Sheerness (0325 after HW Dover)

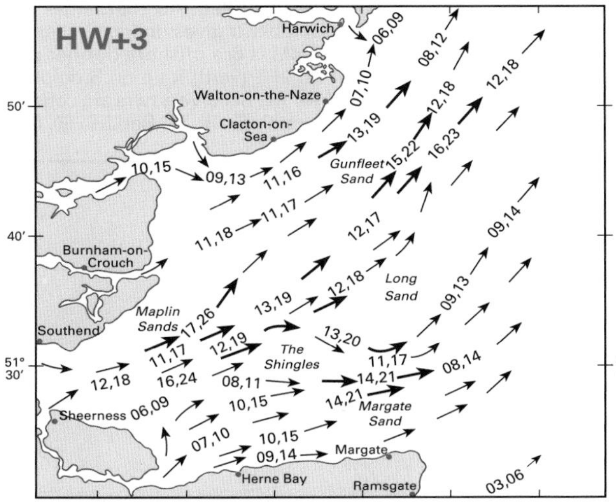
HW+3
Harwich
Walton-on-the-Naze
Clacton-on-Sea
Gunfleet Sand
Burnham-on-Crouch
Long Sand
Maplin Sands
Southend
The Shingles
Sheerness
Margate Sand
Margate
Herne Bay
Ramsgate

3 Hours after HW Sheerness (0425 after HW Dover)

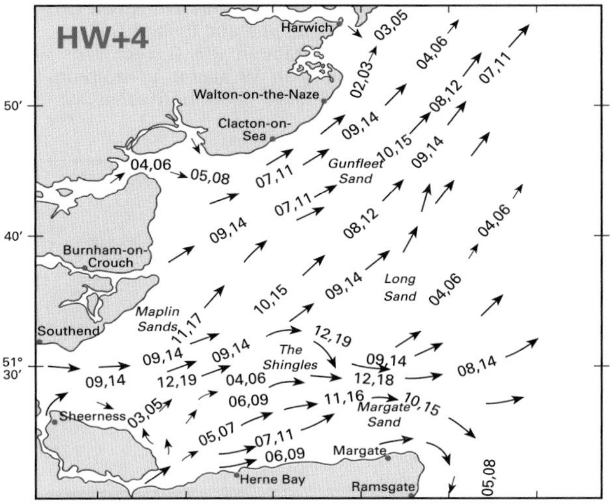
HW+4
Harwich
Walton-on-the-Naze
Clacton-on-Sea
Gunfleet Sand
Burnham-on-Crouch
Long Sand
Maplin Sands
Southend
The Shingles
Sheerness
Margate Sand
Margate
Herne Bay
Ramsgate

4 Hours after HW Sheerness (0525 after HW Dover)

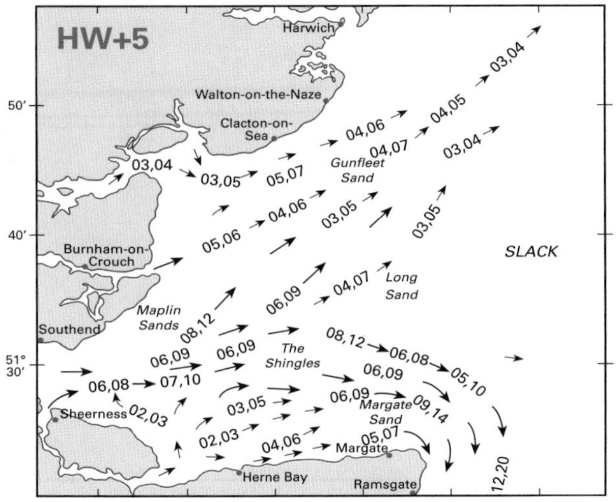
HW+5
Harwich
Walton-on-the-Naze
Clacton-on-Sea
Gunfleet Sand
Burnham-on-Crouch
SLACK
Long Sand
Maplin Sands
Southend
The Shingles
Sheerness
Margate Sand
Margate
Herne Bay
Ramsgate

5 Hours after HW Sheerness (0600 before HW Dover)

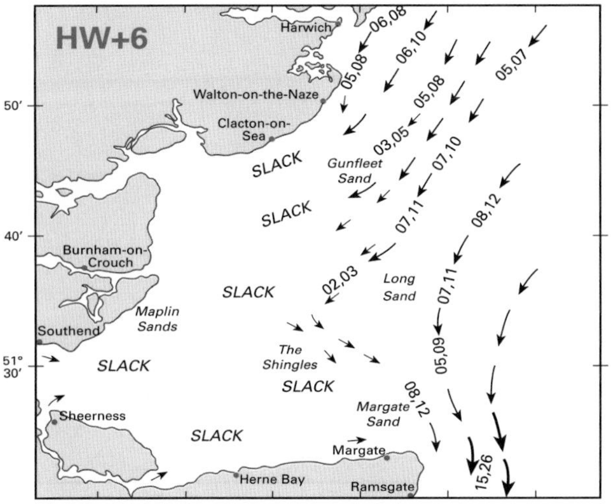
HW+6
Harwich
Walton-on-the-Naze
Clacton-on-Sea
SLACK
Gunfleet Sand
Burnham-on-Crouch
Long Sand
Maplin Sands
Southend
The Shingles
Sheerness
Margate Sand
Margate
Herne Bay
Ramsgate

6 Hours after HW Sheerness (0500 before HW Dover)

9.4.8 WHITSTABLE

Kent **51°21'·86N 01°01'·46E** ❁❁◊◊✿✿

CHARTS AC *5606,* 1607, 2571; Imray Y14, Y7, C1, 2100 Series; Stanfords 5, 8; OS 179

TIDES +0135 Dover; ML 3·0; Duration 0605; Zone 0 (UT)

Standard Port SHEERNESS (⟶)

Times				Height (metres)			
High Water		Low Water		MHWS	MHWN	MLWN	MLWS
0200	0800	0200	0700	5·8	4·7	1·5	0·6
1400	2000	1400	1900				
Differences WHITSTABLE							
–0008	–0011	+0005	0000	–0·3	–0·3	0·0	–0·1
MARGATE							
–0050	–0040	–0020	–0050	–0·9	–0·9	–0·1	0·0
HERNE BAY							
–0025	–0015	0000	–0025	–0·5	–0·5	–0·1	–0·1

SHELTER Good, except in strong winds from NNW to NE. Hbr dries up to 0·4m; access HW±1 for strangers. Yacht berths are limited since priority is given to commercial shipping. Fender board needed against piled quays or seek a mooring to NW of hbr, (controlled by YC).

NAVIGATION WPT 51°22'·65N 01°01'·10E, 345° to W Quay dolphin, 0·83M. From E keep well seaward of Whitstable Street, a hard drying sandspit, which extends 1M N from the coast; shoals a further 1M to seaward are marked by Whitstable Street NCM lt buoy. From W avoid Columbine and Pollard Spits.

Appr (not before half flood) direct in the G sector or via Whitstable Oyster PHM lt buoy in W sector of dolphin lt. Beware many oyster beds and banks near approaches, which are very shallow.

LIGHTS AND MARKS Off head of W Quay on a dolphin, ☆ Fl WRG 5s 2m 5/3M, covers the approaches, vis W118°-156°, G156°-178°, R178°-201°. At the head of the hbr a Dir lt, Fl WRG 5s, leads 122.5 ° into hbr ent, vis G117·5°-120·5°, W120·5°-123·5°(3°), R123·5°-126·5°. Tfc sigs at NE arm: FW 15m 8M = hbr open; FR 10m 5M = hbr closed.

R/T Call *Whitstable Harbour Radio* VHF Ch **09** 12 16 (Mon-Fri: 0830-1700LT. Other times: HW –3 to HW+1). Tidal info is available on request.

TELEPHONE (Dial code 01227) HM 274086, 📠 265441, whitstable.harbour@canterbury.gov.uk, MRSC (01255) 675518; Marinecall 09066 526239; Police 770055; Dr 594400.

FACILITIES Hbr ☎ 274086, AB £10.00, FW, D.
Whitstable YC ☎ 272942, M, R, Slip, L, FW, Bar.
Services: ME, C, CH, ACA, SM, Gas, Ⓔ.
Town EC Wed; ▣, P, 🛒, R, Bar, ✉, Ⓑ, ⇌, ✈ Lydd/Manston.

MINOR HARBOURS WEST OF NORTH FORELAND

MARGATE, Kent, **51°23'·43N 01°22'·65E**. AC 1827, 1828, 323; Imray Y7, C1; Stanfords 5, 8; OS 179. HW+0045 on Dover; ML 2·6; Duration 0610; see 9.4.8. Small hbr drying 3m, inside bkwtr (Stone Pier) FR 18m 4M; exposed to NW'lies. Appr's: from E, via Longnose NCM buoy, keeping about 5ca offshore; from N, via Margate PHM buoy Fl R 2·5s; from W via Gore Chan and S Chan to SE Margate ECM buoy, Q (3) 10s. VHF none. Facilities: Margate YC ☎ (01843) 292602, Ⓒ, Bar. Town EC Thurs; D & P (cans from garage), R, 🛒, Bar, ✉, Ⓑ, ⇌, ✈ Manston.

HERNE BAY, Kent, **51°22'·40N 01°07'·22E**. AC 1607. Tides see 9.4.8. Close E of pier, a 400m long bkwtr gives drying shelter for dayboats/dinghies. Lts: QW 8m 4M is 6ca offshore (former pier hd); bkwtr hd 2FR (vert); pier hd 2FG (vert); R bn on B dolphin, Fl Y 5s, is approx 1M ENE of bkwtr hd. Reculvers twrs are conspic 3M to the E. Slip. **Town** EC Thurs; P, Ⓔ, R, 🛒, Bar, ✉, Ⓑ, ▣.

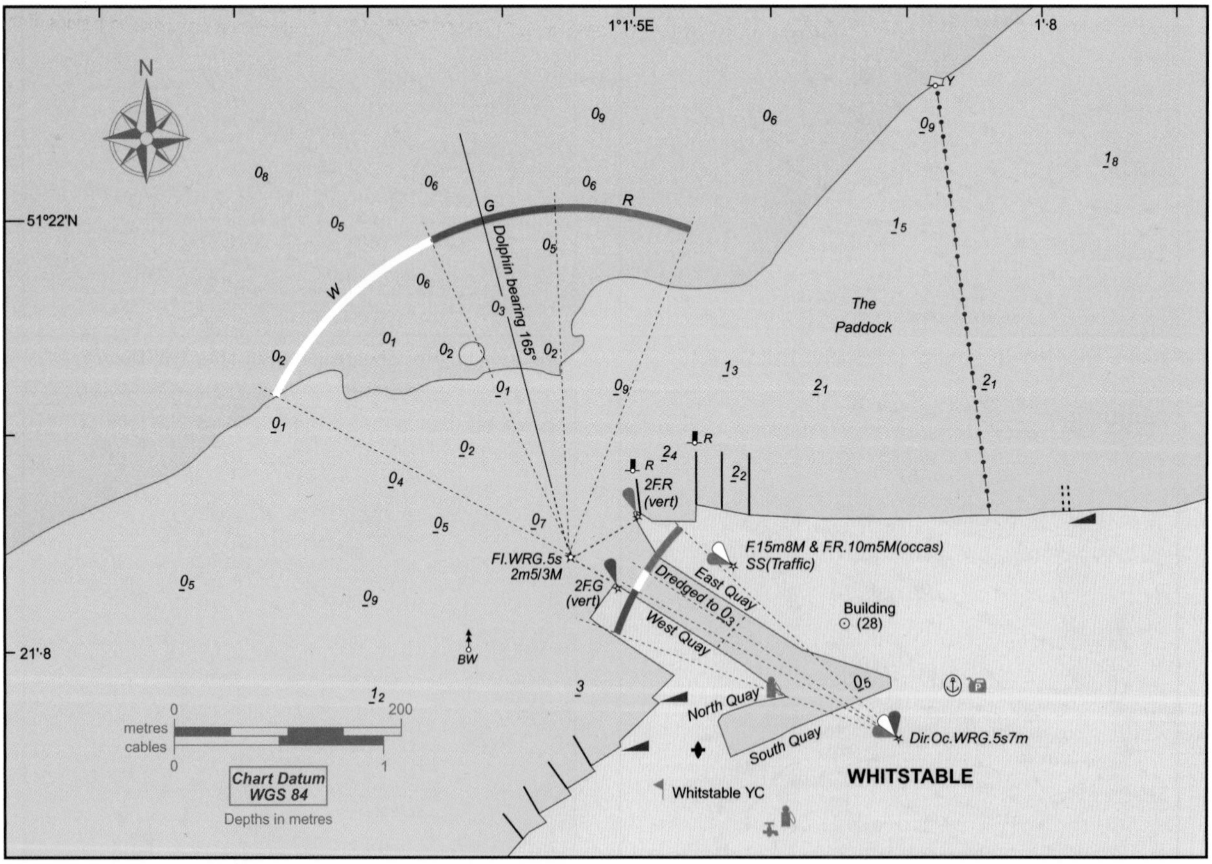
1°1'·5E
1'·8
N
51°22'N
21'·8
G
R
W
Dolphin bearing 165°
The Paddock
2FR (vert)
F.15m8M & F.R.10m5M(occas) SS(Traffic)
Fl.WRG.5s 2m5/3M
2FG (vert)
Dredged to 0.3
East Quay
West Quay
Building ⊙ (28)
North Quay
South Quay
Dir.Oc.WRG.5s7m
WHITSTABLE
Whitstable YC
BW
metres
cables
200
Chart Datum WGS 84
Depths in metres

9.4.9 THE SWALE

Kent ❁❁❁◊◊◊✿✿

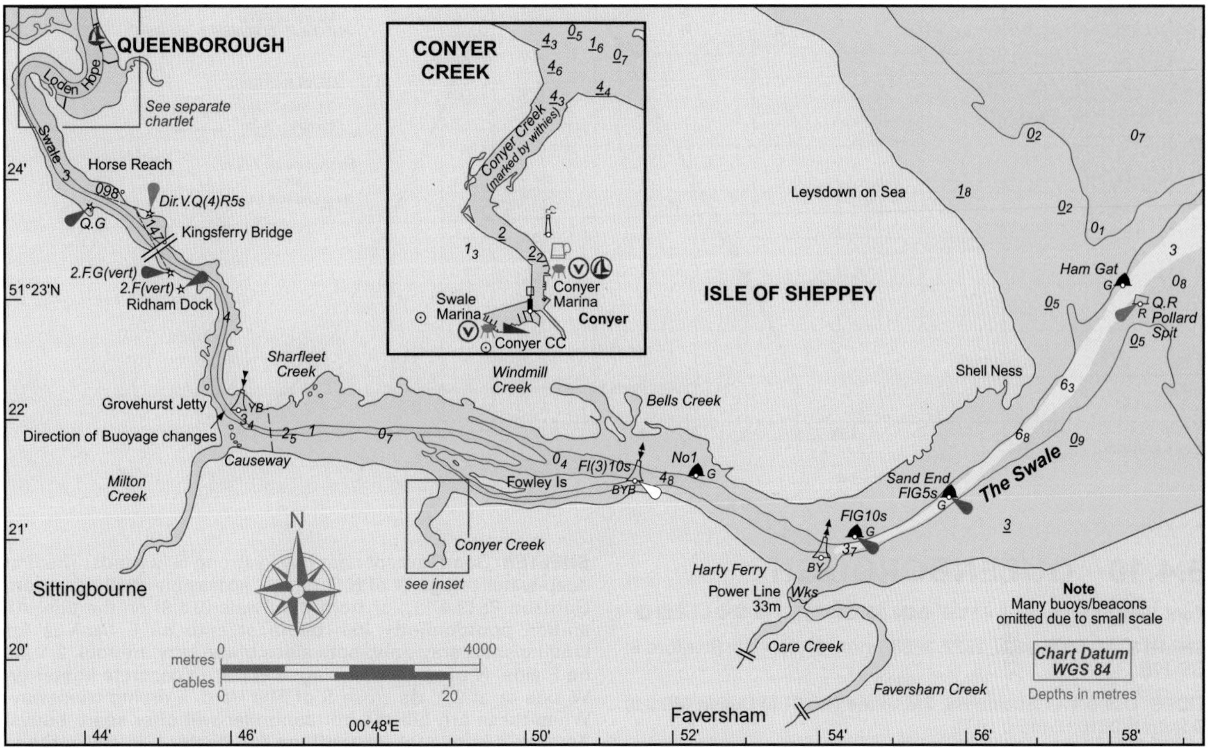
QUEENBOROUGH
See separate chartlet
Loden Hope
Swale
Horse Reach
098°
Dir.V.Q(4)R5s
Q.G
147°
Kingsferry Bridge
2.F.G(vert)
2.F(vert)
Ridham Dock
51°23'N
24'
22'
21'
20'
Sharfleet Creek
Grovehurst Jetty
YB
Direction of Buoyage changes
Causeway
Milton Creek
Sittingbourne
N
metres
cables
4000
20
00°48'E
44'
46'
50'
52'
54'
56'
58'
CONYER CREEK
Conyer Creek (marked by withies)
Swale Marina
Conyer Marina
Conyer
Conyer CC
Windmill Creek
Bells Creek
Fowley Is
Fl(3)10s
BYB
No1
G
Conyer Creek
see inset
Leysdown on Sea
ISLE OF SHEPPEY
Shell Ness
Ham Gat
Q.R
Pollard Spit
Sand End
FlG5s
The Swale
FlG10s
BY
Harty Ferry
Power Line 33m
Wks
Oare Creek
Faversham Creek
Faversham
Note
Many buoys/beacons omitted due to small scale
Chart Datum WGS 84
Depths in metres

CHARTS AC *5606*, 2482, 2571, 2572, *1834*, 3683; Imray Y18, Y14, C1 2100 Series; Stanfords 5, 8; OS 178

TIDES Queenborough +0130 Dover; Harty Ferry +0120 Dover; ML (Harty Ferry) 3·0; Duration 0610; Zone 0 (UT). Faversham HW differences are –0·2m on Sheerness; no other data.

Standard Port SHEERNESS (⟶)

Times				Height (metres)			
High Water		Low Water		MHWS	MHWN	MLWN	MLWS
0200	0800	0200	0700	5·8	4·7	1·5	0·6
1400	2000	1400	1900				
Differences R. SWALE (Grovehurst Jetty)							
–0007	0000	0000	+0016	0·0	0·0	0·0	–0·1

Grovehurst Jetty is close N of the ent to Milton Creek.

SHELTER Excellent in the Swale, the 14M chan between the Isle of Sheppey and the N Kent coast, from Shell Ness in the E to Queenborough in the W. Yachts can enter the drying creeks of Faversham, Oare, Conyer, and Milton. Beware wrecks at ent to Faversham Creek. Many moorings line the chan from Faversham to Conyer Creeks. See 9.4.10 for Queenborough, all-tide access.

NAVIGATION E ent WPT: Columbine Spit SHM, 51°23'·86N 01°00'·03E, 230° to ent to buoyed chan 1·3M. The first chan buoys are Pollard Spit PHM QR and Ham Gat SHM unlit; buoys are moved to suit the shifting chan. Speed limit 8kn. Chan is well marked from Faversham to Milton Creek. The middle section from 1·5M E of Conyer Creek to 0·5M E of Milton Creek is narrowed by drying mudbanks and carries least depths of 0·4m. At Milton Creek direction of buoyage changes. There are numerous oyster beds in the area. Kingsferry Bridge (see opposite) normally opens H and H+30 for masted craft on request, but subject to railway trains; temp anchs off SW bank. The power lines crossing SE of the br have a clearance of 31m.The **W ent** is marked by Queenborough Spit ECM buoy, Q (3) 10s, 1M S of Garrison Pt, at 51°25'·81N 00°43'·93E.

LIGHTS AND MARKS No fixed lts at E ent. In W Swale the following lights are intended for large coasters using the narrow chan:

1. Dir ent lt Q 16m 5M; vis 163°-168°.
2. Round Loden Hope bend: two Q WG and one Q WRG on bns; keep in G sectors. See 9.4.10 chartlet.
3. Horse Reach ldg lts 113°: front QG 7m 5M; rear Fl G 3s 10m 6M. Dir lt 098°, VQ (4) R 5s 6m 5M.
4. Kingsferry Bridge ldg lts 147°: front 2FG(vert) 9m 7M; rear 2 FW (vert) 11m 10M. Lts on bridge: two x 2 FG (vert) on SW buttresses; two x 2 FR (vert) on NE.

Kingsferry Bridge traffic sigs:

No lts	= Bridge down (3·35m MHWS).
Al Q ●/●	= Centre span lifting.
F ●	= Bridge open (29m MHWS).
Q ●	= Centre span lowering. Keep clear.
Q ●	= Bridge out of action.

Best to request bridge opening on VHF Ch 10; normally opens H and H+30.

R/T Call: *Medway Radio* VHF Ch **74** 16 22 (H24); Kingsferry Bridge Ch 10 (H24).

TELEPHONE (Dial code 01795) HM (Medway Ports Ltd) 596593, 📠 581571; MRSC (01255) 675518; Marinecall 09066 526239; Police 477055; Dr or Ⓗ via Medway Navigation Service 663025.

FACILITIES FAVERSHAM: **Services:** BY, AB £5, M, ⛽, FW, Ⓔ, ME, El, ⚒, C (40 ton), SM, D, C (25 ton).
Town EC Thurs; 🛒, R, Bar, Gas, ✉, Ⓑ, ⇌, ✈ Gatwick.
OARE CREEK: **Services:** AB £5, M, C (8 ton), ME, El, ⚒, CH; **Hollow Shore Cruising Club ☎** 533254, Bar.
CONYER CREEK: **Swale Marina ☎** 521562, 📠 520788, AB(dredged 2m) £10, FW, ⛽, D, P, Gas, BH (15 ton), ME, ⚒, C (30ton), Slip, ♿, 🗑; **Conyer CC. Conyer Marina ☎** 521711 AB £5, CH, SM, Rigging, BY, ME, ⚒, El, Ⓔ, Slip, D.
MILTON CREEK (Sittingbourne): **Crown Quay** M, FW.
Town EC Wed; 🛒, R, Bar, ✉, Ⓑ, ⇌, ✈ (Gatwick); also the Dolphin Yard Sailing Barge Museum.
QUEENBOROUGH: See 9.4.10.

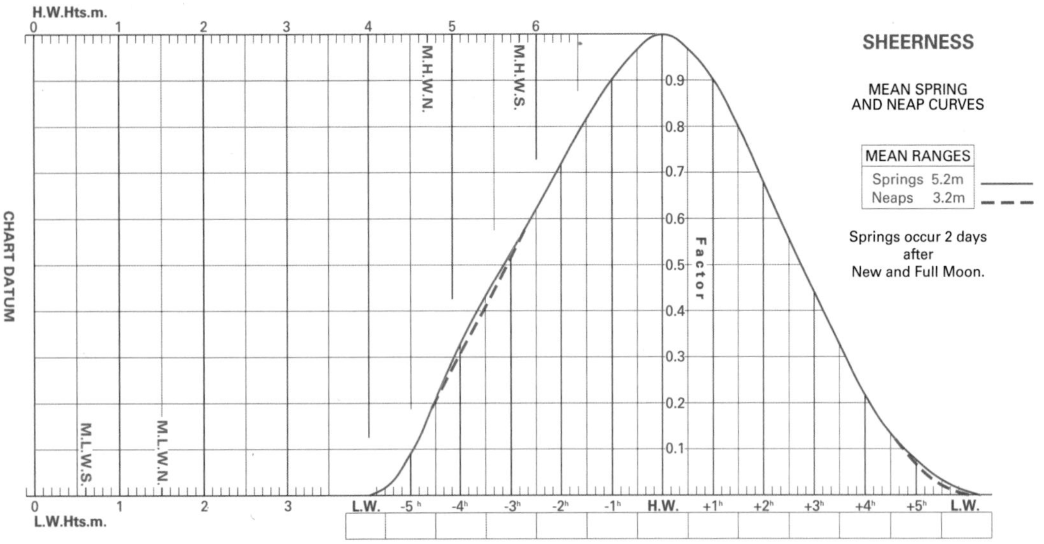
H.W.Hts.m.
0 1 2 3 4 5 6
M.H.W.N.
M.H.W.S.
CHART DATUM
M.L.W.S.
M.L.W.N.
0 1 2 3
L.W.Hts.m.
0.9
0.8
0.7
0.6
0.5
0.4
0.3
0.2
0.1
Factor
L.W. -5h -4h -3h -2h -1h H.W. +1h +2h +3h +4h +5h L.W.
SHEERNESS
MEAN SPRING AND NEAP CURVES
MEAN RANGES
Springs 5.2m
Neaps 3.2m
Springs occur 2 days after New and Full Moon.

9.4.10 QUEENBOROUGH

Kent (Isle of Sheppey) **51°25'·04N 00°44'·19E**

CHARTS AC *5606, 1834,* 2572, 3683; Imray C1, Y14/18; Stanford 8; OS 178

TIDES Use 9.4.11 Sheerness, 2M to the N. +0130 Dover; ML 3·0; Duration 0610; Zone 0 (UT).

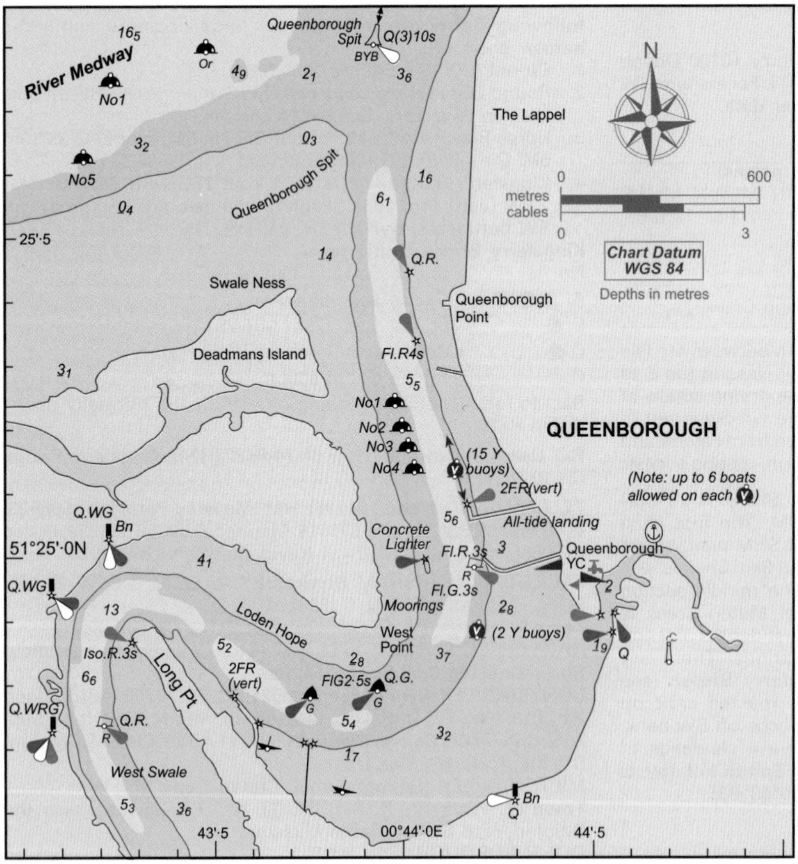
River Medway
No1
No5
Or
Queenborough Spit
Q(3)10s
BYB
The Lappel
Queenborough Spit
Swale Ness
Deadmans Island
Q.R.
Fl.R4s
Queenborough Point
No1
No2
No3
No4
(15 Y buoys)
2F.R(vert)
QUEENBOROUGH
(Note: up to 6 boats allowed on each)
All-tide landing
Concrete Lighter
Fl.R.3s
Fl.G.3s
Moorings
Queenborough
YC
Q.WG
Bn
51°25'·0N
Q.WG
Loden Hope
West Point
(2 Y buoys)
Iso.R.3s
Long Pt
2FR (vert)
FlG2·5s
Q.G.
Q.WRG
Q.R.
West Swale
Bn
Q
43'·5
00°44'·0E
44'·5
25'·5
metres
cables
0 600
0 3
Chart Datum WGS 84
Depths in metres

SHELTER Good, except near HW in strong N'ly winds. The first deep-water refuge W of N Foreland, accessible at all tides from Garrison Pt (9.4.11); or from the Swale (9.4.9) on the tide. An all-tide pontoon/jetty (5m depth at end) on E bank is for landing/short stay only; both sides of the jetty are foul. 2 Y ⓥs on E side, N of all-tide landing; 4 Ⓥ AB on concrete lighter on W side or at 2 Y ⓥs close S of The Hard, a drying causeway. When these are full the hbr controller will offer spare buoys. Smaller R buoys (numbered) are for locals. ⚓ is discouraged due to commercial traffic. Speed limit 8kn.

NAVIGATION WPT: see 9.4.11 for appr via Garrison Pt. Enter the river at Queenborough Spit ECM buoy, Q (3) 10s, 51°25'·75N 00°43'·93E. The chan narrows between drying banks and moorings. See 9.4.9 if approaching from the Swale.

LIGHTS AND MARKS Lights as chartlet. Note: Q 16m 5M lt, vis 163°-168°, on river bend covers the appr chan. All-tide landing 2 FR (vert). Concrete lighter Fl G 3s.

R/T Monitor *Medway Radio* VHF Ch **74** for tfc info. Call Ch 08 *Sheppey One* (Q'boro HM) for berths, also water taxi at weekends only (£1.20 to landing).

TELEPHONE (Dial code 01795) HM 662051; MRSC (01255) 675518; Marinecall 09066 526239; Police 477055; Dr 583828; Ⓗ (01634) 830000 (Gillingham).

FACILITIES Hbr Controller, ⓥ £6.00<11m, ☎/📠 662051, FW on all-tide Landing jetty. **Queenborough YC** Wed, Fri, Sat evenings, Sat, Sun lunchtimes, ☎ 663955, M, R, Bar, ♿, 🚿; **The Creek** ☎ 07974 349018, (HW±1½) Slip, Scrubbing berth (FW, ⛽, D (cans)). **Services:** BY, ME, El, ⚒, CH, C (10 ton), Gas;
Town EC Wed; P & D (cans), 🛒, R, Bar, ✉, ≷, ✈ (Gatwick).

9.4.11 RIVER MEDWAY (SHEERNESS to ROCHESTER)

Kent **51°27'·03N 00°44'·50E** (Off Garrison Pt) ❀❀❀◊◊◊✿✿✿

CHARTS AC *5606*, 1835, *1834, 1185, 2482,* 3683; Imray C1, Y18; Stanfords 5, 8; OS 178

TIDES +0130 Dover; ML 3·1; Duration 0610; Zone 0 (UT)

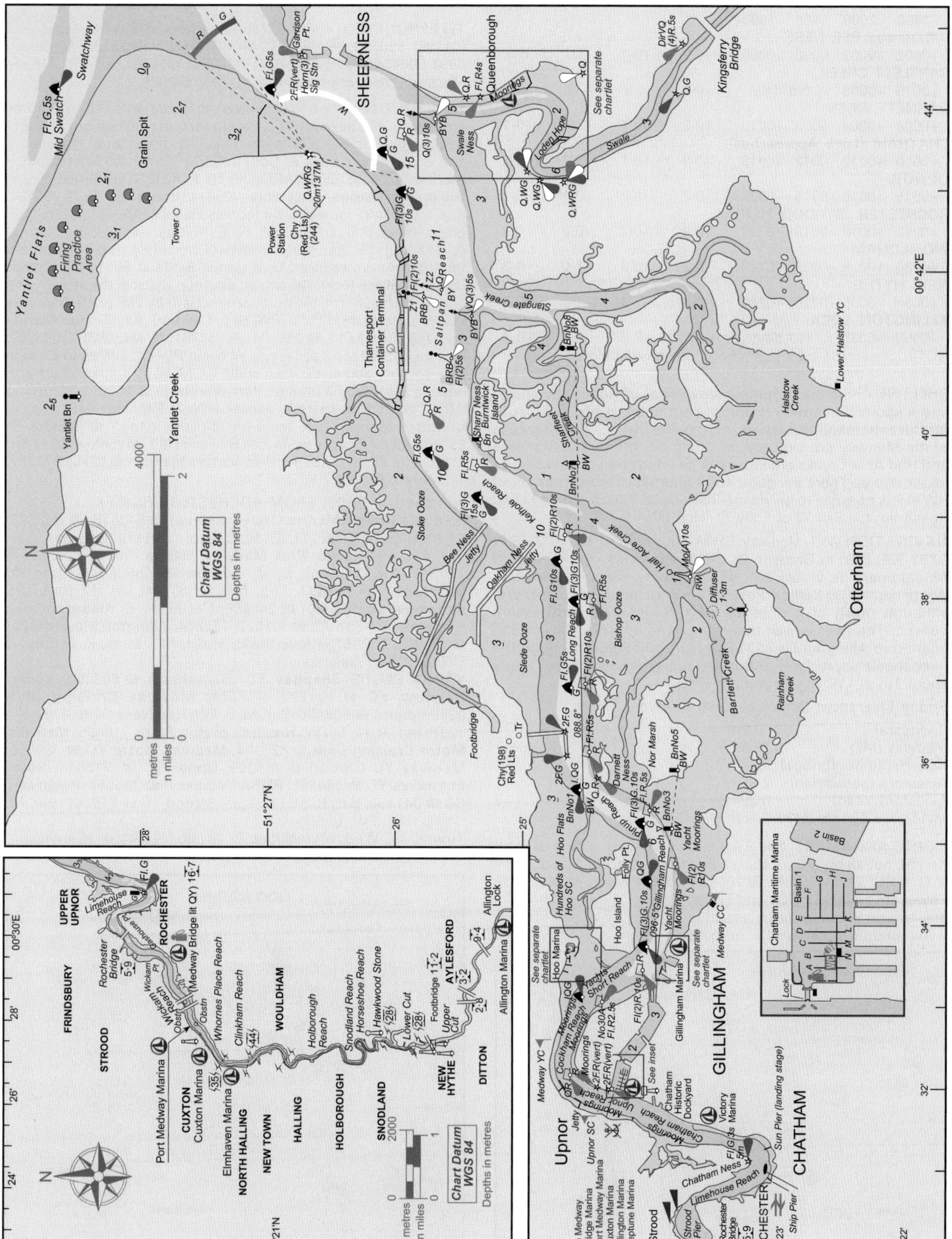
SHEERNESS
Garrison Pt
Queenborough
Kingsferry Bridge
Swale
Swale Ness
Loden Hope
See separate chartlet
Swatchway
Mid Swatch
Grain Spit
Yantlet Flats
Firing Practice Area
Tower
Power Station
Thamesport Container Terminal
Saltpan Reach
Stangate Creek
Yantlet Bn
Yantlet Creek
Chart Datum WGS 84
Depths in metres
metres
n miles
Sharp Ness
Burntwick Island
Stoke Ooze
Kethole Reach
Bee Ness Jetty
Oakham Ness Jetty
Half Acre Creek
Otterham
Halstow Creek
Lower Halstow YC
Slede Ooze
Long Reach
Bishop Ooze
Bartlett Creek
Rainham Creek
Footbridge
Darnett Ness
Nor Marsh
Pinup Reach
Hoo Flats
Hundreds of Hoo
Hoo SC
Folly Pt
Gillingham Reach
Yacht Moorings
Hoo Island
Hoo Marina
Short Reach
Gillingham Marina
Medway CC
GILLINGHAM
Chatham Maritime Marina
Basin 1
Basin 2
Lock
Cockham Reach
Medway YC
Upnor
Upnor SC
Upnor Reach
Chatham Historic Dockyard
Victory Marina
Chatham Reach
Chatham Ness
Limehouse Reach
Sun Pier (landing stage)
CHATHAM
Ship Pier
Strood
Strood Pier
Rochester Bridge
ROCHESTER
To Medway Bridge Marina
Port Medway Marina
Cuxton Marina
Allington Marina
Neptune Marina
UPPER UPNOR
FRINDSBURY
STROOD
Rochester Bridge
Limehouse Reach
Medway Bridge
Wickham Reach
Whornes Place Reach
Clinkham Reach
Port Medway Marina
Cuxton Marina
CUXTON
Elmhaven Marina
NORTH HALLING
NEW TOWN
WOULDHAM
HALLING
Holborough Reach
HOLBOROUGH
Snodland Reach
Horseshoe Reach
Hawkwood Stone
SNODLAND
Lower Cut
Upper Cut
Footbridge
NEW HYTHE
AYLESFORD
DITTON
Allington Marina
Allington Lock

Standard Port SHEERNESS (⟶)

Times				Height (metres)			
High Water		Low Water		MHWS	MHWN	MLWN	MLWS
0200	0800	0200	0700	5·8	4·7	1·5	0·6
1400	2000	1400	1900				
Differences BEE NESS							
+0002	+0002	0000	+0005	+0·2	+0·1	0·0	0·0
BARTLETT CREEK							
+0016	+0008	No data		+0·1	0·0	No data	
DARNETT NESS							
+0004	+0004	0000	+0010	+0·2	+0·1	0·0	−0·1
CHATHAM (Lock Approaches)							
+0010	+0012	+0012	+0018	+0·3	+0·1	−0·1	−0·2
UPNOR							
+0015	+0015	+0015	+0025	+0·2	+0·2	−0·1	−0·1
ROCHESTER (STROOD PIER)							
+0018	+0018	+0018	+0028	+0·2	+0·2	−0·2	−0·3
WOULDHAM							
+0030	+0025	+0035	+0120	−0·2	−0·3	−1·0	−0·3
NEW HYTHE							
+0035	+0035	+0220	+0240	−1·6	−1·7	−1·2	−0·3
ALLINGTON LOCK							
+0050	+0035	No data		−2·1	−2·2	−1·3	−0·4

NOTE: Sheerness tidal predictions are given below.

SHELTER There are 3 marinas downriver of Rochester Bridge and 4 above. Sheerness is solely a commercial hbr. See 9.4.10 for Queenborough and access to/from The Swale. Lower reaches of the Medway are exposed to strong NE winds, but Stangate and Half Acre Creeks are secure in all winds and give access to lesser creeks. There are good ⚓s in Sharfleet Creek; from about HW–4 it is possible to go via the 'back-door' into Half Acre Creek. Speed limit is 6kn W of Folly Pt (Hoo Island).

NAVIGATION WPT Medway SWM buoy, Mo(A) 6s, 51°28′·80N 00°52′·92E, 249° to Garrison Pt, 5·5M. The wreck of the *'Richard Montgomery'* is visible 2M NE of estuary ent and a Military Wreck depth 2_2 in Kethole Reach. There is a huge area to explore, although much of it dries to mud. Some minor creeks are buoyed. The river is well buoyed/marked up to Rochester and tidal up to Allington Lock (21·6M). Above Rochester bridge the river shoals appreciably and in the upper reaches there is only about 1m at LW; access approx HW±3.

Bridge Clearances (MHWS), going up-river:

Rochester	5·9m
Medway (M2)	29·6m
New Hythe (footbridge)	11·3m
Aylesford (pedestrian)	2·87m
Aylesford (road)	3·26m
Maidstone bypass (M20)	9·45m

LIGHTS AND MARKS See 9.4.4 and chartlet for details of most lts. NB: not all buoys are shown due to small scale. Isle of Grain lt Q WRG 20m 13/7/8M R220°-234°, G234°-241°, W241°-013°. Power stn chy (242m) Oc and FR lts. Tfc Sigs: Powerful lt, Fl 7s, at Garrison Pt means large vessel under way: if shown up river = inbound; if to seaward = outbound.

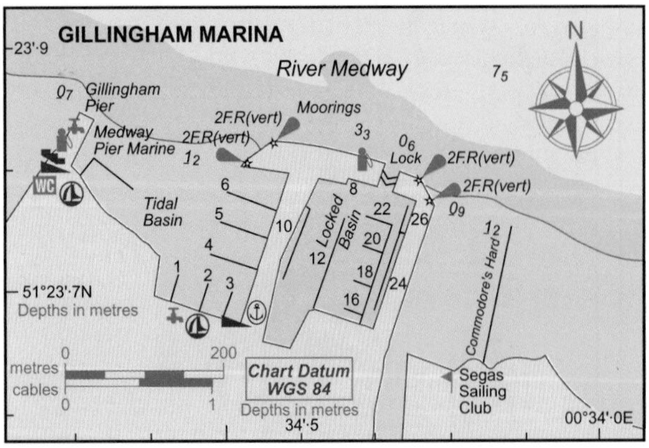
GILLINGHAM MARINA
River Medway
Gillingham Pier
Medway Pier Marine
2F.R(vert)
Moorings
Lock
Tidal Basin
Locked Basin
Commodore's Hard
Segas Sailing Club
51°23′·7N
Depths in metres
Chart Datum WGS 84
Depths in metres
metres
cables
00°34′·0E
34′·5
23′·9

R/T Call: *Medway Radio* VHF Ch **74** 16 (H24). Monitor Ch 74 underway and Ch 16 at ⚓. Radar assistance is available on request Ch 22. Ch **80** M for marinas: Gillingham, Hoo (H24), Medway Bridge (0900-1700LT) and Port Medway (0800-2000LT). Link calls via Thames Radio Ch 02, 83.

TELEPHONE (Dial codes 01795 Sheerness; 01634 Medway) HM (01795) 596593, Fax 581571; MRSC (01255) 675518; Marinecall 0891-500455; Police (01634) 827055, (01795) 661451; Dr via Medway Navigation Service (01795) 663025.

FACILITIES (☎ code 01634, unless otherwise stated) All moorings are run by YCs or marinas. Landing (only) at Gillingham Pier and Dock steps, Sun Pier (Chatham), Ship Pier, Town Quay (Rochester) and Strood Pier. Slips at Commodores Hard, and Gillingham.
Marinas (FROM SEAWARD UP TO ROCHESTER BRIDGE)
Gillingham Marina - see below - (250+12 Ⓥs) ☎ 280022, Fax 280164, pre-book. £1.85 locked basin (access via lock HW±4½), £1.25 tidal basin HW±2, P, D, ⊐D foc, ME, El, Ⓔ, ⚒, Gas, Gaz, CH, BH (65 ton), ⛴, C (1 ton), 🛒, Bar. Note: effects of cross-tide, esp. the ebb, off the lock ent are reduced by a timber baffle at 90° to the stream (close W of the lock). An angled pontoon deflects the stream and is also the fuel berth; the outboard end is lit by 2FR (vert). **Medway Pier Marine** ☎ 851113, D, FW, Slip, C (6 ton), BY, Ⓔ; **Hoo Marina** (120 AB afloat) £12, ☎ 250311, Fax 251761, ⚒, ME, SM, CH, El, Ⓔ, D (cans), C (20 ton), access to W basin HW±1½; HW±3 to E basin (via sill 1m above CD); an unlit WCM buoy marks chan ent; waiting buoy No 53 in river. **Port Werburgh** ☎ 250593; 90 drying AB to W of Hoo marina; access HW±2; FW, fuel, ME, slip, C. **Chatham Marina** - see inset on previous page - ☎ 899200, Fax 899201, (300 AB), access via lock H24 and sill 1.3m below CD (1.5m at MLWS), £2.75, C(15T), P, D, ◙. **Victory Marina** - ☎ 07785 971797, Fax 329783: Ⓥ, FW, ⊐D.

Marinas (UP-RIVER FROM ROCHESTER BRIDGE)
Medway Bridge Marina (160+4 visitors) ☎ 843576, Fax 843820, £1.20, Slip, D, P, ME, El, Ⓔ, ⚒, C (3 ton), BH (10 ton), Gas, Gaz, SM, CH, 🛒, R, Bar; **Port Medway Marina** (50) ☎ 720033, Fax 720315, BH (16 ton), C, ⛴; **Cuxton Marina** (150+some Ⓥ) ☎ 721941, Fax 290853, Slip, ME, El, Ⓔ, ⚒, BH (12 ton), CH; **Elmhaven Marina** (60) ☎ 240489, ME, El, ⚒, C; **Allington Lock** operates HW–3 to +2, ☎ (01622) 752864. **Allington Marina** (120) ☎ (01622) 752057, above the lock; CH, ME, El, ⚒, P, D, Slip, C (10 ton), FW, Gas, Gaz;

YACHT CLUBS Sheppey YC (Sheerness) ☎ 663052; **Lower Halstow YC** ☎ (01227) 458554; **Medway Cruising Club** (Gillingham) ☎ 856489, Bar, M, L, FW; **Hoo Ness YC** ☎ 0181 304 1238, Bar, R, M, L, FW; **Hundred of Hoo SC** ☎ 710405; **Medway Motor Cruising Club** ☎ 827194; **Medway Motor YC** ☎ 389856; **Medway YC** (Upnor) ☎ 718399; **Upnor SC** ☎ 718043; **Royal Engineers YC** ☎ 844555; **RNSA** (Medway) ☎ 744565; **Rochester CC** ☎ 841350, Bar, R, M, FW, L, ◙; **Strood YC** ☎ 718261, Bar, M, C (1·5 ton), FW, L, Slip.
Towns: EC Wed; all facilities R, 🛒, ◙, ✉, ⇌, ✈ (Gatwick).

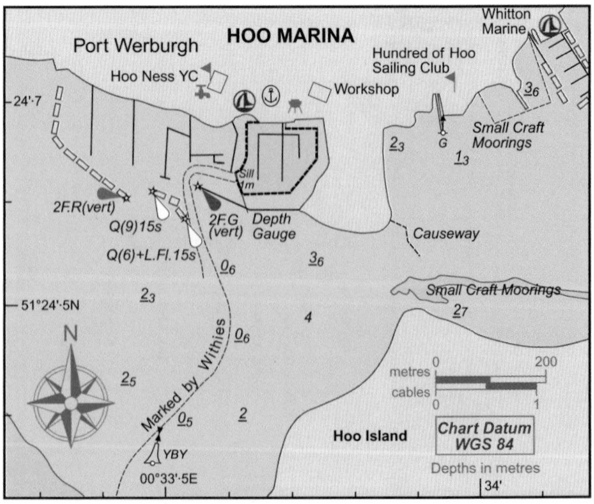
HOO MARINA
Port Werburgh
Hoo Ness YC
Workshop
Whitton Marine
Hundred of Hoo Sailing Club
Small Craft Moorings
Sill 1m
2F.R(vert)
Q(9)15s
2F.G (vert)
Depth Gauge
Q(6)+L.Fl.15s
Causeway
Small Craft Moorings
Marked by Withies
YBY
Hoo Island
Chart Datum WGS 84
Depths in metres
metres
cables
24′·7
51°24′·5N
00°33′·5E
34′

TIME ZONE (UT)
For Summer Time add ONE hour in **non-shaded areas**

ENGLAND – SHEERNESS

LAT 51°27′N LONG 0°45′E

TIMES AND HEIGHTS OF HIGH AND LOW WATERS

SPRING & NEAP TIDES
Dates in red are SPRINGS
Dates in blue are NEAPS

YEAR **2005**

JANUARY

Date	Day	Time	m	Time	m	Time	m	Time	m
1	SA	0327	5.2	0946	1.0	1602	5.1	2145	1.3
2	SU	0405	5.1	1024	1.0	1643	5.0	2224	1.4
3	M	0447	5.0	1104	1.1	1730	4.9	◑ 2309	1.5
4	TU	0536	4.9	1151	1.2	1825	4.9		
5	W	0004	1.6	0635	4.8	1251	1.2	1929	4.8
6	TH	0114	1.6	0747	4.9	1407	1.2	2040	4.9
7	F	0234	1.5	0902	5.0	1525	1.1	2147	5.1
8	SA	0350	1.3	1010	5.2	1633	1.0	2247	5.3
9	SU	0458	1.1	1112	5.5	1733	0.9	2343	5.5
10	M	0601	0.8	1209	5.7	1828	0.8	●	
11	TU	0035	5.6	0701	0.6	1303	5.8	1919	0.7
12	W	0124	5.7	0756	0.4	1355	5.9	2007	0.7
13	TH	0212	5.7	0847	0.3	1444	5.9	2052	0.8
14	F	0258	5.7	0935	0.3	1533	5.8	2134	0.9
15	SA	0343	5.6	1020	0.4	1620	5.6	2215	1.0
16	SU	0429	5.5	1102	0.6	1709	5.4	2255	1.2
17	M	0516	5.3	1144	0.8	1759	5.1	◐ 2341	1.3
18	TU	0608	5.1	1231	1.0	1855	4.9		
19	W	0036	1.5	0708	4.9	1330	1.3	1956	4.7
20	TH	0146	1.6	0818	4.7	1437	1.4	2103	4.7
21	F	0300	1.5	0931	4.7	1542	1.4	2208	4.8
22	SA	0409	1.4	1036	4.9	1638	1.4	2303	5.0
23	SU	0508	1.2	1129	5.0	1726	1.3	2349	5.1
24	M	0557	1.0	1213	5.2	1806	1.2		
25	TU	0028	5.2	0638	0.9	1252	5.3	○ 1840	1.1
26	W	0103	5.3	0715	0.8	1326	5.4	1913	1.0
27	TH	0136	5.4	0749	0.7	1359	5.4	1946	0.9
28	F	0207	5.4	0824	0.7	1432	5.4	2021	0.9
29	SA	0239	5.4	0859	0.6	1505	5.4	2055	0.9
30	SU	0310	5.4	0932	0.7	1539	5.4	2126	1.0
31	M	0343	5.3	1002	0.8	1615	5.2	2156	1.1

FEBRUARY

Date	Day	Time	m	Time	m	Time	m	Time	m
1	TU	0418	5.2	1029	0.9	1655	5.1	2229	1.2
2	W	0459	5.1	1102	1.0	1742	4.9	◑ 2314	1.3
3	TH	0551	5.0	1152	1.2	1842	4.8		
4	F	0017	1.5	0702	4.8	1310	1.3	1958	4.7
5	SA	0151	1.5	0829	4.8	1457	1.4	2118	4.8
6	SU	0330	1.4	0952	5.0	1617	1.2	2231	5.0
7	M	0450	1.1	1104	5.3	1724	1.0	2332	5.3
8	TU	0601	0.7	1204	5.7	1821	0.8	●	
9	W	0026	5.5	0659	0.4	1257	5.9	1911	0.7
10	TH	0114	5.7	0750	0.2	1345	6.0	1956	0.6
11	F	0158	5.8	0836	0.1	1430	6.0	2037	0.6
12	SA	0239	5.8	0917	0.1	1512	5.9	2114	0.7
13	SU	0319	5.8	0954	0.3	1553	5.7	2148	0.8
14	M	0358	5.7	1025	0.5	1633	5.4	2220	1.0
15	TU	0438	5.4	1054	0.8	1713	5.1	2254	1.2
16	W	0521	5.1	1127	1.1	1759	4.8	◐ 2339	1.4
17	TH	0615	4.8	1216	1.4	1856	4.5		
18	F	0045	1.6	0727	4.5	1336	1.7	2010	4.4
19	SA	0220	1.7	0856	4.4	1505	1.7	2133	4.4
20	SU	0346	1.5	1016	4.6	1615	1.6	2239	4.7
21	M	0453	1.2	1113	4.9	1709	1.4	2329	5.0
22	TU	0543	1.0	1156	5.2	1751	1.2		
23	W	0009	5.2	0623	0.8	1233	5.3	1825	1.1
24	TH	0044	5.3	0658	0.7	1306	5.4	○ 1857	0.9
25	F	0116	5.4	0731	0.6	1337	5.5	1930	0.8
26	SA	0147	5.5	0806	0.5	1409	5.6	2004	0.8
27	SU	0217	5.6	0839	0.5	1441	5.6	2036	0.8
28	M	0247	5.6	0911	0.6	1513	5.5	2105	0.9

MARCH

Date	Day	Time	m	Time	m	Time	m	Time	m
1	TU	0318	5.5	0936	0.7	1547	5.4	2130	0.9
2	W	0353	5.4	0958	0.8	1624	5.2	2200	1.0
3	TH	0433	5.3	1028	1.0	1708	5.0	◑ 2244	1.2
4	F	0525	5.0	1119	1.2	1807	4.7	2349	1.4
5	SA	0639	4.8	1245	1.5	1929	4.5		
6	SU	0135	1.5	0815	4.7	1444	1.5	2101	4.6
7	M	0326	1.3	0947	5.0	1608	1.3	2220	4.9
8	TU	0451	0.9	1059	5.4	1716	1.0	2322	5.3
9	W	0557	0.5	1156	5.7	1810	0.8		
10	TH	0012	5.6	0649	0.3	1244	5.9	● 1855	0.6
11	F	0056	5.8	0733	0.1	1327	6.0	1936	0.5
12	SA	0136	5.9	0813	0.1	1407	6.0	2013	0.5
13	SU	0214	5.9	0849	0.2	1445	5.9	2048	0.6
14	M	0251	5.9	0920	0.3	1520	5.7	2119	0.7
15	TU	0327	5.7	0946	0.6	1554	5.4	2147	0.9
16	W	0403	5.5	1009	0.9	1628	5.1	2217	1.1
17	TH	0442	5.1	1038	1.2	1706	4.8	◐ 2255	1.3
18	F	0530	4.7	1122	1.5	1756	4.5	2352	1.6
19	SA	0639	4.4	1235	1.9	1912	4.2		
20	SU	0135	1.7	0815	4.2	1428	1.9	2050	4.2
21	M	0318	1.5	0945	4.5	1546	1.7	2205	4.6
22	TU	0425	1.2	1043	4.9	1642	1.4	2257	4.9
23	W	0515	1.0	1126	5.2	1725	1.2	2338	5.2
24	TH	0555	0.8	1203	5.4	1801	1.0		
25	F	0014	5.4	0630	0.7	1237	5.5	○ 1833	0.9
26	SA	0047	5.5	0705	0.6	1309	5.6	1907	0.8
27	SU	0119	5.6	0740	0.5	1341	5.7	1942	0.7
28	M	0150	5.7	0814	0.5	1414	5.7	2015	0.7
29	TU	0223	5.7	0845	0.6	1447	5.6	2045	0.8
30	W	0257	5.6	0912	0.7	1522	5.5	2113	0.8
31	TH	0335	5.5	0937	0.9	1600	5.3	2148	0.9

APRIL

Date	Day	Time	m	Time	m	Time	m	Time	m
1	F	0419	5.3	1015	1.1	1646	5.0	2237	1.1
2	SA	0517	5.0	1114	1.4	1749	4.7	◑ 2351	1.3
3	SU	0636	4.8	1249	1.6	1915	4.5		
4	M	0147	1.4	0813	4.8	1436	1.6	2049	4.6
5	TU	0326	1.1	0941	5.1	1555	1.3	2205	5.0
6	W	0443	0.7	1047	5.5	1658	1.0	2303	5.3
7	TH	0541	0.4	1139	5.7	1748	0.8	2350	5.6
8	F	0628	0.3	1223	5.9	1831	0.7	●	
9	SA	0031	5.7	0707	0.2	1303	5.9	1909	0.6
10	SU	0110	5.8	0743	0.3	1340	5.9	1945	0.5
11	M	0147	5.9	0815	0.4	1414	5.8	2021	0.5
12	TU	0223	5.8	0844	0.5	1447	5.6	2053	0.7
13	W	0258	5.6	0910	0.8	1519	5.4	2121	0.8
14	TH	0334	5.4	0934	1.0	1550	5.1	2148	1.0
15	F	0412	5.1	1002	1.3	1625	4.8	2223	1.2
16	SA	0458	4.7	1044	1.6	1711	4.5	◐ 2315	1.5
17	SU	0600	4.4	1148	1.9	1819	4.2		
18	M	0041	1.6	0724	4.3	1332	2.0	1954	4.2
19	TU	0233	1.5	0851	4.4	1500	1.8	2114	4.5
20	W	0340	1.2	0955	4.8	1558	1.5	2211	4.8
21	TH	0431	1.0	1043	5.1	1644	1.2	2256	5.1
22	F	0515	0.8	1124	5.4	1724	1.1	2336	5.4
23	SA	0555	0.7	1201	5.5	1802	0.9		
24	SU	0012	5.5	0632	0.6	1237	5.7	○ 1840	0.8
25	M	0048	5.6	0710	0.6	1313	5.7	1918	0.7
26	TU	0124	5.7	0747	0.6	1348	5.7	1956	0.7
27	W	0202	5.7	0822	0.6	1425	5.6	2033	0.7
28	TH	0242	5.7	0855	0.8	1503	5.5	2110	0.8
29	F	0326	5.6	0932	1.0	1546	5.3	2154	0.9
30	SA	0417	5.3	1018	1.2	1638	5.0	2251	1.0

Chart Datum: 2·90 metres below Ordnance Datum (Newlyn)

TIME ZONE (UT)
For Summer Time add ONE hour in **non-shaded areas**

ENGLAND – SHEERNESS

LAT 51°27′N   LONG 0°45′E

TIMES AND HEIGHTS OF HIGH AND LOW WATERS

SPRING & NEAP TIDES
Dates in red are SPRINGS
Dates in blue are NEAPS

YEAR **2005**

MAY

Date	Day	Time	m	Time	m	Time	m	Time	m	Moon
1	SU	0521	5.1	1123	1.5	1745	4.7			◑
2	M	0013	1.1	0640	4.9	1250	1.6	1907	4.7	
3	TU	0150	1.1	0805	5.0	1416	1.5	2030	4.8	
4	W	0311	0.8	0921	5.3	1527	1.3	2139	5.1	
5	TH	0419	0.6	1023	5.5	1628	1.1	2236	5.3	
6	F	0514	0.5	1114	5.6	1718	0.9	2323	5.5	
7	SA	0557	0.5	1157	5.7	1800	0.8			
8	SU	0004	5.6	0634	0.5	1236	5.7	1840	0.7	●
9	M	0044	5.7	0708	0.5	1312	5.7	1919	0.6	
10	TU	0122	5.7	0740	0.6	1346	5.6	1956	0.6	
11	W	0159	5.6	0811	0.8	1418	5.5	2030	0.7	
12	TH	0236	5.5	0839	1.0	1449	5.3	2101	0.9	
13	F	0313	5.3	0906	1.2	1521	5.1	2130	1.0	
14	SA	0352	5.0	0937	1.3	1557	4.9	2204	1.2	
15	SU	0436	4.8	1018	1.6	1641	4.7	2252	1.3	
16	M	0529	4.6	1113	1.8	1740	4.5	2358	1.4	◐
17	TU	0635	4.5	1226	1.9	1855	4.4			
18	W	0124	1.4	0747	4.5	1350	1.8	2011	4.5	
19	TH	0239	1.2	0854	4.8	1458	1.6	2114	4.8	
20	F	0337	1.0	0950	5.0	1552	1.4	2207	5.1	
21	SA	0427	0.9	1039	5.3	1641	1.2	2254	5.3	
22	SU	0514	0.8	1124	5.5	1727	1.0	2338	5.5	
23	M	0559	0.7	1206	5.6	1813	0.9			○
24	TU	0021	5.6	0642	0.7	1247	5.7	1858	0.8	
25	W	0104	5.7	0724	0.7	1328	5.7	1944	0.7	
26	TH	0148	5.8	0806	0.7	1410	5.6	2030	0.6	
27	F	0235	5.7	0848	0.8	1454	5.5	2118	0.6	
28	SA	0325	5.6	0933	1.0	1542	5.3	2210	0.7	
29	SU	0421	5.5	1024	1.2	1637	5.1	2309	0.8	
30	M	0523	5.3	1123	1.3	1740	5.0			◑
31	TU	0019	0.8	0631	5.2	1233	1.4	1850	5.0	

JUNE

Date	Day	Time	m	Time	m	Time	m	Time	m	Moon
1	W	0132	0.8	0742	5.2	1343	1.4	2000	5.0	
2	TH	0240	0.7	0850	5.3	1449	1.3	2106	5.1	
3	F	0343	0.7	0951	5.3	1549	1.2	2204	5.3	
4	SA	0437	0.7	1044	5.4	1643	1.1	2255	5.3	
5	SU	0522	0.8	1130	5.4	1731	0.9	2341	5.4	
6	M	0601	0.8	1211	5.5	1815	0.8			●
7	TU	0024	5.5	0636	0.9	1249	5.5	1857	0.8	
8	W	0105	5.5	0710	0.9	1324	5.4	1937	0.7	
9	TH	0144	5.4	0744	1.0	1357	5.4	2014	0.8	
10	F	0221	5.4	0815	1.1	1430	5.3	2047	0.9	
11	SA	0258	5.2	0846	1.2	1503	5.2	2120	1.0	
12	SU	0336	5.1	0920	1.3	1539	5.0	2155	1.0	
13	M	0416	5.0	0959	1.4	1620	4.9	2237	1.1	
14	TU	0501	4.8	1044	1.5	1707	4.8	2326	1.2	
15	W	0551	4.7	1137	1.6	1802	4.7			◐
16	TH	0023	1.2	0649	4.7	1239	1.7	1905	4.7	
17	F	0128	1.2	0753	4.8	1348	1.6	2013	4.8	
18	SA	0236	1.1	0857	5.0	1456	1.5	2117	5.0	
19	SU	0339	1.0	0956	5.2	1559	1.3	2215	5.2	
20	M	0437	0.9	1050	5.3	1657	1.1	2309	5.4	
21	TU	0530	0.9	1140	5.5	1752	1.0			
22	W	0001	5.6	0621	0.8	1229	5.6	1846	0.8	○
23	TH	0051	5.7	0710	0.8	1315	5.6	1940	0.6	
24	F	0142	5.8	0757	0.8	1402	5.6	2032	0.5	
25	SA	0232	5.9	0845	0.8	1449	5.6	2124	0.4	
26	SU	0324	5.8	0931	0.9	1538	5.5	2215	0.4	
27	M	0416	5.7	1019	1.0	1629	5.4	2307	0.5	
28	TU	0511	5.5	1108	1.1	1722	5.3			◑
29	W	0000	0.6	0607	5.4	1201	1.3	1820	5.2	
30	TH	0056	0.7	0708	5.2	1300	1.3	1922	5.1	

JULY

Date	Day	Time	m	Time	m	Time	m	Time	m	Moon
1	F	0156	0.9	0811	5.1	1404	1.4	2027	5.1	
2	SA	0257	1.0	0914	5.1	1509	1.3	2132	5.1	
3	SU	0356	1.1	1013	5.1	1612	1.2	2232	5.1	
4	M	0448	1.1	1106	5.2	1709	1.1	2326	5.2	
5	TU	0533	1.1	1152	5.3	1800	1.0			
6	W	0013	5.3	0613	1.1	1234	5.3	1845	0.9	●
7	TH	0056	5.3	0650	1.1	1311	5.3	1925	0.8	
8	F	0134	5.3	0724	1.1	1345	5.3	2002	0.8	
9	SA	0210	5.3	0758	1.1	1417	5.3	2036	0.8	
10	SU	0244	5.3	0831	1.1	1450	5.3	2110	0.8	
11	M	0318	5.3	0905	1.1	1523	5.2	2143	0.8	
12	TU	0354	5.2	0940	1.2	1557	5.2	2218	0.9	
13	W	0431	5.1	1016	1.3	1634	5.1	2254	1.0	
14	TH	0512	5.0	1055	1.4	1716	5.0	2333	1.1	◐
15	F	0600	4.9	1141	1.5	1808	4.9			
16	SA	0023	1.2	0658	4.8	1242	1.6	1914	4.8	
17	SU	0133	1.3	0807	4.8	1401	1.6	2030	4.8	
18	M	0256	1.3	0917	5.0	1524	1.5	2143	5.0	
19	TU	0408	1.1	1022	5.2	1635	1.2	2249	5.3	
20	W	0511	1.0	1122	5.4	1741	0.9	2349	5.6	
21	TH	0608	0.9	1215	5.5	1842	0.7			○
22	F	0044	5.8	0700	0.8	1306	5.7	1938	0.4	
23	SA	0136	5.9	0750	0.7	1353	5.7	2030	0.2	
24	SU	0225	6.0	0836	0.7	1439	5.8	2118	0.1	
25	M	0313	6.0	0920	0.8	1523	5.8	2203	0.2	
26	TU	0359	5.9	1001	0.9	1607	5.7	2245	0.3	
27	W	0446	5.6	1040	1.0	1653	5.6	2325	0.6	
28	TH	0534	5.4	1122	1.2	1742	5.3			◑
29	F	0007	0.9	0626	5.1	1212	1.3	1838	5.1	
30	SA	0059	1.2	0725	4.9	1316	1.5	1946	4.9	
31	SU	0206	1.4	0833	4.8	1433	1.5	2103	4.8	

AUGUST

Date	Day	Time	m	Time	m	Time	m	Time	m	Moon
1	M	0317	1.5	0943	4.8	1550	1.4	2216	4.9	
2	TU	0422	1.4	1046	5.0	1658	1.2	2316	5.1	
3	W	0516	1.4	1137	5.1	1752	1.0			
4	TH	0004	5.2	0559	1.3	1219	5.3	1835	0.9	
5	F	0044	5.3	0635	1.2	1256	5.3	1912	0.8	●
6	SA	0120	5.4	0708	1.1	1329	5.4	1946	0.8	
7	SU	0152	5.4	0740	1.0	1400	5.5	2018	0.7	
8	M	0223	5.5	0813	1.0	1430	5.5	2051	0.7	
9	TU	0255	5.5	0846	1.0	1500	5.4	2123	0.7	
10	W	0327	5.4	0918	1.1	1531	5.4	2152	0.8	
11	TH	0400	5.3	0946	1.2	1602	5.3	2219	1.0	
12	F	0435	5.2	1015	1.3	1639	5.2	2247	1.1	
13	SA	0517	5.0	1052	1.4	1726	5.0	2327	1.3	◐
14	SU	0611	4.8	1148	1.6	1829	4.8			
15	M	0035	1.5	0722	4.7	1315	1.7	1954	4.7	
16	TU	0225	1.5	0846	4.7	1503	1.5	2123	4.9	
17	W	0350	1.3	1003	5.0	1625	1.2	2239	5.3	
18	TH	0459	1.1	1108	5.3	1736	0.8	2341	5.6	
19	F	0558	0.9	1203	5.6	1837	0.5			○
20	SA	0035	5.9	0649	0.8	1252	5.8	1928	0.2	
21	SU	0124	6.1	0736	0.7	1336	5.9	2015	0.1	
22	M	0208	6.1	0818	0.6	1418	6.0	2058	0.1	
23	TU	0251	6.1	0858	0.7	1458	6.0	2137	0.2	
24	W	0332	5.9	0934	0.8	1538	5.9	2211	0.4	
25	TH	0413	5.6	1007	1.0	1618	5.6	2241	0.8	
26	F	0454	5.3	1042	1.1	1702	5.3	2313	1.1	◑
27	SA	0538	5.0	1124	1.4	1754	5.0	2357	1.4	
28	SU	0634	4.7	1225	1.6	1904	4.6			
29	M	0110	1.8	0746	4.5	1400	1.7	2034	4.5	
30	TU	0244	1.8	0912	4.5	1533	1.5	2159	4.7	
31	W	0401	1.7	1023	4.8	1644	1.2	2259	5.0	

Chart Datum: 2·90 metres below Ordnance Datum (Newlyn)

TIME ZONE (UT)
For Summer Time add ONE hour in **non-shaded areas**

ENGLAND – SHEERNESS

LAT 51°27′N LONG 0°45′E

TIMES AND HEIGHTS OF HIGH AND LOW WATERS

SPRING & NEAP TIDES
Dates in red are SPRINGS
Dates in blue are NEAPS

YEAR **2005**

SEPTEMBER

Day	Time	m
1 TH	0458	1.5
	1115	5.1
	1735	1.0
	2345	5.3
2 F	0541	1.3
	1157	5.3
	1815	0.9
3 SA	0022	5.4
	0616	1.2
	1232	5.4
	● 1848	0.8
4 SU	0055	5.5
	0647	1.1
	1304	5.5
	1920	0.7
5 M	0126	5.6
	0718	1.0
	1334	5.6
	1952	0.6
6 TU	0155	5.6
	0750	0.9
	1403	5.6
	2024	0.6
7 W	0226	5.6
	0822	0.9
	1432	5.6
	2055	0.7
8 TH	0256	5.6
	0852	1.0
	1502	5.5
	2122	0.8
9 F	0328	5.4
	0917	1.1
	1534	5.4
	2144	1.0
10 SA	0402	5.3
	0943	1.2
	1612	5.3
	2208	1.2
11 SU	0443	5.1
	1020	1.3
	1659	5.1
	◐ 2252	1.4
12 M	0536	4.8
	1119	1.5
	1805	4.8
13 TU	0008	1.7
	0650	4.6
	1258	1.7
	1936	4.7
14 W	0209	1.7
	0824	4.6
	1456	1.5
	2113	4.9
15 TH	0337	1.5
	0948	4.9
	1620	1.1
	2230	5.4
16 F	0446	1.1
	1053	5.3
	1728	0.7
	2329	5.8
17 SA	0542	0.9
	1145	5.6
	1823	0.4
18 SU	0019	6.0
	0630	0.8
	1230	5.9
	○ 1909	0.2
19 M	0103	6.1
	0712	0.7
	1311	6.0
	1950	0.1
20 TU	0144	6.1
	0752	0.6
	1351	6.1
	2028	0.2
21 W	0223	6.0
	0829	0.7
	1429	6.0
	2102	0.4
22 TH	0300	5.8
	0904	0.8
	1507	5.9
	2132	0.7
23 F	0336	5.6
	0935	1.0
	1546	5.6
	2157	1.0
24 SA	0412	5.3
	1006	1.2
	1627	5.3
	2225	1.3
25 SU	0451	4.9
	1043	1.4
	1716	4.9
	◑ 2306	1.7
26 M	0541	4.6
	1139	1.7
	1824	4.5
27 TU	0015	2.0
	0655	4.3
	1325	1.8
	1958	4.4
28 W	0208	2.1
	0831	4.3
	1507	1.6
	2128	4.6
29 TH	0330	1.9
	0949	4.7
	1613	1.3
	2229	5.0
30 F	0427	1.6
	1042	5.0
	1702	1.0
	2313	5.3

OCTOBER

Day	Time	m
1 SA	0510	1.3
	1123	5.3
	1741	0.9
	2350	5.5
2 SU	0546	1.2
	1159	5.5
	1816	0.8
3 M	0022	5.6
	0618	1.0
	1231	5.6
	● 1848	0.7
4 TU	0053	5.6
	0650	1.0
	1302	5.7
	1920	0.7
5 W	0124	5.7
	0723	0.9
	1333	5.7
	1953	0.7
6 TH	0155	5.7
	0756	0.9
	1404	5.7
	2024	0.8
7 F	0227	5.6
	0827	1.0
	1437	5.6
	2052	0.9
8 SA	0300	5.5
	0855	1.1
	1513	5.5
	2117	1.1
9 SU	0336	5.3
	0926	1.2
	1555	5.3
	2149	1.3
10 M	0419	5.1
	1010	1.3
	1648	5.1
	◐ 2242	1.5
11 TU	0515	4.8
	1117	1.5
	1759	4.8
12 W	0006	1.8
	0633	4.6
	1306	1.5
	1931	4.8
13 TH	0156	1.8
	0808	4.7
	1450	1.3
	2102	5.1
14 F	0318	1.5
	0928	5.0
	1607	0.9
	2213	5.5
15 SA	0423	1.2
	1030	5.4
	1709	0.6
	2309	5.8
16 SU	0517	1.0
	1120	5.7
	1759	0.4
	2355	5.9
17 M	0603	0.8
	1203	5.9
	1841	0.4
	○	
18 TU	0037	6.0
	0643	0.7
	1244	6.0
	1919	0.4
19 W	0116	6.0
	0723	0.7
	1323	6.0
	1953	0.5
20 TH	0153	5.9
	0800	0.7
	1401	6.0
	2025	0.6
21 F	0228	5.7
	0836	0.8
	1440	5.8
	2054	0.9
22 SA	0302	5.5
	0908	1.0
	1519	5.5
	2119	1.2
23 SU	0335	5.2
	0938	1.2
	1559	5.2
	2147	1.5
24 M	0411	4.9
	1011	1.4
	1647	4.8
	2227	1.8
25 TU	0457	4.6
	1101	1.6
	1748	4.5
	◑ 2326	2.0
26 W	0604	4.4
	1227	1.8
	1909	4.4
27 TH	0105	2.2
	0735	4.3
	1420	1.6
	2033	4.5
28 F	0240	2.0
	0855	4.5
	1525	1.4
	2139	4.8
29 SA	0340	1.7
	0953	4.9
	1616	1.1
	2227	5.1
30 SU	0427	1.4
	1039	5.2
	1658	0.9
	2307	5.4
31 M	0506	1.2
	1118	5.4
	1736	0.8
	2343	5.5

NOVEMBER

Day	Time	m
1 TU	0543	1.1
	1154	5.5
	1812	0.8
2 W	0018	5.6
	0619	1.0
	1230	5.6
	● 1847	0.8
3 TH	0053	5.7
	0656	0.9
	1305	5.7
	1922	0.8
4 F	0127	5.7
	0733	0.9
	1341	5.7
	1957	0.8
5 SA	0202	5.6
	0810	0.9
	1420	5.7
	2030	1.0
6 SU	0239	5.5
	0847	1.0
	1502	5.6
	2105	1.1
7 M	0320	5.3
	0928	1.0
	1550	5.4
	2148	1.3
8 TU	0408	5.1
	1020	1.2
	1649	5.2
	2246	1.5
9 W	0508	4.9
	1132	1.3
	1800	5.0
	◐	
10 TH	0004	1.7
	0623	4.7
	1307	1.2
	1921	5.0
11 F	0132	1.7
	0746	4.8
	1430	1.0
	2040	5.2
12 SA	0246	1.5
	0859	5.1
	1540	0.8
	2146	5.4
13 SU	0349	1.3
	1000	5.4
	1639	0.7
	2241	5.6
14 M	0443	1.1
	1051	5.6
	1728	0.6
	2328	5.7
15 TU	0531	0.9
	1136	5.7
	1809	0.6
16 W	0010	5.7
	0614	0.8
	1219	5.8
	○ 1844	0.7
17 TH	0049	5.7
	0655	0.7
	1300	5.8
	1919	0.8
18 F	0126	5.7
	0736	0.7
	1340	5.7
	1951	0.9
19 SA	0201	5.6
	0814	0.8
	1420	5.6
	2022	1.1
20 SU	0235	5.4
	0848	1.0
	1500	5.4
	2050	1.3
21 M	0308	5.2
	0918	1.1
	1540	5.1
	2120	1.5
22 TU	0343	5.0
	0951	1.3
	1624	4.9
	2158	1.7
23 W	0426	4.8
	1035	1.4
	1715	4.6
	◑ 2248	1.8
24 TH	0521	4.6
	1135	1.5
	1815	4.5
	2354	2.0
25 F	0631	4.4
	1256	1.6
	1923	4.5
26 SA	0116	2.0
	0745	4.5
	1416	1.4
	2030	4.7
27 SU	0232	1.8
	0850	4.7
	1516	1.3
	2128	4.9
28 M	0330	1.6
	0945	5.0
	1606	1.1
	2218	5.2
29 TU	0420	1.4
	1034	5.2
	1652	1.0
	2303	5.4
30 W	0505	1.2
	1118	5.4
	1735	0.9
	2345	5.5

DECEMBER

Day	Time	m
1 TH	0550	1.1
	1201	5.5
	1817	0.9
	●	
2 F	0025	5.6
	0633	0.9
	1243	5.6
	1857	0.9
3 SA	0106	5.6
	0718	0.9
	1326	5.7
	1938	0.9
4 SU	0146	5.6
	0803	0.8
	1411	5.7
	2020	0.9
5 M	0229	5.5
	0850	0.8
	1459	5.7
	2103	1.0
6 TU	0314	5.4
	0940	0.8
	1551	5.5
	2151	1.2
7 W	0405	5.2
	1035	0.8
	1648	5.4
	2245	1.3
8 TH	0502	5.1
	1137	0.9
	1751	5.2
	◐ 2347	1.5
9 F	0606	5.0
	1246	0.9
	1859	5.1
10 SA	0055	1.5
	0715	5.0
	1355	0.9
	2007	5.2
11 SU	0204	1.5
	0823	5.1
	1501	0.9
	2112	5.2
12 M	0308	1.3
	0926	5.2
	1601	0.9
	2210	5.3
13 TU	0408	1.2
	1023	5.3
	1653	0.9
	2301	5.4
14 W	0502	1.1
	1115	5.4
	1737	1.0
	2347	5.4
15 TH	0552	0.9
	1202	5.5
	1816	1.0
	○	
16 F	0029	5.5
	0638	0.8
	1247	5.5
	1852	1.0
17 SA	0108	5.4
	0721	0.8
	1329	5.5
	1926	1.1
18 SU	0144	5.4
	0800	0.8
	1409	5.4
	1959	1.1
19 M	0218	5.3
	0836	0.9
	1447	5.3
	2030	1.2
20 TU	0251	5.2
	0907	1.0
	1524	5.2
	2101	1.3
21 W	0325	5.1
	0939	1.1
	1602	5.0
	2137	1.4
22 TH	0403	5.0
	1015	1.1
	1643	4.9
	2217	1.5
23 F	0445	4.8
	1058	1.2
	1728	4.7
	◑ 2305	1.7
24 SA	0533	4.7
	1149	1.3
	1820	4.6
25 SU	0000	1.8
	0631	4.6
	1249	1.4
	1920	4.6
26 M	0107	1.8
	0739	4.6
	1400	1.4
	2025	4.7
27 TU	0222	1.7
	0848	4.7
	1511	1.3
	2128	4.9
28 W	0332	1.5
	0951	5.0
	1611	1.2
	2225	5.1
29 TH	0432	1.3
	1047	5.2
	1705	1.0
	2317	5.3
30 F	0527	1.1
	1140	5.4
	1755	0.9
31 SA	0006	5.5
	0619	0.9
	1230	5.6
	● 1842	0.9

Chart Datum: 2·90 metres below Ordnance Datum (Newlyn)

4

9.4.12 RIVER THAMES

London: from Canvey Island to Teddington lock

SEQUENCE Information is arranged as far as possible from seaward, starting abeam Canvey Island and continuing up-river to the head of the tidal Thames at Teddington. See 9.4.13 for Southend-on-Sea and Leigh-on-Sea.

CHARTS AC *5606*, 1185, 1186, 2151, 3337, *2484*, 3319; Imray C1, C2, Y18, 2100 Series; Stanfords 5, 8; OS 176, 177, 178.

Books include: *Nicholsons Guide to the Thames*; *River Thames Book* (Imray). The Port of London Authority (PLA), Bakers Hall, 7 Harp Lane, London EC3R 6LB; ☎ 020 7743 7900, issues free: *General Directions, Permanent Notices: Pleasure Users Guide. Port of London River Byelaws* & *Tide Tables* are available. See www.portoflondon.co.uk. for latest info.

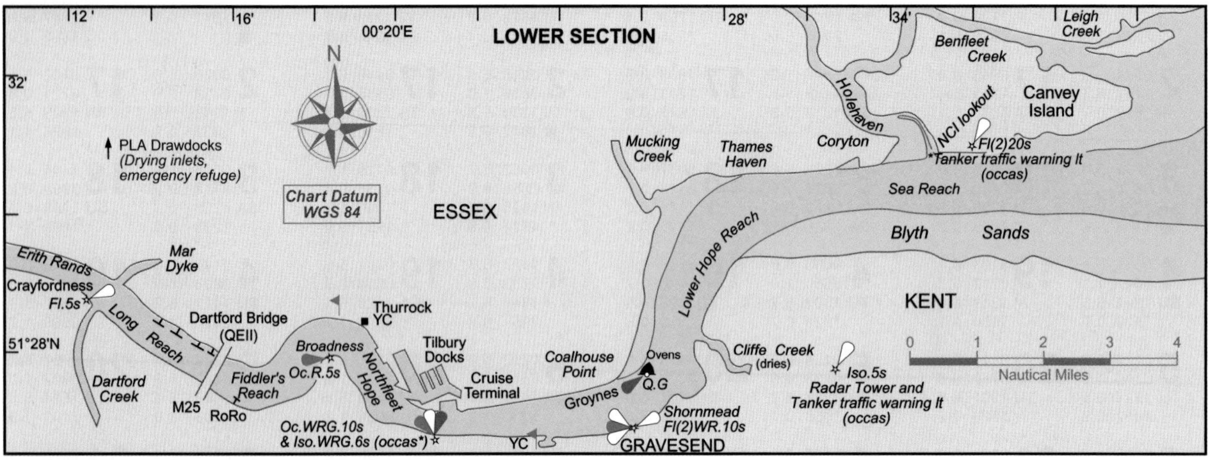
LOWER SECTION
00°20'E
PLA Drawdocks (Drying inlets, emergency refuge)
Chart Datum WGS 84
ESSEX
KENT
Leigh Creek
Benfleet Creek
Canvey Island
Holehaven
Coryton
NCI lookout
Fl(2)20s
Tanker traffic warning lt (occas)
Mucking Creek
Thames Haven
Sea Reach
Blyth Sands
Lower Hope Reach
Erith Rands
Crayfordness
Fl.5s
Mar Dyke
Long Reach
Dartford Bridge (QEII)
Thurrock YC
Broadness
Northfleet Hope
Tilbury Docks
Cruise Terminal
Coalhouse Point
Ovens
Q.G
Cliffe Creek (dries)
Iso.5s
Radar Tower and Tanker traffic warning lt (occas)
Dartford Creek
Fiddler's Reach
Oc.R.5s
M25
RoRo
Oc.WRG.10s & Iso.WRG.6s (occas*)
YC
Groynes
Shornmead Fl(2)WR.10s
GRAVESEND
Nautical Miles

CANVEY ISLAND TO CRAYFORDNESS (AC 1185, 1186, 2484, 2151)

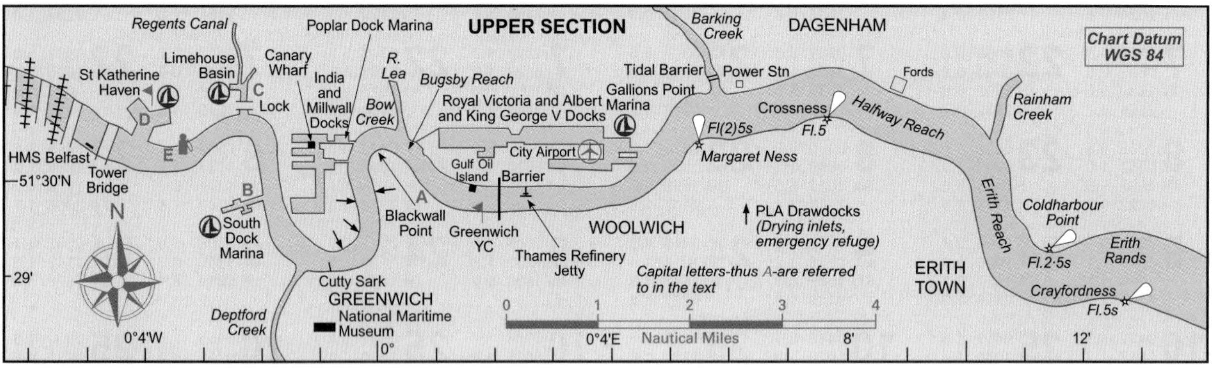
UPPER SECTION
Regents Canal
Poplar Dock Marina
Barking Creek
DAGENHAM
Chart Datum WGS 84
Limehouse Basin
Canary Wharf
R. Lea
St Katherine Haven
India and Millwall Docks
Bow Creek
Bugsby Reach
Tidal Barrier
Power Stn
Fords
Gallions Point
Royal Victoria and Albert and King George V Docks
Marina
Lock
Crossness
Fl(2)5s
Fl.5
Halfway Reach
Rainham Creek
HMS Belfast
Tower Bridge
City Airport
Gulf Oil Island
Barrier
Margaret Ness
South Dock Marina
Blackwall Point
Greenwich YC
Thames Refinery Jetty
WOOLWICH
PLA Drawdocks (Drying inlets, emergency refuge)
Capital letters-thus A-are referred to in the text
Erith Reach
Coldharbour Point
Fl.2·5s
Erith Rands
ERITH TOWN
Crayfordness
Fl.5s
Cutty Sark
GREENWICH
National Maritime Museum
Deptford Creek
Nautical Miles

CRAYFORDNESS TO TOWER BRIDGE (AC 2484, 2151, 3337)

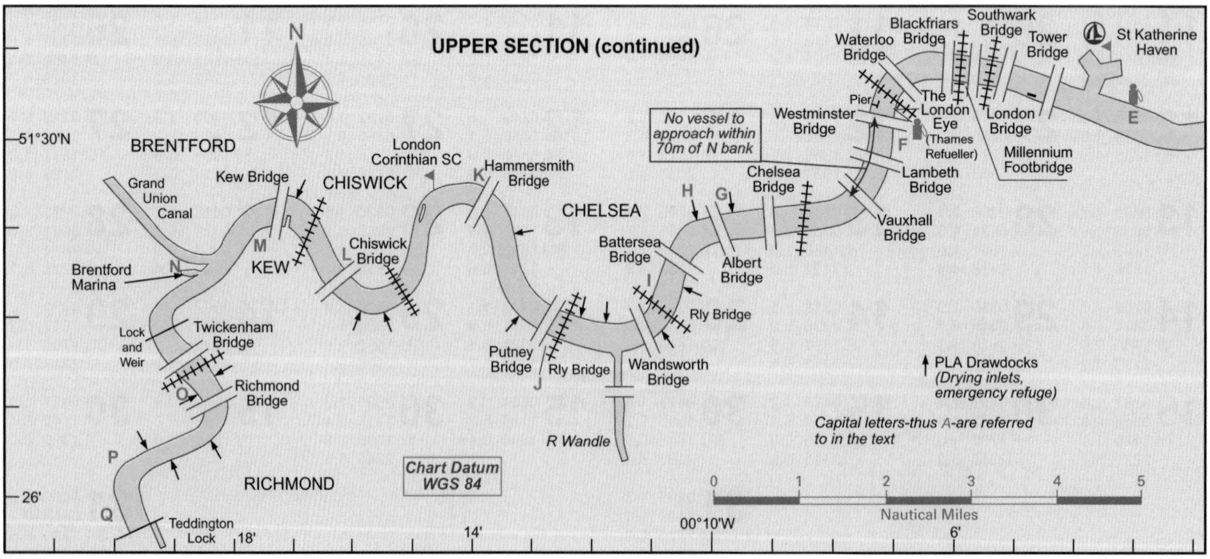
UPPER SECTION (continued)
Blackfriars Bridge
Southwark Bridge
Waterloo Bridge
Tower Bridge
St Katherine Haven
No vessel to approach within 70m of N bank
Westminster Bridge
Pier
The London Eye
(Thames Refueller)
London Bridge
Millennium Footbridge
BRENTFORD
London Corinthian SC
Hammersmith Bridge
Kew Bridge
CHISWICK
Lambeth Bridge
Chelsea Bridge
Grand Union Canal
CHELSEA
Vauxhall Bridge
Brentford Marina
KEW
Chiswick Bridge
Battersea Bridge
Albert Bridge
Rly Bridge
Lock and Weir
Twickenham Bridge
Richmond Bridge
Putney Bridge
Rly Bridge
Wandsworth Bridge
PLA Drawdocks (Drying inlets, emergency refuge)
Capital letters-thus A-are referred to in the text
R Wandle
Chart Datum WGS 84
RICHMOND
Teddington Lock
Nautical Miles

TOWER BRIDGE TO TEDDINGTON (AC 3319)

RIVER THAMES *continued*

HARBOURS IN LOWER REACHES OF RIVER THAMES

HOLEHAVEN, Essex, **51°30′·58N 00°33′·40E.** AC 2484, 1186. HW +0140 on Dover; use differences for CORYTON, see 9.4.13; ML 3·0m; Duration 068. Shelter is good, but beware swell from passing traffic. Note: There is an 8kn speed limit in the river off Coryton and Shellhaven; keep at least 60m clear of berthed tankers and refinery jetties. Keep to Canvey Is side on ent. ⚓ on W edge of chan as long stone groynes extend from E side. 0·5M N of ent an overhead oil pipe crosses chan with clearance of 11m, plus 2 FY lts (horiz). Lts Coryton Refinery Jetty No 4 2 FG (vert). FW from 'The Lobster Smack yard', P & D from Canvey Village (1M); EC Thurs; all other facilities on Canvey Is.

GRAVESEND, Kent, **51°26′·61N 00°22′·90E** (lock into Canal basin). AC 1186, 2151. HW +0150 on Dover; ML 3·3m; Duration 0610. Use Tilbury diffs overleaf. Caution: Off the N bank, from Coalhouse Pt to 7ca E of Gravesend, 6 groynes (tops dry 1·0m) project approx 400m almost into the fairway; their outer ends are marked by SHM bns, Fl G 2·5s. 5 Y buoys downstream of No 6 groyne (the most E'ly) indicate that **no passage exists inshore of the Y buoys and groyne bns.** A SHM buoy *Diver*, L Fl G 10s, between Nos 3 and 2 groynes, marks the N edge of the fairway. ⚓ E of the Sea School jetty, close to S shore, but remote from town. There are Ⓥs off the Club. Lock opens HW $-1\frac{1}{2}$ to HW on request to lock-keeper, ☎ (01474) 352392 (24hrs notice required for night tides). Boats can be left unattended in canal basin but not at ⚓s. Royal Terrace Pier hd FR. Call *Port Control London* (located at Gravesend) VHF Ch 12 if E of Sea Reach No 4 buoy (1.4M SSE of Southend pier); and Ch 68 from No 4 buoy to Crayfordness. Broadcasts on Ch 68 every H & H+30 and on Ch 12 every H+15 and H+45. ⊖537115 (H24); **Gravesend SC** ☎ 533974, Bar, FW, M, P & D (cans); **Services:** C (at canal ent, ask at SC), CH, Ⓔ, ME, El, ⚒. **Town Pier** Projected new development to include Ⓥ opening Spring 2003, max LOA 70m, ☎ (020) 7378 1211. **Town** Tourist info ☎ (01474) 337600, R, 🛒.

Thurrock YC (51°28′·30N 00°19′·57E) at Grays, ☎ (01375) 373720 is 3M upriver on N bank opposite Broadness. 1 Ⓥ, D, P (2M), Bar, R (occas). 1000-1500 M-F; 2000-2300 Thur.

4

THAMES TIDAL BARRIER

51°29′·91N 00°02′·21E (Span G)

Charts AC *5606*, 2484 and 3337.

Description Located at Woolwich Reach, it protects London from floods. There are 9 piers between which gates can be rotated upwards from the river bed to form a barrier. The piers are numbered 1-9 from N to S; the spans are lettered A-K from S to N (see diagram). A, H, J & K are not navigable. C-F, with depth 5·8m and 61m wide, are for larger ships. Spans B and G, with 1·25m, are for small craft/yachts which should lower sail and use engine: W-bound via G and E-bound via B (51°29′·70N 00°02′·33E).

Control & Communications The Thames Barrier Navigation Centre controls all traffic in a Zone from Margaret Ness (51°30′·5N 00°05′·6E) to Blackwall Point (51°30′·3N 00°00′·3E), using the callsign *Woolwich Radio* on VHF Ch **14**, 22, 16. **Inbound** vessels should pass their ETA at the Barrier to *Woolwich Radio* when abeam Crayford Ness (51°28′·9N 00°12′·8E). When passing Margaret Ness they should obtain clearance to proceed through the Barrier. **Outbound** vessels should use the same procedure abeam Tower Bridge (51°30′·3N 00°04′·3E) and Blackwall Point. **Non-VHF** craft should, if possible, pre-notify the Barrier Control ☎ 020 8855 0315; then observe all visual signals, proceed with caution keeping clear of larger vessels and use spans B or G as appropriate. Telephone Barrier Control when passage completed. Sailing vessels should transit the Barrier under power, not sail.

Lights and Signals At Thamesmead and Barking Power Station to the E, and Blackwall Stairs (N bank) and Blackwall Pt (S bank) to the W, noticeboards and lights indicate:
Fl ○ = proceed with extreme caution.
Fl ● = navigation within Zone is prohibited.

On the Barrier piers:
St Andrew's Cross (R lts) = barrier or span closed.
Arrows (G lts) = span indicated is open to traffic.
Spans A, H, J and K are lit with 3 ● in ▽ = No passage.
In addition, in reduced visibility, spans open to navigation are marked by high intensity lts and racons.

Spans open for navigation Information will be included in routine broadcasts by *Woolwich Radio* on VHF Ch 14 at H + 15 and H + 45.

Testing The Barrier is completely closed for testing once a month, for about 3hrs, LW $\pm1\frac{1}{2}$. An annual closure in Sept/Oct lasts about 10 hrs, LW to LW; this may affect passage plans.

Beware On N side of river (Spans E and F) a cross-tide component is reported; expect to lay-off a compensating drift angle. When all spans are closed, keep 200m clear to avoid turbulence. **It is dangerous to transit a closed span, as the gate may be semi-raised.** Small craft should not navigate between Thames Refinery Jetty and Gulf Oil Island, unless intending to transit the Barrier.

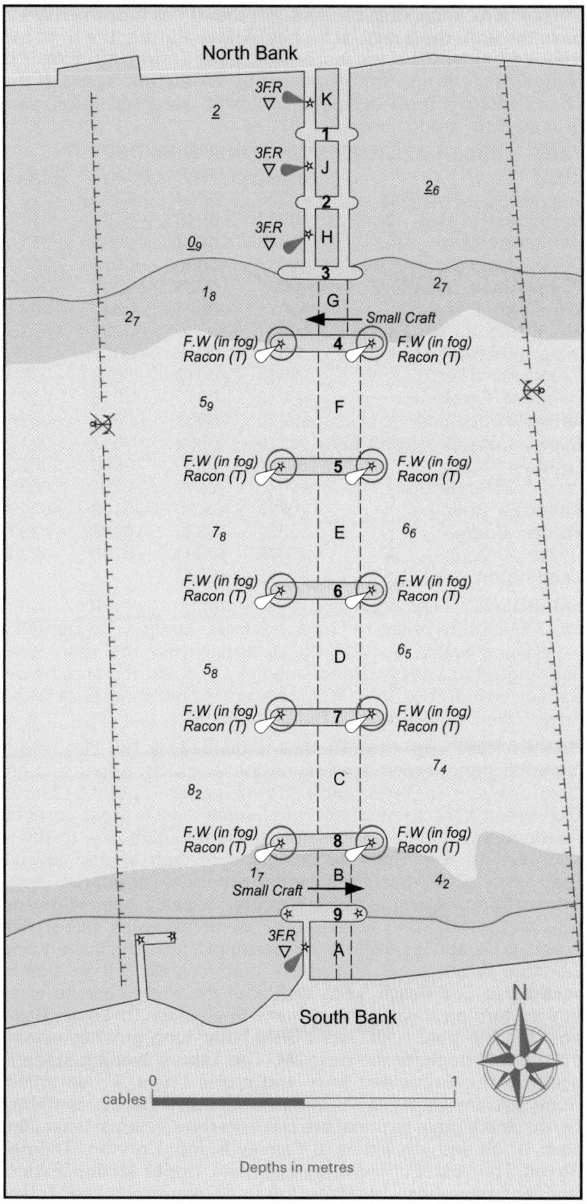
North Bank
3F.R
K
J
H
1
2
3
4
5
6
7
8
9
G
F
E
D
C
B
A
Small Craft
F.W (in fog)
Racon (T)
South Bank
N
cables
0
1
Depths in metres

TIDES +0252 Dover; ML 3·6; Duration 0555; Zone 0 (UT)

Standard Port LONDON BRIDGE (⟶)

Times				Height (metres)			
High Water		Low Water		MHWS	MHWN	MLWN	MLWS
0300	0900	0400	1100	7·1	5·9	1·3	0·5
1500	2100	1600	2300				
Differences TILBURY							
−0055	−0040	−0050	−0115	−0·7	−0·5	+0·1	0·0
WOOLWICH (GALLIONS POINT)							
−0020	−0020	−0035	−0045	−0·1	0·0	+0·2	0·0
ALBERT BRIDGE							
+0025	+0020	+0105	+0110	−0·9	−0·8	−0·7	−0·4
HAMMERSMITH BRIDGE							
+0040	+0035	+0205	+0155	−1·4	−1·3	−1·0	−0·5
KEW BRIDGE							
+0055	+0050	+0255	+0235	−1·8	−1·8	−1·2	−0·5
RICHMOND LOCK							
+0105	+0055	+0325	+0305	−2·2	−2·2	−1·3	−0·5

The river is tidal up to Richmond Footbridge where there is a half-tide lock and a weir with overhead sluice gates. When down, ie closed, these gates maintain at least 1·72m between Richmond and Teddington bridges; the half-tide lock, on the Surrey bank, must then be used. At other times (approx HW ±2) pass through the 3 central arches. Above Putney the ht of LW may be below CD if the water flow over Teddington Weir is reduced; warnings are broadcast by Woolwich Radio. If the Thames Barrier (previous page) is closed, water levels will vary greatly from predictions.

TIDES – TIME DIFFERENCES ON LONDON BRIDGE

Place	MHWS	MHWN	MLWN	MLWS
Gravesend Town Pier	−0059	−0044	−0106	−0125
Broadness Lt Ho	−0052	−0040	−0101	−0119
Stoneness Lt Ho	−0048	−0037	−0059	−0114
Coldharbour Point	−0037	−0030	−0053	−0103
Royal Albert Dock Ent	−0029	−0024	−0043	−0050
Woolwich Ferry	−0028	−0024	−0042	−0047
Royal Victoria Dock Ent	−0021	−0018	−0031	−0025
India & Millwall Dock Ent	−0018	−0015	−0026	−0029
Greenwich Pier	−0014	−0012	−0020	−0023
Deptford Creek	−0012	−0011	−0018	−0021
Millwall Dock Ent	−0010	−0008	−0014	−0016
Surrey Dock Greenland Ent	−0010	−0008	−0013	−0015
London Bridge	0000	0000	0000	0000
Westminster Bridge	+0012	+0011	+0031	+0035
Battersea Bridge	+0023	+0020	+0109	+0110
Putney Bridge	+0032	+0030	+0138	+0137
Chiswick Bridge	+0049	+0044	+0235	+0224
Teddington Lock	+0106	+0056	—	—

EMERGENCY In emergencies call *London Coastguard* on Ch 16; a CG Station is based at Thames Barrier. London CG operates a listening watch on VHF Ch 16 and covers the river from Teddington to Canvey Island. Thames CG cover the area below Canvey Island. Four RNLI LB stations are in operation; Gravesend Tower Pier, Chiswick and Teddington.

NAVIGATION The tidal Thames is divided by the PLA into a lower section: from sea to Crayfordness, and an upper section: Crayfordness to Teddington. **Some general points**: Above Gravesend keep to stbd side of channel - do not cut corners. Boats approaching a bridge against the tide give way to those approaching with the tide; but pleasure craft should always keep clear of commercial vessels, especially tug/barge tows. Above Cherry Garden Pier (Wapping), vessels over 40m and tugs and tows always have priority. Minimise wash, but an 8kn speed limit applies inshore off Southend, off Shellhaven and Coryton, in all creeks and above Wandsworth Bridge. **Lower section**. In Sea Reach, keep well S of the main chan to clear tankers turning abeam Canvey Is and Shellhaven. In Lower Hope hold the NW bank until Ovens SHM buoy; long groynes extend from the N bank for the next 2M. The Tilbury landing stage is used by the Gravesend ferry and cruise liners. In Northfleet Hope beware ships/tugs turning into Tilbury Docks; container berths and a grain terminal are close up-river. Keep at least 60m clear of oil and gas jetties at Canvey Island, Coryton, Thames Haven, Thurrock, Purfleet and Dagenham. **Upper section**. Expect frequent passenger launches from/to Greenwich, The Tower and Westminster. Thames Police and PLA launches are helpful.

BRIDGES

Name of Bridge	Distance from London Bridge Nautical Miles	Clearance below centre span MHWS (m)
Dartford (QEII)	17·68 below	54.1
Tower	0·49 below	8·6 (42·5 open)
ALL BRIDGES UPSTREAM OF TOWER BRIDGE ARE FIXED		
London Bridge	0.00	8·9
Cannon St. Railway	0·16	7·1
Southwark	0·24	7·4
Millennium Bridge	0·41	9·4
Blackfriars Railway	0·62	7·0
Blackfriars	0·63	7·1
Waterloo	1·12	8·5
Charing Cross Railway	1·32	7·0
Westminster	1·64	5·4
Lambeth	2·02	6·5
Vauxhall	2·46	5·6
Victoria Railway	3·31	6·0
Chelsea	3·40	6·6
Albert	4·04	4·9
Battersea	4·27	5·5
Battersea Railway	4·83	6·1
Wandsworth	5·46	5·8
Fulham Railway	6·31	6·9
Putney	6·45	5·5
Hammersmith	7·97	3·7
Barnes Railway	9·55	5·4
Chiswick	10·22	6·9
Kew Railway	10·98	5·6
Kew	11·33	5·3
Richmond Footbridge	13·49	5·5
Twickenham	13·64	5·9
Richmond Railway	13·67	5·3
Richmond	13·97	5·3

Tower Bridge sounds horn for 10s, every 20s, in fog when bascules are open for shipping; standby is Bell 30s. A ▽ of R discs (● lts) below a bridge span = this arch closed.

PIERS WHERE LANDING CAN BE MADE BY ARRANGEMENT Piers with *, contact London River Services ☎ 020 7941 2400, 📠 020 7941 2410: Greenwich Pier*, Tower Pier*, Embankment*, Bankside, Blackfriars, Waterloo Millenium, Westminster Pier*, Festival Pier*, London Bridge City Pier 020 7403 5939; Cadogan Pier (G) 020 7349 8585; Putney Pier 020 7378 1211; Kew Pier, Richmond Lndg Stage 020 7930 2062; Hampton Ct Pier 020 8781 9758.

LIGHTS AND MARKS Glare from shore lts makes navigation by night difficult/risky. Special lts fitted on brs between Tower and Wandsworth: triggered by single large vessel Iso W 4s or by second large vessel VQFl. Other vessels keep clear.

R/T Sea Reach No 4 buoy is 1.35M SSE of Southend pierhead at 51°29'·61N 00°44'·18E. Craft >20m LOA must have VHF radio and call Woolwich Radio on Ch 14 if intending to navigate within the Thames Barrier control zone. Smaller craft with no VHF should call ☎ 020 8855 0315 before and after transiting the Thames Barrier. Routine traffic, weather, tidal and nav info is broadcast by *Port Control London* on Ch 12 at H +15 and H +45 and on Ch 68 at H and H +30; also by *Woolwich Radio* on Ch 14 at H +15 and H +45. The latter will warn if ht of LW upstream of Putney falls below CD. For marina VHF see next page. Avoid using tug VHF Chs: 8, 10, 13, 15, 17, 36, 72, 77.

TELEPHONE (Dial code 020 7 Central London; 020 8 Outer London) PLA: www.portoflondon.co.uk. Operational enquiries 01474 560311; General non-operational enquiries, below Crayfordness: (01474) 562200, 📠 562281; above Crayfordness: 020 7743 7912, 📠 020 7743 7996; Duty Port Controller Gravesend (01474) 560311; Duty Officer Woolwich 020 8855 0315; Port Health Authority (Tilbury 01375) 842663 (H24); London CG 020 8312 7380, email wm_london@mcga.gov.uk; Thames CG (01255) 675518; Marine Support Unit Metropolitan Police HQ (Wapping) 020 7275 4421; London Weather Centre 020 7831 5968; Tower Bridge 020 7407 0922; Richmond Lock 020 8940 0634; **Marinecall** 09066 526239; 🄷 020 7987 7011.

SHELTER Very good in marinas. PLA Drawdocks (⟷) are drying inlets offering emergency refuge, subject to wash.

FACILITIES (Bold red letters in brackets appear on chartlets)
Greenwich YC (A) ☎ 020 88587339; VHF Ch M. FW, ⚓, ME.
Westminster Petroleum Ltd (F) (Fuel barge). Call *Thames Refueller* VHF Ch 14, ☎ 0831 110681, D, Gas, CH, L.
Chelsea Yacht & Boat Co (H) ☎ 020 7352 1427, M, Gas;
Hurlingham YC (J) ☎ 020 8788 5547, M, CH, ME, FW, El, ⚒;
Dove Marina (K).

Chiswick Pier, 51°28'·90N 00°14'·95W. ☎ 020 8742 2713, ℻ 0181 742 0057, £0.95m, long pontoon, 2FG (vert). All tide access, max draft 1·4m. FW, ⚡, ⛽. Visitors welcome.
Chiswick Quay Marina (L) (50) ☎ 020 8994 8743, Access HW±2 via lock, M, FW, BY, M, ME, El, ⚒.
Kew Marina (M) ☎ 020 8940 8364, M, CH, D, P, Gas, SM;
(O), Richmond Slipway BY, CH, D, Gas, M, FW, ME, El, ⚒.
(P) Eel Pie Island BY, CH, ⚡, ME, M, Gas, C (6 ton), ⚒, El, FW;
(Q) Swan Island Hbr, D, M, ME, El, ⚒, FW, Gas, Slip, AB, C (30 ton), CH.

MARINAS ON THE TIDAL THAMES (From seaward: Woolwich to Brentford)

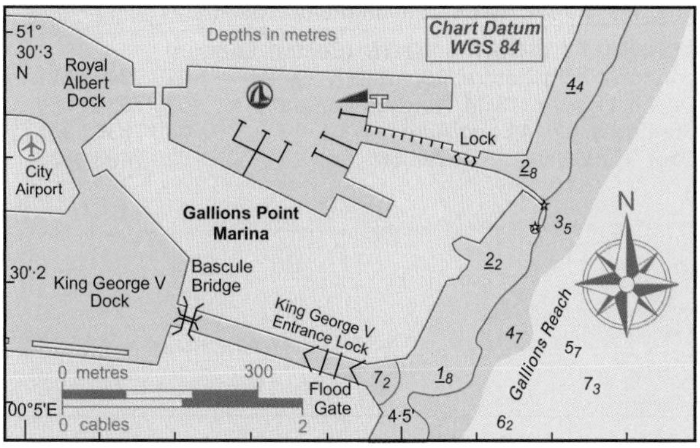
Depths in metres
Chart Datum WGS 84
51° 30'·3 N
Royal Albert Dock
City Airport
Lock
Gallions Point Marina
30'·2
King George V Dock
Bascule Bridge
King George V Entrance Lock
Gallions Reach
Flood Gate
0 metres 300
0 cables 2
00°5'E
N

GALLIONS POINT MARINA, 51°30'·30N 00°04'·66E in entry basin for Royal Albert Dock. AC *2484,* 2151. Tides as for Gallions Pt (9.4.12). Marina ☎ 020 7476 7054 (H24). VHF Ch 80, when vessel expected. Access via lock HW±5; Locking from £5 each way; AB £1.20. Two ☆s 2FG (vert) on river pier. 8m depth in basin. Usual facilities, H24 security. The fuel barge LEONARD is conspic, berthed outside the lock; D, Gas 0900-1600 M-F; ☎ 020 7474 8714 VHF Ch 14. DLR from N Woolwich to central London, until 0030. Woolwich ferry & foot tunnel 15 mins walk. ✈ (City) is adjacent.

SOUTH DOCK MARINA (B), 51°29'·65N 00°01'·97W. AC *2484,* 3337. Tides as for Surrey Dock Greenland Ent (9.4.12). 1·1M above Greenwich, 2·5M below Tower Bridge. Baltic Quay building at SW end of marina is conspic with five arched rooftops. Waiting pontoon at Greenland Pier. Approx access via lock HW-2½ to HW+1½ for 2m draft. **Marina** ☎ 020 7252 2244, ℻ 020 7237 3806, (250 + ⓥ, £15 <15m, £20 >15.5m). VHF Ch **M** 80. **Facilities**: ME, ⚒, El, CH, C (20 ton), Bar, R, 🛒, ⊡, ♿, Dr ☎ 237 1078; ⊞ ⛽ ☎ 020 7955 5000; Police ☎ 020 7252 2836. ⇌, Surrey Quays and Canada Water tube, ✈ City Airport.

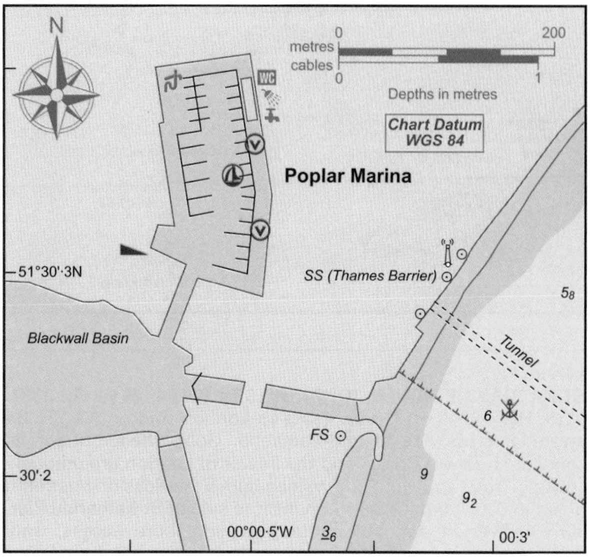
N
metres 0 200
cables 0 1
Depths in metres
Chart Datum WGS 84
Poplar Marina
51°30'·3N
SS (Thames Barrier)
Blackwall Basin
Tunnel
FS
30'·2
00°00·5'W
00·3'

POPLAR DOCK MARINA, 51°30'·07N 00°00'·50W (lock ent). AC *2484,* 3337. Tides: India & Millwall Docks ent (9.4.12). 4·5M below Tower Bridge. Canary Wharf twr (244m) is conspic 4ca W of marina. Lock (200m x 24m) opens 0700-1900LT at HW for outbound and HW-1 to HW+1 for arrivals, foc, but OT £20. Bridge at lock and 2 other bridges open in unison. Least width 12·1m into marina. **Marina** ☎ 0207 5151046, ℻ 0207 5385537, (90 + ⓥ £25, all LOA). VHF Ch 13 (H24). **Facilities**: Slip, Bar, R, 🛒, ⛽, ⊡, ♿; Dr ☎ 020 7237 1078; ⊞ ☎ 020 7955 5000; Police ☎ 252 2836. ⇌, Blackwall DLR, Canary Wharf Tube, ✈ City.

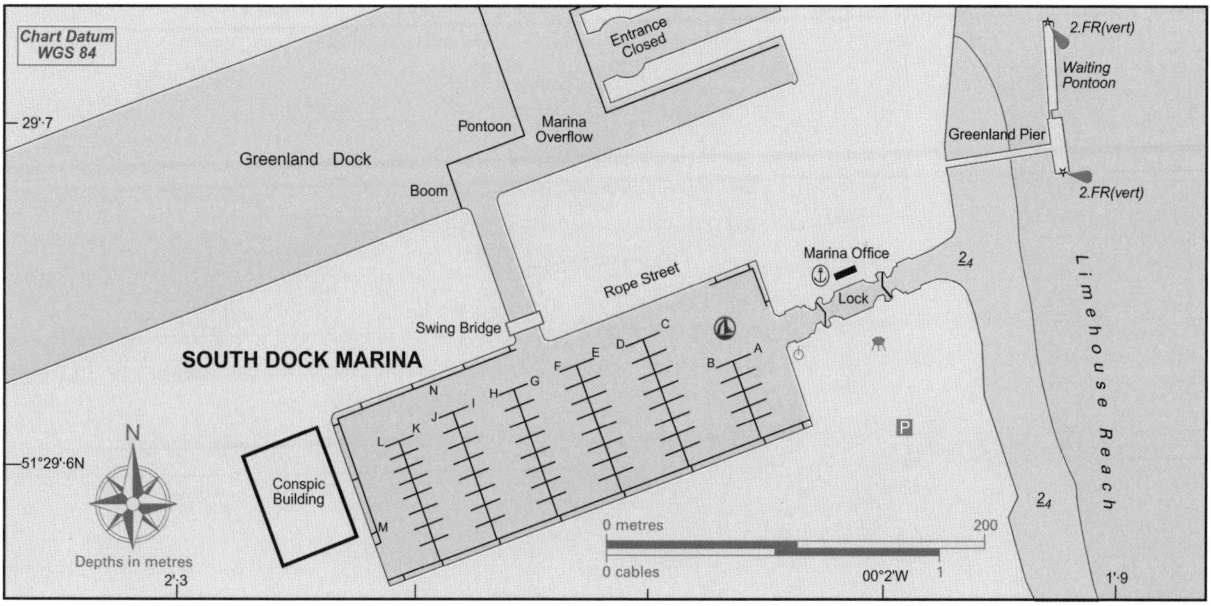
Chart Datum WGS 84
29'·7
Entrance Closed
Pontoon
Marina Overflow
Greenland Dock
Boom
2.FR(vert)
Waiting Pontoon
Greenland Pier
2.FR(vert)
Marina Office
Lock
Rope Street
Swing Bridge
SOUTH DOCK MARINA
Limehouse Reach
51°29'·6N
N
Conspic Building
Depths in metres
0 metres 200
0 cables 1
00°2'W
1'·9

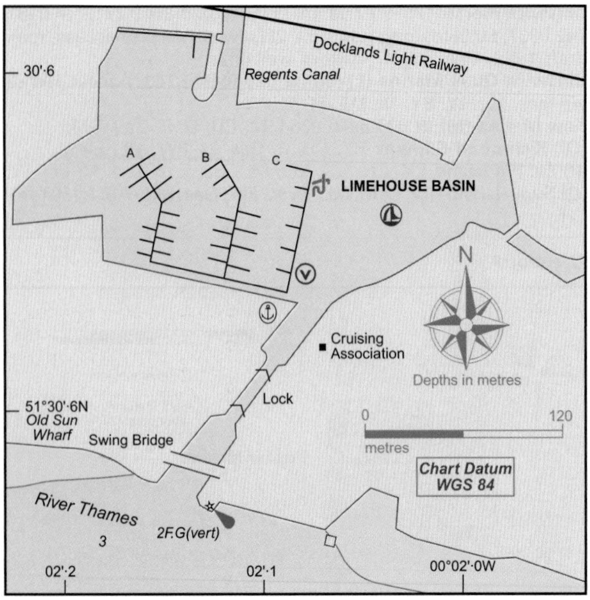
Docklands Light Railway
Regents Canal
30'·6
A
B
C
LIMEHOUSE BASIN
N
Cruising Association
Depths in metres
Lock
51°30'·6N
Old Sun Wharf
Swing Bridge
0
120
metres
Chart Datum WGS 84
River Thames
3
2F.G(vert)
02'·2
02'·1
00°02'·0W

LIMEHOUSE BASIN (C), 51°30'·57N 00°02'·27W. Entry HW±3 via swing bridge/lock, 0800-1800LT daily Apr-Oct; 0800-1630 Nov-Mar; other times by prior arrangement to HM & BWB lock, marina berthing, ☎ 0207 3089930. Waiting pontoon in lock entrance is accessible outside LW±1½. Call VHF Ch 80 *Limehouse Marina*. **Facilities:** (90 berths, £11.75 all LOA) H24 security, ⊡, ⇌, DLR; also entry to Regents Canal and R Lea. *Cruising Association* at: 1 Northey St, Limehouse Basin, E14 8BT, ☎ 020 7537 2828, 📠 020 7537 2266; www.cruising.org.uk; email office@cruising.org.uk; temporary membership, open: 1130-1500 & 1700-2300 Mon-Fri, 1130-2300 Sat, 1200-1500 & 1900-2230 Sun; Bar, R, ♿, ⊡. *Little Ship Club,* Bell Wharf Lane, Upper Thames Street, www.little-ship-club.co.uk.

ADMIRALTY CHART AGENTS (Central London)

London Yacht Centre, 13 Artillery Lane	020 7247 0521
Ocean Leisure, 13/14 Northumberland Av	020 7930 5050
Stanfords, 12/14 Long Acre	020 7836 1321
Capt. O.M.Watts, 7 Dover St	020 7493 4633

ST KATHARINE HAVEN, (D) 51°30'·36N 00°04'·35W. AC 3337, 3319. HW +0245 on Dover. Tides as London Bridge (9.4.12). Be aware of cross tide at mid-flood/ebb. Good shelter under all conditions. Tower Bridge and the Tower of London are uniquely conspic, close up-river. Six Y waiting buoys are close downstream of ent in 0.1 - 1.9m. Or berth on inshore side of St Katharine Pier, 30m upriver of ent, but limited berthing/shore access, only suitable for shoal draft. Pleasure launches berth on S side of pier. **St Katharine Haven** Call St Katharines VHF Ch **80** M. Lock (41m x 12·5m with 2 small lifting bridges), access HW –2 to HW +1½, season 0600-2030, winter 0800-1800LT; other times by prior arrangement. R/G tfc lts at ent. Lock is shut Tues and Wed, Nov to Feb. **Facilities** (100 + 50 ⓥ, usually in Centre Basin or East Dock; give 1 week's notice in season) ☎ 020 7264 5312, 📠 020 7702 2252; £22.40/yacht, ⚒, ⛳, YC, Bar, R, 🛒, ⊖, ⊡. **Fuel Barge (E)** is 400m downstream of lock ent. ☎ 020 7481 1774; VHF Ch 14 *Burgan*. D & Gas, 0900-1600 Mon-Fri; 0900-1300 Sun.

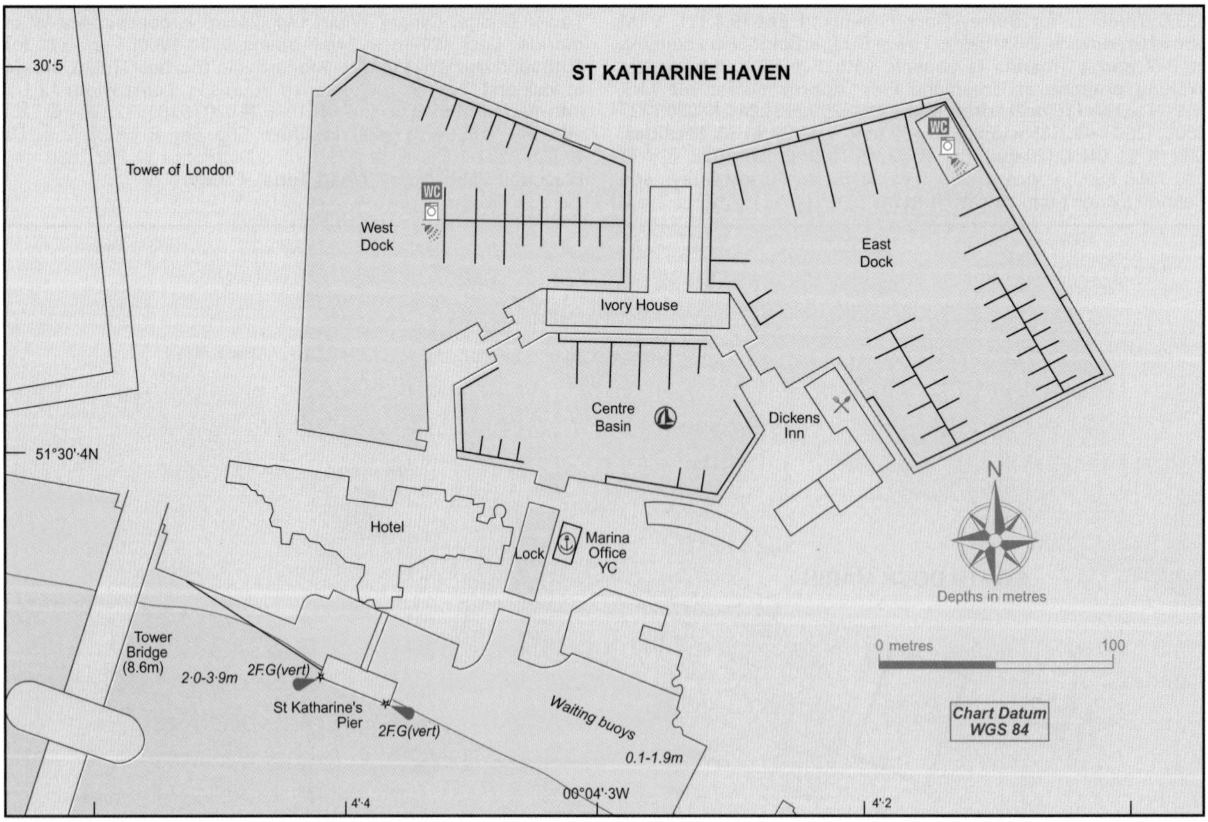
30'·5
ST KATHARINE HAVEN
Tower of London
WC
West Dock
East Dock
Ivory House
Centre Basin
Dickens Inn
51°30'·4N
N
Hotel
Lock
Marina Office YC
Depths in metres
Tower Bridge (8.6m)
2·0-3·9m
2F.G(vert)
St Katharine's Pier
2F.G(vert)
Waiting buoys
0.1-1.9m
0 metres
100
Chart Datum WGS 84
4'·4
00°04'·3W
4'·2

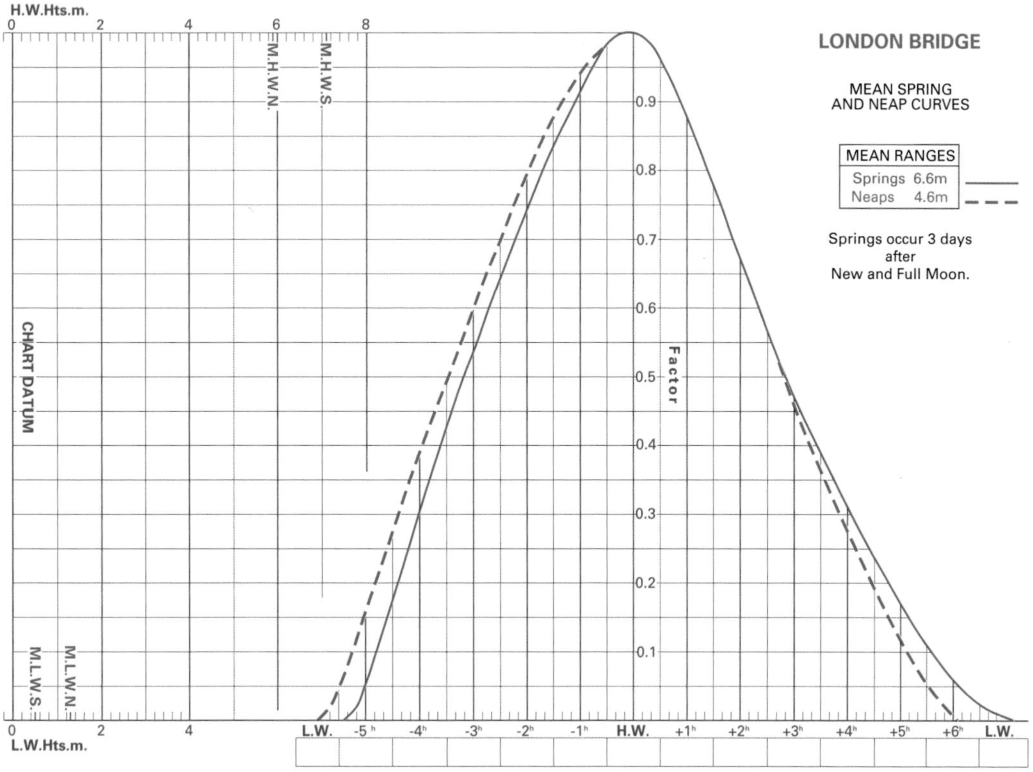
LONDON BRIDGE
MEAN SPRING AND NEAP CURVES
MEAN RANGES
Springs 6.6m
Neaps 4.6m
Springs occur 3 days after New and Full Moon.
H.W.Hts.m.
0
2
4
6
8
M.H.W.N.
M.H.W.S.
CHART DATUM
M.L.W.S.
M.L.W.N.
L.W.Hts.m.
Factor
0.9
0.8
0.7
0.6
0.5
0.4
0.3
0.2
0.1
L.W.
-5h
-4h
-3h
-2h
-1h
H.W.
+1h
+2h
+3h
+4h
+5h
+6h
L.W.

CHELSEA HARBOUR, London, **51°28′·42N 00°10′·82W**. AC 3319. Tides: see 9.4.12. Good shelter in all conditions, 5M above Tower Bridge, reached via 14 fixed bridges. Battersea railway bridge is 120m upstream. Belvedere Tower (80m high with tide ball) is conspic, next to the lock. Basin ent is for max LOA 24m, beam 5·5m, draft 1·8m, with bascule bridge. Lock opens when 2·5m water above sill; tide gauge outside, access HW ±1½, R/G tfc lts. Limited waiting berths and shore access on Chelsea Hbr Pier (1·7m) close upriver. Call Chelsea Hbr VHF Ch 80. **Marina** (50+10 Ⓥ). ☎ 020 7225 9100, fax 020 7352 7868, mobile ☎ 07770 542783, £15.00, Bar, R, Ⓑ, laundrette, showers, WC, disabled, pump-out, shop.

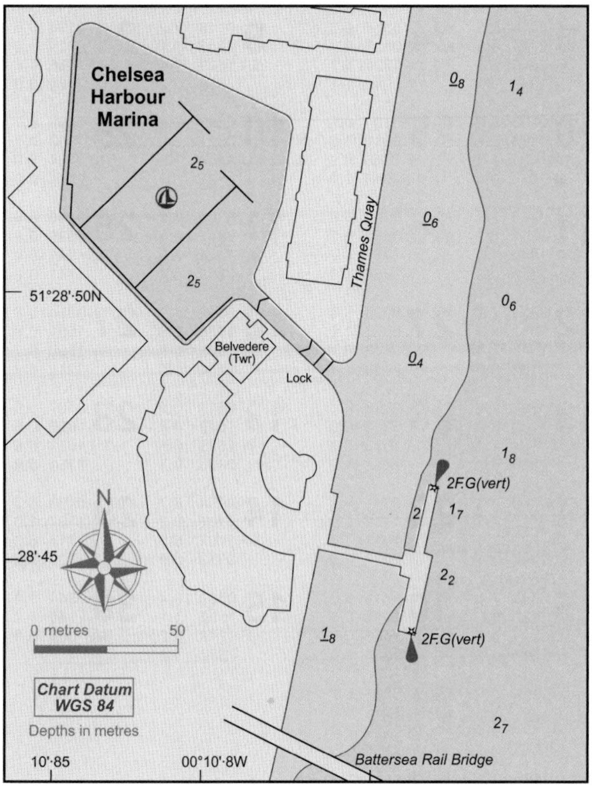
Chelsea Harbour Marina
2₅
2₅
51°28'·50N
Belvedere (Twr)
Lock
Thames Quay
0₈
1₄
0₆
0₆
0₄
1₈
2F.G(vert)
1₇
2
2₂
2F.G(vert)
1₈
2₇
28'·45
0 metres 50
Chart Datum WGS 84
Depths in metres
10'·85
00°10'·8W
Battersea Rail Bridge

BRENTFORD DOCK MARINA (N). 51°28′·88N 00°17′·95W, 1100m beyond Kew bridge. AC 3319. Tides, see Kew Bridge. 60 AB inc Ⓥ, £16.45 all LOA. ☎ 020 8232 8941, fax 020 8560 5486, mobile 07970 143 987. No VHF. Access HW±2½ via lock 4·8m x 9·8m (longer LOA during freeflow); 18m waiting pontoon. **Facilities**: El, ME, Bar, R, shop, ✕; Gunnersbury & Ealing tubes. Ent to Grand Union Canal via lock is nearby: M, AB.

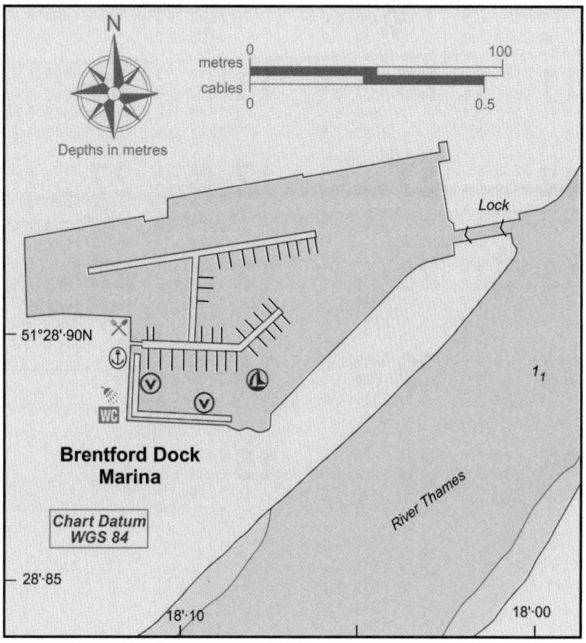
N
metres 0 100
cables 0 0.5
Depths in metres
Lock
51°28'·90N
WC
1₁
Brentford Dock Marina
River Thames
Chart Datum WGS 84
28'·85
18'·10
18'·00

TIME ZONE (UT)
For Summer Time add ONE hour in **non-shaded areas**

ENGLAND – LONDON BRIDGE

LAT 51°30′N LONG 0°05′W

TIMES AND HEIGHTS OF HIGH AND LOW WATERS

SPRING & NEAP TIDES
Dates in red are SPRINGS
Dates in blue are NEAPS

YEAR **2005**

JANUARY

Date	Day	Time	m	Time	m	Time	m	Time	m	Moon
1	SA	0441	6.4	1113	1.0	1723	6.4	2313	1.1	
2	SU	0520	6.3	1149	1.0	1805	6.4	2354	1.2	
3	M	0603	6.2	1231	1.1	1852	6.2			◑
4	TU	0039	1.3	0654	6.1	1321	1.2	1946	6.1	
5	W	0134	1.5	0755	5.9	1424	1.3	2049	5.9	
6	TH	0243	1.7	0906	5.9	1540	1.4	2159	6.0	
7	F	0406	1.6	1019	6.0	1701	1.3	2307	6.2	
8	SA	0525	1.4	1129	6.3	1812	1.1			
9	SU	0008	6.5	0638	1.1	1231	6.7	1912	0.9	
10	M	0103	6.7	0744	0.9	1328	6.9	2008	0.8	●
11	TU	0154	6.9	0844	0.6	1422	7.1	2101	0.7	
12	W	0243	6.9	0939	0.4	1514	7.2	2149	0.7	
13	TH	0331	6.9	1030	0.3	1605	7.2	2234	0.8	
14	F	0418	6.9	1115	0.3	1654	7.1	2315	0.8	
15	SA	0504	6.8	1156	0.4	1742	7.0	2353	0.9	
16	SU	0549	6.7	1233	0.5	1830	6.7			
17	M	0030	1.1	0634	6.5	1309	0.8	1919	6.4	◐
18	TU	0111	1.2	0724	6.3	1349	1.0	2011	6.1	
19	W	0157	1.4	0822	6.1	1438	1.3	2109	5.8	
20	TH	0253	1.6	0929	5.9	1536	1.5	2210	5.7	
21	F	0357	1.7	1038	5.8	1644	1.6	2313	5.8	
22	SA	0511	1.6	1142	6.0	1755	1.5			
23	SU	0011	6.0	0631	1.4	1240	6.2	1853	1.4	
24	M	0102	6.2	0728	1.1	1328	6.4	1941	1.2	
25	TU	0145	6.4	0815	0.9	1410	6.5	2024	1.2	○
26	W	0221	6.5	0857	0.9	1446	6.6	2059	1.2	
27	TH	0253	6.4	0935	0.9	1519	6.5	2128	1.3	
28	F	0323	6.4	1008	1.0	1551	6.5	2154	1.2	
29	SA	0352	6.4	1034	1.0	1625	6.6	2225	1.2	
30	SU	0423	6.5	1100	1.0	1700	6.6	2258	1.1	
31	M	0458	6.5	1128	0.9	1739	6.6	2333	1.0	

FEBRUARY

Date	Day	Time	m	Time	m	Time	m	Time	m	Moon
1	TU	0538	6.5	1201	0.9	1821	6.4			
2	W	0011	1.1	0624	6.4	1241	1.0	1910	6.2	◑
3	TH	0056	1.3	0719	6.1	1331	1.3	2007	5.9	
4	F	0154	1.5	0826	5.9	1442	1.6	2115	5.7	
5	SA	0315	1.8	0943	5.8	1619	1.7	2234	5.7	
6	SU	0455	1.7	1107	5.9	1755	1.5	2349	6.0	
7	M	0637	1.3	1221	6.4	1905	1.1			
8	TU	0051	6.4	0745	0.8	1322	6.8	2002	0.8	●
9	W	0144	6.8	0841	0.4	1414	7.1	2052	0.6	
10	TH	0231	7.0	0931	0.1	1503	7.3	2139	0.5	
11	F	0316	7.1	1017	0.0	1549	7.3	2221	0.5	
12	SA	0358	7.1	1058	0.0	1632	7.3	2259	0.6	
13	SU	0438	7.1	1132	0.2	1713	7.1	2331	0.7	
14	M	0516	7.0	1200	0.5	1752	6.8			
15	TU	0000	0.8	0553	6.8	1226	0.7	1828	6.5	
16	W	0029	1.0	0632	6.5	1256	1.0	1905	6.1	◐
17	TH	0106	1.3	0719	6.1	1338	1.4	1951	5.7	
18	F	0158	1.6	0823	5.6	1438	1.8	2057	5.3	
19	SA	0306	1.8	0958	5.4	1548	2.0	2232	5.3	
20	SU	0419	1.8	1119	5.6	1709	1.9	2344	5.6	
21	M	0604	1.5	1219	6.0	1831	1.5			
22	TU	0039	6.1	0710	1.1	1308	6.4	1923	1.2	
23	W	0124	6.4	0756	0.8	1349	6.6	2007	1.1	
24	TH	0202	6.5	0839	0.7	1425	6.7	2045	1.1	○
25	F	0235	6.5	0918	0.8	1457	6.7	2118	1.2	
26	SA	0305	6.5	0953	0.9	1529	6.6	2145	1.2	
27	SU	0332	6.5	1021	0.9	1601	6.6	2213	1.1	
28	M	0402	6.6	1043	0.9	1635	6.7	2241	1.0	

MARCH

Date	Day	Time	m	Time	m	Time	m	Time	m	Moon
1	TU	0437	6.7	1106	0.9	1712	6.6	2312	0.9	
2	W	0517	6.7	1134	0.9	1753	6.5	2346	0.9	
3	TH	0602	6.5	1210	1.0	1838	6.2			◑
4	F	0027	1.1	0654	6.2	1257	1.3	1931	5.8	
5	SA	0121	1.5	0759	5.8	1403	1.7	2039	5.4	
6	SU	0241	1.8	0921	5.5	1551	2.0	2210	5.4	
7	M	0502	1.8	1102	5.7	1750	1.7	2338	5.8	
8	TU	0640	1.1	1217	6.3	1856	1.1			
9	W	0040	6.3	0736	0.5	1313	6.9	1948	0.7	
10	TH	0130	6.8	0826	0.1	1401	7.3	2035	0.4	●
11	F	0213	7.1	0911	-0.1	1445	7.4	2118	0.3	
12	SA	0254	7.2	0953	-0.1	1526	7.4	2159	0.3	
13	SU	0332	7.2	1030	0.0	1604	7.2	2234	0.4	
14	M	0409	7.2	1100	0.3	1639	7.0	2304	0.6	
15	TU	0444	7.1	1123	0.6	1711	6.8	2328	0.7	
16	W	0519	6.9	1143	0.8	1743	6.5	2351	0.9	
17	TH	0558	6.5	1208	1.1	1817	6.2			◐
18	F	0022	1.1	0642	6.0	1245	1.4	1859	5.7	
19	SA	0112	1.5	0738	5.5	1346	1.9	1954	5.3	
20	SU	0229	1.8	0908	5.2	1506	2.1	2138	5.1	
21	M	0346	1.8	1050	5.4	1628	2.0	2312	5.5	
22	TU	0518	1.5	1152	5.9	1801	1.6			
23	W	0010	6.0	0641	1.0	1240	6.4	1857	1.3	
24	TH	0056	6.3	0728	0.7	1320	6.7	1940	1.1	
25	F	0134	6.5	0810	0.6	1356	6.8	2019	1.0	○
26	SA	0208	6.6	0850	0.7	1429	6.7	2055	1.1	
27	SU	0238	6.5	0927	0.8	1502	6.7	2128	1.1	
28	M	0308	6.6	0958	0.9	1535	6.7	2158	1.0	
29	TU	0341	6.7	1022	0.9	1611	6.7	2227	0.9	
30	W	0419	6.8	1046	0.9	1648	6.6	2256	0.8	
31	TH	0501	6.7	1115	0.9	1729	6.4	2330	0.9	

APRIL

Date	Day	Time	m	Time	m	Time	m	Time	m	Moon
1	F	0547	6.5	1152	1.1	1814	6.1			
2	SA	0012	1.1	0642	6.1	1242	1.5	1907	5.7	◑
3	SU	0109	1.5	0750	5.7	1351	1.9	2021	5.3	
4	M	0242	1.8	0923	5.5	1553	2.1	2202	5.4	
5	TU	0515	1.5	1058	5.9	1734	1.6	2321	5.9	
6	W	0623	0.8	1203	6.5	1834	1.0			
7	TH	0019	6.5	0713	0.2	1255	7.1	1923	0.5	
8	F	0106	6.9	0759	-0.1	1339	7.3	2008	0.3	●
9	SA	0148	7.2	0842	-0.1	1420	7.4	2052	0.2	
10	SU	0228	7.2	0921	0.0	1459	7.2	2132	0.3	
11	M	0306	7.2	0957	0.3	1534	7.0	2208	0.4	
12	TU	0342	7.1	1026	0.5	1605	6.8	2238	0.6	
13	W	0417	6.9	1049	0.8	1635	6.6	2300	0.7	
14	TH	0454	6.7	1107	0.9	1707	6.5	2322	0.9	
15	F	0533	6.4	1132	1.1	1743	6.2	2352	1.1	
16	SA	0617	6.0	1208	1.4	1826	5.8			◐
17	SU	0039	1.4	0710	5.6	1304	1.8	1918	5.4	
18	M	0156	1.7	0822	5.3	1423	2.1	2034	5.2	
19	TU	0313	1.7	1004	5.4	1543	2.0	2225	5.4	
20	W	0430	1.5	1110	5.8	1703	1.8	2329	5.8	
21	TH	0551	1.1	1201	6.3	1811	1.4			
22	F	0017	6.2	0646	0.8	1243	6.6	1900	1.1	
23	SA	0057	6.4	0732	0.7	1321	6.8	1943	1.0	
24	SU	0134	6.6	0814	0.6	1358	6.8	2024	0.9	○
25	M	0209	6.7	0853	0.7	1434	6.8	2104	0.9	
26	TU	0245	6.8	0929	0.8	1511	6.8	2141	0.8	
27	W	0324	6.8	1001	0.8	1550	6.7	2216	0.8	
28	TH	0407	6.8	1032	0.9	1631	6.6	2251	0.8	
29	F	0453	6.7	1107	1.0	1714	6.3	2330	0.9	
30	SA	0544	6.4	1149	1.2	1802	6.0			

Chart Datum: 2·90 metres below Ordnance Datum (Newlyn)

TIME ZONE (UT)
For Summer Time add ONE hour in **non-shaded areas**

ENGLAND – LONDON BRIDGE

LAT 51°30′N LONG 0°05′W

TIMES AND HEIGHTS OF HIGH AND LOW WATERS

SPRING & NEAP TIDES
Dates in red are **SPRINGS**
Dates in blue are **NEAPS**

YEAR **2005**

MAY

Date	Day	Time	m	Time	m	Time	m	Time	m
1	SU	0018	1.1	0644	6.1	1243	1.5	◑ 1901	5.7
2	M	0125	1.4	0758	5.8	1357	1.8	2023	5.5
3	TU	0307	1.5	0924	5.9	1539	1.8	2146	5.7
4	W	0448	1.1	1037	6.3	1702	1.4	2253	6.2
5	TH	0551	0.6	1136	6.7	1802	0.9	2349	6.6
6	F	0641	0.2	1227	7.1	1852	0.5		
7	SA	0037	6.9	0725	0.1	1312	7.2	1938	0.3
8	SU	0122	7.1	0807	0.1	1353	7.1	● 2023	0.3
9	M	0203	7.1	0847	0.3	1432	7.0	2105	0.4
10	TU	0243	6.9	0923	0.6	1506	6.7	2142	0.6
11	W	0321	6.8	0955	0.8	1537	6.6	2215	0.7
12	TH	0358	6.6	1020	1.0	1607	6.5	2240	0.8
13	F	0435	6.5	1041	1.1	1641	6.4	2304	0.9
14	SA	0514	6.3	1108	1.2	1718	6.2	2336	1.0
15	SU	0558	6.0	1145	1.3	1800	6.0		
16	M	0020	1.2	0646	5.8	1234	1.6	◐ 1849	5.7
17	TU	0122	1.4	0744	5.6	1337	1.8	1952	5.4
18	W	0234	1.5	0855	5.5	1451	1.9	2113	5.4
19	TH	0343	1.4	1009	5.8	1604	1.8	2229	5.7
20	F	0453	1.2	1110	6.1	1713	1.5	2327	6.0
21	SA	0556	0.9	1200	6.5	1813	1.2		
22	SU	0015	6.4	0649	0.7	1245	6.7	1905	1.0
23	M	0100	6.6	0736	0.6	1328	6.9	○ 1954	0.8
24	TU	0142	6.8	0821	0.6	1409	6.9	2041	0.7
25	W	0226	6.9	0904	0.7	1452	6.9	2127	0.7
26	TH	0312	6.9	0945	0.7	1536	6.7	2213	0.6
27	F	0400	6.9	1026	0.8	1621	6.6	2258	0.7
28	SA	0452	6.8	1108	1.0	1709	6.4	2344	0.7
29	SU	0547	6.5	1155	1.2	1802	6.2		
30	M	0036	0.9	0647	6.3	1248	1.4	◑ 1902	6.0
31	TU	0138	1.0	0755	6.2	1352	1.5	2011	6.0

JUNE

Date	Day	Time	m	Time	m	Time	m	Time	m
1	W	0252	1.0	0903	6.3	1505	1.5	2118	6.1
2	TH	0407	0.8	1006	6.5	1618	1.3	2219	6.3
3	F	0509	0.7	1103	6.7	1722	1.1	2316	6.6
4	SA	0602	0.5	1155	6.8	1818	0.8		
5	SU	0008	6.7	0649	0.5	1244	6.9	1908	0.7
6	M	0057	6.8	0733	0.5	1328	6.8	● 1956	0.6
7	TU	0143	6.8	0815	0.7	1409	6.7	2040	0.6
8	W	0227	6.7	0854	0.9	1445	6.5	2122	0.7
9	TH	0307	6.6	0929	1.0	1518	6.4	2158	0.8
10	F	0345	6.4	0958	1.2	1549	6.4	2228	0.9
11	SA	0421	6.4	1022	1.2	1622	6.3	2255	0.9
12	SU	0458	6.3	1051	1.2	1658	6.3	2325	1.0
13	M	0538	6.2	1127	1.3	1738	6.1		
14	TU	0002	1.0	0621	6.1	1210	1.4	1822	6.0
15	W	0049	1.1	0710	5.9	1300	1.5	◐ 1913	5.8
16	TH	0146	1.2	0806	5.8	1400	1.7	2016	5.7
17	F	0252	1.3	0910	5.8	1510	1.7	2126	5.7
18	SA	0400	1.2	1017	6.0	1621	1.6	2234	5.9
19	SU	0509	1.1	1118	6.3	1729	1.3	2335	6.2
20	M	0611	0.9	1212	6.6	1832	1.1		
21	TU	0030	6.6	0705	0.7	1302	6.8	1930	0.8
22	W	0122	6.8	0757	0.6	1350	6.9	○ 2026	0.6
23	TH	0212	7.0	0847	0.6	1437	6.9	2121	0.5
24	F	0303	7.1	0936	0.7	1525	6.8	2213	0.4
25	SA	0355	7.0	1023	0.8	1614	6.8	2303	0.4
26	SU	0447	7.0	1109	0.8	1703	6.7	2349	0.4
27	M	0540	6.9	1154	0.9	1753	6.6		
28	TU	0035	0.4	0635	6.7	1240	1.0	◑ 1845	6.5
29	W	0122	0.6	0732	6.6	1329	1.2	1942	6.4
30	TH	0213	0.7	0831	6.4	1423	1.3	2041	6.3

JULY

Date	Day	Time	m	Time	m	Time	m	Time	m
1	F	0310	0.9	0930	6.3	1523	1.4	2142	6.3
2	SA	0412	1.0	1027	6.3	1629	1.4	2242	6.2
3	SU	0515	1.1	1123	6.3	1738	1.3	2342	6.3
4	M	0612	1.0	1217	6.4	1840	1.1		
5	TU	0038	6.4	0702	1.0	1307	6.5	1934	0.9
6	W	0129	6.5	0749	1.0	1352	6.5	● 2023	0.8
7	TH	0215	6.6	0832	1.0	1431	6.5	2107	0.8
8	F	0256	6.5	0911	1.1	1505	6.4	2147	0.8
9	SA	0332	6.5	0944	1.2	1536	6.4	2220	0.9
10	SU	0405	6.4	1009	1.3	1607	6.4	2247	0.9
11	M	0438	6.4	1036	1.2	1639	6.4	2312	0.9
12	TU	0514	6.4	1108	1.2	1714	6.3	2341	0.9
13	W	0552	6.3	1145	1.2	1753	6.3		
14	TH	0015	0.9	0635	6.2	1227	1.3	◐ 1836	6.1
15	F	0058	1.1	0724	6.0	1317	1.4	1930	6.0
16	SA	0154	1.2	0823	5.9	1419	1.6	2034	5.8
17	SU	0306	1.3	0929	5.8	1535	1.7	2146	5.8
18	M	0425	1.3	1039	6.0	1651	1.5	2300	6.0
19	TU	0539	1.1	1144	6.3	1807	1.2		
20	W	0008	6.4	0644	0.9	1243	6.6	1919	0.9
21	TH	0108	6.8	0743	0.7	1335	6.8	○ 2022	0.6
22	F	0202	7.1	0838	0.6	1425	7.0	2118	0.3
23	SA	0254	7.2	0929	0.6	1513	7.0	2210	0.1
24	SU	0344	7.3	1017	0.6	1600	7.0	2256	0.0
25	M	0433	7.2	1100	0.6	1645	7.0	2338	0.1
26	TU	0521	7.1	1140	0.7	1730	7.0		
27	W	0015	0.2	0608	6.9	1218	0.8	1813	6.8
28	TH	0050	0.4	0656	6.6	1256	1.0	◑ 1900	6.6
29	F	0127	0.7	0748	6.3	1339	1.2	1953	6.3
30	SA	0211	1.1	0845	6.0	1430	1.4	2057	6.0
31	SU	0307	1.4	0947	5.8	1531	1.6	2209	5.8

AUGUST

Date	Day	Time	m	Time	m	Time	m	Time	m
1	M	0414	1.6	1051	5.8	1644	1.6	2320	5.9
2	TU	0533	1.5	1153	6.0	1819	1.4		
3	W	0022	6.2	0638	1.3	1248	6.3	1920	1.0
4	TH	0115	6.5	0730	1.1	1335	6.5	2008	0.8
5	F	0200	6.6	0815	1.0	1415	6.6	● 2052	0.7
6	SA	0239	6.7	0856	1.1	1450	6.6	2131	0.7
7	SU	0313	6.6	0931	1.2	1520	6.5	2206	0.8
8	M	0343	6.5	0958	1.3	1548	6.4	2234	0.9
9	TU	0413	6.5	1020	1.3	1616	6.4	2254	1.0
10	W	0445	6.5	1048	1.2	1646	6.5	2314	0.9
11	TH	0520	6.5	1120	1.1	1722	6.5	2341	0.9
12	F	0559	6.4	1155	1.1	1804	6.4		
13	SA	0015	1.0	0644	6.1	1237	1.3	◐ 1853	6.2
14	SU	0100	1.2	0738	5.9	1331	1.6	1955	5.9
15	M	0206	1.5	0844	5.6	1451	1.8	2108	5.7
16	TU	0343	1.7	1003	5.6	1622	1.7	2233	5.8
17	W	0519	1.5	1123	5.9	1803	1.4	2356	6.2
18	TH	0636	1.1	1228	6.4	1920	0.8		
19	F	0059	6.7	0735	0.8	1322	6.8	○ 2016	0.3
20	SA	0152	7.2	0827	0.5	1410	7.1	2108	0.0
21	SU	0240	7.4	0916	0.4	1454	7.2	2155	-0.2
22	M	0326	7.5	1000	0.4	1537	7.3	2237	-0.1
23	TU	0410	7.4	1041	0.4	1618	7.3	2313	0.0
24	W	0452	7.2	1117	0.5	1658	7.2	2344	0.3
25	TH	0532	6.9	1149	0.7	1737	7.0		
26	F	0010	0.6	0611	6.6	1221	0.9	◑ 1816	6.7
27	SA	0039	0.9	0650	6.1	1257	1.2	1901	6.2
28	SU	0118	1.3	0737	5.7	1346	1.5	2003	5.7
29	M	0215	1.8	0852	5.4	1450	1.8	2137	5.4
30	TU	0327	2.0	1019	5.4	1604	1.8	2300	5.6
31	W	0457	1.9	1129	5.7	1804	1.5		

Chart Datum: 2·90 metres below Ordnance Datum (Newlyn)

TIME ZONE (UT)
For Summer Time add ONE hour in **non-shaded areas**

ENGLAND – LONDON BRIDGE

LAT 51°30′N LONG 0°05′W

TIMES AND HEIGHTS OF HIGH AND LOW WATERS

SPRING & NEAP TIDES
Dates in red are SPRINGS
Dates in blue are NEAPS

YEAR **2005**

SEPTEMBER

Date	Day	Time	m	Time	m	Time	m	Time	m	Moon
1	TH	0003	6.1	0620	1.5	1225	6.2	1901	1.0	
2	F	0054	6.5	0711	1.1	1311	6.5	1946	0.7	
3	SA	0137	6.8	0755	1.0	1351	6.7	2028	0.6	●
4	SU	0214	6.8	0835	1.0	1425	6.6	2107	0.6	
5	M	0246	6.7	0911	1.1	1455	6.5	2142	0.8	
6	TU	0315	6.6	0939	1.2	1521	6.4	2211	1.0	
7	W	0344	6.6	1002	1.3	1547	6.5	2229	1.1	
8	TH	0414	6.6	1026	1.2	1618	6.6	2246	1.0	
9	F	0448	6.6	1055	1.1	1655	6.6	2310	0.9	
10	SA	0526	6.4	1127	1.1	1737	6.5	2342	1.0	
11	SU	0609	6.2	1205	1.2	1827	6.2			◐
12	M	0024	1.3	0700	5.8	1257	1.6	1928	5.8	
13	TU	0125	1.7	0806	5.5	1417	1.9	2043	5.5	
14	W	0309	2.0	0933	5.4	1614	1.9	2222	5.6	
15	TH	0512	1.8	1108	5.8	1807	1.3	2349	6.2	
16	F	0626	1.2	1213	6.4	1908	0.6			
17	SA	0047	6.9	0719	0.7	1304	6.9	1959	0.1	
18	SU	0135	7.3	0808	0.4	1348	7.2	2045	-0.2	○
19	M	0219	7.5	0853	0.3	1429	7.4	2129	-0.2	
20	TU	0301	7.5	0936	0.3	1509	7.4	2208	0.0	
21	W	0341	7.4	1015	0.4	1548	7.3	2241	0.2	
22	TH	0418	7.1	1050	0.5	1626	7.2	2308	0.5	
23	F	0453	6.8	1119	0.7	1703	7.0	2330	0.8	
24	SA	0525	6.5	1146	1.0	1742	6.6	2353	1.1	
25	SU	0559	6.1	1218	1.2	1826	6.1			◑
26	M	0027	1.5	0638	5.7	1307	1.6	1922	5.6	
27	TU	0125	2.0	0735	5.3	1418	1.9	2104	5.2	
28	W	0247	2.3	0944	5.2	1534	1.9	2233	5.5	
29	TH	0418	2.1	1058	5.6	1729	1.5	2334	6.0	
30	F	0552	1.7	1154	6.1	1829	1.0			

OCTOBER

Date	Day	Time	m	Time	m	Time	m	Time	m	Moon
1	SA	0024	6.5	0643	1.2	1240	6.5	1913	0.7	
2	SU	0106	6.8	0726	1.0	1319	6.6	1954	0.6	
3	M	0141	6.8	0804	1.0	1353	6.6	2033	0.7	●
4	TU	0213	6.8	0839	1.1	1423	6.6	2109	0.8	
5	W	0243	6.7	0910	1.2	1451	6.5	2138	1.0	
6	TH	0313	6.7	0939	1.2	1521	6.6	2200	1.1	
7	F	0345	6.6	1007	1.1	1556	6.6	2220	1.0	
8	SA	0420	6.6	1036	1.1	1636	6.7	2247	1.0	
9	SU	0459	6.5	1109	1.1	1721	6.5	2323	1.1	
10	M	0543	6.2	1149	1.2	1813	6.2			◐
11	TU	0008	1.4	0634	5.8	1244	1.6	1916	5.8	
12	W	0110	1.9	0742	5.4	1415	1.8	2038	5.5	
13	TH	0258	2.2	0921	5.4	1625	1.6	2219	5.8	
14	F	0455	1.8	1048	5.9	1748	1.0	2332	6.4	
15	SA	0602	1.2	1148	6.5	1843	0.4			
16	SU	0026	7.0	0654	0.6	1237	7.0	1931	0.0	
17	M	0112	7.4	0741	0.3	1321	7.3	2015	-0.1	○
18	TU	0154	7.5	0826	0.2	1402	7.4	2056	0.0	
19	W	0233	7.4	0908	0.3	1442	7.3	2134	0.2	
20	TH	0311	7.2	0948	0.5	1521	7.2	2207	0.5	
21	F	0345	6.9	1023	0.7	1559	7.0	2233	0.8	
22	SA	0417	6.7	1052	0.9	1638	6.7	2254	1.0	
23	SU	0448	6.4	1118	1.0	1718	6.4	2317	1.3	
24	M	0522	6.2	1149	1.3	1802	6.0	2350	1.6	
25	TU	0602	5.8	1237	1.5	1855	5.6			◑
26	W	0039	1.9	0654	5.4	1346	1.8	2010	5.3	
27	TH	0158	2.3	0827	5.2	1500	1.8	2147	5.4	
28	F	0324	2.2	1012	5.4	1617	1.6	2252	5.8	
29	SA	0448	1.9	1111	5.8	1735	1.2	2343	6.2	
30	SU	0555	1.5	1159	6.2	1828	0.9			
31	M	0025	6.5	0641	1.2	1240	6.5	1911	0.8	

NOVEMBER

Date	Day	Time	m	Time	m	Time	m	Time	m	Moon
1	TU	0103	6.7	0722	1.1	1316	6.6	1952	0.8	
2	W	0138	6.8	0801	1.1	1350	6.6	2030	0.8	●
3	TH	0212	6.8	0839	1.0	1424	6.7	2104	0.9	
4	F	0247	6.8	0916	1.0	1501	6.7	2135	1.0	
5	SA	0323	6.7	0952	1.0	1542	6.8	2204	1.0	
6	SU	0401	6.6	1028	1.0	1627	6.7	2238	1.1	
7	M	0443	6.4	1107	1.1	1716	6.5	2318	1.2	
8	TU	0528	6.2	1155	1.2	1811	6.2			
9	W	0007	1.5	0622	5.8	1259	1.4	1917	5.9	◐
10	TH	0112	1.9	0736	5.6	1428	1.5	2038	5.8	
11	F	0247	2.0	0907	5.7	1605	1.3	2158	6.1	
12	SA	0421	1.7	1018	6.1	1715	0.8	2302	6.5	
13	SU	0528	1.2	1116	6.6	1810	0.5	2356	6.9	
14	M	0622	0.8	1207	6.9	1858	0.3			
15	TU	0044	7.2	0711	0.5	1254	7.1	1942	0.3	
16	W	0127	7.2	0757	0.4	1338	7.2	2023	0.4	○
17	TH	0207	7.1	0841	0.5	1420	7.1	2102	0.6	
18	F	0245	6.9	0923	0.7	1501	6.9	2137	0.9	
19	SA	0319	6.7	1000	0.8	1542	6.7	2206	1.1	
20	SU	0350	6.5	1032	1.0	1621	6.5	2228	1.2	
21	M	0421	6.4	1100	1.1	1701	6.3	2253	1.3	
22	TU	0457	6.2	1131	1.2	1742	6.1	2325	1.5	
23	W	0537	6.0	1212	1.4	1829	5.8			◑
24	TH	0009	1.7	0624	5.7	1308	1.6	1922	5.6	
25	F	0105	2.0	0724	5.5	1413	1.6	2027	5.5	
26	SA	0217	2.1	0847	5.4	1519	1.6	2140	5.6	
27	SU	0333	2.0	1006	5.6	1626	1.4	2244	5.9	
28	M	0443	1.8	1105	5.9	1728	1.2	2336	6.3	
29	TU	0544	1.5	1154	6.2	1823	1.0			
30	W	0022	6.6	0637	1.2	1239	6.5	1910	0.9	

DECEMBER

Date	Day	Time	m	Time	m	Time	m	Time	m	Moon
1	TH	0105	6.8	0725	1.0	1321	6.7	1955	0.8	●
2	F	0146	6.9	0812	0.9	1403	6.8	2037	0.8	
3	SA	0227	6.9	0859	0.8	1448	6.9	2118	0.9	
4	SU	0308	6.8	0946	0.8	1534	6.9	2158	1.0	
5	M	0351	6.7	1033	0.8	1624	6.8	2240	1.1	
6	TU	0437	6.5	1121	0.9	1716	6.6	2324	1.2	
7	W	0525	6.3	1211	1.0	1812	6.4			
8	TH	0013	1.4	0620	6.1	1308	1.0	1913	6.3	◐
9	F	0110	1.5	0727	6.0	1413	1.1	2020	6.2	
10	SA	0218	1.6	0838	6.1	1524	1.1	2126	6.3	
11	SU	0333	1.6	0943	6.2	1631	1.0	2228	6.4	
12	M	0444	1.4	1043	6.4	1730	0.9	2324	6.6	
13	TU	0547	1.1	1138	6.6	1823	0.8			
14	W	0015	6.7	0642	0.9	1231	6.7	1910	0.8	
15	TH	0103	6.7	0732	0.8	1320	6.8	1955	0.9	○
16	F	0147	6.7	0820	0.8	1406	6.7	2036	1.0	
17	SA	0227	6.6	0905	0.8	1450	6.6	2115	1.1	
18	SU	0302	6.5	0946	0.9	1531	6.5	2148	1.3	
19	M	0333	6.4	1022	1.0	1608	6.4	2212	1.4	
20	TU	0405	6.3	1051	1.1	1644	6.3	2236	1.4	
21	W	0439	6.3	1117	1.2	1721	6.3	2306	1.3	
22	TH	0516	6.2	1148	1.2	1800	6.2	2343	1.4	
23	F	0557	6.1	1227	1.3	1844	6.0			◑
24	SA	0027	1.5	0644	5.9	1316	1.4	1933	5.9	
25	SU	0120	1.7	0740	5.7	1416	1.5	2031	5.8	
26	M	0226	1.8	0849	5.6	1523	1.5	2137	5.8	
27	TU	0341	1.8	1001	5.7	1632	1.4	2244	6.0	
28	W	0453	1.6	1107	6.0	1738	1.2	2344	6.3	
29	TH	0558	1.3	1206	6.4	1836	1.0			
30	F	0037	6.6	0657	1.0	1259	6.7	1929	0.9	
31	SA	0126	6.8	0755	0.8	1349	6.9	2020	0.8	●

Chart Datum: 2·90 metres below Ordnance Datum (Newlyn)

9.4.13 SOUTHEND-ON-SEA/ LEIGH-ON-SEA

Essex **51°31′·07N 00°42′·57E**

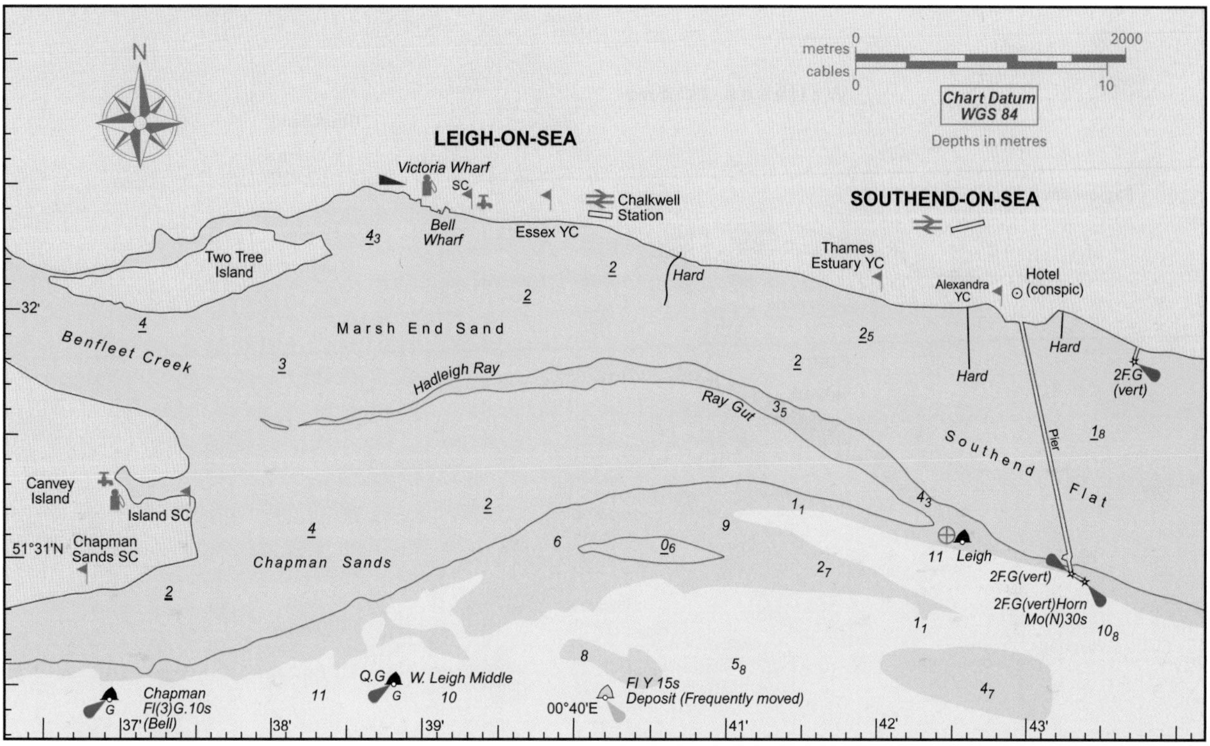
metres 0 2000
cables 0 10
Chart Datum WGS 84
Depths in metres
N
LEIGH-ON-SEA
Victoria Wharf
SC
Bell Wharf
Essex YC
Chalkwell Station
SOUTHEND-ON-SEA
Thames Estuary YC
Alexandra YC
Hotel (conspic)
Two Tree Island
Hard
Hard
Hard
32'
Benfleet Creek
Marsh End Sand
Hadleigh Ray
Ray Gut
Southend Flat
Pier
2F.G (vert)
Canvey Island
Island SC
51°31'N
Chapman Sands SC
Chapman Sands
11 Leigh
2F.G(vert)
2F.G(vert)Horn Mo(N)30s
Chapman Fl(3)G.10s (Bell)
Q.G W. Leigh Middle
Fl Y 15s Deposit (Frequently moved)
00°40'E
37'
38'
39'
41'
42'
43'

CHARTS AC *5606, 1183, 1185*; Imray C1, C2, Y18, 2100 Series; Stanfords 5, 8; OS 178

TIDES +0125 Dover; ML 3·0; Duration 0610; Zone 0 (UT)

Standard Port SHEERNESS (⟵)

Times				Height (metres)			
High Water		Low Water		MHWS	MHWN	MLWN	MLWS
0200	0800	0200	0700	5·8	4·7	1·5	0·6
1400	2000	1400	1900				
Differences SOUTHEND-ON-SEA							
−0005	0000	0000	+0005	0·0	0·0	−0·1	−0·1
CORYTON							
+0005	+0010	+0010	+0015	+0·4	+0·3	+0·1	−0·1

SHELTER The whole area dries soon after half ebb, except Ray Gut (0·4 - 4·8m) which leads to Leigh Creek and Hadleigh Ray, either side of Two Tree Island, thence to Benfleet Creek where the limit of W navigation is the Tidal Barrier just above Benfleet YC; all are buoyed, but echo-sounder is essential. At Leigh-on-Sea some drying moorings are available; or yachts can take the ground alongside Bell Wharf or Victoria Wharf. It is also possible to secure at the end of Southend Pier to collect stores, FW. NOTE: Southend-on-Sea and Leigh-on-Sea are both part of the lower PLA Area and an 8kn speed limit is enforced in inshore areas. Southend BC launches *Alec White II* , *Sidney Bates II* or *Low Way* patrol area (VHF Ch 68 16), Apr-Oct.

NAVIGATION WPT Leigh SHM buoy, 51°31′·07N 00°42′·57E, at ent to Ray Gut; this SHM buoy can be left close to port on entering Ray Gut, since there is now more water NE of it than to the SW. Appr from Shoeburyness, keep outside the W Shoebury SHM buoy, Fl G 2·5s. Beware some 3000 small boat moorings 1M either side of Southend Pier. Speed limit in Canvey Island/Hadleigh Ray areas is 8kn.

LIGHTS AND MARKS Pier lts as on chartlet.

R/T Thames Navigation Service: *Port Control London* VHF Ch 68.

TELEPHONE (Dial code 01702) HM ☎/fax 611889, fax 355110; HM Leigh-on-Sea 710561; MRSC (01255) 675518; Essex Police Marine Section (01268) 775533; Marinecall 09066 526239; Police 431212; Dr 225500; H 348911.

FACILITIES

SOUTHEND-ON-SEA: **Southend Pier** ☎ 215620, AB during day free, £7.70 overnight up to 35′ LOA, M, L, FW, Bar; **Alexandra YC** ☎ 340363, Bar, FW; **Thorpe Bay YC** ☎ 587563, Bar, L, Slip, R, FW; **Thames Estuary YC** ☎ 345967; **Halfway YC** ☎ 582025, pre-book 1 visitor's berth, FW; **Town** EC Wed. CH, ACA, Ⓔ, shops, R, Bar, ✉, Ⓑ, rail, airport.

LEIGH-ON-SEA: **Essex YC** ☎ 478404, FW, Bar; **Leigh on Sea SC** ☎ 476788, FW, Bar; **Bell Wharf**, AB (1st 24hrs free, then £6.60 per subsequent 24 hrs); **Victoria Wharf** AB, SM, Slip; **Town:** EC Wed, P &D (cans), ME, El, ⚒, C, CH, SM.

CANVEY ISLAND: (Dial code 01268) **Services:** Slip, M, D, FW, ME, El, ⚒, C, Gas, CH, Access HW±2; **Island YC** ☎ 683729; **Benfleet YC** (on S side of Benfleet Creek on Canvey Island) ☎ 792278, Access HW±2½, M, Slip, FW, D (by day), CH, ME, El, ⚒, C, Bar, shops, launderette.

NOTES

9.4.14 RIVER ROACH/HAVENGORE

Essex **51°36'·98N 00°52'·14E** (Branklet SPM buoy), R Roach. **51°33'·62N 00°50'·52E**, Havengore Bridge

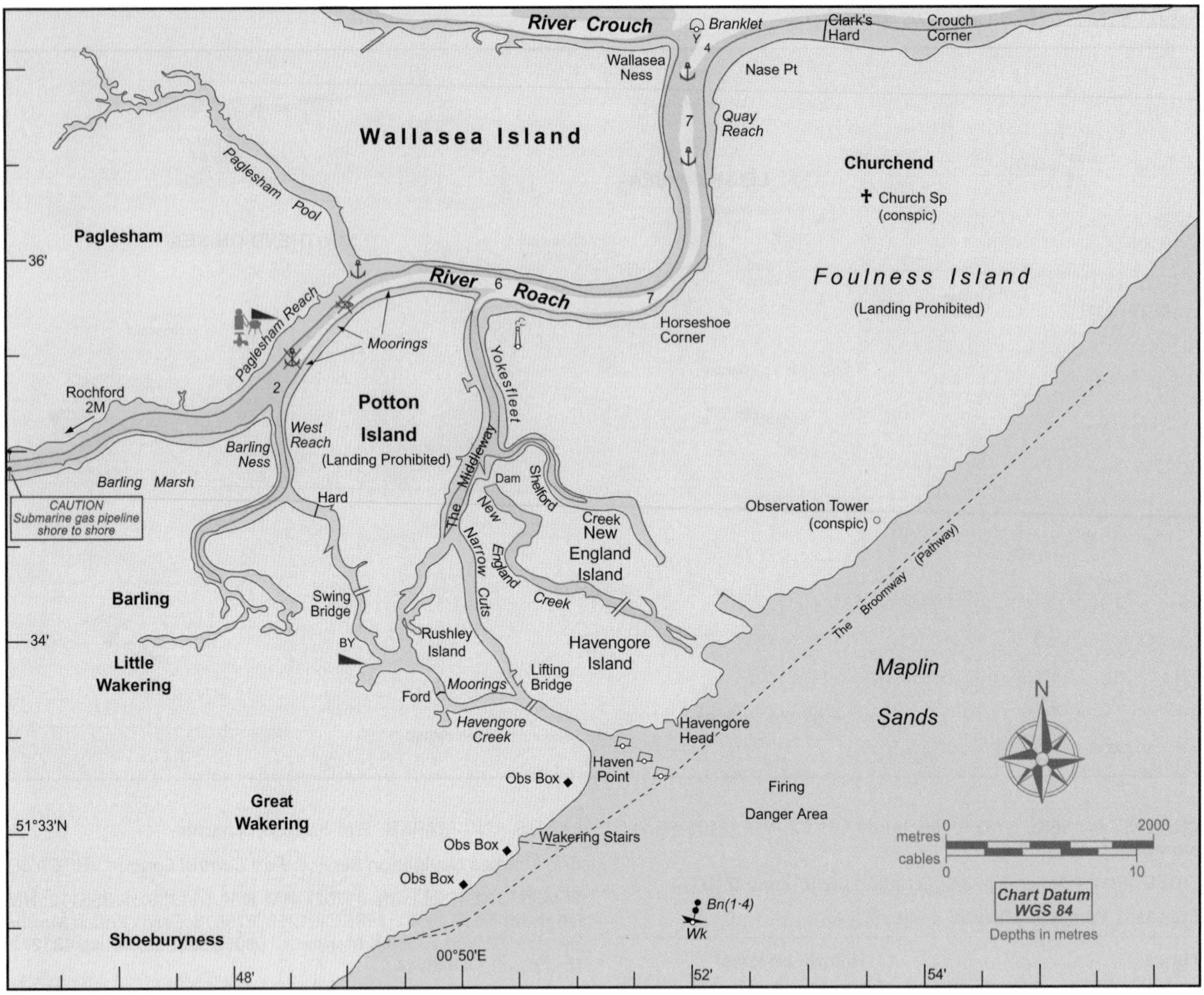
River Crouch
Branklet
Clark's Hard
Crouch Corner
Wallasea Ness
Nase Pt
Quay Reach
Wallasea Island
Churchend
Church Sp (conspic)
Paglesham Pool
Paglesham
36'
River Roach
Foulness Island
(Landing Prohibited)
Paglesham Reach
Moorings
Horseshoe Corner
Yokesfleet
Rochford 2M
Potton Island
West Reach
Barling Ness
(Landing Prohibited)
The Middleway
Dam
Shelford
Barling Marsh
CAUTION Submarine gas pipeline shore to shore
Hard
New Narrow Cuts
Creek
New England Island
Observation Tower (conspic)
New England Creek
The Broomway (Pathway)
Barling
Swing Bridge
34'
Little Wakering
BY
Rushley Island
Havengore Island
Lifting Bridge
Maplin
Sands
Moorings
Ford
Havengore Creek
Havengore Head
Haven Point
Obs Box
Firing Danger Area
Great Wakering
51°33'N
Wakering Stairs
Obs Box
Obs Box
metres 0 2000
cables 0 10
Chart Datum WGS 84
Bn(1·4)
Wk
Depths in metres
Shoeburyness
00°50'E
48'
52'
54'

CHARTS AC *5607, 1185, 3750;* Imray C1, Y17, 2100 Series; Stanfords 5, 4; OS 178

TIDES +0110 Dover; ML 2·7; Duration 0615; Zone 0 (UT)

Standard Port BURNHAM-ON-CROUCH (⟶)

Times				Height (metres)			
High Water		Low Water		MHWS	MHWN	MLWN	MLWS
0000	0600	0500	1100	5·2	4·2	1·0	0·2
1200	1800	1700	2300				
Differences ROCHFORD							
0000	+0005	Dries		−1·8	−1·9	Dries	

SHELTER Good. The Roach gives sheltered sailing and access to a network of secluded creeks, including Havengore (the "backdoor" from the Crouch to the Thames Estuary). No AB available in the area. ⚓s behind sea-walls can be found for all winds at: Quay Reach (often more protected than the Crouch), Paglesham Reach, West Reach, Barling Reach and Yokes Fleet. An ⚓ light is essential due to freighters H24. Speed limit 8kn. Crouch Hbr Authority controls R Roach and Crouch, out to Foulness Pt.

NAVIGATION Normal access H24 to the Roach is from R Crouch (see 9.4.15 for WPT from seaward); the ent between Branklet SPM buoy and Nase Pt is narrowed by mudbanks. Unlit buoys up-river to Barling Ness, above which few boats go. To exit at Havengore Creek, appr via Middleway and Narrow Cuts to reach the bridge before HW.

Entry via **Havengore Creek** is possible in good weather, with great care and adequate rise of tide (max draft 1·5m at HW sp). Shoeburyness Range is usually active Mon-Fri 0600-1700LT; give 24hrs notice to Range Officer by ☎. Subsequent clearance on VHF by Havengore lifting bridge (☎ HW±2, HJ); no passage unless bridge raised. Least water is over the shifting bar, just inside creek ent. From the S, cross Maplin Sands at HW −1 from S Shoebury SHM buoy, Fl G 5s (51°30'·40N 00°52'·50E), leaving Pisces wreck (conspic, 1M from ent) to port.

LIGHTS AND MARKS Unlit, but night entry to R Roach may be possible.

R/T VHF Ch 72 16 is worked by Range Officer (*Shoe Base*) (HO); Radar Control (*Shoe Radar*) (HO); & Bridge keeper (*Shoe Bridge*) (HW±2 by day). Radar guidance may be available.

TELEPHONE (Dial code 01702= Southend) Crouch HM ☎/📠 (01621) 783602; Range Officer 383211; Havengore Bridge 383436; Swing Br to Potton I. ☎ 219491; Marinecall 09066 526239; MRSC (01255) 675518; Dr 218678.

FACILITIES **Paglesham** (East End) FW, D, slip, El, ME (from BY), ⚒, Bar; **Gt Wakering:** Slip, P, D, FW, ME, El, ⚒, C, CH (from BY); at Rochford **Wakering YC** ☎ 530926, M, L, Bar. **Towns** EC Wed Gt Wakering & Rochford; 🛒, R, Bar, ✉ (Great Wakering and Barling); most facilities, Ⓑ and ⇌ in Rochford and Shoeburyness, ✈ (Southend).

9.4.15 BURNHAM-ON-CROUCH

Essex **51°37'·50N 00°48'·23E** (Yacht Hbr) ❁❁❁⛵⛵⛵✿✿

CHARTS AC *5607, 1183, 1975, 3750*; Imray C1, Y17, 2000 Series; Stanfords 1, 19, 5, 4; OS168

TIDES +0115 Dover; ML 2·5; Duration 0610; Zone 0 (UT). Full daily predictions for Burnham are on following pages. Ranges: Sp = 5·0m; Np = 3·2m. Use Walton Tidal Curves (9.4.18)

Standard Port WALTON-ON-THE-NAZE (⟶)

Times				Height (metres)			
High Water		Low Water		MHWS	MHWN	MLWN	MLWS
0000	0600	0500	1100	4·2	3·4	1·1	0·4
1200	1800	1700	2300				
Differences WHITAKER BEACON							
+0022	+0024	+0033	+0027	+0·6	+0·5	+0·2	+0·1
HOLLIWELL POINT							
+0034	+0037	+0100	+0037	+1·1	+0·9	+0·3	+0·1
BURNHAM-ON-CROUCH (but see also full predictions)							
+0050	+0035	+0115	+0050	+1·0	+0·8	−0·1	−0·2
NORTH FAMBRIDGE							
+0115	+0050	+0130	+0100	+1·1	+0·8	0·0	−0·1
HULLBRIDGE							
+0115	+0050	+0135	+0105	+1·1	+0·8	0·0	−0·1
BATTLESBRIDGE							
+0120	+0110	Dries		−1·8	−2·0	Dries	

SHELTER River is exposed to most winds. Cliff Reach (off W edge of lower chartlet) is sheltered from SW'lies. There are six marinas or yacht hbrs. ⚓ prohib in fairway but possible just E or W of the moorings. Speed limit in moorings is 8kn. Ent to Bridge Marsh marina marked by PHM bn, Fl R 10s.

NAVIGATION WPT 51°39'·79N 01°02'·50E, S Buxey SHM buoy, Fl (3) G 15s. Appr from East Swin, or the Wallet via Spitway and N Swallow SWM (more water N of Swallow Tail Bank 2003), into the Whitaker Chan. Near Sunken Buxey seas can be hazardous with strong wind over tide. Ray Sand Chan (dries 1·7m) is usable on the tide by shoal draft boats as a short cut from/to the Blackwater. Shoeburyness Artillery ranges lie E and S of Foulness Pt, clear of the fairway. Landing on Foulness and Bridgemarsh Is (up river) is prohibited. R. Crouch is navigable to Battlesbridge, 10M beyond Burnham.

LIGHTS AND MARKS There are few landmarks to assist entering, but Whitaker Chan and the river are lit/buoyed to 0·5M W of Essex Marina. From Sunken Buxey NCM buoy, Q, the spire of St Mary's ✠ leads 233° to Outer Crouch SCM buoy, Q (6) + L Fl 15s; thence steer 240° past Foulness Pt into the river. There is a 2·2M unlit gap between Inner Crouch SWM buoy, L Fl 10s, and Horse Shoal NCM buoy, Q.

R/T VHF Ch 80 for: Crouch HM Launch (0900-1700LT, w/e); Essex Marina; Burnham Yacht Harbour; W Wick Marina (1000-1700), also Ch M.

TELEPHONE (Dial code Maldon = 01621) HM 783602; MRSC (01255) 675518; Marinecall 09066 526239; Police 773663; Dr 782054.

4

FACILITIES BURNHAM: **Burnham Yacht Hbr** ☎ 782150, 📠 785848, Access H24, (350) £1.75 approx, D, ME, El, ⚒, BH (30 ton), CH, 🗏, R, Bar, Slip; **Royal Corinthian YC** ☎ 782105, AB, FW, M, L, R, Bar; **Royal Burnham YC** ☎ 782044, FW, L, R, Bar; **Crouch YC** ☎ 782252, L, FW, R, Bar; **Services:** AB, BY, C (15 ton), D, P, FW, ME, El, ⚒, M, Slip, CH, ACA, Gas, SM, Gaz. **Town** EC Wed; 🛒, R, Bar, ✉, Ⓑ, ⇌, ✈ (Southend).

WALLASEA (01702): **Essex Marina** (400) ☎ (01702) 258531, 📠 258227, BY, Gas, Bar, C (13 ton), BH (40 ton), CH, D, P, LPG, El, M, ME, R, ⚒, Slip, 🛒; Ferry to Burnham Town Hard at w/ends in season, ☎ 258870; **Essex YC**; ACA.

FAMBRIDGE: **N Fambridge Yacht Stn** (150) ☎ 740370, Access HW±5, M, CH, ⚒, ME, BY, C (5 ton), El, Slip, Gas, Gaz; **W Wick Marina** (Stow Creek) (180) ☎ 741268, Access HW±5, Gas, Gaz, CH, El, Slip, FW, D, C (5 ton), YC, Bar; **Brandy Hole Yacht Stn** (120) ☎ (01702) 230248, L, M, ME, ⚒, Slip, Gas, Gaz, Bar, BY, D, Access HW±4.

ALTHORNE: **Bridge Marsh Marina** (125 + 6 Ⓥ) ☎ 740414, 📠 742216, Access HW±4, ⚒, 🗏, ME, El, C (8 ton), Slip.

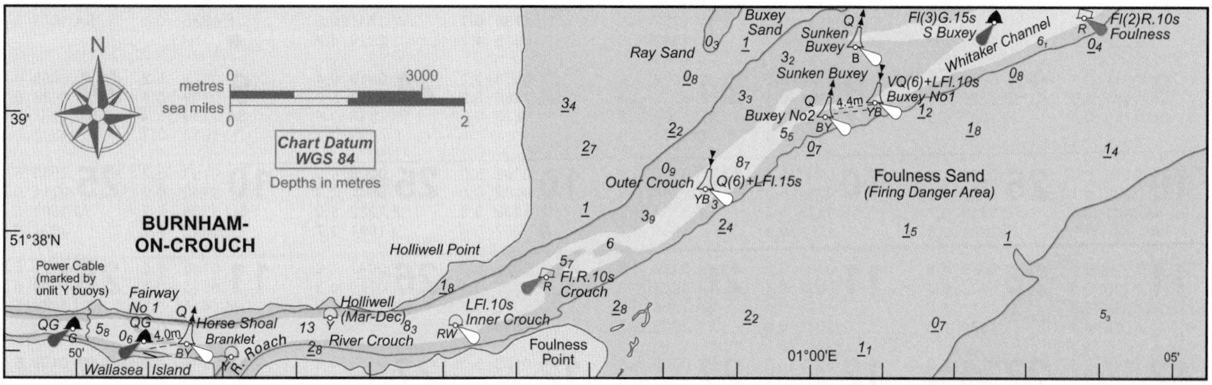
N
metres 0 3000
sea miles 0 2
Chart Datum WGS 84
Depths in metres
BURNHAM-ON-CROUCH
51°38'N
39'
Power Cable (marked by unlit Y buoys)
Fairway No 1
Horse Shoal
Branklet
R. Roach
Wallasea Island
Holliwell (Mar-Dec)
River Crouch
LFl.10s Inner Crouch
Holliwell Point
Fl.R.10s Crouch
Foulness Point
Ray Sand
Buxey Sand
Sunken Buxey
VQ(6)+LFl.10s
Buxey No1
Buxey No2
Outer Crouch
Q(6)+LFl.15s
Fl(3)G.15s S Buxey
Whitaker Channel
Fl(2)R.10s Foulness
Foulness Sand (Firing Danger Area)
01°00'E
05'
50'

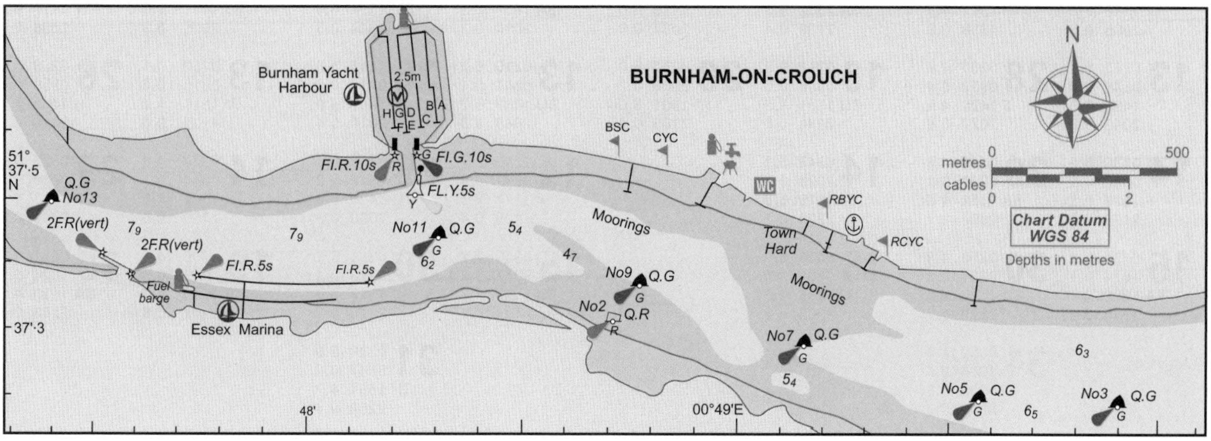
Burnham Yacht Harbour
BURNHAM-ON-CROUCH
N
metres 0 500
cables 0 2
Chart Datum WGS 84
Depths in metres
51° 37'·5 N
37'·3
Q.G No13
2F.R(vert)
Fl.R.10s
Fl.G.10s
Fl.Y.5s
Fl.R.5s
Fuel barge
Essex Marina
No11 Q.G
BSC
CYC
RBYC
RCYC
Moorings
Town Hard
No9 Q.G
No2 Q.R
No7 Q.G
No5 Q.G
No3 Q.G
48'
00°49'E

TIME ZONE (UT)
For Summer Time add ONE hour in **non-shaded areas**

ENGLAND – BURNHAM-ON-CROUCH

LAT 51°37′N LONG 0°48′E

TIMES AND HEIGHTS OF HIGH AND LOW WATERS

SPRING & NEAP TIDES
Dates in red are SPRINGS
Dates in blue are NEAPS

YEAR **2005**

JANUARY

Date	Day	Time	m	Time	m	Time	m	Time	m
1	SA	0318	4.7	0956	0.5	1549	4.6	2151	0.9
2	SU	0357	4.6	1035	0.5	1630	4.6	2233	1.0
3	M	0440	4.5	1120	0.7	1720	4.5	◑ 2321	1.1
4	TU	0532	4.3	1216	0.8	1816	4.3		
5	W	0023	1.1	0633	4.3	1323	0.8	1922	4.3
6	TH	0137	1.1	0744	4.3	1436	0.8	2032	4.3
7	F	0252	1.1	0854	4.5	1547	0.7	2138	4.6
8	SA	0404	0.9	1000	4.7	1651	0.5	2238	4.7
9	SU	0512	0.7	1101	5.0	1750	0.5	2334	4.8
10	M	0616	0.4	1200	5.1	1841	0.4	●	
11	TU	0028	5.0	0709	0.3	1257	5.3	1926	0.4
12	W	0118	5.1	0759	0.1	1348	5.3	2008	0.5
13	TH	0205	5.1	0846	0.0	1435	5.3	2049	0.5
14	F	0250	5.2	0930	0.0	1522	5.3	2129	0.7
15	SA	0334	5.1	1014	0.1	1608	5.1	2209	0.8
16	SU	0417	5.0	1059	0.2	1654	4.8	2253	0.9
17	M	0502	4.8	1146	0.4	1742	4.6	◐ 2343	1.0
18	TU	0553	4.6	1244	0.7	1836	4.3		
19	W	0048	1.1	0653	4.3	1348	0.9	1942	4.1
20	TH	0202	1.2	0804	4.2	1458	1.0	2049	4.1
21	F	0321	1.1	0917	4.2	1602	1.0	2154	4.2
22	SA	0432	0.9	1021	4.5	1658	1.0	2249	4.5
23	SU	0531	0.8	1117	4.6	1746	0.9	2339	4.6
24	M	0621	0.7	1205	4.7	1827	0.9		
25	TU	0021	4.7	0700	0.5	1246	4.7	○ 1901	0.8
26	W	0059	4.8	0733	0.4	1321	4.8	1930	0.8
27	TH	0131	4.8	0803	0.4	1352	4.8	1958	0.8
28	F	0200	4.8	0832	0.4	1420	4.8	2027	0.8
29	SA	0229	4.8	0901	0.4	1451	4.8	2057	0.7
30	SU	0259	4.8	0931	0.3	1525	4.8	2129	0.7
31	M	0332	4.8	1004	0.4	1603	4.8	2204	0.7

FEBRUARY

Date	Day	Time	m	Time	m	Time	m	Time	m
1	TU	0410	4.7	1039	0.4	1645	4.6	2244	0.8
2	W	0453	4.6	1123	0.5	1735	4.3	◑ 2333	1.0
3	TH	0547	4.5	1223	0.8	1834	4.2		
4	F	0043	1.1	0657	4.2	1346	0.9	1950	4.1
5	SA	0211	1.1	0822	4.2	1519	0.9	2110	4.2
6	SU	0346	1.0	0945	4.5	1638	0.8	2223	4.5
7	M	0510	0.7	1056	4.8	1741	0.7	2325	4.7
8	TU	0616	0.3	1157	5.1	1832	0.5	●	
9	W	0020	5.0	0705	0.1	1251	5.3	1914	0.4
10	TH	0108	5.2	0750	0.0	1338	5.5	1953	0.4
11	F	0153	5.2	0832	-0.1	1421	5.5	2031	0.4
12	SA	0233	5.3	0911	-0.1	1502	5.3	2108	0.4
13	SU	0311	5.3	0948	0.0	1541	5.2	2144	0.5
14	M	0349	5.2	1023	0.2	1619	5.0	2220	0.7
15	TU	0426	5.0	1100	0.4	1656	4.6	2300	0.8
16	W	0507	4.7	1142	0.8	1739	4.2	◐ 2348	1.0
17	TH	0558	4.3	1239	1.0	1831	4.0		
18	F	0059	1.1	0712	4.0	1355	1.2	1956	3.8
19	SA	0235	1.2	0846	4.0	1520	1.3	2122	4.0
20	SU	0408	1.0	1004	4.2	1633	1.1	2226	4.2
21	M	0513	0.8	1101	4.5	1727	1.0	2318	4.6
22	TU	0602	0.5	1147	4.7	1810	0.9		
23	W	0000	4.7	0640	0.4	1227	4.8	1842	0.8
24	TH	0039	4.8	0711	0.4	1302	4.8	○ 1911	0.8
25	F	0111	4.8	0740	0.3	1332	4.8	1937	0.7
26	SA	0140	4.8	0808	0.3	1359	5.0	2006	0.7
27	SU	0209	4.8	0837	0.3	1429	5.0	2037	0.5
28	M	0237	5.0	0906	0.2	1501	5.0	2108	0.4

MARCH

Date	Day	Time	m	Time	m	Time	m	Time	m
1	TU	0309	5.0	0935	0.3	1537	5.0	2141	0.4
2	W	0345	5.0	1008	0.4	1616	4.7	2218	0.5
3	TH	0426	4.8	1047	0.5	1701	4.5	◑ 2305	0.8
4	F	0517	4.5	1143	0.9	1757	4.1		
5	SA	0011	1.0	0626	4.2	1314	1.1	1915	3.8
6	SU	0151	1.1	0808	4.1	1506	1.1	2055	4.0
7	M	0351	0.9	0947	4.3	1632	0.9	2216	4.3
8	TU	0510	0.5	1056	4.8	1730	0.7	2315	4.7
9	W	0608	0.2	1150	5.2	1818	0.5		
10	TH	0006	5.0	0652	0.0	1239	5.3	● 1857	0.4
11	F	0052	5.2	0732	-0.1	1322	5.5	1933	0.3
12	SA	0133	5.3	0810	-0.1	1401	5.3	2010	0.3
13	SU	0210	5.3	0845	-0.1	1437	5.2	2045	0.3
14	M	0245	5.3	0917	0.1	1511	5.1	2119	0.4
15	TU	0319	5.2	0947	0.2	1543	4.8	2151	0.4
16	W	0353	5.0	1019	0.5	1614	4.6	2225	0.7
17	TH	0430	4.7	1055	0.8	1650	4.3	◐ 2308	0.9
18	F	0517	4.3	1145	1.1	1733	4.0		
19	SA	0012	1.1	0621	4.0	1303	1.3	1842	3.7
20	SU	0149	1.2	0812	3.8	1439	1.5	2041	3.8
21	M	0336	1.0	0939	4.1	1603	1.2	2155	4.1
22	TU	0443	0.8	1035	4.5	1659	1.0	2247	4.5
23	W	0530	0.5	1119	4.7	1741	0.9	2329	4.7
24	TH	0610	0.4	1157	5.0	1816	0.8		
25	F	0008	4.8	0640	0.3	1232	5.0	○ 1844	0.7
26	SA	0042	4.8	0710	0.3	1304	5.0	1913	0.7
27	SU	0113	4.8	0740	0.3	1334	5.0	1944	0.5
28	M	0145	5.0	0812	0.2	1406	5.0	2016	0.4
29	TU	0216	5.1	0842	0.2	1439	5.0	2050	0.3
30	W	0251	5.1	0913	0.3	1515	5.0	2125	0.3
31	TH	0328	5.0	0947	0.4	1554	4.7	2204	0.4

APRIL

Date	Day	Time	m	Time	m	Time	m	Time	m
1	F	0412	4.8	1029	0.7	1638	4.3	2253	0.7
2	SA	0507	4.5	1127	1.0	1735	4.0	◑	
3	SU	0004	0.9	0623	4.1	1305	1.3	1857	3.8
4	M	0201	1.0	0812	4.1	1459	1.2	2043	4.0
5	TU	0350	0.7	0943	4.5	1616	1.0	2200	4.3
6	W	0457	0.3	1042	5.0	1710	0.7	2254	4.7
7	TH	0549	0.0	1132	5.2	1755	0.5	2343	5.0
8	F	0632	-0.1	1217	5.3	1835	0.4	●	
9	SA	0027	5.2	0709	-0.1	1259	5.3	1912	0.3
10	SU	0107	5.2	0743	0.0	1336	5.2	1947	0.3
11	M	0145	5.2	0815	0.1	1411	5.1	2022	0.3
12	TU	0219	5.2	0846	0.2	1441	5.0	2056	0.3
13	W	0253	5.1	0915	0.4	1511	4.8	2127	0.4
14	TH	0328	4.8	0944	0.7	1541	4.6	2200	0.5
15	F	0405	4.6	1019	0.9	1615	4.3	2242	0.8
16	SA	0449	4.3	1106	1.2	1659	4.1	◐ 2342	1.0
17	SU	0547	4.0	1220	1.5	1802	3.8		
18	M	0110	1.1	0720	3.8	1353	1.5	1941	3.8
19	TU	0247	1.0	0855	4.1	1519	1.3	2106	4.1
20	W	0356	0.8	0954	4.3	1618	1.1	2202	4.3
21	TH	0445	0.5	1039	4.7	1700	0.9	2246	4.6
22	F	0526	0.4	1118	4.8	1737	0.8	2326	4.7
23	SA	0603	0.3	1155	5.0	1813	0.7		
24	SU	0005	4.8	0638	0.3	1231	5.0	○ 1847	0.5
25	M	0043	5.0	0714	0.3	1307	5.0	1923	0.4
26	TU	0120	5.0	0748	0.3	1344	5.0	2000	0.3
27	W	0158	5.1	0823	0.3	1420	5.0	2038	0.3
28	TH	0238	5.1	0859	0.4	1459	4.8	2118	0.3
29	F	0322	5.0	0938	0.5	1542	4.6	2202	0.4
30	SA	0411	4.7	1024	0.9	1630	4.3	2258	0.5

Chart Datum: 2·35 metres below Ordnance Datum (Newlyn)

TIME ZONE (UT)
For Summer Time add ONE hour in **non-shaded areas**

ENGLAND – BURNHAM-ON-CROUCH

LAT 51°37′N LONG 0°48′E

TIMES AND HEIGHTS OF HIGH AND LOW WATERS

SPRING & NEAP TIDES
Dates in **red** are **SPRINGS**
Dates in **blue** are **NEAPS**

YEAR **2005**

MAY

Date	Day	Time m	Phase
1	SU	0512 4.5 / 1126 1.1 / 1731 4.1	◑
2	M	0018 0.8 / 0628 4.2 / 1258 1.3 / 1851 4.0	
3	TU	0205 0.7 / 0801 4.3 / 1435 1.2 / 2017 4.1	
4	W	0332 0.4 / 0917 4.6 / 1547 1.0 / 2127 4.5	
5	TH	0433 0.2 / 1015 5.0 / 1641 0.7 / 2223 4.7	
6	F	0523 0.1 / 1104 5.1 / 1727 0.5 / 2312 5.0	
7	SA	0605 0.0 / 1150 5.1 / 1812 0.4 / 2358 5.0	
8	SU	0642 0.1 / 1231 5.1 / 1850 0.3	●
9	M	0042 5.0 / 0716 0.2 / 1310 5.0 / 1928 0.3	
10	TU	0120 5.0 / 0746 0.3 / 1345 4.8 / 2003 0.3	
11	W	0157 5.0 / 0818 0.4 / 1416 4.7 / 2038 0.3	
12	TH	0232 4.8 / 0848 0.5 / 1445 4.7 / 2110 0.4	
13	F	0307 4.7 / 0919 0.8 / 1517 4.6 / 2144 0.5	
14	SA	0346 4.6 / 0952 0.9 / 1552 4.5 / 2226 0.7	
15	SU	0428 4.3 / 1035 1.1 / 1637 4.2 / 2319 0.8	
16	M	0520 4.1 / 1136 1.3 / 1734 4.1	◐
17	TU	0029 0.9 / 0625 4.0 / 1255 1.5 / 1844 4.0	
18	W	0145 0.9 / 0746 4.1 / 1413 1.3 / 2002 4.1	
19	TH	0254 0.8 / 0854 4.3 / 1518 1.1 / 2103 4.2	
20	F	0350 0.5 / 0947 4.6 / 1608 1.0 / 2155 4.5	
21	SA	0438 0.4 / 1032 4.7 / 1653 0.8 / 2241 4.7	
22	SU	0524 0.3 / 1114 4.8 / 1738 0.7 / 2327 4.8	
23	M	0610 0.3 / 1158 5.0 / 1823 0.5	○
24	TU	0013 5.0 / 0650 0.3 / 1242 5.0 / 1905 0.4	
25	W	0059 5.1 / 0730 0.3 / 1325 5.0 / 1948 0.3	
26	TH	0145 5.1 / 0811 0.4 / 1408 5.0 / 2033 0.2	
27	F	0232 5.1 / 0852 0.5 / 1452 4.8 / 2119 0.2	
28	SA	0321 5.1 / 0934 0.7 / 1538 4.7 / 2208 0.3	
29	SU	0413 4.8 / 1022 0.9 / 1630 4.6 / 2306 0.3	
30	M	0513 4.7 / 1120 1.1 / 1728 4.3	◑
31	TU	0019 0.4 / 0618 4.6 / 1235 1.2 / 1833 4.3	

JUNE

Date	Day	Time m	Phase
1	W	0143 0.4 / 0731 4.6 / 1356 1.1 / 1943 4.3	
2	TH	0259 0.3 / 0839 4.6 / 1508 1.0 / 2049 4.6	
3	F	0400 0.3 / 0940 4.7 / 1607 0.8 / 2148 4.7	
4	SA	0451 0.2 / 1032 4.8 / 1659 0.7 / 2242 4.8	
5	SU	0534 0.3 / 1120 4.8 / 1747 0.5 / 2332 4.8	
6	M	0616 0.4 / 1206 4.8 / 1833 0.4	●
7	TU	0019 4.8 / 0650 0.5 / 1248 4.8 / 1913 0.4	
8	W	0103 4.8 / 0724 0.7 / 1325 4.7 / 1951 0.4	
9	TH	0141 4.7 / 0756 0.7 / 1357 4.7 / 2027 0.4	
10	F	0217 4.7 / 0828 0.8 / 1428 4.7 / 2100 0.4	
11	SA	0252 4.6 / 0858 0.8 / 1459 4.6 / 2132 0.5	
12	SU	0328 4.6 / 0931 0.9 / 1535 4.6 / 2209 0.5	
13	M	0407 4.5 / 1009 1.0 / 1616 4.5 / 2252 0.7	
14	TU	0451 4.3 / 1056 1.2 / 1704 4.3 / 2343 0.8	
15	W	0542 4.2 / 1152 1.2 / 1759 4.2	◐
16	TH	0047 0.8 / 0640 4.2 / 1301 1.2 / 1901 4.2	
17	F	0151 0.7 / 0747 4.3 / 1410 1.2 / 2006 4.2	
18	SA	0255 0.7 / 0849 4.5 / 1514 1.1 / 2106 4.5	
19	SU	0354 0.5 / 0947 4.6 / 1612 0.9 / 2203 4.6	
20	M	0450 0.4 / 1040 4.7 / 1709 0.8 / 2257 4.8	
21	TU	0543 0.4 / 1131 4.8 / 1805 0.5 / 2351 5.0	
22	W	0633 0.4 / 1222 5.0 / 1855 0.4	○
23	TH	0045 5.1 / 0718 0.4 / 1311 5.0 / 1945 0.3	
24	F	0136 5.2 / 0801 0.5 / 1359 5.0 / 2032 0.2	
25	SA	0226 5.2 / 0844 0.5 / 1446 5.0 / 2119 0.1	
26	SU	0316 5.2 / 0927 0.7 / 1532 5.0 / 2207 0.1	
27	M	0407 5.1 / 1012 0.8 / 1620 4.8 / 2259 0.1	
28	TU	0459 5.0 / 1101 0.9 / 1711 4.8 / 2354 0.2	◑
29	W	0554 4.7 / 1157 1.0 / 1805 4.7	
30	TH	0103 0.4 / 0653 4.6 / 1308 1.1 / 1904 4.6	

JULY

Date	Day	Time m	Phase
1	F	0212 0.5 / 0758 4.5 / 1422 1.1 / 2010 4.5	
2	SA	0317 0.5 / 0901 4.5 / 1531 1.0 / 2116 4.5	
3	SU	0414 0.7 / 1001 4.6 / 1634 0.8 / 2217 4.6	
4	M	0505 0.7 / 1054 4.6 / 1730 0.7 / 2313 4.6	
5	TU	0550 0.8 / 1144 4.7 / 1822 0.5	
6	W	0005 4.7 / 0631 0.8 / 1229 4.7 / 1904 0.5	●
7	TH	0051 4.7 / 0706 0.8 / 1310 4.7 / 1942 0.4	
8	F	0131 4.7 / 0739 0.8 / 1344 4.7 / 2016 0.4	
9	SA	0205 4.7 / 0810 0.9 / 1415 4.7 / 2047 0.4	
10	SU	0235 4.7 / 0840 0.9 / 1443 4.7 / 2116 0.4	
11	M	0307 4.6 / 0910 0.9 / 1515 4.7 / 2146 0.4	
12	TU	0341 4.6 / 0943 0.9 / 1550 4.7 / 2220 0.5	
13	W	0419 4.6 / 1021 1.0 / 1629 4.6 / 2301 0.5	
14	TH	0502 4.5 / 1104 1.1 / 1714 4.5 / 2347 0.7	◐
15	F	0553 4.3 / 1159 1.2 / 1807 4.3	
16	SA	0051 0.8 / 0652 4.3 / 1308 1.2 / 1913 4.3	
17	SU	0201 0.8 / 0801 4.3 / 1424 1.2 / 2023 4.3	
18	M	0315 0.8 / 0909 4.5 / 1539 1.1 / 2133 4.5	
19	TU	0423 0.7 / 1014 4.6 / 1651 0.9 / 2237 4.7	
20	W	0525 0.7 / 1113 4.8 / 1757 0.5 / 2339 5.0	
21	TH	0621 0.5 / 1209 5.0 / 1851 0.3	○
22	F	0037 5.2 / 0706 0.5 / 1302 5.1 / 1941 0.1	
23	SA	0129 5.3 / 0749 0.5 / 1349 5.2 / 2027 0.0	
24	SU	0217 5.5 / 0831 0.5 / 1434 5.2 / 2110 -0.1	
25	M	0303 5.5 / 0911 0.5 / 1517 5.3 / 2152 0.0	
26	TU	0349 5.3 / 0952 0.7 / 1559 5.2 / 2234 0.1	
27	W	0434 5.1 / 1033 0.8 / 1642 5.1 / 2319 0.2	
28	TH	0521 4.8 / 1120 0.9 / 1729 4.8	◑
29	F	0009 0.5 / 0611 4.6 / 1217 1.0 / 1823 4.6	
30	SA	0112 0.8 / 0711 4.3 / 1330 1.1 / 1931 4.3	
31	SU	0223 1.0 / 0820 4.2 / 1454 1.1 / 2047 4.2	

AUGUST

Date	Day	Time m	Phase
1	M	0335 1.1 / 0931 4.3 / 1613 1.0 / 2201 4.3	
2	TU	0439 1.0 / 1034 4.5 / 1718 0.8 / 2302 4.6	
3	W	0531 1.0 / 1126 4.7 / 1812 0.7 / 2353 4.7	
4	TH	0616 0.9 / 1213 4.8 / 1852 0.5	
5	F	0038 4.8 / 0650 0.9 / 1253 5.0 / 1928 0.4	●
6	SA	0115 4.8 / 0722 0.9 / 1328 5.0 / 1958 0.4	
7	SU	0148 4.8 / 0751 0.9 / 1357 4.8 / 2025 0.4	
8	M	0215 4.8 / 0818 0.8 / 1422 4.8 / 2051 0.4	
9	TU	0242 4.8 / 0847 0.8 / 1450 4.8 / 2119 0.4	
10	W	0312 4.8 / 0919 0.8 / 1520 4.8 / 2148 0.4	
11	TH	0347 4.8 / 0951 0.8 / 1553 4.8 / 2219 0.5	
12	F	0426 4.7 / 1028 0.9 / 1631 4.7 / 2258 0.7	
13	SA	0511 4.5 / 1114 1.1 / 1721 4.5 / 2349 0.9	◐
14	SU	0606 4.2 / 1218 1.2 / 1825 4.2	
15	M	0110 1.0 / 0716 4.1 / 1344 1.2 / 1948 4.2	
16	TU	0242 1.1 / 0839 4.2 / 1520 1.1 / 2116 4.3	
17	W	0407 1.0 / 0959 4.5 / 1646 0.9 / 2231 4.7	
18	TH	0514 0.8 / 1102 4.7 / 1753 0.4 / 2333 5.1	
19	F	0609 0.7 / 1157 5.1 / 1844 0.2	○
20	SA	0027 5.3 / 0652 0.5 / 1247 5.2 / 1929 0.0	
21	SU	0116 5.5 / 0732 0.5 / 1332 5.3 / 2010 -0.1	
22	M	0201 5.6 / 0812 0.4 / 1414 5.5 / 2050 -0.1	
23	TU	0243 5.5 / 0850 0.5 / 1453 5.5 / 2127 0.0	
24	W	0324 5.3 / 0928 0.5 / 1531 5.3 / 2203 0.1	
25	TH	0403 5.1 / 1005 0.7 / 1610 5.2 / 2238 0.3	
26	F	0442 4.8 / 1046 0.8 / 1651 5.0 / 2319 0.7	◑
27	SA	0524 4.5 / 1133 1.0 / 1740 4.5	
28	SU	0012 1.0 / 0616 4.2 / 1242 1.2 / 1849 4.1	
29	M	0126 1.3 / 0734 4.0 / 1420 1.2 / 2023 4.1	
30	TU	0255 1.5 / 0902 4.1 / 1554 1.1 / 2146 4.2	
31	W	0413 1.3 / 1011 4.3 / 1701 0.9 / 2245 4.6	

Chart Datum: 2·35 metres below Ordnance Datum (Newlyn)

TIME ZONE (UT)
For Summer Time add ONE hour in **non-shaded areas**

ENGLAND – BURNHAM-ON-CROUCH

LAT 51°37′N LONG 0°48′E

TIMES AND HEIGHTS OF HIGH AND LOW WATERS

SPRING & NEAP TIDES
Dates in **red** are **SPRINGS**
Dates in **blue** are **NEAPS**

YEAR **2005**

SEPTEMBER

Date	Day	Time	m	Time	m	Time	m	Time	m	Moon
1	TH	0510	1.1	1104	4.7	1752	0.7	2333	4.8	
2	F	0554	1.0	1149	5.0	1831	0.4			
3	SA	0015	5.0	0630	0.9	1227	5.0	1903	0.4	●
4	SU	0051	5.0	0659	0.9	1302	5.0	1930	0.4	
5	M	0122	5.0	0726	0.9	1330	5.0	1956	0.4	
6	TU	0148	5.0	0754	0.8	1357	5.0	2022	0.4	
7	W	0215	5.0	0824	0.8	1422	5.0	2049	0.4	
8	TH	0243	5.0	0855	0.7	1452	5.0	2117	0.4	
9	F	0316	5.0	0927	0.7	1525	5.0	2146	0.5	
10	SA	0353	4.8	1002	0.8	1602	4.8	2221	0.7	
11	SU	0435	4.6	1046	1.0	1649	4.6	2310	1.0	◐
12	M	0529	4.2	1146	1.2	1754	4.2			
13	TU	0032	1.2	0639	4.0	1324	1.2	1930	4.1	
14	W	0224	1.3	0818	4.1	1519	1.1	2115	4.3	
15	TH	0355	1.1	0946	4.3	1642	0.7	2226	4.8	
16	F	0459	0.9	1047	4.8	1741	0.3	2322	5.2	
17	SA	0549	0.7	1139	5.1	1829	0.0			
18	SU	0011	5.5	0633	0.5	1225	5.3	1909	-0.1	○
19	M	0057	5.6	0710	0.4	1308	5.5	1946	-0.1	
20	TU	0138	5.5	0748	0.4	1348	5.5	2023	0.0	
21	W	0216	5.3	0827	0.4	1425	5.5	2056	0.1	
22	TH	0253	5.2	0903	0.4	1501	5.3	2129	0.3	
23	F	0328	5.1	0939	0.5	1537	5.2	2200	0.5	
24	SA	0402	4.8	1017	0.8	1616	4.8	2236	0.9	
25	SU	0437	4.5	1101	1.0	1702	4.5	2324	1.2	◑
26	M	0522	4.1	1206	1.2	1808	4.0			
27	TU	0039	1.6	0634	3.8	1346	1.2	1955	4.0	
28	W	0216	1.6	0825	4.0	1523	1.1	2120	4.2	
29	TH	0341	1.5	0939	4.3	1629	0.9	2218	4.6	
30	F	0439	1.2	1031	4.7	1717	0.7	2303	4.8	

OCTOBER

Date	Day	Time	m	Time	m	Time	m	Time	m	Moon
1	SA	0524	1.0	1113	4.8	1757	0.4	2342	5.0	
2	SU	0600	0.9	1152	5.0	1828	0.4			
3	M	0017	5.1	0630	0.9	1226	5.0	1856	0.4	●
4	TU	0048	5.0	0658	0.8	1257	5.0	1924	0.4	
5	W	0116	5.0	0728	0.8	1327	5.0	1953	0.4	
6	TH	0146	5.0	0800	0.7	1357	5.0	2022	0.4	
7	F	0216	5.0	0834	0.7	1429	5.1	2052	0.5	
8	SA	0251	5.0	0908	0.7	1504	5.0	2123	0.7	
9	SU	0328	4.8	0946	0.7	1546	4.8	2200	0.9	
10	M	0411	4.6	1033	0.9	1636	4.5	2251	1.1	◐
11	TU	0503	4.2	1139	1.1	1746	4.2			
12	W	0015	1.5	0618	4.0	1324	1.1	1928	4.1	
13	TH	0209	1.5	0802	4.1	1513	0.9	2105	4.5	
14	F	0336	1.2	0924	4.5	1625	0.4	2210	4.8	
15	SA	0435	0.9	1021	4.8	1720	0.2	2301	5.2	
16	SU	0524	0.7	1111	5.1	1806	0.0	2347	5.3	
17	M	0609	0.5	1156	5.3	1845	0.0			○
18	TU	0030	5.5	0648	0.4	1240	5.3	1920	0.1	
19	W	0111	5.3	0726	0.4	1320	5.3	1954	0.2	
20	TH	0148	5.2	0804	0.4	1358	5.3	2027	0.3	
21	F	0223	5.1	0842	0.4	1435	5.2	2057	0.5	
22	SA	0255	5.0	0918	0.5	1512	5.0	2128	0.8	
23	SU	0327	4.7	0954	0.7	1551	4.7	2201	1.0	
24	M	0401	4.5	1038	0.9	1635	4.3	2245	1.3	
25	TU	0443	4.2	1138	1.1	1734	4.1	2352	1.6	◑
26	W	0546	4.0	1306	1.1	1905	3.8			
27	TH	0128	1.7	0726	4.0	1435	1.1	2035	4.1	
28	F	0255	1.6	0847	4.2	1541	0.9	2136	4.5	
29	SA	0356	1.2	0944	4.5	1630	0.7	2221	4.7	
30	SU	0442	1.1	1028	4.7	1711	0.5	2300	5.0	
31	M	0518	0.9	1107	4.8	1747	0.4	2335	5.0	

NOVEMBER

Date	Day	Time	m	Time	m	Time	m	Time	m	Moon
1	TU	0554	0.8	1145	5.0	1822	0.4			
2	W	0010	5.0	0629	0.8	1222	5.0	1854	0.4	●
3	TH	0045	5.0	0704	0.7	1259	5.0	1928	0.5	
4	F	0119	5.0	0741	0.5	1335	5.1	2001	0.5	
5	SA	0156	5.0	0820	0.5	1414	5.1	2035	0.5	
6	SU	0233	5.0	0900	0.5	1456	5.0	2111	0.8	
7	M	0313	4.7	0942	0.5	1542	4.8	2153	1.0	
8	TU	0358	4.5	1034	0.7	1637	4.6	2247	1.2	
9	W	0454	4.2	1143	0.9	1747	4.3			◐
10	TH	0004	1.3	0608	4.1	1319	0.8	1915	4.3	
11	F	0142	1.3	0735	4.2	1449	0.7	2037	4.6	
12	SA	0303	1.2	0848	4.5	1557	0.4	2140	4.8	
13	SU	0404	0.9	0948	4.8	1651	0.2	2231	5.1	
14	M	0455	0.7	1040	5.1	1738	0.1	2318	5.2	
15	TU	0542	0.5	1128	5.1	1819	0.2			
16	W	0002	5.2	0626	0.4	1214	5.2	1854	0.3	○
17	TH	0044	5.1	0706	0.4	1257	5.1	1928	0.4	
18	F	0122	5.0	0746	0.4	1337	5.1	2000	0.5	
19	SA	0157	4.8	0825	0.4	1416	5.0	2032	0.8	
20	SU	0229	4.8	0903	0.5	1453	4.8	2103	0.9	
21	M	0300	4.7	0939	0.7	1531	4.6	2134	1.0	
22	TU	0335	4.6	1019	0.8	1612	4.5	2213	1.2	
23	W	0417	4.3	1110	0.9	1700	4.2	2307	1.5	◑
24	TH	0511	4.2	1213	1.0	1802	4.0			
25	F	0021	1.6	0619	4.1	1326	1.0	1920	4.0	
26	SA	0142	1.5	0737	4.1	1434	0.9	2031	4.2	
27	SU	0251	1.3	0842	4.3	1531	0.8	2125	4.5	
28	M	0345	1.1	0935	4.5	1619	0.7	2211	4.7	
29	TU	0430	1.0	1021	4.7	1704	0.5	2252	4.8	
30	W	0515	0.9	1106	4.8	1748	0.5	2334	5.0	

DECEMBER

Date	Day	Time	m	Time	m	Time	m	Time	m	Moon
1	TH	0601	0.8	1151	5.0	1830	0.5			●
2	F	0017	5.0	0645	0.7	1237	5.1	1909	0.5	
3	SA	0100	5.0	0728	0.5	1321	5.1	1947	0.5	
4	SU	0141	5.0	0813	0.4	1406	5.1	2027	0.7	
5	M	0223	5.0	0858	0.3	1452	5.1	2107	0.8	
6	TU	0307	4.8	0944	0.3	1542	5.0	2151	0.9	
7	W	0355	4.7	1036	0.4	1635	4.7	2241	1.1	
8	TH	0449	4.6	1136	0.5	1737	4.6	2342	1.2	◐
9	F	0551	4.5	1252	0.5	1844	4.5			
10	SA	0059	1.2	0700	4.5	1411	0.5	1957	4.5	
11	SU	0218	1.1	0810	4.6	1520	0.4	2102	4.6	
12	M	0326	1.0	0914	4.7	1619	0.4	2159	4.7	
13	TU	0425	0.8	1011	4.8	1709	0.4	2249	4.8	
14	W	0518	0.7	1105	4.8	1754	0.5	2338	4.8	
15	TH	0611	0.5	1155	5.0	1833	0.5			○
16	F	0023	4.8	0654	0.4	1243	5.0	1908	0.7	
17	SA	0104	4.8	0736	0.4	1325	4.8	1941	0.8	
18	SU	0140	4.8	0815	0.4	1403	4.8	2014	0.9	
19	M	0213	4.7	0852	0.4	1437	4.7	2043	0.9	
20	TU	0243	4.7	0925	0.5	1512	4.6	2113	1.0	
21	W	0316	4.6	0958	0.5	1548	4.5	2147	1.1	
22	TH	0353	4.6	1036	0.7	1627	4.3	2228	1.1	
23	F	0436	4.5	1121	0.8	1713	4.2	2317	1.2	◑
24	SA	0527	4.2	1216	0.9	1806	4.2			
25	SU	0020	1.3	0626	4.2	1320	0.9	1910	4.2	
26	M	0130	1.3	0734	4.2	1424	0.9	2017	4.2	
27	TU	0239	1.2	0840	4.3	1528	0.8	2120	4.5	
28	W	0341	1.1	0940	4.5	1625	0.7	2215	4.6	
29	TH	0441	0.9	1036	4.7	1720	0.7	2306	4.8	
30	F	0539	0.8	1129	5.0	1812	0.5	2356	4.8	
31	SA	0633	0.5	1222	5.1	1856	0.5			●

Chart Datum: 2·35 metres below Ordnance Datum (Newlyn)

9.4.16 RIVER BLACKWATER

Essex **51°45'·33N 00°54'·90E** (5ca S of Nass bn)
Rtgs: Maldon ❀❀◊◊✿✿; Heybridge Basin ❀❀◊✿✿

CHARTS AC *5607, 1183, 1975, 3741*; Imray C1, Y17, 2000 Series; OS 168; Stanfords 5, 6.

TIDES Maldon +0130 Dover; ML 2·8; Duration 0620; Zone 0 (UT)

Standard Port WALTON-ON-THE-NAZE (⟶)

Times				Height (metres)			
High Water		Low Water		MHWS	MHWN	MLWN	MLWS
0000	0600	0500	1100	4·2	3·4	1·1	0·4
1200	1800	1700	2300				
Differences SUNK HEAD							
0000	+0002	–0002	+0002	–0·3	–0·3	–0·1	–0·1
WEST MERSEA							
+0035	+0015	+0055	+0010	+0·9	+0·4	+0·1	+0·1
BRADWELL							
+0035	+0023	+0047	+0004	+1·0	+0·8	+0·2	0·0
OSEA ISLAND							
+0057	+0045	+0050	+0007	+1·1	+0·9	+0·1	0·0
MALDON							
+0107	+0055	No data		–1·3	–1·1	No data	

SHELTER Good, as appropriate to wind. Marinas at Tollesbury, Bradwell and Maylandsea. ⚓ restricted by oyster beds and many moorings. At W Mersea there is a pontoon for landing (limited waiting); also pile moorings in Ray Chan or ⚓ in Mersea Quarters, access approx HW±1½. Berths at Heybridge Basin, access via lock approx HW –1 to HW; a SHM buoy opposite the lock marks the deep water ent. Access to Chelmer & Blackwater Canal (not navigable).

NAVIGATION WPT Knoll NCM, Q, 51°43´·88N 01°05´·07E, 287° to Nass bn, ECM VQ (3) 5s, 6·7M. Speed limit 8kn W of Osea Is.
WEST MERSEA: Avoid oyster beds between Cobmarsh and Packing Marsh Is and in Salcott Chan. ⚓ in Mersea Quarters.
BRADWELL: No dangers, but only suitable for small craft and area gets very crowded; see below under Lts & Marks.
TOLLESBURY FLEET: Proceedings via S Chan up Woodrolfe Creek, a tide gauge shows depth over marina ent sill (approx 2·4m at MHWS and 1·4m at MHWN). Speed limits: Woodrolfe Creek 4kn upper reaches; Tollesbury Fleet S Chan 8kn.

LIGHTS AND MARKS Bradwell Creek ent has SCM bn Q with tide gauge in Creek; leave to **STBD** on entry. 4 PHM buoys, 3 SHM withies and 2 B/W △ ldg bns mark the chan which doglegs past a SHM buoy to marina ent. Power stn is conspic 7ca NNE.
MALDON: From S of Osea Is, 'The Doctor', No 3 SHM buoy on with Blackwater SC lt, Iso G 5s, lead 300° approx up the chan; or No 3 and No 8 buoys in line at 305°. Beyond No 8 buoy, the chan which shifts and carries 0·2m, is lighted and buoyed up to Maldon. Access near HW; pontoons dry to soft mud.

R/T Bradwell and Tollesbury Marinas VHF Ch **80** M (HO). Blackwater Marina VHF Ch M, 0900-2300.Heybridge Lock VHF Ch 80 HW –2+1. Clark and Carter launch - call CC1.

TELEPHONE (Dial code 01621 Maldon; 01206 Colchester/West Mersea) R. Bailiff (Maldon Quay) 856487, Mobile 07818 013723, Office 875837, Mobile 0860 456802; Canal lockmaster 853506; MRSC (01255) 675518; Marinecall 09066 526239; Police (Colchester) 762212, (W Mersea) 382930; Dr 854118, or W Mersea 382015.

FACILITIES
WEST MERSEA (01206): **W Mersea YC** 382947, Fax 386261, Bar, launch service call YC 1; **Town** EC Wed; P, D, FW, ME, EI, CH, 🛒, R, Bar, ✉, Ⓑ, ⇌ (bus to Colchester, Ⓗ ☎ 01206-853535), ✈ (Southend/Stansted).
TOLLESBURY (01621): **Tollesbury Marina** (220+20 Ⓥ) ☎ 869202, Fax 868489, £1.43, marina@woodrolfe.demon.co.uk Access HW±1½, Slip, D, BH (20 ton), Gas, Gaz, LPG, EI, ME, ⚒, C (5 ton), CH, R, Bar, ⊡; **Tollesbury Cruising Club** ☎ 869561, Bar, R, M. **Village** EC Wed; P, 🛒, R, Bar, ✉, Ⓑ (Tues, Thurs 1000-1430), ⇌ (bus to Witham), ✈ (Southend or Cambridge).
BRADWELL (01621): **Bradwell Marina** (280, some Ⓥ) ☎ 776235, Fax 776393, £1.17 approx, Slip, D, P, ME, EI, ⚒, BH (16 ton), CH, R, Bar, Access HW±4½, approx 2m; **Bradwell Quay YC** ☎ 776539, M, FW, Bar, L, Slip. **Town** ✉, ⇌ (bus/taxi to Southminster), ✈ (Southend).
MAYLANDSEA: **Blackwater Marina** (230) ☎ 740264, Fax 742122, £8.50/yacht, Slip, D, ⚒, CH, R, Bar; Access HW±2. 150 moorings in chan. Taxi to Southminster ⇌.
MALDON (01621): **Maldon Quay** HM/River bailiff ☎ 856487, Mobile ☎ 07818 013723; M, P, D, FW, AB < 8m £8, > 8m £10, Slip; **Maldon Little Ship Club** ☎ 854139, Bar; **Services:** Slip, D, ⚒, CH, M, ACA, SM, ME, EI, Ⓔ. **Town** EC Wed; ✉, Ⓑ, ⇌ (bus to Chelmsford, Ⓗ ☎ (01245) 440761), ✈ (Southend, Cambridge or Stansted).
HEYBRIDGE BASIN (01621): **Lockmaster** ☎ 853506, VHF Ch80 opens HW±1 approx. **Blackwater SC** ☎ 853923, L, FW; **Services:** at CRS Marine ☎ 854684, Mobile 07850 543873 (pontoon outside lock), Slip, D, L, M, FW, ME, EI, ⚒, C. Bus to Heybridge/Maldon.

4

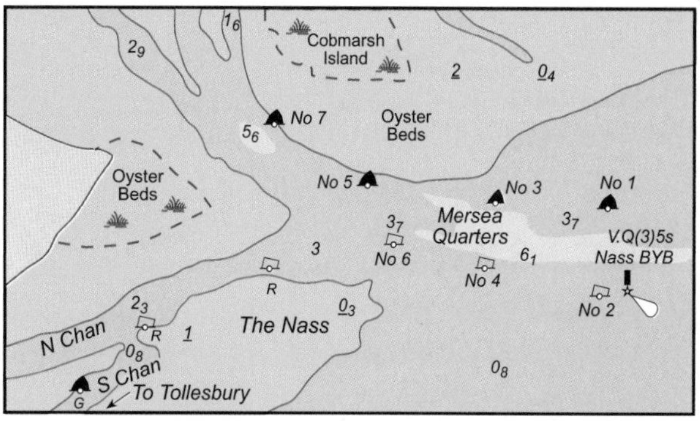
Cobmarsh Island
No 7
Oyster Beds
Oyster Beds
No 5
No 3
No 1
Mersea Quarters
V.Q(3)5s Nass BYB
No 6
No 4
No 2
The Nass
N Chan
S Chan
To Tollesbury

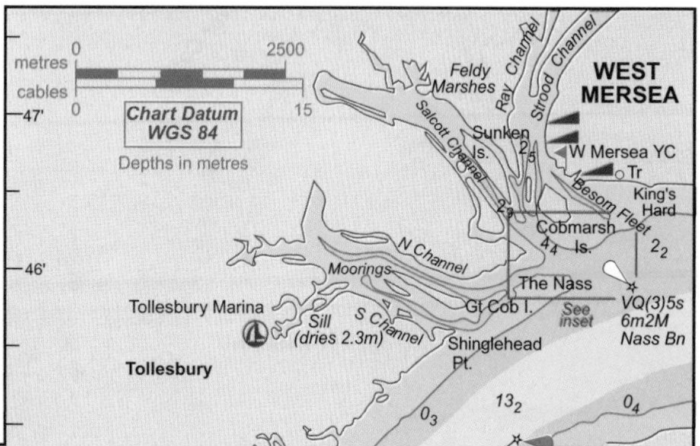

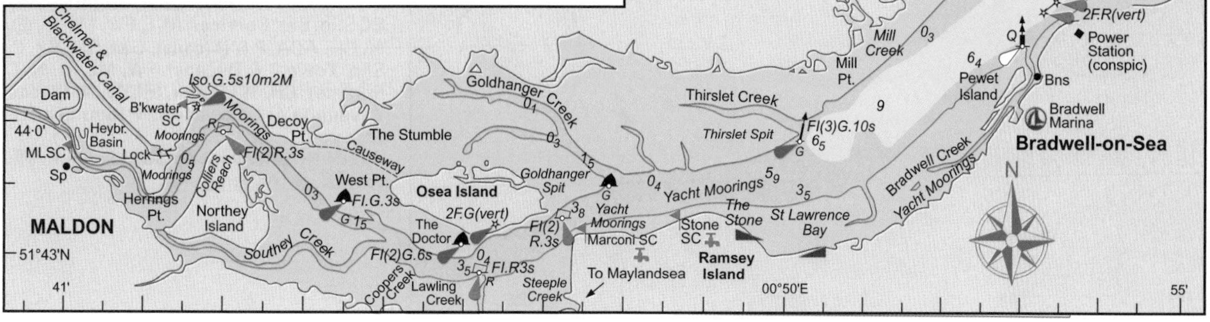
metres 0 2500
cables 0 15
Chart Datum WGS 84
Depths in metres
WEST MERSEA
Feldy Marshes
Ray Channel
Strood Channel
Salcott Channel
Sunken Is.
W Mersea YC
Besom Fleet
King's Hard
Cobmarsh Is.
N Channel
Moorings
The Nass
VQ(3)5s 6m2M Nass Bn
See inset
Gt Cob I.
Tollesbury Marina
Sill (dries 2.3m)
S Channel
Shinglehead Pt.
Tollesbury
2F.R(vert)
Power Station (conspic)
Mill Creek
Mill Pt.
Pewet Island
Bns
Bradwell Marina
Bradwell-on-Sea
Thirslet Creek
Thirslet Spit
Fl(3)G.10s
Chelmer & Blackwater Canal
Dam
Iso G.5s10m2M
B'kwater SC
Moorings
Decoy Pt.
Goldhanger Creek
The Stumble
Heybr. Basin
Lock
MLSC
Sp
Colliers Reach
Fl(2)R.3s
Causeway
West Pt.
Osea Island
Goldhanger Spit
Fl.G.3s
2F.G(vert)
Herrings Pt.
Northey Island
MALDON
Southey Creek
The Doctor
Fl(2)G.6s
Fl(2) R.3s
Yacht Moorings
Yacht Moorings
The Stone
St Lawrence Bay
Stone SC
Marconi SC
Bradwell Creek
Yacht Moorings
Fl.R3s
Lawling Creek
Coopers Creek
Steeple Creek
To Maylandsea
Ramsey Island
44·0'
51°43'N
41'
00°50'E
55'
47'
46'

9.4.17 RIVER COLNE

Essex **51°47'·98N 01°00'·60E** (Brightlingsea) ❁❁◊◊◊✿✿

CHARTS AC *5607, 1183, 1975, 3741*; Imray C1, Y17, 2000 Series; Stan 5, 6; OS 168

TIDES +0050 Dover; ML 2·5; Duration 0615; Zone 0 (UT)

Standard Port WALTON-ON-THE-NAZE (⟶)

Times				Height (metres)			
High Water		Low Water		MHWS	MHWN	MLWN	MLWS
0000	0600	0500	1100	4·2	3·4	1·1	0·4
1200	1800	1700	2300				
Differences BRIGHTLINGSEA							
+0025	+0021	+0046	+0004	+0·8	+0·4	+0·1	0·0
COLCHESTER							
+0035	+0025	Dries		0·0	–0·3	Dries	
CLACTON-ON-SEA							
+0012	+0010	+0025	+0008	+0·3	+0·1	+0·1	+0·1

SHELTER Suitable shelter can be found from most winds, but outer hbr is exposed to W'lies. In the creek S of Cindery Island are moorings (as shown) and long pontoons in about 1·5m, with possible AB for Ⓥs. ⚓ prohib in Brightlingsea Hbr, but there are ⚓s to the NW of Mersea Stone Pt and in Pyefleet Chan, E of Pewit Island. R Colne is navigable for 4·5m draft to Wivenhoe, where the river dries; and to The Hythe, Colchester (3m draft).

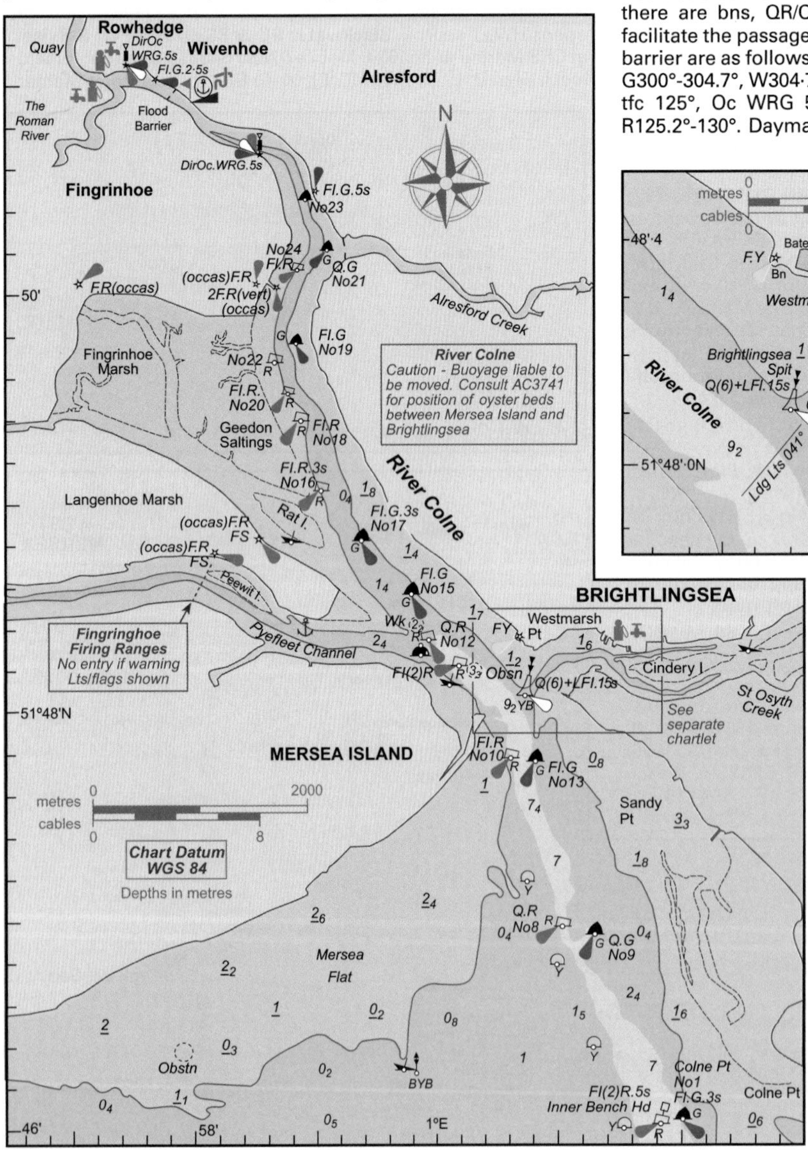
Rowhedge
Quay
DirOc WRG.5s
Wivenhoe
Fl.G.2·5s
The Roman River
Flood Barrier
Alresford
N
DirOc.WRG.5s
Fingrinhoe
Fl.G.5s No23
No24 Fl.R
Q.G No21
F.R(occas)
(occas)F.R
2F.R(vert) (occas)
50'
Alresford Creek
Fl.G No19
Fingrinhoe Marsh
No22
F.R. No20
River Colne
Caution - Buoyage liable to be moved. Consult AC3741 for position of oyster beds between Mersea Island and Brightlingsea
Geedon Saltings
Fl.R No18
Fl.R.3s No16
Langenhoe Marsh
(occas)F.R FS
Rat I.
Fl.G.3s No17
River Colne
(occas)F.R FS
Peewit I.
Fl.G No15
BRIGHTLINGSEA
Westmarsh Pt
Q.R No12
Fingringhoe Firing Ranges
No entry if warning Lts/flags shown
Pyefleet Channel
Fl(2)R
Obsn
Q(6)+LFl.15s
Cindery I
St Osyth Creek
51°48'N
See separate chartlet
MERSEA ISLAND
Fl.R No10
Fl.G No13
metres
cables
2000
Sandy Pt
Chart Datum WGS 84
Depths in metres
Q.R No8
Q.G No9
Mersea Flat
Obstn
BYB
Colne Pt No1
Fl(2)R.5s
Inner Bench Hd
Fl.G.3s
Colne Pt
46'
58'
1°E

NAVIGATION WPT Colne Bar By, SHM Fl (2) G 5s, 51°44'·61N 01°02'·57E, 340° to Mersea Stone, 3·6M. See also 9.4.16. Extensive mud and sand banks flank the ent chan. Large coasters use the Brightlingsea chans. The ent to Brightlingsea Creek is narrow at LW and carries about 1m.

A flood barrier 2ca below Wivenhoe church is normally open (30m wide) allowing unrestricted passage; keep to stbd, max speed 5kn. Tfc lts on N pier are 3FR (vert), vis up/downstream. When lit, they indicate the barrier gates are shut; see also LIGHTS AND MARKS.

Speed limits in approaches and up-river: No13 - 15By(s) = 8kn; No15 - 18By(s) = no spd limit; No18 - 34By(s) = 8kn; No 34 - Colchester = 5kn; Brightlingsea Harbour = 4kn.

LIGHTS AND MARKS Well buoyed/lit up to Wivenhoe. Ldg lts/marks 041° for Brightlingsea: both FR 7/10m 4M; dayglo W □, R stripes on posts; adjusted to suit the chan. Then Spit SCM buoy, Q (6) + L Fl 15s, and chan buoys Fl (3) G 5s and Fl R 5s, plus NCM bn Q where chan is divided by Cindery Is. Bateman's Tr (conspic) by Westmarsh Pt has a FY sodium lt 12m. Pyefleet Chan and other creeks are unlit.

The flood barrier is marked by 2FR/FG (vert) on both sides and there are bns, QR/QG, up/downstream on the river banks. To facilitate the passage of large vessels, Dir lts above and below the barrier are as follows: for up-stream tfc 305°, Oc WRG 5s 5/3M, vis G300°-304.7°, W304·7°-305·3°, R305·3°-310°; and for down-stream tfc 125°, Oc WRG 5s 5/3M, vis G120°-124.8, W°124.8°-125.2°, R125.2°-130°. Daymarks are W ▽ with Or vert stripe.

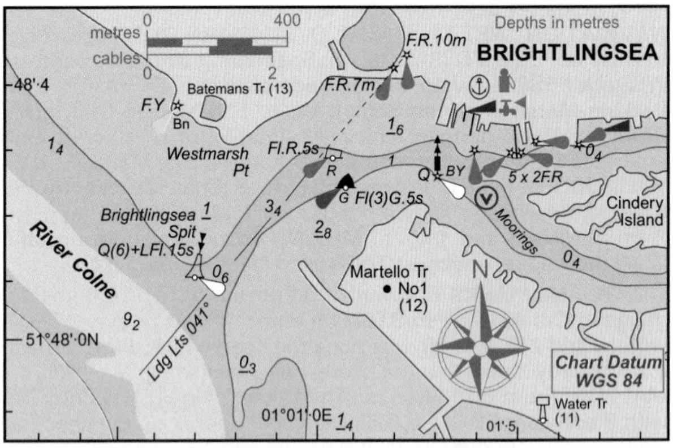
metres
cables
400
Depths in metres
F.R.10m
BRIGHTLINGSEA
48'·4
Batemans Tr (13)
F.R.7m
F.Y
Bn
Westmarsh Pt
Fl.R.5s
BY
5 x 2F.R
Brightlingsea Spit
Q(6)+LFl.15s
Fl(3)G.5s
Moorings
Cindery Island
River Colne
Martello Tr
No1 (12)
51°48'·0N
Ldg Lts 041°
Chart Datum WGS 84
Water Tr (11)
01°01'·0E
01'·5

R/T *Brightlingsea Harbour Radio* VHF Ch 68.

TELEPHONE HM (Brightlingsea) (01206) 302200, mob 07952 734814, 📠 308533; MRSC (01255) 675518; Marinecall 09066 526239; Police (01255) 221312; Dr 302522.

FACILITIES

BRIGHTLINGSEA: **Town Hard** ☎ (01206) 303535, L, FW, Pontoon moorings £7 up to 26ft, £8 up to 36ft, £9 over 36ft, afloat near NCM opposite Town Hard; **Colne YC** ☎ 302594, L, FW, R, Bar; **Brightlingsea SC** Slip, Bar; **Services:** M, L, FW, ME, El, Ⓔ, ⚒, CH, ACA, P & D (cans), Gas, SM, BY, C, Slip. **Town** P & D (cans), FW, ME, El, ⚒, C (mobile), CH, 🛒, R, Bar, ✉, Ⓑ, ⇌ (bus to Wivenhoe or Colchester), ✈ (Southend or Stansted).

WIVENHOE: **Wivenhoe SC. Village** P, 🛒, Bar, ✉, Ⓑ (AM only), ⇌.

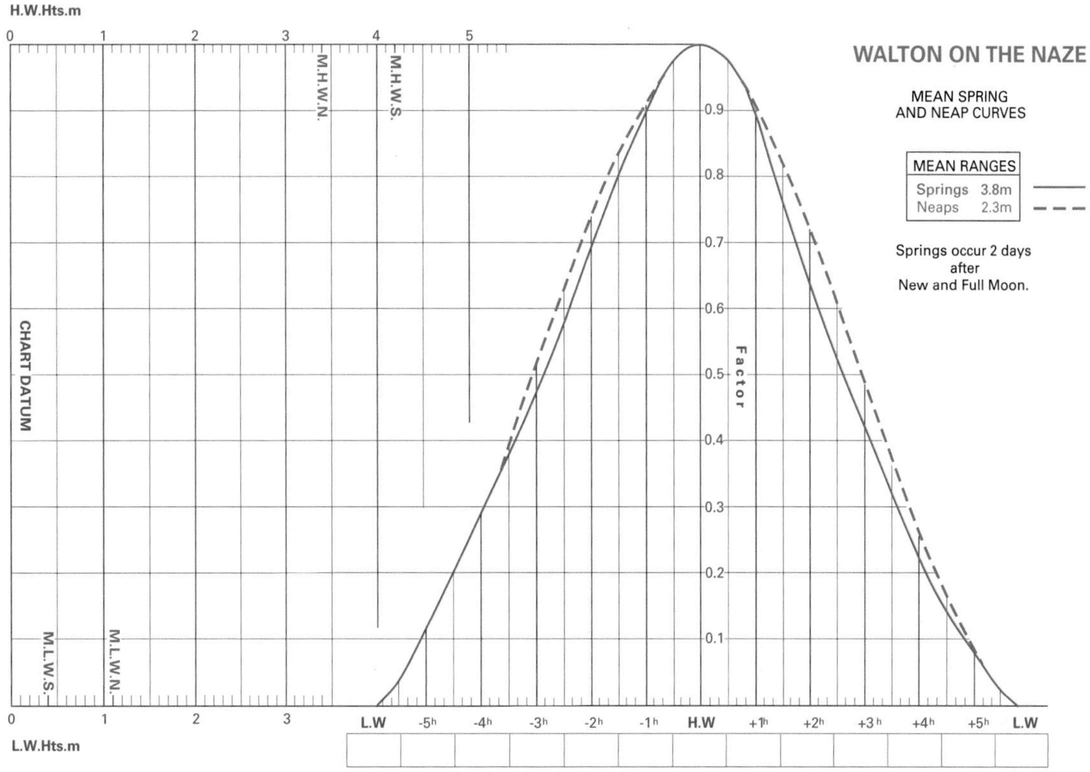
H.W.Hts.m
0
1
2
3
4
5
M.H.W.N.
M.H.W.S.
CHART DATUM
M.L.W.S.
M.L.W.N.
0.9
0.8
0.7
0.6
0.5
0.4
0.3
0.2
0.1
Factor
WALTON ON THE NAZE
MEAN SPRING
AND NEAP CURVES
MEAN RANGES
Springs 3.8m
Neaps 2.3m
Springs occur 2 days
after
New and Full Moon.
0
1
2
3
L.W.Hts.m
L.W
-5h
-4h
-3h
-2h
-1h
H.W
+1h
+2h
+3h
+4h
+5h
L.W

9.4.18 WALTON BACKWATERS

Essex **51°54′·57N 01°16′·79E** (No 2 PHM buoy)

CHARTS AC *5607, 2052, 2695*; Imray C1, Y16, 2000 Series; Stanfords 5, 6; OS 169

TIDES +0030 Dover; ML 2·2; Duration 0615; Zone 0 (UT). Walton is a Standard Port. Predictions are for Walton Pier, ie to seaward. Time differences for Bramble Creek (N of Hamford Water) are +10, –7, –5, +10 mins; height differences are all +0·3m.

SHELTER Good in all weather, but ent not advised if a big sea is running from the NE. Berth HW±5 in Titchmarsh Marina (pontoons lettered A-H from ent), ent dredged 1·3m; or on adjacent pontoons in the Twizzle. Good ⚓s in Hamford Water (keep clear of Oakley Creek) and in N end of Walton Chan, 2ca S of Stone Pt on E side. Walton Yacht Basin more suited for long stay; appr dries.

NAVIGATION WPT Pye End SWM buoy, L Fl 10s, 51°55′·03N 01°17′·89E, 054°/234° from/to buoyed chan ent, 1·0M. NB this stretch carries only 0·9m. From S, appr via Medusa Chan; from N and E via the Harwich recomended yacht track. At narrow ent to Walton Chan leave NCM buoy to stbd, and 3 PHM buoys close to port; after a SHM Fl G 10s buoy abeam Stone Pt best water is on E side. Beware lobster pots off the Naze and Pye Sands and oyster beds in the Backwaters. Buoys may be moved to suit channel changes.

LIGHTS AND MARKS Naze Tr (49m) is conspic 3M S of Pye End buoy. 2M NNE at Felixstowe, cranes and Y flood lts are conspic D/N.

R/T Titchmarsh marina Ch 80, 0800-2000 in season.

TELEPHONE (Dial code 01255) HM 851899; MRSC 675518; Marinecall 09066 526239; Police 851212; Ⓗ 421145.

FACILITIES **Titchmarsh Marina** (450+Ⓥ), ☎ 672185, 📠 851901, £1.37, Access HW±5 over sill 1·3m, D, Gas, Gaz, LPG, ME, CH, El, C (10 ton), BH (35 ton), Slip, R, Bar; **Walton & Frinton YC,** ☎ 675526/678161, R, Bar; **Yacht Basin** (60) run by YC; AB (long stay), FW, ⛽. **Services:** Slip, M, D, C (½ ton), El. **Town** EC Wed; P, SM, 🏧, R, Bar, ✉, Ⓑ, ⇌, ✈ (Southend/Cambridge/Stansted).

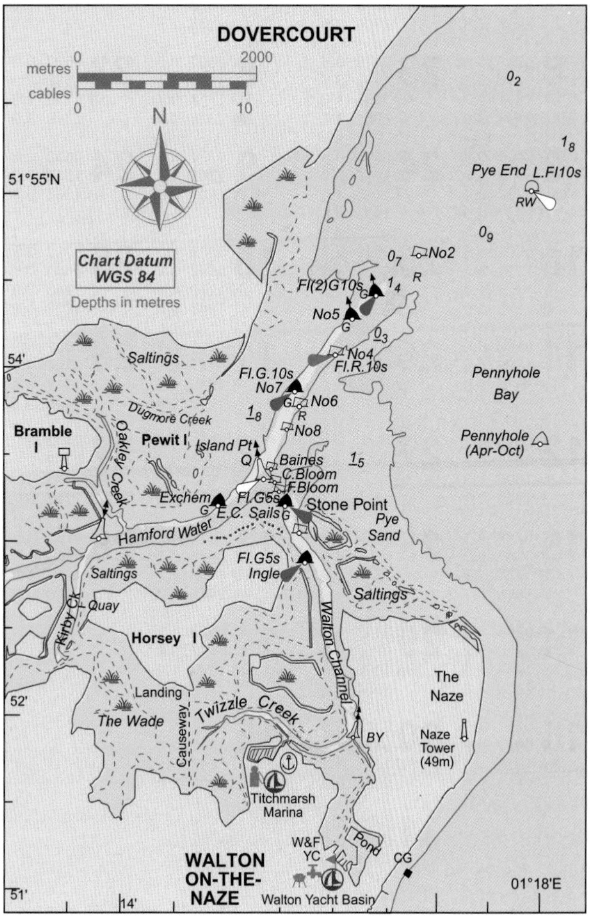
DOVERCOURT
metres 0 2000
cables 0 10
N
Chart Datum
WGS 84
Depths in metres
51°55'N
54'
52'
51'
14'
01°18'E
Pye End L.Fl10s
RW
No2
R
Fl(2)G10s
No5
No4
Fl.R.10s
Fl.G.10s
No7
No6
No8
Pennyhole
Bay
Pennyhole
(Apr-Oct)
Saltings
Dugmore Creek
Bramble
I
Oakley Creek
Pewit I
Island Pt
Q
Baines
C.Bloom
F.Bloom
Exchem
Fl.G5s
E.C. Sails
Stone Point
Pye
Sand
Hamford Water
Fl.G5s
Ingle
Saltings
Quay
Kirby Ck
Horsey I
Walton Channel
The
Naze
Landing
The Wade
Causeway
Twizzle Creek
BY
Naze
Tower
(49m)
Titchmarsh
Marina
W&F
YC
Pond
CG
WALTON
ON-THE-
NAZE
Walton Yacht Basin

TIME ZONE (UT)
For Summer Time add ONE hour in **non-shaded areas**

ENGLAND – WALTON-ON-THE-NAZE

LAT 51°51′N LONG 1°17′E

TIMES AND HEIGHTS OF HIGH AND LOW WATERS

SPRING & NEAP TIDES
Dates in red are SPRINGS
Dates in blue are NEAPS

YEAR **2005**

JANUARY

Date	Day	Time	m	Time	m	Time	m	Time	m
1	SA	0234	3.8	0858	0.7	1506	3.7	2052	1.0
2	SU	0315	3.7	0940	0.7	1550	3.7	2137	1.1
3	M	0400	3.6	1028	0.8	1641	3.6	◑ 2229	1.2
4	TU	0454	3.5	1124	0.9	1740	3.5	2331	1.2
5	W	0558	3.5	1227	0.9	1845	3.5		
6	TH	0040	1.2	0706	3.5	1335	0.9	1952	3.5
7	F	0150	1.2	0813	3.6	1441	0.8	2055	3.7
8	SA	0257	1.0	0916	3.8	1541	0.7	2153	3.8
9	SU	0401	0.8	1015	4.0	1637	0.7	2247	3.9
10	M	0501	0.6	1112	4.1	1728	0.6	● 2339	4.0
11	TU	0558	0.5	1207	4.3	1816	0.6		
12	W	0029	4.1	0651	0.3	1300	4.3	1901	0.7
13	TH	0118	4.1	0742	0.2	1350	4.3	1945	0.7
14	F	0205	4.2	0830	0.2	1438	4.3	2028	0.8
15	SA	0251	4.1	0917	0.3	1526	4.1	2112	0.9
16	SU	0336	4.0	1005	0.4	1614	3.9	2159	1.0
17	M	0423	3.9	1056	0.6	1704	3.7	◐ 2252	1.1
18	TU	0516	3.7	1151	0.8	1801	3.5	2354	1.2
19	W	0617	3.5	1251	1.0	1904	3.3		
20	TH	0104	1.3	0725	3.4	1355	1.1	2009	3.3
21	F	0217	1.2	0835	3.4	1455	1.1	2111	3.4
22	SA	0323	1.0	0937	3.6	1548	1.1	2204	3.6
23	SU	0419	0.9	1030	3.7	1633	1.0	2251	3.7
24	M	0506	0.8	1116	3.8	1713	1.0	2332	3.8
25	TU	0548	0.7	1156	3.8	1749	0.9	○	
26	W	0009	3.9	0624	0.6	1232	3.9	1820	0.9
27	TH	0042	3.9	0656	0.6	1304	3.9	1850	0.9
28	F	0113	3.9	0727	0.6	1334	3.9	1921	0.9
29	SA	0143	3.9	0758	0.6	1406	3.9	1954	0.8
30	SU	0215	3.9	0831	0.5	1441	3.9	2028	0.8
31	M	0249	3.9	0906	0.6	1521	3.9	2106	0.8

FEBRUARY

Date	Day	Time	m	Time	m	Time	m	Time	m
1	TU	0328	3.8	0944	0.6	1605	3.7	2149	0.9
2	W	0413	3.7	1031	0.7	1657	3.5	◑ 2242	1.1
3	TH	0509	3.6	1131	0.9	1759	3.4	2350	1.2
4	F	0621	3.4	1249	1.0	1912	3.3		
5	SA	0112	1.2	0743	3.4	1415	1.0	2029	3.4
6	SU	0240	1.1	0902	3.6	1529	0.9	2139	3.6
7	M	0359	0.8	1010	3.9	1628	0.8	2238	3.8
8	TU	0501	0.5	1109	4.1	1718	0.7	● 2331	4.0
9	W	0554	0.3	1201	4.3	1803	0.6		
10	TH	0019	4.2	0642	0.2	1250	4.4	1845	0.6
11	F	0105	4.2	0727	0.1	1335	4.4	1926	0.6
12	SA	0147	4.3	0809	0.1	1418	4.3	2006	0.6
13	SU	0227	4.3	0849	0.2	1458	4.2	2045	0.7
14	M	0306	4.2	0927	0.4	1538	4.0	2124	0.8
15	TU	0345	4.0	1006	0.6	1617	3.7	2206	0.9
16	W	0428	3.8	1051	0.9	1701	3.4	◐ 2258	1.1
17	TH	0521	3.5	1146	1.1	1756	3.2		
18	F	0005	1.2	0635	3.2	1257	1.3	1917	3.1
19	SA	0134	1.3	0806	3.2	1416	1.4	2040	3.2
20	SU	0301	1.1	0920	3.4	1524	1.2	2142	3.4
21	M	0402	0.9	1015	3.6	1615	1.1	2231	3.7
22	TU	0448	0.7	1059	3.8	1655	1.0	2312	3.8
23	W	0527	0.6	1138	3.9	1729	0.9	2349	3.9
24	TH	0600	0.6	1212	3.9	1800	0.9	○	
25	F	0022	3.9	0631	0.5	1243	3.9	1828	0.8
26	SA	0052	3.9	0701	0.5	1312	4.0	1859	0.8
27	SU	0122	3.9	0732	0.5	1343	4.0	1932	0.7
28	M	0152	4.0	0803	0.4	1417	4.0	2005	0.6

MARCH

Date	Day	Time	m	Time	m	Time	m	Time	m
1	TU	0225	4.0	0835	0.5	1454	4.0	2041	0.6
2	W	0302	4.0	0911	0.6	1535	3.8	2121	0.7
3	TH	0345	3.9	0953	0.7	1622	3.6	◑ 2212	0.9
4	F	0438	3.6	1052	1.0	1720	3.3	2320	1.1
5	SA	0551	3.4	1219	1.2	1838	3.1		
6	SU	0053	1.2	0729	3.3	1403	1.2	2014	3.2
7	M	0245	1.0	0904	3.5	1523	1.0	2132	3.5
8	TU	0359	0.7	1010	3.9	1618	0.8	2229	3.8
9	W	0453	0.4	1102	4.2	1703	0.7	2317	4.0
10	TH	0540	0.2	1149	4.3	1745	0.6	●	
11	F	0002	4.2	0623	0.1	1233	4.4	1824	0.5
12	SA	0044	4.3	0703	0.1	1314	4.3	1903	0.5
13	SU	0123	4.3	0741	0.1	1352	4.2	1941	0.5
14	M	0200	4.3	0815	0.3	1427	4.1	2017	0.6
15	TU	0235	4.2	0848	0.4	1500	3.9	2052	0.6
16	W	0311	4.0	0922	0.7	1533	3.7	2129	0.8
17	TH	0350	3.8	1001	0.9	1610	3.5	◐ 2215	1.0
18	F	0438	3.5	1055	1.2	1655	3.2	2321	1.2
19	SA	0545	3.2	1208	1.4	1807	3.0		
20	SU	0052	1.3	0733	3.1	1338	1.5	2001	3.1
21	M	0231	1.1	0856	3.3	1456	1.3	2112	3.3
22	TU	0334	0.9	0950	3.6	1549	1.1	2202	3.6
23	W	0418	0.7	1032	3.8	1628	1.0	2242	3.8
24	TH	0455	0.6	1109	4.0	1701	0.9	2319	3.9
25	F	0527	0.5	1143	4.0	1731	0.8	○ 2352	3.9
26	SA	0559	0.5	1214	4.0	1802	0.8		
27	SU	0024	3.9	0631	0.5	1246	4.0	1835	0.7
28	M	0057	4.0	0705	0.4	1319	4.0	1910	0.6
29	TU	0130	4.1	0738	0.4	1354	4.0	1946	0.5
30	W	0206	4.1	0811	0.5	1431	4.0	2024	0.5
31	TH	0245	4.0	0848	0.6	1512	3.8	2106	0.6

APRIL

Date	Day	Time	m	Time	m	Time	m	Time	m
1	F	0331	3.9	0933	0.8	1558	3.5	2159	0.8
2	SA	0428	3.6	1035	1.1	1657	3.2	◑ 2313	1.0
3	SU	0547	3.3	1210	1.4	1821	3.1		
4	M	0103	1.1	0733	3.3	1356	1.3	2003	3.2
5	TU	0244	0.8	0900	3.6	1508	1.1	2116	3.5
6	W	0347	0.5	0957	4.0	1559	0.8	2209	3.8
7	TH	0436	0.2	1045	4.2	1641	0.7	2255	4.0
8	F	0518	0.1	1128	4.3	1721	0.6	● 2338	4.2
9	SA	0558	0.1	1209	4.3	1801	0.5		
10	SU	0018	4.2	0634	0.2	1248	4.2	1839	0.5
11	M	0057	4.2	0709	0.3	1324	4.1	1916	0.5
12	TU	0133	4.2	0742	0.4	1356	4.0	1952	0.5
13	W	0208	4.1	0813	0.6	1427	3.9	2026	0.6
14	TH	0244	3.9	0845	0.8	1458	3.7	2102	0.7
15	F	0323	3.7	0922	1.0	1534	3.5	2147	0.9
16	SA	0409	3.5	1013	1.3	1620	3.3	◐ 2251	1.1
17	SU	0510	3.2	1128	1.5	1725	3.1		
18	M	0015	1.2	0643	3.1	1255	1.5	1903	3.1
19	TU	0145	1.1	0814	3.3	1415	1.4	2025	3.3
20	W	0250	0.9	0911	3.5	1510	1.2	2118	3.5
21	TH	0336	0.7	0954	3.8	1550	1.0	2201	3.7
22	F	0414	0.6	1031	3.9	1624	0.9	2239	3.8
23	SA	0449	0.5	1107	4.0	1658	0.8	2316	3.9
24	SU	0525	0.5	1142	4.0	1734	0.7	○ 2353	4.0
25	M	0603	0.5	1218	4.0	1813	0.6		
26	TU	0031	4.0	0640	0.5	1256	4.0	1852	0.5
27	W	0111	4.1	0717	0.5	1334	4.0	1933	0.5
28	TH	0153	4.1	0756	0.6	1415	3.9	2016	0.5
29	F	0238	4.0	0838	0.7	1459	3.7	2104	0.6
30	SA	0330	3.8	0928	1.0	1549	3.5	2204	0.7

Chart Datum: 2·16 metres below Ordnance Datum (Newlyn)

TIME ZONE (UT)
For Summer Time add ONE hour in **non-shaded areas**

ENGLAND – WALTON-ON-THE-NAZE

LAT 51°51′N LONG 1°17′E

TIMES AND HEIGHTS OF HIGH AND LOW WATERS

SPRING & NEAP TIDES
Dates in red are SPRINGS
Dates in blue are NEAPS

YEAR **2005**

MAY

Date	Day	Time	m	Time	m	Time	m	Time	m
1	SU	0433	3.6	1034	1.2	1653	3.3	◑ 2326	0.9
2	M	0553	3.4	1204	1.4	1815	3.2		
3	TU	0106	0.8	0722	3.5	1334	1.3	1938	3.3
4	W	0227	0.6	0835	3.7	1441	1.1	2045	3.6
5	TH	0324	0.4	0931	4.0	1532	0.8	2139	3.8
6	F	0411	0.3	1018	4.1	1615	0.7	2226	4.0
7	SA	0451	0.2	1102	4.1	1657	0.6	2310	4.0
8	SU	0529	0.3	1142	4.1	1737	0.5	● 2352	4.0
9	M	0605	0.4	1221	4.0	1818	0.5		
10	TU	0031	4.0	0638	0.5	1257	3.9	1856	0.5
11	W	0110	4.0	0712	0.6	1329	3.8	1933	0.5
12	TH	0146	3.9	0744	0.7	1400	3.8	2008	0.6
13	F	0223	3.8	0817	0.9	1433	3.7	2045	0.7
14	SA	0303	3.7	0853	1.0	1510	3.6	2130	0.8
15	SU	0347	3.5	0940	1.2	1557	3.4	2227	0.9
16	M	0441	3.3	1045	1.4	1656	3.3	◐ 2337	1.0
17	TU	0549	3.2	1201	1.5	1809	3.2		
18	W	0048	1.0	0708	3.3	1314	1.4	1923	3.3
19	TH	0152	0.9	0813	3.5	1414	1.2	2022	3.4
20	F	0244	0.7	0904	3.7	1501	1.1	2112	3.6
21	SA	0329	0.6	0947	3.8	1543	0.9	2156	3.8
22	SU	0412	0.5	1028	3.9	1625	0.8	2240	3.9
23	M	0455	0.5	1110	4.0	1709	0.7	○ 2324	4.0
24	TU	0537	0.5	1152	4.0	1754	0.6		
25	W	0009	4.1	0620	0.5	1236	4.0	1840	0.5
26	TH	0057	4.1	0704	0.6	1321	4.0	1928	0.4
27	F	0146	4.1	0748	0.7	1407	3.9	2018	0.4
28	SA	0237	4.1	0834	0.8	1455	3.8	2111	0.5
29	SU	0332	3.9	0926	1.0	1549	3.7	2213	0.5
30	M	0434	3.8	1028	1.2	1650	3.5	◑ 2327	0.6
31	TU	0542	3.7	1142	1.3	1758	3.5		

JUNE

Date	Day	Time	m	Time	m	Time	m	Time	m
1	W	0046	0.6	0653	3.7	1258	1.2	1905	3.5
2	TH	0156	0.5	0759	3.7	1405	1.1	2009	3.7
3	F	0253	0.5	0857	3.8	1500	0.9	2105	3.8
4	SA	0341	0.4	0947	3.9	1549	0.8	2157	3.9
5	SU	0422	0.5	1033	3.9	1634	0.7	2245	3.9
6	M	0501	0.6	1117	3.9	1719	0.6	● 2330	3.9
7	TU	0538	0.7	1158	3.9	1802	0.6		
8	W	0013	3.9	0614	0.8	1236	3.8	1843	0.6
9	TH	0053	3.8	0648	0.8	1310	3.8	1921	0.6
10	F	0131	3.8	0722	0.9	1342	3.8	1957	0.6
11	SA	0207	3.7	0755	0.9	1415	3.7	2032	0.7
12	SU	0244	3.7	0831	1.0	1452	3.7	2112	0.7
13	M	0325	3.6	0912	1.1	1535	3.6	2158	0.8
14	TU	0411	3.5	1002	1.3	1625	3.5	2253	0.9
15	W	0504	3.4	1102	1.3	1722	3.4	◐ 2353	0.9
16	TH	0605	3.4	1207	1.3	1825	3.4		
17	F	0053	0.8	0709	3.5	1311	1.3	1927	3.4
18	SA	0153	0.8	0809	3.6	1410	1.2	2025	3.6
19	SU	0248	0.7	0904	3.7	1505	1.0	2119	3.7
20	M	0340	0.6	0955	3.8	1558	0.9	2211	3.9
21	TU	0430	0.6	1044	3.9	1651	0.7	2303	4.0
22	W	0519	0.6	1133	4.0	1743	0.6	○ 2355	4.1
23	TH	0607	0.6	1222	4.0	1836	0.5		
24	F	0048	4.2	0654	0.7	1312	4.0	1927	0.4
25	SA	0140	4.2	0740	0.7	1401	4.0	2018	0.3
26	SU	0232	4.2	0826	0.8	1449	4.0	2110	0.3
27	M	0325	4.1	0915	0.9	1539	3.9	2205	0.3
28	TU	0420	4.0	1007	1.0	1632	3.9	◑ 2304	0.4
29	W	0517	3.8	1107	1.1	1728	3.8		
30	TH	0008	0.6	0617	3.7	1213	1.2	1828	3.7

JULY

Date	Day	Time	m	Time	m	Time	m	Time	m
1	F	0113	0.7	0719	3.6	1322	1.2	1931	3.6
2	SA	0213	0.7	0820	3.6	1426	1.1	2034	3.6
3	SU	0307	0.8	0917	3.7	1525	0.9	2133	3.7
4	M	0354	0.8	1009	3.7	1618	0.8	2227	3.7
5	TU	0437	0.9	1056	3.8	1707	0.7	2316	3.8
6	W	0517	0.9	1140	3.8	1752	0.7	●	
7	TH	0001	3.8	0555	0.9	1221	3.8	1833	0.6
8	F	0042	3.8	0630	0.9	1256	3.8	1910	0.6
9	SA	0118	3.8	0703	1.0	1328	3.8	1943	0.6
10	SU	0150	3.8	0735	1.0	1358	3.8	2014	0.6
11	M	0223	3.7	0808	1.0	1431	3.8	2047	0.6
12	TU	0258	3.7	0844	1.0	1507	3.8	2124	0.7
13	W	0338	3.7	0925	1.1	1548	3.7	2207	0.7
14	TH	0423	3.6	1011	1.2	1635	3.6	◐ 2257	0.8
15	F	0516	3.5	1108	1.3	1731	3.5	2357	0.9
16	SA	0616	3.5	1213	1.3	1836	3.5		
17	SU	0103	0.9	0722	3.5	1324	1.3	1944	3.5
18	M	0211	0.9	0828	3.6	1434	1.2	2050	3.6
19	TU	0315	0.8	0930	3.7	1541	1.0	2152	3.8
20	W	0413	0.8	1027	3.9	1643	0.7	2251	4.0
21	TH	0506	0.7	1120	4.0	1739	0.5	○ 2347	4.2
22	F	0555	0.7	1212	4.1	1832	0.3		
23	SA	0040	4.3	0641	0.7	1301	4.2	1921	0.2
24	SU	0131	4.4	0726	0.7	1348	4.2	2008	0.1
25	M	0219	4.4	0809	0.7	1433	4.3	2054	0.2
26	TU	0306	4.3	0853	0.8	1517	4.2	2139	0.3
27	W	0354	4.1	0938	0.9	1602	4.1	2227	0.4
28	TH	0442	3.9	1028	1.0	1651	3.9	◑ 2318	0.7
29	F	0535	3.7	1125	1.1	1747	3.7		
30	SA	0017	0.9	0634	3.5	1234	1.2	1853	3.5
31	SU	0123	1.1	0741	3.4	1352	1.2	2007	3.4

AUGUST

Date	Day	Time	m	Time	m	Time	m	Time	m
1	M	0230	1.2	0849	3.5	1506	1.1	2117	3.5
2	TU	0330	1.1	0949	3.6	1607	0.9	2216	3.7
3	W	0419	1.1	1039	3.8	1657	0.8	2305	3.8
4	TH	0501	1.0	1124	3.9	1740	0.7	2348	3.9
5	F	0538	1.0	1203	4.0	1818	0.6	●	
6	SA	0026	3.9	0612	1.0	1239	4.0	1850	0.6
7	SU	0100	3.9	0643	1.0	1309	3.9	1919	0.6
8	M	0128	3.9	0712	0.9	1336	3.9	1947	0.6
9	TU	0157	3.9	0743	0.9	1405	3.9	2017	0.6
10	W	0228	3.9	0817	0.9	1436	3.9	2049	0.6
11	TH	0304	3.9	0852	0.9	1511	3.9	2123	0.7
12	F	0345	3.8	0932	1.0	1551	3.8	2204	0.8
13	SA	0432	3.6	1021	1.2	1642	3.6	◐ 2259	1.0
14	SU	0530	3.4	1126	1.3	1749	3.4		
15	M	0015	1.1	0639	3.3	1247	1.3	1910	3.4
16	TU	0141	1.2	0759	3.4	1416	1.2	2034	3.5
17	W	0300	1.1	0915	3.6	1537	1.0	2146	3.8
18	TH	0403	0.9	1016	3.8	1639	0.6	2246	4.1
19	F	0454	0.8	1109	4.1	1731	0.4	○ 2338	4.3
20	SA	0540	0.7	1157	4.2	1819	0.2		
21	SU	0027	4.4	0623	0.7	1243	4.3	1903	0.1
22	M	0114	4.5	0705	0.6	1327	4.4	1946	0.1
23	TU	0158	4.4	0746	0.7	1408	4.4	2026	0.2
24	W	0240	4.3	0827	0.7	1448	4.3	2105	0.3
25	TH	0321	4.1	0908	0.8	1528	4.2	2143	0.5
26	F	0402	3.9	0951	0.9	1611	4.0	◑ 2227	0.8
27	SA	0446	3.6	1042	1.1	1702	3.6	2321	1.1
28	SU	0540	3.4	1149	1.3	1813	3.3		
29	M	0030	1.4	0656	3.2	1320	1.3	1944	3.3
30	TU	0153	1.5	0821	3.3	1448	1.2	2103	3.4
31	W	0306	1.4	0927	3.5	1551	1.0	2200	3.7

Chart Datum: 2·16 metres below Ordnance Datum (Newlyn)

TIME ZONE (UT)
For Summer Time add ONE hour in **non-shaded areas**

ENGLAND – WALTON-ON-THE-NAZE

LAT 51°51′N LONG 1°17′E

TIMES AND HEIGHTS OF HIGH AND LOW WATERS

SPRING & NEAP TIDES
Dates in red are SPRINGS
Dates in blue are NEAPS

YEAR **2005**

SEPTEMBER

Date	Day	Time	m	Time	m	Time	m	Time	m
1	TH	0359	1.2	1018	3.8	1638	0.8	2246	3.9
2	F	0440	1.1	1101	4.0	1717	0.6	2326	4.0
3	SA	0516	1.0	1138	4.0	1751	0.6	●	
4	SU	0001	4.0	0547	1.0	1212	4.0	1820	0.6
5	M	0033	4.0	0616	1.0	1241	4.0	1848	0.6
6	TU	0100	4.0	0646	0.9	1309	4.0	1916	0.6
7	W	0128	4.0	0718	0.9	1336	4.0	1945	0.6
8	TH	0158	4.0	0751	0.8	1407	4.0	2015	0.6
9	F	0232	4.0	0826	0.8	1441	4.0	2047	0.7
10	SA	0311	3.9	0904	0.9	1520	3.9	2125	0.8
11	SU	0355	3.7	0951	1.1	1609	3.7	◐ 2217	1.1
12	M	0451	3.4	1056	1.3	1717	3.4	2339	1.3
13	TU	0604	3.2	1228	1.3	1852	3.3		
14	W	0124	1.4	0739	3.3	1415	1.2	2033	3.5
15	TH	0249	1.2	0903	3.5	1533	0.8	2142	3.9
16	F	0349	1.0	1002	3.9	1628	0.5	2235	4.2
17	SA	0436	0.8	1051	4.1	1715	0.2	2322	4.4
18	SU	0519	0.7	1136	4.3	1758	0.1	○	
19	M	0007	4.5	0559	0.6	1219	4.4	1838	0.1
20	TU	0050	4.4	0640	0.6	1300	4.4	1917	0.2
21	W	0130	4.3	0721	0.6	1339	4.4	1953	0.3
22	TH	0208	4.2	0800	0.6	1417	4.3	2028	0.5
23	F	0245	4.1	0839	0.7	1454	4.2	2102	0.7
24	SA	0320	3.9	0920	0.9	1535	3.9	2141	1.0
25	SU	0357	3.6	1008	1.1	1623	3.6	◑ 2232	1.3
26	M	0443	3.3	1115	1.3	1732	3.2	2346	1.6
27	TU	0559	3.1	1249	1.3	1916	3.2		
28	W	0117	1.6	0745	3.2	1419	1.2	2038	3.4
29	TH	0236	1.5	0856	3.5	1521	1.0	2134	3.7
30	F	0330	1.3	0946	3.8	1606	0.8	2217	3.9

OCTOBER

Date	Day	Time	m	Time	m	Time	m	Time	m
1	SA	0412	1.1	1027	3.9	1643	0.6	2254	4.0
2	SU	0446	1.0	1104	4.0	1714	0.6	2328	4.1
3	M	0516	1.0	1137	4.0	1744	0.6	● 2358	4.0
4	TU	0546	0.9	1207	4.0	1814	0.6		
5	W	0027	4.0	0618	0.9	1238	4.0	1845	0.6
6	TH	0058	4.0	0653	0.8	1309	4.0	1916	0.6
7	F	0130	4.0	0729	0.8	1343	4.1	1948	0.7
8	SA	0206	4.0	0806	0.8	1420	4.0	2022	0.8
9	SU	0245	3.9	0847	0.8	1503	3.9	2102	1.0
10	M	0329	3.7	0938	1.0	1556	3.6	◐ 2157	1.2
11	TU	0424	3.4	1048	1.2	1708	3.4	2323	1.5
12	W	0542	3.2	1228	1.2	1850	3.3		
13	TH	0110	1.5	0723	3.3	1409	1.0	2024	3.6
14	F	0231	1.3	0842	3.6	1517	0.6	2126	3.9
15	SA	0326	1.0	0937	3.9	1608	0.4	2215	4.2
16	SU	0412	0.8	1025	4.1	1652	0.2	2259	4.3
17	M	0454	0.7	1108	4.3	1732	0.2	○ 2341	4.4
18	TU	0535	0.6	1150	4.3	1810	0.3		
19	W	0022	4.3	0616	0.6	1231	4.3	1846	0.4
20	TH	0100	4.2	0657	0.6	1311	4.3	1921	0.5
21	F	0137	4.1	0737	0.6	1349	4.2	1954	0.7
22	SA	0210	4.0	0816	0.7	1428	4.0	2027	0.9
23	SU	0243	3.8	0856	0.8	1508	3.8	2103	1.1
24	M	0319	3.6	0943	1.0	1555	3.5	2150	1.4
25	TU	0403	3.4	1047	1.2	1656	3.3	◑ 2302	1.6
26	W	0508	3.2	1211	1.2	1829	3.1		
27	TH	0032	1.7	0649	3.2	1334	1.2	1955	3.3
28	F	0153	1.6	0807	3.4	1436	1.0	2053	3.6
29	SA	0250	1.3	0901	3.6	1522	0.8	2137	3.8
30	SU	0333	1.2	0944	3.8	1600	0.7	2214	4.0
31	M	0407	1.0	1021	3.9	1634	0.6	2248	4.0

NOVEMBER

Date	Day	Time	m	Time	m	Time	m	Time	m
1	TU	0440	0.9	1057	4.0	1707	0.6	2321	4.0
2	W	0515	0.9	1133	4.0	1742	0.6	● 2355	4.0
3	TH	0553	0.8	1209	4.0	1818	0.7		
4	F	0030	4.0	0632	0.7	1247	4.1	1854	0.7
5	SA	0108	4.0	0714	0.7	1327	4.1	1930	0.7
6	SU	0147	4.0	0757	0.7	1411	4.0	2009	0.9
7	M	0229	3.8	0843	0.7	1459	3.9	2055	1.1
8	TU	0316	3.6	0939	0.8	1557	3.7	2153	1.3
9	W	0415	3.4	1052	1.0	1710	3.5	◐ 2313	1.4
10	TH	0532	3.3	1223	0.9	1838	3.5		
11	F	0045	1.4	0657	3.4	1347	0.8	1957	3.7
12	SA	0200	1.3	0808	3.6	1451	0.6	2057	3.9
13	SU	0257	1.0	0905	3.9	1541	0.4	2146	4.1
14	M	0345	0.8	0955	4.1	1625	0.3	2231	4.2
15	TU	0429	0.7	1041	4.1	1704	0.4	2314	4.2
16	W	0512	0.6	1125	4.2	1742	0.5	○ 2354	4.1
17	TH	0555	0.6	1207	4.1	1818	0.6		
18	F	0033	4.0	0638	0.6	1249	4.1	1853	0.7
19	SA	0110	3.9	0719	0.6	1329	4.0	1927	0.9
20	SU	0143	3.9	0800	0.7	1408	3.9	2000	1.0
21	M	0216	3.8	0839	0.8	1448	3.7	2034	1.1
22	TU	0252	3.7	0923	0.9	1531	3.6	2116	1.3
23	W	0336	3.5	1017	1.0	1621	3.4	◑ 2214	1.5
24	TH	0432	3.4	1122	1.1	1725	3.2	2329	1.6
25	F	0543	3.3	1230	1.1	1843	3.2		
26	SA	0045	1.5	0659	3.3	1333	1.0	1951	3.4
27	SU	0149	1.4	0802	3.5	1426	0.9	2043	3.6
28	M	0239	1.2	0852	3.6	1511	0.8	2127	3.8
29	TU	0322	1.1	0937	3.8	1553	0.7	2207	3.9
30	W	0404	1.0	1020	3.9	1635	0.7	2247	4.0

DECEMBER

Date	Day	Time	m	Time	m	Time	m	Time	m
1	TH	0447	0.9	1103	4.0	1716	0.7	● 2328	4.0
2	F	0532	0.8	1147	4.1	1758	0.7		
3	SA	0010	4.0	0618	0.7	1232	4.1	1839	0.7
4	SU	0053	4.0	0706	0.6	1319	4.1	1921	0.8
5	M	0137	4.0	0755	0.5	1407	4.1	2004	0.9
6	TU	0223	3.9	0845	0.5	1459	4.0	2052	1.0
7	W	0313	3.8	0941	0.6	1555	3.8	2146	1.2
8	TH	0409	3.7	1045	0.7	1659	3.7	◐ 2251	1.3
9	F	0514	3.6	1158	0.7	1809	3.6		
10	SA	0005	1.3	0624	3.6	1312	0.7	1918	3.6
11	SU	0118	1.2	0731	3.7	1416	0.6	2021	3.7
12	M	0222	1.1	0832	3.8	1511	0.6	2115	3.8
13	TU	0317	0.9	0927	3.9	1558	0.6	2204	3.9
14	W	0407	0.8	1019	3.9	1640	0.7	2250	3.9
15	TH	0456	0.7	1107	4.0	1719	0.7	○ 2334	3.9
16	F	0542	0.6	1153	4.0	1757	0.8		
17	SA	0014	3.9	0627	0.6	1236	3.9	1832	0.9
18	SU	0052	3.9	0709	0.6	1316	3.9	1907	1.0
19	M	0126	3.8	0748	0.6	1352	3.8	1939	1.0
20	TU	0158	3.8	0824	0.7	1428	3.7	2011	1.1
21	W	0232	3.7	0900	0.7	1505	3.6	2048	1.2
22	TH	0311	3.7	0941	0.8	1546	3.5	2132	1.2
23	F	0356	3.6	1029	0.9	1634	3.4	◑ 2225	1.3
24	SA	0449	3.4	1124	1.0	1729	3.4	2328	1.4
25	SU	0551	3.4	1224	1.0	1833	3.4		
26	M	0034	1.4	0656	3.4	1324	1.0	1938	3.4
27	TU	0138	1.3	0800	3.5	1423	0.9	2038	3.6
28	W	0236	1.2	0857	3.6	1517	0.8	2131	3.7
29	TH	0332	1.0	0951	3.8	1608	0.8	2220	3.9
30	F	0426	0.9	1042	4.0	1657	0.7	2308	3.9
31	SA	0519	0.7	1133	4.1	1744	0.7	● 2356	4.0

Chart Datum: 2·16 metres below Ordnance Datum (Newlyn)

9.4.19, 20 & 21 RIVERS STOUR, ORWELL AND DEBEN

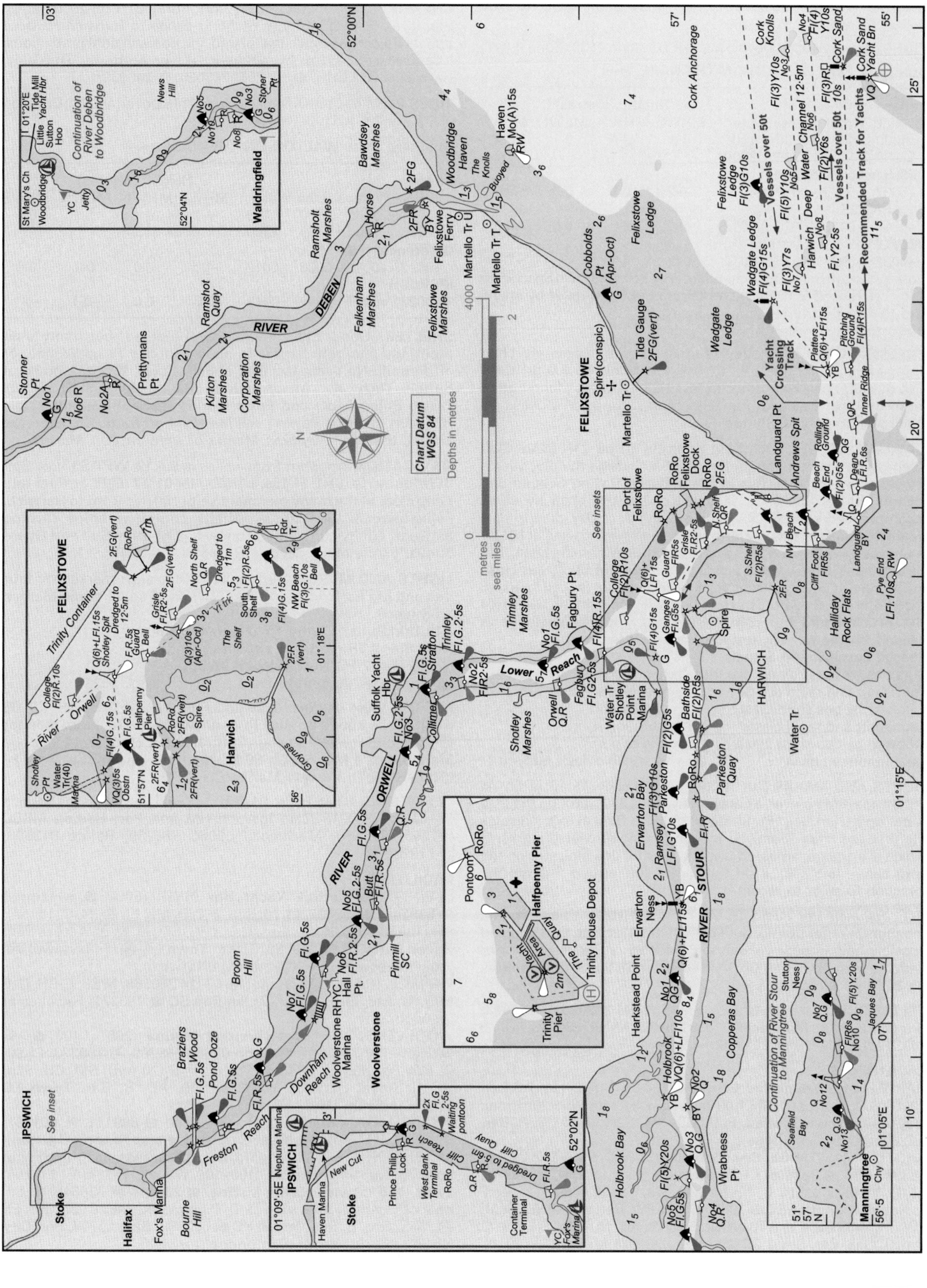
RIVER DEBEN
RIVER ORWELL
RIVER STOUR
FELIXSTOWE
HARWICH
IPSWICH
Chart Datum WGS 84
Depths in metres
Continuation of River Deben to Woodbridge
Waldringfield
Woodbridge Haven
Bawdsey Marshes
Ramsholt Marshes
Falkenham Marshes
Felixstowe Marshes
Kirton Marshes
Corporation Marshes
Trimley Marshes
Shotley Marshes
Lower Reach
Suffolk Yacht Hbr
Woolverstone
Woolverstone Marina
Fox's Marina
Freston Reach
Downham Reach
Halfpenny Pier
Trinity House Depot
Trinity Pier
Port of Felixstowe
Landguard Pt
Andrews Spit
Cobbolds Pt
Felixstowe Ledge
Wadgate Ledge
Cork Anchorage
Harwich Deep Water Channel 12·5m
Vessels over 50t
Recommended Track for Yachts
Yacht Crossing Track
Rolling Ground
Pitching Ground
Halliday Rock Flats
Erwarton Bay
Erwarton Ness
Harkstead Point
Holbrook Bay
Copperas Bay
Parkeston Quay
Wrabness Pt
Continuation of River Stour to Manningtree
Manningtree
Seafield Bay
Jaques Bay
Stutton Ness

9.4.19 RIVER STOUR

Essex/Suffolk **51°57′·06N 01°17′·77E** (Guard PHM buoy)

CHARTS AC *5607, 2052, 2693*, 1491, 1594; Imray C1, Y16, 2000 Series; Stanfords 5, 6; OS 169

TIDES Harwich+0050 Dover; ML 2·1; Duration 0630; Zone 0 (UT)

Standard Port WALTON-ON-THE-NAZE (⟵)

Times				Height (metres)			
High Water		Low Water		MHWS	MHWN	MLWN	MLWS
0000	0600	0500	1100	4·2	3·4	1·1	0·4
1200	1800	1700	2300				
Differences HARWICH							
+0007	+0002	–0010	–0012	–0·2	0·0	0·0	0·0
WRABNESS							
+0017	+0015	–0010	–0012	–0·1	0·0	0·0	0·0
MISTLEY							
+0032	+0027	–0010	–0012	0·0	0·0	–0·1	–0·1

Note: Although Harwich is a Standard Port, it has only two Secondary Ports referenced to it. Harwich HW and LW times differ by only 5 and 10 minutes from Walton-on-the-Naze.

SHELTER Good at Shotley Marina; all tide access via chan dredged 2m, outer limits lit, to lock. Enter only on F.G tfc lt. AB also at Halfpenny Pier (dries; access H24), Mistley, Manningtree (both dry). No yachts at Parkeston Quay. ⚓s off Wrabness Pt, Holbrook Creek and Stutton Ness.

NAVIGATION WPT Cork Sand Yacht Bn, 51°55′·21N 01°25′·20E. Keep clear of commercial shipping/HSS. Outside the hbr, yachts should cross the DW chan at 90° between Rolling Ground and Platters buoys. See 9.4.5. Stay out of the DW chan by using recommended yacht track, running S and W of DW chan to past Harwich. **Caution**: Bkwtr, ESE of Blackman's Hd, covers at HW; it is marked by a PHM bn 2F.R (vert), only 5ca W of main chan. The Guard shoal (0·8m), about 2ca S of Guard PHM buoy, lies close to the recommended yacht track. The R Stour is well marked; speed limit 8kn. Beware 'The Horse' 4ca NE and a drying bank 1½ca NW of Wrabness Pt. From Mistley Quay local knowledge is needed for the narrow, tortuous chan to Manningtree.

Special Local Sound Signals

Commercial vessels may use these additional sigs:

Four short and rapid blasts followed by one short blast	=	I am turning short around to stbd.
Four short and rapid blasts followed by two short blasts)	=	I am turning short around to port.
One prolonged blast	=	I am leaving a dock, quay or ⚓.

LIGHTS AND MARKS The R Stour to Mistley Quay is lit. At Cattawade, 8M up river, a conspic chy leads 270° through the best water up to Harkstead Pt. Shotley Marina: a Dir lt at lock indicates the dredged chan (2·0m) by Inogen (or Moiré) visual marker lt which is a square, ambered display; a vert B line indicates on the appr centre line 339°. If off the centre line, arrows indicate the direction to steer to regain it.

R/T *Harwich Hbr Radio* Ch **71** 11 14 16 (H24). Yachts should monitor Ch 71 for tfc info, but not transmit. Weather, tidal info and possibly help in poor vis may be available on request. The Hbr Patrol launch listens on Ch 11. Hbr Radar Ch 20. Shotley Marina Ch **80** M (lock master).

TELEPHONE (Dial code 01255) Harwich HM 243030, ℻ 240933; Hbr Ops 243000; Marinecall 08068 500455; MRSC 675518; Police 241312; Dr 201299; Ⓗ 201200.

FACILITIES

HARWICH: **Halfpenny Pier** ☎ mob 07730 804345, L, FW, AB free 0900-1600, else (per 24H) £1.00 up to 20m, flat rate £30 > 20m, max stay 72hrs. **Town** EC Wed; P, D, ME, SM, Gas, El, ⚒, 🛒, R, Bar, ✉, Ⓑ, ⇌, ✈ (Cambridge).

SHOTLEY: (01473) **Shotley Marina** (350, visitors welcome) ☎ 788982 H24, ℻ 788868, £1.75, access H24 via lock; D, ▣, ♿, ME, El, Ⓔ, ⚒, BH (40 ton), C, 🛒, BY, CH, SM, Bar, R, Gas, Gaz, Ferry to Harwich; **Shotley SC** ☎ 787500, Slip, FW, Bar. WRABNESS: M, FW, 🛒. MISTLEY and MANNINGTREE: AB, M, FW, 🛒, P & D (cans), Gas, Bar. **Stour SC** ☎ (01206) 393924 M, Bar.

9.4.20 RIVER ORWELL

Suffolk **51°57′·06N 01°17′·77E** (GuardPHM by)

CHARTS AC *5607, 2052, 2693*, 1491; Imray C1,Y16, 2000 Series; Stanfords 5, 6; OS 169. A *Yachting Guide to Harwich Harbour and its Rivers* has much useful info, inc Harwich tidal predictions; it can be obtained free from Harwich Haven Authority, The Quay, Harwich CO12 3HH; ☎ (01255) 243030, ℻ 240933.

TIDES Pin Mill +0100 Dover; Ipswich +0115 Dover; ML 2·4; Duration 0555; Zone 0 (UT)

Standard Port WALTON-ON-THE-NAZE (⟵)

Times				Height (metres)			
High Water		Low Water		MHWS	MHWN	MLWN	MLWS
0000	0600	0500	1100	4·2	3·4	1·1	0·4
1200	1800	1700	2300				
Differences PIN MILL							
+0012	+0015	–0008	–0012	–0·1	0·0	0·0	0·0
IPSWICH							
+0022	+0027	0000	–0012	0·0	0·0	–0·1	–0·1

SHELTER Good. Ent and river well marked, but many unlit moorings line both banks. ⚓s above Shotley Pt on W side, or off Pinmill. No yacht facilities at Felixstowe. Ⓥ's (pre-book) at Suffolk Yacht Hbr, Woolverstone Marina, Ipswich Dock (via Prince Philip Lock) and Fox's Marina (Ipswich) all accessible H24 as is Ipswich Haven - call *Ipswich Port Radio* Ch 68 before arrival, then call *Neptune Marina* or *Ipswich Port Marina.*

NAVIGATION Appr/ent from sea as in 9.4.19. WPT Shotley Spit SCM buoy, Q (6)+L Fl 15s, 51°57′·21N 01°17′·68E, at river ent. Keep clear of the many merchant ships, ferries from/to Harwich, Felixstowe & Ipswich, especially container ships turning between Trinity container terminal and Shotley Spit and Guard buoys. 6kn is max speed in R Orwell.

LIGHTS AND MARKS Suffolk Yacht Hbr appr marked by four bns and ldg lts: front Iso Y; rear Oc Y 4s. Woolverstone Marina: 2 FR (vert).

A14 bridge lts: Centre FY (clearance 38m)

No 9 Pier 2 FR (vert) } shown up and
No 10 Pier 2 FG (vert) } down stream.

● and ● tfc lts control ent to Ipswich Dock (H24).

R/T Call: *Ipswich Port Radio* and *Prince Philip Lock* VHF Ch 68 (H24). Once above Shotley Pt or anywhere in the area, monitor Ch 68 continuously in fog. Suffolk Yacht Hbr, Woolverstone Marina, Fox's Marina: Ch 80 M. Neptune Marina: Ch M 14 80 (0800-1730LT), Ipswich Marina Ch M 80.

TELEPHONE (Dial code 01473) Orwell Navigation Service 231010 ℻ 230915 (also Ipswich HM and Port Radio); MRSC (01255) 675518; Marinecall 09066 526239; Police 613500; Ⓗ 712233.

FACILITIES

LEVINGTON: **Suffolk Yacht Hbr** (SYH) (500+ Ⓥ welcome) ☎ 659240, ℻ 659632, £1.70, Slip, ♿, P, D, ME, El, Ⓔ, ⚒, C (15 ton), BH (10/60 ton), CH, 🛒, Gas, Gaz, LPG, SM, ▣, ♿, ✚, Access H24; **Haven Ports YC** ☎ 659658, R, Bar. **Town** ✉, Ⓑ (Felixstowe), ⇌ (bus to Ipswich), ✈ (Cambridge/Norwich).

PIN MILL: HM ☎ 780621, mobile 07714 260568, M £6, L, CH, C (6 ton), ⚒, ME, El, FW, Bar, R; **Pin Mill SC** ☎ 780271; Facilities at Ipswich.

WOOLVERSTONE: **Woolverstone Marina** (200 + 120 Ⓜ, Ⓥ welcome) ☎ 780206 (H24)mob 07803 968209, ℻ 780273, £1.90, D, FW, BY, ME, El, ⚒, Gas, Gaz, ▣, ♿, C (20 ton), SM, CH, Slip, 🛒, R; **Royal Harwich YC** ☎ 780319, AB, R, Bar. **Town** EC Chelmondiston Wed; ✉, 🛒.

IPSWICH: **Fox's Marina** (100 + some Ⓥ) ☎ 689111, ℻ 601737, £1.50, D, P (cans), BY, Gas, Gaz, BH (44 and 70 ton), C (7 ton), ME, El, Ⓔ, ⚒, CH, ACA, Rigging, Bar; H24 access via Prince Philip Lock to **Neptune Marina** (100+100 Ⓥ), ☎ 215204 ℻ 215206, £1.68, and **Ipswich Haven Marina**, ☎ 236644 ℻ 236645, £1.80, near city centre, both with ▣, D, P (cans), ⚒, ME, C, BH, BY, El, Ⓔ, Gas, Gaz, R, Bar; **Orwell YC** ☎ 602288, Slip, L, FW, Bar. **City** No EC; ✉, Ⓑ, ⇌, ✈ (Cambridge/Norwich).

9.4.21 RIVER DEBEN

Suffolk **51°59'·38N 01°23'·58E** (Felixstowe Ferry) ❀◊◊◊✿✿✿

CHARTS AC *5607, 2052, 2693*; Imray C1, C28, Y16, 2000 Series; Stan 3, 5, 6; OS 169

TIDES Woodbridge Haven +0025 Dover; Woodbridge +0105 Dover; ML 1·9; Duration 0635; Zone 0 (UT)

Standard Port WALTON-ON-THE-NAZE (←)

Times				Height (metres)			
High Water		Low Water		MHWS	MHWN	MLWN	MLWS
0100	0700	0100	0700	4·2	3·4	1·1	0·4
1300	1900	1300	1900				
Differences FELIXSTOWE PIER							
–0005	–0007	–0018	–0020	–0·5	–0·4	0·0	0·0
BAWDSEY							
–0016	–0020	–0030	–0032	–0·8	–0·6	–0·1	–0·1
WOODBRIDGE HAVEN (Ent)							
0000	–0005	–0020	–0025	–0·5	–0·5	–0·1	+0·1
WOODBRIDGE (Town)							
+0045	+0025	+0025	–0020	–0·2	–0·3	–0·2	0·0

SHELTER Good in Tide Mill Yacht Harbour (TMYH) at Woodbridge. Ent by No 24 PHM buoy; depth over sill, dries 1·5m, is 1·6m @ MHWN and 2·5m MHWS, with very accurate tide gauge and 8 waiting buoys. ⚓s up-river N of Horse Sand, at: Ramsholt, Waldringfield, Methersgate, Kyson Point and Woodbridge (9M from ent), keeping clear of moorings.

NAVIGATION WPT Woodbridge Haven SWM buoy lit Mo(A)15s, 51°58'·55N 01°24'·25E, thence leave G conical Bar buoy to Stbd and in 100m the Red PHM to port, clearing The Knolls, steer for entrance. The shifting shingle bar may be crossed at HW–4 to HW depending on draft. Best to enter after half-flood, and leave on the flood. The ent is only 1ca wide and in strong on-shore winds gets dangerously choppy; chan is well buoyed/marked. Keep to the W shore until PHM opposite the SC, then move E of Horse Sand just up river of the ent. No commercial tfc. Speed limit is 8kn above Green Reach. *For regularly updated local information, including chartlet and aerial photos, see www.debenentrance.com.* For latest info call VHF Ch 08 (call *Odd Times*), ☎ (01394) 270106, mob 07860 191768.

LIGHTS AND MARKS Ldg marks (unlit) are unreliable. No lights.

R/T Pilotage info Ch 08. Tide Mill Yacht Hbr VHF Ch **80** M (some VHF dead spots down-river).

TELEPHONE (Dial code 01394) HM 270106, mob 07860 191768, mob 07778 401105; MRSC (01255) 675518; Marinecall 09066 526239; Police (01986) 855321; Ramsholt HM 07751 034959.

FACILITIES
FELIXSTOWE FERRY (01394) **Quay** Slip, M, L, FW, ME, El, ⚒, CH, 🛒, R, Bar; **Felixstowe Ferry SC** ☎ 283785; **Felixstowe Ferry BY** ☎ 282173, M (200), Gas, Slip. RAMSHOLT **Services:** M, FW, Bar. WALDRINGFIELD (01473) Hbr Mr 0410 598552) **Waldringfield SC** ☎ 736633, Bar; **Services:** BY, C, Slip, D, FW, CH, Gas, Gaz, 🛒. WOODBRIDGE (01394) **Tide Mill Yacht Hbr** (150+50 Ⓥ) ☎ 385745, 📠 380735, £1.55, D, L, ME, El, ⚒, C (10 ton), ⛽, 🛒; Tide Mill is conspic daymark. **Services:** CH, Slip, C, M, ACA; **Deben YC. Town** P, D, L, FW, CH, 🛒, R, Bar, ✉, Ⓑ, ⇌, ✈ (Cambridge or Norwich).

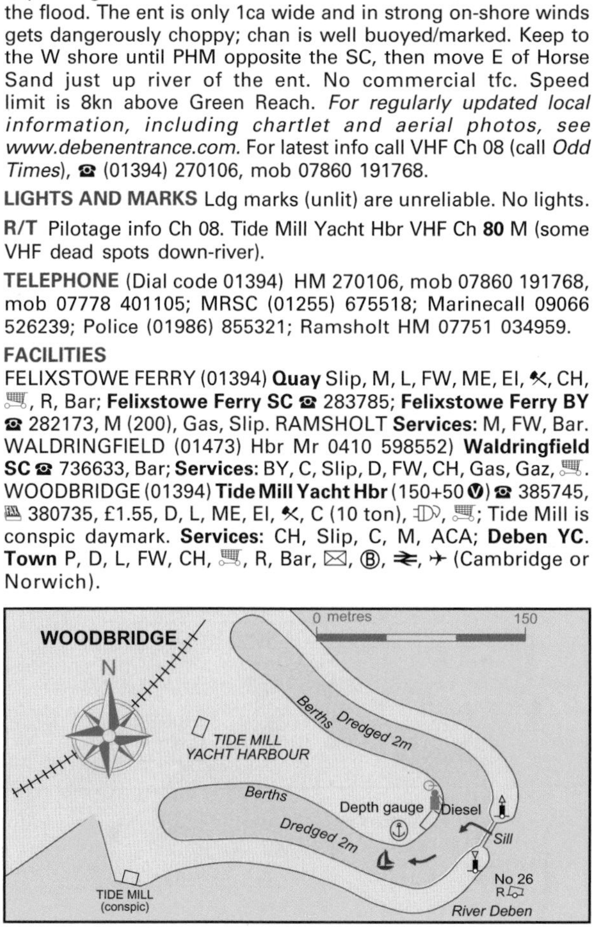
WOODBRIDGE
N
0 metres 150
TIDE MILL
YACHT HARBOUR
Berths
Dredged 2m
Berths
Dredged 2m
Depth gauge
Diesel
Sill
No 26
R
River Deben
TIDE MILL
(conspic)

9.4.22 RIVER ORE/ALDE

Suffolk **52°02'·13N 01°27'·49E** (Ent) ❀◊◊◊✿✿✿

CHARTS AC *5607*, 1543, *2052, 2693, 2695*; Imray C28, 2000 Series; Stanfords 3, 5, 6; OS 169

TIDES Ent. +0015 Dover Slaughden Quay +0155 Dover; ML1·6; Duration 0620; Zone 0 (UT)

Standard Port WALTON-ON-THE-NAZE (←)

Times				Height (metres)			
High Water		Low Water		MHWS	MHWN	MLWN	MLWS
0100	0700	0100	0700	4·2	3·4	1·1	0·4
1300	1900	1300	1900				
Differences ORFORD HAVEN BAR							
–0026	–0030	–0036	–0038	–1·0	–0·8	–0·1	0·0
ORFORD QUAY							
+0040	+0040	+0055	+0055	–1·4	–1·1	0·0	+0·2
SLAUGHDEN QUAY							
+0105	+0105	+0125	+0125	–1·3	–0·8	–0·1	+0·2
IKEN CLIFF							
+0130	+0130	+0155	+0155	–1·3	–1·0	0·0	+0·2

SHELTER Good shelter within the river, but the entrance should not be attempted in strong E/ESE onshore winds and rough seas or at night. Good ⚓s as shown and at Iken; also between Martello Tr and Slaughden Quay. Landing on Havergate Island, a bird sanctuary, is prohib. Visitors' moorings at Orford have small pick-up buoys marked V. Possible use of private mooring via Upson's BY at Slaughden.

NAVIGATION WPT Orford Haven SWM buoy, 52°01'·85N 01°28'·28E may be moved S'wds (May 2004). For latest position call Thames CG ☎ (01255) 675518. The chartlet below depicts a layout of the ent, to which current info can be referred. It is essential to obtain the latest plan of ent and directions. See next page for details.

Navigation *continued overleaf*

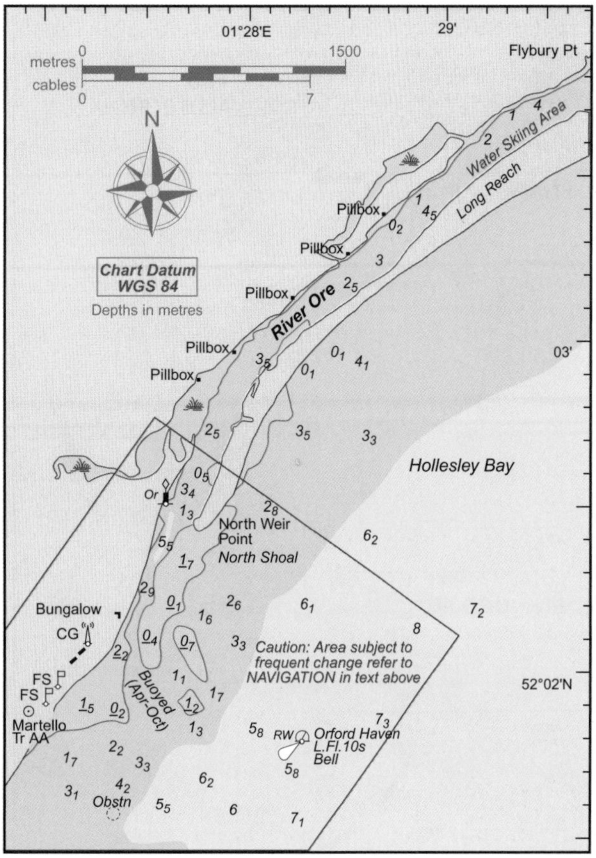
01°28'E
29'
metres 0 1500
cables 0 7
Flybury Pt
N
Water Skiing Area
Long Reach
Pillbox
Pillbox
Pillbox
Pillbox
Pillbox
River Ore
Chart Datum
WGS 84
Depths in metres
03'
Hollesley Bay
North Weir
Point
North Shoal
Bungalow
CG
FS
FS
Martello
Tr AA
Buoyed
(Apr-Oct)
Caution: Area subject to
frequent change refer to
NAVIGATION in text above
52°02'N
RW
Orford Haven
L.Fl.10s
Bell
Obstn

River Ore/Alde *continued*

For regularly updated local information, including chartlet and aerial photos, see www.orfordentrance.com. For latest info call Small Craft Deliveries, 12 Quay St, Woodbridge, Suffolk IP12 1RJ, ☎ (01394) 382655 or local marinas or chandlers.

The bar (approx 0·5m) shifts after onshore gales and is dangerous in rough or confused seas. These result from tidal streams offshore running against those within the shingle banks. Sp ebb reaches 6kn. Without local info do not enter before half flood or at night. For a first visit, appr at about LW+2½ in settled conditions and at nps. See previous warnings. Beware shoals S & SW of Dove Pt (SW tip of Havergate Island). R Ore (re-named R Alde between Orford and Slaughden Quay) is navigable up to Snape. The upper reaches are shallow and winding, and although marked by withies these may have been damaged. There are shelfish beds on the E bank centred on 52°08'·0N 01°35'·6E.

LIGHTS AND MARKS As chartlet. Ent and river are unlit. Shingle Street, about 2ca S of ent, is identified by Martello tr 'AA', CG Stn, terrace houses and DF aerial. Up-river, Orford Ch and Castle are conspic; also Martello Tr 'CC', 3ca S of Slaughden Quay.

R/T Call *Chantry* on Ch 08.

TELEPHONE (Dial codes 01394 Orford; 01728 Aldeburgh) HM Orford 450481; Hbr Office 459950; Small Craft Deliveries (pilotage info) 382655; Marinecall 09066 526239; MRSC (01255) 675518; Police (01473) 613500; Orford Dr 450315 (HO); Aldeburgh Dr 452027 (HO).

FACILITIES

ORFORD **Orford Quay** Slip, AB (1 hour free, then £10/hour), M £5 night, L, FW, D (cans), C (mobile 5 ton), Orford SC (OSC) visitors may use showers (£5 key deposit), R, Bar. **Village** (¼M). EC Wed; P & D (cans), Gas, Gaz, ✉, 🛒, R, Bar, ⇌ (twice daily bus to Woodbridge).

ALDEBURGH **Slaughden Quay** L, FW, Slip, BH (20 ton), CH; **Aldeburgh YC** (AYC) ☎ 452562, ♿, ✂. **Slaughden SC** (SSC). **Services:** M (via Upson's BY if any vacant) £5, ✂, Slip, D, ME, BY, Gas, Gaz, P. **Town** (¾M), EC Wed; P, 🛒, R, Bar, ✉, Ⓑ, ⇌ (bus to Wickham Market), ✈ (Norwich).

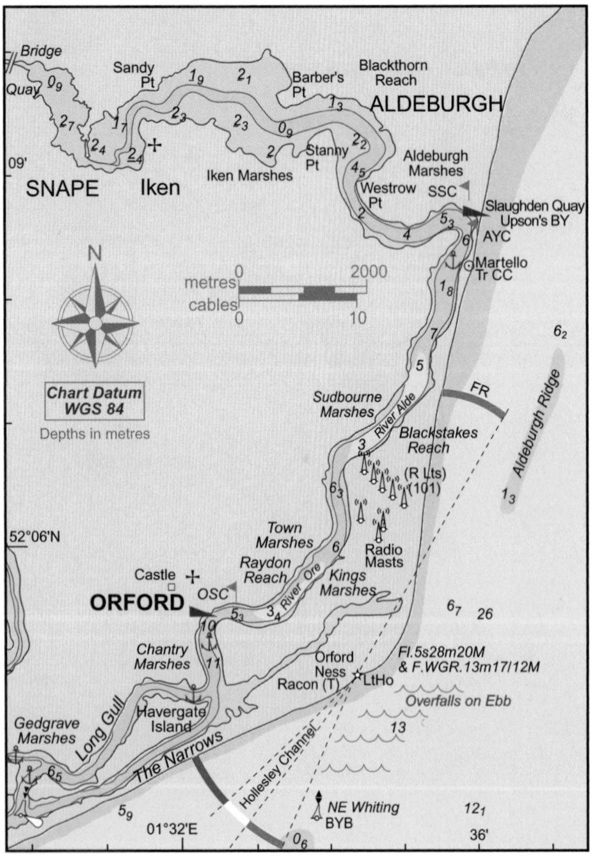
Bridge
Quay
Sandy Pt
Barber's Pt
Blackthorn Reach
ALDEBURGH
Stanny Pt
Aldeburgh Marshes
Iken Marshes
SNAPE
Iken
Westrow Pt
SSC
Slaughden Quay
Upson's BY
AYC
Martello Tr CC
N
metres
cables
2000
10
Chart Datum WGS 84
Depths in metres
Sudbourne Marshes
River Alde
Blackstakes Reach
(R Lts)
(101)
FR
Aldeburgh Ridge
52°06'N
Town Marshes
Radio Masts
Raydon Reach
Castle
River Ore
Kings Marshes
ORFORD
OSC
Chantry Marshes
Orford Ness
Racon (T)
LtHo
Fl.5s28m20M
& F.WGR.13m17/12M
Overfalls on Ebb
Havergate Island
Gedgrave Marshes
Long Gull
The Narrows
Hollesley Channel
NE Whiting
BYB
01°32'E
36'

9.4.23 SOUTHWOLD

Suffolk **52°18'·78N 01°40'·54E**

CHARTS AC 1543, *2695*; Imray C29, C28; Stanfords 3; OS 156

TIDES –0105 Dover; ML 1·5; Duration 0620; Zone 0 (UT)

Standard Port LOWESTOFT (⟶)

Times				**Height (metres)**			
High Water		Low Water		MHWS	MHWN	MLWN	MLWS
0300	0900	0200	0800	2·4	2·1	1·0	0·5
1500	2100	1400	2000				
Differences SOUTHWOLD							
+0105	+0105	+0055	+0055	0·0	0·0	–0·1	0·0
MINSMERE							
+0110	+0110	+0110	+0110	0·0	–0·1	–0·2	–0·2
ALDEBURGH (seaward)							
+0130	+0130	+0115	+0120	+0·3	+0·2	–0·1	–0·2
ORFORD NESS							
+0135	+0135	+0135	+0125	+0·4	+0·6	–0·1	0·0

Note: HW time differences (above) for Southwold apply up the hbr. At the ent mean HW is HW Lowestoft +0035.

SHELTER Good, but the ent is dangerous in strong winds from N through E to S. Visitors berth on a staging 6ca from the ent, on N bank near to the Harbour Inn. If rafted, shore lines are essential due to current.

NAVIGATION WPT 52°18'·09N 01°41'·69E, 315° to N Pier lt, 1M. Enter on the flood since the ebb runs up to 6kn. Some shoals are unpredictable; a sand and shingle bar, extent/depth variable, lies off the hbr ent and a shoal builds inside N Pier. Obtain details of appr chans from HM before entering (Ch 12 or ☎ 724712). Enter between piers in midstream. When chan widens, at The Knuckle (2 FG vert), turn stbd towards LB House; keep within 15m of quay wall until it ends, when resume midstream. Unlit low footbridge ¾M upstream of ent.

LIGHTS AND MARKS Pier 1.1M NNE of hbr has 2F G(vert). Walberswick ✠ in line with N Pier lt = 268°. Hbr ent opens on 300°. 3 FR (vert) at N pier = port closed. Lt ho, W ○ tr, is in Southwold town, 0·86M NNE of hbr ent, Fl (4) WR 20s 37m 16/12M; vis R 204°-215°, W215°-001°.

R/T *Southwold Port Radio* Ch **12** 16 09 (as reqd).

TELEPHONE (Dial code 01502) HM 724712; MRCC (01493) 851338; Marinecall 09066 526239; Weather (01603) 660779; Police (01986) 855321; Dr 722326; Ⓗ 723333.

FACILITIES Hbr AB 20-30ft £12.10, FW, D (cans) also by bowser 100 litres min, BY, CH, ME, ✂, Slip, BH (20 ton), SM. **Southwold SC**; **Town** (¾M), EC Wed (Southwold & Walberswick); Gas, Gaz, Kos, P (cans, 1M), R, 🛒, ✉, Ⓑ, ⇌ (bus to Brampton/Darsham), ✈ (Norwich).

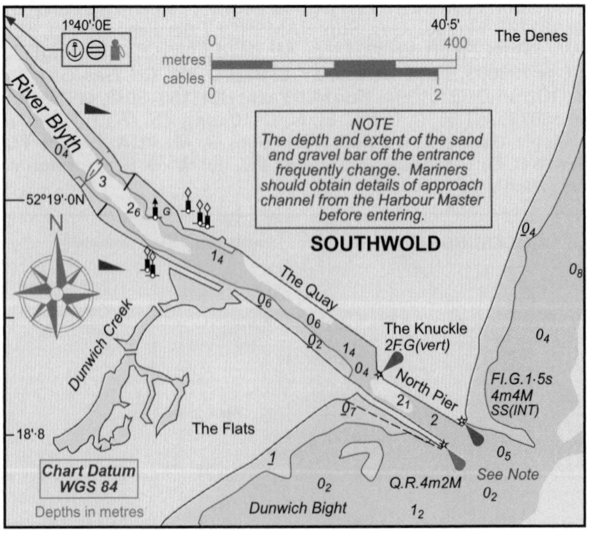
1°40'·0E
40'·5'
The Denes
metres
cables
400
River Blyth
NOTE
The depth and extent of the sand and gravel bar off the entrance frequently change. Mariners should obtain details of approach channel from the Harbour Master before entering.
52°19'·0N
N
SOUTHWOLD
The Quay
Dunwich Creek
The Knuckle
2FG(vert)
North Pier
Fl.G.1·5s
4m4M
SS(INT)
18'·8
The Flats
Chart Datum WGS 84
Depths in metres
Q.R.4m2M
See Note
Dunwich Bight

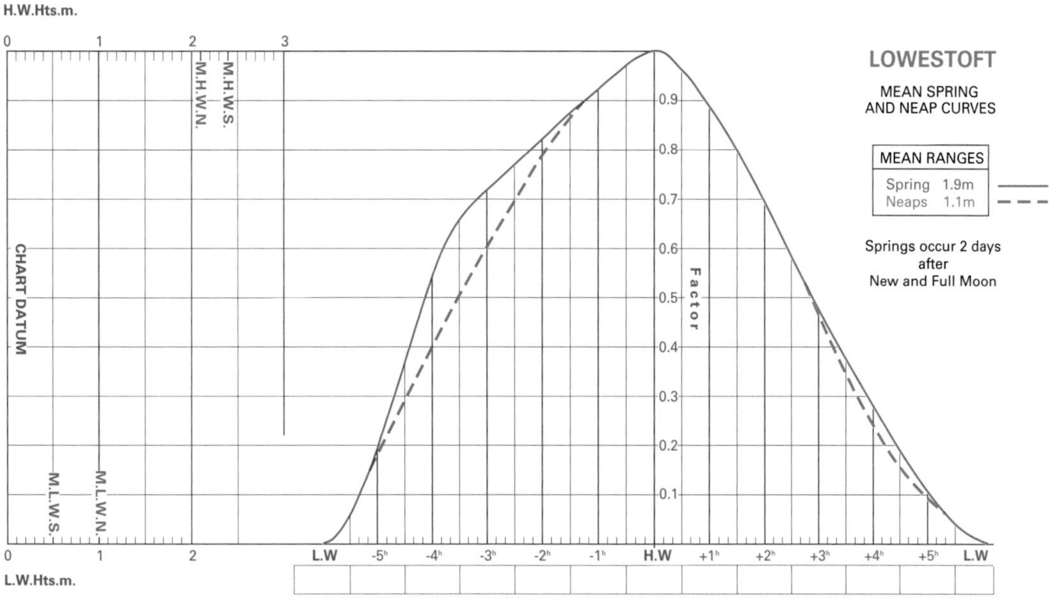
H.W.Hts.m.
0 1 2 3
M.H.W.N.
M.H.W.S.
LOWESTOFT
MEAN SPRING
AND NEAP CURVES
MEAN RANGES
Spring 1.9m
Neaps 1.1m
Springs occur 2 days
after
New and Full Moon
CHART DATUM
Factor
0.9
0.8
0.7
0.6
0.5
0.4
0.3
0.2
0.1
M.L.W.S.
M.L.W.N.
0 1 2
L.W.Hts.m.
L.W -5h -4h -3h -2h -1h H.W +1h +2h +3h +4h +5h L.W

9.4.24 LOWESTOFT

Suffolk **52°28'·31N 01°45'·39E** ❁❁❁◊◊◊✿✿✿

CHARTS AC *1536, 1543*; Imray C28, C29; Stanfords 3; OS 156/134

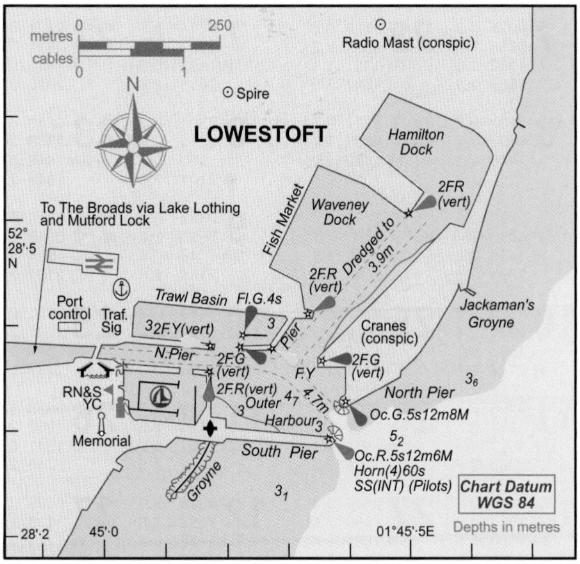
metres 0 250
cables 0 1
Radio Mast (conspic)
N
Spire
LOWESTOFT
Hamilton
Dock
To The Broads via Lake Lothing
and Mutford Lock
52°
28'·5
N
Fish Market
Waveney
Dock
2FR
(vert)
Dredged to
3.9m
2F.R
(vert)
Trawl Basin Fl.G.4s
Port
control
Traf.
Sig
32F.Y(vert)
3
Pier
Jackaman's
Groyne
Cranes
(conspic)
N.Pier
2F.G
(vert)
F.Y
2F.G
(vert)
RN&S
YC
2F.R(vert)
Outer
Harbour
4.7m
North Pier
Oc.G.5s12m8M
Memorial
South Pier
Oc.R.5s12m6M
Horn(4)60s
SS(INT) (Pilots)
Groyne
Chart Datum
WGS 84
28'·2
45'·0
01°45'·5E
Depths in metres

TIDES –0133 Dover; ML 1·6; Duration 0620; Zone 0 (UT).

SHELTER Good; hbr accessible H24. Wind over tide, esp ebb, can make the ent lively. Fairway is dredged 4·7m. Speed limit 4kn. Yacht Basin in SW corner of Outer Hbr is run by RN & S YC with 2 to 2·5m; no berthing on N side of S Pier. Lowestoft Haven Marina 1.5M upriver.

Bridge to Inner Hbr (Lake Lothing and Lowestoft CC) lifts at the following times (20 mins notice required): every day at 0700, 0945, 1115, 1430, 1600, 1800 (W/Es + BH's only), 1900, 2100 and also, by prior arrangement, when ships transit. Small craft may pass under the bridge (clearance 2·2m) at any time but VHF Ch 14 contact advisable.

NAVIGATION Listen on Ch 14 when in vicinity of hbr. Sands continually shift and buoys are moved to suit. Beware shoals and drying areas; do not cross banks in bad weather, nor at mid flood/ ebb. Speed limit in harbour 4 kn.

From S, WPT is E Barnard ECM buoy, Q (3) 10s, 52°25'·15N 01°46'·36E; thence via Stanford Chan E of Newcome Sand QR, Stanford Fl R 2.5s and N Newcome Fl (4) R 15s, all PHM buoys. S Holm SCM, VQ (6)+L Fl 10s, and SW Holm SHM, Fl (2) G 5s, buoys mark the seaward side of this chan.

From E, WPT is Corton ECM buoy, Q (3) 10s Whis, 52°31'·14N 01°51'·37E; then via Holm Chan (buoyed) into Corton Road. Or approach direct to S Holm SCM buoy for Stanford Chan.

From N, appr via Yarmouth, Gorleston and Corton Roads.

LIGHTS AND MARKS N Newcome PHM lt buoy bears 082°/ 6·2ca from hbr ent. Lowestoft lt ho, Fl 15s 37m 23M, is 1M N of hbr ent.

Tfc Sigs: Comply with IPTS (only Nos 2 and 5 are shown) on S pierhead; also get clearance on VHF Ch 14 when entering or leaving, due to restricted vis in appr and ent.

Bridge Sigs (on N side of bridge):

● = bridge operating, keep 150m clear.

● = vessels may enter/leave Inner Hbr.

Yacht Basin tfc sigs on E arm (only visible from inside):
3 FR (vert) = no exit; GWG (vert) = proceed on instruction.

R/T *Lowestoft Hbr Control* (ABP) VHF Ch **14** 16 11 (H24). *Lowestoft Haven Marina* Ch **80**, 37. *Oulton Broad YS and Mutford Lock Control* Ch 73, 9, 14. Pilot Ch 14. RN & SYC Ch 14, 80.

TELEPHONE (Dial code 01502) HM & Bridge Control 572286; Mutford Bridge and Lock 531778 (+Ansafone, checked daily at 0830, 1300 & 1730); Oulton Broad Yacht Stn 574946; MRCC (01493) 851338; Pilot 572286 ext 243; Weather (01603) 660779; Marinecall 09066 526239; Police (01986) 835100; Ⓗ 01493 452452.

FACILITIES **Royal Norfolk & Suffolk YC** ☎ 566726, 📠 517981, £1.75 inc YC facilities, ⚡, D, FW, C (2 ton), ⚓, Slip, R, Bar; **Lowestoft Cruising Club** ☎ 574376 (occas), www.lowestoftcruisingclub.co.uk. AB £1.20, ⚡, FW, Slip (emergency only); **Lowestoft Haven Marina** ☎ 580300, 📠 581851, AB £1.70, ⚡, FW. **Services:** ME, El, ⚒, CH, D, Gas, Gaz, Ⓔ, ACA. **Town** 🛒, R, Bar, ✉, Ⓑ, ⇌, ✈ (Norwich).

Entry to the Broads: www.norfolkbroads.com. Passage to Oulton Broad, from Lake Lothing via two bridges and Mutford Lock (openings are coordinated; fee £7), is available 7 days/wk in working hrs HJ as pre-arranged with Mutford Br/Lock ☎ (01502) 531778/523003 or VHF Ch 73, 9, 14, who will also advise visitors drawing >1·7m. Mutford Control operates in response to bookings and daily Apr-Oct 0800-1800, Nov-Mar 0800-1100. Oulton Broad Yacht Station ☎ (01502) 574946. From Oulton Broad, access into the R. Waveney is via Oulton Dyke. New Cut is a short cut from the R. Waveney to the R Yare for air draft <7·3m. See 9.4.25 for Broads.

TIME ZONE (UT)
For Summer Time add ONE hour in **non-shaded areas**

ENGLAND – LOWESTOFT

LAT 52°28′N LONG 1°45′E

TIMES AND HEIGHTS OF HIGH AND LOW WATERS

SPRING & NEAP TIDES
Dates in red are **SPRINGS**
Dates in blue are **NEAPS**

YEAR **2005**

JANUARY

Date	Day	Time	m	Time	m	Time	m	Time	m
1	SA	0023	2.4	0654	0.8	1305	2.1	1838	1.1
2	SU	0105	2.4	0737	0.8	1348	2.1	1922	1.2
3	M	0148	2.4	0823	0.8	1439	2.0	◑ 2012	1.2
4	TU	0234	2.3	0918	0.8	1554	2.0	2109	1.3
5	W	0328	2.3	1022	0.8	1713	2.1	2220	1.3
6	TH	0439	2.3	1129	0.8	1808	2.2	2342	1.2
7	F	0553	2.3	1228	0.7	1858	2.2		
8	SA	0049	1.1	0654	2.4	1323	0.7	1943	2.3
9	SU	0149	0.9	0753	2.4	1416	0.7	2028	2.4
10	M	0247	0.7	0853	2.5	1508	0.7	● 2114	2.5
11	TU	0343	0.5	0951	2.5	1558	0.7	2200	2.5
12	W	0437	0.3	1046	2.5	1646	0.8	2246	2.6
13	TH	0528	0.2	1137	2.5	1731	0.8	2333	2.6
14	F	0617	0.2	1228	2.4	1813	0.9		
15	SA	0019	2.6	0704	0.3	1321	2.2	1854	1.0
16	SU	0105	2.6	0753	0.4	1420	2.1	1937	1.1
17	M	0154	2.5	0845	0.6	1530	2.1	◐ 2024	1.2
18	TU	0248	2.4	0944	0.7	1635	2.0	2125	1.2
19	W	0359	2.3	1050	0.9	1734	2.1	2256	1.2
20	TH	0516	2.2	1153	1.0	1830	2.1		
21	F	0018	1.2	0630	2.1	1251	1.0	1922	2.2
22	SA	0124	1.0	0744	2.2	1341	1.1	2005	2.2
23	SU	0216	0.9	0839	2.2	1424	1.1	2040	2.3
24	M	0259	0.8	0920	2.2	1500	1.0	2111	2.4
25	TU	0337	0.7	0956	2.2	1531	1.0	○ 2141	2.4
26	W	0413	0.7	1027	2.2	1600	0.9	2214	2.5
27	TH	0447	0.6	1056	2.2	1632	0.9	2249	2.5
28	F	0521	0.6	1127	2.2	1706	0.9	2325	2.5
29	SA	0556	0.6	1159	2.2	1740	0.9		
30	SU	0000	2.5	0629	0.6	1234	2.2	1815	0.9
31	M	0037	2.4	0704	0.6	1311	2.1	1853	1.0

FEBRUARY

Date	Day	Time	m	Time	m	Time	m	Time	m
1	TU	0115	2.4	0742	0.7	1353	2.1	1936	1.0
2	W	0157	2.4	0828	0.8	1445	2.0	◑ 2027	1.1
3	TH	0248	2.3	0927	0.8	1602	2.0	2132	1.2
4	F	0402	2.2	1050	0.9	1726	2.1	2310	1.1
5	SA	0533	2.2	1206	0.9	1826	2.1		
6	SU	0033	1.0	0646	2.3	1309	0.9	1919	2.2
7	M	0140	0.8	0756	2.4	1407	0.8	2010	2.3
8	TU	0242	0.6	0857	2.4	1501	0.8	● 2058	2.4
9	W	0338	0.3	0948	2.5	1549	0.7	2145	2.6
10	TH	0427	0.2	1035	2.5	1633	0.7	2230	2.7
11	F	0513	0.1	1119	2.4	1713	0.7	2313	2.7
12	SA	0556	0.1	1202	2.3	1750	0.7	2356	2.7
13	SU	0637	0.2	1245	2.2	1827	0.8		
14	M	0039	2.6	0717	0.4	1329	2.1	1904	0.9
15	TU	0124	2.5	0758	0.6	1416	2.0	1947	1.0
16	W	0214	2.3	0846	0.9	1520	2.0	◐ 2040	1.1
17	TH	0323	2.2	0954	1.1	1634	2.0	2206	1.2
18	F	0455	2.1	1124	1.2	1740	2.0	2357	1.1
19	SA	0626	2.0	1235	1.2	1845	2.1		
20	SU	0107	1.0	0743	2.1	1333	1.2	1938	2.1
21	M	0159	0.9	0831	2.2	1415	1.1	2017	2.2
22	TU	0240	0.7	0907	2.2	1448	1.0	2049	2.3
23	W	0316	0.6	0936	2.2	1517	0.9	2119	2.4
24	TH	0350	0.6	1003	2.2	1545	0.8	○ 2152	2.5
25	F	0423	0.5	1030	2.3	1616	0.8	2226	2.5
26	SA	0456	0.5	1059	2.3	1648	0.7	2300	2.5
27	SU	0528	0.5	1131	2.3	1721	0.7	2335	2.5
28	M	0600	0.5	1204	2.2	1753	0.8		

MARCH

Date	Day	Time	m	Time	m	Time	m	Time	m
1	TU	0010	2.5	0632	0.6	1240	2.2	1827	0.8
2	W	0047	2.4	0706	0.6	1320	2.1	1908	0.9
3	TH	0131	2.3	0749	0.8	1407	2.1	◑ 1959	1.0
4	F	0228	2.2	0846	0.9	1511	2.0	2107	1.0
5	SA	0352	2.2	1018	1.1	1640	2.0	2300	1.0
6	SU	0534	2.2	1154	1.1	1754	2.1		
7	M	0025	0.8	0655	2.2	1302	1.0	1855	2.2
8	TU	0133	0.6	0803	2.3	1400	0.9	1950	2.3
9	W	0233	0.4	0853	2.4	1450	0.8	2039	2.4
10	TH	0323	0.2	0935	2.4	1533	0.7	● 2124	2.6
11	F	0408	0.1	1015	2.4	1612	0.6	2208	2.7
12	SA	0449	0.1	1054	2.4	1650	0.6	2251	2.7
13	SU	0527	0.2	1132	2.3	1725	0.6	2332	2.6
14	M	0604	0.3	1209	2.2	1801	0.7		
15	TU	0014	2.5	0638	0.5	1245	2.1	1837	0.7
16	W	0057	2.4	0713	0.8	1323	2.1	1918	0.9
17	TH	0147	2.2	0752	1.0	1406	2.0	◐ 2009	1.0
18	F	0259	2.1	0843	1.2	1506	2.0	2127	1.1
19	SA	0440	2.0	1053	1.4	1633	2.0	2330	1.0
20	SU	0608	2.0	1218	1.3	1747	2.0		
21	M	0035	0.9	0720	2.1	1313	1.2	1850	2.1
22	TU	0126	0.8	0805	2.2	1352	1.1	1937	2.2
23	W	0207	0.7	0839	2.2	1423	1.0	2014	2.3
24	TH	0243	0.6	0907	2.2	1450	0.9	2048	2.3
25	F	0317	0.5	0933	2.3	1519	0.8	○ 2123	2.4
26	SA	0350	0.4	1000	2.3	1552	0.7	2158	2.5
27	SU	0424	0.4	1030	2.3	1625	0.6	2233	2.5
28	M	0458	0.4	1102	2.3	1659	0.6	2309	2.5
29	TU	0530	0.5	1136	2.3	1734	0.7	2347	2.5
30	W	0604	0.6	1213	2.3	1810	0.7		
31	TH	0028	2.4	0640	0.7	1254	2.2	1853	0.8

APRIL

Date	Day	Time	m	Time	m	Time	m	Time	m
1	F	0119	2.3	0725	0.9	1343	2.1	1949	0.8
2	SA	0226	2.2	0825	1.1	1446	2.0	◑ 2109	0.9
3	SU	0409	2.1	1004	1.2	1606	2.0	2300	0.8
4	M	0545	2.2	1143	1.2	1724	2.1		
5	TU	0015	0.6	0700	2.3	1250	1.1	1829	2.2
6	W	0119	0.5	0755	2.3	1344	1.0	1926	2.3
7	TH	0214	0.3	0837	2.4	1430	0.8	2015	2.4
8	F	0301	0.2	0914	2.4	1510	0.7	● 2101	2.5
9	SA	0342	0.2	0950	2.4	1548	0.6	2145	2.6
10	SU	0420	0.2	1025	2.4	1625	0.5	2228	2.6
11	M	0456	0.3	1101	2.3	1702	0.6	2310	2.5
12	TU	0530	0.5	1136	2.3	1738	0.6	2352	2.4
13	W	0601	0.7	1209	2.2	1815	0.7		
14	TH	0036	2.2	0632	0.9	1244	2.2	1855	0.8
15	F	0127	2.1	0706	1.1	1325	2.1	1945	0.9
16	SA	0243	2.0	0750	1.3	1417	2.1	◐ 2057	1.0
17	SU	0418	2.0	0854	1.4	1525	2.0	2250	0.9
18	M	0532	2.0	1139	1.4	1647	2.0	2352	0.9
19	TU	0638	2.1	1232	1.3	1753	2.1		
20	W	0040	0.8	0726	2.1	1310	1.2	1846	2.1
21	TH	0123	0.7	0802	2.2	1342	1.1	1931	2.2
22	F	0201	0.6	0831	2.2	1413	0.9	2010	2.3
23	SA	0238	0.5	0859	2.3	1448	0.8	2049	2.4
24	SU	0314	0.4	0929	2.3	1524	0.7	○ 2127	2.5
25	M	0351	0.4	1001	2.4	1602	0.6	2207	2.5
26	TU	0428	0.4	1036	2.4	1641	0.6	2248	2.5
27	W	0505	0.5	1113	2.4	1721	0.6	2331	2.4
28	TH	0543	0.6	1152	2.3	1804	0.6		
29	F	0020	2.4	0624	0.8	1237	2.3	1854	0.6
30	SA	0120	2.3	0714	1.0	1329	2.2	1958	0.7

Chart Datum: 1·50 metres below Ordnance Datum (Newlyn)

TIME ZONE (UT)
For Summer Time add ONE hour in **non-shaded areas**

ENGLAND – LOWESTOFT

LAT 52°28′N LONG 1°45′E

TIMES AND HEIGHTS OF HIGH AND LOW WATERS

SPRING & NEAP TIDES
Dates in **red** are **SPRINGS**
Dates in **blue** are **NEAPS**

YEAR **2005**

MAY

Date	Time	m	Date	Time	m
1 SU	0239 0816 1431 ◑ 2125	2.2 1.2 2.1 0.7	16 M	0341 0807 1441 ◐ 2148	2.0 1.3 2.1 0.9
2 M	0423 0949 1542 2248	2.2 1.3 2.1 0.6	17 TU	0448 0916 1545 2257	2.0 1.4 2.1 0.8
3 TU	0541 1117 1656 2354	2.2 1.2 2.2 0.5	18 W	0545 1103 1655 2348	2.0 1.4 2.1 0.8
4 W	0645 1221 1802	2.3 1.1 2.2	19 TH	0635 1203 1755	2.1 1.3 2.1
5 TH	0054 0734 1316 1900	0.4 2.3 1.0 2.3	20 F	0033 0715 1249 1845	0.7 2.2 1.1 2.2
6 F	0147 0814 1403 1951	0.4 2.3 0.9 2.4	21 SA	0117 0751 1332 1932	0.6 2.2 1.0 2.3
7 SA	0233 0849 1445 2038	0.4 2.3 0.7 2.5	22 SU	0158 0824 1415 2016	0.5 2.3 0.9 2.4
8 SU	0313 0924 1525 ● 2124	0.4 2.4 0.6 2.5	23 M	0240 0859 1459 ○ 2101	0.5 2.3 0.7 2.4
9 M	0350 0959 1605 2209	0.5 2.4 0.6 2.4	24 TU	0322 0935 1543 2146	0.5 2.4 0.6 2.5
10 TU	0425 1034 1643 2253	0.6 2.4 0.6 2.4	25 W	0404 1013 1629 2234	0.5 2.4 0.6 2.5
11 W	0457 1107 1720 2336	0.7 2.3 0.6 2.3	26 TH	0447 1054 1716 2326	0.6 2.4 0.5 2.4
12 TH	0527 1140 1758	0.9 2.3 0.7	27 F	0531 1138 1807	0.7 2.4 0.5
13 F	0021 0557 1215 1839	2.2 1.0 2.3 0.7	28 SA	0022 0617 1226 1902	2.4 0.9 2.4 0.5
14 SA	0112 0631 1255 1927	2.1 1.1 2.2 0.8	29 SU	0126 0708 1318 2006	2.3 1.0 2.3 0.5
15 SU	0218 0713 1344 2027	2.0 1.2 2.2 0.9	30 M	0244 0806 1415 ◑ 2116	2.2 1.2 2.3 0.5
			31 TU	0410 0917 1518 2224	2.2 1.2 2.3 0.5

JUNE

Date	Time	m	Date	Time	m
1 W	0517 1034 1628 2327	2.2 1.2 2.3 0.5	16 TH	0448 0929 1554 2248	2.0 1.3 2.2 0.8
2 TH	0616 1143 1735	2.2 1.2 2.3	17 F	0541 1044 1701 2344	2.1 1.3 2.2 0.7
3 F	0025 0706 1243 1835	0.5 2.2 1.1 2.3	18 SA	0628 1156 1803	2.1 1.2 2.2
4 SA	0118 0748 1336 1930	0.6 2.3 0.9 2.3	19 SU	0036 0711 1255 1858	0.7 2.2 1.1 2.3
5 SU	0204 0826 1424 2022	0.6 2.3 0.8 2.3	20 M	0125 0752 1347 1950	0.6 2.3 0.9 2.3
6 M	0246 0901 1508 ● 2112	0.6 2.4 0.7 2.3	21 TU	0213 0832 1439 2042	0.6 2.3 0.8 2.4
7 TU	0324 0937 1550 2159	0.7 2.4 0.7 2.3	22 W	0300 0913 1530 ○ 2136	0.6 2.4 0.6 2.4
8 W	0359 1011 1631 2244	0.8 2.4 0.6 2.2	23 TH	0348 0956 1622 2230	0.6 2.5 0.5 2.5
9 TH	0431 1044 1710 2327	0.9 2.4 0.6 2.2	24 F	0436 1040 1715 2325	0.7 2.5 0.4 2.5
10 F	0501 1117 1748	1.0 2.4 0.7	25 SA	0523 1127 1807	0.8 2.5 0.3
11 SA	0009 0531 1153 1827	2.1 1.0 2.4 0.7	26 SU	0020 0609 1215 1859	2.4 0.9 2.5 0.3
12 SU	0051 0607 1233 1909	2.1 1.1 2.3 0.7	27 M	0117 0656 1303 1953	2.3 1.0 2.5 0.3
13 M	0137 0648 1318 1955	2.0 1.1 2.3 0.8	28 TU	0223 0744 1355 ◑ 2050	2.2 1.1 2.5 0.4
14 TU	0230 0735 1405 2048	2.0 1.2 2.2 0.8	29 W	0339 0837 1451 2151	2.1 1.1 2.4 0.5
15 W	0343 0827 1456 ◐ 2147	2.0 1.3 2.2 0.8	30 TH	0443 0942 1557 2254	2.1 1.2 2.3 0.6

JULY

Date	Time	m	Date	Time	m
1 F	0541 1059 1709 2354	2.1 1.2 2.3 0.7	16 SA	0439 0945 1608 2256	2.0 1.3 2.2 0.8
2 SA	0635 1212 1816	2.2 1.1 2.2	17 SU	0542 1110 1727	2.1 1.2 2.2
3 SU	0050 0723 1317 1921	0.8 2.2 1.0 2.2	18 M	0001 0634 1226 1833	0.8 2.2 1.1 2.3
4 M	0141 0805 1412 2022	0.9 2.3 0.9 2.2	19 TU	0059 0722 1327 1935	0.8 2.3 0.9 2.3
5 TU	0226 0844 1500 2113	0.9 2.3 0.8 2.2	20 W	0153 0808 1425 2036	0.8 2.3 0.7 2.4
6 W	0306 0919 1543 ● 2158	0.9 2.4 0.7 2.2	21 TH	0246 0854 1522 ○ 2133	0.8 2.4 0.5 2.5
7 TH	0341 0953 1622 2238	1.0 2.4 0.6 2.2	22 F	0337 0940 1616 2226	0.7 2.5 0.3 2.5
8 F	0413 1025 1659 2314	1.0 2.4 0.6 2.2	23 SA	0426 1025 1707 2316	0.7 2.6 0.2 2.5
9 SA	0443 1059 1735 2348	1.0 2.5 0.6 2.2	24 SU	0511 1111 1755	0.7 2.7 0.1
10 SU	0514 1134 1809	1.0 2.5 0.6	25 M	0004 0553 1157 1841	2.4 0.8 2.7 0.2
11 M	0021 0547 1212 1844	2.1 1.0 2.4 0.6	26 TU	0053 0634 1242 1927	2.3 0.9 2.7 0.3
12 TU	0056 0625 1251 1921	2.1 1.0 2.4 0.7	27 W	0145 0715 1329 2015	2.2 0.9 2.6 0.4
13 W	0135 0705 1331 2002	2.1 1.1 2.4 0.7	28 TH	0246 0800 1421 ◑ 2109	2.1 1.0 2.5 0.6
14 TH	0218 0750 1414 ◐ 2049	2.0 1.1 2.3 0.8	29 F	0356 0855 1526 2213	2.1 1.1 2.3 0.8
15 F	0315 0841 1504 2146	2.0 1.2 2.3 0.8	30 SA	0458 1015 1648 2323	2.1 1.1 2.2 1.0
			31 SU	0557 1150 1807	2.1 1.1 2.2

AUGUST

Date	Time	m	Date	Time	m
1 M	0029 0655 1305 1928	1.1 2.2 1.0 2.2	16 TU	0557 1206 1824	2.2 1.1 2.3
2 TU	0128 0745 1404 2028	1.1 2.3 0.9 2.2	17 W	0041 0653 1314 1934	1.0 2.2 0.9 2.4
3 W	0217 0826 1450 2112	1.1 2.3 0.8 2.2	18 TH	0140 0745 1416 2036	0.9 2.4 0.6 2.4
4 TH	0256 0901 1530 2149	1.1 2.4 0.7 2.3	19 F	0235 0833 1512 ○ 2126	0.9 2.5 0.4 2.5
5 F	0329 0932 1606 ● 2221	1.0 2.4 0.6 2.3	20 SA	0325 0920 1603 2212	0.8 2.6 0.2 2.5
6 SA	0358 1004 1639 2250	1.0 2.5 0.6 2.3	21 SU	0410 1005 1649 2255	0.7 2.7 0.1 2.5
7 SU	0426 1037 1711 2319	0.9 2.5 0.5 2.3	22 M	0451 1049 1733 2338	0.7 2.8 0.1 2.4
8 M	0455 1111 1743 2348	0.9 2.6 0.6 2.2	23 TU	0530 1133 1814	0.7 2.8 0.2
9 TU	0527 1146 1814	0.9 2.5 0.6	24 W	0020 0608 1217 1854	2.3 0.8 2.7 0.4
10 W	0020 0600 1221 1846	2.2 0.9 2.5 0.6	25 TH	0103 0646 1302 1934	2.2 0.9 2.6 0.6
11 TH	0055 0636 1257 1920	2.2 1.0 2.4 0.7	26 F	0149 0729 1353 ◑ 2020	2.2 1.0 2.4 0.9
12 F	0134 0716 1337 2001	2.2 1.1 2.4 0.8	27 SA	0244 0822 1501 2119	2.1 1.1 2.3 1.1
13 SA	0220 0804 1425 ◐ 2052	2.1 1.1 2.3 0.9	28 SU	0359 0940 1636 2254	2.1 1.2 2.2 1.3
14 SU	0322 0904 1531 2206	2.1 1.2 2.2 1.0	29 M	0509 1134 1805	2.1 1.1 2.1
15 M	0450 1034 1704 2334	2.1 1.2 2.2 1.0	30 TU	0014 0615 1249 1926	1.3 2.2 1.0 2.2
			31 W	0117 0715 1345 2016	1.3 2.2 0.9 2.3

Chart Datum: 1·50 metres below Ordnance Datum (Newlyn)

TIME ZONE (UT)
For Summer Time add ONE hour in **non-shaded areas**

ENGLAND – LOWESTOFT

LAT 52°28′N LONG 1°45′E

TIMES AND HEIGHTS OF HIGH AND LOW WATERS

SPRING & NEAP TIDES
Dates in red are SPRINGS
Dates in blue are NEAPS

YEAR **2005**

SEPTEMBER

Day	Time	m	Day	Time	m
1 TH	0203 0759 1427 2054	1.2 2.3 0.8 2.3	16 F	0127 0718 1402 2027	1.1 2.4 0.5 2.5
2 F	0238 0833 1504 2125	1.1 2.4 0.7 2.3	17 SA	0219 0808 1455 2110	1.0 2.6 0.3 2.5
3 SA	0307 0904 1537 ● 2153	1.1 2.5 0.6 2.3	18 SU	0305 0855 1541 ○ 2150	0.8 2.7 0.2 2.5
4 SU	0334 0935 1609 2218	1.0 2.5 0.5 2.3	19 M	0347 0940 1624 2229	0.7 2.8 0.1 2.5
5 M	0402 1009 1640 2245	0.9 2.6 0.5 2.3	20 TU	0426 1024 1704 2308	0.7 2.8 0.2 2.5
6 TU	0432 1043 1710 2315	0.8 2.6 0.5 2.3	21 W	0504 1108 1742 2346	0.7 2.8 0.4 2.4
7 W	0503 1117 1740 2347	0.8 2.6 0.6 2.3	22 TH	0542 1152 1818	0.7 2.7 0.6
8 TH	0536 1151 1811	0.9 2.5 0.6	23 F	0024 0621 1238 1854	2.3 0.8 2.5 0.8
9 F	0021 0609 1228 1843	2.3 0.9 2.5 0.7	24 SA	0104 0704 1330 1933	2.3 0.9 2.3 1.1
10 SA	0059 0648 1309 1922	2.3 1.0 2.4 0.9	25 SU	0149 0756 1445 ◑ 2022	2.2 1.0 2.2 1.3
11 SU	0144 0736 1402 ◐ 2013	2.2 1.1 2.3 1.0	26 M	0248 0915 1623 2212	2.2 1.1 2.1 1.5
12 M	0241 0839 1516 2126	2.2 1.1 2.2 1.2	27 TU	0409 1109 1747 2353	2.1 1.1 2.1 1.4
13 TU	0359 1022 1703 2315	2.1 1.1 2.2 1.2	28 W	0521 1216 1901	2.2 1.0 2.2
14 W	0520 1155 1827	2.2 0.9 2.3	29 TH	0051 0624 1308 1949	1.4 2.2 0.8 2.3
15 TH	0028 0623 1302 1935	1.2 2.3 0.7 2.4	30 F	0134 0714 1351 2025	1.3 2.3 0.8 2.3

OCTOBER

Day	Time	m	Day	Time	m
1 SA	0207 0753 1427 2053	1.2 2.4 0.7 2.3	16 SU	0155 0741 1429 2046	1.0 2.6 0.4 2.5
2 SU	0235 0827 1500 2119	1.1 2.5 0.6 2.4	17 M	0239 0829 1514 ○ 2123	0.9 2.7 0.3 2.5
3 M	0302 0902 1532 ● 2144	1.0 2.6 0.6 2.4	18 TU	0321 0915 1555 2200	0.8 2.8 0.3 2.5
4 TU	0332 0937 1603 2212	0.9 2.6 0.5 2.4	19 W	0401 1001 1633 2238	0.7 2.8 0.4 2.5
5 W	0405 1012 1635 2243	0.8 2.6 0.5 2.4	20 TH	0441 1046 1709 2315	0.7 2.7 0.6 2.5
6 TH	0439 1048 1707 2316	0.8 2.6 0.6 2.4	21 F	0520 1131 1743 2351	0.7 2.6 0.8 2.4
7 F	0513 1125 1739 2352	0.8 2.5 0.7 2.4	22 SA	0601 1219 1816	0.8 2.4 1.0
8 SA	0549 1205 1814	0.9 2.5 0.8	23 SU	0028 0644 1314 1851	2.4 0.9 2.2 1.2
9 SU	0031 0631 1253 1856	2.4 0.9 2.4 1.0	24 M	0109 0736 1431 1934	2.3 1.0 2.1 1.4
10 M	0118 0723 1353 ◐ 1950	2.3 1.0 2.3 1.2	25 TU	0201 0850 1600 ◑ 2034	2.2 1.0 2.1 1.5
11 TU	0216 0836 1521 2106	2.2 1.0 2.2 1.3	26 W	0306 1030 1713 2307	2.2 1.0 2.1 1.6
12 W	0327 1022 1710 2257	2.2 1.0 2.3 1.3	27 TH	0423 1133 1818	2.2 0.9 2.2
13 TH	0444 1140 1825	2.2 0.8 2.4	28 F	0007 0527 1223 1909	1.5 2.2 0.9 2.3
14 F	0008 0552 1243 1922	1.3 2.3 0.6 2.4	29 SA	0050 0621 1306 1946	1.4 2.3 0.8 2.3
15 SA	0105 0649 1339 2007	1.1 2.5 0.5 2.5	30 SU	0124 0707 1343 2016	1.2 2.4 0.7 2.3
			31 M	0154 0748 1418 2042	1.1 2.4 0.7 2.4

NOVEMBER

Day	Time	m	Day	Time	m
1 TU	0227 0826 1452 2110	1.0 2.5 0.6 2.4	16 W	0258 0855 1526 ○ 2134	0.8 2.6 0.6 2.5
2 W	0302 0905 1527 ● 2141	0.9 2.5 0.6 2.5	17 TH	0342 0943 1603 2211	0.7 2.6 0.7 2.5
3 TH	0340 0944 1603 2214	0.8 2.6 0.6 2.5	18 F	0424 1031 1639 2248	0.7 2.5 0.8 2.5
4 F	0418 1024 1639 2250	0.8 2.6 0.7 2.5	19 SA	0505 1119 1712 2323	0.7 2.4 1.0 2.5
5 SA	0458 1107 1717 2328	0.8 2.5 0.8 2.5	20 SU	0547 1207 1744 2358	0.8 2.3 1.1 2.4
6 SU	0540 1154 1757	0.8 2.4 0.9	21 M	0631 1259 1817	0.8 2.2 1.2
7 M	0011 0629 1249 1843	2.4 0.8 2.4 1.1	22 TU	0038 0718 1403 1856	2.4 0.9 2.1 1.3
8 TU	0101 0728 1356 1939	2.4 0.8 2.3 1.2	23 W	0126 0816 1519 ◑ 1945	2.3 0.9 2.1 1.4
9 W	0158 0845 1533 ◐ 2051	2.3 0.8 2.2 1.4	24 TH	0220 0927 1626 2045	2.3 1.0 2.1 1.5
10 TH	0303 1009 1702 2223	2.3 0.8 2.3 1.4	25 F	0320 1036 1725 2210	2.2 0.9 2.1 1.5
11 F	0413 1118 1807 2335	2.3 0.6 2.3 1.3	26 SA	0426 1130 1816 2336	2.2 0.9 2.2 1.4
12 SA	0522 1217 1900	2.4 0.6 2.4	27 SU	0529 1215 1858	2.3 0.8 2.2
13 SU	0033 0621 1312 1943	1.2 2.5 0.5 2.4	28 M	0026 0622 1257 1933	1.3 2.3 0.8 2.3
14 M	0126 0715 1401 2021	1.0 2.6 0.5 2.4	29 TU	0110 0709 1337 2006	1.2 2.4 0.7 2.3
15 TU	0213 0806 1445 2057	0.9 2.6 0.5 2.5	30 W	0153 0754 1417 2039	1.0 2.4 0.7 2.4

DECEMBER

Day	Time	m	Day	Time	m
1 TH	0236 0838 1457 ● 2113	0.9 2.5 0.7 2.5	16 F	0331 0938 1541 2151	0.7 2.4 0.9 2.5
2 F	0319 0923 1538 2150	0.8 2.5 0.7 2.5	17 SA	0415 1027 1617 2227	0.7 2.3 1.0 2.5
3 SA	0405 1009 1620 2230	0.7 2.5 0.7 2.5	18 SU	0457 1112 1650 2302	0.7 2.3 1.0 2.5
4 SU	0452 1059 1704 2312	0.7 2.5 0.8 2.5	19 M	0538 1155 1720 2337	0.7 2.2 1.1 2.5
5 M	0542 1152 1749 2358	0.6 2.4 1.0 2.5	20 TU	0617 1236 1752	0.7 2.2 1.1
6 TU	0635 1250 1837	0.6 2.4 1.1	21 W	0015 0656 1318 1829	2.4 0.8 2.1 1.2
7 W	0048 0733 1355 1929	2.5 0.6 2.3 1.2	22 TH	0057 0738 1404 1911	2.4 0.8 2.0 1.2
8 TH	0141 0837 1519 ◐ 2028	2.4 0.6 2.2 1.3	23 F	0143 0825 1504 ◑ 1959	2.3 0.9 2.0 1.3
9 F	0238 0944 1638 2137	2.4 0.6 2.2 1.3	24 SA	0231 0918 1617 2054	2.3 0.9 2.0 1.4
10 SA	0342 1049 1738 2252	2.4 0.6 2.2 1.3	25 SU	0325 1019 1715 2201	2.2 0.9 2.1 1.4
11 SU	0453 1148 1831 2359	2.4 0.6 2.3 1.2	26 M	0431 1120 1805 2324	2.2 0.9 2.1 1.3
12 M	0558 1244 1917	2.4 0.7 2.3	27 TU	0539 1213 1850	2.2 0.9 2.2
13 TU	0059 0656 1335 1958	1.1 2.4 0.7 2.4	28 W	0030 0636 1302 1931	1.2 2.3 0.8 2.3
14 W	0155 0752 1421 2036	0.9 2.4 0.8 2.4	29 TH	0124 0729 1349 2011	1.1 2.3 0.8 2.3
15 TH	0245 0847 1503 ○ 2114	0.8 2.4 0.8 2.5	30 F	0215 0821 1435 2051	0.9 2.4 0.8 2.4
			31 SA	0306 0913 1522 ● 2132	0.8 2.4 0.8 2.5

Chart Datum: 1·50 metres below Ordnance Datum (Newlyn)

9.4.25 GREAT YARMOUTH

Norfolk **52°34'·36N 01°44'·39E** ❁❁⚓✿✿

CHARTS AC *1543, 1536*; Imray C29, C28; Stanfords 3; OS 134

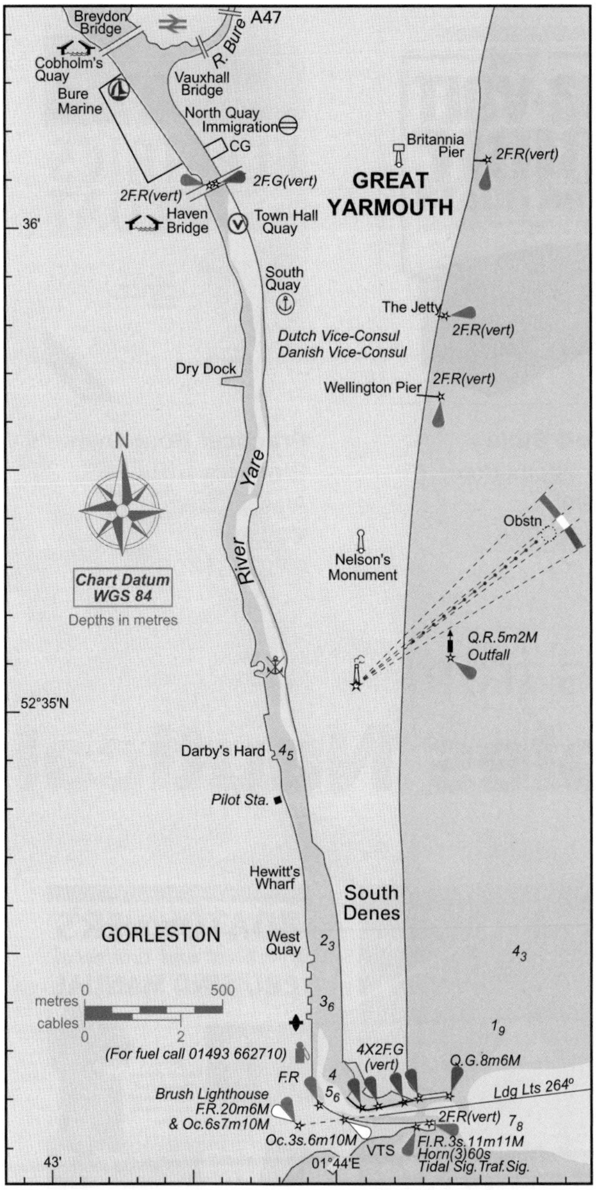
Breydon Bridge
A47
R. Bure
Cobholm's Quay
Bure Marine
Vauxhall Bridge
North Quay
Immigration
CG
Britannia Pier
2F.R(vert)
2F.G(vert)
GREAT YARMOUTH
2F.R(vert)
Haven Bridge
Town Hall Quay
36'
South Quay
The Jetty
2F.R(vert)
Dutch Vice-Consul
Danish Vice-Consul
Dry Dock
Wellington Pier
2F.R(vert)
N
River Yare
Obstn
Nelson's Monument
Chart Datum WGS 84
Depths in metres
Q.R.5m2M
Outfall
52°35'N
Darby's Hard
Pilot Sta.
Hewitt's Wharf
South Denes
GORLESTON
West Quay
metres 0 500
cables 0 2
(For fuel call 01493 662710)
4X2F.G (vert)
Q.G.8m6M
F.R
Ldg Lts 264°
Brush Lighthouse
F.R.20m6M
& Oc.6s7m10M
2F.R(vert)
Oc.3s.6m10M
VTS
Fl.R.3s.11m11M
Horn(3)60s
Tidal Sig.Traf.Sig.
43'
01°44'E

TIDES –0210 Dover; ML 1·5; Duration 0620; Zone 0 (UT)

Standard Port LOWESTOFT (⟵)

Times				**Height (metres)**			
High Water		Low Water		MHWS	MHWN	MLWN	MLWS
0300	0900	0200	0800	2·4	2·1	1·0	0·5
1500	2100	1400	2000				
Differences GORLESTON (To be used for Great Yarmouth)							
–0035	–0035	–0030	–0030	0·0	0·0	0·0	0·0
CAISTER-ON-SEA							
–0120	–0120	–0100	–0100	0·0	–0·1	0·0	0·0
WINTERTON-ON-SEA							
–0225	–0215	–0135	–0135	+0·8	+0·5	+0·2	+0·1

Rise of tide occurs mainly during $3\frac{1}{2}$ hours after LW. From HW Lowestoft –3 until HW the level is usually within 0·3m of predicted HW. Flood tide runs until about HW $+1\frac{1}{2}$ and Ebb until about LW $+2\frac{1}{2}$. See also under NAVIGATION.

SHELTER Excellent on Town Hall Quay, close S of Haven Bridge; ⚓ prohib in hbr which is a busy commercial port.

NAVIGATION WPT 52°34'·43N 01°45'·56E, 264° to front ldg lt, 1·0M. Access is H24, subject to clearance, but small craft must not attempt ent in strong SE winds which cause dangerous seas, especially on the ebb. Except at local slack water, which occurs at HW$+1\frac{1}{2}$ and LW$+1\frac{3}{4}$, tidal streams at the ent are strong. On the flood, the stream eddies NW past S pier, thence up-river; beware being set onto N pier; a QY tidal lt on S pier warns of this D/N. Temp shoaling may occur in the ent during strong E'lies, with depths 1m less than those charted. Beware strong tidal streams that sweep through the Haven Bridge. Slow past Bure Marine.

LIGHTS AND MARKS Main lt Fl R 3s 11m 11M, vis 235°-340°, Horn (3) 60s. (Note: Tfc Sigs and the tidal QY are co-located with the Main lt on a R brick bldg, W lower half floodlit, at S pier). Ldg lts 264°: front Oc 3s 6m 10M; rear Oc 6s 7m 10M, (below the FR 20m 6M on Brush lt ho). N pier lt, QG 8m 6M, vis 176°-078° (262°). Ent and bend marked by five x 2 FG and seven x 2FR (all vert).

TRAFFIC SIGNALS VTS instructions (Ch 12) must always be obeyed. **Inbound**: now IALA sigs on S pier: 3 Fl ● = hbr closed; 3F ● = do not proceed; 3 F ● = vessels may proceed, one-way; ● ○ ● = proceed only when told to; **Outbound**: 3 ● (vert) = no vessel to go down river south of LB shed. Haven and Breydon bridges: 3 ● (vert) = passage prohib.

R/T Call: *Yarmouth* or *Breydon Br* Ch **12** (both H24).

TELEPHONE (Dial code 01493) HM & Port Control 335511, 📠 653464; MRCC 851338; Marinecall 09066 526239; Police 336200; Breydon Bridge 651275.

FACILITIES Town Hall Quay (50m stretch) AB £15/yacht, then £7 for successive days. **Bure Marine Cobholm** ☎ 656996, H24 visitor pontoons planned. D, FW, El, ⛽, BH, C, Slip. **Burgh Castle Marina** (top of Breydon Water 5M) (90+10 visitors) ☎ 780331, £10, Slip, D, ⛽, ME, El, ⚒, ⊡, Gas, CH, 🛒, R, Bar, Access HW ±4 (1m), diving ACA; **Goodchild Marine Services** (top of Breydon Water 5M) (28+6 visitors) ☎ 782301, £12, D, FW, ME, El, C (32 tons, including mast stepping) Gas, ⛽, Access 6ft at LW; **Services:** Slip, Diving, AB, L, M, ⚒, SM, ACA. **Town** EC Thurs; P, D, CH, 🛒, R, Bar, ✉, Ⓑ, ⇌, ✈ (Norwich).

Entry to the Broads: Pass up R Yare at slack LW, under Haven Bridge (2·3m MHWS) thence to Breydon Water via Breydon Bridge (4·0m) or to R Bure. Both bridges lift in co-ordination to pass small craft in groups. All br lifts on request to Hbr Office (01493) 335503 during office hrs. Weekend and bank holiday lifts to be requested working afternoon before. Call the Bridge Officer on VHF Ch 12. R Bure has two fixed bridges (2·3m MHWS).

NORFOLK BROADS: The Broads comprise about 120 miles of navigable rivers and lakes in Norfolk and Suffolk. The main rivers (Bure, Yare and Waveney) are tidal, flowing into the sea at Great Yarmouth. The N Broads have a 2·3m headroom limit. Br clearances restrict cruising to R Yare (Great Yarmouth to Norwich, but note that 3M E of Norwich, Postwick viaduct on S bypass has 10.7m HW clearance) and River Waveney (Lowestoft to Beccles). The Broads may be entered also at Lowestoft (9.4.24). Broads Navigation Authority ☎ (01603) 610734.

Tidal data on the rivers and Broads is based on the time of LW at Yarmouth Yacht Stn (mouth of R Bure), which is LW Gorleston +0100 (see TIDES). Add the differences below to time of LW Yarmouth Yacht Stn to get local LW times:

R Bure		*R Waveney*		*R Yare*	
Acle Bridge	+0230	Berney Arms	+0100	Reedham	+0130
Horning	+0300	St Olaves	+0130	Cantley	+0200
Potter Heigham	+0300	Oulton Broad	+0300	Norwich	+0300
		Beccles	+0300		

LW at Breydon (mouth of R Yare) is LW Yarmouth Yacht Stn +0100. Tide starts to flood on Breydon Water whilst still ebbing from R Bure. Max draft is 1·8m; 2m with care. Tidal range 0·6m to 1·8m.

Licences are compulsory; get temp one from The Broads Authority, 18 Colegate, Norwich NR3 1BQ, ☎ 01603-610734; from Info Centre, Yarmouth Yacht Stn or from River Inspectors. *Hamilton's Guide to the Broads* is recommended. www.hamiltonpublications.com.

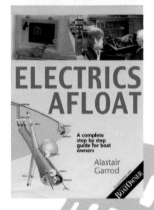

Area 5

North East England
Winterton to Berwick-upon-Tweed

5

9.5.2

North-East England

Blakeney to Berwick-upon-Tweed

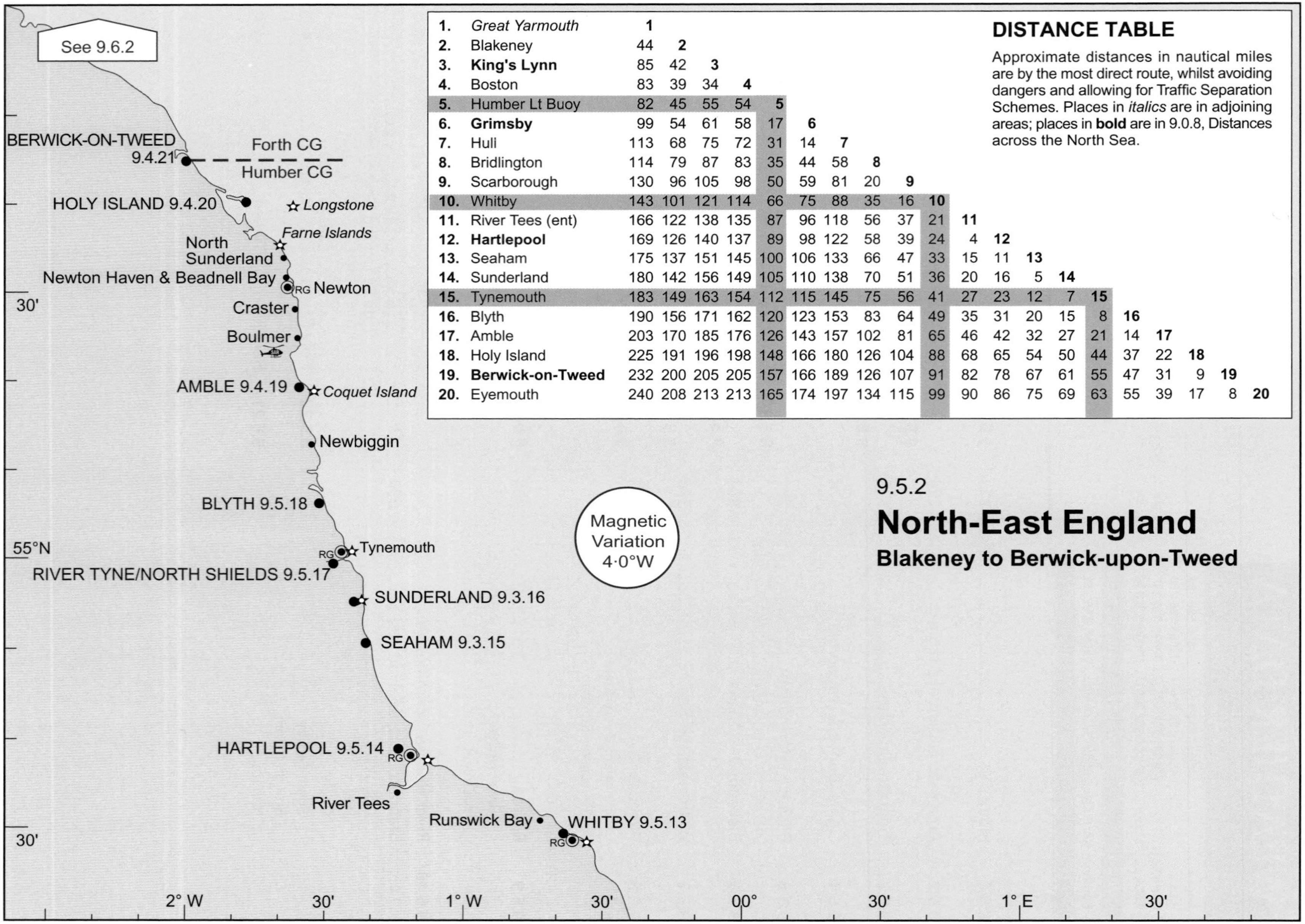

See 9.6.2
BERWICK-ON-TWEED 9.4.21
Forth CG
Humber CG
HOLY ISLAND 9.4.20
Longstone
Farne Islands
North Sunderland
Newton Haven & Beadnell Bay
RG
Newton
Craster
Boulmer
AMBLE 9.4.19
Coquet Island
Newbiggin
BLYTH 9.5.18
55°N
RG
Tynemouth
RIVER TYNE/NORTH SHIELDS 9.5.17
SUNDERLAND 9.3.16
SEAHAM 9.3.15
HARTLEPOOL 9.5.14
RG
River Tees
Runswick Bay
WHITBY 9.5.13
RG
30'
30'
2° W
30'
1° W
30'
00°
30'
1° E
30'
Magnetic Variation 4·0°W

DISTANCE TABLE

Approximate distances in nautical miles are by the most direct route, whilst avoiding dangers and allowing for Traffic Separation Schemes. Places in *italics* are in adjoining areas; places in **bold** are in 9.0.8, Distances across the North Sea.

1.	*Great Yarmouth*	**1**																		
2.	Blakeney	44	**2**																	
3.	**King's Lynn**	85	42	**3**																
4.	Boston	83	39	34	**4**															
5.	Humber Lt Buoy	82	45	55	54	**5**														
6.	**Grimsby**	99	54	61	58	17	**6**													
7.	Hull	113	68	75	72	31	14	**7**												
8.	Bridlington	114	79	87	83	35	44	58	**8**											
9.	Scarborough	130	96	105	98	50	59	81	20	**9**										
10.	Whitby	143	101	121	114	66	75	88	35	16	**10**									
11.	River Tees (ent)	166	122	138	135	87	96	118	56	37	21	**11**								
12.	**Hartlepool**	169	126	140	137	89	98	122	58	39	24	4	**12**							
13.	Seaham	175	137	151	145	100	106	133	66	47	33	15	11	**13**						
14.	Sunderland	180	142	156	149	105	110	138	70	51	36	20	16	5	**14**					
15.	Tynemouth	183	149	163	154	112	115	145	75	56	41	27	23	12	7	**15**				
16.	Blyth	190	156	171	162	120	123	153	83	64	49	35	31	20	15	8	**16**			
17.	Amble	203	170	185	176	126	143	157	102	81	65	46	42	32	27	21	14	**17**		
18.	Holy Island	225	191	196	198	148	166	180	126	104	88	68	65	54	50	44	37	22	**18**	
19.	**Berwick-on-Tweed**	232	200	205	205	157	166	189	126	107	91	82	78	67	61	55	47	31	9	**19**
20.	Eyemouth	240	208	213	213	165	174	197	134	115	99	90	86	75	69	63	55	39	17	8	**20**

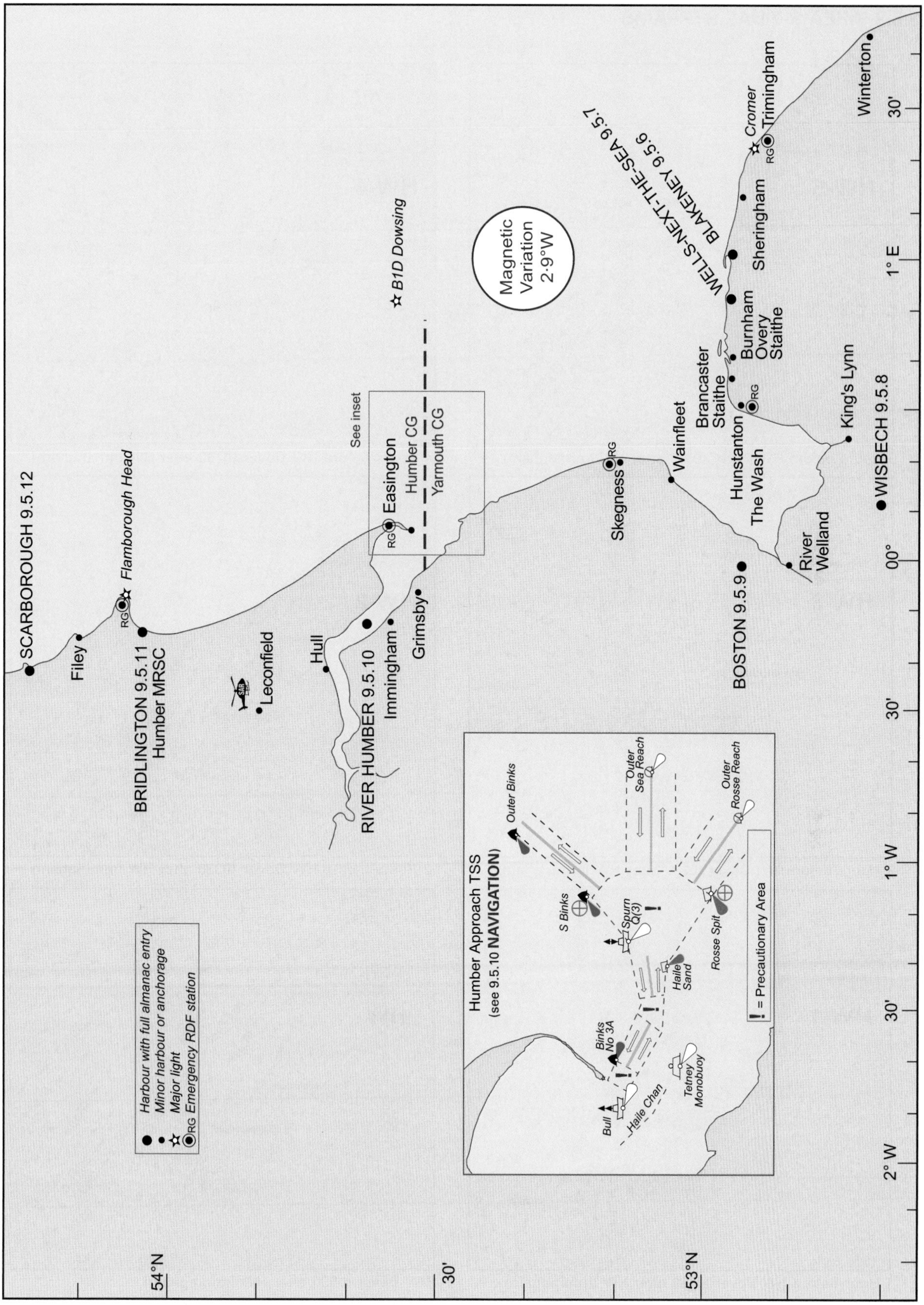
SCARBOROUGH 9.5.12
Filey
Flamborough Head
BRIDLINGTON 9.5.11
Humber MRSC
Leconfield
Hull
RIVER HUMBER 9.5.10
Immingham
Grimsby
Easington
Humber CG
Yarmouth CG
See inset
B1D Dowsing
Magnetic Variation 2·9°W
Skegness
Wainfleet
BOSTON 9.5.9
River Welland
The Wash
Hunstanton
Brancaster Staithe
Burnham Overy Staithe
WELLS-NEXT-THE-SEA 9.5.7
BLAKENEY 9.5.6
Sheringham
Cromer
Trimingham
Winterton
King's Lynn
WISBECH 9.5.8
RG
54°N
30'
53°N
2° W
30'
1° W
30'
00°
30'
1° E
30'
Harbour with full almanac entry
Minor harbour or anchorage
Major light
RG Emergency RDF station
Humber Approach TSS
(see 9.5.10 NAVIGATION)
Outer Binks
S Binks
Spurn Q(3)
Outer Sea Reach
Outer Rosse Reach
Rosse Spit
Haile Sand
Binks No 3A
Bull
Haile Chan
Tetney Monobuoy
! = Precautionary Area

5

9.5.3 AREA 5 TIDAL STREAMS

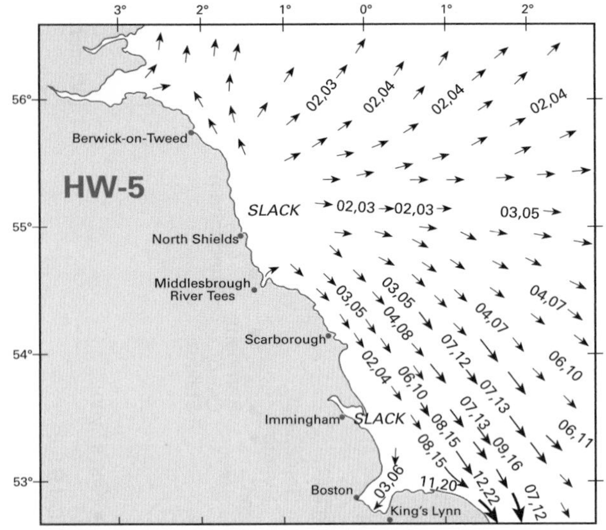
HW-5
Berwick-on-Tweed
North Shields
Middlesbrough
River Tees
Scarborough
Immingham
Boston
King's Lynn
SLACK
SLACK
02,03
02,03
03,05
5 Hours before HW Dover (0030 after HW Immingham)

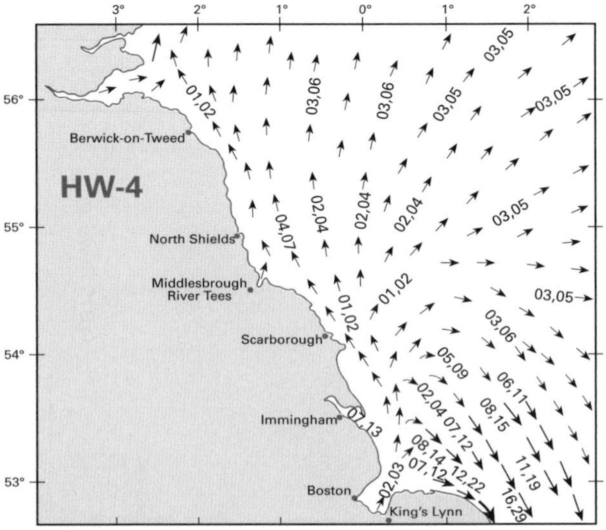
HW-4
Berwick-on-Tweed
North Shields
Middlesbrough
River Tees
Scarborough
Immingham
Boston
King's Lynn
03,05
4 Hours before HW Dover (0130 after HW Immingham)

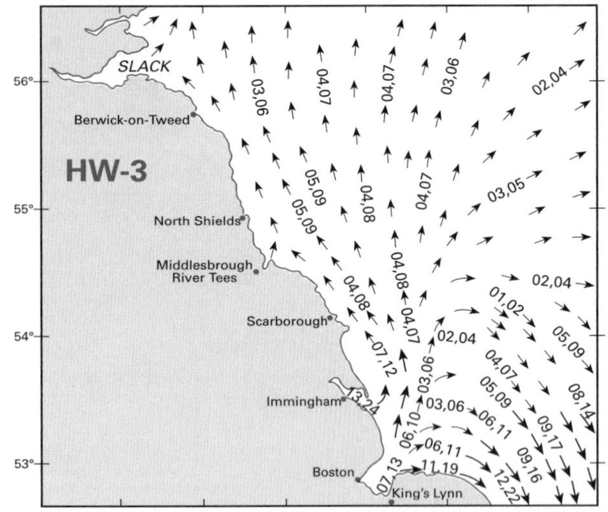
HW-3
SLACK
Berwick-on-Tweed
North Shields
Middlesbrough
River Tees
Scarborough
Immingham
Boston
King's Lynn
02,04
3 Hours before HW Dover (0230 after HW Immingham)

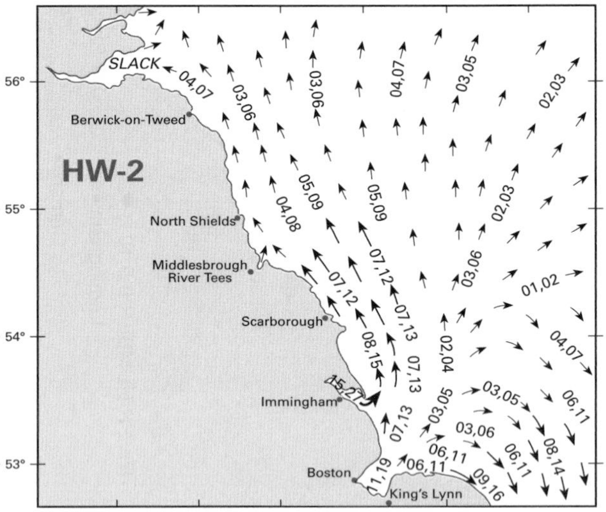
HW-2
SLACK
Berwick-on-Tweed
North Shields
Middlesbrough
River Tees
Scarborough
Immingham
Boston
King's Lynn
2 Hours before HW Dover (0330 after HW Immingham)

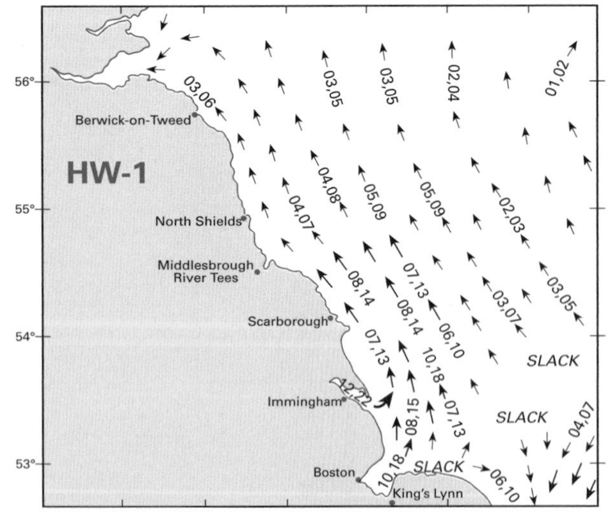
HW-1
Berwick-on-Tweed
North Shields
Middlesbrough
River Tees
Scarborough
Immingham
Boston
King's Lynn
SLACK
SLACK
SLACK
1 Hour before HW Dover (0430 after HW Immingham)

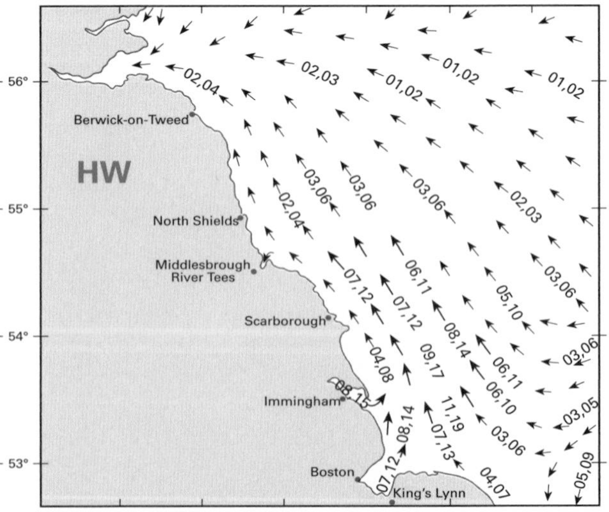
HW
Berwick-on-Tweed
North Shields
Middlesbrough
River Tees
Scarborough
Immingham
Boston
King's Lynn
HW Dover (0530 after HW Immingham)

Northward 9.6.3   Southward 9.4.3

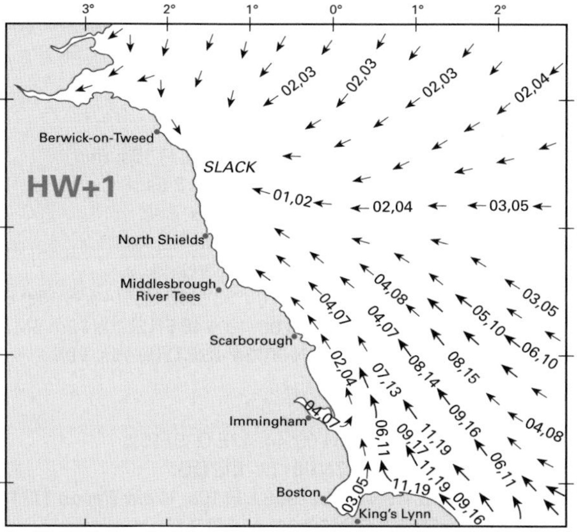
HW+1
SLACK
Berwick-on-Tweed
North Shields
Middlesbrough, River Tees
Scarborough
Immingham
Boston
King's Lynn
3°
2°
1°
0°
1°
2°
56°
55°
54°
53°

1 Hour after HW Dover (0555 before HW Immingham)

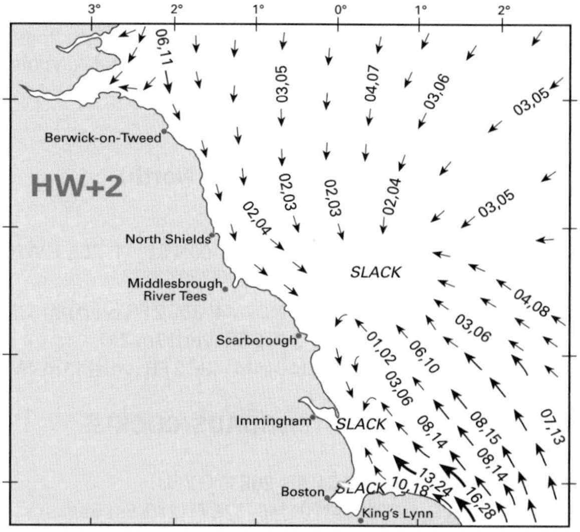
HW+2
SLACK
SLACK
SLACK
Berwick-on-Tweed
North Shields
Middlesbrough, River Tees
Scarborough
Immingham
Boston
King's Lynn

2 Hours after HW Dover (0455 before HW Immingham)

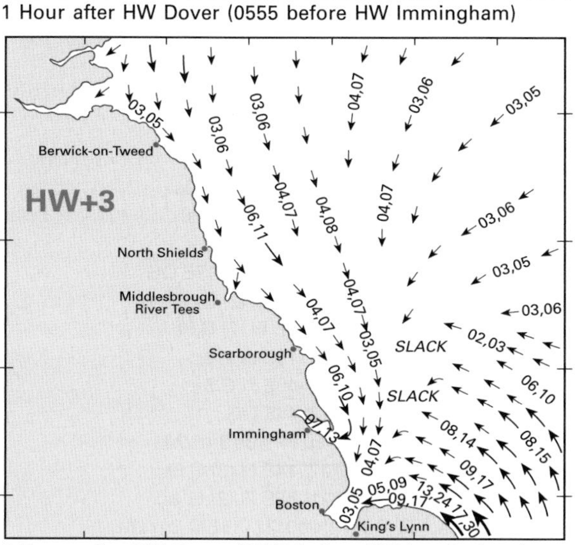
HW+3
SLACK
SLACK
Berwick-on-Tweed
North Shields
Middlesbrough, River Tees
Scarborough
Immingham
Boston
King's Lynn

3 Hours after HW Dover (0355 before HW Immingham)

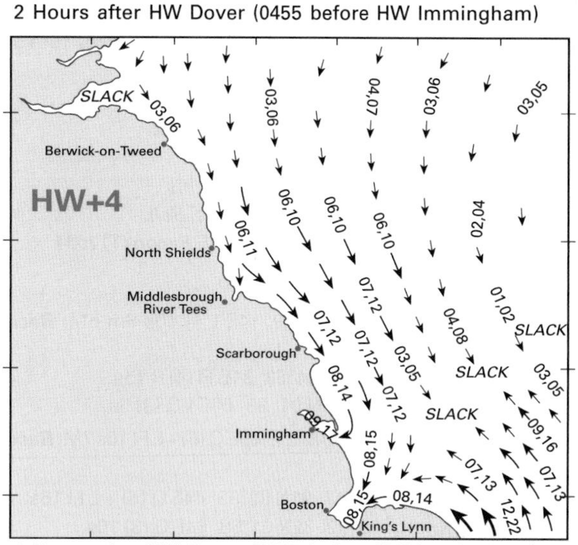
HW+4
SLACK
SLACK
SLACK
SLACK
Berwick-on-Tweed
North Shields
Middlesbrough, River Tees
Scarborough
Immingham
Boston
King's Lynn

4 Hours after HW Dover (0255 before HW Immingham)

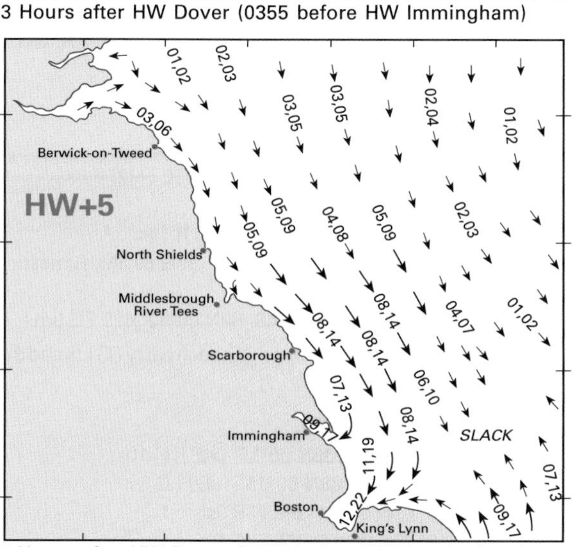
HW+5
SLACK
Berwick-on-Tweed
North Shields
Middlesbrough, River Tees
Scarborough
Immingham
Boston
King's Lynn

5 Hours after HW Dover (0155 before HW Immingham)

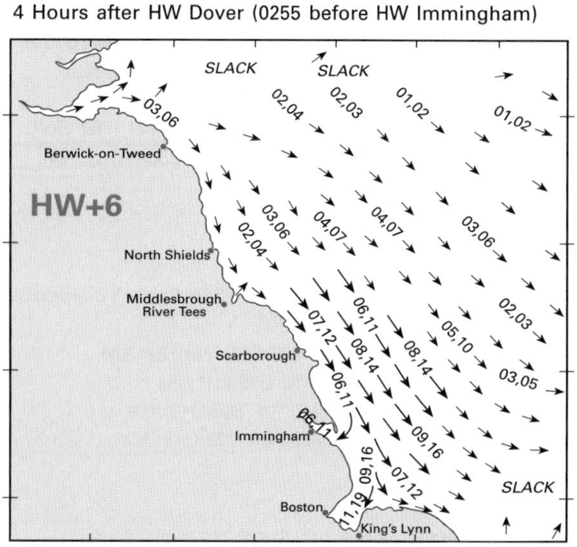
HW+6
SLACK
SLACK
SLACK
Berwick-on-Tweed
North Shields
Middlesbrough, River Tees
Scarborough
Immingham
Boston
King's Lynn

6 Hours after HW Dover (0055 before HW Immingham)

PLOT WAYPOINTS ON YOUR CHART BEFORE USING THEM

9.5.4 LIGHTS, BUOYS AND WAYPOINTS

Blue print = light with a nominal range of 15M or more. CAPITALS = place or feature. *CAPITAL ITALICS* = light-vessel, light float or Lanby. *Italics* = Fog signal. ***Bold italics*** = Racon. Useful waypoints are underlined. Abbreviations are in Chapter 1.

GREAT YARMOUTH TO THE WASH
(Direction of buoyage ⇧ South to North)

▶ **GREAT YARMOUTH**

South Denes Outfall Diffuser ⌕ 52°35'·00N 01°44'·20E F WRG 42m 1M; Vis: R217°-221°, W221°-223°, G223°-227°.

Wellington Pier Hd ⚓ 52°35'·95N 01°44'·30E 2 FR (vert) 8m 3M.
Jetty Hd ⚓ 52°36'·13N 01°44'·34E 2 FR (vert) 7m 2M.
Britannia Pier Hd ⚓ 52°36'·49N 01°44'·43E 2 FR (vert) 11m 4M.

▶ **YARMOUTH & CAISTER ROADS/COCKLE GATEWAY**

SW Scroby ▲ 52°35'·82N 01°46'·26E Fl G 2·5s.
Scroby Elbow ▲ 52°37'·34N 01°46'·37E Fl (2) G 5s; *Bell.*
Mid Caister ⚲ 52°38'·99N 01°45'·66E Fl (2) R 5s; *Bell.*
N Scroby Platform ⊡ 52°40'·21N 01°47'·15E Fl (5) Y 20s 10m 5M and Fl R 3s 50m 3M on mast.
NW Scroby ▲ 52°40'·36N 01°46'·31E Fl (3) G 10s.
N Caister ⚲ 52°40'·77N 01°45'·65E Fl (3) R 10s.
Hemsby ⚲ 52°41'·80N 01°46'·00E Fl R 2·5s.
N Scroby ⚑ 52°41'·58N 01°46'·40E VQ; *Whis.*
Cockle ⚑ 52°44'·03N 01°43'·59E VQ (3) 5s; *Bell.*
Winterton Church 52°42'·92N 01°41'·21E ***Racon (T) 10M.***

▶ **OFFSHORE ROUTE**

Cross Sand ⚑ 52°37'·03N 01°59'·14E L Fl 10s 6m 5M; ***Racon (T)10M.***
E Cross Sand ⚲ 52°37'·87N 01°53'·31E Fl (4) R 15s.
NE Cross Sand ⚑ 52°43'·03N 01°53'·69E VQ (3) 5s.
Smith's Knoll ⚑ 52°43'·52N 02°17'·89E Q (6) + L Fl 15s 7M; ***Racon (T) 10M***; *Whis.*
S Winterton Ridge ⚑ 52°47'·21N 02°03'·44E Q (6) + L Fl 15s.
E Hammond Knoll ⚑ 52°52'·32N 01°58'·64E Q (3) 10s.
Hammond Knoll ⚑ 52°49'·68N 01°57'·54E Q (9) 15s.
Newarp ⚑ 52°48'·37N 01°55'·69E L Fl 10s 7M; ***Racon (O) 10M***.
S Haisbro ⚑ 52°50'·82N 01°48'·29E Q (6) + L Fl 15s; *Bell.*
Mid Haisbro ▲ 52°54'·22N 01°41'·59E Fl (2) G 5s.
N Haisbro ⚑ 53°00'·22N 01°32'·29E Q; ***Racon (T) 10M***; *Bell.*
Happisburgh ☆ 52°49'·21N 01°32'·18E Fl (3) 30s 41m 14M.

(Direction of buoyage ⇧ East to West)

▶ **CROMER**

Cromer ☆ 52°55'·45N 01°19'·01E Fl 5s 84m **21M**; W 8-sided twr; vis: 102°-307° H24; ***Racon (O) 25M***.

Lifeboat ⚓ 52°56'·03N 01°18'·08E 2 FR (vert) 8m 5M.
Tayjack Wk ⚲ 52°57'·61N 01°15'·37E Fl R 2·5s.
E Sheringham ⚑ 53°02'·21N 01°14'·84E Q (3) 10s.
W Sheringham ⚑ 53°02'·95N 01°06'·72E Q (9) 15s.

▶ **BLAKENEY**

Blakeney Overfalls ⚲ 53°03'·01N 01°01'·37E Fl (2) R 5s; *Bell.*
Hjordis Wk ⚲ 52°59'·07N 00°58'·12E QR.

▶ **WELLS-NEXT-THE-SEA/BRANCASTER STAITHE**

Wells Fairway ⚲ 52°59'·81N 00°50'·49E Q.
Bridgirdle ⚲ 53°01'·73N 00°43'·95E.
Brancaster Club Ho ⚓ 52°58'·41N 00°38'·17E Fl 5s 8m 3M; vis: 080°-270°.

▶ **APPROACHES TO THE WASH**

S Race ⚑ 53°07'·81N 00°57'·34E Q (6) + L Fl 15s; *Bell.*
E Docking ⚲ 53°09'·82N 00°50'·39E Fl R 2·5s.
N Race ▲ 53°14'·98N 00°43'·87E Fl G 5s; *Bell.*
N Docking ⚑ 53°14'·82N 00°41'·49E Q.
Scott Patch ⚑ 53°11'·12N 00°36'·39E VQ (3) 5s.
S Inner Dowsing ⚑ 53°12'·12N 00°33'·69E Q (6) + L Fl 15s; *Bell.*
Boygrift Tower ⌕ 53°17'·63N 00°19'·24E Fl (2) 10s 12m 5M.
Burnham Flats ⚑ 53°07'·53N 00°34'·89E Q (9) 15s; *Bell.*

▶ **THE WASH**

West Ridge ⚑ 53°19'·06N 00°44'·47E Q (9) 15s.
Lynn Knock ▲ 53°04'·37N 00°27'·19E QG.
N Well ⚑ 53°03'·02N 00°27'·90E L Fl 10s; *Whis*; ***Racon (T) 10M***.
Woolpack ⚲ 53°02'·68N 00°31'·45E Fl R 10s.
Roaring Middle ⚏ 52°58'·64N 00°21'·08E L Fl 10s 7m 8M.

▶ **CORK HOLE/KING'S LYNN**

Sunk ⚑ 52°56'·29N 00°23'·40E Q (9) 15s.
Seal Sand ⚑ 52°56'·00N 00°20'·00E Q; *Bell.*
No 2 ⚲ 52°55'·00N 00°24'·00E. Fl (2) R 6s.
No. 3 ▲ 52°55'·00N 00°23'·50E Fl (2) G 6s.
No. 5 ⚑ 52°54'·00N 00°23'·95E Q (3) 10s.
No. 7 ▲ 52°53'·20N 00°23'·75E Fl G 5s.
Mid Stylemans ▲ 52°52'·63N 00°23'·17E QG.
No. 8 ⚲ 52°51'·88N 00°22'·54E Fl (2) R 6s.
No. 9 ▲ 52°52'·09N 00°22'·58E Fl (2) G 6s.
No. 11 ▲ 52°51'·83N 00°22'·10E Fl G 3s.
No. 13 ▲ 52°51'·45N 00°22'·40E Fl G 5s.
No. 15 ▲ 52°50'·38N 00°22'·44E QG.
'E' ⚑ 52°48'·15N 00°21'·48E Fl Y 3s 3m 2M.
No. 17 ▲ 52°50'·30N 00°22'·14E Fl (3) G 5s.
No. 21 ▲ 52°50'·24N 00°21'·58E Fl (2) G 4s.
West Stones ⚑ 52°49'·72N 00°21'·15E Q 3m 2M.
West Bank ☆ 52°47'·46N 00°22'·04E Fl Y 2s 3m 4M.
King's Lynn W Bk Ferry Jetty ⚓ 52°45'·37N 00°23'·37E QG.

▶ **WISBECH CHANNEL/RIVER NENE**

(Note: Beacons are moved as required.)
Bar Flat ⚑ 52°55'·25N 00°16'·72E Q (3) 10s.
Westmark Knock ⚲ 52°52'·75N 00°13'·41E Fl (2) R 8s.
Kerr ⚑ 52°51'·74N 00°13'·59E VQ.
Big Tom ⚑ 52°49'·57N 00°13'·11E Fl (2) R 10s.
West End ⚑ 52°49'·39N 00°12'·90E Fl (3) G 5s 3M; B mast.
Marsh ⚑ 52°49'·01N 00°12'·89E QR.
Scottish Sluice West Bk ⚓ 52°48'·52N 00°12'·62E FG 9m.

Masts on W side of River Nene to Wisbech carry FG Lts and those on E side QR or FR Lts.

▶ **FREEMAN CHANNEL**

Boston Roads ⚲ 52°57'·66N 00°16'·04E L Fl 10s.
Boston No. 1 ▲ 52°57'·88N 00°15'·16E Fl G 3s.
Alpha ⚲ 52°57'·65N 00°14'·99E Fl R 3s.
No. 3 ▲ 52°58'·08N 00°14'·07E Fl G 6s.
No. 5 ▲ 52°58'·51N 00°12'·72E Fl G 3s.

Freeman Inner 52°58'·59N 00°11'·36E Q (9) 15s.
Delta 52°58'·38N 00°11'·25E Fl R 6s.

▶ BOSTON LOWER ROAD

Boston No. 7 52°58'·62N 00°10'·00E Fl G 3s.
Boston No. 9 52°57'·58N 00°08'·36E Fl G 3s.
Black Buoy 52°56'·82N 00°07'·74E Fl (2) R 6s.
Boston No.11N 52°56'·66N 00°06'·55E Fl (2) G 6s.
Boston No.13N 52°56'·52N 00°06'·55E Fl G 3s.
Boston No.15 52°56'·34N 00°05'·95E Fl (2) G 6s.
Welland 52°56'·08N 00°05'·27E QR 5m.

Tabs Head 52°56'·00N 00°04'·91E Q WG 4m 1M; R □ on W mast; vis: W shore-251°, G251°-shore.

▶ BOSTON, NEW CUT AND RIVER WITHAM

Ent N side, Dollypeg 52°56'·13N 00°05'·03E QG 4m 1M; B △ on Bn.

New Cut 52°55'·98N 00°04'·67E Fl G 3s; △ on pile.

New Cut Ldg Lts 240°. Front, No. 1 52°55'·85N 00°04'·40E F 5m 5M. Rear, 90m from front, F 8m 5M.

▶ WELLAND CUT/RIVER WELLAND

SE side ☆ 52°55'·72E 00°04'·68E Iso R 2s; NW side Iso G 2s. Lts QR (to port) and QG (to stbd) mark the chan upstream.

(Direction of buoyage North to South)

▶ BOSTON DEEP/WAINFLEET ROADS

Wainfleet Range Control twr ☆ 53°03'·66N 00°14'·11E UQ R (occas), with FR on Trs SW & NE.

Scullridge 52°59'·76N 00°13'·86E.
Friskney 53°00'·59N 00°16'·76E.
Long Sand 53°01'·27N 00°18'·30E.
Pompey 53°02'·19N 00°19'·26E.
Swatchway 53°03'·81N 00°19'·70E.

Off Ingoldmells Point ☆ 53°12'·49N 00°25'·85E Fl Y 5s 22m 5M; Mast; *Mo (U) 30s.*

Boygrift twr 53°17'·63N 00°19'·24E Fl (2) 10s 12m 5M.

THE WASH TO THE RIVER HUMBER

(Direction of buoyage South to North)

Dudgeon 53°16'·62N 01°16'·90E Q (9) 15s 7M; ***Racon (O) 10M***; *Whis.*

E Dudgeon 53°19'·72N 00°58'·69E Q (3) 10s; *Bell.*
Mid Outer Dowsing 53°24'·82N 01°07'·79E Fl (3) G 10s; *Bell.*
N Outer Dowsing 53°33'·52N 00°59'·59E Q.

B.1D Platform Dowsing 53°33'·68N 00°52'·63E Fl (2) 10s 28m **22M**; Morse (U) R 15s 28m 3M; *Horn (2) 60s*; ***Racon (T) 10M.***

▶ RIVER HUMBER APPROACHES

W Ridge 53°19'·04N 00°44'·50E Q (9) 15s.
Inner Dowsing 53°19'·10N 00°34'·80E Q (3) 10s 7M, ***Racon (T) 10M***; *Horn 60s.*
Protector 53°24'·84N 00°25'·12E Fl R 2·5s.
DZ No. 4 53°27'·15N 00°19'·06E Fl Y 5s.
DZ No. 3 53°29'·30N 00°19'·21E Fl Y 2·5s.
Rosse Spit 53°30'·41N 00°16'·91E Fl (2) R 5s.
Haile Sand No. 2 53°32'·42N 00°13'·18E Fl (3) R 10s.

Humber 53°38'·83N 00°20'·17E L Fl 10s 7M; *Horn (2) 30s*; ***Racon (T) 7M.***

N Binks 53°36'·01N 00°18'·28E Fl G 4s.
S Binks 53°34'·74N 00°16'·55E Fl G 2s.

SPURN 53°33'·56N 00°14'·20E Q (3) 10s 10m 8M; *Horn 20s*; ***Racon (M) 5M.***

SE CHEQUER 53°33'·38N 00°12'·55E VQ (6) + L Fl 10s 6m 6M; *Horn 30s.*

Chequer No. 3 53°33'·07N 00°10'·63E Q (6) + L Fl 15s.
No 2B 53°32'·33N 00°09'·10E Fl R 4s.

Tetney 53°32'·35N 00°06'·76E 2 VQ Y (vert); *Horn Mo (A)60s*; QY on 290m floating hose.

▶ RIVERHUMBER/GRIMSBY/HULL

Binks No. 3A 53°33'·92N 00°07'·43E Fl G 4s.
Spurn Pt 53°34'·37N 00°06'·47E Fl G 3s 11m 5M.
BULL 53°33'·54N 00°05'·70E VQ 8m 6M; *Horn (2) 20s.*
North Fort 53°33'·80N 00°04'·19E Q.
South Fort 53°33'·65N 00°03'·96E Q (6) + L Fl 15s.
Haile Sand Fort ☆ 53°32'·07N 00°01'·99E Fl R 5s 21m 3M.
Haile Chan No. 4 53°33'·64N 00°02'·84E Fl R 4s.
Middle No. 7 53°35'·80N 00°01'·50E VQ (6) + L Fl 10s; *Horn 20s.*

Grimsby Royal Dock ent E side ☆ 53°35'·08N 00°04'·04W Fl (2) R 6s 10m 8M; Dn.

Killingholme Lts in line 292°. Front, 53°38'·78N 00°12'·96W Iso R 2s 10m 14M. Rear, 189m from front, Oc R 4s 21m 14M.

Immingham Oil Terminal SE end ☆ 53°37'·70N 00°09'·42W 2 QR (vert) 8m 5M; *Horn Mo (N) 30s.*

Clay Huts No.13 53°38'·54N 00°11'·34W Iso 2s 5m 9M.
Sand End No.16 53°42'·62N 00°14'·50W Fl R 4s 5m 3M.
Hebbles No. 21 53°44'·03N 00°15'·99W Fl G 1·3s.
Lower W Middle No. 24 53°44'·28N 00°18'·35W Fl R 4s.
Hull Marina ☆ 53°44'·24N 00°20'·16W 2 FG (vert).

RIVER HUMBER TO WHITBY

Canada & Giorgios Wreck 53°42'·37N 00°07'·16E VQ (3) 5s.
Hornsea Sewer Outfall 53°55'·01N 00°08'·41W Fl Y 20s.
Atwick Sewer Outfall 53°57'·14N 00°10'·34W Fl Y 10s.

▶ BRIDLINGTON

SW Smithic 54°02'·41N 00°09'·21W Q (9) 15s.

N Pier Hd ☆ 54°04'·77N 00°11'·19W Fl 2s 12m 9M; *Horn 60s*; (Tidal Lts) Fl R or Fl G.

N Smithic 54°06'·22N 00°03'·90W VQ; *Bell.*

Flamborough Hd ☆ 54°06'·98N 00°04'·96W Fl (4) 15s 65m **24M**; W ○ twr; *Horn (2) 90s.*

▶ FILEY/SCARBOROUGH/WHITBY

Filey Brigg 54°12'·74N 00°14'·60W Q (3) 10s; *Bell.*
Scarborough E Pier Hd ☆ 54°16'·88N 00°23'·36W QG 8m 3M.

Scarborough Pier 54°16'·91N 00°23'·40W ☆ Iso 5s 17m 9M; W ○ twr; vis: 219°-039°; vis: 233°-030°; (tide sigs); *Dia 60s.*

Scalby Ness Diffusers 54°18'·59N 00°23'·38W Fl R 5s.
Whitby 54°30'·33N 00°36'·58W Q; *Bell.*

Whitby High ☆ Ling Hill 54°28'·67N 00°34'·10W Fl WR 5s 73m **18M**, R16M; W 8-sided twr and dwellings; vis: R128°-143°, W143°-319°.

Whitby E Pier Hd ☆ 54°29'·64N 00°36'·74W FR 14m 3M; R twr.

Whitby W Pier Hd ☆ 54°29'·65N 00°36'·80W FG (occas) 14m 3M; G twr; *Horn 30s.*

PLOT WAYPOINTS ON YOUR CHART BEFORE USING THEM

WHITBY TO RIVER TYNE

▶ RUNSWICK/REDCAR

Runswick Bay Pier ☆ 54°31'·99N 00°44'·95W 2 FY (occas).

Boulby Outfall 54°34'·52N 00°48'·29W Fl (4) Y 10s.

Redcar Outfall 54°36'·66N 01°00'·37W Fl Y 10s.

Salt Scar 54°38'·12N 01°00'·12W VQ; *Bell.*

Luff Way Ldg Lts 197°. Front, 54°37'·10N 01°03'·71W on Esplanade, FR 8m 7M; vis: 182°-212°. Rear, 115m from front, FR 12m 7M; vis: 182°-212°.

High Stone. Lade Way Ldg Lts 247°. Front, 54°37'·15N 01°03'·92W Oc R 2·5s 9m 7M. Rear, 43m from front, Oc R 2·5s 11m 7M; vis: 232°-262°.

▶ TEES APPROACHES/HARTLEPOOL

Tees Fairway 54°40'·94N 01°06'·48W Iso 4s 8m 8M; ***Racon (B) unknown range***; *Horn (1) 5s.*

Tees N (Fairway) 54°40'·36N 01°07'·19W Q.G.

Tees S (Fairway) 54°40'·29N 01°06'·98W Q.R.

Bkwtr Hd S Gare ☆ 54°38'·85N 01°08'·27W Fl WR 12s 16m **W20M, R17M**; W○ twr; vis: W020°-274°, R274°-357°; Sig Stn; *Horn 30s.*

Ldg Lts 210·1° Front, 54°37'·22N 01°10'·20W FR 18m 13M. **Rear**, 560m from front, FR 20m **16M**.

Longscar 54°40'·86N 01°09'·89W Q (3) 10s; *Bell.*

The Heugh ☆ 54°40'·09N 01°47'·98W Fl (2) 10s 19m **19M**; W twr.

Hartlepool Old Pier Hd ☆ 54°41'·60N 01°11'·09W Q WG 13m 7M; vis: W317°-325°, G325°-317°.

W Hbr N Pier Hd ☆ 54°41'·31N 01°11'·57W Oc G 5s 12m 2M.

Hartlepool Marina Lock Dir Lt 308° 54°41'·45N 01°11'·92W Dir Fl WRG 2s 6m 3M; vis: G305·5°-307°, W307°-309°, R309°-310·5°.

▶ SEAHAM/SUNDERLAND

Seaham N Pier Hd ☆ 54°50'·26N 01°19'·26W Fl G 10s 12m 5M; W col, B bands; *Dia 30s.*

Sunderland Roker Pier Hd ☆ 54°55'·28N 01°21'·15W Fl 5s 25m **23M**; W □ twr, 3 R bands and cupola: vis: 211°-357°; *Siren 20s.*

Old N Pier Hd ☆ 54°55'·13N 01°21'·61W QG 12m 8M; Y twr; *Horn 10s.*

Whitburn Steel 54°56'·30N 01°20'·87W.

Whitburn Firing Range ☆ 54°57'·21N 01°21'·38W and 54°57'·76N 01°21'·35W both FR when firing is taking place.

DZ 54°57'·04N 01°18'·90W and 54°58'·61N 01°19'·90W, both Fl Y 2·5s.

▶ TYNE ENTRANCE/NORTH SHIELDS

Ent North Pier Hd ☆ 55°00'·88N 01°24'·18W Fl (3) 10s 26m 26M; Gy □ twr, W lantern; *Horn 10s.*

South Pier Hd ☆ 55°00'·68N 01°24'·07W Oc WRG 10s 15m W13M, R9M, G8M; Gy □ twr, R&W lantern; vis: W075°-161°, G161°-179° over Bellhues rock, W179°-255°, R255°-075°; *Bell (1) 10s.*

Herd Groyne Hd Ldg Lt 249°. 55°00'·49N 01°25'·44W Oc RG 10s 13m, R11M, G11M; R pile structure, R&W lantern; vis: G224°-246·5°, R251·5°-277°; FR (unintens) 080°-224°. Same structure Dir Oc 10s 14m **19M**; vis: W246·5°°-251·5°; *Bell (1) 5s.*

Royal Quay Marina ent (SS Tfc ⊙) 54°59'·78N 01°26'·98E.

Saint Peter's Marina ent (SS Tfc ⊙) 54°57'·93N 01°34'·35E.

RIVER TYNE TO BERWICK-ON-TWEED

▶ CULLERCOATS/BLYTH/NEWBIGGIN

Cullercoats Ldg Lts 256°. Front, 55°02'·06N 01°25'·91W FR 27m 3M. Rear, 38m from front, FR 35m 3M.

Blyth Ldg Lts 324°. Front, 55°07'·42N 01°29'·82W F Bu 11m 10M. Rear, 180m from front, F Bu 17m 10M. Both Or on twr.

Blyth Fairway 55°06'·59N 01°28'·60W Fl G 3s; *Bell.*

Blyth E Pier H1 Hd ☆ 55°06'·98N 01°29'·37W 2 FR (vert) 7m 8M.

Newbiggin Outfall 55°10'·13N 01°29'·60W Fl Y 5s.

Newbiggin Bkwtr Hd ☆ 55°10'·99N 01°30'·37W Fl G 10s 4M.

▶ COQUET ISLAND/WARKWORTH AND AMBLE

Coquet ☆ 55°20'·03N 01°32'·39W Fl (3) WR 30s 25m **W23M, R19M;** W□ twr, turreted parapet, lower half Gy; vis: R330°-140°, W140°-163°, R163°-180°, W180°-330°; sector boundaries are indeterminate and may appear as Alt WR; *Horn 30s.*

Pan Rocks Outfall 55°20'·32N 01°33'·74W Fl Y; *Bell.*

Amble S Pier Head ☆ 55°20'·34N 01°34'·26W Fl R 5s 9m 5M.

N Pier Head ☆ 55°20'·39N 01°34'·25W Fl G 6s 12m 6M.

▶ BOULMER/CRASTER/NEWTON HAVEN/ BEADNELL BAY

Boulmer Haven 55°25'·00N 01°34'·93W.

Craster Harbour 55°28'·37N 01°35'·59W (unmarked).

Newton Rock 55°32'·15N 01°35'·85W.

▶ N SUNDERLAND (SEAHOUSES) BAMBURGH/ FARNE ISLANDS

The Falls 55°34'·61N 01°37'·12W Fl R 2·5s.

N Sunderland NW Pier Hd ☆ 55°35'·03N 01°38'·94W FG 11m 3M; W twr; vis: 159°-294°; Tfc Sigs; *Siren 90s* (occas).

N. Sunderland Bkwtr Hd ☆ 55°35'·05N 01°38'·89W Fl R 2·5s 6m.

Shoreston Outcars 55°35'·88N 01°39'·34W QR.

Bamburgh Black Rocks Point ☆ 55°36'·99N 01°43'·45W Oc(2) WRG 8s 12m **W14M**, R11M, G11M; W bldg; vis: G122°-165°, W165°-175°, R175°-191°, W191°-238°, R238°-275°, W275°-289°, G289°-300°.

Inner Farne ☆ 55°36'·92N 01°39'·35W Fl (2) WR 15s 27m W10M, R7M; W○ twr; vis: R119°-280°, W280°-119°.

Longstone ☆ W side 55°38'·62N 01°36'·65W Fl 20s 23m **24M**; R twr, W band; *Horn (2) 60s.*

Swedman 55°37'·65N 01°41'·63W Fl G 2·5s.

▶ HOLY ISLAND

Goldstone 55°40'·22N 01°43'·69W.

Ridge 55°39'·70N 01°45'·97W Q (3) 10s.

Triton Shoal 55°39'·61N 01°46'·59W QG.

Plough Rock 55°40'·24N 01°46'·00W.

Old Law E Bn ☆ (Guile Pt) 55°39'·49N 01°47'·60W Oc WRG 6s 9m 4M; vis: G179°-259°, W259°-261°, R261°-shore.

Heugh ☆ 55°40'·09N 01°47'·99W Oc WRG 6s 24m 5M; vis: G135°-308°, W308°-311°, R311°-shore.

Plough Seat 55°40'·37N 01°44'·97W QR.

▶ BERWICK-ON-TWEED

Bkwtr Hd ☆ 55°45'·88N 01°59'·06W Fl 5s 15m 6M; vis: 201°-009°, (obscured 155°-201°); W ○ twr, R cupola and base; FG (same twr) 8m 1M; vis G009°-155°.

9.5.5 PASSAGE INFORMATION

For directions and pilotage refer to: Tidal Havens of the Wash and Humber (Imray/Irving) carefully documents the hbrs of this little-frequented cruising ground. N from R Humber see the Royal Northumberland YC's Sailing Directions, Humber to Rattray Head. The Admiralty Pilot North Sea (West) covers the whole coast. North Sea Passage Pilot (Imray/Navin) goes as far N as Cromer and across to Den Helder.

NORTH NORFOLK COAST (charts 1503, 108) The coast of N Norfolk is unfriendly in bad weather, with no hbr accessible when there is any N in the wind. The hbrs all dry, and seas soon build up in the entrances or over the bars, some of which are dangerous even in a moderate breeze and an ebb tide. But in settled weather and moderate offshore winds it is a peaceful area to explore, particularly for boats which can take the ground. At Blakeney and Wells (see 9.5.6 and 9.5.7) chans shift almost every year, so local knowledge is essential and may best be acquired in advance from the HM; or in the event by following a friendly FV of suitable draft.

Haisborough Sand (buoyed) lies parallel to and 8M off the Norfolk coast at Happisburgh lt ho, with depths of less than 1m in many places, and drying 0·4m near the mid-point. The shoal is steep-to, on its NE side in particular, and there are tidal eddies. Even a moderate sea or swell breaks on the shallower parts. There are dangerous wks near the S end. Haisborough Tail and Hammond Knoll (with wk depth 1.6m) lie to the E of S end of Haisborough Sand. Newarp lt F is 5M SE. Similar banks lie parallel to and up to 60M off the coast.

▶ *The streams follow the generally NW/SE direction of the coast and offshore chans. But in the outer chans the stream is somewhat rotatory: when changing from SE-going to NW-going it sets SW, and when changing from NW-going to SE-going it sets NE, across the shoals. Close S of Haisborough Sand the SE-going stream begins at HW Immingham –0030; the NW-going at HW Immingham +0515, sp rates up to 2·5kn. It is possible to carry a fair tide from Gt Yarmouth to the Wash.* ◀

▶ *If proceeding direct from Cromer to the Humber, pass S of Sheringham Shoal (buoyed) where the ESE-going stream begins at HW Immingham –0225, and the WNW-going at +0430.* ◀ Proceed to NE of Blakeney Overfalls and Docking Shoal, and to SW of Race Bank, so as to fetch Inner Dowsing lt tr (lt, fog sig). Thence pass E of Protector Overfalls, and steer for Rosse Spit buoy at SE ent to R Humber (9.5.10).

THE WASH (charts 108,1200) The Wash is formed by the estuaries of the rivers Great Ouse, Nene, Welland and Witham; it is an area of shifting sands, most of which dry. ▶ *Important features are the strong tidal streams, the low-lying shore, and the often poor vis. Keep a careful watch on the echo sounder, because buoys may (or may not) have been moved to accommodate changes in the chan. Near North Well, the in-going stream begins at HW Immingham –0430, and the out-going at HW Immingham +0130, sp rates about 2kn. The in-going stream is usually stronger than the out-going, but its duration is less. Prolonged NE winds cause an in-going current, which can increase the rate and duration of the in-going stream and raise the water level at the head of the estuary. Do not attempt entry to the rivers too early on the flood, which runs hard in the rivers.* ◀ North Well SWM lt buoy and Roaring Middle lt F are the keys to entering the Wash from N or E. But from the E it is also possible to appr via a shallow route N of Stiffkey Overfalls and Bridgirdle PHM buoy; thence via Sledway and Woolpack PHM lt buoy to North Well and into Lynn Deeps. Near north end of Lynn Deeps there are overfalls over Lynn Knock at sp tides. For King's Lynn (9.5.8) follow either the buoyed/lit Cork Hole or Bulldog chan. For R Nene (Wisbech) (9.5.8) follow the Wisbech Chan. Boston (9.5.9) and R Welland are reached via Freeman Chan, westward from Roaring Middle; or via Boston Deep, all lit.

The NW shore of The Wash is fronted by mudflats extending 2–3M offshore and drying more than 4m; a bombing range is marked by Y bns and buoys. Wainfleet Swatchway should only be used in good vis; the buoyed chan shifts constantly, and several shoals (charted depths unreliable) off Gibraltar Pt obstruct access to Boston Deep. For Wainfleet, see 9.5.9.

THE WASH TO THE RIVER HUMBER (charts 108, 107) Inner Dowsing is a narrow N/S sandbank with a least depth of 1·2m, 8M offshore between Skegness and Mablethorpe. There are overfalls off the W side of the bank at the N end. Inner Dowsing lt float (fog sig) is 1M NE of the bank.

In the outer approaches to The Wash and R. Humber there are many offlying banks, but few of them are of direct danger to yachts. The sea however breaks on some of them in bad weather, when they should be avoided. Fishing vessels may be encountered, and there are many oil/gas installations offshore (see over).

RIVER HUMBER (charts *109*, 1188, 3497) R. Humber is formed by R. Ouse and R. Trent, which meet 13M above Kingston-upon-Hull. It is commercially important and gives access to these rivers and inland waterways; it also drains most of Yorkshire and the Midlands. Where the Humber estuary reaches the sea between Northcoates Pt and Spurn Hd it is 4M wide. A VTS scheme is in operation to regulate commercial shipping in the Humber, Ouse and Trent and provide full radar surveillance. Yachts are advised to monitor the appropriate Humber VTS frequency.

Approaching from the S, a yacht should make good Rosse Spit and then Haile Sand No 2, both PHM lt buoys, before altering westward leading SW of Bull Ch.

If bound to/from the N, avoid The Binks, a shoal (dries 1·6m in places) extending 3M E from Spurn Hd, with a rough sea when wind is against tide. Depths offshore are irregular and subject to frequent change; it would be best to round the S Binks SPM buoy, unless in calm conditions and with local knowledge.

Haile Sand and Bull Sand Forts are both conspic to the SW of Spurn Head; beyond them it is advisable to keep just outside one of the buoyed chans, since shoals are liable to change. Hawke Chan (later Sunk) is the main dredged chan to the N. Haile Chan favours the S side and Grimsby. Bull Chan takes a middle course before merging with Haile Chan. There are good yachting facilities at Grimsby and Hull (9.5.10). ⚓ inside Spurn Head.

▶ *Streams are strong, even fierce at sp; local info suggests that they are stronger than shown in 9.5.3, which is based upon NP 251 (Admiralty Tidal Stream Atlas). 5ca S of Spurn Hd the flood sets NW from about HW Immingham –0520, sp*

5

rate 3·5kn; the ebb sets SE from about HW Immingham, sp rate 4kn. The worst seas are experienced in NW gales against a strong flood tide. 10M E of Spurn Hd the tidal streams are not affected by the river; relative to HW Immingham, the S-going stream begins at –0455, and the N-going at +0130. Nearer the entrance the direction of the S-going stream becomes more W'ly, and that of the N-going stream more E'ly. ◀

R HUMBER TO HARTLEPOOL (charts 107, 121, 129, 134) Air gunnery and bombing practice is carried out 3M off Cowden, 17M S of Bridlington. The range is marked by 6 SPM buoys; 3 seaward ones Fl Y 10s, the 3 inner ones Fl Y 2s or 5s. Bridlington Bay (chart 1882) is clear of dangers apart from Smithic Shoals (marked by N and S cardinal lt buoys), about 3M off Bridlington (9.5.11); the seas break on these shoals in strong N or E winds even at HW.

Flamborough Head (lt, fog sig, RC) is a steep, W cliff with conspic lt ho on summit. The lt may be obsc by cliffs when close inshore. An old lt ho, also conspic, is 2½m WNW. ▶ *Tides run hard around the Head which, in strong winds against a sp tide, is best avoided by 2M.* ◀ From here the coast runs NW, with no offshore dangers until Filey Brigg where rky ledges extend 5ca ESE, marked by an ECM lt buoy. There is anch in Filey B (9.5.11) in N or offshore winds. NW of Filey Brigg beware Old Horse Rks and foul ground 5ca offshore; maintain this offing past Scarborough (9.5.12) to Whitby High lt. Off Whitby (9.5.13) beware Whitby Rk and The Scar (dry in places) to E of hbr, and Upgang Rks (dry in places) 1M to WNW; swell breaks heavily on all these rocks.

From Whitby to Hartlepool (9.5.14) there are no dangers more than 1M offshore. Runswick B (9.5.13 and AC 1612), 5M NW of Whitby, provides anch in winds from S and W but is dangerous in onshore winds. 2½M further NW the little hbr of Staithes is more suitable for yachts which can take the ground, but only in good weather and offshore winds.

Redcliff, dark red and 205m high is a conspic feature of this coast which, along to Hunt Cliff, is prone to landslides and is fringed with rky ledges which dry for about 3ca off. There is a conspic radio mast 4ca SSE of Redcliff. Off Redcar and Coatham beware Salt Scar and West Scar, drying rky ledges lying 1 – 8ca offshore. Other ledges lie close SE and S of Salt Scar which has NCM lt buoy. Between R. Tees (9.5.13) and Hartlepool beware Long Scar, detached rky ledge (dries 2m) with extremity marked by ECM lt buoy. Tees and Hartlepool Bays are exposed to strong E/SE winds. The R. Tees and Middlesbrough are highly industrialised at Hartlepool there is a centre specialising in the maintenance and restoration of Tall Ships.

HARTLEPOOL TO COQUET ISLAND (charts 134, 152, 156) From The Heugh an offing of 1M clears all dangers until past Seaham (9.5.15) and approaching Sunderland (9.5.16), where White Stones, rky shoals with depth 1·8m, lie 1·75M SSE of Roker Pier lt ho, and Hendon Rk, depth 0·9m, lies 1·25M SE of the lt ho. 1M N of Sunderland is Whitburn Steel, a rky ledge with less than 2m over it; a dangerous wreck (buoyed) lies 1ca SE of it. A firing range at Souter Pt is marked by R flags (R lts) when active. Along this stretch of coast industrial smoke haze may reduce vis and obscure lights.

The coast N of Tynemouth (9.5.17) is foul, and on passage to Blyth (9.5.18) it should be given an offing of 1M. 3·5M N of Tynemouth is St Mary's Island (with disused lt ho), joined to mainland by causeway. The small, drying hbr of Seaton Sluice, 1M NW of St Mary's Island, is accessible only in offshore winds via a narrow ent.

Proceeding N from Blyth, keep well seaward of The Sow and Pigs rks, and set course to clear Newbiggin Pt and Beacon Pt by about 1M. There are conspic measured mile bns here. Near Beacon Pt are conspic chys of aluminium smelter and power stn. 2M NNW of Beacon Pt is Snab Pt where rks extend 3ca seaward. Further offshore Cresswell Skeres, rky patches with depth 3m, lie about 1·5M NNE of Snab Pt.

COQUET ISLAND TO FARNE ISLANDS (chart 156) Coquet Is (lt, fog sig) lies about 5ca offshore at SE end of Alnmouth B, and nearly 1M NNE of Hauxley Pt, off which dangerous rks extend 6ca offshore, drying 1·9m. On passage, normally pass 1M E of Coquet Is in the W sector of the lt. ▶ *Coquet chan may be used in good vis by day; but it is only 2ca wide, not buoyed, has least depth of 0·3m near the centre; and the stream runs strongly: S-going from HW Tyne – 0515 and N-going from HW Tyne + 0045.* ◀ In S or W winds, there are good anchs in Coquet Road, W and NW of the Island.

Amble (Warkworth) hbr ent (9.5.19) is about 1M W of Coquet Is, and 1·5M SE of Warkworth Castle (conspic). 4ca NE and ENE of ent is Pan Bush, rky shoal with least depth of 0·3m on which dangerous seas can build in any swell. The bar has varying depths, down to less than 1m. The entrance is dangerous in strong winds from N/E when broken water may extend to Coquet Is. Once inside, the hbr is safe.

Between Coquet Is and the Farne Is, 19M to N, keep at least 1M offshore to avoid various dangers. To seaward, Craster Skeres lie 5M E of Castle Pt, and Dicky Shad and Newton Skere lie 1·75M and 4·5M E of Beadnell Pt; these are three rky banks on which the sea breaks heavily in bad weather. For Newton Haven and N Sunderland (Seahouses), see 9.5.19.

FARNE ISLANDS (charts 111, 160) The coast between N Sunderland Pt (Snook) and Holy Island, 8M NW, has fine hill (Cheviots) scenery fronted by dunes and sandy beaches. The Farne Is and offlying shoals extend 4·5M offshore, and are a mini-cruising ground well worth visiting in good weather. The islands are a bird sanctuary, owned and operated by the National Trust, with large colonies of sea birds and grey seals. AC 111 is essential.

Inner Sound separates the islands from the mainland. In good conditions it is a better N/S route than keeping outside the whole group; but the stream runs at 3kn at sp, and with strong wind against tide there is rough water. If course is set outside Farne Is, pass 1M E of Longstone (lt, fog sig) to clear Crumstone Rk 1M to S, and Knivestone (dries 3·6m) and Whirl Rks (depth 0·6m) respectively 5 and 6ca NE of Longstone lt ho. The sea breaks on these rks.

The islands, rks and shoals are divided by Staple Sound, running NW/SE, into an inner and outer group. The former comprises Inner Farne, W and E Wideopens and Knock's Reef. Inner Farne (lt) is the innermost Is; close NE there is anch called The Kettle, sheltered except from NW, but anch out of stream close to The Bridges connecting Knock's Reef and W Wideopen. 1M NW of Inner Farne Is and separated by Farne Sound, which runs NE/SW, lies the Megstone, a rk

5m high. Beware Swedman reef (dries 0·5m), marked by SHM buoy 4ca WSW of Megstone.

The outer group of Islands comprises Staple and Brownsman Islands, N and S Wamses, the Harcars and Longstone. There is occas anch between Staple and Brownsman Is. ▶ *Piper Gut and Crafords Gut may be negotiated in calm weather and near HW, stemming the S-going stream.* ◀

HOLY ISLAND TO BERWICK (charts 1612, 111, 160) ▶ *Near the Farne Is and Holy Is the SE-going stream begins at HW Tyne –0430, and the NW-going at HW Tyne +0130. Sp rates are about 2.5kn in Inner Sound, 4kn in Staple Sound and about 3·5kn 1M NE of Longstone, decreasing to seaward. There is an eddy S of Longstone on NW-going stream.* ◀

Holy Is (or Lindisfarne; 9.5.20) lies 6M WNW of Longstone, and is linked to mainland by a causeway covered at HW. There is a good anch on S side (chart 1612) with conspic daymarks and dir lts. The castle and a W obelisk at Emanuel Head are also conspic. ▶ *The stream runs strongly in and out of hbr, W-going from HW Tyne + 0510, and E-going from HW Tyne –0045. E of Holy Is, Goldstone chan runs N/S between Goldstone Rk (dries) SHM buoy on E side and Plough Seat Reef and Plough Rk (both dry) on W side, with PHM buoy.* ◀

Berwick Bay has some offlying shoals. Berwick-upon-Tweed (9.5.21) is easily visible against the low shoreline, which rises again to high cliffs further north. The hbr entrance is restricted by a shallow bar, dangerous in onshore winds.

OIL AND GAS INSTALLATIONS Any yacht going offshore in the N Sea is likely to encounter oil or gas installations. These are shown on Admiralty charts, where scale permits; the position of mobile rigs is updated in weekly NMs. Safety zones of radius 500m are established round all permanent platforms, mobile exploration rigs, and tanker loading moorings, as described in the Annual Summary of Admiralty Notices to Mariners No 20. Some of these platforms are close together or inter-linked. Unauthorised vessels, including yachts, must not enter these zones except in emergency or due to stress of weather.

Platforms show a main lt, Fl Mo (U) 15s 15M. In addition secondary lts, Fl Mo (U) R 15s 2M, synchronised with the main lt, may mark projections at each corner of the platform if not marked by a W lt. The fog signal is Horn Mo (U) 30s. See the Admiralty List of Lights and Fog Signals, Vol A.

NORTH SEA PASSAGES See 9.0.8 for Distances across the North Sea. There are also further passage Notes in 9.4.5 for the Southern North Sea TSS; in 9.6.5 for crossing to Norway and the Baltic; in 9.16.5 for crossings from the Frisian Is and German Bight; and in 9.17.5 for crossings from Belgium and the Netherlands.

HARTLEPOOL TO SOUTHERN NETHERLANDS (charts 2182A, 1191, *1190*, 1503, 1408, 1610, 3371, 110) From abeam Whitby the passage can, theoretically, be made on one direct course, but this would conflict with oil/gas activities and platforms including Rough and Amethyst fields off Humber, Hewett off Cromer and very extensive fields further offshore. Commercial, oil-rig support and fishing vessels may be met S of Flamborough Hd and particularly off NE Norfolk where it is advisable to follow an inshore track.

After passing Flamborough Hd, Dowsing B1D, Dudgeon lt buoy and Newarp lt F, either:

Proceed SxE'ly to take departure from the Outer Gabbard; thence cross N Hinder South TSS at right angles before heading for Roompotsluis via Middelbank and subsequent buoyed chan.

Or set course ESE from the vicinity of Cross Sand lt buoy and Smith's Knoll, so as to cross the N/S deep-water traffic routes to the E (see 9.16.5). Thence alter SE toward Hoek van Holland, keeping N of Maas Approaches TSS.

HARTLEPOOL TO THE GERMAN BIGHT (charts 2182A, 1191, 266, 1405) Taking departure eastward from abeam Whitby High lt, skirt the SW Patch off Dogger Bank, keeping clear S of Gordon Gas Field and then N of German Bight W Approach TSS. Thence head for the Elbe or Helgoland; the latter may also serve as a convenient haven in order to adjust the passage for Elbe tides and streams (9.16.5), without greatly increasing passage distance. ▶ *Tidal streams are less than 1kn away from the coast and run E/W along much of the route.* ◀

5

NOTES

9.5.6 BLAKENEY

Norfolk **52°59'·19N 00°57'·90E** (ent shifts) ❀❀◊◊✿✿✿

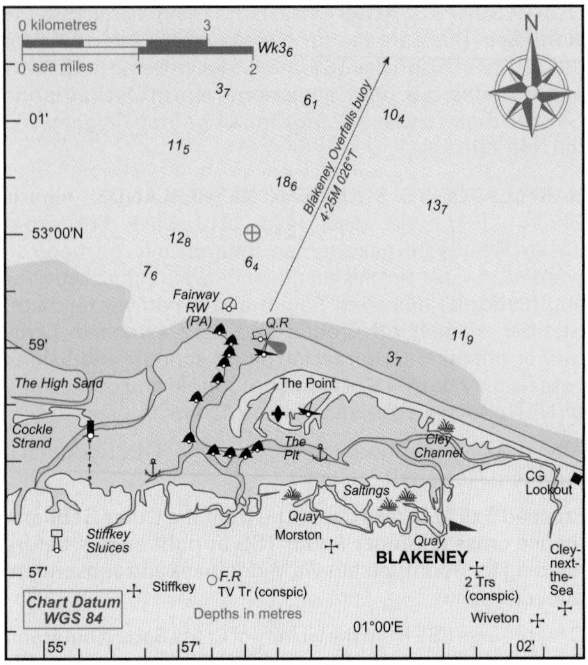
0 kilometres 3
0 sea miles 1 2
N
Wk3₆
01'
53°00'N
59'
57'
Blakeney Overfalls buoy 4·25M 026°T
Fairway RW (PA)
Q.R
The High Sand
Cockle Strand
The Point
The Pit
Cley Channel
CG Lookout
Saltings
Quay
Morston
Quay
BLAKENEY
Stiffkey Sluices
Stiffkey
F.R TV Tr (conspic)
2 Trs (conspic)
Cley-next-the-Sea
Wiveton
Chart Datum WGS 84
Depths in metres
01°00'E
55'
57'
02'

CHARTS AC 1190, 108; Imray C28; Stanfords 19, 3; OS 133

TIDES –0445 Dover; ML Cromer 2·8; Duration 0530; Zone 0 (UT)

Standard Port IMMINGHAM (⟶)

Times				Height (metres)			
High Water		Low Water		MHWS	MHWN	MLWN	MLWS
0100	0700	0100	0700	7·3	5·8	2·6	0·9
1300	1900	1300	1900				
Differences BLAKENEY BAR (approx 52°59'N 00°59'E)							
+0035	+0025	+0030	+0040	–1·6	–1·3	No data	
BLAKENEY (approx 52°57'N 01°01'E)							
+0115	+0055	No data		–3·9	–3·8	No data	
CROMER							
+0050	+0030	+0050	+0130	–2·1	–1·7	–0·5	–0·1

SHELTER Very good. Entry, sp HW ±2, nps HW ±1½. But no access in fresh on-shore winds when conditions at the entrance deteriorate very quickly, especially on the ebb. Moorings in The Pit area dry out. Speed limit 8kn.

NAVIGATION WPT 53°00'·00N 00°58'·20E, approx 225° 1M to Fairway RW buoy which may not be on station or which may shift at entrance to channel. Large dangerous wreck, close E of entrance, marked by lit Q.R PHM buoy. The bar is shallow and shifts often. The channel is marked by unlit SHM buoys, relaid each spring. Strangers are best advised to follow local boats in. Beware mussel lays, drying, off Blakeney Spit.

LIGHTS AND MARKS Conspic marks: Blakeney and Langham churches; a chy on the house on Blakeney Pt neck; TV mast (R lts) approx 2M S of ent.

R/T None.

TELEPHONE (Dial code 01263) MRCC (01493) 851338; Marinecall 09066 526239; Dr 740314.

FACILITIES Quay AB (Free), Slip, M, D, FW, C (15 ton);
Services: CH (Stratton Long) ☎ 740362, AB, BY, M, P & D (cans), FW, ME, El, ⚒, SM, Gaz, AC.
Village EC Wed; 🛒, R, Bar, ✉, Ⓑ, ⇌ (Sheringham), ✈ (Norwich).

9.5.7 WELLS-NEXT-THE-SEA

Norfolk **52°59'·30N 00°49'·75E** (ent shifts) ❀❀◊◊◊✿✿✿

CHARTS AC 1190, 108; Imray C28, Y9; Stanfords 19, 3; OS 132

TIDES –0445 Dover; ML 1·2 Duration 0540; Zone 0 (UT)

Standard Port IMMINGHAM (⟶)

Times				Height (metres)			
High Water		Low Water		MHWS	MHWN	MLWN	MLWS
0100	0700	0100	0700	7·3	5·8	2·6	0·9
1300	1900	1300	1900				
Differences WELLS BAR (approx 52°59'N 00°49'E)							
+0020	+0020	+0020	+0020	–1·3	–1·0	No data	
WELLS-NEXT-THE-SEA (approx 52°57'N 00°51'E)							
+0035	+0045	+0340	+0310	–3·8	–3·8	Not below CD	

Note: LW time differences at Wells are for the end of a LW stand which lasts about 4 hrs at sp and about 5 hrs at nps.

SHELTER Good, but in strong N'lies swell renders entry impossible for small craft. Max draft 3m at sp. Access from HW –1½ to HW +1, but best on the flood. Quay berths mostly dry, some pontoon berths at W end of Fish Quay.

NAVIGATION WPT Fairway SWM buoy, Q, 52°59'·82N 00°50'·51E. The drying bar and ent vary in depth and position; buoys are altered to suit. Initially keep to W side of chan to counter E-going tide at HW–2; and to E side of chan from No 12 PHM lt buoy to quay. Best to seek HM's advice (send SAE for latest free plan) or follow FV of appropriate draft. Speed limits: W end of quay to LB house 8kn; above this 5kn.

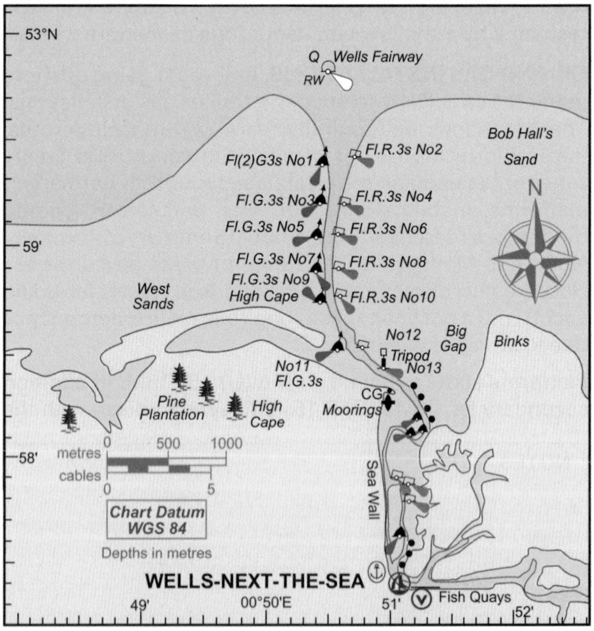
53°N
Q Wells Fairway RW
Bob Hall's Sand
N
Fl(2)G3s No1
Fl.R.3s No2
Fl.G.3s No3
Fl.R.3s No4
Fl.G.3s No5
Fl.R.3s No6
59'
Fl.G.3s No7
Fl.R.3s No8
Fl.G.3s No9
High Cape
Fl.R.3s No10
West Sands
No12
Big Gap
Binks
Tripod
No13
No11 Fl.G.3s
Pine Plantation
High Cape
CG
Moorings
58'
metres 0 500 1000
cables 0 5
Sea Wall
Chart Datum WGS 84
Depths in metres
WELLS-NEXT-THE-SEA
Fish Quays
49'
00°50'E
51'
52'

LIGHTS AND MARKS As plan. Temp buoys may be laid when chan changes. A pine plantation is conspic W of hbr ent; ditto white LB ho with R roof.

R/T *Wells Hbr Radio* Ch 12 16, HW–2 and when vessel due. Hbr launch may escort visitors into hbr and up to Quay.

TELEPHONE (Dial code 01328 Fakenham) HM 711646, mob 07775 507284, ⛴ 711623; MRCC (01493) 851338; Marinecall 09066 526239; Police (01493) 336200; Dr 710741; Ⓗ 710097.

FACILITIES **Main Quay** AB (£11/yacht), ⚓ drying (£8/yacht), ⛽, Showers, WC, ⊡, FW, ME, El, ⚒, BH (7·5 ton), C (25 ton mobile), CH, 🛒, R, Bar; **E Quay** Slip, M, L; **Wells SC** ☎ 710622, Slip, Bar; **Services:** Ⓔ, ACA, SM, LB. **Town:** P(cans) & D (bowser on quay; up to 500 galls), Gas, ⊡, 🛒, R, Bar, ✉, Ⓑ, ⇌ (bus to Norwich/King's Lynn), ✈ (Norwich).

9.5.8 WISBECH

Cambridgeshire **52°40′·02N 00°09′·55E**❀❀◊✿✿

CHARTS AC 108, 1200. Imray Y9

TIDES –0450 Dover, +0025 Immingham; ML 3·5; Duration 0520; Zone 0 (UT)

Standard Port IMMINGHAM (⟶)

Times				**Height (metres)**			
High Water		Low Water		MHWS	MHWN	MLWN	MLWS
0100	0700	0100	0700	7·3	5·8	2·6	0·9
1300	1900	1300	1900				
Differences WISBECH CUT							
+0020	+0025	+0200	+0030	–0·3	–0·7	–0·4	No data
KING'S LYNN							
+0030	+0030	+0305	+0140	–0·5	–0·8	–0·8	+0·1
BURNHAM OVERY STAITHE							
+0045	+0055	No data		–5·0	–4·9	No data	
HUNSTANTON							
+0010	+0020	+0105	+0025	+0·1	–0·2	–0·1	0·0
WEST STONES							
+0025	+0025	+0115	+0040	–0·3	–0·4	–0·3	+0·2

SHELTER Excellent shelter in river with Wisbech Yacht Harbour pontoon berths and shower/toilet facilities immediately below Freedom Bridge in Wisbech town. Vessels of 4·8m draft can reach Wisbech at sp (3·4m at nps), but depths vary. Ent to inland waterways above Wisbech to Peterborough, Oundle, Northampton. Mast lift out service available.

NAVIGATION WPT Roaring Middle NCM Lt Flt 52° 58′.64N 00° 21′.08E 7M 220° to Wisbech No 1 SHM Fl G 5s. Monitor Ch 09 and call HM when you reach Holbeach RAF No 4 ECM to check commercial traffic and opening of Cross Keys Sw Br in river. Red flags and lights shown when Firing Range in use. Ent to R Nene from The Wash well marked with lit buoys/bns from Wisbech No 1 Fl G 5s. Best ent HW–3. ✪s for waiting at Holbeach RAF No 4 ECM. Cross Keys Sw Br in river opens by request given notice. Waiting pontoon 0.5M downstream from bridge thence 6M to Wisbech with FG lts to stbd. Call HM and Cross Keys Sw Br HW –3 to HW. 24H prior notice of visit recommended. Departure best at HW, unless draught >3m; if so, aim to clear Kerr NCM by HW+3. For local pilotage notes ☎ Hbr Office or visit www.fenland.gov.uk.

LIGHTS AND MARKS Big Tom Fl(2)R 10s10m PHM Lt bn and West End SHM Lt bn Fl(3)G 5s 7m3M.

R/T HM Call *'Wisbech Harbour'*, VHF Ch 16 **09**.

TELEPHONE Dial code (01945) HM 588059 (Hbr Office 24H); Cross Keys Swing Bridge 01406 350364; MRCC (01493) 851338;Marinecall 09066 526239; Police (01354) 652561; Dr 582133; Ⓗ 585781.

FACILITIES Yacht Hbr (60AB + 15Ⓥ), £0.90, min charge £5, FW, ⏚, D barge. **Town** P (cans), Bar, R, ⛟, Gas.

ADJACENT HARBOURS

BURNHAM OVERY STAITHE, Norfolk, **52°58′·95N 00°46′·55E** ❀❀◊✿✿✿. AC 1190, 108. HW –0420 on Dover. See 9.5.8. Small drying hbr; ent chan has 0·3m MLWS. ⚓ off the Staithe only suitable in good weather. No lts. Scolt Hd is conspic to W and Gun Hill to E; Scolt Hd Island is conspic 3M long sandbank which affords some shelter. Chan varies constantly and buoys are moved to suit. Local knowledge advisable. Facilities: (01328) **Burnham Overy Staithe SC** ☎ 738348, M, L; **Services:** CH, M, ME, ⚒, Slip, FW; **Burnham Market** EC Wed; Bar, P and D (cans), R, ⛟.

BRANCASTER STAITHE, Norfolk, **52°59′·02N 00°37′·65E** ❀❀◊◊✿✿✿. AC 1190, 108. HW –0425 on Dover; as Burnham. Small drying hbr, dangerous to enter except by day in settled weather. Spd limit 6kn. Appr from due N. Conspic golf club house with lt, Fl 5s 8m 3M, is 0·5M S of chan ent and Fairway buoy. Beware wk shown on chart. Sandbanks shift; buoys changed to suit. Scolt Hd conspic to E. Local knowledge or Pilot advised. Possible ✪ in The Hole. HM ☎ (01485) 210638. Facilities: **Brancaster Staithe SC** ☎ 210249, R, Bar; **Services:** BY, CH, El, FW, P & D (cans), ME, R, ⚒, Bar, ⛟.

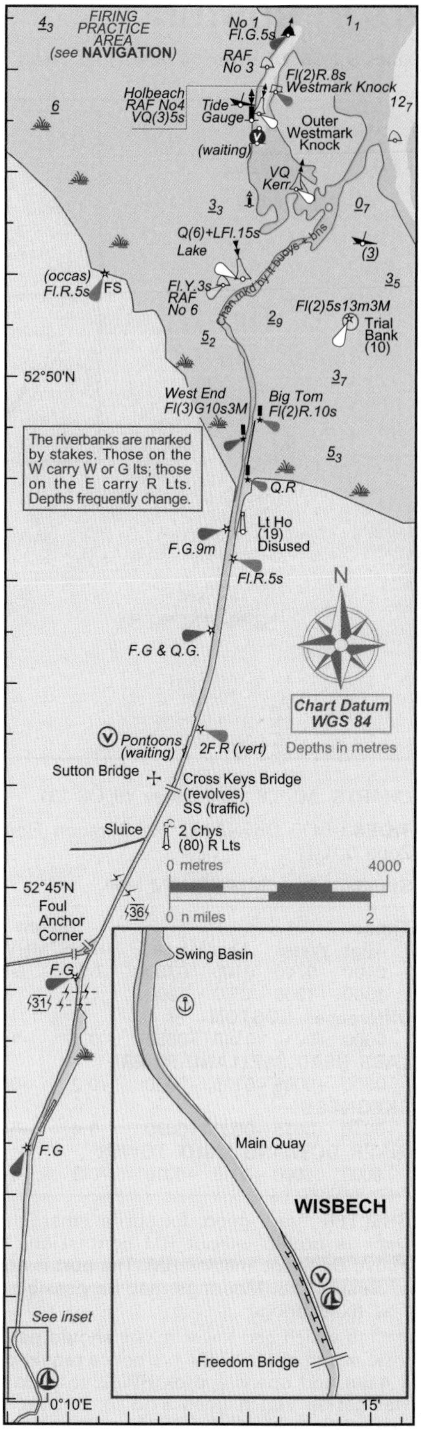
FIRING PRACTICE AREA
(see NAVIGATION)
No 1
Fl.G.5s
RAF No 3
Fl(2)R.8s
Westmark Knock
Holbeach RAF No4 VQ(3)5s
Tide Gauge
Outer Westmark Knock
(waiting)
VQ
Kerr
Q(6)+LFl.15s
Lake
Chan mkd by lit buoys & bns
(occas)
Fl.R.5s
FS
Fl.Y.3s
RAF No 6
Fl(2)5s13m3M
Trial Bank
(10)
52°50′N
West End
Fl(3)G10s3M
Big Tom
Fl(2)R.10s
The riverbanks are marked by stakes. Those on the W carry W or G lts; those on the E carry R Lts. Depths frequently change.
Q.R
Lt Ho
(19)
Disused
F.G.9m
Fl.R.5s
N
F.G & Q.G.
Chart Datum
WGS 84
Depths in metres
Pontoons
(waiting)
2F.R (vert)
Sutton Bridge
Cross Keys Bridge
(revolves)
SS (traffic)
Sluice
2 Chys
(80) R Lts
0 metres
4000
52°45′N
Foul Anchor Corner
0 n miles
2
Swing Basin
F.G
Main Quay
F.G
WISBECH
See inset
Freedom Bridge
0°10′E
15′

KING'S LYNN Norfolk **52°49′·71N 00°21′·14E** (West Stones bn) ❀❀◊✿✿ AC 1190, 108, 1200; Imray Y9; OS 132. HW –0443 Dover; see 9.5.8. Port is well sheltered; entry only recommended HW–3. A busy commercial and fishing port with very limited facilities. River moorings available from local clubs; keep clear of FV moorings. From Sunk WCM follow Cork Hole or Bulldog chan buoyed/lit apprs to King's Lynn. From there to Denver Sluice (ent to inland routes) 6 bridges span river, min cl 9·15m less ht of tide at King's Lynn above Dock sill. Allow 1½H for passage. The sand banks are forever shifting and extend several miles into the Wash. Contact HM 1 week prior for latest info or visit www.portauthoritykingslynn.fsnet.co.uk for charts. Conspic white lt ho (disused, 18m) on Hunstanton cliffs. West Stones bn NCM, Q 3m 2M. Lynn Cut low lt Iso R 2s 11m 3M.HM VHF Ch **14** 16 11 (Mon-Fri: 0800-1730 LT. Other times: HW –4 to HW+1.) (ABP) Ch **14** 16 11 (HW–2½ to HW). HM ☎ 01553 773411 **Docks** ☎ 01553 691555, AB £42 (9m LOA) for 48 hrs, FW, C (32 ton); **Services:** CH, ⚒, ME, El, Ⓔ, D. **Town** EC Wed; P, D, ⛟, R, Bar, ✉, Ⓑ, ⇌, ✈ (Norwich). **Note:** 24M up the Great Ouse river, Ely Marina ☎ (01353) 664622, Slip, M, P, D, FW, ME, El, ⚒, C (10 ton), CH. Lock half-way at Denver Sluice ☎ (01366) 382340/VHF Ch 73, and low bridges beyond.

9.5.9 BOSTON

Lincs **52°56'·00N 00°04'·92E** (Tabs Head bn)

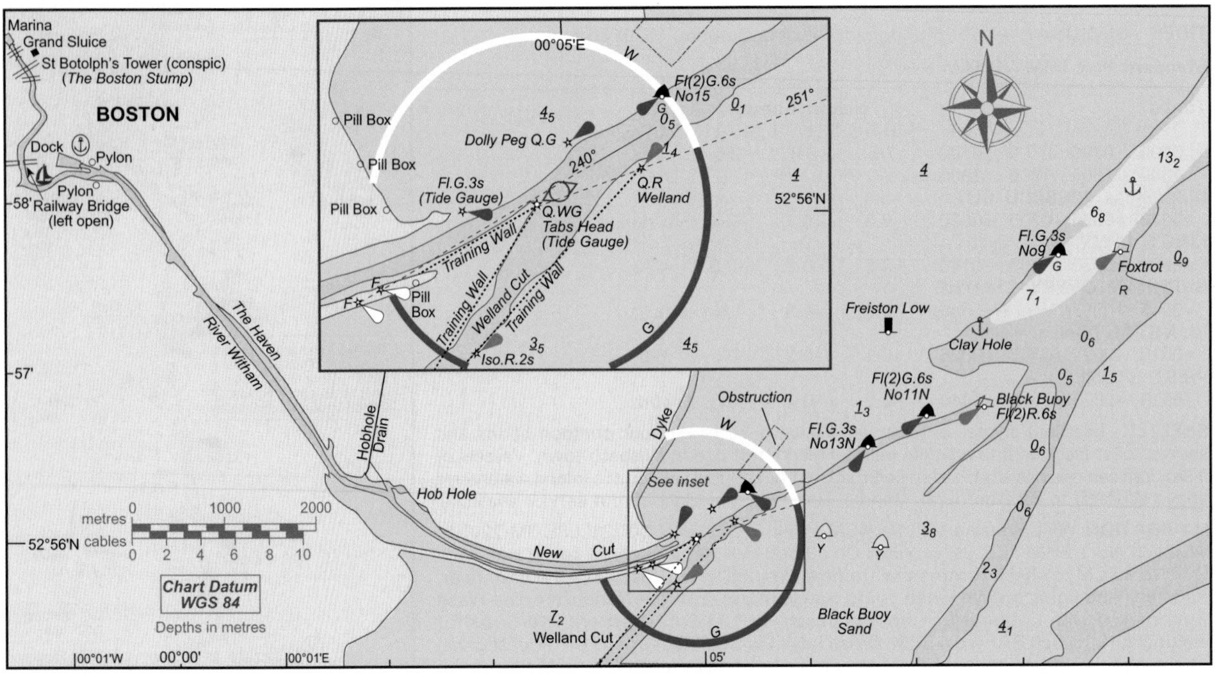
Marina
Grand Sluice
St Botolph's Tower (conspic)
(The Boston Stump)
BOSTON
Dock
Pylon
Pylon
58' Railway Bridge
(left open)
The Haven
River Witham
57'
Hobhole Drain
Hob Hole
New Cut
Welland Cut
metres
0 1000 2000
cables
0 2 4 6 8 10
52°56'N
Chart Datum
WGS 84
Depths in metres
00°01'W
00°00'
00°01'E
05'
00°05'E
Pill Box
Pill Box
Pill Box
Dolly Peg Q.G
Fl.G.3s
(Tide Gauge)
Training Wall
Training Wall
Welland Cut
Training Wall
Q.WG
Tabs Head
(Tide Gauge)
Q.R
Welland
Fl(2)G.6s
No15
240°
251°
Iso.R.2s
52°56'N
N
Freiston Low
Clay Hole
Fl.G.3s
No9
Foxtrot
Fl(2)G.6s
No11N
Fl.G.3s
No13N
Black Buoy
Fl(2)R.6s
Obstruction
Dyke
See inset
Black Buoy
Sand

CHARTS AC 108, 1200; Imray Y9; OS 131

TIDES –0415 Dover; ML 3·3; Duration Flood 0500, Ebb 0700; Zone 0 (UT)

Standard Port IMMINGHAM (⟶)

Times				Height (metres)			
High Water		Low Water		MHWS	MHWN	MLWN	MLWS
0100	0700	0100	0700	7·3	5·8	2·6	0·9
1300	1900	1300	1900				
Differences BOSTON							
0000	+0010	+0140	+0050	–0·5	–1·0	–0·9	–0·5
TABS HEAD (WELLAND RIVER)							
0000	+0005	+0125	+0020	+0·2	–0·2	–0·2	–0·2
SKEGNESS							
+0010	+0015	+0030	+0020	–0·4	–0·5	–0·1	0·0
INNER DOWSING LIGHT TOWER							
0000	0000	+0010	+0010	–0·9	–0·7	–0·1	+0·3

SHELTER Very good. Except in emergency berthing in the Dock is prohib wthout HM permission. Yachts secure just above Dock ent and see HM. The port is administered by Port of Boston Ltd. Moorings may be possible (on S side) below first fixed bridge.

Yachts which can lower masts should pass the Grand Sluice lock into fresh water (24 hrs notice required); the lock is 22·7m x 4·6m and opens approx HW±2. It leads into the R Witham Navigation which goes 31M to Lincoln. Marina is to stbd immediately beyond the sluice. British Waterways have 50 moorings, with FW and ⛽, beyond Grand Sluice, which can be manned at 6H notice.

NAVIGATION WPT Boston Rds SWM lt buoy, L Fl 10s, 52°57'·63N 00°16'·03E, 280° to Freeman Chan ent, 0·70M. Thence Bar Chan is well marked, but liable to change. SW of Clay Hole a new chan has formed which dries 0.6m at entr; it is marked by SHM lt buoys Nos 11N, 13N, and 15. Tabs Head marks the ent to the river; it should be passed not earlier than HW–3 to enable the Grand Sluice to be reached before the start of the ebb. On reaching Boston Dock, masts should be lowered to negotiate swing bridge (cannot always be opened) and three fixed bridges. Chan through town is un-navigable at LW.

LIGHTS AND MARKS St Boltoph's ch tr, (the Boston Stump) is conspic from afar. New Cut and R Witham are marked by bns with topmarks. FW lts mark ldg lines: three pairs going upstream and six pairs going downstream.

R/T All vessels between No9 buoy and Grand Sluice must listen Ch 12. Call: *Boston Port Control* VHF Ch 12 16 (Mon-Fri 0700-1700 LT & HW –2½ to HW +1½). Ch 11 used by dock staff as required. *Grand Sluice* Ch 74.

TELEPHONE (Dial code 01205) HM 362328, ℻ 351852; Dock office 365571, Grand Sluice Control 364864 (not always manned but has answerphone) mob 07712 010920, ℻ 310126; MRCC (01493) 851338; Marinecall 09066 526239; Police 366222; Ⓗ 364801.

FACILITIES **Boston Marina** (50 + some Ⓥ) ☎ 364420, £4 per night any size, access HW±2; FW, ⛽, D, CH, ACA, C in dock, see HM (emergency); **Grand Sluice** showers and toilets; **BWB** moorings: 1st night free, then £4. **Services:** El, ME, ⚒, Gas. **Town** EC Thurs; 🛒, R, Bar, ✉, Ⓑ, ⇌, ✈ (Humberside).

ADJACENT HARBOURS

RIVER WELLAND, Lincolnshire, **52°56'·00N 00°04'·92E** (Tabs Head bn). AC 1190, 1200. At Welland Cut HW –0440 on Dover; ML 0·3m; Duration 0520. See 9.5.9. At Tabs Head bn HW ±3, ent Welland Cut which is defined by training walls and lt bns. Beware sp flood of up to 5kn. Berth 6M up, at Fosdyke on small quay 300m NE of bridge on stbd side. Recommended for short stay only. Very limited facilities but new marina planned for 2004 at Fosdyke ☎ 01205 260240.

WAINFLEET, Lincolnshire, **53°04'·79N 00°19'·89E** (chan ent). AC 108. Skegness HW +0500 on Dover. See 9.5.9 (Skegness). ML 4·0m; Duration 0600. Shelter good, but emergency only. Drying channel starts close S of Gibraltar Point. Swatchway buoyed but not lit; chan through saltings marked by posts with radar reflectors and lateral topmarks. Enter HW ±1½. No lts. Facilities: M, AB (larger boats at fishing jetties, smaller at YC), FW at Field Study Centre on stbd side of ent. All shore facilities at Skegness (3½ miles), EC Thurs.

TIME ZONE (UT)
For Summer Time add ONE hour in **non-shaded areas**

ENGLAND – IMMINGHAM

LAT 53°38′N LONG 0°11′W

TIMES AND HEIGHTS OF HIGH AND LOW WATERS

SPRING & NEAP TIDES
Dates in red are SPRINGS
Dates in blue are NEAPS

YEAR **2005**

JANUARY

Date	Day	Time	m	Date	Day	Time	m
1		0312	1.8	16		0419	1.2
		0916	6.2			1029	6.5
	SA	1509	2.2		SU	1619	2.0
		2112	6.5			2222	6.8
2		0351	2.0	17		0504	1.6
		0958	6.1			1120	6.1
	SU	1549	2.4		M	1704	2.3
		2153	6.4		◐	2316	6.5
3		0436	2.1	18		0552	2.0
		1046	5.9			1214	5.8
	M	1637	2.5		TU	1757	2.6
	◑	2243	6.2				
4		0529	2.2	19		0018	6.1
		1144	5.8			0647	2.4
	TU	1735	2.7		W	1314	5.7
		2343	6.1			1903	2.8
5		0631	2.2	20		0129	5.9
		1252	5.8			0753	2.6
	W	1844	2.7		TH	1417	5.7
						2027	2.8
6		0054	6.1	21		0240	5.8
		0741	2.2			0900	2.6
	TH	1403	5.9		F	1518	5.8
		2000	2.6			2139	2.5
7		0211	6.3	22		0346	5.9
		0850	2.0			0957	2.5
	F	1507	6.2		SA	1610	6.1
		2114	2.3			2234	2.2
8		0322	6.5	23		0440	6.1
		0953	1.8			1045	2.3
	SA	1604	6.5		SU	1654	6.4
		2219	1.9			2320	1.9
9		0425	6.8	24		0525	6.3
		1050	1.6			1128	2.1
	SU	1655	6.8		M	1733	6.7
		2319	1.5				
10		0524	7.0	25		0003	1.7
		1143	1.4			0604	6.5
	M	1744	7.1		TU	1208	1.9
	●				○	1809	6.8
11		0015	1.1	26		0043	1.5
		0620	7.2			0639	6.6
	TU	1234	1.3		W	1245	1.8
		1831	7.4			1844	6.9
12		0109	0.8	27		0120	1.4
		0714	7.3			0713	6.6
	W	1323	1.2		TH	1318	1.8
		1917	7.5			1917	6.9
13		0200	0.7	28		0154	1.4
		0806	7.2			0746	6.6
	TH	1410	1.3		F	1348	1.8
		2003	7.5			1949	6.9
14		0248	0.7	29		0226	1.4
		0854	7.1			0818	6.6
	F	1454	1.4		SA	1417	1.8
		2047	7.4			2019	6.9
15		0334	0.8	30		0255	1.5
		0941	6.8			0850	6.5
	SA	1536	1.7		SU	1448	1.8
		2133	7.2			2050	6.8
				31		0324	1.6
						0924	6.4
					M	1522	1.9
						2124	6.7

FEBRUARY

Date	Day	Time	m	Date	Day	Time	m
1		0356	1.7	16		0452	2.1
		1002	6.2			1104	5.8
	TU	1600	2.1		W	1701	2.5
		2206	6.6		◐	2326	5.9
2		0438	2.0	17		0538	2.6
		1047	6.0			1206	5.5
	W	1649	2.3		TH	1758	2.8
	◑	2258	6.3				
3		0534	2.2	18		0045	5.5
		1147	5.8			0643	3.0
	TH	1754	2.6		F	1325	5.4
						1922	3.0
4		0006	6.1	19		0212	5.4
		0651	2.4			0817	3.1
	F	1311	5.7		SA	1441	5.5
		1920	2.7			2120	2.8
5		0140	5.9	20		0328	5.6
		0819	2.4			0937	2.8
	SA	1438	5.9		SU	1544	5.9
		2052	2.4			2219	2.3
6		0313	6.1	21		0427	5.9
		0935	2.2			1030	2.4
	SU	1547	6.2		M	1634	6.3
		2211	1.9			2305	1.9
7		0427	6.5	22		0511	6.2
		1039	1.9			1114	2.1
	M	1645	6.7		TU	1714	6.6
		2315	1.4			2346	1.6
8		0528	6.9	23		0548	6.5
		1135	1.5			1153	1.9
	TU	1736	7.1		W	1749	6.8
	●						
9		0011	0.9	24		0025	1.4
		0622	7.2			0620	6.6
	W	1226	1.2		TH	1230	1.7
		1822	7.4		○	1822	6.9
10		0102	0.5	25		0101	1.2
		0709	7.3			0651	6.7
	TH	1312	1.1		F	1301	1.6
		1905	7.6			1854	7.0
11		0148	0.4	26		0135	1.2
		0753	7.4			0722	6.8
	F	1355	1.0		SA	1330	1.5
		1947	7.7			1925	7.1
12		0230	0.4	27		0204	1.2
		0832	7.2			0752	6.8
	SA	1434	1.1		SU	1359	1.5
		2028	7.6			1955	7.1
13		0309	0.7	28		0231	1.2
		0909	6.9			0821	6.8
	SU	1510	1.3		M	1428	1.5
		2107	7.4			2025	7.1
14		0344	1.1				
		0944	6.6				
	M	1544	1.7				
		2147	6.9				
15		0417	1.6				
		1021	6.2				
	TU	1619	2.1				
		2230	6.4				

MARCH

Date	Day	Time	m	Date	Day	Time	m
1		0256	1.4	16		0333	1.7
		0852	6.6			0929	6.3
	TU	1459	1.6		W	1542	1.9
		2059	6.9			2152	6.3
2		0325	1.6	17		0404	2.2
		0927	6.4			1002	5.9
	W	1534	1.8		TH	1620	2.3
		2140	6.7		◐	2240	5.7
3		0402	1.9	18		0447	2.7
		1009	6.1			1052	5.5
	TH	1619	2.1		F	1715	2.8
	◑	2231	6.3				
4		0456	2.3	19		0007	5.3
		1105	5.8			0550	3.2
	F	1725	2.5		SA	1235	5.3
		2343	5.8			1836	3.0
5		0618	2.7	20		0146	5.2
		1233	5.5			0725	3.3
	SA	1901	2.7		SU	1405	5.4
						2053	2.8
6		0140	5.7	21		0304	5.5
		0803	2.7			0913	3.0
	SU	1420	5.7		M	1514	5.7
		2049	2.4			2153	2.3
7		0320	6.0	22		0403	5.9
		0928	2.4			1007	2.6
	M	1535	6.2		TU	1605	6.1
		2210	1.8			2237	1.9
8		0430	6.5	23		0446	6.2
		1032	1.9			1050	2.2
	TU	1633	6.7		W	1645	6.5
		2309	1.1			2317	1.5
9		0525	6.9	24		0521	6.5
		1123	1.5			1128	1.9
	W	1721	7.2		TH	1720	6.7
		2359	0.7			2355	1.3
10		0611	7.2	25		0552	6.7
		1210	1.1			1203	1.6
	TH	1805	7.5		F	1753	6.9
	●				○		
11		0045	0.4	26		0031	1.1
		0651	7.4			0622	6.9
	F	1253	0.9		SA	1236	1.5
		1846	7.7			1825	7.1
12		0127	0.3	27		0106	1.0
		0728	7.4			0652	6.9
	SA	1333	0.8		SU	1307	1.4
		1925	7.7			1857	7.2
13		0204	0.4	28		0137	1.0
		0801	7.2			0722	7.0
	SU	1409	0.9		M	1338	1.3
		2003	7.6			1930	7.2
14		0237	0.8	29		0205	1.1
		0832	7.0			0753	6.9
	M	1442	1.2		TU	1409	1.3
		2039	7.3			2004	7.2
15		0306	1.2	30		0234	1.3
		0901	6.6			0825	6.8
	TU	1512	1.5		W	1443	1.4
		2114	6.8			2042	7.0
				31		0305	1.6
						0902	6.6
					TH	1520	1.6
						2126	6.6

APRIL

Date	Day	Time	m	Date	Day	Time	m
1		0345	2.0	16		0411	2.7
		0946	6.2			1008	5.6
	F	1610	2.0		SA	1649	2.6
		2223	6.1		◐	2331	5.3
2		0443	2.5	17		0512	3.1
		1046	5.8			1139	5.3
	SA	1724	2.4		SU	1806	2.8
	◑	2352	5.6				
3		0611	2.9	18		0109	5.2
		1223	5.6			0637	3.3
	SU	1907	2.4		M	1320	5.4
						1943	2.7
4		0155	5.7	19		0225	5.4
		0755	2.8			0818	3.1
	M	1406	5.8		TU	1430	5.6
		2048	2.0			2104	2.3
5		0318	6.1	20		0323	5.8
		0915	2.4			0925	2.7
	TU	1517	6.3		W	1523	6.0
		2157	1.5			2154	1.9
6		0420	6.6	21		0408	6.2
		1014	1.8			1011	2.3
	W	1612	6.8		TH	1605	6.3
		2250	0.9			2237	1.5
7		0507	7.0	22		0444	6.5
		1102	1.4			1050	1.9
	TH	1659	7.2		F	1642	6.6
		2336	0.6			2317	1.3
8		0548	7.2	23		0517	6.7
		1147	1.1			1127	1.6
	F	1741	7.4		SA	1718	6.9
	●					2356	1.1
9		0019	0.5	24		0549	6.9
		0624	7.3			1204	1.4
	SA	1229	0.9		SU	1754	7.1
		1822	7.5		○		
10		0058	0.5	25		0032	1.0
		0657	7.2			0622	7.0
	SU	1308	0.9		M	1241	1.2
		1901	7.5			1831	7.2
11		0133	0.7	26		0108	1.0
		0728	7.1			0655	7.1
	M	1343	1.0		TU	1318	1.1
		1938	7.3			1909	7.2
12		0204	1.0	27		0142	1.1
		0757	6.9			0730	7.0
	TU	1415	1.2		W	1356	1.1
		2014	7.0			1950	7.1
13		0232	1.4	28		0218	1.3
		0824	6.7			0807	6.9
	W	1444	1.5		TH	1436	1.3
		2048	6.6			2035	6.8
14		0259	1.8	29		0256	1.6
		0851	6.4			0849	6.7
	TH	1515	1.8		F	1522	1.5
		2124	6.1			2127	6.4
15		0330	2.3	30		0343	2.1
		0923	6.0			0938	6.3
	F	1554	2.2		SA	1621	1.9
		2210	5.6			2235	6.0

Chart Datum: 3·90 metres below Ordnance Datum (Newlyn)

TIME ZONE (UT)
For Summer Time add ONE hour in **non-shaded areas**

ENGLAND – IMMINGHAM

LAT 53°38′N LONG 0°11′W

TIMES AND HEIGHTS OF HIGH AND LOW WATERS

SPRING & NEAP TIDES
Dates in red are SPRINGS
Dates in blue are NEAPS

YEAR **2005**

MAY

Date	Day	Time	m	Time	m	Time	m	Time	m
1 ◑	SU	0446	2.5	1045	6.0	1739	2.1		
2	M	0018	5.8	0609	2.7	1219	5.9	1907	2.0
3	TU	0147	5.9	0736	2.6	1344	6.1	2027	1.7
4	W	0258	6.2	0847	2.3	1450	6.4	2129	1.3
5	TH	0355	6.6	0945	1.9	1545	6.8	2221	1.0
6	F	0440	6.8	1035	1.5	1633	7.0	2306	0.9
7	SA	0519	7.0	1120	1.2	1717	7.2	2348	0.9
8 ●	SU	0554	7.0	1203	1.1	1758	7.2		
9	M	0026	1.0	0626	7.0	1243	1.1	1838	7.1
10	TU	0102	1.2	0658	6.9	1319	1.2	1917	6.9
11	W	0134	1.4	0728	6.8	1353	1.3	1954	6.7
12	TH	0204	1.7	0757	6.6	1425	1.6	2030	6.4
13	F	0233	1.9	0828	6.4	1458	1.8	2108	6.0
14	SA	0306	2.3	0903	6.2	1539	2.1	2153	5.7
15	SU	0346	2.6	0947	5.8	1631	2.4	2255	5.4
16 ◐	M	0440	2.9	1053	5.6	1737	2.5		
17	TU	0014	5.4	0549	3.1	1219	5.5	1848	2.5
18	W	0126	5.5	0706	3.0	1329	5.6	1958	2.3
19	TH	0227	5.7	0817	2.8	1426	5.9	2058	2.0
20	F	0317	6.0	0916	2.4	1515	6.2	2149	1.7
21	SA	0400	6.3	1005	2.1	1600	6.5	2236	1.4
22	SU	0439	6.6	1050	1.7	1644	6.8	2319	1.2
23 ○	M	0518	6.8	1134	1.4	1727	7.0		
24	TU	0002	1.1	0555	7.0	1218	1.2	1811	7.1
25	W	0044	1.1	0635	7.1	1303	1.1	1858	7.2
26	TH	0126	1.2	0715	7.1	1349	1.0	1946	7.0
27	F	0209	1.4	0758	7.0	1438	1.1	2038	6.8
28	SA	0255	1.6	0845	6.8	1531	1.3	2137	6.5
29	SU	0346	2.0	0939	6.6	1631	1.5	2250	6.2
30 ◑	M	0446	2.3	1044	6.4	1738	1.6		
31	TU	0009	6.1	0553	2.4	1200	6.2	1847	1.6

JUNE

Date	Day	Time	m	Time	m	Time	m	Time	m
1	W	0119	6.1	0704	2.4	1311	6.3	1953	1.6
2	TH	0223	6.2	0811	2.3	1416	6.4	2053	1.5
3	F	0320	6.3	0912	2.0	1514	6.5	2146	1.4
4	SA	0407	6.5	1006	1.8	1607	6.7	2234	1.4
5	SU	0448	6.6	1054	1.6	1654	6.7	2317	1.4
6	M	0525	6.7	1140	1.4	1739	6.7	● 2358	1.5
7	TU	0600	6.7	1222	1.4	1822	6.7		
8	W	0035	1.6	0634	6.7	1302	1.4	1902	6.6
9	TH	0111	1.7	0707	6.7	1339	1.5	1940	6.5
10	F	0144	1.8	0741	6.7	1414	1.6	2017	6.3
11	SA	0216	2.0	0815	6.5	1449	1.7	2054	6.1
12	SU	0249	2.2	0850	6.3	1528	1.9	2134	6.0
13	M	0327	2.4	0930	6.1	1612	2.1	2221	5.8
14	TU	0410	2.6	1018	5.9	1703	2.2	2316	5.7
15 ◐	W	0503	2.7	1116	5.8	1800	2.2		
16	TH	0018	5.6	0604	2.8	1222	5.8	1900	2.2
17	F	0122	5.7	0710	2.7	1325	5.9	2002	2.1
18	SA	0222	5.9	0817	2.5	1426	6.1	2102	1.9
19	SU	0316	6.2	0920	2.2	1523	6.4	2157	1.7
20	M	0406	6.4	1017	1.9	1617	6.7	2249	1.5
21	TU	0452	6.7	1110	1.5	1710	6.9	2338	1.3
22 ○	W	0537	6.9	1203	1.2	1803	7.0		
23	TH	0027	1.2	0621	7.1	1255	1.0	1856	7.1
24	F	0115	1.2	0707	7.2	1348	0.8	1949	7.1
25	SA	0203	1.3	0754	7.2	1439	0.8	2044	7.0
26	SU	0251	1.4	0842	7.2	1531	0.8	2140	6.8
27	M	0339	1.6	0933	7.0	1623	1.0	2238	6.5
28	TU	0430	1.9	1029	6.8	1718	1.2	◑ 2338	6.3
29	W	0525	2.1	1130	6.6	1814	1.5		
30	TH	0037	6.1	0624	2.3	1234	6.4	1913	1.7

JULY

Date	Day	Time	m	Time	m	Time	m	Time	m
1	F	0137	6.0	0730	2.4	1338	6.2	2013	1.9
2	SA	0235	6.0	0838	2.3	1442	6.2	2112	2.0
3	SU	0330	6.1	0940	2.2	1544	6.2	2205	2.0
4	M	0418	6.2	1034	1.9	1638	6.3	2252	2.0
5	TU	0500	6.4	1123	1.7	1727	6.4	2336	1.9
6 ●	W	0539	6.6	1208	1.6	1810	6.4		
7	TH	0017	1.9	0615	6.7	1251	1.5	1849	6.4
8	F	0055	1.8	0651	6.8	1330	1.5	1926	6.4
9	SA	0131	1.8	0727	6.8	1406	1.5	2001	6.4
10	SU	0203	1.9	0801	6.7	1440	1.6	2035	6.4
11	M	0233	2.0	0835	6.6	1513	1.7	2110	6.3
12	TU	0305	2.1	0908	6.5	1547	1.8	2146	6.1
13	W	0340	2.2	0945	6.3	1624	1.9	2228	6.0
14	TH	0421	2.4	1028	6.2	1707	2.1	◐ 2317	5.8
15	F	0511	2.5	1120	6.0	1802	2.2		
16	SA	0018	5.7	0612	2.6	1226	6.0	1908	2.3
17	SU	0130	5.8	0726	2.6	1342	6.0	2020	2.2
18	M	0239	5.9	0843	2.4	1457	6.2	2128	2.0
19	TU	0340	6.2	0954	2.0	1604	6.5	2228	1.8
20	W	0435	6.6	1057	1.6	1705	6.8	2324	1.5
21 ○	TH	0525	6.9	1156	1.2	1803	7.0		
22	F	0016	1.3	0612	7.2	1252	0.8	1857	7.2
23	SA	0107	1.2	0659	7.4	1343	0.5	1948	7.3
24	SU	0154	1.1	0745	7.5	1431	0.4	2036	7.2
25	M	0238	1.2	0830	7.5	1517	0.5	2122	7.0
26	TU	0321	1.3	0915	7.4	1601	0.8	2207	6.8
27	W	0404	1.6	1002	7.1	1644	1.2	2255	6.4
28	TH	0447	2.0	1054	6.7	1730	1.7	◑ 2347	6.0
29	F	0537	2.3	1153	6.3	1822	2.2		
30	SA	0044	5.8	0638	2.6	1301	5.9	1927	2.5
31	SU	0148	5.6	0803	2.7	1415	5.8	2040	2.6

AUGUST

Date	Day	Time	m	Time	m	Time	m	Time	m
1	M	0253	5.7	0922	2.5	1527	5.8	2143	2.5
2	TU	0351	6.0	1021	2.2	1629	6.0	2235	2.3
3	W	0440	6.3	1111	1.9	1718	6.2	2320	2.1
4	TH	0521	6.6	1155	1.6	1758	6.4		
5	F	0002	1.9	0558	6.8	1237	1.4	● 1833	6.5
6	SA	0041	1.8	0633	6.9	1315	1.3	1906	6.6
7	SU	0116	1.7	0707	6.9	1350	1.3	1938	6.6
8	M	0146	1.7	0740	6.9	1421	1.4	2009	6.6
9	TU	0213	1.8	0811	6.9	1449	1.5	2040	6.6
10	W	0240	1.8	0841	6.8	1515	1.6	2111	6.4
11	TH	0310	1.9	0912	6.6	1542	1.8	2144	6.3
12	F	0344	2.1	0949	6.5	1616	2.0	2225	6.0
13	SA	0427	2.3	1036	6.2	1705	2.3	◐ 2318	5.8
14	SU	0526	2.6	1139	5.9	1817	2.5		
15	M	0038	5.6	0647	2.7	1313	5.8	1947	2.6
16	TU	0211	5.8	0821	2.6	1448	6.0	2110	2.4
17	W	0323	6.1	0947	2.1	1604	6.4	2217	2.0
18	TH	0422	6.6	1054	1.5	1706	6.8	2314	1.6
19 ○	F	0513	7.1	1150	1.0	1800	7.2		
20	SA	0005	1.3	0559	7.4	1242	0.5	1848	7.4
21	SU	0052	1.0	0644	7.7	1328	0.3	1932	7.5
22	M	0136	0.9	0726	7.8	1411	0.2	2012	7.4
23	TU	0217	0.9	0808	7.8	1451	0.5	2050	7.2
24	W	0255	1.1	0849	7.5	1528	0.9	2127	6.8
25	TH	0331	1.5	0931	7.1	1603	1.4	2205	6.4
26	F	0407	1.9	1017	6.6	1638	2.0	◑ 2249	6.0
27	SA	0447	2.4	1114	6.1	1721	2.6	2348	5.6
28	SU	0542	2.8	1229	5.6	1825	3.0		
29	M	0104	5.4	0721	3.0	1353	5.5	2010	3.1
30	TU	0220	5.6	0910	2.7	1511	5.6	2126	2.9
31	W	0326	5.9	1007	2.3	1615	6.0	2218	2.5

Chart Datum: 3·90 metres below Ordnance Datum (Newlyn)

TIME ZONE (UT)
For Summer Time add ONE hour in **non-shaded areas**

ENGLAND – IMMINGHAM

LAT 53°38′N LONG 0°11′W

TIMES AND HEIGHTS OF HIGH AND LOW WATERS

SPRING & NEAP TIDES
Dates in red are SPRINGS Dates in blue are NEAPS

YEAR **2005**

SEPTEMBER

Date	Day	Time	m	Time	m	Time	m	Time	m	Moon
1	TH	0418	6.3	1053	1.9	1701	6.3	2303	2.1	
2	F	0459	6.6	1134	1.5	1737	6.5	2343	1.9	
3	SA	0535	6.9	1213	1.3	1809	6.7			●
4	SU	0019	1.7	0608	7.0	1249	1.2	1839	6.8	
5	M	0053	1.6	0641	7.1	1323	1.2	1909	6.8	
6	TU	0122	1.6	0712	7.1	1353	1.3	1938	6.8	
7	W	0148	1.6	0742	7.1	1419	1.4	2006	6.8	
8	TH	0214	1.6	0811	7.0	1442	1.5	2035	6.7	
9	F	0243	1.7	0842	6.8	1507	1.7	2106	6.5	
10	SA	0315	1.9	0919	6.6	1539	2.0	2145	6.2	
11	SU	0357	2.2	1006	6.2	1626	2.4	2236	5.8	◐
12	M	0457	2.6	1115	5.8	1742	2.8	2359	5.6	
13	TU	0629	2.8	1313	5.6	1930	2.9			
14	W	0153	5.7	0818	2.6	1451	6.0	2101	2.6	
15	TH	0309	6.2	0945	1.9	1602	6.5	2207	2.1	
16	F	0406	6.7	1044	1.3	1657	7.0	2259	1.6	
17	SA	0455	7.2	1135	0.7	1744	7.3	2346	1.2	
18	SU	0539	7.6	1221	0.4	1826	7.5			○
19	M	0030	0.9	0620	7.8	1304	0.3	1904	7.5	
20	TU	0112	0.8	0702	7.9	1343	0.4	1940	7.4	
21	W	0150	0.9	0742	7.8	1419	0.7	2013	7.2	
22	TH	0226	1.1	0821	7.5	1450	1.1	2045	6.8	
23	F	0258	1.5	0900	7.0	1519	1.7	2117	6.5	
24	SA	0330	1.9	0942	6.4	1549	2.3	2152	6.0	
25	SU	0407	2.4	1037	5.9	1629	2.8	2245	5.6	◑
26	M	0501	2.8	1201	5.4	1731	3.3			
27	TU	0022	5.4	0630	3.1	1330	5.3	1923	3.4	
28	W	0148	5.5	0846	2.8	1446	5.6	2101	3.1	
29	TH	0256	5.9	0940	2.3	1547	6.0	2153	2.6	
30	F	0349	6.3	1024	1.9	1631	6.3	2236	2.2	

OCTOBER

Date	Day	Time	m	Time	m	Time	m	Time	m	Moon
1	SA	0430	6.6	1102	1.5	1707	6.6	2314	1.9	
2	SU	0505	6.9	1139	1.3	1737	6.8	2349	1.7	
3	M	0537	7.1	1215	1.2	1807	6.9			●
4	TU	0021	1.6	0609	7.1	1249	1.2	1836	7.0	
5	W	0052	1.5	0641	7.2	1319	1.2	1905	7.0	
6	TH	0121	1.5	0713	7.2	1347	1.3	1935	7.0	
7	F	0150	1.5	0745	7.1	1413	1.5	2005	6.8	
8	SA	0222	1.6	0820	6.9	1442	1.7	2038	6.6	
9	SU	0258	1.9	0902	6.6	1518	2.1	2119	6.3	
10	M	0344	2.2	0955	6.1	1610	2.6	2214	5.9	◐
11	TU	0452	2.5	1119	5.7	1730	3.0	2343	5.7	
12	W	0630	2.6	1321	5.7	1917	3.0			
13	TH	0133	5.9	0814	2.3	1443	6.1	2043	2.6	
14	F	0246	6.3	0928	1.7	1546	6.6	2145	2.1	
15	SA	0342	6.9	1022	1.1	1636	7.0	2235	1.6	
16	SU	0430	7.3	1109	0.7	1719	7.3	2321	1.2	
17	M	0513	7.6	1152	0.6	1757	7.4			○
18	TU	0004	1.0	0555	7.7	1233	0.6	1832	7.4	
19	W	0045	0.9	0636	7.7	1311	0.8	1906	7.3	
20	TH	0123	1.0	0716	7.5	1344	1.1	1938	7.1	
21	F	0158	1.2	0756	7.2	1415	1.5	2009	6.9	
22	SA	0230	1.5	0835	6.8	1443	1.9	2039	6.6	
23	SU	0302	1.9	0916	6.3	1513	2.4	2112	6.2	
24	M	0340	2.3	1007	5.8	1552	2.8	2158	5.8	
25	TU	0434	2.7	1128	5.4	1650	3.2	2328	5.5	◑
26	W	0554	2.9	1254	5.3	1817	3.4			
27	TH	0102	5.5	0745	2.8	1406	5.5	2006	3.2	
28	F	0212	5.8	0853	2.4	1505	5.9	2111	2.8	
29	SA	0307	6.2	0940	2.0	1552	6.3	2156	2.4	
30	SU	0350	6.5	1020	1.7	1629	6.6	2235	2.1	
31	M	0427	6.8	1059	1.4	1701	6.8	2311	1.8	

NOVEMBER

Date	Day	Time	m	Time	m	Time	m	Time	m	Moon
1	TU	0501	7.0	1136	1.3	1732	7.0	2346	1.6	
2	W	0536	7.1	1212	1.2	1804	7.1			●
3	TH	0020	1.5	0612	7.2	1246	1.3	1836	7.1	
4	F	0056	1.4	0649	7.2	1319	1.4	1909	7.1	
5	SA	0132	1.4	0728	7.1	1352	1.5	1944	7.0	
6	SU	0211	1.5	0811	6.9	1429	1.8	2023	6.8	
7	M	0255	1.7	0900	6.5	1512	2.2	2108	6.5	
8	TU	0349	2.0	1002	6.1	1608	2.6	2208	6.2	
9	W	0500	2.2	1134	5.8	1724	2.9	2332	6.0	◐
10	TH	0626	2.2	1306	5.9	1852	2.9			
11	F	0103	6.1	0749	1.9	1418	6.2	2009	2.6	
12	SA	0213	6.5	0855	1.6	1518	6.5	2112	2.1	
13	SU	0311	6.8	0950	1.3	1608	6.8	2205	1.7	
14	M	0402	7.1	1038	1.1	1650	7.0	2253	1.4	
15	TU	0448	7.3	1121	1.0	1728	7.1	2338	1.2	
16	W	0532	7.4	1202	1.1	1803	7.2			○
17	TH	0020	1.2	0615	7.3	1240	1.2	1837	7.1	
18	F	0100	1.2	0657	7.1	1314	1.5	1911	7.0	
19	SA	0137	1.4	0737	6.9	1346	1.7	1943	6.9	
20	SU	0211	1.6	0817	6.6	1416	2.0	2015	6.7	
21	M	0245	1.9	0858	6.2	1449	2.3	2050	6.4	
22	TU	0324	2.2	0943	5.9	1527	2.7	2132	6.1	
23	W	0414	2.4	1042	5.6	1616	3.0	2233	5.8	◑
24	TH	0517	2.6	1154	5.5	1721	3.2	2354	5.7	
25	F	0627	2.6	1303	5.5	1837	3.2			
26	SA	0106	5.7	0736	2.5	1405	5.7	1952	3.0	
27	SU	0206	5.9	0837	2.2	1458	6.0	2055	2.7	
28	M	0258	6.2	0929	2.0	1543	6.3	2145	2.4	
29	TU	0343	6.5	1014	1.7	1622	6.6	2230	2.0	
30	W	0426	6.8	1057	1.5	1700	6.8	2312	1.7	

DECEMBER

Date	Day	Time	m	Time	m	Time	m	Time	m	Moon
1	TH	0508	7.0	1138	1.4	1737	7.0	2355	1.5	●
2	F	0551	7.1	1218	1.4	1814	7.1			
3	SA	0038	1.3	0635	7.1	1259	1.4	1853	7.2	
4	SU	0123	1.3	0722	7.1	1340	1.5	1933	7.1	
5	M	0209	1.3	0811	6.9	1424	1.7	2017	7.0	
6	TU	0259	1.4	0905	6.6	1511	2.0	2106	6.9	
7	W	0355	1.5	1008	6.4	1605	2.3	2203	6.6	
8	TH	0457	1.7	1121	6.2	1708	2.5	2311	6.5	◐
9	F	0604	1.8	1233	6.1	1817	2.6			
10	SA	0025	6.4	0711	1.8	1339	6.1	1928	2.5	
11	SU	0134	6.5	0816	1.7	1439	6.3	2035	2.3	
12	M	0237	6.6	0914	1.7	1533	6.4	2135	2.1	
13	TU	0335	6.7	1006	1.6	1620	6.6	2228	1.8	
14	W	0428	6.8	1052	1.6	1701	6.7	2317	1.6	
15	TH	0516	6.8	1135	1.6	1740	6.9			○
16	F	0002	1.5	0601	6.8	1216	1.7	1816	6.9	
17	SA	0045	1.4	0645	6.8	1253	1.8	1852	6.9	
18	SU	0125	1.5	0725	6.6	1327	1.9	1927	6.9	
19	M	0201	1.6	0804	6.5	1359	2.0	2001	6.8	
20	TU	0236	1.7	0841	6.3	1432	2.2	2035	6.6	
21	W	0312	1.9	0918	6.1	1506	2.3	2112	6.4	
22	TH	0351	2.1	0959	5.9	1545	2.5	2154	6.2	
23	F	0437	2.2	1047	5.8	1631	2.8	2244	6.0	◑
24	SA	0530	2.4	1145	5.7	1727	2.9	2345	5.9	
25	SU	0629	2.4	1249	5.6	1833	3.0			
26	M	0052	5.9	0731	2.4	1353	5.8	1943	2.9	
27	TU	0159	6.0	0834	2.3	1453	6.0	2051	2.6	
28	W	0301	6.2	0931	2.1	1545	6.3	2151	2.3	
29	TH	0357	6.5	1023	1.8	1632	6.6	2245	1.9	
30	F	0449	6.7	1112	1.6	1717	6.9	2337	1.5	
31	SA	0541	6.9	1159	1.5	1800	7.1			●

Chart Datum: 3·90 metres below Ordnance Datum (Newlyn)

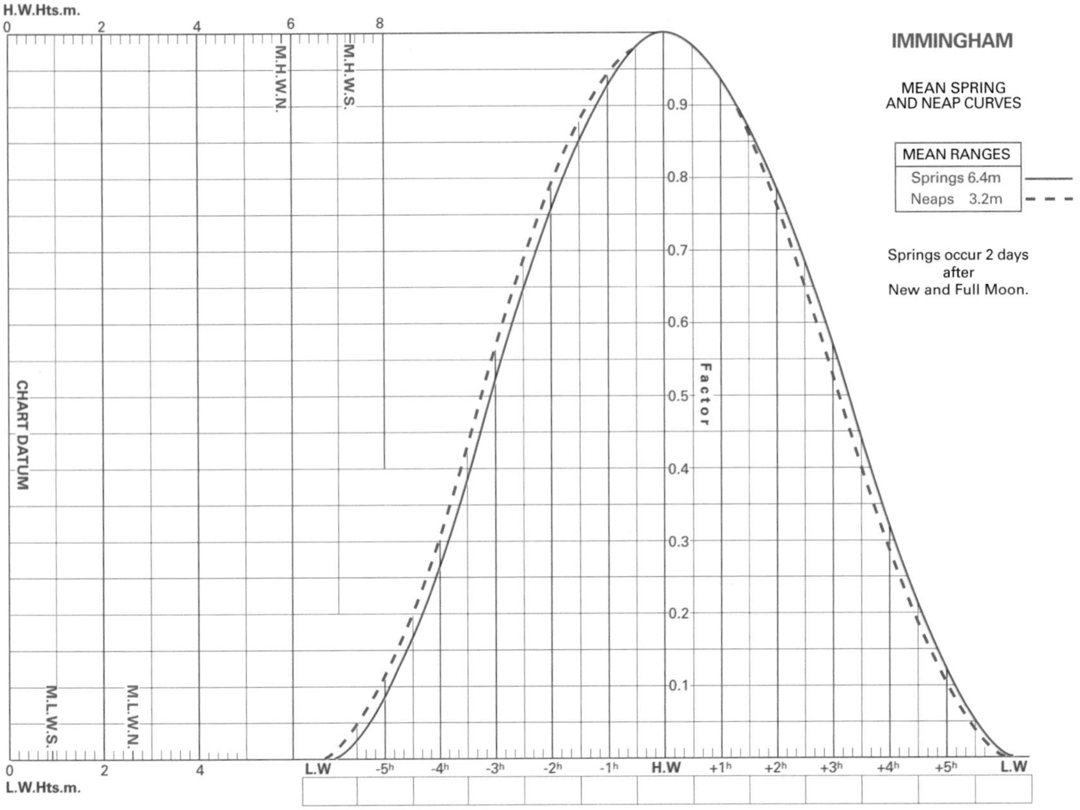
H.W.Hts.m.
IMMINGHAM
MEAN SPRING AND NEAP CURVES
MEAN RANGES
Springs 6.4m
Neaps 3.2m
Springs occur 2 days after New and Full Moon.
M.H.W.N.
M.H.W.S.
CHART DATUM
M.L.W.S.
M.L.W.N.
Factor
L.W.Hts.m.
L.W
H.W

9.5.10 RIVER HUMBER

S bank: NE and N Lincolnshire
N bank: E Riding of Yorks and City of Kingston-upon-Hull
Hull marina: **53°44'·24N 00°20'·15W** Rtg

CHARTS AC 1190, 109, 3497, 1188; Imray C29; OS 107; ABP (local)

TIDES –0510 Immingham, –0452 Hull, Dover; ML 4·1; Duration 0555; Zone 0 (UT)

Standard Port IMMINGHAM (⟵)

Times				Height (metres)			
High Water		Low Water		MHWS	MHWN	MLWN	MLWS
0100	0700	0100	0700	7·3	5·8	2·6	0·9
1300	1900	1300	1900				
Differences BULL SAND FORT							
–0020	–0030	–0035	–0015	–0·4	–0·3	+0·1	+0·2
GRIMSBY							
–0012	–0012	–0015	–0015	–0·2	–0·1	0·0	+0·2
HULL (ALBERT DOCK)							
+0019	+0019	+0033	+0027	+0·3	+0·1	–0·1	–0·2
HUMBER BRIDGE							
+0027	+0022	+0049	+0039	–0·1	–0·4	–0·7	–0·6
BURTON STATHER (R. Trent)*							
+0105	+0045	+0335	+0305	–2·1	–2·3	–2·3	Dries
KEADBY (R. Trent)*							
+0135	+0120	+0425	+0410	–2·5	–2·8	Dries	
BLACKTOFT (R. Ouse)†							
+0100	+0055	+0325	+0255	–1·6	–1·8	–2·2	–1·1
GOOLE (R. Ouse)†							
+0130	+0115	+0355	+0350	–1·6	–2·1	–1·9	–0·6

NOTE: Daily predictions for Immingham are given above.

*Normal river level at Burton Stather is about 0·1m below CD, and at Keadby 0·1m to 0·2m below CD.
†Heights of LW can increase by up to 0·3m at Blacktoft and 0·6m at Goole when river in spate. HW hts are little affected.

SHELTER R Humber is the estuary of R Ouse and R Trent. ABP is the Authority for the Humber and owns the ports of Hull, Grimsby, Immingham and Goole. The Humber estuary has strong tides, and a strong NW'ly against a sp flood of 3-4kts causes a short steep sea. Likewise the ebb in a SE'ly. Off Hull marina the sea also cuts up rough with fresh winds over sp tides. Note: no waiting pontoon here and ent is prone to silting.

Anchorages. ⚓ inside Spurn Hd only with winds from NE to ESE. ⚓ close off Haile Sand Fort only in fair weather. Immingham should be used by yachts only in emergency. If unable to reach Hull on the tide, in S to W winds there is a good ⚓ off the SW bank 8ca above N Killingholme Oil jetty, well out of main chan. In N'lies ⚓ off Hawkin's Pt, N of S9 buoy.

Marinas at Hull, S Ferriby and the docks at Goole are all entered by lock, access HW±3 and Grimsby also by lock HW±2. S Ferriby should not be attempted without up-to-date ABP charts which cover the ever-changing buoyed chan above Hull.

Do not attempt entry to Winteringham (HW±½) or Brough Havens (HW±1) without contacting Humber Yawl Club for details of approach chan and mooring availability. Both dry to soft mud. Winteringham prone to bad silting, but is dredged.

NAVIGATION Note TSS on chartlet and on AC 109. **From S**, WPT 53°30'·44N 00°16'·94E, Rosse Spit PHM buoy, Fl (2) R 5s. Thence make Haile Sand No 2, then via No 2B, Tetney monobuoy and No 2C into Haile Chan.

From N, WPT 53°34'·74N 00°16'·55E, S Binks SPM buoy, Fl G 2s. Thence passing N of Spurn Lt Float, SE Chequer and Chequer No 3 to make Binks 3A; then enter the estuary to the S of Spurn Hd outside Bull Chan. Best arrival at LW. Sp tides are fierce: 4·4kn ebb off Spurn Head and Immingham. There is a big ship ⚓ S of Spurn Hd. Keep clear of large commercial vessels using Hawke (8·4m) and Sunk (8·8m) Chans; these are marked by S1-S9 SHM buoys, all Fl G 1·5s (S8 is a SHM bn, Fl G 1·5s with tide gauge); and by P2-P9 PHM buoys, all Fl R 1·5s.

For **Grimsby** (lock into Fish Dock) make good 255°/1·35M from Lower Burcom No 6 Lt Float, Fl R 4s.

Off **Kingston-upon-Hull** there is a tidal eddy and streams can be rotatory, ie the flood makes W up Hull Roads for ¾hr whilst the ebb is already running down-river over Skitter Sand on the opposite bank (reaches 2½kn at sp). Humber br (conspic) has 30m clearance.

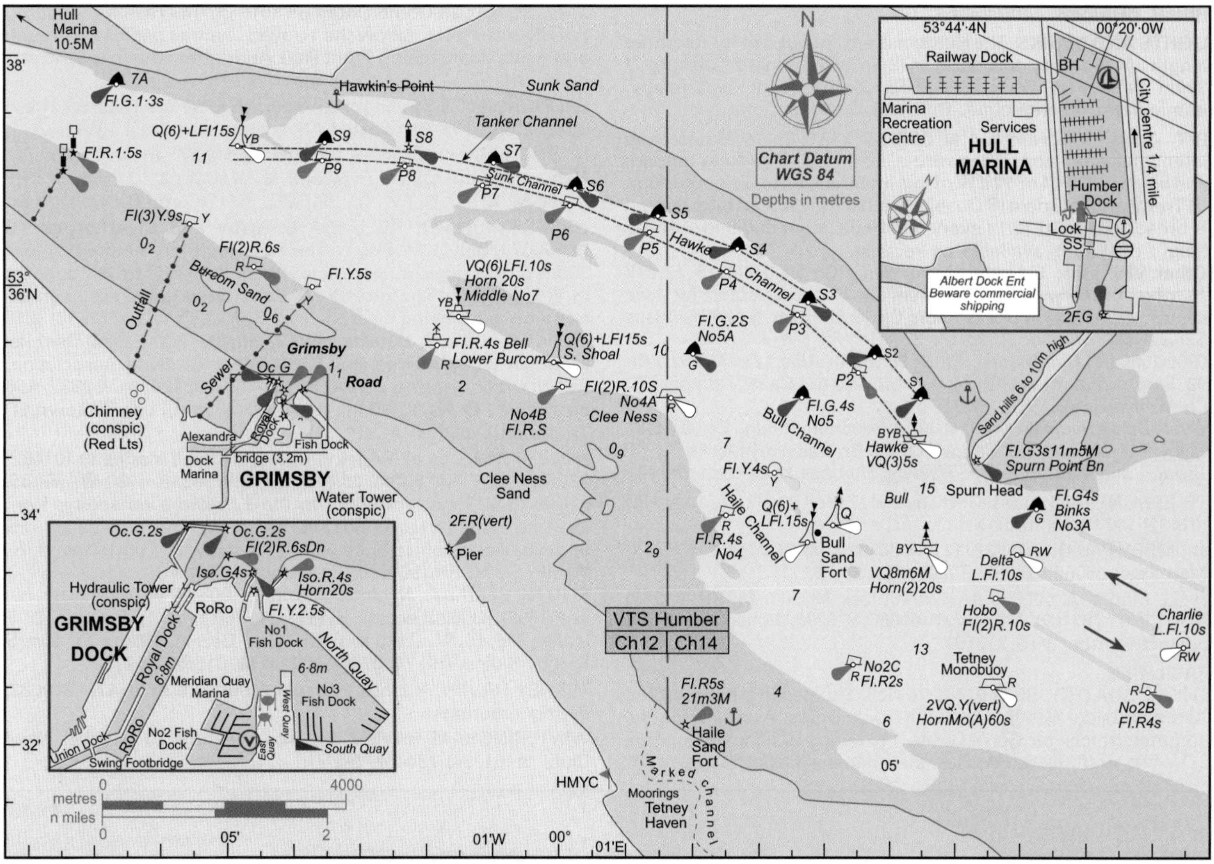
Hull Marina 10·5M
38'
7A
Fl.G.1·3s
Hawkin's Point
Sunk Sand
Q(6)+LFl15s
YB
S9
S8
Fl.R.1·5s
11
P9
P8
Tanker Channel
S7
Sunk Channel
P7
S6
Fl(3)Y.9s
Y
P6
S5
Hawke
P5
S4
Fl(2)R.6s
R
Burcom Sand
Fl.Y.5s
Y
Outfall
53° 36'N
Channel
P4
S3
VQ(6)LFl.10s
Horn 20s
Middle No7
YB
Fl.R.4s Bell
Lower Burcom
R
Q(6)+LFl15s
S. Shoal
10
Fl.G.2S
No5A
G
P3
S2
S1
P2
Grimsby
Road
Sewer
Oc G
2
Fl(2)R.10S
No4A
Clee Ness
R
No4B
Fl.R.S
Fl.G.4s
No5
Bull Channel
BYB
Hawke
VQ(3)5s
Sand hills 6 to 10m high
Fl.G3s11m5M
Spurn Point Bn
Chimney (conspic) (Red Lts)
Alexandra Dock
Royal Dock
Fish Dock
Dock Marina
bridge (3.2m)
GRIMSBY
7
Fl.Y.4s
Y
Clee Ness Sand
Water Tower (conspic)
Bull
15
Spurn Head
Fl.G4s
Binks
No3A
G
34'
Oc.G.2s
Oc.G.2s
Fl(2)R.6sDn
2F.R(vert)
Pier
Haile Channel
Q(6)+LFl.15s
Fl.R.4s
No4
R
Q
Bull Sand Fort
BY
VQ8m6M
Horn(2)20s
RW
Delta
L.Fl.10s
Hydraulic Tower (conspic)
Iso.G4s
Iso.R.4s
Horn20s
RoRo
Fl.Y.2.5s
GRIMSBY DOCK
No1 Fish Dock
North Quay
Royal Dock 6·8m
6·8m
7
Hobo
Fl(2)R.10s
Charlie
L.Fl.10s
RW
VTS Humber
Ch12
Ch14
13
Tetney Monobuoy
R
No2C
Fl.R2s
Meridian Quay Marina
West Quay
No3 Fish Dock
Fl.R5s
21m3M
Haile Sand Fort
4
2VQ.Y(vert)
HornMo(A)60s
6
No2B
Fl.R4s
R
32'
Union Dock
RoRo
No2 Fish Dock
East Quay
South Quay
Swing Footbridge
05'
HMYC
Marked channel
Moorings
Tetney Haven
metres
n miles
0
4000
2
05'
01'W
00°
01'E
N
Chart Datum WGS 84
Depths in metres
53°44'·4N
00°20'·0W
Railway Dock
BH
Marina Recreation Centre
Services
HULL MARINA
City centre 1/4 mile
Humber Dock
Lock
SS
Albert Dock Ent
Beware commercial shipping
2F.G

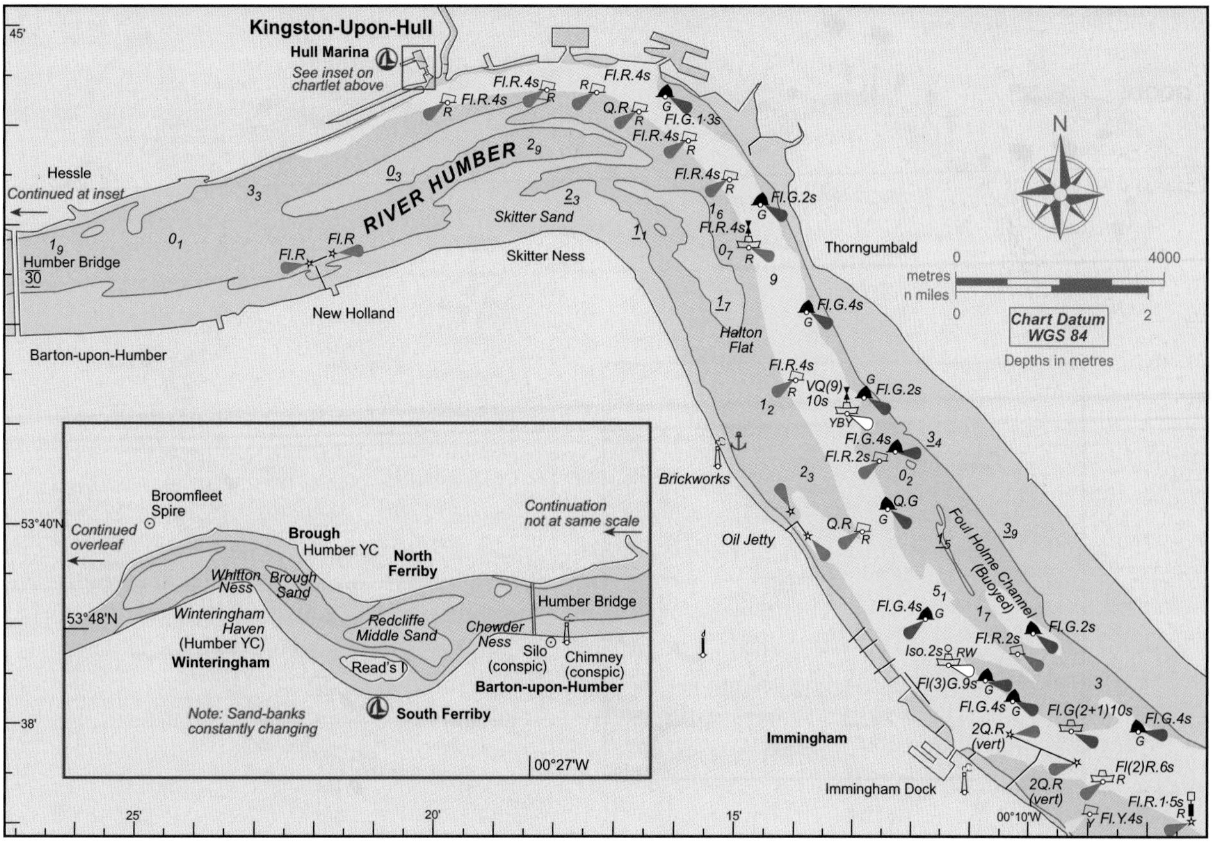
45'
Kingston-Upon-Hull
Hull Marina
See inset on chartlet above
Fl.R.4s
Fl.R.4s
R
Fl.R.4s
Fl.R.4s
R
Q.R
R
G
Fl.G.1·3s
Fl.R.4s
R
Hessle
Continued at inset
RIVER HUMBER
Fl.R.4s
R
Skitter Sand
Fl.G.2s
G
Humber Bridge
30
Fl.R
Fl.R
New Holland
Skitter Ness
Fl.R.4s
R
9
Thorngumbald
Barton-upon-Humber
Halton Flat
Fl.G.4s
G
Fl.R.4s
R
VQ(9) 10s
YBY
Fl.G.2s
G
Fl.G.4s
Fl.R.2s
Brickworks
Q.G
G
Oil Jetty
Q.R
R
Foul Holme Channel (Buoyed)
Fl.G.4s
G
Fl.G.2s
Fl.R.2s
Iso.2s
RW
Fl(3)G.9s
G
3
Fl.G.4s
G
Fl.G(2+1)10s
Fl.G.4s
G
Immingham
2Q.R (vert)
Fl(2)R.6s
R
2Q.R (vert)
Immingham Dock
Fl.R.1·5s
R
Fl.Y.4s
N
0
4000
metres
n miles
0
2
Chart Datum WGS 84
Depths in metres
Broomfleet Spire
Continuation not at same scale
53°40'N
Continued overleaf
Brough
Humber YC
North Ferriby
Whitton Ness
Brough Sand
Humber Bridge
53°48'N
Winteringham Haven (Humber YC)
Winteringham
Redcliffe Middle Sand
Chowder Ness
Read's I
Silo (conspic)
Chimney (conspic)
Barton-upon-Humber
South Ferriby
Note: Sand-banks constantly changing
00°27'W
38'
25'
20'
15'
00°10'W

5

RIVER HUMBER *continued*

LIGHTS AND MARKS The Humber is well buoyed/lit for its whole length. At Grimsby a conspic tr (94m with 'minaret' on top) is 300m W of Fish Dock lock. IPTS control entry to Grimsby, Immingham, Killingholme, Hull and Goole.

R/T Advise *VTS Humber* (☎ 01482-212191) Ch 14 of posn and intentions when appr if seaward of 00°01´·8E (Clee Ness lt float); and listen on Ch 14 or 12 if W of this meridian, up to Gainsborough (R Trent) and to Goole (R Ouse). Weather, nav & tidal information is broadcast on Ch 12/14 every odd H+03; more detailed info, inc height of tide, is available on request.

Other VHF stns: *Grimsby Docks Radio* Ch **74** (H24) 18 79 call *Humber Cruising* for marina staff or *Fishdock Island* for lock keeper. *Immingham Docks Radio* Ch 19 68 (H24). R Hull Port Ops Service call *Drypool Radio* Ch 22 (Mon-Fri HW–2 to HW+1; Sat 0900-1100 LT).*Hull Marina*, Ch M **80** (H24); *Albert Dock Radio* Ch 09. *Ferriby Sluice*(Lock)Ch 74. *S.Ferriby Marina* Ch 80, Humber YC, Ch M (if racing).

Goole Docks Radio Ch 14 (H24) 09 19. Boothferry Bridge Ch 09 (H24). Selby Railway and Toll Bridges Ch 09. Br Waterways locks Ch 74. *Brough and Winteringham Havens, Humber Yawl Club* Ch 37.

TELEPHONE (Dial codes: Grimsby 01472; Hull 01482) Humber HM (01482) 327171 controls whole estuary/river.

GRIMSBY Port Director 327171, 📠 325819; MRSC (01262) 672317; Marinecall 09066 526238; Police (01482) 881111.

HULL Marina ☎ 609960, 📠 224148; lock 330508; MRSC (01262) 672317; ⊖ 782107; Marinecall 09066 526238; Police 26111; Dr contact Humber VTS 212191.

FACILITIES

GOOLE BOATHOUSE ☎ 01405 763985. Situated in a basin off the Aire and Calder Canal near to the Goole Docks. Access is via the commercial lock for Goole Docks. 140 berths £2.58 any size, max LOA 40ft, draft 6ft, D, FW, Gas, El. Other facilities include Dry Dk, Slip, CH, ♿. Call Goole Docks on VHF Ch 14. Take the flood up the River Humber, follow the buoyed channel past Hull, Brough and when approaching Trent Falls Apex alter course to stbd and follow the River Ouse to Goole.

BROUGH HAVEN, E Riding of Yorkshire, **Humber Yawl Club** ☎ (01482) 667224, Slip, FW, Bar, limited AB; contact club. Enter HW±1½.

NABURN (R Ouse, 4M S of York and 80M above Spurn Pt). **Naburn Marina** (300+50 visitors) ☎ (01904) 621021; £6.95; VHF Ch **80** M; CH, P, D, FW, ⚡, ⚒, ME, BH (16 ton), R.

GRIMSBY (01472; NE Lincs) **Grimsby and Cleethorpes YC** ☎ 356678, Bar, R, M, FW, ▣. The **Fish Docks** are entered by lock 300m E of conspic tr. Access is HW±3, with R/G tfc lts, but best to enter without charge HW±2 , when both gates are open for free flow after being cleared in by *Fish Dock Island* Ch 74; (£10 locking fee for Ⓥ outside HW±2). Inside No 2 Fish Dock is: **Meridian Quay Marina** (run by Humber Cruising Association, call *Humber Cruising* Ch 74) ☎ (01472) 268424, 📠 269832, 160 berths + 30 Ⓥ AB, £1.30 inc ⚡, D, BH (35ton), bar, ▣. **Town** EC Thurs; all facilities, ACA.

HULL (01482; City of Kingston-upon-Hull) **Hull Marina** ☎ (01482) 330508, lock ent 53°44'·28N 00°20'·10W, (310 + 20 Ⓥ), £1.55, access HW±3 via lock 150m to the E, beware no shelter from adverse weather/sea conditions when waiting outside of lock in river, Marina office open 0900-1700 daily; D, P, CH, Gas, ⊖, ♿, ⚓, ME, El, ⚒, BH (50 ton), C (2 ton), ▣, SM, ACA.

SOUTH FERRIBY, N Lincs. **Marina** (100+20 visitors) VHF 80, ☎ (01652) 635620; access HW±3, £14 (60 hrs) inc lock fee, D, P (cans), ME, El, ⚒, C (30 ton), CH, Gas, Gaz, ⚓. **Village** 🛒, Bar. S Ferriby Sluice VHF 74: 0730-1600, or ☎ 01652 635219.

TETNEY HAVEN, N Lincs. Humber Mouth YC ☎ (01472) 812063, drying moorings.

WINTERINGHAM HAVEN, N Lincs (belongs to Humber Yawl Club) ☎ (01724) 734452, ✉.

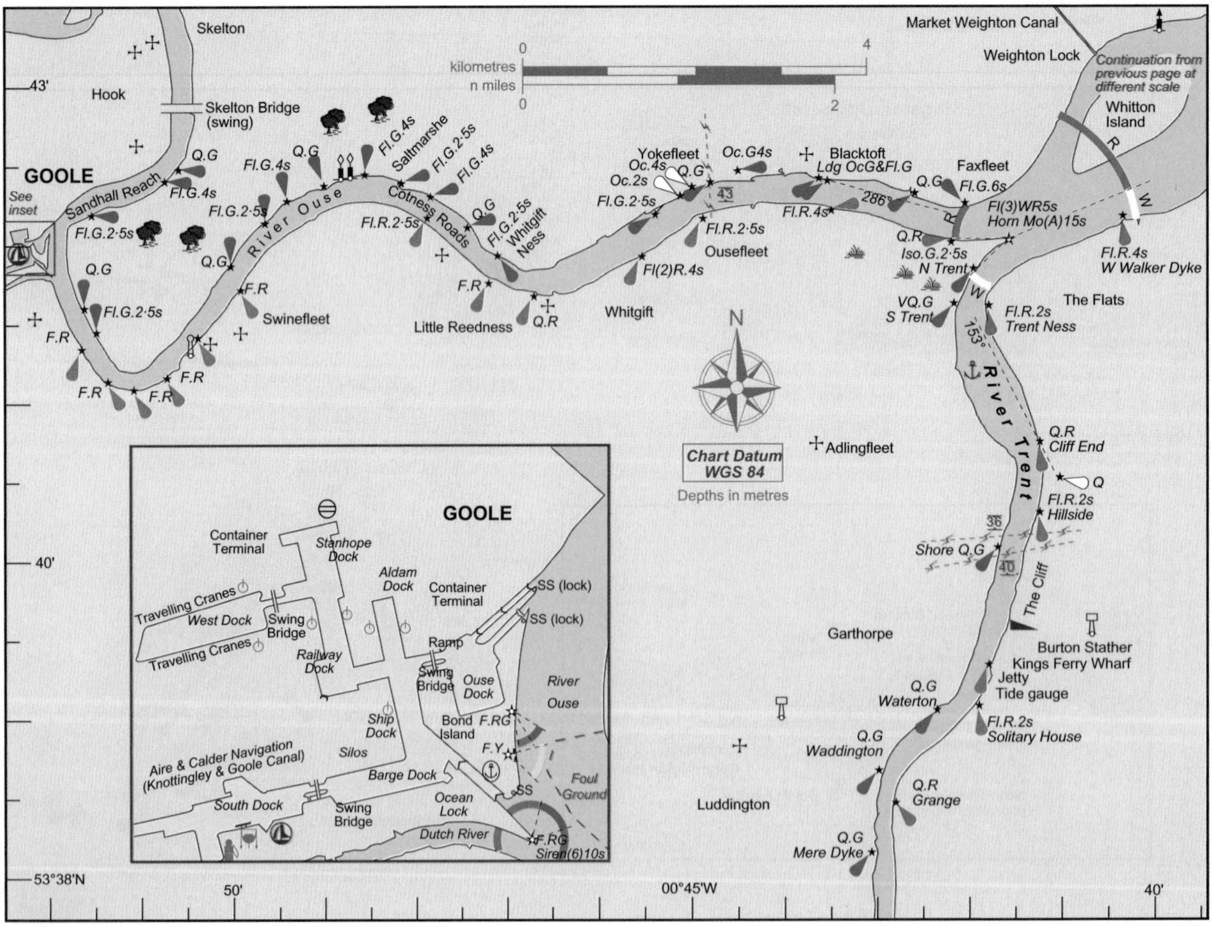
Skelton
Hook
GOOLE
See inset
Skelton Bridge (swing)
Sandhall Reach
River Ouse
Saltmarshe
Cotness Roads
Whitgift Ness
Swinefleet
Little Reedness
Whitgift
Yokefleet
Blacktoft
Ldg OcG&Fl.G
Ousefleet
Faxfleet
Market Weighton Canal
Weighton Lock
Continuation from previous page at different scale
Whitton Island
Fl(3)WR5s Horn Mo(A)15s
Fl.R.4s W Walker Dyke
N Trent
S Trent
The Flats
Fl.R.2s Trent Ness
River Trent
Q.R Cliff End
Fl.R.2s Hillside
Shore Q.G
The Cliff
Adlingfleet
Garthorpe
Burton Stather
Kings Ferry Wharf
Jetty
Tide gauge
Fl.R.2s Solitary House
Waterton
Waddington
Luddington
Q.R Grange
Q.G Mere Dyke
kilometres
n miles
Chart Datum WGS 84
Depths in metres
43'
40'
53°38'N
50'
00°45'W
40'
GOOLE
Container Terminal
Stanhope Dock
Aldam Dock
Container Terminal
SS (lock)
Travelling Cranes
West Dock
Swing Bridge
Railway Dock
Ramp
Ouse Dock
River Ouse
Ship Dock
Bond Island
F.RG
F.Y.
Aire & Calder Navigation (Knottingley & Goole Canal)
Silos
Barge Dock
Foul Ground
South Dock
Swing Bridge
Ocean Lock
Dutch River
Siren(6)10s

9.5.11 BRIDLINGTON

E Riding of Yorkshire **54°04'·78N 00°11'·21W** ❀❀◊◊✿✿✿

CHARTS AC 1191, 1190, 129, 121, 1882; Imray C29; OS 101

TIDES +0553 Dover; ML 3·6; Duration 0610; Zone 0 (UT)

Standard Port NORTH SHIELDS (⟶)

Times				**Height (metres)**			
High Water		Low Water		MHWS	MHWN	MLWN	MLWS
0200	0800	0100	0800	5·0	3·9	1·8	0·7
1400	2000	1300	2000				
Differences BRIDLINGTON							
+0119	+0109	+0109	+0104	+1·1	+0·8	+0·5	+0·4
FILEY BAY							
+0101	+0101	+0101	+0048	+0·8	+1·0	+0·6	+0·3

SHELTER Good, except in E, SE and S winds. Hbr dries completely to soft black mud; access HW±3 (for draft of 2·7m). Visitors normally berth on S pier or near HM's Office. A marina is planned but agreement not reached (mid 2003).

NAVIGATION WPT SW Smithic WCM, Q (9) 15s, 54°02'·41N 00°09'·21W, 333° to ent, 2·6M. Close-in appr is with N pier hd lt on brg 002° to keep W of drying patch (The Canch). Beware bar, 1m at MLWN, could dry out at MLWS.

LIGHTS AND MARKS Hbr is 4M WSW of Flamborough Hd lt, Fl (4) 15s 65m 24M. Y racing marks are laid in the Bay, Apr-Oct. Tidal sigs, by day from S pier: R flag = >2·7m in hbr; No flag = < 2·7m. At night from N pier: Fl ● = >2·7m in hbr; Fl ● = < 2·7m.

R/T Call on VHF Ch 16, then Ch **12**, 67 for working.

TELEPHONE (Dial code 01262) HM 670148/9, 📠 602041, mobile 0860 275150; MRSC 672317; Marinecall 09066 526238; Police (01482) 881111; Ⓗ 673451.

FACILITIES S Pier FW, AB £2.80 /sq m/week or £15/yacht <3days, D (tank/hose), C (5 ton), BH (70 ton), Slip; M, see HM; **Royal Yorks YC** ☎ 672041, L, FW, R, Bar. **Town** EC Thurs; P (cans), CH, ME, El, 🛒, R, Bar, ✉, Ⓑ, ⇌, ✈ (Humberside).

ADJACENT ANCHORAGE (7M SE of Scarborough)

FILEY, N Yorkshire, 54°12'·80N 00°16'·20W, AC 1882, 129. HW +0532 on Dover; ML 3·5m; Duration 0605. See 9.5.11. Good ⚓ in winds from S to NNE in 4 – 5m on hard sand. Lt on cliff above CG Stn, G metal column, FR 31m 1M vis 272°-308°. Filey Brigg, a natural bkwtr, is marked by ECM buoy, Q(3)10s, Bell. Beware Old Horse Rks, 2M WNW of Filey Brigg, foul ground extending ½M offshore. An unmarked Historic Wreck (see 9.0.3h) lies at 54°11'·51N 00°13'·48W. Facilities: EC Wed; 🛒, R, Bar, L, Ⓗ ☎ (01723) 68111, ✉, Ⓑ, ⇌.

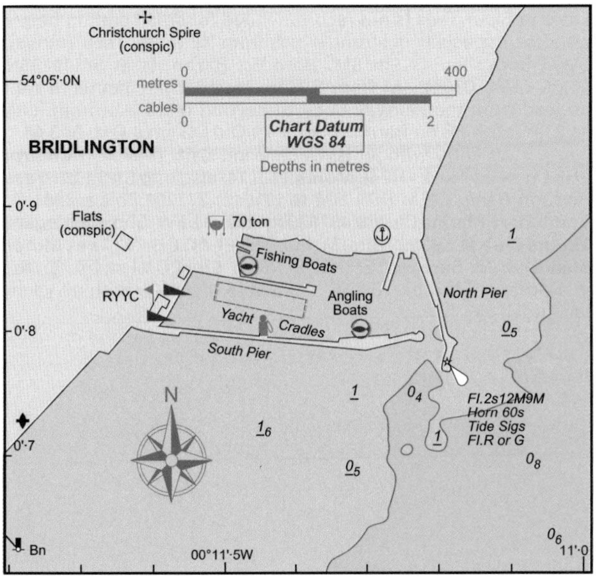
Christchurch Spire
(conspic)
54°05'·0N
metres
cables
400
2
BRIDLINGTON
Chart Datum
WGS 84
Depths in metres
0'·9
Flats
(conspic)
70 ton
Fishing Boats
RYYC
Angling
Boats
North Pier
Yacht
Cradles
0'·8
South Pier
Fl.2s12M9M
Horn 60s
Tide Sigs
Fl.R or G
0'·7
Bn
00°11'·5W
11'·0

9.5.12 SCARBOROUGH

N. Yorkshire **54°16'·88N 00°23'·36W** ❀❀◊◊◊✿✿✿

CHARTS AC 1191, 129, 1612; Imray C29; OS 101

TIDES +0527 Dover; ML 3·5; Duration 0615; Zone 0 (UT)

Standard Port NORTH SHIELDS (⟶)

Times				**Height (metres)**			
High Water		Low Water		MHWS	MHWN	MLWN	MLWS
0200	0800	0100	0800	5·0	3·9	1·8	0·7
1400	2000	1300	2000				
Differences SCARBOROUGH							
+0059	+0059	+0044	+0044	+0·7	+0·7	+0·5	+0·2

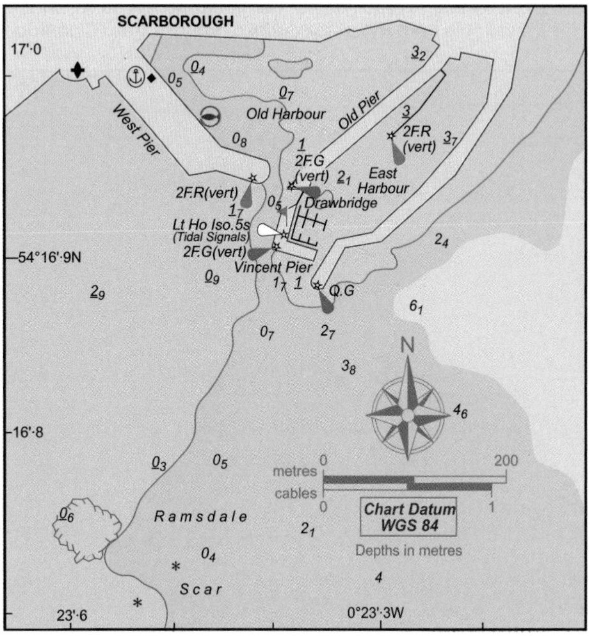
SCARBOROUGH
17'·0
Old Harbour
Old Pier
West Pier
2F.R
(vert)
2F.G
(vert)
East
Harbour
2F.R(vert)
Drawbridge
Lt Ho Iso.5s
(Tidal Signals)
2F.G(vert)
Vincent Pier
54°16'·9N
Q.G
N
16'·8
metres
cables
200
Chart Datum
WGS 84
Ramsdale
Depths in metres
Scar
23'·6
0°23'·3W

SHELTER Good in E Hbr, access HW±3 via narrow (10m) ent by E pier, but not in strong E/SE'lies. 5 Ⓥ pontoon berths, (max LOA 10.3m, draft 1.8m), in the SW corner of E Hbr, just below lt ho. 4 Ⓥ drying AB on Old Pier just N of the drawbridge. In winter months access to East Hbr is via the drawbridge only.

NAVIGATION WPT 54°16'·50N 00°22'·00W, 302° to E pier lt, 0·83M. Appr from the E to avoid Ramsdale Scar, rky shoal 0·9m. Keep careful watch for salmon nets E & SE of ent. Beware rks extending approx 20m SW of E pier head. Give Castle Headland close N of hbr a wide berth due to coastal defence work.

LIGHTS AND MARKS Lt ho (conspic), Iso 5s, Dia 60s, on Vincent Pier is shown by night or B ● by day when there is more than 3·7m over bar in entrance. Other lts as shown on plan.

R/T Call *Scarborough hbr* VHF Ch **12** 16 (H24). Watchkeeper will offer guidance to approaching visitors.

TELEPHONE (Dial code 01723) HM (HO) ☎ 373530, 373877 (OT), 📠 350035; Port Control 373877; CG 372323; MRSC (01262) 672317; Marinecall 09066 526238; Police 500300; Ⓗ 368111.

FACILITIES East Hbr AB £11.75 <10m LOA, M, FW, ⊐D, D, C (3 ton), Slip; **Scarborough YC** ☎ 373821, AB, Slip, M*, FW, ME, El, Ⓛ; **Services:** ME, El, ⚒, CH, P & D (cans), Ⓔ. **Town** EC Wed; P, D, 🛒, R, Bar, ✉, Ⓑ, ⇌, ✈ (Humberside).

9.5.13 WHITBY

N. Yorkshire **54°29'·65N 00°36'·78W** ❀❀⛵⛵⛵✿✿✿

CHARTS AC 129, 134, 1612; Imray C29, C24; OS 94

TIDES +0500 Dover; ML 3·3; Duration 0605; Zone 0 (UT)

Standard Port NORTH SHIELDS (⟶)

Times				Height (metres)			
High Water		Low Water		MHWS	MHWN	MLWN	MLWS
0200	0800	0100	0800	5·0	3·9	1·8	0·7
1400	2000	1300	2000				
Differences WHITBY							
+0034	+0049	+0034	+0019	+0·6	+0·4	+0·1	+0·1

SHELTER Good, except in lower hbr in strong NW to NE winds. Hbr is available from HW±4 for drafts of approx 2m. YC pontoon below br. Marina (dredged approx 2m) is 2ca beyond swing bridge; visitor berths at seaward end of long pontoon. Bridge opens on request HW±2 every H and H+30; extra openings in summer as arranged with WYC. FG lts = open; FR lts = shut.

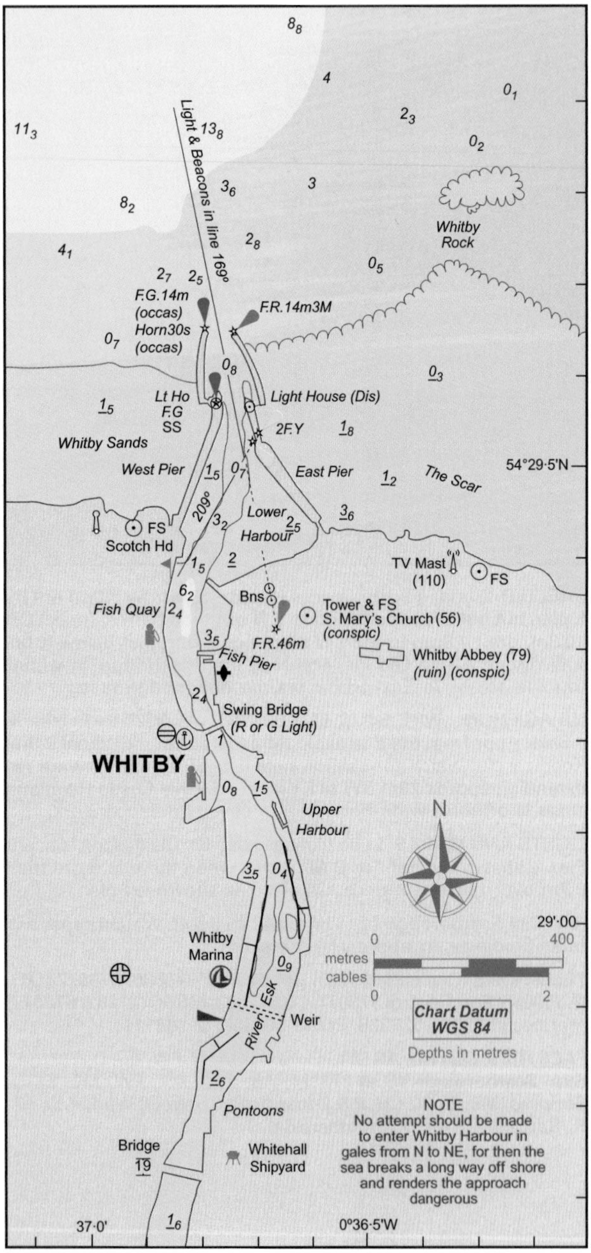
Light & Beacons in line 169°
F.G.14m (occas) Horn30s (occas)
F.R.14m3M
Whitby Rock
Lt Ho F.G SS
Light House (Dis)
2F.Y
Whitby Sands
West Pier
East Pier
The Scar
54°29·5'N
Scotch Hd
FS
Lower Harbour
TV Mast (110)
Bns
Tower & FS S. Mary's Church (56) (conspic)
Fish Quay
F.R.46m
Fish Pier
Whitby Abbey (79) (ruin) (conspic)
Swing Bridge (R or G Light)
WHITBY
Upper Harbour
N
Whitby Marina
29'·00
metres
cables
400
River Esk
Weir
Chart Datum WGS 84
Depths in metres
Pontoons
Whitehall Shipyard
Bridge
NOTE
No attempt should be made to enter Whitby Harbour in gales from N to NE, for then the sea breaks a long way off shore and renders the approach dangerous
37·0'
0°36·5'W

NAVIGATION WPT 54°30'·21N 00°36'96W, 169° to ent, 0·57M. Hbr can be approached safely from any direction except when note on chartlet applies. From the SE beware Whitby Rk; leave Whitby NCM buoy, Q, to port. Beware strong set to E from HW –2 to HW, when nearing piers. Vessels >37m LOA must embark pilot; via HM.

LIGHTS AND MARKS TV mast to E of entr. Whitby High lt ho, Fl WR 5s 73m 18/16M, (R128°-143°, W143°-319°), is 2M ESE of hbr ent.

Ldg lines:

(1) Chapel spire in line 176° with E pier disused lt ho.

(2) FR lt or 2 bns, seen between disused lt houses, lead 169° into hbr. Hold this line until bns (W △ and W ○ with B stripe) on E pier (two FY lts) are abeam.

(3) On course 209° keep these same bns in line astern.

R/T Hbr and Marina VHF Ch **11** 16 12 (H24). Whitby Bridge Ch **11** 16 06 (listens on Ch 16 HW–2 to HW+2).

TELEPHONE (Dial code 01947) HM ☎ 602354, 📠 600380; MRSC (01262) 672317;s Marinecall 09066 526238/453; Police (01653) 692424; Dr 820888.

FACILITIES **Whitby Marina** (200+10 visitors) ☎ 600165, £1.82, D, P (cans), Slip, ME, El, ⚒, C, CH; **Fish Quay** M, D (in commercial quantities only), L, FW, C (1 ton), CH, AB, R, Bar; **Whitby YC** ☎ 603623, M, L, Bar; **Services:** ME, El, ⚒, CH, BH, ACA, SM, Gas, Gaz. **Town** EC Wed; usual amenities, ✉, Ⓑ, ⇌, ✈ (Teesside).

ADJACENT ANCHORAGE (5M WNW of Whitby)

RUNSWICK BAY, N. Yorkshire, **54°32'·11N 00°44'·20W.** AC 1612. HW +0505 on Dover: Differences on R Tyne are approx as Whitby; ML 3·1m; Duration 0605. Good shelter in all winds from SSE thru W to NW. Enter bay at 225° keeping clear of many rks at base of cliffs. Two W posts (2FY by night when required by lifeboat) 18m apart are ldg marks 270° to LB ho and can be used to lead into ⚓. Good holding in 6m to 9m in middle of bay. Facilities: **Runswick Bay Rescue Boat Station** ☎ (01947) 840965. **Village** Bar, R, 🛒.

ADJACENT PORT (3M SSE of Hartlepool)

RIVER TEES/MIDDLESBROUGH, Middlesbrough/Stockton, **54°38'·94N 01°08'·48W.** ❀❀⛵✿. AC 152, 2567, 2566; Imray C29; OS 93. HW +0450 Dover; Differences see 9.5.14. ML 3·1; Duration 0605. R. Tees & Middlesbrough are a major industrial area. 5M upriver from the hbr ent a Tall Ships Centre is planned in the former Middlesborough Dock.

Entry to River Tees is not recommended for small craft in heavy weather, especially in strong winds from NE to SE. Tees Fairway SWM buoy, Iso 4s 9m 8M, Horn 5s, Racon, is at 54°40'·93N 01°06'·38W, 030°/2·4M from S Gare bkwtr. The channel is well buoyed from the Fairway buoy to beyond Middlesbrough. Ldg lts 210°, both FR on framework trs. At Old CG stn a Q lt, or 3 ● (vert), = no entry without HM's consent. Call: *Tees Port Control* VHF Ch **14** 22 16 12 (H24). Monitor Ch 14; also info Ch 14 22. *Tees Barrage Radio* Ch M (37). HM ☎ (01642) 277201;Police 248184. **South Gare Marine Club** ☎ 491039 (occas), M, FW, Slip; **Castlegate Marine Club** ☎ 583299 Slip, M, FW, ME, El, ⚒, CH, 🛒; **Tees Motor Boat Club** M; **Services:** El, ME, Ⓔ, ACA. **City** EC Wed; ✉, Ⓑ, ⇌, ✈. Hartlepool marina (9.5.14) lies 3M to the NNW with all yacht facilities.

9.5.14 HARTLEPOOL

Hartlepool **54°41'·26N 01°11'·90W** (West Hbr ent)

CHARTS AC 152, 2567, 2566; Imray C24; OS 93

TIDES +0437 Dover; ML 3·0; Duration 0600; Zone 0 (UT)

Standard Port NORTH SHIELDS (→)

Times				Height (metres)			
High Water		Low Water		MHWS	MHWN	MLWN	MLWS
0200	0800	0100	0800	5·0	3·9	1·8	0·7
1400	2000	1300	2000				
Differences HARTLEPOOL							
+0015	+0015	+0008	+0008	+0·4	+0·3	0·0	+0·1
MIDDLESBROUGH							
+0019	+0021	+0014	+0011	+0·6	+0·6	+0·3	+0·1

SHELTER Excellent in marina (5m), access HW±5 via chan dredged 0·8m and lock H24 over tidal cill 0.8m below CD. Speed limit 4kn in W Hbr and marina. Strong E/SE winds raise broken water and swell in the bay, making ent channel hazardous, but possible. In such conditions, call VHF Ch M or 80 for advice. Or call *Tees Port Control* Ch 14 for short-stay in Victoria Hbr (commercial dock, not normally for yachts), access H24.

NAVIGATION WPT Longscar ECM buoy, Q (3) 10s, Bell, 54°40'·86N 01°09'·90W, 295° to W Hbr ent 1·06M; (or, for Victoria Hbr, 128°/308° from/to Nos 1/2 buoys, 0·65M). From S, beware Longscar Rks, only 4ca WSW of WPT. Note: Tees Fairway SWM buoy, Iso 4s 8M, (54°40'·94N 01°06'·48W) is 2M E of Longscar ECM buoy and may assist the initial landfall.

LIGHTS AND MARKS The Heugh lt ho Fl (2) 10s 19m 19M, H24. Dir lt Fl WRG 2s 6m 3M leads 308° to W Hbr/marina lock; vis G305·5°-307°, W307°-309°, R309°-38·5°. W Hbr outer piers, Oc R/G 5s 12m 2M; bright street lts on S pier. Inner piers, FR/FG 7m 2M.
Lock sigs: ● = Proceed; ● = Wait; ● ● = Lock closed.
Dir lt Iso WRG 3s 42m, W324·4°-325·4°, leads 325° via lit buoyed chan to Victoria Hbr. 2 FG (vert) on Kafiga pontoons.

R/T Marina Ch **M** 37 80. *Tees Port Control* info Ch 14 22 (H24). *Hartlepool Dock Radio* Ch 12, only for ship docking.

TELEPHONE (Dial code 01429) Marina 865744; ; MRSC (0191) 257 2691; Tees Port Authority (01642) 277205 Fax 277227; Marinecall 09066 526237; Customs (0191) 257 9441; Police 221151; Dr 272679.

FACILITIES **Hartlepool Marina** H24 (500+100 Ⓥ) ☎ 865744, Fax 865947, £1.80, D (H24), P (cans), LPG, BY, El, ME, Launderette, Disabled, Pump-out, BH (40 and 300 tons), C (13 tons), Gas, Gaz; **Tees & Hartlepool YC** ☎ 233423, Bar, Slip; **Services:** CH, ME, EL, ME, C (mobiles). **Town:** P (cans), Supermarket (H24), R, Bar, ✉, Ⓑ, ⇌, ✈ (Teesside).

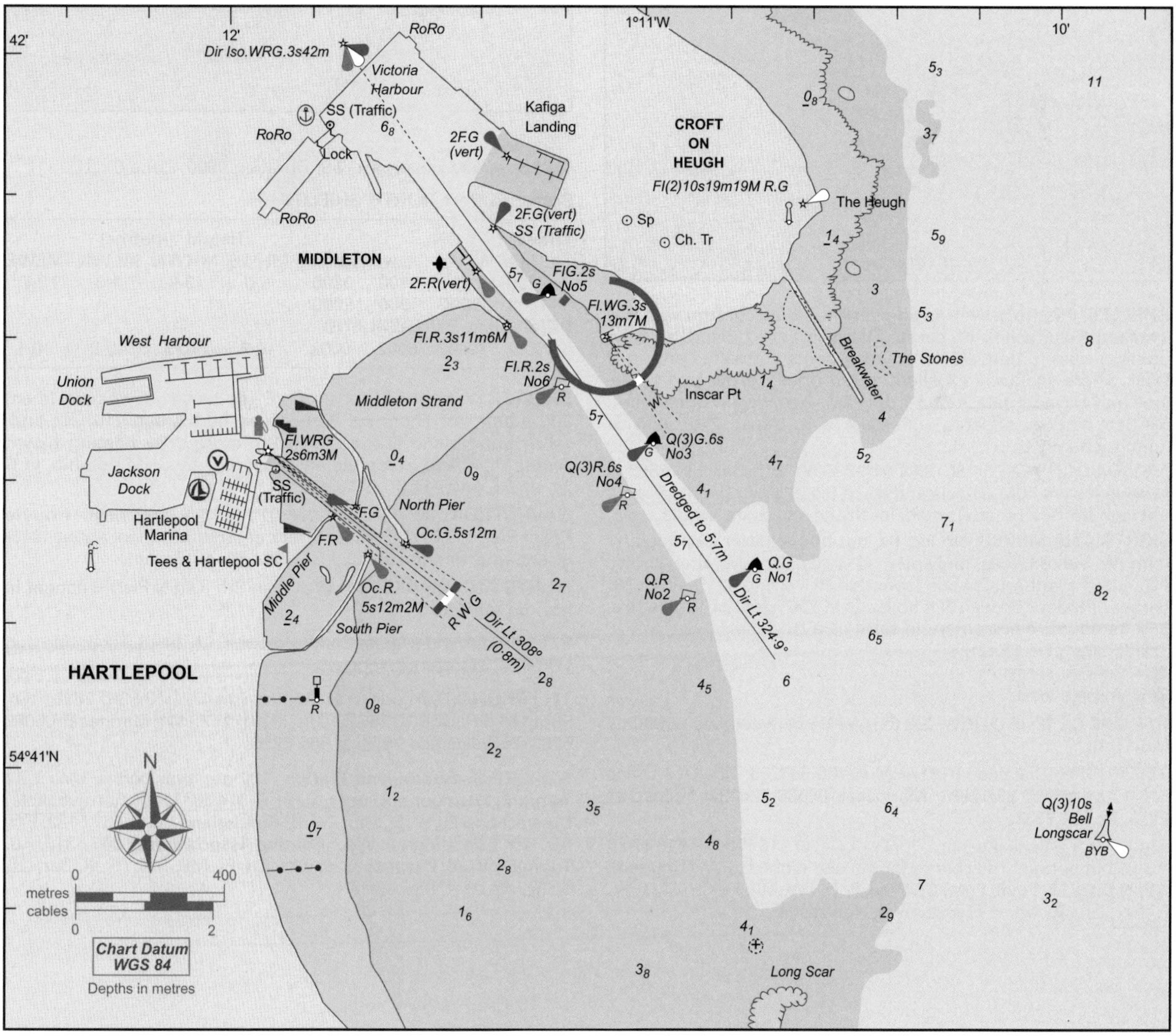
Victoria Harbour
Dir Iso.WRG.3s42m
RoRo
SS (Traffic)
Lock
Kafiga Landing
2F.G (vert)
2F.G(vert)
SS (Traffic)
CROFT ON HEUGH
Fl(2)10s19m19M R.G
The Heugh
Sp
Ch. Tr
MIDDLETON
2F.R(vert)
Fl.G.2s No5
Fl.WG.3s 13m7M
Fl.R.3s11m6M
Fl.R.2s No6
Breakwater
The Stones
Inscar Pt
West Harbour
Union Dock
Middleton Strand
Q(3)G.6s No3
Fl.WRG 2s6m3M
Jackson Dock
SS (Traffic)
Q(3)R.6s No4
Dredged to 5.7m
North Pier
F.G
Hartlepool Marina
Oc.G.5s12m
F.R
Tees & Hartlepool SC
Middle Pier
Oc.R. 5s12m2M
South Pier
Dir Lt 308° (0.8m)
Q.G No1
Q.R No2
Dir Lt 324.9°
HARTLEPOOL
1°11'W
12'
10'
42'
54°41'N
N
metres
cables
0
400
2
Chart Datum WGS 84
Depths in metres
Q(3)10s Bell Longscar
BYB
Long Scar

9.5.15 SEAHAM

Durham **54°50′·24N 01°19′·28W** ❀◊✿

CHARTS AC 152, 1627; Imray C24; OS 88

TIDES +0435 Dover; ML 3·0; Duration 0600; Zone 0 (UT)

Standard Port NORTH SHIELDS (⟶)

Times				**Height (metres)**			
High Water		Low Water		MHWS	MHWN	MLWN	MLWS
0200	0800	0100	0800	5·0	3·9	1·8	0·7
1400	2000	1300	2000				
Differences SEAHAM							
+0004	+0004	–0001	–0001	+0·2	+0·2	+0·2	0·0

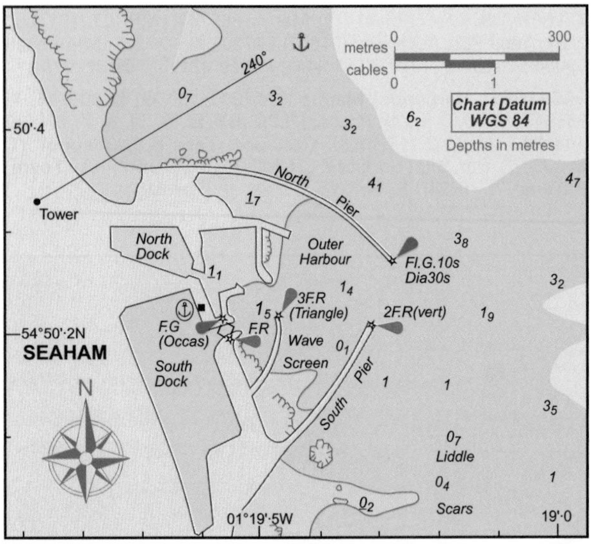
metres 0 300
cables 0 1
Chart Datum WGS 84
Depths in metres
240°
North Pier
Tower
North Dock
Outer Harbour
Fl.G.10s Dia30s
3F.R (Triangle)
2F.R(vert)
F.G (Occas)
F.R
Wave Screen
South Pier
South Dock
SEAHAM
54°50′·2N
50′·4
Liddle Scars
01°19′·5W
19′·0

SHELTER Prior to arrival visiting yachts should confirm with HM availability/suitability of berth. There is very limited, (if any) public access to berths(2004). Small boats normally berth in N Dock where shelter is excellent, but it dries. Larger boats may lock into S Dock; gates open from HW –2 to HW+1. Speed limit 5kn. Or ⚓ 2½ca offshore with clock tr in transit 240° with St John's church tr.

NAVIGATION WPT 54°50′·36N 01°18′·60W (off chartlet), 256° to N bkwtr lt ho, 0·40M. Shoals and rks to S of S bkwtr (Liddle Scars). Ent should not be attempted in strong on-shore winds.

LIGHTS AND MARKS No ldg lts, but hbr is easily identified by lt ho (W with B bands) on N pier, Fl G 10s 12m 5M (often shows FG in bad weather), Dia 30s (sounded HW–2½ to +1½). FS at NE corner of S dock on with N lt ho leads in 256° clear of Tangle Rks. 3FR lts on wave screen are in form of a △.
Traffic sigs at S Dock:
● = Vessels enter
● = Vessels leave

R/T VHF Ch **12** 16 06 (HW–2½ to HW+1½ between 0800–1800 LT Mon-Fri).

TELEPHONE (Dial code 0191) HM 07786 565208; Hbr Ops Office 516 1700; MRSC 257 2691; Marinecall 09066 526237; Police 581 2255; Dr 581 2332.

FACILITIES S Dock (Seaham Hbr Dock Co) ☎ 516 1700, 📠 516 1701, AB £5 but normally no charge for the odd night, L, FW, C (40 ton), AB; **N Dock** M. **Town** (½M) EC Wed; P, D, FW, ME, El, CH (5M), 🛒, R, Bar, ✉, Ⓑ, ≠, ✈ (Teesside or Newcastle).

9.5.16 SUNDERLAND

Tyne and Wear **54°55′·23N 01°21′·15W** ❀❀❀◊◊✿✿

CHARTS AC 152, 1627; Imray C24; OS 88

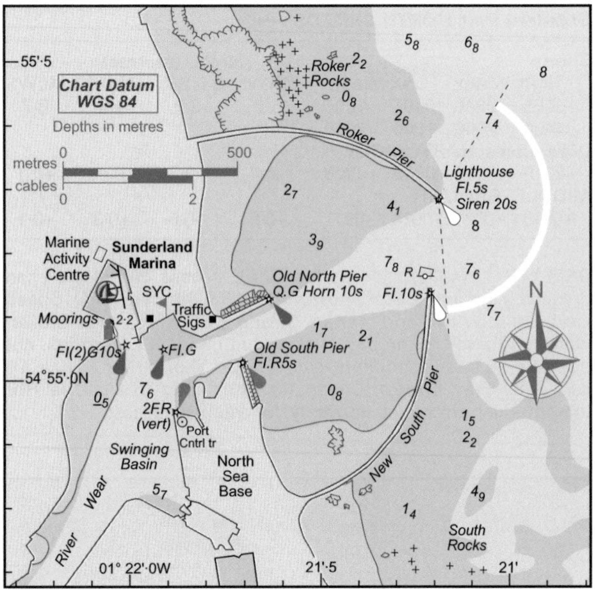
Chart Datum WGS 84
Depths in metres
metres 0 500
cables 0 2
55′·5
Roker Rocks
Roker Pier
Lighthouse Fl.5s Siren 20s
Marine Activity Centre
Sunderland Marina
SYC
Traffic Sigs
Moorings
Fl(2)G10s
Fl.G
Old North Pier Q.G Horn 10s
Fl.10s
Old South Pier Fl.R5s
54°55′·0N
2F.R (vert)
Port Cntrl tr
Swinging Basin
North Sea Base
River Wear
New South Pier
South Rocks
01° 22′·0W
21′·5
21′

TIDES +0430 Dover; ML 2·9; Duration 0600; Zone 0 (UT)

Standard Port NORTH SHIELDS (⟶)

Times				**Height (metres)**			
High Water		Low Water		MHWS	MHWN	MLWN	MLWS
0200	0800	0100	0800	5·0	3·9	1·8	0·7
1400	2000	1300	2000				
Differences SUNDERLAND							
+0002	–0002	–0002	–0002	+0·2	+0·3	+0·2	+0·1

SHELTER Very good, but strong E'lies cause heavy swell in ent and outer hbr. There are 88 pontoon berths and 110 fore-and-aft in Sunderland Marina (2·3m), protected by floating bkwtr; access H24. App to marina ent is marked by SHM dolphin, Fl G 5s, and E jetty, Fl (2) G 10s.

NAVIGATION WPT 54°55′·21N 01°20′·10W, 098°/278° from/to Roker Pier lt, 0·61M. Beware wreck at Whitburn Steel about 1M N of ent, and Hendon Rk (0·9m), 1.2M SE of hbr ent.

LIGHTS AND MARKS 3 Fl ● at Pilot Stn (Old N Pier) = danger in hbr; no ent/dep.

R/T *Sunderland Marina* Ch M. Port VHF Ch 14 16 (H24); tide and visibility reports on request.

TELEPHONE (Dial code 0191) Marina 514 4721; HM 567 2626 (HO), 567 0161 (OT); MRSC 257 2691; ⊜ (0191) 257 9441; Marinecall 09066 526237; Police 454 7555; 🅗 565 6256.

FACILITIES **Sunderland Marina** (120 pontoon berths, max LOA 15m; and 110 moorings) ☎ 514 4721, 📠 514 1847, Ⓥ(when available) £15/yacht, M £9, ♿, D, Slip, FW, ⚓; **Sunderland YC** ☎ 567 5133, FW, AB, Bar, Slip (dinghy); **Wear Boating Association** ☎ 567 5313, AB. **Town** EC Wed; P (cans), Gas, Gaz, CH, El, ME, SM, 🛒, R, Bar, ✉, 🅓, Ⓑ, ≠, ✈ (Newcastle).

9.5.17 R. TYNE/NORTH SHIELDS

Tyne and Wear **55°00'·89N 01°24'·10W** ❁❁◊◊◊✿✿

CHARTS AC 152, 1191, 1934; Imray C24; OS 88

TIDES +0430 Dover; ML 3·0; Duration 0604; Zone 0 (UT)

Standard Port NORTH SHIELDS (⟶)

Times				Height (metres)			
High Water		Low Water		MHWS	MHWN	MLWN	MLWS
0200	0800	0100	0800	5·0	3·9	1·8	0·7
1400	2000	1300	2000				
Differences NEWCASTLE-UPON-TYNE							
+0003	+0003	+0008	+0008	+0·3	+0·2	+0·1	+0·1

SHELTER Good in all weathers. Access H24, but in strong E and NE winds appr may be difficult for smaller craft due to much backwash off the piers; confused seas can build at the ent in severe weather, and a large swell can steepen and break dangerously when meeting an ebb tide up to half a mile inside the harbour. Royal Quays marina (in former Albert Edward Dock) is 2M upriver from pierheads. St Peter's Marina is 8M upriver, and 1M E of city. As a refuge or in emergency yachts may berth on Fish Quay; contact HM. A one-off £10 conservancy fee may be levied by the Port Authority on all visiting craft.

NAVIGATION WPT 55°01'·01N 01°22'·32W, 258° to hbr ent, 1·1M. From S, no dangers. From N, beware Bellhues Rk (approx 1M N of hbr and ¾M off shore); give N pier a wide berth. Dredged chan in Lower Hbr is buoyed. The six bridges at Newcastle have least clearance 25m, or 4m when swing bridge closed.

LIGHTS AND MARKS Dir lt 249°, Oc GWR 10s,. Castle conspic on cliff, N of ent.

R/T Call: *Tyne Hbr Radio* VHF Ch **12** 16 11 (H24). Royal Quays marina Ch 80. St Peter's Marina Ch **80** M.

TELEPHONE (Dial code 0191) HM 257 0407, ℻ 258 3238; Port Ops 257 2080; MRSC 257 2681; Marinecall 09066 526237; Met 2326453; Police 214 6555; Dr via Tyne Hbr Radio 257 2080; Ⓗ (Tynemouth) 259 6660; Ⓗ (Newcastle) 232 5131.

FACILITIES (from seaward)
Tynemouth SC (dinghies) ☎ 2572617
South Shields SC (dinghies) ☎ 4565821

Royal Quays marina 54°59'·79N 01°26'·84W ☎ 272 8282, ℻ 272 8288. 245 berths in 7·9m depth; £1.75. S lock (42.5m x 8·0m) operates locking-out H and H+30, locking-in H+15 and H+45 or on request at quiet times. H24. Waiting pontoon outside lock. Call *Royal Quays marina* VHF Ch 80. BY, BH (30 ton), D, P (H24), FW, ⊡, CH, Bar, El, Gas, Gaz, 🛒.

St Peter's marina 54°57'·94N 01°34'·35W (140 + 20 Ⓥ) ☎ 265 4472, ℻ 276 2618; £1.48. Access approx HW±3½ over sill 0·8m below CD; 2·5m retained within; tfc lts at ent; ⊡. D, P on pontoon outside ent in 2m.

Services: Slip, M, L, FW, ME, El, ⚒, C, CH, AB, ACA, Ⓔ. **City** EC Wed; All amenities, ⇌ (Newcastle/S Shields), ✈ (Newcastle). N Sea ferries see 9.0.5.

5

ADJACENT HARBOUR

CULLERCOATS, Tyne and Wear, **55°02'·08N 01°25'·81W.** AC 1191. +0430 Dover. Tides as 9.5.17. Small drying hbr 1·6M N of R Tyne ent. Appr on ldg line 256°, two bns (FR lts), between drying rks. An occas fair weather ⚓ or dry against S pier. Facilities at Tynemouth.

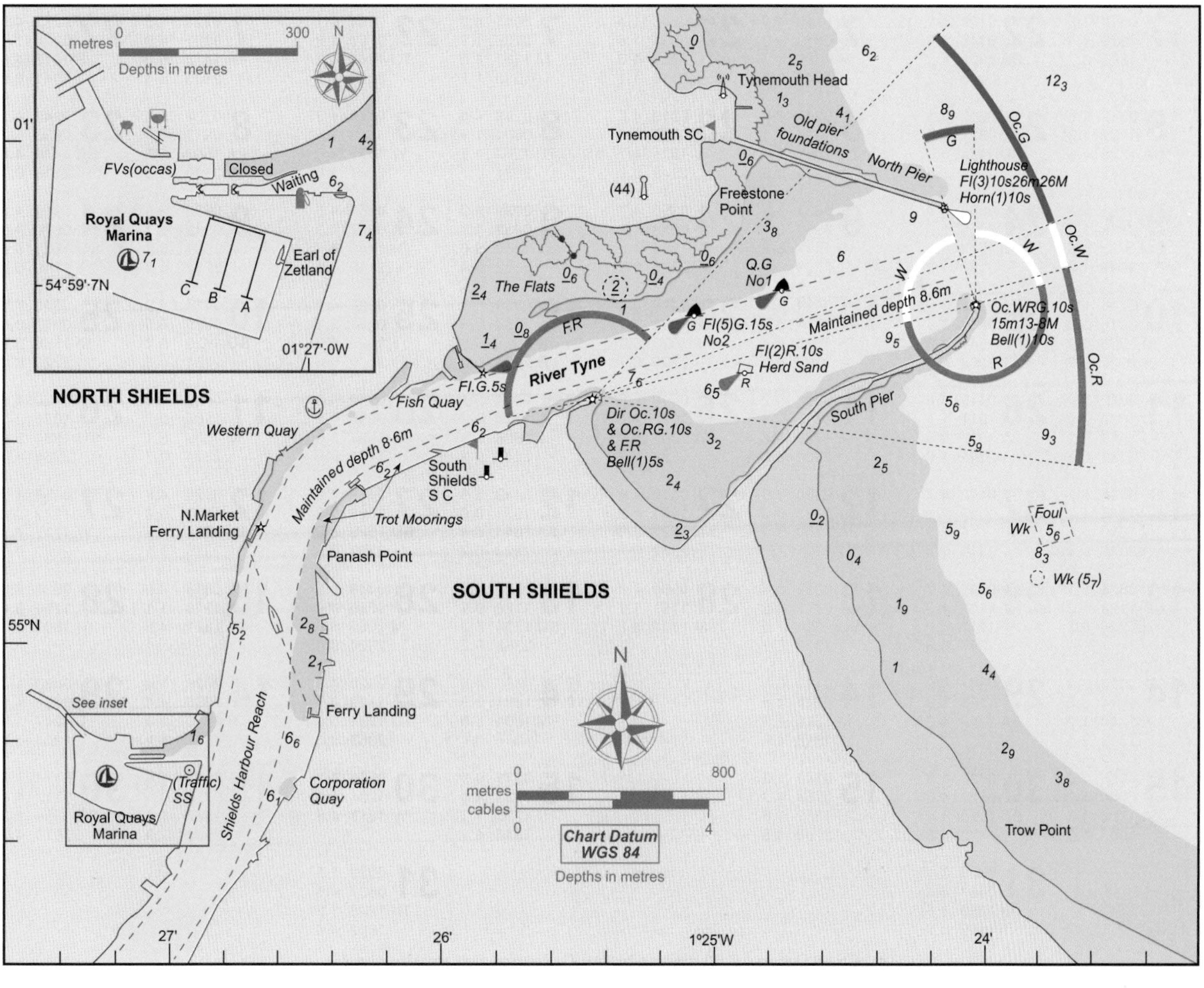

Depths in metres
Royal Quays Marina
Closed
Waiting
FVs(occas)
Earl of Zetland
54°59'·7N
01°27'·0W
NORTH SHIELDS
Western Quay
Fish Quay
N.Market Ferry Landing
Maintained depth 8·6m
River Tyne
The Flats
South Shields S C
Trot Moorings
Panash Point
SOUTH SHIELDS
See inset
Royal Quays Marina
(Traffic) SS
Ferry Landing
Corporation Quay
Shields Harbour Reach
Tynemouth Head
Old pier foundations
Tynemouth SC
Freestone Point
North Pier
Lighthouse Fl(3)10s26m26M Horn(1)10s
Q.G No1
Fl(5)G.15s No2
Fl(2)R.10s Herd Sand
Fl.G.5s
Dir Oc.10s & Oc.RG.10s & F.R Bell(1)5s
South Pier
Oc.WRG.10s 15m13-8M Bell(1)10s
Oc.G
Oc.W
Oc.R
Foul Wk
Wk
Trow Point
Chart Datum WGS 84
Depths in metres
metres
cables
55°N
1°25'W

TIME ZONE (UT)
For Summer Time add ONE hour in **non-shaded areas**

ENGLAND – RIVER TYNE/NORTH SHIELDS

LAT 55°01′N LONG 1°26′W

TIMES AND HEIGHTS OF HIGH AND LOW WATERS

SPRING & NEAP TIDES
Dates in red are **SPRINGS**
Dates in blue are **NEAPS**

YEAR **2005**

JANUARY

Day		Time	m	Time	m	Time	m	Time	m
1	SA	0045	1.3	0651	4.3	1240	1.7	1852	4.6
2	SU	0127	1.4	0734	4.2	1322	1.9	1936	4.4
3	M	0213	1.5	0823	4.1	1411	2.0	◑ 2026	4.4
4	TU	0306	1.6	0919	4.1	1512	2.1	2125	4.3
5	W	0407	1.6	1022	4.1	1623	2.1	2232	4.3
6	TH	0514	1.6	1127	4.2	1738	1.9	2341	4.4
7	F	0620	1.5	1229	4.4	1847	1.7		
8	SA	0049	4.6	0721	1.3	1326	4.6	1949	1.4
9	SU	0151	4.8	0818	1.2	1417	4.8	2046	1.0
10	M	0248	5.0	0910	1.0	1506	5.0	● 2140	0.7
11	TU	0342	5.1	1000	1.0	1553	5.2	2231	0.5
12	W	0434	5.2	1048	1.0	1639	5.3	2322	0.4
13	TH	0524	5.1	1133	1.0	1726	5.3		
14	F	0010	0.4	0614	5.0	1218	1.2	1813	5.2
15	SA	0059	0.6	0704	4.8	1302	1.3	1903	5.0
16	SU	0146	0.8	0754	4.5	1349	1.6	1955	4.8
17	M	0236	1.1	0848	4.3	1440	1.8	◐ 2052	4.5
18	TU	0331	1.5	0947	4.1	1544	2.0	2158	4.3
19	W	0435	1.7	1052	4.0	1700	2.1	2310	4.1
20	TH	0545	1.9	1158	4.0	1818	2.0		
21	F	0022	4.1	0650	1.9	1300	4.1	1922	1.8
22	SA	0126	4.2	0743	1.8	1351	4.3	2014	1.6
23	SU	0217	4.3	0827	1.7	1434	4.5	2056	1.4
24	M	0259	4.4	0905	1.6	1511	4.6	2134	1.2
25	TU	0336	4.5	0939	1.5	1544	4.8	○ 2208	1.1
26	W	0410	4.6	1011	1.4	1615	4.8	2241	1.0
27	TH	0442	4.7	1042	1.3	1646	4.9	2314	0.9
28	F	0514	4.7	1112	1.3	1717	4.9	2347	0.9
29	SA	0547	4.6	1143	1.3	1749	4.9		
30	SU	0020	1.0	0621	4.5	1216	1.4	1822	4.8
31	M	0055	1.1	0657	4.4	1250	1.5	1859	4.7

FEBRUARY

Day		Time	m	Time	m	Time	m	Time	m
1	TU	0133	1.2	0738	4.3	1330	1.6	1943	4.5
2	W	0217	1.4	0828	4.2	1420	1.8	◑ 2038	4.4
3	TH	0314	1.6	0929	4.1	1528	1.9	2148	4.2
4	F	0428	1.7	1043	4.0	1658	2.0	2314	4.2
5	SA	0554	1.7	1202	4.1	1830	1.7		
6	SU	0040	4.3	0710	1.6	1311	4.4	1943	1.4
7	M	0150	4.6	0812	1.3	1408	4.7	2042	0.9
8	TU	0247	4.9	0904	1.1	1457	5.0	● 2135	0.5
9	W	0337	5.1	0951	0.9	1542	5.2	2223	0.3
10	TH	0424	5.2	1034	0.8	1625	5.4	2308	0.2
11	F	0508	5.2	1115	0.8	1708	5.4	2350	0.2
12	SA	0550	5.0	1153	0.9	1750	5.3		
13	SU	0031	0.4	0632	4.8	1231	1.0	1833	5.1
14	M	0110	0.8	0714	4.5	1310	1.3	1918	4.8
15	TU	0149	1.2	0758	4.3	1352	1.6	2008	4.5
16	W	0234	1.6	0850	4.0	1446	1.9	◐ 2109	4.1
17	TH	0331	2.0	0953	3.8	1604	2.1	2226	3.8
18	F	0452	2.2	1112	3.8	1745	2.1	2356	3.8
19	SA	0624	2.2	1232	3.9	1906	1.9		
20	SU	0113	3.9	0729	2.0	1333	4.1	2000	1.6
21	M	0206	4.2	0814	1.8	1418	4.3	2041	1.4
22	TU	0246	4.4	0851	1.6	1454	4.6	2116	1.1
23	W	0319	4.5	0923	1.4	1525	4.7	2149	0.9
24	TH	0350	4.7	0953	1.2	1554	4.9	○ 2220	0.8
25	F	0419	4.7	1022	1.1	1623	5.0	2250	0.7
26	SA	0449	4.8	1051	1.0	1652	5.0	2321	0.7
27	SU	0519	4.8	1121	1.0	1722	5.0	2352	0.7
28	M	0550	4.7	1151	1.1	1754	4.9		

MARCH

Day		Time	m	Time	m	Time	m	Time	m
1	TU	0024	0.9	0623	4.6	1224	1.2	1830	4.8
2	W	0059	1.1	0702	4.4	1301	1.4	1915	4.6
3	TH	0140	1.3	0750	4.2	1350	1.6	◑ 2012	4.3
4	F	0237	1.7	0851	4.0	1500	1.8	2130	4.1
5	SA	0402	1.9	1014	3.9	1644	1.9	2310	4.0
6	SU	0546	1.9	1146	4.0	1827	1.6		
7	M	0041	4.2	0705	1.7	1301	4.3	1938	1.2
8	TU	0148	4.6	0804	1.4	1357	4.7	2034	0.7
9	W	0239	4.9	0852	1.1	1443	5.0	2122	0.4
10	TH	0324	5.1	0934	0.8	1525	5.3	● 2205	0.2
11	F	0404	5.1	1014	0.7	1605	5.4	2246	0.1
12	SA	0443	5.1	1051	0.6	1644	5.4	2323	0.2
13	SU	0520	5.0	1126	0.7	1724	5.3	2358	0.5
14	M	0557	4.8	1201	0.9	1804	5.0		
15	TU	0031	0.9	0633	4.6	1237	1.1	1846	4.7
16	W	0105	1.3	0712	4.3	1315	1.4	1933	4.3
17	TH	0142	1.7	0757	4.0	1404	1.8	◐ 2029	4.0
18	F	0232	2.1	0856	3.8	1516	2.0	2145	3.7
19	SA	0356	2.4	1018	3.6	1703	2.1	2324	3.6
20	SU	0552	2.4	1154	3.7	1837	1.9		
21	M	0048	3.8	0704	2.1	1303	4.0	1932	1.6
22	TU	0141	4.1	0750	1.8	1349	4.2	2012	1.3
23	W	0219	4.3	0825	1.5	1425	4.5	2047	1.0
24	TH	0251	4.5	0857	1.3	1456	4.7	2119	0.8
25	F	0320	4.7	0927	1.1	1525	4.9	○ 2150	0.6
26	SA	0349	4.8	0956	0.9	1553	5.0	2221	0.5
27	SU	0418	4.9	1026	0.8	1623	5.0	2252	0.5
28	M	0448	4.9	1056	0.8	1655	5.0	2324	0.6
29	TU	0520	4.8	1129	0.9	1731	5.0	2357	0.8
30	W	0556	4.7	1204	1.0	1813	4.8		
31	TH	0033	1.1	0637	4.5	1246	1.2	1902	4.5

APRIL

Day		Time	m	Time	m	Time	m	Time	m
1	F	0119	1.4	0727	4.3	1341	1.5	2007	4.2
2	SA	0222	1.8	0833	4.0	1502	1.7	◑ 2134	4.0
3	SU	0358	2.0	1001	3.9	1648	1.6	2314	4.0
4	M	0540	2.0	1133	4.0	1820	1.3		
5	TU	0036	4.3	0652	1.7	1245	4.3	1925	0.9
6	W	0135	4.6	0746	1.3	1339	4.7	2016	0.6
7	TH	0221	4.8	0831	1.0	1423	5.0	2100	0.4
8	F	0302	5.0	0911	0.8	1503	5.2	● 2140	0.3
9	SA	0339	5.0	0948	0.7	1541	5.3	2217	0.3
10	SU	0414	5.0	1025	0.6	1620	5.2	2251	0.5
11	M	0449	4.9	1100	0.7	1659	5.1	2324	0.7
12	TU	0523	4.8	1135	0.9	1739	4.8	2355	1.1
13	W	0558	4.6	1210	1.1	1821	4.5		
14	TH	0026	1.4	0635	4.4	1250	1.4	1906	4.2
15	F	0102	1.8	0718	4.1	1337	1.6	2000	3.9
16	SA	0149	2.1	0812	3.9	1441	1.9	◐ 2109	3.7
17	SU	0304	2.4	0925	3.7	1611	2.0	2235	3.6
18	M	0456	2.4	1055	3.7	1744	1.8	2359	3.7
19	TU	0618	2.2	1212	3.9	1845	1.6		
20	W	0056	4.0	0708	1.9	1304	4.1	1929	1.3
21	TH	0137	4.2	0746	1.6	1343	4.4	2006	1.0
22	F	0211	4.5	0820	1.3	1416	4.6	2041	0.8
23	SA	0243	4.7	0853	1.1	1448	4.8	2115	0.7
24	SU	0314	4.8	0925	0.9	1521	5.0	○ 2148	0.6
25	M	0346	4.9	0959	0.8	1556	5.0	2223	0.6
26	TU	0420	4.9	1035	0.7	1634	5.0	2259	0.7
27	W	0456	4.9	1113	0.8	1717	4.9	2337	0.9
28	TH	0537	4.8	1156	0.9	1807	4.7		
29	F	0020	1.2	0623	4.6	1247	1.1	1904	4.5
30	SA	0114	1.5	0718	4.4	1351	1.3	2015	4.2

Chart Datum: 2·60 metres below Ordnance Datum (Newlyn)

TIME ZONE (UT)
For Summer Time add ONE hour in **non-shaded areas**

ENGLAND – RIVER TYNE/NORTH SHIELDS

LAT 55°01′N LONG 1°26′W

TIMES AND HEIGHTS OF HIGH AND LOW WATERS

SPRING & NEAP TIDES
Dates in red are SPRINGS
Dates in blue are NEAPS

YEAR **2005**

MAY

Date	Day	Time	m	Time	m	Time	m	Time	m
1	SU	0224	1.8	0827	4.2	1512	1.4	◑ 2139	4.1
2	M	0353	2.0	0950	4.1	1642	1.3	2304	4.1
3	TU	0519	1.9	1112	4.2	1759	1.1		
4	W	0014	4.3	0625	1.6	1220	4.4	1900	0.9
5	TH	0110	4.5	0719	1.4	1313	4.7	1950	0.7
6	F	0155	4.7	0804	1.1	1358	4.9	2033	0.6
7	SA	0235	4.8	0845	0.9	1439	5.0	2112	0.6
8	SU	0311	4.9	0924	0.8	1519	5.0	● 2147	0.7
9	M	0346	4.9	1002	0.8	1559	4.9	2221	0.8
10	TU	0421	4.8	1039	0.8	1639	4.8	2253	1.0
11	W	0455	4.7	1115	0.9	1719	4.6	2325	1.3
12	TH	0531	4.6	1152	1.1	1801	4.4	2358	1.5
13	F	0608	4.4	1231	1.3	1846	4.2		
14	SA	0034	1.8	0650	4.2	1317	1.5	1935	4.0
15	SU	0120	2.0	0740	4.0	1413	1.7	2034	3.8
16	M	0221	2.2	0841	3.9	1521	1.8	◐ 2142	3.7
17	TU	0344	2.3	0952	3.8	1636	1.7	2253	3.8
18	W	0507	2.2	1103	3.9	1742	1.6	2354	3.9
19	TH	0609	1.9	1202	4.1	1835	1.3		
20	F	0043	4.2	0656	1.7	1250	4.3	1919	1.1
21	SA	0125	4.4	0737	1.4	1332	4.5	2000	0.9
22	SU	0203	4.6	0817	1.2	1412	4.7	2039	0.8
23	M	0240	4.8	0856	1.0	1453	4.9	○ 2119	0.7
24	TU	0318	4.9	0937	0.8	1536	5.0	2200	0.7
25	W	0357	4.9	1021	0.7	1622	5.0	2243	0.8
26	TH	0440	4.9	1107	0.7	1713	4.9	2328	1.0
27	F	0526	4.9	1158	0.7	1808	4.8		
28	SA	0018	1.2	0616	4.7	1254	0.8	1908	4.6
29	SU	0114	1.5	0713	4.6	1356	0.9	2014	4.4
30	M	0218	1.7	0818	4.4	1505	1.0	◑ 2125	4.2
31	TU	0330	1.8	0929	4.4	1618	1.1	2236	4.2

JUNE

Date	Day	Time	m	Time	m	Time	m	Time	m
1	W	0443	1.8	1041	4.4	1727	1.1	2341	4.3
2	TH	0549	1.6	1147	4.5	1828	1.0		
3	F	0037	4.4	0646	1.5	1244	4.6	1920	1.0
4	SA	0126	4.5	0736	1.3	1334	4.6	2004	1.0
5	SU	0208	4.6	0822	1.2	1420	4.7	2044	1.0
6	M	0247	4.7	0904	1.0	1503	4.7	● 2121	1.1
7	TU	0324	4.7	0945	1.0	1544	4.7	2157	1.2
8	W	0400	4.7	1023	1.0	1625	4.6	2231	1.3
9	TH	0435	4.7	1101	1.0	1705	4.5	2304	1.4
10	F	0511	4.6	1138	1.1	1745	4.4	2338	1.5
11	SA	0547	4.5	1216	1.2	1826	4.3		
12	SU	0015	1.6	0627	4.4	1258	1.3	1909	4.1
13	M	0056	1.8	0711	4.3	1344	1.4	1957	4.0
14	TU	0143	1.9	0800	4.2	1436	1.5	2051	3.9
15	W	0240	2.0	0855	4.1	1533	1.6	◐ 2149	3.9
16	TH	0346	2.1	0955	4.0	1634	1.5	2249	3.9
17	F	0455	2.0	1057	4.1	1734	1.4	2346	4.1
18	SA	0557	1.8	1155	4.2	1830	1.3		
19	SU	0039	4.3	0653	1.6	1251	4.4	1921	1.1
20	M	0127	4.5	0744	1.3	1343	4.6	2010	1.0
21	TU	0213	4.7	0834	1.1	1434	4.8	2059	0.9
22	W	0257	4.9	0924	0.8	1526	4.9	○ 2147	0.9
23	TH	0342	5.0	1014	0.6	1618	5.0	2235	0.9
24	F	0429	5.0	1106	0.5	1711	5.0	2323	1.0
25	SA	0517	5.0	1158	0.4	1805	4.9		
26	SU	0012	1.1	0607	5.0	1251	0.5	1900	4.7
27	M	0103	1.3	0700	4.9	1345	0.6	1957	4.5
28	TU	0156	1.4	0757	4.7	1442	0.8	◑ 2056	4.4
29	W	0254	1.6	0859	4.6	1542	1.0	2158	4.2
30	TH	0358	1.7	1004	4.5	1646	1.2	2300	4.2

JULY

Date	Day	Time	m	Time	m	Time	m	Time	m
1	F	0506	1.7	1112	4.4	1750	1.4		
2	SA	0001	4.2	0613	1.7	1217	4.3	1849	1.4
3	SU	0057	4.3	0714	1.5	1316	4.3	1940	1.4
4	M	0146	4.4	0806	1.4	1408	4.4	2025	1.4
5	TU	0230	4.5	0852	1.2	1454	4.5	2104	1.4
6	W	0309	4.6	0934	1.1	1536	4.5	● 2141	1.4
7	TH	0345	4.7	1012	1.0	1614	4.5	2215	1.4
8	F	0420	4.7	1048	1.0	1650	4.5	2248	1.4
9	SA	0453	4.7	1123	1.0	1726	4.5	2321	1.4
10	SU	0527	4.7	1157	1.0	1802	4.4	2354	1.4
11	M	0603	4.6	1233	1.1	1839	4.3		
12	TU	0029	1.5	0640	4.5	1312	1.2	1919	4.2
13	W	0108	1.6	0720	4.4	1353	1.3	2002	4.1
14	TH	0150	1.8	0805	4.3	1439	1.4	◐ 2051	4.0
15	F	0242	1.9	0857	4.2	1534	1.5	2148	4.0
16	SA	0346	1.9	0959	4.2	1637	1.6	2252	4.0
17	SU	0501	1.9	1109	4.2	1746	1.5	2358	4.2
18	M	0617	1.7	1221	4.3	1853	1.4		
19	TU	0059	4.4	0723	1.5	1328	4.5	1953	1.3
20	W	0154	4.6	0823	1.1	1427	4.8	2047	1.1
21	TH	0244	4.9	0917	0.7	1521	5.0	○ 2138	0.9
22	F	0331	5.1	1009	0.4	1612	5.1	2226	0.9
23	SA	0417	5.2	1059	0.2	1702	5.2	2312	0.8
24	SU	0503	5.3	1147	0.2	1750	5.1	2356	0.9
25	M	0550	5.3	1234	0.3	1839	4.9		
26	TU	0039	1.0	0638	5.2	1321	0.5	1927	4.7
27	W	0125	1.2	0728	5.0	1408	0.8	2018	4.4
28	TH	0213	1.5	0823	4.7	1500	1.2	◑ 2114	4.2
29	F	0311	1.7	0925	4.4	1559	1.5	2216	4.0
30	SA	0423	1.9	1037	4.2	1709	1.8	2324	4.0
31	SU	0546	1.9	1154	4.1	1823	1.9		

AUGUST

Date	Day	Time	m	Time	m	Time	m	Time	m
1	M	0032	4.1	0700	1.7	1305	4.1	1924	1.8
2	TU	0130	4.3	0758	1.5	1402	4.2	2013	1.7
3	W	0217	4.4	0844	1.3	1447	4.4	2053	1.6
4	TH	0256	4.6	0922	1.1	1525	4.5	2128	1.5
5	F	0331	4.7	0957	1.0	1559	4.6	● 2200	1.3
6	SA	0402	4.8	1030	0.9	1630	4.6	2230	1.3
7	SU	0433	4.9	1101	0.8	1702	4.7	2300	1.2
8	M	0503	4.9	1133	0.8	1733	4.6	2330	1.2
9	TU	0535	4.9	1204	0.9	1806	4.6		
10	W	0001	1.3	0607	4.8	1237	1.0	1839	4.5
11	TH	0034	1.4	0641	4.7	1312	1.2	1917	4.3
12	F	0110	1.5	0722	4.5	1352	1.4	2002	4.2
13	SA	0156	1.7	0812	4.3	1443	1.6	◐ 2057	4.1
14	SU	0257	1.9	0917	4.2	1551	1.8	2207	4.0
15	M	0422	2.0	1041	4.1	1717	1.8	2327	4.1
16	TU	0557	1.8	1210	4.2	1840	1.7		
17	W	0041	4.3	0715	1.4	1324	4.5	1944	1.4
18	TH	0141	4.6	0815	1.0	1422	4.8	2038	1.2
19	F	0231	5.0	0908	0.6	1512	5.1	○ 2125	0.9
20	SA	0316	5.2	0957	0.2	1558	5.3	2209	0.8
21	SU	0359	5.4	1042	0.1	1642	5.3	2251	0.7
22	M	0442	5.5	1126	0.1	1725	5.2	2331	0.7
23	TU	0525	5.5	1207	0.2	1808	5.0		
24	W	0010	0.9	0609	5.3	1248	0.6	1850	4.7
25	TH	0050	1.1	0656	5.0	1328	1.0	1935	4.5
26	F	0134	1.4	0747	4.6	1412	1.5	◑ 2026	4.2
27	SA	0228	1.7	0848	4.2	1508	1.9	2128	4.0
28	SU	0343	2.0	1004	3.9	1627	2.2	2246	3.9
29	M	0523	2.0	1135	3.8	1802	2.2		
30	TU	0008	4.0	0648	1.9	1256	4.0	1912	2.1
31	W	0113	4.2	0745	1.6	1351	4.2	1959	1.9

Chart Datum: 2·60 metres below Ordnance Datum (Newlyn)

TIME ZONE (UT)
For Summer Time add ONE hour in **non-shaded areas**

ENGLAND – RIVER TYNE/NORTH SHIELDS

LAT 55°01′N LONG 1°26′W

TIMES AND HEIGHTS OF HIGH AND LOW WATERS

SPRING & NEAP TIDES
Dates in red are **SPRINGS**
Dates in blue are **NEAPS**

YEAR **2005**

SEPTEMBER

Date	Day	Time	m	Time	m	Time	m	Time	m
1	TH	0200	4.4	0827	1.3	1432	4.4	2036	1.6
2	F	0237	4.6	0902	1.1	1505	4.6	2108	1.4
3	SA	0309	4.8	0933	0.9	1535	4.7	● 2138	1.3
4	SU	0338	4.9	1003	0.8	1603	4.8	2206	1.1
5	M	0406	5.0	1033	0.7	1632	4.8	2234	1.1
6	TU	0434	5.0	1102	0.7	1701	4.8	2303	1.1
7	W	0504	5.0	1132	0.8	1731	4.8	2332	1.1
8	TH	0535	4.9	1202	0.9	1803	4.7		
9	F	0004	1.3	0609	4.8	1235	1.1	1838	4.5
10	SA	0040	1.4	0650	4.6	1313	1.4	1923	4.3
11	SU	0125	1.7	0744	4.3	1405	1.7	◐ 2020	4.1
12	M	0231	1.9	0857	4.1	1523	2.0	2138	4.0
13	TU	0408	2.0	1035	4.0	1707	2.1	2310	4.0
14	W	0553	1.7	1209	4.2	1833	1.8		
15	TH	0028	4.3	0707	1.3	1319	4.6	1933	1.5
16	F	0127	4.7	0804	0.8	1411	4.9	2022	1.2
17	SA	0214	5.1	0852	0.4	1456	5.2	2106	0.9
18	SU	0256	5.4	0937	0.2	1537	5.3	○ 2146	0.7
19	M	0337	5.6	1018	0.1	1616	5.3	2225	0.6
20	TU	0417	5.6	1058	0.2	1655	5.2	2303	0.7
21	W	0459	5.5	1135	0.5	1733	5.0	2341	0.9
22	TH	0541	5.2	1210	0.8	1812	4.8		
23	F	0019	1.1	0626	4.9	1247	1.3	1853	4.5
24	SA	0101	1.4	0715	4.5	1325	1.7	1940	4.2
25	SU	0153	1.8	0815	4.1	1417	2.1	◑ 2040	4.0
26	M	0306	2.0	0932	3.8	1540	2.4	2201	3.8
27	TU	0453	2.1	1109	3.7	1734	2.5	2334	3.9
28	W	0623	1.9	1232	3.9	1847	2.2		
29	TH	0044	4.1	0716	1.6	1325	4.2	1932	1.9
30	F	0131	4.4	0756	1.4	1403	4.4	2008	1.7

OCTOBER

Date	Day	Time	m	Time	m	Time	m	Time	m
1	SA	0207	4.6	0830	1.1	1434	4.6	2039	1.4
2	SU	0238	4.8	0901	0.9	1503	4.8	2108	1.2
3	M	0307	5.0	0931	0.8	1531	4.9	● 2137	1.1
4	TU	0335	5.1	1000	0.7	1559	4.9	2206	1.0
5	W	0404	5.1	1030	0.7	1628	5.0	2236	1.0
6	TH	0435	5.1	1101	0.8	1658	4.9	2308	1.1
7	F	0508	5.0	1132	1.0	1732	4.8	2342	1.2
8	SA	0547	4.8	1206	1.3	1811	4.7		
9	SU	0022	1.4	0635	4.6	1249	1.6	1858	4.4
10	M	0114	1.6	0736	4.3	1347	1.9	◐ 2000	4.2
11	TU	0229	1.8	0858	4.1	1515	2.2	2122	4.1
12	W	0410	1.8	1036	4.1	1700	2.1	2255	4.2
13	TH	0544	1.5	1201	4.3	1818	1.9		
14	F	0009	4.5	0651	1.1	1303	4.7	1913	1.5
15	SA	0106	4.8	0744	0.8	1351	4.9	2000	1.2
16	SU	0152	5.1	0830	0.5	1433	5.1	2042	1.0
17	M	0233	5.4	0912	0.4	1511	5.2	○ 2121	0.8
18	TU	0313	5.5	0950	0.4	1548	5.2	2200	0.7
19	W	0354	5.5	1027	0.5	1624	5.2	2238	0.8
20	TH	0435	5.3	1102	0.8	1701	5.0	2316	0.9
21	F	0517	5.0	1136	1.1	1738	4.8	2355	1.2
22	SA	0602	4.7	1209	1.5	1817	4.6		
23	SU	0036	1.5	0650	4.4	1246	1.9	1901	4.3
24	M	0126	1.7	0746	4.1	1334	2.2	1957	4.1
25	TU	0232	2.0	0856	3.8	1448	2.5	◑ 2110	3.9
26	W	0401	2.1	1022	3.7	1637	2.5	2239	3.9
27	TH	0529	1.9	1143	3.9	1759	2.3	2354	4.1
28	F	0629	1.7	1240	4.1	1850	2.1		
29	SA	0046	4.3	0712	1.5	1321	4.4	1928	1.8
30	SU	0126	4.5	0749	1.2	1355	4.6	2003	1.5
31	M	0200	4.8	0823	1.0	1427	4.8	2035	1.3

NOVEMBER

Date	Day	Time	m	Time	m	Time	m	Time	m
1	TU	0232	4.9	0855	0.9	1457	4.9	2107	1.2
2	W	0303	5.0	0928	0.8	1527	5.0	● 2139	1.1
3	TH	0337	5.1	1001	0.8	1559	5.0	2214	1.0
4	F	0413	5.1	1035	0.9	1633	5.0	2251	1.0
5	SA	0453	5.0	1111	1.1	1711	4.9	2332	1.1
6	SU	0539	4.8	1152	1.4	1755	4.8		
7	M	0020	1.3	0634	4.6	1241	1.7	1846	4.6
8	TU	0120	1.4	0740	4.4	1345	2.0	1951	4.4
9	W	0235	1.6	0858	4.2	1508	2.1	◐ 2108	4.3
10	TH	0400	1.5	1023	4.2	1635	2.1	2230	4.4
11	F	0520	1.3	1137	4.4	1748	1.9	2341	4.6
12	SA	0625	1.1	1236	4.6	1845	1.6		
13	SU	0039	4.8	0718	0.9	1325	4.8	1933	1.4
14	M	0128	5.0	0804	0.8	1407	4.9	2017	1.1
15	TU	0212	5.2	0845	0.7	1446	5.0	2059	1.0
16	W	0254	5.2	0924	0.8	1523	5.1	○ 2140	0.9
17	TH	0336	5.2	1000	1.0	1559	5.1	2220	0.9
18	F	0418	5.0	1035	1.2	1636	5.0	2259	1.0
19	SA	0501	4.8	1109	1.4	1713	4.8	2338	1.2
20	SU	0545	4.6	1143	1.7	1751	4.7		
21	M	0019	1.4	0630	4.4	1219	1.9	1833	4.5
22	TU	0105	1.6	0720	4.1	1303	2.1	1922	4.3
23	W	0159	1.8	0816	3.9	1359	2.3	◑ 2021	4.1
24	TH	0303	1.9	0922	3.8	1516	2.4	2130	4.0
25	F	0415	1.9	1032	3.9	1640	2.4	2242	4.1
26	SA	0522	1.8	1135	4.0	1747	2.2	2343	4.2
27	SU	0617	1.6	1227	4.2	1838	2.0		
28	M	0033	4.4	0702	1.4	1310	4.4	1921	1.7
29	TU	0117	4.6	0743	1.3	1348	4.6	2000	1.5
30	W	0157	4.7	0821	1.1	1424	4.8	2039	1.3

DECEMBER

Date	Day	Time	m	Time	m	Time	m	Time	m
1	TH	0237	4.9	0859	1.0	1500	4.9	● 2119	1.1
2	F	0318	5.0	0939	1.0	1537	5.0	2200	1.0
3	SA	0401	5.0	1019	1.1	1617	5.0	2244	0.9
4	SU	0449	5.0	1102	1.2	1700	5.0	2332	0.9
5	M	0540	4.9	1149	1.4	1747	4.9		
6	TU	0025	1.0	0635	4.7	1240	1.6	1839	4.8
7	W	0123	1.1	0737	4.5	1338	1.8	1939	4.7
8	TH	0226	1.2	0844	4.4	1444	1.9	◐ 2045	4.6
9	F	0335	1.3	0954	4.3	1556	2.0	2157	4.5
10	SA	0445	1.3	1101	4.3	1706	1.9	2306	4.6
11	SU	0551	1.3	1203	4.4	1811	1.7		
12	M	0009	4.7	0648	1.2	1257	4.5	1907	1.6
13	TU	0106	4.7	0739	1.2	1344	4.7	1958	1.4
14	W	0157	4.8	0823	1.2	1426	4.8	2045	1.2
15	TH	0243	4.8	0904	1.3	1506	4.9	○ 2128	1.1
16	F	0327	4.8	0941	1.3	1543	4.9	2210	1.1
17	SA	0410	4.8	1017	1.4	1620	4.9	2249	1.1
18	SU	0450	4.7	1051	1.5	1656	4.8	2327	1.1
19	M	0530	4.6	1125	1.6	1732	4.8		
20	TU	0004	1.2	0609	4.4	1200	1.7	1810	4.6
21	W	0043	1.4	0651	4.3	1237	1.9	1851	4.5
22	TH	0125	1.5	0736	4.1	1319	2.0	1937	4.4
23	F	0213	1.6	0826	4.0	1409	2.1	◑ 2029	4.2
24	SA	0306	1.7	0921	3.9	1510	2.2	2127	4.1
25	SU	0406	1.8	1021	3.9	1621	2.3	2230	4.1
26	M	0509	1.8	1123	4.0	1732	2.2	2333	4.2
27	TU	0609	1.7	1219	4.2	1835	2.0		
28	W	0033	4.3	0703	1.5	1311	4.4	1928	1.7
29	TH	0128	4.5	0753	1.4	1357	4.6	2018	1.4
30	F	0219	4.7	0840	1.2	1440	4.8	2106	1.1
31	SA	0308	4.9	0926	1.1	1523	5.0	● 2154	0.9

Chart Datum: 2·60 metres below Ordnance Datum (Newlyn)

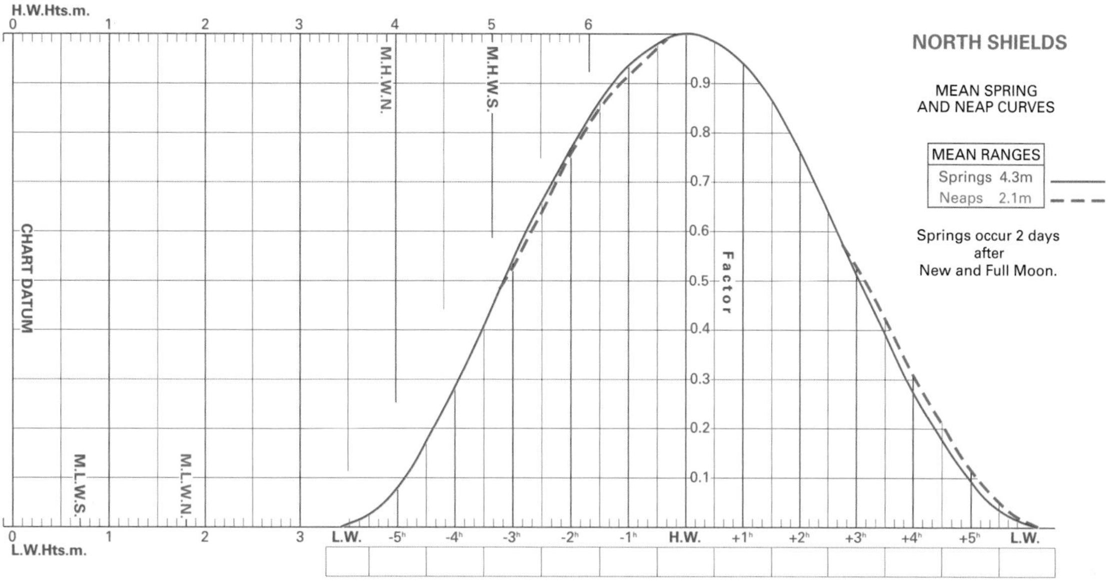
H.W.Hts.m.
NORTH SHIELDS
MEAN SPRING AND NEAP CURVES
MEAN RANGES
Springs 4.3m
Neaps 2.1m
Springs occur 2 days after New and Full Moon.
CHART DATUM
M.H.W.N.
M.H.W.S.
M.L.W.S.
M.L.W.N.
Factor
L.W.Hts.m.
L.W. -5h -4h -3h -2h -1h H.W. +1h +2h +3h +4h +5h L.W.

9.5.18 BLYTH

Northumberland **55°06'·98N 01° 29'·27W**

CHARTS AC 152, 156, 1626; Imray C24; OS 81, 88

TIDES +0430 Dover; ML 2·8; Duration 0558; Zone 0 (UT)

Standard Port NORTH SHIELDS (⟵)

Times				Height (metres)			
High Water		Low Water		MHWS	MHWN	MLWN	MLWS
0200	0800	0100	0800	5·0	3·9	1·8	0·7
1400	2000	1300	2000				
Differences BLYTH							
+0005	–0007	–0001	+0009	0·0	0·0	–0·1	+0·1

SHELTER Very good; access H24. Yachts go to SE part of South Hbr; Ⓥ on N side of RNYC pontoons on E side of Middle Jetty (4·4m least depth).

NAVIGATION WPT Fairway SHM buoy, Fl G 3s, Bell, 55°06'·58N 01°28'·60W, 320° to E pier lt, 0·53M. From N, beware The Pigs, The Sow and Seaton Sea Rks. No dangers from S. At LW in strong SE winds, seas break across ent. There are two wind turbines Fl. Y 2·5s Horn Mo(U)30s on North Spit centred on 55°08'·2N 01°29'·3W. See RNYC Sailing Instructions £25 incl postage from RNYC, House Yacht Tyne, S Hbr, Blyth NE24 3PB.

LIGHTS AND MARKS 9 wind turbines are conspic on the E pier. Outer ldg lts 324°, F Bu 11/17m 10M, Or ◇ on framework trs. Inner ldg lts 338°, F Bu 5/11m 10M, front W 6-sided tr; rear W △ on mast.

R/T Call: *Blyth Hbr Control* VHF Ch **12** 11 16 (H24) for clearance to enter or depart.

TELEPHONE (Dial code 01670) HM 352678 📠 540674; MRSC (0191) 257 2691; Marinecall 09066 526237; Police (01661) 872555; Dr 363334.

FACILITIES **R Northumberland YC** ☎ 353636, www.rnyc.org.uk, email: honsec@rnyc.org.uk, (50) AB £1.00, FW, C (1½ ton), Bar; **South Hbr** ☎ 352678, FW, C (50 ton). **Town** EC Wed; P & D (cans), 🛒, R, Bar, ✉, Ⓑ, Gas, Gaz, bus to Newcastle ⇌, ✈.

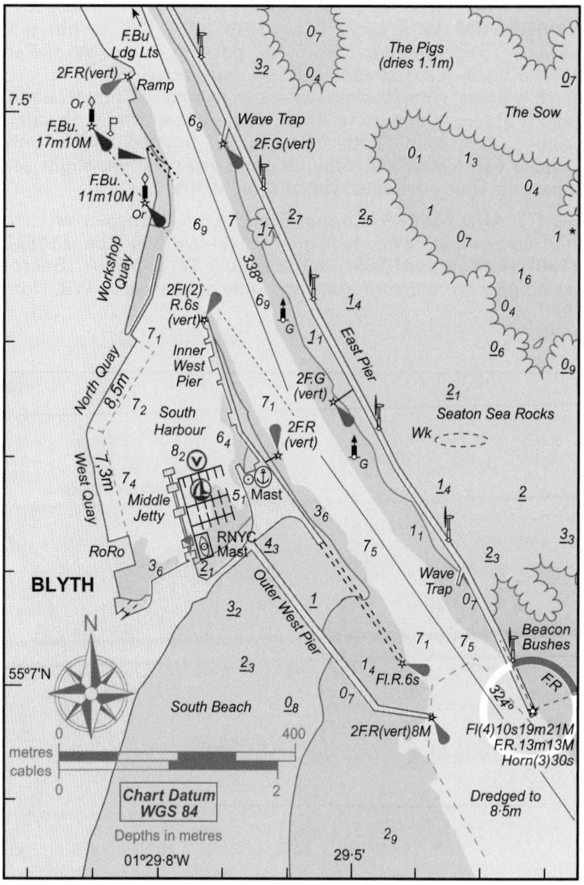
F.Bu Ldg Lts
2F.R(vert)
Ramp
F.Bu. 17m10M
F.Bu. 11m10M
Wave Trap
2F.G(vert)
The Pigs (dries 1.1m)
The Sow
Workshop Quay
North Quay 8.5m
West Quay 7.3m
2Fl(2) R.6s (vert)
Inner West Pier
South Harbour
East Pier
2F.G (vert)
2F.R (vert)
Seaton Sea Rocks
Wk
Middle Jetty
Mast
RNYC Mast
RoRo
BLYTH
Outer West Pier
Wave Trap
Beacon Bushes
Fl.R.6s
324°
338°
F.R
South Beach
2F.R(vert)8M
Fl(4)10s19m21M F.R.13m13M Horn(3)30s
Dredged to 8·5m
metres
cables
Chart Datum WGS 84
Depths in metres
55°7'N
7.5'
01°29·8'W
29·5'

ADJACENT ANCHORAGE

NEWBIGGIN, Northumberland, **55°10'·75N 01°30'·10W**. AC 156. Tides approx as for Blyth, 3·5M to the S. Temp, fair weather ⚓ in about 4m in centre of Bay, sheltered from SW to N winds. Caution: offlying rky ledges to N and S. Conspic church on N side of bay; bkwtr lt Fl G 10s 4M. Facilities: **SC** (dinghies). **Town** 🛒, R, Bar.

9.5.19 AMBLE

Northumberland **55°20'·37N 01°34'·25W**

CHARTS AC 156, 1627; Imray C24; OS 81

TIDES +0412 Dover; ML 3·1; Duration 0606; Zone 0 (UT)

Standard Port NORTH SHIELDS (←)

Times				Height (metres)			
High Water		Low Water		MHWS	MHWN	MLWN	MLWS
0200	0800	0100	0800	5·0	3·9	1·8	0·7
1400	2000	1300	2000				
Differences AMBLE							
–0013	–0013	–0016	–0020	0·0	0·0	+0·1	+0·1
COQUET ISLAND							
–0010	–0010	–0020	–0020	+0·1	+0·1	0·0	+0·1

SHELTER The hbr (alias Warkworth Hbr) is safe in all winds. But ent is dangerous in strong N to E winds or in swell, when heavy seas break on Pan Bush shoal and on the bar at hbr ent, where least depth is 0·8m.
Once inside the N bkwtr, beware drying banks to stbd, ie on N side of channel; keep close (15m) to S quays. 4kn speed limit in hbr. Amble marina is about 5ca from ent. Tidal gauge shows depth over sill; access approx HW±4 between PHM buoy and ECM bn, both unlit. Pontoons are 'A' to 'F' from sill; Ⓥ berth on 'B' initially.

NAVIGATION WPT 55°21'·00N 01°33'·10W, 225° to hbr ent, 0·9M. Ent recommended from NE, passing N and W of Pan Bush. The S-going stream sets strongly across ent.
In NE'ly gales, when broken water can extend to Coquet Island, keep E of island and go to Blyth where app/ent may be safer. Coquet Chan (min depth 0·3m) is not buoyed and is only advised with caution, by day, in good vis/ weather, slight sea state and with adequate rise of tide, ie HW–2.

LIGHTS AND MARKS Coquet Island lt ho, (conspic) W □ tr, turreted parapet, lower half grey; Fl (3) WR 30s 25m 23/19M, R330°-140°, W140°-163°, R163°-180°, W180°-330°. Sector boundaries are indeterminate and may appear as Al WR. Horn 30s.

R/T Call *Amble Marina* Ch **80** (seven days 0900-1700). *Warkworth Hbr* VHF, listens Ch 16, works Ch 14 (Mon-Fri 0900-1700 LT). Coquet YC Ch M (occas).

TELEPHONE (Dial code 01665) HM ☎/📠710306; MRSC (01262) 672317; local CG 710575; Police (01661) 872555; Marinecall 09066 526237; Ⓗ (01670) 521212.

FACILITIES Amble Marina (200+40Ⓥ) ☎ 712168, 📠 713363, £2.00, BY, C, D, Slip, BH (20 ton), ME, El, ⚒, Ⓔ, SM, R, Bar, 🛒, CH, ▣, ♿; **Hbr** D, AB; **Coquet YC** ☎ 711179 Slip, Bar, M, FW, L; **Services:** ME, Slip, CH, El, ⚒, SM, Gas, Gaz, Ⓔ. **Town** 🛒, R, Bar, ✉, ⇌ (Alnmouth), ✈ (Newcastle).

HARBOURS AND ANCHORAGES BETWEEN AMBLE AND HOLY ISLAND

BOULMER, Northumberland, **55°25'·00N 01°33'·90W**. AC 156. Tides approx as for Amble, 4·5M to the S. A small haven almost enclosed by N and S Rheins, rky ledges either side of the narrow (30m) ent, Mar mouth; only advised in settled offshore weather. 2 unlit bns lead approx 262° through the ent, leaving close to stbd a bn on N Rheins. ⚓ just inside in about 1·5m or dry out on sand at the N end. Few facilities: Pub, ✉ in village. Alnwick is 4M inland.

CRASTER, Northumberland, **55°28'·40N 01°35'·30W**. AC 156. Tidal differences: interpolate between Amble (9.5.19) and N Sunderland (9.5.20). Strictly a fair weather ⚓ in offshore winds, 1M S of the conspic Dunstanburgh Castle (ru). The ent, 40m wide, is N of Muckle Carr and S of Little Carr which partly covers and has a bn on its S end. ⚓ in about 3·5m just inshore of these 2 rocky outcrops; or berth at the E pier on rk/sand inside the tiny drying hbr. Facilities: 🛒, R, Bar.

NEWTON HAVEN and BEADNELL BAY, Northumberland, **55°30'·90N 01° 36'·70W**. AC 156. HW +0342 on Dover; Tidal differences: interpolate between Amble (9.5.20) and N Sunderland (9.5.20). ML 2·6m; Duration 0625. A safe ⚓ in winds from NNW to SE via S but susceptible to swell. Ent to S of Newton PHM buoy and Newton Pt. Beware Fills Rks. ⚓ between Fills Rks and Low Newton by the Sea in 4/5m. A very attractive ⚓ with no lts, marks or facilities except a pub. Further ⚓ S of Beadnell Pt (1M N of Newton Pt) in 4-6m; small, fishing hbr whose wall is newly rebuilt; Beadnell SC. Village 0·5M.

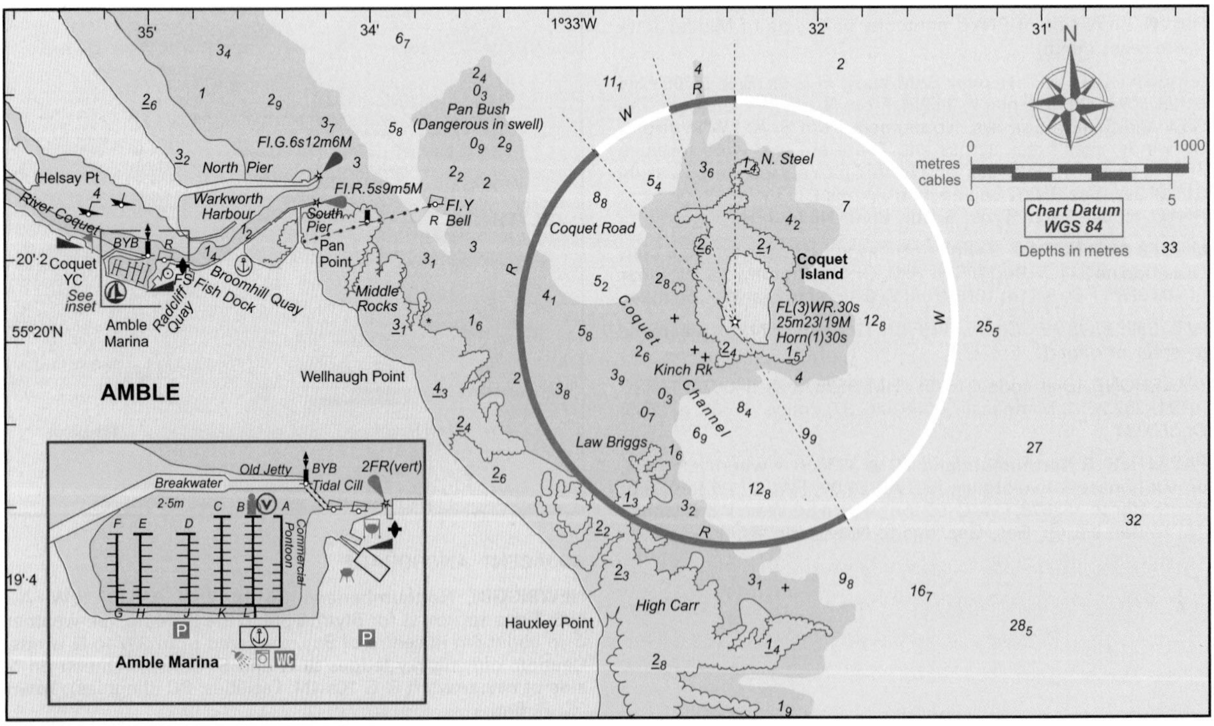
35'
34'
1°33'W
32'
31'
N
Pan Bush
(Dangerous in swell)
Fl.G.6s12m6M
North Pier
Fl.R.5s9m5M
Fl.Y
R Bell
Helsay Pt
River Coquet
Warkworth Harbour
South Pier
Pan Point
Middle Rocks
BYB
Coquet YC
See inset
Amble Marina
Radcliffe Quay
Fish Dock
Broomhill Quay
20'·2
55°20'N
19'·4
AMBLE
Wellhaugh Point
Coquet Road
N. Steel
Coquet Island
FL(3)WR.30s
25m23/19M
Horn(1)30s
Kinch Rk
Coquet Channel
Law Briggs
High Carr
Hauxley Point
metres
cables
1000
Chart Datum
WGS 84
Depths in metres
Old Jetty
Breakwater
BYB
2FR(vert)
Tidal Cill
2·5m
Commercial Pontoon
Amble Marina

HARBOURS AND ANCHORAGES BETWEEN AMBLE AND HOLY ISLAND *continued*

NORTH SUNDERLAND (Seahouses), Northumberland, **55°35′·04N 01°38′·91W**. AC 1612. HW +0340 on Dover; ML No data; Duration 0618. See 9.5.20. Good shelter except in onshore winds when swell makes outer hbr berths (0·7m) very uncomfortable and dangerous. Access HW±3. Inner hbr has excellent berths but usually full of FVs. Beware The Tumblers (rks) to the W of ent and rks protruding NE from bkwtr hd Fl R 2·5s 6m; NW pier hd FG 11m 3M; vis 159°-294°, on W tr; traffic sigs; Siren 90s when vessels expected. When it is dangerous to enter a ● is shown over the FG lt (or R flag over a Bu flag) on NW pier hd. Facilities: EC Wed; Gas; all facilities.

FARNE ISLANDS, Northumberland, **55°37′·15N 01°39′·37W**. AC 160, 156, 111. HW +0345 on Dover; ML 2·6m; Duration 0630. See 9.5.20. The islands are a NT nature reserve in a beautiful area; they should only be attempted in good weather. Landing is only allowed on Farne Island, Staple Is and Longstone. In the inner group, ⚓ in The Kettle on the NE side of Inner Farne; near the Bridges (which connect Knocks Reef to West Wideopen); or to the S of West Wideopen. In the outer group, ⚓ in Pinnacle Haven (between Staple Is and Brownsman). Beware turbulence over Knivestone and Whirl Rks and eddy S of Longstone during NW tidal streams. Lts and marks: Black Rocks Pt, Oc (2) WRG 8s 12m 14/11M; G122°-165°, W165°-175°, R175°-191°, W191°-238°, R238°-275°, W275°-289°, G289°-300°. Bamburgh Castle is conspic 6ca to the SE. Farne Is lt ho at SW Pt, Fl (2) WR 15s 27m 8/6M; W ○ tr; R119°-280°, W280°-119°. Longstone Fl 20s 23m 24M, R tr with W band (conspic), RC, horn (2) 60s. Caution: reefs extend about 7ca seaward. No facilities.

NATIONAL NATURE RESERVE (Holy Island) A National Nature Reserve (NNR) extends from Budle Bay (**55°37′N 01°45′W**, close to Black Rocks Point lt ho) along the coast to Cheswick Black Rocks, 3M SE of Berwick-upon-Tweed. The NNR extends seaward from the HW shoreline to the drying line; it includes Holy Island and the adjacent islets.
Yachtsmen are asked to respect two constraints:

a. Landing is prohib on the small island of Black Law (55°39′·68N 01°47′·50W) from April to August inclusive.
b. Boats should not be landed or recovered any where in the NNR except at the designated and buoyed watersports zone on the SE side of Budle Bay.

9.5.20 HOLY ISLAND

Northumberland **55°39′·57N 01°46′·81W** ❁❁⚓✿✿✿

CHARTS AC 1111, 612; Imray C24; OS 75

TIDES +0344 Dover; ML No data; Duration 0630; Zone 0 (UT)

Standard Port NORTH SHIELDS (⟵)

Times				**Height (metres)**			
High Water		Low Water		MHWS	MHWN	MLWN	MLWS
0200	0800	0100	0800	5·0	3·9	1·8	0·7
1400	2000	1300	2000				
Differences HOLY ISLAND							
−0043	−0039	−0105	−0110	−0·2	−0·2	−0·3	−0·1
NORTH SUNDERLAND (Seahouses)							
−0048	−0044	−0058	−0102	−0·2	−0·2	−0·2	0·0

SHELTER Good S of The Heugh in 3-6m, but ⚓ is uncomfortable in fresh W/SW winds esp at sp flood. Better shelter in The Ouse on sand/mud if able to dry out; but not in S/SE winds.

NAVIGATION WPT 55°39′·76N 01°44′·88W, 260° to Old Law E bn 1·55M. From N identify Emanuel Hd, conspic W △ bn, then appr via Goldstone Chan leaving Plough Seat PHM buoy to stbd. From S, clear Farne Is thence to WPT. Outer ldg bns lead 260° close past Ridge ECM and Triton SHM buoys. Possible overfalls in chan across bar (1·6m) with sp ebb up to 4kn. Inner ldg marks lead 310° to ⚓. Inshore route, round Castle Pt via Hole Mouth and The Yares, may be more sheltered, but is not for strangers.

LIGHTS AND MARKS Outer ldg marks/lts are Old Law bns (conspic), 2 reddish obelisks 21/25m on 260°; E bn has dir lt, Oc WRG 6s 9m 4M, G179°-259°, W259°-261°, R261°-shore. Inner ldg marks/lts are The Heugh tr, B △, on with St Mary's ch belfry 310°. The Heugh has dir lt, Oc WRG 6s 24m 5M, G135°-308°, W308°-311°, R311°-shore. Dir lts Oc WRG are aligned on 263° and 309·5° respectively.

R/T None.

TELEPHONE (Dial code 01289) HM 389248; CG 0191-257 2691; Marinecall 09066 526237.

FACILITIES Limited. FW on village green, R, Bar, limited 🛒, P & D from Beal (5M); bus (occas) to Berwick. Note Lindisfarne is ancient name; Benedictine Abbey (ruins) and Castle (NT) are worth visiting. Causeway to mainland covers at HW. It is usable by vehicles HW+3½ to HW–2; less in adverse weather.

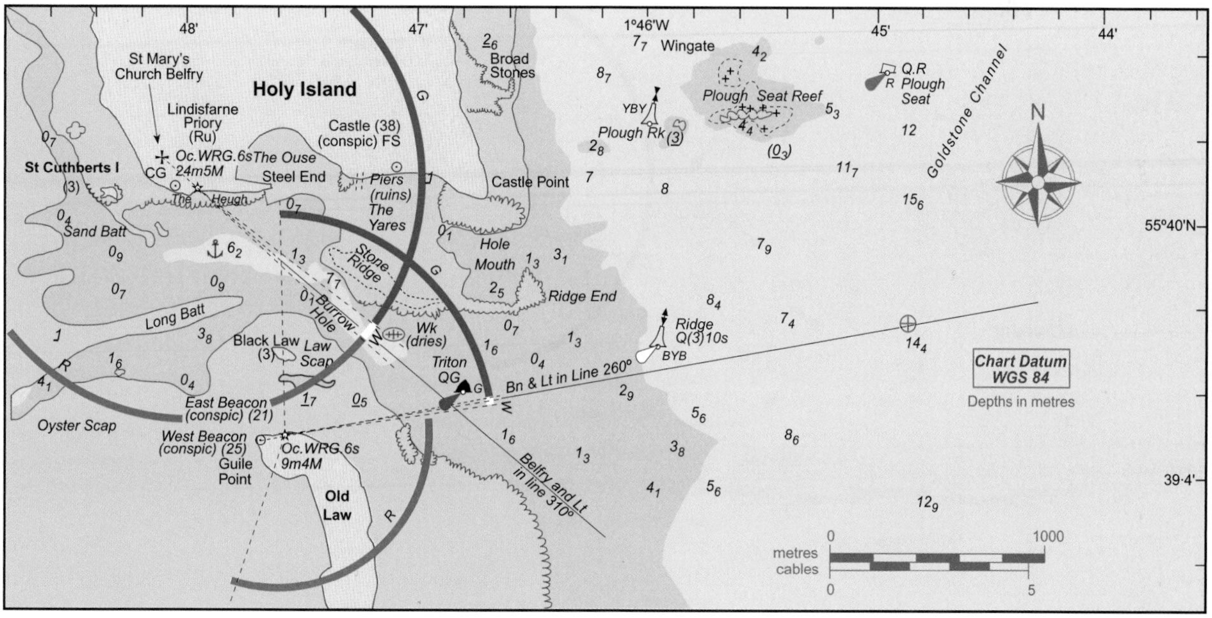
48'
47'
1°46'W
45'
44'
55°40'N
39·4'
Holy Island
St Mary's Church Belfry
Lindisfarne Priory (Ru)
Castle (38) (conspic) FS
Broad Stones
St Cuthberts I
CG
Oc.WRG.6s 24m5M
The Ouse
Steel End
The Heugh
Piers (ruins)
The Yares
Castle Point
Hole Mouth
Ridge End
Stone Ridge
Sand Batt
Long Batt
Burrow Hole
Black Law
Law Scap
Wk (dries)
Triton QG
Bn & Lt in Line 260°
East Beacon (conspic) (21)
West Beacon (conspic) (25)
Oc.WRG.6s 9m4M
Guile Point
Oyster Scap
Old Law
Belfry and Lt in line 310°
Wingate
YBY
Plough Rk
Plough Seat Reef
Q.R
Plough Seat
Goldstone Channel
N
Ridge Q(3)10s
BYB
Chart Datum WGS 84
Depths in metres
metres
cables
0
1000
5

9.5.21 BERWICK-UPON-TWEED

Northumberland **55°45'·87N 01°59'·05W** ❀❀◊◊✿✿

CHARTS AC 111, 160, 1612; Imray C24; OS 75

TIDES +0348 Dover; ML 2·5; Duration 0620; Zone 0 (UT)

Standard Port NORTH SHIELDS (⟵)

Times				Height (metres)			
High Water		Low Water		MHWS	MHWN	MLWN	MLWS
0200	0800	0100	0800	5·0	3·9	1·8	0·7
1400	2000	1300	2000				
Differences BERWICK-UPON-TWEED							
–0053	–0053	–0109	–0109	–0·3	–0·1	–0·5	–0·1

SHELTER Good shelter or ⚓ except in strong E/SE winds. Yachts lie in Tweed Dock (the dock gates have been removed; 0·6m in ent, approx 1·2m inside at MLWS) or temporarily at W end of Fish Jetty (1·2m).

NAVIGATION WPT 55°45'·65N 01°58'·10W, 294° to bkwtr lt ho, 0·58M. On-shore winds and ebb tides cause very confused state over the bar (0·6m). Access HW ±4 at sp. From HW–2 to HW+1 strong flood tide sets S across the ent; keep well up to bkwtr. The sands at the mouth of the Tweed shift so often that local knowledge is essential. The Berwick bridge (first and lowest) has about 3m clearance.

LIGHTS AND MARKS Town hall clock tr and lt ho in line at 294°. When past Crabwater Rk, keep bns at Spittal in line at 207°. Bns are B and Orange with △ top marks (both FR). Caution: The 207° ldg line may not clear the sands off Spittal Point which may encroach W'wards; best water is further W. Other lights as chartlet.

R/T HM VHF Ch 12 16 (HO).

TELEPHONE (Dial code 01289) HM 307404, 📠 332854; MRSC 01333 450666; Marinecall 09066 526237/236; Police 01661 872555; Dr 307484.

FACILITIES **Tweed Dock** ☎ 307404, AB £6.00, M, P(cans), D(cans), FW, Showers, ME, El, ⚒, C (Mobile 3 ton), Slip, SM. **Town** EC Thurs; P, 🛒, R, Bar, ✉, Ⓑ, ⇌ and ✈ (Newcastle or Edinburgh).

AGENTS WANTED If you are interested in becoming our agent for any of the following ports, please write to: The Editor, Reeds OKI Nautical Almanac, A&C Black Publishers Ltd, 37 Soho Square, London, W1D 3QZ – and get your free copy of the Almanac annually. You do not have to live in a port to be the agent, but should at least be a fairly regular visitor.

Keyhaven	Le Légué
Shetland Isles/Lerwick	St Helier/Gorey
Rothesay	Bénodet
Dunmore East	Concarneau
Baltimore	Lézardrieux
Belfast Lough	Lannion River
All Danish ports	Loctudy
Borkum	River Loire
Langeoog	Pornic
Zeebrugge	St Gilles-Croix-de-Vie
Hoek van Holland	Les Sables d'Olonne
Rotterdam	La Rochelle
Blankenberge	Rochefort
IJsselmeer	Capbreton
Le Havre	Port d'Anglet

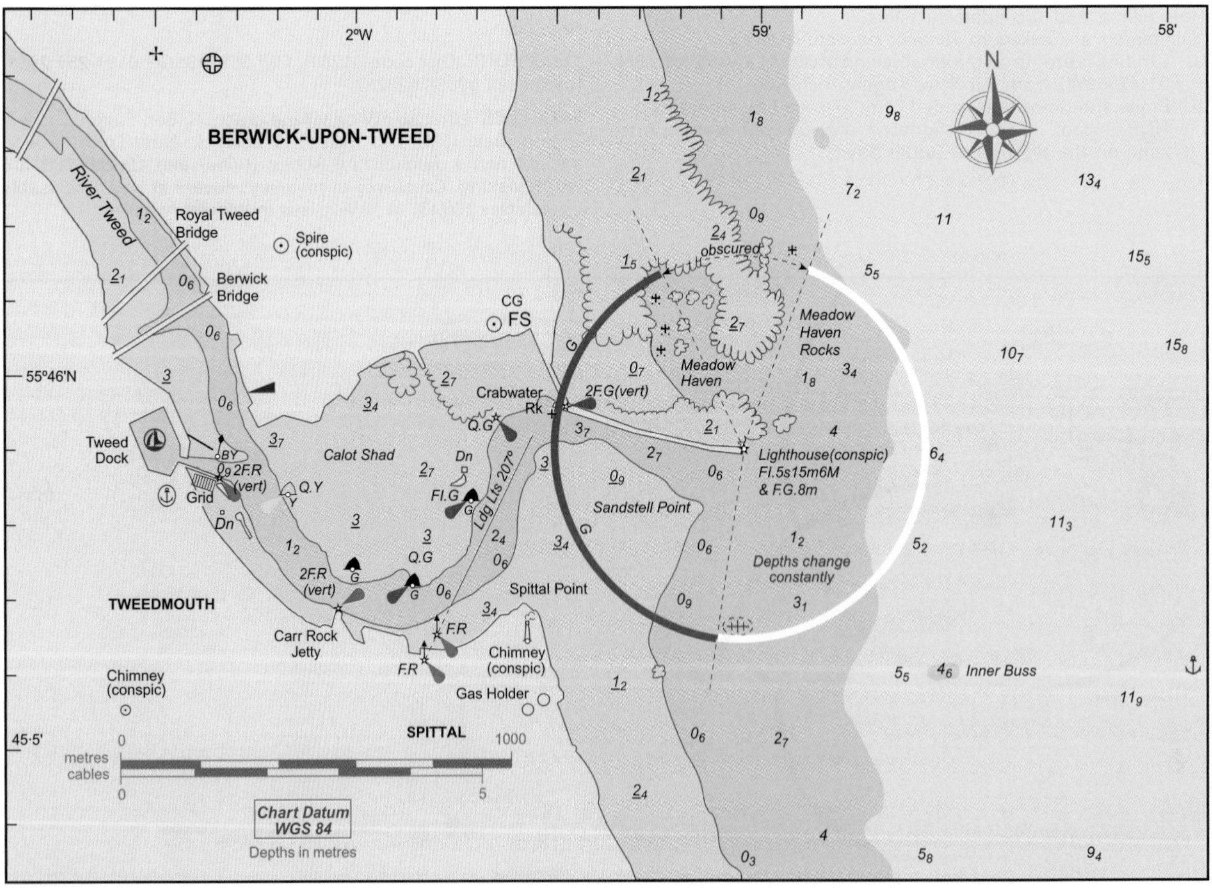
2°W
59'
58'
N
BERWICK-UPON-TWEED
River Tweed
Royal Tweed Bridge
Spire (conspic)
Berwick Bridge
CG
FS
55°46'N
Tweed Dock
BY
2F.R (vert)
Grid
Dn
Q.Y
Calot Shad
Crabwater Rk
Q.G
2F.G(vert)
Fl.G
Ldg Lts 207°
Q.G
2F.R (vert)
obscured
Meadow Haven
Meadow Haven Rocks
Lighthouse(conspic)
Fl.5s15m6M
& F.G.8m
Sandstell Point
Depths change constantly
Spittal Point
TWEEDMOUTH
Carr Rock Jetty
F.R
Chimney (conspic)
Gas Holder
Chimney (conspic)
SPITTAL
Inner Buss
45·5'
metres
cables
1000
5
Chart Datum WGS 84
Depths in metres

WEATHER DATA

WEATHER FORECASTS BY FAX & TELEPHONE

Coastal/Inshore	2-day by Fax	5-day by Phone
Scotland East	09061 502 114	09066 526 236
Scotland North	09061 502 110	09066 526 235
Minch	09061 502 126	09066 526 248
National (3-5 day)	09061 502 109	09066 526 234

Offshore	2-5 day by Fax	2-5 day by Phone
Northern North Sea	09061 502 166	09066 526 256

09066 CALLS COST 60P PER MIN. 09061 CALLS COST £1.50 PER MIN.

Area 6

South-East Scotland
Eyemouth to Rattray Head

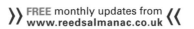

6

DISTANCE TABLE

Approximate distances in nautical miles are by the most direct route, whilst avoiding dangers and allowing for Traffic Separation Schemes. Places in italics are in adjoining areas; places in **bold** are in 9.0.8, Distances across the North Sea.

No.	Place	1	2	3	4	5	6	7	8	9	10	11	12	13	14	15	16	17	18	19	20
1.	*Great Yarmouth*	**1**																			
2.	***Berwick-on-Tweed***	232	**2**																		
3.	Eyemouth	240	10	**3**																	
4.	Dunbar	257	26	17	**4**																
5.	North Berwick	266	35	25	9	**5**															
6.	Granton	285	54	44	27	19	**6**														
7.	**Port Edgar**	290	58	50	34	26	7	**7**													
8.	Burntisland	283	53	43	26	18	5	8	**8**												
9.	Methil	276	45	36	20	13	14	20	12	**9**											
10.	Anstruther	269	38	29	14	10	23	29	22	11	**10**										
11.	Fife Ness	269	38	29	17	14	28	34	27	16	5	**11**									
12.	Bell Rock	276	43	36	27	25	40	47	39	28	17	12	**12**								
13.	**Dundee**	289	58	49	37	34	48	54	47	36	25	20	20	**13**							
14.	Arbroath	284	51	44	34	31	45	51	44	33	22	17	10	15	**14**						
15.	Montrose	291	59	51	43	41	55	61	54	43	32	27	17	27	12	**15**					
16.	Stonehaven	300	72	66	60	58	72	78	71	60	49	44	32	45	30	20	**16**				
17.	**Aberdeen**	308	82	78	73	70	84	90	83	72	61	56	44	57	42	32	13	**17**			
18.	Peterhead	318	105	98	93	95	106	108	105	94	83	78	68	80	64	54	35	25	**18**		
19.	***Fraserburgh***	334	121	114	109	108	122	128	121	110	99	94	83	96	79	68	51	39	16	**19**	
20.	***Wick***	391	178	171	166	165	179	185	178	167	156	151	140	153	136	125	108	96	72	57	**20**

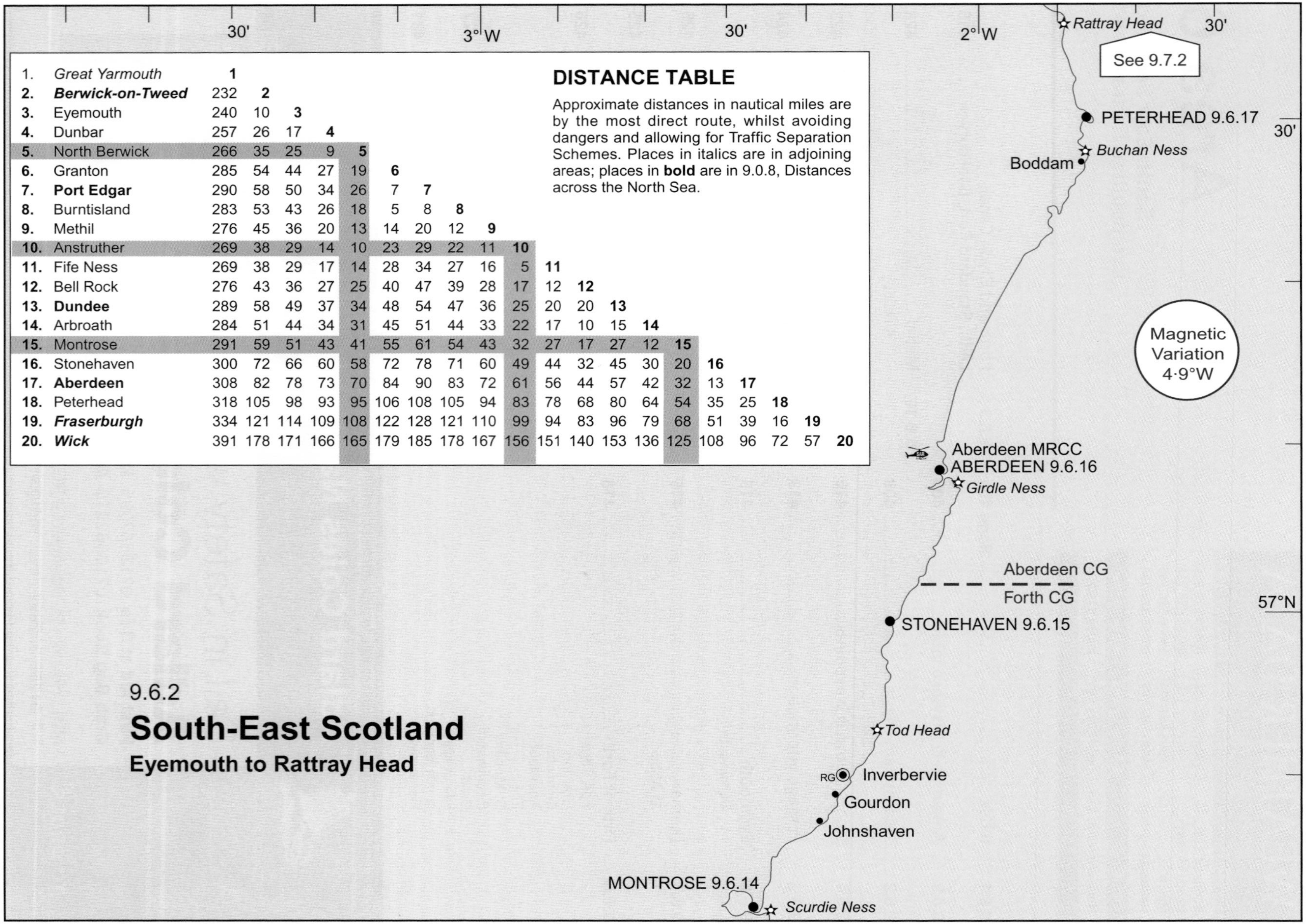

30'
3° W
30'
2° W
30'
30'
57°N
Rattray Head
See 9.7.2
PETERHEAD 9.6.17
Buchan Ness
Boddam
Magnetic Variation 4·9°W
Aberdeen MRCC
ABERDEEN 9.6.16
Girdle Ness
Aberdeen CG
Forth CG
STONEHAVEN 9.6.15
Tod Head
RG
Inverbervie
Gourdon
Johnshaven
MONTROSE 9.6.14
Scurdie Ness

9.6.2

South-East Scotland

Eyemouth to Rattray Head

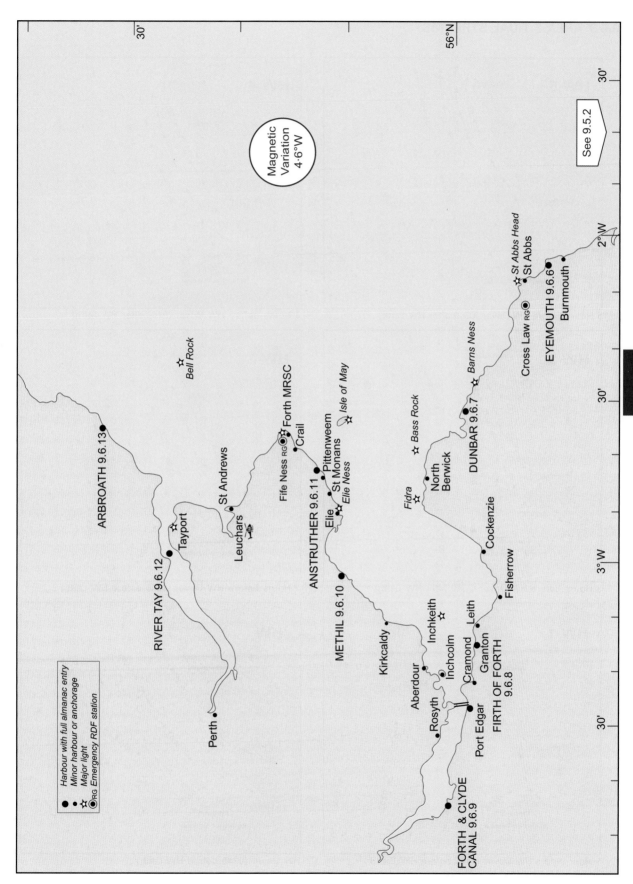

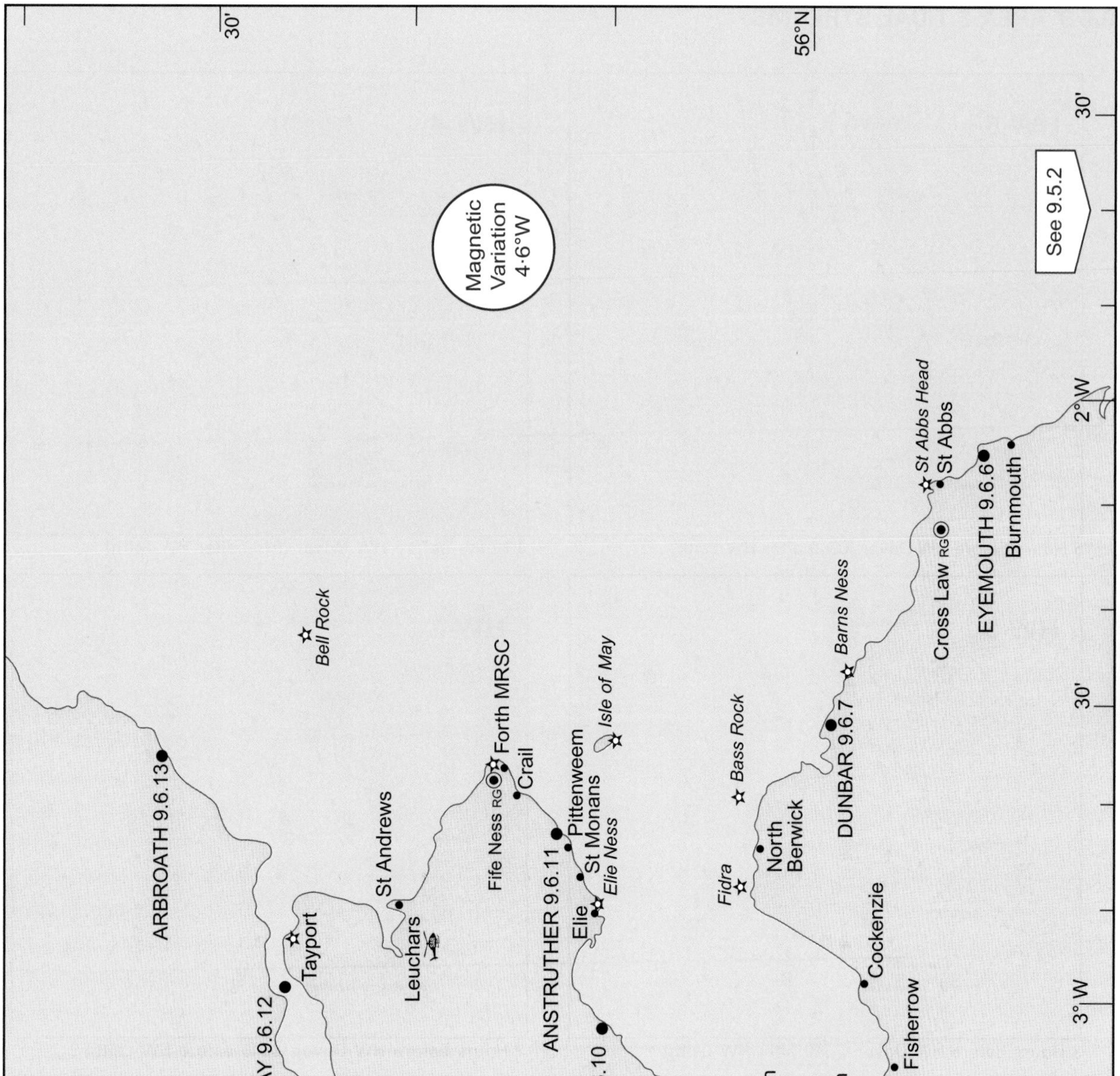
30'
56°N
30'
30'
3° W
30'
2° W
See 9.5.2
Magnetic Variation 4·6°W
Harbour with full almanac entry
Minor harbour or anchorage
Major light
RG Emergency RDF station
ARBROATH 9.6.13
Bell Rock
RIVER TAY 9.6.12
Tayport
Perth
St Andrews
Leuchars
Fife Ness RG
Forth MRSC
Crail
Isle of May
Pittenweem
St Monans
Elie Ness
Elie
ANSTRUTHER 9.6.11
METHIL 9.6.10
Kirkcaldy
Inchkeith
Inchcolm
Aberdour
Rosyth
Cramond
Granton
Leith
Port Edgar
FIRTH OF FORTH 9.6.8
FORTH & CLYDE CANAL 9.6.9
Fisherrow
Cockenzie
Fidra
North Berwick
Bass Rock
DUNBAR 9.6.7
Barns Ness
Cross Law RG
St Abbs Head
St Abbs
EYEMOUTH 9.6.6
Burnmouth

9.6.3 AREA 6 TIDAL STREAMS

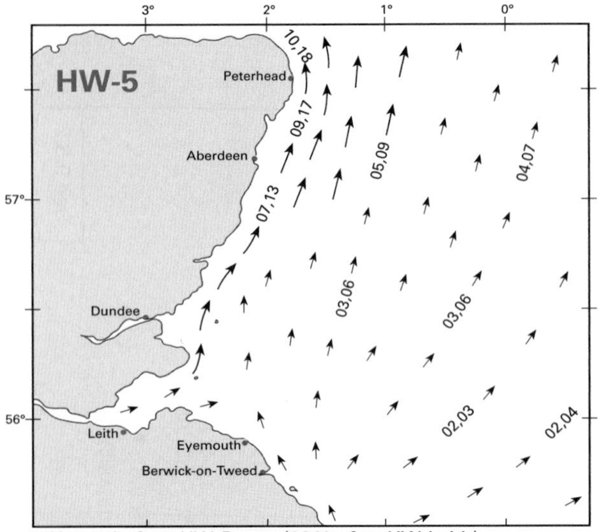
HW-5
Peterhead
Aberdeen
Dundee
Leith
Eyemouth
Berwick-on-Tweed
10,18
09,17
07,13
05,09
04,07
03,06
03,06
02,03
02,04
5 Hours before HW Dover (0340 after HW Leith)

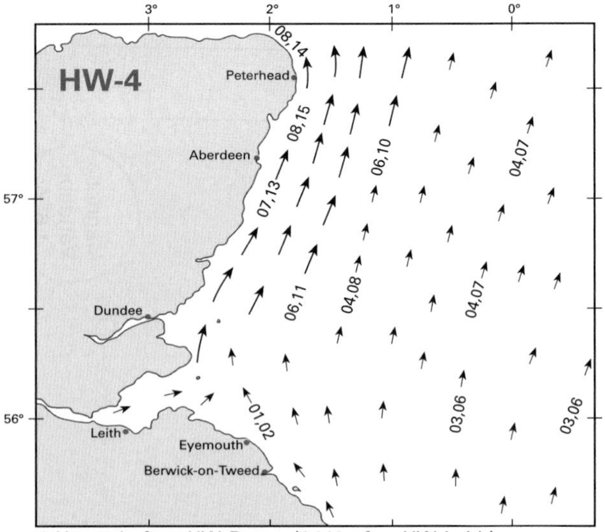
HW-4
Peterhead
Aberdeen
Dundee
Leith
Eyemouth
Berwick-on-Tweed
08,14
08,15
07,13
06,10
04,07
06,11
04,08
04,07
01,02
03,06
03,06
4 Hours before HW Dover (0440 after HW Leith)

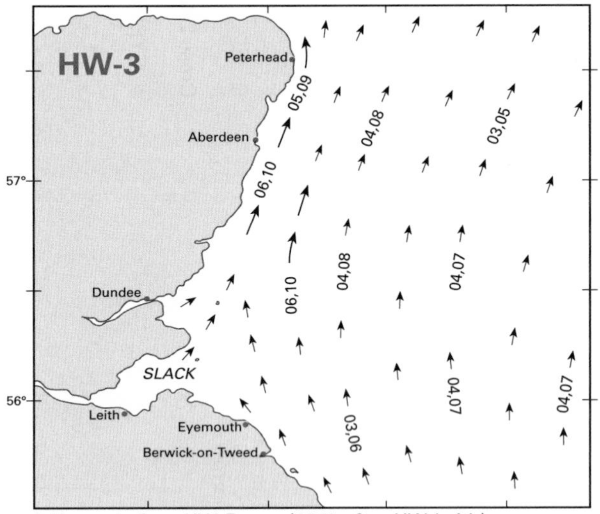
HW-3
Peterhead
Aberdeen
Dundee
Leith
Eyemouth
Berwick-on-Tweed
SLACK
05,09
04,08
03,05
06,10
06,10
04,08
04,07
04,07
04,07
03,06
3 Hours before HW Dover (0540 after HW Leith)

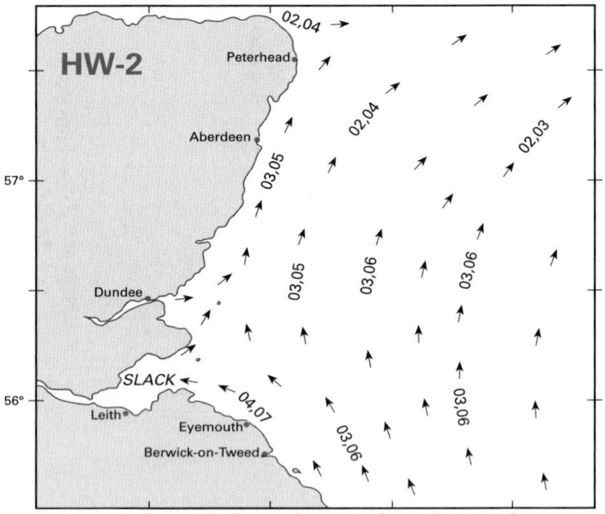
HW-2
Peterhead
Aberdeen
Dundee
Leith
Eyemouth
Berwick-on-Tweed
SLACK
02,04
02,04
02,03
03,05
03,05
03,06
03,06
04,07
03,06
03,06
2 Hours before HW Dover (0545 before HW Leith)

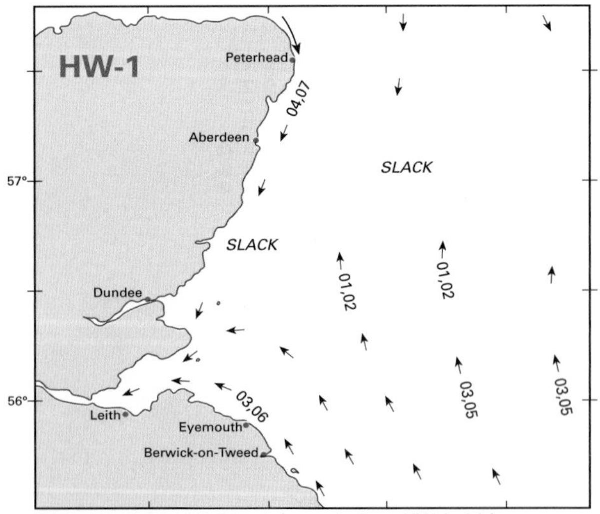
HW-1
Peterhead
Aberdeen
Dundee
Leith
Eyemouth
Berwick-on-Tweed
SLACK
SLACK
04,07
01,02
01,02
03,06
03,05
03,05
1 Hour before HW Dover (0445 before HW Leith)

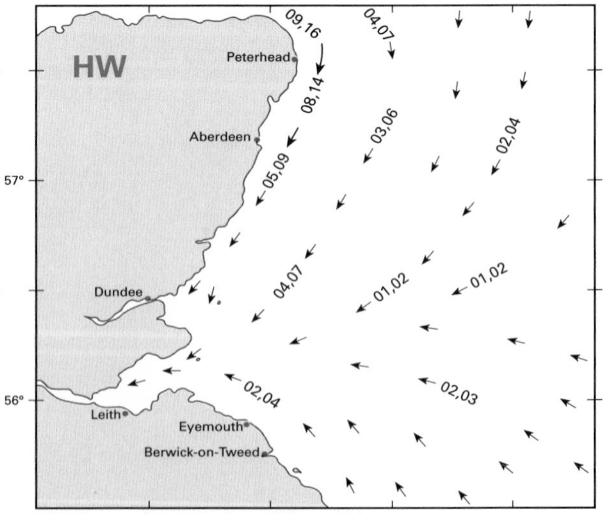
HW
Peterhead
Aberdeen
Dundee
Leith
Eyemouth
Berwick-on-Tweed
09,16
04,07
08,14
03,06
05,09
02,04
04,07
01,02
01,02
02,04
02,03
HW Dover (0345 before HW Leith)

Northward 9.7.3 Southward 9.5.3

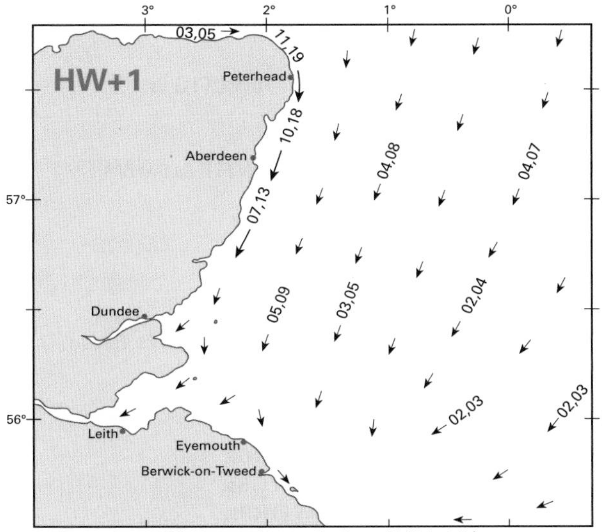
HW+1
Peterhead
Aberdeen
Dundee
Leith
Eyemouth
Berwick-on-Tweed
03,05
11,19
10,18
07,13
04,08
04,07
05,09
03,05
02,04
02,03
02,03

1 Hour after HW Dover (0245 before HW Leith)

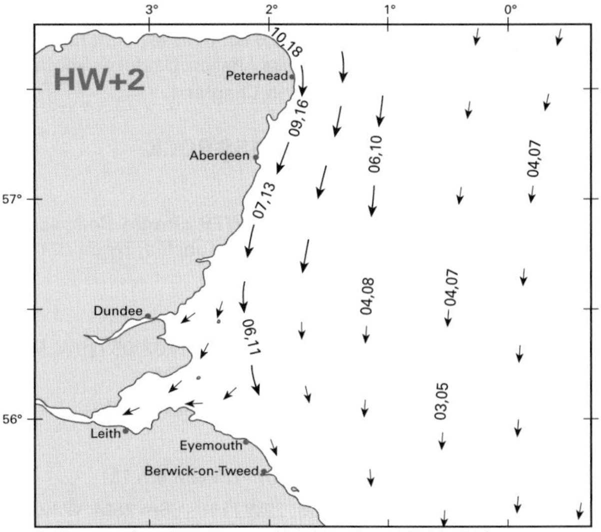
HW+2
Peterhead
Aberdeen
Dundee
Leith
Eyemouth
Berwick-on-Tweed
10,18
09,16
07,13
06,10
04,07
04,08
04,07
06,11
03,05

2 Hours after HW Dover (0145 before HW Leith)

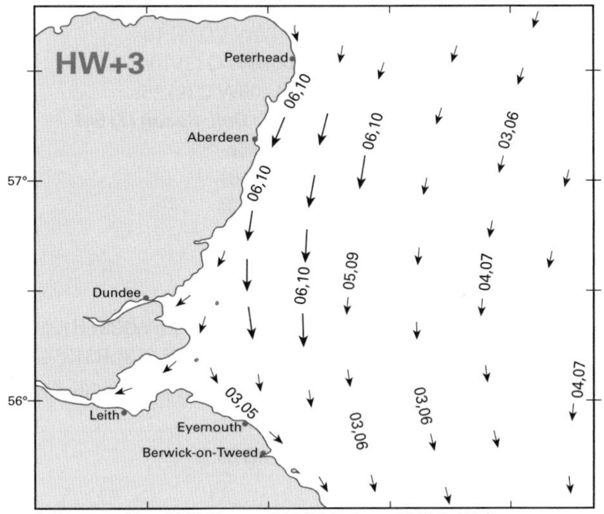
HW+3
Peterhead
Aberdeen
Dundee
Leith
Eyemouth
Berwick-on-Tweed
06,10
06,10
03,06
06,10
06,10
05,09
04,07
04,07
03,05
03,06
03,06

3 Hours after HW Dover (0045 before HW Leith)

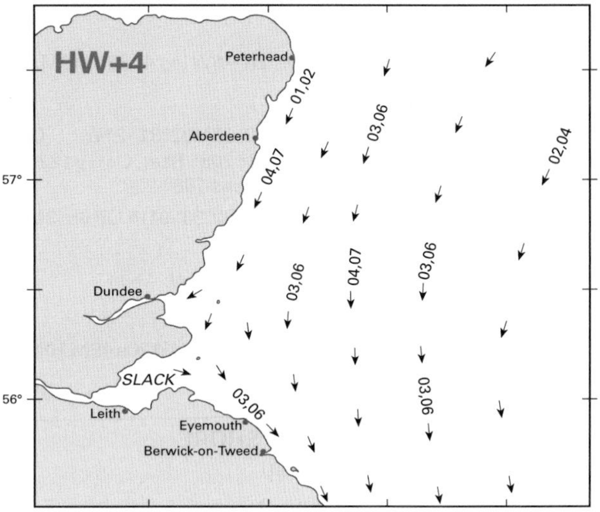
HW+4
Peterhead
Aberdeen
Dundee
Leith
Eyemouth
Berwick-on-Tweed
01,02
03,06
02,04
04,07
03,06
04,07
03,06
SLACK
03,06
03,06

4 Hours after HW Dover (0015 after HW Leith)

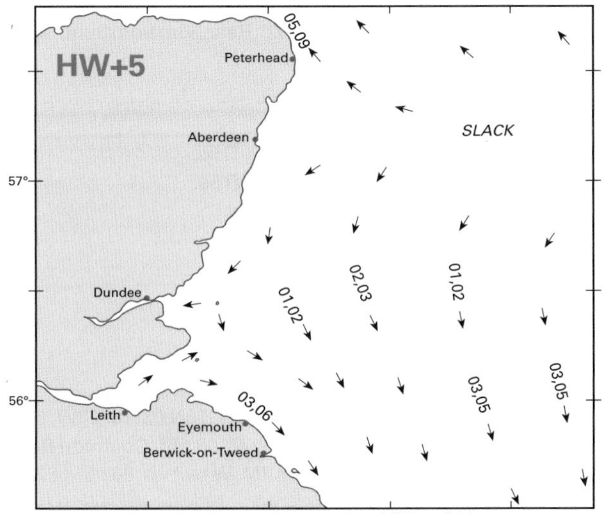
HW+5
Peterhead
Aberdeen
Dundee
Leith
Eyemouth
Berwick-on-Tweed
05,09
SLACK
02,03
01,02
01,02
03,05
03,05
03,06

5 Hours after HW Dover (0115 after HW Leith)

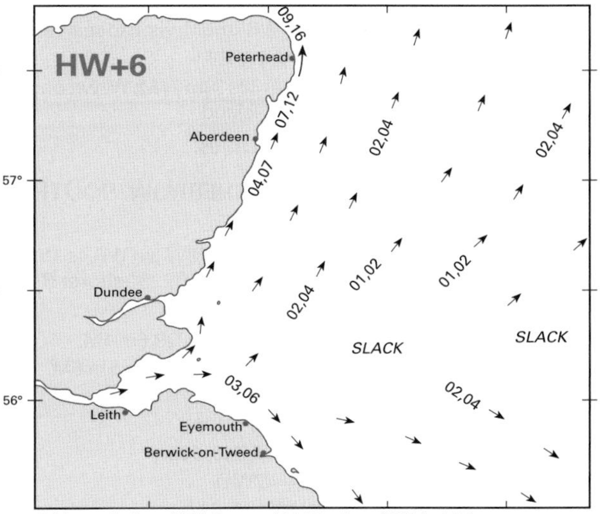
HW+6
Peterhead
Aberdeen
Dundee
Leith
Eyemouth
Berwick-on-Tweed
09,16
07,12
02,04
02,04
04,07
02,04
01,02
01,02
SLACK
SLACK
03,06
02,04

6 Hours after HW Dover (0215 after HW Leith)

PLOT WAYPOINTS ON YOUR CHART BEFORE USING THEM

9.6.4 LIGHTS, BUOYS AND WAYPOINTS

Blue print = light with a nominal range of 15M or more. CAPITALS = place or feature. *CAPITAL ITALICS* = light-vessel, light float or Lanby. *Italics* = Fog signal. ***Bold italics*** = Racon. Useful waypoints are underlined. Abbreviations are in Chapter 1.

BERWICK-UPON-TWEED TO BASS ROCK

▶ BURNMOUTH

Ldg lts 241°. Front, 55°50'·53N 02°04'·25W FR 29m 4M. Rear, 45m from front, FR 35m 4M. Both on W posts (unclear by day).

▶ EYEMOUTH

Blind Buss 55°52'·80N 02°05'·25E Q.

Ldg Lts 174°. Front, W Bkwtr Hd ☆, 55°52'·47N 02°05'·29W FG 9m 6M. Rear, elbow 55m from front, FG 10m 6M.

E Bkwtr Head ☆ 55°52'·50N 02°05'·29W Iso R 2s 8m 8M.

▶ ST ABB'S

Hd of inside Jetty ☆ 55°53'·94N 02°07'·73W FR 4m 1M.

St Abb's Hd ☆ 55°54'·96N 02°08'·29W Fl 10s 68m **26M**; W twr; ***Racon (T) 18M***.

Torness Power Station Pier Head ☆ 55°58'·40N 02°24'·45W Fl R 5s 10m 5M.

Barns Ness Tower ☆ 55°59'·22N 02°26'·76W Iso 4s 36m 10M.

▶ DUNBAR

Bayswell Hill Ldg Lts 198°. Front, 56°00'·25N 02°31'·21W Oc G 6s 15m 3M; W △ on Or col; intens 188°-208°. Rear, Oc G 6s 22m 3M; ▽ on Or col; synch with front, intens 188°-208°.

Victoria Hbr, Middle Quay ☆ 56°00'·31N 02°30'·91W QR 6m 3M; vis over hbr ent.

Bellhaven Bay Outfall 56°00'·99N 02°33'·09W.

S Carr (12) 56°03'·43N 02°37'·77W.

Bass Rock, S side, ☆ 56°04'·61N 02°38'·48W Fl (3) 20s 46m 10M; W twr; vis: 241°-107°.

FIRTH OF FORTH AND SOUTH SHORE

(Direction of buoyage East to West)

▶ NORTH BERWICK

Outfall 56°04'·29N 02°40'·89W Fl Y.

N Pier Hd ☆ 56°03'·66N 02°43'·23W FWR 7m 3M; vis: R to seaward, W over hbr. Not lit if ent closed by weather.

Fidra ☆ 56°04'·39N 02°47'·13W Fl (4) 30s 34m **24M**; W twr; obsc by Bass Rock, Craig Leith and Lamb Island.

Wreck 56°04'·39N 02°52'·39W Fl (2) R 10s.

▶ PORT SETON/COCKENZIE/FISHERROW/SOUTH CHANNEL

Port Seton, E Pier Hd ☆ 55°58'·40N 02°57'·23W Iso WR 4s 10m W9M, R6M; vis: R shore-105°, W105°-225°, R225°-shore; *Bell (occas)*.

Cockenzie Jetty Hd ☆ 55°58'·25N 02°58'·43W QR 6m 1M.

Fisherrow E Pier Hd ☆ 55°56'·79N 03°04'·11W Oc 6s 5m 6M.

Narrow Deep 56°01'·46N 03°04'·59W Fl (2) R 10s.

Herwit 56°01'·05N 03°06'·52W Fl (3) G 10s.

North Craig 56°01'·02N 03°03'·52W Q (3) 10s.

Craigh Waugh 56°00'·26N 03°04'·47W Q.

Diffuser Hds (Outer) 55°59'·81N 03°07'·84W.

Diffuser Hds (Inner) 55°59'·34N 03°08'·04W.

▶ LEITH

Leith Approach 55°59'·95N 03°11'·51W Fl R 3s.

East Bkwtr Hd ☆ 55°59'·48N 03°10'·94W Iso R 4s 7m 9M; *Horn (3) 30s.*

W Bkwtr Hd ☆ 55°59'·36N 03°11'·10W L Fl G 6s.

▶ GRANTON

E Pier Head ☆ 55°59'·28N 03°13'·27W Fl R 2s 5m 6M.

▶ CRAMOND

Church twr 55°58'·67N 03°17'·92W.

▶ NORTH CHANNEL/MIDDLE BANK

Inchkeith Fairway 56°03'·49N 03°00'·10W Iso 2s; ***Racon (T) 5M***.

No. 1 56°03'·22N 03°03'·71W Fl G 9s.

No. 2 56°02'·90N 03°03'·72W Fl R 9s.

No. 3 56°03'·22N 03°06'·10W Fl G 6s.

No. 4 56°02'·89N 03°06'·11W Fl R 6s.

No. 5 56°03'·18N 03°07'·88W Fl G 3s.

No. 6 56°03'·05N 03°08'·44W Fl R 3s.

No. 8 56°02'·95N 03°09'·62W Fl R 9s.

Inchkeith ☆ 56°02'·01N 03°08'·17W Fl 15s 67m **22M**; stone twr.

Pallas Rock 56°01'·50N 03°09'·30W VQ (9) 10s.

East Gunnet 56°01'·41N 03°10'·38W Q (3) 10s.

West Gunnet 56°01'·34N 03°11'·06W Q (9) 15s.

No. 7 56°02'·80N 03°10'·97W QG; *Bell;* ***Racon (T) 5M.***

No. 9 56°02'·32N 03°13'·48W Fl G 6s.

No. 10 56°02'·07N 03°13'·32W Fl R 6s.

No. 11 56°02'·08N 03°15'·26W Fl G 3s.

No. 12 56°01'·78N 03°15'·15W Fl R 3s.

No. 13 56°01'·77N 03°16'·94W Fl G 9s.

No. 14 56°01'·52N 03°16'·82W Fl R 9s.

Oxcars ☆ 56°01'·36N 03°16'·84W Fl (2) WR 7s 16m W13M, R12M; W twr, R band; vis: W072°-087°, R087°-196°, W196°-313°, R313°-072°.

Inchcolm E Pt ☆ 56°01'·72N 03°17'·83W Fl (3) 15s 20m 10M; Gy twr; part obsc by land 075°-145·5°.

No. 15 56°01'·43N 03°18'·78W Fl G 6s.

▶ MORTIMER'S DEEP

Hawkcraig Point Ldg Lts 292°. Front, 56°03'·03N 03°17'·07W Iso 5s 12m 14M; W twr; vis: 282°-302°. Rear, 96m from front, Iso 5s 16m 14M; W twr; vis: 282°-302°.

No. 1 56°02'·66N 03°15'·26W QG.

No. 2 56°02'·70N 03°15'·83W QR.

No. 3 56°02'·50N 03°17'·52W Fl (2) G 5s.

No. 4 56°02'·38N 03°17'·43W Fl (2) R 5s.

No. 5 56°02'·37N 03°17'·94W Fl G 4s.

No. 6 56°02'·28N 03°17'·86W Fl R 4s.

No. 8 56°02'·10N 03°18'·25W Fl R 2s.

No. 7 56°01'·93N 03°19'·00W Fl (2) G 5s.

No. 10 56°01'·83N 03°18'·56W Fl (2) R 5s.

No. 9 56°01'·69N 03°19'·16W QG.

No. 14 56°01'·55N 03°19'·04W Q (9) 15s.

Inchcolm S Lts in line 066°. Front 56°01'·78N 03°18'·28W, 84m from rear, Q 7m 7M; W twr; vis: 062·5°-082·5°. Common Rear, 56°01'·80N 03°18'·13W Iso 5s 11m 7M; W twr; vis: 062·5°-082·5°.

N Lts in line 076·7°. Front, 80m from rear, Q 7m 7M; W twr; vis: 062·5°-082·5°.

▶ APPROACHES TO FORTH BRIDGES

<u>No. 17</u> ▲ 56°01'·23N 03°19'·84W Fl G 3s.
<u>No. 16</u> ◿ 56°00'·87N 03°19'·60W Fl R 3s.
<u>No. 19</u> ▲ 56°00'·71N 03°22'·47W Fl G 9s.
Hound Pt Terminal NE Dn ☆ 56°00'·46N 03°21'·34W 2 FR 7m 5M.
Centre Pier 56°00'·33N 03°21'·79W 2 Aero FR 47m 5M.
Hound Pt SW Dn ☆ 56°00'·28N 03°21'·92W FR 7m 5M.
Inch Garvie, NW end ☆ 56°00'·10N 03°23'·37W L Fl 5s 9m 11M.
N Queensferry ☆ Oc 5s and QR or QG tfc signals.

Forth Rail Bridge. Centres of spans have W Lts and ends of cantilevers R Lts, defining N and S chans.

Forth Road Bridge. N suspension twr Iso G 4s 7m 6M on E and W sides; 2 Aero FR 155m 11M and 2 FR 109m 7M on same twr. Main span, N part QG 50m 6M on E and W sides. Main span, centre Iso 4s 52m 8M on E and W sides. Main span, S part QR 50m 6M on E and W sides. S suspension twr Iso R 4s 7m 6M on E and W sides; 2 Aero FR 155m and 2 Fr 109m 7M on same twr.
Beamer Rk ☆ 56°00'·28N 03°24'·74W Fl 3s 6m 9M; W twr, R top.

▶ PORT EDGAR

W Bkwtr Head ☆ 55°59'·86N 03°24'·78W Fl R 4s 4m 8M; W blockhouse; 3 QY mark floating bkwtr.

3 x 2 FR (vert) mark N ends of Marina pontoons inside hbr.

FIRTH OF FORTH – NORTH SHORE (INWARD)

▶ BURNTISLAND

W Pier Outer Hd ☆ 56°03'·22N 03°14'·26W Fl (2) R 6s 7m; W twr.
E Pier Outer Hd ☆ 56°03'·24N 03°14'·17W Fl (2) G 6s 7m 5M.

▶ ABERDOUR/BRAEFOOT BAY/INCHCOLM

Hawkcraig Pt ☆ (see **MORTIMER'S DEEP** above).
Aberdour Bay Outfall ⊥ Bn 56°02'·96N 03°17'·71W; Y Bn.

Braefoot Bay Terminal, W Jetty. Ldg Lts 247·3°. **Front,** 56°02'·16N 03°18'·71W Fl 3s 6m **15M**; W △ on E dolphin; vis: 237·2°-257·2°; four dolphins marked by 2 FG (vert). **Rear,** 88m from front, Fl 3s 12m **15M**; W ▽ on appr gangway; vis: 237·2°-257·2°; synch with front.

Inchcolm Abbey twr 56°01'·81N 03°18'·11W.

▶ INVERKEITHING BAY

St David's Dir lt 098° ⌡ 56°01'·37N 03°22'·29W Fl G 5s 3m 7M; Or ☐, on pile.

<u>Channel</u> ▲ 56°01'·43N 03°23'·02W QG.
<u>Channel</u> ◿ 56°01'·41N 03°23'·15W QR.
<u>Channel</u> ⌡ 56°01'·43N 03°23'·34W Fl R 3s.

▶ HM NAVAL BASE, ROSYTH

Main Chan Dir lt 323·5°. Bn 'A' 56°01'·19N 03°25'·61W Oc WRG 7m 4M; R ☐ on W post with R bands; vis: G318°-321°, W321°-326°, R326°-328° (H24).

Dir lt 115°, Bn 'C' 56°00'·61N 03°24'·25W Oc WRG 6s 7m 4M; W ▽ on W Bn; vis: R110°-113°, W113°-116·5°, G116·5°-120°.

<u>No. 1</u> ▲ 56°00'·54N 03°24'·56W Fl (2) G 10s.
<u>Whale Bank No. 2</u> ⌡ 56°00'·70N 03°25'·19W Q (3) 10s.
<u>No. 3</u> ▲ 56°00'·87N 03°25'·05W Fl G 5s.
<u>No. 4</u> ◿ 56°00'·82N 03°25'·25W Fl R 3s.
<u>No. 5</u> ▲ 56°01'·08N 03°25'·89W QG.
<u>No. 6</u> ◿ 56°01'·02N 03°25'·96W QR.

S Arm Jetty Hd ☆ 56°01'·09N 03°26'·58W L Fl (2) WR 12s 5m W9M; R6M; vis: W010°-280°, R280°-010°.

RIVER FORTH

▶ ROSYTH TO GRANGEMOUTH

<u>Dhu Craig</u> ▲ 56°00'·74N 03°27'·23W Fl G 5s.
<u>Blackness</u> ◿ 56°01'·06N 03°30'·30W QR.

Charlestown. Lts in line. Front 56°02'·21N 03°30'·68W FG 4m 10M; Y △ on Y pile; vis: 017°-037°; marks line of HP gas main. Rear FG 6m 10M; Y ▽ on Y pile; vis: 017°-037°.

Crombie Jetty, downstream dolphin ☆ 56°01'·94N 03°31'·84W 2 FG (vert) 8m 4M.

Crombie Jetty, upstream dolphin ☆ 56°02'·00N 03°32'·12W 2 FG (vert) 8m 4M.

<u>Tancred Bank</u> ◿ 56°01'·58N 03°31'·91W Fl (2) R 10s.
<u>Dods Bank</u> ◿ 56°02'·03N 03°34'·07W Fl R 3s.
<u>Bo'ness</u> ◿ 56°02'·23N 03°35'·38W Fl R 10s.

Bo'ness. Carriden outfall ⌡ 56°01'·33N 03°33'·71W Fl Y 5s 3M; Y ☐ on Y Bn.

Torry ☆ 56°02'·46N 03°35'·28W Fl G 10s 5m 7M; G ○ structure.
Bo'ness Platform ◿ 56°01'·85N 03°36'·22W 2 QR 3m 2M.

▶ GRANGEMOUTH

<u>Grangemouth App No. 1</u> ⌡ 56°02'·12N 03°38'·10W Fl (3) R 20s 4m 6M.

<u>Hen & Chickens</u> ▲ 56°02'·35N 03°38'·08W Fl (3) G 20s.
No. 2 ▲ 56°02'·35N 03°39'·21W Fl G 5s.
No. 3 ⌡ 56°02'·26N 03°39'·22W Fl R 5s 4m 6M.
No. 4 ☆ 56°02'·37N 03°39'·91W Fl G 2s 4m 5M.
No. 5 ⌡ 56°02'·26N 03°39'·92W Fl R 2s 4m 5M.
<u>Grangemouth SW</u> ▲ 56°02'·23N 03°40'·44W Fl (2) R 5s.
<u>Grangemouth W</u> ◿ 56°02'·38N 03°40'·59W QG.
Dock entrance, E Jetty; *Horn 30s;* docking signals.
Longannet Power Station ☆ 56°02'·78N 03°40'·99W L Fl G 10s 5m 6M.

<u>Inch Brake</u> ▲ 56°03'·61N 03°43'·27W.

FIRTH OF FORTH – NORTH SHORE (OUTWARD)

▶ KIRKCALDY

East Pier Hd ☆ 56°06'·78N 03°08'·90W Fl WG 10s 12m 8M; vis: G156°-336°, W336°-156°.

<u>Kirkcaldy Wreck</u> ▲ 56°07'·27N 03°05'·32W Fl (3) G 20s.

▶ METHIL

Outer Pier Hd ☆ 56°10'·76N 03°00'·48W Oc G 6s 8m 5M; W twr; vis: 280°-100°.

▶ ELIE

<u>Thill Rock</u> ◿ 56°10'·87N 02°49'·70W Fl (4) R 10s.
Elie Ness ☆ 56°11'·04N 02°48'·77W Fl 6s 15m **18M**; W twr.

▶ ST MONANCE

Bkwtr Hd ☆ 56°12'·20N 02°45'·94W Oc WRG 6s 5m W7M, R4M, G4M; vis: G282°-355°, W355°-026°, R026°-038°.

E Pier Hd ☆ 2 FG (vert) 6m 4M; Or tripod; *Bell (occas).*
W Pier near Hd ☆ 2 FR (vert) 6m 4M.

▶ PITTENWEEM

Ldg Lts 037° Middle Pier Hd. Front, 56°12'·69N 02°43'·69W FR 4m 5M. Rear, FR 8m 5M. Both Gy Cols, Or stripes.

E Bkwtr Hd ☆ 56°12'·63N 02°43'·74W Fl (2) RG 5s 9m R9M, G6M; vis: R265°-345°, G345°-055°; *Horn 90s (occas).*

Beacon Rk ☆ 56°12'·62N 02°43'·82W QR 3m 2M.

PLOT WAYPOINTS ON YOUR CHART BEFORE USING THEM

▶ ANSTRUTHER EASTER

Ldg Lts 019°. Front 56°13'·28N 02°41'·76W FG 7m 4M. Rear, 38m from front, FG 11m 4M, (both W masts).

W Pier Hd ☆ 56°13'·18N 02°41'·84W 2 FR (vert) 5m 4M; Gy mast; *Horn (3) 60s (occas).*

E Pier Hd ☆ 56°13'·14N 02°41'·83W Fl G 3s 6m 4M.

▶ MAY ISLAND

Isle of May ☆, Summit 56°11'·12N 02°33'·46W Fl (2) 15s 73m **22M**; □ twr on stone dwelling.

▶ CRAIL

Ldg Lts 295°. Front, 56°15'·46N 02°37'·84W FR 24m 6M (not lit when hbr closed). Rear, 30m from front, FR 30m 6M.

Fife Ness ☆ 56°16'·74N 02°35'·19W Iso WR 10s 12m **W21M, R20M**; W bldg; vis: W143°-197°, R197°-217°, W217°-023°.

▶ FIFE NESS TO MONTROSE

N Carr 56°18'·05N 02°32'·94W Q (3) 10s 3m 5M.
Bell Rk ☆ 56°26'·08N 02°23'·21W Fl 5s 28m **18M**; ***Racon (M) 18M.***

▶ RIVER TAY/TAYPORT/DUNDEE/PERTH

Tay Fairway 56°29'·24N 02°38'·26W L Fl 10s; *Bell.*
Middle Green (N) 56°28'·47N 02°39'·55W Fl (3) G 20s.
Middle Red (S) 56°28'·34N 02°38'·86W Fl (2) R 12s.
Abertay N 56°27'·39N 02°40'·36W Q (3) 10s; ***Racon (T) 8M.***
Abertay S (Elbow) 56°27'·13N 02°39'·83W Fl R 6s.
Inner 56°27'·09N 02°44'·33W Fl (2) R 12s.
N Lady 56°27'·39N 02°46'·85W Fl (2) G 20s.
S Lady 56°27'·20N 02°46'·84W Fl (3) R 20s.
Pool 56°27'·14N 02°48'·53W Fl R 6s.

Tentsmuir Pt 56°26'·59N 02°49'·61W Fl Y 5s; Y◊ on Y Bn; vis: 198°-208°; marks gas pipeline.

Monifieth 56°28'·83N 02°47'·90W Fl Y 5s; Y◊ on Y Bn; vis: 018°-028°; marks gas pipeline.

Horse Shoe 56°27'·27N 02°50'·22W Q (6) + L Fl 15s.
Scalp 56°27'·17N 02°51'·60W Fl (2) R 12s.

Broughty Castle ☆ 56°27'·75N 02°52'·21W 2 FG (vert) 10m 4M; FR is shown at foot of old Lt Ho at Buddon Ness, 4M to E, and at other places on firing range when practice is taking place.

Craig 56°27'·47N 02°53'·00W QR.
Newcombe 56°27'·71N 02°53'·53W Fl R 6s.

Tayport High Lt Ho ☆ Dir lt 269°, 56°27'·17N 02°53'·96W Iso WRG 3s 24m **W22M, R17M, G16M**; W twr; vis: G267°-268°, W268°-270°, R270°-271°.

Dundee Tidal Basin E Ent ☆ 56°27'·91N 02°56'·00W 2 FG (vert).
Middle Bank 56°27'·40N 02°56'·53W Q (3) 10s.

West Deep 56°27'·14W 02°56'·26W Fl R 3s.

Tay Road Bridge N navigation span, centre ☆ 56°27'·04N 02°56'·55W 2 x VQ 27m 4M.

Tay Road Bridge S navigation span, centre ☆ 56°27'·01N 02°56'·48W 2 x VQ 28m 4M.

Tay Railway Bridge navigation ☆ 56°26'·26N 02°59'·31W 2 x 2 F (vert) 23m.

Jock's Hole ☆ 56°21'·75N 03°12'·28W QR 3m 2M.
Cairnie Pier ☆ 56°21'·46N 03°17'·96W 2 X QY.
Elcho Castle ☆ 56°22'·47N 03°20'·95W Iso R 4s 4m 4M.

▶ ARBROATH

Outfall 56°32'·65N 02°35'·07W Fl Y 3s.

Ldg lts 299·2°. Front, 56°33'·29N 02°35'·16W FR 7m 5M; W col. Rear, 50m from front, FR 13m 5M; W col.

W Bkwtr E end, VQ (2) 6s 6m 4M; W post.

E Pier S Elbow ☆ 56°33'·25N 02°34'·97W Fl G 3s 8m 5M; W twr; shows FR when hbr closed; *Siren (3) 60s* (occas).

▶ MONTROSE

Scurdie Ness ☆ 56°42'·10N 02°26'·24W Fl (3) 20s 38m **23M**; W twr; ***Racon (T) 14-16M.***

Ldg Lts 271·5°. Front 56°42'·21N 02°27'·41W, FR 11m 5M; W twin pillars, R bands. Rear, 272m from front, FR 18m 5M; W twr, R cupola.

Annat Shoal 56°42'·37N 02°25'·19W QG.
Annat 56°42'·23N 02°25'·95W Fl G 3s.

MONTROSE TO RATTRAY HEAD

▶ JOHNSHAVEN

Ldg Lts 316°. Front, 56°47'·62N 02°20'·26W FR 5m. Rear, 85m from front, FG 20m; shows R when unsafe to enter hbr.

▶ GOURDON HARBOUR

Ldg Lts 358°. Front, 56°49'·69N 02°17'·24W FR 5m 5M; W twr; shows G when unsafe to enter; *Siren (2) 60s* (occas). Rear, 120m from front, FR 30m 5M; W twr.

W Pier Hd ☆ 56°49'·62N 02°17'·30W Fl WRG 3s 5m W9M, R7M, G7M; vis: G180°-344°, W344°-354°, R354°-180°.

E Bkwtr Hd ☆ 56°49'·58N 02°17'·18W Q 3m 7M.
Todhead ☆ 56°53'·00N 02°12'·97W Fl (4) 30s 41m **18M**; W twr.

▶ STONEHAVEN

Outer Pier Hd ☆ 56°57'·59N 02°12'·00W Iso WRG 4s 7m W11M, R7M, G8M; vis: G214°-246°, W246°-268°, R268°-280°.

Girdle Ness ☆ 57°08'·34N 02°02'·91W Fl (2) 20s 56m **22M**; obsc by Greg Ness when brg more than about 020°; ***Racon (G) 25M.***

▶ ABERDEEN

Fairway 57°09'·31N 02°01'·95W Mo (A) 5s; ***Racon (T) 7M.***

Torry Ldg lts 235·7°. Front, 57°08'·37N 02°04'·51W FR or G 14m 5M; R when ent safe, FG when dangerous to navigation; vis: 195°-279°. Rear, 205m from front, FR 19m 5M; W twr; vis: 195°-279°.

S Bkwtr Hd ☆ 57°08'·69N 02°03'·34W Fl (3) R 8s 23m 7M.

N Pier Hd ☆ 57°08'·74N 02°03'·69W Oc WR 6s 11m 9M; W twr; vis: W145°-055°, R055°-145°. In fog FY 10m (same twr) vis: 136°-336°; *Bell (3) 12s.*

River Don Ent ☆ 57°10'·42N 02°04'·71W Fl 3s 16m 5M.

Buchan Ness ☆ 57°28'·23N 01°46'·51W Fl 5s 40m **28M**; W twr, R bands; ***Racon (O) 14-16M.***

Cruden Skares 57°23'·17N 01°50'·36W Fl R 10s; *Bell.*

▶ PETERHEAD

Kirktown Ldg lts 314°. Front, 57°30'·22N 01°47'·21W FR 13m 8M; R mast, Or △ on R mast. Rear, 91m from front, FR 17m 8M.

S Bkwtr Hd ☆ 57°29'·79N 01°46'·54W Fl (2) R 12s 24m 7M.

N Bkwtr Hd ☆ 57°29'·84N 01°46'·32W Iso RG 6s 19m 11M; W tripod; vis: R171°-236°, G236°-171°; *Horn 30s.*

Marina N Bkwtr Hd ☆ 57°29'·81N 01°47'·49W QG 5m 2M; vis: 185°-300°.

Marina S Bkwtr Hd ☆ 57°29'·80N 01°47'·43W Fl R 4s 6m 2M.

Rattray Hd ☆ 57°36'·61N 01°49'·03W Fl (3) 30s 28m **24M**; W twr; ***Racon (M) 15M.***

9.6.5 PASSAGE INFORMATION

For these waters refer to the Admiralty *North Sea (West) Pilot*; R Northumberland YC's *Sailing Directions Humber to Rattray Head*, and the *Forth Yacht Clubs Association Pilot Handbook* (edition 2001), which covers the Firth of Forth in detail.

A *'Rover Ticket'*, £20 from Aberdeenshire Council or £21 from Moray Council allows berthing (subject to availability) for one week from the date of arrival at the first harbour. Scheme includes, Johnshaven, Gourdon, Stonehaven, Rosehearty, Banff, Portsoy, Cullen, Portknockie, Findochty, Hopeman and Burghead.

BERWICK-UPON-TWEED TO BASS ROCK (charts 160,175) From Berwick-upon-Tweed to the Firth of Forth there is no good hbr which can be approached with safety in strong onshore winds. So, if on passage with strong winds from N or E, plan accordingly and keep well to seaward. In late spring and early summer fog (haar) is likely in onshore winds.

The coast N from Berwick is rky with cliffs rising in height to Burnmouth, then diminishing gradually to Eyemouth (9.6.6). Keep 5ca offshore to clear outlying rks. Burnmouth, although small, has more alongside space than Eyemouth, which is a crowded fishing hbr. 2M NW is St Abb's Hbr (9.6.7), with temp anch in offshore winds in Coldingham B close to the S.

St Abb's Hd (lt) is a bold, steep headland, 92m high, with no offlying dangers. ▶ *The stream runs strongly round the Hd, causing turbulence with wind against tide; this can be largely avoided by keeping close inshore. The ESE-going stream begins at HW Leith –0345, and the WNW-going at HW Leith +0240.* ◀ There is a good anch in Pettico Wick, on NW side of Hd, in S winds, but dangerous if the wind shifts onshore. There are no off-lying dangers between St Abb's Hd and Fast Castle Hd, 3M WNW. Between Fast Castle Hd and Barns Ness, about 8M NW, is the attractive little hbr of Cove; but it dries and should only be approached in ideal conditions.

Torness Power Station (conspic; lt on bkwtr) is 1·75M SE of Barns Ness (lt) which lies 2·5M ESE of Dunbar (9.6.7) and is fringed with rks; tidal streams as for St Abb's Hd. Conspic chys are 7½ca WSW inland of Barns Ness. Between here and Dunbar keep at least 2½ca offshore to clear rky patches. Sicar Rk (7·9m depth) lies about 1·25M ENE of Dunbar, and sea breaks on it in onshore gales.

The direct course from Dunbar to Bass Rk (lt) is clear of all dangers; inshore of this line beware Wildfire Rks (dry) on NW side of Bellhaven B. In offshore winds there is anch in Scoughall Road. Great Carr is ledge of rks, nearly covering at HW, 1M ESE of Gin Hd, with Carr bn (stone tr surmounted by cross) at its N end. Drying ledges of rks extend 1M SE of Great Carr, up to 3ca offshore. Keep at least 5ca off Carr bn in strong onshore winds. Tantallon Castle (ruins) is on cliff edge 1M W of Great Car. Bass Rk (lt) lies 1·25M NNE of Gin Hd, and is a sheer, conspic rk (115m) with no offlying dangers; landing difficult due to swell.

FIRTH OF FORTH, SOUTH SHORE (chart 734, 735) Westward of Bass Rk, Craigleith (51m), Lamb Is (24m) and Fidra (31m) lie 5ca or more offshore, while the coast is generally foul. Craigleith is steep-to, and temporary anchorage can be found on SE and SW sides; if passing inshore of it keep well to N side of chan. N Berwick hbr (dries) lies S of Craigleith, but is unsafe in onshore winds. Between Craigleith and Lamb Is, beware drying rks up to 3ca from land. Lamb Is is 1·5M WNW of N Berwick (9.6.8) and has a rky ledge extending 2½ca SW. Fidra Is (lt) is a bird reserve, nearly connected to the shore by rky ledges, and should be passed to the N; passage and anch on S side are tricky. Anchor on E or W sides, depending on wind, in good weather.

In the B between Fidra and Edinburgh some shelter can be found in SE winds in Aberlady B and Gosford B. The best anch is SW of Craigielaw Pt. Port Seton is a drying fishing hbr 7½ca E of the conspic chys of Cockenzie Power Station; the E side of the hbr can be entered HW ±3, but not advisable in strong onshore wind or sea. Cockenzie (dries) is close to power station; beware Corsik Rk 400m to E. Access HW ±2·5, but no attractions except boatyard. For Fisherrow, see 9.6.8.

There are no dangers on the direct course from Fidra to Inchkeith (lt), which stands between the buoyed deep water chans. Rks extend 7½ca SE from Inchkeith, and 5ca off the W side where there is a small hbr below the lt ho; landing is forbidden without permission. N Craig and Craig Waugh (least depth 0·2m) are buoyed shoals 2·5M SE from Inchkeith lt ho. For Cramond and Inchcolm, see 9.6.8.

▶ *In N Chan, close to Inchkeith the W-going (flood) stream begins about HW Leith –0530, and the E-going at HW Leith +0030, sp rates about 1kn. The streams gather strength towards the Forth bridges, where they reach 2·25kn and there may be turbulence.* ◀

Leith is wholly commercial; Granton has yacht moorings in the E hbr; Port Edgar (9.6.8) is a major yacht hbr close W of Forth road bridge. Hound Point oil terminal is an artificial 'island-jetty' almost in mid-stream, connected to the shore by underwater pipeline (no ⚓). Yachts may pass the terminal on either side at least 30m off and well clear of tankers berthing.

6

RIVER FORTH TO KINCARDINE (charts 736, 737, 738) The main shipping chan under the N span of the rail bridge is busy with commercial traffic for Grangemouth and warships to/from Rosyth dockyard. In the latter case a Protected Chan may be activated; see 9.6.8 for details. W of Beamer Rk the Firth widens as far as Bo'ness (small drying hbr) on the S shore where the chan narrows between drying mudbanks. Charlestown (N bank) dries, but is a secure hbr. Grangemouth is industrially conspic. Caution: gas carriers, tankers, cargo vessels; no yacht facilities. Few yachts go beyond Kincardine swing bridge, clearance 9m, which is no longer opened.

FIRTH OF FORTH, NORTH SHORE (charts 734, 190) From Burntisland the N shore of Firth of Forth leads E to Kinghorn Ness. 1M SSW of Kinghorn Ness Blae Rk (SHM lt buoy) has least depth of 4·1m, and seas break on it in E gales. ▶ *Rost Bank lies halfway between Kinghorn Ness and Inchkeith, with tide rips at sp tides or in strong winds.* ◀

From Kinghorn Ness to Kirkcaldy, drying rks lie up to 3ca offshore. Kirkcaldy hbr (9.6.10) is effectively closed, but yachts can enter inner dock near HW by arrangement; ent is dangerous in strong E'lies, when seas break a long way out.

Between Kirkcaldy and Methil (9.6.10) the only dangers more than 2ca offshore are The Rockheads, extending 4ca SE of Dysart, and marked by 2 SHM buoys. Largo B is anch, well sheltered from N and E, but avoid gaspipes near E side. Close SW of Elie, beware W Vows (dries) and E Vows (dries, bn). There is anch close W of Elie Ness (9.6.8). Ox Rk (dries 2m) lies 5ca ENE of Elie Ness, and 2½ca offshore; otherwise there are no dangers more than 2ca offshore past St Monance, Pittenweem (9.6.8) and Anstruther (9.6.11), but in bad weather the sea breaks on Shield Rk 4ca off Pittenweem. From Anstruther to Crail (9.6.8) and on to Fife Ness keep 3ca offshore to clear Caiplie Rk and other dangers.

May Island (lt) (9.6.8) lies about 5M S of Fife Ness; its shores are bold except at NW end where rks extend 1ca off. Anch near N end at E or W Tarbert, on lee side according to winds; in good weather it is possible to land. Lt ho boats use Kirkhaven, close SE of lt ho.

FIFE NESS TO MONTROSE (chart 190) Fife Ness is fringed by rky ledges, and a reef extends 1M NE to N Carr Rk (dries 1·4m, marked by bn). In strong onshore winds keep to seaward of N Carr ECM lt buoy. From here keep 5ca offshore to clear dangers entering St Andrews B, where there is anch; the little hbr (9.6.13) dries, and should not be approached in onshore winds.

Northward from Firth of Forth to Rattray Hd the coast is mostly rky and steep-to, and there are no out-lying dangers within 2M of the coast except those off R. Tay and Bell Rk. But in an onshore blow there are few safe havens; both yachts and crews need to be prepared for offshore cruising rather than coast-crawling.

R. Tay (9.6.12 and chart 1481) is approached from the NE via Fairway buoy; it is dangerous to cut corners from the S. The Bar, NE of Abertay lt buoy, is dangerous in heavy weather, particularly in strong onshore wind or swell. Abertay Sands extend nearly 4M E of Tentsmuir Pt on S side of chan (buoyed); Elbow is a shoal extension eastward. Gaa Sands running 1·75M E from Buddon Ness, are marked by Abertay lt buoy (Racon) on N side of chan. Passage across Abertay and Gaa Sands is very dangerous. The estuary is shallow, with many shifting sandbanks; Tayport is a good passage stop and best yacht hbr (dries) in the Tay. ▶ *S of Buddon Ness the W-going (flood) stream begins about HW Aberdeen – 0400, and the E-going at about HW Aberdeen + 0230, sp rates 2kn.* ◀

Bell Rk (lt, Racon) lies about 11·5M E of Buddon Ness. ▶ *2M E of Bell Rk the S-going stream begins HW Aberdeen – 0220, and the N-going at HW Aberdeen + 0405, sp rates 1kn. W of Bell Rk the streams begin earlier.* ◀

N from Buddon Ness the coast is sandy. 1·25M SW of Arbroath (9.6.13) beware Elliot Horses, rky patches with depth 1·9m, which extend about 5ca offshore. Between Whiting Ness and Scurdie Ness, 9·5M NNE, the coast is clear of out-lying dangers, but is mostly fringed with drying rks up to 1ca off. In offshore winds there is temp anch in SW of Lunan B, off Ethie Haven.

Scurdie Ness (lt, Racon) is conspic on S side of ent to Montrose (9.6.14). Scurdie Rks (dry) extend 2ca E of the Ness. On N side of chan Annat Bank dries up to about 5ca E of the shore, opposite Scurdie Ness (chart 1438). ▶ *The in-going stream begins at HW Aberdeen – 0500, and the outgoing at HW Aberdeen + 0115;* ***both streams are very strong, up to 7kn at sp,*** *and there is turbulence off the ent on the ebb. The ent is dangerous in strong onshore winds, with breaking seas extending to Scurdie Ness on the ebb. In marginal conditions the last quarter of the flood is best time to enter.* ◀

MONTROSE TO ABERDEEN (chart 210) N from Montrose the coast is sandy for 5M to Milton Ness, where there is anch on S side in N winds. Johnshaven (9.6.15), 2M NE, is a small hbr (dries) with tight entrance, which should not be approached with onshore wind or swell. 5ca NE, off Brotherton Cas, drying rks extend 4ca offshore. Gourdon (9.6.15) has a small hbr (mostly dries) approached on ldg line between rky ledges; inner hbr has storm gates. Outside the hbr rks extend both sides of entrance, and the sea breaks heavily in strong E winds. Keep a sharp lookout for lobster pot dan buoys between Montrose and Stonehaven.

North to Inverbervie the coast is fringed with rky ledges up to 2ca offshore. Just N of Todhead Pt (lt) is Catterline, a small B which forms a natural anch in W winds, but open to E. Downie Pt, SE of Stonehaven (9.6.15) should be rounded 1ca off. The Bay is encumbered by rky ledges up to 2ca from shore and exposed to the E; anch 6ca E of Bay Hotel or berth afloat in outer hbr.

From Garron Pt to Girdle Ness the coast is mostly steep-to. Fishing nets may be met off headlands during fishing season. Craigmaroinn and Seal Craig (dry) are parts of reef 3ca offshore SE of Portlethen, a fishing village with landing sheltered by rks. Cove B has a very small fishing hbr, off which there is anch in good weather; Mutton Rk (dries 2·1m) lie 1½ca offshore. From Cove to Girdle Ness keep 5ca offshore, avoiding Hasman Rks (dries 3·4m) 1ca off Altens .

Greg Ness and Girdle Ness (lt, RC, Racon), at SE corner of Aberdeen B (9.6.16), are fringed by rks. Girdlestone is a rky patch, depth less than 2m, 2ca ENE of lt ho. A drying patch lies 2ca SE of lt ho. ▶ *Off Girdle Ness the S-going stream begins at HW Aberdeen – 0430, and the N-going at HW Aberdeen + 0130, sp rates 2·5kn. A race forms on S-going stream.* ◀

ABERDEEN TO RATTRAY HEAD (chart 213) From Aberdeen there are few offshore dangers to Buchan Ness. Drums Links Firing Range lies 8¾M N of Aberdeen; red flags and lights are shown when firing is taking place. R. Ythan, 1·75M SSW of Hackley Hd, is navigable by small craft, but chan shifts constantly. 3M North is the very small hbr of Collieston (mostly dries), only accessible in fine weather. 4·75M NNE of Hackley Head lie The Skares, rks (marked by PHM lt buoy) extending 3½ca from S point of Cruden B, where there is anch in offshore winds. On N side of Cruden B is Port Erroll (dries 2·5m).

Buchan Ness (lt, fog sig, Racon) is a rky peninsula. 2ca N is Meikle Mackie islet, close W of which is the small hbr of Boddam (dries) (9.6.17). 3ca NE of Meikle Mackie is The Skerry, a rk 6m high on S side of Sandford B; rks on which the sea breaks extend 2ca NNE. The chan between The Skerry and the coast is foul with rks and not advised. Peterhead (9.6.17) is easy to enter in almost all conditions and is an excellent passage port with marina at SW corner of the Bay.

Rattray Bay has numerous submarine pipelines leading ashore to St Fergus Gas Terminal.

For notes on offshore oil/gas installations, see 9.5.5.

Rattray Hd (with lt, fog sig on The Ron, rk 2ca E of Hd) has rky foreshore, drying for 2ca off. Rattray Briggs is a detached reef, depth 0·2m, 2ca E of lt ho. Rattray Hard is a rky patch, depth 10·7m, 1·5M ENE of lt ho, which raises a dangerous sea during onshore gales. ▶ *Off Rattray Hd the S-going stream begins at HW Aberdeen – 0420, and the N-going at HW Aberdeen + 0110, sp rates 3kn. In normal conditions keep about 1M E of Rattray Hd, but pass 5M off in bad weather, preferably at slack water.* ◀ Conspic radio masts with R lts lie 2·5M WNW and 2·2M W of lt ho.

NORTH SEA PASSAGE For distances across the N Sea, see 9.0.8.

FORTH TO NORWAY AND BALTIC (charts 2182B, 2182C) Heading ENE'ly from the Firth of Forth the main hazards result from offshore industrial activities and their associated traffic. In summer particularly, oil/gas exploration, movement of drilling rigs, pipe laying etc create situations which could endanger other vessels. Rig movements and many of the more intense activities are published in Notices to Mariners, but even so it is wise to avoid the gas and oil fields where possible and never to approach within 500m of installations (see 9.5.5). There are TSS to be avoided off the S and SW coast of Norway. Strong currents and steep seas may be experienced in the approaches to the Skagerrak.

9.6.6 EYEMOUTH

Borders **55°52′·52N 02°05′·29W**

CHARTS AC 160, 1612; Imray C24; OS 67

TIDES +0330 Dover; ML No data; Duration 0610; Zone 0 (UT)

Standard Port LEITH (⟶)

Times				Height (metres)			
High Water		Low Water		MHWS	MHWN	MLWN	MLWS
0300	0900	0300	0900	5·6	4·4	2·0	0·8
1500	2100	1500	2100				
Differences EYEMOUTH							
–0003	+0008	+0011	+0005	–0·5	–0·4	–0·1	0·0

SHELTER Good in all weathers, though uncomfortable surge in N over F5, and entry should not be attempted in strong N to E winds. Caution, the entrance is 17m wide. Busy FV hbr which encourages yachtsman to visit. Berth as directed by HM, either (a) on the 100m pontoon along Middle Quay, depth 3m; (b) on the W wall of the N-pointing jetty by the LB; or (c) on the W wall of the centre jetty W of Gunsgreen House (conspic). ⚓ in bay only in offshore winds. F.R (occas) lt indicates unsafe to enter bay or hbr.

NAVIGATION WPT 55°52′·80N 02°05′·34W, 174° to E bkwtr lt, 3ca. Appr can be made N or S of Hurkars; from the N, beware Blind Buss 1·2m, marked by NCM buoy, Q 55°52'·79N 02°05'·14W, about 200m ENE of WPT. From the S, approach on 250° midway between Hurkars and Hettle Scar; there are no ldg marks, hbr ent is dredged to 3·0m.

LIGHTS AND MARKS St. Abbs Hd lt ho Fl 10s 68m 26M is 3M NW. Ldg lts 174° both FG 9/10m 6M, orange columns on W pier. ● or R flag = unsafe to enter.

R/T VHF Ch 16 12 (HO).

TELEPHONE (Dial code 01890) HM 750223, Mobile 07885 742505; MRSC (01333) 450666; Marinecall 09066 526236; Police 750217; Dr 750599, Ⓗ (0131) 536 1000.

FACILITIES **Hbr** AB(quay) £12/yacht, AB(pontoon) £15/yacht (any LOA +7 days for the price of 5), FW, D (see HM for 25 ltr cans or larger quantities by delivery), P (cans), Slip, BY, ME, ⚒, El, C (12 ton mobile), Ⓔ. Gunsgreen House (£2) Showers, ⊡, visitors domestic facilities (new 2004) see www.eyemouth.com
Town LB, P, CH, 🛒, R, Bar, ✉, ⊡, Gas, Gaz, Ⓑ, ⇌ (bus to Berwick -on-Tweed and Edinburgh), ✈ (Edinburgh).

ADJACENT HARBOUR

BURNMOUTH, Borders, **55°50′·61N 02°04′·10W**. AC 160. HW +0315 on Dover, –0025 on Leith; Duration 0615. Use Eyemouth tides 9.6.6. From S beware Quarry Shoal Rks; and E & W Carrs from N. 2 W posts (unclear by day, FR 29/35m 4M) 45m apart, lead 253° to close N of the hbr; as hbr mouth opens, enter on about 185° with outer hbr ent in line with 2FG (vert). Min depth at ent at LWS is 0·6m. Shelter is good especially in inner hbr (dries). With on-shore winds, swell makes outer hbr uncomfortable. HM (018907) 81283 (home); also via Gull's Nest (bar at top of valley) 81306. Facilities: AB £7 (all LOA), FW, limited 🛒.

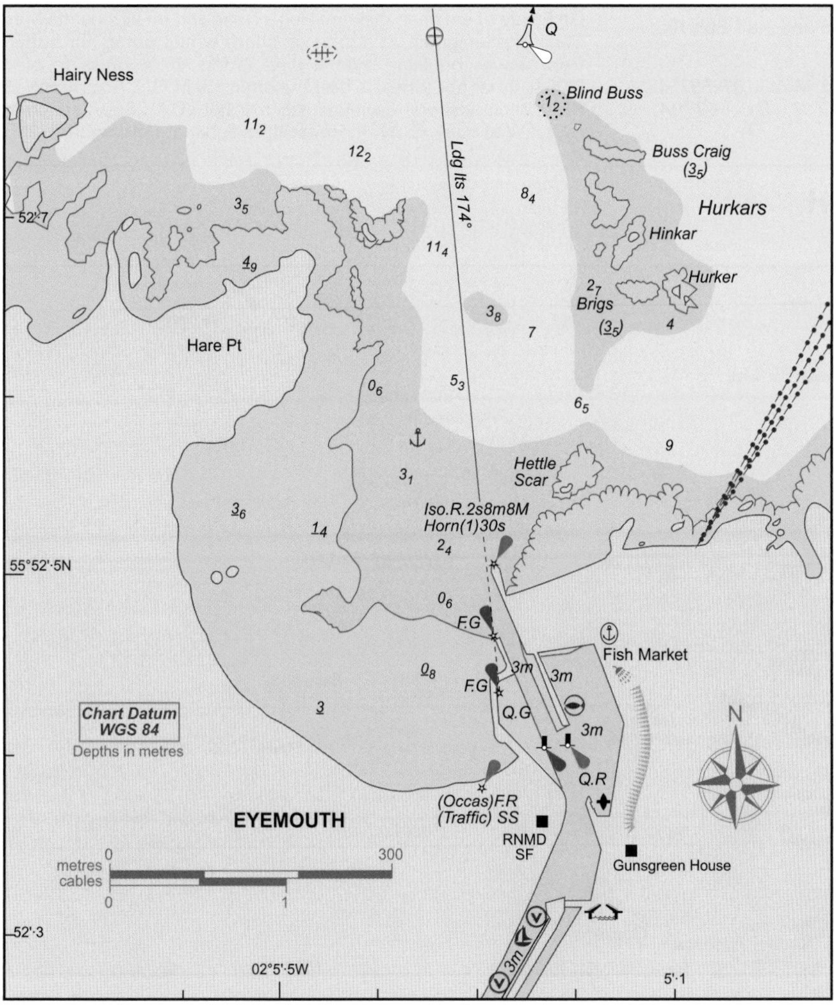
Q
Hairy Ness
Blind Buss
Buss Craig
Hurkars
Hinkar
Hurker
Brigs
Ldg lts 174°
52'·7
Hare Pt
Hettle Scar
Iso.R.2s8m8M
Horn(1)30s
55°52'·5N
F.G
F.G
Q.G
Q.R
Fish Market
3m
3m
3m
Chart Datum
WGS 84
Depths in metres
(Occas)F.R
(Traffic) SS
RNMD
SF
EYEMOUTH
Gunsgreen House
N
metres
cables
0
300
0
1
52'·3
02°5'·5W
5'·1

9.6.7 DUNBAR

East Lothian **56°00′·39N 02°31′·09W** ❁❁❁◊◊✿✿✿

CHARTS AC 175, 734; Imray C23, C27; OS 67

TIDES +0330 Dover; ML 3·0; Duration 0600; Zone 0 (UT)

Standard Port LEITH (⟶)

Times				**Height (metres)**			
High Water		Low Water		MHWS	MHWN	MLWN	MLWS
0300	0900	0300	0900	5·6	4·4	2·0	0·8
1500	2100	1500	2100				
Differences DUNBAR							
–0003	+0003	+0003	–0003	–0·3	–0·3	0·0	+0·1
FIDRA							
–0001	0000	–0002	+0001	–0·2	–0·2	0·0	0·0

SHELTER Outer (Victoria) Hbr is subject to surge in strong NW to NE winds. N side dries; berth on S quay and contact HM. Keep steps clear. Inner (Old or Cromwell) Hbr dries and is safe in strong onshore conditions; entry is through a bridge, lifted on request to HM.

NAVIGATION WPT 56°00′·60N 02°31′·49W, 132° to hbr ent, 0·30M, (preferable in marginal conditions). Beware Wallace's Head Rock , Half Ebb Rock ($\underline{2}_1$m), 1½ca from ent. and Outer Buss 4ca E of ent. Entry is dangerous in heavy on-shore swell. Min depth at ent 0·9m, but may be much less in abnormal circumstances. Keep to port on entry to avoid rockfall off castle.

LIGHTS AND MARKS Church and Castle ruin both conspic. From NE, ldg lts, Oc G 6s 15/22m 3M, synch, intens 188°-208°, 2 W △ on Or cols, lead 198° through the outer rks to the Roads; thence narrow ent opens with QR brg 132°. From NW, appr on brg 132° between bns on Wallaces Head and Half Ebb Rk.

R/T None.

TELEPHONE (Dial code 01368) HM 865404, Mobile 07958754858; MRSC (01333) 450666; Police 862718; Dr 863704; Ⓗ (0131) 536 1000.

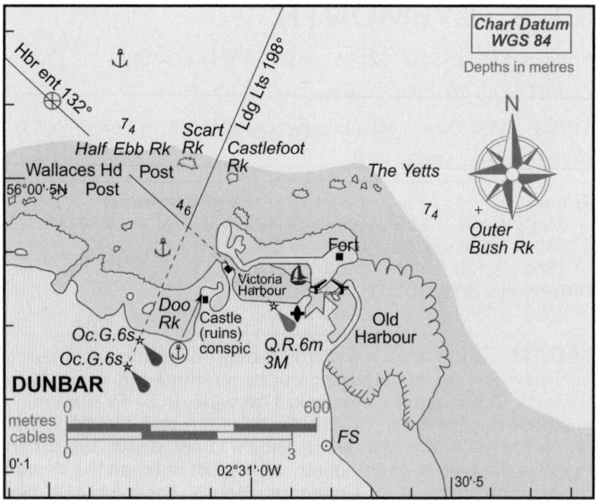

Chart Datum WGS 84
Depths in metres
N
Hbr ent 132°
Ldg Lts 198°
Half Ebb Rk
Scart Rk
Castlefoot Rk
Wallaces Hd
Post
56°00'·5N
The Yetts
Outer Bush Rk
Fort
Victoria Harbour
Doo Rk
Castle (ruins) conspic
Oc.G.6s
Q.R.6m 3M
Old Harbour
DUNBAR
metres
cables
FS
02°31'·0W
30'·5

FACILITIES Quay AB £8 (any length), Slip, FW, D (delivery), P (cans); **N Wall** M, AB; **Inner Hbr** Slip, AB; **Services** ME, Gas, Gaz. **Town** EC Wed; LB, P, ⊡, 🛒, R, Bar, ✉, Ⓑ, ⇌, ✈ Edinburgh.

ADJACENT HARBOUR

ST ABBS, Borders, **55°54′·10N 02°07′·74W**. AC 175. HW +0330 on Dover, –0017 on Leith; HW –0·6m on Leith; Duration 0605. Ldg line (about 228°) S face of Maw Carr on village hall (conspic R roof) leads SW until the hbr ent opens to port and the 2nd ldg line (about 167°) can be seen 2FR 4/8m 1M, or Y LB ho visible thru' ent. On E side of ent chan, beware Hog's Nose and on W side the Maw Carr. Shelter good. In strong on-shore winds outer hbr suffers from waves breaking over E pier. Works in progress to piers (2004). Inner hbr (dries) is best but often full of FVs. Access HW±3. HM directs visitors. Facilities: AB £10 (all LOA), Slip (launching £10), FW at quay, R, 🛒, more facilities & bar at Coldingham (2M).

9.6.8 FIRTH OF FORTH

E and W Lothian/City of Edinburgh/Fife

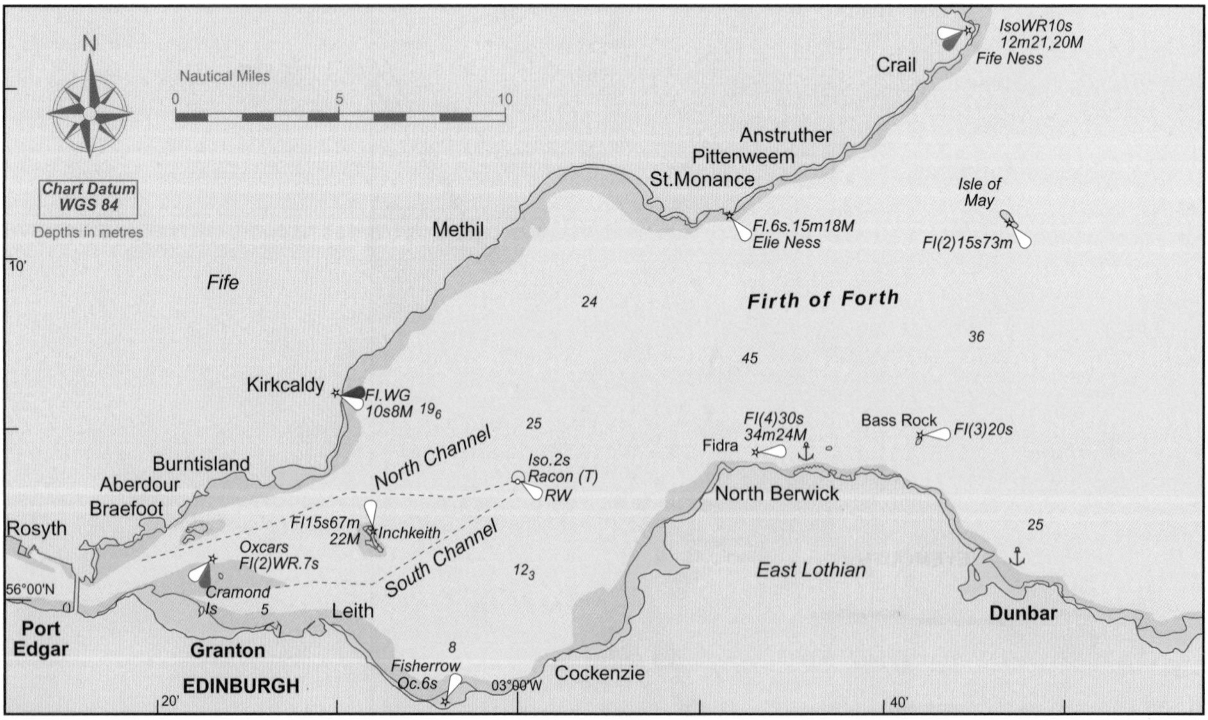

N
Nautical Miles
Chart Datum WGS 84
Depths in metres
IsoWR10s 12m21,20M
Fife Ness
Crail
Anstruther
Pittenweem
St.Monance
Isle of May
Fl(2)15s73m
Fl.6s.15m18M
Elie Ness
Methil
Fife
Firth of Forth
Kirkcaldy
Fl.WG 10s8M
Fl(4)30s 34m24M
Fidra
Bass Rock
Fl(3)20s
Burntisland
Aberdour
Braefoot
North Channel
Iso.2s Racon (T) RW
North Berwick
Rosyth
Fl15s67m 22M
Inchkeith
Oxcars Fl(2)WR.7s
South Channel
East Lothian
56°00'N
Cramond Is
Leith
Dunbar
Port Edgar
Granton
EDINBURGH
Fisherrow Oc.6s
03°00'W
Cockenzie
20'
40'

FIRTH OF FORTH *continued*

CHARTS AC 734, 735, 736, 737, 741; Imray C23, C27; OS 66, 59

TIDES +0350 (Granton) Dover; ML 3·3; Duration 0620; Zone 0 (UT)

Standard Port LEITH (⟶)

Times				Height (metres)			
High Water		Low Water		MHWS	MHWN	MLWN	MLWS
0300	0900	0300	0900	5·6	4·4	2·0	0·8
1500	2100	1500	2100				
Differences COCKENZIE							
−0007	−0015	−0013	−0005	−0·2	0·0	No data	
GRANTON: Same as LEITH							
GRANGEMOUTH							
+0025	+0010	−0052	−0015	−0·1	−0·2	−0·3	−0·3
KINCARDINE							
+0015	+0030	−0030	−0030	0·0	−0·2	−0·5	−0·3
ALLOA							
+0040	+0040	+0025	+0025	−0·2	−0·5	No data	−0·7
STIRLING							
+0100	+0100	No data		−2·9	−3·1	−2·3	−0·7

SHELTER Granton mostly dries but is open to violent swell in N'lies. There are pontoons on E side of Middle pier in about 2m and the RFYC welcomes visitors. Pilot boats berth at seaward end. W hbr is planned for development as a marina. Port Edgar marina offers good shelter, except for a surge at LW esp in E winds, but prone to silting. Caution: strong tidal streams. Do not enter E of wavebreak; 3kn speed limit. Leith is wholly commercial. Rosyth Dockyard should only be used in emergency. Note: Forth Ports plc controls the Firth of Forth, Granton Hbr and all commercial impounded docks.

NAVIGATION WPT Granton 56°00′·00N 03°13′·31W, 180° to ent, 0·72M. WPT Port Edgar 56°N 03°24′·3W, 244° to Dir Lt, Fl R 4s, on W bkwtr, 3ca. Beware Hound Pt terminal; Forth railway and road bridges; vessels bound to/from Rosyth and Grangemouth especially in local fog (haar). On N shore, no vessel may enter Mortimer's Deep (Braefoot gas terminal) without prior approval from Forth Navigation Service. 12kn speed limit W of Forth Rly Bridge. A Protected Chan runs from Nos 13 & 14 buoys (NNW of Oxcars) under the bridges (N of Inch Garvie and Beamer Rk), to Rosyth. When activated (occas) via Forth Ports plc, other vessels must clear the chan for Rosyth traffic.

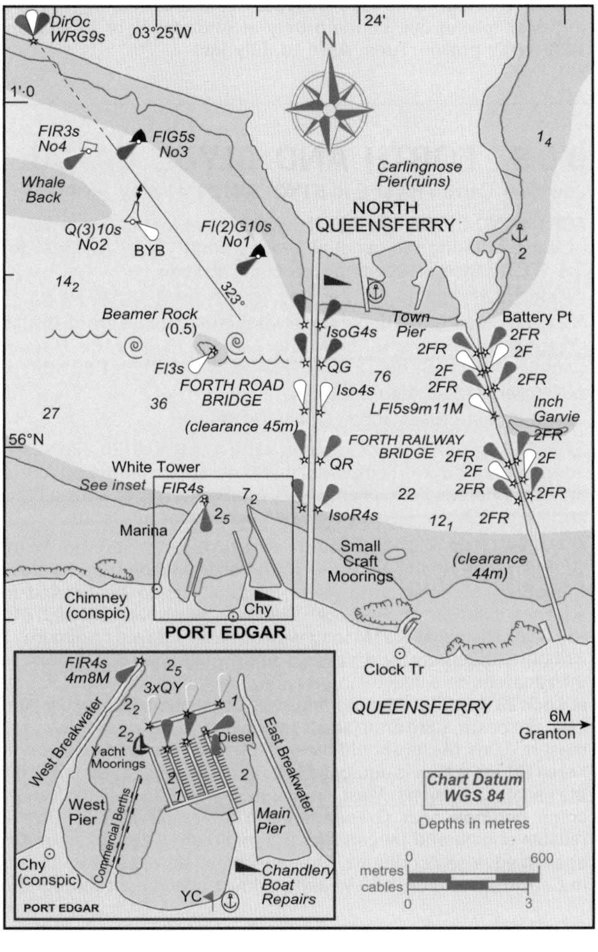
DirOc WRG9s
03°25'W
24'
N
1'·0
FlR3s No4
FlG5s No3
Whale Back
Carlingnose Pier(ruins)
NORTH QUEENSFERRY
Q(3)10s No2
BYB
Fl(2)G10s No1
323°
Beamer Rock (0.5)
Town Pier
Battery Pt
IsoG4s
QG
Fl3s
FORTH ROAD BRIDGE
Iso4s
LFl5s9m11M
Inch Garvie
(clearance 45m)
FORTH RAILWAY BRIDGE
56°N
White Tower
See inset
QR
IsoR4s
Marina
Small Craft Moorings
(clearance 44m)
Chimney (conspic)
Chy
PORT EDGAR
Clock Tr
QUEENSFERRY
6M Granton
FlR4s 4m8M
3xQY
West Breakwater
East Breakwater
Diesel
Yacht Moorings
West Pier
Commercial Berths
Main Pier
Chy (conspic)
Chandlery Boat Repairs
YC
PORT EDGAR
Chart Datum WGS 84
Depths in metres
metres
cables

LIGHTS AND MARKS Granton: R flag with W diagonal cross (or ● lt) on signal mast at middle pier hd = Entry prohib. Port Edgar: On W pier Dir lt Fl R 4s 4m 8M 244°; 3 QY lts mark floating bkwtr; 3 x 2 FR (vert) mark N ends of marina pontoons.

R/T Call *Forth Navigation* (at Grangemouth) Ch **71** (calling and short messages, H24) 16; **20** 12 will be requested if necessary. Traffic, nav and weather info available on request. Leith Hbr Radio Ch 12. Granton marina, call *Boswell* Ch M. Port Edgar Marina Ch M **80** (Apl-Sept 0900-1930; Oct-Mar 0900-1630 LT). Rosyth Dockyard, call *QHM* Ch 74 13 73 (Mon-Fri: 0730-1700). Grangemouth Docks Ch 14 (H24).

TELEPHONE (Dial code 0131) Forth Navigation Service 555 8700; QHM Rosyth (01383) 425050; MRSC (01333) 450666; Weather (0141) 248 3451; Marinecall 09066 526236; Police (S. Queensferry) 331 1798; Ⓗ Edinburgh Royal Infirmary 229-2477; Flag Officer Scotland/Northern Ireland (01436) 674321 ext 3206, for Naval activities off N and E Scotland; Forth Yacht Clubs Ass'n 552 3452.

FACILITIES

GRANTON Extensive development of the W hbr is proposed. HM via Leith, ☎ 555 8866, Access HW±3½, FW, Slip; **Royal Forth YC** ☎ 552 3006, 📠 552 8560, Slip, M, L, FW, C (5 ton), D, El, Bar; **Forth Corinthian YC** ☎ 552 5939, Slip, M, L, Bar; **Services:** Gas, Gaz, ⚒, CH, ME. **Town** D, P, 🛒, R, Bar, ✉, Ⓑ, ≷, ✈ (Buses to Edinburgh).

SOUTH QUEENSFERRY

Port Edgar Marina (300+8 visitors) ☎ 331 3330, 📠 331 4878, £1.50, Access H24, M, Slip, CH, D, C (5 ton) on N end of main pier, El, Ⓔ, ME, ⚒, SM, Gas, Gaz, FW, R; Port Edgar YC, Bar. **Town** EC Wed; P, 🛒, R, Bar, ✉, Ⓑ, ≷ (Dalmeny), ✈ Edinburgh.

EDINBURGH: ACA.

GRANGEMOUTH: HM ☎ 01324 498566 (H24); Port Office ☎ 498597 (HO). VHF Ch 14 16. Commercial port.

Continued overleaf

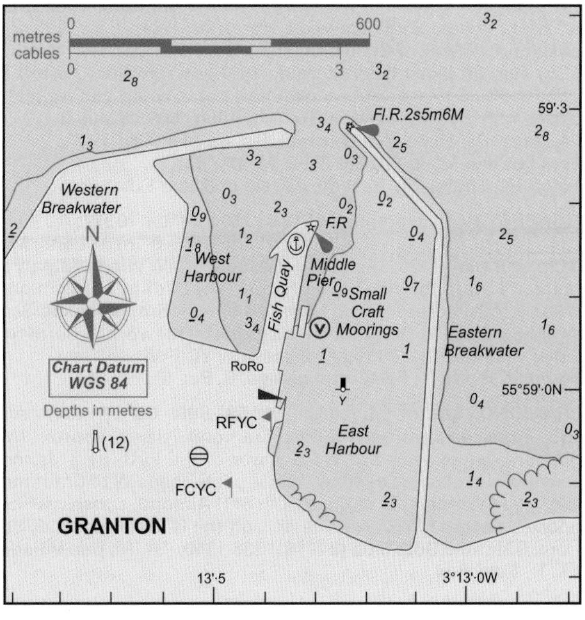
metres
cables
600
Fl.R.2s5m6M
59'·3
Western Breakwater
West Harbour
Fish Quay
Middle Pier
F.R
Small Craft Moorings
Eastern Breakwater
55°59'·0N
Chart Datum WGS 84
Depths in metres
RoRo
RFYC
East Harbour
FCYC
GRANTON
13'·5
3°13'·0W

6

HARBOURS AND ANCHORAGES ON THE NORTH SHORE OF THE FIRTH OF FORTH

INCHCOLM, Fife, **56°01´·85N 03°17´·89W**. AC 736. Tides see 9.6.8. Best ⚓ in 4m, N of abbey (conspic); appr from NW or ESE, to land at pier close E (small fee). Meadulse Rks (dry) on N side. Ends of island foul. At SE end, lt Fl (3) 15s, obsc 075°-145°. No facilities. ☎ 0131-244 3101. Keep clear of large ships under way in Mortimer's Deep.

ABERDOUR, Fife, **56°03´·00N 03°17´·49W**. AC 735, 736. HW +0345 on Dover; +0005 on Leith; HW 0·5m on Leith; ML 3·3m; Duration 0630. See 9.6.8. Good shelter except in SE winds when a swell occurs. The ⚓ between The Little Craigs and the disused pier is good but exposed to winds from E to SW. Temp berths £2 are available in hbr (dries) alongside the quay wall. Beware Little Craigs (dries 2·2m) and outfall 2ca N marked by bn. There are no lts/ marks. Facilities: FW (tap on pier), P, R, 🛒, Bar in village, EC Wed; **Aberdour BC** ☎ (01592) 202827.

KIRKCALDY: See 9.6.10
METHIL: See 9.6.10

ELIE, Fife, **56°11´·20N 02°49´·29W**. AC 734. HW +0325 on Dover, –0015 on Leith; HW –0·1m on Leith; ML 3·0m; Duration 0620; Elie B provides good shelter from N winds for small craft but local knowledge is needed. Hbr dries; 3 short term waiting buoys available. Beware ledge off end of pier which dries. From E beware Ox Rk (dries 1m) 5M ENE of Elie Ness; from W beware rks off Chapel Ness, W Vows, E Vows (surmounted by cage bn) and Thill Rk, marked by PHM Fl(4)R.10s buoy. Lt: Elie Ness Fl 6s 15m 18M, W tr. HM (01333) 330051; AB (3) drying £5, M, ⛽, FW, CH, SC, Slip. Police 592100. Dr ☎ 330302; **Services:** P & D (tanker), Gas, Gaz. El. In Elie & Earlsferry: R, 🛒, Bar, ✉, Ⓑ.

ST MONANS, Fife, **56°12´·25 N 02°45´·94W**. AC 734. HW +0335 on Dover, –0020 on Leith; HW –0·1m on Leith; ML 3·0m; Duration 0620. Shelter good except in strong SE to SW winds when scend occurs in the hbr (dries). Berth alongside E pier until contact with HM. From NE keep at least 2½ca from coast. Bkwtr hd Oc WRG 6s 5m 7/4M; E pier hd 2 FG (vert) 6m 4M. W pier hd 2 FR (vert) 6m 4M. Facilities: HM ☎ 07836 703014 if no reply, 01333 310836 (Anstruther HM assists); AB £11.30 then £5.65 thereafter, FW, ⛽, El; **Services:** Gas, P & D (tanker), AC. Police ☎ (01333) 592100. **Village** R, Bar, 🛒, ✉, Ⓑ.

PITTENWEEM, Fife, **56°12'·60N 02°43'·79W**. AC 734. HW +0325 Dover; –0015 and –0·1m on Leith; ML 3m. Duration 0620. Busy fishing hbr, dredged 1-2m, access all tides, but not in onshore winds. Yachts not encouraged; contact HM for berth at W end of inner hbr, but only for emergency use. Outer hbr dries to rock; is only suitable for temp stop in calm weather. Appr 037° on ldg marks/lts, Gy cols/Y stripe, both FR 3/8m 5M. Rks to port marked by bn, QR 3m 2M, and 3 unlit bns. E bkwtr lt Fl (2) RG 5s 9m 9/6M, R265°-345°, G345°-055°. **R/T** VHF Ch 11 16 (Mon-Fri) or Forth CG Ch 16 (other times). HM ☎/📠 (01333) 312591. Facilities: FW, CH, D & P (tanker), Gas, 🛒, Bar.

ANSTRUTHER: See 9.6.11

CRAIL, Fife, **56°15´·35N 02°37´·29W**. AC 175. HW +0320 on Dover, –0020 on Leith; HW –0·2m on Leith; ML 3·0m; Duration 0615. Good shelter but only for boats able to take the ground alongside. Appr between S pier and bn on rks to S following ldg line 295°, two W concrete pillars with FR lts, 24/30m 6M. Turn 150° to stbd for ent. Call Forth CG on VHF Ch 16 before entering. HM ☎ (01333) 450820. Facilities: AB £11.75, El, FW, ⛽, Slip, P. **Village** EC Wed; Bar, R, 🛒, ✉, Ⓑ.

ISLE OF MAY, Fife, **56°11´·40N 02°33´·69W**. AC 734. HW +0325 on Dover, –0025 on Leith. In settled weather only, and depending on the wind, ⚓ at E or W Tarbert in 4m; landing at Altarstanes. Near the SE tip there is a tiny hbr at Kirkhaven, with narrow, rky ent; yachts can moor fore-and-aft to rings in rks, in about 1-1·5m. SDs are needed. Beware Norman Rk to N of Island, and Maiden Hair Rk to S. At the summit, a □ tr on stone ho, Fl (2) 15s 73m 22M. The island is a bird sanctuary, owned by Scottish Natural Heritage ☎ (01334) 654038. Avoid the breeding season, mid-Mar to end Jul. Landing only at Altarstanes or Kirkhaven, 1000-1700; not on Tues, April to July inc.

HARBOURS AND ANCHORAGES ON THE SOUTH SHORE OF THE FIRTH OF FORTH

NORTH BERWICK, East Lothian, **56°03´·74N 02°43´·04W**. AC 734. Fidra HW +0344 on Dover; ML 3·0m; Duration 0625. See 9.6.8 Fidra. Shelter good with winds from S to W but dangerous with on-shore winds. Ent is 8m wide. Hbr dries. From E or W, from position 0·25M S of Craigleith, steer S for Plattock Rks, thence SSW 40m off bkwtr before turning 180° port into hbr. Bkwtr lt F WR 7m 3M, R to seaward, W over hbr; not lit when bad weather closes hbr. Beware Maiden Rks (bn) 100m NW of this lt. Facilities: AB £5.70, P & D (cans), FW on pier, CH;
East Lothian YC ☎ (01620) 2698, M, ⚓s, Bar.
Town EC Thurs; 🛒, Gas, Ⓑ, ✉, ⇌ and bus Edinburgh.

FISHERROW, East Lothian, **55°56´·79N 03°04´·09W**. AC 734, 735. HW +0345 on Dover, –0005 on Leith; HW –0·1m on Leith; ML 3·0m; Duration 0620. Shelter good except in NW winds. Mainly a pleasure craft hbr, dries 5ca offshore. Appr dangerous in on-shore winds. Access HW±2. High-rise block (38m) is conspic 9ca W of hbr. E pier lt, Oc 6s 5m 6M on metal framework tr. Berth on E pier. HM ☎ (0131) 665 5900; **Fisherrow YC** FW.
Town EC Wed; 🛒, P & D from garage, R, Bar, Ⓑ, ✉, SM.

CRAMOND, City of Edinburgh, **55°59´·80N 03°17´·49W**. AC 736. Tides as Leith (see 9.6.8). Cramond Island, approx 1M offshore, is connected to the S shore of the Firth by a drying causeway. A chan, marked by 7 SHM posts, leads W of Cramond Island to Cramond hbr at the mouth of R Almond, conspic white houses. Access HW±2; AB free or ⚓ off the Is. Seek local advice from: **Cramond Boat Club** ☎ (0131) 336 1356, FW, M, Bar. **Village** 🛒, R, Pub, Bus.

9.6.9 FORTH AND CLYDE CANAL

Lowland Carron River Ent. **51°02'·30N 03°41·46W** ✿◇◇✿✿

FORTH AND CLYDE CANAL These notes are for the convenience of those entering the canal at Grangemouth. Refer to 9.9.21 for the W entrance at Bowling Sea Lock, R.Clyde.

CHARTS AC 737; Imray C27; OS 65, 64; BWB *Skipper's Guide* Forth & Clyde and Union Canal essential. Obtain from British Waterways Scotland, Lowland Canals, Rosebank House, Camelon, Main Street, Falkirk. FK1 4DS . ☎(01324) 671217 or www.scottishcanals.co.uk

TIDES Carron River +0325 Dover, 0030 Leith

SHELTER Carron Sea Lock operates HW-4 to HW+0130, 0800-2000 and daylight hours. Temporary berthing at Grangemouth YC or at nearby Refuge Posts. Temporary ⚓s close WNW of Carron PHM and close SSW of Carron Bn SHM dependant on depth.

NAVIGATION Carron River entrance approached from Grangemouth Roads via Small Craft Recommended Tracks close N of Ship Manoeuvering Area. Passage has to be booked in advance, call "Carron Sea Lock" VHF Ch74, ☎ (01324)483034/07810 0794468. The canal is 31M long with 39 locks. Allow a minimum of 21 hours underway for a passage to Bowling Sea Lock. Transit of the canal can be achieved in 2 days by reaching the Summit Pound at Lock 20 Wyndford on the first day. Canal can take vessels 20m LOA, 6m beam, 1.8m draft (add 0.1m/4inches to draft for freshwater), mast ht 3.0m. Masts should be unstepped before passing through Kerse Bridge which is equipped with air draft gauges calibrated for the canal dimensions. Mast craneage at Port Edgar or BWB mast crane pontoon near Grangemouth YC. Vessels should have a reliable engine and be capable of a minimum waterspeed of 4kn against adverse conditions. Ebb tide can attain rates of up to 6kn in Carron River after heavy rainfall. 4mph speed limit throughout

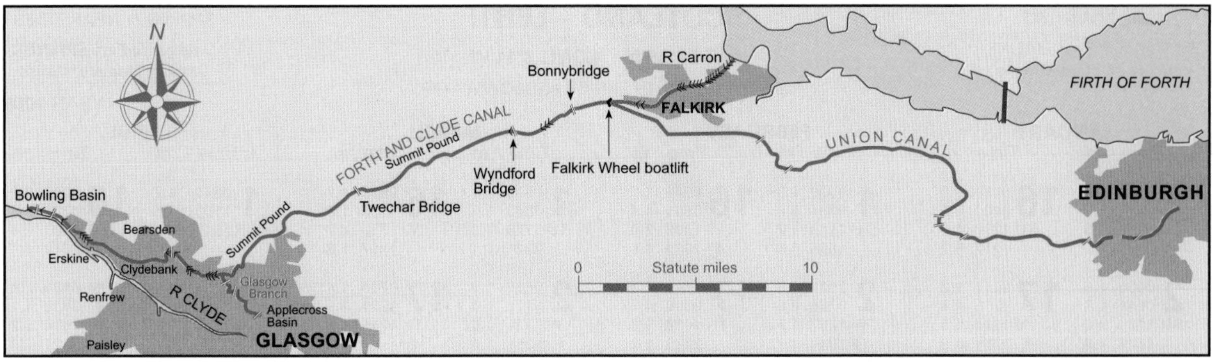
N
R Carron
Bonnybridge
FIRTH OF FORTH
FALKIRK
FORTH AND CLYDE CANAL
Summit Pound
UNION CANAL
Wyndford Bridge
Falkirk Wheel boatlift
EDINBURGH
Bowling Basin
Twechar Bridge
Bearsden
Summit Pound
Erskine
Clydebank
Statute miles
0
10
Renfrew
R CLYDE
Glasgow Branch
Applecross Basin
Paisley
GLASGOW

the canal. Access via Falkirk Wheel to Union Canal and Edinburgh, refer to BWB *Skipper's Guide.*

LOCKS Carron Sea Lock and 9.9.21 Bowling Sea Lock are operated by BW Staff. At other locks BW Staff available to assist. 5 day passage licence costs £5/m and £3.50/m return including access to the Falkirk Wheel, Union Canal and Edinburgh

LIGHTS & MARKS Carron River channel is marked by lighted By PHM & Bn SHM and unlit By(s) PHM & SHM. Bkwtr/Training Bank to W & N of channel marked with Bn(s) & Bol(s).

BOAT SAFETY SCHEME BWB *Skipper's Guide* refers. At Carron Sea Lock transient/visiting craft staying no more than 28 days will be subject to a Dangerous Boat Check of gas and fuel systems. Also required to complete a boat condition declaration and provide evidence of insurance for £1M third party liability.

R/T Call *Carron Sea Lock* VHF Ch 74 .

TELEPHONE Carron Sea Lock (01324) 483034/07810794468. British Waterways Lowlands Canals (01324) 671271.

FACILITIES **Carron Sea Lock** ⚓, P, 🗑, WC, 🚿, Slip. **Falkirk Wheel (on Forth & Clyde)** FW, P, D, 🗑, WC, 🚿 . For details throughout the canal refer to BWB *Skipper's Guide* (using maps).

6

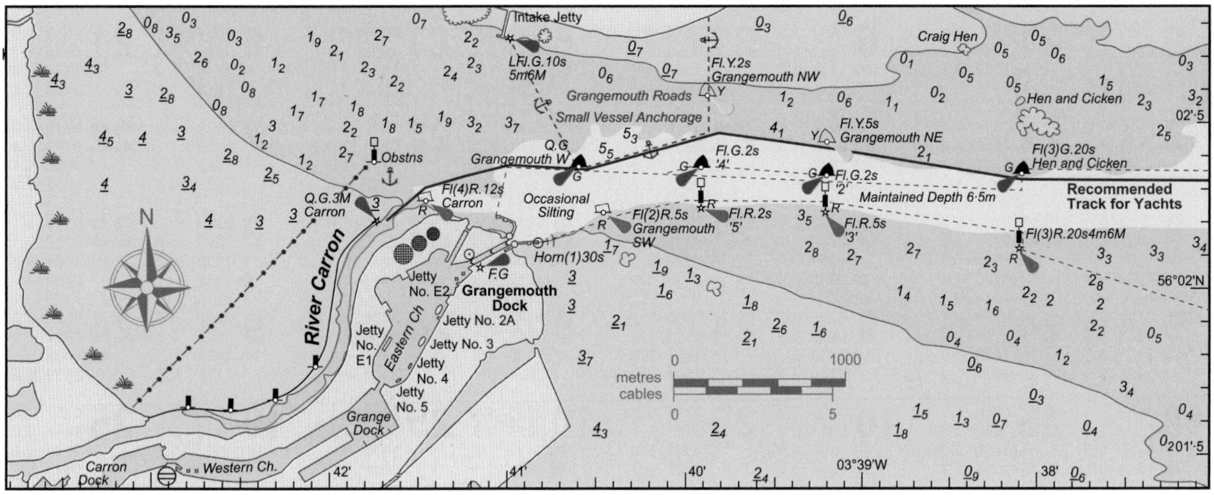
Intake Jetty
LFl.G.10s 5m6M
Fl.Y.2s Grangemouth NW
Craig Hen
Grangemouth Roads
Small Vessel Anchorage
Hen and Cicken
02'·5
Fl.Y.5s Grangemouth NE
Q.G Grangemouth W
Fl.G.2s '4'
Fl(3)G.20s Hen and Cicken
Obstns
Fl.G.2s '2'
Maintained Depth 6·5m
Recommended Track for Yachts
Q.G.3M Carron
Fl(4)R.12s Carron
Occasional Silting
Fl(2)R.5s Grangemouth SW
Fl.R.2s '5'
Fl.R.5s '3'
Fl(3)R.20s4m6M
N
River Carron
Horn(1)30s
F.G
Grangemouth Dock
Jetty No. E2
Jetty No. 2A
Jetty No. E1
Eastern Ch
Jetty No. 3
Jetty No. 4
Jetty No. 5
56°02'N
metres
cables
0
1000
0
5
Grange Dock
Carron Dock
Western Ch.
42'
41'
40'
03°39'W
38'
0201'·5

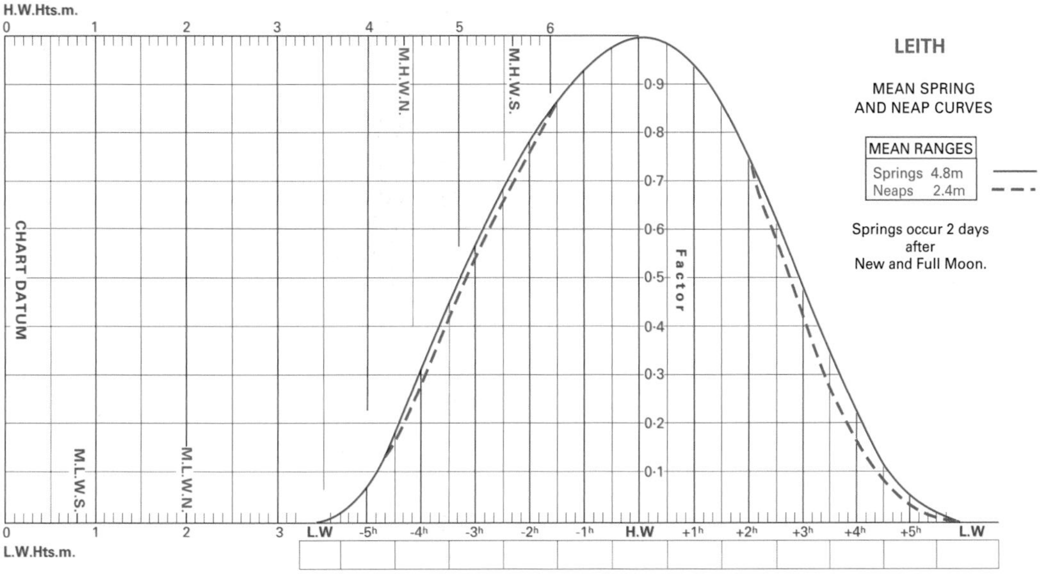
H.W.Hts.m.
0
1
2
3
4
5
6
M.H.W.N.
M.H.W.S.
CHART DATUM
Factor
0·9
0·8
0·7
0·6
0·5
0·4
0·3
0·2
0·1
M.L.W.S.
M.L.W.N.
0
1
2
3
L.W
-5h
-4h
-3h
-2h
-1h
H.W
+1h
+2h
+3h
+4h
+5h
L.W
L.W.Hts.m.
LEITH
MEAN SPRING AND NEAP CURVES
MEAN RANGES
Springs 4.8m
Neaps 2.4m
Springs occur 2 days after New and Full Moon.

TIME ZONE (UT)
For Summer Time add ONE hour in **non-shaded areas**

SCOTLAND – LEITH

LAT 55°59′N LONG 3°11′W

TIMES AND HEIGHTS OF HIGH AND LOW WATERS

SPRING & NEAP TIDES
Dates in red are SPRINGS
Dates in blue are NEAPS

YEAR **2005**

JANUARY

Date	Day	Time	m	Time	m	Time	m	Time	m
1	SA	0558	4.8	1113	1.8	1806	4.9		
2	SU	0000	1.5	0641	4.7	1150	2.0	1848	4.8
3	M	0044	1.6	0729	4.6	1237	2.1	◑ 1937	4.7
4	TU	0136	1.7	0823	4.5	1343	2.2	2036	4.6
5	W	0238	1.8	0924	4.6	1505	2.2	2145	4.6
6	TH	0352	1.8	1029	4.6	1625	2.1	2255	4.7
7	F	0506	1.6	1132	4.8	1734	1.8		
8	SA	0001	5.0	0610	1.5	1230	5.0	1836	1.5
9	SU	0102	5.2	0709	1.3	1324	5.3	1936	1.1
10	M	0157	5.5	0804	1.1	1413	5.5	● 2033	0.8
11	TU	0248	5.7	0856	1.0	1501	5.7	2127	0.5
12	W	0338	5.8	0944	1.0	1549	5.7	2218	0.4
13	TH	0427	5.8	1030	1.0	1637	5.7	2306	0.4
14	F	0517	5.6	1113	1.1	1726	5.6	2351	0.6
15	SA	0608	5.3	1152	1.4	1818	5.4		
16	SU	0034	0.9	0700	5.0	1230	1.6	1912	5.2
17	M	0117	1.3	0755	4.8	1314	1.9	◐ 2011	4.9
18	TU	0205	1.7	0852	4.5	1416	2.1	2113	4.7
19	W	0312	2.0	0953	4.4	1539	2.2	2219	4.5
20	TH	0431	2.1	1058	4.4	1657	2.1	2328	4.5
21	F	0536	2.1	1204	4.5	1803	2.0		
22	SA	0034	4.5	0625	2.0	1301	4.7	1857	1.7
23	SU	0127	4.7	0705	1.8	1346	4.9	1940	1.5
24	M	0209	4.8	0741	1.7	1424	5.0	2017	1.3
25	TU	0245	5.0	0815	1.5	1458	5.1	○ 2051	1.1
26	W	0317	5.1	0849	1.4	1529	5.2	2125	1.0
27	TH	0348	5.1	0923	1.3	1601	5.3	2158	0.9
28	F	0421	5.1	0956	1.3	1632	5.3	2232	0.9
29	SA	0455	5.1	1026	1.3	1704	5.2	2303	1.0
30	SU	0531	5.0	1051	1.4	1737	5.1	2332	1.1
31	M	0609	4.9	1116	1.5	1814	5.0		

FEBRUARY

Date	Day	Time	m	Time	m	Time	m	Time	m
1	TU	0000	1.3	0651	4.8	1149	1.7	1856	4.9
2	W	0037	1.5	0738	4.6	1237	1.9	◑ 1948	4.7
3	TH	0130	1.7	0835	4.5	1347	2.1	2057	4.5
4	F	0248	1.9	0946	4.4	1535	2.1	2224	4.5
5	SA	0442	1.9	1101	4.5	1721	1.9	2345	4.7
6	SU	0603	1.7	1212	4.8	1835	1.5		
7	M	0054	5.1	0705	1.5	1313	5.1	1937	1.0
8	TU	0150	5.4	0759	1.2	1404	5.5	● 2032	0.6
9	W	0239	5.7	0846	0.9	1450	5.7	2120	0.3
10	TH	0325	5.8	0931	0.7	1534	5.9	2205	0.1
11	F	0410	5.8	1011	0.7	1619	5.9	2247	0.2
12	SA	0454	5.6	1048	0.8	1703	5.8	2324	0.4
13	SU	0539	5.4	1119	1.0	1748	5.5	2355	0.8
14	M	0623	5.0	1145	1.3	1835	5.2		
15	TU	0018	1.3	0710	4.7	1218	1.6	1925	4.8
16	W	0049	1.7	0801	4.4	1308	2.0	◐ 2025	4.5
17	TH	0141	2.1	0900	4.2	1436	2.3	2133	4.2
18	F	0323	2.4	1008	4.1	1630	2.3	2252	4.1
19	SA	0505	2.4	1128	4.2	1754	2.1		
20	SU	0016	4.3	0611	2.2	1241	4.5	1852	1.8
21	M	0114	4.5	0656	2.0	1329	4.7	1933	1.5
22	TU	0155	4.8	0731	1.7	1407	5.0	2007	1.2
23	W	0227	5.0	0804	1.5	1439	5.1	2038	1.0
24	TH	0256	5.1	0835	1.2	1509	5.3	○ 2109	0.8
25	F	0326	5.2	0907	1.1	1539	5.4	2140	0.7
26	SA	0356	5.3	0938	1.0	1608	5.4	2211	0.7
27	SU	0429	5.3	1005	1.0	1638	5.4	2239	0.7
28	M	0503	5.2	1027	1.1	1711	5.3	2300	0.9

MARCH

Date	Day	Time	m	Time	m	Time	m	Time	m
1	TU	0539	5.1	1048	1.2	1748	5.2	2321	1.1
2	W	0619	4.9	1119	1.4	1831	5.0	2354	1.4
3	TH	0704	4.7	1204	1.6	1924	4.7	◑	
4	F	0046	1.8	0759	4.5	1313	2.0	2036	4.5
5	SA	0219	2.1	0915	4.3	1527	2.1	2210	4.4
6	SU	0442	2.1	1043	4.4	1724	1.8	2339	4.7
7	M	0559	1.8	1201	4.7	1836	1.3		
8	TU	0048	5.1	0656	1.5	1302	5.1	1932	0.8
9	W	0140	5.4	0745	1.1	1350	5.5	2021	0.4
10	TH	0225	5.7	0828	0.8	1432	5.8	● 2104	0.1
11	F	0306	5.7	0908	0.6	1514	5.9	2143	0.1
12	SA	0346	5.7	0946	0.5	1555	5.9	2220	0.2
13	SU	0427	5.5	1020	0.6	1637	5.7	2251	0.5
14	M	0507	5.3	1048	0.9	1719	5.5	2312	0.9
15	TU	0547	5.0	1110	1.1	1802	5.1	2328	1.3
16	W	0629	4.7	1138	1.5	1850	4.7	2357	1.8
17	TH	0716	4.4	1221	1.9	1945	4.3	◐	
18	F	0044	2.2	0812	4.2	1338	2.2	2050	4.1
19	SA	0219	2.6	0921	4.0	1605	2.3	2207	4.0
20	SU	0438	2.5	1042	4.1	1733	2.1	2344	4.1
21	M	0549	2.3	1206	4.3	1828	1.8		
22	TU	0047	4.4	0634	2.0	1259	4.6	1908	1.5
23	W	0126	4.7	0709	1.7	1337	4.9	1941	1.2
24	TH	0158	5.0	0740	1.4	1409	5.1	2011	0.9
25	F	0227	5.1	0811	1.1	1440	5.3	○ 2042	0.7
26	SA	0256	5.3	0843	0.9	1509	5.4	2113	0.6
27	SU	0327	5.4	0914	0.8	1540	5.5	2143	0.5
28	M	0400	5.4	0941	0.8	1613	5.5	2210	0.7
29	TU	0435	5.3	1005	0.9	1650	5.4	2232	0.9
30	W	0512	5.2	1030	1.0	1731	5.2	2255	1.2
31	TH	0554	5.0	1105	1.3	1819	5.0	2332	1.5

APRIL

Date	Day	Time	m	Time	m	Time	m	Time	m
1	F	0641	4.7	1155	1.6	1917	4.7		
2	SA	0034	2.0	0739	4.5	1321	1.9	◑ 2034	4.4
3	SU	0247	2.3	0902	4.3	1550	1.9	2206	4.5
4	M	0436	2.1	1032	4.4	1720	1.5	2330	4.7
5	TU	0542	1.8	1147	4.8	1824	1.1		
6	W	0034	5.1	0635	1.4	1244	5.2	1915	0.7
7	TH	0123	5.4	0720	1.1	1329	5.5	1959	0.4
8	F	0204	5.5	0802	0.8	1410	5.7	● 2039	0.3
9	SA	0242	5.6	0842	0.6	1451	5.8	2115	0.3
10	SU	0320	5.5	0919	0.5	1532	5.7	2148	0.5
11	M	0359	5.4	0953	0.6	1613	5.5	2215	0.8
12	TU	0437	5.2	1022	0.9	1654	5.3	2233	1.1
13	W	0515	5.0	1045	1.1	1736	5.0	2250	1.5
14	TH	0554	4.7	1112	1.4	1822	4.6	2319	1.8
15	F	0638	4.5	1154	1.8	1913	4.3		
16	SA	0005	2.2	0732	4.2	1301	2.1	◐ 2012	4.1
17	SU	0130	2.6	0839	4.1	1514	2.2	2121	4.0
18	M	0352	2.6	0954	4.1	1650	2.0	2238	4.1
19	TU	0504	2.3	1110	4.2	1743	1.7	2351	4.3
20	W	0552	2.0	1209	4.5	1825	1.5		
21	TH	0038	4.6	0629	1.7	1253	4.8	1900	1.2
22	F	0115	4.9	0704	1.4	1330	5.1	1933	0.9
23	SA	0149	5.1	0738	1.1	1404	5.3	2006	0.7
24	SU	0223	5.3	0812	0.9	1438	5.4	○ 2039	0.6
25	M	0257	5.4	0846	0.8	1513	5.5	2113	0.6
26	TU	0332	5.4	0920	0.7	1552	5.5	2146	0.7
27	W	0410	5.4	0954	0.8	1634	5.4	2218	1.0
28	TH	0451	5.2	1031	0.9	1721	5.2	2254	1.3
29	F	0536	5.0	1117	1.2	1814	5.0	2346	1.7
30	SA	0628	4.8	1224	1.4	1917	4.7		

Chart Datum: 2·90 metres below Ordnance Datum (Newlyn)

TIME ZONE (UT)
For Summer Time add ONE hour in **non-shaded areas**

SCOTLAND – LEITH

LAT 55°59′N LONG 3°11′W

TIMES AND HEIGHTS OF HIGH AND LOW WATERS

SPRING & NEAP TIDES
Dates in red are **SPRINGS**
Dates in blue are **NEAPS**

YEAR **2005**

MAY

Date	Day	Time	m	Time	m	Time	m	Time	m
1	SU	0108	2.1	0733	4.6	1400	1.6	◑ 2034	4.6
2	M	0249	2.2	0856	4.5	1544	1.5	2155	4.6
3	TU	0411	2.0	1016	4.6	1659	1.3	2309	4.8
4	W	0512	1.8	1124	4.9	1759	1.0		
5	TH	0009	5.0	0603	1.5	1219	5.1	1849	0.8
6	F	0058	5.2	0649	1.2	1306	5.3	1931	0.7
7	SA	0139	5.3	0733	0.9	1348	5.4	2009	0.6
8	SU	0218	5.4	0815	0.8	1430	5.5	● 2043	0.7
9	M	0256	5.3	0854	0.7	1512	5.4	2114	0.8
10	TU	0334	5.3	0930	0.8	1553	5.3	2140	1.1
11	W	0411	5.1	1002	1.0	1634	5.1	2202	1.3
12	TH	0448	5.0	1029	1.2	1715	4.9	2227	1.6
13	F	0526	4.8	1100	1.4	1757	4.6	2259	1.9
14	SA	0608	4.6	1141	1.6	1844	4.4	2345	2.1
15	SU	0658	4.4	1236	1.9	1936	4.3		
16	M	0053	2.4	0757	4.2	1352	2.0	◐ 2034	4.2
17	TU	0227	2.5	0904	4.2	1533	2.0	2137	4.2
18	W	0358	2.3	1009	4.3	1640	1.8	2240	4.3
19	TH	0455	2.1	1109	4.5	1728	1.5	2337	4.6
20	F	0541	1.8	1200	4.7	1810	1.3		
21	SA	0026	4.8	0621	1.5	1246	5.0	1849	1.1
22	SU	0109	5.1	0701	1.2	1328	5.2	1928	0.9
23	M	0149	5.2	0741	1.0	1409	5.3	○ 2008	0.8
24	TU	0229	5.4	0823	0.8	1452	5.5	2050	0.8
25	W	0309	5.4	0908	0.7	1537	5.5	2134	0.9
26	TH	0352	5.4	0956	0.7	1624	5.5	2221	1.1
27	F	0437	5.3	1047	0.8	1715	5.4	2311	1.4
28	SA	0526	5.2	1143	0.9	1811	5.2		
29	SU	0007	1.6	0622	5.0	1246	1.1	1913	4.9
30	M	0111	1.8	0727	4.9	1358	1.2	◑ 2022	4.8
31	TU	0223	1.9	0841	4.8	1516	1.3	2132	4.7

JUNE

Date	Day	Time	m	Time	m	Time	m	Time	m
1	W	0332	1.9	0951	4.8	1624	1.3	2238	4.8
2	TH	0433	1.8	1054	4.9	1725	1.2	2338	4.9
3	F	0528	1.6	1152	5.0	1817	1.2		
4	SA	0030	5.0	0619	1.4	1243	5.1	1900	1.1
5	SU	0116	5.1	0707	1.2	1330	5.1	1937	1.1
6	M	0157	5.1	0752	1.0	1414	5.1	● 2011	1.1
7	TU	0236	5.2	0833	1.0	1456	5.1	2043	1.2
8	W	0314	5.1	0911	1.0	1537	5.1	2113	1.3
9	TH	0350	5.1	0945	1.0	1616	5.0	2143	1.4
10	F	0426	5.0	1017	1.1	1654	4.9	2214	1.6
11	SA	0504	4.9	1051	1.3	1733	4.7	2249	1.7
12	SU	0543	4.8	1129	1.4	1815	4.6	2329	1.9
13	M	0627	4.6	1214	1.6	1901	4.5		
14	TU	0018	2.1	0715	4.5	1307	1.7	1950	4.4
15	W	0120	2.2	0810	4.4	1408	1.8	◐ 2046	4.4
16	TH	0232	2.2	0910	4.4	1515	1.7	2144	4.4
17	F	0344	2.1	1011	4.5	1621	1.6	2243	4.5
18	SA	0446	1.9	1109	4.6	1717	1.5	2339	4.7
19	SU	0540	1.7	1205	4.8	1808	1.3		
20	M	0032	4.9	0629	1.4	1258	5.1	1857	1.1
21	TU	0121	5.1	0719	1.1	1348	5.3	1948	1.0
22	W	0207	5.3	0812	0.9	1438	5.5	○ 2039	0.9
23	TH	0252	5.4	0905	0.6	1527	5.6	2130	0.9
24	F	0339	5.5	0959	0.5	1616	5.6	2220	1.0
25	SA	0427	5.5	1052	0.5	1708	5.5	2309	1.1
26	SU	0517	5.4	1144	0.6	1801	5.4	2358	1.3
27	M	0611	5.3	1236	0.7	1858	5.1		
28	TU	0047	1.5	0710	5.2	1332	1.0	◑ 1958	4.9
29	W	0142	1.7	0813	5.0	1432	1.2	2059	4.7
30	TH	0243	1.8	0918	4.9	1538	1.4	2201	4.6

JULY

Date	Day	Time	m	Time	m	Time	m	Time	m
1	F	0350	1.9	1022	4.8	1643	1.6	2302	4.6
2	SA	0454	1.8	1124	4.7	1741	1.6		
3	SU	0001	4.7	0554	1.6	1225	4.8	1829	1.6
4	M	0055	4.8	0649	1.5	1318	4.8	1909	1.6
5	TU	0141	4.9	0737	1.3	1405	4.9	1946	1.5
6	W	0222	5.0	0820	1.2	1446	5.0	● 2020	1.5
7	TH	0300	5.1	0857	1.1	1523	5.0	2054	1.4
8	F	0335	5.1	0931	1.0	1558	5.0	2128	1.4
9	SA	0409	5.1	1004	1.0	1633	5.0	2201	1.4
10	SU	0443	5.1	1038	1.1	1709	4.9	2235	1.5
11	M	0519	5.0	1112	1.1	1746	4.8	2308	1.6
12	TU	0556	4.9	1148	1.3	1827	4.7	2341	1.7
13	W	0636	4.8	1226	1.4	1910	4.6		
14	TH	0020	1.9	0719	4.7	1310	1.6	◐ 1958	4.5
15	F	0113	2.0	0810	4.6	1404	1.7	2053	4.5
16	SA	0224	2.1	0913	4.5	1511	1.8	2155	4.5
17	SU	0348	2.1	1023	4.5	1631	1.7	2259	4.6
18	M	0506	1.9	1133	4.7	1742	1.6		
19	TU	0002	4.8	0611	1.6	1238	5.0	1843	1.4
20	W	0100	5.0	0711	1.2	1336	5.3	1939	1.2
21	TH	0152	5.3	0809	0.8	1428	5.6	○ 2032	1.0
22	F	0240	5.5	0904	0.5	1516	5.8	2122	0.8
23	SA	0326	5.7	0955	0.2	1604	5.8	2209	0.8
24	SU	0413	5.8	1043	0.2	1652	5.7	2253	0.8
25	M	0501	5.8	1128	0.3	1741	5.5	2334	1.0
26	TU	0550	5.6	1211	0.6	1831	5.2		
27	W	0013	1.3	0641	5.4	1253	0.9	1924	5.0
28	TH	0054	1.5	0738	5.1	1336	1.4	◑ 2020	4.7
29	F	0147	1.8	0841	4.8	1433	1.8	2120	4.5
30	SA	0303	2.0	0947	4.6	1553	2.0	2224	4.4
31	SU	0429	2.0	1058	4.4	1710	2.1	2333	4.5

AUGUST

Date	Day	Time	m	Time	m	Time	m	Time	m
1	M	0544	1.9	1210	4.5	1810	2.0		
2	TU	0038	4.6	0646	1.7	1311	4.6	1855	1.9
3	W	0129	4.8	0734	1.4	1357	4.8	1932	1.7
4	TH	0210	5.0	0812	1.2	1434	5.0	2005	1.5
5	F	0246	5.1	0845	1.1	1507	5.0	● 2038	1.4
6	SA	0318	5.2	0916	0.9	1537	5.1	2111	1.3
7	SU	0348	5.3	0947	0.8	1608	5.1	2144	1.2
8	M	0420	5.3	1018	0.8	1641	5.1	2214	1.2
9	TU	0451	5.2	1049	0.9	1716	5.0	2240	1.3
10	W	0524	5.1	1117	1.0	1753	4.9	2304	1.5
11	TH	0559	5.0	1143	1.2	1832	4.8	2331	1.6
12	F	0639	4.9	1213	1.5	1916	4.7		
13	SA	0011	1.8	0726	4.7	1259	1.7	◐ 2008	4.5
14	SU	0113	2.0	0829	4.5	1410	2.0	2113	4.4
15	M	0255	2.2	0951	4.4	1606	2.1	2228	4.5
16	TU	0453	2.0	1114	4.6	1735	1.9	2342	4.7
17	W	0608	1.6	1227	5.0	1838	1.6		
18	TH	0046	5.1	0710	1.1	1326	5.4	1931	1.2
19	F	0139	5.4	0805	0.6	1415	5.7	○ 2020	0.9
20	SA	0224	5.7	0854	0.2	1501	5.9	2105	0.7
21	SU	0308	5.9	0940	0.0	1545	5.9	2148	0.6
22	M	0352	6.0	1023	0.0	1629	5.8	2228	0.6
23	TU	0437	6.0	1102	0.2	1713	5.6	2304	0.8
24	W	0523	5.8	1138	0.6	1759	5.3	2335	1.1
25	TH	0610	5.4	1207	1.1	1846	4.9		
26	F	0007	1.5	0702	5.0	1236	1.6	◑ 1938	4.6
27	SA	0054	1.9	0804	4.6	1323	2.1	2038	4.4
28	SU	0217	2.2	0913	4.3	1458	2.4	2146	4.3
29	M	0415	2.2	1030	4.2	1650	2.4	2303	4.3
30	TU	0544	2.0	1156	4.3	1801	2.3		
31	W	0018	4.5	0642	1.7	1259	4.6	1845	2.0

Chart Datum: 2·90 metres below Ordnance Datum (Newlyn)

TIME ZONE (UT)
For Summer Time add ONE hour in **non-shaded areas**

SCOTLAND – LEITH

LAT 55°59′N LONG 3°11′W

TIMES AND HEIGHTS OF HIGH AND LOW WATERS

SPRING & NEAP TIDES
Dates in red are SPRINGS
Dates in blue are NEAPS

YEAR **2005**

SEPTEMBER

Date	Day	Time	m	Time	m	Time	m	Time	m
1	TH	0111	4.8	0723	1.5	1341	4.8	1918	1.8
2	F	0151	5.0	0756	1.2	1414	5.0	1948	1.5
3	SA	0223	5.2	0825	1.0	1443	5.1	● 2019	1.3
4	SU	0253	5.3	0853	0.8	1511	5.2	2050	1.1
5	M	0322	5.4	0922	0.7	1540	5.3	2120	1.0
6	TU	0351	5.4	0952	0.7	1611	5.3	2148	1.0
7	W	0422	5.4	1019	0.8	1644	5.2	2211	1.1
8	TH	0454	5.3	1040	1.0	1720	5.1	2231	1.3
9	F	0530	5.1	1059	1.2	1758	5.0	2258	1.5
10	SA	0611	5.0	1127	1.5	1841	4.8	2337	1.7
11	SU	0702	4.7	1211	1.9	1934	4.6	◐	
12	M	0039	2.0	0808	4.5	1336	2.2	2042	4.4
13	TU	0247	2.2	0936	4.4	1608	2.3	2209	4.5
14	W	0455	1.9	1104	4.7	1729	2.0	2328	4.7
15	TH	0606	1.4	1217	5.1	1826	1.6		
16	F	0031	5.2	0702	0.9	1312	5.5	1914	1.2
17	SA	0121	5.6	0751	0.5	1357	5.8	1959	0.9
18	SU	0204	5.9	0836	0.2	1439	5.9	○ 2041	0.6
19	M	0245	6.1	0917	0.0	1520	5.9	2121	0.5
20	TU	0328	6.1	0956	0.1	1601	5.8	2159	0.6
21	W	0411	6.0	1031	0.4	1643	5.5	2233	0.8
22	TH	0456	5.7	1059	0.9	1726	5.3	2301	1.1
23	F	0542	5.3	1118	1.3	1810	4.9	2329	1.5
24	SA	0632	4.9	1142	1.8	1859	4.6		
25	SU	0012	1.9	0730	4.5	1228	2.3	◑ 1958	4.4
26	M	0133	2.3	0839	4.2	1402	2.7	2108	4.2
27	TU	0402	2.3	0956	4.1	1626	2.7	2227	4.3
28	W	0524	2.1	1127	4.3	1735	2.4	2346	4.5
29	TH	0616	1.8	1231	4.6	1818	2.1		
30	F	0039	4.8	0654	1.5	1312	4.8	1851	1.8

OCTOBER

Date	Day	Time	m	Time	m	Time	m	Time	m
1	SA	0119	5.1	0725	1.2	1343	5.1	1921	1.5
2	SU	0151	5.3	0753	1.0	1411	5.2	1951	1.3
3	M	0221	5.4	0822	0.8	1439	5.3	● 2022	1.1
4	TU	0251	5.5	0850	0.7	1509	5.4	2052	1.0
5	W	0321	5.5	0919	0.7	1540	5.4	2120	1.0
6	TH	0353	5.5	0945	0.8	1614	5.4	2145	1.1
7	F	0429	5.4	1006	1.0	1650	5.3	2209	1.2
8	SA	0509	5.2	1028	1.3	1730	5.1	2240	1.4
9	SU	0556	5.0	1101	1.7	1816	4.9	2325	1.7
10	M	0651	4.8	1153	2.1	1911	4.6	◐	
11	TU	0044	2.0	0801	4.6	1400	2.4	2026	4.5
12	W	0309	2.0	0929	4.5	1600	2.3	2155	4.6
13	TH	0447	1.7	1052	4.8	1710	2.0	2311	4.9
14	F	0550	1.2	1200	5.2	1803	1.6		
15	SA	0010	5.3	0643	0.8	1252	5.5	1849	1.3
16	SU	0058	5.6	0729	0.5	1335	5.7	1932	0.9
17	M	0141	5.9	0810	0.4	1415	5.8	○ 2014	0.7
18	TU	0222	6.0	0849	0.3	1454	5.8	2055	0.6
19	W	0305	5.9	0925	0.5	1534	5.7	2133	0.7
20	TH	0348	5.8	0957	0.8	1614	5.5	2208	0.9
21	F	0433	5.5	1020	1.2	1655	5.2	2236	1.2
22	SA	0518	5.2	1036	1.6	1737	5.0	2304	1.5
23	SU	0606	4.8	1103	2.0	1824	4.7	2345	1.9
24	M	0700	4.5	1148	2.4	1921	4.4		
25	TU	0051	2.2	0801	4.2	1308	2.7	◑ 2029	4.3
26	W	0316	2.3	0910	4.1	1532	2.8	2141	4.3
27	TH	0438	2.1	1026	4.2	1646	2.5	2253	4.4
28	F	0530	1.8	1137	4.5	1733	2.2	2351	4.7
29	SA	0610	1.6	1224	4.7	1811	1.9		
30	SU	0035	5.0	0643	1.3	1300	5.0	1845	1.6
31	M	0112	5.2	0714	1.1	1332	5.2	1918	1.4

NOVEMBER

Date	Day	Time	m	Time	m	Time	m	Time	m
1	TU	0146	5.3	0745	0.9	1404	5.3	1951	1.2
2	W	0219	5.5	0816	0.9	1437	5.4	● 2024	1.0
3	TH	0254	5.5	0847	0.9	1512	5.5	2057	1.0
4	F	0331	5.5	0918	1.0	1548	5.4	2130	1.0
5	SA	0412	5.4	0948	1.2	1627	5.3	2206	1.2
6	SU	0457	5.3	1022	1.5	1710	5.2	2250	1.3
7	M	0547	5.1	1108	1.8	1800	5.0	2352	1.6
8	TU	0646	4.9	1225	2.2	1859	4.8		
9	W	0118	1.8	0756	4.7	1403	2.3	◐ 2014	4.7
10	TH	0300	1.7	0916	4.7	1531	2.2	2137	4.8
11	F	0421	1.5	1030	4.9	1637	2.0	2246	5.0
12	SA	0523	1.2	1134	5.1	1731	1.7	2344	5.3
13	SU	0616	1.0	1226	5.3	1819	1.4		
14	M	0034	5.5	0702	0.9	1311	5.5	1905	1.1
15	TU	0120	5.6	0742	0.8	1351	5.5	1949	1.0
16	W	0203	5.7	0819	0.8	1431	5.6	○ 2032	0.9
17	TH	0247	5.6	0854	1.0	1511	5.5	2113	0.9
18	F	0331	5.5	0924	1.2	1551	5.4	2149	1.0
19	SA	0415	5.3	0949	1.4	1630	5.2	2221	1.3
20	SU	0458	5.0	1013	1.7	1710	5.0	2251	1.5
21	M	0542	4.8	1044	2.0	1753	4.8	2329	1.7
22	TU	0629	4.6	1126	2.2	1843	4.6		
23	W	0020	2.0	0721	4.4	1226	2.5	◑ 1943	4.4
24	TH	0130	2.1	0819	4.3	1351	2.6	2047	4.4
25	F	0312	2.1	0920	4.3	1529	2.6	2150	4.4
26	SA	0423	2.0	1020	4.4	1634	2.4	2248	4.6
27	SU	0512	1.8	1117	4.6	1723	2.1	2341	4.8
28	M	0554	1.6	1207	4.8	1805	1.8		
29	TU	0027	5.0	0632	1.4	1251	5.0	1844	1.6
30	W	0111	5.2	0708	1.2	1332	5.2	1923	1.3

DECEMBER

Date	Day	Time	m	Time	m	Time	m	Time	m
1	TH	0152	5.3	0746	1.1	1410	5.4	● 2003	1.1
2	F	0233	5.4	0825	1.1	1449	5.5	2045	1.0
3	SA	0316	5.5	0906	1.1	1529	5.5	2131	0.9
4	SU	0401	5.5	0951	1.2	1612	5.4	2220	1.0
5	M	0449	5.4	1039	1.4	1659	5.3	2313	1.1
6	TU	0541	5.3	1132	1.7	1750	5.2		
7	W	0011	1.2	0637	5.1	1231	1.9	1847	5.1
8	TH	0116	1.3	0741	4.9	1337	2.1	◐ 1955	5.0
9	F	0228	1.4	0851	4.8	1447	2.1	2108	4.9
10	SA	0341	1.5	0959	4.8	1554	2.0	2215	5.0
11	SU	0447	1.4	1102	4.9	1655	1.8	2317	5.1
12	M	0545	1.4	1158	5.0	1751	1.6		
13	TU	0013	5.2	0634	1.3	1249	5.1	1843	1.4
14	W	0105	5.2	0716	1.3	1334	5.2	1932	1.2
15	TH	0152	5.3	0754	1.3	1416	5.3	○ 2018	1.1
16	F	0237	5.3	0829	1.4	1456	5.3	2100	1.1
17	SA	0320	5.2	0901	1.4	1535	5.3	2137	1.1
18	SU	0400	5.1	0931	1.5	1612	5.2	2210	1.2
19	M	0439	5.0	1000	1.6	1649	5.1	2240	1.3
20	TU	0518	4.9	1032	1.8	1727	5.0	2314	1.5
21	W	0559	4.7	1109	1.9	1809	4.8	2353	1.6
22	TH	0642	4.6	1150	2.1	1855	4.7		
23	F	0040	1.8	0729	4.5	1242	2.3	◑ 1947	4.5
24	SA	0135	1.9	0822	4.4	1348	2.4	2044	4.5
25	SU	0239	2.0	0919	4.4	1506	2.4	2145	4.5
26	M	0352	1.9	1018	4.4	1621	2.3	2246	4.5
27	TU	0457	1.8	1116	4.6	1722	2.1	2345	4.7
28	W	0552	1.7	1212	4.8	1814	1.8		
29	TH	0040	4.9	0640	1.5	1303	5.0	1903	1.5
30	F	0132	5.2	0728	1.3	1350	5.2	1952	1.2
31	SA	0220	5.4	0815	1.2	1434	5.4	● 2043	0.9

Chart Datum: 2·90 metres below Ordnance Datum (Newlyn)

9.6.10 METHIL

Fife **56°10'·75N 03°00'·55W** ❁♁✿

CHARTS AC 734, 741; Imray C23, C27; OS 59

TIDES +0330 Dover; ML 3·0; Duration 0615; Zone 0 (UT)

Standard Port LEITH (⟵)

Times				Height (metres)			
High Water		Low Water		MHWS	MHWN	MLWN	MLWS
0300	0900	0300	0900	5·6	4·4	2·0	0·8
1500	2100	1500	2100				
Differences METHIL							
−0005	−0001	−0001	−0001	−0·1	−0·1	−0·1	−0·1
KIRKCALDY							
+0005	0000	−0004	−0001	−0·3	`−0·3	−0·2	−0·2

SHELTER Commercial port only suitable as an emergency shelter in No 2 dock and dangerous to enter in bad weather.

NAVIGATION WPT 56°10'·49N 03°00'·10W, 320° to pier hd lt, 0·34M. Beware silting. A sand bar forms rapidly to seaward of the lt ho and dredged depth is not always maintained.

LIGHTS AND MARKS
By day and night (vert lts):

● ● = Dangerous to enter; heave to in roads.

● ○ = Clear to enter No 2 dock.

● = Remain in roads until another signal is made.

R/T *Methil Docks Radio* VHF Ch 14 16 (HW–3 to +1). Forth Navigation Ch 71 (H24).

TELEPHONE (Dial code 01592) HM (Port Manager) (01333) 426725 📠 424873; MRSC (01333) 450666; Marinecall 09066 526236; Police 418888; Dr (01333) 426913.

FACILITIES Hbr No 2 Dock £25.00 per week, FW, C (10 ton). **Town** EC Thurs; P, D, Gas, Gaz, 🛒, R, Bar, ✉, Ⓑ, ⇌ (bus to Markinch or Kirkcaldy), Ⓗ Kirkcaldy, ✈ Edinburgh.

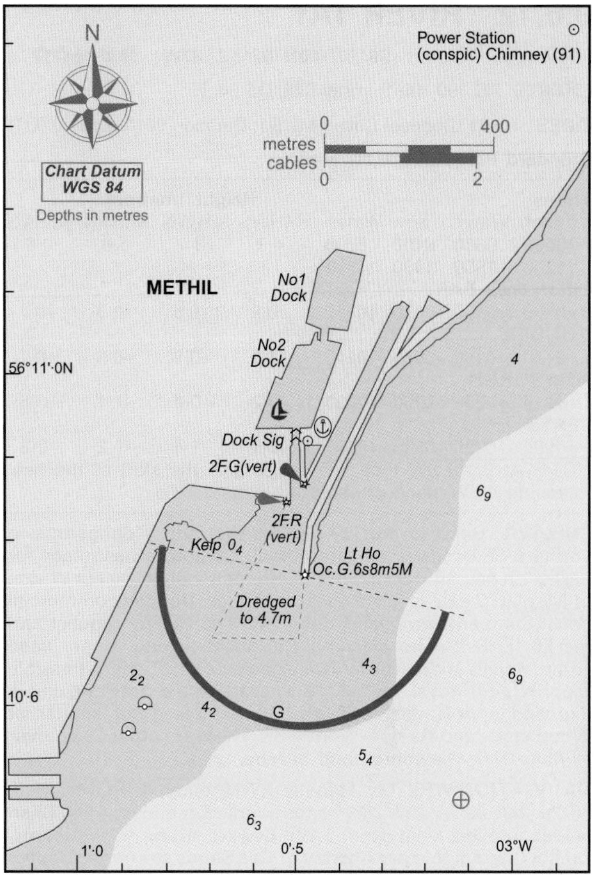
N
Power Station (conspic) Chimney (91)
metres
cables
0
400
0
2
Chart Datum WGS 84
Depths in metres
METHIL
No1 Dock
No2 Dock
56°11'·0N
Dock Sig
2F.G(vert)
2F.R (vert)
Kelp
Lt Ho
Oc.G.6s8m5M
Dredged to 4.7m
10'·6
G
1'·0
0'·5
03°W

ADJACENT HARBOURS

KIRKCALDY, Fife, **56°06'·80N 03°08'·96W**. AC 741. HW +0345 on Dover, −0005 on Leith; HW −0·1m on Leith; ML 3·2m; Duration 0620. See 9.6.10. Shelter good except in strong E winds; an emergency refuge. Officially the hbr is closed (no commercial tfc, but some local FVs) and not manned; depths may be less than charted due to silting. The only hbr light is on E Pier head, Fl WG 10s 12m 8M. Small craft should contact Forth Ports Authority ☎ (01333) 426725, or call Forth Navigation Ch 71 (H24) or Methil Docks Radio Ch 16 14 for advice.

9.6.11 ANSTRUTHER

Fife **56°13'·15N 02°41'·82W** ❁❁♁♁♁✿✿✿

CHARTS AC 175, 734; Imray C23, C27; OS 59

TIDES +0315 Dover; ML 3·1; Duration 0620; Zone 0 (UT)

Standard Port LEITH (⟵)

Times				Height (metres)			
High Water		Low Water		MHWS	MHWN	MLWN	MLWS
0300	0900	0300	0900	5·6	4·4	2·0	0·8
1500	2100	1500	2100				
Differences ANSTRUTHER EASTER							
−0018	−0012	−0006	−0008	−0·3	−0·2	0·0	0·0

SHELTER Good, but dangerous to enter in strong E & S winds. Hbr dries; access approx HW±2. Caution: ledge at base of W pier. No ⚓ to W of hbr; do not go N of W pier lt due to rks. Beware of creels in the area.

NAVIGATION WPT 56°12'·59N 02°42'·20W, 019° to ent, 0·60M. Beware lobster pots and FVs.

LIGHTS AND MARKS Conspic tr on W pier. Ldg lts 019°, both FG 7/11m 4M. Pier lts as chartlet. Horn (3) 60s in conspic tr.

R/T Call *Anstruther Hbr* VHF Ch 11 16 (HO) or Forth CG 16 (OT).

TELEPHONE (Dial code 01333) HM ☎/📠 310836 (HO); MRSC (01333) 450666; Marinecall 09066 526236; Police: 592100, St Andrews 592100; Dr 310352; Ⓗ St Andrews 01334 472327, Kirkaldy 01592 643355.

FACILITIES Harbour: wall AB (22 + 8Ⓥ) £11.95 then £5.98 per day; pontoons (no fin keels) (24 + 16Ⓥ) £16.90 then £8.41 per day for 10m LOA, Slip, FW, ⛽, ♿, Shwrs 0800-2100; **Services:** D (tanker ☎ 312263), ACA, Gas, Gaz, El, Ⓔ, ▣, LB. **Town** EC Wed; P, 🛒, R, Bar, ✉, Ⓑ, ⇌ (bus Cupar or Leuchars), ✈ Edinburgh/Dundee.

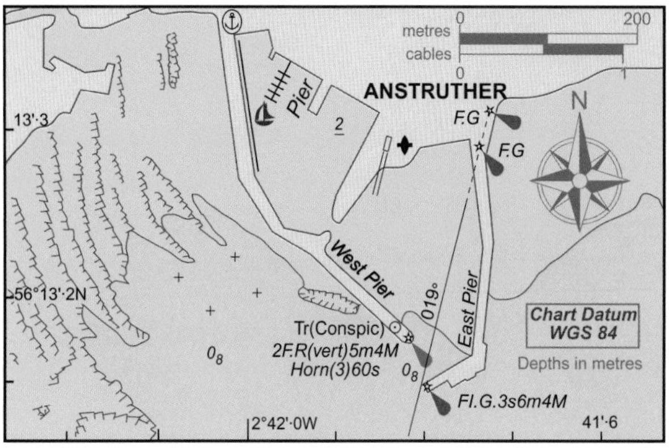
metres
cables
0
200
0
1
ANSTRUTHER
Pier
2
F.G
F.G
N
13'·3
West Pier
East Pier
019°
56°13'·2N
Tr(Conspic)
2F.R(vert)5m4M
Horn(3)60s
Chart Datum WGS 84
Depths in metres
Fl.G.3s6m4M
2°42'·0W
41'·6

9.6.12 RIVER TAY

Fife/Angus Tayport **(56°27'·10N 02°52'·87W)** ❁❁⛆⛆✿✿

CHARTS AC 190, 1481; Imray C23; OS 54, 59

TIDES +0401 (Dundee) Dover; ML 3·1; Duration 0610; Zone 0 (UT)

Standard Port ABERDEEN (⟶)

Times				**Height (metres)**			
High Water		Low Water		MHWS	MHWN	MLWN	MLWS
0000	0600	0100	0700	4·3	3·4	1·6	0·6
1200	1800	1300	1900				
Differences BAR							
+0100	+0100	+0050	+0110	+0·9	+0·8	+0·3	+0·1
DUNDEE							
+0140	+0120	+0055	+0145	+1·1	+0·9	+0·3	+0·1
NEWBURGH							
+0215	+0200	+0250	+0335	−0·2	−0·4	−1·1	−0·5
PERTH							
+0220	+0225	+0510	+0530	−0·9	−1·4	−1·2	−0·3

NOTE: At Perth LW time differences give the start of the rise, following a LW stand of about 4 hours.

SHELTER Good in the Tay Estuary, but ent is dangerous in strong E/SE winds or on-shore swell. **Tayport** is best place for yachts on passage, access HW±4. Hbr partly dries except W side of NE pier; S side is full of yacht moorings. **Dundee** commercial dock (Camperdown), gates open HW–2 to HW by request and fee £6 (Fl R lt = no ent/exit). The docks are no longer used commercially and will be re-developed over next 5 years. Possible moorings off Royal Tay YC. ⚓s as chartlet: the ⚓ off the city is exposed and landing difficult. Off S bank good shelter at Woodhaven and Øs from Wormit BC. There are other ⚓s up river at Balmerino, Newburgh and Inchyra.

NAVIGATION WPT Tay Fairway SWM buoy, L Fl 10s, Bell, 56°29'·24N 02°38'·29W, 209° to the Middle Bar buoys, 1·0M. Chan is well buoyed, least depth 5·2m. Beware strong tidal streams. Do not attempt to cross Abertay or Gaa Sands as charted depths are unreliable.

LIGHTS AND MARKS Tayport High lt Dir 269° Iso WRG 3s, W sector 268°-270°. The HFP "Abertay" ECM buoy, Q (3) 10s (Racon), at E end of Gaa Sands is a clear visual mark. Keep N of Larick, a conspic disused lt bn.

R/T *Dundee Hbr Radio* VHF Ch **12** 16 (H24); local nav warnings, weather, vis and tides on request. Royal Tay YC, Ch M.

TELEPHONE (Dial code 01382): Forth Tay Navigation Service (01324) 498584, 📠 668480; HM (Dundee) 224121, 📠 200834; HM (Perth) (01738) 624056; MRSC (01333) 450666; Marinecall 09066 526236; Tayport Boatowners' Ass'n 553679; Police (Tayport) 542222, (Dundee) 223200; Dr 221953; Ⓗ 223125.

FACILITIES N BANK: **Camperdown Dock**, AB £18 all LOA, £36 for week; FW, ME, EI, C (8 ton); **Victoria Dock**, AB, FW, ME, C (8 ton); **Royal Tay YC** (Broughty Ferry) ☎ 477516, Øs free, R, Bar; **Services:** CH, M, L, ME, EI, ⚒, C (2 ton), ACA. **Dundee City** EC Wed; P, D, CH, 🛒, R, Bar, ✉, Ⓑ, ⇌, ✈. S BANK: **Tayport Hbr** AB £6.60, Slip, L, FW, AC; **Wormit Boating Club** ☎ 541400 Øs free, Slip, L, FW, 🛒.

ADJACENT HARBOURS

PERTH, Perth & Kinross, **56°22'·89N 03°25'·74W**. AC 1481; OS 53, 58. Tides, see 9.6.12. FYCA Pilot Handbook is needed. Leave Tay rly bridge at about HW Dundee –2 to carry a fair tide the 16·5M to Perth. Keep clear of coasters which have to travel at speed and are constrained by their draft. The lit chan favours the S bank for 9M to Newburgh. Here care is needed due to mudbanks in mid-stream; keep S of Mugdrum Is. Up-river, power cables have clearance of 33m and Friarton bridge 26m. Keep S of Willow Is, past the gasworks to hbr on the W bank. Hbr has approx 1·5m. See HM, ☎ (01738) 624056, for berth. VHF Ch 09 16. FW, D & P (cans), usual city amenities, ⇌, ✈.

ST ANDREWS, Fife, **56°20'·32N 02°46'·79W**. AC 190. HW–0015 Leith. Small drying hbr 7M S of Tay Estuary and 8M NW of Fife Ness. In strong onshore winds breaking seas render appr/ent impossible. Appr at HW±2 on 270°, N bkwtr bn in transit with conspic cathedral tr; no lights. A recce by dinghy is useful. Keep about 10m S of the bkwtr for best water. 8m wide ent to inner hbr (drying 2·5m) has lock gates, usually open, and sliding footbridge; berth on W side. Facilities: FW, SC. EC Thurs; all amenities of university town, inc golf course.

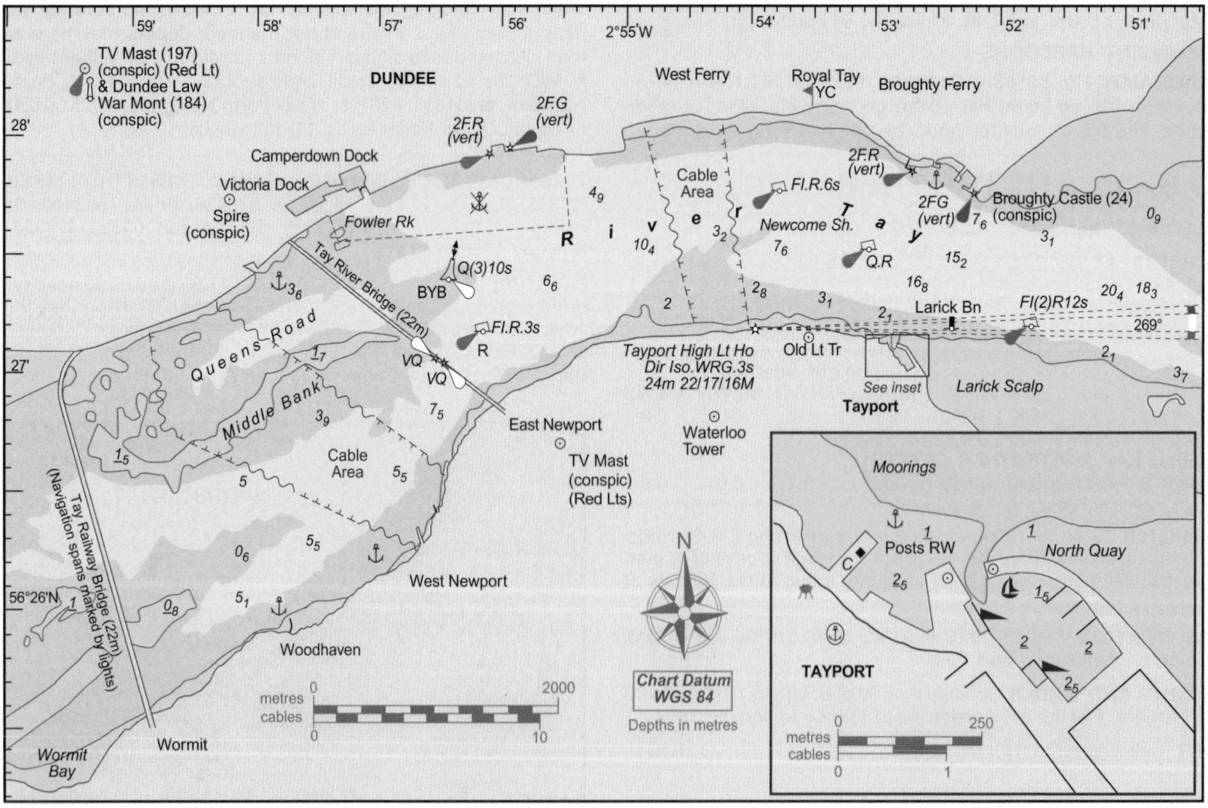
DUNDEE
TV Mast (197) (conspic) (Red Lt) & Dundee Law War Mont (184) (conspic)
Camperdown Dock
Victoria Dock
Spire (conspic)
Fowler Rk
Tay River Bridge (22m)
Queens Road
Middle Bank
Tay Railway Bridge (22m) (Navigation spans marked by lights)
West Ferry
Royal Tay YC
Broughty Ferry
Broughty Castle (24) (conspic)
Cable Area
River Tay
Newcome Sh.
Q(3)10s
BYB
Fl.R.3s
Fl.R.6s
Q.R
Larick Bn
Fl(2)R12s
Tayport High Lt Ho Dir Iso.WRG.3s 24m 22/17/16M
Old Lt Tr
See inset
Tayport
Larick Scalp
East Newport
TV Mast (conspic) (Red Lts)
Waterloo Tower
West Newport
Woodhaven
Wormit
Wormit Bay
Chart Datum WGS 84
Depths in metres
Moorings
Posts RW
North Quay
TAYPORT

9.6.13 ARBROATH

Angus **56°33′·22N 02°34′·99W** ❀❀◊◊✿✿

CHARTS AC 190, 1438; Imray C23; OS 54

TIDES +0317 Dover; ML 2·9; Duration 0620; Zone 0 (UT)

Standard Port ABERDEEN (⟶)

Times				Height (metres)			
High Water		Low Water		MHWS	MHWN	MLWN	MLWS
0000	0600	0100	0700	4·3	3·4	1·6	0·6
1200	1800	1300	1900				
Differences ARBROATH							
+0056	+0037	+0034	+0055	+0·7	+0·7	+0·2	+0·1

SHELTER Good, especially in Inner Basin with lock gates, afloat pontoon berths with 2.5m depth maintained. Ent can be dangerous in moderate SE swell. Small craft can also dry out in the SW corner of inner hbr; inside ent, turn stbd and stbd again.

NAVIGATION WPT 56°32′·98N 02°34′·21W, 299° to ent, 0·5M. Entry should not be attempted LW±2½. Beware Knuckle rks to stbd and Cheek Bush rks to port on entering.

LIGHTS AND MARKS Ldg lts 299°, both FR 7/13m 5M; or twin trs of St Thomas' ✠ visible between N pier lt ho and W bkwtr bn.Hbr entry sigs: Fl G 3s on E pier = Entry safe. Same lt shows FR when hbr closed, entry dangerous. Siren (3) 60s at E pier lt is occas, for FVs. Inner Basin Lock Gates, FR = closed, FG = open >2.5m over sill.

R/T Ch 11 16.

TELEPHONE (Dial code 01241) HM 872166, 📠 878472; MRCC (01224) 592334 MRSC 01333 452000; Marinecall 09066 526236; Police 872222; Dr 876836.

FACILITIES **Inner Basin** 30 + 6Ⓥ, £11/yacht, Showers, WC, **Pier** AB £9/yacht, Slip, D, FW; **Services:** BY, Slip, L, ME, El, ⚒, C (8 ton) Ⓔ, M, Gas, CH. **Town** EC Wed; P, D, 🛒, R, Bar, ✉, Ⓑ, ⇌, ✈ (Dundee).

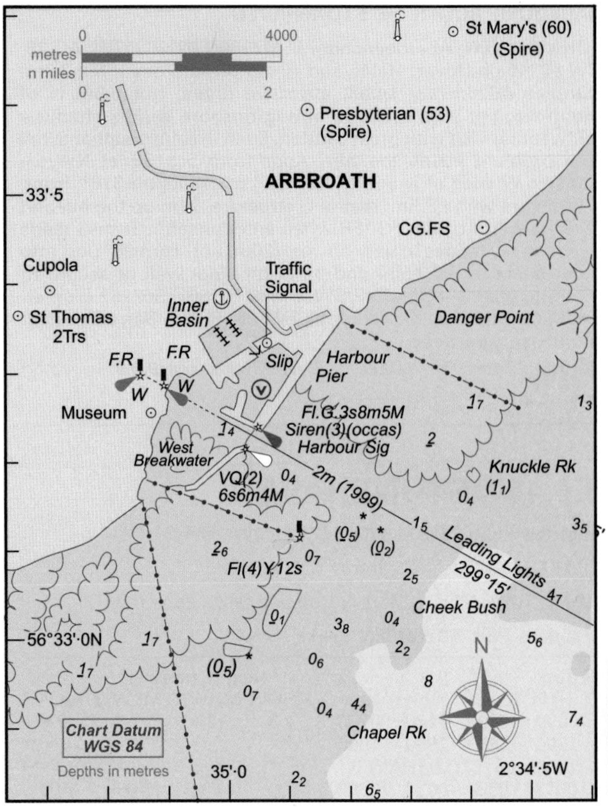
metres
n miles
0
4000
2
St Mary's (60) (Spire)
Presbyterian (53) (Spire)
ARBROATH
33'·5
CG.FS
Cupola
Traffic Signal
St Thomas 2Trs
Inner Basin
Danger Point
F.R
F.R
W
W
Slip
Harbour Pier
Museum
Fl.G.3s8m5M
Siren(3)(occas)
Harbour Sig
West Breakwater
Knuckle Rk
VQ(2) 6s6m4M
2m (1999)
Leading Lights 299°15'
Fl(4)Y.12s
Cheek Bush
56°33'·0N
Chapel Rk
Chart Datum WGS 84
Depths in metres
35'·0
2°34'·5W
N

9.6.14 MONTROSE

Angus **56°42′·19N 02°26′·60W** ❀❀◊◊✿✿

CHARTS AC 190, 1438; Imray C23; OS 54

TIDES +0320 Dover; ML 2·9; Duration 0645; Zone 0 (UT)

Standard Port ABERDEEN (⟶)

Times				Height (metres)			
High Water		Low Water		MHWS	MHWN	MLWN	MLWS
0000	0600	0100	0700	4·3	3·4	1·6	0·6
1200	1800	1300	1900				
Differences MONTROSE							
+0055	+0055	+0030	+0040	+0·5	+0·4	+0·2	0·0

SHELTER Good; yachts are welcome in this busy commercial port. Contact HM for AB, usually available, but beware wash from other traffic. Double mooring lines advised due to strong tidal streams (up to 6kn).

NAVIGATION WPT 56°42′·18N 02°25′·11W, 271° to front ldg lt, 1·25M. Beware Annat Bank to N and Scurdie Rks to S of ent chan. In quiet weather best access is LW to LW+1, but in strong onshore winds only safe access would be from HW –2 to HW. Ent is dangerous with strong onshore winds against ebb tide when heavy overfalls develop.

LIGHTS AND MARKS Scurdie Ness lt ho Fl (3) 20s 38m 23M (conspic). Two sets of ldg lts: Outer 271·5°, both FR 11/18m 5M, front W twin pillars, R bands; rear W tr, R cupola. Inner 265°, both FG 21/33m 5M, Orange △ front and ▽ rear. For position of outer SHM chan buoy (off chartlet), see 9.6.4.

R/T VHF Ch 12 16 (H24).

TELEPHONE (Dial code 01674) HM 672302, 📠 675530; MRSC (01333) 450666; Marinecall 09066 526236; Police 672222; Dr 672554.

FACILITIES **N Quay** ☎ 672302, AB £6.00, D (by tanker via HM), FW, ME, El, C (1½ to 40 ton), CH, Gas. **Town** EC Wed; 🛒, R, P, Bar, ✉, Ⓑ, ⇌, ✈ (Aberdeen).

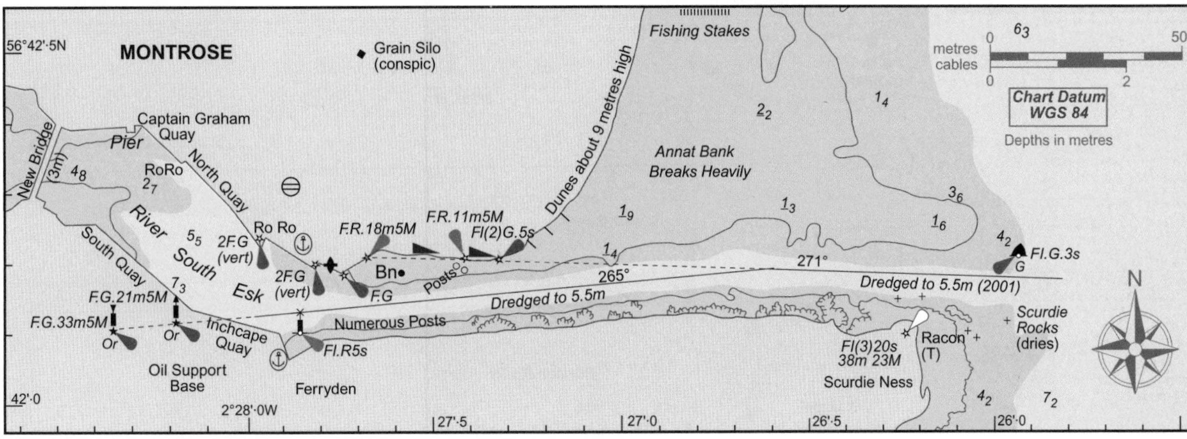
56°42'·5N
MONTROSE
Grain Silo (conspic)
Fishing Stakes
Dunes about 9 metres high
metres
cables
500
Chart Datum WGS 84
Depths in metres
Captain Graham Quay
Pier
New Bridge (3m)
RoRo
North Quay
Annat Bank Breaks Heavily
River South Esk
South Quay
Ro Ro
2F.G (vert)
2F.G (vert)
F.R.18m5M
F.R.11m5M
Fl(2)G.5s
Bn
Posts
265°
271°
Fl.G.3s
G
Dredged to 5.5m (2001)
Dredged to 5.5m
F.G
F.G.21m5M
F.G.33m5M
Or
Or
Inchcape Quay
Numerous Posts
Fl.R5s
Oil Support Base
Ferryden
Fl(3)20s 38m 23M
Racon (T)
Scurdie Ness
Scurdie Rocks (dries)
N
42'·0
2°28'·0W
27'·5
27'·0
26'·5
26'·0

HARBOURS SOUTH OF STONEHAVEN

JOHNSHAVEN, Aberdeenshire, 56°47'·60N 02°20'·07W. AC 28. HW +0245 on Dover; +0045 and +0·4m on Aberdeen; ML 2·7m; Duration 0626. Very small, attractive drying hbr 6·5M N of Montrose. Ent impossible in strong onshore winds; strictly a fair weather visit with great caution. Even in calm weather swell is a problem inside the hbr. Appr from 5ca SE at HW±2½. Conspic W shed at N end of hbr. Ldg marks/lts on 316°: front, R structure with FR 5m; rear is G structure, 20m up the hill and 85m from front, with FG (FR when entry unsafe). Transit leads between rky ledges to very narrow (20m) ent. Turn 90° port into Inner Basin (dries 2·5m) and berth on outer wall or secure to mooring chains, rigged NE/SW. HM ☎ (01561) 362262 (home). Facilities: Slip, AB, ⛽, C (5 ton), FW, 🛒, R, ME, Bar, ✉. Bus to Montrose/Aberdeen.

Berthing Fees: *For details of Rover Ticket see 9.6.5.*

GOURDON, Aberdeenshire, 56°49′·49N 02°17′·21W. AC 28. HW +0240 on Dover; +0035 on Aberdeen; HW +0·4m on Aberdeen; ML 2·7m; Duration 0620. Shelter good in inner W hbr (drys about 2m; protected by storm gates); access from about mid-flood. E (or Gutty) hbr is rky, with difficult access. Beware rky ledges marked by bn and extending 200m S from W pier end. A dangerous rk dries on the ldg line about 1⅓ca S of pier heads. Ldg marks/lts 358°, both FR 5/30m 5M, 2 W trs; front lt shows G when not safe to enter. W pier hd Fl WRG 3s 5m 9/7M, vis G180°-344°, W344°-354° (10°), R354°-180°. E bkwtr hd Q 3m 7M. HM ☎ (01569) 762741 (part-time, same as 9.6.15). Facilities: Slip, FW from standpipe, D, ME, ⛽, M, 🛒, R, Bar. Fish market held Mon-Fri 1130 and 1530. See Rover Ticket, 9.6.5.

Berthing Fees: *For details of Rover Ticket see 9.6.5.*

9.6.15 STONEHAVEN

Aberdeenshire **56°57'·57N 02°12'·02W** ✪✪✪◊✿✿

CHARTS AC 210, 1438; Imray C23; OS 45

TIDES +0235 Dover; ML 2·6; Duration 0620; Zone 0 (UT)

Standard Port ABERDEEN (⟶)

Times				Height (metres)			
High Water		Low Water		MHWS	MHWN	MLWN	MLWS
0000	0600	0100	0700	4·3	3·4	1·6	0·6
1200	1800	1300	1900				
Differences STONEHAVEN							
+0013	+0008	+0013	+0009	+0·2	+0·2	+0·1	0·0

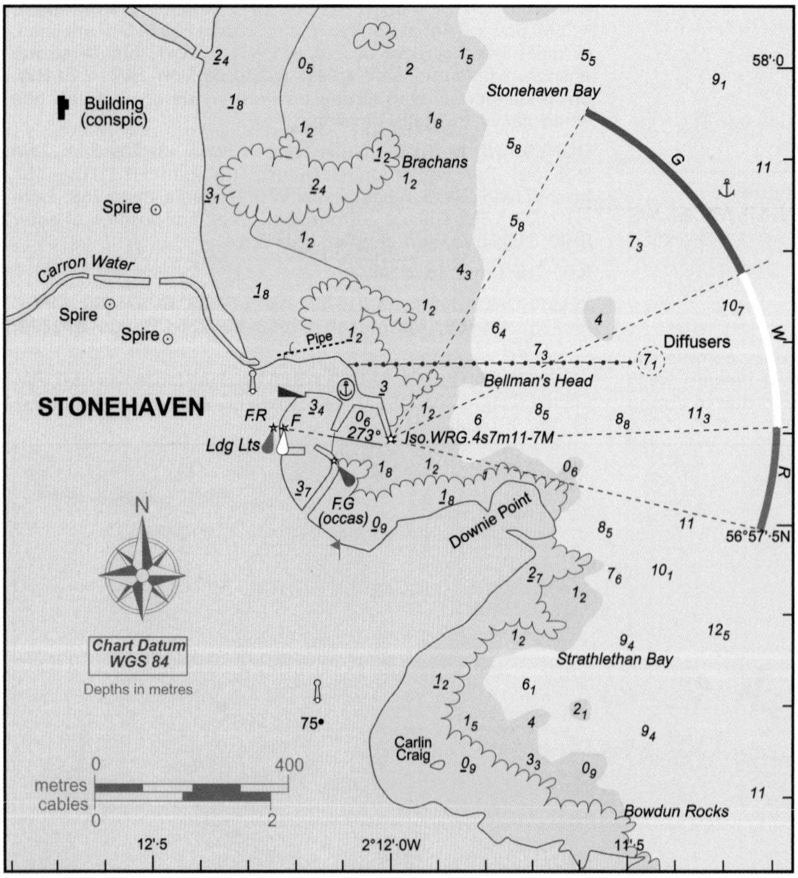
Building (conspic)
Spire
Carron Water
Spire
Spire
STONEHAVEN
FR
F
Ldg Lts
273°
Iso.WRG.4s7m11-7M
FG (occas)
Pipe
Brachans
Stonehaven Bay
Bellman's Head
Diffusers
Downie Point
G
W
R
N
Chart Datum WGS 84
Depths in metres
75•
Strathlethan Bay
Carlin Craig
Bowdun Rocks
0
400
metres
cables
0
2
12'·5
2°12'·0W
11'·5
58'·0
56°57'·5N

SHELTER Good, especially from offshore winds. Berth in outer hbr (1·2 to1·0m) on bkwtr or N wall; sandbank forms in middle to W side. Or ⚓ outside in fair weather. Hbr speed limit 3kn. Inner hbr dries 3·4m and in bad weather is closed, indicated by FG(occas) lt as shown. Do not go S of ldg line, to clear rks close E of inner hbr wall.

NAVIGATION WPT 56°57′·69N 02°11′·11W, 258° to bkwtr lt, 0·50M. Give Downie Pt a wide berth. Do not enter in strong on-shore winds.

LIGHTS AND MARKS N pier Iso WRG 4s 7m 11/7M; appr in W sector, 246°-268°. Inner hbr ldg lts 273°, only apply to inner hbr: front FW 6m 5M; rear FR 8m 5M. FG on SE pier is shown when inner hbr is closed by a boom in bad weather. Conspic monument on hill top to S of hbr.

R/T HM VHF Ch 11.

TELEPHONE (Dial code 01569) HM (part-time) 762741, Mobile 07741050210; MRCC (01224) 592334; Marinecall 09066 526236; Police 762963; Dr 762945; Maritime Rescue International ☎ 764065.

FACILITIES **Hbr** AB £10.00, L, M, FW, ⛽, Slip, ♿, C (1·5 ton), LB, D by tanker, Fri early am; **Aberdeen & Stonehaven SC** Slip, Bar. **Town** EC Wed; P, Gas, 🛒, R, Bar, Ⓗ, ✉, Ⓑ, ≋, ✈ (Aberdeen).

Berthing Fees: *For details of a Rover Ticket see 9.6.5.*

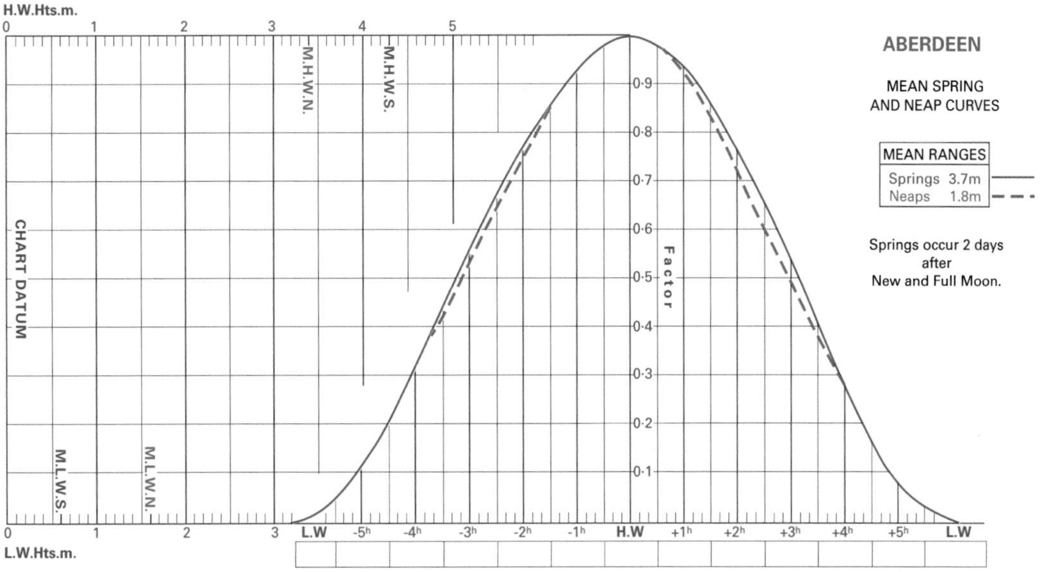
H.W.Hts.m.
M.H.W.N.
M.H.W.S.
CHART DATUM
Factor
M.L.W.S.
M.L.W.N.
L.W.Hts.m.
L.W
-5h
-4h
-3h
-2h
-1h
H.W
+1h
+2h
+3h
+4h
+5h
L.W
ABERDEEN
MEAN SPRING AND NEAP CURVES
MEAN RANGES
Springs 3.7m
Neaps 1.8m
Springs occur 2 days after New and Full Moon.

9.6.16 ABERDEEN

Aberdeenshire **57°08'·70N 02°03'·59W**

CHARTS AC 210, 1446; Imray C23; OS 38

TIDES +0231 Dover; ML 2·5; Duration 0620; Zone 0 (UT)

SHELTER Good in hbr; open at all tides, but do not enter in strong NE/ESE winds. Call HM VHF Ch 12 for berthing details. Yachts are not encouraged in this busy commercial port, but usually lie on N side of Albert Basin alongside floating linkspan. ⚓ in Aberdeen Bay gives some shelter from S and W winds. Peterhead is 25M to N; Stonehaven is 13M S.

NAVIGATION WPT Fairway SWM buoy, Mo (A) 5s, Racon, 57°09'·31N 02°01'·96W, 056°/236° from/to hbr ent 1·05M. Give Girdle Ness a berth of at least ¼M (more in bad weather) and do not pass close round pier hds. Strong tidal streams and, with river in spate, possible overfalls. Chan dredged to 6m on ldg line.

LIGHTS AND MARKS Ldg lts 236° (FR = port open; FG = port closed). Traffic sigs at root of N pier:

● = Entry prohib
● = Dep prohib
● & ● = Port closed

R/T VHF Ch**12** 16 (H24).

TELEPHONE (Dial code 01224) HM 597000, ℻ 571507; MRCC 592334, ℻ 575920; Weather 722334; Marinecall 09066 526236/ 0839 406189; Police 386000.

FACILITIES **Services:** AB £17 for a period of up to 5 days , El, (E), ME, ACA. **City** EC Wed/Sat; all amenities, Train, Airport.

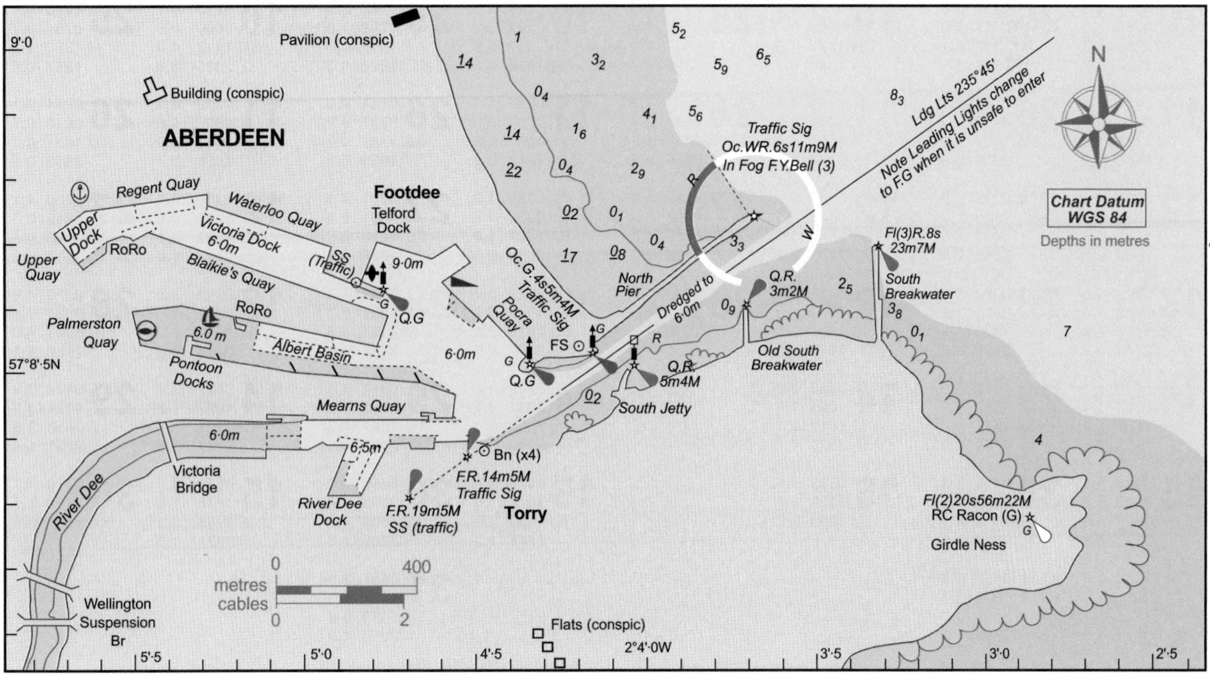
Pavilion (conspic)
Building (conspic)
ABERDEEN
Footdee
Telford Dock
Regent Quay
Waterloo Quay
Upper Dock
Upper Quay
Victoria Dock 6·0m
RoRo
Blaikie's Quay
SS (Traffic)
Palmerston Quay
Albert Basin
Pontoon Docks
Mearns Quay
Victoria Bridge
River Dee
River Dee Dock
Wellington Suspension Br
Oc.G.4s5m4M Traffic Sig
Pocra Quay
Q.G
FS
North Pier
Dredged to 6·0m
Traffic Sig Oc.WR.6s11m9M In Fog F.Y.Bell (3)
Ldg Lts 235°45'
Note Leading Lights change to F.G when it is unsafe to enter
Q.R. 3m2M
Fl(3)R.8s 23m7M
South Breakwater
Old South Breakwater
Q.R. 5m4M
South Jetty
Bn (x4)
F.R.14m5M Traffic Sig
F.R.19m5M SS (traffic)
Torry
Fl(2)20s56m22M RC Racon (G)
Girdle Ness
Flats (conspic)
Chart Datum WGS 84
Depths in metres
metres
cables
9'·0
57°8'·5N
2°4'·0W

TIME ZONE (UT)
For Summer Time add ONE hour in **non-shaded areas**

SCOTLAND – ABERDEEN

LAT 57°09′N LONG 2°05′W

TIMES AND HEIGHTS OF HIGH AND LOW WATERS

SPRING & NEAP TIDES
Dates in red are SPRINGS
Dates in blue are NEAPS

YEAR **2005**

JANUARY

Day	Time	m	Time	m	Time	m	Time	m
1 SA	0446	3.7	1020	1.6	1645	3.9	2303	1.3
2 SU	0531	3.6	1102	1.7	1729	3.8	2350	1.3
3 M ◑	0621	3.5	1153	1.8	1821	3.7		
4 TU	0044	1.4	0716	3.5	1256	1.9	1921	3.6
5 W	0146	1.4	0818	3.5	1407	1.9	2028	3.7
6 TH	0251	1.4	0923	3.6	1518	1.7	2138	3.7
7 F	0356	1.3	1025	3.8	1625	1.5	2246	3.9
8 SA	0458	1.2	1120	3.9	1727	1.3	2346	4.1
9 SU	0555	1.1	1210	4.1	1822	1.0		
10 M	0042	4.3	0646	1.0	1258	4.3	● 1914	0.7
11 TU	0136	4.4	0735	0.9	1345	4.4	2005	0.5
12 W	0228	4.4	0822	0.9	1431	4.5	2054	0.4
13 TH	0319	4.4	0908	1.0	1519	4.5	2144	0.4
14 F	0409	4.3	0953	1.1	1607	4.4	2233	0.6
15 SA	0458	4.1	1039	1.2	1657	4.3	2322	0.8
16 SU	0549	3.8	1127	1.4	1749	4.1		
17 M	0013	1.1	0642	3.6	1221	1.6	◐ 1846	3.9
18 TU	0109	1.3	0741	3.5	1324	1.8	1951	3.6
19 W	0212	1.6	0848	3.4	1438	1.9	2106	3.5
20 TH	0326	1.7	0955	3.4	1601	1.8	2219	3.5
21 F	0435	1.7	1055	3.6	1705	1.7	2321	3.6
22 SA	0526	1.7	1144	3.7	1754	1.5		
23 SU	0012	3.7	0607	1.6	1226	3.8	1834	1.3
24 M	0054	3.8	0644	1.5	1302	4.0	1911	1.1
25 TU	0130	3.9	0717	1.4	1336	4.1	○ 1945	1.0
26 W	0204	3.9	0749	1.3	1407	4.1	2018	0.9
27 TH	0236	3.9	0820	1.2	1438	4.2	2050	0.9
28 F	0308	3.9	0851	1.2	1509	4.2	2122	0.9
29 SA	0341	3.9	0922	1.2	1541	4.1	2156	0.9
30 SU	0415	3.8	0954	1.3	1615	4.1	2230	1.0
31 M	0452	3.7	1029	1.4	1653	4.0	2308	1.1

FEBRUARY

Day	Time	m	Time	m	Time	m	Time	m
1 TU	0534	3.7	1109	1.5	1738	3.8	2355	1.3
2 W ◑	0625	3.5	1202	1.6	1834	3.7		
3 TH	0053	1.4	0727	3.5	1313	1.8	1946	3.6
4 F	0207	1.5	0839	3.5	1439	1.8	2111	3.6
5 SA	0329	1.6	0956	3.6	1608	1.6	2234	3.7
6 SU	0448	1.4	1103	3.8	1721	1.2	2343	4.0
7 M	0549	1.3	1159	4.0	1818	0.9		
8 TU	0040	4.2	0640	1.1	1249	4.3	● 1908	0.5
9 W	0131	4.4	0726	0.9	1334	4.5	1956	0.3
10 TH	0217	4.4	0809	0.8	1417	4.6	2040	0.2
11 F	0301	4.4	0849	0.8	1500	4.6	2123	0.2
12 SA	0343	4.3	0929	0.8	1543	4.5	2205	0.4
13 SU	0425	4.1	1007	1.0	1627	4.4	2245	0.7
14 M	0508	3.8	1048	1.2	1712	4.1	2327	1.1
15 TU	0553	3.6	1133	1.4	1803	3.8		
16 W	0013	1.4	0644	3.4	1230	1.7	◐ 1904	3.5
17 TH	0112	1.8	0748	3.3	1347	1.9	2023	3.3
18 F	0233	2.0	0908	3.2	1532	1.9	2155	3.2
19 SA	0413	2.0	1026	3.3	1650	1.7	2309	3.4
20 SU	0511	1.8	1124	3.5	1739	1.5		
21 M	0000	3.5	0553	1.6	1209	3.7	1818	1.2
22 TU	0039	3.7	0628	1.5	1244	3.9	1852	1.0
23 W	0112	3.8	0700	1.3	1316	4.0	1924	0.9
24 TH	0143	3.9	0730	1.1	1346	4.1	○ 1955	0.7
25 F	0212	4.0	0759	1.0	1415	4.2	2025	0.6
26 SA	0241	4.0	0827	0.9	1445	4.2	2056	0.6
27 SU	0312	4.0	0857	0.9	1516	4.2	2126	0.7
28 M	0343	4.0	0927	1.0	1549	4.2	2158	0.8

MARCH

Day	Time	m	Time	m	Time	m	Time	m
1 TU	0418	3.9	1000	1.1	1626	4.1	2233	1.0
2 W	0457	3.8	1039	1.2	1711	3.9	2317	1.2
3 TH ◑	0545	3.6	1129	1.4	1809	3.7		
4 F	0016	1.5	0648	3.4	1243	1.6	1928	3.5
5 SA	0141	1.7	0809	3.3	1424	1.7	2104	3.4
6 SU	0322	1.7	0937	3.4	1606	1.4	2235	3.6
7 M	0445	1.5	1052	3.7	1717	1.1	2341	3.9
8 TU	0542	1.3	1148	4.0	1810	0.7		
9 W	0032	4.1	0628	1.0	1235	4.2	1856	0.4
10 TH	0116	4.3	0709	0.8	1317	4.5	● 1938	0.2
11 F	0157	4.4	0748	0.6	1357	4.6	2018	0.2
12 SA	0235	4.3	0825	0.6	1437	4.6	2056	0.3
13 SU	0312	4.2	0901	0.7	1516	4.5	2131	0.5
14 M	0349	4.0	0937	0.8	1557	4.3	2206	0.8
15 TU	0426	3.8	1013	1.0	1639	4.0	2241	1.2
16 W	0506	3.6	1054	1.3	1727	3.7	2321	1.5
17 TH ◐	0552	3.4	1145	1.6	1826	3.3		
18 F	0015	1.9	0652	3.2	1301	1.8	1943	3.1
19 SA	0140	2.1	0813	3.1	1454	1.9	2121	3.1
20 SU	0344	2.1	0945	3.2	1624	1.7	2244	3.2
21 M	0448	1.9	1053	3.4	1713	1.4	2335	3.4
22 TU	0530	1.6	1139	3.6	1751	1.2		
23 W	0011	3.6	0603	1.4	1215	3.8	1824	0.9
24 TH	0043	3.8	0633	1.2	1247	3.9	1854	0.8
25 F	0112	3.9	0702	1.0	1317	4.1	○ 1924	0.6
26 SA	0141	4.0	0731	0.9	1347	4.2	1955	0.5
27 SU	0211	4.1	0801	0.8	1418	4.3	2026	0.5
28 M	0241	4.1	0831	0.7	1451	4.3	2057	0.6
29 TU	0314	4.1	0903	0.8	1527	4.2	2130	0.8
30 W	0350	4.0	0939	0.9	1609	4.0	2208	1.0
31 TH	0431	3.8	1022	1.1	1659	3.8	2255	1.3

APRIL

Day	Time	m	Time	m	Time	m	Time	m
1 F	0520	3.6	1119	1.3	1804	3.6		
2 SA	0001	1.6	0627	3.4	1242	1.5	◑ 1930	3.4
3 SU	0137	1.8	0753	3.3	1428	1.5	2107	3.4
4 M	0319	1.8	0923	3.4	1601	1.2	2231	3.6
5 TU	0432	1.5	1036	3.7	1703	0.9	2329	3.9
6 W	0524	1.2	1130	3.9	1752	0.6		
7 TH	0014	4.1	0607	1.0	1214	4.2	1835	0.4
8 F	0054	4.2	0646	0.7	1255	4.4	● 1914	0.3
9 SA	0130	4.2	0724	0.6	1334	4.4	1951	0.3
10 SU	0205	4.2	0800	0.6	1412	4.4	2025	0.5
11 M	0240	4.1	0835	0.6	1451	4.3	2058	0.7
12 TU	0315	4.0	0911	0.8	1532	4.1	2131	1.0
13 W	0350	3.8	0947	1.0	1614	3.8	2204	1.3
14 TH	0427	3.7	1027	1.2	1701	3.5	2242	1.6
15 F	0511	3.5	1116	1.5	1758	3.3	2331	1.9
16 SA ◐	0608	3.3	1224	1.7	1908	3.1		
17 SU	0050	2.1	0721	3.1	1359	1.7	2031	3.1
18 M	0242	2.1	0847	3.1	1533	1.6	2155	3.2
19 TU	0404	1.9	1003	3.3	1630	1.4	2251	3.4
20 W	0450	1.7	1055	3.5	1711	1.1	2330	3.6
21 TH	0526	1.4	1134	3.7	1745	0.9		
22 F	0004	3.7	0558	1.2	1210	3.9	1817	0.7
23 SA	0036	3.9	0629	1.0	1243	4.0	1849	0.6
24 SU	0108	4.0	0701	0.8	1316	4.2	○ 1923	0.5
25 M	0140	4.1	0734	0.7	1352	4.2	1957	0.5
26 TU	0214	4.1	0810	0.7	1431	4.2	2033	0.6
27 W	0250	4.1	0848	0.7	1513	4.1	2112	0.8
28 TH	0329	4.0	0931	0.8	1601	4.0	2156	1.1
29 F	0415	3.8	1022	0.9	1659	3.8	2251	1.4
30 SA	0510	3.7	1128	1.1	1811	3.6		

Chart Datum: 2·25 metres below Ordnance Datum (Newlyn)

TIME ZONE (UT)
For Summer Time add ONE hour in **non-shaded areas**

SCOTLAND – ABERDEEN

LAT 57°09′N LONG 2°05′W

TIMES AND HEIGHTS OF HIGH AND LOW WATERS

SPRING & NEAP TIDES
Dates in red are **SPRINGS**
Dates in blue are **NEAPS**

YEAR **2005**

MAY

Date	Day	Time	m	Time	m	Time	m	Time	m	Moon
1	SU	0003	1.6	0620	3.5	1251	1.2	1932	3.4	◑
2	M	0133	1.8	0741	3.4	1422	1.2	2058	3.5	
3	TU	0258	1.7	0903	3.5	1540	1.0	2211	3.6	
4	W	0405	1.5	1011	3.7	1639	0.8	2305	3.8	
5	TH	0457	1.2	1105	3.9	1728	0.6	2349	3.9	
6	F	0542	1.0	1150	4.1	1810	0.6			
7	SA	0027	4.0	0622	0.8	1232	4.2	1847	0.6	
8	SU	0103	4.1	0700	0.7	1312	4.2	1923	0.6	●
9	M	0138	4.1	0738	0.7	1352	4.1	1957	0.8	
10	TU	0212	4.0	0815	0.7	1432	4.0	2031	0.9	
11	W	0247	4.0	0852	0.8	1513	3.9	2104	1.2	
12	TH	0322	3.8	0930	1.0	1556	3.7	2138	1.4	
13	F	0400	3.7	1010	1.1	1642	3.5	2216	1.6	
14	SA	0442	3.5	1057	1.3	1734	3.3	2303	1.8	
15	SU	0535	3.4	1154	1.5	1833	3.2			
16	M	0005	1.9	0637	3.3	1305	1.5	1937	3.1	◐
17	TU	0129	2.0	0745	3.2	1420	1.5	2046	3.2	
18	W	0248	1.9	0855	3.3	1524	1.4	2150	3.3	
19	TH	0349	1.7	0956	3.4	1615	1.2	2239	3.5	
20	F	0436	1.5	1045	3.6	1658	1.0	2320	3.7	
21	SA	0516	1.3	1128	3.8	1737	0.8	2358	3.8	
22	SU	0554	1.1	1208	3.9	1815	0.7			
23	M	0035	4.0	0632	0.9	1250	4.1	1854	0.7	○
24	TU	0113	4.1	0713	0.7	1332	4.2	1935	0.7	
25	W	0151	4.2	0756	0.6	1418	4.2	2018	0.8	
26	TH	0233	4.1	0842	0.6	1508	4.1	2104	0.9	
27	F	0317	4.1	0932	0.7	1603	4.0	2154	1.1	
28	SA	0408	4.0	1029	0.7	1704	3.8	2251	1.3	
29	SU	0506	3.8	1133	0.8	1810	3.7	2358	1.5	
30	M	0612	3.7	1244	0.9	1919	3.6			◑
31	TU	0110	1.6	0721	3.7	1357	1.0	2030	3.5	

JUNE

Date	Day	Time	m	Time	m	Time	m	Time	m	Moon
1	W	0222	1.6	0832	3.7	1506	1.0	2137	3.6	
2	TH	0328	1.5	0940	3.7	1607	0.9	2233	3.7	
3	F	0426	1.3	1038	3.8	1659	0.9	2320	3.8	
4	SA	0516	1.2	1128	3.9	1744	0.9			
5	SU	0002	3.8	0601	1.0	1214	3.9	1823	0.9	
6	M	0040	3.9	0643	0.9	1257	3.9	1900	1.0	●
7	TU	0117	4.0	0723	0.9	1339	3.9	1936	1.1	
8	W	0152	4.0	0801	0.9	1420	3.8	2011	1.2	
9	TH	0228	3.9	0839	0.9	1500	3.8	2045	1.3	
10	F	0303	3.9	0916	1.0	1541	3.7	2120	1.4	
11	SA	0340	3.8	0955	1.0	1623	3.6	2157	1.5	
12	SU	0420	3.7	1036	1.1	1707	3.4	2238	1.6	
13	M	0505	3.6	1123	1.2	1755	3.3	2325	1.7	
14	TU	0556	3.5	1215	1.3	1848	3.3			
15	W	0023	1.8	0651	3.4	1314	1.4	1943	3.3	◐
16	TH	0131	1.8	0750	3.4	1414	1.3	2043	3.3	
17	F	0237	1.7	0851	3.4	1512	1.3	2142	3.4	
18	SA	0337	1.6	0952	3.5	1607	1.2	2235	3.6	
19	SU	0432	1.4	1048	3.7	1658	1.0	2323	3.8	
20	M	0523	1.2	1140	3.9	1747	0.9			
21	TU	0007	3.9	0611	1.0	1231	4.0	1835	0.9	
22	W	0051	4.1	0700	0.8	1321	4.2	1923	0.8	○
23	TH	0136	4.2	0749	0.6	1413	4.2	2011	0.8	
24	F	0221	4.2	0840	0.5	1506	4.2	2059	0.9	
25	SA	0309	4.2	0932	0.4	1600	4.1	2149	1.0	
26	SU	0400	4.2	1026	0.5	1656	4.0	2241	1.2	
27	M	0454	4.1	1122	0.6	1752	3.8	2336	1.3	
28	TU	0552	4.0	1220	0.7	1850	3.7			◑
29	W	0035	1.4	0652	3.9	1321	0.9	1951	3.5	
30	TH	0138	1.5	0757	3.7	1424	1.1	2056	3.5	

JULY

Date	Day	Time	m	Time	m	Time	m	Time	m	Moon
1	F	0245	1.5	0906	3.6	1530	1.2	2158	3.5	
2	SA	0354	1.5	1012	3.6	1631	1.3	2253	3.6	
3	SU	0456	1.4	1112	3.6	1722	1.3	2341	3.7	
4	M	0547	1.2	1204	3.7	1806	1.3			
5	TU	0024	3.8	0632	1.1	1250	3.7	1845	1.3	
6	W	0103	3.9	0712	1.0	1332	3.8	1921	1.3	●
7	TH	0139	3.9	0750	0.9	1410	3.8	1956	1.2	
8	F	0213	4.0	0826	0.9	1447	3.8	2029	1.2	
9	SA	0247	4.0	0901	0.9	1522	3.8	2102	1.3	
10	SU	0321	3.9	0935	0.9	1558	3.7	2135	1.3	
11	M	0356	3.9	1011	0.9	1635	3.6	2210	1.4	
12	TU	0434	3.8	1049	1.0	1715	3.5	2248	1.5	
13	W	0515	3.7	1130	1.1	1759	3.5	2332	1.6	
14	TH	0600	3.6	1217	1.3	1849	3.4			◐
15	F	0025	1.7	0654	3.5	1313	1.3	1945	3.4	
16	SA	0131	1.7	0756	3.5	1416	1.4	2049	3.4	
17	SU	0244	1.7	0906	3.5	1523	1.4	2154	3.5	
18	M	0356	1.6	1019	3.6	1630	1.3	2254	3.7	
19	TU	0502	1.3	1124	3.8	1731	1.2	2347	3.9	
20	W	0600	1.0	1222	4.0	1825	1.0			
21	TH	0036	4.1	0653	0.7	1316	4.2	1914	0.9	○
22	F	0124	4.3	0743	0.4	1407	4.3	2001	0.8	
23	SA	0210	4.4	0832	0.2	1457	4.4	2047	0.8	
24	SU	0256	4.5	0921	0.2	1545	4.3	2132	0.8	
25	M	0344	4.5	1009	0.3	1633	4.1	2217	1.0	
26	TU	0432	4.4	1057	0.5	1722	3.9	2303	1.1	
27	W	0523	4.2	1146	0.8	1813	3.7	2354	1.3	
28	TH	0618	3.9	1238	1.1	1908	3.5			◑
29	F	0053	1.5	0719	3.7	1337	1.4	2011	3.4	
30	SA	0204	1.7	0833	3.5	1449	1.6	2121	3.4	
31	SU	0329	1.7	0952	3.4	1608	1.7	2228	3.5	

AUGUST

Date	Day	Time	m	Time	m	Time	m	Time	m	Moon
1	M	0444	1.5	1103	3.5	1708	1.6	2324	3.6	
2	TU	0539	1.4	1159	3.6	1754	1.6			
3	W	0010	3.8	0622	1.2	1244	3.7	1832	1.4	
4	TH	0049	3.9	0700	1.0	1321	3.8	1907	1.3	
5	F	0124	4.0	0734	0.9	1354	3.8	1939	1.2	●
6	SA	0155	4.1	0807	0.8	1426	3.9	2009	1.1	
7	SU	0226	4.1	0838	0.7	1457	3.9	2039	1.1	
8	M	0257	4.1	0909	0.7	1528	3.9	2109	1.1	
9	TU	0328	4.1	0941	0.8	1600	3.8	2140	1.2	
10	W	0401	4.0	1013	0.9	1635	3.7	2212	1.3	
11	TH	0437	3.9	1048	1.0	1714	3.7	2250	1.4	
12	F	0518	3.8	1129	1.2	1759	3.5	2336	1.6	
13	SA	0609	3.6	1221	1.4	1856	3.5			◐
14	SU	0041	1.7	0716	3.5	1331	1.6	2005	3.4	
15	M	0206	1.8	0839	3.5	1455	1.6	2122	3.5	
16	TU	0337	1.6	1005	3.6	1618	1.5	2234	3.6	
17	W	0455	1.3	1118	3.8	1724	1.3	2333	3.9	
18	TH	0554	0.9	1216	4.1	1816	1.1			
19	F	0023	4.2	0644	0.5	1307	4.3	1902	0.9	○
20	SA	0109	4.4	0731	0.2	1353	4.4	1945	0.7	
21	SU	0153	4.6	0816	0.1	1437	4.5	2027	0.7	
22	M	0236	4.7	0859	0.1	1519	4.4	2107	0.7	
23	TU	0319	4.6	0941	0.3	1602	4.2	2147	0.8	
24	W	0404	4.5	1023	0.6	1645	4.0	2228	1.0	
25	TH	0451	4.2	1105	0.9	1730	3.7	2314	1.3	
26	F	0543	3.9	1152	1.3	1822	3.5			◑
27	SA	0011	1.6	0644	3.6	1249	1.7	1925	3.4	
28	SU	0126	1.8	0802	3.3	1407	2.0	2042	3.3	
29	M	0311	1.8	0935	3.3	1551	2.0	2202	3.4	
30	TU	0434	1.6	1054	3.4	1655	1.9	2305	3.6	
31	W	0525	1.4	1147	3.6	1739	1.7	2351	3.8	

Chart Datum: 2·25 metres below Ordnance Datum (Newlyn)

TIME ZONE (UT)
For Summer Time add ONE hour in **non-shaded areas**

SCOTLAND – ABERDEEN

LAT 57°09′N LONG 2°05′W

TIMES AND HEIGHTS OF HIGH AND LOW WATERS

SPRING & NEAP TIDES
Dates in red are SPRINGS
Dates in blue are NEAPS

YEAR **2005**

SEPTEMBER

Date	Day	Time	m
1		0605	1.2
		1226	3.7
	TH	1814	1.5
2		0028	3.9
		0639	1.0
	F	1259	3.8
		1846	1.3
3		0100	4.1
		0710	0.8
	SA	1329	3.9
	●	1915	1.2
4		0130	4.2
		0740	0.7
	SU	1357	4.0
		1944	1.0
5		0159	4.2
		0809	0.7
	M	1426	4.0
		2012	1.0
6		0228	4.3
		0838	0.7
	TU	1455	4.0
		2040	1.0
7		0258	4.2
		0907	0.7
	W	1525	4.0
		2109	1.0
8		0331	4.2
		0938	0.9
	TH	1558	3.9
		2141	1.1
9		0406	4.0
		1010	1.0
	F	1635	3.8
		2217	1.3
10		0449	3.9
		1050	1.3
	SA	1720	3.7
		2304	1.5
11		0543	3.7
		1143	1.6
	SU	1818	3.5
	◐		
12		0012	1.7
		0658	3.5
	M	1304	1.8
		1936	3.4
13		0150	1.8
		0830	3.4
	TU	1445	1.9
		2102	3.5
14		0334	1.6
		1004	3.6
	W	1614	1.7
		2220	3.7
15		0448	1.2
		1113	3.9
	TH	1714	1.4
		2319	4.0
16		0542	0.8
		1205	4.2
	F	1801	1.1
17		0006	4.3
		0628	0.4
	SA	1250	4.4
		1843	0.9
18		0049	4.5
		0711	0.2
	SU	1331	4.5
	○	1923	0.7
19		0130	4.7
		0752	0.1
	M	1410	4.5
		2001	0.6
20		0211	4.7
		0831	0.2
	TU	1448	4.4
		2039	0.7
21		0252	4.6
		0909	0.4
	W	1526	4.2
		2117	0.8
22		0335	4.4
		0946	0.8
	TH	1606	4.0
		2157	1.0
23		0421	4.1
		1024	1.2
	F	1648	3.8
		2240	1.3
24		0512	3.8
		1105	1.6
	SA	1736	3.6
		2334	1.6
25		0614	3.5
		1200	1.9
	SU	1839	3.4
	◑		
26		0051	1.8
		0732	3.2
	M	1324	2.2
		1958	3.3
27		0243	1.9
		0908	3.2
	TU	1524	2.2
		2126	3.4
28		0410	1.7
		1030	3.4
	W	1631	2.0
		2234	3.5
29		0458	1.4
		1120	3.6
	TH	1713	1.8
		2321	3.7
30		0536	1.2
		1157	3.7
	F	1747	1.5
		2357	3.9

OCTOBER

Date	Day	Time	m
1		0609	1.0
		1227	3.9
	SA	1817	1.3
2		0029	4.1
		0639	0.9
	SU	1256	4.0
		1846	1.2
3		0059	4.2
		0708	0.7
	M	1324	4.1
	●	1914	1.0
4		0129	4.3
		0736	0.7
	TU	1353	4.2
		1943	1.0
5		0159	4.3
		0806	0.7
	W	1422	4.2
		2012	0.9
6		0231	4.3
		0836	0.8
	TH	1454	4.2
		2044	1.0
7		0306	4.2
		0907	0.9
	F	1528	4.1
		2118	1.1
8		0346	4.1
		0942	1.1
	SA	1606	3.9
		2158	1.2
9		0433	3.9
		1025	1.4
	SU	1653	3.8
		2252	1.4
10		0534	3.7
		1126	1.7
	M	1755	3.6
	◐		
11		0008	1.6
		0656	3.5
	TU	1256	2.0
		1918	3.5
12		0150	1.6
		0829	3.5
	W	1439	1.9
		2045	3.6
13		0325	1.4
		0956	3.7
	TH	1558	1.7
		2201	3.8
14		0432	1.0
		1058	4.0
	F	1654	1.4
		2258	4.1
15		0523	0.7
		1145	4.2
	SA	1739	1.1
		2344	4.3
16		0607	0.5
		1226	4.3
	SU	1820	0.9
17		0026	4.5
		0647	0.4
	M	1304	4.4
	○	1858	0.8
18		0107	4.6
		0725	0.4
	TU	1341	4.4
		1936	0.7
19		0147	4.6
		0802	0.5
	W	1417	4.4
		2014	0.7
20		0229	4.5
		0838	0.8
	TH	1454	4.2
		2053	0.9
21		0312	4.3
		0913	1.1
	F	1531	4.1
		2132	1.1
22		0357	4.0
		0948	1.4
	SA	1611	3.9
		2215	1.3
23		0448	3.7
		1027	1.7
	SU	1656	3.7
		2307	1.6
24		0547	3.4
		1117	2.0
	M	1755	3.5
25		0016	1.8
		0657	3.3
	TU	1234	2.2
	◑	1908	3.4
26		0148	1.8
		0818	3.2
	W	1420	2.3
		2030	3.4
27		0318	1.7
		0940	3.3
	TH	1543	2.1
		2144	3.5
28		0415	1.5
		1035	3.5
	F	1632	1.9
		2237	3.7
29		0455	1.3
		1115	3.7
	SA	1709	1.6
		2317	3.9
30		0530	1.1
		1148	3.9
	SU	1742	1.4
		2352	4.0
31		0602	1.0
		1219	4.0
	M	1813	1.2

NOVEMBER

Date	Day	Time	m
1		0025	4.2
		0632	0.9
	TU	1250	4.2
		1844	1.1
2		0059	4.3
		0704	0.8
	W	1321	4.2
	●	1916	1.0
3		0133	4.3
		0736	0.8
	TH	1354	4.3
		1950	0.9
4		0210	4.3
		0810	0.9
	F	1428	4.3
		2027	1.0
5		0250	4.2
		0847	1.1
	SA	1506	4.2
		2108	1.0
6		0336	4.1
		0929	1.3
	SU	1548	4.1
		2156	1.2
7		0430	3.9
		1019	1.5
	M	1639	3.9
		2256	1.3
8		0537	3.7
		1124	1.8
	TU	1744	3.7
9		0013	1.4
		0654	3.6
	W	1249	1.9
	◐	1902	3.7
10		0140	1.4
		0816	3.6
	TH	1415	1.9
		2021	3.7
11		0300	1.2
		0933	3.8
	F	1527	1.7
		2133	3.9
12		0405	1.0
		1032	3.9
	SA	1624	1.5
		2232	4.1
13		0457	0.9
		1119	4.1
	SU	1713	1.3
		2321	4.3
14		0542	0.7
		1201	4.2
	M	1756	1.1
15		0005	4.4
		0622	0.7
	TU	1239	4.3
		1837	0.9
16		0048	4.4
		0701	0.8
	W	1316	4.3
	○	1917	0.9
17		0130	4.4
		0737	0.9
	TH	1352	4.3
		1957	0.9
18		0212	4.3
		0813	1.1
	F	1428	4.2
		2036	1.0
19		0256	4.1
		0848	1.3
	SA	1505	4.1
		2116	1.1
20		0340	3.9
		0924	1.5
	SU	1544	4.0
		2158	1.3
21		0428	3.7
		1002	1.7
	M	1627	3.8
		2245	1.4
22		0520	3.5
		1046	1.9
	TU	1718	3.6
		2340	1.6
23		0617	3.4
		1143	2.1
	W	1819	3.5
	◑		
24		0046	1.7
		0718	3.3
	TH	1301	2.2
		1924	3.4
25		0159	1.7
		0826	3.3
	F	1421	2.1
		2033	3.5
26		0305	1.6
		0930	3.4
	SA	1528	2.0
		2136	3.6
27		0358	1.5
		1022	3.6
	SU	1618	1.8
		2228	3.7
28		0442	1.3
		1104	3.8
	M	1700	1.6
		2312	3.9
29		0521	1.2
		1142	3.9
	TU	1739	1.4
		2352	4.0
30		0558	1.1
		1218	4.1
	W	1816	1.2

DECEMBER

Date	Day	Time	m
1		0032	4.2
		0635	1.0
	TH	1254	4.2
	●	1855	1.1
2		0114	4.3
		0714	1.0
	F	1331	4.3
		1936	0.9
3		0157	4.3
		0755	1.0
	SA	1410	4.3
		2020	0.9
4		0244	4.3
		0839	1.1
	SU	1452	4.3
		2108	0.9
5		0335	4.2
		0926	1.3
	M	1539	4.2
		2200	0.9
6		0431	4.0
		1018	1.5
	TU	1632	4.1
		2258	1.0
7		0533	3.9
		1117	1.6
	W	1732	4.0
8		0004	1.1
		0638	3.7
	TH	1225	1.7
	◐	1839	3.9
9		0114	1.2
		0747	3.7
	F	1336	1.8
		1948	3.9
10		0223	1.2
		0856	3.7
	SA	1445	1.7
		2058	3.9
11		0329	1.2
		0958	3.8
	SU	1550	1.6
		2203	4.0
12		0428	1.1
		1051	3.9
	M	1647	1.4
		2300	4.0
13		0518	1.1
		1138	4.0
	TU	1738	1.3
		2350	4.1
14		0603	1.1
		1219	4.1
	W	1824	1.1
15		0037	4.1
		0643	1.2
	TH	1259	4.2
	○	1906	1.1
16		0122	4.1
		0720	1.2
	F	1336	4.2
		1947	1.0
17		0204	4.1
		0756	1.3
	SA	1412	4.2
		2026	1.0
18		0246	4.0
		0832	1.4
	SU	1449	4.1
		2104	1.1
19		0326	3.9
		0906	1.5
	M	1525	4.1
		2142	1.1
20		0407	3.8
		0941	1.6
	TU	1603	4.0
		2221	1.2
21		0449	3.6
		1019	1.7
	W	1645	3.8
		2304	1.3
22		0534	3.5
		1101	1.8
	TH	1732	3.7
		2352	1.5
23		0623	3.4
		1151	1.9
	F	1824	3.6
	◑		
24		0046	1.6
		0717	3.4
	SA	1254	2.0
		1922	3.5
25		0147	1.6
		0816	3.4
	SU	1404	2.0
		2024	3.5
26		0247	1.6
		0918	3.5
	M	1512	1.9
		2129	3.6
27		0346	1.5
		1016	3.6
	TU	1613	1.8
		2230	3.7
28		0440	1.4
		1105	3.8
	W	1707	1.6
		2324	3.9
29		0530	1.3
		1150	4.0
	TH	1755	1.3
30		0014	4.0
		0616	1.2
	F	1234	4.1
		1842	1.1
31		0103	4.2
		0702	1.1
	SA	1316	4.3
	●	1929	0.8

Chart Datum: 2·25 metres below Ordnance Datum (Newlyn)

9.6.17 PETERHEAD

Aberdeenshire **57°29'·81N 01°46'·42W** ❁❁❁⚓⚓✿✿

CHARTS AC 213, 1438; Imray C23; OS 30

TIDES +0140 Dover; ML 2·3; Duration 0620; Zone 0 (UT)

Standard Port ABERDEEN (⟵⟶)

Times				Height (metres)			
High Water		Low Water		MHWS	MHWN	MLWN	MLWS
0000	0600	0100	0700	4·3	3·4	1·6	0·6
1200	1800	1300	1900				
Differences PETERHEAD							
−0035	−0045	−0035	−0040	−0·5	−0·3	−0·1	−0·1

SHELTER Good in marina (2·8m). A useful passage hbr, also a major fishing and oil/gas industry port. Access any weather/tide.

NAVIGATION WPT 57°29'·44N 01°45'·75W, 314° to ent, 0·5M. No dangers. 5kn speed limit in Bay; 4kn in marina. Chan between marina bkwtr and SHM lt buoy is <30m wide.

LIGHTS AND MARKS Power stn chy (183m) is conspic 1·25M S of ent, with Fl W lts H24. Ldg marks 314°, front △, rear ▽ on cols; lts as chartlet. Marina E bkwtr ☆ Fl R 4s 6m 2M; W bkwtr hd, QG 5m 2M, vis 185°-300°. Buchan Ness ☆ Fl 5s 40m 28M is 1·6M S of entr.

R/T All vessels, including yachts, **must** call *Peterhead Harbour Radio* VHF Ch **14** for clearance to enter/depart the Bay.

TELEPHONE (Dial code 01779) Marina Mr (Bay Authority: www.peterhead-bay.co.uk) 474020, ℻ 475712; Hr Control (H24) 483630; MRCC (01224) 592334; Marinecall 09066 526236; Police 472571; Dr 474841; Ⓗ 472316.

FACILITIES Peterhead Bay Marina ☎ via 474020 (HO)/℻ 475712, ☎ 483630 (after hrs), 150 AB £10 for 6m LOA, £1 per m thereafter (7 days for price of 5), max LOA 20m; access all tides, 2·3m at ent. Pontoons are 'E' to 'A' from ent. Gas, CH; D from bowser at end of Princess Royal jetty (☆ Oc WRG 4s); R, 🛒 and ⊡ at caravan site. **Peterhead SC** ☎ (01358) 751340 (Sec); **Services:** Slip, ME, El, Ⓔ, ⚒, C, Gas. **Town** EC Wed; P, 🛒, R, ✉, bus to Aberdeen for ⇌ & ✈Ⓨ.

ADJACENT HARBOUR

BODDAM, Aberdeenshire, **57°28'·47N 01°46'·56W**. AC 213. HW +0145 on Dover; Tides as 9.6.17. Good shelter in the lee of Meikle Mackie, the island just N of Buchan Ness, Fl 5s 40m 28M Horn (3) 60s. Inner hbr dries/unlit. Beware rks around Meikle Mackie and to the SW of it. Appr from 1½ca NW of The Skerry. Yachts on S side of outer hbr. All facilities at Peterhead, 2M N.

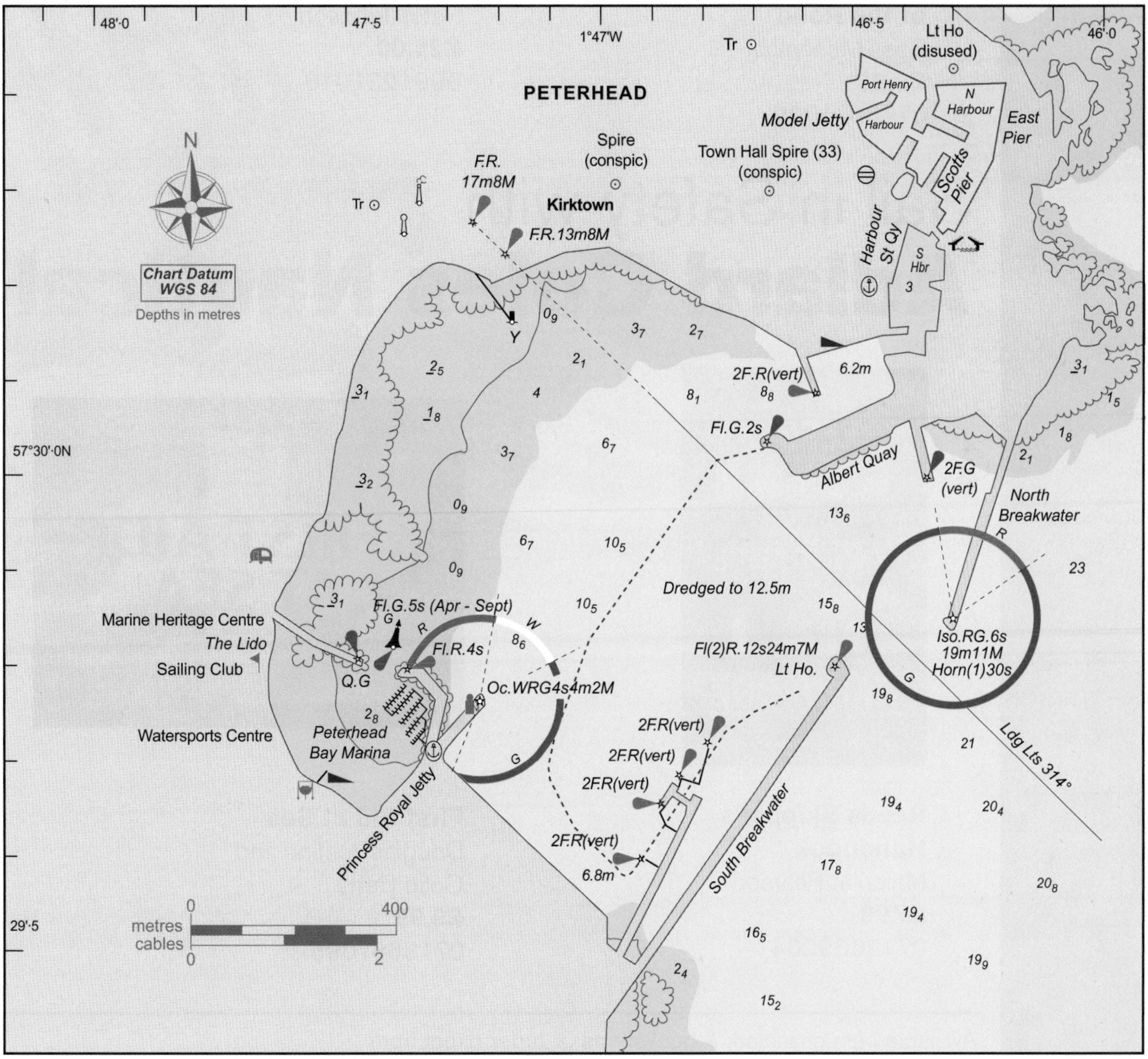
48'·0
47'·5
1°47'W
46'·5
46'·0
57°30'·0N
29'·5
PETERHEAD
Lt Ho (disused)
Tr
Port Henry
Harbour
N Harbour
East Pier
Model Jetty
Spire (conspic)
Town Hall Spire (33) (conspic)
Scotts Pier
Harbour St Qy
S Hbr
F.R. 17m8M
F.R.13m8M
Kirktown
N
Chart Datum WGS 84
Depths in metres
2F.R(vert)
6.2m
Fl.G.2s
Albert Quay
2F.G (vert)
North Breakwater
Dredged to 12.5m
Marine Heritage Centre
The Lido
Sailing Club
Fl.G.5s (Apr - Sept)
Fl.R.4s
Q.G
Oc.WRG4s4m2M
Fl(2)R.12s24m7M
Lt Ho.
Iso.RG.6s 19m11M Horn(1)30s
Watersports Centre
Peterhead Bay Marina
Princess Royal Jetty
2F.R(vert)
6.8m
South Breakwater
Ldg Lts 314°
metres 0 400
cables 0 2

LEARNING
THE RULE OF THE
ROAD
BASIL MOSENTHAL
A GUIDE FOR THE SKIPPERS AND CREWS OF SMALL CRAFT
LIGHTS · SHAPES · SOUND SIGNALS & COLLISION AVOIDANCE

Learning the Rule of the Road
Basil Mosenthal
£9.99
0713671009

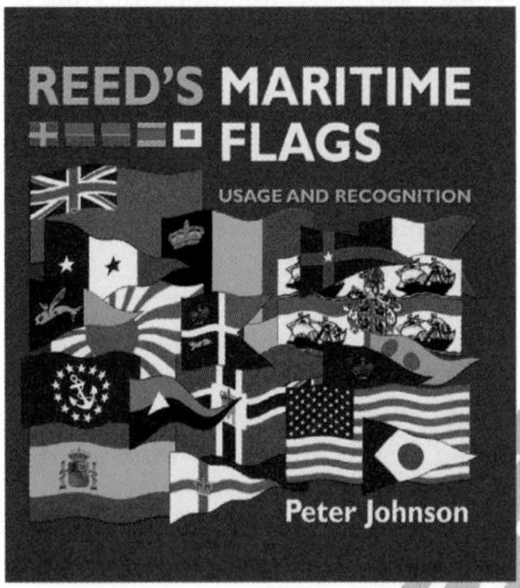
REED'S MARITIME FLAGS
USAGE AND RECOGNITION
Peter Johnson

Reeds Maritime Flags
Peter Johnson
£25.00
0901281018

Sail in Safety with **Adlard Coles Nautical**

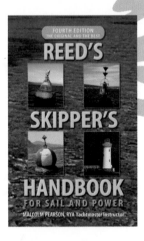

FOURTH EDITION
THE ORIGINAL AND THE BEST
REED'S
SKIPPER'S
HANDBOOK
FOR SAIL AND POWER
MALCOLM PEARSON, RYA Yachtmaster Instructor

Reeds Skipper's Handbook
Malcolm Pearson
£7.99
0713669004

RECOMMENDED BY THE RORC
FIRST AID AT SEA
4th edition
DOUGLAS JUSTINS & COLIN BERRY

First Aid at Sea
Douglas Justins and Colin Berry
£9.99
0713667095

TO ORDER

Available from chandlers & bookshops or order direct from:
MDL, Houndmills, Basingstoke RG21 6XS
Tel: **01256 302692** email: **mdl@macmillan.co.uk** or **www.adlardcoles.com**

Area 7

North-East Scotland
Rattray Head to Cape Wrath
including Orkney and Shetland Islands

DISTANCE TABLE

Approximate distances in nautical miles are by the most direct route, whilst avoiding dangers and allowing for Traffic Separation Schemes. Places in *italics* are in adjoining areas; places in **bold** are in 9.0.8, Distances across the North Sea

1.	*Peterhead*	**1**																			
2.	Fraserburgh	16	**2**																		
3.	Banff/Macduff	33	18	**3**																	
4.	Buckie	46	31	15	**4**																
5.	Lossiemouth	56	41	25	11	**5**															
6.	Findhorn	69	54	38	24	13	**6**														
7.	Nairn	79	64	48	34	23	10	**7**													
8.	Inverness	90	75	59	45	34	23	13	**8**												
9.	Tarbat Ness	72	57	41	27	18	14	17	27	**9**											
10.	Helmsdale	74	59	44	33	26	28	32	43	16	**10**										
11.	Wick	72	57	50	46	44	51	58	69	42	29	**11**									
12.	Duncansby Head	82	67	62	58	57	64	71	81	54	41	13	**12**								
13.	Scrabster	100	85	80	76	75	82	89	99	72	59	31	18	**13**							
14.	Kirkwall	115	100	95	91	90	97	104	114	87	74	46	34	50	**14**						
15.	Stromness	104	89	84	80	79	85	92	103	76	63	35	22	25	32	**15**					
16.	Fair Isle	122	111	116	118	120	130	137	148	121	108	79	68	85	55	77	**16**				
17.	Lerwick	160	150	156	160	162	172	170	190	162	148	120	109	124	95	110	42	**17**			
18.	Loch Eriboll (ent)	137	122	117	113	112	119	126	136	109	96	68	55	37	80	50	110	150	**18**		
19.	Cape Wrath	145	130	125	121	120	127	126	144	117	104	76	63	47	79	58	120	155	13	**19**	
20.	*Ullapool*	198	183	178	174	173	180	179	197	170	157	129	116	100	132	111	173	208	66	53	**20**

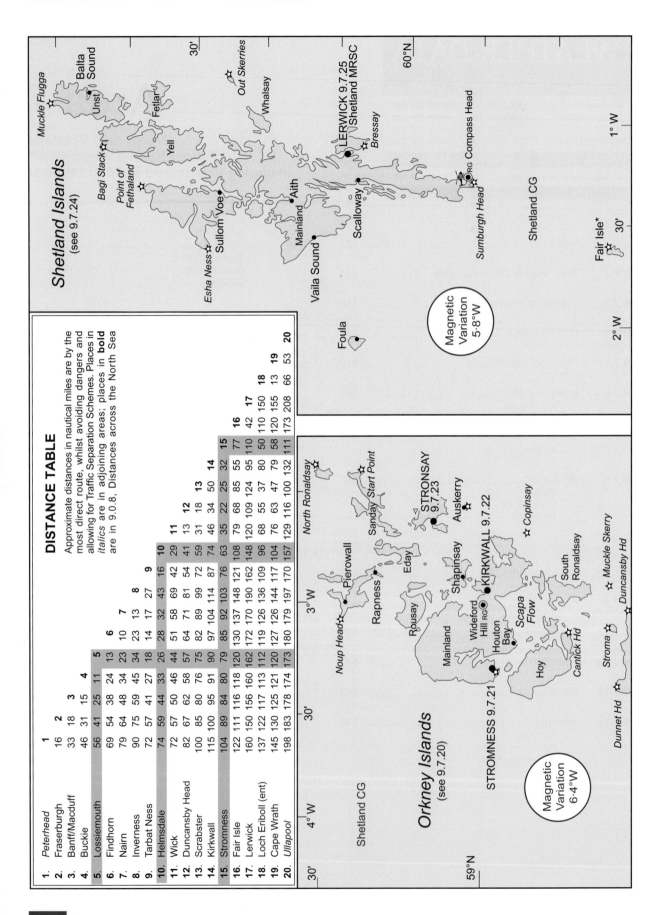

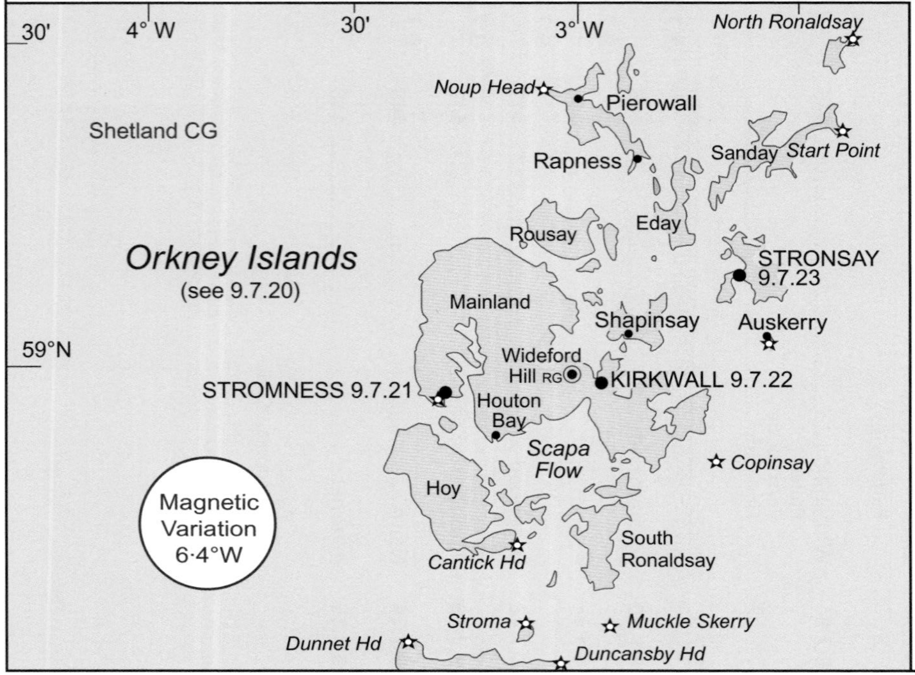

30'
4° W
30'
3° W
59°N
Orkney Islands
(see 9.7.20)
Shetland CG
North Ronaldsay
Noup Head
Pierowall
Rapness
Sanday
Start Point
Eday
Rousay
STRONSAY
9.7.23
Mainland
Shapinsay
Auskerry
Wideford
Hill RG
KIRKWALL 9.7.22
STROMNESS 9.7.21
Houton
Bay
Scapa
Flow
Copinsay
Hoy
Cantick Hd
South
Ronaldsay
Magnetic
Variation
6·4°W
Stroma
Muckle Skerry
Dunnet Hd
Duncansby Hd

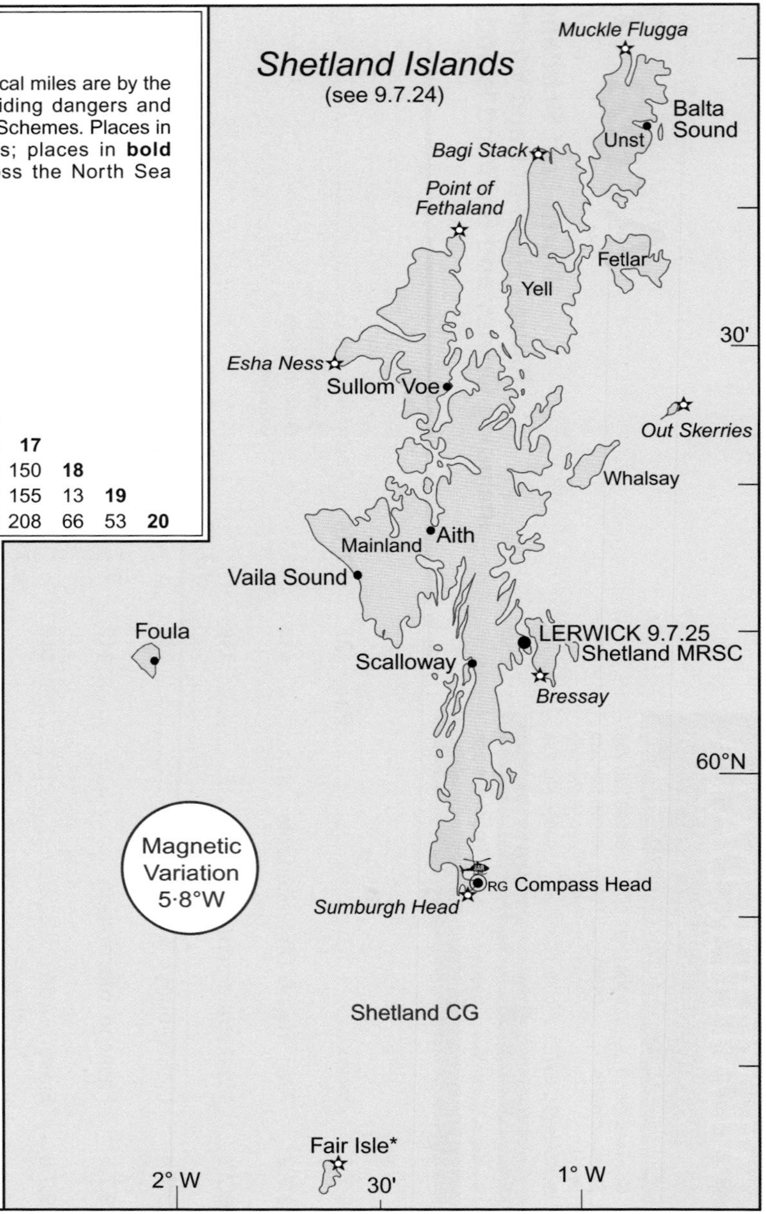

Shetland Islands
(see 9.7.24)
Muckle Flugga
Balta
Sound
Unst
Bagi Stack
Point of
Fethaland
Fetlar
Yell
30'
Esha Ness
Sullom Voe
Out Skerries
Whalsay
Mainland
Aith
Vaila Sound
Foula
LERWICK 9.7.25
Shetland MRSC
Scalloway
Bressay
60°N
Magnetic
Variation
5·8°W
RG Compass Head
Sumburgh Head
Shetland CG
Fair Isle*
2° W
30'
1° W

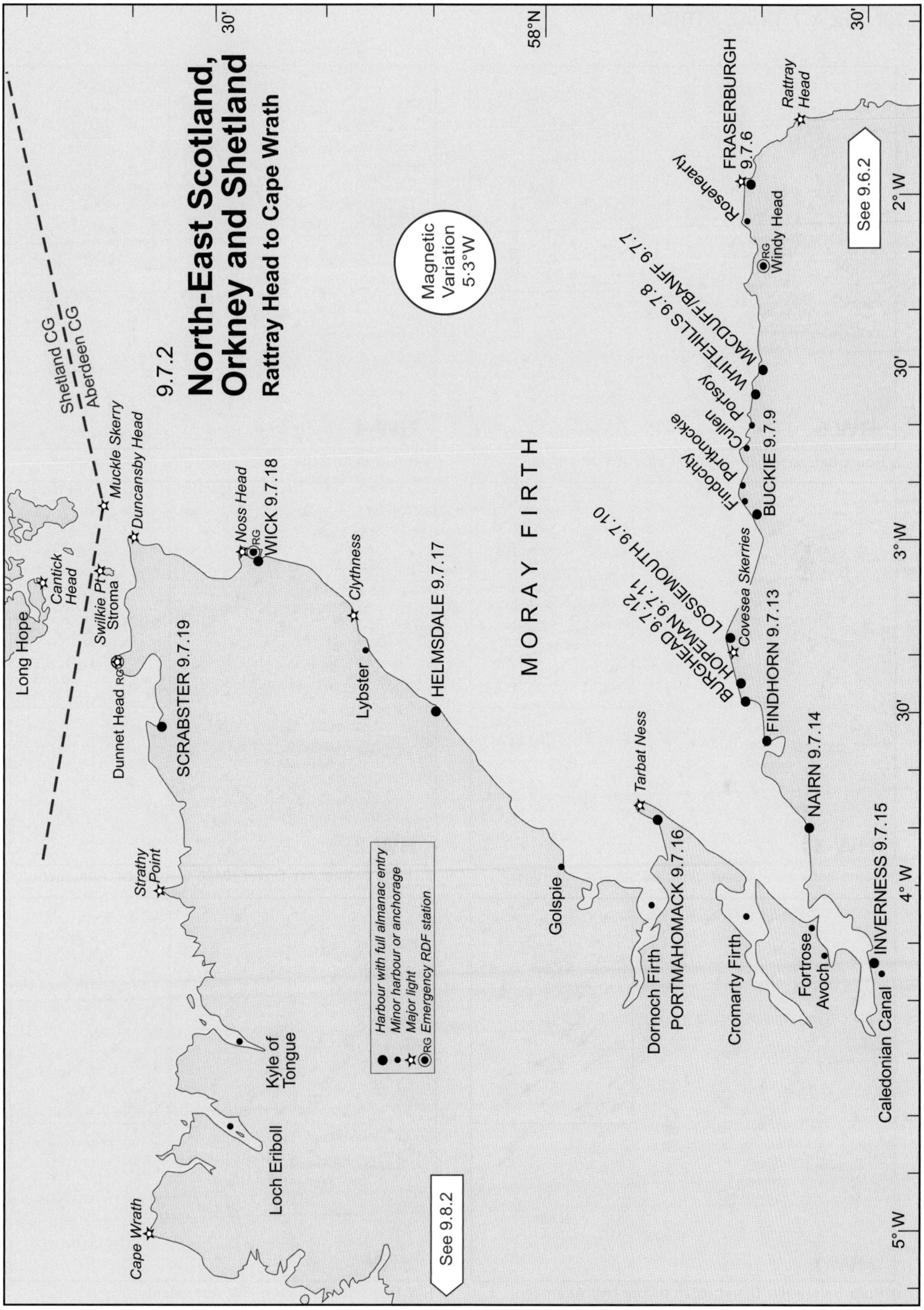
9.7.2
North-East Scotland, Orkney and Shetland
Rattray Head to Cape Wrath
Magnetic Variation 5·3°W
MORAY FIRTH
Shetland CG
Aberdeen CG
Long Hope
Cantick Head
Swilkie Pt
Stroma
Muckle Skerry
Duncansby Head
Dunnet Head RG
SCRABSTER 9.7.19
Noss Head
RG
WICK 9.7.18
Clythness
Lybster
HELMSDALE 9.7.17
Strathy Point
Golspie
Tarbat Ness
PORTMAHOMACK 9.7.16
Dornoch Firth
Cromarty Firth
Fortrose
Avoch
INVERNESS 9.7.15
Caledonian Canal
NAIRN 9.7.14
FINDHORN 9.7.13
BURGHEAD 9.7.12
HOPEMAN 9.7.11
LOSSIEMOUTH 9.7.10
Covesea Skerries
BUCKIE 9.7.9
Findochty
Portknockie
Cullen
Portsoy
WHITEHILLS 9.7.8
MACDUFF/BANFF 9.7.7
Windy Head
RG
Rosehearty
FRASERBURGH 9.7.6
Rattray Head
See 9.6.2
Kyle of Tongue
Loch Eriboll
Cape Wrath
See 9.8.2
Harbour with full almanac entry
Minor harbour or anchorage
Major light
RG Emergency RDF station
58°N
30'
2°W
3°W
4°W
5°W
7

9.7.3 AREA 7 TIDAL STREAMS

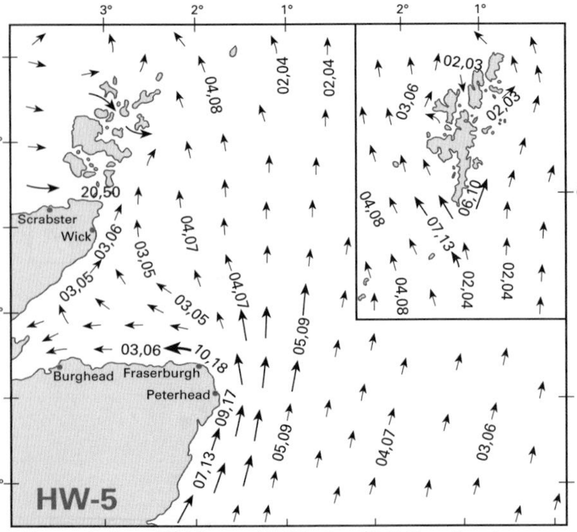
Scrabster
Wick
Burghead
Fraserburgh
Peterhead
HW-5

5 Hours before HW Dover (0500 after HW Aberdeen)

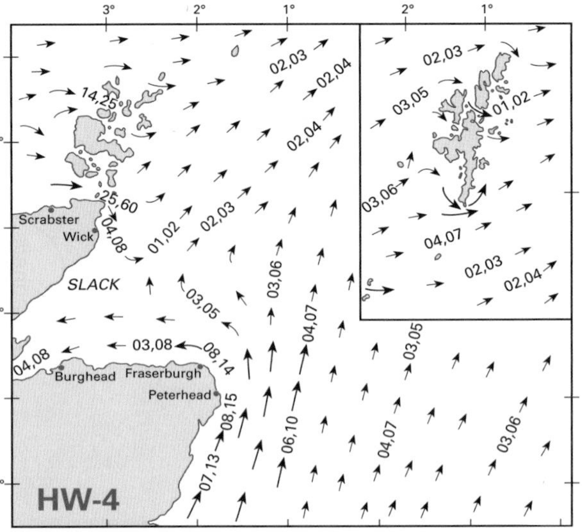
Scrabster
Wick
SLACK
Burghead
Fraserburgh
Peterhead
HW-4

4 Hours before HW Dover (0600 after HW Aberdeen)

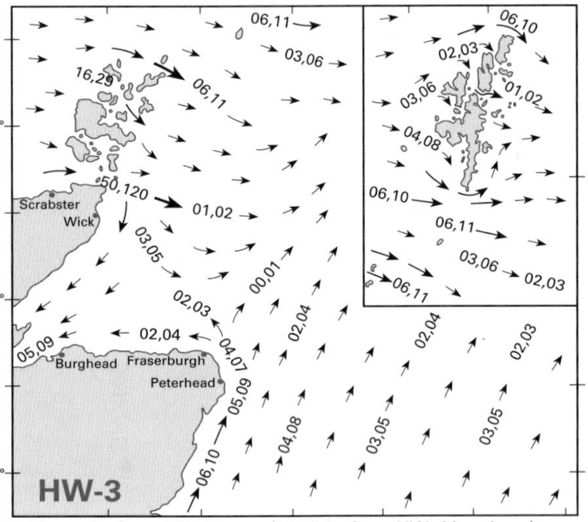
Scrabster
Wick
Burghead
Fraserburgh
Peterhead
HW-3

3 Hours before HW Dover (0520 before HW Aberdeen)

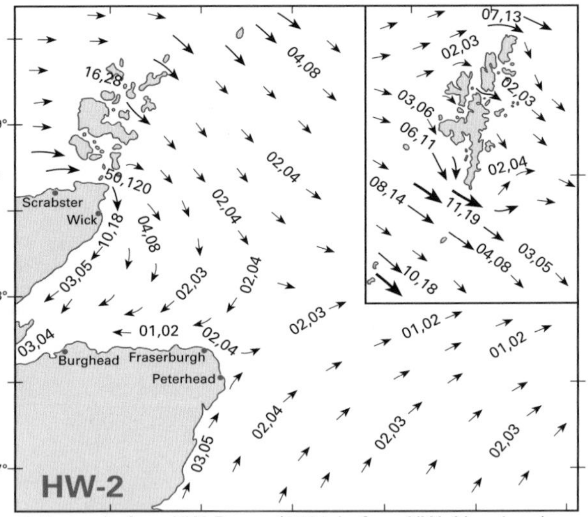
Scrabster
Wick
Burghead
Fraserburgh
Peterhead
HW-2

2 Hours before HW Dover (0420 before HW Aberdeen)

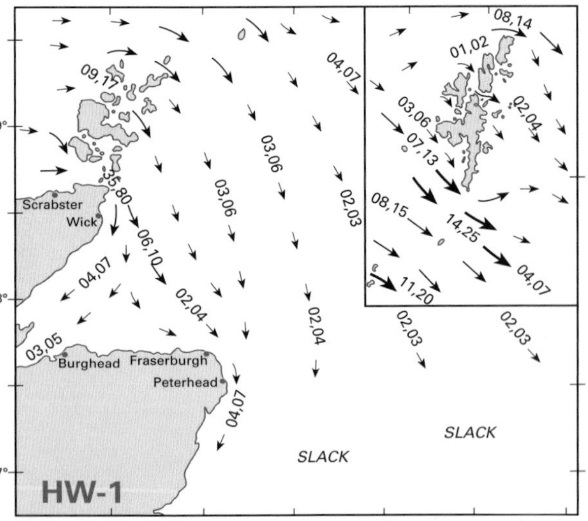
Scrabster
Wick
Burghead
Fraserburgh
Peterhead
SLACK
SLACK
HW-1

1 Hour before HW Dover (0320 before HW Aberdeen)

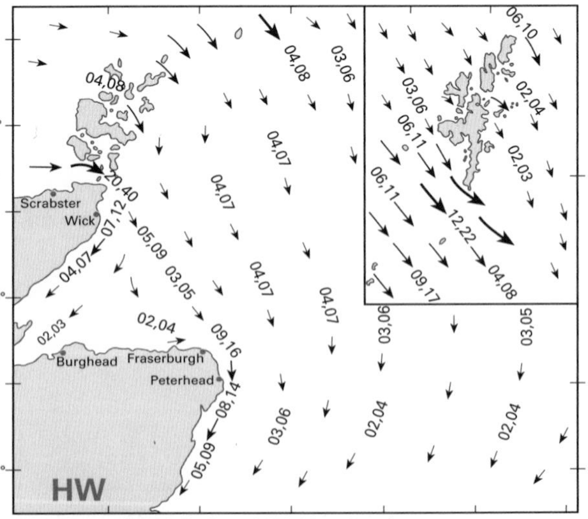
Scrabster
Wick
Burghead
Fraserburgh
Peterhead
HW

HW Dover (0220 before HW Aberdeen)

Southward 9.6.3 Westward 9.8.3

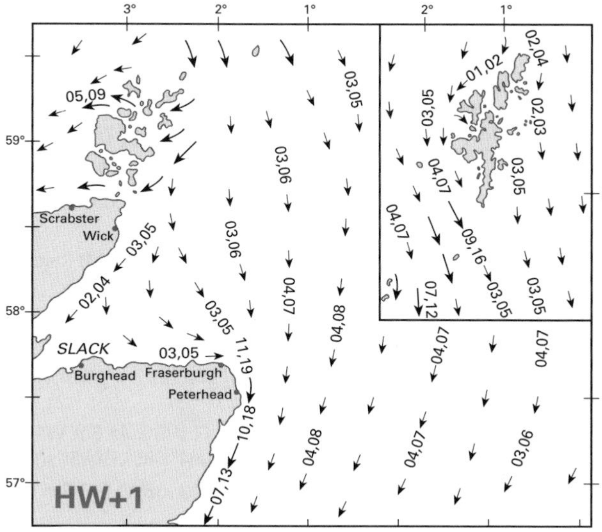
HW+1
Scrabster
Wick
Burghead
Fraserburgh
Peterhead
SLACK
05,09
03,05
02,04
03,05
11,19
10,18
07,13
03,06
03,06
03,05
04,07
04,08
04,08
03,05
04,07
04,07
03,06
01,02
02,04
02,03
03,05
04,07
03,05
04,07
09,16
07,12
03,05
03,05
1 Hour after HW Dover (0120 before HW Aberdeen)

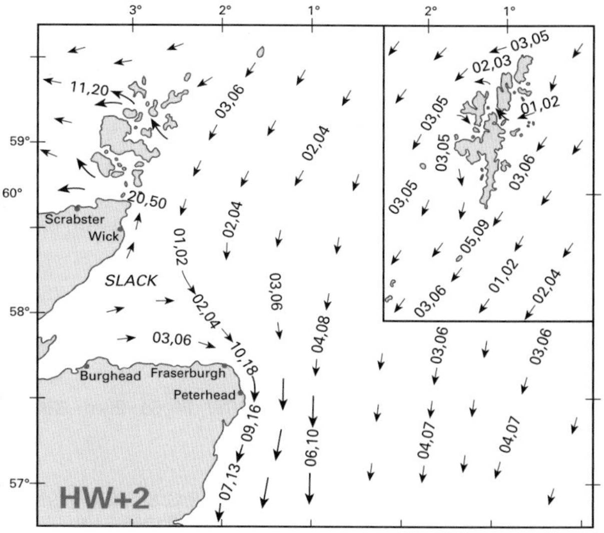
HW+2
Scrabster
Wick
Burghead
Fraserburgh
Peterhead
SLACK
11,20
20,50
03,06
01,02
02,04
10,18
09,16
07,13
02,04
02,04
03,06
04,08
06,10
03,06
04,07
03,06
04,07
03,05
02,03
01,02
03,05
03,05
03,06
03,05
05,09
01,02
02,04
03,06
2 Hours after HW Dover (0020 before HW Aberdeen)

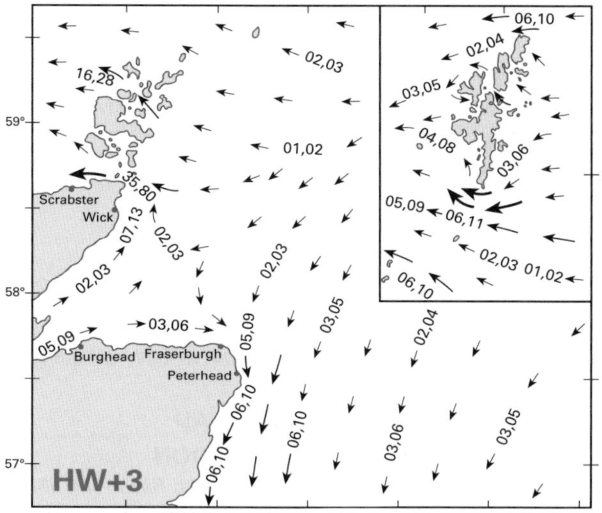
HW+3
Scrabster
Wick
Burghead
Fraserburgh
Peterhead
16,28
35,80
07,13
02,03
02,03
05,09
03,06
05,09
06,10
06,10
06,10
02,03
01,02
02,03
03,05
02,04
03,06
03,05
06,10
02,04
03,05
04,08
03,06
05,09
06,11
02,03
01,02
06,10
3 Hours after HW Dover (0040 after HW Aberdeen)

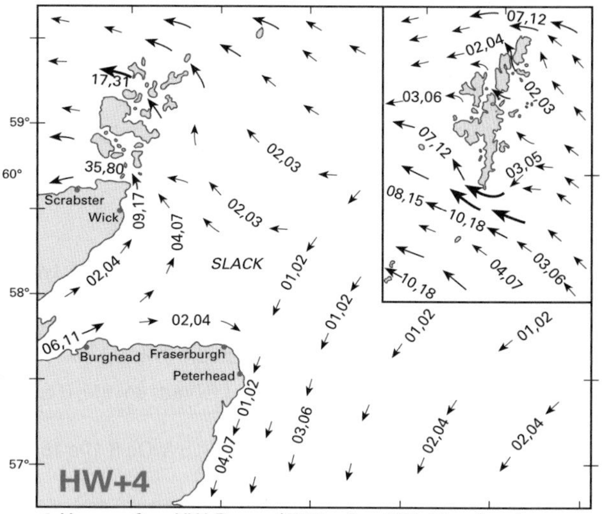
HW+4
Scrabster
Wick
Burghead
Fraserburgh
Peterhead
SLACK
17,31
35,80
09,17
04,07
02,04
06,11
02,04
01,02
04,07
03,06
02,03
02,03
01,02
01,02
01,02
01,02
02,04
02,04
07,12
02,04
03,06
02,03
07,12
03,05
08,15
10,18
04,07
03,06
10,18
4 Hours after HW Dover (0140 after HW Aberdeen)

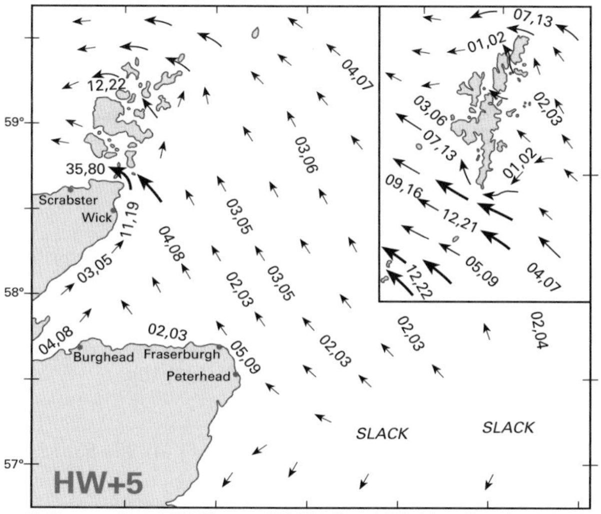
HW+5
Scrabster
Wick
Burghead
Fraserburgh
Peterhead
SLACK
SLACK
12,22
35,80
11,19
03,05
04,08
04,08
02,03
05,09
03,06
03,05
02,03
03,05
02,03
04,07
02,03
02,04
07,13
01,02
03,06
02,03
07,13
01,02
09,16
12,21
05,09
04,07
12,22
5 Hours after HW Dover (0240 after HW Aberdeen)

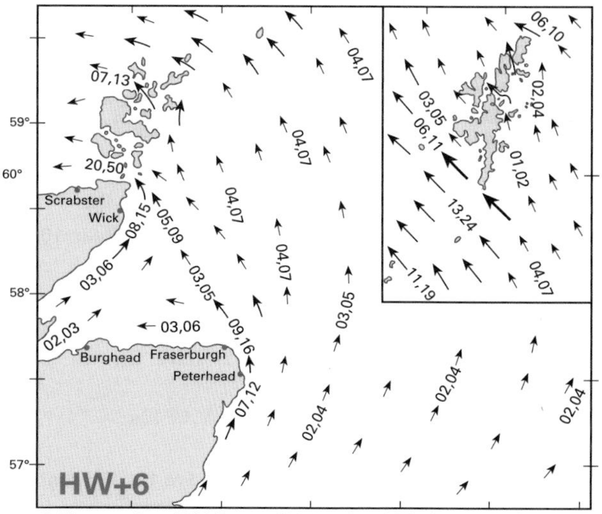
HW+6
Scrabster
Wick
Burghead
Fraserburgh
Peterhead
07,13
20,50
08,15
03,06
02,03
05,09
03,05
03,06
09,16
07,12
04,07
04,07
04,07
04,07
03,05
02,04
02,04
02,04
06,10
03,05
02,04
06,11
01,02
13,24
11,19
04,07
6 Hours after HW Dover (0340 after HW Aberdeen)

PLOT WAYPOINTS ON YOUR CHART BEFORE USING THEM

9.7.4 LIGHTS, BUOYS AND WAYPOINTS

Blue print = light with a nominal range of 15M or more. CAPITALS = place or feature. *CAPITAL ITALICS* = light-vessel, light float or Lanby. *Italics* = Fog signal. ***Bold italics*** = Racon. Useful waypoints are underlined. Abbreviations are in Chapter 1.

RATTRAY HEAD TO INVERNESS

Rattray Hd ☆ 57°36'·61N 01°49'·03W Fl (3) 30s 28m **24M**; W twr; ***Racon (M) 15M***; *Horn (2) 45s.*

Cairnbulg Briggs 57°41'·10N 01°56'·46W Fl (2) 10s 9m 6M.

▶ FRASERBURGH

Ldg lt 291°. 57°41'·57N 02°00'·13W Iso R 2s 12m 9M. Rear, 75m from front, Iso R 2s 17m 9M.

Balaclava Bkwtr Head ☆ 57°41'·51N 01°59'·70W Fl (2) G 8s 26m 6M; dome on W twr; vis: 178°-326°.

Kinnaird Hd ☆ 57°41'·87N 02°00'·26W Fl 5s 25m **22M**; vis: 092°-297°.

▶ MACDUFF/BANFF/WHITEHILLS

Pier Hd ☆ 57°40'·25N 02°30'·02W Fl (2) WRG 6s 12m W9M, R7M; W twr; vis: G shore-115°, W115°-174°, R174°-210°.

Macduff Ldg Lts 127° 57°40'·12N 02°29'·75W Front FR 44m 3M. Rear, 60m from front, FR 55m 3M; both Or △ on mast.

Macduff W Pier Head ☆ 57°40'·22N 02°29'·98W QG 4m 5M.

Whitehills Pier Head ☆ 57°40'·80N 02°34'·88W Fl WR 3s 7m W9M, R6M; W twr; vis: R132°-212°, W212°-245°.

Banff N Pier Head ☆ 57°40'·22N 02°31'·27W Fl 4s.

Banff Ldg Lts 295° Front 57°40·30N 02°31·36N Fl R 4s. Rear, QR; both vis: 210-345°.

▶ PORTSOY

Pier Ldg Lts 160°. Front 57°41'·17N 02°41'·49W F 12m 5M; twr. Rear FR 17m 5M; mast.

▶ BUCKIE

West Muck ☆ 57°41'·06N 02°58'·01W QR 5m 7M; tripod.

N Pier Head ☆ 57°40'·83N 02°57'·71W 2 FR (vert) 6m 9M; R col. (3 FR when Hbr closed.)

N Pier 60m from head ☆ 57°40'·9N 02°57'·5W Oc R 10s 15m **15M** W twr.

Ldg Lts 120°. **Front**, W Pier elbow ☆ 57°40'·80N 02°57'·65W 2 FG (vert) 4m 9M. **Rear**, Iso WG 2s 20m **W16M**, G12M; vis: G090°-110°, W110°-225°.

▶ LOSSIEMOUTH

S Pier Hd ☆ 57°43'·42N 03°16'·69W Fl R 6s 11m 5M; *Siren 60s.*

Covesea Skerries ☆ 57°43'·47N 03°20'·45W Fl WR 20s 49m **W24M, R20M**; W twr; vis: W076°-267°, R267°-282°.

▶ HOPEMAN

W Pier Head ☆ 57°42'·69N 03°26'·29W Oc G 4s 8m 4M.

Ldg Lts 081°. Front, 57°42'·71N 03°26'·18W FR 3m. Rear, 10m from front, FR 4m.

▶ BURGHEAD/FINDHORN

Burghead N Bkwtr Hd ☆ 57°42'·09N 03°30'·03W Oc 8s 7m 5M.

Burghead Spur Hd ☆57°42'·08N 03°30'·03W QR 3m 5M; vis: from SW only.

<u>Findhorn Landfall</u> 57°40'·33N 03°38'·65W. LF 10s.

▶ NAIRN

W Pier Head ☆ 57°35'·60N 03°51'·63W QG 5m 1M; Gy post.

E Pier Head ☆ 57°35'·62N 03°51'·65W Oc WRG 4s 6m 5M; 8-sided twr; vis: Gshore-100°, W100°-207°, R207°-shore.

▶ INVERNESS FIRTH

<u>Riff Bank E</u> 57°38'·38N 03°58'·18W Fl Y 10s 3m 5M.
<u>Navity Bank</u> 57°38'·16N 04°01'·18W Fl (3) G 15s 3m 4M.
<u>Riff Bank N</u> 57°37'·22N 04°02'·75W Fl (2) R 12s 3m 4M.
<u>Riff Bank W</u> 57°35'·78N 04°04'·08W Fl Y 5s 3m 4M.

SOUTH CHANNEL

<u>Riff Bank S</u> 57°36'·73N 04°00'·97W Q (6) + L Fl 15s.
<u>Craigmee</u> 57°35'·30N 04°05'·04W Fl R 6s 3m 4M.

Chanonry ☆ 57°34'·44N 04°05'·57W Oc 6s 12m **15M**; W twr; vis: 148°-073°.

Avoch ☆ 57°34'·02N 04°09'·93W 2 FR (vert) 7/5m 5M; (occas).
<u>Munlochy</u> 57°32'·91N 04°07'·65W L Fl 10s.
<u>Petty Bank</u> 57°31'·58N 04°08'·98W Fl R 5s.
<u>Meikle Mee</u> 57°30'·26N 04°12'·02W Fl G 3s.

Longman Pt 57°29'·99N 04°13'·31W Fl WR 2s 7m W5M, R4M; vis: W078°-258°, R258°-078°.

Craigton Point ☆ 57°30'·05N 04°14'·09W Fl WRG 4s 6m W11M, R7M, G7M; vis: W312°-048°, R048°-064°, W064°-085°, G085°-shore.

Kessock Bridge N Trs ☆ 57°30'·01N 04°13'·88W; QG 3m 3M; S Trs QR 3m 3M.

Bridge Centre mark 57°29'·97N 04°13'·79W; Or △; ***Racon (K) 6M.***
Main Chan North side ☆ Oc G 6s 28m 5M.
South side ☆ 57°29'·93N 04°13'·74W Oc R 6s 28m 5M.

▶ INVERNESS

R. Ness Outer 57°29'·83N 04°13'·93W QR 3m 4M.
Inner Bn 57°29'·72N 04°14'·11W QR 3m 4M.

Embankment Head ☆ 57°29'·72N 04°14'·25W Fl G 2s 8m 4M; G framework twr.

E side ☆ 57°29'·56N 04°14'·21W Fl R 3s 7m 6M.

▶ CALEDONIAN CANAL

Clachnaharry, S Training Wall Head 57°29'·43N 04°15'·86W Iso G 4s 5m 2M; tfc signals.

N Training Wall Head 57°29'·45N 04°15'·82W QR 5m 2M.

INVERNESS TO DUNCANSBY HEAD

▶ CROMARTY FIRTH/INVERGORDON

<u>Fairway</u> 57°39'·96N 03°54'·19W L Fl 10s; ***Racon (M) 5M.***
<u>Cromarty Bank</u> 57°40'·66N 03°56'·78W Fl (2) G 10s.
<u>Buss Bank</u> 57°40'·97N 03°59'·54W Fl R 3s.

The Ness ☆ 57°40'·98N 04°02'·20W Oc WR 10s 18m **W15M**, R11M; W twr; vis: R079°-088°, W088°-275°, obsc by N Sutor when brg less than 253°.

Nigg Oil Terminal Pier Head ☆ 57°41'·54N 04°02'·60W Oc G 5s 31m 5M; Gy twr, floodlit.

<u>Nigg Sands E</u> 57°41'·60N 04°04'·35W Fl (2) G 10s.
<u>Nigg Sands W</u> 57°41'·28N 04°07'·24W Fl G 3s.
<u>Newhall</u> 57°40'·93N 04°07'·95W Fl (2) R 10s.

Invergordon Dockyard Pier Head ☆ 57°41'·15N 04°09'·75W Fl (3) G 10s 15m 4M.

Supply Base ☆ 57°41'·09N 04°10'·37W Oc G 8s 9m 6M.
Queen's Dock W ☆ 57°41'·10N 04°10'·78W ☆ Iso G 2s 9m 6M.
<u>Three Kings</u> 57°43'·73N 03°54'·25W Q (3) 10s.

▶ DORNOCH FIRTH/TAIN

Tarbat Ness ☆ 57°51'·88N 03°46'·76W Fl (4) 30s 53m **24M**; W twr, R bands; ***Racon (T) 14-16M.***

Tain Range 57°52'·96N 03°47'·24W Fl Y 5s.
Range ☆ 57°49'·46N 03°57'·54W Fl R 5s, when firing occurs.

▶ HELMSDALE/LYBSTER

Ben-a-Chielt ☆ 58°19'·69N 03°22'·36W Aero 5 FR (vert) (461).
Lybster, S Pier Hd ☆ 58°17'·79N 03°17'·41W Oc R 6s 10m 3M.
Clyth Ness ☆ 58°18'·64N 03°12'·74W Fl (2) 30s 45m 14M.

▶ WICK

S Pier Head ☆ 58°26'·34N 03°04'·73W Fl WRG 3s 12m W12M, R9M, G9M; W 8-sided twr; vis: G253°-270°, W270°-286°, R286°-329°; *Bell (2) 10s* (occas).

Dir lt 288·5° 58°26'·54N 03°05'·34W F WRG 9m W10M, R7M, G7M; col on N end of bridge; vis: G283·5°-287·2°, W287·2°-289·7°, R289·7°-293·5°.

Noss Head ☆ 58°28'·71N 03°03'·09W Fl WR 20s 53m **W25M, R 21M**; W twr; vis: R shore-191°, W191°-shore.

DUNCANSBY HEAD TO CAPE WRATH

Duncansby Head ☆ 58°38'·65N 03°01'·58W Fl 12s 67m **22M**; W twr; ***Racon (T)***.

Pentland Skerries ☆ 58°41'·41N 02°55'·49W Fl (3) 30s 52m **23M**; W twr; *Horn 45s*.

Lother Rock ☆ 58°43'·80N 02°58'·68W Q 13m 6M; ***Racon (M) 10M***.

S Ronaldsay, Burwick Bkwtr Head ☆ 58°44'·35N 02°58'·31W 2FR (vert) 8m 5M.

Swona ☆ 58°44'·25N 03°04'·24W Fl 8s 17m 9M; vis: 261°-210°.
Swona N Head ☆ 58°45'·11N 03°03'·10W Fl (3) 10s 16m 10M.

Stroma ☆, Swilkie Point 58°41'·75N 03°07'·01W Fl (2) 20s 32m **26M**; W twr; *Horn (2) 60s*.

Inner sound, John O'Groats, Pier Head ☆ 58°38'·72N 03°04'·23W Fl R 3s 4m 2M; W post.

Dunnet Head ☆ 58°40'·28N 03°22'·60W Fl (4) 30s 105m **23M**.

▶ THURSO/SCRABSTER

Thurso Bkwtr Head ☆ 58°35'·97N 03°30'·48W QG 5m 4M; G post; shown 1/9-30/4.

Thurso Ldg Lts 195°. Front, 58°35'·96N 03°30'·76W FG 5m 4M; Gy post. Rear, FG 6m 4M; Gy mast.

Scrabster Queen Elizabeth Pier Hd ☆ 58°36'·66N 03°32'·31W Fl (2) 4s 8m 8M.

Scrabster Outer Pier Hd ☆ 58°36'·61N 03°32'·58W Q (2) G 6s 8m 4M.

Strathy Point ☆ 58°36'·04N 04°01'·12W Fl 20s 45m **26M**; W twr on W dwelling. F.R. on chimney 100° 8·5M.

Sule Skerry ☆ 59°05'·09N 04°24'·38W Fl (2) 15s 34m **21M**; W twr; ***Racon (T)***.

North Rona ☆ 59°07'·27N 05°48'·91W Fl (3) 20s 114m **24M**.

Sula Sgeir ☆ 59°05'·61N 06°09'·57W Fl 15s 74m 11M; □ structure.

Loch Eriboll, White Head ☆ 58°31'·01N 04°38'·90W Fl WR 10s 18m W13M, R12M; W twr and bldg; vis: W030°-172°, R172°-191°, W191°-212°.

Cape Wrath ☆ 58°37'·54N 04°59'·94W Fl (4) 30s 122m **22M**; W twr.

ORKNEY ISLANDS

Tor Ness ☆ 58°46'·78N 03°17'·86W Fl 5s 21m **17M**; W twr.

Cantick Head (S Walls, SE end) ☆ 58°47'·23N 03°07'·88W Fl 20s 35m **18M**; W twr.

SCAPA FLOW AND APPROACHES

Ruff Reef, off Cantick Hd ☆ 58°47'·43N 03°07'·80W Fl (2) 10s 10m 6M.

Long Hope, S Ness Pier Hd ☆ 58°48'·05N 03°12'·35W Fl WRG 3s 6m W7M, R5M, G5M; vis: G082°-242°, W242°-252°, R252°-082°.

Hoxa Head ☆ 58°49'·31N 03°02'·09W Fl WR 3s 15m W9M, R6M; W twr; vis: W026°-163°, R163°-201°, W201°-215°.

Stanger Head ☆ 58°48'·96N 03°04'·74W Fl R 5s 25m 8M.
Roan Head ☆ 58°50'·72N 03°03'·94W Fl (2) R 6s 12m 7M.
Nevi Skerry 58°50'·67N 03°02'·70W Fl (2) 6s 7m 6M.
Calf of Flotta ☆ 58°51'·27N 03°03'·92W QR 8m 4M.
Flotta E Jetty ☆ 58°50'·75N 03°03'·91W 2 FR (vert) 10m 3M.
Mooring dolphins, E and W, both QR 8m 3M.

SPM twr No. 1 58°52'·14N 03°07'·46W Fl Y 5s 12m 3M; *Horn Mo (A) 60s*.

SPM twr No. 2 58°52'·23N 03°05'·96W Fl (4) Y 15s 12m 3M; *Horn Mo (N) 60s*.

Gibraltar Pier ☆ 58°50'·27N 03°07'·88W 2 FG (vert) 7m 3M.
Sutherland Pier ☆ 58°50'·19N 03°08'·07W QG 8m 3M.
Golden Wharf ☆ 58°50'·16N 03°11'·46W 2 FR (vert) 7m 3M.
Lyness Wharf ☆ 58°50'·02N 03°11'·42W 2 FR (vert) 7m 3M.
Needle Point 58°50'·09N 02°57'·46W Fl G 3s 6m 3M.

St Margaret's Hope Pier Head ☆ 58°49'·93N 02°57'·67W 2 FG (vert) 6m 2M.

Ldg Lts 196°, 58°49'·57N 02°57'·64W both FR 7/11m.
Rose Ness ☆ 58°52'·33N 02°49'·97W Fl 6s 24m 8M; W twr.
Scapa Pier ☆ 58°57'·39N 02°58'·42W Fl G 3s 6m 8M.
Scapa Skerry 58°56'·87N 02°59'·16W Fl (2) R 12s.
Barrel of Butter ☆ 58 53'·40N 03°07'·62W Fl (2) 10s 6m 7M.

Cava ☆ 58°53'·21N 03°10'·70W Fl WR 3s 11m W10M, R8M; W ○ twr; vis: W351°-143°, R143°-196°, W196°-251°, R251°-271°, W271°-298°.

Houton Bay Ldg Lts 316°. Front, 58°54'·97N 03°11'·56W Fl G 3s 8m. Rear, 200m from front, FG 16m; vis: 312°-320°.

▶ CLESTRAN SOUND

<u>Peter Skerry</u> 58°55'·25N 03°13'·51W Fl G 6s.
<u>Riddock Shoal</u> 58°55'·86N 03°15'·15W Fl (2) R 12s.

▶ HOY SOUND

<u>Ebbing Eddy Rocks</u> 58°56'·60N 03°17'·00W Q.

Graemsay Is Hoy Sound Low ☆ Ldg Lts 104°. **Front**, 58°56'·42N 03°18'·60W Iso 3s 17m **15M**; W twr; vis: 070°-255°. **High Rear**, 1·2M from front, Oc WR 8s 35m **W20M, R16M**; W twr; vis: R097°-112°, W112°-163°, R163°-178°, W178°-332°; obsc on Ldg line within 0·5M.

Skerry of Ness ☆ 58°56'·95N 03°17'·83W Fl WG 4s 7m W7M, G4M; vis: W shore-090°, G090°-shore.

▶ STROMNESS

<u>Stromness</u> 58°57'·25N 03°17'·61W QR.
<u>Stromness</u> 58°57'·38N 03°17'·65W Fl G 3s.

Ldg Lts 317°. Front, 58°57'·61N 03°18'·15W FR 29m 11M; post on W twr. Rear, 55m from front, FR 39m 11M; vis: 307°-327°; H24.

N Pier Head ☆ 58°57'·75N 03°17'·71W Fl R 3s 8m 5M.

▶ AUSKERRY

Copinsay ☆ 58°53'·77N 02°40'·35W Fl (5) 30s 79m **21M**; W twr;
Auskerry ☆ 59°01'·51N 02°34'·34W Fl 20s 34m **20M**; W twr.

Helliar Holm, S end ☆ 59°01'·13N 02°54'·09W Fl WRG 10s 18m W14M, R11M, G11M; W twr; vis: G256°-276°, W276°-292°, R292°-098°, W098°-116°, G116°-154°.

Balfour Pier Shapinsay ☆ 59°01'·86N 02°54'·49W Fl (2) WRG 5s 5m W3M, R2M, G2M; vis: G270°-010°, W010°-020°, R020°-090°.

▶ KIRKWALL

<u>Scargun Shoal</u> 59°00'·69N 02°58'·58W.

PLOT WAYPOINTS ON YOUR CHART BEFORE USING THEM

Thieves Holm, ✦ 59°01'·09N 02°56'·21W Q.R8M

Pier N end ☆ 58°59'·29N 02°57'·72W Iso WRG 5s 8m **W15M**, R13M, G13M; W twr; vis: G153°-183°, W183°-192°, R192°-210°.

▶ **WIDE FIRTH**

Linga Skerry ⚓ 59°02'·39N 02°57'·56W Q (3) 10s.
Boray Skerries ⚓ 59°03'·65N 02°57'·66W Q (6) + L Fl 15s.
Skertours ⚓ 59°04'·11N 02°56'·72W Q.
Galt Skerry ⚓ 59°05'·21N 02°54'·20W Q.
Brough of Birsay ☆ 59°08'·19N 03°20'·41W Fl (3) 25s 52m **18M**.

Papa Stronsay NE end, The Ness 59°09'·34N 02°34'·93W Fl(4)20s 8m 9M; W twr.

▶ **STRONSAY, PAPA SOUND**

Quiabow ▲ 59°09'·82N 02°36'·30W Fl (2) G 12s.
No. 1 ▲ (off Jacks Reef) 59°09'·16N 02°36'·51W Fl G 5s.
No. 2 ⬱ 59°08'·92N 02°36'·61W Fl R 5s.
No. 4 ⬱ 59°08'·77N 02°36'·46W Fl (2) R 5s.
No. 3 ▲ 59°08'·70N 02°36'·18W Fl (2) G 5s.
Whitehall Pier Hd ✦ 50°08'·61N 02°35'·96W 2 FG (vert) 8m 4M.

▶ **SANDAY ISLAND/NORTH RONALDSAY**

Start Point ☆ 59°16'·69N 02°22'·71W Fl (2) 20s 24m **18M**.

Kettletoft Pier Head ✦ 59°13'·80N 02°35'·86W Fl WRG 3s 7m W7M, R5M, G5M; vis: W351°-011°, R011°-180°, G180°-351°.

N Ronaldsay ☆ NE end, 59°23'·37N 02°23'·03W Fl 10s 43m **24M**; R twr, W bands; *Racon (T) 14-17M; Horn 60s.*

Nouster Pier Head ✦ 59°21'·30N 02°26'·48W QR 5m.

▶ **EDAY/EGILSAY**

Calf Sound ✦ 59°14'·30N 02°45'·83W Fl(3)WRG 10s 8m W8M, R6M, G6M; W twr; vis: R shore-216°, W216°-223°, G223°-302°, W302°-307°.

Backaland Pier ✦ 59°09'·43N 02°44'·88W Fl R 3s 5m 4M; vis: 192°-250°.

Egilsay Graand ⚓ 59°06'·86N 02°54'·42W Q (6) + L Fl 15s.
Egilsay Pier, S end ✦ 59°09'·29N 02°56'·81W Fl G 3s 4m 4M.

▶ **WESTRAY/PIEROWALL**

Noup Head ☆ 59°19'·86N 03°04'·23W Fl 30s 79m **20M**; W twr; vis: about 335°-282° but partially obsc 240°-275°.

Pierowall E Pier Head ✦ 59°19'·35N 02°58'·53W Fl WRG 3s 7m W11M, R7M, G7M; vis: G254°-276°, W276°-291°, R291°-308°, G308°-215°.

Papa Westray, Moclett Bay Pier Head ✦ 59°19'·60N 02°53'·52W Fl WRG 5s 7m W5M, R3M, G3M; vis: G306°-341°, W341°-040°, R040°-074°.

SHETLAND ISLES

▶ **FAIR ISLE**

Skadan South ☆, 59°30'·84N 01°39'·16W Fl (4) 30s 32m **22M**; W twr; vis: 260°-146°, obsc inshore 260°-282°; *Horn (2) 60s.*

Skroo ☆ N end 59°33'·13N 01°36'·58W Fl (2) 30s 80m **22M**; W twr; vis: 086°·7°-358°.

▶ **MAINLAND, SOUTH**

Sumburgh Head ☆ 59°51'·21N 01°16'·58W Fl (3) 30s 91m **23M**.
Pool of Virkie, Marina E Bkwtr Head ✦ 59°53'·01N 01°17'·16W 2 FG (vert) 6m 5M.
Mousa, Perie Bard ✦ 59°59'·84N 01°09'·51W Fl 3s 20m 10M.
Aithsvoe ✦ 60°02'·26N 01°12'·97W Fl R 3s 3m 2M; vis: 305°-339°.

▶ **BRESSAY/LERWICK**

Bressay, Kirkabister Ness ☆ 60°07'·20N 01°07'·29W Fl (2) 20s 32m **23M**.

Cro of Ham ✦ 60°08'·26N 01°07'·57W Fl 3s 12m 3M.
Twageos Point ✦ 60°08'·91N 01°07'·95W L Fl 6s 8m 6M.

Maryfield Ferry Terminal ✦ 60°09'·43N 01°07'·45W Oc WRG 6s 5m 5M; vis: W008°-013°, R013°-111°, G111°-008°.

Bkwtr N Head ✦ 60°09'·24N 01°08'·41W 2 FR (vert) 5m 4M.

North Ness ☆ 60°09'·57N 01°08'·77W Iso WG 4s 4m 5M; vis: Wshore-158°, G158°-216°, W216°-301°.

Loofa Baa ⚓ 60°09'·72N 01°08'·79W Q (6) + L Fl 15s 4m 5M.
Soldian Rock ⚓ 60°12'·51N 01°04'·73W Q (6) + L Fl 15s.

N ent Dir lt 215°. 60°10'·47N 01°09'·53W Oc WRG 6s 27m 8M; Y △, Or stripe; vis: R211°-214°, W214°-216°, G216°-221°.

Gremista Marina S Hd ✦ 60°10'·20N 01°09'·61W Iso R 4s 3m 2M.
Greenhead ✦ 60°10'·84N 01°09'·10W Q (4) R 10s 4m 3M.

Rova Hd ✦ 60°11'·46N 01°08'·60W Fl (3) WRG 18s 12m W12M, R9M, G9M; W twr; vis: R 090°-182°, W182°-191°, G191°-213°, R213°-241°, W241°-261·5°, G261·5°-009°, R009°-040°. Same structure and synhcronised: Fl (3) WRG 18s 14m **W16M**, R13M, G13M; vis: R176·5°-182°, W182°-191°, G191°-196·5°.

The Brethren Rock ⚓ 60°12'·35N 01°08'·24W Q (9) 15s.
The Unicorn Rock ⚓ 60°13'·51N 01°08'·48W VQ (3) 5s.

Dales Voe ✦ 60°11'·79N 01°11'·23W Fl (2) WRG 8s 5m W4M, R3M, G3M; vis: G220°-227°, W227°-233°, R233°-240°.

Dales Voe Quay ✦ 60°11'·60N 01°10'·48W 2 FR (vert) 9m 3M.
Laxfirth Pier Hd ✦ 60°12'·74N 01°12'·14W 2 FG (vert) 4m 2M.

Hoo Stack ✦ 60°14'·96N 01°05'·38W Fl (4) WRG 12s 40m W7M, R5M, G5M; W pylon; vis: R169°-180°, W180°-184°, G184°-193°, W193°-169°. Same structure, Dir lt 182°. Fl (4) WRG 12s 33m W9M, R6M, G6M; vis: R177°-180°, W180°-184°, G184°-187°; synch with upper lt.

Mull (Moul) of Eswick ✦ 60°15'·74N 01°05'·90W Fl WRG 3s 50m W9M, R6M, G6M; W twr; vis: R028°-200°, W200°-207°, G207°-018°, W018°-028°.

▶ **WHALSAY/SKERRIES**

Symbister Ness ✦ 60°20'·43N 01°02'·29W Fl (2) WG 12s 11m W8M, G6M; W twr; vis: W shore-203°, G203°-shore.

Symbister Bay N Bkwtr Head ✦ 60°20'·63N 01°01'·72W Oc G 7s 3m 3M.
E Bkwtr Head ✦ 60°20'·67N 01°01'·66W Oc R 7s 3m 3M.
S Bkwtr Hd ✦ 60°20'·58N 01°01'·63W QG 4m 2M.
Marina N pontoon ✦ 60°20'·50N 01°01'·59W 2 FG (vert) 2m 3M.
Skate of Marrister ✦ 60°21'·35N 01°01'·39W Fl G 6s 4m 4M.

Suther Ness ✦ 60°22'·12N 01°00'·20W Fl WRG 3s 10m W10M, R8M, G7M; vis: W shore-038°, R038°-173°, W173°-206°, G206°-shore.

Mainland, Laxo Voe ferry terminal ✦ 60°21'·13N 01°10'·27W 2 FG (vert) 4m 2M.

Bound Skerry ☆ 60°25'·47N 00°43'·72W Fl 20s 44m **20M**; W twr.

South Mouth. Ldg Lts 014°. Front, 60°25'·33N 00°45'·01W FY 3m 2M. Rear, FY 12m 2M.
Bruray Bn 'D' ✦ Fl (3) R 6s 3m 3M.
Bruray Bn 'B' ✦ VQ R 3m 3M.
Housay Bn 'A' ✦ VQ G 3m 3M.
Bruray ferry berth ✦ 60°25'·36N 00°45'·12W 2 FG (vert) 6m 4M.

Muckle Skerry ✦ 60°26'·41N 00°51'·84W Fl (2) WRG 10s 15m W7M, R5M, G5M; W twr; vis: W046°-192°, R192°-272°, G272°-348°, W348°-353°, R353°-046°.

▶ **YELL SOUND**

S ent, Lunna Holm ✦ 60°27'·34N 01°02'·52W Fl (3) WRG 15s 19m W10M, R7M, G7M; W ◯ twr; vis: R shore-090°, W090°-094°, G094°-209°, W209°-275°, R275°-shore.

Firths Voe ☆, N shore 60°27'·21N 01°10'·63W Oc WRG 8s 9m **W15M**, R10M, G10M; W twr; vis: W189°-194°, G194°-257°, W257°-261°, R261°-339°, W339°-066°.

Linga Is. Dir lt 150° ☆ 60°26'·80N 01°09'·13W Q (4) WRG 8s 10m W9M, R9M, G9M; vis: R145°-148°, W148°-152°, G152°-155°. Q (4) WRG 8s 10m W7M, R4M, G4M; same structure; vis: R052°-146°, G154°-196°, W196°-312°; synch.

The Rumble Bn ☆ 60°28'·16N 01°07'·26W; R Bn; Fl 10s 8m 4M; ***Racon (O)***.

Yell, Ulsta Ferry Terminal Breakwater Head ☆ 60°29'·74N 01°09'·52W Oc RG 4s 7m R5M, G5M; vis: G shore-354°, R044°-shore. Same structure; Oc WRG 4s 5m W8M, R5M, G5M; vis: G shore-008°, W008°-036°, R036°-shore.

Toft ferry terminal ☆ 60°28'·02N 01°12'·40W 2 FR (vert) 5m 2M.

Ness of Sound, W side ☆ 60°31'·34N 01°11'·28W Fl (3) WRG 12s 18m W9M, R6M, G6M; vis: G shore-345°, W345°-350°, R350°-160°, W160°-165°, G165°-shore.

Brother Is. Dir lt 329°. 60°30'·95N 01°14'·11W Fl (4) WRG 8s 16m W10M, R7M, G7M; vis: G323·5°-328°, W328°-330°, R330°-333·5°.

Mio Ness ☆ 60°29'·66N 01°13'·68W Q (2) WR 10s 12m W7M, R4M; W ○ twr; vis: W282°-238°, R238°-282°.

Tinga Skerry ☆ 60°30'·48N 01°14'·86W Q (2) G 10s 9m 5M. W ○ twr.

▶ YELL SOUND, NORTH ENTRANCE

Bagi Stack ☆ 60°43'·53N 01°07'·54W Fl (4) 20s 45m 10M.

Gruney Is ☆ 60°39'·15N 01°18'·17W Fl WR 5s 53m W8M, R6M; W twr; vis: R064°-180°, W180°-012°; ***Racon (T) 14M***.

Pt of Fethaland ☆ 60°38'·05N 01°18'·70W Fl (3) WR 15s 65m **W24M, R20M**; vis R080°-103°, W103°-160°, R160°-206°, W206°-340°.

Muckle Holm ☆ 60°34'·83N 01°16'·01W Fl (4) 10s 32m 10M.

Little Holm ☆ 60°33'·42N 01°15'·88W Iso 4s 12m 6M; W twr.

Outer Skerry ☆ 60°33'·03N 01°18'·32W Fl 6s 12m 8M.

Quey Firth ☆ 60°31'·43N 01°19'·58W Oc WRG 6s 22m W12M, R8M, G8M; W twr; vis: W shore (through S and W-290°, G290°-327°, W327°-334°, R334°-shore.

Lamba, S side ☆ 60°30'·73N 01°17'·84W Fl WRG 3s 30m W8M, R5M, G5M; W twr; vis: G shore-288°, W288°-293°, R293°-327°, W327°-044°, R044°-140°, W140°-shore. Dir lt 290·5° Fl WRG 3s 24m W10M, R7M, G7M; vis: 285·5°-288°, W288°-293°, R293°-295·5°.

▶ SULLOM VOE

Gluss Is ☆ Ldg Lts 194·7° (H24). **Front**, 60°29'·77N 01°19'·44W F 39m **19M**; □ on Gy twr; H24. **Rear**, 0·75M from front, F 69m **19M**; □ on Gy twr.; H24. Both Lts 9M by day.

Little Roe ☆ 60°29'·99N 01°16'·46W Fl (3) WR 10s 16m W5M, R4M; W structure, Or band; vis: R036°-095·5°, W095·5°-036°.

Skaw Taing ☆ Ldg Lts 150·5°. Front, 60°29'·10N 01°16'·86W Fl (2) WRG 5s 21m W8M, R5M, G5M; Or and W structure; vis: W049°-078°, G078°-147°, W147°-154°, R154°-169°, W169°-288°. Rear, 195m from front, Fl (2) 5s 35m 8M; vis: W145°-156°.

Ness of Bardister ☆ 60°28'·19N 01°19'·63W Oc WRG 8s 20m W9M, R6M, G6M; Or and W structure; vis: W180·5°-240°, R240°-310·5°, W310·5°-314·5°, G314·5°-030·5°.

Fugla Ness. Lts in line 212·3°. Rear, 60°27'·25N 01°19'·74W Iso 4s 45m 14M. Common front 60°27'·45N 01°19'·57W Iso 4s 27m 14M; synch with rear Lts. Lts in line 203°. Rear, 60°27'·26N 01°19'·81W Iso 4s 45m 14M.

Sella Ness ☆ Dir lt 133·5° 60°26'·76N 01°16'·66W Oc WRG 10s 19m **W16M**, R3M, G3M; vis: G123·5°-130·5°, Al WG 130·5°-132·5°, white phase increasing with brg, W132·5°-134·5°. Al WR134·5°-136·5°, R phase inc with brg. R136·5°-143·5°; H24. By day Oc WRG 10s 19m W2M, R1M, G1M as above.

Tug Jetty Pier Head ☆ 60°26'·81N 01°16'·30W Iso G 4s 4m 3M.

Garth Pier N arm Head ☆ 60°26'·69N 01°16'·35W Fl (2) G 5s 4m 3M.

▶ EAST YELL/UNST/BALTA SOUND

Whitehill ☆ 60°34'·80N 01°00'·25W Fl WR 3s 24m W9M, R6M; vis: W shore-163°, R163°-211°, W211°-349°, R349°-shore.

Uyea Sound ☆ 60°41'·15N 00°55'·48W Fl (2) 8s 6m 7M.

Balta Sound ☆ 60°44'·48N 00°47'·56W Fl WR 10s 17m 10M, R7M; vis: W249°-008°, R008°-058°, W058°-154°.

Balta Marina Bkwtr Hd ☆ 60°45'·57N 00°50'·38W Fl R 6s 2m 2M.

Holme of Skaw ☆ 60°49'·87N 00°46'·33W Fl 5s 8m 8M.

Muckle Flugga ☆ 60°51'·32N 00°53'·14W Fl (2) 20s 66m **22M**.

Yell. Cullivoe Bkwtr Hd ☆ 60°41'·91N 00°59'·66W Fl (2) WRG 10s 3m 4M; vis: G080°-294°, W294°-355°, R355°-080°.

▶ MAINLAND, WEST

Esha Ness ☆ 60°29'·34N 01°37'·65W Fl 12s 61m **25M**.

Ness of Hillswick ☆ 60°27'·21N 01°29'·80W Fl (4) WR 15s 34m W9M, R6M; vis: W217°-093°, R093°-114°.

Muckle Roe, Swarbacks Minn ☆ 60°20'·98N 01°27'·07W Fl WR 3s 30m W9M, R6M; vis: W314°-041°, R041°-075°, W075°-137°.

W Burra Firth Outer ☆ 60°17'·79N 01°33'·56W Oc WRG 8s 27m W9M, R7M, G7M; vis: G136°-142°, W142°-150°, R150°-156°. H24.

W Burra Firth Inner ☆ 60°17'·78N 01°32'·17W F WRG 9m **W15M**, R9M, G9M; vis: G095°-098°, W098°-102°, W098°-102°, R102°-105°; H24.

Aith Breakwater ☆ 60°17'·22N 01°22'·43W QG 5m 3M.

W Burra Firth Transport Pier Head ☆ 60°17'·71N 01°32'·41W Iso G 4s 4m 4M.

Ve Skerries ☆ 60°22'·36N 01°48'·78W Fl (2) 20s 17m 11M; W twr; ***Racon (T) 15M***.

Papa Stour Housa Voe Dir lt 228° ☆ 60°19'·58N 01°40'·47W F WRG 2m W9M, R7M, G7M; vis: G219°-226°, W226°-230°, R230°-239°.

Rams Head ☆ 60°11'·96N 01°33'·47W Fl WRG 8s 16m W9M, R6M; G6M; W house; vis: G265°-355°, W355°-012°, R012°-090°, W090°-136°, obsc by Vaila I when brg more than 030°.

North Havra ☆ 60°09'·85N 01°20'·31W Fl WRG 12s 24m W11M, R8M, G8M; W twr; vis: G001°-053·5°, W053·5°-060·5°, R060·5°-182°, G274°-334°, W334°-337·5°, R337·5°-001°.

▶ SCALLOWAY

Point of the Pund ☆ 60°07'·99N 01°18'·31W Fl WRG 5s 20m W7M, R5M, G5M; W twr; vis: R350°-090°, G090°-111°, R111°-135°, W135°-140°, G140°-177°, W267°-350°.

Whaleback Skerry ⚓ 60°07'·95N 01°18'·90W Q.

Blacks Ness Pier SW corner ☆ 60°08'·02N 01°16'·59W Oc WRG 10s 10m W11M, G8M, R8M; vis: G052°-063·5°, W063·5°-065·5°, R065·5°-077°.

Fugla Ness ☆ 60°06'·38N 01°20'·85W Fl (2) WRG 10s 20m W10M, R7M, G7M; W twr; vis: G014°-032°, W032°-082°, R082°-134°, W134°-shore.

▶ FOULA

South Ness ☆ 60°06'·75N 02°03'·87W Fl (3) 15s 36m **18M**; W twr; vis: obscured 123°-221°.

9.7.5 PASSAGE INFORMATION

Refer to the *N Coast of Scotland Pilot*; the CCC's SDs (3 vols) for *N and NE coasts of Scotland; Orkney;* and *Shetland.*

A *'Rover Ticket'*, £20 from Aberdeenshire Council or £21 from Moray Council allows berthing(subject to availability) for one week from arrival at the first harbour. Scheme includes: Johnshaven, Gourdon, Stonehaven, Rosehearty, Banff, Portsoy, Cullen, Portknockie, Findochty, Hopeman and Burghead. A *"Rover Ticket"*, £9.44/4days or £19.41/14days from Orkney Is Council includes: Stromness, Pierowall, Stronsay, Westray, Shapinsay, Kirkwall, Burray, S.Ronaldsay, Hoy and Holm.

MORAY FIRTH: SOUTH COAST (charts 115, 222, 223) Crossing the Moray Firth from Rattray Hd (lt, fog sig) to Duncansby Hd (lt, Racon) heavy seas may be met in strong W winds. Most hbrs in the Firth are exposed to NE-E winds. For oil installations, see 9.5.5; the Beatrice Field is 20M S of Wick. ▶ *Tidal streams attain 3kn at sp close off Rattray Hd, but 5M NE of the Head the NE-going stream begins at HW Aberdeen + 0140, and the SE-going stream at HW Aberdeen – 0440, sp rates 2kn. Streams are weak elsewhere in the Moray Firth, except in the inner part.* ◀ In late spring/early summer fog (haar) is likely in onshore winds.

In strong winds the sea breaks over Steratan Rk and Colonel Rk, respectively 3M E and 1M ENE of Fraserburgh (9.7.6). Rosehearty firing range is N & W of Kinnairds Hd (lt); tgt buoys often partially submerged. Banff B is shallow; N of Macduff (9.7.7) beware Collie Rks. Banff hbr dries, and should not be approached in fresh NE-E winds, when seas break well offshore; Macduff would then be a feasible alternative.

From Meavie Pt to Scar Nose dangers extend up to 3ca from shore in places. Beware Caple Rk (depth 0·2m) 7½ca W of Logie Hd. Spey B is clear of dangers more than 7½ca from shore; anch here, but only in offshore winds. Beware E Muck (dries) 5ca SW of Craigenroan, an above-water rky patch 5ca SW of Craig Hd, and Middle Muck and W Muck in approach to Buckie (9.7.9); Findochty & Portknockie are 2 and 3.5M ENE. Halliman Skerries (dry; bn) lie 1·5M WNW of Lossiemouth (9.7.10). Covesea Skerries (dry) lie 5ca NW of their lt ho.

Inverness Firth is approached between Nairn (9.7.15) and S Sutor. In heavy weather there is a confused sea with overfalls on Guillam Bank, 9M S of Tarbat Ness. The sea also breaks on Riff Bank (S of S Sutor) which dries in places. Chans run both N and S of Riff Bank. ▶ *Off Fort George, on E side of ent to Inverness Firth (chart 1078), the SW-going stream begins HW Aberdeen + 0605, sp rate 2·5kn; the NE-going stream begins at HW Aberdeen – 0105, sp rate 3·5kn. There are eddies and turbulence between Fort George and Chanonry Pt when stream is running hard.* ◀ There is a firing range between Nairn and Inverness marked, when in operation, by flags at Fort George. Much of Inverness Firth is shallow, but a direct course from Chanonry Pt to Kessock Bridge, via Munlochy SWM and Meikle Mee SHM lt buoys, carries a least depth of 2·1m. Meikle Mee bank dries 0·2m. For Fortrose and Avoch, see 9.7.15.

MORAY FIRTH: NORTH WEST COAST (chart 115) Cromarty Firth (charts 1889, 1890) is entered between N Sutor and S Sutor, both fringed by rks, some of which dry. ▶ *Off the entrance the in-going stream begins at HW Aberdeen + 0605, and the out-going at HW Aberdeen – 0105, sp rates 1·5 kn.* ◀ Good sheltered anchs within the firth, see 9.7.16.

The coast NE to Tarbat Ness (lt) is fringed with rks. Beware Three Kings (dries) about 3M NE of N Sutor. ▶ *Culloden Rk, a shoal with depth of 1·8m, extends 2½ca NE of Tarbat Ness, where stream is weak.* ◀ Beware salmon nets between Tarbat Ness and Portmahomack (9.7.16). Dornoch Firth (9.7.16) is shallow, with shifting banks, and in strong E winds the sea breaks heavily on the bar E of Dornoch Pt.

At Lothbeg Pt, 5M SW of Helmsdale (9.7.17), a rky ledge extends 5ca offshore. Near Berriedale, 7M NE of Helmsdale, The Pinnacle, a detached rk 61m high, stands close offshore. The Beatrice oil field lies on Smith Bank, 28M NE of Tarbat Ness, and 11M off Caithness coast. Between Dunbeath and Lybster (9.7.17) there are no dangers more than 2ca offshore. Clyth Ness (lt) is fringed by detached and drying rks. From here to Wick (9.7.18) the only dangers are close inshore. There is anch in Sinclair's B in good weather, but Freswick B further N is better to await the tide in Pentland Firth (beware wreck in centre of bay). Stacks of Duncansby and Baxter Rk (depth 2·7m) lie 1M and 4ca S of Duncansby Hd.

PENTLAND FIRTH (charts 2162, 2581) ▶ ***This potentially dangerous chan should only be attempted with moderate winds (less than F4), good vis, no swell and a fair np tide; when it presents few problems.*** *A safe passage depends on a clear understanding of tidal streams and correct timing. The Admiralty Tidal Stream Atlas for Orkney and Shetland (NP 209) gives large scale vectors and is essential. Even in ideal conditions the races off Duncansby Hd, Swilkie Pt (N end of Stroma), and Rks of Mey (Merry Men of Mey) must be avoided as they are always dangerous to small craft. Also avoid the Pentland Skerries, Muckle Skerry, Old Head, Lother Rock (S Ronaldsay), and Dunnet Hd on E-going flood. For passages across the Firth see CCC SDs for Orkney.* ◀

At E end the Firth is entered between Duncansby Hd and Old Hd (S Ronaldsay), between which lie Muckle Skerry and the Pentland Skerries. Near the centre of Firth are the Islands of Swona (N side) and Stroma (S side). Outer Sound (main chan, 2·5M wide) runs between Swona and Stroma; Inner Sound (1·5M wide) between Stroma and the mainland. Rks of Mey extend about 2ca N of St John's Pt. The W end of the Firth is between Dunnet Hd and Tor Ness (Hoy).

▶ ***Tidal streams reach 8-9kn at sp in the Outer Sound, and 9-12kn between Pentland Skerries and Duncansby Hd. The resultant dangerous seas, very strong eddies and violent races should be avoided by yachts at all costs.*** *Broadly the E-going stream begins at HW Aberdeen + 0500, and the W-going at HW Aberdeen – 0105.* ***Duncansby Race*** *extends ENE towards Muckle Skerry on the SE-going stream, but by HW Aberdeen – 0440 it extends NW from Duncansby Hd. Note: HW at Muckle Skerry is the same time as HW Dover. A persistent race off* ***Swilkie Pt*** *at N end of Stroma,* ***is very dangerous with a strong W'ly wind over a W-going stream. The most dangerous and extensive race in the Firth is Merry Men of Mey.*** *It forms off St John's Pt on W-going stream at HW Aberdeen – 0150 and for a while extends right across to Tor Ness with heavy breaking seas even in fine weather.* ◀

Passage Westward: This is the more difficult direction due to prevailing W winds. ▶ *Freswick B, 3·5M S of Duncansby Hd, is a good waiting anch; here an eddy runs N for 9 hrs. Round Duncansby Hd close in at HW Aberdeen –0220, as the ebb starts to run W. Take a mid-course through the Inner Sound to appr the Rks of Mey from close inshore. Gills Bay is a temp anch if early; do not pass Rks of Mey until ebb has run for at least 2 hrs. Pass 100m N of the Rks (awash).*◀

Passage Eastward: ► *With a fair wind and tide, no race forms and the passage is easier. Leave Scrabster at local LW+1 so as to be close off Dunnet Hd not before HW Aberdeen +0340 when the E-going flood starts to make. If late, give the Hd a wide berth. Having rounded the Rks of Mey, steer S initially to avoid being set onto the rky S tip of Stroma, marked by unlit SCM bn.*◄ Then keep mid-chan through the Inner Sound and maintain this offing to give Duncansby Hd a wide berth.

PENTLAND FIRTH TO CAPE WRATH (chart 1954) Dunnet B, S of Dunnet Hd (lt) gives temp anch in E or S winds, but dangerous seas enter in NW'lies. On W side of Thurso B is Scrabster (9.7.19) sheltered from S and W. ► *Between Holborn Hd and Strathy Pt the E-going stream begins at HW Ullapool – 0150, and the W-going at HW Ullapool + 0420, sp rates 1·8kn. Close to Brims Ness off Ushat Hd the sp rate is 3kn, and there is often turbulence.* ◄

SW of Ushat Hd the Dounreay power stn is conspic, near shore. Dangers extend 2½ca seaward off this coast.

► *Along E side of Strathy Pt (lt) an eddy gives almost continuous N-going stream, but there is usually turbulence off the Pt where this eddy meets the main E or W stream.*◄ Several small B's along this coast give temp anch in offshore winds, but must not be used or approached with wind in a N quarter.

Kyle of Tongue (9.7.19) is entered from E through Caol Raineach, S of Eilean nan Ron, or from N between Eilean Iosal and Cnoc Glass. There is no chan into the kyle W of Rabbit Is,to which a drying spit extends 0·5M NNE from the mainland shore. Further S there is a bar across entrance to inner part of kyle. There are anchs on SE side of Eilean nan Ron, SE side of Rabbit Is, off Skullomie, or S of Eilean Creagach off Talmine. Approach to the latter runs close W of Rabbit Islands, but beware rks to N and NW of them.

Loch Eriboll, (chart 2076 and 9.7.19), provides secure anchs, but in strong winds violent squalls blow down from mountains. Eilean Cluimhrig lies on W side of entrance; the E shore is fringed with rks up to 2ca offshore. At White Hd (lt) the loch narrows to 6ca. There are chans W and E of Eilean Choraidh. Best anchs in Camas an Duin (S of Ard Neackie) or in Rispond B close to entrance (but not in E winds, and beware Rispond Rk which dries).

The coast to C. Wrath (9.8.5) is indented, with dangers extending 3ca off the shore and offlying rks and Is. Once a yacht has left Loch Eriboll she is committed to a long and exposed passage until reaching Loch Inchard. The Kyle of Durness is dangerous if the wind or sea is onshore. ► *Give Cape Wrath a wide berth when wind-against-tide which raises a severe sea.*◄ A firing exercise area extends 8M E of C. Wrath, and 4M offshore. When in use, R flags or pairs of R lts (vert) are shown from E and W limits, and yachts should keep clear.

ORKNEY ISLANDS (9.7.20 and charts 2249, 2250) The Islands are mostly indented and rky, but with sandy beaches especially on NE sides. ►*Pilotage is easy in good vis, but in other conditions great care is needed since tides run strongly. For details refer to* Clyde Cruising Club's *Orkney Sailing Directions and the* Admiralty *Tidal Atlas NP 209.*◄

► *When cruising in Orkney it is essential to understand and use the tidal streams to the best advantage, avoiding the various tide races and overfalls, particularly near sp.*◄ A good engine is needed since, for example, there are many places where it is dangerous to get becalmed. Swell from the Atlantic or North Sea can contribute to dangerous sea conditions, or penetrate to some of the anchorages. During summer months winds are not normally unduly strong, and can be expected to be Force 7 or more on about two days a month. But in winter the wind reaches this strength for 10-15 days per month, and gales can be very severe in late winter and early spring. Cruising conditions are best near midsummer, when of course the hours of daylight are much extended.

Stronsay Firth and Westray Firth run SE/NW through the group. The many good anchs, include: Deer Sound (W of Deer Ness); B of Firth, B of Isbister, and off Balfour in Elwick B (all leading from Wide Firth); Rysa Sound, B of Houton, Hunda Sound (in Scapa Flow); Rousay Sound; and Pierowall Road (Westray). Plans for some of these are on chart 2622. For Houton Bay, Shapinsay, Auskerry and Pierowall see 9.7.20. There is a major oil terminal and prohibited area at Flotta, on the S side of Scapa Flow.

► ***Tide races or dangerous seas occur at the entrances to most of the firths or sounds when the stream is against strong winds. This applies particularly to Hoy Sound, Eynhallow Sound, Papa Sound (Westray), Lashy Sound, and North Ronaldsay Firth. Also off Mull Head, over Dowie Sand, between Muckle Green Holm and War Ness (where violent turbulence may extend right across the firth), between Faraclett Head and Wart Holm, and off Sacquoy Hd. Off War Ness the SE-going stream begins at HW Aberdeen + 0435, and the NW-going at HW Aberdeen – 0200, sp rates 7kn.*** ◄

7

SHETLAND ISLANDS (9.7.24 and charts 3281, 3282, 3283) ► *These Islands mostly have bold cliffs and are relatively high, separated by narrow sounds through which the tide runs strongly, so that in poor vis great care is needed. Avoid sp tides, swell and wind against tide conditions.*◄ Although there are many secluded and attractive anchs, remember that the weather can change very quickly, with sudden shifts of wind. Also beware salmon fisheries and mussel rafts (unlit) in many Voes, Sounds and hbrs. Lerwick (9.7.25) is the busy main port and capital; for Scalloway, Vaila Sound and Balta Sound see 9.7.25. Refer to the CCC's *Shetland Sailing Directions.*

► *Coming from the S, beware a most violent and dangerous race (roost) off Sumburgh Hd (at S end of Mainland) on both streams. Other dangerous areas include between Ve Skerries and Papa Stour; the mouth of Yell Sound with strong wind against N-going stream; and off Holm of Skaw (N end of Unst). Tidal streams run mainly NW/SE and are not strong except off headlands and in the major sounds; the Admiralty Tidal Atlas NP 209 gives detail. The sp range is about 2m.*◄

The 50M passage from Orkney can conveniently be broken by a stop at Fair Isle (North Haven). ► *Note that races form off both ends of the Is, especially S (Roost of Keels); see 9.7.25.* ◄

Recommended Traffic Routes: NW-bound ships pass to the NE (no closer than 10M to Sumburgh Hd) or SW of Fair Isle; SE-bound ships pass no closer than 5M off N Ronaldsay (Orkney). Lerwick to Bergen, Norway is about 210M.

9.7.6 FRASERBURGH

Aberdeenshire 57°41'·50N 01°59'·79W ❀❀◊◊✿✿

CHARTS AC 115, *222*, 1462; Imray C23, C22; OS 30

TIDES +0120 Dover; ML 2·3; Duration 0615; Zone 0 (UT)

Standard Port ABERDEEN (⟵)

Times				Height (metres)			
High Water		Low Water		MHWS	MHWN	MLWN	MLWS
0000	0600	0100	0700	4·3	3·4	1·6	0·6
1200	1800	1300	1900				
Differences FRASERBURGH							
–0105	–0115	–0120	–0110	–0·6	–0·5	–0·2	0·0

SHELTER A safe refuge, but ent is dangerous in NE/SE gales. A very busy FV hbr; yachts are not encouraged but may find a berth in S Hbr (3.2m). FVs come and go H24.

NAVIGATION WPT 57°41'·30N 01°58'·80W, 291° to ent, 0·57M. The ent chan is dredged 5·9m. Good lookout on entering/ leaving. Yachts can enter under radar control in poor vis.

LIGHTS AND MARKS Kinnairds Hd lt ho, Fl 5s 25m 22M, is 0·45M NNW of ent. Cairnbulg Briggs bn, Fl (2) 10s 9m 6M, is 1·8M ESE of ent. Ldg lts 291°: front Iso R 2s 12m 9M; rear Iso R 2s 17m 9M.

R/T Call on approach VHF Ch **12** 16 (H24) for directions/berth.

TELEPHONE (Dial code 01346) Port Office 515858; Watch Tr 515926; MRCC (01224) 592334; Marinecall 09066 526235; Police 513121; Dr 518088.

FACILITIES **Port** ☎ 515858, AB £10 (in S Hbr) any LOA, Slip, P (cans), D, FW, CH, ME, El, ⚒, C (30 ton & 70 ton mobile), SM, 🛒, R, Bar; **Town** EC Wed; ⊠, Ⓑ, ⇌, ✈ (bus to Aberdeen).

ADJACENT HARBOURS

ROSEHEARTY, Aberdeen, **57°42'·08N 02°06'·87W**. ❀❀◊✿✿. AC 222, 213. HW Aberdeen –1. E pier and inner hbr dry, but end of W pier is accessible at all tides. Ent exposed in N/E winds; in E/SE winds hbr can be uncomfortable. Ldg marks B/W now (2001) lit on approx 220°; rks E of ldg line. When 30m from pier, steer midway between ldg line and W pier. Port Rae, close to E, has unmarked rks; local knowledge. AB £10 any LOA. *For details of Rover berting ticket see 9.7.5.* **Town** 🛒, R, Bar, ⊠. Firing range: for info ☎ (01346) 571634; see also 9.7.5. **Pennan Bay**, 5M W: ⚓ on sand between Howdman ($\underline{2}$·9m) and Tamhead ($\underline{2}$·1m) rks, 300m N of hbr (small craft only). **Gardenstown** (Gamrie Bay). Appr from E of Craig Dagerty rk (4m, conspic). Access HW±3 to drying hbr or ⚓ off.

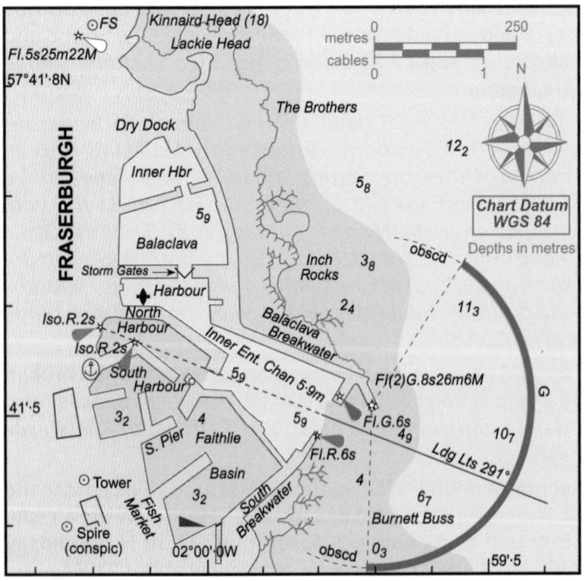
Kinnaird Head (18)
Lackie Head
Fl.5s25m22M
57°41'·8N
FRASERBURGH
Dry Dock
The Brothers
Inner Hbr
Balaclava
Storm Gates
Harbour
North Harbour
Iso.R.2s
Iso.R.2s
South Harbour
Inch Rocks
Balaclava Breakwater
Inner Ent. Chan 5·9m
Fl(2)G.8s26m6M
Fl.G.6s
Fl.R.6s
Ldg Lts 291°
S. Pier
Faithlie Basin
Fish Market
South Breakwater
Burnett Buss
Tower
Spire (conspic)
02°00'·0W
59'·5
41'·5
obscd
Chart Datum WGS 84
Depths in metres
metres
cables

9.7.7 MACDUFF/BANFF

Aberdeenshire Macduff **57°40'·25N 02°30'·03W** ❀❀◊◊✿✿
Banff **57°40'·22N 02°31'·27W** ❀❀◊◊✿✿

CHARTS AC 115, *222*, 1462; Imray C23, C22; OS 29

TIDES + 0055 Dover; ML 2·0; Duration 0615; Zone 0 (UT)

Standard Port ABERDEEN (⟵)

Times				Height (metres)			
High Water		Low Water		MHWS	MHWN	MLWN	MLWS
0200	0900	0400	0900	4·3	3·4	1·6	0·6
1400	2100	1600	2100				
Differences BANFF							
–0100	–0150	–0150	–0050	–0·4	–0·2	–0·1	+0·2

SHELTER **Macduff**: Reasonably good, but ent not advised in strong NW winds. Slight/moderate surge in outer hbr with N/ NE gales. Hbr ent is 17m wide with 3 basins; approx 2·6m in outer hbr and 2m inner hbr. A busy cargo/fishing port with limited space for yachts. **Banff**: Popular hbr (dries); access HW±4. When Macduff ent is very rough in strong NW/N winds, Banff can be a safe refuge; berth in outer basin and contact HM. In strong E/ ENE winds Banff is unusable.

NAVIGATION WPT 57°40'·48N 02°30'·59W, 127° to **Macduff** ent, 0·4M. WPT 57°40'·11N 02°30'·85W, 115° to **Banff** ent, 0·25M. Beware Feachie Craig, Collie Rks and rky coast N and S of hbr ent.

LIGHTS AND MARKS **Macduff**: Ldg lts/marks 127° both FR 44/ 55m 3M, orange △s. Pier hd lt, Fl (2) WRG 6s 12m 9/7M, W tr; W115°-174°, Horn (2) 20s. **Banff**: Fl 4s end of New Quay and ldg lts 295° rear Fl R 2s, front Fl R 4s.

R/T **Macduff** Ch 12 16 (H24); **Banff** Ch 14 (part-time).

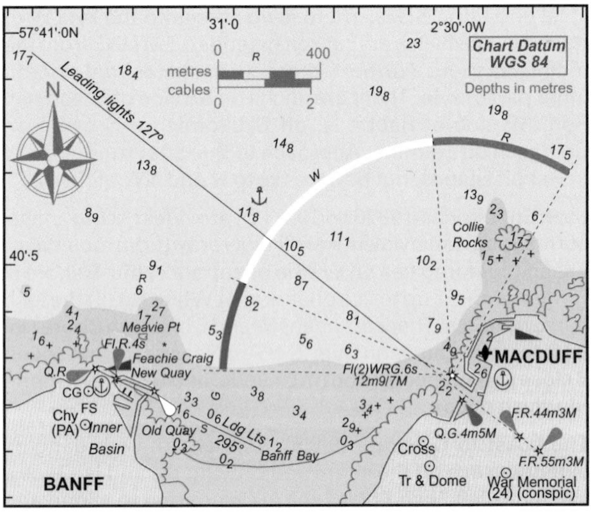
57°41'·0N
31'·0
2°30'·0W
Chart Datum WGS 84
Depths in metres
metres
cables
Leading lights 127°
Collie Rocks
Meavie Pt
Fl.R.4s
Feachie Craig
New Quay
Q.R
CG
FS
Chy (PA)
Inner Basin
Old Quay
Ldg Lts 295°
Banff Bay
Fl(2)WRG.6s 12m9/7M
MACDUFF
Q.G.4m5M
F.R.44m3M
F.R.55m3M
Cross
Tr & Dome
War Memorial (24) (conspic)
BANFF
40'·5

TELEPHONE (Dial code 01261) HM (**Macduff**) 832236, 📠 833612, Watch tr 833962; HM (**Banff**) 815544 (part time); MRCC (01224) 592334; Marinecall 09066 526235; Police 812555; Dr (**Banff**) 812027.

FACILITIES Macduff: **Hbr** £10 any LOA, Slip, P (cans), D, FW, ME, El, ⚒, CH. **Town** EC Wed; 🛒, R, Bar, ⊠, ⇌ (bus to Keith). Banff: **Hbr** £10 any LOA, *for details of Rover berthing ticket see 9.7.5.*, FW, ⊐D, Slip, new toilet block; **Banff SC**: showers. **Town**, P, D, 🛒, R, Bar, ⇌, Ⓑ, ✈ (Aberdeen).

ADJACENT HARBOURS

PORTSOY, Aberdeenshire, **57°41'·34N 02°41'·59W**. ❀❀◊✿✿✿. AC 222. HW +0047 on Dover; –0132 and Ht –0·3m on Aberdeen. Small drying hbr; ent exposed to NW/NE'lies. New Hbr to port of ent partially dries; inner hbr dries to clean sand. Ldg lts 160°, front FW 12m 5M on twr; rear FR 17m 5M. HM ☎ (01261) 815544. Facilities: few. AB £10, *for details of Rover berthing ticket see 9.7.5.*, FW, Slip, 🛒, R, Bar, ⊠. **Sandend Bay**, 1·7M W (57°41'N 02°44'·5W). ⚓ on sand E of hbr.

9.7.8 WHITEHILLS

Aberdeenshire **57°40'·80N 02°34'·87W**

CHARTS AC 115, *222*; Imray C23, C22; OS 29

TIDES +0050 Dover; ML 2·4; Duration 0610; Zone 0 (UT)

Standard Port ABERDEEN (⟵)

Times				Height (metres)			
High Water		Low Water		MHWS	MHWN	MLWN	MLWS
0200	0900	0400	0900	4·3	3·4	1·6	0·6
1400	2100	1600	2100				
Differences WHITEHILLS							
–0122	–0137	–0117	–0127	–0·4	–0·3	+0·1	+0·1

SHELTER Safe. In strong NW/N winds beware surge in the narrow ent and outer hbr, when ent is best not attempted. See HM for vacant pontoon berth. Ent dredged to 1·5m and inner hbr 1·5m (2002).

NAVIGATION WPT 57°41'·98N 02°34'·89W, 180° to bkwtr lt, 1·2M. Reefs on S side of chan marked by 2 rusty/white SHM bns. Beware fishing floats.

LIGHTS AND MARKS Fl WR 3s on pier hd, vis R132°–212°, W212°–245°; appr in R sector.

R/T Whitehills Hbr Radio VHF Ch 14 16.

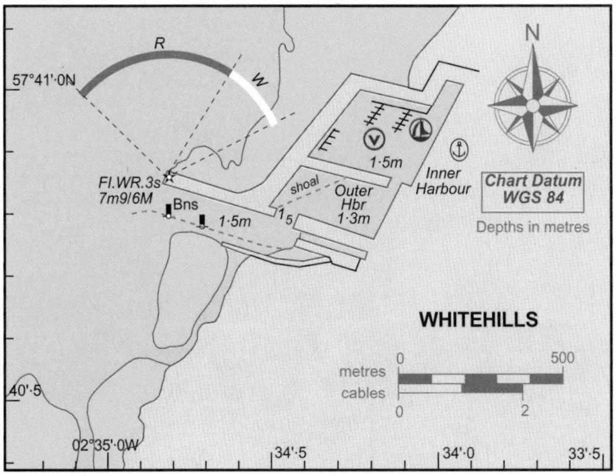
57°41'·0N
R
W
N
Fl.WR.3s
7m9/6M
Bns
1·5m
shoal
Outer Hbr
1·3m
1·5m
Inner Harbour
Chart Datum WGS 84
Depths in metres
WHITEHILLS
metres
cables
0
500
2
40'·5
02°35'·0W
34'·5
34'·0
33'·5

TELEPHONE (Dial code 01261) HM 861291 or home 861435; MRCC (01224) 592334; Marinecall 09066 526235; Police Banff 812555; Dr 812027.

FACILITIES **Marina** (38,+ welcome), ☎ 861291 £15 (decreasing to £30/3nights), Quayside £12, D, FW, ME, El, CH; email: enquiries@whitehillsharbour.co.uk. **Town** , R, Bar, ✉, ⇌ (bus to Keith), ✈ (Aberdeen).

ADJACENT HARBOURS

CULLEN, Moray, **57°41'·63N 02°49'·29W**. AC 222. HW +0045 on Dover, HW –0135 & –0·3m on Aberdeen; Duration 0555; ML 2·4m. Shelter good, but ent hazardous in strong W/N winds. Appr on 180° toward conspic viaduct and W bn on N pier. Caple Rk, 0·2m, is 5ca NE of hbr. Access HW ±2 approx. Small drying unlit hbr, best for shoal draft. Moor S of Inner jetty if < 1m draft. Beware moorings across inner basin ent. Pontoons in inner hbr. *For details of Rover berthing ticket see 9.7.5.* HM ☎ (01261) 842477 (home,part-time). **Town** ,R,Bar, ✉.

PORTKNOCKIE, Moray, **57°42'·28N 02°51'·79W**. AC 222. HW +0045 on Dover; –0135 and ht –0·3m Aberdeen; ML 2·3m; Duration 0555; access H24. Good shelter in one of the safest hbrs on S side of Moray Firth, but scend is often experienced; care needed in strong NW/N winds. FW ldg lts, on white-topped poles, lead approx 143°, to ent. Orange street lts surround the hbr. Berth N quay of outer hbr on firm sand; most of inner hbr dries. HM ☎ (01542) 840833 (home, p/time); Facilities: Slip, AB, *for details of Rover berthing ticket see 9.7.5.*, FW, ⚒; Dr ☎ 840272. **Town** EC Wed; Ⓑ, P & D, ✉, , Bar.

ADJACENT HARBOUR (2M ENE of BUCKIE)

FINDOCHTY, Moray, **57°41'·94N 02°54'·29W**. AC 222. HW +0045 on Dover, HW –0140 & ht –0·2m on Aberdeen; ML 2·3m; Duration 0550. Ent is about 2ca W of conspic church belfry. 1ca N of ent, leave Beacon Rock (3m high) to stbd. Ldg lts, FR, lead approx 166° into Outer Basin which dries 0·2m and has many rky outcrops; access HW ±2 for 1·5m draft. Ent faces N and is 20m wide; unlit white bn at hd of W pier. Good shelter in inner basin for 100 small craft/yachts on 3 pontoons (the 2 W'ly pontoons dry); AB, *for details of Rover berthing ticket see 9.7.5.* HM ☎ (01542) 832560 (home, part-time). **Town** , R, Bar, ✉, Ⓑ.

9.7.9 BUCKIE

Moray **57°40'·84N 02°57'·63W**

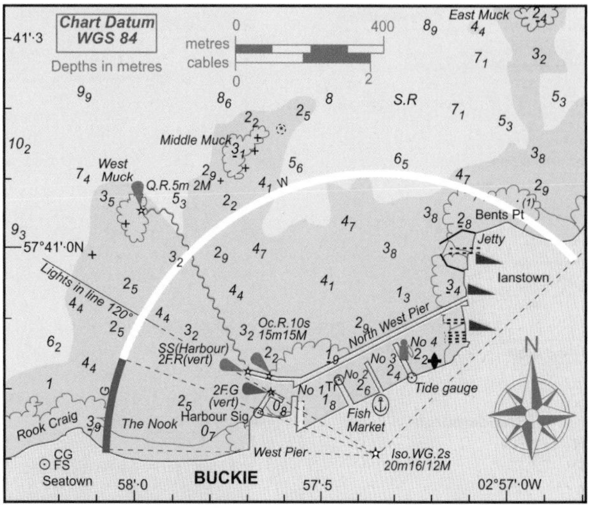
Chart Datum WGS 84
Depths in metres
metres
cables
0
400
2
East Muck
41'·3
S.R
Middle Muck
West Muck
Q.R.5m 2M
57°41'·0N
Lights in line 120°
Bents Pt
Jetty
Ianstown
Oc.R.10s 15m15M
SS(Harbour)
2F.R(vert)
North West Pier
No 4
No 3
No 2
No 1
2F.G (vert)
Harbour Sig
Tide gauge
Fish Market
Rook Craig
The Nook
West Pier
Iso.WG.2s 20m16/12M
CG
FS
Seatown
BUCKIE
58'·0
57'·5
02°57'·0W
N

CHARTS AC 115, *222*, 1462; Imray C23, C22; OS 28

TIDES +0040 Dover; ML 2·4; Duration 0550; Zone 0 (UT)

Standard Port ABERDEEN (⟵)

Times				Height (metres)			
High Water		Low Water		MHWS	MHWN	MLWN	MLWS
0200	0900	0400	0900	4·3	3·4	1·6	0·6
1400	2100	1600	2100				
Differences BUCKIE							
–0130	–0145	–0125	–0140	–0·2	–0·2	0·0	+0·1

SHELTER Good in all weathers, but in strong NNW to NE winds there is a dangerous swell over the bar at hbr ent, which is 24m wide and dredged to 4m, but subject to silting. Entrance dredged to 4m but subject to silting. Access H24. Berth in No 4 basin as directed by HM.

NAVIGATION WPT 57°41'·30N 02°58'·89W, 126° to ent, 0·80M. Beware W Muck (QR 5m tripod, 2M), Middle Muck and E Muck Rks, 3ca off shore.

LIGHTS AND MARKS The Oc R 10s 15m 15M, W tr on N bkwtr, 2FG(vert) in line 120° with Iso WG 2s 20m 16/12M, W tr, R top, leads clear of W Muck. White tr of ice plant on pier No. 2 is conspic. Entry sigs on N pier: 3 ● lts = hbr closed. Traffic is controlled by VHF.

R/T VHF Ch 12 16 (H24).

TELEPHONE (Dial code 01542) HM 831700 834742; MRCC (01224) 592334; Marinecall 09066 526235; Police 832222; Dr 831555.

FACILITIES **No 4 Basin** AB £10.58 or £5.29 <12hrs, FW; **Services:** D & P (delivery), BY, ME, El, ⚒, CH, Slip, C (15 ton), Gas. **Town** EC Wed; , Bar, Ⓑ, ✉, at Strathlene caravan site 1·5M E, ⇌ (bus to Elgin), ✈ (Aberdeen or Inverness).

7

9.7.10 LOSSIEMOUTH

Moray **57°43'·41N 03°16'·63W** ✲✲⚓⚓✿✿✿

CHARTS AC *223*, 1462; Imray C23, C22; OS 28

TIDES +0040 Dover; ML 2·3; Duration 0605; Zone 0 (UT)

Standard Port ABERDEEN (⟵)

Times				Height (metres)			
High Water		Low Water		MHWS	MHWN	MLWN	MLWS
0200	0900	0400	0900	4·3	3·4	1·6	0·6
1400	2100	1600	2100				
Differences LOSSIEMOUTH							
–0125	–0200	–0130	–0130	–0·2	–0·2	0·0	0·0

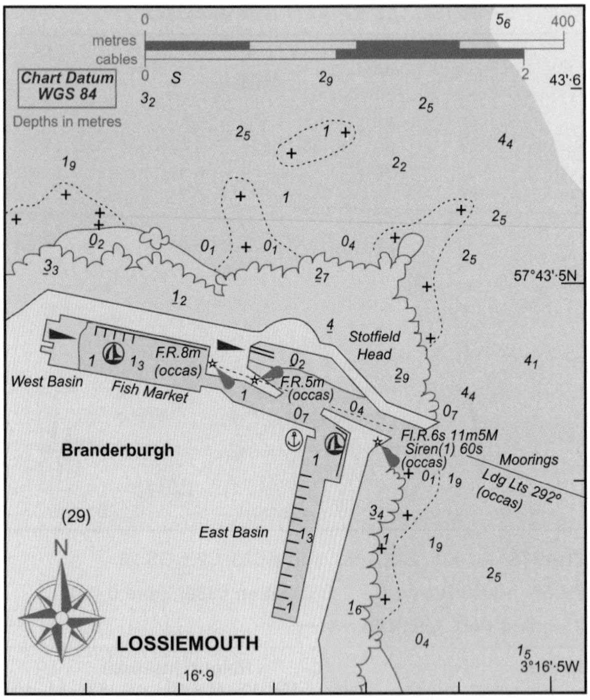
metres
cables
Chart Datum WGS 84
Depths in metres
43'·6
57°43'·5N
Stotfield Head
F.R.8m (occas)
F.R.5m (occas)
West Basin
Fish Market
Fl.R.6s 11m5M Siren(1) 60s (occas)
Moorings
Ldg Lts 292° (occas)
Branderburgh
(29)
East Basin
N
LOSSIEMOUTH
16'·9
3°16'·5W

SHELTER Very good in winds from SSE to NW. In N to SE winds >F6 appr to ent can be dangerous, with swell in outer hbr. Pontoon berths in both basins, dredged 2m; access HW±4. But chan and Basins are prone to silting; a vessel drawing 2m would have little clearance at LWS ±1. West basin also used by FV's.

NAVIGATION WPT 57°43'·38N 03°16'·09W, 277° to ent, 0·30M. Rks to N and S of hbr ent; appr from E. Near ent, beware current from R Lossie setting in N'ly direction, causing confused water in N to SE winds at sp.

LIGHTS AND MARKS Covesea Skerries, W lt ho, Fl WR 20s 49m 24M, is 2M W of the hbr ent. Ldg lts 292°, both FR 5/8m; S pier hd Fl R 6s 11m 5M. Traffic sigs: B ● at S pier (● over Fl R 6s) = hbr shut.

R/T VHF Ch 12 16 HO.

TELEPHONE (Dial code 01343) HM ☎/📠 813066; MRCC (01224) 592334; Marinecall 09066 526235; Police 812022; Dr 812277.

FACILITIES Marina (43), ☎ 813066, £15.00 inc ⚡, FW, ⊡, ♿; **Hbr** ME, El, ⚒, C, SM; **Lossiemouth CC** ☎ 814519; **Hbr Service Stn** ☎ 813001, Mon-Fri 0800-2030, Sat 0800-1930, Sun 0930-1900, P & D cans, Gas. **Town** EC Thurs; 🛒, R, Bar, ✉, Ⓑ, ⇌ (bus to Elgin), ✈ (Inverness).

9.7.11 HOPEMAN

Moray **57°42'·70N 03°26'·31W** ✲✲⚓⚓✿✿

CHARTS AC *223*, 1462; Imray C23, C22; OS 28

TIDES +0050 Dover; ML 2·4; Duration 0610; Zone 0 (UT)

Standard Port ABERDEEN (⟵)

Times				Height (metres)			
High Water		Low Water		MHWS	MHWN	MLWN	MLWS
0200	0900	0400	0900	4·3	3·4	1·6	0·6
1400	2100	1600	2100				
Differences HOPEMAN							
–0120	–0150	–0135	–0120	–0·2	–0·2	0·0	0·0

SHELTER Once in Inner basin, shelter good from all winds; but hbr dries, access HW ± 2 (for 1·5m draft). Ent is difficult in winds from NE to SE. A popular yachting hbr with AB. For details of Rover berthing see 9.7.5.

NAVIGATION WPT 57°42'·66N, 03°26'·59W, 083° to ent, 0·17M. Dangerous rks lie off hbr ent. Do not attempt entry in heavy weather. Beware lobster pot floats E and W of hbr (Mar-Aug).

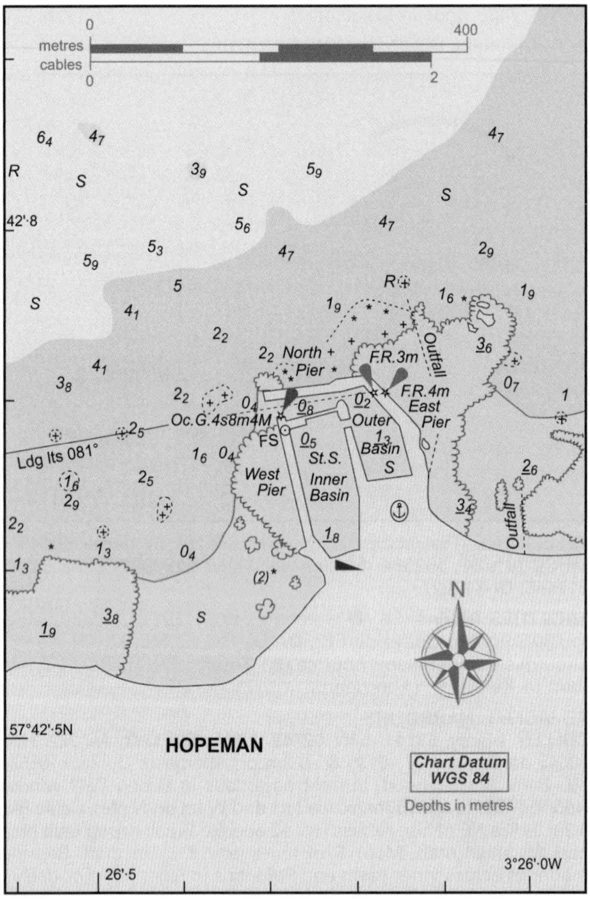
metres
cables
42'·8
North Pier
F.R.3m
Outfall
F.R.4m
East Pier
Oc.G.4s8m4M
FS
Outer Basin
Ldg lts 081°
West Pier
St.S.
Inner Basin
N
57°42'·5N
HOPEMAN
Chart Datum WGS 84
Depths in metres
26'·5
3°26'·0W

LIGHTS AND MARKS Ldg lts 081°, FR 3/4m; S pier hd FG 4s 8m 4M.

R/T Call *Burghead Radio* Ch 14 (HX).

TELEPHONE (Dial code 01343) HM ☎/📠 835337 (part-time); MRCC (01224) 592334; Marinecall 09066 526235; Police 830222; Dr 543141.

FACILITIES Hbr AB £9, *for details of Rover Ticket see 9.7.5.*, FW, Slip. **Services:** CH, ME, Gas, ⚒, El, P (cans). **Town** EC Wed; 🛒, R, Bar, ✉, Ⓑ, ⇌ (bus to Elgin), ✈ (Inverness).

9.7.12 BURGHEAD

Moray **57°42'·06N 03°30'·02W**

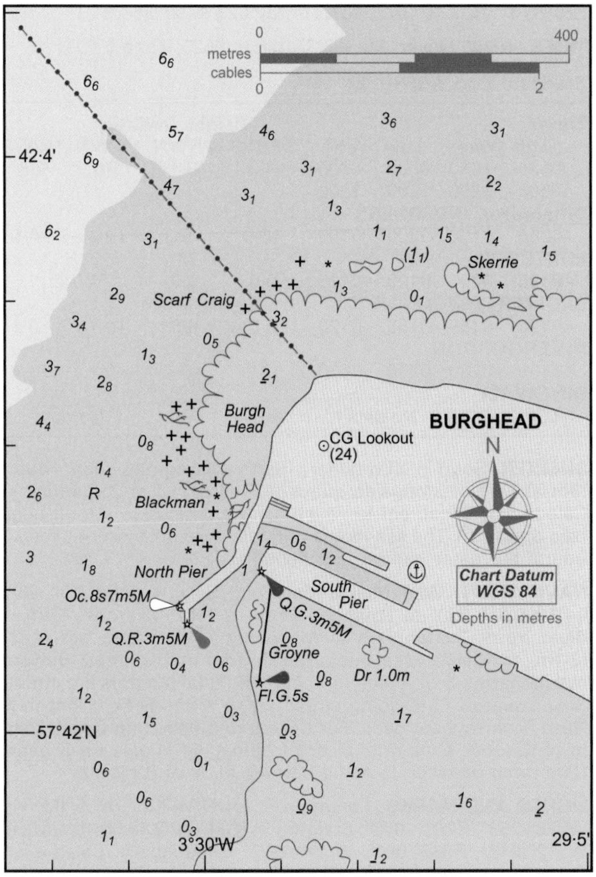
metres
cables
Scarf Craig
Burgh Head
BURGHEAD
CG Lookout (24)
Blackman
North Pier
Oc.8s7m5M
Q.R.3m5M
South Pier
Q.G.3m5M
Groyne
Dr 1.0m
Fl.G.5s
Skerrie
Chart Datum WGS 84
Depths in metres
42·4'
57°42'N
3°30'W
29·5'

CHARTS AC 1462, *223*; Imray C22, C23; OS 28

TIDES +0035 Dover; ML 2·4; Duration 0610; Zone 0 (UT)

Standard Port ABERDEEN (⟵)

Times				Height (metres)			
High Water		Low Water		MHWS	MHWN	MLWN	MLWS
0200	0900	0400	0900	4·3	3·4	1·6	0·6
1400	2100	1600	2100				
Differences BURGHEAD							
–0120	–0150	–0135	–0120	–0·2	–0·2	0·0	0·0

SHELTER One of the few Moray Firth hbrs accessible in strong E winds. 0·6m depth in ent chan and 1·4m in hbr. Go alongside where available and contact HM. Can be very busy with FVs.

NAVIGATION WPT 57°42'·28N 03°30'·39W, 137° to N pier lt QR, 0·28M. Access HW ±4. Chan is variable due to sand movement. Advisable to contact HM if entering at LW.

LIGHTS AND MARKS No ldg lts but night ent is safe after identifying the N pier lts: QR 3m 5M and Oc 8s 7m 5M.

R/T Call *Burghead Radio* VHF Ch **14** 12 (HO and when vessel due).

TELEPHONE (Dial code 01343) HM 835337; MRCC (01224) 592334; Marinecall 09066 526235; Dr 812277.

FACILITIES **Hbr** AB £9, *for details of Rover Ticket see 9.7.5.*, FW, AB, C (50 ton mobile), L, Slip, BY, ⚒. **Town** EC Thurs; Bar, ✉, 🛒, Ⓑ, ⇌ (bus to Elgin), ✈ (Inverness).

9.7.13 FINDHORN

Moray **57°39'·64N 03°37'·47W**

CHARTS AC *223*; Imray C22, C23; OS 27

TIDES +0110 Dover; ML 2·5; Duration 0615; Zone 0 (UT)

Standard Port ABERDEEN (⟵)

Times				Height (metres)			
High Water		Low Water		MHWS	MHWN	MLWN	MLWS
0200	0900	0400	0900	4·3	3·4	1·6	0·6
1400	2100	1600	2100				
Differences FINDHORN							
–0120	–0150	–0135	–0130	0·0	–0·1	0·0	+0·1

SHELTER ⚓ in pool off boatyard or off N pier or dry out alongside, inside piers and ask at YC; or pick up Y 🅜 off N pier. Do not attempt entry in strong NW/NE winds or with big swell running; expect breakers/surf either side of ent.

NAVIGATION WPT 57°40'·33N 03°38'·65W, SWM Landfall Buoy. Access HW±2. 100m SE of the Landfall Buoy there is 1 Y waiting 🅜 in 4m. From WPT, the bar is marked (Fl R marker) and thence by Fl R or G buoys all of which are moved to suit the channel into the bay, and may be lifted Nov to early Apr. Once past The Ee, turn port inside G buoys. The S part of Findhorn Bay dries extensively.

LIGHTS AND MARKS Unlit. There is a windsock on FS by The Ee. Boatyard building is conspic.

R/T VHF Ch M *Chadwick Base* (when racing in progress). Findhorn BY: Ch 80.

TELEPHONE (Dial code 01309) Fairways Committee (via BY) 690099; MRCC (01224) 592334; Findhorn Pilot (Derek Munro) 690802, mob 07747 840916; Marinecall 09066 526235; Police 0845 6005000700; Dr 678866/678888; Findhorn BY 690099.

FACILITIES **Royal Findhorn YC** ☎ 690247, M, 🅜 (free), FW, Bar; **Services:** BY, L, M, ⛽, FW, Slip, C (16 ton), P & D (cans), El, ME, CH, ACA, Gas, ⚒. **Town** 🛒, R, Bar, ✉, Ⓑ, ⇌ (Forres), ✈ (Inverness).

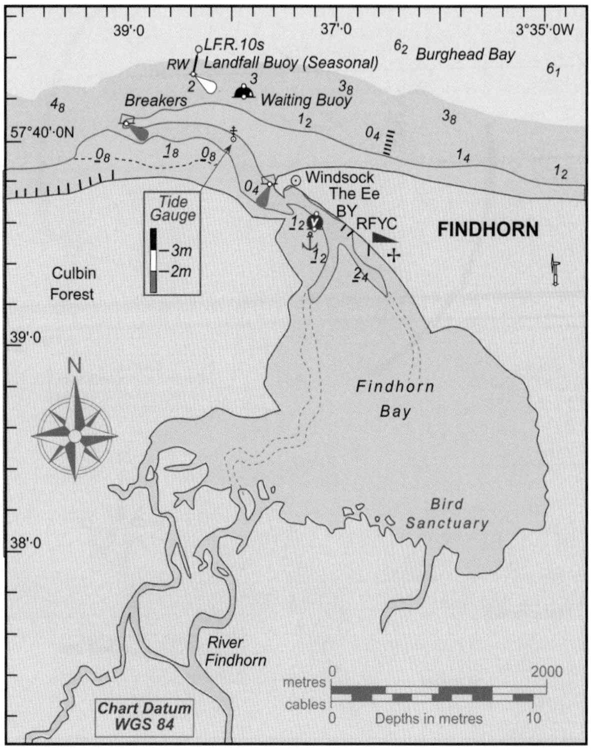
39'·0
37'·0
3°35'·0W
L.F.R.10s
RW Landfall Buoy (Seasonal)
Burghead Bay
Breakers
Waiting Buoy
57°40'·0N
Windsock
The Ee
BY
RFYC
FINDHORN
Tide Gauge
3m
2m
Culbin Forest
Findhorn Bay
Bird Sanctuary
38'·0
River Findhorn
metres
cables
Depths in metres
Chart Datum WGS 84

9.7.14 NAIRN

Highland **57°35'·61N 03°51'·65W**

CHARTS AC *223*, 1462; Imray C23, C22; OS 27

TIDES +0110 Dover; ML 2·2; Duration 0615; Zone 0 (UT)

Standard Port ABERDEEN (←→)

Times				Height (metres)			
High Water		Low Water		MHWS	MHWN	MLWN	MLWS
0200	0900	0400	0900	4·3	3·4	1·6	0·6
1400	2100	1600	2100				
Differences NAIRN							
–0120	–0150	–0135	–0130	0·0	–0·1	0·0	+0·1
McDERMOTT BASE							
–0110	–0140	–0120	–0115	–0·1	–0·1	+0·1	+0·3

SHELTER Good, but entry difficult in fresh NNE'ly. Pontoons in hbr with Ⓥ berths. Best entry HW ± 1½. A Y Ⓐ is close to the WPT, approx 400m NNW of the pierheads; the W'ly buoy in 2·5m, the E'ly in 1·5m. No commercial shipping.

NAVIGATION WPT 57°35'·88N 03°51'·89W, 155° to ent, 0·3M. The approach dries to 100m off the pierheads. Inside, the best water is to the E side of the river chan.

LIGHTS AND MARKS Lt ho on E pier hd, Oc WRG 4s 6m 5M, vis G shore-100°, W100°-207°, R207°-shore. Keep in W sector. McDermott Base, 4·5M to the W, has a large conspic cream-coloured building; also useful if making for Inverness Firth.

R/T None. Ch M (weekends only).

TELEPHONE (Dial code 01667) HM 454330; MRCC (01224) 592334; Clinic 455092; Marinecall 09066 526235; Police 452222; Dr 453421.

FACILITIES **Nairn Basin** AB £15.28 - 48hrs, Slip(launching £5), AC (110 volts), P(cans), D; **Nairn SC** ☎ 453897, Bar. **Town** EC Wed; 🛒, R, Bar, ✉, Ⓑ, ⇌, ✈ (Inverness).

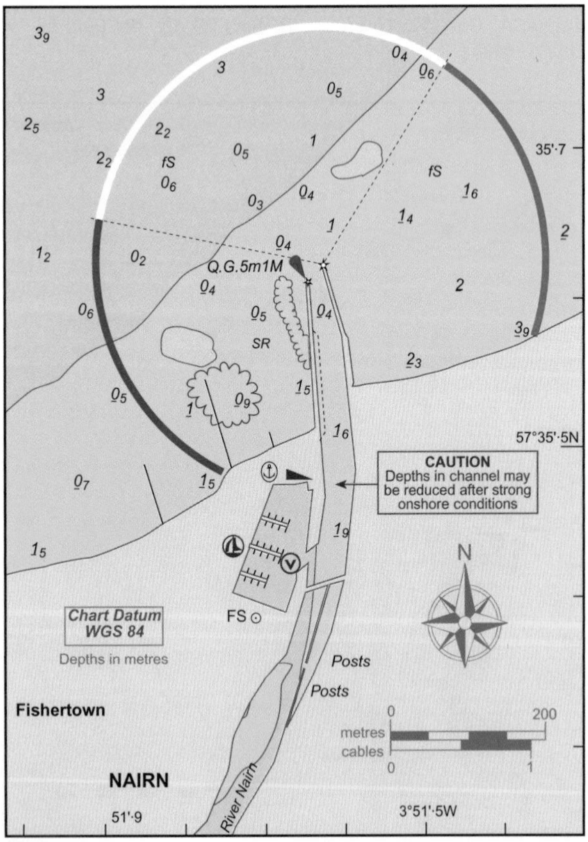
Q.G.5m1M
CAUTION
Depths in channel may be reduced after strong onshore conditions
Chart Datum WGS 84
Depths in metres
FS
SR
fS
Posts
Posts
Fishertown
NAIRN
River Nairn
N
metres
cables
0
200
0
1
35'·7
57°35'·5N
51'·9
3°51'·5W

9.7.15 INVERNESS

Highland **57°29'·73N 04°14'·17W**

CHARTS AC *223*, 1077, 1078; Imray C23, C22; OS 26/27

TIDES +0100 Dover; ML 2·7; Duration 0620; Zone 0 (UT)

Standard Port ABERDEEN (←→)

Times				Height (metres)			
High Water		Low Water		MHWS	MHWN	MLWN	MLWS
0300	1000	0000	0700	4·3	3·4	1·6	0·6
1500	2200	1200	1900				
Differences INVERNESS							
–0050	–0150	–0200	–0150	+0·5	+0·3	+0·2	+0·1
FORTROSE							
–0125	–0125	–0125	–0125	0·0	0·0	No data	
CROMARTY							
–0120	–0155	–0155	–0120	0·0	0·0	+0·1	+0·2
INVERGORDON							
–0105	–0200	–0200	–0110	+0·1	+0·1	+0·1	+0·1
DINGWALL							
–0045	–0145	No data		+0·1	+0·2	No data	

SHELTER Good in all weathers. Berth at Longman Yacht Haven (3m at LW) or alongside quays in R Ness; or at 2 marinas in Caledonian Canal, ent to which can be difficult in strong tides (see opposite). The sea lock is normally available HW±4 in canal hours; the gates cannot be opened LW±2.

NAVIGATION WPT Meikle Mee SHM By Fl G 3s, 57°30'·25N 04°12'·03W, 250° to Longman Pt bn, 0·74M. Inverness Firth is deep from Chanonry Pt to Munlochy SWM buoy, but shoal (2·1m) to Meikle Mee buoy. Meikle Mee partly dries. Beware marine farms S of Avoch (off chartlet). Tidal streams are strong S of Craigton Pt (E-going stream at sp exceeds 5kn). Ent to R Ness is narrow but deep. For the ent to Caledonian Canal, keep to N Kessock bank until clear of unmarked shoals on S bank. Care must be taken to avoid Carnare Pt W of R mouth.

LIGHTS AND MARKS Longman Pt bn Fl WR 2s 7m 5/4M, vis W078°-258°, R258° -078°. Craigton Pt lt, Fl WRG 4s 6m 11/7M vis W312°-048°, R048°-064°, W064°-085°, G085°-shore. Caledonian Canal ent marked by QR and Iso G 4s on ends of training walls.

R/T Call: *Inverness Hbr Office* VHF Ch 12 (Mon-Fri: 0900 -1700 LT). Inverness Boat Centre Ch 80 M (0900-1800 LT). Caledonian Canal: Ch 74 is used by all stations. Call: *Clachnaharry Sea Lock*; or for office: *Caledonian Canal*.

TELEPHONE (Dial code 01463) HM 715715; Clachnaharry Sea Lock 713896; Canal Office 233140; MRCC (01224) 592334; Marinecall 09066 526235; Police 715555; Dr 234151.

FACILITIES **Longman Yacht Haven** (18+4 visitors), £12, ☎ 715715, FW, access H24 (3m at LW); **Citadel and Shore Street Quays** (R Ness) ☎ 715715, AB £12, P, D, FW, ME, El; (For commercial ships unless directed by HM). **Services:** Slip, M, ME, El, C (100 ton), CH, FW, P, SM, Gas. **Town** EC Wed; 🛒, R, Bar, ✉, Ⓑ, ⇌, ✈.

MINOR HARBOURS IN INVERNESS FIRTH

FORTROSE, Highland, **57°34'·71N 04°08'·04W**. AC 1078. Tides 9.7.15. HW +0055 on Dover; ML 2·5m; Duration 0620. Small drying unlit hbr, well protected by Chanonry Ness to E; access HW±2, limited space. Follow ldg line 296°, Broomhill Ho (conspic on hill to NW) in line with school spire until abeam SPM buoy; then turn W to avoid Craig an Roan rks (1·8m) ESE of ent. Chanonry Pt lt, Oc 6s 12m 15M, obscd 073°-shore. HM ☎ (01381) 620861; Dr ☎ 620909. Facilities: EC Thurs; AB £5, L, M, P, D, Slip, Gas, R, 🛒, ✉, Ⓑ; **Chanonry SC** (near pier) ☎ 01381 621973.

AVOCH, Highland, **57°34'·03N 04°09'·94W**. AC 1078. Tides as Fortrose (1·25M to the ENE). Hbr dries, mostly on the N side, but is bigger than Fortrose; access HW±2. Small craft may stay afloat at nps against the S pier, which has 2FR (vert) at E-facing ent. HM ☎ (mobile) 07779 833951. Facilities: AB £7, FW, ⛽. **Village**: ✉, 🛒, R, Bar, P & D (cans), ME.

INVERNESS *continued*

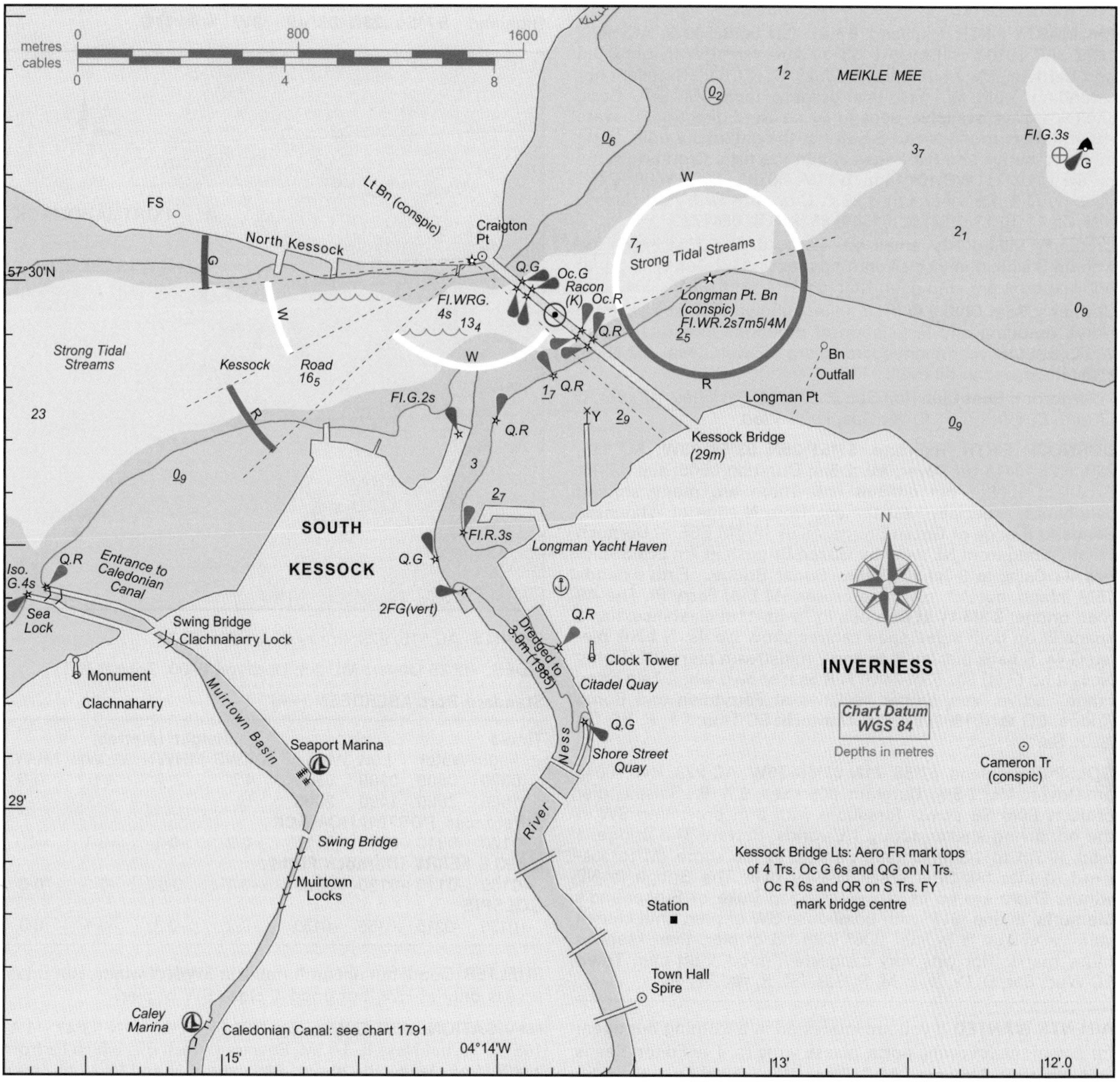
metres
cables
0
800
1600
4
8
MEIKLE MEE
Fl.G.3s
G
FS
Lt Bn (conspic)
Craigton Pt
North Kessock
57°30'N
Strong Tidal Streams
Q.G
Oc.G
Racon (K)
Oc.R
Longman Pt. Bn (conspic) Fl.WR.2s7m5/4M
Fl.WRG. 4s
Q.R
Bn
Outfall
Longman Pt
Kessock
Road
Fl.G.2s
Kessock Bridge (29m)
SOUTH
KESSOCK
Fl.R.3s
Longman Yacht Haven
Iso. G.4s
Q.R
Entrance to Caledonian Canal
Sea Lock
Swing Bridge
Clachnaharry Lock
2FG(vert)
Dredged to 3.0m (1985)
Clock Tower
Citadel Quay
Monument
Clachnaharry
Muirtown Basin
Seaport Marina
Shore Street Quay
River Ness
INVERNESS
Chart Datum WGS 84
Depths in metres
Cameron Tr (conspic)
29'
Swing Bridge
Muirtown Locks
Kessock Bridge Lts: Aero FR mark tops of 4 Trs. Oc G 6s and QG on N Trs. Oc R 6s and QR on S Trs. FY mark bridge centre
Station
Town Hall Spire
Caley Marina
Caledonian Canal: see chart 1791
04°14'W
15'
13'
12'.0

CALEDONIAN CANAL (Sea lock 57°29'·44N 04°15'·84W). These notes are for the convenience of those entering the Canal at Inverness. They supplement and partly duplicate the main information and chartlet in 9.8.17.

CHARTS AC 1791, 1078; OS 26, 27, 34, 41. *BWB Skipper's Guide* essential.

TIDES Differences: Clachnaharry +0116 on Dover; see 9.7.15.

SHELTER Clachnaharry sea lock operates HW±4 (sp) within canal hours. The road and rail swing bridges may cause delays up to 25 mins. Seaport and Caley marinas: see Facilities.

NAVIGATION The 60M Caledonian Canal consists of 38M through three lochs, (Lochs Ness, Oich and Lochy), connected by 22M through canals. It can take vessels 45m LOA, 10m beam, 4m draft and max mast ht 27·4m. The passage normally takes two full days, possibly longer in the summer; 14 hrs is absolute minimum. Speed limit is 5kn in canal sections. There are 10 swing bridges; road tfc has priority at peak hrs. Do not pass bridges without the keeper's instructions. From Clachnaharry sea lock to Loch Ness (Bona Ferry lt ho) is approx 7M, via Muirtown and Dochgarroch locks.

LOCKS All 29 locks are manned and operate early May to early Oct, 0800-1800LT daily. Dues: see 9.8.17. For regulations and *BWB Skipper's Guide* apply: Canal Manager, Muirtown Wharf, Inverness IV3 5LS, ☎ (01463) 233140; 📠 710942. www.scottishcanals.co.uk

LIGHTS & MARKS Chans are marked by posts, cairns and unlit buoys, PHM on the NW side of the chan and SHM on the SE side.

BOAT SAFETY SCHEME Transient/visiting vessels will be checked for apparent dangerous defects eg leaking gas or fuel, damaged electrical cables, taking in water, risk of capsize. £1M 3rd party insurance is required. For details see 9.8.17.

R/T Sea locks and main lock flights operate VHF Ch **74** (HO).

TELEPHONE Clachnaharry sea lock (01463) 713896; Canal Office, Inverness (01463) 233140.

FACILITIES **Seaport marina** (20+ 20 Ⓥ), ☎ (01463) 239745, ⊐D, FW, D, El, ME, ✕, Gas, Gaz, ⊡, C (40 ton), ⚲, ♿. **Caley marina** (25+25 Ⓥ) ☎ (01463) 236539, FW, ⊐D, CH, D, ME, El, ✕, C (20 ton), ACA.

OTHER HARBOURS ON THE NORTH WEST SIDE OF THE MORAY FIRTH

CROMARTY FIRTH, Highland, **57°41'·18N 04°02'·09W**. AC 1889, 1890. HW +0100 on Dover -0135 on Aberdeen;HW height 0.0m on Aberdeen; ML 2·5m; Duration 0625. See 9.7.15. Excellent hbr extending 7·5M W, past Invergordon, then 9M SW. Good shelter always available, depending on wind direction. Beware rks and reefs round N and S Sutor at the ent; many unlit oil rig mooring buoys and fish cages within the firth. Cromarty lt ho, on the Ness, Oc WR 10s 18m 15/11M, R079°–088°, W088°–275°, obsc by N Sutor when brg < 253°. *Cromarty Firth Port Control* VHF Ch 11 16 13 (H24) ☎ (01349) 852308 📠 854172.

Cromarty Village Hbr, small hbr, partly drying, just inside the firth on S side. Many small craft on moorings; ⚓ 2ca W of S pier hd in approx 6m with good holding. HM ☎ (01381) 600479.

Cromarty Boat Club 2 Ⓥ (free) in 3m, showers, ⊡, key at Royal Hotel; dredging and installation of pontoons intended during 2003; see www.cromartyboatclub.org. Ferry: Local to Nigg; also Invergordon-Kirkwall.

Invergordon Boat Club Hon Sec ☎ 877612. Facilities: AB, Bar, C (3 ton), D, FW, ✉, P, R, 🛒, Gas, L; EC Wed.

DORNOCH FIRTH, Highland. **57°51'·28N 03°59'·39W**. AC 115, 223. HW +0115 on Dover; ML 2·5m; Duration 0605; see 9.7.16. Excellent shelter but difficult ent. There are many shifting sandbanks, especially near the ent, from N edge of Whiteness Sands to S edge of Gizzen Briggs. ⚓s in 7m ¾M ESE of Dornoch Pt (sheltered from NE swell by Gizzen Briggs); in 7m 2ca SSE of Ard na Cailc; in 3·3m 1M below Bonar Bridge. Firth extends 15M inland, but AC coverage ceases ¼M E of Ferry Pt. The A9 road bridge, 3·3M W of Dornoch Pt, with 11m clearance, has 3 spans lit on both sides; span centres show Iso 4s, N bank pier Iso G 4s, S bank pier Iso R 4s and 2 midstream piers QY. Tarbat Ness lt ho Fl (4) 30s 53m 24M. Fl R 5s lt shown when Tain firing range active. Very limited facilities at Ferrytown and Bonar Bridge. CG ☎ (01862) 810016. **Dornoch**: EC Thur; 🛒, P, ✉, Dr, Ⓑ, R, Bar.

GOLSPIE, Highland, **57°58'·71N 03°56'·79W**. AC 223. HW +0045 on Dover; ML 2·3m; Duration 068. See 9.7.16. Golspie pier projects 60m SE across foreshore with arm projecting SW at the hd, giving shelter during NE winds. Beware The Bridge, a bank (0·3m to 1·8m) running parallel to the shore ¼M to seaward of pier hd. Seas break heavily over The Bridge in NE winds. There are no lts. To enter, keep Duke of Sutherland's Memorial in line 316° with boathouse SW of pier, until church spire in village is in line 006° with hd of pier, then keep on those marks. Hbr gets very congested; good ⚓ off pier. **Town** EC Wed; Bar, D, Dr, Ⓗ, L, M, P, Gas, ✉, R, ⇌, 🛒, Ⓑ.

AGENTS WANTED If you are interested in becoming our agent for any of the following ports, please write to: The Editor, Reeds OKI Nautical Almanac, A&C Black Publishers Ltd, 37 Soho Square, London, W1D 3QZ – and get your free copy of the Almanac annually. You do not have to live in a port to be the agent, but should at least be a fairly regular visitor.

Keyhaven	Le Légué
Shetland Isles/Lerwick	St Helier/Gorey
Rothesay	Bénodet
Dunmore East	Concarneau
Baltimore	Lézardrieux
Belfast Lough	Lannion River
All Danish ports	Loctudy
Borkum	River Loire
Langeoog	Pornic
Zeebrugge	St Gilles-Croix-de-Vie
Hoek van Holland	Les Sables d'Olonne
Rotterdam	La Rochelle
Blankenberge	Rochefort
IJsselmeer	Capbreton
Le Havre	Port d'Anglet

9.7.16 PORTMAHOMACK

Highland **57°50'.28N 03°49'·79W** ❁❁♿✿✿

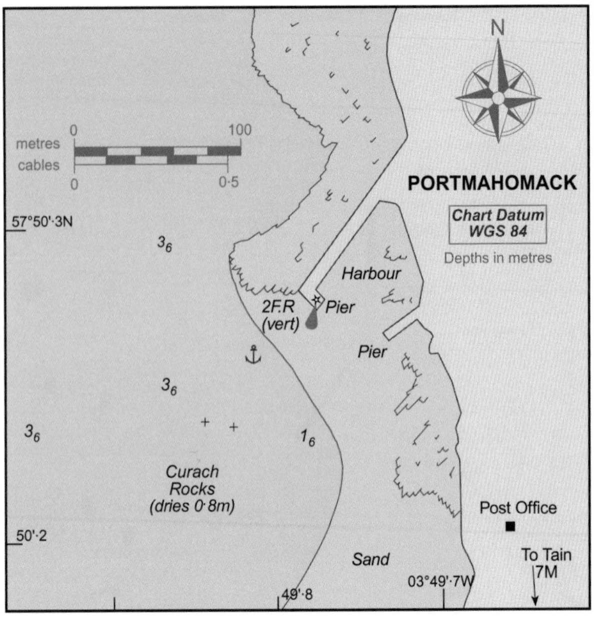
N
PORTMAHOMACK
Chart Datum WGS 84
Depths in metres
metres
cables
0
100
0
0·5
57°50'·3N
50'·2
Harbour
Pier
Pier
2F.R (vert)
Curach Rocks (dries 0·8m)
Post Office
Sand
To Tain 7M
03°49'·7W
49'·8

CHARTS AC 115, 223; Imray C23, C22; OS 21

TIDES +0035 Dover; ML 2·5; Duration 0600; Zone 0 (UT)

Standard Port ABERDEEN (⟵)

Times				Height (metres)			
High Water		Low Water		MHWS	MHWN	MLWN	MLWS
0300	0800	0200	0800	4·3	3·4	1·6	0·6
1500	2000	1400	2000				
Differences PORTMAHOMACK							
–0120	–0210	–0140	–0110	–0·2	–0·1	+0·1	+0·1
MEIKLE FERRY (Dornoch Firth)							
–0100	–0140	–0120	–0055	+0·1	0·0	–0·1	0·0
GOLSPIE							
–0130	–0215	–0155	–0130	–0·3	–0·3	–0·1	0·0

SHELTER Good, but uncomfortable in SW/NW winds. Hbr dries, access only at HW, but good ⚓ close SW of pier.

NAVIGATION WPT SPM buoy, Fl Y 5s, 57°53'·01N 03°47'·11W, 166° to Tarbat Ness lt, 1·13M. Beware Curach Rks which lie from 2ca SW of pier to the shore. Rks extend N and W of the pier. Beware lobster pot floats and salmon nets N of hbr. Tain firing & bombing range is about 3M to the W, S of mouth of Dornoch Firth; R flags, R lts, shown when active.

LIGHTS AND MARKS Tarbert Ness lt ho Fl (4) 30s 53m 24M, W twr R bands, is 2·6M to NE of hbr. Pier hd 2 FR (vert) 7m 5M.

R/T None.

TELEPHONE (Dial code 01862) HM 871353; MRCC (01224) 592334; Marinecall 09066 526235; Dr 892759.

FACILITIES **Hbr**, AB <5m £8.23, 5-7m £11.16, 7-10m £15.28, M, L, FW. Showers, WC. **Town** EC Wed; R, 🛒, Bar, ✉, ⇌ (bus to Tain), ✈ (Inverness).

9.7.17 HELMSDALE

Highland **58°06'·83N 03°38'·89W**

CHARTS AC 115, 1462; Imray C22; OS 17

TIDES +0035 Dover; ML 2·2; Duration 0615; Zone 0 (UT)

Standard Port WICK (⟶)

Times				Height (metres)			
High Water		Low Water		MHWS	MHWN	MLWN	MLWS
0000	0700	0200	0700	3·5	2·8	1·4	0·7
1200	1900	1400	1900				
Differences HELMSDALE							
+0025	+0015	+0035	+0030	+0·4	+0·3	+0·1	0·0

SHELTER Good, except in strong E/SE'lies. AB on NW pier, approx 1m. 30m of Pontoon berths through HM. Limited depths at LWS.

NAVIGATION WPT 58°06'·59N 03°38'·39W, 313° to ent, 0·35M, ldg marks are dark poles with Or topmarks. Beware spate coming down river after heavy rain. Shoal both sides of chan and bar builds up when river in spate. Silting reported 2003.

LIGHTS AND MARKS Ldg lts 313° (occas).

R/T VHF Ch 13 16.

TELEPHONE (Dial code 01431) HM 821692 (Office), 821386 (Home); MRCC (01224) 592334; Police 821222; Marinecall 09066 526235; Dr 821221, or 821225 (Home).

FACILITIES **Hbr** AB <5m £8.23, 5m-7m £11.16, 7m-10m £15.28, M (See HM), FW, Slip. **Town** EC Wed; P, D, Gas, ⊠, R, Bar, ⊠, Ⓑ (Brora), ⇌ (Wick).

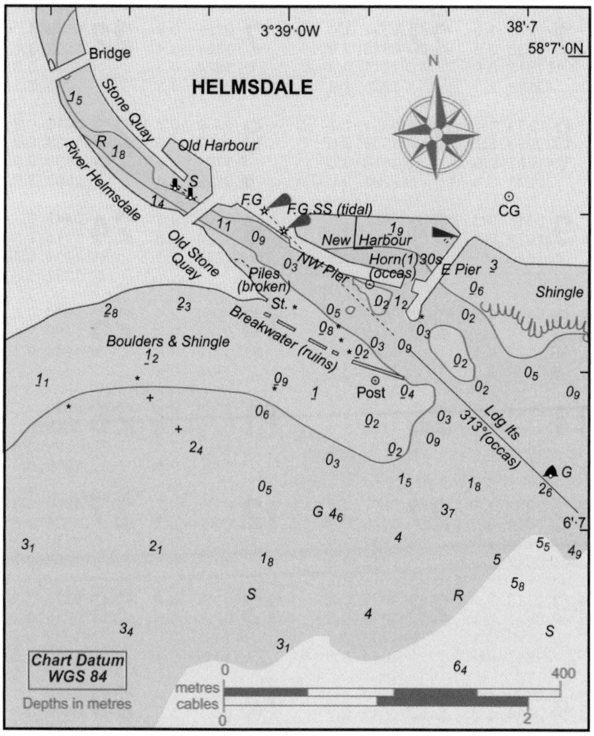
3°39'·0W
38'·7
58°7'·0N
HELMSDALE
Bridge
Stone Quay
Old Harbour
River Helmsdale
F.G
F.G.SS (tidal)
New Harbour
Horn(1)30s (occas)
E Pier
NW Pier
Old Stone Quay
Piles (broken)
Breakwater (ruins)
Shingle
Boulders & Shingle
Post
Ldg lts 313°(occas)
CG
6'·7
Chart Datum WGS 84
Depths in metres
metres
cables

ADJACENT HARBOUR

LYBSTER, Highland, **58°17'·72N 03°17'·39W**. AC 115. HW +0020 on Dover; HW –0150 sp, –0215 np; HW ht –0·6m on Aberdeen; ML 2·1m; Duration 0620. Excellent shelter in basin (SW corner of inner hbr); AB on W side of pier in about 1·2m. Most of hbr dries to sand/mud and is much used by FVs; no bollards on N wall. Appr on about 350°. Beware rks close on E side of ent; narrow (10m) ent is difficult in strong E to S winds. Min depth 2·5m in ent. S pier hd, Oc R 6s 10m 3M, occas in fishing season. AB £7.00 per week, FW on W quay. **Town** EC Thurs; Bar, D, P, R.

9.7.18 WICK

Highland **58°26'·38N 03°04'·72W**

CHARTS AC 115, 1462; Imray C22, C68; OS 12

TIDES +0010 Dover; ML 2·0; Duration 0625; Zone 0 (UT). Wick is a Standard Port. Daily tidal predictions are given below.

Standard Port WICK (⟶)

Times				Height (metres)			
High Water		Low Water		MHWS	MHWN	MLWN	MLWS
0000	0700	0200	0700	3·5	2·8	1·4	0·7
1200	1900	1400	1900				
Differences DUNCANSBY HEAD							
–0115	–0115	–0110	–0110	–0·4	–0·4	No data	

SHELTER Good, except in strong NNE to SSE winds. A good hbr to await right conditions for W-bound passage through the Pentland Firth (see 9.7.5). Berth where directed in the Inner Hbr, 2·4m. NB: The River Hbr (commercial) is leased and must **not** be entered without prior approval.

NAVIGATION WPT 58°26'·18N 03°03'·39W, 284° to S pier, 0·72M. From the N, open up hbr ent before rounding North Head so as to clear drying Proudfoot Rks. Hbr ent is dangerous in strong E'lies as boats have to turn port 90° at the end of S pier. On S side of bay, an unlit bn, 300m ENE of LB slip, marks end of ruined bkwtr.

LIGHTS AND MARKS S pier lt, Fl WRG 3s 12m 12/9M, G253°-270°, W270°-286°, R286°-329°, Bell (2) 10s (fishing). Ldg lts , both FR 5/8m, lead 234° into outer hbr. Traffic signals:
- B ● (●) at CG stn on S Head = hbr closed by weather.
- B ● (●) at S pier head = caution; hbr temp obstructed.

R/T VHF Ch 14 16 (when vessel expected).

TELEPHONE (Dial code 01955) HM 602030, 605936; MRSC (01224) 592334; Police 603551; Ⓗ 602434, 602261.

FACILITIES **Inner and Outer Hbr** AB £7, £35 per week (showers available), Slip, ME; **Fish Jetty** D, FW, CH; **Services:** ME, El, Slip, Gas, C (15/ 100 ton). **Town** EC Wed; P, R, Bar, ⊠, Ⓑ, ⇌, ✈.

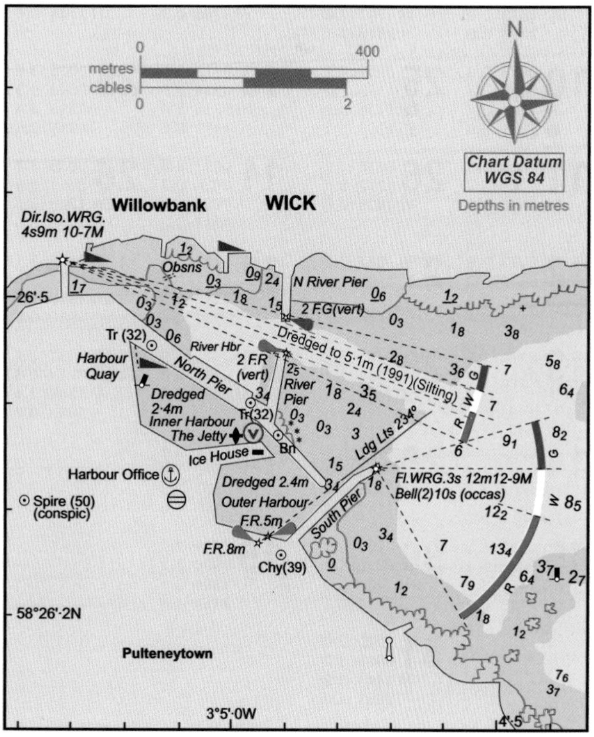
metres
cables
Chart Datum WGS 84
Depths in metres
Dir.Iso.WRG. 4s9m 10-7M
Willowbank
WICK
Obsns
N River Pier
2 F.G(vert)
26'·5
Dredged to 5·1m (1991)(Silting)
Tr (32)
River Hbr
2 F.R (vert)
Harbour Quay
North Pier
River Pier
Dredged 2·4m
Inner Harbour
The Jetty
Ldg Lts 234°
Ice House
Harbour Office
Dredged 2.4m
Outer Harbour
F.R.5m
F.R.8m
South Pier
Fl.WRG.3s 12m12-9M
Bell(2)10s (occas)
Spire (50) (conspic)
Chy(39)
58°26'·2N
Pulteneytown
3°5'·0W

TIME ZONE (UT)
For Summer Time add ONE hour in **non-shaded areas**

SCOTLAND – WICK

LAT 58°26′N LONG 3°05′W

TIMES AND HEIGHTS OF HIGH AND LOW WATERS

SPRING & NEAP TIDES
Dates in red are SPRINGS
Dates in blue are NEAPS

YEAR **2005**

JANUARY

Date	Time	m	Time	m	Time	m	Time	m
1 SA	0231	2.9	0758	1.4	1433	3.2	2048	1.1
2 SU	0314	2.9	0838	1.4	1516	3.1	2135	1.2
3 M	0403	2.8	0925	1.5	1606	3.0	◑ 2233	1.2
4 TU	0501	2.8	1028	1.6	1706	3.0	2342	1.2
5 W	0604	2.8	1153	1.6	1815	3.0		
6 TH	0049	1.2	0708	2.9	1311	1.5	1925	3.0
7 F	0153	1.2	0811	3.0	1418	1.4	2035	3.2
8 SA	0251	1.1	0909	3.2	1518	1.1	2139	3.3
9 SU	0344	1.0	1003	3.4	1613	0.9	2236	3.5
10 M	0435	0.9	1053	3.6	1704	0.7	● 2331	3.6
11 TU	0523	0.9	1141	3.7	1755	0.5		
12 W	0023	3.6	0609	0.9	1229	3.8	1844	0.4
13 TH	0114	3.6	0654	0.9	1317	3.8	1933	0.4
14 F	0203	3.4	0737	1.0	1404	3.7	2023	0.5
15 SA	0252	3.3	0821	1.1	1452	3.6	2113	0.7
16 SU	0341	3.1	0906	1.3	1542	3.4	2206	1.0
17 M	0432	2.9	0958	1.4	1637	3.2	◐ 2304	1.2
18 TU	0528	2.8	1107	1.5	1738	3.0		
19 W	0010	1.4	0629	2.8	1232	1.6	1846	2.9
20 TH	0122	1.4	0737	2.8	1356	1.5	2001	2.8
21 F	0225	1.5	0840	2.9	1458	1.4	2106	2.9
22 SA	0314	1.4	0932	3.0	1546	1.3	2158	3.0
23 SU	0354	1.4	1015	3.2	1626	1.1	2241	3.1
24 M	0431	1.3	1054	3.3	1702	1.0	2319	3.1
25 TU	0504	1.2	1129	3.4	1736	0.9	○ 2354	3.2
26 W	0535	1.2	1202	3.4	1808	0.8		
27 TH	0027	3.2	0605	1.1	1234	3.4	1839	0.8
28 F	0100	3.2	0634	1.1	1305	3.4	1910	0.8
29 SA	0132	3.1	0704	1.1	1336	3.4	1941	0.8
30 SU	0205	3.1	0735	1.1	1408	3.3	2014	0.9
31 M	0240	3.0	0809	1.2	1444	3.2	2051	1.0

FEBRUARY

Date	Time	m	Time	m	Time	m	Time	m
1 TU	0321	2.9	0847	1.3	1527	3.1	2135	1.1
2 W	0410	2.8	0934	1.4	1621	3.0	◑ 2236	1.2
3 TH	0511	2.8	1045	1.5	1733	2.9		
4 F	0002	1.3	0623	2.8	1235	1.5	1857	2.9
5 SA	0128	1.3	0739	2.9	1406	1.3	2023	3.0
6 SU	0241	1.2	0850	3.1	1516	1.1	2135	3.2
7 M	0340	1.1	0950	3.3	1611	0.8	2233	3.4
8 TU	0429	1.0	1043	3.5	1700	0.5	● 2325	3.5
9 W	0513	0.8	1130	3.7	1746	0.3		
10 TH	0012	3.6	0554	0.8	1216	3.8	1829	0.2
11 F	0057	3.6	0634	0.7	1300	3.8	1911	0.3
12 SA	0140	3.4	0712	0.8	1342	3.7	1952	0.4
13 SU	0220	3.3	0749	0.9	1424	3.6	2030	0.7
14 M	0301	3.1	0826	1.0	1507	3.3	2109	1.0
15 TU	0343	2.9	0906	1.2	1554	3.1	2154	1.3
16 W	0432	2.7	1002	1.4	1652	2.8	◐ 2257	1.5
17 TH	0532	2.6	1139	1.6	1805	2.6		
18 F	0028	1.6	0648	2.6	1332	1.6	1936	2.6
19 SA	0202	1.6	0809	2.7	1444	1.4	2053	2.7
20 SU	0300	1.5	0910	2.9	1531	1.2	2145	2.8
21 M	0341	1.4	0956	3.0	1609	1.0	2226	3.0
22 TU	0416	1.3	1034	3.2	1643	0.9	2301	3.1
23 W	0447	1.1	1109	3.3	1714	0.7	2334	3.1
24 TH	0516	1.0	1141	3.4	1744	0.6	○	
25 F	0005	3.2	0543	0.9	1213	3.4	1813	0.6
26 SA	0036	3.2	0611	0.8	1243	3.5	1842	0.6
27 SU	0106	3.2	0641	0.8	1313	3.4	1912	0.6
28 M	0137	3.2	0711	0.8	1344	3.4	1943	0.7

MARCH

Date	Time	m	Time	m	Time	m	Time	m
1 TU	0210	3.1	0744	0.9	1419	3.3	2018	0.9
2 W	0248	3.0	0820	1.1	1502	3.1	2058	1.0
3 TH	0333	2.9	0905	1.2	1556	2.9	◑ 2153	1.3
4 F	0432	2.8	1013	1.4	1713	2.8	2335	1.5
5 SA	0551	2.7	1228	1.4	1851	2.7		
6 SU	0120	1.5	0718	2.8	1407	1.2	2025	2.9
7 M	0238	1.3	0838	3.0	1512	0.9	2133	3.1
8 TU	0333	1.1	0939	3.2	1602	0.6	2225	3.3
9 W	0416	0.9	1029	3.5	1646	0.3	2311	3.5
10 TH	0456	0.7	1114	3.7	1727	0.2	● 2353	3.5
11 F	0533	0.6	1157	3.8	1806	0.2		
12 SA	0033	3.5	0609	0.6	1238	3.8	1842	0.3
13 SU	0110	3.4	0645	0.6	1316	3.7	1917	0.5
14 M	0146	3.2	0719	0.7	1354	3.5	1949	0.7
15 TU	0220	3.1	0754	0.9	1434	3.2	2021	1.0
16 W	0257	2.9	0831	1.1	1517	2.9	2056	1.3
17 TH	0339	2.8	0920	1.3	1611	2.7	◐ 2143	1.6
18 F	0436	2.6	1055	1.5	1727	2.5	2328	1.7
19 SA	0556	2.5	1257	1.5	1906	2.4		
20 SU	0131	1.7	0727	2.6	1416	1.3	2030	2.6
21 M	0237	1.6	0837	2.7	1504	1.1	2121	2.7
22 TU	0318	1.4	0926	2.9	1541	0.9	2200	2.9
23 W	0351	1.2	1005	3.0	1614	0.8	2233	3.0
24 TH	0420	1.0	1039	3.2	1644	0.6	2305	3.1
25 F	0448	0.9	1112	3.3	1714	0.5	○ 2336	3.2
26 SA	0516	0.7	1144	3.4	1743	0.5		
27 SU	0007	3.3	0545	0.7	1217	3.4	1812	0.5
28 M	0038	3.3	0616	0.6	1249	3.4	1844	0.5
29 TU	0110	3.2	0649	0.7	1324	3.3	1917	0.7
30 W	0145	3.2	0725	0.8	1403	3.2	1953	0.9
31 TH	0223	3.1	0805	0.9	1450	3.0	2036	1.1

APRIL

Date	Time	m	Time	m	Time	m	Time	m
1 F	0310	2.9	0856	1.1	1551	2.8	2138	1.4
2 SA	0411	2.8	1028	1.2	1717	2.7	◑ 2335	1.5
3 SU	0535	2.7	1234	1.2	1857	2.7		
4 M	0115	1.5	0705	2.7	1359	0.9	2021	2.9
5 TU	0225	1.3	0822	2.9	1457	0.7	2120	3.1
6 W	0315	1.1	0921	3.2	1544	0.5	2207	3.2
7 TH	0355	0.9	1009	3.4	1624	0.3	2249	3.3
8 F	0432	0.7	1053	3.5	1701	0.2	● 2328	3.4
9 SA	0508	0.6	1134	3.6	1737	0.3		
10 SU	0004	3.4	0544	0.5	1213	3.6	1810	0.4
11 M	0039	3.3	0619	0.6	1251	3.4	1843	0.6
12 TU	0112	3.2	0655	0.7	1328	3.3	1914	0.8
13 W	0145	3.1	0730	0.8	1406	3.0	1944	1.1
14 TH	0219	3.0	0809	1.0	1448	2.8	2017	1.3
15 F	0259	2.8	0858	1.2	1540	2.6	2100	1.5
16 SA	0350	2.6	1021	1.4	1652	2.4	◐ 2228	1.7
17 SU	0504	2.5	1204	1.4	1821	2.4		
18 M	0030	1.7	0631	2.5	1328	1.2	1945	2.5
19 TU	0151	1.6	0747	2.6	1421	1.1	2040	2.6
20 W	0238	1.4	0841	2.8	1501	0.9	2121	2.8
21 TH	0313	1.2	0924	2.9	1536	0.7	2156	2.9
22 F	0345	1.0	1002	3.1	1608	0.6	2230	3.1
23 SA	0415	0.8	1038	3.2	1639	0.5	2303	3.2
24 SU	0447	0.7	1114	3.3	1711	0.4	○ 2337	3.3
25 M	0520	0.6	1150	3.4	1744	0.5		
26 TU	0011	3.3	0555	0.6	1229	3.4	1819	0.6
27 W	0047	3.3	0634	0.6	1310	3.3	1858	0.7
28 TH	0126	3.2	0716	0.7	1356	3.2	1940	0.9
29 F	0209	3.1	0805	0.8	1451	3.0	2031	1.2
30 SA	0300	3.0	0912	0.9	1559	2.8	2147	1.4

Chart Datum: 1·71 metres below Ordnance Datum (Newlyn)

TIME ZONE (UT)
For Summer Time add ONE hour in **non-shaded areas**

SCOTLAND – WICK

LAT 58°26′N LONG 3°05′W

TIMES AND HEIGHTS OF HIGH AND LOW WATERS

SPRING & NEAP TIDES
Dates in red are SPRINGS
Dates in blue are NEAPS

YEAR **2005**

MAY

Date	Time	m	Date	Time	m
1 SU	0405	2.8	16 M	0418	2.6
	1053	1.0		1107	1.2
	1723	2.7		1727	2.4
	◑ 2328	1.5		◐ 2314	1.6
2 M	0526	2.8	17 TU	0531	2.6
	1223	0.9		1219	1.2
	1848	2.7		1838	2.5
3 TU	0052	1.4	18 W	0035	1.6
	0645	2.8		0641	2.6
	1337	0.8		1321	1.1
	2000	2.8		1939	2.6
4 W	0157	1.2	19 TH	0137	1.4
	0756	3.0		0742	2.7
	1433	0.6		1410	0.9
	2055	3.0		2029	2.7
5 TH	0247	1.0	20 F	0224	1.2
	0855	3.1		0833	2.8
	1519	0.5		1451	0.8
	2141	3.1		2111	2.9
6 F	0329	0.9	21 SA	0304	1.1
	0944	3.3		0919	3.0
	1558	0.5		1528	0.7
	2222	3.2		2151	3.0
7 SA	0408	0.7	22 SU	0342	0.9
	1029	3.3		1002	3.1
	1634	0.5		1605	0.6
	2300	3.2		2229	3.2
8 SU	0445	0.6	23 M	0420	0.8
	1110	3.4		1045	3.3
	1708	0.5		1642	0.6
	● 2336	3.3		○ 2308	3.3
9 M	0523	0.6	24 TU	0500	0.6
	1150	3.3		1129	3.3
	1742	0.6		1722	0.6
				2348	3.3
10 TU	0011	3.3	25 W	0542	0.6
	0600	0.6		1215	3.3
	1229	3.2		1804	0.7
	1815	0.8			
11 W	0044	3.2	26 TH	0030	3.4
	0638	0.7		0628	0.5
	1306	3.1		1304	3.3
	1847	1.0		1849	0.8
12 TH	0118	3.1	27 F	0114	3.3
	0716	0.8		0719	0.6
	1345	2.9		1356	3.2
	1919	1.2		1939	1.0
13 F	0152	3.0	28 SA	0202	3.2
	0756	1.0		0817	0.6
	1427	2.7		1455	3.0
	1954	1.3		2035	1.2
14 SA	0231	2.9	29 SU	0257	3.1
	0844	1.1		0927	0.7
	1516	2.6		1600	2.9
	2036	1.5		2144	1.3
15 SU	0318	2.7	30 M	0400	3.0
	0948	1.2		1044	0.8
	1616	2.5		1710	2.8
	2139	1.6		◑ 2301	1.4
			31 TU	0509	2.9
				1157	0.8
				1819	2.7

JUNE

Date	Time	m	Date	Time	m
1 W	0013	1.3	16 TH	0535	2.7
	0617	2.9		1213	1.1
	1304	0.8		1831	2.6
	1924	2.8			
2 TH	0119	1.2	17 F	0026	1.4
	0724	3.0		0637	2.7
	1402	0.7		1311	1.0
	2021	2.9		1929	2.7
3 F	0216	1.1	18 SA	0128	1.3
	0825	3.0		0738	2.8
	1450	0.7		1403	0.9
	2111	3.0		2023	2.8
4 SA	0304	1.0	19 SU	0223	1.2
	0919	3.1		0837	2.9
	1531	0.8		1451	0.9
	2155	3.1		2113	3.0
5 SU	0348	0.9	20 M	0312	1.0
	1008	3.1		0932	3.1
	1609	0.8		1537	0.8
	2235	3.1		2200	3.1
6 M	0429	0.8	21 TU	0400	0.8
	1052	3.1		1025	3.2
	1645	0.8		1623	0.7
	● 2313	3.2		2246	3.3
7 TU	0510	0.8	22 W	0449	0.7
	1133	3.1		1117	3.3
	1721	0.9		1710	0.7
	2349	3.2		○ 2332	3.4
8 W	0550	0.7	23 TH	0538	0.5
	1213	3.1		1208	3.4
	1756	1.0		1757	0.8
9 TH	0024	3.2	24 F	0018	3.5
	0628	0.8		0628	0.4
	1251	3.0		1301	3.4
	1829	1.1		1845	0.8
10 F	0059	3.1	25 SA	0106	3.5
	0706	0.8		0721	0.4
	1329	2.9		1354	3.3
	1903	1.2		1934	0.9
11 SA	0134	3.1	26 SU	0156	3.4
	0745	0.9		0817	0.4
	1409	2.8		1448	3.1
	1938	1.2		2024	1.0
12 SU	0211	3.0	27 M	0248	3.3
	0826	0.9		0915	0.5
	1451	2.7		1544	3.0
	2015	1.3		2119	1.1
13 M	0251	2.9	28 TU	0343	3.2
	0913	1.0		1016	0.6
	1538	2.6		1641	2.9
	2100	1.4		◑ 2219	1.2
14 TU	0338	2.8	29 W	0442	3.1
	1008	1.1		1119	0.8
	1632	2.5		1739	2.8
	2158	1.5		2326	1.3
15 W	0433	2.7	30 TH	0543	3.0
	1111	1.1		1222	0.9
	1731	2.5		1840	2.7
	◐ 2313	1.5			

JULY

Date	Time	m	Date	Time	m
1 F	0036	1.3	16 SA	0541	2.8
	0648	2.9		1213	1.1
	1325	1.0		1833	2.7
	1942	2.8			
2 SA	0146	1.3	17 SU	0036	1.4
	0756	2.9		0652	2.8
	1422	1.1		1320	1.1
	2040	2.8		1938	2.8
3 SU	0247	1.2	18 M	0151	1.3
	0859	2.9		0805	2.9
	1510	1.1		1424	1.1
	2130	3.0		2041	2.9
4 M	0337	1.0	19 TU	0256	1.1
	0953	2.9		0914	3.0
	1552	1.1		1521	1.0
	2215	3.1		2138	3.1
5 TU	0422	0.9	20 W	0353	0.9
	1040	3.0		1015	3.2
	1630	1.1		1613	0.9
	2256	3.2		2230	3.3
6 W	0502	0.9	21 TH	0444	0.6
	1122	3.0		1109	3.4
	1707	1.1		1702	0.8
	● 2333	3.2		○ 2319	3.5
7 TH	0540	0.8	22 F	0534	0.4
	1201	3.0		1201	3.5
	1741	1.1		1748	0.8
8 F	0009	3.2	23 SA	0007	3.6
	0616	0.8		0622	0.2
	1238	3.0		1252	3.5
	1814	1.1		1833	0.7
9 SA	0043	3.2	24 SU	0055	3.7
	0651	0.7		0710	0.2
	1313	3.0		1340	3.4
	1846	1.1		1916	0.8
10 SU	0116	3.2	25 M	0141	3.7
	0725	0.8		0758	0.3
	1347	2.9		1428	3.3
	1918	1.1		1959	0.9
11 M	0150	3.1	26 TU	0228	3.6
	0759	0.8		0846	0.4
	1423	2.8		1515	3.1
	1950	1.1		2043	1.0
12 TU	0224	3.1	27 W	0317	3.4
	0835	0.9		0936	0.7
	1500	2.8		1603	2.9
	2025	1.2		2132	1.1
13 W	0302	3.0	28 TH	0409	3.2
	0915	1.0		1031	0.9
	1543	2.7		1655	2.8
	2106	1.3		◑ 2234	1.3
14 TH	0345	2.9	29 F	0507	3.0
	1003	1.0		1133	1.2
	1632	2.7		1754	2.7
	◐ 2157	1.4		2355	1.4
15 F	0437	2.8	30 SA	0614	2.8
	1104	1.1		1245	1.3
	1730	2.6		1901	2.7
	2310	1.5			
			31 SU	0125	1.4
				0732	2.7
				1359	1.4
				2011	2.8

AUGUST

Date	Time	m	Date	Time	m
1 M	0239	1.3	16 TU	0138	1.3
	0846	2.7		0752	2.8
	1456	1.4		1413	1.3
	2111	2.9		2019	2.9
2 TU	0331	1.1	17 W	0252	1.1
	0944	2.8		0909	3.0
	1541	1.3		1515	1.1
	2159	3.1		2122	3.1
3 W	0413	1.0	18 TH	0348	0.8
	1030	2.9		1009	3.2
	1618	1.2		1605	1.0
	2240	3.2		2216	3.4
4 TH	0450	0.9	19 F	0436	0.5
	1109	3.0		1101	3.4
	1652	1.2		1650	0.8
	2317	3.3		○ 2305	3.6
5 F	0524	0.8	20 SA	0521	0.2
	1145	3.1		1148	3.5
	1724	1.1		1732	0.7
	● 2351	3.3		2351	3.8
6 SA	0557	0.7	21 SU	0605	0.1
	1218	3.1		1233	3.6
	1754	1.0		1812	0.6
7 SU	0023	3.3	22 M	0035	3.8
	0627	0.6		0647	0.1
	1250	3.1		1316	3.5
	1823	1.0		1850	0.7
8 M	0054	3.3	23 TU	0119	3.8
	0657	0.6		0728	0.3
	1321	3.1		1358	3.3
	1852	1.0		1929	0.7
9 TU	0124	3.3	24 W	0202	3.7
	0727	0.7		0808	0.5
	1352	3.0		1439	3.2
	1921	1.0		2007	0.9
10 W	0155	3.2	25 TH	0246	3.4
	0758	0.8		0848	0.8
	1424	2.9		1521	3.0
	1953	1.1		2050	1.1
11 TH	0228	3.1	26 F	0334	3.2
	0831	0.9		0933	1.1
	1501	2.9		1609	2.8
	2028	1.2		◑ 2146	1.3
12 F	0307	3.0	27 SA	0431	2.9
	0909	1.0		1033	1.4
	1544	2.8		1707	2.7
	2110	1.3		2321	1.5
13 SA	0355	2.9	28 SU	0544	2.7
	1000	1.2		1202	1.6
	1639	2.7		1821	2.7
	◐ 2210	1.4			
14 SU	0500	2.8	29 M	0111	1.5
	1120	1.3		0714	2.6
	1748	2.7		1341	1.7
	2359	1.5		1943	2.7
15 M	0623	2.7	30 TU	0228	1.3
	1253	1.4		0837	2.7
	1904	2.8		1444	1.6
				2049	2.9
			31 W	0317	1.2
				0931	2.8
				1526	1.4
				2138	3.1

Chart Datum: 1·71 metres below Ordnance Datum (Newlyn)

TIME ZONE (UT)
For Summer Time add ONE hour in **non-shaded areas**

SCOTLAND – WICK

LAT 58°26′N LONG 3°05′W

TIMES AND HEIGHTS OF HIGH AND LOW WATERS

SPRING & NEAP TIDES
Dates in red are SPRINGS
Dates in blue are NEAPS

YEAR **2005**

SEPTEMBER

Day	Time	m	Day	Time	m
1	0355	1.0	16	0335	0.6
	1013	3.0		0958	3.3
TH	1601	1.3	F	1550	1.0
	2218	3.2		2200	3.5
2	0428	0.8	17	0420	0.4
	1048	3.1		1044	3.5
F	1631	1.1	SA	1630	0.8
	2253	3.3		2246	3.7
3	0459	0.7	18	0501	0.2
	1121	3.1		1127	3.6
SA	1700	1.0	SU	1708	0.7
	● 2326	3.4		○ 2330	3.9
4	0529	0.6	19	0540	0.2
	1151	3.2		1208	3.6
SU	1728	0.9	M	1746	0.6
	2357	3.4			
5	0558	0.6	20	0012	3.9
	1221	3.2		0618	0.2
M	1756	0.9	TU	1247	3.5
				1823	0.6
6	0026	3.4	21	0053	3.8
	0625	0.6		0655	0.4
TU	1250	3.2	W	1324	3.4
	1824	0.9		1900	0.7
7	0056	3.4	22	0134	3.6
	0654	0.6		0730	0.7
W	1320	3.2	TH	1401	3.2
	1853	0.9		1937	0.9
8	0126	3.4	23	0215	3.4
	0723	0.8		0804	1.0
TH	1351	3.1	F	1439	3.1
	1924	1.0		2018	1.1
9	0159	3.2	24	0301	3.1
	0755	0.9		0840	1.4
F	1426	3.0	SA	1523	2.9
	1959	1.1		2111	1.4
10	0239	3.1	25	0358	2.8
	0831	1.1		0929	1.6
SA	1508	2.9	SU	1621	2.8
	2041	1.3		◑ 2251	1.5
11	0329	2.9	26	0515	2.6
	0919	1.3		1114	1.8
SU	1602	2.8	M	1739	2.7
	◐ 2141	1.4			
12	0440	2.8	27	0046	1.5
	1048	1.5		0651	2.5
M	1716	2.8	TU	1314	1.8
	2355	1.5		1907	2.7
13	0616	2.7	28	0202	1.4
	1245	1.5		0815	2.7
TU	1843	2.8	W	1420	1.7
				2018	2.9
14	0137	1.3	29	0249	1.2
	0752	2.9		0906	2.8
W	1408	1.4	TH	1501	1.5
	2004	3.0		2108	3.0
15	0245	1.0	30	0326	1.0
	0904	3.1		0944	3.0
TH	1505	1.2	F	1534	1.3
	2108	3.2		2147	3.2

OCTOBER

Day	Time	m	Day	Time	m
1	0358	0.9	16	0357	0.4
	1018	3.1		1021	3.5
SA	1603	1.2	SU	1606	0.8
	2222	3.3		2223	3.7
2	0428	0.7	17	0435	0.4
	1049	3.2		1101	3.6
SU	1631	1.0	M	1643	0.7
	2255	3.4		○ 2306	3.8
3	0456	0.6	18	0512	0.4
	1119	3.3		1139	3.6
M	1659	0.9	TU	1721	0.7
	● 2326	3.5		2348	3.8
4	0524	0.6	19	0548	0.5
	1149	3.3		1216	3.5
TU	1728	0.8	W	1759	0.7
	2357	3.5			
5	0553	0.6	20	0028	3.7
	1218	3.4		0623	0.7
W	1757	0.8	TH	1252	3.5
				1837	0.8
6	0029	3.5	21	0109	3.5
	0622	0.7		0656	1.0
TH	1250	3.3	F	1327	3.3
	1829	0.9		1915	1.0
7	0103	3.4	22	0150	3.2
	0653	0.8		0729	1.2
F	1322	3.3	SA	1404	3.2
	1903	0.9		1958	1.2
8	0140	3.3	23	0235	3.0
	0727	1.0		0803	1.5
SA	1359	3.2	SU	1445	3.0
	1941	1.1		2051	1.4
9	0224	3.1	24	0330	2.8
	0807	1.2		0846	1.7
SU	1443	3.1	M	1539	2.9
	2029	1.2		2216	1.5
10	0321	2.9	25	0442	2.6
	0901	1.5		1011	1.9
M	1540	2.9	TU	1653	2.8
	◐ 2147	1.4		◑ 2353	1.5
11	0440	2.8	26	0608	2.6
	1048	1.7		1209	1.9
TU	1659	2.8	W	1816	2.7
	2359	1.3			
12	0619	2.8	27	0113	1.4
	1237	1.6		0728	2.7
W	1828	2.9	TH	1333	1.8
				1929	2.8
13	0125	1.1	28	0207	1.2
	0746	2.9		0824	2.8
TH	1351	1.5	F	1421	1.6
	1945	3.1		2024	3.0
14	0227	0.8	29	0246	1.1
	0849	3.2		0905	3.0
F	1444	1.2	SA	1457	1.4
	2047	3.3		2107	3.1
15	0315	0.6	30	0320	0.9
	0938	3.4		0940	3.1
SA	1527	1.0	SU	1529	1.2
	2138	3.5		2144	3.3
			31	0351	0.8
				1013	3.2
			M	1559	1.1
				2220	3.4

NOVEMBER

Day	Time	m	Day	Time	m
1	0421	0.8	16	0447	0.7
	1045	3.4		1113	3.5
TU	1629	1.0	W	1702	0.8
	2254	3.5		○ 2328	3.6
2	0452	0.7	17	0522	0.8
	1117	3.4		1150	3.5
W	1701	0.9	TH	1743	0.8
	● 2330	3.5			
3	0523	0.7	18	0009	3.5
	1150	3.5		0557	1.0
TH	1735	0.8	F	1226	3.5
				1823	0.9
4	0007	3.5	19	0050	3.3
	0556	0.8		0632	1.2
F	1225	3.5	SA	1302	3.4
	1812	0.9		1903	1.0
5	0047	3.4	20	0131	3.2
	0632	1.0		0706	1.4
SA	1302	3.4	SU	1339	3.3
	1852	0.9		1946	1.1
6	0131	3.3	21	0214	3.0
	0713	1.1		0740	1.5
SU	1343	3.3	M	1418	3.1
	1939	1.0		2033	1.3
7	0222	3.1	22	0303	2.8
	0800	1.4		0821	1.7
M	1431	3.2	TU	1505	3.0
	2039	1.1		2133	1.4
8	0324	3.0	23	0402	2.7
	0903	1.6		0915	1.8
TU	1531	3.1	W	1603	2.9
	2210	1.2		◑ 2247	1.4
9	0444	2.9	24	0509	2.6
	1041	1.7		1041	1.9
W	1647	3.0	TH	1713	2.8
	◐ 2344	1.2			
10	0607	2.9	25	0000	1.4
	1210	1.6		0618	2.6
TH	1807	3.0	F	1209	1.8
				1822	2.8
11	0100	1.0	26	0103	1.3
	0722	3.0		0721	2.7
F	1320	1.5	SA	1316	1.7
	1918	3.2		1923	2.9
12	0201	0.8	27	0154	1.2
	0822	3.1		0812	2.9
SA	1415	1.3	SU	1407	1.5
	2020	3.3		2015	3.0
13	0250	0.7	28	0235	1.1
	0911	3.3		0855	3.0
SU	1501	1.1	M	1449	1.4
	2113	3.5		2102	3.2
14	0332	0.7	29	0313	1.0
	0955	3.4		0933	3.2
M	1542	1.0	TU	1527	1.2
	2201	3.6		2144	3.3
15	0410	0.7	30	0348	0.9
	1035	3.5		1011	3.3
TU	1622	0.9	W	1604	1.1
	2245	3.6		2226	3.4

DECEMBER

Day	Time	m	Day	Time	m
1	0423	0.9	16	0505	1.1
	1048	3.5		1132	3.5
TH	1642	1.0	F	1735	0.9
	● 2309	3.5		2358	3.3
2	0501	0.9	17	0542	1.2
	1127	3.5		1209	3.5
F	1722	0.9	SA	1815	0.9
	2353	3.5			
3	0541	0.9	18	0038	3.2
	1207	3.6		0616	1.3
SA	1806	0.8	SU	1246	3.4
				1854	1.0
4	0039	3.5	19	0117	3.1
	0623	1.0		0650	1.3
SU	1250	3.5	M	1321	3.4
	1853	0.8		1932	1.0
5	0129	3.4	20	0155	3.0
	0709	1.2		0723	1.4
M	1335	3.5	TU	1357	3.3
	1946	0.8		2011	1.1
6	0223	3.2	21	0235	2.9
	0800	1.3		0758	1.5
TU	1426	3.4	W	1436	3.2
	2048	0.9		2052	1.2
7	0324	3.1	22	0319	2.8
	0859	1.4		0836	1.6
W	1523	3.3	TH	1518	3.0
	2200	1.0		2141	1.3
8	0430	3.0	23	0408	2.7
	1011	1.5		0923	1.6
TH	1629	3.2	F	1609	2.9
	◐ 2314	1.0		◑ 2240	1.3
9	0538	2.9	24	0504	2.7
	1127	1.6		1028	1.7
F	1737	3.2	SA	1708	2.9
				2345	1.4
10	0024	1.0	25	0605	2.7
	0644	3.0		1151	1.7
SA	1238	1.5	SU	1812	2.9
	1844	3.2			
11	0127	1.0	26	0047	1.3
	0746	3.0		0705	2.8
SU	1341	1.4	M	1305	1.7
	1949	3.2		1915	2.9
12	0222	1.0	27	0144	1.3
	0841	3.1		0802	2.9
M	1437	1.3	TU	1406	1.5
	2049	3.3		2017	3.0
13	0308	1.0	28	0234	1.2
	0929	3.2		0853	3.1
TU	1526	1.1	W	1458	1.4
	2143	3.3		2114	3.1
14	0349	1.0	29	0320	1.1
	1013	3.3		0941	3.2
W	1611	1.0	TH	1546	1.2
	2231	3.4		2206	3.3
15	0428	1.1	30	0405	1.1
	1054	3.4		1026	3.4
TH	1654	1.0	F	1632	1.0
	○ 2316	3.3		2256	3.4
			31	0449	1.0
				1110	3.5
			SA	1718	0.8
				● 2345	3.5

Chart Datum: 1·71 metres below Ordnance Datum (Newlyn)

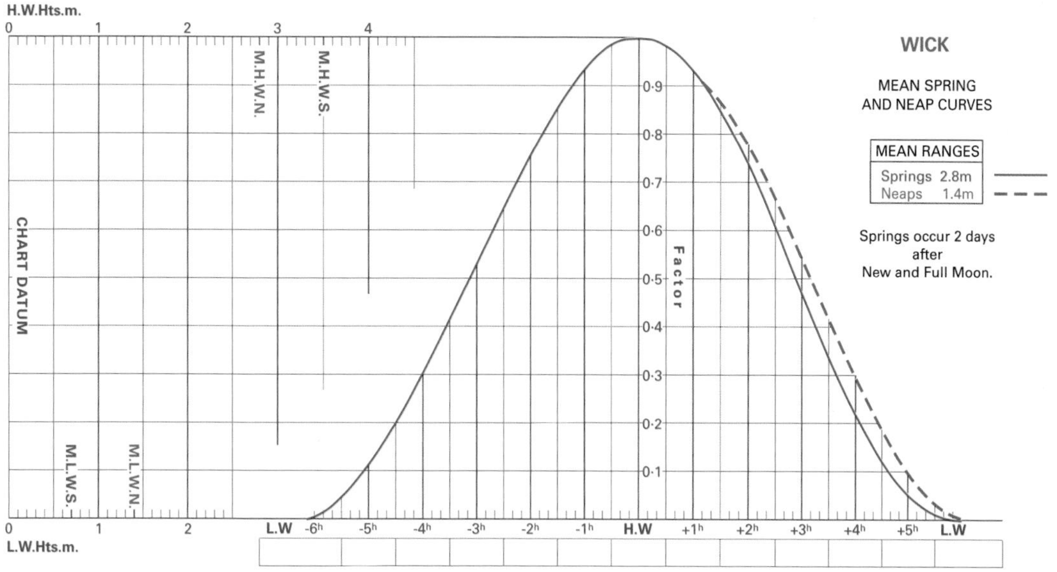
H.W.Hts.m.
0 1 2 3 4
M.H.W.N.
M.H.W.S.
CHART DATUM
M.L.W.S.
M.L.W.N.
Factor
0·9
0·8
0·7
0·6
0·5
0·4
0·3
0·2
0·1
WICK
MEAN SPRING AND NEAP CURVES
MEAN RANGES
Springs 2.8m
Neaps 1.4m
Springs occur 2 days after New and Full Moon.
0 1 2
L.W.Hts.m.
L.W -6h -5h -4h -3h -2h -1h H.W +1h +2h +3h +4h +5h L.W

9.7.19 SCRABSTER

Highland **58°36'·61N 03°32'·61W**

CHARTS AC 1954, 2162, 1462; Imray C68; OS 12

TIDES -0240 Dover; ML 3·2; Duration 0615; Zone 0 (UT)

Standard Port WICK (←)

Times				**Height (metres)**			
High Water		Low Water		MHWS	MHWN	MLWN	MLWS
0200	0700	0100	0700	3·5	2·8	1·4	0·7
1400	1900	1300	1900				
Differences SCRABSTER							
–0255	–0225	–0240	–0230	+1·5	+1·2	+0·8	+0·3
GILLS BAY							
–0150	–0150	–0202	–0202	+0·7	+0·7	+0·6	+0·3
STROMA							
–0115	–0115	–0110	–0110	–0·4	–0·5	–0·1	–0·2
LOCH ERIBOLL (Portnancon)							
–0340	–0255	–0315	–0255	+1·6	+1·3	+0·8	+0·4
KYLE OF DURNESS							
–0350	–0350	–0315	–0315	+1·1	+0·7	+0·4	–0·1
SULE SKERRY (59°05'N 04°24'W)							
–0320	–0255	–0315	–0250	+0·4	+0·3	+0·2	+0·1
RONA (59°08'N 05°49'W)							
–0410	–0345	–0330	–0340	–0·1	–0·2	–0·2	–0·1

SHELTER Very good except for swell in NW and N winds. Yachts usually lie in the Inner (0·9 - 1·2m) or Centre Basins (0·9 - 2·7m). ⚓ is not advised. A good hbr to await the right conditions for E-bound passage through Pentland Firth (see 9.7.5). Beware floating creel lines in W of hbr. New jetty works for RoRo finished late 2003.

NAVIGATION WPT 58°36'·58N 03°32'·09W, 278° to E pier lt, 0·25M. Can be entered H24 in all weathers. Beware FVs and the Orkney ferries.

LIGHTS AND MARKS No ldg marks/lts. Entry is simple once the conspic ice plant tr and/or pier lts have been located. Do not confuse hbr lts with the shore lts of Thurso.

R/T Call HM VHF Ch 12 16 (H24) for berthing directions, before entering hbr. From the W reception is very poor due to masking by Holborn Head.

TELEPHONE (Dial code 01847) HM 892779, 📠 892353, Mobile 07803 290366, harbour@scrabster.co.uk, www.scrabster.co.uk; MRSC (01224) 592334; Marinecall 09066 526235; Police 893222; Dr 893154.

FACILITIES **Hbr** AB £8.00 (£35/week), FW, D, P (cans), ME, El, C (15, 30 & 100 ton mobiles), Slip, CH, ♿; **Pentland Firth YC** M, R, Bar, Showers (keys held by Duty HM). **Thurso** EC Thurs; 🛒, R, Bar, ✉, Ⓑ, ⇌, ✈ (Wick). Ferries to Stromness, Kirkwall.

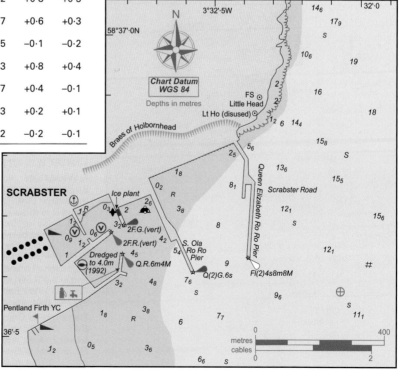

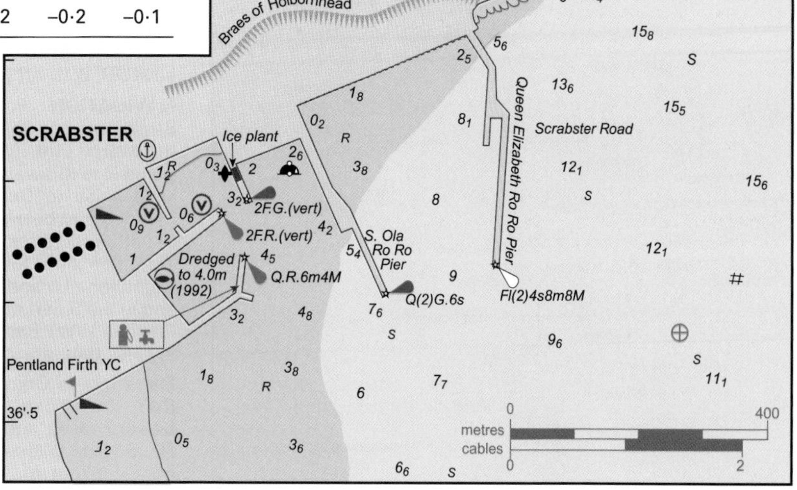
3°32'·5W
32'·0
58°37'·0N
N
Chart Datum WGS 84
Depths in metres
FS
Little Head
Lt Ho (disused)
Braes of Holbornhead
SCRABSTER
Ice plant
2F.G.(vert)
2F.R.(vert)
Dredged to 4.0m (1992)
Q.R.6m4M
S. Ola Ro Ro Pier
Q(2)G.6s
Queen Elizabeth Ro Ro Pier
Fl(2)4s8m8M
Scrabster Road
Pentland Firth YC
36'·5
metres
cables
0
400
2

ANCHORAGES BETWEEN SCRABSTER AND CAPE WRATH

KYLE OF TONGUE, Highland, **58°31'·97N 04°22'·67W** (ent). AC 2720, 1954. HW +0050 on Ullapool; HW ht –0·4m; see 9.7.19. The Kyle runs about 7M inland. Entry (see 9.7.5) should not be attempted in strong N winds. ⚓ at Talmine (W of Rabbit Is) protected from all but NE winds; at Skullomie Hr, protected from E'lies; off Mol na Coinnle, a small bay on SE side of Eilean nan Ron, protected from W and N winds; off S of Rabbit Is, protected from W to N winds. No ldg lts/marks. Facilities: Limited 🛒 at Talmine (½M from slip) or at Coldbachie (1½M from Skullomie).

LOCH ERIBOLL, Highland, **58°32'·58N 04°37'·48W**. AC 2076. HW –0345 on Dover; ML 2·7m. See 9.7.19. Enter between Whiten Hd and Klourig Is in W sector of White Hd lt, Fl WR10s, vis W030°-172°, R172°-191°, W191°-212°. In SW winds fierce squalls funnel down the loch. Yachts can enter Rispond Hbr, access approx HW ± 3, and dry out alongside; no lts/marks and very limited facilities. Good ⚓s: at Rispond Bay on W side of loch, ent good in all but E winds, in approx 5m; off Portnancon in 5·5m; at the head of the loch; at Camus an Duin and in bays to N and S of peninsula at Heilam on E side of loch.

9.7.20 ORKNEY ISLANDS

The Orkney Islands number about 70, of which some 24 are inhabited. They extend from Duncansby Hd 5 to 50M NNE, and are mostly low-lying, but Hoy in the SW of the group reaches 475m (1560ft). Coasts are generally rky and much indented, but there are many sandy beaches. A passage with least width of about 3M runs NW/SE through the group. The islands are separated from Scotland by the Pentland Firth, a very dangerous stretch of water. The principal island is Mainland (or Pomona) on which stands Kirkwall, the capital.

Severe gales blow in winter and early spring. The climate is mild but windy, and very few trees grow. There are LBs at Longhope, Stromness and Kirkwall. *"Rover Ticket"* for 4 or 14 day berthing fees, good value, refer to 9.7.5.

CHARTS AC 2162, 2250 and 2249, at medium scale. For larger scale charts, see under individual hbrs. Imray C68; OS sheets 5 and 6.

TIDES Wick (9.7.18) is the Standard Port. Tidal streams are strong, particularly in Pentland Firth and in the firths and sounds among the islands.

SHELTER There are piers (fender board advised) at all main islands. Yachts can pay 4 or 14 day hbr dues (£10.77 or £22.15) to berth on all Council-operated piers, except St Margaret's Hope. Some of the many ⚓s are listed below:

Mainland SCAPA BAY: good except in S winds. No yacht berths alongside pier due to heavy hbr traffic. Only ents to Scapa Flow are via Hoy Snd, Hoxa Snd or W of Flotta.

ST MARYS (known as Holm, pronounced Ham): Piermaster ☎ 01856 731365; N side of Kirk Sound; ⚓ in B of Ayre or berth E side of pier HW±4. P & D (cans), ✉, Bar, R, Bus to Kirkwall and Burwick Ferry.

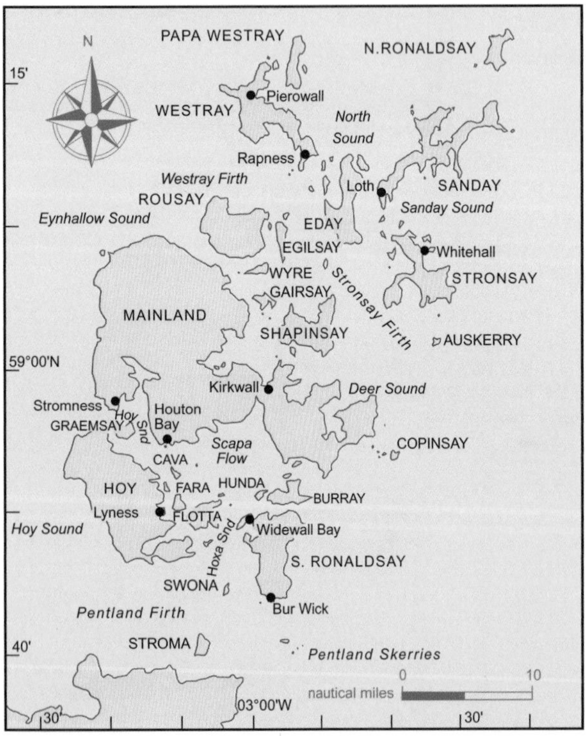
N
PAPA WESTRAY
N.RONALDSAY
15'
Pierowall
WESTRAY
North
Sound
Rapness
Westray Firth
Loth
SANDAY
ROUSAY
Sanday Sound
Eynhallow Sound
EDAY
EGILSAY
Whitehall
WYRE
Stronsay Firth
STRONSAY
GAIRSAY
MAINLAND
SHAPINSAY
AUSKERRY
59°00'N
Kirkwall
Deer Sound
Stromness
Houton
Bay
GRAEMSAY
Hoy Snd
Scapa
Flow
COPINSAY
CAVA
HOY
FARA
HUNDA
BURRAY
Lyness
FLOTTA
Hoxa Snd
Widewall Bay
Hoy Sound
S. RONALDSAY
SWONA
Bur Wick
Pentland Firth
40'
STROMA
Pentland Skerries
0
10
nautical miles
03°00'W
30'
30'

KIRK SOUND (E ent): ⚓ N of Lamb Holm; beware fish cages.

DEER SOUND: ⚓ in Pool of Mirkady or off pier on NW side of sound; very good shelter, no facilities.

Burray E WEDDEL SOUND: ⚓ to E of pier in E'lies, sheltered by No 4 Churchill Barrier; Piermaster ☎ 01856 731365, 📠 731254; pier is exposed in strong W'lies. P & D (cans), BY, Slip, 🛒, ✉, Bar, R, Bus to Kirkwall.

HUNDA SOUND: good ⚓ in all winds.

S Ronaldsay ST MARGARET'S HOPE: ❁❁⚓⚓✿✿. ⚓ in centre of bay; or AB £6.50 at pier, (keep clear of ferry berth on S side of pier), beware salmon farm. HM ☎ 01856 831440, mob 07879 688040; Dr 831206. FW, P & D (cans), 🛒, R, Bar, ✉, Bus Kirkwall, Vehicle ferry to Gill's Bay/Caithness. WIDEWALL B: ⚓ sheltered except SWlies.

Flotta Berth on Sutherland Pier, SW of oil terminal. HM ☎ 701411. P & D (cans), 🛒, ✉.

Hoy LONG HOPE: ⚓ E of S Ness pier, used by steamers, or berth on pier (safest at slack water) ☎ 701263; Dr 701209. Facilities: FW, P & D (cans), ✉, 🛒, Bar.

LYNESS: berth on pier; avoid disused piles; ⚓ in Ore Bay. HM ☎ 791387. FW, P & D (cans), Bar, ✉. Beware fish cages.

PEGAL B: good ⚓ except in strong W winds.

Rousay WYRE SOUND: ⚓ E of Rousay pier, or berth on it ✉, 🛒, R. Piermaster ☎ 7821261.

Eday FERSNESS Bay: good holding, sheltered from S winds. Piermaster ☎ 01857 622265;

BACKALAND Bay: berth on pier clear of ferry or ⚓ to NW. Beware cross tides. FW, P & D, 🛒, ✉.

CALF SOUND: ⚓ in Carrick B; good shelter from SW-NW'lies.

Papa Westray B OF MOCLETT: Good ⚓ but open to S. Piermaster ☎ 01857 644259;

SOUTH WICK: ⚓ off the old pier or ESE of pier off Holm of Papa. Backaskaill: P & D (cans), 🛒, ✉.

Sanday LOTH B: berth on pier, clear of ferry. Piermaster ☎ 01857 600227; Beware strong tides.

KETTLETOFT B: ⚓ in bay or berth on pier; very exposed to SE'lies. HM ☎ 600227. P & D (cans), FW, Gas, ✉, Ⓑ, 🛒, hotel.

NORTH BAY: on NW side of island, exposed to NW.

OTTERSWICK: good ⚓ except in N or E winds.

N Ronaldsay SOUTH B: ⚓ in middle of bay or berth on pier; Piermaster ☎ 01857 633239; open to S & W and swell. 🛒, ✉.

LINKLET B: ⚓ off jetty at N of bay, open to E.

NAVIGATION From the mainland, appr from Scrabster to Stromness and Scapa Flow via Hoy Mouth and Hoy Sound. From the Moray Firth (Wick) keep well E of the Pentland Skerries if going N to Kirkwall. Or, if bound for Scapa Flow via Hoxa Sound, keep close to Duncansby Head, passing W of the Pentland Skerries and between Swona and S Ronaldsay. Keep well clear of Lother Rk (dries 1·8m; lt, Q, Racon) off SW tip of S Ronaldsay. Time this entry for slack water in the Pentland Firth (about HW Aberdeen –1¾ and +4). Be aware of tankers off Flotta oil terminal and in the S part of Scapa Flow, where also lie the remains of the German WW1 Battle Fleet lie; classified as Historic Wrecks (see 9.0.3h), they are protected, but authorised diving is allowed.

Elsewhere in Orkney navigation is easy in clear weather, apart from the strong tidal streams in all the firths and sounds. Beware races and overfalls off Brough of Birsay (Mainland), Noup Head (Westray) and Dennis Head (N Ronaldsay). Keep a good lookout for the many lobster pots (creels).

LIGHTS AND MARKS The main hbrs and sounds are well lit; for details see 9.7.4. Powerful lts are shown offshore from Cantick Hd, Graemsay Island, Copinsay, Auskerry, Kirkwall, Brough of Birsay, Sanday Island, N Ronaldsay and Noup Hd.

R/T Orkney Hbrs Navigation Service (call: *Orkney Hbr Radio*, Ch 09 11 20 16 (H24)) covers Scapa Flow and appr's, Wide Firth, Shapinsay Sound and Kirkwall Bay.

TELEPHONE Area Code for islands SW of Stronsay and Westray Firths is 01856; islands to the NE are 01857.

MEDICAL SERVICES Doctors are available at Kirkwall, Stromness, Rousay, Hoy, Shapinsay, Eday, S and N Ronaldsay, Stronsay, Sanday and Westray (Pierowall); Papa Westray is looked after by Westray. The only hospital (and dentist) are at Kirkwall. Serious cases are flown to Aberdeen (1 hour).

FISH FARMS Fish cages/farms approx 30m x 50m may be found anywhere in sheltered waters within anchoring depths. Some are well buoyed, others are marked only by poles. Too many to list but the following will show the scale of the operations:

Beware **salmon cages** (may be marked by Y buoys/lts) at:

Kirkwall Bay	Toy Ness (Scapa Flow)
Rysa Sound	St Margaret's Hope
Bring Deeps	Backaland Bay (Eday)
Pegal Bay (Hoy)	Hunda Sound
Lyrawa Bay	Kirk Sound
Ore Bay (Hoy)	Carness Bay
Widewall Bay (S Ronaldsay)	Bay of Ham
	Bay of London (Eday)

Beware **oysters and longlines** at:

Widewall Bay	Bay of Firth
Swanbister Bay	Damsay Sound
Water Sound	Millburn Bay (Gairsay)
Hunda Sound	Pierowall
Deer Sound	Bay of Skaill (Westray)
Inganess Bay	Longhope

MINOR HARBOURS IN THE ORKNEY ISLANDS

HOUTON BAY, Mainland, **58°54'·85N 03°11'·33W**. AC 35, 2568. HW –0140 on Dover, –0400 on Aberdeen; HW ht +0·3m on Kirkwall; ML 1·8m; Duration 0615. ⚓ in the bay in approx 5·5m at centre, sheltered from all winds. Ent is to the E of Holm of Houton; ent chan dredged 3·5m for 15m each side of ldg line. Keep clear of shipping/ferries plying to Flotta. Ldg lts 316°: front Fl G 3s 8m, rear FG 16m; both R △ on W pole, B bands. Ro Ro terminal in NE corner marked by Iso R 4s with SHM Fl G on edge of ldg line. Bus to Kirkwall; Slip close E of piers. Yachtsmen may contact **M. Grainger** ☎ 01856 811397 for help.

SHAPINSAY, Orkney Islands, **59°01'·97N 02°54'·10W**. AC 2249, 2584. HW –0015 on Dover, –0330 on Aberdeen; HW ht –1·0m on Aberdeen. Good shelter in Elwick Bay off Balfour on SW end of island in 2·5-3m. Enter bay passing W of Helliar Holm which has lt Fl WRG 10s on S end. Keep mid-chan. Balfour Pier lt Q WRG 5m 3/2M; vis G270°–010°, W010°–020°, R020°–090°. Piermaster ☎ 01856 711358; Tides in The String reach 5kn at sp. Facilities: FW, P & D (cans), ✉, shop, Bar.

AUSKERRY, Orkney Islands, **59°02'·02N 02°34'·65W**. AC 2250. HW –0010 on Dover, –0315 on Aberdeen, HW ht –1m on Aberdeen. Small island at ent to Stronsay Firth with small hbr on W side. Safe ent and good shelter except in SW winds. Ent has 3·5m; 1·2m alongside pier. Yachts can lie secured between ringbolts at ent and the pier. Auskerry Sound and Stronsay Firth are dangerous with wind over tide. Auskerry lt at S end, Fl 20s 34m 18M, W tr. No facilities.

PIEROWALL, Westray, **59°19'·32N 02°58'·51W**. AC 2250, 2622. HW –0135 on Dover; ML 2·2m; Duration 0620. See 9.7.23. The bay is a good ⚓ in 2-7m and well protected. Marina pontoons in deep water alongside pier at Gill Pt. From S, beware Skelwick Skerry rks, and from the N the rks extending approx 1ca off Vest Ness. The N ent via Papa Sound needs local knowledge; tide race on the ebb. A dangerous tide race runs off Mull Hd at the N of Papa Westray. Lights: E pier hd Fl WRG 3s 7m 11/7M, G254°–276°, W276°–291°, R291°–308°. W pier hd 2 FR (vert) 4/6m 3M. VHF Ch 16. HM ☎ (01857) 677216. **Marina** AB, FW, ⛽D. Facilities: P & D (cans), Gas, Bar, ✉, Ⓑ, R, 🛒.

RAPNESS: Berth on pier, clear of Ro-Ro. Piermaster ☎ 01857 677212; Open to SSW.

9.7.21 STROMNESS

Orkney Islands, Mainland **58°57'·78N 03°17'·72W** ❁❁◊◊◊✿✿✿

CHARTS AC 2249, 2568; Imray C68; OS 6

TIDES -0145 Dover; ML 2·0; Duration 0620; Zone 0 (UT)

Standard Port WICK (←)

Times				Height (metres)			
High Water		Low Water		MHWS	MHWN	MLWN	MLWS
0000	0700	0200	0700	3·5	2·8	1·4	0·7
1200	1900	1400	1900				
Differences STROMNESS							
–0225	–0135	–0205	–0205	+0·1	–0·1	0·0	0·0
ST MARY'S (Scapa Flow)							
–0140	–0140	–0140	–0140	–0·2	–0·2	0·0	–0·1
BURRAY NESS (Burray)							
+0005	+0005	+0015	+0015	–0·2	–0·3	–0·1	–0·1
WIDEWALL BAY (S Ronaldsay)							
–0155	–0155	–0150	–0150	+0·1	–0·1	–0·1	–0·3
BUR WICK (S Ronaldsay)							
–0100	–0100	–0150	–0150	–0·1	–0·1	+0·2	+0·1
MUCKLE SKERRY (Pentland Firth)							
–0025	–0025	–0020	–0020	–0·9	–0·8	–0·4	–0·3

SHELTER Very good. Northern Lights Board have sole use of pier near to ldg lts. Marina in N of hbr; or ⚓ where shown.

NAVIGATION WPT 58°56'·93N 03°17'·00W, 317° to front ldg lt, 0·88M. Entry from the W should not be attempted with strong wind against tide due to heavy overfalls; if entering against the ebb, stand on to avoid being swept onto Skerry of Ness. Tides in Hoy Sound are very strong (>7kn sp). No tidal stream in hbr.

LIGHTS AND MARKS For Hoy Sound, ldg lts 104° on Graemsay Is: front Iso 3s 17m 15M, W tr; rear Oc WR 8s 35m 20/16M, ldg sector is R097°-112°. Skerry of Ness, Fl WG 4s 7m 7/4M; W shore-090°, G090°-shore. Hbr ldg lts 317°, both FR 29/39m 11M (H24), W trs, vis 307°-327°. Stromness Marina ent. Fl(2)R 5s.

R/T VHF Ch 12 16 (0900-1700 LT). (See also 9.7.22).

TELEPHONE (Dial code 01856) HM 850744; Fuel 851286; MRSC 01595 692976; Marinecall 09066 526235; Police 850222; Dr 850205; Dentist 850658.

FACILITIES **Stromness Marina:** 10⓿ £1.00, ⛽D, FW, Showers, WC, ⚒, El, Ⓔ, ME, C (mobile, 30 ton), Slip. **Town** EC Thurs; FW, D, 🛒, R, Bar, Gas, ✉, ▣, Ⓑ, ⇌ (ferry to Scrabster, bus to Thurso), ✈ (Kirkwall). Yachtsmen may contact for help/advice: **Mr S. Mowat** ☎ 850624 or **Capt A. Johnston** ☎ 850366.

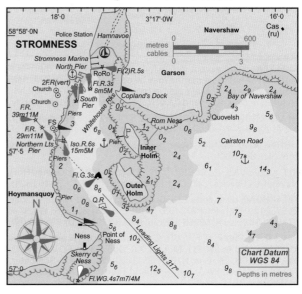

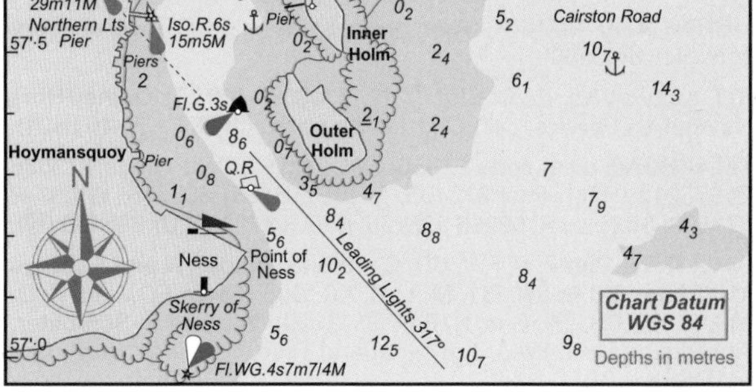

18'·0
3°17'·0W
16'·0
58°58'·0N
STROMNESS
Police Station
Hamnavoe
Navershaw
Cas (ru)
metres
cables
600
Stromness Marina
North Pier
RoRo
Fl(2)R.5s
Garson
2F.R(vert)
Church
Fl.R.3s 8m5M
Copland's Dock
Church
South Pier
Bay of Navershaw
F.R. 39m11M
Piers
Whitehouse Rks
Rom Ness
Quovelsh
F.R. 29m11M
Northern Lts
57'·5 Pier
Iso.R.6s 15m5M
Pier
Inner Holm
Cairston Road
Piers
Fl.G.3s
Outer Holm
Hoymansquoy
Pier
Q.R
N
Ness
Point of Ness
Leading Lights 317°
Skerry of Ness
57'·0
Fl.WG.4s7m7/4M
Chart Datum WGS 84
Depths in metres

9.7.22 KIRKWALL

Orkney Islands, Mainland **58°59'·30N 02°57'·70W** ❁❁❁◊◊✿✿✿

CHARTS AC 2250, 2249, 2584, 1553; Imray C68; OS 6

TIDES –0045 Dover; ML 1·8; Duration 0620; Zone 0 (UT)

Standard Port WICK (⟵)

Times				Height (metres)			
High Water		Low Water		MHWS	MHWN	MLWN	MLWS
0000	0700	0200	0700	3·5	2·8	1·4	0·7
1200	1900	1400	1900				
Differences KIRKWALL							
–0042	–0042	–0041	–0041	–0·5	–0·4	–0·1	–0·1
DEER SOUND							
–0040	–0040	–0035	–0035	–0·3	–0·3	–0·1	–0·1
TINGWALL							
–0200	–0125	–0145	–0125	–0·4	–0·4	–0·1	–0·1

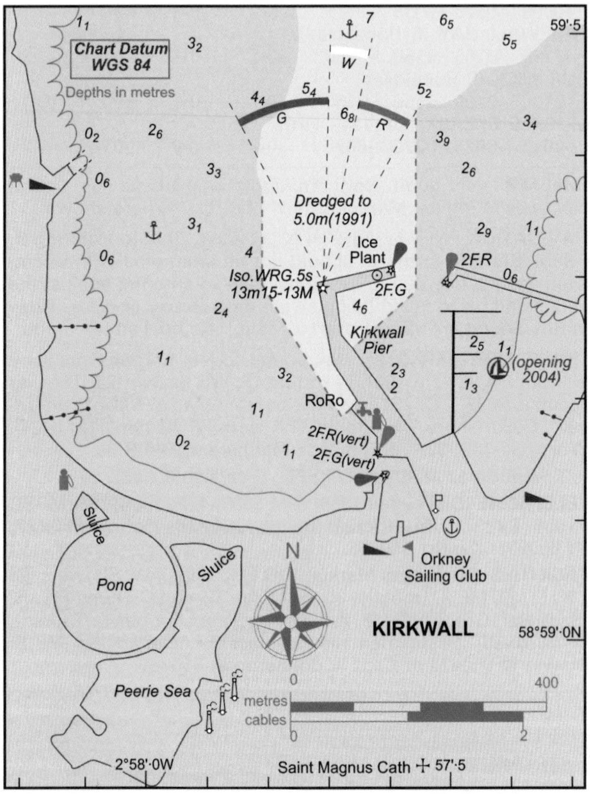
Chart Datum WGS 84
Depths in metres
59'·5
Dredged to 5.0m(1991)
Iso.WRG.5s 13m15-13M
Ice Plant
2F.R
2F.G
Kirkwall Pier
(opening 2004)
RoRo
2F.R(vert)
2F.G(vert)
Sluice
Pond
Sluice
Orkney Sailing Club
KIRKWALL
58°59'·0N
Peerie Sea
metres
cables
2°58'·0W
Saint Magnus Cath 57'·5

SHELTER Good except in N winds or W gales when there is a surge at the ent. New marina may be open Jun 2004 on E of main pier; or SW end of main pier in inner hbr (very full in Jun/Jul); or safe ⚓ between pier and Crow Ness Pt. New RoRo in NW of bay.

NAVIGATION WPT 59°01'·37N 02°57'·10W, 188° to pier hd lt, 2·2M. Appr in W sector of pier hd lt. Bay is shoal to SW.

LIGHTS AND MARKS Appr with St Magnus Cathedral (very conspic) brg 190°.

R/T *Kirkwall Hbr Radio* VHF Ch 12 16 (0800-1700 LT). Orkney Hbrs Navigation Service, call: *Orkney Hbr Radio* Ch 09 11 20 16 (H24).

TELEPHONE (Dial code 01856) HM 872292; Port Office 873636 📠 873012 (H24); Fuel 873105; MRSC (01595) 692976; Weather 873802; Marinecall 09066 526235; Police 872241; Dr 885400 (Ⓗ).

FACILITIES Pier P, D, FW, CH, C (mobile, 25 ton); **N and E Quays** M; **Orkney SC** ☎ 872331, M, L, C, AB, Slip. **Town** EC Wed; P, D, ME, El, ⚒, CH, 🛒, Gas, R, Bar, Ⓑ, ⊡, ✉, ⇌ (ferry to Scrabster, Aberdeen (Mon, Wed, Fri), Shetland (Tue, Thu, Sat, Sun), bus to Thurso), ✈.

9.7.23 STRONSAY

Orkney Islands, Stronsay **59°08'·57N 02°36'·01W** ❁❁◊◊✿✿

CHARTS AC 2250, 2622; Imray C68; OS 6

TIDES As Dover; ML 1·7; Duration 0620; Zone 0 (UT)

Standard Port WICK (⟵)

Times				Height (metres)			
High Water		Low Water		MHWS	MHWN	MLWN	MLWS
0000	0700	0200	0700	3·5	2·8	1·4	0·7
1200	1900	1400	1900				
Differences LOTH (Sanday)							
–0052	–0052	–0058	–0058	–0·1	0·0	+0·3	+0·4
KETTLETOFT PIER (Sanday)							
–0025	–0025	–0015	–0015	0·0	0·0	+0·2	+0·2
RAPNESS (Westray)							
–0205	–0205	–0205	–0205	+0·1	0·0	+0·2	0·0
PIEROWALL (Westray)							
–0150	–0150	–0145	–0145	+0·2	0·0	0·0	–0·1

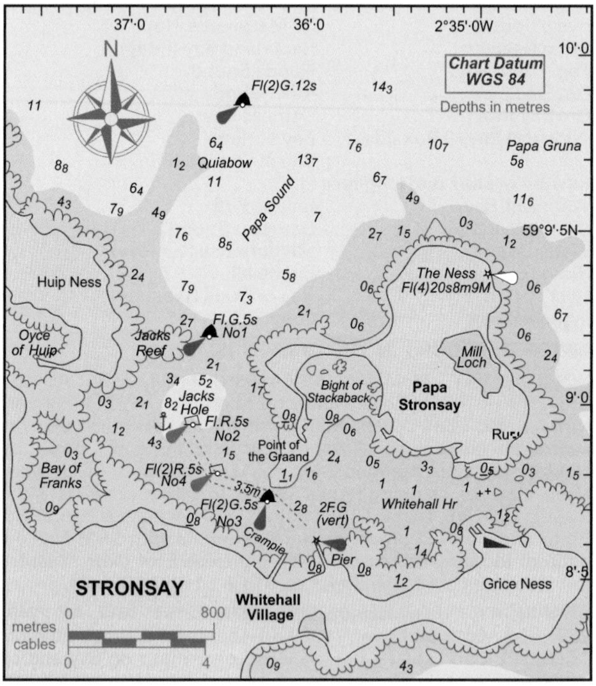
37'·0
36'·0
2°35'·0W
10'·0
Chart Datum WGS 84
Depths in metres
Fl(2)G.12s
Quiabow
Papa Sound
Papa Gruna
59°9'·5N
Huip Ness
The Ness Fl(4)20s8m9M
Oyce of Huip
Jacks Reef
Fl.G.5s No1
Mill Loch
Jacks Hole
Bight of Stackaback
Papa Stronsay
9'·0
Fl.R.5s No2
Point of the Graand
Bay of Franks
Fl(2)R.5s No4
Fl(2)G.5s No3
3.5m
Crampie
2F.G (vert)
Whitehall Hr
Pier
Grice Ness
8'·5
STRONSAY
Whitehall Village
metres
cables

SHELTER Good from all winds. Good ⚓ between seaward end of piers, or berth on outer end of W pier and contact HM. The extended E pier head is berth for Ro-Ro ferry. There are many other sheltered ⚓s around the bay.

NAVIGATION WPT 59°09'·82N 02°36'·31W, Quiabow SHM By, Fl (2) G 12s, 189° to No 1 lt buoy, 6·5ca. 800m NE of Huip Ness is Quiabow, a submerged rk. Jack's Reef extends 400m E from Huip Ness, and is marked by No 1 SHM buoy Fl G 5. A bank extends 350m SW from Papa Stronsay. Crampie Shoal is in mid-chan, marked by No 3 buoy. The buoyed chan to Whitehall pier is dredged 3·5m. Spit to E of Whitehall pier extends 400m N. The E ent is narrow and shallow and should not be attempted.

LIGHTS AND MARKS As chartlet. Pier hd lts, 2FG (vert).

R/T See Kirkwall.

TELEPHONE (Dial code 01857) Piermaster 616317; MRSC (01595) 692976; Marinecall 09066 526235; Police (01856) 872241; Dr 616321.

FACILITIES W Pier M, L, AB; **Main (E) Pier** M, L, FW, AB clear of ferry. **Village (Whitehall)** EC Thurs; P, D, 🛒, Bar, ✉, Ⓑ, ⇌ (ferry to Scrabster, bus to Thurso), ✈.

TIME ZONE (UT)
For Summer Time add ONE hour in **non-shaded areas**

SCOTLAND – LERWICK

LAT 60°09′N LONG 1°08′W

TIMES AND HEIGHTS OF HIGH AND LOW WATERS

SPRING & NEAP TIDES
Dates in red are SPRINGS
Dates in blue are NEAPS

YEAR **2005**

JANUARY

Date	Time	m	Time	m	Time	m	Time	m
1 SA	0213	1.8	0750	1.0	1412	2.0	2039	0.8
2 SU	0256	1.8	0831	1.0	1456	1.9	2125	0.8
3 M	0344	1.7	0921	1.1	1547	1.9	◑ 2218	0.8
4 TU	0439	1.7	1023	1.1	1647	1.8	2323	0.9
5 W	0541	1.7	1146	1.1	1756	1.8		
6 TH	0032	0.8	0648	1.8	1305	1.0	1910	1.9
7 F	0135	0.8	0751	1.9	1407	0.9	2017	2.0
8 SA	0232	0.8	0846	2.0	1503	0.8	2117	2.1
9 SU	0325	0.7	0937	2.2	1555	0.6	2215	2.2
10 M	0416	0.7	1027	2.3	1646	0.5	● 2311	2.2
11 TU	0504	0.7	1116	2.3	1735	0.3		
12 W	0004	2.3	0551	0.7	1205	2.4	1823	0.3
13 TH	0055	2.2	0636	0.7	1253	2.4	1911	0.3
14 F	0143	2.1	0721	0.7	1341	2.3	1959	0.4
15 SA	0229	2.0	0806	0.8	1429	2.2	2049	0.5
16 SU	0316	1.9	0853	0.9	1518	2.1	2142	0.7
17 M	0405	1.8	0946	1.0	1611	1.9	◐ 2243	0.8
18 TU	0500	1.7	1056	1.0	1714	1.8	2358	0.9
19 W	0606	1.7	1227	1.0	1831	1.7		
20 TH	0110	1.0	0714	1.7	1344	1.0	1945	1.7
21 F	0210	1.0	0815	1.8	1443	0.9	2048	1.8
22 SA	0258	1.0	0906	1.9	1530	0.9	2139	1.8
23 SU	0340	1.0	0950	2.0	1611	0.8	2221	1.9
24 M	0417	0.9	1029	2.1	1646	0.7	2259	1.9
25 TU	0450	0.9	1105	2.1	1720	0.6	○ 2334	2.0
26 W	0521	0.8	1138	2.1	1752	0.6		
27 TH	0007	2.0	0551	0.8	1210	2.2	1823	0.5
28 F	0040	2.0	0622	0.8	1240	2.1	1855	0.5
29 SA	0111	1.9	0653	0.8	1312	2.1	1929	0.5
30 SU	0144	1.9	0726	0.8	1346	2.1	2005	0.6
31 M	0220	1.8	0802	0.8	1423	2.0	2044	0.7

FEBRUARY

Date	Time	m	Time	m	Time	m	Time	m
1 TU	0301	1.8	0843	0.9	1508	1.9	2129	0.8
2 W	0351	1.7	0935	1.0	1604	1.8	◑ 2227	0.8
3 TH	0450	1.7	1047	1.0	1715	1.8	2345	0.9
4 F	0602	1.7	1229	1.0	1842	1.8		
5 SA	0110	0.9	0721	1.8	1352	0.9	2006	1.8
6 SU	0220	0.9	0829	1.9	1456	0.7	2115	2.0
7 M	0319	0.8	0927	2.1	1550	0.5	2213	2.1
8 TU	0409	0.7	1018	2.2	1639	0.3	● 2305	2.2
9 W	0454	0.6	1107	2.3	1724	0.2	2352	2.2
10 TH	0536	0.5	1152	2.4	1807	0.1		
11 F	0036	2.2	0616	0.5	1236	2.4	1849	0.2
12 SA	0117	2.1	0656	0.5	1319	2.3	1931	0.3
13 SU	0157	2.0	0736	0.6	1401	2.2	2012	0.5
14 M	0236	1.9	0817	0.7	1443	2.0	2055	0.7
15 TU	0317	1.8	0901	0.8	1529	1.9	2141	0.9
16 W	0402	1.7	1000	0.9	1623	1.7	◐ 2244	1.0
17 TH	0500	1.6	1141	1.0	1742	1.6		
18 F	0024	1.1	0628	1.6	1321	1.0	1925	1.6
19 SA	0148	1.1	0749	1.7	1429	0.9	2039	1.6
20 SU	0245	1.0	0847	1.8	1517	0.8	2127	1.7
21 M	0327	1.0	0932	1.9	1555	0.7	2205	1.8
22 TU	0402	0.9	1010	2.0	1627	0.6	2240	1.9
23 W	0432	0.8	1045	2.0	1657	0.5	2313	1.9
24 TH	0501	0.7	1117	2.1	1726	0.4	○ 2343	2.0
25 F	0529	0.6	1147	2.1	1756	0.4		
26 SA	0013	2.0	0559	0.6	1217	2.1	1827	0.4
27 SU	0042	2.0	0629	0.6	1248	2.1	1859	0.4
28 M	0112	1.9	0702	0.6	1320	2.1	1933	0.5

MARCH

Date	Time	m	Time	m	Time	m	Time	m
1 TU	0145	1.9	0737	0.6	1356	2.0	2011	0.6
2 W	0222	1.8	0818	0.7	1439	1.9	2055	0.7
3 TH	0308	1.8	0909	0.8	1537	1.8	◑ 2151	0.9
4 F	0408	1.7	1022	0.9	1655	1.7	2316	1.0
5 SA	0526	1.6	1217	0.9	1836	1.6		
6 SU	0102	1.0	0701	1.7	1347	0.8	2009	1.7
7 M	0216	0.9	0819	1.8	1450	0.6	2114	1.9
8 TU	0311	0.7	0917	2.0	1540	0.4	2205	2.0
9 W	0356	0.6	1006	2.1	1624	0.2	2250	2.1
10 TH	0436	0.5	1051	2.3	1705	0.1	● 2331	2.1
11 F	0514	0.4	1133	2.3	1744	0.1		
12 SA	0009	2.1	0552	0.4	1213	2.3	1821	0.2
13 SU	0046	2.0	0630	0.4	1252	2.2	1859	0.3
14 M	0120	2.0	0708	0.5	1331	2.1	1936	0.5
15 TU	0154	1.9	0746	0.6	1410	1.9	2011	0.7
16 W	0230	1.8	0827	0.7	1453	1.8	2048	0.9
17 TH	0310	1.7	0920	0.9	1543	1.6	◐ 2136	1.0
18 F	0400	1.6	1055	1.0	1653	1.5	2326	1.1
19 SA	0515	1.5	1244	0.9	1903	1.4		
20 SU	0115	1.1	0715	1.6	1359	0.9	2018	1.5
21 M	0220	1.0	0818	1.7	1448	0.7	2102	1.6
22 TU	0302	0.9	0904	1.8	1524	0.6	2137	1.7
23 W	0335	0.8	0941	1.9	1555	0.5	2210	1.8
24 TH	0404	0.7	1015	1.9	1624	0.4	2241	1.9
25 F	0432	0.6	1047	2.0	1654	0.3	○ 2311	1.9
26 SA	0502	0.5	1118	2.1	1725	0.3	2341	2.0
27 SU	0533	0.4	1150	2.1	1757	0.3		
28 M	0011	2.0	0606	0.4	1223	2.1	1830	0.3
29 TU	0042	2.0	0641	0.4	1258	2.0	1906	0.4
30 W	0115	1.9	0719	0.5	1338	2.0	1946	0.6
31 TH	0153	1.9	0804	0.6	1427	1.8	2032	0.7

APRIL

Date	Time	m	Time	m	Time	m	Time	m
1 F	0240	1.8	0900	0.7	1532	1.7	2133	0.9
2 SA	0343	1.7	1020	0.8	1656	1.6	◑ 2310	1.0
3 SU	0506	1.6	1216	0.7	1844	1.6		
4 M	0055	1.0	0647	1.6	1337	0.6	2004	1.7
5 TU	0202	0.8	0803	1.8	1435	0.4	2059	1.8
6 W	0253	0.7	0859	1.9	1521	0.3	2145	1.9
7 TH	0335	0.5	0946	2.1	1602	0.2	2226	2.0
8 F	0413	0.4	1029	2.1	1640	0.1	● 2303	2.0
9 SA	0451	0.3	1109	2.2	1717	0.2	2338	2.0
10 SU	0528	0.3	1148	2.2	1753	0.3		
11 M	0011	2.0	0605	0.3	1226	2.1	1827	0.4
12 TU	0044	2.0	0643	0.4	1304	2.0	1901	0.6
13 W	0117	1.9	0721	0.5	1343	1.8	1934	0.7
14 TH	0151	1.8	0803	0.7	1426	1.7	2007	0.9
15 F	0230	1.7	0856	0.8	1515	1.5	2050	1.0
16 SA	0319	1.6	1017	0.9	1617	1.4	◐ 2228	1.1
17 SU	0422	1.5	1148	0.9	1810	1.4		
18 M	0017	1.1	0609	1.5	1303	0.8	1933	1.5
19 TU	0132	1.0	0734	1.5	1359	0.7	2020	1.5
20 W	0220	0.9	0822	1.6	1439	0.6	2057	1.7
21 TH	0255	0.8	0902	1.7	1513	0.5	2130	1.8
22 F	0327	0.6	0937	1.9	1546	0.4	2203	1.9
23 SA	0359	0.5	1012	2.0	1619	0.3	2235	1.9
24 SU	0433	0.4	1047	2.0	1653	0.3	○ 2308	2.0
25 M	0508	0.4	1124	2.1	1729	0.3	2342	2.0
26 TU	0545	0.4	1202	2.1	1806	0.4		
27 W	0017	2.0	0625	0.4	1245	2.0	1846	0.5
28 TH	0054	2.0	0709	0.4	1333	1.9	1930	0.6
29 F	0137	1.9	0800	0.5	1431	1.8	2022	0.8
30 SA	0229	1.8	0903	0.6	1540	1.6	2129	0.9

Chart Datum: 1·22 metres below Ordnance Datum (Local)

7

TIME ZONE (UT)
For Summer Time add ONE hour in **non-shaded areas**

SCOTLAND – LERWICK

LAT 60°09′N LONG 1°08′W

TIMES AND HEIGHTS OF HIGH AND LOW WATERS

SPRING & NEAP TIDES
Dates in red are **SPRINGS**
Dates in blue are **NEAPS**

YEAR **2005**

MAY

Date	Day	Time	m	Time	m	Time	m	Time	m
1	SU	0337	1.7	1028	0.6	1700	1.6	◑ 2304	1.0
2	M	0457	1.6	1202	0.6	1831	1.6		
3	TU	0032	0.9	0627	1.7	1314	0.5	1939	1.7
4	W	0136	0.8	0737	1.8	1410	0.4	2031	1.7
5	TH	0227	0.7	0833	1.9	1456	0.3	2116	1.8
6	F	0310	0.5	0921	2.0	1537	0.3	2156	1.9
7	SA	0350	0.4	1005	2.0	1614	0.3	2233	1.9
8	SU	0428	0.4	1046	2.0	1650	0.4	● 2307	2.0
9	M	0507	0.4	1126	2.0	1725	0.4	2341	2.0
10	TU	0545	0.4	1204	1.9	1800	0.6		
11	W	0014	2.0	0624	0.4	1244	1.8	1833	0.7
12	TH	0049	1.9	0704	0.5	1324	1.7	1906	0.8
13	F	0124	1.8	0747	0.6	1406	1.6	1942	0.9
14	SA	0204	1.7	0837	0.7	1454	1.5	2027	1.0
15	SU	0251	1.7	0939	0.7	1547	1.5	2135	1.0
16	M	0346	1.6	1051	0.8	1652	1.4	◐ 2310	1.0
17	TU	0452	1.5	1157	0.7	1820	1.4		
18	W	0024	1.0	0617	1.5	1256	0.7	1922	1.5
19	TH	0122	0.9	0725	1.6	1344	0.6	2006	1.6
20	F	0208	0.8	0813	1.7	1426	0.5	2045	1.7
21	SA	0247	0.7	0855	1.8	1506	0.4	2122	1.8
22	SU	0326	0.6	0937	1.9	1545	0.4	2200	1.9
23	M	0405	0.5	1020	2.0	1625	0.4	○ 2239	2.0
24	TU	0446	0.4	1104	2.0	1706	0.4	2318	2.1
25	W	0530	0.3	1151	2.0	1749	0.5	2359	2.1
26	TH	0616	0.3	1241	2.0	1835	0.6		
27	F	0043	2.0	0705	0.3	1337	1.9	1924	0.7
28	SA	0133	2.0	0800	0.4	1436	1.8	2018	0.8
29	SU	0230	1.9	0903	0.4	1538	1.7	2121	0.9
30	M	0333	1.8	1016	0.5	1645	1.6	◑ 2235	0.9
31	TU	0442	1.8	1133	0.5	1757	1.6	2353	0.8

JUNE

Date	Day	Time	m	Time	m	Time	m	Time	m
1	W	0557	1.7	1242	0.5	1901	1.6		
2	TH	0101	0.8	0705	1.8	1341	0.5	1956	1.7
3	F	0158	0.7	0805	1.8	1429	0.5	2043	1.8
4	SA	0246	0.6	0857	1.8	1511	0.5	2126	1.8
5	SU	0330	0.5	0944	1.9	1550	0.5	2206	1.9
6	M	0411	0.5	1029	1.9	1627	0.6	● 2243	1.9
7	TU	0452	0.5	1110	1.9	1704	0.6	2320	2.0
8	W	0532	0.5	1151	1.8	1740	0.7	2355	2.0
9	TH	0612	0.5	1230	1.8	1815	0.8		
10	F	0030	1.9	0651	0.5	1309	1.7	1849	0.8
11	SA	0107	1.9	0731	0.6	1348	1.7	1926	0.9
12	SU	0145	1.8	0814	0.6	1430	1.6	2006	0.9
13	M	0227	1.7	0901	0.6	1515	1.5	2053	0.9
14	TU	0315	1.7	0954	0.7	1605	1.5	2151	1.0
15	W	0407	1.6	1053	0.7	1701	1.5	◐ 2305	1.0
16	TH	0506	1.6	1153	0.7	1804	1.5		
17	F	0019	0.9	0613	1.6	1250	0.7	1906	1.6
18	SA	0118	0.8	0719	1.7	1341	0.6	1958	1.7
19	SU	0209	0.8	0816	1.8	1429	0.6	2045	1.8
20	M	0257	0.6	0909	1.9	1517	0.5	2131	1.9
21	TU	0344	0.5	1000	2.0	1604	0.5	2217	2.0
22	W	0432	0.4	1052	2.0	1652	0.5	○ 2303	2.1
23	TH	0521	0.3	1146	2.1	1739	0.5	2350	2.1
24	F	0610	0.2	1240	2.0	1827	0.6		
25	SA	0039	2.1	0701	0.2	1334	2.0	1915	0.6
26	SU	0130	2.1	0753	0.2	1427	1.9	2005	0.7
27	M	0223	2.0	0847	0.3	1520	1.8	2057	0.7
28	TU	0318	2.0	0947	0.4	1615	1.7	◑ 2156	0.8
29	W	0416	1.9	1053	0.5	1714	1.6	2305	0.8
30	TH	0521	1.8	1204	0.6	1816	1.6		

JULY

Date	Day	Time	m	Time	m	Time	m	Time	m
1	F	0023	0.8	0631	1.7	1308	0.7	1917	1.6
2	SA	0131	0.8	0738	1.7	1404	0.7	2012	1.7
3	SU	0229	0.7	0838	1.7	1451	0.7	2102	1.8
4	M	0319	0.7	0932	1.8	1534	0.8	2147	1.9
5	TU	0403	0.6	1019	1.8	1614	0.8	2228	1.9
6	W	0444	0.6	1101	1.8	1651	0.8	● 2306	2.0
7	TH	0523	0.5	1140	1.8	1727	0.8	2342	2.0
8	F	0559	0.5	1217	1.8	1801	0.8		
9	SA	0017	2.0	0634	0.5	1252	1.8	1833	0.8
10	SU	0051	2.0	0709	0.5	1326	1.8	1905	0.8
11	M	0124	1.9	0745	0.5	1401	1.7	1940	0.8
12	TU	0201	1.9	0822	0.6	1439	1.7	2017	0.8
13	W	0240	1.8	0903	0.6	1521	1.6	2059	0.9
14	TH	0326	1.7	0949	0.7	1609	1.6	◐ 2151	0.9
15	F	0418	1.7	1045	0.7	1704	1.6	2301	0.9
16	SA	0520	1.7	1153	0.8	1808	1.6		
17	SU	0028	0.9	0632	1.7	1302	0.8	1915	1.7
18	M	0138	0.8	0747	1.7	1403	0.7	2016	1.8
19	TU	0237	0.7	0852	1.8	1459	0.7	2110	1.9
20	W	0332	0.6	0951	2.0	1553	0.6	2202	2.1
21	TH	0423	0.4	1047	2.1	1642	0.6	○ 2252	2.2
22	F	0513	0.2	1140	2.1	1729	0.5	2341	2.2
23	SA	0600	0.1	1230	2.1	1814	0.5		
24	SU	0029	2.3	0647	0.1	1318	2.1	1857	0.5
25	M	0117	2.3	0733	0.2	1404	2.0	1941	0.6
26	TU	0204	2.2	0820	0.3	1450	1.9	2027	0.6
27	W	0253	2.1	0910	0.5	1537	1.7	2117	0.7
28	TH	0344	1.9	1006	0.6	1627	1.7	◑ 2218	0.8
29	F	0443	1.8	1115	0.8	1727	1.6	2346	0.9
30	SA	0556	1.7	1234	0.9	1838	1.6		
31	SU	0112	0.9	0718	1.6	1343	0.9	1946	1.7

AUGUST

Date	Day	Time	m	Time	m	Time	m	Time	m
1	M	0220	0.8	0829	1.6	1439	0.9	2045	1.8
2	TU	0313	0.8	0925	1.7	1525	0.9	2133	1.9
3	W	0356	0.7	1009	1.8	1604	0.9	2214	2.0
4	TH	0433	0.6	1048	1.8	1639	0.8	2252	2.0
5	F	0507	0.5	1123	1.9	1711	0.7	● 2326	2.1
6	SA	0539	0.5	1156	1.9	1740	0.7	2358	2.1
7	SU	0610	0.4	1227	1.9	1810	0.7		
8	M	0028	2.1	0640	0.4	1257	1.9	1839	0.7
9	TU	0059	2.0	0712	0.5	1328	1.8	1911	0.7
10	W	0130	2.0	0746	0.5	1400	1.8	1944	0.7
11	TH	0205	1.9	0822	0.6	1438	1.8	2023	0.8
12	F	0246	1.9	0903	0.7	1522	1.7	2109	0.9
13	SA	0337	1.8	0954	0.8	1617	1.7	◐ 2213	1.0
14	SU	0442	1.7	1103	0.9	1722	1.7	2349	1.0
15	M	0603	1.7	1234	0.9	1841	1.7		
16	TU	0121	0.9	0734	1.7	1350	0.9	1956	1.8
17	W	0228	0.7	0847	1.9	1451	0.8	2057	2.0
18	TH	0324	0.5	0946	2.0	1543	0.7	2151	2.1
19	F	0414	0.3	1038	2.1	1629	0.6	○ 2239	2.3
20	SA	0459	0.2	1126	2.2	1712	0.5	2326	2.4
21	SU	0542	0.1	1210	2.2	1753	0.4		
22	M	0010	2.4	0624	0.1	1253	2.1	1833	0.4
23	TU	0054	2.4	0706	0.2	1333	2.0	1914	0.5
24	W	0138	2.3	0748	0.4	1413	1.9	1956	0.6
25	TH	0222	2.1	0831	0.6	1455	1.8	2041	0.7
26	F	0310	1.9	0918	0.8	1540	1.7	◑ 2139	0.9
27	SA	0405	1.7	1019	1.0	1635	1.7	2317	1.0
28	SU	0520	1.6	1159	1.1	1756	1.6		
29	M	0058	1.0	0706	1.6	1325	1.1	1924	1.7
30	TU	0209	0.9	0825	1.6	1426	1.1	2027	1.8
31	W	0259	0.8	0913	1.7	1510	1.0	2114	1.9

Chart Datum: 1·22 metres below Ordnance Datum (Local)

TIME ZONE (UT)
For Summer Time add ONE hour in **non-shaded areas**

SCOTLAND – LERWICK

LAT 60°09′N LONG 1°08′W

TIMES AND HEIGHTS OF HIGH AND LOW WATERS

SPRING & NEAP TIDES
Dates in red are SPRINGS
Dates in blue are NEAPS

YEAR **2005**

SEPTEMBER

Date	Day	Time	m	Time	m	Time	m	Time	m
1	TH	0338	0.7	0951	1.8	1546	0.9	2153	2.0
2	F	0411	0.6	1025	1.9	1617	0.8	2229	2.1
3	SA	0441	0.5	1057	1.9	1646	0.7	● 2301	2.1
4	SU	0510	0.5	1127	2.0	1713	0.6	2331	2.1
5	M	0539	0.4	1156	2.0	1742	0.6		
6	TU	0000	2.2	0608	0.4	1224	2.0	1811	0.6
7	W	0029	2.1	0639	0.5	1252	2.0	1843	0.6
8	TH	0100	2.1	0711	0.5	1323	1.9	1917	0.7
9	F	0135	2.0	0747	0.7	1358	1.9	1956	0.8
10	SA	0216	1.9	0827	0.8	1440	1.8	2044	0.9
11	SU	0309	1.8	0919	0.9	1536	1.8	◐ 2150	1.0
12	M	0422	1.7	1034	1.1	1649	1.7	2339	1.0
13	TU	0555	1.7	1226	1.1	1819	1.7		
14	W	0115	0.9	0736	1.8	1344	1.0	1944	1.8
15	TH	0220	0.7	0843	1.9	1442	0.8	2045	2.0
16	F	0312	0.5	0935	2.0	1528	0.7	2135	2.2
17	SA	0357	0.3	1021	2.2	1610	0.6	2221	2.3
18	SU	0438	0.2	1103	2.2	1649	0.5	○ 2305	2.4
19	M	0518	0.1	1143	2.2	1728	0.4	2346	2.4
20	TU	0557	0.2	1221	2.2	1807	0.4		
21	W	0027	2.4	0636	0.3	1257	2.1	1846	0.5
22	TH	0109	2.2	0714	0.5	1334	2.0	1928	0.6
23	F	0152	2.1	0753	0.8	1412	1.9	2013	0.8
24	SA	0239	1.9	0833	1.0	1454	1.8	2109	0.9
25	SU	0333	1.7	0925	1.2	1547	1.7	◑ 2248	1.0
26	M	0445	1.6	1116	1.3	1702	1.7		
27	TU	0031	1.0	0649	1.6	1257	1.2	1854	1.7
28	W	0143	0.9	0804	1.6	1401	1.1	1959	1.8
29	TH	0231	0.8	0846	1.7	1443	1.0	2045	1.9
30	F	0308	0.7	0920	1.8	1517	0.9	2123	2.0

OCTOBER

Date	Day	Time	m	Time	m	Time	m	Time	m
1	SA	0339	0.6	0953	1.9	1547	0.8	2158	2.1
2	SU	0408	0.5	1023	2.0	1615	0.7	2229	2.1
3	M	0436	0.5	1053	2.1	1643	0.6	● 2300	2.2
4	TU	0505	0.4	1121	2.1	1714	0.6	2330	2.2
5	W	0536	0.5	1150	2.1	1746	0.6		
6	TH	0002	2.2	0608	0.5	1220	2.1	1819	0.6
7	F	0036	2.2	0642	0.6	1252	2.1	1857	0.7
8	SA	0114	2.1	0720	0.8	1328	2.0	1940	0.8
9	SU	0200	2.0	0803	0.9	1412	1.9	2033	0.9
10	M	0301	1.8	0900	1.1	1511	1.8	◐ 2146	0.9
11	TU	0421	1.7	1024	1.2	1630	1.8	2339	0.9
12	W	0559	1.7	1218	1.1	1805	1.8		
13	TH	0103	0.8	0729	1.8	1329	1.0	1927	1.9
14	F	0204	0.6	0827	1.9	1422	0.9	2026	2.1
15	SA	0252	0.4	0914	2.1	1506	0.7	2115	2.2
16	SU	0335	0.3	0956	2.1	1547	0.6	2159	2.3
17	M	0414	0.3	1036	2.2	1625	0.5	○ 2241	2.4
18	TU	0452	0.3	1112	2.2	1704	0.5	2322	2.4
19	W	0530	0.4	1148	2.2	1744	0.5		
20	TH	0003	2.3	0607	0.5	1223	2.2	1824	0.6
21	F	0045	2.2	0643	0.7	1259	2.1	1906	0.7
22	SA	0128	2.0	0720	0.9	1336	2.0	1951	0.8
23	SU	0214	1.9	0757	1.1	1418	1.9	2048	0.9
24	M	0306	1.7	0843	1.2	1509	1.8	2209	1.0
25	TU	0410	1.6	1017	1.3	1613	1.7	◑ 2338	1.0
26	W	0554	1.6	1200	1.3	1755	1.7		
27	TH	0051	1.0	0714	1.6	1313	1.2	1915	1.8
28	F	0145	0.9	0802	1.7	1402	1.1	2005	1.9
29	SA	0225	0.8	0840	1.8	1439	1.0	2045	1.9
30	SU	0258	0.7	0914	1.9	1511	0.9	2121	2.0
31	M	0329	0.6	0945	2.0	1542	0.8	2155	2.1

NOVEMBER

Date	Day	Time	m	Time	m	Time	m	Time	m
1	TU	0400	0.6	1016	2.1	1614	0.7	2229	2.2
2	W	0433	0.5	1048	2.2	1648	0.6	● 2304	2.2
3	TH	0507	0.6	1121	2.2	1724	0.6	2341	2.2
4	F	0543	0.6	1155	2.2	1803	0.6		
5	SA	0021	2.2	0621	0.7	1231	2.2	1845	0.7
6	SU	0107	2.1	0704	0.8	1311	2.1	1934	0.7
7	M	0201	2.0	0753	1.0	1400	2.0	2033	0.8
8	TU	0307	1.9	0853	1.1	1504	1.9	2147	0.8
9	W	0421	1.8	1014	1.2	1620	1.9	◐ 2322	0.8
10	TH	0547	1.8	1150	1.1	1744	1.9		
11	F	0038	0.7	0702	1.8	1301	1.0	1900	2.0
12	SA	0139	0.6	0759	1.9	1356	0.9	2000	2.1
13	SU	0228	0.5	0846	2.0	1442	0.8	2051	2.2
14	M	0311	0.5	0929	2.1	1525	0.7	2138	2.2
15	TU	0350	0.5	1008	2.2	1605	0.6	2222	2.3
16	W	0428	0.6	1045	2.2	1646	0.6	○ 2304	2.2
17	TH	0506	0.6	1121	2.2	1727	0.6	2346	2.2
18	F	0543	0.8	1157	2.2	1809	0.6		
19	SA	0028	2.1	0619	0.9	1234	2.2	1851	0.7
20	SU	0111	2.0	0656	1.0	1312	2.1	1936	0.8
21	M	0155	1.9	0733	1.1	1353	2.0	2026	0.9
22	TU	0242	1.8	0816	1.2	1439	1.9	2125	0.9
23	W	0334	1.7	0916	1.2	1533	1.8	◑ 2232	1.0
24	TH	0436	1.6	1042	1.3	1636	1.8	2339	1.0
25	F	0558	1.6	1201	1.2	1758	1.7		
26	SA	0039	0.9	0704	1.7	1303	1.1	1909	1.8
27	SU	0129	0.9	0751	1.8	1352	1.0	1959	1.9
28	M	0211	0.8	0830	1.9	1432	0.9	2041	2.0
29	TU	0249	0.7	0906	2.0	1510	0.8	2121	2.1
30	W	0327	0.7	0942	2.1	1548	0.8	2202	2.1

DECEMBER

Date	Day	Time	m	Time	m	Time	m	Time	m
1	TH	0405	0.7	1020	2.2	1628	0.7	● 2244	2.2
2	F	0445	0.7	1058	2.3	1710	0.6	2329	2.2
3	SA	0527	0.7	1138	2.3	1754	0.6		
4	SU	0017	2.2	0610	0.8	1221	2.3	1841	0.6
5	M	0110	2.1	0657	0.9	1307	2.2	1933	0.6
6	TU	0206	2.0	0748	0.9	1359	2.1	2030	0.6
7	W	0304	1.9	0843	1.0	1459	2.1	2133	0.7
8	TH	0406	1.8	0947	1.1	1603	2.0	◐ 2247	0.7
9	F	0514	1.8	1104	1.1	1714	2.0		
10	SA	0003	0.7	0622	1.8	1222	1.0	1827	2.0
11	SU	0108	0.7	0723	1.9	1326	0.9	1932	2.0
12	M	0202	0.7	0816	1.9	1421	0.9	2030	2.0
13	TU	0249	0.7	0903	2.0	1509	0.8	2122	2.1
14	W	0331	0.8	0946	2.1	1554	0.7	2211	2.1
15	TH	0411	0.8	1026	2.2	1637	0.7	○ 2255	2.1
16	F	0450	0.8	1105	2.2	1719	0.7	2338	2.1
17	SA	0528	0.9	1143	2.2	1800	0.7		
18	SU	0018	2.0	0604	0.9	1220	2.2	1840	0.7
19	M	0058	2.0	0640	1.0	1257	2.1	1920	0.7
20	TU	0137	1.9	0714	1.0	1334	2.1	2000	0.8
21	W	0216	1.8	0750	1.1	1413	2.0	2042	0.8
22	TH	0257	1.7	0831	1.1	1456	1.9	2130	0.9
23	F	0343	1.7	0920	1.1	1545	1.8	◑ 2225	0.9
24	SA	0435	1.7	1026	1.2	1641	1.8	2328	0.9
25	SU	0536	1.7	1151	1.2	1745	1.8		
26	M	0029	0.9	0643	1.7	1259	1.1	1857	1.8
27	TU	0124	0.9	0740	1.8	1354	1.0	1959	1.9
28	W	0212	0.9	0828	1.9	1442	0.9	2052	2.0
29	TH	0259	0.8	0914	2.1	1528	0.8	2143	2.1
30	F	0346	0.8	0958	2.2	1615	0.7	2233	2.1
31	SA	0432	0.7	1043	2.3	1702	0.5	● 2324	2.2

Chart Datum: 1·22 metres below Ordnance Datum (Local)

9.7.24 SHETLAND ISLANDS

The Shetland Islands consist of approx 100 islands, holms and rks of which fewer than 20 are inhabited. They lie 90 to 150M NNE of the Scottish mainland. By far the biggest island is Mainland with Lerwick (9.7.25), the capital, on the E side and Scalloway (overleaf), the only other town and old capital, on the W side. At the very S is Sumburgh airport and there are airstrips at Baltasound, Scalsta and Tingwall. Two islands of the Shetland group not shown on the chartlet are Fair Isle (see overleaf), 20M SSW of Sumburgh Hd and owned by the NT for Scotland, and Foula (see below) 12M WSW of Mainland. There are LBs at Lerwick and Aith. The CG MRSC is at Lerwick ☎ (01595) 692976, with an Auxiliary Station (Watch & Rescue) at Fair Isle.

CHARTS AC: medium scale 3281, 3282, 3283; larger scale 3271, 3272, 3292, 3293, 3294, 3295, 3297, 3298; OS sheets 1-4.

TIDES Lerwick is the Standard Port. Tidal streams run mostly N/ S or NW/SE and in open waters to the E and W are mostly weak. But rates >6kn can cause dangerous disturbances at the N and S extremities of the islands and in the two main sounds (Yell Sound and BlueMull/Colgrave Sounds). Keep 3M off Sumburgh Head to clear a dangerous race (roost) or pass close inshore.

SHELTER Weather conditions are bad in winter; yachts should only visit Apr – Sept. Around mid-summer it is day light H24. Some 12 small, non-commercial "marinas" are asterisked below; they are mostly full of local boats but supposedly each reserves 1 berth for visitors. Often only 1 boat lies between 2 fingers so that she can be held off by warps all round. Of the many ⚓s, the following are safe to enter in most weathers:

Mainland (anti-clockwise from Sumburgh Head)

GRUTNESS VOE*: 1·5M N of Sumburgh Hd, a convenient passage ⚓ , open to NE. Beware 2 rks awash in mid-ent.

CAT FIRTH: excellent shelter, ⚓ in approx 6m. Facilities: ✉ (Skellister), FW, 🛒 (both at Lax Firth).

GRUNNA VOE: off S side of Dury Voe, good shelter and holding, ⚓ in 5-10m; beware prohib ⚓ areas. Facilities: 🛒, FW, ✉ (Lax Firth).

WHALSAY*: FV hbr at Symbister. FW, D, 🛒, ✉.

OUT SKERRIES*: Quay and ⚓ at Bruray. FW, D, 🛒, ✉.

S OF YELL SOUND*: Tides –0025 on Lerwick. W of Lunna Ness, well-protected ⚓s with good holding include: Boatsroom Voe, W Lunna Voe (small hotel, FW), Colla Firth* (excellent pier) and Dales Voe. Facilities: none.

SULLOM VOE: tides –0130 on Lerwick. 6·5M long deep water voe, partly taken over by the oil industry. ⚓ S of the narrows. Facilities at Brae: FW, 🛒, ✉, D, ME, El, ⚒, Bar.

HAMNA VOE: Tides –0200 on Lerwick; very good shelter. Ldg line 153° old house on S shore with prominent rk on pt of W shore 3ca within ent. Almost land-locked; ⚓ in 6m approx, but bottom foul with old moorings. Facilities: ✉ (0·5M), Vs, D (1·5M), L (at pier).

URA FIRTH: NE of St Magnus Bay, ⚓ off Hills Wick on W side or in Hamar Voe on E side, which has excellent shelter in all weathers and good holding, but no facilities. Facilities: Hills Wick FW, ✉, D, ME, El, ⚒, 🛒, R, Bar.

OLNA FIRTH: NE of Swarbacks Minn, beware rk 1ca off S shore which dries. ⚓ in firth, 4-8m or in Gon Firth or go alongside pier at Voe. Facilities: (Voe) FW, 🛒, D, ✉, Bar.

SWARBACKS MINN*: a large complex of voes and isles SE of St Magnus Bay. Best ⚓ Uyea Sound or Aith Voe*, both well sheltered and good holding. Facilities: former none; Aith FW, ✉, 🛒, Bar, LB.

VAILA SOUND: on SW of Mainland, ent via Easter Sound (do not attempt Wester Sound); very good shelter, ⚓ N of Salt Ness in 4-5m in mud. See WALLS* overleaf: FW, 🛒, ✉.

GRUTING VOE*: HW –0150 on Lerwick, ⚓ in main voe or in Seli, Scutta or Browland* voes. Facilities: 🛒 and ✉ at Bridge of Walls (hd of Browland Voe).

Yell. MID YELL VOE: tides –0040 on Lerwick, enter through S Sd or Hascosay Sd, good ⚓ in wide part of voe 2·5-10m. Facilities: ✉, FW at pier on S side, D, 🛒, ME, ⚒, El.

BASTA VOE: good ⚓ above shingle bank in 5-15m; good holding in places. Facilities: FW, 🛒, Hotel, ✉.

BLUE MULL SND*: ⚓ at Cullivoe, pier and slip. D, FW, 🛒.

BURRA VOE*: small marina on N shore, FW, ⛽, 🛒, ✉.

Foula: Ham Voe on E side has tiny hbr/pier, unsafe in E'ly; berth clear of mailboat. Avoid Hoevdi Grund, 2M ESE.

NAVIGATION A careful lookout must be kept for salmon farming cages, mostly marked by Y buoys and combinations of Y lts. The Clyde Cruising Club's *Shetland Sailing Directions and Anchorages* are essential for visitors. For general passage information see 9.7.5. Weather forecasting and avoiding wind-over-tide conditions are more significant than elsewhere in the UK. Local magnetic anomalies may be experienced.

Note: There are two Historic Wrecks (*Kennemerland* and *Wrangels Palais*) on Out Skerries at 60°25'·2N 00°45'·0W and 60°25'·5N 00°43'·3W (see 9.0.3h).

LIGHTS AND MARKS See 9.7.4. Powerful lights show offshore from Fair Isle, Sumburgh Head, Kirkabister Ness, Bound Skerry, Muckle Flugga, Pt of Fethaland, Esha Ness and Foula.

R/T For Port Radio services see 9.7.25. There is no Coast Radio Station.

TELEPHONE (Dial code 01595; 01806 for Sullom Voe) MRSC 692976; Sullom Voe Port Control (01806) 242551, 📠 242237; Weather 692239; Forecaster (01806) 242069; Sumburgh Airport (01950) 460654.

FACILITIES See SHELTER. All stores can be obtained in Lerwick and to a lesser extent in Scalloway. Elsewhere in Shetland there is little available and yachts should be well provisioned for extended offshore cruising.

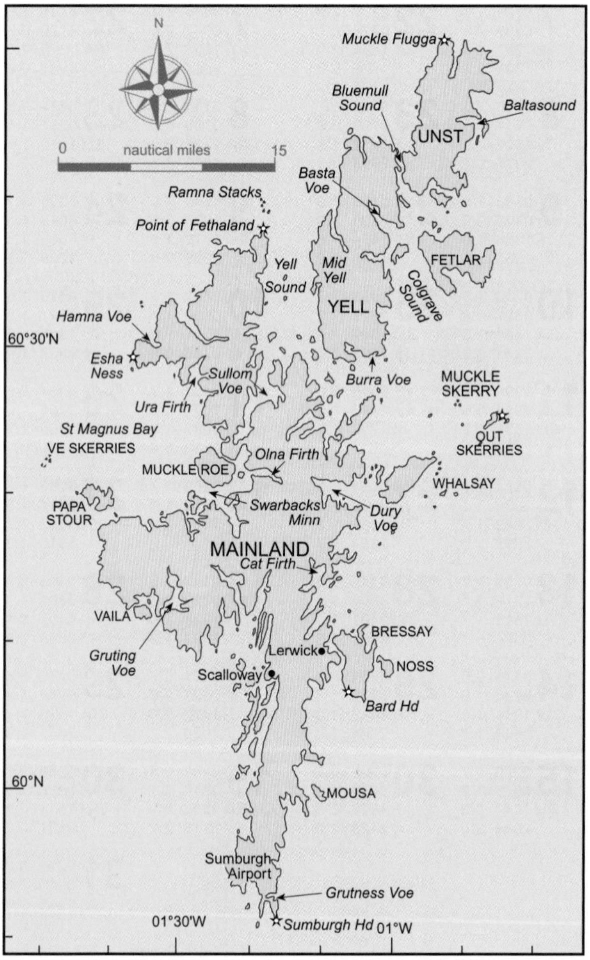
N
Muckle Flugga
Bluemull Sound
Baltasound
UNST
0 nautical miles 15
Basta Voe
Ramna Stacks
Point of Fethaland
FETLAR
Yell Sound
Mid Yell
Colgrave Sound
YELL
Hamna Voe
60°30'N
Esha Ness
Sullom Voe
Burra Voe
MUCKLE SKERRY
Ura Firth
St Magnus Bay
OUT SKERRIES
VE SKERRIES
Olna Firth
MUCKLE ROE
WHALSAY
PAPA STOUR
Swarbacks Minn
Dury Voe
MAINLAND
Cat Firth
VAILA
BRESSAY
Gruting Voe
Lerwick
NOSS
Scalloway
Bard Hd
60°N
MOUSA
Sumburgh Airport
Grutness Voe
01°30'W
Sumburgh Hd
01°W

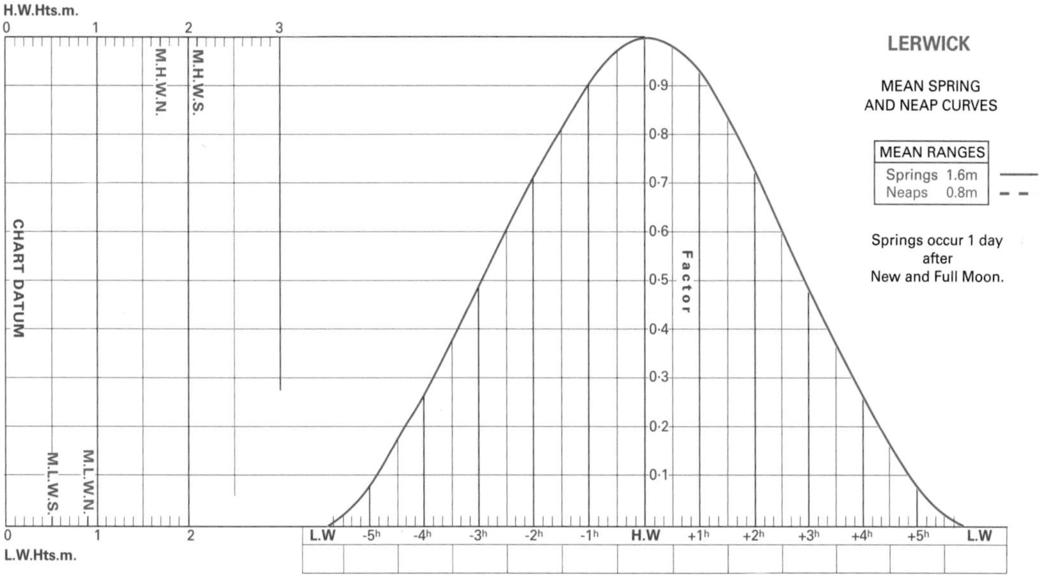
H.W.Hts.m.
0
1
2
3
M.H.W.N.
M.H.W.S.
CHART DATUM
M.L.W.S.
M.L.W.N.
L.W.Hts.m.
0·9
0·8
0·7
0·6
0·5
0·4
0·3
0·2
0·1
Factor
L.W
-5h
-4h
-3h
-2h
-1h
H.W
+1h
+2h
+3h
+4h
+5h
L.W
LERWICK
MEAN SPRING AND NEAP CURVES
MEAN RANGES
Springs 1.6m
Neaps 0.8m
Springs occur 1 day after New and Full Moon.

9.7.25 LERWICK

Shetland Is, Mainland 60°09'·26N 01°08'·42W

CHARTS AC 3283, 3272, 3271; OS 4

TIDES –0001 Dover; ML 1·4; Duration 0620; Zone 0 (UT)

Standard Port LERWICK (⟵)

Times				Height (metres)			
High Water		Low Water		MHWS	MHWN	MLWN	MLWS
0000	0600	0100	0800	2·1	1·7	0·9	0·5
1200	1800	1300	2000				
Differences FAIR ISLE							
–0006	–0015	–0031	–0037	+0·1	0·0	+0·1	+0·1
SUMBURGH (Grutness Voe)							
+0006	+0008	+0004	–0002	–0·3	–0·3	–0·2	–0·1
DURY VOE							
–0015	–0015	–0010	–0010	0·0	–0·1	0·0	–0·2
BURRA VOE (YELL SOUND)							
–0025	–0025	–0025	–0025	+0·2	+0·1	0·0	–0·1
BALTA SOUND							
–0055	–0055	–0045	–0045	+0·2	+0·1	0·0	–0·1
BLUE MULL SOUND							
–0135	–0135	–0155	–0155	+0·5	+0·2	+0·1	0·0
SULLOM VOE							
–0135	–0125	–0135	–0120	0·0	0·0	–0·2	–0·2
HILLSWICK (URA FIRTH)							
–0220	–0220	–0200	–0200	–0·1	–0·1	–0·1	–0·1
SCALLOWAY							
–0150	–0150	–0150	–0150	–0·5	–0·4	–0·3	0·0
FOULA (23M West of Scalloway)							
–0140	–0130	–0140	–0120	–0·1	–0·1	0·0	0·0

SHELTER Good. HM allocates berths in Small Dock or Albert Dock. FVs occupy most alongside space. ⚓ prohib for about 2ca off the waterfront. Gremista marina in N hbr, is mainly for local boats, and is about 1M from the town.

NAVIGATION WPT 60°05'·97N 01°08'·62W, 010° to Maryfield lt, 3·5M, in W sector. From S, Bressay Sound is clear of dangers. From N, WPT 60°11'·60N 01°07'·88W, 035°/215° from/to N ent Dir lt, 1·34M; lt Oc WRG 6s, W sector 214°-216°. Beware Soldian Rk (dries), Nive Baa (0·6m), Green Holm (10m) and The Brethren (two rks 2m and 1·5m).

LIGHTS AND MARKS Kirkabister Ness, Fl (2) 20s 32m 23M; Cro of Ham, Fl 3s 3M; Maryfield, Oc WRG 6s, W 008°-013°; all on Bressay. Twageos Pt, L Fl 6s 8m 6M. Loofa Baa SCM lt bn, as on chartlet. 2 SHM lt buoys mark Middle Ground in N Hbr.

R/T *Lerwick Harbour* VHF Ch **12** 11 16 (H24) for VTS, radar and information. Other stns: *Sullom Voe Hbr Radio* broadcasts traffic info and local forecasts on request Ch **14** 12 20 16 (H24).

TELEPHONE (Dial code 01595) HM 692991, 🖷 693452; MRSC 692976; Weather 692239; Police 692110; Dr 693201.

FACILITIES **Hbr** Slip, M, P, D, L, FW, ME, ⚒, Gas; **Lerwick Hbr Trust** ☎ 692991, AB(pontoon 6Ⓥs) £0.50, ⚡, M, FW, D, P, ♿ ramps/toilet; **Lerwick Boating Club** ☎ 692407, L, C, Bar, ⊡; **Services:** ME, El, Ⓔ, ⚒, Slip, BY, CH, SM, Gas, ACA. **Town** EC Wed (all day); 🛒, R, Bar, ✉, Ⓑ, ⇄, (ferry to Aberdeen), ✈. www.shetland.news.co.uk.

7

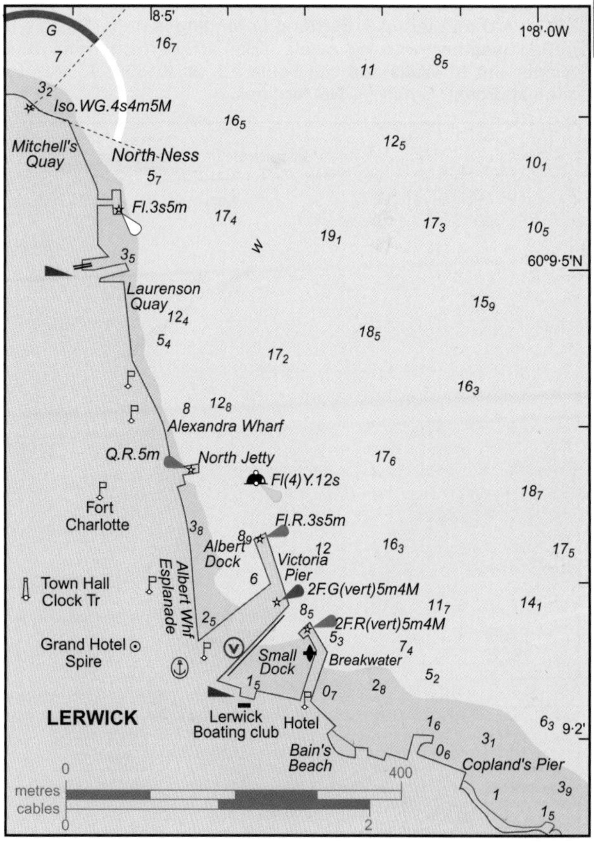
1°8'·0W
60°9·5'N
9·2'
Iso.WG.4s4m5M
Mitchell's Quay
North Ness
Fl.3s5m
Laurenson Quay
Alexandra Wharf
Q.R.5m
North Jetty
Fl(4)Y.12s
Fort Charlotte
Fl.R.3s5m
Albert Dock
Victoria Pier
Town Hall Clock Tr
Albert Whf Esplanade
2F.G(vert)5m4M
2F.R(vert)5m4M
Grand Hotel Spire
Small Dock
Breakwater
LERWICK
Lerwick Boating club
Hotel
Bain's Beach
Copland's Pier
metres
cables
0
400
2

OTHER HARBOURS IN THE SHETLAND ISLANDS

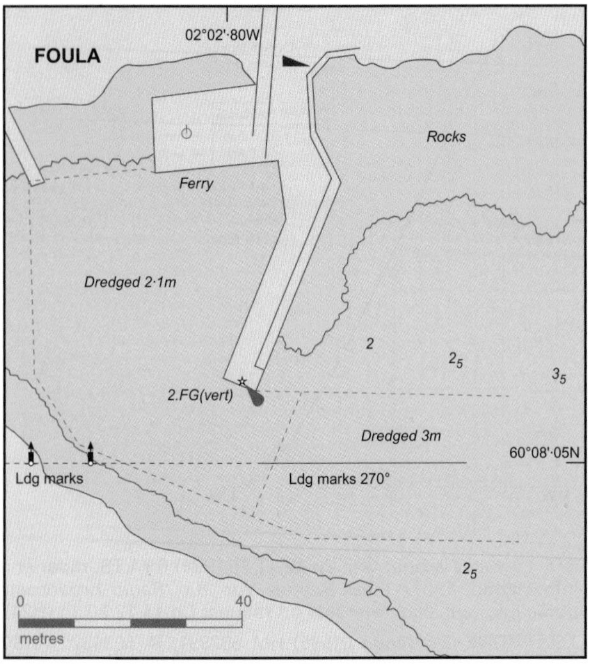
FOULA
02°02'·80W
Rocks
Ferry
Dredged 2·1m
2
2₅
3₅
2.FG(vert)
Dredged 3m
60°08'·05N
Ldg marks
Ldg marks 270°
2₅
0
40
metres

FOULA, Shetland Islands, **60°08'·02N 02°02'·92W** (Ham Voe). AC 3283. HW –0150 on Dover; ML 1·3m. See 9.7.25. Foula is 12M WSW of Mainland. Highest ground is 416m. S Ness lt ho, Fl (3) 15s, is at the S tip. Beware Foula Shoal (7·6m) and Hœvdi Grund (1·4m), respectively 4·3M E and 2M SE of Ham Voe.

Ham Voe is a narrow inlet on the E coast with a quay; rks on both sides. Two R ▲ ldg marks, approx 270°, are hard to see. ☆ 2 FG (vert) on pierhead. Berthing or landing is only possible in settled weather with no swell. Take advice from mail boat skipper out of Walls and call Foula ✉, ☎ (01595) 753222 for prior approval. Small ✈. No facilities.

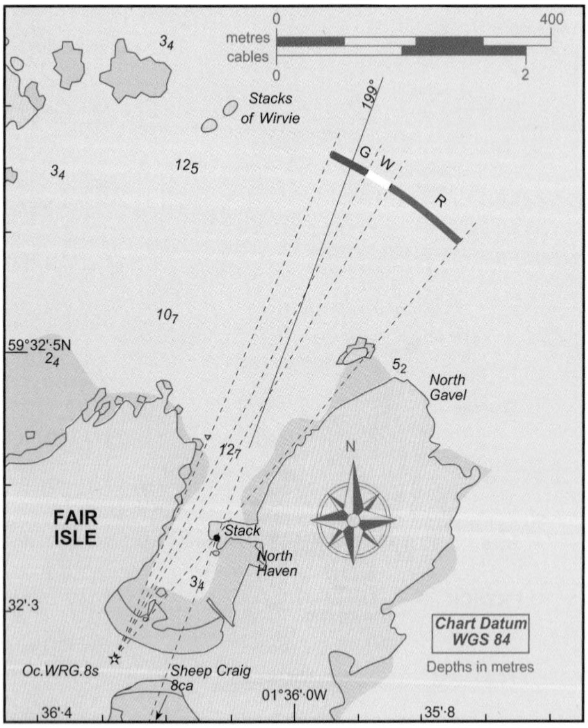
0
400
metres
cables
0
2
3₄
Stacks of Wirvie
199°
G
W
R
3₄
12₅
10₇
59°32'·5N
2₄
5₂
North Gavel
N
12₇
FAIR ISLE
Stack
North Haven
3₄
32'·3
Chart Datum WGS 84
Depths in metres
Oc.WRG.8s
Sheep Craig
8ca
01°36'·0W
36'·4
35'·8

BALTA SOUND, Unst, **60°44'·32N 00°48'·12W**. AC 3293. HW –0105 on Dover; ML 1·3; Duration 0640. See 9.7.25. Balta Sound is a large almost landlocked inlet with good shelter from all winds. Beware fish farms and bad holding on kelp. Safest and main entry is via S Chan between Huney Is and Balta Is; inner chan marked by two PHM lt buoys. N Chan is deep but narrow; keep to Unst shore. ⚓ off Sandisons Wharf (2FG vert) in approx 6m or enter marina close W (one Ⓥ, very shallow); pier has Oc WRG 10s 5m 2M, G272°–282°, W282°–287°, R287°–297°. VHF Ch 16; 20 (HO or as required). Facilities: BY, FW, D, El, ME, ⚒; Hotel by pier. **Baltasound village**, Bar, R, 🛒, ✉.

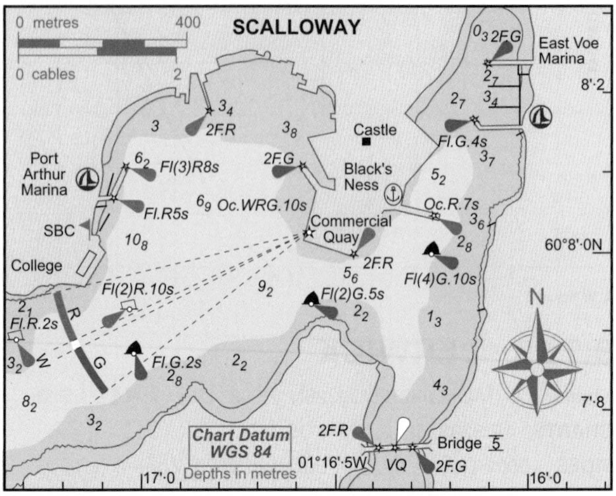
0 metres 400
0 cables 2
SCALLOWAY
0₃ 2FG
East Voe Marina
8'·2
2₇
3₄
2₇
3₄
3
2FR
3₈
Castle
Fl.G.4s
3₇
Port Arthur Marina
6₂ Fl(3)R8s
2FG
Black's Ness
5₂
Fl.R5s
6₉ Oc.WRG.10s
Commercial Quay
Oc.R.7s
3₆
SBC
10₈
2₈
60°8'·0N
College
2FR
5₆
Fl(4)G.10s
Fl(2)R.10s
9₂
Fl(2)G.5s
2₁
2₂
Fl.R.2s
1₃
R
W
G
Fl.G.2s
2₂
2₈
N
4₃
8₂
7·8
3₂
Chart Datum WGS 84
2FR
Bridge 5
01°16'·5W
VQ
2FG
17'·0
Depths in metres
16'·0

SCALLOWAY, Mainland, **60°08'·02N 01°16'·59W**. AC 3294. HW –0200 on Dover; ML 0·9m; Duration 0620. See 9.7.25. A busy fishing port; good shelter and ⚓ in all weathers. Care is needed negotiating the islands in strong SW'lies. The N Chan is easier and safer than the S Chan, both are well lit and marked. Castle and warehouse (both conspic) lead 054° through S Chan. Dir Oc WRG 10s on hbr quay leads 064·5° into hbr. Hbr lts as chartlet. Ⓥ pontoon in 3m off SBC is best option; marina close N or new marina in E Voe (though mostly full of local boats. ⚓s in hbr 6 -10m or in Hamna Voe (W Burra). Call *Scalloway Hbr Radio* VHF Ch **12** 09 16 (Mon-Fri 0600-1800; Sat 0600-1230LT). Piermaster ☎ (01595) 880574, 📠 880566 (H24). **Facilities**: **Scalloway Boat Club** (SBC) ☎ 880409 welcomes visitors; AB (free), Bar. **Town** EC Thurs; Slip, P, D, FW, SM, BY, CH, C, El, ME, ⚒, ✉, R, 🛒, Bar.

VAILA SOUND (WALLS), Mainland, **60°13'·65N 01°33'·87W**. AC 3295. Tides approx as Scalloway (above); see 9.7.25. Appr to E of Vaila island (do not attempt Wester Sound) in the W sector (355°-012°) of Rams Head lt, Fl WRG 8s 16m 9/6M. Gruting Voe lies to the NE. Enter Easter Sound and go N for 1·5M, passing E of Linga islet, to Walls at the head of Vaila Voe. Navigate by echo sounder. Beware fish farms. Temp'y AB on Bayhaa pier (covers). Close E of this, AB £1 on pontoon of Peter Georgeson **marina**; Sec ☎ (01595) 809273, FW. **Walls Regatta Club** welcomes visitors; showers, Bar, Slip. **Village**: P & D (cans), 🛒, ✉.

FAIR ISLE, Shetland Islands, **59°32'·37N 01°36'·21W** (North Haven). AC 2622. HW –0030 on Dover; ML 1·4m; Duration 0620. See 9.7.25 Good shelter in North Haven, except in NE winds. AB on pier or ⚓ in approx 2m. Beware strong cross-tides in the apprs; beware also rocks all round Fair Isle, particularly in S Haven and South Hbr which are not recommended. Ldg marks 199° into North Haven: front, Stack of N Haven (only visible as a dark "tooth" sticking up from the jumble of blocks which form the bkwtr) in transit with conspic summit of Sheep Craig (rear). Dir lt, 209·5° into N Haven, Oc WRG 8s 10m 6M, vis G204°-208°, W208°- 211°, R211°-221°. Other lts: At N tip, Skroo Fl (2) 30s 80m **22**M, vis 086·7°–358°, Horn (3) 45s. At S tip, Skadan Fl (4) 30s 32m **22**M, vis 260°–146°, but obscd close inshore from 260°–282°, Horn (2) 60s. **Facilities**: 🛒, ✉ at N Shriva, ✈ and a bi-weekly mail boat (*Good Shepherd*) to Shetland.

Area 8

North-West Scotland
Cape Wrath to Crinan Canal

8

1. Mull of Kintyre	232	203	189	175	159	133	143	121	105	120	89	87	98	72	78	62	57	54	51	**1**
2. Crinan	187	157	158	129	112	95	95	74	63	97	42	30	54	25	45	14	9	6	**2**	
3. Loch Craignish	188	158	159	131	118	95	96	76	64	98	44	31	55	26	46	17	14	**3**		
4. Craobh Haven	184	155	155	117	114	93	92	70	60	93	40	27	50	21	43	5	**4**			
5. Loch Melfort	184	154	155	117	114	92	93	69	61	92	40	27	45	18	45	**5**				
6. Loch Lathaich	160	130	124	98	91	62	67	49	35	56	31	53	77	48	**6**					
7. Oban	169	138	139	111	100	76	77	56	44	77	24	13	29	**7**						
8. Fort William	198	161	162	134	121	99	98	75	63	96	43	34	**8**							
9. Loch Aline	157	127	128	100	87	65	66	45	33	66	13	**9**								
10. Tobermory	144	114	115	87	74	52	53	32	20	53	**10**									
11. Castlebay (Barra)	133	105	92	69	97	43	76	59	46	**11**										
12. Eigg	123	98	97	75	54	34	35	14	**12**											
13. Mallaig	112	82	83	84	42	33	21	**13**												
14. Kyle of Lochalsh	91	63	62	63	21	53	**14**													
15. Loch Harport	110	82	65	45	66	**15**														
16. Portree	83	57	53	42	**16**															
17. East Loch Tarbert	75	56	33	**17**																
18. Stornoway	53	45	**18**																	
19. Ullapool	54	**19**																		
20. *Cape Wrath*	**20**																			

DISTANCE TABLE

Approximate distances in nautical miles are by the most direct route, keeping East of Skye and Mull where appropriate, and avoiding dangers. Places in *italics* are in adjoining areas.

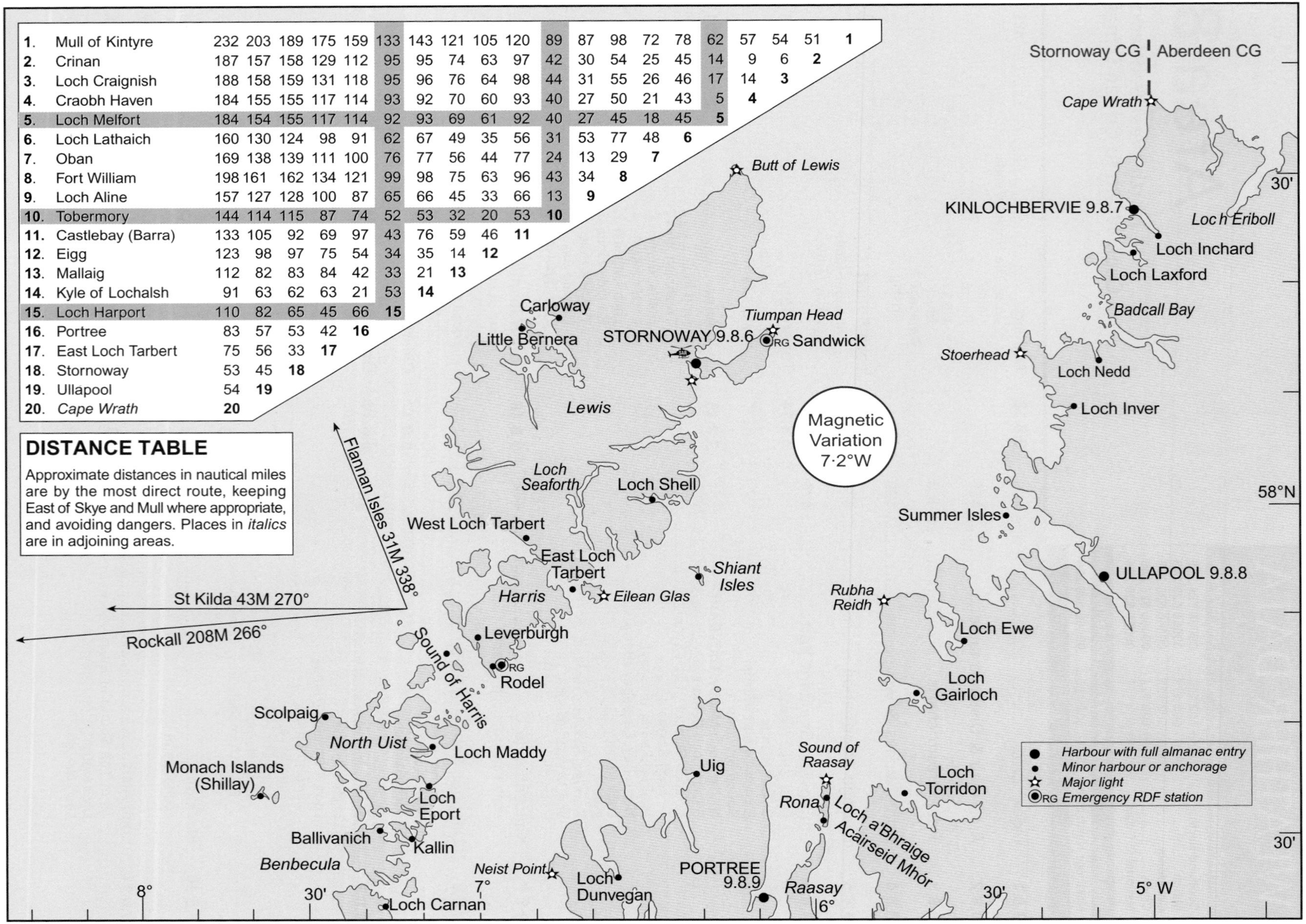
Stornoway CG
Aberdeen CG
Cape Wrath
KINLOCHBERVIE 9.8.7
Loch Eriboll
Loch Inchard
Loch Laxford
Badcall Bay
Stoerhead
Loch Nedd
Loch Inver
Butt of Lewis
Tiumpan Head
STORNOWAY 9.8.6
RG Sandwick
Carloway
Little Bernera
Lewis
Magnetic Variation 7·2°W
Loch Seaforth
Loch Shell
Summer Isles
58°N
ULLAPOOL 9.8.8
West Loch Tarbert
East Loch Tarbert
Shiant Isles
Rubha Reidh
Harris
Eilean Glas
Flannan Isles 31M 338°
St Kilda 43M 270°
Rockall 208M 266°
Leverburgh
RG
Rodel
Sound of Harris
Loch Ewe
Loch Gairloch
Scolpaig
North Uist
Loch Maddy
Monach Islands (Shillay)
Uig
Sound of Raasay
Loch Torridon
Loch Eport
Rona
Loch a'Bhraige
Acairseid Mhór
Ballivanich
Kallin
Benbecula
Neist Point
Loch Dunvegan
PORTREE 9.8.9
Raasay
Loch Carnan
8°
30'
7°
6°
5° W
Harbour with full almanac entry
Minor harbour or anchorage
Major light
RG Emergency RDF station

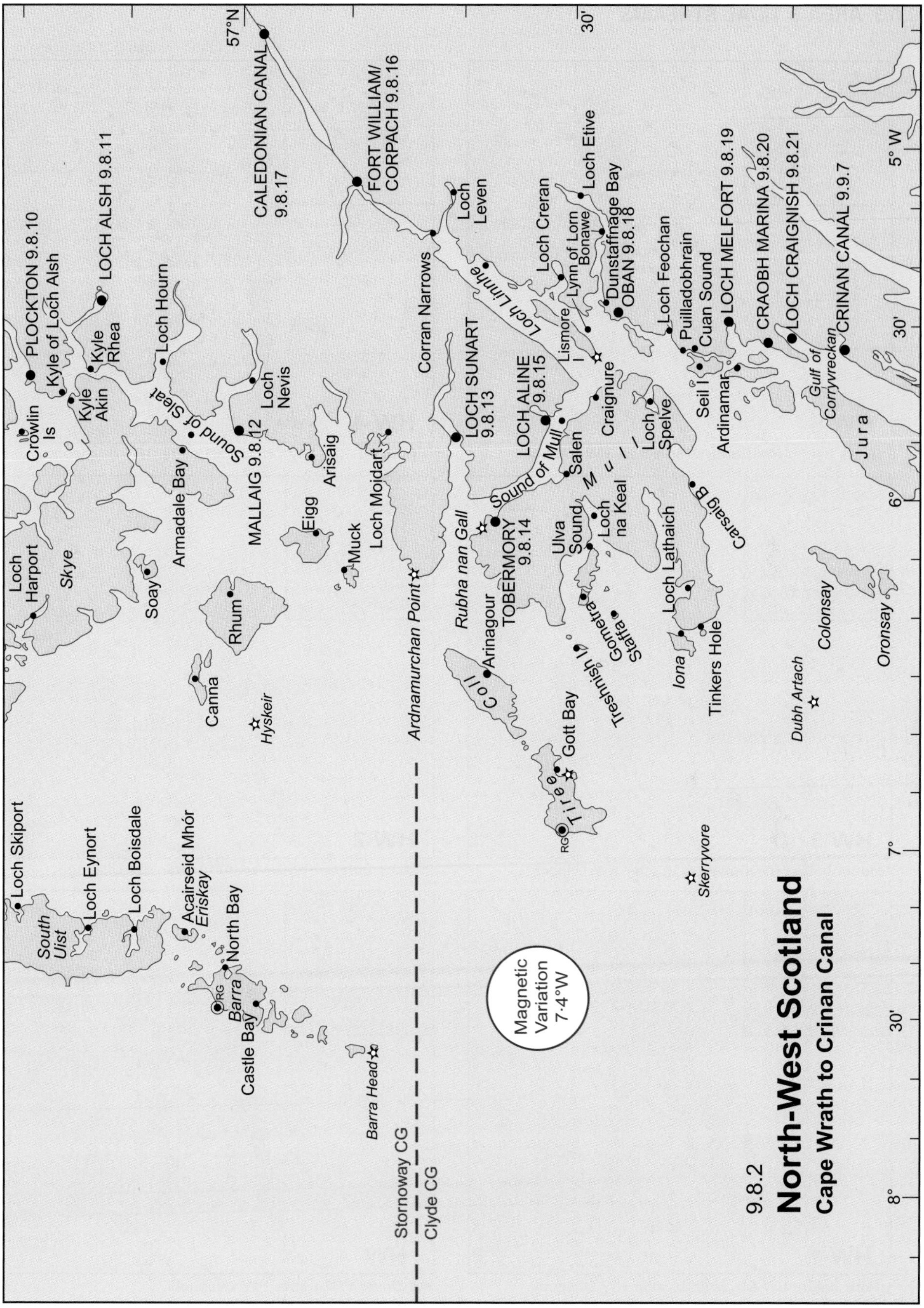
57°N
30'
5° W
30'
6°
30'
7°
30'
8°
CALEDONIAN CANAL 9.8.17
FORT WILLIAM/ CORPACH 9.8.16
PLOCKTON 9.8.10
Kyle of Loch Alsh
LOCH ALSH 9.8.11
Kyle Rhea
Kyle Akin
Loch Hourn
Crowlin Is
Sound of Sleat
Loch Nevis
MALLAIG 9.8.12
Armadale Bay
Arisaig
Loch Moidart
Eigg
Muck
Loch Harport
Skye
Soay
Rhum
Canna
Hyskeir
Corran Narrows
Loch Leven
Loch Linnhe
LOCH SUNART 9.8.13
LOCH ALINE 9.8.15
Sound of Mull
Salen
Craignure
Lismore I
Loch Creran
Lynn of Lorn
Bonawe
Loch Etive
Dunstaffnage Bay
OBAN 9.8.18
Loch Feochan
Puilladobhrain
Cuan Sound
LOCH MELFORT 9.8.19
CRAOBH MARINA 9.8.20
LOCH CRAIGNISH 9.8.21
CRINAN CANAL 9.9.7
Gulf of Corryvreckan
Jura
Seil I
Ardinamar
Loch Spelve
Mull
Carsaig B
Loch na Keal
Ulva Sound
Loch Lathaich
Tinkers Hole
Iona
Staffa
Gometra
Treshnish Is
Rubha nan Gall
TOBERMORY 9.8.14
Arinagour
Coll
Gott Bay
Tiree
RG
Ardnamurchan Point
Colonsay
Oronsay
Dubh Artach
Skerryvore
Loch Skiport
South Uist
Loch Eynort
Loch Boisdale
Acairseid Mhór
Eriskay
North Bay
Barra
RG
Castle Bay
Barra Head
Stornoway CG
Clyde CG
Magnetic Variation 7·4°W

9.8.2

North-West Scotland

Cape Wrath to Crinan Canal

9.8.3 AREA 8 TIDAL STREAMS

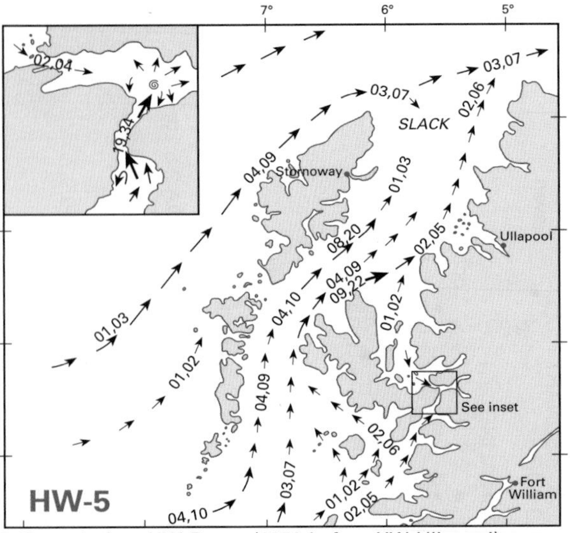

7°
6°
5°
58°
57°
02,04
19,34
03,07
03,07
SLACK
02,06
04,09
Stornoway
01,03
08,20
01,03
02,05
Ullapool
04,09
09,22
04,10
01,02
01,02
04,09
See inset
02,06
03,07
01,02
02,05
Fort William
04,10
HW-5

5 Hours before HW Dover (0050 before HW Ullapool)

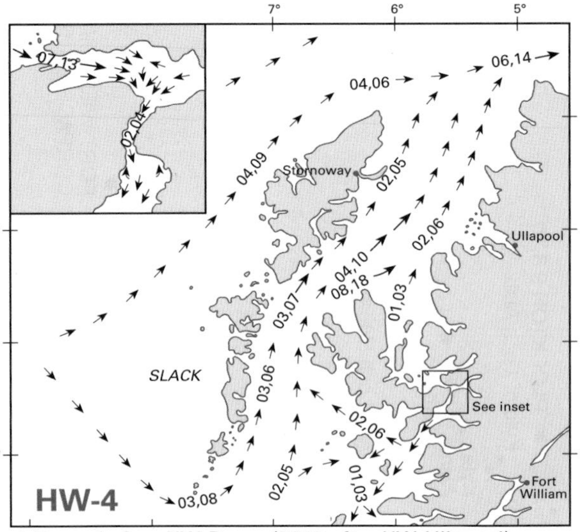

7°
6°
5°
58°
57°
07,13
02,04
06,14
04,06
04,09
Stornoway
02,05
02,06
Ullapool
04,10
08,18
03,07
01,03
SLACK
03,06
See inset
02,06
02,05
01,03
Fort William
03,08
HW-4

4 Hours before HW Dover (0010 after HW Ullapool)

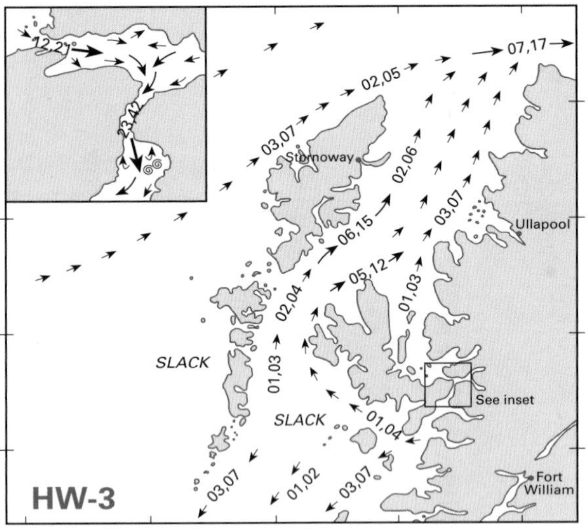

58°
57°
12,21
23,42
07,17
02,05
03,07
Stornoway
02,06
06,15
03,07
Ullapool
05,12
01,03
02,04
SLACK
01,03
See inset
SLACK
01,04
03,07
01,02
03,07
Fort William
HW-3

3 Hours before HW Dover (0110 after HW Ullapool)

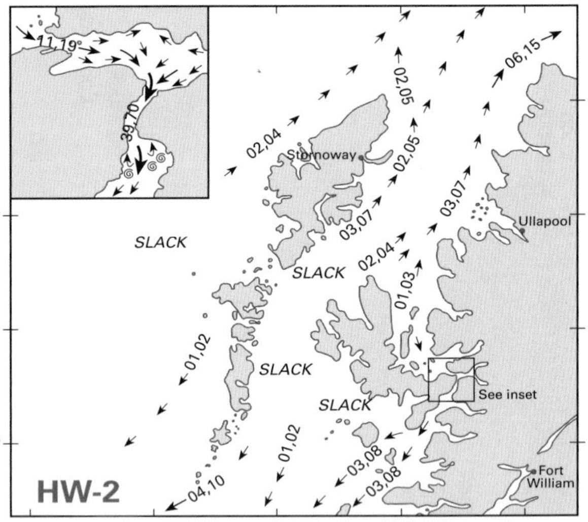

58°
57°
11,19
39,70
02,05
06,15
02,04
Stornoway
02,05
03,07
03,07
Ullapool
SLACK
SLACK
02,04
01,03
01,02
SLACK
See inset
SLACK
01,02
03,08
03,08
04,10
Fort William
HW-2

2 Hours before HW Dover (0210 after HW Ullapool)

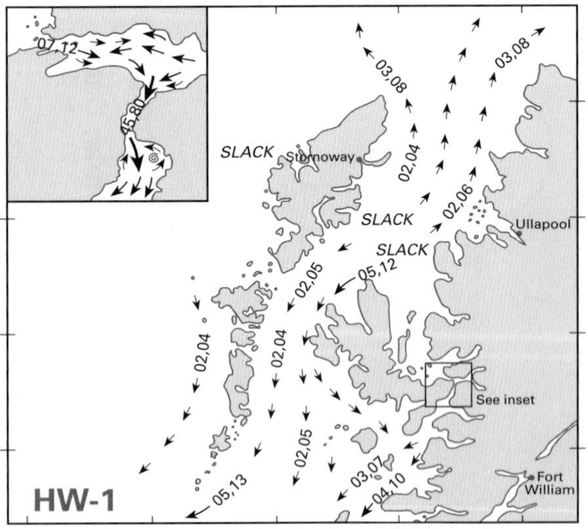

58°
57°
07,12
45,80
03,08
03,08
SLACK
Stornoway
02,04
02,06
SLACK
Ullapool
SLACK
02,05
05,12
02,04
02,04
See inset
02,05
03,07
04,10
05,13
Fort William
HW-1

1 Hour before HW Dover (0310 after HW Ullapool)

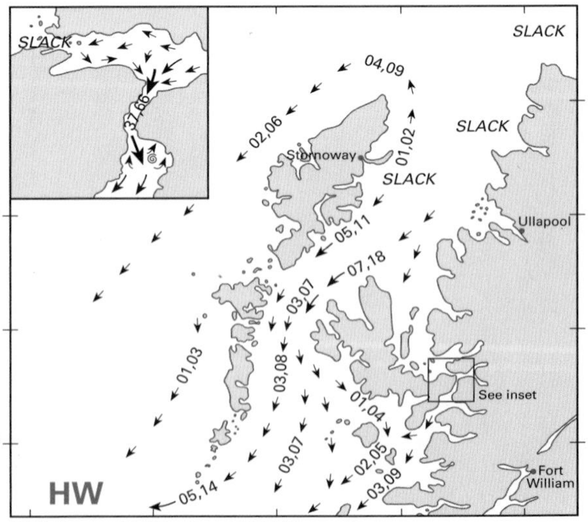

58°
57°
SLACK
SLACK
37,66
04,09
02,06
01,02
SLACK
Stornoway
SLACK
Ullapool
05,11
07,18
03,07
01,03
03,08
See inset
01,04
03,07
02,05
03,09
05,14
Fort William
HW

HW Dover (0410 after HW Ullapool)

Eastward 9.7.3 Southward 9.9.3 Mull of Kintyre 9.9.12

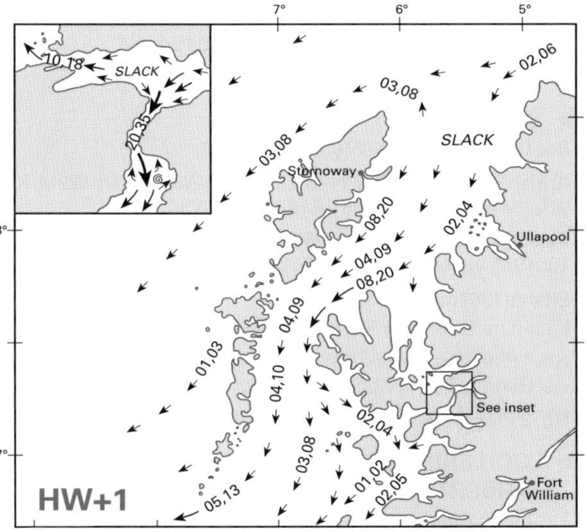

7°
6°
5°
58°
57°
10,18
SLACK
20,35
03,08
02,06
SLACK
03,08
Stornoway
08,20
02,04
Ullapool
04,09
08,20
04,09
01,03
04,10
02,04
See inset
03,08
01,02
02,05
05,13
Fort William
HW+1

1 Hour after HW Dover (0510 after HW Ullapool)

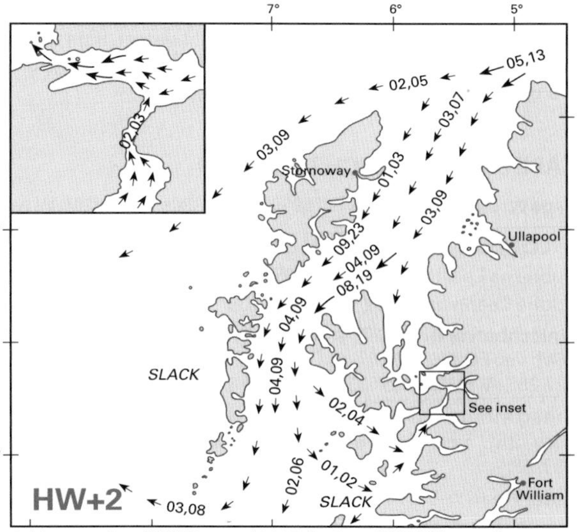

7°
6°
5°
58°
57°
02,03
02,05
05,13
03,07
03,09
Stornoway
01,03
03,09
09,23
Ullapool
04,09
08,19
04,09
SLACK
04,09
02,04
See inset
02,06
01,02
SLACK
03,08
Fort William
HW+2

2 Hours after HW Dover (0615 before HW Ullapool)

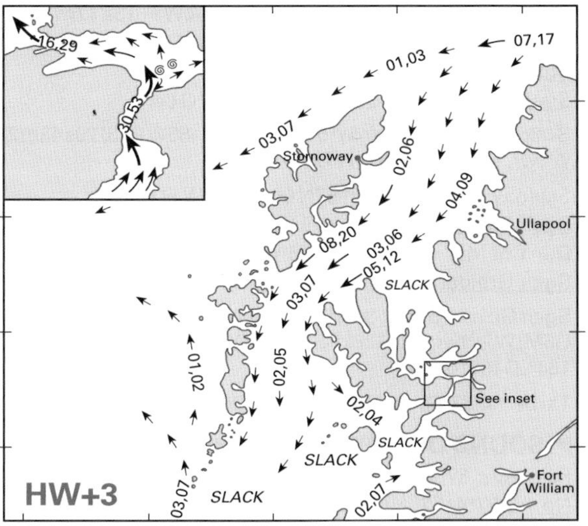

16,29
30,53
01,03
07,17
03,07
Stornoway
02,06
04,09
58°
Ullapool
08,20
03,06
05,12
SLACK
03,07
01,02
02,05
See inset
02,04
57°
SLACK
SLACK
03,07
SLACK
02,07
Fort William
HW+3

3 Hours after HW Dover (0515 before HW Ullapool)

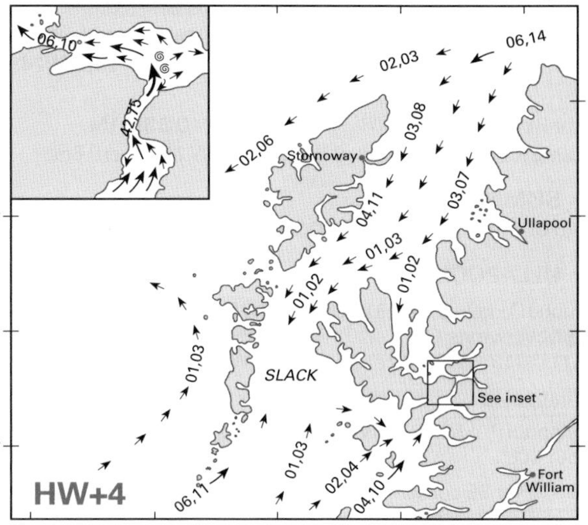

06,10
42,75
02,03
06,14
03,08
02,06
Stornoway
03,07
58°
04,11
Ullapool
01,03
01,02
01,02
01,03
SLACK
See inset
57°
01,03
02,04
04,10
06,11
Fort William
HW+4

4 Hours after HW Dover (0415 before HW Ullapool)

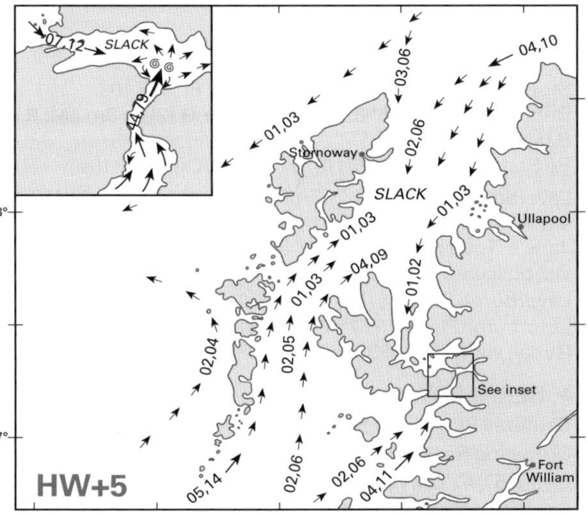

07,12
SLACK
44,79
03,06
04,10
01,03
Stornoway
02,06
SLACK
01,03
58°
Ullapool
01,03
04,09
01,03
01,02
02,04
02,05
See inset
57°
02,06
02,06
04,11
05,14
Fort William
HW+5

5 Hours after HW Dover (0315 before HW Ullapool)

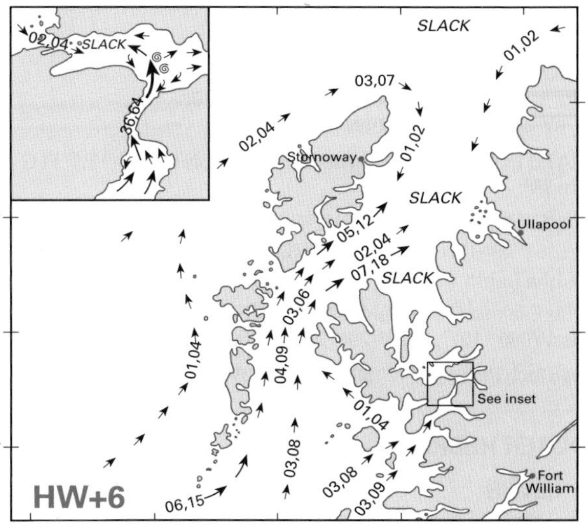

02,04
SLACK
36,64
SLACK
01,02
03,07
02,04
Stornoway
01,02
SLACK
58°
Ullapool
05,12
02,04
07,18
SLACK
03,06
01,04
04,09
See inset
01,04
57°
03,08
03,08
03,09
06,15
Fort William
HW+6

6 Hours after HW Dover (0215 before HW Ullapool)

8

PLOT WAYPOINTS ON YOUR CHART BEFORE USING THEM

9.8.4 LIGHTS, BUOYS AND WAYPOINTS

Blue print = light with a nominal range of 15M or more. CAPITALS = place or feature. *CAPITAL ITALICS* = light-vessel, light float or Lanby. *Italics* = Fog signal. ***Bold italics*** = Racon. Useful waypoints are underlined. Abbreviations are in Chapter 1.

CAPE WRATH TO LOCH TORRIDON

Cape Wrath ☆ 58°37'·54N 04°59'·99W Fl (4) 30s 122m **22M**; W twr.

▶ LOCH INCHARD/LOCH LAXFORD

Rubha na Lecaig ☆ 58°27'·41N 05°04'·58W Fl (2) 10s 30m 8M.
Bodha Ceann na Saile 58°27'·24N 05°04'·01W Q.

Kinlochbervie Dir lt 327° ☆. 58°27'·49N 05°03'·08W WRG 15m **16M**; vis: FG326°-326·5°, Al GW326·5°-326·75°, FW326·75°-327·25°, Al RW327·25°-327·5°, FR327·5°-328°.

Creag Mhòr Dir lt 147°. 58°26'·99N 05°02'·45W Oc WRG 2·8s 16m 9M; vis: R136·5°-146·5°, W146·5°-147·5°, G147·5°-157·5°.

Stoer Head ☆ 58°14'·43N 05°24'·07W Fl 15s 59m **24M**; W twr.

▶ LOCH INVER

Soyea I ☆ 58°08'·56N 05°19'·67W Fl (2) 10s 34m 6M.
Glas Leac ☆ 58°08'·68N 05°16'·36W Fl WRG 3s 7m 5M; vis: W071°-078°, R078°-090°, G090°-103°, W103°-111°, R111°-243°, W243°-247°, G247°-071°.

Hbr Bkwtr Head ☆ 58°08'·93N 05°15'·08W QG 3m 1M.
Culag Pier Head ☆ 58°08'·90N 05°14'·89W 2 FG (vert) 6m.

▶ SUMMER ISLES

Old Dornie Pier Head ☆ 58°02'·56N 05°25'·39W Fl G 3s 5m.

▶ ULLAPOOL

Rubha Cadail ☆ 57°55'·51N 05°13'·40W Fl WRG 6s 11m W9M, R6M, G6M; W twr; vis: G311°-320°, W320°-325°, R325°-103°, W103°-111°, G111°-118°, W118°-127°, R127°-157°, W157°-199°.

Ullapool Pt 57°53'·70N 05°10'·68W QR.

Ullapool Pt ☆ 57°53'·59N 05°09'·93W Iso R 4s 8m 6M; W twr; vis: 258°-108°.

Ferry Pier SE corner ☆ 57°53'·70N 05°09'·43W Fl R 3s 6m 1M.

Cailleach Head ☆ 57°55'·81N 05°24'·23W Fl (2) 12s 60m 9M; W twr; vis: 015°-236°.

▶ LOCH EWE/LOCH GAIRLOCH

Fairway 57°51'·98N 05°40'·09W L Fl 10s.
No. 1 57°50'·97N 05°40'·09W Fl (3) G 10s.
57°49'·84N 05°35'·49W Fl (4) R 10s.

NATO POL Jetty, NW corner ☆ 57°49'·66N 05°35'·12W Fl G 4s 5m 3M.

E 57°49'·42N 05°35'·51W Fl R 2s.
D 57°49'·11N 05°36'·11W Fl (2) R 10s.
Rubha Reidh ☆ 57°51'·52N 05°48'·72W Fl (4) 15s 37m **24M**.

Glas Eilean ☆ 57°42'·79N 05°42'·42W Fl WRG 6s 9m W6M, R4M; vis: W080°-102°, R102°-296°, W296°-333°, G333°-080°.

Gairloch Pier ☆ 57°42'·59N 05°41'·03W QR 6m 2M.

OUTER HEBRIDES – EAST SIDE

▶ LEWIS

Butt of Lewis ☆ 58°30'·89N 06°15'·84W Fl 5s 52m **25M**; R twr; vis: 056°-320°.

Tiumpan Head ☆ 58°15'·66N 06°08'·29W Fl (2) 15s 55m **25M**; W twr.

Broad Bay Tong Anch. Ldg Lts 320° 58°14'·48N 06°19'·98W Oc R 8s 8m 4M. Rear, 70m from front, Oc R 8s 9m 4M.

Airport app lts 58°13'·87N 06°20'·04W Q 3m 2M.

▶ STORNOWAY

Reef Rock 58°11'·58N 06°21'·97W QR.

Arnish Point ☆ 58°11'·50N 06°22'·16W Fl WR 10s 17m W9M, R7M; W ○ twr; vis: W088°-198°, R198°-302°, W302°-013°.

Sandwick Bay, NW side ☆ 58°12'·20N 06°22'·11W Oc WRG 6s 10m 9M; vis: G334°-341°, W341°-347°, R347°-354°.

Eitshal (367m) ☆ 58°10'·74N 06°35'·13W 4 FR (vert) on mast.
Eilean na Gobhail ☆ 58°12'·14N 06°22'·99W Fl G 6s 8m.

No. 1 Pier SW corner ☆ 58°12'·36N 06°23'·43W Q WRG 5m 11M; vis: Gshore-335°, W335°-352°, R352°-shore.

No. 3 Pier ☆ 58°12'·31N 06°23'·28W Q (2) G 10s 7m 2M.

▶ LOCH ERISORT/LOCH SHELL/EAST LOCH TARBERT

Tabhaidh Bheag ☆ 58°07'·19N 06°23'·06W Fl 3s 13m 3M.
Eilean Chalabrigh ☆ 58°06'·82N 06°26'·67W QG 5m 3M.
Gob na Milaid Pt ☆ 58°01'·08N 06°22'·04W Fl 15s 17m 10M.
Rubh' Uisenis ☆ 57°56'·25N 06°28'·36W Fl 5s 24m 11M; W twr.
Shiants 57°54'·57N 06°25'·70W QG.
Sgeir Inoe 57°50'·93N 06°33'·93W Fl G 6s.

Scalpay, **Eilean Glas** ☆ 57°51'·41N 06°38'·55W Fl (3) 20s 43m **23M**; W twr, R bands; ***Racon (T) 16-18M***.

Scalpay N Hbr 57°52'·57N 06°42'·22W Fl G 2s.
Sgeir Bràigh Mor 57°51'·51N 06°43'·84W Fl G 6s.
Dun Cor Mòr ☆ 57°51'·03N 06°44'·01W Fl R 5s 10m 5M.
Sgeir Graidach 57°50'·36N 06°41'·37W Q (6) + L Fl 15s.

Sgeir Ghlas ☆ 57°52'·36N 06°45'·24W Iso WRG 4s 9m W9M, R6M, G6M; W ○ twr; vis: G282°-319°, W319°-329°, R329°-153°, W153°-164°, G164°-171°.

Tarbert ☆ 57°53'·82N 06°47'·93W Oc WRG 6s 10m 5M

▶ SOUND OF HARRIS/LEVERBURGH

Fairway 57°40'·35N 07°02'·15W L Fl 10s.
No. 1 57°41'·20N 07°02'·67W QG.
No. 3 57°41'·86N 07°03'·44W Fl G 5s.
No. 4 57°41'·76N 07°03'·63W Fl R 5s.
L1 57°42'·59N 07°03'·21W Fl (2) G 5s.
Grocis Sgeir 57°44'·15N 07°01'·52W Fl (3) R 10s.
Stumbles Rk 57°45'·13N 07°01'·79W Fl (2) R 10s.
Dubh Sgeir 57°45'·52N 07°s02'·62W Q (2) 5s 9m 6M; R twr, B bands.
Bo Stainan 57°45'·76N 07°02'·40W VQ(6) + LF 10s.

Leverburgh Ldg Lts 014·7°. Front, 57°46'·23N 07°02'·04W Q 10m 4M. Rear, Oc 3s 12m 4M.
Jane's Tower 57°45'·76N 07°02'·12W Q (2) G 5s 6m 4M; vis: obscured 273°-318°.
Leverburgh Reef 57°45'·97N 07°01'·86W Fl R 2s 4m.
Leverburgh Pier Hd ☆ 57°46'·01N 07°01'·62W Oc WRG 8s 5m 2M; Gy col; vis: G305°-059°, W059°-066°, R066°-125°.

▶ BERNERAY

Berneray Bkwtr Hd ☆ 57°42'·87N 07°10'·07W Iso R 4s 6m 4M.
Drowning Rock 57°42'·47N 07°09'·34W Q (2) G 8s 2m 2M.
BA3 57°41'·74N 07°08'·14W Fl (2) R.
Reef Chan No. 1 ☆ 57°42'·95N 07°09'·08W QG 2m 4M.
Reef Chan No. 2 ☆ 57°42'·96N 07°09'·06W Iso G 4s 2m 4M.

▶ NORTH UIST

Fairway 57°40'·23N 07°01'·39W L Fl 10s.
No.1 57°41'·20N 07°02'·67W QG.
No. 3 57°41'·86N 07°03'·44W Fl G 5s.
No. 4 57°41'·76N 07°03'·63W Fl R 5s.
NF 3 57°41'·47N 07°06'·68W Fl G 10s.
NF 6 57°41'·57N 07°08'·03W Fl R.
Eilean Fuam ☆ 57°41'·93N 07°10'·69W Q 6m 2M; W col.
Newton Jetty Root ☆ 57°41'·54N 07°11'·63W 2 FG (vert) 9m 4M.

Vallay Island ☆ 57°39'·69N 07°26'·42W Fl WRG 3s 4m 8M; vis: W206°-085°, G085°-140°, W140°-145°, R145°-206°.

Griminish Hbr Ldg Lts 183°. Front, 57°39'·38N 07°26'·75W QG 6m 4M. Rear, 110m from front, QG 7m 4M.

Pier Hd ☆ 57°39'·26N 07°26'·36W 2 FG (vert) 6m 4M; Gy col.

▶ LOCH MADDY

Weaver's Pt ☆ 57°36'·49N 07°06'·00W Fl 3s 24m 7M; W hut.
Glas Eilean Mòr ☆ 57°35'·95N 07°06'·70W Fl (2) G 4s 8m 5M.
Rubna Nam Pleàc ☆ 57°35'·76N 07°06'·76W Fl R 4s 7m 5M.

Ruigh Liath E Islet ☆ 57°35'·72N 07°08'·42W QG 6m 5M.

Vallaquie I ☆ 57°35'·50N 07°09'·40W Fl (3) WRG 8s 11m W7M, R5M, G5M; W pillar; vis: G shore-205°, W205°-210°, R210°-240°, G240°-254°, W254°-257°, R257°-shore.

Lochmaddy Ldg Lts 298°. Front, Ro-Ro Pier 57°35'·76N 07°09'·36W 2 FG (vert) 8m 4M. Rear, 110m from front, Oc G 8s 10m 4M; vis: 284°-304°.

57°35'·92N 07°08'·68W Fl R 3s 4M.

▶ GRIMSAY

No. 1 57°28'·26N 07°11'·82W Fl (2) R 8s.
No. 2 57°28'·62N 07°11'·80W Fl R 5s.
No. 3 57°28'·71N 07°11'·84W Fl G 2s.

Kallin Harbour Bkwtr NE corner ☆, 57°28'·88N 07°12'·31W 2 FR (vert) 6m 5M; Gy col.

▶ SOUTH UIST, LOCH CARNAN

Landfall 57°22'·27N 07°11'·52W L Fl 10s.
No. 1 57°22'·42N 07°14'·93W Fl G 2·5s.
No. 2 57°22'·39N 07°14'·93W Fl R 2s.
No. 3 57°22'·32N 07°15'·61W Fl R 5s.
No. 4 57°22'·25N 07°15'·88W QR.
No. 2 57°22'·11N 07°16'·20W QG.

Ldg Lts 222°. Front 57°22'·00N 07°16'·34W Fl R 2s 7m 5M; W ◊ on post. Rear, 58m from front, Iso R 10s 11m 5M; W ◊ on post.

Ushenish ☆ (S Uist) 57°17'·89N 07°11'·58W Fl WR 20s 54m **W19M, R15M**; W twr; vis: W193°-356°, R356°-018°.

▶ LOCH BOISDALE

MacKenzie Rk 57°08'·24N 07°13'·71W Fl (3) R 15s 3m 4M.

Calvay E End ☆ 57°08'·53N 07°15'·38W Fl (2) WRG 10s 16m W7M, R4M, G4M; W twr; vis: W111°-190°, G190°-202°, W202°-286°, R286°-111°.

N side ☆ 57°08'·99N 07°17'·05W Fl G 6s 3m 3M.
Eilean Dubh ☆ 57°09'·07N 07°18'·18W Fl (2) R 5s 2m 3M.

Gasay I ☆ 57°08'·93N 07°17'·39W Fl WR 5s 10m W7M, R4M; W twr; vis: W120°-284°, R284°-120°.

Gasay Spar 57°09'·02N 07°17'·45W QG 4m 5M.
Sgeir Rock 57°09'·09N 07°17'·76W Fl G 3s 2m 4M.
Eilean Dubh ☆ 57°09'·07N 07°18'·18W Fl (2) R 5s 2m 3M.

Ro-Ro Jetty Head ☆ 57°09'·12N 07°18'·22W Iso RG 4s 8m 2M; vis: G shore-283°, R283°-shore; 2 FG (vert) 8m 3M on dn.

▶ LUDAIG

The Witches 57°05'·72N 07°20'·84W Fl R 5s.
Off Ludaig 57°05'·94N 07°19'·56W.
Ludaig Bwtr ☆ 57°06'·17N 07°19'·49W 2 FR (vert) 6m 3M.

▶ ERISKAY

Bank Rk ☆ 57°05'·56N 07°17'·60W Q (2) 4s 5m 4M.
Pier ☆ 57°05'·25N 07°18'·17W 2 FR (vert) 5m 5M.

Acairseid Mhor Ldg Lts 285°. Front, 57°03'·89N 07°17'·25W Oc R 6s 9m 4M. Rear, 24m from front, Oc R 6s 10m 4M.

57°03'·89N 07°17'·10W Fl G 5s.
Acairseid Pier ☆ 57°04'·03N 07°17'·61W 2 FG (vert) 5m 4M.

▶ BARRA/CASTLEBAY, VATERSAY SOUND

Drover Rocks 57°04'·08N 07°23'·54W Q (6) + L Fl 15s.
Binch Rock 57°01'·71N 07°17'·16W Q (6) + L Fl 15s.
Curachan 56°58'·56N 07°20'·51W Q (3) 10s.

Ardveenish ☆ 57°00'·21N 07°24'·43W Oc WRG 6m 9/6M; vis: G300°-304°, W304°-306°, R306°-310°.

Aird Mhor RoRo terminal ☆ 57°00'·54N 07°24'·09W Fl G 2·5s 3M
Bo Vich Chuan 56°56'·15N 07°23'·31W Q (6) + L Fl 15s; ***Racon (M) 5M***.

Channel Rk ☆ 56°56'·24N 07°28'·94W Fl WR 6s 4m W6M, R4M; vis: W121·5°-277°, R277°-121·5°.

Castle Bay S 56°56'·09N 07°27'·21W Fl (2) R 8s; ***Racon (T) 7M***.

Sgeir Dubh ☆ 56°56'·40N 07°28'·92W Q (3) WG 6s 6m W6M, G4M; vis: W280°-117°, G117°-280°.

Castlebay ☆ 56°57'·16N 07°29'·63W Fl R 5s 2m 3M.

Rubha Glas. Ldg Lts 295°. Front 56°56'·77N 07°30'·64W FG 9m 11M; Or △ on W twr. Rear, 457m from front, FG 15m 11M; Or ▽ on W twr.

Barra Hd ☆ 56°47'·11N 07°39'·26W Fl 15s 208m **18M**; W twr; obsc by islands to NE.

OUTER HEBRIDES – WEST SIDE

8

Flannan I ☆, Eilean Mór 58°17'·32N 07°35'·23W Fl (2) 30s 101m **20M**; W twr; obsc in places by Is to W of Eilean Mór.

Rockall ☆ 57°35'·76N 13°41'·27W Fl 15s 19m 8M (unreliable).
Whale Rock 57°54'·40N 07°59·91W Q (3) 10s 5m 5M.
Haskeir I ☆ 57°41'·98N 07°41·36W Fl 20s 44m **23M**; W twr.

▶ EAST LOCH ROAG

Aird Laimishader Carloway ☆ 58°17'·06N 06°49'·50W Fl 6s 63m 8M; W hut; obsc on some brgs.

Ardvanich Pt ☆ 58°13'·48N 06°47'·68W Fl G 3s 4m 2M.

Tidal Rk ☆ 58°13'·45N 06°47'·57W Fl R 3s 2m 2M (synch with Ardvanich Pt above).

Gt Bernera Kirkibost Jetty ☆ 2 FG (vert) 7m 2M.

Grèinam ☆ 58°13'·30N 06°46'·16W Fl WR 6s 8m W8M, R7M; W Bn; vis: R143°-169°, W169°-143°.

Rubha Arspaig Jetty Hd ☆ 2 FR (vert) 10m 4M.

▶ NORTH UIST/SOUTH UIST

Vallay I ☆ 57°39'·70N 07°26'·34W Fl WRG 3s 8M; vis: W206°-085°, G085°-140°, W140°-145°, R145°-206°.

Falconet twr ☆ 57°22'·04N 07°23'·58W FR 25m 8M (3M by day); shown 1h before firing, changes to Iso R 2s 15 min before firing until completion.

▶ ST KILDA

Ldg Lts 270°. Front, 57°48'·32N 08°34'·31W Oc 5s 26m 3M. Rear, 100m from front, Oc 5s 38m 3M; synch.

PLOT WAYPOINTS ON YOUR CHART BEFORE USING THEM

LOCHTORRIDONTO MULL

▶ SKYE

Eilean Trodday ☆ 57°43'·64N 06°17'·89W Fl (2) WRG 10s 52m W12M, R9M, G9M; W Bn; vis: W062°-088°, R088°-130°, W130°-322°, G322°-062°.

Comet Rock 57°44'·60N 06°20'·50W Fl R 6s.

▶ RONA/LOCH A'BHRAIGE

Rona NE Point ☆ 57°34'·68N 05°57'·56W Fl 12s 69m **19M**; W twr; vis: 050°-358°.

Loch A'Bhraige, Sgeir Shuas ☆ 57°35'·02N 05°58'·61W Fl R 2s 6m 3M; vis: 070°-199°.

Jetty, SW corner ☆ 57°34'·66N 05°57'·93W 2 FR (vert).

Rock 57°34'·59N 05°58'·01W QR 4m 3M.

Ldg Lts 136·5°. Front, No. 9 57°34'·41N 05°58'·09W Q WRG 3m W4M, R3M; vis: W135°-138°, R138°-318°, G318°-135°. Rear, No. 10 Iso 6s 28m 5M.

No. 1 57°34'·27N 05°58'·34W Fl G 3s 91m 3M; Or bn.

Rubha Chùiltairbh 57°34'·12N 05°57'·17W Fl 3s 6m 5M.

No. 11 57°33'·12N 05°57'·60W QY 6m 4M.

No. 3 57°32'·59N 05°57'·86W Fl (2) 10s 9m 4M.

No. 12 57°32'·04N 05°58'·15W QR 5m 3M.

Garbh Eilean SE Pt No. 8 57°30'·67N 05°58'·60W Fl 3s 8m 5M; W Bn.

▶ INNER SOUND

Ru Na Lachan ☆ 57°29'·02N 05°52'·15W Oc WR 8s 21m 10M; twr; vis: W337°-022°, R022°-117°, W117°-162°.

▶ SOUND OF RAASAY, PORTREE

Sgeir Mhór 57°24'·57N 06°10'·53W Fl G 5s.

Portree Pier Head ☆ 57°24'·64N 06°11'·42W 2 FR (vert) 6m 4M; (occas).

▶ CROWLIN ISLANDS

Eilean Beag ☆ 57°21'·21N 05°51'·42W Fl 6s 32m 6M; W Bn.

▶ RAASAY/LOCH SLIGACHAN

Suisnish ☆ 57°19'·87N 06°03'·91W 2 FG (vert) 8m 2M.

Eyre Point ☆ 57°20'·01N 06°01'·29W Fl WR 3s 6m W9M, R6M; W twr; vis: W215°-266°, R266°-288°, W288°-063°.

Sconser Ferry Terminal ☆ 57°18'·88N 06°06'·67W QR 8m 3M.

McMillan's Rock 57°21'·11N 06°06'·32W Fl (2) G 12s.

Penfold Rock 57°20'·62N 06°05'·54W Fl R 5s.

Jackal Rock 57°20'·34N 06°04'·76W Fl G 5s.

▶ LOCH CARRON

Sgeir Golach 57°21'·20N 05°39'·01W.

Bogha Dubh Sgeir 57°20°·92N 05°37'·85W.

Old Lt Ho (13) 57°20'·95N 05°38'·88W (unlit).

▶ KYLE AKIN AND KYLE OF LOCH ALSH

Carragh Rk 57°17'·18N 05°45'·36W Fl (2) G 12s; ***Racon (T) 5M***.

Bow Rk 57°16'·71N 05°45'·85W Fl (2) R 12s.

Fork Rks 57°16'·85N 05°44'·93W Fl G 6s.

Black Eye Rk 57°16'·72N 05°45'·31W Fl R 6s.

Skye Bridge Centre ☆ 57°16'·57N 05°44'·58W Oc 6s.

Eileanan Dubha East ☆ 57°16'·56N 05°42'·32W Fl (2) 10s 9m 8M; vis: obscured 104°-146°.

8 Metre Rock ☆ 57°16'·60N 05°42'·69W Fl G 6s 5m 4M.

String Rock 57°16'·50N 05°42'·89W Fl R 6s.

Allt-an-Avaig Jetty ☆ 2 FR (vert) 10m; vis: 075°-270°.

S shore, Ferry slipway ☆ 57°16'·42N 05°43'·40W QR 6m.

Ferry Pier, W and E sides ☆ 2 FG (vert) 6/5m 5/4M.

Butec Jetty W end, N corner ☆ 57°16'·74N 05°42'·53W Oc G 6s 5m 3M each end, synch.

Sgeir-na-Caillich ☆ 57°15'·59N 05°38'·90W Fl (2) R 6s 3m 4M.

▶ SOUND OF SLEAT

Kyle Rhea ☆ 57°14'·22N 05°39'·93W Fl WRG 3s 7m W11M, R9M, G8M; W Bn; vis: Rshore-219°, W219-228°, G228°-338°, W338°-346°, R346°-shore.

Sandaig I, NW point ☆ 57°10'·05N 05°42'·29W Fl 6s 13m 8M; W twr.

Ornsay, N end ☆ 57°09'·08N 05°46'·95W Fl R 6s 8m 4M; W twr.

Ornsay, SE end ☆ 57°08'·59N 05°46'·88W Oc 8s 18m **15M**; W twr; vis: 157°-030°.

Eilean Iarmain, off Pier Hd ☆ 57°08'·78N 05°47'·89W 2 FR (vert) 3m 2M.

Armadale Bay Pier Centre ☆ 57°03'·86N 05°53'·58W Oc R 6s 6m 6M.

Pt. of Sleat ☆ 57°01'·08N06°01'·08W Fl 3s 20m9M; W twr.

Elgol ☆ 57°08'·78N 06°06'·53W Fl G 3s 4m 4M.

▶ MALLAIG, ENTRANCETO LOCH NEVIS

Sgeir Dhearg 57°00'·74N 05°49'·50W QG.

Northern Pier E end ☆ 57°00'·47N 05°49'·50W Iso WRG 4s 6m W9M, R6M, G6M; Gy twr; vis: G181°-185°, W185°-197°, R197°-201°. Fl G 3s 14m 6M; same structure.

Sgeir Dhearg ☆ 57°00'·63N 05°49'·61W Fl (2) WG 8s 6m 5M; Gy Bn; vis: G190°-055°, W055°-190°.

▶ NW SKYE, UIG/LOCH DUNVEGAN/LOCH HARPORT

Uig, Edward Pier Hd ☆ 57°35'·09N 06°22'·29W Iso WRG 4s 9m W7M, R4M, G4M; vis: W180°-008°, G008°-052°, W052°-075°, R075°-180°.

Bo Na Farmachd 57°26'·79N 06°35'·86W Fl G 5s.

Waternish Pt ☆ 57°36'·48N 06°37'·99W Fl 20s 21m 8M; W twr.

Loch Dunvegan, Uiginish Pt ☆ 57°26'·84N 06°36'·53W Fl WRG 3s 16m W7M, R5M, G5M; W metal-framed Twr; vis: G041°-132°, W132°-145°, R145°-148°, W148°-253°, R253°-263°, W263°-273°, G273°-306°, obsc by Fiadhairt Pt when brg > 148°.

Neist Point ☆ 57°25'·41N 06°47'·30W Fl 5s 43m **16M**; W twr.

Loch Harport, Ardtreck Pt ☆ 57°20'·38N 06°25'·80W Fl 6s 18m 9M; small W twr.

SMALL ISLES AND WEST OF MULL

▶ CANNA, RHUM

E end, Sanday Is ☆ 57°02'·82N 06°28'·02W Fl 6s 32m 9M; W twr; vis: 152°-061°.

Loch Scresort ☆ 57°00'·71N 06°15'·72W 2F.R(vert) 7m 2M.

Loch Scresort 57°00'·79N 06°14'·61W Q

▶ ÒIGH SGEIR/EIGG/MUCK/ARISAIG

Humla 57°00'·46N 06°37'·39W Fl G 6s 3m 4M.

Hyskeir ☆ 56°58'·14N 06°40'·87W Fl (3) 30s 41m **24M**; W twr.

N end *Horn 30s*; ***Racon (T) 14-17M***.

SE point Eigg (Eilean Chathastail) ☆ 56°52'·25N 06°07'·28W Fl 6s 24m 8M; W twr; vis: 181°-shore.

Eigg (Ferry Terminal) ☆ 56°52'·80N 06°07'·60W Dir Fl WRG 3s 9m W14, R11, G11; H24; steel pole; vis: G252·5°-254°, W254°-256°, R256°-257·5°. 2FR(vert) on same structure.

Isle of Muck (Port Mor) ☆ 56°49'·96N 06°13'·64W Dir Fl WRG 3s 7m W14, R11, G11, by day W1, R1, G1; steel twr; vis: G319·5°-321°, W321°-323°, R323°-324·5°.

Bogha Ruadh ☆ 56°49'·56N 06°13'·05W Fl G 5s 4m 3M

Bo Faskadale 56°48'·18N 06°06'·37W Fl (3) G 18s.

Ardnamurchan ☆ 56°43'·63N 06°13'·58W Fl (2) 20s 55m **24M**; Gy twr; vis: 002°-217°; *Horn (2) 20s*.

Cairns of Coll, Suil Ghorm ☆ 56°42'·26N 06°26'·75W Fl 12s 23m 10M; W twr.

▶ COLL/ARINAGOUR

Loch Eatharna, Bogha Mór 56°36'·63N 06°30'·95W Fl G 6s.
Arinagour Pier ☆ 56°36'·85N 06°31'·31W 2 FR (vert) 12m.

▶ TIREE

Roan Bogha 56°32'·23N 06°40'·18W Q (6) + L Fl 15s 3m 5M.
Placaid Bogha 56°33'·22N 06°44'·06W Fl G 4s.

Scarinish ☆, S side of ent 56°30'·01N 06°48'·27W Fl 3s 11m **16M**; W □ twr; vis: 210°-030°.

Gott Bay Ldg Lts 286·5°. Front 56°30'·61N 06°47'·82W FR 8m. Rear 30m from front FR 11m.

Skerryvore ☆ 56°19'·36N 07°06'·88W Fl 10s 46m **23M**; Gy twr; ***Racon (M) 18M***; *Horn 60s*.

▶ LOCH NA LÀTHAICH (LOCH LATHAICH)

Eileanan na Liathanaich, SE end ☆ 56°20'·56N 06°16'·38W, Fl WR 6s 12m W8M, R6M; vis: R088°-108°, W108°-088°.

Dubh Artach ☆ 56°07'·94N 06°38'·08W Fl (2) 30s 44m **20M**; Gy twr, R band.

SOUND OF MULL

▶ LOCH SUNART/TOBERMORY/LOCH ALINE

Ardmore Pt ☆ 56°39'·37N 06°07'·70W Fl (2) 10s 18m 13M.
New Rks 56°39'·05N 06°03'·30W Fl G 6s.

Rubha nan Gall ☆ 56°38'·33N 06°04'·00W Fl 3s 17m **15M**, W twr.

Bogha Bhuilg 56°36'·13N 05°59'·13W Fl G 5s.
Hispania Wreck 56°34'·95N 05°59'·12W Fl (2) R 10s.
Bo Rocks 56°31'·53N 05°55'·53W Fl (2) G 6s.

Eileanan Glasa (Dearg Sgeir) ☆ 56°32'·25N 05°54'·80W Fl 6s 7m 8M; W ○ twr.

Fiunary Spit 56°32'·66N 05°53'·17W Fl G 6s.
Avon Rock 56°30'·78N 05°46'·80W Fl (4) R 12s.
Lochaline 56°32'·09N 05°46'·48W QR.

Lochaline Ldg Lts 356°. Front, 56°32'·39N 05°46'·49W F 2m. Rear, 88m from front, F 4m; both H24.

Ardtornish Pt ☆ 56°31'·10N 05°45'·23W Fl (2) WRG 10s 8m W8M, R6M, G6M; W twr; vis: G shore-302°, W302°-308°, R308°-342°, W342°-057°, R057°-095°, W095°-108°, G108°-shore.

Yule Rocks 56°30'·01N 05°43'·96W Fl R 15s.

Glas Eileanan Gy Rks ☆ 56°29'·77N 05°42'·83W Fl 3s 11m 6M; W ○ twr on W base.

Craignure Ldg Lts 240·9°. Front, 56°28'·26N 05°42'·28W FR 10m. Rear, 150m from front, FR 12m; vis: 225·8°-255·8°.

MULL TO CALEDONIAN CANAL AND OBAN

Lismore ☆, SW end 56°27'·34N 05°36'·45W Fl 10s 31m **17M**; W twr; vis: 237°-208°.

Lady's Rk 56°26'·92N 05°37'·05W Fl 6s 12m 5M.

Duart Pt ☆ 56°26'·84N 05°38'·77W Fl (3) WR 18s 14m W5M, R3M; vis: W162°-261°, R261°-275°, W275°-353°, R353°-shore.

▶ LOCH LINNHE

Corran Shoal 56°43'·69N 05°14'·39W QR.

Ent W side, Corran Pt ☆ 56°43'·25N 05°14'·54W Iso WRG 4s 12m W10M, R7M; W twr; vis: R shore-195°, W195°-215°, G215°-305°, W305°-030°, R030°-shore.

Corran Narrows NE ☆ 56°43'·62N 05°13'·90W Fl 5s 4m 4M; W twr; vis: S shore-214°.

Jetty ☆ 56°43'·40N 05°14'·64W Fl R 5s 7m 3M; Gy mast.

56°42'·85N 05°14'·93W Fl (2) R 10s.
Clovullin Spit 56°42'·29N 05°15'·56W Fl (2) R 15s.
Cuil-cheanna Spit 56°41'·17N 05°15'·72W Fl G 6s.

▶ FORT WILLIAM/CALEDONIAN CANAL

Corpach, Caledonian Canal Lock ent ☆ 56°50'·52N 05°07'·44W Iso WRG 4s 6m 5M; W twr; vis: G287°-310°, W310°-335°, R335°-030°.
Eilean na Creiche 56°50'·40N 05°07'·38W Fl R 3s 3m 4M.
Lochy Flat S 56°49'·53N 05°07'·02W QG.
McLean Rock 56°49'·81N 05°07'·04W Fl (2) R 12s 3m 4M.

▶ LYNN OF LORN

Sgeir Bhuidhe Appin 56°33'·63N 05°24'·65W Fl (2) WR 7s 8m W9M R6M; W Bn; vis: W013·5°-184°, R184°-220°.

Appin Point 56°32'·69N 05°25'·97W Fl G 6s.

Dearg Sgeir, off Aird's Point 56°32'·20N 05°25'·22W, Fl WRG 2s 2m W3M, R1M, G1M; vis: R196°-246°, W246°-258°, G258°-041°, W041°058°, R058°-093°, W093°-139°.

Rubha nam Faoileann (Eriska) 56°32'·20N 05°24'·11W, QG 2m 2M; G col; vis 128°-329°.

▶ DUNSTAFFNAGE BAY

Pier Hd ☆, NE end 56°27'·21N 05°26'·18W 2 FG (vert) 4m 2M.

▶ OBAN

N spit of Kerrera ☆ 56°25'·49N 05°29'·56W Fl R 3s 9m 5M; W col, R bands.

Dunollie ☆ 56°25'·37N 05°29'·05W Fl (2) WRG 6s 7m W5M, G4M, R4M; vis: G351°-009°, W009°-047°, R047°-120°, W120°-138°, G138°-143°.

Rubbh'a' Chruidh ☆ 56°25'·32N 05°29'·29W QR 3m 2M.
Corran Ledge 56°25'·19N 05°29'·11W VQ (9) 10s.
Oban N Pier Mid ☆ 56°24'·87N 05°28'·49W 2 FG (vert) 8m 5M.

OBAN TO LOCH CRAIGNISH

Sgeir Rathaid North 56°24'·92N 05°29'·24W Q.
Sgeir Rathaid South 56°24'·74N 05°29'·37W Q (6) + L Fl 15s.
Ardbhan 56°24'·18N 05°30'·39W Fl G 5s.
Ferry Rocks NW 56°24'·11N 05°30'·70W QG.
Ferry Rocks SE 56°23'·99N 05°30'·53W Fl R 5s.
Little Horse Shoe 56°23'·22N 05°31'·83W Fl (4) R 12s.

Kerrera Sound, Dubha Sgeirean ☆ 56°22'·81N 05°32'·27W Fl (2) 12s 7m 5M; W ○ twr.

Bogha Nuadh 56°21'·69N 05°37'·88W Q (6) + LFl 15s
Bono Rock 56°16'·23N 05°40'·98W Fl (4) R 12s.

Fladda ☆ 56°14'·89N 05°40'·83W Fl (2) WRG 9s 13m W11M, R9M, G9M; W twr; vis: R169°-186°, W186°-337°, G337°-344°. W344°-356°, R356°-026°.

Dubh Sgeir (Luing) ☆ 56°14'·76N 05°40'·20W Fl WRG 6s 9m W6M, R4M. G4M; W twr; vis: W000°-010°, R010°-025°, W025°-199°, G199°-000°; ***Racon (M) 5M***.

The Garvellachs, Eileach an Naoimh, SW end ☆ 56°13'·04N 05°49'·06W Fl 6s 21m 9M; W Bn; vis: 240°-215°.

▶ LOCH MELFORT/CRAOBH HAVEN

Melfort Pier ☆ 56°16'·14N 05°30'·19W Dir FR 6m 3M; (Private shown 1/4 to 31/10).

56°12'·88N 05°33'·59W.

Craobh Marina Bkwtr Hd ☆ 56°12'·78N 05°33'·52W Iso WRG 5s 10m W5M, R3M, G3M; vis: G114°-162°, W162°-183°, R183°-200°.

For Colonsay, and Sounds of Jura and Islay see 9.9.4.

9.8.5 PASSAGE INFORMATION

It is essential to carry large scale charts, and current Pilots, ie Admiralty *W Coast of Scotland Pilot*; Clyde Cruising Club's *Sailing Directions, Pt 2 Kintyre to Ardnamurchan* and *Pt 3 Ardnamurchan to Cape Wrath*; and the *Yachtsman's Pilot to W Coast of Scotland (Vol 2 Crinan to Canna), (Vol 3 The Western Isles), (Vol 4 Skye & NW Scotland)*, Lawrence/ Imray.

The West coast of Scotland provides splendid, if sometimes boisterous, sailing and matchless scenery. In summer the long daylight hours and warmth of the Gulf Stream compensate for the lower air temperatures and higher wind speeds experienced when depressions run typically north of Scotland. Inshore winds are often unpredictable, due to geographical effects of lochs, mountains and islands offshore; calms and squalls can alternate rapidly.

Good anchors, especially on kelp/weed, are essential. Øs are listed, but it should not be assumed that these will always be available. Particularly in N of area, facilities are very dispersed. A *'Rover Ticket'*, 5m/£15+£5/additional 1mLOA from Highland Council allows berthing for 15 days and scheme includes: Kinlochbervie, Lochinver, Gairloch, Kyle of Lochalsh, Kyleakin, Portree and Uig.VHF communications with shore stations may be limited by high ground. Beware ever more fish farms in many inlets. Local magnetic anomalies occur in Kilbrannan Sound, Passage of Tiree, Sound of Mull, Canna, and East Loch Roag. Submarines exercise throughout these waters; see 9.8.22.

CAPE WRATH TO ULLAPOOL (charts 1785, 1794) C Wrath (lt, fog sig) is a steep headland (110m). ▶ *To N of it the E-going stream begins at HW Ullapool – 0350, and W- going at HW Ullapool + 0235, sp rates 3kn. Eddies close inshore cause almost continuous W-going stream E of Cape, and N-going stream SW of it. Where they meet is turbulence, with dangerous seas in bad weather.* ◀ Duslic Rk, 7ca NE of lt ho, dries $\underline{3}$·4m. 6M SW of C Wrath, islet of Am Balg (45m) is foul for 2ca around.

There are anchs in Loch Inchard (chart 2503), the best shelter being in Kinlochbervie (9.8.7) on N shore; also good anchs among Is along S shore of Loch Laxford, entered between Ardmore Pt and Rubha Ruadh. Handa Is to WSW is a bird sanctuary. Handa Sound is navigable with care, but beware Bogha Morair in mid-chan and associated overfalls. ▶ *Tide turns 2hrs earlier in the Sound than offshore.* ◀

▶ *Strong winds against tide raise a bad sea off Pt of Stoer.* ◀ The best shelter is 8M S at Loch Inver (chart 2504), with good anch off hotel near head of loch. S lies Enard Bay.

ULLAPOOL TO LOCH TORRIDON (charts 1794, 2210) The Summer Isles (chart 2501), 12M NW of the major fishing port of Ullapool (9.8.8), offer some sheltered anchs and tight approaches. The best include the Bay on E side of Tanera Mor; off NE of Tanera Beg (W of Eilean Fada Mor); and in Caolas Eilean Ristol, between the Is and mainland.

Loch Ewe (9.8.8 and chart 3146) provides good shelter and easy access. Best anchs are in Poolewe Bay (beware Boor Rks off W shore) and in SW corner of Loch Thuirnaig (entering, keep close to S shore to avoid rks extending from N side). Off Rubha Reidh (lt) seas can be dangerous. ▶ *The NE-going stream begins at HW Ullapool – 0335; the SW-going at HW Ullapool + 0305. Sp rates 3kn, but slacker to SW of point.* ◀ Longa Is lies N of ent to Loch Gairloch (9.8.8 and chart 2528). The chan N of it is navigable but narrow at E end. Outer loch is free of dangers, but exposed to swell. Best anch is on S side of loch in Caolas Bad a' Chrotha, W of Eilean Horrisdale.

Entering L Torridon (chart 2210) from S or W beware Murchadh Breac (dries $\underline{1}$·5m) 3ca NNW of Rubha na Fearna. Best anchs are SW of Eilean Mor (to W of Ardheslaig); in Loch a 'Chracaich, 7ca further SE; E of Shieldaig Is; and near head of Upper L Torridon. ▶ *Streams are weak except where they run 2-3 kn in narrows between L Shieldaig and Upper L Torridon.* ◀

OUTER HEBRIDES (charts 1785, 1794, 1795) The E sides of these Is have many good, sheltered anchs, but W coasts give little shelter. The CCC's *Outer Hebrides SDs* or *The Western Isles* (Imray) are advised. ▶ *The Minches and Sea of the Hebrides can be very rough, particularly in the Little Minch between Skye and Harris, and around Shiant Is where tide runs locally 4kn at sp, and heavy overfalls can be met. The NE-going stream begins at HW Ullapool – 0335; the SW-going stream at HW Ullapool + 0250, sp rates 2·5kn.* ◀

From N to S, the better hbrs in Outer Hebrides include:

Lewis. Stornoway (9.8.6); Loch Grimshader (beware Sgeir a'Chaolais, dries in entrance); Loch Erisort; Loch Odhairn; Loch Shell (9.8.6). Proceeding S from here, or to E Loch Tarbert beware Sgeir Inoe (dries $\underline{2}$·3m) 3M ESE of Eilean Glas lt ho at SE end of Scalpay.

Harris. E Loch Tarbert; Loch Scadaby; Loch Stockinish; Loch Finsby; W Loch Tarbert; Loch Rodel (Ø). A well buoyed/lit ferry chan connects Leverburgh (South Harris) to Berneray.

N Uist. Loch Maddy (Ø); Loch Eport, Kallin Hbr (Ø).

S Uist. Loch Carnan (Ø); Loch Skiport; Loch Eynort; Loch Boisdale (Ø).

Barra. Castlebay (Ø), see 9.8.6, and Berneray, on N side, E of Shelter Rk.

Activity at the Hebrides Range, S. Uist ☎ (01870) 604441, is broadcast daily at 0950LT and Mon-Fri 1100-1700LT on VHF Ch **12** (Ch 73 in emergency) and on MF 2660 kHz.

SKYE TO ARDNAMURCHAN PT (charts 1795, 2210, 2209, 2208, 2207) Skye and the islands around it provide many good and attractive anchs, of which the most secure are: Acairseid Mhor on the W side of Rona; Portree (9.8.9); Isleornsay; Portnalong, near the ent to Loch Harport, and Carbost at the head; Loch Dunvegan; and Uig Bay in Loch Snizort. Øs at Stein (Loch Dunvegan), Portree, Acairseid Mhor (Rona), Churchton Bay (Raasay) and Armadale Bay (S tip).

▶ *Tides are strong off Rubha Hunish at N end of Skye, and heavy overfalls occur with tide against fresh or strong winds.* ◀ Anch behind Fladday Is near the N end of Raasay can be squally and uncomfortable; and Loch Scavaig (S. Skye, beneath the Cuillins) more so, though the latter is so spectacular as to warrant a visit in fair weather. Soay Is has a small, safe hbr on its N side, but the bar at ent almost dries at LW sp.

Between N Skye and the mainland there is the choice of Sound of Raasay or Inner Sound. **The direction of buoyage**

in both Sounds is Northward. In the former, coming S from Portree, beware Sgeir Chnapach (3m) and Ebbing Rk (dries 2·9m), both NNW of Oskaig Pt. ► *At the Narrows (chart 2534) the SE-going stream begins at HW Ullapool – 0605, and the NW-going at HW Ullapool + 0040; sp rate 1·4kn in mid-chan, but more near shoals each side.*◄ Beware McMillan's Rk (0·4m depth) in mid-chan, marked by SHM lt buoy.

The chan between Scalpay and Skye narrows to 2½ca with drying reefs each side and least depth 0·1m. ► *Here the E-going stream begins at HW Ullapool + 0550, and W-going at HW Ullapool – 0010, sp rate 1kn.*◄

Inner Sound, which is a Submarine exercise area, is wider and easier than Sound of Raasay; the two are connected by Caol Rona and Caol Mor, respectively N and S of Raasay. Dangers extend about 1M N of Rona, and Cow Is lies off the mainland 8M to S; otherwise approach from N is clear to Crowlin Is, which should be passed to W. There is a good anch between Eilean Mor and Eilean Meadhonach.

A torpedo range in the Inner Sound does not normally restrict passage, but vessels may be requested to keep to the E side of the Sound if the range is active. Range activity is broadcast at 0800 and 1800LT first on VHF Ch 16 and then on Ch 8, and is indicated by Red Flags flown at the range building at Applecross, by all range vessels and at the naval pier at Kyle of Lochalsh (9.8.11), ☎ (01599) 534262.

Approaching Kyle Akin (chart 2540) from W, beware dangerous rks to N, off Bleat Is (at S side of entrance to Loch Carron); on S side of chan, Bogha Beag (dries 0·6m) and Black Eye Rk (depth 3·8m), respectively 6ca and 4ca W of bridge. For Plockton (Loch Carron), see 9.8.10. Pass at least 100m N or S of Eileanan Dubha in Kyle Akin. On S side of chan String Rk (dries) is marked by PHM lt buoy. For Loch Alsh, see 9.8.11.

Kyle Rhea connects Loch Alsh with NE end of Sound of Sleat. ► ***The tidal streams are very strong: N-going stream begins HW Ullapool + 0600, sp rate 6-7kn; S-going stream begins at HW Ullapool, sp rate 8kn.*** *Eddies form both sides of the Kyle and there are dangerous overfalls off S end in fresh S'ly winds on S-going stream.*◄ Temp anch in Sandaig Bay, 3M to SW.

The Sound of Sleat widens to 4M off Point of Sleat and is exposed to SW winds unless Eigg and Muck give a lee. Mallaig (9.8.12) is a busy fishing and ferry hbr, convenient for supplies. Further S the lochs require intricate pilotage. 6M NE of Ardnamurchan Pt (lt, fog sig) are Bo Faskadale rks, drying 0·5m and marked by SHM lt buoy, and Elizabeth Rk with depth of 0·7m. ► *Ardnamurchan Pt is an exposed headland onto which the ebb sets. With onshore winds, very heavy seas extend 2M offshore and it should be given a wide berth. Here the N-going stream begins at HW Oban – 0525, and the S-going at HW Oban + 0100, sp rates 1·5kn.*◄

THE SMALL ISLES (charts 2207, 2208) These consist of Canna, Rhum, Eigg (9.8.12) and Muck. Dangers extend SSW from Canna: at 1M Jemina Rk (depth 1·5m) and Belle Rk (depth 3·6m); at 2M Humla Rk (5m high), marked by buoy and with offlying shoals close W of it; at 5M Oigh Sgeir (lt, fog sig), the largest of a group of small islands; and at 7M Mill Rks (with depths of 1·8m).

► *The tide runs hard here, and in bad weather the sea breaks heavily up to 15M SW of Canna. Between Skerryvore and Neist Pt the stream runs generally N and S, starting N-going at HW Ullapool + 0550, and S-going at HW Ullapool – 0010. It rarely exceeds 1kn, except near Skerryvore, around headlands of The Small Isles, and over rks and shoals.*◄

1M off the N side of Muck are Godag Rks, some above water but with submerged dangers extending 2ca further N. Most other dangers around the Small Isles are closer inshore, but there are banks on which the sea breaks heavily in bad weather. A local magnetic anomaly exists about 2M E of Muck. The hbrs at Eigg (SE end), Rhum (Loch Scresort) and Canna (between Canna and Sanday) are all exposed to E'lies; Canna has best shelter and is useful for the Outer Hebrides.

ARDNAMURCHAN TO CRINAN (charts 2171, 2169) S of Ardnamurchan the route lies either W of Mull via Passage of Tiree (where headlands need to be treated with respect in bad weather); or via the more sheltered Sound of Mull and Firth of Lorne. The former permits a visit to Coll and Tiree, where best anchs are at Arinagour (🜨s) and Gott Bay respectively. Beware Cairns of Coll, off the N tip.

The W coast of Mull is rewarding in settled weather, but careful pilotage is needed. Beware tide rip off Caliach Pt (NW corner) and Torran Rks off SW end of Mull (large scale chart 2617 required). Apart from the attractions of Iona and of Staffa (Fingal's Cave), the remote Treshnish Is are worth visiting. The best anchs in this area are at Ulva, Gometra, Bull Hole and Tinker's Hole in Iona Sound. The usual passage through Iona Sound avoids overfalls W of Iona, but heed shoal patches. Loch Lathaich on the N side of Ross of Mull is 5M to the E; a good base with anch at Bunessan.

The Sound of Mull gives access to Tobermory (9.8.14, 🜨), Dunstaffnage Bay, Oban (9.8.18), and up Loch Linnhe through Corran Narrows (where tide runs strongly) to Fort William (9.8.16) and to Corpach for the Caledonian Canal (9.8.17). But, apart from these places, there are dozens of lovely anchs in the sheltered lochs inside Mull, as for example in Loch Sunart (9.8.13)with 🜨s at Kilchoan; also at Craignure and Salen Bays on Sound of Mull. For Loch Aline see 9.8.15.

On the mainland shore Puilladobhrain is a sheltered anch. Cuan Sound (see 9.8.18 for details) is a useful short cut to Loch Melfort, (9.8.19) and Craobh Marina (9.8.20). Good shelter, draft permitting, in Ardinamar B, SW of Torsa.

Sound of Luing (chart *2326*) between Fladda (lt), Lunga and Scarba on the W side, and Luing and Dubh Sgeir (lt) on the E side, is the normal chan to or from Sound of Jura, despite dangers at the N end and strong tidal streams.► *The N and W-going flood begins at HW Oban + 0430; the S and E-going ebb at HW Oban –0155.* ***Sp rates are 2·5kn at S end of Sound, increasing to 6kn or more in Islands off N entrance, where there are eddies, races and overfalls.***◄

► ***From the N, beware very strong streams, eddies and whirlpools in Dorus Mór, off Craignish Pt. Streams begin to set W and N away from Dorus Mór at HW Oban + 0345, and E and S towards Dorus Mór at HW Oban – 0215, sp rates 7kn.***◄ At N end of Sound of Jura (chart *2326*) is Loch Craignish (9.8.21).For Gulf of Corryvreckan, Colonsay, Islay, Loch Crinan and passage south through the Sound of Jura, see 9.9.5.

8

9.8.6 STORNOWAY

Lewis (Western Isles) **58°11′·58N 06°21′·82W** ✾✾✾◌◌✿✿

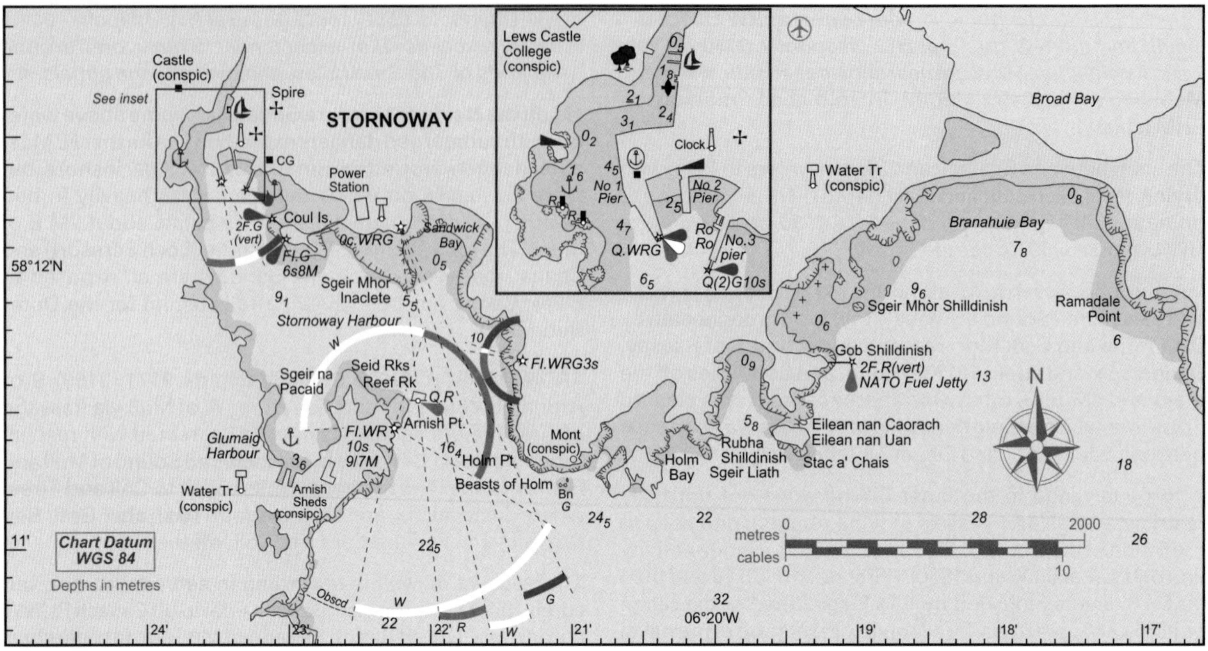
STORNOWAY
Castle (conspic)
See inset
Spire
CG
Power Station
Coul Is.
2F.G (vert)
Fl.G 6s8M
Oc.WRG
Sandwick Bay
Sgeir Mhor Inaclete
Stornoway Harbour
Seid Rks
Reef Rk
Sgeir na Pacaid
Q.R
Fl.WRG3s
Glumaig Harbour
Fl.WR 10s 9/7M
Arnish Pt.
Holm Pt.
Beasts of Holm
Bn G
Mont (conspic)
Water Tr (conspic)
Arnish Sheds (conspic)
Chart Datum WGS 84
Depths in metres
Obscd
58°12′N
11′
24′
23′
22′
21′
06°20′W
19′
18′
17′
Lews Castle College (conspic)
Clock
No 1 Pier
No 2 Pier
No.3 pier
Q.WRG
Q(2)G10s
Water Tr (conspic)
Broad Bay
Branahuie Bay
Sgeir Mhòr Shilldinish
Ramadale Point
Gob Shilldinish
2F.R(vert)
NATO Fuel Jetty
Eilean nan Caorach
Eilean nan Uan
Stac a' Chais
Rubha Shilldinish
Sgeir Liath
Holm Bay
metres
cables
2000
10
N

CHARTS AC 1785, 1794, 2529; Imray C67; OS 8

TIDES –0428 Dover; ML 2·8; Duration 0610; Zone 0 (UT)

Standard Port STORNOWAY (⟶)

Times				Height (metres)			
High Water		Low Water		MHWS	MHWN	MLWN	MLWS
0100	0700	0300	0900	4·8	3·7	2·0	0·7
1300	1900	1500	2100				
East side of Outer Hebrides, N to S							
Differences LOCH SHELL (Harris)							
–0013	0000	0000	–0017	0·0	–0·1	–0·1	0·0
EAST LOCH TARBERT (Harris)							
–0025	–0010	–0010	–0020	+0·2	0·0	+0·1	+0·1
LOCH MADDY (N Uist)							
–0044	–0014	–0016	–0030	0·0	–0·1	–0·1	0·0
LOCH CARNAN (S Uist)							
–0050	–0010	–0020	–0040	–0·3	–0·5	–0·1	–0·1
LOCH SKIPORT (S Uist)							
–0100	–0025	–0024	–0024	–0·2	–0·4	–0·3	–0·2
LOCH BOISDALE (S Uist)							
–0055	–0030	–0020	–0040	–0·7	–0·7	–0·3	–0·2
BARRA (North Bay)							
–0103	–0031	–0034	–0048	–0·6	–0·5	–0·2	–0·1
CASTLE BAY (Barra)							
–0115	–0040	–0045	–0100	–0·5	–0·6	–0·3	–0·1
BARRA HEAD (Berneray)							
–0115	–0040	–0045	–0055	–0·8	–0·7	–0·2	+0·1
West side of Outer Hebrides, N to S							
CARLOWAY (W Lewis)							
–0040	+0020	–0035	–0015	–0·6	–0·5	–0·4	–0·1
LITTLE BERNERA (W Lewis)							
–0021	–0011	–0017	–0027	–0·5	–0·6	–0·4	–0·2
WEST LOCH TARBERT (W Harris)							
–0015	–0015	–0046	–0046	–1·1	–0·9	–0·5	0·0
SCOLPAIG (W North Uist)							
–0033	–0033	–0040	–0040	–1·0	–0·9	–0·5	0·0
SHILLAY (Monach Islands)							
–0103	–0043	–0047	–0107	–0·6	–0·7	–0·7	–0·3
BALIVANICH (W Benbecula)							
–0103	–0017	–0031	–0045	–0·7	–0·6	–0·5	–0·2

SHELTER Good. A small marina, max LOA 12m, at the N end of the Inner Hbr, beyond the LB berth, has depths 1·4 - 3·3m. Or AB for larger boats on adjacent Cromwell St Quay, close S; or lie alongside FVs in the inner hbr. Visitors should report to HM. Ullapool ferries use the new No 3 pier and commercial vessels on Nos 1 and 2 Piers. S'ly swells can make anchoring uncomfortable. Much of the hbr is foul with old wire hawsers. ⚓s as on chartlet at: Poll nam Portan on the W side of inner chan, opposite No 1 Pier; Glumaig Hbr is best ⚓, but oil works may preclude this; in bay NW of Coul Island (Eilean na Gobhail).

NAVIGATION WPT 58°09′·98N 06°20′·87W, 343° to Oc WRG lt, 2·3M. Reef Rk, N of Arnish Pt on W side of ent, is marked by PHM buoy, QR. At the E side of ent an unlit G bn marks the Beasts of Holm, a rky patch off Holm Pt, on which is a conspic memorial. A local magnetic anomaly exists over a small area in mid-hbr, 1·75ca N of Seid Rks PHM bn.

LIGHTS AND MARKS Arnish sheds are conspic 3ca SW of Arnish Pt lt, Fl WR 10s 17m 19/15M, W tr; W sector 302°-013° covers ent. Then in turn follow W sectors of: Sandwick Bay lt, (close E of water tr, 3 power stn chys and fuel tanks; all conspic) Oc WRG 6s 10m 9M, W341°-347°; then Stoney Field Fl WRG 3s 8m 11M, vis W102°-109° across hbr; and finally No 1 Pier, Q WRG 5m 11M, W335°-352°.

R/T VHF Ch 12 16 (H24).

TELEPHONE (Dial code 01851) HM 702688, 📠 705714; MRSC 702013; ⊜ 703626; Marinecall 09066 526248; Police 702222; Dr 703145.

FACILITIES **Marina** 27 berths, inc 8 Ⓥ, £9.05 via HM Ch 12; FW. **Nos 1 & 2 Piers** FW, C (10 ton), CH, AB, Slip, P.**No3 Pier** AB(E side)FW, C (Mobile10+ ton), D(road tanker) **Services:** ACA, ME, El, ⚒. **Town** EC Wed; P (cans), D, El, 🛒, 🧺, R, Bar, Gas, ✉, Ⓑ, ⇌ (ferry to Ullapool, bus to Garve), ✈.

HARBOURS AND ANCHORAGES ON THE EAST SIDE OF THE OUTER HEBRIDES (Western Isles), from N to S:

For information, 🅥s mentioned in this section are inspected annually, have pick up buoys, can take yachts <15tons, and there is no charge <7days. Refer to www.w-isles.gov.uk/harbourmaster

LOCH SHELL, Lewis, **57°59´·98N 06°25´·07W**. AC 1794. HW –0437 on Dover; ML 2·7m. See 9.8.6. Pass S of Eilean Iuvard; beware rks to W of Is. ⚓ in Tob Eishken, 2½M up loch on N shore (beware rk awash on E side of ent), or at head of loch (exposed to E winds; dries some distance). Facilities: ✉/Stores at Lemreway.

SHIANT ISLANDS, Lewis, **57°53´·68N 06°21´·37W**. AC 1794, 1795. Tides as Loch Shell 9.8.6. Beware strong tidal streams and overfalls in Sound of Shiant. Strictly a fair weather ⚓ ; in W winds ⚓ E of Mol Mor, isthmus between Garbh Eileen (160m) and Eileen an Tighe. In E winds ⚓ W of Mol Mor. No lights or facilities.

EAST LOCH TARBERT, Harris, **57°49´·98N 06°41´·07W**. AC 2905. HW –0446 on Dover; ML 3·0m; Duration 0605. See 9.8.6. Appr via Sound of Scalpay; beware Elliot Rk (2m) 2½ca SSW of Rubha Crago. A bridge (20m cl'nce) at 57°52'·80N 06°41'·73W joins Scalpay to Harris. Bridge lts: Centre Oc 6s; N side Iso G 4s 35m; S side Iso R 4s 35m. Eilean Glas lt ho at E end of Scalpay, Fl (3) 20s 43m 23M; W tr, R bands. In Sound of Scalpay, stream sets W from HW +3, and E from HW –3. ⚓ off Tarbert WSW of steamer pier in about 2·5m. ☎ (01589) 502444. Facilities: EC Thurs; Bar, D, Dr, FW, P, ✉, R, 🛒, ferry to Uig. Alternatively Scalpay N Hbr gives good shelter. Beware rk 5ca off Aird an Aiseig, E side of ent. SHM buoy marks wk off Coddem; 5ca E of the buoy is a rk, depth 1·1m. Ldg Lt Oc WRG 6s 10m 5M. Both piers have 2FG (vert) lts; ⚓ 7ca N, in about 3m. Facilities: FW at pier, ✉, 🛒, ferry to Harris.

SOUND OF HARRIS, 57°43'N 06°58'W. Passages through this difficult Sound are detailed in the *W Coast of Scotland Pilot*. The Stanton and Outer Stromay Chans off the Harris shore are the most feasible for yachts. AC 2642 shows the newly marked ferry routes from Leverburgh to Berneray and ***beware of the orientation of N on this chart***.

LOCH MADDY, North Uist, **57°35´·98N 07°06´·07W**. AC 2825. HW –0500 on Dover. See 9.8.6. With strong wind against tide there can be bad seas off ent. Appr clear, but from S beware submerged rk ½ca N of Leacnam Madadh. Lts: Weaver's Pt Fl 3s 21m 7M; Glas Eilean Mor Fl (2) G 4s 8m 5M; Rubna Nam Pleac Fl R 4s 7m 5M. Inside loch: Ruigh Liath QG 6m 5M; Vallaquie Is Dir Fl (3) WRG 8s. Ferry pier ldg lts 298°: front 2FG(vert) 4M; rear Oc G 8s 10m 4M, vis 284°-304°. 2 🅥s Bagh Aird nam Madadh; 2 🅥s W of and 4 🅥s SW of ferry pier ☎ (01870) 602425; 2 🅥s E of Oronsay. ⚓s: clear S of ferry pier; NE of Vallaquie Is; Charles Hbr; Oronsay (⚓ not advised due to moorings), tidal berth on private pier; Sponish Hbr; Loch Portain. VHF Ch 12 16. Port Manager ☎ (01876) 5003337 (day), 5003226 (night). Facilities: Lochmaddy, EC Wed; Shop, Ⓑ, Gas, ✉, P, D, FW; Loch Portain ✉, Shop.

LOCH EPORT, North Uist, **57°33'·45N 07°08'·12W**. AC 2825, but not the head of loch. Tides, approx as L Maddy; 3kn sp stream. On the S side of ent are rks, some drying. The ent proper is clean but very narrow (about 100m) for 5ca, then widens. Follow the charted clearing line 082°. Best ⚓s are: Bàgh a' Bhiorain (S of chan; line up cairn and Bu boulder on 129°); and Acairseid Lee (N bank) E or W of Deer Is. 🛒, R, Bar, ✉ at Clachan, hd of loch.

LOCH CARNAN, South Uist, **57°22'·03N 07°16'·39W**. AC 2825. Tides, see 9.8.6. SWM buoy, L Fl 10s, at 57°22'·30N 07°11'·57W is almost 2M E of app chan proper, marked by Nos 1 and 2 buoys, Fl G 2·5s and Fl R 2s, at 57°22'·45N 07°14'·90W. Round No 3 PHM buoy, Fl R 5s, between Gasay and Taigh Iamain, then pick up ldg lts 222° to Sandwick quay; front Fl R 2s, rear Iso R 10s, both 5M, W ◇s on posts. Power stn and 2 chys are conspic close to SE of quay. Call ☎ (01870) 602425 for permission to berth on the quay (MoD property). There is ⚓ or 2 🅥s about 2ca WNW of the quay in deep water. ☎ (01870) 610238. The passage S of Gasay is unmarked and needs careful pilotage. FW, D available.

LOCH SKIPPORT, South Uist, **57°19'·98N 07°13'·67W**. AC 2904, 2825. HW –0602 on Dover; see 9.8.6. Easy ent 3M NNE of Hecla (604m). No lights, but 2¼M SSE is Usinish lt ho Fl WR 20s 54m 19/15M. ⚓s at: Wizard Pool in 7m; beware Float Rk, dries 2·3m; on N side of Caolas Mor in 7m; Bagh Charmaig in 5m. Linne Arm has narrow ent, many fish farms and poor holding. No facilities.

LOCH EYNORT, South Uist, **57°13'·13N 07°16'·87W**. AC 2825. Tides: interpolate between Lochs Skipport and Boisdale, see 9.8.6. ⚓s in the outer loch at Cearcdal Bay and on the N side just before the narrows are exposed to the E. The passage to Upper L Eynort is very narrow and streams reach 5-7kn; best not attempted unless local fishermen offer guidance. Good ⚓ inside at Bàgh Lathach.

LOCH BOISDALE, South Uist, **57°08'·78N 07°16'·07W**. AC 2770. HW –0455 on Dover; ML 2·4m; Duration 0600. See 9.8.6. Good shelter except in SE gales when swell runs right up the 2M loch. From N, appr between Rubha na Cruibe and Calvay Is; ldg line 245°: Hollisgeir (0·3m) on with pier (ru). From S beware Clan Ewan Rk, dries 1·2m, and McKenzie Rk (2·4m), marked by PHM lt buoy Fl (3) R 15s. Chan to Boisdale Hbr lies N of Gasay Is; beware rks off E end. ⚓ off pier in approx 4m, or SW of Gasay Is in approx 9m. 4 🅥s NE of pier ☎ (01870) 602425. There are fish cages W of Rubha Bhuailt. Lts: E end of Calvay Is Fl (2) WRG 10s 16m 7/4M. Gasay Is Fl WR 5s 10m 7/4M. N side of loch, opp Gasay Is, Fl G 6s. Ro-Ro terminal Iso RG 4s 8m 2M; and close SE, Fl (2) R 5s. See 9.8.4. ☎ (0187) 700288. Facilities: EC Tues; Bar, FW (on pier), P, ✉, R, ferry to mainland.

ACAIRSEID MHÓR, Eriskay, ⊕ **57°03'·78N 07°16'·35W**. AC 2770. Tides approx as for North Bay (Barra), see 9.8.6. Ben Scrien (183m) is conspic, pointed peak N of hbr. Ldg lts 285°, both Oc R 6s 9/10m 4M, W △ ▽ on orange posts, lead for 0·5M from the above lat/long between two drying rks into the outer loch. A SHM buoy, Fl G 6s, marks a rk drying 3m. 3 🅥s are at 57°03'·95N 07°17'·40W on S side of inner loch, opp pier, 2 FG (vert). ☎ (01870) 602425. 🛒, R, Bar, ✉ at Haun, 1·5M at N end of island.

NORTH BAY, Barra, **57°00'·11N 07°24'·67W**. AC 2770. Tides see 9.8.6. Well marked approach to inlet sheltered from S and W winds. WPT 56°58'·68N 07°20'·31W is about 200m NE of Curachan ECM buoy, Q (3) 10s, and in the white sector (304°-306°) of Ardveenish dir ☆ 305°, Oc WRG 3s, 2·5M to the WNW. ⚓ 1ca WNW of Black Island or in N part of Bay Hirivagh where there are 🅥s; or tempy AB on the quay in 4·5m. FW, Bar, 🛒, bus to Castlebay.

CASTLEBAY, Barra, **56°56´·78N 07°29´·67W**. AC 2769. HW –0525 on Dover; ML 2·3m; Duration 0600. See 9.8.6. Very good shelter & holding. Best ⚓ in approx 8m NW of Kiessimul Castle (on an island); NE of castle are rks. 8 🅥s lie to W of pier ☎ (01870) 602425. Or ⚓ in Vatersay Bay in approx 9m. W end of Vatersay Sound is closed by a causeway. Beware rks NNW of Sgeir Dubh a conspic W/G tr, Q(3)WG 6s 6m 6/4M, vis W280°-117°, G117°-280°; which leads 283° in transit with Sgeir Liath bn. Chan Rk, 2ca to the S, is marked by Fl WR 6s 4m 6/4M. Close-in ldg lts 295°, both FG 11M on W framework trs: front 9m Or △ on Rubha Glas; rear, 457m from front, 15m Or ▽. ☎ (01871) 810306. Facilities: Bar, D, FW, P, ✉, R, 🛒, Ferry to mainland.

HIE 🅥s are also located in the Outer Hebrides at:

Loch Rodel, Harris. AC 2642. 3 🅥s at 57°44'·2N 06°57'·4W in Poll an Tigh-mhàil; enter from SW past jetties. No lts.

Kallin, Grimsay. AC 2904. 1 🅥 at 57°28'·9N 07°12'·2W, NE of hbr. 3 chan lt buoys and 2 FR (vert) on hbr bkwtr. ☎ (01870) 602425.

TIME ZONE (UT)
For Summer Time add ONE hour in **non-shaded areas**

SCOTLAND – STORNOWAY

LAT 58°12′N LONG 6°23′W

TIMES AND HEIGHTS OF HIGH AND LOW WATERS

SPRING & NEAP TIDES
Dates in red are SPRINGS Dates in blue are NEAPS

YEAR **2005**

JANUARY

Date	Day	Time	m	Time	m	Time	m	Time	m
1	SA	0404	1.6	1009	4.1	1650	1.5	2251	3.7
2	SU	0447	1.7	1056	3.9	1737	1.6	2347	3.6
3	M	0537	1.9	1152	3.9	1829	1.6	◑	
4	TU	0048	3.6	0634	2.0	1254	3.8	1927	1.7
5	W	0151	3.7	0738	2.0	1358	3.9	2031	1.6
6	TH	0252	3.8	0846	1.9	1505	4.0	2136	1.5
7	F	0351	4.0	0954	1.7	1609	4.1	2237	1.4
8	SA	0445	4.3	1059	1.5	1709	4.3	2333	1.2
9	SU	0536	4.6	1158	1.2	1805	4.5		
10	M	0024	1.0	0624	4.9	1253	0.9	● 1856	4.7
11	TU	0113	0.9	0712	5.1	1344	0.6	1945	4.7
12	W	0159	0.8	0758	5.2	1432	0.5	2031	4.7
13	TH	0243	0.8	0844	5.1	1517	0.5	2117	4.5
14	F	0327	0.9	0931	5.0	1603	0.6	2204	4.3
15	SA	0411	1.1	1021	4.8	1649	0.9	2256	4.0
16	SU	0458	1.4	1116	4.5	1738	1.2	2358	3.7
17	M	0551	1.7	1219	4.2	1831	1.5	◐	
18	TU	0111	3.5	0652	1.9	1330	3.9	1932	1.8
19	W	0229	3.5	0808	2.0	1443	3.7	2046	1.9
20	TH	0338	3.5	0932	2.0	1551	3.7	2159	1.9
21	F	0434	3.7	1041	1.9	1648	3.7	2256	1.8
22	SA	0518	3.9	1135	1.7	1734	3.8	2342	1.6
23	SU	0556	4.1	1219	1.5	1813	3.9		
24	M	0022	1.4	0629	4.3	1258	1.3	1847	4.0
25	TU	0059	1.2	0701	4.4	1333	1.1	○ 1919	4.1
26	W	0133	1.1	0730	4.5	1406	1.0	1950	4.2
27	TH	0204	1.0	0759	4.5	1437	0.9	2020	4.2
28	F	0236	1.0	0827	4.5	1508	0.9	2052	4.2
29	SA	0307	1.0	0856	4.4	1541	0.9	2124	4.1
30	SU	0340	1.1	0927	4.3	1617	1.0	2201	3.9
31	M	0415	1.3	1003	4.1	1656	1.2	2245	3.8

FEBRUARY

Date	Day	Time	m	Time	m	Time	m	Time	m
1	TU	0456	1.5	1049	4.0	1741	1.4	2344	3.6
2	W	0544	1.6	1153	3.8	1834	1.6	◑	
3	TH	0055	3.6	0644	1.8	1314	3.7	1941	1.7
4	F	0211	3.6	0801	1.9	1439	3.7	2103	1.7
5	SA	0326	3.8	0935	1.8	1601	3.9	2224	1.6
6	SU	0431	4.1	1056	1.5	1708	4.1	2327	1.3
7	M	0527	4.5	1157	1.1	1803	4.4		
8	TU	0019	1.0	0616	4.8	1249	0.7	● 1849	4.6
9	W	0105	0.7	0701	5.1	1335	0.4	1931	4.7
10	TH	0147	0.6	0742	5.3	1417	0.2	2010	4.8
11	F	0227	0.5	0822	5.3	1457	0.2	2048	4.6
12	SA	0306	0.6	0902	5.1	1536	0.4	2126	4.4
13	SU	0345	0.8	0942	4.8	1615	0.7	2205	4.1
14	M	0425	1.1	1027	4.5	1655	1.1	2251	3.8
15	TU	0509	1.5	1121	4.0	1739	1.5	2355	3.5
16	W	0600	1.8	1238	3.7	1830	1.9	◐	
17	TH	0137	3.4	0710	2.1	1411	3.4	1944	2.2
18	F	0304	3.4	0904	2.2	1532	3.4	2131	2.2
19	SA	0411	3.6	1033	2.0	1636	3.5	2242	2.0
20	SU	0501	3.8	1127	1.7	1723	3.7	2330	1.7
21	M	0540	4.0	1208	1.5	1800	3.8		
22	TU	0009	1.5	0613	4.2	1243	1.2	1830	4.0
23	W	0044	1.2	0642	4.4	1314	0.9	1859	4.2
24	TH	0115	1.0	0708	4.6	1343	0.8	○ 1926	4.4
25	F	0144	0.8	0733	4.6	1411	0.6	1953	4.4
26	SA	0213	0.7	0759	4.7	1440	0.6	2020	4.4
27	SU	0242	0.7	0825	4.6	1511	0.6	2049	4.3
28	M	0313	0.8	0854	4.5	1544	0.8	2121	4.2

MARCH

Date	Day	Time	m	Time	m	Time	m	Time	m
1	TU	0346	0.9	0927	4.3	1619	1.0	2159	4.0
2	W	0424	1.2	1010	4.0	1700	1.3	2251	3.8
3	TH	0509	1.4	1114	3.7	1751	1.6	◑	
4	F	0015	3.6	0608	1.7	1257	3.5	1902	1.9
5	SA	0149	3.5	0739	1.9	1440	3.5	2051	1.9
6	SU	0314	3.7	0941	1.7	1605	3.7	2222	1.7
7	M	0423	4.1	1057	1.3	1706	4.1	2320	1.3
8	TU	0517	4.5	1151	0.9	1754	4.4		
9	W	0007	1.0	0602	4.9	1236	0.5	1834	4.6
10	TH	0050	0.7	0643	5.2	1316	0.3	● 1910	4.8
11	F	0129	0.5	0720	5.3	1354	0.1	1944	4.8
12	SA	0206	0.4	0756	5.3	1430	0.2	2017	4.7
13	SU	0242	0.5	0831	5.1	1505	0.4	2049	4.5
14	M	0318	0.7	0907	4.8	1540	0.8	2122	4.2
15	TU	0355	1.0	0945	4.4	1615	1.2	2159	3.9
16	W	0435	1.4	1032	3.9	1653	1.6	2245	3.6
17	TH	0521	1.8	1143	3.5	1738	2.0	◐	
18	F	0029	3.4	0623	2.2	1339	3.3	1840	2.4
19	SA	0223	3.4	0833	2.3	1506	3.3	2058	2.4
20	SU	0338	3.5	1015	2.1	1614	3.4	2219	2.2
21	M	0433	3.7	1105	1.8	1700	3.6	2306	1.9
22	TU	0513	4.0	1142	1.5	1735	3.9	2344	1.6
23	W	0546	4.2	1214	1.2	1804	4.1		
24	TH	0016	1.3	0613	4.4	1244	0.9	1830	4.4
25	F	0047	1.0	0639	4.6	1311	0.7	○ 1856	4.6
26	SA	0115	0.8	0704	4.8	1340	0.5	1923	4.7
27	SU	0145	0.6	0730	4.8	1409	0.5	1951	4.7
28	M	0215	0.6	0758	4.8	1441	0.5	2021	4.6
29	TU	0248	0.7	0830	4.6	1514	0.7	2054	4.4
30	W	0323	0.8	0907	4.3	1550	1.0	2134	4.2
31	TH	0403	1.1	0956	4.0	1632	1.4	2231	3.9

APRIL

Date	Day	Time	m	Time	m	Time	m	Time	m
1	F	0451	1.4	1114	3.7	1724	1.7		
2	SA	0006	3.7	0557	1.7	1307	3.5	◑ 1846	2.0
3	SU	0140	3.6	0753	1.9	1445	3.5	2050	2.0
4	M	0303	3.8	0941	1.6	1601	3.8	2210	1.7
5	TU	0409	4.2	1045	1.2	1655	4.1	2303	1.4
6	W	0501	4.5	1133	0.8	1738	4.4	2347	1.0
7	TH	0543	4.8	1214	0.5	1814	4.6		
8	F	0027	0.7	0621	5.0	1252	0.4	● 1846	4.7
9	SA	0105	0.6	0656	5.1	1327	0.3	1917	4.7
10	SU	0141	0.6	0729	5.0	1400	0.4	1947	4.7
11	M	0217	0.6	0803	4.8	1434	0.7	2018	4.5
12	TU	0253	0.8	0838	4.5	1507	1.0	2050	4.3
13	W	0330	1.1	0916	4.2	1541	1.3	2126	4.1
14	TH	0409	1.5	1003	3.8	1617	1.7	2213	3.8
15	F	0455	1.8	1110	3.5	1659	2.1	2333	3.6
16	SA	0555	2.1	1254	3.3	1757	2.4	◐	
17	SU	0127	3.5	0741	2.3	1425	3.3	1952	2.5
18	M	0248	3.5	0928	2.1	1535	3.4	2135	2.3
19	TU	0348	3.7	1022	1.8	1624	3.7	2227	2.0
20	W	0433	3.9	1101	1.5	1700	3.9	2305	1.7
21	TH	0507	4.2	1135	1.2	1729	4.2	2338	1.4
22	F	0537	4.4	1205	1.0	1757	4.4		
23	SA	0010	1.1	0605	4.6	1236	0.7	1825	4.6
24	SU	0042	0.9	0634	4.7	1307	0.6	○ 1855	4.8
25	M	0116	0.7	0705	4.8	1340	0.5	1927	4.8
26	TU	0151	0.7	0739	4.8	1415	0.6	2001	4.7
27	W	0228	0.7	0818	4.6	1452	0.8	2041	4.6
28	TH	0309	0.9	0905	4.3	1531	1.1	2129	4.3
29	F	0355	1.1	1006	3.9	1617	1.5	2238	4.0
30	SA	0452	1.4	1135	3.7	1716	1.8		

Chart Datum: 2·71 metres below Ordnance Datum (Newlyn)

TIME ZONE (UT)
For Summer Time add ONE hour in **non-shaded areas**

SCOTLAND – STORNOWAY

LAT 58°12′N LONG 6°23′W

TIMES AND HEIGHTS OF HIGH AND LOW WATERS

SPRING & NEAP TIDES
Dates in red are SPRINGS
Dates in blue are NEAPS

YEAR **2005**

MAY

Date	Day	Time	m	Time	m	Time	m	Time	m	Moon
1	SU	0005	3.9	0612	1.6	1307	3.5	1847	2.0	◑
2	M	0127	3.9	0753	1.6	1432	3.6	2029	2.0	
3	TU	0242	4.0	0918	1.4	1543	3.8	2142	1.7	
4	W	0346	4.2	1019	1.1	1635	4.0	2235	1.4	
5	TH	0437	4.4	1106	0.9	1716	4.2	2321	1.2	
6	F	0520	4.6	1146	0.8	1750	4.4			
7	SA	0002	1.0	0557	4.7	1224	0.7	1821	4.5	
8	SU	0041	0.9	0633	4.7	1259	0.7	1852	4.6	●
9	M	0119	0.8	0707	4.6	1333	0.8	1923	4.5	
10	TU	0156	0.9	0742	4.5	1407	1.0	1955	4.5	
11	W	0234	1.1	0819	4.3	1441	1.2	2030	4.3	
12	TH	0312	1.3	0901	4.0	1515	1.4	2111	4.1	
13	F	0353	1.5	0949	3.7	1552	1.7	2200	3.9	
14	SA	0439	1.7	1050	3.5	1635	2.0	2306	3.7	
15	SU	0534	1.9	1202	3.4	1729	2.2			
16	M	0020	3.6	0644	2.0	1320	3.3	1844	2.3	◐
17	TU	0135	3.6	0809	2.0	1433	3.4	2015	2.3	
18	W	0241	3.7	0918	1.8	1530	3.6	2123	2.1	
19	TH	0335	3.8	1006	1.6	1612	3.8	2210	1.9	
20	F	0417	4.0	1045	1.4	1647	4.1	2250	1.6	
21	SA	0454	4.3	1122	1.1	1721	4.4	2329	1.3	
22	SU	0530	4.5	1159	0.9	1755	4.6			
23	M	0009	1.1	0607	4.6	1238	0.8	1830	4.7	○
24	TU	0051	0.9	0647	4.7	1317	0.7	1909	4.8	
25	W	0134	0.8	0731	4.6	1357	0.8	1951	4.8	
26	TH	0218	0.8	0819	4.5	1439	0.9	2038	4.7	
27	F	0306	0.8	0914	4.3	1524	1.1	2133	4.5	
28	SA	0359	1.0	1018	4.0	1614	1.4	2239	4.3	
29	SU	0501	1.2	1131	3.8	1716	1.7	2351	4.2	
30	M	0611	1.3	1245	3.7	1832	1.8			◑
31	TU	0102	4.1	0724	1.4	1401	3.6	1951	1.9	

JUNE

Date	Day	Time	m	Time	m	Time	m	Time	m	Moon
1	W	0211	4.1	0837	1.3	1511	3.7	2103	1.7	
2	TH	0315	4.1	0940	1.3	1607	3.8	2202	1.6	
3	F	0410	4.2	1033	1.2	1651	4.0	2253	1.4	
4	SA	0456	4.3	1118	1.1	1728	4.1	2339	1.3	
5	SU	0538	4.3	1158	1.1	1802	4.2			
6	M	0022	1.2	0616	4.3	1236	1.1	1835	4.3	●
7	TU	0104	1.1	0654	4.2	1313	1.1	1909	4.4	
8	W	0144	1.1	0732	4.1	1348	1.2	1943	4.4	
9	TH	0222	1.2	0811	4.0	1424	1.2	2020	4.3	
10	F	0301	1.2	0851	3.9	1459	1.4	2100	4.2	
11	SA	0340	1.4	0935	3.8	1536	1.5	2144	4.1	
12	SU	0422	1.5	1023	3.6	1616	1.7	2233	3.9	
13	M	0508	1.6	1117	3.5	1703	1.9	2328	3.8	
14	TU	0559	1.7	1215	3.4	1758	2.0			
15	W	0025	3.7	0654	1.8	1316	3.5	1859	2.1	◐
16	TH	0123	3.7	0754	1.7	1417	3.6	2003	2.1	
17	F	0221	3.7	0853	1.6	1512	3.7	2104	1.9	
18	SA	0318	3.9	0949	1.5	1600	4.0	2200	1.7	
19	SU	0410	4.0	1040	1.3	1645	4.2	2252	1.5	
20	M	0501	4.2	1128	1.2	1729	4.4	2344	1.2	
21	TU	0550	4.4	1215	1.0	1813	4.7			
22	W	0035	1.0	0640	4.5	1302	0.9	1858	4.8	○
23	TH	0126	0.8	0730	4.5	1348	0.9	1944	4.9	
24	F	0216	0.7	0821	4.5	1433	0.9	2033	4.9	
25	SA	0306	0.6	0913	4.4	1519	1.0	2125	4.8	
26	SU	0357	0.7	1007	4.2	1608	1.2	2221	4.6	
27	M	0450	0.8	1106	4.0	1701	1.4	2323	4.4	
28	TU	0546	1.0	1210	3.8	1800	1.6			◑
29	W	0027	4.2	0644	1.2	1319	3.6	1906	1.7	
30	TH	0134	4.1	0748	1.4	1430	3.6	2018	1.8	

JULY

Date	Day	Time	m	Time	m	Time	m	Time	m	Moon
1	F	0241	4.0	0855	1.5	1535	3.6	2129	1.8	
2	SA	0344	3.9	0959	1.5	1629	3.8	2232	1.6	
3	SU	0439	3.9	1054	1.5	1712	3.9	2325	1.5	
4	M	0527	3.9	1140	1.4	1750	4.1			
5	TU	0013	1.4	0609	3.9	1222	1.4	1825	4.2	
6	W	0057	1.3	0648	4.0	1301	1.3	1900	4.3	●
7	TH	0136	1.2	0725	4.0	1337	1.2	1934	4.4	
8	F	0213	1.1	0800	4.0	1412	1.2	2007	4.4	
9	SA	0248	1.1	0835	4.0	1445	1.2	2040	4.3	
10	SU	0322	1.1	0911	3.9	1519	1.3	2115	4.2	
11	M	0357	1.2	0949	3.8	1553	1.4	2152	4.1	
12	TU	0434	1.3	1032	3.7	1632	1.6	2233	3.9	
13	W	0516	1.4	1120	3.6	1714	1.7	2322	3.8	
14	TH	0601	1.5	1215	3.5	1804	1.9			◐
15	F	0019	3.7	0652	1.6	1314	3.6	1901	1.9	
16	SA	0122	3.7	0751	1.7	1416	3.6	2006	1.9	
17	SU	0229	3.7	0858	1.7	1518	3.8	2118	1.8	
18	M	0339	3.8	1007	1.6	1617	4.0	2229	1.6	
19	TU	0446	4.0	1109	1.4	1711	4.3	2333	1.3	
20	W	0545	4.2	1204	1.2	1801	4.6			
21	TH	0029	1.0	0637	4.5	1254	1.0	1848	4.9	○
22	F	0122	0.7	0726	4.6	1340	0.8	1934	5.1	
23	SA	0209	0.4	0811	4.7	1424	0.7	2019	5.2	
24	SU	0255	0.3	0856	4.6	1506	0.7	2105	5.1	
25	M	0339	0.4	0941	4.4	1549	0.9	2152	4.9	
26	TU	0424	0.6	1030	4.2	1634	1.1	2245	4.6	
27	W	0510	0.9	1125	3.9	1723	1.4	2346	4.3	
28	TH	0600	1.3	1232	3.7	1820	1.7			◑
29	F	0057	4.0	0656	1.6	1349	3.5	1932	2.0	
30	SA	0213	3.7	0807	1.9	1506	3.5	2103	2.0	
31	SU	0326	3.6	0931	1.9	1611	3.7	2223	1.9	

AUGUST

Date	Day	Time	m	Time	m	Time	m	Time	m	Moon
1	M	0430	3.6	1039	1.9	1701	3.8	2321	1.7	
2	TU	0521	3.7	1130	1.7	1740	4.0			
3	W	0008	1.5	0602	3.8	1212	1.5	1815	4.2	
4	TH	0048	1.3	0637	3.9	1249	1.3	1847	4.4	
5	F	0123	1.1	0710	4.1	1323	1.2	1917	4.5	●
6	SA	0154	1.0	0740	4.2	1355	1.0	1945	4.5	
7	SU	0224	0.9	0809	4.2	1425	1.0	2012	4.5	
8	M	0254	0.9	0839	4.2	1454	1.0	2040	4.4	
9	TU	0324	0.9	0911	4.1	1525	1.1	2108	4.3	
10	W	0357	1.0	0945	4.0	1557	1.3	2139	4.1	
11	TH	0433	1.2	1024	3.8	1634	1.5	2217	3.9	
12	F	0514	1.4	1116	3.7	1718	1.7	2314	3.8	
13	SA	0602	1.6	1222	3.6	1812	1.9			◐
14	SU	0036	3.6	0702	1.8	1336	3.6	1922	2.0	
15	M	0205	3.6	0821	1.9	1451	3.7	2056	1.9	
16	TU	0332	3.7	0952	1.8	1601	4.0	2226	1.6	
17	W	0444	4.0	1101	1.5	1700	4.4	2330	1.2	
18	TH	0540	4.3	1155	1.2	1751	4.8			
19	F	0022	0.8	0628	4.6	1242	0.9	1835	5.1	○
20	SA	0109	0.5	0710	4.8	1325	0.7	1917	5.4	
21	SU	0152	0.2	0750	4.9	1405	0.5	1957	5.4	
22	M	0232	0.2	0829	4.8	1445	0.6	2037	5.3	
23	TU	0312	0.3	0908	4.6	1524	0.7	2119	5.0	
24	W	0351	0.6	0949	4.4	1604	1.0	2204	4.6	
25	TH	0432	1.0	1036	4.0	1648	1.4	2301	4.2	
26	F	0515	1.5	1143	3.7	1738	1.8			◑
27	SA	0022	3.8	0605	1.9	1313	3.5	1848	2.2	
28	SU	0151	3.6	0715	2.2	1438	3.5	2049	2.3	
29	M	0312	3.5	0911	2.3	1551	3.7	2222	2.1	
30	TU	0421	3.6	1028	2.1	1645	3.9	2314	1.8	
31	W	0511	3.7	1116	1.9	1724	4.1	2354	1.5	

Chart Datum: 2·71 metres below Ordnance Datum (Newlyn)

TIME ZONE (UT)
For Summer Time add ONE hour in **non-shaded areas**

SCOTLAND – STORNOWAY

LAT 58°12′N LONG 6°23′W

TIMES AND HEIGHTS OF HIGH AND LOW WATERS

SPRING & NEAP TIDES
Dates in red are **SPRINGS**
Dates in blue are **NEAPS**

YEAR **2005**

SEPTEMBER

Date	Day	Time	m	Time	m	Time	m	Time	m	Moon
1	TH	0547	3.9	1154	1.6	1757	4.3			
2	F	0027	1.3	0617	4.1	1229	1.4	1825	4.5	
3	SA	0058	1.1	0645	4.3	1301	1.1	1852	4.6	●
4	SU	0126	0.9	0712	4.4	1329	1.0	1917	4.7	
5	M	0153	0.8	0738	4.5	1357	0.9	1941	4.7	
6	TU	0221	0.7	0805	4.5	1425	0.9	2005	4.6	
7	W	0250	0.8	0833	4.4	1454	1.0	2031	4.5	
8	TH	0321	0.9	0902	4.3	1526	1.2	2100	4.3	
9	F	0355	1.1	0937	4.1	1601	1.4	2137	4.1	
10	SA	0434	1.4	1025	3.9	1643	1.6	2234	3.8	
11	SU	0521	1.7	1146	3.7	1738	1.9			◐
12	M	0023	3.6	0624	2.0	1316	3.7	1900	2.1	
13	TU	0209	3.6	0806	2.2	1439	3.8	2105	2.0	
14	W	0336	3.8	0950	2.0	1552	4.1	2227	1.6	
15	TH	0440	4.1	1052	1.6	1649	4.6	2321	1.1	
16	F	0529	4.4	1140	1.2	1736	5.0			
17	SA	0007	0.7	0611	4.7	1224	0.9	1817	5.3	
18	SU	0048	0.4	0649	4.9	1304	0.7	1855	5.5	○
19	M	0127	0.2	0724	5.0	1342	0.6	1932	5.5	
20	TU	0204	0.3	0759	5.0	1419	0.6	2009	5.3	
21	W	0241	0.5	0834	4.8	1457	0.8	2047	5.0	
22	TH	0317	0.8	0910	4.5	1535	1.1	2128	4.6	
23	F	0354	1.2	0951	4.2	1616	1.5	2219	4.1	
24	SA	0434	1.7	1050	3.9	1704	2.0	2348	3.7	
25	SU	0520	2.1	1235	3.7	1812	2.3			◑
26	M	0125	3.5	0624	2.5	1403	3.6	2031	2.4	
27	TU	0248	3.5	0843	2.6	1518	3.7	2204	2.2	
28	W	0359	3.6	1004	2.3	1615	3.9	2250	1.9	
29	TH	0446	3.8	1049	2.0	1656	4.2	2325	1.6	
30	F	0520	4.0	1126	1.7	1729	4.4	2356	1.3	

OCTOBER

Date	Day	Time	m	Time	m	Time	m	Time	m	Moon
1	SA	0549	4.3	1200	1.5	1757	4.6			
2	SU	0025	1.1	0615	4.5	1230	1.2	1822	4.7	
3	M	0052	0.9	0641	4.6	1258	1.0	1846	4.8	●
4	TU	0119	0.8	0706	4.7	1326	0.9	1911	4.9	
5	W	0147	0.7	0733	4.8	1356	0.9	1937	4.8	
6	TH	0218	0.8	0802	4.7	1427	1.0	2006	4.7	
7	F	0250	0.9	0833	4.5	1501	1.1	2039	4.4	
8	SA	0325	1.2	0910	4.3	1539	1.4	2123	4.1	
9	SU	0405	1.5	1004	4.0	1624	1.6	2235	3.8	
10	M	0454	1.9	1137	3.8	1726	1.9			◐
11	TU	0035	3.6	0607	2.2	1307	3.8	1910	2.1	
12	W	0210	3.6	0807	2.3	1427	4.0	2105	1.8	
13	TH	0328	3.9	0937	2.0	1536	4.3	2213	1.4	
14	F	0426	4.2	1033	1.6	1631	4.7	2302	1.0	
15	SA	0511	4.5	1118	1.3	1716	5.0	2344	0.7	
16	SU	0549	4.8	1200	1.0	1756	5.2			
17	M	0022	0.5	0624	4.9	1239	0.8	1832	5.3	○
18	TU	0059	0.5	0658	5.0	1317	0.8	1908	5.3	
19	W	0135	0.6	0730	4.9	1355	0.8	1944	5.1	
20	TH	0210	0.8	0804	4.8	1433	1.0	2021	4.8	
21	F	0246	1.1	0839	4.6	1512	1.3	2102	4.4	
22	SA	0322	1.5	0919	4.3	1553	1.7	2152	4.0	
23	SU	0400	1.9	1014	4.0	1641	2.0	2311	3.7	
24	M	0444	2.2	1146	3.8	1745	2.3			
25	TU	0044	3.5	0544	2.5	1313	3.7	1935	2.4	◑
26	W	0205	3.5	0739	2.6	1427	3.8	2113	2.2	
27	TH	0315	3.6	0916	2.5	1529	3.9	2205	2.0	
28	F	0407	3.8	1009	2.2	1615	4.1	2243	1.7	
29	SA	0444	4.1	1048	1.9	1652	4.3	2316	1.5	
30	SU	0515	4.3	1122	1.6	1722	4.5	2346	1.2	
31	M	0542	4.5	1153	1.4	1749	4.7			

NOVEMBER

Date	Day	Time	m	Time	m	Time	m	Time	m	Moon
1	TU	0015	1.0	0609	4.7	1224	1.2	1816	4.8	
2	W	0046	0.9	0637	4.8	1257	1.1	1845	4.8	●
3	TH	0118	0.8	0708	4.9	1331	1.0	1917	4.8	
4	F	0152	0.9	0741	4.8	1407	1.0	1954	4.7	
5	SA	0228	1.0	0819	4.7	1446	1.1	2037	4.4	
6	SU	0306	1.3	0904	4.5	1530	1.3	2133	4.1	
7	M	0350	1.6	1008	4.2	1623	1.6	2259	3.8	
8	TU	0445	1.9	1132	4.1	1735	1.8			
9	W	0031	3.7	0604	2.2	1251	4.1	1909	1.8	◐
10	TH	0152	3.7	0745	2.2	1404	4.2	2037	1.6	
11	F	0305	3.9	0905	1.9	1510	4.4	2143	1.4	
12	SA	0403	4.1	1003	1.7	1606	4.6	2233	1.1	
13	SU	0448	4.4	1052	1.4	1653	4.8	2316	1.0	
14	M	0527	4.6	1135	1.2	1734	4.9	2355	0.9	
15	TU	0602	4.7	1217	1.1	1812	4.9			
16	W	0033	0.9	0635	4.8	1257	1.0	1849	4.8	○
17	TH	0110	1.0	0709	4.8	1337	1.1	1926	4.7	
18	F	0146	1.1	0744	4.7	1417	1.2	2005	4.5	
19	SA	0222	1.3	0821	4.6	1457	1.4	2048	4.2	
20	SU	0259	1.5	0903	4.4	1539	1.6	2136	4.0	
21	M	0337	1.8	0953	4.2	1625	1.8	2236	3.7	
22	TU	0420	2.1	1056	4.0	1720	2.0	2345	3.6	
23	W	0514	2.3	1206	3.9	1827	2.2			◑
24	TH	0059	3.5	0624	2.4	1315	3.8	1946	2.2	
25	F	0211	3.6	0751	2.4	1421	3.8	2057	2.0	
26	SA	0312	3.7	0904	2.3	1518	3.9	2147	1.8	
27	SU	0357	3.9	0954	2.1	1602	4.1	2228	1.6	
28	M	0433	4.2	1035	1.8	1640	4.3	2304	1.4	
29	TU	0506	4.4	1114	1.6	1715	4.4	2340	1.2	
30	W	0539	4.6	1153	1.4	1751	4.6			

DECEMBER

Date	Day	Time	m	Time	m	Time	m	Time	m	Moon
1	TH	0017	1.1	0613	4.8	1233	1.2	1829	4.7	●
2	F	0055	1.0	0650	4.9	1315	1.1	1910	4.7	
3	SA	0135	1.0	0731	4.9	1358	1.0	1955	4.6	
4	SU	0216	1.1	0815	4.8	1444	1.0	2045	4.4	
5	M	0259	1.2	0906	4.7	1533	1.1	2143	4.2	
6	TU	0347	1.4	1005	4.5	1629	1.2	2251	4.0	
7	W	0442	1.7	1113	4.4	1732	1.4			
8	TH	0004	3.8	0548	1.9	1222	4.3	1840	1.5	◐
9	F	0117	3.8	0704	1.9	1330	4.2	1952	1.5	
10	SA	0228	3.8	0820	1.9	1436	4.2	2100	1.4	
11	SU	0331	3.9	0927	1.7	1537	4.3	2159	1.4	
12	M	0423	4.1	1025	1.6	1630	4.3	2249	1.3	
13	TU	0507	4.2	1116	1.4	1717	4.4	2334	1.2	
14	W	0545	4.4	1202	1.3	1759	4.4			
15	TH	0014	1.2	0622	4.5	1247	1.2	1839	4.4	○
16	F	0054	1.2	0658	4.6	1329	1.2	1919	4.3	
17	SA	0132	1.2	0734	4.6	1409	1.2	1957	4.2	
18	SU	0209	1.3	0811	4.6	1448	1.2	2036	4.1	
19	M	0245	1.4	0849	4.5	1527	1.3	2117	4.0	
20	TU	0322	1.5	0929	4.3	1607	1.5	2200	3.9	
21	W	0401	1.7	1014	4.1	1649	1.6	2249	3.7	
22	TH	0444	1.9	1104	4.0	1736	1.8	2345	3.6	
23	F	0534	2.1	1158	3.8	1828	1.9			◑
24	SA	0046	3.5	0631	2.2	1257	3.8	1925	1.9	
25	SU	0150	3.6	0735	2.2	1356	3.8	2027	1.9	
26	M	0250	3.7	0839	2.1	1456	3.8	2127	1.8	
27	TU	0343	3.9	0941	2.0	1553	3.9	2221	1.6	
28	W	0429	4.1	1037	1.8	1646	4.1	2310	1.4	
29	TH	0513	4.4	1129	1.5	1735	4.3	2357	1.3	
30	F	0556	4.6	1219	1.2	1823	4.4			
31	SA	0042	1.1	0640	4.8	1309	1.0			●

Chart Datum: 2·71 metres below Ordnance Datum (Newlyn)

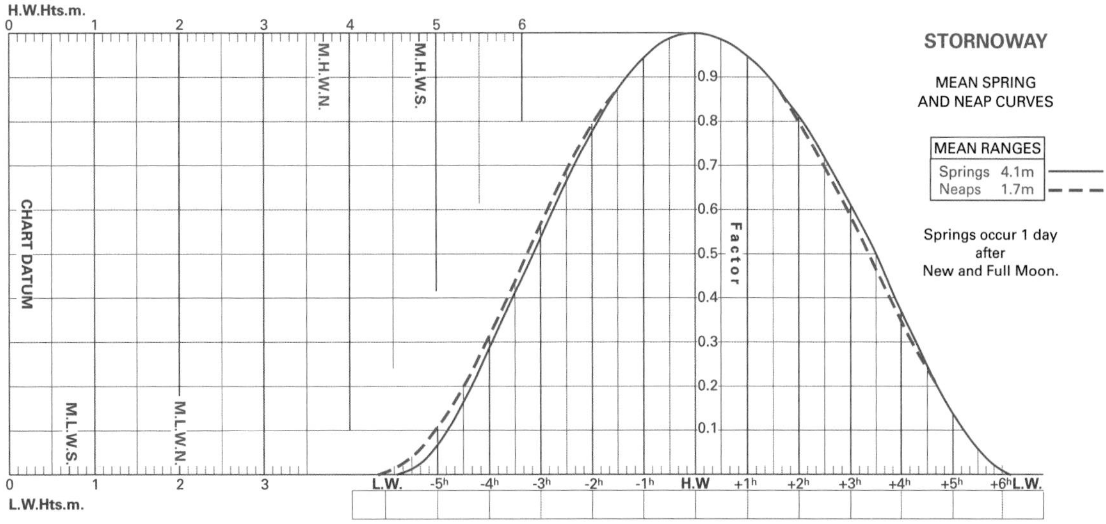
H.W.Hts.m.
M.H.W.N.
M.H.W.S.
CHART DATUM
M.L.W.S.
M.L.W.N.
L.W.Hts.m.
Factor
L.W. -5h -4h -3h -2h -1h H.W +1h +2h +3h +4h +5h +6h L.W.
STORNOWAY
MEAN SPRING AND NEAP CURVES
MEAN RANGES
Springs 4.1m
Neaps 1.7m
Springs occur 1 day after New and Full Moon.

ISLANDS WEST OF THE OUTER HEBRIDES (N to S)

TIDES

Standard Port STORNOWAY (⟵)

Times				Height (metres)			
High Water		Low Water		MHWS	MHWN	MLWN	MLWS
0100	0700	0300	0900	4·8	3·7	2·0	0·7
1300	1900	1500	2100				
Differences FLANNAN ISLES							
–0026	–0016	–0016	–0026	–0·9	–0·7	–0·6	–0·2
VILLAGE BAY (St Kilda)							
–0040	–0040	–0045	–0045	–1·4	–1·2	–0·8	–0·3
ROCKALL							
–0055	–0055	–0105	–0105	–1·8	–1·5	–0·9	–0·2

FLANNAN ISLES, Western Isles, centred on **58°17´·28N 07°35´·27W** (Eilean Mór). AC 2524, 2721. Tides, as above. Uninhabited group of several rky islets, 18M WNW of Gallan Head (Lewis). The main islet is Eilean Mór where landing can be made on SW side in suitable conditions. Lt ho, Fl (2) 30s 101m 20M, is a 23m high W tr on NE tip of Eilean Mór; the lt is obscured by islets to the W which are up to 57m high. No recommended ⚓s and the few charted depths are by lead-line surveys.

ST KILDA, Western Isles, **57°48´·28N 08°33´·07W.** AC 2721, 2524. Tides at Village Bay, Hirta: HW –0510 on Dover; ML 1·9m; Duration 0615; see above. A group of four isles and three stacks, the main island is Hirta from which the Army withdrew in April 1998 after 30 years. The facility is now manned by a civilian company, Serco ☎ (01870) 604443, based at South Uist. Hirta is owned by National Trust for Scotland and leased to Scottish National Heritage who employ a Seasonal Warden, ☎ 01870 604628. ⚓ in Village Bay, SE-facing, in approx 5m about 1·5ca off the pier. Ldg lts 270°, both Oc 5s 26/38m 3M. If wind is between NE and SSW big swells enter the bay; good holding, but untenable if winds strong. Levenish Is (55m) is 1·5M E of Hirta with offlying rks. Call *Kilda Radio* VHF Ch 16 12 73 (HJ) for permission to land; ☎ (01870) 604406 (HO), 604612 (OT); 📠 604601. Alternative ⚓ at Glen Bay on N side is only safe in S & E winds. Facilities: FW from wells near landings.

ROCKALL, 57°35´·7N 13°41´·2W. AC 1128, 2524. Tides, as above. A 19m high granite rock, 200M W of N Uist. Best access by helicopter. Lt, Fl 15s 13M, is often extinguished for long periods due to weather damage. Helen's Reef, 1·4m, on which the sea breaks is 2M ENE.

MONACH ISLANDS (or Heisker Is), centred on 57°31´·28N 07°38´·07W. AC 2721, 2722. Tides, see 9.8.6 Shillay. The group lies 5M SW of N Uist and 8M WNW of Benbecula. The 5 main islands (W-E) are Shillay, Ceann Iar, Shivinish, Ceann Ear and Stockay; all uninhabited. There are many rky offliers from NW through N to SE of the group. On Shillay there is a conspic, disused, red brick lt ho. ⚓s at: E of disused lt ho; Croic Hbr, bay N of Shivinish; and S Hbr on W side of Shivinish.

9.8.7 KINLOCHBERVIE

Highland **58°27′·26N 05°02′·78W**

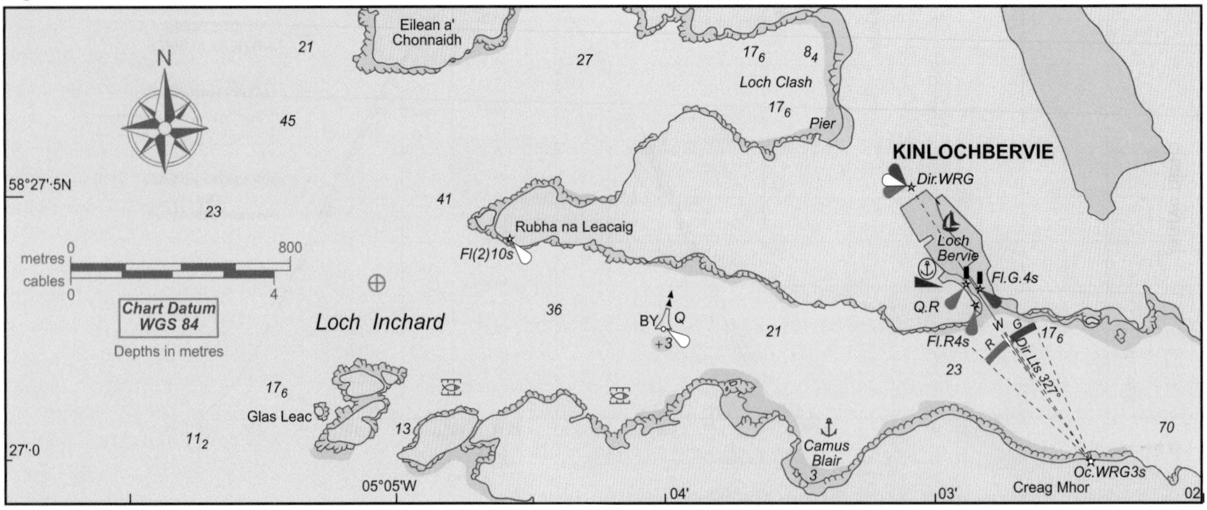
Eilean a' Chonnaidh
21
27
17₆
8₄
Loch Clash
17₆
Pier
45
KINLOCHBERVIE
Dir.WRG
58°27'·5N
41
23
Rubha na Leacaig
Fl(2)10s
Loch Bervie
Fl.G.4s
metres 0 800
cables 0 4
Chart Datum WGS 84
Depths in metres
Loch Inchard
36
BY Q
+3
Q.R
21
Fl.R4s
Dir Lts 327°
17₆
23
17₆
Glas Leac
13
Camus Blair
3
70
27'·0
11₂
05°05'W
04'
03'
Oc.WRG3s
Creag Mhor
02

CHARTS AC 1954, 1785, 2503; Imray C67; OS 9

TIDES –0400 Dover; ML 2·7; Duration 0610; Zone 0 (UT)

Standard Port ULLAPOOL (⟼)

Times				Height (metres)			
High Water		Low Water		MHWS	MHWN	MLWN	MLWS
0000	0600	0300	0900	5·2	3·9	2·1	0·7
1200	1800	1500	2100				
Differences LOCH BERVIE							
+0030	+0010	+0010	+0020	–0·3	–0·3	–0·2	0·0
LOCH LAXFORD							
+0015	+0015	+0005	+0005	–0·3	–0·4	–0·2	0·0
BADCALL BAY							
+0005	+0005	+0005	+0005	–0·7	–0·5	–0·5	+0·2
LOCH NEDD							
0000	0000	0000	0000	–0·3	–0·2	–0·2	0·0
LOCH INVER							
–0005	–0005	–0005	–0005	–0·2	0·0	0·0	+0·1

SHELTER Very good in Kinlochbervie Hbr off the N shore of Loch Inchard. A useful passage port, only 14.5 track miles S of Cape Wrath. It is also a busy FV port, but in NNE corner yachts AB on 18m long pontoon in 4m on SW side only; NE side is shoal/foul. If full, ⚓ at Loch Clash, open to W; landing jetty in 2·7m. Other ⚓s at: Camus Blair on S shore, 5ca SW of hbr ent, and up the loch at L Sheigra, Achriesgill Bay and 5ca short of the head of the loch.

NAVIGATION WPT 58°27′·34N 05°05′·08W (at mouth of Loch Inchard), 100° to hbr ent, 1·3M. The sides of the loch are clean, but keep to N side of Loch Inchard to clear Bodha Ceann na Saile NCM and rk (3m depth) almost in mid-chan.

LIGHTS AND MARKS From offshore in good vis Ceann Garbh, a conspic mountain 899m (6M inland), leads 110° toward ent of Loch Inchard. Rubha na Leacaig, Fl (2) 10s 30m 8M, marks N side of loch ent. Dir ☆ WRG (H24) 15m 16M, Y framework tr (floodlit) leads 327° into hbr; see 9.8.4 for vis sectors. The 25m wide ent chan (and hbr) is dredged 4m and marked by 2 PHM poles, Fl R 4s and QR, and by a SHM pole, Fl G 4s. On S shore of loch Creag Mhòr, Dir Oc lt WRG 2.8s 16m 9M, is aligned 147°/327° with hbr ent chan; see 9.8.4.

R/T VHF Ch **14** 16 HX. Ch 06 is used by FVs in the Minches.

TELEPHONE (Dial code 01971) HM ☎ 521235, 📠 521718, mob 07787 151446; MRSC (01851) 702013; ⊖ (0141) 887 9369 (H24); Marinecall 09066 526248; Police 521222; Dr 502002.

FACILITIES AB(pontoon) £1.30<10m for 48hrs, FW, D at FV quay, P (cans), Gas, CH, ME, ✉, Bar, 🛒, R, Showers (Mission & Hbr Office), ♿. In summer, bus to Inverness.

⚓ & HBR BETWEEN KINLOCHBERVIE AND ULLAPOOL

LOCH LAXFORD Highland, **58°24′·78N 05°07′·18W**. AC 2503. HW –0410 on Dover. ML 2·7m. See 9.8.7. Ent between Rubha Ruadh and Ardmore Pt, 1M ENE, clearly identified by 3 isolated mountains (N-S) Ceann Garbh, Ben Arkle and Ben Stack. The many ⚓s in the loch include: Loch a'Chadh-fi, on N/NE sides of islet (John Ridgeway's Adventure School on Pt on W side of narrows has moorings); Bagh nah-Airde Beag, next bay to E, (beware rk 5ca off SE shore which covers at MHWS); Weaver's Bay on SW shore, 3M from ent (beware drying rk off NW Pt of ent); Bagh na Fionndalach Mor on SW shore (4-6m); Fanagmore Bay on SW shore (beware head of bay foul with old moorings). Beware many fish farming cages. Facilities: none, nearest stores at Scourie (5M).

LOCH INVER Highland, **58°08′·98N 05°15′·08W**. AC 2504. HW –0433 on Dover; ML 3·0m. See 9.8.7. Good shelter in all weathers at head of loch in busy fishing hbr on S side. Appr N or S of Soyea Is, Fl (2) 10s 34m 6M; beware rk drying 1·7m about 50m off Kirkaig Point (S side of ent). Glas Leac, a small islet 7ca WSW of hbr, may be passed on either side. Its ☆, Fl WRG 3s, has 3 WRG sectors (see 9.8.4) covering the chans N and S of Soyea Is and into the hbr. The church, hotel (S side) and white ho (N side) are all conspic. A pontoon for yachts, <12m LOA, is in 5m between the bkwtr (QG) and the first FV pier. Or, in W'ly gales, ⚓ in the lee of bkwtr in about 8m; or where HM directs. Other ⚓s on S shore of Loch Inver. VHF Ch 09 16. HM ☎ (01571) 844265. **Facilities**: FW, P, D, ◙, 🛒, ✉, Gas.

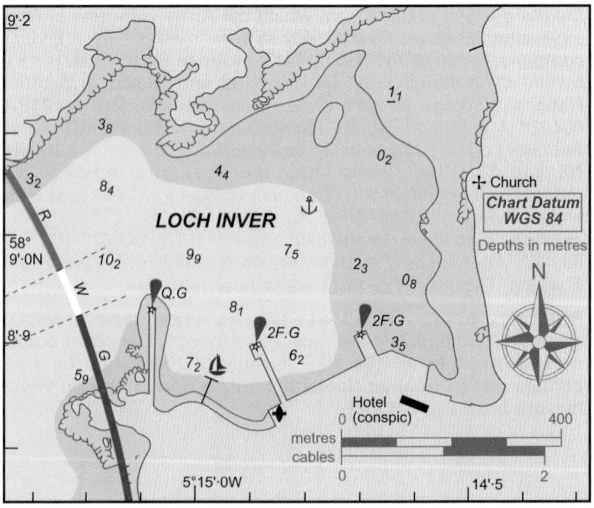
9'·2
1₁
3₈
0₂
4₄
3₂
8₄
Church
Chart Datum WGS 84
LOCH INVER
58° 9'·0N
10₂
9₉
7₅
2₃
Depths in metres
0₈
N
Q.G
8₁
2F.G
2F.G
8'·9
6₂
3₅
7₂
5₉
Hotel (conspic)
metres 0 400
cables 0 2
5°15'·0W
14'·5

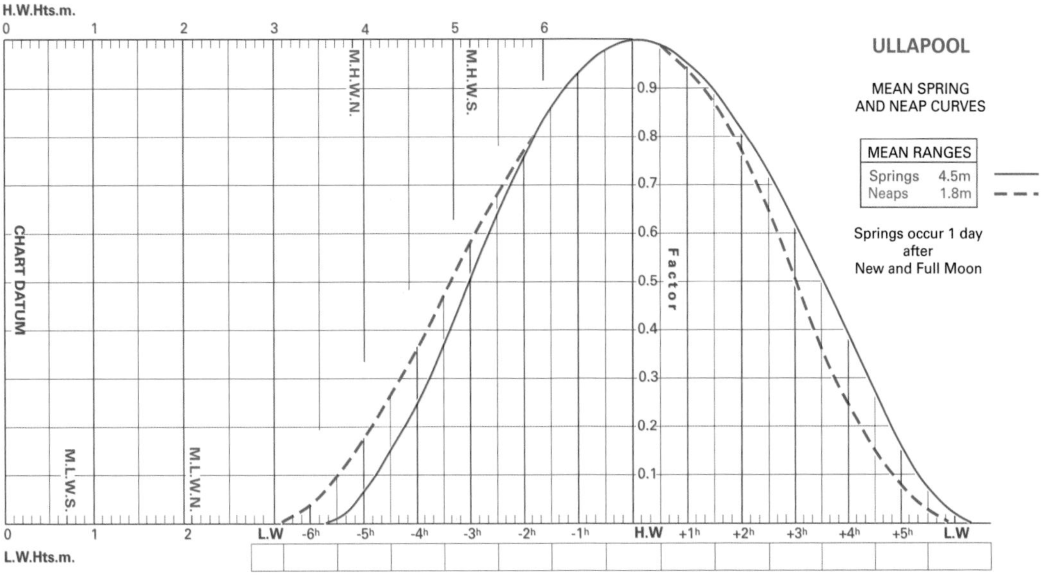
H.W.Hts.m.
0 1 2 3 4 5 6
M.H.W.N.
M.H.W.S.
CHART DATUM
M.L.W.S.
M.L.W.N.
0.9
0.8
0.7
0.6
0.5
0.4
0.3
0.2
0.1
Factor
0 1 2
L.W.Hts.m.
L.W -6h -5h -4h -3h -2h -1h H.W +1h +2h +3h +4h +5h L.W
ULLAPOOL
MEAN SPRING AND NEAP CURVES
MEAN RANGES
Springs 4.5m
Neaps 1.8m
Springs occur 1 day after New and Full Moon

9.8.8 ULLAPOOL

Highland **57°53′·70N 05°09′·38W** ❁❁❁✿✿✿

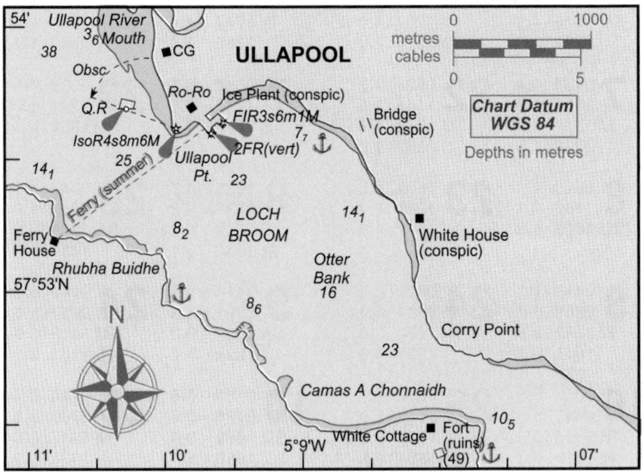
Ullapool River
Mouth
CG
ULLAPOOL
metres
cables
0 1000
0 5
Obsc.
Q.R
Ro-Ro
Ice Plant (conspic)
FIR3s6m1M
Bridge (conspic)
Chart Datum WGS 84
Depths in metres
IsoR4s8m6M
2FR(vert)
Ullapool Pt.
Ferry (summer)
LOCH BROOM
Ferry House
White House (conspic)
Rhubha Buidhe
57°53'N
Otter Bank
Corry Point
Camas A Chonnaidh
White Cottage
Fort (ruins)
5°9'W
11'
10'
07'
54'

CHARTS AC 1794, 2500, 2501, 2509; Imray C67; OS 19

TIDES –0415 Dover; ML 3·0; Duration 0610; Zone 0 (UT)

Standard Port ULLAPOOL (⟶)

Times				Height (metres)			
High Water		Low Water		MHWS	MHWN	MLWN	MLWS
0000	0600	0300	0900	5·2	3·9	2·1	0·7
1200	1800	1500	2100				
Differences SUMMER ISLES (Tanera Mor)							
–0005	–0005	–0010	–0010	–0·1	+0·1	0·0	+0·1
LOCH EWE (Mellon Charles, 57°51′N 05°38′W)							
–0010	–0010	–0010	–0010	–0·1	–0·1	–0·1	0·0
LOCH GAIRLOCH							
–0020	–0020	–0010	–0010	0·0	+0·1	–0·3	–0·1

SHELTER Good in ⚓ E of pier. A commercial port and may be congested. Visiting yachts are welcome but consult HM for berth. Loch Kanaird (N of ent to Loch Broom) has good ⚓ E of Isle Martin. Possible ⚓s 6ca S of Ullapool Pt, and beyond the narrows 3ca ESE of W cottage. The upper loch is squally in strong winds.

NAVIGATION WPT L Broom ent 57°55′·78N 05°15′·08W, 129° to Ullapool Pt lt, 3.5M. N of Ullapool Pt extensive drying flats off the mouth of Ullapool R are marked by QR buoy. Beware fish pens and unlit buoys SE of narrows off W shore.

LIGHTS AND MARKS Rhubha Cadail, N of L. Broom ent, Fl WRG 6s 11m 9/6M. Cailleach Hd, W of ent, Fl (2) 12s 60m 9M. Ullapool Pt Iso R 4s 8m 6M; grey mast, vis 258°-108°.

R/T VHF Ch 14 16 12 (Jul-Nov: H24. Dec-Jun: HO).

TELEPHONE (Dial code 01854) HM 612091/612724, 📠 612678; MRSC (01851) 702013; ⊜ (0141) 887 9369; Marinecall 09066 526248; Police 612017; Dr 612015.

FACILITIES **Pier** AB - consult HM, D, FW, CH; **Ullapool YC Services:** Gas, ME, El, Ⓔ, ⚒. **Town** EC Tues (winter); P, ⊡, 🛒, R, Bar, ✉, Ⓑ, ⇌ (bus to Garve). Daily buses to Inverness (✈), ferries three times a day (summer) to Stornoway. No Sunday bus, train or ferry services.

ADJACENT ANCHORAGES

SUMMER ISLES, 58°01′N 05°25′W. AC 2509, 2501. HW –0425 Dover; See 9.8.8; streams are weak and irreg. In the N apps to Loch Broom some 30 islands and rks, the main ones being Eilean Mullagrach, Isle Ristol, Glas-leac Mor, Tanera Beg, Eilean a' Char, Eilean Fada Mor. Beware rks at S end of Horse Sound. ⚓s: Isle Ristol, ⚓ to S of drying causeway; close to slip is lt Fl G 3s. Tanera Beg, ⚓ in the chan to the E inside Eilean Fada Mor . Tanera More on E side, ⚓ in bay ; new pier but many moorings; or in NW, ⚓ close E of Eilean na Saille, but N of drying rk. Beware of fish pens and activities in ⚓'s around Tanera More. Temp ⚓ at Badentarbat B for Achiltibuie on mainland. Facilities: 🛒, R, Gas, FW, D (emerg) ☎ (01854) 622261.

LOCH EWE, 57°52′·0N 05°40′·0W (SWM buoy, L Fl 10s). AC 2509, 3146. Tides: See 9.8.8; HW –0415 on Dover; ML 2·9m; Duration 0610. Shelter in all winds. Easy ent with no dangers in loch. Rhubha Reidh lt, Fl (4) 15s 37m 24M, W tr, is 4·5M W of ent. No 1 buoy Fl (3) G 10s. Loch approx 7M long with Isle Ewe and 2 small islets about 2M from ent in centre; can be passed on either side. Temp ⚓ in bay of Isle of Ewe. Beware unlit buoys E side Isle Ewe. Aultbea Pier, 2 FG (vert), to NE. NATO fuelling jetty and dolphins, all Fl G 4s. Sheltered ⚓ in Loch Thurnaig to S. **Aultbea**: Dr, P, ✉, R, 🛒, Bar. Poolewe Bay (3·5m, at head of loch): Boor Rks off W shore about 7ca from loch hd. **Inverewe Gdns** on NE side. Poolewe: FW, D, L on pier, P (at garage), ✉, R, Bar, 🛒, Gas.

LOCH GAIRLOCH, 57°43′N 05°45′W. AC 228, 2528. HW –0440 on Dover. See 9.8.8. A wide loch facing W. Ent clear of dangers. Quite heavy seas enter in bad weather. Good shelter in Badachro, SW of Eilean Horrisdale on S side of loch or in Loch Shieldaig at SE end of the loch. Or ⚓ in Flowerdale Bay in approx 6m near Gairloch pier. Lts: Glas Eilean Fl WRG 6s 9m 6/4M, W080°-102°, R102°-296°, W296°-333°, G333°-080°. Pier hd, QR 9m. HM ☎ (01445) 712377. VHF Ch 16 (occas). Gairloch Pier: AB fees charged. P (cans), D, FW, Hotel, Gas, 🛒, CH, Bar, ✉.

8

TIME ZONE (UT)
For Summer Time add ONE hour in **non-shaded areas**

SCOTLAND – ULLAPOOL

LAT 57°54′N LONG 5°10′W

TIMES AND HEIGHTS OF HIGH AND LOW WATERS

SPRING & NEAP TIDES
Dates in red are SPRINGS
Dates in blue are NEAPS

YEAR **2005**

JANUARY

Day	Time	m	Day	Time	m
1 SA	0409	1.8	16 SU	0511	1.5
	1005	4.6		1122	4.8
	1650	1.8		1745	1.4
	2250	4.3			
2 SU	0451	2.0	17 M	0006	4.3
	1051	4.5		0602	1.9
	1735	1.9		1225	4.5
	2345	4.1		◐ 1837	1.8
3 M	0540	2.1	18 TU	0114	4.1
	1146	4.3		0703	2.1
	1827	2.0		1335	4.2
◑				1938	2.1
4 TU	0049	4.1	19 W	0231	4.0
	0638	2.2		0818	2.3
	1254	4.2		1450	4.1
	1928	2.0		2052	2.2
5 W	0157	4.1	20 TH	0345	4.0
	0747	2.3		0941	2.3
	1404	4.3		1601	4.1
	2037	2.0		2207	2.2
6 TH	0302	4.2	21 F	0443	4.2
	0900	2.2		1052	2.2
	1512	4.4		1659	4.2
	2145	1.8		2307	2.1
7 F	0401	4.5	22 SA	0529	4.4
	1009	2.0		1144	2.0
	1617	4.5		1745	4.3
	2247	1.6		2353	1.9
8 SA	0455	4.8	23 SU	0606	4.6
	1110	1.7		1227	1.8
	1716	4.8		1824	4.5
	2341	1.4			
9 SU	0544	5.1	24 M	0032	1.8
	1205	1.3		0638	4.8
	1811	5.0		1305	1.6
				1858	4.6
10 M	0032	1.2	25 TU	0108	1.6
	0631	5.3		0707	4.9
	1258	1.0		1340	1.4
	● 1902	5.2		○ 1929	4.8
11 TU	0120	1.0	26 W	0141	1.5
	0718	5.6		0736	5.0
	1348	0.8		1412	1.3
	1951	5.3		1959	4.8
12 W	0207	1.0	27 TH	0212	1.4
	0804	5.6		0803	5.0
	1437	0.7		1444	1.2
	2039	5.2		2029	4.8
13 TH	0253	1.0	28 F	0243	1.3
	0850	5.6		0832	5.0
	1524	0.7		1515	1.2
	2127	5.1		2100	4.8
14 F	0338	1.1	29 SA	0315	1.3
	0938	5.4		0902	5.0
	1610	0.8		1546	1.2
	2215	4.8		2132	4.7
15 SA	0424	1.3	30 SU	0347	1.4
	1028	5.2		0935	4.9
	1657	1.1		1619	1.3
	2307	4.5		2209	4.5
			31 M	0423	1.5
				1012	4.7
				1656	1.5
				2253	4.4

FEBRUARY

Day	Time	m	Day	Time	m
1 TU	0503	1.7	16 W	0005	4.0
	1056	4.5		0610	2.1
	1738	1.7		1241	4.0
	2348	4.2		◐ 1834	2.1
2 W	0552	1.9	17 TH	0131	3.8
	1153	4.3		0720	2.4
	1831	1.9		1409	3.8
◑				1947	2.4
3 TH	0101	4.1	18 F	0307	3.8
	0653	2.2		0909	2.5
	1314	4.1		1538	3.8
	1942	2.1		2138	2.5
4 F	0221	4.1	19 SA	0421	3.9
	0815	2.2		1041	2.3
	1445	4.1		1645	3.9
	2112	2.1		2254	2.3
5 SA	0337	4.2	20 SU	0512	4.2
	0948	2.1		1134	2.0
	1610	4.3		1733	4.1
	2234	1.9		2341	2.0
6 SU	0443	4.6	21 M	0550	4.4
	1103	1.7		1214	1.7
	1718	4.6		1809	4.4
	2335	1.6			
7 M	0537	4.9	22 TU	0018	1.8
	1202	1.3		0620	4.6
	1812	4.9		1249	1.4
				1839	4.6
8 TU	0026	1.2	23 W	0052	1.5
	0623	5.3		0648	4.8
	1254	0.9		1320	1.2
	● 1857	5.2		1908	4.8
9 W	0113	0.9	24 TH	0123	1.3
	0707	5.6		0714	5.0
	1340	0.5		1351	1.0
	1939	5.3		○ 1935	4.9
10 TH	0156	0.7	25 F	0152	1.1
	0748	5.7		0739	5.1
	1424	0.4		1419	0.9
	2019	5.3		2002	4.9
11 F	0237	0.6	26 SA	0221	1.0
	0829	5.7		0806	5.2
	1505	0.4		1448	0.8
	2059	5.2		2030	4.9
12 SA	0317	0.7	27 SU	0251	0.9
	0910	5.5		0834	5.1
	1544	0.6		1517	0.8
	2138	4.9		2100	4.9
13 SU	0357	0.9	28 M	0322	1.0
	0952	5.2		0905	5.0
	1623	0.9		1548	1.0
	2219	4.6		2134	4.7
14 M	0437	1.2			
	1036	4.8			
	1702	1.3			
	2304	4.3			
15 TU	0520	1.6			
	1130	4.4			
	1744	1.7			

MARCH

Day	Time	m	Day	Time	m
1 TU	0356	1.2	16 W	0444	1.5
	0941	4.8		1044	4.2
	1623	1.2		1659	1.7
	2214	4.5		2255	4.0
2 W	0434	1.4	17 TH	0529	2.0
	1023	4.5		1154	3.8
	1702	1.5		1742	2.1
	2305	4.3	◐		
3 TH	0520	1.7	18 F	0021	3.7
	1120	4.2		0630	2.3
	1751	1.9		1329	3.6
◑				1844	2.5
4 F	0020	4.0	19 SA	0215	3.6
	0619	2.0		0830	2.5
	1253	3.9		1505	3.6
	1904	2.2		2101	2.6
5 SA	0155	4.0	20 SU	0345	3.7
	0752	2.2		1018	2.3
	1442	3.9		1619	3.8
	2100	2.3		2231	2.4
6 SU	0323	4.1	21 M	0442	4.0
	0946	2.0		1109	1.9
	1614	4.1		1707	4.0
	2231	2.0		2316	2.0
7 M	0433	4.4	22 TU	0521	4.2
	1102	1.6		1146	1.6
	1717	4.5		1742	4.3
	2329	1.5		2352	1.7
8 TU	0526	4.9	23 W	0551	4.5
	1156	1.1		1219	1.3
	1803	4.8		1811	4.5
9 W	0015	1.1	24 TH	0024	1.4
	0609	5.2		0617	4.7
	1242	0.6		1250	1.0
	1841	5.1		1837	4.8
10 TH	0058	0.8	25 F	0055	1.1
	0648	5.5		0643	5.0
	1323	0.3		1319	0.8
	● 1918	5.3		○ 1904	4.9
11 F	0137	0.5	26 SA	0124	0.9
	0726	5.7		0709	5.1
	1401	0.2		1348	0.6
	1952	5.3		1931	5.0
12 SA	0215	0.4	27 SU	0154	0.7
	0803	5.6		0736	5.2
	1438	0.3		1417	0.6
	2027	5.2		2000	5.1
13 SU	0252	0.5	28 M	0225	0.7
	0839	5.4		0807	5.1
	1513	0.5		1448	0.6
	2100	5.0		2032	5.0
14 M	0328	0.8	29 TU	0258	0.8
	0917	5.1		0841	5.0
	1547	0.8		1520	0.8
	2134	4.7		2107	4.8
15 TU	0405	1.1	30 W	0334	1.0
	0957	4.6		0920	4.8
	1622	1.2		1556	1.1
	2210	4.3		2149	4.6
			31 TH	0414	1.2
				1008	4.4
				1637	1.5
				2243	4.3

APRIL

Day	Time	m	Day	Time	m
1 F	0503	1.6	16 SA	0558	2.2
	1119	4.1		1250	3.5
	1729	1.9		1803	2.4
			◐		
2 SA	0007	4.0	17 SU	0113	3.6
	0608	1.9		0738	2.4
	1305	3.8		1416	3.5
	◑ 1852	2.3		1957	2.6
3 SU	0143	3.9	18 M	0246	3.7
	0755	2.1		0926	2.2
	1446	3.8		1532	3.7
	2059	2.2		2142	2.4
4 M	0309	4.1	19 TU	0352	3.8
	0943	1.8		1024	1.9
	1607	4.1		1625	3.9
	2219	1.9		2234	2.0
5 TU	0416	4.4	20 W	0437	4.1
	1049	1.3		1105	1.6
	1702	4.4		1703	4.2
	2311	1.4		2312	1.7
6 W	0506	4.8	21 TH	0510	4.3
	1137	0.9		1139	1.3
	1744	4.8		1734	4.4
	2355	1.0		2347	1.4
7 TH	0548	5.1	22 F	0539	4.6
	1219	0.6		1211	1.0
	1819	5.0		1802	4.7
8 F	0035	0.7	23 SA	0019	1.1
	0625	5.3		0607	4.8
	1258	0.4		1243	0.8
	● 1852	5.1		1831	4.9
9 SA	0114	0.5	24 SU	0052	0.9
	0701	5.4		0637	5.0
	1334	0.3		1315	0.6
	1924	5.2		○ 1901	5.1
10 SU	0150	0.5	25 M	0126	0.7
	0736	5.3		0709	5.1
	1408	0.4		1348	0.6
	1956	5.1		1934	5.1
11 M	0226	0.6	26 TU	0201	0.7
	0812	5.1		0746	5.1
	1442	0.6		1422	0.6
	2027	4.9		2010	5.0
12 TU	0302	0.8	27 W	0238	0.7
	0849	4.8		0826	4.9
	1515	1.0		1459	0.8
	2100	4.6		2050	4.9
13 W	0338	1.1	28 TH	0319	0.9
	0929	4.4		0915	4.6
	1548	1.3		1539	1.2
	2134	4.4		2139	4.6
14 TH	0416	1.5	29 F	0405	1.2
	1017	4.1		1017	4.3
	1624	1.7		1626	1.5
	2216	4.1		2244	4.4
15 F	0500	1.9	30 SA	0501	1.5
	1124	3.8		1141	4.0
	1705	2.1		1727	1.9
	2324	3.8			

Chart Datum: 2·75 metres below Ordnance Datum (Newlyn)

TIME ZONE (UT)
For Summer Time add ONE hour in **non-shaded areas**

SCOTLAND – ULLAPOOL

LAT 57°54′N LONG 5°10′W

TIMES AND HEIGHTS OF HIGH AND LOW WATERS

SPRING & NEAP TIDES
Dates in red are SPRINGS
Dates in blue are NEAPS

YEAR **2005**

MAY

Date	Day	Time	m	Time	m	Time	m	Time	m	Moon
1	SU	0007	4.2	0615	1.7	1309	3.9	1857	2.2	◑
2	M	0130	4.1	0754	1.8	1433	3.9	2038	2.1	
3	TU	0246	4.2	0920	1.5	1545	4.1	2150	1.8	
4	W	0351	4.4	1021	1.2	1638	4.4	2243	1.4	
5	TH	0441	4.7	1110	1.0	1719	4.6	2329	1.1	
6	F	0524	4.9	1152	0.8	1755	4.8			
7	SA	0010	0.9	0602	5.0	1231	0.7	1828	4.9	
8	SU	0050	0.8	0639	5.0	1307	0.7	1900	4.9	●
9	M	0128	0.8	0715	4.9	1341	0.8	1931	4.9	
10	TU	0205	0.9	0752	4.8	1415	1.0	2003	4.8	
11	W	0241	1.0	0831	4.5	1448	1.2	2037	4.6	
12	TH	0318	1.3	0913	4.3	1523	1.5	2113	4.4	
13	F	0357	1.5	1002	4.0	1600	1.7	2157	4.2	
14	SA	0441	1.8	1101	3.8	1642	2.0	2255	3.9	
15	SU	0535	2.0	1208	3.7	1736	2.3			
16	M	0014	3.8	0646	2.1	1318	3.6	1852	2.4	◐
17	TU	0134	3.7	0810	2.1	1427	3.6	2024	2.3	
18	W	0242	3.8	0919	1.9	1527	3.8	2132	2.1	
19	TH	0336	4.0	1009	1.6	1613	4.1	2221	1.8	
20	F	0419	4.2	1051	1.4	1651	4.3	2302	1.5	
21	SA	0456	4.4	1129	1.1	1726	4.6	2341	1.2	
22	SU	0532	4.7	1206	0.9	1800	4.8			
23	M	0020	1.0	0610	4.8	1244	0.8	1836	5.0	○
24	TU	0101	0.8	0650	4.9	1323	0.7	1915	5.1	
25	W	0143	0.7	0735	4.9	1404	0.8	1957	5.1	
26	TH	0227	0.7	0826	4.8	1447	1.0	2045	5.0	
27	F	0314	0.9	0923	4.6	1533	1.2	2140	4.8	
28	SA	0406	1.0	1029	4.4	1626	1.5	2245	4.6	
29	SU	0505	1.3	1140	4.2	1728	1.7	2355	4.4	
30	M	0614	1.4	1251	4.0	1843	1.9			◑
31	TU	0106	4.3	0729	1.5	1404	4.0	2000	1.9	

JUNE

Date	Day	Time	m	Time	m	Time	m	Time	m	Moon
1	W	0216	4.3	0841	1.5	1511	4.1	2110	1.7	
2	TH	0320	4.4	0944	1.4	1608	4.2	2210	1.6	
3	F	0415	4.5	1037	1.3	1654	4.4	2302	1.4	
4	SA	0502	4.5	1123	1.2	1734	4.5	2348	1.3	
5	SU	0545	4.6	1205	1.1	1810	4.7			
6	M	0031	1.2	0625	4.6	1244	1.1	1843	4.7	●
7	TU	0112	1.1	0704	4.6	1320	1.2	1917	4.7	
8	W	0150	1.1	0743	4.5	1356	1.3	1950	4.7	
9	TH	0228	1.2	0822	4.4	1431	1.4	2024	4.6	
10	F	0305	1.3	0902	4.3	1506	1.5	2101	4.5	
11	SA	0344	1.4	0944	4.2	1544	1.7	2140	4.3	
12	SU	0425	1.6	1030	4.0	1624	1.8	2226	4.2	
13	M	0509	1.7	1122	3.9	1709	2.0	2320	4.0	
14	TU	0600	1.8	1220	3.8	1803	2.1			
15	W	0023	3.9	0658	1.9	1322	3.7	1907	2.1	◐
16	TH	0129	3.9	0801	1.9	1422	3.8	2016	2.1	
17	F	0229	4.0	0902	1.8	1518	4.0	2120	2.0	
18	SA	0324	4.1	0958	1.6	1607	4.2	2216	1.7	
19	SU	0416	4.3	1048	1.4	1653	4.5	2307	1.5	
20	M	0505	4.5	1135	1.2	1736	4.7	2356	1.2	
21	TU	0554	4.7	1221	1.0	1820	5.0			
22	W	0044	1.0	0643	4.8	1308	0.9	1904	5.1	○
23	TH	0133	0.8	0734	4.9	1354	0.9	1951	5.2	
24	F	0222	0.7	0827	4.9	1441	0.9	2041	5.2	
25	SA	0312	0.7	0922	4.8	1530	1.1	2133	5.1	
26	SU	0403	0.8	1018	4.6	1620	1.2	2230	4.9	
27	M	0457	0.9	1117	4.4	1714	1.4	2330	4.7	
28	TU	0552	1.1	1219	4.2	1813	1.6			◑
29	W	0034	4.5	0651	1.4	1325	4.1	1916	1.8	
30	TH	0140	4.3	0754	1.5	1433	4.0	2026	1.9	

JULY

Date	Day	Time	m	Time	m	Time	m	Time	m	Moon
1	F	0247	4.2	0900	1.7	1537	4.1	2136	1.8	
2	SA	0351	4.2	1004	1.7	1633	4.2	2240	1.7	
3	SU	0448	4.2	1100	1.6	1719	4.3	2334	1.6	
4	M	0537	4.3	1147	1.6	1800	4.5			
5	TU	0021	1.5	0619	4.4	1230	1.5	1835	4.6	
6	W	0104	1.4	0658	4.4	1308	1.5	1908	4.7	●
7	TH	0142	1.3	0734	4.5	1344	1.4	1940	4.7	
8	F	0218	1.2	0809	4.5	1418	1.4	2012	4.7	
9	SA	0253	1.2	0843	4.5	1452	1.4	2043	4.7	
10	SU	0327	1.2	0918	4.4	1526	1.5	2116	4.6	
11	M	0402	1.3	0954	4.3	1601	1.5	2152	4.5	
12	TU	0438	1.4	1034	4.1	1639	1.6	2233	4.3	
13	W	0517	1.5	1121	4.0	1721	1.8	2320	4.2	
14	TH	0601	1.7	1218	3.9	1811	1.9			◐
15	F	0019	4.0	0653	1.8	1323	3.9	1911	2.1	
16	SA	0128	4.0	0756	1.9	1428	3.9	2022	2.1	
17	SU	0239	4.0	0908	1.9	1531	4.1	2136	2.0	
18	M	0348	4.1	1017	1.7	1629	4.4	2243	1.7	
19	TU	0453	4.3	1117	1.5	1721	4.7	2342	1.4	
20	W	0550	4.6	1210	1.3	1810	5.0			
21	TH	0036	1.0	0641	4.9	1300	1.0	1856	5.2	○
22	F	0127	0.7	0730	5.0	1347	0.8	1941	5.4	
23	SA	0215	0.5	0817	5.1	1432	0.8	2027	5.5	
24	SU	0302	0.4	0903	5.0	1517	0.8	2113	5.4	
25	M	0348	0.5	0950	4.8	1602	0.9	2202	5.2	
26	TU	0433	0.7	1040	4.6	1647	1.1	2255	4.9	
27	W	0518	1.0	1136	4.3	1736	1.4	2354	4.5	
28	TH	0607	1.4	1239	4.1	1832	1.8			◑
29	F	0102	4.2	0702	1.7	1353	3.9	1941	2.0	
30	SA	0218	4.0	0812	2.0	1510	3.9	2107	2.2	
31	SU	0334	3.9	0935	2.1	1617	4.0	2229	2.1	

AUGUST

Date	Day	Time	m	Time	m	Time	m	Time	m	Moon
1	M	0440	4.0	1045	2.0	1709	4.2	2328	1.9	
2	TU	0531	4.1	1137	1.9	1751	4.4			
3	W	0014	1.6	0612	4.3	1220	1.7	1825	4.6	
4	TH	0054	1.4	0646	4.5	1257	1.5	1855	4.7	
5	F	0129	1.2	0718	4.6	1330	1.4	1923	4.8	●
6	SA	0202	1.1	0747	4.7	1402	1.3	1950	4.9	
7	SU	0233	1.0	0816	4.7	1433	1.2	2018	4.9	
8	M	0303	1.0	0845	4.6	1503	1.2	2046	4.9	
9	TU	0333	1.1	0916	4.6	1534	1.3	2117	4.7	
10	W	0403	1.2	0950	4.4	1607	1.4	2151	4.6	
11	TH	0437	1.3	1029	4.3	1644	1.6	2231	4.4	
12	F	0515	1.5	1119	4.1	1728	1.8	2322	4.2	
13	SA	0601	1.8	1227	4.0	1823	2.0			◐
14	SU	0037	4.0	0702	2.0	1348	3.9	1938	2.2	
15	M	0212	3.9	0830	2.1	1506	4.0	2113	2.1	
16	TU	0341	4.0	1003	2.0	1615	4.3	2236	1.8	
17	W	0453	4.3	1110	1.7	1712	4.7	2337	1.3	
18	TH	0548	4.7	1202	1.3	1759	5.1			
19	F	0029	0.9	0633	5.0	1249	1.0	1842	5.4	○
20	SA	0116	0.5	0715	5.2	1333	0.7	1923	5.7	
21	SU	0200	0.2	0755	5.3	1414	0.5	2004	5.7	
22	M	0241	0.2	0835	5.2	1455	0.5	2045	5.6	
23	TU	0321	0.3	0915	5.0	1535	0.7	2128	5.3	
24	W	0401	0.6	0957	4.7	1616	1.0	2214	4.9	
25	TH	0440	1.0	1044	4.4	1700	1.4	2310	4.4	
26	F	0523	1.5	1146	4.1	1750	1.9			◑
27	SA	0024	4.0	0611	2.0	1310	3.9	1858	2.2	
28	SU	0152	3.8	0721	2.4	1443	3.8	2045	2.4	
29	M	0320	3.7	0912	2.5	1600	3.9	2224	2.2	
30	TU	0429	3.9	1036	2.3	1654	4.2	2318	1.9	
31	W	0518	4.1	1125	2.0	1733	4.4	2359	1.6	

Chart Datum: 2·75 metres below Ordnance Datum (Newlyn)

TIME ZONE (UT)
For Summer Time add ONE hour in **non-shaded areas**

SCOTLAND – ULLAPOOL

LAT 57°54′N LONG 5°10′W

TIMES AND HEIGHTS OF HIGH AND LOW WATERS

SPRING & NEAP TIDES
Dates in red are SPRINGS
Dates in blue are NEAPS

YEAR **2005**

SEPTEMBER

Date	Day	Time	m	Time	m	Time	m	Time	m
1	TH	0555	4.3	1203	1.8	1805	4.6		
2	F	0033	1.4	0625	4.6	1237	1.5	1832	4.8
3	SA	0105	1.1	0652	4.7	1308	1.3	● 1857	5.0
4	SU	0135	1.0	0719	4.8	1337	1.1	1922	5.1
5	M	0204	0.9	0745	4.9	1406	1.0	1947	5.1
6	TU	0232	0.8	0811	4.9	1435	1.0	2014	5.1
7	W	0300	0.9	0840	4.8	1505	1.1	2044	4.9
8	TH	0329	1.0	0911	4.7	1537	1.2	2116	4.8
9	F	0401	1.2	0948	4.5	1613	1.5	2155	4.5
10	SA	0437	1.5	1035	4.3	1656	1.8	2248	4.2
11	SU	0522	1.9	1146	4.1	1751	2.1	◐	
12	M	0018	3.9	0626	2.2	1325	4.0	1915	2.3
13	TU	0211	3.8	0816	2.4	1452	4.1	2112	2.2
14	W	0344	4.0	1000	2.1	1604	4.4	2233	1.7
15	TH	0449	4.4	1101	1.7	1658	4.8	2328	1.2
16	F	0536	4.8	1148	1.3	1742	5.2		
17	SA	0014	0.7	0616	5.1	1231	0.9	1821	5.6
18	SU	0056	0.4	0652	5.3	1311	0.6	○ 1900	5.8
19	M	0136	0.2	0728	5.4	1350	0.5	1937	5.8
20	TU	0214	0.2	0803	5.3	1429	0.5	2016	5.6
21	W	0250	0.4	0838	5.1	1507	0.7	2055	5.2
22	TH	0327	0.8	0915	4.8	1546	1.1	2138	4.8
23	F	0403	1.2	0954	4.5	1627	1.5	2230	4.3
24	SA	0442	1.7	1045	4.1	1715	2.0	2348	3.9
25	SU	0526	2.2	1220	3.9	1821	2.4	◑	
26	M	0122	3.7	0632	2.6	1406	3.8	2020	2.5
27	TU	0254	3.7	0843	2.7	1530	3.9	2202	2.3
28	W	0405	3.9	1013	2.4	1626	4.1	2252	2.0
29	TH	0452	4.1	1059	2.1	1704	4.4	2329	1.7
30	F	0526	4.4	1135	1.8	1735	4.6		

OCTOBER

Date	Day	Time	m	Time	m	Time	m	Time	m
1	SA	0002	1.4	0555	4.6	1207	1.5	1801	4.8
2	SU	0033	1.1	0621	4.8	1237	1.3	1826	5.0
3	M	0102	0.9	0647	5.0	1307	1.1	● 1851	5.2
4	TU	0130	0.8	0712	5.1	1336	1.0	1917	5.2
5	W	0158	0.8	0740	5.1	1406	1.0	1945	5.2
6	TH	0227	0.9	0809	5.1	1438	1.0	2017	5.0
7	F	0258	1.0	0842	4.9	1512	1.2	2053	4.8
8	SA	0332	1.3	0921	4.7	1551	1.4	2138	4.5
9	SU	0411	1.6	1011	4.4	1637	1.8	2243	4.2
10	M	0500	2.0	1131	4.2	1738	2.1	◐	
11	TU	0031	3.9	0612	2.4	1312	4.1	1915	2.2
12	W	0211	3.9	0816	2.4	1436	4.2	2107	2.0
13	TH	0334	4.2	0946	2.1	1545	4.5	2217	1.6
14	F	0433	4.5	1041	1.7	1637	4.9	2308	1.1
15	SA	0516	4.9	1126	1.3	1720	5.3	2351	0.8
16	SU	0554	5.2	1208	0.9	1759	5.5		
17	M	0031	0.5	0628	5.3	1248	0.7	○ 1836	5.6
18	TU	0109	0.4	0701	5.4	1326	0.6	1913	5.6
19	W	0145	0.5	0734	5.3	1404	0.7	1951	5.4
20	TH	0221	0.8	0808	5.2	1442	1.0	2030	5.1
21	F	0256	1.1	0842	4.9	1521	1.3	2112	4.7
22	SA	0331	1.5	0920	4.6	1602	1.7	2204	4.3
23	SU	0409	1.9	1005	4.3	1649	2.0	2315	3.9
24	M	0453	2.3	1120	4.0	1751	2.4		
25	TU	0041	3.7	0552	2.6	1307	3.9	◑ 1929	2.5
26	W	0206	3.7	0742	2.8	1436	3.9	2110	2.3
27	TH	0319	3.9	0922	2.6	1539	4.1	2207	2.1
28	F	0411	4.1	1016	2.3	1623	4.3	2248	1.8
29	SA	0449	4.3	1055	1.9	1656	4.5	2323	1.5
30	SU	0520	4.6	1129	1.7	1725	4.8	2354	1.3
31	M	0548	4.8	1202	1.4	1752	5.0		

NOVEMBER

Date	Day	Time	m	Time	m	Time	m	Time	m
1	TU	0025	1.1	0615	5.0	1234	1.2	1820	5.1
2	W	0056	1.0	0643	5.2	1307	1.1	● 1851	5.2
3	TH	0128	0.9	0714	5.2	1341	1.0	1924	5.2
4	F	0201	1.0	0747	5.2	1417	1.1	2002	5.0
5	SA	0236	1.1	0825	5.1	1456	1.2	2047	4.8
6	SU	0315	1.4	0910	4.9	1540	1.4	2143	4.5
7	M	0359	1.7	1009	4.6	1633	1.7	2300	4.3
8	TU	0454	2.1	1128	4.4	1740	1.9		
9	W	0030	4.1	0612	2.3	1253	4.3	◐ 1911	2.0
10	TH	0154	4.1	0753	2.3	1410	4.4	2040	1.8
11	F	0309	4.3	0912	2.1	1517	4.6	2147	1.5
12	SA	0407	4.5	1011	1.7	1611	4.9	2239	1.3
13	SU	0452	4.8	1059	1.4	1657	5.1	2324	1.0
14	M	0531	5.0	1144	1.2	1739	5.3		
15	TU	0005	0.9	0606	5.2	1226	1.0	1818	5.3
16	W	0044	0.9	0640	5.2	1306	1.0	○ 1856	5.3
17	TH	0121	1.0	0714	5.2	1346	1.1	1935	5.1
18	F	0157	1.1	0748	5.1	1425	1.2	2016	4.9
19	SA	0232	1.4	0824	5.0	1504	1.4	2059	4.6
20	SU	0309	1.7	0901	4.7	1545	1.7	2146	4.3
21	M	0347	1.9	0944	4.5	1630	1.9	2242	4.1
22	TU	0429	2.2	1038	4.3	1723	2.2	2347	3.9
23	W	0521	2.5	1152	4.1	1830	2.3	◑	
24	TH	0057	3.8	0631	2.6	1314	4.0	1948	2.3
25	F	0209	3.9	0758	2.6	1426	4.0	2058	2.2
26	SA	0311	4.0	0909	2.4	1522	4.2	2152	2.0
27	SU	0400	4.2	1002	2.2	1607	4.4	2235	1.8
28	M	0439	4.5	1046	1.9	1644	4.6	2313	1.5
29	TU	0513	4.7	1125	1.7	1720	4.8	2350	1.3
30	W	0546	4.9	1203	1.5	1755	4.9		

DECEMBER

Date	Day	Time	m	Time	m	Time	m	Time	m
1	TH	0026	1.2	0620	5.1	1243	1.3	● 1833	5.1
2	F	0104	1.1	0657	5.3	1323	1.1	1915	5.1
3	SA	0143	1.1	0736	5.3	1405	1.1	2001	5.0
4	SU	0224	1.2	0820	5.3	1450	1.1	2053	4.9
5	M	0308	1.4	0910	5.1	1539	1.3	2151	4.7
6	TU	0357	1.6	1007	4.9	1634	1.4	2257	4.5
7	W	0453	1.9	1113	4.8	1736	1.6		
8	TH	0007	4.3	0559	2.0	1224	4.6	◐ 1845	1.7
9	F	0120	4.3	0714	2.1	1334	4.6	1958	1.7
10	SA	0231	4.3	0828	2.1	1442	4.6	2106	1.7
11	SU	0335	4.4	0935	1.9	1544	4.7	2206	1.6
12	M	0428	4.6	1033	1.7	1638	4.8	2258	1.5
13	TU	0513	4.8	1125	1.6	1726	4.9	2344	1.4
14	W	0553	4.9	1212	1.4	1809	4.9		
15	TH	0026	1.4	0630	5.0	1256	1.4	○ 1850	4.9
16	F	0105	1.4	0705	5.1	1336	1.3	1930	4.9
17	SA	0142	1.4	0740	5.1	1416	1.4	2009	4.8
18	SU	0218	1.5	0814	5.0	1454	1.4	2047	4.7
19	M	0254	1.6	0849	4.9	1532	1.6	2126	4.5
20	TU	0331	1.8	0925	4.7	1611	1.7	2207	4.3
21	W	0409	1.9	1004	4.6	1653	1.8	2252	4.2
22	TH	0450	2.1	1051	4.4	1738	2.0	2347	4.0
23	F	0538	2.3	1148	4.2	1831	2.1	◑	
24	SA	0050	3.9	0635	2.4	1256	4.1	1931	2.2
25	SU	0157	3.9	0743	2.4	1405	4.1	2036	2.2
26	M	0259	4.1	0853	2.4	1506	4.2	2138	2.0
27	TU	0353	4.3	0956	2.2	1602	4.3	2232	1.9
28	W	0440	4.5	1051	2.0	1653	4.5	2320	1.7
29	TH	0524	4.8	1140	1.7	1741	4.7		
30	F	0005	1.5	0605	5.0	1227	1.4	1827	4.9
31	SA	0050	1.3	0647	5.3	1314	1.1	● 1914	5.1

Chart Datum: 2·75 metres below Ordnance Datum (Newlyn)

9.8.9 PORTREE

Skye (Highland) **57°24'·73N 06°11'·07W** ❀❀❀◊◊✿✿✿

CHARTS AC 2209, 2534; Imray C66; OS 23

TIDES –0445 Dover; ML no data; Duration 0610; Zone 0 (UT)

Standard Port ULLAPOOL (⟵)

Times				Height (metres)			
High Water		Low Water		MHWS	MHWN	MLWN	MLWS
0000	0600	0300	0900	5·2	3·9	2·1	0·7
1200	1800	1500	2100				
Differences PORTREE (Skye)							
–0025	–0025	–0025	–0025	+0·1	–0·2	–0·2	0·0
SHIELDAIG (Loch Torridon)							
–0020	–0020	–0015	–0015	+0·4	+0·3	+0·1	0·0
LOCH A'BHRAIGE (Rona)							
–0020	0000	–0010	0000	–0·1	–0·1	–0·1	–0·2
PLOCKTON							
+0005	–0025	–0005	–0010	+0·5	+0·5	+0·5	+0·2
LOCH SNIZORT (Uig Bay, Skye)							
–0045	–0020	–0005	–0025	+0·1	–0·4	–0·2	0·0
LOCH DUNVEGAN (Skye)							
–0105	–0030	–0020	–0040	0·0	–0·1	0·0	0·0
LOCH HARPORT (Skye)							
–0115	–0035	–0020	–0100	–0·1	–0·1	0·0	+0·1
SOAY (Camus nan Gall)							
–0055	–0025	–0025	–0045	–0·4	–0·2	No data	
KYLE OF LOCHALSH							
–0040	–0020	–0005	–0025	+0·1	0·0	0·0	–0·1
DORNIE BRIDGE (Loch Alsh)							
–0040	–0010	–0005	–0020	+0·1	–0·1	0·0	0·0
GLENELG BAY (Kyle Rhea)							
–0105	–0035	–0035	–0055	–0·4	–0·4	–0·9	–0·1
LOCH HOURN							
–0125	–0050	–0040	–0110	–0·2	–0·1	–0·1	+0·1

SHELTER Secure in all but strong SW'lies, when Camas Bàn is more sheltered. In the N of the bay there are 8 HIE Øs for <15 tons. Short stay pontoon on pier.

NAVIGATION WPT 57°24'·58N 06°10'·07W, 275° to pier, 0·72M. From the S, avoid rks off An Tom Pt (1·5M to E, off chartlet).

LIGHTS AND MARKS Only lts are a SHM buoy Fl G 5s marking Sgeir Mhór, 2 FR (vert) 6m 4M (occas) on the pier and a SPM buoy Fl Y 5s.

R/T VHF Ch 16 12 (occas).

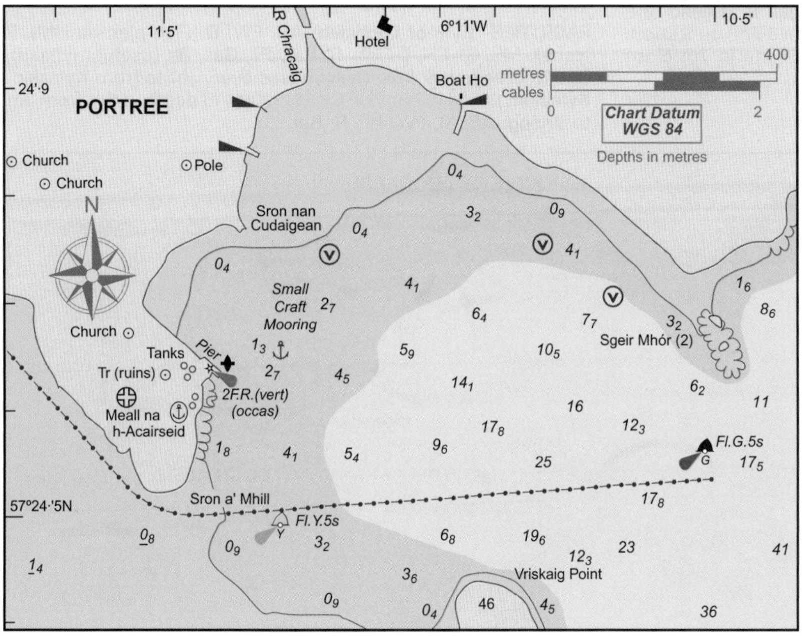
11·5'
6°11'W
10·5'
24'·9
PORTREE
R Chracaig
Hotel
Boat Ho
metres
cables
400
Chart Datum WGS 84
Depths in metres
Church
Church
Pole
Sron nan Cudaigean
Small Craft Mooring
Church
Tanks
Pier
Tr (ruins)
2F.R.(vert) (occas)
Meall na h-Acairseid
Sgeir Mhór (2)
Fl.G.5s
G
Sron a' Mhill
Fl.Y.5s
Y
57°24·5N
Vriskaig Point

TELEPHONE (Dial code 01478) HM ☎ 612926; Moorings 612341; MRSC (01851) 702013; ⊖ (0141) 887 9369; Marinecall 09066 526248; Police 612888; Dr 612013; Ⓗ 612704.

FACILITIES Pier AB £8, D (cans), L, FW. **Town** EC Wed; P, 🛒, Gas, Gaz, ⊡, R, Bar, ✉, Ⓑ, bus to Kyle of Lochalsh, ⇌.

ANCHORAGES AROUND OR NEAR SKYE

LOCH TORRIDON, Highland, **57°36'N 05°49'W**. AC 228. Tides, see 9.8.9. Three large lochs: ent to outer loch (Torridon) is 3M wide, with isolated Sgeir na Trian (2m) almost in mid-chan; ⚓s on SW side behind Eilean Mór and in L Beag. L Sheildaig is middle loch with good ⚓ between the Is and village. 1M to the N, a 2ca wide chan leads into Upper L Torridon; many fish cages and prone to squalls. Few facilities, except Shieldaig: FW, 🛒, R, Bar, ✉, Garage.

LOCH A'BHRAIGE, Rona (Highland), **57°34'·6N 05°57'·9W**. AC 2479, 2534. HW –0438 on Dover; ML 2·8m; Duration 0605. See 9.8.9. A good ⚓ in NW of the island, safe except in NNW winds. Beware rks on NE side up to 1ca off shore. Hbr in NE corner of loch head. Ldg lts 137°, see 9.8.4. Facilities: jetty, FW and a helipad, all owned by MOD (DRA). Before ent, call *Rona* Range Control VHF Ch 13.

Acarseid Mhor is ⚓ on W of Rona. App S of Eilean Garbh marked by W arrow. SD sketch of rks at ent is necessary. FW (cans), showers. At **Churchton Bay**, SW tip of Raasay, there are 4 HIE Øs; ☎ (01478) 612341; Slip, showers, R, ⊡.

LOCH DUNVEGAN, 4 Øs off Stein, **57°30'·9N 06°34'·5W**. 3 Øs off Dunvegan, 57°26'·3N 06°35'·2W. Fuel, FW, R. ☎ (01478) 612341.

LOCH HARPORT, Skye (Highland), **57°20'·6N 06°25'·8W**. AC 1795. HW –0447 (sp), –0527 (np) on Dover. See 9.8.9. On E side of Loch Bracadale, entered between Oronsay Is and Ardtreck Pt (W lt ho, Fl 6s 18m 9M). SW end of Oronsay has conspic rk pillar, called The Castle; keep ¼M off-shore here and off E coast of Oronsay which is joined to Ullinish Pt by drying reef. ⚓ Oronsay Is, N side of drying reef (4m), or on E side, but beware rk (dries) 0·5ca off N shore of Oronsay. Fiskavaig Bay 1M S of Ardtreck (7m); Loch Beag on N side of loch, exposed to W winds; Port na Long E of Ardtreck, sheltered except from E winds (beware fish farm); 1 Ø off the distillery and 2 Ø off *The Old Inn* at Carbost on SW shore. Facilities: EC Wed (Carbost); 🛒, Bar, R, P (garage), ✉, FW. (Port na Long) Bar, FW, 🛒.

SOAY HARBOUR, Skye (Highland), **57°09'·5N 06°13'·4W**. AC 2208. Tides see 9.8.9. Narrow inlet on NW side of Soay; enter from Soay Sound above half flood to clear bar, dries 0·6m. Appr on 135° from 5ca out to avoid reefs close each side of ent. Cross bar slightly E of mid-chan, altering 20° stbd for best water; ent is 15m wide between boulder spits marked by W poles with Or tops. ⚓ in 3m mid-pool or shoal draft boats can enter inner pool. Good shelter and holding. Camas nan Gall (poor holding) has public ☎; no other facilities.

ARMADALE BAY, Skye (Highland), 4M NW of Mallaig. AC 2208. 6 Øs at **57°04'·0N 05°53'·6W**, ☎ (01478) 612341. Bay is sheltered from SE to N winds but subject to swell in winds from N to SE. From S, beware the Eilean Maol and Sgorach rocks. Ferry pier, Oc R 6s 6m 6M, with conspic W shed. Facilities, Skye Yachts ☎ 01471 844216, 📠 844387: M (£5 <10m, £10 >10m), FW at ferry pier or by hose to charter M's, D, 🛒, ⊡, showers, Gas, free pontoon for tenders, ferry to Mallaig for ⇌. Ardvasar ¾ mile: P (cans), Gaz at ¼ mile; R, Bar.

CROWLIN ISLANDS, Highland, **57°21'·1N 05°50'·6W**. AC 2209, 2498. HW –0435 on Dover, –0020 on Ullapool; HW +0·3m on Ullapool. See 9.8.8. ⚓ between Eilean Meadhonach and Eilean Mor, appr from N, keep E of Eilean Beg. Excellent shelter except in strong N winds. There is an inner ⚓ with 3½m but ent chan dries. Eilean Beg lt ho Fl 6s 32m 6M, W tr. No facilities.

8

9.8.10 PLOCKTON

Highland **57°20′·52N 05°38′·47W**

CHARTS AC 2209, 2528; Imray C66; OS 24, 33

TIDES –0435 Dover; ML 3·5m; Duration 0600; See 9.8.9

SHELTER Good, exposed only to N/NE'lies. 5 Y 🅐s or ⚓ in centre of bay in approx 3·5m. Inner part of bay shoals and dries to the SW.

NAVIGATION WPT 57°21′·16N 05°39′·44W; thence track towards Bogha Dubh Sgeir PHM bn, between Cat Is disused ltho and Sgeir Golach PHM bn and High Stone (1m) to the N. Hawk (0.1m) will be cleared when Duncraig Castle bears 158°. Alter S to the ⚓. Beware Plockton Rks (3·1m) on E side of bay.

LIGHTS AND MARKS No lts or buoys. Old lt ho (13m) on Cat Is is conspic, as is Duncraig Castle.

R/T None.

TELEPHONE HM (01599) 534589, 534167, Mobile 07802 367253 (at Kyle of Lochalsh); MRSC (01851) 702013; ⊜ (0141) 887 9369; Marinecall 09066 526248; Police/Dr via HM.

FACILITIES **Village** FW, M £5, L at 24m long pontoon, D (cans), CH, R, Bar, ✉, ⇌, airstrip, (bus to Kyle of Lochalsh).

LOCH CARRON. Strome Narrows are no longer buoyed or lit. At head of loch are 3 Y 🅐s (max LOA 14m) in 3m off drying jetty at 57°23′·95N 05°29′·0W; call ☎ 01520 722321. Appr on 328° between Sgeir Chreagach and Sgeir Fhada.

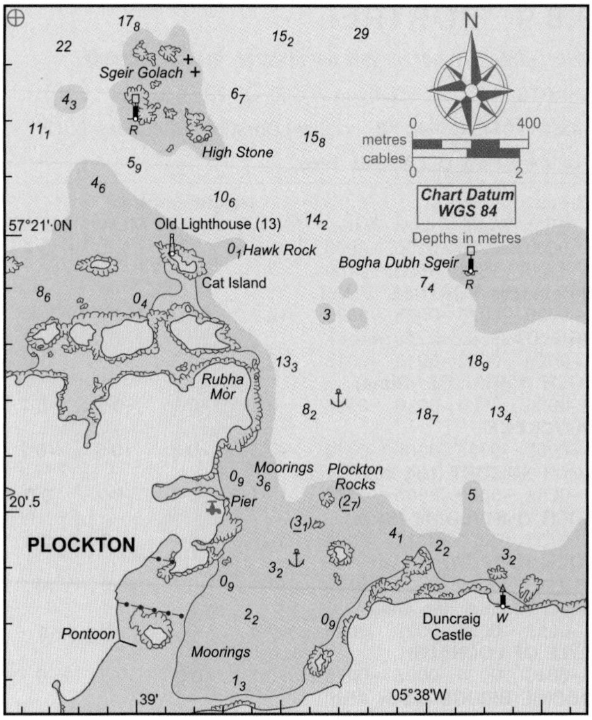
Sgeir Golach
High Stone
Chart Datum WGS 84
Depths in metres
metres
cables
57°21'·0N
Old Lighthouse (13)
Hawk Rock
Bogha Dubh Sgeir
Cat Island
Rubha Mòr
Moorings
Plockton Rocks
Pier
20'.5
PLOCKTON
Pontoon
Moorings
Duncraig Castle
39'
05°38'W

9.8.11 LOCH ALSH

Highland **57°16′·68N 05°42′·87W**

CHARTS AC 2540, 2541; Imray C66; OS 33

TIDES –0450 Dover; ML 3·0m; Duration 0555; See 9.8.9

SHELTER **Kyle (of Lochalsh):** AB on Railway Pier, with FVs, or on 40m L-shaped pontoon (seasonal), close W of Railway Pier; or ⚓ off the hotel there in 11m. **Kyleakin:** 4 free 🅐s are subject to tidal stream. Lit pontoon on NW side of hbr.

⚓s, safe depending on winds, are (clockwise from Kyle): Avernish B, (2ca N of Racoon Rk) in 3m clear of power cables, open to SW; NW of Eilean Donnan Cas (conspic); in Ratagan B at head of L Duich in 7m; in Totaig B facing Loch Long ent in 3·5m; on S shore in Ardintoul B in 5·5m; at head of Loch na Béiste in 7m close inshore and W of fish cages.

NAVIGATION WPT (from Inner Sound) 57°16′·98N 05°45′·77W, 303°/123° from/to bridge, 7½ca. Chan to bridge is marked by 2 PHM and 2 SHM lt buoys. Bridge to Skye, 30m clearance, is lit Oc 6s in centre of main span, Iso R 4s on S pier and Iso G4s on N pier. The secondary NE span is lit, but has only 4.5m clearance.

LIGHTS AND MARKS Lts/marks as chartlet. Direction of buoyage is N in Kyle Rhea, thence E up Loch Alsh; but W through Kyle Akin and the bridge, ie SHMs are on N side of chan.

R/T VHF Ch 11 16. Sky br VHF Ch 12.

TELEPHONE (Dial code 01599) HM 534589, 534167, Mobile 07802 367253; MRSC (01851) 702013; ⊜ (0141) 887 9369; Marinecall 09066 526248; Police, Dr, Ⓗ : via HM. Sky br ☎ 534844, 534969.

FACILITIES **Kyle of Lochalsh**: AB, FW, D (Fish pier via HM), P (cans), ME, Ⓔ, CH, ✉, Ⓑ, R, Bar, Gas, ⇌ (useful railhead), Bus to Glasgow & Inverness; buses every ½hr to/from Kyleakin. **Kyleakin:** ☎ 534167 or VHF Ch 11, 120m AB depth varies from 3m to drying: AB, M, FW, R, Bar.

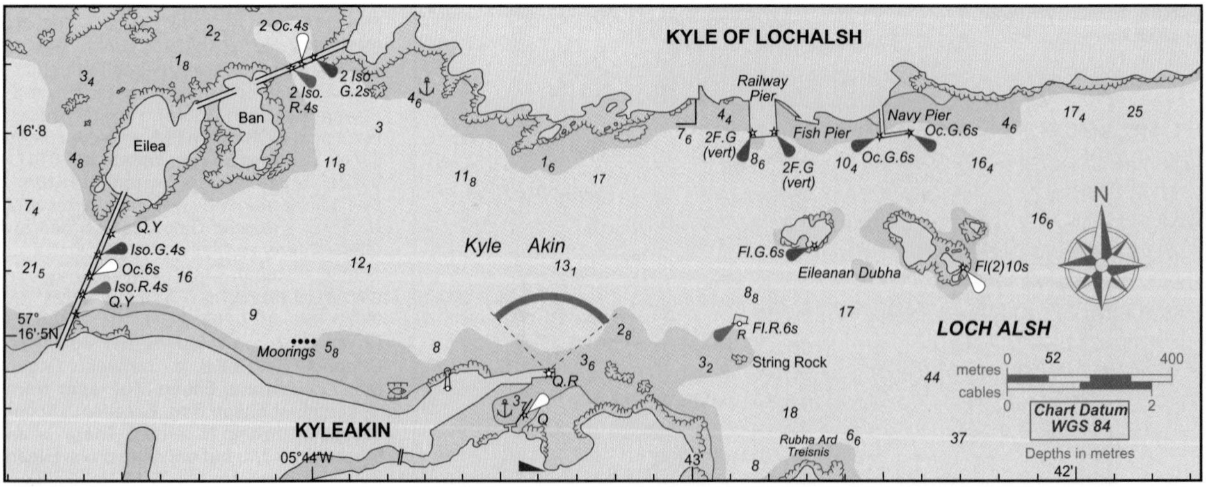
KYLE OF LOCHALSH
2 Oc.4s
2 Iso. G.2s
2 Iso. R.4s
Ban
Eilea
16'·8
Railway Pier
2F.G (vert)
Fish Pier
2F.G (vert)
Navy Pier
Oc.G.6s
Oc.G.6s
Q.Y
Iso.G.4s
Oc.6s
Iso.R.4s
Q.Y
Kyle Akin
Fl.G.6s
Eileanan Dubha
Fl(2)10s
57° 16'·5N
Moorings
Fl.R.6s
String Rock
LOCH ALSH
Q.R
Q
metres
cables
Chart Datum WGS 84
KYLEAKIN
05°44'W
43'
Rubha Ard Treisnis
Depths in metres
42'

ANCHORAGES IN THE SOUND OF SLEAT (see also 9.8.9)

SOUND OF SLEAT: There are ⚓s at: **Glenelg Bay (57°12'·57N 05°37'·95W)** SW of pier out of the tide, but only moderate holding. Usual facilities in village. At **Sandaig Bay** (57°10'·0N 05°41'·4W), exposed to SW. Sandaig Is are to NW of the bay; beware rks off Sgeir nan Eun. Eilean Mór has lt Fl 6s. At **Isleornsay Hbr** (57°09'N 05°48'W) 2ca N of pier, 2FR (vert) and floodlit. Give drying N end of Ornsay Is a wide berth. Lts: SE tip of Ornsay, Oc 8s 18m 15M, W tr; N end, Fl R 6s 8m 4M. Facilities: FW, ✉, Hotel.

LOCH HOURN, Highland, **57°08'N 05°42'W**. AC 2208, 2541. Tides see 9.8.9. Ent is S of Sandaig Is and opposite Isle Ornsay, Skye. Loch extends 11M inland via 4 narrows to Loch Beag; it is scenically magnificent, but violent squalls occur in strong winds. Sgeir Ulibhe, drying 2·1m, bn, lies almost in mid-ent; best to pass S of it to clear Clansman Rk, 2·1m, to the N. ⚓s on N shore at Eilean Ràrsaidh and Camas Bàn, within first 4M. For pilotage further E, consult SDs. Facilities at Arnisdale (Camas Bàn): FW, 🛒, R, Bar, ✉. Doune Marine (01687 462667) FW, D.

LOCH NEVIS, Highland, **57°02'·2N 05°43'·3W**. AC 2208, 2541. HW –0515 on Dover. See 9.8.9. Beware rks Bogha cas Sruth (dries 1·8m), Bogha Don and Sgeirean Glasa both marked by bns. ⚓ NE of Eilean na Glaschoille, good except in S winds; or 9 Or Ⓥs off Inverie, £5 (free if dining), 10m max LOA. Call *Old Forge* VHF Ch 16, 12; FW, Bar, R, showers, ▣. In strong winds expect violent unpredictable squalls. Enter the inner loch with caution, and ⚓ N or SE of Eilean Maol.

ANCHORAGES IN THE SMALL ISLANDS

CANNA, The Small Islands, **57°03'·3N 06°29'·4W**. AC 1796, 2208. HW –0457 (Sp), –0550 (Np) on Dover; HW –0035 and –0·4m on Ullapool; Duration 0605. Good shelter, except in strong E'lies, in hbr between Canna and Sanday Is but holding is poor due to kelp. Appr along Sanday shore, keeping N of Sgeir a' Phuirt, dries 4·6m. Ldg marks as in SDs. ⚓ in 3 - 4m W of Canna pier, off which beware drying rky patch. ⚓ Lt is advised due to FVs. Conspic W lt bn, Fl 6s 32m 9M, vis 152°-061°, at E end of Sanday Is. Magnetic anomaly off NE Canna. Facilities: FW, shower at farm, R(☎01687 462937) with limited 🛒, ✉, Note: NT manage island.

RUM, The Small Islands, **57°00'·1N 06°15'·7W**. AC 2207, 2208. HW –0500 on Dover; –0035 and –0·3m on Ullapool; ML 2·4m; Duration 0600. SNH owns Is. The mountains (809m) are unmistakeable. Landing is only allowed at L Scresort on E side; no dogs beyond village limit. Beware drying rks 1ca off N point of ent and almost 3ca off S point. The head of the loch dries 2ca out; ⚓ off slip on S side or further in, to NE of jetty. Hbr is open to E winds/swell. Facilities: Hotel, ✉, FW, 🛒 (limited), R, Bar, ferry to Mallaig.

EIGG HARBOUR, The Small Islands, **56°52'·6N 06°07'·6W**. AC 2207. HW –0523 on Dover. See 9.8.12. Coming from N or E enter between Garbh Sgeir and Flod Sgeir (bn, ○ top-mark), drying rks. An Sgùrr is a conspic 391m high peak/ridge brg 290°/1·3M from pier. New pier works (2003). Most of hbr dries, but good ⚓ 1ca NE of Galmisdale Pt pier, except in NE winds when yachts should go through the narrows and ⚓ in South Bay in 6-8m; tide runs hard in the narrows. Also ⚓ in 2·5m at Poll nam Partan, about 2ca N of Flod Sgeir. SE point of Eilean Chathastail Fl 6s 24m 8M, vis 181°-shore, W tr. VHF Ch 08 *Eigg Hbr*. HM ☎ via (01687) 482428. FW, repairs. **Pierhead** Showers, ✉, R, 🛒, Gas. **Cleadale village** (2M to N) Bar.

MUCK, The Small Islands, **56°49'·8N 06°13'·3W**. AC 2207. Tides approx as Eigg, 9.8.12. Port Mór at SE end is the main hbr, with a deep pool inside offlying rks, but open to S'lies. Approach: Dir lt Fl WRG 3s 7m vis 1M by day leads between Dubh Sgeir (Fl(2) R 10s) and Bogha Ruadh (Fl G 5s) rks; see 9.8.4. ⚓ towards the NW side of inlet; NE side has drying rks. To N of Is, Bagh a' Ghallanaich is ⚓ protected from S; ent needs SDs and careful identification of marks. Few facilities.

9.8.12 MALLAIG

Highland **57°00'·47N 05°49'·47W** ❀❀❀◊◊◊✿✿

CHARTS AC 2208, 2541; Imray C65, C66; OS 40

TIDES –0515 Dover; ML 2·9; Duration 0605; Zone 0 (UT)

Standard Port OBAN (⟶)

Times				Height (metres)			
High Water		Low Water		MHWS	MHWN	MLWN	MLWS
0000	0600	0100	0700	4·0	2·9	1·8	0·7
1200	1800	1300	1900				
Differences MALLAIG							
+0017	+0017	+0017	+0017	+1·0	+0·7	+0·3	+0·1
INVERIE BAY (Loch Nevis)							
+0030	+0020	+0035	+0020	+1·0	+0·9	+0·2	0·0
BAY OF LAIG (Eigg)							
+0015	+0030	+0040	+0005	+0·7	+0·6	–0·2	–0·2
LOCH MOIDART							
+0015	+0015	+0040	+0020	+0·8	+0·6	–0·2	–0·2
LOCH EATHARNA (Coll)							
+0025	+0010	+0015	+0025	+0·4	+0·3	No data	
GOTT BAY (Tiree)							
0000	+0010	+0005	+0010	0·0	+0·1	0·0	0·0

SHELTER Good in SW'lies but open to N. Access H24. ⚓ in SE part of hbr or find a berth on Fish Pier. No Ⓥs. Hbr is often full of FVs; also Skye ferry.

NAVIGATION WPT 57°00'·75N 05°49'·49W, 191° to Steamer Pier lt, 540m, passing E of Sgeir Dhearg lt bn. The former W chan is now permanently closed to navigation.

LIGHTS AND MARKS As chartlet & 9.8.4. Town lts may obscure Sgeir Dhearg lt. IPTS (3 FR vert at pier hd) indicate ferries operating, no other traffic allowed except by HM's permission.

R/T Call: *Mallaig Hbr Radio* VHF Ch 09 16 (HO).

TELEPHONE (Dial code 01687) HM 462154, outside office hrs 462411; MRSC (01851) 702013; ⊜ (0141) 887 9369; Marinecall 09066 526248; Police 462177.

FACILITIES Hbr AB £6 whenever alongside for FW/fuel/stores (⚓ is free), M, P (cans), D, FW, ME, El, ⚒, C (mobile 10 ton), CH, Ⓔ, ACA, Slip; a busy FV hbr, yacht berths may be provided at a later date near root of the Fish Pier. **Town** EC Wed; Dr 462202. 🛒, R, Gas, Gaz, Bar, ✉, Ⓑ, ⇌.

ADJACENT ANCHORAGE

ARISAIG, (Loch nan Ceall), Highland, **56°53'·64N 05°55'·77W** (ent). AC 2207. HW –0515 on Dover; +0030 and +0·9m on Oban. S side of ent is identifiable by W mark on Rubh' Arisaig. SDs essential. S Chan is winding, but marked by 8 perches; each must be identified. Appr HW±4 to avoid strongest streams LW±1½. Caution: many unmarked rks; no lts. Sheltered ⚓ at head of loch, clear of moorings. Call **Arisaig Marine** ☎ (01687) 450224, 📠 450678, VHF Ch 16, M; few Ⓥs, C (10 ton), CH, D & FW at ferry pier (HW), P (cans), El, ME, ⚒, Slip. **Village** EC Thurs; FW at hotel, Bar, ✉, R, Gas, 🛒, ⇌.

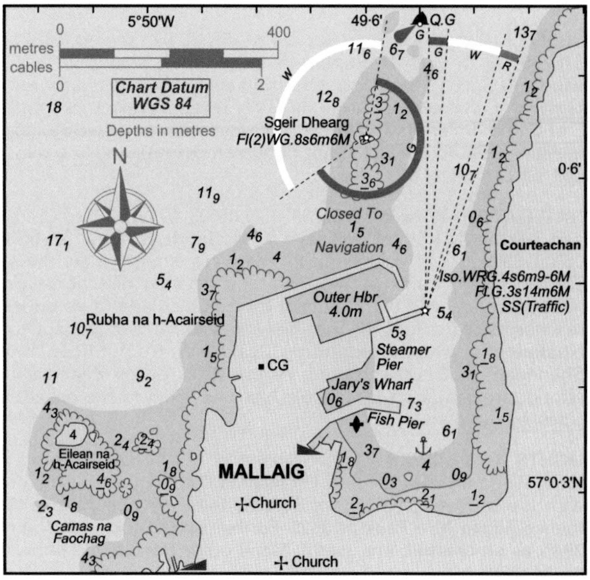
5°50'W
49·6'
Q.G
metres
cables
400
Chart Datum
WGS 84
Depths in metres
N
Sgeir Dhearg
Fl(2)WG.8s6m6M
Closed To
Navigation
Courteachan
Iso.WRG.4s6m9-6M
Fl.G.3s14m6M
SS(Traffic)
Rubha na h-Acairseid
Outer Hbr
4.0m
Steamer
Pier
CG
Jary's Wharf
Fish Pier
Eilean na
h-Acairseid
MALLAIG
Church
Camas na
Faochag
Church
57°0·3'N
0·6'

9.8.13 LOCH SUNART

Highland **56°39'·49N 06°00'·07W** ❁❁◊◊✿✿

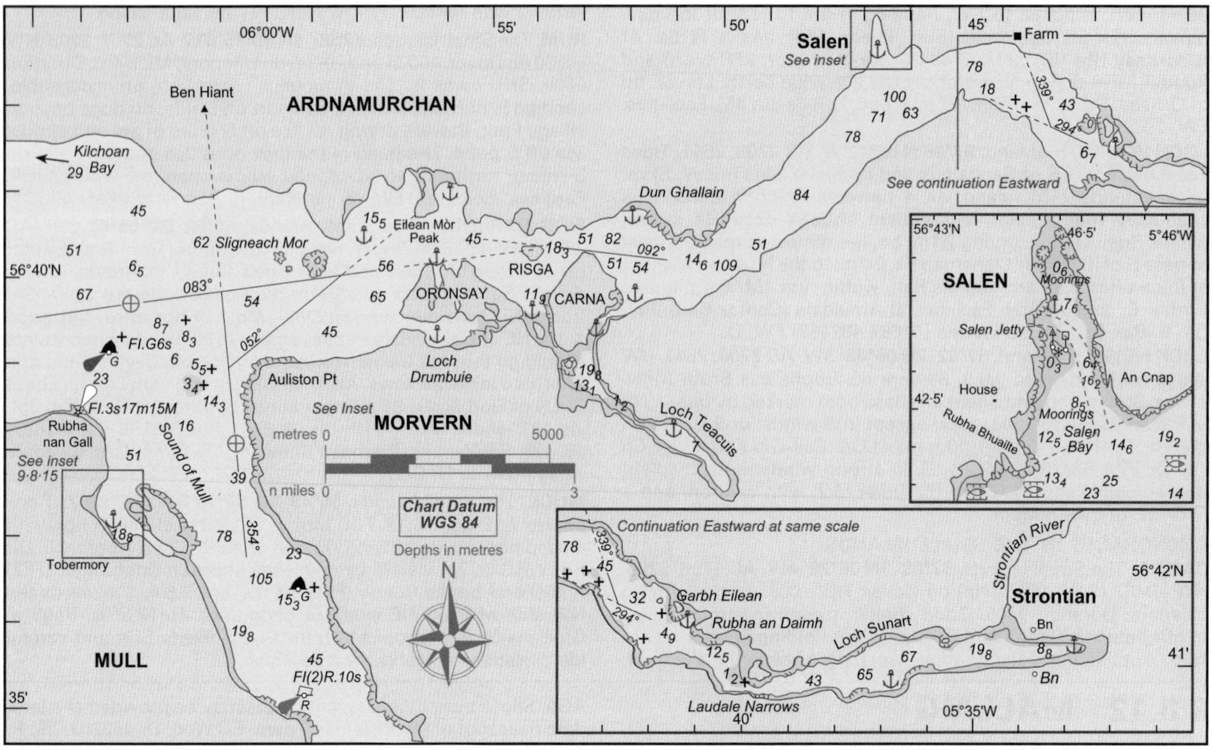
ARDNAMURCHAN
Ben Hiant
Kilchoan Bay
Sligneach Mor
Eilean Mòr Peak
ORONSAY
RISGA
CARNA
Dun Ghallain
Loch Drumbuie
Auliston Pt
See Inset
MORVERN
Loch Teacuis
Rubha nan Gall
See inset 9·8·15
Tobermory
Sound of Mull
MULL
Fl.G6s
Fl.3s17m15M
Fl(2)R.10s
Chart Datum WGS 84
Depths in metres
metres 0 5000
n miles 0 3
Salen
See inset
Farm
See continuation Eastward
SALEN
Salen Jetty
Moorings
House
Rubha Bhuaile
An Cnap
Salen Bay
Continuation Eastward at same scale
Garbh Eilean
Rubha an Daimh
Loch Sunart
Strontian River
Strontian
Laudale Narrows
06°00'W
55'
50'
45'
56°40'N
35'
56°43'N
5°46'W
42·5'
46·5'
56°42'N
41'
05°35'W
40'

CHARTS AC *2171*, 2392, 2394; Imray C65; OS 45, 47, 49

TIDES Salen –0500 Dover; ML 2·0; Zone 0 (UT)

Standard Port OBAN (⟶)

Times				Height (metres)			
High Water		Low Water		MHWS	MHWN	MLWN	MLWS
0100	0700	0100	0800	4·0	2·9	1·8	0·7
1300	1900	1300	2000				
Differences SALEN (Loch Sunart)							
–0015	+0015	+0010	+0005	+0·6	+0·5	–0·1	–0·1

SHELTER 8 Øs at Kilchoan Bay (56°41'·5N 06°07'·3W); ☎ (01972) 510209. ⚓s in Loch Drumbuie (S of Oronsay) sheltered in all winds; in Sailean Mór (N of Oronsay) convenient and easy ent; between Oronsay and Carna; in Loch Teacuis (very tricky ent); E of Carna; Salen Bay, with Øs and jetty, open only to SSE (see facilities); Garbh Eilean (NW of Rubha an Daimh), and E of sand spit by Strontian R.

NAVIGATION West WPT, 56°39'·69N 06°03'·07W, 083° to Creag nan Sgarbh (NW tip of Orinsay), 3·7M. **South WPT**, 56°38'·00N 06°00'·65W, 1M S of Auliston Pt; there are extensive rky reefs, The Stirks W of this pt. AC 2394 and detailed directions are needed to navigate the 17M long loch, particularly in its upper reaches. Beware Ross Rk, S of Risga; Broad Rk, E of Risga; Dun Ghallain Rk; shoals extending 3ca NNW from Eilean mo Shlinneag off S shore; drying rk 1ca W of Garbh Eilean and strong streams at sp in Laudale Narrows. Fish farms on both sides of the loch.

LIGHTS AND MARKS Unlit. Transits as on the chart: from W WPT, Risga on with N tip of Oronsay at 083°; N pt of Carna on with top of Risga 092°. From S WPT, Ben Hiant bearing 354°, thence Eilean Mor Peak at 052°. Further up the loch, 339° and 294°, as on chartlet, are useful. Many other transits are shown on AC 2394.

R/T None, except under Salen Bay below.

TELEPHONE (Dial code 01967) MRSC (01475) 729014; ⊖ (0141) 887 9369; Marinecall 09066 526247; Dr 431231.

FACILITIES SALEN BAY jetty (56°42'·39N 05°46'·17W). ☎ 01967 431333. VHF Ch 16 (occas). Access HW±2 to jetty, keeping on E side of ent to avoid a drying reef on W side; two R Øs (15 ton) £10 (other moorings are private); ⚓ buoy advised as bottom is generally foul. L (£2 unless on Ø), FW, D by hose, ⊐D, Slip, SM, ME, El, CH, Gas, Gaz, Diver, ▣, 🛒, R, Bar. **Acharacle** (2½M), P, 🛒, ✉, Ⓑ (Tues/Wed, mobile), ⇌ (bus to Loch Ailort/Fort William), ✈ (Oban). STRONTIAN FW, P, 🛒, hotel, ✉, Gas, Gaz, Bar. Bus to Fort William.

ANCHORAGES IN COLL AND TIREE (Argyll and Bute)

ARINAGOUR, Loch Eatharna, Coll, **56°37'·0N 06°31'·2W**. AC 2171, 2474. HW –0530 on Dover; ML 1·4m; Duration 0600; see 9.8.12. Good shelter except with SE swell or strong winds from ENE to SSW. Enter at SHM buoy, Fl G 6s, marking Bogha Mòr. Thence NW to Arinagour ferry pier, 2 FR(vert) 10m. Beware McQuarrie's Rk (dries 2·9m) 1ca E of pier hd and unmarked drying rks further N on E side of fairway. Ch and hotel are conspic ahead. Continue N towards old stone pier; ⚓ S of it or pick up a buoy. Six Øs on W side of hbr, between the two piers. Also ⚓ E of Eilean Eatharna. Piermaster ☎ (01879) 230347; VHF Ch 31. **Facilities:** HIE Trading Post ☎ 230349, M, D, FW, Gas, 🛒, CH, R. **Village** ▣, FW, P, ✉, ferry to Oban (⇌).

GOTT BAY, Tiree, **56°30'·74N 06°48'·07W**. AC 2474. Tides as 9.8.12; HW –0540 on Dover. HM ☎ (01879) 230337, VHF Ch 31. Adequate shelter in calm weather, but exposed in winds ENE to S. (in which case use Wilson hbr in Balephetrish Bay IM W, Ldg lts F.G/Oc.G). The bay, at NE end of island, can be identified by conspic latticed tr at Scarinish about 8ca SW of ent, with lt Fl 3s 11m 16M close by (obscd over hbr). Appr on NW track, keeping to SW side of bay which is obstructed on NE side by Soa Is and drying rks. The ferry pier at S side of ent has FR ldg lts 286½°. ⚓ 1ca NW of pier head in 3m on sand; L at pier. Facilities: P & D (cans), Gas, 🛒, R, Bar, ✉ at Scarinish (½M), ferry to Oban (⇌).

9.8.14 TOBERMORY

Mull (Argyll and Bute) **56°37'·19N 06°03'·87W**

CHARTS AC *2171, 2390,* 2474; Imray C65; OS 47

TIDES –0519 Dover; ML 2·4; Duration 0610; Zone 0 (UT)

Standard Port OBAN (⟶)

Times				Height (metres)			
High Water		Low Water		MHWS	MHWN	MLWN	MLWS
0100	0700	0100	0800	4·0	2·9	1·8	0·7
1300	1900	1300	2000				
Differences TOBERMORY (Mull)							
+0025	+0010	+0015	+0025	+0·4	+0·4	0·0	0·0
CARSAIG BAY (S Mull)							
–0015	–0005	–0030	+0020	+0·1	+0·2	0·0	–0·1
IONA (SW Mull)							
–0010	–0005	–0020	+0015	0·0	+0·1	–0·3	–0·2
BUNESSAN (Loch Lathaich, SW Mull)							
–0015	–0015	–0010	–0015	+0·3	+0·1	0·0	–0·1
ULVA SOUND (W Mull)							
–0010	–0015	0000	–0005	+0·4	+0·3	0·0	–0·1

SHELTER Good, but some swell in strong N/NE winds. 22 visitor moorings are marked by a blue buoy with a Y pick-up. ⚓ clear of fairway, where marked; at SE end of The Doirlinn.

NAVIGATION WPT 56°37'·59N 06°03'·17W, 224° to moorings 0·5M. N ent is wide and clear of dangers. S ent via The Doirlinn is only 80m wide at HW, and dries at LW; at HW±2 least depth is 2m. Enter between 2 bns on 300°.

LIGHTS AND MARKS Rhubha nan Gall, Fl 3s 17m 15M, W tr is 1M N of ent. Ch spire and hotel turret are both conspic.

R/T VHF Ch 16 12 (HO), M.

TELEPHONE (Dial code 01688) Piermaster 302017, ⛴ 302660; MRSC (01475) 729014; Local CG 302200; Marinecall 09066 526247; Police 302016; Dr 302013.

FACILITIES **Cal-Mac Pier**, only short stay AB for P, D; landing stage FW £2; **Western Isles YC** ☎ 302371; **Services:** visitor moorings £9 <8m £12 >8m or, 10 nights/£70-£90, ME, CH, ACA, Gaz, Gas, Divers. **Town** EC Wed (winter); FW, P, Dr, 🛒, R, Bar, ✉, Ⓑ, ⇌ (ferry to Oban), ✈ (grass strip; helipad on golf course).

SOUND OF MULL (Mull, **56°31'·44N 05°56'·82W**). Beware drying rks 6ca E of the bay; ent on SE side. **Salen Jetty,** visitor moorings £10. Landing from yacht at ⚓ £1 per person/H24. FW, D. **Village,** 🛒, ME, Ⓔ, CH, R, Dr, ✉. Land at jetty in SW corner.

CRAIGNURE, (Mull, **56°28'·37N 05°42'·25W**) ldg lts 241°, both FR 10/12m. Facilities: 🛒, Bar, ✉, Gas, ferry to Oban. Tides, see 9.8.15.

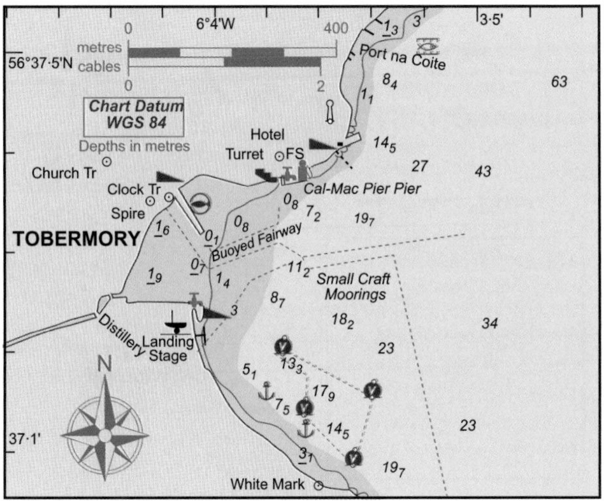
6°4'W
56°37·5'N
37·1'
3·5'
metres
cables
Chart Datum WGS 84
Depths in metres
Port na Coite
Hotel Turret
Church Tr
Clock Tr
Spire
TOBERMORY
Cal-Mac Pier Pier
Buoyed Fairway
Small Craft Moorings
Distillery
Landing Stage
White Mark
N

9.8.15 LOCH ALINE

Highland **56°32'·09N 05°46'·47W**

CHARTS AC *2390*; Imray C65; OS 49

TIDES –0523 Dover; Duration 0610; Zone 0 (UT)

Standard Port OBAN (⟶)

Times				Height (metres)			
High Water		Low Water		MHWS	MHWN	MLWN	MLWS
0100	0700	0100	0800	4·0	2·9	1·8	0·7
1300	1900	1300	2000				
Differences LOCH ALINE							
+0012	+0012	No data		+0·5	+0·3	No data	
SALEN (Sound of Mull)							
+0045	+0015	+0020	+0030	+0·2	+0·2	–0·1	0·0
CRAIGNURE (Sound of Mull)							
+0030	+0005	+0010	+0015	0·0	+0·1	–0·1	–0·1

SHELTER Very good. ⚓s in SE end of loch and in N and E part of loch. Temp berth on the old stone slip in the ent on W side, depth and ferries permitting.

NAVIGATION WPT 56°31'·49N 05°46'·37W, 176° to front ldg bn, 0·9M. Bns (not easily seen) lead 356°, 100m W of Bogha Lurcain, drying rk off Bolorkle Pt on E side of ent. The buoyed ent is easy, but narrow with a bar (min depth 2·1m); stream runs 2½kn at sp. Beware coasters from the sand mine going to/from the jetty (which completely fill the entr) and ferries to/from Mull. Last 5ca of loch dries.

LIGHTS AND MARKS Ardtornish Pt lt ho, 1M SSE of ent, Fl (2) WRG 10s 7m 8/5M. Lts and buoys as chartlet. War memorial (conspic, 9m high) stands on W side of ent. Ldg lts are FW 2/4m (H24). 1M up the loch on E side a Y bn with Y ○ topmark marks a reef, and ½M further up similar bn marks a larger reef on W side. Both top marks need new coat of paint. Clock tr is very conspic at head of loch.

R/T None.

TELEPHONE (Dial code 01967) MRSC (01475) 729014; ⊖ (0141) 887 9369; Marinecall 09066 526247; Ⓗ (01631) 563727; Dr 421252.

FACILITIES **Village** FW at pier, Gas, 🛒, R, Bar, P, ✉, (Ⓑ, ⇌, ✈ at Oban), Ferry to Fishnish Bay (Mull).

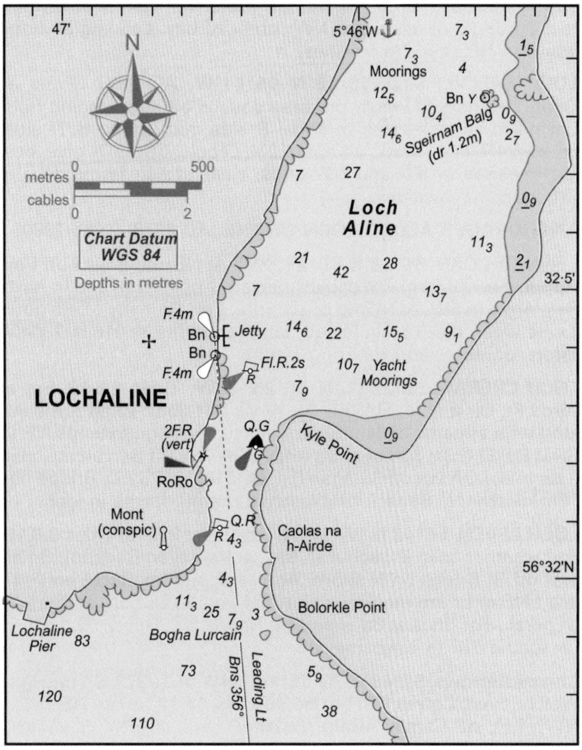
47'
5°46'W
32·5'
56°32'N
N
metres
cables
Chart Datum WGS 84
Depths in metres
Moorings
Bn Y
Sgeirnam Balg (dr 1.2m)
Loch Aline
F.4m
Bn
Jetty
Fl.R.2s
Yacht Moorings
LOCHALINE
2F.R (vert)
Q.G
Kyle Point
RoRo
Mont (conspic)
Q.R
Caolas na h-Airde
Bolorkle Point
Lochaline Pier
Bogha Lurcain
Leading Lt
Bns 356°

ANCHORAGES on WEST and SOUTH COASTS OF MULL (Anti-clockwise from the North. SDs essential)

TRESHNISH ISLES, 56°29'N 06°31'W. AC 2652. The main Is (N to S) are: Cairn na Burgh, Fladda, Lunga, Bac Mòr and Bac Beag. Tides run hard and isles are exposed to swell, but merit a visit in calm weather. Appr with caution on ldg lines as in CCC SDs; temp ⚓ off Lunga's N tip in 4m.

STAFFA, 56°25'·96N 06°20'·34W. AC 2652. Spectacular isle with Fingal's Cave, but same caveats as above. Very temp ⚓ off SE tip where there is landing; beware unmarked rks.

GOMETRA, 56°28'·85N 06°23'W. AC 2652. Tides as 9.8.14. The narrow inlet between Gometra and Ulva Is offers sheltered ⚓, except in S'lies. Appr on 020° between Staffa and Little Colonsay, or N of the former. Beware rks drying 3·2m, to stbd and 5ca S of ent. Inside, E side is cleaner.

LOCH NA KEAL, 56°26'N 06°18'W (ent). AC 2652. Tides in 9.8.14. Appr S of Geasgill Is and N of drying rks off **Inch Kenneth**; E of this Is and in **Sound of Ulva** are sheltered ⚓s, except in S'lies. Beware MacQuarrie's Rk, dries 0·8m.

LOCH LATHAICH, Mull, **56°19'·29N 06°15'·47W.** AC 2617. HW –0545 on Dover; ML 2·4. See 9.8.14. Excellent shelter with easy access; good base for cruising W Mull. Eilean na Liathanaich (a group of islets) lie off the ent, marked by a W bn at the E end, Fl WR 6s 12m 8/6M, R088°-108°, W108°-088°. Keep to W side of loch and ⚓ off Bendoran BY in SW, or SE of Eilean Ban off the pier in approx 5m. **Facilities**: (Bunessan) Shop, ✉, Bar, R, FW.

SOUND OF IONA, 56°19'·45N 06°23'·12W. AC 2617. Tides see 9.8.14. From N, enter in mid-chan; from S keep clear of Torran Rks. Cathedral brg 012° closes the Iona shore past 2 SHM buoys and SCM buoy. Beware a bank 0·1m in mid-sound, between cathedral and Fionnphort; also tel cables and ferries. ⚓ S of ferry close in to Iona, or in Bull Hole. Consult SDs. Crowded in season; limited facilities.

TINKER'S HOLE, Ross of Mull, **56°17'·49N 06°23'·07W.** AC 2617. Beware Torran Rks, reefs extending 5M S and SW of Erraid. Usual app from S, avoiding Rankin's Rks, drying 0·8m, and rk, dries 2·3m, between Eilean nam Muc and Erraid. Popular ⚓ in mid-pool between Eilean Dubh and Erraid.

CARSAIG BAY, Ross of Mull, **56°19'·19N 05°59'·07W.** Tides see 9.8.14. AC 2386. Temp, fair weather ⚓s to N of Gamhnach Mhòr, reef 2m high, or close into NW corner of bay. Landing at stone quay on NE side. No facilities.

LOCH SPELVE, Mull, **56°23'N 05°41'W.** AC 2387. Tides as Oban. Landlocked water, prone to squalls off surrounding hills. Ent narrows to ½ca due to shoal S side and drying rk N side, 56°23'·24N 05°41'·95W, ☆ QG 3m 2M, G pole. CCC SDs give local ldg lines. ⚓s in SW and NW arms, clear of fish farms. Pier at Croggan; no facilities.

ANCHORAGES ALONG LOCH LINNHE (AC 2378, 2379, 2380)

LYNN OF LORN, 56°33'N 05°25'·2W: At NE end are ⚓s off **Port Appin**, clear of ferry and cables (beware Appin Rks); and in **Airds Bay**, open to SW. At NW tip of Lismore, **Port Ramsey** offers good ⚓s between the 3 main islets. **Linnhe Marina** ☎ 01631 730401 offers pontoon and mooring berths.

LOCH CRERAN, 56°32'·14N 05°25'·22W. Tides 9.8.16. Ent at Airds Pt, Dir lt 050°, Fl WRG 2s, W vis 041-058°. Chan turns 90° stbd with streams of 4kn. Sgeir Callich, rky ridge extends NE to SHM By, Fl G 3s; ⚓ W of it. Ⓜs (max LOA 7m) off Barcaldine; also 3 Ⓜs max LOA 9m off Creagan Inn, ☎ (01631) 573250. Bridge has 12m clearance. Beware of extensive marine farms in loch.

LOCH LEVEN, 56°42'N 05°12'W. (see inset 9.8.16) Tides 9.8.16. Fair weather ⚓s in Ballachulish Bay, at Kentallen B (deep), Onich and off St Brides on N shore. App bridge (17m clnce) on 114°; 4ca ENE of br are moorings and ⚓ at Poll an Dùnan, entered W of perch. Facilities at Ballachulish: Hotels, 🛒, R, ✉, Ⓑ. Loch is navigable 7M to Kinlochleven.

Corran Narrows, 56°43'·27N 05°14'·34W. AC 2372. Sp rate 6kn. Well buoyed; Corran Pt lt ho, Iso WRG 4s, and lt bn 5ca NE. ⚓ 5ca NW of Pt, off Camas Aiseig pier/slip.

9.8.16 FORT WILLIAM/CORPACH

Highland 56°48'·99N 05°07'·07W (off Fort William)

CHARTS AC 2372, 2380; Imray C65, C23; OS 41

TIDES –0535 Dover; ML 2·3; Duration 0610; Zone 0 (UT)

Standard Port OBAN (⟶)

Times				**Height (metres)**			
High Water		Low Water		MHWS	MHWN	MLWN	MLWS
0100	0700	0100	0800	4·0	2·9	1·8	0·7
1300	1900	1300	2000				
Differences CORPACH							
0000	+0020	+0040	0000	0·0	0·0	–0·2	–0·2
LOCH EIL (Head)							
+0025	+0045	+0105	+0025		No data		No data
CORRAN NARROWS							
+0007	+0007	+0004	+0004	+0·4	+0·4	–0·1	0·0
LOCH LEVEN (Head)							
+0045	+0045	+0045	+0045		No data		No data
LOCH LINNHE (Port Appin)							
–0005	–0005	–0030	0000	+0·2	+0·2	+0·1	+0·1
LOCH CRERAN (Barcaldine Pier)							
+0010	+0020	+0040	+0015	+0·1	+0·1	0·0	+0·1
LOCH CRERAN (Head)							
+0015	+0025	+0120	+0020	–0·3	–0·3	–0·4	–0·3

SHELTER Exposed to winds SW thro' N to NE. ⚓s off Fort William pier; in Camus na Gall; SSW of Eilean A Bhealaidh; and off Corpach Basin, where there is also a waiting pontoon; or inside the canal where it is more sheltered. The sea lock is normally available HW±4 during canal hrs. For Caledonian Canal see 9.8.17.

NAVIGATION Corpach WPT 56°50'·29N 05°07'·07W, 315° to lock ent, 0·30M. Beware McLean Rk, dries 0·3m, buoyed, 8ca N of Fort William. Lochy Flats dry 3ca off the E bank. In Annat Narrows at ent to Loch Eil streams reach 5kn.

LIGHTS AND MARKS Iso WRG 4s lt is at N jetty of sea-lock ent, W310°-335°. A long pier/viaduct off Ft William is unlit.

R/T Call: *Corpach Lock* VHF Ch **74** 16 (during canal hours).

TELEPHONE (Dial code 01397) HM 772249, ⛴ 772484 (Corpach); MRSC (01475) 729014; ⊖ 702948; Marinecall 09066 526247; Police 702361; Dr 703136.

FACILITIES Fort William. Pier ☎ 703881, AB; **Services**: Slip, L, CH, ACA. **Town** EC Wed; P, ME, El, ⚒, YC, 🛒, R, Bar, Ⓗ, ✉, Ⓑ, ⇌. CORPACH. **Corpach Basin** ☎ 772249, AB, L, FW, D; **Lochaber YC** ☎ 703576, M, FW, L, Slip; **Services:** ME, El, ⚒, D (cans), M, CH, Slip, Divers. **Village** P, 🛒, R, Bar, ✉, Ⓑ, ⇌.

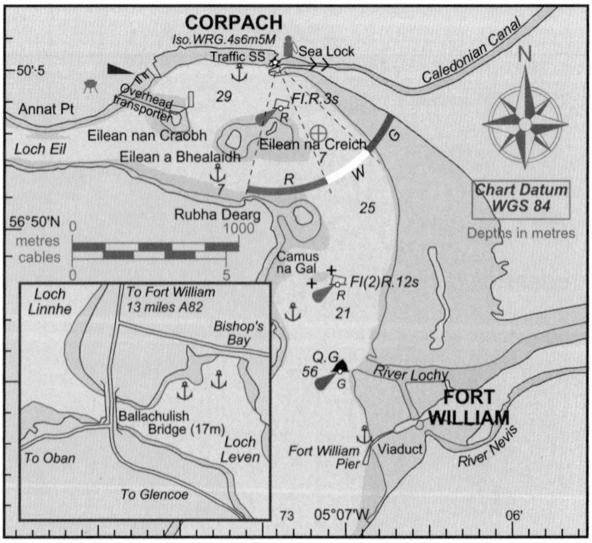
CORPACH
Iso.WRG.4s6m5M
Traffic SS
Sea Lock
Caledonian Canal
N
50'·5
Overhead transporter
29
Fl.R.3s
R
Annat Pt
Eilean nan Craobh
Eilean na Creich
G
Loch Eil
Eilean a Bhealaidh
7
7
R
W
Chart Datum WGS 84
25
Rubha Dearg
56°50'N
0
1000
metres
cables
0
5
Depths in metres
Camus na Gal
Fl(2)R.12s
R
21
Loch Linnhe
To Fort William 13 miles A82
Bishop's Bay
Q.G
56
G
River Lochy
FORT WILLIAM
Ballachulish Bridge (17m)
Loch Leven
To Oban
Fort William Pier
Viaduct
River Nevis
To Glencoe
73
05°07'W
06'

9.8.17 CALEDONIAN CANAL

Highland ❁❁◊◊◊✿✿✿

CHARTS AC 1791; Imray C23; OS 41, 34, 26; *BWB Skippers Guide*

TIDES Tidal differences: Corpach –0455 on Dover; See 9.8.16. Clachnaharry: +0116 on Dover; See 9.7.15.

SHELTER Corpach is at the SW ent of the Caledonian Canal, see 9.8.16; the sea locks at both ends do not open LW±2 at springs. For best shelter transit the sea lock and lie above the double lock. Numerous pontoons along the canal; cost is included in the canal dues. For Inverness see 9.7.15.

NAVIGATION The 60M canal consists of 38M through 3 lochs, (Lochs Lochy, Oich and Ness), connected by 22M through canals. Loch Oich is part of a hydro-electric scheme which may vary the water level. The passage normally takes two full days, possibly longer in the summer; absolute minimum is 14 hrs. Speed limit is 5kn in the canal sections. There are 10 swing bridges; road tfc has priority at peak hrs. Do not pass bridges without the keeper's instructions.

LOCKS There are 29 locks: 14 between Loch Linnhe (Corpach), via Lochs Lochy and Oich up to the summit (106′ above sea level); and 15 locks from the summit down via Loch Ness to Inverness.

2004 information

Hours: 31 Mar to 1 Jun Mon-Sun 0830-1730
2 Jun to 7 Sep Mon-Sun 0800-1730
8 Sep to 2 Nov Mon-Sun 0830-1730
3 Nov to 29 Mar Mon-Sun 0900-1600

Dues payable at Corpach: transit/lock fee Outward £15 per metre for 8 day passage or less; Return £10.50 per metre. £20 per metre is charged for a 2 week sojourn. For regulations and useful booklet *BWB Skipper's Guide* apply: Canal Manager, Canal Office, Seaport Marina, Muirtown Wharf, Inverness IV3 5LE, ☎ (01463) 233140/℻ 710942. www.scottishcanals.co.uk

LIGHTS & MARKS See 9.8.16 and 9.7.15 for ent lts. Channel is marked by posts, cairns and unlit buoys, PHM on the NW side of the chan and SHM on the SE side.

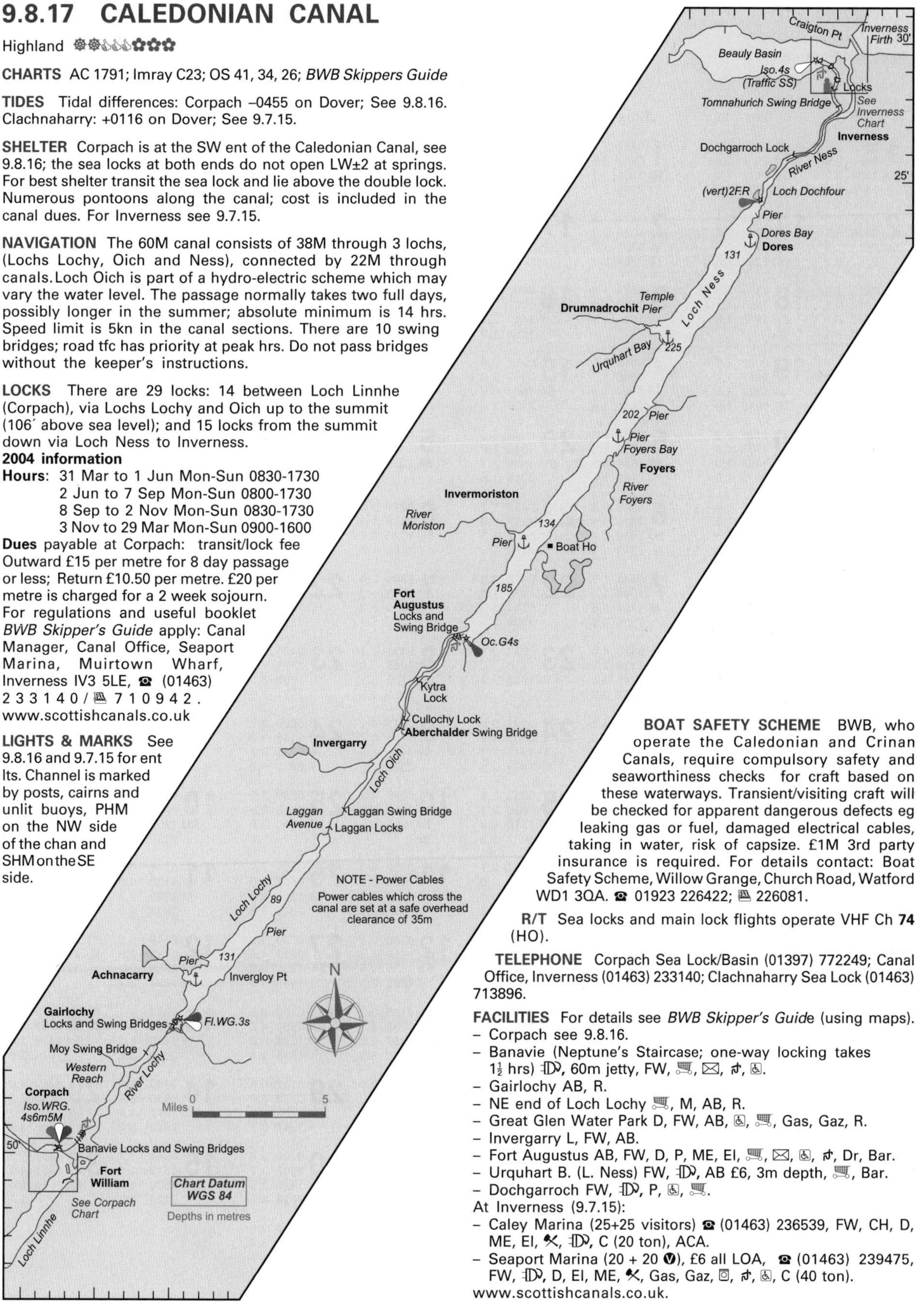
Craigton Pt
Inverness Firth
30'
Beauly Basin
Iso.4s
(Traffic SS)
Locks
Tomnahurich Swing Bridge
See Inverness Chart
Inverness
Dochgarroch Lock
River Ness
25'
(vert)2F.R
Loch Dochfour
Pier
Dores Bay
Dores
131
Temple
Drumnadrochit Pier
Loch Ness
Urquhart Bay
225
202
Pier
Pier
Foyers Bay
Foyers
River Foyers
Invermoriston
River Moriston
134
Pier
Boat Ho
185
Fort Augustus
Locks and Swing Bridge
Oc.G4s
Kytra Lock
Cullochy Lock
Aberchalder Swing Bridge
Invergarry
Loch Oich
Laggan Avenue
Laggan Swing Bridge
Laggan Locks
NOTE - Power Cables
Power cables which cross the canal are set at a safe overhead clearance of 35m
Loch Lochy
89
Pier
Pier
131
Achnacarry
Invergloy Pt
N
Gairlochy
Locks and Swing Bridges
Fl.WG.3s
Moy Swing Bridge
Western Reach
River Lochy
Corpach
Iso.WRG.
4s6m5M
Miles 0 5
50'
Banavie Locks and Swing Bridges
Fort William
See Corpach Chart
Chart Datum
WGS 84
Depths in metres
Loch Linnhe

BOAT SAFETY SCHEME BWB, who operate the Caledonian and Crinan Canals, require compulsory safety and seaworthiness checks for craft based on these waterways. Transient/visiting craft will be checked for apparent dangerous defects eg leaking gas or fuel, damaged electrical cables, taking in water, risk of capsize. £1M 3rd party insurance is required. For details contact: Boat Safety Scheme, Willow Grange, Church Road, Watford WD1 3QA. ☎ 01923 226422; ℻ 226081.

R/T Sea locks and main lock flights operate VHF Ch **74** (HO).

TELEPHONE Corpach Sea Lock/Basin (01397) 772249; Canal Office, Inverness (01463) 233140; Clachnaharry Sea Lock (01463) 713896.

FACILITIES For details see *BWB Skipper's Guide* (using maps).
- Corpach see 9.8.16.
- Banavie (Neptune's Staircase; one-way locking takes 1½ hrs) ⊣D, 60m jetty, FW, 🛒, ✉, ⛽, ♿.
- Gairlochy AB, R.
- NE end of Loch Lochy 🛒, M, AB, R.
- Great Glen Water Park D, FW, AB, ♿, 🛒, Gas, Gaz, R.
- Invergarry L, FW, AB.
- Fort Augustus AB, FW, D, P, ME, EI, 🛒, ✉, ♿, ⛽, Dr, Bar.
- Urquhart B. (L. Ness) FW, ⊣D, AB £6, 3m depth, 🛒, Bar.
- Dochgarroch FW, ⊣D, P, ♿, 🛒.

At Inverness (9.7.15):
- Caley Marina (25+25 visitors) ☎ (01463) 236539, FW, CH, D, ME, EI, ⚒, ⊣D, C (20 ton), ACA.
- Seaport Marina (20 + 20 Ⓥ), £6 all LOA, ☎ (01463) 239475, FW, ⊣D, D, EI, ME, ⚒, Gas, Gaz, ⊡, ⛽, ♿, C (40 ton).

www.scottishcanals.co.uk.

TIME ZONE (UT)
For Summer Time add ONE hour in **non-shaded areas**

SCOTLAND – OBAN

LAT 56°25′N LONG 5°29′W

TIMES AND HEIGHTS OF HIGH AND LOW WATERS

SPRING & NEAP TIDES
Dates in red are SPRINGS
Dates in blue are NEAPS

YEAR **2005**

JANUARY

Date	Day	Time	m	Time	m	Time	m	Time	m	Moon
1	SA	0254	1.5	0850	3.6	1531	1.9	2115	3.3	
2	SU	0332	1.6	0928	3.5	1611	1.9	2157	3.2	
3	M	0416	1.6	1014	3.4	1705	2.0	2248	3.1	◑
4	TU	0509	1.7	1111	3.3	1812	2.0	2355	3.0	
5	W	0613	1.7	1226	3.3	1922	1.9			
6	TH	0124	3.1	0722	1.6	1356	3.4	2028	1.7	
7	F	0244	3.2	0833	1.5	1508	3.5	2127	1.5	
8	SA	0344	3.5	0941	1.3	1605	3.7	2221	1.2	
9	SU	0435	3.8	1043	1.1	1656	3.8	2311	1.0	
10	M	0522	4.0	1139	0.9	1743	3.9	2358	0.8	●
11	TU	0608	4.1	1230	0.7	1827	3.9			
12	W	0045	0.6	0653	4.2	1320	0.7	1910	3.9	
13	TH	0132	0.6	0738	4.2	1407	0.8	1952	3.7	
14	F	0218	0.6	0822	4.0	1454	0.9	2034	3.6	
15	SA	0304	0.8	0907	3.8	1540	1.1	2116	3.4	
16	SU	0352	1.0	0954	3.6	1627	1.4	2159	3.2	
17	M	0441	1.2	1046	3.3	1717	1.6	2249	3.0	◐
18	TU	0536	1.5	1154	3.1	1813	1.8			
19	W	0002	2.9	0641	1.7	1328	3.0	1916	1.9	
20	TH	0134	2.9	0807	1.8	1452	3.0	2025	1.9	
21	F	0247	3.0	0938	1.8	1550	3.1	2130	1.7	
22	SA	0342	3.2	1037	1.7	1629	3.3	2220	1.6	
23	SU	0427	3.4	1121	1.6	1703	3.4	2303	1.4	
24	M	0508	3.6	1158	1.5	1738	3.6	2342	1.2	
25	TU	0546	3.7	1231	1.4	1814	3.7			○
26	W	0019	1.1	0621	3.8	1303	1.3	1848	3.8	
27	TH	0055	1.0	0655	3.9	1334	1.3	1920	3.8	
28	F	0127	1.0	0726	3.9	1403	1.3	1948	3.7	
29	SA	0156	1.1	0755	3.8	1429	1.4	2014	3.6	
30	SU	0224	1.1	0823	3.8	1449	1.5	2043	3.5	
31	M	0256	1.2	0854	3.6	1518	1.6	2117	3.4	

FEBRUARY

Date	Day	Time	m	Time	m	Time	m	Time	m	Moon
1	TU	0335	1.3	0932	3.5	1601	1.7	2159	3.2	
2	W	0424	1.5	1020	3.3	1701	1.8	2254	3.1	◑
3	TH	0527	1.6	1126	3.1	1824	1.9			
4	F	0019	3.0	0648	1.7	1317	3.0	1951	1.8	
5	SA	0228	3.1	0816	1.6	1510	3.2	2109	1.6	
6	SU	0345	3.4	0939	1.4	1616	3.4	2213	1.3	
7	M	0438	3.7	1046	1.1	1704	3.6	2306	0.9	
8	TU	0523	4.0	1139	0.8	1745	3.8	2353	0.6	●
9	W	0605	4.2	1226	0.6	1823	3.9			
10	TH	0037	0.4	0644	4.3	1309	0.5	1859	3.9	
11	F	0120	0.3	0723	4.3	1350	0.6	1934	3.9	
12	SA	0201	0.4	0801	4.2	1428	0.7	2008	3.7	
13	SU	0241	0.6	0837	3.9	1506	0.9	2041	3.5	
14	M	0321	0.8	0913	3.6	1544	1.2	2112	3.3	
15	TU	0402	1.2	0951	3.3	1627	1.5	2147	3.1	
16	W	0448	1.5	1036	3.0	1718	1.7	2232	2.9	◐
17	TH	0545	1.8	1154	2.7	1821	1.9			
18	F	0003	2.7	0707	2.0	1449	2.7	1938	1.9	
19	SA	0227	2.8	0947	2.0	1601	2.9	2108	1.8	
20	SU	0342	3.0	1040	1.8	1632	3.1	2210	1.6	
21	M	0422	3.2	1117	1.5	1657	3.3	2253	1.3	
22	TU	0458	3.5	1148	1.4	1726	3.5	2328	1.1	
23	W	0532	3.7	1216	1.2	1758	3.7			
24	TH	0001	0.9	0605	3.8	1243	1.1	1829	3.8	○
25	F	0033	0.8	0636	3.9	1310	1.0	1857	3.8	
26	SA	0101	0.7	0703	4.0	1335	1.0	1921	3.8	
27	SU	0128	0.7	0728	3.9	1356	1.0	1944	3.7	
28	M	0156	0.8	0754	3.8	1416	1.1	2012	3.6	

MARCH

Date	Day	Time	m	Time	m	Time	m	Time	m	Moon
1	TU	0228	0.9	0825	3.7	1446	1.3	2045	3.5	
2	W	0306	1.1	0900	3.5	1526	1.4	2125	3.3	
3	TH	0354	1.3	0944	3.2	1622	1.6	2218	3.1	◑
4	F	0502	1.6	1049	2.9	1752	1.8	2351	2.9	
5	SA	0638	1.7	1326	2.8	1933	1.8			
6	SU	0234	3.0	0818	1.6	1525	3.0	2100	1.5	
7	M	0343	3.4	0945	1.3	1620	3.3	2205	1.2	
8	TU	0431	3.7	1043	1.0	1700	3.5	2255	0.8	
9	W	0511	4.0	1129	0.7	1734	3.8	2339	0.5	
10	TH	0549	4.2	1210	0.5	1806	3.9			●
11	F	0020	0.3	0624	4.3	1248	0.4	1837	4.0	
12	SA	0100	0.3	0659	4.3	1323	0.5	1908	3.9	
13	SU	0139	0.3	0732	4.1	1357	0.6	1938	3.8	
14	M	0215	0.6	0804	3.9	1431	0.9	2006	3.7	
15	TU	0250	0.9	0835	3.6	1506	1.1	2035	3.5	
16	W	0327	1.2	0908	3.2	1547	1.4	2108	3.2	
17	TH	0411	1.6	0945	2.9	1638	1.7	2149	3.0	◐
18	F	0508	1.9	1042	2.6	1742	1.9	2252	2.7	
19	SA	0633	2.1	1426	2.6	1901	1.9			
20	SU	0219	2.7	0944	2.0	1533	2.8	2037	1.8	
21	M	0333	2.9	1025	1.7	1606	3.0	2145	1.6	
22	TU	0403	3.2	1055	1.5	1631	3.2	2226	1.3	
23	W	0434	3.4	1121	1.2	1700	3.5	2301	1.0	
24	TH	0506	3.7	1146	1.0	1731	3.7	2332	0.8	
25	F	0538	3.8	1210	0.9	1800	3.8			○
26	SA	0001	0.7	0607	4.0	1236	0.8	1826	3.8	
27	SU	0030	0.6	0633	4.0	1301	0.8	1849	3.9	
28	M	0100	0.6	0659	4.0	1324	0.8	1915	3.8	
29	TU	0132	0.6	0728	3.9	1352	0.9	1947	3.7	
30	W	0208	0.8	0802	3.7	1426	1.1	2023	3.5	
31	TH	0250	1.0	0840	3.4	1509	1.3	2107	3.3	

APRIL

Date	Day	Time	m	Time	m	Time	m	Time	m	Moon
1	F	0345	1.3	0927	3.1	1610	1.5	2207	3.0	
2	SA	0504	1.5	1045	2.7	1743	1.7			◑
3	SU	0002	2.9	0640	1.6	1353	2.7	1919	1.6	
4	M	0221	3.1	0822	1.5	1513	2.9	2045	1.4	
5	TU	0323	3.4	0936	1.2	1603	3.2	2147	1.0	
6	W	0409	3.7	1026	0.9	1639	3.5	2235	0.7	
7	TH	0448	4.0	1107	0.7	1709	3.7	2318	0.5	
8	F	0524	4.1	1144	0.6	1739	3.8	2358	0.4	●
9	SA	0559	4.2	1219	0.5	1809	3.9			
10	SU	0037	0.4	0631	4.1	1253	0.6	1839	3.9	
11	M	0114	0.5	0702	4.0	1325	0.7	1908	3.9	
12	TU	0149	0.8	0733	3.8	1359	0.9	1937	3.7	
13	W	0224	1.1	0804	3.5	1435	1.1	2008	3.5	
14	TH	0300	1.4	0838	3.2	1517	1.4	2044	3.3	
15	F	0344	1.7	0915	2.9	1608	1.6	2126	3.0	
16	SA	0444	2.0	1012	2.6	1710	1.8	2229	2.8	◐
17	SU	0612	2.1	1338	2.6	1823	1.9			
18	M	0126	2.7	0907	2.0	1443	2.7	1944	1.8	
19	TU	0247	2.9	0947	1.7	1522	2.9	2054	1.6	
20	W	0324	3.1	1014	1.5	1554	3.2	2141	1.3	
21	TH	0357	3.4	1039	1.3	1625	3.4	2218	1.1	
22	F	0430	3.6	1105	1.0	1656	3.6	2251	0.9	
23	SA	0503	3.8	1131	0.9	1725	3.7	2324	0.7	
24	SU	0533	3.9	1158	0.7	1752	3.8	2359	0.6	○
25	M	0603	4.0	1227	0.7	1820	3.9			
26	TU	0035	0.5	0634	3.9	1259	0.7	1852	3.8	
27	W	0115	0.6	0710	3.8	1336	0.8	1930	3.7	
28	TH	0159	0.8	0749	3.6	1418	1.0	2014	3.6	
29	F	0250	1.0	0835	3.3	1509	1.2	2106	3.3	
30	SA	0353	1.2	0933	2.9	1614	1.4	2215	3.1	

Chart Datum: 2·10 metres below Ordnance Datum (Newlyn)

TIME ZONE (UT)
For Summer Time add ONE hour in **non-shaded areas**

SCOTLAND – OBAN

LAT 56°25′N LONG 5°29′W

TIMES AND HEIGHTS OF HIGH AND LOW WATERS

SPRING & NEAP TIDES
Dates in red are **SPRINGS** Dates in blue are **NEAPS**

YEAR **2005**

MAY

Date	Time	m	Date	Time	m
1 SU ◑	0509 1102 1734	1.4 2.7 1.5	16 M	0539 1147 1737 ◐ 2335	2.1 2.7 1.8 2.9
2 M	0012 0636 1330 1859	3.0 1.5 2.7 1.5	17 TU	0715 1338 1841	2.0 2.7 1.8
3 TU	0152 0805 1444 2018	3.2 1.4 2.9 1.3	18 W	0120 0830 1428 1943	2.9 1.8 2.9 1.7
4 W	0253 0910 1533 2119	3.4 1.2 3.1 1.0	19 TH	0224 0912 1508 2037	3.1 1.6 3.1 1.5
5 TH	0340 0958 1608 2209	3.6 1.0 3.4 0.8	20 F	0308 0946 1543 2124	3.3 1.4 3.3 1.2
6 F	0420 1038 1638 2253	3.8 0.9 3.6 0.7	21 SA	0347 1018 1616 2207	3.5 1.2 3.5 1.0
7 SA	0457 1114 1709 2334	3.9 0.8 3.7 0.7	22 SU	0425 1050 1649 2249	3.7 1.0 3.6 0.8
8 SU ●	0531 1148 1741	3.9 0.8 3.8	23 M	0502 1124 1723 ○ 2333	3.8 0.8 3.8 0.7
9 M	0013 0604 1222 1812	0.7 3.9 0.8 3.9	24 TU	0540 1201 1800	3.9 0.7 3.9
10 TU	0051 0636 1257 1844	0.9 3.8 0.9 3.8	25 W	0018 0619 1242 1840	0.6 3.8 0.7 3.9
11 W	0127 0710 1333 1917	1.1 3.6 1.0 3.7	26 TH	0106 0701 1327 1925	0.7 3.7 0.7 3.8
12 TH	0203 0744 1412 1952	1.3 3.4 1.2 3.6	27 F	0157 0747 1415 2014	0.8 3.5 0.8 3.7
13 F	0242 0822 1454 2031	1.6 3.2 1.4 3.4	28 SA	0252 0838 1508 2110	0.9 3.3 1.0 3.5
14 SA	0328 0905 1542 2115	1.8 3.0 1.6 3.2	29 SU	0353 0938 1608 2216	1.1 3.0 1.1 3.3
15 SU	0425 1002 1636 2212	2.0 2.8 1.7 3.0	30 M	0501 1056 1715 ◑ 2345	1.3 2.8 1.3 3.2
			31 TU	0615 1240 1828	1.4 2.8 1.3

JUNE

Date	Time	m	Date	Time	m
1 W	0112 0728 1357 1941	3.2 1.4 2.9 1.3	16 TH	0656 1301 1834	1.9 2.9 1.7
2 TH	0217 0832 1451 2046	3.3 1.3 3.0 1.2	17 F	0052 0755 1405 1932	3.1 1.7 3.0 1.6
3 F	0309 0923 1531 2142	3.4 1.2 3.2 1.1	18 SA	0204 0846 1455 2031	3.2 1.6 3.1 1.4
4 SA	0354 1006 1606 2230	3.5 1.2 3.4 1.1	19 SU	0303 0933 1541 2129	3.4 1.4 3.3 1.2
5 SU	0433 1044 1642 2314	3.6 1.1 3.5 1.1	20 M	0354 1017 1625 2224	3.5 1.2 3.5 1.0
6 M	0509 1121 1717 ● 2355	3.6 1.1 3.7 1.1	21 TU	0442 1101 1709 2318	3.7 1.0 3.7 0.8
7 TU	0545 1157 1753	3.6 1.0 3.7	22 W ○	0528 1146 1753	3.7 0.8 3.9
8 W	0034 0620 1236 1829	1.2 3.6 1.1 3.7	23 TH	0010 0614 1232 1839	0.7 3.8 0.7 3.9
9 TH	0113 0657 1314 1905	1.3 3.5 1.1 3.7	24 F	0103 0700 1320 1926	0.7 3.7 0.6 3.9
10 F	0151 0735 1354 1943	1.4 3.4 1.2 3.6	25 SA	0155 0747 1408 2014	0.7 3.6 0.6 3.9
11 SA	0231 0814 1434 2022	1.6 3.3 1.3 3.5	26 SU	0247 0836 1459 2105	0.8 3.4 0.7 3.7
12 SU	0313 0856 1515 2102	1.7 3.1 1.5 3.4	27 M	0341 0927 1551 2201	1.0 3.2 0.9 3.5
13 M	0400 0941 1559 2147	1.8 3.0 1.6 3.2	28 TU	0437 1025 1648 ◑ 2304	1.1 3.0 1.1 3.3
14 TU	0453 1034 1646 2237	1.9 2.9 1.7 3.1	29 W	0536 1134 1749	1.3 2.9 1.2
15 W	0553 1141 1738 ◐ 2338	1.9 2.8 1.7 3.1	30 TH	0018 0639 1251 1855	3.2 1.4 2.8 1.4

JULY

Date	Time	m	Date	Time	m
1 F	0133 0743 1359 2007	3.1 1.5 2.9 1.5	16 SA	0643 1238 1844	1.8 2.9 1.7
2 SA	0239 0844 1455 2117	3.1 1.5 3.0 1.5	17 SU	0057 0753 1414 1955	3.1 1.7 3.0 1.6
3 SU	0335 0936 1542 2216	3.2 1.5 3.2 1.4	18 M	0233 0859 1524 2108	3.2 1.5 3.2 1.4
4 M	0421 1021 1624 2306	3.3 1.4 3.3 1.4	19 TU	0343 0958 1619 2215	3.4 1.3 3.5 1.2
5 TU	0500 1102 1704 2349	3.4 1.3 3.5 1.4	20 W	0440 1050 1707 2315	3.5 1.0 3.8 0.9
6 W ●	0538 1142 1743	3.4 1.2 3.6	21 TH ○	0529 1139 1753	3.7 0.7 4.0
7 TH	0028 0614 1222 1821	1.4 3.5 1.1 3.7	22 F	0009 0613 1226 1837	0.7 3.8 0.5 4.1
8 F	0105 0651 1300 1857	1.4 3.6 1.1 3.7	23 SA	0059 0656 1311 1921	0.6 3.8 0.4 4.2
9 SA	0141 0727 1337 1933	1.4 3.5 1.1 3.7	24 SU	0146 0738 1357 2004	0.5 3.7 0.4 4.1
10 SU	0217 0803 1412 2007	1.4 3.5 1.2 3.7	25 M	0232 0819 1442 2047	0.6 3.6 0.5 3.9
11 M	0252 0836 1446 2040	1.5 3.4 1.3 3.6	26 TU	0317 0901 1528 2131	0.8 3.4 0.7 3.7
12 TU	0325 0909 1519 2114	1.6 3.3 1.4 3.5	27 W	0403 0943 1616 2219	1.0 3.2 1.0 3.4
13 W	0358 0944 1557 2151	1.7 3.1 1.5 3.4	28 TH	0451 1031 1708 ◑ 2315	1.3 3.0 1.3 3.1
14 TH	0438 1027 1642 ◐ 2237	1.8 3.0 1.6 3.3	29 F	0545 1136 1808	1.5 2.8 1.5
15 F	0534 1121 1738 2335	1.8 2.9 1.6 3.2	30 SA	0039 0647 1308 1924	2.9 1.7 2.8 1.7
			31 SU	0220 0759 1432 2111	2.8 1.7 2.9 1.8

AUGUST

Date	Time	m	Date	Time	m
1 M	0343 0913 1536 2223	2.9 1.7 3.0 1.7	16 TU	0241 0844 1529 2107	3.0 1.6 3.3 1.5
2 TU	0429 1010 1620 2310	3.1 1.5 3.2 1.6	17 W	0356 0951 1621 2220	3.2 1.3 3.6 1.2
3 W	0500 1053 1658 2348	3.2 1.3 3.5 1.4	18 TH	0446 1045 1705 2315	3.5 1.0 3.9 0.8
4 TH	0532 1132 1735	3.4 1.1 3.6	19 F ○	0527 1131 1746	3.7 0.6 4.2
5 F	0021 0604 1209 ● 1810	1.3 3.6 1.0 3.8	20 SA	0002 0605 1215 1824	0.6 3.9 0.4 4.3
6 SA	0053 0638 1244 1844	1.2 3.7 0.9 3.9	21 SU	0046 0641 1257 1903	0.4 3.9 0.3 4.4
7 SU	0123 0711 1316 1915	1.2 3.7 0.9 3.9	22 M	0127 0716 1339 1941	0.4 3.9 0.3 4.3
8 M	0153 0740 1346 1944	1.2 3.7 1.0 3.8	23 TU	0206 0751 1420 2017	0.5 3.8 0.4 4.0
9 TU	0221 0806 1413 2010	1.3 3.6 1.1 3.8	24 W	0245 0825 1500 2054	0.7 3.6 0.7 3.7
10 W	0243 0831 1441 2038	1.4 3.5 1.2 3.6	25 TH	0324 0859 1543 2132	1.0 3.4 1.0 3.4
11 TH	0304 0901 1515 2109	1.5 3.3 1.3 3.5	26 F	0408 0935 1630 ◑ 2215	1.3 3.1 1.4 3.0
12 F	0338 0939 1558 2149	1.6 3.2 1.5 3.3	27 SA	0459 1022 1727 2326	1.6 2.9 1.8 2.7
13 SA	0429 1027 1655 ◐ 2243	1.7 3.0 1.6 3.1	28 SU	0602 1215 1850	1.8 2.7 2.0
14 SU	0549 1141 1813	1.9 2.9 1.8	29 M	0226 0721 1532 2131	2.7 1.9 2.8 2.0
15 M	0013 0721 1410 1940	2.9 1.8 3.0 1.7	30 TU	0352 0857 1620 2227	2.8 1.8 3.0 1.8
			31 W	0426 0958 1617 2302	3.0 1.5 3.3 1.6

Chart Datum: 2·10 metres below Ordnance Datum (Newlyn)

TIME ZONE (UT)
For Summer Time add ONE hour in **non-shaded areas**

SCOTLAND – OBAN

LAT 56°25′N LONG 5°29′W

TIMES AND HEIGHTS OF HIGH AND LOW WATERS

SPRING & NEAP TIDES
Dates in red are SPRINGS
Dates in blue are NEAPS

YEAR **2005**

SEPTEMBER

Date	Day	Time	m	Time	m	Time	m	Time	m	Moon
1	TH	0446	3.3	1040	1.3	1645	3.5	2332	1.4	
2	F	0512	3.5	1115	1.1	1717	3.7			
3	SA	0000	1.2	0542	3.7	1149	0.9	1748	3.9	●
4	SU	0027	1.1	0614	3.8	1220	0.8	1819	4.0	
5	M	0054	1.0	0643	3.9	1248	0.8	1848	4.0	
6	TU	0121	1.0	0708	3.8	1315	0.8	1913	4.0	
7	W	0144	1.1	0730	3.8	1340	0.9	1937	3.9	
8	TH	0203	1.2	0755	3.6	1409	1.1	2003	3.8	
9	F	0227	1.3	0826	3.5	1443	1.2	2034	3.6	
10	SA	0302	1.5	0903	3.3	1527	1.5	2112	3.3	
11	SU	0350	1.7	0952	3.1	1629	1.7	2205	3.0	◐
12	M	0517	1.9	1116	2.9	1804	1.9			
13	TU	0010	2.8	0704	1.9	1419	3.0	1945	1.8	
14	W	0258	2.9	0834	1.6	1522	3.4	2115	1.5	
15	TH	0355	3.2	0941	1.3	1608	3.8	2216	1.1	
16	F	0437	3.5	1031	0.9	1648	4.1	2302	0.8	
17	SA	0512	3.8	1114	0.5	1726	4.3	2343	0.5	
18	SU	0543	3.9	1156	0.3	1802	4.4			○
19	M	0022	0.4	0615	4.0	1237	0.3	1836	4.4	
20	TU	0059	0.5	0647	4.0	1316	0.3	1910	4.3	
21	W	0135	0.6	0719	3.9	1354	0.5	1943	4.0	
22	TH	0210	0.8	0750	3.8	1432	0.9	2016	3.7	
23	F	0248	1.1	0821	3.5	1512	1.2	2049	3.4	
24	SA	0330	1.4	0855	3.3	1558	1.6	2127	3.0	
25	SU	0422	1.7	0938	3.0	1657	2.0	2224	2.7	◑
26	M	0526	1.9	1103	2.8	1833	2.2			
27	TU	0209	2.6	0647	2.0	1504	2.9	2130	2.0	
28	W	0320	2.8	0827	1.8	1540	3.1	2209	1.8	
29	TH	0353	3.1	0930	1.6	1554	3.3	2237	1.6	
30	F	0416	3.3	1012	1.3	1619	3.6	2303	1.3	

OCTOBER

Date	Day	Time	m	Time	m	Time	m	Time	m	Moon
1	SA	0442	3.5	1046	1.1	1648	3.8	2327	1.2	
2	SU	0512	3.7	1117	0.9	1719	4.0	2352	1.0	
3	M	0542	3.9	1147	0.8	1748	4.1			●
4	TU	0018	0.9	0609	3.9	1215	0.8	1815	4.1	
5	W	0044	0.9	0633	3.9	1243	0.8	1840	4.1	
6	TH	0108	1.0	0657	3.9	1312	0.9	1907	3.9	
7	F	0133	1.1	0726	3.8	1345	1.1	1937	3.8	
8	SA	0203	1.2	0801	3.6	1425	1.3	2011	3.5	
9	SU	0243	1.4	0842	3.4	1515	1.5	2053	3.2	
10	M	0337	1.6	0939	3.2	1630	1.8	2156	2.9	◐
11	TU	0507	1.8	1125	3.0	1808	1.9			
12	W	0115	2.7	0647	1.8	1401	3.2	1947	1.7	
13	TH	0243	3.0	0814	1.6	1459	3.5	2104	1.4	
14	F	0335	3.3	0918	1.2	1544	3.9	2156	1.1	
15	SA	0413	3.5	1008	0.9	1623	4.1	2238	0.8	
16	SU	0445	3.8	1052	0.6	1700	4.3	2317	0.7	
17	M	0515	3.9	1133	0.5	1734	4.4	2353	0.6	○
18	TU	0546	4.1	1213	0.5	1808	4.3			
19	W	0028	0.6	0618	4.1	1252	0.6	1840	4.2	
20	TH	0103	0.7	0649	4.0	1330	0.9	1912	4.0	
21	F	0139	0.9	0721	3.9	1408	1.2	1945	3.7	
22	SA	0217	1.2	0754	3.7	1447	1.5	2019	3.4	
23	SU	0300	1.4	0831	3.4	1534	1.9	2058	3.1	
24	M	0352	1.7	0917	3.2	1635	2.1	2154	2.8	
25	TU	0454	1.9	1030	3.0	1811	2.3			◑
26	W	0122	2.7	0607	2.0	1348	3.0	2049	2.1	
27	TH	0227	2.9	0731	1.9	1443	3.1	2129	1.9	
28	F	0307	3.1	0842	1.7	1515	3.3	2158	1.7	
29	SA	0338	3.3	0929	1.5	1543	3.6	2223	1.5	
30	SU	0407	3.5	1006	1.3	1613	3.8	2248	1.3	
31	M	0438	3.7	1038	1.1	1644	3.9	2314	1.1	

NOVEMBER

Date	Day	Time	m	Time	m	Time	m	Time	m	Moon
1	TU	0508	3.8	1109	1.0	1715	4.0	2341	1.0	
2	W	0536	3.9	1142	0.9	1744	4.1			●
3	TH	0009	0.9	0602	4.0	1216	0.9	1813	4.0	
4	F	0040	0.9	0633	3.9	1253	0.9	1846	3.9	
5	SA	0114	1.0	0708	3.9	1334	1.1	1923	3.7	
6	SU	0153	1.2	0749	3.7	1422	1.3	2005	3.5	
7	M	0240	1.3	0839	3.5	1520	1.5	2056	3.2	
8	TU	0340	1.5	0943	3.3	1634	1.7	2208	2.9	
9	W	0456	1.6	1127	3.2	1759	1.7			◐
10	TH	0036	2.8	0620	1.6	1326	3.4	1925	1.6	
11	F	0209	3.0	0741	1.5	1427	3.6	2035	1.4	
12	SA	0303	3.2	0848	1.3	1515	3.8	2127	1.2	
13	SU	0342	3.5	0941	1.1	1556	4.0	2209	1.1	
14	M	0414	3.7	1028	0.9	1634	4.1	2248	1.0	
15	TU	0446	3.8	1111	0.8	1709	4.1	2324	0.9	
16	W	0519	4.0	1152	0.9	1743	4.1			○
17	TH	0000	0.9	0553	4.0	1232	1.0	1816	4.0	
18	F	0037	1.0	0627	4.0	1311	1.2	1850	3.8	
19	SA	0115	1.1	0702	3.9	1350	1.4	1926	3.6	
20	SU	0155	1.3	0739	3.8	1431	1.7	2004	3.4	
21	M	0238	1.4	0819	3.6	1517	1.9	2046	3.2	
22	TU	0326	1.6	0905	3.4	1613	2.1	2138	3.0	
23	W	0419	1.8	1002	3.2	1723	2.2	2259	2.8	◑
24	TH	0519	1.9	1123	3.1	1855	2.2			
25	F	0114	2.9	0622	1.9	1319	3.1	2013	2.1	
26	SA	0210	3.0	0726	1.9	1416	3.3	2058	1.9	
27	SU	0251	3.2	0823	1.7	1456	3.4	2132	1.7	
28	M	0327	3.4	0910	1.5	1533	3.6	2203	1.5	
29	TU	0401	3.5	0952	1.4	1609	3.8	2235	1.3	
30	W	0435	3.7	1033	1.2	1645	3.9	2307	1.1	

DECEMBER

Date	Day	Time	m	Time	m	Time	m	Time	m	Moon
1	TH	0508	3.8	1114	1.1	1721	4.0	2342	1.0	●
2	F	0543	3.9	1157	1.0	1758	4.0			
3	SA	0021	1.0	0621	4.0	1243	1.0	1837	3.9	
4	SU	0103	0.9	0703	3.9	1331	1.0	1920	3.7	
5	M	0148	1.0	0749	3.9	1423	1.2	2006	3.5	
6	TU	0238	1.1	0841	3.7	1520	1.3	2059	3.3	
7	W	0333	1.2	0941	3.6	1622	1.5	2200	3.1	
8	TH	0436	1.4	1056	3.4	1731	1.6	2320	3.0	◐
9	F	0546	1.4	1232	3.4	1844	1.6			
10	SA	0102	3.0	0659	1.4	1346	3.5	1951	1.6	
11	SU	0214	3.1	0811	1.4	1444	3.6	2050	1.5	
12	M	0304	3.3	0913	1.3	1533	3.7	2138	1.4	
13	TU	0345	3.5	1007	1.3	1615	3.7	2221	1.3	
14	W	0423	3.6	1055	1.2	1653	3.8	2300	1.2	
15	TH	0501	3.8	1140	1.2	1729	3.8	2339	1.2	○
16	F	0538	3.9	1221	1.3	1805	3.8			
17	SA	0018	1.1	0616	3.9	1302	1.4	1841	3.7	
18	SU	0059	1.2	0653	3.9	1341	1.5	1918	3.7	
19	M	0139	1.2	0731	3.8	1420	1.7	1956	3.5	
20	TU	0219	1.3	0809	3.7	1500	1.8	2034	3.4	
21	W	0300	1.5	0848	3.6	1543	1.9	2115	3.3	
22	TH	0342	1.6	0930	3.4	1630	2.0	2201	3.1	
23	F	0426	1.7	1016	3.3	1725	2.1	2255	3.0	◑
24	SA	0515	1.8	1112	3.2	1825	2.1			
25	SU	0009	3.0	0609	1.9	1225	3.2	1927	2.0	
26	M	0135	3.0	0708	1.8	1347	3.2	2024	1.9	
27	TU	0237	3.1	0810	1.7	1450	3.4	2115	1.7	
28	W	0327	3.3	0910	1.6	1542	3.5	2200	1.5	
29	TH	0412	3.5	1006	1.4	1628	3.7	2243	1.3	
30	F	0455	3.7	1059	1.2	1712	3.8	2326	1.0	
31	SA	0537	3.9	1150	1.0	1754	3.9			●

Chart Datum: 2·10 metres below Ordnance Datum (Newlyn)

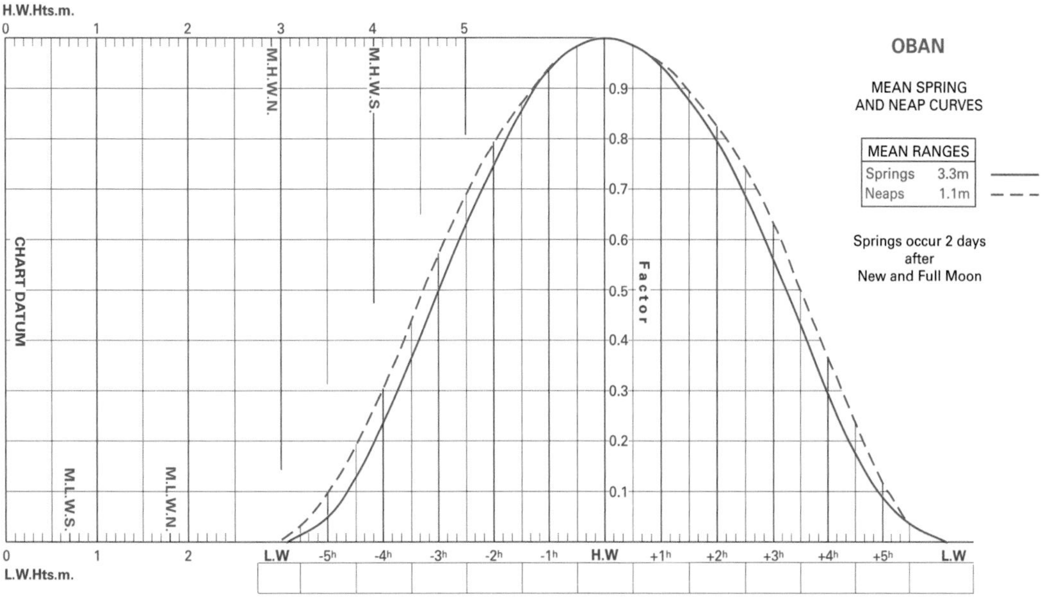
H.W.Hts.m.
OBAN
MEAN SPRING
AND NEAP CURVES
MEAN RANGES
Springs 3.3m
Neaps 1.1m
Springs occur 2 days after New and Full Moon
M.H.W.N.
M.H.W.S.
CHART DATUM
Factor
M.L.W.S.
M.L.W.N.
L.W.Hts.m.
L.W -5h -4h -3h -2h -1h H.W +1h +2h +3h +4h +5h L.W

ADJACENT MARINA/ANCHORAGES

DUNSTAFFNAGE BAY, Argyll & Bute, **56°27´·04N 05°25´·97W**. ❀❀❀◊◊◊✿✿✿ AC 2387, 2378. HW –0530 on Dover; see 9.8.18. Good shelter at marina pontoons, SE side of bay entered 'twixt Rubha Garbh and Eilean Mór; little room to ⚓, within the bay the tidal stream is rotary but sets E through the marina most of the time. No navigational hazards, speed limit 4kn in bay/⚓. Do not approach marina through moorings, use buoyed fairway. W and SW sides of bay dry. Private pier on NW side has 2 FG (vert) 4m 2M. **Dunstaffnage Marina** (150 inc 10Ⓥ AB £2.00) ☎ (01631) 566555, 📠 567422, VHF Ch M, D, Gas, Slip, BH (18 ton), CH, C (masting), ME, BY, Showers, WC, ▣, SM, R, Bar; Facilities: P (cans, ¾M), 🛒 (½M), Bus, ⇄ Oban (2M) & Connel (airstrip).

LOCH ETIVE, AC 2378 to Bonawe, thence AC 5076. Connel Bridge, 15m clrnce, and Falls of Lora can be physical and tidal barriers. HT cables at Bonawe have 13m clearance. See *Clyde Cruising Club Sailing Directions.*

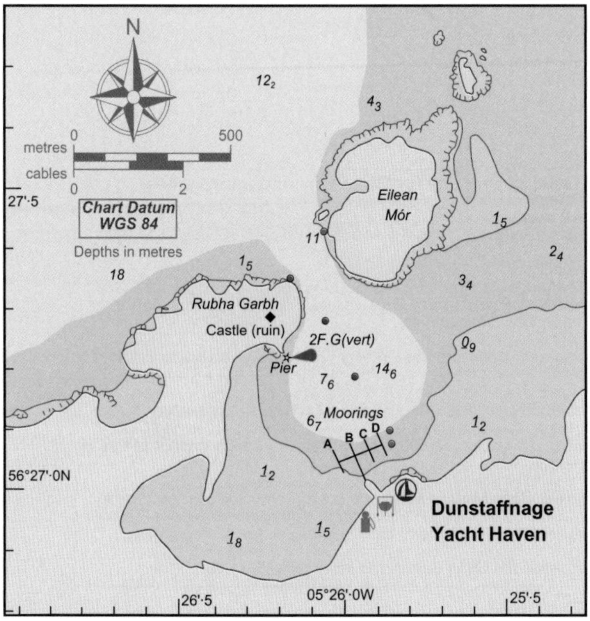
N
metres 0 500
cables 0 2
27'·5
Chart Datum WGS 84
Depths in metres
Eilean Mór
Rubha Garbh
Castle (ruin)
2F.G(vert)
Pier
Moorings
A B C D
56°27'·0N
Dunstaffnage Yacht Haven
26'·5
05°26'·0W
25'·5

9.8.18 OBAN

Argyll and Bute **56°24'·99N 05°29'·07W** ❀❀❀◊◊◊✿✿

CHARTS AC *2171*, 2387, 1790; Imray C65; OS 49

TIDES –0530 Dover; ML 2·4; Duration 0610; Zone 0 (UT)

Standard Port OBAN (⟶)

Times				Height (metres)			
High Water		Low Water		MHWS	MHWN	MLWN	MLWS
0100	0700	0100	0800	4·0	2·9	1·8	0·7
1300	1900	1300	2000				
Differences DUNSTAFFNAGE BAY							
+0005	0000	0000	+0005	+0·1	+0·1	+0·1	+0·1
CONNEL							
+0020	+0005	+0010	+0015	–0·3	–0·2	–0·1	+0·1
BONAWE							
+0150	+0205	+0240	+0210	–2·0	–1·7	–1·3	–0·5

SHELTER Good except in strong SW/NW winds, but Ardantrive Bay (30 Ⓥs, 56 pontoon berths and water taxi 0800-2300) is sheltered from these winds. See chartlet for Ⓥs. ⚓s off town, but in deep water. ⚓ or M off Brandystone and in Kerrera Sound at: Horseshoe Bay, Gallanachbeg (rk dries 0·3m) and Little Horseshoe Bay. Dunstaffnage Bay, 3M NE: see facing column.

NAVIGATION WPT (N) 56°25´·84N 05°30´·07W, 129° to Dunollie lt, 0·73M and WPT (S) 56°21´·99N 05°32´·95W, 030° to 140m ESE of Sgeirean Dubha 9 cables. Beware Sgeir Rathaid, buoyed, in middle of the bay; also CalMac ferries running to/from Railway Quay. Ferry Rks in mid-channel at 56°24´·0N can be passed on either side but note the direction of the buoyage is NE, thus pass to the E'ward of the port-hand unlit buoy or to the W'ward of the stbd-conical QG buoy. The N'ly stbd-hand buoy must always be passed to the W'ward.

LIGHTS AND MARKS N Spit of Kerrera Fl R 3s 9m 5M, W col, R bands. Dunollie Fl (2) WRG 6s 7m 5/4M; G351°-009°, W009°-047°, R047°- 120°, W120°-138°, G138°-143°. N Pier 2FG (vert). S Quay 2FG (vert). Northern Lights Wharf Oc G 6s.

R/T Call *North Pier* Ch 12 16 (0900-1700). For Railway Quay, call *CalMac* Ch 06 12 16. For Ardantrive Bay, call *Oban Yachts* and Water taxi Ch 80.

TELEPHONE (Dial code 01631) Pier 562892; Marinecall 09066 526247; ⊖ 563079; MRSC (01475) 729014; Police 562213; Dr 563175.

OBAN *continued*

FACILITIES N Pier ☎ 562892, L, FW, C (15 ton mobile) via Piermaster; **Rly Quay,** L, Slip, D, FW, CH; **Services:** BY, Slip, ACA, Gas, ME, El, divers.

Ardantrive Bay Oban Yachts ☎ 565333, (fax) 565888, www.obanyachts.com, 56 (inc 30 (visitors)) AB(pontoons) £1.65, 30 (visitor's buoys) £1.65; Water taxi Ch 80; D, FW, Showers, WC, ME, ⚒, C, CH, Slip, BH (16 ton), Gas. **Town** P, R, Bar, ≷, ✈.

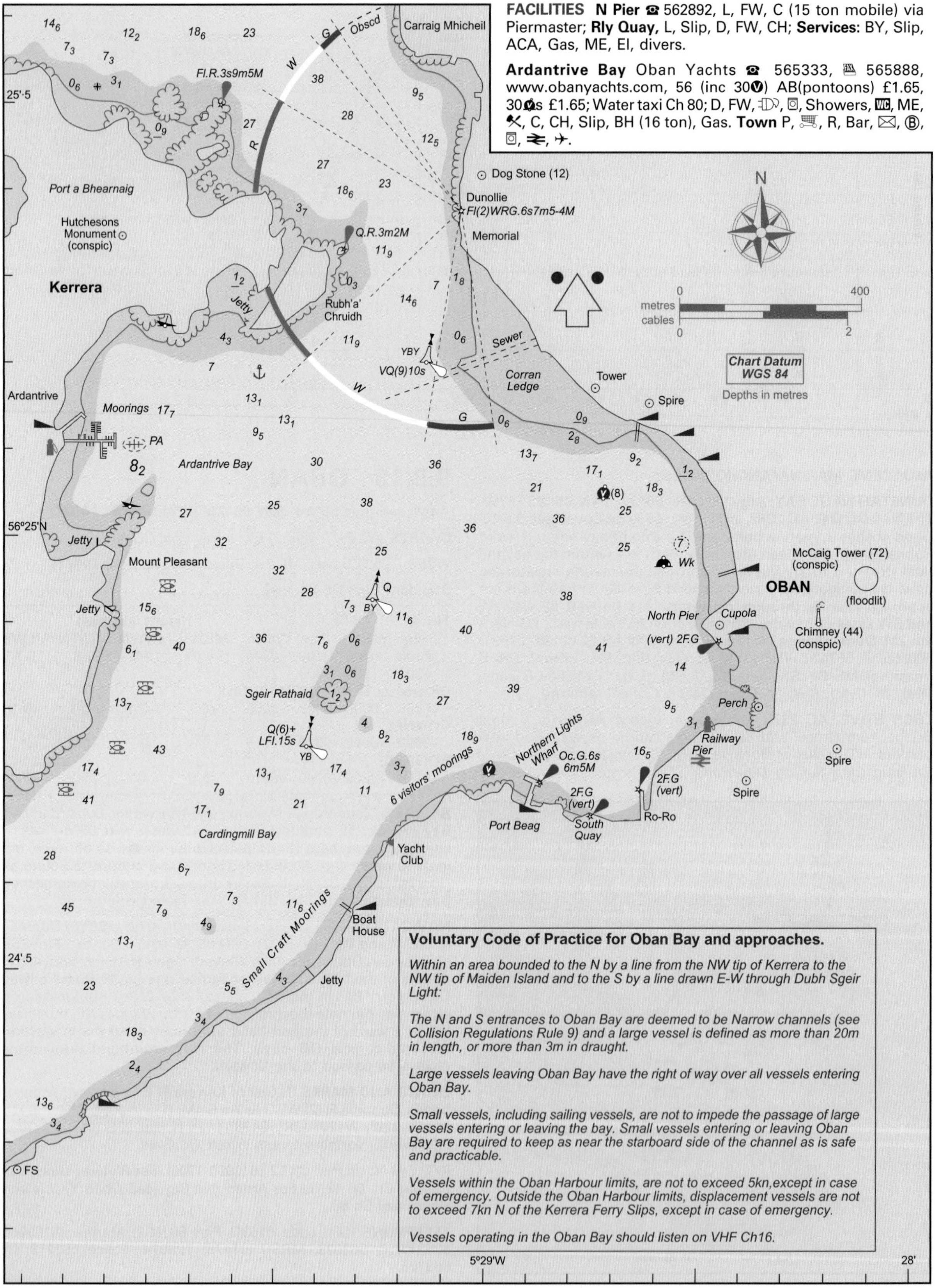
Carraig Mhicheil
Fl.R.3s9m5M
Port a Bhearnaig
Hutchesons Monument (conspic)
Kerrera
Q.R.3m2M
Rubh'a' Chruidh
Jetty
Dog Stone (12)
Dunollie
Fl(2)WRG.6s7m5-4M
Memorial
N
metres
cables
Chart Datum WGS 84
Depths in metres
Sewer
YBY
VQ(9)10s
Corran Ledge
Tower
Spire
Ardantrive
Moorings
PA
Ardantrive Bay
56°25'N
Mount Pleasant
McCaig Tower (72) (conspic)
OBAN
(floodlit)
Wk
Q
BY
North Pier
(vert) 2F.G
Cupola
Chimney (44) (conspic)
Perch
Sgeir Rathaid
Q(6)+ LFl.15s
YB
Railway Pier
Spire
Northern Lights Wharf
Oc.G.6s 6m5M
6 visitors' moorings
2F.G (vert)
South Quay
Ro-Ro
Port Beag
Cardingmill Bay
Yacht Club
Boat House
Small Craft Moorings
Jetty
24'.5
25'.5
FS
5°29'W
28'

Voluntary Code of Practice for Oban Bay and approaches.

Within an area bounded to the N by a line from the NW tip of Kerrera to the NW tip of Maiden Island and to the S by a line drawn E-W through Dubh Sgeir Light:

The N and S entrances to Oban Bay are deemed to be Narrow channels (see Collision Regulations Rule 9) and a large vessel is defined as more than 20m in length, or more than 3m in draught.

Large vessels leaving Oban Bay have the right of way over all vessels entering Oban Bay.

Small vessels, including sailing vessels, are not to impede the passage of large vessels entering or leaving the bay. Small vessels entering or leaving Oban Bay are required to keep as near the starboard side of the channel as is safe and practicable.

Vessels within the Oban Harbour limits, are not to exceed 5kn,except in case of emergency. Outside the Oban Harbour limits, displacement vessels are not to exceed 7kn N of the Kerrera Ferry Slips, except in case of emergency.

Vessels operating in the Oban Bay should listen on VHF Ch16.

ANCHORAGES ON MAINLAND SHORE OF FIRTH OF LORN

LOCH FEOCHAN, Argyll and Bute, **56°21'.39N 05°29'·77W**. AC 2387. HW = HW Oban; flood runs 4 hrs, ebb for 8 hrs. Caution: strong streams off Ardentallan Pt. Good shelter, 5M S of Oban and 1·5M SE of Kerrera. Best appr at local slack LW = LW Oban +0200. Narrow chan marked by 3 PHM buoys, 2 PHM perches on shore and 5 SHM buoys. ⚓ off pier, or moor off **Ardoran Marine** ☎ (01631) 566123, 📠 566611; 4 🅥s £10 <11m, D, FW, ME, CH, Slip, Showers.

PUILLADOBHRAIN, Argyll & Bute, **56°19'·47N 05°35'·22W**. AC 2386/2387. Tides as Oban. Popular ⚓ on the SE shore of the Firth of Lorne, approx 7M S of Oban, sheltered by the islets to the W of it. At N end of Ardencaple Bay identify Eilean Dùin (18m) and steer SE keeping 1½ca off to clear a rk awash at its NE tip. Continue for 4ca between Eilean nam Beathach, with Orange drum on N tip, and Dun Horses rks drying 2·7m. Two W cairns on E side of Eilean nam Freumha lead approx 215° into the inner ⚓ in about 4m. Landing at head of inlet. Nearest facilities: Bar, ☎, at Clachan Br (½M); ☎, ✉ at Clachan Seil.

CUAN SOUND, Argyll & Bute, **56°15'·84N 05°37'·47W**. AC 2386, 2326. Tides see 9.8.19 SEIL SOUND. Streams reach 6kn at sp; N-going makes at HW Oban +0420, S-going at HW Oban –2. The Sound is a useful doglegged short cut from Firth of Lorne to Lochs Melfort and Shuna, but needs care due to rks and tides. There are ⚓s at either end to await the tide. At the 90° dogleg, pass close N of Cleit Rk onto which the tide sets; it is marked by a Y △ perch. The chan is only ¾ca wide here due to rks off Seil. Overhead cables (35m) cross from Seil to Luing. There are ⚓s out of the tide to the S of Cleit Rk. No lts/facilities. See CCC SDs.

ARDINAMAR, Luing/Torsa, **56°14'·92N 05°37'·04W**. AC *2326*. HW –0555 on Dover; ML 1·7m; see 9.8.19 SEIL SOUND. A small cove and popular ⚓ between Luing and Torsa, close W of ent to L. Melfort. Appr on brg 290°. Narrow, shallow (about 1m CD) ent has drying rks either side, those to N marked by 2 SHM perches. Keep about 15m S of perches to ⚓ in 2m in centre of cove; S part dries. Few facilities: 🛒, ✉, ☎, at Cullipool 1·5M WNW. Gas at Cuan Sound ferry 2M NNW.

9.8.19 LOCH MELFORT

Argyll and Bute **56°14'·59N 05°34'·07W** ❁❁❁◊◊◊✿✿✿

CHARTS AC *2169, 2326*; Imray C65; OS 55

TIDES Loch Shuna –0615 Dover; ML Loch Melfort 1·7; Duration Seil Sound 0615; Zone 0 (UT)

Standard Port OBAN (⟵)

Times				Height (metres)			
High Water		Low Water		MHWS	MHWN	MLWN	MLWS
0100	0700	0100	0800	4·0	2·9	1·8	0·7
1300	1900	1300	2000				
Differences LOCH MELFORT							
–0055	–0025	–0040	–0035	–1·2	–0·8	–0·5	–0·1
SEIL SOUND							
–0035	–0015	–0040	–0015	–1·3	–0·9	–0·7	–0·3

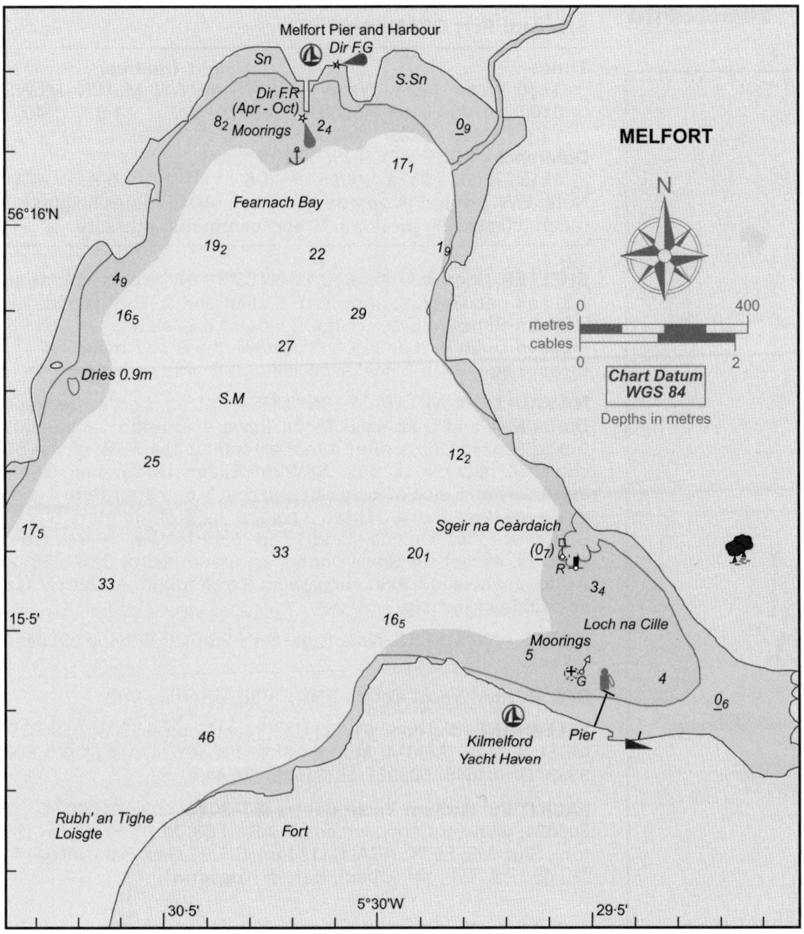
Melfort Pier and Harbour
Dir F.G
Sn
S.Sn
Dir F.R
(Apr - Oct)
Moorings
MELFORT
Fearnach Bay
56°16'N
Dries 0.9m
S.M
metres
cables
Chart Datum
WGS 84
Depths in metres
Sgeir na Ceàrdaich
R
Loch na Cille
Moorings
G
Kilmelford
Yacht Haven
Pier
Rubh' an Tighe
Loisgte
Fort
15·5'
30·5'
5°30'W
29·5'

SHELTER Good at Kilmelford Yacht Haven in Loch na Cille; access at all tides for 3m draft, but no lights. Or at Melfort Pier (Fearnach Bay at N end of loch): pier/pontoon in 2m, but chan to inner hbr dries; good ⚓ in N winds. ⚓s sheltered from S–W at: a bay with one or two private moorings ½M inside the ent on S shore, but beware rk drying 1·5m; in Kames Bay (1·5M further E) clear of moorings, rks and fish farm.

NAVIGATION WPT 56°13'·99N 05°35'·07W, 030° to summit Eilean Gamhna, 4ca. Pass either side of Eilean Gamhna. 8ca NE lies Campbell Rk (1·8m). A rk drying 1m lies 1½ca ESE of the FS on Eilean Coltair. The S side of L Melfort is mostly steep-to, except in Kames Bay. At Loch na Cille, beware drying reef ¾ca off NE shore (PHM perch), and rk near S shore (SHM perch); boats may obscure perches.

LIGHTS AND MARKS A Dir FR ☆ 6m 3M on Melfort pier (also depth gauge) and a Dir FG ☆ close NE on the shore are not ldg lts, nor do they form a safe transit. Approach on a N'ly track keeping them an equal angle off each bow.

R/T Kilmelford VHF Ch **80** M (HO).

TELEPHONE (Dial code 01852) MRSC (01475) 729014; ⊖ (0141) 887 9369; Police (01631) 562213; Marinecall 09066 526247; 🄷 (01546) 602323.

FACILITIES Kilmelford Yacht Haven ☎ 200248, 📠 200343, £12.50 (any LOA), D, FW, ⊡, BH (20 ton), Slip, ME, El, ⚒, Gas, ♿; **Melfort Pier** ☎ 200333, 📠 200329, AB £12, 🅥£12(any LOA), M, D, FW, ME, Slip, R, Bar, ⊡. **Village** (¾M) 🛒, Bar, ✉.

9.8.20 CRAOBH MARINA (L Shuna)

Argyll & Bute **56°12′·80N 05°33′·54W**

CHARTS AC *2169, 2326*; Imray C65; OS 55

TIDES HW Loch Shuna –0100 Oban; –0615 Dover; Seil Sound Duration 0615, ML 1·4; Zone 0 (UT). For tidal figures see 9.8.19.

SHELTER Very good. Craobh (pronounced Croove) Marina (access H24) on SE shore of Loch Shuna is enclosed by N and S causeways between islets. The ent is between 2 bkwtrs on the N side. In the marina, a shoal area S of the E bkwtr is marked by 9 PHM and 2 SHM buoys. A Y perch in W corner of hbr marks a spit; elsewhere ample depth. There are ⚓s in Asknish Bay 1M to the N, and in the bays E of Eilean Arsa and at Bàgh an Tigh-Stòir, S of Craobh.

NAVIGATION WPT 56°13′·01N 05°33′·57W, 173° to ent, 2ca. Tidal streams in Loch Shuna are weak. Beware fish farm 2ca N of Shuna, lobster pots in appr's and unmarked rks (dr 1·5m) 4ca NNE of ent. An unlit SHM buoy marks a rk (1m) 150m NNW of the W bkwtr. 1M N of marina, Eich Donna, an unmarked reef (dr 1·5m), lies between Eilean Creagach and Arduaine Pt.

LIGHTS AND MARKS The W sector, 162°-183°, of Dir Lt, Iso WRG 5s 10m 5/3M, on E bkwtr hd leads 172° between the close-in rks above. Multi coloured marina buildings are conspic.

R/T VHF Ch M, 80 (summer 0830-2000; winter 0830-1800).

TELEPHONE (Dial code 01852) HM 500222, Fax 500252; MRSC (01475) 729014; Customs (0141) 887 9369; Marinecall 09066 526247; Police (01546) 602222; Hospital (01546) 602323.

FACILITIES **Craobh Marina** (200+50 visitors) ☎ 500222, Fax 500252, £2.00, D, SM, BY, CH, Slip, BH (15 ton), C (12 ton), Gas, Gaz, ME, El, ⚒, R, SC, Ⓔ, Divers. **Village** shop, Bar, Ⓑ (Fri), ✉ (Kilmelford), ⇌ (Oban by bus), ✈ (Glasgow).

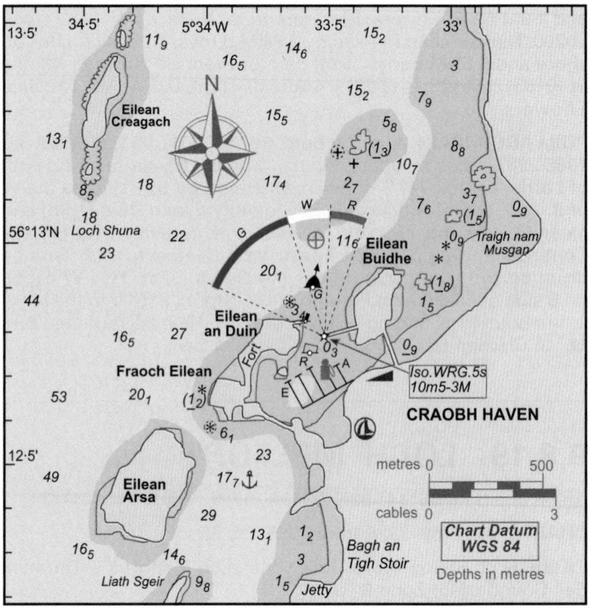

34·5'
5°34'W
33·5'
33'
13·5'
Eilean Creagach
Loch Shuna
56°13'N
Eilean Buidhe
Traigh nam Musgan
Eilean an Duin
Fraoch Eilean
Fort
Iso.WRG.5s 10m5-3M
CRAOBH HAVEN
12·5'
Eilean Arsa
Liath Sgeir
Bagh an Tigh Stoir
Jetty
metres 0 500
cables 0 3
Chart Datum WGS 84
Depths in metres

9.8.21 LOCH CRAIGNISH

Argyll and Bute **56°07′·99N 05°35′·07W** (Ardfern)

CHARTS AC *2169, 2326*; Imray C65, C63; OS 55

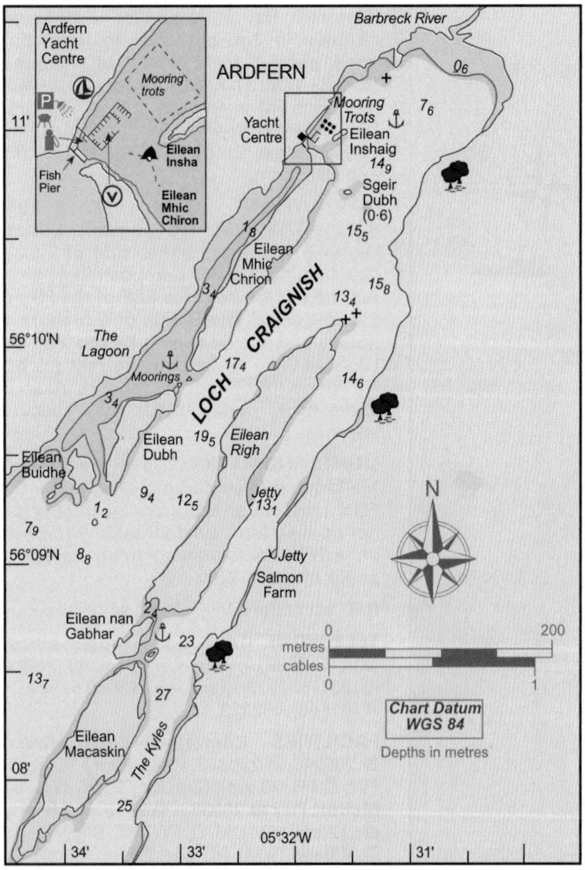

Ardfern Yacht Centre
Mooring trots
Eilean Insha
Fish Pier
Eilean Mhic Chiron
Barbreck River
ARDFERN
Yacht Centre
Mooring Trots
Eilean Inshaig
Sgeir Dubh (0·6)
Eilean Mhic Chrion
LOCH CRAIGNISH
56°10'N
The Lagoon
Moorings
Eilean Dubh
Eilean Righ
Eilean Buidhe
Jetty
Salmon Farm
56°09'N
Eilean nan Gabhar
metres 0 200
cables 0 1
Chart Datum WGS 84
Depths in metres
Eilean Macaskin
The Kyles
08'
34'
33'
05°32'W
31'

TIDES +0600 Dover; ML (Loch Beag)1·2; Duration (Seil Sound) 0615; Zone 0 (UT)

Standard Port OBAN (⟵)

Times				Height (metres)			
High Water		Low Water		MHWS	MHWN	MLWN	MLWS
0100	0700	0100	0800	4·0	2·9	1·8	0·7
1300	1900	1300	2000				
Differences LOCH BEAG (Sound of Jura)							
–0110	–0045	–0035	–0045	–1·6	–1·2	–0·8	–0·4

Note: HW Ardfern is approx HW Oban –0045; times/heights much affected by local winds and barometric pressure

SHELTER Good at Ardfern, 56°11′·0N 05°31′·8W, access H24; ⚓s at:
- Eilean nan Gabhar; appr from E chan and ⚓ E of island.
- Eilean Righ; midway up the E side of the island.
- Eilean Dubh in the "lagoon" between the Is and mainland.

Beware squalls in E'lies, especially on E side of loch.

NAVIGATION WPT 56°07′·59N 05°35′·37W (off chartlet) between Dorus Mór and Liath-sgier Mhòr. Beware: strong tidal streams (up to 8kn) in Dorus Mór; a reef extending 1ca SSW of the SE chain of islands; rk 1½ca SSW of Eilean Dubh; fish cages especially on E side of loch; a drying rk at N end of Ardfern ⚓ with a rk awash ¼ca E of it. (These 2 rks are ½ca S of the more S'ly of little islets close to mainland). The main fairway is free from hazards, except for Sgeir Dhubh, an unmarked rk 3½ca SSE of Ardfern, with a reef extending about ½ca all round. Ardfern is 1ca W of Eilean Inshaig.

LIGHTS AND MARKS Note: unlit SHM 25m off SW end of Eilean Inshaig.

R/T Ardfern Yacht Centre VHF Ch 80 M (office hrs).

TELEPHONE (Dial code 01852) HM (Yacht Centre) 500247/500636; MRSC (01475) 729014; Marinecall 09066 526247; Customs (0141) 887 9369; Dr (01546) 602921; Hospital (01546) 602449.

FACILITIES **Ardfern Yacht Centre** (87+20 visitors, 12 visitors' moorings); ☎ 500247, Fax 500624, www.ardfernyacht.co.uk, AB £1.53, M £1.10, D, BH (20 ton), Slip, ME, El, ⚒, ACA, C (12 ton), CH, Ⓢ, Gas, Gaz. **Village** R, shop, Ⓑ (Fri), ✉, ⇌ (Oban), Bar, ✈ (Glasgow).

9.8.22 SUBMARINE EXERCISE AREAS (SUBFACTS)

Areas North of Mull in which submarine activity is planned for the next 16 hrs are broadcast by CG Coordination Centres on a notified VHF Ch after an initial announcement on VHF Ch 16 at the times below. The areas are referred to by names given below, rather than by numbers indicated. For Areas 22 – 81 (South of Mull), see 9.9.19.

Stornoway	0110 0510 0910 1310 1710 and 2110 UT
Clyde	0020 0420 0820 1220 1620 and 2020 UT

During notified NATO exercises, Subfacts are also broadcast on MF by **Stornoway** 1743 kHz and **Clyde** 1883 kHz, at the same times as above.

General information on Subfacts is also broadcast twice daily at 0620 & 1820 UT by **Portpatrick** Navtex **(O)**. **Stornoway** and **Clyde** CG will also supply Subfacts on request Ch 16.

A Fisherman's hotline ☎ (01436) 674321 deals with queries. FOSNNI Ops ☎ (01436) 674321 ext 3206/6778, may help. Submarines on the suface and at periscope depth always listen on Ch 16. See also 9.9.19.

1	Tiumpan	**14**	Raasay
2	Minch North	**15**	Neist
3	Stoer	**16**	Bracadale
4	Shiant	**17**	Ushenish
5	Minch South	**18**	Hebrides North
6	Ewe	**19**	Canna
7	Trodday	**20**	Rhum
8	Rona West	**21**	Sleat
9	Rona North	**22**	Barra
10	Lochmaddy	**23**	Hebrides Central
11	Dunvegan	**24**	Hawes
12	Portree	**25**	Eigg
13	Rona South	**26**	Hebrides South

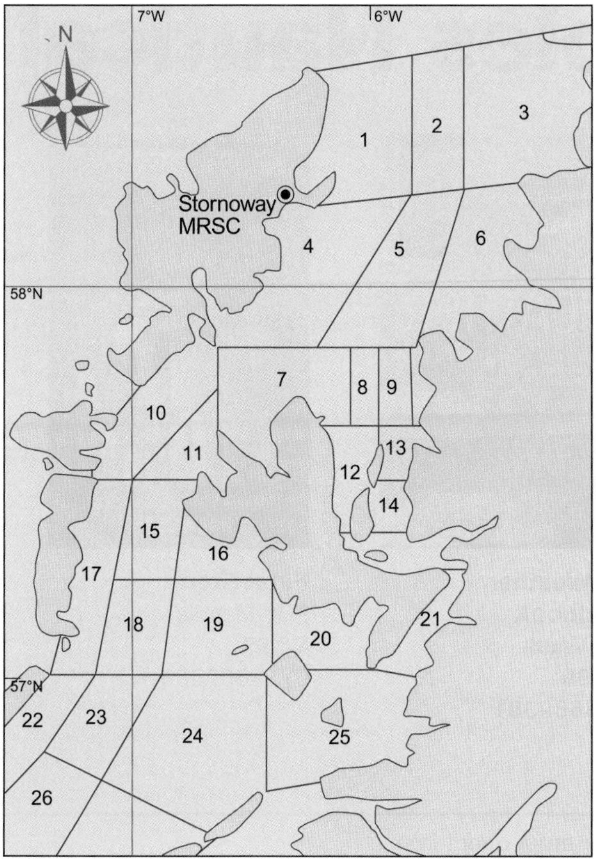
7°W
6°W
N
1
2
3
Stornoway
MRSC
4
5
6
58°N
7
8
9
10
11
12
13
14
15
16
17
18
19
20
21
57°N
22
23
24
25
26

9.8.23 FERRIES ON THE WEST COAST OF SCOTLAND

The following is a brief summary of the many ferries plying between mainland and island harbours. It supplements the UK and Continental ferry services listed in 9.0.5, and may prove useful when cruise plans or crews change, often in remote places. It covers Area 8 (Stornoway to Oban) and Area 9 (Jura to the Clyde).

The major operator is Caledonian MacBrayne: Head Office, The Ferry Terminal, Gourock PA19 1QP; ☎ 08705-650000 for reservations, (08705) 650000. www.calmac.co.uk

Many routes are very short and may not be pre-bookable; seasonal routes are *asterisked.

From	**To**	**Time**	**Remarks**
Area 8			
Berneray	Leverburgh	1¼	Not Sun
Ullapool	Stornoway	2¾ hrs	
Uig (Skye)	Tarbert (Harris)	1¾ hrs	Not Sun
Uig	Lochmaddy (N Uist)	1¾ hrs	
Oban	Castlebay/Lochboisdale	5-7 hrs	
Sconser (Skye)	Raasay	15 mins	Not Sun
Mallaig*	Armadale (Skye)	20 mins	
Mallaig	Eigg-Muck-Rhum-Canna	Varies	Not Sun
Oban	Coll-Tiree	Varies	Not Thurs
Tobermory	Kilchoan	35 mins	
Fionnphort	Iona	5 mins	
Lochaline	Fishnish (Mull)	15 mins	
Oban	Craignure (Mull)	45 mins	
Oban	Lismore	50 mins	Not Sun
Areas 8/9			
Oban	Colonsay	2¼ hrs	Sun/W/Fri
Area 9			
Kennacraig	Port Askaig/Colonsay	Varies	Wed
Kennacraig	Port Ellen	2h 10m	
Kennacraig	Port Askaig	2 hrs	
Tayinloan	Gigha	20 mins	
Ardrossan	Brodick	55 mins	
Claonaig	Lochranza (Arran)	30 mins	
Largs	Cumbrae Slip	10 mins	
Tarbert (L Fyne)	Portavadie*	25 mins	
Colintraive	Rhubodach (Bute)	5 mins	
Wemyss Bay	Rothesay (Bute)	35 mins	
Gourock	Dunoon	20 mins	

Other Island Ferry Operators

Area	**From**	**Operator**	**Telephone**
Corran - V	Ardgour	Highland Council	01855 841243
Easdale - P	Seil	Area Manager	01631 562125
Firth of Lorn - P	Colonsay Uisken (Ross of Mull) Scalasaig (Colonsay) Tarbert (Jura) Port Askaig (Islay)	K & C Byrne	01951 200320
Jura - V	Port Askaig (Islay)	Serco Denholm	01496 840681
Kerrara - P	Oban	D McEachan	01631 563665
Kilgregan - P	Gourock	Clyde Marine Motoring	01475 721281
Lismore - P	Port Appin	Area Manager	01631 562125
Loch Nevis - P	Mallaig	Bruce Watt	01687 462233
Luing - P/V	Seil	Area Manager	01631 562125
Morvern	Sunart	Pre-book via	01688 302851
Mull	Drimnin	Sound of Mull	or mobile
Ardnamurchan	Tobermoray Kilchoan	Transport	07799 608199
Skye - V	Gleneig	R Macleod	01599 511302
Staffa - P	Iona	D Kirkpatrick	01681 700373
Staffa - P	Mull	Gordon Grant	01681 700338
Staffa - P	Mull	Turus Mara	01688 400242

P = Passenger only V = Cars and Passengers

8

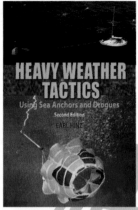

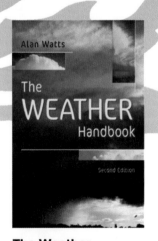

Area 9

South-West Scotland
Crinan Canal to Mull of Galloway

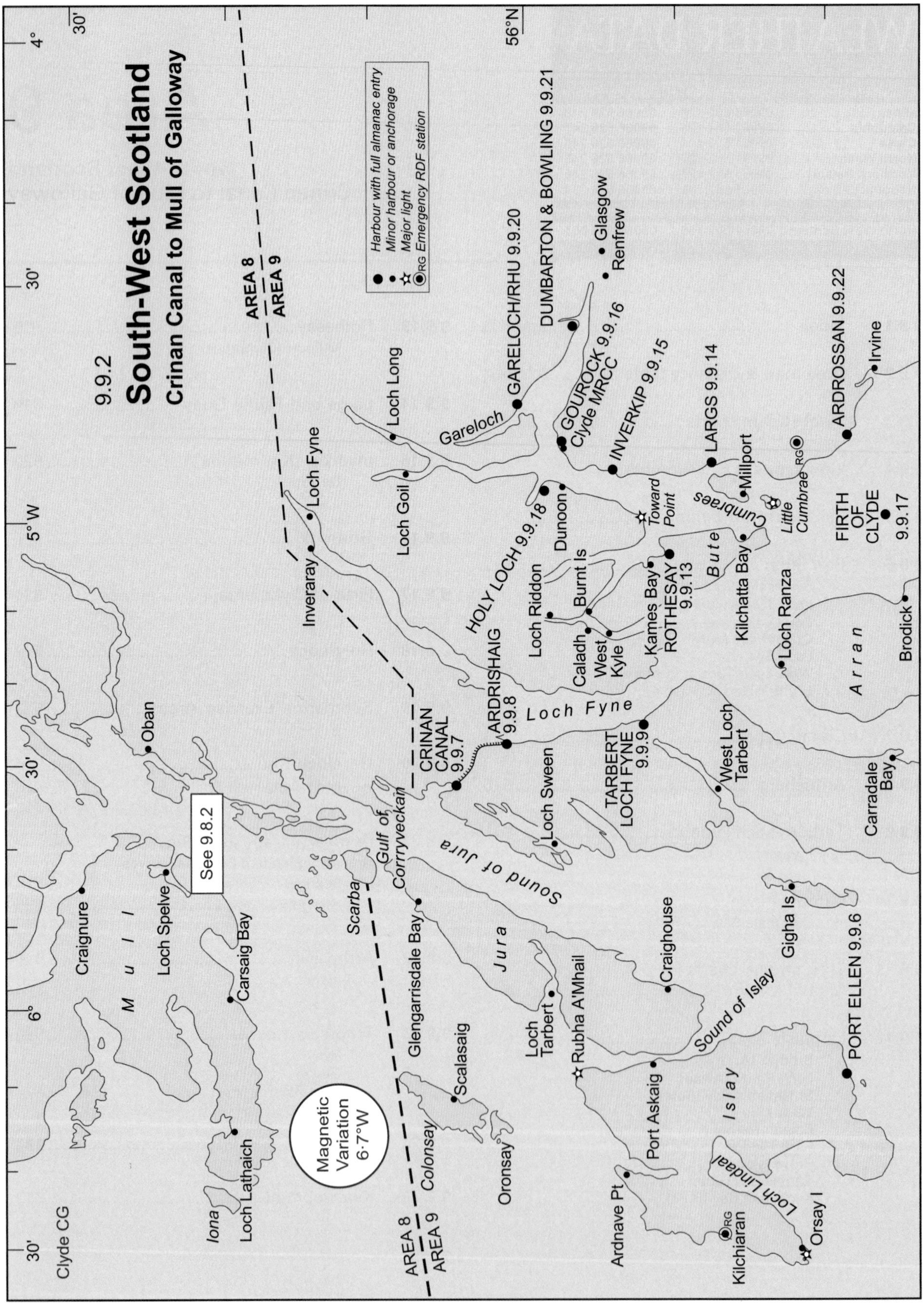
9.9.2
South-West Scotland
Crinan Canal to Mull of Galloway
Harbour with full almanac entry
Minor harbour or anchorage
Major light
RG Emergency RDF station
Magnetic Variation 6·7°W
AREA 8
AREA 9
See 9.8.2
Clyde CG
Mull
Craignure
Loch Spelve
Carsaig Bay
Iona
Loch Lathaich
Oban
Colonsay
Oronsay
Scalasaig
Glengarrisdale Bay
Scarba
Gulf of Corryvreckan
Jura
Sound of Jura
Loch Tarbert
Rubha A'Mhail
Craighouse
Sound of Islay
Port Askaig
Islay
PORT ELLEN 9.9.6
Loch Indaal
Ardnave Pt
Kilchiaran
Orsay I
Gigha Is
CRINAN CANAL 9.9.7
ARDRISHAIG 9.9.8
Loch Sween
TARBERT LOCH FYNE 9.9.9
West Loch Tarbert
Carradale Bay
Loch Fyne
Inveraray
Loch Goil
Loch Long
Gareloch
GARELOCH/RHU 9.9.20
DUMBARTON & BOWLING 9.9.21
Glasgow
Renfrew
GOUROCK 9.9.16
Clyde MRCC
INVERKIP 9.9.15
LARGS 9.9.14
Millport
Cumbraes
Little Cumbrae
ARDROSSAN 9.9.22
Irvine
FIRTH OF CLYDE 9.9.17
HOLY LOCH 9.9.18
Dunoon
Toward Point
Loch Riddon
Burnt Is
Caladh
West Kyle
Kames Bay
ROTHESAY 9.9.13
Bute
Kilchatta Bay
Loch Ranza
Arran
Brodick
4°
30'
5°W
6°
56°N

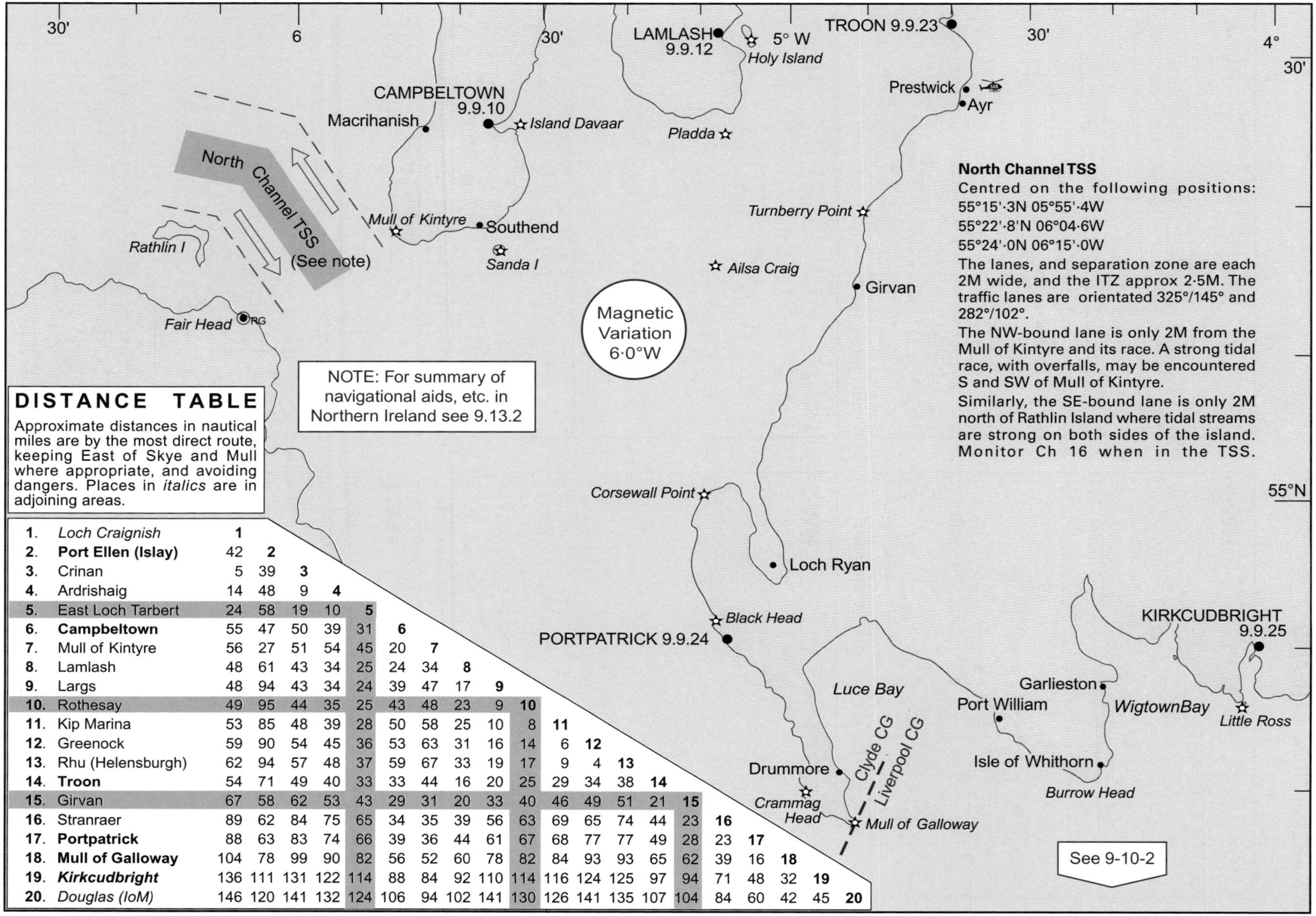
30'
6
30'
5° W
30'
4°
30'
55°N
LAMLASH
9.9.12
Holy Island
TROON 9.9.23
Prestwick
Ayr
CAMPBELTOWN
9.9.10
Macrihanish
Island Davaar
Pladda
North Channel TSS
(See note)
Mull of Kintyre
Southend
Sanda I
Rathlin I
Fair Head
RG
Turnberry Point
Ailsa Craig
Girvan
Magnetic
Variation
6·0°W
Corsewall Point
Loch Ryan
Black Head
PORTPATRICK 9.9.24
Luce Bay
Drummore
Crammag
Head
Clyde CG
Liverpool CG
Mull of Galloway
Port William
Garlieston
WigtownBay
Isle of Whithorn
Burrow Head
KIRKCUDBRIGHT
9.9.25
Little Ross
See 9-10-2

NOTE: For summary of navigational aids, etc. in Northern Ireland see 9.13.2

North Channel TSS

Centred on the following positions:
55°15'·3N 05°55'·4W
55°22'·8'N 06°04·6W
55°24'·0N 06°15'·0W

The lanes, and separation zone are each 2M wide, and the ITZ approx 2·5M. The traffic lanes are orientated 325°/145° and 282°/102°.

The NW-bound lane is only 2M from the Mull of Kintyre and its race. A strong tidal race, with overfalls, may be encountered S and SW of Mull of Kintyre.

Similarly, the SE-bound lane is only 2M north of Rathlin Island where tidal streams are strong on both sides of the island. Monitor Ch 16 when in the TSS.

DISTANCE TABLE

Approximate distances in nautical miles are by the most direct route, keeping East of Skye and Mull where appropriate, and avoiding dangers. Places in *italics* are in adjoining areas.

		1	2	3	4	5	6	7
1.	*Loch Craignish*	1						
2.	**Port Ellen (Islay)**	42	2					
3.	Crinan	5	39	3				
4.	Ardrishaig	14	48	9	4			
5.	East Loch Tarbert	24	58	19	10	5		
6.	**Campbeltown**	55	47	50	39	31	6	
7.	Mull of Kintyre	56	27	51	54	45	20	7
8.	Lamlash	48	61	43	34	25	24	34
9.	Largs	48	94	43	34	24	39	47
10.	Rothesay	49	95	44	35	25	43	48
11.	Kip Marina	53	85	48	39	28	50	58
12.	Greenock	59	90	54	45	36	53	63
13.	Rhu (Helensburgh)	62	94	57	48	37	59	67
14.	**Troon**	54	71	49	40	33	33	44
15.	Girvan	67	58	62	53	43	29	31
16.	Stranraer	89	62	84	75	65	34	35
17.	**Portpatrick**	88	63	83	74	66	39	36
18.	**Mull of Galloway**	104	78	99	90	82	56	52
19.	***Kirkcudbright***	136	111	131	122	114	88	84
20.	*Douglas (IoM)*	146	120	141	132	124	106	94

		8	9	10	11	12	13	14
8.	Lamlash	8						
9.	Largs	17	9					
10.	Rothesay	23	9	10				
11.	Kip Marina	25	10	8	11			
12.	Greenock	31	16	14	6	12		
13.	Rhu (Helensburgh)	33	19	17	9	4	13	
14.	**Troon**	16	20	25	29	34	38	14
15.	Girvan	20	33	40	46	49	51	21
16.	Stranraer	39	56	63	69	65	74	44
17.	**Portpatrick**	44	61	67	68	77	77	49
18.	**Mull of Galloway**	60	78	82	84	93	93	65
19.	***Kirkcudbright***	92	110	114	116	124	125	97
20.	*Douglas (IoM)*	102	141	130	126	141	135	107

		15	16	17	18	19	20
15.	Girvan	15					
16.	Stranraer	23	16				
17.	**Portpatrick**	28	23	17			
18.	**Mull of Galloway**	62	39	16	18		
19.	***Kirkcudbright***	94	71	48	32	19	
20.	*Douglas (IoM)*	104	84	60	42	45	20

9.9.3 AREA 9 TIDAL STREAMS

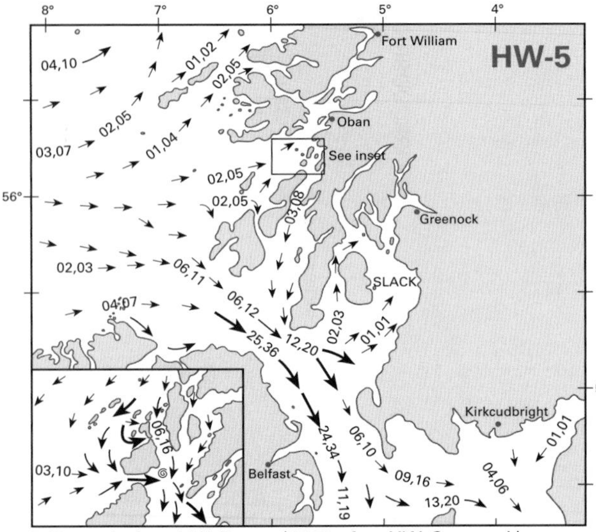
HW-5
Fort William
Oban
See inset
Greenock
SLACK
Kirkcudbright
Belfast

5 Hours before HW Dover (0605 after HW Greenock)

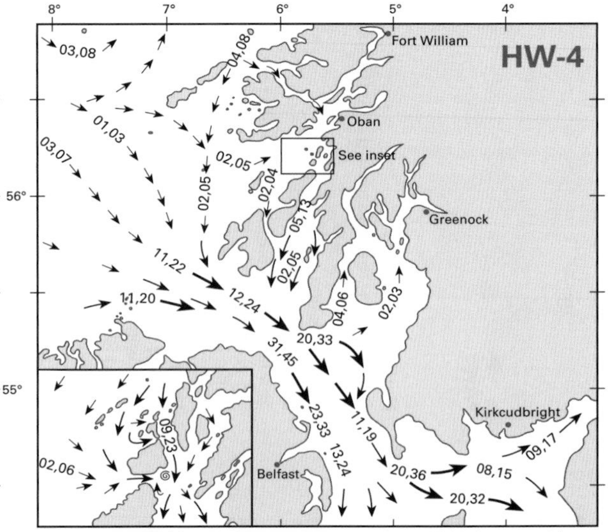
HW-4
Fort William
Oban
See inset
Greenock
Kirkcudbright
Belfast

4 Hours before HW Dover (0520 before HW Greenock)

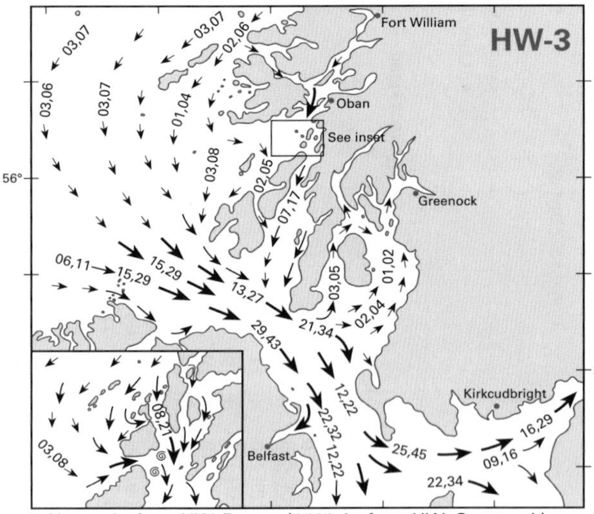
HW-3
Fort William
Oban
See inset
Greenock
Kirkcudbright
Belfast

3 Hours before HW Dover (0420 before HW Greenock)

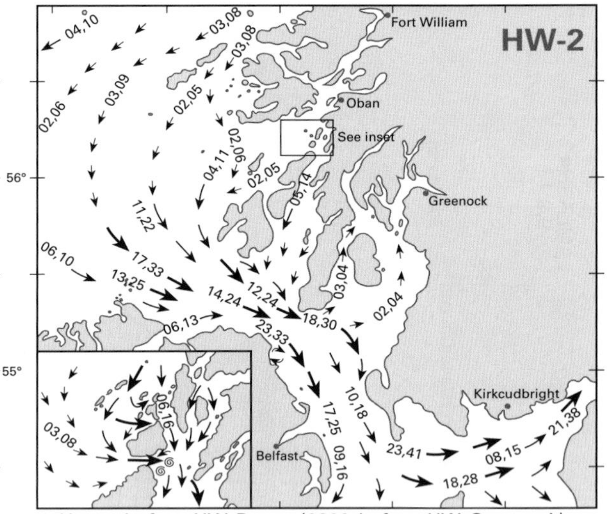
HW-2
Fort William
Oban
See inset
Greenock
Kirkcudbright
Belfast

2 Hours before HW Dover (0320 before HW Greenock)

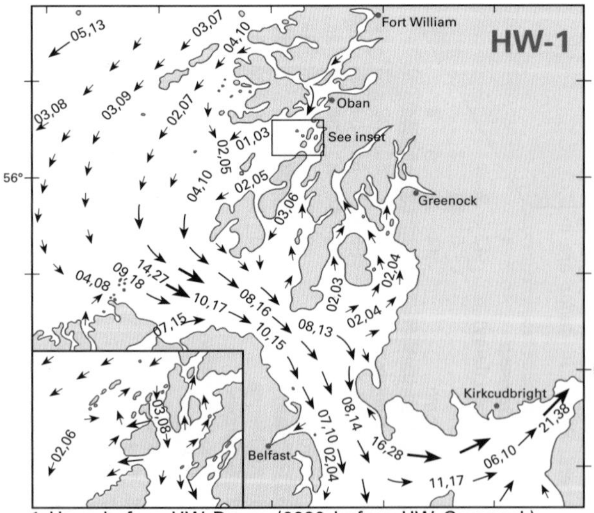
HW-1
Fort William
Oban
See inset
Greenock
Kirkcudbright
Belfast

1 Hour before HW Dover (0220 before HW Greenock)

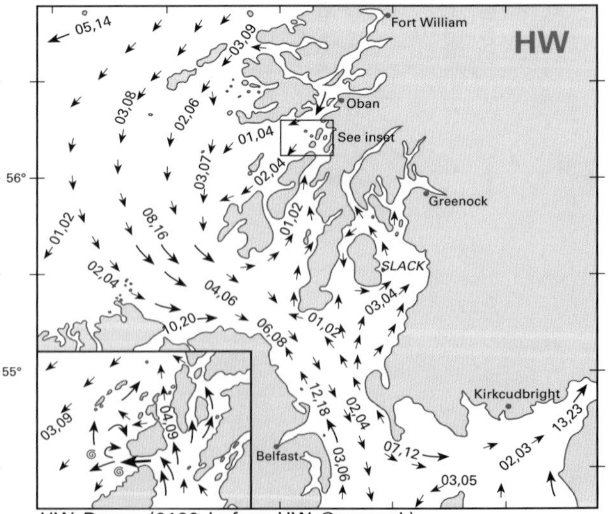
HW
Fort William
Oban
See inset
Greenock
SLACK
Kirkcudbright
Belfast

HW Dover (0120 before HW Greenock)

Northward 9.8.3 Mull of Kintyre 9.9.12 Irish Sea 9.10.3 Northern Ireland 9.13.3

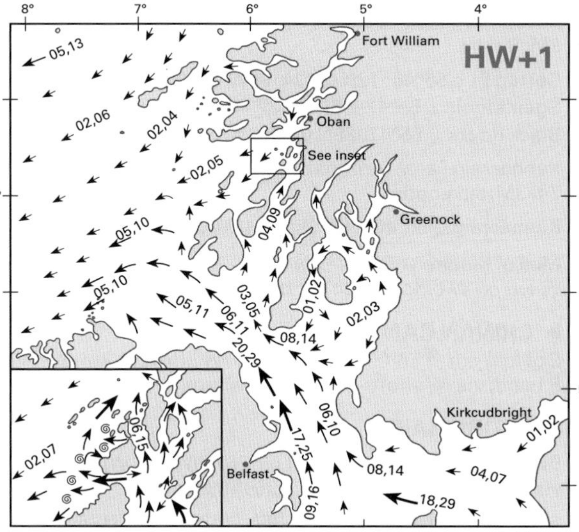
8°
7°
6°
5°
4°
56°
Fort William
HW+1
Oban
See inset
Greenock
Kirkcudbright
Belfast
05,13
02,06
02,04
02,05
04,09
05,10
05,10
05,11
06,11
03,05
01,02
02,03
08,14
20,29
17,25
06,10
08,14
04,07
18,29
09,16
01,02
02,07
06,15

1 Hour after HW Dover (0020 before HW Greenock)

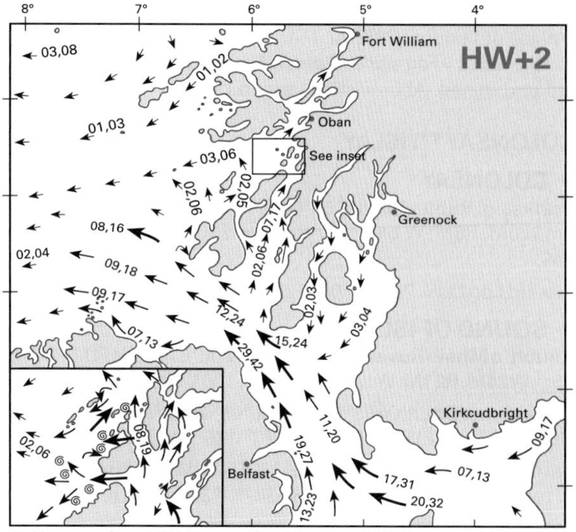
8°
7°
6°
5°
4°
56°
55°
Fort William
HW+2
Oban
See inset
Greenock
Kirkcudbright
Belfast
03,08
01,02
01,03
03,06
02,05
02,06
07,17
02,06
08,16
02,04
09,18
09,17
07,13
12,24
29,42
15,24
02,03
03,04
11,20
19,27
13,23
17,31
20,32
07,13
09,17
02,06
06,19

2 Hours after HW Dover (0040 after HW Greenock)

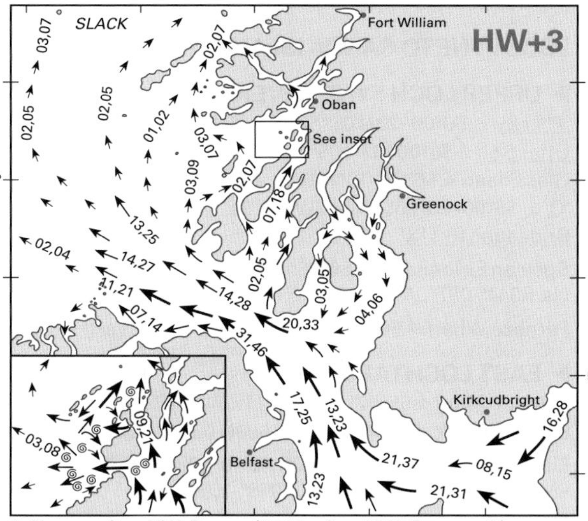
56°
SLACK
Fort William
HW+3
Oban
See inset
Greenock
Kirkcudbright
Belfast
03,07
02,07
02,05
02,05
01,02
03,07
03,09
02,07
07,18
13,25
02,04
14,27
11,21
14,28
02,05
03,05
04,06
20,33
07,14
31,46
17,25
13,23
21,37
08,15
16,28
21,31
13,23
03,08
09,21

3 Hours after HW Dover (0140 after HW Greenock)

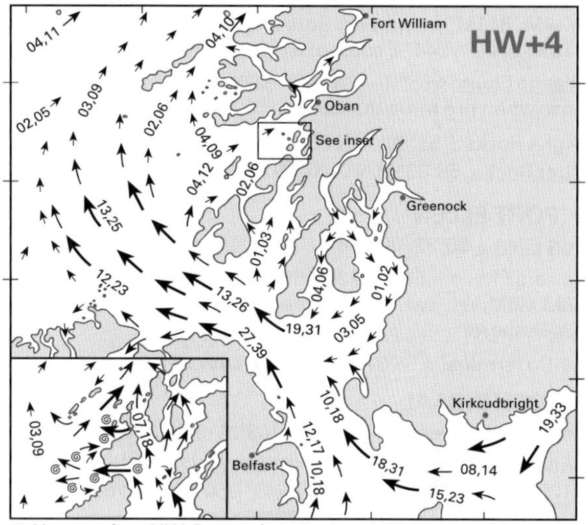
56°
55°
Fort William
HW+4
Oban
See inset
Greenock
Kirkcudbright
Belfast
04,11
04,10
02,05
03,09
02,06
04,09
04,12
02,06
13,25
01,03
12,23
13,26
04,06
01,02
19,31
27,39
03,05
10,18
12,17
10,18
18,31
08,14
19,33
15,23
03,09
07,18

4 Hours after HW Dover (0240 after HW Greenock)

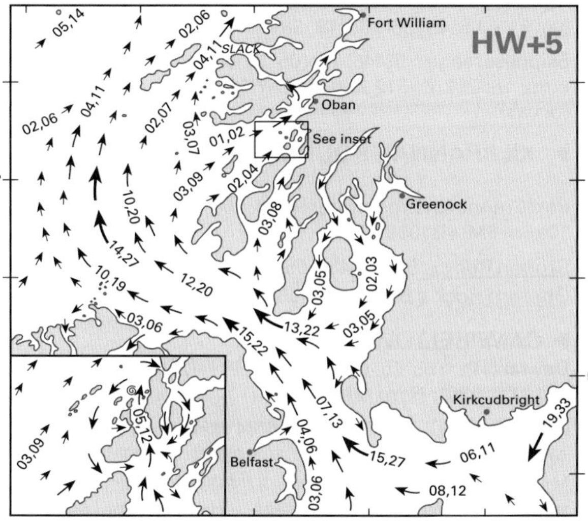
56°
Fort William
HW+5
SLACK
Oban
See inset
Greenock
Kirkcudbright
Belfast
05,14
02,06
04,11
04,11
02,06
02,07
03,07
01,02
10,20
03,09
02,04
03,08
14,27
10,19
12,20
03,05
02,03
03,06
13,22
03,05
15,22
07,13
04,06
15,27
06,11
19,33
08,12
03,06
03,09
05,12

5 Hours after HW Dover (0340 after HW Greenock)

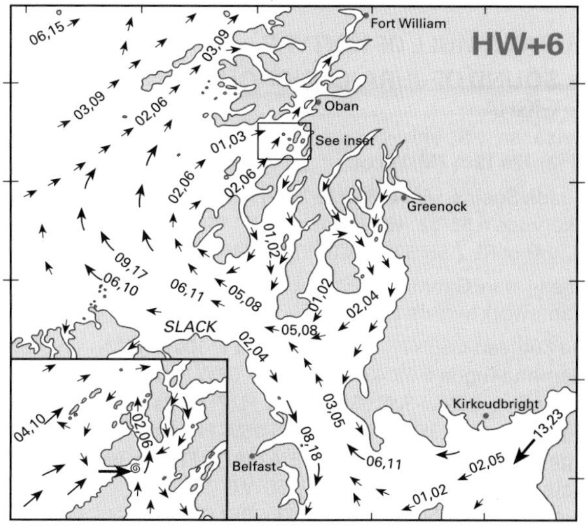
56°
55°
Fort William
HW+6
Oban
See inset
Greenock
Kirkcudbright
Belfast
06,15
03,09
03,09
02,06
01,03
02,06
02,06
01,02
09,17
06,10
06,11
05,08
01,02
02,04
SLACK
05,08
02,04
03,05
08,18
06,11
13,23
02,05
01,02
04,10
02,06

6 Hours after HW Dover (0440 after HW Greenock)

9

PLOT WAYPOINTS ON YOUR CHART BEFORE USING THEM

9.9.4 LIGHTS, BUOYS AND WAYPOINTS

Blue print = light with a nominal range of 15M or more. CAPITALS = place or feature. *CAPITAL ITALICS* = light-vessel, light float or Lanby. *Italics* = Fog signal. ***Bold italics*** = Racon. Useful waypoints are underlined. Abbreviations are in Chapter 1.

COLONSAY TO ISLAY

▶ COLONSAY

Scalasaig, Rubha Dubh ☆ 56°04'·01N 06°10'·90W Fl (2) WR 10s 8m W8M, R6M; W bldg; vis: R shore-230°, W230°-337°, R337°-354°.

Pier Hd Ldg Lts ☆ 262° 56°04'·12N 06°11'·02W FR 8/10m (occas).

▶ SOUND OF ISLAY

Rhubh' a Mháil (Ruvaal) ☆ 55°56'·18N 06°07'·46W Fl (3) WR 15s 45m **W24M, R21M**; W twr; vis: R075°-180°, W180°-075°.

Carragh an t'Struith ☆ 55°52'·30N 06°05'·78W Fl WG 3s 8m W9M, G6M, W twr; vis: W354°-078°, G078°-170°, W170°-185°.

Carraig Mòr ☆ 55°50'·42N 06°06'·13W Fl (2) WR 6s 7m W8M, R6M; W twr; vis: R shore-175°, W175°-347°, R347°-shore.

Black Rocks 55°47'·50N 06°04'·09W Fl G 6s.

McArthur's Hd ☆ 55°45'·84N 06°02'·90W Fl (2) WR 10s 39m W14M, R11M; W twr; W in Sound of Islay from NE coast-159°, R159°-244°, W244°-E coast of Islay.

Eilean a Chùirn ☆ 55°40'·12N 06°01'·22W Fl (3) 18s 26m 8M; W Bn; obsc when brg more than 040°.

Gigha Rocks 55°39'·20N 05°43'·65W Q (9) 15s.

Otter Rock 55°33'·86N 06°07'·92W Q (6) + L Fl 15s.

▶ PORT ELLEN

Port Ellen 55°37'·00N 06°12'·27W QG.

Carraig Fhada ☆ 55°37'·22N 06°12'·71W Fl WRG 3s 20m W8M, R6M, G6M; W□twr; vis: W shore-248°, G248°-311°, W311°-340°, R340°-shore.

Ro-Ro terminal ☆ 55°37'·61N 06°11'·44W 2 FG (vert) 7m 3M.

▶ LOCH INDAAL

Bruichladdich Pier Hd ☆ 55°45'·83N 06°21'·67 W 2 FR (vert) 6m 5M.

Rubh'an Dùin ☆ 55°44'·70N 06°22'·28 W Fl (2) WR 7s 15m W13M, R12M; W twr; vis: W218°-249°, R249°-350°, W350°-036°.

Orsay Is, **Rhinns of Islay** ☆ 55°40'·40N 06°30'·84W Fl 5s 46m **24M**; W twr; vis: 256°-184°.

JURA TO MULL OF KINTYRE

▶ SOUND OF JURA/CRAIGHOUSE/LOCH SWEEN/GIGHA

Reisa an t-Struith, S end of Is ☆ 56°07'·77N 05°38'·91W Fl (2) 12s 12m 7M; W col.

Ruadh Sgeir ☆ 56°04'·32N 05°39'·77W Fl 6s 15m 9M; W○ twr.

Skervuile ☆ 55°52'·46N 05°49'·85W Fl 15s 22m 9M; W twr.

Ninefoot Rk 55°52'·46N 05°52'·95W Q (3) 10s.

Eilean nan Gabhar ☆ 55°50'·04N 05°56'·25W Fl 5s 7m 8M; framework twr; vis: 225°-010°.

Na Cùiltean ☆ 55°48'·64N 05°54'·90W Fl 10s 9m 9M.

Gamhna Gigha ☆ 55°43'·78N 05°41'·08W Fl (2) 6s 7m 5M.

Badh Rk 55°42'·30N 05°41'·24W Fl (2) G 12s.

Sgeir Nuadh 55°41'·78N 05°42'·06W Fl R 6s.

Sgeir Gigalum 55°39'·96N 05°42'·67W Fl G 6s 3m 4M.

Cath Sgeir 55°39'·66N 05°47'·50W Q (9) 15s.

Gigalum Rks 55°39'·20N 05°43'·70W Q (9) 15s.

Caolas Gigalum 55°39'·15N 05°44'·57W.

▶ WEST LOCH TARBERT

Dunskeig Bay ☆ 55°45'·22N 05°35'·00W Q (2) 10s 11m 8M.

Eileen Tráighe (off S side) 55°45'·37N 05°35'·75W Fl (2) R 5s 5m 3M; R post.

Corran Pt 55°46'·12N 05°34'·35W QG 3m 3M; G post.

Sgeir Mhein 55°47'·06N 05°32'·42W QR 3m 3M; R post.

Black Rocks 55°47'·89N 05°30'·20W QG 3M; G post.

Kennacraig Ferry Terminal ☆ 55°48'·40N 05°29'·01W 2 FG (vert) 7m 3M; silver post.

Kennacraig 55°48'·66N 05°29'·18W QR; unreliable.

Mull of Kintyre ☆ 55°18'·64N 05°48'·25W Fl (2) 20s 91m **24M**; W twr on W bldg; vis: 347°-178°; *Horn Mo (N) 90s*.

▶ CRINAN CANAL

E of lock ent ☆ 56°05'·48N 05°33'·37W Fl WG 3s 8m 4M; W twr, R band; vis: W shore-146°, G146°-shore.

▶ ARDRISHAIG

Breakwater Hd ☆ 56°00'·76N 05°26'·59W L Fl WRG 6s 9m 4M; vis: G287°-339°, W339°-350°, R350°-035°.

Sgeir Sgalag No. 49 56°00'·36N 05°26'·30W Fl G 5s.

Gulnare Rk No. 48 56°00'·18N 05°26'·31W Fl R 4s.

LOCH FYNE TO SANDA ISLAND

▶ UPPER LOCH FYNE/INVERARY

'P' Lt By 56°00'·23N 05°22'·07W Fl R 3s.

Otter Spit ☆ 56°00'·63N 05°21'·10W Fl G 3s 7m 8M.

Glas Eilean ☆ 56°01'·10N 05°21'·16W Fl R 5s 12m 7M.

'Q' 56°00'·95N 05°20'·67W Fl R 3s.

Brideagan Rks 'X' 56°06'·32N 05°14'·06W Fl R 3s.

Sgeir an Eirionnaich ☆ 56°06'·47N 05°13'·55W Fl WR 3s 7m 8M; vis: R044°-087°, W087°-192°, R192°-210°, W210°-044°.

Furnace Wharf ☆ 56°09'·05N 05°10'·45W 2 FR (vert) 9m 5M.

▶ EAST LOCH TARBERT

Madadh Maol ☆ 55°52'·02N 05°24'·25W Fl R 2·5s 4m 3M.

Eilean a'Choic, SE side ☆ 55°51'·99N 05°24'·37W QG 3m 2M.

Eilean na Beithe ☆ 55°52'·68N 05°19'·62W Fl WRG 3s 7m 5M; vis: G036°-065°, W065°-078°, R078°-106°.

Portavadie Bkwtr ☆ 55°52'·52N 05°19'·24W 2 FG (vert) 6/4m 4M.

Sgat Mór ☆ 55°50'·85N 05°18'·50W Fl 3s 9m 12M; W○ twr.

No. 51 55°45'·56N 05°19'·68W Fl R 4s.

Skipness range ☆ 55°46'·72N 05°19'·06W Iso R 8s 7m 10M; Y ◇ on bldg; vis 292·2°-312·2°. Oc (2) Y 10s **24M** when range in use (occas).

▶ KILBRANNAN SOUND/CRANNAICH/CARRADALE BAY

Port Crannaich Breakwater Head ☆ 55°35'·60N 05°27'·84W Fl R 10s 5m 6M; vis: 099°-279°.

Crubon Rock 55°34'·48N 05°27'·07W Fl (2) R 12s.

Otterard Rock 55°27'·07N 05°31'·11W Q (3) 10s.

▶ CAMPBELTOWN LOCH

Davaar N Pt ☆ 55°25'·69N 05°32'·42W Fl (2) 10s 37m **23M**; W twr; vis: 073°-330°; *Horn (2) 20s*.

Methe Bank 'C' 55°25'·30N 05°34'·42W Fl (2) 6s.

Arranman's Barrels 55°19'·40N 05°32'·87W Fl (2) R 12s.

Macosh Rock 55°17'·95N 05°37'·00W Fl R 6s.

Sanda Island ☆ 55°16'·50N 05°35'·01W Fl 10s 50m **15M**; W twr.

Patersons Rock 55°16'·90N 05°32'·48W Fl (3) R 18s.

KYLES OF BUTE TO RIVER CLYDE

▶ KYLES OF BUTE/CALADH

Ardlamont Point No. 47 ⌐ 55°49'·59N 05°11'·76W Fl R 4s.

Carry Point No. 46 ⌐ 55°51'·39N 05°12'·24W Fl R 4s.

Rubha Ban ⌐ 55°54'·95N 05°12'·40W Fl R 4s.

Burnt Is ▲ (NE of Eilean Fraoich) 55°55'·78N 05°10'·49W Fl G 3s.

Burnt I No. 42 ⌐ (S of Eilean Buidhe) 55°55'·76N 05°10'·39W Fl R 2s.

Creyke Rock No. 45 ⌐ 55°55'·67N 05°10'·89W.

Beere Rock No. 44 ▲ 55°55'·55N 05°10'·63W.

Wood Farm Rock No. 43 ▲ 55°55'·41N 05°10'·34W.

Rubha á Bhodaich ▲ 55°55'·38N 05°09'·59W Fl G.

Ardmaleish Point No. 41 ↨ 55°53'·02N 05°04'·70W Q.

▶ ROTHESAY

Front Pier, E end ↯ 55°50'·32N 05°03'·10W 2 FG (vert) 7m 5M.

Pier W end ↯ 55°50'·35N 05°03'·32W 2 FR (vert) 7m 5M.

Albert Pier near N end ↯ 2 FR (vert) 8m 5M.

▶ FIRTH OF CLYDE

Ascog Patches No. 13 ↨ 55°49'·71N 05°00'·25W Fl (2) 10s 5m 5M.

Toward Pt ☆ 55°51'·73N 04°58'·79W Fl 10s 21m **22M**; W twr.

No. 34 ↧ 55°51'·44N 04°59'·11W.

Toward Bank No. 35 ▲ 55°51'·04N 05°00'·01W Fl G 3s.

Skelmorlie ↨ 55°51'·65N 04°56'·34W Iso 5s.

▶ WEMYSS/INVERKIP

Wemyss Bay Pier ↯ 55°52'·56N 04°53'·47W 2 FG (vert) 7m 5M.

'M' ▲ 55°53'·52N 04°54'·41W Fl G 5s.

'O' ▲ 55°54'·55N 04°54'·55W Fl G 2·5s.

Kip ▲ 55°54'·49N 04°52'·98W QG.

Warden Bank ▲ 55°54'·77N 04°54'·54W Fl G 2s.

Cowal ↨ 55°56'·00N 04°54'·83W L Fl 10s.

The Gantocks ↧ 55°56'·45N 04°55'·08W Fl R 6s 12m 6M; ◯ twr.

▶ DUNOON

Dunoon Pier, S end 55°56'·76N 04°55'·31W and N end ↯ both 2 FR (vert) 5m 6M.

Cloch Point ↯ 55°56'·55N 04°52'·74W Fl 3s 24m 8M; W ◯ twr, B band, W dwellings.

McInroy's Point, Ro-Ro Ferry terminal Head ↯ 55°57'·08N 04°51'·26W 2 FG (vert) 5/3m 6M.

▶ HOLY LOCH

Hunter's Quay, Ro-Ro terminal ↯ 55°58'·26N 04°54'·50W 2 FR (vert) 6/4m 6M.

Holy Loch Marina 55°59'·00N 04°56'·80W 2 FR (vert) 4m 1M.

▶ LOCH LONG/LOCH GOIL

Loch Long ↨ 55°59'·15N 04°52'·42W Oc 6s.

Baron's Pt No. 3 ↯ 55°59'·18N 04°51'·12W Oc (2) Y 10s 5m 3M.

Ravenrock Pt ↯ 56°02'·14N 04°54'·39W Fl 4s 12m 10M; W twr on W col. Dir lt 204°, WRG 9m (same twr); vis: F R201·5°-203°, Al WR203°-203·5° (W phase incr with brg), F 203·5°-204·5°, Al WG204·5°-205° (G phase incr with brg), FG205°-206·5°.

Port Dornaige ↯ 56°03'·75N 04°53'·65W Fl 6s 8m 11M; W col; vis: 026°-206°.

Carraig nan Ron (Dog Rock) ↯ 56°06'·00N 04°51'·71W Fl 2s 7m 11M; W col.

Rubha Ardnahein ↯ 56°06'·15N 04°53'·60W Fl R 5s 3m 3M; vis: 132°-312°.

The Perch, Ldg Lts 318° Front, 56°06'·90N 04°54'·31W F WRG 3m 5M; vis: G311°-317°, W317°-320°, R320°-322°. Same structure, Fl R 3s 3m 3M; vis: 187°-322°. Rear, 700m from front, F 7m 5M; vis: 312°-322·5°.

Cnap Pt ↯ 56°07'·40N 04°49'·97W Ldg Lts 031°. Front, Q 8m 10M; W col. Rear, 87m from front F 13m; R line on W twr.

Ashton ↨ 55°58'·10N 04°50'·65W Iso 5s.

▶ GOUROCK

Railway Pier Hd ↯ 55°57'·77N 04°49'·06W 2 FG (vert) 10m 3M.

Kempock Pt No. 4 ↯ 55°57'·71N 04°49'·37W Oc (2) Y 10s 6m 3M.

Whiteforeland ⌐ 55°58'·11N 04°47'·28W L Fl 10s.

Rosneath Patch ↨ 55°58'·52N 04°47'·45W Fl (2) 10s 5m 10M.

▶ ROSNEATH/RHU NARROWS/GARELOCH

Ldg Lts 356°. **Front, No. 7N** ↨ 56°00'·05N 04°45'·36W Dir lt 356°. WRG 5m **W16M**, R13M, G13M; vis: Al WG 353°-355°, FW 355°-357°, Al WR 357°-000°, FR000°-002°.

Dir lt 115° WRG 5m **W16M**, R13M, G13M; vis: Al WG 111°-114°; F 114°-116°, Al WR 116°-119°; F R119°-121°. Passing lt Oc G 6s 6m 3M; G △ on G pile. Rear, Ardencaple Castle Centre ↯ 56°00'·54N 04°45'·43W 2 FG (vert) 26m 12M; twr on Castle NW corner; vis: 335°-020°.

No. 8N Lt Bn ↨ 56°59'·09N 04°44'·21W Dir lt 080° WRG 4m; **W16M**, R13M, G13M; vis: F G 075°-077·5°, Al WG077·5°-079·5°, F079·5°-080·5°, Alt WR080·5°-082·5°, FR082·5°-085°. Dir lt 138° WRG 4m **W16M**, R13M, G13M; vis: FG132°-134°, Al WG134°-137°, F 137°-139°, Al WR139°-142°. Passing lt Fl Y 3s 6m 3M.

Gareloch No. 1 Lt Bn ↨ 55°59'·12N 04°43'·89W VQ (4) Y 5s 9m; Y 'X' on Y structure.

Row ▲ 55°59'·84N 04°45'·13W Fl G 5s.

Cairndhu ▲ 56°00'·35N 04°46'·00W Fl G 2·5s.

Castle Pt ↯ 56°00'·19N 04°46'·50W Fl (2) R 10s 8m 6M; R mast.

▲ 56°00'·61N 04°46'·53W Fl G 4s.

No. 3 N Lt Bn ↨ 56°00'·07N 04°46'·72W Dir lt 149° WRG 9m **W16M**, R13M, G13M F & Al; vis: FG144°-145°, Al WG145°-148°, F148°-150°, Al WR150°-153°, FR153°-154°. Passing lt Oc R 8s 9m 3M.

Rosneath DG Jetty ↯ 56°00'·39N 04°47'·51W 2 FR (vert) 5M; W col; vis: 150°-330°.

Rhu SE ▲ 56°00'·64N 04°47'·17W Fl G 3s.

Rhu Pt ↧ 56°00'·95N 04°47'·19W Q (3) WRG 6s 9m W10M, R7M, G7M; vis: G270°-000°, W000°-114°, R114°-188°.

Dir lt 318° WRG **W16M**, R13M, G13M; vis: Al WG 315°-317°, F317°-319°, Al WR319°-321°, FR321°-325°.

Limekiln No. 2N Lt Bn ↨ 56°00'·67N 04°47'·64W Dir lt 295° WRG 5m **W16M**, R13M, G13M F & Al; R □ on R Bn; vis: Al WG291°-294°, F294°-296°, Al WR 296°-299°, FR299°-301°.

Rhu NE ▲ 56°01'·02N 04°47'·58W QG.

Rhu Spit ↧ 56°00'·84N 04°47'·34W Fl 3s 6m 6M.

Mambeg Dir lt 331° 56°03'·74N 04°50'·47W Q (4) WRG 8s 10m 14M; vis: G328·5°-330°, W330°-332°, R332°-333°; H24.

▶ GREENOCK

Anchorage Lts in line 196°. Front, 55°57'·62N 04°46'·58W FG 7m 12M; Y col. Rear, 32m from front, FG 9m 12M. Y col.

Lts in line 194·5°. Front, 55°57'·45N 04°45'·91W FG 18m. Rear, 360m from front, FG 33m.

Clydeport Container Terminal NW corner ↯ QG 8m 8M.

Victoria Hbr W side ↯ 55°56'·77N 04°44'·70W 2 FG 5m (vert).

Garvel W end ↯ 55°56'·81N 04°43'·55W Oc G 10s 9m 4M.

E end, Maurice Clark Pt ↯ 55°56'·60N 04°42'·85W QG 7m 2M.

▶ PORT GLASGOW

Beacon off ent ↧ 55°56'·25N 04°41'·26W FG 7m 9M.

Steamboat Quay, W end ↯ 55°56'·25N 04°41'·44W FG 12m 12M;

9

PLOT WAYPOINTS ON YOUR CHART BEFORE USING THEM

B&W chequered col; vis 210°-290°. From here to Glasgow Lts on S bank are Fl G and Lts on N bank are Fl R.

CLYDE TO MULL OF GALLOWAY

▶ LARGS

Approach 55°46'·40N 04°51'·85W L Fl 10s.
Marina S Bkwtr Hd ☆ 55°46'·36N 04°51'·73W Oc G 10s 4m 4M.
W Bkwtr Hd ☆ 55°46'·37N 04°51'·67W Oc R 10s 4m 4M.

▶ FAIRLIE

Fairlie Patch 55°45'·38N 04°52'·34W Fl G 1·5s.
Hunterston Jetty S ☆ 55°45'·10N 04°52'·88W 2 FG (vert) 11m 5M.
Pier N ☆ 55°45'·30N 04°52'·65W 2 FG (vert) 11m 5M.
Fairlie Quay Pier Hd N ☆ 55°46'·06N 04°51'·78W 2 FG (vert).

▶ MILLPORT, GREAT CUMBRAE

The Eileans, W end ☆ 55°44'·89N 04°55'·59W QG 5m 2M.

Ldg Lts 333°. Pier Head front, 55°45'·04N 04°55'·85W FR 7m 5M. Rear, 137m from front, FR 9m 5M.

Mountstuart 55°48'·00N 04°57'·57W L Fl 10s.
Portachur 55°44'·35N 04°58'·52W Fl G 3s.

Runnaneun Pt (Rubha'n Eun) ☆ 55°43'·79N 05°00'·23W Fl R 6s 8m 12M; W twr.

Sheanawally Point ☆ 55°44'·12N 04°56'·37W Fl 10s 6m 5M; vis: 061°300°.

Little Cumbrae I Cumbrae Elbow ☆ 55°43'·22N 04°58'·06W Fl 6s 28m 14M; W twr; vis: 334°-193°.

▶ ARDROSSAN

Approach Dir lt 055° 55°38'·66N 04°49'·22W WRG 15m W14M, R11M, G11M; vis: F G050°-051·2°, Alt WG 051·2°-053·8°, W phase inc with Brg; F W053·8°-056·2°; Alt WR 056·2°-058·8°. R phase inc with brg; F R058·8°-060°. Same structure FR 13m 6M; vis: 325°-145°.

N Bkwtr Hd ☆ 55°38'·53N 04°49'·64W Fl R 5s 7m 5M; R gantry.
W Crinan Rk 55°38'·47N 04°49'·89W Fl R 4s.

Lighthouse Pier Head ☆ 55°38'·47N 04°49'·57W Iso WG 4s 11m 9M; W twr; vis: W035°-317°, G317°-035°.

Eagle Rock 55°38'·21N 04°49'·69W Fl G 5s.

▶ IRVINE

Ent N side ☆ 55°36'·21N 04°42'·09W Fl R 3s 6m 5M; R col.
S side ☆ 55°36'·17N 04°42'·04W Fl G 3s 6m 5M; G col.

Ldg Lts 051°. Front, 55°36'·40N 04°41'·57W FG 10m 5M. Rear, 101m from front, FR 15m 5M; G masts, both vis: 019°-120°.

▶ TROON

Troon 55°33'·06N 04°41'·35W Fl G 4s.
Troon Approach 55°33'·06N 04°41'·35W Fl R 2s 4m 3M.

West Pier Head ☆ 55°33'·07N 04°41'·02W Fl (2) WG 5s 11m 9M; W twr; vis: G036°-090°, W090°-036°.

East Pier Head ☆ 55°33'·03N 04°40'·96W Fl R 10s 6m 3M.
Lady I 55°31'·63N 04°44'·04W Fl 2s 19m 8M; W Bn.

▶ ARRAN/RANZA/LAMLASH/BRODICK

Brodick Pier Hd ☆ 55°32'·64N 05°08'·28W 2 FR (vert) 9m 4M.
Hamilton Rk 55°32'·63N 05°04'·90W Fl R 6s.
Pillar Rk Pt ☆ (Holy Island), 55°31'·04N 05°03'·67W Fl (2) 20s 38m **25M**; W □ twr.
Fullarton Rk 55°30'·64N 05°04'·57W Fl (2) R 12s.

Holy I SW end ☆ 55°30'·73N 05°04'·21W Fl G 3s 14m 10M; W twr; vis: 282°-147°.

Pladda ☆ 55°25'·50N 05°07'·12W Fl (3) 30s 40m **17M**; W twr.

▶ AYR

S. Nicholas 55°28'·12N 04°39'·44W Fl G 2s.
North Breakwater Head ☆ 55°28'·21N 04°38'·78W QR 9m 5M.

South Pier Head ☆ 55°28'·17N 04°38'·74W Q 7m 7M; R twr; vis: 012°-161°. Also FG 5m 5M; vis: 012°-082°.

Ldg Lts 098°. Front, 55°28'·15N 04°38'·38W FR 10m 5M; Tfc sigs. Rear, 130m from front Oc R 10s 18m 9M.

Turnberry Point ☆, near castle ruins 55°19'·56N 04°50'·71W Fl 15s 29m **24M**; W twr.

Ailsa Craig ☆ 55°15'·12N 05°06'·52W Fl 4s 18m **17M**; W twr; vis: 145°-028°.

▶ GIRVAN

S Pier Hd ☆ 55°14'·72N 04°51'·90W 2 FG (vert) 8m 4M; W twr.
N Bkwtr Hd 55°14'·74N 04°51'·85W Fl (2) R 6s 7m 4M.
N Groyne Hd 55°14'·71N 04°51'·71W Iso 4s 3m 4M.

▶ LOCH RYAN

Milleur Point 54°01'·28N 05°05'·66W Q.
Forbes Shoal 54°59'·47N 05°02'·96W QR.
Loch Ryan W 54°59'·23N 05°03'·24W QG.
Cairn Pt ☆ 54°58'·46N 05°01'·85W Fl (2) R 10s 14m 12M; W twr.
Cairnryan ☆ 54°57'·77N 05°00'·99W Fl R 5s 5m 5M.
Stranraer No.1 54°56'·67N 05°01'·32W Oc G 6s.
No. 3 54°55'·87N 05°01'·60W QG.
No. 5 54°55'·08N 05°01'·86W Fl G 3s.

▶ STRANRAER

Ross Pier Head ☆ 54°54'·54N 05°01'·64W 2 F Bu (vert).
E Pier Head ☆ 54°54'·61N 05°01'·60W 2 FR (vert) 9m.
W Pier Head ☆ 54°54'·51N 05°01'·75W 2 FG (vert) 8m 4M; Gy col.

Corsewall Point ☆ 55°00'·41N 05°09'·58W Fl (5) 30s 34m **22M**; W twr; vis: 027°-257°.

Killantringan Black Head ☆ 54°51'·70N 05°08'·85W Fl (2) 15s 49m **25M**; W twr.

▶ PORTPATRICK

Ldg Lts 050·5°. Front, 54°50'·50N 05°07'·02W FG (occas). Rear, 68m from front, FG 8m (occas).

Crammag Hd ☆ 54°39'·90N 04°57'·92W Fl 10s 35m **18M**; W twr.

Mull of Galloway ☆, SE end 54°38'·08N 04°51'·45W Fl 20s 99m **28M**; W twr; vis: 182°-105°.

▶ ISLE OF WHITHORN/GARLIESTON

Port William Ldg Lts 105°. Front, Pier Head 54°45'·66N 04°35'·28W Fl G 3s 7m 3M. Rear, 130m from front, FG 10m 2M.

Whithorn Hbr E Pier Head ☆ 54°41'·88N 04°21'·86W QG 4m 5M.

Ldg Lts 335°. Front, 54°42'·01N 04°22'·05W Oc R 8s 7m 7M; Or ♦. Rear, 35m from front, Oc R 8s 9m 7M; Or ♦, synch.

Garlieston Pier Hd ☆ 54°47'·32N 04°21'·81W 2 FR (vert) 8m 3M.

Little Ross ☆ 54°45'·93N 04°05'·10W Fl 5s 50m 12M; W twr; obsc in Wigtown B when brg more than 103°.

▶ KIRKCUDBRIGHT BAY/KIPPFORD

No. 1 Lifeboat House ☆ 54°47'·68N 04°03'·74W Fl 3s 7m 3M.0
No.12 54°49'·15N 04°04'·83W Fl R 3s.
Perch No.14 ☆ 54°49'·24N 04°04'·83W Fl 3s 5m.
No. 22 54°50'·08N 04°04'·02W Fl R 3s 2m.
Outfall 54°50'·18N 04°03'·84W Fl Y 5s 3m 2M; Y twr.
Hestan I, E end ☆ 54°49'·95N 03°48'·53W Fl (2) 10s 42m 9M.
Barnkirk Pt ☆ 54°58'·00N 03°16'·02W Fl 2s 18m 2M.

9.9.5 PASSAGE INFORMATION

Although conditions in the South-West of Scotland are in general less rugged than from Mull northwards, some of the remarks at the start of 9.8.5 are equally applicable to this area. Refer to the Admiralty *West Coast of Scotland Pilot*; to *Yachtsman's Pilot to the W Coast of Scotland, Clyde to Colonsay* (Imray/Lawrence) and to the Clyde Cruising Club's SDs. Submarines exercise throughout these waters; see 9.8.22 for information on active areas (Subfacts).

Some of the following more common Gaelic terms may help with navigation: *Acairseid*: anchorage. *Ailean*: meadow. *Aird, ard*: promontory. *Aisir, aisridh*: passage between rocks. *Beag*: little. *Beinn*: mountain. *Bo, boghar, bodha*: rock. *Cala*: harbour. *Camas*: channel, bay. *Caol*: strait. *Cladach*: shore, beach. *Creag*: cliff. *Cumhamn*: narrows. *Dubh, dhubh*: black. *Dun*: castle. *Eilean, eileanan*: island. *Garbh*: rough. *Geal, gheal*: white. *Glas, ghlas*: grey, green. *Inis*: island. *Kyle*: narrow strait. *Linn, Linne*: pool. *Mor, mhor*: large. *Mull*: promontory. *Rinn, roinn*: point. *Ruadh*: red, brown. *Rubha, rhu*: cape. *Sgeir*: rock. *Sruth*: current. *Strath*: river valley. *Tarbert*: isthmus. *Traigh*: beach. *Uig*: bay.

CORRYVRECKAN TO CRINAN (charts *2326*, 2343) ▶***Between Scarba and Jura is the Gulf of Corryvreckan (chart 2343) which is best avoided, and should never be attempted by yachts except at slack water and in calm conditions.*** *(In any event the Sound of Luing is always a safer and not much longer alternative). The Gulf has a least width of 6ca and is free of dangers, other than its very strong tides which, in conjunction with a very uneven bottom, cause extreme turbulence. This is particularly dangerous with strong W winds over a W-going (flood) tide which spews out several miles to seaward of the gulf, with overfalls extending 5M from the W of ent (The Great Race). Keep to the S side of the gulf to avoid the worst turbulence and the whirlpool known as The Hag, caused by depths of only 29m, as opposed to more than 100m in the fairway.* ***The W-going stream in the gulf begins at HW Oban + 0410, and the E-going at HW Oban – 0210. Sp rate W-going is 8·5kn, and E-going about 6kn.*** ◀

▶ *The range of tide at sp can vary nearly 2m between the E end of the gulf (1·5m) and the W end (3·4m), with HW ½ hr earlier at the E end. Slack water occurs at HW Oban +4 and –2½ and lasts almost 1 hr at nps, but only 15 mins at sps. On the W-going (flood) stream eddies form both sides of the gulf, but the one on the N (Scarba) shore is more important. Where this eddy meets the main stream off Camas nam Bairneach there is violent turbulence, with heavy overfalls extending W at the division of the eddy and the main stream.* ◀There are temp anchs with the wind in the right quarter in Bàgh Gleann a' Mhaoil in the SE corner of Scarba, and in Bàgh Gleann nam Muc at N end of Jura but the latter has rks in approaches E and SW of Eilean Beag.

SE of Corryvreckan is Loch Crinan, which leads to the Crinan Canal (9.9.7). Beware Black Rk, 2m high and 2ca N of the canal sea lock, and dangers extending 100m from the rk.

WEST OF JURA TO ISLAY (charts 2481, 2168) The W coasts of Colonsay and Oronsay (chart *2169*) are fringed with dangers up to 2M offshore. The two islands are separated by a narrow chan which dries and has an overhead cable (10m). There are HIE ⚓s at Scalasaig; see 9.9.6.

The Sound of Islay presents no difficulty; hold to the Islay shore, where all dangers are close in.▶ *The N-going stream begins at HW Oban + 0440, and the S-going at HW Oban – 0140. The sp rates are 2·5kn at N entrance and 1·5kn at S entrance, but reaching 5kn in the narrows off Port Askaig.*◀ There are anchs in the Sound, but mostly holding ground is poor. The best places are alongside at Port Askaig (9.9.6), or at anch off the distillery in Bunnahabhain B, 2·5M to N. ▶ *There are overfalls off McArthur's Hd (Islay side of S entrance) during the S-going stream.* ◀

The N coast of Islay and Rhinns of Islay are very exposed. In the N there is anch SE of Nave Island at entrance to Loch Gruinart; beware Balach Rks which dry, just to N.▶ *To the SW off Orsay (lt), Frenchman's Rks and W Bank there is a race and overfalls which should be cleared by 3M. Here the NW-going stream begins at HW Oban + 0530, and the SE-going at HW Oban – 0040;* ***sp rates are 6-8kn inshore,*** *but decrease to 3kn 5M offshore.* ◀ Loch Indaal gives some shelter; beware rks extending from Laggan Pt on E side of ent. Off the Mull of Oa there are further overfalls. Port Ellen, the main hbr on Islay, has HIE ⚓s; there are some dangers in approach, and it is exposed to S; see 9.9.6 and chart 2474.

SOUND OF JURA TO GIGHA (charts 2397, 2396, 2168) From Crinan to Gigha the Sound of Jura is safe if a mid-chan course is held. Ruadh Sgeir (lt) are rky ledges in mid-fairway, about 3M W of Crinan. Loch Sween (chart 2397) can be approached N or SE of MacCormaig Islands, where there is an attractive anch on NE side of Eilean Mor, but exposed to NE. Coming from N beware Keills Rk and Danna Rk. Sgeirean a Mhain is a rk in fairway 1·5M NE of Castle Sween (conspic on SE shore). Anch at Tayvallich, near head of loch on W side.

W Loch Tarbert (chart 2477) is long and narrow, with good anchs and lts near ent, but unmarked shoals. On entry give a berth of at least 2½ca to Eilean Traighe off N shore, E of Ardpatrick Pt. Dun Skeig, an isolated hill, is conspic on S shore. Good anch near head of loch, 1M by road from E Loch Tarbert, Loch Fyne; see 9.9.9.

On W side of Sound, near S end of Jura, are The Small Is (chart 2396) across the mouth of Loch na Mile. Beware Goat Rk (dries 0·3m) 1½ca off southernmost Is, Eilean nan Gabhar, behind which is good anch. Also possible to go alongside Craighouse Pier (HIE ⚓) (9.9.6). Another anch is in Lowlandman's B, about 3M to N, but exposed to S winds; Ninefoot Rks with depth of 2·4m and ECM lt buoy lie off ent. Skervuile (lt) is a reef to the E, in middle of the Sound.

S of W Loch Tarbert, and about 2M off the Kintyre shore, is Gigha Is (chart 2475 and 9.9.6). Good anchs on E side in Druimyeon B and Ardminish B (HIE ⚓s), respectively N and S of Ardminish Pt. Outer and Inner Red Rks (least depth 2m) lie 2M SW of N end of Gigha Is. Dangers extend 1M W off S end of Gigha Is. Gigalum Is and Cara Is are off the S end. Gigha Sound needs very careful pilotage, since there are several dangerous rks, some buoyed/lit, others not.▶ *The N-going stream begins at HW Oban + 0430, and S-going at HW Oban – 0155, sp rates 1·3kn.* ◀

MULL OF KINTYRE (charts 2126, 2199, 2798) From Crinan to Mull of Kintyre is about 50M.▶ *This long peninsula much affects the tidal streams in North Chan. Off Mull of Kintyre (lt, fog sig) the N-going stream begins at HW Oban + 0400, and the S-going at HW Oban – 0225, sp rate 5kn. A strong race and overfalls exist S and SW of Mull of Kintyre, dangerous in strong S winds against S-going tide. Careful timing is needed, especially W-bound (9.9.11).*◀ The Traffic Separation Scheme in the North Channel, is only 2M W of the Mull and may limit sea-room in the ITZ.

Sanda Sound separates Sanda Is (lt) and its rks and islets, from Kintyre. On the mainland shore beware Macosh Rks (dry, PHM lt buoy) forming part of Barley Ridges, 2ca offshore; Arranman Barrels, drying and submerged, marked by PHM lt buoy; and Blindman Rk (depth 2m) 1·3M N of Ru Stafnish, where 3 radio masts are 5ca inland. Sanda Is has Sheep Is 3ca to the N; Paterson's Rk (dries) is 1M E. There is anch in Sanda hbr on N side.▶ *In Sanda Sound the E-going stream begins at HW Greenock + 0340, and the W-going at HW Greenock – 0230, sp rates 5kn. Tide races extend W, N and NE from Sanda, and in strong S or SW winds the Sound is dangerous.*◀ In these conditions pass 2M S of Mull of Kintyre and Sanda and E of Paterson's Rk.

MULL OF KINTYRE TO UPPER LOCH FYNE (charts *2126*, 2383, 2381, 2382).▶ *Once E of Mull of Kintyre, tidal conditions and pilotage much improve.*◀ Campbeltown (9.9.10) is entered N of Island Davaar (lt, fog sig). 1·5M N of lt ho is Otterard Rk (depth 3·8m), with Long Rk (dries 1·1m) 5ca W of it; only Otterard Rock is buoyed.▶ *E of Island Davaar tide runs 3kn at sp, and there are overfalls.*◀

Kilbrannan Sound runs 21M from Island Davaar to Skipness Pt, where it joins Inchmarnock Water, Lower Loch Fyne and Bute Sound.▶ *There are few dangers apart from overfalls on Erins Bank, 10M S of Skipness, on S-going stream.*◀ Good anch in Carradale B (9.9.10), off Torrisdale Castle. ▶ *There are overfalls off Carradale Pt on S-going stream.*◀

Lower L. Fyne (chart 2381) is mainly clear of dangers to East L. Tarbert (9.9.9). On E shore beware rks off Ardlamont Pt; 4M to NW is Skate Is which is best passed to W. 3M S of Ardrishaig (9.9.8) beware Big Rk (depth 2·1m). Further N, at entrance to Loch Gilp (mostly dries) note shoals (least depth 1·5m) round Gulnare Rk, PHM lt buoy; also Duncuan Is with dangers extending SW to Sgeir Sgalag (depth 0·6m), buoyed.

Where Upper L. Fyne turns NE (The Narrows) it is partly obstructed by Otter Spit (dries 0·9m), extending 8ca WNW from E shore and marked by lt bn. The stream runs up to 2kn here. A buoyed/lit rk, depth less than 2m, lies about 7ca SW of Otter Spit bn. In Upper L. Fyne (chart 2382) off Minard Pt, the chan between rks and islands in the fairway is buoyed/lit. For Inveraray, see 9.9.9.

ARRAN, BUTE AND FIRTH OF CLYDE (charts 1906, 1907) Bute Sound leads into Firth of Clyde, and is clear in fairway. Arran's mountains tend to cause squalls or calms, but it has good anchs at Lamlash (9.9.12), Brodick and Loch Ranza. Sannox Rock (depth 1·5m) is 2½ca off Arran coast 8M N of Lamlash (9.9.12). 1ca off W side of Inchmarnock is Tra na-h-uil, a rk drying 1·5m. In Inchmarnock Sound, Shearwater Rk (depth 0·9m) lies in centre of S entrance.

Kyles of Bute are attractive chan N of Bute from Inchmarnock Water to Firth of Clyde, and straightforward apart from Burnt Islands. Here it is best to take the north channel, narrow but well buoyed, passing S of Eilean Buidhe, and N of Eilean Fraoich and Eilean Mor.▶ *Care is needed, since sp stream may reach 5kn.*◀ Caladh Hbr is a beautiful anch 7ca NW of Burnt Is.

The N lochs in Firth of Clyde are less attractive. Loch Goil is worth a visit; Loch Long is squally and has few anchs but has no hidden dangers, while Gareloch (9.9.20) has Rhu marina, the submarine base and hotel with mooring near the northern end (west shore).▶ *Navigation in Firth of Clyde is easy since tidal streams are weak, seldom exceeding 1kn.*◀ Channels are well marked; but beware unlit moorings commercial and naval shipping; see 9.9.19. There are marinas on the mainland at Largs (9.9.14) and Inverkip (9.9.15). Rothesay hbr (9.9.13) on E Bute, and Kilchattan B (anch 6M to S) are both sheltered from SSE to WNW.

FIRTH OF CLYDE TO MULL OF GALLOWAY (charts *2131*, *2126*, 2199, 2198) Further S the coast is less inviting, with mostly commercial hbrs until reaching Ardrossan (9.9.22) and Troon (9.9.23), NW of which there are various dangers: beware Troon Rk (depth 5·6m, but sea can break), Lappock Rk (dries 0·6m, marked by bn), and Mill Rk (dries 0·4m, buoyed). Lady Isle (lt), shoal to NE, is 2M WSW of Troon.

▶ *There is a severe race off Bennane Hd (8M SSE of Ailsa Craig, conspic) when tide is running strongly.*◀ Loch Ryan offers little for yachtsmen but there is anch S of Kirkcolm Pt, inside the drying spit which runs in SE direction 1·5M from the point. There is also useful anch in Lady Bay, sheltered except from NE.▶ *Between Corsewall Pt and Mull of Galloway the S-going stream begins HW Greenock + 0310, and the N-going at HW Greenock – 0250. Sp rate off Corsewall Pt is 2-3 kn, increasing to 5kn off and S of Black Hd. Portpatrick (9.9.24) is a useful passage hbr, but not in onshore winds. Races occur off Morroch B, Money Hd and Mull of Logan.*◀

▶ *A race SSE of Crammag Hd is bad if wind against tide. Mull of Galloway (lt) is a high (82m), steep-to headland. Beware dangerous race extending nearly 3M to S. On E-going stream the race extends NNE into Luce B; on W-going stream it extends SW and W. Best to give the race a wide berth, or pass close inshore at slack water nps and calm weather. SW wind >F4 against W-going stream, do not attempt inshore route.*◀

SCOTLAND – SW COAST The Scares, two groups of rocks, lie at the mouth of Luce Bay which elsewhere is clear more than 3ca offshore; but the whole bay is occupied by a practice bombing range, marked by 12 DZ SPM lt buoys. Good anch at E Tarbert B to await the tide around the Mull of Galloway, or dry out alongside in shelter of Drummore. Off Burrow Hd there is a bad race in strong W winds with W-going tide. Luce Bay Firing Range (D402/403) lies at the NW end. For info on activity ☎ (01776) 888792. In Wigtown B the best anch is in Isle of Whithorn B, but exposed to S. It is also possible to dry out in Garlieston, see 9.9.25.

A tank firing range, between the E side of ent to Kirkcudbright Bay (9.9.25) and Abbey Hd, 4M to E, extends 14M offshore. If unable to avoid the area, cross it at N end close inshore. For information contact the Range safety boat "Gallovidian" on VHF Ch 16, 73. The range operates 0900-1600LT Mon-Fri, but weekend and night firing may also occur.

See 9.10.5 for continuation E into Solway Firth and S into the Irish Sea. For notes on crossing the Irish Sea, see 9.13.5.

HARBOURS AND ANCHORAGES IN COLONSAY, JURA, ISLAY AND THE SOUND OF JURA

SCALASAIG, Colonsay, **56°04'·14N 06°10'·86W**. AC *2169*, 2474. HW +0542 on Dover; ML 2·2m. See 9.9.6. Conspic monument ½M SW of hbr. Beware group of rks N of pier hd marked by bn. 2 HIE Ⓥ berths on N side of pier, inner end approx 2·5m. Inner hbr to SW of pier is safe, but dries. Ldg lts 262°, both FR 8/10m on pier. Also ⚓ clear of cable in **Loch Staosnaig**; SW of Rubha Dubh lt, Fl (2) WR 10s 8m 8/6M; R shore-230°, W230°-337°, R337°-354°. Facilities: D, P, 🛒 (all at ✉), FW, Hotel ☎ (01951) 200316, Dr (0951) 200328.

LOCH TARBERT, W Jura, **55°57'·69N 06°00'·06W**. AC *2169*, 2481. Tides as Rubha A'Mhàil (N tip of Islay). See 9.9.6. HW –0540 on Dover; ML 2·1m; Duration 0600. Excellent shelter inside the loch, but subject to squalls in strong winds; ⚓ outside in Glenbatrick Bay in approx 6m in S winds, or at Bagh Gleann Righ Mor in approx 2m in N winds. To enter inner loch via Cumhann Beag, there are four pairs of ldg marks (W stones) at approx 120°, 150°, 077°, and 188°, the latter astern, to be used in sequence; pilot book required. There are no facilities.

PORT ASKAIG, Islay, **55°50'·87N 06°06'·26W**. AC 2168, 2481. HW +0610 on Dover; ML 1·2m. See 9.9.6. Hbr on W side of Sound of Islay. ⚓ close inshore in 4m or secure to ferry pier. Beware strong tide/eddies. ☆ FR at LB. Facilities: FW (hose on pier), Gas, P, R, Hotel, 🛒, ✉, ferries to Jura and Kintyre. Other ⚓s in the Sound at: Bunnahabhain (2M N); Whitefarland Bay, Jura, opp Caol Ila distillery; NW of Am Fraoch Eilean (S tip of Jura); Aros Bay, N of Ardmore Pt.

CRAIGHOUSE, SE Jura, **55°49'·99N 05°56'·31W**. AC 2168, 2481, 2396. HW +0600 on Dover; ML 0·5m; Duration 0640 np, 0530 sp. See 9.9.6. Good shelter, but squalls occur in W winds. Enter between lt bn on SW end of Eilean nan Gabhar, Fl 5s 7m 8M vis 225°-010°, and unlit bn close SW. There are 8 HIE Ⓥs N of pier (☎ (01496) 810332), where yachts may berth alongside; or ⚓ in 5m in poor holding at the N end of Loch na Mile. Facilities: very limited, Bar, FW, ✉, R, 🛒, Gas, P & D (cans). **Lowlandman's Bay** is 1M further N, with ECM buoy, Q (3) 10s, marking Nine Foot Rk (2·4m) off the ent. ⚓ to SW of conspic houses, off stone jetty.

LOCH SWEEN, Argyll and Bute, **55°55'·69N 05°41'·26W**. AC 2397. HW +0550 on Dover; ML 1·5m; Duration = 0610. See 9.9.7 Carsaig Bay. Off the ent to loch, **Eilean Mòr** (most SW'ly of MacCormaig Isles) has tiny ⚓ on N side in 3m; local transit marks keep clear of two rks, 0·6m and 0·9m. Inside the loch, beware Sgeirean a'Mhain, a rk in mid-chan to S of Taynish Is, 3M from ent. Good shelter in Loch a Bhealaich (⚓ outside **Tayvallich** in approx 7m on boulders) or enter inner hbr to ⚓ W of central reef. There are no lts. Facilities: Gas, Bar, ✉, FW (🚰 by ✉), R, 🛒. Close to NE are ⚓s at **Caol Scotnish** and **Fairy Is**, the former obstructed by rks 3ca from ent.

WEST LOCH TARBERT, Argyll and Bute, (Kintyre), **55°45'N 05°36'W**. AC 2477. Tides as Gigha Sound, 9.9.6. Good shelter. Ent is S of Eilean Traighe, Fl (2) R 5s, and NW of Dun Skeig, Q (2) 10s, where there is also conspic conical hill (142m). Loch is lit for 5M by 3 bns, QG, QR and QG in sequence, up to Kennacraig ferry pier, 2FG (vert). PHM buoy, QR, is 2½ca NW of pier. Caution: many drying rks and fish farms outside the fairway and near head of loch. ⚓s are NE of Eilean Traighe (beware weed & ferry wash); near Rhu Pt, possible Ⓥs; NE of Eilean dà Gallagain, and at loch hd by pier (ru). Tarbert (9.9.9) is 1·5M walk/bus.

GIGHA ISLAND, Argyll and Bute, **55°40'·6N 05°44'·0W**. AC 2168, 2475. HW +0600 on Dover; ML 0·9m; Duration 0530. See 9.9.6. Main ⚓ is **Ardminish Bay**: 12 HIE Ⓥs in the centre. Reefs extend off both points, the S'ly reef marked by an unlit PHM buoy. Kiln Rk (dries 1·5m) is close NE of the old ferry jetty. **Druimyeon Bay** is more sheltered in E'lies, but care needed entering from S. ⚓s sheltered from winds in ( ): Port Mór (S-W), Bàgh na Dòirlinne (SE-S), W Tarbert Bay (NE). Caolas Gigalum (⚓ 50m SE of pier) is safe in all but NE-E winds. Beware many rks in Gigha Sound. Lts: Fl (2) 6s, on Gamhna Gigha (off NE tip); WCM buoy Fl (9) 15s marks Gigalum Rks, at S end of Gigha. **Ardminish** ☎/📠 (01583) 505254: FW, Gas, P & D (cans), 🗑, ✉, Bar, R, 🛒.

9.9.6 PORT ELLEN

Islay (Argyll and Bute) **55°37'·29N 06°12'·26W** ✿✿✿✿✿✿

CHARTS AC 2168, 2474; Imray C64

TIDES HW +0620 np, +0130 sp on Dover; ML 0·6. Sea level is much affected by the weather, rising by 1m in S/E gales; at nps the tide is sometimes diurnal and range negligible.

Standard Port OBAN (⟵)

Times				Height (metres)			
High Water		Low Water		MHWS	MHWN	MLWN	MLWS
0100	0700	0100	0800	4·0	2·9	1·8	0·7
1300	1900	1300	2000				
Differences PORT ELLEN (S Islay)							
–0530	–0050	–0045	–0530	–3·1	–2·1	–1·3	–0·4
SCALASAIG (E Colonsay)							
–0020	–0005	–0015	+0005	–0·1	–0·2	–0·2	–0·2
GLENGARRISDALE BAY (N Jura)							
–0020	0000	–0010	0000	–0·4	–0·2	0·0	–0·2
CRAIGHOUSE (SE Jura)							
–0230	–0250	–0150	–0230	–3·0	–2·4	–1·3	–0·6
RUBHA A'MHÀIL (N Islay)							
–0020	0000	+0005	–0015	–0·3	–0·1	–0·3	–0·1
ARDNAVE POINT (NW Islay)							
–0035	+0010	0000	–0025	–0·4	–0·2	–0·3	–0·1
ORSAY ISLAND (SW Islay)							
–0110	–0110	–0040	–0040	–1·4	–0·6	–0·5	–0·2
BRUICHLADDICH (Islay, Loch Indaal)							
–0105	–0035	–0110	–0110	–1·8	–1·3	–0·4	+0·1
PORT ASKAIG (Sound of Islay)							
–0110	–0030	–0020	–0020	–1·9	–1·4	–0·8	–0·3
GIGHA SOUND (Sound of Jura)							
–0450	–0210	–0130	–0410	–2·5	–1·6	–1·0	–0·1
MACHRIHANISH							
–0520	–0350	–0340	–0540	Mean range 0·5 metres.			

SHELTER Good shelter on pontoons, but in S winds swell sets into the bay. 10 HIE Ⓥs to W of Rubha Glas; adjacent rks marked by 3 perches with reflective topmarks. In W'lies ⚓ in Kilnaughton Bay, N of Carraig Fhada lt ho; or 4M ENE at Loch-an-t-Sàilein.

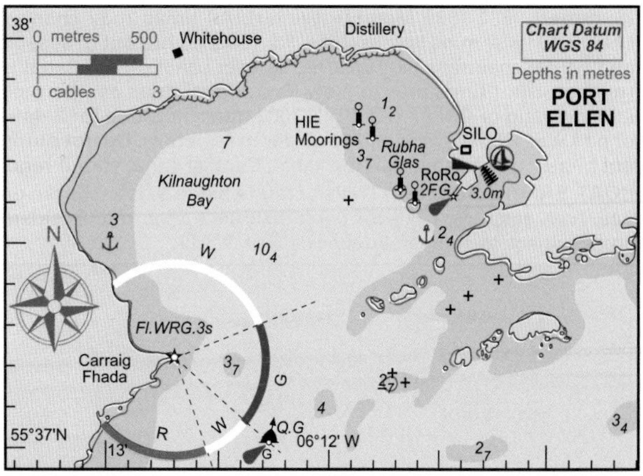
38'
0 metres 500
0 cables 3
Whitehouse
Distillery
Chart Datum WGS 84
Depths in metres
PORT ELLEN
HIE Moorings
Rubha Glas
SILO
RoRo 2F.G
3.0m
Kilnaughton Bay
N
W
Fl.WRG.3s
Carraig Fhada
G
R
W
Q.G
G
55°37'N
13'
06°12' W

NAVIGATION WPT 55°36'·69N 06°12'·06W, 326° to Carraig Fhada lt ho, 0·63M. Beware Otter Rk 4M SE of hbr, rks on both sides of ent and in NE corner of bay. Keep close to pier.

LIGHTS AND MARKS On W side 10 Radio masts (103m) and Carraig Fhada lt ho (conspic), Fl WRG 3s 20m 8/6M; W shore-248°, G248°-311°, W311°-340°, R340°-shore; keep in W sector until past the SHM buoy, QG. Ro-Ro pier shows 2 FG (vert) and Marina pontoon Fl G 4s. Limits of dredged area around Ro-Ro Pier and pontoon area marked by buoys.

R/T. None.

TELEPHONE Moorings (01496) 302441/300131; MRCC (01475) 729988.

FACILITIES **Marina** (24 inc Ⓥ - visitors welcome), £12<10m, £14 >10m, D, FW, ⚡, Slip; **Village** Bar, FW, ✉, R, 🛒, Gas. 7 malt whisky distilleries in or near Port Ellen.

9.9.7 CRINAN CANAL

Argyll and Bute **56°05'·50N 05°33'·38W** Crinan

CHARTS AC *2326*, 2320; Imray C65; OS 55

TIDES –0608 Dover; ML 2·1; Duration 0605; Zone 0 (UT) HW Crinan is at HW Oban –0045

Standard Port OBAN (⟵)

Times				Height (metres)			
High Water		Low Water		MHWS	MHWN	MLWN	MLWS
0100	0700	0100	0800	4·0	2·9	1·8	0·7
1300	1900	1300	2000				
Differences CARSAIG BAY (56°02'N 05°38'W)							
–0105	–0040	–0050	–0050	–2·1	–1·6	–1·0	–0·4

Note: In the Sound of Jura, S of Loch Crinan, the rise of tide occurs mainly during the 3½hrs after LW; the fall during the 3½hrs after HW. At other times the changes in level are usually small and irregular.

SHELTER Complete shelter in canal basin; yachts are welcome, but often full of FVs. Good shelter in Crinan Hbr (E of Eilean da Mheinn) but full of moorings. Except in strong W/N winds, ⚓ E of the canal ent, clear of fairway. Gallanach Bay on N side of L Crinan has good holding in about 3m. Berths may be reserved at Bellanoch Bay.

NAVIGATION WPT 56°05'·70N 05°33'·64W, 146° to Fl WG 3s lt, 0·27M. Beware Black Rock (2m high) in appr NE of ldg line 146° to dir Fl WG 3s lt. Off NW corner of chartlet, no ⚓ in a nearly rectangular shellfish bed, 6ca by 6ca. SPM lt buoys mark each corner: Fl (4) Y 12s at the NE and NW corners, Fl Y 6s at the SW and SE corners; the latter being about 100m NE of Black Rock.

CANAL Canal is 9M long with 15 locks and 7 opening bridges. Least transit time is 5 to 6 hrs, observing 4kn speed limit. If short-handed, helpers may be available via canal staff or 01546 602458. Entry at all tides. Max LOA: 26·82m, 6.09m beam, 2·89m draft (add 0.10m to your salt water draft), mast 28.95m. Vessels NW-bound have right of way. **Lock hrs**: In season sea locks open 0830-1900 if tide allows daily. Sea lock outer gates are left open after hours for yachts to shelter. Inland locks and bridges operate 0830-1630 Mon-Sat (Spring and Autumn), 0830-1730 Mon-Sun (Summer) 0830-1530 Mon-Fri (Winter). All times may change. **Last locking 30 mins before close.** For reduced hrs out of season and winter maintenance closures, contact canal office. Canal is routinely shut Christmas to New Year. **Canal dues** can be paid at Ardrishaig or Crinan sea locks. 2003 transit/lock fee for 3 days or part was £9 per metre and £6.30 per m for return. **Do not** pump out bilge water or toilets in the canal. Contact canal staff if reqd.

BOAT SAFETY SCHEME Transit craft liable to safety checks on gas, fuel, electrics; £1M 3rd party insurance required. Resident craft subject to full safety checks. See 9.8.17.

LIGHTS AND MARKS Crinan Hotel is conspic W bldg. A conspic chy, 3ca SW of hotel, leads 187° into Crinan Hbr. E of sea-lock: Dir Fl WG 3s 8m 4M, vis W 114°-146°, G146°-280°. Ent: 2 FG (vert) and 2FR (vert).

R/T VHF Ch **74** 16 only at sea locks.

TELEPHONE (Dial code 01546) Sea lock 830285; Canal HQ 603210; MRCC (01475) 729988; Marinecall 09068 500463; Police 602222; Dr 602921.

FACILITIES Canal HQ ☎ 603210, www.scottishcanals.co.uk, M, L, FW, *Skippers Brief* is essential reading; **Sea Basin** AB (overnight rate available), D. **Services:** BY, Slip, ME, El, ⚒, Gas, ACA, C (5 ton), ▣, CH, P (cans), 🛒, R, Bar. Use shore toilets, not yacht heads, whilst in canal. **Village** ✉, Ⓑ (Ardrishaig), ⇌ (Oban), ✈ (Glasgow or Macrihanish). There is a wintering park, plus BY and CH, at Cairnbaan for yachts <10m LOA.

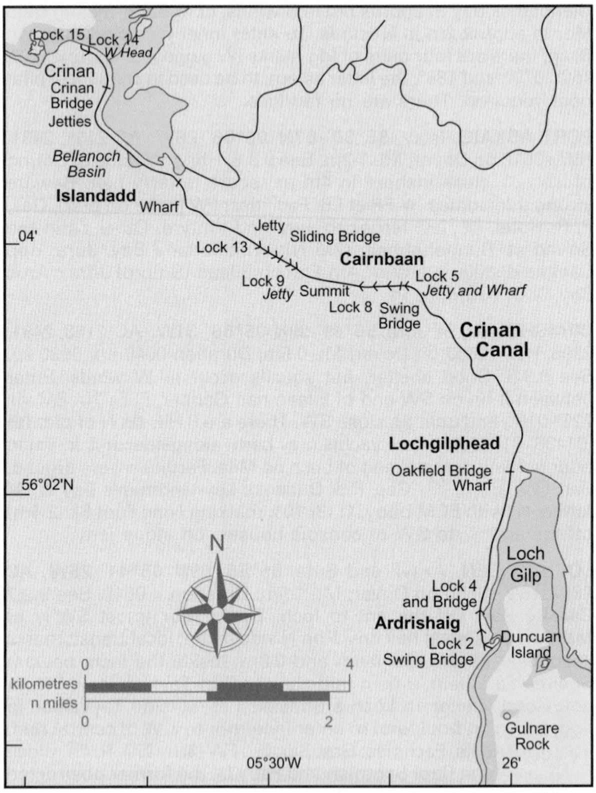
Lock 15
Lock 14
W Head
Crinan
Crinan Bridge Jetties
Bellanoch Basin
Islandadd
Wharf
04'
Jetty
Sliding Bridge
Lock 13
Cairnbaan
Lock 9
Jetty
Summit
Lock 5
Jetty and Wharf
Lock 8
Swing Bridge
Crinan Canal
Lochgilphead
Oakfield Bridge
Wharf
56°02'N
N
Loch Gilp
Lock 4 and Bridge
Ardrishaig
Lock 2
Swing Bridge
Duncuan Island
kilometres
n miles
0
4
2
Gulnare Rock
05°30'W
26'

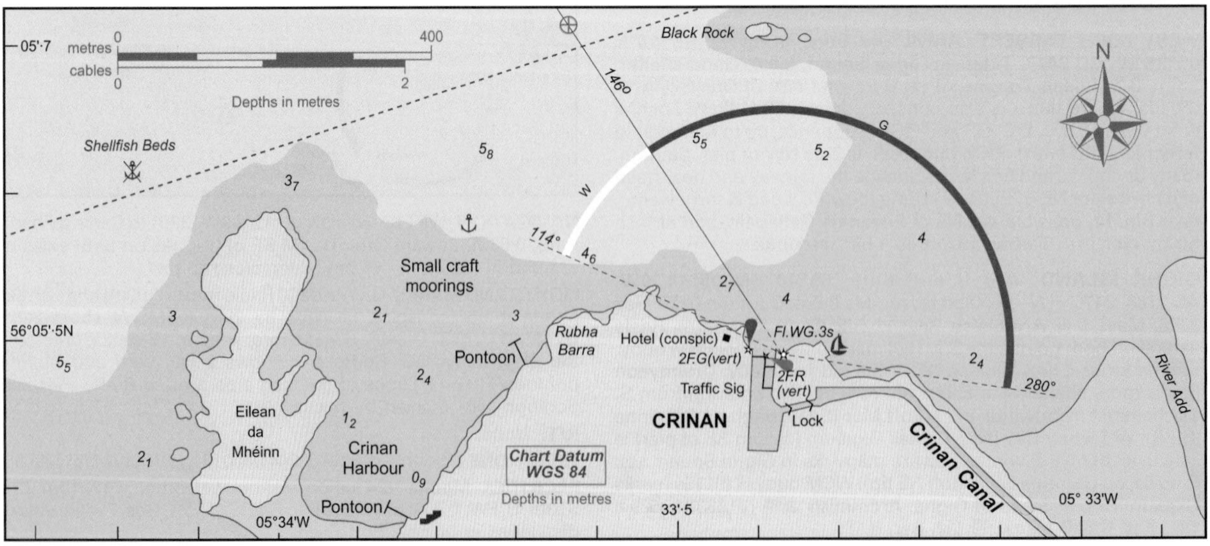
05'·7
metres
cables
0
400
2
Depths in metres
Black Rock
146°
N
Shellfish Beds
W
G
114°
Small craft moorings
56°05'·5N
Rubha Barra
Hotel (conspic)
Fl.WG.3s
2F.G(vert)
2F.R (vert)
Traffic Sig
Pontoon
280°
River Add
Eilean da Mhéinn
Crinan Harbour
CRINAN
Lock
Crinan Canal
Chart Datum WGS 84
Depths in metres
Pontoon
05°34'W
33'·5
05° 33'W

9.9.8 ARDRISHAIG

Argyll and Bute **56°00'·78N 05°26'·62W** ❁❁⛵⛵✿✿

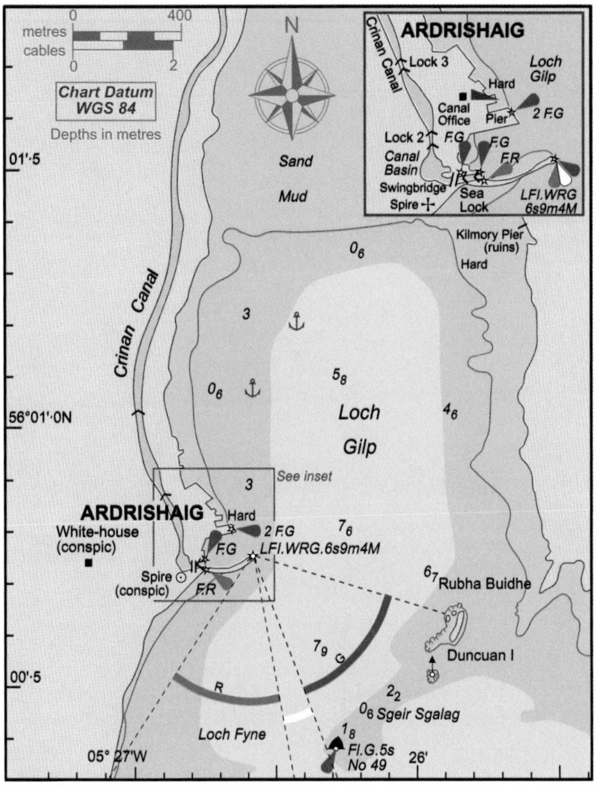
metres
cables
0
400
0
2
Chart Datum
WGS 84
Depths in metres
N
01'·5
Sand
Mud
ARDRISHAIG
Crinan Canal
Lock 3
Loch Gilp
Hard
Canal Office
Pier
2 F.G
Lock 2
F.G
F.G
F.R
Canal Basin
Swingbridge
Spire
Sea Lock
LFl.WRG 6s9m4M
Kilmory Pier (ruins)
Hard
Crinan Canal
56°01'·0N
Loch
Gilp
See inset
ARDRISHAIG
Hard
White-house (conspic)
2 F.G
F.G
LFl.WRG.6s9m4M
Spire (conspic)
F.R
Rubha Buidhe
Duncuan I
00'·5
R
G
Sgeir Sgalag
Loch Fyne
Fl.G.5s
No 49
05° 27'W
26'

CHARTS AC *2131,* 2381; Imray C63; OS 55

TIDES +0120 Dover; ML 1·9; Duration 0640; Zone 0 (UT)

Standard Port GREENOCK (⟶)

Times				Height (metres)			
High Water		Low Water		MHWS	MHWN	MLWN	MLWS
0000	0600	0000	0600	3·4	2·8	1·0	0·3
1200	1800	1200	1800				
Differences ARDRISHAIG							
+0006	+0006	-0015	+0020	0·0	0·0	+0·1	–0·1
INVERARAY							
+0011	+0011	+0034	+0034	–0·1	+0·1	–0·5	–0·2

SHELTER Hbr is sheltered except from strong E'lies; do not berth on pier or ⚓ due to commercial vessels H24. Sea lock into the Crinan Canal is usually left open, however, a waiting pontoon has been installed outside the lock, with restricted depth, for use in fair weather only. Access at all tides. Complete shelter in the canal basin, or beyond lock No 2; see 9.9.7. Also ⚓ 2ca N of hbr, off the W shore of L Gilp.

NAVIGATION WPT No 48 PHM buoy, Fl R 4s, 56°00'·18N 05°26'·31W, 345° to bkwtr lt, 0·61M. Dangerous drying rks to E of appr chan are marked by No 49 Fl.G.5s SHM buoy.

LIGHTS AND MARKS Conspic W Ho on with block of flats leads 315°between Nos 48 and 49 buoys. Bkwtr lt, L Fl WRG 6s, W339°-350°. Pier is floodlit. Other lights as plan.

R/T VHF Ch **74** 16.

TELEPHONE (Dial code 01546) HM 603210, 📠 603941; Sea lock 602458; MRCC (01475) 729988; Marinecall 09066 526246; Police 602222; Dr 602921.

FACILITIES **Pier/Hbr** ☎ 603210, AB, Slip, FW; **Sea Lock** ☎ 602458; **Crinan Canal** www.scottishcanals.co.uk, AB, M, L, FW, R, Bar; dues, see 9.9.7. **Services:** BY, ME, El, ⚒, CH, D (cans), Gas; C (20 ton) at Lochgilphead (2M). **Village** EC Wed; P & D (cans), 🛒, R, Bar, ✉, Ⓑ, ⇌ (bus to Oban), ✈ (Glasgow or Campbeltown).

9.9.9 TARBERT, LOCH FYNE

Also known as East Loch Tarbert

Argyll and Bute **55°52'·05N 05°24'·22W** ❁❁❁⛵⛵⛵✿✿

CHARTS AC *2131,* 2381; Imray C63; OS 62

TIDES +0120 Dover; ML 1·9; Duration 0640; Zone 0 (UT)

Standard Port GREENOCK (⟶)

Times				Height (metres)			
High Water		Low Water		MHWS	MHWN	MLWN	MLWS
0000	0600	0000	0600	3·4	2·8	1·0	0·3
1200	1800	1200	1800				
Differences EAST LOCH TARBERT							
–0005	–0005	0000	–0005	+0·2	+0·1	0·0	0·0

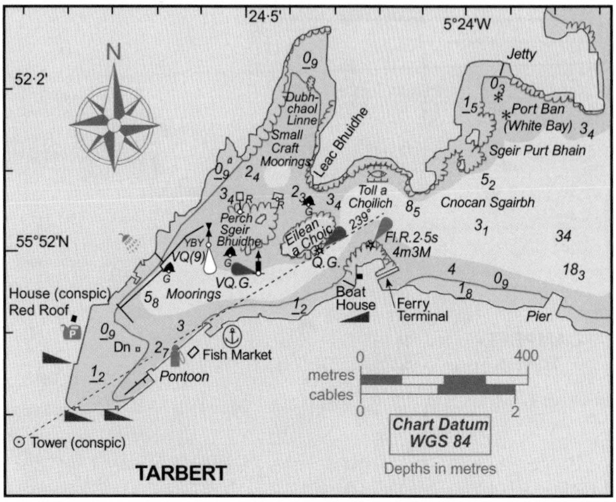
24·5'
5°24'W
Jetty
N
52·2'
Dubh-chaol Linne
Small Craft Moorings
Leac Bhuidhe
Port Ban (White Bay)
Sgeir Purt Bhain
Toll a Choilich
Cnocan Sgairbh
Perch
Sgeir Bhuidhe
Eilean a Choic
55°52'N
YBY
VQ(9)
VQ.G.
Q.G.
Fl.R.2·5s 4m3M
239°
Moorings
House (conspic)
Red Roof
Boat House
Ferry Terminal
Pier
Dn
Fish Market
Pontoon
metres
cables
0
400
0
2
Chart Datum
WGS 84
Depths in metres
Tower (conspic)
TARBERT

SHELTER Very good in all weathers but gets crowded. Access H24. Visitors berth only on SE side of yacht pontoons in 5m.

NAVIGATION WPT 55°52'·02N 05°23'·03W, 270° to Fl R 2·5s lt, 0·70M. Ent is very narrow. Cock Isle divides the ent in half: Main hbr to the S, Buteman's Hole to the N, where ⚓s are fouled by heavy moorings and lost chains. Speed limit 3kn.

LIGHTS AND MARKS Outer ldg lts 252° to S ent: Fl R 2·5s on with Cock Is lt QG. Inner ldg line 239°: same QG, G column, on with conspic ✠ tr. Note: The W sector, 065°-078°, of Eilean na Beithe ☆, Fl WRG 3s 7m 5M (on E shore of Lower Loch Fyne), could be used to position for the initial appr to Tarbert.

R/T Call VHF Ch 16; work Ch 14 (0900-1700LT).

TELEPHONE (Dial code 01880) HM 820344, 📠 820719; MRCC (01475) 729988; Marinecall 09066 526246; Police 820200; Ⓗ (01546) 602323.

FACILITIES **Yacht Berthing Facility** 100 visitors, AB £1.50, FW, AC; **Old Quay** D, FW; **Tarbert YC** Slip, L; **Services:** SM, ⓔ, ACA, ⚒, CH. **Town** EC Wed; P & D (cans), Gas, Gaz, L, 🛒, R, Bar, ✉, Ⓑ, ⇌ (bus to Glasgow), ✈ (Glasgow/Campbeltown).

ANCHORAGES IN LOCH FYNE

(beware discarded wires on sea bed throughout the area)

INVERARAY, Argyll and Bute, **56°13'·95N 05°04'·07W**. AC *2131,* 2382. HW +0126 on Dover. See 9.9.8. In Upper Loch Fyne (see 9.9.5) 4 🅐 laid at the head of the loch are for patrons of the oyster Bar. Beyond Otter Spit, are ⚓s on NW bank at Port Ann, Loch Gair and Minard Bay; and on SE bank at Otter Ferry, Strachur Bay (5 🅐s off Creggans Inn, ☎ (01369) 860279) and St Catherine's. Inveraray: beware An Oitir drying spit 2ca offshore, ½M S of pier. ⚓ SSW of pier in 4m or dry out NW of the pier. FW (on pier), ✉, 🛒, R, Bar, Gas, bus to Glasgow. In Lower L Fyne, 6M NNE of East Loch Tarbert there is a 🅐 at Kilfinan Bay, ☎ (01700) 821201.

9.9.10 CAMPBELTOWN

Argyll & Bute **55°25'·90N 05°32'·56W** Hbr ent

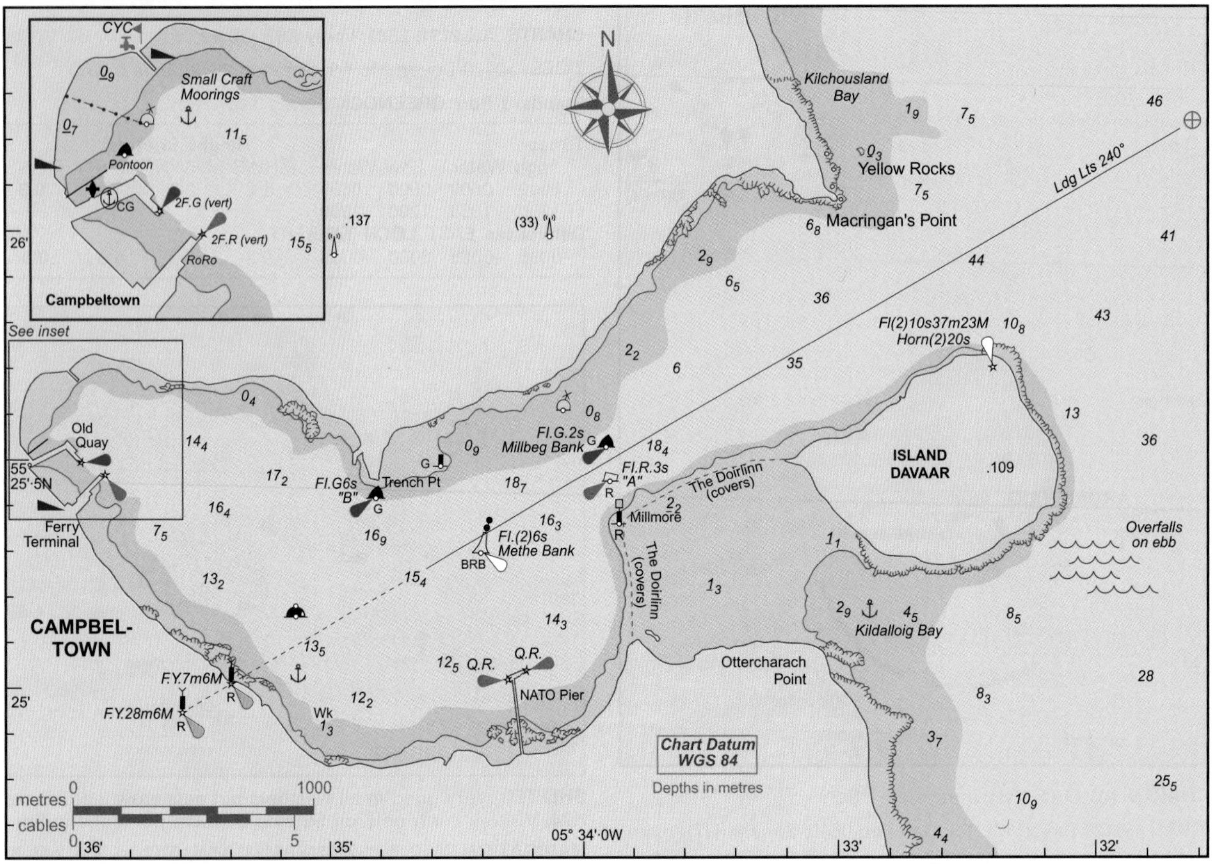
CYC
Small Craft Moorings
Pontoon
CG
2F.G (vert)
2F.R (vert)
RoRo
Campbeltown
See inset
Old Quay
Ferry Terminal
CAMPBEL- TOWN
Kilchousland Bay
Yellow Rocks
Macringan's Point
Ldg Lts 240°
Fl(2)10s37m23M
Horn(2)20s
ISLAND DAVAAR
Fl.G.2s
Millbeg Bank
Trench Pt
Fl.G6s "B"
Fl.R.3s "A"
The Doirlinn (covers)
Millmore
Fl.(2)6s
Methe Bank
BRB
Q.R.
NATO Pier
F.Y.7m6M
F.Y.28m6M
Wk
Kildalloig Bay
Otterchararch Point
Overfalls on ebb
Chart Datum WGS 84
Depths in metres
metres
cables
05° 34'·0W

CHARTS AC *2126*, 1864; Imray C63; OS 68

TIDES +0125 Dover; ML 1·8; Duration 0630; Zone 0 (UT)

Standard Port GREENOCK (⟶)

Times				Height (metres)			
High Water		Low Water		MHWS	MHWN	MLWN	MLWS
0000	0600	0000	0600	3·4	2·8	1·0	0·3
1200	1800	1200	1800				
Differences CAMPBELTOWN							
−0025	−0005	−0015	+0005	−0·5	−0·3	+0·1	+0·2
CARRADALE BAY							
−0015	−0005	−0005	+0005	−0·3	−0·2	+0·1	+0·1
SOUTHEND, (Mull of Kintyre)							
−0030	−0010	+0005	+0035	−1·3	−1·2	−0·5	−0·2

SHELTER Good, but gusts off the hills in strong SW'lies. Yacht pontoon (10+20Ⓥ) dredged 3·0m is close NW of Old Quay and gives excellent sheltered berthing. Yachts >12m LOA should notify ETA to Berthing Master by ☎ (below). Excellent ⚓ close E of front ldg lt (240°); ⚓ near moorings NNE of the hbr is cluttered and exposed to SE winds: use only in settled conditions and do not pick up private mooring buoy. S of Island Davaar there is a temp ⚓ in Kildalloig Bay, but no access to the loch.

NAVIGATION WPT 55°26'·24N 05°31'·61W, 240° to first chan buoys, 1·4M. The ent is easily identified by radio masts N and NE of Trench Pt (conspic W bldg) and conspic lt ho on N tip of Island Davaar off which streams are strong (4kn sp). Caution: The Dhorlin, a bank drying 2·5m which covers at HW, is close S of the ldg line.

LIGHTS AND MARKS Davaar Fl (2) 10s 37m 23M. Otterard Rk (3·8m depth, off chartlet, 1·5M NNE of Island Davaar), is marked by ECM buoy Q (3) 10s. Ldg lts 240°, both FY 7/28m 6M, are sodium vapour lts, H24. The ☆ 2FR (vert) at the NE end of the ferry terminal pier is on a dolphin, standing clear of the pier head.

R/T VHF Ch 12 13 16 (Mon-Fri 0900-1700).

TELEPHONE (Dial code 01586) HM 552552, 📠 554739; Yacht pontoon Berthing Master ☎ & 📠 552131, mobile 07798 524821, night 554266; MRCC (01475) 729988; Marinecall 09066 526246; Police 552253; Dr 552105.

FACILITIES **Yacht pontoon** £1.10 (3rd day free), FW, AC; Bath/shower in hotel opposite. **Old Quay** ☎ 552552, D, FW, AB, LB; **New Quay** Slip; **Campbeltown SC** Slip (dinghies), Bar, regular racing. **Town** EC Wed; ME, ACA, C (25 ton), P, D, El, CH, Ⓔ, Gas, Gaz, 🛒 (2 supermarkets), R, Bar, ✉, Ⓑ, ⓛ, Ⓗ, ♿ toilet about 100m from yacht pontoon, key at Tourist office or police station (H24). Bus thrice daily to Glasgow, ✈ twice daily to Glasgow, ⇌ (nearest is Arrochar, 90 miles N by road). Car hire/taxi.

ADJACENT ANCHORAGE IN KILBRANNAN SOUND

CARRADALE BAY, Argyll and Bute, **55°34'·40N 05°28'·66W.** AC *2131*, HW+0115 on Dover. ML 1·8m. See 9.9.10. Good ⚓ in 7m off Torrisdale Castle in SW corner of Carradale Bay. In N & E winds ⚓ in NE corner of bay, W of Carradale Pt. 3ca E of this Pt, a PHM buoy Fl (2) R 12s marks Cruban Rk. With S & SE winds a swell sets into bay, when good shelter can be found 1M N in **Carradale Harbour** (Port Crannaich); if full of FVs, ⚓ 100m N of Hbr. Bkwtr lt, Fl R 10s 5m 6M. Piermaster ☎ (01586) 431228. Facilities: FW on pier, D (cans), Gas, 🛒, R, Bar, ✉.

9.9.11 TIDAL STREAMS AROUND THE MULL OF KINTYRE

HW DOVER –6

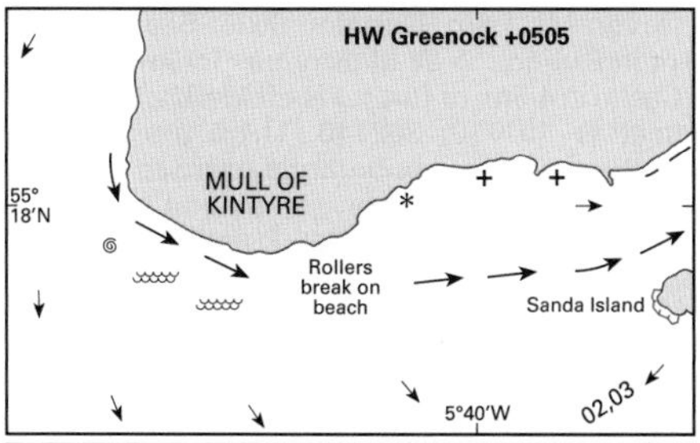
HW Greenock +0505
MULL OF KINTYRE
55° 18'N
Rollers break on beach
Sanda Island
5°40'W
02,03

HW –5

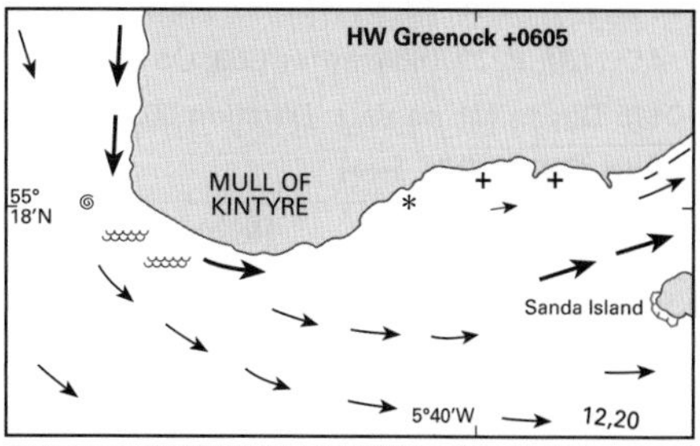
HW Greenock +0605
MULL OF KINTYRE
55° 18'N
Sanda Island
5°40'W
12,20

HW –4

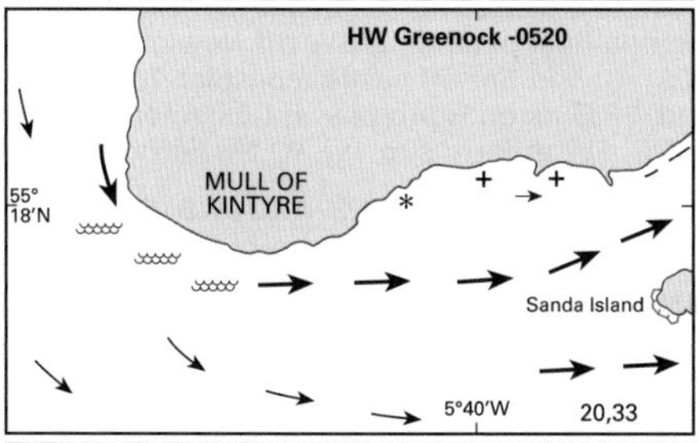
HW Greenock -0520
MULL OF KINTYRE
55° 18'N
Sanda Island
5°40'W
20,33

HW –3

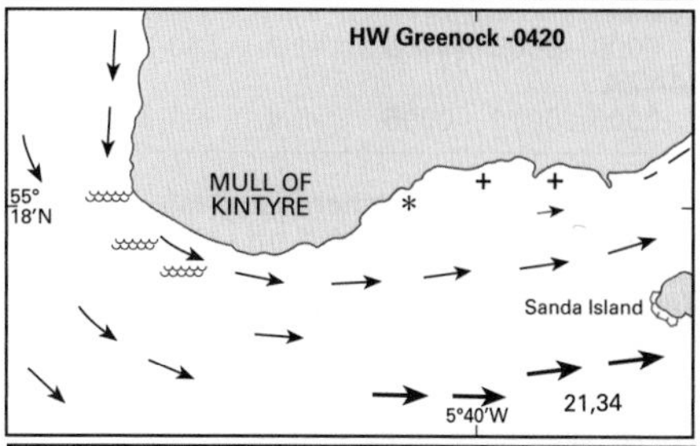
HW Greenock -0420
MULL OF KINTYRE
55° 18'N
Sanda Island
5°40'W
21,34

HW –2

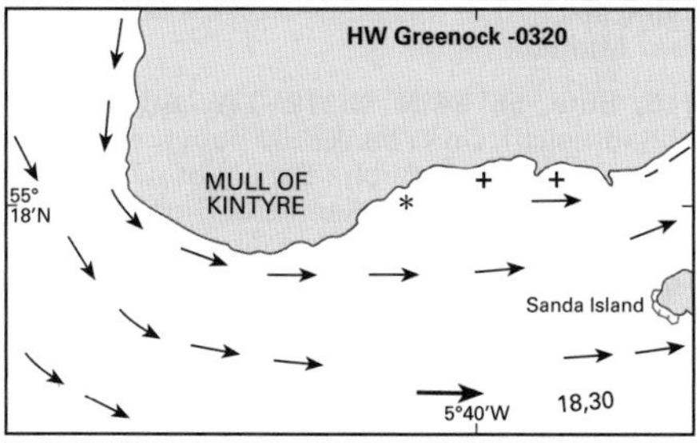
HW Greenock -0320
MULL OF KINTYRE
55° 18'N
Sanda Island
5°40'W
18,30

HW –1

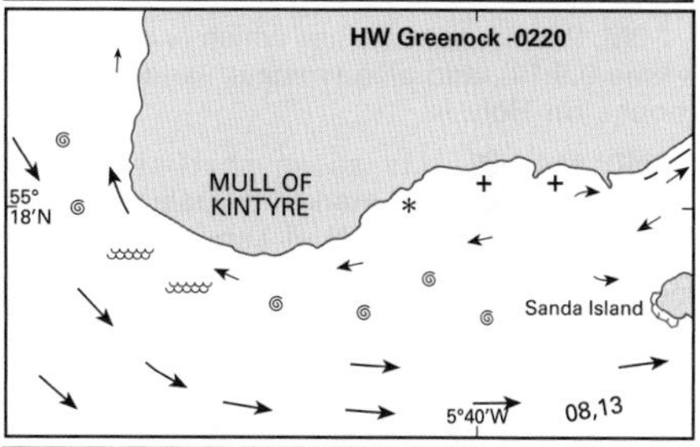
HW Greenock -0220
MULL OF KINTYRE
55° 18'N
Sanda Island
5°40'W
08,13

HW DOVER

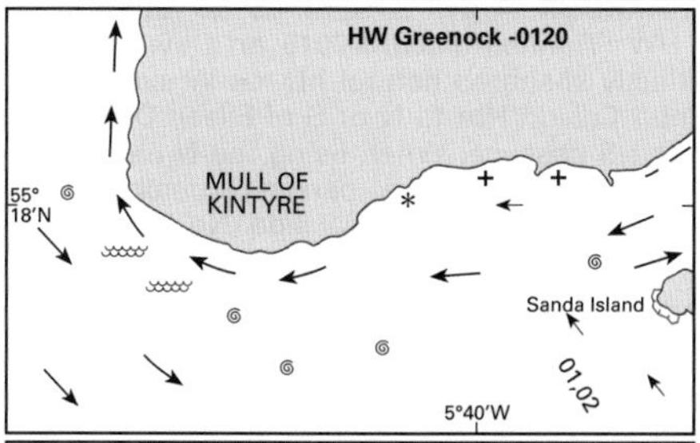
HW Greenock -0120
MULL OF KINTYRE
55° 18'N
Sanda Island
5°40'W
01,02

HW +1

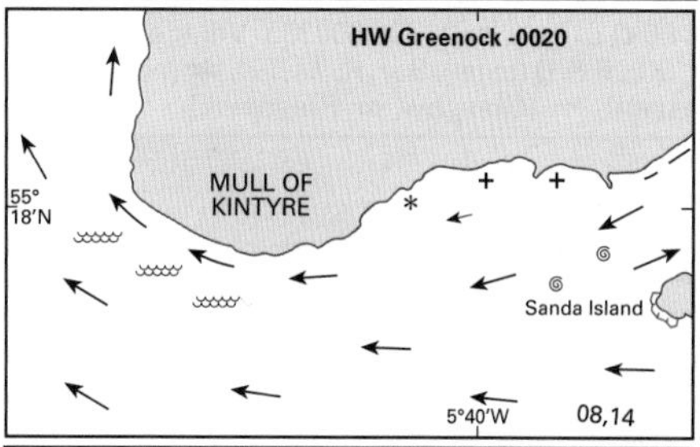
HW Greenock -0020
MULL OF KINTYRE
55° 18'N
Sanda Island
5°40'W
08,14

HW +2

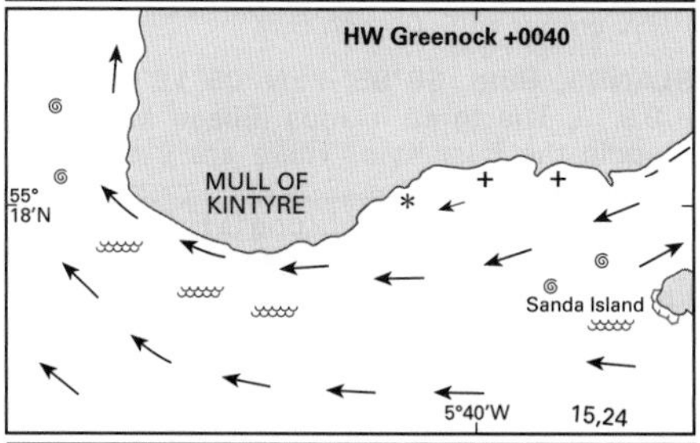
HW Greenock +0040
MULL OF KINTYRE
55° 18'N
Sanda Island
5°40'W
15,24

HW +3

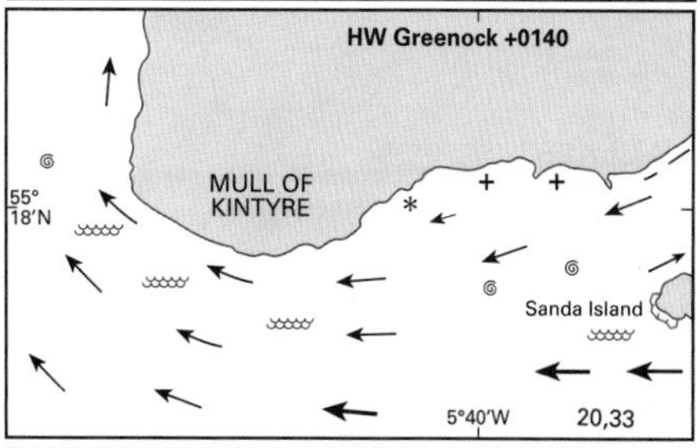
HW Greenock +0140
MULL OF KINTYRE
55° 18'N
Sanda Island
5°40'W
20,33

HW +4

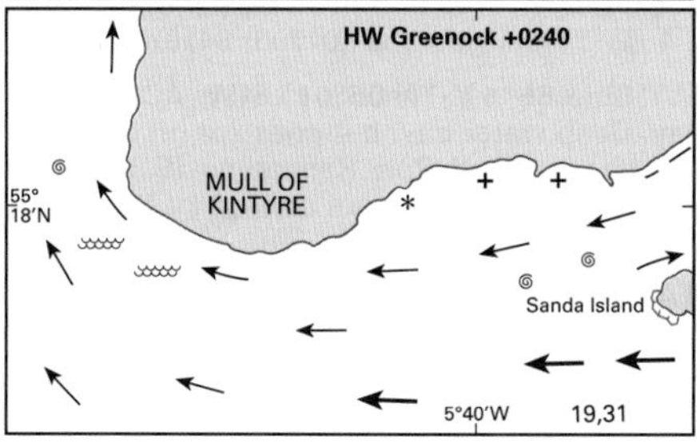
HW Greenock +0240
MULL OF KINTYRE
55° 18'N
Sanda Island
5°40'W
19,31

HW DOVER +5

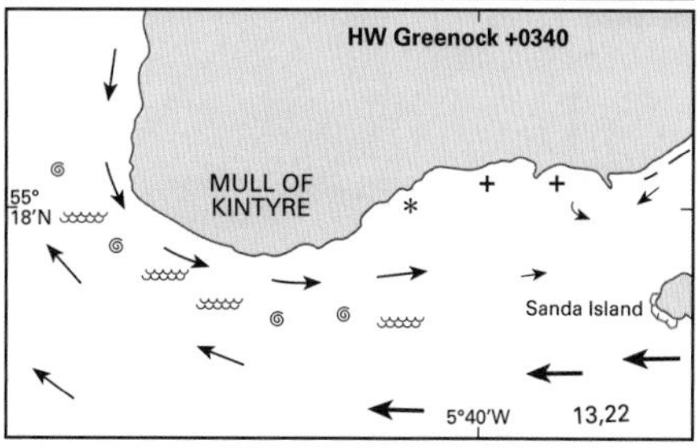
HW Greenock +0340
MULL OF KINTYRE
55° 18'N
Sanda Island
5°40'W
13,22

9

9.9.12 LAMLASH

Isle of Arran, N Ayrshire **55°32'·00N 05°07'·06W** ❀❀❀⛵⛵⛵✿✿✿

CHARTS AC *2131, 2220,* 1864; Imray C63; OS 69

TIDES +0115 Dover; ML no data; Duration 0635; Zone 0 (UT)

Standard Port GREENOCK (⟶)

Times				Height (metres)			
High Water		Low Water		MHWS	MHWN	MLWN	MLWS
0000	0600	0000	0600	3·4	2·8	1·0	0·3
1200	1800	1200	1800				
Differences LAMLASH							
–0016	–0036	–0024	–0004	–0·2	–0·2	No data	
BRODICK BAY							
0000	0000	+0005	+0005	–0·2	–0·2	0·0	0·0
LOCH RANZA							
–0015	–0005	–0010	–0005	–0·4	–0·3	–0·1	0·0

SHELTER Very good in all weathers. Lamlash is a natural hbr and sheltered anchorages as follows: ⚓ off Lamlash except in E'lies - note depth may be 20m; off Kingscross Point, good except in strong N/NW winds; off the Farm at NW of Holy Island in E'lies. Or pick up Ⓥ off Lamlash Pier. Or dry out against pier if in need of repairs. See also Brodick 5M N, and Loch Ranza 14M N (RH col).

NAVIGATION WPT 55°32'·63N 05°03'·06W, 270° to N Chan buoy (Fl R 6s), 1·0M. Beware submarines which exercise frequently in this area (see 9.9.19), and also wreck of landing craft (charted) off farmhouse on Holy Is.

LIGHTS AND MARKS Lts as on chartlet. There are two consecutive measured miles marked by poles north of Sannox, courses 322°/142° (about 12M N of Lamlash).

R/T None.

TELEPHONE (Dial code 01770) MRCC (01475) 729988; Marinecall 09066 526246; Police 302573; Ⓗ 600777.

FACILITIES **Lamlash Old Pier** Slip, L, FW, CH, ⚒ (hull repairs); **Arran YC** 25 Ⓥ £10 via: ☎ 01770 600333. **Village** EC Wed (Lamlash/Brodick); ME, P & D (cans), Bar, R, 🛒, ✉, ⇌ (bus to Brodick, ferry to Ardrossan), ✈ (Glasgow or Prestwick).

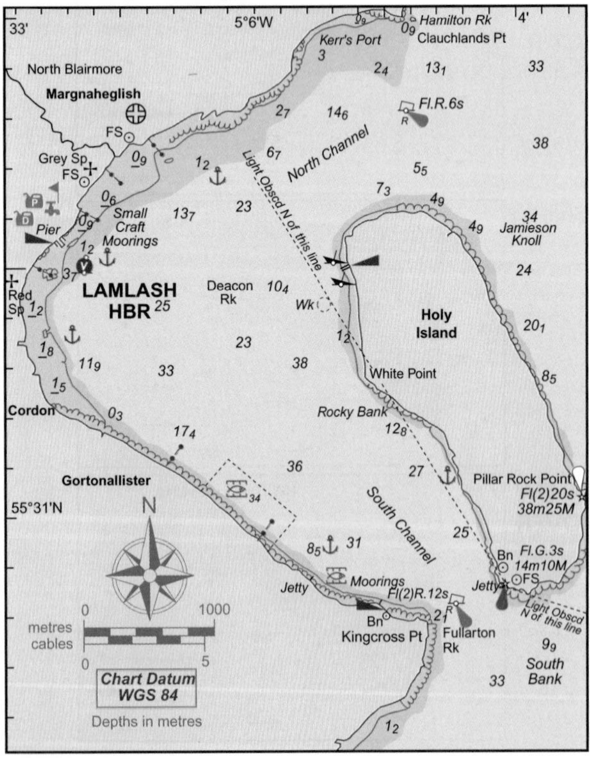

33'
5°6'W
4'
Hamilton Rk
Clauchlands Pt
Kerr's Port
North Blairmore
Margnaheglish
FS
Grey Sp
Pier
Small Craft Moorings
LAMLASH HBR
Deacon Rk
Red Sp
Cordon
Gortonallister
55°31'N
N
Fl.R.6s
North Channel
Light Obscd N of this line
Jamieson Knoll
Holy Island
Wk
White Point
Rocky Bank
Pillar Rock Point
Fl(2)20s 38m25M
South Channel
Moorings
Jetty
Fl(2)R.12s
Bn
Fl.G.3s 14m10M
Kingcross Pt
Fullarton Rk
Light Obscd N of this line
South Bank
metres
cables
0
1000
5
Chart Datum WGS 84
Depths in metres

OTHER HARBOURS ON ARRAN

BRODICK, Arran, **55°35'·50N 05°08'·66W.** AC *2131,* 2220, 1864. HW +0115 on Dover; ML 1·8m; Duration 0635. See 9.9.12. Shelter is good except in E winds. ⚓ W of ferry pier in 3m; on NW side just below the Castle in 4·5m, or further N off Merkland Pt in 3-4m. Also 5 Ⓥs: contact ☎ (01770) 302140. There are no navigational dangers but the bay is in a submarine exercise area; see 9.9.19. Only lts are 2FR (vert) 9/7m 4M on pier hd and Admiralty buoy, Fl Y 2s, 5ca N of pier. Facilities: Ⓑ, Bar, P and D (cans), FW (at pier hd), ME, ✉, R, 🛒. Ferry to Rothesay and Ardrossan.

LOCH RANZA, Arran, **55°42'·60N 05°17'·96W.** AC *2131,* 2383, 2221. HW +0120 on Dover; ML 1·7m; Duration 0635. See 9.9.12. Good shelter, but swell enters loch with N'lies. The 850m mountain 4M to S causes fierce squalls in the loch with S winds. Beware Screda Reef extending SW off Newton Pt. 5 Ⓥs; call ☎ (01770) 302140. ⚓ in 5m off castle (conspic); holding is suspect in soft mud. 2F.G lts on RoRo pier at Coillemore. S shore dries. Facilities: Bar, FW at ferry slip, ✉, R, 🛒. Ferry to Claonaig.

HARBOURS AND ANCHORAGES AROUND BUTE
(Clockwise from Garroch Head, S tip of Bute)

ST NINIAN'S BAY, Bute, **55°48'·15N 05°07'·86W.** AC 2221, 2383. Inchmarnock Is gives some shelter from the W, but Sound is exposed to S'lies. At S end, beware Shearwater Rk, 0·9m, almost in mid-sound. ⚓ in about 7m, 2ca E of St Ninian's Pt; beware drying spit to S of this Pt. Or ⚓ off E side of Inchmarnock, close abeam Midpark Farm.

WEST KYLE, Bute, **55°54'N 05°12'·7W.** AC1906. Tides, see 9.9.13 (Tighnabruaich). On W bank PHM buoys, each Fl R 4s, mark Ardlamont Pt, Carry Pt and Rubha Ban; N of which are two Fl Y buoys (fish farms). ⚓ close off Kames or Tighnabruaich, where space allows; or in Black Farland Bay (N of Rubha Dubh). There are some Ⓥs on W side, some of which may not be safe though some are maintained by hotels: Karnes Hotel ☎ (01700) 811489; Kyles of Bute Hotel 811350; Royal Hotel 811239; and Tighnabruaich Hotel 811615. Facilities: FW, D (cans), BY, 🛒.

CALADH HARBOUR, Argyll & Bute, **55°56'·00N, 05°11'·73W.** AC 1906. HW (Tighnabruaich) +0015 on Dover; ML 2·1m. See 9.9.13. Perfectly sheltered natural hbr on W side of ent to Loch Riddon. Enter Caladh Hbr to N or S of Eilean Dubh; keep to the middle of the S passage. When using the N ent, keep between R and G bns to clear a drying rk marked by perch. ⚓ in the middle of hbr; land at a stone slip on SW side. No facilities/stores; see West Kyle above.

LOCH RIDDON, Argyll & Bute, **55°57'N 05°11'·6W.** AC 1906. Tides, see 9.9.13. Water is deep for 1·3M N of Caladh and shore is steep-to; upper 1·5M of loch dries. ⚓ on W side close N of Ormidale pier; on E side at Salthouse; off Eilean Dearg (One Tree Is); and at NW corner of Fearnoch Bay.

BURNT ISLANDS, Bute, **55°55'·76N 05°10'·39W.** AC 1906. Tides, see 9.9.13. The three islands (Eilean Mor, Fraoich and Buidhe) straddle the East Kyle. There are 2 channels: North, between Buidhe and the other 2 islets, is narrow, short and marked by 2 SHM buoys (the NW'ly one is Fl G 3s), and one PHM buoy, Fl R 2s. South chan lies between Bute and Fraoich/Mor; it is unlit, but marked by one PHM and two SHM buoys. A SHM buoy, Fl G 3s, is off Rubha a' Bhodaich, 4ca ESE. Direction of buoyage is to SE. Sp streams reach 5kn in N Chan and 3kn in S Chan. ⚓ in Wreck Bay, Balnakailly Bay or in the lee of Buidhe and Mor in W'lies; also W of Colintraive Pt, clear of ferry and cables. There are 4 Ⓥs off the hotel, ☎ (01700) 84207.

KAMES BAY, Bute, **55°51'·7N 05°04'·81W.** AC 1906, 1867. Tides as Rothesay. Deep water bay, but dries 2ca off head of loch and 1ca off NW shore. ⚓ off Port Bannatyne (S shore) as space permits W of ruined jetty. Beware drying rks 1ca off Ardbeg Pt. No lts. Facilities: BY, FW, Gas, 🛒, Bar, ✉.

KILCHATTAN BAY, Bute, **55°45'N 05°01'·1W.** AC 1907. Bay is deep, but dries 3ca off the W shore. Temp ⚓s only in offshore winds: off the village on SW side, or on N side near Kerrytonlia Pt. Ⓥs for hotel guests. Rubh' an Eun Lt, Fl R 6s, is 1·1M to SSE. Facilities: FW, 🛒, ✉, bus Rothesay.

9.9.13 ROTHESAY

Isle of Bute, Argyll & Bute **55°50´·32N 05°03´·08W**

CHARTS AC *2131, 1907, 1906, 1867;* Imray C63, 2900 Series; OS 63

TIDES +0100 Dover; ML 1·9; Duration 0640; Zone 0 (UT)

Standard Port GREENOCK (⟷)

Times				**Height (metres)**			
High Water		Low Water		MHWS	MHWN	MLWN	MLWS
0000	0600	0000	0600	3·4	2·8	1·0	0·3
1200	1800	1200	1800				
Differences ROTHESAY BAY							
−0020	−0015	−0010	−0002	+0·2	+0·2	+0·2	+0·2
RUBHA BHODACH (Burnt Is)							
−0020	−0010	−0007	−0007	−0·2	−0·1	+0·2	+0·2
TIGHNABRUAICH							
+0007	−0010	−0002	−0015	0·0	+0·2	+0·4	+0·5

SHELTER Good on yacht pontoons in Outer Hbr (2m) and at W end inside the Front pier (2m) (Mar-Oct) but subject to ferry wash. 40 ⚓s WNW of pier or good ⚓ in bay ¼M W, off Isle of Bute SC; except in strong N/NE'lies when Kyles of Bute or Kames Bay offer better shelter.

NAVIGATION WPT 55°51´·00N 05°02´·76W, 194° to Outer hbr ent, 0·69M. From E keep 1ca off Bogany Pt, and off Ardbeg Pt from N.

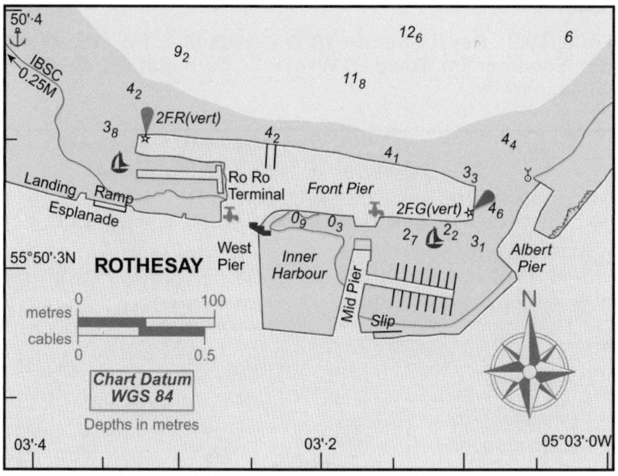
50'·4
IBSC 0.25M
9_2
12_6
6
11_8
4_2
2F.R(vert)
3_8
4_2
4_1
4_4
Ro Ro Terminal
Landing Ramp
Esplanade
Front Pier
3_3
2F.G(vert)
4_6
0_9
0_3
2_7
2_2
3_1
55°50'·3N
ROTHESAY
West Pier
Inner Harbour
Mid Pier
Slip
Albert Pier
N
metres 0 100
cables 0 0.5
Chart Datum WGS 84
Depths in metres
03'·4
03'·2
05°03'·0W

LIGHTS AND MARKS Lts as chartlet, hard to see against shore lts. Conspicuous church spire leads 190° to outer hbr; at night beware large, unlit Admiralty buoy "MK" on this bearing 5½ca from harbour. 3½ca N of hbr is Rothesay 'A' mooring buoy, Fl Y 2s.

R/T VHF Ch 12 16 (1 May-30 Sept: 0600-2100; 1 Oct-30 Apl: 0600-1900 LT).

TELEPHONE (Dial code 01700) HM 503842; Berthing 500630; Moorings 504750; MRCC (01475) 729988; Marinecall 09066 526246; Police 502121; Dr 503985; Ⓗ 503938.

FACILITIES Outer Hbr AB £2.00, ⊐D, FW, Slip, D*, L, FW, ME, El, CH, ⓢ; **Inner Hbr** L, FW, AB; **Front Pier (W)** FW, ⊐D, R, ⓢ; **Albert Pier** D*, L, FW, C (4 ton mobile). **Town** EC Wed; P, D, CH, 🛒, R, Bar, ✉, Ⓑ, ⇌ (ferry to Wemyss Bay), ✈ (Glasgow). *By arrangement (min 200 galls).

GREAT CUMBRAE ISLAND

MILLPORT, Great Cumbrae, N Ayrshire, 55°45´·00N 04°55´·82W. AC 1867, 1907. HW +0100 on Dover; ML 1·9m; Duration 0640. See 9.9.14. Good shelter, except in S'lies. ⚓ in approx 3m S of pier or E of the Eileans. 12 HIE ⚓s 1½ca SSE of pier; call ☎ (01475) 530741. Ldg marks: pier hd on with ✠ twr 333°; or ldg lts 333°, both FR 7/9m 5M, between the Spoig and the Eileans, QG. Unmarked, drying rk is close E of ldg line. HM ☎ (01475) 530826. **Town** EC Wed; CH, Bar, Gas, D, P, FW, ✉, R, Slip, 🛒.

9.9.14 LARGS AND FAIRLIE QUAY

N Ayrshire **55°46'·40N 04°51'·84W**

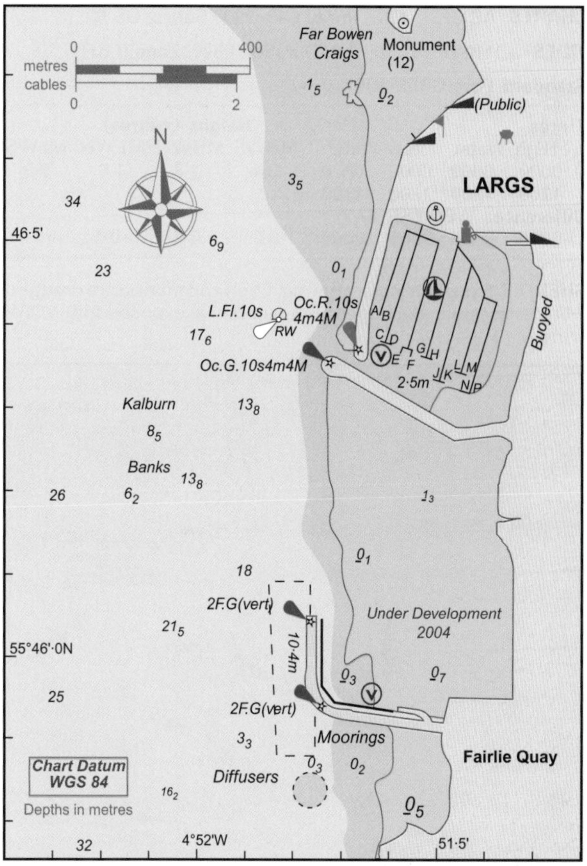
metres 0 400
cables 0 2
Far Bowen Craigs
Monument (12)
1_5
0_2
(Public)
N
34
3_5
LARGS
46·5'
6_9
23
0_1
L.Fl.10s
RW
Oc.R.10s 4m4M
17_6
Oc.G.10s4m4M
Buoyed
2·5m
Kalburn
13_8
8_5
Banks
13_8
26
6_2
1_3
0_1
18
2F.G(vert)
Under Development 2004
21_5
10·4m
55°46'·0N
0_3
0_7
25
2F.G(vert)
3_3
Moorings
Fairlie Quay
0_3
0_2
Diffusers
Chart Datum WGS 84
16_2
Depths in metres
0_5
32
4°52'W
51·5'

CHARTS AC *2131*, 1907, 1867; Imray C63, 2900 Series; OS 63

TIDES +0105 Dover; ML 1·9; Duration 0640; Zone 0 (UT)

Standard Port GREENOCK (⟷)

Times				**Heights (metres)**			
High Water		Low Water		MHWS	MHWN	MLWN	MLWS
0000	0600	0000	0600	3·4	2·8	1·0	0·3
1200	1800	1200	1800				
Differences MILLPORT							
−0005	−0025	−0025	−0005	0·0	−0·1	0·0	+0·1

SHELTER Excellent in Largs Yacht Haven, access all tides (2·5m in ent; 3m deep berths). 6 pontoons; Ⓥ on 'C/D'. At Fairlie Quay, good on pontoon, access all tides (2.6m deep berths). Cumbrae Is gives shelter from W'lies; Largs Chan is open to S or N winds.

NAVIGATION WPT 55°46´·40N 04°51´·84W, SWM buoy, L Fl 10s, off ent. From S beware Hunterston and Southannan sands and outfalls from Hunterston Power Stn (conspic). From the S bkwtr to Fairlie Quay is a restricted, no ⚓ area.

LIGHTS AND MARKS 'Pencil' monument (12m) conspic 4ca N of ent. Lts as on chartlet. Largs Pier, 2 FG (vert) when vessel expected.

R/T *Largs Yacht Haven* Ch **80** M (H24). *Fairlie Quay Marina* Ch **80** M (H24).

TELEPHONE (Dial code 01475) Largs Yacht Haven 675333, 📠 672245; Fairlie Quay 568267; Largs SC 670000; MRCC 729988; Dr 673380; Ⓗ 733777; Marinecall 09066 526246; Police 674651.

FACILITIES Largs Yacht Haven (670, some Ⓥ), £2.18, Fuel H24: D, P, ⓢ, SM, BY, C (17 ton), ME, El, ⚒, BH (70 ton), Divers, Ⓔ, CH, ⓢ, Gas, Gaz, Slip (access H24), Bar, R; **Fairlie Quay** (Facilities being developed 2004) Some Ⓥ £10/yacht, Fuel H24: D, SM, BY, ME, El, ⚒, BH (80 ton), CH, Gas. **Fairlie YC**; **Town** 🛒, R, Bar, ✉, Ⓑ, ⇌ (dep Largs every H −10; 50 mins to Glasgow), ✈.

9

9.9.15 INVERKIP (KIP MARINA)

Inverclyde **55°54'·50N 04°53'·00W**

CHARTS AC *2131, 1907;* Imray C63, 2900 Series; OS 63

TIDES +0110 Dover; ML 1·8; Duration 0640; Zone 0 (UT)

Standard Port GREENOCK (⟶)

Times				**Height (metres)**			
High Water		Low Water		MHWS	MHWN	MLWN	MLWS
0000	0600	0000	0600	3·4	2·8	1·0	0·3
1200	1800	1200	1800				
Differences WEMYSS BAY							
−0005	−0005	−0005	−0005	0·0	0·0	+0·1	+0·1

SHELTER Excellent inside marina. Chan and marina are dredged 3·5m; accessible at all tides. Inverkip Bay is exposed to SW/NW winds.

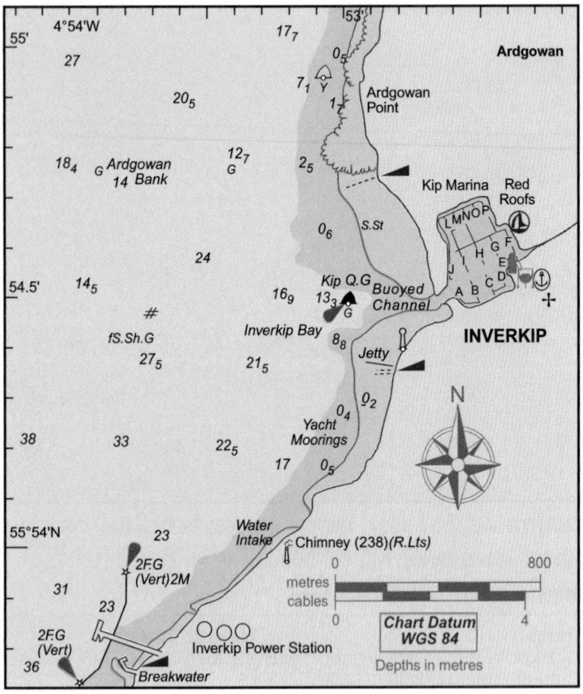
4°54'W
55'
Ardgowan
Ardgowan Point
Ardgowan 14 Bank
Kip Marina
Red Roofs
S.St
Kip Q.G
Buoyed Channel
INVERKIP
Inverkip Bay
Jetty
fS.Sh.G
Yacht Moorings
54.5'
55°54'N
Water Intake
Chimney (238)(R.Lts)
2F.G (Vert)2M
2F.G (Vert)
metres
cables
Chart Datum WGS 84
Inverkip Power Station
Breakwater
Depths in metres

NAVIGATION WPT 55°54'·49N 04°52'·95W, Kip SHM buoy, QG, at ent to buoyed chan; beware shifting bank to the N.

LIGHTS AND MARKS SHM 55°54'·55N 04°54'·47W Fl G 1·06M 093° to entr which is ½M N of conspic chmy (238m). SPM buoy marks sewer outfall off Ardgowan Pt. From Kip SHM buoy, 3 SHM and 3 PHM buoys mark 365m long appr chan.

R/T VHF Ch **80** M (H24).

TELEPHONE (Dial code 01475) HM 521485; MRCC 729988; Marinecall 09066 526246; Police 521222; Dr 520248; Ⓗ 33777.

FACILITIES Kip Marina (540+40 Ⓥ), ☎ 521485, Fax 521298, £1.80, £10 <5hrs,s D, P (cans), ⚒, C, ME, El, Ⓔ, SM, CH, Diver, BH (50 ton), 🛒, R, Bar, Ⓛ, Gas, Gaz, YC. **Town** ✉, Ⓑ (Gourock), ⇌, ✈ (Glasgow).

ADJACENT ANCHORAGES

DUNOON, Argyll and Bute, **55°56'·70N 04°55'·20W**. AC *2131,* 1907, 1994. Use Greenock tides. Temp ⚓ in West or East Bays (S and N of Dunoon Pt). The former is open to the S; the latter more shoal. Six HIE Ⓜs (free) in each bay; call ☎ (01369) 703785. The Gantocks, drying rks 3ca SE of Dunoon Pt, have W ○ bn tr, Fl R 6s 12m 6M. 2FR (vert) on ferry pier. Facilities: P & D (cans), 🛒, R, Bar, ✉, Gas, ferry to Gourock. 3 Ⓜs off Inellan, 3·7M S of Dunoon, ☎ (01369) 830445.

GOUROCK 9.9.16

Inverclyde **55°58'·00N 04°49'·00W** (As WPT)

CHARTS AC *2131, 1994;* Imray C63, 2900 Series; OS 63.

TIDES +0122 Dover; ML 2·0; Duration 0640; Zone 0 (UT)

Standard Port GREENOCK (⟶)

SHELTER Gourock: good ⚓ in West Bay, but open to N/NE winds. Greenock is a large port with a major container terminal (Clydeport) and other commercial facilities. Hbrs are controlled by Clyde Port Authority.

NAVIGATION Gourock WPT 55°57'·90N 04°49'·00W, 000°/180° from/to Kempock Pt, 1ca. No navigational dangers, but much shipping and ferries in the Clyde. The S edge of the Firth of Clyde recommended channel lies 2ca N of Kempock Pt. Beware foul ground in Gourock Bay. The pier at the S end of Gourock Bay is disused and unsafe.

LIGHTS AND MARKS as chartlet. Note Ashton and Whiteforeland SWM buoys.

R/T Call: *Clydeport Estuary Radio* VHF Ch 12 16 (H24). Info on weather and traffic available on request.

TELEPHONE (Dial codes: Gourock/Greenock 01475; Glasgow 0141) General Mgr Marine 725775; Estuary Control 726221; MRCC 729988; Police 724444; Marinecall 09066 526246; Dr 634617.

FACILITIES Royal Gourock YC ☎ 632983 M, L, FW, ME, 🛒, R, Bar; **Services:** SM. **Town** EC Wed; P, D, 🛒, R, Bar, ✉, Ⓑ, ⇌, ✈ (Glasgow).

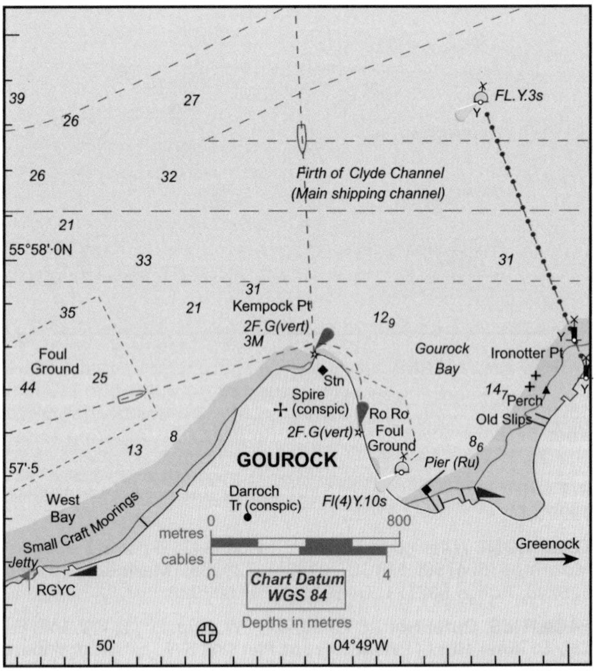
FL.Y.3s
Firth of Clyde Channel (Main shipping channel)
55°58'·0N
Kempock Pt
2F.G(vert) 3M
Foul Ground
Gourock Bay
Ironotter Pt
Perch
Old Slips
Stn
Spire (conspic)
Ro Ro
Foul Ground
2F.G(vert)
GOUROCK
Pier (Ru)
57'·5
West Bay
Darroch Tr (conspic)
Fl(4)Y.10s
Small Craft Moorings
Jetty
RGYC
metres
cables
Chart Datum WGS 84
Depths in metres
Greenock
50'
04°49'W

9.9.17 FIRTH OF CLYDE AREA

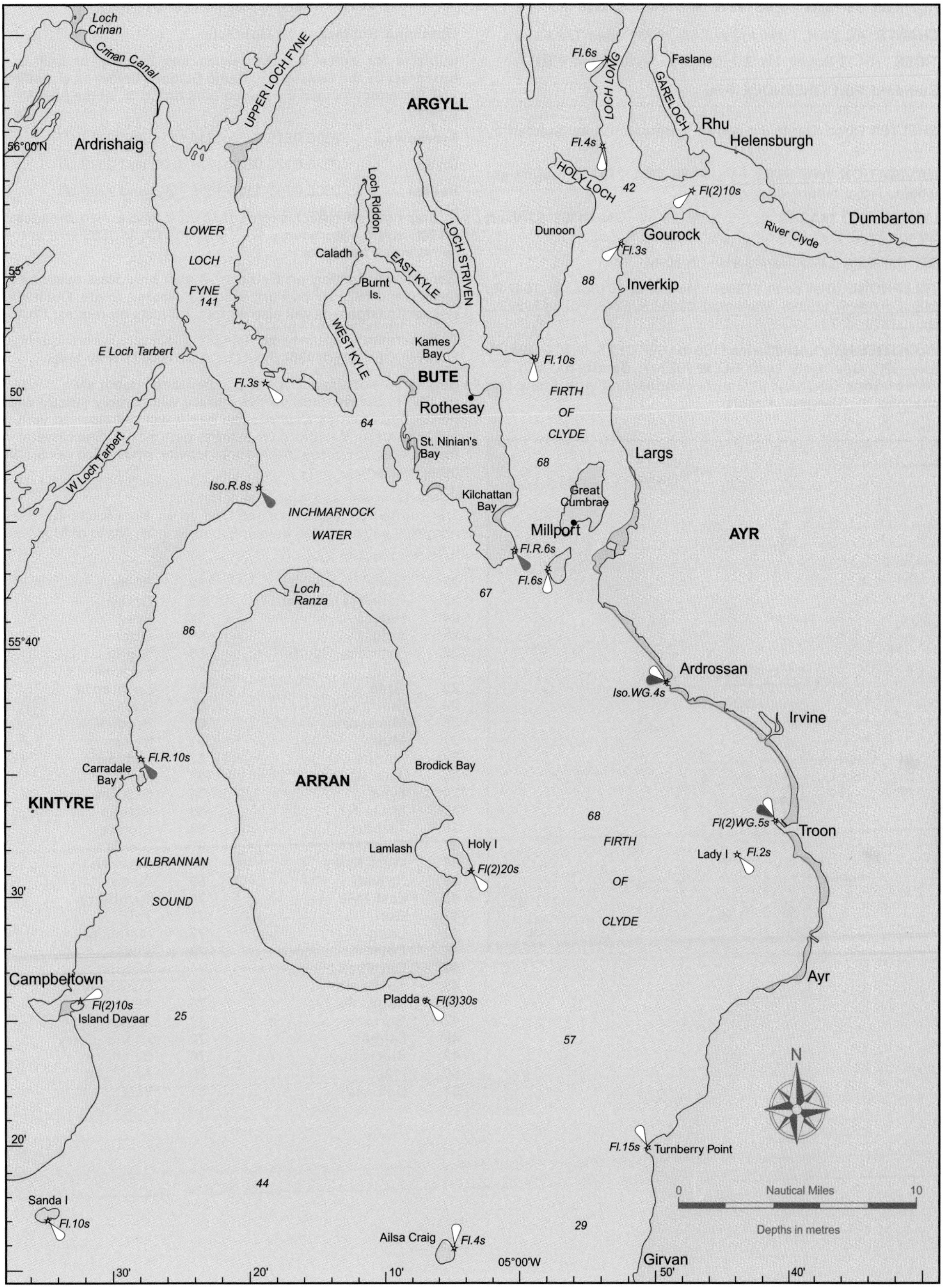
Loch Crinan
Crinan Canal
UPPER LOCH FYNE
ARGYLL
Fl.6s
LOCH LONG
Faslane
GARELOCH
Rhu
Helensburgh
56°00'N
Ardrishaig
Fl.4s
HOLY LOCH
42
Fl(2)10s
Dumbarton
River Clyde
Loch Riddon
LOCH STRIVEN
Dunoon
Gourock
LOWER LOCH FYNE 141
Caladh
EAST KYLE
Fl.3s
55'
Burnt Is.
88
Inverkip
WEST KYLE
Kames Bay
E Loch Tarbert
Fl.10s
BUTE
Fl.3s
50'
Rothesay
FIRTH OF CLYDE
64
St. Ninian's Bay
Largs
68
W Loch Tarbert
Iso.R.8s
Kilchattan Bay
Great Cumbrae
INCHMARNOCK WATER
Millport
AYR
Fl.R.6s
Fl.6s
Loch Ranza
67
86
55°40'
Ardrossan
Iso.WG.4s
Irvine
Fl.R.10s
Carradale Bay
Brodick Bay
ARRAN
KINTYRE
68
Fl(2)WG.5s
Troon
Holy I
Lamlash
FIRTH OF CLYDE
Lady I
Fl.2s
KILBRANNAN SOUND
Fl(2)20s
30'
Campbeltown
Ayr
Fl(2)10s
Island Davaar
25
Pladda
Fl(3)30s
57
N
20'
Fl.15s
Turnberry Point
44
0
Nautical Miles
10
Sanda I
Fl.10s
Depths in metres
29
Ailsa Craig
Fl.4s
05°00'W
Girvan
30'
20'
10'
50'
40'

9

9.9.18 HOLY LOCH

Argyll **55°59'·03N 04°56'·82W**

CHARTS AC *2131, 1994;* Imray C63, 2900 Series; OS 63

TIDES +0122 Dover; ML 2·0; Duration 0640; Zone 0 (UT)

Standard Port GREENOCK (⟶)

SHELTER Good. Depth 3m within marina. Berth as directed by HM.

NAVIGATION WPT 55°59'·03N 04°55'·75W 270° to marina ent 0.60M. No offshore dangers.

LIGHTS AND MARKS No 30 SCM 55°58'·75N 04°53'·82W off Strone Pt. 2FR at SE end of pier. Marina floodlit.

R/T Call *Holy Loch Marina* VHF Ch 80 M.

TELEPHONE (Dial code 01369) Marina ☎ 701800, 📠 704749; MRCC (01475) 729988; Marinecall 09066 526246; Police 702222; Dr 703279; Ⓗ 704341.

FACILITIES **Holy Loch Marina** (100 inc 6Ⓥ) £1.55, D, P, C, BH (23 ton), BY, Gas, Holy Loch SC ☎ 702707. **Sandbank**: PO, 🛒. Ferries from Sandbank to Gourock connecting with trains and coaches to Glasgow Airport.

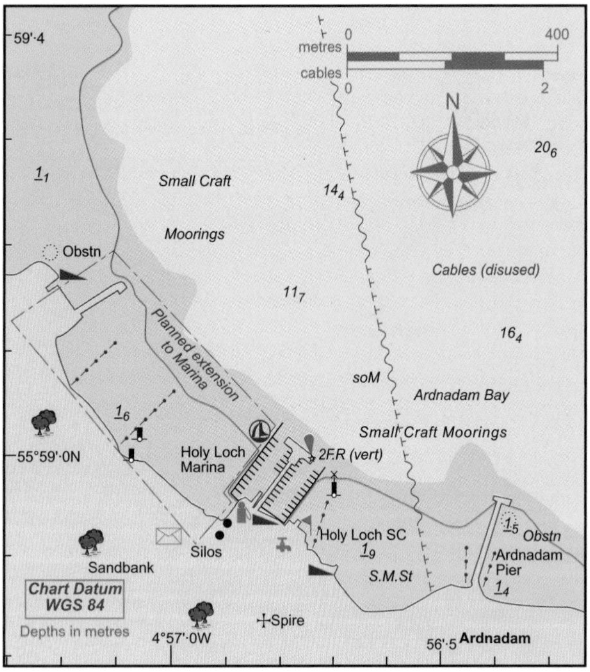
59'·4
metres
0
400
cables
0
2
N
2_{0_6}
1_1
Small Craft
Moorings
14_4
Obstn
Cables (disused)
11_7
16_4
Planned extension to Marina
soM
Ardnadam Bay
1_6
Small Craft Moorings
55°59'·0N
Holy Loch Marina
2F.R (vert)
1_5 Obstn
Silos
Holy Loch SC
1_9
Ardnadam Pier
Sandbank
S.M.St
1_4
Chart Datum WGS 84
Depths in metres
4°57'·0W
Spire
56'·5
Ardnadam

9.9.19 SUBMARINE EXERCISE AREAS

Obtaining Subfacts and Gunfacts

Subfacts for areas between Barra and the Isle of Man are broadcast by the Coastguard Radio Stations below on a notified VHF Ch, after an initial announcement on Ch 16, at the following times:

Stornoway	0110 0510 0910 1310 1710 and 2110 UT
Clyde	0020 0420 0820 1220 1620 and 2020 UT
Belfast	0305 0705 1105 1505 1905 and 2305 UT

During notified NATO exercises, Subfacts are also broadcast on MF SSB by Stornoway 1743 kHz, and Clyde 1883 kHz, at the same times as above.

General information on Subfacts is also broadcast twice daily at 0620 and 1820 UT by Portpatrick (O) Navtex. Clyde, Oban and Belfast Coastguards will also supply Subfacts on request Ch 16.

A Fisherman's Hotline, ☎ (01436) 674321, answers queries. FOSNNI Ops, ☎ (01436) 674321 ext 3206/6778 may help.

Submarines on the surface and at periscope depth always listen on Ch 16. Submarines on the surface will comply strictly with IRPCS; Submarines at periscope depth will not close to within 1500 yds of a FV without its express permission. See Chapter 7 for general advice on submarine activity which also occurs in other sea areas.

Subfacts areas (see map opposite).
The numbered areas are referred to in broadcasts by their names; these are listed below. For areas 1-26, North of Mull, see 9.8.22.

22	Barra	**52**	Boyle
23	Hebrides Central	**53**	Orsay
24	Hawes	**54**	Islay
25	Eigg	**55**	Otter
26	Hebrides South	**56**	Gigha
27	Ford	**57**	Earadale
28	Tiree	**58**	Lochranza
29	Staffa	**59**	Davaar
30	Mackenzie	**60**	Brodick
31	Mull	**61**	Irvine
32	Linnhe	**62**	Lamlash
33	Jura Sound	**63**	Ayr
34	Fyne	**64**	Skerries
35	Minard	**65**	Rathlin
36	Tarbert	**66**	Kintyre
37	Skipness	**67**	Sanda
38	West Kyle	**68**	Stafnish
39	Striven	**69**	Pladda
40	East Kyle	**70**	Turnberry
41	Goil	**71**	Torr
42	Long	**72**	Mermaid
43	Cove	**73**	Ailsa
44	Gareloch	**74**	Maiden
45	Rosneath	**75**	Corsewall
46	Cumbrae	**76**	Ballantrae
47	Garroch	**77**	Magee
48	Laggan	**78**	Londonderry
49	Blackstone	**79**	Beaufort
50	Place	**80**	Ardglass
51	Colonsay	**81**	Peel

SUBMARINE EXERCISE AREA MAP

Those areas in which submarine activity is planned for the next 16 hrs are broadcast by Coastguard Coordination Centres at the times and on the VHF channels shown below. The areas are referred to not by numbers, but by names as listed on the previous page; see also 9.8.22 for areas to the North of Mull. Subfacts/Gunfacts are also broadcast by Stornoway on Ch 10 or 73 and 1743 kHz at 0110 UT and ev 4 hrs.

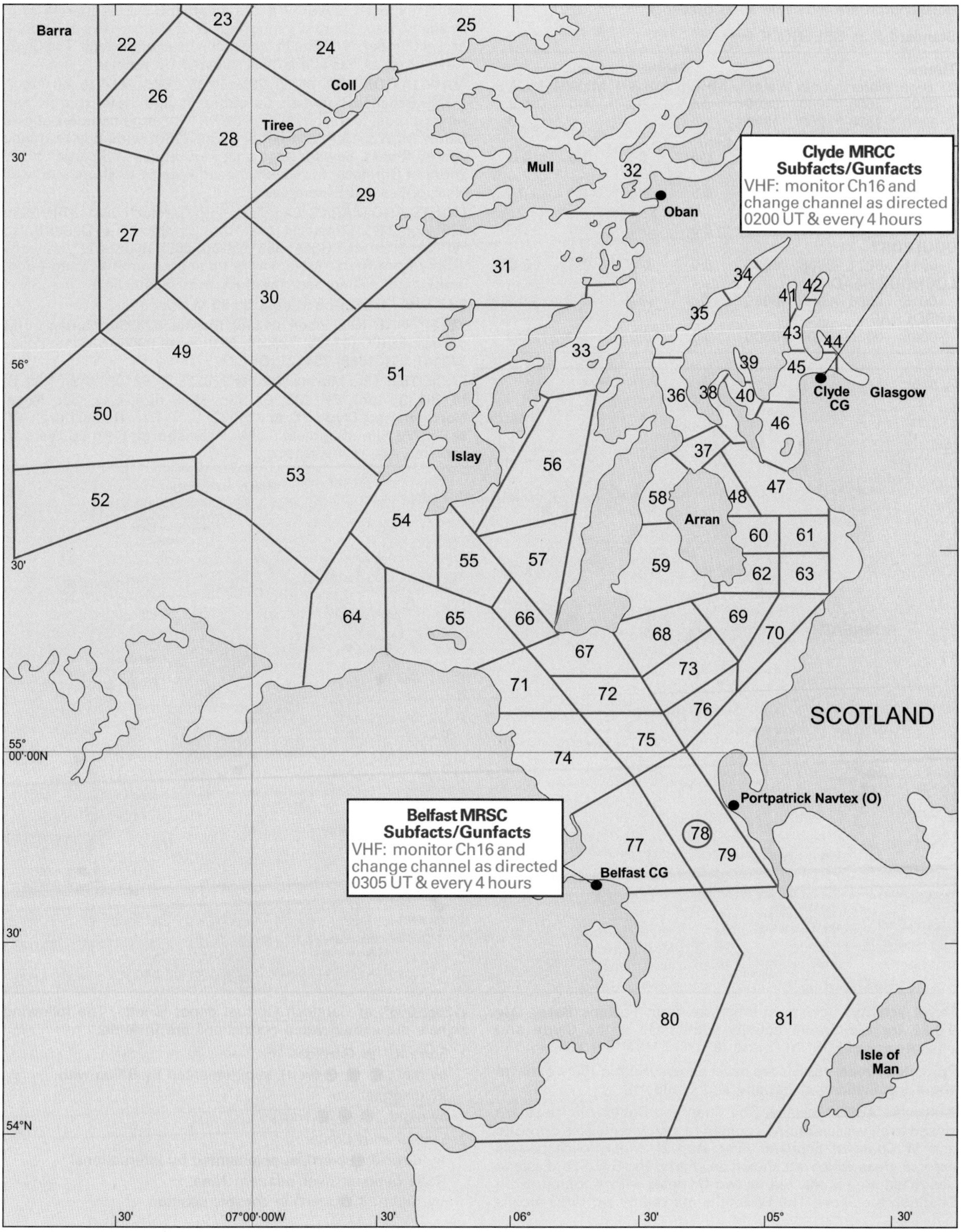
Barra
Coll
Tiree
Mull
Oban
Islay
Arran
Clyde CG
Glasgow
SCOTLAND
Portpatrick Navtex (O)
Belfast CG
Isle of Man
Clyde MRCC
Subfacts/Gunfacts
VHF: monitor Ch16 and change channel as directed
0200 UT & every 4 hours
Belfast MRSC
Subfacts/Gunfacts
VHF: monitor Ch16 and change channel as directed
0305 UT & every 4 hours
22 23 24 25 26 27 28 29 30 31 32 33 34 35 36 37 38 39 40 41 42 43 44 45 46 47 48 49 50 51 52 53 54 55 56 57 58 59 60 61 62 63 64 65 66 67 68 69 70 71 72 73 74 75 76 77 78 79 80 81
30'
56°
30'
55° 00'·00N
30'
54°N
30'
07°00'·00W
30'
06°
30'
05°
30'

9.9.20 GARELOCH/RHU

Argyll & Bute **56°00'·70N 04°46'·57W** (Rhu marina)
Rhu ❁❁❁◊◊✿✿; Sandpoint (W Dunbartonshire) ❁❁❁◊✿

CHARTS AC *2131, 1994, 2000;* Imray C63, 2900 Series; OS 56, 63

TIDES +0110 Dover; ML 1·9; Duration 0640; Zone 0 (UT). Tides at Helensburgh are the same as at Greenock

Standard Port GREENOCK (⟶)

Times				Height (metres)			
High Water		Low Water		MHWS	MHWN	MLWN	MLWS
0000	0600	0000	0600	3·4	2·8	1·0	0·3
1200	1800	1200	1800				
Differences ROSNEATH (Rhu pier)							
−0005	−0005	−0005	−0005	0·0	−0·1	0·0	0·0
FASLANE							
−0010	−0010	−0010	−0010	0·0	0·0	−0·1	−0·2
GARELOCHHEAD							
0000	0000	0000	0000	0·0	0·0	0·0	−0·1
COULPORT							
−0011	−0011	−0008	−0008	0·0	0·0	0·0	0·0
LOCHGOILHEAD							
+0015	0000	−0005	−0005	−0·2	−0·3	−0·3	−0·3
ARROCHAR							
−0005	−0005	−0005	−0005	0·0	0·0	−0·1	−0·1

BYELAWS Loch Long and Gareloch are classified as Dockyard Ports under the jurisdiction of the Queen's Harbour Master. Do not impede the passage of submarines or other warships.

SHELTER Rhu Marina is entered between low, floating wavebreaks on its S and W sides, not easy to find at night; caution cross-tides. On E/SE sides a rock bkwtr 1m above MHWS protects from strong SE'lies. Helensburgh Pier is only a temp drying berth, rather exposed, used by occas steamers. ⚓ E of marina or in Rosneath Bay. There are moorings N of the narrows at Stroul B and at Clynder; N of Rhu Pt; and at the head of the loch. The Clyde Naval Base at Faslane is best avoided by yachts.

NAVIGATION WPT 55°59'·29N 04°45'·26W, 356° to bn No 7, 1·3M. Beaches between Cairndhu Pt and Helensburgh Pier (dries almost to the head) are strewn with large boulders above/below MLWS. Gareloch ent is about 225m wide due to drying spit off Rhu Pt. Beware large unlit MoD buoys and barges off W shore of Gareloch; for Garelochhead keep to W shore until well clear of Faslane Base area.

LIGHTS AND MARKS Ldg/dir lts into Gareloch 356°, 318°, 295°, 329° and 331°. Conspic ✠ tr at Rhu. Gareloch Fuel Depot lt, Iso WRG 4s 10m 14M, G351°-356°, W356°-006°, R006°-011°, is clearly visible from the S. Many shore lts and an unlit floating boom make night sailing near the Base area inadvisable.

R/T VHF Ch 16. Rhu Marina Ch **80** M (H24).

TELEPHONE (Dial code 01436) Marina 820238; Queen's HM 674321; MRCC (01475) 729014; Marinecall 09066 526246; Police 672141; Ⓗ (01389) 754121; Dr 672277.

FACILITIES **Rhu Marina** (200) ☎ 820238, 📠 821039, AB £1.60, D, M, BH (35 ton), CH, ME, El, Slip, M, C hire, Gas, Gaz; **Royal Northern and Clyde YC** ☎ 820322, L, R, Bar; **Helensburgh SC** ☎ 672778 Slip (dinghies) L, FW; **Helensburgh** (1M) EC Wed; all services, ⇌, ✈ (Glasgow).

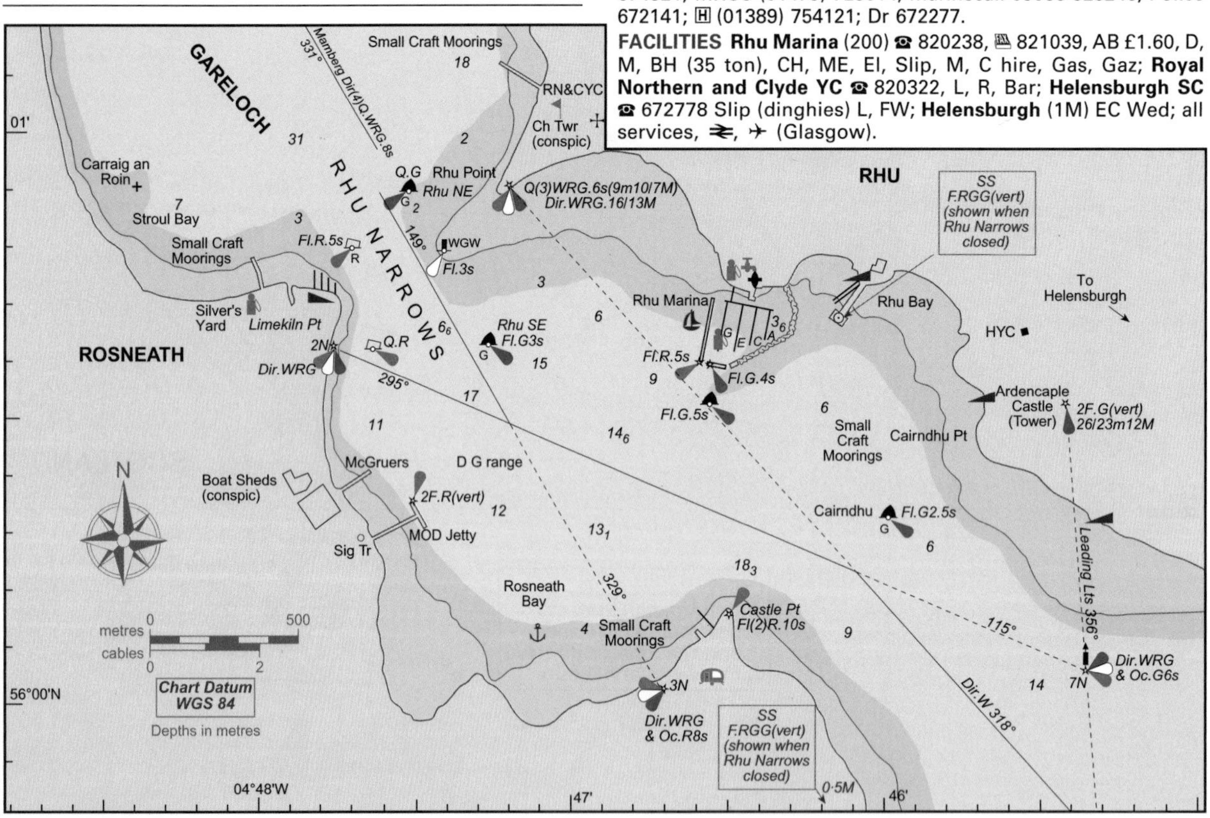
GARELOCH
RHU NARROWS
Small Craft Moorings
Mamberg Dir(4)Q.WRG.8s
331°
RN&CYC
Ch Twr (conspic)
Carraig an Roin
Stroul Bay
Small Craft Moorings
Q.G Rhu Point
Rhu NE
Q(3)WRG.6s(9m10/7M) Dir.WRG.16/13M
RHU
SS F.RGG(vert) (shown when Rhu Narrows closed)
Fl.R.5s
WGW
Fl.3s
149°
Silver's Yard
Limekiln Pt
Rhu Marina
Rhu Bay
To Helensburgh
HYC
ROSNEATH
2N
Dir.WRG
Q.R
Rhu SE Fl.G3s
Fl.R.5s
Fl.G.4s
Fl.G.5s
295°
Ardencaple Castle (Tower)
2F.G(vert) 26/23m12M
Small Craft Moorings
Cairndhu Pt
McGruers
D G range
Boat Sheds (conspic)
2F.R(vert)
MOD Jetty
Sig Tr
Cairndhu
Fl.G2.5s
Leading Lts 356°
Rosneath Bay
329°
Castle Pt Fl(2)R.10s
Small Craft Moorings
115°
3N
Dir.WRG & Oc.R8s
Dir.WRG & Oc.G6s
7N
Dir.W 318°
SS F.RGG(vert) (shown when Rhu Narrows closed)
metres 0 500
cables 0 2
Chart Datum WGS 84
Depths in metres
01'
56°00'N
04°48'W
47'
46'
0·5M

Naval activity: Beware submarines from Faslane Base. See 9.9.22 for submarine activity (Subfacts) in the Clyde and offshore or call FOSNNI Ops ☎ (01436) 674321 Ext 3206.

Protected Areas: Vessels are never allowed within 150m of naval shore installations at Faslane and Coulport.

Restricted Areas (Faslane, Rhu Chan and Coulport): These are closed to all vessels during submarine movements (see opposite and *W Coast of Scotland Pilot*, App 2). MoD Police patrols enforce areas which are shown on charts. The S limit of Faslane Restricted area is marked by two Or posts with X topmarks on Shandon foreshore. The W limit is marked by Iso WRG 4s, vis W356°-006°, at Gareloch Oil fuel depot N jetty. The following signals are shown when restrictions are in force:

1. Entrance to Gareloch
   by day : ● ● ● (vert), supplemented by R flag with W diagonal bar.
   by night : ● ● ● (vert).
2. Faslane and Coulport
   by day : 3 ● (vert), supplemented by International Code pendant over pendant Nine.
   by night : 3 ● (vert) in conspic position.

HOLY LOCH, Argyll & Bute, 55°58'·5N 04°54'·0W: Controlled by QHM Clyde but navigation is not restricted. See marina 9.9.18.

LOCH LONG/LOCH GOIL, Argyll and Bute, approx 56°00'N 04°52'·5W to 56°12'·00N 04°45'·00W. AC 3746. Tides: See 9.9.20 for differences. ML 1·7m; Duration 0645.

Shelter: Loch Long is about 15M long. Temp ⚓s (S→N) at Cove, Blairmore (not in S'lies), Ardentinny, Portincaple, Coilessan (about 1M S of Ardgartan Pt), and near head of loch (Arrochar) on either shore. In Loch Goil ⚓ at Swines Hole and off Carrick Castle (S of the pier, in N'lies a swell builds). Avoid ⚓ near Douglas Pier. The head of the loch is crowded with private/dinghy moorings, and is either too steep-to or too shallow to ⚓. The loch is frequently closed to navigation due to the trial range half way down.

Lights: Coulport Jetty, 2FG (vert) each end and two Fl G 12s on N jetty; Port Dornaige Fl 6s 8m 11M, vis 026°-206°; Dog Rock (Carraig nan Ron) Fl 2s 11M; Finnart Oil Terminal has FG lts and ldg lts 031° QW/FW on Cnap Pt. Upper Loch Long is unlit. Loch Goil ent is marked by 2 PHM buoys (Fl R 3s and QR), a SHM buoy (QG) and ldg lts 318°: front (The Perch) Dir FWRG and Fl R 3s; rear FW. Rubha Ardnahein Fl R5s.

Facilities: Loch Long (Cove), Cove SC, FW, Bar; 🛒, FW (pier); (Portincaple) shops, hotel, ✉, FW; (Ardentinny) shop, 🛒, R, hotel, M; (Blairmore) shops, ✉, Slip, FW; (Arrochar) shops, hotel, FW, Gas, ✉. Loch Goil (Carrick Castle) has ✉, shop, hotel; (Lochgoilhead) has a store, ✉, hotel, FW, Gas.

9.9.21 DUMBARTON (SANDPOINT) AND BOWLING

Inverclyde **55°56'·50N 04°34'·27W** ❀❀❀⚓✿

CHARTS AC *2131, 2007, 1994:* BW Skipper's Guide for Forth and Clyde Canal, BW Skipper's Brief for Lowland Canals; Imray 63, 2900 Series.

TIDES +0122 Dover; ML 2·0; Duration 0640; Zone 0 (UT)

Standard Port GREENOCK (⟶)

Times				Height (metres)			
High Water		Low Water		MHWS	MHWN	MLWN	MLWS
0000	0600	0000	0600	3·4	2·8	1·0	0·3
1200	1800	1200	1800				
Differences PORT GLASGOW (55°56'·10N 04°40'·50W)							
+0010	+0005	+0010	+0020	+0·2	+0·1	0·0	0·0
DUMBARTON							
+0015	+0010	+0020	+0040	+0·4	+0·3	+0·1	0·0
BOWLING							
+0020	+0010	+0030	+0055	+0·6	+0·5	+0·3	+0·1
RENFREW							
+0025	+0015	+0035	+0100	+0·9	+0·8	+0·5	+0·2
GLASGOW							
+0025	+0015	+0035	+0105	+1·3	+1·2	+0·6	+0·4

SHELTER Good. From seaward, AB at: Dumbarton (Sandpoint Marina), Bowling Hbr (within HO, lock access HW±2 to Basin and Forth & Clyde Canal); pontoon 8M upriver at Renfrew (waterbus stop). Hbrs are controlled by Clyde Port Authority.

NAVIGATION WPT No 1 SHM buoy, FL G 5s, 55°57'·61N 04°45'·96W, 2ca NNW of Clydeport container terminal (conspic blue cranes). No navigational dangers, but much shipping and ferries in the Clyde. Keep just inboard of chan lateral marks as depths shoal rapidly outboard. For Dumbarton (see plan) follow buoyed ch closely. For Bowling Hbr (N bank) cross the river at 90° abeam No 45 SHM buoy, Fl G 2s; follow ldg marks as plan.

LIGHTS AND MARKS The R Clyde is well buoyed/lit, but yachts may not transit at night.

R/T Call *Clydeport Estuary Control* VHF Ch **12** 16 (H24) when appr No 1 buoy on way up river. Weather and traffic info on request. Marina Ch M. Lock Keeper Ch 16 74, HW±2.

TELEPHONE (Dial codes: Greenock 01475; Glasgow 0141, followed by 7 digit Tel No). General Mgr Marine 725775; Estuary Control 01475 726221; British Waterways Board 332 6936, in emergency dial 100 and ask for Freephone Canals; MRCC 729988; Police 01389 822000; Dr 634617; Marinecall 09066 526246; Ⓗ (01389) 754121.

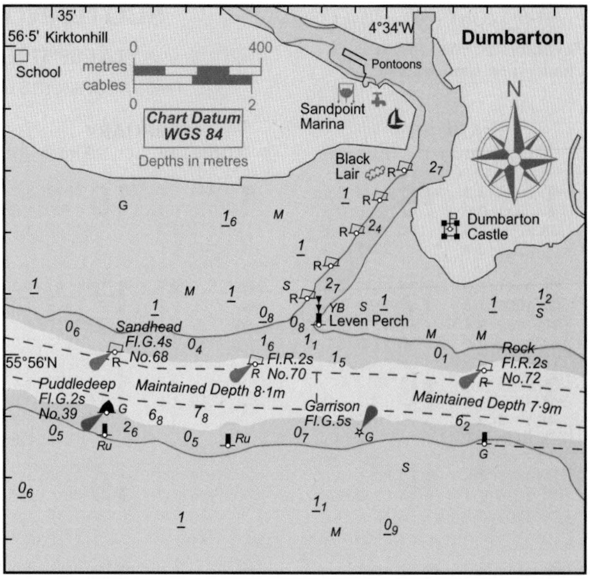
Dumbarton
56·5' Kirktonhill
School
metres
cables
Chart Datum
WGS 84
Depths in metres
4°34'W
Pontoons
Sandpoint Marina
Black Lair
Dumbarton Castle
Leven Perch
Sandhead
Fl.G.4s
No.68
55°56'N
Fl.R.2s
No.70
Puddledeep
Fl.G.2s
No.39
Maintained Depth 8·1m
Garrison
Fl.G.5s
Rock
Fl.R.2s
No.72
Maintained Depth 7·9m

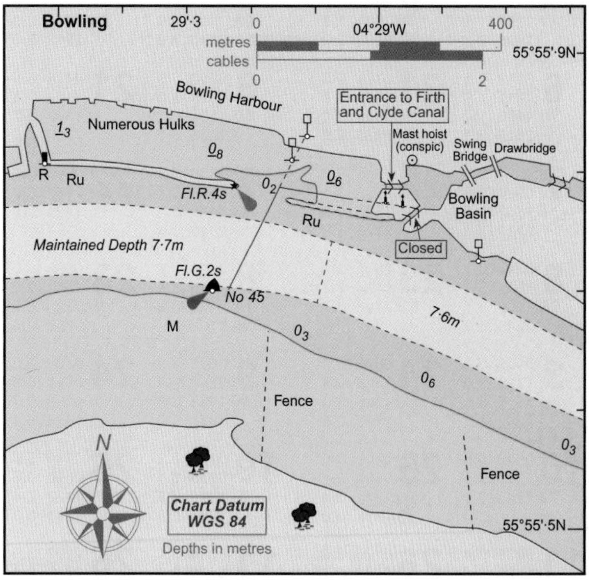
Bowling
29'·3
metres
cables
04°29'W
55°55'·9N
Bowling Harbour
Entrance to Firth and Clyde Canal
Numerous Hulks
Mast hoist (conspic)
Swing Bridge
Drawbridge
Fl.R.4s
Bowling Basin
Closed
Maintained Depth 7·7m
Fl.G.2s
No 45
7·6m
Fence
Chart Datum
WGS 84
Depths in metres
55°55'·5N

FACILITIES Sandpoint Marina ☎ (01389) 762396, 731500, 📠 732605. £5 any LOA. Limited visitors berths. Call marina on Ch M and report to office on arrival. BH (40T), ⛽, FW, BY, D (can), CH, slip. **Town** 🛒, R, Bar, Ⓑ, ✉, ⇌ 30 mins to Glasgow. www.scottishcanals.co.uk.

Bowling Basin 55°55'·8N 04°29'·0W; ☎ (01389) 877969. W end of Forth and Clyde Canal, see 9.6.9. For lock hrs call VHF Ch 16, 74 HW±2 as far ahead as possible for current position. *Skipper's Brief* is essential. **Facilities:** AB £2.25, FW, Showers, WC, D by prior notice; Mast crane. **Town** P&D (cans), 🛒, R, Bar, ✉, Ⓑ, ⇌.

RENFREW 55°55'·94N 04°34'·25W; 4 Ⓥ(contact ☎ 0141 8861013 for availability) AB £15 on *SS Kyle* pontoon; Renfrew Hbr for laying-up/repairs.

GLASGOW 55°55'·94N 04°34'·25W; Clyde Yacht Clubs Association is at 8 St James St, Paisley. ☎ 8878296. Clyde Cruising Club is at Suite 408, Pentagon Centre, 36 Washington Street, Glasgow G3 8AZ, ☎ 221 2774, 📠 221 2775. **Services:** ACA, CH.

TIME ZONE (UT)
For Summer Time add ONE hour in **non-shaded areas**

SCOTLAND – GREENOCK

LAT 55°57′N LONG 4°46′W

TIMES AND HEIGHTS OF HIGH AND LOW WATERS

SPRING & NEAP TIDES
Dates in red are SPRINGS
Dates in blue are NEAPS

YEAR **2005**

JANUARY

Day	Time	m	Time	m	Time	m	Time	m
1 SA	0358	3.0	0921	0.9	1552	3.4	2135	0.7
2 SU	0441	3.0	1006	1.0	1633	3.4	2223	0.7
3 M	0527	2.9	1057	1.0	1718	3.3	◑ 2318	0.7
4 TU	0616	2.8	1154	1.1	1809	3.2		
5 W	0018	0.8	0710	2.8	1256	1.1	1908	3.1
6 TH	0119	0.8	0817	2.8	1400	1.0	2019	3.1
7 F	0220	0.7	0934	2.9	1503	0.9	2137	3.1
8 SA	0319	0.7	1037	3.1	1602	0.7	2243	3.2
9 SU	0415	0.6	1129	3.3	1655	0.5	2342	3.3
10 M ●	0508	0.6	1216	3.5	1745	0.3		
11 TU	0038	3.4	0559	0.6	1303	3.6	1833	0.2
12 W	0133	3.4	0649	0.6	1349	3.8	1922	0.1
13 TH	0225	3.4	0739	0.6	1434	3.8	2011	0.1
14 F	0314	3.4	0828	0.6	1518	3.8	2100	0.2
15 SA	0400	3.3	0916	0.7	1603	3.8	2151	0.3
16 SU	0444	3.3	1006	0.8	1649	3.6	2247	0.5
17 M	0528	3.2	1100	1.0	1737	3.5	◐ 2349	0.7
18 TU	0613	3.1	1203	1.1	1829	3.2		
19 W	0056	0.8	0702	3.0	1316	1.2	1930	3.0
20 TH	0201	0.9	0803	2.9	1431	1.2	2108	2.9
21 F	0301	0.9	0931	2.9	1534	1.0	2228	2.9
22 SA	0355	0.9	1036	3.1	1625	0.9	2322	3.0
23 SU	0442	0.8	1124	3.2	1708	0.7		
24 M	0008	3.0	0523	0.8	1206	3.3	1745	0.6
25 TU	0049	3.0	0601	0.7	1242	3.4	○ 1818	0.6
26 W	0126	3.0	0634	0.7	1314	3.4	1848	0.5
27 TH	0159	3.0	0706	0.7	1345	3.5	1918	0.5
28 F	0229	3.0	0739	0.6	1418	3.5	1950	0.4
29 SA	0300	3.0	0814	0.6	1452	3.5	2025	0.4
30 SU	0332	3.0	0851	0.6	1529	3.5	2103	0.4
31 M	0406	3.0	0931	0.6	1606	3.4	2146	0.4

FEBRUARY

Day	Time	m	Time	m	Time	m	Time	m
1 TU	0441	3.0	1016	0.7	1645	3.3	2236	0.5
2 W	0520	2.9	1108	0.9	1729	3.2	◑ 2333	0.7
3 TH	0605	2.8	1210	1.0	1822	3.0		
4 F	0036	0.8	0706	2.7	1320	1.0	1930	2.9
5 SA	0145	0.9	0850	2.7	1438	0.9	2110	2.9
6 SU	0258	0.9	1019	2.9	1551	0.7	2236	3.0
7 M	0405	0.8	1116	3.2	1647	0.4	2340	3.1
8 TU ●	0501	0.6	1205	3.4	1736	0.2		
9 W	0035	3.2	0550	0.5	1253	3.6	1821	0.0
10 TH	0127	3.3	0635	0.4	1338	3.8	1905	0.0
11 F	0214	3.4	0720	0.4	1421	3.8	1949	0.0
12 SA	0255	3.4	0803	0.4	1502	3.9	2032	0.1
13 SU	0332	3.4	0846	0.5	1542	3.8	2117	0.3
14 M	0407	3.3	0929	0.6	1620	3.7	2204	0.5
15 TU	0443	3.3	1013	0.8	1700	3.4	2257	0.8
16 W ◐	0522	3.1	1105	1.0	1742	3.1		
17 TH	0007	1.0	0605	3.0	1220	1.2	1831	2.9
18 F	0129	1.1	0658	2.8	1403	1.2	1938	2.6
19 SA	0238	1.1	0811	2.8	1513	1.1	2220	2.6
20 SU	0336	1.0	1012	2.9	1606	0.9	2312	2.8
21 M	0424	0.9	1106	3.1	1649	0.7	2354	2.9
22 TU	0505	0.7	1147	3.2	1724	0.5		
23 W	0033	3.0	0540	0.6	1223	3.3	1755	0.4
24 TH	0109	3.0	0611	0.5	1253	3.3	○ 1824	0.4
25 F	0140	3.0	0640	0.5	1322	3.4	1851	0.3
26 SA	0207	3.0	0710	0.4	1354	3.4	1921	0.3
27 SU	0232	3.0	0743	0.4	1429	3.4	1954	0.2
28 M	0300	3.1	0818	0.4	1504	3.5	2032	0.2

MARCH

Day	Time	m	Time	m	Time	m	Time	m
1 TU	0330	3.1	0857	0.4	1540	3.4	2114	0.3
2 W	0402	3.0	0941	0.5	1617	3.3	2201	0.4
3 TH	0437	2.9	1033	0.7	1659	3.1	◑ 2257	0.7
4 F	0520	2.8	1138	0.8	1751	2.9		
5 SA	0003	0.9	0619	2.7	1255	0.9	1900	2.7
6 SU	0121	1.0	0816	2.6	1429	0.8	2111	2.7
7 M	0251	1.0	1006	2.9	1544	0.5	2239	2.9
8 TU	0400	0.8	1103	3.2	1636	0.3	2336	3.1
9 W	0451	0.6	1151	3.4	1721	0.0		
10 TH	0026	3.2	0535	0.4	1237	3.6	● 1801	-0.1
11 F	0111	3.3	0616	0.3	1321	3.7	1842	-0.1
12 SA	0151	3.3	0655	0.3	1402	3.8	1921	0.0
13 SU	0226	3.4	0734	0.3	1440	3.8	2001	0.1
14 M	0258	3.4	0812	0.3	1516	3.7	2041	0.3
15 TU	0330	3.4	0851	0.4	1551	3.5	2122	0.5
16 W	0404	3.3	0931	0.6	1628	3.3	2206	0.8
17 TH	0440	3.2	1015	0.8	1708	3.0	◐ 2301	1.1
18 F	0523	3.0	1113	1.1	1756	2.7		
19 SA	0046	1.3	0614	2.8	1328	1.2	1900	2.5
20 SU	0208	1.3	0722	2.7	1442	1.1	2200	2.5
21 M	0309	1.1	0933	2.7	1535	0.9	2248	2.7
22 TU	0357	0.9	1036	2.9	1617	0.6	2328	2.8
23 W	0437	0.7	1117	3.1	1653	0.5		
24 TH	0005	2.9	0510	0.6	1152	3.2	1723	0.4
25 F	0039	3.0	0540	0.4	1221	3.2	○ 1751	0.3
26 SA	0109	3.0	0609	0.4	1253	3.3	1819	0.2
27 SU	0134	3.0	0639	0.3	1327	3.3	1851	0.1
28 M	0200	3.1	0713	0.2	1404	3.4	1926	0.1
29 TU	0228	3.1	0750	0.2	1441	3.4	2006	0.1
30 W	0259	3.2	0831	0.2	1518	3.4	2050	0.3
31 TH	0332	3.2	0918	0.4	1557	3.2	2138	0.5

APRIL

Day	Time	m	Time	m	Time	m	Time	m
1 F	0409	3.0	1013	0.6	1641	3.0	2235	0.8
2 SA	0454	2.9	1122	0.7	1737	2.8	◑ 2345	1.0
3 SU	0600	2.7	1249	0.8	1903	2.6		
4 M	0113	1.1	0816	2.6	1423	0.6	2121	2.6
5 TU	0244	1.0	0948	2.9	1527	0.4	2230	2.9
6 W	0347	0.8	1043	3.2	1616	0.1	2321	3.1
7 TH	0435	0.5	1130	3.4	1659	0.0		
8 F	0005	3.2	0515	0.4	1215	3.5	● 1738	-0.1
9 SA	0045	3.2	0553	0.3	1258	3.6	1816	0.0
10 SU	0121	3.3	0629	0.2	1338	3.6	1853	0.1
11 M	0153	3.3	0705	0.2	1415	3.5	1931	0.3
12 TU	0225	3.4	0742	0.3	1450	3.5	2010	0.4
13 W	0257	3.4	0819	0.4	1525	3.3	2049	0.6
14 TH	0331	3.4	0858	0.5	1602	3.1	2132	0.9
15 F	0407	3.2	0942	0.7	1644	2.9	2222	1.1
16 SA	0448	3.0	1037	1.0	1735	2.6	◐ 2335	1.3
17 SU	0541	2.8	1218	1.1	1841	2.5		
18 M	0118	1.3	0647	2.7	1356	1.0	2031	2.4
19 TU	0226	1.2	0811	2.7	1451	0.8	2204	2.6
20 W	0317	1.0	0941	2.8	1536	0.6	2248	2.8
21 TH	0359	0.8	1029	3.0	1613	0.5	2325	2.9
22 F	0435	0.6	1106	3.1	1646	0.3		
23 SA	0000	3.0	0506	0.4	1142	3.2	1716	0.2
24 SU	0031	3.0	0538	0.3	1220	3.2	○ 1748	0.1
25 M	0101	3.1	0612	0.2	1300	3.3	1824	0.1
26 TU	0131	3.2	0649	0.1	1341	3.3	1904	0.1
27 W	0203	3.3	0730	0.1	1422	3.3	1948	0.2
28 TH	0238	3.3	0815	0.2	1503	3.3	2036	0.4
29 F	0314	3.3	0907	0.3	1547	3.1	2128	0.6
30 SA	0355	3.1	1008	0.5	1639	2.9	2229	0.8

Chart Datum: 1·62 metres below Ordnance Datum (Newlyn)

TIME ZONE (UT)
For Summer Time add ONE hour in **non-shaded areas**

SCOTLAND – GREENOCK

LAT 55°57′N LONG 4°46′W

TIMES AND HEIGHTS OF HIGH AND LOW WATERS

SPRING & NEAP TIDES
Dates in red are SPRINGS
Dates in blue are NEAPS

YEAR **2005**

MAY

Day	Time	m	Day	Time	m
1	0446	3.0	16	0511	2.9
	1122	0.6		1125	0.9
SU	1750	2.7	M	1821	2.6
	◑ 2341	1.0		◐	
2	0604	2.8	17	0007	1.2
	1247	0.6		0611	2.8
M	1929	2.6	TU	1247	0.9
				1928	2.5
3	0102	1.1	18	0118	1.2
	0801	2.8		0719	2.8
TU	1402	0.4	W	1352	0.8
	2103	2.7		2042	2.6
4	0221	1.0	19	0219	1.0
	0921	3.0		0828	2.8
W	1501	0.3	TH	1442	0.6
	2205	2.9		2147	2.7
5	0323	0.8	20	0310	0.8
	1016	3.2		0929	2.9
TH	1550	0.1	F	1525	0.5
	2253	3.0		2236	2.8
6	0412	0.6	21	0353	0.7
	1105	3.3		1020	3.0
F	1634	0.1	SA	1604	0.3
	2336	3.1		2317	2.9
7	0454	0.4	22	0433	0.5
	1150	3.4		1105	3.1
SA	1714	0.1	SU	1642	0.2
				2354	3.0
8	0014	3.2	23	0511	0.3
	0531	0.3		1150	3.2
SU	1233	3.4	M	1722	0.2
	● 1752	0.2		○	
9	0050	3.2	24	0031	3.1
	0607	0.3		0550	0.2
M	1313	3.3	TU	1236	3.3
	1830	0.3		1803	0.2
10	0124	3.3	25	0109	3.2
	0643	0.3		0633	0.1
TU	1351	3.3	W	1323	3.3
	1908	0.5		1849	0.3
11	0157	3.4	26	0147	3.3
	0719	0.3		0718	0.1
W	1428	3.2	TH	1410	3.3
	1947	0.6		1938	0.4
12	0231	3.4	27	0226	3.4
	0756	0.4		0809	0.1
TH	1504	3.1	F	1459	3.2
	2028	0.7		2031	0.5
13	0305	3.4	28	0308	3.4
	0837	0.5		0904	0.2
F	1543	3.0	SA	1552	3.1
	2112	0.8		2126	0.6
14	0341	3.3	29	0354	3.3
	0922	0.7		1006	0.3
SA	1628	2.8	SU	1653	2.9
	2200	1.0		2226	0.8
15	0422	3.1	30	0452	3.1
	1015	0.8		1115	0.4
SU	1720	2.7	M	1802	2.8
	2258	1.1		◑ 2330	0.9
			31	0605	3.0
				1226	0.4
			TU	1914	2.8

JUNE

Day	Time	m	Day	Time	m
1	0038	0.9	16	0013	1.0
	0730	3.0		0631	2.9
W	1332	0.3	TH	1245	0.7
	2024	2.8		1937	2.6
2	0148	0.9	17	0113	1.0
	0845	3.1		0731	2.8
TH	1431	0.3	F	1342	0.6
	2126	2.9		2037	2.7
3	0253	0.8	18	0213	0.9
	0946	3.2		0836	2.9
F	1523	0.3	SA	1435	0.5
	2218	3.0		2141	2.7
4	0348	0.6	19	0310	0.7
	1039	3.2		0939	3.0
SA	1610	0.3	SU	1525	0.4
	2304	3.0		2237	2.9
5	0434	0.5	20	0402	0.6
	1127	3.2		1035	3.1
SU	1653	0.3	M	1613	0.4
	2346	3.1		2325	3.0
6	0516	0.4	21	0450	0.4
	1212	3.1		1128	3.2
M	1734	0.4	TU	1701	0.3
	●				
7	0024	3.2	22	0010	3.2
	0553	0.4		0535	0.2
TU	1254	3.1	W	1220	3.2
	1814	0.5		○ 1749	0.4
8	0100	3.3	23	0054	3.3
	0629	0.4		0623	0.1
W	1334	3.0	TH	1313	3.2
	1853	0.6		1839	0.4
9	0135	3.3	24	0137	3.4
	0705	0.4		0712	0.0
TH	1412	3.0	F	1407	3.2
	1933	0.7		1932	0.4
10	0210	3.4	25	0221	3.5
	0742	0.5		0803	0.0
F	1450	2.9	SA	1502	3.2
	2014	0.7		2024	0.5
11	0245	3.4	26	0306	3.5
	0822	0.5		0856	0.1
SA	1530	2.9	SU	1556	3.1
	2056	0.7		2116	0.5
12	0321	3.3	27	0354	3.5
	0904	0.6		0952	0.1
SU	1614	2.8	M	1650	3.1
	2139	0.8		2210	0.6
13	0400	3.2	28	0446	3.4
	0951	0.6		1053	0.2
M	1701	2.7	TU	1744	3.0
	2226	0.9		◑ 2305	0.7
14	0444	3.1	29	0544	3.2
	1045	0.7		1157	0.3
TU	1752	2.7	W	1836	2.9
	2317	0.9			
15	0534	2.9	30	0006	0.8
	1144	0.7		0648	3.1
W	1843	2.7	TH	1301	0.4
	◐			1930	2.9

JULY

Day	Time	m	Day	Time	m
1	0112	0.9	16	0021	0.9
	0801	3.0		0641	2.9
F	1401	0.5	SA	1250	0.7
	2032	2.8		1936	2.6
2	0222	0.9	17	0123	0.9
	0915	3.0		0748	2.8
SA	1457	0.5	SU	1351	0.7
	2138	2.9		2049	2.7
3	0326	0.8	18	0231	0.8
	1018	3.0		0904	2.9
SU	1550	0.5	M	1452	0.6
	2235	2.9		2205	2.8
4	0420	0.6	19	0338	0.7
	1112	3.0		1015	3.0
M	1638	0.6	TU	1552	0.6
	2323	3.0		2304	3.0
5	0506	0.5	20	0436	0.4
	1200	3.0		1116	3.1
TU	1723	0.6	W	1647	0.5
				2354	3.2
6	0005	3.2	21	0526	0.2
	0546	0.5		1213	3.1
W	1245	2.9	TH	1739	0.5
	● 1804	0.6		○	
7	0044	3.2	22	0042	3.4
	0622	0.4		0614	0.0
TH	1326	2.9	F	1310	3.2
	1843	0.6		1829	0.4
8	0120	3.3	23	0128	3.5
	0656	0.4		0701	-0.1
F	1404	2.9	SA	1404	3.2
	1920	0.6		1919	0.4
9	0153	3.3	24	0214	3.6
	0729	0.4		0748	-0.1
SA	1440	2.8	SU	1455	3.2
	1956	0.6		2007	0.4
10	0227	3.3	25	0258	3.7
	0804	0.5		0836	0.0
SU	1516	2.8	M	1542	3.2
	2032	0.6		2054	0.4
11	0301	3.3	26	0341	3.7
	0840	0.5		0926	0.1
M	1553	2.8	TU	1625	3.2
	2110	0.6		2142	0.5
12	0337	3.3	27	0425	3.6
	0919	0.5		1020	0.3
TU	1631	2.8	W	1706	3.2
	2151	0.7		2232	0.6
13	0416	3.2	28	0511	3.4
	1003	0.5		1120	0.5
W	1712	2.8	TH	1748	3.1
	2235	0.7		◑ 2328	0.8
14	0458	3.1	29	0602	3.2
	1054	0.6		1227	0.6
TH	1755	2.8	F	1833	2.9
	◐ 2325	0.8			
15	0546	3.0	30	0034	0.9
	1151	0.6		0700	2.9
F	1841	2.7	SA	1334	0.8
				1924	2.8
			31	0156	1.0
				0836	2.7
			SU	1437	0.8
				2041	2.8

AUGUST

Day	Time	m	Day	Time	m
1	0310	0.9	16	0202	0.9
	1011	2.8		0840	2.7
M	1535	0.8	TU	1429	0.9
	2211	2.9		2144	2.8
2	0408	0.8	17	0325	0.7
	1108	2.8		1010	2.9
TU	1626	0.8	W	1540	0.8
	2306	3.0		2250	3.0
3	0455	0.6	18	0426	0.4
	1155	2.9		1115	3.1
W	1710	0.7	TH	1638	0.7
	2351	3.2		2341	3.3
4	0534	0.5	19	0515	0.1
	1237	2.9		1210	3.2
TH	1750	0.7	F	1727	0.5
				○	
5	0030	3.2	20	0028	3.5
	0608	0.4		0559	0.0
F	1317	2.9	SA	1302	3.3
	● 1825	0.6		1813	0.4
6	0105	3.3	21	0114	3.7
	0638	0.4		0642	-0.1
SA	1352	2.9	SU	1350	3.3
	1857	0.6		1857	0.4
7	0135	3.3	22	0158	3.8
	0707	0.4		0725	-0.1
SU	1423	2.9	M	1434	3.4
	1928	0.6		1941	0.4
8	0205	3.3	23	0240	3.8
	0736	0.4		0808	0.0
M	1452	2.9	TU	1512	3.4
	2001	0.5		2024	0.4
9	0237	3.3	24	0319	3.8
	0808	0.4		0852	0.2
TU	1521	2.9	W	1548	3.4
	2036	0.5		2107	0.5
10	0311	3.3	25	0358	3.6
	0842	0.4		0940	0.4
W	1553	3.0	TH	1623	3.3
	2113	0.5		2152	0.6
11	0347	3.3	26	0437	3.4
	0922	0.4		1033	0.7
TH	1627	2.9	F	1701	3.2
	2154	0.6		◑ 2242	0.9
12	0424	3.2	27	0520	3.1
	1008	0.5		1146	1.0
F	1703	2.9	SA	1744	3.1
	2242	0.7		2349	1.1
13	0506	3.1	28	0610	2.8
	1103	0.7		1309	1.2
SA	1745	2.8	SU	1833	2.9
	◐ 2338	0.9			
14	0557	2.9	29	0134	1.2
	1207	0.8		0721	2.6
SU	1839	2.7	M	1418	1.2
				1938	2.8
15	0044	1.0	30	0252	1.1
	0705	2.8		1009	2.7
M	1315	0.9	TU	1517	1.1
	2000	2.6		2149	2.9
			31	0349	0.9
				1100	2.8
			W	1607	0.9
				2248	3.1

Chart Datum: 1·62 metres below Ordnance Datum (Newlyn)

TIME ZONE (UT)
For Summer Time add ONE hour in **non-shaded areas**

SCOTLAND – GREENOCK

LAT 55°57′N LONG 4°46′W

TIMES AND HEIGHTS OF HIGH AND LOW WATERS

SPRING & NEAP TIDES
Dates in red are SPRINGS
Dates in blue are NEAPS

YEAR **2005**

SEPTEMBER

Date	Day	Time	m	Time	m	Time	m	Time	m	Moon
1	TH	0434	0.7	1141	3.0	1650	0.8	2332	3.2	
2	F	0511	0.5	1218	3.0	1726	0.7			
3	SA	0009	3.3	0542	0.4	1255	3.0	1758	0.6	●
4	SU	0042	3.3	0611	0.4	1327	3.0	1827	0.6	
5	M	0110	3.3	0637	0.4	1355	3.0	1855	0.6	
6	TU	0139	3.4	0703	0.4	1419	3.1	1926	0.5	
7	W	0210	3.4	0733	0.3	1445	3.1	1959	0.5	
8	TH	0244	3.4	0807	0.3	1514	3.1	2037	0.5	
9	F	0319	3.4	0846	0.4	1546	3.1	2118	0.6	
10	SA	0355	3.3	0930	0.6	1620	3.0	2207	0.7	
11	SU	0434	3.1	1025	0.8	1659	2.9	2307	0.9	◐
12	M	0524	2.9	1133	1.1	1754	2.8			
13	TU	0020	1.0	0636	2.7	1251	1.2	1926	2.7	
14	W	0152	1.0	0840	2.7	1420	1.2	2131	2.9	
15	TH	0317	0.7	1014	2.9	1533	1.0	2234	3.2	
16	F	0412	0.4	1111	3.1	1625	0.7	2324	3.4	
17	SA	0457	0.1	1159	3.3	1710	0.6			
18	SU	0010	3.6	0537	0.0	1244	3.4	1751	0.4	○
19	M	0054	3.8	0617	0.0	1325	3.4	1831	0.4	
20	TU	0137	3.8	0657	0.0	1403	3.5	1911	0.4	
21	W	0216	3.8	0737	0.2	1437	3.5	1951	0.4	
22	TH	0254	3.8	0817	0.4	1510	3.5	2031	0.5	
23	F	0330	3.6	0900	0.7	1545	3.5	2113	0.7	
24	SA	0407	3.4	0946	1.0	1622	3.4	2159	0.9	
25	SU	0447	3.1	1048	1.3	1704	3.2	2259	1.2	◑
26	M	0537	2.8	1237	1.5	1755	3.0			
27	TU	0106	1.3	0647	2.6	1350	1.5	1900	2.9	
28	W	0222	1.2	0952	2.7	1449	1.3	2106	2.9	
29	TH	0317	1.0	1036	2.9	1539	1.1	2218	3.1	
30	F	0401	0.8	1113	3.1	1620	0.9	2302	3.2	

OCTOBER

Date	Day	Time	m	Time	m	Time	m	Time	m	Moon
1	SA	0438	0.6	1149	3.1	1656	0.8	2338	3.3	
2	SU	0510	0.5	1222	3.2	1726	0.7			
3	M	0008	3.3	0537	0.4	1254	3.2	1754	0.6	●
4	TU	0038	3.4	0603	0.4	1320	3.2	1822	0.6	
5	W	0109	3.4	0630	0.4	1344	3.2	1854	0.5	
6	TH	0143	3.4	0702	0.4	1412	3.3	1929	0.5	
7	F	0219	3.5	0739	0.4	1442	3.3	2008	0.5	
8	SA	0256	3.4	0820	0.5	1515	3.3	2053	0.6	
9	SU	0333	3.3	0907	0.8	1550	3.2	2145	0.8	
10	M	0415	3.1	1003	1.0	1632	3.1	2251	1.0	◐
11	TU	0508	2.9	1114	1.3	1731	2.9			
12	W	0011	1.0	0635	2.7	1241	1.4	1919	2.8	
13	TH	0146	0.9	0847	2.8	1409	1.3	2111	3.0	
14	F	0257	0.6	1003	3.0	1515	1.1	2212	3.3	
15	SA	0349	0.4	1053	3.2	1606	0.8	2301	3.6	
16	SU	0433	0.2	1137	3.4	1648	0.6	2347	3.7	
17	M	0513	0.1	1217	3.5	1728	0.5			○
18	TU	0030	3.8	0551	0.1	1255	3.5	1806	0.5	
19	W	0113	3.8	0629	0.3	1330	3.6	1844	0.5	
20	TH	0152	3.7	0708	0.4	1404	3.6	1922	0.5	
21	F	0229	3.7	0748	0.7	1438	3.7	2002	0.6	
22	SA	0305	3.5	0829	0.9	1514	3.6	2043	0.8	
23	SU	0343	3.3	0914	1.1	1551	3.5	2129	1.0	
24	M	0425	3.1	1008	1.4	1633	3.4	2227	1.2	
25	TU	0517	2.8	1140	1.6	1724	3.2			◑
26	W	0010	1.3	0628	2.6	1305	1.6	1827	3.0	
27	TH	0136	1.3	0856	2.7	1407	1.5	1949	3.0	
28	F	0233	1.1	0952	2.9	1459	1.3	2122	3.1	
29	SA	0319	0.9	1033	3.1	1543	1.1	2215	3.2	
30	SU	0358	0.7	1110	3.2	1620	0.9	2254	3.3	
31	M	0431	0.6	1145	3.3	1652	0.8	2329	3.3	

NOVEMBER

Date	Day	Time	m	Time	m	Time	m	Time	m	Moon
1	TU	0501	0.5	1216	3.3	1723	0.7			
2	W	0003	3.4	0530	0.5	1245	3.3	1754	0.6	●
3	TH	0041	3.4	0602	0.5	1314	3.4	1829	0.5	
4	F	0120	3.5	0639	0.5	1346	3.5	1908	0.5	
5	SA	0200	3.5	0720	0.6	1420	3.5	1951	0.5	
6	SU	0240	3.4	0806	0.7	1456	3.5	2041	0.6	
7	M	0322	3.3	0857	0.9	1535	3.4	2138	0.7	
8	TU	0411	3.1	0956	1.1	1622	3.3	2246	0.9	
9	W	0515	2.9	1107	1.3	1729	3.1			◐
10	TH	0005	0.9	0648	2.8	1227	1.4	1908	3.1	
11	F	0123	0.8	0825	2.9	1343	1.3	2039	3.2	
12	SA	0227	0.6	0933	3.1	1448	1.1	2143	3.4	
13	SU	0320	0.4	1024	3.3	1541	0.9	2235	3.5	
14	M	0406	0.3	1108	3.4	1627	0.7	2323	3.6	
15	TU	0449	0.3	1148	3.5	1708	0.6			
16	W	0008	3.6	0528	0.4	1226	3.5	1746	0.6	○
17	TH	0051	3.6	0608	0.5	1302	3.6	1824	0.6	
18	F	0131	3.5	0647	0.7	1338	3.7	1902	0.6	
19	SA	0210	3.5	0728	0.8	1414	3.7	1942	0.7	
20	SU	0247	3.3	0810	1.0	1450	3.7	2024	0.8	
21	M	0327	3.2	0855	1.2	1528	3.6	2110	0.9	
22	TU	0411	3.1	0945	1.3	1609	3.5	2202	1.1	
23	W	0503	2.9	1045	1.4	1656	3.3	2308	1.2	◑
24	TH	0604	2.8	1156	1.5	1752	3.1			
25	F	0026	1.2	0711	2.8	1305	1.5	1854	3.1	
26	SA	0132	1.1	0827	2.8	1405	1.4	2001	3.1	
27	SU	0225	1.0	0933	3.0	1455	1.2	2107	3.1	
28	M	0310	0.8	1023	3.1	1539	1.0	2202	3.2	
29	TU	0349	0.7	1104	3.2	1618	0.9	2249	3.3	
30	W	0426	0.6	1140	3.3	1655	0.7	2333	3.3	

DECEMBER

Date	Day	Time	m	Time	m	Time	m	Time	m	Moon
1	TH	0503	0.6	1215	3.4	1733	0.6			●
2	F	0017	3.4	0541	0.6	1251	3.5	1813	0.5	
3	SA	0102	3.4	0624	0.6	1328	3.6	1856	0.4	
4	SU	0148	3.4	0710	0.7	1407	3.6	1944	0.4	
5	M	0234	3.4	0800	0.8	1448	3.6	2036	0.5	
6	TU	0323	3.3	0854	0.9	1532	3.6	2133	0.5	
7	W	0418	3.1	0951	1.0	1624	3.5	2236	0.6	
8	TH	0521	3.0	1053	1.1	1726	3.4	2343	0.6	◐
9	F	0630	3.0	1201	1.2	1839	3.3			
10	SA	0051	0.6	0740	3.0	1310	1.2	1957	3.3	
11	SU	0154	0.6	0848	3.1	1417	1.1	2109	3.3	
12	M	0251	0.6	0948	3.2	1517	1.0	2210	3.4	
13	TU	0342	0.6	1038	3.3	1608	0.8	2303	3.4	
14	W	0429	0.6	1123	3.4	1654	0.7	2351	3.4	
15	TH	0513	0.6	1203	3.5	1735	0.6			○
16	F	0037	3.3	0555	0.7	1242	3.6	1814	0.6	
17	SA	0120	3.3	0636	0.8	1320	3.6	1852	0.6	
18	SU	0200	3.2	0717	0.9	1356	3.7	1931	0.7	
19	M	0238	3.2	0757	0.9	1433	3.7	2010	0.7	
20	TU	0317	3.1	0838	1.0	1510	3.6	2051	0.8	
21	W	0357	3.1	0920	1.1	1548	3.5	2134	0.8	
22	TH	0441	3.0	1005	1.1	1629	3.4	2222	0.9	
23	F	0528	2.9	1055	1.2	1714	3.3	2316	1.0	◑
24	SA	0618	2.9	1151	1.3	1804	3.2			
25	SU	0015	1.0	0711	2.8	1252	1.3	1859	3.1	
26	M	0116	1.0	0812	2.8	1354	1.3	2001	3.0	
27	TU	0212	0.9	0921	2.9	1453	1.1	2110	3.0	
28	W	0305	0.9	1021	3.0	1545	0.9	2214	3.1	
29	TH	0354	0.8	1110	3.2	1633	0.7	2309	3.2	
30	F	0441	0.7	1153	3.3	1718	0.6			
31	SA	0001	3.3	0527	0.6	1235	3.5	1803	0.4	●

Chart Datum: 1·62 metres below Ordnance Datum (Newlyn)

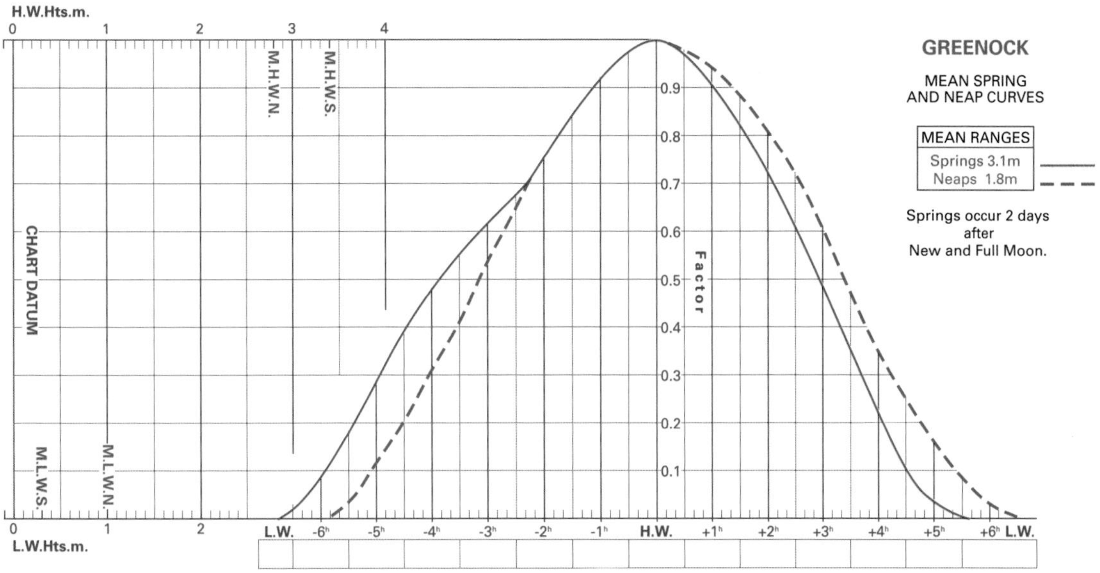
GREENOCK
MEAN SPRING AND NEAP CURVES
MEAN RANGES
Springs 3.1m
Neaps 1.8m
Springs occur 2 days after New and Full Moon.
H.W.Hts.m.
L.W.Hts.m.
CHART DATUM
M.H.W.N.
M.H.W.S.
M.L.W.S.
M.L.W.N.
Factor
L.W. -6h -5h -4h -3h -2h -1h H.W. +1h +2h +3h +4h +5h +6h L.W.

9.9.22 ARDROSSAN

N Ayrshire **55°38'·50N 04°49'·61W**

CHARTS AC *2126*, 2221, *2491*, *1866*; Imray C63; OS 63/70

TIDES +0055 Dover; ML 1·9; Duration 0630; Zone 0 (UT)

Standard Port GREENOCK (←)

Times				Height (metres)			
High Water		Low Water		MHWS	MHWN	MLWN	MLWS
0000	0600	0000	0600	3·4	2·8	1·0	0·3
1200	1800	1200	1800				
Differences ARDROSSAN							
−0020	−0010	−0010	−0010	−0·2	−0·2	+0·1	+0·1
IRVINE							
−0020	−0020	−0030	−0010	−0·3	−0·3	−0·1	0·0

SHELTER Good in marina (formerly Eglinton Dock), access at all tides over sill, 5·2m least depth. A storm gate is fitted; max acceptable beam is 8·6m (28ft). Strong SW/NW winds cause heavy seas in the apprs and the hbr may be closed in SW gales. Ferries berth on both sides of Winton Pier.

NAVIGATION WPT 55°38'·13N 04°50'·55W, 055° to hbr ent, 0·65M. From the W/NW keep clear of low-lying Horse Isle (conspic W tower on its S end) ringed by drying ledges. The passage between Horse Isle and the mainland is obstructed by unmarked drying rks and should not be attempted. Be aware of following dangers: From the S/SE, Eagle Rk 3ca S of hbr ent, marked by SHM buoy, Fl G 5s. 3ca SE of Eagle Rk lies unmarked Campbell Rk (0·2m). W Crinan Rk (1·1m) is 300m W of hbr ent, marked by PHM buoy, Fl R 4s.

LIGHTS AND MARKS Dir lt WRG 15m W14M, R/G11M (see 9.9.4); W sector leads 055° to hbr ent between lt ho and detached bkwtr. Lt ho Iso WG 4s 11m 9M, G317°-035°, W elsewhere. On S end of detached bkwtr, Fl WR 2s 7m 5M, R041°-126°, W elsewhere.

Tfc signals, shown H24 from control twr at ent to marina:

3 F ● lts (vert) = hbr and marina closed; no entry/exit for commercial and pleasure vessels.

3 F ● lts (vert) = marina open, hbr closed; pleasure craft may enter/exit the marina, no commercial movements.

2 F ● lts over 1 F ● = hbr open, marina closed; in severe weather marina storm gate is closed. Commercial vessels may enter/exit hbr, subject to approval by Hbr Control on VHF. Pleasure craft must clear the approach channel, ferry turning area (between the detached bkwtr and Winton Pier) and the outer basin. Yachts may not manoeuvre under sail alone until to seaward of the outer breakwater.

R/T *Clyde Marina* VHF Ch **80** M. *Hbr Control* Ch 12 14 16 (H24).

TELEPHONE (Dial code 01294) Marina 607077, Fax 607076; Control Twr 463972, Fax 601289; MRCC (01475) 729988; Marinecall 09066 526246; Police 468236; Dr 463011; H (01563) 521133.

FACILITIES **Clyde Marina** (250 inc 50 visitors) ☎ 607077, Fax 607076, £1.95, access all tides, Marina Office hrs 0900-1800, D, ME, El, (E), CH, BH (50 ton). **Town** EC Wed; R, Bar, Gas, ✉, (B), ⇌, ✈ (Prestwick/Glasgow). Ferry to Brodick (Arran).

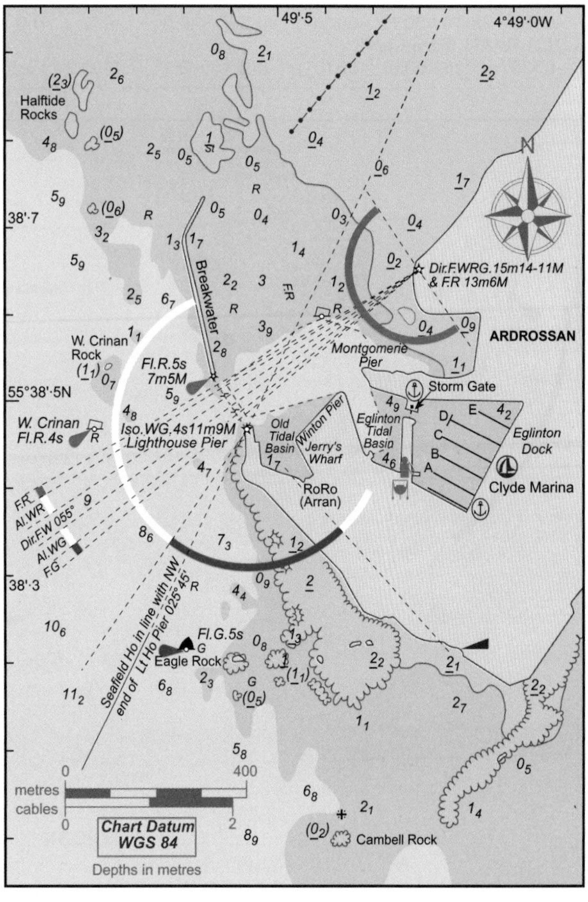
49'·5
4°49'·0W
Halftide Rocks
38'·7
55°38'·5N
38'·3
Breakwater
W. Crinan Rock
Fl.R.5s 7m5M
W. Crinan Fl.R.4s
Iso.WG.4s11m9M Lighthouse Pier
Old Tidal Basin
Winton Pier
Jerry's Wharf
RoRo (Arran)
Eglinton Tidal Basin
Montgomerie Pier
Storm Gate
Eglinton Dock
Clyde Marina
ARDROSSAN
Dir.F.WRG.15m14-11M & F.R 13m6M
Dir.FW 055°
Al.WR
Al.WG
F.R
F.G
Seafield Ho in line with NW end of Lt Ho Pier 025·45°
Fl.G.5s
Eagle Rock
Campbell Rock
metres 0 400
cables 0 2
Chart Datum WGS 84
Depths in metres

HARBOUR BETWEEN ARDROSSAN AND TROON

IRVINE, N Ayrshire, 55°36'·17N 04°42'·07W. AC *2126,* 2220, 1866. HW +0055 on Dover. Tides: see 9.9.22. Good shelter once across the bar (0·5m CD); access approx HW ±3½ for 1·4m draft. Do not attempt ent in heavy onshore weather. The IB-B SPM buoy, Fl Y 3s, is 1·15M from hbr ent, close NW of ldg line. 5 blocks of flats and chys are conspic ENE of ent. Ldg lts 051°: front, FG 10m 5M; rear, FR 15m 5M. The ent groynes have bns, Fl R 3s and Fl G 3s; groynes inside the ent have unlit perches. White Pilot tr with mast is conspic 3ca inside ent. Visitors' pontoons on N side or on S side at visitors' quay (2·2m). ⚓ prohib. VHF Ch 12 (0800-1600 Tues and Thurs; 0800-1300 Wed). HM ☎ (01294) 487286, 📠 487111. Berths available above opening footbridge which opens at 5 mins notice ☎ 08708 403123 or VHF Ch 12 (call *Irvine Bridge*). Facilities: **Quay** AB < 5m £4, >5m <10m £6, >10m <15m £9, FW, Slip, C (3 ton), Showers, SM. **Town** P & D (cans, 1·5km), Gas, 🛒, R, ⇌, ✈ (Prestwick).

9.9.23 TROON

S Ayrshire **55°33'·10N 04°40'·97W** ❀❀❀◊◊◊✿✿

CHARTS AC *2126, 2220, 1866*; Imray C63; OS 70

TIDES +0050 Dover; ML 1·9; Duration 0630; Zone 0 (UT)

Standard Port GREENOCK (⟵)

Times				Height (metres)			
High Water		Low Water		MHWS	MHWN	MLWN	MLWS
0000	0600	0000	0600	3·4	2·8	1·0	0·3
1200	1800	1200	1800				
Differences TROON							
−0025	−0025	−0020	−0020	−0·2	−0·2	0·0	0·0
AYR							
−0025	−0025	−0030	−0015	−0·4	−0·3	+0·1	+0·1
GIRVAN							
−0025	−0040	−0035	−0010	−0·3	−0·3	−0·1	0·0
LOCH RYAN (Stranraer)							
−0030	−0025	−0010	−0010	−0·2	−0·1	0·0	+0·1

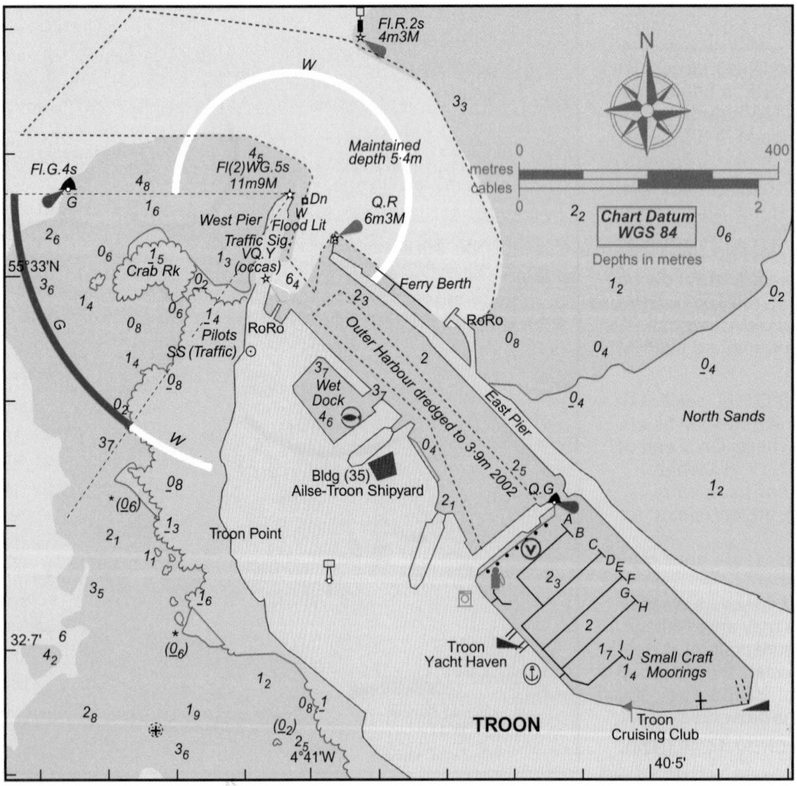
Fl.R.2s
4m3M
W
Maintained depth 5·4m
Fl.G.4s
G
Fl(2)WG.5s
11m9M
Dn
Q.R
6m3M
West Pier
Flood Lit
Traffic Sig.
VQ.Y
(occas)
Crab Rk
55°33'N
Ferry Berth
RoRo
Pilots
SS (Traffic)
Outer Harbour dredged to 3·9m 2002
East Pier
Wet Dock
Bldg (35)
Ailse-Troon Shipyard
Q.G
Troon Point
Troon Yacht Haven
Small Craft Moorings
Troon Cruising Club
TROON
North Sands
Chart Datum WGS 84
Depths in metres
metres
cables
N
32·7'
4°41'W
40·5'

SHELTER Complete in marina (2·4m at ent, 1·6m at SE end); speed limit 5kn. Strong SW/NW winds cause heavy seas in the apprs. Inside hbr.

NAVIGATION WPT 55°33'·20N 04°42'·00W, 103° to W pier lt, 0·61M. Appr in sector SW to NW. Beware Lady Isle, Fl (4) 30s 19m 8M, W bn, 2·2M SW; Troon Rock (5·6m, occas breaks) 1·1M W; Lappock Rock (0·6m, bn with G barrel topmark) 1·6M NNW; Mill Rock (0·4m) ½M NNE of hbr ent, marked by unlit PHM buoy.

LIGHTS AND MARKS No ldg lts. Sheds (35m) at Ailsa Shipyard are conspic and floodlit at night. Traffic signals VQ.Y. occas when Fast Ferries arriving/departing . W pier hd Fl (2) WG 5s 11m 9M, G036°-090°, W090°-036°. 14m SE of this lt there is a floodlit dolphin, W with dayglow patches. A SHM lt buoy, FG, marks the chan in the ent to marina.

R/T HM VHF Ch 16 14. Marina VHF Ch **80** M (H24).

TELEPHONE (Dial code 01292) HM 281687, 📠 287787; Marina 315553; MRCC (01475) 729988; Marinecall 09066 526246; Police 313100; Dr 313593; Ⓗ 610555 (Ayr).

FACILITIES **Troon Yacht Haven** (300+50 Ⓥ) ☎ 315553, 📠 312836, £1.93, access all tides. Ⓥ on pontoon A, first to stbd. AB for LOA 36m x 3m draft at pontoon ends. D (H24), ME, El, Ⓔ, CH, ⚒, SM (daily pick-up), BH (50 ton), C (20 ton), Slip, 🛒, R ☎ 311523, Bar, ⊡, Gas, Gaz; **Troon CC** ☎ 311865; **Troon YC** ☎ 316770. **Town** EC Wed; ✉, Ⓑ, ⇌, ✈ (Prestwick/Glasgow). Fast RoRo ferry to Belfast.

HARBOURS ON THE FIRTH OF CLYDE SOUTH OF TROON

AYR, S Ayrshire, **55°28'·22N 04°38'·78W**. AC *2126,* 2220, 1866. HW +0050 on Dover; ML 1·8m. Duration 0630. See 9.9.23. After heavy rains large amounts of debris may be washed down the R Ayr. From the W, hbr ent lies between conspic gasholder to the N and townhall spire to the S. Outer St Nicholas SHM buoy, Fl G 2s, warns of shoals and eponymous Rock (0·8m) 150m S of ent. Ldg lts 098°: front, by Pilot Stn, FR 10m 5M R tr, also tfc sigs; rear (130m from front), Oc R 10s 18m 9M. N bkwtr hd, QR 9m 5M. S pier hd, Q 7m 7M, vis 012°-161°, and FG 5m 5M, same structure, vis 012°-082°, over St Nicholas Rk. Tfc sigs (near front ldg lt): 2 ● (vert) = hbr closed to incoming traffic. HM ☎ (01292) 281687; VHF Ch 14 16; **Ayr Y & CC** at S dock, M. **Services:** ⚒, ME, El, CH. **Town** EC Wed; Ⓑ, Bar, Gas, P & D, FW, ✉, R, ⇌, 🛒.

GIRVAN, S Ayrshire, **55°14'·77N 04°51'·87W**. AC 2199, 1866. HW +0043 on Dover; ML 1·8m; Duration 0630. See 9.9.23. Good shelter at inner hbr for 16 yachts on 60m pontoon (1·7m) beyond LB. Coasters and FVs berth on adjacent quay. No access LW±2 over bar 1·5m. Beware Girvan Patch, 1·7m, 4ca SW of ent, and Brest Rks, 3·5M N of hbr extending 6ca offshore. Ch spire (conspic) brg 104° leads between N bkwtr, Fl (2) R 6s 7m 4M, and S pier, 2 FG (vert) 8m 4M. Inner N groyne, Iso 4s 3m 4M. Tfc sigs at root of S pier: 2 B discs (hor), at night 2 ● (hor) = hbr shut. VHF Ch 12 16 (HO). HM ☎ (01465) 713648, 📠 714454; FW, Slip. **Town** EC Wed; Ⓑ, ✉, 🛒, R, ⇌, P & D (cans).

ANCHORAGES WITHIN LOCH RYAN

LOCH RYAN, Dumfries and Galloway, **55°01'N 05°05'W**. AC 2198, 1403. HW (Stranraer) +0055 on Dover; ML 1·6m; Duration 0640. See tides 9.9.23. See adjacent chartlet. Very good shelter except in strong NW winds. Ent between Milleur Pt and Finnarts Pt. ⚓s in Lady Bay, 1·3M SSE of Milleur Pt, but exposed to heavy wash from fast catamaran ferries; in The Wig in 3m (avoid weed patches); or off Stranraer 3ca NW of W pier hd. Larger yachts berth on NE side of E pier, by arrangement with HM, VHF Ch 14 (H24) or ☎ (01776) 702460. Beware The Beef Barrel, rk 1m high 6ca SSE of Milleur Pt; the sand spit running 1·5M to SE from W shore opposite Cairn Pt lt ho Fl (2) R10s 14m 12M. Lt at Cairnryan ferry terminal Fl R 5s 5m 5M. Lts at Stranraer: centre pier hd 2FBu (vert), E pier hd 2FR (vert), W pier hd 2 FG (vert) 8m 4M. Facilities (Stranraer): EC Wed; Ⓑ, Bar, D, FW, P, ✉, R, ⇌, 🛒.

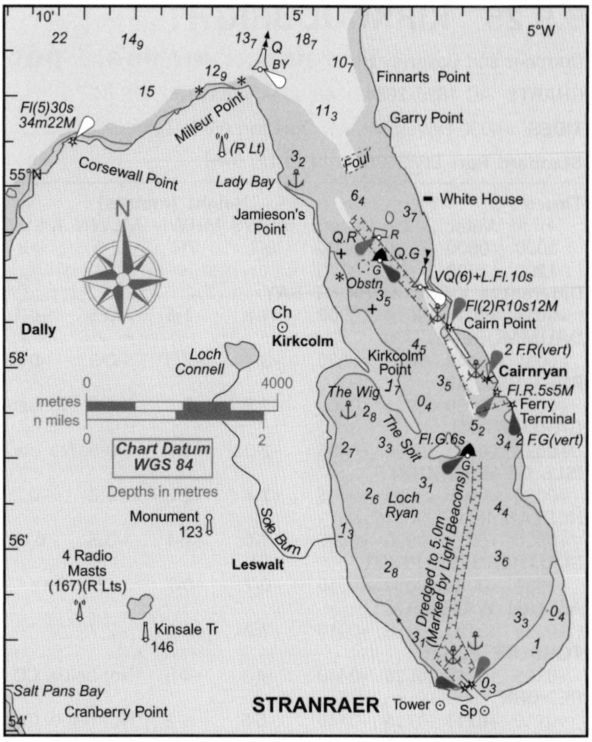
Finnarts Point
Garry Point
Fl(5)30s 34m22M
Milleur Point
Corsewall Point
Lady Bay
(R Lt)
Foul
White House
Jamieson's Point
Q.R
Q.G
Obstn
VQ(6)+L.Fl.10s
Fl(2)R10s12M Cairn Point
Dally
Ch
Kirkcolm
Loch Connell
Kirkcolm Point
2 F.R(vert)
Cairnryan
Fl.R.5s5M Ferry Terminal
F.G(vert)
The Wig
The Spit
Fl.G.6s
Loch Ryan
metres
n miles
Chart Datum WGS 84
Depths in metres
Monument 123
4 Radio Masts (167)(R Lts)
Leswalt
Soleburn
Dredged to 5.0m (Marked by Light Beacons)
Kinsale Tr 146
Salt Pans Bay
Cranberry Point
STRANRAER
Tower
Sp
5°W
55°N
58'
56'
54'

9.9.24 PORTPATRICK

Dumfries and Galloway **54°50'·42N 05°07'·18W**

CHARTS AC *2724*, 2198; Imray C62; OS 82

TIDES +0032 Dover; ML 2·1; Duration 0615; Zone 0 (UT)

Standard Port LIVERPOOL (⟶)

Times				Heights (metres)			
High Water		Low Water		MHWS	MHWN	MLWN	MLWS
0000	0600	0200	0800	9·3	7·4	2·9	0·9
1200	1800	1400	2000				
Differences PORTPATRICK							
+0018	+0026	0000	−0035	−5·5	−4·4	−2·0	−0·6

SHELTER Good in tiny Inner hbr, but ent is difficult in strong SW/NW winds. Beware cross tides off ent, up to 3kn springs.

NAVIGATION WPT 54°50'·00N 05°08'·07W, 055° to ent, 0·70M. Ent to outer hbr by short narrow chan with hazards either side, including rky shelf covered at HW. Barrel buoy (a mooring buoy) marks end of Half Tide Rk; do not cut inside.

LIGHTS AND MARKS Killantringan lt ho, Fl (2) 15s 49m 25M, is 1.6M NW of ent. Ldg lts 050°, FG (H24) 6/8m: Front on sea wall; rear on bldg; 2 vert orange stripes by day. Conspic features include: TV mast 1M NE, almost on ldg line; large hotel on cliffs about 1½ca NNW of hbr ent; Dunskey Castle (ru) 4ca SE of hbr.

R/T None.

TELEPHONE (Dial code 01776) HM 810355; MRSC (01475) 729988; Marinecall 09066 526246; Police 702112; ⊞ 702323.

FACILITIES Hbr Slip (small craft), AB £9, M, FW, L. Note: Pontoons are planned in inner hbr, to be dredged approx 2·5m. **Village** EC Thurs; P (cans), D (bulk tanker), Gas, 🛒, R, Bar, ✉, Ⓑ (Stranraer), ⇌ (bus to Stranraer), ✈ (Carlisle).

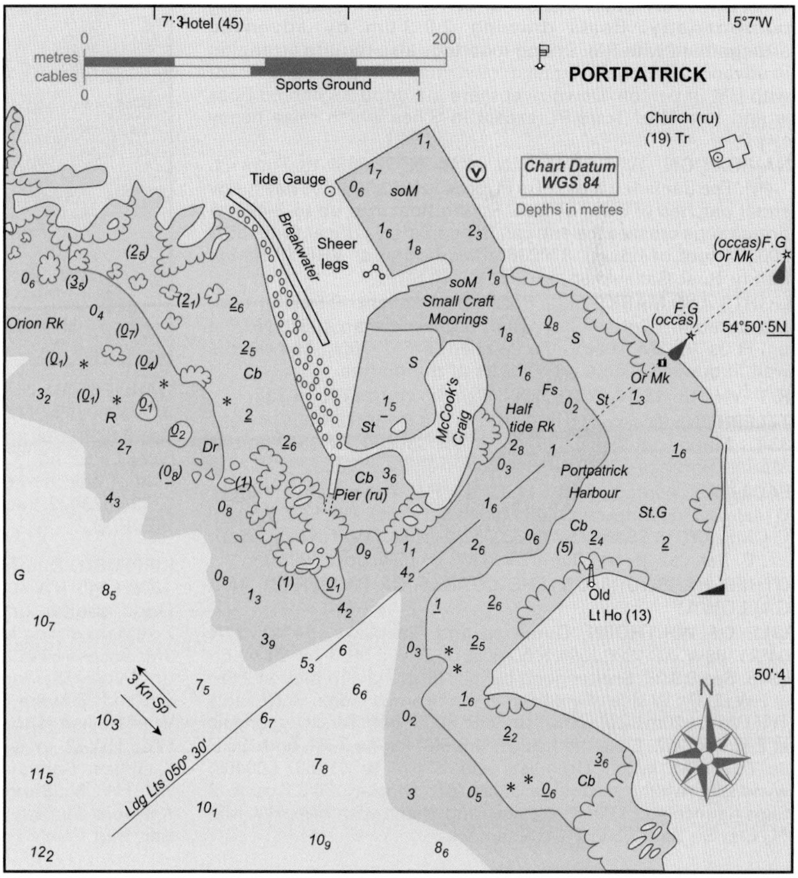
7'·3
Hotel (45)
5°7'W
metres
cables
Sports Ground
PORTPATRICK
Church (ru) (19) Tr
Chart Datum WGS 84
Depths in metres
Tide Gauge
Breakwater
soM
Sheer legs
Small Craft Moorings
(occas)F.G Or Mk
F.G (occas)
54°50'·5N
Orion Rk
Or Mk
McCook's Craig
Half tide Rk
Pier (ru)
Portpatrick Harbour
St.G
Old Lt Ho (13)
3 Kn Sp
Ldg Lts 050° 30'
50'·4

9.9.25 KIRKCUDBRIGHT

Dumfries and Galloway **54°50'·31N 04°03'·48W** ❁❁❁◊◊◊✿✿✿

CHARTS AC *1826*, 2094, 1346, 1344; Imray C62; OS 84

TIDES +0030 Dover; ML 4·1; Duration 0545; Zone 0 (UT)

Standard Port LIVERPOOL (9.10.12) (⟷)

Times				**Height (metres)**			
High Water		Low Water		MHWS	MHWN	MLWN	MLWS
0000	0600	0200	0800	9·3	7·4	2·9	0·9
1200	1800	1400	2000				
Differences KIRKCUDBRIGHT BAY							
+0015	+0015	+0010	0000	−1·8	−1·5	−0·5	−0·1
DRUMMORE							
+0030	+0040	+0015	+0020	−3·4	−2·5	−0·9	−0·3
PORT WILLIAM							
+0030	+0030	+0025	0000	−2·9	−2·2	−0.8	No data
GARLIESTON							
+0025	+0035	+0030	+0005	−2·3	−1·7	−0·5	No data
ISLE OF WHITHORN							
+0020	+0025	+0025	+0005	−2·4	−2·0	−0·8	−0.2
HESTAN ISLET (Kippford)							
+0025	+0025	+0020	+0025	−1·0	−1·1	−0.5	0.0
SOUTHERNESS POINT							
+0030	+0030	+0030	+0010	−0·7	−0·7	No data	
ANNAN WATERFOOT							
+0050	+0105	+0220	+0310	−2·2	−2·6	−2·7	*
TORDUFF POINT							
+0105	+0140	+0520	+0410	−4·1	−4·9	*Not below CD	
REDKIRK							
+0110	+0215	+0715	+0445	−5·5	−6·2	*Not below CD	

Notes: At Annan Waterfoot, Torduff Pt and Redkirk the LW time differences are for the start of the rise, which at sp is very sudden. *At LW the tide does not usually fall below CD.

SHELTER Very good. Depths at LW: 1·0-2·0m at the floating pontoon/jetty. Boats drawing 2·0-3·0m by advanced arrangement with HM. Drying moorings also require arranging in advance. Drying out against town quay only by arrangement with HM in person. Down-river there are good ⚓s behind Ross Is and ½ca N of Torrs Pt, except in S'lies which raise heavy swell.

NAVIGATION WPT 54°45'·51N 04°04'·08W, 005° to Torrs Pt, 1·4M. The Bar is 1ca N of Torrs Pt; access HW±3. R Dee has many shoal patches of 0·3m or less. Spring tides run up to 3-4kn. A firing range crosses the ent; call Range Safety Officer ☎ (01557) 500271 (out of hours), 830236 office hours) or VHF 73 Range Safety Boat Gallavidian on Ch 16.

LIGHTS AND MARKS Little Ross lt ho, W of ent, Fl 5s 50m 12M, (obscured in Wigtown bay when brg more than 103°). No 1 lt bn, Fl 3s 7m 3M, is atop the LB shed (54°47'·70N). The river is well lit/buoyed. There are Fl G lts at the marina.

R/T VHF Ch 12 16 (0730-1700). *Range Control* Ch 16 73.

TELEPHONE (Dial code 01557) HM ☎/📠 331135; MRCC 0151-931 3341; Marinecall 09066 526246; Police 330600; Dr 330755; GM Marine Services 07970 109814.

FACILITIES Pontoon/jetty £11.00, ⛽, FW; **Town Quay** P (hose), D (delivery to pontoon via GM Marine Services), FW, El, C (15 ton) CH, ME. **KYC** ☎ 330963; **SC** ☎ 330032, Slip, M, FW; **Town** EC Thur; 🛒, R, Bar, ✉, Ⓑ, ⇌ (Dumfries 30M), ✈ (Glasgow 100M).

OTHER HARBOURS ON THE COASTS OF DUMFRIES AND GALLOWAY

ISLE OF WHITHORN, Dumfries and Galloway, **54°41'·91N 04°21'·88W.** AC *1826*, 2094. HW +0035 on Dover; ML 3·7m; Duration 0545. See 9.9.25. Shelter good but hbr dries, having approx 2·5m at HW±3. On W side of ent beware the Skerries ledge. St Ninian's Tr (Fl WR 3s 20m 6/4M viz: W310°-005° R005°-040° W□tr) is conspic at E side of ent. E pier hd has QG 4m 5M; ldg lts 335°, both Oc R 8s 7/9m 7M, synch, Or masts and ◊. HM ☎ (01988) 500468, www.isleofwhithorn.com; Facilities: AB on quay £4.83/yacht, 2 Slips (launching £1.00), P, D (by arrangementt with HM), FW, ME, ⚒, CH, 🛒, Bar, ✉, VHF Ch08 (occas).

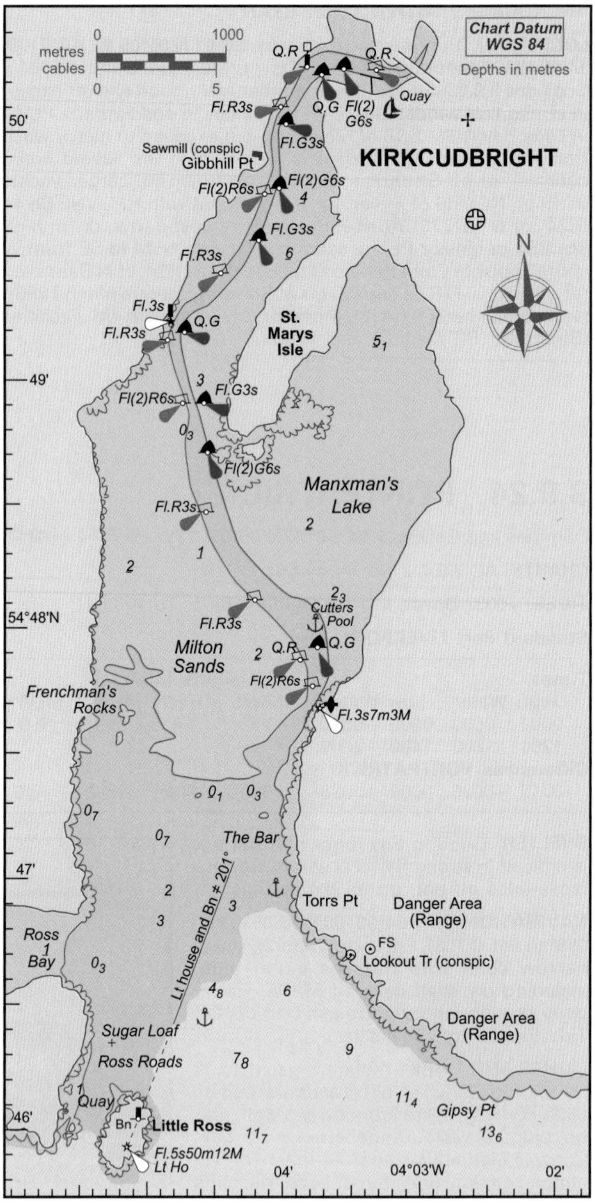
metres
cables
0
1000
5
Chart Datum
WGS 84
Depths in metres
KIRKCUDBRIGHT
Q.R
Q.G
Fl(2) G6s
Quay
Fl.R3s
Fl.G3s
Sawmill (conspic)
Gibbhill Pt
Fl(2)R6s
Fl(2)G6s
St. Marys Isle
Fl.3s
Manxman's Lake
Cutters Pool
Milton Sands
Frenchman's Rocks
Fl.3s7m3M
The Bar
Lt house and Bn ≠ 201°
Torrs Pt
Danger Area (Range)
FS
Lookout Tr (conspic)
Ross Bay
Sugar Loaf
Ross Roads
Quay
Bn
Little Ross
Fl.5s50m12M
Lt Ho
Gipsy Pt
50'
49'
54°48'N
47'
46'
04'
04°03'W
02'

GARLIESTON, Dumfries and Galloway, **54°47'·36N 04°21'·83W.** AC *1826*, 2094. HW +0035 on Dover; ML no data; Duration 0545. See 9.9.25. Hbr affords complete shelter but dries. Access (2m) HW±3. Pier hd lt 2FR (vert) 5m 3M. Beware rky outcrops in W side of bay marked by a perch. HM ☎ (01988) 600295, Mobile 07734 073422. Facilities: M £3, FW, AC on quay, Slip. **Town:** 🛒, ME, P, D.

KIPPFORD, Dumfries & Galloway, **54°52'·36N 03°48'·93W.** AC *1826*, 1346. HW +0040 on Dover; ML 4·2m (Hestan Is). See 9.9.25. Good shelter on drying moorings/pontoons off Kippford, 2·75M up drying Urr Estuary from Hestan Is lt ho Fl (2) 10s 42m 9M. Access HW±2 via marked, unlit chan. *Clyde Cruising Club* or *Solway Sailing Directions* (from Solway YC) are strongly advised. Beware Craig Roan on E side of ent. Temp ⚓s NE or W of Hestan Is to await tide. VHF: Ch M call *Kippford Startline* (YC) HW±2 in season. Ch 16 *Kippford Slipway* (Pilotage). Facilities: **Solway YC** (01556) 600221, www.thesyc.com; AB, ⛽, FW, M; **Services:** AB £6, M, Slip, D (cans), CH, Gaz, BY *Kippford Slipway Ltd*(01556) 620249, ME. **Town** P, SM, 🛒, ✉, Bar, Slip.

Area 10

North-West England, Isle of Man and North Wales

Mull of Galloway to Bardsey Island

10

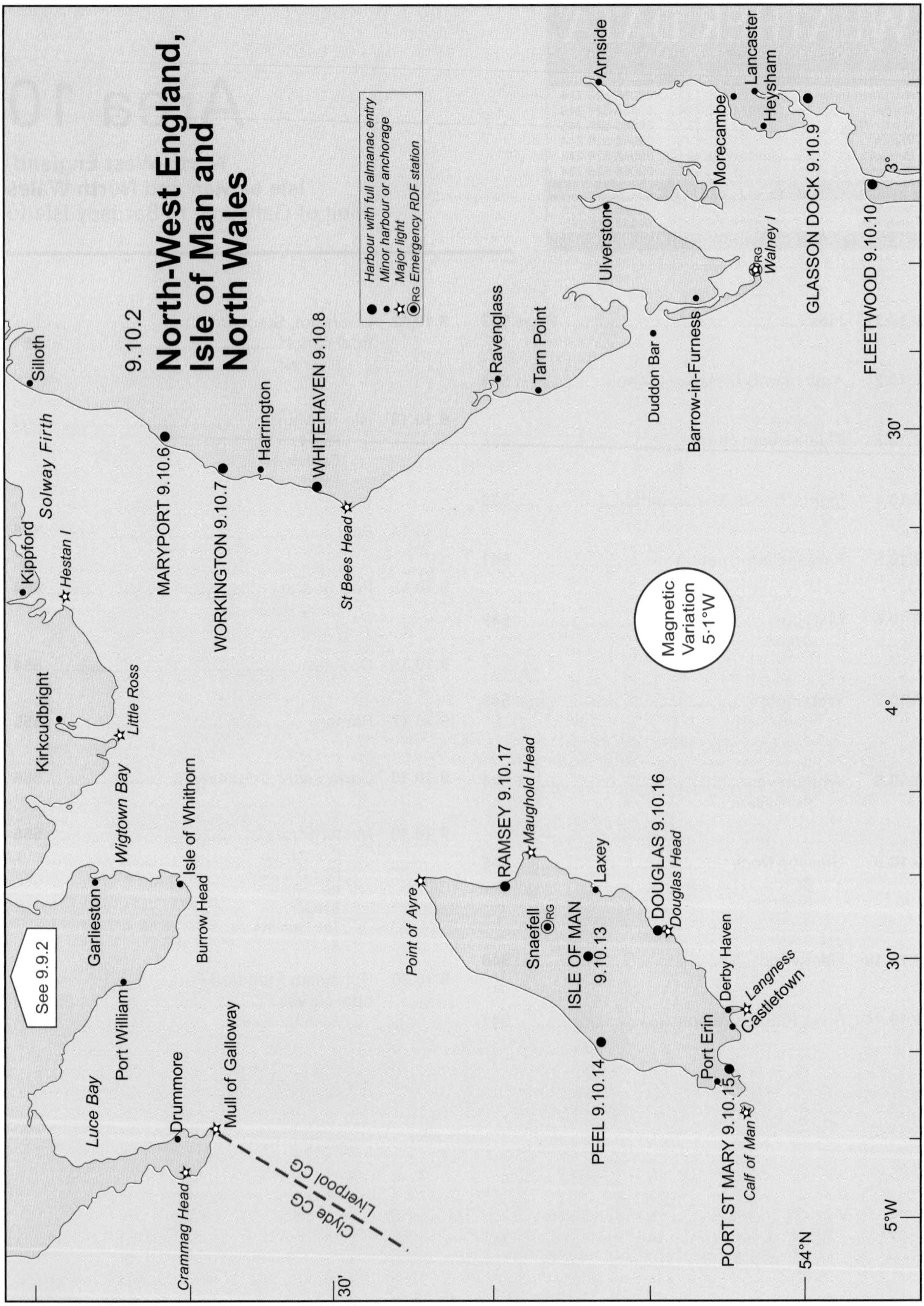
9.10.2
North-West England, Isle of Man and North Wales
Harbour with full almanac entry
Minor harbour or anchorage
Major light
RG Emergency RDF station
See 9.9.2
Luce Bay
Port William
Garlieston
Wigtown Bay
Kirkcudbright
Little Ross
Kippford
Hestan I
Solway Firth
Silloth
Crammag Head
Drummore
Mull of Galloway
Burrow Head
Isle of Whithorn
Clyde CG
Liverpool CG
MARYPORT 9.10.6
WORKINGTON 9.10.7
Harrington
WHITEHAVEN 9.10.8
St Bees Head
Ravenglass
Tarn Point
Duddon Bar
Barrow-in-Furness
Walney I
RG
Ulverston
Morecambe
Heysham
Lancaster
Arnside
GLASSON DOCK 9.10.9
FLEETWOOD 9.10.10
Magnetic Variation 5·1°W
Point of Ayre
RAMSEY 9.10.17
Maughold Head
Snaefell
RG
ISLE OF MAN 9.10.13
Laxey
DOUGLAS 9.10.16
Douglas Head
PEEL 9.10.14
Derby Haven
Langness
Castletown
Port Erin
PORT ST MARY 9.10.15
Calf of Man
54°N
30'
5°W
30'
4°
30'
3°

Off Skerries TSS

Centred on:
53°22·8'N 04°52'·0W
53°31'·3N 04°41'·7W
53°32'·1N 04°31'·6W

The separation zone and traffic lanes are 2M wide and orientated 263°-083° and 216°-036°.

The passage outside the Skerries is preferable to the inside passage, except in strong offshore winds. The inside passage should not be used at night. When passing outside the Skerries allow a distance off of at least 1M to avoid the worst of the strong tidal stream.

Monitor Ch 16 when in the TSS.

1.	***Fishguard***	171	158	175	175	169	160	153	140	126	134	144	153	147	136	100	88	78	89	45	**1**
2.	Bardsey Island	127	113	129	129	123	114	107	94	80	88	98	107	101	90	53	41	31	43	**2**	
3.	**Holyhead**	93	81	94	96	90	69	68	62	46	50	65	79	73	68	36	32	26	**3**		
4.	Caernarfon	117	103	104	105	99	82	81	73	68	68	80	76	70	59	22	10	**4**			
5.	Beaumaris	109	93	94	95	89	72	71	73	58	58	70	66	60	49	12	**5**				
6.	**Conwy**	111	95	95	92	86	58	72	72	57	59	68	62	56	46	**6**					
7.	**Liverpool**	118	102	97	89	83	60	80	86	76	70	77	52	46	**7**						
8.	**Fleetwood**	95	79	68	59	53	30	58	80	63	57	55	10	**8**							
9.	Glasson Dock	101	85	74	66	60	37	64	85	69	63	61	**9**								
10.	Ramsey	44	28	34	41	35	34	6	24	27	15	**10**									
11.	Douglas	60	42	46	50	44	39	19	30	13	**11**										
12.	**Port St Mary**	56	41	61	63	57	50	35	18	**12**											
13.	Peel	41	26	46	55	49	52	18	**13**												
14.	**Point of Ayre**	38	22	28	37	31	34	**14**													
15.	Ravenglass	70	54	40	30	23	**15**														
16.	Workington	63	47	25	6	**16**															
17.	**Maryport**	65	49	26	**17**																
18.	**Kirkcudbright**	48	32	**18**																	
19.	***Mull of Galloway***	16	**19**																		
20.	***Portpatrick***	**20**																			

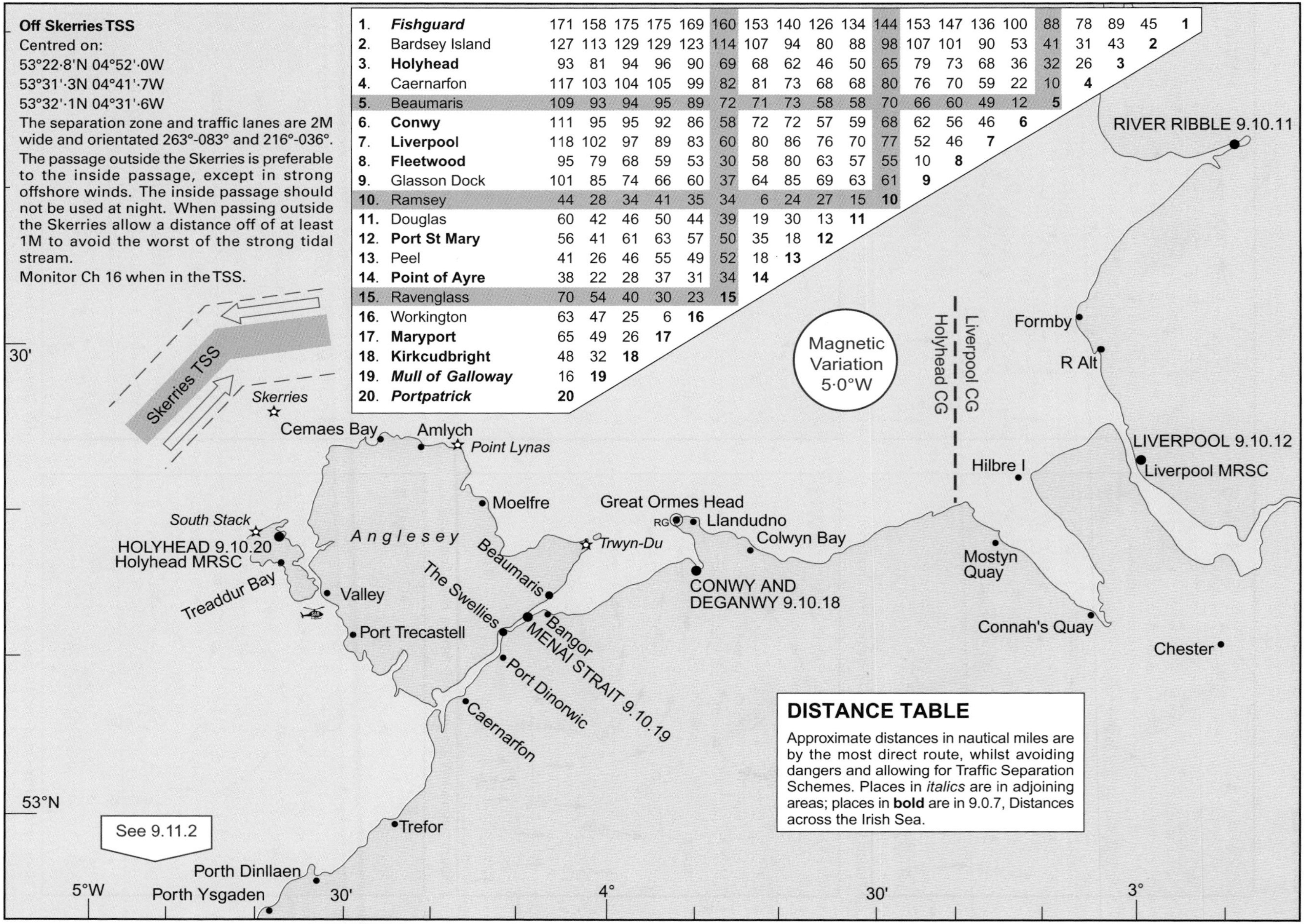
Skerries TSS
Skerries
Cemaes Bay
Amlych
Point Lynas
Moelfre
South Stack
HOLYHEAD 9.10.20
Holyhead MRSC
Anglesey
Treaddur Bay
Valley
Port Trecastell
The Swellies
Beaumaris
Trwyn-Du
Bangor
MENAI STRAIT 9.10.19
Port Dinorwic
Caernarfon
Trefor
Porth Dinllaen
Porth Ysgaden
Great Ormes Head
RG
Llandudno
Colwyn Bay
CONWY AND DEGANWY 9.10.18
Magnetic Variation 5·0°W
Liverpool CG
Holyhead CG
Hilbre I
Mostyn Quay
Connah's Quay
Chester
Formby
R Alt
RIVER RIBBLE 9.10.11
LIVERPOOL 9.10.12
Liverpool MRSC
30'
53°N
5°W
30'
4°
30'
3°

See 9.11.2

DISTANCE TABLE

Approximate distances in nautical miles are by the most direct route, whilst avoiding dangers and allowing for Traffic Separation Schemes. Places in *italics* are in adjoining areas; places in **bold** are in 9.0.7, Distances across the Irish Sea.

9.10.3 AREA 10 TIDAL STREAMS

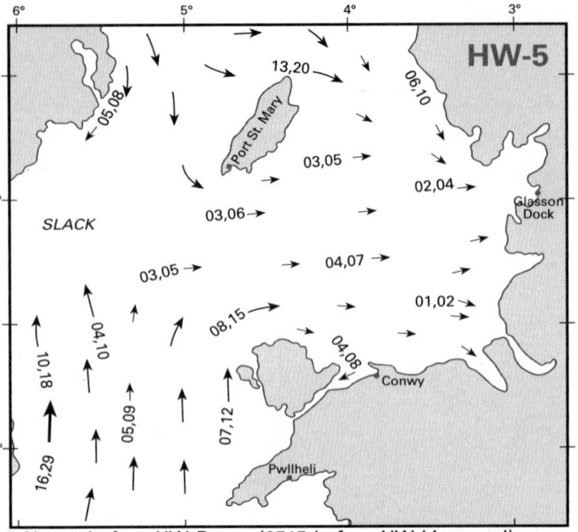
HW-5
6°
5°
4°
3°
54°
53°
SLACK
Port St. Mary
Glasson Dock
Conwy
Pwllheli
13,20
06,10
05,08
03,05
02,04
03,06
03,05
04,07
01,02
08,15
04,10
10,18
04,08
05,09
07,12
16,29
5 Hours before HW Dover (0515 before HW Liverpool)

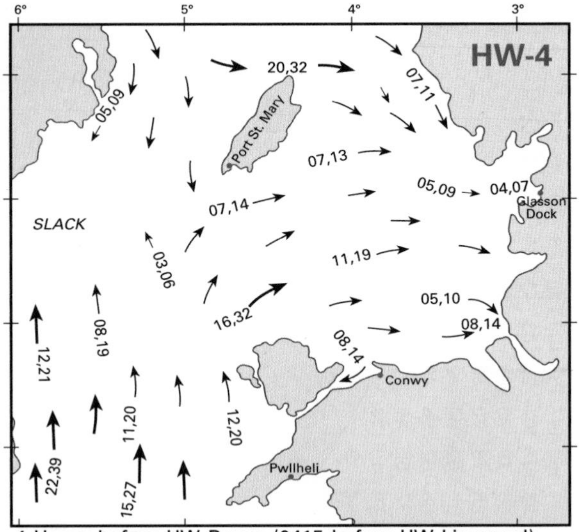
HW-4
6°
5°
4°
3°
54°
53°
SLACK
Port St. Mary
Glasson Dock
Conwy
Pwllheli
20,32
07,11
05,09
07,13
05,09
04,07
07,14
03,06
11,19
16,32
05,10
08,14
08,14
08,19
12,21
11,20
12,20
22,39
15,27
4 Hours before HW Dover (0415 before HW Liverpool)

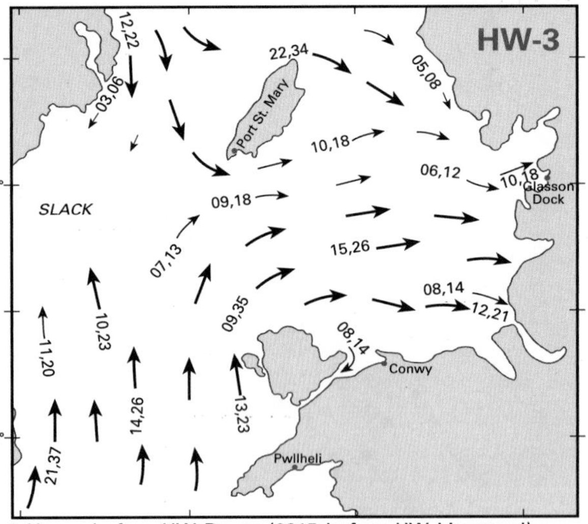
HW-3
54°
53°
SLACK
Port St. Mary
Glasson Dock
Conwy
Pwllheli
12,22
22,34
05,08
03,06
10,18
06,12
10,18
09,18
07,13
15,26
08,14
12,21
09,35
08,14
10,23
11,20
14,26
13,23
21,37
3 Hours before HW Dover (0315 before HW Liverpool)

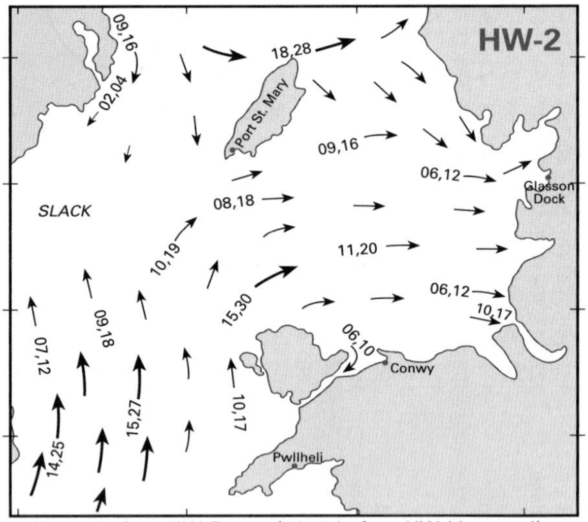
HW-2
54°
53°
SLACK
Port St. Mary
Glasson Dock
Conwy
Pwllheli
09,16
18,28
02,04
09,16
06,12
08,18
10,19
11,20
06,12
10,17
15,30
06,10
09,18
07,12
15,27
10,17
14,25
2 Hours before HW Dover (0215 before HW Liverpool)

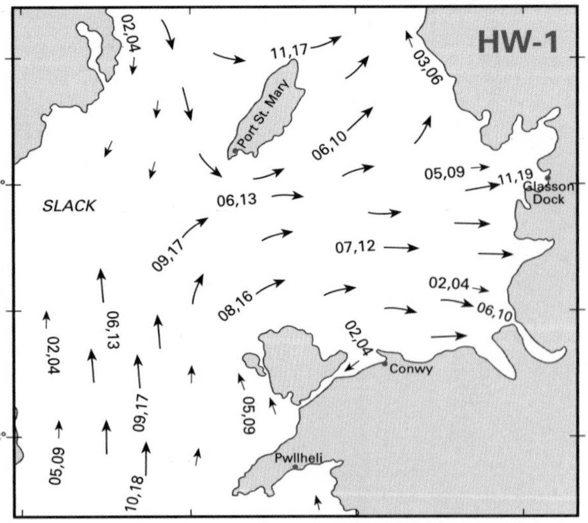
HW-1
54°
53°
SLACK
Port St. Mary
Glasson Dock
Conwy
Pwllheli
02,04
11,17
03,06
06,10
05,09
11,19
06,13
09,17
07,12
02,04
06,10
08,16
02,04
06,13
02,04
09,17
05,09
05,09
10,18
1 Hour before HW Dover (0115 before HW Liverpool)

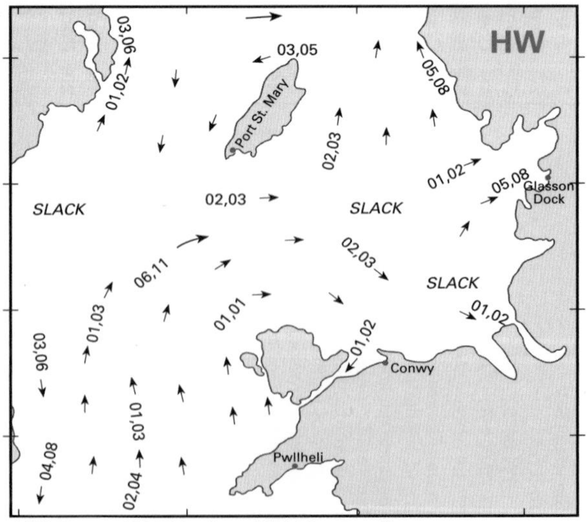
HW
54°
53°
SLACK
SLACK
SLACK
Port St. Mary
Glasson Dock
Conwy
Pwllheli
03,06
03,05
05,08
01,02
02,03
01,02
05,08
02,03
02,03
06,11
01,03
01,01
01,02
01,02
03,06
01,03
04,08
02,04
HW Dover (0015 before HW Liverpool)

Northward 9.9.3 Southward 9.11.3 North Ireland 9.13.3 Mull of Kintyre 9.9.12 South Ireland 9.12.3

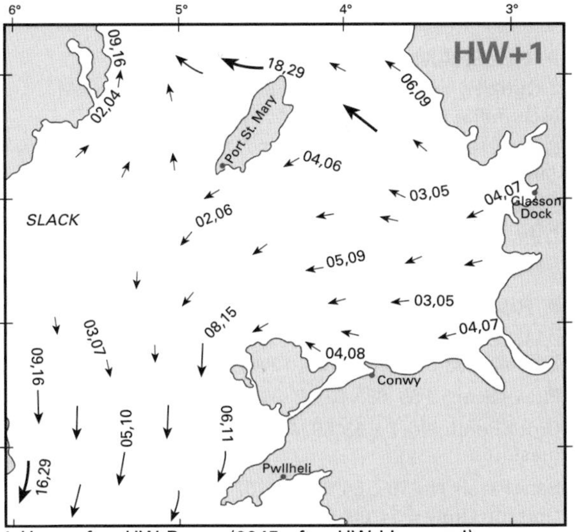
HW+1
6°
5°
4°
3°
54°
53°
Port St. Mary
Glasson Dock
Conwy
Pwllheli
SLACK
09,16
02,04
18,29
06,09
04,06
03,05
04,07
02,06
05,09
03,05
04,07
08,15
03,07
04,08
09,16
05,10
06,11
16,29

1 Hour after HW Dover (0045 after HW Liverpool)

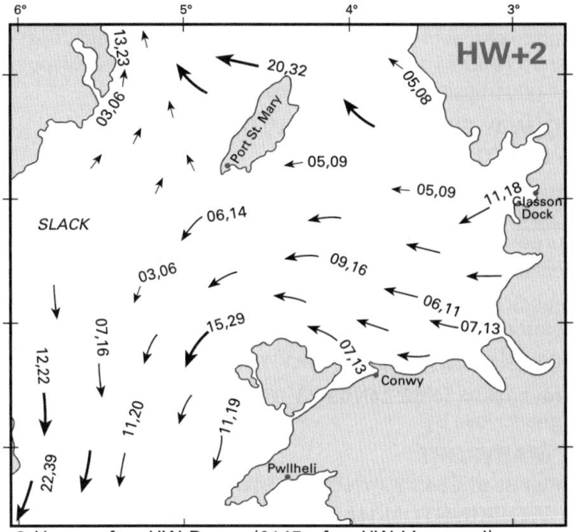
HW+2
6°
5°
4°
3°
54°
53°
Port St. Mary
Glasson Dock
Conwy
Pwllheli
SLACK
13,23
20,32
05,08
03,06
05,09
05,09
11,18
06,14
09,16
03,06
06,11
07,13
15,29
07,16
07,13
12,22
11,20
11,19
22,39

2 Hours after HW Dover (0145 after HW Liverpool)

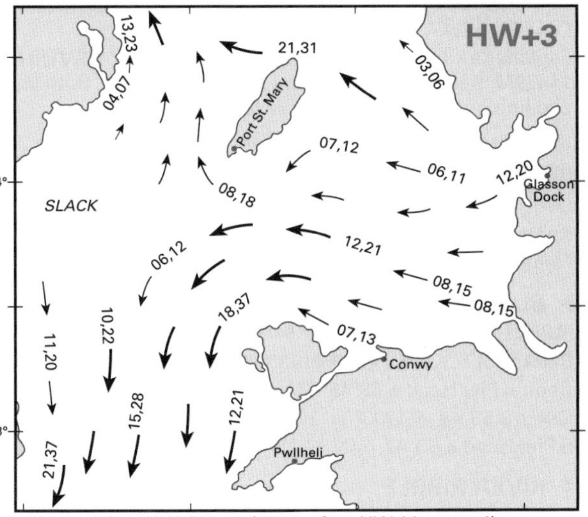
HW+3
Port St. Mary
Glasson Dock
Conwy
Pwllheli
SLACK
13,23
21,31
03,06
04,07
07,12
06,11
12,20
08,18
12,21
06,12
08,15
08,15
18,37
10,22
07,13
11,20
15,28
12,21
21,37

3 Hours after HW Dover (0245 after HW Liverpool)

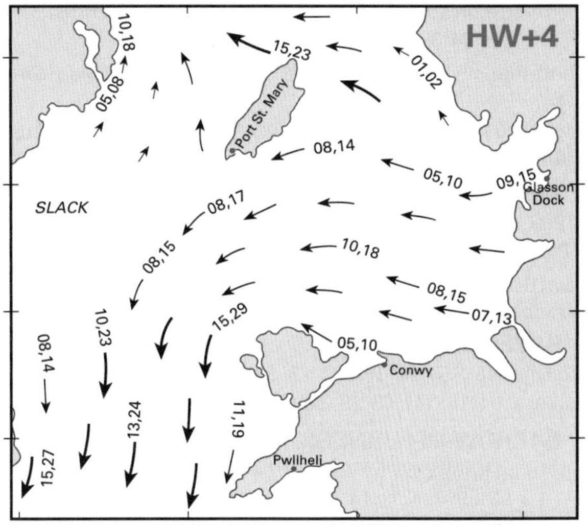
HW+4
Port St. Mary
Glasson Dock
Conwy
Pwllheli
SLACK
10,18
15,23
01,02
05,08
08,14
05,10
09,15
08,17
10,18
08,15
08,15
07,13
15,29
10,23
05,10
08,14
13,24
11,19
15,27

4 Hours after HW Dover (0345 after HW Liverpool)

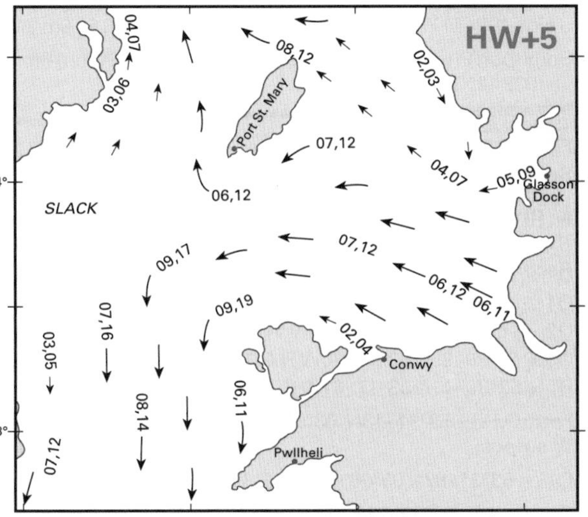
HW+5
Port St. Mary
Glasson Dock
Conwy
Pwllheli
SLACK
04,07
08,12
02,03
03,06
07,12
04,07
05,09
06,12
09,17
07,12
06,12
06,11
09,19
02,04
07,16
03,05
08,14
06,11
07,12

5 Hours after HW Dover (0445 after HW Liverpool)

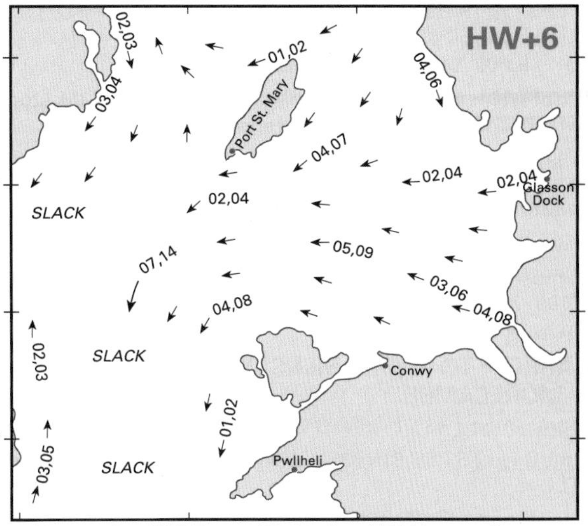
HW+6
Port St. Mary
Glasson Dock
Conwy
Pwllheli
SLACK
SLACK
SLACK
02,03
01,02
04,06
03,04
04,07
02,04
02,04
02,04
05,09
07,14
03,06
04,08
04,08
02,03
01,02
03,05

6 Hours after HW Dover (0545 after HW Liverpool)

10

PLOT WAYPOINTS ON YOUR CHART BEFORE USING THEM

9.10.4 LIGHTS, BUOYS AND WAYPOINTS

Blue print = light with a nominal range of 15M or more. CAPITALS = place or feature. *CAPITAL ITALICS* = light-vessel, light float or Lanby. *Italics* = Fog signal. ***Bold italics*** = Racon. Useful waypoints are underlined. Abbreviations are in Chapter 1.

SOLWAY FIRTHTO BARROW-IN-FURNESS

▶ SILLOTH

Two Feet Bank 54°42'·40N 03°44'·46W Q (9) 15s.

Solway 54°46'·80N 03°30'·14W Fl G 4s.

Corner 54°48'·85N 03°29'·71W Fl (2) G 6s.

Beckfoot 54°50'·28N 03°27'·12W Fl (3) G 10s.

Lees Scar Lt Bn ☆ 54°51'·78N 03°24'·79W Fl G 10s 11m 2M; W structure on piles; vis: 005°-317°.

E Cote ☆ 54°52'·78N 03°22'·89W FG 15m 12M; vis: 046°-058°.

Groyne Hd ☆ 54°52'·14N 03°23'·93W 2 FG (vert) 4m 4M; Fl Bu tfc signals close by.

▶ MARYPORT

S Pier Head ☆ 54°43'·07N 03°30'·64W Fl 1·5s 10m 6M.

▶ WORKINGTON/HARRINGTON

N Workington 54°40'·10N 03°38'·18W.

S Workington 54°37'·01N 03°38'·58W VQ (6) + L Fl 10s.

Pier Head ☆ 54°39'·14N 03°34'·80W QG 5m.

South Pier ☆ 54°39'·12N 03°34'·67W Fl 5s 11m 8M; R bldg; *Siren 20s.*

Ldg Lts 131·8°. Front, 54°38'·92N 03°34'·19W FR 10m 3M. Rear, 134m from front, FR 12m 3M.

▶ WHITEHAVEN

W Pier Hd ☆ 54°33'·17N 03°35'·92W Fl G 5s 16m 13M; W ○ twr.

N Pier Hd ☆ 54°33'·17N 03°35'·75W 2 FR (vert) 8m 9M; W ○ twr.

Saint Bees Hd ☆ 54°30'·81N 03°38'·23W Fl (2) 20s 102m **18M**; W ○ twr; obsc shore-340°.

▶ RAVENGLASS

Blockhouse ☆ 54°20'·16N 03°25'·34W FG; (Eskdale Range).

Selker 54°16'·14N 03°29'·58W Fl (3) G 10s; *Bell.*

▶ BARROW-IN-FURNESS

Lightning Knoll 53°59'·83N 03°14'·28W L Fl 10s; *Bell.*

Sea 1 53°59'·75N 03°14'·09W Fl G 2·5s.

Halfway Shoal 54°01'·46N 03°11'·88W QR 19m 10s; R&W chequered Bn; ***Racon (B) 10M.***

Outer Bar 54°02'·00N 03°11'·10W Fl (4) R 10s.

Bar 54°02'·54N 03°10'·31W Fl (2) R 5s.

Isle of Walney ☆ 54°02'·92N 03°10'·64W Fl 15s 21m **23M**; stone twr; obsc 122°-127° within 3M of shore.

Walney Chan Ldg Lts 040·7°. No.1 Front, 54°03'·19N 03°09'·22W Q 7m 10M; B Pile. No. 2 Rear, 0·61M from front, Iso 2s 13m 10M; Pile.

Haws Point W 54°02'·99N 03°10'·11W QR 8m 6M.

Rampside Sands Ldg Lts 005·1°. No. 3 Front, 54°04'·41N 03°09'·79W Q 9m10M; W ○ twr. No. 4 Rear, 0·77M from front, Iso 2s 14m 6M; R col, W face.

BARROW TO RIVERS MERSEY AND DEE

▶ MORECAMBE

Morecambe 53°51'·99N 03°24'·10W Q (9) 15s; *Whis.*

Lune Deep 53°55'·81N 03°11'·08W Q (6) + L Fl 15s; *Whis;* ***Racon (T).***

Shell Wharf 53°55'·46N 03°08'·96W Fl G 2·5s.

King Scar 53°56'·96N 03°04'·38W Fl (2) G 5s.

Sewer outfall ☆ 54°04'·33N 02°53'·84W Fl G 2s 4m 2M; twr.

Lts in line about 090°. Front, 54°04'·41N 02°52'·63W FR 10m 2M; G mast. Rear, 140m from front, FR 14m 2M; G mast.

▶ HEYSHAM

S Outfall 54°01'·73N 02°55'·80W Fl (2) G 10s 5m 2M.

N Outfall ☆ 54°01'·85N 02°55'·77W Fl G 5s 5m 2M.

S Bkwtr Head ☆ 54°01'·90N 02°55'·72W 2 FG (vert) 9m 5M; W twr; *Siren 30s.*

SW Quay Ldg Lts 102·2°. Front, 54°01'·91N 02°55'·22W both F Bu 11/14m 2M; Or & B ♦ on masts.

S Pier Head ☆ 54°01'·91N 02°55'·43W Oc G 7·5s 9m 6M.

▶ RIVER LUNE/GLASSON DOCK

R Lune No.1 53°58'·63N 03°00'·03W Q (9) 15s.

S Bank 53°58'·12N 02°56'·12W Fl (2) G 4s.

Plover Scar 53°58'·89N 02°52'·96W Fl 2s 6m 6M; W twr, B lantern.

Crook Perch, No. 7 53°59'·46N 02°52'·36W Fl G 5s 3M; G △ on mast.

Bazil Perch, No.16 54°00'·20N 02°51'·65W Fl (3) R 10s 3M.

Glasson Quay ☆ 54°00'·03N 02°51·03W FG 1M.

▶ FLEETWOOD

Fairway No. 1 53°57'·67N 03°02'·03W Q; *Bell.*

Esplanade Ldg Lts 156°. Front, 53°55'·71N 03°00'·56W Iso G 2s 14m 9M. Rear, 320m from front, Iso G 4s 28m 9M. Both vis on Ldg line only. (H24) (chan liable to change).

Steep Breast Perch ☆ 53°55'·75N 03°00'·56W Iso G 2s 3m 2M.

Black Scar Perch No. 11 53°56'·24N 03°01'·06W QG 4m 2M *Horn (1) 15s.*

Knott End slip Hd ☆ 53°55'·73N 03°00'·10W 2 FR (vert) 3m 2M.

Fleetwood Yacht Hbr ☆ 53°55'·13N 03°00'·50W 2 FR (vert).

▶ BLACKPOOL

N Pier Head ☆ 53°49'·16N 03°03'·77W 2 FG (vert) 3M.

Blackpool Tower 53°48'·95N 03°03'·30W Aero FR 158m.

Central Pier Head ☆ 53°48'·65N 03°03'·67W 2 FG (vert) 4M.

Obstn 53°48'·45N 03°04'·30W.

S Pier Head ☆ 53°47'·74N 03°03'·71W 2 FG (vert) 4M.

▶ RIVER RIBBLE

Gut 53°41'·74N 03°08'·98W L Fl 10s.

Perches show Fl R on N side, and Fl G on S side of chan.

S side, 14¼M Perch ☆ 53°42'·75N 03°04'·90W Fl G 5s 6m 3M.

Southport Pier Head ☆ 53°39'·33N 03°01'·31W 2 FG (vert) 6m 5M; vis: 033°-213°.

Jordan's Spit 53°35'·76N 03°19'·28W Q (9) 15s.

FT 53°34'·56N 03°13'·20W Q.

Spoil Ground 53°34'·25N 03°17'·41W Fl Y 3s.

▶ RIVER MERSEY/LIVERPOOL

BAR 53°32'·01N 03°20'·98W Fl 5s 10m 12M; *Horn (2) 20s;* ***Racon (T) 10M.***

Q1 53°31'·00N 03°16'·72W VQ.

Q2 53°31'·47N 03°14'·95W VQ R.

Q3 53°30'·95N 03°15'·10W Fl G 3s.

BT 53°30'·41N 03°17'·61W Fl (3) G 9s.

Formby 53°31'·13N 03°13'·50W Iso 4s 11m 6M; R hull, W stripes.

C4 53°31'·82N 03°08'·51W Fl R 3s R hull.

Crosby 53°30'·72N 03°06'·29W Oc 5s 11m 8M; R hull, W stripes.

C14 ▬ 53°29'·91N 03°05'·34W Fl R 3s; R hull.
Brazil ▲ 53°26'·84N 03°02'·24W QG; G hull.

Seacombe Ferry N and S corners ☆ 53°24'·63N 03°00'·91W 3 FG 5m 5M; near N corner FY 8m 6M; *Bell (3) 20s.*

Birkenhead, Woodside Ferry N end ☆ 53°23'·76N 03°00'·49W 3 FG 5m 4M and S end 2 FG (vert) with *Bell (4) 15s.*

Pluckington Bank ⊥ 53°23'·00N 02°59'·56W VQ (9)10s.
Brombro ⊥ 53°21'·83N 02°58'·68W Q (3) 10s.
Eastham Locks E Dn ☆ 53°19'·58N 02°57'·00W Fl (2) R 6s 5m 8M.

Garston NW Dn ☆ 53°20'·89N 02°54'·63W 2 FG (vert) 12m 9M; *Horn 11s.*

▶ RIVER DEE

HE1 ⊥ 53°26'·33N 03°18'·08W Q (9) 15s.
HE2 ⊥ 53°25'·13N 03°12'·96W Q (3) 10s.
HE3 ▲ 53°24'·67N 03°12'·88W QG.
Hilbre I ☆ 53°22'·99N 03°13'·72W Fl R 3s 14m 5M; W twr.
HE4 ▲ 53°22'·32N 03°14'·29W.

▶ MOSTYN/CONNAH'S QUAY

Dir Lt 174°. ☆ 53°19'·33N 03°16'·12W Iso WRG 2s 16m 7M; vis: G174·8°-176·8°, W176·8°-177·8°, R177·8°-179·8°; H24.

M1 ▲ 53°20'·98N 03°16'·39W QG.
M2 ▬ 53°20'·72N 03°16'·20W QR.
Mostyn S Bkwtr Hd ☆ 53°19'·22N 03°15'·67W Fl G 5s.
M8 ▬ 53°19'·61N 03°15'·52W Fl R 5s.

Flint Sands, N Training wall Head ☆ 53°15'·07N 03°06'·52W Fl R 3s 4m 6M; twr.

Connah's Quay, South Training Wall Head ☆ 53°13'·97N 03°04'·48W Fl G 5s 3m 6M.

▶ WELSH

Salisbury Middle ▬ 53°21'·30N 03°16'·39W Fl (3) R 10s.
NE Mostyn ▲ 53°21'·50N 03°17'·81W Fl (3) G 10s.
Dee ⊥ 53°21'·99N 03°18'·68W Q (6) + L Fl 15s.
Air ▲ 53°21'·85N 03°19'·29W.
East Hoyle ▬ 53°22'·05N 03°21'·11W Fl (4) R 15s.
Talacre ▲ 53°21'·74N 03°21'·68W.
SH7 ▲ 53°21'·82N 03°22'·23W Fl (4) G 15s.
SH3 ▲ 53°21'·23N 03°24'·43W Fl (2) G 5s.
SH1 ▲ 53°21'·30N 03°25'·96W Fl G 2·5s.
South Hoyle Outer ▬ 53°21'·47N 03°27'·48W Fl R 2·5s.

▶ MID HOYLE CHANNEL

E Hoyle Spit ▲ 53°22'·52N 03°19'·07W Fl G 5s.
Mid Hoyle ▬ 53°22'·92N 03°19'·50W Fl R 2·5s.
Hoyle ▬ 53°23'·16N 03°21'·38W QR.
NW Hoyle ▬ 53°23'·32N 03°23'·89W Fl R 2·5s.
N Hoyle ⊥ 53°26'·68N 03°30'·58W VQ.

ISLE OF MAN

Whitestone Bank ☆ 54°24'·58N 04°20'·41W Q (9) 15s.

Point of Ayre ★ 54°24'·94N 04°22'·13W Fl (4) 20s 32m **19M**; W twr, two R bands, *Horn (3) 60s*, ***Racon (M) 13-15M.***

Low Lt ☆ 54°25'·03N 04°21'·86W Fl 3s 10m 8M; R twr, lower part W, on B Base; part obsc 335°-341°.

▶ PEEL

Peel Bkwtr Head ☆ 54°13'·67N 04°41'·69W Oc 7s 11m 6M; W twr; *Bell (4) 12s* (occas).

Peel Groyne Head ☆ 54°13'·56N 04°41'·67W Oc R 2s 4m.

▶ PORT ERIN

Ldg Lts 099·1°. Front, 54°05'·23N 04°45'·57W FR 10m 5M; W twr, R band. Rear, 39m from front, FR 19m 5M; W col, R band.

Raglan Pier Head ☆ 54°05'·12N 04°45'·86W Oc G 5s 8m 5M.
Thousla Rock ☆ 54°03'·73N 04°48'·05W Fl R 3s 9m 4M.
Calf of Man ★ W Pt 54°03'·19N 04°49'·78W Fl 15s 93m **26M**; W 8-sided twr; vis 274°-190°; *Horn 45s.*
Chicken Rock ☆ 54°02'·26N 04°50'·32W Fl 5s 38m 13M; twr; *Horn 60s.*

▶ PORT ST MARY

The Carrick ⊥ 54°04'·30N 04°42'·68W Q (2) 5s 6m 3M.
Alfred Pier Head ☆ 54°04'·33N 04°43'·82W Oc R 10s 8m 6M; W twr, R band.
Inner Pier Head ☆ 54°04'·42N 04°44'·15W Oc R 3s 8m 5M.

▶ CASTLETOWN/DERBY HAVEN

Dreswick Pt ☆ 54°03'·29N 04°37'·45W Fl (2) 30s 23m 12M; W twr.
▬ 54°03'·73N 04°38'·62W Fl R 3s: *Bell.*
New Pier Head ☆ 54°04'·33N 04°38'·97W Oc R 15s 8m 5M.
Derby Haven, Bkwtr SW end ☆ 54°04'·58N 04°37'·06W Iso G 2s 5m 5M; W twr, G band.

▶ DOUGLAS

Douglas Head ★ 54°08'·60N 04°27'·95W Fl 10s 32m **24M**; W twr; obsc brg more than 037°. FR Lts on radio masts 1 and 3M West.
No. 1 ▲ 54°09'·04N 04°27'·68W Q (3) G 5s.
No. 3 ▲ 54°08'·94N 04°27'·91W Fl G 3s.
Princess Alexandra Pier Head ☆ 54°08'·84N 04°27'·85W Fl R 5s 16m 8M; R mast; *Whis (2) 40s.*
Ldg Lts 229·3°, Front ⊥, 54°08'·72N 04°28'·25W Oc 10s 9m 5M; W △ R border on mast. Rear ⊥, 62m from front, Oc 10s 12m 5M; W ▽ on R border; synch with front.
Victoria Pier Head ☆ 54°08'·84N 04°28'·08W Iso G 10s 10m 3M; W col; vis: 225°-327°; Intnl Port Tfc Signals.
Conister Rock Refuge twr 54°09'·03N 04°28'·12W Q 3M; vis: 234°-312°.

▶ LAXEY

Pier Head ☆ 54°13'·50N 04°23'·43W Oc R 3s 7m 5M; W twr, R band; obsc when brg less than 318°.
Bkwtr Hd ☆ 54°13'·45N 04°23'·32W Oc G 3s 7m; W twr, G band.
Maughold Head ★ 54°17'·72N 04°18'·58W Fl (3) 30s 65m **21M**.
Bahama ⊥ 54°20'·01N 04°08'·57W VQ (6) + L Fl 10s; *Bell.*

▶ RAMSEY

Queens Pier Dn ☆ 54°19'·28N 04°21'·95W Fl R 5s.
S Pier Head ☆ 54°19'·43N 04°22'·50W QR 8m 10M; W twr, R band, B base.
N Pier Hd ☆ 54°19'·46N 04°22'·50W QG 9m 10M; W twr, B base.
King William Bank ⊥ 54°26'·01N 04°00'·08W Q (3) 10s.

WALES – NORTH COAST & INNER PASSAGE

West Hoyle Spit Bn ⊥ 53°21'·20N 03°24'·08W QG 5M. Outer Dir Lt 096·5° Iso WRG 2s 7M; vis G094°-096°, W096°-097°, R097°-099°; Occas when vessels expected; By day 3M
SH3 ▲ 53°21'·23N 03°24'·43W Fl (2) G 5s.
SH2 ▬ 53°21'·28N 03°24'·48W Fl R 5s.
South Hoyle Outer ▬ 53°21'·47N 03°24'·70W Fl R 2·5s.
Prestatyn ▲ 53°21'·51N 03°28'·51W QG.
Inner Passage ▬ 53°21'·91N 03°31'·95W Fl R 5s.
Rhyl Flats ▲ 53°22'·03N 03°32'·37W Fl G 5s.
Mid Patch Spit ▬ 53°22'·25N 03°32'·67W QR.
N Rhyl ⊥ 53°22'·76N 03°34'·58W Q.
North Hoyle Wind Farm (30 turbines, see 9.10.5) centred on 53°25'·00N 03°27'·00W. NW, NE, SW, SE extremities (F.R Lts) Fl Y 2.5s 5M Horn Mo (U) 30s.
W Constable ⊥ 53°23'·14N 03°49'·26W Q (9) 15s; ***Racon (M) 10M***

PLOT WAYPOINTS ON YOUR CHART BEFORE USING THEM

▶ RHYL/LLANDUDNO/CONWY

River Clwyd Outfall ▲ 53°19'·59N 03°30'·63W.

River Clwyd Bkwtr Head ⳑ 53°19'·46N 03°30'·35W QR 7m 2M.

Kimmel Bay Outfall ▲ 53°20'·22N 03°34'·20W.

Llanddulas, Llysfaen Jetty ☆ 53°17'·59N 03°39'·49W Fl G 10s.

Raynes Quarry Jetty Hd ☆ 53°17'·62N 03°40'·37W 2 FG (vert).

Llandudno Pier Hd ☆ 53°19'·90N 03°49'·51W 2 FG (vert) 8m 4M.

Great Ormes Hd Lt Ho 53°20'·56N 03°52'·17W (unlit).

Conwy Fairway ⌀ 53°17'·95N 03°55'·58W L Fl 10s.

C2 ⌀ 53°17'·60N 03°54'·32W Fl (2) R 10s.

C6 ⌀ 53°17'·78N 03°52'·27W Fl (6) R 30s.

C8 ⌀ 53°18'·00N 03°52'·05W Fl (8) R 10s.

C7 ▲ 53°18'·06N 03°50'·75W QG.

Conway R ent S side ☆ 53°18'·07N 03°50'·86W Fl WR 5s 5m 2M; vis: W076°-088°, R088°-171°, W171°-319°, R319°-076°.

Conwy Marina Bkwtr S End ☆ 53°17'·50N 03°50'·20W (PA) Fl G 3s 3m 1M; Tfc and tidal gate at Marina ent.

▶ ANGLESEY

Pilot Station Pier ☆ 53°24'·90N 04°17'·20W 2 FR (vert).

Point Lynas ☆ 53°24'·98N 04°17'·35W Oc 10s 39m **18M**; W castellated twr; vis: 109°-315°; *Horn 45s;* H24.

▶ AMLWCH

Main Bkwtr ☆ 53°25'·02N 04°19'·91W Fl G 15s 11m 3M; W mast; vis: 141°-271°.

Inner Bkwtr ☆ 53°24'·99N 04°19'·95W 2 FR (vert) 12m 5M; W mast; vis: 164°-239°.

Wylfa power station 53°25'·09N 04°29'·29W 2 FG (vert) 13m 6M.

Furlong ▲ 53°25'·41N 04°30'·47W Fl G 2·5s.

Archdeacon Rock ⳑ 53°26'·71N 04°30'·87W Q.

Victoria Bank ⳑ 53°25'·61N 04°31'·37W VQ.

Coal Rk ⳑ 53°25'·91N 04°32'·79W Q (6) + L Fl 15s.

Ethel Rk ⳑ 53°26'·64N 04°33'·67W VQ.

W Mouse ⳑ 53°25'·05N 04°33'·27W.

The Skerries ☆ 53°25'·27N 04°36'·55W Fl (2) 10s 36m **22M**; W ○ twr, R band; ***Racon (T) 25M.*** FR 26m 16M; same twr; vis: 231°-254°; *Horn (2) 20s;* H24.

Langdon ⳑ 53°22'·74N 04°38'·74W Q (9) 15s.

Bolivar ▲ 53°21'·51N 04°35'·33W FL G 2·5s.

Wk ⌀ 53°20'·43N 04°36'·60W Fl (2) R 10s.

Clipera ⌀ 53°20'·10N 04°36'·20W Fl (4) R 15s; *Bell.*

▶ HOLYHEAD

Bkwtr Head ☆ 53°19'·86N 04°37'·16W Fl (3) G 10s 21m 14M; W □ twr, B band; Fl Y vis: 174°-226°; *Siren 20s.*

⌀ 53°19'·41N 04°37'·57W Fl (4) R 15s.

⌀ 53°19'·38N 04°37'·69W Oc R 3s.

Marina Bkwter Hd ☆ 53°18'·40N 04°38'·63W 2 FR (vert).

Old Hbr, Admiralty Pier Dn ☆ 53°18'·87N 04°37'·07W 2 FG (vert) 8m 5M; *Horn 15s (occas).*

South Stack ☆ 53°19'·31N 04°41'·98W Fl 10s 60m **24M**; (H24); W ○ twr; obsc to N by N Stack and part obsc in Penrhos bay; *Horn 30s.* Fog Det lt vis: 145°-325°.

Llanddwyn I ☆ 53°08'·05N 04°24'·79W Fl WR 2·5s 12m W7M, R4M; W twr; vis: R280°-015°, W015°-120°.

MENAI STRAIT TO BARDSEY ISLAND

Trwyn-Du ☆ 53°18'·77N 04°02'·44W Fl 5s 19m 12M; W ○ castellated twr, B bands; vis: 101°-023°; *Bell (1) 30s,* sounded continuously. FR on radio mast 2M SW.

Ten Feet Bank ⌀ 53°19'·47N 04°02'·82W QR.

Dinmor ▲ 53°19'·34N 04°03'·32W QG.

▶ BEAUMARIS/BANGOR

(Direction of buoyage ⌂ NE to SW)

Perch Rock ⳑ 53°18'·73N 04°02'·09W Fl R 5s.

B2 ⌀ 53°18'·32N 04°02'·07W Fl (2) R 5s.

B1 ▲ 53°18'·12N 04°02'·37W Fl (2) G 10s.

B3 ▲ 53°17'·72N 04°02'·77W QG.

B8 ⌀ 53°16'·47N 04°04'·47W Fl (3) R 10s.

B5 ▲ 53°15'·77N 04°04'·91W Fl G 5s.

Beaumaris Pier ☆ 53°15'·67N 04°05'·41W F WG 5m 6M; vis: G212°-286°, W286°-041°, G041°-071°.

B10 ⌀ 53°15'·60N 04°05'·22W Fl (2) R 10s.

B12 ⌀ 53°15'·47N 04°05'·58W QR.

B7 ▲ 53°15'·10N 04°06'·13W Fl (2) G 5s.

Bangor ⌀ 53°14'·47N 04°07'·59W.

St George's Pier ☆ 53°13'·53N 04°09'·54W Fl G 10s.

Price's Point ☆ 53°13'·11N 04°10'·53W Fl WR 2s 5m 3M; W Bn; vis: R059°-239°, W239°-259°.

Britannia Tubular Bridge, S chan Ldg Lts 231° E side. Front, 53°12'·92N 04°11'·05W FW. Rear, 45m from front, FW (shown Apr-Sep). Centre span of bridge Iso 5s 27m 3M, one either side (shown Apr-Sep). SE end of bridge, FR 21m 3M either side, NW end of bridge section FG 21m 3M either side.

▶ PORT DINORWIC

Pier Head ☆ 53°11'·18N 04°12'·64W F WR 5m 2M; vis: R225°-357°, W357°-225°.

C9 ▲ 53°08'·52N 04°16'·87W.

Channel ▲ 53°10'·34N 04°15'·19W.

C14 ⌀ 53°10'·19N 04°15'·37W.

C11 ▲ 53°09'·92N 04°15'·67W.

C13 ▲ 53°09'·52N 04°15'·92W.

(Direction of buoyage ⌂ SW to NE)

Change ⳑ 53°08'·82N 04°16'·72W.

▶ CAERNARFON

Caernarfon N Pier Hd ☆ 53°08'·72N 04°16'·56W 2 FG (vert) 5m 2M.

C10 ⌀ 53°07'·96N 04°18'·27W QR.

Abermenai Point ☆ 53°07'·62N 04°19'·72W Fl WR 3·5s 6m 3M; W mast; vis: R065°-245°, W245°-065°.

Mussel Bank ⌀ 53°07'·27N 04°20'·81W Fl (2) R 5s.

C6 ⌀ 53°07'·20N 04°21'·93W Fl R 5s.

C5 ▲ 53°07'·05N 04°22'·67W.

C4 ⌀ 53°07'·22N 04°23'·12W QR.

C3 ▲ 53°07'·35N 04°23'·87W QG.

C1 ▲ 53°07'·18N 04°24'·43W Fl G 5s.

C2 ⌀ 53°07'·28N 04°24'·49W Fl R 10s.

Poole ⌀ 53°00'·02N 04°34'·10W Fl Y 6s; (Apr-Oct).

▶ PORTH DINLLÄEN

CG Stn ☆ 52°56'·82N 04°33'·89W FR when firing taking place 10M North.

Careg y Chwislen ⳑ 52°56'·99N 04°33'·51W.

Bardsey I ☆ 52°44'·97N 04°48'·02W Fl (5) 15s 39m **26M**; W □ twr, R bands; obsc by Bardsey I 198°-250° and in Tremadoc B when brg less than 260°; *Horn Mo (N) 45s;* H24.

9.10.5 PASSAGE INFORMATION

For detailed directions covering these waters and harbours refer to the Admiralty Pilot *W Coast of England and Wales*; *Lundy and Irish Sea Pilot* (Taylor/Imray).

SOLWAY FIRTH (chart 1346) Between Abbey Head and St Bees Head lies the Solway Firth, most of which is encumbered by shifting sandbanks.The *Solway SDs* (see above) are virtually essential. Off the entrances to the Firth, and in the approaches to Workington (9.10.7) beware shoals over which strong W winds raise a heavy sea. There are navigable, buoyed chans as far as Annan on the N shore, but buoys are laid primarily for the aid of Pilots.

▶ *Local knowledge is required, particularly in the upper Firth, where streams run very strongly in the chans when the banks are dry, and less strongly over the banks when covered. In Powfoot chan for example the in-going stream begins at HW Liverpool – 0300, and the outgoing at HW Liverpool + 0100,* ***sp rates up to 6kn.*** ◀ For Silloth and Maryport see 9.10.6; Workington and Harrington 9.10.7, Whitehaven and Ravenglass 9.10.8. South along the Cumbrian coast past St Bees Hd to Walney Is there are no dangers more than 2M offshore, but no shelter either.

BARROW TO CONWY (AC 2010, 1981, *1978*) Ent to Barrow-in-Furness (9.10.9 and chart 3164) is about 1M S of Hilpsford Pt at S end of Walney Island where the lt ho is prominent. ▶*The stream sets across the narrow chan, which is well marked but shallow in patches.*◀ W winds cause rough sea in the ent. Moorings and anch off Piel and Roa Islands, but space is limited . ▶ *Stream runs hard on ebb. Coming from the S it is possible with sufficient rise of tide to cross the sands between Fleetwood and Barrow.* ◀

Lune Deep, 2M NW of Rossall Pt, is ent to Morecambe B (chart 2010), and gives access to the ferry/commercial port of Heysham, Glasson Dock (9.10.9), and Fleetwood (9.10.10); it is well buoyed. ▶ *Streams run 3·5kn at sp.*◀ Most of Bay is encumbered with drying sands, intersected by chans which are subject to change. S of Morecambe B, beware shoals and drying outfall (2·0m) extending 3M W of Rossall Pt. Further S, R. Ribble (9.10.11) gives access via a long drying chan to the marina at Preston.

Queen's Chan and Crosby Chan (charts 1951 and *1978*) are entered E of the Bar Lanby. They are well buoyed, dredged and preserved by training banks, and give main access to R. Mersey and Liverpool (9.10.12). Keep clear of commercial shipping. From the N the old Formby chan is abandoned, but possible near HW. Towards HW and in moderate winds a yacht can cross the training bank (level of which varies between 2m and 3m above CD) E of Great Burbo Bank, if coming from the W. Rock Chan, parts of which dry and which is unmarked, may also be used but beware wrecks.

In good weather and at nps, the Dee Estuary (charts 1953, *1978*) is accessible for boats able to take the ground. But most of estuary dries and banks extend 6M seaward. Chans shift, and buoys are moved as required. ▶ *Stream runs hard in chans when banks are dry.* ◀ Main ent is Welsh Chan, but if coming from N, Hilbre Swash runs W of Hilbre Is (lit). This area is being extensively dredged and developed.

Sailing W from the Dee on the ebb, it is feasible to take the Inner Passage (buoyed) S of West Hoyle Spit, and this enjoys some protection from onshore winds at half tide or below. Rhyl is a tidal hbr, not accessible in strong onshore winds, but gives shelter for yachts able to take the ground. Abergele Road, Colwyn B and Llandudno B are possible anchs in settled weather and S winds. Conwy (9.10.18) offer good shelter in both marina and harbour. ▶ *Between Point of Ayr and Great Ormes Head the E-going stream begins at HW Liverpool + 0600, and the W-going at HW Liverpool – 0015, sp rates 3kn.* ◀

North Hoyle Wind Farm consists of 30 turbines and is centred on 53°25'·00N 03°27'·00W. Each turbine is 58m high, with 80m diameter blades and clearance of 18m. Many of them are lit. Vessels to keep well clear and not enter the area.

ISLE OF MAN (IOM) (charts 2094, 2696) For general pilotage information, tidal streams and hbr details of IOM, see *IOM Sailing Directions, Tidal Streams and Anchorages*, published by Hunter Publications (9.10.13). For notes on crossing the Irish Sea, see 9.13.5.

There are four choices when rounding South of Isle of Man: **a**, In bad weather, or at night, keep S of Chicken Rk (lt, fog sig). **b**, In good conditions, pass between Chicken Rk and Calf of Man (lt, fog sig). **c**, With winds of Force 3 or less and a reliable engine giving at least 5kn, and only by day use Calf Sound between Calf of Man and IOM, passing W of Kitterland Island but E of Thousla Rock, which is marked by lt bn and is close to Calf of Man shore. **d**, Little Sound, a minor chan, runs E of Kitterland Is.

▶ *The stream runs strongly through Calf Sound, starting N-going at HW Liverpool – 0145, and S-going at HW Liverpool + 0345, sp rates 3·5kn. W of Calf of Man the stream runs N and S, but changes direction off Chicken Rk and runs W and E between Calf of Man and Langness Pt 6M to E. Overfalls extend E from Chicken Rk on E-going stream, which begins at HW Liverpool + 0610, and N from the rk on W-going stream, which begins at HW Liverpool.* ◀

▶ *Off Langness Pt (lt) the Skerranes (dry) extend 1ca SW, and tidal stream runs strongly, with eddies and a race. E side of Langness peninsula is foul ground, over which a dangerous sea can build in strong winds. Here the NE-going stream begins at HW Liverpool + 0545, and the SW-going at HW Liverpool – 0415, sp rates 2·25kn.* ◀

There is anch in Derby Haven, N of St Michael's Is, but exposed to E. From here to Douglas (9.10.16) and on to Maughold Hd (lt), there are no dangers more than 4ca offshore. ▶ *Near the coast the SW-going stream runs for 9 hours and the NE-going for 3 hours, since an eddy forms during the second half of the main NE-going stream. Off Maughold Hd the NE-going stream begins at HW Liverpool + 0500, and the SW-going at HW Liverpool – 0415.* ◀

SE, E and NW of Pt of Ayre are dangerous banks, on which seas break in bad weather. These are Whitestone Bk (least depth 2·0m), Bahama Bk (1·5m, buoy), Ballacash Bk (2·7 m), King William Bks (3·3m, buoy), and Strunakill Bk (6·7m).

The W coast of IOM has few pilotage hazards. A spit with depth of 1·4m runs 2ca offshore from Rue Pt. Jurby Rk (depth 2·7m) lies 3ca off Jurby Hd. Craig Rk (depth 4 m) and shoals lie 2·5M NNE of Peel (9.10.14).

MENAI STRAIT (9.10.19 and chart *1464*) The main features of this narrow chan include: Puffin Is, seaward of NE end; Beaumaris; Garth Pt at Bangor, where NE end of Strait begins; Menai Suspension Bridge (30·5m); The Swellies, a narrow 1M stretch with strong tide and dangers mid-stream; Britannia Rail Bridge (27·4m), with cables close W at elevation of 22m; Port Dinorwic and Caernarfon (9.10.19); Abermenai Pt and Fort Belan, where narrows mark SW end of Strait; and Caernarfon Bar.

The following brief notes only cover very basic pilotage. For detailed directions see *W Coasts of England and Wales Pilot*, or *Cruising Anglesey and N Wales* (NW Venturers Yacht Club). ▶ *For tidal streams 'Arrowsmiths' is recommended, from Arrowsmiths, Winterstoke Rd., Bristol, BS3 2NT, cost £3.00. The Swellies should be taken near local HW slack, and an understanding of tidal streams is essential. The tide is about 1 hour later, and sp range about 2·7m more, at NE end of Strait than at SW end. Levels differ most at about HW+1 (when level at NE end is more than 1·8m above level at SW end); and at about HW – 0445 (when level at NE end is more than 1·8m below level at SW end). Normally the stream runs as follows (times referred to HW Holyhead). HW – 0040 to HW + 0420: SW between Garth Pt and Abermenai Pt. HW + 0420 to HW + 0545: outwards from about The Swellies, ie NE towards Garth Pt and SW towards Abermenai Pt. HW + 0545 to HW – 0040: NE between Abermenai Pt and Garth Pt. Sp rates are generally about 3kn,* ***but more in narrows, eg 5kn off Abermenai Pt, 6kn between the bridges, and 8kn at The Swellies.*** *The timings and rates of streams may be affected by strong winds in either direction.* ◀

▶ *From NE, enter chan W of Puffin Island, taking first of ebb to reach the Swellies at slack HW (HW Holyhead – 0100). Slack HW only lasts about 20 mins at sps, a little more at nps.* ◀ Pass under centre of suspension bridge span, and steer to leave Platters (dry) on mainland shore to port and Swellies lt bn close to stbd. From Swellies lt bn to Britannia Bridge hold mainland shore, leaving bn on Price Pt to port, and Gored Goch and Gribbin Rk to stbd. Leave Britannia Rk (centre pier of bridge) to stbd. Thence to SW hold to buoyed chan near mainland shore. (A Historic Wreck (see 9.0.3h) is 4ca SW of Britannia Bridge at 53°12'·77N 04°11'·72W). Port Dinorwic is useful to await right tidal conditions for onward passage in either direction. **Note: Direction of buoyage becomes NE off Caernarfon.**

▶ *Caernarfon Bar is impassable even in moderately strong winds against ebb, and narrows at Abermenai Pt demand a fair tide, or slackish water, since tide runs strongly here. Going seaward on first of ebb, when there is water over the banks, it may not be practicable to return to the Strait if conditions on the bar are bad.* ◀ Then it is best to anch near Mussel Bank buoy and await slack water, before returning to Caernarfon (say). Leaving Abermenai Pt on last of ebb means banks to seaward are exposed and there is little water in chan or over bar.

Going NE'ward it is safe to reach the Swellies with last of flood, leaving Caernarfon about HW Holyhead – 0230. Do not leave too late, or full force of ebb will be met before reaching Bangor.

ANGLESEY TO BARDSEY ISLAND (AC *1977*, 1970, 1971) On N coast of Anglesey, a race extends 5ca off Pt Lynas (lt, fog sig, RC) on E-going stream. Amlwch is a small hbr (partly dries) 1·5M W of Pt Lynas. A drying rk lies 100m offshore on W side of appr, which should not be attempted in strong onshore winds. From here to Carmel Hd beware E Mouse (and shoals to SE), Middle Mouse, Harry Furlong's Rks (dry), Victoria Bank (least depth 1·8m), Coal Rk (awash), and W Mouse (with dangers to W and SW). The outermost of these dangers is 2M offshore. There are overfalls and races at headlands and over many rks and shoals along this coast.

▶ *Between Carmel Hd and The Skerries (lt, fog sig, Racon) the NE-going stream begins at HW Holyhead + 0550, and the SW-going at HW Holyhead – 0010,* ***sp rates 5kn.*** *1M NW of Skerries the stream turns $1\frac{1}{2}$ hours later, and runs less strongly.* ◀ Simplest passage, or at night or in bad weather, is to pass 1M off Skerries, in the TSS ITZ. In good conditions by day and at slack water, Carmel Hd can be rounded close inshore; but beware short, steep, breaking seas here in even moderate winds against tide.

Holyhead (9.10.20) is a port of refuge, access H24 in all weathers, within New Hbr; beware fast ferries. ▶ *Races occur off N Stack and (more severe) off S Stack (lt, fog sig), up to 1·5M offshore on NNE-going stream which begins at HW Holyhead – 0605, sp rate 5kn. Races do not extend so far on SSW-going stream which begins at HW Holyhead + 0020,* ***sp rate 5kn.*** ◀ The W coast of Anglesey is rugged with rks, some drying, up to 1·5M offshore. There are races off Penrhyn Mawr and Rhoscolyn Hd. Pilot's Cove, E of Llanddwyn Is, is good anch to await the right conditions for Menai Strait.

On the Lleyn Peninsula Porth Dinllaen (9.10.20) is good anch, but exposed to N and NE. Braich y Pwll is the steep, rky point at end of Lleyn Peninsula (chart 1971). About 1M N of it and up to 1M offshore lie The Tripods, a bank on which there are overfalls and a bad sea with wind against tide.

▶ *Bardsey Sound, 1·5M wide, can be used by day in moderate winds.* ***Stream reaches 6kn at sp, and passage should be made at slack water,*** *– 0015 HW or + 0035 LW Holyhead.* ◀ Avoid Carreg Ddu on N side and Maen Bugail Rk (dries 4·1m) on S side of Sound, where there are dangerous races. If passing outside Bardsey Is (lt, fog sig) make a good offing to avoid overfalls which extend 1·5M W and 2·5M S of Island. Turbulence occurs over Bastram Shoal, Devil's Tail and Devil's Ridge, which lie SSE and E of Bardsey Is.

NOTES

9.10.6 MARYPORT

Cumbria **54°43'·03N 03°30'·38W**

CHARTS AC*1826,* 1346, 2013; Imray C62; OS 89

TIDES +0038 Dover; ML no data; Duration 0550; Zone 0 (UT)

Standard Port LIVERPOOL (⟶)

Times				Height (metres)			
High Water		Low Water		MHWS	MHWN	MLWN	MLWS
0000	0600	0200	0800	9·3	7·4	2·9	0·9
1200	1800	1400	2000				
Differences MARYPORT							
+0017	+0032	+0020	+0005	−0·7	−0·8	−0·4	0·0
SILLOTH							
+0030	+0040	+0045	+0055	−0·1	−0·3	−0·6	−0·1

SHELTER Good in marina, access HW ±2½ nps over sill 1·75m; at other times Workington is a refuge. Elizabeth Basin dries 2m, access HW±1½; commercial, not used by yachts.

NAVIGATION WPT 54°43´·09N 03°32´·47W, 090° to S pier, 1M. Overfalls at ent with W/SW winds over ebb. At HW–3 1·8m over bar at ent and in river chan; mud banks cover HW –2.

LIGHTS AND MARKS As chartlet. SHM bn Fl G 5s marks outfall 6ca SW of S pier.

R/T Port VHF Ch 12 (occas) 16. Marina (H24) Ch M1 M2 80 16.

TELEPHONE (Dial code 01900) HM 817440; Hbr Authority 604351; CG 812782; MRSC (0151) 931 3341; Marinecall 09066 526245; Police 602422; Dr 815544; Ⓗ 812634.

FACILITIES Maryport Marina (200) ☎ 814431, 818672, £13/ yacht, BY, BH, El, CH, ◙, ME, Slip (±3HW), P (cans), (fresh fish from Fisherman's Co-op); **Maryport Yachting Ass'n** ☎ 64964. **Town** EC Wed; P, D, ME, 🛒, R, Bar, ✉, Ⓑ, ≹, ✈ (Newcastle).

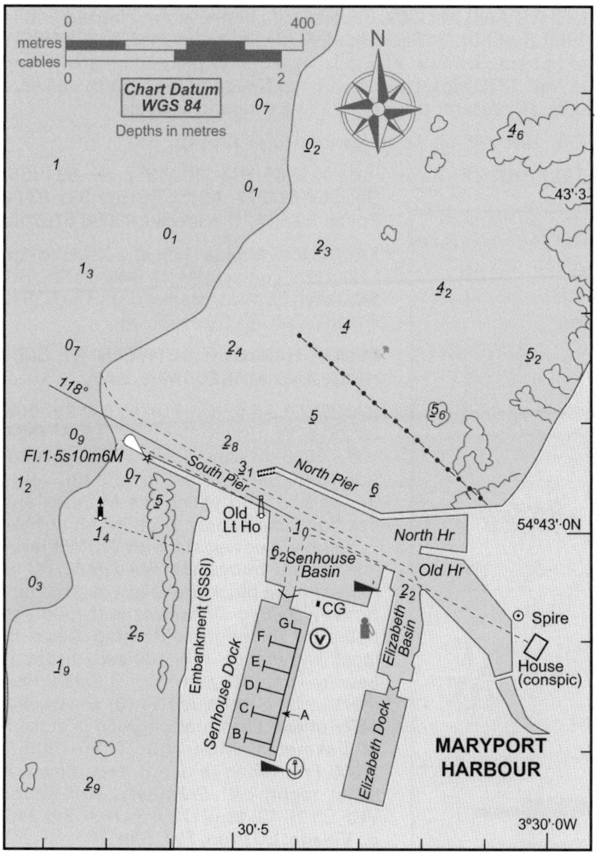
metres
cables
0
400
2
Chart Datum WGS 84
Depths in metres
N
43'·3
118°
Fl.1·5s10m6M
South Pier
North Pier
Old Lt Ho
North Hr
54°43'·0N
Senhouse Basin
Old Hr
CG
Spire
House (conspic)
Embankment (SSSI)
Senhouse Dock
Elizabeth Basin
Elizabeth Dock
MARYPORT HARBOUR
30'·5
3°30'·0W

9.10.7 WORKINGTON

Cumbria 54°39'·03N 03°34'·38W

CHARTS AC *1826,* 1346, 2013; Imray C62; OS 89

TIDES +0025 Dover; ML 4·5; Duration 0545; Zone 0 (UT)

Standard Port LIVERPOOL (⟶)

Times				Height (metres)			
High Water		Low Water		MHWS	MHWN	MLWN	MLWS
0000	0600	0200	0800	9·3	7·4	2·9	0·9
1200	1800	1400	2000				
Differences WORKINGTON							
+0020	+0020	+0020	+0010	−1·2	−1·1	−0·3	0·0

SHELTER Good; ent and chan to Prince of Wales Dock are dredged 1·8m. Berth where you can (free) or ⚓ in Turning Basin. Lock (HW±1½) into PoW Dock 1·8m (for coasters). Low (1·8m) fixed railway bridge across ent to inner tidal hbr.

NAVIGATION WPT 54°39´·59N 03°35´·38W, 131° to front ldg lt, 1·0M. Tide sets strongly across ent. In periods of heavy rain a strong freshet from R Derwent may be encountered in the hbr ent.

LIGHTS AND MARKS Workington Bank, least depth 5·5m, is 2M W of hbr ent; it is marked by a NCM buoy Q.Fl and a SCM buoy, VQ (6) + L Fl 10s, (see 9.10.4). A SHM buoy, Fl G 5s, 1·3M NW of hbr ent is a mark for English Chan. Ldg lts 132°, both FR 10/12m 3M, on W pyramidal trs with Y bands. Two sets of F Bu lts in line mark NE and SW edges of chan. There are 16 wind-turbines between ¾M and 2M NE of hbr ent.

R/T VHF Ch 14 16 (HW–2½ to HW+2 approx).

TELEPHONE (Dial code 01900) HM 602301 604696 ; CG 2238; MRSC (0151) 931 3341; Marinecall 09066 526245; Police 602422; Dr 64866; Ⓗ 602244.

FACILITIES Dock D, FW, ME, El; **Vanguard SC** ☎ 826886, M, FW. **Town** EC Thurs; P, 🛒, R, Bar, ✉, Ⓑ, ≹, ✈ (Carlisle).

See Workington chartlet overleaf

MINOR HARBOUR 10M NNE OF MARYPORT

SILLOTH, Cumbria, **54°52´·16N 03°23´·86W**. AC*1826,* 1346, 2013. HW –0050 on Dover; ML no data; Duration 0520. See 9.10.6. Appr via English or Middle Chans, approx 8M long, requires local knowledge. Beware constantly shifting chans and banks. Yachts are not encouraged. ⚓ SW of ent in about 4m off Lees Scar, Fl G 10s 11m 2M; exposed to SW winds. Outer hbr dries; lock into New Dock (note sill 1.2 above CD), which is mainly commercial. East Cote Dir lt 052° FG 15m 12M; vis 046°-058°, intens 052°. Ldg lts, both F, 115°. Groyne 2 FG (vert). Tfc sigs on mast at New Dock: no entry unless Y signal arm raised by day or Q Bu lt by night. VHF Ch 16 12 (HW–2½ to HW+1½). HM ☎ (016973) 31358. Facilities: EC Tues; FW, Ⓑ, Bar, ✉, R, 🛒.

MINOR HARBOUR 2M SOUTH OF WORKINGTON

HARRINGTON, Cumbria, **54°36´·77N 03°34´·29W**. AC *1826,* 1346, 2013. HW +0025 on Dover; Duration 0540; Use Diff's Workington 9.10.7. Good shelter in small hbr only used by local FVs and yachts; dries 3ca offshore. Ent difficult in strong W winds. Berth on N wall of inner hbr (free). Call ☎ (01946) 823741 Ext 148 for moorings. Limited facilities. **SC**.

WORKINGTON *continued*

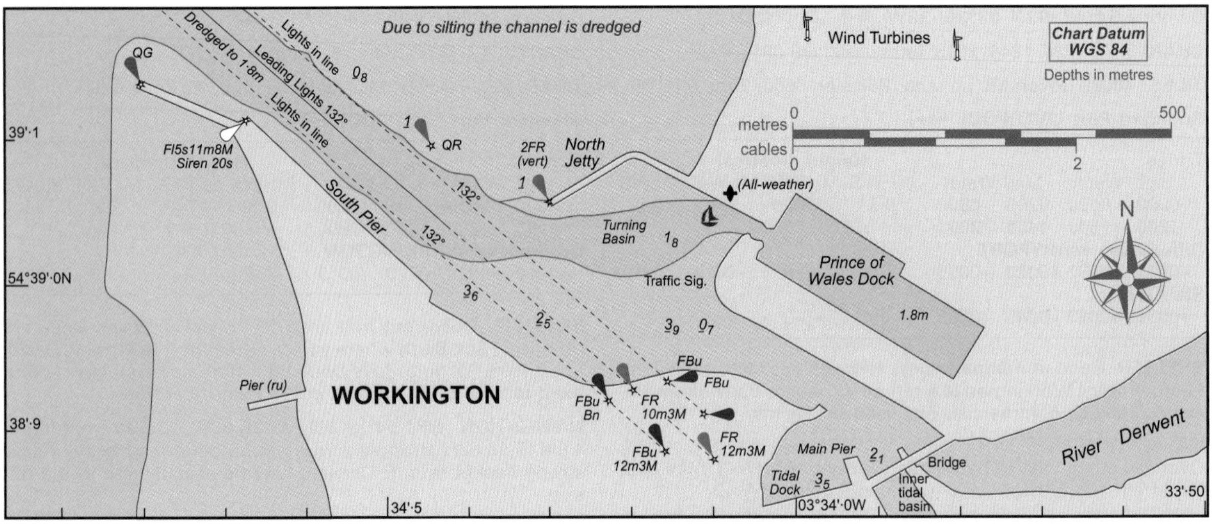
Due to silting the channel is dredged
Dredged to 1·8m
Lights in line
Leading Lights 132°
Lights in line
QG
Fl5s11m8M
Siren 20s
QR
2FR (vert)
North Jetty
South Pier
Wind Turbines
Chart Datum WGS 84
Depths in metres
metres
cables
(All-weather)
Turning Basin
Traffic Sig.
Prince of Wales Dock
1.8m
FBu
FBu Bn
FR 10m3M
FBu 12m3M
FR 12m3M
Pier (ru)
WORKINGTON
Main Pier
Tidal Dock
Inner tidal basin
Bridge
River Derwent
39'·1
54°39'·0N
38'·9
34'·5
03°34'·0W
33'·50

9.10.8 WHITEHAVEN

Cumbria **54°33'·18N 03°35'·82W** ❁❁❁◊◊✿✿

CHARTS AC *1826*, 1346, 2013; Imray C62; OS 89

TIDES +0015 Dover; ML 4·5; Duration 0550; Zone 0 (UT)

Standard Port LIVERPOOL (⟶)

Times				Height (metres)			
High Water		Low Water		MHWS	MHWN	MLWN	MLWS
0000	0600	0200	0800	9·3	7·4	2·9	0·9
1200	1800	1400	2000				
Differences WHITEHAVEN							
+0005	+0015	+0010	+0005	−1·3	−1·1	−0·5	+0·1
TARN POINT (54°17'N 03°25'W)							
+0005	+0005	+0010	0000	−1·0	−1·0	−0·4	0·0
DUDDON BAR (54°09'N 03°20'W)							
+0003	+0003	+0008	+0002	−0·8	−0·8	−0·3	0·0

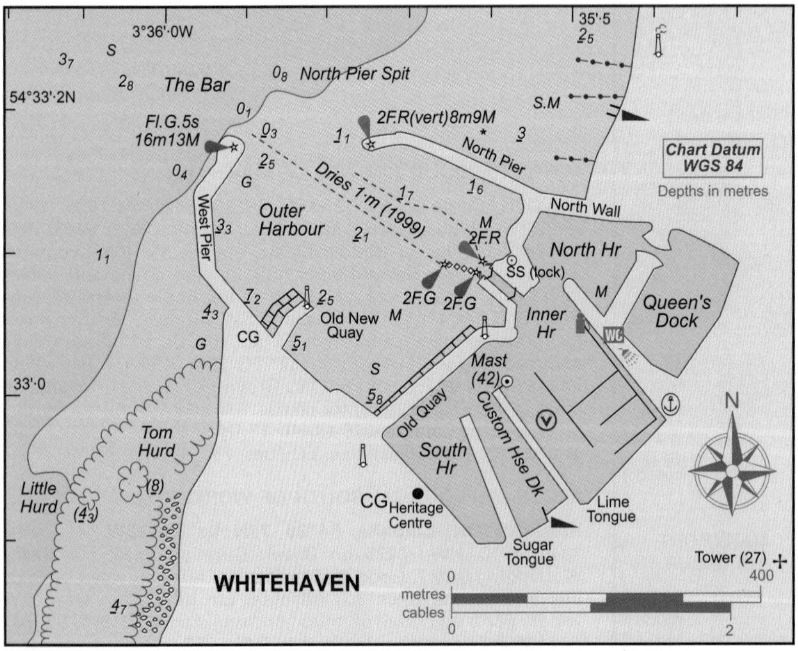
3°36'·0W
54°33'·2N
The Bar
North Pier Spit
Fl.G.5s 16m13M
2F.R(vert)8m9M
North Pier
S.M
Chart Datum WGS 84
Depths in metres
Dries 1·m (1999)
Outer Harbour
West Pier
North Wall
2F.R
SS (lock)
North Hr
Queen's Dock
2F.G
2F.G
Old New Quay
Inner Hr
CG
Mast (42)
Old Quay
Custom Hse Dk
South Hr
CG Heritage Centre
Lime Tongue
Sugar Tongue
Tom Hurd
Little Hurd
33'·0
35'·5
WHITEHAVEN
metres
cables
Tower (27)

SHELTER Very good, entry safe in most weathers. One of the more accessible ports of refuge in NW England, with a new marina in the inner hbr. Appr chan across the outer hbr is dredged to 1·0m above CD giving access approx HW±4. Sea lock (30m x 13.7m), with sill at CD, maintains 7m within inner hbr. Yacht pontoons are in Inner Hbr. Queen's Dock (from which the lock gates have been decommissioned) and N Hbr remain for commercial and FV use.

NAVIGATION WPT 54°33'·34N 03°36'·21W, 133° to W pier hd, 4½ca. There are no hazards in the offing. Hold closer to the North Pier, and beware stone bar at end of W Pier.

LIGHTS AND MARKS Several tall chimneys are charted within 1·5M S of hbr. St Bees Head, Fl (2) 20s 102m 21M, is 2·7M SSW of hbr ent. SHM bn, Fl G 2·5s, 4½ca S of W pierhead marks sewer outfall. IPTS sigs 1-3 shown from N side of lock ent to seaward only at present: priority to inward bound vessels.

R/T HM VHF Ch 12 16 (as for access times).

TELEPHONE (Dial code 01946)HM 692435, 691135; Sealock 694672; MRSC (0151) 931 3341; Police 692616; Marinecall 09066 526245.

FACILITIES **Marina** (155) ☎ 692435, <12m £12, >12m contact HM, D, Slip, FW, BH, **SC**. **Town** EC Wed, Market days Thurs, Sat; P (cans), Bar, Ⓑ, ✉, R, ⇌.

MINOR HARBOUR BETWEEN ST BEES HEAD AND MORECAMBE BAY

RAVENGLASS, Cumbria, **54°20'·00N 03°26'·80W** (drying line). AC 1346, *1826*. HW +0020 on Dover; ML no data; Duration 0545. See 9.10.8 (Tarn Point). Large drying hbr, into which R's Mite, Irt and Esk flow; has approx 2·5m in ent at HW–2. Sellafield power stn with WCM lt buoy and outfall buoys are 5M NNW. FG ☆ (occas) is on blockhouse at S side of ent. *Solway Sailing Directions* with pilotage notes by Ravenglass Boating Ass'n or local knowledge are advised. From N beware Drigg Rk and from S Selker Rks, marked by SHM buoy Fl (3) G 10s, 5M SSW of ent. Firing range D406 is close S at Eskmeals; Mon-Thur 0800-1600LT (1500 Fri). When in use R flags flown, R lts at night; call *Eskmeals Gun Range* VHF Ch 16 13, ☎ (01229) 717631 Ext 245/6. **Village**: EC Wed; FW, Slip, Bar, ✉.

9.10.9 GLASSON DOCK

Lancashire **53°59'·98N 02°50'·93W** ❁❁◊◊◊✿✿

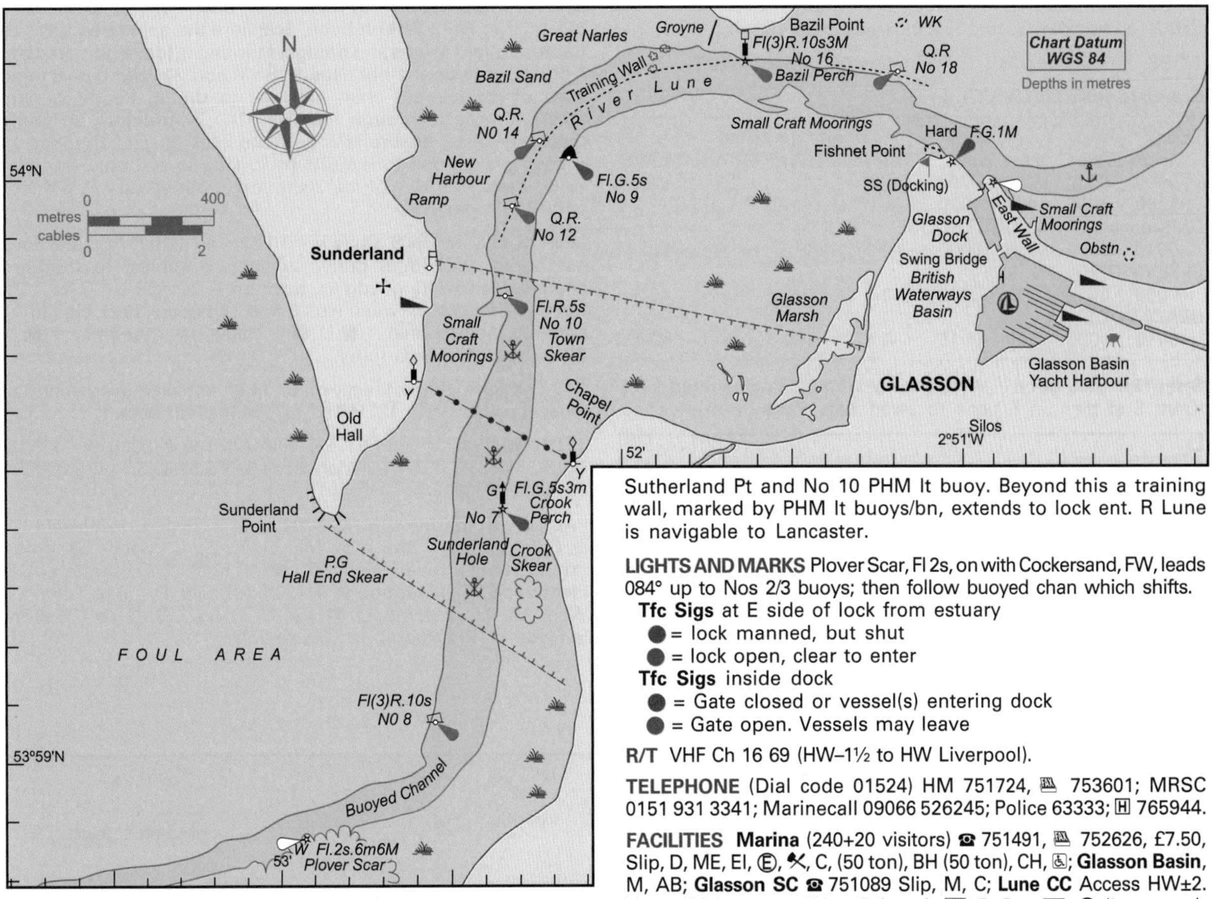
Chart Datum WGS 84
Depths in metres
Great Narles
Groyne
Bazil Point
Fl(3)R.10s3M No 16
WK
Q.R No 18
Bazil Sand
Training Wall
River Lune
Bazil Perch
Q.R. NO 14
Small Craft Moorings
Hard
F.G.1M
Fishnet Point
SS (Docking)
New Harbour
Ramp
Fl.G.5s No 9
Q.R. No 12
Glasson Dock
East Wall
Small Craft Moorings
Obstn
Swing Bridge
British Waterways Basin
54°N
metres
cables
0
400
2
Sunderland
Fl.R.5s No 10
Town Skear
Small Craft Moorings
Glasson Marsh
Glasson Basin Yacht Harbour
GLASSON
Chapel Point
Old Hall
Y
Silos
2°51'W
52'
G
Fl.G.5s3m
Crook Perch
No 7
Sunderland Point
Sunderland Hole
Crook Skear
P.G
Hall End Skear
FOUL AREA
Fl(3)R.10s NO 8
53°59'N
Buoyed Channel
W Fl.2s.6m6M
Plover Scar
53'

CHARTS AC *1826,* 1552, 2010; Imray C62; OS 102, 97

TIDES +0020 Dover; ML No data; Duration 0535; Zone 0 (UT)

Standard Port LIVERPOOL (⟶)

Times				Height (metres)			
High Water		Low Water		MHWS	MHWN	MLWN	MLWS
0000	0600	0200	0700	9·3	7·4	2·9	0·9
1200	1800	1400	1900				
Differences BARROW-IN-FURNESS (Ramsden Dock)							
+0015	+0015	+0015	+0015	0·0	−0·3	+0·1	+0·2
ULVERSTON							
+0020	+0040	No data		0·0	−0·1	No data	
ARNSIDE							
+0100	+0135	No data		+0·5	+0·2	No data	
MORECAMBE							
+0005	+0010	+0030	+0015	+0·2	0·0	0·0	+0·2
HEYSHAM							
+0005	+0005	+0015	0000	+0·1	0·0	0·0	+0·2
GLASSON DOCK							
+0020	+0030	+0220	+0240	−2·7	−3·0	No data	
LANCASTER							
+0110	+0030	Dries out		−5·0	−4·9	Dries out	

Note: At Glasson Dock LW time differences give the end of a LW stand which lasts up to 2 hours at sp.

SHELTER Very good in marina; also sheltered ⚓ in R Lune to await sea lock, opens HW-1 (Liverpool) to HW, into Glasson Dock. Inner lock/swing bridge lead into BWB basin.

NAVIGATION WPT 53°58′·41N 03°00′·09W (2ca S of R Lune No 1 WCM By), 084° to front ldg lt 084°, 4·2M. Leave WPT at HW–2 via buoyed/lit chan. Plover Scar lt bn has a tide gauge showing depth over the lock sill at Glasson Dock. ⚓ is prohib between Sutherland Pt and No 10 PHM lt buoy. Beyond this a training wall, marked by PHM lt buoys/bn, extends to lock ent. R Lune is navigable to Lancaster.

LIGHTS AND MARKS Plover Scar, Fl 2s, on with Cockersand, FW, leads 084° up to Nos 2/3 buoys; then follow buoyed chan which shifts.

Tfc Sigs at E side of lock from estuary
● = lock manned, but shut
● = lock open, clear to enter

Tfc Sigs inside dock
● = Gate closed or vessel(s) entering dock
● = Gate open. Vessels may leave

R/T VHF Ch 16 69 (HW–1½ to HW Liverpool).

TELEPHONE (Dial code 01524) HM 751724, 📠 753601; MRSC 0151 931 3341; Marinecall 09066 526245; Police 63333; Ⓗ 765944.

FACILITIES **Marina** (240+20 visitors) ☎ 751491, 📠 752626, £7.50, Slip, D, ME, El, Ⓔ, ⚒, C, (50 ton), BH (50 ton), CH, ♿; **Glasson Basin,** M, AB; **Glasson SC** ☎ 751089 Slip, M, C; **Lune CC** Access HW±2. **Town** EC Lancaster Wed; P (cans), 🛒, R, Bar, ✉, Ⓑ (Lancaster), ⇌ (bus to Lancaster 4M), ✈ (Blackpool).

ADJACENT HARBOURS IN MORECAMBE BAY

BARROW-IN-FURNESS, Cumbria, **54°05′·64N 03°13′·44W.** AC *1826,* 2010, 3164. HW +0030 on Dover; See 9.10.9. ML 5·0m; Duration 0530. Good shelter but open to SE winds. Drying moorings off Piel and Roa Islands or ⚓ clear of fairway. Marks/lts: Walney Island lt ho (conspic stone tr), Fl 15s 21m 23M (obsc 122°-127° within 3M of shore), RC. Directions: From Lightning Knoll SWM buoy (L Fl 10s), ldg lts, front Q 7m 10M; rear (6ca from front), Iso 2s 13m 10M (lattice structures) lead 041°/3·7M past Halfway Shoal bn, QR 16m 10M with RY chequers, Racon, to Bar buoy Fl (2) R 5s (abeam Walney Island lt ho). Inner Channel ldg lts, front Q 9m 10M, rear Iso 2s 14m 6M, lead 006° past Piel Is with least charted depth 1·7m. Piel Island has conspic ruined castle, slip and moorings on E side. Roa Island, 5ca N, has jetty at S end and moorings on E side; a causeway joins it to mainland. Commercial docks, 3M NW at Barrow, reached via buoyed/lit Walney Chan, dredged to 2·5m, which must be kept clear. HM (Barrow) ☎ (01229) 822911, 📠 835822; VHF *Barrow Port Control* Ch 12 16 (H24). Facilities: Piel Is, Bar; Roa, Hotel, 🛒. **Barrow** EC Thurs.

HEYSHAM, Lancashire, **54°02′·01N 02°55′·96W.** AC *1826,* 2010, 1552. HW +0015 on Dover; ML 5·1m; Duration 0545. See 9.10.9. Good shelter, but yachts not normally accepted without special reason. Beware high speed ferries and oil rig supply ships. Ldg lts 102°, both F Bu 11/14m 2M, Y+B ◊ on masts. S jetty lt 2 FG (vert), Siren 30s. S pier hd ,Oc G 7·5s 9m 6M. N pier hd, 2FR (vert) 11m, obsc from seaward. Ent sigs: R flag or ● = no entry; no sig = no dep; 2 R flags or 2 ● = no ent or dep. VHF Ch 14 74 16 (H24). HM ☎ (01524) 852373. Facilities: EC Wed (Morecambe also); Bar, FW, R, 🛒 at Morecambe (2M).

9.10.10 FLEETWOOD

Lancashire **53°55'·49N 03°00'·15W**

CHARTS AC *1826,* 2010, 1552; Imray C62; OS 102

TIDES +0015 Dover; ML 5.2; Duration 0530; Zone 0 (UT)

Standard Port LIVERPOOL (⟶)

Times				Height (metres)			
High Water		Low Water		MHWS	MHWN	MLWN	MLWS
0000	0600	0200	0700	9·3	7·4	2·9	0·9
1200	1800	1400	1900				
Differences WYRE LIGHTHOUSE							
−0010	−0010	+0005	0000	−0·1	−0·1	No data	
FLEETWOOD							
−0008	−0008	−0003	−0003	−0·1	−0·1	+0·1	+0·3
BLACKPOOL							
−0015	−0005	−0005	−0015	−0·4	−0·4	−0·1	+0·1

SHELTER Very good in Wyre Dock Marina 5·5m. Sheltered ⚓ off Knott End pier on E bank to await tide. Passage up-river to Skippool (5M) needs local knowledge and shoal draft; access HW±1 (if ht of tide is >8·0m).

NAVIGATION WPT 53°57´·57N 03°02´·33W, Fairway NCM buoy, VQ, 143° to No 3 SHM lt buoy, 3ca; here the appr chan turns S. Caution: avoid ferries and dredgers turning in lower hbr, dredged 4·5m. Further up the hbr, Nos 23 SHM and 24 PHM buoys mark start of marina ent chan dredged to drying height of $\underline{3}$m. Freeflow access through lock HW±1½. In addition, on many dates specified by the HM between Mar 29 and October 13 access is extended to HW±2½ by locking in and out . For best water keep 15m NW of the 300m long training wall (5 perches with R □ topmarks).

LIGHTS AND MARKS Chan is well buoyed/lit, but AC 1552 does not depict individual buoys which are subject to frequent change due to silting. Ldg lts, front Iso G 2s; rear Iso G 4s, 156° (only to be used between Nos 8 and 13 buoys). Lock sigs (only enter on instructions): 1 ● (1 ●) = Gates open for entry; 2 ● (2 ●) = open for departures.

R/T Call *RoRo Ships* directly on Ch 11 for info on movements. Call *Fleetwood Dock* Ch **12**, HW±2 for marina/Fish Dock.

TELEPHONE (Dial code 01253) HM (ABP) ☎ 879056, ℻ 777549; MRSC (0151) 931 3341/3; Marinecall 09066 526245; Police (01524) 63333; Dr 873312.

FACILITIES **Marina** (210) ☎ 879062, ℻ 777549, £16.45/yacht, D, C (25 ton), CH, SM, ACA, ME, El, ⚒, Ⓔ, C (mobile 50 ton by arrangement). **River Wyre YC** ☎ 811948, 1 Ⓥ. **Blackpool & Fleetwood YC** (Skippool) ☎ 884205, AB, Slip, FW, Bar; **Town** EC Wed; P & D (cans), ME, El, ⚒, CH, R, Bar, ✉, Ⓑ, ⇌ (Poulton-le-Fylde or Blackpool), ✈ (Blackpool).

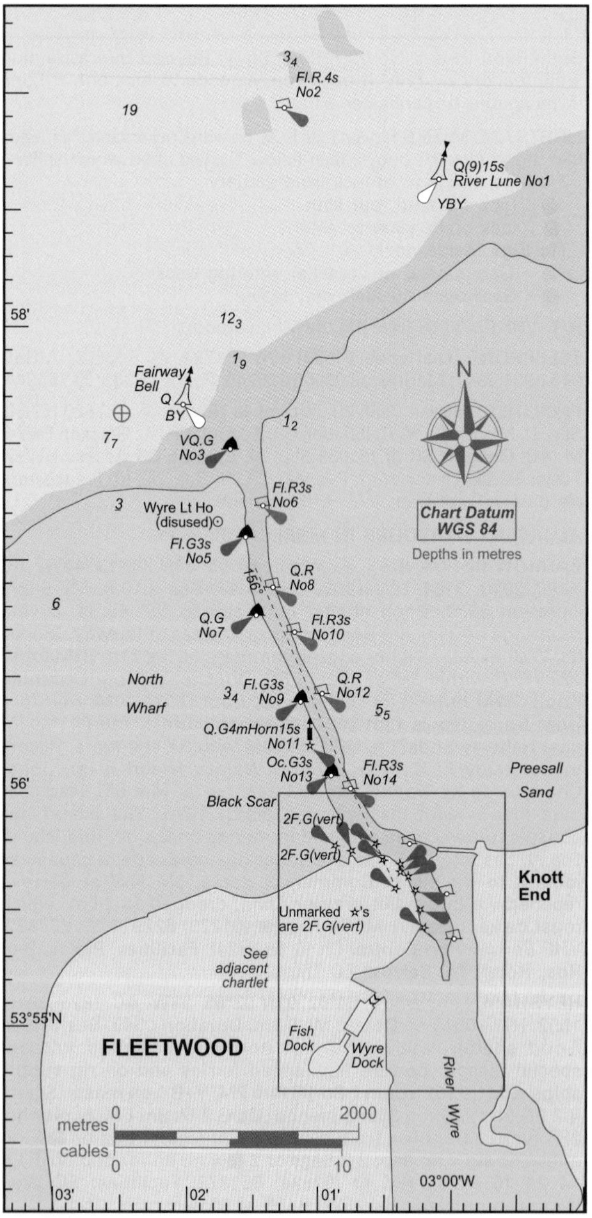
Fl.R.4s
No2
19
Q(9)15s
River Lune No1
YBY
58'
Fairway
Bell
Q
BY
VQ.G
No3
Fl.R3s
No6
Wyre Lt Ho
(disused)
Fl.G3s
No5
Q.R
No8
Q.G
No7
Fl.R3s
No10
North
Wharf
Fl.G3s
No9
Q.R
No12
Q.G4mHorn15s
No11
Oc.G3s
No13
Fl.R3s
No14
56'
Black Scar
Preesall
Sand
2F.G(vert)
Knott
End
Unmarked ☆'s
are 2F.G(vert)
See
adjacent
chartlet
Chart Datum
WGS 84
Depths in metres
N
53°55'N
FLEETWOOD
Fish
Dock
Wyre
Dock
River
Wyre
metres
cables
2000
10
03'
02'
01'
03°00'W

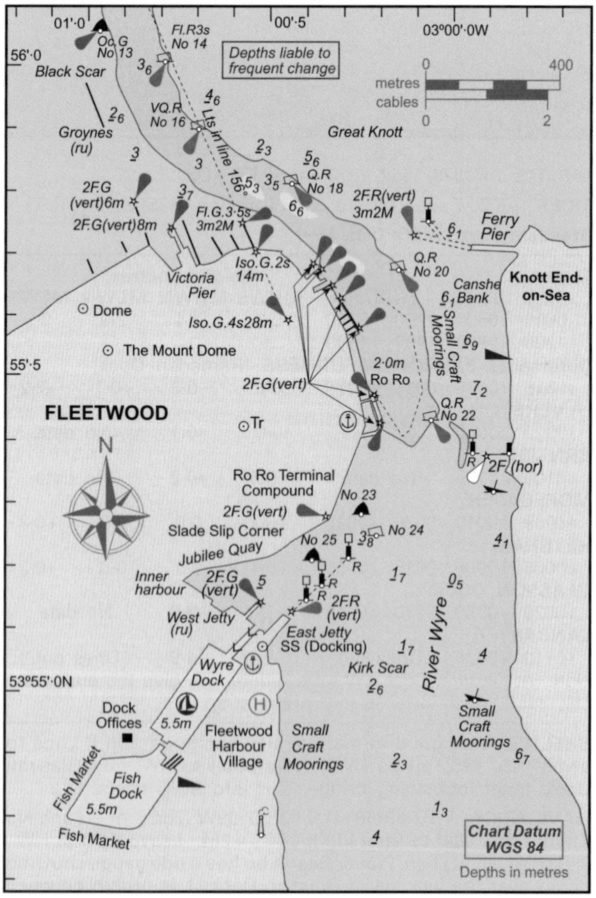
01'·0
Fl.R3s
No 14
00'·5
03°00'·0W
56'·0
Oc.G
No 13
Black Scar
Depths liable to
frequent change
metres
cables
400
VQ.R
No 16
Lts in line 156°
Groynes
(ru)
Great Knott
Q.R
No 18
2F.G
(vert)6m
2F.R(vert)
3m2M
Ferry
Pier
2F.G(vert)8m
Fl.G.3·5s
3m2M
Iso.G.2s
14m
Q.R
No 20
Victoria
Pier
Canshe
Bank
Knott End-
on-Sea
Dome
Iso.G.4s28m
Small Craft
Moorings
The Mount Dome
55'·5
2·0m
Ro Ro
2F.G(vert)
Q.R
No 22
FLEETWOOD
Tr
2F(hor)
N
Ro Ro Terminal
Compound
No 23
2F.G(vert)
Slade Slip Corner
No 24
No 25
Jubilee Quay
Inner
harbour
2F.G
(vert)
2F.R
(vert)
West Jetty
(ru)
East Jetty
SS (Docking)
River Wyre
Kirk Scar
Wyre
Dock
53°55'·0N
Dock
Offices
5.5m
Fleetwood
Harbour
Village
Small
Craft
Moorings
Small
Craft
Moorings
Fish Market
Fish
Dock
5.5m
Fish Market
Chart Datum
WGS 84
Depths in metres

9.10.11 RIVER RIBBLE/PRESTON

Lancashire **53°43'·51N 03°00'·08W**

CHARTS AC *1826,* 1981; Imray C62; OS 102

TIDES +0013 Dover; ML No data; Duration 0520; Zone 0 (UT)

Standard Port LIVERPOOL (⟶)

Times				**Height (metres)**			
High Water		Low Water		MHWS	MHWN	MLWN	MLWS
0000	0600	0200	0700	9·3	7·4	2·9	0·9
1200	1800	1400	1900				
Differences PRESTON							
+0010	+0010	+0335	+0310	−4·0	−4·1	−2·8	−0·8

LW time differences give the end of a LW stand lasting 3½ hrs.

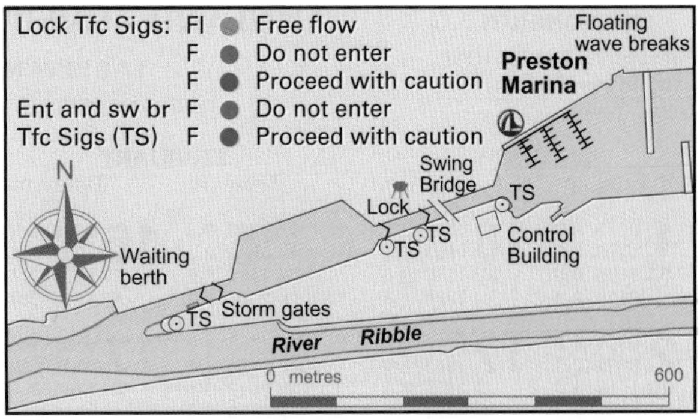
Lock Tfc Sigs: Fl Free flow
F Do not enter
F Proceed with caution
Ent and sw br F Do not enter
Tfc Sigs (TS) F Proceed with caution
Floating wave breaks
Preston Marina
N
Swing Bridge
Lock
TS
Control Building
Waiting berth
Storm gates
River Ribble
0 metres 600

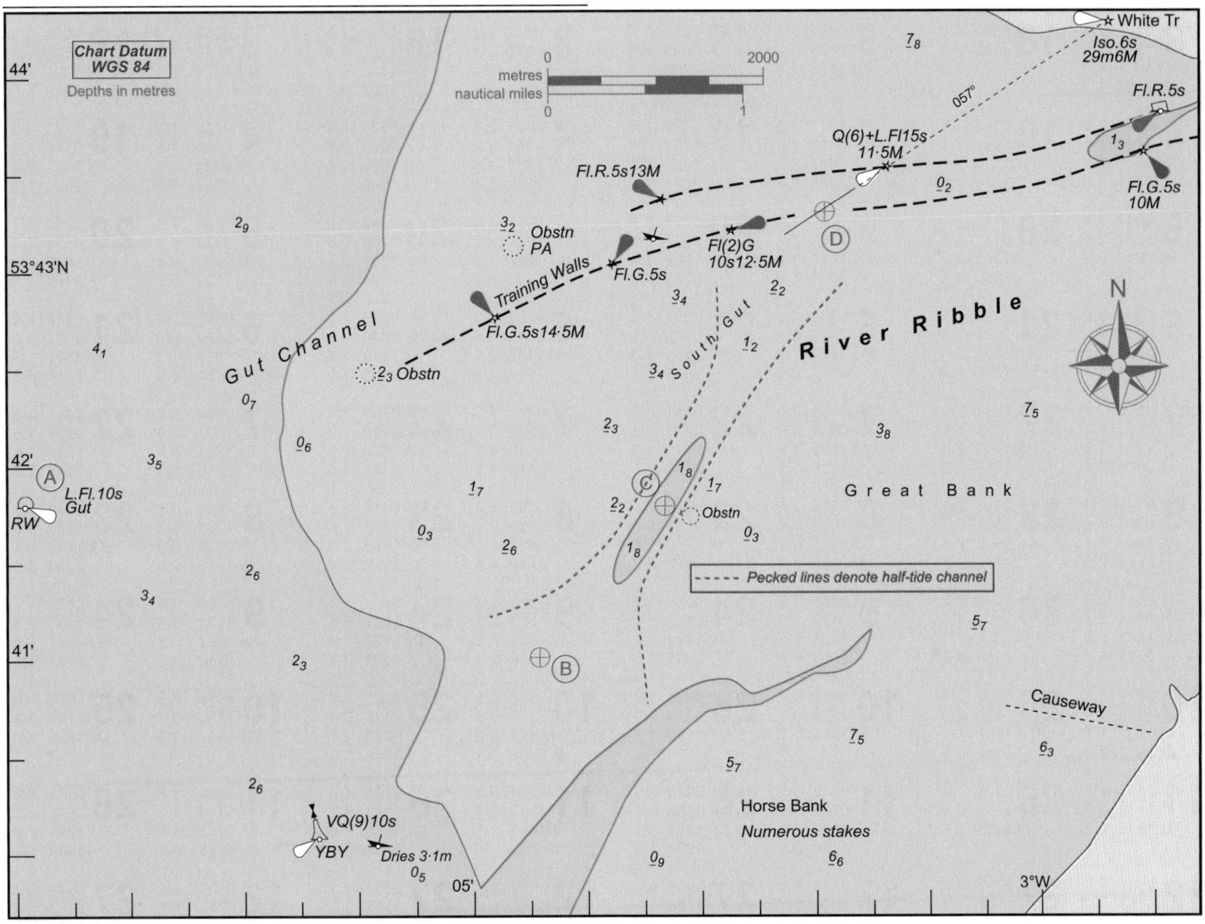
Chart Datum WGS 84
Depths in metres
0 metres 2000
nautical miles 0 1
44'
53°43'N
42'
41'
White Tr
Iso.6s 29m6M
057°
Fl.R.5s
Q(6)+L.Fl15s 11·5M
Fl.R.5s13M
Fl.G.5s 10M
Obstn PA
Fl(2)G 10s12·5M
Training Walls
Fl.G.5s
Fl.G.5s14·5M
Gut Channel
Obstn
South Gut
River Ribble
N
Great Bank
L.Fl.10s Gut
RW
Obstn
Pecked lines denote half-tide channel
Causeway
Horse Bank
Numerous stakes
VQ(9)10s
YBY
Dries 3·1m
05'
3°W

SHELTER Good in Preston marina (5m depth) 15M upriver. Lock in HW-1 to +2, 0700-2100 Apr-Oct (no commercial tfc); lay-by berth outside storm gates for 2m draft. Swing bridge opens in unison with locks. Possible drying berths on the N bank at Lytham or Freckleton, or 2M up R Douglas access HW±1.

NAVIGATION WPT **A** 53°41'·75N 03°08'·90W, Gut SWM buoy, L Fl 10s. The seaward 2·5M of original lit chan has silted up; best water is now via South Gut chan (liable to shift), navigable HW±2. Not before HW Liverpool −2, leave WPT **A** tracking 105° 2·9M to WPT **B** 53°40'·96N 03°04'·22W, then tracking 032° 0·9M to WPT **C** 53°41'·70N 03°03'·43W. Then tracking 026° 1·8M to WPT **D** 53°43'·29N 03°02'·10W to the transit of the 11½M perch Q(6) + LFl 15s with conspic W Tr. Enter via the gap, leaving 11½M perch 100m to port. If draught less than 2m leave WPT **A** tracking 3·2M E to WPT **C**. Then tracking 026° 1·8M to WPT **D**. The river trends 080° between training walls, drying 3m, marked by perches, lit as below, but night appr not advised. Note: The chartlet shows only the seaward end of the estuary. Remaining 15M is straightforward.

LIGHTS AND MARKS 14½M perch, Fl G 5s, is the most seaward chan mark. Up-river from 11½M perch there is a PHM buoy and perch (off chartlet), both Fl R 5s. 4 SHM perches, Fl G 5s, lead to 5M perch, Fl (2) G 10s, marking mouth of unlit R Douglas. 3M and 2M perches are Fl G 5s; 1M perch is Fl G 10s. Tfc lts at locks into marina. Warton airfield beacon, Mo (WQ) G 9s, is N abeam 6M perch, Fl G 5s.

R/T At Preston, for locks call *Riversway* Ch 16 14; Marina Ch **80**, both (HW±2). Douglas BY Ch 16 when vessel due.

TELEPHONE (Dial code 01772) Preston locks 726871; MRSC (0151) 9313341; Marinecall 09066 526245; Police 203203; H 710408.

FACILITIES **Preston Marina** (125) ☎ 733595, mob 07770 505094 Fax 731881, £5/yacht, D, CH, ME, ⚒, Gas, C (25 ton, 45 ton by arrangement), R, ⛟, ACA, ♿. **Douglas BY,** ☎/Fax 812462, mob 07740 780899, AB, £0.98, C (20 ton), CH, D, FW, ⚒, Slip, ME. **Freckleton BY** ☎ 632439, mob 07957 820881, AB, £5/yacht, slip, FW, CH, ME. **Ribble Cruising Club** ☎ (01253) 739983.

TIME ZONE (UT)
For Summer Time add ONE hour in **non-shaded areas**

ENGLAND – LIVERPOOL (ALFRED DOCK)

LAT 53°24′N LONG 3°01′W

TIMES AND HEIGHTS OF HIGH AND LOW WATERS

SPRING & NEAP TIDES
Dates in red are SPRINGS
Dates in blue are NEAPS

YEAR **2005**

JANUARY

Date	Day	Time m	Time m	Time m	Time m
1	SA	0219 8.3	0839 2.5	1436 8.5	2119 2.4
2	SU	0301 8.0	0922 2.7	1519 8.3	2202 2.6
3	M	0347 7.8	1010 2.9	1608 8.1	◑ 2253 2.7
4	TU	0442 7.6	1107 3.1	1705 7.9	2355 2.8
5	W	0546 7.6	1212 3.1	1810 7.9	
6	TH	0104 2.8	0654 7.7	1325 2.9	1917 8.1
7	F	0215 2.5	0800 8.1	1437 2.6	2023 8.4
8	SA	0320 2.1	0901 8.6	1543 2.1	2126 8.8
9	SU	0417 1.7	0956 9.1	1643 1.6	2223 9.1
10	M	0510 1.4	1048 9.5	1739 1.1	● 2317 9.4
11	TU	0601 1.1	1139 9.7	1833 0.8	
12	W	0008 9.5	0650 1.0	1229 9.9	1923 0.6
13	TH	0059 9.5	0738 1.0	1318 9.9	2012 0.6
14	F	0147 9.4	0824 1.2	1405 9.7	2057 0.8
15	SA	0233 9.1	0908 1.5	1452 9.4	2142 1.2
16	SU	0319 8.7	0953 1.9	1539 9.0	2226 1.7
17	M	0407 8.2	1040 2.4	1629 8.4	◐ 2313 2.3
18	TU	0501 7.7	1133 2.8	1727 7.9	
19	W	0007 2.8	0605 7.4	1237 3.1	1836 7.6
20	TH	0111 3.1	0720 7.3	1349 3.2	1950 7.5
21	F	0220 3.1	0828 7.6	1503 3.0	2054 7.7
22	SA	0324 2.9	0922 7.9	1602 2.6	2146 8.0
23	SU	0413 2.6	1007 8.3	1648 2.3	2230 8.3
24	M	0455 2.3	1047 8.6	1729 2.0	2308 8.5
25	TU	0533 2.1	1123 8.8	1807 1.9	○ 2344 8.6
26	W	0608 1.9	1157 8.9	1843 1.7	
27	TH	0017 8.7	0641 1.8	1231 9.0	1917 1.7
28	F	0050 8.7	0714 1.8	1304 9.0	1949 1.7
29	SA	0123 8.7	0746 1.8	1337 9.0	2020 1.7
30	SU	0157 8.7	0819 1.9	1412 8.9	2051 1.9
31	M	0232 8.5	0854 2.1	1448 8.7	2124 2.1

FEBRUARY

Date	Day	Time m	Time m	Time m	Time m
1	TU	0310 8.3	0933 2.3	1530 8.5	2204 2.4
2	W	0357 8.0	1019 2.7	1622 8.1	◑ 2256 2.8
3	TH	0457 7.7	1121 3.0	1728 7.8	
4	F	0011 3.0	0611 7.5	1243 3.1	1844 7.7
5	SA	0142 3.0	0731 7.7	1414 2.9	2005 7.9
6	SU	0302 2.6	0846 8.2	1533 2.3	2118 8.4
7	M	0408 2.0	0947 8.9	1638 1.6	2218 8.9
8	TU	0504 1.4	1040 9.4	1734 0.9	● 2310 9.4
9	W	0554 1.0	1129 9.9	1825 0.5	2358 9.6
10	TH	0641 0.7	1215 10.1	1912 0.2	
11	F	0042 9.7	0725 0.6	1300 10.1	1954 0.2
12	SA	0125 9.6	0806 0.7	1342 10.0	2034 0.5
13	SU	0206 9.3	0844 1.0	1423 9.6	2111 1.0
14	M	0244 8.9	0921 1.5	1504 9.1	2146 1.6
15	TU	0323 8.4	1000 2.1	1545 8.4	2224 2.3
16	W	0406 7.8	1045 2.7	1634 7.7	◐ 2311 3.0
17	TH	0501 7.2	1146 3.3	1741 7.1	
18	F	0015 3.5	0623 6.9	1303 3.5	1913 6.9
19	SA	0132 3.6	0757 7.1	1432 3.3	2033 7.2
20	SU	0254 3.3	0901 7.6	1546 2.8	2129 7.7
21	M	0357 2.9	0949 8.1	1635 2.3	2213 8.1
22	TU	0442 2.4	1029 8.5	1714 1.9	2251 8.5
23	W	0520 2.0	1105 8.8	1750 1.6	2325 8.7
24	TH	0554 1.7	1138 9.0	1824 1.4	○ 2357 8.9
25	F	0626 1.5	1210 9.1	1856 1.3	
26	SA	0028 8.9	0656 1.4	1241 9.2	1925 1.3
27	SU	0059 9.0	0726 1.4	1313 9.2	1953 1.3
28	M	0131 9.0	0757 1.4	1345 9.1	2021 1.5

MARCH

Date	Day	Time m	Time m	Time m	Time m
1	TU	0203 8.9	0829 1.6	1421 9.0	2052 1.8
2	W	0239 8.6	0904 1.9	1501 8.6	2128 2.2
3	TH	0323 8.2	0948 2.4	1551 8.1	◑ 2217 2.8
4	F	0421 7.7	1049 2.9	1659 7.5	2333 3.3
5	SA	0542 7.3	1220 3.2	1828 7.3	
6	SU	0122 3.3	0716 7.4	1407 2.9	2003 7.6
7	M	0254 2.7	0838 8.1	1530 2.1	2116 8.2
8	TU	0400 2.0	0938 8.8	1632 1.3	2210 8.9
9	W	0453 1.3	1027 9.5	1723 0.6	2256 9.4
10	TH	0540 0.8	1113 9.9	1808 0.2	● 2339 9.7
11	F	0624 0.5	1155 10.1	1850 0.1	
12	SA	0019 9.7	0704 0.4	1236 10.1	1928 0.2
13	SU	0058 9.6	0741 0.6	1315 9.8	2003 0.6
14	M	0134 9.3	0816 0.9	1353 9.4	2035 1.1
15	TU	0209 8.9	0848 1.4	1429 8.9	2104 1.7
16	W	0243 8.4	0921 2.0	1507 8.2	2134 2.4
17	TH	0321 7.9	1001 2.7	1550 7.5	◐ 2215 3.1
18	F	0409 7.3	1100 3.3	1652 6.9	2321 3.7
19	SA	0527 6.8	1223 3.6	1836 6.6	
20	SU	0048 3.8	0719 6.8	1356 3.4	2004 6.9
21	M	0219 3.6	0830 7.3	1515 2.9	2101 7.5
22	TU	0330 3.0	0920 7.9	1606 2.3	2145 8.0
23	W	0416 2.4	1001 8.4	1645 1.8	2222 8.4
24	TH	0454 1.9	1037 8.7	1720 1.4	2256 8.7
25	F	0528 1.6	1110 9.0	1753 1.2	○ 2328 8.9
26	SA	0600 1.3	1141 9.1	1825 1.0	2359 9.1
27	SU	0631 1.1	1213 9.2	1856 1.0	
28	M	0031 9.1	0702 1.1	1247 9.3	1925 1.1
29	TU	0104 9.1	0735 1.1	1322 9.2	1955 1.3
30	W	0139 9.0	0809 1.3	1400 9.0	2027 1.7
31	TH	0218 8.7	0846 1.7	1443 8.5	2107 2.2

APRIL

Date	Day	Time m	Time m	Time m	Time m
1	F	0304 8.2	0934 2.3	1536 7.9	2200 2.8
2	SA	0405 7.7	1041 2.8	1650 7.3	◑ 2322 3.3
3	SU	0532 7.3	1219 3.0	1828 7.1	
4	M	0115 3.2	0708 7.5	1404 2.6	1958 7.6
5	TU	0242 2.6	0823 8.1	1519 1.8	2102 8.3
6	W	0343 1.9	0920 8.8	1614 1.1	2151 8.9
7	TH	0434 1.2	1007 9.4	1701 0.6	2235 9.3
8	F	0518 0.8	1051 9.7	1744 0.3	● 2315 9.5
9	SA	0600 0.5	1131 9.8	1822 0.3	2352 9.5
10	SU	0638 0.5	1210 9.7	1857 0.5	
11	M	0028 9.3	0713 0.7	1247 9.5	1928 0.9
12	TU	0102 9.1	0746 1.1	1323 9.1	1956 1.4
13	W	0136 8.8	0817 1.5	1358 8.6	2023 1.9
14	TH	0209 8.4	0849 2.0	1434 8.1	2052 2.5
15	F	0246 7.9	0928 2.6	1517 7.4	2133 3.1
16	SA	0332 7.4	1024 3.1	1613 6.9	◐ 2235 3.6
17	SU	0438 6.9	1143 3.4	1748 6.6	
18	M	0001 3.8	0628 6.8	1306 3.3	1920 6.8
19	TU	0126 3.6	0745 7.2	1421 2.9	2020 7.3
20	W	0238 3.1	0838 7.7	1518 2.3	2105 7.9
21	TH	0330 2.5	0921 8.2	1601 1.8	2144 8.3
22	F	0412 2.0	0958 8.6	1639 1.4	2219 8.7
23	SA	0449 1.6	1033 8.9	1716 1.1	2253 8.9
24	SU	0526 1.2	1108 9.1	1751 1.0	○ 2327 9.1
25	M	0603 1.0	1144 9.2	1826 0.9	
26	TU	0003 9.2	0640 0.9	1223 9.2	1900 1.0
27	W	0041 9.2	0717 1.0	1304 9.1	1935 1.3
28	TH	0122 9.1	0757 1.2	1348 8.8	2014 1.7
29	F	0207 8.7	0842 1.6	1437 8.4	2100 2.2
30	SA	0259 8.3	0936 2.1	1536 7.8	2200 2.7

Chart Datum: 4·93 metres below Ordnance Datum (Newlyn)

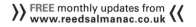

TIME ZONE (UT)
For Summer Time add ONE hour in **non-shaded areas**

ENGLAND – LIVERPOOL (ALFRED DOCK)

LAT 53°24'N LONG 3°01'W

TIMES AND HEIGHTS OF HIGH AND LOW WATERS

SPRING & NEAP TIDES
Dates in red are SPRINGS
Dates in blue are NEAPS

YEAR **2005**

MAY

Date	Day	Time	m	Time	m	Time	m	Time	m	Moon
1	SU	0405	7.9	1048	2.5	1652	7.4	2323	3.0	◑
2	M	0528	7.6	1218	2.5	1820	7.4			
3	TU	0058	2.9	0649	7.8	1344	2.2	1936	7.8	
4	W	0216	2.4	0757	8.3	1453	1.7	2035	8.3	
5	TH	0316	1.9	0853	8.8	1548	1.2	2125	8.7	
6	F	0407	1.4	0942	9.1	1634	0.9	2208	9.0	
7	SA	0452	1.1	1026	9.3	1714	0.8	2248	9.1	
8	SU	0533	0.9	1107	9.3	1751	0.9	2325	9.1	●
9	M	0611	1.0	1145	9.2	1824	1.1			
10	TU	0000	9.0	0646	1.1	1222	9.0	1854	1.4	
11	W	0034	8.9	0719	1.4	1257	8.7	1922	1.7	
12	TH	0108	8.7	0752	1.7	1332	8.4	1950	2.1	
13	F	0143	8.4	0826	2.1	1410	8.0	2023	2.5	
14	SA	0222	8.0	0906	2.5	1453	7.6	2104	2.9	
15	SU	0307	7.6	0958	2.9	1544	7.1	2201	3.3	
16	M	0403	7.3	1102	3.1	1651	6.9	2313	3.5	◐
17	TU	0518	7.1	1210	3.1	1815	6.9			
18	W	0025	3.4	0638	7.2	1316	2.8	1922	7.2	
19	TH	0131	3.1	0740	7.6	1415	2.4	2014	7.7	
20	F	0230	2.6	0829	8.0	1508	2.0	2058	8.2	
21	SA	0322	2.1	0913	8.4	1555	1.6	2139	8.6	
22	SU	0409	1.7	0955	8.7	1638	1.3	2218	8.9	
23	M	0454	1.4	1037	9.0	1720	1.1	2258	9.1	○
24	TU	0538	1.1	1120	9.1	1801	1.0	2340	9.3	
25	W	0622	1.0	1205	9.2	1842	1.1			
26	TH	0025	9.3	0707	1.0	1253	9.1	1924	1.3	
27	F	0113	9.1	0755	1.1	1344	8.8	2010	1.6	
28	SA	0204	8.9	0847	1.4	1437	8.5	2102	2.0	
29	SU	0300	8.6	0944	1.7	1536	8.1	2202	2.4	
30	M	0402	8.3	1048	1.9	1643	7.8	2311	2.6	◑
31	TU	0510	8.2	1157	2.0	1754	7.7			

JUNE

Date	Day	Time	m	Time	m	Time	m	Time	m	Moon
1	W	0025	2.6	0619	8.1	1309	2.0	1902	7.8	
2	TH	0138	2.4	0724	8.2	1417	1.9	2002	8.0	
3	F	0242	2.1	0823	8.4	1514	1.7	2055	8.3	
4	SA	0336	1.8	0915	8.6	1602	1.6	2141	8.5	
5	SU	0424	1.6	1002	8.7	1644	1.5	2223	8.7	
6	M	0506	1.5	1045	8.7	1720	1.6	2301	8.8	●
7	TU	0546	1.5	1124	8.7	1754	1.6	2337	8.7	
8	W	0623	1.6	1202	8.6	1826	1.8			
9	TH	0012	8.7	0659	1.7	1238	8.5	1857	2.0	
10	F	0048	8.6	0735	1.9	1314	8.3	1929	2.2	
11	SA	0125	8.4	0811	2.1	1352	8.1	2004	2.4	
12	SU	0204	8.2	0850	2.3	1432	7.9	2044	2.6	
13	M	0246	8.0	0933	2.5	1516	7.6	2132	2.9	
14	TU	0333	7.8	1022	2.7	1606	7.4	2227	3.1	
15	W	0426	7.6	1118	2.8	1705	7.3	2329	3.1	◐
16	TH	0527	7.5	1217	2.7	1810	7.3			
17	F	0033	3.0	0629	7.6	1319	2.6	1912	7.6	
18	SA	0136	2.8	0730	7.9	1419	2.3	2009	8.0	
19	SU	0237	2.4	0826	8.2	1515	1.9	2100	8.4	
20	M	0334	2.0	0920	8.5	1607	1.6	2149	8.8	
21	TU	0428	1.6	1012	8.8	1656	1.4	2236	9.1	
22	W	0521	1.3	1104	9.0	1744	1.2	2325	9.3	○
23	TH	0613	1.0	1155	9.1	1832	1.2			
24	F	0015	9.4	0705	0.9	1247	9.1	1920	1.2	
25	SA	0106	9.4	0757	0.8	1339	9.1	2009	1.4	
26	SU	0158	9.4	0848	0.9	1431	8.9	2059	1.6	
27	M	0250	9.2	0938	1.1	1523	8.6	2150	1.9	
28	TU	0344	8.9	1030	1.4	1617	8.2	2245	2.2	◑
29	W	0440	8.5	1124	1.8	1716	7.9	2344	2.4	
30	TH	0541	8.2	1222	2.1	1821	7.7			

JULY

Date	Day	Time	m	Time	m	Time	m	Time	m	Moon
1	F	0049	2.6	0646	8.0	1327	2.4	1925	7.7	
2	SA	0200	2.6	0750	7.9	1432	2.4	2025	7.8	
3	SU	0305	2.4	0850	8.0	1529	2.3	2118	8.1	
4	M	0400	2.2	0943	8.2	1615	2.2	2204	8.3	
5	TU	0447	2.0	1029	8.3	1655	2.1	2245	8.5	
6	W	0529	1.9	1111	8.4	1732	2.1	2322	8.6	●
7	TH	0609	1.8	1149	8.4	1808	2.0	2358	8.7	
8	F	0647	1.8	1224	8.4	1842	2.0			
9	SA	0033	8.7	0723	1.8	1259	8.4	1914	2.1	
10	SU	0109	8.6	0757	1.9	1334	8.3	1948	2.1	
11	M	0145	8.5	0831	2.0	1410	8.2	2024	2.2	
12	TU	0222	8.4	0905	2.1	1447	8.1	2103	2.4	
13	W	0301	8.2	0943	2.3	1527	7.9	2146	2.6	
14	TH	0344	8.1	1027	2.5	1614	7.7	2237	2.9	◐
15	F	0435	7.9	1120	2.7	1710	7.5	2338	3.0	
16	SA	0535	7.7	1225	2.8	1816	7.5			
17	SU	0049	3.0	0641	7.7	1336	2.7	1924	7.7	
18	M	0202	2.7	0750	7.9	1445	2.4	2030	8.1	
19	TU	0311	2.3	0857	8.2	1546	2.0	2129	8.6	
20	W	0414	1.8	0958	8.6	1642	1.6	2223	9.1	
21	TH	0512	1.3	1054	9.0	1735	1.3	2314	9.5	○
22	F	0608	0.9	1147	9.2	1826	1.1			
23	SA	0004	9.7	0700	0.5	1238	9.4	1914	0.9	
24	SU	0054	9.8	0749	0.4	1326	9.4	2000	1.0	
25	M	0142	9.8	0835	0.5	1412	9.2	2044	1.1	
26	TU	0229	9.6	0918	0.7	1457	8.9	2127	1.5	
27	W	0316	9.2	1001	1.2	1543	8.5	2212	1.9	
28	TH	0404	8.7	1045	1.8	1632	8.0	2303	2.4	◑
29	F	0458	8.1	1136	2.4	1730	7.5			
30	SA	0004	2.9	0603	7.6	1236	2.9	1843	7.3	
31	SU	0118	3.1	0719	7.4	1346	3.1	1958	7.4	

AUGUST

Date	Day	Time	m	Time	m	Time	m	Time	m	Moon
1	M	0239	3.0	0831	7.5	1459	3.0	2059	7.7	
2	TU	0346	2.6	0928	7.7	1557	2.7	2149	8.1	
3	W	0437	2.3	1016	8.1	1641	2.4	2232	8.5	
4	TH	0519	2.0	1058	8.3	1720	2.2	2309	8.7	
5	F	0557	1.8	1134	8.5	1756	2.0	2344	8.8	●
6	SA	0633	1.7	1208	8.5	1829	1.9			
7	SU	0017	8.9	0705	1.6	1240	8.6	1859	1.8	
8	M	0049	8.8	0736	1.6	1311	8.6	1929	1.8	
9	TU	0121	8.8	0805	1.7	1342	8.5	2000	1.9	
10	W	0153	8.7	0834	1.8	1414	8.4	2034	2.0	
11	TH	0227	8.6	0905	2.0	1449	8.3	2110	2.3	
12	F	0305	8.4	0940	2.3	1531	8.0	2152	2.6	
13	SA	0353	8.0	1025	2.7	1623	7.7	2248	3.0	◐
14	SU	0454	7.7	1132	3.1	1732	7.4			
15	M	0009	3.2	0607	7.4	1302	3.2	1853	7.5	
16	TU	0140	3.0	0730	7.6	1426	2.8	2012	7.9	
17	W	0301	2.4	0849	8.0	1536	2.3	2118	8.6	
18	TH	0408	1.7	0952	8.6	1634	1.7	2213	9.2	
19	F	0506	1.0	1045	9.1	1726	1.1	2302	9.7	○
20	SA	0558	0.5	1134	9.5	1814	0.8	2349	10.0	
21	SU	0646	0.2	1219	9.6	1859	0.6			
22	M	0034	10.1	0730	0.1	1303	9.6	1941	0.6	
23	TU	0118	10.0	0810	0.3	1345	9.4	2020	0.9	
24	W	0201	9.7	0849	0.7	1425	9.0	2058	1.3	
25	TH	0242	9.2	0925	1.3	1504	8.5	2138	1.9	
26	F	0325	8.5	1004	2.1	1547	8.0	2223	2.6	◑
27	SA	0414	7.8	1050	2.8	1638	7.4	2324	3.1	
28	SU	0519	7.2	1151	3.4	1757	7.0			
29	M	0044	3.4	0653	6.9	1309	3.6	1933	7.1	
30	TU	0221	3.3	0814	7.1	1437	3.4	2041	7.6	
31	W	0335	2.8	0911	7.6	1543	3.0	2131	8.1	

Chart Datum: 4·93 metres below Ordnance Datum (Newlyn)

TIME ZONE (UT)
For Summer Time add ONE hour in **non-shaded areas**

ENGLAND – LIVERPOOL (ALFRED DOCK)

LAT 53°24′N LONG 3°01′W

TIMES AND HEIGHTS OF HIGH AND LOW WATERS

SPRING & NEAP TIDES
Dates in **red** are **SPRINGS**
Dates in **blue** are **NEAPS**

YEAR **2005**

SEPTEMBER

Date	Day	Time	m	Time	m	Time	m	Time	m
1	TH	0422	2.3	0957	8.0	1628	2.5	2212	8.5
2	F	0501	1.9	1036	8.4	1706	2.1	2249	8.8
3	SA	0536	1.6	1111	8.6	1739	1.8	● 2322	9.0
4	SU	0609	1.4	1143	8.7	1809	1.7	2353	9.0
5	M	0639	1.4	1213	8.8	1837	1.6		
6	TU	0022	9.0	0707	1.4	1242	8.8	1905	1.5
7	W	0051	9.0	0734	1.4	1311	8.8	1935	1.6
8	TH	0122	8.9	0802	1.6	1342	8.7	2006	1.8
9	F	0155	8.8	0831	1.9	1416	8.5	2040	2.1
10	SA	0233	8.5	0904	2.3	1456	8.2	2120	2.5
11	SU	0321	8.0	0947	2.8	1550	7.7	◐ 2215	3.0
12	M	0425	7.5	1056	3.3	1704	7.3	2347	3.3
13	TU	0551	7.2	1243	3.5	1837	7.3		
14	W	0133	3.1	0727	7.4	1418	3.0	2004	7.9
15	TH	0257	2.3	0845	8.0	1527	2.2	2107	8.7
16	F	0400	1.5	0941	8.8	1622	1.5	2158	9.4
17	SA	0453	0.7	1029	9.3	1711	0.9	2244	9.9
18	SU	0539	0.3	1113	9.6	1755	0.6	○ 2327	10.2
19	M	0623	0.1	1155	9.7	1837	0.4		
20	TU	0009	10.2	0703	0.1	1235	9.6	1916	0.6
21	W	0051	9.9	0740	0.5	1313	9.4	1952	0.9
22	TH	0130	9.5	0814	1.0	1350	9.0	2028	1.4
23	F	0208	9.0	0847	1.7	1426	8.5	2104	2.0
24	SA	0248	8.3	0921	2.4	1504	8.0	2146	2.7
25	SU	0333	7.6	1003	3.1	1552	7.4	◑ 2247	3.3
26	M	0437	6.9	1107	3.7	1710	6.9		
27	TU	0013	3.6	0625	6.6	1234	3.9	1902	6.9
28	W	0153	3.4	0748	7.0	1409	3.6	2012	7.4
29	TH	0306	2.8	0844	7.5	1517	3.1	2102	8.0
30	F	0352	2.3	0928	8.0	1601	2.5	2143	8.5

OCTOBER

Date	Day	Time	m	Time	m	Time	m	Time	m
1	SA	0430	1.8	1006	8.5	1638	2.1	2219	8.8
2	SU	0503	1.5	1040	8.7	1710	1.7	2252	9.0
3	M	0535	1.3	1111	8.9	1740	1.5	● 2321	9.1
4	TU	0605	1.2	1141	9.0	1810	1.4	2351	9.1
5	W	0635	1.2	1210	9.0	1841	1.3		
6	TH	0021	9.1	0704	1.3	1241	9.0	1912	1.4
7	F	0055	9.0	0734	1.6	1315	8.9	1945	1.6
8	SA	0132	8.8	0805	1.9	1352	8.6	2021	2.0
9	SU	0214	8.4	0842	2.4	1436	8.2	2104	2.5
10	M	0305	7.9	0930	2.9	1534	7.8	◐ 2207	3.0
11	TU	0415	7.3	1046	3.4	1652	7.4	2344	3.2
12	W	0548	7.1	1234	3.4	1828	7.5		
13	TH	0126	2.8	0722	7.5	1404	2.9	1948	8.1
14	F	0244	2.1	0830	8.2	1509	2.1	2048	8.8
15	SA	0342	1.3	0922	8.9	1602	1.5	2137	9.4
16	SU	0431	0.7	1007	9.3	1649	0.9	2222	9.8
17	M	0515	0.4	1048	9.6	1731	0.7	○ 2304	10.0
18	TU	0555	0.3	1128	9.6	1812	0.6	2344	9.9
19	W	0633	0.5	1205	9.5	1850	0.8		
20	TH	0023	9.6	0707	0.9	1242	9.3	1925	1.1
21	F	0101	9.2	0739	1.4	1317	8.9	2000	1.6
22	SA	0138	8.7	0810	2.0	1353	8.5	2036	2.1
23	SU	0217	8.1	0843	2.6	1431	8.0	2117	2.7
24	M	0301	7.5	0924	3.2	1517	7.5	2215	3.3
25	TU	0359	6.9	1025	3.7	1623	7.1	◑ 2333	3.5
26	W	0538	6.6	1148	4.0	1811	7.0		
27	TH	0057	3.4	0705	6.9	1314	3.7	1927	7.3
28	F	0212	3.0	0803	7.4	1426	3.3	2021	7.8
29	SA	0305	2.5	0849	7.9	1516	2.7	2104	8.3
30	SU	0346	2.0	0928	8.4	1556	2.2	2141	8.6
31	M	0422	1.6	1003	8.7	1631	1.8	2215	8.9

NOVEMBER

Date	Day	Time	m	Time	m	Time	m	Time	m
1	TU	0456	1.4	1036	8.9	1706	1.6	2247	9.1
2	W	0530	1.2	1108	9.1	1742	1.4	● 2321	9.2
3	TH	0605	1.2	1141	9.2	1818	1.3	2357	9.2
4	F	0639	1.4	1217	9.1	1855	1.4		
5	SA	0036	9.1	0714	1.6	1257	9.0	1933	1.6
6	SU	0119	8.8	0751	1.9	1341	8.8	2016	1.9
7	M	0207	8.4	0835	2.4	1430	8.4	2107	2.3
8	TU	0303	8.0	0930	2.8	1531	8.1	2214	2.6
9	W	0413	7.6	1045	3.2	1645	7.8	◐ 2338	2.7
10	TH	0538	7.4	1213	3.1	1808	7.9		
11	F	0103	2.5	0658	7.7	1335	2.8	1920	8.3
12	SA	0216	2.0	0803	8.2	1441	2.2	2020	8.8
13	SU	0315	1.5	0856	8.7	1536	1.7	2112	9.2
14	M	0404	1.1	0941	9.1	1623	1.3	2158	9.4
15	TU	0448	0.9	1023	9.3	1707	1.1	2241	9.5
16	W	0527	0.9	1103	9.3	1747	1.1	○ 2322	9.4
17	TH	0603	1.1	1140	9.3	1826	1.2		
18	F	0000	9.2	0637	1.4	1216	9.1	1903	1.5
19	SA	0038	8.9	0710	1.8	1252	8.9	1940	1.8
20	SU	0115	8.6	0742	2.2	1329	8.6	2017	2.2
21	M	0154	8.2	0816	2.6	1409	8.3	2058	2.6
22	TU	0237	7.7	0855	3.1	1453	7.9	2148	3.0
23	W	0327	7.3	0947	3.4	1547	7.5	◑ 2248	3.2
24	TH	0432	7.0	1054	3.7	1655	7.3	2353	3.3
25	F	0553	6.9	1205	3.6	1815	7.3		
26	SA	0058	3.1	0704	7.2	1311	3.4	1920	7.6
27	SU	0158	2.7	0758	7.6	1411	3.0	2011	7.9
28	M	0251	2.3	0843	8.1	1504	2.6	2055	8.3
29	TU	0337	2.0	0923	8.5	1551	2.1	2136	8.7
30	W	0419	1.7	1001	8.8	1635	1.8	2216	8.9

DECEMBER

Date	Day	Time	m	Time	m	Time	m	Time	m
1	TH	0500	1.5	1040	9.1	1718	1.5	● 2258	9.1
2	F	0541	1.4	1120	9.2	1802	1.4	2341	9.2
3	SA	0622	1.4	1202	9.3	1846	1.3		
4	SU	0026	9.1	0704	1.6	1248	9.3	1932	1.4
5	M	0115	8.9	0748	1.8	1337	9.1	2021	1.6
6	TU	0206	8.7	0837	2.1	1429	8.9	2114	1.8
7	W	0301	8.4	0931	2.4	1526	8.7	2213	2.0
8	TH	0402	8.1	1032	2.6	1628	8.4	◐ 2316	2.2
9	F	0510	7.8	1140	2.7	1735	8.3		
10	SA	0025	2.3	0621	7.8	1252	2.7	1844	8.3
11	SU	0136	2.2	0728	8.0	1403	2.5	1948	8.5
12	M	0241	2.0	0827	8.3	1505	2.2	2046	8.7
13	TU	0335	1.8	0918	8.6	1559	1.9	2138	8.8
14	W	0422	1.7	1003	8.8	1646	1.7	2224	8.9
15	TH	0502	1.6	1044	9.0	1729	1.6	○ 2306	8.9
16	F	0540	1.7	1123	9.0	1810	1.6	2345	8.8
17	SA	0616	1.8	1200	9.0	1850	1.7		
18	SU	0023	8.7	0651	2.0	1237	8.9	1928	1.9
19	M	0100	8.5	0725	2.2	1314	8.8	2005	2.1
20	TU	0138	8.3	0758	2.4	1352	8.6	2042	2.3
21	W	0217	8.1	0834	2.7	1432	8.3	2120	2.5
22	TH	0258	7.8	0915	2.9	1515	8.1	2203	2.8
23	F	0344	7.6	1004	3.1	1603	7.8	◑ 2253	2.9
24	SA	0438	7.3	1100	3.3	1659	7.6	2351	3.0
25	SU	0541	7.2	1204	3.4	1801	7.5		
26	M	0054	3.0	0647	7.4	1310	3.2	1905	7.7
27	TU	0157	2.8	0749	7.7	1415	2.9	2005	8.0
28	W	0256	2.4	0843	8.1	1515	2.5	2101	8.3
29	TH	0349	2.1	0932	8.6	1610	2.1	2152	8.7
30	F	0438	1.8	1019	9.0	1702	1.7	2242	9.0
31	SA	0526	1.5	1106	9.3	1753	1.3	● 2332	9.2

Chart Datum: 4·93 metres below Ordnance Datum (Newlyn)

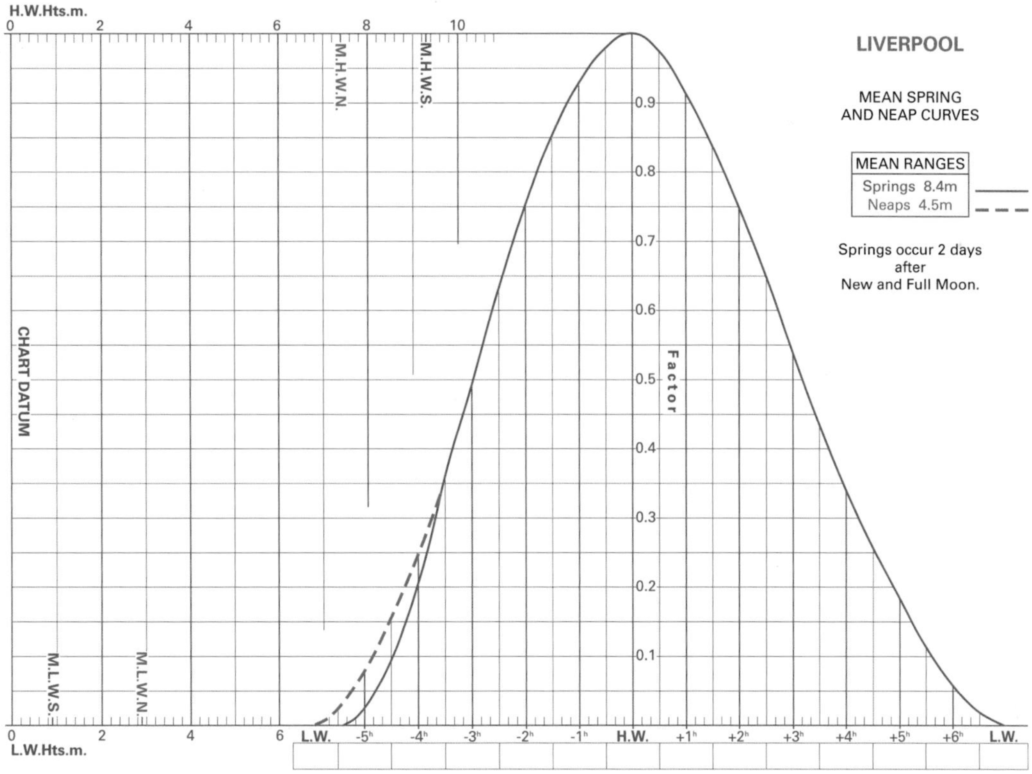
H.W.Hts.m.
0
2
4
6
8
10
M.H.W.N.
M.H.W.S.
CHART DATUM
0.9
0.8
0.7
0.6
0.5
0.4
0.3
0.2
0.1
Factor
M.L.W.S.
M.L.W.N.
L.W.Hts.m.
L.W.
-5h
-4h
-3h
-2h
-1h
H.W.
+1h
+2h
+3h
+4h
+5h
+6h
L.W.
LIVERPOOL
MEAN SPRING AND NEAP CURVES
MEAN RANGES
Springs 8.4m
Neaps 4.5m
Springs occur 2 days after New and Full Moon.

9.10.12 LIVERPOOL

Merseyside **53°24'·22N 03°00'·28W** (Liver Bldg)

CHARTS AC *1826, 1978,* 1951, 3490; Imray C62; OS 108

TIDES +0015 Dover; ML 5·2; Duration 0535; Zone 0 (UT)

Standard Port LIVERPOOL (ALFRED DOCK) (⟵)

Times					Height (metres)			
	High Water		Low Water		MHWS	MHWN	MLWN	MLWS
	0000	0600	0200	0700	9·3	7·4	2·9	0·9
	1200	1800	1400	1900				
Differences SOUTHPORT								
	−0020	−0010	No data		−0·3	−0·3	No data	
FORMBY								
	−0015	−0010	−0020	−0020	−0·3	−0·1	0·0	+0·1
GLADSTONE DOCK								
	−0003	−0003	−0003	−0003	−0·1	−0·1	0·0	−0·1
EASTHAM (River Mersey)								
	+0010	+0010	+0009	+0009	+0·3	+0·1	−0·1	−0·3
HALE HEAD (River Mersey)								
	+0030	+0025	No data		−2·4	−2·5	No data	
WIDNES (River Mersey)								
	+0040	+0045	+0400	+0345	−4·2	−4·4	−2·5	−0·3
FIDDLER'S FERRY (River Mersey)								
	+0100	+0115	+0540	+0450	−5·9	−6·3	−2·4	−0·4
HILBRE ISLAND (River Dee)								
	−0015	−0012	−0010	−0015	−0·3	−0·2	+0·2	+0·4
MOSTYN DOCKS (River Dee)								
	−0020	−0015	−0020	−0020	−0·8	−0·7	No data	
CONNAH'S QUAY (River Dee)								
	0000	+0015	+0355	+0340	−4·6	−4·4	Dries	
CHESTER (River Dee)								
	+0105	+0105	+0500	+0500	−5·3	−5·4	Dries	
COLWYN BAY								
	−0020	−0020	No data		−1·5	−1·3	No data	
LLANDUDNO								
	−0020	−0020	−0035	−0040	−1·7	−1·4	−0·7	−0·3

NOTE: LW time differences at Connah's Quay give the end of a LW stand lasting about 3¾hrs at sp and 5hrs at nps. A bore occurs in the R Dee at Chester.

SHELTER Good at marina in Brunswick and Coburg docks. Ent is 1M S of Liver Bldg, abeam Pluckington Bank (PB) WCM buoy; access approx HW ±2¼ sp, ±1½ nps, 0600-2200 Mar-Oct. Good shelter also in Canning and Albert Docks but access HW–2 to HW, and not on every tide. ⚓ on the SW side of river but only in fair weather.

NAVIGATION WPT Bar PHM lt F 53°32′·02N 03°20′·98W, 111° to Q1 NCM lt F, 2·8M. From Q1 to marina is 15·5M via Queen's and Crosby Chans. Both chans have training banks which cover and it is unwise to navigate between the floats/buoys and the trng banks. In strong NW'lies there is swell on the bar. Wind against tide causes steep, breaking seas in outer reaches of River Mersey. Inside the buoyed chan is safe; elsewhere local knowledge and great caution needed as the whole area (R Dee, R Mersey to R Alt and N to Morecambe Bay) is littered with sandbanks. Sp tidal streams exceed 5kn within the river. For **R Dee**: WPT 53°25′·13N 03°13′·17W, Hilbre Swash HE2 ECM buoy, Q(3) 10s, (chan shifts). From the W use Welsh Chan. The Dee estuary mostly dries.

Leeds & Liverpool Canal (BWB) gives access to E Coast, ent at Stanley Dock. Max draft 1·0m, air draft 2·2m, beam 4·3m, LOA 18·3m. Liverpool to Goole 161M, 103 locks.

Manchester Ship Canal, ent at Eastham Locks, leads 31M to Salford Quays or R Weaver for boatyards at Northwich. Obtain licence from MSC Co ☎ 0151 327 1461.

LIGHTS AND MARKS Bar PHM lt F, Fl 5s 12m 21M, Horn (2) 20s, Racon. Formby SWM lt F, Iso 4s, is at the ent to Queen's Chan which is marked by PHM lt Flts and SHM buoys, and 3 NCM buoys, numbered Q1-Q12. Crosby Chan is similarly marked, C1-C23. From Crosby SWM lt F, Oc 5s, the track up-river is approx 145°. See also 9.10.3. The Liver Bldg (twin spires) and Port of Liverpool Bldg (dome) are conspic on the E bank opposite Birkenhead Docks.

Liverpool continued overleaf

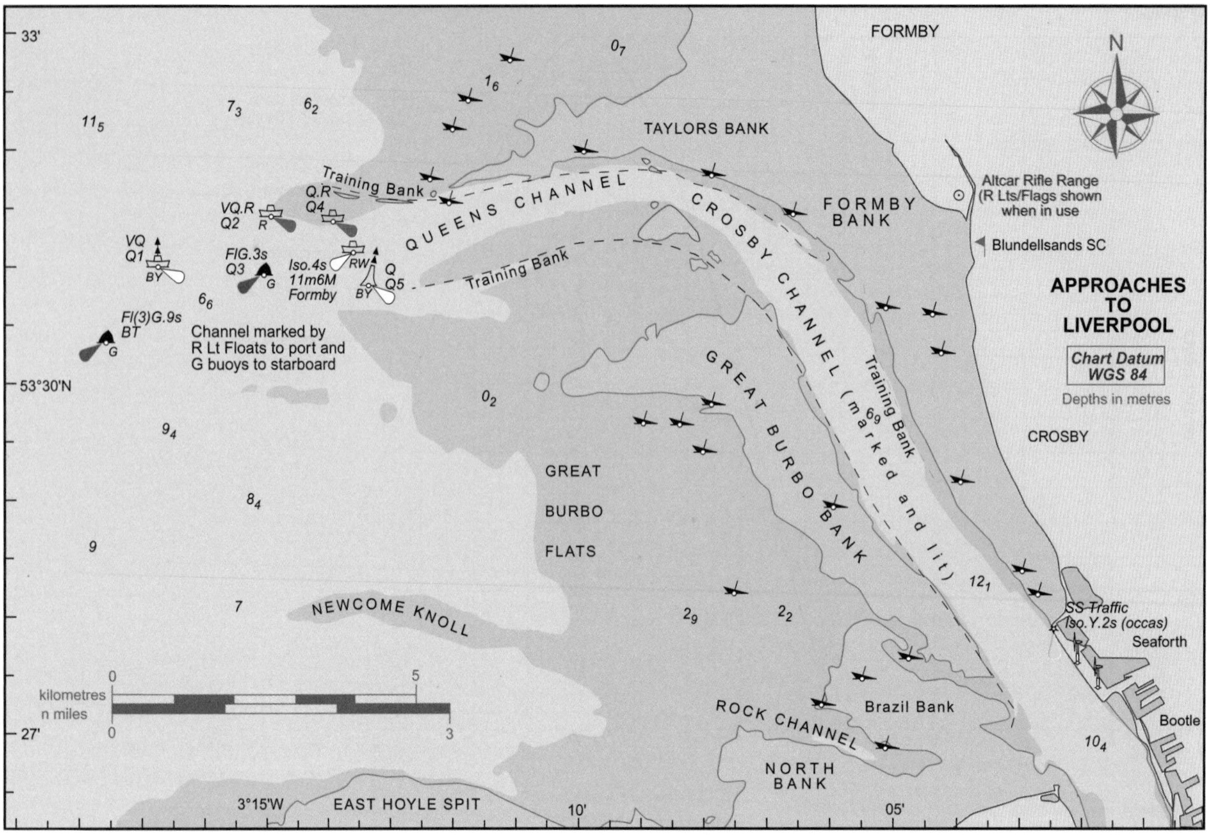
FORMBY
TAYLORS BANK
APPROACHES TO LIVERPOOL
Chart Datum WGS 84
Depths in metres
Altcar Rifle Range (R Lts/Flags shown when in use
Blundellsands SC
FORMBY BANK
QUEENS CHANNEL
CROSBY CHANNEL
Training Bank
Training Bank (marked and lit)
GREAT BURBO BANK
GREAT BURBO FLATS
NEWCOME KNOLL
ROCK CHANNEL
Brazil Bank
NORTH BANK
EAST HOYLE SPIT
CROSBY
Seaforth
Bootle
SS Traffic Iso.Y.2s (occas)
Channel marked by R Lt Floats to port and G buoys to starboard
VQ Q1 BY
VQ.R Q2 R
Q.R Q4
Fl.G.3s Q3 G
Iso.4s 11m6M Formby RW
Q Q5 BY
Fl(3)G.9s BT G
kilometres
n miles
33'
53°30'N
27'
3°15'W
10'
05'

R/T Monitor *Mersey Radio* VHF Ch **12** 16 (H24). Local nav and gale warnings are broadcast on receipt on Ch 12. Traffic movements, nav warnings and weather reports are broadcast on Ch 09 at HW–3 and –2. Radar Ch 18 covers a radius of 20M and in poor vis can offer continuous fixing. *Liverpool Marina* Ch **37M**. Eastham Locks Ch 07 (H24). Manchester Ship Canal Ch 14.

TELEPHONE (Dial code 0151) Port Ops 949 6134/5, 📠 949 56090; MRSC 931 3341; Marinecall 09066 526245; Police 709 6010; Ⓗ 709 0141.

FACILITIES **Liverpool Marina** (300 + 50) ☎ 707 6777 , (0600-2200 Mar–Oct), 📠 707 6770; harbourside@liverpoolmarina.com. £1.65. Ent via Brunswick Dock lock, pontoons inside, min depth 3·5m; night locking as pre-arranged. Conspic black control bldg at lock ent has IPTS (sigs 2, 3 & 5). £1.76, D, P (½M), BH (60 ton), Slip, CH, SM, ⌼, ♿, Bar, R (☎ 707 6888); **Albert Dock** ☎ 709 6558; access through Canning Dock, VHF Ch M when ent manned, AB, FW, AC; **Royal Mersey YC** ☎ 645 3204, Slip, M, P, D, L, FW, R, Bar. **W Kirby SC** ☎ 625 5579, AB (at HW), Slip, M (in Dee Est), L, FW, C (30ton), Bar; **Hoylake SC** ☎ 632 2616, Slip, M, FW, Bar; **Services:** CH, SM, ME, El, ⚒, ACA, Ⓔ. **City** EC Wed; all facilities, ✉, Ⓑ, ⇌, ✈.

ADJACENT ANCHORAGE

RIVER ALT, Merseyside, **53°31′·42N 03°03′·80W**. AC *1978*, 1951. HW –0008 on Dover; see 9.10.12. Good shelter but only for LOA <8·5m x 1·2m draft on a HW of at least 8m. Mersey E training wall can be crossed HW±2. Ent to chan (shifts frequently) is E of C14 PHM lt float, thence marked by locally-laid Y Fairway buoy and perches on the training wall. Unsafe to ⚓ in R Alt; pick up a free mooring off the SC and contact club. Local knowledge advised. Facilities very limited. **Blundellsands SC** ☎ (0151) 929 2101 (occas), Slip, L (at HW), FW, Bar.

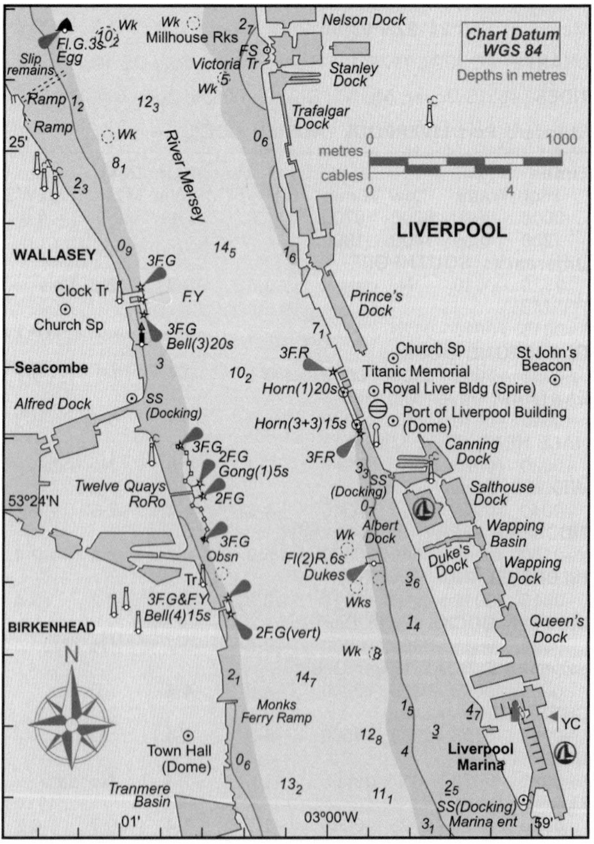
Chart Datum WGS 84
Depths in metres
Nelson Dock
Stanley Dock
Trafalgar Dock
Millhouse Rks
Victoria Tr
River Mersey
LIVERPOOL
metres
cables
WALLASEY
Clock Tr
Church Sp
Seacombe
Alfred Dock
Twelve Quays RoRo
BIRKENHEAD
Town Hall (Dome)
Tranmere Basin
Monks Ferry Ramp
Prince's Dock
Church Sp
St John's Beacon
Titanic Memorial
Royal Liver Bldg (Spire)
Port of Liverpool Building (Dome)
Canning Dock
Salthouse Dock
Albert Dock
Wapping Basin
Wapping Dock
Duke's Dock
Queen's Dock
Liverpool Marina
SS(Docking) Marina ent
YC
Fl.G.3s Egg
Slip remains
Ramp
3F.G
F.Y
3F.G Bell(3)20s
SS (Docking)
3F.G
2F.G Gong(1)5s
2F.G
3F.G Obsn
3F.G&F.Y Bell(4)15s
2F.G(vert)
3F.R
Horn(1)20s
Horn(3+3)15s
3F.R
SS (Docking)
Fl(2)R.6s Dukes
Wk
Wks
25'
53°24'N
01'
03°00'W
59'

9.10.13 ISLE OF MAN

CHARTS AC Irish Sea *1826, 1411*; 2094 (small scale); 2696 (ports). *Imray, C26, Y70. OS 95.*

The Isle of Man is one of the British Islands, set in the Irish Sea roughly equidistant from England, Scotland, Wales and Ireland but it is not part of the UK. It has a large degree of self-government. Lights are maintained by the Commissioners of Northern Lighthouses in Scotland. Manx hbrs are administered by the IOM Government.

Directions. *Isle of Man - Tides, Directions and anchorages (1997)* is recommended; from Hunter Publications, Wild Boar Cottage, Rawcliffe Rd, St Michaels, Preston PR3 0UH, ☎ 01995-679240, 📠 679740.

Passage information. See 9.10.5.

Distances. See 9.10.2 for distances between ports in Area 10 and 9.0.7 for distances across the Irish Sea, North Channel and St George's Channel.

Harbours and anchorages. Most of the hbrs are on the E and S sides, but a visit to the W coast with its characteristic cliffs is worth while. The four main hbrs are treated below in an anti-clockwise direction from Peel on the W coast to Ramsey in the NE. There are good ⚓s at: Port Erin in the SW, Castletown and Derby Haven in the SE, and Laxey Bay in the E. All IOM hbrs charge the same overnight berthing fee, ie £7.47 regardless of LOA. In addition, a charge of £11.75 is levied on all visiting craft using the pontoons in Douglas Harbour; a weekly fee allows use of all hbrs.

R/T. If contact with local HMs cannot be established on VHF, vessels should call *Douglas Hbr Control* Ch 12 16 for urgent messages or other info.

Coastguard. Call Liverpool MRSC Ch 16 67; the Snaefell (IoM) aerial is linked to Liverpool by land line.

Customs. The IOM is under the same customs umbrella as the rest of the UK, and there are no formalities on landing from or returning to UK.

Weather. Forecasts can be obtained direct from the forecaster at Ronaldsway Met Office ☎ 0900 624 3200, H24. **Douglas Hbr** Control (9.10.16) can supply visibility and wind info on request.

MINOR HARBOURS IN THE ISLE OF MAN

PORT ERIN, Isle of Man, **54°05'·31N 04°46'·34W**. AC 2094, 2696. HW –0020 on Dover; ML 2·9m; Duration 0555. See 9.10.15. From S and W, Milner's Twr on Bradda Hd is conspic. Ldg lts, both FR 10/19m 5M, lead 099° into the bay. Beware the ruined bkwtr (dries 2·9m) extending N from the SW corner, marked by an unlit SHM buoy. A small hbr on the S side dries 0·8m. Raglan Pier (E arm of hbr), Oc G 5s 8m 5M. Two ⚓s W of Raglan Pier. Good ⚓ in 3-8m N of Raglan Pier, but exposed to W'lies. Call HM Port St. Mary (VHF Ch 12) ☎ 833205

CASTLETOWN BAY, Isle of Man, **54°03'·51N 04°38'·57W**. AC 2094, 2696. HW +0025 on Dover; ML 3·4m; Duration 0555. The bay gives good shelter except in SE to SW winds. From the E, keep inside the race off Dreswick Pt, or give it a wide berth. Beware Lheeah-rio Rks in W of bay, marked by PHM buoy, Fl R 3s, Bell. Hbr dries 3·1m to level sand. Access HW±2½. Berth in outer hbr or go via swing footbridge (manually opened) into inner hbr below fixed bridge. ⚓ between Lheeah-rio Rks and pier in 3m; or NW of Langness Pt. Lts: Langness lt, on Dreswick Pt, Fl (2) 30s 23m 12M. Hbr S (New) Pier, Oc R 15s 8m 5M; Inner S pier (Irish Quay), Oc R 4s 5m 5M, vis 142°-322°. 150m NW is swing bridge marked by 2 FR (hor). N pier, Oc G 4s 3m (W metal post on concrete column). VHF Ch 12 16 (when vessel due). HM ☎ 823549; Dr 823597. Facilities: **Outer hbr** Slip, L, C (20 ton) AB; **Irish Quay** AB, C, FW; **Inner hbr** AB, C, FW; **Town** P, D, Gas, ME.

LAXEY, Isle of Man, **54°13'·46N 04°23'·32W**. AC 2094. HW +0025 on Dover; +0010 and –2·0m on Liverpool; ML 4m; Duration 0550. The bay gives good shelter in SW to N winds. 2 orange ⚓s (seasonal) are close E of hbr ent; 2 more are 1M S in Garwick Bay. ⚓ about 2ca S of pierhds or in Garwick Bay. The hbr dries 3·0m to rk and is only suitable for small yachts; access HW±3 for 1·5m draft. Beware rks on N side of the narrow ent. Keep close to pier after entering to avoid training wall on NE side. AB on inside of pier; inner basin is full of local boats. Pier hd lt Oc R 3s 7m 5M, obsc when brg <318°. Bkwtr hd lt Oc G 3s 7m. HM ☎ 861663. Facilities: FW, R, ✉, Ⓑ, Bar.

9.10.14 PEEL

Isle of Man 54°13'·61N 04°41'·68W ❁❁⛵✿✿✿

CHARTS AC 2094, 2696; Imray C62; Y70; OS 95

TIDES +0005 Dover; ML 2·9; Duration 0545; Zone 0 (UT)

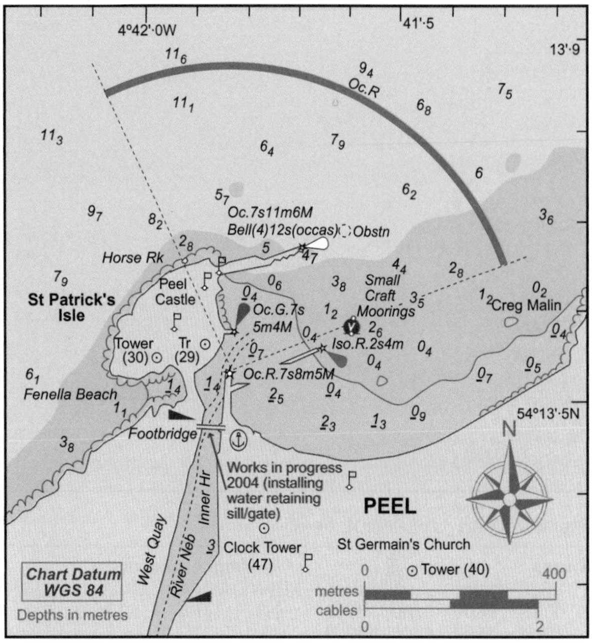
4°42'·0W
41'·5
13'·9
Oc.R
Oc.7s11m6M
Bell(4)12s(occas)
Obstn
Horse Rk
St Patrick's Isle
Peel Castle
Tower (30)
Tr (29)
Oc.G.7s 5m4M
Small Craft Moorings
Iso.R.2s4m
Oc.R.7s8m5M
Creg Malin
Fenella Beach
Footbridge
54°13'·5N
Works in progress 2004 (installing water retaining sill/gate)
PEEL
Inner Hr
West Quay
River Neb
Clock Tower (47)
St Germain's Church
Tower (40)
Chart Datum WGS 84
Depths in metres
metres
cables
0
400
2

Standard Port LIVERPOOL (⟵)

Times				Height (metres)			
High Water		Low Water		MHWS	MHWN	MLWN	MLWS
0000	0600	0200	0700	9·3	7·4	2·9	0·9
1200	1800	1400	1900				
Differences PEEL							
+0005	+0005	-0015	–0025	–4·1	–3·1	–1·4	–0·5

SHELTER Good, except in strong NW to NE winds when ent should not be attempted. 4 Y ⚓s (lifted mid Sep) off S groyne in about 2m. Hbr dries. Fin keelers may be able to berth on N bkwtr in 5m. Inner hbr dries approx 2·8m, flat sand; access HW±3, possible AB on W quay. A water retention scheme similar to Douglas is under construction, completion due spring 2005.

NAVIGATION WPT 54°13'·97N 04°41'·43W, 200° to groyne lt, 0·42M. When close in, beware groyne on S side of hbr ent, submerged at half tide.

LIGHTS AND MARKS Power stn chy (80m, grey with B top) at S end of inner hbr is conspic from W and N, R Lts are unreliable; chy brg 203° leads to hbr ent. Groyne lt and Clock Tr (conspic) in transit 200° are almost on same line. Peel Castle and 2 twrs are conspic on St Patrick's Isle to NW of hbr. No ldg lts. N bkwtr Oc 7s 11m 6M. Groyne Iso R 2s 4m. S pier hd Oc R 7s 8m 5M; vis 156°-249°. Castle jetty Oc G 7s 5m 4M.

R/T VHF Ch 12 16 (when vessel expected; at other times call *Douglas Hbr Control* Ch 12).

TELEPHONE (Dial code 01624) HM ☎/📠 842338, Mobile 07624 495036; MRSC 0151-931 3341; Weather 0696 888322; Marinecall 09066 526245; Police 631212; Dr 843636.

FACILITIES **Outer & Inner Hbrs**, AB see 9.10.13, M, Slip, FW, ME, El, ⚒, C (30 ton mobile); **Peel Sailing and Cruising Club** ☎ 842390, Showers (key via HM), R, ▣, Bar; **Services:** Gas, BY, CH, ACA. **Town** EC Thurs; P & D (cans), 🛒, R, Bar, ✉, Ⓑ, ⇌ (bus to Douglas, qv for ferries), ✈ Ronaldsway. Facilities: EC Thurs; Bar, D, P, FW, R, Slip, 🛒.

10

9.10.15 PORT ST MARY

Isle of Man **54°04'·43N 04°43'·73W**

CHARTS AC 2094, 2696; Imray C62; Y70; OS 95

TIDES +0020 Dover; ML 3·2; Duration 0605; Zone 0 (UT)

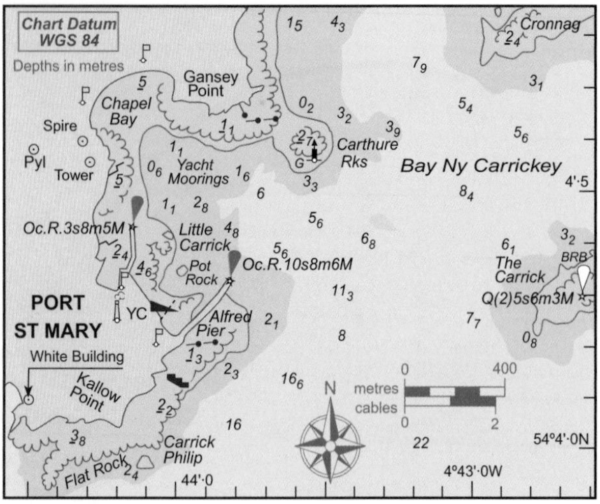
Chart Datum WGS 84
Depths in metres
Gansey Point
Chapel Bay
Spire
Pyl
Tower
Yacht Moorings
Carthure Rks
Bay Ny Carrickey
Cronnag
Oc.R.3s8m5M
Little Carrick
Pot Rock
Oc.R.10s8m6M
The Carrick
Q(2)5s6m3M
BRB
PORT ST MARY
YC
Alfred Pier
White Building
Kallow Point
Carrick Philip
Flat Rock
metres
cables
44'·0
4°43'·0W
54°4'·0N

Standard Port LIVERPOOL (⟵)

Times				Height (metres)			
High Water		Low Water		MHWS	MHWN	MLWN	MLWS
0000	0600	0200	0700	9·3	7·4	2·9	0·9
1200	1800	1400	1900				
Differences PORT ST MARY							
+0005	+0015	–0010	–0030	–3·4	–2·6	–1·3	–0·4
CALF SOUND							
+0005	+0005	–0015	–0025	–3·2	–2·6	–0·9	–0·3
PORT ERIN							
–0005	+0015	–0010	–0050	–4·1	–3·2	–1·3	–0·5

SHELTER Very good except in E or SE winds. ⚓ S of Gansey Pt, but poor holding. 6 Or Ⓥs between Alfred Pier and Little Carrick.

NAVIGATION WPT 54°04'·21N 04°43'·37W, 295° to Alfred Pier lt, 0·30M. Rky outcrops to SE of pier to 2ca offshore. Beware lobster/crab pots, especially between Calf Island and Langness Pt.

LIGHTS AND MARKS Alfred Pier, Oc R 10s 8m 6M. Inner pier, Oc R 3s 8m 5M; both lts on W trs + R band, in transit 295° lead clear S of The Carrick Rk, in centre of bay, which is marked by IDM bn, Q (2) 5s 6m 3M. A conspic TV mast (133m), 5ca WNW of hbr, in transit with Alfred Pier lt leads 290° towards the hbr and also clears The Carrick rock.

R/T Call *Port St Mary Hbr* VHF Ch 12 16 (when vessel due or through Douglas Hbr Control Ch 12).

TELEPHONE (Dial code 01624) HM 833205; MRSC 0151 931 3341; Marinecall 09066 526245; Police 631212; Dr 832281.

FACILITIES **Alfred Pier** AB see 9.10.13, Slip, D (road tanker), L, FW, C (20 ton mobile); **Inner Hbr** dries 2·4m on sand; AB, Slip, D, L, FW; **Isle of Man YC** ☎ 832088, FW, Showers, Bar; **Services:** ME, CH, D, El, SM. **Town** EC Thurs; CH, 🛒, R, Bar, ✉, Ⓑ, ⇌ (bus to Douglas, qv for ferries), ✈ Ronaldsway.

MINOR HARBOUR EAST OF CASTLETOWN

DERBY HAVEN, Isle of Man, **54°04'·65N 04°36'·45W**. Tides & charts as above. Rather remote bay exposed only to NE/E winds. ⚓ in centre of bay, NW of St Michael's Island, in 3-5m. A detached bkwtr on NW side of the bay gives shelter to craft able to dry out behind it. Lts: Iso G 2s on S end of bkwtr. Aero FR (occas) at Ronaldsway airport, NW of bay. Facilities: at Castletown (1½M) or Port St Mary.

9.10.16 DOUGLAS

Isle of Man **54°08'·87N 04°27'·96W**

CHARTS AC 2094, 2696; Imray C62; Y70; OS 95

TIDES +0009 Dover; ML 3·8; Duration 0600; Zone 0 (UT)

Standard Port LIVERPOOL (⟵)

Times				Height (metres)			
High Water		Low Water		MHWS	MHWN	MLWN	MLWS
0000	0600	0200	0700	9·3	7·4	2·9	0·9
1200	1800	1400	1900				
Differences DOUGLAS							
+0005	+0015	–0015	–0025	–2·4	–2·0	–0·5	–0·1

SHELTER Good except in NE winds. Very heavy seas run in during NE gales. Outer hbr: Victoria and King Edward VIII piers are for commercial vessels/ferries. At inner end of Battery Pier in summer about 18 boats can raft up on pontoon; untenable in NE/E winds. Complete shelter in inner hbr, with possible pontoon berths, flapgate lowers on the flood and rises on the ebb at 4·4m above CD, lifting bridge opens every ½H subject to tide/road traffic conditions (request opening on VHF Ch12).

NAVIGATION WPT 54°09'·01N 04°27'·67W (abeam No 1 SHM buoy, Q (3) G 5s), 229° to front ldg lt, 0·47M. Appr from NE of No 1 buoy (to avoid overfalls E of Princess Alexandra Pier) and await port entry sig, or call on VHF Ch 12. There is no bar. Keep clear of large vessels and ferries. Beware concrete step at end of dredged area (◊ mark on King Edward VIII Pier) and cill at ent to inner hbr.

LIGHTS AND MARKS Douglas Head Fl 10s 32m 24M. Ldg lts 229°, both Oc 10s 9/12m 5M, synch; front W △; rear W ▽, both on R border. IPTS Nos 2, 3 & 5 shown from mast on Victoria Pier. Dolphin at N end of Alexandra Pier 2FR (vert).

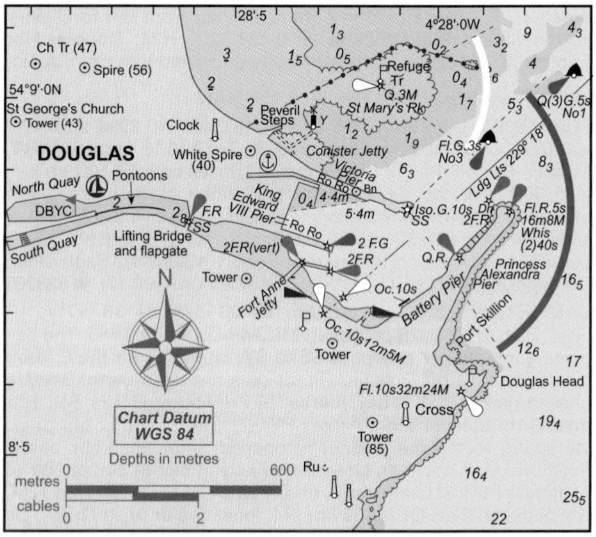
28'·5
4°28'·0W
Ch Tr (47)
Spire (56)
54°9'·0N
St George's Church Tower (43)
Clock
Peveril Steps
Refuge Tr Q.3M
St Mary's Rk
Q(3)G.5s No1
DOUGLAS
White Spire (40)
Conister Jetty
Fl.G.3s No3
Ldg Lts 229°18'
North Quay
Pontoons
DBYC
King Edward VIII Pier
Victoria Pier
Ro Ro
4·4m
5·4m
Iso.G.10s
2FR
Fl.R.5s 16m8M Whis (2)40s
South Quay
Lifting Bridge and flapgate
2FR(vert)
2FG
Q.R.
Princess Alexandra Pier
Tower
Fort Anne Jetty
Oc.10s
Battery Pier
Port Skillion
Oc.10s12m5M
Douglas Head
Fl.10s32m24M
Cross
Tower (85)
Chart Datum WGS 84
Depths in metres
metres
cables
600
8'·5

R/T *Douglas Hbr Control* VHF Ch **12** 16 (H24); also broadcasts nav warnings for IoM ports and coastal waters on Ch 12 including weather and tidal info on request.

TELEPHONE (Dial code 01624) Hr Control 686628 📠 626403 (H24); MRSC 0151-931 3341; Marinecall 09066 526245; Police 631212; Ⓗ 642642.

FACILITIES **Outer Hbr** AB see 9.10.13, M, FW at pontoon, ME, El, ⚒, C (10, 5 ton), Slip; **Inner Hbr (Pontoons and N and S Quays)** (68); Ⓥ according to space (no reservations), AB, M, ⛽, FW, ME, C, El, ⚒, CH, Slip; **Douglas Bay YC** ☎ 673965, Bar, Slip, L, showers 0930-2300. **Services:** P & D (cans), CH, ACA, El, Divers, Gas, Gaz, Kos. **Town** www.gov.im, EC Thurs; 🛒, R, Bar, ✉, Ⓑ, Ⓓ, Ferry to Heysham and Liverpool; also in summer to Dublin and Belfast; ✈ Ronaldsway.

9.10.17 RAMSEY

Isle of Man **54°19'·44N 04°22'·49W**

CHARTS AC 2094, 2696; Imray C62; Y70; OS 95

TIDES +0020 Dover; ML 4·2; Duration 0545; Zone 0 (UT)

Standard Port LIVERPOOL (←)

Times				Height (metres)			
High Water		Low Water		MHWS	MHWN	MLWN	MLWS
0000	0600	0200	0700	9·3	7·4	2·9	0·9
1200	1800	1400	1900				
Differences RAMSEY							
+0005	+0015	–0005	–0015	–1·9	–1·5	–0·6	0·0

SHELTER Very good except in strong NE winds. Hbr dries 1·8m-6m. Access and ent only permitted HW –2½ to HW +2. Berth on Town quay (S side) or as directed by HM on entry. 2 orange 🅥s are close NW of Queen's Pier hd (only in summer). Note: Landing on Queen's Pier is prohibited.

NAVIGATION WPT 54°19´·44N 04°21´·89W, 270° to ent, 0·37M. The foreshore dries out 1ca to seaward of the pier hds.

LIGHTS AND MARKS No ldg lts/marks. Relative to hbr ent, Pt of Ayre, Fl (4) 20s 32m 19M, is 5·5M N; Maughold Hd, Fl (3) 30s 65m 21M, is 3M SE; Albert Tr (□ stone tr 14m, on hill 130m) is conspic 7ca S; and Snaefell (617m) bears 220°/5M. Inside the hbr an Iso G 4s, G SHM post, marks the S tip of Mooragh Bank; it is not visible from seaward. 2FR (hor) on each side mark the centre of swing bridge.

R/T *Ramsey Hbr* VHF Ch **12** 16 (0700-1600LT and when a vessel is due); OT call *Douglas Hbr Control* Ch **12**.

TELEPHONE (Dial code 01624) HM (non-resident) 812245, mob 07624 460304; MRSC 0151 931 3341; Marinecall 09066 526245; Police 631212; Dr 813881; H 811811.

FACILITIES **Outer Hbr: E Quay** ☎ 812245, strictly for commercial vessels (frequent movements H24), no AB for yachts, FW; **Town Quay** (S side) AB see 9.10.13, D, FW. **Inner Hbr, W Quay** AB, D, FW, Slip (Grid); **N Quay** AB, FW; **Shipyard Quay** Slip; **Old Hbr** AB, Slip, M; **Manx S&CC:** ☎ 813494 AB £7.26; **Services:** P & D (cans) from garages; none located at hbr. ME, El, Ⓔ, ⚒, ♿. **Town** EC Wed; ⛟, R, Gas, Gaz, Kos, Bar, ⊡, ✉, Ⓑ, ⇌ (bus to Douglas, which see for ferries), ✈ Ronaldsway.

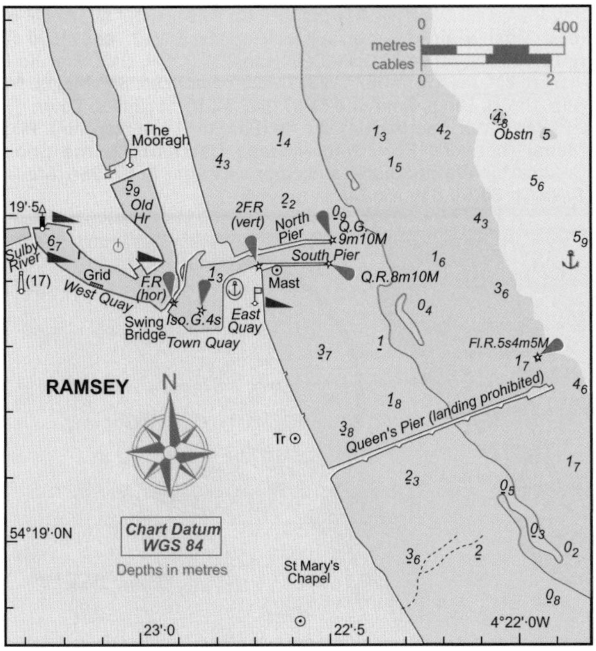
metres
cables
0
400
2
The Mooragh
Old Hr
Sulby River
(17)
Grid
West Quay
F.R (hor)
Swing Bridge
Iso.G.4s
Town Quay
East Quay
Mast
2F.R (vert)
North Pier
South Pier
Q.G. 9m10M
Q.R.8m10M
Obstn
Fl.R.5s4m5M
Queen's Pier (landing prohibited)
RAMSEY
N
Tr
Chart Datum WGS 84
Depths in metres
St Mary's Chapel
54°19'·0N
19'·5
23'·0
22'·5
4°22'·0W

9.10.18 CONWY AND DEGANWY

Conwy **53°17'·25N 03°50'·00W** (marina)

CHARTS AC *1826, 1977, 1978, 1463*; Imray C52; OS 115; Stanfords 27

TIDES –0015 Dover; ML 4·3; Duration 0545; Zone 0 (UT)

Standard Port HOLYHEAD (→)

Times				Height (metres)			
High Water		Low Water		MHWS	MHWN	MLWN	MLWS
0000	0600	0500	1100	5·6	4·4	2·0	0·7
1200	1800	1700	2300				
Differences CONWY							
+0025	+0035	+0120	+0105	+2·3	+1·8	+0·6	+0·4

NOTE: HW Conwy is approx HW Liverpool –0040 sp and –0020 nps.

SHELTER Good, except in strong NW'lies. Conwy Marina is to stbd past the Narrows, Deganwy Quay Marina to port, accesses via half-tide gates; contact HM for pontoon berths between marina and castle and 🅥's. 10kn spd limit above LFl.G.

NAVIGATION 'Inshore Passage' (close SW of Gt Orme's Hd), only advised with local knowledge otherwise use WPT Fairway buoy (L.Fl.10s), 53°17´·95N 03°55´·58W, 115° to No C2 PHM (Fl(2)R10s), 0·80M. From C2 channel is marked C1 (Fl.G10s) SHM, C4 (Fl(4)R20s) PHM, C6 (Fl(6)R30s) PHM, C8 (Fl(8)R30s) PHM, C3 (Fl(3)G15s) SHM, C5 (Fl(5)G20s) SHM, Perch Lt (L.Fl.G15s) at 53°18'·06N 03°50'·84W, C7 (Q.G) SHM, PHM unlit at narrows. Access HW±2; if Conwy Sands (to N) are covered, there is enough water in chan for 2m draft boat. After C5 leave Perch lt approx 30m to stbd. Pass unlit PHM. Conwy Marina ent to stbd has R/G entry lts. Beware unlit moorings. Deganwy Quay Marina to port, channel marked by 3 PHM, keep close to these. Min depth in chan 2.5m when Marina gate open. Sp ebb reaches 5kn.

LIGHTS AND MARKS Penmaenmawr Sewer Outfall (Fl.Y.5s) is not a ch mark. Ent ch buoyage is lit as above up to C7. PHMs are unlit bns. Jetty unlit to stbd. Conwy Marina Bkwtr lt Fl.G.3s. Deganwy Quay Marina Out. App. Chan. PHM Fl R (2+1) 10s. 2 unlit pontoons in hbr.

R/T HM Ch **14** 16 (Summer 0900-1700LT daily; winter, same times Mon-Fri). Conwy Marina Ch 80 (H24). Deganwy Quay Ch 80. N Wales CC launch Ch M, water taxi.

TELEPHONE (Dial code 01492) HM 596253 📠 585222; MRSC (01407) 762051; Marinecall 09066 526244; Police 517171; Dr 592424.

FACILITIES **Conwy Marina** (500) access LW ±3½ ☎ 593000, 📠 572111, £25<10m, D & P (0700-2200), BH (30 ton), ⛽, CH, Gas, ⊡, SM, R, Bar, BY, ⚒; **Harbour** ☎ 596253, Pontoon AB £11.00, Quay AB dries (12·3m max LOA; short stay for loading), M, D, P, FW, ♿; **Deganwy Quay Marina** ,(200 inc 🅥) access LW ±3½ ☎ 583984 , AB £3.00, FW, D, ♿, ⚒,ME, El, Ⓔ, Slip, BH; **Conwy YC** ☎ 583690, Slip, M, L, FW, R, Bar; **N Wales Cruising Club** ☎ 593481, AB, M, FW, Bar. **Services:** ME, Gas, Gaz, ⚒, El, Ⓔ. **Town** EC Wed; P & D (cans), ⛟, R, Bar, ✉, Ⓑ, ⇌, ✈ (Liverpool).

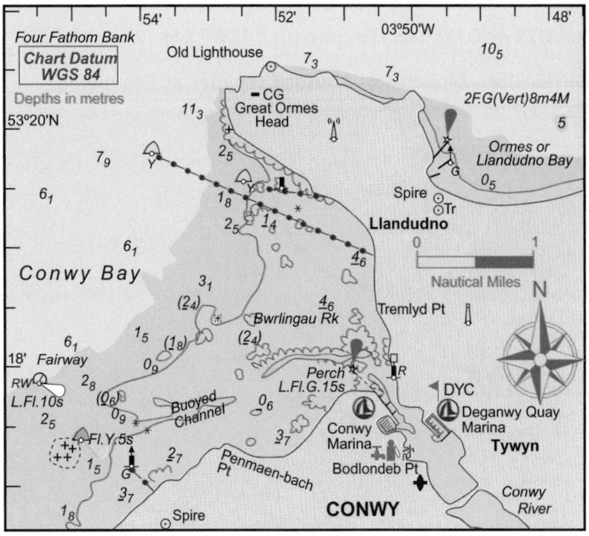
Four Fathom Bank
Chart Datum WGS 84
Depths in metres
54'
52'
03°50'W
48'
53°20'N
Old Lighthouse
CG
Great Ormes Head
2F.G(Vert)8m4M
Ormes or Llandudno Bay
Spire
Tr
Llandudno
Nautical Miles
0
1
Conwy Bay
Tremlyd Pt
Bwrlingau Rk
18' Fairway
RW
L.Fl.10s
Buoyed Channel
Perch
L.Fl.G.15s
Fl.Y.5s
DYC
Deganwy Quay Marina
Conwy Marina
Tywyn
Penmaen-bach Pt
Bodlondeb Pt
CONWY
Spire
Conwy River
N

9.10.19 MENAI STRAIT

Gwynedd/Isle of Anglesey

CHARTS AC *1464*, Imray C52; Stanfords 27; OS 114, 115. NOTE: The definitive Pilot book is *Cruising Anglesey and the North Wales Coast* by R Morris, 5th edition 1995: North West Venturers YC

TIDES Beaumaris –0025 Dover; ML Beaumaris 4·2; Duration 0540
Standard Port HOLYHEAD (⟶)

Times				**Height (metres)**			
High Water		Low Water		MHWS	MHWN	MLWN	MLWS
0000	0600	0500	1100	5·6	4·4	2·0	0·7
1200	1800	1700	2300				
Differences BEAUMARIS							
+0025	+0010	+0055	+0035	+2·0	+1·6	+0·5	+0·1
MENAI BRIDGE							
+0030	+0010	+0100	+0035	+1·7	+1·4	+0·3	0·0
PORT DINORWIC							
–0015	–0025	+0030	0000	0·0	0·0	0·0	+0·1
CAERNARFON							
–0030	–0030	+0015	–0005	–0·4	–0·4	–0·1	–0·1
FORT BELAN							
–0040	–0015	–0025	–0005	–1·0	–0·9	–0·2	–0·1
LLANDDWYN ISLAND							
–0115	–0055	–0030	–0020	–0·7	–0·5	–0·1	0·0

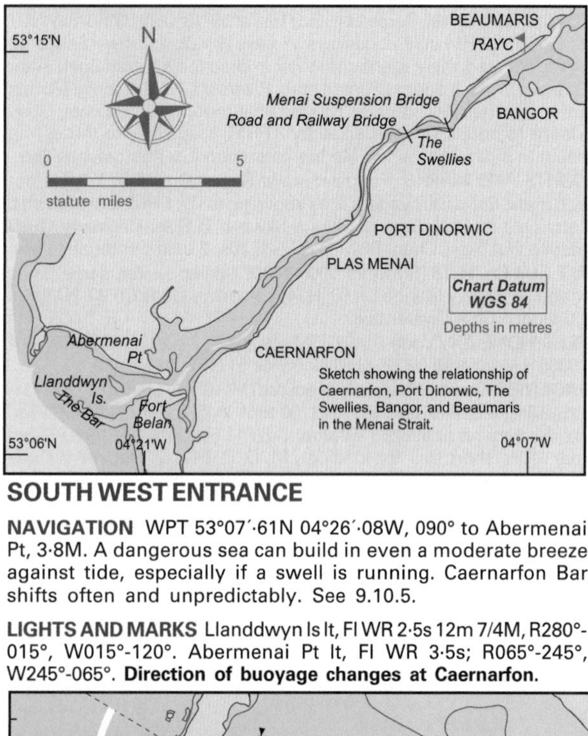
BEAUMARIS
RAYC
53°15'N
N
Menai Suspension Bridge
Road and Railway Bridge
The Swellies
BANGOR
0
5
statute miles
PORT DINORWIC
PLAS MENAI
Chart Datum WGS 84
Depths in metres
Abermenai Pt
CAERNARFON
Llanddwyn Is.
The Bar
Fort Belan
Sketch showing the relationship of Caernarfon, Port Dinorwic, The Swellies, Bangor, and Beaumaris in the Menai Strait.
53°06'N
04°21'W
04°07'W

SOUTH WEST ENTRANCE

NAVIGATION WPT 53°07´·61N 04°26´·08W, 090° to Abermenai Pt, 3·8M. A dangerous sea can build in even a moderate breeze against tide, especially if a swell is running. Caernarfon Bar shifts often and unpredictably. See 9.10.5.

LIGHTS AND MARKS Llanddwyn Is lt, Fl WR 2·5s 12m 7/4M, R280°-015°, W015°-120°. Abermenai Pt lt, Fl WR 3·5s; R065°-245°, W245°-065°. **Direction of buoyage changes at Caernarfon.**

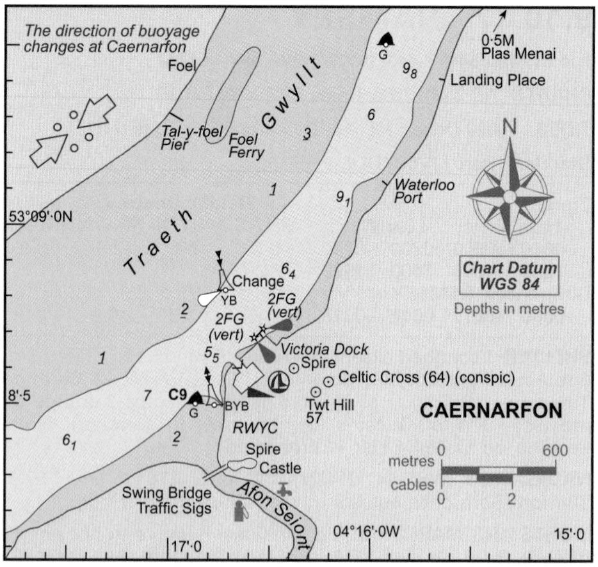
The direction of buoyage changes at Caernarfon
Foel
Tal-y-foel Pier
Foel Ferry
Gwyllt
Traeth
0·5M Plas Menai
Landing Place
Waterloo Port
N
53°09'·0N
Change
YB
2FG (vert)
2FG (vert)
Chart Datum WGS 84
Depths in metres
Victoria Dock
Spire
Celtic Cross (64) (conspic)
C9
G
BYB
Twt Hill 57
CAERNARFON
RWYC
Spire
Castle
metres 0 600
cables 0 2
Swing Bridge Traffic Sigs
Afon Seiont
8'·5
17'·0
04°16'·0W
15'·0

CAERNARFON 53°08'·51N 04°16'·83W

SHELTER Good in Victoria Dock marina, access HW±2 via gates, trfc lts; pontoons at SW end in 2m. Or in river hbr (S of conspic castle), dries to mud/gravel, access HW±3 via swing bridge; for opening sound B (–···). ⚓ off Foel Ferry, with local knowledge; or temp ⚓ in fair holding off Abermenai Pt, sheltered from W'lies, but strong streams. 🅐 waiting 1½ca SW of C9.

R/T Victoria Dock marina VHF Ch 80. Port Ch 14 16 (HJ).

TELEPHONE (Dial code 01286) HM 672118, 📠 678729, Mobile 0410 541364; Police 673333; 🄷 01248 384384 Emergency 01248 384001.

FACILITIES **Dock** £1.49 **River Hbr** £11.65/yacht, 0700-2300 (Summer), FW, Slip, C (2 ton), 🛒, ME, El, Ⓔ, ⛵; **Caernarfon SC** ☎ (01248) 672861, L, Bar; **Royal Welsh YC** ☎ (01248) 672599, Bar; **Town** P (cans), ✉, Ⓑ.

PORT DINORWIC 53°11'·23N 04°13'·70W

TELEPHONE (Dial code 01248) Marina 671500; MRSC (01407) 762051; Dr 670423.

FACILITIES **Port Dinorwic Marina** (230 berths in fresh water) £15 any LOA. Call *Dinorwic Marina* VHF Ch **80** M (HO)3 🅐 1ca NE of lock. **Tidal basin** dries at sp; lock opens HW±2. ☎ 671500 📠 671252, Lock office 671335, D, P (cans), ⛽, CH, SM; Pier hd F WR 5m 2M, vis R225°-357°, W357°-225°. **Services:** SM, ME, El, ⚒, Slip, C, CH. Dinas Boatyard ☎ 671642 all BY facilities. **Town** Ⓔ, ✉ (Bangor or Caernarfon), Ⓑ, ⇌ (Bangor), ✈ (Liverpool). **Plas Menai** (between Port Dinorwic and Caernarfon), the Sport Council for Wales Sailing and Sports Centre: ☎ 670964. *Menai Base* Ch **80** M; day moorings only; ♿.

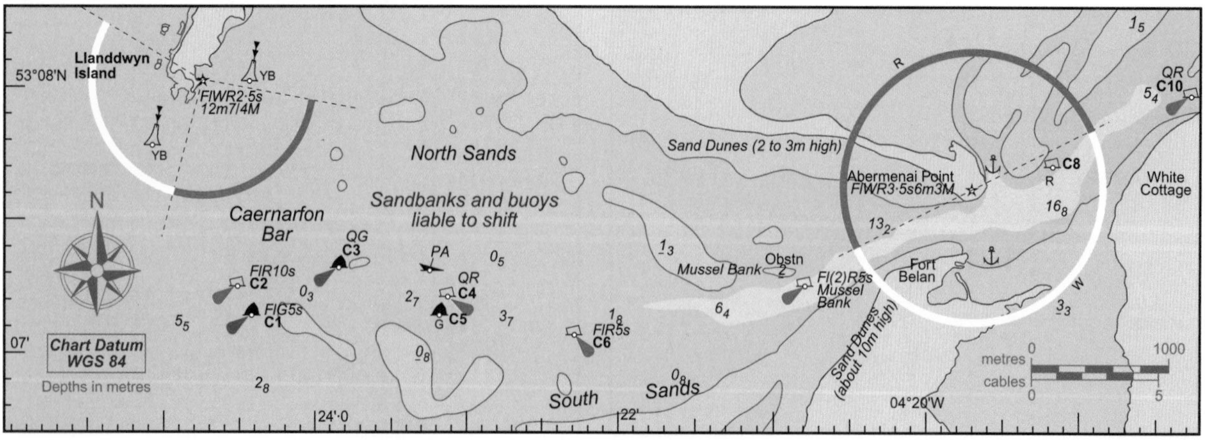
Llanddwyn Island
53°08'N
YB
FlWR2·5s 12m7/4M
YB
North Sands
Sandbanks and buoys liable to shift
Caernarfon Bar
N
QG C3
Fl R10s C2
Fl G5s C1
PA
QR C4
C5
Fl R5s C6
Chart Datum WGS 84
Depths in metres
07'
South Sands
Sand Dunes (2 to 3m high)
Abermenai Point FlWR3·5s6m3M
Mussel Bank
Obstn
Fl(2)R5s Mussel Bank
Fort Belan
Sand Dunes (about 10m high)
QR C10
C8
White Cottage
metres 0 1000
cables 0 5
24'·0
22'
04°20'W

NORTH EAST ENTRANCE

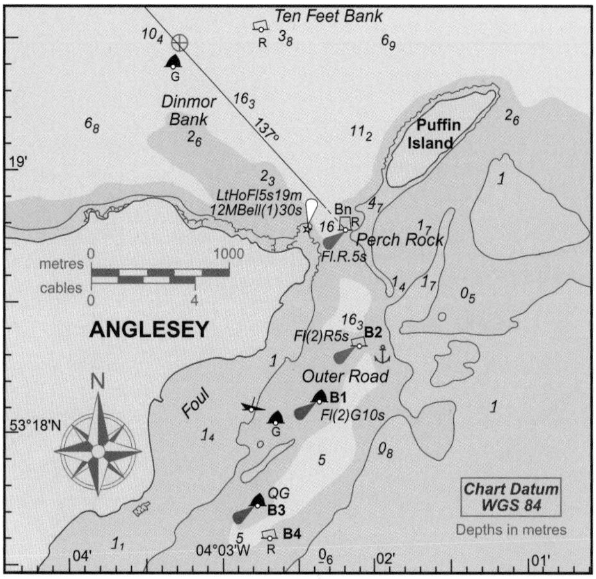
Ten Feet Bank
Dinmor Bank
Puffin Island
LtHoFl5s19m 12MBell(1)30s
Bn
Perch Rock
Fl.R.5s
metres
cables
ANGLESEY
Fl(2)R5s
B2
Outer Road
B1
Fl(2)G10s
Foul
QG
B3
B4
Chart Datum WGS 84
Depths in metres
53°18'N
04°03'W

NAVIGATION WPT 53°19'·48N 04°03'·28W, 137° to Perch Rk PHM bn, 1·0M. In N'ly gales seas break on Ten Foot Bank. In N Strait keep to buoyed chan, nearer Anglesey. Night pilotage not advised due to many unlit buoys/moorings.

LIGHTS AND MARKS At NE end of Strait, Trwyn-Du lt, W tr/B bands, Fl 5s 19m 12M, vis 101°-023° (282°), Bell 30s. Conspic tr on Puffin Is. Chan is laterally buoyed, some lit. Beaumaris pier has FWG sectored lt (see 9.10.4).

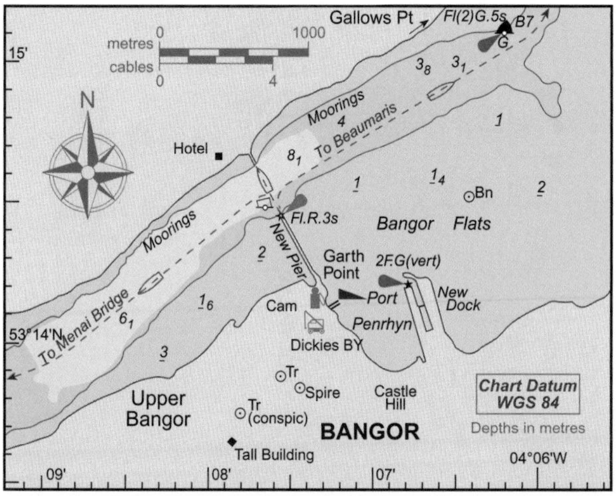
Gallows Pt
Fl(2)G.5s
B7
metres
cables
Hotel
Moorings
To Beaumaris
Fl.R.3s
New Pier
Bangor Flats
Garth Point
2F.G(vert)
Port Penrhyn
New Dock
Cam
Dickies BY
To Menai Bridge
Upper Bangor
Spire
Castle Hill
Tr (conspic)
BANGOR
Tall Building
Chart Datum WGS 84
Depths in metres
53°14'N
04°06'W

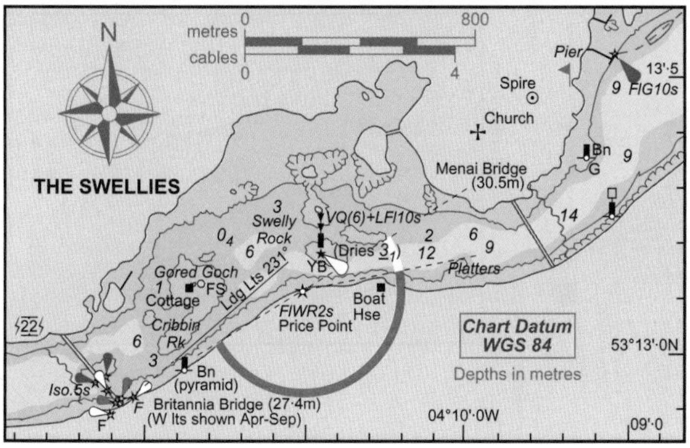
metres
cables
Pier
Fl G10s
Spire
Church
Menai Bridge (30.5m)
THE SWELLIES
Swelly Rock
VQ(6)+LFl10s
(Dries 3₁)
YB
Platters
Gored Goch
Cottage
Cribbin Rk
Ldg Lts 231°
FlWR2s Price Point
Boat Hse
Iso.5s
Bn (pyramid)
Britannia Bridge (27·4m) (W lts shown Apr-Sep)
Chart Datum WGS 84
Depths in metres
53°13'·0N
04°10'·0W

MENAI BRIDGE/BEAUMARIS 53°15'·66N 04°05'·38W

SHELTER Reasonable off Beaumaris except from NE winds. ⚓ S of B10 PHM buoy or call YCs for mooring. At Menai Bridge, call HM VHF Ch 69 16 for mooring or temp'y berth on St George's Pier (S of which a marina is planned).

TELEPHONE (Dial code 01248) HM Menai 712312, mobile 07990 531595; MRSC (01407) 762051; Marinecall 09066 526244; Police (01286) 673333; Dr 810501.

FACILITIES **St George's Pier** (Fl G 10s) L at all tides; **Royal Anglesey YC** ☎ 810295, Slip, M, L, R, Bar, P; **North West Venturers YC** ☎ 810023, M, L, FW, water taxi at w/ends only; **Menai Bridge SC. Services:** Slip, P & D (cans), FW, ME, BH (20 ton), ⚒, C (2 ton), CH, El, Ⓔ, Gas. **Both towns** EC Wed; ✉, Ⓑ, ⇌ (bus to Bangor), ✈ (Liverpool).

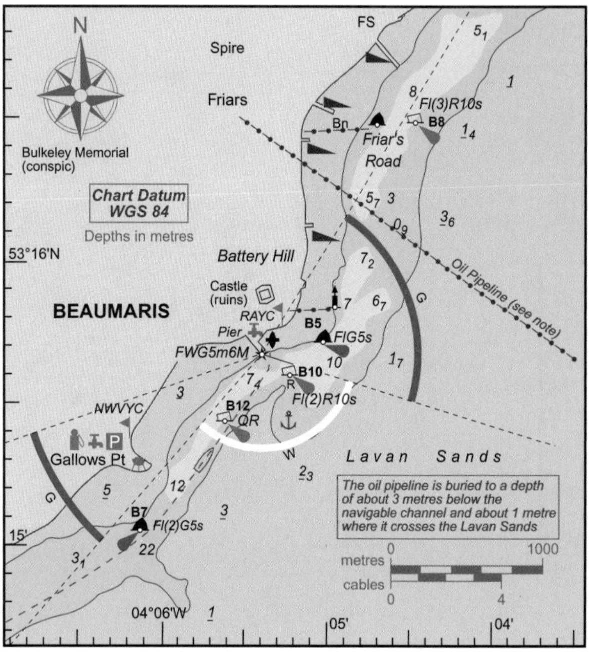
FS
Spire
Friars
Fl(3)R10s
B8
Bn
Friar's Road
Bulkeley Memorial (conspic)
Chart Datum WGS 84
Depths in metres
Battery Hill
Oil Pipeline (see note)
Castle (ruins)
RAYC
BEAUMARIS
Pier
B5
FlG5s
FWG5m6M
B10
Fl(2)R10s
NWVYC
B12
QR
Gallows Pt
Lavan Sands
The oil pipeline is buried to a depth of about 3 metres below the navigable channel and about 1 metre where it crosses the Lavan Sands
B7
Fl(2)G5s
metres
cables
53°16'N
04°06'W

BANGOR 53°14'·46N 04°07'·58W

SHELTER Good, except in E'lies, at Dickies BY or Port Penrhyn dock (both dry; access HW±2).

R/T *Dickies* VHF Ch 09 M 16 (0930-1730), all year.

TELEPHONE (Dial code 01248) Penrhyn HM 352525, 📠 352525; MRSC (01407) 762051; Police (01286) 673333; Dr (emergency) 384001.

FACILITIES **Services:** Slip, D, P (cans), FW, ME, El, ⚒, C, CH, Ⓔ, SM, BH (30 ton), Gas, Gaz, ACA; **Port Penrhyn**, Slip, AB, D. **Town** ✉, Ⓑ, ⇌, ✈ (Chester).

THE SWELLIES 53°13'·14N 04°10'·46W

NAVIGATION For pilotage notes, see 9.10.5. The passage should only be attempted at slack HW, which is –0200 HW Liverpool. The shallow rky narrows between the bridges are dangerous for yachts at other times, when the stream can reach 8kn. At slack HW there is 3m over The Platters and the outcrop off Price Pt, which can be ignored. For shoal-draft boats passage is also possible at slack LW nps, but there are depths of 0·5m close E of Britannia Bridge. The bridges and power cables have a least clearance of 22m at MHWS. Night passage is not recommended.

LIGHTS AND MARKS SE side of chan QR 4m, R mast, vis 064°-222°. Price Pt, Fl WR 2s 5m 3M, W Bn, vis R059°-239°, W239°-259°. Britannia Bridge, E side, ldg lts 231°, both FW (shown Apr-Sep). Bridge lts, both sides: Centre span Iso 5s 27m 3M; S end, FR 21m 3M; N end, FG 21m 3M.

9.10.20 HOLYHEAD

Isle of Anglesey **53°19'·72N 04°37'·07W** ❁❁❁⛵⛵⛵✿✿

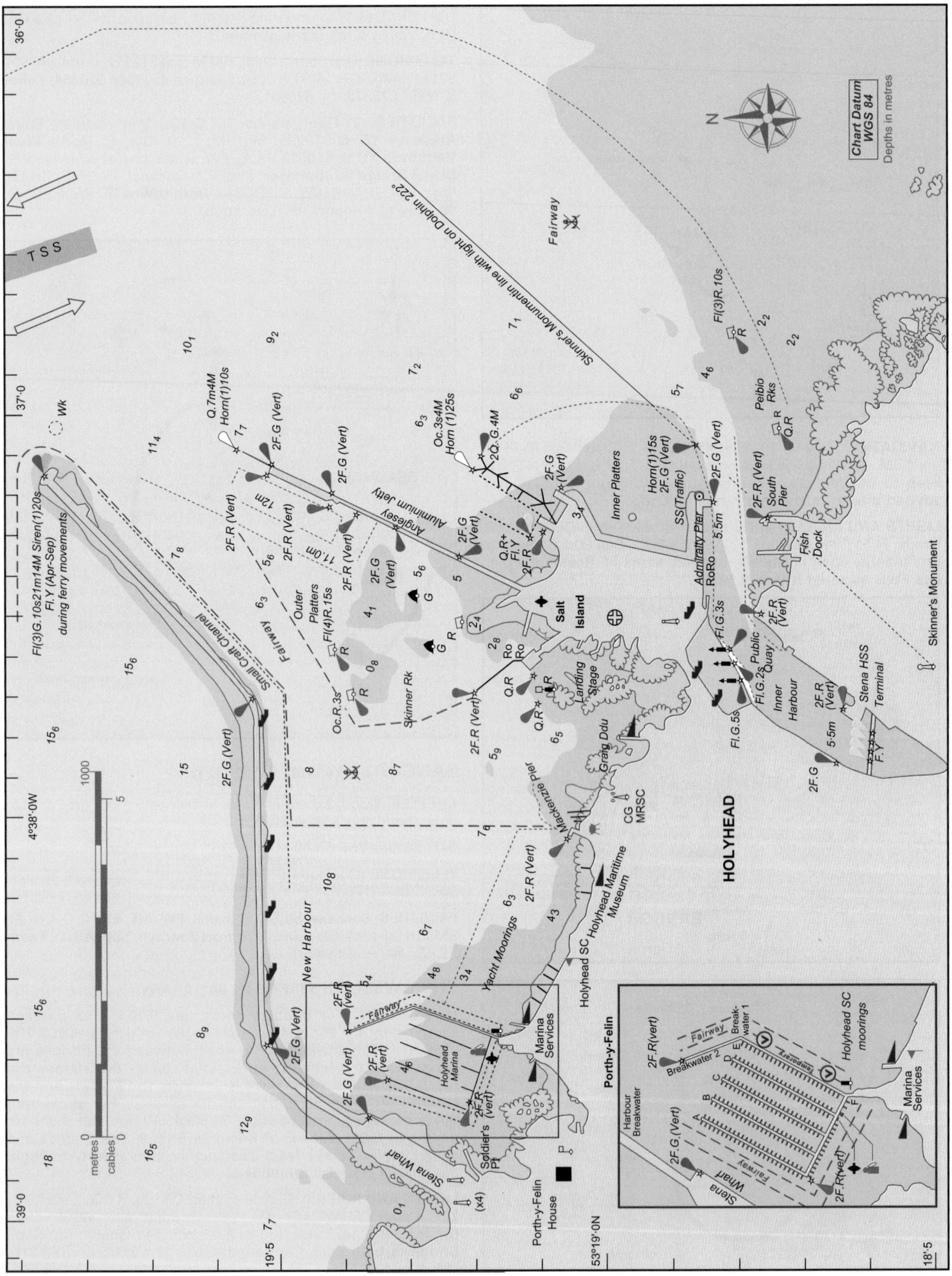
Chart Datum WGS 84
Depths in metres
N
TSS
Fairway
Skinner's Monument line with light on Dolphin 222°
Fl(3)R.10s
Peibio Rks
Q.R
Inner Platters
Horn(1)15s
2F.G (Vert)
SS(Traffic)
Admiralty Pier
RoRo
5.5m
2F.R (Vert)
South Pier
Fish Dock
Skinner's Monument
Q.7m4M
Horn(1)10s
2F.G (Vert)
Oc.3s4M
Horn (1)25s
2Q.G.4M
Anglesey Aluminium Jetty
Q.R+
Fl.Y
2F.R
12m
11.0m
Outer Platters
Fl(4)R.15s
Oc.R.3s
Skinner Rk
Salt Island
Ro Ro
Landing Stage
Graig Ddu
CG MRSC
Mackenzie Pier
Holyhead Maritime Museum
HOLYHEAD
Fl.G.3s
Public Quay
Fl.G.2s
Fl.G.5s
Inner Harbour
Stena HSS Terminal
F.Y
2F.G
Fl(3)G.10s21m14M Siren(1)20s
Fl.Y (Apr-Sep)
during ferry movements
Wk
Small Craft Channel
New Harbour
Yacht Moorings
Holyhead SC
Holyhead Marina
Marina Services
Soldier's Pt
Stena Wharf
Porth-y-Felin House
metres
cables
4°38'·0W
53°19'·0N
36'·0
37'·0
39'·0
19'·5
18'·5
Porth-y-Felin
Harbour Breakwater
Breakwater 2
Break-water 1
Holyhead SC moorings
2F.R(vert)
2F.G.(Vert)

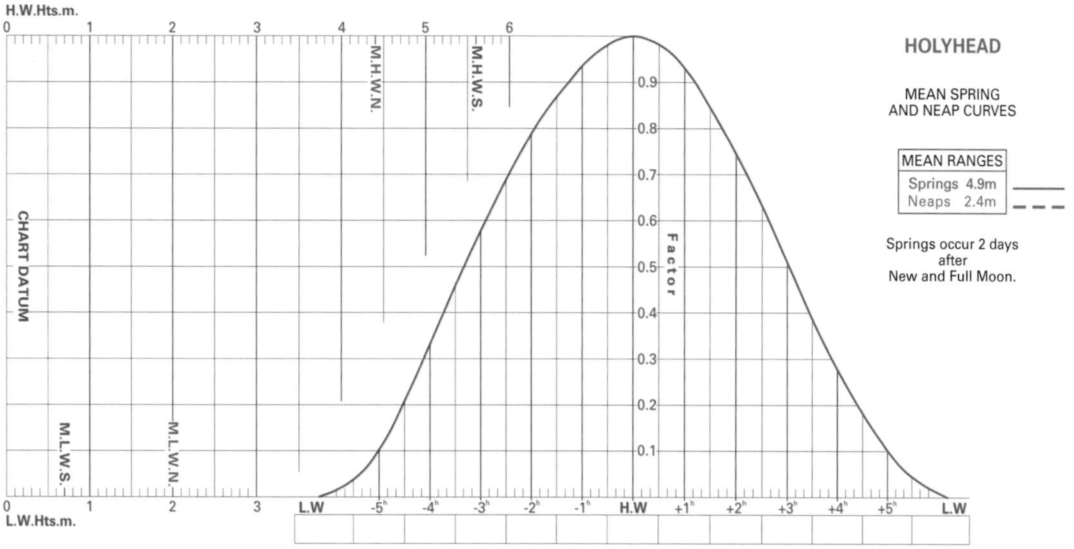
H.W.Hts.m.
0 1 2 3 4 5 6
M.H.W.N.
M.H.W.S.
CHART DATUM
M.L.W.S.
M.L.W.N.
0 1 2 3
L.W.Hts.m.
0.9
0.8
0.7
0.6
0.5
0.4
0.3
0.2
0.1
Factor
L.W -5h -4h -3h -2h -1h H.W +1h +2h +3h +4h +5h L.W
HOLYHEAD
MEAN SPRING AND NEAP CURVES
MEAN RANGES
Springs 4.9m
Neaps 2.4m
Springs occur 2 days after New and Full Moon.

CHARTS AC *1826,* 1970, *1977,* 1413, 2011; Imray C61, C52; Stanfords 27; OS 114

TIDES –0035 Dover; ML 3·2; Duration 0615; Zone 0 (UT)

Standard Port HOLYHEAD (⟶)

Times				Height (metres)			
High Water		Low Water		MHWS	MHWN	MLWN	MLWS
0000	0600	0500	1100	5·6	4·4	2·0	0·7
1200	1800	1700	2300				
Differences TRWYN DINMOR (W of Puffin Is)							
+0025	+0015	+0050	+0035	+1·9	+1·5	+0·5	+0·2
MOELFRE (NE Anglesey)							
+0025	+0020	+0050	+0035	+1·9	+1·4	+0·5	+0·2
AMLWCH (N Anglesey)							
+0020	+0010	+0035	+0025	+1·6	+1·3	+0·5	+0·2
CEMAES BAY (N Anglesey)							
+0020	+0025	+0040	+0035	+1·0	+0·7	+0·3	+0·1
TREARDDUR BAY (W Anglesey)							
–0045	–0025	–0015	–0015	–0·4	–0·4	0·0	+0·1
PORTH TRECASTELL (SW Anglesey)							
–0045	–0025	–0005	–0015	–0·6	–0·6	0·0	0·0
TREFOR (Lleyn peninsula)							
–0115	–0100	–0030	–0020	–0·8	–0·9	–0·2	–0·1
PORTH DINLLAEN (Lleyn peninsula)							
–0120	–0105	–0035	–0025	–1·0	–1·0	–0·2	–0·2
PORTH YSGADEN (Lleyn peninsula)							
–0125	–0110	–0040	–0035	–1·1	–1·0	–0·1	–0·1
BARDSEY ISLAND							
–0220	–0240	–0145	–0140	–1·2	–1·2	–0·5	–0·1

SHELTER Good in marina, least depth 2m, but temp'y visitors berths on E side of floating bwtr are exposed to fresh E'lies. Alternatively ⚓ or pick up Y ⓥ off HSC; or drying AB on bkwtr in emergency only; or in Fish Dock. Strong NE winds raise an uncomfortable sea.

NAVIGATION WPT 53°20'·12N 04°37'·27W, 165° to bkwtr lt ho, 0·28M. Yachts entering New Hbr should use the Small Craft Chan, parallel to and within 70m of the bkwtr; but beware shoal, drying 0·5m, which extends 35m SE of bkwtr head. Use Small Craft Ch. close SE of the breakwater until clear of the Fairway area in the New Harbour. There are frequent HSS and Ro-Ro ferries to and from Dun Laoghaire. No anchoring in fairways. Ferries comply with a mini-TSS at the hbr ent by entering within 100-500m of bkwtr hd for Ro-Ro terminals in New Hbr or the Inner Hbr; outbound ferries pass within 2½ca WSW of Clipera PHM buoy, Fl(4) R 15s. Yachts keep clear as High speed ferries operate in the area.

LIGHTS AND MARKS Ldg marks 165°: bkwtr lt ho on with chy (127m, grey + B top; R lts); chy and Holyhead Mountain (218m) are conspic from afar. Cranes on aluminium jetty conspic closer to. Inner hbr tfc sigs from old lt ho at E end of Admiralty pier: ● = Ent is impracticable. ○ = Ent is clear.

R/T *Holyhead Marina* and *Holyhead SC*: Ch **37**. Monitor *Holyhead* VHF Ch 14 16 (H24) for ferry traffic. Broadcast of local nav info/ warnings1200UT daily on Ch 14.

TELEPHONE (Dial code 01407) Marina 764242; Port Control 763071 🖷 606622; MRSC 762051; Marinecall 09066 526244; Police (01286) 673333; Dr via MRSC.

FACILITIES **Holyhead Marina** ☎ 764242, mob 07714 292990, 🖷 769152, £1.73, ⓥ 20 approx, D, FW, ⊡, Gas, Gaz, BY, CH, ME, Ⓔ, El, ⚒, BH, Slip, R. **Holyhead SC (HSC)** ☎ 762526, M £8.00, L, FW, launch (call Ch M: 0900-2100, Fri/Sat to 2330), Slip, R (Wed, Fri, Sat, Sun only), Bar ☎ 762496; **Fish Dock** ☎ 760139 AB on pontoons,but little room,FW, D by hose. **Inner Hbr** ☎ 762304, used by Stena HSS; not advised for yachts. **Services:** BY, ACA, CH, ME, El, ⚒, C (100 ton), BH, Slip, Ⓔ. **Town** EC Tues; P, 🛒, R, Bar, ⊡, ✉, Ⓑ, ⇌, ✈ (Liverpool/Manchester). Ferry/HSS to Dun Laoghaire and Dublin. **Trearddur Bay** (3M south) M (small craft only), L; **BY** ☎ 860501, D, FW, ⚒, CH. **Village** P, 🛒, R, Bar.

MINOR HARBOUR ON THE LLEYN PENINSULA

PORTH DINLLAEN, Gwynedd, **52°56'·68N 04°33'·66W**. AC 1971, 1512. HW –0240 on Dover; ML 2·5m; Duration 0535. See 9.10.20. Shelter good in S to W winds but strong NNW to NNE winds cause heavy seas in the bay. Beware Carreg-y-Chad (1·8m) 0·75M SW of the point, and Carreg-y-Chwislen (dries, with unlit IDM Bn) 2ca ENE of the point. From N, Garn Fadryn (369m) brg 182° leads into the bay. Best ⚓ 1ca S of LB ho in approx 2m. HM ☎ (01758) 720276; CG ☎ 01407 762051. Facilities: EC Wed; Bar, 🛒 by landing stage. At Morfa Nefyn (1M), Bar, P, R, 🛒.

NOTES

TIME ZONE (UT)
For Summer Time add ONE hour in **non-shaded areas**

WALES – HOLYHEAD

LAT 53°19′N LONG 4°37′W

TIMES AND HEIGHTS OF HIGH AND LOW WATERS

SPRING & NEAP TIDES
Dates in red are **SPRINGS**
Dates in blue are **NEAPS**

YEAR **2005**

JANUARY

Date	Day	Time	m	Time	m	Time	m	Time	m
1	SA	0128	4.8	0724	1.7	1340	5.1	2002	1.6
2	SU	0211	4.7	0808	1.9	1423	5.0	2048	1.7
3	M	0259	4.6	0857	2.0	1513	4.9	◑ 2141	1.8
4	TU	0357	4.5	0956	2.1	1612	4.8	2242	1.8
5	W	0504	4.5	1102	2.1	1720	4.8	2348	1.7
6	TH	0612	4.6	1211	1.9	1831	4.9		
7	F	0052	1.6	0715	4.9	1317	1.7	1936	5.0
8	SA	0151	1.4	0811	5.1	1416	1.4	2035	5.2
9	SU	0246	1.2	0902	5.4	1512	1.1	2130	5.5
10	M	0337	1.0	0951	5.7	1604	0.8	● 2222	5.6
11	TU	0426	0.9	1039	5.9	1655	0.6	2312	5.7
12	W	0514	0.8	1127	6.0	1745	0.5		
13	TH	0001	5.6	0601	0.8	1216	6.0	1834	0.5
14	F	0051	5.5	0649	0.9	1304	5.9	1923	0.7
15	SA	0140	5.3	0738	1.1	1353	5.7	2014	0.9
16	SU	0230	5.0	0828	1.4	1444	5.4	2107	1.3
17	M	0324	4.7	0924	1.7	1540	5.1	◐ 2205	1.6
18	TU	0425	4.5	1028	2.0	1643	4.8	2309	1.9
19	W	0535	4.4	1140	2.1	1755	4.6		
20	TH	0017	2.0	0647	4.5	1253	2.1	1909	4.5
21	F	0123	2.0	0750	4.6	1359	2.0	2012	4.6
22	SA	0220	1.9	0841	4.8	1453	1.8	2102	4.8
23	SU	0305	1.8	0922	5.0	1535	1.5	2143	4.9
24	M	0343	1.6	0958	5.2	1612	1.4	2218	5.0
25	TU	0416	1.4	1030	5.3	1645	1.2	○ 2250	5.1
26	W	0447	1.3	1101	5.4	1716	1.1	2321	5.2
27	TH	0519	1.2	1132	5.5	1748	1.1	2353	5.2
28	F	0550	1.2	1204	5.5	1820	1.1		
29	SA	0026	5.1	0623	1.2	1238	5.4	1853	1.1
30	SU	0100	5.1	0657	1.3	1312	5.3	1927	1.2
31	M	0136	5.0	0734	1.4	1348	5.2	2006	1.3

FEBRUARY

Date	Day	Time	m	Time	m	Time	m	Time	m
1	TU	0216	4.8	0816	1.6	1430	5.0	2051	1.5
2	W	0304	4.7	0907	1.8	1521	4.8	◑ 2148	1.7
3	TH	0405	4.5	1013	2.0	1630	4.7	2301	1.9
4	F	0525	4.5	1135	2.0	1759	4.6		
5	SA	0023	1.9	0647	4.6	1257	1.8	1924	4.8
6	SU	0137	1.7	0756	4.9	1408	1.4	2032	5.0
7	M	0238	1.3	0853	5.3	1507	1.0	2127	5.3
8	TU	0330	1.0	0943	5.6	1558	0.6	● 2216	5.6
9	W	0417	0.8	1029	5.9	1645	0.4	2301	5.7
10	TH	0501	0.6	1113	6.1	1730	0.2	2344	5.7
11	F	0544	0.5	1157	6.1	1813	0.3		
12	SA	0026	5.6	0625	0.6	1240	6.0	1855	0.5
13	SU	0108	5.4	0708	0.8	1323	5.7	1938	0.8
14	M	0150	5.1	0751	1.1	1406	5.4	2022	1.2
15	TU	0233	4.8	0838	1.5	1453	5.0	2110	1.7
16	W	0323	4.5	0935	1.9	1550	4.6	◐ 2209	2.1
17	TH	0429	4.3	1051	2.2	1706	4.3	2328	2.3
18	F	0557	4.2	1220	2.3	1844	4.2		
19	SA	0053	2.3	0724	4.4	1341	2.1	2001	4.3
20	SU	0203	2.2	0824	4.6	1438	1.8	2053	4.6
21	M	0252	1.9	0906	4.9	1519	1.5	2130	4.8
22	TU	0328	1.6	0940	5.1	1553	1.3	2202	5.0
23	W	0358	1.3	1010	5.3	1623	1.0	2230	5.1
24	TH	0427	1.1	1039	5.4	1652	0.9	○ 2258	5.3
25	F	0456	1.0	1108	5.5	1721	0.8	2327	5.3
26	SA	0526	0.9	1139	5.6	1751	0.8	2358	5.3
27	SU	0557	0.9	1211	5.5	1822	0.8		
28	M	0030	5.3	0629	0.9	1244	5.5	1854	0.9

MARCH

Date	Day	Time	m	Time	m	Time	m	Time	m
1	TU	0105	5.2	0704	1.1	1319	5.3	1931	1.1
2	W	0142	5.0	0745	1.3	1359	5.1	2015	1.4
3	TH	0227	4.8	0835	1.6	1450	4.8	◑ 2111	1.7
4	F	0327	4.6	0943	1.9	1604	4.5	2232	2.0
5	SA	0454	4.4	1117	2.0	1751	4.4		
6	SU	0009	2.0	0631	4.5	1251	1.8	1925	4.6
7	M	0130	1.8	0746	4.9	1403	1.3	2030	5.0
8	TU	0231	1.4	0842	5.3	1459	0.9	2120	5.3
9	W	0319	1.0	0929	5.6	1545	0.5	2202	5.5
10	TH	0401	0.7	1011	5.9	1627	0.3	● 2242	5.7
11	F	0441	0.5	1053	6.1	1707	0.2	2320	5.7
12	SA	0520	0.4	1133	6.0	1746	0.3	2358	5.6
13	SU	0559	0.5	1213	5.9	1824	0.5		
14	M	0035	5.4	0637	0.7	1253	5.6	1901	0.9
15	TU	0112	5.2	0717	1.0	1332	5.2	1939	1.3
16	W	0149	4.9	0800	1.4	1413	4.8	2021	1.7
17	TH	0231	4.6	0852	1.9	1504	4.4	◐ 2113	2.2
18	F	0328	4.3	1003	2.2	1619	4.1	2231	2.5
19	SA	0457	4.1	1141	2.3	1811	4.0		
20	SU	0015	2.5	0643	4.2	1310	2.1	1938	4.2
21	M	0135	2.3	0752	4.5	1409	1.8	2028	4.5
22	TU	0224	2.0	0836	4.8	1449	1.5	2104	4.8
23	W	0259	1.6	0910	5.0	1522	1.2	2133	5.0
24	TH	0329	1.3	0940	5.2	1552	0.9	2200	5.2
25	F	0358	1.0	1009	5.4	1620	0.7	○ 2228	5.3
26	SA	0427	0.8	1039	5.5	1650	0.6	2258	5.4
27	SU	0457	0.7	1110	5.6	1720	0.6	2329	5.4
28	M	0529	0.7	1143	5.6	1752	0.7		
29	TU	0003	5.4	0603	0.7	1219	5.5	1827	0.8
30	W	0039	5.3	0642	0.9	1257	5.3	1906	1.1
31	TH	0119	5.1	0726	1.2	1342	5.0	1953	1.4

APRIL

Date	Day	Time	m	Time	m	Time	m	Time	m
1	F	0207	4.9	0821	1.5	1439	4.7	2055	1.8
2	SA	0312	4.6	0937	1.8	1605	4.4	◑ 2224	2.1
3	SU	0444	4.4	1115	1.8	1757	4.4		
4	M	0001	2.1	0619	4.6	1244	1.6	1920	4.6
5	TU	0118	1.7	0730	4.9	1350	1.2	2018	5.0
6	W	0214	1.3	0824	5.3	1442	0.8	2103	5.2
7	TH	0300	1.0	0909	5.6	1524	0.5	2141	5.4
8	F	0340	0.7	0949	5.8	1603	0.4	● 2217	5.5
9	SA	0418	0.5	1029	5.9	1641	0.4	2253	5.6
10	SU	0456	0.5	1108	5.8	1717	0.5	2329	5.5
11	M	0533	0.6	1147	5.6	1753	0.7		
12	TU	0005	5.4	0611	0.8	1225	5.4	1828	1.0
13	W	0040	5.2	0650	1.1	1303	5.1	1904	1.4
14	TH	0116	5.0	0732	1.5	1343	4.7	1944	1.8
15	F	0156	4.7	0821	1.8	1431	4.4	2033	2.2
16	SA	0247	4.4	0925	2.1	1540	4.1	◐ 2141	2.5
17	SU	0403	4.2	1053	2.2	1720	4.0	2319	2.6
18	M	0541	4.2	1218	2.1	1849	4.1		
19	TU	0042	2.4	0657	4.4	1320	1.8	1944	4.4
20	W	0137	2.0	0748	4.6	1405	1.5	2022	4.7
21	TH	0217	1.7	0827	4.9	1440	1.2	2054	4.9
22	F	0250	1.4	0901	5.1	1513	1.0	2124	5.1
23	SA	0322	1.1	0933	5.3	1544	0.8	2155	5.3
24	SU	0355	0.8	1007	5.5	1617	0.6	○ 2228	5.4
25	M	0429	0.7	1042	5.6	1651	0.6	2303	5.5
26	TU	0505	0.7	1120	5.6	1728	0.7	2340	5.5
27	W	0545	0.7	1201	5.4	1808	0.9		
28	TH	0021	5.4	0629	0.9	1247	5.2	1853	1.2
29	F	0107	5.2	0721	1.1	1339	4.9	1946	1.5
30	SA	0202	5.0	0824	1.4	1446	4.6	2055	1.8

Chart Datum: 3·05 metres below Ordnance Datum (Newlyn)

TIME ZONE (UT)
For Summer Time add ONE hour in **non-shaded areas**

WALES – HOLYHEAD

LAT 53°19'N LONG 4°37'W

TIMES AND HEIGHTS OF HIGH AND LOW WATERS

SPRING & NEAP TIDES
Dates in red are SPRINGS
Dates in blue are NEAPS

YEAR **2005**

MAY

Date	Day	Time	m	Time	m	Time	m	Time	m
1	SU	0311	4.8	0942	1.6	1615	4.4	◑ 2219	2.0
2	M	0437	4.7	1108	1.6	1747	4.5	2344	1.9
3	TU	0559	4.8	1224	1.4	1900	4.7		
4	W	0052	1.7	0705	5.0	1326	1.1	1954	4.9
5	TH	0148	1.4	0759	5.2	1416	0.9	2038	5.1
6	F	0235	1.1	0844	5.4	1459	0.7	2116	5.3
7	SA	0316	0.9	0925	5.5	1538	0.7	2152	5.4
8	SU	0355	0.8	1006	5.6	1615	0.7	● 2228	5.4
9	M	0434	0.8	1045	5.5	1651	0.8	2304	5.4
10	TU	0513	0.8	1124	5.3	1726	1.0	2340	5.3
11	W	0551	1.0	1202	5.1	1802	1.2		
12	TH	0015	5.2	0630	1.2	1241	4.9	1838	1.5
13	F	0052	5.0	0712	1.5	1321	4.7	1918	1.8
14	SA	0132	4.8	0758	1.7	1408	4.4	2005	2.1
15	SU	0220	4.6	0854	1.9	1506	4.2	2103	2.3
16	M	0321	4.4	1001	2.0	1622	4.1	◐ 2216	2.4
17	TU	0437	4.3	1114	2.0	1739	4.2	2332	2.3
18	W	0549	4.4	1218	1.8	1841	4.3		
19	TH	0034	2.1	0648	4.6	1309	1.6	1929	4.6
20	F	0124	1.8	0736	4.8	1352	1.3	2009	4.8
21	SA	0206	1.5	0818	5.0	1431	1.1	2046	5.0
22	SU	0245	1.2	0858	5.2	1509	0.9	2123	5.3
23	M	0324	1.0	0938	5.4	1547	0.8	○ 2201	5.4
24	TU	0405	0.8	1020	5.5	1628	0.7	2241	5.5
25	W	0449	0.7	1104	5.5	1711	0.8	2325	5.6
26	TH	0536	0.7	1152	5.4	1758	0.9		
27	F	0012	5.5	0626	0.8	1245	5.2	1848	1.2
28	SA	0103	5.4	0723	0.9	1343	5.0	1945	1.4
29	SU	0200	5.2	0826	1.1	1449	4.8	2050	1.6
30	M	0306	5.0	0935	1.2	1604	4.6	◑ 2201	1.8
31	TU	0417	5.0	1046	1.3	1719	4.6	2313	1.8

JUNE

Date	Day	Time	m	Time	m	Time	m	Time	m
1	W	0528	4.9	1154	1.3	1826	4.7		
2	TH	0019	1.6	0633	5.0	1255	1.2	1922	4.8
3	F	0118	1.5	0730	5.1	1347	1.2	2010	4.9
4	SA	0209	1.3	0819	5.1	1433	1.1	2052	5.1
5	SU	0255	1.2	0905	5.2	1515	1.1	2131	5.2
6	M	0338	1.1	0947	5.2	1554	1.1	● 2209	5.2
7	TU	0419	1.1	1028	5.1	1631	1.2	2246	5.3
8	W	0459	1.1	1107	5.1	1707	1.3	2322	5.2
9	TH	0537	1.2	1145	5.0	1742	1.4	2357	5.2
10	F	0615	1.3	1223	4.8	1819	1.5		
11	SA	0034	5.1	0654	1.4	1302	4.7	1858	1.7
12	SU	0113	4.9	0736	1.5	1345	4.6	1940	1.8
13	M	0155	4.8	0822	1.6	1432	4.4	2028	2.0
14	TU	0244	4.7	0913	1.7	1527	4.3	2122	2.1
15	W	0339	4.5	1010	1.8	1629	4.3	◐ 2223	2.1
16	TH	0441	4.5	1110	1.8	1733	4.3	2327	2.1
17	F	0544	4.6	1208	1.6	1831	4.5		
18	SA	0027	1.9	0643	4.7	1302	1.5	1923	4.7
19	SU	0122	1.7	0737	4.9	1352	1.3	2011	4.9
20	M	0213	1.4	0828	5.0	1440	1.1	2056	5.2
21	TU	0301	1.1	0917	5.2	1526	1.0	2141	5.4
22	W	0350	0.9	1006	5.4	1613	0.9	○ 2227	5.5
23	TH	0440	0.7	1056	5.4	1701	0.8	2315	5.7
24	F	0531	0.6	1148	5.4	1751	0.9		
25	SA	0004	5.7	0623	0.6	1241	5.3	1841	1.0
26	SU	0056	5.6	0717	0.6	1335	5.2	1935	1.1
27	M	0150	5.5	0813	0.8	1433	5.0	2031	1.3
28	TU	0246	5.3	0911	1.0	1534	4.8	◑ 2131	1.5
29	W	0347	5.1	1013	1.2	1638	4.6	2235	1.7
30	TH	0451	5.0	1116	1.4	1744	4.6	2342	1.7

JULY

Date	Day	Time	m	Time	m	Time	m	Time	m
1	F	0557	4.8	1219	1.5	1847	4.6		
2	SA	0047	1.7	0702	4.8	1318	1.6	1943	4.7
3	SU	0148	1.6	0801	4.8	1412	1.6	2033	4.9
4	M	0242	1.5	0852	4.8	1459	1.5	2117	5.0
5	TU	0329	1.4	0937	4.9	1540	1.4	2156	5.1
6	W	0411	1.3	1018	4.9	1618	1.4	● 2232	5.2
7	TH	0449	1.2	1055	5.0	1652	1.4	2307	5.2
8	F	0524	1.2	1130	5.0	1726	1.3	2341	5.2
9	SA	0559	1.2	1205	4.9	1801	1.4		
10	SU	0015	5.2	0633	1.2	1240	4.9	1835	1.4
11	M	0050	5.1	0709	1.3	1317	4.8	1912	1.5
12	TU	0127	5.0	0747	1.4	1355	4.7	1952	1.6
13	W	0206	4.9	0828	1.5	1438	4.6	2035	1.8
14	TH	0249	4.8	0914	1.6	1527	4.5	◐ 2126	1.9
15	F	0340	4.7	1008	1.7	1626	4.4	2227	2.0
16	SA	0443	4.6	1111	1.8	1734	4.4	2336	2.0
17	SU	0555	4.6	1218	1.7	1843	4.6		
18	M	0046	1.8	0706	4.7	1323	1.6	1944	4.8
19	TU	0150	1.5	0810	4.9	1421	1.4	2038	5.1
20	W	0248	1.2	0907	5.1	1514	1.1	2128	5.4
21	TH	0342	0.9	1000	5.3	1604	0.9	○ 2216	5.7
22	F	0432	0.6	1049	5.5	1651	0.7	2304	5.8
23	SA	0521	0.4	1138	5.5	1738	0.7	2351	5.9
24	SU	0610	0.3	1226	5.5	1825	0.7		
25	M	0039	5.9	0658	0.4	1314	5.3	1912	0.8
26	TU	0127	5.8	0747	0.6	1402	5.1	2001	1.1
27	W	0217	5.5	0837	0.9	1453	4.9	2054	1.4
28	TH	0310	5.2	0932	1.3	1550	4.6	◑ 2154	1.7
29	F	0410	4.9	1033	1.7	1656	4.5	2304	1.9
30	SA	0521	4.6	1141	1.9	1811	4.4		
31	SU	0020	2.0	0639	4.5	1253	2.0	1922	4.5

AUGUST

Date	Day	Time	m	Time	m	Time	m	Time	m
1	M	0134	1.9	0751	4.5	1358	1.9	2021	4.7
2	TU	0235	1.7	0848	4.6	1449	1.8	2107	4.9
3	W	0322	1.5	0932	4.8	1531	1.6	2145	5.1
4	TH	0400	1.3	1008	4.9	1605	1.5	2218	5.2
5	F	0434	1.2	1040	5.0	1636	1.3	● 2249	5.3
6	SA	0505	1.1	1110	5.1	1706	1.2	2319	5.4
7	SU	0535	1.0	1140	5.1	1737	1.2	2350	5.4
8	M	0606	1.0	1211	5.1	1808	1.2		
9	TU	0022	5.3	0637	1.1	1244	5.0	1841	1.2
10	W	0055	5.3	0710	1.2	1318	4.9	1915	1.4
11	TH	0129	5.1	0745	1.3	1355	4.8	1954	1.5
12	F	0207	5.0	0825	1.5	1438	4.7	2040	1.8
13	SA	0253	4.8	0916	1.7	1532	4.5	◐ 2140	2.0
14	SU	0354	4.6	1023	1.9	1646	4.4	2259	2.1
15	M	0521	4.4	1146	2.0	1813	4.5		
16	TU	0025	1.9	0652	4.6	1306	1.8	1927	4.8
17	W	0140	1.6	0805	4.8	1411	1.5	2026	5.1
18	TH	0241	1.2	0902	5.2	1504	1.2	2117	5.5
19	F	0333	0.7	0951	5.4	1551	0.8	○ 2202	5.8
20	SA	0419	0.4	1036	5.6	1635	0.6	2247	6.1
21	SU	0504	0.2	1119	5.7	1718	0.5	2331	6.1
22	M	0547	0.2	1201	5.6	1801	0.5		
23	TU	0015	6.1	0630	0.4	1244	5.5	1843	0.7
24	W	0059	5.9	0713	0.7	1327	5.2	1928	1.0
25	TH	0144	5.5	0758	1.1	1411	5.0	2016	1.4
26	F	0232	5.1	0847	1.5	1501	4.7	◑ 2113	1.8
27	SA	0329	4.7	0945	2.0	1605	4.4	2228	2.1
28	SU	0445	4.3	1102	2.3	1732	4.3	2357	2.2
29	M	0623	4.2	1229	2.4	1902	4.4		
30	TU	0121	2.1	0745	4.4	1344	2.2	2005	4.7
31	W	0222	1.8	0839	4.6	1435	2.0	2050	4.9

Chart Datum: 3·05 metres below Ordnance Datum (Newlyn)

TIME ZONE (UT)
For Summer Time add ONE hour in **non-shaded areas**

WALES – HOLYHEAD

LAT 53°19′N LONG 4°37′W

TIMES AND HEIGHTS OF HIGH AND LOW WATERS

SPRING & NEAP TIDES
Dates in **red** are **SPRINGS**
Dates in **blue** are **NEAPS**

YEAR **2005**

SEPTEMBER

Date	Day	Time	m	Time	m	Time	m	Time	m
1	TH	0305	1.5	0917	4.8	1513	1.7	2125	5.1
2	F	0339	1.3	0948	5.0	1544	1.4	2155	5.3
3	SA	0409	1.1	1016	5.1	1612	1.2	● 2223	5.4
4	SU	0437	1.0	1042	5.2	1639	1.1	2251	5.5
5	M	0505	0.9	1110	5.3	1708	1.0	2321	5.5
6	TU	0533	0.9	1140	5.3	1738	1.0	2351	5.5
7	W	0603	0.9	1211	5.3	1809	1.1		
8	TH	0023	5.4	0633	1.1	1244	5.2	1842	1.2
9	F	0056	5.3	0707	1.3	1320	5.0	1921	1.4
10	SA	0134	5.1	0748	1.5	1402	4.8	2008	1.7
11	SU	0221	4.8	0839	1.8	1457	4.6	◐ 2112	2.0
12	M	0329	4.5	0954	2.1	1618	4.5	2242	2.1
13	TU	0513	4.4	1132	2.2	1757	4.5		
14	W	0018	1.9	0653	4.6	1257	2.0	1915	4.9
15	TH	0133	1.5	0801	4.9	1400	1.6	2013	5.3
16	F	0230	1.0	0852	5.3	1450	1.1	2100	5.7
17	SA	0317	0.6	0935	5.5	1533	0.8	2143	6.0
18	SU	0359	0.3	1015	5.7	1614	0.6	○ 2225	6.2
19	M	0440	0.2	1054	5.8	1654	0.5	2306	6.2
20	TU	0520	0.3	1133	5.7	1734	0.5	2348	6.1
21	W	0600	0.5	1212	5.6	1815	0.7		
22	TH	0030	5.8	0639	0.9	1252	5.3	1857	1.1
23	F	0112	5.4	0719	1.3	1332	5.1	1943	1.5
24	SA	0157	5.0	0804	1.8	1418	4.8	2038	1.9
25	SU	0251	4.5	0858	2.2	1517	4.5	◑ 2152	2.3
26	M	0410	4.2	1017	2.6	1646	4.3	2329	2.4
27	TU	0600	4.1	1158	2.6	1828	4.4		
28	W	0054	2.2	0723	4.3	1316	2.4	1935	4.6
29	TH	0153	1.9	0813	4.6	1407	2.1	2019	4.9
30	F	0234	1.6	0848	4.8	1443	1.8	2053	5.1

OCTOBER

Date	Day	Time	m	Time	m	Time	m	Time	m
1	SA	0307	1.3	0918	5.1	1513	1.5	2123	5.3
2	SU	0336	1.1	0944	5.2	1540	1.2	2151	5.5
3	M	0403	0.9	1011	5.4	1608	1.1	● 2220	5.6
4	TU	0431	0.9	1039	5.4	1638	1.0	2250	5.6
5	W	0500	0.9	1109	5.5	1709	1.0	2322	5.6
6	TH	0531	0.9	1141	5.5	1742	1.0	2355	5.5
7	F	0604	1.1	1216	5.4	1818	1.2		
8	SA	0032	5.3	0640	1.3	1255	5.2	1900	1.4
9	SU	0115	5.1	0725	1.6	1341	5.0	1953	1.7
10	M	0209	4.8	0822	2.0	1442	4.7	◐ 2105	2.0
11	TU	0328	4.5	0945	2.3	1608	4.6	2240	2.0
12	W	0518	4.4	1123	2.3	1744	4.7		
13	TH	0009	1.8	0646	4.7	1242	2.0	1857	5.1
14	F	0118	1.4	0747	5.0	1341	1.6	1952	5.4
15	SA	0211	1.0	0833	5.3	1429	1.2	2038	5.7
16	SU	0255	0.7	0913	5.6	1511	0.9	2120	6.0
17	M	0336	0.5	0951	5.7	1550	0.7	○ 2201	6.1
18	TU	0414	0.5	1028	5.8	1630	0.6	2242	6.0
19	W	0452	0.6	1106	5.7	1710	0.7	2323	5.9
20	TH	0530	0.8	1144	5.6	1751	0.9		
21	F	0004	5.6	0608	1.1	1222	5.4	1832	1.2
22	SA	0046	5.2	0647	1.5	1301	5.2	1917	1.6
23	SU	0129	4.9	0729	1.9	1344	4.9	2010	2.0
24	M	0220	4.5	0819	2.3	1437	4.6	2117	2.2
25	TU	0332	4.2	0929	2.6	1555	4.4	◑ 2243	2.4
26	W	0510	4.1	1104	2.7	1727	4.4		
27	TH	0004	2.2	0634	4.3	1225	2.5	1841	4.6
28	F	0105	2.0	0728	4.5	1320	2.2	1932	4.8
29	SA	0149	1.7	0807	4.8	1401	1.9	2011	5.1
30	SU	0225	1.4	0839	5.0	1434	1.6	2044	5.3
31	M	0257	1.2	0909	5.2	1505	1.4	2116	5.4

NOVEMBER

Date	Day	Time	m	Time	m	Time	m	Time	m
1	TU	0327	1.0	0938	5.4	1537	1.2	2148	5.5
2	W	0358	1.0	1009	5.5	1610	1.0	● 2222	5.6
3	TH	0431	0.9	1042	5.6	1645	1.0	2258	5.6
4	F	0505	1.0	1118	5.6	1723	1.0	2337	5.5
5	SA	0543	1.1	1157	5.5	1806	1.2		
6	SU	0020	5.3	0626	1.4	1242	5.4	1854	1.4
7	M	0111	5.1	0716	1.7	1334	5.2	1953	1.6
8	TU	0212	4.8	0819	2.0	1438	5.0	2107	1.8
9	W	0334	4.6	0939	2.2	1558	4.9	◐ 2230	1.8
10	TH	0506	4.6	1103	2.1	1720	5.0	2347	1.6
11	F	0623	4.8	1215	1.9	1830	5.2		
12	SA	0051	1.3	0721	5.0	1314	1.6	1926	5.4
13	SU	0145	1.1	0808	5.3	1404	1.3	2014	5.6
14	M	0231	0.9	0849	5.4	1448	1.1	2058	5.8
15	TU	0312	0.8	0928	5.6	1530	0.9	2141	5.8
16	W	0351	0.9	1006	5.6	1612	0.9	○ 2223	5.7
17	TH	0429	1.0	1044	5.6	1653	1.0	2304	5.6
18	F	0507	1.1	1122	5.6	1734	1.1	2345	5.4
19	SA	0545	1.4	1200	5.4	1816	1.4		
20	SU	0026	5.1	0623	1.6	1239	5.2	1859	1.6
21	M	0108	4.8	0704	1.9	1319	5.0	1946	1.8
22	TU	0155	4.6	0750	2.2	1406	4.8	2041	2.0
23	W	0251	4.4	0846	2.4	1505	4.6	◑ 2145	2.2
24	TH	0403	4.2	0955	2.6	1616	4.5	2256	2.2
25	F	0518	4.3	1110	2.5	1728	4.6		
26	SA	0000	2.0	0622	4.4	1215	2.4	1829	4.7
27	SU	0053	1.8	0713	4.7	1307	2.1	1919	4.9
28	M	0137	1.6	0755	4.9	1350	1.8	2003	5.1
29	TU	0216	1.4	0832	5.1	1430	1.6	2042	5.2
30	W	0253	1.3	0908	5.3	1509	1.3	2121	5.4

DECEMBER

Date	Day	Time	m	Time	m	Time	m	Time	m
1	TH	0330	1.1	0944	5.5	1548	1.2	● 2201	5.5
2	F	0409	1.1	1022	5.6	1629	1.0	2243	5.5
3	SA	0449	1.1	1103	5.7	1714	1.0	2329	5.5
4	SU	0533	1.1	1148	5.7	1802	1.0		
5	M	0017	5.4	0621	1.3	1236	5.6	1854	1.1
6	TU	0112	5.2	0714	1.5	1330	5.4	1952	1.2
7	W	0211	5.0	0813	1.7	1429	5.3	2056	1.4
8	TH	0320	4.8	0919	1.9	1536	5.2	◐ 2205	1.5
9	F	0434	4.7	1030	1.9	1647	5.1	2314	1.5
10	SA	0545	4.8	1139	1.9	1755	5.1		
11	SU	0018	1.4	0647	4.9	1243	1.7	1856	5.2
12	M	0116	1.4	0741	5.0	1339	1.6	1952	5.3
13	TU	0207	1.3	0828	5.2	1431	1.4	2042	5.4
14	W	0253	1.3	0911	5.3	1518	1.3	2128	5.4
15	TH	0335	1.3	0951	5.4	1602	1.2	○ 2212	5.4
16	F	0415	1.3	1030	5.5	1644	1.2	2253	5.3
17	SA	0453	1.4	1108	5.5	1724	1.2	2332	5.2
18	SU	0529	1.4	1145	5.4	1803	1.3		
19	M	0010	5.1	0605	1.6	1221	5.3	1841	1.4
20	TU	0049	4.9	0643	1.7	1258	5.2	1921	1.6
21	W	0128	4.8	0723	1.9	1338	5.0	2004	1.7
22	TH	0211	4.6	0807	2.0	1422	4.9	2051	1.8
23	F	0301	4.5	0857	2.2	1513	4.7	◑ 2144	2.0
24	SA	0359	4.4	0954	2.3	1612	4.6	2243	2.0
25	SU	0504	4.4	1058	2.3	1718	4.6	2345	2.0
26	M	0609	4.5	1204	2.2	1822	4.6		
27	TU	0043	1.9	0706	4.6	1304	2.0	1921	4.8
28	W	0136	1.7	0757	4.9	1358	1.8	2014	5.0
29	TH	0225	1.5	0842	5.1	1447	1.5	2102	5.2
30	F	0310	1.3	0926	5.4	1534	1.2	2149	5.3
31	SA	0355	1.1	1009	5.6	1621	0.9	● 2236	5.5

Chart Datum: 3·05 metres below Ordnance Datum (Newlyn)

Area 11

South Wales and Bristol Channel
Bardsey Island to Lands End

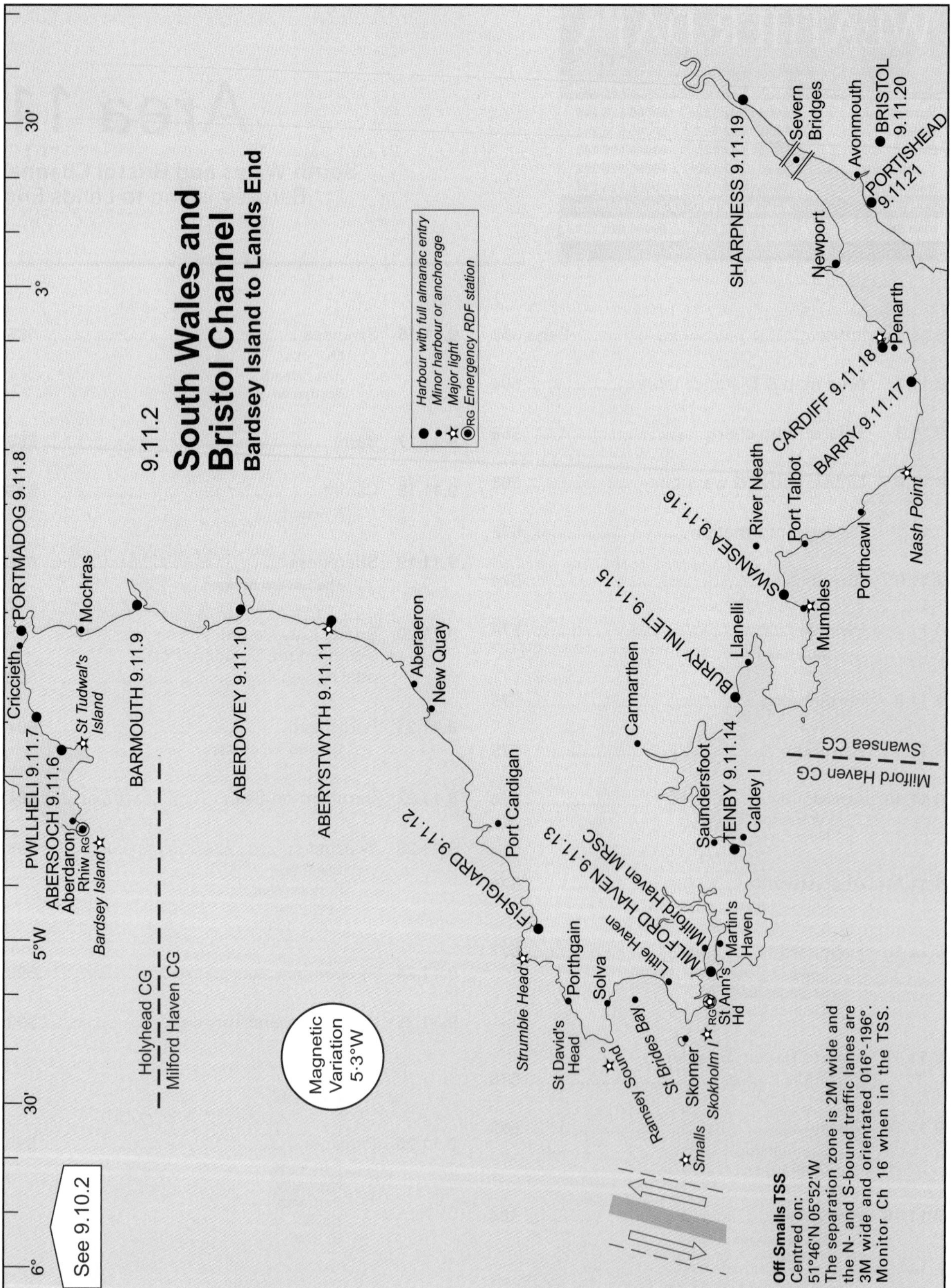
9.11.2
South Wales and Bristol Channel
Bardsey Island to Lands End
Harbour with full almanac entry
Minor harbour or anchorage
Major light
RG Emergency RDF station
Magnetic Variation 5·3°W
See 9.10.2
Holyhead CG
Milford Haven CG
Milford Haven CG
Swansea CG
PORTMADOG 9.11.8
Criccieth
Mochras
PWLLHELI 9.11.7
ABERSOCH 9.11.6
Aberdaron
Rhiw RG
Bardsey Island
St Tudwal's Island
BARMOUTH 9.11.9
ABERDOVEY 9.11.10
ABERYSTWYTH 9.11.11
Aberaeron
New Quay
Port Cardigan
FISHGUARD 9.11.12
Strumble Head
Porthgain
St David's Head
Solva
Ramsey Sound
St Brides Bay
Skomer
Skokholm I
Smalls
Little Haven
St Ann's Hd
RG
MILFORD HAVEN 9.11.13
Milford Haven MRSC
Martin's Haven
Saundersfoot
TENBY 9.11.14
Caldey I
Carmarthen
BURRY INLET 9.11.15
Llanelli
Mumbles
SWANSEA 9.11.16
River Neath
Port Talbot
Porthcawl
Nash Point
BARRY 9.11.17
CARDIFF 9.11.18
Penarth
Newport
SHARPNESS 9.11.19
Severn Bridges
Avonmouth
PORTISHEAD 9.11.21
BRISTOL 9.11.20
6°
30'
5°W
30'
3°
30'
52°N
30'
30'
Off Smalls TSS
Centred on:
51°46'N 05°52'W
The separation zone is 2M wide and the N- and S-bound traffic lanes are 3M wide and orientated 016°-196°. Monitor Ch 16 when in the TSS.

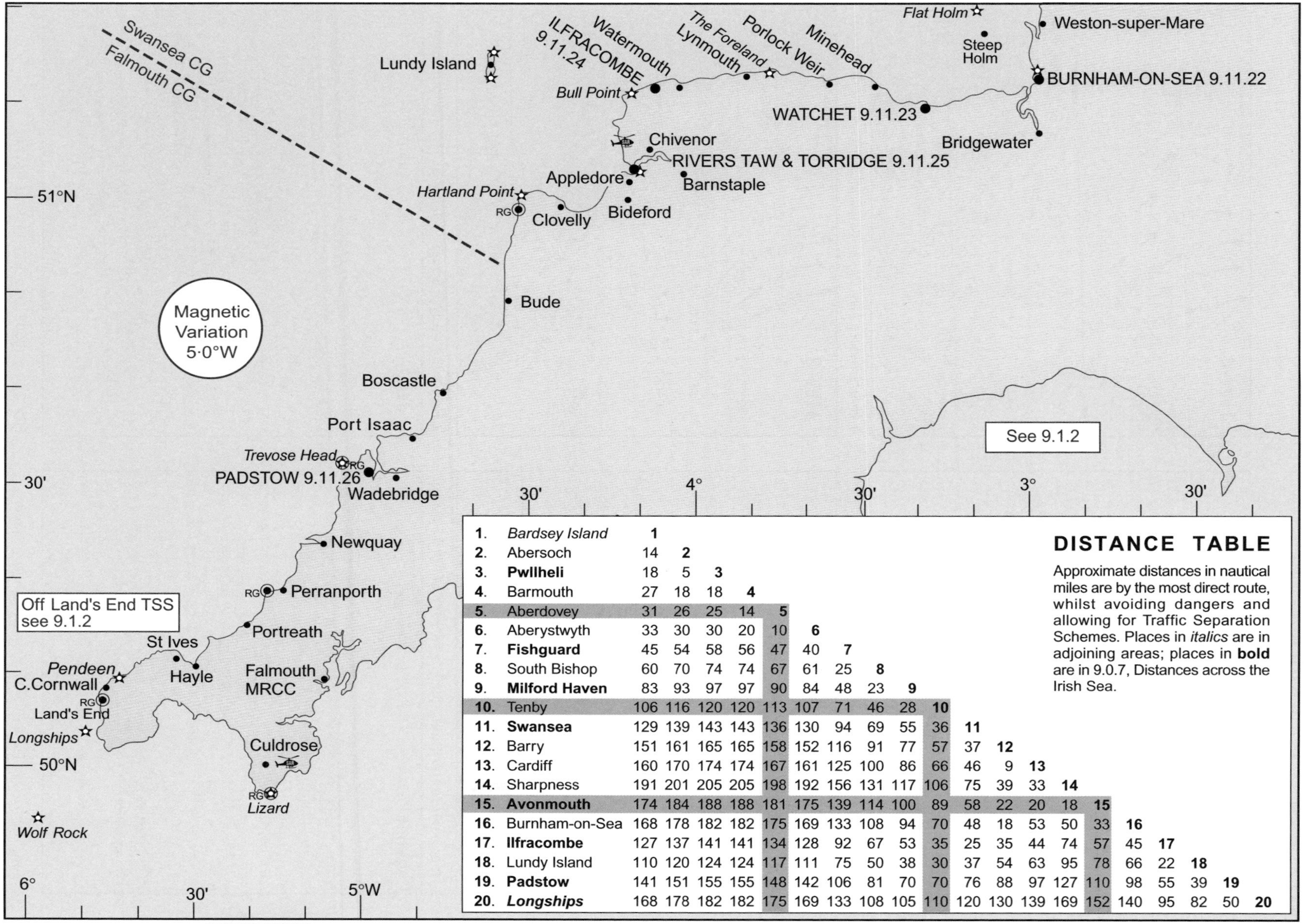

Swansea CG
Falmouth CG
Lundy Island
ILFRACOMBE 9.11.24
Watermouth
The Foreland
Lynmouth
Porlock Weir
Minehead
Flat Holm
Steep Holm
Weston-super-Mare
BURNHAM-ON-SEA 9.11.22
WATCHET 9.11.23
Bridgewater
Bull Point
Chivenor
RIVERS TAW & TORRIDGE 9.11.25
Appledore
Barnstaple
Bideford
Hartland Point
Clovelly
51°N
Bude
Magnetic Variation 5·0°W
Boscastle
Port Isaac
Trevose Head
PADSTOW 9.11.26
Wadebridge
30'
4°
3°
See 9.1.2
Newquay
Perranporth
Off Land's End TSS see 9.1.2
Portreath
St Ives
Hayle
Falmouth MRCC
Pendeen
C.Cornwall
Land's End
Longships
Culdrose
50°N
Lizard
Wolf Rock
6°
5°W
RG

DISTANCE TABLE

Approximate distances in nautical miles are by the most direct route, whilst avoiding dangers and allowing for Traffic Separation Schemes. Places in *italics* are in adjoining areas; places in **bold** are in 9.0.7, Distances across the Irish Sea.

1.	*Bardsey Island*	**1**																			
2.	Abersoch	14	**2**																		
3.	**Pwllheli**	18	5	**3**																	
4.	Barmouth	27	18	18	**4**																
5.	Aberdovey	31	26	25	14	**5**															
6.	Aberystwyth	33	30	30	20	10	**6**														
7.	**Fishguard**	45	54	58	56	47	40	**7**													
8.	South Bishop	60	70	74	74	67	61	25	**8**												
9.	**Milford Haven**	83	93	97	97	90	84	48	23	**9**											
10.	Tenby	106	116	120	120	113	107	71	46	28	**10**										
11.	**Swansea**	129	139	143	143	136	130	94	69	55	36	**11**									
12.	Barry	151	161	165	165	158	152	116	91	77	57	37	**12**								
13.	Cardiff	160	170	174	174	167	161	125	100	86	66	46	9	**13**							
14.	Sharpness	191	201	205	205	198	192	156	131	117	106	75	39	33	**14**						
15.	**Avonmouth**	174	184	188	188	181	175	139	114	100	89	58	22	20	18	**15**					
16.	Burnham-on-Sea	168	178	182	182	175	169	133	108	94	70	48	18	53	50	33	**16**				
17.	**Ilfracombe**	127	137	141	141	134	128	92	67	53	35	25	35	44	74	57	45	**17**			
18.	Lundy Island	110	120	124	124	117	111	75	50	38	30	37	54	63	95	78	66	22	**18**		
19.	**Padstow**	141	151	155	155	148	142	106	81	70	70	76	88	97	127	110	98	55	39	**19**	
20.	***Longships***	168	178	182	182	175	169	133	108	105	110	120	130	139	169	152	140	95	82	50	**20**

11

9.11.3 AREA 11 TIDAL STREAMS

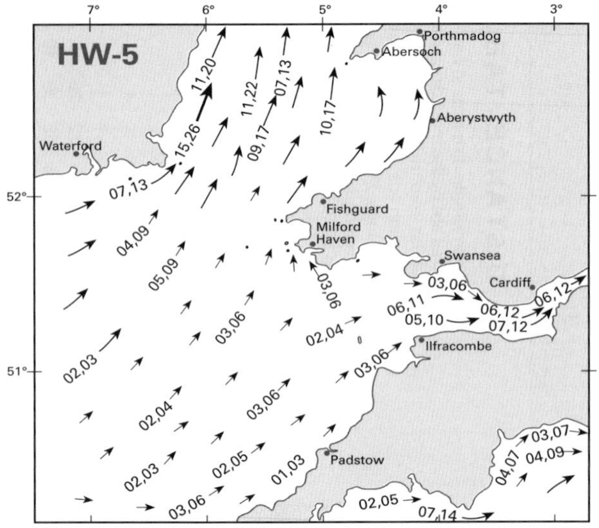
HW-5
Porthmadog
Abersoch
Aberystwyth
Waterford
Fishguard
Milford Haven
Swansea
Cardiff
Ilfracombe
Padstow
5 Hours before HW Dover (HW Milford Haven)

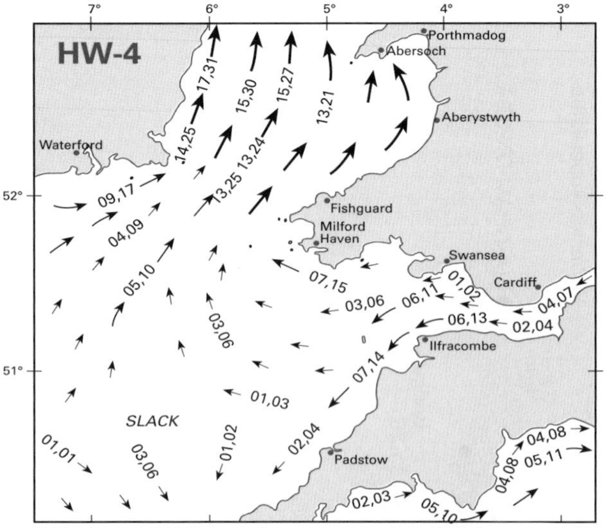
HW-4
Porthmadog
Abersoch
Aberystwyth
Waterford
Fishguard
Milford Haven
Swansea
Cardiff
Ilfracombe
SLACK
Padstow
4 Hours before HW Dover (0100 after HW Milford Haven)

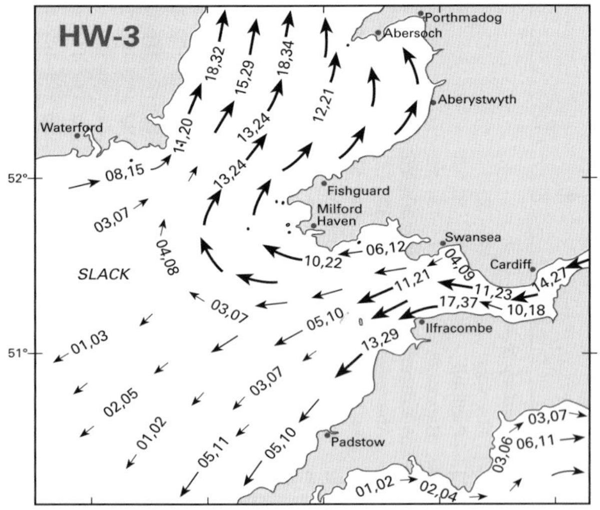
HW-3
Porthmadog
Abersoch
Aberystwyth
Waterford
Fishguard
Milford Haven
SLACK
Swansea
Cardiff
Ilfracombe
Padstow
3 Hours before HW Dover (0200 after HW Milford Haven)

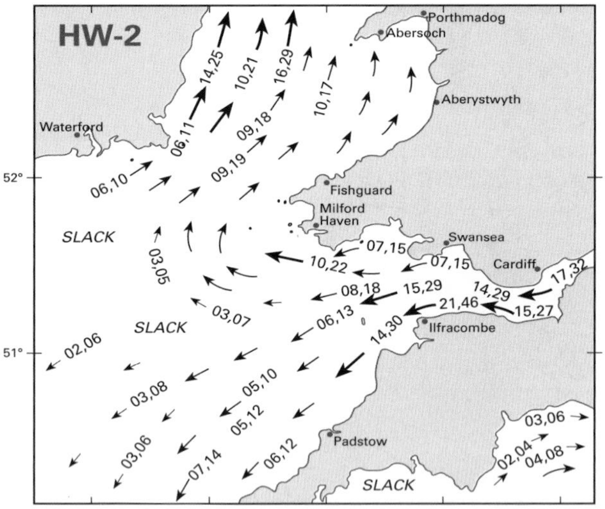
HW-2
Porthmadog
Abersoch
Aberystwyth
Waterford
Fishguard
Milford Haven
SLACK
Swansea
Cardiff
SLACK
Ilfracombe
Padstow
SLACK
2 Hours before HW Dover (0300 after HW Milford Haven)

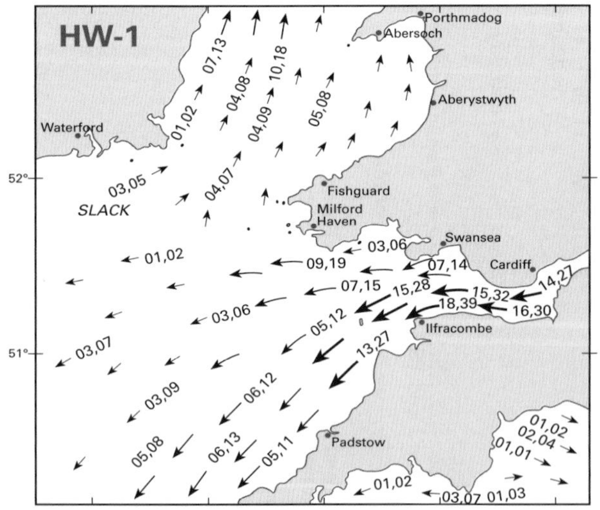
HW-1
Porthmadog
Abersoch
Aberystwyth
Waterford
SLACK
Fishguard
Milford Haven
Swansea
Cardiff
Ilfracombe
Padstow
1 Hour before HW Dover (0400 after HW Milford Haven)

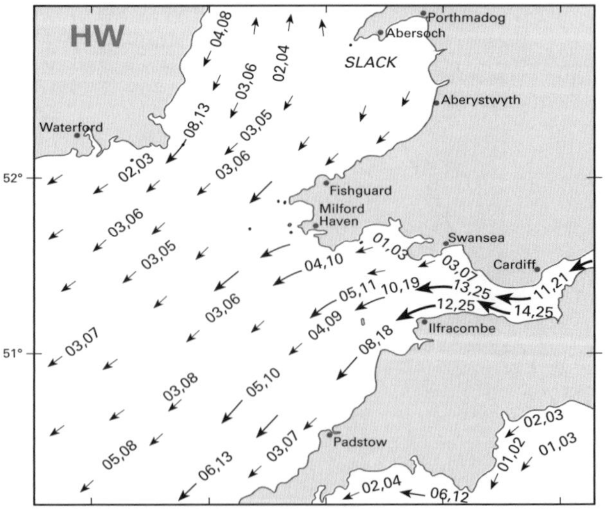
HW
Porthmadog
Abersoch
SLACK
Aberystwyth
Waterford
Fishguard
Milford Haven
Swansea
Cardiff
Ilfracombe
Padstow
HW Dover (0500 after HW Milford Haven)

Southward 9.1.3 Northward 9.10.3 South Ireland 9.12.3

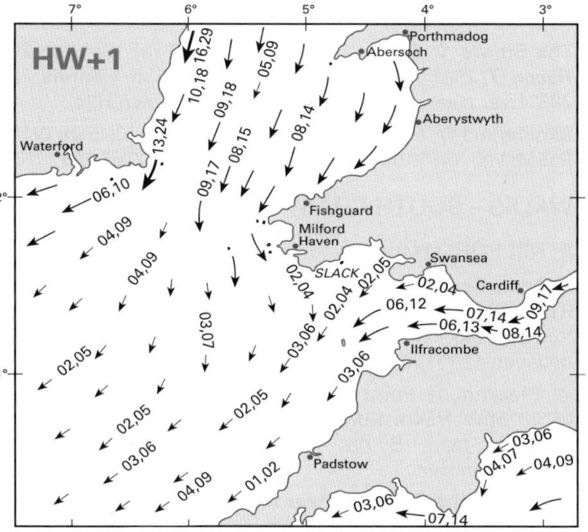
HW+1
Porthmadog
Abersoch
Aberystwyth
Waterford
Fishguard
Milford Haven
Swansea
Cardiff
Ilfracombe
Padstow
SLACK

1 Hour after HW Dover (0600 after HW Milford Haven)

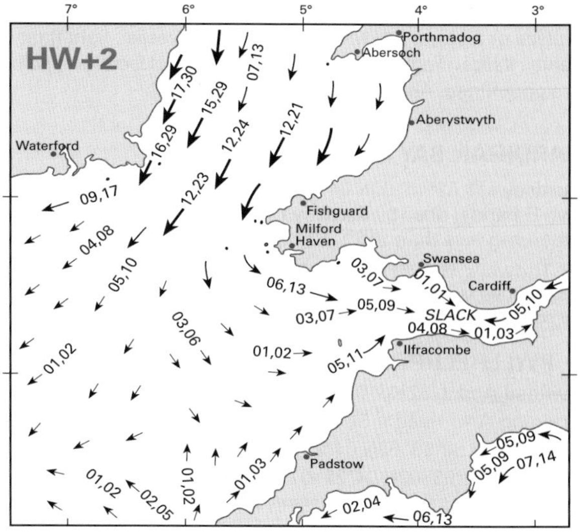
HW+2
Porthmadog
Abersoch
Aberystwyth
Waterford
Fishguard
Milford Haven
Swansea
Cardiff
Ilfracombe
Padstow
SLACK

2 Hours after HW Dover (0525 before HW Milford Haven)

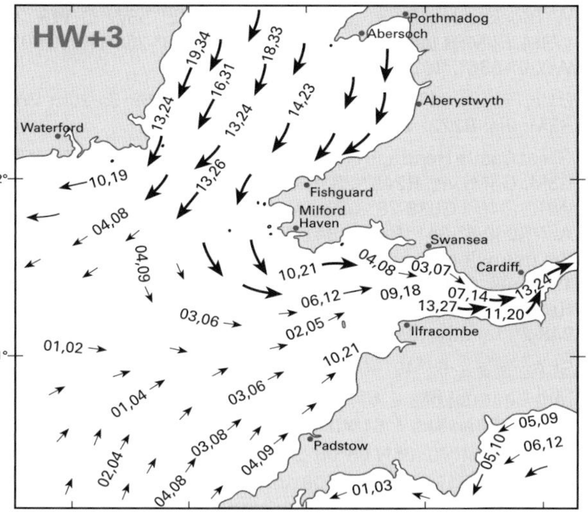
HW+3
Porthmadog
Abersoch
Aberystwyth
Waterford
Fishguard
Milford Haven
Swansea
Cardiff
Ilfracombe
Padstow

3 Hours after HW Dover (0425 before HW Milford Haven)

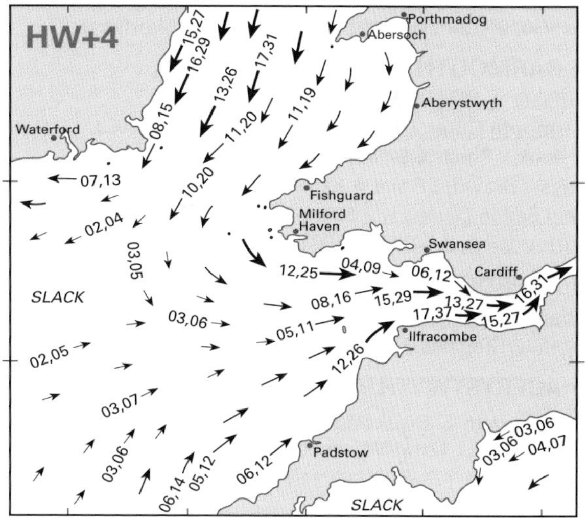
HW+4
Porthmadog
Abersoch
Aberystwyth
Waterford
Fishguard
Milford Haven
Swansea
Cardiff
Ilfracombe
Padstow
SLACK
SLACK

4 Hours after HW Dover (0325 before HW Milford Haven)

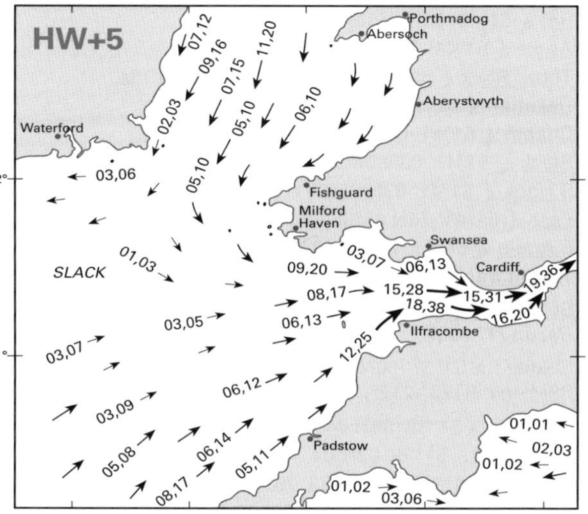
HW+5
Porthmadog
Abersoch
Aberystwyth
Waterford
Fishguard
Milford Haven
Swansea
Cardiff
Ilfracombe
Padstow
SLACK

5 Hours after HW Dover (0225 before HW Milford Haven)

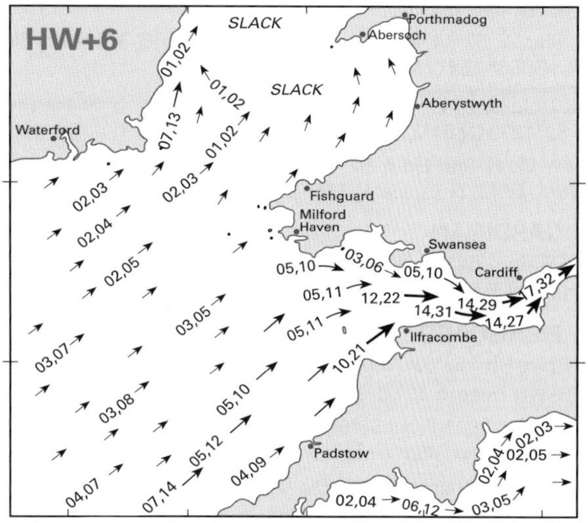
HW+6
Porthmadog
Abersoch
Aberystwyth
Waterford
Fishguard
Milford Haven
Swansea
Cardiff
Ilfracombe
Padstow
SLACK
SLACK

6 Hours after HW Dover (0125 before HW Milford Haven)

11

PLOT WAYPOINTS ON YOUR CHART BEFORE USING THEM

9.11.4 LIGHTS, BUOYS AND WAYPOINTS

Blue print = light with a nominal range of 15M or more. CAPITALS = place or feature. *CAPITAL ITALICS* = light-vessel, light float or Lanby. *Italics* = Fog signal. ***Bold italics*** = Racon. Useful waypoints are underlined. Abbreviations are in Chapter 1.

CARDIGAN BAY (see also 9.10.4)

Bardsey I ☆ 52°45'·00N 04°47'·98W Fl (5) 15s 39m **26M**; W □ twr, R bands; obsc by Bardsey I 198°-250° and in Tremadoc B when brg less than 260°; *Horn Mo(N) 45s.*

St Tudwal's ☆ 52°47'·92N 04°28'·30W Fl WR 15s 46m W14, R10M; vis: W349°-169°, R169°-221°, W221°-243°, R243°-259°, W259°-293°, R293°-349°; obsc by East I 211°-231°.

▶ PWLLHELI/PORTHMADOG/MOCHRAS LAGOON

Pwllheli App 52°53'·02N 04°23'·07W Iso 2s.
Training Arm Head ☆ 52°53'·25N 04°23'·74W QG 3m 3M.
Abererch 52°53'·52N 04°23'·07W; (Apr-Oct).
Butlins 52°53'·02N 04°22'·07W; (Apr-Oct).
West End 52°52'·42N 04°25'·57W; (Apr-Oct).
Porthmadog Fairway 52°52'·97N 04°11'·18W L Fl 10s.

Shell I, NE Corner ☆ 52°49'·56N 04°07'·71W Fl WRG 4s; vis: G079°-124°, W124°-134°, R134°-179°; (Mar-Nov).

◀ BARMOUTH

Diffuser 52°43'·19N 04°05'·38W Fl Y 5s.
Barmouth Outer 52°42'·62N 04°04'·83W L Fl 10s.
N Bank Y Perch ☆ 52°42'·83N 04°03'·74W QR 4m 5M.
Ynys y Brawd, SE end ☆ 52°42'·99N 04°03'·12W Fl R 5s 5M.
Sarn Badrig Causeway 52°41'·19N 04°25'·36W Q (9) 15s; *Bell.*
Sarn-y-Bwch 52°34'·81N 04°13'·58W VQ (9) 10s.

◀ ABERDOVEY

Aberdovey Outer 52°32'·00N 04°05'·56W; Iso 4s.
Cynfelyn Patches, Patches 52°25'·83N 04°16'·41W Q (9) 15s.

▶ ABERYSTWYTH/ABERAERON/NEW QUAY

Aberystwyth S Breakwater Head ☆ 52°24'·40N 04°05'·52W Fl (2) WG 10s 12m 10M; vis: G030°-053°, W053°-210°.

Ldg Lts 133°. Front, 52°24'·37N 04°05'·39W FR 4m 5M. Rear, 52m from front, FR 7m 6M.

Aberaeron S Pier ☆ 52°14'·61N 04°15'·94W Fl (3) G 10s 11m 6M; vis: 050°-243°.

N Pier ☆ 52°14'·61N 04°15'·87W Fl (4) WRG 15s 10m 6M; vis: G050°-104°, W104°-178°, R178°-232°.

Carreg Ina 52°13'·25N 04°20'·75W Q.
52°12'·94N 04°21'·29W Q (3) 10s.

New Quay Pier Hd ☆ 52°12'·95N 04°21'·35W Fl WG 3s 12m W8M, G5M; G △; vis: W135°-252°, G252°-295.

▶ CARDIGAN

CG Bldg ☆ 52°06'·98N 04°41'·21W 2 FR (vert).
Channel 52°06'·44N 04°41'·43W Fl (2) 5s.

▶ FISHGUARD

N Bkwtr Hd ☆ 52°00'·76N 04°58'·23W Fl G 4·5s 18m 13M; *Bell (1) 8s.*
E Bkwtr Head ☆ 52°00'·31N 04°58'·86W Fl R 3s 10m 5M.

Lts in line 282°. Front 52°00'·68N 04°59'·27W FG 77m 5M W ◇ on mast. Rear, 46m from front, FG 89m 5M.

Penanglas, 152m S of Pt, *Dia (2) 60s*; W obelisk.

Strumble Head ☆ 52°01'·79N 05°04'·43W Fl (4) 15s 45m **26M**; vis: 038°-257°; (H24).

BISHOPS AND SMALLS

South Bishop ☆ 51°51'·14N 05°24'·74W Fl 5s 44m **16M**; W ○ twr; *Horn (3) 45s;* ***Racon (O) 10M***; (H24).

The Smalls ☆ 51°43'·28N 05°40'·19W Fl (3) 15s 36m **25M**; ***Racon (T) 25M***; *Horn (2) 60s.* Same twr, FR 33m 13M; vis: 253°-285° over Hats and Barrels Rk; both Lts shown H24.

Skokholm I ☆, 51°41'·64N 05°17'·22W Fl WR 10s 54m **W18M, R15M**; vis: 301°-154°, R154°-129°; part obsc 226°-258°; (H24).

WALES – SOUTH COAST – BRISTOL CHANNEL

▶ MILFORD HAVEN

St Ann's Head ☆ 51°40'·87N 05°10'·42W Fl WR 5s 48m **W18M, R17M**, R14M; W 8-sided twr; vis: W233°-247°, R247°-285°, R(intens)285°-314°, R314°-332°, W332°-131°, partially obscured between 124°-129°; *Horn (2) 60s.*

W Blockhouse Point Ldg Lts 022·5°. Front, 51°41'·31N 05°09'·56W F 54m 13M; B stripe on W twr; vis: 004·5°-040·5°; intens on lead. By day 10M; vis: 004·5°-040·5°; ***Racon (Q) range unknown.***

Watwick Point Common Rear ☆, 0·5M from front, F 80m **15M**; vis: 013·5°-031·5°. By day 10M; vis: 013·5°-031·5°; ***Racon (Y) range unknown.***

W Blockhouse Point 51°41'·31N 05°09'·56W Q WR 21m W9M, R7M; R lantern on W base: vis: W220°-250°, R250°-020°, W020°-036°, R036°-049°.

Dale Fort ☆ 51°42'·16N 05°09'·01W Fl (2) WR 5s 20m W5M, R3M; vis: R222°-276°, W276°-019°.

Great Castle Head 51°42'·67N 05°07'·07W F WRG 27m W5M, R3M, G3M; vis: R243°-281°, G281°-299°, W299°-029°; also Dir WRG (040°) G038·25°-039°, Al WG039°-039·5° W039·5°-040·5° AlWR040·5°-041° R041°-041·75° (not used in conjunction with the following front light) also Ldg Lts 039·7° **Front**, Oc 4s 27m **15M**; vis: 031·2°-048·2°. **Rear**, 890m from front, **Little Castle Head** 51°43'·03N 05°06'·60W Oc 8s 53m **15M**; vis: 031·2°-048·2°; by day 10M vis: 032·2°-047·2°.

St Anne's 51°40'·25N 05°10'·51W Fl R 2·5s.
Mid Channel Rks 51°40'·18N 05°10'·14W Q (9) 15s.
Middle Chan Rks ☆ 51°40'·32N 05°09'·83W Fl (3) G 7s 18m 8M.
Sheep 51°40'·06N 05°08'·31W QG.
Millbay 51°41'·05N 05°09'·45W Fl (2) R 5s.
W Chapel 51°40'·98N 05°08'·67W Fl G 10s.
E Chapel 51°40'·87N 05°08'·15W Fl R 5s.
Rat 51°40'·80N 05°07'·86W Fl G 5s.
Angle 51°41'·63N 05°08'·27W VQ.
Thorn Rock 51°41'·53N 05°07'·76W Q (9) 15s.
Dakotian 51°42'·15N 05°08'·29W Q (3) 10s.
Chapel 51°41'·66N 05°06'·86W Fl G 5s.
Stack 51°42'·03N 05°06'·52W Fl R 2·5s.
S Hook 51°41'·83N 05°06'·10W Q (6) +L Fl 15s.
Esso 51°41'·74N 05°05'·24W Q.
E Angle 51°41'·72N 05°04'·26W Fl (3) G 10s.
Turbot Bank 51°37'·41N 05°10'·08W VQ (9) 10s.

St Gowan 51°31'·93N 04°59'·77W Q (6) + L Fl 15s, *Whis,* ***Racon (T) 10M.***

Caldey I ☆ 51°37'·90N 04°41'·08W Fl (3) WR 20s 65m W13M, R9M; vis: R173°-212°, W212°-088°, R088°-102°.

Eel Point 51°38'·86N 04°42'·24W.
Giltar Spit 51°39'·03N 04°42'·10W.
Spaniel 51°38'·06N 04°39'·75W.
Woolhouse 51°39'·33N 04°39'·69W.
North Highcliff 51°39'·38N 04°40'·77W.

▶ TENBY/SAUNDERSFOOT/CARMARTHEN BAY/ BURRY INLET

Tenby Pier Head ☆ 51°40'·40N 04°41'·89W FR 7m 7M.
Saundersfoot Pier Hd ☆ 51°42'·59N 04°41'·73W Fl R 5s 6m 7M.
DZ1 51°42'·05N 04°36'·00W.
DZ2 51°39'·98N 04°37'·73W Fl Y 2·5s.
DZ3 51°37'·37N 04°37'·84W.
DZ7 51°38'·09N 04°30'·12W Fl Y 10s.
DZ4 51°35'·73N 04°30'·05W Fl Y 5s.
DZ8 51°41'·51N 04°24'·42W.
DZ6 51°38'·02N 04°24'·37W.
DZ5 51°36'·37N 04°24'·39W Fl Y 2·5s.
Burry Port Barrel Post ☆ 51°40'·49N 04°15'·01W Fl R 3s 5M.
Burry Port Inlet ☆ 51°40'·62N 04°15'·06W Fl 5s 7m **15M**.
Llanelli Ent N side ☆ Fl R 5s 2M.

West Helwick (W HWK) 51°31'·40N 04°23'·65W Q (9) 15s; ***Racon (T) 10M***; *Whis.*

East Helwick 51°31'·80N 04°12'·68W VQ (3) 5s; *Bell.*

▶ SWANSEA BAY/SWANSEA

Ledge 51°29'·93N 03°58'·77W VQ (6) + L Fl 10s.
Mixon 51°33'·12N 03°58'·78W Fl (2) R 5s; *Bell.*
Outer Spoil Gnd 51°32'·11N 03°55'·73W Fl Y 2·5s.
Grounds 51°32'·81N 03°53'·47W VQ (3) 5s.

Mumbles ☆ 51°34'·01N 03°58'·27W Fl (4) 20s 35m **15M**; W twr; *Horn (3) 60s.*

Railway Pier Hd ☆ 51°34'·21N 03°58'·44W 2 FR (vert) 11m 9M.

SW Inner Green Grounds 51°34'·06N 03°57'·03W Q (6) + L Fl 15s; *Bell.*

Outer Fairway 51°35'·52N 03°56'·09W QG; *Bell.*
Swansea West Fairway 51°35'·56N 03°56'·24W QR.
Swansea Inner Fairway 51°36'·23N 03°55'·67W Fl G 2·5s; *Bell.*

E Bkwtr Head ☆ 51°36'·38N 03°55'·62W 2 FG (vert) 10m 6M; *Siren 30s.*

W Pier Head ☆ 51°36'·50N 03°55'·73W Fl (2) R 10s 11m 9M.

Lts in line 020°. Jetty Head Front, 51°36'·55N 03°55'·52W Oc G 4s 5m 2M. Rear, 260m from front, FG 6M.

▶ SWANSEA BAY/RIVER NEATH/PORT TALBOT

Neath App Chan 51°35'·71N 03°52'·83W Fl G 5s.
Monkstone ☆ 51°36'·32N 03°51'·97W Fl (2) G 6s 6m 5M.

Neath SE Trg Wall N End ☆ 51°37'·09N 03°50'·85W Fl (3) G 10s 6m 5M.

Neath SE Trg Wall Middle ☆ 51°36'·70N 03°51'·41W Fl G 1·5s 6m 5M.

Neath SE Trg Wall N end inner ☆ 51°37'·09N 03°50'·85W Fl(3)G 10s 6m 5M.

Cabenda 51°33'·36N 03°52'·23W VQ (6) + L Fl 10s; ***Racon (Q) range unknown***.
P Talbot S Outer 51°33'·71N 03°51'·30W Fl G 5s.
P Talbot N Outer 51°33'·78N 03°51'·38W Fl R 5s.
North Inner 51°34'·22N 03°50'·25W Fl R 3s.

Ldg Lts 059·8° (occas). Front 51°34'·92N 03°48'·10W Oc R 3s 12m 6M. Rear, 400m from front, Oc R 6s 32m 6M.

N Bkwtr Head ☆ 51°34'·77N 03°49'·00W Fl (4) R 10s 11m 3M.
S Bkwtr Head ☆ 51°34'·46N 03°49'·04W Fl G 3s 11m 3M.

BRISTOL CHANNEL – EASTERN PART (NORTH SHORE)

Kenfig 51°29'·44N 03°46'·06W VQ (3) 5s.
W Scar 51°28'·31N 03°55'·57W Q (9) 15s, *Bell*, ***Racon (T) 10M***.
South Scar (S SCAR) 51°27'·61N 03°51'·58W Q (6) + L Fl 15s.
Hugo 51°28'·63N 03°48'·07W QR.
East Scarweather 51°27'·98N 03°46'·76W Q (3) 10s; *Bell.*

▶ PORTHCAWL

Fairy 51°27'·86N 03°42'·07W Q (9) 15s; *Bell.*
Tusker 51°26'·85N 03°40'·74W Fl (2) R 5s *Bell.*

Porthcawl Bkwtr Head ☆ 51°28'·39N 03°41'·98W F WRG 10m W6M, R4M, G4M; vis: G302°-036°, W036°-082°, R082°-122°.

W Nash 51°25'·99N 03°45'·95W VQ (9) 10s ; *Bell.*
Middle Nash 51°24'·83N 03°39'·41W Q (6) + L Fl 15s.
East Nash 51°24'·06N 03°34'·10W Q (3) 10s.

Nash ☆ 51°24'·03N 03°33'·06W Fl (2) WR 15s 56m **W21M**, **R16M**; vis: R280°-290°, W290°-100°, R100°-120°, W120°-128°.

Saint Hilary ☆ 51° 27'·43N 03°24'·18W Aero QR 346m 11M; radio mast; 4 FR (vert) on same mast 6M.

Breaksea Point intake ☆ 51°22'·51N 03°24'·53W Fl R 11m.

BREAKSEA 51°19'·88N 03°19'·08W Fl 15s 11m 12M; ***Racon (T) 10M***; *Horn (2) 30s.*

Wenvoe ☆ 51°27'·55N 03°16'·93W Aero Q 365m 12M; radio mast (H24).

Merkur 51°21'·88N 03°15'·95W QR.
Welsh Water Barry W 51°22'·27N 03°16'·94W Fl R 5s.

▶ BARRY

W Breakwater Head ☆ 51°23'·46N 03°15'·52W Fl 2·5s 12m 10M.
E Breakwater Head ☆ 51°23'·50N 03°15'·43W QG 7m 8M.
Lavernock Spit 51°23'·02N 03°10'·82W VQ (6) + L Fl 10s.
North One Fathom 51°20'·94N 03°12'·17W Q.
Mackenzie 51°21'·75N 03°08'·24W QR.
Holm Middle 51°21'·71N 03°06'·72W Fl G 2·5s.
Wolves 51°23'·13N 03°08'·88W VQ.

Flat Holm ☆, SE Pt 51°22'·54N 03°07'·14W Fl (3) WR 10s 50m **W15M**, R12M; W ○ twr; vis: R106°-140°, W140°-151°, R151°-203°, W203°-106°; (H24).

Weston 51°22'·60N 03°05'·75W Fl (2) R 5s.
Monkstone Rock ☆ 51°24'·89N 03°06'·02W Fl 5s 13m 12M.

▶ CARDIFF and PENARTH ROADS

Lavernock Outfall 51°23'·95N 03°09'·50W Fl Y 5s.
Ranie 51°24'·23N 03°09'·39W Fl (2) R 5s.
S Cardiff 51°24'·18N 03°08'·57W Q (6) + L Fl 15s; *Bell.*
Mid Cardiff 51°25'·60N 03°08'·09W Fl (3) G 10s.
Cardiff Spit 51°24'·57N 03°07'·12W QR.
N Cardiff 51°26'·52N 03°07'·19W QG.

▶ PENARTH/CARDIFF

Penarth Pier near Head ☆ 51°26'·08N 03°09'·90W 2 FR (vert) 8/6m 3M; *Reed Mo (BA) 60s.* when vessel expected.

Wrach Chan Dir lt 348·5°. 51°27'·16N 03°09'·75W Oc WRG 10s 5m; W3M, R3M, G3M; vis: G344·5°-347°, W347°-350°, R350°-352°; H24.

Outer Wrach 51°26'·20N 03°09'·46W Q (9) 15s.
Inner Wrach 51°26'·74N 03°09'·65W Fl G 2·5s.

Queen Alexandra Dock ent South Jetty Head ☆ 51°27'·09N 03°09'·58W 2 FG (vert); Tfc sigs; *Dia 60s.*

Tail Patch 51°23'·53N 03°03'·65W QG.
Hope 51°24'·84N 03°02'·68W Q (3) 10s.
NW Elbow 51°26'·28N 02°59'·93W VQ (9) 10s; *Bell.*
EW Grounds 51°27'·12N 02°59'·95W L Fl 10s 7M, *Whis,* ***Racon (T) 7M***.

PLOT WAYPOINTS ON YOUR CHART BEFORE USING THEM

▶ NEWPORT DEEP

Newport Deep 51°29'·36N 02°59'·12W Fl (3) G 10s; *Bell.*

▶ RIVER USK/NEWPORT

East Usk ☆ 51°32'·40N 02°58'·01W Fl (2) WRG 10s 11m **W15M**, R11M, G11M; vis: W284°-290°, R290°-017°, W017°-037°, G037°-115°, W115°-120°. Also Oc WRG 10s 10m W11M, R9M, G9M; vis: G018°-022°, W022°-024°, R024°-028°.

Alexandra Dock, S Lock W Pier Hd ☆ 51°32'·87N 02°59'·26W 2 FR (vert) 9m 6M; *Horn 60s.*

E Pier Head ☆ 51°32'·96N 02°59'·11W 2 FG (vert) 9m 6M.

Julians Pill Ldg Lts 062°. Front, 51°33'·30N 02°57'·94W FG 5m 4M. Rear, 61m from front, FG 8m 4M.

Birdport Jetty ☆ 51°33'·66N 02°58'·10W 2 FG (vert) 6m.
Dallimores Wharf ☆ 51°33'·88N 02°58'·60W 2 FG (vert).

Transporter Bridge, W side ☆ 51°34'·25N 02°59'·23W 2 FR (vert); 2 FY (vert) shown on transporter car.

E side ☆ 2 FG (vert). Centres of George Street and Newport Bridges marked by FY Lts.

BRISTOL CHANNEL – E. PART (SOUTH SHORE)

▶ BRISTOL DEEP

N Elbow 51°26'·97N 02°58'·65W QG; *Bell.*
S Mid Grounds 51°27'·62N 02°58'·68W VQ (6) + L Fl 10s.
E Mid Grounds 51°28'·14N 02°53'·56W Fl R 5s.
Clevedon 51°27'·39N 02°54'·93W VQ.
Welsh Hook 51°28'·53N 02°51'·86W Q (6) + L Fl 15s; *Bell.*
Avon 51°27'·92N 02°51'·73W Fl G 2·5s.

Black Nore Point ☆ 51°29'·09N 02°48'·05W Fl (2) 10s 11m **17M**; obsc by Sand Pt when brg less than 049°; vis: 044°-243°.

Newcome 51°30'·01N 02°46'·71W Fl (3) R 10s.
Denny Shoal 51°30'·15N 02°45'·45W VQ (6) + L Fl 10s.
Firefly 51°29'·96N 02°45'·35W Fl (2) G 5s.
Outer 51°29'·99N 02°44'·79W Fl G 5s.
Middle 51°29'·93N 02°44'·22W QG.
Inner 51°29'·86N 02°43'·87W Fl (3) G 15s.
Cockburn 51°30'·46N 02°44'·07W Fl R 2·5s.

Portishead Point ☆ 51°29'·68N 02°46'·42W Q (3) 10s 9m **16M**; B twr, W base; vis: 060°-262°; *Horn 20s.*

▶ PORTISHEAD

Pier Head ☆ 51°29'·69N 02°45'·27W Iso G 2s 5m 3M.

Seabank. Lts in line 086·8°. Front, 51°30'·07N 02°43'·81W IQ 13m 5M; vis: 070·3°-103·3°; by day 1M vis: 076·8°-096·8°. Rear, 500m from front, IQ 16m 5M; vis: 070·3°-103·3°; by day 1M, vis: 076·8°-096·8°.

Royal Portbury Dock ☆ 51°30'·15N 02°43'·75W L Fl G 15s 5m 6M.

Pier corner ☆ 51°30'·12N 02°43'·84W Fl G 2s 7m 7M; Gy pillar; *Dia 30s*, sounded HW–4 to HW+3.

Knuckle Lts in line 099·6° 51°29'·94N 02°43'·67W Oc G 5s 6m 6M. Rear, 165m from front, FG 13m 6M; vis: 044°-134°.

▶ AVONMOUTH

Royal Edward Dock N Pier Head ☆ 51°30'·49N 02°43'·09W Fl 4s 15m 10M; vis: 060°-228·5°.

King Road Ldg Lts 072·4°. N Pier Head ☆ Front, 51°30'·49N 02°43'·09W Oc R 5s 5m 9M; W obelisk, R bands; vis: 062°-082°. Rear ☆, 546m from front, QR 15m 10M; vis: 066°-078°.

▶ RIVER AVON

S Pier Head ☆ 51°30'·37N 02°43'·10W Oc RG 30s 9m 10M; vis: R294°-036°, G036°-194°.

Ldg Lts 127·2°. Front, 51°30'·10N 02°42'·59W Iso R 2s 6m 3M, vis: 010°-160°. Rear, Iso R 2s10m 3M, vis: 048°-138°.

Monoliths 51°30'·25N 02°42'·76W Fl R 5s 5m 3M; vis: 317°-137°.

Saint George Ldg Lts 173·3°, 51°29'·76N 02°42'·67W both Oc G 5s 7/13m 1M, vis: 158°-305°; synchronised.

Nelson Point ☆ 51°29'·86N 02°42'·50W Fl R 3s 9m 3M.
Broad Pill ☆ 51°29'·68N 02°41'·97W QR 4m 1M.

Avonmouth Bridge, NE end ☆ 51°29'·39N 02°41'·55W L Fl R 10s 5m 3M, SW end L Fl G 10s 5m 3M, show up and downstream. From here to City Docks, G Lts are shown on S bank, and R Lts on N bank.

▶ CUMBERLAND BASIN

Ent N side ☆ 51°26'·98N 02°37'·44W 2 FR (vert) 6m 1M; S side W end 2 FG (vert) 7m 1M.

▶ AVON BRIDGE

N side ☆ 51°26'·83N 02°37'·43W FR 6m 1M on Bridge pier.
Centre of span ☆ 51°26'·82N 02°37'·44W Iso 5s 6m 1M.
S side ☆ 51°26'·81N 02°37'·44W FG 6m 1M on Bridge pier.

SEVERN ESTUARY

▶ THE SHOOTS

Redcliffe Ldg Lts 012·9° Front 51°36'·20N 02°41'·37W F Bu 16m; vis: 358°-028°. Rear, 320m from front, F Bu 33m 10M.

Lower Shoots 51°33'·85N 02°42'·05W Q (9) 15s 6m 7M.
North Mixoms 51°34'·04N 02°42'·61W Fl (3) R 10s 6m 6M.

Second Severn Crossing, Centre span ☆ 51°34'·45N 02°42'·03W Q Bu 5M; ***Racon (O) (3cm) range unknown.***

Old Man's Hd 51°34'·74N 02°41'·69W VQ (9) W 10s 6m 7M.

Lady Bench (Lts in line 234°) 51°34'·85N 02°42'·20W QR 6m 6M. Rear, Oc R 5s 38m 3M.

Charston Rock ☆ 51°35'·35N 02°41'·68W Fl 3s 5m 8M.

Chapel Rock ☆ 51°36'·44N 02°39'·21W Fl WRG 2·6s 6m 8M, vis: W213°-284°, G284°-049°, W049°-051·5°, R051·5°-160°.

▶ RIVER WYE

Wye Bridge ☆ 51°37'·05N 02°39'·65W 2 F Bu (hor); centre span.

▶ SEVERN BRIDGE

Aust ☆ 51°36'·16N 02°38'·00W 2 QG (vert) 11m 6M.

West Tower ☆ 51°36'·73N 02°38'·80W 3 QR (hor) on upstream/downstream sides; *Siren (3) 30s*; obscured 040°-065°.

Centre of span ☆ 51°36'·59N 02°38'·43W Q Bu, each side.

East Tower ☆ 51°36'·46N 02°38'·07W 3 QG (hor) on upstream/downstream sides.

Lyde Rock ☆ 51°36'·89N 02°38'·67W Q WR 5m 5M; vis: R148°-237°, W237°-336°, R336°-067°.

Sedbury ☆ 51°37'·81N 02°39'·04W 2 FR (vert) 10m 3M.

Slime Road Ldg Lts 210·4°. Front, 51°37'·24N 02°39'·08W F Bu 9m 5M. Rear, 91 m from front, F Bu 16m 5M; B twr,

Inward Rocks Ldg Lts 252·5°. Front, 51°39'·26N 02°37'·47W F 6m 6M; B twr. Rear, 183m from front, F 23m 2M.

COUNTS 51°39'·48N 02°35'·84W .

Sheperdine Ldg Lts 070·4°. Front, 51°40'·06N 02°33'·31W F 8m 5M. Rear, 168m from front, F 13m 5M.

LEDGES 51°39'·77N 02°34'·15W Fl (3) G 10s.

Narlwood Rocks Ldg Lts 224·9°. Front, 51°39'·57N 02°34'·77W Fl 2s 5m 8M. Rear, 198m from front Fl 2s 9m 8M.

Hills Flats 51°40'·68N 02°32'·67W Fl G 4s.

Hayward Rock ⚓ 51°41'·24N 02°31'·18W Q 6m 4M.

Conigre Ldg Lts 077·5°. Front, 51°41'·46N 02°30'·03W F Bu 21m 8M. Rear, 213m from front, F Bu 29m 8M.

Fishing House Ldg Lts 217·7°. Front, 51°40'·98N 02°31'·00W F 5m 2M. Rear, F 11m 2M.

▶ BERKELEY

Bull Rock ☆ 51°41'·80N 02°29'·89W Fl 3s 6m 8M.

Berkeley Pill Ldg Lts 187·8°. Front, 51°41'·99N 02°29'·41W FG 5m 2M. Rear, 152m from front, FG 11m 2M.

Panthurst Pill ☆ 51°42'·59N 02°29'·02W F Bu 6m 1M; Y pillar.
Lydney Pier Hd ☆ 51°42'·63N 02°30'·35W 2 FR (vert) 6m.

▶ SHARPNESS DOCKS

S Pier Hd ☆ 51°42'·97N 02°29'·12W 2 FG (vert) 6m 3M; *Siren 20s.*
N Pier ☆ 51°43'·07N 02°29'·10W 2 FR (vert) 6m 3M.
Old ent, S side 51°43'·52N 02°28'·93W; *Siren 5s* (tidal).

BRISTOL CHANNEL (SOUTH SHORE)

▶ WESTON-SUPER-MARE

Pier Head ☆ 51°20'·88N 02°59'·26W 2 FG (vert) 6m.
E Culver ⚓ 51°18'·00N 03°15'·44W Q (3) 10s.
W Culver ⚓ 51°17'·37N 03°18'·68W VQ (9) 10s.
Gore ⚓ 51°13'·94N 03°09'·79W Iso 5s; *Bell.*

▶ BURNHAM-ON-SEA/RIVER PARRETT

Ent ☆ 51°14'·89N 03°00'·36W Fl 7·5s 7m 12M; vis: 074°-164°.

Dir lt 076°. F WRG 4m W12M, R10M, G10M; vis: G071°-075°, W075°-077°, R077°-081°.

Bridgewater Bar No. 1 ⚓ 51°14'·53N 03°03'·75W QR.

Seafront Lts in line 112°, moved for changing chan, Front, 51°14'·39N 02°59'·95W FR 6m 3M W □, Or stripe on sea wall. Rear, FR 12m 3M; on church twr.

Stert Reach ☆ 51°13'·53N 03°00'·29W Fl 3s 4m 7M; vis: 187°-217°.
Brue Bn ☆ 51°13'·53N 03°00'·29W Fl R 3s 4m 3M.
DZ No. 1 ⚓ 51°15'·28N 03°09'·49W Fl Y 2·5s.
Hinkley Point ☆ 51°12'·93N 03°08'·05W 2 FG (vert) 7m 3M.
DZ No. 2 ⚓ 51°13'·77N 03°17'·19W Fl Y 10s.
DZ No. 3 ⚓ 51°15'·52N 03°14'·98W Fl Y 5s.

▶ WATCHET

W Bkwtr Head ☆ 51°11'·03N 03°19'·74W Oc G 3s 9m 9M.
E Pier ☆ 51°11'·01N 03°19'·72W 2 FR (vert) 3M.

▶ MINEHEAD/PORLOCK WEIR

Bkwtr Hd ☆ 51°12'·81N 03°28'·36W Fl (2) G 5s 4M; vis: 127°-262°.
Sewer Outfall ⚓ 51°12'·97N 03°28'·31W QG 6m 7M.

Lynmouth Foreland ☆ 51°14'·73N 03°47'·21W Fl (4) 15s 67m **18M**; W ○ twr; vis: 083°-275°; (H24).

▶ LYNMOUTH/WATERMOUTH

River Training Arm ☆ 51°13'·90N 03°49'·83W 2 FR (vert) 6m 5M.
Harbour Arm ☆ 51°13'·92N 03°49'·84W 2 FG (vert) 6m 5M.
Sand Ridge ⚓ 51°15'·01N 03°49'·78W.
Copperas Rock ⚓ 51°13'·78N 04°00'·60W.

Watermouth ☆ 51°12'·93N 04°04'·60W Oc WRG 5s 1m 3M; W △; vis: G149·5°-151·5°, W151·5°-154·5°, R154·5°-156·5°.

▶ ILFRACOMBE

Lantern Hill ☆ 51°12'·66N 04°06'·78W Fl G 2·5s 39m 6M.
Promenade Pier N end ☆ 51°12'·69N 04°06'·68W 2 FG (vert).

Ldg Lts 188°. Front, 51°12'·53N 04°06'·65W Oc 10s 8m 3M. Rear, Oc 10s 6m 3M.

Horseshoe ⚓ 51°15'·02N 04°12'·96W Q.

Bull Point ☆ 51°11'·94N 04°12'·09W Fl (3) 10s 54m **20M**; W ○ twr, obscd shore-056°. Same twr; FR 48m 12M; vis: 058°-096°.

Morte Stone ⚓ 51°11'·30N 04°14'·95W.
Baggy Leap ⚓ 51°08'·92N 04°16'·97W.

▶ BIDEFORD, RIVERS TAW AND TORRIDGE

Bideford Fairway ⚓ 51°05'·25N 04°16'·25W L Fl 10s; *Bell.*
Bar ⚓ 51°04'·96N 04°14'·83W QG.
Middle Ridge ⚓ 51°04'·62N 04°13'·82W Fl G 5s.
Pulley ⚓ 51°04'·08N 04°12'·74W Fl G 10s.

Instow ☆ Ldg Lts 118°. **Front**, 51°03'·62N 04°10'·67W Oc 6s 22m **15M**; vis: 104·5°-131·5°. **Rear**, 427m from front, Oc 10s 38m **15M**; vis: 104°-132°; (H24).

Crow Pt ☆ 51°03'·96N 04°11'·40W Fl WR 5s 8m W6M R5M; vis: R225°-232°, W232°-237°, R237°-358°, W358°-015°, R 015°-045°.

Clovelly Hbr Quay Hd ☆ 50°59'·92N 04°23'·83W Fl G 5s 5m 5M.

▶ LUNDY

Near North Point ☆ 51°12'·10N 04°40'·65W Fl 15s 48m **17M**; vis: 009°-285°.

South East Point ☆ 51°09'·72N 04°39'·37W Fl 5s 53m **15M**; vis: 170°-073°; *Horn 25s.*

Jetty Head ☆ 51°09'·80N 04°39'·20W Fl R 3s 8m 3M.

Hartland Point ☆ 51°01'·29N 04°31'·59W Fl (6) 15s 37m **25M**; (H24); *Horn 60s.*

NORTH CORNWALL

▶ BUDE

Compass Point twr 50°49'·71N 04°33'·42W.

▶ PADSTOW

Stepper Point ☆ 50°34'·12N 04°56'·72W L Fl 10s 12m 4M.
Greenaway ⚓ 50°33'·78N 04°56'·06W Fl (2) R 10s.
Bar ⚓ 50°33'·46N 04°56'·12W Fl G 5s.
St Saviour's Pt ☆ 50°32'·76N 04°56'·06W L Fl G 10s 1m.
N Quay Head ☆ 50°32'·50N 04°56'·16W 2 FG (vert) 6m 2M.

Trevose Head ☆ 50°32'·94N 05°02'·13W Fl 7·5s 62m **21M**; *Horn (2) 30s.*

▶ NEWQUAY

North Pier Head ☆ 50°25'·07N 05°05'·19W 2 FG (vert) 5m 2M.
South Pier Head ☆ 50°25'·05N 05°05'·20W 2 FR (vert) 4m 2M.
The Stones ⚓ 50°15'·64N 05°25'·51W Q.

Godrevy I ☆ 50°14'·54N 05°24'·04W Fl WR 10s 37m W12M, R9M; vis: W022°-101°, R101°-145°, W145°-272°.

▶ HAYLE

App ⚓ 50°12'·26N 05°26'·30W QR.

Lts in line 180°. Front, 50°11'·50N 05°26'·18W F 17m 4M. Rear, 110m from front, F 23m 4M.

▶ ST IVES

App ⚓ 50°12'·85N 05°28'·42W
East Pier Head ☆ 50°12'·80N 05°28'·61W 2 FG (vert) 8m 5M.
West Pier Head ☆ 50°12'·77N 05°28'·73W 2 FR (vert) 5m 3M.

Pendeen ☆ 50°09'·90N 05°40'·32W Fl (4) 15s 59m **16M**; vis: 042°-240°; in bay between Gurnard Hd and Pendeen it shows to coast; *Horn 20s.*

For Lts further SW see 9.1.4.

9.11.5 PASSAGE INFORMATION

For directions on this coast refer to the Admiralty *W Coasts of England and Wales Pilot*; *Lundy and Irish Sea Pilot* (Imray/Taylor). For additional tidal information for east of Ilfracombe/Swansea, *Arrowsmith's Bristol Channel Tide Tables,* from J.W.Arrowsmith Ltd ☎ (0117) 9667545.

It is useful to know some Welsh words with navigational significance. *Aber:* estuary. *Afon:* river. *Bach, bychan, fach:* little. *Borth:* cove. *Bryn:* hill. *Careg, craig:* rock. *Coch, goch:* red. *Dinas:* fort. *Ddu:* black. *Fawr, Mawr:* big. *Ffrydiau:* tiderip. *Llwyd:* grey. *Moel:* bare conical hill. *Mor:* sea. *Morfa:* sandy shore. *Mynydd:* mountain. *Penrhyn:* headland. *Porth:* cove. *Ynys, Ynysoedd*: island(s).

CARDIGAN BAY (charts 1971, 1972, 1973) Hbrs are mostly on a lee shore, and/or have bars which make them dangerous to approach in bad weather. Abersoch (9.11.6) and Pwllheli (9.11.7) offer best shelter from prevailing W'lies. There may be overfalls off Trwyn Cilan, SW of St Tudwal's Is (lit). In N part of bay there are three major dangers to coasting yachts, as described briefly below: St Patrick's Causeway (Sarn Badrig) runs 12M SW from Mochras Pt. It is mostly large loose stones, and dries (up to 1·5m) for much of its length. In strong winds the sea breaks heavily at all states of tide. The outer end is marked by a WCM lt buoy. At the inner end there is a chan about 5ca offshore, which can be taken with care at half tide.

Sarn-y-Bwch runs 4M WSW from Pen Bwch Pt. It is composed of rky boulders, drying in places close inshore and with least depth 0·3m over 1M offshore. There is a WCM buoy off W end. NW of Aberystwyth (9.11.11), Sarn Cynfelyn and Cynfelyn Patches extend a total of 6·5M offshore, with depths of 1·5m in places. A WCM buoy is at the outer end. Almost halfway along the bank is Main Channel, 3ca wide, running roughly N/S, but not marked.

A military firing area occupies much of Cardigan B. Beware targets and buoys, some unlit. Range activity is broadcast on VHF Ch 16, 0800-1600LT Mon-Fri or ☎ (01239) 813462.

If on passage N/S through St George's Chan (ie not bound for Cardigan B or Milford Haven) the easiest route, and always by night, is W of the Bishops and the Smalls, noting the TSS. If bound to/from Milford Haven or Cardigan Bay, passage inside both the Smalls and Grassholm is possible.

RAMSEY SOUND AND THE BISHOPS (chart 1482) The Bishops and the Clerks are islets and rks 2·5M W and NW of Ramsey Is, a bird sanctuary SSW of St David's Hd. N Bishop is the N'ly of the group, 3ca ENE of which is Bell Rk (depth 1·9m). S Bishop (Lt, fog sig, RC) is 3M to the SSW.

Between S Bishop and Ramsey Is the dangers include Daufraich with offliers to the E and heavy overfalls; Llech Isaf and Llech Uchaf drying rks are further ENE. Carreg Rhoson and offliers are between Daufraich and N Bishop. The navigable routes between most of these islets and rks trend NE/SW, but use only by day, in good visibility and with local knowledge. The N/S route close W of Ramsey I is said to be easier than Ramsey Snd (see below).

► *2M W of The Bishops the S-going stream begins at HW Milford Haven +4, and the N-going at HW –2½, sp rates 2kn. Between The Bishops and Ramsey Is the SW-going stream begins at HW Milford Haven +3½, and the NE-going at HW –3,* ***sp rates 5kn.*** ◄

► *Ramsey Sound should be taken at slack water. The S-going stream begins at HW Milford Haven +3, and the N-going at HW –3½,* ***sp rates 6kn at The Bitches,*** *where chan is narrowest (2ca), decreasing N and S.* ◄ The Bitches are rks up to 4m high and extending 2ca from E side of Ramsey Is. Other dangers are: Gwahan and Carreg-gafeiliog, both 3m high at N end of Sound, to W and E; Horse Rk (dries 0·9m) almost in mid-chan about 5ca NNE of The Bitches, with associated overfalls; Shoe Rk (dries 3m) at SE end of chan; and rks extending 5ca SSE from S end of Ramsey Is.

THE SMALLS TO MILFORD HAVEN (chart *1478*) St Brides Bay (9.11.12) provides anch in settled weather/offshore winds, it is also a regular anchorage for tankers, but is a trap in westerlies. Solva is a little hbr with shelter for boats able to take the ground, or anch behind Black Rk (dries 3·6m) in the middle of the entrance.

The Smalls Lt, where there is a Historic Wreck (see 9.0.3h) is 13M W of the Welsh mainland (Wooltack Pt). 2M and 4M E of The Smalls are the Hats and Barrels, rky patches on which the sea breaks. ► *7M E of The Smalls is Grassholm Island with a race either end and strong tidal eddies so that it is advisable to pass about 1M off. The chan between Barrels and Grassholm is 2·5M wide, and here the S-going stream begins at HW Milford Haven + 0440, and the N-going at HW Milford Haven – 0135,* ***sp rates 5kn.*** ◄ 5M of clear water lie between Grassholm and Skomer Is/Skokholm Is to the E. But Wildgoose Race, which forms W of Skomer and Skokholm is very dangerous, so keep 2M W of these two Islands.

To E of Skomer is Midland Is, and between here and Wooltack Pt is Jack Sound, least width about 1ca. Do not attempt it without AC 1482, detailed pilotage directions, and only at slack water nps. Correct timing is important. The S-going stream begins at HW Milford Haven +2, and the N-going at HW –4½, sp rates 6-7kn. Rocks which must be identified include, from N to S: On E side of chan off Wooltack Pt, Tusker Rk (2m), steep-to on its W side; and off Anvil Pt, The Cable (dries 2·4m), The Anvil and Limpet Rks (3·7m). On the W side lie the Crabstones (3·7m) and the Blackstones (1·5m).

MILFORD HAVEN TO MUMBLES HD (charts *1179*, 1076) Milford Haven (9.11.13) is a long natural, all-weather hbr with marinas beyond the oil terminals. 3M S of the ent, beware Turbot Bank (WCM lt buoy). Crow Rk (dries 5·5m) is 5ca SSE of Linney Hd, and The Toes are dangerous submerged rks close W and SE of Crow Rk. There is a passage inshore of these dangers. There are overfalls on St Gowan Shoals which extend 4M SW of St Govan's Hd, and the sea breaks on the shallow patches in bad weather. For firing areas from Linney Hd to Carmarthen Bay, see 9.11.15.

Caldey Is (Lt) lies S of Tenby (9.11.14). Off its NW pt is St Margaret's Is connected by a rky reef. Caldey Sound, between St Margaret's Is and Giltar Pt (chart 1482), is buoyed, but beware Eel Spit near W end of Caldey Is where there can be a nasty sea with wind against tide, and Woolhouse Rks (dry 3·6m) 1ca NE of Caldey Is. Saundersfoot hbr (dries) is 2M N of Tenby, with anch well sheltered from N and W but subject to swell. Streams are weak here. Carmarthen Bay has no offshore dangers for yachts, other than the extensive drying sands at head of B and on its E side off Burry Inlet (9.11.15).

S of Worms Head, Helwick Sands (buoyed at each end) extend 7M W from Port Eynon Pt; least depth of 1·3m is near their W end. Stream sets NE/SW across the sands. There is a narrow chan inshore, close to Port Eynon Pt. ▶ *Between here and Mumbles Hd the stream runs roughly along coast, sp rates 3kn off Pts, but there are eddies in Port Eynon B and Oxwich B (both yacht anchs), and overfalls SSE of Oxwich Pt.* ◀

MUMBLES HEAD TO CARDIFF (charts 1165, 1182) Off Mumbles Hd (Lt, fog sig) beware Mixon Shoal (dries 0·3m), marked by PHM buoy. In good conditions pass N of shoal, 1ca off Mumbles Hd. Anch N of Mumbles Hd, good holding but exposed to swell. At W side of Swansea Bay, Green Grounds, rky shoals, lie in appr's to Swansea (9.11.16).

Scarweather Sands, much of which dry (up to 3·3m) and where sea breaks heavily, extend 7M W from Porthcawl (9.11.16) and are well buoyed (chart 1161). There is a chan between the sands and coast to E, but beware Hugo Bank (dries 2·6m) and Kenfig Patches (0·5m) with overfalls up to 7ca offshore between Sker Pt and Porthcawl.

Nash Sands extend 7·5M WNW from Nash Pt. Depths vary and are least at inshore end (dries 3m), but Nash Passage, 1ca wide, runs close inshore between E Nash ECM buoy and ledge off Nash Pt. ▶ *On E-going stream there are heavy overfalls off Nash Pt and at W end of Nash Sands. Between Nash Pt and Breaksea Pt the E-going stream begins at HW Avonmouth + 0535, and the W-going at HW Avonmouth – 0035, sp rates 3kn. Off Breaksea Pt there may be overfalls.* ◀

From Rhoose Pt to Lavernock Pt the coast is fringed with foul ground. Lavernock Spit extends 1·75M S of Lavernock Pt, and E of the spit is main chan to Cardiff (9.11.18); the other side of the chan being Cardiff Grounds, a bank drying 5·4m which lies parallel with the shore and about 1·5M from it.

SEVERN ESTUARY (charts 1176, 1166) Near the centre of Bristol Chan, either side of the buoyed fairway are the islands of Flat Holm (Lt, fog sig) and Steep Holm. 7M SW of Flat Holm lies Culver Sand (0·9m), 3M in length, with W & ECM bys. Monkstone Rk (Lt, dries) is 2M NW of the buoyed chan to Avonmouth and Bristol (9.11.20). Extensive drying banks cover the N shore of the estuary, beyond Newport and the Severn bridges (chart 1176).

▶ *The range of tide in the Bristol Chan is exceptionally large, 12·2m sp and 6·0m np, and tidal streams are very powerful, particularly above Avonmouth. Between Flat Holm and Steep Holm the E-going stream begins at HW Avonmouth – 0610, sp 3kn, and the W-going at HW Avonmouth + 0015, sp 4kn.* ◀

The ent to the R. Avon is just to the S of Avonmouth S Pier Hd. Bristol City Docks lie some 6M up river. Approach the ent via King Road and the Newcombe and Cockburn lt buoys and thence via the Swash chan into the Avon. The ent dries at LW but the river is navigable at about half tide. ▶ *Tidal streams are strong in the approaches to Avonmouth, up to **5kn at sp.** The tide is also strong in the R. Avon which is best entered no earlier than HW Avonmouth – 0200.* ◀

From Avonmouth it is 16M to Sharpness which yachts should aim to reach at about HW Avonmouth. ▶ ***Spring streams can run 8kn at the Shoots, and 6kn at the Severn** bridges (9.11.19). At the Shoots the flood begins at HW Avonmouth –0430 and the ebb at HW Avonmouth + 0045. The Severn Bore can usually be seen if Avonmouth range is 13·5m or more.* ◀

AVONMOUTH TO HARTLAND POINT (AC 1152, 1165) From Avonmouth to Sand Pt, the part-drying English Grounds extend 3M off the S shore. Portishead Dock (9.11.21) is being developed as a marina. Extensive mud flats fill the bays S to Burnham-on-Sea (9.11.22). Westward, the S shore of Bristol Chan is cleaner than N shore. But there is less shelter since the approaches to hbrs such as Watchet (9.11.23), Minehead, Porlock Weir and Watermouth dry out, see 9.11.23. ▶ *In bad weather dangerous overfalls occur NW and NE of Foreland Pt. 5M to W there is a race off Highveer Pt. Between Ilfracombe (9.11.24) and Bull Pt the E-going stream begins at HW Milford Haven + 0540, and the W-going at HW Milford Haven – 0025, sp rates 3kn. Overfalls occur up to 1·5M N of Bull Pt and over Horseshoe Rks, which lie 3M N. There is a dangerous race off Morte Pt, 1·5M to W of Bull Pt.* ◀

Shelter is available under lee of Lundy Is (9.11.25); but avoid bad races to NE (White Horses), the NW (Hen and Chickens), and to SE; also overfalls over NW Bank. ▶ *W of Lundy streams are moderate, but strong around the Is and much stronger towards Bristol Chan proper.* ◀

Proceeding WSW from Rivers Taw/Torridge (9.11.25), keep 3M off to avoid the race N of Hartland Pt (Lt, fog sig, conspic radome). There is shelter off Clovelly in S/SW winds.

HARTLAND POINT TO LAND'S END (charts 1156, 1149) The N coast of Cornwall and SW approaches to Bristol Chan are very exposed. Yachts need to be sturdy and well equipped, since if bad weather develops no shelter may be at hand. Bude (9.11.25) dries, and is not approachable in W winds; only accessible in calm weather or offshore winds. Boscastle is a tiny hbr (dries) 3M NE of Tintagel Hd. Only approach in good weather or offshore winds; anch off or dry out alongside.

Padstow is a refuge, but in strong NW winds the sea breaks on bar and prevents entry. Off Trevose Hd (Lt) beware Quies Rks which extend 1M to W. From here S the coast is relatively clear to Godrevy Is, apart from Bawden Rks 1M N of St Agnes Hd. Newquay B (9.11.26) is good anch in offshore winds, and the hbr (dries) is sheltered but uncomfortable in N winds. Off Godrevy Is (Lt) are The Stones, drying rky shoals extending 1·5M offshore and marked by NCM lt buoy.

In St Ives Bay (chart 1168), Hayle (9.11.26) is a commercial port (dries); seas break heavily on bar at times, especially with a ground swell. ▶ *Stream is strong, so enter just before HW.* ◀ The bottom is mostly sand. St Ives (dries) (9.11.26) gives shelter from winds E to SW, but is very exposed to N; there is sometimes a heavy breaking sea if there is ground swell.

From St Ives to Land's End coast is rugged and exposed. There are overfalls SW of Pendeen Pt (lt, fog sig). Vyneck Rks lie awash about 3ca NW of C Cornwall. The Brisons are two high rky islets 5ca SW of C Cornwall, with rky ledges inshore and to the S. The Longships (lt, fog sig) group of rks is about 1M W of Land's End. The inshore passage (001° on Brisons) is about 4ca wide with unmarked drying rks on the W side; only to be considered in calm weather. See 9.1.5 for tides.

For Isles of Scilly and South Cornwall, see 9.1.5.

9.11.6 ABERSOCH

Gwynedd **52°49'·29N 04°29'·20W**

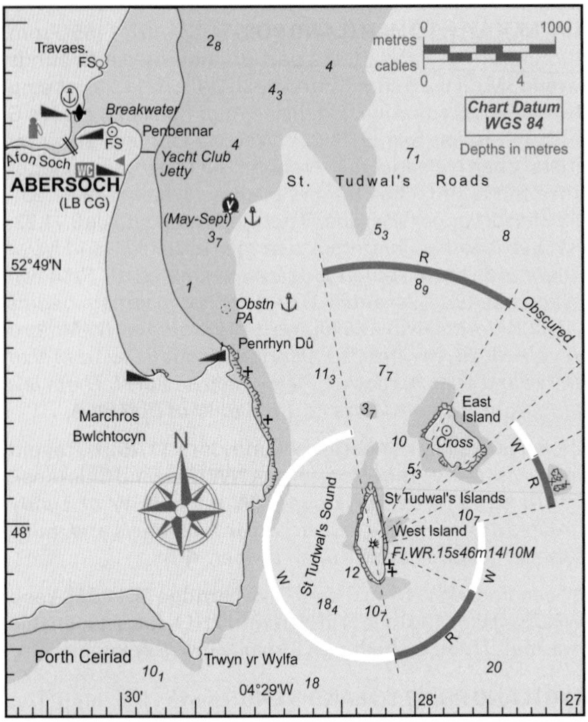
Travaes.
FS
Breakwater
Penbennar
FS
Afon Soch
ABERSOCH
(LB CG)
Yacht Club Jetty
(May-Sept)
St. Tudwal's Roads
metres
cables
Chart Datum WGS 84
Depths in metres
52°49'N
Obstn PA
Penrhyn Dû
Obscured
Marchros
Bwlchtocyn
N
East Island
Cross
St Tudwal's Islands
West Island
Fl.WR.15s46m14/10M
St Tudwal's Sound
48'
Porth Ceiriad
Trwyn yr Wylfa
04°29'W
30'
28'
27

CHARTS AC *1410,* 1971, 1512; Imray C61, C52; Stanfords 27; OS 123

TIDES –0315 Dover; ML 2·5; Duration 0520; Zone 0 (UT)

Standard Port MILFORD HAVEN (⟶)

Times				Height (metres)			
High Water		Low Water		MHWS	MHWN	MLWN	MLWS
0100	0800	0100	0700	7·0	5·2	2·5	0·7
1300	2000	1300	1900				
Differences ST TUDWAL'S ROADS							
+0155	+0145	+0240	+0310	–2·2	–1·9	–0·7	–0·2
ABERDARON							
+0210	+0200	+0240	+0310	–2·4	–1·9	–0·6	–0·2

SHELTER There are few moorings for visitors. Apply to HM or SC. ⚓ in St Tudwal's Roads clear of moored yachts; sheltered from SSE through S to NE.

NAVIGATION WPT 52°48'·52N 04°26'·13W, 293° to YC jetty, 2·4M. There are no navigational dangers, but steer well clear of the drying rks to the E of East Island; an unlit PHM buoy is 2ca E of these rks (just off chartlet). St Tudwal's islands themselves are fairly steep-to, except at N ends. St Tudwal's Sound is clear of dangers.

LIGHTS AND MARKS The only lt is on St Tudwal's West Island, Fl WR 15s 46m 14/10M (see chartlet and 9.11.4).

R/T S Caernarfon YC Ch **80** M.

TELEPHONE (Dial code 01758) HM 712203; MRSC (01407) 762051; Marinecall 09066 526244; Police (01286) 673333; Dr 612535.

FACILITIES **South Caernarvonshire YC** ☎ 712338, Slip, M, L, FW, R, Bar (May-Sept), D; **Abersoch Power Boat Club** ☎ 812027. **Services:** BY, Slip, ME, El, ⚒, ACA, CH, P, C (12 ton), LPG. **Town** EC Wed; CH, 🛒, R, Bar, ✉, Ⓑ, ≷ (Pwllheli), ✈ (Chester).

9.11.7 PWLLHELI

Gwynedd **52°53´·23N 04°23´·75W**

CHARTS AC *1410,* 1971, 1512; Imray C61, C52; OS 123; Stanfords 27

TIDES –0315 Dover; ML 2·6; Duration 0510; Zone 0 (UT)

Standard Port MILFORD HAVEN (⟶)

Times				Height (metres)			
High Water		Low Water		MHWS	MHWN	MLWN	MLWS
0100	0800	0100	0700	7·0	5·2	2·5	0·7
1300	2000	1300	1900				
Differences PWLLHELI							
+0210	+0150	+0245	+0320	–2·0	–1·8	–0·6	–0·2
CRICCIETH							
+0210	+0155	+0255	+0320	–2·0	–1·8	–0·7	–0·3

SHELTER Good in hbr & marina, pontoons are numbered 4–12 from S–N. Pile berths on S side of appr chan. Drying moorings in inner hbr (SW and NW bights).

NAVIGATION WPT 52°53'·02N 04°23'·07W, SWM lt buoy, Iso 2s, 299° to QG lt at head of Training Arm, 0·47M. Ent is safe in most winds, but in strong E to SW winds sea breaks on offshore shoals. Ent subject to silting and Bar and hbr chan are dredged but only to to 0·6m below CD ; 3 tide gauges. No ⚓ in hbr; 4kn speed limit. Max tidal stream 2kn.

LIGHTS AND MARKS No ldg lts/marks, but ent chan well marked (see chartlet). Gimblet Rock (30m) is conspic conical rock 3ca SW of ent.

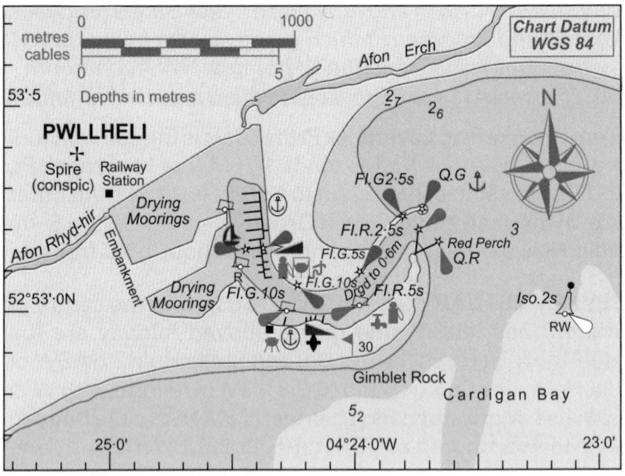
metres
cables
Chart Datum WGS 84
Afon Erch
53'·5
Depths in metres
PWLLHELI
Spire (conspic)
Railway Station
Drying Moorings
Afon Rhyd-hir
Embankment
N
Fl.G.2·5s
Q.G
Fl.R.2·5s
Red Perch Q.R
Fl.G.5s
Fl.G.10s
Dgd to 0·6m
Fl.R.5s
52°53'·0N
Iso.2s
RW
Gimblet Rock
Cardigan Bay
25·0'
04°24·0'W
23·0'

R/T Marina: Ch **80** M H24. HM: VHF Ch **12** 16 (0900-1715).

TELEPHONE (Dial code 01758) HM 704081, mob 07879 433145; MRSC (01407) 762051; Ⓗ Bangor (A&E) 01248 384384; Marinecall 09066 526244; Police (01286) 673333; Dr 701457.

FACILITIES **Marina** (400) ☎ 701219, 📠 701443, £2.12, £9.40 <4hrs, P, D, LPG, BH (40 ton), C, Slip, Ⓞ, ♿, 🚿; **Marina Boat Club** ☎ 612271, Slip, FW; **Hbr Authority** Slip, M, L, FW, AB; **Pwllheli SC** ☎ 614442, 📠 612134; pwllhelisailingclub@bt internet.com; **Services:** BY, Slip, L, FW, ME, Gas, Gaz, LPG, ⚒, CH, ACA, D, C (14 ton), El, Ⓔ, SM. **Town** EC Thurs; 🛒, R, Bar, ✉, Ⓑ, ≷, ✈ (Chester).

ADJACENT HARBOUR

MOCHRAS, Gwynedd, **52°49´·57N 04°07´·77W**. AC 1971, 1512. HW –0245 on Dover. Small yacht hbr on SE side of Shell Is. Mochras lagoon dries. Bar, about 2ca seaward. Entry advised HW±2. Tide runs strongly in the narrows on the ebb; at sp beware severe eddies inside ent. Ent between Shell Is (lt Fl WRG 4s; G079°-124°, W124°-134°, R134°-179°; shown mid Mar-Nov) and sea wall. 3 grey posts, R topmarks, mark N side of chan. Shifting chan, marked by posts & buoys, runs NE to Pensarn, where permanent moorings limit space. To S, buoyed chan runs to Shell Is Yacht Hbr ☎ (0134123) 453 with facilities: M, FW, Slip, R, Bar, shwrs. Pensarn: drying AB, ≷.

9.11.8 PORTHMADOG

Gwynedd **52°55'·32N 04°07'·77W** ❁◊◊◊✿✿✿

CHARTS AC *1410*, 1971, 1512,; Imray C61, C51; Stanfords 27; OS 124

TIDES –0247 Dover; ML no data; Duration 0455; Zone 0 (UT)

Standard Port MILFORD HAVEN (⟶)

Times				Height (metres)			
High Water		Low Water		MHWS	MHWN	MLWN	MLWS
0100	0800	0100	0700	7·0	5·2	2·5	0·7
1300	2000	1300	1900				
Differences PORTHMADOG							
+0235	+0210	No data		–1·9	–1·8	No data	

SHELTER Inner hbr (N of Cei Ballast): Good all year round; visitors' drying AB adjacent Madoc YC or afloat rafted on moored yachts off YC. Outer hbr: Summer only, exposed to S winds. Speed limit 6kn in hbr upstream of No 8 buoy.

NAVIGATION WPT Fairway SWM buoy, 52°52'·97N 04°11'·09W, 041° to conspic white Ho at W side of ent, 1·91M; chan shifts and may divide. Bar changes frequently, but is near to No 3 and 4 buoys; dries approx 0·3m. Latest info from HM on request. Advise entering HW±1½. In SW'lies, waves are steep-sided and close, especially on the ebb.

LIGHTS AND MARKS Fairway buoy RW, L Fl 10s. Chan marker buoys (14) have R/G reflective top marks and numbers in W reflective tape. Moel-y-Gest is conspic hill (259m) approx 1M WNW of hbr. Harlech Castle (ru) is about 3M SE of appr chan.

R/T HM Ch 12 16 (0900-1715 and when vessel due). Madoc YC: Ch M.

TELEPHONE (Dial code 01766) HM 512927, mobile (07879) 433147; MRSC (01407) 762051; Pilot 530684; Hbr Authority Gwynedd Council (01758) 613131; Marinecall 09066 526244; Police (01286) 673333; Dr 512284.

FACILITIES **Hbr** (265 berths) ☎ 512927, £6.80 < 12m, £7.20 >12m; D, FW, C, Slip(launching £8.50); **Madoc YC** ☎ 512976, AB, M, FW, Bar; **Porthmadog SC** ☎ 513546, AB, M, FW, Slip; **Services:** CH, ACA, ⚒, D, P (cans), C (8 ton), M, BY, El, Pilot. **Town** EC Wed; ✉, Ⓑ, ⇌, ✈ (Chester).

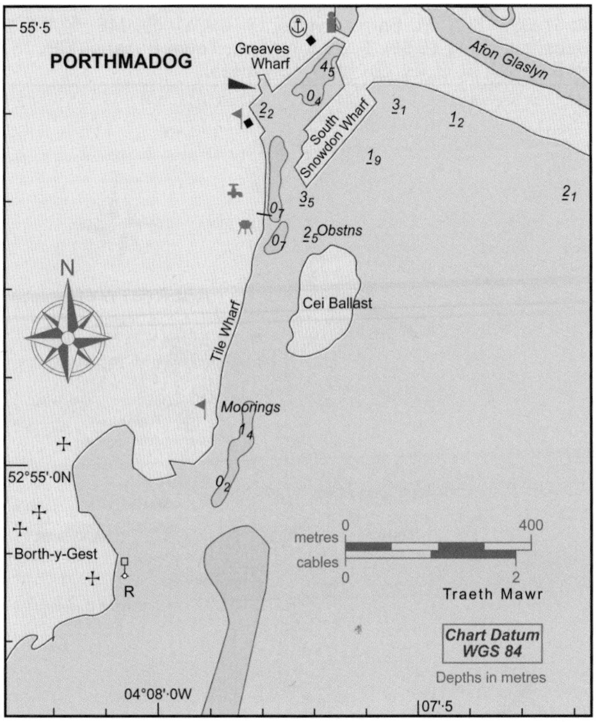
PORTHMADOG
55'·5
Greaves Wharf
Afon Glaslyn
South Snowdon Wharf
Obstns
Cei Ballast
Tile Wharf
Moorings
N
52°55'·0N
Borth-y-Gest
R
metres
cables
400
Traeth Mawr
Chart Datum WGS 84
Depths in metres
04°08'·0W
07'·5

9.11.9 BARMOUTH

Gwynedd **52°42'·97N 04°03'·07W** ❁❁◊◊✿✿✿

CHARTS AC *1410*, 1971, 1484; Imray C61, C51; Stanfords 27; OS 124

TIDES –0305 Dover; ML 2·6; Duration 0515; Zone 0 (UT)

Standard Port MILFORD HAVEN (⟶)

Times				Height (metres)			
High Water		Low Water		MHWS	MHWN	MLWN	MLWS
0100	0800	0100	0700	7·0	5·2	2·5	0·7
1300	2000	1300	1900				
Differences BARMOUTH							
+0215	+0205	+0310	+0320	–2·0	–1·7	–0·7	0·0

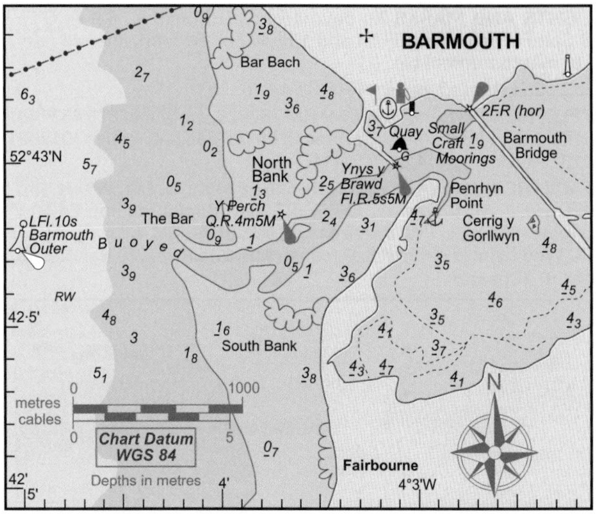
BARMOUTH
Bar Bach
North Bank
Y Perch
Q.R.4m5M
The Bar
Quay
Small Craft Moorings
Ynys y Brawd
Fl.R.5s5M
2F.R (hor)
Barmouth Bridge
Penrhyn Point
Cerrig y Gorllwyn
52°43'N
LFl.10s
Barmouth Outer
Buoyed
RW
42·5'
South Bank
metres
cables
1000
Chart Datum WGS 84
Depths in metres
Fairbourne
4°3'W
42'
N

SHELTER Good. Entry HW±2½ safe, but impossible with strong SW'lies. Exposed ⚓ W of Barmouth Outer buoy in 6 to 10m. Serious silting reported. In hbr there are 5 Ⓥs; secure as directed by HM, because of submarine cables and strong tidal streams. A Ⓥ berth is marked at W end of quay, dries at half-tide. The estuary and river (Afon Mawddach) are tidal and can be navigated for about 7M above rly br (clearance approx 5·5m); but chan is not buoyed, and sandbanks move constantly - local knowledge essential. Drying ⚓ inside Penrhyn Pt.

NAVIGATION WPT, Barmouth Outer SWM buoy, L Fl 10s, 52°42'·72N 04°05'·02W, 082° to Y perch lt, QR, 0·78M. Appr from SW between St Patrick's Causeway (Sarn Badrig) and Sarn-y-Bwch (see 9.11.5). Barmouth can be identified by Cader Idris, a mountain 890m high, 5M ESE. Fegla Fawr, a rounded hill, lies on S side of hbr. The Bar, 0·75M W of Penrhyn Pt, with min depth 0·3m is subject to considerable change. Chan is marked by buoys, all unlit, fitted with radar reflectors and reflective tape and moved as required. Spring ebb runs 3 - 5kn. Note: Historic Wrecks (see 9.0.3h) lie at 52°46'·73N 04°07'·53W and 52°46'·53N 04°11'·03W, 4·5 and 5·5M NNW of Barmouth Outer SWM buoy.

LIGHTS AND MARKS Outer SWM L Fl 10s. SHM Q Fl G. Bar No2 PHM Fl R. Inner buoy. Y perch QR 4m 5M on R framework tr, marks S end of stony ledge extending 3ca SW from Ynys y Brawd across N Bank. Ynys y Brawd groyne, SE end, marked by lit bn, Fl R 5s 5M. NW end of rly bridge 2 FR (hor).

R/T Call *Barmouth Hbr* VHF Ch **12** 16 (Apr-Sep 0900-1700 later for HW; Oct-Mar 0900-1600); wind and sea state are available.

TELEPHONE (Dial code 01341) HM 280671 mob 07879 433146; MRSC (01407) 762051; Marinecall 09066 526244; Police (01286) 673333; Dr 280521.

FACILITIES Quay £7.00 < 9m £10.50 > 9m, M (incl 3 drying Ⓥ) contact HM in advance if deep water Ⓥ required, D, FW, El, ⛽, Slip(launching £8.50); Merioneth YC ☎ 280000; Services: CH, ACA. **Town** EC Wed; P, D, 🛒, R, Bar, ✉, Ⓑ, ⇌, ✈ (Chester), ferry to Penrhyn Pt. **Fairbourne** ✉, 🛒, ⇌, ferry to Barmouth.

11

9.11.10 ABERDOVEY

Gwynedd **52°32'·57N 04°02'·72W** (Jetty) ❁❁◊◊✿✿✿

CHARTS AC *1410*, 1972, 1484; Imray C61, C51; Stanfords 27; OS 135

TIDES –0320 Dover; ML 2·6; Duration 0535; Zone 0 (UT). For differences see 9.11.11.

SHELTER Good except in strong W/SW winds. Berth on jetty in 3m; to the E there is heavy silting.

NAVIGATION WPT Aberdovey Outer SWM buoy, Iso.4s, 52°32'·00N 04°05'·56W, 093° to Bar buoy, 0.43M. Bar and channel constantly shift and are hazardous below half-tide; buoys moved accordingly. Enter the channel at gateway between Bar SHM and PHM Fl R 5s. Visitors should call HM on VHF before entering. Submarine cables (prohib ⚓s) marked by bns with R ◊ topmarks.

LIGHTS AND MARKS No daymarks. 3 SHM buoys (Bar Fl G 5s, S Spit Fl G and Inner Fl G) and 1 PHM Fl R 5s mark chan to jetty. Lts may be unreliable.

R/T Call *Aberdovey Hbr* VHF Ch 12 16.

TELEPHONE (Dial code 01654) HM 767626, mobile 07879 433148; MRSC (01646) 690909; Marinecall 09066 526244; Police (01286) 673333; Dr 710414; Ⓗ 710411.

FACILITIES Jetty AB £7.00 <9m, £10.50 >9m; M, FW; **Wharf** Slip, AB, L, FW, C; **Dovey YC** ☎ 767607, Bar, Slip(launching £4.50 if engine <10hp), L, FW; **Services:** BY, ME, El, ✕, CH, ACA, Ⓔ. **Town** EC Wed (winter only); P & D (cans), ME, El, CH, 🛒, R, Bar, ✉, Ⓑ, ⇌, ✈ (Chester).

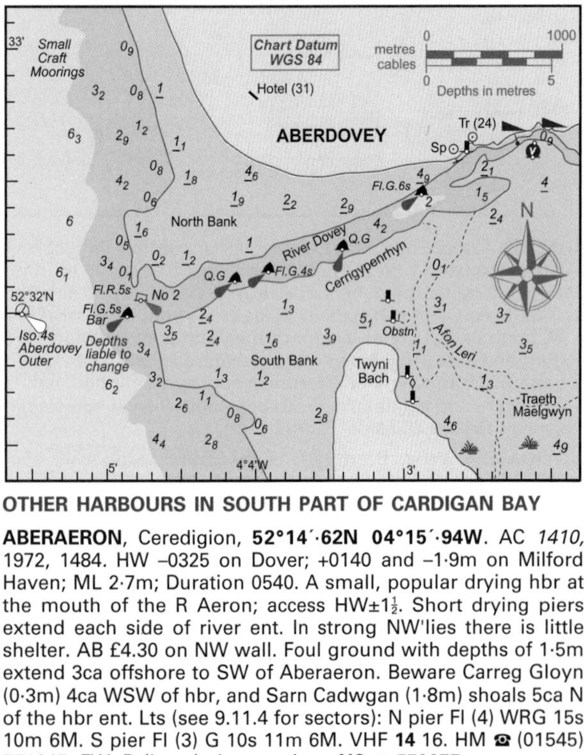
Chart Datum WGS 84
metres
cables
Depths in metres
Small Craft Moorings
Hotel (31)
ABERDOVEY
Tr (24)
Sp
North Bank
River Dovey
Fl.G.6s
Q.G
Fl.G.4s
Cerrigypenrhyn
Fl.R.5s
No 2
Fl.G.5s Bar
Iso.4s Aberdovey Outer
Depths liable to change
52°32'N
South Bank
Obstn
Afon Leri
Twyni Bach
Traeth Maelgwyn
4°4'W

OTHER HARBOURS IN SOUTH PART OF CARDIGAN BAY

ABERAERON, Ceredigion, **52°14'·62N 04°15'·94W**. AC *1410*, 1972, 1484. HW –0325 on Dover; +0140 and –1·9m on Milford Haven; ML 2·7m; Duration 0540. A small, popular drying hbr at the mouth of the R Aeron; access HW±1½. Short drying piers extend each side of river ent. In strong NW'lies there is little shelter. AB £4.30 on NW wall. Foul ground with depths of 1·5m extend 3ca offshore to SW of Aberaeron. Beware Carreg Gloyn (0·3m) 4ca WSW of hbr, and Sarn Cadwgan (1·8m) shoals 5ca N of the hbr ent. Lts (see 9.11.4 for sectors): N pier Fl (4) WRG 15s 10m 6M. S pier Fl (3) G 10s 11m 6M. VHF **14** 16. HM ☎ (01545) 571645; FW, D (hose) via aquarium. **YC** ☎ 570077.

NEW QUAY, Ceredigion, **52°12'·92N 04°21'·22W**. AC *1410*, 1972, 1484. HW –0335 on Dover; Duration 0540; see 9.11.11. Good shelter in offshore winds, but untenable in NW'lies. On E side of bay Carreg Ina, rks drying 1·3m, are marked by NCM buoy, Q. Two Y bns mark a sewer outfall running 7ca NNW from Ina Pt. The hbr (dries 1·6m) is protected by a pier with lt, Fl WG 3s 12m 8/5M; W135°-252°, G252°-295°. Groyne extends 80m SSE of pierhd to a SHM bn; close ENE of which is a ECM bn, Q (3) 10s. ⚓s are 1ca E of pier; £4.30. VHF Ch **14** 16. HM ☎ (01545) 560368. MRSC (01646) 690909; Dr ☎ 560203; YC ☎ 560516. Facilities: FW, D (from fishermen). **Town** P (3M), ✉, R, Bar.

9.11.11 ABERYSTWYTH

Ceredigion **52°24'·42N 04°05'·47W** ❁❁◊◊◊✿✿✿

CHARTS AC *1410*, 1972, 1484; Imray C61, C51; Stanfords 27; OS 135

TIDES –0330 Dover; ML 2·7; Duration 0540; Zone 0 (UT)

Standard Port MILFORD HAVEN (⟶)

Times				Height (metres)			
High Water		Low Water		MHWS	MHWN	MLWN	MLWS
0100	0800	0100	0700	7·0	5·2	2·5	0·7
1300	2000	1300	1900				
Differences ABERDOVEY							
+0215	+0200	+0230	+0305	–2·0	–1·7	–0·5	0·0
ABERYSTWYTH							
+0145	+0130	+0210	+0245	–2·0	–1·7	–0·7	0·0
NEW QUAY							
+0150	+0125	+0155	+0230	–2·1	–1·8	–0·6	–0·1
ABERPORTH							
+0135	+0120	+0150	+0220	–2·1	–1·8	–0·6	–0·1

SHELTER Good, in marina (1·7m) on E side of chan; or dry against Town Quay. Access approx HW±3 (HW±2 for strangers). The Bar, close off S pier hd, has 0·7m least depth. E edge of inner hbr chan 0·3m is defined by WCM beacon which in line with Y day mark gives a daytime lead into the Hbr.

NAVIGATION WPT 52°24'·83N 04°06'·22W, 313°/133° from/to ent, 0·6M. Approach dangerous in strong on-shore winds. From N, beware Castle Rks, within R sector 141°-175° of N bkwtr lt, QWR 9m 2M; also rks drying 0·5m W of N bkwtr and boulders below S pier hd. Turn 90° port inside narrow ent.

LIGHTS AND MARKS N bkwtr hd ≠ 140° Wellington Mon't (on top Pendinas, conspic hill 120m high) clears to S of Castle Rks. Ldg lts 133°, both FR on Ystwyth Bridge, white daymarks. WCM bn on with Y daymark leads 100° across bar into hbr ent.

R/T HM VHF Ch 14 16. Marina Ch 80.

TELEPHONE (Dial code 01970) HM ☎/📠 611433 Mobile 07974 023965; Marina 611422; MRSC (01646) 690909; Marinecall 09066 526244; Police 612791; Dr 624855.

FACILITIES Marina (Y Lanfa), ☎ 611422, 📠 624122, (88 + 15 Ⓥ), £1.35, access HW±2, D, Slip, BH (10 ton), C (max 15 ton by arrangement), ⛽, ♿; **Town Quay** AB £5.50, C (3 ton), L, FW; **YC** ☎ 612907, Slip, M, Bar; **Services:** El, CH, D, Ⓔ, ME, ✕, M, 2 Slips(launching £5.50), C (25 ton), Gas. **Town** P (cans), CH, 🛒, R, Bar, SM, ♿, 🅾, ✉, Ⓑ, ⇌, ✈ (Swansea).

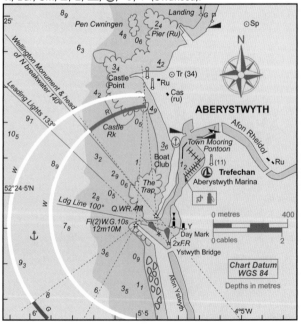

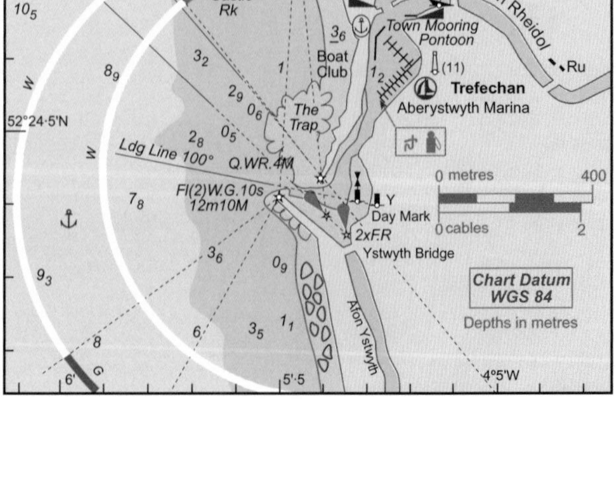
Landing
Pen Cwningen
Pier (Ru)
Sp
Wellington Monument & head of N breakwater 140°
Leading Lights 133°
Castle Point
Tr (34)
Ru
Cas (ru)
ABERYSTWYTH
Afon Rheidol
Castle Rk
Town Mooring Pontoon
Boat Club
Trefechan
Aberystwyth Marina
The Trap
Ldg Line 100°
Q.WR.4M
52°24·5'N
Fl(2)W.G.10s 12m10M
Day Mark
2xF.R
Ystwyth Bridge
Afon Ystwyth
metres
cables
Chart Datum WGS 84
Depths in metres
4°5'W

MINOR HARBOUR, 12M NE of Fishguard

PORT CARDIGAN, Ceredigion, **52°07′·02N 04°42′·07W**. AC 1973, 1484. HW –0405 on Dover; ML 2·4m; Duration 0550. Shelter is good, but ent dangerous in strong N/NW winds. Large scale chart (1484) and local advice essential. Bar has 0·3m or less; breakers form esp on sp ebb. ⚓ near Hotel (conspic) on E side of ent. Chan is usually close to E side; IDM bn, Fl (2) 5s, should be left to stbd when clear of the bar. From Pen-yr-Ergyd to Bryn-Du chan is marked with mid channel markers but shifts constantly. St Dogmaels has ⚓ or a 🅥 via Mooring Master ☎ (01329) 621437 mob 07774 126342. Or ⚓ in pools off Pen-yr-Ergyd. Possible 🅥s off Teifi Boating Club. **Moorings:** administered by Afon Teifi Fairway Committee, Mooring Master ☎ (01239) 613966, Sec ☎ 613704;
Teifi Boating Club ☎ 613846, FW, Bar; **Services:** ME, ⚒. **Town** EC Wed; Ⓑ, 🛒, CH, P&D (cans), FW, ME, Bar, R.

9.11.12 FISHGUARD

Pembrokeshire **52°00'·12N 04°58'·40W**
Commercial Hbr ❀❀❀◊◊✿; Lower Hbr ❀❀◊✿✿✿

CHARTS AC *1178, 1410,* 1973, 1484; Imray C61, C51, C60; Stanfords 27; OS 157

TIDES –0400 Dover; ML 2·6; Duration 0550; Zone 0 (UT)

Standard Port MILFORD HAVEN (⟶)

Times				Height (metres)			
High Water		Low Water		MHWS	MHWN	MLWN	MLWS
0100	0800	0100	0700	7·0	5·2	2·5	0·7
1300	2000	1300	1900				
Differences FISHGUARD							
+0115	+0100	+0110	+0135	–2·2	–1·8	–0·5	+0·1
PORT CARDIGAN							
+0140	+0120	+0220	+0130	–2·3	–1·8	–0·5	0·0
CARDIGAN (Town)							
+0220	+0150	No data		–2·2	–1·6	No data	
PORTHGAIN							
+0055	+0045	+0045	+0100	–2·5	–1·8	–0·6	0·0
RAMSEY SOUND							
+0030	+0030	+0030	+0030	–1·9	–1·3	–0·3	0·0
SOLVA							
+0015	+0010	+0035	+0015	–1·5	–1·0	–0·2	0·0
LITTLE HAVEN							
+0010	+0010	+0025	+0015	–1·1	–0·8	–0·2	0·0
MARTIN'S HAVEN							
+0010	+0010	+0015	+0015	–0·8	–0·5	+0·1	+0·1
SKOMER IS							
–0005	–0005	+0005	+0005	–0·4	–0·1	0·0	0·0

SHELTER Good, except in strong NW/NE winds. Access H24 to Goodwick (upper, commercial) hbr with only 2 Ⓥ berths; no ⚓, except SW of ferry quay. Lower Town (Fishguard) dries 3·2m; access HW±1, limited AB. Good holding in most of the bay; ⚓ off Saddle Pt in 2m or as shown. Strong S'lies funnel down the hbr.

NAVIGATION WPT 52°01′·02N 04°57′·57W, 237° to N bkwtr lt, 0·48m. Beware large swell, especially in N winds. Keep clear of ferries and high-speed SeaCat manoeuvring.

LIGHTS AND MARKS Strumble Hd lt, Fl (4) 15s 45m 26M, is approx 4M WNW of hbr. N bkwtr Fl G 4·5s 18m 13M, Bell 8s. E bkwtr Fl R 3s 10m 5M. Ldg lts 282° (to ferry berths), both FG; W ◊ on masts. The SHM (bn) at Aber gwavn is very small.

R/T HM Ch 14 16. Goodwick Marine Ch M (occas).

TELEPHONE (Dial code 01348) Commercial Hbr Supervisor 404425; HM (Lower hbr) 873369; MRSC (01646) 690909; Marinecall 09066 526244; Police 873073; Dr 872802.

FACILITIES **Goodwick Hbr** AB £10 all LOA, D from bowser; **Lower Town, Fishguard** M (£5 AB) via HM mob 07775 523846; **Fishguard Bay YC**, FW, Bar, Ⓢ; **Services:** BY, ⚒, FW, ME, ACA, Slip, CH, El. **Town** EC Wed; P & D (cans), 🛒, R, Gas, Bar, ✉, Ⓓ, Ⓑ, ⇌, ✈ (Cardiff), Ferry–Rosslare.

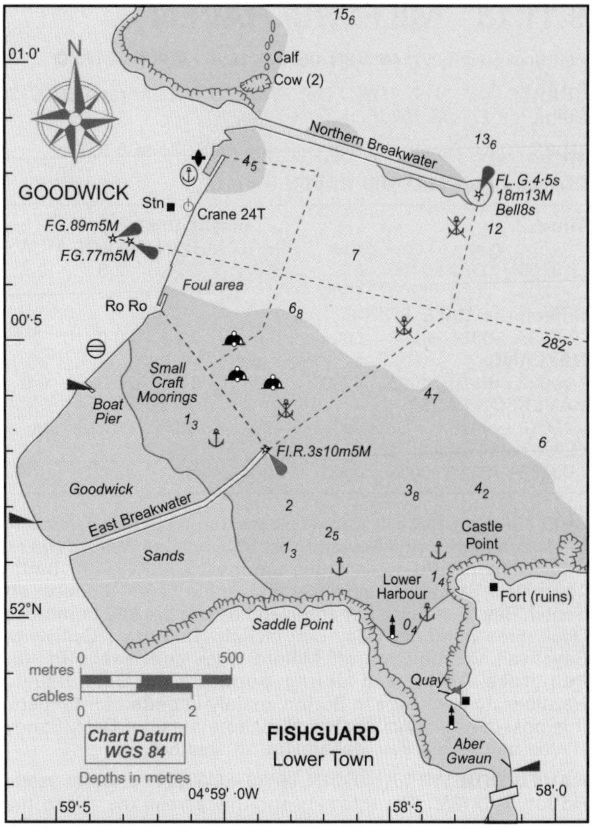
01·0'
N
15₆
Calf
Cow (2)
Northern Breakwater
13₆
4₅
FL.G.4·5s 18m13M Bell8s
12
GOODWICK
Stn
Crane 24T
F.G.89m5M
F.G.77m5M
7
Foul area
Ro Ro
6₈
00'·5
282°
Small Craft Moorings
Boat Pier
1₃
4₇
6
Fl.R.3s10m5M
Goodwick
East Breakwater
3₈
4₂
2
Castle Point
Sands
2₅
1₃
Lower Harbour
1₄
Fort (ruins)
52°N
Saddle Point
0₄
metres
0
500
cables
0
2
Quay
Chart Datum WGS 84
FISHGUARD
Lower Town
Aber Gwaun
Depths in metres
04°59'·0W
59'·5
58'·5
58'·0

HARBOURS IN ST BRIDES BAY

SOLVA, Pembrokeshire, **51°52′02N 05°11′·67W**. AC *1478*. HW –0450 on Dover; ML 3·2m; Duration 0555. See 9.11.12. Good shelter for small boats that can take the ground; access HW±3. Avoid in strong S winds. Black Scar, Green Scar and The Mare are rks 5ca S. Ent via SSE side; best water near Black Rk in centre of ent. Beware stone spit at Trwyn Caws on W just inside ent. There are 9 Or 🅥s drying on hard sand (£5.00), drying/rafting ABs for <9·5m LOA; or ⚓ behind the rk in approx 3m. Yachts can go up to the quay (£6.50) Facilities: showers, 🛒, Bar, R in village. FW on quay, Slip (launching £5). HM (01437) 721703 mob 07974 020139, VHF Ch 16 8, M, CH. **Solva Boat Owners Assn** ☎ 721489 mob 07974 020139.

ST BRIDES BAY, Pembrokeshire, **51°49′02N 05°10′·07W**. AC *1478.* HW (Little Haven) –0450 on Dover; ML 3·2m; Duration 0555. See 9.11.12. A SPM buoy, Fl (5) Y 20s, is midway between Ramsey and Skomer islands at 51°48'·2N 05°20'·0W. Keep at least 100m offshore 1/9-28/2 to avoid disturbing seals, and ditto nesting sea birds 1/3-31/7. Many good ⚓s, especially between Little Haven and Borough Head in S or E winds or between Solva and Dinas Fawr in N or E winds. In W'lies boats should shelter in Solva (above), Skomer (below) or Pendinas Bach. Tankers anchor in mouth of B. For apprs from the N or S see 9.11.5. Facilities: (Little Haven) CH, 🛒, R, Bar, FW (cans).

SKOMER, Pembrokeshire, **51°44′·42N 05°16′·77W**. AC *1478,* 2878. HW –0455 Dover. See 9.11.12. The island is a National Nature Reserve (fee payable to Warden on landing) and also a Marine Nature Reserve, extending to Marloes Peninsula. Keep at least 100m offshore 1/9-28/2 to avoid disturbing seals and ditto nesting sea birds 1/3-31/7. There is a 5kn speed limit within 100m of the island. ⚓ in S Haven (N Haven ⚓ prohibited due to eel grass). Enter N Haven close to W shore, and land on W side of bay on beach or at steps. In N Haven pick up 🅥s provided or ⚓ to seaward of them. No access to the island from S Haven. For Jack Sound see 9.11.5. There are no lts, marks or facilities. For info, Marine Conservation Officer ☎ (01646) 636736.

11

9.11.13 MILFORD HAVEN

Pembrokeshire **51°40'·13N 05°08'·16W** ❁❁❁◊◊◊✿✿

CHARTS AC *1410, 1178, 1478, 2878,* 3273/4/5; Imray C60, C13; Stanfords 27; OS 157

TIDES –0500 Dover; ML 3·8; Duration 0605; Zone 0 (UT)

Standard Port MILFORD HAVEN (⟶)

Times				**Height (metres)**			
High Water		Low Water		MHWS	MHWN	MLWN	MLWS
0100	0800	0100	0700	7·0	5·2	2·5	0·7
1300	2000	1300	1900				
Differences DALE ROADS							
–0005	–0005	–0008	–0008	0·0	0·0	0·0	–0·1
NEYLAND							
+0002	+0010	0000	0000	0·0	0·0	0·0	0·0
HAVERFORDWEST							
+0010	+0025	Dries out		–4·8	–4·9	Dries out	
LLANGWM (Black Tar)							
+0010	+0020	+0005	0000	+0·1	+0·1	0·0	–0·1

SHELTER Very good in various places round the hbr, especially in Milford Marina and Neyland Yacht Haven. Call *Milford Haven Radio Port Control* to ascertain the most suitable ⚓ or berth. ⚓s in Dale Bay; off Chapel Bay and Angle Pt on S shore; off Scotch Bay, E of Milford marina; and others beyond Pembroke Dock. Free pontoons (May-Oct) include: Dale Bay, Gelliswick Bay; waiting pontoons off Milford Dock and Hobbs Pt (for Pembroke Dock); and drying pontoons at Dale Beach, Hazelbeach, Neyland and Burton; mainly intended for tenders. It is possible to dry out safely at inshore areas of Dale, Sandy Haven and Angle Bay, depending on weather.

NAVIGATION WPT 51°40'·21N, 05°10'·28W, 220° to Great Castle Hd ldg lt, 3·18M. The tide sets strongly across the ent to the Haven particularly at sp. In bad weather avoid passing over Mid Chan Rks and St Ann's Hd shoal, where a confused sea and swell will be found (see AC 3273). Give St Ann's Head a wide berth especially on the ebb, when East Chan by Sheep Island is better. Beware large tankers entering and leaving the Haven and ferries moving at high speed in the lower Haven. Caution: Only 15m clearance below cables between Thorn Island and Thorn Pt. NB: Milford Haven Port Authority has a jetty, Port Control and offices near Hubberston Pt. Their launches have G hulls and W upperworks with 'PILOT' in black letters and fly a Pilot flag (HOTEL) while on patrol; Fl Bu lt at night. Their instructions must be obeyed. No vessel may pass within 100m of any terminal or any tanker, whether at ⚓ or under way.

River Cleddau is navigable 6M to Picton Pt, at junction of West and East arms, at all tides for boats of moderate draught. Clearance under Cleddau Bridge above Neyland is 37m; and 25m under power cable 1M upstream. Chan to Haverfordwest has 2m at HW and clearances of only 6m below cables and bridge; only feasible for shoal draft/lifting keel and unmasted craft.

Firing Ranges to the S and SE, see 9.11.14 and AC 1076.

Call Port Control VHF Ch 12 or tel/fax as below for navigational advice or port operational information.

LIGHTS AND MARKS See 9.11.4 for details. Many ldg lts have deliberately been omitted from the chartlet for clarity, since virtually all are specifically for Very Large Crude Carriers heading to and from the oil refinery. The Haven is very well buoyed and lit as far as Cleddau bridge. Milford Dock ldg lts 348°, both F.Bu, with W ○ daymarks. Dock entry sigs on E side of lock: 2 FG (vert) = gates open, vessels may enter. Exit sigs are given via VHF Ch 14. VHF is normally used for ent/exit by day and night.

R/T Within the Haven keep a listening watch on Ch 12. Port Authority: *Milford Haven Port Control*, Ch **12** 11 14 16 (H24); 09 10 67. *Milford Haven Patrol* launches, Ch 11 12 (H24). To lock into Milford Marina first call *Milford Pier Head* Ch **14** for instructions (for lock hrs see Facilities); then call *Milford Marina* Ch M for a berth. Neyland Yacht Haven Ch **80**, M.

Broadcasts: Local forecasts on Ch 12 14 at 0300, 0900, 1500 and 2100 (all UT). Nav warnings follow on Ch14. Gale warnings issued on receipt Ch 12 14. Expected shipping movements for next 24 hours on Ch 12, 0800–0830, 2000–2030LT and on request. Tide hts and winds on request. Bcsts on Ch 16 67 at 0335 then every 4 hrs to 2335.

TELEPHONE (Dial code 01646) Lock 696310; Port Ctrl 696100, ℻ 696125; MRSC 690909; Marinecall 09066 526243; Police (01437) 763355; Ⓗ Haverfordwest (01437) 764545; Dr 690674.

FACILITIES Marinas/ Berthing (from seaward):

Dale Bay 🛒, FW, R, Slip, Pontoon, YC.

Milford Haven Port Authority jetty ☎ 696133 (occas use by visitors with approval from HM), AB, FW.

Milford Marina (280) ☎ 696312, ℻ 696314, Pierhead ☎ 696310; £1.30. VHF Ch M. Lock hrs: ent HW–4, exit –3½, free flow HW –2¼ to HW–¼, ent +1½, exit +1¾, ent +2¾, exit +3¼; waiting pontoon or shelter in lock, 3·5m water at MLWS. D (H24), C, BH (16 ton), CH, EI, ME, ⚒, Ⓔ, Gas, Gaz, 🛒, R, Bar, Ice, ⊡, ♿, ✉, Ⓑ.

Neyland Yacht Haven (420 inc Ⓥ) ☎ 601601, ℻ 600713, £1.59, D, CH, Ⓔ, Gas, Gaz, ⊡, C (20 ton), SM, SC, ME, EI, ⚒, R, 🛒; Access lower basin H24, upper basin HW±3½ (sill + depth gauges and R/G lit perches); marina and approaches dredged annually Oct/March - proceed with extreme caution.

Lawrenny Yacht Station (100) ☎ 651212/651065, ⚓ £5, L, FW, BY, CH, D, P, ⚒, C (15 ton), ME, Slip(launching £5.00), ⊡, Bar, R, 🛒, ♿, ✉, Gas.

Services: All marine services available; check with HM, marinas or YC/SC. **Dale Sailing Co** (@ Neyland), BY, CH, ME, ⚒, D, LPG, BH (35T). **East Llannion Marine**: access HW±3, Slip, scrubbing piles, BH (30 ton), fuel. **Rudder's BY**, small but useful, is just upstream of Burton Pt.

Yacht Clubs: Dale YC ☎ 636362; Pembrokeshire YC ☎ 692799; Neyland YC ☎ 600267; Pembroke Haven YC ☎ 684403; Lawrenny YC ☎ 651212.

Towns: Milford Haven, EC Thurs; ✉, Ⓑ, ⇌. Pembroke Dock, EC Wed; ✉, Ⓑ, ⇌, Ⓗ. Neyland, EC Wed; ✉, Ⓑ. Haverfordwest, EC Thurs; ✉, Ⓗ, Ⓑ, ⇌, ✈ (Swansea or Cardiff). Ferry: Pembroke Dock–Rosslare.

SMALL BOAT PASSAGES The following small boat passages, suitable for dinghies, canoes etc, are in operation in the port of Milford Haven in the following positions:

Herbrandston Jetty	51°42'·32N	05°04'·70W approx
Elf Jetty	51°42'·29N	05°03'·72W approx
Texaco West end	51°41'·76N	05°03'·06W approx
Texaco Jetty centre	51°41'·83N	05°02'·25W approx
Texaco East end	51°41'·82N	05°01'·69W approx

All the above small boat passages exhibit all round fixed yellow lights at night and are marked by day with high visibility orange on the jetty legs. The maximum headroom above MHWS for the small boat passages are:

Herbrandston	3.40m	Texaco Centre	3.35m
Elf	2.78m	Texaco East	4.60m
Texaco West	4.36m		

NOTES

MILFORD HAVEN *continued*

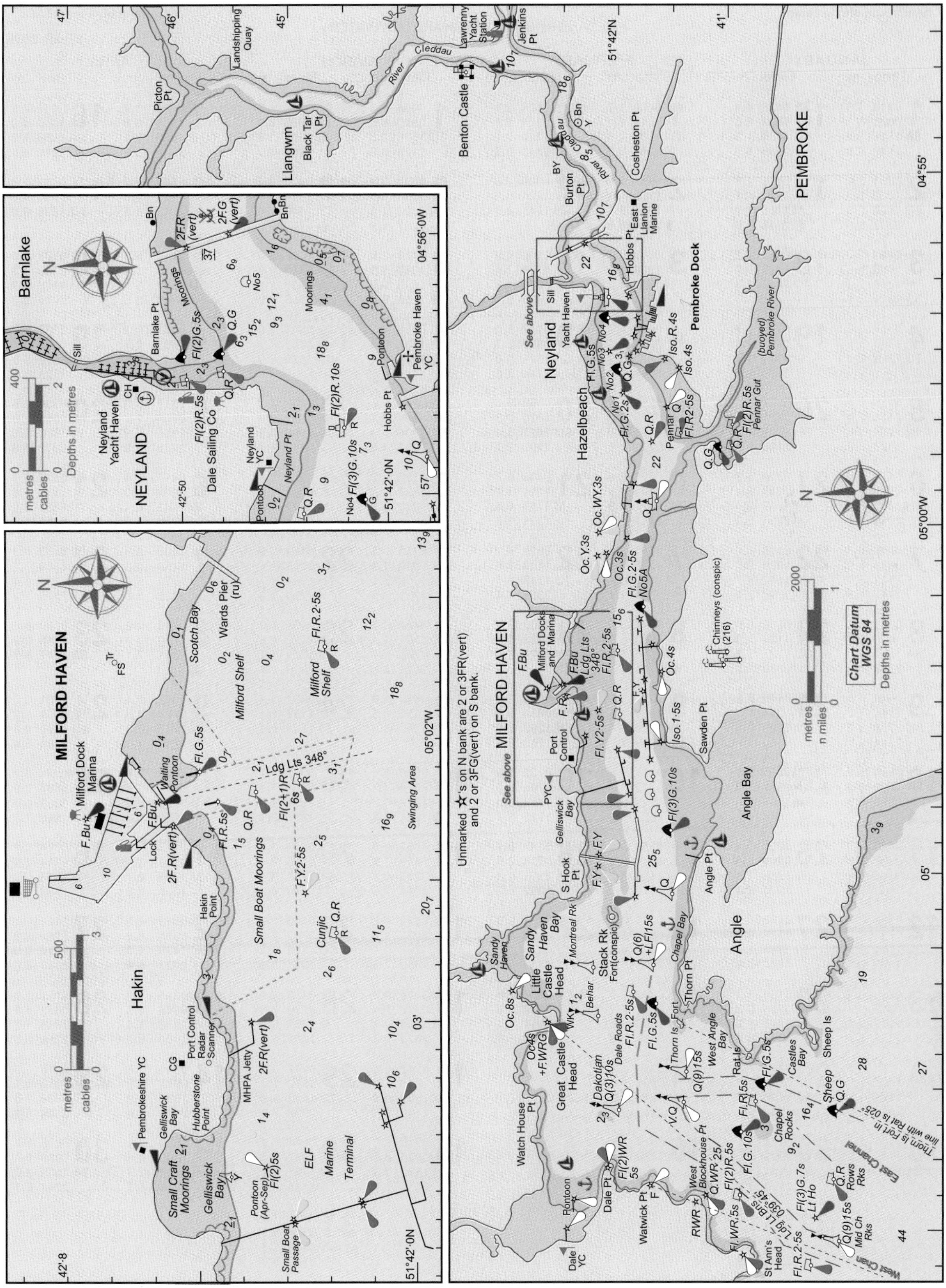
MILFORD HAVEN
Milford Dock Marina
Hakin
Scotch Bay
Wards Pier (ru)
Milford Shelf
Small Boat Moorings
Swinging Area
ELF Marine Terminal
Gelliswick Bay
Small Craft Moorings
Pembrokeshire YC
Hubberstone Point
MHPA Jetty
Port Control Radar Scanner
Ldg Lts 348°
51°42'·0N
05°02'W
NEYLAND
Neyland Yacht Haven
Dale Sailing Co
Barnlake
Barnlake Pt
Neyland Pt
Pembroke Haven YC
Hobbs Pt
Depths in metres
04°56'·0W
Llangwm
Black Tar Pt
Picton Pt
Landshipping Quay
Lawrenny Yacht Station
Jenkins Pt
River Cleddau
Benton Castle
Burton Pt
Cosheston Pt
PEMBROKE
East Llanion Marine
Pembroke Dock
Pembroke River
Pennar Gut
Hazelbeach
Unmarked ☆'s on N bank are 2 or 3FR(vert) and 2 or 3FG(vert) on S bank.
Chimneys (conspic) (216)
Chart Datum WGS 84
Depths in metres
Sawden Pt
Angle Bay
Angle Pt
Angle
Chapel Bay
Thorn Pt
Thorn Is
West Angle Bay
Rat Is
Castles Bay
Sheep Is
Chapel Rocks
Sheep
Rows Rks
Mid Ch Rks
St Ann's Head
West Blockhouse Pt
Watwick Pt
Dale Pt
Dale YC
Watch House Pt
Great Castle Head
Little Castle Head
Sandy Haven
Sandy Haven Bay
S Hook Pt
Gelliswick Bay
Stack Rk
Dale Roads
Dakotian
East Channel
West Chan
Thorn Is Fort in line with Rat Is 025°
Ldg Lt Bns 039·45°
05°00'W
04°55'W
05'
51°42'N

TIME ZONE (UT)
For Summer Time add ONE hour in **non-shaded areas**

WALES – MILFORD HAVEN

LAT 51°42′N LONG 5°03′W

TIMES AND HEIGHTS OF HIGH AND LOW WATERS

SPRING & NEAP TIDES
Dates in red are SPRINGS
Dates in blue are NEAPS

YEAR **2005**

JANUARY

Date	Day	Time	m	Time	m	Time	m	Time	m
1	SA	0318	1.8	0925	6.1	1546	1.9	2149	5.8
2	SU	0357	2.0	1006	5.9	1628	2.0	2233	5.6
3	M	0443	2.2	1053	5.8	1716	2.2	◑ 2324	5.4
4	TU	0537	2.3	1149	5.6	1816	2.3		
5	W	0026	5.4	0644	2.4	1255	5.6	1927	2.3
6	TH	0137	5.4	0759	2.3	1407	5.7	2040	2.1
7	F	0248	5.7	0911	2.0	1517	5.9	2147	1.8
8	SA	0351	6.1	1015	1.6	1620	6.3	2247	1.5
9	SU	0449	6.5	1114	1.2	1718	6.6	2341	1.1
10	M	0544	6.9	1209	0.9	1812	6.9	●	
11	TU	0032	0.9	0635	7.2	1301	0.6	1903	7.0
12	W	0122	0.7	0725	7.3	1351	0.5	1952	7.1
13	TH	0209	0.7	0813	7.3	1439	0.6	2039	6.9
14	F	0255	0.8	0900	7.2	1525	0.8	2124	6.7
15	SA	0340	1.1	0946	6.9	1610	1.1	2209	6.3
16	SU	0425	1.4	1033	6.5	1656	1.5	2255	6.0
17	M	0513	1.8	1122	6.1	1745	1.9	◐ 2346	5.6
18	TU	0608	2.2	1217	5.7	1842	2.3		
19	W	0048	5.3	0713	2.4	1324	5.4	1950	2.4
20	TH	0201	5.2	0831	2.5	1436	5.3	2104	2.4
21	F	0314	5.3	0943	2.4	1545	5.4	2206	2.2
22	SA	0416	5.6	1039	2.1	1642	5.7	2256	2.0
23	SU	0505	5.9	1126	1.9	1727	5.9	2338	1.7
24	M	0545	6.2	1205	1.6	1806	6.1		
25	TU	0015	1.5	0621	6.4	1241	1.4	○ 1841	6.3
26	W	0050	1.4	0655	6.5	1314	1.3	1914	6.4
27	TH	0122	1.3	0727	6.6	1345	1.2	1946	6.4
28	F	0154	1.2	0758	6.6	1416	1.2	2017	6.4
29	SA	0225	1.2	0830	6.6	1448	1.2	2049	6.3
30	SU	0258	1.3	0903	6.5	1521	1.4	2122	6.2
31	M	0332	1.5	0937	6.3	1555	1.6	2158	6.0

FEBRUARY

Date	Day	Time	m	Time	m	Time	m	Time	m
1	TU	0408	1.7	1016	6.1	1633	1.8	2240	5.7
2	W	0451	2.0	1103	5.8	1721	2.1	◑ 2334	5.5
3	TH	0548	2.2	1204	5.5	1828	2.3		
4	F	0046	5.3	0710	2.4	1326	5.4	2001	2.4
5	SA	0215	5.4	0845	2.2	1455	5.5	2129	2.1
6	SU	0335	5.8	1004	1.8	1611	5.9	2237	1.6
7	M	0441	6.3	1108	1.3	1713	6.4	2334	1.1
8	TU	0537	6.8	1203	0.8	1806	6.8	●	
9	W	0024	0.7	0627	7.3	1252	0.4	1853	7.1
10	TH	0111	0.5	0713	7.5	1338	0.2	1937	7.2
11	F	0154	0.4	0757	7.5	1420	0.2	2018	7.2
12	SA	0235	0.5	0838	7.4	1459	0.5	2057	6.9
13	SU	0313	0.7	0918	7.1	1536	0.9	2135	6.6
14	M	0350	1.1	0956	6.6	1613	1.3	2212	6.1
15	TU	0427	1.6	1036	6.1	1650	1.9	2253	5.7
16	W	0508	2.1	1121	5.5	1735	2.3	◐ 2343	5.2
17	TH	0605	2.6	1221	5.1	1841	2.7		
18	F	0100	4.9	0736	2.8	1353	4.8	2020	2.8
19	SA	0242	5.0	0919	2.7	1525	5.0	2144	2.6
20	SU	0358	5.3	1025	2.3	1627	5.4	2239	2.2
21	M	0448	5.7	1111	1.9	1711	5.8	2321	1.8
22	TU	0528	6.1	1149	1.5	1748	6.1	2358	1.4
23	W	0602	6.4	1222	1.3	1821	6.4		
24	TH	0030	1.2	0634	6.6	1253	1.0	○ 1852	6.6
25	F	0102	1.0	0705	6.8	1323	0.9	1922	6.7
26	SA	0132	0.9	0735	6.9	1353	0.8	1952	6.7
27	SU	0203	0.8	0806	6.9	1423	0.9	2023	6.7
28	M	0234	0.9	0837	6.8	1454	1.0	2054	6.5

MARCH

Date	Day	Time	m	Time	m	Time	m	Time	m
1	TU	0306	1.1	0910	6.6	1525	1.3	2128	6.3
2	W	0340	1.4	0946	6.3	1600	1.6	2207	5.9
3	TH	0420	1.8	1030	5.9	1645	2.0	◑ 2258	5.6
4	F	0516	2.2	1131	5.4	1751	2.4		
5	SA	0014	5.2	0644	2.4	1304	5.1	1942	2.6
6	SU	0158	5.2	0837	2.3	1449	5.3	2122	2.2
7	M	0329	5.7	1000	1.8	1609	5.8	2231	1.6
8	TU	0434	6.3	1101	1.1	1706	6.4	2324	1.0
9	W	0526	6.9	1151	0.6	1753	6.9		
10	TH	0010	0.6	0611	7.3	1236	0.3	● 1835	7.2
11	F	0053	0.3	0653	7.5	1316	0.1	1914	7.3
12	SA	0132	0.2	0733	7.5	1353	0.2	1951	7.2
13	SU	0208	0.3	0810	7.4	1428	0.4	2026	7.0
14	M	0242	0.6	0846	7.0	1501	0.8	2100	6.6
15	TU	0315	1.1	0920	6.5	1532	1.3	2132	6.2
16	W	0347	1.6	0955	6.0	1603	1.8	2208	5.7
17	TH	0422	2.1	1034	5.4	1640	2.4	◐ 2251	5.2
18	F	0510	2.6	1126	4.9	1737	2.8	2358	4.8
19	SA	0641	2.9	1303	4.6	1929	3.0		
20	SU	0202	4.7	0847	2.8	1457	4.8	2113	2.7
21	M	0328	5.1	0957	2.4	1601	5.2	2212	2.3
22	TU	0419	5.6	1043	1.9	1644	5.7	2254	1.8
23	W	0458	6.0	1120	1.5	1719	6.1	2329	1.4
24	TH	0532	6.4	1153	1.2	1752	6.4		
25	F	0002	1.1	0604	6.7	1224	0.9	○ 1822	6.7
26	SA	0034	0.8	0635	6.9	1254	0.7	1853	6.8
27	SU	0106	0.7	0707	7.0	1325	0.7	1924	6.9
28	M	0138	0.7	0739	7.0	1357	0.7	1956	6.9
29	TU	0211	0.8	0812	6.9	1429	0.9	2029	6.7
30	W	0244	1.0	0847	6.6	1502	1.2	2105	6.4
31	TH	0321	1.3	0926	6.2	1540	1.6	2148	6.0

APRIL

Date	Day	Time	m	Time	m	Time	m	Time	m
1	F	0406	1.7	1014	5.8	1628	2.1	2244	5.6
2	SA	0508	2.2	1122	5.3	1743	2.5	◑	
3	SU	0007	5.3	0647	2.4	1302	5.0	1940	2.5
4	M	0153	5.3	0833	2.1	1445	5.3	2112	2.1
5	TU	0317	5.8	0948	1.6	1556	5.9	2215	1.5
6	W	0417	6.4	1043	1.0	1647	6.4	2305	1.0
7	TH	0506	6.9	1130	0.6	1731	6.8	2348	0.6
8	F	0549	7.2	1210	0.4	1811	7.1	●	
9	SA	0027	0.4	0628	7.3	1248	0.3	1847	7.1
10	SU	0105	0.4	0705	7.3	1323	0.4	1922	7.1
11	M	0139	0.5	0741	7.1	1356	0.7	1955	6.9
12	TU	0213	0.8	0815	6.8	1428	1.0	2027	6.6
13	W	0245	1.2	0848	6.3	1458	1.4	2100	6.2
14	TH	0316	1.6	0922	5.9	1528	1.9	2134	5.8
15	F	0351	2.1	1000	5.4	1603	2.3	2216	5.3
16	SA	0437	2.5	1050	4.9	1655	2.7	◐ 2316	4.9
17	SU	0557	2.8	1211	4.6	1835	3.0		
18	M	0101	4.8	0749	2.8	1406	4.7	2019	2.8
19	TU	0237	5.0	0908	2.4	1516	5.1	2126	2.4
20	W	0334	5.5	0959	2.0	1602	5.5	2212	1.9
21	TH	0416	5.9	1038	1.6	1639	6.0	2250	1.5
22	F	0453	6.3	1114	1.2	1714	6.4	2326	1.2
23	SA	0527	6.6	1148	0.9	1747	6.7		
24	SU	0001	0.9	0602	6.8	1223	0.8	○ 1821	6.9
25	M	0037	0.7	0637	7.0	1258	0.7	1856	7.0
26	TU	0114	0.7	0714	7.0	1333	0.7	1933	6.9
27	W	0151	0.8	0752	6.8	1410	0.9	2012	6.8
28	TH	0231	1.0	0833	6.5	1449	1.2	2054	6.5
29	F	0315	1.3	0919	6.1	1534	1.6	2144	6.1
30	SA	0408	1.7	1015	5.7	1630	2.0	2248	5.7

Chart Datum: 3·71 metres below Ordnance Datum (Newlyn)

TIME ZONE (UT)
For Summer Time add ONE hour in **non-shaded areas**

WALES – MILFORD HAVEN

LAT 51°42′N LONG 5°03′W

TIMES AND HEIGHTS OF HIGH AND LOW WATERS

SPRING & NEAP TIDES
Dates in red are SPRINGS
Dates in blue are NEAPS

YEAR **2005**

MAY

Date	Day	Time	m	Time	m	Time	m	Time	m
1	SU	0517	2.0	1128	5.3	1751	2.3	◑	
2	M	0009	5.5	0649	2.1	1258	5.2	1929	2.3
3	TU	0137	5.6	0814	1.9	1423	5.5	2048	1.9
4	W	0251	6.0	0922	1.5	1528	5.9	2148	1.5
5	TH	0350	6.4	1016	1.2	1619	6.3	2238	1.1
6	F	0438	6.7	1101	0.9	1703	6.6	2321	0.9
7	SA	0522	6.9	1141	0.8	1743	6.8		
8	SU	0000	0.8	0601	6.9	1219	0.8	● 1819	6.8
9	M	0038	0.8	0638	6.8	1254	0.8	1854	6.8
10	TU	0113	0.9	0714	6.7	1328	1.0	1928	6.6
11	W	0148	1.1	0749	6.4	1400	1.3	2002	6.4
12	TH	0221	1.4	0823	6.1	1432	1.6	2036	6.1
13	F	0255	1.7	0859	5.8	1505	1.9	2112	5.8
14	SA	0332	2.0	0938	5.4	1542	2.2	2154	5.5
15	SU	0417	2.3	1026	5.1	1631	2.5	2248	5.2
16	M	0520	2.6	1129	4.8	1744	2.7	◐ 2359	5.0
17	TU	0642	2.6	1250	4.8	1910	2.7		
18	W	0122	5.1	0757	2.4	1409	5.0	2020	2.4
19	TH	0230	5.4	0857	2.1	1505	5.4	2116	2.1
20	F	0322	5.7	0946	1.8	1550	5.8	2203	1.7
21	SA	0406	6.1	1029	1.4	1631	6.2	2246	1.4
22	SU	0448	6.4	1111	1.1	1711	6.5	2328	1.1
23	M	0530	6.7	1152	0.9	1752	6.8	○	
24	TU	0011	0.9	0612	6.8	1234	0.8	1833	6.9
25	W	0055	0.8	0656	6.9	1316	0.8	1917	6.9
26	TH	0140	0.8	0741	6.7	1359	1.0	2003	6.8
27	F	0226	0.9	0829	6.5	1446	1.2	2052	6.6
28	SA	0317	1.2	0921	6.2	1536	1.5	2147	6.3
29	SU	0413	1.4	1019	5.9	1635	1.8	2248	6.1
30	M	0519	1.7	1123	5.6	1746	2.0	◑ 2356	5.9
31	TU	0631	1.8	1234	5.5	1901	2.0		

JUNE

Date	Day	Time	m	Time	m	Time	m	Time	m
1	W	0107	5.9	0741	1.7	1346	5.6	2011	1.9
2	TH	0215	6.0	0845	1.6	1450	5.8	2113	1.7
3	F	0315	6.1	0941	1.5	1545	6.0	2206	1.5
4	SA	0407	6.3	1029	1.4	1633	6.2	2253	1.4
5	SU	0454	6.4	1112	1.3	1716	6.4	2335	1.3
6	M	0537	6.4	1152	1.2	1756	6.4	●	
7	TU	0015	1.3	0617	6.4	1230	1.3	1833	6.5
8	W	0053	1.3	0655	6.3	1306	1.3	1909	6.4
9	TH	0130	1.4	0731	6.2	1341	1.4	1945	6.3
10	F	0205	1.5	0807	6.0	1415	1.6	2020	6.2
11	SA	0241	1.6	0843	5.8	1449	1.8	2057	6.0
12	SU	0317	1.8	0921	5.6	1527	2.0	2137	5.8
13	M	0358	2.0	1003	5.4	1609	2.2	2221	5.6
14	TU	0445	2.2	1051	5.2	1701	2.3	2313	5.4
15	W	0541	2.3	1146	5.1	1803	2.4	◐	
16	TH	0012	5.3	0645	2.3	1251	5.1	1910	2.4
17	F	0117	5.4	0749	2.2	1357	5.3	2014	2.2
18	SA	0221	5.6	0850	2.0	1457	5.6	2114	1.9
19	SU	0319	5.9	0945	1.7	1550	6.0	2209	1.6
20	M	0412	6.2	1038	1.4	1640	6.3	2301	1.3
21	TU	0504	6.4	1127	1.1	1730	6.6	2352	1.0
22	W	0555	6.7	1216	1.0	1819	6.9	○	
23	TH	0043	0.8	0645	6.8	1305	0.9	1908	7.0
24	F	0133	0.7	0736	6.8	1354	0.9	1958	7.0
25	SA	0224	0.7	0826	6.7	1443	1.0	2049	6.9
26	SU	0315	0.8	0917	6.5	1533	1.1	2141	6.7
27	M	0407	1.0	1008	6.2	1625	1.4	2234	6.5
28	TU	0501	1.3	1101	6.0	1721	1.6	◑ 2329	6.2
29	W	0558	1.6	1159	5.7	1822	1.8		
30	TH	0029	6.0	0657	1.8	1302	5.6	1926	2.0

JULY

Date	Day	Time	m	Time	m	Time	m	Time	m
1	F	0133	5.8	0801	1.9	1407	5.5	2033	2.0
2	SA	0237	5.7	0903	1.9	1510	5.6	2135	2.0
3	SU	0338	5.8	1000	1.9	1607	5.8	2230	1.8
4	M	0433	5.9	1050	1.7	1657	6.0	2318	1.7
5	TU	0521	6.0	1133	1.6	1741	6.2		
6	W	0001	1.6	0603	6.1	1214	1.5	● 1820	6.3
7	TH	0041	1.5	0642	6.1	1251	1.4	1857	6.3
8	F	0117	1.4	0718	6.2	1326	1.4	1932	6.3
9	SA	0151	1.4	0752	6.1	1359	1.4	2005	6.3
10	SU	0224	1.4	0826	6.1	1432	1.5	2039	6.2
11	M	0258	1.5	0900	5.9	1506	1.6	2114	6.1
12	TU	0332	1.6	0935	5.8	1543	1.7	2150	6.0
13	W	0409	1.8	1013	5.6	1622	1.9	2231	5.8
14	TH	0451	2.0	1057	5.5	1708	2.1	◐ 2318	5.6
15	F	0540	2.1	1149	5.3	1804	2.3		
16	SA	0015	5.5	0642	2.2	1255	5.3	1915	2.3
17	SU	0125	5.4	0757	2.2	1408	5.4	2031	2.2
18	M	0240	5.6	0910	2.0	1518	5.7	2142	1.9
19	TU	0348	5.9	1015	1.7	1620	6.1	2245	1.4
20	W	0450	6.2	1113	1.3	1717	6.6	2342	1.0
21	TH	0546	6.6	1206	1.0	1810	6.9	○	
22	F	0035	0.7	0638	6.8	1256	0.7	1900	7.2
23	SA	0126	0.5	0727	7.0	1345	0.6	1949	7.3
24	SU	0214	0.4	0814	7.0	1431	0.6	2036	7.3
25	M	0300	0.5	0900	6.8	1516	0.8	2122	7.1
26	TU	0345	0.7	0944	6.6	1601	1.0	2207	6.7
27	W	0429	1.1	1029	6.2	1646	1.4	2254	6.3
28	TH	0515	1.6	1117	5.8	1736	1.8	◑ 2345	5.9
29	F	0607	2.0	1212	5.4	1836	2.2		
30	SA	0047	5.5	0710	2.3	1322	5.2	1952	2.4
31	SU	0201	5.2	0827	2.4	1440	5.2	2113	2.4

AUGUST

Date	Day	Time	m	Time	m	Time	m	Time	m
1	M	0317	5.3	0939	2.3	1551	5.5	2218	2.2
2	TU	0421	5.5	1035	2.1	1646	5.8	2309	1.9
3	W	0511	5.8	1121	1.8	1730	6.1	2351	1.6
4	TH	0552	6.0	1200	1.6	1808	6.3		
5	F	0027	1.4	0627	6.2	1235	1.4	● 1841	6.5
6	SA	0101	1.3	0700	6.3	1308	1.3	1913	6.5
7	SU	0132	1.2	0732	6.4	1339	1.2	1944	6.6
8	M	0202	1.2	0802	6.4	1410	1.2	2015	6.5
9	TU	0232	1.2	0832	6.3	1441	1.3	2045	6.4
10	W	0302	1.3	0903	6.2	1513	1.4	2117	6.3
11	TH	0334	1.5	0936	6.0	1546	1.7	2152	6.1
12	F	0408	1.8	1014	5.8	1624	1.9	2233	5.8
13	SA	0450	2.1	1100	5.5	1714	2.2	◐ 2327	5.5
14	SU	0547	2.3	1205	5.3	1826	2.4		
15	M	0042	5.3	0714	2.5	1333	5.2	2005	2.4
16	TU	0216	5.3	0851	2.3	1501	5.6	2131	2.0
17	W	0339	5.7	1005	1.8	1611	6.1	2238	1.5
18	TH	0444	6.2	1104	1.3	1709	6.7	2334	0.9
19	F	0538	6.7	1156	0.9	1800	7.2	○	
20	SA	0024	0.5	0626	7.1	1244	0.5	1846	7.5
21	SU	0111	0.2	0711	7.2	1328	0.3	1931	7.6
22	M	0154	0.2	0753	7.2	1410	0.4	2013	7.5
23	TU	0235	0.3	0834	7.1	1450	0.6	2054	7.2
24	W	0314	0.7	0913	6.7	1528	0.9	2134	6.8
25	TH	0351	1.2	0951	6.3	1607	1.4	2215	6.3
26	F	0429	1.7	1032	5.8	1649	2.0	◑ 2259	5.7
27	SA	0513	2.2	1121	5.3	1744	2.5	2357	5.2
28	SU	0616	2.7	1233	5.0	1913	2.8		
29	M	0125	4.8	0754	2.9	1417	5.0	2059	2.7
30	TU	0303	5.0	0924	2.6	1539	5.3	2208	2.4
31	W	0410	5.4	1022	2.2	1631	5.8	2255	1.9

Chart Datum: 3·71 metres below Ordnance Datum (Newlyn)

TIME ZONE (UT)
For Summer Time add ONE hour in **non-shaded areas**

WALES – MILFORD HAVEN

LAT 51°42′N LONG 5°03′W

TIMES AND HEIGHTS OF HIGH AND LOW WATERS

SPRING & NEAP TIDES
Dates in red are SPRINGS
Dates in blue are NEAPS

YEAR **2005**

SEPTEMBER

Date	Day	Time	m	Time	m	Time	m	Time	m	Phase
1	TH	0455	5.8	1105	1.8	1712	6.1	2333	1.6	
2	F	0532	6.1	1141	1.5	1746	6.4			
3	SA	0006	1.3	0605	6.4	1214	1.3	1818	6.6	●
4	SU	0037	1.1	0635	6.5	1244	1.1	1848	6.8	
5	M	0105	1.0	0705	6.6	1314	1.0	1917	6.8	
6	TU	0134	1.0	0733	6.7	1343	1.0	1946	6.8	
7	W	0203	1.0	0802	6.6	1413	1.1	2015	6.7	
8	TH	0232	1.2	0832	6.5	1444	1.3	2046	6.5	
9	F	0302	1.4	0904	6.3	1516	1.5	2120	6.2	
10	SA	0334	1.7	0940	6.0	1553	1.9	2200	5.9	
11	SU	0414	2.1	1026	5.6	1643	2.3	2255	5.4	◐
12	M	0513	2.5	1135	5.3	1803	2.6			
13	TU	0020	5.1	0656	2.7	1318	5.2	2000	2.5	
14	W	0211	5.2	0847	2.4	1455	5.6	2127	2.0	
15	TH	0336	5.7	0959	1.8	1603	6.3	2230	1.3	
16	F	0435	6.3	1054	1.2	1656	6.9	2321	0.8	
17	SA	0524	6.9	1141	0.7	1743	7.4			
18	SU	0006	0.4	0607	7.2	1224	0.4	1826	7.6	○
19	M	0049	0.2	0648	7.4	1305	0.3	1907	7.7	
20	TU	0128	0.2	0726	7.4	1343	0.4	1946	7.5	
21	W	0205	0.4	0803	7.1	1420	0.6	2024	7.2	
22	TH	0240	0.8	0839	6.8	1456	1.1	2100	6.7	
23	F	0314	1.3	0914	6.4	1531	1.6	2137	6.1	
24	SA	0348	1.9	0951	5.9	1608	2.2	2218	5.5	
25	SU	0426	2.4	1036	5.3	1659	2.7	2312	5.0	◑
26	M	0524	2.9	1146	4.9	1834	3.0			
27	TU	0049	4.6	0717	3.1	1348	4.9	2037	2.9	
28	W	0242	4.8	0900	2.8	1513	5.3	2144	2.5	
29	TH	0346	5.3	0956	2.4	1604	5.7	2228	2.0	
30	F	0428	5.8	1037	1.9	1642	6.2	2304	1.6	

OCTOBER

Date	Day	Time	m	Time	m	Time	m	Time	m	Phase
1	SA	0503	6.2	1112	1.5	1716	6.5	2335	1.3	
2	SU	0535	6.5	1144	1.2	1747	6.7			
3	M	0005	1.1	0604	6.7	1215	1.0	1817	6.9	●
4	TU	0035	1.0	0634	6.8	1245	0.9	1847	7.0	
5	W	0105	0.9	0703	6.9	1316	0.9	1917	7.0	
6	TH	0135	1.0	0734	6.8	1348	1.0	1949	6.8	
7	F	0205	1.1	0806	6.7	1421	1.2	2022	6.6	
8	SA	0237	1.4	0840	6.4	1456	1.6	2059	6.3	
9	SU	0313	1.8	0920	6.1	1538	1.9	2144	5.8	
10	M	0358	2.2	1012	5.7	1636	2.3	2246	5.4	◐
11	TU	0506	2.6	1130	5.3	1808	2.6			
12	W	0020	5.1	0700	2.7	1314	5.4	1958	2.4	
13	TH	0208	5.3	0837	2.3	1443	5.8	2115	1.8	
14	F	0323	5.9	0943	1.8	1546	6.4	2212	1.3	
15	SA	0417	6.4	1034	1.2	1636	7.0	2300	0.8	
16	SU	0502	6.9	1119	0.8	1721	7.3	2343	0.5	
17	M	0543	7.2	1200	0.6	1802	7.5			○
18	TU	0022	0.4	0622	7.3	1240	0.5	1841	7.5	
19	W	0100	0.5	0659	7.2	1317	0.6	1919	7.3	
20	TH	0135	0.8	0734	7.1	1353	0.9	1955	6.9	
21	F	0209	1.1	0809	6.7	1428	1.3	2031	6.5	
22	SA	0242	1.6	0844	6.3	1503	1.8	2107	6.0	
23	SU	0315	2.0	0921	5.9	1541	2.3	2148	5.5	
24	M	0352	2.5	1005	5.4	1629	2.7	2240	5.0	
25	TU	0446	2.9	1108	5.1	1752	3.0			◑
26	W	0002	4.7	0625	3.1	1252	4.9	1942	2.9	
27	TH	0151	4.8	0807	2.9	1423	5.2	2057	2.6	
28	F	0301	5.2	0912	2.5	1519	5.6	2145	2.2	
29	SA	0347	5.6	0957	2.1	1601	6.0	2224	1.8	
30	SU	0424	6.0	1035	1.7	1637	6.4	2258	1.5	
31	M	0458	6.4	1109	1.4	1711	6.6	2331	1.2	

NOVEMBER

Date	Day	Time	m	Time	m	Time	m	Time	m	Phase
1	TU	0530	6.7	1143	1.2	1744	6.8			
2	W	0003	1.1	0602	6.9	1217	1.0	1817	6.9	●
3	TH	0037	1.0	0636	6.9	1252	1.0	1852	6.9	
4	F	0111	1.0	0711	6.9	1329	1.1	1929	6.8	
5	SA	0147	1.2	0748	6.8	1407	1.2	2008	6.6	
6	SU	0225	1.4	0829	6.6	1450	1.5	2052	6.3	
7	M	0308	1.8	0916	6.2	1540	1.9	2145	5.8	
8	TU	0401	2.2	1016	5.9	1644	2.2	2253	5.5	
9	W	0513	2.5	1132	5.7	1811	2.3			◐
10	TH	0017	5.3	0649	2.5	1259	5.7	1938	2.1	
11	F	0144	5.5	0812	2.2	1416	6.0	2048	1.8	
12	SA	0254	5.9	0916	1.8	1518	6.4	2145	1.4	
13	SU	0349	6.3	1008	1.4	1609	6.8	2233	1.1	
14	M	0436	6.7	1054	1.1	1656	7.0	2316	0.9	
15	TU	0518	6.9	1136	1.0	1738	7.1	2356	0.9	
16	W	0558	7.0	1216	0.9	1818	7.0			○
17	TH	0034	1.0	0635	7.0	1255	1.0	1856	6.9	
18	F	0111	1.1	0712	6.8	1332	1.2	1934	6.6	
19	SA	0146	1.4	0748	6.6	1409	1.5	2011	6.3	
20	SU	0220	1.7	0824	6.3	1445	1.8	2048	6.0	
21	M	0255	2.0	0902	6.0	1524	2.2	2128	5.6	
22	TU	0332	2.3	0945	5.7	1608	2.5	2215	5.3	
23	W	0420	2.6	1037	5.4	1708	2.7	2314	5.0	◑
24	TH	0527	2.9	1143	5.2	1825	2.8			
25	F	0031	4.9	0650	2.9	1304	5.2	1940	2.7	
26	SA	0150	5.1	0802	2.7	1414	5.4	2042	2.4	
27	SU	0249	5.4	0901	2.4	1507	5.7	2132	2.1	
28	M	0336	5.8	0948	2.0	1552	6.0	2215	1.8	
29	TU	0417	6.1	1031	1.7	1633	6.3	2255	1.5	
30	W	0456	6.5	1112	1.4	1713	6.6	2334	1.3	

DECEMBER

Date	Day	Time	m	Time	m	Time	m	Time	m	Phase
1	TH	0535	6.7	1153	1.2	1754	6.8			●
2	F	0014	1.1	0615	6.9	1235	1.1	1835	6.8	
3	SA	0055	1.1	0656	7.0	1318	1.0	1919	6.8	
4	SU	0137	1.2	0740	6.9	1404	1.1	2005	6.6	
5	M	0222	1.3	0828	6.8	1452	1.3	2055	6.4	
6	TU	0310	1.5	0919	6.6	1544	1.5	2149	6.1	
7	W	0404	1.8	1017	6.3	1644	1.7	2248	5.9	
8	TH	0508	2.0	1120	6.1	1752	1.9	2354	5.7	◐
9	F	0620	2.1	1228	6.0	1903	1.9			
10	SA	0105	5.7	0732	2.1	1338	6.0	2010	1.9	
11	SU	0214	5.8	0839	1.9	1442	6.2	2111	1.7	
12	M	0315	6.0	0938	1.7	1540	6.3	2205	1.6	
13	TU	0409	6.2	1031	1.6	1632	6.4	2253	1.5	
14	W	0457	6.4	1118	1.4	1720	6.5	2336	1.4	
15	TH	0540	6.6	1201	1.4	1803	6.5			○
16	F	0016	1.4	0621	6.6	1242	1.4	1843	6.5	
17	SA	0055	1.4	0659	6.6	1320	1.4	1921	6.4	
18	SU	0131	1.5	0736	6.5	1357	1.5	1958	6.3	
19	M	0206	1.6	0812	6.4	1433	1.7	2034	6.1	
20	TU	0240	1.8	0848	6.2	1508	1.8	2111	5.9	
21	W	0315	2.0	0925	6.0	1545	2.0	2149	5.6	
22	TH	0354	2.2	1006	5.8	1627	2.2	2232	5.4	
23	F	0439	2.4	1052	5.6	1717	2.4	2322	5.2	◑
24	SA	0534	2.6	1145	5.4	1817	2.5			
25	SU	0021	5.1	0641	2.6	1249	5.3	1924	2.5	
26	M	0131	5.2	0751	2.6	1357	5.4	2030	2.4	
27	TU	0237	5.4	0856	2.3	1501	5.6	2130	2.1	
28	W	0334	5.8	0954	2.0	1557	5.9	2223	1.8	
29	TH	0425	6.1	1047	1.7	1648	6.3	2312	1.5	
30	F	0514	6.5	1136	1.3	1738	6.6	2359	1.2	
31	SA	0601	6.8	1225	1.0	1827	6.8			●

Chart Datum: 3·71 metres below Ordnance Datum (Newlyn)

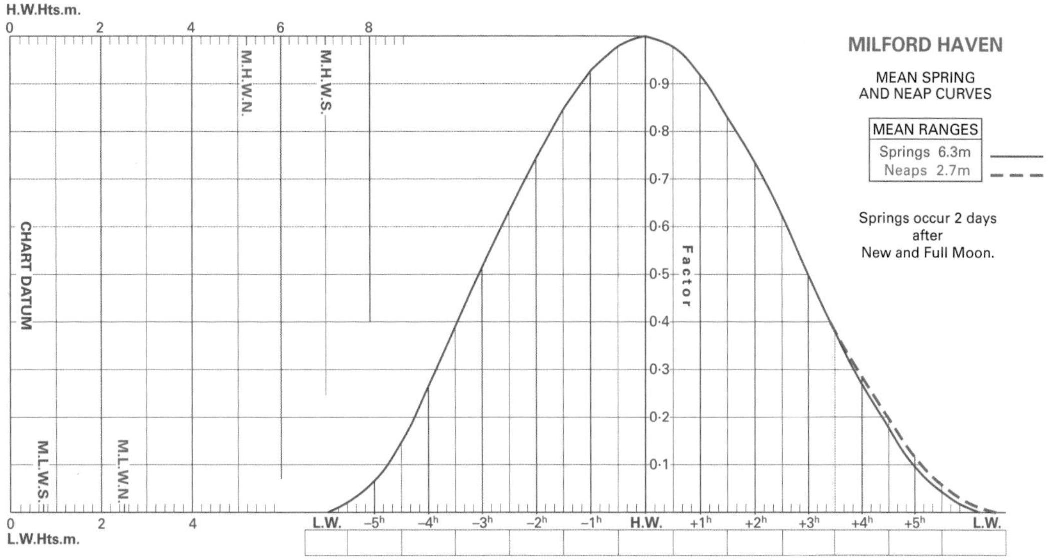
H.W.Hts.m.
M.H.W.N.
M.H.W.S.
CHART DATUM
M.L.W.S.
M.L.W.N.
L.W.Hts.m.
Factor
MILFORD HAVEN
MEAN SPRING
AND NEAP CURVES
MEAN RANGES
Springs 6.3m
Neaps 2.7m
Springs occur 2 days
after
New and Full Moon.
L.W. -5h -4h -3h -2h -1h H.W. +1h +2h +3h +4h +5h L.W.

9.11.14 TENBY

Pembrokeshire **51·40'·42N 04°41'·93W**

CHARTS AC *1179, 1076,* 1482*;* Imray C60; Stanfords 14; OS 158

TIDES –0510 Dover; ML 4·5; Duration 0610; Zone 0 (UT)

Standard Port MILFORD HAVEN (←)

Times				**Height (metres)**			
High Water		Low Water		MHWS	MHWN	MLWN	MLWS
0100	0800	0100	0700	7·0	5·2	2·5	0·7
1300	2000	1300	1900				
Differences TENBY							
–0015	–0010	–0015	–0020	+1·4	+1·1	+0·5	+0·2
STACKPOLE QUAY (7M W of Caldey Island)							
–0005	+0025	–0010	–0010	+0·9	+0·7	+0·2	+0·3

SHELTER Good, but hbr dries up to 5m; access HW±2½. Sheltered ⚓s, depending on wind direction, to NE in Tenby Roads, in Lydstep Haven (2·5M SW), and around Caldey Island as follows: Priory Bay (shallow, to the N), Jone's Bay (NE), Drinkim Bay (E) or Sandtop Bay (W). Also at Saundersfoot about 2M to the N; see below.

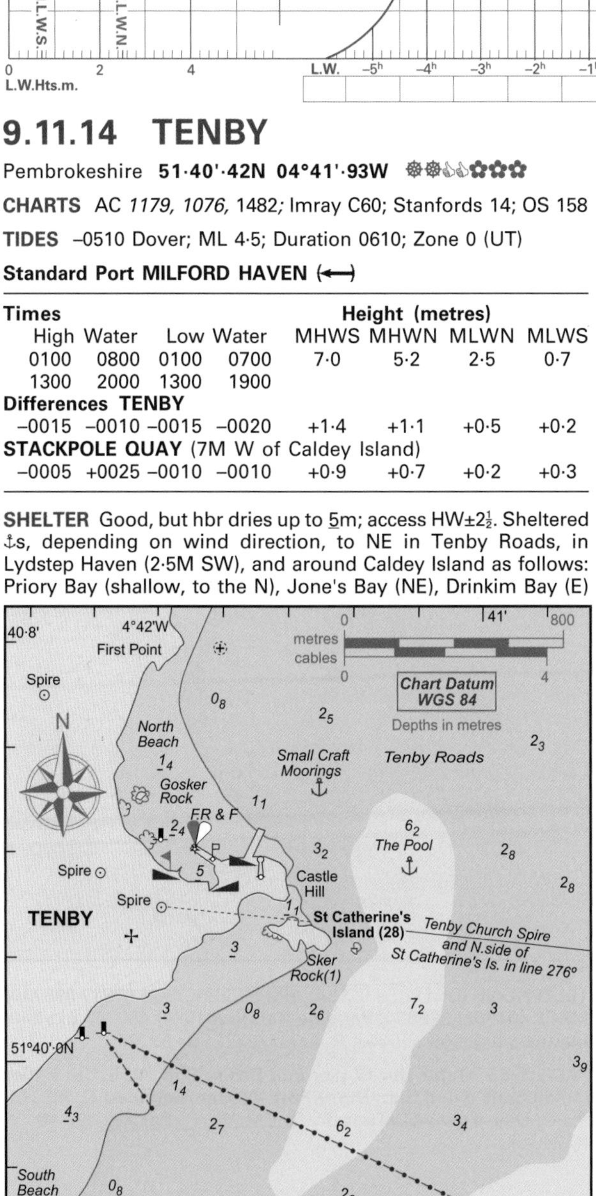
40·8'
4°42'W
First Point
41'
metres
cables
0
800
4
Chart Datum
WGS 84
Depths in metres
Spire
N
North
Beach
Gosker
Rock
Small Craft
Moorings
Tenby Roads
FR & F
The Pool
Spire
Castle
Hill
TENBY
Spire
St Catherine's
Island (28)
Tenby Church Spire
and N.side of
St Catherine's Is. in line 276°
Sker
Rock(1)
51°40'·0N
South
Beach
Giltar Spit

NAVIGATION WPT 51°40´·02N 04°38´·08W, 279° to monument on Castle Hill, 2·2M. The ⊕ WPT (off chartlet) is 2ca W of DZ2 SPM buoy, Fl Y 2·5s. Beware Woolhouse Rks (3·6m) 1·5M SExE of the hbr, marked by unlit SCM buoy; and Sker Rk (1m high) closer in off St Catherine's Island (28m). From the W, Caldey Sound is navigable with care by day between Eel Pt SHM and Giltar Spit PHM unlit buoys. Approaching Tenby Roads, keep outside the line of mooring buoys. For adjacent Firing ranges, see overleaf. Caldey Island is private and landing not allowed.

LIGHTS AND MARKS Church spire and N side of St Catherine's Is in line at 276°. FR 7m 7M on pier hd. Inside hbr, FW 6m 1M marks landing steps PHM beacon (unlit) marks outcrop from Gosker Rk on beach close N of hbr ent. Hbr is floodlit.

R/T VHF Ch 16 80 (listening during HO).

TELEPHONE (Dial code 01834) HM 842717 (end May-end Sept), Mobile 07977 609947; MRSC (01646) 690909; Marinecall 09066 526243; Police (01437) 763355 ; Dr 844161; Ⓗ 842040.

FACILITIES Hbr ☎/📠 842717, Slip (up to 4·2m), L, AB, ⚒, FW; **Tenby YC** ☎ 842762; **Town** EC Wed; P & D (cans), ⊡, CH, 🛒, R, Bar, Gas, ✉, Ⓑ, ⇌, ✈ (Swansea; and a small airfield at Haverfordwest).

OTHER ADJACENT HARBOURS

SAUNDERSFOOT, Pembrokeshire, **51°42´·60N 04°41´·76W.** AC *1179,* 1076, 1482. HW–0510 on Dover; ML 4·4m; Duration 0605. See 9.11.14. A half-tide hbr with good shelter, but there may be a surge in prolonged E winds. On appr, beware buoys marking restricted area (power boats, etc) between Coppett Hall Pt and Perry's Pt. AB may be available (see HM), or moorings in the middle. Pier hd lt Fl R 5s 6m 7M on stone cupola. VHF: HM 11 16. HM ☎/📠 (01834) 812094/(Home 831389). Facilities: 6 AB, CH, FW (on SW wall), Slip, P & D (cans), ME, BH. **Town** EC Wed; 🛒, R, Bar, ✉, Ⓑ, ⇌ (Tenby/Saundersfoot).

CARMARTHEN, Carmarthenshire, **51°46´·27N 04°22´·53W.** AC *1179,* 1076. HW –0455 on Dover. See 9.11.15. R Towy & Taf dry; access HW±2. Beware Carmarthen Bar in S winds F4 and over with strong sp streams. Nav info is available from Carmarthen Bar Navigation Commitee ☎ (01267) 231250 or YC's. Appr on N'ly hdg toward Wharley Pt, leaving DZ8 & 9 buoys 5ca to stbd. Chan shifts frequently and is unmarked so local knowledge reqd unless conditions ideal. ⚓ in mid-stream or 🅰s at R Towy YC off Ferryside (7M below Carmarthen) or R Towey Boat Club 1M N on W bank. Access for both HW±2 . 4 power lines cross in last 2·5M before Carmarthen, clearance 7·4m. **R Towy YC** ☎ (01267) 238356, M, FW, Bar. **R Towy BC** ☎ (01267) 238316. **Town** Ⓑ, Bar, Gas, ✉, 🛒, ⇌, ✈ (Cardiff).

FIRING RANGES between LINNEY HEAD and BURRY INLET

For daily info on all range firing times call *Milford Haven CG* Ch 16/67 or ☎ 01646 690909.

Castlemartin Range Danger Area extends 12M WNW from Linney Hd, thence in an anti-clockwise arc to a point 12M S of St Govan's Hd. The exact Danger Area operative on any one day depends on the ranges/ammunition used; it is primarily a tank range. When firing is in progress R flags are flown (Fl R lts at night) along the coast from Freshwater West to Linney Hd to St Govan's Hd. Yachts are requested to keep clear of ranges when active.
Firing takes place on weekdays 0900 -1630, exceptionally to 1700. Night firing takes place on Mon to Thurs, up to 2359, depending on the hours of darkness. In Jan only small arms are usually fired and the danger area is reduced.
Days/times of firing are published locally and can be obtained by VHF from *Castlemartin Range* Ch 16 or ☎ 01646 662367 (H24 answering service); Range safety launches Ch 16 or 12; and Milford Haven CG Ch 16. Also from the Range Office ☎ (01646) 662287 or Warren Tower 01646 662336.

Manorbier Range (further E) covers a sector arc radius 12M centred on Old Castle Hd; E/W extent is approx between St Govan's Hd and Caldey Is (see AC Q6402). It is usually active Mon-Fri 0900-1700LT, occas Sat/Sun, and is primarily a surface to air missile range, but active parts depend on the weapons in use on any given day. On firing days warnings are broadcast on Ch 16, 73 at 0830, 1430 and on completion; R flags are flown either side of Old Castle Hd. Yachts on passage should either stay 12M offshore or close inshore via Stackpole Hd, Trewent Pt, Priest's Nose and Old Castle Hd. Firing days/times are available from local HMs and YCs. For further info call: *Manorbier Range Control* Ch 16, 73 (also manned by Range safety launches); *Milford Haven CG* Ch 16; or Range Control ☎ (01834) 871282 ext 209, fax 871283.

Penally Range (further E at Giltar Pt) is for small arms only and seldom interferes with passage through Caldey Sound. Info ☎ (01834) 843522.

Pendine Range (between Tenby and Burry Inlet) is a MOD range for testing explosive devices. It is usually possible to steer the rhumb line course from Tenby to Worms Hd without interference. Info ☎ (01994) 453243. Broadcasts on VHF Ch 16, 73 at 0900 and 1400LT. Range active 0800-1615.

Pembrey Range (approx 5M NW of Burry Inlet) is used for bombing practice by the RAF. Info ☎ (01554) 891224.

9.11.15 BURRY INLET

Carmarthenshire **51°40'·52N 04°14'·93W** (Burry Port)

CHARTS AC *1179*, 1076, 1167; Imray C59, C60; Stanfords 14; OS 159

TIDES –0500 Dover; ML 4·7; Duration 0555; Zone 0 (UT)

Standard Port MILFORD HAVEN (←→)

Times				Height (metres)			
High Water		Low Water		MHWS	MHWN	MLWN	MLWS
0100	0800	0100	0700	7·0	5·2	2·5	0·7
1300	2000	1300	1900				
Differences BURRY PORT							
+0003	+0003	+0007	+0007	+1·6	+1·4	+0·5	+0·4
LLANELLI							
–0003	–0003	+0150	+0020	+0·8	+0·6	No data	
FERRYSIDE							
0000	–0010	+0220	0000	–0·3	–0·7	–1·7	–0·6
CARMARTHEN							
+0010	0000	Dries		–4·4	–4·8	Dries	

SHELTER Good in Burry Port via new lock with flapgate controlled by R/G lts, waiting buoys outside, access HW±1½. Depth over sill 2·5m. Pontoons expected for 2004. ⚓ 1 to 2ca E of barrel post. Sp tides run hard. Note: If bad weather precludes access to Burry Inlet, see 9.11.14 for ⚓s around Caldey Island, especially in W'lies. Call hbr office (01554 935691 mob 07817 395710). Visitors welcome but few facilities.

NAVIGATION WPT 51°36'·37N 04°24'·38W, 087° to Burry Holms 3·3M; thence 4·5M to Burry Port. Carmarthen Bar, extending from the R Towy ent SE to Burry Holms, should not be attempted in W winds >F5 nor at night. Best entry is close NW of Burry Holms at HW–2; thence track 018° with Worms Hd on a stern transit (198°) between Burry Holms and Limekiln Pt. When Whiteford lt ho (disused) bears about 082°, alter to approx 050° into deeper water and steer to leave the barrel post at least 1½ ca to port as a large sand bank is forming. Continue on this line to ⚓ in deep water beyond hbr ent, as shown. Chan is not buoyed/lit and is liable to shift. Before appr, check Firing Range activity (above).

LIGHTS AND MARKS Whiteford lt ho is conspic, but no longer lit. On head of W bkwtr is Barrel post, Fl R 3s 5M; 1½ca N is conspic old lt ho (W tr, R top) Fl 5s 7m 15M, and flagstaff.

R/T Ch 16

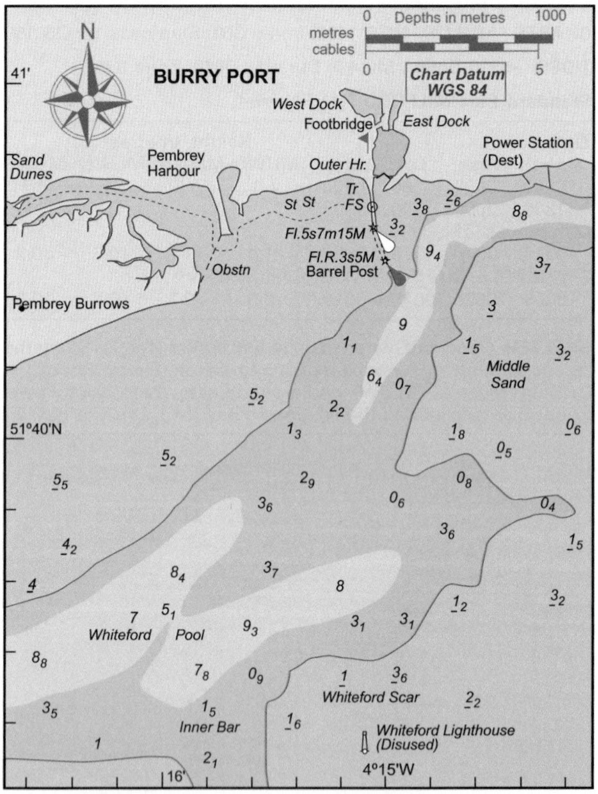
0 Depths in metres 1000
metres
cables
0
5
N
41'
BURRY PORT
Chart Datum WGS 84
West Dock
Footbridge
East Dock
Power Station (Dest)
Sand Dunes
Pembrey Harbour
Outer Hr
Tr
St St
FS
Fl.5s7m15M
Fl.R.3s5M Barrel Post
Obstn
Pembrey Burrows
Middle Sand
51°40'N
Whiteford
Pool
Whiteford Scar
Inner Bar
Whiteford Lighthouse (Disused)
16'
4°15'W

TELEPHONE (Dial code 01554); HM 835691, mob 07817 395710; MRCC (01792) 366534; Pendine Range (01994) 453243 Ext 240; Marinecall 09066 526243; Police 772222; Dr 832240.

FACILITIES **Outer Hbr W pier and Basin**: Slip, M, L, CH; **E Pier** (small craft only): Slip; **Burry Port YC** Bar; **Services:** D, ME, El, ✗, C, Gas. **Town** EC Tues; P, D, CH, ✉, R, Bar, ✉, Ⓑ, ⇌, ✈ (Cardiff).

9.11.16 SWANSEA

Swansea 51°36'·43N 03°55'·67W ❀❀❀⚓⚓⚓✿✿✿

CHARTS AC *1179, 1165,* 1161; Imray C59; Stanfords 14; OS 159

TIDES –0500 Dover; ML 5·2; Duration 0620; Zone 0 (UT)

Standard Port MILFORD HAVEN (⟵)

Times				Height (metres)			
High Water		Low Water		MHWS	MHWN	MLWN	MLWS
0100	0800	0100	0700	7·0	5·2	2·5	0·7
1300	2000	1300	1900				
Differences SWANSEA							
+0004	+0006	–0006	–0003	+2·6	+2·1	+0·7	+0·3
MUMBLES							
+0005	+0010	–0020	–0015	+2·3	+1·7	+0·6	+0·2
PORT TALBOT							
+0003	+0005	–0010	–0003	+2·6	+2·2	+1·0	+0·5
PORTHCAWL							
+0005	+0010	–0010	–0005	+2·9	+2·3	+0·8	+0·3

SHELTER Very good in marina; enter via R Tawe barrage lock, which operates on request HW±4½ (co-ordinated with the marina lock), 0700-2200BST; out of season, 0700-1900UT, but to 2200 at w/ends. Lock fee £2.40 per week. There are pontoons in both locks. Yachts usually exit Tawe barrage lock at H+00, and enter at H+30. Locks are closed when ht of tide falls to 1·5m above CD, usually at MLWS. At sp, do not enter river until LW+1½. Two large Or holding buoys below barrage in mid-stream; also, at W side of barrage lock, a landing pontoon (dries, foul ground). No Ⓥ berths at SY & SAC pontoons close N of marina ent.

NAVIGATION WPT SHM By, QG, Bell, 51°35'·53N 03°56'·08W, 020° to E bkwtr lt, 0·92M. In Swansea Bay tidal streams flow anti-clockwise for 9½ hrs (Swansea HW –3½ to +6), with at times a race off Mumbles Hd. From HW–6 to –3 the stream reverses, setting N past Mumbles Hd towards Swansea. Keep seaward of Mixon Shoal. When N of SW Inner Green Grounds (SWIGG) SCM lt buoy, Q (6)+L Fl 15s, keep to W of dredged chan and clear of commercial ships. Yachts must motor in hbr and appr, max speed 4kn.

LIGHTS AND MARKS Mumbles Hd, Fl (4) 20s35m16M, is 3M SSW of hbr ent. A conspic TV mast (R lts) NNE of hbr is almost aligned with the fairway. Ldg lts 020°: front Oc G 4s 5m 2M; rear FG 6M; these mark E side of chan dredged 3m. When N of QR and QG chan buoys stay inside dredged chan. **Port Traffic sigs** are conspic at W side of ent to King's Dock; there are 9 lts, ● or ●, arranged in a 3 x 3 frame. Yachts arriving must obey the middle lt in left column:

- ● = Do not enter the river; hold SW of W Pier.
- ● = Yachts may enter the river, keeping to mid-chan, then to W of holding buoys.

Lock Master will advise on tfc movements Ch 18.
Lock sigs for barrage and marina locks alike are:

- ●● = Lock closed. Do not proceed
- ● = Wait
- ● = Enter with caution
- ●● = Free flow operating; proceed with caution

Barrage lock lit by 2FR/FG (vert) to seaward.

R/T For barrage, call *Tawe Lock* Ch 18. For marina call *Swansea Marina* Ch **80**. For commercial docks call *Swansea Docks Radio* VHF Ch14 (H24).

TELEPHONE (Dial code 01792) HM 653787 🖷 650729; Barrage 456014; MRCC 366534; Police 456999; Marinecall 09066 526243; Ⓗ 205666; Dr 653452; DVLA (for SSR) 783355.

FACILITIES **Swansea Marina** (350+50 visitors) ☎ 470310, 🖷 463948, £1.40, D (no P), C (1 ton), BH (25 ton), ⛽, Gas, Gaz, Ice, CH, ME, El, Ⓔ, ⚒, ▣, ♿, Bar, R; **Swansea Yacht & Sub Aqua Club (SY & SAC)** ☎ 654863, M, L, (no visitors' berths), FW, C (5 ton static), R, Bar; **Services:** ME, SM, ACA, CH, El, Ⓔ, ⚒. **City** ⚒, 🛒, R, Bar, ✉, Ⓑ, ⇌, ✈.

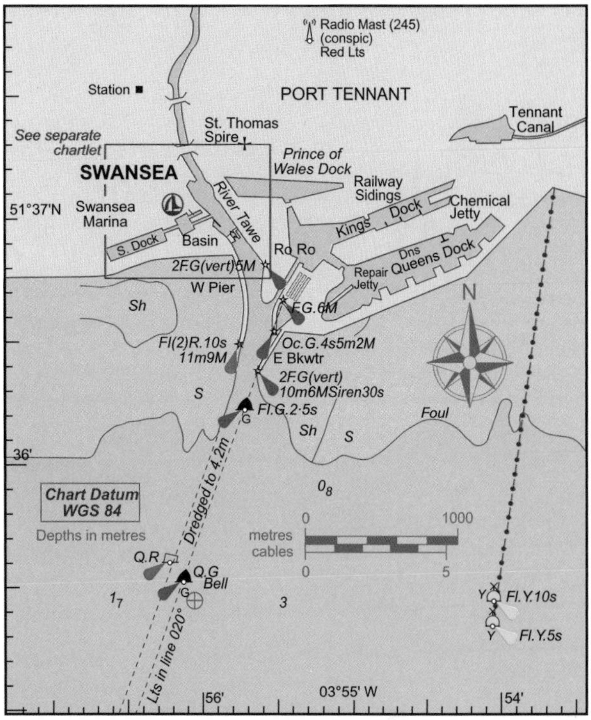
Radio Mast (245) (conspic) Red Lts
Station
PORT TENNANT
Tennant Canal
See separate chartlet
St. Thomas Spire
Prince of Wales Dock
SWANSEA
Railway Sidings
Chemical Jetty
51°37'N
Swansea Marina
River Tawe
Kings Dock
S. Dock
Basin
Ro Ro
Dns Queens Dock
Repair Jetty
2F.G(vert)5M
W Pier
F.G.6M
N
Sh
Fl(2)R.10s 11m9M
Oc.G.4s5m2M
E Bkwtr
2F.G(vert) 10m6MSiren30s
S
Fl.G.2·5s
Foul
Sh
S
36'
Chart Datum WGS 84
Depths in metres
Dredged to 4·2m
metres cables
0 1000
0 5
Q.R
Q.G Bell
Fl.Y.10s
Fl.Y.5s
3
Lts in line 020°
56'
03°55' W
54'

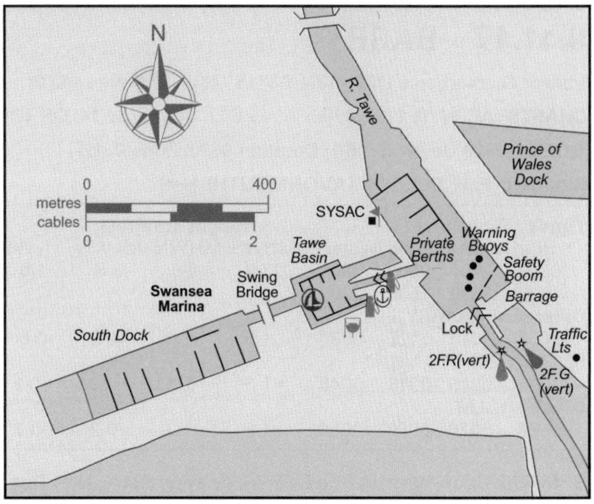
N
R. Tawe
Prince of Wales Dock
metres cables
0 400
0 2
SYSAC
Tawe Basin
Private Berths
Warning Buoys
Safety Boom
Barrage
Swing Bridge
Swansea Marina
Lock
South Dock
Traffic Lts
2F.R(vert)
2F.G (vert)

ADJACENT HARBOURS AND ANCHORAGES

MUMBLES, 51°34'·2N 03°58'·2W. Good ⚓ in W'lies 5ca N of Mumbles Hd lt ho. **Bristol Chan YC** ☎ (01792) 366000, Slip, M; **Mumbles YC** ☎ 369321, Slip, M, L, FW, C (hire).

R NEATH, 51°37'·88N 03°49'·97W. Ent over bar HW±2½ via 1·5M chan, marked/lit training wall to stbd. Tfc info from *Neath Pilot* VHF Ch 77, if on stn. **Monkstone Marina,** W bank just S of bridge, dries 4m: AB, 2 Y Ⓥs, D, FW, Slip, BH (15 ton), R, Bar, Visitors welcome. **Monkstone C & SC,** ☎ (01792) 812229; VHF Ch M (occas).

PORTHCAWL, Bridgend, **51°28'·48N 03°42'·02W.** AC *1165,* 1169. HW –0500 on Dover; ML 5·3m. See 9.11.16. A tiny drying hbr (access HW±2) protected by bkwtr running SE from Porthcawl Pt. Beware rk ledge (dries) W of bkwtr. Porthcawl lt ho, F WRG (see 9.11.4) in line 094° with St Hilary radio mast (QR & FR) leads through Shord chan. Tidal streams can reach 6kn at sp off end of bkwtr. 3 Ⓥs or ⚓ approx 3ca SSE of lt ho. HM ☎ (01656) 782756. Facilities: **Porthcawl Hbr B C** ☎ 782342. **Town** EC Wed; P & D (cans), CH, 🛒, R, Bar, ✉, Ⓑ, ⇌ (Bridgend), ✈ (Cardiff).

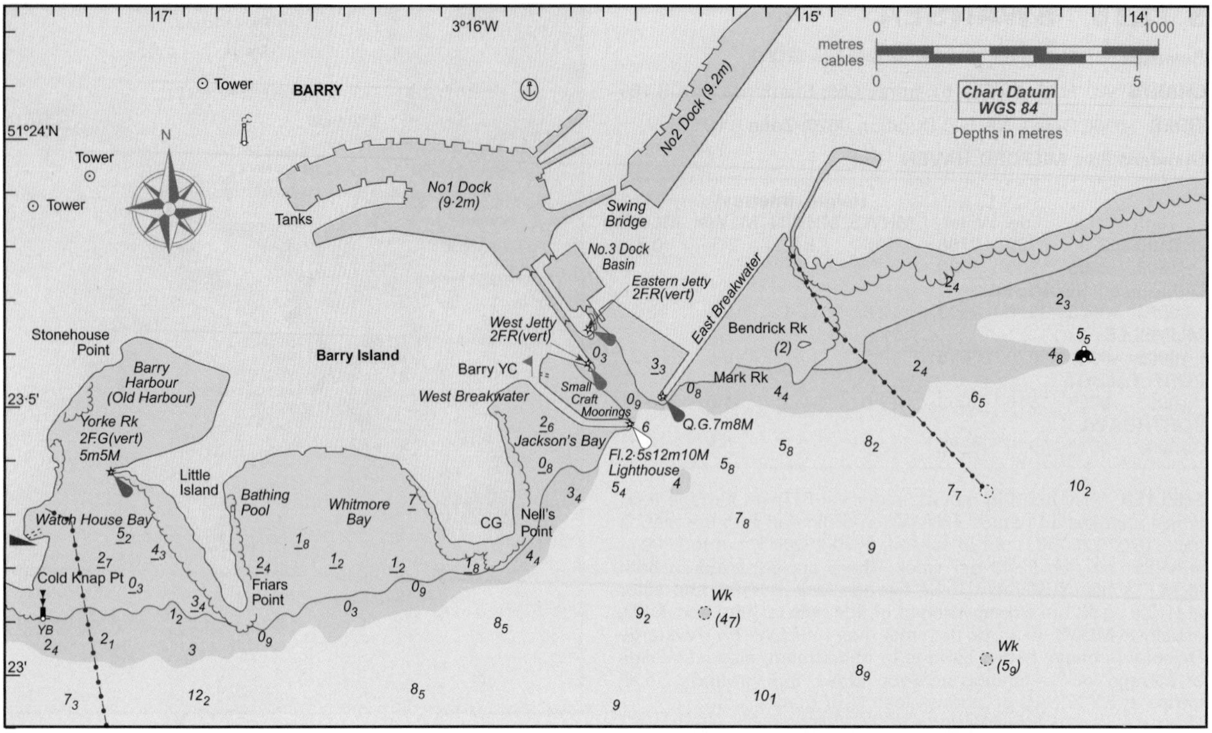
BARRY
Tower
Tower
Tower
51°24'N
23·5'
23'
17'
3°16'W
15'
14'
metres
cables
1000
Chart Datum WGS 84
Depths in metres
No2 Dock (9·2m)
No1 Dock (9·2m)
Tanks
Swing Bridge
No.3 Dock Basin
Eastern Jetty 2F.R(vert)
West Jetty 2F.R(vert)
East Breakwater
Bendrick Rk
Mark Rk
Q.G.7m8M
Barry YC
West Breakwater
Small Craft Moorings
Jackson's Bay
Fl.2·5s12m10M Lighthouse
Stonehouse Point
Barry Harbour (Old Harbour)
Barry Island
Yorke Rk 2F.G(vert) 5m5M
Little Island
Bathing Pool
Whitmore Bay
CG
Nell's Point
Watch House Bay
Cold Knap Pt
Friars Point
YB
Wk
Wk

9.11.17 BARRY

Vale of Glamorgan **51°23'·48N 03°15'·45W**

CHARTS AC *1179, 1152, 1182*; Imray C59; Stanfords 14; OS 171

TIDES –0423 Dover; ML 6·1; Duration 0630; Zone 0 (UT)

Standard Port BRISTOL (AVONMOUTH) (→)

Times				Height (metres)			
High Water		Low Water		MHWS	MHWN	MLWN	MLWS
0600	1100	0300	0800	13·2	9·8	3·8	1·0
1800	2300	1500	2000				
Differences BARRY							
–0030	–0015	–0125	–0030	–1·8	–1·3	+0·2	0·0
FLAT HOLM							
–0015	–0015	–0045	–0045	–1·3	–1·1	–0·2	+0·2
STEEP HOLM							
–0020	–0020	–0050	–0050	–1·6	–1·2	–0·2	–0·2

SHELTER Good, but in strong E/SE winds avoid Barry; No 1 Dock is no longer available to pleasure craft. Access H24 to the Outer hbr. No AB; pick up a mooring (free) and see YC. The Old Hbr to W of Barry Island dries and is not used.

NAVIGATION WPT 51°23'·03N 03°15'·08W, 332° to ent, 0·53M. Beware heavy merchant traffic. Approaching from E keep well out from the shore. Strong tidal stream across ent.

LIGHTS AND MARKS Welsh Water Barry West PHM buoy, Fl R 5s, and Merkur PHM buoy, Fl R 2·5s, lie respectively 217°/1·5M and 191°/1·65M from hbr ent. W bkwtr Fl 2·5s 10M. E bkwtr QG 8M.

R/T *Barry Radio* VHF Ch **11** 10 16 (HW–4 to HW+3); tidal info on request. *Bristol Pilot* via Ch 16 may advise on vacant moorings.

TELEPHONE (Dial code 01446) HM 732665 fax 700100; MRCC (01792) 366534; Marinecall 09066 526243; Police 734451; Dr 739543.

FACILITIES **Barry YC** (130) ☎ 735511, access HW±3½, Slip, M, Bar, FW; **Services:** Slip, D, FW, Gas, ME, El, ⚒, CH, SM. **Town** EC Wed; P (cans, 1M away), D, CH, 🛒, R, Bar, ✉, Ⓑ, ⇌, ✈ (Cardiff).

9.11.18 CARDIFF (Penarth)

Vale of Glamorgan **51°26'·74N 03°09'·92W** (marina)

CHARTS AC *1179, 1176, 1182*; Imray C59; Stanfords 14; OS 171

TIDES –0425 Dover; ML 6·4; Duration 0610; Zone 0 (UT)

Standard Port BRISTOL (AVONMOUTH) (→)

Times				Height (metres)			
High Water		Low Water		MHWS	MHWN	MLWN	MLWS
0600	1100	0300	0800	13·2	9·8	3·8	1·0
1800	2300	1500	2000				
Differences CARDIFF							
–0015	–0015	–0100	–0030	–1·0	–0·6	+0·1	0·0
NEWPORT							
–0020	–0010	0000	–0020	–1·1	–1·0	–0·6	–0·7
CHEPSTOW (River Wye)							
+0020	+0020	No data		No data		No data	

Note: At Newport the ht of LW does not normally fall below MLWS. Tidal hts are based on a minimum river flow; max flow may raise ht of LW by as much as 0·3m.

SHELTER Very good in marina. Access via barrage not LW ± 1 and marina lock usually H24 but see below. Depth gauge shows ht of water above sill. See opposite for barrage locks. Waiting trot berths in outer hbr; or ⚓ off Penarth seafront in W'lies; in E'lies cramped ⚓ off Alexandra Dock ent in 2m.

NAVIGATION WPT 51°24'·03N 03°08'·81W (2½ca SW of S Cardiff SCM lt buoy), 349° to barrage locks, 2·9M. The outer appr's from W or SW are via Breaksea lt float and N of One Fathom Bank. Keep S of Lavernock Spit (SCM lt buoy) and NW of Flat Holm and Wolves drying rk (NCM lt buoy). From NE, drying ledges and shoals extend >1M offshore. From E, appr via Monkstone lt ho and S Cardiff SCM buoy. Ranny Spit (dries 0·4m) is 3½ca to the W, and Cardiff Grounds (dries 5·4m) 3½ca to the E. The Wrach Chan is buoyed/lit and dredged 1·2m; it passes 1½ca E of Penarth Head. Do not impede merchant ships, especially those entering/leaving Alexandra Dock. The appr chan to the locks is dredged 0·7m below CD. Contact Barrage Control for up-to-date depths if entering at LW.

CARDIFF *continued*

Cardiff Bay Barrage

a. Call *Barrage Control* VHF Ch 18 or ☎ 029 2070 0234 to request lock-in or lock-out. Waiting berth on a barge in outer hbr.
b. Subject to VHF instructions, enter the outer hbr (Wpt 51°26'·71N 03°09'·84W) and lock in.
c. IPTS (sigs 1, 2, 3, 5 in 9.0.4) are shown at lock ent.
d. Outbound locks run on the hour and half hour. Inbound locks run on quarter past and quarter to the hour.

LIGHTS AND MARKS Ldg lts 348·5°, both FW 4/24m 17M, hard to identify due to other adjacent lts; front ldg lt is obscured by the Barrage at certain states of the tide.

R/T Port VHF Ch **14** 16 (HW–4 to HW+3). *Barrage Control* Ch 18 H24. Penarth marina Ch 80 H24.

TELEPHONE (Dial code 029) HM 2040 0500; 📠 2047 1071 Barrage control 2070 0234; Marina 2070 5021; MRCC (01792) 366534; Marinecall 09066 526243; Weather Centre 2039 7020; Police (01446) 734451; Dr 2041 5258; Cardiff Bay Authority 2087 7900.

FACILITIES **Penarth Marina** (350+ Ⓥ welcome); max draft 3m), ☎ 2070 5021 H24, 📠 2071 2170, www.crestnicholsonmarinas.co.uk; £2.00, £10.00 < 5 hrs, P (0930-1730, F pontoon), D (Daily 0900-1730, E pontoon), El, ME, ⚒, C, CH, BY, BH (20T) Gas, LPG, ⊡, R; **Penarth YC** ☎ 2070 8196, Slip, FW, Bar; **Cardiff YC** ☎ 2046 3697, Slip, M, FW, L (floating pontoon), Bar; **Cardiff Bay YC** ☎ 2022 6575, M, L, C, FW, Bar, Slip; **Services:** D, SM, ⚒, C (20 ton), CH, ACA, ME, El, Ⓔ, BY, Slip, BH (20 ton), Gas. **City** P, D, ME, El, 🛒, R, Bar, ✉, Ⓑ, ⇌, ✈ (15 mins).

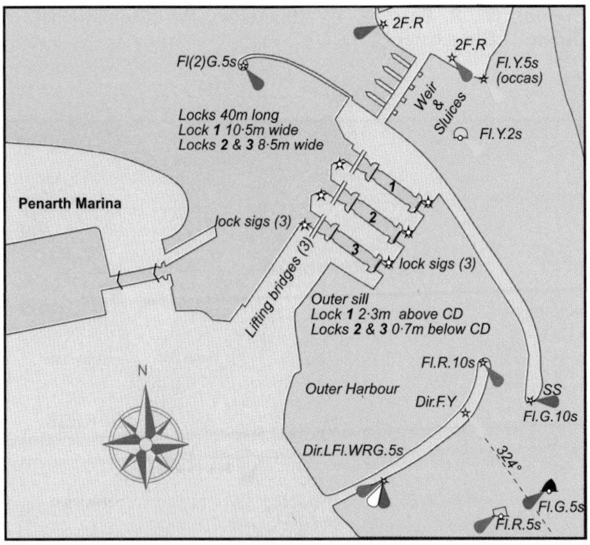

2F.R
2F.R
Fl.Y.5s (occas)
Fl(2)G.5s
Weir & Sluices
Fl.Y.2s
Locks 40m long
Lock 1 10·5m wide
Locks 2 & 3 8·5m wide
Penarth Marina
lock sigs (3)
lock sigs (3)
Lifting bridges (3)
Outer sill
Lock 1 2·3m above CD
Locks 2 & 3 0·7m below CD
Fl.R.10s
SS
Fl.G.10s
Outer Harbour
Dir.F.Y
N
Dir.LFl.WRG.5s
324°
Fl.G.5s
Fl.R.5s

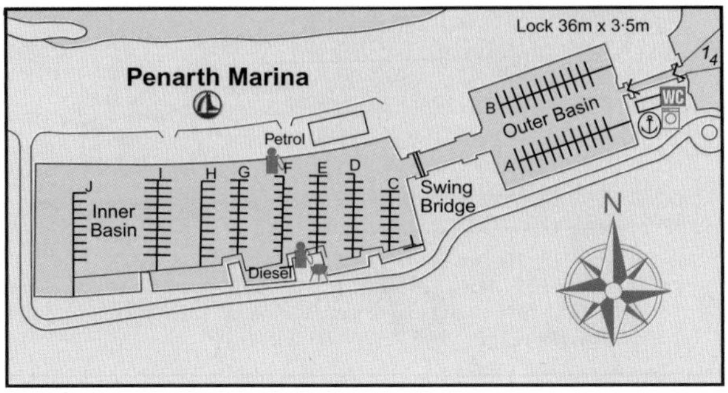

Lock 36m x 3·5m
Penarth Marina
Outer Basin
Petrol
Inner Basin
Swing Bridge
Diesel
N

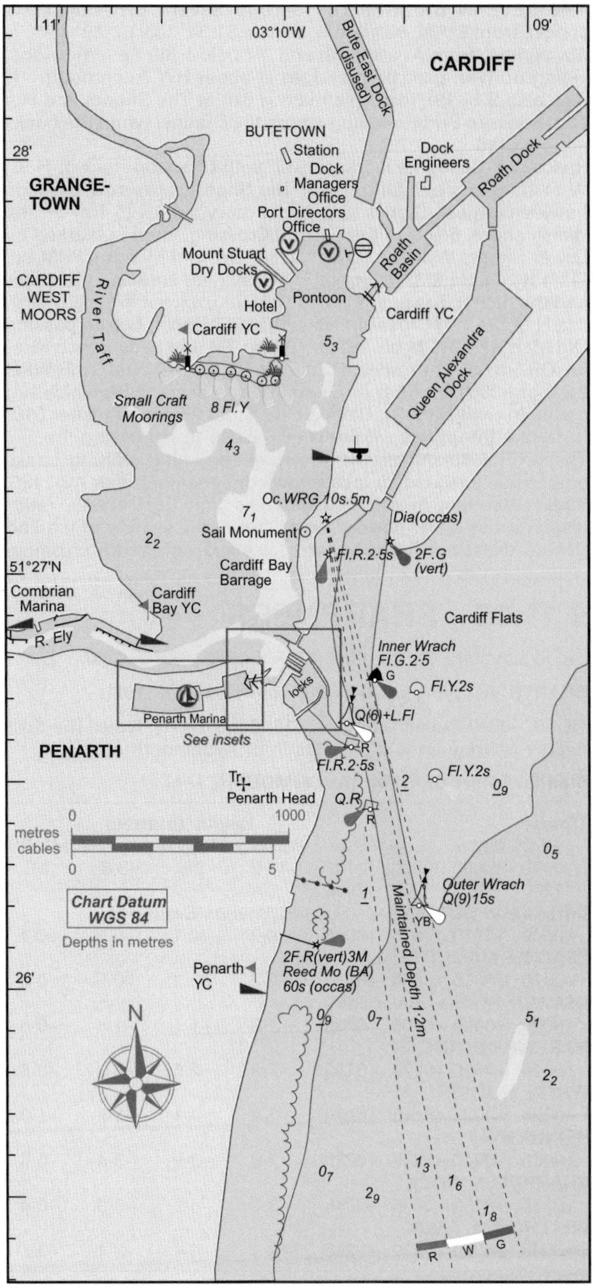

11'
03°10'W
09'
Bute East Dock (disused)
CARDIFF
BUTETOWN
Station
Dock Managers Office
Port Directors Office
Dock Engineers
Roath Dock
28'
GRANGE-TOWN
Mount Stuart Dry Docks
Roath Basin
CARDIFF WEST MOORS
River Taff
Hotel
Pontoon
Cardiff YC
Cardiff YC
Queen Alexandra Dock
Small Craft Moorings
8 Fl.Y
Oc.WRG.10s.5m
Dia(occas)
Sail Monument
Fl.R.2·5s
2F.G (vert)
51°27'N
Cardiff Bay Barrage
Combrian Marina
Cardiff Bay YC
Cardiff Flats
R. Ely
Inner Wrach Fl.G.2·5
Fl.Y.2s
locks
Q(6)+L.Fl
Penarth Marina
See insets
PENARTH
Fl.R.2·5s
Fl.Y.2s
Penarth Head
Q.R
metres 0 1000
cables 0 5
Outer Wrach Q(9)15s
Chart Datum WGS 84
Depths in metres
Maintained Depth 1·2m
Penarth YC
2F.R(vert)3M
Reed Mo (BA) 60s (occas)
26'
N
R W G

ADJACENT HARBOUR

NEWPORT, Newport, **51°32'·95N 02°59'·13W**. AC *1179, 1152, 1176*. HW –0425 on Dover; ML 6·0m; Duration 0620. See 9.11.18. A commercial port controlled by ABP, but a safe shelter for yachts. Enter R Usk over bar (approx 0·5m) E of West Usk buoy, QR Bell) and follow buoyed and lit chan to S Lock ent; turn NE (ldg lts 057°) for yacht moorings on S side between power stn pier and YC. Beware overhead cables in Julian's Pill, clearance 38m. East Usk lt ho Fl (2) WRG 10s 11m 15/11M, W284°-290°, R290°-017°, W017°-037°, G037°-115°, W115°-120°. Ldg lts 057°, both FG. Alexandra Dock, S lock W pier head 2 FR (vert) 9/7m 6M. E pier head 2 FG (vert) 9/7m 6M. Port VHF Ch 16 09 69 **71** (HW ±4). VTS, not compulsory for yachts, is on same chans/times, call *Newport Radio*. HM (ABP) ☎ (01633) 244411, 📠 221285. Facilities: **Newport and Uskmouth SC** Bar, M; **Services:** CH, El, ME, ⚒, Ⓔ. **Town** EC Thurs; all facilities.

THE SEVERN BRIDGES The Second Severn Crossing (37m cl'nce), from 51°34'·88N 02°43'·80W to 51°34'·14N 02°39'·82W, is 4M upriver from Avonmouth and 3M below the Severn Bridge. Going upriver, pass both bridges at about HW Avonmouth –1¾ (see also 9.11.19); max sp stream is 8kn at The Shoots and 6kn at the Severn Bridge, setting across the channel when the banks are covered.

Redcliffe F Bu ldg lts in transit 013° with Charston Rock lt, Fl 3s, W ○ tr, B stripe, lead through The Shoots, a narrow passage between English Stones (6·2m) and rocky ledges (5·1m) off the Welsh shore. 5ca S of the Second Crossing, chan is marked by Lower Shoots WCM bn, Q (9) 15s 6m 7M, and Mixoms PHM bn, Fl (3) R 10s 6m 6M. No vessel may navigate between the shore and the nearer Tower of the 2nd Crossing, except in emergency. 4ca N of the 2nd Crossing, leave the 013° transit before passing Old Man's Hd WCM bn, VQ (9) 10s 6m 7M and Lady Bench PHM bn, QR 6m 6M. From abeam Charston Rk, keep Chapel Rk, Fl WRG 2·6s, brg 050° until E tr of Severn Bridge bears 068°; which brg maintain until Lyde Rk, QWR, bears about 355°, when alter 010° to transit the bridge (36·6m cl'nce) close to rks drying 1m.

These brief directions, the strong streams and shifting banks emphasise the need for local knowledge together with AC 1166.

Radar Warning, In certain conditions and tidal states, radar displays may show misleading echoes in the vicinity of the 2nd Severn Crossing. Racon (o) at centre span of centre crossing.

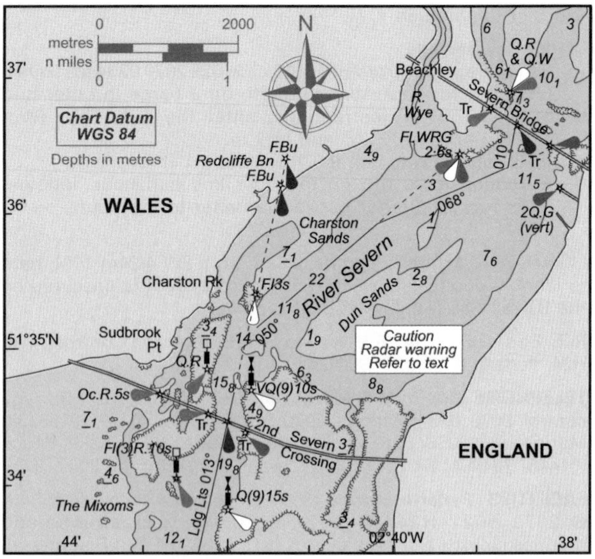
metres
n miles
0
2000
1
N
37'
36'
34'
51°35'N
44'
02°40'W
38'
Chart Datum WGS 84
Depths in metres
WALES
ENGLAND
Beachley
R. Wye
Severn Bridge
Q.R & Q.W
Fl.WRG 2·6s
Redcliffe Bn
F.Bu
Charston Sands
River Severn
Dun Sands
Charston Rk
Fl.3s
Sudbrook Pt
Q.R
Caution
Radar warning
Refer to text
Oc.R.5s
VQ(9)10s
2nd Severn Crossing
Fl(3)R.10s
The Mixoms
Q(9)15s
Ldg Lts 013°
2Q.G (vert)
Tr
068°
050°
010°

9.11.19 SHARPNESS

Gloucestershire **51°43'·03N 02°29'·08W**

CHARTS AC *1166*, Imray C59; Stanfords 14; OS 162

TIDES –0315 Dover; Duration 0415; Zone 0 (UT). Note: The tidal regime is irregular and deviates from Avonmouth curve.

Standard Port BRISTOL (AVONMOUTH) (⟶)

Times				Height (metres)			
High Water		Low Water		MHWS	MHWN	MLWN	MLWS
0000	0600	0000	0700	13·2	9·8	3·8	1·0
1200	1800	1200	1900				
Differences SUDBROOK (Second Severn Crossing)							
+0010	+0010	+0025	+0015	+0·2	+0·1	–0·1	+0·1
BEACHLEY/AUST (Severn Bridge)							
+0010	+0015	+0040	+0025	–0·2	–0·2	–0·5	–0·3
INWARD ROCKS (River Severn)							
+0020	+0020	+0105	+0045	–1·0	–1·1	–1·4	–0·6
NARLWOOD ROCKS							
+0025	+0025	+0120	+0100	–1·9	–2·0	–2·3	–0·8
WHITE HOUSE							
+0025	+0025	+0145	+0120	–3·0	–3·1	–3·6	–1·0
BERKELEY							
+0030	+0045	+0245	+0220	–3·8	–3·9	–3·4	–0·5
SHARPNESS DOCK							
+0035	+0050	+0305	+0245	–3·9	–4·2	–3·3	–0·4
WELLHOUSE ROCK							
+0040	+0055	+0320	+0305	–4·1	–4·4	–3·1	–0·2

SHELTER Very good. The sea lock into the commercial dock is generally open HW-2 to HW but this is dependent on commercial shipping movements. The advice is plan your passage to arrive no sooner than HW-1 and no later than HW. For more detailed information on lock fees, canal licences and the passage from Avonmouth contact the HM at Sharpness on 01453 811862. The fog signal on Sharpness Point is available on request to Sharpness Radio on VHF channel 13 or 01453 511968.

NAVIGATION WPT 51°42'·83N 02°29'·28W, 028° to ent, 2ca. Leave King Road, Avonmouth (17M downriver) not before HW Sharpness –3, to be off hbr ent about HW –½. Stem strong flood S of F Bu lt; beware Tidal eddy. Do not proceed above the Severn Bridge except HW±2. There is a 5H flood and a 7H ebb. Use the transits shown on AC 1166. Request pilot notes from Sharpness HM in good time.

LIGHTS AND MARKS Lts as chartlet, but night passage not advised without local knowledge/pilot (07774 226143).

R/T Call *Sharpness Radio* VHF Ch 13 (HW –6 to +1) for lock. Gloucester & Sharpness Canal Ch 74 for bridges (no locks). Call *Bristol VTS* VHF Ch 12 when passing reporting points inwards/outwards: E/W Grounds PHM, Welsh Hook SCM and at Lower Shoots Bcn.

TELEPHONE (Dial code 01453) Pierhead 511968 (HW–5 to HW+1); HM 811862/64 (HO), 811863; Police (01452) 521201; Ⓗ 810777.

FACILITIES **Sharpness Marine** (170 inc 2Ⓥ) ☎ 811476, £7 all LOA, Ⓓ, El, D, FW, ⚒, CH, Gas, ME, C. **Town** D (above Fretherne Bridge), R, Bar, ✉, Ⓑ (Berkeley), ⇌ (Stonehouse), ✈ (Bristol). Gloucester: D, ACA.

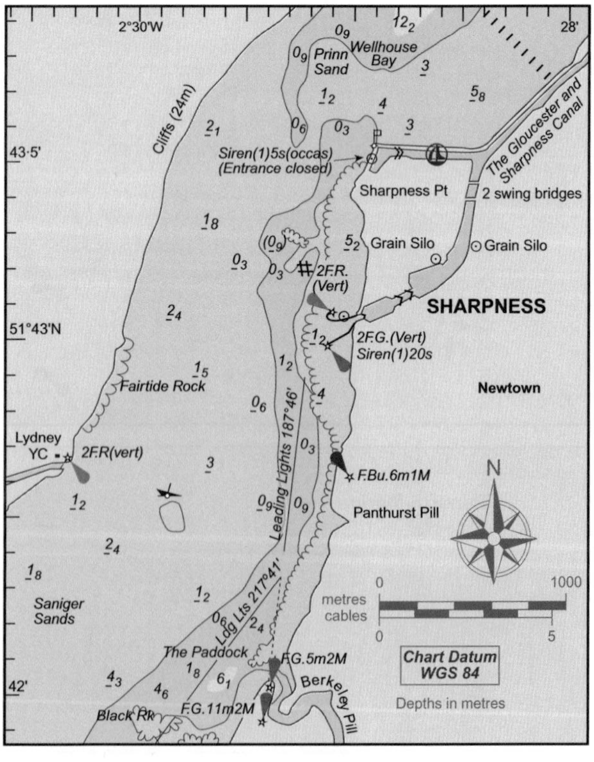
2°30'W
28'
43·5'
51°43'N
42'
Prinn Sand
Wellhouse Bay
The Gloucester and Sharpness Canal
Cliffs (24m)
Siren(1)5s(occas)
(Entrance closed)
Sharpness Pt
2 swing bridges
Grain Silo
Grain Silo
2F.R.(Vert)
SHARPNESS
2F.G.(Vert)
Siren(1)20s
Fairtide Rock
Newtown
Lydney YC
2F.R(vert)
Leading Lights 187°46'
F.Bu.6m1M
N
Panthurst Pill
Ldg Lts 217°41'
Saniger Sands
metres
cables
0
1000
5
The Paddock
F.G.5m2M
Berkeley Pill
Black Rk
F.G.11m2M
Chart Datum WGS 84
Depths in metres

TIME ZONE (UT)
For Summer Time add ONE hour in **non-shaded areas**

ENGLAND – PORT OF BRISTOL (AVONMOUTH)

LAT 51°30′N LONG 2°44′W

TIMES AND HEIGHTS OF HIGH AND LOW WATERS

SPRING & NEAP TIDES
Dates in red are SPRINGS
Dates in blue are NEAPS

YEAR **2005**

JANUARY

Date	Day	Time	m	Time	m	Time	m	Time	m
1	SA	0422	2.6	1015	11.4	1644	2.7	2238	11.1
2	SU	0458	2.7	1052	11.2	1722	2.8	2318	10.8
3	M ◑	0539	2.9	1138	11.0	1806	3.0		
4	TU	0006	10.6	0628	3.2	1233	10.7	1858	3.3
5	W	0106	10.3	0728	3.5	1340	10.5	2003	3.6
6	TH	0219	10.3	0847	3.6	1456	10.7	2132	3.5
7	F	0340	10.7	1016	3.3	1613	11.1	2258	3.1
8	SA	0451	11.4	1129	2.7	1719	11.8		
9	SU	0004	2.4	0550	12.2	1232	2.0	1817	12.5
10	M ●	0104	1.9	0644	12.9	1331	1.5	1912	13.0
11	TU	0200	1.5	0735	13.4	1427	1.2	2004	13.3
12	W	0253	1.2	0825	13.7	1519	0.9	2053	13.4
13	TH	0340	1.1	0913	13.7	1606	0.9	2139	13.3
14	F	0422	1.2	0958	13.5	1646	1.0	2223	13.0
15	SA	0459	1.5	1042	13.1	1722	1.4	2303	12.4
16	SU	0531	2.0	1124	12.4	1754	2.0	2344	11.7
17	M ◐	0603	2.5	1209	11.6	1829	2.5		
18	TU	0027	11.0	0640	3.0	1302	10.8	1910	3.1
19	W	0123	10.3	0728	3.6	1408	10.3	2004	3.6
20	TH	0235	9.9	0834	4.0	1518	10.1	2117	3.8
21	F	0347	10.1	1004	3.9	1624	10.3	2239	3.5
22	SA	0449	10.5	1118	3.4	1721	10.8	2342	2.9
23	SU	0542	11.2	1214	2.8	1811	11.3		
24	M	0035	2.4	0628	11.8	1304	2.3	1855	11.7
25	TU ○	0124	2.0	0710	12.1	1351	2.1	1936	12.0
26	W	0210	1.9	0749	12.3	1436	2.1	2014	12.0
27	TH	0252	1.9	0826	12.3	1515	2.2	2048	12.0
28	F	0327	2.1	0859	12.2	1547	2.3	2120	11.9
29	SA	0353	2.2	0929	12.1	1610	2.4	2149	11.9
30	SU	0415	2.2	0959	12.1	1632	2.3	2219	11.8
31	M	0442	2.2	1032	11.9	1700	2.3	2252	11.6

FEBRUARY

Date	Day	Time	m	Time	m	Time	m	Time	m
1	TU	0515	2.3	1110	11.7	1735	2.5	2333	11.2
2	W ◑	0554	2.6	1156	11.2	1817	2.9		
3	TH	0023	10.7	0642	3.2	1255	10.6	1910	3.5
4	F	0129	10.2	0750	3.7	1412	10.2	2030	3.9
5	SA	0259	10.1	0940	3.8	1547	10.4	2234	3.7
6	SU	0431	10.7	1114	3.1	1708	11.1	2352	2.8
7	M	0540	11.7	1224	2.2	1811	12.1		
8	TU ●	0056	2.0	0636	12.8	1326	1.4	1905	13.0
9	W	0154	1.3	0727	13.6	1422	0.8	1955	13.6
10	TH	0246	0.7	0815	14.0	1512	0.4	2040	13.8
11	F	0332	0.5	0859	14.2	1554	0.3	2122	13.8
12	SA	0410	0.6	0940	14.0	1630	0.5	2200	13.5
13	SU	0441	1.0	1016	13.5	1657	1.1	2233	12.9
14	M	0503	1.5	1050	12.8	1718	1.7	2303	12.1
15	TU	0524	2.1	1122	11.8	1743	2.3	2334	11.2
16	W ◐	0552	2.7	1159	10.8	1816	3.0		
17	TH	0013	10.3	0630	3.4	1250	9.8	1903	3.8
18	F	0113	9.5	0729	4.2	1418	9.2	2014	4.3
19	SA	0258	9.2	0858	4.5	1552	9.4	2151	4.2
20	SU	0420	9.8	1049	3.9	1659	10.1	2316	3.4
21	M	0521	10.7	1154	3.0	1752	11.0		
22	TU	0014	2.6	0608	11.5	1246	2.3	1836	11.7
23	W	0106	2.0	0651	12.1	1335	1.9	1916	12.1
24	TH ○	0154	1.7	0729	12.5	1421	1.8	1953	12.3
25	F	0238	1.7	0806	12.6	1502	1.8	2027	12.4
26	SA	0315	1.7	0839	12.6	1535	1.9	2058	12.4
27	SU	0343	1.9	0908	12.6	1557	2.1	2126	12.4
28	M	0401	1.9	0937	12.5	1612	2.1	2155	12.3

MARCH

Date	Day	Time	m	Time	m	Time	m	Time	m
1	TU	0422	1.9	1009	12.4	1634	2.0	2227	12.1
2	W	0450	1.9	1045	12.0	1705	2.2	2305	11.6
3	TH ◑	0525	2.3	1128	11.3	1742	2.7	2352	10.8
4	F	0608	3.1	1224	10.4	1832	3.6		
5	SA	0056	10.0	0712	3.9	1345	9.7	1950	4.3
6	SU	0239	9.6	0930	4.1	1541	9.9	2230	3.9
7	M	0425	10.4	1110	3.1	1704	11.0	2345	2.7
8	TU	0533	11.7	1216	2.0	1803	12.2		
9	W	0045	1.7	0626	12.9	1313	1.0	1853	13.2
10	TH ●	0139	0.9	0713	13.8	1405	0.4	1938	13.8
11	F	0228	0.3	0757	14.2	1451	0.0	2019	14.1
12	SA	0311	0.2	0837	14.3	1531	0.1	2057	14.0
13	SU	0347	0.4	0914	14.0	1603	0.5	2131	13.5
14	M	0414	0.9	0947	13.4	1625	1.1	2159	12.9
15	TU	0431	1.5	1015	12.6	1641	1.7	2225	12.2
16	W	0446	2.0	1042	11.7	1700	2.2	2251	11.3
17	TH ◐	0510	2.5	1112	10.7	1729	2.9	2323	10.4
18	F	0544	3.3	1151	9.6	1809	3.8		
19	SA	0010	9.4	0637	4.2	1310	8.7	1922	4.6
20	SU	0207	8.8	0814	4.7	1519	8.9	2111	4.5
21	M	0349	9.4	1017	4.1	1631	9.7	2251	3.6
22	TU	0452	10.4	1130	3.1	1724	10.8	2350	2.7
23	W	0540	11.3	1221	2.3	1807	11.6		
24	TH	0040	2.0	0622	12.1	1309	1.8	1846	12.2
25	F ○	0128	1.7	0701	12.5	1355	1.6	1923	12.6
26	SA	0212	1.5	0737	12.7	1436	1.6	1958	12.7
27	SU	0250	1.6	0811	12.8	1510	1.7	2030	12.7
28	M	0320	1.6	0843	12.9	1534	1.8	2101	12.7
29	TU	0341	1.7	0915	12.8	1550	1.8	2132	12.6
30	W	0403	1.7	0949	12.6	1612	1.9	2206	12.3
31	TH	0430	1.8	1027	12.0	1642	2.2	2245	11.6

APRIL

Date	Day	Time	m	Time	m	Time	m	Time	m
1	F	0505	2.3	1111	11.2	1720	2.8	2333	10.7
2	SA ◑	0550	3.1	1209	10.1	1812	3.8		
3	SU	0043	9.8	0702	4.0	1342	9.5	1953	4.5
4	M	0244	9.7	0934	3.8	1538	10.0	2221	3.6
5	TU	0414	10.7	1055	2.7	1650	11.2	2326	2.4
6	W	0515	11.9	1155	1.6	1744	12.3		
7	TH	0021	1.4	0605	13.0	1248	0.8	1830	13.2
8	F ●	0112	0.7	0650	13.7	1337	0.3	1912	13.7
9	SA	0159	0.4	0732	14.0	1421	0.2	1951	13.8
10	SU	0241	0.4	0810	13.9	1500	0.4	2027	13.6
11	M	0317	0.7	0845	13.5	1531	0.9	2059	13.2
12	TU	0343	1.2	0917	12.9	1551	1.5	2127	12.6
13	W	0359	1.7	0944	12.2	1606	1.9	2151	12.0
14	TH	0414	2.1	1010	11.4	1626	2.3	2217	11.2
15	F	0439	2.5	1037	10.5	1653	2.9	2246	10.4
16	SA	0511	3.2	1113	9.6	1731	3.6	◐ 2329	9.5
17	SU	0600	4.0	1218	8.8	1836	4.4		
18	M	0104	8.9	0733	4.5	1431	8.8	2026	4.6
19	TU	0306	9.3	0915	4.2	1548	9.6	2202	3.9
20	W	0410	10.2	1044	3.3	1643	10.6	2310	2.9
21	TH	0501	11.1	1141	2.5	1729	11.4		
22	F	0002	2.3	0545	11.8	1231	2.0	1810	12.1
23	SA	0051	1.8	0625	12.4	1317	1.7	1849	12.6
24	SU	0136	1.6	0704	12.7	1400	1.6	○ 1926	12.9
25	M	0216	1.5	0742	12.9	1437	1.6	2002	13.0
26	TU	0251	1.4	0819	13.0	1507	1.6	2038	13.0
27	W	0322	1.4	0857	12.9	1534	1.7	2114	12.8
28	TH	0351	1.5	0936	12.5	1601	1.9	2154	12.3
29	F	0424	1.8	1019	11.9	1634	2.3	2237	11.6
30	SA	0503	2.4	1108	11.1	1716	3.0	2331	10.7

Chart Datum: 6·50 metres below Ordnance Datum (Newlyn)

TIME ZONE (UT)
For Summer Time add ONE hour in **non-shaded areas**

ENGLAND – PORT OF BRISTOL (AVONMOUTH)

LAT 51°30′N LONG 2°44′W

TIMES AND HEIGHTS OF HIGH AND LOW WATERS

SPRING & NEAP TIDES
Dates in red are SPRINGS
Dates in blue are NEAPS

YEAR **2005**

MAY

Date	Day	Time	m	Time	m	Time	m	Time	m	Moon
1	SU	0556	3.1	1211	10.2	1817	3.8			◑
2	M	0050	10.1	0727	3.6	1347	9.9	2023	4.0	
3	TU	0235	10.2	0912	3.2	1516	10.4	2152	3.2	
4	W	0348	11.0	1023	2.4	1621	11.3	2254	2.3	
5	TH	0446	11.9	1121	1.7	1714	12.2	2347	1.5	
6	F	0536	12.7	1213	1.1	1801	12.8			
7	SA	0037	1.0	0621	13.2	1301	0.8	1842	13.2	
8	SU	0124	0.9	0702	13.3	1346	0.8	1921	13.2	●
9	M	0207	0.9	0741	13.1	1426	1.0	1957	13.0	
10	TU	0245	1.2	0818	12.8	1458	1.4	2030	12.7	
11	W	0314	1.7	0851	12.3	1523	1.8	2100	12.2	
12	TH	0334	2.0	0921	11.7	1542	2.1	2128	11.7	
13	F	0353	2.3	0949	11.1	1605	2.4	2155	11.1	
14	SA	0420	2.6	1019	10.5	1634	2.8	2228	10.5	
15	SU	0455	3.0	1057	9.9	1712	3.3	2312	9.9	
16	M	0543	3.6	1153	9.4	1808	3.9			◐
17	TU	0019	9.4	0654	4.0	1317	9.2	1932	4.2	
18	W	0157	9.5	0816	3.9	1444	9.6	2056	3.9	
19	TH	0312	10.0	0932	3.4	1549	10.3	2209	3.3	
20	F	0410	10.8	1042	2.9	1643	11.1	2311	2.6	
21	SA	0501	11.5	1142	2.4	1730	11.8			
22	SU	0006	2.1	0547	12.1	1234	2.0	1814	12.4	
23	M	0056	1.7	0632	12.6	1322	1.7	1856	12.8	○
24	TU	0142	1.4	0716	12.8	1406	1.5	1938	13.0	
25	W	0226	1.3	0800	12.9	1447	1.5	2021	13.1	
26	TH	0308	1.3	0846	12.8	1525	1.6	2105	12.9	
27	F	0349	1.4	0932	12.5	1603	1.8	2151	12.5	
28	SA	0430	1.7	1019	12.1	1643	2.2	2240	11.9	
29	SU	0517	2.1	1111	11.5	1731	2.7	2336	11.3	
30	M	0613	2.6	1212	10.9	1833	3.2			◑
31	TU	0047	10.9	0720	2.8	1326	10.6	1953	3.3	

JUNE

Date	Day	Time	m	Time	m	Time	m	Time	m	Moon
1	W	0205	10.9	0832	2.7	1438	10.7	2108	3.0	
2	TH	0311	11.2	0939	2.5	1541	11.1	2212	2.6	
3	F	0409	11.6	1039	2.2	1637	11.6	2309	2.1	
4	SA	0502	12.0	1134	1.9	1726	12.0			
5	SU	0001	1.8	0549	12.2	1225	1.7	1810	12.3	
6	M	0050	1.6	0634	12.3	1311	1.6	1852	12.4	●
7	TU	0135	1.6	0716	12.3	1354	1.6	1931	12.4	
8	W	0216	1.8	0755	12.1	1432	1.8	2008	12.2	
9	TH	0252	2.0	0832	11.8	1503	2.1	2042	11.9	
10	F	0321	2.3	0907	11.4	1530	2.3	2115	11.6	
11	SA	0346	2.5	0939	11.1	1556	2.5	2147	11.2	
12	SU	0414	2.7	1012	10.8	1626	2.7	2220	10.9	
13	M	0448	2.8	1048	10.5	1703	2.9	2259	10.5	
14	TU	0530	3.0	1131	10.2	1748	3.2	2348	10.2	
15	W	0621	3.2	1224	10.0	1845	3.5			◐
16	TH	0050	10.1	0721	3.4	1329	9.9	1954	3.6	
17	F	0200	10.2	0829	3.4	1440	10.2	2108	3.4	
18	SA	0309	10.6	0942	3.2	1548	10.7	2220	3.0	
19	SU	0413	11.1	1054	2.8	1649	11.4	2325	2.4	
20	M	0512	11.7	1156	2.3	1743	12.1			
21	TU	0022	1.9	0605	12.2	1252	1.9	1833	12.6	
22	W	0117	1.6	0657	12.6	1345	1.6	1922	13.0	○
23	TH	0210	1.3	0749	12.9	1436	1.4	2011	13.2	
24	F	0302	1.2	0839	12.9	1524	1.4	2100	13.2	
25	SA	0351	1.1	0929	12.9	1609	1.5	2149	13.0	
26	SU	0437	1.2	1017	12.6	1652	1.7	2237	12.7	
27	M	0521	1.4	1105	12.2	1735	2.0	2327	12.2	
28	TU	0605	1.8	1154	11.7	1820	2.4			◑
29	W	0022	11.7	0651	2.2	1250	11.2	1910	2.8	
30	TH	0124	11.2	0742	2.6	1351	10.8	2009	3.1	

JULY

Date	Day	Time	m	Time	m	Time	m	Time	m	Moon
1	F	0228	10.9	0841	2.9	1455	10.6	2118	3.2	
2	SA	0329	10.9	0948	3.0	1556	10.7	2228	3.1	
3	SU	0427	11.0	1053	2.9	1653	11.0	2327	2.8	
4	M	0522	11.2	1150	2.5	1744	11.4			
5	TU	0020	2.4	0610	11.5	1242	2.2	1829	11.8	
6	W	0109	2.2	0656	11.6	1329	2.0	1912	12.0	●
7	TH	0155	2.1	0739	11.7	1413	2.0	1953	12.0	
8	F	0239	2.2	0819	11.7	1453	2.1	2030	11.9	
9	SA	0316	2.3	0855	11.6	1527	2.3	2105	11.8	
10	SU	0348	2.5	0929	11.4	1555	2.4	2137	11.6	
11	M	0414	2.6	1000	11.3	1620	2.5	2208	11.4	
12	TU	0440	2.6	1030	11.1	1650	2.5	2240	11.2	
13	W	0511	2.6	1104	10.9	1725	2.7	2317	11.0	
14	TH	0549	2.7	1145	10.7	1807	2.9			◐
15	F	0005	10.7	0634	3.0	1236	10.4	1859	3.3	
16	SA	0104	10.4	0730	3.3	1340	10.2	2008	3.6	
17	SU	0215	10.4	0844	3.5	1457	10.3	2135	3.5	
18	M	0333	10.6	1015	3.3	1616	10.8	2255	2.9	
19	TU	0446	11.2	1130	2.8	1722	11.6			
20	W	0002	2.3	0549	11.8	1235	2.2	1818	12.4	
21	TH	0105	1.7	0647	12.5	1335	1.7	1912	13.1	○
22	F	0204	1.2	0741	13.0	1432	1.3	2003	13.5	
23	SA	0300	0.8	0832	13.3	1523	1.0	2052	13.7	
24	SU	0349	0.6	0919	13.4	1608	0.9	2138	13.7	
25	M	0432	0.6	1004	13.3	1647	1.0	2222	13.4	
26	TU	0509	0.9	1045	12.9	1720	1.4	2304	12.9	
27	W	0542	1.4	1125	12.3	1751	2.0	2346	12.1	
28	TH	0613	2.0	1206	11.5	1823	2.6			◑
29	F	0034	11.2	0649	2.7	1255	10.7	1905	3.3	
30	SA	0134	10.4	0737	3.4	1401	10.0	2004	3.9	
31	SU	0248	9.9	0843	3.8	1516	9.9	2135	4.1	

AUGUST

Date	Day	Time	m	Time	m	Time	m	Time	m	Moon
1	M	0358	10.0	1011	3.8	1625	10.2	2300	3.6	
2	TU	0500	10.4	1123	3.2	1723	10.9	2359	2.9	
3	W	0554	11.0	1219	2.6	1813	11.5			
4	TH	0051	2.4	0641	11.5	1311	2.1	1857	12.0	
5	F	0140	2.1	0723	11.8	1359	1.9	1937	12.2	●
6	SA	0227	2.0	0802	11.9	1443	1.9	2015	12.3	
7	SU	0308	2.0	0838	11.9	1521	2.0	2049	12.2	
8	M	0342	2.2	0910	11.8	1551	2.2	2119	12.0	
9	TU	0407	2.4	0938	11.7	1610	2.3	2146	11.9	
10	W	0424	2.4	1005	11.6	1630	2.3	2214	11.7	
11	TH	0445	2.4	1034	11.4	1657	2.4	2247	11.5	
12	F	0515	2.5	1110	11.1	1732	2.7	2328	11.1	
13	SA	0552	2.8	1155	10.7	1814	3.2			◐
14	SU	0021	10.5	0639	3.4	1255	10.1	1914	3.8	
15	M	0133	10.0	0750	3.9	1419	9.9	2058	4.0	
16	TU	0307	10.0	0950	3.9	1557	10.3	2242	3.4	
17	W	0436	10.7	1120	3.1	1711	11.4	2356	2.4	
18	TH	0543	11.7	1228	2.2	1811	12.5			
19	F	0059	1.5	0639	12.7	1329	1.5	1902	13.4	○
20	SA	0157	0.8	0730	13.4	1423	0.8	1951	14.0	
21	SU	0249	0.3	0817	13.8	1512	0.5	2036	14.3	
22	M	0335	0.1	0900	13.9	1553	0.4	2118	14.2	
23	TU	0414	0.3	0940	13.7	1628	0.7	2157	13.8	
24	W	0445	0.8	1016	13.2	1654	1.3	2233	13.0	
25	TH	0509	1.5	1049	12.4	1714	2.0	2306	12.0	
26	F	0530	2.2	1120	11.4	1737	2.7	2341	10.9	◑
27	SA	0559	3.0	1157	10.4	1811	3.5			
28	SU	0029	9.8	0640	3.8	1256	9.5	1904	4.3	
29	M	0203	9.1	0748	4.5	1443	9.2	2039	4.8	
30	TU	0336	9.2	0936	4.4	1603	9.7	2246	4.1	
31	W	0442	10.0	1105	3.5	1704	10.6	2344	3.0	

Chart Datum: 6·50 metres below Ordnance Datum (Newlyn)

TIME ZONE (UT)
For Summer Time add ONE hour in **non-shaded areas**

ENGLAND – PORT OF BRISTOL (AVONMOUTH)

LAT 51°30′N LONG 2°44′W

TIMES AND HEIGHTS OF HIGH AND LOW WATERS

SPRING & NEAP TIDES
Dates in red are SPRINGS
Dates in blue are NEAPS

YEAR **2005**

SEPTEMBER

Date	Day	Time	m	Time	m	Time	m	Time	m
1	TH	0536	10.9	1201	2.6	1754	11.5		
2	F	0033	2.2	0620	11.6	1251	2.0	1836	12.2
3	SA	0120	1.8	0700	12.1	1339	1.7	● 1915	12.5
4	SU	0206	1.6	0737	12.3	1423	1.6	1951	12.6
5	M	0248	1.7	0811	12.3	1502	1.8	2023	12.5
6	TU	0323	1.9	0842	12.2	1533	2.0	2052	12.4
7	W	0348	2.2	0910	12.1	1551	2.2	2119	12.2
8	TH	0400	2.4	0936	12.0	1606	2.3	2147	12.1
9	F	0416	2.4	1005	11.8	1630	2.3	2220	11.8
10	SA	0443	2.5	1040	11.4	1701	2.6	2259	11.2
11	SU	0516	2.9	1124	10.7	1740	3.2	◐ 2351	10.3
12	M	0601	3.6	1224	9.9	1837	4.0		
13	TU	0106	9.6	0710	4.4	1359	9.5	2047	4.4
14	W	0304	9.6	0954	4.2	1553	10.2	2243	3.4
15	TH	0433	10.7	1117	3.0	1704	11.5	2350	2.2
16	F	0535	11.9	1217	1.9	1759	12.8		
17	SA	0046	1.2	0625	13.0	1312	1.1	1846	13.8
18	SU	0139	0.5	0711	13.7	1403	0.5	○ 1931	14.3
19	M	0227	0.1	0754	14.1	1448	0.3	2013	14.5
20	TU	0310	0.1	0834	14.0	1528	0.4	2052	14.2
21	W	0346	0.4	0910	13.7	1600	0.9	2128	13.6
22	TH	0413	1.1	0943	13.1	1622	1.6	2159	12.8
23	F	0431	1.8	1011	12.2	1636	2.2	2228	11.8
24	SA	0448	2.5	1039	11.3	1657	2.9	2257	10.6
25	SU	0514	3.2	1110	10.3	1727	3.6	◑ 2334	9.5
26	M	0551	4.0	1158	9.3	1816	4.5		
27	TU	0104	8.6	0659	4.8	1415	8.8	1957	5.1
28	W	0312	8.8	0903	4.8	1538	9.5	2228	4.3
29	TH	0416	9.8	1044	3.8	1637	10.5	2320	3.1
30	F	0507	10.8	1136	2.7	1725	11.5		

OCTOBER

Date	Day	Time	m	Time	m	Time	m	Time	m
1	SA	0006	2.2	0550	11.7	1224	2.0	1806	12.2
2	SU	0052	1.7	0629	12.3	1310	1.6	1844	12.6
3	M	0136	1.6	0705	12.6	1353	1.6	● 1920	12.8
4	TU	0217	1.6	0739	12.6	1432	1.7	1953	12.7
5	W	0252	1.8	0811	12.5	1504	1.9	2023	12.6
6	TH	0318	2.1	0840	12.4	1526	2.1	2053	12.5
7	F	0334	2.3	0909	12.3	1544	2.2	2124	12.3
8	SA	0352	2.3	0942	12.0	1609	2.3	2200	11.8
9	SU	0420	2.5	1020	11.5	1641	2.7	2242	11.1
10	M	0455	3.0	1106	10.7	1722	3.3	◐ 2336	10.2
11	TU	0541	3.8	1210	9.8	1825	4.2		
12	W	0058	9.4	0658	4.6	1405	9.6	2058	4.3
13	TH	0304	9.8	0949	4.0	1542	10.6	2227	3.1
14	F	0419	10.9	1058	2.8	1645	11.8	2327	1.9
15	SA	0515	12.2	1153	1.7	1737	13.0		
16	SU	0020	1.0	0602	13.1	1245	1.0	1823	13.8
17	M	0110	0.5	0645	13.7	1333	0.6	○ 1905	14.2
18	TU	0156	0.3	0726	13.9	1417	0.5	1946	14.1
19	W	0238	0.5	0804	13.8	1457	0.8	2024	13.8
20	TH	0313	0.9	0839	13.4	1528	1.3	2059	13.2
21	F	0339	1.5	0911	12.7	1550	2.0	2130	12.3
22	SA	0357	2.1	0939	12.0	1605	2.5	2158	11.4
23	SU	0416	2.6	1006	11.2	1627	3.0	2226	10.5
24	M	0442	3.2	1037	10.3	1658	3.6	2301	9.6
25	TU	0517	3.9	1121	9.4	1744	4.4	◑	
26	W	0007	8.7	0617	4.7	1321	8.9	1914	4.9
27	TH	0228	8.8	0806	4.9	1458	9.4	2114	4.6
28	F	0335	9.6	0953	4.1	1557	10.3	2237	3.6
29	SA	0428	10.5	1056	3.2	1646	11.2	2327	2.7
30	SU	0512	11.4	1145	2.4	1729	11.9		
31	M	0013	2.1	0552	12.1	1231	2.0	1808	12.4

NOVEMBER

Date	Day	Time	m	Time	m	Time	m	Time	m
1	TU	0057	1.8	0630	12.5	1314	1.8	1846	12.7
2	W	0139	1.7	0706	12.7	1355	1.7	● 1922	12.8
3	TH	0216	1.8	0741	12.8	1431	1.8	1957	12.8
4	F	0248	1.9	0815	12.7	1502	1.9	2033	12.7
5	SA	0314	2.0	0851	12.6	1531	2.0	2111	12.4
6	SU	0341	2.2	0929	12.2	1603	2.2	2153	11.9
7	M	0413	2.5	1012	11.6	1640	2.7	2239	11.2
8	TU	0452	3.1	1103	10.9	1728	3.3	2336	10.4
9	W	0545	3.8	1212	10.3	1843	3.8	◐	
10	TH	0058	9.9	0720	4.2	1355	10.3	2033	3.7
11	F	0239	10.2	0915	3.7	1514	11.0	2151	2.9
12	SA	0348	11.1	1023	2.8	1615	11.9	2252	2.1
13	SU	0444	12.0	1119	2.0	1708	12.7	2346	1.4
14	M	0533	12.7	1211	1.4	1755	13.2		
15	TU	0036	1.1	0616	13.2	1259	1.1	1838	13.5
16	W	0122	0.9	0657	13.3	1344	1.1	○ 1919	13.4
17	TH	0204	1.1	0736	13.2	1425	1.4	1959	13.1
18	F	0242	1.4	0813	12.9	1500	1.8	2036	12.6
19	SA	0311	1.9	0847	12.4	1527	2.3	2110	11.9
20	SU	0334	2.3	0919	11.9	1547	2.7	2141	11.3
21	M	0357	2.7	0949	11.2	1612	3.0	2212	10.6
22	TU	0425	3.1	1023	10.6	1646	3.4	2248	10.0
23	W	0501	3.5	1105	10.0	1730	3.9	◑ 2338	9.5
24	TH	0552	4.1	1209	9.5	1833	4.2		
25	F	0056	9.2	0705	4.4	1344	9.5	1951	4.3
26	SA	0226	9.4	0828	4.2	1457	10.0	2109	3.9
27	SU	0331	10.1	0944	3.7	1553	10.6	2222	3.4
28	M	0424	10.8	1049	3.1	1644	11.3	2322	2.8
29	TU	0511	11.5	1143	2.5	1730	11.9		
30	W	0013	2.3	0554	12.2	1233	2.1	1813	12.4

DECEMBER

Date	Day	Time	m	Time	m	Time	m	Time	m
1	TH	0100	1.9	0636	12.6	1319	1.8	● 1856	12.7
2	F	0143	1.8	0717	12.9	1403	1.7	1939	12.8
3	SA	0225	1.7	0759	12.9	1446	1.7	2023	12.8
4	SU	0304	1.8	0842	12.9	1528	1.7	2108	12.6
5	M	0342	2.0	0927	12.6	1609	1.9	2154	12.3
6	TU	0422	2.3	1014	12.2	1653	2.2	2242	11.8
7	W	0505	2.7	1105	11.7	1742	2.6	2335	11.2
8	TH	0557	3.1	1206	11.3	1842	2.9	◐	
9	F	0039	10.8	0704	3.4	1321	11.0	1950	3.0
10	SA	0156	10.7	0823	3.4	1434	11.1	2101	3.0
11	SU	0306	10.9	0936	3.1	1537	11.5	2208	2.7
12	M	0407	11.3	1040	2.7	1634	11.8	2308	2.4
13	TU	0501	11.8	1136	2.3	1726	12.2		
14	W	0001	2.0	0548	12.2	1228	2.0	1813	12.4
15	TH	0051	1.8	0633	12.5	1316	1.9	○ 1858	12.5
16	F	0136	1.7	0715	12.6	1401	1.9	1941	12.4
17	SA	0218	1.8	0755	12.5	1441	2.1	2021	12.1
18	SU	0254	2.1	0833	12.2	1516	2.4	2058	11.8
19	M	0324	2.3	0908	11.9	1543	2.7	2131	11.5
20	TU	0351	2.6	0941	11.6	1609	2.8	2203	11.1
21	W	0418	2.7	1014	11.2	1639	3.0	2236	10.7
22	TH	0450	2.9	1049	10.8	1715	3.1	2313	10.4
23	F	0529	3.2	1130	10.5	1758	3.4	◑ 2358	10.1
24	SA	0617	3.5	1222	10.1	1850	3.6		
25	SU	0055	9.8	0717	3.8	1328	10.0	1953	3.8
26	M	0206	9.8	0830	3.9	1440	10.2	2109	3.8
27	TU	0320	10.2	0948	3.6	1549	10.6	2226	3.4
28	W	0426	10.8	1058	3.1	1651	11.2	2332	2.8
29	TH	0522	11.6	1158	2.4	1746	11.9		
30	F	0028	2.3	0612	12.3	1253	2.0	1837	12.4
31	SA	0121	1.9	0701	12.8	1346	1.6	● 1927	12.8

Chart Datum: 6·50 metres below Ordnance Datum (Newlyn)

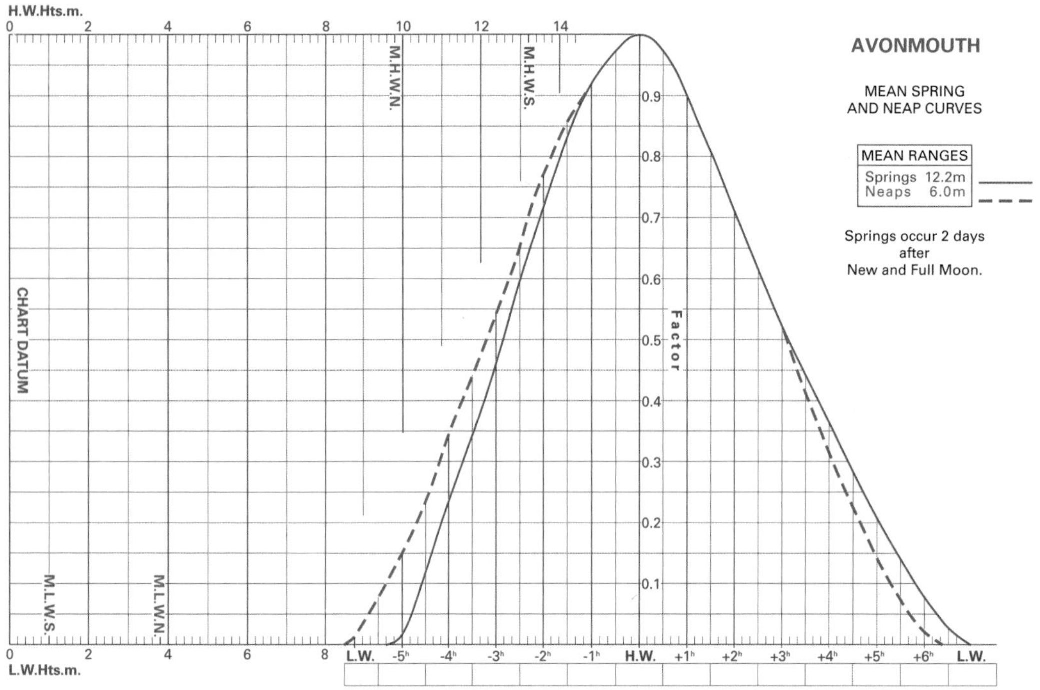
H.W.Hts.m.
0 2 4 6 8 10 12 14
M.H.W.N.
M.H.W.S.
CHART DATUM
M.L.W.S.
M.L.W.N.
0 2 4 6 8
L.W.Hts.m.
0.9
0.8
0.7
0.6
0.5
0.4
0.3
0.2
0.1
Factor
L.W. -5h -4h -3h -2h -1h H.W. +1h +2h +3h +4h +5h +6h L.W.
AVONMOUTH
MEAN SPRING AND NEAP CURVES
MEAN RANGES
Springs 12.2m
Neaps 6.0m
Springs occur 2 days after New and Full Moon.

9.11.20 BRISTOL (CITY DOCKS)

City of Bristol **51°26'·95N 02°37'·44W** ❀❀◊◊◊✿✿✿

CHARTS AC *1179, 1176,* 1859; Imray C59; Stanfords 14; OS 172

TIDES –0410 on Dover; ML 7·0; Duration 0620; Zone 0 (UT)

Standard Port BRISTOL (AVONMOUTH) (⟵)

Times				**Height (metres)**			
High Water		Low Water		MHWS	MHWN	MLWN	MLWS
0200	0800	0300	0800	13·2	9·8	3·8	1·0
1400	2000	1500	2000				
Differences SHIREHAMPTON (R Avon, 51°29'N 02°41'W)							
0000	0000	+0035	+0010	–0·7	–0·7	–0·8	0·0
SEA MILLS (R Avon, 51°29'N 02°39'W)							
+0005	+0005	+0105	+0030	–1·4	–1·5	–1·7	–0·1
CUMBERLAND BASIN (Ent)							
+0010	+0010	Dries		–2·9	–3·0	Dries	

SHELTER Excellent in Bristol Floating Harbour and in Bristol marina. Avonmouth and Royal Portbury Docks are prohib to yachts, except in emergency. Crockerne Pill has drying moorings and a grid for emergency repairs. Speed limit in R Avon = 6kn. Drying moorings (soft mud) may be found at Lamplighters Quay just up stream of the M5 motorway br. and convenient when carrying the ebb from Sharpness. ☎ 0117 9381757 📠 0117 9382085. For R Avon, Cumberland Basin and Bristol Hbr refer to *Bristol Harbour: Info for Boat Owners*, from HM, Underfall Yard, Cumberland Rd, Bristol BS1 6XG.

NAVIGATION Avonmouth WPT 51°30'·45N 02°43'·33W, 127° to front ldg lt, 0·61M. The chan from Flatholm is buoyed. See R/T below for compliance with VTS and reporting. Sp tidal stream across ent reaches 5kn.

Locking in: Best to reach Cumberland Basin by HW (approx 7M upriver from WPT); waiting pontoon (dries). Ent lock opens approx HW–2½, –1½ and –¼hr for arrivals; departing craft lockout approx 15 mins after these times. Swing bridge opens in unison with lock, but not Mon-Fri during road tfc rush hrs 0800-0900 and 1700-1800. Inner (Junction) lock is always open, unless ht of HW >9·6m ('stopgate' tide) when it closes; read special instructions. If you miss the last lock-in, call VHF Ch 12 for advice. Options: dry out in soft mud at pontoons, or on N Wall (bow abreast ladder No 4 Survey Mark; no nearer the lock gate). Other areas are foul.

Bridges: Prince St bridge is manned 0915-2215 summer, by appointment only in winter; openings are normally at H+15. Pre-notify Bridgemaster ☎ 9299338, call VHF Ch 73 or sound •—•(R). Redcliffe bridge opening: pre-arrange with HM. Clearances above hbr datum: Prince St 2·2m; Redcliffe 3·6m; St Augustine 3·1m. Water level can be 0·5m above hbr datum.

LIGHTS AND MARKS R Avon ent is abeam S pier lt Oc RG 30s, vis R294°-036°, G036°-194°. Ldg lts 127° both Iso.R.2s. St George ldg lts 173°, both Oc G 5s synch; front R/Or post; rear W/Or chequers on Or post. Upriver, G or R ☆s mark the outside of bends.

Ent sigs to Bristol Hbr may be shown from E bank, 1½ and 2½ca beyond Clifton Suspension Bridge: ● = continue with caution; ● = stop and await orders.

R/T W of Flatholm/Steepholm, *Severn VTS* Ch **69**, E of this line *Bristol VTS* Ch **12**. Yachts bound for Bristol **must** call *Bristol VTS* at English and Welsh Grounds SWM buoy and at Welsh Hook PHM buoy; comply with VTS instructions. If no radio , ☎ *Bristol VTS* (0117) 9822257 by mobile phone. On entering R Avon call again, low power, confirming bound for City Docks. Keep well clear of large vessels. At Black Rks (0·8M to run) call *City Docks Radio*, low power, Ch **14** 11 (HW–3 to HW+1) for instructions. For berths, call *Bristol Hbr* Ch 73 16 (HO), and/or Bristol Marina Ch **80** M. Prince St br and Netham lock Ch 73.

TELEPHONE (Dial code 0117) HM 9031484, 📠 9031487; Dock Master 9273633; Prince St and Redcliffe Bridges 9299338; Netham Lock 9776590; MRCC (01792) 366534; Bristol weather centre 9279298; Marinecall 09066 526243; Police 9277777; Ⓗ 9230000.

FACILITIES Portishead CC (Crockerne Pill), drying M; **Lamplighters Quay** ½M above M5 br on E Bank; drying AB, VHF Ch 80, C (20 ton), BH (9 ton) ☎ 938 1757 📠 938 2085; **Bristol Hbr** ☎ 9031484, 📠 9031487, approx 40 ⓥ AB £0.85 inc licence fee, FW, D, ⊕, ⚓, Slip(launching £0.85/m), CH, Gas, 🛒, R, Bar; ferries ply around the hbr. **Bristol Marina** access HW–3 to +1, (80, inc ⓥ; 20m max LOA) ☎ 9213198, 📠 9297672, £1.55 incl licence fee, FW, D, ⚓, El, Ⓔ, ME, ⚒, Gas, Gaz, SM, Slip, CH, C (6&12 ton), BH (30 ton), ♿, ⊡; **Baltic Wharf Leisure Centre** contact Hbr Office ☎ 9031484, Slip, L, Bar; **Cabot Cruising Club** ☎ 9268318, 📠 9812458, M, L, FW, AB,Bar; **Portavon Marina** ☎ 9861626, 📠 986 6455, Bitton Road, Keynsham BS18 2DD; Slip, M, ME, ⚒, CH, R; **Bathurst Basin** Shower block; **City** EC Wed/Sat; all facilities, ACA, P, D, ✉, Ⓑ, ⇌, ✈.

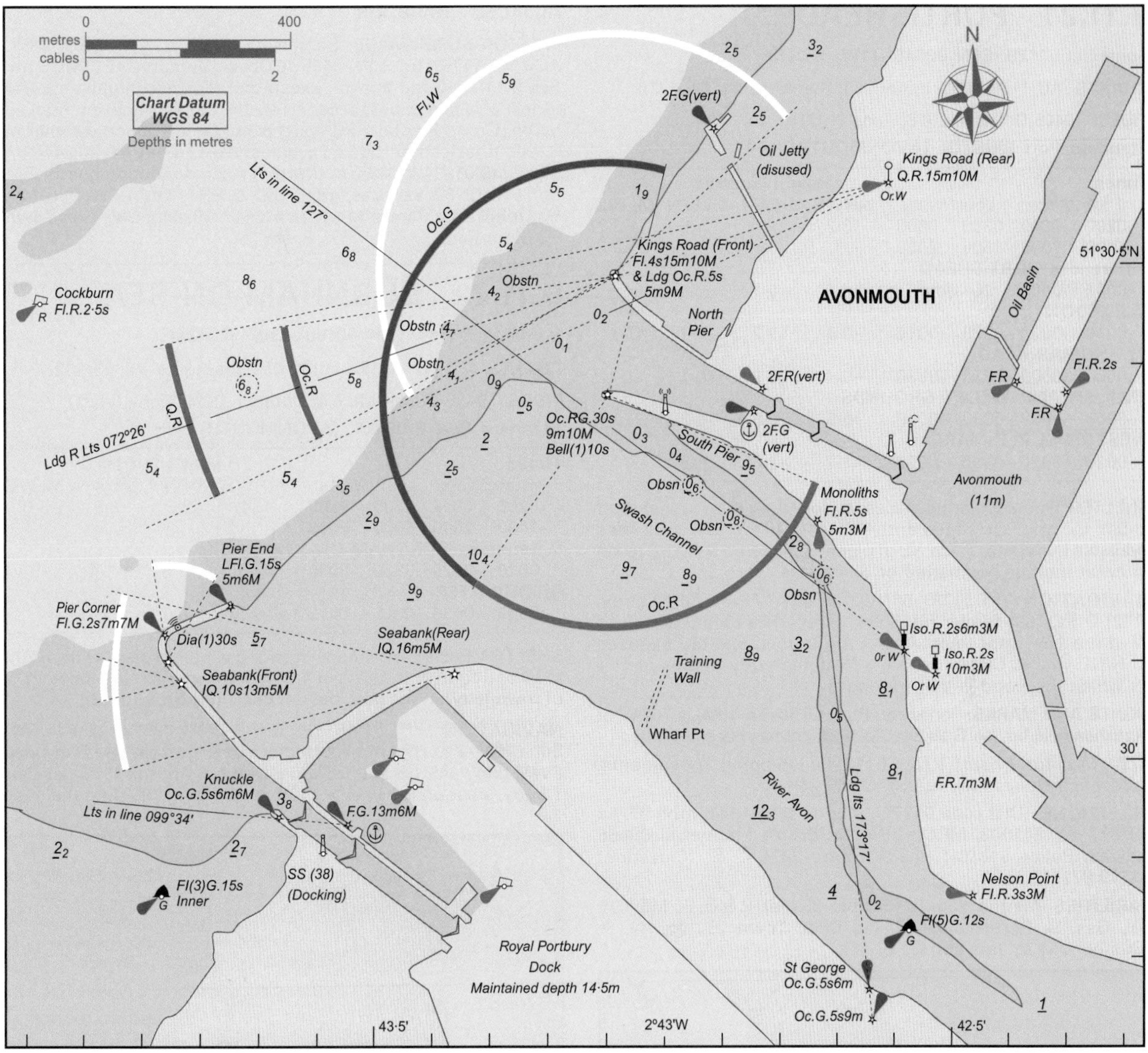
metres 0 400
cables 0 2
Chart Datum WGS 84
Depths in metres
Fl.W
Oc.G
Lts in line 127°
2F.G(vert)
Oil Jetty (disused)
Kings Road (Rear) Q.R.15m10M
Or.W
Kings Road (Front) Fl.4s15m10M & Ldg Oc.R.5s 5m9M
AVONMOUTH
51°30·5'N
Cockburn Fl.R.2·5s
R
Obstn
North Pier
Oil Basin
Q.R
Oc.R
Ldg R Lts 072°26'
2F.R(vert)
F.R
Fl.R.2s
Oc.RG.30s 9m10M Bell(1)10s
2F.G (vert)
South Pier
Obsn
Swash Channel
Monoliths Fl.R.5s 5m3M
Avonmouth (11m)
Pier End LFl.G.15s 5m6M
Pier Corner Fl.G.2s7m7M
Dia(1)30s
Seabank(Rear) IQ.16m5M
Seabank(Front) IQ.10s13m5M
Oc.R
Training Wall
Wharf Pt
Iso.R.2s6m3M
Iso.R.2s 10m3M
Or W
30'
F.R.7m3M
River Avon
Ldg lts 173°17'
Knuckle Oc.G.5s6m6M
Lts in line 099°34'
F.G.13m6M
Fl(3)G.15s Inner
G
SS (38) (Docking)
Nelson Point Fl.R.3s3M
Fl(5)G.12s
Royal Portbury Dock
Maintained depth 14·5m
St George Oc.G.5s6m
Oc.G.5s9m
43·5'
2°43'W
42·5'

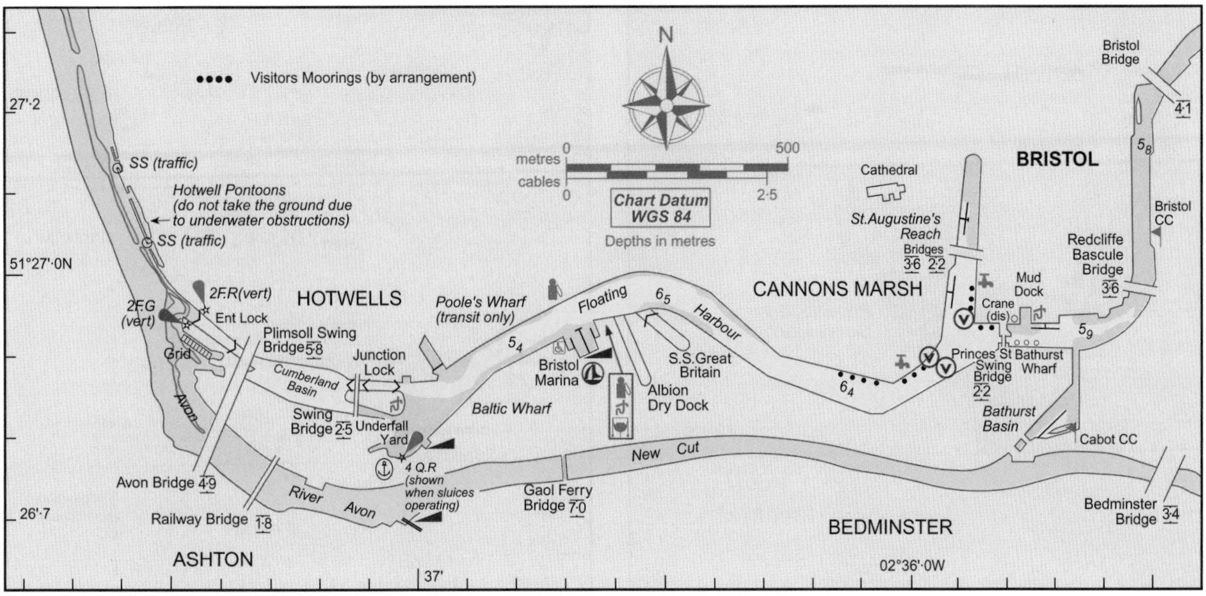
Visitors Moorings (by arrangement)
27'·2
metres 0 500
cables 0 2·5
Chart Datum WGS 84
Depths in metres
Bristol Bridge
BRISTOL
Cathedral
St.Augustine's Reach
Bridges 3·6 2·2
SS (traffic)
Hotwell Pontoons (do not take the ground due to underwater obstructions)
SS (traffic)
51°27'·0N
2F.R(vert)
2F.G (vert)
Ent Lock
HOTWELLS
Poole's Wharf (transit only)
Floating Harbour
CANNONS MARSH
Mud Dock
Crane (dis)
Bristol CC
Redcliffe Bascule Bridge 3·6
Grid
Plimsoll Swing Bridge 5·8
Cumberland Basin
Junction Lock
Bristol Marina
S.S.Great Britain
Albion Dry Dock
Princes St Swing Bridge 2·2
Bathurst Wharf
Bathurst Basin
Cabot CC
Swing Bridge 2·5
Underfall Yard
Baltic Wharf
Avon
4 Q.R (shown when sluices operating)
New Cut
Avon Bridge 4·9
River Avon
Gaol Ferry Bridge 7·0
Railway Bridge 1·8
26'·7
ASHTON
BEDMINSTER
Bedminster Bridge 3·4
37'
02°36'·0W

9.11.21 PORTISHEAD

Somerset **51°29'·56N 02°45'·41W**

CHARTS AC *1176,* 1859; Imray C59; Stanfords 14; OS 171/2

TIDES –0405 Dover; ML 6·8; Zone 0 (UT)

Standard Port BRISTOL (AVONMOUTH) (⟵)

Times				Height (metres)			
High Water		Low Water		MHWS	MHWN	MLWN	MLWS
0200	0800	0300	0800	13·2	9·8	3·8	1·0
1400	2000	1500	2000				
Differences PORTISHEAD							
–0002	0000	No data		–0·1	–0·1	No data	
CLEVEDON							
–0010	–0020	–0025	–0015	–0·4	–0·2	+0·2	0·0
ST THOMAS HEAD							
0000	0000	–0030	–0030	–0·4	–0·2	+0·1	+0·1
ENGLISH AND WELSH GROUNDS							
–0008	–0008	–0030	–0030	–0·5	–0·8	–0·3	0·0
WESTON-SUPER-MARE							
–0020	–0030	–0130	–0030	–1·2	–1·0	–0·8	–0·2

SHELTER Good in marina. Access by lock 9m x 40m x 3·5m draft (5·5m by prior arrangement) HW ±4½ (nps) ±3¾ (sp). ⓥ's available in marina. ⚓ 1ca NE of pier hd (sheltered from SE to W) to await the tide for marina or Sharpness.

NAVIGATION WPT 51°29'·96N 02°45'·35W, Firefly SHM buoy, Fl (2) G 5s, 168° to pier hd, 500m. Firefly Rks (0·9m) are close W of the 168° appr track. Appr's dry to mud and are exposed to N/NE winds. Close inshore a W-going eddy begins at HW –3 whilst the flood is still making E.

LIGHTS AND MARKS Portishead Pt, Q (3) 10s9m 16M, is 7ca W of Portishead pierhd, Iso G 2s 5m 3M. Lock ent has FG and FR lts.

R/T Monitor *Bristol VTS* Ch **12** for shipping movements. Portishead Quays Marina VHF Ch 80 24H.

TELEPHONE (Dial code 01275) Marina ☎ 841941, mob 07764 635877, 📠 841942; MRCC (01792) 366534; Marinecall 09066 526243; Police 818181; Health centre 847474; Ⓗ (Clevedon) 01179 872212.

FACILITIES **Marina** (200+) £1.50, BH (35 ton), P & D, El, ME, CH, BY, Gas, ⊡. **Portishead Cruising Club**; **Town** ✉, Ⓑ, ⇌, ✈ (Bristol). 3M to Junction 19 of M5.

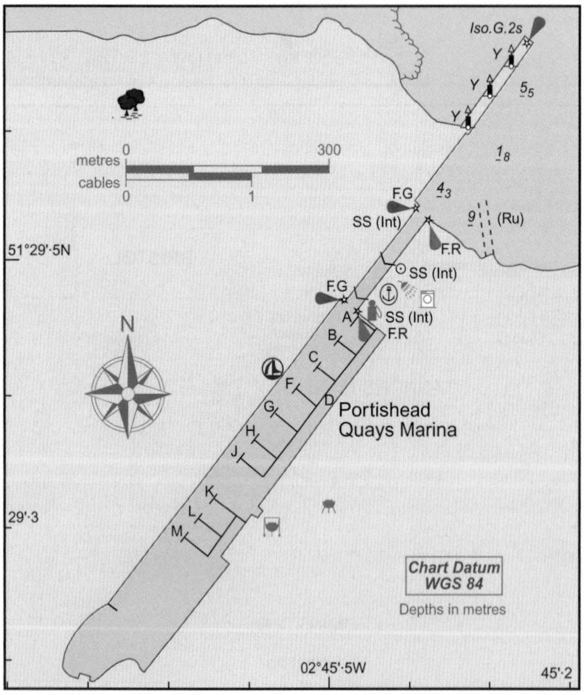
Iso.G.2s
metres 0 300
cables 0 1
51°29'·5N
29'·3
F.G
SS (Int)
(Ru)
F.R
SS (Int)
SS (Int)
F.R
Portishead Quays Marina
Chart Datum WGS 84
Depths in metres
02°45'·5W
45'·2

ADJACENT HARBOUR

WESTON-SUPER-MARE, Somerset, **51°21'·03N 02°59'·28W.** AC *1179,* 1176,1152. HW –0435 on Dover; Duration 0655; ML 6·1m. See 9.11.21. Good shelter, except in S'lies, in Knightstone Hbr (dries) at N end of bay; access HW±1½. Causeway at ent marked by bn. Grand Pier hd 2 FG (vert) 6/5m. Or ⚓ in good weather in R Axe (dries), entry HW±2. Facilities: **Weston Bay YC** (located on beach) ☎ 01934 413366, M (lower R Axe), dry out on beach, FW, Bar, VHF Ch 80; **Services**: AB, CH, El, D, BH (10 ton), FW, Slip, ME, ⚒; **Uphill Boat Centre** ☎ 01934 418617 AB, slip, Gas, Gaz; **Town** EC Mon; Bar, Ⓑ, FW, P, ✉, R, ⇌, 🛒.

9.11.22 BURNHAM-ON-SEA

Somerset **51°14'·23N 03°00'·33W**

CHARTS AC *1179, 1152*; Imray C59; Stanfords 14; OS 182

TIDES –0435 Dover; ML 5·4; Duration 0620; Zone 0 (UT)

Standard Port BRISTOL (AVONMOUTH) (⟵)

Times				Height (metres)			
High Water		Low Water		MHWS	MHWN	MLWN	MLWS
0200	0800	0300	0800	13·2	9·8	3·8	1·0
1400	2000	1500	2000				
Differences BURNHAM-ON-SEA							
–0020	–0025	–0030	0000	–2·3	–1·9	–1·4	–1·1
BRIDGWATER							
–0015	–0030	+0305	+0455	–8·6	–8·1	Dries	

SHELTER Ent is very choppy in strong winds, especially from SW to W and from N to NE. ⚓ in 4m about 40m E of No 1 buoy or S of town jetty or, for best shelter, ⓥ/⚓ in R Brue (dries).

NAVIGATION WPT 51°15'·32N 03°08'·22W, 095° to Low lt, 5M. Enter HW –3 to HW; not advised at night. Or from ½M S of Gore SWM buoy pick up brg 076° on Low lt ho. Approx 1½M past No 1 buoy, steer on ldg line/lts 112°; thence alter 180° into the river

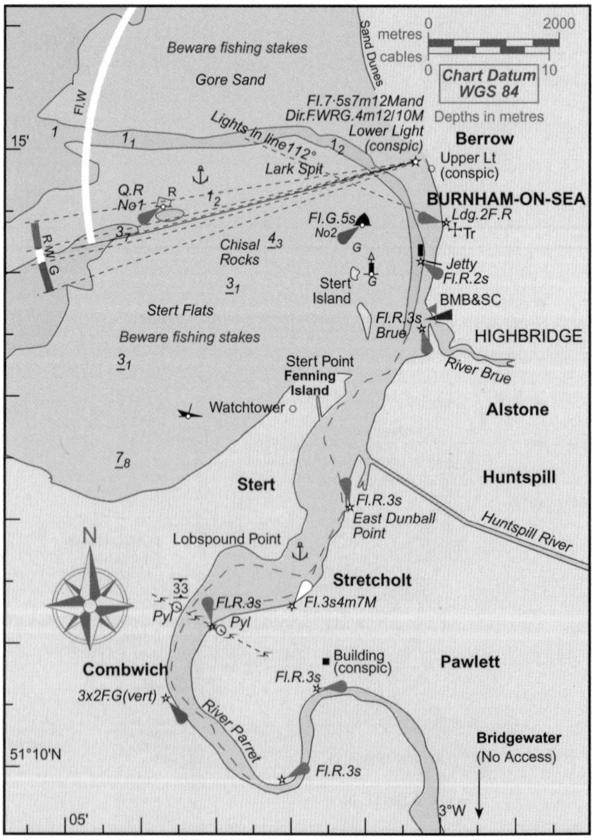
Beware fishing stakes
Gore Sand
Sand Dunes
metres 0 2000
cables 0 10
Chart Datum WGS 84
Depths in metres
Fl.7·5s7m12Mand
Dir.F.WRG.4m12/10M
Lower Light (conspic)
Lights in line 112°
Lark Spit
Berrow
Upper Lt (conspic)
BURNHAM-ON-SEA
Ldg.2F.R
Tr
F.W
15'
Q.R No1
R
Fl.G.5s No2
G
Chisal Rocks
Stert Island
G
Jetty Fl.R.2s
BMB&SC
Stert Flats
Fl.R.3s
Brue
HIGHBRIDGE
Beware fishing stakes
Stert Point
Fenning Island
River Brue
Watchtower
Alstone
Stert
Fl.R.3s
East Dunball Point
Huntspill
Lobspound Point
Huntspill River
Stretcholt
Fl.R.3s
Fl.3s4m7M
Pyl
Pyl
Building (conspic)
Pawlett
Combwich
Fl.R.3s
3x2F.G(vert)
River Parrett
Bridgewater (No Access)
51°10'N
Fl.R.3s
05'
3°W

BURNHAM *continued*

chan but banks and depths change frequently. Beware unmarked fishing stakes outside appr chan.

LIGHTS AND MARKS Low lt ho Dir 076° as chartlet. Ldg lts/marks 112° (moved as chan shifts): front FR 6m 3M, Or stripe on □ W background on sea wall; rear FR 12m 3M, church tr.

R/T HM and Pilot VHF Ch 08 16 (when vessel expected).

TELEPHONE (Dial code 01278) HM and Pilot 782180; MRCC (01792) 366534; Marinecall 09066 526243; Police (01823) 337911; Ⓗ 782262.

FACILITIES **Burnham-on-Sea MB&SC** ☎ 792911, M, few drying Ⓥs in River Brue, L, Slip, Bar; **Brue Yachts** ☎ 783275 mob 07810 622209, drying pontoon £7, FW, D, 🛒. **Services:** ME, El, ⚒, ACA (Bridgwater). **Town** EC Wed; Gas, ✉, Ⓑ, ⇌ (Highbridge), ✈ (Bristol). Note: No access to Bridgwater marina from sea/R Parrett.

9.11.23 WATCHET

Somerset **51°11´·03N 03°19´·72W**

CHARTS AC *1179, 1152, 1160*; Imray C59; Stanfords 14; OS 181

TIDES –0450 Dover; ML 5·9; Duration 0655; Zone 0 (UT)

Standard Port BRISTOL (AVONMOUTH) (⟵)

Times				Height (metres)			
High Water		Low Water		MHWS	MHWN	MLWN	MLWS
0200	0800	0300	0800	13·2	9·8	3·8	1·0
1400	2000	1500	2000				
Differences HINKLEY POINT							
–0020	–0025	–0100	–0040	–1·7	–1·4	–0·2	–0·2
WATCHET							
–0035	–0050	–0145	–0040	–1·9	–1·5	+0·1	+0·1
MINEHEAD							
–0037	–0052	–0155	–0045	–2·6	–1·9	–0·2	0·0
PORLOCK BAY							
–0045	–0055	–0205	–0050	–3·0	–2·2	–0·1	–0·1
LYNMOUTH							
–0055	–0115	No data		–3·6	–2·7	No data	

SHELTER Good, but open to N and E winds. The outer hbr ent dries 6·5m, but has about 6m depth at MHWS; access approx HW±2½. Marina entered through a dropping sill gate which is open when the tide level is at or above CD +6.92m (retained water

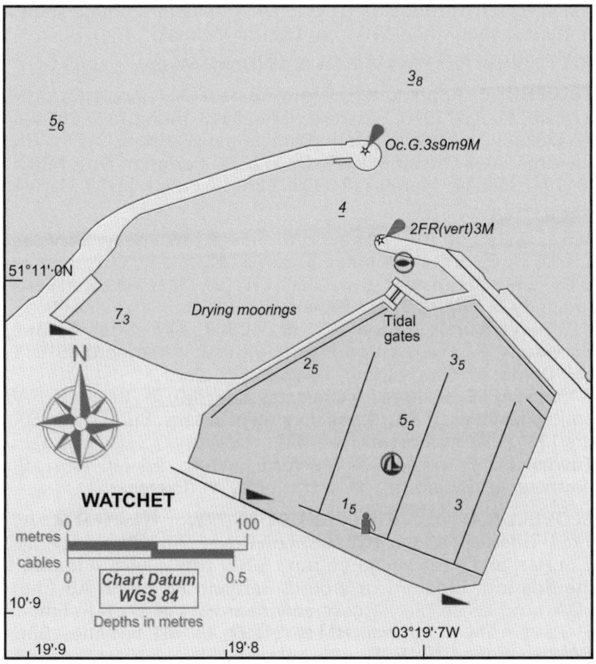
3_8
5_6
Oc.G.3s9m9M
4
2F.R(vert)3M
51°11'·0N
7_3
Drying moorings
Tidal gates
2_5
3_5
N
5_5
WATCHET
1_5
3
0
100
metres
cables
0
0.5
Chart Datum WGS 84
Depths in metres
10'·9
19'·9
19'·8
03°19'·7W

level). Min clearance over the gate, when it has just opened or is about to close 2.5m. Approx gate opening times HW ±2½H sp, HW ±1½H np. Movement through the entrance is controlled by stop/go R/G lts. Entrance max width 8m. Min retained water depths vary 1.5–3.0m.

NAVIGATION WPT 51°12´·03N 03°18´·88W, 208° to hbr ent, 1·1M. Rks/mud dry 5ca to seaward. Beware tidal streams 4-5kn at sp offshore and around W pier hd. Culver Sand (0·9m) is approx 6M NNE, marked by ECM and WCM lt buoys. 5M E of hbr are Lilstock range target buoys. DZ No 2 SPM buoy, Fl Y 10s, bears 030°/3·2M from Watchet. 3kn speed limit in marina.

LIGHTS AND MARKS Two unlit radio masts (206m) bearing 208° 1·6M from hbr ent are conspic approach marks. Hinkley Pt nuclear power stn is conspic 7·5M to the E. W pier hd Oc G 3s 9m 9M on Red (R) tr. E pier hd 2 FR (vert) 3M.

R/T VHF Ch 80 (from HW–2, but occas).

TELEPHONE (Dial code 01984) HM 631264 📠 639238 mob 077477 785508; Watchet Boat Owners Association (01643) 702569; MRCC (01792) 366534; Marinecall 09066 526243; Police (01823) 337911 (Minehead).

FACILITIES **Services:** AB (250 inc Ⓥ) £2.25 inc ⚡, D, ⊡, CH, Gaz, Slip(launching £5.00), ACA (Bridgwater). **Town** EC Wed; ✉, Ⓑ, 🛒, R, Bar. At Williton (2M): Gas, D & P (cans); Ⓗ (Minehead 8M), ⇌ (Taunton 18M), ✈ (Bristol).

OTHER HARBOURS ON S SHORE OF BRISTOL CHANNEL

MINEHEAD, Somerset, **51°12´·79N 03°28´·37W**. AC *1179*, 1165, 1160. HW–0450 on Dover. ML 5·7m. See 9.11.23. Small hbr, dries 7·5m; access HW±2. Good shelter within pier curving E and then SE, over which seas may break in gales at MHWS; exposed to E'lies. Best appr from N or NW; beware The Gables, shingle bank (dries 3·7m) about 5ca ENE of pier. Keep E of a sewer outfall which passes ½ca E of pierhd and extends 1¾ca NNE of it; outfall is protected by rk covering, drying 2·8m and N end marked by SHM bn QG 6m 7M. There are 6 pairs of fore and aft R Ⓥs at hbr ent just seaward of 3 posts or drying alongside berth, £1.00 at inner end of pier. Hbr gets very crowded. Holiday camp is conspic 6ca SE. Pierhd lt Fl (2) G 5s 4M, vis 127°-262°. VHF Ch 16 12 14 (occas). HM ☎ (01643) 702566; Facilities: **Hbr** FW, Slip (launching £5.00). **Town** EC Wed; D, P, El, Gas, ME, ⚒, R, Bar, 🛒, ✉, Ⓑ, ⇌ (Taunton).

PORLOCK WEIR, Somerset, **51°13´·17N 03°37´·64W**. AC *1179*, 1165, 1160. HW –0500 on Dover; ML 5·6m. See 9.11.23. Access HW±1½. Ent chan (250°), about 15m wide marked by withies (3 PHM and 1 SHM), between shingle bank/wood pilings to stbd and sunken wooden wall to port is difficult in any seas. A small pool (1m) just inside ent is for shoal draft boats; others dry out on pebble banks. Or turn 90° stbd, via gates (but opening bridge usually closed), into inner drying dock with good shelter. No lts. HM ☎ 01643 863187 (not local). **Porlock Weir SC**. Facilities: FW and limited 🛒.

LYNMOUTH, Devon, **51°14'·16N 03°49'·79W**. AC 1160,1165. HW–0515 on Dover. See 9.11.23. Tiny hbr, dries approx 5m; access HW±1, but not with particularly low Nps, but only in settled offshore weather. Appr from Sand Ridge SHM buoy, 1·6M W of Foreland Pt and 9ca N of hbr ent. The narrow appr chan between drying boulder ledges is marked by 7 unlit posts. After first 2 posts keep 10m away from next SH post then next 2PH posts keep to middle of ent. Hbr ent is between piers, 2FR/FG lts, on W side of river course. Berth on E pier, which covers (beware) at MHWS. Resort facilities. Admin by Council ☎ 01598 752384.

WATERMOUTH, Devon, **51°13´·03N 04°04´·6W**. AC *1179*, 1165. HW –0525 on Dover; ML 4·9m; Duration 0625. Use 9.11.24. Good shelter in drying hbr, but heavy surge runs in strong NW winds. Access HW±3 at sp; only as far as inner bkwtr at np. Dir lt 153° Oc WRG 5s 1m, vis W151·5°-154·5°, W △ on structure, 1½ca inside ent on S shore. Bkwtr, covered at half tide, has Fl G 5s 2M. 9 Y Ⓥs with B handles £6.50. HM ☎ (01271) 865422 mob 07977 363179. Facilities: **Hbr** D (cans), FW (cans), CH, C (12 ton), Slip (launching £5.00); **YC** ☎ 865048, Bar. **Combe Martin** 1½M all facilities.

11

9.11.24 ILFRACOMBE

Devon **51°12'·65N 04°06'·65W**

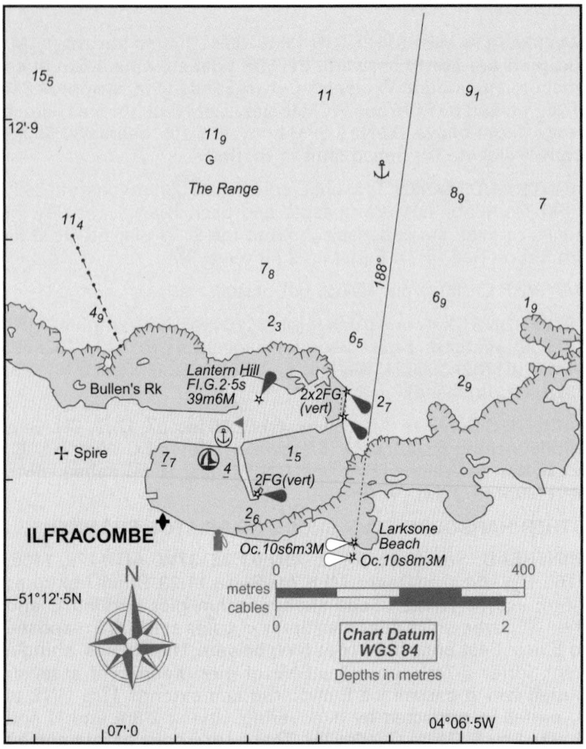

The Range
Bullen's Rk
Lantern Hill
Fl.G.2·5s
39m6M
2x2FG
(vert)
2FG(vert)
Spire
ILFRACOMBE
Oc.10s6m3M
Oc.10s8m3M
Larksone
Beach
188°
metres
cables
400
Chart Datum
WGS 84
Depths in metres
12'·9
51°12'·5N
07'·0
04°06'·5W

CHARTS AC *1179, 1165,* 1160; Imray C59; Stanfords 14; OS 180

TIDES –0525 Dover; ML 5·0; Duration 0625; Zone 0 (UT)

Standard Port MILFORD HAVEN (⟵)

Times				Height (metres)			
High Water		Low Water		MHWS	MHWN	MLWN	MLWS
0100	0700	0100	0700	7·0	5·2	2·5	0·7
1300	1900	1300	1900				
Differences ILFRACOMBE							
–0016	–0016	–0041	–0031	+2·3	+1·8	+0·6	+0·3
LUNDY ISLAND							
–0025	–0025	–0020	–0035	+1·0	+0·7	+0·2	0·0

SHELTER Good except in NE/E winds. SW gales can cause surge in hbrs, which dry. 8 Ⓥs in outer hbr, access HW±3. Or ⚓ clear of pier. Visitors AB on N wall of inner hbr, access HW±2 or dry out on chains off foot of N Pier.

NAVIGATION WPT 51°13´·23N 04°06´·67W, 180° to pier hd, 0·55M. From E, beware Copperas Rks (4M to E), and tiderips on Buggy Pit, 7ca NE of ent. On entry keep toward Pier to clear drying ledges and lobster keep-pots obstructing hbr ent on SE side.

LIGHTS AND MARKS Oc 10s Ldg Lts 188°. Lantern Hill lt, Fl G 2·5s 39m 6M, on small conspic chapel. Pier has 2 FG (vert).

R/T Call: *Ilfracombe Hbr* VHF Ch 12 16 (when manned).

TELEPHONE (Dial code 01271) HM 862108 mob 07775 532606; MRCC (01792) 366534; Marinecall 09066 526243; Police 08705 777444; Dr 863119.

FACILITIES **Hbr** AB and Ⓥs £1.02, M, D (S Quay), FW, CH, Slip(launching £10.50/week), ME, El, ⚒; **Ilfracombe YC** ☎ 863969, M, Ⓢ, Bar, C (35 ton, as arranged) **Town** EC Thurs, 🛒, R, Bar, ✉, Ⓑ, bus to Barnstaple (⇌), ✈ (Exeter).

9.11.25 RIVERS TAW & TORRIDGE

Devon **51°04'·37N 04°12'·88W**

CHARTS AC *1179, 1164, 1160*; Imray C58; Stanfords 14; OS 180

TIDES –0525 (Appledore) Dover; ML 3·6; Duration 0600; Zone 0 (UT)

Standard Port MILFORD HAVEN (⟵)

Times				Height (metres)			
High Water		Low Water		MHWS	MHWN	MLWN	MLWS
0100	0700	0100	0700	7·0	5·2	2·5	0·7
1300	1900	1300	1900				
Differences APPLEDORE							
–0020	–0025	+0015	–0045	+0·5	0·0	–0·9	–0·5
YELLAND MARSH (R Taw)							
–0010	–0015	+0100	–0015	+0·1	–0·4	–1·2	–0·6
FREMINGTON (R Taw)							
–0010	–0015	+0030	–0030	–1·1	–1·8	–2·2	–0·5
BARNSTAPLE (R Taw)							
0000	–0015	–0155	–0245	–2·9	–3·8	–2·2	–0·4
BIDEFORD (R Torridge)							
–0020	–0025	0000	0000	–1·1	–1·6	–2·5	–0·7
CLOVELLY							
–0030	–0030	–0020	–0040	+1·3	+1·1	+0·2	+0·2

SHELTER Very well protected, but ent is dangerous in strong on-shore winds and/or swell. Yachts can ⚓ or pick up RNLI buoy (please donate to RNLI, Boathouse ☎ 473969) or Appledore Shipbuilders buoy (☎ 473281 ℻ 462500) in Appledore Pool, N of Skern Pt where sp stream can reach 5kn. Bideford quay dries to soft mud; used by coasters.

NAVIGATION WPT 51°05´·43N 04°16´·11W, 118° to Bar, 0·9M. Bar and sands constantly shift; buoys are moved occasionally to comply. For advice on bar contact Pilot Ch 12 or Swansea CG. Least depths over bar 0·1 and 0·4m. Estuary dries and access is only feasible from HW–2 to HW. Night entry not advised for strangers. Once tide is ebbing, breakers quickly form between Bar SHM buoy and Middle Ridge SHM buoy. Hold the ldg line 118° only up to Outer Pulley where chan deviates stbd toward Pulley buoy and Grey Sand Hill, thence to Appledore Pool. 2M passage to Bideford is not difficult. Barnstaple (7M): seek local advice or take pilot.

LIGHTS AND MARKS Entry: Bideford fairway buoy L Fl 10s, Middle Ridge SHM Fl G 5s, Outer Pulley SHM Fl G 2·5s, Pulley SHM Fl G 10s. Crow Pt and Ldg lts as chartlet. Ldg marks are W trs, lit H24. R Torridge: Lt QY at E end of Bideford bridge shows preferred chan; then SHM bn, QG, on W bank.

R/T *2 Rivers Port/Pilots* VHF Ch 12 16 (From HW–2).

TELEPHONE Appledore/Bideford: Code 01237. Appledore HM 474569; Pilot 477928; Bideford HM 428816, mob 07977 287404, ℻ 478849; Dr 474994. Instow/Barnstaple: Dial code 01271. HM via Amenities Officer 388327; Dr 372672. Common Nos: MRCC (01792) 366534; Marinecall 09066 526243; Police 08705 777444.

FACILITIES
APPLEDORE: no AB - contact HM; slips at town quay. **Services:** CH, D, El, Ⓔ, BY, C (70 tons), Slip, ME, ⚒.
BIDEFORD: AB on new Town Quay, FW, CH, 🛒, R, Gas, Bar. Ferry to Lundy Is. HM ☎ 07977 287404.
INSTOW: **North Devon YC**, ☎ 860367, FW, Slip, R, Bar; **Services:** AB and a few moorings, £5 via Instow Marine ☎ 861081, CH, D, ME, M, Ⓔ, C (4 ton). **Town** R, FW, Bar.
BARNSTAPLE: AB (free for short stay, see HM), 🛒, Bar, Gas. FW: limited facilities; P & D: small quantities in cans. Bulk D (min 500 ltrs/110 galls) by bowser, see HM.
Towns: EC Barnstaple & Bideford = Wed; ✉ (all four), Ⓑ (Barnstaple, Bideford), ⇌ (Barnstaple, ✈ (Exeter).

CLOVELLY, Devon, **51°00'·18N 04°23'·77W**. AC *1164*. Tides see above. HW –0524 on Dover. Tiny drying hbr, 5M E of Hartland Pt, is sheltered from S/SW winds; useful to await the tide into Bideford or around Hartland Pt. Some AB (max LOA 12m) £5 on pier, access only near HW; or ⚓ off in 5m. Lt Fl G 5s 5m 5M on hbr wall. HM ☎ (01237) 431761. Facilities: Slip, FW, ✉, limited 🛒, P, D.

RIVERS TAW & TORRIDGE *continued*

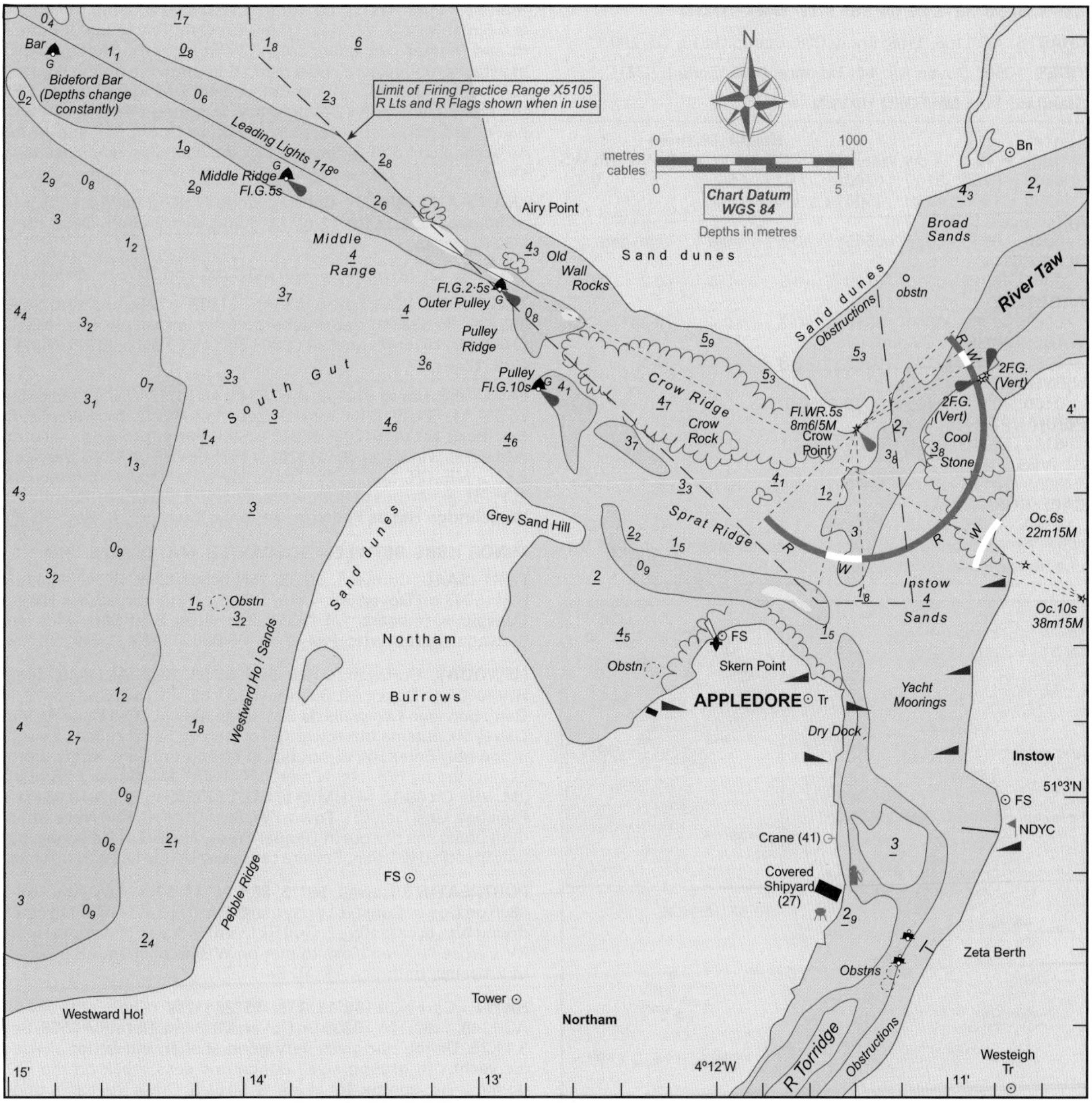
Bar
Bideford Bar
(Depths change constantly)
Limit of Firing Practice Range X5105
R Lts and R Flags shown when in use
Leading Lights 118°
Middle Ridge
Fl.G.5s
Middle
Range
Fl.G.2·5s
Outer Pulley
Pulley Ridge
Pulley
Fl.G.10s
South Gut
Old Wall Rocks
Airy Point
Sand dunes
Chart Datum
WGS 84
Depths in metres
metres
cables
Broad Sands
River Taw
Obstructions
obstn
Crow Ridge
Crow Rock
Fl.WR.5s
8m6/5M
Crow Point
2F.G.
(Vert)
Cool Stone
Oc.6s
22m15M
Oc.10s
38m15M
Sprat Ridge
Grey Sand Hill
Instow Sands
Northam Burrows
Obstn
FS
Skern Point
APPLEDORE
Tr
Yacht Moorings
Dry Dock
Instow
51°3'N
NDYC
Westward Ho! Sands
Crane (41)
Covered Shipyard (27)
Zeta Berth
Obstns
Pebble Ridge
Tower
Westward Ho!
Northam
R Torridge
Obstructions
Westeigh Tr
4°12'W
15'
14'
13'
11'
4'
Bn

ISLAND IN BRISTOL CHANNEL, 10M NNW of Hartland Pt

LUNDY ISLAND, Devon, **51°09´·83N 04°39´·27W**. AC *1179, 1164*. HW –0530 on Dover; ML 4·3m; Duration 0605. See 9.11.24 ☎ 01237 470074. Beware bad tide races, esp on E-going flood, off the N and SE tips of the island; and to the SW on the W-going ebb. A violent race forms over Stanley Bank 3M NE of the N tip. Shelter good in lee of island's high ground (145m). In SSW to NW winds, usual ⚓ is close inshore to NW of SE Pt and Rat Island, clear of ferry. In N'lies ⚓ in The Rattles, small bay on S side. In E'lies Jenny's Cove is safe if no W'ly swell. Lts: NW Pt, Fl 15s 48m 17M, vis 009°-285°, W ○ tr. On SE Pt, Fl 5s 53m 15M, vis 170°-073°, W ○ tr, horn 25s. Two Historic Wrecks (see 9.0.3h) lie on the E side of island, at 51°11'N 04°39'·4W, and 4ca further E. Facilities: Landing by the ⚓ off SE end of island or using N side of jetty to disembark passengers only, boats may not remain alongside; £3.50, £10 season per head landing fee. The waters around Lundy are a Marine Nature Reserve. **Lundy Co**: Gas, Bar.

MINOR HARBOURS ON THE NW COAST OF CORNWALL

BUDE, Cornwall, **50°49´·93N 04°33´·37W**. AC 1156. HW–0540 on Dover. Duration 0605. See 9.11.26. Limited shelter in drying hbr, access HW±2 in daylight, quiet weather, no swell conditions but sea-lock gives access to canal basin with 2m. Conspic W radar dish aerials 3·3M N of hbr. Outer ldg marks 075°, front W spar with Y ◊ topmark, rear W flagstaff; hold this line until inner ldg marks in line at 131°, front W pile, rear W spar, both with Y △ topmarks. There are no lts. VHF Ch 16 12 (when vessel expected). Advise HM of ETA with 24H notice ☎ (01288) 353111; FW on quay; **Town** (½M); Ⓑ, Bar, ✉, R, 🛒, Gas.

BOSCASTLE, Cornwall, **50°41'·48N 04°42·17W**. AC 1156. HW –0543 on Dover; see 9.11.26. A tiny, picturesque hbr, almost a land-locked cleft in the cliffs. Access HW±2, but not in onshore winds when swell causes surge inside. An E'ly appr, S of Meachard Rk (37m high, 2ca NW of hbr), is best. 2 short bkwtrs at ent; moor bows-on to drying S quay. HM ☎ 01840 250453.

9.11.26 PADSTOW

Cornwall **50°32'·51N 04°56'·17W**

CHARTS AC 1156, 1168; Imray C58; Stanfords 13; OS 200

TIDES –0550 Dover; ML 4·0; Duration 0600; Zone 0 (UT)

Standard Port MILFORD HAVEN (⟵)

Times				Height (metres)			
High Water		Low Water		MHWS	MHWN	MLWN	MLWS
0100	0700	0100	0700	7·0	5·2	2·5	0·7
1300	1900	1300	1900				
Differences BUDE							
–0040	–0040	–0035	–0045	+0·7	+0·6	No data	
BOSCASTLE							
–0045	–0010	–0110	–0100	+0·3	+0·4	+0·2	+0·2
PADSTOW							
–0055	–0050	–0040	–0050	+0·3	+0·4	+0·1	+0·1
WADEBRIDGE (R Camel)							
–0052	–0052	+0235	+0245	–3·8	–3·8	–2·5	–0·4
NEWQUAY							
–0100	–0110	–0105	–0050	0·0	+0·1	0·0	–0·1
PERRANPORTH							
–0100	–0110	–0110	–0050	–0·1	0·0	0·0	+0·1
ST IVES							
–0050	–0115	–0105	–0040	–0·4	–0·3	–0·1	+0·1
CAPE CORNWALL							
–0130	–0145	–0120	–0120	–1·0	–0·9	–0·5	–0·1

Note: At Wadebridge LW time differences give the start of the rise, following a LW stand of about 5 hours.

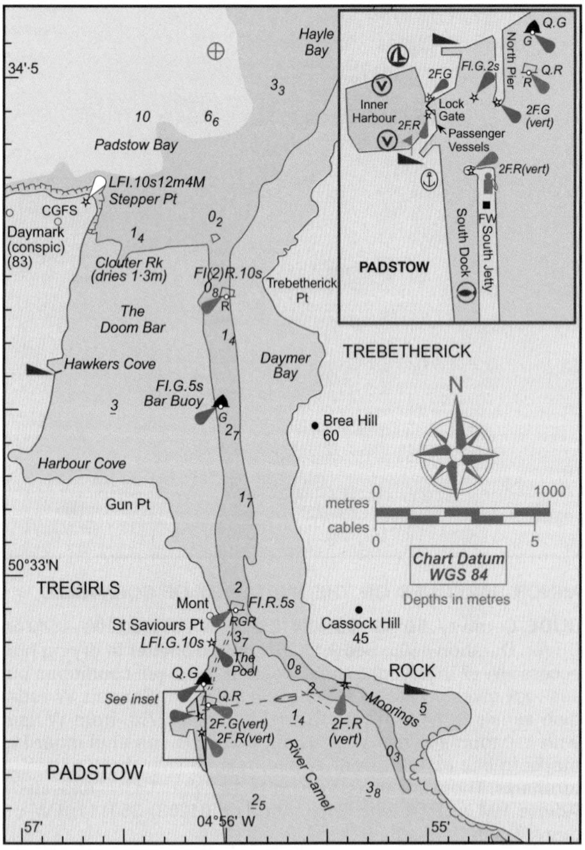
Hayle Bay
Padstow Bay
LFl.10s12m4M
Stepper Pt
CGFS
Daymark (conspic) (83)
Clouter Rk (dries 1·3m)
Fl(2)R.10s
Trebetherick Pt
The Doom Bar
Hawkers Cove
Fl.G.5s Bar Buoy
Daymer Bay
TREBETHERICK
Brea Hill 60
Harbour Cove
Gun Pt
metres
cables
Chart Datum WGS 84
Depths in metres
50°33'N
TREGIRLS
Mont
Fl.R.5s
St Saviours Pt
LFl.G.10s
The Pool
Cassock Hill 45
ROCK
Moorings
Q.G
Q.R
See inset
2F.G(vert)
2F.R(vert)
2F.R (vert)
River Camel
PADSTOW
04°56' W
57'
55'
34'·5
Inner Harbour
Lock Gate
Passenger Vessels
North Pier
South Dock
South Jetty
FW
Fl.G.2s
2F.G
2F.R
2F.G (vert)
2F.R(vert)

SHELTER Good in inner hbr 3m+, access via tidal gate HW±2 sp, ±1½ nps via tidal gate. If too late for gate, moor in the Pool or ⚓ close N in 1·5m LWS. Drying moorings available for smaller craft. Good AB at Wadebridge 4.5M up R Camel.

NAVIGATION WPT 50°34'·56N 04°56'·07W, 044° to Stepper Pt, 0·6M. From SW, beware Quies Rks, Gulland Rk, The Hen, Gurley Rk, Chimney Rks and a wreck 5ca W of Stepper Pt (all off the chartlet). From N, keep well off Newland Island and its offlying reef. Best appr HW–2½, do not try LW±1½; least depth on the bar is 0·5m at MLWS. Waiting ⚓s in Port Quin Bay in lee of Rumps Pt and Mother Ivey's Bay 3M WSW Stepper Pt. Shifting banks in estuary require care and a rising tide (ditto the drying R Camel to Wadebridge, 4M). If in doubt, consult HM. Identify/align 180° the first 2 chan buoys before entry. In strong onshore winds or heavy ground swell, seas can break on Doom Bar and in the adjacent chan. S of St Saviour's Pt the chan lies very close to W shore.

LIGHTS AND MARKS Conspic stone tr (83m daymark), 3ca W of Stepper Pt, L Fl 10s 12m 4M, marks river mouth. Outer hbr 2 FG/FR (vert).

R/T VHF Ch 12 16 (Mon-Fri 0800–1700 and HW±2). Water taxi.

TELEPHONE (Dial codes 01841; 01208 = Wadebridge) HM 532239 Fax 533346 padstowharbour@compuserve.com; MRCC (01326) 317575; Marinecall 09068 500 458; Police 08705 777444; Dr 532346.

FACILITIES Hbr ☎ 532239, Fax 533346, AB £1.20, ♿, Slip(launching £5.00), M, FW, El, C (60 ton), D, Gas, Gaz, ME, launderette, showers, 🛒, R, Bar; **Rock SC** ☎ (01208) 862431, Slip; **Ferry 1** to Rock, also on request as water taxi, ☎ (01326) 317575 or VHF Ch 12 16. **Services:** BY, C, ME, CH, Slip, L, ⚒. **Town** www.padstow-harbour.co.uk; launderette, P, ✉, Ⓑ, ⇌ (bus to Bodmin Parkway), ✈ (Newquay/Plymouth). **Wadebridge** HM as Padstow; AB only; **Town** 🛒, R, Bar, ✉, Ⓑ.

MINOR HBRS BETWEEN BOSCASTLE AND LAND'S END

PORT ISAAC, Cornwall, **50°35'·75N 04°49'·57W.** AC 1156, 1168. HW –0548 on Dover; ML 4·1m. Small drying hbr, access HW±2. Conspic ✠ tr bears 171°/1·3M. Rks close E of 50m wide ent between short bkwtrs. HM ☎ 01208 880607; 🛒, R, Bar, ✉, LB.

NEWQUAY, Cornwall, **50°25'·06N 05°05'·19W.** AC 1149, 1168. HW –0604 on Dover; ML 3·7m; see 9.11.26. Ent to drying hbr ('The Gap') between two walls, is 23m wide. Beware Old Dane Rk and Listrey Rk outside hbr towards Towan Hd. Swell causes a surge in the hbr. Enter HW±2 but not in strong onshore winds. Berth as directed by HM. Lts: N pier 2 FG (vert) 2M; S pier 2 FR (vert) 2M. VHF Ch 08 16 14. HM ☎ (01637) 872809 mob 07813 064412. Facilities: Gas, Gaz, CH. **Town**; FW, Slip, D, 🛒, R, Bar. Note: Shoal draft boats can dry out in Gannel Creek, close S of Newquay, but only in settled weather. Beware causeway bridge half way up creek.

PORTREATH, Cornwall, **50°15'·88N 05°17'·57W.** AC 1149. HW –0600 on Dover. Conspic W daymark (38m) at E side of ent to small drying hbr, access HW±2. Gull Rk (23m) is 3ca W of ent and Horse Rk is close N. Keep close to pier on W side of chan. AB in either of 2 basins, both dry. 🛒, R, Bar, ✉.

HAYLE, Cornwall, **50°11'·77N 05°26'·17W** (Chan ent). AC 1149, 1168. HW –0605 on Dover; ML 3·6m; Duration 0555. See 9.11.26. Drying hbr gives very good shelter, but is not advised for yachts. In ground swell dangerous seas break on the bar, drying 2·7m; approx 4m at ent @ MHWS. Cross the bar in good weather HW±1. Charted aids do not necessarily indicate best water. Ldg marks/lts 180°: both W □ R horiz band, ☆ FW 17/23m 4M. PHM buoy, QR is about 8ca N of the front ldg lt. Training wall on W side of ent chan is marked by 4 perches (FG lts). The hbr is divided by long central island (about 700m long, with lt bn QG at NW end) which should be left to stbd. Follow the SE arm of hbr to Hayle; the S arm leads to Lelant Quay. HM ☎ (01736) 754043, AB £5. Facilities: EC Thurs; Ⓑ, Bar, FW (can), ⇌, R, 🛒, Gas, P & D (cans).

ST IVES, Cornwall, **50°12'·79N 05°28'·67W**. AC 1149, 1168. HW –0610 on Dover; ML 3·6m; Duration 0555. See 9.11.26. Drying hbr with about 4·5m @ MHWS. Good shelter except in on-shore winds when heavy swell works in. Ⓥs and ⚓ in 3m between the hbr and Porthminster Pt to S and drying Or Ⓥs in hbr. From the NW beware Hoe Rk off St Ives Hd, and from SE The Carracks. Keep E of SHM buoy about 1½ ca ENE of E pier. Lts: E pier hd 2 FG (vert) 8m 5M. W pier hd 2 FR (vert) 5m 3M. VHF Ch 12 16 (occas). HM ☎ (01736) 795018. Facilities: Ⓥs £12.13; **E Pier** FW. **Town** EC Thurs; Gas, Gaz, Ⓑ, launderette, Bar, ✉, R, 🛒, ⇌.

Area 12

South Ireland
Malahide clockwise to Liscannor Bay

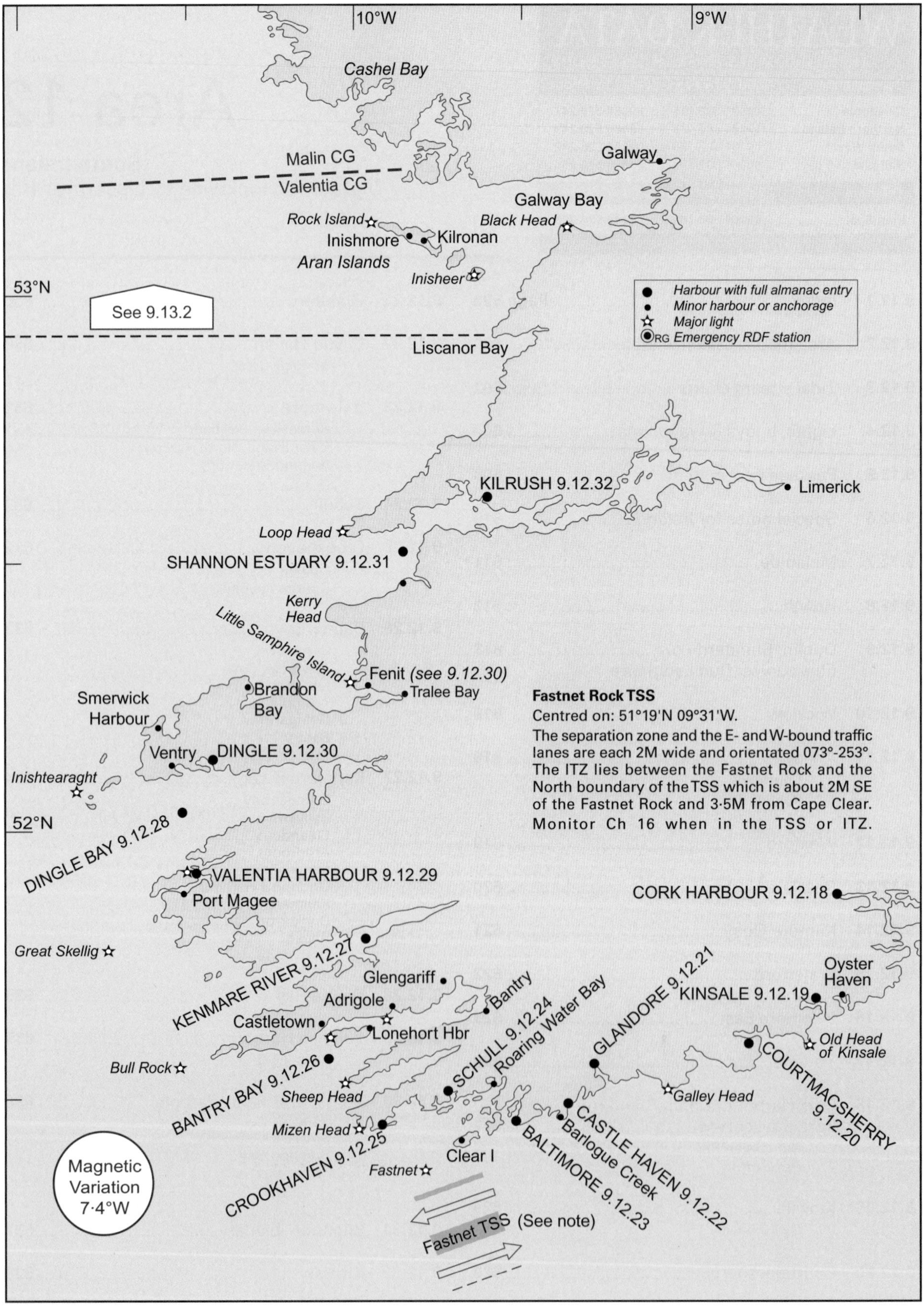
10°W
9°W
Cashel Bay
Malin CG
Valentia CG
Galway
Galway Bay
Rock Island
Black Head
Inishmore
Kilronan
Aran Islands
Inisheer
53°N
See 9.13.2
Liscanor Bay
Harbour with full almanac entry
Minor harbour or anchorage
Major light
RG Emergency RDF station
KILRUSH 9.12.32
Limerick
Loop Head
SHANNON ESTUARY 9.12.31
Kerry Head
Little Samphire Island
Fenit (see 9.12.30)
Tralee Bay
Smerwick Harbour
Brandon Bay
Ventry
DINGLE 9.12.30
Inishtearaght
52°N
DINGLE BAY 9.12.28
VALENTIA HARBOUR 9.12.29
Port Magee
Fastnet Rock TSS
Centred on: 51°19'N 09°31'W.
The separation zone and the E- and W-bound traffic lanes are each 2M wide and orientated 073°-253°. The ITZ lies between the Fastnet Rock and the North boundary of the TSS which is about 2M SE of the Fastnet Rock and 3·5M from Cape Clear. Monitor Ch 16 when in the TSS or ITZ.
CORK HARBOUR 9.12.18
Great Skellig
KENMARE RIVER 9.12.27
Glengariff
Adrigole
Bantry
Castletown
Lonehort Hbr
SCHULL 9.12.24
Roaring Water Bay
GLANDORE 9.12.21
KINSALE 9.12.19
Oyster Haven
Old Head of Kinsale
COURTMACSHERRY 9.12.20
Bull Rock
BANTRY BAY 9.12.26
Sheep Head
Galley Head
Mizen Head
CASTLE HAVEN 9.12.22
Barlogue Creek
BALTIMORE 9.12.23
Clear I
CROOKHAVEN 9.12.25
Fastnet
Magnetic Variation 7·4°W
Fastnet TSS (See note)

		1	2	3	4	5	6	7	8	9	10	11	12	13	14	15	16	17	18	19	20
1.	***Carlingford Lough***	**1**																			
2.	Howth	39	**2**																		
3.	**Dun Laoghaire**	48	8	**3**																	
4.	**Wicklow**	63	25	21	**4**																
5.	**Arklow**	75	37	36	15	**5**															
6.	**Tuskar Rock**	113	73	70	52	37	**6**														
7.	**Rosslare**	108	70	66	47	34	8	**7**													
8.	**Dunmore East**	139	101	102	84	69	32	32	**8**												
9.	**Youghal**	172	134	133	115	100	63	65	34	**9**											
10.	**Crosshaven**	192	154	155	137	122	85	85	59	25	**10**										
11.	Kinsale	202	164	168	150	135	98	95	69	35	17	**11**									
12.	**Baltimore**	239	201	196	177	164	128	132	102	70	54	42	**12**								
13.	**Fastnet Rock**	250	212	207	189	174	137	144	112	78	60	49	10	**13**							
14.	Bantry	281	243	241	223	208	171	174	146	112	94	83	42	34	**14**						
15.	Darrynane	283	245	240	221	208	172	176	146	114	98	86	44	39	38	**15**					
16.	Valentia	295	257	252	242	227	184	188	165	131	113	102	56	48	55	16	**16**				
17.	Dingle	308	270	265	246	233	197	201	171	139	123	111	69	61	63	29	13	**17**			
18.	Kilrush	361	323	318	299	286	250	254	224	192	176	164	122	114	116	82	66	64	**18**		
19.	*Galway*	366	362	357	339	324	287	291	262	228	210	199	159	150	155	119	103	101	76	**19**	
20.	*Slyne Head*	317	351	346	328	313	276	283	251	217	199	188	153	139	144	113	97	95	75	49	**20**

DISTANCE TABLE

Approximate distances in nautical miles are by the most direct route, whilst avoiding dangers and allowing for Traffic Separation Schemes. Places in *italics* are in adjoining areas; places in **bold** are in 9.0.7, Distances across the Irish Sea.

9.12.2

South Ireland

Malahide clockwise to Liscanor Bay

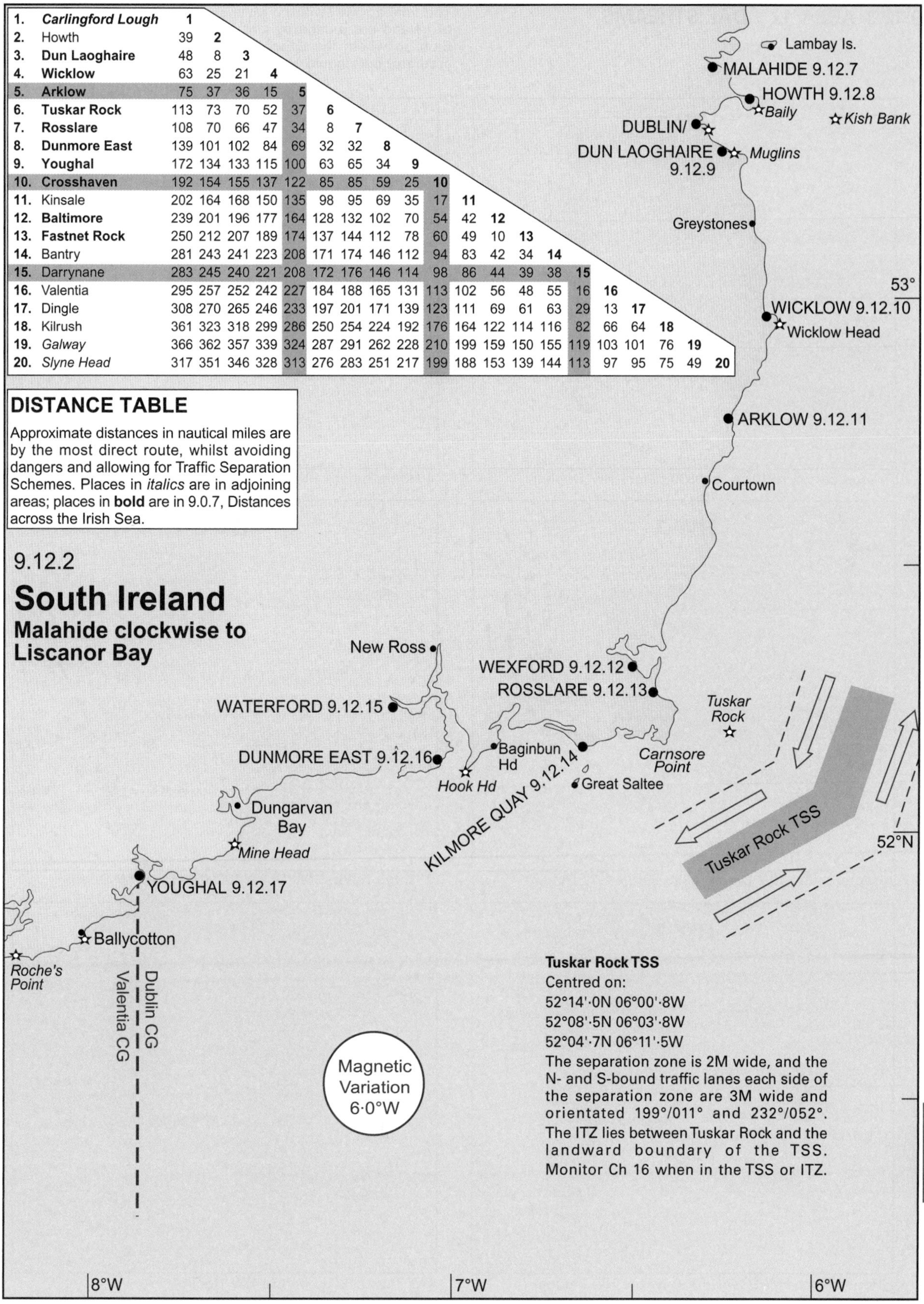

Lambay Is.
MALAHIDE 9.12.7
HOWTH 9.12.8
Baily
Kish Bank
DUBLIN/
DUN LAOGHAIRE 9.12.9
Muglins
Greystones
53°
WICKLOW 9.12.10
Wicklow Head
ARKLOW 9.12.11
Courtown
New Ross
WEXFORD 9.12.12
ROSSLARE 9.12.13
WATERFORD 9.12.15
Tuskar Rock
DUNMORE EAST 9.12.16
Baginbun Hd
Carnsore Point
Hook Hd
Great Saltee
KILMORE QUAY 9.12.14
Dungarvan Bay
Tuskar Rock TSS
Mine Head
52°N
YOUGHAL 9.12.17
Ballycotton
Roche's Point
Dublin CG
Valentia CG
Magnetic Variation 6·0°W
8°W
7°W
6°W

Tuskar Rock TSS

Centred on:
52°14'·0N 06°00'·8W
52°08'·5N 06°03'·8W
52°04'·7N 06°11'·5W

The separation zone is 2M wide, and the N- and S-bound traffic lanes each side of the separation zone are 3M wide and orientated 199°/011° and 232°/052°. The ITZ lies between Tuskar Rock and the landward boundary of the TSS. Monitor Ch 16 when in the TSS or ITZ.

9.12.3 AREA 12 TIDAL STREAMS

The tidal arrows (with no rates shown) off the S and W coasts of Ireland are printed by kind permission of the Irish Cruising Club, to whom the Editor is indebted. They have been found accurate, but should be used with caution.

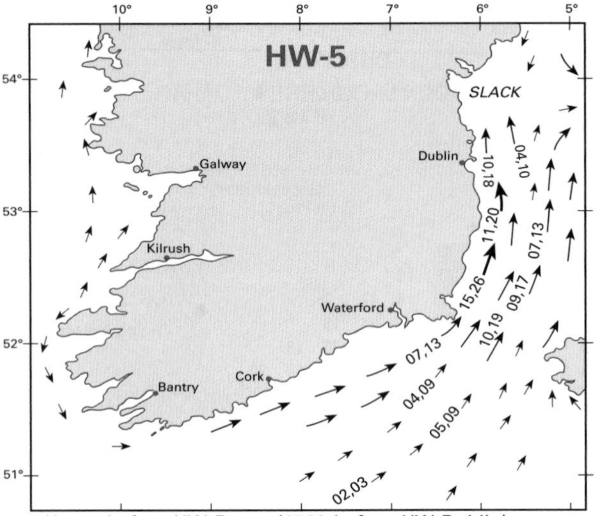
HW-5
SLACK
Galway
Dublin
Kilrush
Waterford
Cork
Bantry
04,10
10,18
11,20
07,13
15,26
09,17
10,19
07,13
04,09
05,09
02,03
5 Hours before HW Dover (0530 before HW Dublin)

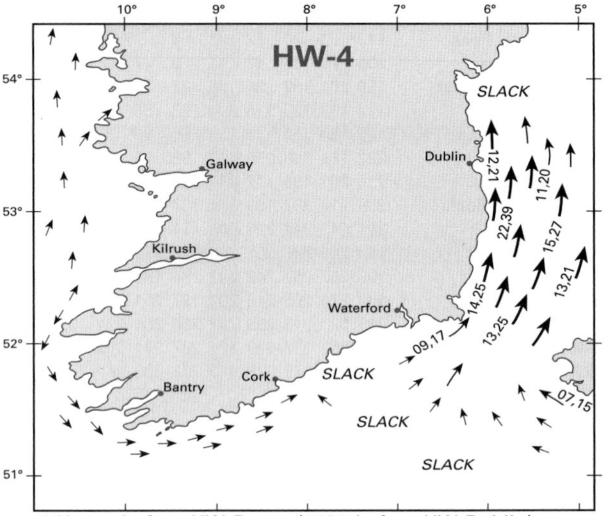
HW-4
SLACK
Galway
Dublin
Kilrush
Waterford
Cork
Bantry
12,21
11,20
22,39
15,27
14,25
13,21
13,25
09,17
07,15
4 Hours before HW Dover (0430 before HW Dublin)

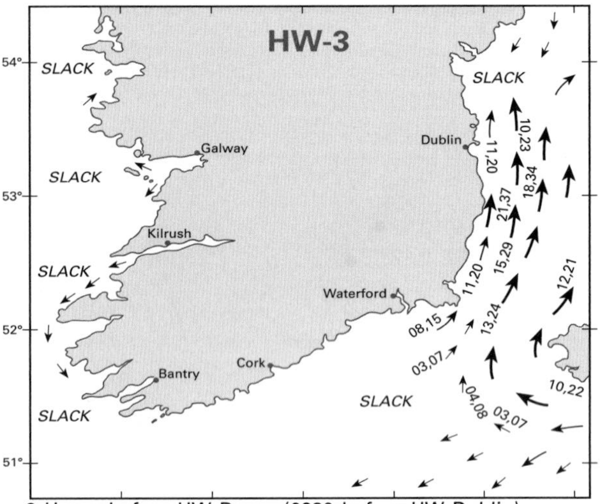
HW-3
SLACK
Galway
Dublin
Kilrush
Waterford
Cork
Bantry
10,23
11,20
18,34
21,37
15,29
11,20
12,21
08,15
13,24
03,07
10,22
04,08
03,07
3 Hours before HW Dover (0330 before HW Dublin)

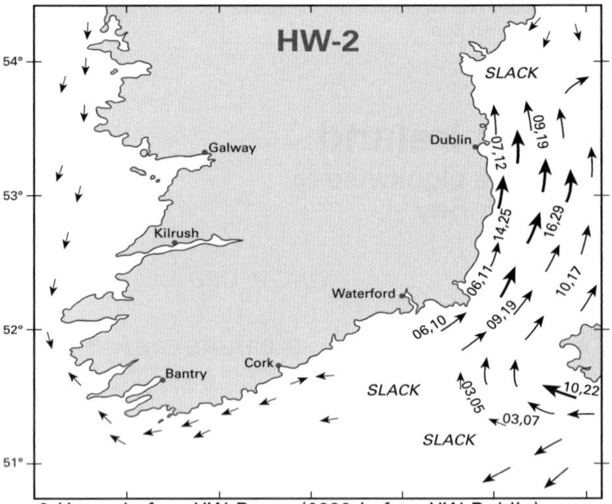
HW-2
SLACK
Galway
Dublin
Kilrush
Waterford
Cork
Bantry
09,19
07,12
16,29
14,25
06,11
10,17
06,10
09,19
03,05
10,22
03,07
2 Hours before HW Dover (0230 before HW Dublin)

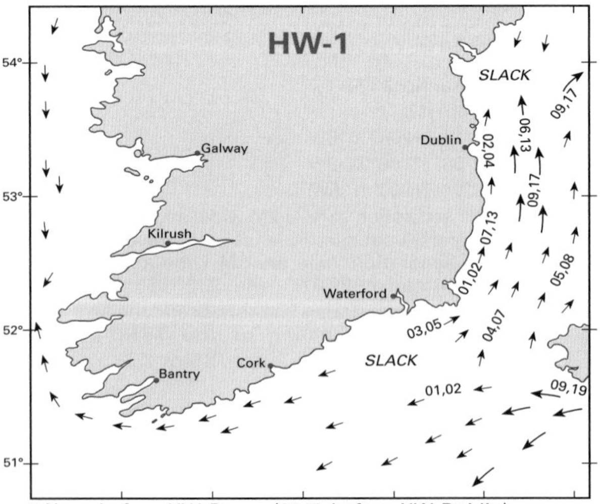
HW-1
SLACK
Galway
Dublin
Kilrush
Waterford
Cork
Bantry
09,17
06,13
02,04
09,17
07,13
05,08
01,02
03,05
04,07
01,02
09,19
1 Hour before HW Dover (0130 before HW Dublin)

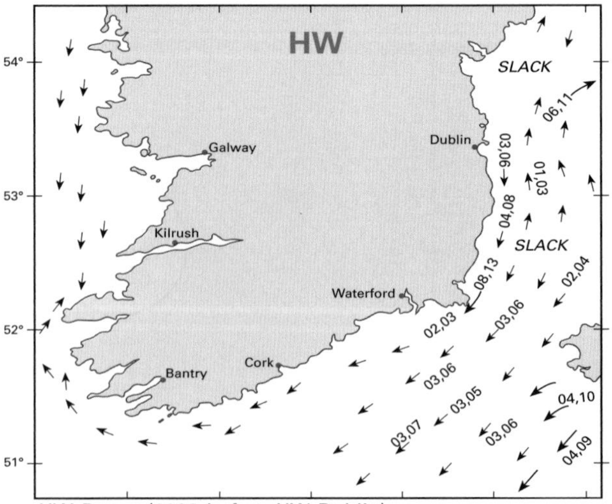
HW
SLACK
Galway
Dublin
Kilrush
Waterford
Cork
Bantry
06,11
03,06
01,03
04,08
08,13
02,04
02,03
03,06
03,06
03,05
04,10
03,07
03,06
04,09
HW Dover (0030 before HW Dublin)

Northward 9.13.3 South Irish Sea 9.11.3

The tidal arrows (with no rates shown) off the S and W coasts of Ireland are printed by kind permission of the Irish Cruising Club, to whom the Editor is indebted. They have been found accurate, but should be used with caution.

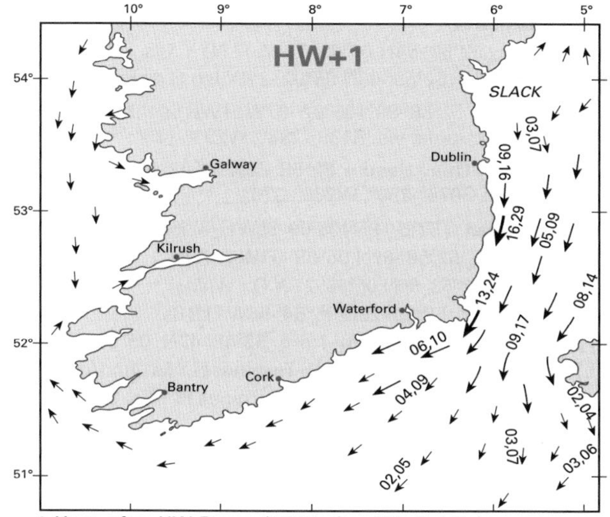
HW+1
SLACK
Dublin
Galway
Kilrush
Waterford
Cork
Bantry
03,07
09,16
16,29
05,09
13,24
08,14
06,10
09,17
04,09
02,04
03,07
03,06
02,05

1 Hour after HW Dover (0030 after HW Dublin)

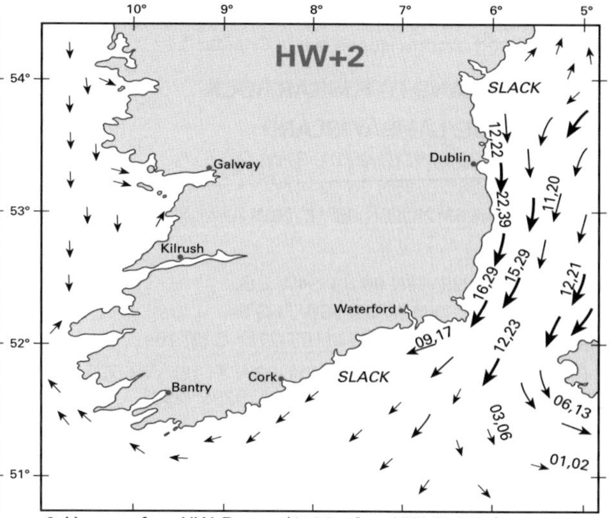
HW+2
SLACK
Dublin
Galway
Kilrush
Waterford
Cork
Bantry
12,22
22,39
11,20
15,29
16,29
12,21
09,17
12,23
SLACK
06,13
03,06
01,02

2 Hours after HW Dover (0130 after HW Dublin)

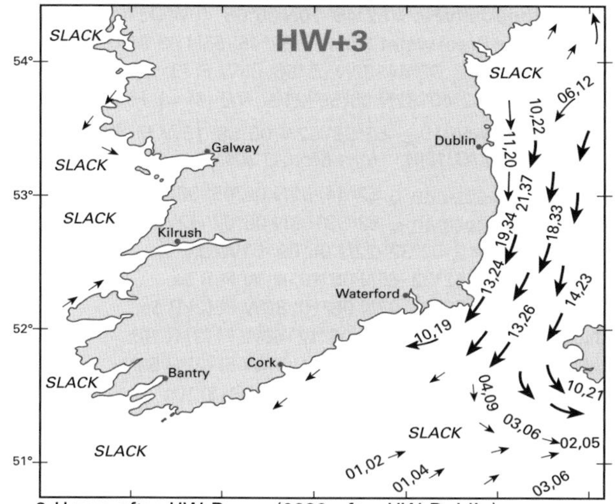
HW+3
SLACK
SLACK
SLACK
SLACK
SLACK
Dublin
Galway
Kilrush
Waterford
Cork
Bantry
06,12
10,22
11,20
21,37
19,34
18,33
13,24
14,23
10,19
13,26
10,21
04,09
03,06
02,05
SLACK
SLACK
01,02
01,04
03,06

3 Hours after HW Dover (0230 after HW Dublin)

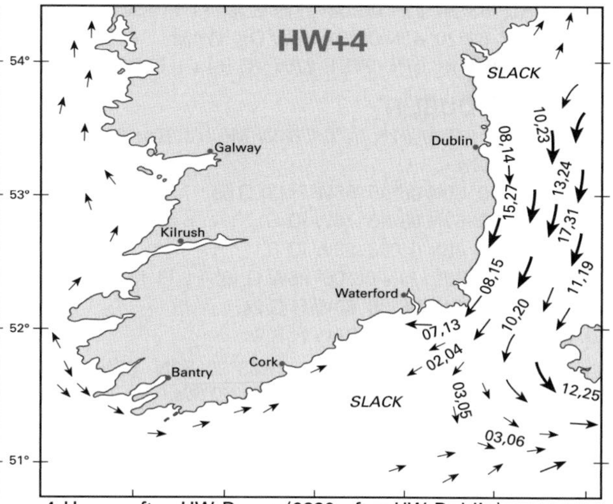
HW+4
SLACK
Dublin
Galway
Kilrush
Waterford
Cork
Bantry
10,23
08,14
13,24
15,27
17,31
08,15
11,19
10,20
07,13
02,04
12,25
SLACK
03,05
03,06

4 Hours after HW Dover (0330 after HW Dublin)

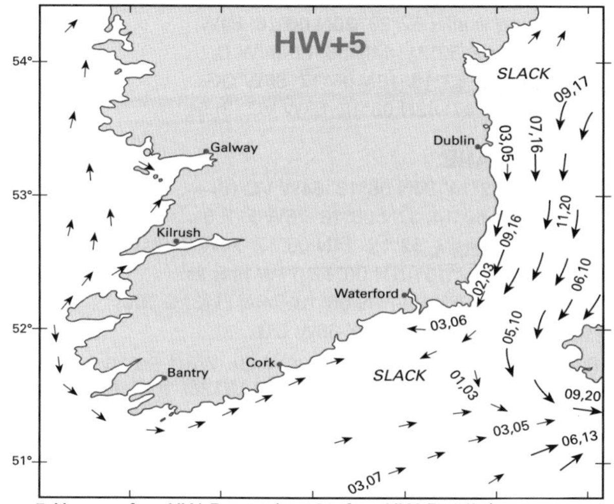
HW+5
SLACK
Dublin
Galway
Kilrush
Waterford
Cork
Bantry
09,17
07,16
03,05
11,20
09,16
06,10
02,03
03,06
05,10
SLACK
01,03
09,20
03,05
06,13
03,07

5 Hours after HW Dover (0430 after HW Dublin)

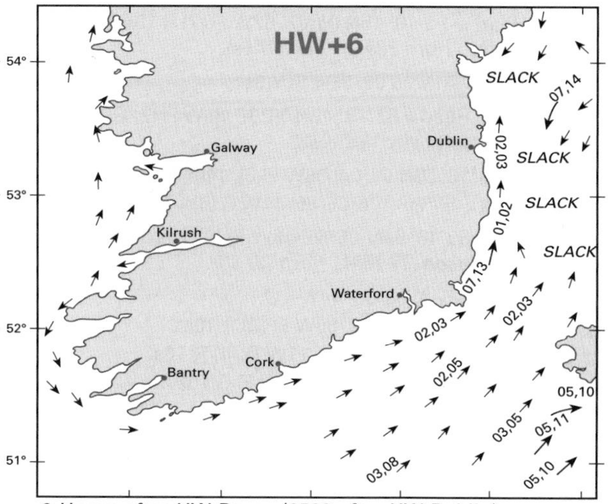
HW+6
SLACK
Dublin
Galway
Kilrush
Waterford
Cork
Bantry
07,14
02,03
SLACK
SLACK
01,02
SLACK
07,13
02,03
02,03
02,05
05,10
03,05
05,11
03,08
05,10

6 Hours after HW Dover (0530 after HW Dublin)

12

PLOT WAYPOINTS ON YOUR CHART BEFORE USING THEM

9.12.4 LIGHTS, BUOYS AND WAYPOINTS

Blue print = light with a nominal range of 15M or more. CAPITALS = place or feature. *CAPITAL ITALICS* = light-vessel, light float or Lanby. *Italics* = Fog signal. ***Bold italics*** = Racon. Useful waypoints are underlined. Abbreviations are in Chapter 1.

LAMBAY ISLAND TO TUSKAR ROCK

▶ MALAHIDE/LAMBAY ISLAND

Taylor Rks 53°30'·21N 06°01'·87W; Q.
Burren Rks 53°29'·35N 06°02'·47W.
Dublin Airport 53°25'·28N 06°16'·20W Aero Al Fl WG 4s 95m.

▶ HOWTH

S Rowan 53°23'·78N 06°03'·94W QG.
Howth 53°23'·74N 06°03'·59W Fl G 5s.
Rowan Rocks 53°23'·88N 06°03'·27W Q (3) 10s.

E Pier Head ☆ 53°23'·66N 06°04'·03W Fl (2) WR 7·5s 13m W12M, R9M; W twr; vis: W256°-295°, R295°-256°.

W Pier Ext Mole Head ☆ 53°23'·53N 06°04'·09W Fl G 3s 7m 6M.
Trawler Pier Head ☆ 53°23'·50N 06°04'·11W QR 7m 6M.

Baily ☆ 53°21'·70N 06°03'·14W Fl 15s 41m **26M**; twr.
Rosbeg E 53°21'·02N 06°03'·45W Q (3) 10s.
Rosbeg S 53°20'·22N 06°04'·17W Q (6) + L Fl 15s.
N Burford 53°20'·52N 06°01'·49W Q; *Whis.*
S Burford 53°18'·07N 06°01'·27W VQ (6) + L Fl 10s; *Whis.*

▶ PORT OF DUBLIN

Dublin Bay 53°19'·92N 06°04'·64W Mo (A) 10s; ***Racon (M) range unknown.***
No. 1 53°20'·30N 06°05'·56W Fl (3) G 5s.
No. 3 53°20'·57N 06°06'·76W IQ G.
No. 4 53°20'·48N 06°06'·93W IQ R.
Bar Obstn 53°20'·70N 06°06'·96W Q (6) + L Fl 15s.
No. 5 53°20'·64N 06°08'·60W Fl G 2s.
No. 6 53°20'·56N 06°08'·75W Fl R 2s.

Great S Wall Hd **Poolbeg** ☆ 53°20'·53N 06°09'·08W Oc (2) R 20s 20m **15M**; R ○ twr; *Horn (2) 60s.*

N Bull ☆ 53°20'·70N 06°08'·98W Fl (3) G 10s 15m 12M; G ○ twr.
No. 9 53°20'·68N 06°10'·16W Fl G 2s.
N Bank ☆ 53°20'·69N 06°10'·59W Oc G 8s 10m **16M**; G □ twr.

▶ DUN LAOGHAIRE

E Bkwtr Head ☆ 53°18'·15N 06°07'·62W Fl (2) R 10s 16m **17M**; twr, R lantern; *Horn 30s* (or *Bell (1) 6s*).

Outfall 53°18'·41N 06°08'·35W Fl Y 5s.

W Breakwater Head ☆ 53°18'·19N 06°07'·85W Fl (3) G 7·5s 11m 7M; twr, G lantern; vis: 188°-062°.

Muglins ☆ 53°16'·55N 06°04'·58W Fl 5s 14m 11M.
Bennett Bank 53°20'·17N 05°55'·11W Q (6) + L Fl 15s.

Kish Bank ☆ 53°18'·64N 05°55'·48W Fl (2) 20s 29m **22M**; W twr, R band; ***Racon (T) 15M***; *Horn (2) 30s.*

N Kish 53°18'·56N 05°56'·44W VQ.
E Kish 53°14'·35N 05°53'·56W Fl (2) R 10s.
E Codling 53°08'·54N 05°47'·11W Fl (4) R 10s.
W Codling 53°06'·97N 05°54'·51W Fl G 10s.
S Codling 53°04'·74N 05°49'·76W VQ (6) + L Fl 10s.
Greystones 53°08'·42N 06°02'·54W Fl Y 5s.
Mouldltch Bk 53°08'·42N 06°01'·22W Fl R 10s.
Breaches Shoal 53°05'·67N 05°59'·81W Fl (2) R 6s.
North India 53°03'·12N 05°53'·46W Q.
South India 53°00'·36N 05°53'·31W Q (6) + L Fl 15s.

CODLING LANBY 53°03'·02N 05°40'·76W Fl 4s 12m **15M**; tubular structure on By; ***Racon (G)10M***; *Horn 20s.*

▶ WICKLOW

Wicklow 52°59'·54N 06°01'·29W; Fl (4) Y 10s.
W Pier Head ☆ 52°59'·00N 06°02'·21W Iso G 4s 5m 6M.

E Pier Head ☆ 52°58'·99N 06°02'·07W Fl WR 5s 11m 6M; W twr, R base and cupola; vis: R136°-293°, W293°-136°.

West Packet Quay Head ☆ 52°58'·88N 06°02'·08W Fl WG 10s 5m 6M; vis: G076°-256°, W256°-076°.

Wicklow Head ☆ 52°57'·95N 05°59'·89W Fl (3) 15s 37m **23M**; W twr.
Horseshoe 52°56'·62N 05°59'·31W Fl R 3s.
N Arklow 52°53'·86N 05°55'·21W Q; *Whis.*
No. 2 Arklow 52°50'·22N 05°54'·56W Fl R 6s.
Arklow Bank Wind Farm from 52°48'·47N 05°56'·57W to 52°46'·47N 05°57'·11W, N and S Turbines Fl Y 5s 14m 10M + Fl W Aero lts. AIS transmitters. Other turbines Fl Y 5s. See 9.12.5.

▶ ARKLOW

S Pier Head ☆ 52°47'·61N 06°08'·22W Fl WR 6s 11m 13M; twr; vis: R shore-223°, W223°-350°; R350°-shore.

N Pier Head ☆ 52°47'·63N 06°08'·29W L Fl G 7s 7m 10M.
Roadstone Jetty Hd ☆ 52°46'·70N 06°08'·46W Oc R 10s 9m 9M.
Roadstone Breakwater Head ☆ 52°46'·65N 06°08'·23W QY.
No. 1 Arklow 52°44'·32N 05°56'·05W Fl (3) R 10s.
S Arklow 52°40'·82N 05°59'·21W VQ (6) + L Fl 10s.

ARKLOW LANBY 52°39'·52N 05°58'·16W Fl (2) 12s 12m **15M**; ***Racon (O)10M***; *Horn Mo (A) 30s.*

No. 2 Glassgorman 52°44'·52N 06°05'·36W Fl (4) R 10s.
No. 1 Glassgorman 52°39'·08N 06°07'·42W Fl (2) R 6s.
N Blackwater 52°32'·22N 06°09'·51W Q.
No. 6 Rusk 52°32'·65N 06°10'·41W Fl R 3s.
No. 4 Rusk 52°31'·07N 06°10'·86W Fl (2) R 5s.
No. 2 Rusk 52°28'·62N 06°12'·66W Fl (3) R 10s.
No. 1 Rusk 52°28'·52N 06°11'·76W Fl (2) G 5s.
E Blackwater 52°28'·02N 06°08'·06W Q (3) 10s.
W Blackwater 52°25'·87N 06°13'·56W Fl G 6s.
SE Blackwater 52°25'·64N 06°09'·66W Fl R 10s.
S Blackwater 52°22'·76N 06°12'·86W Q (6) + L Fl 15s; *Whis.*

▶ WEXFORD

N Training Wall 52°20'·20N 06°26'·84W.
North Long 52°21'·44N 06°17'·04W Q.
West Long 52°18'·18N 06°17'·96W QG.
Lucifer 52°17'·02N 06°12'·67W VQ (3) 5s.

▶ ROSSLARE

S Long 52°14'·84N 06°15'·64W VQ (6) + L Fl 10s; *Whis.*
Splaugh 52°14'·37N 06°16'·76W Fl R 6s.
South Holdens 52°15'·14N 06°17'·24W Fl (2) G 6s.
Calmines 52°15'·01N 06°17'·77W Fl R 2s.
W Holdens 52°15'·77N 06°18'·74W Fl (3) G 10s.
No. 3 52°15'·38N 06°20'·68W QG.

Pier Hd ☆ 52°15'·43N 06°20'·29W Oc WRG 5s 15m W13M, R10M, G10M; R twr; vis: G098°-188°, W188°-208°, R208°-246°, G246°-283°, W283°-286°, R286°-320°.

Ballygeary ☆ 52°15'·25N 06°20'·48W Oc WR 1·7s 7m 4M vis: Rshore-152°, W152°-200°, W(unintens)200°-205°.

Tuskar ☆ 52°12'·17N 06°12'·42W Q (2) 7·5s 33m **24M**; W twr; *Horn (4) 45s*, ***Racon (T) 18M.***

TUSKAR ROCK TO OLD HEAD OF KINSALE

S Rock ♦ 52°10'·80N 06°12'·84W Q (6) + L Fl 15s.
Fundale ▬ 52°10'·64N 06°20'·26W Fl (2) R 10s.
Barrels ♦ 52°08'·32N 06°22'·05W Q (3) 10s; *Whis.*

▶ CARNA

Pier Head ✧ 52°11'·92N 06°20'·89W Fl R 3s 6m 4M.

▶ KILMORE

St Patrick's Bridge ▬ 52°09'·30N 06°34'·71W Fl R 6s; (Apr-Sep).
St Patrick's Bridge ▲ 52°09'·13N 06°34'·71W Fl G 6s; (Apr-Sep)

Kilmore Breakwater Head ✧ 52°10'·20N 06°35'·15W Q RG 7m 5M; vis: R269°-354°, G354°-003°, R003°-077°.

Ldg lts 007·9°, Front 52°10'·37N 06°35'·08W Oc 4s 3m 6M. Rear, 100m from front, Oc 4s 6m 6M; sync with front.

CONINGBEG ⛴ 52°02'·40N 06°39'·49W Fl (3) 30s 12m **24M**; R hull, and twr, ***Racon (M) 13M***; *Horn (3) 60s.*

▶ WATERFORD

Hook Head ☆ 52°07'·32N 06°55'·85W Fl 3s 46m **23M**; W twr, two B bands; ***Racon (K) 10M vis 237°-177°***; *Horn (2) 45s.*

Waterford ♦ 52°08'·95N 06°57'·00W Fl R 3s. Fl (3) R 10s.
Duncannon No. 1 ▲ 52°11'·02N 06°56'·28W Fl G 2s.
Duncannon No. 2 ▬ 52°11'·02N 06°56'·47W QR.
Duncannon No. 3 ▲ 52°12'·02N 06°56'·21W Fl G 4s.
Duncannon No. 4 ▬ 52°12'·02N 06°56'·42W Fl R 3s.
Duncannon No. 5 ▲ 52°12'·42N 06°56'·20W Fl (2) G 4s.

Duncannon Dir lt 002°. 52°13'·23N 06°56'·25W Oc WRG 4s 13m W11M, R8M, G8M; W twr on fort; vis: G358°-001·7°, W001·7°-002·2°, R002·2°-006°. Same twr, Oc WR 4s 13m W9M, R7M; vis: R119°-149°, W149°-172°.

Drumroe Bank ▬ 52°13'·56N 06°56'·70W QR.

Passage Point ✧ 52°14'·26N 06°57'·77W Fl WR 5s 7m W6M, R5M; R pile structure; vis: W shore-127°, R127°-302°.

Seedes Bank ▲ 52°15'·27N 06°59'·63W Fl G 2s.

Cheek Point ✧ 52°16'·12N 06°59'·38W Q WR 6m 5M; W mast; vis: W007°-289°, R289°-007°.

Sheagh ✧ 52°16'·29N 06°59'·34W Fl R 3s 29m 3M; Gy twr; vis: 090°-318°.

Kilmokea ✧ 52°16'·50N 06°58'·93W Fl 5s.
River Barrow Railway Bridge ✧ 2 FR (Hor); tfc sigs.
Garraunbaun Rock No. 2 ✧ 52°17'·38N 07°00'·94W.

Snowhill Point Ldg lts 255°. Front, 52°16'·39N 07°00'·91W Fl WR 2·5s 5m 3M; vis: W222°-020°, R020°-057°, W057°-107°. Rear, Flour Mill, 750m from front, Q 12m 5M.

Queen's Chan Ldg lts 098°. Front, 52°15'·32N 07°02'·38W QR 8m 5M; B twr, W band; vis: 030°-210°. Rear, 550m from front, Q 15m 5M; W mast.

Beacon Quay ✧ 52°15'·50N 07°04'·21W Fl 3s 9m; vis: 255°-086°.

Cove ✧ 52°15'·05N 07°05'·16W Fl WRG 6s 6m 2M; W twr; vis: R111°-161°, G161°-234°, W234°-111°.

Smelting Ho Pt ✧ 52°15'·15N 07°05'·27W Q 8m 3M; W mast.

Ballycar ✧ 52°15'·06N 07°05'·51W Fl RG 3s 5m; vis: G127°-212°, R212°-284°.

▶ DUNMORE EAST

East Pier Head ☆ 52°08'·93N 06°59'·37W Fl WR 8s 13m **W17M**, R13M; Gy twr, vis: W225°-310°, R310°-004°.

East Breakwater extn ✧ 52°08'·98N 06°59'·37W Fl R 2s 6m 4M; vis: 000°-310°.

West Wharf ✧ 52°08'·97N 06°59'·45W Fl G 2s 6m 4M; vis: 165°-246°.

▶ DUNGARVAN

Ballinacourty Point ✧ 52°04'·69N 07°33'·18W Fl (2) WRG 10s 16m W10M, R8M, G8M; W twr; vis: G245°-274°, W274°-302°, R302°-325°, W325°-117°.

Helvick ♦ 52°03'·61N 07°32'·25W Q (3) 10s.

Mine Head ☆ 51°59'·52N 07°35'·25W Fl (4) 20s 87m **20M**; W twr, B band; vis: 228°-052°.

▶ YOUGHAL

Bar Rocks ♦ 51°54'·85N 07°50'·05W Q (6) + L Fl 15s.
Blackball Ledge ♦ 51°55'·34N 07°48'·53W Q (3) 10s.

W side of ent ☆ 51°56'·57N 07°50'·53W Fl WR 2·5s 24m **W17M**, R13M; W twr; vis: W183°-273°, R273°-295°, W295°-307°, R30§7°-351°, W351°-003°.

▶ BALLYCOTTON

Ballycotton ☆ 51°49'·52N 07° 59'·09W Fl WR 10s 59m **W21M**, **R17M**; B twr, within W walls, B lantern; vis: W238°-048°, R048°-238°; *Horn (4) 90s.*

The Smiths ▬ 51°48'·62N 08°00'·71W Fl (3) R 10s.
Power ♦ 51°45'·59N 08°06'·67W Q (6) + L Fl 15s.
Pollock Rock ▬ 51°46'·22N 08°07'·85W Fl R 6s.

▶ CORK

Cork ♦ 51°42'·92N 08°15'·60W L Fl 10s; ***Racon (T) 7M.***
Daunt Rock ▬ 51°43'·52N 08°17'·65W Fl (2) R 6s.

Fort Davis Ldg lts 354·1°. **Front,** 51°48'·82N 08°15'·80W Dir WRG 29m **17M**; vis: FG351·5°-352·25°, AlWG352·25°-353°, FW353°-355°, AlWR355°-355·75°, FR355·75°-356·5°. Rear, Dognose Quay, 203m from front, Oc 5s 37m 10M; Or 3, synch with front.

Roche's Point ☆ 51°47'·59N 08°15'·29W Fl WR 3s 30m **W20M**, **R16M**; vis: Rshore-292°, W292°-016°, R016°-033°, W(unintens) 033°-159°, R159°-shore.

Outer Hbr Rk E2 ▬ 51°47'·52N 08°15'·67W Fl R 2·5s.
Chicago Knoll E1 ▲ 51°47'·66N 08°15'·54W Fl G 5s.
W1 ▲ 51°47'·69N 08°16'·05W Fl G 10s.
W2 ▬ 51°47'·69N 08°16'·34W Fl R 10s.
The Sound E4 ♦ 51°47'·92N 08°15'·77W Q.
W4 ▬ 51°48'·02N 08°15'·94W Fl R 5s.
W3 ▲ 51°48'·12N 08°15'·61W Fl G 2·5s.

White Bay Ldg lts 034·6°. Front, 51°48'·53N 08°15'·22W Oc R 5s 11m 5M; W hut. Rear, 113m from front, Oc R 5s 21m 5M; W hut; synch with front.

W6 ▬ 51°48'·28N 08°15'·94W Fl R 2·5s.

Dognose Bk ▲ 51°49'·02N 08°16'·20W Fl G 5s.

Spit Bank Pile ✧ 51°50'·72N 08°16'·45W Iso WR 4s 10m W10M, R7M; W house on R piles; vis: R087°-196°, W196°-221°, R221°358°.

C1 ▲ 51°48'·82N 08°16'·97W Fl G 10s.
C2 ▬ 51°48'·70N 08°17'·34W Fl R 5s.

East Ferry Marina, E Passage ✧ 51°51'·91N 08°12'·82W 2 FR (vert) at N and S ends.

▶ KINSALE/OYSTER HAVEN

Bulman ♦ 51°40'·14N 08°29'·74W Q (6) + L Fl 15s.

Charle's Fort ✧ 51°41'·74N 08°29'·97W Fl WRG 5s 18m W9M, R6M, G7M; vis: G348°-358°, W358°-004°, R004°-168°; H24.
Spur ▬ 51°41'·80N 08°30'·31W Fl (2) R 6s.
Split ▬ 51°42'·17N 08°30'·48W QR.s
Crohague ▬ 51°42'·21N 08°30'·81W QR.

PLOT WAYPOINTS ON YOUR CHART BEFORE USING THEM

OLD HEAD OF KINSALE TO MIZEN HEAD

Old Head of Kinsale ☆, S point 51°36'·28N 08°32'·03W Fl (2) 10s 72m **25M**; B twr, two W bands; *Horn (3) 45s*.

▶ COURTMACSHERRY

Barrel Rock 51°37'·01N 08°37'·30W.

Black Tom 51°36'·41N 08°37'·95W, Fl G 5s.

Courtmacsherry 51°38'·29N 08°40'·90W Fl G 3s.

Wood Point (Land Pt) ☆ 51°38'·16N 08°41'·00W Fl (2) WR 5s 15m 5M; vis: W315°-332°, R332°-315°.

Galley Head ☆ summit 51°31'·80N 08°57'·19W Fl (5) 20s 53m **23M**; W twr; vis: 256°-065°.

Wind Rock 51°35'·66N 08°51'·01W.

▶ GLANDORE

51°33'·09N 09°06'·60W GRG Fl(2+1)7s.

Sunk Rock 51°33'·52N 09°06'·84W Q.

▶ CASTLE HAVEN

Reen Point ☆ 51°30'·98N 09°10'·50W Fl WRG 10s 9m W5M, R3M, G3M; W twr; vis: G shore-338°, W338°-001°, R001°-shore.

Kowloon Bridge 51°27'·58N 09°13'·75W Q (6) + L Fl 15s.

▶ BALTIMORE

Barrack Point ☆ 51°28'·33N 09°23'·65W Fl (2) WR 6s 40m W6M, R3M; vis: R168°-294°, W294°-038°.

Loo Rock 51°28'·43N 09°23'·45W Fl G 3s.

Lousy Rocks 51°28'·95N 09°23'·03W

Wallis Rock 51°28'·95N 09°23'·02W QR.

Fastnet ☆, W end 51°23'·35N 09°36'·19W Fl 5s 49m **27M**; Gy twr, *Horn (4) 60s*, ***Racon (G) 18M***.

Copper Point Long Island, E end ☆ 51°30'·24N 09°32'·08W Q (3)10s 16m 8M; W □ twr.

Amelia Rk 51°29'·97N 09°31'·45W Fl G 3s.

▶ SCHULL/LONG ISLAND CHANNEL

Bull Rock 51°30'·75N 09°32'·20W Fl (2) R 6s 4m 4M.

Ldg lts 346° Front, 51°31'·68N 09°32'·43W Oc 5s 5m 11M, W mast. Rear, 91m from front, Oc 5s 8m11M; W mast.

Cush Spit 51°30'·29N 09°33'·01W Q.

▶ CROOKHAVEN

Black Horse Rocks 51°28'·44N 09°41'·66W.

Rock Island Point ☆ 51°28'·59N 09°42'·29W L Fl WR 8s 20m W13M, R11M; W twr; vis: W over Long Island B to 281°, R281°-340°; inside harbour R281°-348°, W348° towards N shore.

Mizen Head ☆ 51°27'·00N 09°49'·24W Iso 4s 55m **15M**; vis: 313°-133°.

MIZEN HEAD TO DINGLE BAY

Sheep's Head ☆ 51°32'·60N 09°50'·95W Fl (3) WR 15s 83m **W18M, R15M**; W bldg; vis: R007°-017°, W017°-212°.

▶ BANTRY BAY/CASTLETOWN BEARHAVEN/ WHIDDY ISLE/BANTRY/GLENGARIFF

Roancarrigmore ☆ 51°39'·19N 09°44'·83W Fl WR 3s 18m **W18M**, R14M; W □ twr, B band; vis: W312°-050°, R050°-122°, R(unintens) 122°-242°, R242°-312°. Reserve lt W8M, R6M obsc 140°-220°.

Ardnakinna Pt ☆ 51°37'·11N 09°55'·08W Fl (2) WR 10s 62m **W17M**, R14M; W ○ twr; vis: R319°-348°, W348°-066°, R066°-shore.

Walter Scott Rock 51°38'·54N 09°54'·24W Q (6) + L Fl 15s.

Castletown Dir lt 024° ☆ 51°38'·79N 09°54'·30W Oc WRG 5s 4m W14M, R11M, G11M; W hut, R stripe; vis: G020·5°-024°, W024°-024·5°, R024·5°-027·5°.

Oilean na g Cadrach (Sheep Islands) ☆ 51°38'·38N 09°53'·90W Q 3m 3M.

Castletown Ldg lts 010°. Front, 51°39'·16N 09°54'·40W Oc 3s 4m 1M; W col, R stripe; vis: 005°-015°. Rear, 80m from front, Oc 3s 7m 1M; W with R stripe; vis: 005°-015°.

Perch Rock ☆ 51°38'·84N 09°54'·47W QG 4m 1M; G col.

Cametringane Spit 51°38'·94N 09°54'·48W QR.

Bull Rock ☆ 51°35'·51N 10°18'·08W Fl 15s 83m **21M**; W twr; vis: 220°-186°.

▶ KENMARE RIVER/DARRYNANE/BALLYCROVANE

Ballycrovane Hbr ☆ 51°42'·63N 09° 57'·53W Fl R 3s.

Darrynane Ldg lts 034°. Front, 51°45'·90N 10°09'·20W Oc 3s 10m 4M. Rear, Oc 3s 16m 4M.

Skelligs Rock ☆ 51°46'·12N 10°32'·51W Fl (3) 15s 53m **19M**; W twr; vis: 262°-115°; part obsc within 6M 110°-115°.

▶ VALENTIA/PORTMAGEE

Fort (Cromwell) Point ☆ 51°56'·02N 10°19'·27W Fl WR 2s 16m **W17M, R15M**; W twr; vis: R304°-351°, W102°-304°; obsc from seaward by Doulus Head when brg more than 180°.

FR lts on radio masts on Geokaun hill 1·20M WSW.

Harbour Rock 51°55'·82N 10°18'·92W Q (3) 10s 4m 5M; vis: 080°-040°.

Ldg lts 141°. Front, 51°55'·52N 10°18'·41W Oc WRG 4s 25m W11M, R8M, G8M; W twr, R stripe; vis: G134°-140°, W140°-142°, R142°-148°. Rear, 122m from front, Oc 4s 43m 5M; vis: 128°-157·5° synch with front.

The Foot 51°55'·73N 10°17'·10W VQ (3) 5s.

DINGLE BAY TO LOOP HEAD

▶ DINGLE BAY/VENTRY/DINGLE

Dingle, NE side of entrance ☆ 52°07'·30N 10°15'·51W Fl G 3s 20m 6M.

Black Point 52°07'·40N 10°15'·84W Fl (3) G 5s.

Flaherty Point 52°07'·51N 10°16'·05W QR.

East Pier Head ☆ 52°08'·22N 10°16'·52W 2 FG (vert) 5m 2M.

Ldg lts 182°. Front 52°07'·41N 10°16'·59W, rear 100m from front, both Oc 3s.

Inishtearaght ☆, W end Blasket Islands 52°04'·55N 10°39'·68W Fl (2) 20s 84m **19M**; W twr; vis: 318°-221°; ***Racon (O)***.

▶ BRANDON BAY

Brandon Pier Head ☆ 52°16'·00N 10°09'·61W 2 FG (vert) 5m 4M.

▶ TRALEE BAY

Little Samphire I ☆ 52°16'·26N 09°52'·91W Fl WRG 5s 17m **W16M**, R13M; G13M; Bu ○ twr; vis: R262°-275°, R280°-090°, G090°-140°, W140°-152°, R152°-172°.

Great Samphire I ☆ 52°16'·15N 09°51'·82W QR 15m 3M; vis: 242°-097°.

Fenit Hbr Pier Head ☆ 52°16'·24N 09°51'·55W 2 FR (vert) 12m 3M; vis: 148°-058°.

Fenit Marina Ent Hd ☆ 52°16'·25N 09°51'·66W Iso G 6s 6m.

▶ SHANNON ESTUARY

Ballybunnion 52°32'·52N 09°46'·93W VQ; ***Racon (M) 6M***.
Kilstiffin 52°33'·80N 09°43'·83W Fl R 3s.

Kilcredaune Head 52°34'·82N 09°42'·64W Fl 6s 41m 13M; W twr; obsc 224°-247° by hill within 1M.

Kilcredaune 52°34'·44N 09°41'·70W Fl (2+1) R 10s.
Tail of Beal 52°34'·39N 09°40'·75W Q (9) 15s.
Carrigaholt 52°34'·92N 09°40'·51W Fl (2) R 6s.
Beal Spit 52°34'·82N 09°39'·98W VQ (9) 10s.
Beal Bar 52°35'·18N 09°39'·23W Q.
Doonaha 52°35'·46N 09°38'·50W Q (3) R 5s.
Letter Point 52°35'·44N 09°35'·89W Fl R 7s.
Asdee 52°35'·09N 09°34'·55W Fl R 5s.
Rineanna 52°35'·59N 09°31'·24W QR.
North Carraig 52°35'·60N 09°29'·76W Q.

Scattery I, Rineanna Point 52°36'·32N 09°31'·03W Fl (2) 8s 15m 10M; W twr; vis: 208°-092°.

▶ KILRUSH

Off Cappagh Pier 52°37'·64N 09°30'·21WL Fl 10s.

Marina Ent Chan Ldg lts 355°. Front, 52°37'·99N 09°30'·27W Oc 3s. Rear, 75m from front, Oc 3s.

Tarbert I North Point 52°35'·52N 09°21'·83W Q WR 4s 18m W14M, R10M; W○twr; vis: W069°-277°, R277°-287°, W287°-339°.

Tarbert (Ballyhoolahan Pt) Ldg lts 128·2°. Front, 52°34'·35N 09°18'·80W Iso 3s 13m 3M; △ on W twr; vis: 123·2°-133·2°. Rear, 400m from front, Iso 5s 18m 3M; G stripe on W Bn.

Kilkerin 52°35'·53N 09°21'·02W Fl (2) R 6s.
Gorgon 52°35'·18N 09°20'·84W Fl (2) G 6s.
Bolands 52°34'·96N 09°19'·63W Fl (2) R 6s.
Carraig Fada 52°35'·26N 09°16'·03W Fl G 5s.

Garraunbaun Point 52°35'·62N 09°13'·94W Fl (3) WR 10s 16m W8M, R5M; W□col, vis: R shore-072°, W072°-242°, R242°-shore.

Loghill 52°36'·32N 09°12'·85W Fl G 3s.

Rinealon Point 52°37'·12N 09°09'·82W Fl 2·5s 4m 7M; B col, W bands; vis: 234°-088°.

▶ FOYNES

W Chan Ldg lts 107·9° (may be moved for changes in chan). Front, 52°36'·91N 09°06'·59W Oc 4s 34m 12M. Rear, Oc 4s 39m 12M.

Carrigeen No. 4 52°37'·02N 09°07'·00W IQ R 7m 2M.

▶ RIVER SHANNON

Beeves Rock 52°39'·01N 09°01'·35W Fl WR 5s 12m W12M, R9M; vis: W064·5°-091°, R091°-238°, W238°-265°, W(unintens) 265°-064·5°.

Shannon Airport 52°42'·12N 08°55'·48W Aero Al Fl WG 7·5s 40m.

Dernish I Pier Head 52°40'·73N 08°55'·09W 2 FR (vert) 4m 2M each end.

Conor Rock 52°40'·93N 08°54'·24W Fl R 4s 6m 6M; W twr; vis: 228°-093°.

North Channel Ldg lts 093°. Front, Tradree Rock 52°41'·00N 08°49'·87W Fl R 2s 6m 5M; W Trs; vis: 246°-110°. Rear 0·65M from front, Iso 6s 14m 5M; W twr, R bands; vis: 327°-190°.

Bird Rock 52°40'·95N 08°50'·26W QG 6m 5M; W twr.
Grass I 52°40'·43N 08°48'·45W Fl G 2s 6m 4M.
Logheen Rock 52°40'·33N 08°48'·15W QR 4m 5M.
S side Spilling Rock 52°40'·04N 08°47'·07W Fl G 5s 5m 5M.

N side, Ldg lts 061°. Front, 52°40'·72N 08°45'·27W, Crawford Rock 490m from rear, Fl R 3s 6m 5M. Crawford No. 2, Common Rear, 52°40'·85N 08°44'·88W Iso 6s 10m 5M.

Ldg lts 302·1°. 52°40'·66N 08°44'·40W Flagstaff Rock, 670m from rear, Fl R 7s 7m 5M.

The Whelps 52°40'·68N 08°45'·09W Fl G 3s 5m 5M; W pile.

Ldg lts 106·5°. Meelick Rock, Front 52°40'·25N 08°42'·36W Iso 4s 6m 3M. Meelick No. 2, rear 275m from front Iso 6s 9m 5M; both W pile structures.

Braemar Point 52°39'·17N 08°41'·94W Iso 4s 5m 5M W pile structure.

N side Clonmacken Point 52°39'·52N 08°40'·69W Fl R 3s 7m 4M.

E side Spillane's Tower 52°39'·34N 08°39'·70W Fl 3s 11m 6M; turret on twr.

▶ LIMERICK DOCK

Lts in line 098·5°. Front, 52°39'·49N 08°38'·80W F 8m. Rear, 100m from front; F 7m R ◇ on cols; occas.

Loop Head ☆ 52°33'·68N 09°55'·96W Fl (4) 20s 84m **23M**.

List below any other waypoints that you use regularly

Description	Latitude	Longitude	Description	Latitude	Longitude

9.12.5 PASSAGE INFORMATION

For all Irish waters the Sailing Directions published by the Irish Cruising Club are strongly recommended, and particularly on the W coast, where other information is scarce. They are published in two volumes: *E and N coasts of Ireland* which runs anti-clockwise from Carnsore Pt to Bloody Foreland, and *S and W coasts of Ireland* which goes clockwise. For notes on crossing the Irish Sea, see 9.13.5; and for Distances across it see 9.0.7.

MALAHIDE TO TUSKAR ROCK (charts 1468, 1787) Malahide (9.12.7), 4M from both Lambay Is and Howth, can be entered in most weather via a channel which constantly shifts through drying sandbanks. Ireland's Eye, a rky island which rises steeply to a height of 99m, lies about 7½ca N of Howth (9.12.8) with reefs running SE and SW from Thulla Rk at its SE end. Ben of Howth, on N side of Dublin Bay, is steep-to, with no dangers more than 1ca offshore.

Rosbeg Bank lies on the N side of Dublin Bay. Burford Bank, on which the sea breaks in E gales, and Kish Bank lie offshore in the approaches. ▶ *The N-going stream begins at HW Dublin – 0600, and the S-going at HW Dublin, sp rates 3kn.* ◀

From Dublin (9.12.9) to Carnsore Pt the shallow offshore banks cause dangerous overfalls and dictate the route which is sheltered from the W winds. ▶ *Tidal streams run mainly N and S, but the N-going flood sets across the banks on the inside, and the S-going ebb sets across them on the outside.* ◀ As a cruising area, hbr facilities are being improved.

Leaving Dublin Bay, yachts normally use Dalkey Sound, but with a foul tide or light wind it is better to use Muglins Sound. Muglins (lt) is steep-to except for a rk about 1ca WSW of the lt. Beware Leac Buidhe (dries) 1ca E of Clare Rk. The inshore passage is best as far as Wicklow (9.12.10).

Thereafter yachts may either route offshore, passing east of Arklow Bank and its Lanby to fetch Tuskar Rock or Greenore Pt. Or keep inshore of Arklow Bank, avoiding Glassgorman Banks; through the Rusk Channel, inside Blackwater and Lucifer Banks, to round Carnsore Pt NW of Tuskar Rock. Arklow (9.12.11) is safe in offshore winds; Wexford (9.12.12) has a difficult entrance. Rosslare (9.12.13) lacks yacht facilities, but provides good shelter to wait out a SW'ly blow.

Arklow Bank Wind Farm is on the bank in the area W of No.2 and No1 Arklow buoys. It has 7 wind turbines, each 72.8m high with 104m diameter blades. They are lit, N'most and S'most are fitted with AIS (Automatic Identification System for radar) transmitters. See 9.12.4.

TUSKAR ROCK TO OLD HEAD OF KINSALE (chart 2049) Dangerous rks lie up to 2ca NW and 6½ca SSW of Tuskar Rk and there can be a dangerous race off Carnsore Pt. In bad weather or poor visibility, use the Inshore Traffic Zone of the Tuskar Rock TSS, passing to seaward of Tuskar Rk (lt), the Barrels ECM lt buoy and Coningbeg lt float.

If taking the inshore passage from Greenore Pt, stay inside The Bailies to pass 2ca off Carnsore Pt. Watch for lobster pots in this area. Steer WSW to pass N of Black Rk and the Bohurs, S of which are extensive overfalls. The little hbr of Kilmore Quay (9.12.14) has been rebuilt with a new marina, but beware rks and shoals in the approaches.

Saltee Sound (chart 2740) is a safe passage, least width 3ca, between Great and Little Saltee, conspic islands to S and N. ▶ *Sebber Bridge extends 7½ca N from the NE point of Great Saltee and Jackeen Rk is 1M NW of the S end of Little Saltee, so care is needed through the sound, where the stream runs 3·5 kn at sp.* ◀ There are several rks S of the Saltees, but yachts may pass between Coningbeg Rk and the lt float. There are no obstructions on a direct course for a point 1M S of Hook Head, to avoid the overfalls and Tower Race, which at times extend about 1M S of the Head.

Dunmore East (9.12.16 and chart 2046) is a useful passage port at the mouth of Waterford Hbr (9.12.15). To the W, beware salmon nets and Falskirt, a dangerous rk off Swines Pt. There are few offlying rks from Tramore Bay to Ballinacourty Pt on the N side of Dungarvan Bay (9.12.18 and chart 2017). Helvick is a small sheltered hbr approached along the S shore of the bay, keeping S of Helvick Rk (ECM lt buoy) and other dangers to the N.

Mine Hd (lt) has two dangerous rks, The Rogue about 2½ca E and The Longship 1M SW. To the W, there is a submerged rk 100m SE of Ram Hd. ▶ *Here the W-going stream starts at HW Cobh + 0230, and the E-going at HW Cobh –0215, sp rates 1·5 kn.* ◀ For Youghal, see 9.12.17. Pass 1ca S of Capel Island. The sound is not recommended.

The N side of Ballycotton B is foul up to 5ca offshore. Ballycotton Hbr (9.12.18) is small and crowded, but usually there is sheltered anch outside. Sound Rk and Small Is lie between the mainland and Ballycotton Is (lt, fog sig). From Ballycotton to Cork keep at least 5ca off for dangers including The Smiths (PHM lt buoy) 1·5M WSW of Ballycotton Island. Pass between Hawk Rk, close off Power Hd, and Pollock Rk (PHM lt buoy) 1.25M SE.

Near the easy entrance and excellent shelter of Cork Harbour (9.12.18 and chart 1777), Ringabella Bay offers temp anch in good weather. 7ca SE of Robert's Hd is Daunt Rk (3·5m) on which seas break in bad weather; marked by PHM lt buoy. Little Sovereign on with Reanies Hd 241° leads inshore of it. The Sovereigns are large rks off Oyster Haven, a good hbr but prone to swell in S'lies. The ent is clear except for Harbour Rk which must be passed on its W side, see 9.12.19. Bulman Rk (SCM lt buoy) is 4ca S of Preghane Pt at the ent to Kinsale's fine harbour (9.12.19).

▶ *Old Head of Kinsale (lt, fog sig) is quite steep-to, but a race extends 1M to SW on W-going stream, and to SE on E-going stream.* ◀ There is an inshore passage in light weather, but in strong winds keep 2M off.

OLD HEAD OF KINSALE TO MIZEN HEAD (chart 2424) From Cork to Mizen Hd there are many natural hbrs. Only the best are mentioned here. ▶ *Offshore the stream seldom exceeds 1·5kn, but it is stronger off headlands causing races and overfalls with wind against tide. Prolonged W winds increase the rate/duration of the E-going stream, and strong E winds have a similar effect on the W-going stream.* ◀

In the middle of Courtmacsherry Bay are several dangers, from E to W: Blueboy Rk, Barrel Rk (with Inner Barrels closer inshore), and Black Tom; Horse Rk is off Barry's Pt at the W side of the bay. These must be avoided going to or from Courtmacsherry, where the bar breaks in strong S/SE winds, but the river carries 2·3m; see 9.12.20. Beware Cotton Rk and Shoonta Rk close E of Seven Heads, off which rks extend 50m. Clonakilty B has little to offer. Keep at least 5ca off Galley Hd to clear Dhulic Rk, and further off in fresh winds. ▶ *Offshore the W-going stream makes at HW Cobh + 0200, and the E-going at HW Cobh – 0420, sp rates 1·5 kn.* ◀

Across Glandore Bay there are good anchs off Glandore (9.12.21), or off Union Hall. Sailing W from Glandore, pass outside or inside High Is and Low Is, but if inside beware Belly Rk (awash) about 3ca S of Rabbit Is. On passage Toe Head has foul ground 100m S, and 7½ca S is a group of rks called the Stags. Castle Haven (9.12.22), a sheltered and attractive hbr, is entered between Reen Pt (lt) and Battery Pt. Baltimore (9.12.23) is 10M further W.

Fastnet Rk (lt, fog sig) is nearly 4M WSW of C Clear; 2½ca NE of it is an outlying rk. An E/W TSS lies between 2 and 8M SSE of the Fastnet. Long Island Bay can be entered from C Clear or through Gascanane Sound, between Clear Is and Sherkin Is. Carrigmore Rks lie in the middle of this chan, with Gascanane Rk 1ca W of them. The chan between Carrigmore Rks and Badger Island is best. If bound for Crookhaven, beware Bullig Reef, N of Clear Is.

Schull (9.12.24) is N of Long Island, inside which passage can be made W'ward to Crookhaven (9.12.25). This is a well sheltered hbr, accessible at all states of tide, entered between Rock Is lt Ho and Alderman Rks, ENE of Streek Hd. Anch off the village.

▶ *Off Mizen Hd (lt ho) the W-going stream starts at HW Cobh + 0120, and the E-going at HW Cobh – 0500. The sp rate is 4 kn, which with wind against tide forms a dangerous race, sometimes reaching to Brow Hd or Three Castle Hd , with broken water right to the shore.* ◀

THE WEST COAST

This coast offers wonderful cruising, although exposed to the Atlantic and any swell offshore; but this diminishes mid-summer. In bad weather however the sea breaks dangerously on shoals with quite substantial depths. There is usually a refuge close by, but if caught out in deteriorating weather and poor vis, a stranger may need to make an offing until conditions improve, so a stout yacht and good crew are required. Even in mid-summer at least one gale may be meet in a two-week cruise. Fog is less frequent than in the Irish Sea.

▶ *Tidal streams are weak, except round headlands.* ◀ There are few lights, so inshore navigation is unwise after dark. Coastal navigation is feasible at night in good visibility. Keep a good watch for drift nets off the coast, and for lobster pots in inshore waters. Stores, fuel and water are not readily available.

MIZEN HEAD TO DINGLE BAY (chart 2423) At S end of Dunmanus Bay Three Castle Hd has rks 1ca W, and sea can break on S Bullig 4ca off Hd. Dunmanus B (chart 2552) has three hbrs: Dunmanus, Kitchen Cove and Dunbeacon. Carbery, Cold and Furze Is lie in middle of B, and it is best to keep N of them. Sheep's Hd (lt) is at the S end of Bantry Bay (9.12.26; charts 1838, 1840) which has excellent hbrs, notably Glengariff and Castletown. There are few dangers offshore, except around Bear and Whiddy Islands. ▶ *Off Blackball Hd at W entrance to Bantry B there can be a nasty race, particularly on W-going stream against the wind. Keep 3ca off Crow Is to clear dangers.* ◀

Dursey Island is steep-to except for rk 7½ca NE of Dursey Hd and Lea Rk (1·4m)1½ca SW . The Bull (lt, fog sig, Racon) and two rks W of it lie 2·5M WNW of Dursey Hd. The Cow is midway between The Bull and Dursey Hd, with clear water each side. Calf and Heifer Rks are 7½ca SW of Dursey Hd, where there is often broken water. ▶ *2M W of The Bull the stream turns NW at HW Cobh + 0150, and SE at HW Cobh – 0420. Dursey Sound (chart 2495) is a good short cut, but the stream runs 4kn at sp; W-going starts at HW Cobh + 0135, and E-going at HW Cobh – 0450.* ◀ Flag Rk lies almost awash in mid-chan at the narrows, which are crossed by cables 25m above MHWS. Hold very close to the Island shore. Beware wind changes in the sound, and broken water at N entrance.

Kenmare R. (chart 2495 and 9.12.27) has attractive hbrs and anchs, but its shores are rky, with no lights. The best places are Sneem, Kilmakilloge and Ardgroom. Off Lamb's Head, Two Headed Island is steep-to; further W is Moylaun Is with a rk 300m SW of it. Little Hog (or Deenish) Island is rky 1·5M to W, followed by Great Hog (or Scariff) Is which has a rk close N, and a reef extending 2ca W.

Darrynane is an attractive, sheltered hbr NNW of Lamb Hd. The entrance has ldg lts and marks, but is narrow and dangerous in bad weather. Ballinskelligs Bay has an anch N of Horse Is, which has two rks close off E end. Centre of bay is a prohib anch (cables reported).

Rough water is met between Bolus Hd and Bray Hd with fresh onshore winds or swell. The SW end of Puffin Island is steep-to, but the sound to the E is rky and not advised. Great Skellig (lit) is 6M, and Little Skellig 5M WSW of Puffin Is. Lemon Rk lies between Puffin Is and Little Skellig. ▶ *Here the stream turns N at HW Cobh + 0500, and S at HW Cobh – 0110.* ◀ There is a rk 3ca SW of Great Skellig. When very calm it is possible to go alongside at Blind Man's Cove on NE side of Great Skellig, where there are interesting ruins.

DINGLE BAY TO LISCANNOR BAY (chart 2254) Dingle Bay (charts 2789, 2790) is wide and deep, with few dangers around its shores. Cahersiveen (9.12.29) and Dingle (9.12.30) have small marinas. The best anchs are at Portmagee and Ventry. At the NW ent to the bay, 2·5M SSW of Slea Hd, is Wild Bank (or Three Fathom Pinnacle), a shallow patch with overfalls. 3M SW of Wild Bank is Barrack Rk, which breaks in strong winds.

▶ *The Blasket Islands are very exposed, with strong tides and overfalls, but worth a visit in settled weather (chart 2790).* ◀ Great Blasket and Inishvickillane each have anch and landing on their NE side. Inishtearaght is the most W'ly Is (lt), but further W lie Tearaght Rks, and 3M S are Little Foze and Gt Foze Rks. Blasket Sound is the most convenient N-S route, 1M wide, and easy in daylight and reasonable weather with fair wind or tide; extensive rks and shoals form its W side. ▶ *The N-going stream starts at HW Galway + 0430, and the S-going at HW Galway – 0155, with sp rate 3 kn.* ◀

Between Blasket Sound and Sybil Pt there is a race in W or NW winds with N-going tide, and often a nasty sea. Sybil Pt has steep cliffs, and offlying rks extend 3½ca.

Smerwick hbr, entered between Duncapple Is and the E Sister is sheltered, except from NW or N winds. From here the scenery is spectacular to Brandon Bay on the W side of which there is an anch, but exposed to N winds and to swell.

There is no lt from Inishtearaght to Loop Hd, apart from Little Samphire Is in Tralee B, where Fenit hbr provides the only secure refuge until entering the Shannon Estuary. The coast from Loop Hd to Liscanor Bay has no safe anchs, and no lts. Take care not to be set inshore, although there are few offlying dangers except near Mutton Is and in Liscanor Bay.

THE SHANNON ESTUARY (charts 1819, 1547, 1548, 1549) The estuary and lower reaches of the Shannon (9.12.31), are tidal for 50M, from its mouth between Loop Hd and Kerry Hd up to Limerick Dock, some 15M beyond the junction with R. Fergus. ▶ *The tides and streams are those of a deep-water inlet, with roughly equal durations of rise and fall, and equal rates of flood and ebb streams. In the entrance the flood stream begins at HW Galway – 0555, and the ebb at HW Galway + 0015.* ◀

There are several anchs available for yachts on passage up or down the coast. Kilbaha Bay (chart 1819) is about 3M E of Loop Hd, and is convenient in good weather or in N winds, but exposed to SE and any swell. Carrigaholt B (chart 1547), entered about 1M N of Kilcredaun Pt, is well sheltered from W winds and has little tidal stream. In N winds there is anch SE of Querrin Pt (chart 1547), 4·5M further up river on N shore. At Kilrush (9.12.32) there is a marina and anchs E of Scattery Is and N of Hog Is. ▶ *Note that there are overfalls 0·75M S of Scattery Is with W winds and ebb tide.* ◀

▶ *Off Kilcredaun Pt the ebb reaches 4kn at sp, and in strong winds between S and NW a bad race forms. This can be mostly avoided by keeping near the N shore, which is free from offlying dangers, thereby cheating the worst of the tide. When leaving the Shannon in strong W winds, aim to pass Kilcredaun Pt at slack water, and again keep near the N shore. Loop Hd (lt) marks the N side of Shannon est, and should be passed 3ca off. Here the stream runs SW from HW Galway + 0300, and NE from HW Galway – 0300.* ◀

▶ *Above the junction with R. Fergus (chart 1540) the tidal characteristics become more like those of most rivers, ie the flood stream is stronger than the ebb, but it runs for a shorter time. In the Shannon the stream is much affected by the wind. S and W winds increase the rate and duration of the flood stream, and reduce the ebb. Strong N or E winds have the opposite effect. Prolonged or heavy rain increases the rate and duration of the ebb.* ◀ The Shannon is the longest river in Ireland, rising at Lough Allen 100M above Limerick, thence 50M to the sea.

9.12.6 SPECIAL NOTES FOR IRELAND

Céad Míle Fáilte! One hundred thousand Welcomes!

Lifejackets: ***It is compulsory to wear lifejackets in Irish (Eire) waters on all craft of<7m LOA. On Children age under 16, must at all times wear a lifejacket or personal floatation device on deck when underway. Every vessel, irrespective of size, must carry a lifejacket or personal flotation device for each person on board. These regulations are mandatory from June 2004.***

Ordnance Survey map numbers refer to the Irish OS maps, scale 1:50,000 or 1¼ inch to 1 mile, which cover the whole island, including Ulster, in 89 sheets.

Irish Customs: First port of call should preferably be at Customs posts in one of the following hbrs: Dublin, Dun Laoghaire, Waterford, New Ross, Cork, Ringaskiddy, Bantry, Foynes, Limerick, Galway, Sligo and Killybegs. Yachts may, in fact, make their first call anywhere and if no Customs officer arrives within a reasonable time, the skipper should inform the nearest Garda (Police) station of the yacht's arrival. Only non-EC members should fly flag Q or show ● over ○ lts on arrival. Passports are not required by UK citizens. All current Northern Ireland 5 and 6 digit telephone numbers have become 8 digits **028 90**12 3456

Telephone: To call the Irish Republic from the UK, dial **00 - 353**, then the area code (given in UK ☎ directories and below) minus the initial 0, followed by the ☎ number. To call UK from the Irish Republic: dial 00-44, followed by the area code minus the initial 0, then the number.

Salmon drift nets are everywhere along the S and W coasts, off headlands and islands during the summer and especially May-Jul. They may be $1\frac{1}{2}$ to 3M long and are hard to see. FVs may give warnings on VHF Ch 16, 06, 08.

Liquified petroleum gas: In Eire LPG is supplied by Kosan, a sister company of Calor Gas Ltd, but the bottles have different connections, and the smallest bottle is taller than the normal Calor one fitted in most yachts. Calor Gas bottles can be filled in most larger towns. Camping Gaz is widely available. The abbreviation Kos indicates where Kosan gas is available.

Information: The Irish Cruising Club publishes 2 highly recommended books of Sailing Directions, one for the S and W coasts of Ireland, the other for the N and E coasts. They are distributed by Imray and are available in good UK bookshops and chandleries. Further info is available from: Irish Sailing Association, 3 Park Road, Dun Laoghaire, Co Dublin, ☎ (01) 2800239, 📠 2807558; or the Irish Tourist Board, 150 New Bond St, London W1Y 0AQ, ☎ (020 7) 518 0800.

Email/Websites:

Commissioners of Irish Lights	www.cil.ie
Irish Sailing Association	www.sailing.ie
Irish Tourist Board (Eire)	www.ireland.travel.ie
Irish Forecasts from RTE	www.rte.ie/aertel/p160.htm

Currency is the Euro (€). Cash is most readily obtained via Euro or Travellers' cheques.

ACCESS BY AIR: There are airports in Eire at Dublin, Waterford, Cork, Kerry, Shannon, Galway, Connaught, Sligo and Donegal/Carrickfin. See also Ferries in 9.0.5.

Northern Ireland: Belfast CG (MRSC) is at Bangor, Co Down, ☎ (028 91) 463933, 📠 465886. HM Customs (⊜) should be contacted H24 on ☎ (028 90) 358250 at the following ports, if a local Customs Officer is not available: Belfast, Warrenpoint, Kilkeel, Ardglass, Portavogie, Larne, Londonderry, Coleraine. Northern Ireland's main airport is Belfast (Aldergrove).

Gaelic: It helps to understand some of the commoner words for navigational features (courtesy of the Irish Cruising Club):

Ail, alt	cliff, height	*Inish, illaun*	island
Aird, ard	height, high	*Inver*	river mouth
Anna, annagh	marsh	*Keal, keel*	narrow place, sound
Ath	ford		
Bal, Bally	town	*Kill*	church, cell
Barra	sandbank	*Kin, ken*	promontory, head
Bel, beal	mouth, strait		
Beg	little	*Knock*	hill
Ben, binna	hill	*Lag*	hollow
Bo	sunken rock	*Lahan*	broad
Boy, bwee	yellow	*Lea*	grey
Bullig	shoal, round rock, breaker	*Lenan*	weed-covered rock
Bun	end, river mouth	*Lis*	ancient fort
		Long, luing	ship
Caher	fort	*Maan*	middle
Camus	bay, river bend	*Maol, mwee*	bare
		Mara	of the sea
Carrick	rock	*More, mor*	big
Cladach	shore	*Rannagh*	point
Cuan, coon	harbour	*Ron, roan*	seal
Derg, dearg	red	*Roe, ruadh*	red
Drum	hill, ridge	*Scolt*	split, rky gut
Duff, dubh	black	*Scrow*	boggy, grassy sward
Dun, doon	fort		
Ennis	island	*Slieve*	mountain
Fad, fadda	long	*Slig*	shells
Fan	slope	*Stag, stac*	high rock
Fin	white	*Tawney*	low hill
Freagh, free	heather	*Tigh, ti*	house
Gall	stranger	*Togher*	causeway
Glas, glass	green	*Tra, traw*	strand
Glinsk	clear water	*Turlin*	boulder beach
Gorm	blue		
Gub	point of land	*Vad, bad*	boat
Hassans	swift current		

9.12.7 MALAHIDE

Dublin **53°27'·20N 06°08'·90W**

CHARTS AC 1468, 633; Imray C61, C62; Irish OS 50

TIDES +0030 Dover; ML 2·4; Duration 0615; Zone 0 (UT)

Standard Port DUBLIN (NORTH WALL) ⟼

Times				Height (metres)			
High Water		Low Water		MHWS	MHWN	MLWN	MLWS
0000	0700	0000	0500	4·1	3·4	1·5	0·7
1200	1900	1200	1700				
Differences MALAHIDE							
+0002	+0003	+0009	+0009	+0·1	−0·2	−0·4	−0·2

SHELTER Good in the marina, dredged approx 2·3m. Access HW±4. Visitors berth on pontoon F. ⚓ between marina and Grand Hotel on S edge of fairway, clear of moorings.

NAVIGATION WPT: SWM LFl 10s 53°27'·10N 06°06'·81W. The approach channel lies between drying sandbanks with constantly changing depths. It is strongly recommended that visiting yachtsmen obtain up-to-date information by ☎ or VHF from the marina on the latest depths / buoyage and refer this to AC 633. Channel is marked by 4 PHM buoys and 4 SHM buoys which are lit. Entry not advised in strong onshore winds against the ebb. The flood reaches 3kn sp, and the ebb 3½kn. Speed limit 4kn in fairway and marina.

LIGHTS AND MARKS The marina and apartment blocks close S of it are visible from the WPT. The Grand Hotel is no longer conspic from seaward, due to trees and bldgs.

R/T Marina Ch **M** 80 (H24) . MYC, call *Yacht Base* Ch M (occas).

TELEPHONE (Dial code 01) Marina 8454129, [fax] 8454255; MRCC 6620922/3; ⊖ 8746571; Police 666 4600; Dr 845 5994; Ⓗ 837 7755.

FACILITIES **Marina** (350)☎ 8454129, [fax] 8454255, [V] (20) €2.60, D, P, Gas, BH (30 ton), BY, R, Bar, Ice; **Malahide YC** ☎ 8453372, Slip, Scrubbing posts for <10m LOA; **Services:** Ⓔ, Kos. **Town** , Ⓑ, ⇌, ✈ (Dublin).

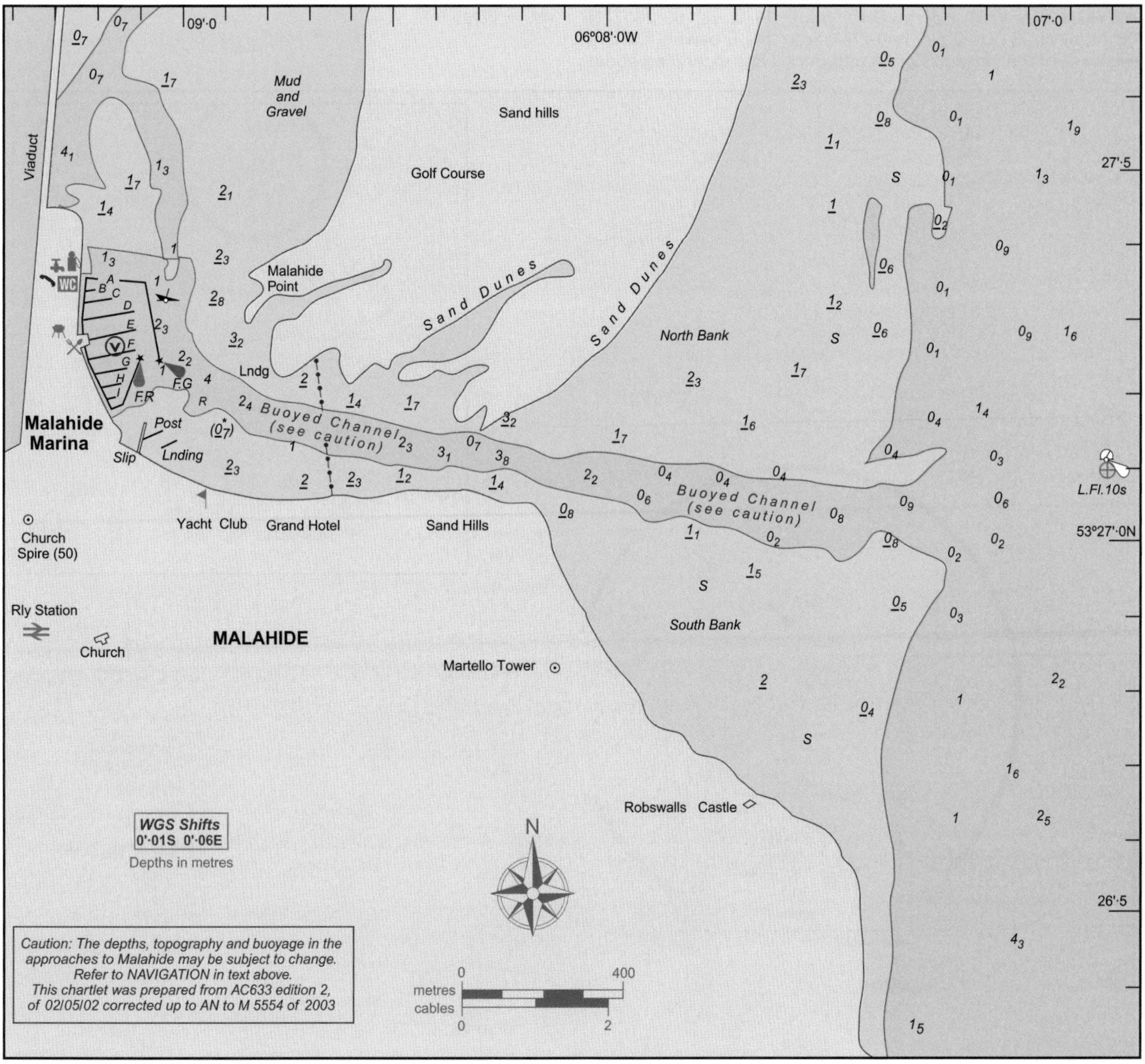
09'·0
06°08'·0W
07'·0
Mud and Gravel
Sand hills
Golf Course
Viaduct
27'·5
Malahide Point
Sand Dunes
Sand Dunes
North Bank
Lndg
F.G
F.R
Buoyed Channel (see caution)
Buoyed Channel (see caution)
Malahide Marina
Post
Slip
Lnding
L.Fl.10s
53°27'·0N
Church Spire (50)
Yacht Club
Grand Hotel
Sand Hills
South Bank
Rly Station
Church
MALAHIDE
Martello Tower
Robswalls Castle
WGS Shifts
0'·01S 0'·06E
Depths in metres
N
26'·5
Caution: The depths, topography and buoyage in the approaches to Malahide may be subject to change. Refer to NAVIGATION in text above. This chartlet was prepared from AC633 edition 2, of 02/05/02 corrected up to AN to M 5554 of 2003
metres
cables
0
400
0
2

9.12.8 HOWTH

Dublin **53°23'·60N 06°04'·00W** ❁❁❁◊◊✿✿✿

CHARTS AC 1468, 1415; Imray C61, C62; Irish OS 50

TIDES +0025 Dover; ML 2·4; Duration 0625; Zone 0 (UT)

Standard Port DUBLIN (NORTH WALL) (⟶)

Times				**Height (metres)**			
High Water		Low Water		MHWS	MHWN	MLWN	MLWS
0000	0700	0000	0500	4·1	3·4	1·5	0·7
1200	1900	1200	1700				
Differences HOWTH							
−0007	−0005	+0001	+0005	0·0	−0·1	−0·2	−0·2

SHELTER Good, available at all tides and in almost any conditions. After a severe ENE'ly storm, expect a dangerous scend in the app chan. Caution: many moorings in E part of outer hbr. No ent to FV basin for yachts. Inside the inner hbr keep strictly to chan to avoid drying shoals either side and a substantial wavebreak (gabion). Marina dredged to 2·5m. Visitors should check depth of berth offered by marina against depth drawn; R PHM posts mark the outer limit of dredging around the marina. 4kn speed limit. There is a fair weather ⚓ in 2-3m at Carrigeen Bay, SW side of Ireland's Eye.

NAVIGATION WPT Howth SHM buoy, Fl G 5s, 53°23'·72N 06°03'·53W, 251° to E pier lt, 0·27M. From the S beware Casana Rk 4ca S of the Nose of Howth and Puck's Rks extending about 50m off the Nose. Ireland's Eye is 0·6M N of hbr, with the Rowan Rks SE and SW from Thulla, marked by Rowan Rks ECM, and S Rowan SHM lt buoys. The usual appr passes S of Ireland's Eye. Between the Nose and the hbr, watch out for lobster pots. Beware rks off both pier hds. Howth Sound has 2·4m min depth. Give way to FVs (constrained by draft) in the Sound and hbr entrance.

LIGHTS AND MARKS Baily lt ho, Fl 15s 41m 26M, is 1·5M S of Nose of Howth. Disused lt ho on E pier is conspic. E pier lt, Fl (2) WR 7·5s 13m 12/9M; W 256°–295°, R elsewhere. W sector leads safely to NE pierhead which should be rounded 50m off. Ent to FV Basin has QR and Fl G 3s. The chan to marina is marked by 8 R & G floating perches (some lit) with W reflective tape (2 bands = port, 1 = stbd).

R/T Marina Ch M 80 (H24). HM VHF Ch 16 11 (Mon-Fri 0700–2300LT; Sat/Sun occas).

TELEPHONE (Dial code 01) HM 832 2252; MRCC 6620922/3; ⊖ 8746571; Police 666 4900; Dr 832 3191; Ⓗ 837 7755.

FACILITIES Howth YC Marina (350 inc Ⓥ) ☎ 839 2777, 📠 839 2430; €2.50, M, D (H24), Slip, C (12 ton), ⊕, ▣, ♿. **Howth YC** ☎ 832 2141, Scrubbing posts <20m LOA, R (☎ 839 2100), Bar (☎ 832 0606), ▣, ♿. **Howth Boat Club** (no facilities). **Services:** LB, Gas, Kos, ME, SM, CH, El, Ⓔ. **Town** P & D (cans), ✉, Ⓑ, ▣, ⇌, ✈ (Dublin).

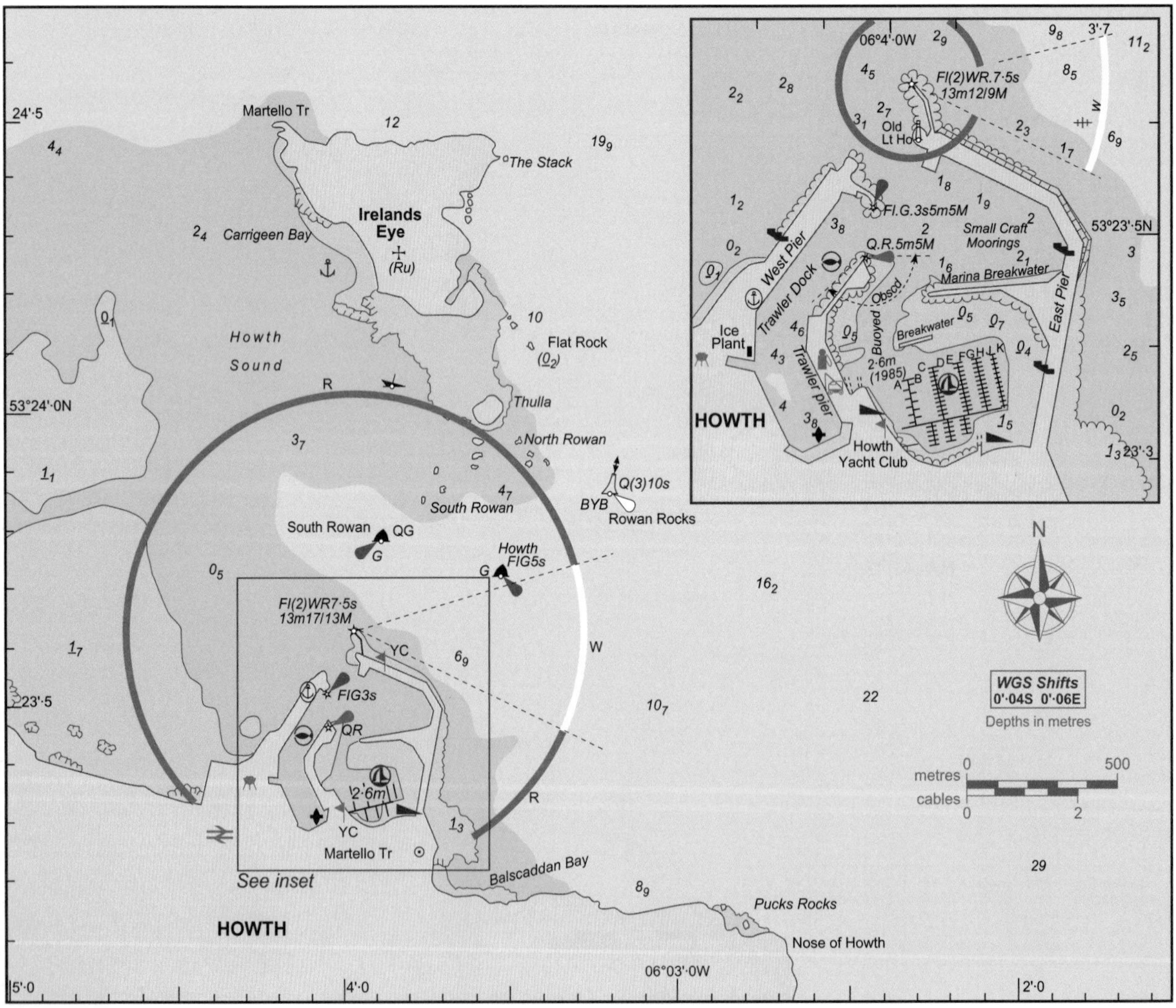
Martello Tr
Ireland's Eye
Carrigeen Bay
The Stack
Howth Sound
Flat Rock
Thulla
North Rowan
South Rowan
Q(3)10s
BYB
Rowan Rocks
South Rowan QG
Howth FlG5s
Fl(2)WR7·5s 13m17/13M
FlG3s
QR
YC
See inset
HOWTH
Balscaddan Bay
Pucks Rocks
Nose of Howth
53°24'·0N
06°03'·0W
WGS Shifts 0'·04S 0'·06E
Depths in metres
metres
cables
06°4'·0W
Fl(2)WR.7·5s 13m12/9M
Old Lt Ho
Fl.G.3s5m5M
Q.R.5m5M
Small Craft Moorings
Marina Breakwater
West Pier
Trawler Dock
East Pier
Ice Plant
Buoyed Chan
Breakwater
Trawler pier
Howth Yacht Club
53°23'·5N

9.12.9 DUBLIN/DUN LAOGHAIRE

Dublin City moorings **53°20'·85N 06°14'·80W**
Dun Laoghaire (Port ent) **53°18'·16N 06°07'·68W**

Dun Laoghaire ✿✿✿◊◊◊✿✿; Dublin ✿✿✿◊◊✿✿✿

CHARTS AC 1468, 1415, 1447; Imray C61, C62; Irish OS 50

TIDES +0042 Dover; ML 2·4; Duration 0640; Zone 0 (UT)

Standard Port DUBLIN (NORTH WALL) (⟶)

Times				Height (metres)			
High Water		Low Water		MHWS	MHWN	MLWN	MLWS
0000	0700	0000	0500	4·1	3·4	1·5	0·7
1200	1900	1200	1700				
Differences DUBLIN BAR and DUN LAOGHAIRE							
−0006	−0001	−0002	−0003	0·0	0·0	0·0	+0·1
GREYSTONES (53°09'N 06°04'W)							
−0008	−0008	−0008	−0008	−0·5	−0·4	No data	

SHELTER Dublin Port Excellent on N side 1ca below Matt Talbot br on pontoons. Poolbeg YBC Marina new 2004, S of Alexandra Basin W. **Dun Laoghaire** Excellent. Breakwaters within main hbr protect 475 berth marina from ferry wash. Ⓥ berths on end of pontoons or as directed. In addition all YCs advertise Ⓥs and/or pontoon berths.

NAVIGATION Both Dublin Port and Dun Laoghaire are accesssible H24, but the ent to R Liffey roughs up in E'ly F5+ against an ebb tide. **Dublin Port** WPT 53°20'·50N 06°06'·71W, 275° to hbr ent, 1·35M. Note that Bull Wall covers 0.6 to 2.7m at HW. For clearance to enter call *Dublin Port Radio* Ch 12. River is very busy 0600-1000 and 1800-1000. Keep sharp lookout for coasters and ferries, esp astern. East Link Lifting Br (2·2m closed) opens 1100, 1500 and 2100, or on request HO and Bank Holidays. Call 00 353 1 855 5779. **Dun Laoghaire** WPT 53°18'·40N06°07'·00W, 060°/240° from/to ent to Dun Laoghaire, 0·47M. Keep clear of coasters, ferries and the HSS catamarans (41kn), which turn off St Michael's Pier. Beware drying rks approx 10m off the E Pierhead.

TSS: Two TSS ½M long, one at either end of the Burford Bank lead to/from an anti-clockwise circular TSS radius 2·3ca centred on Dublin Bay SWM buoy, Mo (A) 10s, (53°19'·90N 06°04'·58W, 2·5M NE of Dun Laoghaire and 2·75M ESE of Dublin Port). Do not impede large vessels and keep clear of the TSS and fairway.

LIGHTS AND MARKS Dublin Port: No ldg lts/marks. Poolbeg power stn 2 R/W chimneys (VQ R) are conspic from afar.
Dun Laoghaire: On Ro Ro Berth 2 x Fl.W = 'HSS under way; small craft keep clear of No 1 Fairway' (extends 600m seaward of ent).

R/T DUBLIN call *Dublin Port Radio* Ch **12** 13 16 (H24). Lifting bridge (call *Eastlink*) Ch 12. *Poolbeg Marina* Ch **37** 12 16. DUN LAOGHAIRE call *Dun Laoghaire Hbr* VHF Ch **14** 16 (H24); Marina Ch M; YCs Ch M. Dublin Coast Radio Stn 16 67 83.

TELEPHONE (Dial code 00 353 1) HM Dublin 8748771; HM Dun Laoghaire 2801130, 📠 2809607; MRCC 6620922/3; Coast/Cliff Rescue Service 2803900; ⊜ 2803992; Weather 1550 123855; Police (Dublin) 6668000, (Dun Laoghaire) 6665000; Dr 2859244; Ⓗ 2806901.

FACILITIES DUBLIN **Dublin City Moorings** ☎ 818 3300, mobile 086856 8113, 20 Ⓥ's AB in 3·3m,€2.50, FW, ⛽, Showers. **Poolbeg YBC Marina** ☎ 6604681, 📠 56 7790295, www.poolbegmarina.ie, 35 Ⓥ's for 20m max LOA in 2.4m,€2.30, D, FW, ⛽, Showers, ▣, Slip, Bar, R. Ferry to Holyhead. City of Dublin, all needs, ⇄, ✈.

DUN LAOGHAIRE **Dun Laoghaire Hbr Marina** ☎ 202 0040, (475 AB inc 20Ⓥ) €3.75, ▣, ♿; **Yacht Clubs** (E to W): **National YC** ☎ 2805725, 📠 2807837, Slip, M, L, C (12 ton), FW, D, R, Bar; **Royal St George YC** ☎ 2801811, 📠 2843002, Boatman ☎ 2801208; AB by prior agreement, €3.00, Slip, M, D, L, FW, C (5 ton), R, Bar; **Royal Irish YC** ☎ 2809452, 📠 2809723, Slip, M, D, L, FW, C (5 ton), R, Bar; **Dun Laoghaire Motor YC** ☎ 2801371, 📠 2800870, Slip, FW, AB, Bar, R. **Services** SM, CH, ACA, ⚒, Ⓔ, El, Gas. **Irish National SC** ☎ 28444195. HSS to Holyhead.

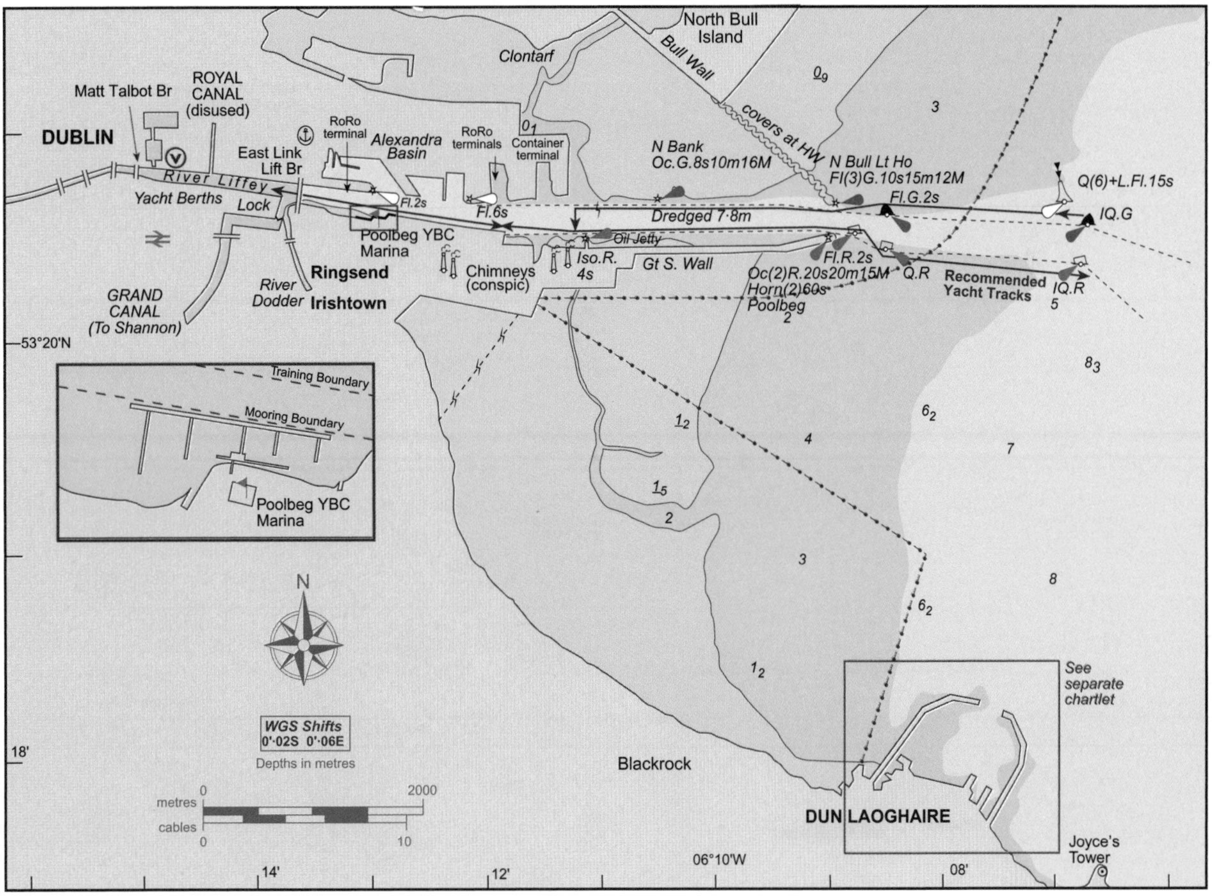
North Bull Island
Bull Wall
Clontarf
covers at HW
N Bank Oc.G.8s10m16M
N Bull Lt Ho Fl(3)G.10s15m12M
Fl.G.2s
Q(6)+L.Fl.15s
IQ.G
Dredged 7·8m
Oil Jetty
Matt Talbot Br
ROYAL CANAL (disused)
DUBLIN
East Link Lift Br
RoRo terminal
Alexandra Basin
RoRo terminals
Container terminal
River Liffey
Yacht Berths
Lock
Fl.2s
Fl.6s
Poolbeg YBC Marina
Chimneys (conspic)
Iso.R. 4s
Gt S. Wall
Fl.R.2s
Oc(2)R.20s20m15M
Horn(2)60s
Poolbeg
Q.R
Recommended Yacht Tracks
IQ.R
Ringsend
Irishtown
River Dodder
GRAND CANAL (To Shannon)
53°20'N
Training Boundary
Mooring Boundary
Poolbeg YBC Marina
N
WGS Shifts 0'·02S 0'·06E
Depths in metres
metres
cables
2000
10
18'
14'
12'
06°10'W
08'
Blackrock
DUN LAOGHAIRE
See separate chartlet
Joyce's Tower

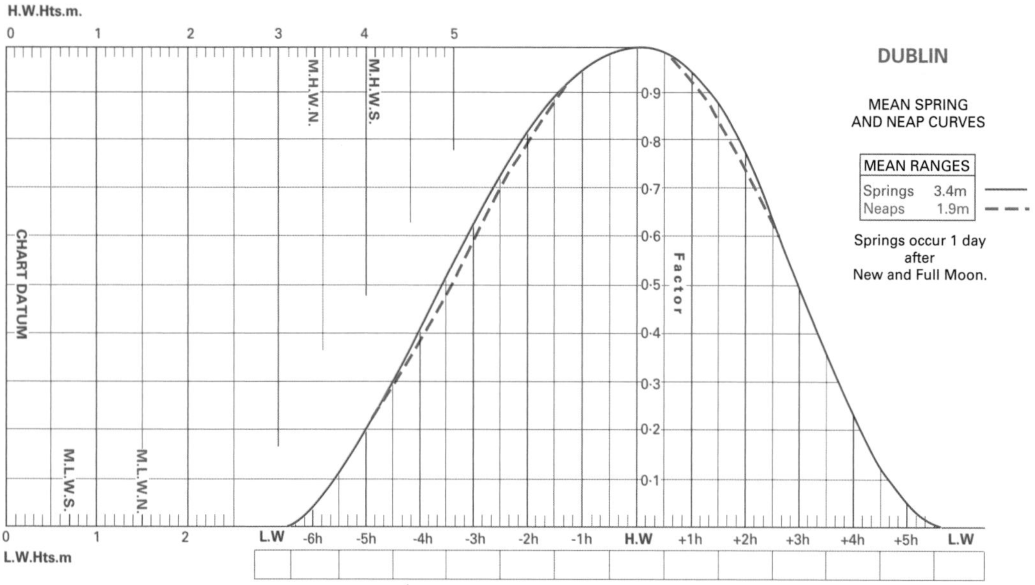
H.W.Hts.m.
L.W.Hts.m
CHART DATUM
M.L.W.S.
M.L.W.N.
M.H.W.N.
M.H.W.S.
Factor
L.W -6h -5h -4h -3h -2h -1h H.W +1h +2h +3h +4h +5h L.W
DUBLIN
MEAN SPRING AND NEAP CURVES
MEAN RANGES
Springs 3.4m
Neaps 1.9m
Springs occur 1 day after New and Full Moon.

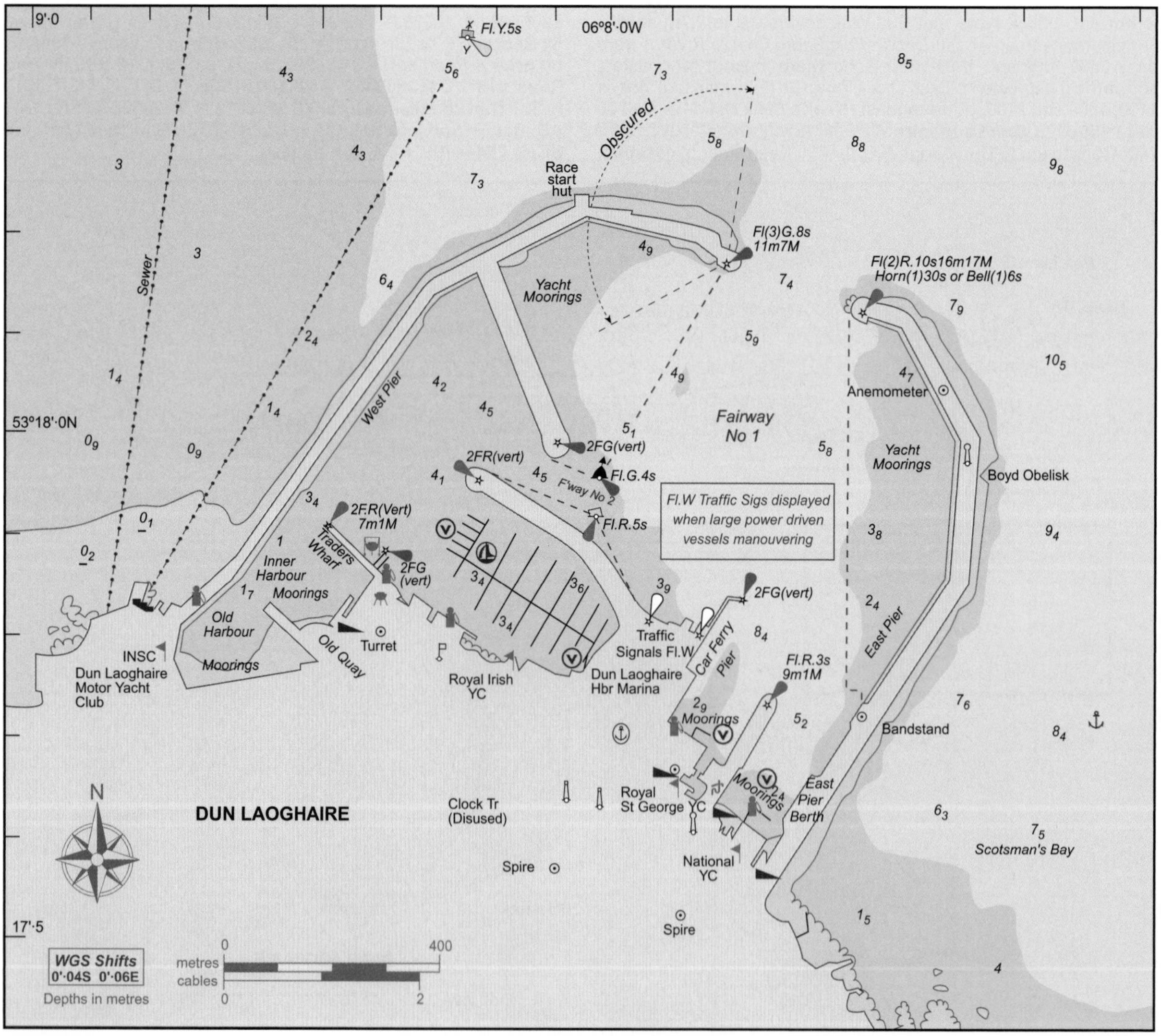
9'·0
06°8'·0W
53°18'·0N
17'·5
Fl.Y.5s
Sewer
Obscured
Race start hut
Fl(3)G.8s 11m7M
Fl(2)R.10s16m17M Horn(1)30s or Bell(1)6s
Yacht Moorings
West Pier
Anemometer
Fairway No 1
2FG(vert)
2FR(vert)
Fl.G.4s
F'way No 2
Fl.R.5s
Boyd Obelisk
Fl.W Traffic Sigs displayed when large power driven vessels manouvering
2F.R(Vert) 7m1M
Traders Wharf
2FG (vert)
Inner Harbour Moorings
Old Harbour
Moorings
Old Quay
Turret
INSC
Dun Laoghaire Motor Yacht Club
Royal Irish YC
Traffic Signals Fl.W
Dun Laoghaire Hbr Marina
Car Ferry Pier
2FG(vert)
Fl.R.3s 9m1M
East Pier
Moorings
Bandstand
Royal St George YC
East Pier Berth
DUN LAOGHAIRE
Clock Tr (Disused)
Spire
National YC
Scotsman's Bay
WGS Shifts 0'·04S 0'·06E
Depths in metres
metres
cables

TIME ZONE (UT)
For Summer Time add ONE hour in **non-shaded areas**

IRELAND – DUBLIN (NORTH WALL)

LAT 53°21′N LONG 6°13′W

TIMES AND HEIGHTS OF HIGH AND LOW WATERS

SPRING & NEAP TIDES
Dates in red are SPRINGS
Dates in blue are NEAPS

YEAR **2005**

JANUARY

Date	Day	Time	m	Time	m	Time	m	Time	m
1	SA	0253	3.5	0822	1.3	1509	3.8	2103	1.1
2	SU	0340	3.5	0908	1.4	1555	3.7	2150	1.1
3	M	0431	3.4	1000	1.5	1645	3.6	◑ 2243	1.2
4	TU	0527	3.4	1058	1.5	1740	3.6	2342	1.2
5	W	0627	3.4	1202	1.5	1841	3.6		
6	TH	0045	1.2	0729	3.5	1309	1.4	1947	3.6
7	F	0148	1.1	0828	3.6	1411	1.3	2052	3.7
8	SA	0246	1.0	0923	3.8	1509	1.0	2152	3.9
9	SU	0339	0.9	1014	4.0	1603	0.8	2247	4.0
10	M	0428	0.8	1103	4.2	1654	0.6	● 2338	4.1
11	TU	0514	0.7	1150	4.3	1743	0.4		
12	W	0028	4.1	0559	0.7	1238	4.4	1832	0.4
13	TH	0118	4.0	0645	0.7	1327	4.3	1922	0.4
14	F	0210	3.9	0734	0.8	1417	4.3	2014	0.5
15	SA	0302	3.8	0825	1.0	1510	4.1	2107	0.7
16	SU	0357	3.6	0920	1.1	1606	4.0	2202	0.9
17	M	0456	3.5	1019	1.3	1705	3.8	◐ 2300	1.1
18	TU	0557	3.4	1122	1.5	1810	3.6		
19	W	0004	1.3	0700	3.4	1232	1.5	1917	3.5
20	TH	0118	1.5	0803	3.4	1348	1.5	2024	3.4
21	F	0229	1.5	0901	3.5	1456	1.4	2126	3.5
22	SA	0325	1.4	0953	3.7	1550	1.3	2218	3.5
23	SU	0409	1.3	1036	3.8	1632	1.2	2259	3.6
24	M	0444	1.2	1113	3.9	1708	1.0	2333	3.6
25	TU	0515	1.2	1145	3.9	1741	1.0	○	
26	W	0004	3.6	0543	1.1	1216	3.9	1811	0.9
27	TH	0034	3.7	0610	1.0	1246	3.9	1840	0.8
28	F	0105	3.7	0638	1.0	1320	3.9	1910	0.8
29	SA	0140	3.7	0710	1.0	1356	3.9	1944	0.8
30	SU	0218	3.7	0747	1.0	1436	3.9	2023	0.8
31	M	0300	3.6	0829	1.0	1519	3.8	2106	0.9

FEBRUARY

Date	Day	Time	m	Time	m	Time	m	Time	m
1	TU	0346	3.6	0915	1.1	1605	3.7	2154	1.0
2	W	0437	3.5	1007	1.3	1657	3.6	◑ 2250	1.2
3	TH	0536	3.4	1111	1.4	1801	3.5	2359	1.3
4	F	0647	3.4	1230	1.4	1920	3.4		
5	SA	0118	1.3	0801	3.5	1352	1.3	2039	3.5
6	SU	0232	1.2	0907	3.7	1503	1.0	2146	3.7
7	M	0333	1.0	1003	3.9	1601	0.7	2242	3.9
8	TU	0422	0.8	1053	4.1	1650	0.4	● 2331	4.0
9	W	0506	0.6	1139	4.3	1735	0.3		
10	TH	0016	4.0	0546	0.5	1223	4.4	1817	0.2
11	F	0100	4.0	0627	0.5	1307	4.3	1901	0.2
12	SA	0142	3.9	0710	0.6	1351	4.2	1945	0.4
13	SU	0226	3.8	0755	0.7	1437	4.1	2031	0.6
14	M	0311	3.6	0844	0.9	1526	3.9	2119	0.9
15	TU	0401	3.5	0938	1.1	1619	3.7	2210	1.2
16	W	0459	3.3	1038	1.3	1723	3.4	◐ 2309	1.5
17	TH	0608	3.2	1147	1.5	1838	3.2		
18	F	0021	1.7	0718	3.2	1313	1.6	1953	3.2
19	SA	0202	1.7	0826	3.3	1439	1.5	2103	3.2
20	SU	0309	1.6	0926	3.5	1534	1.3	2200	3.3
21	M	0353	1.4	1013	3.7	1614	1.1	2241	3.5
22	TU	0426	1.2	1051	3.8	1647	0.9	2313	3.6
23	W	0455	1.1	1123	3.9	1716	0.8	2341	3.6
24	TH	0520	0.9	1151	3.9	1742	0.7	○	
25	F	0007	3.7	0543	0.8	1219	3.9	1807	0.6
26	SA	0034	3.8	0609	0.7	1250	4.0	1836	0.6
27	SU	0106	3.8	0640	0.7	1326	4.0	1910	0.6
28	M	0143	3.8	0716	0.7	1405	3.9	1948	0.6

MARCH

Date	Day	Time	m	Time	m	Time	m	Time	m
1	TU	0224	3.8	0757	0.8	1447	3.9	2031	0.7
2	W	0308	3.7	0843	0.9	1534	3.7	2119	1.0
3	TH	0358	3.5	0936	1.1	1629	3.5	◑ 2216	1.2
4	F	0459	3.4	1044	1.3	1738	3.3	2331	1.4
5	SA	0616	3.3	1214	1.4	1911	3.3		
6	SU	0103	1.5	0744	3.4	1347	1.2	2036	3.4
7	M	0226	1.3	0856	3.6	1500	0.9	2144	3.6
8	TU	0326	1.0	0954	3.9	1555	0.6	2237	3.8
9	W	0413	0.8	1043	4.1	1639	0.3	2321	3.9
10	TH	0453	0.6	1126	4.2	1720	0.2	●	
11	F	0000	4.0	0530	0.4	1206	4.3	1758	0.1
12	SA	0036	3.9	0607	0.4	1244	4.2	1836	0.2
13	SU	0111	3.9	0646	0.4	1324	4.1	1915	0.4
14	M	0148	3.8	0727	0.6	1406	4.0	1956	0.6
15	TU	0228	3.6	0813	0.7	1451	3.8	2039	0.9
16	W	0311	3.5	0905	1.0	1541	3.5	2127	1.2
17	TH	0402	3.3	1003	1.2	1641	3.3	◐ 2223	1.5
18	F	0512	3.2	1110	1.4	1801	3.1	2333	1.8
19	SA	0636	3.1	1232	1.5	1922	3.0		
20	SU	0111	1.8	0750	3.2	1408	1.4	2036	3.1
21	M	0240	1.6	0854	3.4	1504	1.2	2133	3.3
22	TU	0325	1.4	0944	3.5	1544	1.0	2213	3.4
23	W	0358	1.2	1023	3.7	1615	0.8	2245	3.6
24	TH	0425	1.0	1055	3.8	1642	0.6	2312	3.7
25	F	0449	0.8	1122	3.9	1707	0.5	○ 2335	3.8
26	SA	0513	0.7	1149	3.9	1734	0.4		
27	SU	0001	3.8	0539	0.5	1221	4.0	1804	0.4
28	M	0034	3.9	0612	0.5	1258	4.0	1839	0.5
29	TU	0112	3.9	0650	0.5	1339	3.9	1919	0.6
30	W	0154	3.8	0733	0.6	1425	3.8	2005	0.8
31	TH	0241	3.7	0824	0.8	1516	3.7	2057	1.0

APRIL

Date	Day	Time	m	Time	m	Time	m	Time	m
1	F	0334	3.6	0924	1.0	1617	3.5	2201	1.3
2	SA	0438	3.4	1041	1.2	1736	3.3	◑ 2321	1.5
3	SU	0602	3.3	1213	1.2	1911	3.3		
4	M	0053	1.5	0730	3.4	1341	1.0	2031	3.4
5	TU	0212	1.3	0842	3.6	1447	0.8	2134	3.6
6	W	0309	1.0	0940	3.9	1538	0.5	2224	3.8
7	TH	0354	0.8	1029	4.0	1621	0.3	2306	3.9
8	F	0434	0.6	1111	4.1	1700	0.2	● 2341	3.9
9	SA	0511	0.5	1148	4.1	1737	0.3		
10	SU	0012	3.9	0547	0.4	1224	4.1	1812	0.4
11	M	0043	3.8	0625	0.5	1302	4.0	1848	0.6
12	TU	0118	3.8	0706	0.6	1342	3.8	1926	0.8
13	W	0156	3.7	0751	0.7	1426	3.7	2007	1.0
14	TH	0237	3.6	0841	0.9	1514	3.4	2053	1.3
15	F	0325	3.4	0938	1.1	1611	3.2	2149	1.5
16	SA	0426	3.3	1042	1.3	1726	3.0	◐ 2257	1.7
17	SU	0552	3.1	1154	1.4	1846	3.0		
18	M	0016	1.8	0710	3.2	1314	1.3	1956	3.1
19	TU	0142	1.7	0813	3.3	1416	1.2	2052	3.3
20	W	0238	1.4	0904	3.5	1459	1.0	2134	3.4
21	TH	0315	1.2	0945	3.6	1533	0.8	2208	3.6
22	F	0345	1.0	1018	3.7	1603	0.6	2235	3.7
23	SA	0412	0.8	1048	3.8	1631	0.5	2301	3.8
24	SU	0440	0.6	1119	3.9	1702	0.4	○ 2331	3.9
25	M	0512	0.5	1155	4.0	1737	0.4		
26	TU	0007	4.0	0549	0.5	1237	4.0	1815	0.5
27	W	0048	4.0	0631	0.5	1323	3.9	1859	0.7
28	TH	0134	3.9	0721	0.6	1414	3.8	1949	0.9
29	F	0226	3.8	0819	0.8	1511	3.6	2048	1.1
30	SA	0324	3.7	0928	0.9	1619	3.5	2156	1.3

Chart Datum: 0·20 metres above Ordnance Datum (Dublin)

TIME ZONE (UT)
For Summer Time add ONE hour in **non-shaded areas**

IRELAND – DUBLIN (NORTH WALL)

LAT 53°21′N LONG 6°13′W

TIMES AND HEIGHTS OF HIGH AND LOW WATERS

SPRING & NEAP TIDES
Dates in red are SPRINGS
Dates in blue are NEAPS

YEAR **2005**

MAY

Date	Day	Time	m	Time	m	Time	m	Time	m
1	SU	0432	3.6	1045	1.0	1739	3.4	◑ 2313	1.4
2	M	0553	3.5	1205	1.0	1901	3.4		
3	TU	0032	1.4	0712	3.6	1320	0.9	2012	3.5
4	W	0143	1.3	0821	3.7	1422	0.7	2112	3.6
5	TH	0241	1.1	0919	3.9	1514	0.6	2202	3.7
6	F	0329	0.9	1010	4.0	1558	0.5	2245	3.8
7	SA	0412	0.7	1053	4.0	1639	0.5	2320	3.8
8	SU	0452	0.7	1132	4.0	1716	0.6	● 2351	3.8
9	M	0531	0.6	1207	3.9	1751	0.7		
10	TU	0021	3.8	0609	0.7	1244	3.8	1825	0.8
11	W	0055	3.8	0651	0.7	1324	3.7	1902	1.0
12	TH	0133	3.7	0735	0.8	1406	3.6	1942	1.1
13	F	0214	3.7	0823	1.0	1453	3.4	2027	1.3
14	SA	0300	3.5	0916	1.1	1545	3.3	2120	1.5
15	SU	0354	3.4	1014	1.2	1647	3.1	2222	1.6
16	M	0502	3.3	1115	1.3	1758	3.1	◐ 2330	1.7
17	TU	0616	3.2	1217	1.3	1905	3.1		
18	W	0036	1.6	0720	3.3	1316	1.2	2000	3.2
19	TH	0134	1.5	0813	3.4	1404	1.0	2045	3.4
20	F	0220	1.3	0857	3.6	1445	0.9	2122	3.6
21	SA	0258	1.1	0936	3.7	1522	0.7	2155	3.7
22	SU	0334	0.9	1014	3.8	1558	0.6	2229	3.9
23	M	0410	0.7	1054	3.9	1635	0.5	○ 2306	4.0
24	TU	0450	0.6	1137	4.0	1715	0.5	2347	4.0
25	W	0534	0.5	1223	4.0	1759	0.6		
26	TH	0032	4.1	0622	0.5	1315	3.9	1846	0.8
27	F	0123	4.0	0717	0.6	1410	3.8	1940	0.9
28	SA	0218	4.0	0819	0.7	1511	3.7	2040	1.1
29	SU	0318	3.9	0926	0.8	1616	3.6	2145	1.2
30	M	0425	3.8	1035	0.8	1726	3.5	◑ 2253	1.3
31	TU	0537	3.8	1144	0.9	1837	3.5		

JUNE

Date	Day	Time	m	Time	m	Time	m	Time	m
1	W	0001	1.3	0647	3.8	1250	0.9	1942	3.5
2	TH	0108	1.3	0752	3.8	1352	0.8	2041	3.6
3	F	0209	1.2	0853	3.8	1446	0.8	2134	3.7
4	SA	0303	1.1	0947	3.8	1535	0.8	2219	3.7
5	SU	0352	1.0	1035	3.8	1618	0.9	2258	3.8
6	M	0436	0.9	1116	3.8	1657	0.9	● 2332	3.8
7	TU	0518	0.9	1153	3.7	1733	1.0		
8	W	0003	3.8	0558	0.9	1229	3.7	1807	1.0
9	TH	0037	3.8	0638	0.9	1306	3.6	1843	1.1
10	F	0114	3.8	0720	0.9	1346	3.5	1920	1.2
11	SA	0153	3.8	0804	1.0	1429	3.5	2001	1.3
12	SU	0236	3.7	0850	1.1	1514	3.4	2046	1.4
13	M	0323	3.6	0939	1.1	1603	3.3	2137	1.5
14	TU	0414	3.5	1030	1.2	1658	3.2	2234	1.5
15	W	0510	3.4	1123	1.2	1756	3.2	◐ 2333	1.5
16	TH	0610	3.4	1216	1.2	1854	3.3		
17	F	0030	1.5	0709	3.4	1309	1.1	1947	3.4
18	SA	0123	1.4	0805	3.5	1358	1.0	2035	3.5
19	SU	0213	1.2	0857	3.6	1445	0.9	2120	3.7
20	M	0301	1.0	0947	3.8	1531	0.8	2205	3.9
21	TU	0348	0.8	1037	3.9	1616	0.7	2249	4.0
22	W	0436	0.7	1126	4.0	1701	0.7	○ 2334	4.1
23	TH	0525	0.5	1216	4.0	1747	0.7		
24	F	0022	4.2	0616	0.5	1308	4.0	1835	0.8
25	SA	0113	4.2	0711	0.5	1402	3.9	1927	0.9
26	SU	0207	4.2	0809	0.5	1459	3.8	2023	1.0
27	M	0304	4.1	0910	0.6	1558	3.7	2122	1.1
28	TU	0405	4.0	1011	0.7	1659	3.6	◑ 2222	1.2
29	W	0509	3.9	1112	0.9	1803	3.5	2325	1.3
30	TH	0616	3.8	1215	1.0	1906	3.5		

JULY

Date	Day	Time	m	Time	m	Time	m	Time	m
1	F	0030	1.4	0721	3.7	1318	1.1	2006	3.5
2	SA	0137	1.4	0825	3.7	1419	1.2	2103	3.6
3	SU	0240	1.3	0924	3.7	1514	1.2	2154	3.7
4	M	0337	1.2	1017	3.6	1601	1.2	2237	3.7
5	TU	0425	1.1	1102	3.6	1642	1.2	2313	3.8
6	W	0507	1.0	1139	3.6	1718	1.1	● 2346	3.8
7	TH	0546	1.0	1212	3.6	1751	1.1		
8	F	0018	3.9	0623	0.9	1246	3.6	1822	1.1
9	SA	0052	3.9	0659	0.9	1321	3.6	1855	1.1
10	SU	0128	3.9	0735	0.9	1358	3.5	1929	1.1
11	M	0207	3.8	0812	1.0	1438	3.5	2007	1.2
12	TU	0248	3.7	0851	1.0	1520	3.5	2049	1.2
13	W	0332	3.7	0934	1.1	1606	3.4	2135	1.3
14	TH	0420	3.6	1022	1.1	1656	3.4	◐ 2226	1.4
15	F	0513	3.5	1115	1.2	1752	3.3	2325	1.5
16	SA	0614	3.4	1215	1.2	1854	3.4		
17	SU	0030	1.4	0722	3.5	1317	1.2	1957	3.5
18	M	0137	1.3	0830	3.6	1417	1.1	2055	3.6
19	TU	0239	1.1	0931	3.7	1513	1.0	2148	3.8
20	W	0336	0.9	1026	3.9	1603	0.9	2236	4.0
21	TH	0429	0.6	1117	4.0	1650	0.7	○ 2323	4.2
22	F	0518	0.4	1206	4.0	1735	0.6		
23	SA	0009	4.3	0606	0.3	1254	4.0	1820	0.6
24	SU	0056	4.3	0656	0.3	1343	4.0	1907	0.7
25	M	0146	4.3	0748	0.4	1434	3.9	1957	0.8
26	TU	0238	4.2	0842	0.5	1526	3.7	2050	1.0
27	W	0332	4.1	0937	0.7	1621	3.6	2146	1.1
28	TH	0432	3.9	1033	1.0	1720	3.5	◑ 2247	1.3
29	F	0538	3.7	1133	1.2	1824	3.4	2353	1.4
30	SA	0649	3.5	1240	1.4	1930	3.4		
31	SU	0108	1.5	0759	3.5	1354	1.5	2032	3.5

AUGUST

Date	Day	Time	m	Time	m	Time	m	Time	m
1	M	0226	1.4	0906	3.5	1458	1.5	2129	3.6
2	TU	0328	1.3	1004	3.5	1547	1.4	2217	3.7
3	W	0416	1.2	1049	3.5	1627	1.3	2255	3.8
4	TH	0454	1.0	1123	3.6	1700	1.2	2327	3.9
5	F	0528	0.9	1153	3.6	1731	1.1	● 2357	3.9
6	SA	0600	0.9	1222	3.6	1758	1.0		
7	SU	0027	3.9	0628	0.8	1252	3.6	1825	1.0
8	M	0059	3.9	0657	0.8	1325	3.7	1855	1.0
9	TU	0134	3.9	0728	0.8	1401	3.7	1929	1.0
10	W	0213	3.9	0804	0.9	1440	3.6	2008	1.0
11	TH	0254	3.8	0846	0.9	1523	3.6	2051	1.1
12	F	0339	3.7	0932	1.0	1610	3.5	2140	1.3
13	SA	0430	3.5	1025	1.2	1705	3.4	◐ 2238	1.4
14	SU	0533	3.4	1130	1.4	1812	3.3	2353	1.5
15	M	0654	3.3	1247	1.4	1929	3.4		
16	TU	0118	1.4	0816	3.4	1402	1.3	2038	3.6
17	W	0232	1.2	0923	3.6	1504	1.1	2135	3.9
18	TH	0333	0.8	1019	3.8	1555	0.9	2224	4.1
19	F	0423	0.5	1107	4.0	1639	0.7	○ 2309	4.3
20	SA	0508	0.3	1151	4.1	1720	0.5	2352	4.4
21	SU	0551	0.2	1234	4.1	1801	0.5		
22	M	0034	4.4	0634	0.2	1317	4.0	1843	0.5
23	TU	0119	4.4	0719	0.3	1401	3.9	1927	0.7
24	W	0205	4.2	0807	0.5	1446	3.7	2016	0.8
25	TH	0255	4.0	0857	0.8	1535	3.6	2110	1.1
26	F	0350	3.8	0950	1.1	1630	3.5	◑ 2210	1.3
27	SA	0457	3.5	1048	1.4	1738	3.3	2318	1.5
28	SU	0617	3.3	1157	1.6	1851	3.3		
29	M	0041	1.6	0735	3.2	1328	1.7	2002	3.4
30	TU	0214	1.5	0851	3.3	1441	1.6	2105	3.6
31	W	0315	1.3	0950	3.4	1530	1.5	2155	3.7

Chart Datum: 0·20 metres above Ordnance Datum (Dublin)

TIME ZONE (UT)
For Summer Time add ONE hour in **non-shaded areas**

IRELAND – DUBLIN (NORTH WALL)

LAT 53°21′N LONG 6°13′W

TIMES AND HEIGHTS OF HIGH AND LOW WATERS

SPRING & NEAP TIDES
Dates in red are SPRINGS
Dates in blue are NEAPS

YEAR **2005**

SEPTEMBER

Day	Time	m
1 TH	0358 1032 1607 2234	1.1 3.5 1.3 3.9
2 F	0433 1103 1638 2305	0.9 3.6 1.1 3.9
3 SA	0502 1130 1705 ● 2333	0.8 3.7 1.0 4.0
4 SU	0529 1156 1730 2359	0.7 3.7 0.9 4.0
5 M	0554 1221 1754	0.7 3.8 0.8
6 TU	0028 0619 1251 1822	4.0 0.7 3.8 0.8
7 W	0102 0649 1326 1856	4.0 0.7 3.8 0.8
8 TH	0139 0725 1405 1934	3.9 0.8 3.8 0.9
9 F	0221 0807 1447 2017	3.8 0.9 3.7 1.0
10 SA	0307 0854 1535 2108	3.7 1.1 3.6 1.2
11 SU	0400 0951 1631 ◐ 2212	3.5 1.3 3.4 1.4
12 M	0509 1104 1742 2339	3.3 1.5 3.3 1.5
13 TU	0643 1232 1910	3.3 1.6 3.4
14 W	0113 0811 1353 2023	1.4 3.4 1.4 3.6
15 TH	0230 0918 1455 2122	1.1 3.6 1.2 3.9
16 F	0326 1010 1543 2210	0.7 3.9 0.9 4.2
17 SA	0412 1055 1624 2253	0.4 4.0 0.6 4.3
18 SU	0453 1135 1702 ○ 2333	0.2 4.1 0.5 4.4
19 M	0532 1212 1740	0.1 4.1 0.4
20 TU	0012 0610 1249 1819	4.4 0.2 4.0 0.5
21 W	0053 0650 1328 1901	4.3 0.4 3.9 0.6
22 TH	0137 0732 1409 1948	4.1 0.7 3.8 0.8
23 F	0224 0818 1454 2041	3.9 1.0 3.7 1.0
24 SA	0316 0909 1546 2140	3.6 1.3 3.5 1.3
25 SU	0421 1008 1653 ◑ 2248	3.4 1.6 3.4 1.5
26 M	0544 1118 1813	3.2 1.8 3.3
27 TU	0011 0708 1250 1928	1.6 3.1 1.9 3.4
28 W	0148 0828 1413 2035	1.5 3.2 1.7 3.5
29 TH	0248 0925 1502 2126	1.3 3.4 1.5 3.7
30 F	0329 1003 1539 2205	1.0 3.6 1.3 3.8

OCTOBER

Day	Time	m
1 SA	0402 1034 1609 2238	0.9 3.7 1.1 3.9
2 SU	0430 1102 1636 2305	0.7 3.8 0.9 4.0
3 M	0455 1126 1700 ● 2330	0.7 3.8 0.8 4.0
4 TU	0519 1149 1725 2359	0.6 3.9 0.8 4.0
5 W	0545 1219 1754	0.6 3.9 0.7
6 TH	0033 0617 1255 1828	4.0 0.7 3.9 0.8
7 F	0112 0654 1335 1909	4.0 0.8 3.9 0.8
8 SA	0156 0738 1420 1956	3.8 1.0 3.8 1.0
9 SU	0247 0829 1511 2054	3.7 1.2 3.7 1.2
10 M	0347 0932 1611 ◐ 2207	3.5 1.4 3.5 1.4
11 TU	0504 1052 1726 2337	3.3 1.6 3.5 1.4
12 W	0640 1221 1852	3.3 1.6 3.5
13 TH	0106 0801 1337 2005	1.2 3.5 1.4 3.7
14 F	0216 0904 1436 2104	0.9 3.7 1.2 4.0
15 SA	0309 0955 1523 2154	0.6 3.9 0.9 4.2
16 SU	0353 1038 1605 2237	0.4 4.0 0.7 4.3
17 M	0434 1116 1644 ○ 2316	0.3 4.1 0.6 4.3
18 TU	0511 1151 1722 2354	0.3 4.1 0.5 4.3
19 W	0548 1224 1801	0.4 4.0 0.6
20 TH	0034 0625 1301 1843	4.2 0.6 4.0 0.7
21 F	0116 0704 1341 1929	4.0 0.8 3.9 0.8
22 SA	0202 0747 1425 2020	3.8 1.1 3.8 1.0
23 SU	0253 0837 1515 2117	3.6 1.4 3.6 1.2
24 M	0355 0935 1616 2222	3.3 1.6 3.5 1.4
25 TU	0511 1043 1733 ◑ 2334	3.2 1.8 3.4 1.5
26 W	0631 1201 1848	3.1 1.9 3.4
27 TH	0057 0743 1324 1952	1.5 3.2 1.8 3.5
28 F	0203 0840 1420 2046	1.3 3.4 1.6 3.6
29 SA	0248 0923 1501 2128	1.1 3.6 1.4 3.8
30 SU	0323 0958 1533 2204	0.9 3.7 1.2 3.9
31 M	0352 1028 1602 2234	0.8 3.8 1.0 3.9

NOVEMBER

Day	Time	m
1 TU	0419 1053 1629 2302	0.7 3.9 0.9 4.0
2 W	0446 1120 1658 ● 2334	0.7 4.0 0.8 4.0
3 TH	0517 1152 1732	0.7 4.0 0.8
4 F	0012 0552 1231 1810	4.0 0.7 4.0 0.8
5 SA	0055 0633 1315 1856	4.0 0.9 4.0 0.8
6 SU	0144 0720 1404 1949	3.8 1.1 3.9 1.0
7 M	0240 0816 1459 2053	3.7 1.3 3.8 1.1
8 TU	0346 0924 1601 2206	3.5 1.5 3.7 1.2
9 W	0503 1040 1714 ◐ 2326	3.5 1.6 3.7 1.2
10 TH	0625 1158 1830	3.5 1.6 3.7
11 F	0043 0737 1309 1939	1.1 3.6 1.4 3.8
12 SA	0149 0839 1408 2040	0.9 3.7 1.2 4.0
13 SU	0244 0931 1459 2134	0.7 3.9 1.1 4.1
14 M	0332 1017 1545 2221	0.6 4.0 0.9 4.1
15 TU	0414 1057 1628 2303	0.6 4.0 0.8 4.1
16 W	0453 1133 1709 ○ 2342	0.6 4.0 0.7 4.1
17 TH	0530 1207 1750	0.7 4.0 0.7
18 F	0021 0606 1243 1831	4.0 0.9 4.0 0.8
19 SA	0103 0644 1321 1916	3.9 1.0 4.0 0.9
20 SU	0146 0725 1404 2004	3.7 1.2 3.9 1.0
21 M	0234 0811 1450 2056	3.6 1.4 3.8 1.2
22 TU	0328 0905 1543 2152	3.4 1.6 3.6 1.3
23 W	0432 1006 1646 ◑ 2252	3.2 1.7 3.5 1.4
24 TH	0542 1113 1754 2356	3.2 1.8 3.4 1.4
25 F	0648 1220 1859	3.2 1.8 3.4
26 SA	0058 0745 1321 1954	1.4 3.3 1.7 3.5
27 SU	0151 0834 1410 2041	1.2 3.5 1.5 3.6
28 M	0234 0914 1450 2123	1.1 3.6 1.4 3.7
29 TU	0311 0949 1525 2200	1.0 3.8 1.2 3.8
30 W	0345 1021 1600 2238	0.9 3.9 1.0 3.9

DECEMBER

Day	Time	m
1 TH	0419 1055 1637 ● 2317	0.8 4.0 0.9 4.0
2 F	0456 1133 1717	0.8 4.1 0.8
3 SA	0000 0536 1215 1801	4.0 0.8 4.1 0.7
4 SU	0048 0621 1302 1851	4.0 0.9 4.1 0.7
5 M	0140 0710 1353 1946	3.9 1.0 4.1 0.8
6 TU	0237 0806 1449 2048	3.8 1.2 4.0 0.9
7 W	0339 0909 1549 2153	3.7 1.3 4.0 0.9
8 TH	0447 1016 1654 ◐ 2301	3.6 1.4 3.9 1.0
9 F	0557 1125 1802	3.6 1.5 3.9
10 SA	0010 0704 1233 1908	1.0 3.6 1.4 3.9
11 SU	0116 0806 1337 2013	1.0 3.7 1.3 3.9
12 M	0217 0903 1436 2113	1.0 3.8 1.2 3.9
13 TU	0310 0954 1529 2207	1.0 3.9 1.1 3.9
14 W	0358 1039 1617 2254	1.0 3.9 1.0 3.9
15 TH	0440 1119 1701 ○ 2335	1.0 4.0 0.9 3.9
16 F	0518 1154 1742	1.0 4.0 0.9
17 SA	0013 0553 1229 1822	3.8 1.1 4.0 0.9
18 SU	0050 0628 1305 1903	3.7 1.1 4.0 0.9
19 M	0129 0705 1343 1945	3.7 1.2 3.9 1.0
20 TU	0211 0745 1424 2028	3.6 1.3 3.9 1.1
21 W	0255 0829 1508 2114	3.5 1.4 3.7 1.1
22 TH	0343 0918 1555 2202	3.4 1.5 3.6 1.2
23 F	0436 1013 1646 ◑ 2254	3.3 1.6 3.5 1.3
24 SA	0535 1113 1743 2350	3.3 1.7 3.4 1.4
25 SU	0637 1213 1844	3.3 1.7 3.4
26 M	0046 0733 1310 1944	1.4 3.4 1.6 3.4
27 TU	0140 0824 1403 2040	1.3 3.5 1.5 3.5
28 W	0230 0910 1451 2132	1.2 3.7 1.3 3.7
29 TH	0316 0954 1537 2220	1.1 3.8 1.1 3.8
30 F	0400 1036 1623 2307	1.0 4.0 0.9 3.9
31 SA	0443 1119 1708 ● 2353	0.9 4.1 0.7 4.0

Chart Datum: 0·20 metres above Ordnance Datum (Dublin)

9.12.10 WICKLOW

Wicklow **52°58'·98N 06°02'·70W** ❀❀❀◊◊✿✿

CHARTS AC 1468, 633; Imray C61; Irish OS 56

TIDES –0010 Dover; ML 1·7; Duration 0640; Zone 0 (UT)

Standard Port DUBLIN (NORTH WALL) (⟵)

Times				Height (metres)			
High Water		Low Water		MHWS	MHWN	MLWN	MLWS
0000	0700	0000	0500	4·1	3·4	1·5	0·7
1200	1900	1200	1700				
Differences WICKLOW							
–0019	–0019	–0024	–0026	–1·4	–1·1	–0·4	0·0

SHELTER Very safe, and access H24. Outer hbr is open to NE winds which cause a swell. Moorings in NW of hbr belong to SC and may not be used without permission. 4 berths on E Pier (2·5m) are convenient except in strong winds NW to NE, with fender boards/ladders provided. W pier is not recommended. ⚓ in hbr is restricted by ships' turning circle. Inner hbr (river) gives excellent shelter in 2·5m on N and S Quays, which are used by FVs. Packet Quay is for ships (2·5m), but may be used if none due; fender board needed. Yachts should berth on N or S quays as directed and/or space available.

NAVIGATION WPT 52°59'·20N 06°01'·80W, 220° to ent, 0·27M. Appr presents no difficulty; keep in the R sector of the E pier lt to avoid Planet Rk and Pogeen Rk.

LIGHTS AND MARKS No ldg marks/lts; lts are as on the chartlet. W pier head lt, Iso G 4s, is shown H24. ☆ Fl WG 10s on Packet Quay hd is vis G076°-256°, W256°-076°.

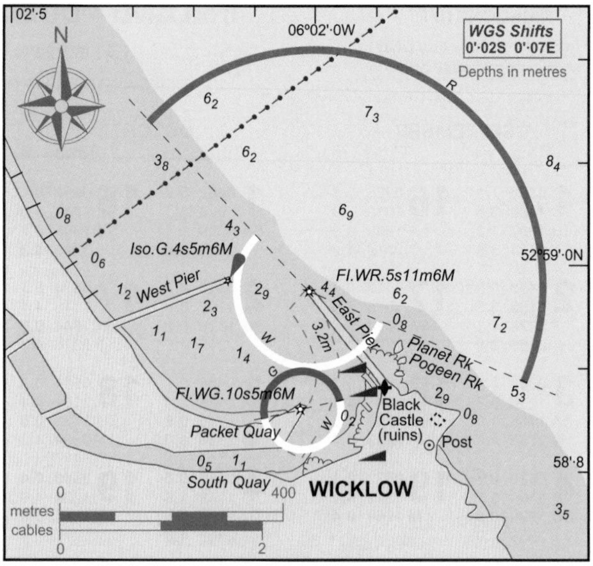
WGS Shifts
0'·02S 0'·07E
Depths in metres
06°02'·0W
52°59'·0N
58'·8
Iso.G.4s5m6M
West Pier
Fl.WR.5s11m6M
East Pier
Planet Rk
Pogeen Rk
Fl.WG.10s5m6M
Packet Quay
Black Castle (ruins)
Post
South Quay
WICKLOW
metres
cables

R/T VHF Ch 12, **14**, 16. Wicklow SC Ch M 16 (occas).

TELEPHONE (Dial code 0404) HM ☎/📠 67455; MRCC (01) 6620922; Coast/Cliff Rescue Service 69962; ⊖ 67222; Police 67107; Dr 67381.

FACILITIES East Pier, S and N Quays, L, FW, AB €4.44, reductions for longer stay, P & D (cans; bulk: see HM); **Wicklow SC** ☎ 67526, Slip (HW), M, L, FW, Bar; **Services**: ME, El, C, Kos, Gaz. **Town** CH, 🛒, R, Bar, ✉, Ⓑ, ⇌, ✈ (Dublin).

9.12.11 ARKLOW

Wicklow **52°47'·60N 06°08'·20W** ❀❀❀◊◊✿✿

CHARTS AC 1468, 633; Imray C61; Irish OS 62

TIDES –0150 Dover; ML 1·0; Duration 0640; Zone 0 (UT)

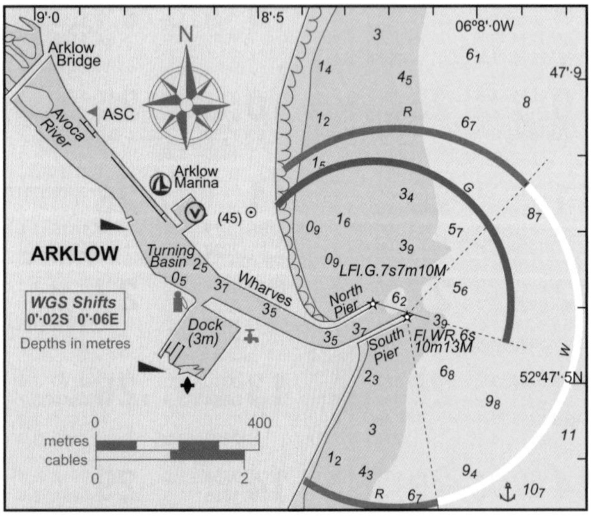
Arklow Bridge
Avoca River
ASC
Arklow Marina
ARKLOW
Turning Basin
WGS Shifts
0'·02S 0'·06E
Depths in metres
Dock (3m)
Wharves
North Pier
LFl.G.7s7m10M
South Pier
Fl.WR.6s 10m13M
06°8'·0W
47'·9
52°47'·5N
metres
cables

Standard Port DUBLIN (NORTH WALL) (⟵)

Times				Height (metres)			
High Water		Low Water		MHWS	MHWN	MLWN	MLWS
0000	0700	0000	0500	4·1	3·4	1·5	0·7
1200	1900	1200	1700				
Differences ARKLOW (Note small Range)							
–0315	–0201	–0140	–0134	–2·7	–2·2	–0·6	–0·1
COURTOWN							
–0328	–0242	–0158	–0138	–2·8	–2·4	–0·5	0·0

SHELTER Good, access H24; but ent unsafe in strong or prolonged NE to SE winds, when seas break across the bar. A 60 berth marina lies on NE side of river. Good ⚓ in bay; avoid whelk pots. One AB for Ⓥ (1.4m) at ASC quay. AB on SE wall of Dock (ent is 13·5m wide; 3m depth) in perfect shelter, but amidst FVs. **Arklow Roadstone Hbr**, 1M S of Arklow, is not for yachts.

NAVIGATION WPT 52°47'·60N 06°07'·50W, 270° to ent, 0·40M. No navigational dangers, but beware ebb setting SE across hbr ent; give S pierhd a wide berth. Ent is difficult without power, due to blanking by piers. 3kn speed limit. Night entry, see below. Caution: Up-river of Dock ent keep to NE side of river. Work in progress on windfarm on SW bank (2003).

LIGHTS AND MARKS No ldg lts/marks. Conspic factory chy 2·5ca NW of piers. N pier L Fl G 7s 7m 10M, vis shore-287°. S pier Fl WR 6s 11m 13M; vis R shore–223°, W223°–350°, R350°–shore. **Caution**: The pier head lts are very difficult to see due to powerful orange flood lts near the root of both piers shining E/ENE onto the piers (to assist pilotage of departing commercial vessels). Best advice to visitors is to approach from the NE with R sector just showing, or enter by day.

R/T Marina Ch 16 12 (HJ); Arklow SC Ch 10.

TELEPHONE (Dial code 0402) HM 32466, 📠 31068; MRCC (01) 6620922/3; Coast/Cliff Rescue Service 32430; RNLI 32901; ⊖ 32553; Police 32304/5; Dr 32421.

FACILITIES (from seaward) **Dock** €10.00, use showers and toilets in LB Hse; **Marina** (60) €2.40/m, ☎ 39901/32610. **Arklow SC** (NE bank, 500m up-river from Dock), showers, pontoon €14.00, 1 Ⓥ. **Services:** FW, ME, El, ⚒, C (20 ton mobile), Kos. **Town** EC Wed; limited CH for yachts, 🛒, R, P & D (cans), Bar, ✉, Ⓑ, ⇌, ✈ (Dublin).

MINOR HARBOURS S of ARKLOW

COURTOWN, Cork, **52°38'·55N 06°13'·50W**. AC 1787. 10M S of Arklow is feasible in settled weather and offshore winds. Caution: 10m wide ent; only 1m (maintained by local YC) at MLWS due to silting. AB on E wall or pick up vacant mooring.

Minor hbrs S of Arklow *continued*

POLDUFF PIER, Cork, **52°34'·15N 06°11'·97W**. AC 1787. 14M S of Arklow. Pier, 100m long, extends in NE direction from shore. NW side of pier has slipway from shore and 1m depth alongside. Local moorings W of pier. Good shelter for small boats in S to W winds. Swell in winds E of S. Appr in daylight only. Appr is clear from NE to E. Rks extend from shore E'ward 200m N of pier but steering along line of pier will clear them. Pub near pier. Village 1M W.

9.12.12 WEXFORD

Wexford **52°20'·10N 06°27'·00W**

CHARTS AC 1787, 1772; Imray C61; Irish OS 77

TIDES –0450 Dover; ML 1·3; Duration 0630; Zone 0 (UT)

Standard Port COBH (⟶)

Times				Height (metres)			
High Water		Low Water		MHWS	MHWN	MLWN	MLWS
0500	1100	0500	1100	4·1	3·2	1·3	0·4
1700	2300	1700	2300				
Differences WEXFORD							
+0126	+0126	+0118	+0108	–2·1	–1·7	–0·3	+0·1

SHELTER 250m of AB available just below bridge. Sheltered ⚓ off town quays in 2·3m, but streams are strong. Some 🅥s are provided by WHBC, close N of Ballast Bank. There are no commercial users, other than FVs. Work continues on new waterfront on W side of river.

NAVIGATION For regularly updated local information visit www.whbtc.com/harbour.htm or ☎ 053 22039. Entry is hazardous in fresh/strong conditions between S and NE when the sea breaks on the bar. It is also difficult at any time for craft with a draft >1.3m. The Bar Buoy (lit PHM) 52°19'·59N 06°19·57W (2004 position) marks the entrance to the channel marked by 15 lit PHMs and 3 lit SHMs. Do not confuse channel markers with those of mussel beds. From Rossiter's PHM about 1 ca north of the S training wall steer approximately 280° to pass well south of the *Black Man* marking the end of the N training wall. Proceed either to the quays or by arrangement with WHBTC to a visitor's mooring.

LIGHTS AND MARKS The marks and tracks on chartlet should be treated with great caution. The white marks on the embankment along the N side of hbr have only limited relevance to the shifting chan. There are no ldg lts. The 2 church spires at Wexford give useful general orientation.

R/T Wexford Hbr BC VHF Ch 16 (best time to try 1000-1200 Hrs).

TELEPHONE (Dial code 053) Wexford Hbr BC 22039; MRSC (01) 6620922/3; ⊖ 33116; Police 053 22333; Dr 31154; ⊞ 42233.

FACILITIES **Wexford Quays,** AB (free), Slip, P, D, FW, ME, El, 🛒, CH; **Wexford Hbr Boat Club**, Slip, C (5 ton), Bar; **Town** ✉, Ⓑ, ⇌, ✈ (Waterford).

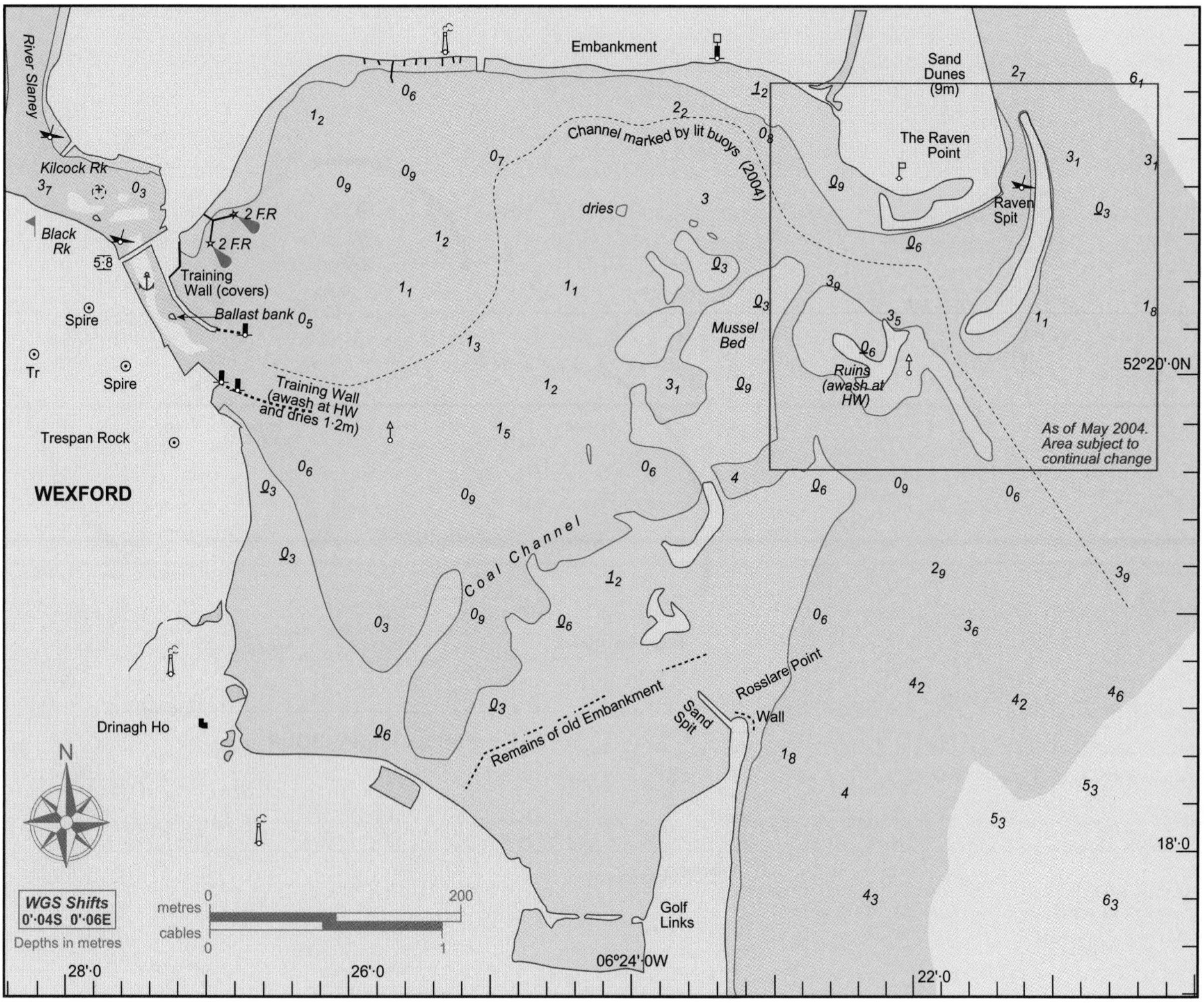
River Slaney
Embankment
Sand Dunes (9m)
The Raven Point
Raven Spit
Kilcock Rk
Black Rk
2 F.R
2 F.R
Training Wall (covers)
Ballast bank
Channel marked by lit buoys (2004)
dries
Mussel Bed
Ruins (awash at HW)
Spire
Tr
Spire
Training Wall (awash at HW and dries 1·2m)
Trespan Rock
WEXFORD
52°20'·0N
As of May 2004. Area subject to continual change
Coal Channel
Rosslare Point
Sand Spit
Wall
Remains of old Embankment
Drinagh Ho
N
Golf Links
WGS Shifts
0'·04S 0'·06E
Depths in metres
metres
cables
0
200
0
1
28'·0
26'·0
06°24'·0W
22'·0
18'·0

9.12.13 ROSSLARE HARBOUR

Dublin **52°15'·30N 06°20'·90W** ❀❀❀◊◊✿

CHARTS AC 1787, 1772,; Imray C61, C57; Irish OS 77

TIDES –0510 Dover; ML 1·1; Duration 0640; Zone 0 (UT)

Standard Port COBH (⟶)

Times				**Height (metres)**			
High Water		Low Water		MHWS	MHWN	MLWN	MLWS
0500	1100	0500	1100	4·1	3·2	1·3	0·4
1700	2300	1700	2300				
Differences ROSSLARE HARBOUR							
+0045	+0035	+0015	–0005	–2·2	–1·8	–0·5	–0·1

SHELTER Useful passage shelter from SW'lies, but few facilities for yachts which may berth on E wall of marshalling area (⛵ on the chartlet, 3·7m), or ⚓ about 0·5M W of hbr. Small craft hbr not advised. In winds from WNW-NNE it is often uncomfortable and, if these winds freshen, dangerous; leave at once, via S Shear. Rosslare has 160 ferry/high-speed catamaran (41kn) movements per week.

NAVIGATION WPT 52°14'·82N 06°15·60W, (abeam S Long SCM buoy, VQ (6)+L Fl 10s), 285° to bkwtr lt, 2·92M. Main appr from E, S and W is via S Shear, buoyed/lit chan to S of Holden's Bed, a shoal of varying depth; the tide sets across the chan. From S, beware rks off Greenore Pt, and overfalls here and over The Baillies. From the N, appr via N Shear. Tuskar TSS is approx 8M ESE of hbr. Yachts, bound N/S, will usually navigate to the W of Tuskar Rk where the 3·5M wide chan lies to seaward of The Bailies. A passage inshore of The Bailies requires local knowledge and should not be attempted at night. In heavy weather or poor vis, passage E of Tuskar Rk is advised.

LIGHTS AND MARKS Tuskar Rk, Q (2) 7·5s 33m 28M, is 5·8M SE of hbr. Water tr (R lt, 35m) is conspic 0·8M SSE of hbr ent. Bkwtr lt, Oc WRG 5s 15m 13/10M, see 9.12.4. Its two W sectors (188°-208° and 283°–286°) cover N and S Shear respectively. Note: Powerful floodlights in the hbr make identification of navigational lights difficult.

R/T Call: *Rosslare Hbr* VHF Ch **12** (H24) before entering hbr.

TELEPHONE (Dial code 053) HM 57921, mobile 087 598535, 📠 33206; MRCC (01) 6620922/3; LB Lookout Stn 33205; ⊖ 33116; Police 053 33204; Dr 31154; 🄷 42233.

FACILITIES **Hbr Ops** ☎ 33162, No dues, P&D (cans), L, FW (by hose on Berths 2 & 3), ME, C, Divers, Kos, El. **Village;** 🛒, R, Bar, ✉, Ⓑ, ⇌, ✈ (Dublin). Ferries to Fishguard, Pembroke Dock, Cherbourg and Roscoff.

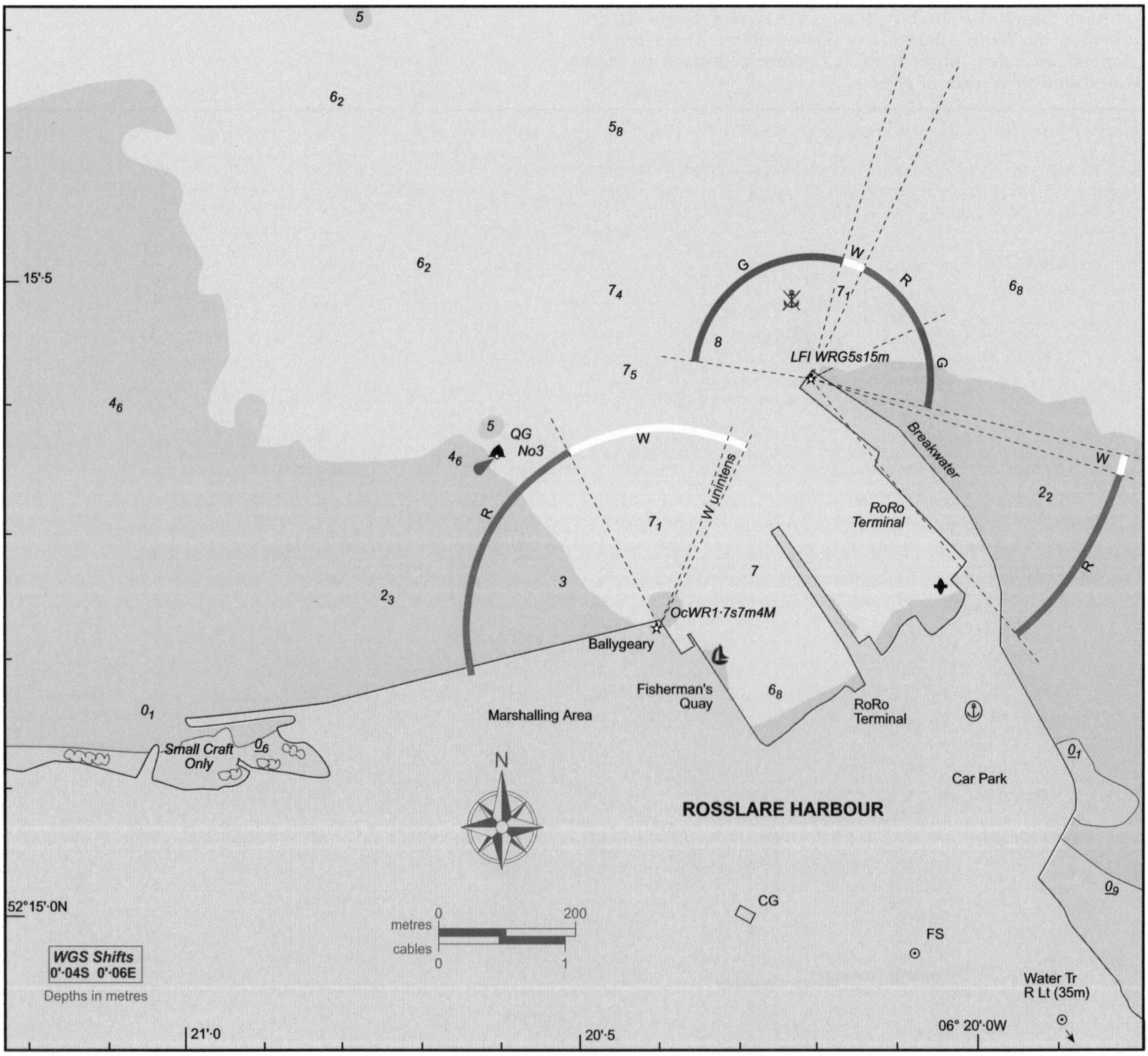
15'·5
LFl WRG5s15m
Breakwater
RoRo Terminal
QG
No3
W unintens
OcWR1·7s7m4M
Ballygeary
Fisherman's Quay
Marshalling Area
RoRo Terminal
Small Craft Only
N
ROSSLARE HARBOUR
Car Park
CG
FS
Water Tr
R Lt (35m)
52°15'·0N
WGS Shifts
0'·04S 0'·06E
Depths in metres
metres
cables
21'·0
20'·5
06° 20'·0W

9.12.14 KILMORE QUAY

Wexford **52°10'·25N 06°35'·15W** ❁❁❁◊◊✿✿✿

CHARTS AC *2049,* 2740; Imray C61, C57; Irish OS 77

TIDES –0535 Dover; ML No data; Duration 0605; Zone 0 (UT)

Standard Port COBH (⟶)

Times				**Height (metres)**			
High Water		Low Water		MHWS	MHWN	MLWN	MLWS
0500	1100	0500	1100	4·1	3·2	1·3	0·4
1700	2300	1700	2300				
Differences BAGINBUN HEAD (5M NE of Hook Hd)							
+0003	+0003	–0008	–0008	–0·2	–0·1	+0·2	+0·2
GREAT SALTEE							
+0019	+0009	–0004	+0006	–0·3	–0·4	No data	
CARNSORE POINT							
+0029	+0019	–0002	+0008	–1·1	–1·0	No data	

SHELTER Excellent in marina (3·0m depth), but hbr ent is exposed to SE'lies. FVs berth on W and E piers, close S of marina.

NAVIGATION WPT 52°09'·20N 06°35'·28W, 007° to pierhd lt, 1·0M, on ldg line. Great (57m) and Little (35m) Saltee Islands lie 3M and 1·7M to SSW and S, respectively, of hbr, separated by Saltee Sound. From the E, safest appr initially is via Saltee Sound, then N to WPT. Caution: In bad weather seas break on the Bohurs and The Bore, rks 2M E of Saltee Islands. Beware Goose Rk (2·6m) close W of Little Saltee and Murroch's Rk (2·1m) 6ca NW of Little Saltee. St Patrick's Bridge, 650m E of the WPT, is a 300m wide E/W chan used by FVs and yachts, but carrying only 2·4m; care needed in strong onshore winds. It is marked by a PHM buoy, Fl R 6s, and a SHM buoy, Fl G 6s, (laid Apr to mid-Sep); general direction of buoyage is E. From the W, appr is clear but keep at least 5ca off Forlorn Pt to avoid Forlorn Rk (1·5m).

LIGHTS AND MARKS Ldg lts/marks, both Oc 4s 3/6m 6M, W pylons with R stripe, lead 008° to the hbr. From W, ldg lts are obsc'd by piers until S of hbr ent. Turn 90° port into hbr ent, just past ☆ QRG at head of W Quay; do not overshoot into shoal water ahead. The R sectors of this ☆, QRG 7m 5M, R269°-354°, G354°-003°(9°), R003°-077°, warn of Forlorn Rock and The Lings to W of the ldg line and shingle banks drying 0·6m close E of the ldg line. A white-gabled church is conspic from afar, as are two 20m high flood lt pylons on the E quay. A disused lt ship at the inner end of W quay is a museum; its lt housing is of no navigational significance. Ballyteige Castle (AC 2740) is hard to see and of no navigational use.

R/T VHF Ch 09 (occas).

TELEPHONE (Dial code 053) HM ☎/📠 29955; ⊖ 33741; MRCC (01) 6620922/3; Emergency/Dr/Police 999.

FACILITIES Marina (35+20 Ⓥ) ☎/📠 29955, €2.20, Slip, ⛽, LB; **Village** Showers at Stella Maris (10 mins walk), Gaz, CH, ME, El, D & P (cans) is 3M away, R, Bar, 🛒, ✉, Ⓗ (Wexford 15M).

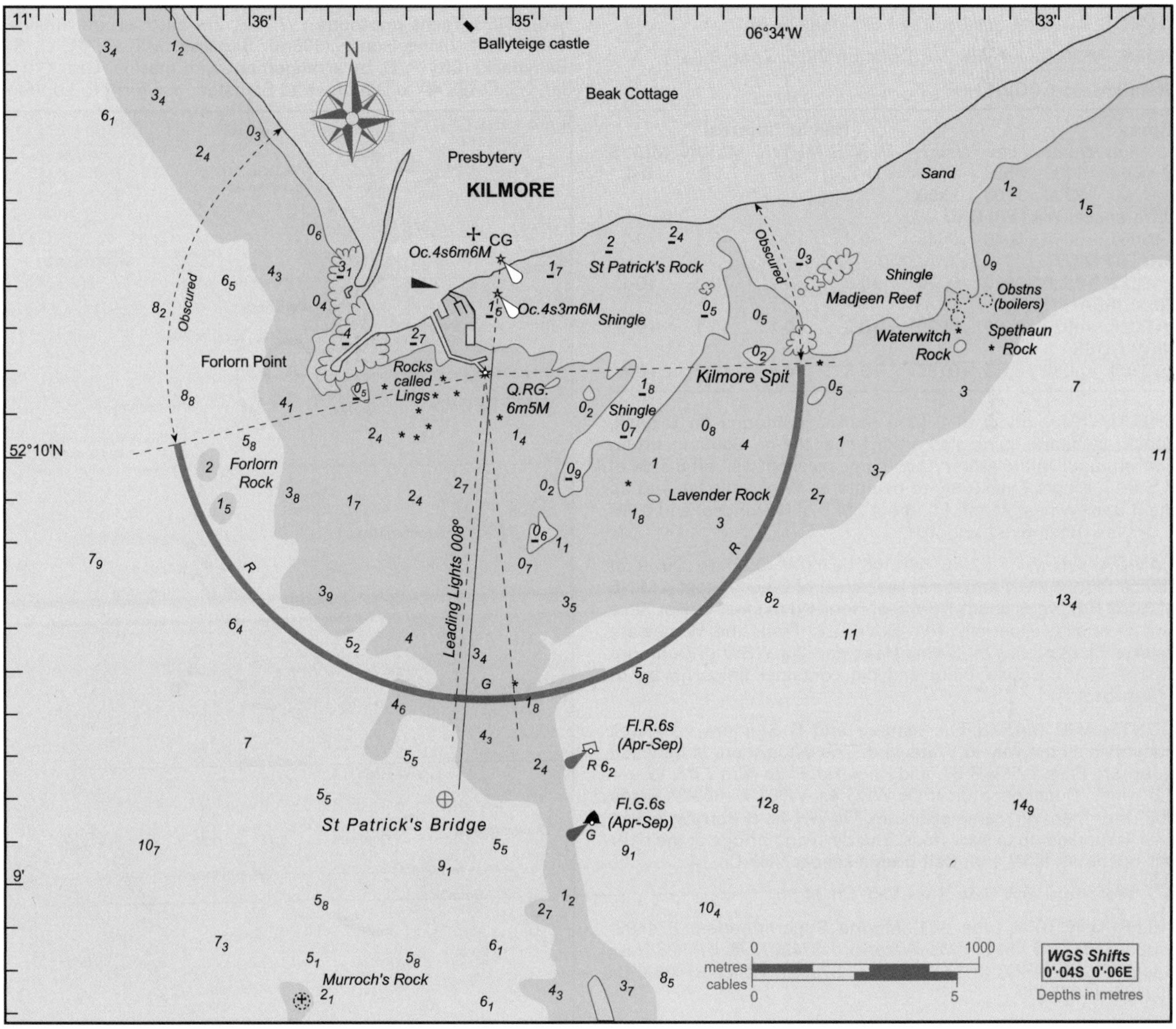

36'
35'
06°34'W
33'
11'
52°10'N
9'
N
Ballyteige castle
Beak Cottage
Presbytery
KILMORE
CG
Oc.4s6m6M
Oc.4s3m6M
St Patrick's Rock
Shingle
Obscured
Madjeen Reef
Obstns (boilers)
Waterwitch Rock
Spethaun Rock
Sand
Forlorn Point
Rocks called Lings
Q.RG. 6m5M
Kilmore Spit
Forlorn Rock
Lavender Rock
Leading Lights 008°
Fl.R.6s (Apr-Sep)
Fl.G.6s (Apr-Sep)
St Patrick's Bridge
Murroch's Rock
metres
cables
1000
WGS Shifts
0'·04S 0'·06E
Depths in metres

9.12.15 WATERFORD

Waterford **52°15'·50N 07°06'·00W** ❀❀❀◊◊✿✿

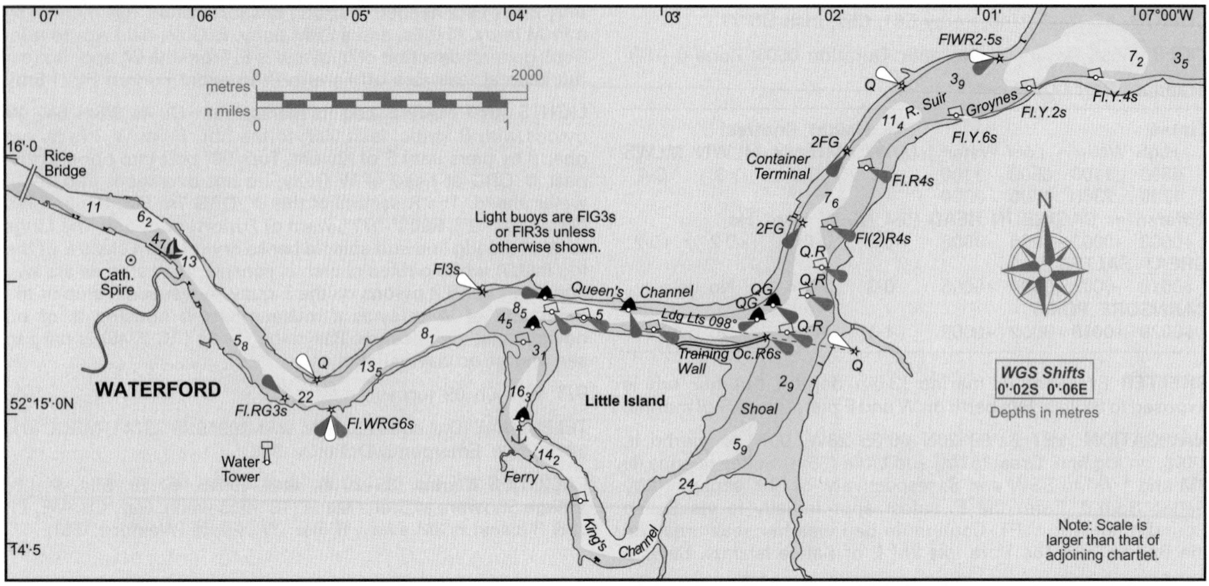
07'
06'
05'
04'
03'
02'
01'
07°00'W
metres
n miles
0
2000
1
16'·0
Rice Bridge
Cath. Spire
WATERFORD
52°15'·0N
Water Tower
14'·5
Light buoys are FlG3s or FlR3s unless otherwise shown.
Fl3s
Queen's Channel
Ldg Lts 098°
Training Wall
Oc.R6s
Q
Fl.RG3s
Fl.WRG6s
Little Island
Ferry
King's Channel
Shoal
Container Terminal
2FG
R. Suir
Groynes
FlWR2·5s
Fl.Y.2s
Fl.Y.4s
Fl.Y.6s
Fl.R4s
Fl(2)R4s
Q.R
QG
WGS Shifts
0'·02S 0'·06E
Depths in metres
Note: Scale is larger than that of adjoining chartlet.

CHARTS AC *2049, 2046;* Imray C57; Irish OS 76

TIDES –0520 Dover; ML 2·4; Duration 0605; Zone 0 (UT)

Standard Port COBH (⟶)

Times				Height (metres)			
High Water		Low Water		MHWS	MHWN	MLWN	MLWS
0500	1100	0500	1100	4·1	3·2	1·3	0·4
1700	2300	1700	2300				
Differences WATERFORD							
+0057	+0057	+0046	+0046	+0·4	+0·3	–0·1	+0·1
CHEEKPOINT							
+0022	+0020	+0020	+0020	+0·3	+0·2	+0·2	+0·1
KILMOKEA POINT							
+0026	+0022	+0020	+0020	+0·2	+0·1	+0·1	+0·1
NEW ROSS							
+0100	+0030	+0055	+0130	+0·3	+0·4	+0·3	+0·4

SHELTER Very good on 2 long marina pontoons on S bank, abeam cathedral spire, also a third near the br. Caution: strong tidal stream. Up the estuary are many excellent ⚓s: off S side of R Suir in King's Chan (only to be entered W of Little Is); and up the R Barrow near Marsh Pt (about 2M S of New Ross) and 0·5M S of New Ross fixed bridge.

NAVIGATION WPT 52°06'·50N 06°56'·50W, 002° to Dir lt at Duncannon, 6·7M. From the E, keep clear of Brecaun reef (2M NE of Hook Hd). Keep about 1·5M S of Hook Hd to clear Tower Race and overfalls, especially HW Dover ±2. From the W beware Falskirt Rk (3m), 2ca off Swine Head and 2M WSW of Dunmore East (9.12.16). Cruise liners and big container ships go up to Waterford.

LIGHTS AND MARKS The estuary and R Suir are very well buoyed/lit all the way to Waterford. The estuary ent is between Dunmore East, L Fl WR 8s, and Hook Hd, Fl 3s 46m 23M, W tr + 2 B bands. Duncannon dir lt Oc WRG 4s, W001·7°–002·2°, leads 002° into the river; same structure, Oc WR 4s. R Barrow is also well lit/marked up to New Ross. The rly swing bridge at the river ent opens at its W end. Call bridge-keeper VHF Ch 14.

R/T Waterford and New Ross VHF Ch 14 16.

TELEPHONE (Dial code 051) Marina Superintendent 874499, mobile 087 238 4944; HMs Waterford 874907, 🏛 874908/New Ross 421303; MRCC (01) 6620922; ⊜ 875391; Police 874888; Dr 883194; Ⓗ 875429.

FACILITIES Yacht pontoons FW, ⛽, 2m all tides on outside; showers at Viking House (300m). **Services:** ME, El, ✂, C, BY (Ballyhack). **City** P, D, by arrangement with marina, Gaz, 🛒, R, Bar, ✉, 🅾, Ⓑ, ⇌ to Dublin, ✈ to Stansted, bus/ferry to London.

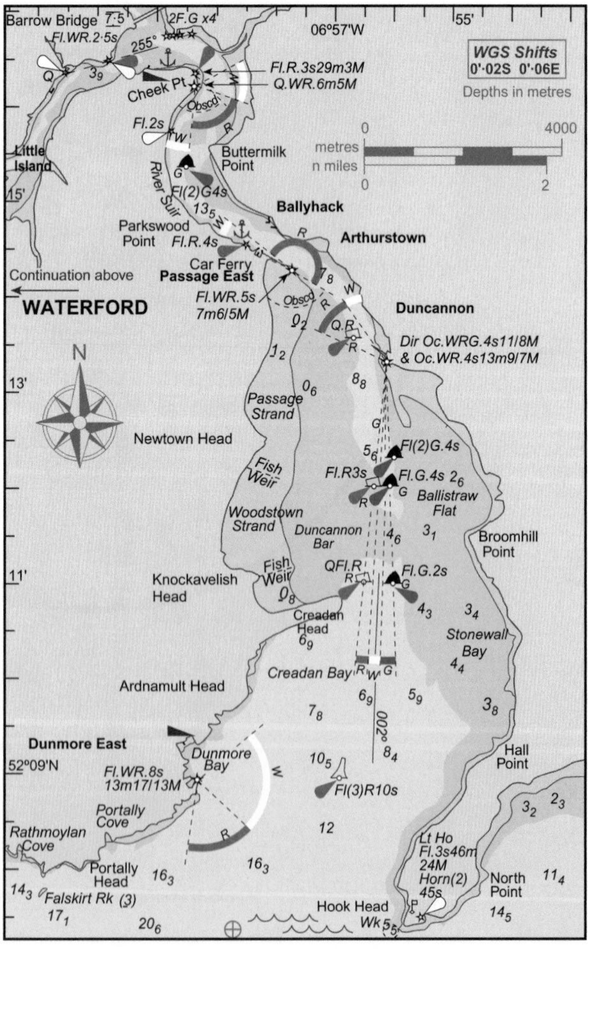
Barrow Bridge 7·5
Fl.WR.2·5s
255°
2F.G x4
06°57'W
55'
Fl.R.3s29m3M
Q.WR.6m5M
Cheek Pt
WGS Shifts
0'·02S 0'·06E
Depths in metres
Fl.2s
Little Island
Buttermilk Point
metres
n miles
0
4000
2
15'
River Suir
Fl(2)G4s
Ballyhack
Parkswood Point
Fl.R.4s
Arthurstown
Car Ferry
Passage East
Continuation above
WATERFORD
Fl.WR.5s 7m6/5M
Duncannon
Dir Oc.WRG.4s11/8M & Oc.WR.4s13m9/7M
13'
Passage Strand
Newtown Head
Fish Weir
Fl.R3s
Fl(2)G.4s
Fl.G.4s
Ballistraw Flat
Woodstown Strand
Duncannon Bar
Broomhill Point
11'
Knockavelish Head
QFl.R
Fl.G.2s
Creadan Head
Stonewall Bay
Creadan Bay
Ardnamult Head
002°
Dunmore East
Dunmore Bay
52°09'N
Fl.WR.8s 13m17/13M
Hall Point
Fl(3)R10s
Portally Cove
Rathmoylan Cove
Lt Ho Fl.3s46m 24M Horn(2) 45s
Portally Head
Falskirt Rk (3)
North Point
Hook Head
Wk

9.12.16 DUNMORE EAST

Waterford **52°08'·95N 06°59'·37W** ❁❁❁◊◊✿

CHARTS AC *2049, 2046*; Imray C57, C61; Irish OS 76

TIDES –0535 Dover; ML 2·4; Duration 0605; Zone 0 (UT)

Standard Port COBH (⟶)

Times				**Height (metres)**			
High Water		Low Water		MHWS	MHWN	MLWN	MLWS
0500	1100	0500	1100	4·1	3·2	1·3	0·4
1700	2300	1700	2300				
Differences DUNMORE EAST							
+0008	+0003	0000	0000	+0·1	0·0	+0·1	+0·2
DUNGARVAN HARBOUR							
+0004	+0012	+0007	–0001	0·0	+0·1	–0·2	0·0

SHELTER Very good in hbr, but yacht moorings are exposed to E'lies. ⚓ N of the hbr. Visitors welcome but call HM before arrival. A useful passage port and refuge, but primarily a busy FV hbr. In bad weather berth on FVs at W Wharf, clear of ice plant, in at least 2m. Or go up R Suir to Waterford (9.12.15).

NAVIGATION WPT (see also 9.12.15) 52°08'·00N, 06°58'·00W, 317° to bkwtr lt, 1·2M. Enter under power. From E, stay 1·5M off Hook Hd to clear Tower Race; then alter course for hbr in R sector of E pier lt ho. In calm weather Hook Hd can be rounded 1ca off. From W, beware Falskirt Rk (off Swines Hd, 2M WSW) dries 3·0m. By night track E for Hook Hd until in R sector of E pier lt, then alter to N.

LIGHTS AND MARKS Lts as chartlet and see 9.12.4.

R/T VHF Ch 14 16 (Pilot Station).

TELEPHONE (Dial code 051) HM 383166, Fax 383607; Pilot 383119; Police 383112; ⊖ 875391; MRCC (01) 6620922/3; Coast Life Saving Service 383115; Dr 383194.

FACILITIES Hbr ☎ 383166, D, FW (E pier), Slip, Kos, CH, BH (230 ton); **Waterford Hbr SC ☎** 83389, R, Bar; **Village** P (cans), Bar, R, ⛟, Ⓑ, ✉, ⇌ (Waterford), ✈ (Dublin).

DUNGARVAN BAY (22M W of Dunmore East): See 9.12.18.

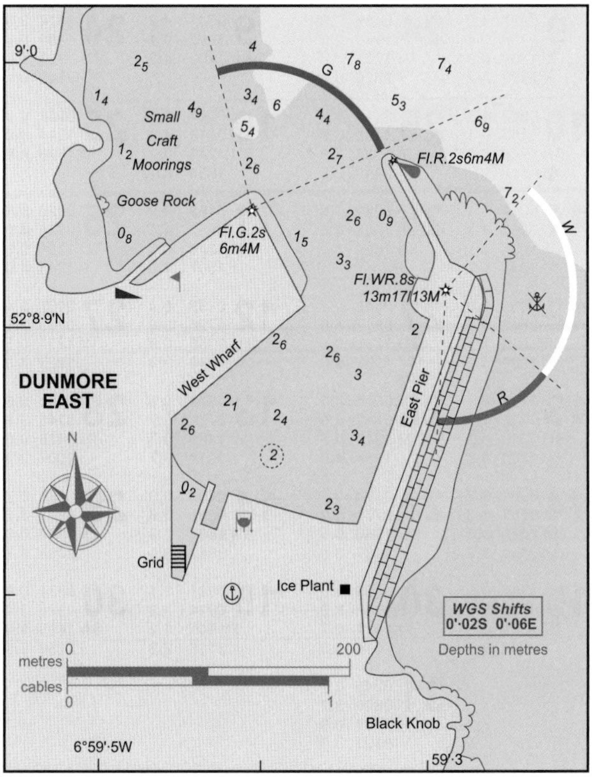
DUNMORE EAST
Small Craft Moorings
Goose Rock
Fl.G.2s 6m4M
Fl.R.2s6m4M
Fl.WR.8s 13m17/13M
West Wharf
East Pier
Ice Plant
Grid
Black Knob
52°8·9'N
6°59'·5W
WGS Shifts 0'·02S 0'·06E
Depths in metres

9.12.17 YOUGHAL

Cork **51°56'·54N 07°50'·20W** ❁❁◊◊◊✿✿

CHARTS AC *2049*, 2071; Imray C57; Irish OS 81, 82

TIDES –0556 Dover; ML 2·1; Duration 0555; Zone 0 (UT)

Standard Port COBH (⟶)

Times				**Height (metres)**			
High Water		Low Water		MHWS	MHWN	MLWN	MLWS
0500	1100	0500	1100	4·1	3·2	1·3	0·4
1700	2300	1700	2300				
Differences YOUGHAL							
0000	+0010	+0010	0000	–0·2	–0·1	–0·1	–0·1

SHELTER Good, but strong S'lies cause swell inside the hbr. Only drying AB. ⚓ as chartlet; no dues. Strong tides run throughout anchorages.

NAVIGATION WPT, East Bar, 51°55'·62N 07°48'·00W, 302° to Fl WR 2·5s lt, 1·8M. Beware Blackball Ledge (ECM buoy Q(3)10s) and Bar Rks (SCM buoy Q(6)+L.Fl.15s), both outside hbr ent in R sector of lt ho. From W, appr via West Bar (1·7m) is shorter; E Bar has 2·0m. In winds E to SSW >F6 both Bars are likely to have dangerous seas. Beware salmon nets set throughout June-July, Mon-Thurs 0400-2100.

LIGHTS AND MARKS W of ent, Fl WR 2·5s 24m 17/14M, W tr (15m), has two W sectors ldg over the bars (see 9.12.4). Water tr is conspic from seaward; clock tr and ✠ tr within hbr. Up-river, 175° transit of convent belfry tr/town hall clears W of Red Bank.

R/T VHF Ch 14 16 HW±3 (Youghal Shipping)

TELEPHONE (Dial code 024) HM Mobile 0872511143 MRCC (066) 9476109; Coast Guard 93252; ⊖ (021) 968783; Police 92200; Dr 92702. Youghal Shipping 92577(for poss. drying AB)

FACILITIES Services: L, FW , Slip. AB(☎Youghal Shipping) **Town** P & D (cans), ⛟, R, Bar, ✉, Ⓑ, Bus (Cork/W'ford), ✈(Cork).

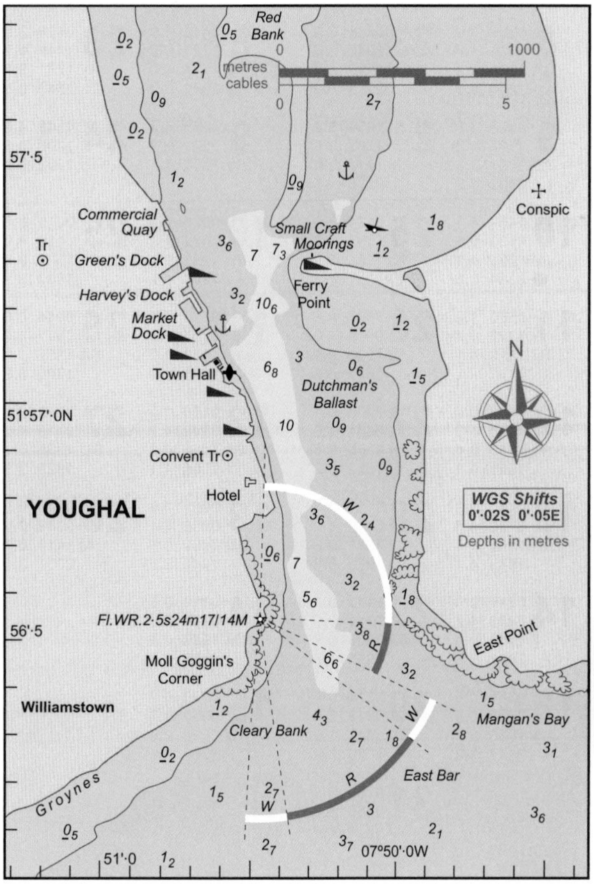
YOUGHAL
Red Bank
Commercial Quay
Green's Dock
Harvey's Dock
Market Dock
Town Hall
Small Craft Moorings
Ferry Point
Conspic
Dutchman's Ballast
Convent Tr
Hotel
Fl.WR.2·5s24m17/14M
Moll Goggin's Corner
Williamstown
Cleary Bank
East Point
Mangan's Bay
East Bar
Groynes
57'·5
51°57'·0N
56'·5
51'·0
07°50'·0W
WGS Shifts 0'·02S 0'·05E
Depths in metres

TIME ZONE (UT)
For Summer Time add ONE hour in **non-shaded areas**

IRELAND – COBH

LAT 51°51′N LONG 8°18′W

TIMES AND HEIGHTS OF HIGH AND LOW WATERS

SPRING & NEAP TIDES
Dates in red are SPRINGS
Dates in blue are NEAPS

YEAR **2005**

JANUARY

Date	Day	Time	m	Time	m	Time	m	Time	m
1	SA	0240	1.1	0844	3.8	1510	1.2	2057	3.7
2	SU	0325	1.2	0927	3.7	1556	1.3	2144	3.6
3	M	0414	1.2	1015	3.7	1646	1.3	◑ 2236	3.6
4	TU	0510	1.3	1109	3.6	1746	1.4	2335	3.5
5	W	0614	1.3	1210	3.6	1853	1.4		
6	TH	0041	3.5	0721	1.3	1316	3.6	2000	1.3
7	F	0148	3.6	0829	1.2	1422	3.7	2106	1.1
8	SA	0255	3.8	0935	1.0	1526	3.8	2207	0.9
9	SU	0359	3.9	1037	0.8	1627	3.9	2303	0.7
10	M	0457	4.1	1132	0.6	1722	4.1	● 2354	0.5
11	TU	0550	4.2	1222	0.4	1812	4.1		
12	W	0042	0.4	0638	4.3	1310	0.4	1859	4.1
13	TH	0130	0.3	0726	4.3	1357	0.4	1945	4.1
14	F	0217	0.4	0813	4.2	1443	0.5	2031	3.9
15	SA	0305	0.5	0900	4.0	1530	0.7	2117	3.8
16	SU	0353	0.7	0947	3.9	1618	0.8	2203	3.6
17	M	0443	0.8	1036	3.7	1708	1.0	◐ 2253	3.5
18	TU	0538	1.0	1129	3.5	1804	1.2	2350	3.3
19	W	0638	1.2	1230	3.4	1906	1.3		
20	TH	0058	3.3	0743	1.3	1337	3.3	2012	1.3
21	F	0209	3.3	0850	1.3	1441	3.4	2116	1.3
22	SA	0314	3.5	0951	1.2	1539	3.5	2213	1.1
23	SU	0408	3.6	1042	1.0	1629	3.7	2258	1.0
24	M	0454	3.8	1123	0.9	1711	3.8	2335	0.8
25	TU	0534	3.9	1157	0.8	1748	3.9	○	
26	W	0007	0.8	0609	4.0	1228	0.8	1821	3.9
27	TH	0036	0.7	0641	4.0	1259	0.8	1852	3.9
28	F	0107	0.7	0712	4.0	1331	0.8	1923	3.9
29	SA	0140	0.8	0744	3.9	1405	0.9	1955	3.8
30	SU	0216	0.8	0818	3.9	1441	1.0	2030	3.8
31	M	0255	0.9	0855	3.8	1519	1.0	2109	3.8

FEBRUARY

Date	Day	Time	m	Time	m	Time	m	Time	m
1	TU	0337	1.0	0936	3.8	1600	1.2	2154	3.7
2	W	0425	1.1	1024	3.6	1650	1.3	◑ 2248	3.6
3	TH	0524	1.3	1123	3.5	1758	1.4	2355	3.4
4	F	0639	1.4	1236	3.4	1922	1.4		
5	SA	0114	3.4	0801	1.3	1356	3.4	2043	1.2
6	SU	0236	3.5	0921	1.1	1514	3.5	2154	0.9
7	M	0350	3.8	1028	0.8	1620	3.8	2253	0.6
8	TU	0449	4.0	1123	0.5	1714	4.0	● 2344	0.3
9	W	0539	4.2	1211	0.3	1801	4.1		
10	TH	0029	0.2	0624	4.3	1255	0.2	1844	4.2
11	F	0113	0.1	0707	4.3	1337	0.2	1925	4.2
12	SA	0156	0.2	0749	4.2	1418	0.3	2005	4.1
13	SU	0237	0.3	0830	4.1	1458	0.5	2044	3.9
14	M	0318	0.5	0910	3.9	1538	0.7	2123	3.7
15	TU	0400	0.7	0950	3.7	1619	0.9	2204	3.5
16	W	0446	1.0	1035	3.4	1707	1.2	◐ 2252	3.3
17	TH	0541	1.3	1130	3.2	1807	1.4	2358	3.1
18	F	0649	1.4	1247	3.0	1923	1.5		
19	SA	0131	3.1	0808	1.4	1412	3.1	2044	1.4
20	SU	0251	3.2	0927	1.3	1520	3.3	2154	1.2
21	M	0350	3.5	1025	1.0	1612	3.5	2243	0.9
22	TU	0436	3.7	1107	0.8	1654	3.7	2320	0.7
23	W	0515	3.9	1140	0.7	1731	3.8	2349	0.6
24	TH	0549	4.0	1208	0.6	1803	3.9	○	
25	F	0015	0.6	0619	4.0	1237	0.6	1832	3.9
26	SA	0044	0.6	0647	4.0	1307	0.6	1900	3.9
27	SU	0115	0.6	0716	4.0	1338	0.7	1929	3.9
28	M	0149	0.6	0748	3.9	1411	0.7	2001	3.9

MARCH

Date	Day	Time	m	Time	m	Time	m	Time	m
1	TU	0226	0.7	0822	3.9	1446	0.8	2037	3.8
2	W	0306	0.8	0901	3.8	1525	1.0	2119	3.7
3	TH	0352	1.0	0948	3.6	1614	1.2	◑ 2213	3.5
4	F	0452	1.2	1049	3.3	1722	1.4	2323	3.3
5	SA	0610	1.4	1209	3.1	1854	1.4		
6	SU	0053	3.2	0741	1.3	1343	3.2	2026	1.2
7	M	0229	3.4	0910	1.0	1508	3.4	2142	0.9
8	TU	0342	3.7	1018	0.7	1611	3.7	2241	0.5
9	W	0437	4.0	1109	0.4	1701	4.0	2329	0.2
10	TH	0523	4.2	1153	0.1	1744	4.2	●	
11	F	0011	0.1	0604	4.3	1234	0.1	1823	4.2
12	SA	0051	0.0	0643	4.3	1312	0.1	1900	4.2
13	SU	0129	0.1	0721	4.2	1349	0.2	1936	4.1
14	M	0207	0.3	0757	4.0	1425	0.4	2010	3.9
15	TU	0244	0.5	0832	3.8	1500	0.6	2045	3.8
16	W	0322	0.7	0909	3.6	1537	0.9	2123	3.5
17	TH	0404	1.0	0949	3.4	1620	1.2	◐ 2207	3.3
18	F	0456	1.3	1038	3.1	1719	1.4	2308	3.0
19	SA	0605	1.5	1153	2.9	1840	1.5		
20	SU	0052	2.9	0728	1.5	1342	2.9	2007	1.4
21	M	0225	3.1	0852	1.3	1455	3.1	2123	1.2
22	TU	0324	3.4	0954	1.0	1546	3.4	2214	0.9
23	W	0408	3.6	1036	0.8	1628	3.6	2250	0.7
24	TH	0446	3.8	1110	0.6	1703	3.8	2320	0.6
25	F	0519	3.9	1139	0.5	1735	3.9	○ 2347	0.5
26	SA	0549	4.0	1208	0.5	1804	3.9		
27	SU	0016	0.4	0617	4.0	1239	0.5	1833	4.0
28	M	0049	0.4	0647	4.0	1312	0.5	1904	4.0
29	TU	0124	0.5	0721	3.9	1346	0.6	1937	3.9
30	W	0203	0.6	0758	3.9	1424	0.7	2016	3.9
31	TH	0246	0.7	0840	3.7	1507	0.9	2101	3.7

APRIL

Date	Day	Time	m	Time	m	Time	m	Time	m
1	F	0337	0.9	0930	3.5	1600	1.1	2157	3.5
2	SA	0439	1.1	1034	3.2	1712	1.3	◑ 2312	3.3
3	SU	0559	1.3	1159	3.1	1843	1.3		
4	M	0049	3.2	0732	1.2	1337	3.1	2014	1.1
5	TU	0221	3.4	0857	0.9	1456	3.4	2127	0.7
6	W	0326	3.7	0959	0.6	1553	3.7	2222	0.4
7	TH	0417	4.0	1048	0.3	1640	4.0	2308	0.2
8	F	0501	4.2	1130	0.2	1722	4.1	● 2349	0.1
9	SA	0541	4.2	1209	0.1	1800	4.2		
10	SU	0027	0.1	0617	4.2	1246	0.2	1834	4.1
11	M	0103	0.2	0652	4.1	1320	0.3	1907	4.0
12	TU	0138	0.4	0726	3.9	1355	0.5	1940	3.9
13	W	0213	0.6	0759	3.7	1429	0.7	2014	3.7
14	TH	0250	0.8	0835	3.6	1504	0.9	2052	3.5
15	F	0331	1.1	0914	3.3	1546	1.2	2136	3.3
16	SA	0422	1.3	1001	3.1	1643	1.4	◐ 2232	3.1
17	SU	0529	1.4	1107	2.9	1800	1.5	2359	2.9
18	M	0647	1.4	1251	2.9	1922	1.4		
19	TU	0141	3.0	0801	1.3	1412	3.1	2031	1.2
20	W	0242	3.3	0901	1.1	1505	3.3	2124	1.0
21	TH	0327	3.5	0948	0.8	1547	3.6	2205	0.7
22	F	0406	3.7	1027	0.7	1625	3.7	2240	0.6
23	SA	0441	3.8	1103	0.5	1659	3.9	2314	0.5
24	SU	0514	3.9	1138	0.5	1733	3.9	○ 2349	0.4
25	M	0548	4.0	1214	0.4	1808	4.0		
26	TU	0026	0.4	0624	4.0	1251	0.5	1843	4.0
27	W	0107	0.4	0703	3.9	1331	0.5	1923	4.0
28	TH	0151	0.5	0745	3.8	1415	0.6	2007	3.9
29	F	0239	0.7	0833	3.6	1504	0.8	2058	3.7
30	SA	0334	0.9	0928	3.4	1603	1.0	2158	3.5

Chart Datum: 0·13 metres above Ordnance Datum (Dublin)

TIME ZONE (UT)
For Summer Time add ONE hour in **non-shaded areas**

IRELAND – COBH

LAT 51°51′N LONG 8°18′W

TIMES AND HEIGHTS OF HIGH AND LOW WATERS

SPRING & NEAP TIDES
Dates in red are SPRINGS
Dates in blue are NEAPS

YEAR **2005**

MAY

Day	Time	m	Day	Time	m
1 SU	0438 1035 1714 ◑ 2313	1.0 3.2 1.1 3.3	16 M	0454 1034 1719 ◐ 2311	1.3 3.1 1.3 3.1
2 M	0555 1155 1836	1.1 3.2 1.1	17 TU	0602 1146 1830	1.4 3.0 1.3
3 TU	0041 0720 1320 1956	3.3 1.0 3.3 0.9	18 W	0029 0707 1303 1933	3.1 1.3 3.1 1.2
4 W	0159 0833 1430 2102	3.5 0.8 3.5 0.6	19 TH	0137 0805 1404 2027	3.3 1.1 3.3 1.0
5 TH	0259 0931 1526 2156	3.7 0.6 3.7 0.4	20 F	0230 0856 1454 2115	3.5 0.9 3.5 0.8
6 F	0350 1020 1613 2243	3.9 0.4 3.9 0.3	21 SA	0315 0943 1539 2200	3.6 0.8 3.7 0.7
7 SA	0434 1104 1656 2325	4.0 0.3 4.0 0.3	22 SU	0358 1028 1622 2244	3.8 0.6 3.8 0.6
8 SU ●	0515 1144 1735	4.0 0.3 4.0	23 M	0441 1112 1705 ○ 2328	3.9 0.5 3.9 0.5
9 M	0003 0552 1221 1810	0.3 4.0 0.4 4.0	24 TU	0524 1155 1748	3.9 0.5 4.0
10 TU	0039 0627 1255 1843	0.4 3.9 0.5 3.9	25 W	0012 0608 1240 1831	0.4 3.9 0.5 4.0
11 W	0113 0700 1329 1916	0.6 3.8 0.6 3.8	26 TH	0058 0653 1326 1917	0.4 3.9 0.5 4.0
12 TH	0147 0733 1403 1951	0.7 3.7 0.8 3.7	27 F	0147 0742 1415 2007	0.5 3.8 0.6 3.9
13 F	0224 0809 1439 2030	0.9 3.5 1.0 3.5	28 SA	0239 0834 1507 2101	0.6 3.7 0.7 3.8
14 SA	0305 0849 1521 2114	1.1 3.4 1.1 3.4	29 SU	0335 0930 1605 2201	0.7 3.5 0.8 3.6
15 SU	0354 0936 1613 2206	1.2 3.2 1.3 3.2	30 M	0436 1031 1709 ◑ 2307	0.8 3.4 0.8 3.5
			31 TU	0544 1139 1819	0.9 3.4 0.9

JUNE

Day	Time	m	Day	Time	m
1 W	0017 0655 1249 1928	3.5 0.9 3.4 0.8	16 TH	0612 1158 1835	1.2 3.3 1.2
2 TH	0125 0800 1353 2030	3.5 0.8 3.5 0.7	17 F	0028 0712 1300 1934	3.4 1.2 3.4 1.1
3 F	0224 0857 1451 2125	3.6 0.7 3.6 0.6	18 SA	0129 0808 1359 2030	3.5 1.1 3.5 1.0
4 SA	0317 0949 1542 2215	3.7 0.7 3.7 0.6	19 SU	0225 0904 1455 2126	3.6 0.9 3.6 0.8
5 SU	0405 1037 1629 2300	3.8 0.6 3.8 0.6	20 M	0320 0959 1550 2221	3.7 0.8 3.8 0.7
6 M	0449 1119 1711 ● 2341	3.8 0.6 3.8 0.6	21 TU	0415 1052 1643 2313	3.8 0.6 3.9 0.5
7 TU	0530 1158 1750	3.8 0.6 3.8	22 W ○	0507 1142 1734	3.9 0.5 4.0
8 W	0017 0606 1234 1825	0.7 3.8 0.7 3.8	23 TH	0003 0557 1232 1823	0.4 3.9 0.4 4.1
9 TH	0051 0640 1308 1859	0.8 3.7 0.8 3.8	24 F	0053 0647 1320 1913	0.4 3.9 0.4 4.1
10 F	0125 0715 1342 1935	0.8 3.7 0.8 3.7	25 SA	0143 0737 1410 2003	0.4 3.9 0.4 4.0
11 SA	0201 0751 1418 2013	0.9 3.6 0.9 3.6	26 SU	0234 0828 1501 2055	0.4 3.8 0.4 3.9
12 SU	0241 0830 1458 2054	1.0 3.5 1.0 3.5	27 M	0326 0920 1554 2148	0.5 3.7 0.5 3.8
13 M	0326 0914 1543 2140	1.1 3.4 1.1 3.4	28 TU	0420 1013 1649 ◑ 2243	0.6 3.6 0.6 3.7
14 TU	0416 1003 1635 2231	1.2 3.3 1.2 3.4	29 W	0518 1108 1748 2341	0.8 3.5 0.8 3.6
15 W	0512 1058 1733 ◐ 2328	1.2 3.3 1.2 3.4	30 TH	0618 1208 1850	0.9 3.4 0.8

JULY

Day	Time	m	Day	Time	m
1 F	0043 0719 1311 1952	3.5 0.9 3.4 0.9	16 SA	0615 1207 1842	1.2 3.4 1.2
2 SA	0145 0819 1412 2052	3.5 1.0 3.4 0.9	17 SU	0038 0723 1314 1951	3.4 1.2 3.4 1.1
3 SU	0243 0917 1511 2148	3.5 0.9 3.5 0.9	18 M	0145 0831 1421 2100	3.5 1.1 3.5 1.0
4 M	0337 1012 1605 2239	3.5 0.9 3.6 0.9	19 TU	0253 0937 1528 2204	3.6 0.9 3.7 0.8
5 TU	0427 1100 1652 2322	3.6 0.8 3.7 0.8	20 W	0357 1037 1629 2302	3.7 0.7 3.9 0.6
6 W	0511 1141 1734 ● 2359	3.7 0.8 3.8 0.8	21 TH	0456 1131 1724 ○ 2354	3.9 0.5 4.1 0.4
7 TH	0550 1216 1811	3.7 0.8 3.8	22 F	0548 1220 1814	4.0 0.3 4.2
8 F	0032 0626 1249 1845	0.8 3.7 0.8 3.8	23 SA	0043 0636 1308 1901	0.3 4.0 0.2 4.2
9 SA	0105 0700 1321 1919	0.8 3.7 0.8 3.8	24 SU	0130 0724 1355 1948	0.2 4.0 0.2 4.2
10 SU	0139 0734 1354 1953	0.9 3.7 0.8 3.7	25 M	0217 0810 1441 2034	0.3 4.0 0.3 4.1
11 M	0215 0809 1430 2030	0.9 3.6 0.9 3.7	26 TU	0304 0856 1528 2121	0.4 3.9 0.4 3.9
12 TU	0255 0848 1510 2109	1.0 3.6 1.0 3.6	27 W	0351 0942 1616 2207	0.6 3.7 0.6 3.7
13 W	0336 0929 1553 2151	1.1 3.5 1.0 3.6	28 TH	0439 1029 1706 ◑ 2258	0.7 3.6 0.8 3.5
14 TH	0421 1015 1641 ◐ 2239	1.1 3.5 1.1 3.5	29 F	0531 1122 1802 2355	1.0 3.4 1.0 3.3
15 F	0513 1107 1737 2334	1.2 3.5 1.2 3.5	30 SA	0631 1224 1907	1.1 3.3 1.1
			31 SU	0102 0738 1337 2017	3.2 1.2 3.2 1.2

AUGUST

Day	Time	m	Day	Time	m
1 M	0212 0848 1447 2126	3.2 1.2 3.3 1.1	16 TU	0116 0806 1401 2041	3.3 1.3 3.4 1.1
2 TU	0315 0953 1547 2224	3.3 1.1 3.5 1.0	17 W	0237 0920 1517 2152	3.4 1.0 3.6 0.8
3 W	0409 1046 1636 2309	3.5 0.9 3.6 0.9	18 TH	0347 1023 1619 2250	3.6 0.7 3.9 0.5
4 TH	0455 1127 1718 2344	3.6 0.8 3.8 0.8	19 F	0444 1116 1711 ○ 2340	3.9 0.4 4.1 0.3
5 F ●	0534 1200 1755	3.7 0.7 3.9	20 SA	0533 1203 1758	4.1 0.2 4.3
6 SA	0014 0609 1229 1827	0.7 3.8 0.7 3.9	21 SU	0025 0618 1248 1841	0.1 4.2 0.1 4.3
7 SU	0043 0640 1256 1857	0.7 3.8 0.7 3.9	22 M	0109 0701 1331 1923	0.1 4.2 0.1 4.3
8 M	0113 0711 1326 1927	0.8 3.8 0.7 3.8	23 TU	0151 0743 1413 2005	0.2 4.1 0.2 4.1
9 TU	0146 0742 1359 1958	0.8 3.7 0.8 3.8	24 W	0233 0824 1455 2046	0.3 3.9 0.4 3.9
10 W	0220 0815 1435 2033	0.9 3.7 0.8 3.8	25 TH	0314 0905 1538 2127	0.6 3.8 0.6 3.7
11 TH	0257 0851 1513 2111	1.0 3.7 0.9 3.7	26 F	0357 0947 1622 ◑ 2211	0.8 3.6 0.9 3.5
12 F	0336 0932 1556 2155	1.1 3.6 1.1 3.6	27 SA	0445 1035 1715 2304	1.1 3.3 1.2 3.2
13 SA	0421 1021 1649 ◐ 2249	1.2 3.5 1.2 3.5	28 SU	0544 1139 1821	1.3 3.1 1.4
14 SU	0521 1123 1758 2357	1.3 3.4 1.3 3.3	29 M	0019 0659 1310 1943	3.0 1.4 3.0 1.4
15 M	0642 1239 1920	1.4 3.3 1.3	30 TU	0149 0824 1431 2108	3.0 1.3 3.2 1.3
			31 W	0258 0938 1531 2208	3.2 1.1 3.4 1.1

Chart Datum: 0·13 metres above Ordnance Datum (Dublin)

TIME ZONE (UT)
For Summer Time add ONE hour in **non-shaded areas**

IRELAND – COBH

LAT 51°51′N LONG 8°18′W

TIMES AND HEIGHTS OF HIGH AND LOW WATERS

SPRING & NEAP TIDES
Dates in red are SPRINGS
Dates in blue are NEAPS

YEAR **2005**

SEPTEMBER

Date	Day	Time	m	Time	m	Time	m	Time	m	Phase
1	TH	0352	3.5	1030	0.9	1618	3.7	2250	0.9	
2	F	0435	3.7	1108	0.7	1657	3.8	2323	0.7	
3	SA	0513	3.8	1137	0.6	1732	3.9	2350	0.7	●
4	SU	0546	3.9	1202	0.6	1802	4.0			
5	M	0015	0.6	0615	3.9	1226	0.6	1829	4.0	
6	TU	0043	0.7	0642	3.9	1254	0.6	1855	3.9	
7	W	0114	0.7	0710	3.8	1327	0.7	1925	3.9	
8	TH	0147	0.8	0741	3.8	1402	0.8	1957	3.9	
9	F	0221	0.9	0815	3.8	1440	0.9	2034	3.8	
10	SA	0300	1.0	0856	3.7	1524	1.1	2118	3.6	
11	SU	0346	1.2	0946	3.5	1618	1.2	2215	3.4	◐
12	M	0450	1.4	1053	3.3	1731	1.4	2330	3.2	
13	TU	0618	1.4	1219	3.2	1901	1.4			
14	W	0101	3.2	0750	1.3	1354	3.4	2029	1.1	
15	TH	0230	3.4	0907	1.0	1509	3.7	2140	0.8	
16	F	0337	3.7	1008	0.6	1606	4.0	2235	0.5	
17	SA	0429	4.0	1058	0.3	1653	4.2	2321	0.2	
18	SU	0514	4.2	1143	0.1	1737	4.4			○
19	M	0003	0.1	0555	4.3	1225	0.0	1817	4.4	
20	TU	0043	0.1	0635	4.2	1305	0.1	1855	4.3	
21	W	0122	0.2	0714	4.1	1344	0.3	1933	4.1	
22	TH	0201	0.4	0751	4.0	1423	0.5	2010	3.9	
23	F	0240	0.6	0829	3.8	1503	0.7	2048	3.7	
24	SA	0320	0.9	0909	3.5	1545	1.0	2129	3.4	
25	SU	0406	1.2	0955	3.3	1636	1.3	2218	3.1	◑
26	M	0505	1.4	1058	3.1	1744	1.5	2332	2.9	
27	TU	0625	1.5	1243	3.0	1911	1.6			
28	W	0123	2.9	0756	1.4	1410	3.1	2039	1.4	
29	TH	0236	3.2	0910	1.2	1506	3.4	2137	1.1	
30	F	0326	3.4	0959	0.9	1550	3.7	2218	0.9	

OCTOBER

Date	Day	Time	m	Time	m	Time	m	Time	m	Phase
1	SA	0407	3.7	1035	0.8	1628	3.8	2250	0.7	
2	SU	0443	3.8	1104	0.7	1701	4.0	2318	0.7	
3	M	0515	3.9	1129	0.6	1730	4.0	2344	0.6	●
4	TU	0544	3.9	1155	0.6	1757	4.0			
5	W	0013	0.6	0612	4.0	1226	0.6	1825	4.0	
6	TH	0046	0.7	0642	4.0	1300	0.7	1856	4.0	
7	F	0120	0.8	0714	3.9	1337	0.8	1931	3.9	
8	SA	0157	0.9	0752	3.8	1419	0.9	2011	3.8	
9	SU	0239	1.0	0836	3.7	1507	1.1	2059	3.6	
10	M	0332	1.2	0932	3.5	1606	1.3	2200	3.4	◐
11	TU	0442	1.4	1043	3.3	1722	1.4	2319	3.2	
12	W	0609	1.4	1213	3.3	1852	1.3			
13	TH	0053	3.2	0737	1.2	1346	3.5	2017	1.1	
14	F	0218	3.5	0851	0.9	1453	3.8	2122	0.8	
15	SA	0319	3.8	0948	0.5	1546	4.1	2213	0.5	
16	SU	0408	4.1	1037	0.3	1632	4.3	2258	0.3	
17	M	0452	4.2	1121	0.2	1713	4.3	2339	0.2	○
18	TU	0532	4.3	1201	0.2	1752	4.3			
19	W	0017	0.3	0610	4.2	1240	0.3	1829	4.2	
20	TH	0055	0.4	0647	4.1	1318	0.5	1904	4.1	
21	F	0132	0.6	0723	4.0	1355	0.7	1939	3.9	
22	SA	0209	0.8	0759	3.8	1433	0.9	2015	3.7	
23	SU	0249	1.0	0839	3.6	1515	1.2	2055	3.4	
24	M	0333	1.3	0925	3.3	1605	1.4	2142	3.2	
25	TU	0432	1.5	1024	3.1	1710	1.6	2248	3.0	◑
26	W	0548	1.6	1156	3.0	1830	1.6			
27	TH	0030	3.0	0711	1.5	1328	3.2	1947	1.5	
28	F	0153	3.2	0819	1.3	1426	3.4	2046	1.2	
29	SA	0246	3.4	0910	1.1	1511	3.6	2130	1.0	
30	SU	0328	3.6	0950	0.9	1549	3.8	2208	0.9	
31	M	0405	3.8	1024	0.8	1624	3.9	2242	0.7	

NOVEMBER

Date	Day	Time	m	Time	m	Time	m	Time	m	Phase
1	TU	0440	3.9	1056	0.7	1656	4.0	2315	0.7	
2	W	0513	4.0	1129	0.6	1727	4.0	2349	0.7	●
3	TH	0547	4.1	1205	0.6	1801	4.1			
4	F	0025	0.7	0622	4.1	1243	0.7	1837	4.0	
5	SA	0104	0.7	0700	4.0	1325	0.8	1917	3.9	
6	SU	0147	0.8	0743	3.9	1411	0.9	2003	3.8	
7	M	0236	1.0	0833	3.8	1504	1.1	2056	3.6	
8	TU	0333	1.1	0932	3.6	1605	1.2	2159	3.4	
9	W	0441	1.2	1042	3.5	1717	1.3	2313	3.3	◐
10	TH	0600	1.2	1204	3.5	1840	1.2			
11	F	0037	3.4	0719	1.1	1323	3.6	1955	1.0	
12	SA	0152	3.6	0827	0.9	1427	3.8	2057	0.8	
13	SU	0252	3.8	0924	0.6	1520	4.0	2148	0.6	
14	M	0343	4.0	1014	0.5	1607	4.1	2234	0.5	
15	TU	0428	4.1	1059	0.4	1650	4.2	2317	0.5	
16	W	0511	4.2	1141	0.5	1730	4.2	2356	0.5	○
17	TH	0550	4.1	1220	0.6	1807	4.1			
18	F	0033	0.6	0626	4.1	1257	0.7	1842	4.0	
19	SA	0109	0.8	0702	4.0	1333	0.9	1916	3.8	
20	SU	0145	0.9	0739	3.8	1410	1.1	1951	3.7	
21	M	0223	1.1	0819	3.7	1450	1.2	2031	3.5	
22	TU	0306	1.2	0903	3.5	1537	1.4	2116	3.4	
23	W	0358	1.4	0955	3.3	1634	1.5	2211	3.2	◑
24	TH	0502	1.5	1058	3.2	1740	1.6	2320	3.2	
25	F	0612	1.5	1213	3.3	1847	1.5			
26	SA	0038	3.2	0717	1.4	1321	3.4	1947	1.4	
27	SU	0143	3.4	0812	1.2	1414	3.5	2038	1.2	
28	M	0235	3.6	0900	1.1	1500	3.7	2125	1.0	
29	TU	0320	3.8	0945	0.9	1542	3.8	2209	0.9	
30	W	0404	3.9	1028	0.8	1623	4.0	2251	0.8	

DECEMBER

Date	Day	Time	m	Time	m	Time	m	Time	m	Phase
1	TH	0446	4.0	1111	0.7	1704	4.0	2333	0.7	●
2	F	0529	4.1	1153	0.7	1746	4.0			
3	SA	0015	0.7	0611	4.1	1237	0.7	1828	4.0	
4	SU	0059	0.7	0656	4.1	1323	0.7	1914	4.0	
5	M	0146	0.7	0743	4.0	1412	0.8	2003	3.8	
6	TU	0236	0.8	0835	3.9	1504	0.9	2056	3.7	
7	W	0332	0.9	0932	3.8	1601	1.0	2154	3.6	
8	TH	0432	1.0	1033	3.7	1704	1.1	2257	3.5	◐
9	F	0539	1.0	1139	3.6	1814	1.1			
10	SA	0005	3.5	0649	1.0	1247	3.7	1922	1.1	
11	SU	0114	3.6	0756	1.0	1351	3.7	2025	1.0	
12	M	0217	3.7	0856	0.9	1448	3.8	2121	0.9	
13	TU	0314	3.8	0951	0.8	1541	3.9	2212	0.8	
14	W	0406	3.9	1040	0.8	1629	3.9	2258	0.8	
15	TH	0453	4.0	1125	0.8	1712	3.9	2339	0.8	○
16	F	0535	4.0	1205	0.8	1751	3.9			
17	SA	0017	0.8	0613	4.0	1242	0.9	1826	3.9	
18	SU	0052	0.8	0649	4.0	1316	1.0	1900	3.8	
19	M	0126	0.9	0725	3.9	1351	1.1	1935	3.7	
20	TU	0201	1.0	0802	3.8	1427	1.2	2012	3.7	
21	W	0239	1.1	0842	3.7	1508	1.3	2053	3.6	
22	TH	0322	1.2	0925	3.6	1554	1.4	2138	3.5	
23	F	0411	1.3	1012	3.5	1645	1.4	2230	3.4	◑
24	SA	0507	1.4	1104	3.5	1744	1.5	2328	3.4	
25	SU	0609	1.4	1203	3.4	1846	1.4			
26	M	0031	3.4	0712	1.4	1305	3.5	1947	1.4	
27	TU	0135	3.5	0812	1.3	1405	3.6	2045	1.2	
28	W	0236	3.6	0910	1.1	1503	3.7	2141	1.1	
29	TH	0333	3.8	1006	1.0	1557	3.8	2233	0.9	
30	F	0427	3.9	1058	0.8	1649	3.9	2322	0.7	
31	SA	0517	4.1	1147	0.7	1737	4.0			●

Chart Datum: 0·13 metres above Ordnance Datum (Dublin)

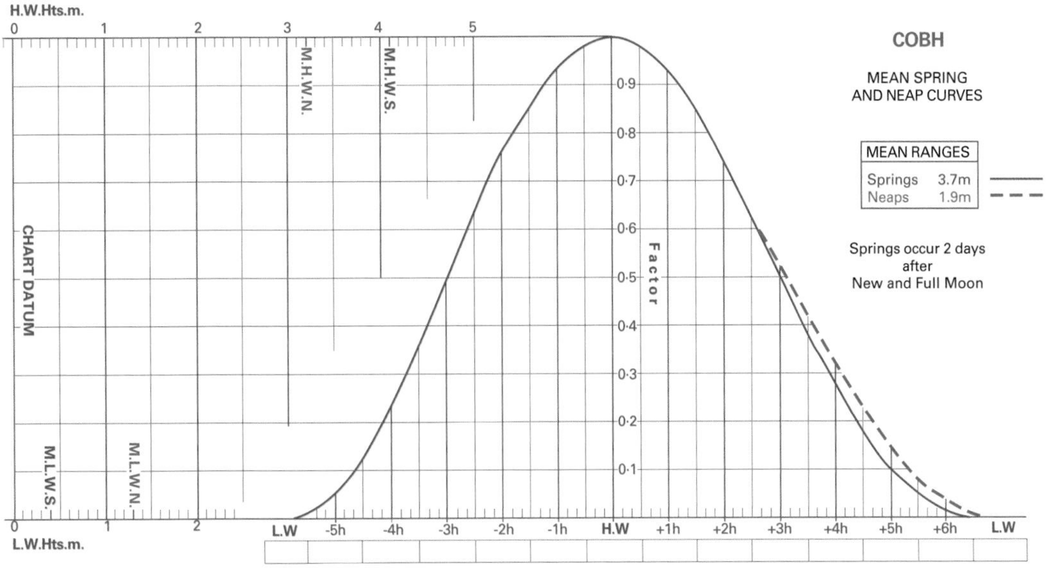
H.W.Hts.m.
COBH
MEAN SPRING AND NEAP CURVES
MEAN RANGES
Springs 3.7m
Neaps 1.9m
Springs occur 2 days after New and Full Moon
M.H.W.N.
M.H.W.S.
CHART DATUM
M.L.W.S.
M.L.W.N.
Factor
L.W.Hts.m.
L.W -5h -4h -3h -2h -1h H.W +1h +2h +3h +4h +5h +6h L.W

9.12.18 CORK HARBOUR

Cork **51°47'·50N 08°15'·54W**

CHARTS AC 1765, *1777*, 1773; Imray C57, C56; Irish OS 81, 87

TIDES −0523 Dover; ML 2·3; Duration 0555; Zone 0 (UT)

Standard Port COBH (⟵)

Times				**Height (metres)**			
High Water		Low Water		MHWS	MHWN	MLWN	MLWS
0500	1100	0500	1100	4·1	3·2	1·3	0·4
1700	2300	1700	2300				
Differences BALLYCOTTON (15M ENE of Roche's Point)							
−0011	+0001	+0003	−0009	0·0	0·0	−0·1	0·0
RINGASKIDDY							
+0005	+0020	+0007	+0013	+0·1	+0·1	+0·1	+0·1
MARINO POINT							
0000	+0010	0000	+0010	+0·1	+0·1	0·0	0·0
CORK CITY							
+0005	+0010	+0020	+0010	+0·4	+0·4	+0·3	+0·2
ROBERTS COVE (approx 4M SW of Roche's Point)							
−0005	−0005	−0005	−0005	−0·1	0·0	0·0	+0·1

SHELTER Very good in all conditions, esp in Crosshaven and East Passage. There are 3 main marinas at Crosshaven (see Facilities), plus a small private marina and several ⚓s up the Owenboy River, in particular at Drake's Pool. There is a marina at E Ferry in E Passage at the E end of Great Island. Cobh, Ringaskiddy and Cork City are commercial and ferry ports; contact Port Ops for advice on yacht berths.

NAVIGATION WPT 51°46'·57N, 08°15'·39W, 005° to Roche's Pt lt, 1M; also on 354°ldg line. Safe hbr with no dangers for yachts; ent is deep and well marked. Sp rate is about 1½kn in ent. Main chan up to Cork and the chan to E Ferry are marked, but shoal outside navigable chan. Ent to Owenboy River carries at least 3m at LWS, and the chan is buoyed. Head for Cage buoy (C1), Fl G 5s, to pick up the ldg marks/lts 252°, close S of pink ho, R roof.

LIGHTS AND MARKS The 24·5m high hammerhead water tr S of Crosshaven and the R/W power stn chy NE of Corkbeg Is are conspic from seaward. Two set Ldg lts/marks lead through The Sound, either side of Hbr Rk (5·2m), not a hazard for yachts; but do not impede merchant ships. The chan is marked by C1 SHM buoy Fl G 10s, C1A SHM buoy Fl G 5s; C2A PHM buoy Fl R 7·5s, C2 PHM buoy Fl R 5s; and C4 PHM buoy Fl R 10s.

R/T Call: *Cork Hbr Radio* (Port Ops) VHF Ch 12 14 16 (H24); *Crosshaven BY* Ch M (Mon– Fri: 0830– 1700LT). *Royal Cork* YC Marina Ch M (0900– 2359LT); also Ch M for RC water taxi.

TELEPHONE (Dial code 021) HM 4273125, Fax 4276284, info@portofcork.ie; Port Ops 4811380; MRCC (066) 9476109; IMES 4831448; ⊜ 4311024; Police 4831222; Dr 4831716; Ⓗ 4546400.

FACILITIES **Crosshaven BY Marina** (100 + 20 Ⓥ) ☎ 4831161, Fax 4831603, cby@eircom.net, €2.00, BH (40 ton), C (1.5 tons), M, Ⓔ, CH, D, P (cans), El, Gas, Gaz, Kos, SM, ME, ⚒; **Salve Marine** (45 + 12 Ⓥ) ☎ 4831145, Fax 4831747, AB €2.00, M, BY, El, ME, C, CH, R, D, P (cans), Slip; **Royal Cork YC Marina** (170 + 30 Ⓥ) ☎ 4831023, Fax 4831586, www.royalcork.com, €2.40, P , Bar, R, Slip, ♿; **Crosshaven Pier/Pontoon** AB €19.05 any size. **East Ferry Marina** (85 + 15 Ⓥ) ☎ 4813390, €2.00, D, Bar, R, Slip; access all tides, max draft 5·5m. **Crosshaven Village** FV pier in 3·5m at Town quay, L, Slip, Grid, SM, ACA, Bar, Dr, ✉, R, 🛒, Ⓑ. **Cork City** All facilities. Ferries (to UK and France), ⇌, ✈.

MINOR HARBOUR 16M ENE of YOUGHAL

DUNGARVAN BAY, Waterford, **52°05'·15N 07°36'·70W**. AC 2017. HW −0540 on Dover; Duration 0600. See 9.12.16. A large bay, drying to the W, entered between Helvick Hd to the S and to the N Ballynacourty Pt, Fl (2) WRG 10s; see 9.12.4. Appr in W sector (274°–302°) of this lt, to clear Carricknamoan islet to the N, and Carrickapane Rk and Helvick Rk (ECM buoy Q (3) 10s) to the S. 5ca W of this buoy are The Gainers, a large unmarked rky patch (dries 0·8m). Beware salmon nets. Off Helvick hbr are 8 Y Ⓥs or ⚓ in approx 4m. Dungarvan town hbr is accessible HW+3, via buoyed (FlG/FlR) chan which shifts, the buoys being moved to suit; there are now no ldg lts. Appr is difficult in SE'lies >F6. ⚓ in the pool below the town or AB on pontoon (dries to soft mud), S bank below bridge; craft can stay overnight beyond double Y lines. Facilities: D & P (cans), Bar, Ⓑ, ✉, Ⓑ, R, 🛒, Kos.

MINOR HARBOUR 15M ENE of ROCHE'S POINT

BALLYCOTTON, Cork, **51°49'·70N 08°00·19W**. AC 2424. HW −0555 on Dover; Duration 0550. See above. Small, NE-facing hbr at W end of bay suffers from scend in strong SE winds; 3m in ent and about 1·5m against piers. Many FVs alongside piers, on which yachts should berth, rather than ⚓ in hbr, which is foul with old ground tackle. 6 Y Ⓥs are outside hbr, or good ⚓ in offshore winds in 6m NE of pier, protected by Ballycotton Is. Lt ho Fl WR 10s 59m 21/17M, B tr in W walls; W238°–048°, R048°–238°; Horn (4) 90s. Facilities: FW on pier. **Village** Hotel, R, ✉, 🛒, LB, Kos.

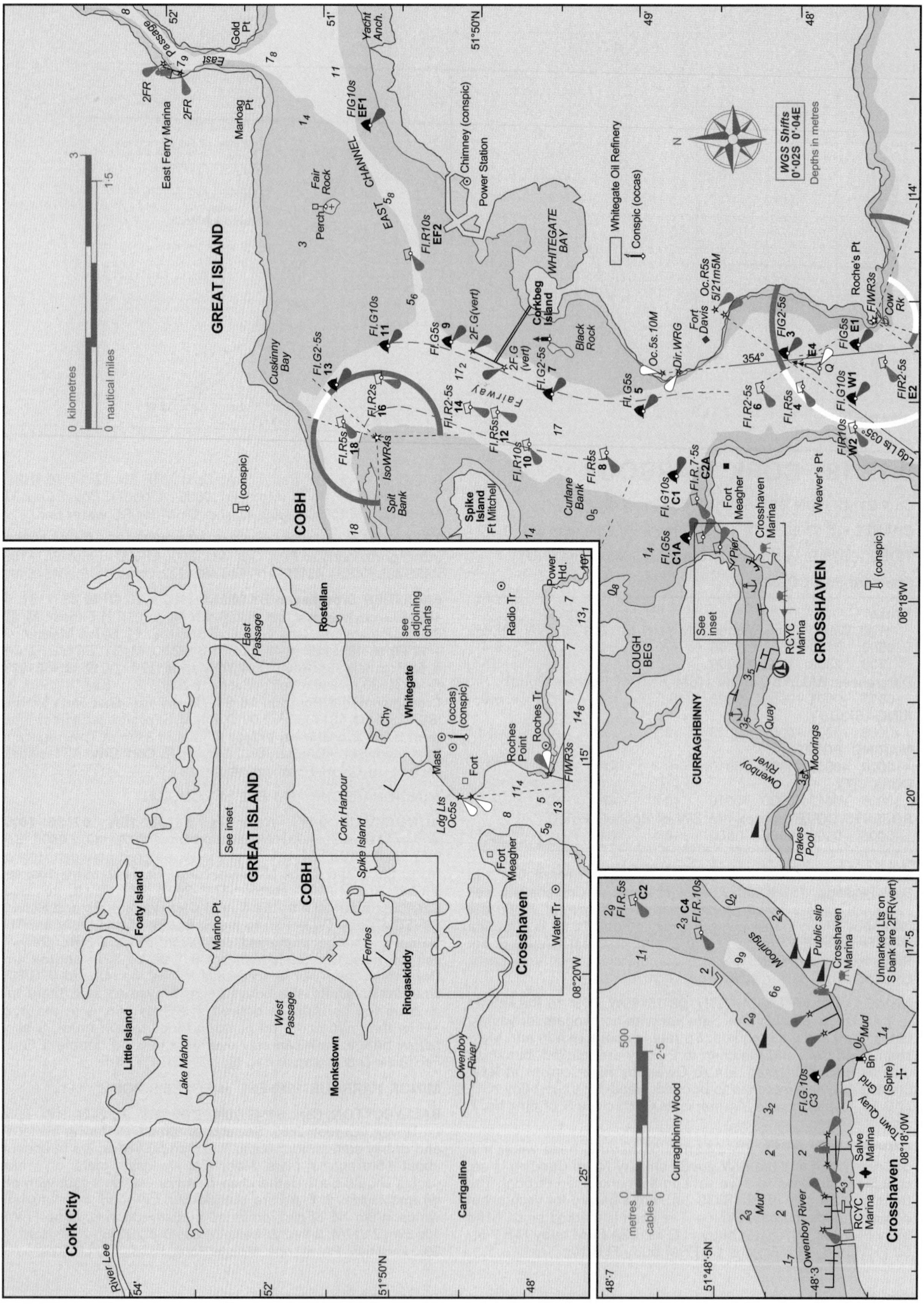
GREAT ISLAND
COBH
Cuskinny Bay
Spit Bank
Spike Island
Ft Mitchell
Curlane Bank
East Ferry Marina
Marloag Pt
Gold Pt
East Passage
EAST CHANNEL
Fair Rock
Perch
Chimney (conspic)
Power Station
WHITEGATE BAY
Corkbeg Island
Black Rock
Whitegate Oil Refinery
Conspic (occas)
Fort Davis
Roche's Pt
Cow Rk
Weaver's Pt
Fort Meagher
Crosshaven Marina
CROSSHAVEN
RCYC Marina
CURRAGHBINNY
LOUGH BEG
Owenboy River
Drakes Pool
Moorings
Quay
Pier
See inset
Fairway
Yacht Anch.
WGS Shifts 0'·02S 0'·04E
Depths in metres
0 kilometres 3
0 nautical miles 1·5
51°50'N
08°18'W
Cork City
River Lee
Little Island
Lake Mahon
Foaty Island
Marino Pt.
Monkstown
West Passage
Ringaskiddy
Ferries
Carrigaline
Spike Island
Cork Harbour
Rostellan
Whitegate
see adjoining charts
Radio Tr
Roches Point
Roches Tr
Power Hd.
Water Tr
Crosshaven
Owenboy River
08°20'W
Curraghbinny Wood
Public slip
Salve Marina
Town Quay
Grid
(Spire)
Unmarked Lts on S bank are 2FR(vert)
metres 0 500
cables 0 2·5
51°48'·5N
08°18'·0W

9.12.19 KINSALE

Cork **51°40'·80N 08°30'·00W** ✿✿✿◊◊◊✿✿✿

CHARTS AC 1765, 2053; Imray C56; Irish OS 87

TIDES –0600 Dover; ML 2·2; Duration 0600; Zone 0 (UT)

Standard Port COBH (⟵)

Times				Height (metres)			
High Water		Low Water		MHWS	MHWN	MLWN	MLWS
0500	1100	0500	1100	4·1	3·2	1·3	0·4
1700	2300	1700	2300				
Differences KINSALE							
–0019	–0005	–0009	–0023	–0·2	0·0	+0·1	+0·2

SHELTER Excellent, except in very strong SE winds. Access H24 in all weathers/tides. Marinas at Kinsale YC and Castlepark; Ⓥ's berth on outside of pontoons in 10m in both cases; NNW of latter is FV pontoon and no ⚓ area. Hbr speed limit 6kn. Possible AB (Sun-Thurs) at Trident Hotel. No ⚓ allowed in main channel or within 700m of Town Pier. Contact HM prior to ⚓.

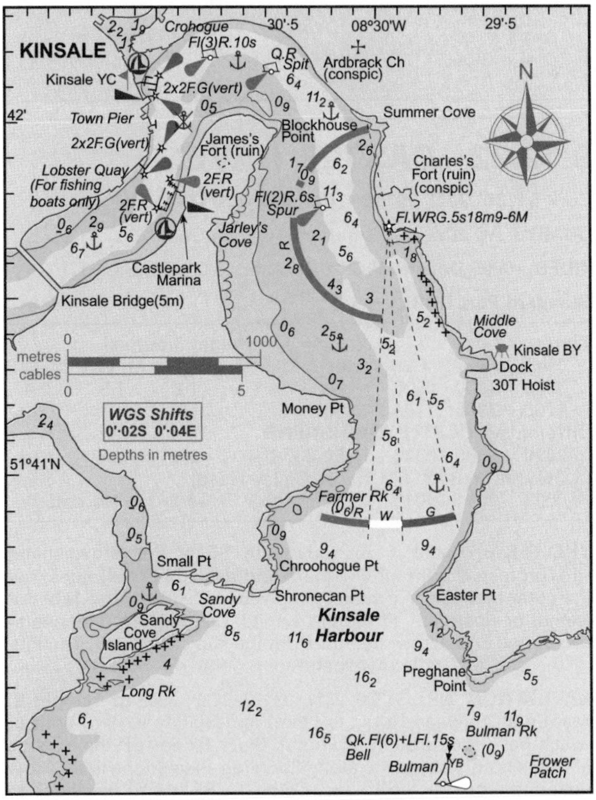
KINSALE
Kinsale YC
Crohogue
Fl(3)R.10s
Q.R
Spit
Ardbrack Ch (conspic)
08°30'W
30'·5
29'·5
2x2F.G(vert)
Town Pier
2x2F.G(vert)
Blockhouse Point
Summer Cove
James's Fort (ruin)
Charles's Fort (ruin) (conspic)
Lobster Quay (For fishing boats only)
2F.R (vert)
Fl(2)R.6s
Spur
Fl.WRG.5s18m9-6M
Jarley's Cove
Castlepark Marina
Kinsale Bridge(5m)
Middle Cove
Kinsale BY
Dock
30T Hoist
metres
cables
WGS Shifts
0'·02S 0'·04E
Depths in metres
Money Pt
51°41'N
42'
Farmer Rk
Small Pt
Chroohogue Pt
Sandy Cove
Sandy Cove Island
Shronecan Pt
Kinsale Harbour
Easter Pt
Long Rk
Preghane Point
Bulman Rk
Qk.Fl(6)+LFl.15s Bell
Bulman YB
Frower Patch

NAVIGATION WPT 51°40'·00N 08°30'·00W, 001° to Charles's Fort lt, 1·7M. Beware: Bulman Rk (0·9m; SCM lt buoy) 4ca S of Preghane Pt; and Farmer Rk (0·6m) ¾ca off W bank.

LIGHTS AND MARKS Charles's Fort Dir 001°, Fl WRG 5s 18m 9/6M, vis W358°-004° (H24). Chan is marked by PHM lt buoys. Marina lts are 2 FG or FR as appropriate.

R/T KYC VHF Ch M 16. Castlepark marina 06 16 M. HM **14** 16.

TELEPHONE (Dial code 021) HM 4772503 (HO), 4773047 (OT), 📠 4774695; MRCC (066) 9476109; Coast/Cliff Rescue Service 4772346; ⊖ 4311044/4315422; Police 4772302; Dr 4772253; Ⓗ 4546400.

FACILITIES (from seaward) **Kinsale BY**, ☎ 4774774, 📠 4775405. D, Ⓥ, FW, ME, ✗, El, BH (30 ton). **Kinsale YC Marina** (170 + 50 Ⓥ; 10m depth), ☎ 4772196, 📠 4774455, €1.90, Slip, D, R, Bar, ♿; **Trident Hotel**, D, FW, AB, Sun-Thur try Sail Ireland ☎ 4772927, 📠 4774170. **Castlepark Marina** (70+20 Ⓥ) ☎ 4774959, 📠 4774958 €1.85, D, Slip, R, Bar, El, ⊡; ferry (3 mins) to town. **Services:** ME, El, Ⓔ, Divers, C (30 ton), D, SM, Gas, Gaz. **Town** P (cans), 🛒, R, Bar, ✉, Ⓑ, (bus to Cork), ⇌, ✈.

MINOR HARBOUR 2M EAST OF KINSALE

OYSTER HAVEN, Cork, **51°41'·20N 08°26'·90W**. ✿✿◊✿✿. AC 1765, 2053. HW –0600 on Dover; ML 2·2m; Duration 0600. Use 9.12.19. Good shelter but subject to swell in S winds. Enter 0·5M N of Big Sovereign, a steep islet divided into two. Keep to S of Little Sovereign on E side of ent. There is foul ground off Ballymacus Pt on W side, and off Kinure Pt on E side. Pass W of Hbr Rk (0·9m) off Ferry Pt, the only danger within hbr. ⚓ NNW of Ferry Pt in 4–6m on soft mud/weed. NW arm shoals suddenly about 5ca NW of Ferry Pt. Also ⚓ up N arm of hbr in 3m off the W shore. Weed in higher reaches may foul ⚓. No lts, marks or VHF radio. Coast/Cliff Rescue Service ☎ (021) 4770711. Facilities at Kinsale. See 9.12.19.

9.12.20 COURTMACSHERRY

Cork **51°38'·22N 08°40'·90W** ✿✿◊◊✿✿✿

CHARTS AC *2092*, 2081; Imray C56; Irish OS 87

TIDES HW –0610 on Dover; Duration 0545; Zone 0 (UT)

Standard Port COBH (⟵)

Times				Height (metres)			
High Water		Low Water		MHWS	MHWN	MLWN	MLWS
0500	1100	0500	1100	4·1	3·2	1·3	0·4
1700	2300	1700	2300				
Differences COURTMACSHERRY							
–0029	–0007	+0005	–0017	–0·4	–0·3	–0·2	–0·1

SHELTER Good shelter up-river, but in strong S/SE winds seas break on the bar (2·3m), when ent must not be attempted. Dry out in small inner hbr or AB afloat on jetty (FVs) or on yacht pontoon (18·5m). ⚓ NE of Ferry Pt in about 2·5m or N of pontoon. Weed may foul ⚓; best to moor using two ⚓s.

NAVIGATION WPT, 51°37'·50N 08°40'·17W, 324° to Wood Pt, 0·8M. Appr in the W sector of Wood Pt lt, between Black Tom and Horse Rk (dries 3·6m); the latter is 3-4½ca E of Barry Pt on the W shore. Black Tom (2·3m), with SHM buoy Fl.G.5s 5ca SSE, is close NE of the appr. Further to NE, in centre of bay, Barrel Rk (dries 2·6m), has unlit SCM perch (no topmark). To NNW and E of it are Inner Barrels (0·5m) and Blueboy Rk. Hbr ent is between Wood Pt and SHM buoy 2ca NE, Fl G 3s. Chan (2m) is marked by 3 unlit SHM spar buoys after these; keep close N of moorings.

LIGHTS AND MARKS Wood Pt, Fl (2) WR 5s 15m 5M, W315°–332°, R332°–315°.

R/T None.

TELEPHONE (023) HM/RNLI 46600/40394; Dr 46186; Police 46122; Coast Rescue Service ☎ 40110.

FACILITIES Quay AB €1.27, min €12.70. ⊐D, FW, ♿, D, Slip, LB, R. **Village**, Bar, R, 🛒, (bus to Cork), ⇌, ✈.

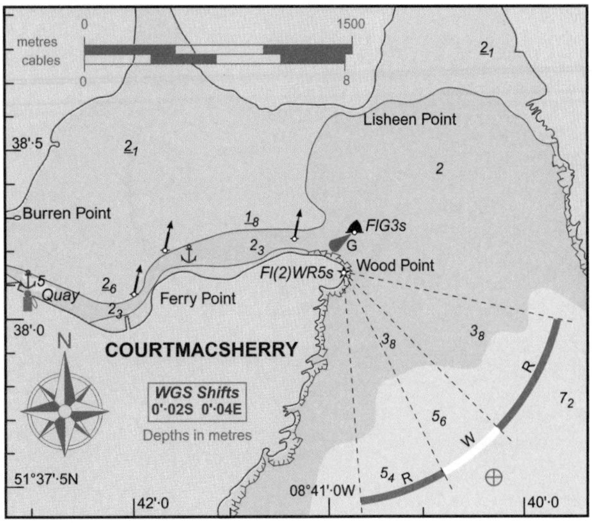
metres
cables
1500
Lisheen Point
38'·5
Burren Point
FlG3s
G
Wood Point
Fl(2)WR5s
Quay
Ferry Point
38'·0
COURTMACSHERRY
WGS Shifts
0'·02S 0'·04E
Depths in metres
51°37'·5N
08°41'·0W
42'·0
40'·0

9.12.21 GLANDORE

Cork, **51°33'·70N 09°07'·20W**

CHARTS AC *2092*; Imray C56; Irish OS 89

TIDES Approx as for 9.12.22 Castletownshend. Zone 0 (UT)

SHELTER Excellent. 12 Y ⚓s or ⚓ 1½ca SW of Glandore Pier in 2m or 1ca NE of the New pier at Unionhall in 3m.

NAVIGATION WPT 51°32'·35N 09°05'·10W, 129° to Outer Dangers 1·2M. Approach between Adam Is and Goat's Hd, thence keep E of Eve Is and W of the chain of rks: Outer, Middle and Inner Dangers and Sunk Rk. Before altering W for Unionhall, stand on to clear mudbank 1ca off S shore.

LIGHTS AND MARKS Galley Hd, Fl (5) 20s, is 5M E of the ent. Outer Dangers are marked by a preferred-chan-to-port buoy (GRG), Fl (2+1) G 7s, and a PHM bn; Middle and Inner Dangers by 2 SHM bns; and Sunk Rk by a NCM lt buoy, Q.

R/T None. No HM.

TELEPHONE (Dial code 028) Hbr Mr 33419; Police (023) 48162; Dr 23456; Coast Rescue ☎ 33115.

FACILITIES FW at both piers; **Glandore** GHYC, ✉, R, Bar, Kos. **Unionhall** D, P, ME, Gas, ✉, R, Bar, 🛒.

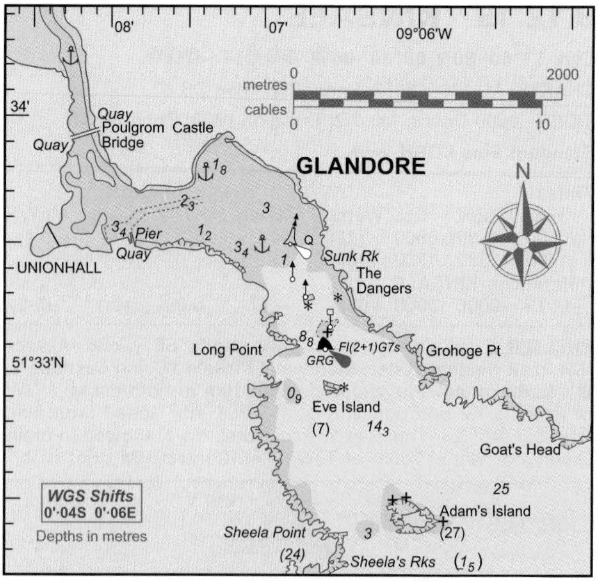
08'
07'
09°06'W
34'
metres
cables
0
2000
10
Quay
Poulgrom Castle
Bridge
GLANDORE
N
Pier
Quay
UNIONHALL
Sunk Rk
The Dangers
Fl(2+1)G7s
GRG
Grohoge Pt
Long Point
51°33'N
Eve Island
Goat's Head
WGS Shifts
0'·04S 0'·06E
Depths in metres
Adam's Island
Sheela Point
Sheela's Rks

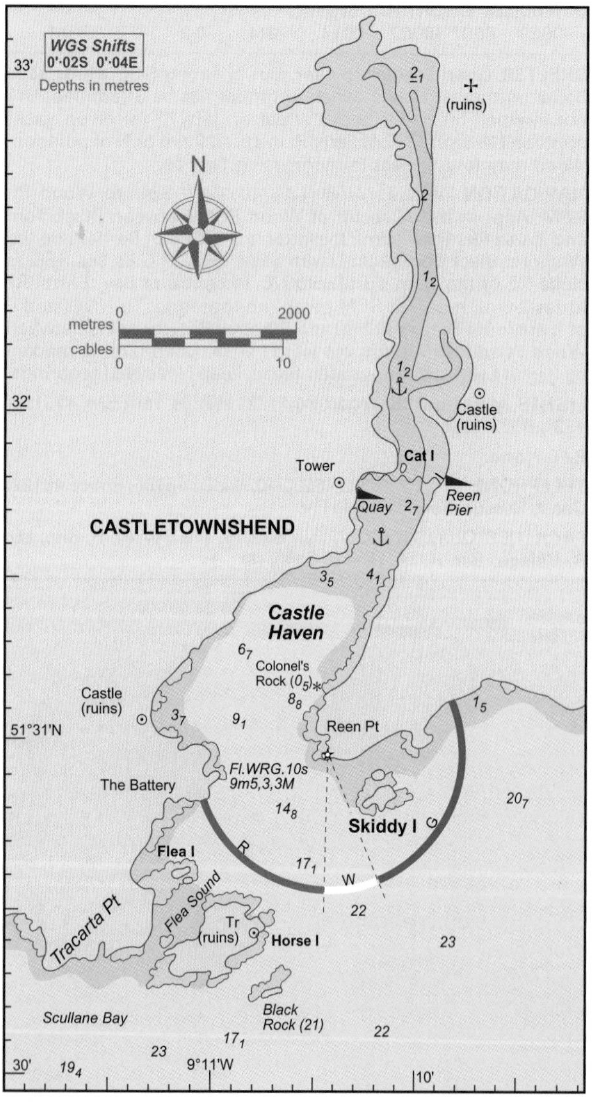
WGS Shifts
0'·02S 0'·04E
Depths in metres
33'
(ruins)
N
metres
cables
0
2000
10
32'
Castle (ruins)
Cat I
Tower
Reen Pier
Quay
CASTLETOWNSHEND
Castle Haven
Colonel's Rock (0₅)
Castle (ruins)
Reen Pt
51°31'N
Fl.WRG.10s 9m5,3,3M
The Battery
Skiddy I
Flea I
Flea Sound
Tracarta Pt
Tr (ruins)
Horse I
Scullane Bay
Black Rock (21)
30'
9°11'W
10'

9.12.22 CASTLE HAVEN

Cork **51°30'·90N 09°10'·70W**

CHARTS AC *2092, 2129*; Imray C56; Irish OS 88, 89

TIDES +0605 Dover; ML 2·2; Duration 0605; Zone 0 (UT)

Standard Port COBH (⟵)

Times				Height (metres)			
High Water		Low Water		MHWS	MHWN	MLWN	MLWS
0500	1100	0500	1100	4·1	3·2	1·3	0·4
1700	2300	1700	2300				
Differences CASTLETOWNSHEND							
−0020	−0030	−0020	−0050	−0·4	−0·2	+0·1	+0·3
CLONAKILTY BAY (5M NE of Galley Head)							
−0033	−0011	−0019	−0041	−0·3	−0·2	No data	

SHELTER Excellent ⚓ in midstream SE of Castletownshend slip, protected from all weathers and available at all tides; but the outer part of hbr is subject to swell in S winds. Or ⚓ N of Cat Island, or upstream as depth permits. Caution: An underwater cable runs E/W across the hbr from the slip close N of Reen Pier to the slip at Castletownshend.

NAVIGATION WPT 51°30'·28N, 09°10'·26W, 351° to Reen Pt lt, 7ca. Enter between Horse Is (35m) and Skiddy Is (9m) both of which have foul ground all round. Black Rk lies off the SE side of Horse Is and is steep-to along its S side. Flea Sound is a narrow boat chan, obstructed by rks. Colonel's Rk (0·5m) lies close to the E shore, 2ca N of Reen Pt. Beware salmon nets.

LIGHTS AND MARKS Reen Pt, Fl WRG 10s; a small slender W bn; vis G shore-338°, W338°-001°, R001°-shore. A ruined tr is on Horse Is.

R/T None.

TELEPHONE (Dial code 028) MRCC (066) 9746109; Coast/Cliff Rescue Service 21039; ⊖ Bantry (027) 50061; Police 36144; Dr 23456; Ⓗ 21677.

FACILITIES Reen Pier L, FW; **Sailing Club** ☎ 36100; **Castletownsend Village** Slip, Bar, R, 🛒, FW, ✉, Ⓑ (Skibbereen), ⇌, ✈ (Cork).

BARLOGE CREEK, Cork, **51°29'·57N 09°17'·58W**. AC 2129. Tides approx as Castletownsend. A narrow creek, well sheltered except from S/SE winds. Appr with Gokane Pt brg 120°. Enter W of Bullock Is, keeping to the W side to clear rks S of the island. ⚓ W of the Is in 3m but weedy. No facilities.

9.12.23 BALTIMORE

Cork **51°28'·30N 09°23'·40W** ❀❀❀⚓⚓✿✿✿

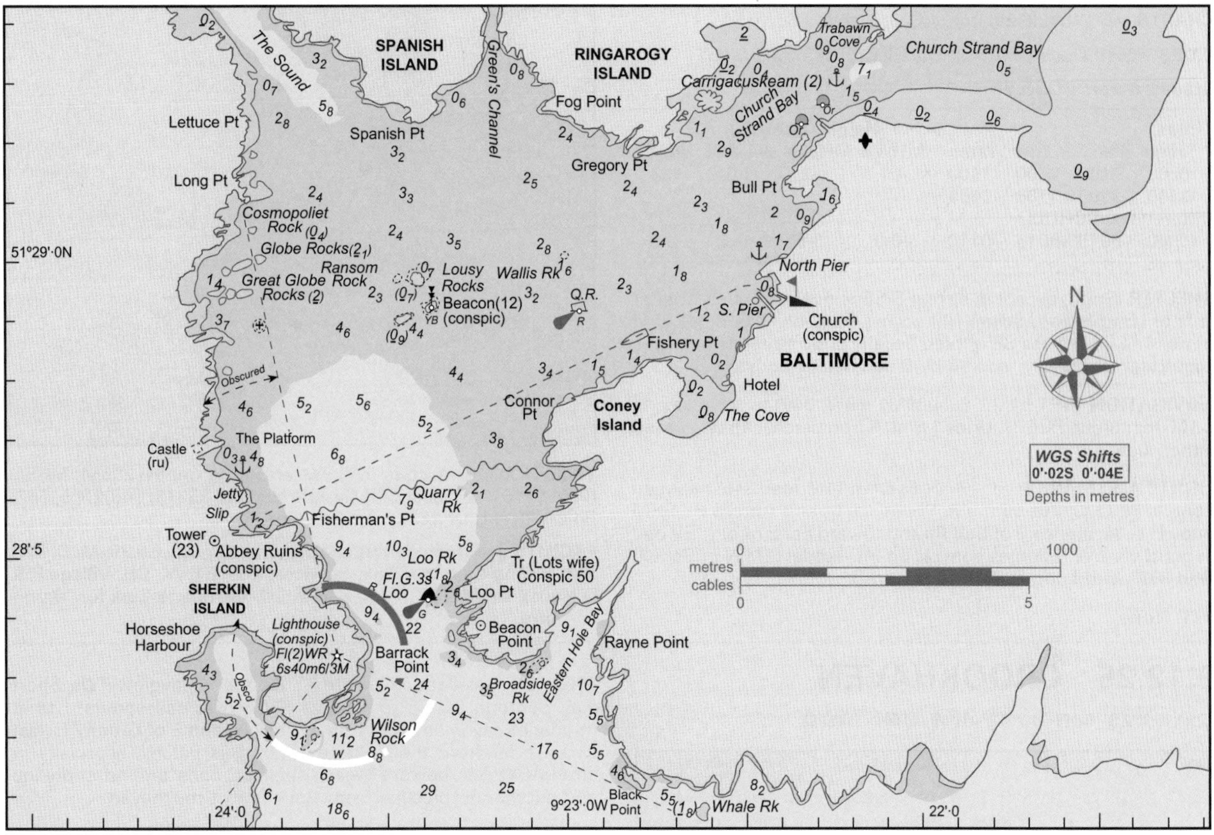
The Sound
SPANISH ISLAND
Green's Channel
RINGAROGY ISLAND
Fog Point
Trabawn Cove
Church Strand Bay
Carrigacuskeam (2)
Church Strand Bay
Lettuce Pt
Spanish Pt
Gregory Pt
Long Pt
Bull Pt
Cosmopoliet Rock
Globe Rocks
Ransom Rocks (2)
Great Globe Rock
Lousy Rocks
Wallis Rk
Beacon(12) YB (conspic)
Q.R.
North Pier
S. Pier
Church (conspic)
Fishery Pt
BALTIMORE
Hotel
The Cove
Obscured
Connor Pt
Coney Island
The Platform
Castle (ru)
WGS Shifts
0'·02S 0'·04E
Depths in metres
Jetty
Slip
Quarry Rk
Fisherman's Pt
Tower (23)
Abbey Ruins (conspic)
Loo Rk
Tr (Lots wife) Conspic 50
Fl.G.3s
Loo
Loo Pt
SHERKIN ISLAND
metres
cables
Horseshoe Harbour
Lighthouse (conspic)
Fl(2)WR 6s40m6/3M
Barrack Point
Beacon Point
Eastern Hole Bay
Rayne Point
Broadside Rk
Obscd
Wilson Rock
Black Point
Whale Rk
51°29'·0N
28'·5
24'·0
9°23'·0W
22'·0

CHARTS AC 2129, 3725; Imray C56; Irish OS 88

TIDES –0605 Dover; ML 2·1; Duration 0610; Zone 0 (UT)

Standard Port COBH (⟵)

Times				Height (metres)			
High Water		Low Water		MHWS	MHWN	MLWN	MLWS
0500	1100	0500	1100	4·1	3·2	1·3	0·4
1700	2300	1700	2300				
Differences BALTIMORE							
–0025	–0005	–0010	–0050	–0·6	–0·3	+0·1	+0·2

SHELTER Excellent; access H24 from the S. At Baltimore a large water barge secured to outer end of the S pier provides AB for up to 20 yachts in 1·5m depth. Inner Hbr, partly drying between N and S piers, is mostly used by local boats and FVs; the latter also berth on N pier. ⚓ SW of S pier, or N of N pier; or in strong NW'lies in Church Strand Bay as shown. ⚓ lts are required. Do not ⚓ in the dredged chan between Wallis Rk buoy and N pier. In strong W winds ⚓ in lee of Sherkin Is off Castle ruins. A similar water barge with AB is secured to the jetty.

NAVIGATION WPT 51°27'·80N 09°23'·42W, 000° to Loo Rk SHM buoy, Fl G 3s, 0·62M. Do not cut between this buoy and mainland. Beware Lousy Rks (SCM bn) and Wallis Rk (PHM buoy, QR) in the middle of the bay. From/to the N The Sound needs careful pilotage; AC 3725 and ICC SDs essential. R Ilen is navigable on the flood for at least 4M above The Sound. Speed limit 6kn within hbr.

LIGHTS AND MARKS Ent easily identified by conspic W tr (Lot's Wife) to stbd on Beacon Pt and Barrack Pt lt ho, Fl (2) WR 6s, to port.

R/T VHF Ch 06, HM 09, 16.

TELEPHONE (Dial code 028) Hr Board sec ☎/📠 20014; MRSC and Coast/Cliff Rescue Service (066) 9476109; ⊖ (027) 53210; Police 20102; Dr 23456/after hrs 1850 335999, Ⓗ 21677.

FACILITIES Berthing barges (up to 20 Ⓥ) ☎ (021) 774959, to book 087 2351485/www.atlanticboat.ie 📠 (021) 774958, (May-Sept), €15.00, Slip, AB, FW, AC; **Baltimore SC** ☎/📠 20426, visitors welcome, bar, showers; **Glenans Irish Sailing School** ☎ (01) 6611481. **Services:** D (hose), P (cans), BY, ME, El, CH, 🛒, Gas, Gaz, Kos, ⚒, ACA; **Village** Bar, ✉, bus to Cork for ⇌, ✈.

ADJACENT ANCHORAGES

HORSESHOE HARBOUR, 51°28'·20N 09°23'·86W. Small unlit hbr on Sherkin Is, 3ca WSW of ent to Baltimore. Keep to the W at narrow ent. ⚓ in about 5m in centre of cove.

CLEAR ISLAND, NORTH HARBOUR, 51°26'·60N 09°30'·20W. AC 2129. Tides approx as Schull, 9.12.24. A tiny, partly drying inlet on N coast of Clear Is, exposed to N'ly swell. There are rks either side of the outer appr 196°. Inside the narrow (30m), rky ent keep to the E. Lie to 2⚓s on E side in about 1·5m or berth at inner end of pier. Few facilities.

ROARING WATER BAY Long Island Bay, entered between Cape Clear and Mizen Hd, extends NE into Roaring Water Bay (AC 2129). The Fastnet Rk, Fl 5s 49m 28M, Horn (4) 60s, is 4M to seaward. Safest appr, S of Schull, is via Carthy's Sound (51°30'N 09°30'W). From the SE appr via Gascanane Sound, but beware Toorane Rks, Anima Rk and outlying rks off many of the islands. Shelter in various winds at ⚓s clockwise from Horse Island: 3ca E and 7ca NE of E tip of Horse Is; in Ballydehob B 2m; Poulgorm B 2m; 5ca ENE of Mannin Is in 4m; 2ca SE of Carrigvalish Rks in 6m. Rincolisky Cas (ru) is conspic on S side of bay. The narrow chan E of Hare Is and N of Sherkin Is has two ⚓s; it also leads via The Sound into Baltimore hbr. Local advice is useful. There are temp fair weather ⚓s in the Carthy's Islands. Rossbrin Cove, 2·5M E of Schull, is a safe ⚓, but many local moorings; no access from E of Horse Is due to drying Horse Ridge. No facilities at most of the above ⚓s.

9.12.24 SCHULL

Cork **51°30'·80N 09°32'·00W**

CHARTS AC 2184, 2129; Imray C56; Irish OS 88

TIDES +0610 Dover; ML 1·8; Duration 0610; Zone 0 (UT)

Standard Port COBH (⟵)

Times				Height (metres)			
High Water		Low Water		MHWS	MHWN	MLWN	MLWS
0500	1100	0500	1100	4·1	3·2	1·3	0·4
1700	2300	1700	2300				
Differences SCHULL							
−0040	−0015	−0015	−0110	−0·9	−0·6	−0·2	0·0

SHELTER Good, except in strong S/SE winds when best shelter is N of Long Island. Schull Hbr access H24. 12 Y ✪s in NE part of hbr or ⚓ in 3m 1ca SE of pier, usually lit by street lts all night; keep clear of fairway marked by 8 unlit lateral buoys.

NAVIGATION WPT 51°29'·60N 09°31'·60W, 346° to front ldg lt, 2·1M. In hbr ent, Bull Rk (dries 1·8m), R iron perch, can be passed either side.

LIGHTS AND MARKS Ldg lts, Oc 5s 5/8m 11M, lead 346° between Long Is Pt, Q (3) 10s 16m 8M, W conical tr, and Amelia Rk SHM buoy Fl G 3s; thence E of Bull Rk and toward head of bay. By day in good vis 2 W radomes conspic on Mt Gabriel (2M N of Schull) lead 355° with Long Is Pt lt ho in transit.

R/T None.

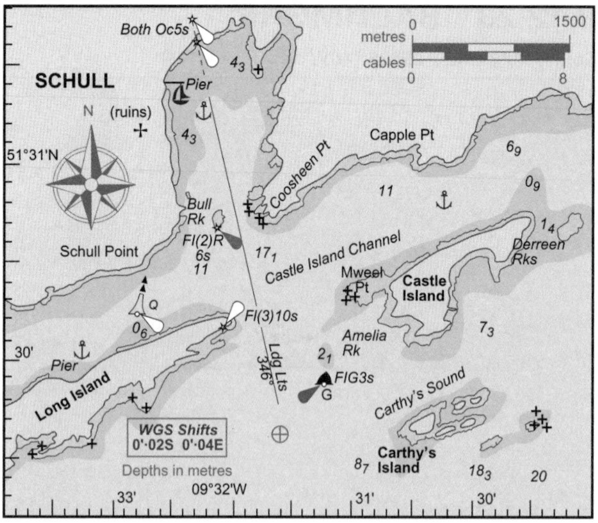
SCHULL
Both Oc5s
Pier
Schull Point
Bull Rk
Fl(2)R 6s 11
Castle Island Channel
Coosheen Pt
Capple Pt
Castle Island
Mweel Pt
Derreen Rks
Amelia Rk
Fl(3)10s
FlG3s
Ldg Lts 346°
Long Island
Carthy's Sound
Carthy's Island
WGS Shifts 0'·02S 0'·04E
Depths in metres
09°32'W
51°31'N

TELEPHONE (Dial code 028) Water Sports Centre 28554; MRSC (066) 9476109; Coast/Cliff Rescue Service 35318; ⊖ (027) 51562; Police 28111; Dr 28311; Ⓗ (027) 50133.

FACILITIES **Schull Pier/Hbr** Slip, AB tempy, ✪s €6.35, M, D, FW, SM; **Sailing Club** ☎ 37352; **Services:** Kos, BY, ⚒, CH. **Village** P & D (cans), Dr, ME, El, 🛒, R, Bar, ▣, ✉, Ⓑ, bus to Cork for: ⇌, ✈, car ferry.

9.12.25 CROOKHAVEN

Cork **51°28'·50N 09°42'·00W**

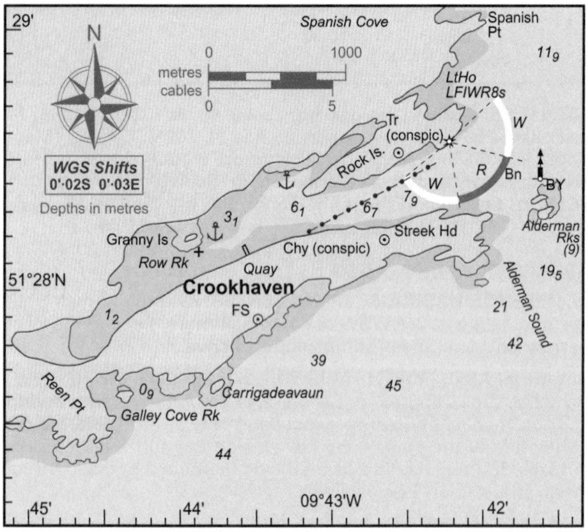
Spanish Cove
Spanish Pt
LtHo LFlWR8s
Tr (conspic)
Rock Is.
Granny Is
Row Rk
Quay
Crookhaven
Chy (conspic)
Streek Hd
Alderman Rks (9)
Alderman Sound
Bn
BY
FS
Reen Pt
Galley Cove Rk
Carrigadeavaun
WGS Shifts 0'·02S 0'·03E
Depths in metres
09°43'W
51°28'N

CHARTS AC 2184; Imray C56; Irish OS 88

TIDES +0550 Dover; ML 1·8; Duration 0610; Zone 0 (UT)

Standard Port COBH (⟵)

Times				Height (metres)			
High Water		Low Water		MHWS	MHWN	MLWN	MLWS
0500	1100	0500	1100	4·1	3·2	1·3	0·4
1700	2300	1700	2300				
Differences CROOKHAVEN							
−0057	−0033	−0048	−0112	−0·8	−0·6	−0·4	−0·1
DUNMANUS HARBOUR							
−0107	−0031	−0044	−0120	−0·7	−0·6	−0·2	0·0
DUNBEACON HARBOUR							
−0057	−0025	−0032	−0104	−0·8	−0·7	−0·3	−0·1

SHELTER Excellent. There are 8 Y ✪s and 10 dayglow R ✪s. Short stay pontoon for up to 4 boats (FW/stores/passengers). ⚓s in middle of bay in 3m; off W tip of Rock Is; and E of Granny Is; last two are far from the svillage. Holding is patchy, especially in strong SW'lies; beware weed, shellfish beds around shoreline and submarine pipeline from Rock Is to Crookhaven.

NAVIGATION WPT 51°28'·50N 09°40'·50W, 274° to Rock Is lt ho, 1M. Ent between this lt and NCM bn on Black Horse Rks (3½ca ESE). From S, keep 1ca E of Alderman Rks and ½ca off Black Horse Rks bn. Passage between Streek Hd and Alderman Rks is not advised for strangers. Inside the bay the shores are steep to.

LIGHTS AND MARKS Lt ho on Rock Is (conspic W tr) L Fl WR 8s 20m 13/11M; vis outside hbr: W over Long Is Bay–281°, R281°–340°; vis inside hbr: R 281°–348°, W348°–N shore.

R/T None.

TELEPHONE (Dial code 028) HM (O'Sullivan's Bar) 35319; MRSC (066) 9476109; Coast/Cliff Rescue at Goleen 35318; ⊖ (027) 50061; Dr 35148; ✉ 35200.

FACILITIES **Village** ✪s €8.00, Bar, R, FW, 🛒, Kos, ✉, D (cans), ME, Gas, Ⓑ (Schull), taxi to Goleen then bus to Cork, ✈, ⇌.

ADJACENT HARBOURS

GOLEEN (Kireal-coegea), Cork, **51°29'·65N 09°42'·21W**. AC 2184. Tides as Crookhaven. A narrow inlet 6ca N of Spanish Pt; good shelter in fair weather, except from SE. 2 churches are easily seen, but ent not visible until close. Keep to S side of ent and ⚓ fore-and-aft just below quay, where AB also possible. Facilities: P, 🛒, Bar.

DUNMANUS BAY, Cork. AC 2552. Tides see 9.12.25. Appr between Three Castle Hd and Sheep's Hd, Fl (3) WR 15s 83m 18/15M; no other lts. Ent to **Dunmanus Hbr**, 51°32'·70N 09°39'·86W, is 1ca wide; breakers both sides. ⚓ in 4m centre of B. **Kitchen Cove**, 51°35'·50N 09°38'·05W, is the best of the 3 hbrs; enter W of Owens Is and ⚓ 1ca NNW of it or 2ca further N in 3m. Exposed to S, but good holding. Quay at Ahakista village: 🛒, R, Bar. **Dunbeacon Hbr**, 51°36'·35N 09°33'·60W, is shallow and rock-girt. ⚓ E or SE of Mannion Is. At Durrus (1¼M): Fuel (cans), R, Bar.

9.12.26 BANTRY BAY

Cork **51°34'N 09°57'W**

CHARTS AC *2552*, 1840, 1838; Imray C56; Irish OS 84, 85, 88

TIDES +0600 Dover; ML 1·8; Duration 0610; Zone 0 (UT)

Standard Port COBH (⟵)

Times				**Height (metres)**			
High Water		Low Water		MHWS	MHWN	MLWN	MLWS
0500	1100	0500	1100	4·1	3·2	1·3	0·4
1700	2300	1700	2300				
Differences BANTRY							
−0045	−0025	−0040	−0105	−0·9	−0·8	−0·2	0·0
CASTLETOWN (Bearhaven)							
−0048	−0012	−0025	−0101	−0·9	−0·6	−0·1	0·0
BLACK BALL HARBOUR (51°36N 10°02W)							
−0115	−0035	−0047	−0127	−0·7	−0·6	−0·1	+0·1

SHELTER/NAVIGATION Bantry Bay extends 20M ENE from Sheep's Hd, Fl (3) WR 15s 83m 18/15M. Access is easy, but the Bay is exposed to W'lies. The shore is clean everywhere except off Bear Is and Whiddy Is. Some of the many well sheltered ⚓s on the N shore are detailed on this page. The S shore has few ⚓s.

CASTLETOWN, 51°38'·80N 09°54'·45W. AC 1840. Sheltered ⚓ in 2·4m NW of Dinish Is, to E of 010° ldg line, but never far from FVs; also ⚓ at **Dunboy Bay,** W of Piper Sound (open to E). 4 Y 🅥s are laid Apr-Sep 3ca E of Dinish Is. Lts: At W ent, Ardnakinna Pt, Fl (2) WR 10s 62m 17/14M, H24. At E ent to Bearhaven: Roancarrigmore, Fl WR 3s 18m 18/14M. Appr W of Bear Is on 024° Dir lt, Oc WRG 5s 4m 14/11M (W024°–024·5°); then inner ldg lts 010°, both Oc 3s 4/7m 1M, vis 005°-015°, via ent chan which narrows to 50m abeam Perch Rk lt bn, QG. Beware Walter Scott Rk (2·7m), SCM buoy, Q (6) + L Fl 15s, and Carrigaglos (0·6m high) S of Dinish Is. VHF Ch 14 16. HM ☎ (027) 70220, ℻ 70329. Facilities: FW & D on quay; BH on Dinish Is. **Town** El, ME, ⚒, P (cans), Bar, Ⓑ, ✉, 🛒, R, Kos.

LAWRENCE COVE, 51°38'·28N 09°49'·28W; AC 1840. *See inset on chartlet below.* Good shelter on N side of Bear Island. Marina on S side of cove has NE/SW pontoon 90m long (40 AB in 3-3·5m). From E keep clear of Palmer Rk and a shoal patch, both 1·8m. ☎/℻ 027 75044; VHF Ch 16 M. AB (€1.52), FW, ⛽, D, BH, ▣. Friendly welcome at the only marina between Kinsale and Dingle. There are 4 Y 🅥s in 3m close S of Ardagh Pt, or ⚓ in 4m to W of Turk Is. At Rerrin village: BY, Slip, 🛒, R, Bar, ✉, storage facilities. Bus to Cork and all storage facilities.

LONEHORT HARBOUR, 51°38'·12N 09°47'·80W. AC 1840. At E tip of Bear Is, good shelter but keep S at ent to clear unmarked rks; then turn ENE to ⚓ in 2·7m at E end of cove.

ADRIGOLE, 51°40'·51N 09°43'·22W. AC 1840. Good shelter, but squally in W/N gales. Beware Doucallia Rk, dries 1·2m, 1M SSW of ent. Beyond the 2ca wide ent, keep E of Orthons Is (rks on W side). 7 Y 🅥s NE of Orthons Is. ⚓s to suit wind direction: off pier on E shore 4m; N or NW of Orthons Is. Drumlave (½M E): 🛒.

Trafrask Bay, 2M to the E, has 1 Y 🅥 at **51°40'·8N 09°40'·1W**.

GLENGARRIFF, 51°44'·20N 09°31'·90W. AC 1838. Tides as Bantry. Beautiful ⚓ S of Bark Is in 7-10m; or to NE in 3m, where there are 6 Y 🅥s. Better for yachts than Bantry hbr. Ent between Big Pt and Gun Pt. No lts/marks. Keep 1ca E of rks off Garinish Island (Illnacullen) and Ship Is; beware marine farms. Rky chan W of Garinish, with HT cable 15m clearance, should not be attempted. Facilities: Eccles hotel, showers. **Village** FW, Bar, D & P (cans), ✉, R, 🛒, Kos.

BANTRY, 51°40'·85N 09°27'·85W. AC 1838. Beware Gerane Rks ½M W of Whiddy Is. Appr via the buoyed/lit N chan (10m) to E of Horse and Chapel Is; keep 2ca off all islands to clear unlit mussel rafts. The S chan, fair weather only, has a bar 2m; ldg marks 091°, front RW post, FW lt; rear W post, FR lt. 🅥 call Bantry Hbr Ch 14 or ☎ 027 51253; VHF Ch 14 11 16 (H24). HM (027) 53277; ⊜ 50061; Police 50045; Dr 50405; Ⓗ 50133. MRCC (066) 9476109. Facilities: **Pier** L, FW; **Bantry Bay SC** ☎ 50081 Slip, L; **Town** EC Wed; P & D (cans), Kos, ME, CH, 🛒, R, Bar, ✉, Ⓑ, bus to Cork.

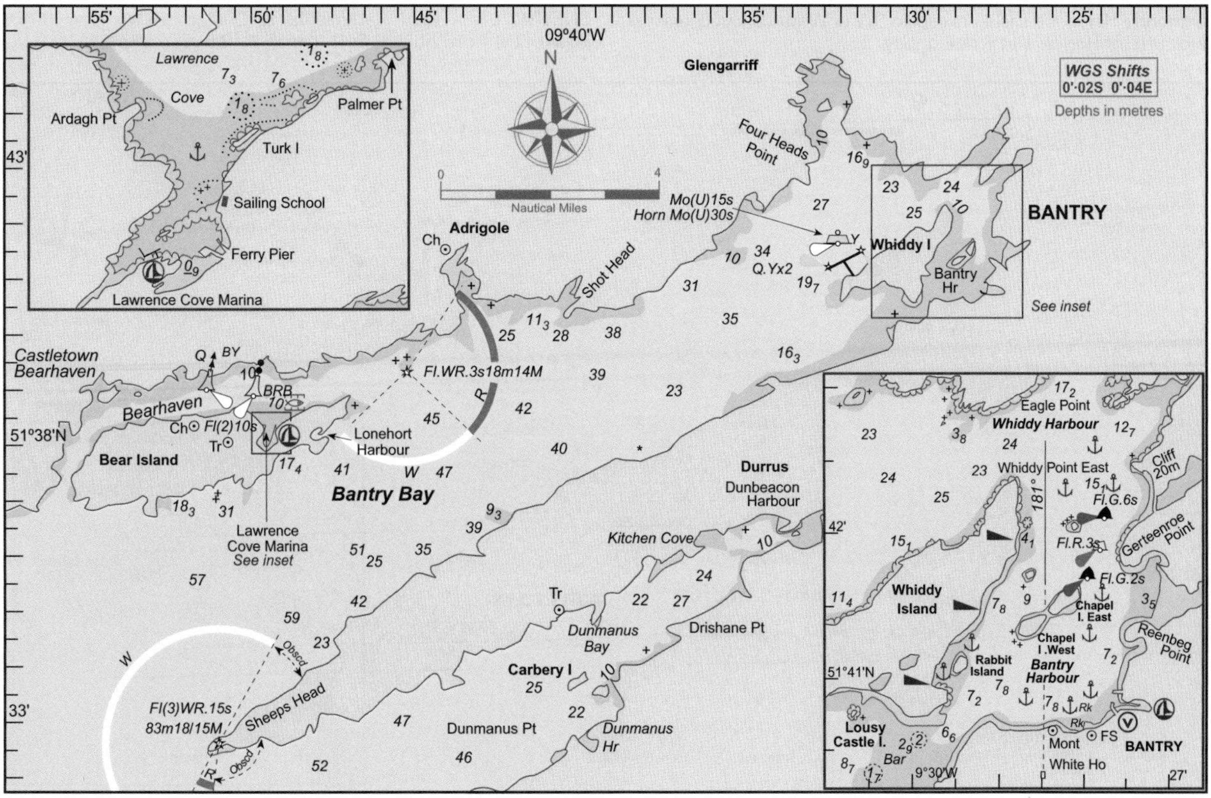
09°40'W
N
Glengarriff
WGS Shifts
0'·02S 0'·04E
Depths in metres
Lawrence
Cove
Ardagh Pt
Palmer Pt
Turk I
Sailing School
Ferry Pier
Lawrence Cove Marina
Nautical Miles
Four Heads Point
Mo(U)15s
Horn Mo(U)30s
Whiddy I
Bantry Hr
BANTRY
See inset
Adrigole
Shot Head
Castletown Bearhaven
Bearhaven
Fl(2)10s
BRB
Fl.WR.3s18m14M
Lonehort Harbour
Bear Island
Bantry Bay
Lawrence Cove Marina
See inset
Durrus
Dunbeacon Harbour
Kitchen Cove
Dunmanus Bay
Drishane Pt
Carbery I
Dunmanus Pt
Dunmanus Hr
Fl(3)WR.15s
83m18/15M
Sheeps Head
Obscd
Eagle Point
Whiddy Harbour
Whiddy Point East
Cliff 20m
Fl.G.6s
Fl.R.3s
Gerteenroe Point
Fl.G.2s
Whiddy Island
Chapel I. East
Chapel I. West
Reenbeg Point
Rabbit Island
Bantry Harbour
Lousy Castle I.
Bar
Mont
White Ho
FS
BANTRY
51°38'N
51°41'N

9.12.27 KENMARE RIVER

Kerry **51°45'·00N 10°00'·00W** ❀❀❀◊✿✿

CHARTS AC *2495*; Imray C56; Irish OS 84

TIDES +0515 Dover; Duration Dunkerron 0620; West Cove 068. Zone 0 (UT)

Standard Port COBH (⟵)

Times				Height (metres)			
High Water		Low Water		MHWS	MHWN	MLWN	MLWS
0500	1100	0500	1100	4·1	3·2	1·3	0·4
1700	2300	1700	2300				
Differences BALLYCROVANE HARBOUR (Coulagh Bay)							
–0116	–0036	–0053	–0133	–0·6	–0·5	–0·1	0·0
DUNKERRON HARBOUR							
–0117	–0027	–0050	–0140	–0·2	–0·3	+0·1	0·0
WEST COVE (51°46'N 10°03'W)							
–0113	–0033	–0049	–0129	–0·6	–0·5	–0·1	0·0
BALLINSKELLIGS BAY							
–0119	–0039	–0054	–0134	–0·5	–0·5	–0·1	0·0

SHELTER Garnish Bay (S of Long I): is only good in settled weather and W'ly winds. ⚓ either W or 1ca S of the Carrigduff concrete bn.

Ballycrovane: in NE of Coulagh B is a good x, but open to W'ly swell which breaks on submerged rks in SE. N and E shores are foul. x 5ca NE of Bird Is.

Cleanderry: Ent NE of Illaunbweeheen (Yellow Is) is only 7m wide and rky. ⚓ ENE of inner hbr. Beware mussel farms.

Ardgroom: excellent shelter, but intricate ent over rky bar. Appr with B bn brg 135°; then 2 W bns (front on Black Rk, rear ashore) lead 099° through bar. Alter 206° as two bns astern come in transit. When clear, steer WNW to ⚓ ½ ca E of Reenavade pier; power needed. Beware fish farms.

Kilmakilloge: is a safe ⚓ in all winds. Beware mussel beds and rky shoals. On appr keep S side of ent, steer W of Spanish Is, but pass N of it. Bunaw Hbr ldg lts 041°, front Oc R 3s, rear Iso R 2s, (access only near HW; AB for shoal draft). Keep S side of ent; ⚓ 2ca W of Carrigwee bn; S of Eskadawer Pt; or Collorus Hbr W side only.

Ormond's Hbr: good shelter except in SW or W winds, but beware rk 2½ca ENE of Hog Is. ⚓ in S half of bay.

Kenmare: Good shelter. Access only near HW via narrow ch marked by withies. AB at pier at N side of river, just below town.

Dunkerron Hbr: Ent between Cod Rks and The Boar to ⚓ 1ca NW of Fox Is in 3·2m; land at Templenoe pier. 4ca E of Reen Pt behind pier, AB (€8.89) at floating jetty in 1·8m but appr may be less at LW.

Sneem: enter between Sherky Is and Rossdohan Is. Hotel conspic NE of hbr. 3 Y ●s and ⚓ NE of Garinish Is, but uncomfortable if swell enters either side of Sherky Is.

Darrynane: 1½M NW of Lamb's Hd, is appr'd from the S between Deenish and Moylaun Islands, but not with high SW swell. Enter with care on the ldg marks/lts 034°, 2 W bns, both Oc 3s 10/16m 4M. 3 Y ●s and safe ⚓ (3m) NE of Lamb's Is. Also ⚓s in Lehid Hbr, R Blackwater, Coongar Hbr & W Cove.

NAVIGATION WPT 51°40'·00N 10°17'·20W, 065° to 0.5M S of Sherky Island, 15·6M. From SW, keep NW of The Bull and Dursey Is. From SE, Dursey Sound is possible in fair wx but narrow (beware Flag Rk 0·3m) and with cable car, 21m clearance. To clear dangerous rks off Coulagh Bay, keep twr on Dursey Is well open of Cod's Head 220°. From NW, there are 3 deep chans off Lamb's Head: between Scarriff Is and Deenish Is which is clear; between Deenish and Moylaun Is which has rky shoals; and between Moylaun and Two Headed Is which is clear and 4½ca wide. A night appr into the river is possible, but close appr to hbrs or ⚓s is not advised. Up-river from Sneem Hbr, keep N of Maiden Rk, dries 0·5m, and Church Rks; also Lackeen Rks and Carrignarona beg. Beware salmon nets Jun–Sep. See 9.12.5.

LIGHTS AND MARKS On Dursey Is: Old Watch Twr (conspic) 250m. Eagle Hill (Cod's Hd) 216m. lights are as on chartlet.

R/T None.

TELEPHONE (Dial code 064) MRCC (066) 9476109; Coast/Cliff Rescue Service (Waterville) (066) 74320; ⊖ Bantry (027) 50061; Ⓗ 4108; Police 41177.

FACILITIES
ARDGROOM (Pallas Hbr): D & P (cans), 🛒, R, Bar, Kos, ✉ at Ardgroom village (2M SSW of Reenavade pier).
KILMAKILLOGE: **Bunaw Pier**, AB, 🛒, Bar; 2M to D, Kos, ✉.
KENMARE: AB. **Town** D & P (cans), Kos, Gaz, R, 🛒, Bar, Ⓗ, ✉, Ⓑ, ⇌ (bus to Killarney), ✈ (Cork or Killarney).
SNEEM: L at Hotel Parknasilla & Oysterbed Ho pier (FW). **Town** (2M from hbr), P & D (cans), R, Bar, ✉, Slip, 🛒, Kos.

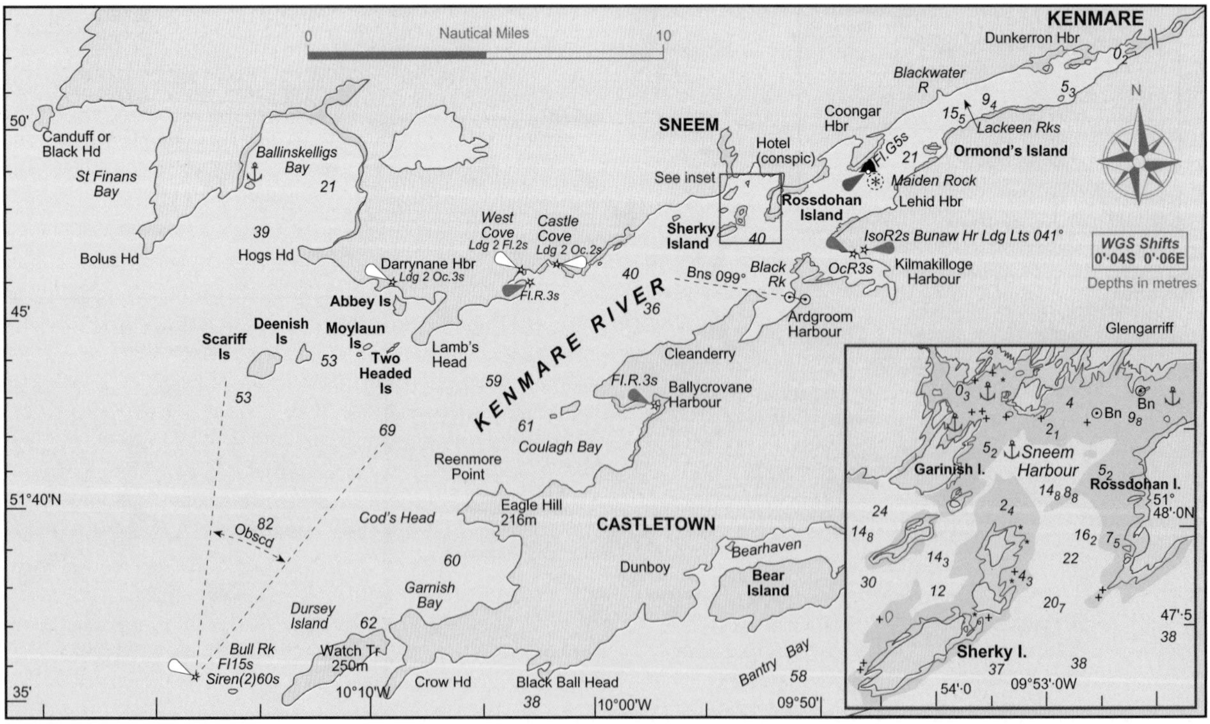
KENMARE
Dunkerron Hbr
Nautical Miles
0
10
Blackwater R
Coongar Hbr
SNEEM
Hotel (conspic)
Lackeen Rks
Ormond's Island
Maiden Rock
Lehid Hbr
See inset
Rossdohan Island
Sherky Island
IsoR2s Bunaw Hr Ldg Lts 041°
OcR3s
Kilmakilloge Harbour
Black Rk
Bns 099°
Ardgroom Harbour
WGS Shifts
0'·04S 0'·06E
Depths in metres
Glengarriff
Candouff or Black Hd
St Finans Bay
Ballinskelligs Bay
Bolus Hd
Hogs Hd
West Cove Ldg 2 Fl.2s
Castle Cove Ldg 2 Oc.2s
Darrynane Hbr Ldg 2 Oc.3s
Fl.R.3s
Abbey Is
Scariff Is
Deenish Is
Moylaun Is
Two Headed Is
Lamb's Head
KENMARE RIVER
Cleanderry
Fl.R.3s
Ballycrovane Harbour
Coulagh Bay
Reenmore Point
Eagle Hill 216m
Cod's Head
CASTLETOWN
Bearhaven
Bear Island
Dunboy
Garnish Bay
Dursey Island
Obscd
Bull Rk Fl15s Siren(2)60s
Watch Tr 250m
Crow Hd
Black Ball Head
Bantry Bay
50'
45'
51°40'N
35'
10°10'W
10°00'W
09°50'
Sneem Harbour
Garinish I.
Rossdohan I.
Sherky I.
Bn
51° 48'·0N
47'·5
54'·0
09°53'·0W

9.12.28 DINGLE BAY

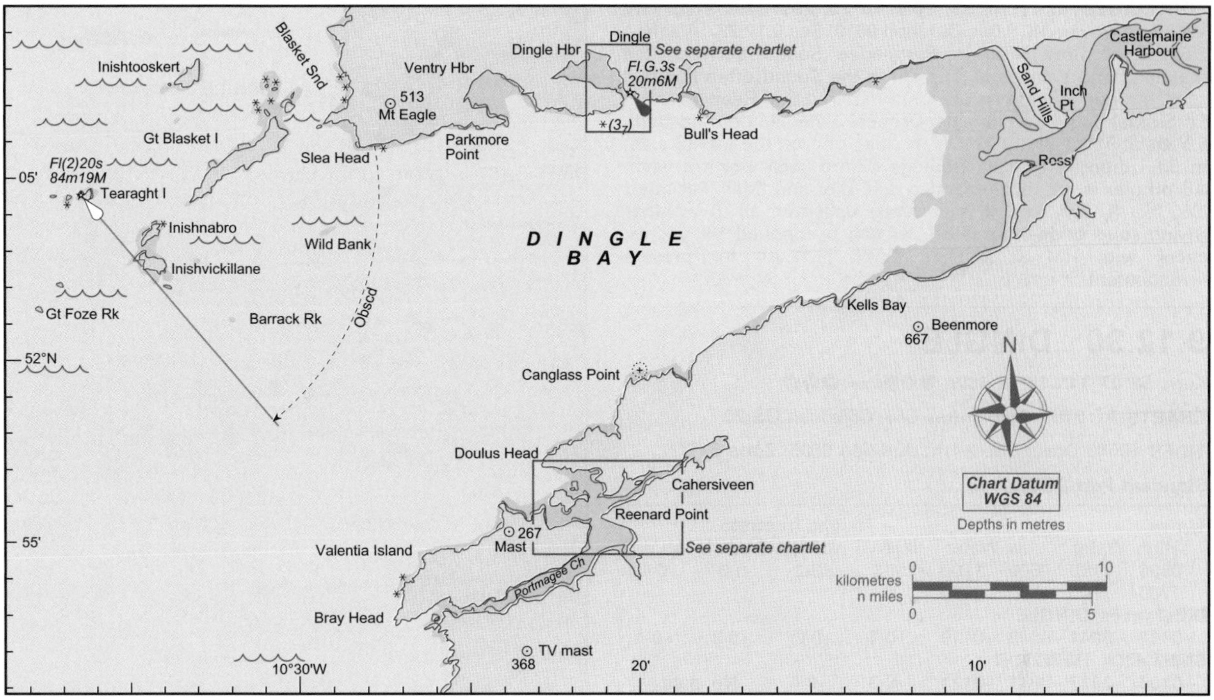

Inishtooskert
Blasket Snd
Ventry Hbr
Dingle Hbr
Dingle
See separate chartlet
Fl.G.3s 20m6M
Castlemaine Harbour
Sand Hills
Inch Pt
513 Mt Eagle
Gt Blasket I
Slea Head
Parkmore Point
Bull's Head
Fl(2)20s 84m19M
05'
Tearaght I
Inishnabro
Wild Bank
Inishvickillane
DINGLE BAY
Ross
Gt Foze Rk
Barrack Rk
Obscd
Kells Bay
Beenmore 667
52°N
Canglass Point
N
Doulus Head
Cahersiveen
Chart Datum WGS 84
Reenard Point
Depths in metres
55'
267 Mast
Valentia Island
See separate chartlet
Portmagee Ch
kilometres
n miles
Bray Head
TV mast 368
10°30'W
20'
10'

9.12.29 VALENTIA HARBOUR

Kerry **51°55'·7N 10°17'·1W** ❁❁⛵⛵✿✿✿

CHARTS AC 2125; Imray C56; Irish OS 84

TIDES +0515 Dover; Zone 0 (UT)

Standard Port COBH (⟵)

Times				Height (metres)			
High Water		Low Water		MHWS	MHWN	MLWN	MLWS
0500	1100	0500	1100	4·1	3·2	1·3	0·4
1700	2300	1700	2300				
Differences VALENTIA HARBOUR (Knight's Town)							
−0118	−0038	−0056	−0136	−0·6	−0·4	−0·1	0·0

SHELTER Good ⚓s at: Glanleam B, 6ca S of Fort Pt in 4m; 1ca NW of LB slip in 2·5m, with 6 Y ♦s (beware The Foot, spit drying 1·2m, marked by ECM buoy, Q (3) 5s); SE of the ferry pier at Knight's Town (E end of the island) in 4m; in bay on the S side of Beginish Is in 3m.

NAVIGATION Wpt 51°56'·84N 10°20'·15W 147° to Fort Pt lt 1M. Appr the NE end of Valentia Is, either (a) via Doulus Bay, N of Beginish Is (avoid if swell is running) or better (b) between Fort Pt and Beginish Is (easy access except in strong NW'lies). For (a) clear Black Rks by ½ ca then head for the E end of Beginish Is as soon as Reenard Pt opens to port of it. When Lamb Is and the N point of Beginish are about to open astern, alter course to keep them so till Reenard Point opens to the E of Church Is. Then steer to pass 50m E of Church Is to avoid Passage Rk ($\underline{1}_5$) 1 ca E of Is. For (b): beware Hbr Rk, 2·6m, 3ca SE of Fort Pt and 100m SW of ldg line and marked by ECM bn Q (3) 10s. For appr S of Island via Portmagee chan see **Portmagee** overleaf for info on availability of the swing bridge across the chan. For Cahersiveen marina from Valentia Is start as early on the tide as you can to cross the Caher Bar, follow the ldg lts/lines 019°–199°, 100°–280°, 076°–256°, 053°–233°, 035°–215° and then keep to the middle of the river.

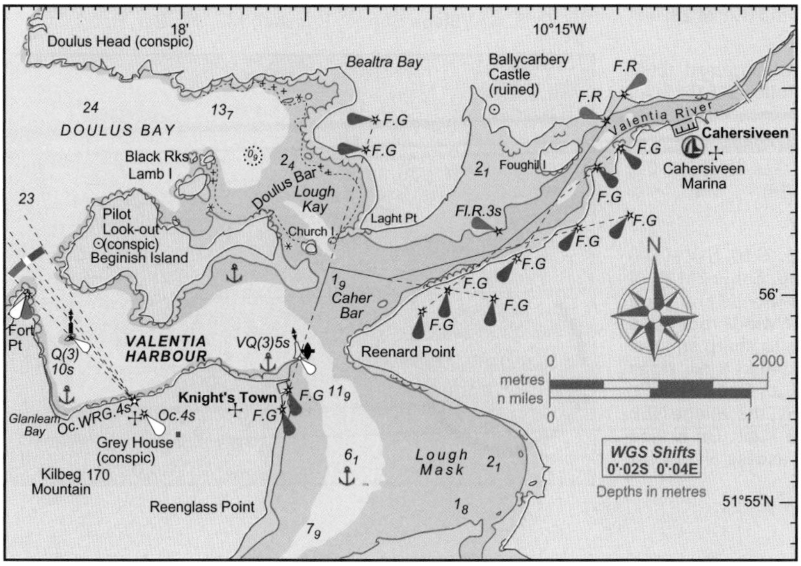

18'
10°15'W
Doulus Head (conspic)
Bealtra Bay
Ballycarbery Castle (ruined)
F.R
F.R
24
13_7
DOULUS BAY
F.G
F.G
Valentia River
Cahersiveen
Black Rks
Lamb I
2_4
Doulus Bar
Lough Kay
2_1
Foughil I
F.G
Cahersiveen Marina
23
Pilot Look-out (conspic)
Beginish Island
Church I
Laght Pt
Fl.R.3s
F.G
F.G
F.G
N
F.G
1_9
Caher Bar
F.G
F.G
F.G
56'
Fort Pt
Q(3) 10s
VALENTIA HARBOUR
VQ(3)5s
Reenard Point
0
2000
metres
n miles
0
1
Glanleam Bay
Oc.WRG.4s
Knight's Town
F.G 11_9
Oc.4s
F.G
Grey House (conspic)
6_1
Lough Mask
2_1
WGS Shifts 0'·02S 0'·04E
Kilbeg 170 Mountain
Depths in metres
51°55'N
Reenglass Point
1_8
7_9

LIGHTS AND MARKS Fort Pt lt, Fl WR 2s 16m 17/15M, W102°-304°, R304°-351°, obsc'd from seaward when E of Doulus Head. Ldg lts 141°: Front Dir Oc WRG 4s 25m 11/8M, W sector 140°-142°; rear, Oc 4s 43m 5M, synch. 12 F.G and 2 F.R lights on B & W poles (see chartlet).

R/T Cahersiveen Marina VHF Ch 80.

TELEPHONE Knightstown HM (066) 9476124, 📠 9476309; CG 9476109; ⊖ 7128540; Dr 9472121; Police 9472111; Ⓗ 9472100; Cahersiveen Marina ☎ 947 2777, 📠 9472993, www.cahersiveenmarina.ie.

FACILITIES **Knight's Town**: 6 Y ♦s; BY, ⚒, ME, Gas, P & D (cans), Kos, 🛒, R, Bar, 🗏. Ferry/bus to Cahersiveen (2½M) for usual shops; EC Thurs. Bus to ⇄ (Tralee and Killarney), ✈ (Kerry, Shannon, Cork). **Cahersiveen Marina** (2M upriver): (80 incl V) €1.50, BH(14T), ME, El, Ch, Ⓔ, ⚒, P & D, 🗏, 🛒, Ⓑ, ✉, R, Bar.

ANCHORAGES SW VALENTIA ISLAND

PORTMAGEE, Kerry, **51°53'·20N 10°22'·29W**. AC 2125. HW +0550 on Dover; ML 2·0m; Duration 0610; See 9.12.29. A safe ⚓ 2·5M E of Bray Head in Portmagee Sound between the mainland and Valentia Is. The ent to the Sound often has bad seas, but dangers are visible. Care required E of Reencaheragh Pt (S side) due rks either side. Deepest water is N of mid-chan. 6 Y 🅐s at 51°53'·3N 10°22'·5W (N side), or ⚓ off the pier (S side) in 5m, opposite Skelling Heritage Centre (well worth a visit). AB on pier is not recommended due to strong tides. Facilities: FW, 🛒, R, Bar, Kos. It is currently uncertain as to whether Swing road bridge 1ca E of pier can be opened for yachts; check with HM at Knight's Town (9.12.29) for present arrangement, if any.

9.12.30 DINGLE

Kerry **52°07'·14N 10°15'·48W** ❀❀❀◊◊◊✿✿✿

CHARTS AC 2789, 2790; Imray C55, C56; Irish OS 70

TIDES +0540 Dover; ML 2·1m; Duration 0605; Zone 0 (UT)

Standard Port COBH (⟵)

Times				Height (metres)			
High Water		Low Water		MHWS	MHWN	MLWN	MLWS
0500	1100	0500	1100	4·1	3·2	1·3	0·4
1700	2300	1700	2300				
Differences DINGLE							
−0111	−0041	−0049	−0119	−0·1	0·0	+0·3	+0·4
SMERWICK HARBOUR							
−0107	−0027	−0041	−0121	−0·3	−0·4	No data	
FENIT PIER (Tralee Bay)							
−0057	−0017	−0029	−0109	+0·5	+0·2	+0·3	+0·1

SHELTER Excellent at marina (5m depth) in landlocked hbr. A busy fishing port. There are 4 Y 🅐s at **Kells Bay** (52°01'·6N 10°06'·3W), 8M SE of Dingle ent.

NAVIGATION WPT 52°06'·20N 10° 15'·48W, 360° to lt Fl G 3s, 1·06M. Easy ent H24. Beware Crow Rk (dries 3·7m), 0·8M SW of Reenbeg Pt; and rky ledge SW of Black Pt.
Note: **Castlemaine Hbr**, approx 15M E at the head of Dingle Bay, largely dries and should not be attempted without local knowledge or inspection at LW.

LIGHTS AND MARKS Eask Twr (195m, with fingerpost pointing E) is conspic 0·85M WSW of ent. Lt tr, Fl G 3s 20m 6M, on NE side of ent. Ent chan, dredged 2·6m, is marked by 5 SHM lt buoys and 3 PHM lt buoys, as chartlet. Ldg lts, both Oc 3s, (W ◊s on B poles) lead from astern 182° to hbr bkwtrs.

R/T Ch **14** 16, but no calls required. Valentia Radio (Ch 24 28) will relay urgent messages to Dingle HM.

TELEPHONE (Dial code 066) HM 9151629; Coastguard (066) 9476109; ⊖ 7121480; Dr 9152225; ⊞ 9151455; Police 9151522. All emergencies: 999 or 112.

FACILITIES Marina (60 + 20 Ⓥ) ☎ 9151629, 📠 9152629, €1.80, D, Slip, ⊡, ♿, C (hire). **Town** P (cans), Kos, ME, Ⓔ, Gas, Gaz, SM, ✉, R, Bar, 🛒, Ⓑ, ⇌ Tralee (by bus), ✈ (Kerry 30M).

ANCHORAGE CLOSE WEST OF DINGLE BAY

VENTRY Kerry, **52°06·70N 10°20'·30W**. AC 2789, 2790. HW +0540 on Dover; ML 2·1m; Duration 0605; Use 9.12.30. Ent is 2M W of conspic Eask Tr. A pleasant hbr with easy ent 1M wide and good holding on hard sand; sheltered from SW to N winds, but open to swell from the SE, and in fresh W'lies prone to sharp squalls. Beware Reenvare Rks 1ca SE of Parkmore Pt; also a rky ridge 2·9m, on which seas break, extends 2·5ca SSE of Ballymore Pt. No lts. ⚓s in about 4m off Ventry Strand (⊕ brg W, the village NE); or in 3m SW side of bay, 1ca N of pier; also 3 Y 🅐s. On N side 3 Y 🅐s off pier at Ventry village. Both piers access HW±3 for landing. Facilities: P, Slip, 🛒, Kos, Bar, R, ✉.

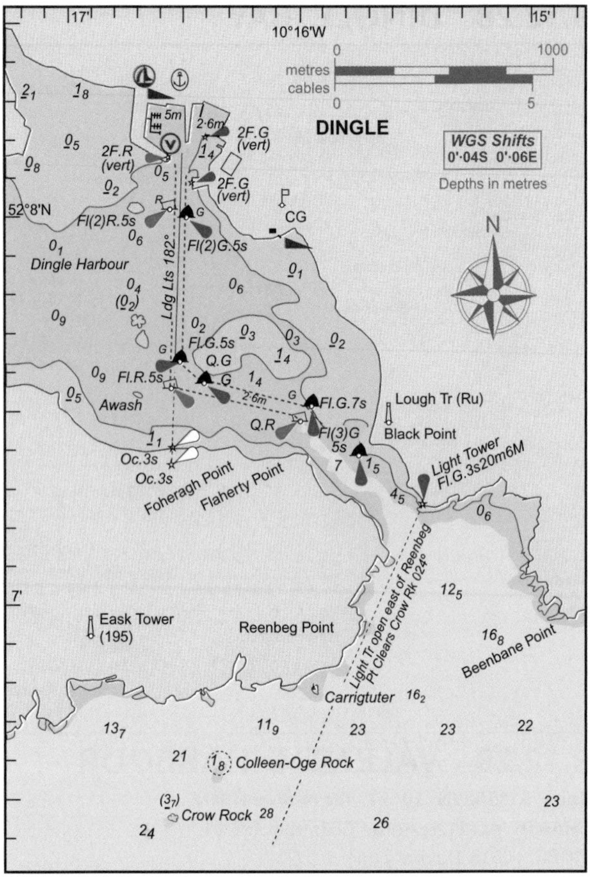
DINGLE
10°16'W
WGS Shifts
0'·04S 0'·06E
Depths in metres
Dingle Harbour
Ldg Lts 182°
Fl(2)R.5s
Fl(2)G.5s
Fl.G.5s
Fl.R.5s
Q.G
Q.R
Fl.G.7s
Fl(3)G 5s
Oc.3s
Awash
Lough Tr (Ru)
Black Point
Light Tower Fl.G.3s20m6M
Foheragh Point
Flaherty Point
Eask Tower (195)
Reenbeg Point
Light Tr open east of Reenbeg Pt Clears Crow Rk 024°
Beenbane Point
Carrigtuter
Colleen-Oge Rock
Crow Rock
52°8'N

SIGNIFICANT HARBOUR BETWEEN THE BLASKETS AND KERRY HEAD

FENIT HARBOUR, 52°16'·20N 09°51'·61W, is in SE corner of Tralee Bay. *See chartlet below.* Appr on 146° to Little Samphire Is, conspic lt ho, Fl WRG 5s 17m 16/13M, thence 7ca E to Samphire Is; lt QR 15m 3M vis 242°–097°. Good shelter in marina, but a few berths exposed to SE winds. Fenit Pier head 2 FR (vert) 12m 3M, vis 148°–058°. For 🅐s call *Neptune* (Tralee SC) VHF Ch 14 16. Port Manager: VHF Ch 16 14 M (0900-2100UT), ☎ (066) 7136231, 📠 (066) 7136473; ⊖ ☎ (066) 7121480. **Marina** (140 inc 20 Ⓥ); max LOA 15m), €1.60 (min €16.00), FW, ⚡, D, ⊡, ♿; **Village** Slip, C, P (cans), ME, 🛒, Bar, R, ✉.

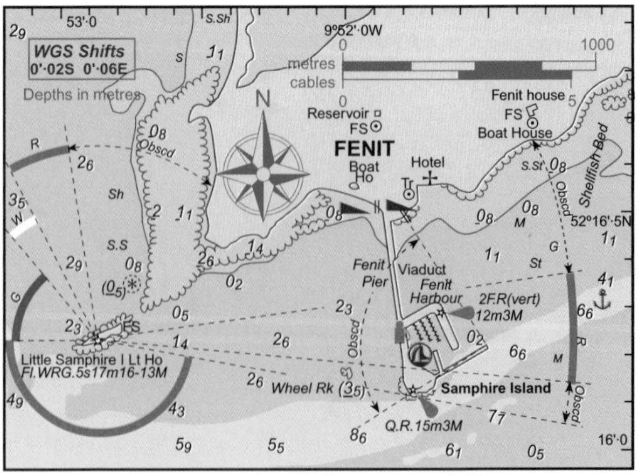
FENIT
9°52'·0W
WGS Shifts
0'·02S 0'·06E
Depths in metres
Fenit house
Reservoir
Boat House
Hotel
Boat Ho
Fenit Pier
Viaduct
Fenit Harbour
2FR(vert) 12m3M
Little Samphire I Lt Ho Fl.WRG.5s17m16-13M
Wheel Rk
Samphire Island
Q.R.15m3M
Shellfish Bed
52°16'·5N
Obscd

ANCHORAGES BETWEEN THE BLASKETS AND KERRY HD

SMERWICK HARBOUR, Kerry, **52°13'·00N 10°24'·00W**. AC 2789. Tides 9.12.30. Adequate shelter in 1M wide bay, except from NW'ly when considerable swell runs in. Ent between The Three Sisters (150m hill) and Dunacapple Is to the NE. Beacon Fl.R.3s at pier end at Ballnagall Pt. ⚓s at: the W side close N or S of the Boat Hr in 3-10m; to the S, off Carrigveen Pt in 2·5m; or in N'lies at the bay in NE corner inside 10m line. Facilities at Ballynagall village on SE side: 4 Y Ⓥs, pier (0·5m), limited 🛒, Bar, Bus.

BRANDON BAY, Kerry, **52°16'·10N 10°09'·92**W. AC 2739. Tides as Fenit 9.12.30. A 4M wide bay, very exposed to the N, but in moderate SW-W winds there is safe ⚓ in 6m close E of drying Brandon Pier, 2FG (vert). Cloghane Inlet in SW of Bay is not advised. Facilities at Brandon: limited 🛒, P (1M), ✉, R, Bar, bus.

TRALEE BAY, Kerry, **52°18'·00N 09°56'·00W**. AC 2739. HW –0612 on Dover; ML 2·6m; Duration 0605. See 9.12.30. Enter the bay passing 3M N of Magharee Islands. Pick up the W sector (W140°–152°) of Little Samphire Is lt, Fl WRG 5s 17m 16/13M; see 9.12.4 for sectors. Approach between Magharee Is and Mucklaghmore (30m high).

9.12.31 SHANNON ESTUARY

Clare (N); Kerry and Limerick (S) **52°35'·00N 09°40'·00W**

CHARTS AC 1819, 1547, 1548, 1549, 1540; L. Derg 5080; L. Ree 5078. Imray C55. OS 63, 64. The ICC's *Sailing Directions for S & W Ireland* and/or Admiralty *Irish Coast Pilot* are essential.

TIDES

HW at	HW Galway	HW Dover
Kilbaha & Carrigaholt	–0015	+0605
Tarbert Island	+0035	–0530
Foynes	+0050	–0515
Limerick	+0130	–0435

At Limerick strong S-W winds increase the height and delay the times of HW; strong N-E winds do the opposite.

SHELTER The Shannon Estuary is 50M long, (Loop Hd to Limerick). For boats on passage N/S the nearest ⚓ is Kilbaha Bay, 3M inside Loop Hd; it has Ⓥs sheltered in winds from W to NE, but is exposed to swell and holding is poor. 6M further E, Carrigaholt Bay has Ⓥs and good shelter from W'lies; ⚓ just N of the new quay, out of the tide. Kilrush marina (9.12.32) with all facilities is 7M further E. From Kilcredaun Head in the W to the R Fergus ent (about 25M) there are ⚓s or Ⓥs, protected from all but E winds, at Tarbert Is, Glin, Labasheeda, Killadysert (pontoon) and among the islands in the Fergus mouth. There is a pontoon off the YC S of Foynes Is and drying quays at Ballylongford Creek (Saleen), Knock and Clarecastle (S of Ennis, off chartlet). Yachts may enter Limerick Dock, but this is a commercial port with usual problems; major improvements planned.

NAVIGATION WPT 52°32'·50N 09°46'·90W, Ballybunnion NCM By VQ, 064° to Tail of Beal Bar buoy WCM, Q (9) 15s, 4·2M. For notes on ent and tidal streams see 9.12.5. The ebb can reach 4kn. Ldg lts, Oc. 5s, 046·4°' on Corlis Pt. The lower estuary between Kerry and Loop Heads is 9M wide, narrowing to 2M off Kilcredaun Pt. Here the chan is well buoyed in mid-stream and then follows the Kerry shore, S of Scattery Is. From Tarbert Is to Foynes Is the river narrows to less than 1M in places, before widening where the R Fergus joins from the N, abeam Shannon airport. Above this point the buoyed chan narrows and becomes shallower although there is a minimum of 2m at LWS. AC 1540 is essential for the final 15M stretch to Limerick.

RIVER SHANNON The Shannon, the longest navigable river in the UK or Ireland, is managed by Limerick Hbr Commissioners up to Limerick. Up-stream it effectively becomes an inland waterway; progress is restricted by locks and bridges. Info on navigation and facilities can be obtained from the Waterways Service, Dept of Art, Culture & the Gaeltacht, 51 St Stephen's Green, Dublin 2, ☎ 01-6613111; or from the Inland Waterways Association of Ireland, Kingston House, Ballinteer, Dublin 4, ☎ 01-983392; also from Tourist Offices and inland marinas.

LIGHTS AND MARKS Principal lts are listed in 9.12.4. There are QW (vert) aero hazard lts on tall chimneys at Money Pt power station 3M ESE of Kilrush. 2 chys at Tarbert Is are conspic (R lts).

R/T Foynes Ch 12 13 16 (occas). *Shannon Estuary Radio* Ch 12 13 16 (HO).

FACILITIES Marine facilities are available at several communities on the Shannon; M, P & D (cans), FW, 🛒, can be found at many villages. Ⓥs are being laid at Labasheeda, Glin Pier (pontoon) and Foynes. E of Aughanish Is on S shore, R Deal is navigable 3M to Askeaton. Ent, marked by RW bn, is 8ca SE of Beeves Rk with 1m in buoyed chan. BY at Massey's Pier ☎ 069 73100, 📠 392344, Ⓥs, FW, C, CH, ⛽, D, Slip. Facilities at Foynes and Limerick include: **Foynes** Slip, L, AB, P & D (cans), FW, ✉, Ⓑ, Dr, 🛒, R, Bar; **Foynes YC** ☎ (069) 65261, AB (pontoon), Bar, R. **Limerick**: **Hbr Commission** ☎ (061) 315377; ⊖ ☎ 415366. **City** Slip, AB, L, FW, P & D (cans), Kos, Gas, Gaz, ME, El, Dr, Ⓗ, ✉, all usual city amenities, ⇌, ✈ (Shannon).

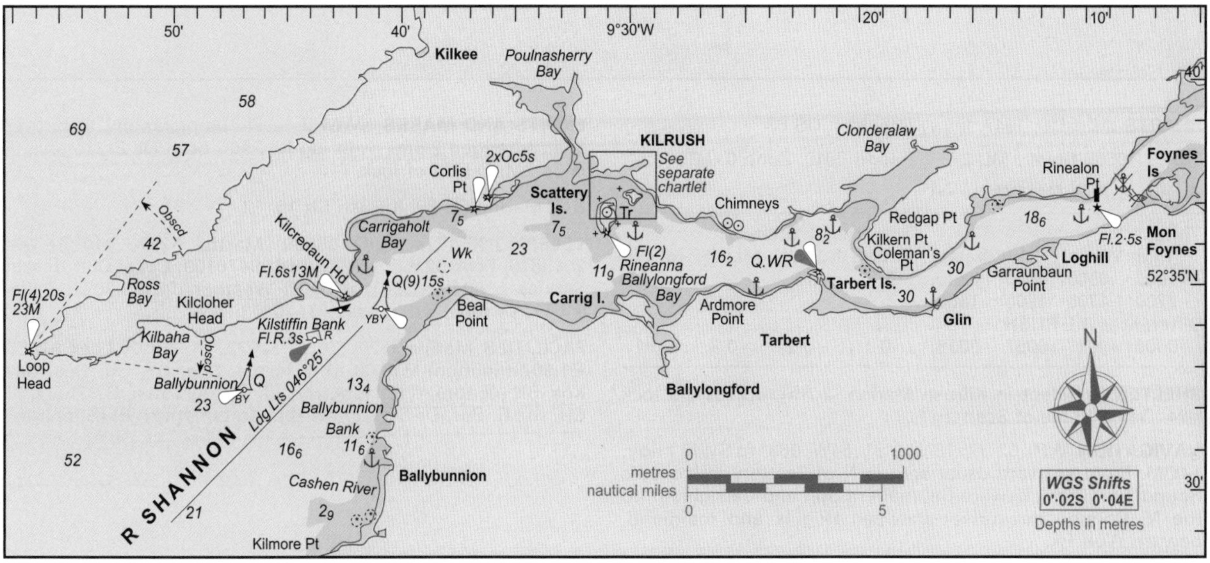
50'
40'
9°30'W
20'
10'
Kilkee
Poulnasherry Bay
KILRUSH
See separate chartlet
Clonderalaw Bay
Foynes Is
Rinealon Pt
Corlis Pt
2xOc5s
Scattery Is.
Chimneys
Redgap Pt
Kilkern Pt
Coleman's Pt
Carrigaholt Bay
Kilcredaun Hd
Fl.6s13M
Q(9)15s
Wk
Fl(2)
Rineanna
Ballylongford Bay
Q.WR
Tarbert Is.
Fl.2·5s
Mon
Foynes
Loghill
Garraunbaun Point
52°35'N
Ross Bay
Kilcloher Head
Kilstiffin Bank
Fl.R.3s
Fl(4)20s 23M
Loop Head
Kilbaha Bay
Ballybunnion
Q
BY
Beal Point
Carrig I.
Ardmore Point
Tarbert
Glin
YBY
Obscd
Ldg Lts 046°25'
Ballybunnion Bank
Ballylongford
Ballybunnion
Cashen River
Kilmore Pt
R SHANNON
metres
nautical miles
0
1000
5
N
WGS Shifts
0'·02S 0'·04E
Depths in metres
30'
40'

9.12.32 KILRUSH

Clare **52°37'·90N 09°29'·70W** ❁❁❁⛵⛵⛵✿✿✿

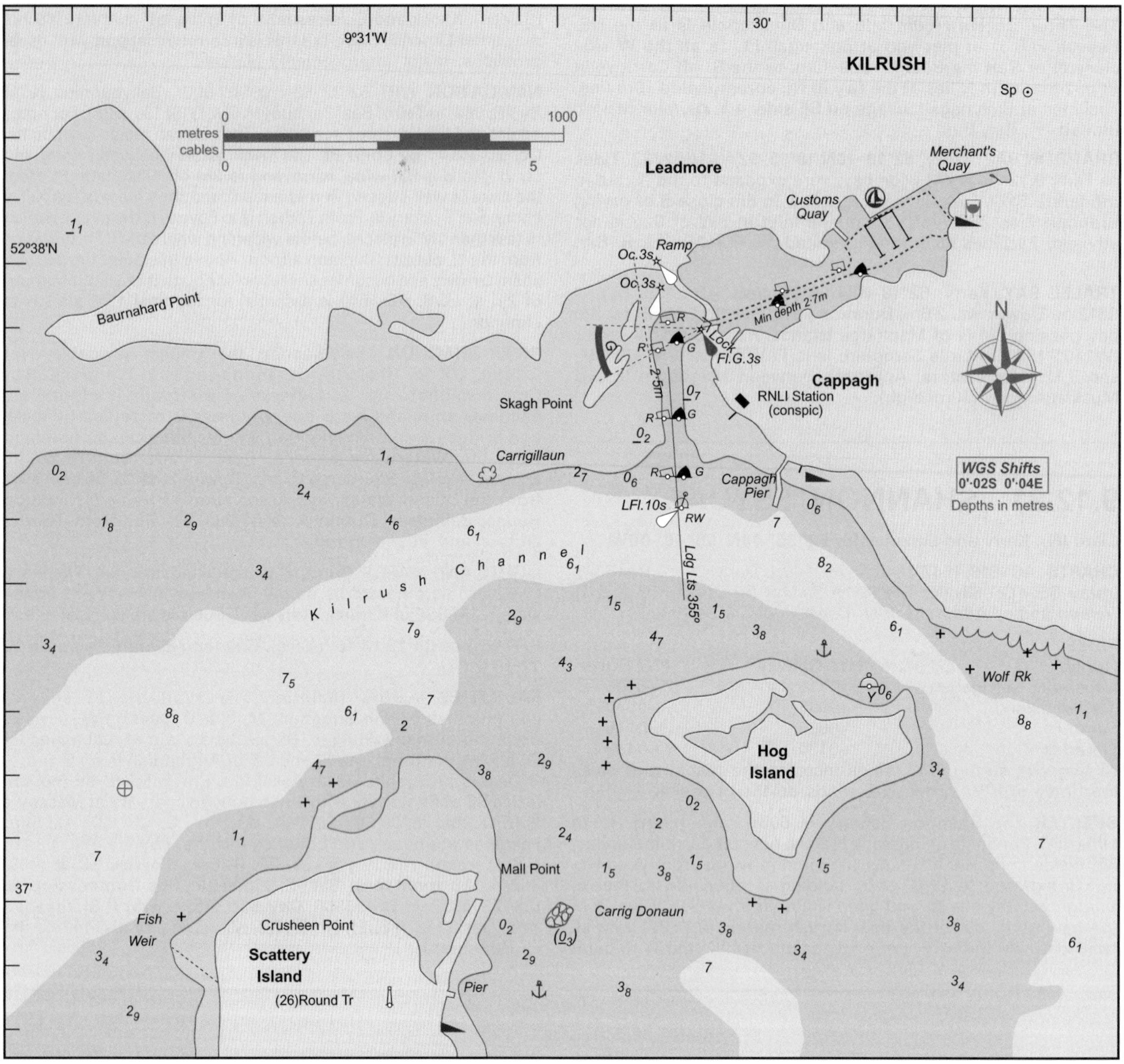
9°31'W
30'
KILRUSH
Sp
metres
cables
0
1000
0
5
Leadmore
Merchant's Quay
Customs Quay
Ramp
Oc.3s
Oc.3s
Lock
Min depth 2·7m
Fl.G.3s
2·5m
Cappagh
RNLI Station (conspic)
N
52°38'N
Baurnahard Point
Skagh Point
Carrigillaun
Cappagh Pier
LFl.10s
RW
Ldg Lts 355°
WGS Shifts
0'·02S 0'·04E
Depths in metres
Kilrush Channel
Wolf Rk
Hog Island
Mall Point
Carrig Donaun
37'
Fish Weir
Crusheen Point
Scattery Island
(26)Round Tr
Pier

CHARTS AC 1819, 1547; Imray C55; Irish OS 63

TIDES –0555 Dover; ML 2·6; Duration 0610; Zone 0 (UT)

Standard Port GALWAY (⟶)

Times				Height (metres)			
High Water		Low Water		MHWS	MHWN	MLWN	MLWS
1000	0500	0000	0600	5·1	3·9	2·0	0·6
2200	1700	1200	1800				
Differences KILRUSH							
–0006	+0027	+0057	–0016	–0·1	–0·2	–0·3	–0·1

SHELTER Excellent in Kilrush Marina (2·7m), access via lock H24. Day ⚓ in lee of Scattery Is.

NAVIGATION WPT 52°37'·18N 09°31'·64W, 063° to SWM buoy, 1·00M. From seaward usual appr is N of Scattery Is (conspic Round Twr, 26m); beware Baurnahard Spit and Carrigillaun to the N. Coming down-river between Hog Is and mainland, beware Wolf Rk.

LIGHTS AND MARKS SWM By L Fl 10s marks ent to buoyed chan (dredged 2·5m), with ldg lts 355°, both Oc 3s, to lock. Fl G 3s 2M, S side of lock.

R/T Marina Ch 80. Kilrush Ch 16, 12.

TELEPHONE (Dial code 06590) Marina 52072 Mobile 086 2313870; Lock 52155; MRCC (066) 9476109; Coast/Cliff Rescue Service 51004; ⊖ (061) 415366; Weather (061) 62677; Police 51017; Dr (065) 51581 also 51470.

FACILITIES Marina (120+50) ☎ 52072, 📠 51692, Lock 52155, €1.90, minimum €16.00, D, P (cans), Slip, BY, CH, Gas, Gaz, Kos, BH (45 ton), C (26 ton), ME, El, 🄴, 🛒; **Town** EC Thurs; El, CH, 🛒, R, Bar, Dr, ✉, Ⓑ, ⇌ (bus to Limerick), ✈ (Shannon).

Area 13

North Ireland

Lambay Island anti-clockwise to Liscannor Bay

1.	*Kilrush*	318	361	364	335	332	323	309	291	276	270	251	220	203	191	183	142	119	75	76	**1**
2.	Galway	348	366	338	309	307	297	284	266	253	245	227	192	178	166	163	104	94	49	**2**	
3.	Slyne Head	352	317	289	260	257	248	234	217	201	195	178	143	128	117	114	55	44	**3**		
4.	Westport	337	323	295	266	249	240	226	207	193	187	168	137	120	108	100	57	**4**			
5.	Eagle Island	297	262	234	205	198	193	175	162	147	136	123	88	72	62	59	**5**				
6.	Sligo	281	246	218	189	179	177	156	146	123	117	107	72	51	30	**6**					
7.	Killybegs	267	232	204	175	171	163	148	132	115	109	93	58	43	**7**						
8.	Burtonport	218	182	153	130	130	116	108	90	74	68	49	18	**8**							
9.	**Tory Island**	209	174	146	117	113	105	90	74	57	51	35	**9**								
10.	L Swilly (Fahan)	200	166	138	109	104	96	81	65	48	42	**10**									
11.	**Lough Foyle**	157	121	92	72	73	55	47	30	11	**11**										
12.	**Portrush**	150	115	87	58	60	48	35	19	**12**											
13.	Altacarry Head	135	102	74	45	45	31	21	**13**												
14.	**Carnlough**	118	78	50	25	26	11	**14**													
15.	**Larne**	108	73	45	16	16	**15**														
16.	**Carrickfergus**	101	66	39	6	**16**															
17.	**Bangor**	96	61	34	**17**																
18.	**Strangford Lough**	71	36	**18**																	
19.	**Carlingford Lough**	50	**19**																		
20.	***Dun Laoghaire***	**20**																			

DISTANCE TABLE

Approximate distances in nautical miles are by the most direct route, whilst avoiding dangers and allowing for Traffic Separation Schemes. Places in *italics* are in adjoining areas; places in **bold** are in 9.0.7, Distances across the Irish Sea.

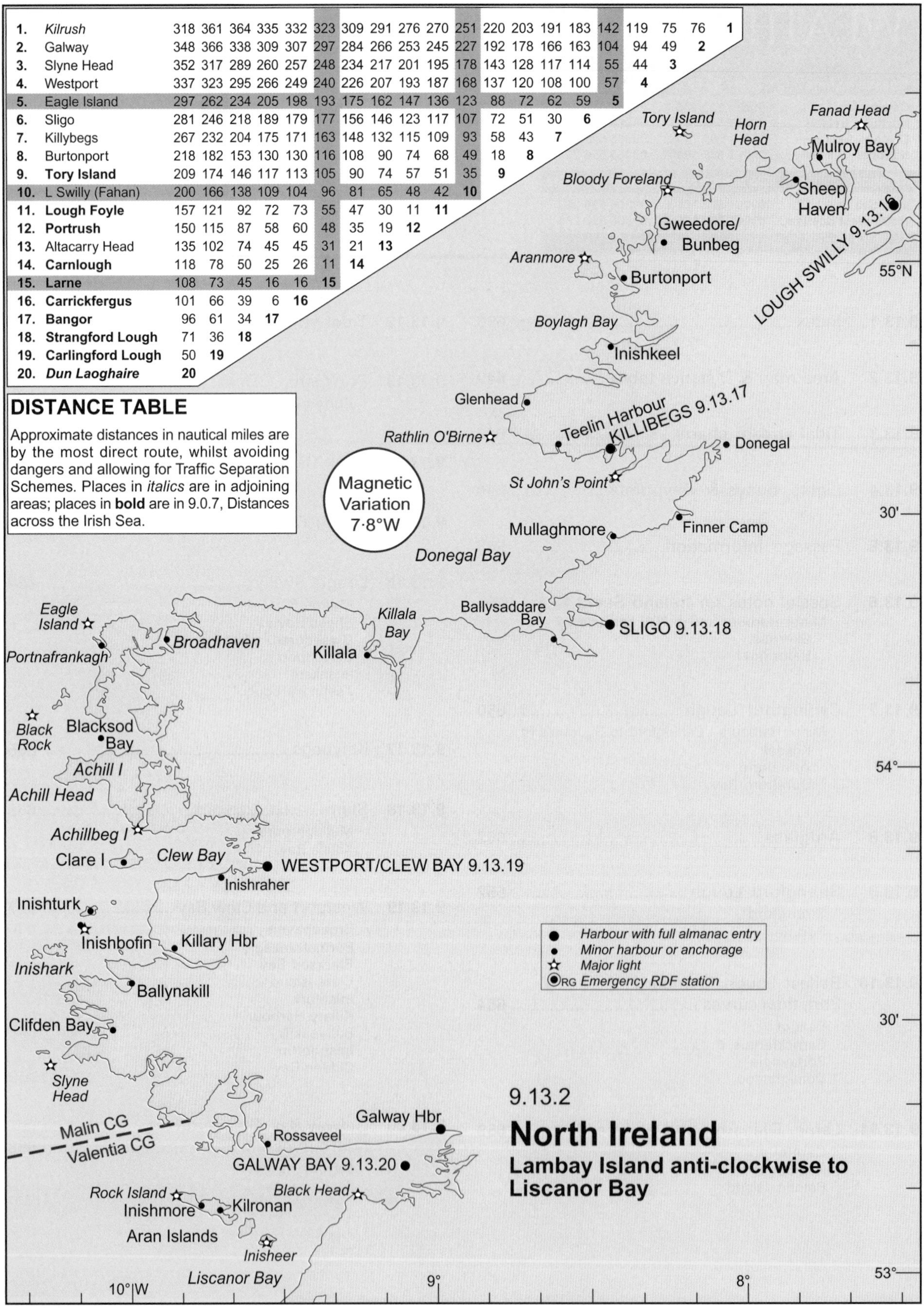
Magnetic Variation 7·8°W
Tory Island
Horn Head
Fanad Head
Mulroy Bay
Bloody Foreland
Sheep Haven
LOUGH SWILLY 9.13.16
Gweedore/ Bunbeg
Aranmore
Burtonport
55°N
Boylagh Bay
Inishkeel
Glenhead
Teelin Harbour
KILLIBEGS 9.13.17
Rathlin O'Birne
Donegal
St John's Point
Mullaghmore
Finner Camp
30'
Donegal Bay
Eagle Island
Killala Bay
Ballysaddare Bay
SLIGO 9.13.18
Portnafrankagh
Broadhaven
Killala
Black Rock
Blacksod Bay
Achill I
Achill Head
54°
Achillbeg I
Clare I
Clew Bay
WESTPORT/CLEW BAY 9.13.19
Inishraher
Inishturk
Inishbofin
Killary Hbr
Inishark
Ballynakill
Clifden Bay
30'
Slyne Head
Malin CG
Valentia CG
Galway Hbr
Rossaveel
GALWAY BAY 9.13.20
Rock Island
Black Head
Inishmore
Kilronan
Aran Islands
Inisheer
Liscanor Bay
10°W
9°
8°
53°

Harbour with full almanac entry
Minor harbour or anchorage
Major light
RG Emergency RDF station

9.13.2

North Ireland

Lambay Island anti-clockwise to Liscanor Bay

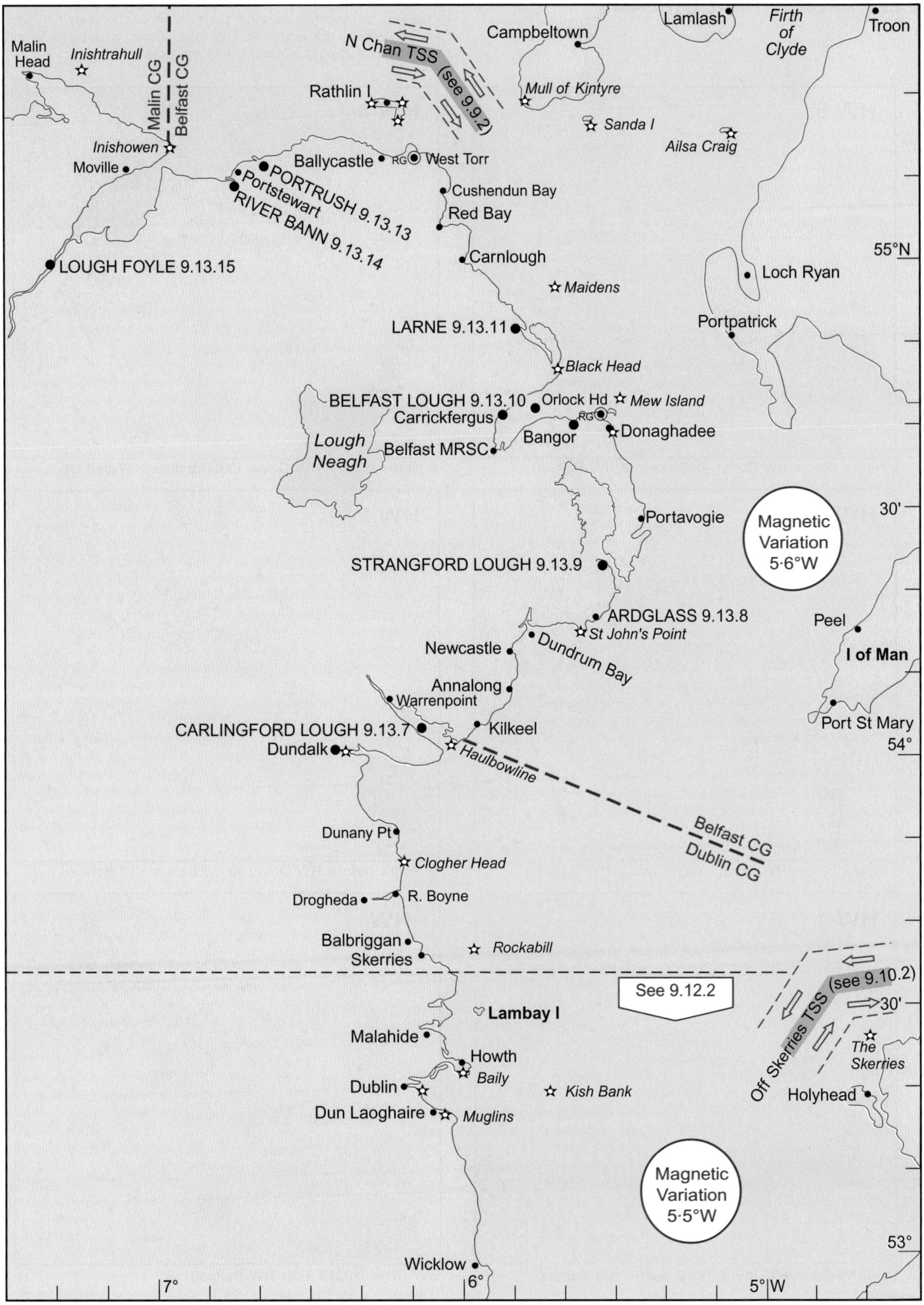
Malin Head
Inishtrahull
Malin CG
Belfast CG
Inishowen
Moville
LOUGH FOYLE 9.13.15
Portstewart
PORTRUSH 9.13.13
RIVER BANN 9.13.14
Ballycastle
RG
West Torr
Rathlin I
N Chan TSS
(see 9.9.2)
Campbeltown
Mull of Kintyre
Sanda I
Lamlash
Firth of Clyde
Troon
Ailsa Craig
Cushendun Bay
Red Bay
Carnlough
Maidens
55°N
Loch Ryan
Portpatrick
LARNE 9.13.11
Black Head
BELFAST LOUGH 9.13.10
Orlock Hd
Mew Island
Carrickfergus
RG
Donaghadee
Bangor
Lough Neagh
Belfast MRSC
Portavogie
Magnetic Variation 5·6°W
30'
STRANGFORD LOUGH 9.13.9
ARDGLASS 9.13.8
St John's Point
Peel
I of Man
Newcastle
Dundrum Bay
Annalong
Warrenpoint
Kilkeel
CARLINGFORD LOUGH 9.13.7
Dundalk
Haulbowline
Port St Mary
54°
Belfast CG
Dublin CG
Dunany Pt
Clogher Head
Drogheda
R. Boyne
Balbriggan
Skerries
Rockabill
See 9.12.2
(see 9.10.2)
Off Skerries TSS
30'
Lambay I
Malahide
Howth
Baily
The Skerries
Dublin
Kish Bank
Holyhead
Dun Laoghaire
Muglins
Magnetic Variation 5·5°W
53°
Wicklow
7°
6°
5°W

9.13.3 AREA 13 TIDAL STREAMS

The tidal arrows (with no rates shown) off the S and W coasts of Ireland are printed by kind permission of the Irish Cruising Club, to whom the Editor is indebted. They have been found accurate, but should be used with caution.

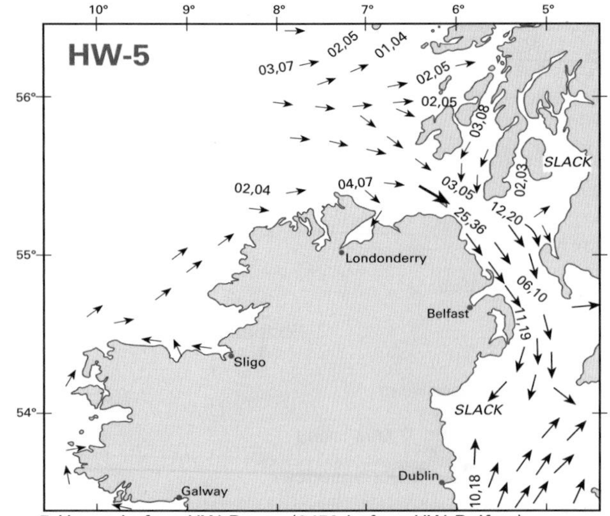
HW-5
10°
9°
8°
7°
6°
5°
56°
55°
54°
03,07
02,05
01,04
02,05
02,05
03,08
02,04
04,07
03,05
02,03
SLACK
25,36
12,20
06,10
11,19
SLACK
10,18
Londonderry
Belfast
Sligo
Dublin
Galway
5 Hours before HW Dover (0450 before HW Belfast)

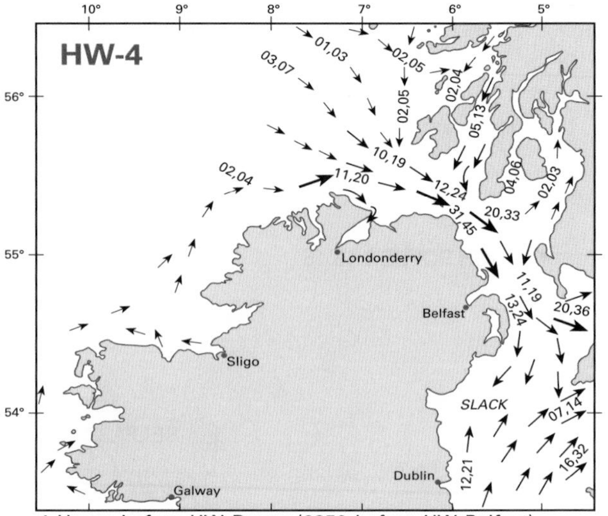
HW-4
10°
9°
8°
7°
6°
5°
56°
55°
54°
01,03
03,07
02,05
02,05
02,04
05,13
10,19
02,04
11,20
12,24
31,45
20,33
04,06
02,03
11,19
13,24
20,36
SLACK
07,14
16,32
12,21
Londonderry
Belfast
Sligo
Dublin
Galway
4 Hours before HW Dover (0350 before HW Belfast)

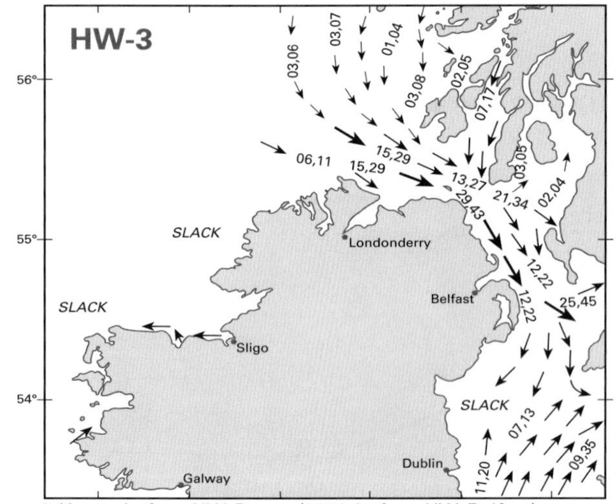
HW-3
56°
55°
54°
03,06
03,07
01,04
03,08
02,05
07,17
06,11
15,29
15,29
13,27
03,05
29,43
21,34
02,04
SLACK
12,22
12,22
25,45
SLACK
SLACK
07,13
09,35
11,20
Londonderry
Belfast
Sligo
Dublin
Galway
3 Hours before HW Dover (0250 before HW Belfast)

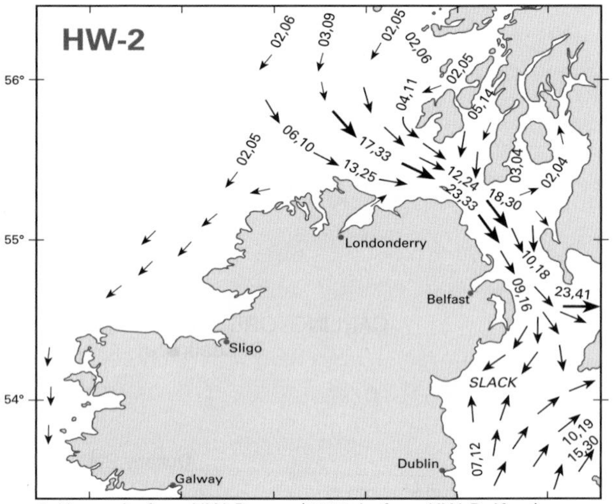
HW-2
56°
55°
54°
02,06
03,09
02,05
02,06
02,05
04,11
05,14
06,10
17,33
02,05
13,25
12,24
23,33
03,04
02,04
18,30
10,18
09,16
23,41
SLACK
07,12
10,19
15,30
Londonderry
Belfast
Sligo
Dublin
Galway
2 Hours before HW Dover (0150 before HW Belfast)

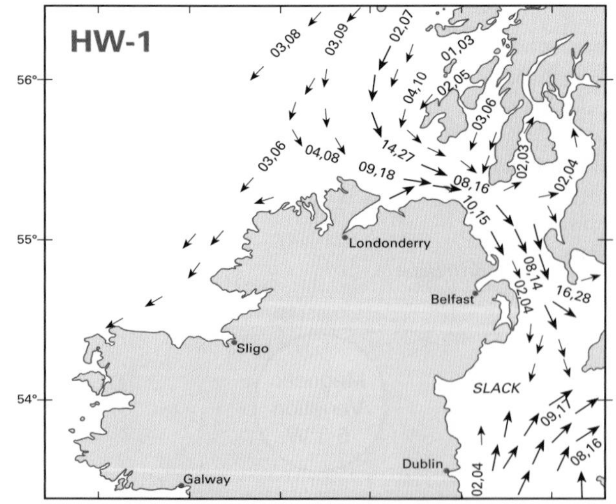
HW-1
56°
55°
54°
03,08
03,09
02,07
01,03
02,05
04,10
03,06
03,06
04,08
14,27
09,18
08,16
02,03
02,04
10,15
08,14
02,04
16,28
SLACK
09,17
08,16
02,04
Londonderry
Belfast
Sligo
Dublin
Galway
1 Hour before HW Dover (0050 before HW Belfast)

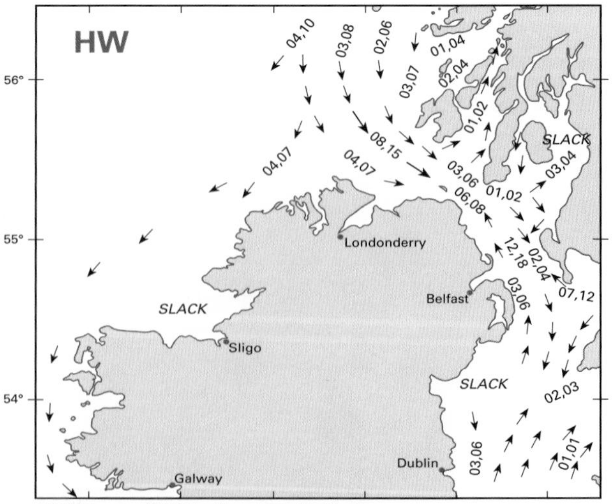
HW
56°
55°
54°
04,10
03,08
02,06
01,04
03,07
02,04
01,02
SLACK
08,15
04,07
04,07
03,06
03,04
01,02
06,08
12,18
02,04
03,06
07,12
SLACK
SLACK
02,03
03,06
01,01
Londonderry
Belfast
Sligo
Dublin
Galway
HW Dover (0010 after HW Belfast)

Rathlin Island 9.13.13
Mull of Kintyre 9.9.12
North Irish Sea 9.10.3
SW Scotland 9.9.3
South Ireland 9.12.3

The tidal arrows (with no rates shown) off the S and W coasts of Ireland are printed by kind permission of the Irish Cruising Club, to whom the Editor is indebted. They have been found accurate, but should be used with caution.

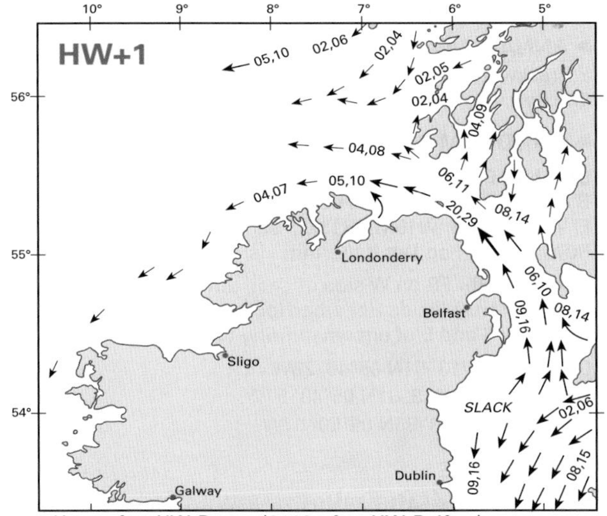
HW+1
10°
9°
8°
7°
6°
5°
56°
55°
54°
05,10
02,06
02,04
02,05
02,04
04,09
04,08
06,11
05,10
04,07
20,29
08,14
06,10
09,16
08,14
SLACK
02,06
09,16
08,15
Londonderry
Belfast
Sligo
Dublin
Galway

1 Hour after HW Dover (0110 after HW Belfast)

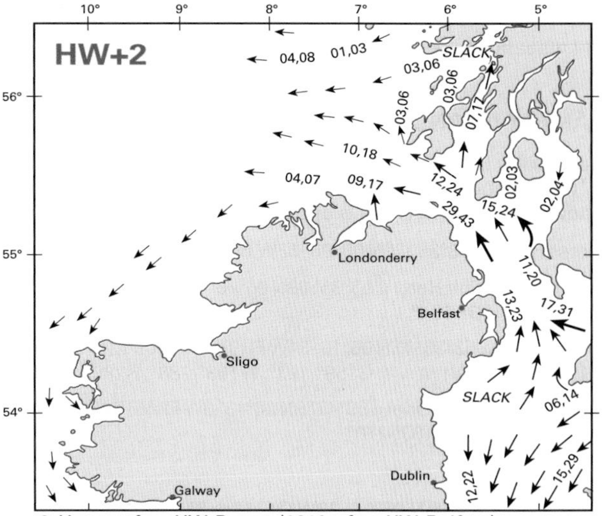
HW+2
10°
9°
8°
7°
6°
5°
56°
55°
54°
04,08
01,03
SLACK
03,06
03,06
03,06
07,12
10,18
04,07
09,17
12,24
15,24
02,03
02,04
29,43
11,20
13,23
17,31
SLACK
06,14
12,22
15,29
Londonderry
Belfast
Sligo
Dublin
Galway

2 Hours after HW Dover (0210 after HW Belfast)

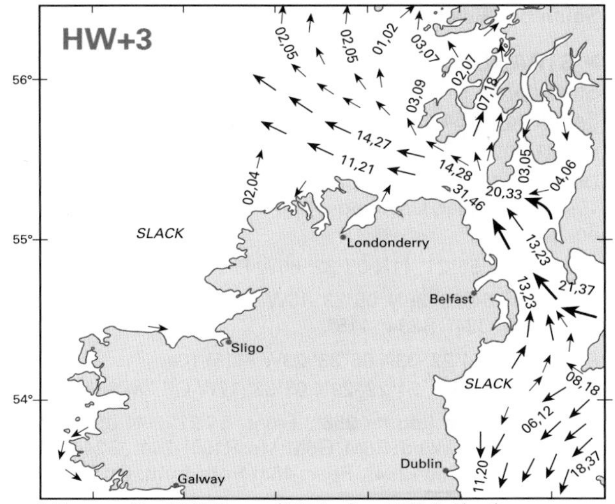
HW+3
56°
55°
54°
02,05
02,05
01,02
03,07
02,07
03,09
07,18
14,27
11,21
14,28
03,05
04,06
02,04
31,46
20,33
SLACK
13,23
21,37
13,23
SLACK
08,18
06,12
11,20
18,37
Londonderry
Belfast
Sligo
Dublin
Galway

3 Hours after HW Dover (0310 after HW Belfast)

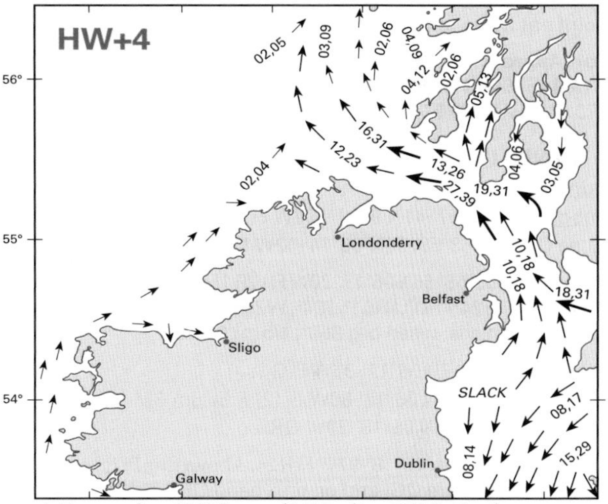
HW+4
56°
55°
54°
02,05
03,09
02,06
04,09
02,06
04,12
05,13
16,31
12,23
13,26
02,04
27,39
19,31
04,06
03,05
10,18
10,18
18,31
SLACK
08,17
08,14
15,29
Londonderry
Belfast
Sligo
Dublin
Galway

4 Hours after HW Dover (0410 after HW Belfast)

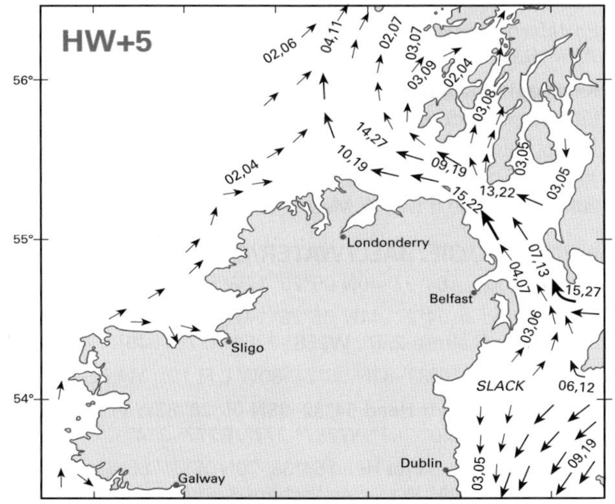
HW+5
56°
55°
54°
02,06
04,11
02,07
03,07
03,09
02,04
03,08
14,27
10,19
09,19
03,05
02,04
13,22
03,05
15,22
07,13
04,07
15,27
03,06
SLACK
06,12
03,05
09,19
Londonderry
Belfast
Sligo
Dublin
Galway

5 Hours after HW Dover (0510 after HW Belfast)

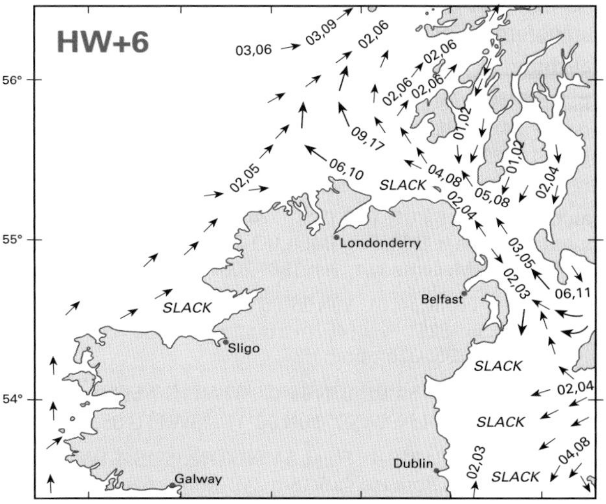
HW+6
56°
55°
54°
03,06
03,09
02,06
02,06
02,06
02,06
01,02
09,17
06,10
01,02
02,05
SLACK
04,08
05,08
02,04
02,04
03,05
02,03
06,11
SLACK
SLACK
02,04
SLACK
02,03
SLACK
04,08
Londonderry
Belfast
Sligo
Dublin
Galway

6 Hours after HW Dover (0610 after HW Belfast)

PLOT WAYPOINTS ON YOUR CHART BEFORE USING THEM

9.13.4 LIGHTS, BUOYS AND WAYPOINTS

Blue print = light with a nominal range of 15M or more. CAPITALS = place or feature. *CAPITAL ITALICS* = light-vessel, light float or Lanby. *Italics* = Fog signal. ***Bold italics*** = Racon. Useful waypoints are underlined. Abbreviations are in Chapter 1.

LAMBAY ISLANDTO DONAGHADEE

Rockabill ☆ 53°35'·82N 06°00'·25W Fl WR 12s 45m **W22M, R18M;** W twr, B band; vis: W178°-329°, R329°-178°; *Horn (4) 60s.* Also shown by day when horn is operating.

Cross Rock 53°35'·30N 06°06'·55W Fl R 10s.

Skerries Bay Pier Head ☆ 53°35'·09N 06°06'·49W Oc R 6s 7m 7M; W col; vis: 103°-154°.

Balbriggan ☆ 53°36'·76N 06°10'·84W Fl (3) WRG 20s 12m W13M, R10M, G10M; W twr; vis: G159°-193°, W193°-288°, R288°-305°.

Clogher Head Port Oriel ☆ 53°47'·9N 06°13'·3W Fl WR 4s 10m 6M; vis: W170°-180°, R180°-270°.

▶ DROGHEDA

Aleria 53°43'·35N 06°14'·33W QG 18m 3M.

Lyons 53°43'·24N 06°14'·26W Fl (3) R 5s 10m 3M. Above this Point ent lts on stbd hand are G, and on port hand R.

Port Approach Dir lt 53°43'·30N 06°14'·73W WRG 10m **W19M, R15M,** G15M; vis: FG268°-269°, Al WG269°-269·5°, FW269·5°-270·5°, Al WR270·5°-271°, FR271°-272°; H24.

▶ DUNDALK

Dunany 53°53'·56N 06°09'·47W Fl R 3s.
Imogene 53°57'·41N 06°07'·02W Fl (2) R 10s.
Giles Quay ☆ 53°59'·05N 06°14'·42W Fl G 3s.

Pile Light ☆ 53°58'·56N 06°17'·70W Fl WR 15s 10m **W21M, R18M;** W Ho; vis: W124°-151°, R151°-284°, W284°-313°, R313°-124°. Fog Det lt VQ 7m, vis: when brg 358°; *Horn (3) 60s.*

No. 1 53°58'·17N 06°17'·36W Fl G 3s.
No. 2 53°58'·33N 06°17'·80W Fl (2) R 5s 5m 3M.
No. 6 53°58'·04N 06°18'·70W QR.

No. 8 53°59'·31N 06°18'·97W Fl R 2s. Above this Pt lts on stbd hand when ent are QG, and on port hand QR.

▶ CARLINGFORD LOUGH/NEWRY RIVER

Carlingford 53°58'·76N 06°01'·06W L Fl 10s.

Hellyhunter 54°00'·35N 06°02'·10W Q (6) + L Fl 15s; ***Racon*.**

No. 1 54°00'·73N 06°03'·41W Fl (3) G 6s.
No. 4 54°01'·08N 06°04'·07W Fl R 4s.
No. 6 54°01'·24N 06°04'·39W Fl R 2s.
No. 5 54°01'·38N 06°04'·50W Fl R 2s.

Haulbowline ☆ 54°01'·19N 06°04'·74W Fl (3) 10s 32m **17M;** Gy twr; reserve lt 15M; Fog Det lt VQ 26m; vis: 330°. Turning lt ☆ FR 21m 9M; same twr; vis: 196°-208°; *Horn 30s.*

Ldg lts 310·4° Front, 54°01'·80N 06°05'·43W Oc 3s 7m 11M; R △ on twr; vis: 295°-325°. Rear, 457m from front, Oc 3s 12m 11M; R ▽ on twr; vis: 295°-325°; both H24.

Greenore Pier Hd ☆ 54°02'·07N 06°07'·97W Fl R 7·5s 10m 5M.
Carlingford Quay Hd ☆ 54°02'·60N 06°11'·09W Fl G 3s 5m 3M.

Newry River Ldg lts 310·4°. Front, 54°06'·37N 06°16'·51W. Rear, 274m from front. Both Iso 4s 5/15m 2M; stone cols.

Warren Pt Bkwtr Hd ☆ 54°05'·79N 06°15'·26W Fl G 3s 6m 3M.

▶ KILKEEL

Pier Head ☆ 54°03'·46N 05°59'·30W Fl WR 2s 8m 8M; vis: R296°-313°, W313°-017°.

Meeney's Pier Head ☆ 54°03'·48N 05°59'·31W Fl G 3s 6m 2M.

▶ ANNALONG

E Breakwater Head ☆ 54°06'·51N 05°53'·73W Oc WRG 5s 8m 9M; twr; vis: G204°-249°, W249°-309°, R309°-024°.

▶ DUNDRUM BAY

St John's Point ☆ 54°13'·61N 05°39'·30W Q (2) 7·5s 37m **25M;** B twr, Y bands; H24 when horn is operating. **Auxiliary Light** ☆ Fl WR 3s 14m **W15M,** R11M; same twr, vis: W064°-078°, R078°-shore; Fog Det lt VQ 14m vis: 270°; *Horn (2) 60s.*

Dundrum Hbr FR on W side of chan outside Hbr and 3 FR on W side of chan inside Hbr when local vessels expected. FR on flagstaffs S and E of ent when firing takes place.

DZ East 54°13'·51N 05°46'·23W.
DZ Middle 54°13'·01N 05°48'·57W.
DZ West 54°13'·35N 05°50'·07W.

▶ ARDGLASS

Inner Pier Head ☆ 54°15'·79N 05°36'·33W Iso WRG 4s 10m W8M, R7M, G5M; twr; vis: G shore-308°, W308°-314°, R314°-shore.

South Pier Head ☆ 54°15'·67N 05°36'·16W Fl R 3s 10m 5M.

▶ STRANGFORD LOUGH

Strangford 54°18'·61N 05°28'·67W L Fl 10s.
Bar Pladdy 54°19'·34N 05°30'·51W Q (6) + L Fl 15s.
Angus Rock ☆ 54°19'·84N 05°31'·56W Fl R 5s 15m 6M.

Dogtail Pt Ldg lts 341° Front, 54°20'·79N 05°31'·83W Oc (4) G 10s 2m 5M. Rear, Gowlands Rk, 0·8M from front, Oc (4) G 10s 6m 5M.

Salt Rock ☆ 56°21'·41N 05°32'·66W Fl R 3s 8m 3M.

Swan I ☆ 54°22'·38N 05°33'·16W Fl (2) WR 6s 5m; W col; vis: W115°-334°, R334°-115°.

S Pladdy ☆ 54°22'·33N 05°33'·23W Fl (3) 10s.
Watch Ho Pt Rk ☆ 54°22'·29N 05°33'·17W QR 3m 3M.

Strangford East Ldg lts 256°. Front, 54°22'·29N 05°33'·27W Oc WRG 5s 6m W9M, R6M, G6M: vis: R190°-244°, G244°-252°, W252°-260°, R260°-294°. Rear, 46m from front, Oc R 5s 10m 6M; vis: 250°-264°.

Church Point Bn 54°22'·59N 05°33'·40W Fl (4) R 10s.

Portaferry Pier Head ☆ 54°22'·82N 05°33'·03W Oc WR 10s 9m W9M, R6M; Or mast; vis: W335°-005°, R005°-017°, W017°-128°.

Killyleagh Town Rock 54°23'·61N 05°38'·54W Q 4M.
Limestone Rock ☆ 54°25'·14N 05°36'·11W QR 3m 3M.
Butter Pladdy 54°22'·45N 05°25'·74W Q (3) 10s.

SOUTH ROCK 54°24'·49N 05°22'·02W Fl (3) R 30s 12m **20M;** R hull and lt twr, W Mast, *Horn (3) 45s,* ***Racon (T) 13M.***

▶ PORTAVOGIE/BALLYWATER/DONAGHADEE

Plough Rock 54°27'·40N 05°25'·12W Fl R 3s.

S Pier Head ☆ 54°27'·44N 05°26'·14W, Iso WRG 5s 9m 9M; □ twr; vis: G shore-258°, W258°-275°, R275°-348°.

Skulmartin 54°31'·82N 05°24'·80W L Fl 10s; *Whis.*

Ballywalter, Bkwtr Head 54°32'·68N 05°28'·83W Fl WRG 1·5s 5m 9M; vis: G240°-267°, W267°-277°, R277°-314°.

Donaghadee ☆, S Pier Head 54°38'·70N 05°31'·86W Iso WR 4s 17m **W18M,** R14M; W twr; vis: W shore-326°, R326°-shore; *Siren 12s.*

DONAGHADEE TO RATHLIN ISLAND

Governor Rocks 54°39'·36N 05°31'·99W Fl R 3s.
Deputy Reefs 54°39'·51N 05°31'·94W Fl G 2s.
Foreland Spit 54°39'·63N 05°32'·31W Fl R 6s.

▶ BELFAST LOUGH

Mew I ☆ NE end 54°41'·91N 05°30'·79W Fl (4) 30s 37m; B twr, W band; ***Racon (O) 14M***.

S Briggs 54°41'·19N 05°35'·72W Fl (2) R 10s.

▶ BANGOR

N Pier Head ☆ 54°40'·03N 05°40'·34W Iso R 12s 9m14M.

Dir lt 105°. 54°39'·98N 05°40'·15W Oc WRG 10s 1M; vis: G093°-104·8°, W104·8°-105·2°, R105·2°-117°.

Marina ent ☆ 54°39'·97N 05°40'·29W Fl G 3s 5m 1M.

Belfast Fairway 54°41'·71N 05°46'·24W L Fl 10s; *Horn (1) 16s*; ***Racon (G) range unknown***.

Cloghan Jetty 54°44'·10N 05°41'·58W QG.

Kilroot power station intake ☆ 54°43'·20N 05°45'·88W Oc G 4s; 2 QR on chy 500m N.

▶ CARRICKFERGUS

E Pier Head ☆ 54°42'·63N 05°48'·37W Fl G 7·5s 5m 4M; G col.
Marina E Bkwtr Head ☆ 54°42'·58N 05°48'·69W QG 8m 3M.
W Breakwater ☆ 54°42'·58N 05°48'·78W QR 7m 3M; R □ pillar.

Marina Ent Appr ☆ 54°42'·58N 05°48'·78W Dir Oc WRG 3s 5m 3M; vis: G308°-317·5°, W317·5°-322·5°, R322·5°-332°.

Black Hd ☆ 54°45'·99N 05°41'·33W Fl 3s 45m **27M**; W 8-sided twr.
N Hunter Rock 54°53'·04N 05°45'·13W Q.
S Hunter Rock 54°52'·69N 05°45'·22W VQ (6) + L Fl 10s; *Whis*.

▶ LARNE

Barr Pt ☆ 54°51'·50N 05°46'·81W; *Horn 30s*. Fog Det lt VQ.
Larne No. 1 54°51'·68N 05°47'·67W QG.
Larne No. 3 54°51'·27N 05°47'·64W Fl (2) G 6s.
Larne No. 5 54°50'·48N 05°47'·74W QG.
Larne No. 7 54°50'·46N 05°47'·46W QG.
Chaine Twr ☆ 54°51'·27N 05°47'·90W Iso WR 5s 23m 16M; Gy twr; vis: W230°-240°, R240°-shore.
Larne No. 2 54°51'·07N 05°47'·55W Fl R 3s.

Ent Ldg lts 184°, No. 11 Front, 54°49'·60N 05°47'·81W Oc 4s 6m 12M; W 2 with R stripe on R pile structure; vis: 179°-189°. No. 12 Rear, 610m from front, Oc 4s 14m 12M; W 2 with R stripe on R □ twr; synch with front, vis: 5° either side of Ldg line.

East Maiden ☆ 54°55'·74N 05°43'·65W Fl (3) 20s 29m 24M; W twr, B band; ***Racon (M) 11-21M***. Auxiliary lt Fl R 5s 15m 8M; same twr; vis:142°-182° over Russel and Highland Rks.

▶ CARNLOUGH/RED BAY

Carnlough Hbr N Pier ☆ 54°59'·59N 05°59'·29W Fl G 3s 4m 5M.
Red Bay Pier ☆ 55°03'·93N 06°03'·21W Fl 3s 10m 5M.

RATHLIN ISLAND TO INISHTRAHULL

▶ RATHLIN ISLAND

Rue Point ☆ 55°15'·53N 06°11'·47W Fl (2) 5s 16m 14M; W 8-sided twr, B bands.

Drake Wreck 55°17'·00N 06°12'·48W Q (6) + L Fl 15s.

Altacarry Head Rathlin East ☆ 55°18'·06N 06°10'·30W Fl (4) 20s 74m **26M**; W twr, B band; vis: 110°-006° and 036°-058°; ***Racon (G) 15-27M***.

Rathlin W 0·5M NE of Bull Pt ☆ 55°18'·05N 06°16'·82W Fl R 5s 62m **22M**; W twr, lantern at base; vis: 015°-225°; H24.

Manor House ☆ 55°17'·52N 06°11'·73W Oc WRG 4s 5M; vis: G020°-023°, W023°-026°, R026°-029°.

Rathlin Hbr Bkwtr ☆ 55°17'·5N 06°11'·8W Fl (3) G 6s 6m 6M.

Rathlin Hbr S Breakwater ☆ 55°17'·5N 06°11'·72W Fl (2) R 4s 5m 1M: vis: 130°-062°

▶ PORTRUSH

N Pier Hd ☆ 55°12'·34N 06°39'·58W Fl R 3s 6m 3M; vis: 220°-160°.
Portstewart Point ☆ 55°11'·33N 06°43'·26W Oc R 10s 21m 5M; R □ hut; vis: 040°-220°.

▶ RIVER BANN/COLERAINE

Ldg lts 165°. Front, 55°09'·96N 06°46'·23W Oc 5s 6m 2M; W twr. Rear, 245m from front, Oc 5s 14m 2M; W □ twr. River Bann marked by Fl G on stbd hand, and Fl R on port.

W Mole ☆ 56°10'·25N 06°46'·45W Fl G 5s 4m 2M; Gy mast; vis: 170°-000°.

Foyle 55°15'·32N 06°52'·60W L Fl 10s; *Whis*.
Tuns 55°14'·00N 06°53'·46W Fl R 3s.

Inishowen ☆ 55°13'·56N 06°55'·75W Fl (2) WRG 10s 28m **W18M**, R14M, G14M; W twr, 2 B bands; vis: G197°-211°, W211°-249°, R249°-000°; *Horn (2) 30s*. Fog Det lt VQ 16m vis: 270°.

▶ LOUGH FOYLE

Greencastle S Bkwtr Dir lt 042·5°. Front, 55°12'·17N 06°59'·13W Fl (2) WRG 3s 4m W11M, R9M, G9M; vis G307°-040° W040°-045° R045°-055°

Warren Point lt Bn twr ☆ 55°12'·58N 06°57'·14W Fl 1·5s 11m 4M; twr, G abutment; vis: 232°-061°.

Magilligan Point ☆ 55°11'·73N 06°58'·06W QR 7m 4M; R structure. FR, 700m SE, when firing taking place.

McKinney's 55°10'·9N 07°00'·5W Fl R 5s

Moville 55°10'·98N 07°02'·13W Fl WR 2·5s 11m 4M; W house on G piles vis: W240°-064°, R064°-240°.

Above this point the channel to R.Foyle is marked by lts Fl G, when entering, on stbd hand, and Fl R on port hand. G lts are shown from W structures on G or B piles; R lts from W structures on R piles.

Kilderry 55°04'·10N 07°14'·03W Fl G 2s 4m 3M; G △.
Muff 55°03'·62N 07°14'·28W Fl G 2s 4m 3M; G △.
Coneyburrow 55°03'·32N 07°14'·49W QG 4m 3M.
Faughan 55°03'·12N 07°14'·50W Fl R 4s 5m 3M.
Culmore Pt ☆ 55°02'·77N 07°15'·22W Q 6m 3M; G ○ twr.
Culmore Bay 55°02'·71N 07°15'·70W QG.

Ballynagard 55°02'·27N 07°16'·43W Fl 3s 6m 3M; W lantern on G □ house.

Otterbank 55°01'·94N 07°16'·71W Fl R 4s 6m 3M; W structure on R □ twr.

Brookhall ☆ 55°01'·69N 07°17'·11W QG 6m 3M.
Mountjoy ☆ 55°01'·25N 07°17'·54W QR 5m 3M.

Inishtrahull ☆ 55°25'·86N 07°14'·62W Fl (3) 15s 59m **19M**; W twr; obscd 256°-261° within 3M; ***Racon (T) 24M 060°-310°***.

INISHTRAHULL TO BLOODY FORELAND

▶ LOUGH SWILLY/BUNCRANA/RATHMULLAN

Fanad Head ☆ 55°16'·57N 07°37'·91W Fl (5) WR 20s 39m **W18M**, R14M; W twr; vis R100°-110°, W110°-313°, R313°-345°, W345°-100°.

Swilly More 55°15'·12N 07°35'·79W Fl G 3s.

PLOT WAYPOINTS ON YOUR CHART BEFORE USING THEM

Dunree ☆ 55°11'·88N 07°33'·25W Fl (2) WR 5s 46m W12M, R9M; vis: R320°-328°, W328°-183°, R183°-196°.

Colpagh 55°10'·42N 07°31'·55W Fl R 6s.

White Strand Rocks 55°09'·06N 07°29'·95W Fl R 10s.

Buncrana Pier near Head ☆ 55°07'·60N 07°27'·86W Iso WR 4s 8m W14M, R11M; vis: R shore-052° over Inch spit, W052°-139°, R139°-shore over White Strand Rock.

Rathmullan Pier Head ☆ 55°05'·70N 07°31'·66W Fl G 3s 5M; vis: 206°-345°.

▶ MULROY BAY

Limeburner 55°18'·54N 07°48'·40W Q Fl; *Whis.*

Ravedy Island ☆ 55°15'·14N 07°46'·90W Fl 3s 9m 3M; twr; vis: 177°-357°.

Dundooan Rocks ☆ 55°13'·13N 07°47'·98W QG 4m 1M; G twr.

Crannoge Point 55°12'·28N 07°48'·43W Fl G 5s 5m 2M; G twr.

▶ SHEEPHAVEN

Downies Bay Pier Head ☆ 55°11'·35N 07°50'·51W Fl R 3s 5m 2M; vis: 283° through N till obsc by Downies Pt.

Portnablahy Ldg lts 125·3°. Front 55°10'·79N 07°55'·65W Oc 6s 7m 2M; B col, W bands. Rear, 81m from front, Oc 6s 12m 2M; B col, W bands.

Tory Island ☆ 55°16'·36N 08°14'·97W Fl (4) 30s 40m **27M**; B twr, W band; vis: 302°-277°; ***Racon (M) 12-23M***; H24.

West town Ldg lts 001° ☆ 55°15'·79N 08°13'·50W Iso 2s 9m 7M △ on Y structure R stripe Rear Iso 2s 11m 7M ▽ ditto (synchronised)

Inishbofin Pier ☆ 55°10'·08N 08°10·57W Fl 8s 3m 3M; part obsc.

Ballyness Hbr. Ldg lts 119·5°. Front, 55°09'·06N 08°06'·98W Iso 4s 25m 1M. Rear, 61m from front, Iso 4s 26m 1M.

Bloody Foreland ☆ 55°09'·51N 08°17'·03W Fl WG 7·5s 14m W6M, G4M; vis: W062°-232°, G232°-062°.

BLOODY FORELAND TO RATHLIN O'BIRNE

Glassagh. Ldg lts 137·4°. Front, 55°06'·83N 08°18'·97W Oc 8s 12m 3M. Rear, 46m from front, Oc 8s 17m 3M; synch.

Inishsirrer, NW end ☆ 55°07'·40N 08°20'·93W Fl 3·7s 20m 4M; W □ twr vis: 083°-263°.

▶ BUNBEG/MULLAGHDOO/OWEY SOUND

Gola I Ldg lts 171·2°. Front, 55°05'·11N 08°21'·07W Oc 3s 9m 2M; W Bn, B band. Rear, 86m from front, Oc 3s 13m 2M; B Bn, W band; synch with front.

Middle Rock 55°04'·50N 08°21'·02W Fl R 3s.

Gola Spit 55°04'·91N 08°20'·39W Fl (2) R 6s.

Bo I East Point 55°04'·78N 08°20'·15W Fl G 3s 3m; G Bn.

Inishinny No. 1 ☆ 55°04'·47N 08°19'·84W QG 3m 1M; G □ col.

Carrickbullog No. 2 ☆ 55°04'·38N 08°19'·60W QR.

Inishcoole No. 4 ☆ 55°03'·91N 08°18'·91W QR 4m 2M; R □ col.

Yellow Rks No. 6 ☆ 55°03'·66N 08°18'·95W QR 3m 1M; □ col with steps; Neon.

Cruit I. Owey Sound Ldg lts 068·3°. Front, 55°03'·06N 08°25'·85W Oc 10s. Rear, 107m from front, Oc 10s.

Rinnalea Point ☆ 55°02'·59N 08°23'·72W Fl 7·5s 19m 9M; □ twr; vis: 132°-167°.

Aranmore, Rinrawros Pt ☆ 55°00'·90N 08°33'·66W Fl (2) 20s 71m **29M**; W twr; obsc by land about 234°-007° and about 013°. Auxiliary lt Fl R 3s 61m 13M, same twr; vis: 203°-234°.

▶ NORTH SOUND OF ARAN/RUTLAND NORTH CHANNEL

Ldg lts 186°. Front, 54°58'·94N 08°29'·27W Oc 8s 8m 3M; B Bn, W band. Rear, 395m from front, Oc 8s 17m 3M; B Bn.

Ballagh Rocks ☆ 54°59'·96N 08°28'·86W Fl 2·5s 13m 5M.

Black Rocks ☆ 54°59'·43N 08°29'·63W Fl R 3s 3m 1M; R col.

Inishcoo Ldg lts 119·3°. Front, 54°59'·12N 08°27'·74W Iso 6s 6m 1M; W Bn, B band. Rear, 248m from front, Iso 6s 11m 1M.

Carrickatine No. 2 Bn ☆ 54°59'·26N 08°28'·06W QR 6m 1M.

Rutland I Ldg lts 137·6°. Front, 54°58'·97N 08°27'·68W Oc 6s 8m 1M; W Bn, B band. Rear, 330m from front, Oc 6s 14m 1M.

▶ BURTONPORT

Ldg lts 068·1°. Front 54°58'·95N 08°26'·40W FG 17m 1M; Gy Bn, W band. Rear, 355m from front, FG 23m 1M; Gy Bn, Y band.

▶ SOUTH SOUND OF ARAN/RUTLAND SOUTH CHANNEL

Illancrone I ☆ 54°56'·27N 08°28'·57W Fl 5s 7m 6M; W □ twr.

Wyon Point ☆ 54°56'·51N 08°27'·54W Fl (2) WRG 10s 8m W6M, R3M; W □ twr; vis: G shore-021°, W021°-042°, R042°-121°, W121°-150°, R 150°-shore.

Turk Rocks ☆ 54°57'·30N 08°28'·18W Fl G 5s 6m 2M; G □ twr.

Aileen Reef ☆ 54°58'·18N 08°28'·82W QR 6m 1M. R □ Bn.

Leac na bhFear ☆ 54°58'·19N 08°29'·22W Q (2) 5s 4m 2M.

Carrickbealatroha, Upper ☆ 54°58'·64N 08°28'·63W Fl 5s 3m 2M; W □ brickwork twr.

Corren's Rock ☆ 54°58'·11N 08°26'·68W Fl R 3s 4m 2M; R □ twr.

Teige's Rock ☆ 54°58'·60N 08°26'·81W Fl 3s 4m 2M.

Dawros Hd ☆ 54°49'·62N 08°33'·69W L Fl 10s 39m 4M; W □ col.

Dawros Bay ☆ 54°49'·3N 08°32'W Fl (2) 10s 5m 3M.

Rathlin O'Birne, W side ☆ 54°39'·80N 08°49'·94W Fl WR 15s 35m **W18M**, R14M; W twr; vis: R195°-307°, W307°-195°; ***Racon (O) 13M, vis 284°-203°.***

RATHLIN O'BIRNE TO EAGLE ISLAND

▶ DONEGAL BAY, TEELIN/KILLYBEGS

Teelin Hbr ☆ 54°37'·33N 08°37'·76W Fl R 10s; R structure.

St John's Pt ☆ 54°34'·16N 08°27'·64W Fl 6s 30m 14M; W twr.

Bullockmore 54°33'·98N 08°30'·14W Qk Fl (9) 15s.

Rotten I ☆ 54°36'·97N 08°26'·41W Fl WR 4s 20m **W15M**, R11M; W twr; vis: W255°-008°, R008°-039°, W039°-208°.

New Landing Dir lt 338°. 54°38'·14N 08°26'·38W Oc WRG 6s 17m; vis: G328°°-334°, Al WG334°-336°, W336°-340°, Al WR340°-342°, R342°-348°.

Killybegs Outer 54°37'·92N 08°29'·15W VQ (6) + L Fl 10s.

Killybegs Inner 54°38'·02N 08°26'·09W VQ.

Black Rock Pier ☆ 54°38'·03N 08°26'·59W 2 FR (vert) 7m.

Finner Camp ☆ 54°29'·70N 08°13'·90W Aero Q WRG 67m.

▶ SLIGO

Wheat Rock 54°18'·84N 08°39'·10W Q (6) + LFl 15s.

Black Rock ☆ 54°18'·45N 08°37'·06W Fl 5s 24m 13M; W twr, B band. Auxiliary lt Fl R 3s 12m 5M; same twr; vis: 107°-130° over Wheat and Seal rks.

Lower Rosses, (N of Cullaun Bwee) ☆ 54°19'·72N 08°34'·41W Fl (2) WRG 10s 8m 13-10M; W hut on piles; vis: G over Bungar bank-066°, W066°-070°, R070° over Drumcliff bar; shown H24.

Bungar Bank 54°19'·06N 08°36'·66W Fl (2) G 5s.

Ldg lts 125°. Front, Metal Man 54°18'·24N 08°34'·56W Fl (3) 6s 13m 7M. Rear, Oyster I, 365m from front, fL (3) 6s 13m 7M (synchronised); H24.

▶ KILLALA

Inishcrone Pier Root ☆ 54°13'·21N 09°05'·79W Fl WRG 1·5s 8m 2M; vis: W098°-116°, G116°-136°, R136°-187°.

Ldg lts 230°. Rinnaun Point, Front No. 1, 54°13'·53N 09°12'·27W Oc 10s 7m 5M; □ twr. Rear, 150m from front, No. 2 Oc 10s 12m 5M; □ twr.

Dir lt 215°, Inch I, 54°13'·29N 09°12'·30W Fl WRG 2s 6m 3M; □ twr; vis: G205°-213°, W213°-217°, R217°-225°.

Ldg lts 196°. Kilroe, Front, 54°12'·63N 09°12'·33W Oc 4s 5m 2M; □ twr. Rear,120m from front, Oc 4s 10m 2M; □ twr.

Ldg lts 236°. Pier, Front, 54°13'·02N 09°12'·84W Iso 2s 5m 2M; W ◊ on twr. Rear, 200m from front, Iso 2s 7m 2M; W ◊ on pole.

Killala Bay. Bone Rock, NE end 54°15'·80N 09°11'·24W Q 7m.

▶ BROAD HAVEN BAY

Gubacashel Point ☆ 54°16'·06N 09°53'·33W Iso WR 4s 27m W17M, R12M; R110°-133°, W133°-355° R355°-021° W twr.

Ballyglass ☆ 54°15'·27N 09°53'·41W Fl G 3s.

EAGLE ISLAND TO SLYNE HEAD

Eagle I, W end ☆ 54°17'·02N 10°05'·56W Fl (3) 15s 67m **19M**; W twr.

Black Rock ☆ 54°04'·03N 10°19'·25W Fl WR 12s 86m **W20M, R16M**; W twr; vis: W276°-212°, R212°-276°.

▶ BLACKSOD BAY

Blacksod 54°05'·89N 10°03'·01W Q (3) 10s.

Blacksod Pier Root ☆ 54°05'·91N 10°03'·63W Fl (2) WR 7·5s 13m W12M, R9M; W twr on dwelling; vis: R189°-210°, W210°-018°.

Achill I Ridge Point ☆ 54°01'·78N 09°58'·50W Fl 5s 21m 5M.

▶ ACHILL SOUND

Achill Sound ☆ 53°56'·05N 09°55'·30W QR; R Bn.

Ldg lts 330° 53°52'·50N 09°56'·91W Whitestone Point, Front and rear both Oc 4s 5/6m; W ◊, B stripe.

Saulia Pier ☆ 53°57'·03N 09°55'·56W Fl G 3s 12m.

Achillbeg E lt Bn 53°52'·11N 09°56'·60W Fl R 2s 5m; R □ twr.

Carrigin-a-tShrutha ☆ 53°52'·28N 09°56'·78W Q (2) R 5s; R Bn.

Achill I Ldg lts 310° Purteen 53°57'·83N 10°05'·93W (PA) Oc 8s 5m. Rear, 46m from front Oc 8s 6m.

▶ CLEW BAY/WESTPORT

Achillbeg I S Point ☆ 53°51'·51N 09°56'·85W Fl WR 5s 56m **W18M, R18M, R15M**; W □ twr on □ building; vis: R262°-281°, W281°-342°, R342°-060°, W060°-092°, R(intens) 092°-099°, W099° -118°.

Clare I, E Pier ☆ 53°48'·04N 09°57'·06W Fl R 3s 5m 3M.

Cloughcormick 53°50'·56N 09°43'·20W Q (9) 15s.

Dorinish 53°49'·48N 09°40'·50W Fl G 3s.

Inishgort S Point ☆ 53°49'·61N 09°40'·25W L Fl 10s 11m 10M; W twr. Shown H24.

Westport Appr ☆ 53°47'·98N 09°34'·33W Fl 3s.

Roonagh Quay Ldg lts 144°. Front 53°45'·75N 09°54'·23W. Rear, 54m from front, both Iso 10s 9/15m.

▶ INISHBOFIN/CLIFDEN BAY

Inishlyon Lyon Head ☆ 53°36'·74N 10°09'·56W Fl WR 7·5s 13m W7M, R4M; W post; vis: W036°-058°, R058°-184°, W184°-325°, R325°-036°.

Gun Rock ☆ 53°36'·59N 10°13'·23W Fl (2) 6s 8m 4M; W col; vis: 296°-253°.

Cleggan Point ☆ 53°34'·49N 10°07'·73W Fl (3) WRG 15s 20m W6M, R3M, G3M; W col on W hut; vis: W shore-091°, R091°-124°, G124°-221°.

Carrickrana Rocks Bn 53°29'·24N 10°09'·48W; large W Bn.

Slyne Head, North twr, Illaunamid ☆ 53°23'·99N 10°14'·06W Fl (2) 15s 35m **19M**; B twr.

SLYNE HEAD TO BLACK HEAD

Inishnee ☆ 53°22'·75N 09°54'·53W Fl (2) WRG 10s 9m W5M, R3M, G3M; W col on W □ base; vis: G314°-017°, W017°-030°, R030°-080°, W080°-194°.

Croaghnakeela Is ☆ 53°19'·40N 09°58'·21W Fl 3·7s 7m 5M; W col; vis: 034°-045°, 218°-286°, 311°-325°.

▶ GALWAY BAY/INISHMORE

Eeragh, Rock Is ☆ 53°08'·10N 09°51'·39W Fl 15s 35m **23M**; W twr, two B bands; vis: 297°-262°.

Killeany 53°07'·26N 09°38'·24W Fl G 3s.

Straw Is ☆ 53°07'·06N 09°37'·85W Fl (2) 5s 11m **15M**; W twr.

Killeany Ldg lts 192°. Front, 53°06'·25N 09°39'·74W Oc 5s 6m 3M; W col on W □ base; vis: 142°-197°. Rear, 43m from front, Oc 5s 8m 2M; W col on W □ base; vis: 142°-197°.

Kilronan Pier Head ☆ 53°07'·10N 09°39'·98W Fl WG 1·5s 5m 3M; W col; vis: G240°-326°, W326°-000°.

▶ KIGGAUL BAY

Kiggaul Bay ☆ 53°14'·02N 09°43'·04W Fl WR 3s 5m W5M, R3M; vis: W329°-359°, R359°-059°, part obsc by W shore of bay.

▶ CASHLA BAY/SPIDDLE

Ship Rock 53°15'·73N 09°34'·28W Fl R 3s.

Lion Rock 53°15'·79N 09°34'·16W Fl G 3s.

Ent W side ☆ 53°14'·23N 09°35'·20W Fl (3) WR 10s 8m W6M, R3M; W col on concrete structure; vis: W216°-000°, R000°-069°.

Cannon Rock 53°14'·09N 09°34'·35W Fl G 5s.

Lion Pt Dir lt 53°15'·83N 09°33'·95W Iso WRG 4s 6m W8M, R6M, G6M; vis: G357·5°-008·5°, W008·5°-011·5°, R011·5°-017·5°.

Rossaveel Pier Ldg lts 116° Front, 53°16'·02N 09°33'·38W Oc 3s 7m 3M; W mast. Rear, 90m from front, Oc 3s 8m 3M.

Spiddle Pier Head ☆ 53°14'·42N 09°18'·55W Fl WRG 3·5s 11m W6M, R4M, G4M; Y col; vis: G102°-282°, W282°-024°, R024°-066°.

▶ GALWAY

Margaretta Shoal 53°13'·68N 09°05'·99W Fl G 3s; *Whis.*

Black Rock 53°14'·00N 09°06'·55W Fl R 3s.

Tawin Shoals 53°14'·30N 09°04'·26W Fl (3) G 10s.

Mutton Is 53°15'·07N 09°02'·93W Fl (2)R 6s.

Peter Rock 53°15'·17N 09°01'·09W.

Leverets ☆ 53°15'·33N 09°01'·90W Q WRG 9m 10M; B □ twr, W bands; vis: G015°-058°, W058°-065°, R065°-103°, G103°-143·5°, W143·5°-146·5°, R146·5°-015°.

Rinmore ☆ 53°16'·12N 09°01'·97W Iso WRG 4s 7m 5M; W □ twr; vis: G359°-008°, W008°-018°, R018°-027°.

Nimmo's Pier Head ☆ 53°16'·00N 09°02'·81W Fl Y 2s 7m 7M.

Approach chan Dir lt 325°. 53°16'·12N 09°02'·83W WRG 7m 3M; vis: FG322·25°-323·75°, AlGW323·75°-324·75°, F324·75°-325·25°, AlRW325·25°-326·25°, FR326·25°-331·25° Fl R 331·25°-332·25°.

Black Head ☆ 53°09'·26N 09°15'·83W Fl WR 5s 20m W11M, R8M, W □ twr; vis: 045°-268°, R268°-276°.

Finnis Rock 53°02'·82N 09°29'·14W Q (3) 10s.

Inisheer ☆ 53°02'·78N 09°31'·58W Iso WR 12s 34m **W20M, R16M**; vis: 225°-231°, W231°-245°, R245°-269°, W269°-115°; ***Racon (K) 13M.***

9.13.5 PASSAGE INFORMATION

For all Irish waters the Sailing Directions published by the Irish Cruising Club are strongly recommended, and particularly on the N and W coasts, where other information is scarce. They are published in 2 volumes: *E and N coasts of Ireland* which runs anti-clockwise from Carnsore Pt to Bloody Foreland, and *S and W coasts of Ireland* which goes clockwise.

CROSSING THE IRISH SEA (charts 1123, 1121, 1411) Passages across the Irish Sea can range from the fairly long haul from Land's End to Cork (140M), to the relatively short hop from Mull of Kintyre to Torr Pt (11M). Such distances are deceptive, because the average cruising yacht needs to depart from and arrive at a reasonably secure hbr. ► *In the North Chan strong tidal streams can cause heavy overfalls.* ◄ Thus each passage needs to be treated on its merits. See 9.0.7 for distances across the Irish Sea.

Many yachts use the Land's End/Cork route on their way to (and from) the delightful cruising ground along the S coast of Ireland, see 9.12.5. Penzance Bay, or one of the Scilly Is anchs, make a convenient place from which to leave, with good lights to assist departure.

► *Although the Celtic Sea is exposed to the Atlantic, there are no dangers on passage and the tidal streams are weak.* ◄ A landfall between Ballycotton and Old Hd of Kinsale (both have good lights) presents no offlying dangers, and in poor vis decreasing soundings indicate approach to land. There is a likelihood, outward bound under sail, that the boat will be on the wind – a possible benefit on the return passage. If however the wind serves, and if it is intended to cruise along the southern coast, a landfall at the Fastnet with arrival at (say) Baltimore will place the yacht more to windward, for little extra distance.

From Land's End the other likely destination is Dun Laoghaire. A stop at (say) Milford Haven enables the skipper to select the best time for passing the Smalls or Bishops (see 9.11.5) and roughly divides the total passage into two equal parts. From S Bishop onwards there are the options of making the short crossing to Tuskar Rk and going N inside the banks (theoretically a good idea in strong W winds), or of keeping to seaward. ► *But in bad weather the area off Tuskar is best avoided; apart from the Traffic Separation Scheme, the tide is strong at sp and the sea can be very rough.* ◄

The ferry route Holyhead/Dun Laoghaire is another typical crossing, and is relatively straightforward with easy landfalls either end. ► *The tide runs hard round Anglesey at sp, so departure just before slack water minimises the set N or S.* ◄ Beware also the TSS off The Skerries.

The Isle of Man (9.10.5) is a good centre for cruising in the Irish Sea, and its hbrs provide convenient staging points whether bound N/S or E/W.

CROSSING TO SCOTLAND (charts 2198, 2199, 2724) Between Scotland and Northern Ireland there are several possible routes, but much depends on weather and tide. ► *Time of departure must take full advantage of the stream, and avoid tide races and overfalls (see 9.9.5). Conditions can change quickly, so a flexible plan is needed.* ◄

► *From Belfast Lough ent, the passage distance to Mull of Kintyre is about 35M and, with a departure at HW Dover (also local HW) providing at least 6hrs of N-going tides, fair winds make it possible to get past the Mull or Sanda Is on one tide. But to be more confident of reaching Port Ellen or Gigha Is a departure from Carnlough or Red Bay at HW makes a shorter passage with better stream advantage.The inshore side of the TSS coincides with the outer limit of the race S and SW off the Mull of Kintyre; this occurs between HW Dover + 0430 and + 0610 when a local S-going stream opposes the main N-going stream (9.9.11).* ◄

For information on submarine hazards see 7.14.1.

LAMBAY ISLAND TO FAIR HEAD (AC 44, 2093, 2198/9) The coast is fairly steep-to except in larger bays, particularly Dundalk. ► *Streams offshore run up to 2·5kn as far as Rockabill, but are weaker further N until approaching Belfast Lough.* ◄ Lambay Island is private, and steep-to except on W side, where there can be overfalls. Skerries Islands (Colt, Shenick's and St Patrick's) are 1M E and SE of Red Island, to E of Skerries hbr. Shenick's Island is connected to shore at LW. Pass between Colt and St Patrick's Islands, but the latter has offliers 3ca to S. Rockabill, two steep-to rks with lt ho, is 2·5M E of St Patrick's Island.

Going NE from Carlingford Lough (9.13.7), after rounding Hellyhunter By, there are no offshore dangers until Strangford Lough (9.13.9). For Ardglass, see 9.13.8. N of Strangford keep 5ca off Ballyquintin Pt. 3M to NE are Butter Pladdy Rks; keep to E of these. 2M further N is South Rk, with disused lt ho, part of group of rks to be avoided in poor vis or bad weather by closing South Rk lt float. In good vis pass inshore of South Rk, between it and North Rks (chart 2156), rounding South Ridge PHM buoy.

Three routes lead into Belfast Lough (9.13.10): **a**. E of Mew Is, but beware Ram Race (to the N on the ebb, and the S on the flood); **b**. Copeland Sound, between Mew Is and Copeland Is, is passable but not recommended; **c**. Donaghadee Sound is buoyed and a good short cut for yachts. ► *Here the stream runs SSE from HW Belfast + 0530 and NW from HW Belfast – 0030, 4·5kn max. An eddy extends S to Ballyferris Pt, and about 1M offshore.* ◄ For Donaghadee, see chart 3709.

N from Belfast Lough, Black Hd is clean. Pass E of Muck Is, which is steep-to. Hunter Rk (0·8m), 2·5M NE of Larne, is marked by N & S cardinals. 2M further N are the Maidens, two dangerous groups of rks extending 2·5M N/S; E Maiden is lit.

The very small hbr of Carnlough (9.13.11) provides shelter for small yachts, but should not be approached in strong onshore winds. Other anchs in offshore winds are at Red Bay (9.13.11) 5M further N, and in Cushendun B, 5M NNW of Garron Pt. All provide useful anch on passage to/from the Clyde or Western Is. Fair Hd is a bold 190m headland, steep-to all round, but with extensive overfalls in Rathlin Sound.

FAIR HEAD TO BLOODY FORELAND (chart 2723) This is a good cruising area, under the lee of land in SW'lies, but very exposed to NW or N. Beware fishing boats and nets in many places and the North Channel TSS.

► *A fair tide is essential through Rathlin Sound (9.13.12), as sp rates reach 6kn, with dangerous overfalls. The main stream sets W from HW Dover +½ for 5 hrs, and E from HW Dover –5½ for 5 hrs. The worst overfalls are S of Rue Pt (Slough-na-more) from HW Dover +1½ to +2½, and it is best to enter W-bound at the end of this period, on the last of fair tide. E-bound enter the Sound at HW Dover –5. Close inshore between Fair Hd and Carrickmannanon Rk a counter eddy runs W from HW Dover – 3, and an E-going eddy runs from HW Dover +2 to +3.* ◄ Pass outside Carrickmannanon Rk (0·3m) and Sheep Is. There are small hbrs in Church Bay (Rathlin Is) and at Ballycastle.

Proceeding to Portrush (9.13.13), use Skerries Sound in good weather. ► *Enter Lough Foyle by either the North Chan W of The Tuns, or S chan passing 2ca N of Magilligan Pt and allowing for set towards The Tuns on the ebb (up to 3·5kn).* ◄

Tor Rks, Inishtrahull and Garvan Isles lie NE and E of Malin Hd. In bad weather it is best to pass at least 3M N of Tor Rks. Inishtrahull is lit and about 1M long; rks extend N about 3ca into Tor Sound. ► *Inishtrahull Sound, between Inishtrahull and Garvan Isles, is exposed; tidal streams up to 4kn sp can raise a dangerous sea with no warning. Stream also sets hard through Garvan Isles, S of which Garvan Sound can be passed safely in daylight avoiding two sunken rks, one 1½ca NE of Rossnabarton, and the other 5ca NW. The main stream runs W for only 3hrs, from HW Galway – 0500 to – 0200. W of Malin Hd a W-going eddy starts at HW Galway + 0400, and an E-going one at HW Galway – 0300.* ◄

W of Malin Head the direction of buoyage changes to E. From Malin Head SW to Dunaff Head, at ent to Lough Swilly (9.13.16), keep 5ca offshore. Trawbreaga Lough (AC 2697) gives shelter, but is shallow, and sea can break on bar; only approach when no swell, and at half flood. Ent to L Swilly is clear except for Swilly Rks off the W shore, SSE of Fanad Hd.

W from Lough Swilly the coast is very foul. Beware Limeburner Rk (2m), 6·8M WNW of Fanad Hd. Mulroy Bay (9.13.16) has good anchs but needs accurate pilotage, as in *ICC SDs*.

Between Mulroy B and Sheephaven there is inshore passage S of Frenchman's Rk, and between Guill Rks and Carnabollion, safe in good weather; otherwise keep 1M offshore. Sheep Haven B (9.13.16) is easy to enter between Rinnafaghla Pt and Horn Hd, and has good anchs except in strong NW or N winds. Beware Wherryman Rks, dry 1·5m, 1ca off E shore.

Between Horn Hd and Bloody Foreland (chart 2752) are three low-lying islands: Inishbeg, Inishdooey and Inishbofin. The latter is almost part of the mainland; it has a temp anch on S side and a more sheltered anch on NE side in Toberglassan B. 6M offshore is Tory Is (lt, fog sig, RC) with rks for 5ca off SW side. Temp anch in good weather in Camusmore B. ▶ *In Tory Sound the stream runs W from HW Galway + 0230, and E from HW Galway – 0530, sp rates 2kn.* ◀

BLOODY FORELAND TO EAGLE ISLAND (chart 2725) Off low-lying Bloody Foreland (lt) there is often heavy swell. The coast and islands 15M SW to Aran Is give good cruising (chart 1883). An inshore passage avoids offlying dangers: Buniver and Brinlack shoals, which can break; Bullogconnell 1M NW of Gola Is; and Stag Rks 2M NNW of Owey Is. Anchs include Bunbeg and Gweedore hbr, and Cruit B which has easier access. Behind Aran Is are several good anchs. Use N ent, since S one is shallow (chart 2792). Rutland N Chan is main appr to Burtonport (9.13.16).

Boylagh B has shoals and rks N of Roaninish Is. Connell Rk (0·3m) is 1M N of Church Pool, a good anch, best approached from Dawros Hd 4·5M to W. On S side of Glen B a temp anch (but not in W or NW winds) is just E of Rinmeasa Pt. Rathlin O'Birne Is has steps E side; anch SE of them 100m offshore. Sound is 5ca wide; hold Is side to clear rks off Malin Beg Hd.

In Donegal B (chart 2702) beware uncharted rks W of Teelin, a good natural hbr but exposed to S/SW swell. Killybegs (9.13.17) has better shelter and is always accessible. Good shelter with fair access in Donegal Hbr (chart 2715). Good anch or ⚓ via YC at Mullaghmore in fair weather; sea state is calm with winds from SE through S to NW. Inishmurray is worth a visit in good weather, anch off S side. There are shoals close E and NE of the Is, and Bomore Rks 1·5M to N. Keep well clear of coast S to Sligo (9.13.18) in onshore winds, and watch for lobster pots.

Killala B has temp anch 1M S of Kilcummin Hd, on W side. Proceeding to Killala beware St Patrick's Rks. Ent has ldg lts and marks, but bar is dangerous in strong NE winds.

The coast W to Broadhaven is inhospitable. Only Belderg and Portacloy give a little shelter. Stag Rks are steep-to and high. Broadhaven (chart 2703) is good anch and refuge, but in N/NW gales sea can break in ent. In approaches beware Slugga Rk on E side with offlier, and Monastery Rk (0·3m) on S side.

EAGLE ISLAND TO SLYNE HEAD (chart 2420) This coast has many inlets, some sheltered. ▶ *Streams are weak offshore.* ◀ There are few lights. Keep 5ca off Erris Hd, and further in bad weather. Unless calm, keep seaward of Eagle Is (lt) where there is race to N. Frenchport (chart 2703) is good temp anch except in strong W winds. Inishkea Is (chart 2704) can be visited in good weather; anch N or S of Rusheen Is. On passage keep 5ca W of Inishkea to avoid bad seas if wind over tide. The sound off Mullett Peninsula is clear, but for Pluddany Rk 6ca E of Inishkea N.

Blacksod B (chart 2704 and 9.13.19) has easy ent (possible at night) and good shelter. In the approaches Black Rk (lt) has rks up to 1·25M SW. From N, in good weather, there is chan between Duvillaun Beg and Gaghta Is, but in W gales beware breakers 1M SE of Duvillaun More.

Rough water is likely off impressive Achill Hd. Achill Sound (chart 2667) is restricted by cables 11m high at swing bridge. ▶*Anchs each end of Sound, but the stream runs strongly.* ◀

Clare Is has Two Fathom Rk (3·4m) 5ca off NW coast, and Calliaghcrom Rk 5ca to the N; anch on NE side. In Clew Bay Newport and Westport (AC 2667, 2057 and 9.13.19) need detailed pilotage directions. S of Clare Is beware Meemore Shoal 1·5M W of Roonagh Hd. 2M further W is the isolated rk Mweelaun. The islands of Caher, Ballybeg, Inishturk (with anch on E side) and Inishdalla have few hidden dangers, but the coast to the E must be given a berth of 1·5M even in calm weather; in strong winds seas break much further offshore.

Killary B (chart 2706) and Little Killary both have good anchs in magnificent scenery. Consult sailing directions, and only approach in reasonable weather and good vis.

Ballynakill Hbr (chart 2706), easily entered either side of Freaghillaun South, has excellent shelter; Tully mountain is conspic to N. Beware Mullaghadrina and Ship Rk in N chan. Anch in Fahy, Derryinver or Barnaderg B. There is anch on S side of Inishbofin (lt), but difficult access/exit in strong SW wind or swell (9.13.19). Rks and breakers exist E of Inishbofin and S of Inishshark; see chart 2707 for clearing lines. Lecky Rks lie 1M SSE of Davillaun. Carrickmahoy is a very dangerous rk (1·9m) between Inishbofin and Cleggan Pt.

Cleggan B is moderate anch, open to NW but easy access. High Is Sound is usual coasting route, not Friar Is Sound or Aughrus Passage. Clifden B (chart 2708) has offlying dangers with breakers; enter 3ca S of Carrickrana Bn and anch off Drinagh Pt, in Clifden Hbr or Ardbear B; see 9.13.19.

Slyne Hd (lt, Racon) marks SW end of the rocks and islets stretching 2M WSW from coast. ▶ *Here the stream turns N at HW Galway – 0320, and S at HW Galway + 0300. It runs 3kn at sp, and in bad weather causes a dangerous race; keep 2M offshore.* ◀ Seas break on Barret Shoals, 3M NW of Slyne Hd.

SLYNE HEAD TO LISCANNOR BAY (chart 2173) In good visibility the Connemara coast (charts 2709, 2096) and Aran Islands (chart 3339) give excellent cruising. But there are many rks, and few navigational marks. Between Slyne Head and Roundstone B are many offlying dangers. If coasting, keep well seaward of Skerd Rks. A conspic twr (24m) on Golan Head is a key feature. Going E the better hbrs are Roundstone B, Cashel B, Killeany B, Greatman B and Cashla B. Kilronan (Killeany B) on Inishmore is only reasonable hbr in Aran Islands, but is exposed in E winds. Disused lt ho on centre of island is conspic.

Normal approach to Galway B is through N Sound or S Sound. N Sound is 4M wide from Eagle Rk and other dangers off Lettermullan shore, to banks on S side which break in strong winds. S Sound is 3M wide, with no dangers except Finnis Rk (0·4m) 5ca SE of Inisheer. The other channels are Gregory Sound, 1M wide between Inishmore and Inishmaan, and Foul Sound between Inishmaan and Inisheer. The latter has one danger, Pipe Rk and the reef inshore of it, extending 3ca NW of Inisheer.

The N side of Galway Bay is exposed, with no shelter. Galway (9.13.20) is a commercial port, with possible marina plans. 3M SE, New Hbr (chart 1984) is a more pleasant anch with moorings off Galway Bay SC. Westward to Black Hd there are many bays and inlets, often poorly marked, but providing shelter and exploration. The coast SW to Liscannor Bay is devoid of shelter. O'Brien's Twr is conspic just N of the 199m high Cliffs of Moher.

9.13.6 Special notes for Ireland: See 9.12.6.

MINOR HARBOURS AND ANCHORAGES TO THE NORTH WEST OF LAMBAY ISLAND

SKERRIES, Dublin, **53°35'·09N 06°06'·49W**. AC 633. Tides as Balbriggan, 9.13.7. E & SE of Red Island (a peninsula) lie Colt, Shenick's and St Patrick's Is, the latter foul to S and SW. Inshore passage between Colt and St Patrick's Is uses transit/brg as on chart to clear dangers. Good shelter and holding in 3m at Skerries Bay, W of Red Is. Appr from E or NE outside PHM buoy, Fl R 10s, off Red Is. ⚓ WNW of pier, Oc R 6s 7m 7M, vis 103°-154°; clear of moorings. Most facilities; Skerries SC ☎ 1-849 1233. Rockabill Lt, Fl WR 12s 45m 22/18M, is conspic 2·4M ExN of St Patrick's Is.

BALBRIGGAN, Dublin, **53°36'·76N 06°10'·84W**. AC 4414, 68. Tides see 9.13.7. Good shelter in small hbr, dries about 0·9m, access approx HW ±2. Hbr unattractive, mainly FV's. Appr on SW, to open the outer hbr which is entered on SE; thence to inner hbr and AB on SE quay. Beware shoaling on both sides of outer hbr. Lt, Fl (3) WRG 20s 12m 13/10M, conspic W tr on E bkwtr head, vis G159°-193°, W193°-288°, R288°-305°. Facilities: FW, D (by tanker from skerries), Gas, Slip, BH, R, Bar, 🛒.

9.13.7 CARLINGFORD LOUGH

Louth/Down **54°01'·25N 06°04'·30W** ❀❀⚓⚓✿✿✿

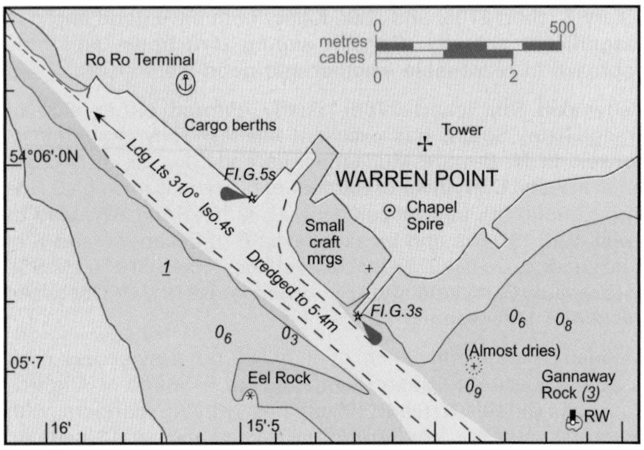
metres
cables
0
500
2
Ro Ro Terminal
Cargo berths
Tower
54°06'·0N
Ldg Lts 310°
Iso.4s
Fl.G.5s
WARREN POINT
Chapel Spire
Small craft mrgs
Dredged to 5·4m
Fl.G.3s
Eel Rock
(Almost dries)
Gannaway Rock (3)
RW
05'·7
16'
15'·5

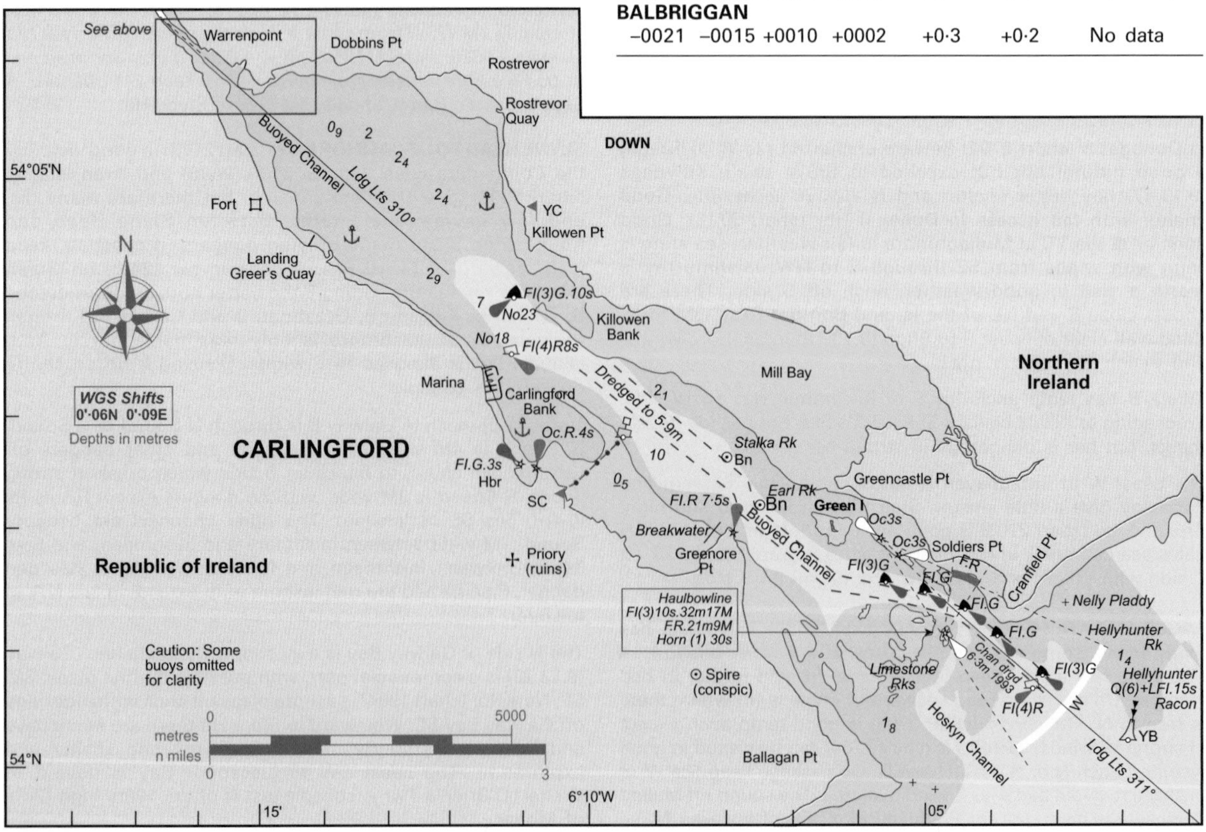
See above
Warrenpoint
Dobbins Pt
Rostrevor
Rostrevor Quay
DOWN
54°05'N
Buoyed Channel
Ldg Lts 310°
Fort
Landing Greer's Quay
YC
Killowen Pt
N
Fl(3)G.10s
No23
Killowen Bank
No18
Fl(4)R8s
Marina
Carlingford Bank
Mill Bay
Northern Ireland
WGS Shifts
0'·06N 0'·09E
Depths in metres
CARLINGFORD
Oc.R.4s
Dredged to 5·9m
Stalka Rk
Bn
Fl.G.3s
Hbr
SC
Fl.R 7·5s
Earl Rk
Green I
Greencastle Pt
Oc3s
Breakwater
Greenore Pt
Soldiers Pt
Cranfield Pt
Republic of Ireland
Priory (ruins)
Haulbowline
Fl(3)10s.32m17M
F.R.21m9M
Horn (1) 30s
Nelly Pladdy
Hellyhunter Rk
Fl(3)G
Hellyhunter
Q(6)+LFl.15s
Racon
Caution: Some buoys omitted for clarity
Spire (conspic)
Limestone Rks
Chan dred 6·3m 1993
Fl(4)R
YB
metres
n miles
0
5000
3
Ballagan Pt
Hoskyn Channel
Ldg Lts 311°
54°N
15'
6°10'W
05'

CHARTS AC 44, 2800; Imray C62; Irish OS 29, 36

TIDES Cranfield Pt +0025 and Warrenpoint +0035 Dover; ML 2·9; Duration Cranfield Pt 0615, Warrenpoint 0540; Zone 0 (UT)

Standard Port DUBLIN (NORTH WALL) (⟵)

Times				Height (metres)			
High Water		Low Water		MHWS	MHWN	MLWN	MLWS
0000	0700	0000	0500	4·1	3·4	1·5	0·7
1200	1900	1200	1700				
Differences CRANFIELD POINT							
−0027	−0011	+0005	−0010	+0·7	+0·9	+0·3	+0·2
WARRENPOINT							
−0020	−0010	+0025	+0035	+1·0	+0·7	+0·2	0·0
NEWRY (VICTORIA LOCK)							
−0005	−0015	+0045	Dries	+1·2	+0·9	+0·1	Dries
DUNDALK (SOLDIERS POINT)							
−0010	−0010	0000	+0045	+1·0	+0·8	+0·1	−0·1
DUNANY POINT							
−0028	−0018	−0008	−0006	+0·7	+0·9	No data	
RIVER BOYNE BAR							
−0005	0000	+0020	+0030	+0·4	+0·3	−0·1	−0·2
BALBRIGGAN							
−0021	−0015	+0010	+0002	+0·3	+0·2	No data	

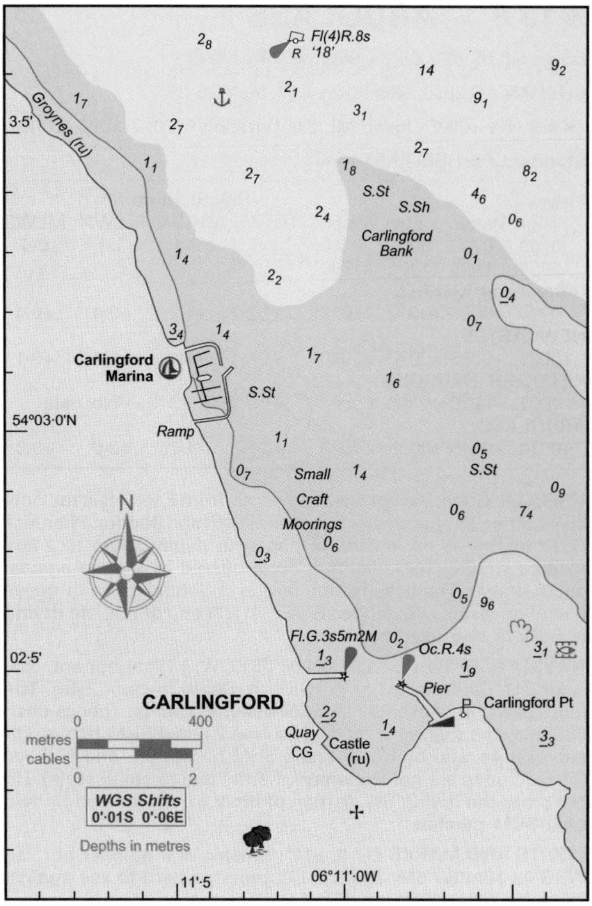
Fl(4)R.8s
R '18'
Groynes (ru)
3·5'
S.St
S.Sh
Carlingford Bank
Carlingford Marina
S.St
54°03·0'N
Ramp
Small Craft Moorings
S.St
N
Fl.G.3s5m2M
Oc.R.4s
02·5'
Pier
CARLINGFORD
Carlingford Pt
0
400
metres
cables
0
2
Quay
CG
Castle (ru)
WGS Shifts
0'·01S 0'·06E
Depths in metres
11'·5
06°11'·0W

SHELTER Good. **Carlingford Marina** protected on S side by sunken barge; depths 1·4m – 3·5m. Visitors should check depth of berth offered by marina against depth drawn. Appr from N with Nos 18 and 23 buoys in transit astern 012°, to clear the tail of Carlingford Bank (dries).

There are harbours at: **Carlingford Hbr** (dries 2·2m), AB at piers. **Warrenpoint** has pontoons on NW side of bkwtr (Fl G 3s); access dredged 1·1m. ⚓s clockwise from ent include: at Greenore Pt, between SW end of quay and bkwtr, in 3m clear of commercial tfc; off Greer's Quay in 2m; off Rostrevor Quay, Killowen Pt (YC) and off derelict pier at Greencastle Pt (beware rks).

NAVIGATION WPT 54°00'·09N 06°02'·00W, (2½ ca S of Hellyhunter SCM lt buoy) 311° to first chan buoys, 1M. The main chan is Carlingford Cut (6·3m), about 3ca SW of Cranfield Pt, and passing 2ca NE of Haulbowline lt ho. Drying rks and shoals obstruct most of the ent. The lough becomes choppy in S winds: due to the funnelling effect of the mountains NW winds cause a worse sea state within the lough than outside it. The ent is impassable in strong on-shore winds. Tides run up to 5kn off Greenore Pt and entry is impracticable against the ebb. Beware sudden squalls and waterspouts. Caution: Yachts should at all times keep clear of commercal shipping in the narrow dredged channel. The head of the lough is shallow. Note: The NE bank is Ulster, SW bank is the Republic of Ireland. Yachts may be stopped by Naval vessels.

LIGHTS AND MARKS Haulbowline Fl (3) 10s 32m 17M; granite tr; also turning lt FR 21m 9M, vis 196°-208°, horn 30s. Ldg lts 310°26': both Oc 3s 7/12m 11M, vis 295°-325°; R △ front, ▽ rear, on framework trs. Greenore Pier Fl R 7·5s 10m 5M. Newry R: Ldg lts 310°, both Iso 4s 5/15m 2M, stone columns.

R/T Greenore (*Ferry Greenore*) Ch 12 16 (HJ). Carlingford marina Ch M 16. Warrenpoint Ch 12 16 (H24); call Ch 12 at By No. 23 to enter dredged chan. Dundalk Ch 14 16 (HW±3).

TELEPHONE (Dial code Greenore/Carlingford 042; Warrenpoint 028). MRCC (01) 6620922/3 or (02891) 463933; Irish ⊖: Dundalk (042) 34114; Marinecall 09066 526249; Dr (042) 73110; Ⓗ Newry (028) 3026 5511, Dundalk (042) 34701; Police (042) 9373102, (028) 4172 2222.

FACILITIES **Carlingford Marina** (200), ☎ (042)937 3073, 📠 (042)937 3075, mob 0872 321567, €2.50, D, C, CH, BH (50T), Divers, Slip, ⊡, Bar, R. **Carlingford YC** ☎ (041) 685 1951, Slip, Bar, M, FW; **Village** P (cans), 🛒, R, Bar, Ⓑ, ✉. **Hbr** AB, Slip; **Dundalk SC** FW, Slip; **Services:** ME, El, ⚒, Kos, Gas. **Warrenpoint** HM ☎ (02841) 752878, 📠 (02841) 773962; EC Wed; AB, M (but no access at LW), FW, P, D, ✉ (also at Rostrevor, Carlingford), Ⓑ (also Dundalk), ≷ (Dundalk, Newry), ✈ (Dublin).

MINOR HARBOURS BETWEEN CARLINGFORD LOUGH AND ST. JOHN'S POINT

KILKEEL, Down, **54°03'·47N 05°59'·26W**. AC 44, 2800. HW +0015 on Dover; ML 2·9m; Duration 0620. See 9.13.8. Inner basin is completely sheltered, but gets crowded by FVs; depth off quays approx 1m. Secure in inner basin and see HM. There are drying banks both sides of ent chan and SW gales cause a sandbank right across ent. This is dredged or slowly eroded in E winds. S bkwtr lt Fl WR 2s 8m 8M, R296°-313°, W313°-017°, storm sigs. Meeney's pier (N bkwtr) Fl G 3s 6m 2M. VHF Ch **12** 14 16 (Mon-Fri: 0900-2000). HM ☎ (028 417) 62287; Facilities: FW on quay, BY (between fish market and dock), El, ME, ⚒, Slip. **Town** (¾M) EC Thurs; Bar, ✉, R, 🛒, Gas, ⊡.

ANNALONG HBR, Down, **54°06'·50N 05°53'·65W**. AC 44. Tides as Kilkeel, see 9.13.8. Excellent shelter in small drying hbr, dredged to 1·5m 80m beyond pier with 30m pontoon, ⛽, FW. Appr in W sector of S bkwtr lt, Oc WRG 5s 8m 9M, vis G204°-249°, W249°-309°, R309°-024°. Hug N side of the bkwtr to avoid rky shore to stbd. Surge gate at hbr ent may be closed in SE winds (3R lts vert shown). IPTS shown at ent. HM ☎ mob 07739 527036 Facilities: 🛒, Bar, ✉.

DUNDRUM BAY, Down. AC 44. Tides see 9.13.8. This 8M wide bay to the W of St John's Pt is shoal to 5ca offshore and unsafe in onshore winds. The small drying hbr at **Newcastle** (54°11'·8N 05°53'·0W) is for occas use in fair weather. HM ☎ (02843) 722804, mob 07803 832515. **Dundrum Hbr** (**54°14'·2N 05°49'·4W**) No longer used by commercial tfc, provides ⚓ in 2m for shoal draft; the bar carries about 0·3m. A steep sea can run at the bar in onshore winds. HW Dundrum is approx that of HW Liverpool; see also 9.13.8 Newcastle. *The Irish Cruising Club's Sailing Directions* are essential for the 1M long, buoyed appr chan. 3 unlit DZ buoys offshore are part of the Ballykinler firing range, 2M E of hbr; R flag/lts indicate range active.

9.13.8 ARDGLASS

Down 54°15′·63N 05°35′·96W ❁❁❁◊◊✿✿

CHARTS AC 2093, 633; Imray C62; Irish OS 21

TIDES HW +0025 Dover; ML 3·0; Duration 0620; Zone 0 (UT)

Standard Port BELFAST (⟶)

Times				Height (metres)			
High Water		Low Water		MHWS	MHWN	MLWN	MLWS
0100	0700	0000	0600	3·5	3·0	1·1	0·4
1300	1900	1200	1800				
Differences KILKEEL							
+0040	+0030	+0010	+0010	+1·2	+1·1	+0·4	+0·4
NEWCASTLE							
+0025	+0035	+0020	+0040	+1·6	+1·1	+0·4	+0·1
KILLOUGH HARBOUR							
0000	+0020	No data		+1·8	+1·6	No data	
ARDGLASS							
+0010	+0015	+0005	+0010	+1·7	+1·2	+0·6	+0·3

SHELTER Good, except in strong winds from E to S. It is the only all-weather, all-tide shelter between Howth and Bangor. Phennick Cove marina is on W side of hbr, with depths 1·0m to 2·8m. Visitors should check depth of berth offered by marina against depth drawn. The busy fishing port is in South Hbr, with quays (2·1m) on inside of extended S pier. At NW end of hbr, old drying N Dock is also used by FVs.

NAVIGATION WPT 54°15′·30N 05°35′·32W, 131° to hbr ent, 5ca. Appr 311° in W sector of WRG Dir lt. Depth in chan 2·4m. The inner bkwtr is marked by an ECM buoy, VQ (3) 4s. Thence chan 232° into the marina is marked by Nos 2 and 4 PHM buoys, QR and Fl R 4s; and by Nos 3 and 5 SHM buoys, QG and Fl G 4s. (These buoys are not shown on chartlet due to small scale). Do not cross the drying SW portion of inner bkwtr, marked by two unlit SCM perches.

LIGHTS AND MARKS Dir lt, 311°, conspic W tr at inner hbr, Iso WRG 4s 10m 8/7/5M, W308°-314°; reported hard to see against shore lts. S bkwtr Fl R 3s 10m 5M. W roof of shed on S bkwtr is conspic. If entering S Hbr, avoid Churn Rk, unlit SCM bn. Entrance to marina is buoyed. Castle, spire and water tr (off plan) are conspic to W.

R/T Hbr VHF Ch 12 14 16. Marina Ch M, 80.

TELEPHONE (Dial code 028) HM 4484 1291, mob 07790 648274; MRSC 9046 3933; Marinecall 09066 526249; Police 4461 5011; Dr 9084 1242.

FACILITIES Marina (55, inc 20 Ⓥ), ☎/📠 4484 2332, £1·60, D (in 20 & 25 ltr cans), ⛽, 🅾, ♿. **Town** P (cans), Bar, ✉, R, 🛒, Gas.

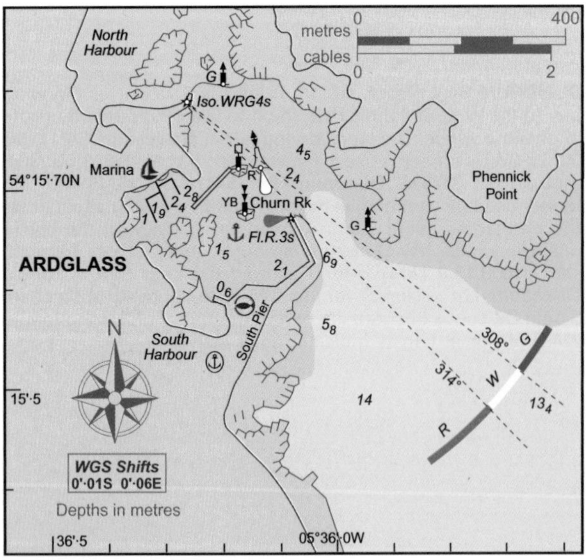
North Harbour
metres
0
400
cables
0
2
G
Iso.WRG4s
Marina
54°15′·70N
R
YB
Churn Rk
Fl.R.3s
Phennick Point
G
ARDGLASS
South Harbour
South Pier
N
308°
314°
G
W
R
14
WGS Shifts
0′·01S 0′·06E
Depths in metres
15′·5
36′·5
05°36′·0W

9.13.9 STRANGFORD LOUGH

Down **54°19′·33N 05°30′·85W** (Narrows) ❁❁◊◊✿✿✿

CHARTS AC 2156, 2159; Imray C62; Irish OS 21

TIDES Killard Pt 0000, Strangford Quay +0200 Dover; ML 2·0; Duration 0610; Zone 0 (UT)

Standard Port BELFAST (⟶)

Times				Height (metres)			
High Water		Low Water		MHWS	MHWN	MLWN	MLWS
0100	0700	0000	0600	3·5	3·0	1·1	0·4
1300	1900	1200	1800				
Differences STRANGFORD (The Narrows)							
+0147	+0157	+0148	+0208	+0·1	+0·1	−0·2	0·0
KILLARD POINT (Entr)							
+0011	+0021	+0005	+0025	+1·0	+0·8	+0·1	+0·1
QUOILE BARRIER							
+0150	+0200	+0150	+0300	+0·2	+0·2	−0·3	−0·1
KILLYLEAGH							
+0157	+0207	+0211	+0231	+0·3	+0·3	No data	
SOUTH ROCK							
+0023	+0023	+0025	+0025	+1·0	+0·8	+0·1	+0·1
PORTAVOGIE							
+0010	+0020	+0010	+0020	+1·2	+0·9	+0·3	+0·2

SHELTER Excellent, largest inlet on E coast. Good ⚓s in the Narrows at Cross Roads seldom used; in Strangford Creek (NW of Swan Island, which is marked by 3 lt bns to S, E and N); in Audley Rds and Ballyhenry Bay. 3 Ⓐs at Strangford. Portaferry has a small marina with visitors' berths. Many good ⚓s and some Ⓐs up the lough, by villages and YCs; dues, if applicable, are seldom collected.

NAVIGATION WPT Strangford SWM buoy, L Fl 10s, 54°18′·63N 05°28′·62W, 306° to Angus Rk lt tr, 2·05M. Strangers should use the E Chan. Beware St Patricks Rk, Bar Pladdy and Pladdy Lug; also overfalls in the SE apprs and at the bar, which can be dangerous when ebb from narrows is running against strong onshore winds. During flood the bar presents no special problem, but preferably enter on the young flood or when tide in the Narrows is slack. Strong (up to 7kn at sp) tidal streams flow through the Narrows. The flood starts in the Narrows at HW Belfast -3½ and runs for about 6 hrs; the ebb starts at HW Belfast +2½. Beware car ferry plying from Strangford, S and E of Swan Is, to Portaferry. Swan Island, seen as a grassy mound at HW, is edged with rks and a reef extends 32m E ending at W bn, Fl (2) WR 6s. Further up the lough, AC 2156 is essential; pladdies are drying patches, often un-marked.

LIGHTS AND MARKS See chartlet. Ent identified by Fairway buoy (SWM), W tr with R top on Angus Rk, Pladdy Lug bn (W), Bar Pladdy SCM lt buoy and St Patrick's Rock perch. See chartlet for clearance lines.

R/T *Strangford FerryTerminal HM* Ch 12 14 16 M (Mon-Fri 0900-1700LT). YC's and Riordan Marine Ch **80** M. Portaferry Ch M2 80.

TELEPHONE (Dial code 028) Strangford HM 4488 1637; MRSC 9146 3933; Marinecall 09066 526249; Police 4461 5011; Medical Clinic 4431 3016; Casualty 4461 3311.

FACILITIES
STRANGFORD: 3 Ⓐs SE of Swan Is. **Riordan Marine** ☎ 4488 1449: FW, El, Ⓔ, ⚒, D (cans). Village: 🛒, R, Bar, ✉.
PORTAFERRY: **Marina** ☎ 4272 9598, 📠 4272 9784, mobile 07703 209780. £1.20, ⛽, FW, Gas, Gaz, P & D (cans), 🛒, R, Bar, ✉, Ⓑ. **Cook Street Pier** (2½ca S) has limited AB, FW.
QUOILE RIVER: **Quoile YC** ☎ 4461 2266. AB, M, Slip, FW.
KILLYLEAGH: M, P & D (cans), L, CH, 🛒, Gas, Gaz, Kos, R, Ⓑ, Bar, ✉; **Killyleagh YC** ☎ 4482 8250; N of village, **East Down YC** ☎ 4482 8375, AB.
RINGHADDY QUAY: CC, M, AB drying, FW, Slip.
SKETRICK ISLAND: To the SW in White Rk B, **Strangford Lough YC**, ☎ 9754 1202, L, AB, FW, BY, CH, R, Bar. To the NW, **Down CC**, FW, D, Bar, SM (Irish Spars & Rigging ☎ 9754 1727.
KIRCUBBIN: Gas, P & D (cans), Ⓑ, R, Bar, 🛒, ✉.

STRANGFORD LOUGH *continued*

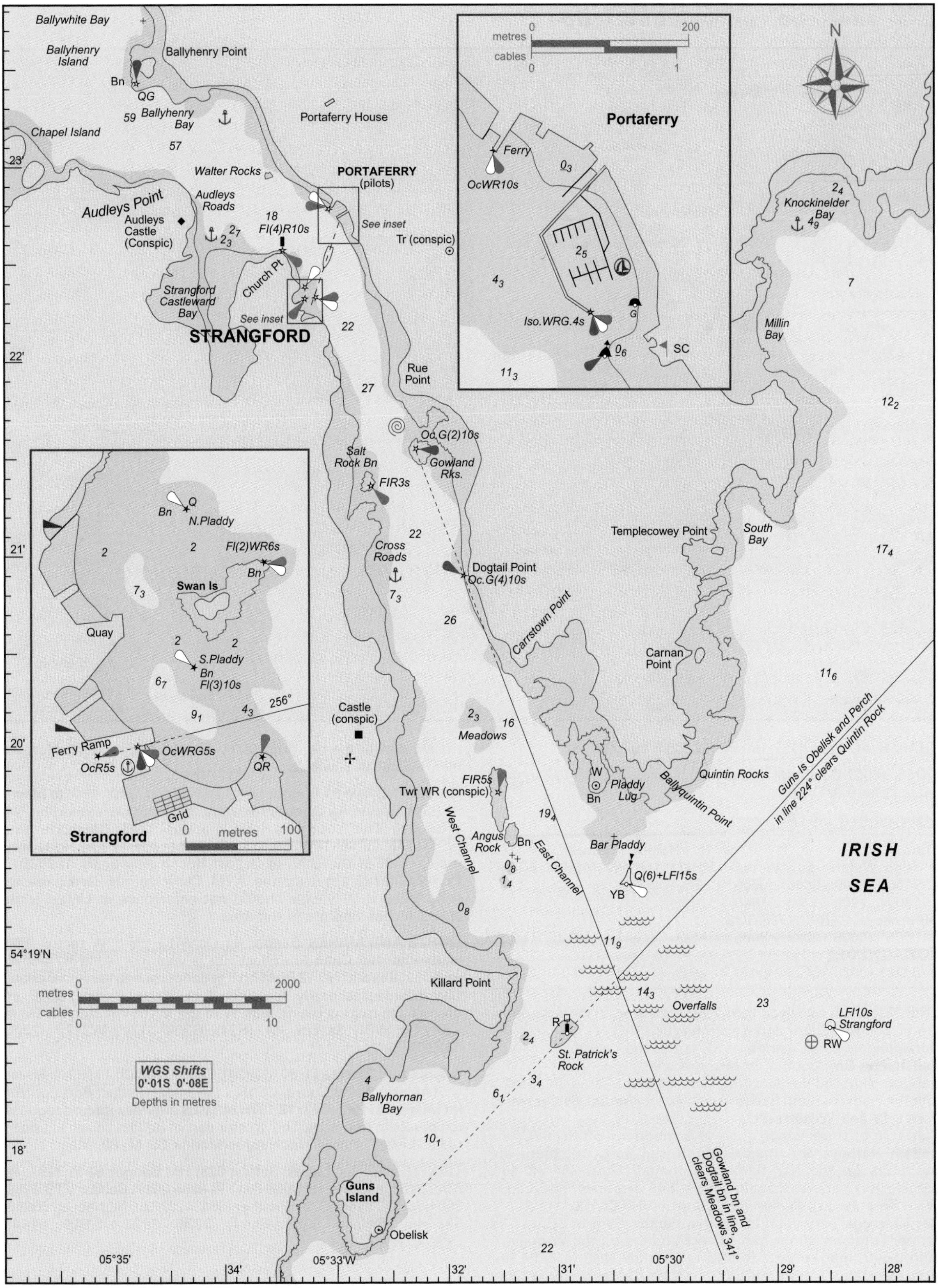
Ballywhite Bay
Ballyhenry Island
Ballyhenry Point
Bn
QG
59
Ballyhenry Bay
Chapel Island
57
Portaferry House
Walter Rocks
PORTAFERRY
(pilots)
Audleys Point
Audleys Roads
Audleys Castle (Conspic)
18
Fl(4)R10s
See inset
Tr (conspic)
Church Pt
Strangford Castleward Bay
STRANGFORD
22
Rue Point
27
Salt Rock Bn
Oc.G(2)10s
Gowland Rks.
FlR3s
22
Cross Roads
Dogtail Point
Oc.G(4)10s
26
Carrstown Point
Castle (conspic)
Meadows
16
FlR5s
Twr WR (conspic)
West Channel
Angus Rock
Bn
East Channel
Pladdy Lug
Ballyquintin Point
Quintin Rocks
Bar Pladdy
Q(6)+LFl15s
YB
Killard Point
Overfalls
23
LFl10s Strangford
RW
St. Patrick's Rock
Ballyhornan Bay
Guns Island
Obelisk
22
Gowland bn and Dogtail bn in line, clears Meadows 341°
Guns Is Obelisk and Perch in line 224° clears Quintin Rock
IRISH SEA
Templecowey Point
South Bay
Carnan Point
Millin Bay
Knockinelder Bay
N
Portaferry
metres 0 200
cables 0 1
Ferry
OcWR10s
Iso.WRG.4s
SC
Strangford
N.Pladdy
Fl(2)WR6s
Swan Is
Quay
S.Pladdy
Bn
Fl(3)10s
256°
Ferry Ramp
OcR5s
OcWRG5s
QR
Grid
metres 0 100
metres 0 2000
cables 0 10
WGS Shifts
0'·01S 0'·08E
Depths in metres
54°19'N
05°35'
05°33'W
05°30'

9.13.10 BELFAST LOUGH

County Down and County Antrim **54°42'N 05°45'W**
Bangor ⚙⚙⚙◊◊◊✿✿; Carrickfergus ⚙⚙⚙◊◊◊✿✿

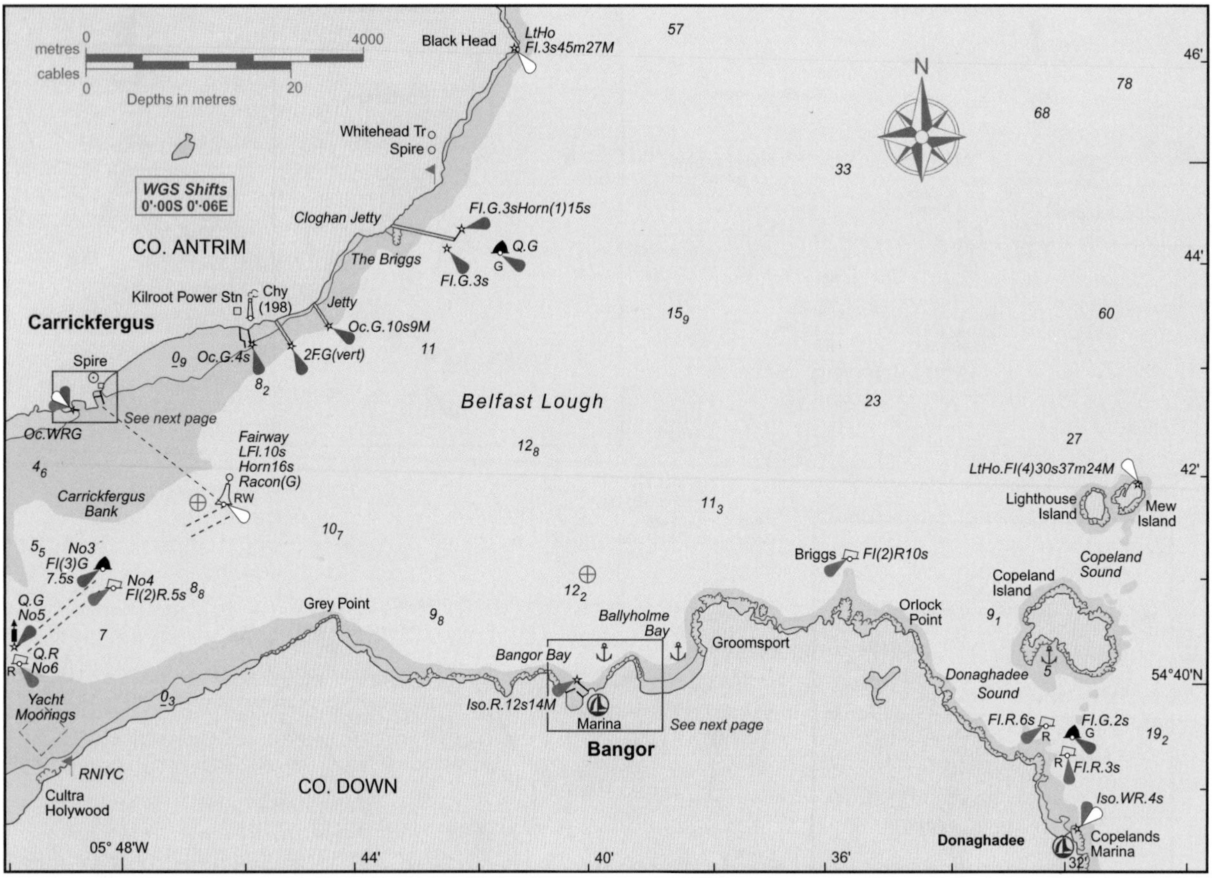
metres 0 4000
cables 0 20
Depths in metres
WGS Shifts
0'·00S 0'·06E
Black Head
LtHo
Fl.3s45m27M
Whitehead Tr
Spire
Cloghan Jetty
Fl.G.3sHorn(1)15s
Q.G
G
The Briggs
Fl.G.3s
CO. ANTRIM
Kilroot Power Stn
Chy
(198)
Jetty
Carrickfergus
Oc.G.10s9M
11
Spire
Oc.G.4s
2F.G(vert)
See next page
Oc.WRG
Fairway
LFl.10s
Horn16s
Racon(G)
RW
Belfast Lough
Carrickfergus
Bank
No3
Fl(3)G
7.5s
No4
Fl(2)R.5s
Q.G
No5
Q.R
No6
Yacht
Moorings
Grey Point
RNIYC
Cultra
Holywood
CO. DOWN
05° 48'W
44'
40'
36'
Ballyholme
Bay
Bangor Bay
Iso.R.12s14M
Marina
Bangor
See next page
Groomsport
Briggs
Fl(2)R10s
Orlock
Point
Copeland
Island
Copeland
Sound
LtHo.Fl(4)30s37m24M
Lighthouse
Island
Mew
Island
Donaghadee
Sound
Fl.R.6s
Fl.G.2s
Fl.R.3s
Iso.WR.4s
Donaghadee
Copelands
Marina
N
46'
44'
42'
54°40'N

CHARTS AC 2198, 1753; Imray C62, C64; Irish OS 15

TIDES +0007 Dover; ML Belfast 2·0, Carrickfergus 1·8; Duration 0620; Zone 0 (UT)

Standard Port BELFAST (⟶)

Times				Height (metres)			
High Water		Low Water		MHWS	MHWN	MLWN	MLWS
0100	0700	0000	0600	3·5	3·0	1·1	0·4
1300	1900	1200	1800				
Differences CARRICKFERGUS							
+0005	+0005	+0005	+0005	−0·3	−0·3	−0·2	−0·1
DONAGHADEE							
+0020	+0020	+0023	+0023	+0·5	+0·4	0·0	+0·1

SHELTER Main sailing centres, clockwise around Belfast Lough, are at Bangor, Cultra and Carrickfergus.
Donaghadee: small marina at SE ent to the Lough.
Ballyholme Bay: good ⚓ in offshore winds.
Bangor: exposed to N winds, but well sheltered in marina (depths 2·9m to 2·2m). Speed limits: 4kn in marina, 8kn between Luke's Pt and Wilson's Pt.
Cultra: in offshore winds good ⚓ & moorings off RNoIYC.
Belfast Harbour is a major commercial port, but there are pontoons on the NW bank at Donegall Quay (54°36'·16N 05°55'·20W) between Lagan Bridge, 8m clearance, and Lagan Weir. To enter call *Belfast Port Control* VHF Ch **12**.
Carrickfergus: very good in marina, depths 1·8m to 2·3m. The former commercial hbr has 10 yacht berths on the W quay. A stub bkwtr, marked by 2 PHM bns, extends NNE into the hbr from the W pier. The ent and SW part of the hbr are dredged 2·3m; the NE part of the hbr dries 0·7m. Good ⚓ SSE of Carrickfergus Pier, except in E winds.

NAVIGATION WPT Bangor 54°41´·00N 05°40´·00W, 190° to bkwtr lt, 1·0M. Rounding Orlock Pt beware Briggs Rocks extending ¾M offshore. The Lough is well marked. **WPT** Carrickfergus 54°41´·71N 05°46´·16W, Fairway SWM buoy, L Fl 10s, Horn 16s, marks start of the chan to Belfast Hbr. It also bears 121°/301° from/to Carrickfergus marina, 1.7M. Carrickfergus Bank liable to shift. Deep draft yachts should not enter/leave at LW±2. High speed ferries operate in the area.

LIGHTS AND MARKS Bangor Dir Oc WRG 10s lt; W sector 105° leads into ent. Chan to Belfast Hbr is well marked/lit by buoys and bns. Beyond No 12 PHM bn it is dangerous to leave the chan. Carrickfergus is easily recognised by conspic castle to E of marina. On marina bkwtr, 30m W of the ☆ QR 7m 3M, is a Dir lt 320°, Oc WRG 3s 5m 3M, (H24), G308°-317½°, W317½°-322½°, R322½°-332°.

R/T Bangor Marina Ch **80** M (H24); Bangor HM Ch 11 (H24). Royal N of Ireland YC (at Cultra) Ch **16**; 11 (H24) 80. *Belfast Port Control* (at Milewater Basin) Ch **12** 16 (H24); VTS provides info on request to vessels in port area. The greater part of Belfast Lough is under radar surveillance. Carrickfergus Marina Ch M, 80, M2.

TELEPHONE (Dial codes: Belfast 028) HM Bangor 9145 3297, 🖷 9145 3450; HM Belfast 9055 3012/🖷 9055 3017; Belfast VTS 9055 3504; MRSC 9146 3933; Weather (08494) 22339; Marinecall 09066 526249; Police 9055 8411, 9336 2021, 9145 4444; Dr 9146 8521.

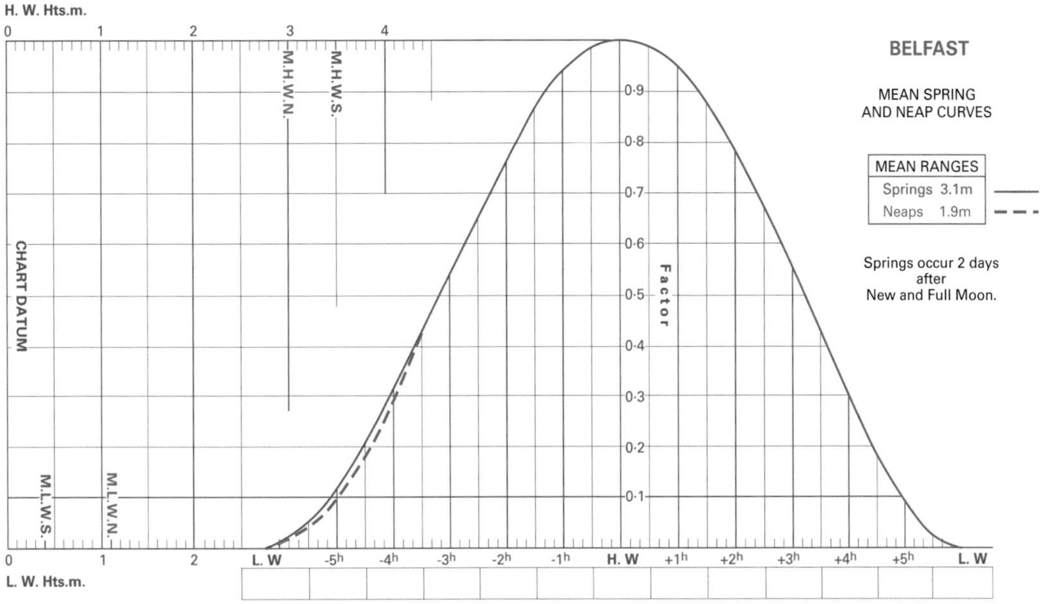
H. W. Hts.m.
0
1
2
3
4
M.H.W.N.
M.H.W.S.
CHART DATUM
M.L.W.S.
M.L.W.N.
0·9
0·8
0·7
0·6
0·5
0·4
0·3
0·2
0·1
Factor
BELFAST
MEAN SPRING AND NEAP CURVES
MEAN RANGES
Springs 3.1m
Neaps 1.9m
Springs occur 2 days after New and Full Moon.
0
1
2
L. W
-5h
-4h
-3h
-2h
-1h
H. W
+1h
+2h
+3h
+4h
+5h
L. W
L. W. Hts.m.

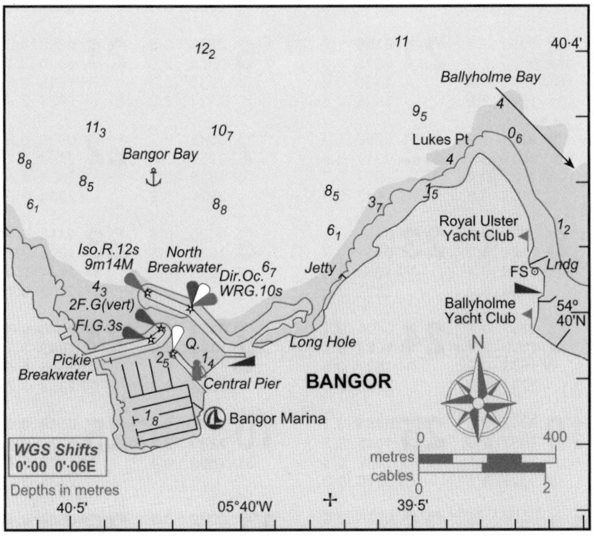
40·4'
Ballyholme Bay
Lukes Pt
Bangor Bay
Royal Ulster Yacht Club
Iso.R.12s 9m14M
North Breakwater
Dir.Oc. WRG.10s
Jetty
FS
Lndg
2F.G(vert)
Fl.G.3s
Q.
Long Hole
Ballyholme Yacht Club
54° 40'N
Pickie Breakwater
Central Pier
BANGOR
Bangor Marina
N
WGS Shifts
0'·00 0'·06E
metres
cables
Depths in metres
40·5'
05°40'W
39·5'

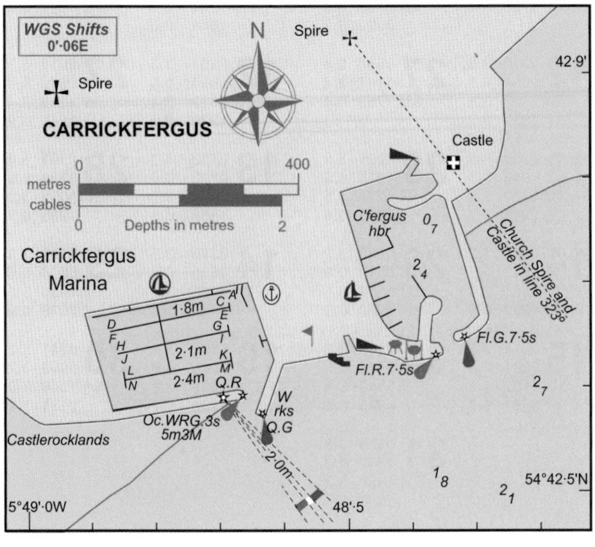
WGS Shifts
0'·06E
N
Spire
Spire
42·9'
CARRICKFERGUS
Castle
metres
cables
Depths in metres
C'fergus hbr
Church Spire and Castle in line 325°
Carrickfergus Marina
1·8m
2·1m
2·4m
Fl.G.7·5s
Fl.R.7·5s
Q.R
W rks
Q.G
Oc.WRG.3s 5m3M
Castlerocklands
2·0m
54°42·5'N
5°49'·0W
48'·5

FACILITIES Clockwise around the Lough:

GROOMSPORT BAY: HM ☎ 9127 8040, M, Slip, FW; **Cockle Island Boat Club**, Slip, M, FW, L, R.

BALLYHOLME BAY: **Ballyholme YC** ☎ 9127 1467, two ⚓s, R, Bar; **Royal Ulster YC** ☎ 9127 0568, M, R, Bar.

BANGOR: **Bangor Marina** (560 + 40 Ⓥ), (£1.75) ☎ 9145 3297, 📠 9145 3450, P, D, C, CH, BH (40 ton), ME, El, Ⓔ, ⚒, Gas, Gaz, Slip, SM, 🛒, ⊡; **Todd Chart Agency** ☎ 9146 6640, 📠 9147 1070 ACA, CH. **Services:** BY, Diving, Gas, ME, El, ⚒. **Town** EC Thurs; 🛒, R, Bar, ⊠, Ⓑ, ≠, ✈ (Belfast).

CULTRA: **Royal North of Ireland YC,** ☎ 9042 8041, M, L, AB, FW, Slip, P (½M), D, R, Bar. **Services:** ME, El, ⚒; **Town** P, CH, 🛒, R, Bar, ⊠, Ⓑ, ≠, ✈.

BELFAST: River manager ☎ 9032 8507, AB, P, D, FW, ME, El, ⚒, CH, C (200 ton), SM, Gas. **City** EC Wed; all facilities, ≠, ✈.

CARRICKFERGUS: **Marina** (280 inc Ⓥ) ☎ 9336 6666, 📠 9335 0505, carrick.marina@virgin.net; £1.75, El, ⚒, Gas, Rigging, ME, Ⓔ. **Carrick SC** ☎ 351402, M, L, FW, C, AB; **Hbr**: 10 AB, D, BH (45 ton).**Town** EC Wed; 🛒, R, Ⓑ, ⊠, ≠, ✈ (Belfast).

MINOR HARBOURS BETWEEN STRANGFORD AND BELFAST LOUGHS

PORTAVOGIE, Down, **54°27´·45N 05°26´·08W**. ✪✪✪✪✪. AC 2156. HW +0016 on Dover; ML 2·6m; Duration 0620. See 9.13.9. Good shelter, but hbr so full of FVs as to risk damage; best only for overnight or emergency. Entrance dangerous in strong onshore winds. Beware Plough Rks to SE marked by PHM buoy, Fl (2) R 10s, and McCammon Rks to NE of ent. Keep in W sector of outer bkwtr lt, Iso WRG 5s 9m 9M, G shore-258°, W258°-275°, R275°-348°. Inner bkwtr 2 FG (vert) 6m 4M. VHF Ch 12 14 16 (Mon-Fri: 0900-1700LT). HM ☎ (028) 4277 1470. Facilities: Slip, FW (on central quay) ⚒, ME, El. **Town** EC Thurs; CH, D & P (cans), ⊠, R, Gas, 🛒. No licenced premises.

DONAGHADEE, Down, **54°38´·71N 05°31´·85W**. ✪✪✪✪✪✪. AC 1753, 3709. HW +0025 on Dover; see 9.13.10; ML no data; Duration 0615. Excellent shelter and basic facilities in tiny marina, access HW±4 over sill; covers approx 1.1m at half tide. Appr on about 275° on ldg marks, orange △s to tricky ent with sharp 90° port turn into marina (pilots available). Appr in strong winds or at night not advised. 3ca to the N, the Old Hbr is small and very full; scend often sets in. Beware rky reef with less than 2m extends 1·5ca ENE from S pier hd. Max depth in hbr is approx 2·5m, dries at SW end; best berth alongside SE quay. S pier lt, Iso WR 4s 17m 18/14M, W shore–326°, R326°–shore. HM ☎/📠 (028) 9188 2377. Police 9188 2526. Facilities: **Copelands Marina** ☎ 9188 2184, mobile 07802 363382; VHF Ch **16** 11 80; AB for 6 Ⓥ, FW, D, ⛽, C (20 ton). **Old Hbr** AB £4. **Town** Bar, D, P, Gas, ⊠, R, 🛒, Ⓑ, ≠ (Bangor), ✈ (Belfast).

TIME ZONE (UT)
For Summer Time add ONE hour in **non-shaded areas**

NORTHERN IRELAND – BELFAST

LAT 54°36′N LONG 5°55′W

TIMES AND HEIGHTS OF HIGH AND LOW WATERS

SPRING & NEAP TIDES
Dates in red are SPRINGS
Dates in blue are NEAPS

YEAR **2005**

JANUARY

Date	Day	Time	m	Time	m	Time	m	Time	m
1	SA	0211	3.0	0817	1.0	1431	3.4	2040	0.8
2	SU	0255	2.9	0901	1.1	1513	3.3	2126	0.8
3	M	0346	2.9	0949	1.1	1602	3.3	◑ 2220	0.9
4	TU	0442	2.9	1045	1.2	1659	3.2	2320	0.9
5	W	0542	2.9	1149	1.2	1803	3.2		
6	TH	0024	0.9	0644	2.9	1301	1.2	1908	3.2
7	F	0129	0.8	0747	3.1	1408	1.0	2012	3.3
8	SA	0227	0.8	0847	3.2	1506	0.9	2112	3.3
9	SU	0320	0.7	0942	3.3	1559	0.7	2208	3.4
10	M	0411	0.7	1035	3.5	1651	0.5	● 2303	3.4
11	TU	0501	0.7	1126	3.6	1742	0.4	2356	3.4
12	W	0552	0.7	1216	3.7	1832	0.3		
13	TH	0050	3.3	0641	0.7	1307	3.7	1922	0.3
14	F	0143	3.3	0731	0.7	1356	3.7	2012	0.3
15	SA	0236	3.2	0820	0.7	1446	3.6	2104	0.4
16	SU	0328	3.1	0910	0.8	1536	3.5	2158	0.5
17	M	0420	3.0	1003	0.9	1629	3.4	◐ 2256	0.7
18	TU	0513	3.0	1104	1.0	1726	3.2	2359	0.9
19	W	0611	2.9	1212	1.1	1833	3.0		
20	TH	0104	1.0	0715	2.9	1324	1.2	1947	3.0
21	F	0205	1.0	0818	3.0	1432	1.1	2053	3.0
22	SA	0259	1.0	0914	3.1	1529	1.0	2145	3.0
23	SU	0344	1.0	1001	3.3	1613	0.9	2229	3.1
24	M	0422	0.9	1042	3.4	1649	0.8	2307	3.1
25	TU	0457	0.9	1119	3.5	1720	0.8	○ 2340	3.1
26	W	0530	0.8	1153	3.5	1752	0.7		
27	TH	0011	3.1	0604	0.8	1225	3.5	1824	0.7
28	F	0037	3.0	0637	0.8	1253	3.5	1856	0.6
29	SA	0103	3.0	0711	0.8	1323	3.5	1930	0.6
30	SU	0136	3.0	0746	0.8	1358	3.5	2006	0.6
31	M	0214	3.0	0824	0.8	1438	3.4	2047	0.6

FEBRUARY

Date	Day	Time	m	Time	m	Time	m	Time	m
1	TU	0259	3.0	0907	0.9	1524	3.3	2136	0.7
2	W	0350	2.9	0959	1.0	1619	3.2	◑ 2234	0.9
3	TH	0450	2.9	1104	1.1	1726	3.1	2344	1.0
4	F	0600	2.8	1230	1.2	1840	3.0		
5	SA	0105	1.0	0716	2.9	1355	1.0	1954	3.1
6	SU	0216	0.9	0829	3.1	1459	0.8	2103	3.2
7	M	0314	0.8	0931	3.3	1554	0.6	2202	3.3
8	TU	0405	0.7	1024	3.4	1645	0.4	● 2254	3.3
9	W	0454	0.6	1114	3.6	1733	0.2	2345	3.3
10	TH	0540	0.6	1202	3.6	1819	0.2		
11	F	0034	3.3	0625	0.5	1250	3.7	1903	0.2
12	SA	0122	3.3	0709	0.5	1336	3.7	1946	0.2
13	SU	0207	3.2	0751	0.6	1421	3.6	2029	0.4
14	M	0251	3.2	0834	0.6	1505	3.5	2113	0.6
15	TU	0334	3.1	0921	0.8	1550	3.3	2204	0.8
16	W	0421	3.0	1015	0.9	1642	3.0	◐ 2308	1.0
17	TH	0514	2.9	1128	1.1	1745	2.8		
18	F	0021	1.2	0623	2.8	1249	1.2	1921	2.7
19	SA	0132	1.2	0749	2.9	1403	1.1	2039	2.8
20	SU	0233	1.1	0853	3.0	1507	0.9	2132	2.9
21	M	0322	1.0	0941	3.2	1551	0.8	2214	3.0
22	TU	0401	0.9	1022	3.3	1626	0.7	2250	3.0
23	W	0436	0.8	1057	3.3	1657	0.6	2321	3.0
24	TH	0509	0.7	1128	3.4	1729	0.5	○ 2346	3.0
25	F	0542	0.7	1153	3.4	1800	0.5		
26	SA	0005	3.0	0613	0.6	1220	3.4	1829	0.5
27	SU	0030	3.1	0643	0.6	1252	3.5	1900	0.4
28	M	0103	3.1	0715	0.6	1328	3.5	1935	0.5

MARCH

Date	Day	Time	m	Time	m	Time	m	Time	m
1	TU	0141	3.1	0752	0.6	1409	3.4	2014	0.6
2	W	0223	3.1	0834	0.7	1456	3.3	2101	0.7
3	TH	0312	3.0	0926	0.9	1552	3.1	◑ 2158	0.9
4	F	0412	2.9	1033	1.1	1703	2.9	2311	1.1
5	SA	0528	2.8	1220	1.1	1824	2.9		
6	SU	0053	1.1	0656	2.8	1349	0.9	1948	2.9
7	M	0211	1.0	0819	3.0	1452	0.6	2100	3.0
8	TU	0308	0.8	0921	3.2	1546	0.4	2154	3.2
9	W	0357	0.7	1010	3.4	1633	0.2	2241	3.2
10	TH	0442	0.5	1057	3.5	1717	0.1	● 2326	3.3
11	F	0524	0.5	1142	3.6	1759	0.1		
12	SA	0010	3.3	0604	0.5	1227	3.6	1837	0.2
13	SU	0053	3.3	0643	0.5	1310	3.6	1915	0.3
14	M	0133	3.3	0721	0.5	1351	3.5	1952	0.5
15	TU	0212	3.2	0801	0.6	1432	3.4	2031	0.7
16	W	0252	3.2	0844	0.7	1515	3.1	2117	0.9
17	TH	0336	3.1	0936	0.9	1604	2.9	◐ 2216	1.1
18	F	0427	2.9	1049	1.1	1704	2.7	2338	1.3
19	SA	0529	2.8	1214	1.1	1847	2.5		
20	SU	0054	1.3	0700	2.8	1327	1.0	2017	2.6
21	M	0159	1.2	0821	2.9	1430	0.9	2108	2.8
22	TU	0252	1.0	0911	3.0	1517	0.7	2147	2.9
23	W	0334	0.9	0950	3.2	1554	0.6	2221	2.9
24	TH	0410	0.7	1022	3.2	1627	0.5	2249	3.0
25	F	0444	0.7	1049	3.3	1659	0.4	○ 2310	3.0
26	SA	0516	0.6	1115	3.4	1730	0.4	2332	3.1
27	SU	0546	0.6	1147	3.4	1759	0.4		
28	M	0001	3.2	0615	0.5	1223	3.5	1831	0.4
29	TU	0036	3.2	0649	0.5	1304	3.5	1907	0.5
30	W	0115	3.3	0728	0.5	1348	3.4	1949	0.6
31	TH	0159	3.2	0812	0.6	1438	3.2	2038	0.8

APRIL

Date	Day	Time	m	Time	m	Time	m	Time	m
1	F	0248	3.1	0907	0.8	1540	3.0	2137	1.0
2	SA	0351	2.9	1023	1.0	1656	2.8	◑ 2254	1.2
3	SU	0513	2.8	1219	1.0	1819	2.8		
4	M	0044	1.2	0646	2.9	1338	0.7	1946	2.9
5	TU	0158	1.0	0807	3.1	1440	0.5	2049	3.0
6	W	0255	0.8	0904	3.3	1530	0.3	2137	3.2
7	TH	0343	0.7	0951	3.4	1615	0.2	2221	3.2
8	F	0425	0.6	1035	3.5	1656	0.2	● 2303	3.3
9	SA	0504	0.5	1118	3.5	1734	0.3	2343	3.3
10	SU	0542	0.5	1200	3.5	1809	0.4		
11	M	0022	3.3	0617	0.5	1242	3.4	1844	0.5
12	TU	0101	3.3	0654	0.5	1322	3.3	1920	0.7
13	W	0139	3.3	0733	0.6	1402	3.2	1958	0.8
14	TH	0218	3.3	0816	0.7	1445	3.0	2042	1.0
15	F	0302	3.2	0906	0.9	1535	2.8	2138	1.2
16	SA	0351	3.0	1016	1.0	1632	2.6	◐ 2256	1.3
17	SU	0450	2.9	1137	1.0	1743	2.5		
18	M	0012	1.3	0557	2.8	1246	1.0	1932	2.6
19	TU	0117	1.2	0716	2.8	1345	0.9	2026	2.7
20	W	0212	1.1	0818	2.9	1434	0.7	2104	2.8
21	TH	0258	0.9	0900	3.1	1515	0.6	2136	2.9
22	F	0338	0.8	0935	3.2	1551	0.5	2204	3.0
23	SA	0413	0.7	1008	3.3	1624	0.4	2232	3.1
24	SU	0446	0.6	1043	3.4	1656	0.4	○ 2303	3.2
25	M	0518	0.6	1121	3.4	1729	0.4	2338	3.3
26	TU	0552	0.5	1202	3.5	1807	0.5		
27	W	0018	3.3	0630	0.5	1249	3.4	1848	0.6
28	TH	0101	3.4	0714	0.5	1338	3.3	1935	0.7
29	F	0148	3.3	0804	0.6	1435	3.2	2028	0.9
30	SA	0241	3.2	0906	0.7	1540	3.0	2131	1.1

Chart Datum: 2·01 metres below Ordnance Datum (Belfast)

TIME ZONE (UT)
For Summer Time add ONE hour in **non-shaded areas**

NORTHERN IRELAND – BELFAST

LAT 54°36′N LONG 5°55′W

TIMES AND HEIGHTS OF HIGH AND LOW WATERS

SPRING & NEAP TIDES
Dates in red are **SPRINGS**
Dates in blue are **NEAPS**

YEAR **2005**

MAY

Date	Day	Time	m	Time	m	Time	m	Time	m
1	SU	0346	3.0	1032	0.8	1654	2.8	◑ 2250	1.2
2	M	0506	3.0	1204	0.7	1815	2.8		
3	TU	0020	1.1	0632	3.0	1317	0.6	1927	2.9
4	W	0133	1.0	0744	3.1	1417	0.4	2024	3.0
5	TH	0231	0.9	0840	3.3	1507	0.3	2112	3.1
6	F	0321	0.7	0928	3.4	1551	0.3	2156	3.2
7	SA	0404	0.6	1013	3.5	1630	0.4	2237	3.3
8	SU	0444	0.6	1055	3.4	1708	0.5	● 2317	3.3
9	M	0522	0.6	1136	3.4	1743	0.6	2355	3.4
10	TU	0558	0.6	1216	3.3	1818	0.7		
11	W	0033	3.4	0634	0.7	1256	3.2	1854	0.9
12	TH	0112	3.4	0712	0.7	1336	3.1	1934	1.0
13	F	0152	3.4	0754	0.8	1420	3.0	2018	1.1
14	SA	0235	3.3	0842	0.8	1508	2.8	2108	1.2
15	SU	0322	3.2	0939	0.9	1603	2.7	2208	1.2
16	M	0415	3.0	1047	1.0	1703	2.6	◐ 2316	1.3
17	TU	0514	2.9	1153	0.9	1807	2.6		
18	W	0022	1.2	0615	2.9	1253	0.9	1908	2.7
19	TH	0121	1.2	0714	3.0	1344	0.8	1959	2.8
20	F	0212	1.0	0806	3.1	1429	0.6	2042	3.0
21	SA	0257	0.9	0852	3.2	1509	0.6	2122	3.1
22	SU	0337	0.8	0934	3.3	1546	0.5	2200	3.2
23	M	0415	0.7	1017	3.4	1625	0.5	○ 2240	3.3
24	TU	0455	0.6	1102	3.4	1706	0.5	2323	3.4
25	W	0537	0.5	1150	3.4	1750	0.6		
26	TH	0008	3.4	0622	0.5	1242	3.4	1838	0.7
27	F	0056	3.4	0711	0.5	1336	3.3	1929	0.8
28	SA	0146	3.4	0807	0.5	1434	3.1	2025	0.9
29	SU	0241	3.3	0912	0.5	1538	3.0	2127	1.0
30	M	0343	3.2	1025	0.6	1646	2.9	◑ 2236	1.0
31	TU	0454	3.2	1138	0.6	1755	2.9	2347	1.0

JUNE

Date	Day	Time	m	Time	m	Time	m	Time	m
1	W	0607	3.2	1245	0.5	1857	2.9		
2	TH	0055	1.0	0713	3.2	1345	0.5	1953	3.0
3	F	0158	0.9	0812	3.3	1438	0.5	2043	3.1
4	SA	0254	0.8	0905	3.3	1524	0.5	2129	3.2
5	SU	0343	0.8	0952	3.3	1606	0.6	2212	3.3
6	M	0427	0.7	1036	3.3	1645	0.7	● 2253	3.3
7	TU	0507	0.7	1117	3.2	1722	0.8	2332	3.4
8	W	0545	0.7	1156	3.2	1758	0.9		
9	TH	0011	3.4	0620	0.8	1234	3.1	1834	1.0
10	F	0050	3.5	0656	0.8	1314	3.0	1912	1.0
11	SA	0130	3.4	0734	0.8	1355	2.9	1953	1.0
12	SU	0210	3.4	0815	0.8	1439	2.9	2037	1.0
13	M	0251	3.3	0901	0.8	1529	2.8	2124	1.1
14	TU	0336	3.2	0951	0.8	1622	2.8	2215	1.1
15	W	0427	3.1	1047	0.9	1717	2.8	◐ 2311	1.2
16	TH	0523	3.0	1146	0.8	1811	2.8		
17	F	0012	1.2	0621	3.0	1244	0.8	1904	2.9
18	SA	0115	1.1	0719	3.1	1339	0.7	1955	3.0
19	SU	0212	1.0	0815	3.2	1429	0.7	2045	3.1
20	M	0304	0.9	0907	3.3	1517	0.6	2132	3.2
21	TU	0353	0.7	0958	3.4	1603	0.6	2220	3.3
22	W	0440	0.6	1049	3.4	1650	0.6	○ 2309	3.4
23	TH	0529	0.5	1140	3.4	1740	0.6	2358	3.5
24	F	0619	0.4	1234	3.3	1831	0.7		
25	SA	0049	3.5	0710	0.3	1329	3.3	1923	0.7
26	SU	0140	3.5	0804	0.3	1426	3.2	2016	0.8
27	M	0234	3.5	0901	0.4	1525	3.1	2112	0.8
28	TU	0330	3.4	1002	0.4	1624	3.0	◑ 2210	0.9
29	W	0430	3.3	1104	0.5	1722	3.0	2311	0.9
30	TH	0533	3.2	1207	0.6	1820	3.0		

JULY

Date	Day	Time	m	Time	m	Time	m	Time	m
1	F	0017	1.0	0638	3.2	1310	0.7	1917	3.0
2	SA	0124	1.0	0743	3.1	1407	0.8	2013	3.0
3	SU	0228	0.9	0844	3.1	1459	0.8	2105	3.1
4	M	0325	0.9	0937	3.1	1545	0.8	2152	3.3
5	TU	0413	0.8	1023	3.1	1626	0.9	2235	3.3
6	W	0456	0.8	1103	3.1	1703	0.9	● 2314	3.4
7	TH	0532	0.8	1141	3.1	1738	0.9	2352	3.4
8	F	0604	0.8	1216	3.0	1813	0.9		
9	SA	0029	3.5	0635	0.7	1251	3.0	1848	0.9
10	SU	0105	3.4	0709	0.7	1325	2.9	1925	0.9
11	M	0139	3.4	0744	0.7	1402	2.9	2003	0.9
12	TU	0214	3.4	0822	0.7	1441	2.9	2044	0.9
13	W	0252	3.3	0904	0.7	1527	2.9	2128	1.0
14	TH	0337	3.2	0953	0.8	1618	2.9	◐ 2218	1.1
15	F	0429	3.1	1048	0.8	1713	2.9	2316	1.1
16	SA	0531	3.1	1151	0.9	1812	2.9		
17	SU	0026	1.1	0637	3.1	1259	0.9	1913	3.0
18	M	0140	1.1	0744	3.1	1402	0.8	2014	3.1
19	TU	0244	0.9	0847	3.2	1458	0.7	2110	3.2
20	W	0340	0.7	0944	3.3	1550	0.7	2203	3.4
21	TH	0431	0.5	1037	3.3	1640	0.7	○ 2254	3.5
22	F	0521	0.4	1129	3.3	1729	0.6	2344	3.5
23	SA	0610	0.3	1222	3.3	1818	0.6		
24	SU	0035	3.6	0659	0.2	1315	3.3	1907	0.6
25	M	0126	3.6	0747	0.2	1407	3.2	1955	0.6
26	TU	0215	3.6	0836	0.3	1458	3.2	2044	0.7
27	W	0305	3.5	0927	0.4	1549	3.1	2135	0.8
28	TH	0357	3.4	1023	0.6	1641	3.0	◑ 2232	0.9
29	F	0453	3.2	1126	0.8	1736	3.0	2339	1.0
30	SA	0558	3.0	1233	0.9	1838	2.9		
31	SU	0052	1.1	0715	2.9	1338	1.0	1944	3.0

AUGUST

Date	Day	Time	m	Time	m	Time	m	Time	m
1	M	0205	1.0	0830	2.9	1436	1.0	2045	3.1
2	TU	0310	0.9	0927	3.0	1526	1.0	2135	3.2
3	W	0402	0.8	1013	3.0	1608	1.0	2218	3.3
4	TH	0442	0.8	1051	3.0	1643	0.9	2257	3.4
5	F	0513	0.7	1126	3.0	1716	0.9	● 2331	3.4
6	SA	0541	0.7	1156	3.0	1749	0.9		
7	SU	0003	3.4	0610	0.7	1223	3.0	1821	0.8
8	M	0033	3.4	0640	0.6	1248	3.0	1854	0.8
9	TU	0102	3.4	0711	0.6	1318	3.0	1928	0.8
10	W	0136	3.4	0745	0.6	1354	3.0	2004	0.8
11	TH	0213	3.4	0822	0.6	1436	3.0	2045	0.9
12	F	0256	3.3	0907	0.7	1524	3.0	2133	1.0
13	SA	0348	3.2	1000	0.9	1621	2.9	◐ 2231	1.1
14	SU	0452	3.0	1105	1.0	1728	2.9	2349	1.2
15	M	0607	3.0	1225	1.1	1840	2.9		
16	TU	0124	1.1	0723	3.0	1347	1.0	1951	3.0
17	W	0234	0.9	0834	3.1	1448	0.9	2054	3.2
18	TH	0331	0.6	0934	3.2	1540	0.8	2148	3.4
19	F	0421	0.4	1026	3.3	1628	0.7	○ 2238	3.5
20	SA	0509	0.3	1115	3.3	1714	0.6	2326	3.6
21	SU	0554	0.2	1203	3.3	1759	0.6		
22	M	0014	3.7	0637	0.2	1251	3.3	1842	0.6
23	TU	0103	3.7	0720	0.2	1338	3.3	1926	0.6
24	W	0149	3.6	0802	0.3	1423	3.2	2010	0.6
25	TH	0235	3.5	0845	0.5	1508	3.2	2056	0.7
26	F	0322	3.3	0935	0.8	1554	3.1	◑ 2150	0.9
27	SA	0414	3.1	1037	1.0	1647	3.0	2300	1.1
28	SU	0516	2.9	1153	1.2	1751	2.9		
29	M	0021	1.2	0652	2.7	1307	1.3	1914	2.9
30	TU	0140	1.1	0819	2.7	1412	1.2	2024	3.0
31	W	0252	1.0	0913	2.9	1505	1.1	2115	3.2

Chart Datum: 2·01 metres below Ordnance Datum (Belfast)

TIME ZONE (UT)
For Summer Time add ONE hour in **non-shaded areas**

NORTHERN IRELAND – BELFAST

LAT 54°36′N LONG 5°55′W

TIMES AND HEIGHTS OF HIGH AND LOW WATERS

SPRING & NEAP TIDES
Dates in red are SPRINGS
Dates in blue are NEAPS

YEAR **2005**

SEPTEMBER

Date	Day	Time	m	Time	m	Time	m	Time	m
1	TH	0342	0.8	0956	3.0	1546	1.0	2157	3.3
2	F	0417	0.7	1032	3.0	1620	0.9	2233	3.4
3	SA	0445	0.7	1103	3.0	1652	0.8	● 2303	3.4
4	SU	0513	0.6	1129	3.0	1723	0.8	2329	3.4
5	M	0541	0.6	1149	3.1	1753	0.8	2355	3.5
6	TU	0609	0.6	1211	3.1	1823	0.8		
7	W	0026	3.5	0637	0.6	1242	3.2	1853	0.7
8	TH	0102	3.5	0709	0.6	1318	3.2	1929	0.8
9	F	0141	3.5	0747	0.7	1358	3.2	2010	0.8
10	SA	0225	3.3	0831	0.8	1444	3.1	2058	1.0
11	SU	0317	3.2	0925	1.0	1541	3.0	◐ 2159	1.1
12	M	0427	3.0	1031	1.2	1654	2.9	2327	1.2
13	TU	0549	2.9	1201	1.3	1818	2.9		
14	W	0116	1.1	0712	2.9	1338	1.2	1937	3.0
15	TH	0224	0.8	0829	3.0	1439	1.0	2042	3.3
16	F	0319	0.5	0924	3.2	1528	0.8	2133	3.5
17	SA	0406	0.3	1011	3.3	1612	0.7	2220	3.6
18	SU	0450	0.2	1055	3.4	1654	0.6	○ 2306	3.7
19	M	0531	0.2	1139	3.4	1735	0.6	2351	3.7
20	TU	0610	0.3	1223	3.4	1815	0.6		
21	W	0037	3.7	0647	0.4	1306	3.4	1855	0.6
22	TH	0121	3.6	0726	0.6	1347	3.4	1937	0.7
23	F	0205	3.4	0806	0.8	1429	3.3	2022	0.8
24	SA	0250	3.2	0852	1.0	1513	3.2	2114	0.9
25	SU	0341	3.0	0949	1.2	1604	3.1	◑ 2225	1.1
26	M	0441	2.8	1112	1.4	1706	2.9	2349	1.2
27	TU	0622	2.6	1230	1.4	1827	2.9		
28	W	0104	1.1	0756	2.7	1338	1.3	1952	3.0
29	TH	0213	1.0	0848	2.8	1434	1.2	2045	3.1
30	F	0304	0.9	0929	2.9	1517	1.0	2126	3.2

OCTOBER

Date	Day	Time	m	Time	m	Time	m	Time	m
1	SA	0340	0.7	1003	3.0	1553	0.9	2200	3.3
2	SU	0411	0.7	1032	3.1	1625	0.9	2228	3.4
3	M	0441	0.6	1055	3.1	1655	0.8	● 2254	3.4
4	TU	0508	0.6	1116	3.2	1724	0.8	2323	3.5
5	W	0535	0.6	1142	3.3	1753	0.7	2357	3.5
6	TH	0605	0.6	1214	3.3	1825	0.7		
7	F	0035	3.5	0640	0.7	1251	3.4	1902	0.8
8	SA	0118	3.5	0720	0.8	1332	3.3	1945	0.8
9	SU	0205	3.3	0807	0.9	1420	3.2	2037	1.0
10	M	0303	3.1	0902	1.1	1518	3.1	◐ 2144	1.1
11	TU	0419	2.9	1012	1.3	1635	3.0	2326	1.1
12	W	0541	2.8	1146	1.4	1803	3.0		
13	TH	0101	1.0	0706	2.9	1321	1.2	1924	3.1
14	F	0207	0.7	0815	3.1	1421	1.0	2026	3.3
15	SA	0259	0.5	0906	3.2	1510	0.9	2116	3.5
16	SU	0345	0.4	0950	3.4	1553	0.7	2201	3.6
17	M	0426	0.4	1033	3.4	1632	0.7	○ 2245	3.7
18	TU	0504	0.4	1114	3.5	1711	0.6	2329	3.7
19	W	0541	0.5	1156	3.5	1750	0.6		
20	TH	0013	3.6	0617	0.7	1237	3.5	1829	0.7
21	F	0056	3.5	0655	0.8	1317	3.5	1911	0.7
22	SA	0139	3.3	0736	1.0	1358	3.5	1956	0.8
23	SU	0224	3.2	0821	1.1	1442	3.4	2048	1.0
24	M	0314	3.0	0916	1.3	1532	3.2	2154	1.1
25	TU	0412	2.8	1031	1.5	1629	3.1	◑ 2311	1.2
26	W	0523	2.6	1147	1.5	1736	3.0		
27	TH	0020	1.1	0710	2.7	1253	1.4	1851	3.0
28	F	0122	1.0	0806	2.8	1351	1.3	1955	3.1
29	SA	0214	0.9	0847	2.9	1439	1.2	2041	3.2
30	SU	0256	0.8	0922	3.1	1518	1.0	2119	3.3
31	M	0332	0.7	0952	3.2	1553	0.9	2152	3.4

NOVEMBER

Date	Day	Time	m	Time	m	Time	m	Time	m
1	TU	0404	0.7	1021	3.3	1625	0.9	2225	3.5
2	W	0434	0.7	1050	3.3	1656	0.8	● 2300	3.5
3	TH	0506	0.7	1121	3.4	1730	0.8	2339	3.5
4	F	0541	0.7	1157	3.5	1807	0.7		
5	SA	0021	3.5	0621	0.8	1238	3.5	1848	0.7
6	SU	0108	3.4	0705	0.9	1322	3.4	1936	0.8
7	M	0201	3.3	0756	1.0	1412	3.3	2032	0.9
8	TU	0303	3.1	0854	1.2	1512	3.2	2144	1.0
9	W	0415	3.0	1004	1.3	1625	3.1	◐ 2314	1.0
10	TH	0533	2.9	1126	1.3	1748	3.1		
11	F	0033	0.9	0647	3.0	1247	1.2	1902	3.2
12	SA	0138	0.7	0749	3.1	1351	1.1	2003	3.4
13	SU	0232	0.6	0841	3.3	1444	0.9	2055	3.5
14	M	0318	0.5	0927	3.4	1530	0.8	2143	3.6
15	TU	0400	0.6	1010	3.5	1612	0.8	2227	3.6
16	W	0439	0.6	1052	3.5	1653	0.7	○ 2311	3.6
17	TH	0517	0.8	1133	3.6	1733	0.7	2354	3.5
18	F	0555	0.9	1214	3.6	1813	0.8		
19	SA	0036	3.4	0634	1.0	1255	3.6	1854	0.8
20	SU	0118	3.2	0715	1.1	1336	3.6	1938	0.9
21	M	0202	3.1	0759	1.2	1419	3.5	2025	0.9
22	TU	0250	3.0	0848	1.3	1505	3.3	2119	1.0
23	W	0343	2.8	0944	1.4	1557	3.2	◑ 2220	1.1
24	TH	0442	2.7	1047	1.4	1654	3.1	2323	1.1
25	F	0546	2.7	1153	1.4	1755	3.0		
26	SA	0023	1.1	0649	2.8	1254	1.4	1854	3.0
27	SU	0118	1.0	0745	2.9	1348	1.3	1949	3.1
28	M	0206	0.9	0831	3.0	1436	1.1	2037	3.2
29	TU	0248	0.8	0913	3.2	1518	1.0	2121	3.3
30	W	0327	0.8	0951	3.3	1557	0.9	2202	3.4

DECEMBER

Date	Day	Time	m	Time	m	Time	m	Time	m
1	TH	0405	0.8	1029	3.4	1636	0.8	● 2244	3.5
2	F	0445	0.8	1108	3.5	1717	0.7	2329	3.5
3	SA	0527	0.8	1149	3.5	1800	0.7		
4	SU	0016	3.5	0612	0.8	1234	3.5	1846	0.6
5	M	0106	3.4	0700	0.9	1320	3.5	1937	0.6
6	TU	0201	3.3	0753	1.0	1411	3.5	2033	0.7
7	W	0300	3.1	0849	1.0	1507	3.4	2138	0.7
8	TH	0405	3.0	0950	1.1	1613	3.3	◐ 2248	0.7
9	F	0513	3.0	1057	1.1	1724	3.3	2358	0.7
10	SA	0618	3.0	1207	1.1	1833	3.3		
11	SU	0103	0.7	0718	3.1	1315	1.1	1936	3.3
12	M	0201	0.7	0813	3.2	1417	1.0	2034	3.4
13	TU	0253	0.7	0904	3.3	1511	0.9	2126	3.4
14	W	0339	0.8	0951	3.4	1559	0.8	2214	3.4
15	TH	0422	0.8	1036	3.5	1644	0.8	○ 2259	3.4
16	F	0502	0.9	1118	3.6	1725	0.8	2341	3.3
17	SA	0541	1.0	1158	3.6	1805	0.8		
18	SU	0021	3.2	0619	1.0	1238	3.6	1842	0.8
19	M	0101	3.1	0657	1.1	1318	3.6	1920	0.8
20	TU	0141	3.0	0736	1.1	1357	3.5	1959	0.8
21	W	0223	3.0	0817	1.1	1438	3.4	2042	0.9
22	TH	0309	2.9	0901	1.2	1521	3.3	2128	0.9
23	F	0359	2.8	0949	1.2	1608	3.2	◑ 2219	1.0
24	SA	0452	2.8	1043	1.3	1701	3.1	2316	1.0
25	SU	0547	2.8	1144	1.3	1758	3.1		
26	M	0016	1.0	0644	2.9	1250	1.3	1857	3.1
27	TU	0116	1.0	0741	3.0	1352	1.2	1957	3.1
28	W	0211	0.9	0836	3.1	1447	1.1	2052	3.2
29	TH	0301	0.8	0925	3.2	1537	0.9	2143	3.3
30	F	0347	0.8	1011	3.3	1623	0.8	2231	3.4
31	SA	0433	0.8	1055	3.4	1709	0.6	● 2320	3.4

Chart Datum: 2·01 metres below Ordnance Datum (Belfast)

9.13.11 LARNE

Antrim **54°51'·20N 05°47'·50W**

CHARTS AC 2198, 1237; Imray C62, C64; Irish OS 9

TIDES +0005 Dover; ML 1·6; Duration 0620; Zone 0 (UT)

Standard Port BELFAST (⟵)

Times				**Height (metres)**			
High Water		Low Water		MHWS	MHWN	MLWN	MLWS
0100	0700	0000	0600	3·5	3·0	1·1	0·4
1300	1900	1200	1800				
Differences LARNE							
+0005	0000	+0010	–0005	–0·7	–0·5	–0·3	0·0
RED BAY							
+0022	–0010	+0007	–0017	–1·9	–1·5	–0·8	–0·2
CUSHENDUN BAY							
+0010	–0030	0000	–0025	–1·7	–1·5	–0·6	–0·2

SHELTER Secure shelter in Larne Lough or ⚓ overnight outside hbr in Brown's Bay (E of Barr Pt) in 2–4m. Hbr can be entered H24 in any conditions. Larne is a busy commercial and ferry port; W side is commercial until Curran Pt where there are two YCs with congested moorings. ⚓ S of Ballylumford Power Stn. No AB available for visitors. Yachts should not berth on any commercial quays, inc Castle Quay, without HM's permission. Boat Hbr (0·6m) 2ca S of Ferris Pt only for shoal draft craft.

NAVIGATION WPT 54°51'·70N 05°47'·47W, 184° to front ldg lt, 2·1M. Beware Hunter Rk 2M NE of hbr ent. Magnetic anomalies exist near Hunter Rk and between it and the mainland. Inside the narrow ent, the recommended chan is close to the E shore. Tide in the ent runs at up to 3½kn.

LIGHTS AND MARKS No1 SHM Q G 1½ca off chartlet N edge; Ldg lts 184°, Oc 4s 6/14m 12M, synch and vis 179°-189°; W ◊ with R stripes. Chaine Tr and fairway lts as chartlet. Note: Many shore lts on W side of ent may be mistaken for nav lts.

R/T VHF Ch 14 11 16 *Larne Port Control.* Traffic, weather and tidal info available on Ch 14.

TELEPHONE (Dial code 02828) HM 872100 📠 872209; MRSC 9146 3933; Pilot 273785; Marinecall 09066 526249; Dr 275331; Police 272266.

FACILITIES Pier ☎ 27 9221, M, L, FW, C (32 ton); **E Antrim Boat Club** ☎ 277204, Visitors should pre-contact Sec'y for advice on moorings; Slip, L, 🛒, FW, Bar; **Services:** D, Gas, ⚒, El. **Town** EC Tues; P & D (delivered, tidal), CH, 🛒, R, Bar, ✉, Ⓑ, ⇌, Ferry to Cairnryan and Stranraer, ✈ (Belfast City and Belfast/Aldergrove).

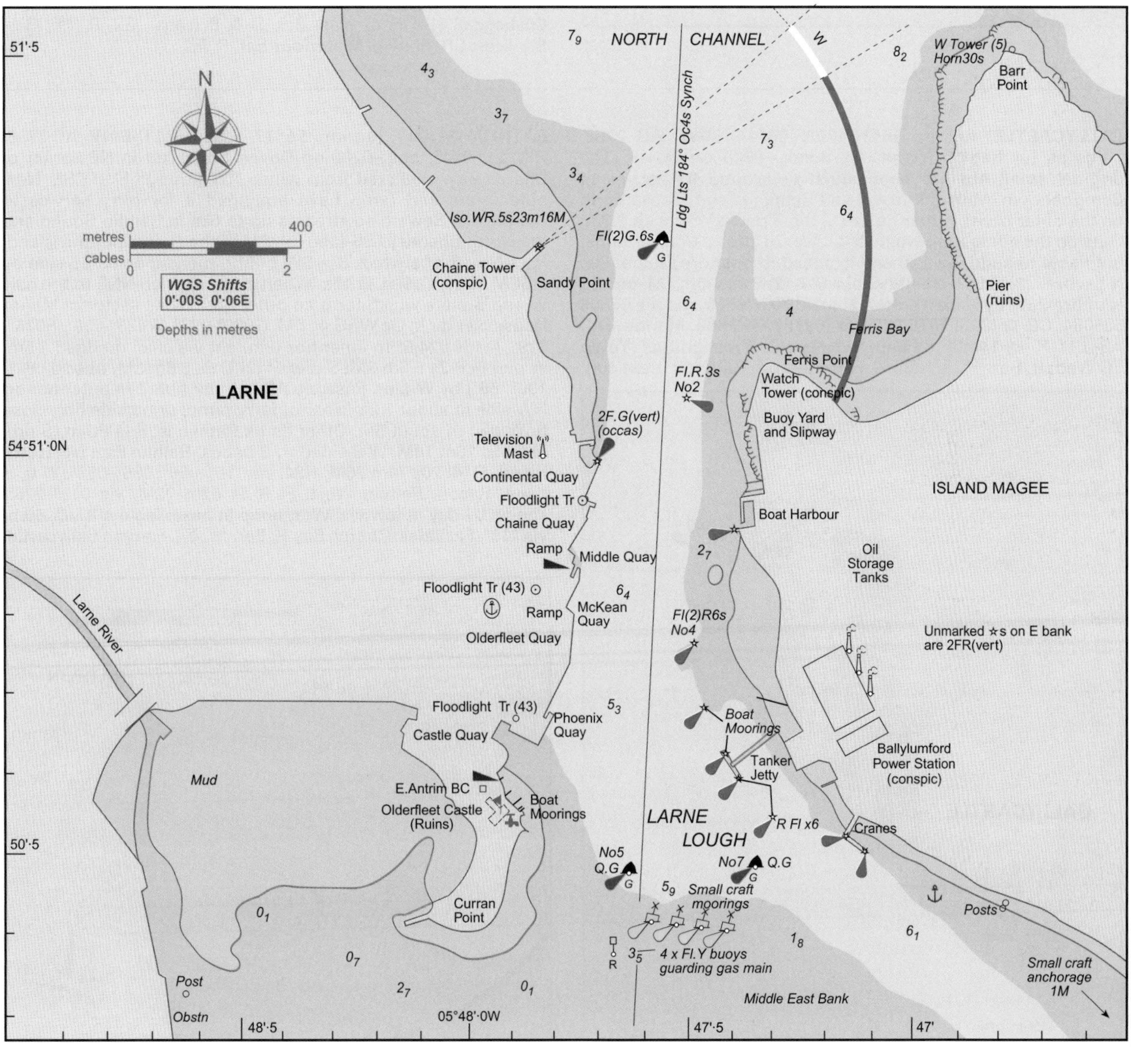
NORTH CHANNEL
W Tower (5)
Horn30s
Barr Point
Iso.WR.5s23m16M
Fl(2)G.6s
G
Ldg Lts 184° Oc4s Synch
metres
cables
400
WGS Shifts
0'·00S 0'·06E
Depths in metres
Chaine Tower
(conspic)
Sandy Point
Pier
(ruins)
Ferris Bay
Ferris Point
Watch Tower (conspic)
Buoy Yard and Slipway
Fl.R.3s
No2
LARNE
2F.G(vert)
(occas)
Television Mast
Continental Quay
Floodlight Tr
Chaine Quay
Boat Harbour
ISLAND MAGEE
Ramp
Middle Quay
Oil Storage Tanks
Floodlight Tr (43)
Ramp
McKean Quay
Olderfleet Quay
Fl(2)R6s
No4
Unmarked ✶s on E bank are 2FR(vert)
Larne River
Floodlight Tr (43)
Phoenix Quay
Castle Quay
Boat Moorings
Tanker Jetty
Ballylumford Power Station (conspic)
Mud
E.Antrim BC
Olderfleet Castle (Ruins)
Boat Moorings
LARNE LOUGH
R Fl x6
Cranes
No5
Q.G
No7
Q.G
Small craft moorings
Curran Point
Posts
4 x Fl.Y buoys guarding gas main
Small craft anchorage 1M
Post
Obstn
Middle East Bank
51'·5
54°51'·0N
50'·5
48'·5
05°48'·0W
47'·5
47'

SIGNIFICANT HARBOURS AND ANCHORAGES BETWEEN LARNE AND PORTRUSH

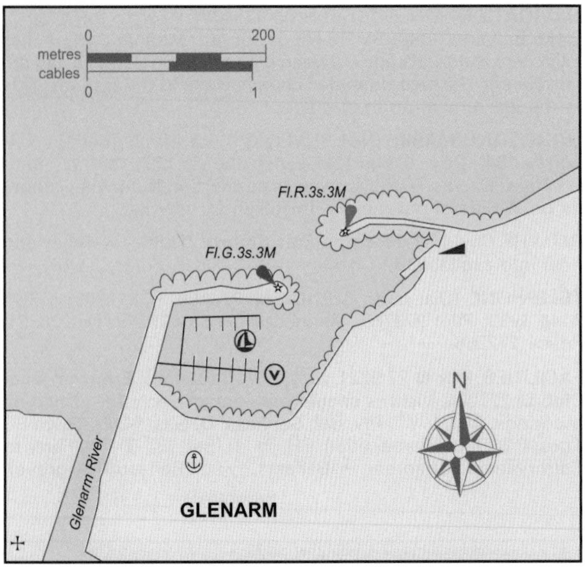
0
200
metres
cables
0
1
Fl.R.3s.3M
Fl.G.3s.3M
N
Glenarm River
GLENARM

GLENARM, Antrim, **54°58′N 05°57′W**. (see chartlet left) AC 2198. HW +0006 on Dover, +0005 on Belfast; HW –1·6m on Belfast; ML no data; Duration 0625. Good shelter in marina. Hbr ent lts Q.G.3s3M and Q.R.3s3M. HM and Marina ☎ 07703 606763. 60+30Ⓥ in 4-6m, £1.00, FW, D (by road tanker), ⛽. **Village** 🛒, P (cans).

CARNLOUGH HARBOUR, Antrim, **54°59′·87N 05°59′·20W**. AC 2198. HW +0006 on Dover, +0005 on Belfast; HW –1·6m on Belfast; ML no data; Duration 0625. Good shelter, except in SE gales; do not enter in fresh/strong onshore winds. Entrance shoaling due to build up of kelp, minimum depth 1m (2004). Ldg marks 310°, Y ▽s on B/W posts. N pier lt, Fl G 3s 4m 5M; S pier Fl R 3s 6m 5M, both lts on B/W columns. Beware fish farms in the bay marked by lt buoys (unreliable); and rks which cover at HW on either side of ent. Small hbr used by yachts and small FVs; visitors welcome. HM ☎ (Mobile) 07703 606763. Facilities: **Quay** AB £1, AC (see HM),D (by arrangement), FW, Slip. **Town** P (cans), Gas, Gaz, ✉, R, 🛒, Bar, ♿.

RED BAY, Antrim, **55°03′·91N 06°03′·13W**. AC 2199. HW +0010 on Dover; ML 1·1m; Duration 0625. See 9.13.11. Good holding, but open to E winds. Beware rks, 2 ruined piers W of Garron Pt and fish farms, marked by lt buoys, on S side of bay, approx ½M from shore. Glenariff pier has lt Fl 3s 10m 5M. In S and E winds ⚓ 2ca off W stone arch near hd of bay in approx 3·5m; in N or W winds ⚓ S of small pier in 2 – 5m, ½M NE of Waterfoot village. Facilities: **Cushendall** (1M N of pier) Bar, D & P (cans), ✉, R, 🛒, Gas; **Services:** CH, El, Slip. **Waterfoot** Bar, R, ✉.

BALLYCASTLE, Antrim, **55°12'·50N 06°14'·30W**. AC 2798. Tides as for Rathlin Island; ML 0·8m; –0320 on Dover. The original small hbr has been much developed for ferries to Campbeltown (Mull of Kintyre) and Rathlin Island. These berth on the outer bkwtr. A marina lies in the S part of hbr with 3·2m. Outside the hbr is a fair weather ⚓, clear of strong tidal streams, but liable to sudden swell and exposed to onshore winds. Lts: N bkwtr Fl (3) G 6s 6·5m 6M; S bkwtr Fl (2) R 4s 4·6m 1M, obsc'd N of brg 261° by N bkwtr. HM ☎ (028) 2076 8525, mobile 07803 505084; CG ☎ (028) 2076 2226; Ⓗ (028) 2076 2666. **Marina**: (74) AB, £11.75 <9·14m, E, L, Slip. **Services:** D, P (cans), Gas. **Town** EC Wed; R, Bar, 🛒, ✉, Ⓑ, ♿. Ferry to/from Rathlin I (next col).

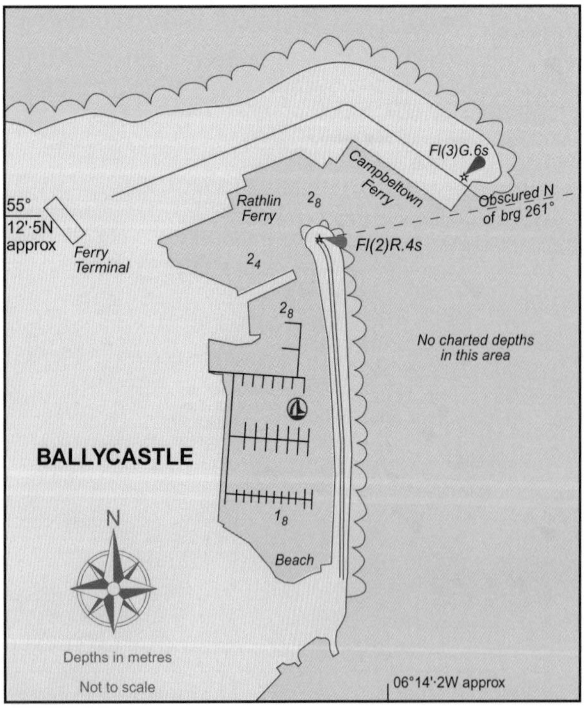
55° 12'·5N approx
Ferry Terminal
Rathlin Ferry
2_8
Campbeltown Ferry
Fl(3)G.6s
Obscured N of brg 261°
Fl(2)R.4s
2_4
2_8
No charted depths in this area
BALLYCASTLE
1_8
Beach
N
Depths in metres
Not to scale
06°14'·2W approx

RATHLIN ISLAND, Antrim, **55°17'·52N 06°11'·60W**. AC 2798. HW sp –0445, nps –0200 on Dover. Small hbr in NE corner of Church Bay, sheltered from winds NW through E to SSE. New outer piers and ramp have equipped it for ferry service to Ballycastle. Beware sp streams up to 6kn in Rathlin Sound and the North Channel TSS (above), 2M to the N and E of the island. Pass N or E of a wreck 6ca SW of hbr, marked on its SE side by a SCM buoy, Q(6)+L Fl 15s. When clear, appr on NNE to the new W and S piers which form an outer hbr. White sector of Manor House pier dir lt, Oc WRG 4s 5M, G020°-023°, W023°-026°, R026°-029°, leads 024·5° to inner hbr (2m) ent via chan dredged 3·5m. W pier Fl R 2s 5·3m 3M; S pier Fl (2) G 6s 3·5m 3M, obsc'd 062°-130° (68°) by W pier. Possible AB in inner hbr. ⚓ in outer hbr on NW side in about 1.2m clear of ferry ramp; or outside hbr, close to W pier in about 5m. Other lts on Rathlin Is: Rue Point (S tip), Fl (2) 5s 16m 14M, W 8-sided tr, B bands. Rathlin East (Altacarry Head), Fl (4) 20s 74m 26M, H24, vis 110°–006°, 036°–058°, W tr, B band, Racon. Rathlin West, Fl R 5s 62m 22M, vis 015°–225°, shown by day in low vis, W tr, lamp at base; fog det lt VQ, 69m, vis 119°. **Facilities:** Church Bay R, Bar, 🛒, ✉. Ferry to Ballycastle.

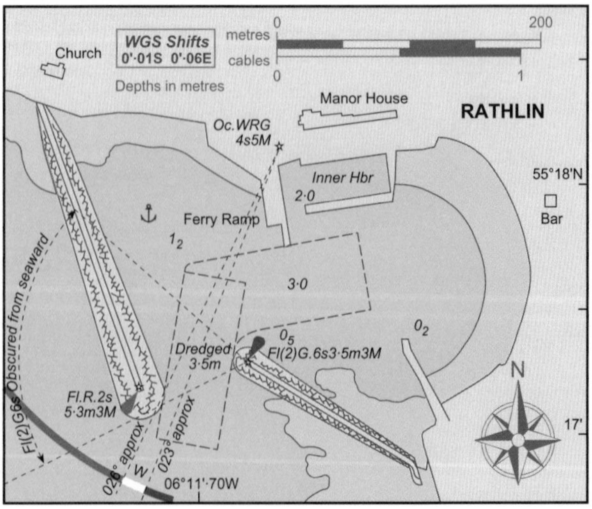
WGS Shifts
0'·01S 0'·06E
Church
metres
cables
0
200
0
1
Depths in metres
Manor House
RATHLIN
Oc.WRG
4s5M
Inner Hbr
2·0
55°18'N
Bar
Ferry Ramp
1_2
3·0
0_5
0_2
Fl(2)G.6s3·5m3M
Dredged
3·5m
Fl.R.2s
5·3m3M
Obscured from seaward
Fl(2)G6s
023° approx
026° approx
W
06°11'·70W
17'
N

9.13.12 TIDAL STREAMS AROUND RATHLIN ISLAND

North Ireland 9.13.3
North Irish Sea 9.10.3
Off Mull of Kintyre 9.9.12
SW Scotland 9.9.3
South Ireland 9.12.3

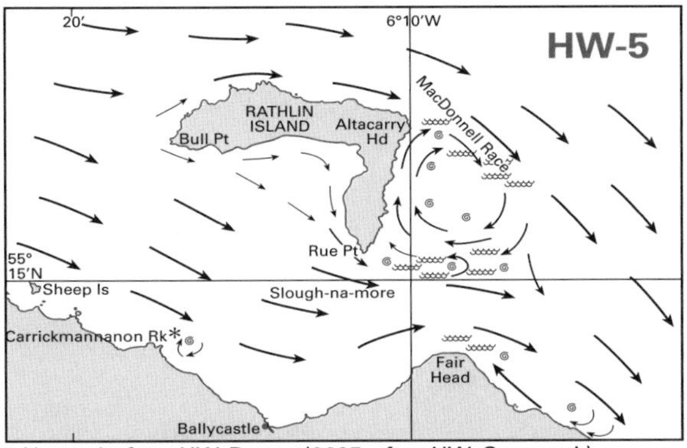
HW-5
20′
6°10′W
55°
15′N
RATHLIN
ISLAND
Bull Pt
Altacarry
Hd
MacDonnell Race
Rue Pt
Sheep Is
Slough-na-more
Carrickmannanon Rk
Fair
Head
Ballycastle
5 Hours before HW Dover (0605 after HW Greenock)

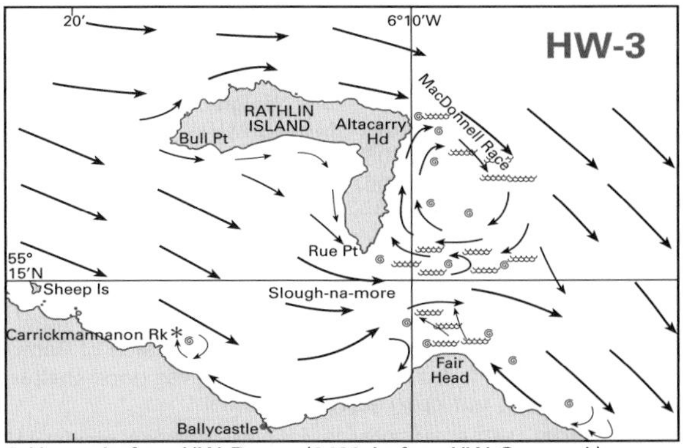
HW-3
20′
6°10′W
55°
15′N
RATHLIN
ISLAND
Bull Pt
Altacarry
Hd
MacDonnell Race
Rue Pt
Sheep Is
Slough-na-more
Carrickmannanon Rk
Fair
Head
Ballycastle
3 Hours before HW Dover (0420 before HW Greenock)

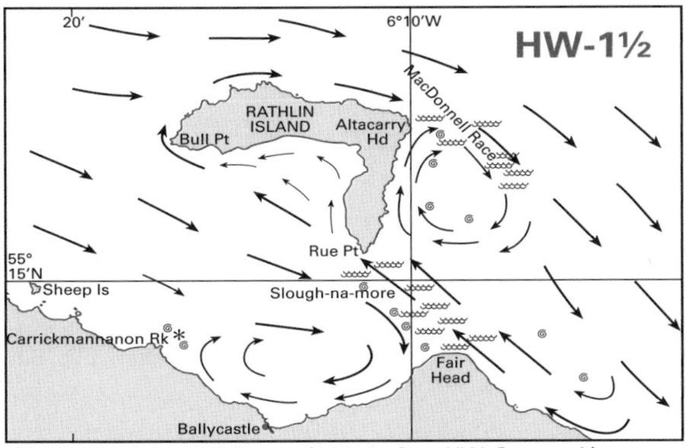
HW-1½
20′
6°10′W
55°
15′N
RATHLIN
ISLAND
Bull Pt
Altacarry
Hd
MacDonnell Race
Rue Pt
Sheep Is
Slough-na-more
Carrickmannanon Rk
Fair
Head
Ballycastle
1½ Hours before HW Dover (0250 before HW Greenock)

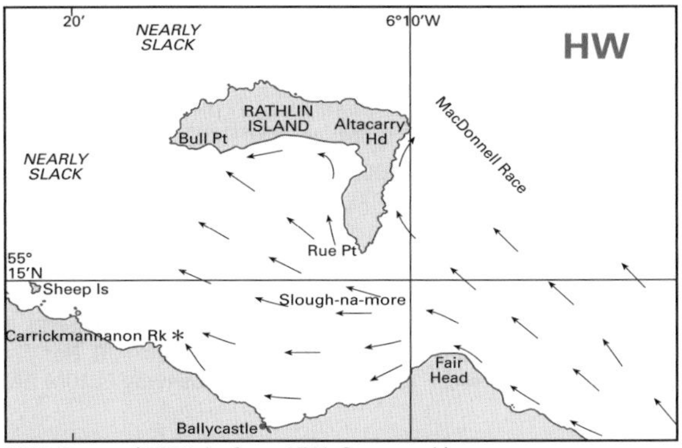
HW
20′
6°10′W
NEARLY
SLACK
NEARLY
SLACK
55°
15′N
RATHLIN
ISLAND
Bull Pt
Altacarry
Hd
MacDonnell Race
Rue Pt
Sheep Is
Slough-na-more
Carrickmannanon Rk
Fair
Head
Ballycastle
HW Dover (0120 before HW Greenock)

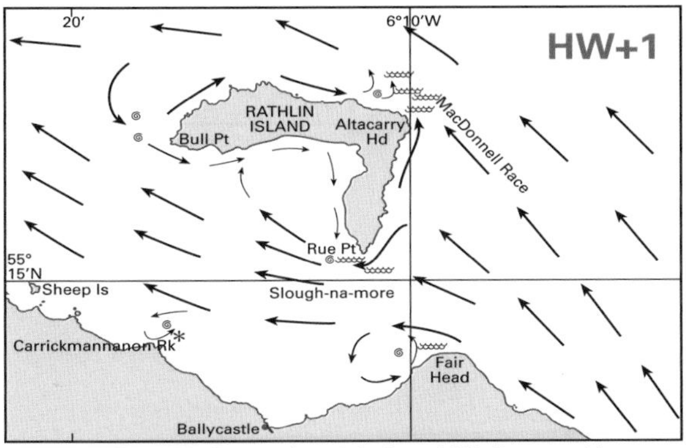
HW+1
20′
6°10′W
55°
15′N
RATHLIN
ISLAND
Bull Pt
Altacarry
Hd
MacDonnell Race
Rue Pt
Sheep Is
Slough-na-more
Carrickmannanon Rk
Fair
Head
Ballycastle
1 Hour after HW Dover (0020 before HW Greenock)

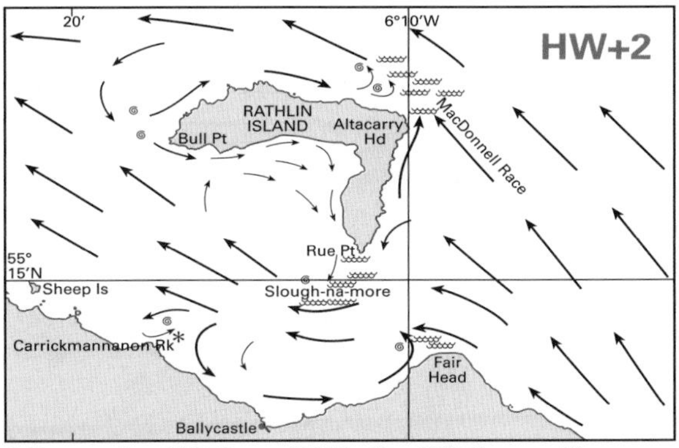
HW+2
20′
6°10′W
55°
15′N
RATHLIN
ISLAND
Bull Pt
Altacarry
Hd
MacDonnell Race
Rue Pt
Sheep Is
Slough-na-more
Carrickmannanon Rk
Fair
Head
Ballycastle
2 Hours after HW Dover (0040 after HW Greenock)

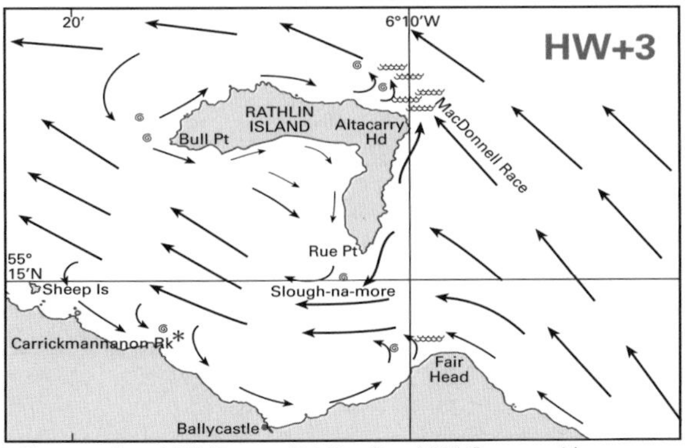
HW+3
20′
6°10′W
55°
15′N
RATHLIN
ISLAND
Bull Pt
Altacarry
Hd
MacDonnell Race
Rue Pt
Sheep Is
Slough-na-more
Carrickmannanon Rk
Fair
Head
Ballycastle
3 Hours after HW Dover (0140 after HW Greenock)

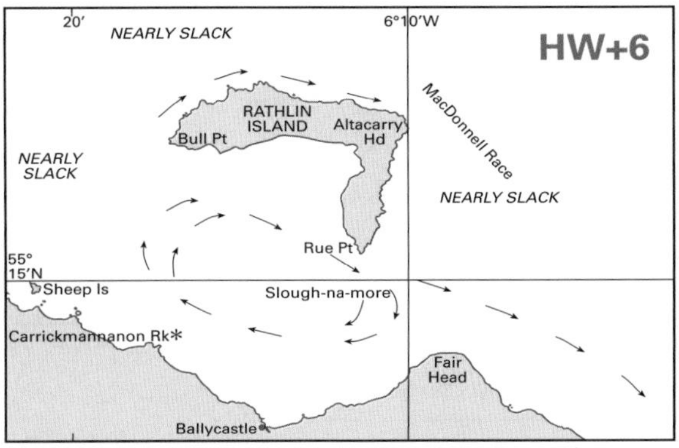
HW+6
20′
6°10′W
NEARLY SLACK
NEARLY
SLACK
NEARLY SLACK
55°
15′N
RATHLIN
ISLAND
Bull Pt
Altacarry
Hd
MacDonnell Race
Rue Pt
Sheep Is
Slough-na-more
Carrickmannanon Rk
Fair
Head
Ballycastle
6 Hours after HW Dover (0440 after HW Greenock)

13

9.13.13 PORTRUSH

Antrim **55°12'·34N 06°39'·49W**

CHARTS AC 2798, 2499, 49; Imray C53, C64; Irish OS 4

TIDES –0400 Dover; ML 1·1; Duration 0610; Zone 0 (UT)

Standard Port BELFAST (⟵)

Times				Height (metres)			
High Water		Low Water		MHWS	MHWN	MLWN	MLWS
0100	0700	0000	0600	3·5	3·0	1·1	0·4
1300	1900	1200	1800				
Differences PORTRUSH							
–0433		–0433		–1·6	–1·6	–0·3	0·0

SHELTER Good in hbr, except in strong NW/N winds. Berth on N pier or on pontoon at NE end of it and see HM. A Ⓥ may be available, but very congested in season. ⚓ on E side of Ramore Hd in Skerries Roads 1ca S of Large Skerrie gives good shelter in most conditions, but open to NW sea/swell.

NAVIGATION WPT 55°13′·00N 06°41′·00W, 128° to N pier lt, 1·1M. Ent with on-shore winds >F 4 is difficult. Beware submerged bkwtr projecting 20m SW from N pier. Depth is 2·8m in hbr entrance.

LIGHTS AND MARKS Ldg lts 028° (occas, for LB use) both FR 6/8m 1M; R △ on metal bn and metal mast. N pier Fl R 3s 6m 3M; vis 220°-160°. S pier Fl G 3s 6m 3M; vis 220°-100°.

R/T VHF Ch 12 16 (0900-1700LT, Mon-Fri; extended evening hrs June-Sept; Sat-Sun: 0900–1700, June-Sept only).

TELEPHONE (Dial code 028) HM 7082 2307; MRSC 9146 3933; Marinecall 09066 526249; Police 7034 4122; Dr 7082 3767; Ⓗ 7034 4177.

FACILITIES Hbr AB £12, D, FW, M, Slip (launching £3), Gas, El, Ⓔ, ♿; Portrush YC ☎ 7082 3932, Bar; Town EC Wed; 🛒, R, Bar, ⊡, D & P (cans), ✉, Ⓑ, ⇌, ✈ (Belfast). Giant's Causeway is 10M ENE.

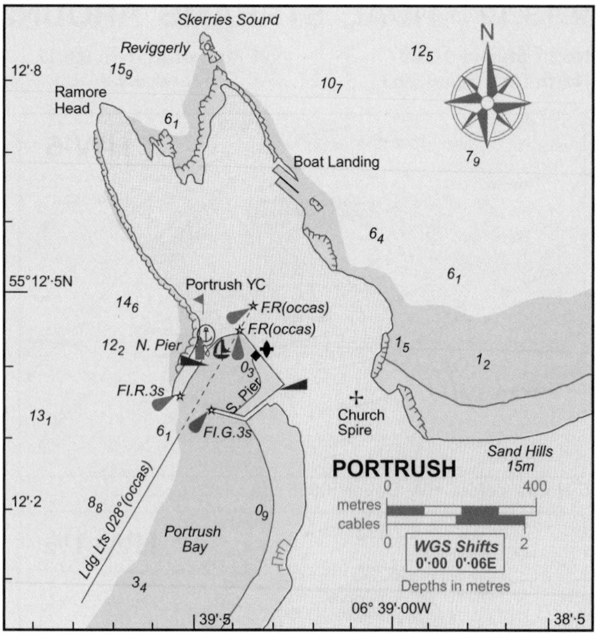
Skerries Sound
Reviggerly
Ramore Head
Boat Landing
Portrush YC
F.R(occas)
F.R(occas)
N. Pier
S. Pier
Fl.R.3s
Fl.G.3s
Church Spire
Ldg Lts 028°(occas)
Portrush Bay
PORTRUSH
Sand Hills 15m
metres
cables
WGS Shifts
0'·00 0'·06E
Depths in metres
55°12'·5N
06° 39'·00W

PORTSTEWART, Antrim, **55°11'·21N 06°43'·21W**. AC 49. Tides as for Portrush. A tiny hbr 1·1ca S of Portstewart Pt lt, Oc R 10s 21m 5M, vis 040°–220°, obscd in final appr. A temp, fair weather berth (£7) at S end of inner basin in 0·8 – 1·7m; the very narrow ent is open to SW wind and swell. Beware salmon nets and rks close to S bkwtr. Facilities: EC Thurs; FW, Gas, D (tanker), Slip, Bar, 🛒, R, handy shops.

9.13.14 RIVER BANN and COLERAINE

Londonderry/Antrim **55°10'·32N 06°46'·35W**

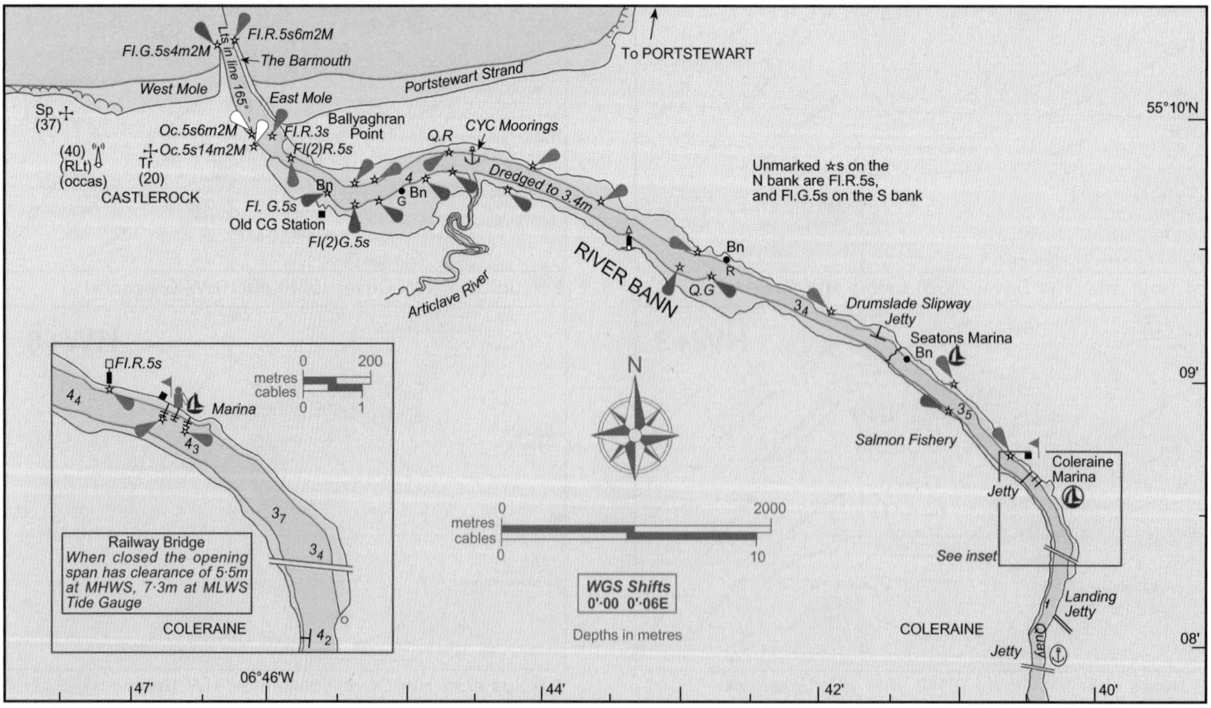
Fl.R.5s6m2M
Fl.G.5s4m2M
The Barmouth
Lts in line 165°
To PORTSTEWART
West Mole
East Mole
Portstewart Strand
Oc.5s6m2M
Oc.5s14m2M
Fl.R.3s
Fl(2)R.5s
Ballyaghran Point
Q.R
CYC Moorings
CASTLEROCK
Fl. G.5s
Old CG Station
Fl(2)G.5s
Dredged to 3·4m
Articlave River
Unmarked ☆s on the N bank are Fl.R.5s, and Fl.G.5s on the S bank
RIVER BANN
Q.G
Drumslade Slipway
Jetty
Seatons Marina
Salmon Fishery
Coleraine Marina
See inset
Landing Jetty
Quay
COLERAINE
Fl.R.5s
Marina
Railway Bridge
When closed the opening span has clearance of 5·5m at MHWS, 7·3m at MLWS
Tide Gauge
WGS Shifts
0'·00 0'·06E
Depths in metres
55°10'N
06°46'W

RIVER BANN *continued*

CHARTS AC 2723, 2798, 2499; Imray C64; Irish OS 4

TIDES –0345 Dover (Coleraine); ML 1·1; Duration 0540; Zone 0 (UT)

Standard Port BELFAST (⟵)

Times				Height (metres)			
High Water		Low Water		MHWS	MHWN	MLWN	MLWS
0100	0700	0000	0600	3·5	3·0	1·1	0·4
1300	1900	1200	1800				
Differences COLERAINE							
–0403		–0403		–1·3	–1·2	–0·2	0·0

SHELTER Good, once inside the river ent (The Barmouth) between 2 training walls, extending 2ca N from the beaches. Do not try to enter in strong on-shore winds or when swell breaks on the pierheads. If in doubt call Coleraine Hbr Radio or ring HM. ⚓ upstream of old CG stn, or berth at Seaton's or Coleraine marinas, 3½M & 4½M from ent, on NE bank.

NAVIGATION WPT 55°11'·00N, 06°46'·65W, 165° to ent, 0·72M. Appr from E of N to bring ldg lts into line at bkwtr ends. The sand bar is constantly moving but ent is dredged to approx 3·5m. Beware salmon nets across the width of the river at 2M or 4M above ent, May to July. Also beware commercial traffic.

LIGHTS AND MARKS Ldg lts 165°, both Oc 5s 6/14m 2M, front on W pyramidal metal tr; rear W □ tr. Portstewart Pt, Oc R 10s, is 2M ENE.

R/T Coleraine Hbr Radio Ch 12 (Mon-Fri: HO and when vessel due). Coleraine Marina Ch M.

TELEPHONE (Dial code 028) HM 7034 2012, ⊜ 7035 2000; MRSC 9146 3933; Marinecall 09066 526249; Rly Bridge 7034 2403; Police 7034 4122; Ⓗ 7034 4177; Dr 7034 4831.

FACILITIES Seatons Marina ☎ 7083 2086 mobile 07733 100915, BH (14 ton), Slip(launching £3). **Coleraine Hbr** ☎ 7034 2012, BH (35 ton); **Coleraine (Borough Council) Marina** (45+15 Ⓥ), ☎ 7034 4768, £13, Slip, D, R, BH (15 ton); **Coleraine YC** ☎ 7034 4503, Bar, M; **Services**: Gas, Kos, El, Ⓔ. **Town** EC Thurs; P & D (cans), 🛒, R, ✉, Ⓑ, ⇌, ✈ (Belfast).

9.13.15 LOUGH FOYLE

Londonderry (to SE)/Donegal (to NW) **55°14'N 06°54W**

CHARTS AC 2723, 2798, 2499; Imray C53, C64; Irish OS 3, 4, 7

TIDES
Warren Point: –0430 Dover
Moville: –0350 Dover; –0055 Londonderry; –0400 Belfast
Culmore Point: –0025 Londonderry
Londonderry: –0255 Dover
ML 1·6; Duration 0615; Zone 0 (UT)

Standard Port GALWAY (⟵)

Times				Height (metres)			
High Water		Low Water		MHWS	MHWN	MLWN	MLWS
0200	0900	0200	0800	5·1	3·9	2·0	0·6
1400	2100	1400	2000				
Differences LONDONDERRY							
+0254	+0319	+0322	+0321	–2·4	–1·8	–0·8	–0·1
INISHTRAHULL							
+0100	+0100	+0115	+0200	–1·8	–1·4	–0·4	–0·2
PORTMORE							
+0120	+0120	+0135	+0135	–1·3	–1·1	–0·4	–0·1
TRAWBREAGA BAY							
+0115	+0059	+0109	+0125	–1·1	–0·8	No data	

SHELTER The SE side of the Lough is low lying and shallow. The NW rises steeply and has several village hbrs between the ent and Londonderry (often referred to as Derry).
White Bay: close N of Dunagree Point is a good ⚓ on passage.
Greencastle: a busy fishing hbr, open to swell in winds SW to E. Only advised for yachts in emergency.
Moville: the pier, with 1·5m at the end, is near the village (shops closed all day Wed), but is much damaged. ⚓ outside hbr is exposed; inside hbr for shoal draft only. 8 Y Ⓥs are about 600m up-stream.
Carrickarory: pier/quay is condemned as unsafe. ⚓ in bay is sheltered in winds from SW to NNW.
Culmore Bay: Complete shelter. ⚓ 1½ca W of Culmore Pt in pleasant cove, 4M from Londonderry.
Londonderry: Little used by yachts, although commercial operations have been transferred to new facilities at Lisahally (55°02'·6N 07°15'·6W). AB on non-commercial quay below Guildhall or ⚓ close below Craigavon Bridge clearance 1·7m.

NAVIGATION WPT Tuns PHM buoy, Fl R 3s, 55°14'·00N 06°53'·49W, 235° to Warren Pt lt, 2·5M. The Tuns bank lies 3M NE of Magilligan Pt and may dry. The main or N Chan, ¾M wide, runs NW of The Tuns; a lesser chan, min depth 4m, runs 3ca off shore around NE side of Magilligan Pt. Beware commercial traffic. Foyle Bridge at Rosses Pt has 32m clearance. In June and July the chan is at times obstructed by salmon nets at night. N Chan tides reach 3½kn, and up-river the ebb runs up to 6kn.

LIGHTS AND MARKS Inishowen Fl (2) WRG 10s 28m 18/14M; W tr, 2 B bands; vis G197°–211°, W211°–249°, R249°–000°; Horn (2) 30s. Warren Pt Fl 1·5s 9m 10M; W tr, G abutment; vis 232°–061°. Magilligan Pt QR 7m 4M; R structure. The main chan up to Londonderry is very well lit. Foyle Bridge centre FW each side; VQ G on W pier; VQ R on E.

R/T VHF Ch 14 12 16 (H24). Traffic and nav info Ch 14.

TELEPHONE (Dial code 028) HM (at Lisahally) 7186 0555, ⊜ 7186 1168; MRSC 9146 3933; ⊖ 7126 1937 or 9035 8250; Marinecall 09066 526249; Police 7776 6797; Dr 7126 4868; Ⓗ 7034 5171.

FACILITIES (Londonderry) **Hbr Mr** ☎ 7186 0555, M, FW; **Prehen Boat Club** ☎ 7034 3405. **City** P & D (cans), ME, El, 🛒, R, Bar, ✉, Ⓑ, ⇌, ✈. CULDAFF BAY (10M W of Foyle SWM buoy) 6 Y Ⓥs are at 55°18'N 07°09'·1W, off Bunnagee Port.

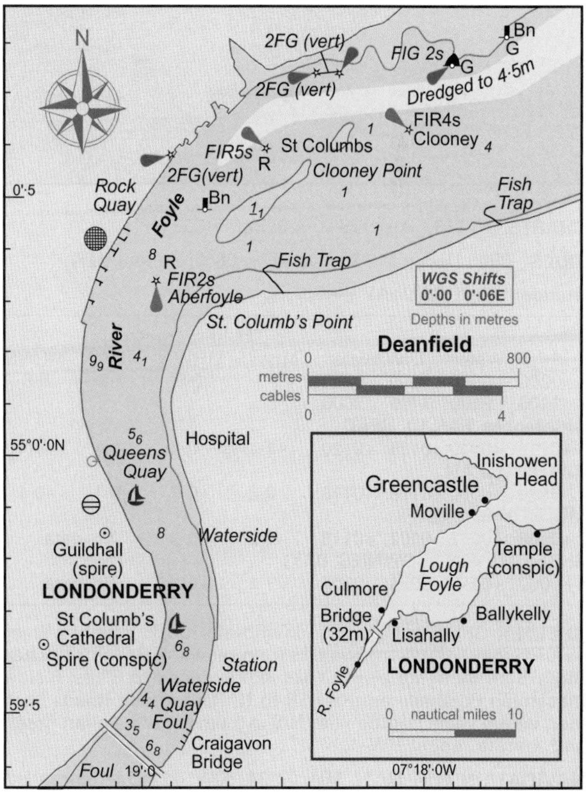
N
2FG (vert)
Fl G 2s
G
Bn
G
2FG (vert)
Dredged to 4·5m
FlR4s
Clooney
St Columbs
R
FlR5s
2FG(vert)
Clooney Point
Rock Quay
Foyle
Bn
Fish Trap
0'·5
R
FlR2s
Aberfoyle
Fish Trap
WGS Shifts
0'·00 0'·06E
St. Columb's Point
Depths in metres
River
Deanfield
metres
cables
Hospital
55°0'·0N
Queens Quay
Waterside
Guildhall (spire)
LONDONDERRY
St Columb's Cathedral Spire (conspic)
Station
Waterside Quay
Foul
59'·5
Craigavon Bridge
Foul
Inishowen Head
Greencastle
Moville
Temple (conspic)
Lough Foyle
Culmore
Bridge (32m)
Ballykelly
Lisahally
LONDONDERRY
R. Foyle
nautical miles
07°18'·0W

9.13.16 LOUGH SWILLY

Donegal **55°17'N 07°34'W**

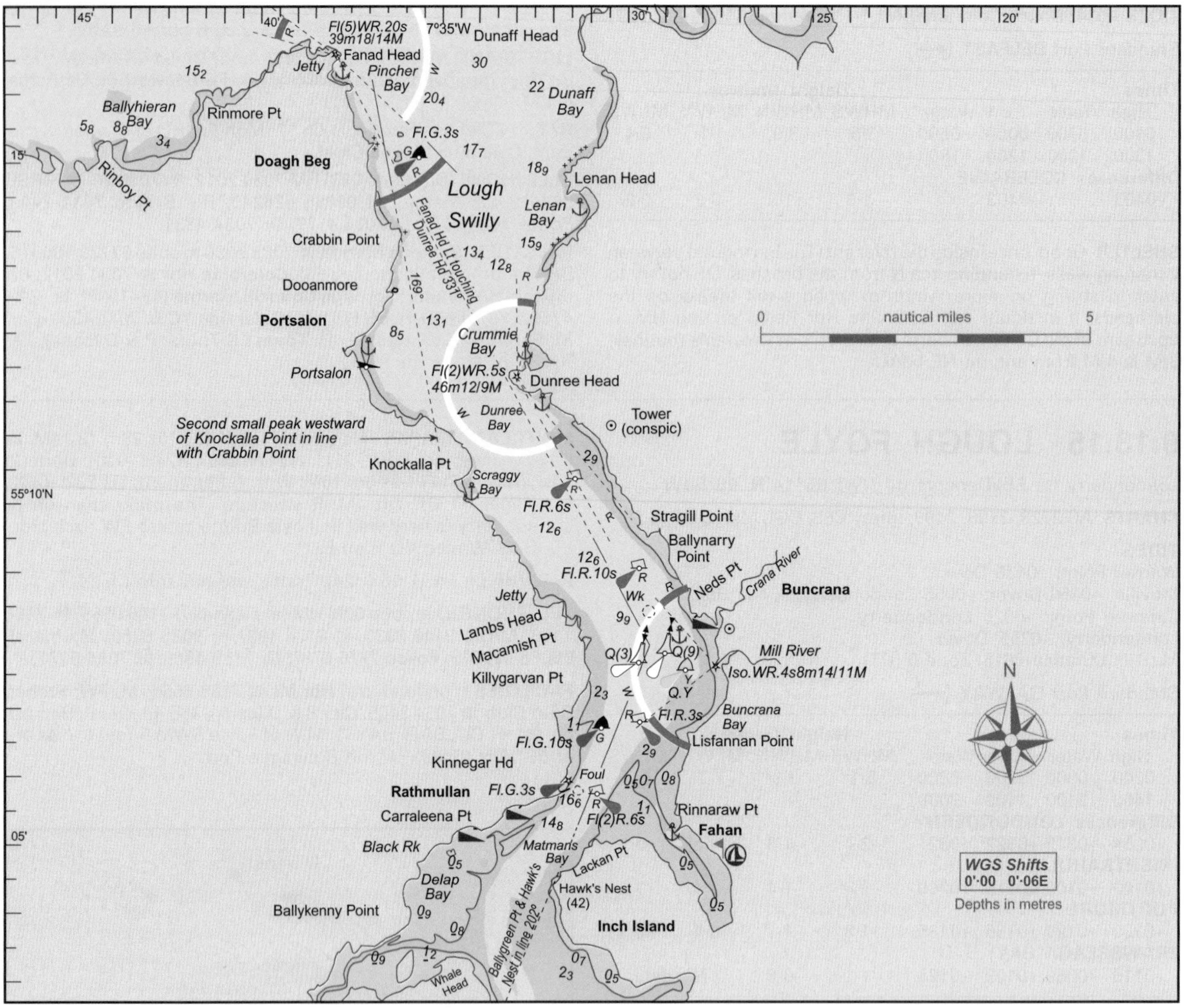
Fl(5)WR.20s 39m18/14M
7°35'W
Dunaff Head
Fanad Head
Jetty
Pincher Bay
30
15₂
Ballyhieran Bay
Rinmore Pt
22 Dunaff Bay
20₄
5₈ 8₈
3₄
Fl.G.3s
Rinboy Pt
Doagh Beg
17₇
18₉
Lenan Head
Lough Swilly
Lenan Bay
Fanad Hd Lt touching Dunree Hd 331°
Crabbin Point
15₉
13₄
12₈
Dooanmore
169°
Portsalon
13₁
8₅
Crummie Bay
Portsalon
Fl(2)WR.5s 46m12/9M
Dunree Head
Dunree Bay
Tower (conspic)
Second small peak westward of Knockalla Point in line with Crabbin Point
Knockalla Pt
2₉
Scraggy Bay
55°10'N
Fl.R.6s
12₆
Stragill Point
Ballynarry Point
12₆
Fl.R.10s
Neds Pt
Crana River
Buncrana
Jetty
Wk
9₉
Lambs Head
Macamish Pt
Mill River
Q(3)
Q(9)
Iso.WR.4s8m14/11M
Killygarvan Pt
2₃
Q.Y
Fl.R.3s
Buncrana Bay
Fl.G.10s
Lisfannan Point
2₉
Kinnegar Hd
Foul
Rathmullan
Fl.G.3s
16₆
14₈
Fl(2)R.6s
Rinnaraw Pt
Carraleena Pt
Fahan
05'
Black Rk
Matmaris Bay
Lackan Pt
Delap Bay
Hawk's Nest (42)
Ballykenny Point
Ballygreen Pt & Hawk's Nest in line 202°
Inch Island
Whale Head
0 nautical miles 5
N
WGS Shifts
0'·00 0'·06E
Depths in metres
45'
40'
30'
25'
20'
15'

CHARTS AC 2697; Irish OS 2, 3, 6; Imray C53

TIDES –0500 Dover; ML 2·3; Duration 0605; Zone 0 (UT)

Standard Port GALWAY (⟶)

Times				Height (metres)			
High Water		Low Water		MHWS	MHWN	MLWN	MLWS
0200	0900	0200	0800	5·1	3·9	2·0	0·6
1400	2100	1400	2000				
Differences FANAD HEAD							
+0115	+0040	+0125	+0120	–1·1	–0·9	–0·5	–0·1
RATHMULLAN							
+0125	+0050	+0126	+0118	–0·8	–0·7	–0·1	–0·1
MULROY BAY (BAR)							
+0108	+0052	+0102	+0118	–1·2	–1·0	No data	
SHEEP HAVEN (DOWNIES BAY)							
+0057	+0043	+0053	+0107	–1·1	–0·9	No data	

SHELTER Good, but beware downdrafts on E side. ⚓s N of 55°05'N may suffer from swell. ⚓s from seaward: Ballymastocher Bay where there are also 8 Y 🅐s, but exposed to E'lies; inside Macamish Pt, sheltered from SE to N; Rathmullan Roads N of pier, where yacht pontoon lies N/S in 3·6m MLWS; Fahan Creek and marina ent at HW–1.

NAVIGATION WPT 55°17'·50N 07°34'·50W, 172° to Dunree Hd lt, 5·7M. Ent is easy and main chan is well lit/buoyed. Beware: off W shore Swilly More Rks, Kinnegar Spit and Strand; off E shore Colpagh Rks and Inch Flats. These dangers are buoyed, as is Fahan Creek. There are mussel lines (badly marked) N of a line Rathmullen to Lisfannon Pt and a salmon farm S of Scraggy Bay (☎ 074 50172/59071 for permission to use their pier).

LIGHTS AND MARKS Fanad Hd lt, Fl (5) WR 20s 39m 18/14M, touching Dunree Hd lt, Fl (2) WR 5s 46m 12/9M, leads 151° into the Lough. Thence Ballygreen Pt and Hawk's Nest in line at 202°.

R/T None.

TELEPHONE (Dial codes: both sides of lough 074) Rathmullan Pontoon 9158131, 9158315 (eves); MRCC 9370243; Police W side 9153114(Milford) and 9361555(Buncrana); Dr 9158416 (Rathmullan) and 9363611 (Buncrana).

FACILITIES **Rathmullan** Pontoon berth €15.00/day, €30.00 overnight, FW, slip. Services: 🗟, R, Hotel, Bar, D & P (cans), Kos, 🛒, ✉, EC Wed. **Ramelton** AB (drying), BY ☎ 9151082, Bar, R, D & P (cans), FW, Kos, 🛒, ✉. **Fahan Marina** ☎ 9368752,145 + 4🅥, €2/m, FW, Showers, WC, ⌖; **Fahan**, Slip, FW, Bar, R, ✉, **Lough Swilly YC** www.loughswillyyc.com. Services (1M SE): 🛒, D & P (cans), ⇄, ✈ (Londonderry 10M bus/taxi). **Buncrana** AB (congested), Hotel, R, Bar, Ⓑ, ✉, 🛒, 🗟, D & P (cans), Kos.

OTHER HARBOURS AND ANCHORAGES IN DONEGAL

MULROY BAY, Donegal, **55°15′·30N 07°46′·30W**. AC 2699; HW (bar) –0455 on Dover. See 9.13.16. Beware Limeburner Rk, (marked by NCM buoy, Q, whis) 3M N of ent and the bar which is dangerous in swell or onshore winds. Ent at half flood (not HW); chan lies between Bar Rks and Sessiagh Rks, thence through First, Second and Third Narrows (with strong tides) to Broad Water. HW at the head of the lough is 2¼ hrs later than at the bar. ⚓s: Close SW of Ravedy Is (Fl 3s 9m 3M); Fanny's Bay (2m), excellent; Rosnakill Bay (3·5m) in SE side; Cranford Bay; Milford Port (3 to 4m). Beware power cable 6m, over Moross chan, barring North Water to masted boats. Facilities: **Milford Port** AB, FW, 🛒; **Fanny's Bay** ✉, Shop at Downings village (1M), hotel at Rosepenna (¾M).

SHEEP HAVEN, Donegal, **55°11′·00N 07°51′·00W**. AC 2699. HW –0515 on Dover. See 9.13.16. Bay is 2M wide with many ⚓s, easily accessible in daylight, but exposed to N winds. Beware rks off Rinnafaghla Pt, and further S: Black Rk (6m) and Wherryman Rks, which dry, 1ca off E shore. ⚓ or 8 Y 🅥s in Downies Bay to SE of pier; in Pollcormick inlet close W in 3m; in Ards Bay for excellent shelter, but beware the bar in strong winds. Lts: Portnablahy ldg lts 125°, both Oc 6s 7/12m 2M, B col, W bands; Downies pier hd, Fl R 3s 5m 2M, R post. Facilities: (Downies) EC Wed; 🛒, FW, P (cans 300m), R, Bar; (Portnablahy Bay) 🛒, P (cans), R, Bar.

GWEEDORE HBR/BUNBEG, Donegal, **55°03'·75N 08°18'·87W**. AC 1883. Tides see 9.13.17. Gweedore hbr, the estuary of the R Gweedore, has sheltered ⚓s or temp AB at Bunbeg Quay, usually full of FVs. Apprs via Gola N or S Sounds are not simple especially in poor visibility. N Sound is easier with ldg lts 171°, both Oc 3s 9/13m 2M, B/W bns, on the SE tip of Gola Is. (There are also ⚓s on the S and E sides of Gola Is). E of Bo Is the bar 0·4m has a Fl G 3s and the chan, lying E of Inishinny Is and W of Inishcoole, is marked by a QG and 3 QR. A QG marks ent to Bunbeg. Night ent not advised. Facilities: FW, D at quay; 🛒, ✉, Ⓑ, Bar at village ½M.

BURTONPORT, Donegal, **54°58′·93N 08°26′·60W**. AC 1879, 2792. HW –0525 on Dover; ML 2·0m; Duration 0605. See 9.13.17. Only appr via N Chan. Ent safe in all weathers except NW gales. Hbr very full, no space to ⚓; berth on local boat at pier or go to Rutland Hbr or Aran Roads: 6 Y 🅥s 250m NE of Black Rks, Fl R 3s. Ldg marks/lts: N Chan ldg lts on Inishcoo 119·3°, both Iso 6s 6/11m 1M; front W bn, B band; rear B bn, Y band. Rutland Is ldg lts 138°, both Oc 6s 8/14m 1M; front W bn, B band; rear B bn, Y band. Burtonport ldg lts 068°, both FG 17/23m 1M; front Gy bn, W band; rear Gy bn, Y band. HM ☎ (075) 42155 (43170 home), 📠 (074) 41205; VHF Ch 06, 12, **14**, 16. Facilities: D (just inside pier), FW (root of pier), P (½M inland). **Village** Bar, ✉, R, 🛒, Kos.

INISHKEEL, Donegal, **54°50′·82N 08°26′·50W**. AC 2792. 6 Y 🅥s in Church Pool, 3ca E of Inishkeel. Open to N/NE'lies.

TEELIN HARBOUR, Donegal, **54°37'·50N 08°37'·87W**. AC 2792. Tides as 9.13.17. A possible passage ⚓, mid-way between Rathlin O'Birne and Killybegs. But Hbr is open to S'ly swell and prone to squalls in NW winds. Ent, 1ca wide, is close E of Teelin Pt lt, Fl R 10s, which is hard to see by day. 4 Y 🅥s and ⚓ on E side in 3m to N of pier, or ⚓ on E side near pier. Many moorings and, in the NE, mussel rafts. Facilities: possible FW, D, 🛒 at Carrick, 3M inland.

9.13.17 KILLYBEGS

Donegal **54°36'·90N 08°26'·80W** ❀❀❀◊◊✿

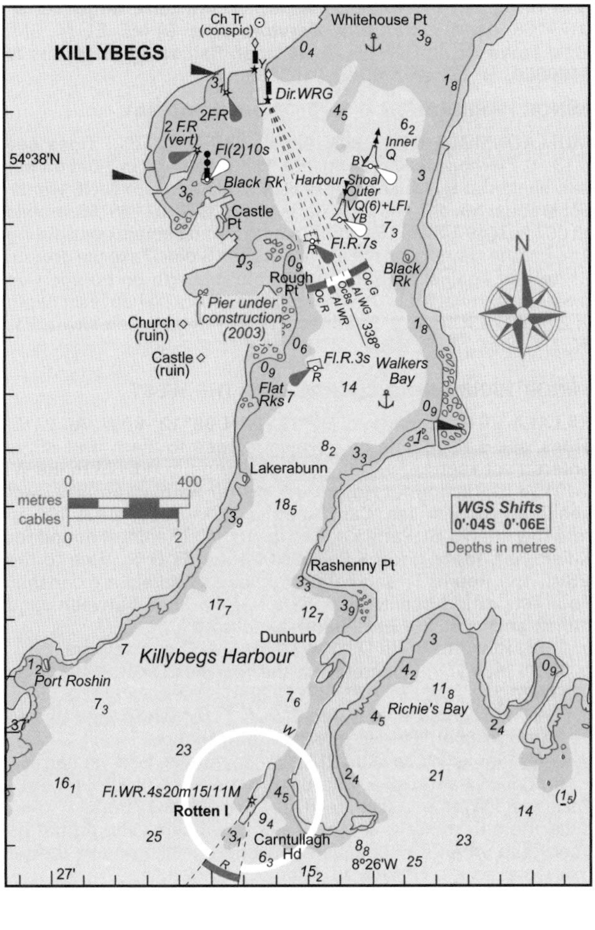
KILLYBEGS
Ch Tr (conspic)
Whitehouse Pt
Dir.WRG
2 F.R (vert)
2F.R
Fl(2)10s
54°38'N
Black Rk
Harbour Shoal
Inner Q
Outer VQ(6)+LFl.
Castle Pt
Fl.R.7s
Black Rk
Rough Pt
Oc G
Oc R
Al WG
Al WR
338°
Pier under construction (2003)
Church (ruin)
Castle (ruin)
Fl.R.3s
Walkers Bay
Flat Rks
Lakerabunn
metres
cables
WGS Shifts 0'·04S 0'·06E
Depths in metres
Rashenny Pt
Dunburb
Killybegs Harbour
Port Roshin
Richie's Bay
Fl.WR.4s20m15/11M
Rotten I
Carntullagh Hd
8°26'W
27'
37'

CHARTS AC 2702, 2792; Irish OS 10; Imray C53

TIDES –0520 Dover; ML 2·2; Duration 0620; Zone 0 (UT)

Standard Port GALWAY (⟶)

Times				Height (metres)			
High Water		Low Water		MHWS	MHWN	MLWN	MLWS
0600	1100	0000	0700	5·1	3·9	2·0	0·6
1800	2300	1200	1900				
Differences KILLYBEGS							
+0040	+0050	+0055	+0035	–1·0	–0·9	–0·5	0·0
GWEEDORE HARBOUR							
+0048	+0100	+0055	+0107	–1·3	–1·0	–0·5	–0·1
BURTONPORT							
+0042	+0055	+0115	+0055	–1·2	–1·0	–0·6	–0·1
DONEGAL HARBOUR (SALTHILL QUAY)							
+0038	+0050	+0052	+0104	–1·2	–0·9	No data	

SHELTER Secure natural hbr, but some swell in SSW winds. A busy major FV port, H24 access. ⚓ about 2½ca NE of the Pier, off blue shed (Gallagher Bros) in 3m, clear of FV wash. Or contact HM and berth at pier. Or **Bruckless Hbr**, about 2M E at the head of McSwyne's Bay, is a pleasant ⚓ in 1·8m, sheltered from all except SW winds. Ent on 038° between rks; ICC SDs are essential.

NAVIGATION WPT 54°36′·00N 08°27′·00W, 022° to Rotten Is lt, 0·94M. From W, beware Manister Rk (covers at HW; dries at LW) off Fintragh B. Keep mid chan until off Rough Pt, then follow the Dir lt or Y ◊ ldg marks 338° into hbr. Pier under construction on Rough Pt (2003).

LIGHTS AND MARKS Rotten Is lt, Fl WR 4s 20m 15/11M, W tr, vis W255°–008°, R008°–039°, W039°–208°. Dir lt 338°, Oc WRG 6s 17m; W sector 336°-340° (see 9.13.4). Harbour Shoal (2·3m) is marked by a SCM and NCM lt buoy.

R/T HM VHF Ch 16 14; essential to request a berth.

TELEPHONE (Dial code 07497) HM 31032, 📠 31840; MRCC (01) 6620922/3; Bundoran Inshore Rescue ☎ (072) 41713; ⊖ 31070; Police 31002; Dr 31148 (Surgery).

FACILITIES **Town Pier** ☎ 31032, AB (free), M, D & P (cans), FW, ME, EI, CH, Slip, 🛒, R, Bar; **Black Rock Pier** AB, M, Slip, D; **Services:** ⚒, C (12 ton), ME, EI, ⚒, Kos, Ⓔ. **Town** EC Wed; ✉, Ⓑ, ⇌ (bus to Sligo), ✈ (Strandhill).

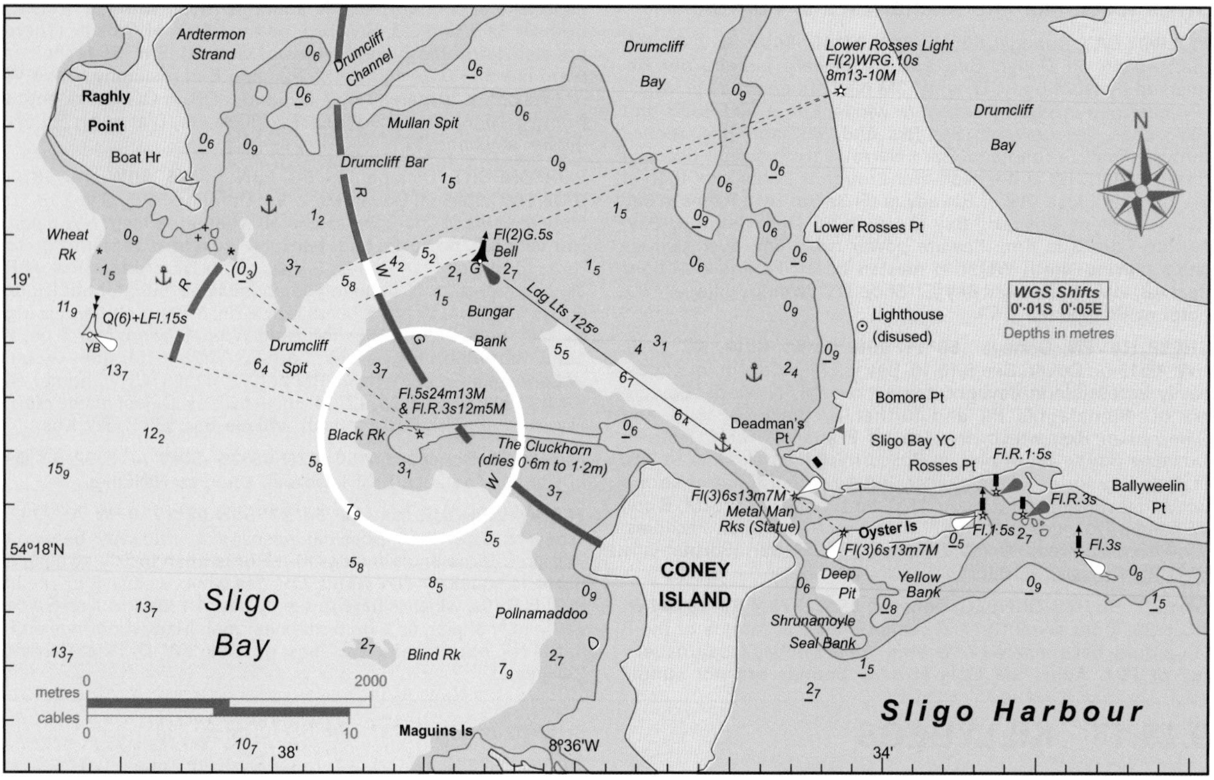
Ardtermon Strand
Drumcliff Channel
Raghly Point
Boat Hr
Mullan Spit
Drumcliff Bar
Drumcliff Bay
Lower Rosses Light Fl(2)WRG.10s 8m13-10M
Drumcliff Bay
N
Wheat Rk
Lower Rosses Pt
Fl(2)G.5s Bell
Ldg Lts 125°
Q(6)+LFl.15s
YB
Bungar Bank
WGS Shifts 0'·01S 0'·05E
Depths in metres
Lighthouse (disused)
Drumcliff Spit
Fl.5s24m13M & Fl.R.3s12m5M
Bomore Pt
Black Rk
The Cluckhorn (dries 0·6m to 1·2m)
Deadman's Pt
Sligo Bay YC
Rosses Pt
Fl.R.1·5s
Fl(3)6s13m7M
Metal Man Rks (Statue)
Fl.R.3s
Ballyweelin Pt
Oyster Is
Fl.1·5s
Fl(3)6s13m7M
Fl.3s
54°18'N
CONEY ISLAND
Deep Pit
Yellow Bank
Sligo Bay
Pollnamaddoo
Shrunamoyle
Seal Bank
Blind Rk
metres
cables
2000
Sligo Harbour
Maguins Is
38'
8°36'W
34'
19'

9.13.18 SLIGO

Sligo **54°18'·30N 08°34'·70W** ❀❀⚓⚓✿✿✿

CHARTS AC 2767, 2852; Imray C54; Irish OS 16, 25

TIDES –0511 Dover; ML 2·3; Duration 0620; Zone 0 (UT)

Standard Port GALWAY (⟶)

Times				Height (metres)			
High Water		Low Water		MHWS	MHWN	MLWN	MLWS
0600	1100	0000	0700	5·1	3·9	2·0	0·6
1800	2300	1200	1900				
Differences SLIGO HARBOUR (Oyster Is)							
+0043	+0055	+0042	+0054	–1·0	–0·9	–0·5	–0·1
MULLAGHMORE							
+0036	+0048	+0047	+0059	–1·4	–1·0	–0·4	–0·2
BALLYSADARE BAY (Culleenamore)							
+0059	+0111	+0111	+0123	–1·2	–0·9	No data	
KILLALA BAY (Inishcrone)							
+0035	+0055	+0030	+0050	–1·3	–1·2	–0·7	–0·2

SHELTER The lower hbr is fairly exposed; ⚓ along N side of Oyster Island, or proceed 4M (not at night) up to the shelter of Sligo town; 2nd berth below bridge for yachts.

NAVIGATION WPT 54°19'·15N 08°36'·77W, 125° to front ldg lt, 1·6M. The passage between Oyster Island and Coney Island is marked 'Dangerous'. Pass N of Oyster Is leaving Blennick Rks to port. Passage up to Sligo town between training walls. Some perches are in bad repair. Pilots at Raghly Pt and Rosses Pt. Approach quays at half tide or higher.

LIGHTS AND MARKS Lower Rosses Lt, Fl (2) WRG 10s 8m 13-10M (H24), W sector 066°-070°. Ldg lts (H24) lead 125° into ent: front, Fl (3) 6s 13m 7M, Metal Man Rks (statue of a man on a twr); rear, Oyster Is lt ho, Fl (3) 6s 13m 7M. Lts up-channel are unreliable.

R/T Pilots VHF Ch 12 16. HM Ch 16.

TELEPHONE (Dial code 071) Hbr Office ☎/📠 9161197, mob 086 8526233; MRCC (01) 6620922/3; ⊜ 9161064; Police 9157000; Dr 9142886; Ⓗ 9171111.

FACILITIES **No 3 berth** (next to bridge) AB 20-30ft €19.00, P & D (in cans), FW, ME, El, ⚒, CH, C (15 ton); **Sligo YC** ☎ 9177168, ♁s, FW, Bar, Slip. **Services:** Slip, D, ME, El, ⚒, SM, Gas; **Town** 🛒, R, Bar, ✉, Ⓑ, ⇌ Irish Rail ☎ 9169888, Bus ☎ 9160066, ✈ (Strandhill) ☎ 9168280.

MINOR HARBOUR ON S SIDE OF DONEGAL BAY

MULLAGHMORE 54°27'·90N 08°26'·80W. AC 2702. Tides see 9.13.18. Pierhead lit Fl G 3s 5m 3M. Fair weather ⚓ in 2-3m off hbr ent, sheltered by Mullaghmore Head, except from N/NE winds. For ♁s near hbr ent, call Liam Carey at BY, ☎/📠 071 66106, mobile ☎ 087 2574497. Keep close to N pier to avoid shingle bank drying 1m, ⅔ of the way across the ent toward the S pier. Take the ground or dry out against the piers inside hbr or berth on pontoon on bkwtr (min 1m at MLWS), access approx HW±2 when least depth is 2m. VHF Ch 16, 8, 6. Facilities: FW at S Pier and on bkwtr, BY, ⚒, D (cans), 🛒, R, Bar.

MINOR HARBOUR/ANCHORAGE TO THE WEST

KILLALA BAY, Sligo/Mayo, **54°13'·02N 09°12'·80W.** AC 2715. Tides, see 9.13.18. The bay, which is open to the N and NE, is entered between Lenadoon Pt and Kilcummin Hd, 6M to the W. 1·1M W of Kilcummin Hd are 8 Y ♁s off Rathlackan pier, well sheltered from W'lies. Carrickpatrick ECM buoy, Q (3) 10s, in mid-bay marks St Patrick's Rks to the W. Thence, if bound for Killala hbr, make good Killala SHM buoy, Fl G 6s, 7½ca to the SSW. The Round Tr and cathedral spire at Killala are conspic. Four sets of ldg bns/lts lead via a narrow chan between sand dunes and over the bar (0·3m) as follows:

a. 230°, Rinnaun Pt lts Oc 10s 7/12m 5M, □ concrete trs.
b. 215°, Inch Is, □ concrete trs; the rear has Dir lt Fl WRG 2s, G205°-213°, W213°-217°, R217°-225°.
c. 196°, Kilroe lts Oc 4s 5/10m 2M, W □ trs, which lead to ⚓ in Bartragh Pool, 6ca NE of Killala hbr; thence
d. 236°, Pier lts Iso 2s 5/7m 2M, W ◇ daymarks, lead via narrow, dredged chan to pier where AB is possible in about 1·5m.

Facilities: FW, P & D (cans), 🛒 in town ½M, EC Thurs.
Other hbrs in the bay: R Moy leading to Ballina should not be attempted without pilot/local knowledge. Inishcrone in the SE has a pier and lt, Fl WRG 1·5s 8m 2M; see 9.13.4.

9.13.19 WESTPORT (CLEW BAY)

Mayo **53°47'·85N 09°35'·40W** ❁❁◊◊◊✿✿✿

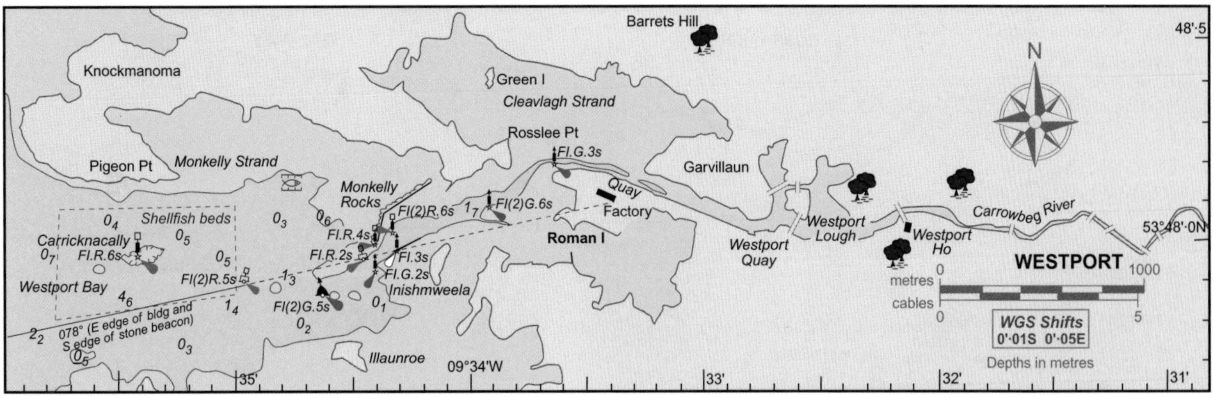
Barrets Hill
48'·5
N
Knockmanoma
Green I
Cleavlagh Strand
Rosslee Pt
Fl.G.3s
Pigeon Pt
Monkelly Strand
Garvillaun
Monkelly Rocks
Quay
Fl(2)R.6s
Fl(2)G.6s
Factory
Shellfish beds
Carricknacally
Fl.R.6s
Fl.R.4s
Roman I
Westport Lough
Westport Quay
Westport Ho
Carrowbeg River
53°48'·0N
Fl.R.2s
Fl.3s
Fl.G.2s
Inishmweela
WESTPORT
Westport Bay
Fl(2)R.5s
metres
cables
1000
078° (E edge of bldg and S edge of stone beacon)
Fl(2)G.5s
WGS Shifts
0'·01S 0'·05E
Illaunroe
09°34'W
Depths in metres
35'
33'
32'
31'

CHARTS AC 2667, 2057; Imray C54; Irish OS 30, 31

TIDES –0545 Dover; ML 2·5; Duration 0610; Zone 0 (UT)

Standard Port GALWAY (⟶)

Times				Height (metres)			
High Water		Low Water		MHWS	MHWN	MLWN	MLWS
0600	1100	0000	0700	5·1	3·9	2·0	0·6
1800	2300	1200	1900				
BROADHAVEN							
+0040	+0050	+0040	+0050	–1·4	–1·1	–0·4	–0·1
BLACKSOD QUAY							
+0025	+0035	+0040	+0040	–1·2	–1·0	–0·6	–0·2
CLARE ISLAND							
+0019	+0013	+0029	+0023	–1·0	–0·7	–0·4	–0·1
KILLARY HARBOUR							
+0021	+0015	+0035	+0029	–1·0	–0·8	–0·4	–0·1
INISHBOFIN HARBOUR							
+0013	+0009	+0021	+0017	–1·0	–0·8	–0·4	–0·1
CLIFDEN BAY							
+0005	+0005	+0016	+0016	–0·7	–0·5	No data	
SLYNE HEAD							
+0002	+0002	+0010	+0010	–0·7	–0·5	No data	

SHELTER Secure ⚓s amongst the islands at all times, as follows: E of Inishlyre in 2m; 2ca NE of Dorinish More, good holding in lee of Dorinish Bar (dries); 6 🅜s in Rosmoney Hbr 53°49'·75N 09°37'·34W; Westport Quay HW±1½, to dry out on S side; Newport Hbr (dries) can be reached above mid-flood with careful pilotage (AC 2667); dry out against N quay or ⚓ at E end of Rabbit Is.

NAVIGATION WPT 53°49'·20N 09°42'·10W, 071° to Inishgort lt ho, 1·2M. Contact Tom Gibbons (Inishlyre Is) ☎ (098) 26381 for pilotage advice. Approaches to Westport Channel between Monkellys Rks and Inishmweela are well marked by lit PHMs and SHMs. Beware fish farms E of Clare I. and in Newport Bay. Do not anchor or ground in the Carricknacally Shellfish Bed Area.

LIGHTS AND MARKS Westport B entered via Inishgort lt, L Fl 10s 11m 10M (H24), and a series of ldg lines, but not advised at night. Final appr line 080° towards lt bn, Fl 3s. but beware of drying patches on this lead inwards from Pigeon PHM. Chan from Westport Bay to Westport Quay, 1½M approx, is marked by bns.

R/T None.

TELEPHONE (Dial code 098) MRCC (01) 6620922/3; ⊖ (094) 21131; Police 25555; Ⓗ (094) 21733.

FACILITIES **Westport Quays** M, AB free, Slip, 🛒, R, Bar; **Services:** Kos, El, Ⓔ; **Town** EC Wed; P & D (cans), ✉, Ⓑ, ⇌, ✈ (Galway/ Knock). **Mayo SC Rosmoney** ☎ 26160, Slip, Bar; **Glénans Irish SC** ☎ 26046 on Collanmore Is;

OTHER ANCHORAGES FROM EAGLE IS TO SLYNE HEAD

BROAD HAVEN, Mayo, **54°16'·00N 09°53'·20W**. AC 2703. See 9.13.19 for tides; ML 1·9m. A safe refuge except in N'lies. Easy appr across Broad Haven Bay to the ent between Brandy Pt and Gubacashel Pt, Iso WR 4s27m 12/9M, W tr. 7ca S of this lt is Ballyglas Fl G 3s on W side. ⚓ close N or S of Ballyglas which has pier (2m) and 8 Y 🅜s. In E'lies ⚓ 3ca S of Inver Pt out of the tide. Further S off Barrett Pt, the inlet narrows and turns W to Belmullet. Facilities: 🛒, ✉.

PORTNAFRANKAGH Mayo, **54°14'·95N 10°06'·00W**. AC 2703. Tides approx as Broad Haven. A safe passage ⚓ , close to the coastal route, but swell enters in all winds. Appr toward Port Pt, thence keep to the N side for better water; middle and S side break in onshore winds. ⚓ in 4–5m on S side, close inshore. L and slip at new pier. Unlit, but Eagle Is lt, Fl (3) 10s 67m 26M H24, W tr, is 2M N. No facilities; Belmullet 4M, 🛒.

BLACKSOD BAY, Mayo, **54°05'·00N 10°02'·00W**. AC 2704. HW –0525 on Dover; ML 2·2m; Duration 0610. See 9.13.19. Easy appr, accessible by night. Safe ⚓s depending on wind: NW of Blacksod Pt (3m) 6 Y 🅜s; at Elly B (1·8m); Elly Hbr 6 Y 🅜s; Saleen B Ldg lts 319°, both Oc 4s, lead to pier 2F.G; N of Claggan Pt. Beware drying rk 3·5ca SSE of Ardmore Pt. Lts: Blacksod Pt, Fl (2) WR 7·5s 13m 9M, see 9.13.4. ECM buoy Q (3) 10s. Blacksod pier hd, 2 FR (vert). Few facilities; nearest town is Belmullet.

CLARE ISLAND, Mayo, **53°48'·1N 09°56'·7W**. 6 🅜s on SE side untenable in E winds. Hotel, Bar, some 🛒.

INISHTURK, Mayo, **53°42'·3N 10°05'·2W**. 8 Y 🅜s Garranty Hbr. sheltered SW to NNW winds. Slip, quay, Bar, R, ✉, 6 🅜s on E side.

KILLARY HARBOUR, Mayo/Galway, **53°37'·83N 09°54'·00W**, 4ca W of Doonee Is. AC 2706. Tides 9.13.19. A spectacular 7M long inlet, narrow and deep. Caution fish farms, some with Fl Y lts. Appr in good vis to identify Doonee Is and Inishbarna bns ldg 099° to ent. ⚓s off Dernasliggaun, Bundorragha and, at head of inlet, Leenaun with 8 Y 🅜s. (Village: L, 🛒, Bar, hotel). Enter **Little Killary Bay** 4ca S of Doonee Is; drying rks at ent. Good ⚓ in 3m at head of bay.

BALLYNAKILL, Galway, **53°34'·95N 10°03'·00W**. AC 2706. Tides as Inishbofin/Killary. Easy appr between Cleggan Pt, Fl (3) WRG 15s and Rinvyle Pt. Then pass N of Freaghillaun South Is, E of which is good passage ⚓ in 7m. Further E, Carrigeen and Ardagh Rks lie in mid-chan. Keep N for ⚓ in Derryinver B. S chan leads to ⚓s: off Ross Pt; S of Roeillaun; in Fahy Bay with 8 Y 🅜s sheltered by bar dries 0[illegible]m. No facilities.

INISHBOFIN, Mayo, **53°36'·60N 10°13'·20W**. AC 1820, 2707.HW –0555 on Dover; ML 1·9m. See 9.13.19. Very safe hbr once inside narrow ent. 2 conspic W trs lead 032°. ⚓ between new pier and Port Is. Old pier to the E dries. Gun Rock, Fl (2) 6s 8m 4M, vis 296°-253°. Facilities: FW, R, Bar, 🛒, Hotel ☎ (095) 45803.

CLIFDEN BAY, Galway, **53°29'·40N 10°05'·90W**. AC 1820, 2708. HW –0600 on Dover; Duration 0610. Tides at 9.13.19. Before entering identify the conspic W bn on Carrickrana Rks. To the E keep clear of Coghan's Rks and Doolick Rks. Ldg marks: W bn at Fishing Pt on 080° with Clifden Castle (ruin); caution bar 2·4m off Fishing Pt. 8 Y 🅜s are 3ca S of Castle ruins, or ⚓ NE of Drinagh Pt. In the drying creek to Clifden beware ruined trng wall; dry out against the quay. Or enter Ardbear Bay to ⚓ SE of Yellow Slate Rks in 3·4m. Keep clear of fish farms. Facilities: **Town** EC Thurs; Bar, Ⓑ, CH, D, P, ✉, R, 🛒, Kos, FW, 🛒, R, Dr, Ⓗ. Bus to Galway.

9.13.20 GALWAY BAY

Galway **53°12'N 09°08'W**

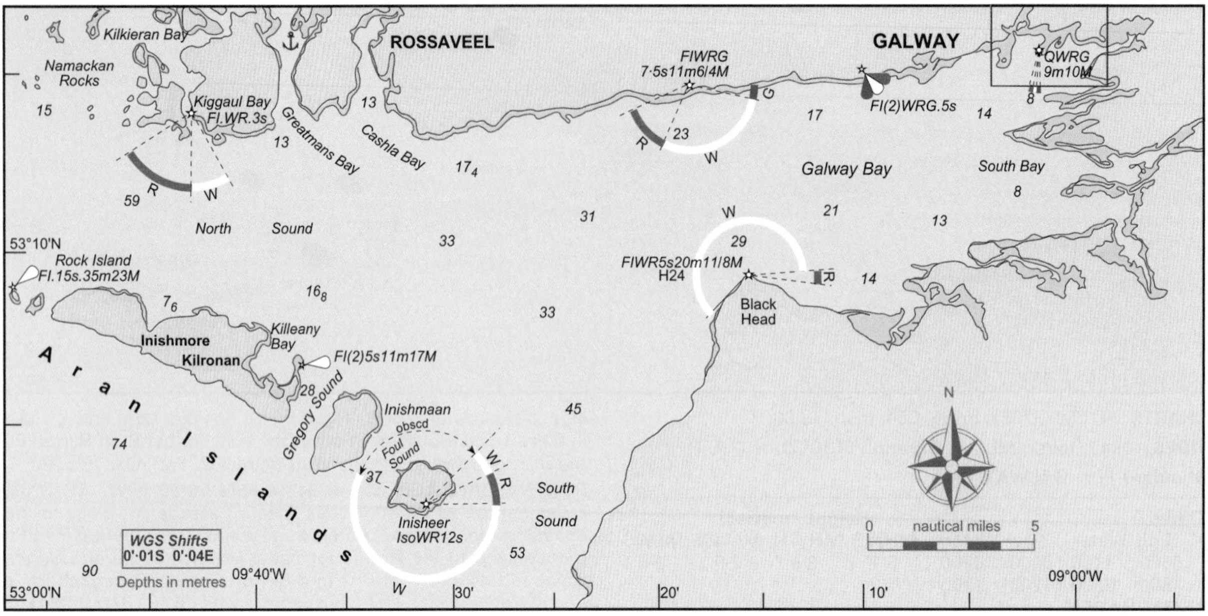
Kilkieran Bay
Namackan Rocks
ROSSAVEEL
GALWAY
FlWRG 7·5s11m6/4M
QWRG 9m10M
Kiggaul Bay Fl.WR.3s
Greatmans Bay
Cashla Bay
Fl(2)WRG.5s
Galway Bay
South Bay
North Sound
53°10'N
Rock Island Fl.15s.35m23M
FlWR5s20m11/8M H24
Black Head
Inishmore
Killeany Bay
Kilronan
Fl(2)5s11m17M
Aran Islands
Gregory Sound
Inishmaan
obscd
Foul Sound
Inisheer IsoWR12s
South Sound
WGS Shifts 0'·01S 0'·04E
Depths in metres
09°40'W
53°00'N
nautical miles
09°00'W

CHARTS AC 2173, 3339, 1984,1903; Imray C55; Irish OS 45, 46, 51

TIDES –0555 Dover; ML 2·9; Duration 0620; Zone 0 (UT)

Standard Port GALWAY (⟶)

Times				Height (metres)			
High Water		Low Water		MHWS	MHWN	MLWN	MLWS
0600	1100	0000	0700	5·1	3·9	2·0	0·6
1800	2300	1200	1900				
Differences KILKIERAN COVE							
+0005	+0005	+0016	+0016	–0·3	–0·2	–0·1	0·0
ROUNDSTONE BAY							
+0003	+0003	+0008	+0008	–0·7	–0·5	–0·3	–0·1
KILLEANY BAY (Aran Islands)							
–0008	–0008	+0003	+0003	–0·4	–0·3	–0·2	–0·1
LISCANNOR							
–0003	–0007	+0006	+0002	–0·4	–0·3	No data	

SHELTER Galway Bay is sheltered from large swells by Aran Is, but seas get up in the 20M from Aran Is to Galway. Beware salmon drift nets in the apps to many bays. The better ⚓s from Slyne Head and clock-wise around Galway Bay are:

Bunowen Bay: (53°24'·6N 10°06'·9W). Sheltered in W-NE winds; unsafe in S'ly. Easy appr with Bunowen House brg 000°, leaving Mullauncarrickscoltia Rk (1·1m) to port. ⚓ in 3-4m below conspic Doon Hill.

Roundstone Bay: AC2709 (Off chartlet at 53°23'N 09°54'·5W). Safe shelter/access, except in SE'ly. 4 Y Øs are 5ca SSE of Roundstone, or ⚓ in 2m off N quay. There are other ⚓s E'ward in Bertraghboy and Cashel Bays.

Kilkieran Bay: Easy ent abm Golam Tr (conspic). 12 Y Øs off Kilkieran. Many ⚓s in 14M long, sheltered bay.

Kiggaul Bay: Easy ent, H24; ⚓ close W/NW of lt Fl WR 3s 5/3M. Depth 3 to 4m; exposed to S/SE winds.

Greatman Bay: Beware English Rk (dries 1·2m), Keeraun Shoal (breaks in heavy weather), Arkeena Rk, Trabaan Rk, Rin Rks and Chapel Rks. ⚓ off Natawny Quay (E side), or on 4 Y Øs off Maumeen Quay (dries), AB possible.

Cashla Bay: Easiest hbr on this coast; ent in all weather. ⚓ and 8 Y Øs (planned) off Sruthan Quay. Rossaveel, on E side, is a busy fishing and ferry hbr.

Note: There is no safe hbr from Cashla to Galway (20M).

Bays between Black Hd and Galway have rks and shoals, but give excellent shelter. Kinvarra B, Aughinish B, South B and Ballyvaghan B are the main ones. Enter Kinvarra B with caution on the flood; beware rks. Berth in small drying hbr. Beware fish farm in South B. Ballvaghan B, entered either side of Illaunloo Rk, leads to two piers (both dry) or ⚓ close NE in pool (3m). Best access HW±2.

NAVIGATION Enter the Bay by one of four Sounds:

1. North Sound between Inishmore and Golam Tr (conspic), 4½M wide, is easiest but beware Brocklinmore Bank in heavy weather.
2. Gregory Sound between Inishmore and Inishmaan, is free of dangers, but give Straw Island a berth of 2-3ca.
3. Foul Sound between Inishmaan and Inisheer; only danger is Pipe Rock (dries) at end of reef extending 3ca NW of Inisheer.
4. South Sound between Inisheer and mainland. Only danger Finnis Rock (dries 0·4m) 4½ca SE of E point of Inisheer (marked by ECM buoy Q (3) 10s). From S, beware Kilstiffin Rocks off Liscanor Bay.

LIGHTS AND MARKS Roundstone Bay: Croaghnakeela Is Fl 3·7s 7m 5M. Inishnee lt Fl (2) WRG 10s 9m 5/3M, W sector 017°-030°. Kiggaul Bay: Fl WR 3s 5m 5/3M, W329°-359°, R359°-059°. Cashla Bay: Killeen Pt Fl (3) WR 10s 6/3M; Lion Pt Dir lt 010°, Iso WRG 4s 8/6M, W008·5°-011·5°. Rossaveel ldg lts 116°, Oc 3s. Black Head lt Fl WR 5s 20m 11/8M H24, vis W045°-268°, R268°-276° covers Illanloo Rk.

FACILITIES

BUNOWEN Bay: No facilities.
ROUNDSTONE Bay: 🛒, FW, Bar, ✉, Bus to Galway.
KILKIERAN Bay: Bar, ☎, P, 🛒, Bus to Galway.
KIGGAUL Bay: Bar (no ☎), shop at Lettermullen (1M).
GREATMAN Bay: Maumeen 🛒, P (1M), Bar.
CASHLA Bay: **Carraroe** (1M SW) 🛒, Hotel, ☎; **Rossaveel** HM ☎ 091 572108, FW, D, ME; **Costelloe** (1½M E), Hotel, ✉, Gge.

ARAN ISLANDS The only reasonable shelter is on Inishmore in Killeany Bay, but exposed to E/NE winds and crowded with FVs. HM ☎ 099 61150; 8 Y Øs available; or ⚓ S of Kilronan pier; or ⚓ E of Killeany Pt; or in good weather ⚓ at Portmurvy. Kilronan, facilities: 8Øs, 🛒, D, FW, ✉; Ferry to Galway, ✈ to Galway from airstrip on beach. **Lights and marks**: Inishmore: Eeragh Island (Rk Is) Fl 15s 35m 23M, W tr, B bands. Killeany Bay: Straw Is, Fl (2) 5s 11m 17M. Kilronan pier Fl WG 1·5s. Ldg lts 192° both Oc 5s for Killeany hbr. Inishmaan is not lit.Inisheer: Iso WR 12s 34m 20/16M, Racon, vis W225°-245° (partially obscd 225°-231° beyond 7M), R245°-269° covers Finnis Rk, W269°-115°; obscd 115°-225°.

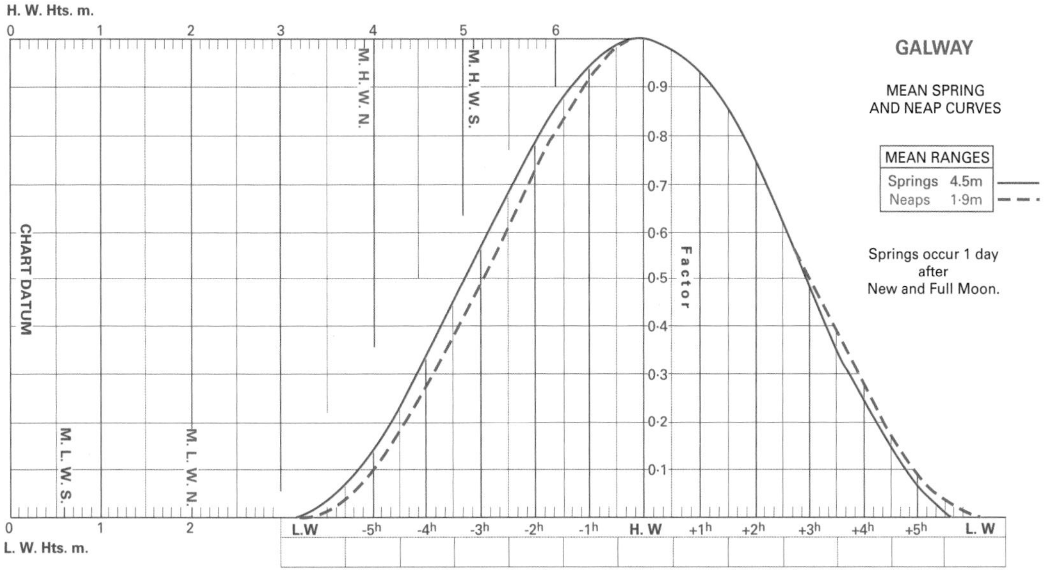
H. W. Hts. m.
0 1 2 3 4 5 6
M. H. W. N.
M. H. W. S.
CHART DATUM
M. L. W. S.
M. L. W. N.
0·9
0·8
0·7
0·6
0·5
0·4
0·3
0·2
0·1
Factor
0 1 2
L. W. Hts. m.
L.W -5h -4h -3h -2h -1h H. W +1h +2h +3h +4h +5h L. W
GALWAY
MEAN SPRING AND NEAP CURVES
MEAN RANGES
Springs 4.5m
Neaps 1·9m
Springs occur 1 day after New and Full Moon.

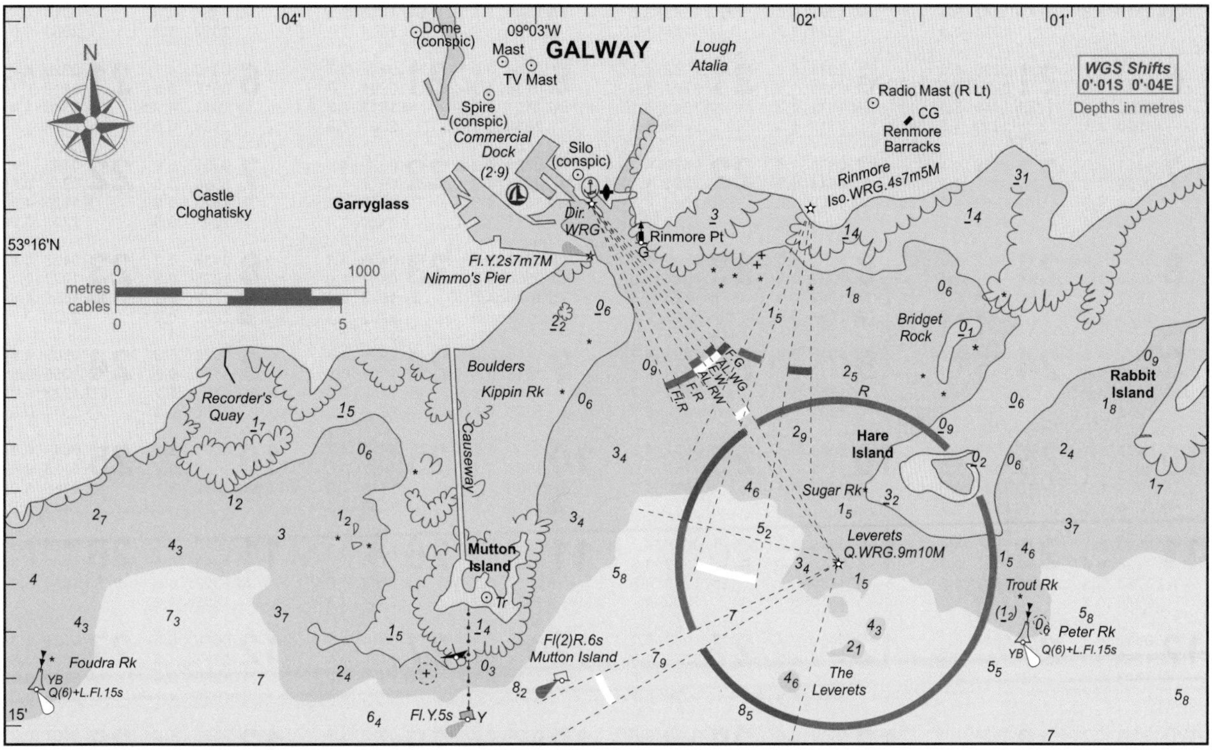
GALWAY
09°03'W
04'
02'
01'
Dome (conspic)
Mast
TV Mast
Spire (conspic)
Commercial Dock
(2·9)
Silo (conspic)
Lough Atalia
Radio Mast (R Lt)
CG
Renmore Barracks
WGS Shifts
0'·01S 0'·04E
Depths in metres
Rinmore Iso.WRG.4s7m5M
Rinmore Pt
Dir. WRG
Castle Cloghatisky
Garryglass
53°16'N
Fl.Y.2s7m7M
Nimmo's Pier
metres 0 1000
cables 0 5
Bridget Rock
Boulders
Kippin Rk
Causeway
Recorder's Quay
Rabbit Island
Hare Island
Sugar Rk
Leverets Q.WRG.9m10M
Mutton Island
Tr
Trout Rk
Peter Rk
Q(6)+L.Fl.15s
YB
Foudra Rk
Q(6)+L.Fl.15s
Fl(2)R.6s Mutton Island
Fl.Y.5s
The Leverets
15'
F.G
Al.WG
F.W
Al.RW
F.R
Fl.R

GALWAY HARBOUR 53°16'·07N 09°02'·74W ☸☸☸👍👍✿✿✿

SHELTER Very good in Galway hbr, protected from SW'lies by Mutton Island. Dock gates open HW–2 to HW, when min depth is 6m. Enter Galway Dock and secure in SW corner of basin, or ask HM for waiting berth on lead-in pier. It is dangerous to lie in the 'Layby' (a dredged cut NE of New pier) when wind is SE or S; if strong from these points, seas sweep round the pierhead. New Harbour (2·5M ESE and home of Galway Bay SC) is nearest safe ⚓ to Galway.

NAVIGATION Galway WPT 53°14´·80N 09°03´·40W, 061° to Leverets lt, 1·1M.

LIGHTS AND MARKS Leverets Q WRG 9m 10M; B tr, W bands; G015°-058°, W058°-065°, R065°-103°, G103°-143°, W143°-146°, R146°-015°. Rinmore Iso WRG 4s 7m 5M; W □ tr ; G359°-008°, W008°-018°, R018°-027°. Appr chan 325° is defined by a Dir lt WRG 7m 3M on New Pier, sectors: FG 322¼°–323¾°, Al GW 3s 323¾°–324¾°, FW 324¾°–325¼°, Al RW 3s 325¼°–326¼°, FR 326¼°–331¼°, Fl R 3s 331¼°–332¼°.

R/T Call *Galway Harbour Radio* VHF Ch **12** 16 (HW–2½ to HW+1). Call Galway Pilots on VHF Ch **12** in case ship movements are imminent or under way and follow their instructions on berthing.

TELEPHONE (Dial code 091) HM 561874, 📠 563738; MRCC (066) 9476109; Coast/Cliff Rescue Service (099) 61107; Police 538000; Dr 562453.

FACILITIES Dock AB €12.70 if space available, FW, El, ME, ⚒, C (35 ton), CH, LB, PV, SM, 🛒, R, Bar; **Galway YC** M, Slip, FW, C, CH, Bar; **Galway Bay SC** ☎ 794527, M, CH, Bar; **Town** EC Mon; P, D, ACA, Gas, Gaz, Kos, 🛒, R, Bar, ✉, Ⓑ, ⇌, ✈ Carnmore (6M to the E of Galway City). The nearest D by pump is Rossaveal.

TIME ZONE (UT)
For Summer Time add ONE hour in **non-shaded areas**

IRELAND – GALWAY

LAT 53°16′N LONG 9°03′W

TIMES AND HEIGHTS OF HIGH AND LOW WATERS

SPRING & NEAP TIDES
Dates in red are SPRINGS
Dates in blue are NEAPS

YEAR **2005**

JANUARY

Date	Day	Time	m	Time	m	Time	m	Time	m
1	SA	0202	1.7	0833	4.4	1431	1.4	2112	4.2
2	SU	0246	1.8	0913	4.3	1514	1.5	2200	4.1
3	M	0335	1.9	1000	4.2	1603	1.7	◑ 2252	4.0
4	TU	0433	2.0	1052	4.2	1701	1.7	2347	4.1
5	W	0539	2.0	1151	4.1	1810	1.8		
6	TH	0047	4.2	0651	1.9	1300	4.2	1926	1.7
7	F	0151	4.3	0759	1.6	1414	4.3	2029	1.4
8	SA	0249	4.6	0856	1.3	1517	4.5	2121	1.2
9	SU	0342	4.9	0948	1.0	1612	4.8	2210	1.0
10	M	0432	5.1	1037	0.7	1704	5.0	● 2258	0.8
11	TU	0523	5.3	1126	0.4	1754	5.1	2345	0.7
12	W	0612	5.3	1212	0.3	1843	5.1		
13	TH	0031	0.7	0700	5.3	1257	0.3	1929	5.0
14	F	0117	0.8	0747	5.2	1341	0.4	2017	4.8
15	SA	0202	1.0	0835	4.9	1426	0.7	2108	4.5
16	SU	0251	1.3	0926	4.6	1514	1.1	2204	4.2
17	M	0348	1.6	1022	4.3	1609	1.5	◐ 2304	4.0
18	TU	0455	1.8	1122	4.0	1715	1.8		
19	W	0007	3.9	0609	2.0	1228	3.9	1837	2.0
20	TH	0118	3.9	0722	2.0	1342	3.8	1954	2.0
21	F	0226	4.0	0826	1.8	1449	3.9	2049	1.8
22	SA	0319	4.1	0917	1.7	1540	4.0	2131	1.7
23	SU	0402	4.3	1001	1.4	1624	4.2	2209	1.5
24	M	0441	4.4	1040	1.2	1703	4.3	2246	1.3
25	TU	0518	4.5	1117	1.0	1741	4.5	○ 2322	1.2
26	W	0555	4.6	1152	0.9	1817	4.5	2357	1.1
27	TH	0630	4.7	1225	0.8	1853	4.6		
28	F	0031	1.0	0704	4.7	1257	0.8	1927	4.6
29	SA	0105	1.1	0736	4.7	1328	0.8	2001	4.5
30	SU	0139	1.1	0806	4.6	1401	1.0	2035	4.4
31	M	0216	1.3	0836	4.5	1438	1.2	2112	4.2

FEBRUARY

Date	Day	Time	m	Time	m	Time	m	Time	m
1	TU	0258	1.5	0915	4.3	1521	1.4	2201	4.1
2	W	0348	1.7	1008	4.2	1613	1.6	◑ 2259	4.0
3	TH	0448	1.9	1113	4.0	1716	1.8		
4	F	0005	3.9	0603	1.9	1229	3.9	1845	1.9
5	SA	0121	4.0	0738	1.8	1358	4.0	2019	1.7
6	SU	0235	4.3	0850	1.4	1512	4.3	2117	1.3
7	M	0334	4.6	0944	0.9	1608	4.6	2206	0.9
8	TU	0426	5.0	1032	0.5	1657	4.9	● 2251	0.6
9	W	0515	5.2	1116	0.2	1744	5.1	2334	0.4
10	TH	0601	5.4	1158	0.1	1828	5.1		
11	F	0016	0.3	0645	5.4	1239	0.1	1910	5.1
12	SA	0057	0.4	0728	5.2	1318	0.2	1952	4.9
13	SU	0138	0.6	0810	5.0	1356	0.6	2034	4.6
14	M	0220	1.0	0853	4.6	1437	1.0	2119	4.3
15	TU	0306	1.4	0939	4.2	1521	1.4	2209	3.9
16	W	0403	1.7	1032	3.9	1616	1.9	◐ 2310	3.7
17	TH	0521	2.0	1138	3.6	1739	2.2		
18	F	0031	3.5	0646	2.1	1311	3.5	1920	2.2
19	SA	0210	3.6	0807	2.0	1441	3.6	2034	2.0
20	SU	0310	3.9	0906	1.7	1533	3.9	2118	1.7
21	M	0352	4.1	0947	1.4	1613	4.1	2154	1.4
22	TU	0429	4.3	1021	1.1	1649	4.3	2229	1.1
23	W	0505	4.5	1055	0.8	1723	4.5	2303	0.9
24	TH	0539	4.7	1128	0.6	1757	4.7	○ 2337	0.7
25	F	0611	4.8	1159	0.5	1830	4.7		
26	SA	0009	0.7	0642	4.8	1230	0.5	1900	4.7
27	SU	0040	0.7	0711	4.8	1259	0.6	1929	4.7
28	M	0113	0.8	0738	4.7	1331	0.7	1957	4.5

MARCH

Date	Day	Time	m	Time	m	Time	m	Time	m
1	TU	0148	0.9	0805	4.6	1407	1.0	2028	4.4
2	W	0228	1.2	0840	4.4	1448	1.3	2112	4.1
3	TH	0316	1.5	0933	4.1	1538	1.7	◑ 2218	3.9
4	F	0416	1.8	1049	3.8	1644	2.0	2336	3.8
5	SA	0537	1.9	1216	3.7	1840	2.1		
6	SU	0106	3.9	0736	1.7	1401	3.9	2018	1.7
7	M	0230	4.2	0846	1.3	1511	4.3	2111	1.3
8	TU	0327	4.6	0936	0.8	1600	4.6	2154	0.9
9	W	0415	5.0	1018	0.4	1644	4.9	2235	0.5
10	TH	0500	5.2	1058	0.2	1726	5.1	● 2316	0.3
11	F	0543	5.4	1137	0.0	1807	5.2	2355	0.2
12	SA	0625	5.4	1214	0.1	1846	5.1		
13	SU	0034	0.3	0704	5.2	1251	0.3	1923	4.9
14	M	0112	0.5	0743	5.0	1326	0.6	1959	4.7
15	TU	0150	0.8	0821	4.6	1401	1.0	2037	4.3
16	W	0231	1.3	0902	4.2	1439	1.5	2119	4.0
17	TH	0322	1.7	0949	3.8	1525	2.0	◐ 2212	3.7
18	F	0445	2.0	1052	3.5	1657	2.3	2329	3.4
19	SA	0614	2.1	1243	3.3	1845	2.3		
20	SU	0148	3.5	0734	2.0	1425	3.5	2004	2.1
21	M	0248	3.7	0838	1.7	1513	3.8	2051	1.8
22	TU	0329	4.0	0917	1.3	1549	4.1	2127	1.4
23	W	0405	4.3	0951	1.0	1623	4.4	2202	1.1
24	TH	0439	4.5	1024	0.7	1656	4.6	2236	0.8
25	F	0512	4.7	1057	0.5	1729	4.8	○ 2309	0.6
26	SA	0544	4.8	1129	0.4	1759	4.9	2341	0.5
27	SU	0614	4.9	1159	0.4	1829	4.9		
28	M	0013	0.5	0643	4.9	1229	0.5	1857	4.8
29	TU	0047	0.6	0713	4.8	1303	0.7	1926	4.7
30	W	0124	0.8	0745	4.6	1340	1.0	2000	4.5
31	TH	0206	1.1	0825	4.3	1422	1.4	2046	4.2

APRIL

Date	Day	Time	m	Time	m	Time	m	Time	m
1	F	0255	1.4	0924	4.0	1515	1.8	2157	3.9
2	SA	0359	1.7	1045	3.8	1629	2.1	◑ 2323	3.8
3	SU	0535	1.8	1217	3.7	1851	2.1		
4	M	0058	3.9	0726	1.6	1356	4.0	2002	1.7
5	TU	0216	4.3	0828	1.2	1456	4.4	2052	1.3
6	W	0310	4.7	0915	0.8	1541	4.7	2134	0.9
7	TH	0355	5.0	0956	0.5	1622	5.0	2214	0.5
8	F	0438	5.2	1035	0.3	1702	5.1	● 2253	0.4
9	SA	0520	5.3	1112	0.3	1740	5.2	2332	0.3
10	SU	0601	5.2	1148	0.4	1818	5.1		
11	M	0010	0.4	0639	5.1	1223	0.6	1853	4.9
12	TU	0048	0.6	0717	4.8	1256	0.9	1929	4.7
13	W	0125	1.0	0755	4.5	1330	1.2	2005	4.4
14	TH	0206	1.3	0835	4.2	1407	1.6	2047	4.1
15	F	0255	1.7	0922	3.8	1450	2.0	2138	3.8
16	SA	0418	2.0	1022	3.5	1622	2.4	◐ 2243	3.5
17	SU	0541	2.0	1154	3.4	1807	2.4		
18	M	0058	3.5	0648	1.9	1344	3.5	1915	2.1
19	TU	0208	3.7	0747	1.7	1437	3.8	2008	1.8
20	W	0252	3.9	0834	1.4	1514	4.1	2050	1.5
21	TH	0329	4.2	0913	1.1	1548	4.4	2128	1.1
22	F	0403	4.4	0949	0.8	1620	4.6	2203	0.9
23	SA	0436	4.6	1023	0.7	1651	4.8	2238	0.7
24	SU	0509	4.8	1055	0.6	1723	5.0	○ 2311	0.5
25	M	0543	4.9	1128	0.5	1755	5.0	2346	0.5
26	TU	0618	4.9	1202	0.6	1830	5.0		
27	W	0025	0.6	0655	4.8	1240	0.8	1907	4.9
28	TH	0107	0.7	0737	4.6	1321	1.1	1949	4.6
29	F	0153	1.0	0825	4.4	1408	1.4	2042	4.4
30	SA	0246	1.3	0927	4.1	1506	1.8	2154	4.1

Chart Datum: 0·20 metres above Ordnance Datum (Dublin)

TIME ZONE (UT)
For Summer Time add ONE hour in **non-shaded areas**

IRELAND – GALWAY

LAT 53°16′N LONG 9°03′W

TIMES AND HEIGHTS OF HIGH AND LOW WATERS

SPRING & NEAP TIDES
Dates in red are SPRINGS
Dates in blue are NEAPS

YEAR **2005**

MAY

Day	Time	m	Day	Time	m
1	0355	1.6	16	0458	1.9
	1044	3.9		1100	3.6
SU	1632	2.0	M	1717	2.3
◑	2317	4.0	◐	2316	3.7
2	0534	1.6	17	0600	1.9
	1209	3.9		1216	3.6
M	1829	1.9	TU	1824	2.2
3	0040	4.1	18	0040	3.7
	0700	1.4		0655	1.7
TU	1331	4.1	W	1331	3.8
	1935	1.6		1919	1.9
4	0150	4.4	19	0150	3.8
	0801	1.2		0746	1.5
W	1430	4.5	TH	1421	4.1
	2026	1.3		2008	1.6
5	0244	4.7	20	0237	4.1
	0849	0.9		0831	1.3
TH	1516	4.7	F	1501	4.3
	2109	1.0		2050	1.3
6	0331	4.9	21	0317	4.3
	0930	0.8		0911	1.1
F	1556	4.9	SA	1536	4.6
	2150	0.8		2129	1.1
7	0414	5.0	22	0354	4.5
	1009	0.7		0948	0.9
SA	1635	5.0	SU	1611	4.8
	2230	0.6		2206	0.8
8	0456	5.0	23	0433	4.7
	1046	0.7		1024	0.8
SU	1713	5.0	M	1648	5.0
●	2310	0.7	○	2245	0.6
9	0536	5.0	24	0515	4.8
	1122	0.8		1102	0.7
M	1750	5.0	TU	1728	5.1
	2349	0.7		2326	0.5
10	0616	4.8	25	0559	4.9
	1156	1.0		1142	0.7
TU	1827	4.8	W	1811	5.1
11	0027	0.9	26	0010	0.5
	0655	4.6		0644	4.8
W	1231	1.2	TH	1226	0.8
	1904	4.6		1855	5.0
12	0107	1.1	27	0057	0.6
	0734	4.4		0731	4.7
TH	1306	1.5	F	1312	1.1
	1942	4.4		1944	4.8
13	0149	1.4	28	0147	0.8
	0815	4.1		0822	4.5
F	1345	1.7	SA	1403	1.3
	2025	4.2		2040	4.6
14	0238	1.6	29	0241	1.0
	0902	3.9		0922	4.3
SA	1430	2.0	SU	1502	1.6
	2113	3.9		2147	4.3
15	0344	1.8	30	0347	1.3
	0956	3.7		1031	4.1
SU	1538	2.2	M	1621	1.8
	2211	3.8	◑	2300	4.2
			31	0507	1.4
				1143	4.1
			TU	1752	1.8

JUNE

Day	Time	m	Day	Time	m
1	0010	4.3	16	0550	1.7
	0623	1.4		1204	3.9
W	1254	4.2	TH	1819	2.0
	1901	1.6			
2	0116	4.4	17	0017	3.9
	0727	1.3		0647	1.7
TH	1356	4.4	F	1304	4.0
	1957	1.4		1917	1.8
3	0214	4.5	18	0121	4.0
	0820	1.2		0742	1.5
F	1447	4.5	SA	1402	4.2
	2045	1.2		2010	1.5
4	0305	4.6	19	0224	4.1
	0905	1.2		0832	1.4
SA	1531	4.7	SU	1451	4.4
	2128	1.1		2057	1.2
5	0350	4.6	20	0317	4.3
	0945	1.1		0917	1.2
SU	1611	4.7	M	1537	4.7
	2210	1.0		2142	1.0
6	0434	4.6	21	0407	4.6
	1024	1.1		1001	1.0
M	1649	4.7	TU	1622	4.9
●	2252	1.0		2227	0.7
7	0516	4.6	22	0456	4.7
	1100	1.2		1046	0.8
TU	1727	4.7	W	1709	5.0
	2333	1.0	○	2314	0.5
8	0557	4.5	23	0546	4.8
	1136	1.3		1132	0.7
W	1806	4.7	TH	1758	5.1
9	0013	1.1	24	0002	0.4
	0637	4.4		0634	4.9
TH	1213	1.4	F	1219	0.7
	1844	4.6		1846	5.1
10	0054	1.2	25	0050	0.4
	0717	4.3		0723	4.8
F	1251	1.5	SA	1306	0.8
	1924	4.4		1936	5.0
11	0134	1.3	26	0138	0.5
	0758	4.2		0812	4.7
SA	1330	1.6	SU	1354	1.0
	2006	4.3		2029	4.8
12	0216	1.4	27	0228	0.7
	0841	4.1		0906	4.5
SU	1412	1.8	M	1447	1.3
	2050	4.1		2128	4.6
13	0302	1.5	28	0323	1.0
	0928	3.9		1005	4.3
M	1500	1.9	TU	1549	1.5
	2138	4.0	◑	2232	4.4
14	0355	1.6	29	0426	1.2
	1018	3.9		1108	4.1
TU	1601	2.0	W	1704	1.7
	2229	3.9		2335	4.2
15	0453	1.7	30	0535	1.4
	1110	3.8		1212	4.1
W	1712	2.1	TH	1821	1.7
◐	2322	3.9			

JULY

Day	Time	m	Day	Time	m
1	0039	4.2	16	0532	1.7
	0645	1.5		1205	4.0
F	1318	4.1	SA	1814	1.9
	1927	1.6			
2	0143	4.1	17	0031	3.9
	0748	1.6		0643	1.8
SA	1419	4.2	SU	1310	4.1
	2024	1.5		1931	1.7
3	0242	4.2	18	0144	4.0
	0841	1.6		0759	1.6
SU	1510	4.3	M	1417	4.3
	2112	1.4		2035	1.4
4	0333	4.2	19	0254	4.2
	0925	1.5		0858	1.4
M	1554	4.4	TU	1515	4.5
	2156	1.2		2128	1.0
5	0419	4.3	20	0352	4.4
	1006	1.4		0949	1.1
TU	1634	4.5	W	1607	4.8
	2238	1.1		2218	0.7
6	0502	4.3	21	0445	4.7
	1045	1.4		1037	0.8
W	1713	4.5	TH	1658	5.0
●	2320	1.0	○	2306	0.4
7	0544	4.4	22	0535	4.9
	1122	1.3		1123	0.6
TH	1752	4.6	F	1747	5.2
	2359	1.0		2352	0.2
8	0623	4.4	23	0623	5.0
	1159	1.3		1208	0.5
F	1831	4.6	SA	1835	5.2
9	0036	1.0	24	0037	0.1
	0701	4.4		0709	5.0
SA	1236	1.3	SU	1252	0.5
	1908	4.5		1922	5.2
10	0112	1.0	25	0121	0.2
	0739	4.4		0754	4.9
SU	1312	1.3	M	1336	0.7
	1945	4.4		2009	5.0
11	0147	1.1	26	0205	0.4
	0817	4.3		0840	4.6
M	1348	1.4	TU	1422	1.0
	2022	4.3		2100	4.7
12	0223	1.2	27	0251	0.8
	0856	4.2		0931	4.4
TU	1426	1.5	W	1512	1.3
	2101	4.2		2156	4.4
13	0302	1.3	28	0343	1.2
	0936	4.1		1026	4.1
W	1509	1.7	TH	1615	1.6
	2144	4.1	◑	2257	4.1
14	0345	1.5	29	0444	1.6
	1020	4.0		1127	3.9
TH	1600	1.8	F	1734	1.8
◐	2233	4.0			
15	0434	1.6	30	0002	3.9
	1109	4.0		0557	1.8
F	1701	1.9	SA	1237	3.8
	2328	3.9		1857	1.9
			31	0115	3.8
				0715	1.9
			SU	1356	3.8
				2009	1.7

AUGUST

Day	Time	m	Day	Time	m
1	0227	3.8	16	0125	3.8
	0820	1.9		0746	1.8
M	1459	4.0	TU	1357	4.1
	2103	1.5		2028	1.5
2	0324	3.9	17	0246	4.1
	0909	1.7		0851	1.5
TU	1546	4.2	W	1505	4.5
	2146	1.3		2122	1.0
3	0409	4.1	18	0345	4.4
	0951	1.5		0940	1.1
W	1626	4.4	TH	1558	4.8
	2224	1.1		2208	0.6
4	0451	4.2	19	0434	4.7
	1029	1.3		1025	0.7
TH	1703	4.5	F	1647	5.1
	2301	0.9	○	2252	0.2
5	0529	4.4	20	0521	5.0
	1105	1.2		1108	0.4
F	1740	4.6	SA	1733	5.3
●	2337	0.8		2334	0.0
6	0606	4.5	21	0605	5.1
	1140	1.0		1150	0.3
SA	1815	4.7	SU	1818	5.4
7	0011	0.7	22	0015	-0.1
	0641	4.5		0647	5.1
SU	1215	1.0	M	1231	0.3
	1848	4.7		1901	5.3
8	0043	0.7	23	0056	0.1
	0716	4.5		0728	5.0
M	1247	1.0	TU	1312	0.5
	1920	4.6		1944	5.1
9	0115	0.8	24	0136	0.4
	0748	4.5		0809	4.8
TU	1319	1.1	W	1353	0.8
	1950	4.5		2027	4.7
10	0146	0.9	25	0217	0.8
	0819	4.4		0851	4.5
W	1353	1.2	TH	1437	1.2
	2019	4.4		2116	4.3
11	0221	1.1	26	0302	1.3
	0851	4.3		0938	4.1
TH	1431	1.4	F	1530	1.6
	2054	4.2	◑	2213	3.9
12	0300	1.4	27	0358	1.8
	0929	4.1		1034	3.8
F	1516	1.6	SA	1650	2.0
	2145	4.0		2324	3.6
13	0346	1.6	28	0519	2.1
	1020	4.0		1154	3.6
SA	1612	1.9	SU	1828	2.1
◐	2250	3.8			
14	0444	1.9	29	0052	3.5
	1122	3.9		0647	2.2
SU	1724	2.0	M	1342	3.7
				2001	1.9
15	0001	3.7	30	0220	3.7
	0559	2.0		0800	2.1
M	1234	3.9	TU	1448	3.9
	1909	1.8		2058	1.6
			31	0313	3.9
				0851	1.8
			W	1533	4.2
				2131	1.3

Chart Datum: 0·20 metres above Ordnance Datum (Dublin)

TIME ZONE (UT)
For Summer Time add ONE hour in **non-shaded areas**

IRELAND – GALWAY

LAT 53°16′N LONG 9°03′W

TIMES AND HEIGHTS OF HIGH AND LOW WATERS

SPRING & NEAP TIDES
Dates in red are SPRINGS
Dates in blue are NEAPS

YEAR **2005**

SEPTEMBER

Date	Day	Time	m	Time	m	Time	m	Time	m
1	TH	0354	4.1	0931	1.5	1610	4.4	2202	1.0
2	F	0431	4.4	1007	1.2	1645	4.6	2235	0.8
3	SA	0507	4.5	1041	1.0	1719	4.7	● 2308	0.6
4	SU	0541	4.7	1115	0.8	1752	4.8	2340	0.6
5	M	0615	4.7	1147	0.8	1823	4.8		
6	TU	0011	0.6	0646	4.7	1218	0.8	1850	4.8
7	W	0041	0.7	0715	4.7	1249	0.9	1915	4.7
8	TH	0111	0.9	0741	4.6	1322	1.0	1940	4.5
9	F	0144	1.1	0808	4.4	1359	1.3	2013	4.3
10	SA	0223	1.4	0843	4.2	1443	1.6	2104	4.0
11	SU	0310	1.8	0937	4.0	1538	1.9	◐ 2224	3.8
12	M	0412	2.1	1052	3.9	1655	2.1	2347	3.7
13	TU	0546	2.2	1213	3.9	1913	1.9		
14	W	0122	3.8	0743	1.9	1350	4.1	2021	1.4
15	TH	0242	4.2	0839	1.5	1457	4.6	2109	0.9
16	F	0333	4.6	0925	1.1	1545	5.0	2151	0.5
17	SA	0417	4.9	1007	0.7	1630	5.3	2231	0.2
18	SU	0459	5.2	1047	0.4	1713	5.5	○ 2310	0.0
19	M	0541	5.3	1127	0.3	1755	5.5	2349	0.1
20	TU	0621	5.3	1207	0.3	1837	5.4		
21	W	0027	0.3	0659	5.1	1246	0.5	1916	5.1
22	TH	0105	0.6	0737	4.9	1325	0.8	1957	4.8
23	F	0143	1.1	0815	4.6	1405	1.3	2040	4.3
24	SA	0224	1.6	0856	4.2	1454	1.7	2134	3.9
25	SU	0317	2.0	0947	3.9	1615	2.1	◑ 2248	3.6
26	M	0451	2.4	1100	3.6	1759	2.2		
27	TU	0034	3.5	0621	2.4	1319	3.6	1935	2.0
28	W	0202	3.7	0730	2.2	1425	3.9	2034	1.7
29	TH	0251	4.0	0822	1.9	1508	4.2	2101	1.4
30	F	0329	4.3	0902	1.6	1545	4.4	2131	1.1

OCTOBER

Date	Day	Time	m	Time	m	Time	m	Time	m
1	SA	0403	4.5	0938	1.2	1618	4.6	2203	0.9
2	SU	0437	4.7	1013	1.0	1650	4.8	2235	0.7
3	M	0509	4.8	1046	0.8	1721	4.9	● 2307	0.6
4	TU	0541	4.9	1117	0.7	1750	4.9	2336	0.7
5	W	0611	4.9	1148	0.7	1818	4.9		
6	TH	0006	0.8	0639	4.9	1220	0.8	1846	4.8
7	F	0039	1.0	0708	4.8	1256	1.0	1917	4.6
8	SA	0115	1.2	0739	4.6	1335	1.2	1956	4.4
9	SU	0157	1.6	0819	4.4	1422	1.5	2053	4.1
10	M	0247	1.9	0917	4.1	1519	1.9	◐ 2216	3.9
11	TU	0356	2.2	1038	4.0	1643	2.0	2342	3.8
12	W	0610	2.3	1204	4.0	1859	1.8		
13	TH	0116	4.0	0725	1.9	1335	4.3	2000	1.4
14	F	0224	4.4	0818	1.5	1437	4.7	2047	1.0
15	SA	0311	4.8	0903	1.1	1525	5.1	2128	0.6
16	SU	0353	5.1	0944	0.7	1608	5.4	2207	0.4
17	M	0434	5.3	1024	0.5	1650	5.5	○ 2245	0.4
18	TU	0513	5.3	1104	0.5	1731	5.5	2322	0.5
19	W	0553	5.3	1143	0.5	1812	5.3		
20	TH	0000	0.7	0630	5.2	1222	0.7	1851	5.1
21	F	0037	1.0	0708	4.9	1301	1.0	1932	4.7
22	SA	0114	1.4	0746	4.6	1342	1.4	2015	4.3
23	SU	0155	1.8	0828	4.3	1430	1.8	2106	4.0
24	M	0246	2.2	0917	4.0	1543	2.1	2215	3.7
25	TU	0419	2.5	1020	3.8	1719	2.2	◑ 2353	3.6
26	W	0546	2.5	1222	3.7	1833	2.1		
27	TH	0119	3.8	0649	2.3	1342	3.9	1933	1.9
28	F	0213	4.0	0742	2.0	1431	4.1	2017	1.6
29	SA	0253	4.3	0826	1.7	1509	4.3	2053	1.3
30	SU	0327	4.5	0905	1.4	1543	4.5	2128	1.1
31	M	0400	4.7	0941	1.2	1615	4.7	2201	0.9

NOVEMBER

Date	Day	Time	m	Time	m	Time	m	Time	m
1	TU	0432	4.9	1015	1.0	1645	4.9	2233	0.9
2	W	0503	5.0	1048	0.9	1716	4.9	● 2304	0.9
3	TH	0535	5.0	1121	0.8	1751	5.0	2337	0.9
4	F	0610	5.0	1158	0.8	1828	4.9		
5	SA	0014	1.1	0646	4.9	1238	0.9	1908	4.7
6	SU	0056	1.3	0726	4.8	1322	1.1	1956	4.5
7	M	0143	1.6	0813	4.6	1412	1.4	2056	4.2
8	TU	0238	2.0	0914	4.4	1512	1.7	2210	4.1
9	W	0352	2.2	1029	4.2	1635	1.8	◐ 2331	4.1
10	TH	0547	2.1	1148	4.3	1826	1.7		
11	F	0050	4.3	0657	1.9	1306	4.5	1930	1.4
12	SA	0155	4.6	0752	1.5	1409	4.8	2021	1.1
13	SU	0245	4.8	0839	1.2	1500	5.0	2104	0.9
14	M	0328	5.1	0922	1.0	1545	5.2	2143	0.8
15	TU	0408	5.2	1003	0.8	1627	5.2	2221	0.8
16	W	0448	5.2	1044	0.8	1709	5.2	○ 2259	0.9
17	TH	0527	5.2	1124	0.9	1750	5.1	2336	1.1
18	F	0607	5.0	1205	1.0	1832	4.9		
19	SA	0014	1.3	0646	4.9	1245	1.2	1913	4.6
20	SU	0054	1.6	0726	4.7	1327	1.4	1957	4.3
21	M	0136	1.9	0808	4.4	1413	1.7	2045	4.1
22	TU	0224	2.1	0854	4.2	1508	1.9	2143	3.9
23	W	0331	2.3	0947	4.0	1621	2.0	◑ 2251	3.8
24	TH	0453	2.4	1048	3.9	1732	2.0		
25	F	0002	3.8	0557	2.3	1200	3.8	1831	2.0
26	SA	0107	4.0	0653	2.2	1318	3.9	1924	1.8
27	SU	0159	4.2	0744	1.9	1414	4.1	2010	1.6
28	M	0241	4.4	0828	1.7	1456	4.3	2051	1.4
29	TU	0317	4.6	0908	1.4	1533	4.5	2128	1.2
30	W	0353	4.8	0946	1.2	1610	4.7	2203	1.1

DECEMBER

Date	Day	Time	m	Time	m	Time	m	Time	m
1	TH	0429	5.0	1024	1.0	1650	4.8	● 2240	1.0
2	F	0508	5.1	1103	0.8	1732	4.9	2320	1.0
3	SA	0550	5.1	1146	0.8	1817	4.9		
4	SU	0003	1.1	0634	5.1	1231	0.8	1904	4.8
5	M	0049	1.2	0720	5.0	1317	0.9	1953	4.7
6	TU	0138	1.4	0810	4.8	1407	1.1	2050	4.5
7	W	0233	1.7	0907	4.6	1503	1.3	2155	4.3
8	TH	0339	1.9	1013	4.5	1611	1.5	◐ 2305	4.2
9	F	0503	1.9	1122	4.4	1735	1.6		
10	SA	0014	4.3	0619	1.8	1232	4.4	1853	1.5
11	SU	0120	4.4	0722	1.7	1337	4.5	1952	1.4
12	M	0217	4.6	0816	1.5	1435	4.7	2041	1.3
13	TU	0305	4.8	0903	1.3	1524	4.8	2124	1.3
14	W	0348	4.9	0948	1.2	1610	4.8	2204	1.3
15	TH	0429	4.9	1031	1.1	1653	4.8	○ 2243	1.3
16	F	0510	4.9	1113	1.1	1736	4.7	2321	1.3
17	SA	0551	4.9	1154	1.1	1818	4.6		
18	SU	0000	1.4	0631	4.8	1235	1.2	1859	4.5
19	M	0040	1.5	0711	4.7	1313	1.2	1941	4.4
20	TU	0120	1.6	0751	4.6	1352	1.4	2024	4.2
21	W	0202	1.8	0832	4.4	1434	1.5	2110	4.1
22	TH	0247	1.9	0914	4.2	1519	1.7	2200	4.0
23	F	0340	2.1	1000	4.1	1612	1.8	◑ 2253	3.9
24	SA	0442	2.2	1048	4.0	1711	1.9	2346	3.9
25	SU	0547	2.2	1140	3.9	1815	1.9		
26	M	0043	4.0	0649	2.1	1241	3.9	1918	1.9
27	TU	0141	4.1	0747	1.9	1353	4.0	2013	1.7
28	W	0234	4.3	0838	1.7	1454	4.2	2100	1.5
29	TH	0320	4.6	0925	1.3	1545	4.5	2144	1.3
30	F	0406	4.8	1010	1.0	1634	4.7	2228	1.1
31	SA	0452	5.0	1055	0.8	1722	4.9	● 2313	0.9

Chart Datum: 0·20 metres above Ordnance Datum (Dublin)

Area 14

West Denmark
Skagen to Rømø

The Danish Flag – Dannebrog

According to legend, Dannebrog (literally 'the cloth of the Danes') fell down from the sky on June 15, 1219 to the Danish King Valdemar II during his crusade to Estonia. With the flag in hand, the King won the battle at Lyndanisse near Reval (Tallin).The flag was given to him as a divine approval. This is the explanation Danes like to give when telling the origin of the Danish national flag. If the legend is true, it would make it the World's oldest national flag still in use.

Up to 1854 the Dannebrog was solely the flag of the Danish King and the Royal Navy. Slowly it also became the Danish symbol of the army and the mercantile marine and in 1854, private persons were allowed to use the rectangular flag.

The Dannebrog exists in various forms. The most famous one is the rectangular form which is a simple white cross on a bright red background. The exact shade of the red color of the background of the rectangular flag has never been established, but rest assured that the Danes will know when it's right or wrong!

The Dannebrog also exists in a swallow-tailed version. The form has been known since the fifteenth century and it also represented the King and the Navy. Today, this version of the flag belongs to the state of Denmark, the Royal House and the Navy. Private persons must have a special permission to fly the swallow-tailed Dannebrog.

The swallow-tailed Dannebrog of the Queen of Denmark is very recognisable, as it has the royal coat of arms in the central field.

The Danish people love their flag and are very proud to use it whenever it is possible, whether as a tiny paper version for the Christmas tree or as facial make-up at a football match.

There are a few rules to follow when it comes to the display of Dannebrog. The two big versions – the rectangular and the swallow-tail – are flown on special occasions and are hoisted at sunrise (usually 8 o'clock) and lowered at sunset. To fly Dannebrog by night is considered an offence, punishable by law. The flag must never touch the ground. The pennant (never called Dannebrog) can be used 24 hours and is only lowered when Dannebrog is hoisted.

1	*Hamburg*	338	317	265	233	216	192	163	167	139	136	110	99	113	90	81	110	88	54	61	**1**
2	*Wangerooge*	283	262	210	178	168	147	109	112	94	90	66	68	52	108	38	27	24	42	**2**	
3	*Cuxhaven*	304	284	232	200	162	138	110	113	85	82	56	56	66	70	58	56	38	**3**		
4	*Helgoland*	259	238	186	154	141	119	83	85	63	60	40	39	47	104	44	43	**4**			
5	*Wilhelmshaven*	414	296	242	310	184	162	125	128	106	103	83	82	82	123	45	**5**				
6	*Bremerhaven*	306	285	233	201	185	163	127	129	107	104	84	83	82	123	**6**					
7	*Kiel/Holtenau*	261	233	281	249	232	208	180	183	189	186	126	126	129	**7**						
8	*Husum*	275	247	195	163	152	131	95	98	68	65	44	45	**8**							
9	*Hörnum*	248	215	163	131	108	86	70	73	29	26	14	**9**								
10	*Föhr*	272	239	187	155	122	100	84	87	43	40	**10**									
11	*List*	230	197	145	113	91	70	27	30	8	**11**										
12	Rømø	233	200	148	116	94	73	30	33	**12**											
13	Fanø	210	177	125	93	79	57	3	**13**												
14	**Esbjerg**	200	174	122	90	76	54	**14**													
15	Hvide Sande	162	179	77	45	24	**15**														
16	Torsminde	141	108	56	24	**16**															
17	Thyborøn	114	84	32	**17**																
18	Hanstholm	85	52	**18**																	
19	Hirtshals	33	**19**																		
20	**Skagen**	**20**																			

DISTANCE TABLE

Approximate distances in nautical miles are by the most direct route, whilst avoiding dangers and allowing for Traffic Separation Schemes. Places in *italics* are in adjoining areas. Places in bold are in 9.0.8 Distances across the North Sea.

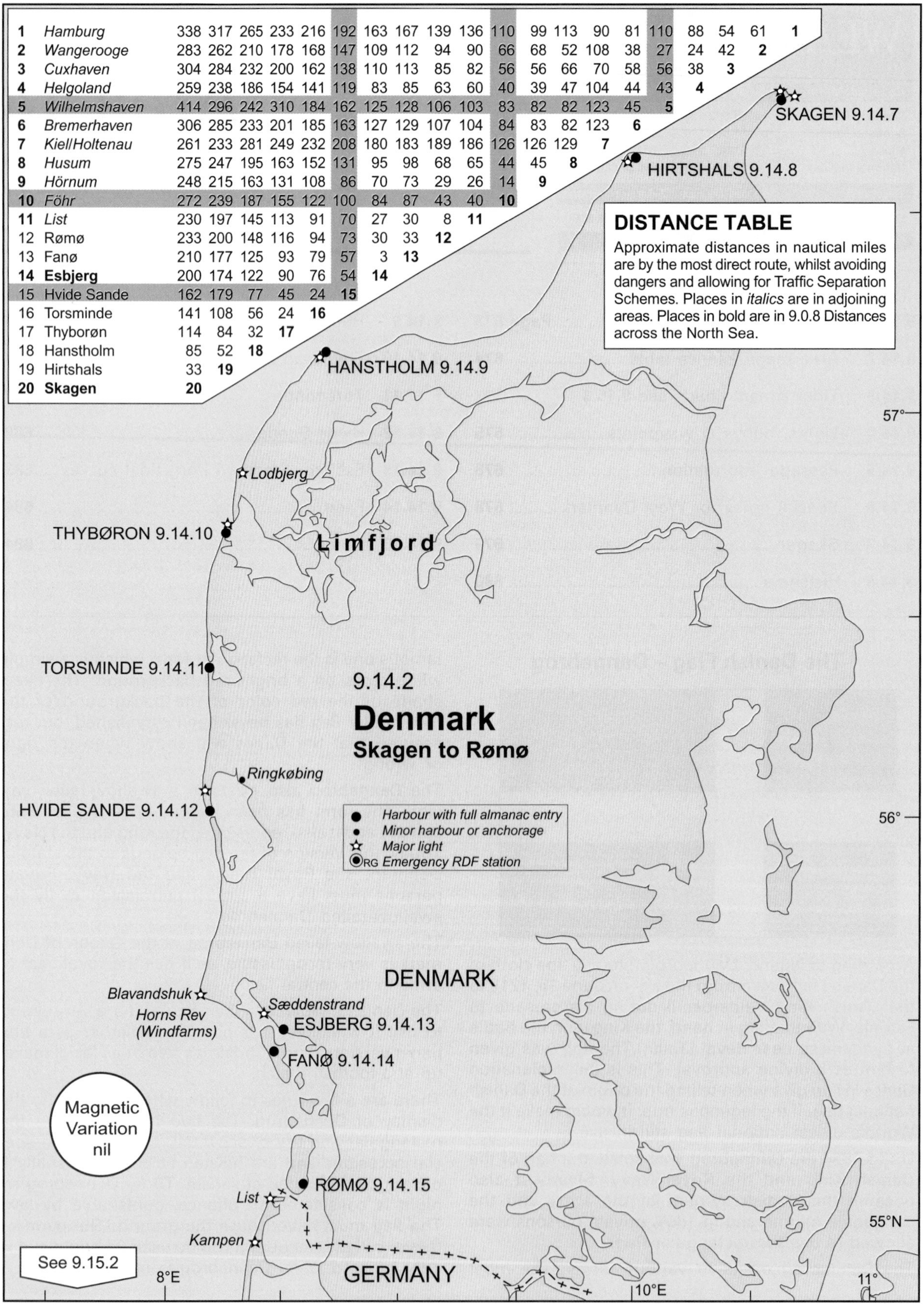

SKAGEN 9.14.7
HIRTSHALS 9.14.8
HANSTHOLM 9.14.9
Lodbjerg
THYBØRON 9.14.10
Limfjord
57°
TORSMINDE 9.14.11
9.14.2
Denmark
Skagen to Rømø
Ringkøbing
HVIDE SANDE 9.14.12
56°
Harbour with full almanac entry
Minor harbour or anchorage
Major light
RG Emergency RDF station
DENMARK
Blavandshuk
Horns Rev
(Windfarms)
Sæddenstrand
ESJBERG 9.14.13
FANØ 9.14.14
Magnetic
Variation
nil
RØMØ 9.14.15
List
Kampen
55°N
See 9.15.2
8°E
GERMANY
10°E
11°

PLOT WAYPOINTS ON YOUR CHART BEFORE USING THEM

9.14.3 TIDAL STREAM CHARTS see 9.15.3

9.14.4 LIGHTS, BUOYS AND WAYPOINTS

Blue print = light with a nominal range of 15M or more. CAPITALS = place or feature. *CAPITAL ITALICS* = light-vessel, light float or Lanby. *Italics* = Fog signal. ***Bold italics*** = Racon. Useful waypoints are underlined. Abbreviations are in Chapter 1. Positions are referenced to the WGS 84 datum. Admiralty charts for this area may be referenced to either WGS84 or ED50.

SKAGEN TO THYBORON

▶ SKAGEN

Skagen W ☆ 57°44'·92N 10°35·66E, Fl (3) WR 10s 31m **W17M**/ R12M; W053°-248°, R248°-323°; W ○ twr.

Skagen ☆ 57°44'·11N 10°37'·76E, Fl 4s 44m **23M**; Gy ○ twr; **Racon G, 20M**.

Skagen No 1A 57°43'·42N 10°53'·51E, L Fl 10s; **Racon N**.

Skagen No. 2 57°37'·59N 11°05'·51E, L Fl 10s.

Skagens Rev 57°45'·95N 10°43'·70E, Q.

57°43'·83N 10°42'·27E, Q (3) 10s.

Skagen Harbour

Ldg Its 334·5°, both Iso R 4s 13/22m 8M. Front 57°43'·06N 10°35'·45E; mast. Rear, 57°43'·2N 10°35'·4E; twr.

E bkwtr knuckle ☆ 57°43'·25N 10°36'·44E, F 4m 2M; Gy lantern.

E bkwtr ☆ 57°42'·88N 10°35'·66E, Fl G 3s 8m 5M; G twr; *Horn (2) 30s.*

W bkwtr ☆ 57°42'·84N 10°35'·59E, Fl R 3s 8m 5M; R twr.

Forhavns SW mole ☆ 57°42'·94N 10°35'·51E, FR 5m 2M; Gy col.

NE mole ☆ 57°42'·96N 10°35'·56E, FG 5m 2M; Gy col.

Inner W mole ☆ 57°43'·08N 10°35'·51E, FR 6m; post; only over the hbr.

Inner E mole ☆ 57°43'·08N 10°35'·55E, FG 6m; post.

▶ HIRTSHALS

Hirtshals ☆ 57°35'·07N 09°56'·45E, F Fl 30s 57m **F 18M; Fl 25M**; W ○ twr, approx 1M SSW of hbr ent.

Ldg Its 166°, both 156°-176°. Front 57°35'·69N 09°57'·64E, Iso R 2s 10m 11M; R △ on twr; Rear, 330m from front, Iso R 4s 18m 11M; R ▽ on twr; marina is close NW of this lt.

Access chan 57°36'·18N 09°56·95E, Fl (3) G 10s.

57°36'·12N 09°57·15E, Fl G 5s.

57°36'·44N 09°57'·68E, Fl R 3s.

57°36'·43N 09°57'·72E, Fl (5) Y 20s.

57°36'·15N 09°57'·72E.

Outer W mole ☆ 57°35'·97N 09°57'·36E, Fl G 3s 14m 6M; G mast; *Horn 15s.*

W mole spur ☆ 57°35'·79N 09°57'·55E, Fl G 5s 9m 4M; G mast.

E mole ☆ 57°35'·85N 09°57'·60E, Fl R 5s 9m 6M; G mast.

Inner hbr ☆ 57°35'·71N 09°57'·77E, FG 6m 4M; G mast.

▶ LØKKEN

Lee bkwtr ☆ 57°22'·47N 09°41'·85E, Fl 5s 5m 5M.

▶ TRANUM STRAND

Y 57°10'·87N 09°20'·86E.

Y 57°12'·03N 09°20'·86E.

Tranum No. 1 ☆ 57°10'·68N 09°26'·56E Al WR 4s 20m **W16M**, R13M; twr; by day Fl; shown when firing is taking place.

Tranum No. 2 ☆ 57°12'·42N 09°30'·14E Al WR 4s by day Fl; shown when firing is taking place.

Y 57°15'·39N 09°28'·16E.

▶ LILD STRAND

Bragerne 57°10'·68N 08°56'·20E, Fl G 5s.

Ldg Its 138°, triple, F 12/22m 7/8M; 127°-149°; 3 masts. Front 57°09'·21N 08°57'·63E; *Siren 30s, fishing (occas).*

▶ HANSTHOLM

Hanstholm ☆ 57°06'·65N 08°35'·74E, Fl (3) 20s 65m **26M**; shown by day in poor vis; W 8-sided twr; approx 1M S of the hbr ent.

Hanstholm 57°08'·10N 08°34'·94E, LFl 10s.

Ldg Its 142·6, both Iso 2s 37/45m 13M; synch. Front 57°07'·12N 08°36'·15E; R △ on mast; 127·6°-157·6°. Rear, 170m from front, R ▽ on mast.

W outer mole ☆ 57°07'·54N 08°35'·46E, Fl G 3s 11m 9M; G pillar.

E outer mole ☆ 57°07'·60N 08°35'·58E, Fl R 3s 11m 9M; R pillar.

W inner mole ☆ 57°07'·41N 08°35'·58E, F G 6m 6M; G col.

E inner mole ☆ 57°07'·35N 08°35'·64E, F R 6m 6M, H24; R col, floodlit.

Roshage ☆ 57°07'·76N 08°37'·22E (1M E of hbr), Fl 5s 7m 5M.

▶ NØRRE VORUPER

Mole ☆ 57°57'·73N 08°21'·64E, Fl G 5s 6m 4M.

Ldg Its, both Iso R 4s 20/39m 9M; vis 22·5° either side of ldg line; synch. Indicate safest landing place. Front 57°57'·44N 08°22'·08E. Rear, 80m from front.

Lodbjerg ☆ 56°49'·39N 08°15'·74E, Fl (2) 20s 48m **23M**; ○ twr.

▶ THYBORØN

Landfall 56°42'·55N 08°08'·70E, L Fl 10s; **Racon T, 10m**.

Agger Tange ldg Its 082°. Front 56°42'·97N 08°14'·11E, Oc WRG 4s 8m W11M, R/G8M; G074·5°-079·5°, W079·5°-084·5°, R084·5°-089·5°; R △ on bn. Rear 804m from front, Iso 4s 17m 11M; 080°-084°; R ▽ on Gy twr.

Off Havmolen 56°43'·25N 08°12'·52E.

Approach ☆ 56°42'·49N 08°12'·90E Fl (3) 10s 24m 12M; intens 023·5°-203·5°; also shown by day in poor vis; lattice twr.

Havrevlen (hbr entry buoys) 56°42'·79N 08°13'·37E.

56°42'·77N 08°13'·72E. 56°42'·53N 08°13'·77E, Fl (2) G 5s.

Langholm ldg Its 120°, both Iso 2s 7/13m 11M; synch; 113°-127°. Front 56°42'·45N 08°14'·53E, R △ on R hut. Rear, R ▽ on Gy twr.

Thyborøn Havn ☆ 56°42'·35N 08°13'·39E, Oc (2) WRG 12s 6m W12M, R/G9M; G122·5°-146·5°, W146·5°-150°, R150°-211·3°, G211·3°-337·5°, W337·5°-340°, R340°-344°; W twr R band.

Yderhavn, N mole ☆ 56°42'·02N 08°13'·52E, Fl G 3s 6m 4M; G pedestal.

S mole ☆ 56°41'·97N 08°13'·53E, Fl R 3s 6m 4M; R pedestal.

LIMFJORD (Limited coverage, only to 08°42'E)

Sælhundeholm Løb, into Nissum Bredning ('Broad').

No. 1 56°41'·14N 08°14'·17E, Fl (2) G 5s.

No. 3 56°40'·75N 08°13'·79E, Fl G 3s.

No. 7 56°40'·31N 08°13'·52E, Fl G 3s.

No. 11 56°39'·83N 08°13'·59E, Fl G 3s.

No. 16 56°38'·51N 08°13'·89E, Fl R 3s.

No. 18 56°38'·20N 08°14'·34E, Fl (2) R 5s.

No. 21 56°38'·98N 08°14'·71E, Fl G 3s.

No. 26 56°38'·71N 08°15'·38E, Fl R 3s.

No. 29 56°38'·40N 08°15'·94E, Fl G 3s.

56°38'·06N 08°16'·70E, Q.

▶ APPROACHES TO LEMVIG (Marina & Havn)

Toftum Dir ☆ 120°; 56°33'·09N 08°18'·33E, Iso WRG 4s 24m, W12M, R/G 8M; G110°-120°, W120°-137°, R137°-144°; hut.

PLOT WAYPOINTS ON YOUR CHART BEFORE USING THEM

Rønnen 56°36'·71N 08°21'·74E, Fl G 3s.
Rønnen 56°35'·58N 08°21'·62E, L Fl 10s.
Søgard Mark ldg lts 243·5°, both FR 20/30m 5M; vis 90° either side of ldg line. Front, 56°34'·39N 08°17'·29E; R △ on W bcn. Rear, 235m from front; R ▽ on W post.
Rønnen Spit 56°35'·34N 08°20'·70E.
Chan 56°33'·27N 08°18'·31E.
Ldg lts, W of hbr 177·7°, both FR 8/20m 5M; 153°-203°. Front 56°33'·04N 08°18'·16E; R △ on twr. Rear, 184m from front; R ▽ on W post.
Marina, N mole ☆ 56°33'·09N 08°18'·33E, FG 3m 5M.
S mole, FR 3m 4M. Marina is on the W side, 9ca N of the Havn.
Ostre Havn 56°33'·17N 08°18'·40E. Havn ent, FG/FR 4m 5M.

▶ THISTED HAVN (Marina)

Outer W mole ☆ 56°57'·10N 08°41'·90E, Fl R 3s 4m 2M.
Outer E mole ☆ 56°57'·10N 08°41'·95E, Fl G 3s 4m 2M.
Thisted Bredning ☆ 56°58'·52N 08°41'·15E, Aero 3 Fl R 1·5s (vert; 45m apart) 183m 10M; TV mast; 1·55M NNW of hbr ent.

THYBORON TO BLÅVANDS HUK

Bovbjerg ☆ 56°30'·74N 08°07'·13E, L Fl (2) 15s 62m **16M**.

▶ TORSMINDE HAVN

(All positions in this section are approximate)
Lt ho ☆ 56°22'·34N 08°06'·99E, F 30m 13M; Gy twr.
N mole ☆ 56°22'·36N 08°06'·62E, Iso R 2s 9m 4M; R hut.
S mole ☆ 56°22'·26N 08°06'·92E, Iso G 2s 9m 4M; G hut.
Groyne, N ☆ 56°22'·46N 08°06'·82E, Fl 5s 8m 5M; gy hut.
West hbr, W mole ☆ 56°22'·36N 08°07'·12E, F G 5m 2M; Gy post.
E mole ☆ 56°22'·26N 08°07'·18E, F R 5m 2M; Gy post.
NW dolphin ☆ 56°22'·26N 08°07'·22E, F G 5m 4M; Gy post.
SE dolphin ☆ 56°22' 26N 08°07' 26E, F G 5m 4M; Gy post.
Lock, E side ☆ 56°22'·36N 08°07'·22E, Iso 4s 12m 4M; Gy mast; 020°-160°.
Road bridge ☆ 56°22'·36N 08°07'·26E, Iso 4s 5m 4M: 200°-340°.

▶ HVIDE SANDE

Lyngvig ☆ 56°02'·95N 08°06'·17E, Fl 5s 53m **22M**; W ○ twr.
N outer bkwtr ☆ 55°59'·94N 08°06'·55E, Fl R 3s 7m 8M; R hut.
N mole ☆ 55°59'·96N 08°06' 85E, Fl R 5s 10m 6M; R structure; *Horn 15s.*
S mole ☆ 55°59'·93N 08°06'·88E, Fl G 5s 10m 6M.
N inner mole ☆ 56°00'·06N 08°07'·22E, FR 5m 3M; Gy col.
S inner mole ☆ 56°00'·06N 08°07'·32E, FG 5m 2M; Gy col.
Lt ho ☆ 56°00'·00N 08°07'·35E, F 27m 14M; Gy twr.
Nordhavn, E pier ☆ 56°00'·16N 08°07'·42E, FG 4m 4M.
W pier ☆ 56°00'·07N 08°07'·12E, 2 FR 3m 2M; W posts; 060°-035°.
Sydhavn, W pier ☆ 56°00'·06N 08°07'·52E, FG 4m 2M.
E Pier ☆ 56°00'·06N 08°07'·53E, FR 4m 2M; Gy post
Lock entrance ldg lts 293·5°, both FR 11/14m 2M; 201·6°-021·6°. Front 56°00'·0N 08°07'·8E; R △ on gy tr. Rear, 72m from front, R ▽ on gy twr.
Fjordhavn ldg lts 246·6°. Front 56°00'·5N 08°07'·9E, Iso G 2s 4m 4M; Or △ on mast. Rear, 128m away, Iso G 4s 6m 4M, Or ▽ on mast.

Coastal marks. 55°48'·47N 07°56'·22E, Fl (5) Y 20s.

▶ HORNS REV (marks westward from coast)

Oskbøl firing range. Two lights (4M apart), both AlFl WR 4s 35m **16M**, R13M, (by day Q 10M), are shown when firing is in progress. North ☆ 55°37'·3N 08°07'·1E. South ☆ 55°33'·6N 08°04'·7E.
Range safety buoys: 55°42'·32N 08°06'·92E, Fl Y 5s.
55°38'·63N 07°50'·91E, Fl Y 3s.
55°37'·35N 07°56'·98E, Fl Y 3s.
55°36'·02N 08°02'·49E.

Blåvands Huk ☆ 55°33'·46N 08°04'·95E Fl (3) 20s 55m **23M**; W □ twr.

Søren Bovbjergs Dyb (unlit side channel, N to S)
55°33'·57N 07°55'·55E.
55°32'·80N 07°55'·30E.
55°32'·19N 07°56'·29E.
55°31'·24N 07°57'·46E.

Slugen Channel (N to S)
55°33'·99N 07°49'·38E, L Fl G 10s.
55°32'·26N 07°53'·65E, Fl G 3s.
55°31'·46N 07°52'·88E, Fl (2) R 5s.
55°30'·52N 07°59'·20E, Fl (2) G 5s.
55°29'·42N 08°02'·56E, Fl (3) R 10s.

Horns Rev is ringed clockwise by:
Tuxen 55°34'·22N 07°41'·92E, Q.
Vyl 55°26'·22N 07°49'·99E, Q (6) + L Fl 15s.
No. 2 55°28'·74N 07°36'·49E, L Fl 10s.
Horns Rev W 55°34'·47N 07°26'·05E, Q (9) 15s; 22M offshore.

Wind farm in □, 2·7M x 2·5M, centred on 55°29'·22N 07°50'·21E: 80 turbines, the 12 perimeter turbines marked by Fl (3) Y 10s. NE turbine (55°30'·28N 07°52'·63E), Racon (U); transformer platform, 55°30'·52N 07°52'·53E, 2 Mo (U) 15s 15m 5M.
SW turbine (55°28'·11N 07°48'·26E), Racon (U).
7 recording stations each marked by SPM buoy Fl (5) Y 20s.
Met mast (60m) ☆ 55°31'·32N 07°47'·33E, 2 Mo (U) 15s 8m 3M.
Met masts 151B (55°29'·21N 07°54'·72E) and 151C (55°29'·24N 07°58'·52E): both 70m, ☆ 2 Mo (U) 15s `12m 5M and Aero QR.

BLÅVANDS HUK TO RØMØ

▶ APPROACHES TO ESBJERG

Grådyb 55°24'·63N 08°11'·59E, L Fl 10s; **Racon G, 10M.**
Sædding Strand ldg lts 053·8°; valid as far as Nos 7/8 buoys; H24.
Front 55°29'·74N 08°23'·87E, Iso 2s 13m **21M**; 052°-056°; R bldg.
Middle, 630m from front, 55°29'·94N 08°24'·33E, Iso 4s 26m **21M**; 051°-057°; R twr, W bands.
Rear, 0·75M from front, 55°30'·18N 08°24'·92E, F 37m **18M**, 052°-056°; R twr.
No. 1 55°25'·49N 08°13'·89E, Q.
No. 2 55°25'·62N 08°13'·73E, Fl (3) R 10s.
No. 3 55°25'·93N 08°14'·84E, Fl G 3s.
No. 4 55°26'·02N 08°14'·72E, Fl R 3s.
Tide Gauge ☆ 55°26'·05N 08°15'·93E, Fl (5) Y 20s 8m 4M.
No. 5 55°26'·32N 08°15'·83E, Fl G 5s.
No. 6 55°26'·44N 08°15'·70E, Fl R 5s.
No. 7 55°26'·76N 08°16'·91E, Q.
No. 8 55°26'·89N 08°16'·81E, Fl (2) R 5s.
Ldg lts 067°, valid as far as Nos 9/10 buoys. Both FG 10/25m **16M**, H24. Front, 55°28'·76N 08°24'·70E, Gy tripod; rear, Gy twr.
No. 9 55°27'·04N 08°18'·21E, Fl (2) G 10s.
No.10 55°27'·20N 08°18'·04E, Fl (2) R 10s.
Ldg lts 049°, valid as far as No 16 buoy/Jerg. Both FR 16/27m **16M**, H24. Front, 55°29'·92N 08°23'·75E, W twr; rear, Gy twr.
No. 11 55°27'·71N 08°19'·59E, Fl G 3s.
No. 12 55°27'·88N 08°19'·39E, Fl R 3s.
No. 13 55°28'·40N 08°20'·99E, Fl G 5s.
No. 14 55°28'·57N 08°20'·73E, Fl R 5s.

Jerg ☆ 55°28'·88N 08°22'·00E, Fl G 3s 7m 5M; G twr, Y base.
No. 16 55°29'·04N 08°21'·80E, Q (6) + L Fl 15s.
No. 15A 55°29'·01N 08°22'·47E, Fl (2) G 5s.
No 18 55°29'·19N 08°22'·71E, Fl (2) R 5s.
Fovrfelt N ☆ 55°29'·29N 08°23'·79E, Oc (2) WRG 6s 7m 5M; G066·5°-073°, W073°-077°, R077°-085·5°, G327°-331°, W331°-333·5°, R333·5°-342°; Y twr.
Fovrfelt ☆ 55°29'·03N 08°23'·75E, Fl (2) R 10s 11m 6M; R twr.
No 15B 55°28'·83N 08°23'·65E, Fl (2) G 10s.

▶ ESBJERG HAVN

Strandby, shelter mole, NW corner ☆ 55°28'·76N 08°24'·63E, Oc WRG 5s 6m W13M, R/G9M; G101·7°-105·5°, W105·5°-109·5°, R109·5°-111·7°; W bldg, R band.
Industrifiskerihavn, W mole ☆ 55°28'·52N 08°24'·96E, Fl R 5s 6m 4M; R structure.
E mole ☆ 55°28'·52N 08°25'·03E, Fl G 5s 6m 4M; G structure.
Nordsøkai 55°28'·45N 08°25'·04E, Q (9) 15s 5m; Y twr, B band.
Konsumfiskerihavn, W mole ☆ 55°28'·31N 08°25'·33E, Fl R 3s 6m; 203°-119°; R tr. Yacht hbr in Basin II, N part.
E mole ☆ 55°28·31N 08°25·40E, Fl G 3s 6m; 023°-256°; G tr.
Trafikhavn, NW corner, ☆ 55°28·22N 08°25·43E, Oc (2) WRG 12s 6m W13M, R/G9M; 118°-G-124·5°-W-129°-R-131°; W bldg, R band.
N mole ☆ 55°28'·13N 08°25'·46E, FR 8m 5M; 232°-135°; R bldg.
S mole ☆ 55°28'·08N 08°25'·51E, FG 8m 4M; 045°-276°; G bldg.
No. 22 55°27'·62N 08°25'·50E, Fl (2)R 5s.

Sønderhavn (industrial) W mole ☆ 55°27'·49N 08°26'·12E, FR 9m 4M. E mole ☆ 55°27'·43N 08°26'·31E, FG 9m 4M.

Aero ☆ 55°27'·27N 08°27'·32E (close ESE of Sonderhavn), 3 x Fl 1·5s (vert, 82m apart) 251m 12M, H24; on chimney.

▶ FANØ

Slunden outer ldg lts 242°, both Iso 2s 5/8m 3M; 227°-257°. Front 55°27'·20N 08°24'·53E; twr. Rear, 106m from front; twr.
E shore, reciprocal ldg lts 062°, both FR 10/13m 3M; 047°-077°. Front 55°27'·65N 08°26'·01E; twr. Rear, 140m from front; twr.
No. 1 ☆ 55°27'·45N 08°25'·28E, Fl (2) G 10s 5m 2M; G pile.
No. 2 ☆ 55°27'·42N 08°25'·32E, Fl (2+1) Y 5s 5m 2M; Y pile.
No. 3 ☆ 55°27'·39N 08°25'·07E, Fl G 3s 5m 2M; G pile.
No. 4 ☆ 55°27'·35N 08°25'·10E, Fl R 3s 5m 2M; R pile.
Nordby ldg lts 214°, both FR 7/9m 4M; 123·7°-303·7°. Front 55°26'·94N 08°24'·44E; W mast. Rear, 84m from front; Gy twr.
Kremer Sand ☆ 55°27'·3N 08°24'·9E, FG 5m 3M; G dolphin.
Næs Søjord ☆ 55°27'·27N 08°24'·86E, FR 5m 3M; R pile.
Nordby marina 55°26'·65N 08°24'·53E.

▶ KNUDEDYB

G 55°20'·50N 08°24'·28E.
K 55°18'·92N 08°20'·06E.
No. 2 55°18'·82N 08°21'·33E.
No. 4 55°18'·81N 08°22'·21E.
No. 6 55°18'·38N 08°24'·63E.
No. 10 55°18'·68N 08°28'·50E.
Knoben 55°18'·71N 08°30'·60E.

▶ JUVRE DYB

No. 4 55°13'·76N 08°24'·73E.
No. 6 55°13'·41N 08°26'·60E.
No. 8 55°12'·69N 08°26'·83E.
No. 10 55°12'·55N 08°28'·72E.
Rejsby Stjært 55°13'·15N 08°30'·55E.

OUTER APPROACH (Lister Tief) TO RØMØ

See also 9.15.4 for details of lights on Sylt.

Rode Klit Sand 55°11'·11N 08°04'·88E, Q (9) 15s, (130°/9M to Lister Tief).
Lister Tief 55°05'·32N 08°16'·80E, Iso 8s, *Whis.*
No. 1 55°05'·21N 08°18'·20E.
No. 3 55°04'·75E 08°18'·73E, Fl G 4s.
No. 2 55°04'·23N 08°22'·32E, Fl (3) R 10s.
No. 9 55°03'·76N 08°23'·05E, Fl (2) G 9s.
Lister Landtief No 5 55°03'·68N 08°24'·73E.
No. 4 55°03'·84N 08°25'·29E, FL (2) R 5s.
G1 55°03'·27N 08°28'·32E, Fl Y 4s.

▶ RØMØ DYB and HAVN

No. 1 55°03'·23N 08°30'·30E, Fl (2) G 10s.
No. 10 ☆ 55°03'·50N 08°31'·10E, Fl (2) R 10s 5m 3M; R pole.
No. 14 ☆ 55°03'·85N 08°32'·55E, Fl R 3s 6m 2M; R pole.
No. 20 ☆ 55°04'·79N 08°34'·13E, Fl R 5s 5m 2M; R pole.
No. 9 55°04'·79N 08°34'·63E.
No. 11 55°05'·17N 08°34'·69E.
Rømø Hbr:
S mole ☆ 55°05'·19N 08°34'·31E, Fl R 3s 7m 2M; Gy twr.
N mole ☆ 55°05'·23N 08°34'·30E, Fl G 3s 7m 2M; Gy twr.
Inner S mole ☆ 55°05'·2N 08°34'·2E, FR 4m 1M.
Inner N mole ☆ 55°05'·3N 08°34'·2E, FG 4m 1M.

9.14.5 PASSAGE INFORMATION

Pilots include the Admiralty *North Sea (East) Pilot* (NP 55) and *Cruising Guide to Germany and Denmark* (Imray/Navin).

Jutland's low, sandy W coast is not a notable cruising ground and lacks genuine harbours of refuge in strong onshore winds. Even Esbjerg is made difficult by a bar on which seas break heavily in strong W or SW winds. Thyborøn should not be approached on the ebb with onshore winds >F5. But in settled weather, these and other ports may break the long passage to the Skagerrak or round Skagen (The Skaw) into the Kattegat.

Coastal dangers include: Horns Rev, a reef extending about 22M W of Blåvands Huk, but with a buoyed channel some 5M offshore; and, extensive sand ridges lying parallel to and some 5 cables off the shore, with depths of 1m to 5.5m. There are many coastal nature reserves, as charted, into which entry is either restricted or prohibited; but they do not deny access to hbrs.

▶*Tidal streams are weak as far N as Thyborøn and imperceptible further N, but expect wind-driven currents such as the N-going Stryget.*◀ The general direction of buoyage is northerly. Navigational marks are excellent. Ldg beacons have △ daymarks on the front beacon and ▽ on the rear. There is much fishing activity, including pairs trawling.

SKAGEN TO HANSTHOLM (*AC 1402*) From/to Skagen (9.14.7) keep outside the cardinal buoys marking Skagen Rev. There are no offshore hazards from here to Hirtshals (9.14.8). In Jammerbugt (The Bay of Woe: Hirtshals to Hanstholm) a firing practice area extends 7M off Tranum Strand, 57°10'N 09°25'E.

HANSTHOLM TO THYBORØN (*AC 1404*). Off Hanstholm (9.14.9) S/SW winds may cause currents up to 4 knots in rough weather, but tidal streams are imperceptible for 15-20M offshore. It is best to round Hanstholm outside the SWM buoy. Underwater obstructions and the slim possibility of former WW2 mines may make anchoring dangerous.

Thyborøn (9.14.10) is the western entrance to the Limfjord (*AC 426 to 430*) which gives access to the Baltic via Aalborg and Hals/ Egense (91 track miles). It is a large area of sheltered water with many harbours, of which Lemvig and Thisted are the most W'ly. Some of the marinas are only suitable for drafts <1·5m, but there are plenty of ⚓s and it is deservedly a popular cruising ground. The Danish word 'Bredning', meaning a Broad (as in Norfolk), aptly describes the stretches of water linked by narrow sounds; least depths are 4m.

THYBORØN TO HVIDE SANDE (*AC 1404*) 'Dangerous anchoring' areas fringe the coast to 1M offshore. Bovbjerg lt ho, a red tower on a 38m high sand dune, is conspic. Torsminde (9.14.11) is a FV hbr between the sea and Nissum Fjord. S of here coastal dunes are high enough to obscure the houses behind them. ▶*Tidal streams (such as they are) divide off Lyngvig lt ho, ie to the S the in-going stream sets S and the out-going stream sets N; the reverse occurs N of Lyngvig.*◀

HVIDE SANDE TO ESBJERG (*AC 1404, 3768, Danish 99*) Firing practice areas extend 9M W and 8M NNW from a pos'n 4M N of Blåvands Huk lt ho; and 7-10M to seaward of Nyminde Gab 55°49'N 08°12'E. Charts warn of the dangers of anchoring and fishing due to wrecks and underwater explosives.

Entrance to Hvide Sande (9.14.12) can be difficult when sluicing causes strong currents in the entrance. Thence Ringkøbing Fjord, a lagoon 15M long by 6M wide, is entered via a lock. There are several attractive hbrs/marinas (Ringkøbing, Bork, Skaven and Stavning) and anchs, but also shallows and conservation areas with prohibited access - see Danish chart *99*.

Off Blåvands Huk, Slugen is the well-buoyed/lit and deep inshore channel through the shallow banks of Horns Rev. The general direction of buoyage is NW'wards. Close SW of Slugen a large rectangular windfarm (80 turbines) is centred on 55°29'·22N 07°50'.21E; there are Racons (U) at the NE and SW corners. 3 meteorological masts (60-70m high) lie close NW and E of the windfarm. See 9.14.4 for light details.

ESBJERG TO RØMØ (*AC 1404, 3768*) Grådyb, the ent channel to Esbjerg, is well buoyed. ▶*In Esbjerg Roads the stream sets ESE from HW Helgoland –0305 and WSW from +0315. Tidal streams in the Fanø Bugt are shown in tables on chart 3768. In the open sea the flood is SE-going and the ebb NW-going; there is no slack water, just a turning of the stream, usually anti-clockwise. The rate is 1½kn at the change; the ebb is often stronger than the flood.*

Abreast Rømø Havn (9.14.15) the ingoing stream begins at HW Helgoland –0215 and runs NNE across the hbr entrance; the outgoing stream begins at +0345 and runs SSW across the entrance; max rate in each direction is about 2kn.◀

From Grådyb SWM buoy/Racon to Lister Tief SWM is 171°/ 19·5M. Approach Rømø via the buoyed channel.

A firing practice range extends 12M seaward of Rømø.

CROSSING THE NORTH SEA (*AC 2182A, 2182B, 2182C*) Important planning considerations to be taken into account:

1. Distances are considerable, eg Harwich to Esbjerg is 330M and Harwich to Skagen is 483M, so experienced crew, used to night passages, and a well found yacht are essential. See 9.0.8 for distances across the North Sea.
2. The many oil/gas rigs must be known and avoided.
3. The extensive Dutch & German TSS south of 54°14'N, ie about Helgoland, must be carefully negotiated.

From the English S coast it may be prudent to coast-hop via Holland and the Frisian Islands, then make for Helgoland, dependent on weather. A suitable departure point from the Thames estuary is S Galloper SCM, and from Lowestoft Smiths Knoll SCM. From further N, ie Hartlepool to the Firth of Forth, a track to Esbjerg avoids Dogger Bank and the densest oil/gas rig concentrations. See also 9.15.5 and 9.16.5 for other options.

9.14.6 SPECIAL NOTES FOR WEST DENMARK

LANGUAGES: English and German are widely spoken (as is Danish). The alphabet contains 3 non-English letters: å, æ and ø. å replaces aa which may still be found, as in Aalborg.

AMTSKOMMUNERS are given in lieu of 'counties' in the UK.

CHARTS: Danish charts are issued by Kort-og Matrikelstyrelsen, Rentemestervej 8, DK-2400 København. Those prefixed 'DK' are standard Danish nautical charts. Leisure charts for W Jutland are not available. Admiralty charts are mostly small scale.

LIGHTS: Navigational marks, buoys and lights are excellent.

SIGNALS: Local port, tidal, distress and traffic signals are given where possible. When motoring under sail, always display a motoring ▼.

HARBOURS: Most yacht hbrs are owned by the state or community and run by a local Yacht Club (as in Germany).

TRAFFIC SEPARATION SCHEMES: There are none off West Jutland, but off Skagen (The Skaw) traffic between the Skaggerak and Kattegat is heavy.

TELEPHONES: To call UK from Denmark: dial 00 44, then the UK area code, minus the initial zero; followed by the number required. To call Denmark, which has no area codes, from the UK: dial 00 (or +) 45, then the required 8 digit number.

EMERGENCIES: Police, Fire and Ambulance: dial 112.

PUBLIC HOLIDAYS: New Year's Day, Maundy Thurs (Thu before Easter) thru' to Easter Monday, Common Prayer Day (4th Fri after Easter), Ascension Day, Whit Monday, Constitution Day (5 Jun), Christmas Eve to Boxing Day. Local festivals are common.

GAS: Propane is the norm. Camping Gaz (butane) is available, but Calor gas, neither butane nor propane, is not.

TIME: DST is kept from the last Sunday in March until the last Sunday in October.

MONEY: The Danish krone (Dkr) = 100 øre. Rate of exchange Spring 2004: £1.00 = approx Dkr 10.70; 1 Dkr = approx £0.09. VAT (*moms*) is 25%, on everything. Banks with ATMs are as common as in the UK. All major credit cards are accepted.

USEFUL ADDRESSES: Danish Tourist Board, 55 Sloane St, London SW1X 9SY; ☎ 020 7259 5959; 📠 020 7495 5955; dtb.london@dt.dk. The Embassy is at the same address.

In Denmark: The main Tourist Office is Vesterbrogade 6D, 1620 København V; ☎ 33 11 14 15; dt@dt.dk; www.dt.dk. There are excellent and very helpful TOs in most fair-sized towns.
British Embassy, Kastelsvej 36-40, DK-2100 København 0; ☎ 33 44 52 00.
British Consulate, Kanalen 1, DK-6700 Esbjerg.
For other addresses see Chapter 1, 1.5.

TRANSPORT: DFDS operate the Harwich-Esbjerg ferry, see 9.0.5. Other ferries run from Hirtshals to Oslo and Kristiansand; and from Hanstholm to Bergen, the Faeroe Is and Iceland.

UK scheduled and low-cost flights go to Billund (35M NE of Esbjerg) and Copenhagen. Internal flights are limited as Denmark is compact and has good trains and buses.

Trains (DSB) are notably reliable and fast, with a broad fare structure. Bicycles are very popular and easy to hire if you do not have a 'folder'.

SHOPPING: Most towns have a market day on either Wed or Sat. Launderettes (*montvaskeri*), coin or token-operated, are to be found in most towns.

9.14.7 SKAGEN

Nordjylland **57°42'·86N 10°35'·63E**

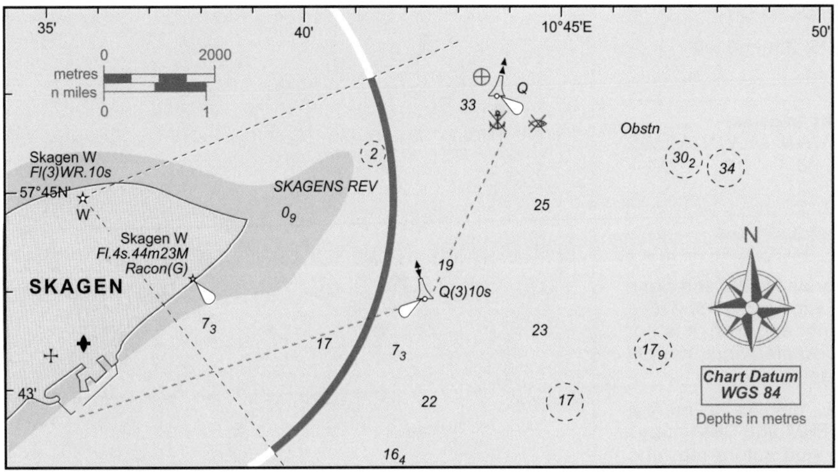
35'
40'
10°45'E
50'
0 2000
metres
n miles
0 1
Skagen W
Fl(3)WR.10s
57°45N'
W
Skagen W
Fl.4s.44m23M
Racon(G)
SKAGEN
SKAGENS REV
Q
33
Obstn
25
19
Q(3)10s
23
22
17
N
Chart Datum
WGS 84
Depths in metres
43'

CHARTS AC 1402, 2107 with 1:12,500 hbr inset.

TIDES Variations in heights are minimal and largely generated by wind. ATT Vol 2 publishes height differences referred to Bergen and advises the use of harmonic constants for time differences. But for all practical purposes Hirtshals differences are adequate. HW heights are: MHWS 0·2m, MHWN 0·1m.

TIDAL STREAMS are perceptible only in calm conditions. Wind usually has an over-riding effect such that the current is E-going for 75% of the year.

SHELTER is good, access at all tides/ weather. Yachts berth in 4m between Old Pier and Pier 1, NE of the central pontoon. FVs berth both sides of Pier 1. There are also yacht pontoons in 3·5m at the E end of Bundgarns Bassin.

NAVIGATION From the W, the WPT is 57°43'·98N 10°43'·67E, a NCM buoy Q, marking the NE tip of Skagens Rev. Thence 200°/2·2M to an ECM buoy, Q(3) 10s, at 57°43'·84N 10°42'·35E. From here the hbr ent bears 258°/3·6M.

LIGHTS AND MARKS As chartlet and 9.14.4. Skagen West lt ho is 2M N of the hbr ent on the N tip of the peninsula; its R sector shows over Skagens Rev. Skagen lt ho is 1.7M NE of the hbr ent, with Racon G, 20M. The peninsula is low-lying, flat and fringed by endless sand dunes.

R/T VHF Ch 16; 12 13, HX.

TELEPHONE (Dial code 00 45) HM 98 44 10 60/98 44 13 46/98 44 14 66, Coastguard 98 44 12 22, Hospital 99 79 79 79, Police (Emergency) 112, Taxi 98 92 47 00.

FACILITIES AB, FW, D; **Services**: WC, Showers, YC Skagen Sejl Klub 98 45 06 79, ME, SM; **Town**: R, PO, ✈ (Aalborg) ☎ 98 17 33 11.

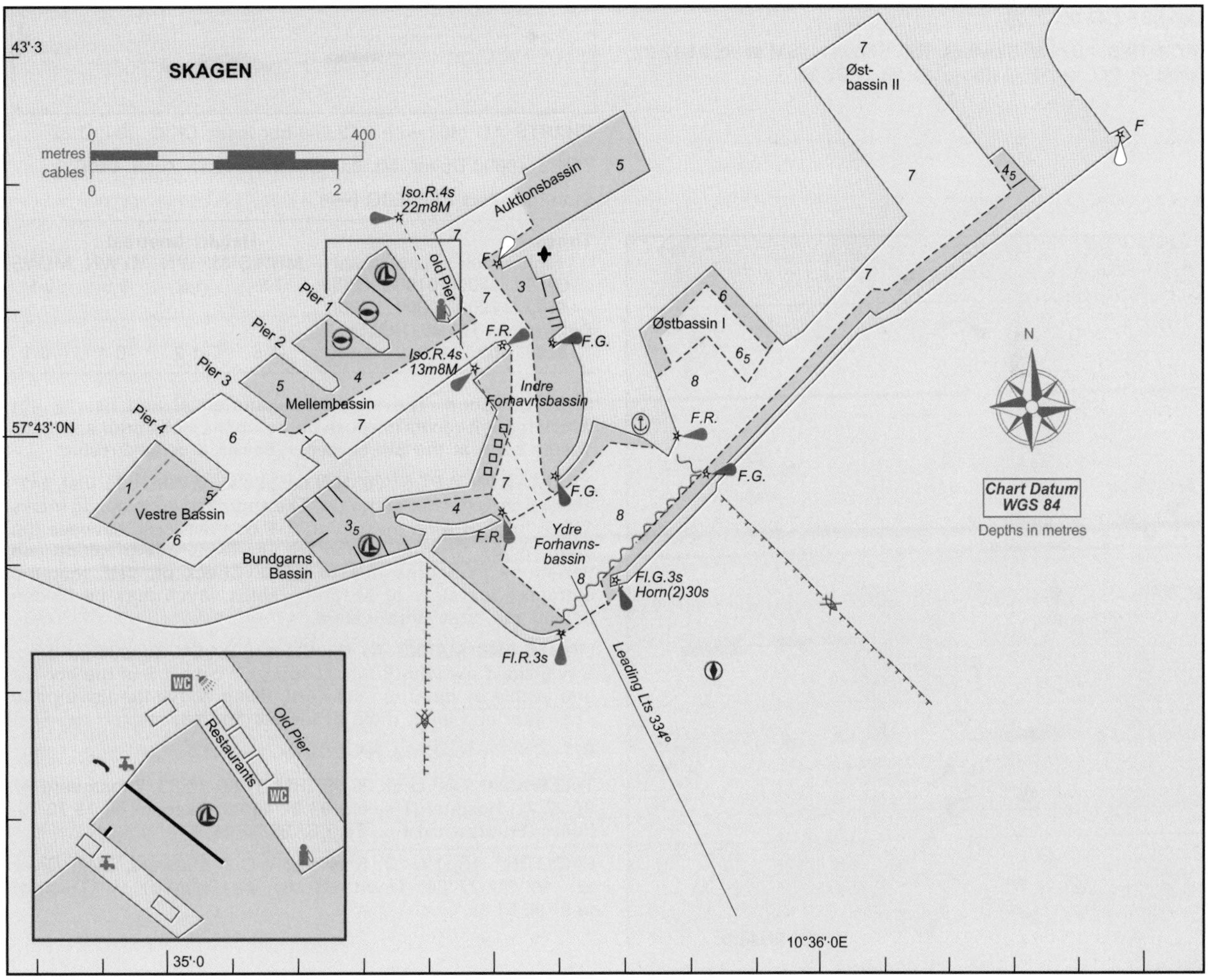
43'·3
SKAGEN
0 400
metres
cables
0 2
Øst-
bassin II
F
Auktionsbassin
Iso.R.4s
22m8M
Old Pier
Pier 1
Pier 2
Pier 3
Pier 4
F.R.
F.G.
Iso.R.4s
13m8M
Østbassin I
Indre
Forhavnsbassin
Mellembassin
57°43'·0N
F.R.
F.G.
Vestre Bassin
Bundgarns
Bassin
F.G.
F.R.
Ydre
Forhavns-
bassin
Fl.G.3s
Horn(2)30s
Fl.R.3s
Leading Lts 334°
N
Chart Datum
WGS 84
Depths in metres
WC
Old Pier
Restaurants
WC
35'·0
10°36'·0E

9.14.8 HIRTSHALS

Nordjylland **57°35'·90N 09°57'·54E**

CHARTS AC 1402 with 1:12,500 hbr inset; DK92; D 63

TIDES +0600 Dover, ML 0·0, Duration 0625, Zone -0100

Standard Port ESBJERG (⟶)

Times				**Height (metres)**			
High Water		Low Water		MHWS	MHWN	MLWN	MLWS
0300	0700	0100	0800	1·9	1·5	0·5	0·1
1500	1900	1300	2000				
Differences HIRTSHALS							
+0055	+0320	+0340	+0100	−1·6	−1·3	−0·4	−0·1

SHELTER Good. Yachts berth in a small marina to stbd and close S of the hbr ent. Hirtshals is a commercial and fishing hbr which foreign yachts may use only with HM's prior approval. It is not advisable to attempt entrance in strong onshore winds from N to NW due to heavy seas and strong E-going current.

NAVIGATION WPT 57°36'·39N 09°57'·32E, 166°/7ca to marina ent in front of rear 166° ldg lt. The outer PHM and SHM buoys funnel vessels into the entrance. Turn to stbd before reaching the Inner Hbr lt FG. Caution: FVs and fast ferries to Norway.

LIGHTS AND MARKS As chartlet and 9.14.4. 166° ldg bcns: front, R ▲ on frame twr; rear, R ▼ on frame twr. The white lt ho is approx 1M SW of the hbr ent.

R/T VHF Ch 16; 14, HX.

TELEPHONE (Dial code 00 45) HM 98 94 42 93, Coastguard 98 92 22 22, Hospital (Hjørring) 98 92 72 44, Police (Emergency) 112, Taxi 98 92 47 00.

FACILITIES AB, FW; **Services**: WC, Showers, SM ☎ 98 94 12 27; **Town**: R, PO, ≷, ✈ (Aalborg) ☎ 98 17 33 11.

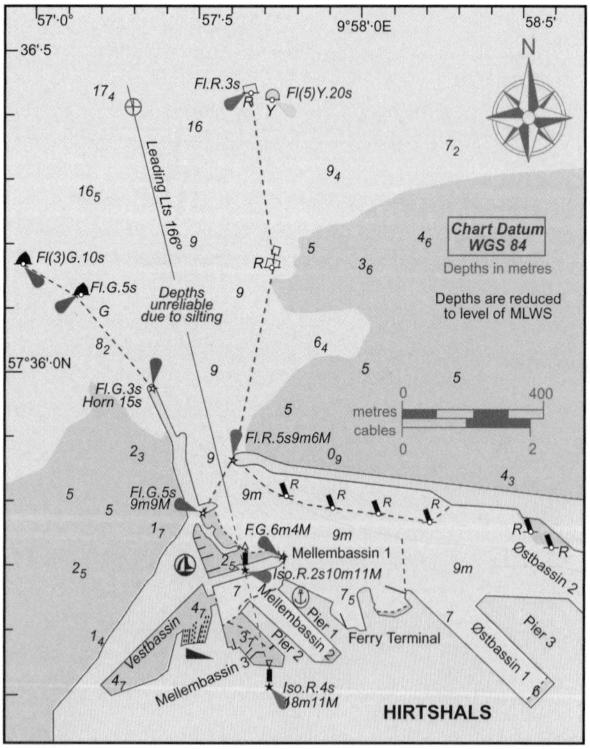
57'·0
57'·5
9°58'·0E
58·5'
36'·5
57°36'·0N
N
Fl.R.3s
Fl(5)Y.20s
Leading Lts 166°
Fl(3)G.10s
Fl.G.5s
Depths unreliable due to silting
Chart Datum WGS 84
Depths in metres
Depths are reduced to level of MLWS
Fl.G.3s Horn 15s
Fl.R.5s9m6M
Fl.G.5s 9m9M
F.G.6m4M
Mellembassin 1
Iso.R.2s10m11M
Vestbassin
Mellembassin 2
Mellembassin 3
Pier 1
Pier 2
Pier 3
Ferry Terminal
Østbassin 1
Østbassin 2
Iso.R.4s 18m11M
HIRTSHALS
metres
cables
0
400
2

9.14.9 HANSTHOLM

Viborg **57°07'·57N 08°35'·51**

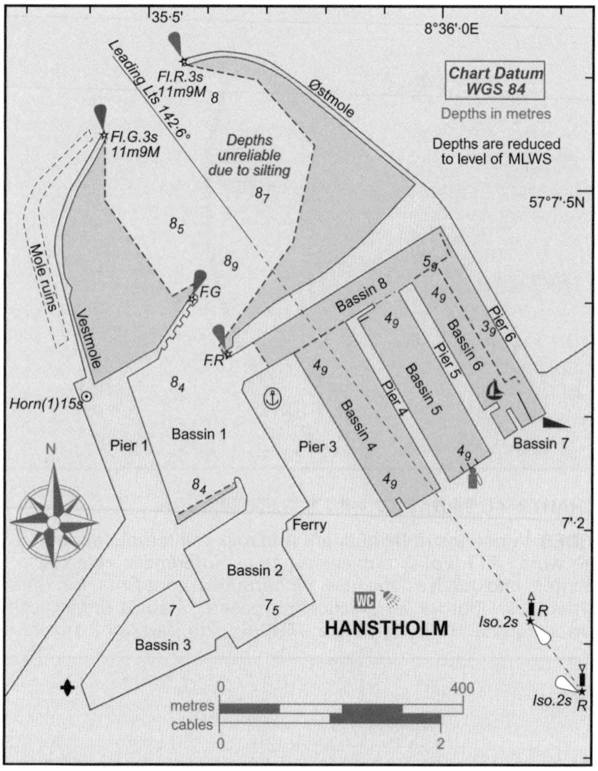
35·5'
8°36'·0E
57°7'·5N
7'·2
Leading Lts 142·6°
Fl.R.3s 11m9M
Fl.G.3s 11m9M
Depths unreliable due to silting
Østmole
Vestmole
Mole ruins
Chart Datum WGS 84
Depths in metres
Depths are reduced to level of MLWS
F.G
F.R
Horn(1)15s
N
Pier 1
Bassin 1
Pier 3
Bassin 8
Bassin 6
Pier 6
Pier 5
Bassin 5
Pier 4
Bassin 4
Bassin 7
Ferry
Bassin 2
Bassin 3
HANSTHOLM
Iso.2s
Iso.2s
R
metres
cables
0
400
2

CHARTS AC 1402 with 1:12,500 hbr inset; DK92, 104; D 82

TIDES +0600 Dover, ML 0.0, Duration 0630, Zone -0100

Standard Port ESBJERG (⟶)

Times				**Height (metres)**			
High Water		Low Water		MHWS	MHWN	MLWN	MLWS
0300	0700	0100	0800	1·9	1·5	0·5	0·1
1500	1900	1300	2000				
Differences HANSTHOLM							
+0100	+0340	+0340	+0130	−1·6	−1·2	−0·4	−0·1

SHELTER Good. The port is a commercial and fishing hbr which foreign yachts may use only with the HM's prior approval. Yachts berth at the SW corner of Bassin 6 or as directed.

NAVIGATION WPT 57°08'·10N 08°34'·94E [SWM, L Fl 10s], 142° about 6 ca to the hbr entrance. The approach is clear. Ldg marks 142·6° front, R ▲ on mast; rear, R ▼ on mast, lead between the outer moles. Charted depths are unreliable due to silting and variations in depths due to wind. Check on VHF that the entrances are clear of departing ships which may be hidden behind the large breakwaters.

LIGHTS AND MARKS As chartlet and 9.14.4. Hanstholm lt ho, a W 8-sided twr with R top, is approx 7 cables S of the hbr ent and visible by day from seaward, rising above the flat terrain. The outer and inner mole heads are floodlit.

R/T VHF Ch 16; 12 13, HX

TELEPHONE (Dial code 00 45) HM 97 96 18 33, Coastguard 97 92 22 22, Hospital (Thisted) 97 92 44 00 (Skagen) 99 79 79 79, Police (Emergency) 112, Taxi 97 96 17 11

FACILITIES AB, FW, D; **Services**: WC & showers, ME, Diver ☎ 97 96 27 00; **Town**: 🛒, R, ≷ (Thisted), ✈ (Thisted) ☎ 97 96 51 66.

9.14.10 THYBORØN

Ringkøbing **56°42'·87N 08°12'·81E** ❁❁◊◊◊✿✿

CHARTS AC 426 (inc 2 hbr plans); DK 108S; D81

TIDES +0530 Dover; ML 0·0; Duration 0620; Zone -0100

Standard Port ESBJERG (⟶)

Times				Heights (metres)			
High Water		Low Water		MHWS	MHWN	MLWN	MLWS
0300	0700	0100	0800	1·9	1·5	0·5	0·1
1500	1900	1300	2000				
Differences THYBORØN							
+0120	+0230	+0410	+0210	–1·5	–1·2	–0·4	–0·1

SHELTER inside is good. Yachts berth in the N'most basin, Nordre Inderhavn, in 3·5m or as directed.

NAVIGATION Entry can be dangerous in near gale force onshore winds which cause breaking seas and violent eddies. Least depth is normally about 6m on approach and 5m-8m within the bar.

WPT 56°42'·55N 08°08'·70E [SWM buoy L Fl 10s, Racon T], 082°/2·5M to abeam unlit SHM buoy at ent. Here turn stbd SSE, past a SHM buoy Fl (2) G 5s, into the main fairway to the Yderhavn ent. Inside the ent turn 90° stbd to Nordre Inderhavn 4 cables N.

LIGHTS AND MARKS As on chartlet and 9.14.4. Outer 082° ldg marks: front, Agger Tange R ▲ on bn; rear, R ▼ on gy frame twr. Langholm 120° ldg marks: front, R ▲ on R hut; rear, R ▼ on gy frame twr. Caution: light sectors and buoys in the approach chans are moved to reflect changes in depths.

The Appr lt, Fl (3) 10s, is an all-round lt ho; in poor vis shown by day. The E mole lt, Oc (2) WRG 12s, has a W sector covering an approach from the NNW.

R/T VHF Ch Ch 16; 12 13, H24

TELEPHONE (Dial code 00 45) HM 97 83 10 50; CG 97 82 13 22; Ⓗ (Thisted) 97 92 44 00; Taxi 97 83 25 11.

FACILITIES AB 60Kr any LOA, D; **Services**: WC, showers, ME, ⚒ Thyborøn Bådebyggeri ☎ 97 83 11 26, SM Thybøron Sejlmageri ☎ 97 83 11 25; **Town**: R, ⊞, PO, ⇌, ✈ (Thisted) ☎ 97 96 51 66.

LIMFJORD cuts across Jutland via Ålborg to the E ent at Hals in the Kattegat, approx 91M; saving about 90M over the offshore route via Skagen. Thyborøn is the W ent to Limfjord, a notable cruising ground in its own right. **Lemvig** (see chartlet below) is 10-13M SSE of Thyborøn. A marina at Vinkel Hage, 56°33'·93N 08°17'·86E, is about 9ca N of Lemvig on the W bank.

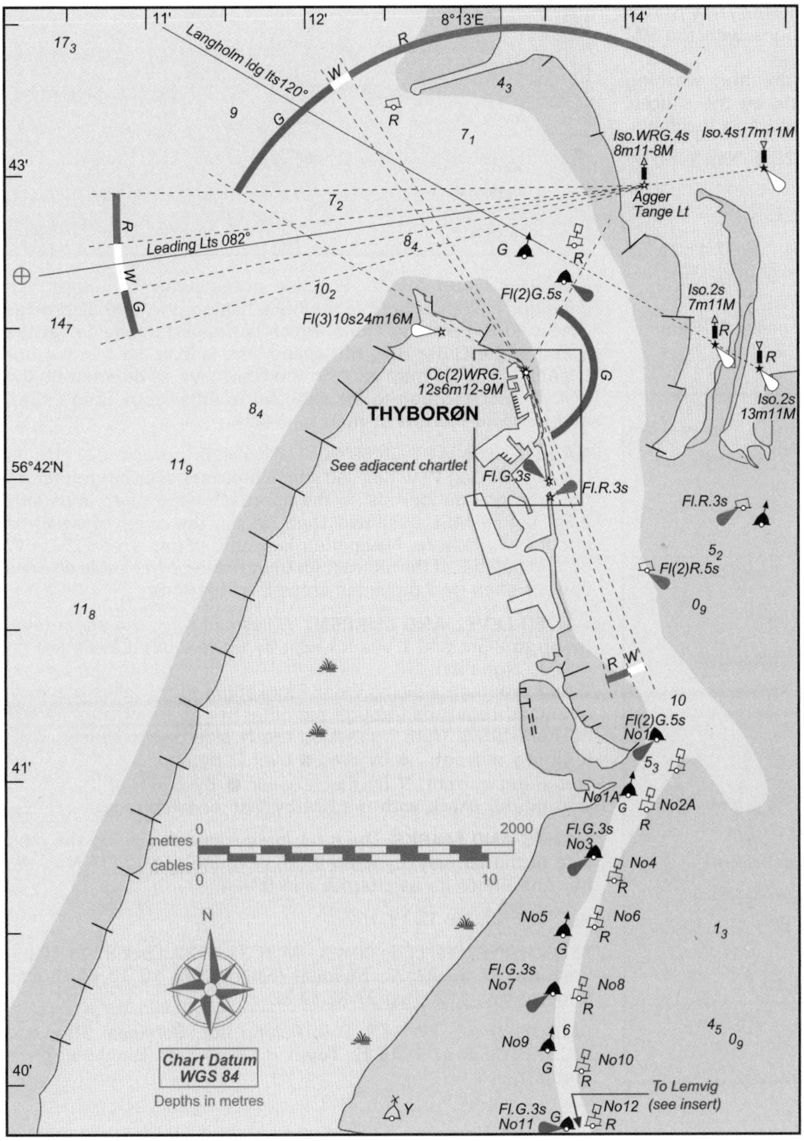
Langholm ldg lts120°
Leading Lts 082°
Iso.WRG.4s 8m11-8M
Iso.4s17m11M
Agger Tange Lt
Fl(2)G.5s
Fl(3)10s24m16M
Iso.2s 7m11M
Iso.2s 13m11M
Oc(2)WRG. 12s6m12-9M
THYBORØN
See adjacent chartlet
Fl.G.3s
Fl.R.3s
Fl(2)R.5s
56°42'N
43'
41'
40'
8°13'E
Fl(2)G.5s No1
No1A
No2A
Fl.G.3s No3
No4
No5
No6
Fl.G.3s No7
No8
No9
No10
Fl.G.3s No11
No12
To Lemvig (see insert)
Chart Datum WGS 84
Depths in metres

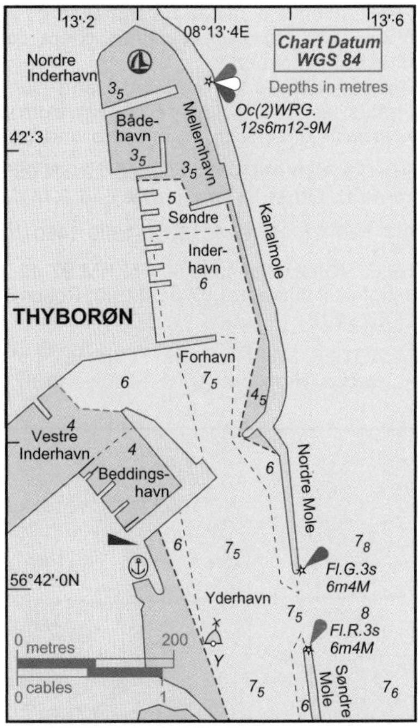
Nordre Inderhavn
Chart Datum WGS 84
Depths in metres
Oc(2)WRG. 12s6m12-9M
Bådehavn
Mellemhavn
Søndre Inderhavn
Kanalmole
THYBORØN
Forhavn
Vestre Inderhavn
Beddingshavn
Nordre Mole
Fl.G.3s 6m4M
Yderhavn
Fl.R.3s 6m4M
Søndre Mole
56°42'·0N

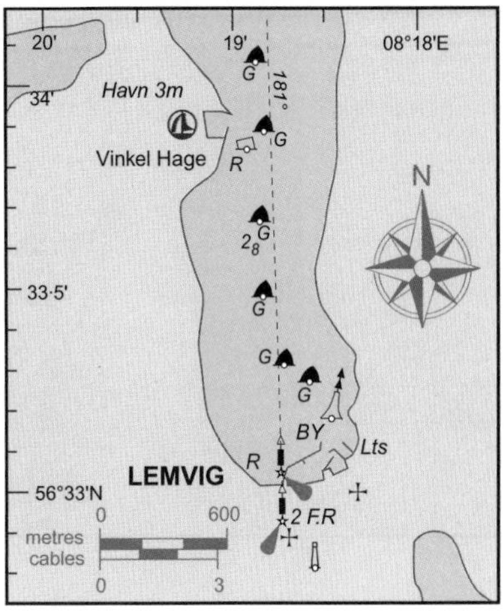
08°18'E
Havn 3m
Vinkel Hage
181°
LEMVIG
56°33'N
33·5'
2 F.R
Lts

9.14.11 TORSMINDE

Ringkøbing **56°22'·32N 08°06'·82E**

CHARTS AC 1404; DK93; D 82

TIDES +0425 Dover; ML 0·1; Duration 0605; Zone -0100

Standard Port ESBJERG (⟶)

Times				**Height (metres)**			
High Water		Low Water		MHWS	MHWN	MLWN	MLWS
0300	0700	0100	0800	1·8	1·4	0·4	0·0
1500	1900	1300	2000				
Differences TORSMINDE							
+0045	+0050	+0040	+0010	–1·3	–1·0	–0·4	–0·1

SHELTER Conditions are similar to Hvide Sande (9.14.12). Shelter is good inside, but see the notes below. Yachts berth in the Vesthavn on pontoons in the S'most basin. There is no access into Nissum Fjord due to drainage sluices which block the hbr immediately W of the road bridge.

NAVIGATION WPT 56°22'·34N 08°05'·49E, approx 090°/1M to hbr ent. Even moderate winds can cause breakers over the bar which normally has less than 2·7m below MSL and the hbr may have less water than charted due to silting. Strong W'lies can raise the water level by up to 3·0m and E'lies lower it by up to 1·8m. Levels are said to be signalled by a complex array of R & W lts, but before approaching, check conditions with the HM and request a berth.
Sluicing causes currents into and out of the hbr; warning signals, as in 9.14.12, are shown from masts by the sluices. Approach directly from seaward and turn stbd into Vesthavn.

LIGHTS AND MARKS Lt Ho 56°22'·5N 08°07'·2E, F 30m 14M, gy frame tr. Other lts as chartlet and 9.14.4.

R/T VHF Ch 16; 12 13, 0300-1300 1400-2400 LT.

TELEPHONE (Dial code 00 45) HM 97 49 70 44; CG 97 41 22 22; Hospital (Holstebro) 97 41 42 00; Police (Emergency) 112; Taxi 97 82 14 15.

FACILITIES FW, D, D, ME; **Town**: R, at campsite, ⇌ (Ramme, Holstebro, Ringkøbing), ✈ (Karup) ☎ 97 10 12 18.

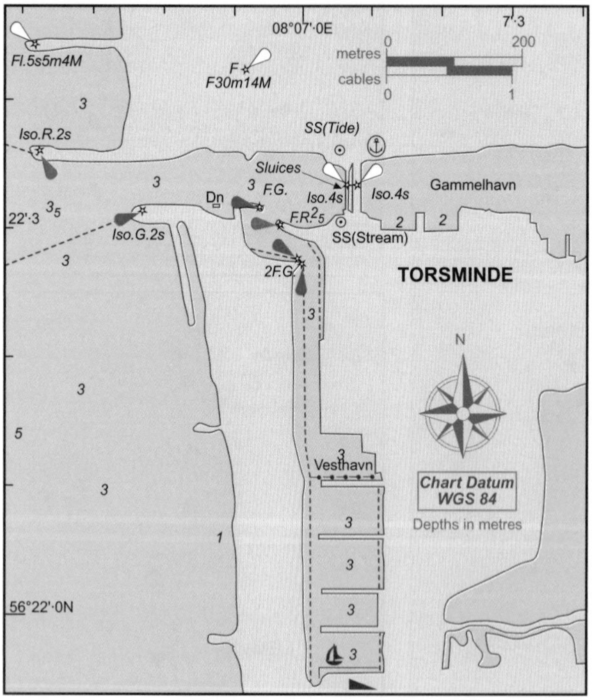
08°07'·0E
Fl.5s5m4M
F30m14M
metres
cables
Iso.R.2s
SS(Tide)
Sluices
F.G.
Iso.4s
Gammelhavn
Dn
F.R.
Iso.G.2s
SS(Stream)
2F.G.
TORSMINDE
N
Vesthavn
Chart Datum
WGS 84
Depths in metres
56°22'·0N

9.14.12 HVIDE SANDE

Ringkøbing **55°59'·93N 08°06'·68E**

CHARTS AC 1404; DK 93, 99; D82

TIDES +0345 Dover, ML 0·2, Duration 0550, Zone -0100. Mean range is about 0·75m.

Standard Port ESBJERG (⟶)

Times				**Height (metres)**			
High Water		Low Water		MHWS	MHWN	MLWN	MLWS
0300	0700	0100	0800	1·9	1·5	0·5	0·1
1500	1900	1300	2000				
Differences HVIDE SANDE							
0000	+0010	–0015	–0025	–1·1	–0·8	–0·3	–0·1

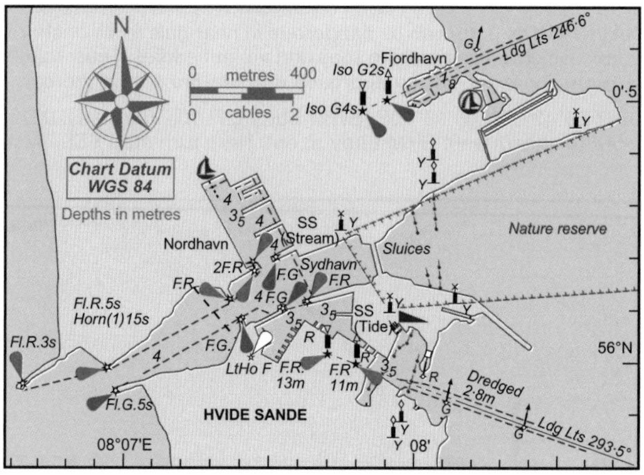
N
metres 400
cables 2
Iso G2s
Fjordhavn
Iso G4s
Ldg Lts 246·6°
Chart Datum
WGS 84
Depths in metres
Nordhavn
SS
(Stream)
Sluices
Nature reserve
Sydhavn
Fl.R.5s
Horn(1)15s
Fl.R.3s
SS
(Tide)
LtHo F
13m
11m
Dredged
2·8m
Fl.G.5s
HVIDE SANDE
08°07'E
56°N
Ldg Lts 293·5°

SHELTER Good inside, but see notes below on approach conditions. The harbour is mainly a fishing port and also gives access to Ringkøbing Fjord, which is drained by sluices at the E end of the Outer Hbr. Hbr speed limit is 3kn. No ⚓ in the hbr channels. Yachts may berth in the Nordhavn as directed by the HM. Or lock through to the Østhavn to enter appr chan (1·8m) and berth in Fjordhavn marina (1·6m).

NAVIGATION WPT 55°59'·80N 08°05'·49E, approx 072°/1M to hbr ent. Strong W winds can cause breakers over bar rendering the entrance dangerous. In the approach chan there is usually 2·5m below MSL over two sand ridges, the outer of which is about 3ca offshore. Navigation is prohib within areas 250m W of, and 500m E of the sluices. An underwate power cable crosses the ent chan and pipelines cross E of the lock.

WATER LEVEL AND CURRENT W'lies can raise the water level by up to 3·5m and E'lies lower it by up to 2·0m. Levels are no longer signalled.
When drainage sluicing from Ringkøbing Fjord takes place, a strong current runs through the outer hbr. Warning signals are hoisted/shown from a mast on the N side of the sluice:
In-going current: ▲ by day; ● over ○ by night.
Out-going current: ▼ by day; ○ over ● by night.
If in doubt, check with the HM by VHF or telephone.

LIGHTS AND MARKS The lt ho, grey frame twr, is on the stbd side of the fairway. Lyngvig lt ho, W round twr, is 3M N of the hbr ent. Other lts as chartlet and 9.14.4.

R/T VHF Ch 16; 12 13, HX

TELEPHONE (Dial code 00 45) HM 97 31 16 33, Lock 97 31 10 93, Customs 97 32 22 22, Hospital (Esbjerg) 75 18 19 00, Police (Emergency) 112, Taxi 97 32 32 32,

FACILITIES AB, FW, D, D in fishing hbr; **Services**: Showers, WC, ME, Ch ☎ 97 31 15 22; **Town**: R, PO, ⇌ (Ringkøbing), ✈ (Esbjerg).

9.14.13 ESBJERG

Ribe **55°28'·11N 08°25'·50E** (Entrance to Trafikhavn)

CHARTS AC 420, 3766; DK 94/5; D83, 109

TIDES ESBJERG is a Standard Port (⟶) +0340 Dover; ML 0·7; Duration 0605; Zone -0100. See differences overleaf, 9.14.14.

SHELTER All tide access. Yachts berth in the FV basin No II as shown. Or at Nordby marina on Fanø, 9.14.14.

NAVIGATION From the N, either pass to seaward of Horns Rev, which extends about 21M W from Blåvands Huk to Horns Rev W WCM buoy, Q(9)15s, 55°34'·49N 07°26'·08E.
Or take the Slugen chan, 9 to 4M W of Blåvands Huk. This is marked near its N end by Tuxen NCM Q, 55°34'·21N 07°41'·93E, and thence by 2 PHM & 3 SHM lt buoys. The general direction of buoyage through the Slugen is NW. From the E'most PHM buoy, Fl(3)R 10s, to Grådyb SWM is 132°/7·1M.

WPT 55°24'·63N 08°11'·61E, Grådyb SWM buoy L Fl 10s, Racon G. From the WPT, three sets of ldg lts lead through Grådyb (buoyed chan dredged 10m), passing between sand banks and into hbr at No 16 SCM buoy marking a Y-junction:

a. Sæding Strand triple ldg lts (Iso 2s, Iso 4s and F) lead 053.8°/3.7M to No 7 and No 8 buoys. There jink stbd onto (b)

b. Sæding Strand South ldg lts, both FG, 067°/8ca to Nos 9 & 10 buoys. Thence

c. Sæding Strand North ldg lts, both FR, 049°/2.8M to abeam No 16 SCM buoy.

Thereafter follow the buoyed chan round onto SSE; this turn is covered by 4 directional lights, should you feel the need. Esbjerg basins lie to port, or deviate stbd at No 21 buoy for Nordby marina.

LIGHTS AND MARKS Blåvands Huk lt ho, W square tr, is 9.6M NNW of Gradyb SWM buoy. On the SW side of the Slugen chan extensive, well lit windfarms are being built in shoal waters; keep well clear.
Hbr daymark: The conspic power stn chimney (251m high) is 7.5 cables E of No 25 SHM lt buoy; see chartlet.
Sæding Strand triple ldg lts 053.8°: Front, Iso 2s , R wooden bldg; Middle, Iso 4s, R metal tr W bands; Rear, FW, R framework tr. All other light details are in 9.14.4 or shown on the chartlet.

R/T VHF Ch 16: 12 13 14, H24

TELEPHONE (Dial code 00 45) HM 75129200; Coastguard 75128299; Hosp 75181900; Customs 75122500; Police (Emergency) 112; Taxi 75126988.

FACILITIES Marina, 60 Kr, D, FW, AC; **Services**: Showers/WC at Esbjerg Søsport (YC) ☎ 75144747; ⚒ A-Z Snedkeriet ☎ 75126599; SM, Vase As ☎ 75123333; Diver, Bjarnes Dykkerservice ☎ 75120444, ME; **Town**: 🛒, R, Bar, PO, ⇌, ✈ (8km NE). Ferries to Harwich and Newcastle.

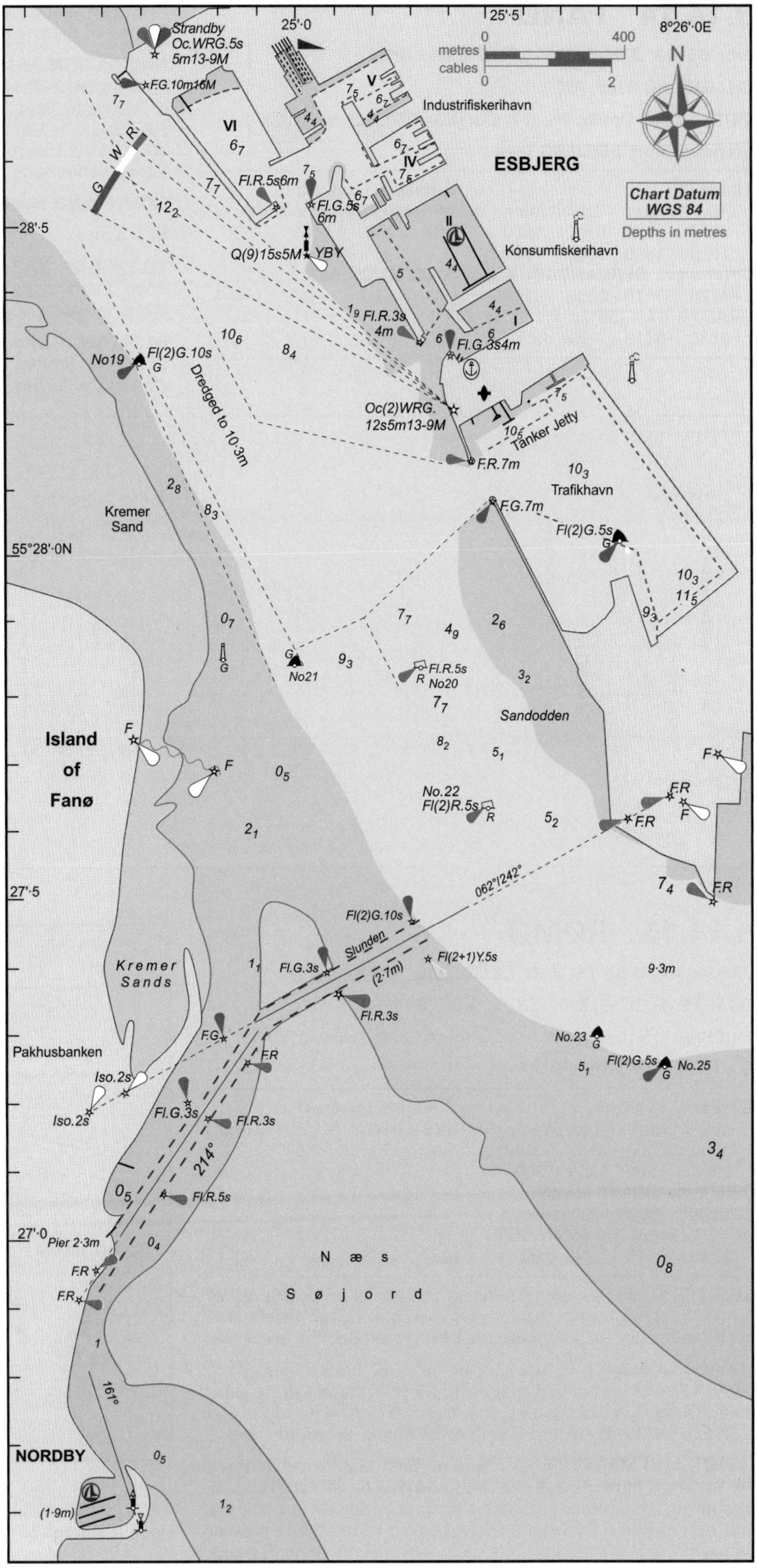
25'·0
25'·5
8°26'·0E
metres
cables
400
Strandby
Oc.WRG.5s
5m13-9M
F.G.10m16M
Industrifiskerihavn
ESBJERG
Chart Datum
WGS 84
Depths in metres
Konsumfiskerihavn
Fl.R.5s6m
Fl.G.5s
6m
Q(9)15s5M YBY
28'·5
Fl.R.3s
4m
Fl.G.3s4m
No19
Fl(2)G.10s
Dredged to 10·3m
Oc(2)WRG.
12s5m13-9M
Tanker Jetty
F.R.7m
Trafikhavn
F.G.7m
Fl(2)G.5s
Kremer
Sand
55°28'·0N
No21
Fl.R.5s
No20
Sandodden
Island
of
Fanø
No.22
Fl(2)R.5s
27'·5
062°/242°
Fl(2)G.10s
Slunden
Fl(2+1)Y.5s
Fl.G.3s
(2·7m)
Fl.R.3s
Kremer
Sands
Pakhusbanken
No.23
Fl(2)G.5s
No.25
Iso.2s
Fl.G.3s
Fl.R.3s
214°
Fl.R.5s
27'·0
Pier 2·3m
N æ s
S ø j o r d
161°
NORDBY
(1·9m)

9.14.14 FANØ

Ribe **55°27'·37N 08°25'·09E**

CHARTS AC 3766, 420.

TIDES +0340 Dover; ML 0·7; Duration 0605; Zone -0100

Standard Port ESBJERG (⟵)

Times				Height (metres)			
High Water		Low Water		MHWS	MHWN	MLWN	MLWS
0300	0700	0100	0800	1·9	1·5	0·5	0·1
1500	1900	1300	2000				
Differences BLÅVANDSHUK (55°33'·0N 08°05'·0E)							
−0120	−0110	−0050	−0100	−0·1	−0·1	−0·2	−0·1
GRADYB BAR (55°26'·0N 08°15'·0E)							
−0130	−0115	No data		−0·4	−0·3	−0·2	−0·1

SHELTER Good, access at all tides. Yachts berth in Nordby Marina in 1·8m via an approach channel with about 1m.

NAVIGATION As for Esbjerg until abeam No 22 buoy; here pick up Slunden 242° ldg lts, both Iso 2s, passing between two pairs of lt bcns to Næs Søjord Bn F R, R pile, then turning to 214° for F R Ldg lts at Nordby. The final appr is on 161·6° transit of two WR bns in the marina. An alternative to Slunden chan is a buoyed chan with 2·1m, ldg S from close to No 21 SHM buoy.

LIGHTS AND MARKS As Esbjerg and see 9.14.4 for lt details.

R/T None

TELEPHONE (Dial code 00 45) HM 75 16 31 00, CG 75 16 36 66, Hosp (Esbjerg) 75 18 19 00, Customs (Esbjerg) 75 12 25 00, Pol (Emergency) 112.

FACILITIES Pontoons with FW; **Services**: Showers and WC at SC; **Town**: limited 🛒 at Nordby, R, Bar. Full services at Esbjerg via regular ferries.

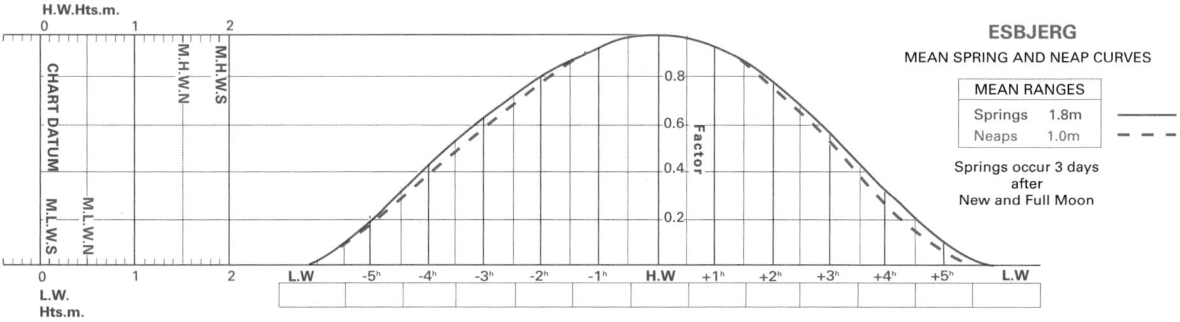
H.W.Hts.m.
0
1
2
CHART DATUM
M.H.W.N
M.H.W.S
M.L.W.S
M.L.W.N
L.W.
Hts.m.
0.8
0.6
0.4
0.2
Factor
L.W
-5h
-4h
-3h
-2h
-1h
H.W
+1h
+2h
+3h
+4h
+5h
ESBJERG
MEAN SPRING AND NEAP CURVES
MEAN RANGES
Springs 1.8m
Neaps 1.0m
Springs occur 3 days after New and Full Moon

9.14.15 RØMØ

Sønderjylland **55°05'·21N 08°34'·31E**

CHARTS AC 3766, 3767; DK 94; BSH 3013/2 & 3

TIDES +0315 Dover; ML 0·9; Duration 0620; Zone -0100

Standard Port ESBJERG (⟵)

Times				Height (metres)			
High Water		Low Water		MHWS	MHWN	MLWN	MLWS
0300	0700	0100	0800	1·9	1·5	0·5	0·1
1500	1900	1300	2000				
Difference RØMØ HAVN							
−0040	−0005	0000	−0020	0·0	+0·1	−0·2	−0·2
HOJER (54°58'·0N 08°40'·0E)							
−0020	+0015	No data		+0·5	+0·6	−0·1	−0·1

SHELTER Good, access at all tides. The hbr is on the SE tip of Rømø. Yachts berth at 3 pontoons in about 4m on the N side of the inner hbr; or ⚓ outside the hbr, close N of the entrance.

NAVIGATION WPT 55°05'·33N 08°16'·83E, Lister Tief SWM buoy, 107°/7M via buoyed channel to G1 Pillar buoy Fl Y 4s. Here enter Rømø Dyb (deep water), marked by 3 PHM lt dolphins and by No 1 SHM lt buoy and 5 unlit SHM buoys to the hbr ent.

LIGHTS AND MARKS On the N end of Sylt: List West [Oc WRG 6s, W twr, R lantern] and List Ost [Iso WRG 6s, W twr, R band, R lantern]. The former provides a narrow W sector to mark the first part of Rømø Dyb and a second part is marked by a further narrow W sector from List Land lt Oc WRG 3s, W mast, R band. See 9.14.4 for lt sectors. Hbr lts as on chartlet.

R/T VHF Ch 16; 10 12 13, HX.

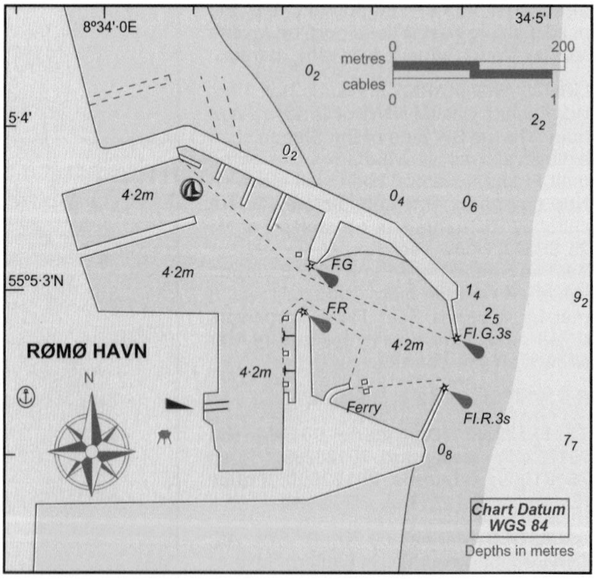
8°34'·0E
34·5'
5·4'
55°5·3'N
metres
cables
200
4·2m
F.G
F.R
Fl.G.3s
Fl.R.3s
Ferry
RØMØ HAVN
N
Chart Datum
WGS 84
Depths in metres

TELEPHONE (Dial code 00 45) HM 74 75 55 92; CG 74 75 22 22; Hosp (Esbjerg) 75 18 19 00; Pol (Emergency) 112; Taxi 74 75 11 00, 74 75 53 94.

FACILITIES D in FV hbr, FW; **Services**: ME, ⚒, CH, Showers at SC on N pier. **Town**: 🛒, Rail at Vibe, ✈ (Esbjerg).

TIME ZONE -0100
(Danish Standard Time)
Subtract 1 hour for UT
For Danish Summer Time add ONE hour in **non-shaded areas**

DENMARK – ESBJERG

LAT 55°28′N LONG 8°27′E

TIMES AND HEIGHTS OF HIGH AND LOW WATERS

SPRING & NEAP TIDES
Dates in **red** are **SPRINGS**
Dates in blue are **NEAPS**

YEAR **2005**

JANUARY

Date	Day	Time	m	Time	m	Time	m	Time	m
1	SA	0545	1.8	1208	0.1	1815	1.5		
2	SU	0013	0.2	0622	1.8	1249	0.1	1857	1.5
3	M	0057	0.2	0707	1.8	1335	0.1	◑ 1945	1.5
4	TU	0147	0.2	0759	1.8	1427	0.1	2041	1.5
5	W	0242	0.2	0857	1.7	1524	0.2	2145	1.5
6	TH	0342	0.2	1006	1.7	1627	0.2	2254	1.5
7	F	0451	0.2	1121	1.6	1734	0.2		
8	SA	0006	1.5	0601	0.2	1236	1.6	1839	0.2
9	SU	0111	1.6	0708	0.1	1344	1.6	1937	0.2
10	M	0209	1.6	0807	0.1	1445	1.6	● 2030	0.1
11	TU	0303	1.7	0902	0.0	1539	1.6	2119	0.1
12	W	0352	1.7	0953	-0.1	1630	1.6	2206	0.1
13	TH	0439	1.8	1041	-0.1	1718	1.5	2251	0.1
14	F	0524	1.8	1129	-0.1	1803	1.5	2337	0.1
15	SA	0610	1.8	1216	-0.1	1848	1.5		
16	SU	0023	0.1	0658	1.8	1305	0.0	1936	1.4
17	M	0112	0.1	0749	1.8	1356	0.1	◐ 2027	1.4
18	TU	0204	0.1	0845	1.7	1451	0.2	2123	1.4
19	W	0303	0.2	0948	1.7	1553	0.2	2224	1.4
20	TH	0411	0.2	1053	1.6	1700	0.2	2325	1.5
21	F	0525	0.2	1157	1.6	1804	0.2		
22	SA	0025	1.5	0633	0.2	1257	1.5	1900	0.2
23	SU	0121	1.6	0730	0.1	1351	1.5	1949	0.2
24	M	0210	1.6	0820	0.1	1438	1.5	2031	0.2
25	TU	0254	1.7	0902	0.1	1520	1.5	○ 2107	0.2
26	W	0333	1.7	0938	0.1	1556	1.5	2139	0.1
27	TH	0405	1.7	1009	0.1	1627	1.4	2209	0.1
28	F	0433	1.7	1039	0.0	1654	1.4	2241	0.1
29	SA	0459	1.7	1110	0.0	1723	1.5	2315	0.0
30	SU	0528	1.7	1145	0.0	1754	1.5	2352	0.0
31	M	0602	1.7	1223	0.0	1830	1.5		

FEBRUARY

Date	Day	Time	m	Time	m	Time	m	Time	m
1	TU	0033	0.0	0642	1.7	1305	0.0	1911	1.5
2	W	0118	0.0	0729	1.7	1352	0.0	◑ 2000	1.4
3	TH	0209	0.0	0824	1.6	1445	0.1	2057	1.4
4	F	0308	0.1	0931	1.5	1548	0.2	2209	1.4
5	SA	0418	0.2	1055	1.4	1700	0.3	2333	1.4
6	SU	0539	0.2	1221	1.4	1817	0.2		
7	M	0049	1.4	0656	0.1	1335	1.4	1922	0.2
8	TU	0154	1.5	0758	0.0	1436	1.5	● 2016	0.1
9	W	0249	1.6	0851	-0.2	1529	1.5	2105	0.0
10	TH	0339	1.7	0939	-0.2	1615	1.5	2150	-0.1
11	F	0424	1.8	1024	-0.2	1657	1.5	2233	-0.1
12	SA	0507	1.8	1108	-0.2	1737	1.5	2315	-0.2
13	SU	0549	1.8	1150	-0.2	1815	1.4	2358	-0.1
14	M	0631	1.7	1233	-0.1	1855	1.4		
15	TU	0042	-0.1	0715	1.7	1316	0.0	1938	1.4
16	W	0128	0.0	0805	1.6	1403	0.1	◐ 2028	1.4
17	TH	0221	0.1	0902	1.5	1458	0.2	2127	1.4
18	F	0326	0.2	1009	1.4	1609	0.3	2237	1.4
19	SA	0452	0.2	1121	1.3	1729	0.3	2346	1.4
20	SU	0611	0.2	1225	1.3	1833	0.2		
21	M	0048	1.5	0711	0.1	1323	1.4	1925	0.2
22	TU	0142	1.5	0759	0.0	1412	1.4	2007	0.1
23	W	0228	1.6	0839	0.0	1456	1.4	2044	0.0
24	TH	0308	1.6	0913	-0.1	1533	1.4	○ 2116	0.0
25	F	0342	1.6	0944	-0.1	1605	1.4	2147	-0.1
26	SA	0412	1.6	1014	-0.1	1633	1.4	2219	-0.1
27	SU	0440	1.6	1045	-0.2	1702	1.4	2253	-0.2
28	M	0509	1.6	1119	-0.2	1731	1.4	2330	-0.2

MARCH

Date	Day	Time	m	Time	m	Time	m	Time	m
1	TU	0542	1.6	1157	-0.2	1803	1.4		
2	W	0009	-0.2	0621	1.6	1237	-0.1	1842	1.4
3	TH	0054	-0.2	0706	1.5	1323	0.0	◑ 1927	1.4
4	F	0144	-0.1	0802	1.4	1415	0.1	2022	1.3
5	SA	0243	0.0	0912	1.3	1518	0.2	2136	1.3
6	SU	0359	0.1	1047	1.3	1638	0.3	2312	1.3
7	M	0530	0.1	1216	1.3	1802	0.2		
8	TU	0034	1.4	0647	0.0	1325	1.3	1906	0.1
9	W	0139	1.5	0745	-0.2	1423	1.4	2000	0.0
10	TH	0233	1.6	0836	-0.3	1511	1.4	● 2046	-0.2
11	F	0321	1.7	0920	-0.3	1554	1.5	2130	-0.2
12	SA	0405	1.7	1002	-0.3	1632	1.5	2211	-0.3
13	SU	0445	1.7	1042	-0.3	1707	1.4	2251	-0.3
14	M	0523	1.7	1120	-0.2	1741	1.4	2331	-0.3
15	TU	0600	1.6	1158	-0.1	1815	1.4		
16	W	0012	-0.2	0639	1.5	1236	0.0	1851	1.4
17	TH	0054	-0.1	0722	1.4	1317	0.1	◐ 1934	1.3
18	F	0142	0.0	0813	1.3	1403	0.2	2027	1.3
19	SA	0240	0.1	0919	1.2	1504	0.3	2139	1.3
20	SU	0409	0.2	1037	1.1	1636	0.3	2259	1.3
21	M	0540	0.1	1148	1.2	1756	0.2		
22	TU	0008	1.3	0640	0.0	1248	1.2	1851	0.1
23	W	0105	1.4	0727	0.0	1339	1.3	1934	0.0
24	TH	0154	1.5	0806	-0.1	1424	1.4	2012	0.0
25	F	0236	1.5	0841	-0.2	1503	1.4	○ 2046	-0.1
26	SA	0312	1.6	0912	-0.2	1537	1.4	2120	-0.2
27	SU	0345	1.6	0945	-0.2	1609	1.4	2154	-0.2
28	M	0418	1.6	1018	-0.3	1639	1.4	2230	-0.3
29	TU	0451	1.6	1054	-0.3	1709	1.4	2308	-0.3
30	W	0526	1.5	1132	-0.2	1742	1.4	2349	-0.3
31	TH	0606	1.5	1213	-0.2	1819	1.4		

APRIL

Date	Day	Time	m	Time	m	Time	m	Time	m
1	F	0035	-0.2	0654	1.4	1259	0.0	1905	1.3
2	SA	0127	-0.1	0753	1.3	1352	0.1	◑ 2003	1.3
3	SU	0230	0.0	0913	1.2	1459	0.2	2126	1.3
4	M	0354	0.0	1048	1.1	1624	0.2	2301	1.3
5	TU	0524	0.0	1206	1.2	1745	0.1		
6	W	0018	1.4	0632	-0.2	1309	1.3	1846	0.0
7	TH	0119	1.5	0726	-0.3	1402	1.4	1937	-0.2
8	F	0212	1.6	0813	-0.4	1447	1.4	● 2024	-0.3
9	SA	0300	1.7	0857	-0.4	1527	1.4	2106	-0.3
10	SU	0342	1.6	0936	-0.3	1603	1.4	2148	-0.4
11	M	0421	1.6	1014	-0.3	1637	1.4	2227	-0.3
12	TU	0457	1.5	1050	-0.2	1709	1.4	2306	-0.3
13	W	0531	1.4	1124	-0.1	1739	1.4	2344	-0.2
14	TH	0606	1.3	1200	0.0	1811	1.4		
15	F	0024	-0.1	0642	1.2	1236	0.1	1849	1.3
16	SA	0108	0.0	0727	1.1	1318	0.1	◐ 1937	1.3
17	SU	0200	0.1	0826	1.1	1410	0.2	2039	1.3
18	M	0314	0.1	0943	1.1	1524	0.3	2158	1.3
19	TU	0447	0.1	1100	1.1	1654	0.2	2315	1.3
20	W	0553	0.0	1204	1.2	1800	0.1		
21	TH	0018	1.4	0642	-0.1	1259	1.3	1851	0.0
22	F	0111	1.4	0724	-0.2	1346	1.3	1933	-0.1
23	SA	0157	1.5	0803	-0.2	1429	1.4	2012	-0.2
24	SU	0239	1.5	0839	-0.3	1507	1.4	○ 2051	-0.2
25	M	0318	1.5	0915	-0.3	1542	1.4	2129	-0.3
26	TU	0356	1.5	0951	-0.3	1617	1.4	2209	-0.3
27	W	0434	1.5	1030	-0.2	1651	1.4	2250	-0.3
28	TH	0515	1.4	1111	-0.2	1727	1.4	2334	-0.3
29	F	0600	1.3	1154	-0.1	1807	1.4		
30	SA	0024	-0.2	0652	1.2	1242	0.0	1857	1.3

Chart Datum: 0·69 metres below Dansk Normal Null

TIME ZONE -0100
(Danish Standard Time)
Subtract 1 hour for UT
For Danish Summer Time add ONE hour in **non-shaded areas**

DENMARK – ESBJERG

LAT 55°28′N LONG 8°27′E

TIMES AND HEIGHTS OF HIGH AND LOW WATERS

SPRING & NEAP TIDES
Dates in red are **SPRINGS**
Dates in blue are **NEAPS**

YEAR **2005**

MAY

Date	Day	Time	m	Time	m	Time	m	Time	m
1	SU	0119	-0.2	0757	1.1	1339	0.1	◑ 2002	1.3
2	M	0227	-0.1	0917	1.1	1447	0.2	2123	1.3
3	TU	0348	-0.1	1037	1.1	1606	0.1	2245	1.4
4	W	0506	-0.1	1145	1.2	1719	0.1	2355	1.5
5	TH	0608	-0.2	1244	1.3	1820	-0.1		
6	F	0055	1.5	0701	-0.3	1335	1.3	1912	-0.2
7	SA	0148	1.6	0748	-0.3	1420	1.4	2000	-0.3
8	SU	0236	1.6	0831	-0.3	1500	1.4	● 2045	-0.3
9	M	0320	1.6	0911	-0.3	1538	1.4	2127	-0.3
10	TU	0359	1.5	0948	-0.2	1612	1.4	2206	-0.3
11	W	0434	1.4	1023	-0.1	1642	1.4	2245	-0.2
12	TH	0506	1.3	1056	-0.1	1711	1.4	2322	-0.2
13	F	0538	1.2	1129	0.0	1741	1.4		
14	SA	0000	-0.1	0611	1.1	1204	0.0	1816	1.4
15	SU	0041	0.0	0651	1.1	1245	0.1	1900	1.4
16	M	0128	0.0	0742	1.1	1333	0.1	◐ 1953	1.3
17	TU	0225	0.1	0846	1.1	1432	0.2	2057	1.3
18	W	0334	0.1	1000	1.1	1543	0.2	2210	1.3
19	TH	0445	0.0	1109	1.2	1655	0.1	2320	1.4
20	F	0545	0.0	1210	1.2	1757	0.0		
21	SA	0021	1.4	0636	-0.1	1303	1.3	1850	0.0
22	SU	0116	1.4	0722	-0.2	1352	1.4	1937	-0.1
23	M	0206	1.5	0805	-0.2	1436	1.4	○ 2023	-0.2
24	TU	0254	1.5	0847	-0.2	1518	1.4	2107	-0.2
25	W	0339	1.4	0929	-0.2	1558	1.4	2152	-0.3
26	TH	0424	1.4	1012	-0.2	1638	1.4	2238	-0.3
27	F	0510	1.3	1055	-0.1	1719	1.4	2326	-0.3
28	SA	0600	1.3	1142	-0.1	1805	1.4		
29	SU	0018	-0.2	0654	1.2	1232	0.0	1858	1.4
30	M	0115	-0.2	0756	1.2	1327	0.1	◑ 2000	1.4
31	TU	0218	-0.1	0903	1.1	1430	0.1	2110	1.4

JUNE

Date	Day	Time	m	Time	m	Time	m	Time	m
1	W	0327	-0.1	1011	1.2	1539	0.1	2221	1.5
2	TH	0436	-0.1	1114	1.2	1648	0.0	2327	1.5
3	F	0538	-0.2	1212	1.3	1751	-0.1		
4	SA	0028	1.5	0633	-0.2	1303	1.4	1847	-0.2
5	SU	0124	1.6	0722	-0.2	1351	1.4	1939	-0.2
6	M	0214	1.5	0808	-0.2	1436	1.5	● 2027	-0.2
7	TU	0300	1.5	0849	-0.2	1516	1.5	2112	-0.2
8	W	0341	1.4	0927	-0.1	1552	1.5	2152	-0.2
9	TH	0417	1.3	1002	0.0	1624	1.5	2230	-0.1
10	F	0449	1.2	1035	0.0	1654	1.4	2306	-0.1
11	SA	0518	1.2	1106	0.0	1721	1.4	2341	0.0
12	SU	0548	1.2	1141	0.0	1753	1.5		
13	M	0018	0.0	0623	1.2	1220	0.0	1831	1.5
14	TU	0100	0.0	0707	1.2	1304	0.0	1918	1.5
15	W	0146	0.0	0759	1.2	1354	0.1	◐ 2011	1.5
16	TH	0240	0.0	0900	1.2	1452	0.1	2112	1.4
17	F	0339	0.0	1006	1.2	1555	0.1	2220	1.4
18	SA	0443	0.0	1114	1.3	1702	0.1	2330	1.4
19	SU	0545	0.0	1217	1.3	1806	0.0		
20	M	0036	1.4	0642	0.0	1315	1.4	1906	0.0
21	TU	0138	1.4	0735	-0.1	1408	1.4	2000	-0.1
22	W	0234	1.4	0824	-0.1	1457	1.5	○ 2051	-0.2
23	TH	0327	1.4	0912	-0.1	1544	1.5	2141	-0.2
24	F	0418	1.4	0957	-0.1	1629	1.5	2230	-0.2
25	SA	0506	1.4	1044	-0.1	1714	1.6	2318	-0.2
26	SU	0556	1.3	1130	-0.1	1801	1.6		
27	M	0009	-0.2	0645	1.3	1218	0.0	1851	1.6
28	TU	0101	-0.2	0738	1.3	1309	0.0	◑ 1946	1.6
29	W	0157	-0.1	0834	1.3	1405	0.0	2046	1.6
30	TH	0256	-0.1	0933	1.3	1506	0.0	2151	1.6

JULY

Date	Day	Time	m	Time	m	Time	m	Time	m
1	F	0359	0.0	1034	1.3	1612	0.0	2256	1.5
2	SA	0503	0.0	1134	1.3	1720	0.0	2359	1.5
3	SU	0603	0.0	1231	1.4	1824	0.0		
4	M	0059	1.5	0658	0.0	1324	1.5	1922	-0.1
5	TU	0153	1.5	0748	0.0	1413	1.5	2015	-0.1
6	W	0242	1.4	0832	0.0	1458	1.5	● 2101	-0.1
7	TH	0325	1.4	0912	0.0	1537	1.5	2142	-0.1
8	F	0403	1.3	0946	0.1	1611	1.5	2218	0.0
9	SA	0435	1.3	1018	0.1	1640	1.5	2251	0.0
10	SU	0503	1.3	1049	0.1	1706	1.5	2321	0.0
11	M	0530	1.3	1121	0.0	1734	1.6	2354	0.0
12	TU	0600	1.3	1157	0.0	1807	1.6		
13	W	0030	0.0	0636	1.3	1237	0.0	1847	1.6
14	TH	0112	0.0	0720	1.3	1322	0.0	◐ 1934	1.6
15	F	0159	0.0	0810	1.3	1412	0.0	2027	1.6
16	SA	0251	0.0	0908	1.3	1509	0.1	2130	1.5
17	SU	0351	0.1	1015	1.3	1615	0.1	2245	1.5
18	M	0458	0.1	1130	1.3	1728	0.1		
19	TU	0004	1.4	0608	0.1	1242	1.4	1840	0.1
20	W	0118	1.4	0712	0.1	1345	1.5	1945	0.0
21	TH	0221	1.5	0807	0.1	1440	1.5	○ 2040	-0.1
22	F	0318	1.5	0857	0.0	1531	1.6	2131	-0.2
23	SA	0409	1.5	0945	0.0	1618	1.7	2219	-0.2
24	SU	0455	1.5	1030	-0.1	1703	1.7	2305	-0.2
25	M	0539	1.5	1114	-0.1	1748	1.8	2351	-0.2
26	TU	0623	1.4	1159	-0.1	1833	1.8		
27	W	0037	-0.2	0707	1.4	1245	-0.1	1921	1.7
28	TH	0126	-0.1	0755	1.4	1336	0.0	◑ 2015	1.7
29	F	0218	0.0	0848	1.4	1430	0.0	2115	1.6
30	SA	0315	0.1	0948	1.4	1535	0.1	2221	1.5
31	SU	0423	0.2	1054	1.4	1651	0.1	2330	1.5

AUGUST

Date	Day	Time	m	Time	m	Time	m	Time	m
1	M	0533	0.2	1157	1.5	1806	0.1		
2	TU	0033	1.5	0636	0.2	1257	1.5	1909	0.1
3	W	0131	1.5	0730	0.2	1351	1.6	2002	0.0
4	TH	0223	1.5	0815	0.1	1439	1.6	2048	0.0
5	F	0307	1.5	0854	0.1	1520	1.7	● 2127	0.0
6	SA	0345	1.4	0929	0.1	1554	1.7	2200	0.0
7	SU	0416	1.4	0959	0.1	1623	1.7	2228	0.0
8	M	0444	1.4	1029	0.1	1648	1.7	2257	0.0
9	TU	0509	1.4	1100	0.0	1715	1.7	2327	0.0
10	W	0536	1.5	1133	0.0	1744	1.7		
11	TH	0002	0.0	0607	1.5	1212	0.0	1820	1.7
12	F	0040	0.0	0645	1.5	1254	0.0	1903	1.7
13	SA	0124	0.0	0730	1.5	1341	0.0	◐ 1954	1.6
14	SU	0213	0.1	0822	1.5	1435	0.1	2055	1.6
15	M	0310	0.2	0926	1.4	1540	0.2	2213	1.5
16	TU	0420	0.3	1049	1.4	1702	0.2	2346	1.4
17	W	0542	0.3	1215	1.5	1826	0.2		
18	TH	0106	1.5	0654	0.3	1325	1.6	1933	0.1
19	F	0209	1.5	0751	0.2	1424	1.7	○ 2027	-0.1
20	SA	0304	1.6	0842	0.1	1515	1.8	2116	-0.2
21	SU	0352	1.6	0927	0.0	1601	1.9	2201	-0.2
22	M	0434	1.6	1010	-0.1	1645	1.9	2244	-0.2
23	TU	0514	1.6	1052	-0.1	1727	1.9	2326	-0.1
24	W	0553	1.6	1135	-0.1	1809	1.9		
25	TH	0008	0.0	0631	1.6	1218	-0.1	1852	1.8
26	F	0051	0.1	0712	1.5	1304	0.0	◑ 1940	1.7
27	SA	0136	0.2	0800	1.5	1355	0.1	2036	1.6
28	SU	0229	0.3	0857	1.5	1457	0.2	2143	1.5
29	M	0335	0.4	1007	1.5	1621	0.3	2257	1.5
30	TU	0459	0.4	1121	1.5	1748	0.3		
31	W	0006	1.5	0611	0.4	1227	1.6	1851	0.2

Chart Datum: 0·69 metres below Dansk Normal Null

TIME ZONE -0100
(Danish Standard Time)
Subtract 1 hour for UT
For Danish Summer Time add ONE hour in **non-shaded areas**

DENMARK – ESBJERG

LAT 55°28'N LONG 8°27'E

TIMES AND HEIGHTS OF HIGH AND LOW WATERS

SPRING & NEAP TIDES
Dates in red are SPRINGS
Dates in blue are NEAPS

YEAR **2005**

SEPTEMBER

Date	Day	Time	m	Time	m	Time	m	Time	m
1	TH	0106	1.5	0706	0.3	1323	1.7	1942	0.2
2	F	0157	1.5	0751	0.2	1412	1.7	2025	0.1
3	SA	0242	1.6	0830	0.2	1454	1.8	● 2101	0.1
4	SU	0319	1.6	0904	0.2	1530	1.8	2132	0.1
5	M	0352	1.6	0934	0.1	1600	1.8	2200	0.1
6	TU	0420	1.6	1004	0.1	1627	1.8	2228	0.1
7	W	0446	1.6	1036	0.1	1653	1.8	2300	0.0
8	TH	0512	1.6	1109	0.0	1723	1.8	2334	0.0
9	F	0542	1.6	1148	0.0	1758	1.8		
10	SA	0012	0.1	0616	1.6	1229	0.0	1840	1.7
11	SU	0054	0.2	0657	1.6	1316	0.1	◐ 1930	1.6
12	M	0143	0.3	0748	1.6	1411	0.2	2034	1.5
13	TU	0240	0.4	0853	1.5	1520	0.3	2201	1.5
14	W	0354	0.5	1024	1.5	1650	0.3	2338	1.5
15	TH	0523	0.5	1156	1.6	1815	0.2		
16	F	0053	1.5	0636	0.4	1306	1.7	1918	0.1
17	SA	0154	1.6	0732	0.2	1404	1.8	2009	0.0
18	SU	0244	1.7	0821	0.1	1454	1.9	○ 2054	-0.1
19	M	0328	1.7	0905	0.0	1540	2.0	2137	-0.1
20	TU	0408	1.7	0948	-0.1	1622	2.0	2218	-0.1
21	W	0445	1.7	1029	-0.1	1702	1.9	2257	0.0
22	TH	0520	1.7	1109	-0.1	1741	1.9	2336	0.1
23	F	0555	1.7	1151	0.0	1821	1.8		
24	SA	0015	0.2	0632	1.7	1235	0.1	1905	1.7
25	SU	0057	0.3	0714	1.6	1323	0.2	◑ 1955	1.6
26	M	0143	0.4	0806	1.6	1421	0.3	2100	1.5
27	TU	0242	0.5	0915	1.6	1547	0.4	2218	1.4
28	W	0410	0.6	1036	1.6	1719	0.4	2330	1.4
29	TH	0534	0.5	1147	1.6	1821	0.3		
30	F	0030	1.5	0632	0.4	1246	1.7	1910	0.2

OCTOBER

Date	Day	Time	m	Time	m	Time	m	Time	m
1	SA	0123	1.6	0718	0.3	1337	1.8	1951	0.2
2	SU	0209	1.6	0758	0.3	1421	1.8	2027	0.1
3	M	0248	1.7	0833	0.2	1458	1.8	● 2058	0.1
4	TU	0322	1.7	0905	0.2	1531	1.8	2128	0.1
5	W	0353	1.7	0937	0.1	1602	1.8	2200	0.1
6	TH	0422	1.7	1012	0.1	1633	1.8	2233	0.1
7	F	0450	1.7	1048	0.1	1706	1.8	2309	0.1
8	SA	0521	1.7	1127	0.1	1743	1.8	2348	0.2
9	SU	0555	1.7	1210	0.1	1827	1.7		
10	M	0032	0.3	0637	1.7	1300	0.2	◐ 1921	1.6
11	TU	0122	0.4	0730	1.7	1358	0.3	2031	1.5
12	W	0222	0.5	0840	1.6	1512	0.3	2202	1.5
13	TH	0339	0.5	1012	1.6	1641	0.3	2327	1.5
14	F	0503	0.5	1137	1.7	1757	0.2		
15	SA	0034	1.6	0612	0.4	1244	1.8	1855	0.1
16	SU	0130	1.7	0707	0.2	1341	1.9	1945	0.0
17	M	0218	1.7	0756	0.1	1431	2.0	○ 2030	0.0
18	TU	0301	1.8	0842	0.0	1517	2.0	2112	0.0
19	W	0340	1.8	0924	0.0	1559	2.0	2151	0.0
20	TH	0417	1.8	1006	0.0	1638	1.9	2230	0.1
21	F	0451	1.8	1047	0.0	1715	1.8	2306	0.2
22	SA	0524	1.8	1128	0.1	1753	1.7	2343	0.3
23	SU	0557	1.7	1210	0.2	1832	1.6		
24	M	0021	0.4	0636	1.7	1256	0.3	1917	1.5
25	TU	0104	0.5	0723	1.7	1350	0.4	◑ 2014	1.4
26	W	0156	0.6	0823	1.6	1501	0.5	2127	1.4
27	TH	0306	0.6	0939	1.6	1628	0.5	2241	1.4
28	F	0433	0.6	1054	1.7	1735	0.4	2345	1.5
29	SA	0541	0.5	1158	1.7	1826	0.3		
30	SU	0039	1.6	0633	0.4	1252	1.8	1909	0.2
31	M	0128	1.7	0717	0.3	1339	1.8	1947	0.2

NOVEMBER

Date	Day	Time	m	Time	m	Time	m	Time	m
1	TU	0211	1.7	0757	0.3	1423	1.8	2022	0.2
2	W	0251	1.8	0834	0.2	1502	1.8	● 2057	0.1
3	TH	0326	1.8	0912	0.2	1539	1.8	2133	0.1
4	F	0400	1.8	0950	0.1	1617	1.8	2209	0.2
5	SA	0433	1.8	1030	0.1	1655	1.7	2248	0.2
6	SU	0506	1.8	1113	0.1	1737	1.7	2331	0.3
7	M	0545	1.8	1200	0.1	1826	1.6		
8	TU	0017	0.3	0631	1.7	1253	0.2	1924	1.5
9	W	0109	0.4	0727	1.7	1354	0.2	◐ 2034	1.5
10	TH	0211	0.5	0839	1.7	1506	0.3	2153	1.5
11	F	0322	0.5	1000	1.7	1622	0.3	2305	1.5
12	SA	0437	0.4	1114	1.8	1730	0.2		
13	SU	0007	1.6	0543	0.3	1218	1.9	1828	0.1
14	M	0101	1.7	0640	0.2	1316	1.9	1918	0.1
15	TU	0151	1.7	0732	0.1	1408	1.9	2005	0.1
16	W	0235	1.8	0820	0.1	1455	1.9	○ 2048	0.1
17	TH	0315	1.8	0905	0.0	1539	1.8	2127	0.2
18	F	0353	1.8	0948	0.1	1618	1.8	2206	0.2
19	SA	0428	1.8	1030	0.1	1655	1.7	2242	0.3
20	SU	0500	1.8	1110	0.2	1730	1.6	2318	0.3
21	M	0533	1.8	1151	0.3	1805	1.5	2354	0.4
22	TU	0607	1.8	1233	0.3	1844	1.5		
23	W	0033	0.4	0649	1.7	1319	0.4	◑ 1931	1.4
24	TH	0120	0.5	0739	1.7	1413	0.4	2030	1.4
25	F	0215	0.5	0839	1.7	1515	0.4	2137	1.4
26	SA	0321	0.5	0948	1.7	1622	0.4	2245	1.5
27	SU	0430	0.5	1057	1.7	1723	0.4	2346	1.6
28	M	0534	0.4	1159	1.7	1815	0.3		
29	TU	0042	1.6	0629	0.4	1255	1.7	1903	0.2
30	W	0132	1.7	0718	0.3	1347	1.8	1946	0.2

DECEMBER

Date	Day	Time	m	Time	m	Time	m	Time	m
1	TH	0218	1.7	0805	0.2	1435	1.8	● 2028	0.2
2	F	0300	1.7	0849	0.2	1521	1.7	2109	0.2
3	SA	0341	1.7	0933	0.1	1606	1.7	2151	0.2
4	SU	0420	1.8	1018	0.1	1651	1.7	2234	0.2
5	M	0500	1.8	1105	0.1	1738	1.6	2319	0.2
6	TU	0543	1.8	1154	0.1	1828	1.6		
7	W	0007	0.3	0632	1.8	1247	0.1	1923	1.5
8	TH	0059	0.3	0727	1.8	1345	0.1	◐ 2024	1.5
9	F	0155	0.3	0830	1.8	1447	0.2	2128	1.5
10	SA	0258	0.3	0938	1.8	1553	0.2	2233	1.5
11	SU	0405	0.3	1047	1.8	1658	0.2	2333	1.6
12	M	0512	0.3	1151	1.8	1758	0.2		
13	TU	0030	1.6	0614	0.2	1252	1.8	1852	0.1
14	W	0122	1.7	0711	0.1	1347	1.8	1942	0.1
15	TH	0211	1.7	0803	0.1	1438	1.8	○ 2027	0.2
16	F	0255	1.8	0852	0.1	1524	1.7	2109	0.2
17	SA	0336	1.8	0937	0.1	1604	1.6	2148	0.2
18	SU	0412	1.8	1018	0.1	1640	1.5	2224	0.3
19	M	0445	1.7	1057	0.2	1712	1.5	2258	0.3
20	TU	0516	1.7	1133	0.2	1743	1.4	2332	0.3
21	W	0546	1.7	1210	0.3	1815	1.4		
22	TH	0009	0.3	0621	1.7	1248	0.3	1853	1.4
23	F	0049	0.3	0703	1.7	1330	0.3	◑ 1939	1.4
24	SA	0136	0.3	0751	1.7	1418	0.3	2034	1.5
25	SU	0228	0.3	0848	1.7	1512	0.3	2136	1.5
26	M	0327	0.4	0951	1.6	1612	0.3	2243	1.5
27	TU	0432	0.4	1101	1.6	1716	0.3	2350	1.5
28	W	0539	0.3	1211	1.6	1817	0.3		
29	TH	0051	1.6	0642	0.3	1315	1.6	1913	0.2
30	F	0147	1.6	0740	0.2	1413	1.6	2004	0.2
31	SA	0238	1.7	0833	0.1	1507	1.6	● 2052	0.2

Chart Datum: 0·69 metres below Dansk Normal Null

Area 15

15

Germany
Danish border to Emden

The official name of the German flag is *Bundesflagge* (federal flag). However this name is mainly used by authorities or in very official announcements. Most Germans simply call the flag *Deutschlandfahne* (Germany flag). It has three equal horizontal bands of black, red, and gold.

1	***Den Helder***	378	322	187	192	198	229	245	192	175	180	159	150	153	148	130	115	125	95	115	**1**
2	***Delfzijl***	327	222	155	119	127	159	173	120	105	100	89	83	81	65	56	41	10	22	**2**	
3	Borkum	305	200	133	97	105	104	163	110	95	88	80	71	67	55	46	31	32	**3**		
4	Emden	337	232	165	129	137	174	190	137	120	115	106	97	85	80	63	47	**4**			
5	Norderney	291	186	123	77	85	81	137	84	69	62	53	44	44	29	18	**5**				
6	Langeoog	308	204	119	72	77	114	130	77	60	47	43	34	35	21	**6**					
7	Wangerooge	283	178	109	60	52	61	108	55	42	38	27	19	24	**7**						
8	**Helgoland**	259	154	83	38	47	88	104	51	38	44	43	35	**8**							
9	Hooksiel	405	301	116	69	73	101	117	64	47	36	9	**9**								
10	**Wilhelmshaven**	414	310	125	78	82	110	123	70	56	45	**10**									
11	**Bremerhaven**	306	201	127	80	82	81	131	78	58	**11**										
12	Cuxhaven	304	200	110	63	66	54	70	17	**12**											
13	**Brunsbüttel**	301	196	126	75	76	37	53	**13**												
14	Kiel/Holtenau	231	249	179	128	129	90	**14**													
15	Hamburg	338	233	163	112	113	**15**														
16	Husum	268	163	95	48	**16**															
17	**Hörnum Lt (Sylt)**	225	120	47	**17**																
18	***Esbjerg***	195	90	**18**																	
19	*Thyboron*	104	**19**																		
20	***Skagen***	**20**																			

DISTANCE TABLE

Approximate distances in nautical miles are by the most direct route, whilst avoiding dangers and allowing for Traffic Separation Schemes. Places in *italics* are in adjoining areas; places in **bold** are in 9.0.8, Distances across the North Sea.

9.15.2

Germany

Danish Border to Emden

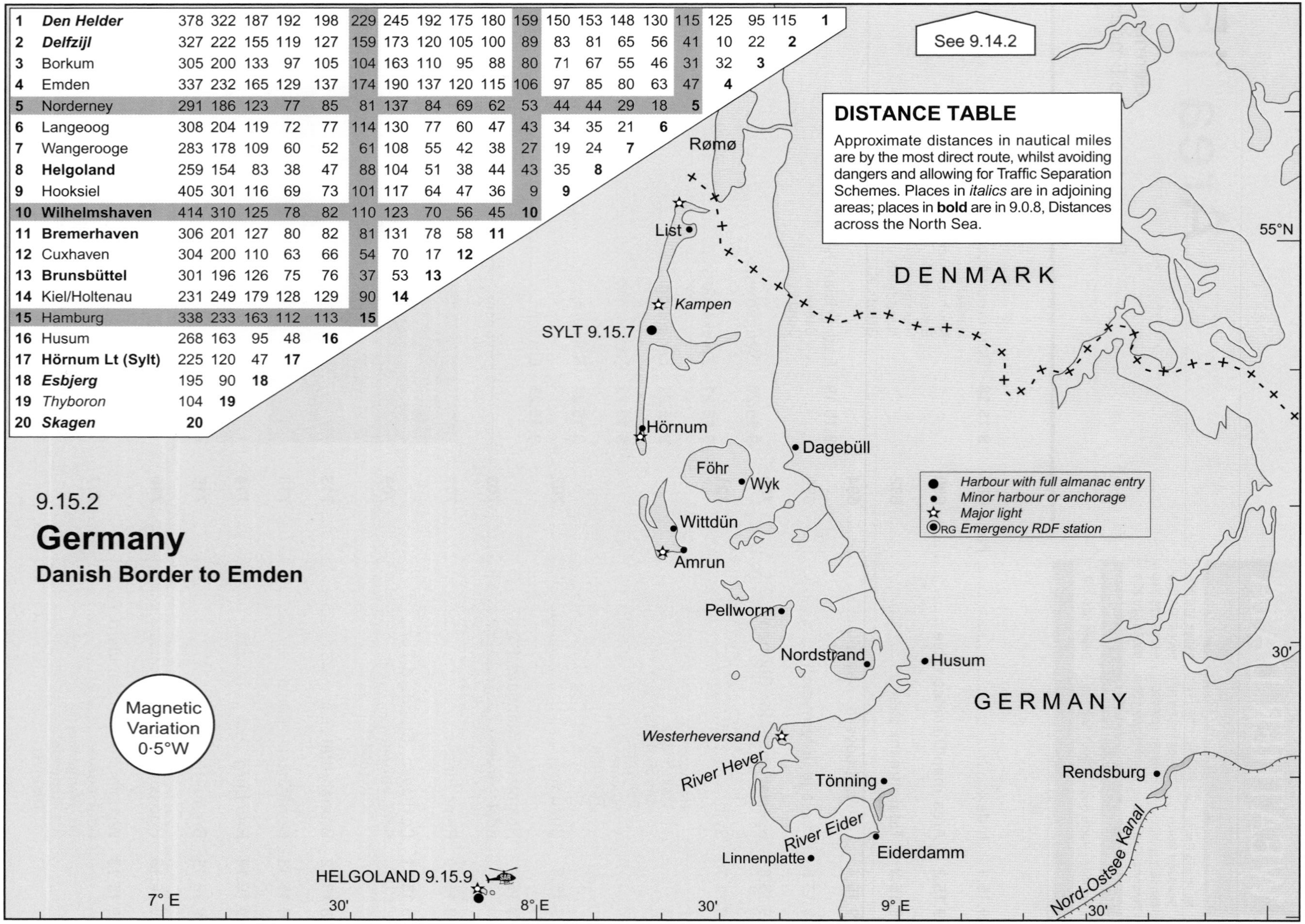
See 9.14.2
Rømø
List
Kampen
SYLT 9.15.7
Hörnum
Dagebüll
Föhr
Wyk
Wittdün
Amrun
Pellworm
Nordstrand
Husum
DENMARK
GERMANY
55°N
30'
Harbour with full almanac entry
Minor harbour or anchorage
Major light
RG Emergency RDF station
Westerheversand
River Hever
Tönning
River Eider
Linnenplatte
Eiderdamm
Rendsburg
Nord-Ostsee Kanal
HELGOLAND 9.15.9
Magnetic
Variation
0·5°W
7° E
30'
8° E
30'
9° E
30'

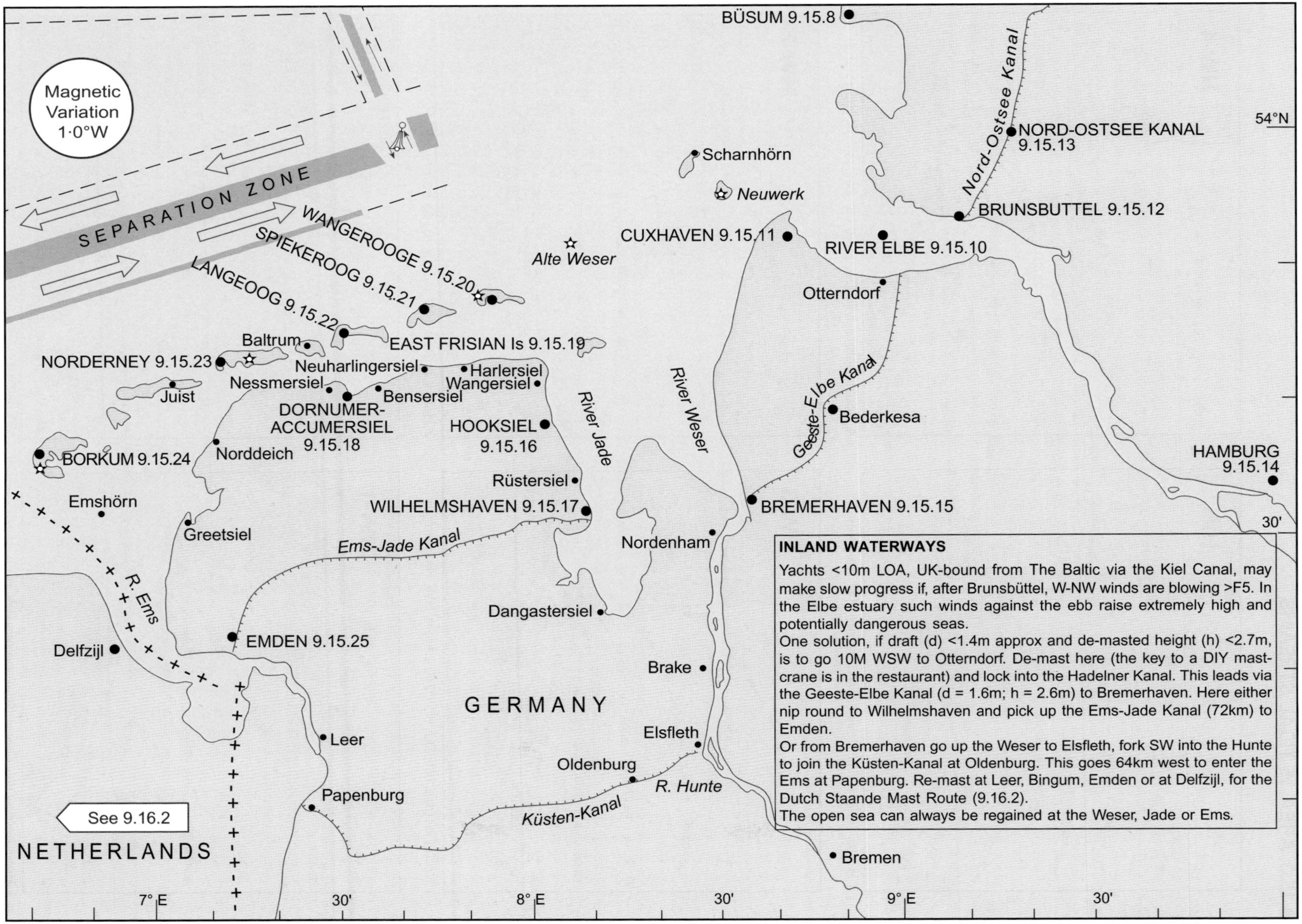
Magnetic
Variation
1·0°W
SEPARATION ZONE
BÜSUM 9.15.8
Nord-Ostsee Kanal
NORD-OSTSEE KANAL
9.15.13
54°N
Scharnhörn
Neuwerk
BRUNSBUTTEL 9.15.12
CUXHAVEN 9.15.11
RIVER ELBE 9.15.10
Alte Weser
WANGEROOGE 9.15.20
SPIEKEROOG 9.15.21
LANGEOOG 9.15.22
Otterndorf
Baltrum
EAST FRISIAN Is 9.15.19
NORDERNEY 9.15.23
Neuharlingersiel
Harlersiel
Wangersiel
Nessmersiel
Bensersiel
Juist
Geeste-Elbe Kanal
River Jade
River Weser
Bederkesa
DORNUMER-
ACCUMERSIEL
9.15.18
HOOKSIEL
9.15.16
BORKUM 9.15.24
Norddeich
HAMBURG
9.15.14
Rüstersiel
Emshörn
WILHELMSHAVEN 9.15.17
BREMERHAVEN 9.15.15
30'
Greetsiel
Nordenham
Ems-Jade Kanal
R. Ems
Dangastersiel
EMDEN 9.15.25
Delfzijl
Brake
GERMANY
Leer
Elsfleth
Oldenburg
R. Hunte
Papenburg
Küsten-Kanal
See 9.16.2
NETHERLANDS
Bremen
7° E
30'
8° E
30'
9° E
30'

INLAND WATERWAYS

Yachts <10m LOA, UK-bound from The Baltic via the Kiel Canal, may make slow progress if, after Brunsbüttel, W-NW winds are blowing >F5. In the Elbe estuary such winds against the ebb raise extremely high and potentially dangerous seas.

One solution, if draft (d) <1.4m approx and de-masted height (h) <2.7m, is to go 10M WSW to Otterndorf. De-mast here (the key to a DIY mast-crane is in the restaurant) and lock into the Hadelner Kanal. This leads via the Geeste-Elbe Kanal (d = 1.6m; h = 2.6m) to Bremerhaven. Here either nip round to Wilhelmshaven and pick up the Ems-Jade Kanal (72km) to Emden.

Or from Bremerhaven go up the Weser to Elsfleth, fork SW into the Hunte to join the Küsten-Kanal at Oldenburg. This goes 64km west to enter the Ems at Papenburg. Re-mast at Leer, Bingum, Emden or at Delfzijl, for the Dutch Staande Mast Route (9.16.2).

The open sea can always be regained at the Weser, Jade or Ems.

9.15.3 AREA 15 TIDAL STREAMS

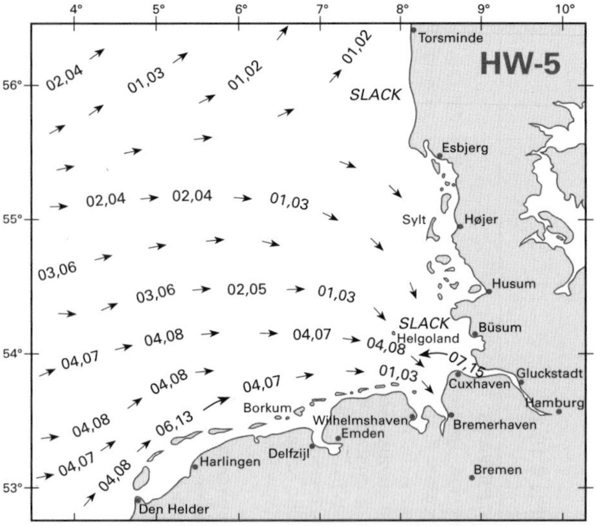
HW-5
Torsminde
Esbjerg
Sylt
Højer
Husum
Büsum
Helgoland
Gluckstadt
Cuxhaven
Hamburg
Borkum
Wilhelmshaven
Emden
Bremerhaven
Harlingen
Delfzijl
Bremen
Den Helder
SLACK

5 Hours before HW Dover (0440 before HW Helgoland)

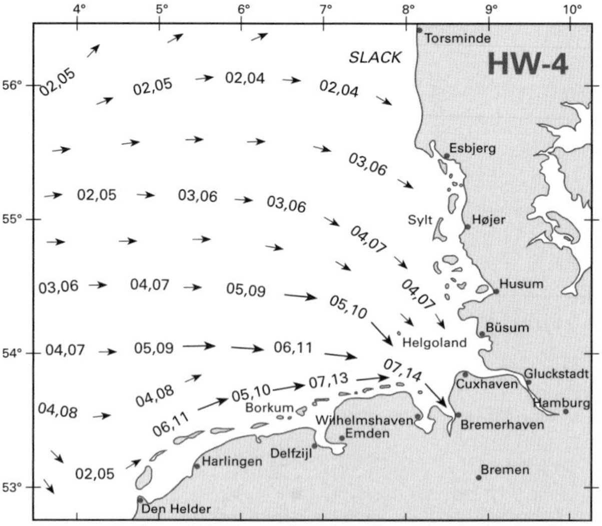
HW-4
Torsminde
Esbjerg
Sylt
Højer
Husum
Büsum
Helgoland
Gluckstadt
Cuxhaven
Hamburg
Borkum
Wilhelmshaven
Emden
Bremerhaven
Harlingen
Delfzijl
Bremen
Den Helder
SLACK

4 Hours before HW Dover (0340 before HW Helgoland)

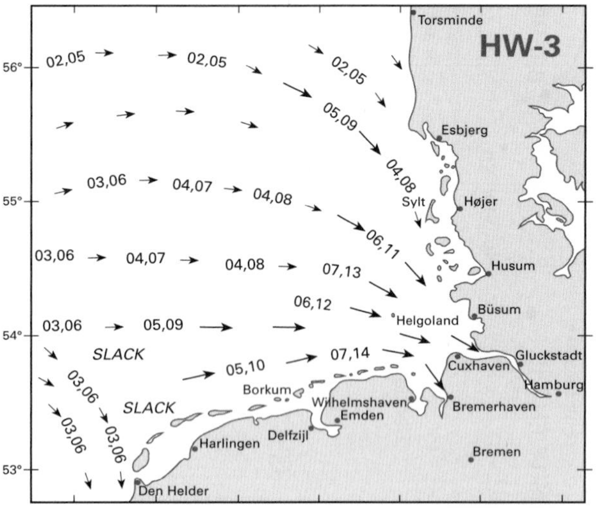
HW-3
Torsminde
Esbjerg
Sylt
Højer
Husum
Büsum
Helgoland
Gluckstadt
Cuxhaven
Hamburg
Borkum
Wilhelmshaven
Emden
Bremerhaven
Harlingen
Delfzijl
Bremen
Den Helder
SLACK

3 Hours before HW Dover (0240 before HW Helgoland)

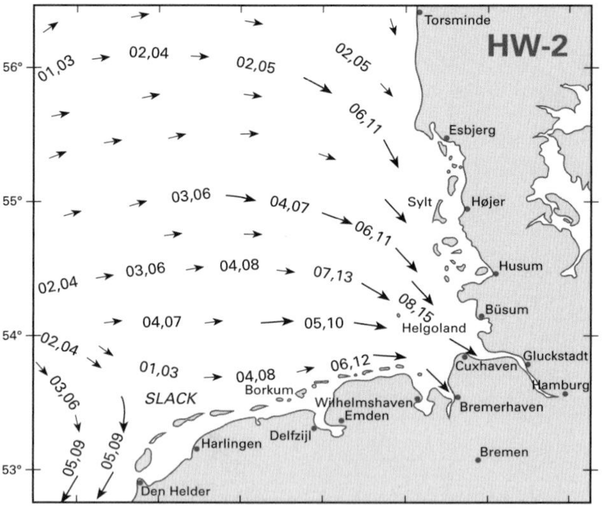
HW-2
Torsminde
Esbjerg
Sylt
Højer
Husum
Büsum
Helgoland
Gluckstadt
Cuxhaven
Hamburg
Borkum
Wilhelmshaven
Emden
Bremerhaven
Harlingen
Delfzijl
Bremen
Den Helder
SLACK

2 Hours before HW Dover (0140 before HW Helgoland)

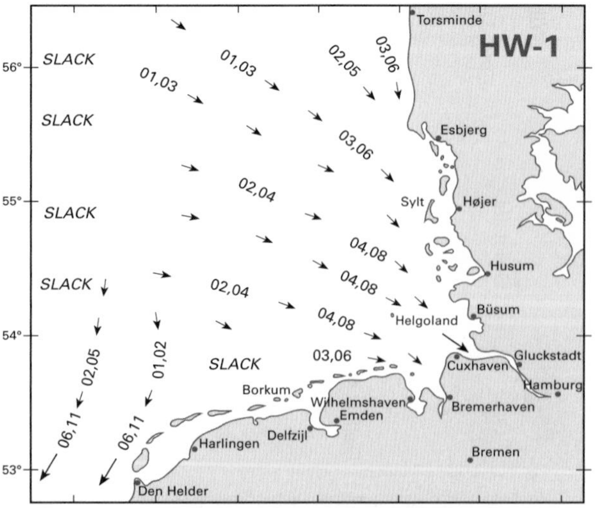
HW-1
Torsminde
Esbjerg
Sylt
Højer
Husum
Büsum
Helgoland
Gluckstadt
Cuxhaven
Hamburg
Borkum
Wilhelmshaven
Emden
Bremerhaven
Harlingen
Delfzijl
Bremen
Den Helder
SLACK

1 Hour before HW Dover (0040 before HW Helgoland)

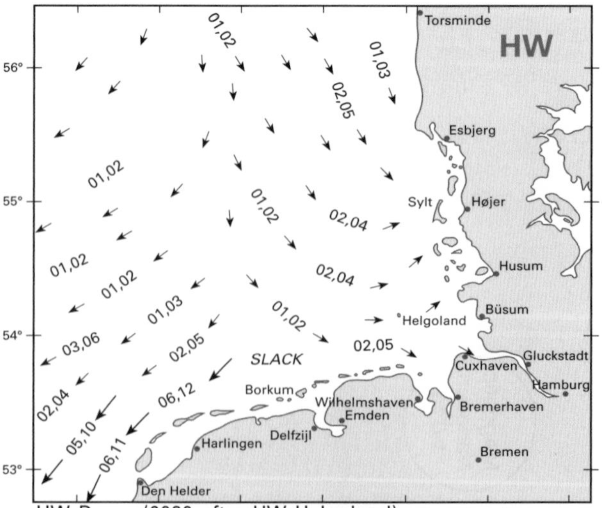
HW
Torsminde
Esbjerg
Sylt
Højer
Husum
Büsum
Helgoland
Gluckstadt
Cuxhaven
Hamburg
Borkum
Wilhelmshaven
Emden
Bremerhaven
Harlingen
Delfzijl
Bremen
Den Helder
SLACK

HW Dover (0020 after HW Helgoland)

South-westward 9.16.3

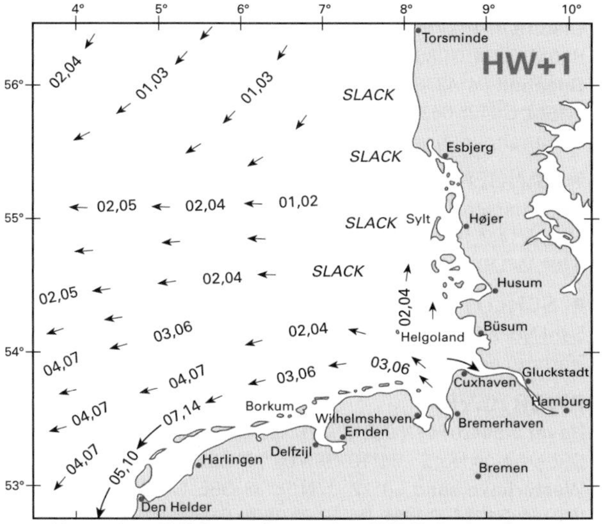
HW+1
SLACK
Torsminde
Esbjerg
Sylt
Højer
Husum
Büsum
Helgoland
Gluckstadt
Cuxhaven
Hamburg
Bremerhaven
Wilhelmshaven
Emden
Borkum
Delfzijl
Harlingen
Bremen
Den Helder
4° 5° 6° 7° 8° 9° 10°
56° 55° 54° 53°

1 Hour after HW Dover (0120 after HW Helgoland)

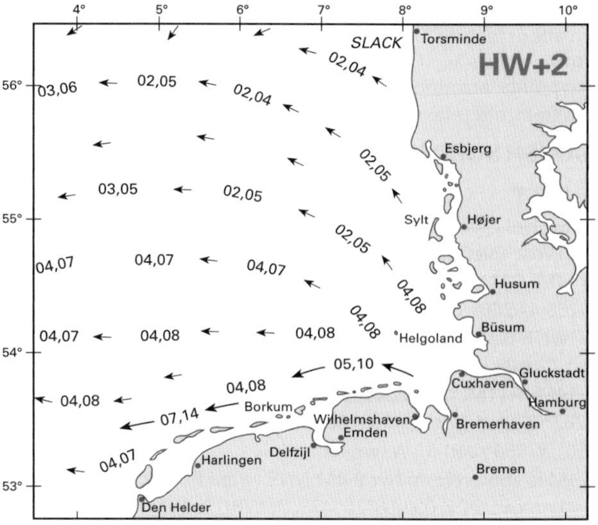
HW+2
SLACK
Torsminde
Esbjerg
Sylt
Højer
Husum
Büsum
Helgoland
Gluckstadt
Cuxhaven
Hamburg
Bremerhaven
Wilhelmshaven
Emden
Borkum
Delfzijl
Harlingen
Bremen
Den Helder
4° 5° 6° 7° 8° 9° 10°
56° 55° 54° 53°

2 Hours after HW Dover (0220 after HW Helgoland)

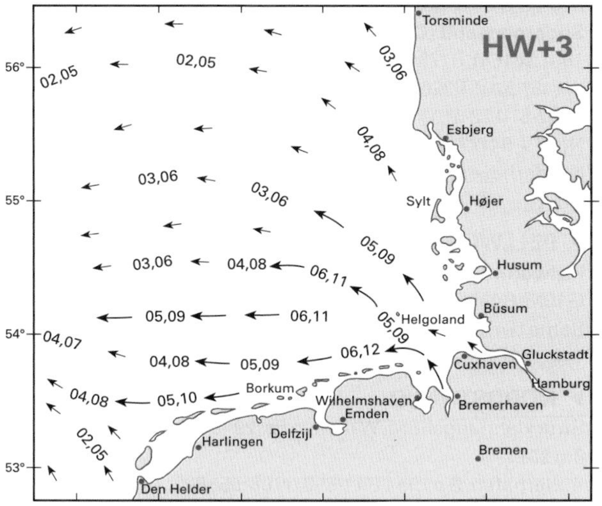
HW+3
Torsminde
Esbjerg
Sylt
Højer
Husum
Büsum
Helgoland
Gluckstadt
Cuxhaven
Hamburg
Bremerhaven
Wilhelmshaven
Emden
Borkum
Delfzijl
Harlingen
Bremen
Den Helder
56° 55° 54° 53°

3 Hours after HW Dover (0320 after HW Helgoland)

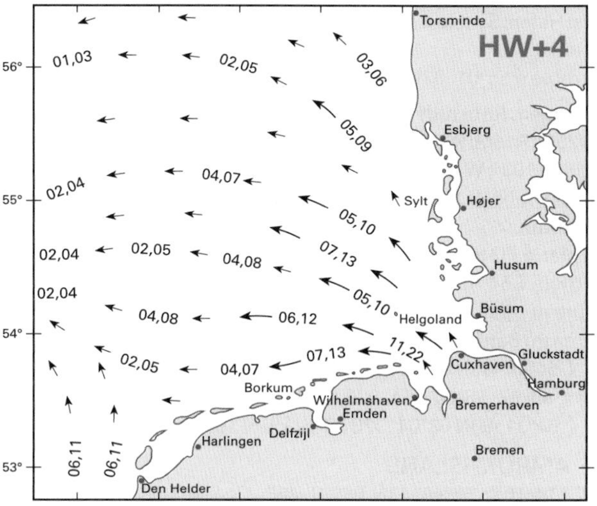
HW+4
Torsminde
Esbjerg
Sylt
Højer
Husum
Büsum
Helgoland
Gluckstadt
Cuxhaven
Hamburg
Bremerhaven
Wilhelmshaven
Emden
Borkum
Delfzijl
Harlingen
Bremen
Den Helder
56° 55° 54° 53°

4 Hours after HW Dover (0420 after HW Helgoland)

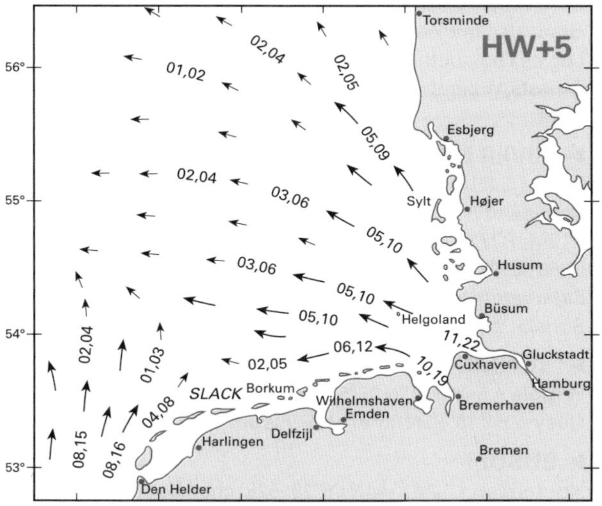
HW+5
SLACK
Torsminde
Esbjerg
Sylt
Højer
Husum
Büsum
Helgoland
Gluckstadt
Cuxhaven
Hamburg
Bremerhaven
Wilhelmshaven
Emden
Borkum
Delfzijl
Harlingen
Bremen
Den Helder
56° 55° 54° 53°

5 Hours after HW Dover (0520 after HW Helgoland)

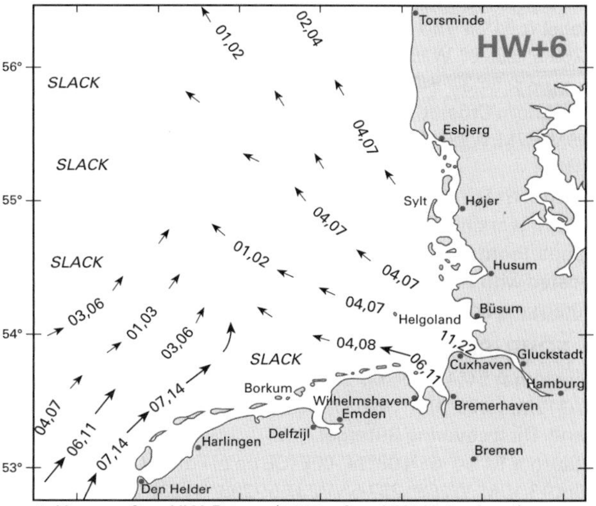
HW+6
SLACK
Torsminde
Esbjerg
Sylt
Højer
Husum
Büsum
Helgoland
Gluckstadt
Cuxhaven
Hamburg
Bremerhaven
Wilhelmshaven
Emden
Borkum
Delfzijl
Harlingen
Bremen
Den Helder
56° 55° 54° 53°

6 Hours after HW Dover (0620 after HW Helgoland)

PLOT WAYPOINTS ON YOUR CHART BEFORE USING THEM

9.15.4 LIGHTS, BUOYS AND WAYPOINTS

Blue print = light with a nominal range of 15M or more. CAPITALS = place or feature. *CAPITAL ITALICS* = light-vessel, light float or Lanby. *Italics* = Fog signal. ***Bold italics*** = Racon. Useful waypoints are underlined. Abbreviations are in Chapter 1. Positions are referenced to the WGS 84 datum.

DANISH BORDER TO BUSUM

▶ SYLT

Lister Tief 55°05'·33N 08°16'·79E, Iso 8s; *Whis.*

List West (Ellenbogen) ☆ 55°03'·15N 08°24'·00E, Oc WRG 6s 19m W14M, R11M, G10M; R040°-133°, W133°-227°, R227°-266·4°, W266·4°-268°, G268°-285°, W285°-310°, W(unintens) 310°-040°; W twr, R lantern.

List Ost (N side), ☆ 55°02'·93N 08°26'·58E, Iso WRG 6s 22m W14M, R11M, G10M; W(unintens) 010·5°-098°, W098°-262°, R262°-278°, W278°-296°, R296°-323·3°, W323·3°-324·5°, G324·5°-350°, W350°-010·5°; W twr, R band.

Q 4M is shown from twr 9·4M NNE when firing takes place.

List Land ☆ 55°01'·03N 08°26'·47E, Oc WRG 3s 14m W13M, R10M, G9M; W170°-203°, G203°-212°, W212°-215·5°, R215·5°-232·5°, W232·5°-234°, G234°-243°, W243°-050°; W mast, R band.

List Hafen, S mole ☆ 55°01'·01N 08°26'·51E, FR 5m 4M; 218°-353°; R mast.

N mole ☆ 55°01'·03N 08°26'·52E, FG 8m 4M; 218°-038°; G mast.

Kampen, Rote Kliff ☆ 54°56'·76N 08°20'·38E, L Fl WR 10s 62m **W20M, R16M**; W193°-260°, W (unintens) 260°-339°, W339°-165°, R165°-193°; W twr, B band.

Theeknobs W 54°43'·51N 08°09'·87E, Q (9) 15s.

Hörnum ☆ 54°45'·23N 08°17'·47E, Fl (2) 9s 48m **20M**.

N pier ☆ FG 6m 4M, 024°-260°.

S mole ☆ 54°45'·57N 08°17'·97E, FR 7m 4M.

Vortrapptief 54°34'·88N 08°12'·97E, Iso 4s; toward Hörnum.

Amrum Bank, offshore:

N 54°44'·96N 08°06'·92E, Q.

W 54°37'·96N 07°54'·92E, Q (9) 15s.

S 54°31'·96N 08°04'·92E, Q (6) + L Fl 15s.

▶ AMRUM ISLAND

Norddorf ☆ 54°40'·13N 08°18'·46E, Oc WRG 6s 22m **W15M**, R12M, G11M; W031-097°, R097°-176·5°, W176·5°-178·5°, G178·5°-188°; W ○ twr, R lantern.

Nebel ☆ 54°38'·75N 08°21'·75E, Oc WRG 5s 16m **W20M, R/G15M**; R255·5°-258·5°, W258·5°-260·5°, G260·5°-263·5°; R twr, W band.

Amrum ☆ 54°37'·84N 08°21'·23E, Fl 7·5s 63m **23M**; R twr, W bands.

Wriakhorn Cross lt, 54°37'·62N 08°21'·22E, L Fl (2) WR 15s 26m W9M, R7M; W297·5°-319·5°, R319·5°-330°, W330°-005·5°, R005·5°-034°.

Amrum Hafen ldg lts 272° have been inoperative since at least 2002. If working, both are Iso R 4s 11/33m 10/**15M**; W masts, R bands. Front, 54°37'·88N 08°22'·92E. **Rear**, 0·9M from front; co-located with Amrum main lt.

Rütergat 54°30'·08N 08°12'·32E, Iso 8s.

▶ FÖHR ISLAND

Nieblum ☆ 54°41'·10N 08°29'·20E, Oc (2) WRG 10s 11m **W19M, R/G15M**; G028°-031°, W031°-032·5°, R032·5°-035·5°; R twr, W band. Dir lt covering Rütergat.

Ohlörn ☆ 54°40'·85N 08°34'·00E (SE tip of Föhr), Oc (4) WR 15s 10m 13/10M, W208°-237·5°, R237·5°-298°, W298°-353°, R353°-080°; R twr, Gy lantern.

Wyk Hbr outer ent, FR 54°41'·55N 08°34'·69E; and FG.

▶ DAGEBÜLL

Oland Is, near W end, ☆ 54°40'·51N 08°41'·28E, F WRG 7m W13M, R10M, G9M; G086°-093°, W093°-160°, R160°-172°; R twr.

Dagebüll 54°43'·82N 08°41'·43E, Iso WRG 8s 23m **W18M, R/G15M**; G042°-043°, W043°-044·5°, R044·5°-047°; G mast.

FW lts shown from N and S moles.

▶ LANGENESS ISLAND

Nordmarsch ☆ 54°37'·58N 08°31'·85E (W end), L Fl (3) WR 20s 13m W14M, R11M; W268°-279°, R279°-306°, W306°-045°, R045°-070°, W070°-218°; dark brown twr.

▶ SCHLÜTTSIEL

Schl No. 2/SA 26 54°36'·84N 08°38'·95E.

Harbour ent, S side ▲ 54°40'·89N 08°45'·10E.

RIVER HEVER

Hever 54°20'·41N 08°18'·82E, Iso 4s; *Whis.*

Süderhever No. 2 54°18'·96N 08°23'·92E.

Westerheversand, 54°22'·37N 08°38'·36E, Oc (3) WRG 15s 41m **W21M, R17M, G16M**; W012·2°-069°, G069°-079·5°°, W079·5°-080·5° (ldg sector for Hever), R080·5°-107°, W107°-233°, R233°-248°; R twr, W bands.

Suderoogsand (Cross lt), 54°22'·37N 08°38'·36E, Iso WRG 6s 18m, **W15M**, R12M, G11M. R240°-244°, W244°-246°, G246°-248°, W248°-320°, R320°-338°, W338°-013°, R013°-048°, W048°-082·5°, R082·5°-122·5°, W122·5°-150°; B pile structure.

No. 7 54°21'·18N 08°27'·40E, Fl G 4s.

Norderhever No. 1 54°22'·46N 08°30'·83E, Fl (2+1) R 15s.

No. 20 54°24'·70N 08°35'·42E, Fl R 4s.

▶ PELLWORM ISLAND

Pellworm ☆ 54°29'·78N 08°39'·98E: Oc WRG 5s 38m **20M, R 16M, G 15M**; G037·5°-040°, W040°-042·5°, R042·5°-045°; R twr, W band.

Same twr, **Cross Light** ☆ Oc WR 5s 38m **W15M**, R12M; R122·6°-140°, W 140°-210·2°, W 255°-307°.

▶ NORDSTRAND

Strucklahnungshörn, W mole ☆ 54°29'·91N 08°48'·29E, Oc G 6s 8m 2M.

Suderhafen, S mole 54°28'·07N 08°55'·62E.

▶ HUSUM

SHM bcn, Fl G 4s, 54°28'·80N 08°58'·60E, marks start of access chan; also marked by two PHM bcns, both Fl (2) R 9s.

Ldg lts 090°, both Iso G 8s 7/9m 3M; intens on ldg line; synch; R masts, W bands. Front, 54°28'·79N 09°00'·32E. Rear, 40m from front.

▶ RIVER EIDER

Eider 54°14'·54N 08°27'·61E, Iso 4s.

St Peter ☆ 54°17'·24N 08°39'·10E, L Fl (2) WR 15s 23m **W15M**, R12M; R271°-280·5°, W280·5°-035°, R035°-055°, W055°-068°, R068°-091°, W091°-120°; R twr, B lantern.

Eiderdamm lock, N mole, W end ☆ Oc (2) R 12s 8m 5M; W twr.

S mole, W end ☆ Oc G 6s 8m 6M; W twr, Gy top.

▶ TÖNNING

W mole ☆ 54°18'·93N 08°57·09E, FR 5m 4M; R col.

Quay ☆ 54°18'·95N 08°57'·12E, FG 5m 4M; G col.

▶ BÜSUM

Norderpiep 54°11'·44N 08°28'·52E; chan buoyed but unlit.

Süderpiep 54°05'·82N 08°25'·70E, Iso 8s; *Whis.*

Büsum ☆ 54°07'·60N 08°51'·48E, Iso WR 6s 22m **W19M**, R12M; W248°-317°, R317°-024°, W024°-148°.
Ldg lts 355·1°, both Iso 4s 9/12m 13M; synch; B masts, W bands. Front, 54°07'·53N 08°51'·48E. Rear, 110m from front.
W mole 54°07'·19N 08°51'·52E Oc (3) R 12s 10m 4M; 186°-120°; R twr. E mole 54°07'·19N 08°51'·65E, Oc (3) G 12s 10m 4M; 260°-168°; G twr.

GERMAN BIGHT TO RIVER ELBE

GB Light V 54°10'·80N 07°27'·60E, Iso 8s 12m **17M**; R hull marked G-B; *Horn Mo (R) 30s*; ***Racon T, 8M.***

▶ HELGOLAND

Seven cardinal buoys mark the outer limit of Nature Reserve:
Helgoland-O 54°08'·96N 07°53'·49E, Q (3) 10s; *Whis.*
Helgoland-W 54°10'·61N 07°48'·17E.
Nathurn-N 54°13'·36N 07°48'·97E.
Sellebrunn W 54°14'·39N 07°49'·76E, Q (9) 15s; *Whis.*
Düne-N 54°13'·50N 07°56'·13E.
Düne-O 54°10'·87N 07°56'·24E.
Düne -S 54°09'·51N 07°55'·94E, Q (6) + L Fl 15s.
Helgoland ☆ 54°10'·91N 07°52'·93E, Fl 5s 82m **28M**; brown □ twr, B lantern, W balcony.
FR on radio masts 180m SSE and 740m NNW of lt ho.
Binnen reede ldg lts 302·2°, both Oc R 6s 8/10m 6M; synch. Front (W pier) 54°10'·78N 07°53'·36E. Rear, 50m from front.
Vorhafen. Ostmole, S elbow 54°10'·31N 07°53'·94E, Oc WG 6s 5m W6M, G3M; W203°-250°, G250°-109°; G post; fog det lt.
Ostmole 54°10'·33N 07°53'·88E, FG 7m 3M; 289°-180°.
Sudmole 54°10'·24N 07°53'·94E, Oc (2) R 12s 7m 4M; 101°-334°; R post.

▶ DÜNE

Ldg lts 020°. Front 54°10'·87N 07°54'·80E, Iso 4s 11m 8M; intens on ldg line. Rear, 120m from front, Iso WRG 4s 17m W11M, R/G10M; synch; G010°-018·5°, W018·5°-021°, R021°-030, G106°-125°, W125°-130°, R130°144°.

RIVER ELBE (LOWER)

▶ APPROACHES

Elbe 53°59'·95N 08°06'·49E, Iso 10s; ***Racon T, 8M.***
No.1 53°59'·21N 08°13'·20E, QG.
No.5 53°59'·31N 08°18'·93E, QG.
Scharnhörnriff N 53°58'·96N 08°11'·17E, Q.
Scharnhörnriff W 53°58'·49N 08°08'·72E, Q (9) 15s.
Westertill N 53°58'·12N 08°06'·67E, Q.
Nordergründe N 53°57'·06N 08°00'·12E, VQ.
No.11 53°58'·65N 08°26'·02E, Fl G 4s.
No.19 53°57'·71N 08°34'·33E, QG.
No.25 53°56'·62N 08°38'·25E, QG.
Neuwerk ☆, S side 53°54'·92N 08°29'·73E, L Fl (3) WRG 20s 38m **W16M**, R12M, G11M; G165·3°-215·3°, W215·3°-238·8°, R238·8°-321°, R343°-100°.

▶ CUXHAVEN

Ldg lts 151·2°, both Iso 4s 58m **17/21M**, 149·2°-154·2°; intens on ldg line; synch. Front, **Baumrönne** ☆, 53°51'·19N 08°44'·15E, 1·55M from rear, W ○ twr, B band on gallery. Same twr, (i) Fl 3s 25m **17M**; 143·8°-149·2°. (ii) Fl (2) 9s **17M**, 154·2°-156·7°. **Rear, Altenbruch (W)**, 53°49'·81N 08°45'·43E. [Same structure, Iso 8s 51m **22M** is the rear 261° ldg lt, for down-river tfc, paired with **Altenbruch (E)**, the front ldg lt, also Iso 8s.]

Note: There are two Altenbruch lts, **(W)** and **(E)**, 1.3M apart.
Ldg lts 130·8°, both Iso 8s 19/31m **19M**/11M; synch; W ○ twrs, B bands. **Front, Altenbruch (E)**, 53°50'·02N 08°47'·66E. Rear, Wehldorf, 53°49'·82N 08°48'·09E. **Altenbruch (E)** also has ☆ Iso WRG 8s, W/G8M, R9M; G117·5°-124°, W124°-135°, R135°-140°; the white sector covers the 130·8° ldg line.
Yacht hbr ent, 53°52'·43N 08°42'·49E, F WR and F WG lts.

▶ OTTERNDORF

No. 43 53°50'·23N 08°52'·24E, Oc (2) G 9s.
Ldg lts 092·8°, both Iso 4s 23/45m 18M, vis on ldg line only; synch; W twr, R bands, R conical roof. Front, Otterndorf/Belum 53°50'·12N 08°56'·16E. Rear, Belum, 0.83M from front.
Medem 53°50'·15N 08°53'·85E, Fl (3) 12s 6m 5M; B △, on B col.
No. 45 53°50'·39N 08°54'·24E, Fl G 4s.
No. 51 53°51'·03N 09°00'·15E, QG.
Balje ☆ ldg lts 081°, both Iso 8s 24/54m **17/21M**; intens on ldg line; synch; W ○ twrs, R bands. **Front**, 53°51'·29N 09°02'·63E. **Rear**, 1·35M from front.

15

NORD-OSTSEE KANAL (KIEL CANAL)

▶ BRUNSBÜTTEL

Ldg lts 065·5°, both Iso 3s 24/46m **16/21M**; synch; R twrs, W bands. Front, **Schleuseninsel** ☆ 53°53'·32N 09°08'·47E; vis N of brg 063·3°; lock sigs close N. Rear, **Industriegebiet** ☆, 0·9M from front.
No. 57a 53°52'·62N 09°07'·93E, Fl G 4s; 030°/8 cables to lock.
Alter Vorhafen S mole (mole 4) 53°53'·27N 09°08'·59E, F WG 14m W10M, G6M; W266·3°-273·9°, G273·9°-088·8°, floodlit.

▶ RENDSBURG

No. 2/Obereider 1 54°18'·91N 09°42'·64E, Fl (2+1) R 15s.
HOLTENAU, No. 13 Roads 54°22'·09N 10°09'·60E, Fl G 4s.
Tiessenkai 54°22'·09N 10°09'·30E, Oc (3) WG 12s 22m.

RIVER ELBE (KIEL CANAL TO HAMBURG)

Listed below are some of the more accessible yacht hbrs, but not the many ldg lts and dir lts for the main river fairway.

▶ FRIEBURG

Reede 1 53°50'·41N 09°19'·45E, Oc (2) Y 9s; off ent.

▶ STÖRLOCH

Stör ldg lts 093·8°, both Fl 3s 7/12m 6M; synch. Front, 53°49'·29N 09°23'·91E; △ on R ○ twr. Rear, 200m from front; ▽ on white mast.

▶ GLÜCKSTADT

Glückstadt ldg lts 131·8°, both Iso 8s 15/30m **19/21M**; intens on ldg line; W twrs, R bands. **Front** ☆, 53°48'·31N 09°24'·24E. **Rear** ☆, 0·68M from front.
Rhinplatte Nord 53°48'·09N 09°23'·36E, Oc WRG 6s 11m W6M, R4M, G3M; G122°-144°, W144°-150°, R150°-177°, W177°-122°.
N mole 53°47'·12N 09°24'·53E, Oc WRG 6s 9m W9M R7M, G6M; R330°-343°, W343°-346°, G346°-008°, G123°-145°, W145°-150°, R150°-170°; W twr with gallery.
N pier hd 53°47'·10N 09°24'·50E, FR 5m 5M. (FG on S mole hd.)

▶ KRUCKAU

S mole, 53°42'·85N 09°30'·72E, Oc WRG 6s 8m, W6M, R4M, G3M; W116·3°-120·7° ldg sector, R120·7°-225°, G225°-315°, R315°-331·9°, W331·9°-335·4° ldg sector, G335·4°-116·3°; B dolphin.

▶ PINNEAU

Ldg lts 112·7°, both Iso 4s 8/13m 6M, intens on ldg line. Front, 53°40'·08N 09°34'·02E; W △ on mast. Rear 400m from front.

PLOT WAYPOINTS ON YOUR CHART BEFORE USING THEM

N training wall, 53°40'·75N 09°32'·34E, Oc (2) WRG 12s 8m, W6M, R4M, G3M; G049°-082·5°, W082·5°-092·5° ldg sector, R092·5°-130°, G130°-156·9°, W156·9°-161·6° ldg sector, R161·6°-049°; R dolphin.

▶ STADE

No. 103 53°37'·96N 09°31'·50E (2ca N of ent), Oc (2) G 9s.
Stadersand ☆ 53°37'·69N 09°31'·64E (at ent), Iso 8s 20m 14M.

HAMBURG

▶ WEDEL, HAMBURGER YACHT HAFEN

No. 119/HN1 53°34'·04N 09°39'·42E, QG.
No. 122 53°34'·15N 09°40'·62E, Oc (2) R 9s.
E ent, E pier hd ☆ 53°34'·25N 09°40'·79E, FG 5m 3M. (Both entrances show FR & FG, May to Oct).

▶ SCHULAU

No. 123 53°33'·85N 09°41'·97E, Fl G 4s.
E pier head ☆ 53°34'·09N 09°41'·95E, FG 5m 3M.

▶ MÜHLENBERG

E pier head 53°33'·19N 09°49'·40E (unmarked).

▶ TEUFELSBRÜCK

W breakwater hd 53°32'·83N 09°52'·04E (unmarked).

▶ RÜSCHKANAL

Ent, W side ☆ 53°32'·65N 09°50'·87E, FY 6m 4M, dolphin.
No. 133 53°32'·92N 09°49'·75E, Oc (2) G 9s.

▶ STEENDIEKKANAL

Ent, W side ☆ 53°32'·49N 09°51'·88E, FG 7m 2M, dolphin.

▶ CITY SPORTHAFEN

Brandenburger Hafen Ent ☆ 53°32'·52N 09°58'·81E, Iso Or 2s.

WESER ESTUARY AND RIVER

▶ APPROACH CHANNELS

ALTE WESER

Schlüsseltonne 53°56'·25N 07°54'·76E, Iso 8s.
Alte Weser ☆ 53°51'·79N 08°07'·65E, F WRG 33m **W23M, R19M, G18M**; W288°-352°, R352°-003°, W003°-017°, ldg sector for Alte Weser, G017°-045°, W045°-074°, G074°-118°, W118°-123° ldg sector for Alte Weser, R123°-140°, G140°-175°, W175°-183°, R183°-196°, W196°-238°; R ○ twr, 2 W bands, B base; Fog det lt; *Horn Mo (AL) 60s.*
16/A15 53°49'·66N 08°06'·44E, Fl (2+1) R 15s (junction with Neuwe Weser)

NEUE WESER

1b/Jade 1 53°52'·40N 07°44'·00E, Oc G 4s.
3/Jade 2 53°52'·40N 07°44'·00E, Fl (2+1) G 15s; ***Racon T, 8M.***
9/Mittelrinne 2 53°50'·68N 08°01'·16E, Fl (2+1) G 15s.
Tegeler Plate ☆, N end, 53°47'·87N 08°11'·45E, Oc (3) WRG 12s 21m **W21M, R17M, G16M**; W329°-340°, R340°-014°, W014°-100°, G100°-116°, W116°-119° ldg sector for Neue Weser, R119°-123°, G123°-144°, W144°-147° ldg sector for Alte Weser, R147°-264°; R ○ twr, gallery, W lantern, R roof; Fog det lt.

▶ RIVER WESER

Robbenplate ldg lts 122·3°, both Oc 6s 15/37m **17/18M. Front** ☆, 53°40'·89N 08°22'·99E, R tripod; intens on ldg line. **Rear** ☆, 0·54M from front; 116°-125·5°; synch; R□ twr, 3 galleries, G lantern with front; fog det lt.
Hohe Weg ☆ 53°42'·74N 08°14'·57E, F WRG 29m **W19M, R16M, G15M**; W102°-138·5°, G138·5°-142·5°, W142·5°-145·5°, R145·5°-184°, W184°-278·5°; R 8-sided twr, 2 galleries, G lamp; fog det lt.
Dwarsgat ☆ ldg lts 320·1°, both Iso 6s 16/35m **15/17M.** Front, 53°43'·12N 08°18'·44E. **Rear** ☆, 0·75M from front; synch; (reciprocal of Wremerloch 140° ldg line).
Robbennordsteert ☆ 53°42'·13N 08°20'·37E, F WR 11m W10M, R7M; W324°-004°, R004°-090°, W090°-121°.
Wremerloch ldg lts 140·1°, both Iso 6s 15/31m 13/14M. Front, 53°38'·42N 08°25'·07E. Rear, 0·57M from front, synch.
Langlütjen ldg lts 305·2°, both Oc 6s 15/31m 13/14M. Front, 53°39'·62N 08°22'·79E; 288°-310°; B mast, B & W gallery. Rear, 930m from front, synch.
Imsum ldg lts 125·2°. Front 53°36'·38N 08°30'·53E, Iso 4s 15m 13M; R tripod with gallery. **Rear** ☆, 1·02M from front, Oc 6s 39m **16M**; synch.
Solthorn ldg lts 320·6°. Front 53°38'·29N 08°27'·32E, Iso 4s 15/31m 13/**17M**; both R&W masts. **Rear** ☆, 700m from front, synch.
Fischereihafen ldg lts 150·8°, both Oc 6s 17/45m **18M. Common front,** 53°31'·88N 08°34'·52E, R △ on W mast. **Rear** ☆, 0·68M from front, 2 R ▽ on W mast, R bands; synch.
Same masts, ldg lts 053·9° (astern), both Oc 6s 17/27m 11/13M. **Common front, as above.** Rear, Geestemünde, 340m from front.

▶ BREMERHAVEN

No. 61 53°32'·26N 08°33'·93E, QG; (Km 66·0).
Vorhafen N pier ☆ 53°32'·15N 08°34'·50E, FR 15m 5M; 245°-166°; F in fog.
S pier hd ☆ 53°32'·09N 08°34'·50E FG 15m 5M; 355°-265°.
Grossensiel Hafen N hd ☆ 53°28'·06N 08°29'·05E, FG 11m 2M.

▶ BREMEN

No. 99/Hunte 53°15'·45N 08°28'·86E, IQ G; (Km 32·7).
Hasenbüren Sporthafen ☆ 53°07'·51N 08°40'·03E, 2 FY (vert).

RIVER JADE

▶ APPROACHES

Jade-Weser, 53°58'·33N 07°38'·83E, Oc 4s; ***Racon T, 8M.***
1b/Jade 1 53°52'·40N 07°44'·00E, Oc G 4s.
Tonne 3/Jade 2 53°52'·07N 07°47'·18E, Fl (2+1) G 15s; ***Racon T, 8M.***
Mellumplate ☆ 53°46'·28N 08°05'·51E, F 28m **24M**; 116·1°-116·4° ldg sector for outer part of Wangerooger Fahrwasser; R □ twr, W band. Four other lts are shown from the same twr: Fl 4s **23M**, 114°-115·2°. Fl (4) 15s, 117·2°-118·4°. Mo (A) 7·5s, 115·2°-116·1° ldg sector. Mo (N) 7·5s; 116·4°-117·2° ldg sector.
No. 7 53°50'·31N 07°51'·30E, Oc (3) G 12s.
No.11 53°49'·19N 07°55'·20E, Fl G 4s.
No.15/Blaue Balje 53°48'·12N 07°58'·72E, IQ G 13s.
No.19 53°47'·10N 08°01'·83E, QG.
No.23/B20 53°45'·16N 08°02'·74E, Oc (3) G 12s.
No. 31/P-Reede/W Siel 1 53°41'·59N 08°04'·51E, Oc (3) G 12s.

▶ HOOKSIEL

Voslapp ldg lts 164·5°, both Iso 6s 15/60m **24/27M**; intens on ldg line, synch. **Front**, 53°37'·18N 08°06'·87E; R ○ twr, W bands, R lantern. **Rear** ☆, 2·35M from front; W ○ twr, R bands.
Tossens ldg lts 146°, both Oc 6s 15/51m **20M. Front**, 53°34'·55N 08°12'·42E, W ○ twr, R band, R lantern. **Rear**, 2M from front; R ○ twr, W stripes, 3 galleries.
No. 37/Hooksiel 1 53°39'·37N 08°06'·58E, IQ G 13s.
H3 53°38'·65N 08°05'·63E, Fl G 4s.
Vorhafen ent ☆ 53°38'·63N 08°05'·25E, L Fl R 6s 9m 3M.

▶ WILHELMSHAVEN

Eckwarden ldg lts 154°. **Front, Solthörner Watt** ☆ 53°32'·40N

08°13'·00E, Iso WRG 3s 15m **W19M**, W12M, R9M, G8M; R346°-348°, W348°-028°, R028°-052°, W (intens) 052°-054° ldg sector, G054°-067·5°, W067·5°-110°, G110°-152·6°, W (intens) 152·6°-across fairway, with undefined limit on E side of ldg line; R ○ twr, W bands. **Rear** ☆, 1·27M from front, Iso 3s 41m **21M**, synch; R pyramidal framework twr & lantern.

Arngast ☆ Dir lt, 53°28'·88N 08°10'·89E, F WRG 30m **W21M**, W10, **R16M**, **G17M**, G7M; W135°-142°, G142°-150°, W150°-152°, G152°-174·6°, R180·5°-191°, W191°-213°, R213°-225°, W(10M) 286°-303°, G(7M) 303°-314°; R ○ twr, W bands. Three other lts on same twr: (i) Fl WG 3s, G174·6°-175·5°, W175·5°-176·4°. (ii) Fl (2) 9s, 177·4°-180·5°. (iii) Oc 6s **20M**, 176·4°-177·4°.

Neuer Vorhafen ldg lts 207·8°, both Iso 4s 17/23m 11M; intens on ldg line. Front, 53°31'·82N 08°09'·60E ; B mast, R lantern. Rear, 180m from front; Y bldg.

W mole ☆ 53°32'·48N 08°10'·08E, Oc G 6s 15m 4M.

E mole ☆ 53°32'·43N 08°10'·24E, Oc R 6s 15m 5M.

Fluthafen N mole ☆ 53°30'·86N 08°09'·32E, F WG 9m; W6M, G3M; W216°-280°, G280°-010°, W010°-020°, G020°-130°; G twr.

S arm ☆ 53°30'·80N 08°09'·17E, FR 6m 5M.

RIVER JADE TO RIVER EMS

▶ NORTH EDGE OF INSHORE TRAFFIC ZONE

TG19/Weser 2 53°54'·99N 07°44'·52E, Fl (2+1) G 15s.
TG17/Weser 1 53°53'·43N 07°33'·13E, IQ G 13s.
TG15 53°52'·17N 07°24'·21E, Fl (2) G 9s.
TG13 53°50'·85N 07°15'·43E, Oc (3) G 12s.
TG11 53°49'·62N 07°06'·53E, Fl (2) G 9s.
TG9 53°48'·35N 06°57'·68E, Oc (3) G 12s.
TG7 53°47'·24N 06°49'·65E, Fl (2) G 9s.
TG5 53°45'·81N 06°39'·99E, Oc (3) G 12s.
TG3 53°44'·62N 06°31'·10E, Fl (2) G 9s.
TG1/Ems 53°43'·36N 06°22'·24E, IQ G 13s.

EAST FRISIAN ISLANDS

▶ WANGEROOGE

Harle 53°49'·24N 07°48'·92E, Iso 8s.

Wangerooge ☆, W end, 53°47'·40N 07°51'·37E, Fl R 5s 60m **23M**; R ○ twr, 2 W bands. Same twr: F WR 24m **W15M**, R11M, W055°-060·5°, R060·5°-065·5°, W065·5°-071°. Same twr: Dir F WRG 24m **W22M**, **G18M**, **R17M**; G119·4°-138·8°, W138·8°-152·2° ldg sector, R152·2°-159·9°.

Buhne W bkwtr head ☆ 53°46'·33N 07°51'·93E, FR 3m 4M.

▶ SPIEKEROOG

Otzumer Balje 53°47'·98N 07°37'·12E, Iso 4s (frequently moved.)

Spiekeroog ☆ 53°45'·0N 07°41'·3E, FR 6m 4M; R mast; 197°-114°.

▶ LANGEOOG

Accumer Ee 53°46·81N 07°26·12E, Iso 8s; (frequently moved).

W mole head ☆ 53°43'·42N 07°30'·13E, Oc WRG 6s 8m W7M, R5M, G4M; G064°-070°, W070°-074°, R074°-326°, W326°-330°, G330°-335°, R335°-064°; R basket on R mast; *Horn Mo (L) 30s* (0730-1800LT).

▶ BALTRUM

Groyne hd ☆ 53°43'·3N 07°21'·7E, Oc WRG 6s 6m; W6M, R4M, G3M; G074·5°-090°, W090°-095°, R095°-074·5°.

▶ NORDERNEY

Norderney N 53°46'·06N 07°17'·12E, Q.

Dovetief 53°45'·25N 07°09'·13E, Iso 4s.

Schluchter 53°44'·45N 07°02'·23E, Iso 8s.

W mole head ☆ 53°41'·9N 07°09'·9E, Oc (2) R 9s 13m 4M.

Norderney ☆ 53°42'·58N 07°13'·83E, Fl (3) 12s 59m **23M**; unintens 067°-077° and 270°-280°; R 8-sided twr.

▶ JUIST

Juist-N 53°43'·82N 06°55'·42E, VQ.

Aero lt 53°40'·85N 07°03'·40E, Fl 5s 14m (occas).

Training wall, S end ☆ 53°39'·65N 06°59'·81E, Oc (2) R 9s 7m 3M; R post.

15

RIVERS JADE TO EMS: MAINLAND HARBOURS

▶ HARLESIEL

Carolinensieler Balje, Leitdamm ☆ 53°44'·13N 07°50'·10E, L Fl 8s 7m 6M; G mast.

N mole head ☆ 53°42'·63N 07°48'·70E, Iso R 4s 6m 7M.

▶ NEUHARLINGERSIEL

Training wall head ☆ 53°43'·22N 07°42'·30E, Oc 6s 6m 5M.

▶ BENSERSIEL

E training wall head ☆ 53° 41'·80N 07°32'·84E, Oc WRG 6s 6m W5M, R3M, G2M; G110°-119°, W119°-121°, R121°-110°.

Ldg lts 138°, both Iso 6s 12/18m 9M, intens on ldg line. Rear, 167m from front. Inner hbr, W mole hd FG; E mole hd FR.

▶ DORNUMER-ACCUMERSIEL

W bkwtr head ☆ 53°41'·25N 07°29'·40E.

▶ NESSMERSIEL

N mole head ☆ 53°41'·9N 07°21'·7E, Oc 4s 6m 5M; G mast.

▶ NORDDEICH

E trng wall head ☆ FR 8m 4M, 327°-237°; R & W △ on R twr.

W trng wall head ☆ 53°38'·7N 07°09'·0E, FG 8m 4M, 021°-327°; G framework twr, W lantern.

Outer ldg lts 144°, both B masts. Front, Iso WR 6s 6m W6M, R5M; R078°-122°, W122°-150°. Rear, 140m from front, Iso 6s 9m 6M; synch. Inner ldg lts 170°: both Iso W 3s 12/23m 10M, synch. Outward (reciprocal) ldg lts 350°: front Iso WR 3s 5m 6/4M; rear, 95m from front, Iso W 3s 8m 6M.

▶ GREETSIEL

Meßstation lt bcn 53°32'·92N 07°02'·16E, Fl Y 4s 15m 3M.

RIVER EMS

▶ APPROACHES

GW/EMS 54°09'·96N 06°20'·72E, Iso 8s 12m **17M**; *Horn Mo (R) 30s (H24)*; ***Racon T, 8M***.

Borkumriff 53°47'·44N 06°22'·05E, Oc 4s; ***Racon T, 8M***.

Osterems 53°41'·91N 06°36'·17E, Iso 4s.

Riffgat 53°38'·96N 06°27'·07E, Iso 8s.

Westerems 53°36'·9N 06°19'·41E, Iso 4s; ***Racon T, 8M***.

H1 53°34'·91N 06°17'·97E.

▶ BORKUM

Borkum Grosser ☆ 53°35'·32N 06°39'·64E, Fl (2) 12s 63m **24M**; Brown ○ twr. Same structure, F WRG 46m **W19M**, **R/G15M**; G107·4°-109°, W109°-111·2°, R111·2°-112·6°.

Fischerbalje ☆ 53°33'·16N 06°42'·86E, Oc (2) WRG 16s 15m **W16M**, R12M, G11M; R260°-313°, G313°-014°, W014°-068°, (ldg sector to Fischerbalje); R068°-123°. Fog det lt; W ○ twr, R top and lantern, on tripod.

Schutzhafen ☆ 53°33'·48N 06°45'·02E, FG10m 4M & FR 8m 5M.

PLOT WAYPOINTS ON YOUR CHART BEFORE USING THEM

▶ ALTE EMS (Unlit secondary channel)

A5 53°33'·75N 06°38'·20E.
A8/AE-Reede 53°30'·52N 06°42'·45E, Fl (2) R 9s.
A16/Dukegat-Reede 53°28'·87N 06°48'·40E, Fl R 4s.

▶ RIVER EMS (LOWER)

No. 27 53°30'·24N 06°47'·52E, Fl G 4s.
No. 30 53°28'·81N 06°50'·37E, Fl (2) R 9s.
Eemshaven, W pier ☆ 53°27'·72N 06°50·02E, FG 8m 3M.
No. 35 53°27'·03N 06°52'·80E, Fl G 4s.
No. 37 53°26'·01N 06°54'·85E, QG.
Campen ☆ 53°24'·33N 07°00'·92E, F 62m **30M**; 126·8°-127·1°; R framework twr, 2 galleries, W central column, G cupola.
Same twr: Fl 5s, 126·3°-126·8°; and Fl (4) 15s, 127·1°-127·6°.
No. 41 53°24'·25N 06°56'·68E, Fl (2) G 9s.
No. 44 53°22'·07N 06°58'·69E, Fl R 4s.
No. 49 53°19'·95N 06°59'·71E, Oc (2) G 9s.

▶ KNOCK

Knock ☆ 53°20'·32N 07°01'·40E, F WRG 28m W12M, R9M, G8M; Gy twr, four galleries, broad top, radar antenna; W270°-299°, R299-008·3°, G008·3°-023°, W023°-026·8°, R026·8°-039°, W039°-073°, R073°-119°, W119°-154°; fog det lt.
K4 53°19'·84N 07°00'·76E, QR.

▶ DELFZIJL (Netherlands; see 9.16.4)

PS3/BW26 53°19'·25N 07°00'·31E, Fl (2+1) G 12s.
W mole, ☆ 53°19'·01N 07°00'·26E, FG.
E mole ☆ 53°18'·93N 07°00'·58E, FR; in fog FY.

▶ EMDEN

Logum ldg lts 075·2°, both Oc (2) 12s 16/28m 12M, synch; W masts, R bands. Front, 53°20'·12N 07°07'·96E. Rear, 630m from front.
Wybelsum ☆ 53°20'·17N 07°06'·52E, F WR 16m W6M, R5M; W295°-320°, R320°-024°, W024°-049°; W ○ twr, R bands; radar antenna; fog detector lt.
Inner ldg lts 087·6°, both Oc 5s 14/30m 14M; synch, intens on ldg line. Front, 53°20'·03N 07°12'·08E. Rear, 0·8M from front.
No. 71 53°19'·92N 07°09'·74E, Oc (2) G 9s.
Outer hbr, W pier ☆ 53°20'·06N 07°10'·49E, FR 10m 4M; R 8-sided twr; *Horn Mo (ED) 30s.*
E pier ☆ 53°20'·05N 07°10'·84E, FG 7m 5M; R twr, B band.

9.15.5 PASSAGE INFORMATION

Refer to: Admiralty Pilot NP 55 *North Sea (East);* and *Cruising Guide to Germany and Denmark* (Imray/Navin).

NORTH FRISIAN ISLANDS TO RIVER ELBE (charts 1875, 3767)

Lister Tief is the chan between the Danish island of Rømø and the N end of Sylt; it gives access to List Roads and hbr as well as to Danish hbrs. Lister Tief is well buoyed, with a least depth over the bar of about 4m. In relative terms it is the safest chan on this coast (after Süderpiep), available for yachts seeking anch under the lee of Sylt in strong W winds (when however there would be a big swell over the bar on the ebb). Beware buoyed obstructions (ODAS), 18M WSW of List West lt ho.

Sylt (9.15.7) is the largest of the N Frisian Islands, almost 20M long from S to N. It has a straight seaward coast, and a peninsula on its E side connects by Hindenburgdamm to the mainland. Vortrapptief is the NNE chan inward between Amrum and Sylt, leading to Hörnum Hafen. It has a depth of about 4m (subject to frequent change) and is buoyed and lit. The area should not be approached in strong W winds. ▶*The flood (ESE-going) stream begins at HW Helgoland –0350, and the ebb (WNW-going) at HW Helgoland +0110, sp rates 2·5kn.*◀

Rütergat and Schmaltief give access to **Amrum** (Wittdün hbr on SE side), to Wyk on the SE corner of **Fohr** and to Dagebüll. The R. Hever consists of several chans on the N side of Eiderstedt Peninsula, and S of the North Frisian Islands of **Süderoogsand** and **Pellworm**. Mittelhever is the most important of the three buoyed chans through the outer grounds, all of which meet SE of Süderoogsand. Here they separate once more into Norderhever, which runs NE between Pellworm and Nordstrand into a number of watt channels; and Heverstrom which leads to Husum (9.15.7).

Approaching R. Eider from seaward, find the Eider SWM lt buoy, about 1·2M W of the buoyed ent chan. The ent can be rough in W winds, and dangerous in onshore gales. St Peter lt ho is conspic on N shore. Here the estuary winds up to the Eiderdamm, a storm barrage with a lock (H24) and sluices. Tönning is about 5M up-river. The upper Eider parallels the Nord-Ostsee Kanal which it joins at Gieselau.

The W coast of Schleswig-Holstein is flat and marshy, with partly-drying banks extending 5 - 10M offshore. Between the banks and islands, the chans change frequently. Süderpiep and Norderpiep join S of Blauort and lead to Büsum (9.15.8) and Meldorfer Hafen (marina). Norderpiep has a bar (depth 3m) and is unlit; Süderpiep is deeper and preferable in W'lies. Landmarks from seaward are Tertius bn and Blauortsand bn, and a conspic silo and tall building at Büsum.

RIVER ELBE (charts 3619, 3625, 3266, 3268) Yachts entering the Elbe are probably bound for Brunsbüttel (9.15.12) at the ent to the Nord-Ostsee Kanal (9.15.13). See 9.15.11 for Cuxhaven and 9.15.10/14 for the River Elbe and Hamburg. From E end of TSS the chan is well marked by buoys and beacon trs. Commercial traffic is very heavy. ▶*At Elbe SWM buoy the E-going (flood) stream begins at HW Helgoland – 0500, and the W-going (ebb) stream at HW Helgoland + 0500, sp rates 2kn. The stream runs harder N of Scharnhörn, up to 3·5kn on the ebb, when the Elbe estuary is dangerous in strong W or NW winds.*◀

RIVER WESER (charts 3368, 3405, 3406, 3407) The R Weser is a major waterway leading to Bremerhaven, Nordenham, Brake and Bremen which connect with the inland waterways. The upper reaches, *Unterweser*, run from Bremen to Bremerhaven (9.15.15) and below Bremerhaven the *Aussenweser* flows into a wide estuary split by two main chans, Neue Weser and Alte Weser. The position and extent of sandbanks vary: on the W side they tend to be steep-to, but on the E side there are extensive drying shoals (eg Tegeler Plate).

The Jade-Weser SWM lt buoy marks the approach from NW to Neue Weser (the main fairway) and Alte Weser which are separated by Roter Sand and Roter Grund, marked by the disused Roter Sand lt tr (conspic). Both chans are well marked and converge about 3M S of Alte Weser lt tr (conspic). From this junction Hohewegrinne (buoyed) leads inward in a SE direction past Tegeler Plate lt tr (conspic) on the NE side and Hohe Weg lt tr (conspic) to the SSE. From Robbenplate to Bremerhaven it is constrained by training walls. ▶*In the Aussenweser the stream, which runs over 3kn at sp, often sets towards the banks and the branch chans which traverse them.*◀

The Weser-Elbe Wattfahrwasser is a demanding, but useful inshore passage between R. Weser and R. Elbe. It leads NNE from the Wurster Arm (E of Hohe Weg), keeping about 3M offshore; SE of Neuwerk and around Cuxhaven training wall. It normally requires two tides, but there are suitable anchs.

RIVER JADE (charts 3368, 3369) To the E of Wangerooge and Minsener Oog lie the estuaries of R. Jade and R. Weser. Although not so hazardous as R. Elbe, the outer parts of both rivers can become very rough with wind against tide, and are dangerous on the ebb in strong NW winds.The Jade is entered from 1n/Jade 1 buoy via the Wangerooger Fahrwasser (buoyed) which leads SSE past Wangersiel and the yachting centre of Hooksiel (9.15.16) to Wilhelmshaven (9.15.17). To the S of Wilhelmshaven, the Jadebusen is a large, shallow area of water, through which chans run to the small hbrs of Dangastersiel and Vareler Siel.

THE EAST FRISIAN ISLANDS (9.15.19 and chart 3761) The East Frisian Islands have fewer facilities for yachtsmen than the West Frisian Islands (Dutch), and most of them are closer to the mainland, with groynes and sea defences on their W and NW sides. Their bare sand dunes are not easy to identify, so the few conspic landmarks must be carefully selected. Shoals extend seaward for 2M or more in places. The seegaten between the islands vary in position and depth, and all of them are dangerous on the ebb tide, even in a moderate onshore wind.There are Nature Reserves (entry prohibited) inshore of the W end of Spiekeroog, Langeoog and Baltrum (chart 1875). For general notes, see 9.16.5.

For navigating inside the islands, in the *wattfahrenwassern* or so-called watt chans, it is essential to have the large scale pleasure craft charts (BSH) and to understand the system of channel marking. Withies, unbound (ŧ with twigs pointing up) are used as PHMs, and withies which are bound (ŧ with twigs pointing down) as SHMs. Inshore of the islands the *conventional direction of buoyage is always Eastward*, even though in places this may conflict with the actual direction of the flood.

The general tactic, whether E or W-bound, is to leave as early as possible on the flood (dependent on distance) so as to reach your destination or negotiate the shallowest part of the *wattfahrenwassern* near HW. Springs occur around midday and give approx 0·5m more water than neaps.

Blau Balje lies between **Minsener Oog** and Wangerooge. Although marked by buoys (prefixed 'B' and moved as necessary) this chan is dangerous in N winds. A prohib area (15/5–31/8) S of the E end of Wangerooge is for the protection of seals.

Harle chan (buoys prefixed by 'H') leads W of **Wangerooge** (9.15.20), but beware Buhne H groyne which extends 7½ca WSW from end of island to edge of fairway. Dove Harle (buoys prefixed by 'D') leads to the hbr. In bad weather Harlesiel, 4M S on the mainland, is a more comfortable berth.

Between **Spiekeroog** (9.15.21) and Langeoog, the buoyed Westerbalje and Otzumer Balje chans lead inward. The latter is usually the deeper (0·7m–2·0m) but both chans may silt up and should be used only in good weather and on a rising tide.

Proceeding W, the next major chan through the islands is Acummer Ee between **Langeoog** and Baltrum. Shoals extend 2M offshore, depths in chan vary considerably and it is prone to silting; it is marked by buoys prefixed with 'A', moved as necessary. In onshore winds the sea breaks on the bar and the chan should not be used. Apart from Langeoog (9.15.22), Accumer Ee gives access to the mainland hbrs of Dornumer-Accumersiel (9.15.18) and Bensersiel.

Baltrum (9.15.19) is about 2·5M long, very low in the E and rising in the W to dunes about 15m high. With local knowledge and only in good weather it could be approached through Wichter Ee, a narrow unmarked channel between Baltrum and Norderney; but it is obstructed by drying shoals and a bar and is not advised. A small pier and groyne extend about 2ca from the SW corner of Baltrum. The little hbr dries, and is exposed to the S and SW. Southwards from Wichter Ee, the Nessmersiel Balje, with buoys on its W side prefixed by 'N', leads to the sheltered hbr of Nessmersiel (9.15.18).

SW of Norderney, Busetief leads in a general S direction to the tidal hbr of Norddeich (9.15.18), which can also be approached with sufficient rise of tide from Osterems through the Norddeich Wattfahrwasser with a depth of about 2m at HW. Busetief is deeper than Dovetief and Schluchter, and is buoyed. ▶*The flood begins at HW Helgoland –0605, and the ebb at HW Helgoland –0040, sp rates 1kn.*◀

Norderneyer Seegat is a deep chan close W of **Norderney**, but it is approached across dangerous offshore shoals, through which lead two shallow buoyed channels, Dovetief and Schluchter. Dovetief is the main chan, but Schluchter is more protected from the NE. Depths vary considerably and at times the chans silt up. Neither should be used in strong winds. Further inshore, Norderneyer Seegat leads round the W end of the island to the harbour of Norderney (9.15.23). Beware groynes and other obstructions along the shore. **Juist** (9.15.19) is the last of the chain of similar, long, narrow and low-lying islands. **Memmert** on the E side of Osterems is a bird sanctuary, and landing is prohibited.

Borkum (9.15.24 and chart 3631) lies between Osterems and Westerems, with high dunes each end so that at a distance it looks like two separate islands. Round the W end of Borkum are unmarked groynes, some extending 2¾ca offshore. Conspic landmarks include Grosse bn and Neue bn, a water tr, Borkum Grosser lt ho and two disused lt houses; all are near the W end of the island.

RIVER JADE TO RIVER EMS (chart 3761) The route to seaward of the Frisian Is from the E end of Wangerooge to abeam Borkum is about 50 miles. This is via the ITZ, S of the Terschellinger-German Bight TSS, the E-going lane of which is marked on its S side by SHM buoys lettered TG17 to TG1/Ems. About 4M S of this line of buoys the landward side of the ITZ is marked by landfall buoys showing the apprs to the eight main seegaten between the East Frisian Is. There are major lts on Wangerooge, Norderney and Borkum. ▶*Near the TSS the E-going stream begins at HW Helgoland –0500, and the W-going at HW Helgoland + 0100,sp rates 1·2kn. Inshore the stream is influenced by the flow through the seegaten.*◀

RIVER EMS (charts 2593, 3632) The River Ems forms the boundary between Germany and the Netherlands, and is a major waterway leading to Eemshaven, Delfzijl (9.16.7), Emden (9.15.25), Leer and Papenburg. Approach through Hubertgat or Westerems, which join W of Borkum; the former is unlit and sparsely buoyed. Both can be dangerous with an ebb stream and a strong W or NW wind. ▶*The flood begins at HW Helgoland + 0530, and the ebb at HW Helgoland – 0030, sp rates 1·5kn.*◀

From close SW of Borkum the chan divides: Randzel Gat to the N and Alte Ems running parallel to it to the S – as far as Eemshaven on the S bank. About 3M further on the chan again divides. Bocht van Watum is always varying so keep in main chan, Ostfriesisches Gatje, for Delfzijl and beyond. Off Eemshaven the stream runs 2-3kn.

Osterems is the E branch of the estuary of R. Ems, passing between Borkum and Memmert. It is poorly marked, unlit and much shallower than Westerems. It also gives access to the Ley chan, leading to the hbr of Greetsiel (9.15.18). But it is not advised without local knowledge and in ideal weather.

FROM GERMAN BIGHT TO UK (charts 2182A, 1405, 3761, 2593, 1505) From the Elbe, Weser and Jade estuaries, skirt the E ends of TSS to depart from Helgoland (9.15.9). Thence parallel the N side of TSS, towards Botney Ground (BG2 buoy) if heading north of the Humber. If bound for the Thames Estuary or down Channel, follow the ITZ westwards until S of Off Texel TSS; thence head west (see 9.16.5). Avoid areas of offshore industrial activity (9.5.5). West of German Bight streams run approx E/W, spring rates under 1kn. For distances across the N Sea, see 9.0.8.

9.15.6 SPECIAL NOTES FOR GERMANY

LANDS are given in lieu of 'counties' in the UK.

CHARTS: German charts are issued by the Bundesamt für Seeschiffahrt und Hydrographie (BSH), Hamburg. In this Almanac German *seekarten* charts are prefixed 'D'. The 3000 Series of leisure-craft charts are prefixed BSH. 3010-3015 cover the N sea coast and 3009 the Kiel Canal. They are a handy size (42 x 59cm), stowed in a large clear polythene envelope; each set has up to 16 sheets at medium/large scale. All charts are referred to WGS 84 and are corrected by *Nachrichten für Seefahrer* (NfS) = Notices to Mariners. Where possible the AC, Imray and Dutch chart numbers are also quoted.

LIGHTS: In coastal waters considerable use is made of light sectors. A leading or directional sector (usually W, and often intens) may be flanked by warning sectors to show the side to which the vessel has deviated: If to port, a FR lt or a Fl W lt with an even number of flashes; if to starboard, a FG lt or a Fl W lt with an odd number of flashes. Crossing lts with R, W and G sectors indicate (eg) the limits of roadsteads, bends in chans etc.

SIGNALS: IPTS are widely used in major ports. Local port, tidal, distress and traffic signals are given where possible. Visual storm warning signals are not used. When motoring under sail, always display a motoring ▼. Rule 25e is strictly enforced and non-compliance will incur a fine.

Lights on movable bridges and locks

●●	=	Passage/entry prohib.
●	=	Prepare to pass or enter; exit from lock prohib.
●	=	Exit from lock permitted.
○ ●●	=	Passage or entry permitted if there is sufficient clearance; beware of oncoming tfc which has right of way.
○○ ●●	=	Lift bridge is at first lift position; and may be passed by vessels for which the vertical clearance is safe.
●●	=	Passage/entry permitted; oncoming tfc stopped.
○ ●●	=	Passage or entry permitted, but beware oncoming traffic which may have right of way.
● ●	=	Bridge, lock or flood barrage closed to navigation.

Signals hoisted at masts

By day	*By night*	*Meaning*
R cylinder	○ ● ○	Reduce speed to minimise wash.
● ● ▼	● ● ●	Unusual obstruction to navigation.
● ▼ ▲	● ● ○	Long term closure of waterway.

HARBOURS: There are no commercially run marinas. Most yacht hbrs are owned by the state or community and run by a local Yacht Club (as in Belgium and the Netherlands).

TRAFFIC SEPARATION SCHEMES: The extensive TSS (off Terschelling, in the German Bight and in the approaches to the Rivers Jade and Elbe) link up with the various Dutch TSS. Information broadcasts by VTS centres and their associated communications are also shown in Areas 15 and 16.
Caution: Vessels in the ITZ to the south of the E-bound lane of the Terschelling-German Bight TSS are forbidden to cross the TSS between the Rivers Jade and Ems. Nor should the S edge of the E-bound lane (well marked by buoys TG1 to TG17) be approached closer than 1M, except in emergency or stress of weather. The German Marine Police can impose on-the-spot fines or confiscate equipment to the value of €1000, pending payment of the fine. Skippers are, therefore, advised to:

- Log their positions, times, courses, wind, weather, seastate, other traffic and use of sail or engine. These records can be important in any dispute or litigation and also keep the skipper alert to any consequences. In addition, they can demonstrate that the yacht is being responsibly navigated.
- Always monitor the appropriate VTS channel. If a deviation from the rules is necessary, inform the VTS centre.
- Beware of deep draught vessels proceeding from the German Bight pilot station to the Jade and E-bound traffic crossing in the TSS. The former have right of way over E-bound traffic. Yachts either E- or W-bound must take this into account.
- Any course/speed changes made by a yacht must be timely, clear and obvious to other shipping.

HIGH SPEED CRAFT: High speed craft ply between Emden and Borkum; and Hamburg to Stadersand, Cuxhaven and Helgoland. Keep a good lookout.

TELEPHONES: To call UK from Germany: dial 00 44; then the UK area code, minus the initial zero; followed by the number required. To call Germany from UK: dial 00-49; then area code minus initial zero; then desired number.

Mobile phone numbers in Germany begin 017 ... etc.

EMERGENCIES: Police: dial 110. Fire, Ambulance: dial 112.

PUBLIC HOLIDAYS: New Year's Day, Good Friday, Easter Monday, Labour Day (1 May), Ascension Day, Whit Monday, Day of German Unity (3 Oct), Christmas Day and Boxing Day.

National Water Parks exist in the Wadden Sea areas (tidal mud flats) of Lower Saxony, (excluding the Jade and Weser rivers and the Ems-Dollart estuary), and along the west coast of Schleswig-Holstein. Since 11 Oct 2002 these conservation areas have the status of Particularly Sensitive Sea Areas (PSSA) in or near which vessels should take the utmost care to avoid damaging the marine environment and marine organisms living therein. Ditch no waste. The Parks (shown on AC & BSH charts) are divided into 3 zones with certain rules:

Zone 1 comprises the most sensitive areas (about 30%) where yachts must keep to buoyed chans, except HW±3. Speed limit 8kn.
Zone 2 is a buffer zone.
Zone 3 is the remainder. No special constraints exist in Zones 2 and 3.

CUSTOMS: Ports of entry are: Borkum, Norderney, Norddeich, Wilhelmshaven, Bremerhaven, Cuxhaven. Not Helgoland.

GAS: Sometimes Calor gas bottles can be re-filled. German 'Flussig' gas can be used with Calor regulators.

CURRENCY: Euro (€).

VISITORS' TAX: of up to €2.56 per person per day may be payable.

USEFUL ADDRESSES: German National Tourist Office, PO Box 2695, London W1A 3TN; ☎ 020 7317 0908; 📠 020 7495 6129. gntolon@dzt.org.uk
German Embassy, 23 Belgrave Sq, London SW1X 8PZ. ☎ 020 7824 1300; 📠 020 7824 1435. info@german-embassy.org.uk
British Consulate-General, Harvesterhude Weg 8a, 20148 Hamburg; and
British Consulate, Herrlichkeiten 6, Postfach 10 38 60, 28199 Bremen.

9.15.7 SYLT

Schleswig-Holstein **54°45'·50N 08°17'·80E** (Hörnum)
Hörnum; List

CHARTS AC 3767; D107, D108; BSH 3013.2/3 List, 3013.4/5 Hörnum

TIDES +0110 Dover; ML 1·8; Duration 0540; Zone –0100

Standard Port HELGOLAND (⟶)

Times				**Height (metres)**			
High Water		Low Water		MHWS	MHWN	MLWN	MLWS
0100	0600	0100	0800	2·7	2·4	0·4	0·0
1300	1800	1300	2000				
Differences LIST							
+0252	+0240	+0201	+0210	–0·7	–0·6	–0·2	0·0
HÖRNUM							
+0223	+0218	+0131	+0137	–0·5	–0·4	–0·2	0·0
AMRUM-HAFEN							
+0138	+0137	+0128	+0134	+0·2	+0·2	–0·1	0·0
DAGEBÜLL							
+0226	+0217	+0211	+0225	+0·5	+0·5	–0·1	–0·1
SUDEROOGSAND							
+0116	+0102	+0038	+0122	+0·5	+0·4	+0·1	0·0
HUSUM							
+0205	+0152	+0118	+0200	+1·2	+1·1	+0·1	0·0

Westerland (the capital) is in the centre of Sylt (about 20M long) where the Hindenburgdamm links it to the mainland. Large areas of Sylt are nature reserves; landing prohib. List is in the N and Hörnum in the S. Two other hbrs which both dry are Munkmarsch (€6.90) and Rantum (€6.60); access HW ±3.

FACILITIES WESTERLAND: CG 85199; Police 70470. Ⓗ 04651 8410. **Town** ⊞, R, Bar, P & D (cans), Gaz, ⊖, ✉, Ⓑ, ⇌, ✈.

LIST

SHELTER The small hbr is sheltered except from NE/E winds. Access by day at all tides, but beware strong cross streams.

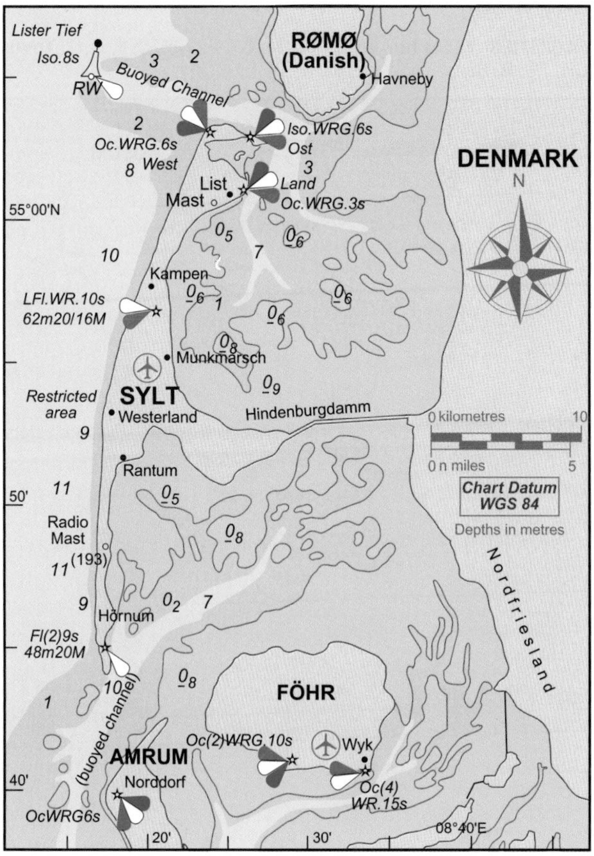
Lister Tief
Iso.8s
RW
Buoyed Channel
RØMØ
(Danish)
Havneby
DENMARK
Iso.WRG.6s
Ost
Oc.WRG.6s
West
List
Land
Oc.WRG.3s
Mast
55°00'N
Kampen
LFl.WR.10s
62m20/16M
Munkmarsch
Restricted area
SYLT
Westerland
Hindenburgdamm
0 kilometres 10
0 n miles 5
Chart Datum
WGS 84
Depths in metres
Rantum
50'
Radio Mast
Nordfriesland
Hörnum
Fl(2)9s
48m20M
(buoyed channel)
FÖHR
Oc(2)WRG.10s
Wyk
AMRUM
Norddorf
Oc(4)
WR.15s
OcWRG6s
40'
20'
30'
08°40'E

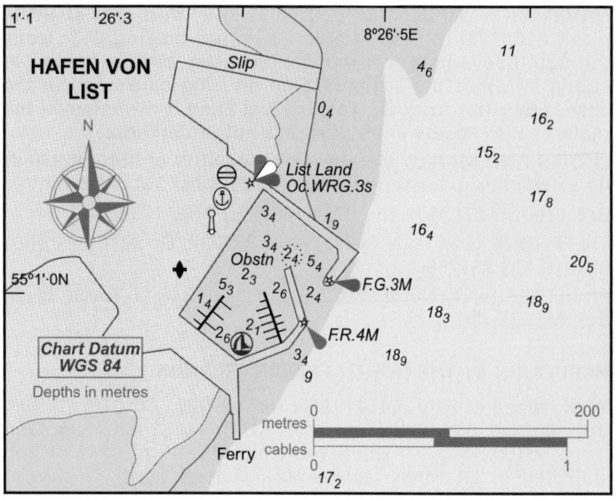
HAFEN VON
LIST
N
Slip
8°26'·5E
26'·3
List Land
Oc.WRG.3s
Obstn
55°1'·0N
F.G.3M
F.R.4M
Chart Datum
WGS 84
Depths in metres
metres
cables
Ferry
0
200
1

Ent is 25m wide; marina at S end carries 1·1m-2·6m. NE quay is open construction, unsuitable for yachts.

NAVIGATION WPT 55°05'·32N 08°16'·67E Lister Tief SWM buoy, 111°/7·0M to No 13 SHM buoy. Thence 214°/2·0M to the hbr via buoyed chan and W sector of List Land dir lt. In strong W/NW winds expect a big swell on the bar (depth 6m) on the ebb, which sets on to Salzsand.

LIGHTS AND MARKS Hbr lts as on the chartlet. See 9.15.4 for lts at List West, List Ost, List Land (overlooks List hbr) and Kampen, 5.4M SW. Rømø church, 7M NNE, is conspic.

R/T VHF Ch 11 (0800-1200, 1600-1800).

TELEPHONE (Dial code 04651)
HM 870374; Police 870510; ⊖ 870413, CG 870365; Dr 870350.

FACILITIES Hbr AB €1.00, FW, ⊖, Slip, SC. **Village** ⊞, R, Bar, P & D (cans), Ferry to Römö (Denmark).

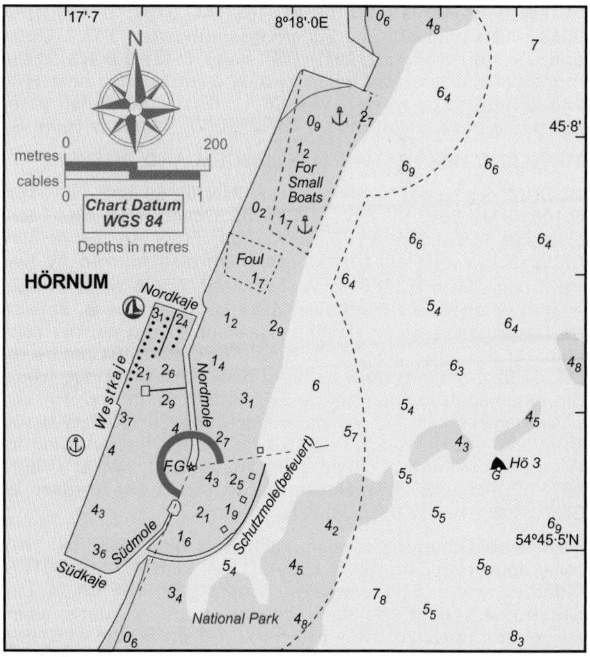
17'·7
8°18'·0E
N
45·8'
metres
cables
0
200
1
Chart Datum
WGS 84
Depths in metres
For
Small
Boats
Foul
HÖRNUM
Nordkaje
Westkaje
Nordmole
Schutzmole(befeuert)
F.G
Südmole
Südkaje
Hö 3
G
54°45'·5'N
National Park

HÖRNUM

SHELTER Good in the small hbr, approx 370m x 90m, protected by outer mole on SE side and by 2 inner moles. Yacht haven at the N end. Good ⚓ in Hörnum Reede in W and N winds and in Hörnumtief in E and S winds.

NAVIGATION WPT: 54°34'·87N 08°12'·97E, Vortrapptief SWM buoy, 016°/10M to S tip of Sylt. Hörnum lt bearing 012° leads through buoyed, lit Vortrapptief between drying banks. In strong W winds the sea breaks on off-lying banks and in the chan. Enter hbr from SE, keeping List Land lt ho between the mole heads. Access at all tides but not in darkness.

LIGHTS AND MARKS Hörnum lt is 3½ca SSW of hbr ent. Other lts as chartlet. Conspic radio mast (5 Fl R lts) 3M N of hbr.

R/T VHF Ch 67; Mon-Thu 0700-1600; Fri 0700-1230, all LT.

TELEPHONE (Dial code 04651) HM 881027; Dr 881016; Police 881510; CG 881256.

FACILITIES Sylter YC ☎ 880274, AB €1.00, Bar, ▣. **Town** 🛒, R, Bar, ME, ✉, Ⓑ.

HARBOURS IN THE NORTH FRISIAN ISLANDS

WYK, Island of Föhr, **54°41'·66N 08°34'·72E**. AC 3767; D 107, BSH 3013.6. HW +0107 on Dover (UT); +0137 on Helgoland (zone –0100); ML 2·8. Good yacht hbr (1·2-1·7m) to N of ent, sheltered in all winds; access H24; visitors berth W side of pontoon 1. Also berths on E quay of inner hbr. Ferry hbr (4m). Lts see 9.15.4: Olhörn (SE point of Föhr), R twr. Mole heads, FR, R mast and FG, G mast. Port VHF Ch **11** 16. Yacht hbr HM ☎ (04681) 3030; Commercial HM ☎ 500430; **Marine Police** ☎ 1280; Dr ☎ 8558; ⊖ ☎ 2594; Facilities: **Hbr road** (500m), CH, ▣, P & D (cans); **Yacht Hbr** €1.00, R, 🛒; **W Quay** D.

AMRUM-HAFEN, 54°37'·90N 08°23'·04E. AC 3767; D 107, BSH 3013.6 & 7. HW +0107 on Dover (UT); +0137 on Helgoland (zone –0100); ML 2·7m; Duration 0540. See 9.15.7. Appr via Rütergat and Norderaue. Make good RGR buoy No 26/AH1, Fl(2+1)R 15s, at 54°37'·76N 08°24'·80E where the hbr chan starts; it carries 2·5m and is marked by PHM withies ⸸. Yachts berth S of stone quay, lying bows to pontoon, stern to posts. Good shelter except in E winds. Ferry quay is 800m to the E. The 272° ldg lts have been inoperative since at least 2002. Lt ho Fl 7·5s, R tr, W bands is same location as rear ldg lt. Wriakhörn, Cross lt, is 1M WSW of hbr, see 9.15.4. It is not advisable to enter at night. HM ☎ (04682) 2294; ⊖ ☎ 2026; Dr ☎ 531; Facilities: AB €1.00, P & D (cans) at Nebel; **Amrum YC** ☎ 2054.

PELLWORM, 54°31'·27N 08°41'·16E. AC 3767; D 106, BSH 3013.11 & 12C. Tides: see Suderoogsand/Husum, 9.15.7. Outer appr via Norderhever to NH18 RGR buoy, Fl (2+1) R 15s, at the mouth of the ent chan which carries 0·2m (access near HW) and is marked by withies. VHF Ch 11, 0700-1700. Small yacht hbr partly dries to soft mud; 2·8m at MHW. Village is 600m S.

MAINLAND HBRS BETWEEN PELLWORM AND BÜSUM

HUSUM, Schleswig-Holstein, **54°28'·74N 08°59'·92E**. AC 3767; D.106, BSH 3013.12. HW + 0036 on Dover (UT); ML 1·9m; Duration 0555. See 9.15.7. SHM bcn, Fl G 4s, 54°28'·80N 08°58'·60E, marks start of access chan; also marked by two PHM bcns, both Fl (2) R 9s. A sluice/lock, 7ca W of rly bridge, is shut when level > 0·3m over MHW, as shown by ●. Beware the canal effect when meeting big ships in the narrow appr chan. In the outer hbr yachts should turn stbd just before rly bridge for pontoons on S bank, or pass through bridge (clnce 5m when shut) to inner hbr by SC Nordsee; both dry. VHF call *Husum Port* Ch 11. Tfc reports broadcast on Ch 11 every H +00 from HW –4 to HW +2. See 9.15.4 for hbr lts; the outer ldg lts have been withdrawn. Night entry not advised. HM ☎ (04841) 667218; Sluice ☎ 2565; **Husum YC** ☎ 65670; **SC Nordsee** ☎ 3436; ⊖ ☎ 61759. AB €0.72, P, D, at hbr.

TÖNNING, Schleswig-Holstein, **54°19'·00N 08°57'·00E**. AC 3767 (only appr from Eider SWM buoy); D.104, BSH 3013.14, 3014.8. Eiderdamm lock, 5·5M down-river, opens H24; VHF Ch 14. Lts, see 9.15.4. Above the dam, beware strong currents when sluices are operated HW +3 to HW+½. AB on S side of drying marina (3m at MHW), or on river quays. Up river, bridge (clnce 5·6m) opens on request Mon-Sat 0600-SS. HM ☎ (04861) 1400; Dr ☎ 389; Ⓗ ☎ 706; Facilities: **Quay** €0.72, FW, P, D, BY, C (5 ton), Slip; **YC** ☎ 754 (all welcome). **Town** Ⓑ, ✉, ⇌, Gaz.

R Eider and the Gieselau Kanal (BSH 3009.7/6/5/2) link Tönning to the Kiel Canal (9.15.13) and Rendsburg.

9.15.8 BÜSUM

Schleswig-Holstein **54°07'·16N 08°51'·52E** ❁❁❁◊◊◊✿✿

CHARTS AC 1875, 3767; D.105, BSH 3014.4.

TIDES HW +0036 on Dover (UT); ML 1·9m; Duration 0625
Standard Port HELGOLAND (⟶)

Times				Height (metres)			
High Water		Low Water		MHWS	MHWN	MLWN	MLWS
0100	0600	0100	0800	2·7	2·4	0·4	0·0
1300	1800	1300	2000				
Differences BÜSUM							
+0054	+0049	–0001	+0027	+0·9	+0·8	+0·1	+0·1
LINNENPLATE							
+0047	+0046	+0034	+0046	+0·7	+0·6	0·0	–0·1
SÜDERHÖFT							
+0103	+0056	+0051	+0112	+0·7	+0·6	–0·1	0·0
EIDERSPERRWERK							
+0120	+0115	+0130	+0155	+0·7	+0·6	–0·1	0·0

SHELTER Very good. Beware strong cross-tides and sudden winds over moles. A flood barrage closes when level exceeds MHW, but craft < 30m LOA can enter via a lock. For opening (H24), call VHF or sound 1 long blast in appr chan; 2 long blasts at lock if not already open; obey R/G lts. Turn 90° stbd into marina (1·8m LW) Basin IV. Meldorf marina is 4M ESE with 2-6m & all facilities. Appr via Kronenloch (1·1m); enter via barrage/lock.

NAVIGATION WPT 54°05'·82N 08°25'·70E, Süderpiep SWM buoy Iso 8s, 096°/1·0M to No 1 SHM buoy, Fl G 4s. Chan is lit/well-buoyed. Norderpiep is buoyed, but unlit; beware bar if wind-over-tide. Both are approx 15M long; night appr not advised.

LIGHTS AND MARKS Lt ho, ldg lts 355·1° and hbr lts as chartlet. A 22 storey bldg is conspic 8ca NW of hbr; silo is conspic in hbr.

R/T Call *Büsum Port* Ch 11 16 for lock opening.

TELEPHONE (Dial code 04834) HM 2183; CG 2246; ⊖ 2376; Dr 2088; YC 2997.

FACILITIES **Yacht hbr** AB €1.00, M, BY, El, ME, C, P, D, ▣. **Town** CH, 🛒, R, Bar, ✉, Ⓑ, ⇌, Ⓗ, ✈ (Hamburg).

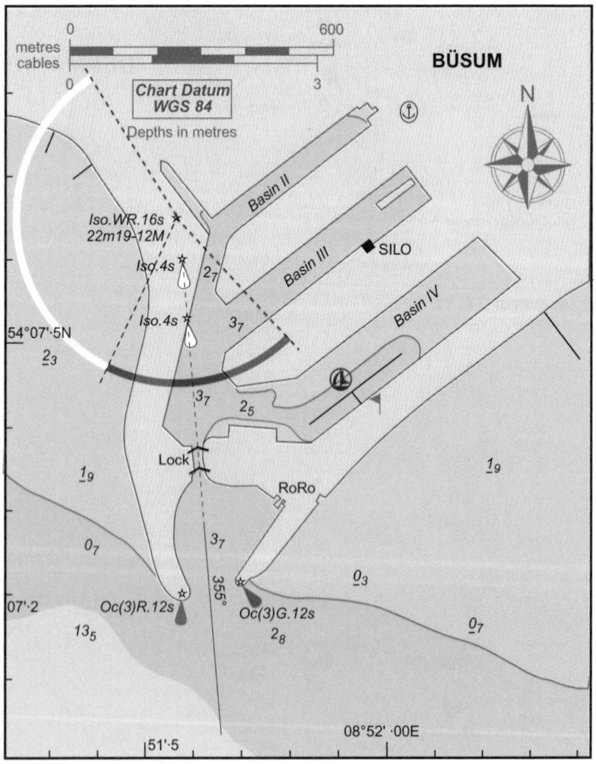
metres
cables
0
600
3
BÜSUM
Chart Datum WGS 84
Depths in metres
N
Basin II
Basin III
Basin IV
SILO
Iso.WR.16s
22m19-12M
Iso.4s
54°07'·5N
Lock
RoRo
Oc(3)R.12s
Oc(3)G.12s
355°
07'·2
08°52'·00E
51'·5

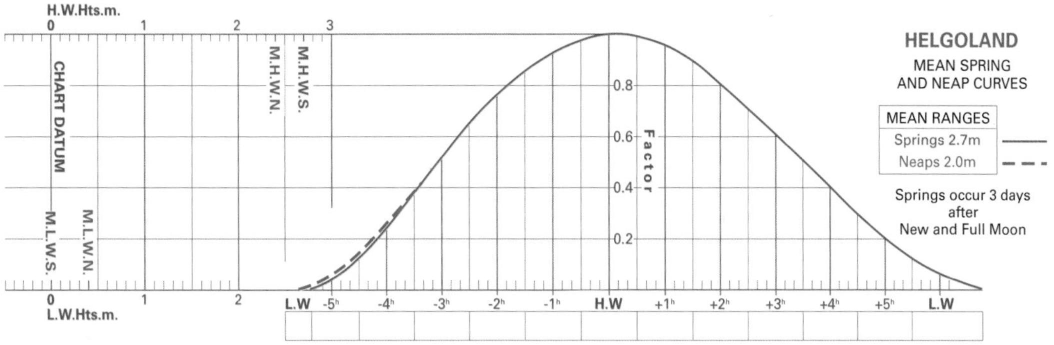
H.W.Hts.m.
0 1 2 3
CHART DATUM
M.H.W.N.
M.H.W.S.
M.L.W.S.
M.L.W.N.
0.8
0.6
0.4
0.2
Factor
0 1 2
L.W.Hts.m.
L.W -5h -4h -3h -2h -1h H.W +1h +2h +3h +4h +5h L.W
HELGOLAND
MEAN SPRING
AND NEAP CURVES
MEAN RANGES
Springs 2.7m
Neaps 2.0m
Springs occur 3 days
after
New and Full Moon

9.15.9 HELGOLAND

Schleswig-Holstein **54°10'·28N 07°53'·93E**

CHARTS AC 3761, 1875; Imray C26; D3, 88; BSH 3014.2/3

TIDES −0030 Dover; ML 1·4; Duration 0540; Zone −0100 Helgoland is a Standard Port ⟷.

SHELTER Good in safe artificial hbr (5m); yachts should berth on pontoons on the NE side of the Südhafen which gets very crowded, rafting 10 deep. Or ⚓ in the SW part of the Vorhafen, sheltered except in SE'lies; get permission from Port Control VHF Ch 67. Yachts are prohib from the Nordost hbr, the Dünen hbr and from landing on Düne Island. NOTE: Helgoland is not a port of entry into Germany. Customs in Helgoland are for passport control. Duty free goods are obtainable; hence many day-trippers by ferry. There is a visitors' tax of €2.56 per person per night.

NAVIGATION WPT 54°08'·96N 07°53'·48E, [Helgoland-O ECM buoy, Q (3) 10s, Whis],020°/1·3M to abeam No 3 buoy. Beware: the Hogstean shoal (1m), 4ca S of Sudmole head lt, and other rky shoals either side of chan; lobster pots around Düne Is and fast ferries using the S appr chan and ent.

Caution: Entry is prohib at all times into Nature Reserves close either side of the appr chans from SSW and NW. These Reserves extend about 2M NE and SW of Helgoland; their limits are marked by 7 cardinal buoys. Marine police are active in this respect. A smaller Reserve, lying to the N, E and S of Düne, is a prohib ⚓, with other restrictions. See BSH 3014.2, AC 3761 and 1875 (plan) for limits.

LIGHTS AND MARKS Lt ho, Fl 5s 82m 28M; brown □ tr, B lantern, W balcony. Düne ldg lts 020°: front Iso 4s; rear Dir Iso WRG 4s, W sector 018·5°-021°. Binnenhafen ldg lts 302°: both Oc R 6s, synch. The general direction of buoyage changes at 54°11'N.

R/T *Helgoland Port Radio* Ch 67 16 (**1/5 – 31/8**. Mon-Thur: 0700-1200,1300-2000; Fri/Sat 0700-2000; Sun 0700-1200LT. **1/9–30/4**. Mon-Thur 0700-1200, 1300-1600; Fri 0700-1200). Coast Radio Ch 03 16 27 88 (H24). Bremen (MRCC) maintains a distress watch via Helgoland on Ch 16 and Ch 70 DSC.

TELEPHONE (Dial code 04725) HM 8159 3583; CG 210; ⊖ 1537 or 304; Met 811007; Police 607; Dr 7345; Ⓗ 8030; Ambulance 7723; SAR 811305; Brit Consul (040) 446071.

FACILITIES **Vorhafen** L, ⚓; **Südhafen** ☎ 504, AB €1.02, D, FW (cans), ME, CH, C (mobile 12 ton), R, Bar; **Binnenhafen** ☎ 504, closed except for fuel; **Wasser Sport Club** ☎ 7422, Berthing <10m with permission; Bar, R, M, C (12 ton), D, P, CH, ME, El, FW. **Town** Gaz, R, Bar, ✉, Ⓑ, ✈ (to Bremen, Hamburg and Cuxhaven). Ferry: Hamburg-Harwich.

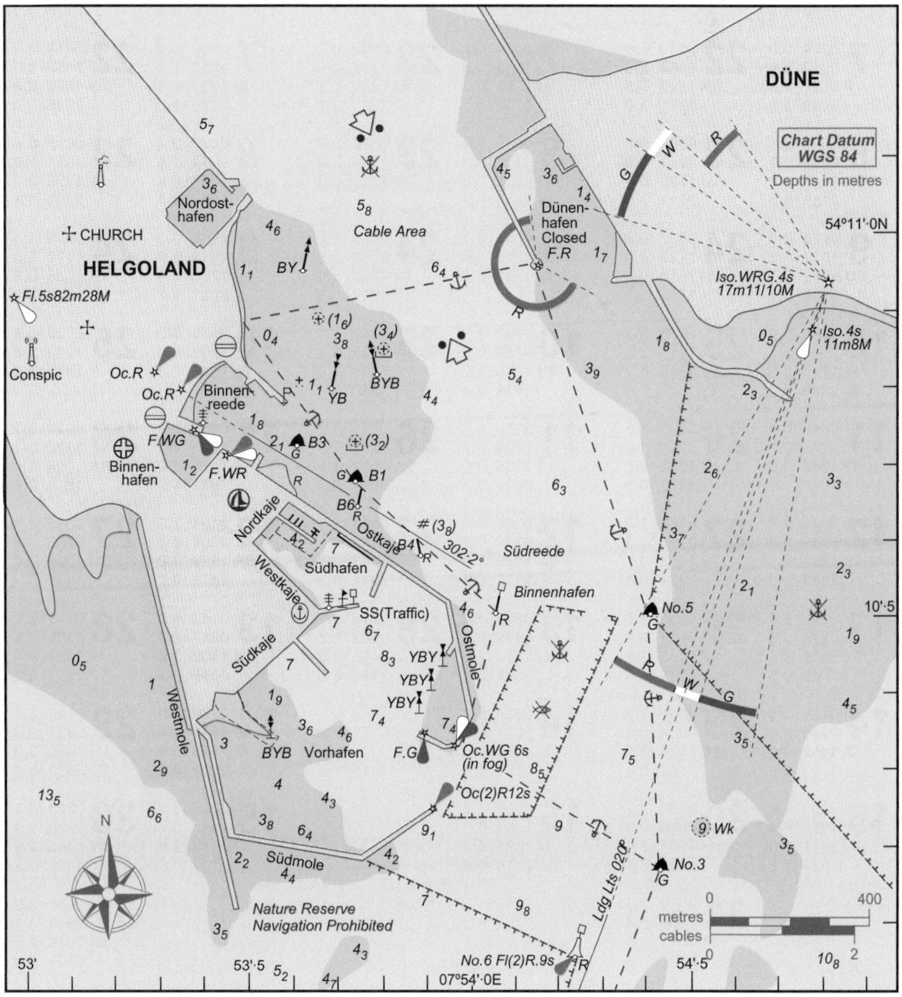
DÜNE
Chart Datum
WGS 84
Depths in metres
54°11'·0N
HELGOLAND
CHURCH
Nordost-
hafen
Fl.5s82m28M
Conspic
Oc.R
Binnen-
reede
F.WG
F.WR
Binnen-
hafen
Cable Area
Dünen-
hafen
Closed
F.R
Iso.WRG.4s
17m11/10M
Iso.4s
11m8M
BY
YB
BYB
B3
B1
B6
B4
Nordkaje
Ostkaje
Westkaje
Südkaje
Südhafen
302·2°
Südreede
Binnenhafen
SS(Traffic)
Ostmole
No.5
YBY
Westmole
Vorhafen
F.G
Oc.WG 6s
(in fog)
Oc(2)R12s
Wk
No.3
Südmole
Ldg Lts 020°
Nature Reserve
Navigation Prohibited
No.6 Fl(2)R.9s
metres
cables
53'
53'·5
07°54'·0E
54'·5
10'·5

TIME ZONE -0100
(German Standard Time)
Subtract 1 hour for UT
For German Summer Time add ONE hour in **non-shaded areas**

GERMANY – HELGOLAND

LAT 54°11′N LONG 7°53′E

TIMES AND HEIGHTS OF HIGH AND LOW WATERS

SPRING & NEAP TIDES
Dates in red are SPRINGS
Dates in blue are NEAPS

YEAR **2005**

JANUARY

Date	Time	m	Time	m	Time	m	Time	m
1 SA	0255	3.2	0943	0.6	1523	2.9	2149	0.7
2 SU	0331	3.1	1021	0.6	1603	2.8	2229	0.7
3 M	0410	3.1	1100	0.6	1646	2.8	◑ 2311	0.8
4 TU	0455	3.0	1143	0.7	1733	2.8		
5 W	0003	0.9	0550	3.0	1240	0.8	1832	2.8
6 TH	0110	1.0	0658	3.0	1350	0.8	1940	2.9
7 F	0224	0.9	0812	3.0	1502	0.8	2049	2.9
8 SA	0337	0.8	0923	3.1	1610	0.8	2155	3.0
9 SU	0446	0.7	1027	3.1	1713	0.7	2255	3.2
10 M	0549	0.6	1126	3.2	1810	0.6	● 2349	3.2
11 TU	0646	0.4	1221	3.1	1905	0.6		
12 W	0040	3.3	0741	0.4	1317	3.1	1958	0.5
13 TH	0131	3.4	0835	0.3	1411	3.0	2048	0.5
14 F	0221	3.4	0925	0.3	1459	3.0	2131	0.5
15 SA	0308	3.4	1008	0.4	1541	2.9	2211	0.5
16 SU	0352	3.3	1049	0.5	1623	2.9	2252	0.6
17 M	0437	3.3	1130	0.6	1707	2.8	◐ 2336	0.7
18 TU	0526	3.2	1213	0.7	1756	2.8		
19 W	0028	0.8	0621	3.0	1306	0.8	1855	2.7
20 TH	0135	0.9	0728	2.9	1415	0.9	2005	2.8
21 F	0254	0.9	0843	2.8	1528	0.9	2118	2.9
22 SA	0408	0.8	0954	2.9	1633	0.9	2221	3.0
23 SU	0508	0.8	1051	3.0	1725	0.9	2311	3.1
24 M	0557	0.8	1137	3.0	1810	0.8	2352	3.2
25 TU	0638	0.7	1217	3.0	1848	0.7	○	
26 W	0029	3.3	0715	0.6	1251	3.0	1923	0.6
27 TH	0103	3.3	0750	0.5	1323	3.0	1957	0.6
28 F	0136	3.2	0823	0.5	1355	3.0	2028	0.5
29 SA	0206	3.2	0854	0.4	1426	2.9	2059	0.4
30 SU	0236	3.1	0926	0.4	1501	2.9	2134	0.4
31 M	0310	3.1	1000	0.4	1537	2.9	2210	0.5

FEBRUARY

Date	Time	m	Time	m	Time	m	Time	m
1 TU	0344	3.1	1032	0.4	1612	2.8	2241	0.6
2 W	0418	3.0	1101	0.5	1646	2.8	◑ 2317	0.7
3 TH	0500	3.0	1145	0.7	1735	2.7		
4 F	0015	0.8	0604	2.9	1254	0.8	1846	2.8
5 SA	0139	0.8	0729	2.8	1421	0.9	2013	2.8
6 SU	0310	0.7	0859	2.9	1547	0.8	2135	3.0
7 M	0434	0.6	1018	3.0	1703	0.7	2246	3.1
8 TU	0545	0.4	1123	3.0	1806	0.6	● 2343	3.2
9 W	0644	0.3	1218	3.0	1900	0.4		
10 TH	0032	3.3	0736	0.2	1308	3.0	1948	0.4
11 F	0119	3.3	0824	0.2	1355	3.0	2033	0.3
12 SA	0205	3.4	0908	0.3	1438	3.0	2113	0.3
13 SU	0248	3.4	0945	0.4	1515	3.0	2148	0.4
14 M	0327	3.3	1018	0.5	1549	3.0	2223	0.5
15 TU	0404	3.2	1049	0.6	1624	2.9	2258	0.6
16 W	0442	3.1	1120	0.7	1702	2.8	◐ 2338	0.7
17 TH	0529	2.9	1204	0.9	1754	2.8		
18 F	0038	0.8	0633	2.7	1312	1.0	1907	2.7
19 SA	0202	0.9	0756	2.6	1439	1.0	2034	2.8
20 SU	0332	0.9	0921	2.7	1602	1.0	2153	2.9
21 M	0447	0.8	1030	2.8	1705	0.8	2251	3.1
22 TU	0540	0.7	1119	2.9	1753	0.7	2333	3.2
23 W	0622	0.6	1158	3.0	1833	0.6		
24 TH	0009	3.2	0658	0.5	1232	3.0	○ 1909	0.5
25 F	0043	3.2	0732	0.4	1303	3.0	1940	0.4
26 SA	0115	3.2	0802	0.3	1332	3.0	2011	0.3
27 SU	0144	3.1	0832	0.3	1403	3.0	2041	0.3
28 M	0213	3.1	0903	0.3	1435	2.9	2114	0.3

MARCH

Date	Time	m	Time	m	Time	m	Time	m
1 TU	0245	3.1	0935	0.3	1508	2.9	2148	0.3
2 W	0318	3.1	1005	0.4	1540	2.9	2216	0.4
3 TH	0351	3.0	1031	0.5	1612	2.8	◑ 2249	0.5
4 F	0431	2.9	1111	0.6	1700	2.7	2346	0.6
5 SA	0537	2.7	1224	0.8	1817	2.7		
6 SU	0117	0.7	0711	2.7	1402	0.9	1954	2.8
7 M	0300	0.6	0850	2.7	1539	0.8	2125	3.0
8 TU	0430	0.4	1014	2.8	1657	0.6	2236	3.1
9 W	0539	0.3	1117	2.9	1758	0.4	2331	3.2
10 TH	0635	0.2	1208	2.9	1848	0.3	●	
11 F	0018	3.2	0723	0.1	1251	3.0	1932	0.2
12 SA	0101	3.3	0804	0.2	1332	3.0	2012	0.2
13 SU	0142	3.3	0841	0.3	1409	3.0	2048	0.3
14 M	0220	3.3	0913	0.4	1442	3.0	2122	0.3
15 TU	0256	3.2	0941	0.4	1513	3.0	2153	0.4
16 W	0330	3.1	1007	0.5	1544	3.0	2224	0.5
17 TH	0405	3.0	1035	0.7	1618	2.9	◐ 2259	0.6
18 F	0447	2.8	1114	0.8	1705	2.8	2352	0.8
19 SA	0547	2.6	1219	1.0	1815	2.7		
20 SU	0113	0.9	0709	2.5	1349	1.0	1945	2.7
21 M	0249	0.8	0841	2.6	1523	1.0	2113	2.9
22 TU	0414	0.7	0958	2.7	1635	0.8	2218	3.0
23 W	0513	0.6	1051	2.8	1726	0.7	2303	3.1
24 TH	0554	0.4	1129	2.9	1806	0.5	2339	3.1
25 F	0630	0.3	1203	3.0	1843	0.4	○	
26 SA	0013	3.1	0702	0.3	1235	3.0	1915	0.3
27 SU	0045	3.2	0733	0.2	1304	3.0	1946	0.3
28 M	0115	3.2	0805	0.2	1334	3.0	2017	0.2
29 TU	0146	3.1	0837	0.2	1406	3.0	2051	0.2
30 W	0220	3.1	0909	0.3	1440	2.9	2125	0.2
31 TH	0258	3.0	0941	0.4	1515	2.9	2201	0.3

APRIL

Date	Time	m	Time	m	Time	m	Time	m
1 F	0338	2.9	1015	0.5	1556	2.9	2243	0.4
2 SA	0427	2.8	1103	0.7	1651	2.8	◑ 2345	0.5
3 SU	0537	2.7	1219	0.8	1810	2.8		
4 M	0117	0.5	0709	2.6	1358	0.8	1945	2.9
5 TU	0258	0.5	0845	2.7	1532	0.7	2113	3.0
6 W	0423	0.3	1004	2.7	1644	0.5	2219	3.1
7 TH	0524	0.2	1100	2.8	1739	0.3	2311	3.1
8 F	0614	0.1	1146	2.9	1826	0.2	● 2357	3.2
9 SA	0659	0.1	1227	2.9	1909	0.2		
10 SU	0040	3.2	0737	0.2	1304	3.0	1947	0.2
11 M	0117	3.2	0809	0.3	1336	3.1	2021	0.3
12 TU	0151	3.2	0838	0.4	1407	3.1	2054	0.3
13 W	0225	3.1	0904	0.4	1439	3.0	2125	0.3
14 TH	0300	2.9	0932	0.5	1512	3.0	2157	0.4
15 F	0337	2.8	1003	0.7	1547	3.0	2233	0.6
16 SA	0418	2.7	1041	0.8	1631	2.9	◐ 2320	0.7
17 SU	0512	2.6	1138	0.9	1733	2.8		
18 M	0030	0.8	0625	2.5	1259	1.0	1854	2.8
19 TU	0158	0.8	0751	2.5	1431	0.9	2020	2.8
20 W	0324	0.6	0909	2.7	1548	0.8	2130	2.9
21 TH	0427	0.5	1007	2.8	1643	0.7	2220	3.0
22 F	0512	0.4	1048	2.9	1727	0.6	2300	3.1
23 SA	0550	0.3	1125	3.0	1807	0.5	2336	3.2
24 SU	0626	0.3	1159	3.1	1843	0.4	○	
25 M	0010	3.2	0700	0.3	1231	3.1	1916	0.3
26 TU	0044	3.2	0734	0.3	1303	3.1	1952	0.3
27 W	0121	3.2	0811	0.3	1340	3.1	2031	0.2
28 TH	0202	3.1	0848	0.4	1420	3.0	2112	0.2
29 F	0248	3.0	0928	0.5	1504	3.0	2159	0.3
30 SA	0339	2.9	1014	0.6	1553	3.0	2252	0.4

Chart Datum: 1·68 metres below Normal Null (German reference level)

TIME ZONE -0100
(German Standard Time)
Subtract 1 hour for UT
For German Summer Time add ONE hour in **non-shaded areas**

GERMANY – HELGOLAND

LAT 54°11′N LONG 7°53′E

TIMES AND HEIGHTS OF HIGH AND LOW WATERS

SPRING & NEAP TIDES
Dates in red are SPRINGS
Dates in blue are NEAPS

YEAR **2005**

MAY

Date	Day	Time	m	Time	m	Time	m	Time	m	Moon
1	SU	0436	2.7	1111	0.7	1654	2.9	2357	0.4	◑
2	M	0545	2.7	1223	0.7	1809	2.9			
3	TU	0119	0.4	0707	2.6	1350	0.7	1934	2.9	
4	W	0248	0.4	0831	2.6	1514	0.6	2053	3.0	
5	TH	0403	0.2	0940	2.7	1620	0.4	2155	3.1	
6	F	0457	0.2	1032	2.8	1710	0.3	2244	3.1	
7	SA	0543	0.2	1116	2.9	1757	0.3	2331	3.1	
8	SU	0627	0.3	1158	3.0	1843	0.3			●
9	M	0016	3.1	0706	0.3	1236	3.1	1921	0.3	
10	TU	0053	3.1	0737	0.4	1307	3.1	1955	0.3	
11	W	0126	3.1	0805	0.5	1338	3.1	2028	0.4	
12	TH	0200	3.0	0835	0.5	1412	3.1	2102	0.4	
13	F	0238	2.9	0906	0.6	1449	3.1	2137	0.5	
14	SA	0317	2.8	0941	0.7	1527	3.1	2215	0.6	
15	SU	0358	2.7	1020	0.8	1608	3.0	2258	0.7	
16	M	0445	2.7	1108	0.8	1659	2.9	2353	0.7	◐
17	TU	0544	2.6	1212	0.9	1803	2.9			
18	W	0104	0.7	0655	2.6	1331	0.9	1918	2.9	
19	TH	0220	0.6	0808	2.7	1447	0.8	2029	2.9	
20	F	0327	0.5	0910	2.8	1548	0.7	2127	3.0	
21	SA	0419	0.5	0958	2.9	1638	0.6	2214	3.1	
22	SU	0504	0.4	1040	3.0	1725	0.6	2257	3.2	
23	M	0546	0.4	1120	3.1	1808	0.5	2336	3.2	○
24	TU	0626	0.4	1158	3.2	1848	0.4			
25	W	0017	3.2	0707	0.4	1239	3.2	1932	0.4	
26	TH	0104	3.2	0752	0.4	1324	3.2	2021	0.3	
27	F	0155	3.1	0839	0.5	1412	3.2	2111	0.2	
28	SA	0248	2.9	0926	0.5	1501	3.1	2203	0.3	
29	SU	0342	2.8	1016	0.6	1553	3.1	2259	0.3	
30	M	0439	2.8	1113	0.6	1653	3.1			◑
31	TU	0000	0.4	0543	2.7	1217	0.6	1801	3.0	

JUNE

Date	Day	Time	m	Time	m	Time	m	Time	m	Moon
1	W	0108	0.4	0652	2.7	1328	0.6	1913	3.0	
2	TH	0220	0.4	0802	2.7	1441	0.6	2023	3.1	
3	F	0328	0.4	0905	2.7	1545	0.5	2124	3.1	
4	SA	0422	0.3	0958	2.8	1639	0.4	2216	3.1	
5	SU	0508	0.4	1045	2.9	1729	0.4	2305	3.1	
6	M	0554	0.5	1130	3.1	1817	0.4	2353	3.1	●
7	TU	0636	0.5	1210	3.1	1858	0.4			
8	W	0033	3.1	0710	0.5	1245	3.2	1935	0.5	
9	TH	0109	3.0	0742	0.6	1319	3.2	2010	0.5	
10	F	0144	3.0	0815	0.6	1355	3.2	2046	0.5	
11	SA	0221	2.9	0849	0.6	1432	3.2	2122	0.5	
12	SU	0259	2.9	0924	0.6	1509	3.2	2159	0.6	
13	M	0337	2.8	1002	0.7	1547	3.1	2238	0.6	
14	TU	0419	2.8	1044	0.7	1629	3.0	2321	0.6	
15	W	0506	2.7	1132	0.8	1718	3.0			◐
16	TH	0011	0.6	0600	2.7	1231	0.8	1816	2.9	
17	F	0112	0.6	0701	2.8	1340	0.8	1923	3.0	
18	SA	0218	0.6	0804	2.8	1446	0.8	2028	3.0	
19	SU	0320	0.6	0902	2.9	1547	0.7	2127	3.1	
20	M	0416	0.6	0954	3.0	1644	0.6	2221	3.2	
21	TU	0509	0.6	1045	3.1	1739	0.6	2311	3.2	
22	W	0600	0.6	1135	3.2	1831	0.5			○
23	TH	0002	3.2	0651	0.5	1225	3.3	1924	0.4	
24	F	0057	3.2	0743	0.5	1316	3.3	2019	0.3	
25	SA	0153	3.1	0836	0.5	1408	3.3	2112	0.2	
26	SU	0246	3.0	0923	0.4	1457	3.3	2202	0.3	
27	M	0336	2.9	1010	0.5	1547	3.3	2252	0.3	
28	TU	0427	2.8	1100	0.6	1640	3.2	2345	0.4	◑
29	W	0522	2.8	1154	0.6	1738	3.2			
30	TH	0039	0.5	0620	2.8	1252	0.6	1839	3.1	

JULY

Date	Day	Time	m	Time	m	Time	m	Time	m	Moon
1	F	0136	0.6	0719	2.8	1357	0.6	1944	3.0	
2	SA	0239	0.6	0821	2.8	1506	0.6	2050	3.0	
3	SU	0342	0.6	0922	2.9	1611	0.6	2151	3.0	
4	M	0437	0.6	1018	3.0	1706	0.6	2245	3.0	
5	TU	0527	0.7	1108	3.1	1756	0.6	2335	3.1	
6	W	0612	0.7	1152	3.2	1841	0.6			●
7	TH	0019	3.1	0652	0.7	1231	3.3	1920	0.6	
8	F	0056	3.0	0728	0.6	1307	3.3	1958	0.6	
9	SA	0130	3.0	0802	0.6	1342	3.3	2033	0.6	
10	SU	0204	3.0	0835	0.6	1415	3.3	2105	0.5	
11	M	0237	2.9	0907	0.6	1448	3.2	2138	0.5	
12	TU	0312	2.9	0942	0.6	1523	3.1	2214	0.5	
13	W	0350	2.9	1020	0.6	1600	3.1	2250	0.5	
14	TH	0430	2.8	1057	0.7	1638	3.1	2325	0.6	◐
15	F	0510	2.8	1139	0.7	1721	3.0			
16	SA	0010	0.7	0558	2.8	1235	0.8	1820	3.0	
17	SU	0111	0.7	0659	2.8	1346	0.8	1931	3.0	
18	M	0223	0.7	0809	2.9	1501	0.8	2046	3.0	
19	TU	0335	0.7	0919	3.0	1614	0.7	2156	3.1	
20	W	0443	0.7	1024	3.1	1722	0.6	2300	3.1	
21	TH	0546	0.7	1124	3.2	1824	0.5	2357	3.1	○
22	F	0644	0.6	1217	3.3	1920	0.3			
23	SA	0053	3.1	0737	0.5	1308	3.4	2014	0.3	
24	SU	0146	3.1	0828	0.4	1358	3.4	2104	0.3	
25	M	0234	3.0	0912	0.4	1445	3.4	2149	0.3	
26	TU	0318	3.0	0952	0.4	1530	3.4	2231	0.4	
27	W	0401	3.0	1035	0.5	1616	3.3	2313	0.5	
28	TH	0447	2.9	1120	0.6	1704	3.2	2355	0.7	◑
29	F	0535	2.9	1209	0.7	1756	3.1			
30	SA	0042	0.8	0628	2.8	1309	0.8	1858	2.9	
31	SU	0144	0.9	0734	2.8	1425	0.8	2012	2.9	

AUGUST

Date	Day	Time	m	Time	m	Time	m	Time	m	Moon
1	M	0300	0.9	0848	2.9	1544	0.8	2128	2.9	
2	TU	0411	0.9	0957	3.0	1651	0.7	2232	2.9	
3	W	0509	0.8	1053	3.2	1743	0.7	2322	3.0	
4	TH	0556	0.8	1137	3.2	1827	0.7			
5	F	0004	3.1	0638	0.7	1216	3.3	1907	0.6	●
6	SA	0041	3.0	0715	0.6	1252	3.3	1942	0.5	
7	SU	0113	3.0	0748	0.6	1325	3.3	2014	0.5	
8	M	0143	3.1	0818	0.5	1354	3.3	2043	0.5	
9	TU	0212	3.0	0847	0.5	1422	3.2	2112	0.5	
10	W	0244	3.0	0919	0.5	1454	3.2	2145	0.5	
11	TH	0319	3.0	0954	0.5	1529	3.1	2217	0.5	
12	F	0353	2.9	1026	0.6	1601	3.1	2244	0.6	
13	SA	0425	2.9	1056	0.7	1637	3.0	2318	0.7	◐
14	SU	0505	2.8	1144	0.8	1731	2.9			
15	M	0016	0.9	0608	2.8	1300	0.8	1851	2.9	
16	TU	0140	0.9	0733	2.9	1432	0.8	2022	2.9	
17	W	0310	0.9	0859	3.0	1600	0.7	2146	3.0	
18	TH	0431	0.8	1014	3.1	1715	0.5	2256	3.1	
19	F	0540	0.7	1115	3.3	1818	0.4	2353	3.1	○
20	SA	0637	0.5	1207	3.4	1912	0.3			
21	SU	0043	3.1	0726	0.4	1255	3.4	2000	0.3	
22	M	0130	3.1	0811	0.4	1341	3.5	2045	0.3	
23	TU	0213	3.1	0852	0.4	1425	3.5	2124	0.4	
24	W	0251	3.1	0929	0.4	1506	3.4	2159	0.5	
25	TH	0328	3.1	1005	0.5	1545	3.3	2232	0.7	
26	F	0405	3.0	1044	0.6	1626	3.2	2306	0.8	◑
27	SA	0447	3.0	1126	0.8	1713	3.0	2348	0.9	
28	SU	0537	2.9	1222	0.9	1814	2.8			
29	M	0051	1.1	0647	2.8	1342	1.0	1934	2.7	
30	TU	0216	1.1	0812	2.9	1514	1.0	2102	2.8	
31	W	0344	1.1	0934	3.0	1633	0.9	2216	2.9	

Chart Datum: 1·68 metres below Normal Null (German reference level)

TIME ZONE -0100
(German Standard Time)
Subtract 1 hour for UT
For German Summer Time add ONE hour in **non-shaded areas**

GERMANY – HELGOLAND

LAT 54°11′N LONG 7°53′E

TIMES AND HEIGHTS OF HIGH AND LOW WATERS

SPRING & NEAP TIDES
Dates in red are **SPRINGS**
Dates in blue are **NEAPS**

YEAR **2005**

SEPTEMBER

Date	Day	Time	m	Time	m	Time	m	Time	m
1	TH	0452	0.9	1036	3.2	1729	0.7	2307	3.0
2	F	0539	0.8	1119	3.2	1809	0.7	2344	3.1
3	SA	0618	0.7	1154	3.3	1844	0.6	●	
4	SU	0017	3.1	0654	0.6	1228	3.3	1917	0.5
5	M	0048	3.1	0726	0.5	1300	3.3	1947	0.5
6	TU	0117	3.1	0755	0.5	1328	3.2	2014	0.5
7	W	0144	3.1	0823	0.5	1354	3.2	2042	0.5
8	TH	0214	3.1	0853	0.5	1423	3.2	2112	0.5
9	F	0245	3.0	0925	0.5	1456	3.1	2142	0.6
10	SA	0317	3.0	0956	0.6	1530	3.1	2209	0.7
11	SU	0349	2.9	1026	0.7	1609	2.9	◐ 2244	0.8
12	M	0432	2.8	1115	0.8	1707	2.8	2346	1.0
13	TU	0541	2.8	1238	0.8	1833	2.8		
14	W	0120	1.1	0714	2.9	1420	0.8	2013	2.8
15	TH	0300	1.0	0849	3.0	1555	0.6	2142	2.9
16	F	0425	0.8	1005	3.2	1708	0.5	2249	3.0
17	SA	0529	0.7	1102	3.3	1805	0.3	2341	3.0
18	SU	0622	0.5	1151	3.3	1854	0.3	○	
19	M	0026	3.1	0707	0.4	1235	3.4	1937	0.3
20	TU	0107	3.1	0748	0.4	1318	3.5	2016	0.4
21	W	0145	3.2	0826	0.4	1358	3.5	2051	0.5
22	TH	0219	3.2	0902	0.5	1437	3.4	2122	0.6
23	F	0252	3.2	0936	0.5	1513	3.2	2151	0.7
24	SA	0326	3.1	1010	0.6	1551	3.1	2222	0.9
25	SU	0405	3.0	1050	0.8	1636	2.9	◑ 2303	1.0
26	M	0454	2.9	1142	0.9	1735	2.7		
27	TU	0003	1.2	0602	2.9	1258	1.1	1854	2.6
28	W	0130	1.3	0730	2.9	1433	1.1	2025	2.7
29	TH	0305	1.2	0858	3.0	1601	0.9	2146	2.8
30	F	0421	1.0	1006	3.1	1701	0.8	2240	2.9

OCTOBER

Date	Day	Time	m	Time	m	Time	m	Time	m
1	SA	0511	0.9	1049	3.2	1739	0.7	2315	3.1
2	SU	0548	0.7	1123	3.2	1811	0.6	2346	3.1
3	M	0623	0.7	1156	3.2	1843	0.5	●	
4	TU	0017	3.1	0656	0.6	1228	3.3	1913	0.5
5	W	0046	3.2	0726	0.6	1258	3.3	1943	0.5
6	TH	0114	3.2	0755	0.5	1326	3.3	2012	0.6
7	F	0143	3.1	0826	0.5	1356	3.2	2042	0.6
8	SA	0215	3.1	0859	0.5	1432	3.1	2113	0.7
9	SU	0250	3.1	0934	0.6	1512	3.0	2148	0.8
10	M	0330	3.0	1015	0.7	1600	2.9	◐ 2232	0.9
11	TU	0421	2.9	1111	0.8	1705	2.8	2340	1.0
12	W	0534	2.9	1234	0.8	1831	2.7		
13	TH	0113	1.1	0705	3.0	1414	0.8	2007	2.8
14	F	0251	1.0	0836	3.1	1545	0.6	2130	2.9
15	SA	0410	0.8	0949	3.2	1652	0.4	2232	2.9
16	SU	0508	0.6	1042	3.3	1742	0.3	2319	3.0
17	M	0557	0.5	1128	3.3	1828	0.4	○	
18	TU	0001	3.1	0642	0.4	1213	3.3	1909	0.4
19	W	0040	3.2	0723	0.5	1253	3.4	1944	0.6
20	TH	0115	3.2	0800	0.5	1331	3.4	2016	0.6
21	F	0148	3.3	0835	0.6	1408	3.3	2047	0.7
22	SA	0221	3.2	0909	0.6	1446	3.1	2117	0.8
23	SU	0256	3.2	0944	0.7	1526	2.9	2150	0.9
24	M	0335	3.1	1023	0.8	1609	2.8	2230	1.1
25	TU	0421	3.0	1111	1.0	1703	2.7	◑ 2324	1.2
26	W	0521	2.9	1216	1.1	1812	2.6		
27	TH	0039	1.3	0639	2.9	1340	1.1	1934	2.7
28	F	0208	1.2	0803	3.0	1505	1.0	2054	2.8
29	SA	0329	1.1	0915	3.1	1611	0.8	2154	2.9
30	SU	0426	1.0	1006	3.2	1655	0.7	2234	3.0
31	M	0507	0.9	1044	3.2	1729	0.7	2307	3.2

NOVEMBER

Date	Day	Time	m	Time	m	Time	m	Time	m
1	TU	0545	0.8	1119	3.3	1803	0.6	2340	3.2
2	W	0621	0.7	1153	3.3	1837	0.6	●	
3	TH	0011	3.2	0654	0.7	1226	3.3	1910	0.6
4	F	0043	3.2	0728	0.6	1301	3.3	1946	0.7
5	SA	0118	3.2	0806	0.6	1340	3.2	2022	0.7
6	SU	0157	3.2	0846	0.6	1422	3.1	2100	0.8
7	M	0238	3.2	0929	0.6	1509	3.0	2142	0.9
8	TU	0324	3.1	1018	0.7	1603	2.9	2234	1.0
9	W	0420	3.1	1118	0.7	1707	2.8	◐ 2340	1.0
10	TH	0530	3.0	1233	0.7	1825	2.7		
11	F	0102	1.0	0652	3.1	1400	0.7	1950	2.7
12	SA	0229	0.9	0814	3.1	1521	0.6	2105	2.8
13	SU	0343	0.8	0923	3.2	1624	0.5	2203	2.9
14	M	0439	0.6	1017	3.2	1712	0.5	2250	3.0
15	TU	0528	0.6	1105	3.2	1757	0.5	2333	3.1
16	W	0616	0.5	1151	3.3	1839	0.6	○	
17	TH	0014	3.2	0658	0.6	1232	3.3	1914	0.7
18	F	0049	3.3	0736	0.6	1309	3.2	1946	0.7
19	SA	0123	3.3	0812	0.7	1347	3.1	2019	0.8
20	SU	0159	3.3	0849	0.7	1427	3.0	2053	0.8
21	M	0236	3.2	0925	0.7	1507	2.9	2128	0.9
22	TU	0314	3.2	1003	0.8	1547	2.8	2206	1.0
23	W	0355	3.2	1045	0.9	1632	2.8	◑ 2251	1.1
24	TH	0443	3.1	1135	1.0	1727	2.7	2349	1.2
25	F	0543	3.0	1239	1.0	1833	2.7		
26	SA	0101	1.2	0655	3.0	1353	1.0	1946	2.8
27	SU	0219	1.2	0807	3.1	1502	0.9	2051	2.9
28	M	0325	1.1	0909	3.1	1557	0.8	2141	3.0
29	TU	0416	1.0	0958	3.2	1642	0.8	2222	3.1
30	W	0502	0.9	1040	3.3	1723	0.8	2301	3.2

DECEMBER

Date	Day	Time	m	Time	m	Time	m	Time	m
1	TH	0546	0.8	1120	3.3	1803	0.7	● 2339	3.3
2	F	0627	0.7	1200	3.3	1843	0.7		
3	SA	0019	3.3	0710	0.7	1245	3.3	1928	0.8
4	SU	0103	3.3	0757	0.6	1334	3.2	2015	0.8
5	M	0150	3.3	0845	0.5	1424	3.1	2059	0.8
6	TU	0236	3.3	0932	0.5	1511	3.0	2143	0.8
7	W	0323	3.3	1022	0.6	1603	2.9	2234	0.8
8	TH	0417	3.2	1119	0.6	1701	2.8	◐ 2332	0.9
9	F	0519	3.2	1221	0.7	1807	2.8		
10	SA	0038	0.9	0628	3.2	1330	0.7	1917	2.8
11	SU	0152	0.9	0741	3.2	1442	0.7	2026	2.8
12	M	0304	0.8	0850	3.2	1546	0.7	2127	2.9
13	TU	0408	0.7	0950	3.1	1640	0.7	2220	3.0
14	W	0503	0.7	1043	3.1	1729	0.7	2309	3.1
15	TH	0554	0.7	1133	3.2	1814	0.8	○ 2353	3.3
16	F	0640	0.7	1218	3.2	1853	0.8		
17	SA	0032	3.3	0719	0.7	1256	3.1	1927	0.8
18	SU	0108	3.3	0757	0.7	1333	3.1	2002	0.8
19	M	0145	3.3	0835	0.7	1411	3.0	2038	0.8
20	TU	0222	3.3	0911	0.7	1448	3.0	2111	0.8
21	W	0256	3.3	0944	0.7	1524	2.9	2145	0.8
22	TH	0331	3.2	1020	0.8	1602	2.9	2223	0.9
23	F	0408	3.1	1058	0.8	1644	2.8	◑ 2305	1.0
24	SA	0452	3.0	1141	0.9	1732	2.8	2357	1.0
25	SU	0546	3.0	1237	0.9	1830	2.8		
26	M	0102	1.1	0652	3.0	1343	1.0	1935	2.9
27	TU	0213	1.1	0801	3.1	1450	0.9	2038	2.9
28	W	0320	1.0	0906	3.1	1550	0.9	2135	3.1
29	TH	0420	0.9	1003	3.2	1645	0.9	2227	3.2
30	F	0517	0.8	1054	3.2	1737	0.8	2317	3.3
31	SA	0610	0.7	1145	3.2	1828	0.8	●	

Chart Datum: 1·68 metres below Normal Null (German reference level)

9.15.10 RIVER ELBE

Niedersachsen/Schleswig-Holstein

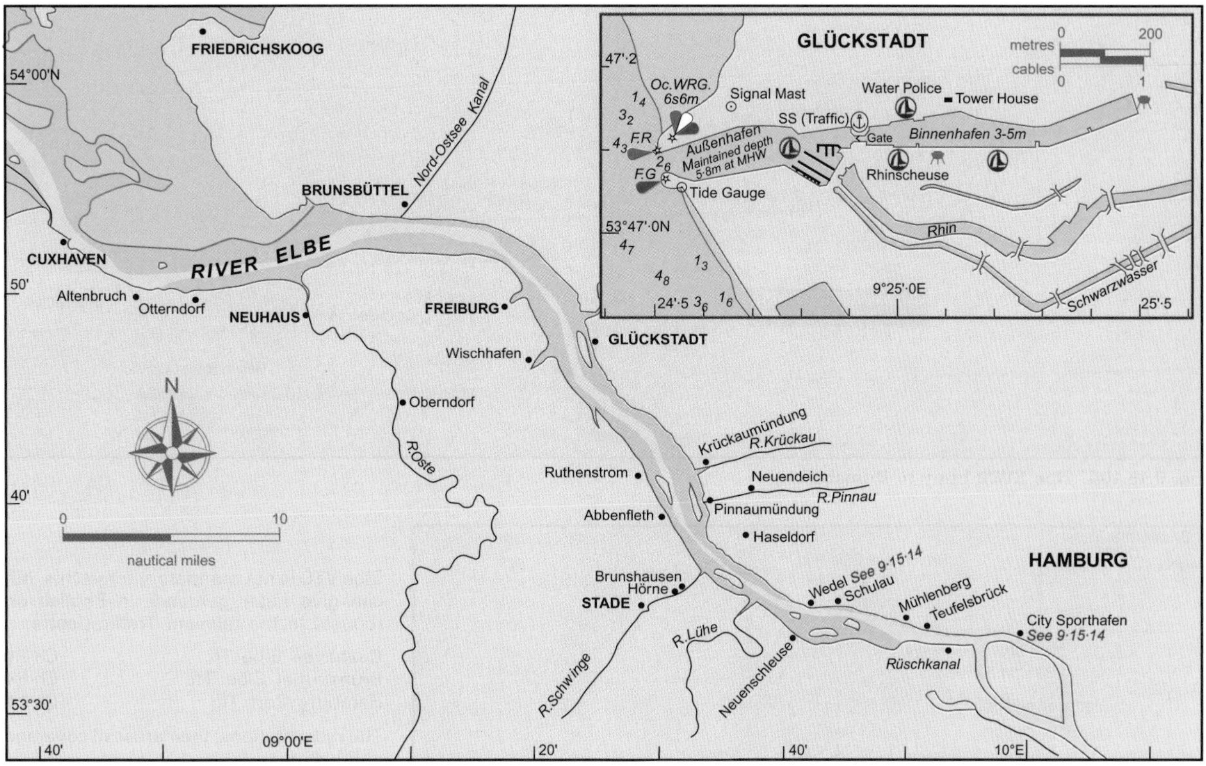
GLÜCKSTADT
metres 0 200
cables 0 1
47'·2
Oc.WRG. 6s6m
Signal Mast
Water Police
Tower House
SS (Traffic)
F.R
Außenhafen
Maintained depth 5·8m at MHW
Gate
Binnenhafen 3-5m
F.G
Tide Gauge
Rhinscheuse
53°47'·0N
Rhin
Schwarzwasser
9°25'·0E
24'·5
25'·5
FRIEDRICHSKOOG
54°00'N
Nord-Ostsee Kanal
BRUNSBÜTTEL
CUXHAVEN
RIVER ELBE
50'
Altenbruch
Otterndorf
NEUHAUS
FREIBURG
Wischhafen
GLÜCKSTADT
Oberndorf
N
R.Oste
Krückaumündung
R.Krückau
Ruthenstrom
Neuendeich
R.Pinnau
Pinnaumündung
Abbenfleth
Haseldorf
40'
0 10
nautical miles
Brunshausen
Hörne
STADE
Wedel See 9·15·14
Schulau
HAMBURG
Mühlenberg
Teufelsbrück
City Sporthafen See 9·15·14
R.Lühe
Neuenschleuse
Rüschkanal
R.Schwinge
53°30'
40'
09°00'E
20'
40'
10°E

CHARTS AC 3619, 3625, 3267, 3268; D 44, 46, 47, 48; BSH 3010.1-13

TIDES

Standard Port CUXHAVEN (⟶)

Times				Height (metres)			
High Water		Low Water		MHWS	MHWN	MLWN	MLWS
0200	0800	0200	0900	3·3	2·9	0·4	0·1
1400	2000	1400	2100				
Differences SCHARHÖRN (11M NW of Cuxhaven)							
−0045	−0047	−0101	−0103	+0·1	+0·1	+0·1	0·0
GROßER VOGELSAND							
−0044	−0046	−0101	−0103	0·0	0·0	+0·1	−0·1
OTTERNDORF							
+0025	+0025	+0022	+0022	−0·1	−0·1	0·0	0·0
GLÜCKSTADT							
+0205	+0214	+0220	+0213	−0·3	−0·2	−0·2	0·0
STADERSAND							
+0241	+0245	+0300	+0254	−0·1	0·0	−0·2	0·0
SCHULAU							
+0304	+0315	+0337	+0321	+0·1	+0·2	−0·3	−0·1
SEEMANNSHÖFT (53°32'·5N 09°52'·7E)							
+0324	+0332	+0403	+0347	+0·2	+0·3	−0·4	−0·2
HAMBURG							
+0338	+0346	+0422	+0406	+0·4	+0·4	−0·4	−0·3

NAVIGATION Distances: Elbe SWM buoy to Cuxhaven = 24M; Cuxhaven to Wedel Yacht Haven = 45M; Wedel to City Sport Hafen = 11·5M. The river is 13m deep up to Hamburg and tidal to Geesthacht, 24M above Hamburg. Strong W winds can raise the level by as much as 4m. Do not try to enter in strong W/NW winds against the ebb. It is a very busy waterway and at night the many lights can be confusing. Yachts should keep to stbd, just outside the marked chan.

SHELTER & FACILITIES Better hbrs are listed below, with BSH 3010 sheet Nos. It is not a particularly salubrious yachting area:

FREIBURG: 7M above Brunsbüttel on the SW bank. Enter at HW, but mainly commercial at Freiburg Reede; little space for small craft. ML 2·2m. HM ☎ (04779) 8314. Facilities: ME, El, ⚒, C, FW, Slip; **Jugendheim & YC Klubheim** 🛒, R, Bar. (Sheet 6).

STÖRLOCH/BORSFLETH: Ent approx 600m above locks on E bank. ML 2·8m. HM ☎ (04124) 71437. Facilities: FW, YC. Stör Bridge VHF Ch 09, 16. (Sheet 6).

STÖR/BEIDENFLETH: ML 2·8m. **Langes Rack YC**. (Sheet 6)

GLÜCKSTADT: E bank, mouth of R Stör (see inset). Good shelter: 1 marina in outer hbr, 5.8m at MHW. Or via entry gate, opens HW −2 to +½, into inner hbr for 3 marinas in 3-5m. VHF Ch 11. HM ☎ (04124) 2087; ⊖ ☎ 2171. YC, FW, C, D, 🛒, R, ⊡, Bar. (Sheet 6).

WISCHHAFEN: HM ☎ (04770) 334; ⊖ 3014 FW, M, Slip, P, D, ML 2·7m. (Sheet 6).

RUTHENSTROM: 197° ldg bns with △ topmarks into hbr. ML 2·6m. HM ☎ (04143) 5282; C, Slip, FW, ME, El, ⚒. (Sheet 7).

KRÜCKAUMÜNDUNG JACHTHAFEN: Entrance via lock gate; ☎ (04125) 1521 Slip, FW. ML 2·7m. ⊖ ☎ 20551. (Sheet 7).

PINNAUMÜNDUNG JACHTHAFEN: Ent via lock gate on N bank after passing through main locks. ML 2·5m. HM ☎ (04101) 22447 Slip, M, FW, YC, C. (Sheets 7/8).

PINNAU-NEUENDEICH: Marina 1½M up the Pinnau from main locks and another at approx 2M. (Sheets 7/8).

ABBENFLETH: Ent marked by two bns in line 221° with △ topmarks. (Sheets 7/8).

HASELDORF Hafen: HM ☎ (04129) 268 Slip, FW, 🛒, YC. (8/9)

R. SCHWINGE on SW bank, 12M up-river from Glückstadt:
- BRUNSHAUSEN (04141) 3085. ML 1·1; Duration 0510. (Sheets 8/9)
- HÖRNE/WÖHRDEN ML 2·8m
- STADE (04141) 101275 C, YC, 🛒; Access HW ±4. Very good shelter in scenic town. ⊖ ☎ 3014. (Sheets 8/9).

LÜHE: Hafen in town of Lühe. (Sheet 8).

RIVER ELBE, VESSEL TRAFFIC SERVICE

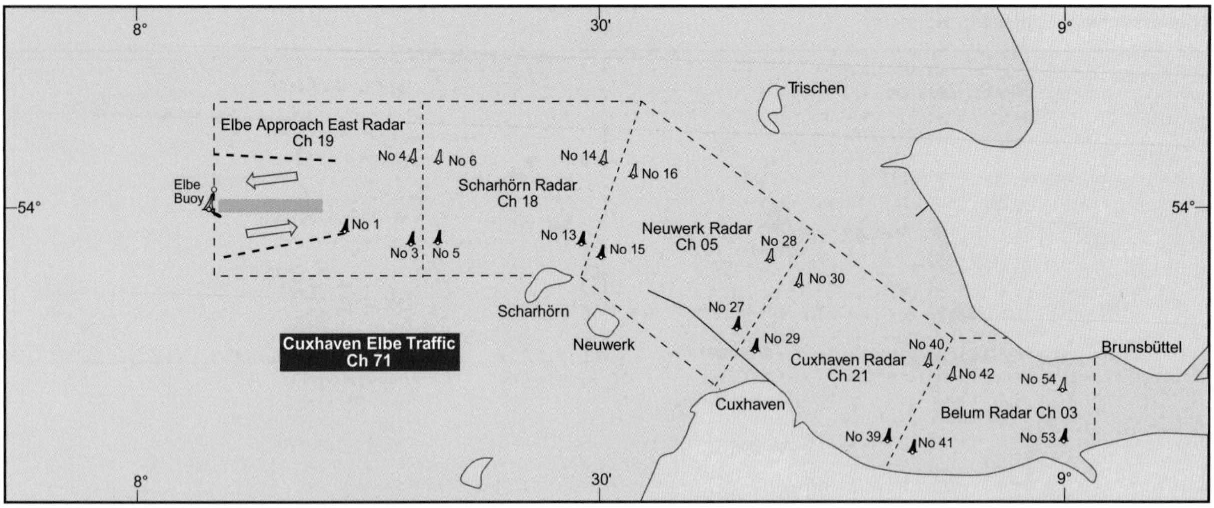
8°
30'
9°
54°
Trischen
Elbe Approach East Radar
Ch 19
Elbe
Buoy
No 4
No 6
No 1
No 3
No 5
Scharhörn Radar
Ch 18
No 14
No 16
No 13
No 15
Neuwerk Radar
Ch 05
No 28
No 30
Scharhörn
Neuwerk
No 27
No 29
Cuxhaven Elbe Traffic
Ch 71
Cuxhaven Radar
Ch 21
No 40
No 42
No 54
Brunsbüttel
Cuxhaven
Belum Radar Ch 03
No 39
No 41
No 53

Fig. 9.15.10A. Elbe SWM buoy to Brunsbüttel

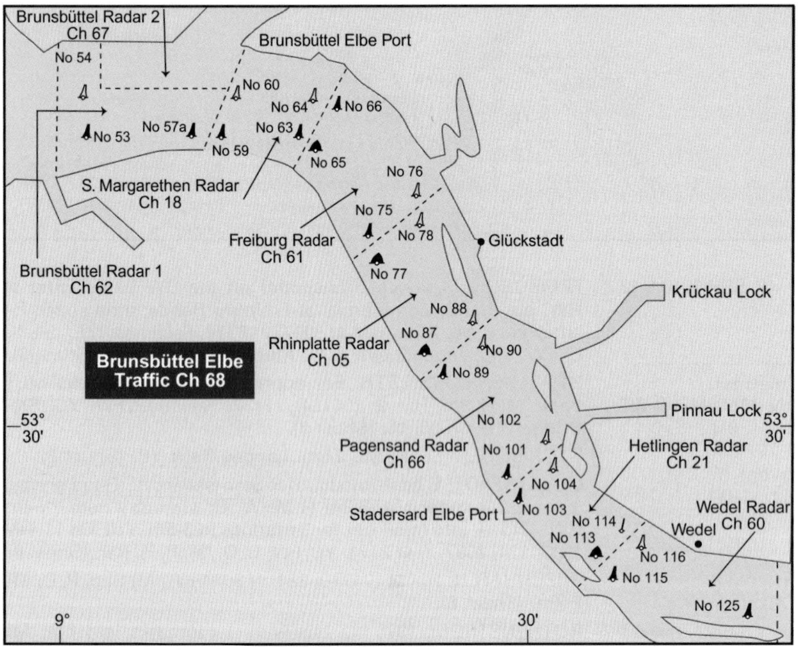
Brunsbüttel Radar 2
Ch 67
Brunsbüttel Elbe Port
No 54
No 60
No 64
No 66
No 53
No 57a
No 63
No 59
No 65
S. Margarethen Radar
Ch 18
No 76
No 75
No 78
Freiburg Radar
Ch 61
Glückstadt
Brunsbüttel Radar 1
Ch 62
No 77
Krückau Lock
No 88
Rhinplatte Radar
Ch 05
No 87
No 90
Brunsbüttel Elbe
Traffic Ch 68
No 89
Pinnau Lock
53°
30'
No 102
Pagensand Radar
Ch 66
No 101
Hetlingen Radar
Ch 21
No 104
Stadersand Elbe Port
No 103
No 114
Wedel Radar
Wedel Ch 60
No 113
No 116
No 115
No 125
9°
30'

Fig. 9.15.10B. Brunsbüttel to 2M east of Wedel

Elbe VTS is not mandatory for yachts, but can give radar guidance in English on request to the relevant Traffic Centre:

Cuxhaven Elbe Tfc	Ch 71
Brunsbuttel Elbe Tfc	Ch 68
Hamburg Port Tfc	Ch 14

The radar stations, their areas of coverage and VHF are:

Elbe SWM-buoy 53	See 9.15.11
Buoys 51-125	See 9.15.12

Then *Hamburg Radar:*

Buoys 125-129	Ch 19
Buoys 129-132	Ch 03
Buoys 134-Vorhafen	Ch 63
09°56'·80E-Norderelbbrücken	Ch 05

Traffic and navigational info is broadcast by:

Cuxhaven Elbe Tfc	See 9.15.11
Brunsbuttel Elbe Tfc	See 9.15.12
Hamburg Port Tfc	See 9.15.14

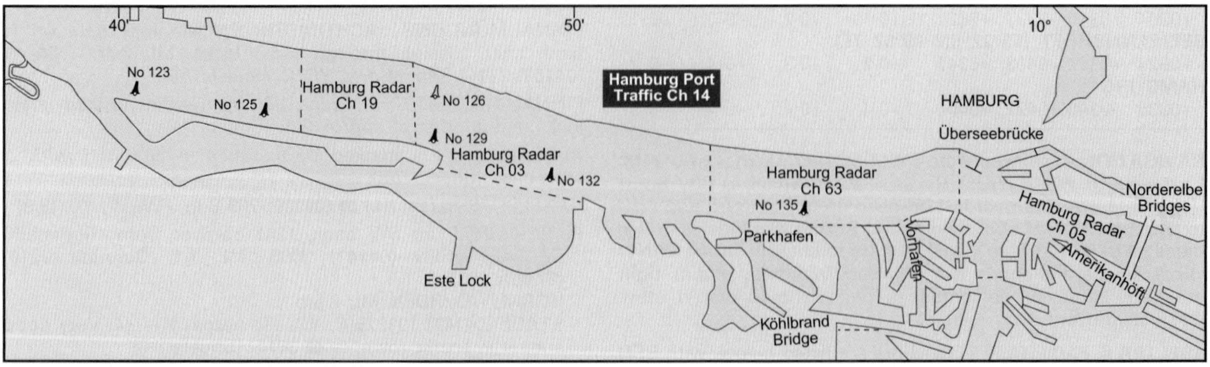
40'
50'
10°
No 123
No 125
Hamburg Radar
Ch 19
No 126
Hamburg Port
Traffic Ch 14
HAMBURG
No 129
Hamburg Radar
Ch 03
No 132
Überseebrücke
Hamburg Radar
Ch 63
No 135
Norderelbe
Bridges
Hamburg Radar
Ch 05
Parkhafen
Vorhafen
Amerikanhöft
Este Lock
Köhlbrand
Bridge

Fig. 9.15.10C. 2M east of Wedel to Hamburg City centre

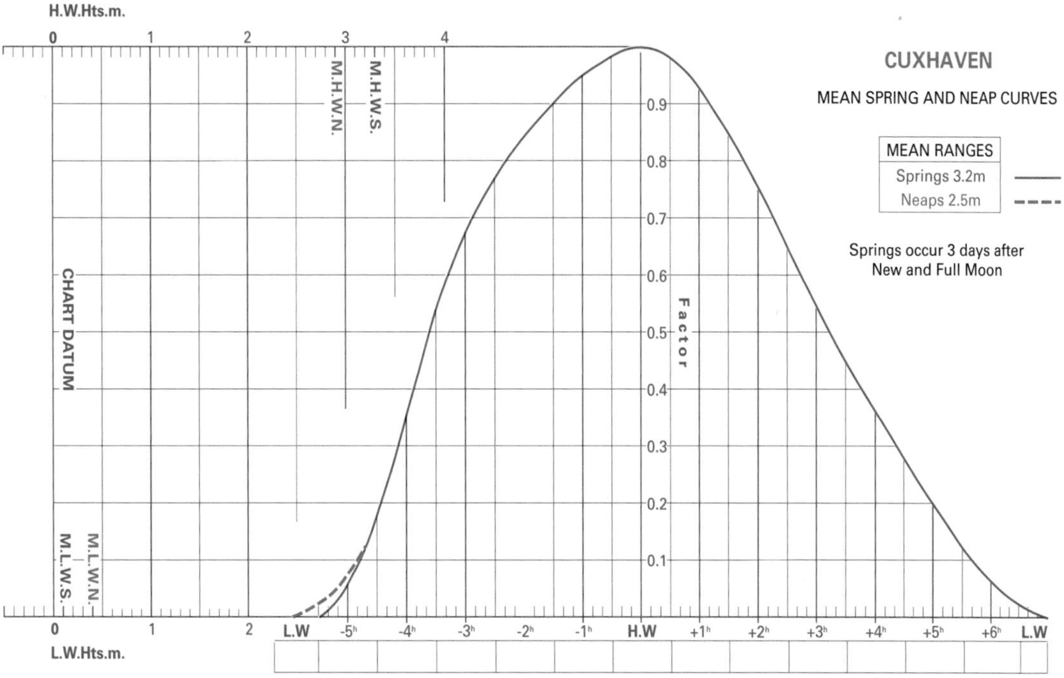
H.W.Hts.m.
0 1 2 3 4
M.H.W.N.
M.H.W.S.
CHART DATUM
M.L.W.S.
M.L.W.N.
0.9
0.8
0.7
0.6
0.5
0.4
0.3
0.2
0.1
Factor
0 1 2
L.W.Hts.m.
L.W -5h -4h -3h -2h -1h H.W +1h +2h +3h +4h +5h +6h L.W
CUXHAVEN
MEAN SPRING AND NEAP CURVES
MEAN RANGES
Springs 3.2m
Neaps 2.5m
Springs occur 3 days after
New and Full Moon

15

9.15.11 CUXHAVEN

Niedersachsen **53°52'·43N 08°42'·49E** (Marina ent)

CHARTS AC 3619; Imray C26; D44, BSH 3010.1/2

TIDES +0103 Dover; ML 1·7; Duration 0535; Zone –0100

CUXHAVEN predictions (⟶)

SHELTER Good in both marinas: YC marina (3·5m; open H24 Apr-Oct) N of radar tr. Marina Cuxhaven, close S of radio mast, is entered from Alter Hafen via bridge which opens (0600-2100) H and H+30, on request Ch 69, not at night nor in winds > F7. Yachts > 20m LOA berth in the Alter Hafen or Alter Fischereihafen.

NAVIGATION WPT 53°53'·92N 08°41'·20E [No 31 SHM buoy, Fl G 4s], 152°/1·7M to marina ent. From No 27 SHM buoy, appr is in W sector (149°-154°) of Baumrönne ldg lt Iso 4s. Chan well marked/lit, see 9.15.4. Ebb runs up to 5kn off Cuxhaven. Much commercial shipping.

LIGHTS AND MARKS Ent to YC Marina is close NW of conspic radar tr, and N of disused lt ho (dark R with copper cupola). YC marina ent, N side FWG; S side FWR, shown 1 Apr-31 Oct.

R/T Cuxhaven Port/lock Ch 69. Radar cover of the outer Elbe is provided as follows:

Elbe West Radar	Ch 65	G. Bight lt float - buoy 1;
Elbe East Radar	Ch 19	Elbe lt float - buoy 5;
Scharhörn Radar	Ch 18	Buoys 3 - 15;
Neuwerk Radar	Ch 05	Buoys 13 - 29;
Cuxhaven Radar	Ch 21	Buoys 27 - 41;
Belum Radar	Ch 03	Buoys 39 - 53.

Cuxhaven Elbe Traffic (VTS) broadcasts nav/weather info for the outer Elbe on Ch 71 in German & English every H + 35. CG & LB: Ch 16. *Cuxhaven Elbe Port* (Sig stn/Distress) Ch **12** 16 (H24).

TELEPHONE (Dial code 04721) HM 34111 (Apr-Oct); LB 34622 and Ch 16; Weather 36400; Port Authority 501450; ⊜ 21085; British Cruising Ass'n and Little Ship Club 57270, ⊞ 572757; Police 110; Waterway Police 745930; CG and MRCC 38011/12, Ch16; Dr & Fire 112; Brit Consul (040) 446071.

FACILITIES Cuxhaven YC Marina (Segler-Vereinigung) ☎ 34111 (summer only), €1.31, Slip, FW, P & D (cans), C (10 ton), AC (free up to 500 watts, then €0.36/kilowatt), BY, ME, El, ⚒, CH, SM, Gaz, chart agent, Ⓔ, R, Bar, ⊡, ⊜, bikes available foc; **Cuxhaven Marina** ☎ 37363, open all year, 90 berths inc approx 45 for Ⓥ, €1.31, usual facilities. Swing bridge opens every H and H+30 during daytime. **City** All facilities, ⇄, ✈ (Bremen, Hamburg, Hanover). Ferry: Hamburg -Harwich.

HARBOUR 7m ESE of CUXHAVEN, on S bank of ELBE

OTTERNDORF, Niedersachsen, **53°50'·10N 08°53'·84E**. AC 3619, 3625; BSH 3014.11. HW +0100 on Dover (UT); ML 2·9m; Duration 0525; see 9.15.10. Ent marked by Medem lt bn & perches. Appr chan (0·8m) from Elbe divides: yachts can take the W branch to Kutterhafen (0·9m) and the R. Medem; or to E, through lock for the Hadelner Kanal and turn hard stbd into yacht hbr. Lockmaster ☎ (04751) 2190; Yacht hbr ☎ 13131 C, Bar. **Town** (3km) ME, Gaz, ⊞, ✉.

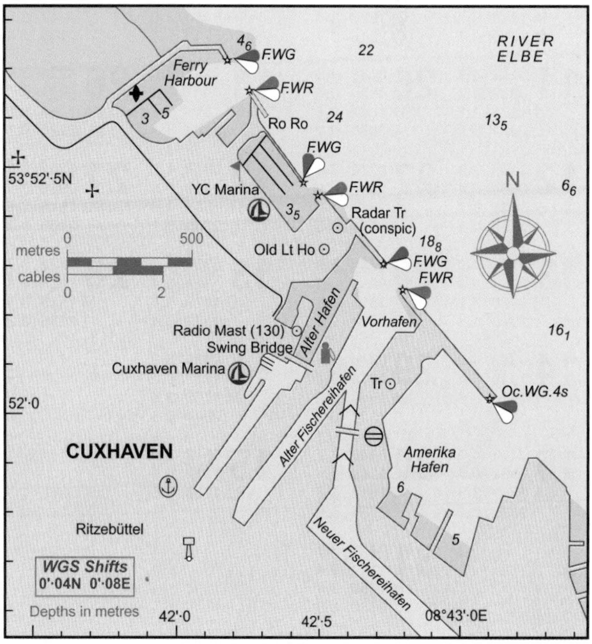
RIVER ELBE
Ferry Harbour
F.WG
F.WR
22
24
13₅
Ro Ro
F.WG
53°52'·5N
YC Marina
F.WR
N
6₆
3₅
Radar Tr (conspic)
18₈
F.WG
F.WR
Old Lt Ho
metres 0 500
cables 0 2
Radio Mast (130)
Swing Bridge
Alter Hafen
Vorhafen
16₁
Cuxhaven Marina
Tr
Oc.WG.4s
52'·0
CUXHAVEN
Alter Fischereihafen
Amerika Hafen
6
5
Ritzebüttel
Neuer Fischereihafen
WGS Shifts
0'·04N 0'·08E
Depths in metres
42'·0
42'·5
08°43'·0E

TIME ZONE -0100
(German Standard Time)
Subtract 1 hour for UT
For German Summer Time add ONE hour in **non-shaded areas**

GERMANY – CUXHAVEN

LAT 53°52′N LONG 8°43′E

TIMES AND HEIGHTS OF HIGH AND LOW WATERS

SPRING & NEAP TIDES
Dates in red are SPRINGS
Dates in blue are NEAPS

YEAR **2005**

JANUARY

Date	Time	m	Date	Time	m
1 SA	0405 1105 1637 2312	3.8 0.6 3.4 0.7	**16** SU	0500 1212 1738	3.9 0.5 3.4
2 SU	0442 1141 1716 2350	3.7 0.6 3.3 0.8	**17** M	0014 0545 1252 ◐ 1820	0.7 3.9 0.6 3.4
3 M ◑	0522 1219 1757	3.6 0.7 3.3	**18** TU	0055 0633 1332 1906	0.7 3.7 0.7 3.3
4 TU	0029 0606 1301 1845	0.8 3.6 0.7 3.3	**19** W	0144 0729 1422 2004	0.8 3.5 0.8 3.2
5 W	0119 0700 1356 1945	1.0 3.5 0.8 3.3	**20** TH	0248 0837 1529 2114	0.9 3.4 0.9 3.3
6 TH	0224 0806 1506 2054	1.0 3.6 0.9 3.4	**21** F	0406 0953 1644 2227	0.9 3.4 1.0 3.4
7 F	0339 0919 1620 2204	1.0 3.6 0.9 3.5	**22** SA	0525 1104 1753 2331	0.9 3.4 0.9 3.6
8 SA	0454 1032 1732 2308	0.8 3.7 0.8 3.6	**23** SU	0628 1202 1850	0.8 3.5 0.9
9 SU	0606 1139 1837	0.7 3.7 0.8	**24** M	0020 0718 1248 1936	3.7 0.8 3.6 0.8
10 M	0007 0711 1240 ● 1936	3.8 0.6 3.7 0.7	**25** TU	0101 0801 1327 ○ 2015	3.8 0.7 3.6 0.7
11 TU	0101 0809 1337 2031	3.9 0.4 3.7 0.6	**26** W	0138 0839 1403 2050	3.9 0.6 3.6 0.7
12 W	0153 0904 1433 2125	3.9 0.4 3.7 0.6	**27** TH	0212 0916 1437 2124	3.9 0.6 3.6 0.6
13 TH	0244 0959 1526 2215	4.0 0.4 3.7 0.5	**28** F	0245 0950 1509 2154	3.9 0.5 3.6 0.5
14 F	0333 1049 1614 2258	4.0 0.4 3.6 0.5	**29** SA	0315 1019 1540 2224	3.8 0.4 3.5 0.4
15 SA	0417 1132 1657 2336	4.0 0.4 3.5 0.6	**30** SU	0346 1048 1614 2256	3.7 0.4 3.4 0.5
			31 M	0421 1121 1650 2330	3.7 0.4 3.4 0.5

FEBRUARY

Date	Time	m	Date	Time	m
1 TU	0457 1153 1723	3.7 0.5 3.4	**16** W	0015 0550 1240 ◐ 1811	0.6 3.6 0.7 3.4
2 W	0000 0530 1221 ◑ 1758	0.6 3.6 0.6 3.3	**17** TH	0050 0637 1317 1902	0.7 3.4 0.8 3.2
3 TH	0032 0611 1301 1848	0.7 3.5 0.7 3.3	**18** F	0145 0741 1421 2015	0.8 3.2 1.0 3.2
4 F	0126 0714 1407 1959	0.8 3.4 0.9 3.3	**19** SA	0307 0905 1548 2142	0.9 3.2 1.0 3.3
5 SA	0247 0838 1535 2124	0.9 3.4 0.9 3.4	**20** SU	0442 1031 1716 2300	0.9 3.2 1.0 3.5
6 SU	0421 1008 1706 2245	0.7 3.5 0.9 3.6	**21** M	0603 1141 1826 2359	0.8 3.4 0.8 3.7
7 M	0549 1129 1826 2355	0.6 3.6 0.7 3.7	**22** TU	0700 1231 1916	0.7 3.5 0.7
8 TU ●	0704 1236 1932	0.4 3.6 0.6	**23** W	0042 0742 1310 1957	3.8 0.6 3.6 0.6
9 W	0053 0805 1333 2027	3.8 0.3 3.6 0.4	**24** TH	0118 0820 1345 ○ 2033	3.8 0.5 3.6 0.5
10 TH	0144 0858 1424 2115	3.9 0.2 3.6 0.4	**25** F	0153 0855 1417 2106	3.8 0.4 3.6 0.4
11 F	0232 0947 1511 2200	4.0 0.2 3.6 0.3	**26** SA	0224 0927 1446 2136	3.8 0.3 3.6 0.3
12 SA	0316 1033 1553 2240	4.0 0.3 3.6 0.4	**27** SU	0252 0956 1515 2205	3.8 0.3 3.6 0.3
13 SU	0357 1111 1629 2313	4.0 0.4 3.6 0.4	**28** M	0322 1025 1546 2235	3.7 0.3 3.5 0.3
14 M	0435 1143 1703 2344	3.9 0.5 3.5 0.5			
15 TU	0512 1212 1735	3.8 0.6 3.5			

MARCH

Date	Time	m	Date	Time	m
1 TU	0356 1056 1620 2307	3.7 0.3 3.5 0.3	**16** W	0439 1130 1654 2338	3.7 0.5 3.5 0.5
2 W	0431 1125 1652 2333	3.7 0.4 3.4 0.4	**17** TH ◐	0514 1154 1726	3.5 0.7 3.4
3 TH ◑	0503 1150 1724	3.6 0.5 3.4	**18** F	0008 0555 1226 1812	0.6 3.3 0.8 3.3
4 F	0002 0543 1226 1811	0.5 3.4 0.7 3.2	**19** SA	0056 0655 1325 1923	0.8 3.1 1.0 3.2
5 SA	0054 0648 1334 1928	0.6 3.3 0.8 3.2	**20** SU	0214 0818 1454 2054	0.9 3.0 1.0 3.3
6 SU	0222 0820 1512 2102	0.7 3.2 0.9 3.4	**21** M	0354 0951 1633 2221	0.9 3.1 1.0 3.4
7 M	0407 1000 1655 2232	0.6 3.3 0.8 3.5	**22** TU	0526 1109 1752 2326	0.7 3.3 0.8 3.6
8 TU	0542 1124 1818 2344	0.4 3.4 0.6 3.7	**23** W	0630 1202 1846	0.5 3.4 0.6
9 W	0656 1230 1922	0.3 3.5 0.4	**24** TH	0012 0712 1241 1928	3.7 0.4 3.5 0.5
10 TH	0041 0754 1322 ● 2013	3.8 0.2 3.5 0.3	**25** F	0048 0749 1316 ○ 2005	3.8 0.3 3.6 0.4
11 F	0130 0843 1408 2057	3.9 0.1 3.6 0.2	**26** SA	0123 0824 1348 2038	3.8 0.3 3.6 0.3
12 SA	0214 0926 1448 2136	3.9 0.2 3.6 0.2	**27** SU	0154 0856 1417 2109	3.8 0.2 3.7 0.3
13 SU	0254 1006 1524 2212	4.0 0.3 3.7 0.3	**28** M	0224 0927 1445 2139	3.8 0.2 3.7 0.2
14 M	0331 1039 1555 2244	4.0 0.4 3.7 0.3	**29** TU	0256 0957 1517 2210	3.8 0.2 3.6 0.2
15 TU	0405 1106 1624 2312	3.8 0.4 3.6 0.4	**30** W	0331 1029 1551 2243	3.7 0.3 3.5 0.2
			31 TH	0410 1100 1628 2316	3.6 0.4 3.5 0.3

APRIL

Date	Time	m	Date	Time	m
1 F	0450 1132 1707 2354	3.5 0.5 3.5 0.4	**16** SA ◐	0527 1154 1738	3.3 0.8 3.4
2 SA ◑	0539 1216 1801	3.3 0.7 3.3	**17** SU	0026 0621 1245 1841	0.7 3.1 0.9 3.3
3 SU	0052 0649 1328 1919	0.5 3.2 0.8 3.3	**18** M	0133 0735 1404 2003	0.8 3.0 1.0 3.3
4 M	0220 0821 1506 2054	0.6 3.2 0.8 3.4	**19** TU	0303 0902 1539 2129	0.8 3.1 0.9 3.4
5 TU	0403 0956 1645 2221	0.5 3.2 0.7 3.6	**20** W	0433 1021 1702 2239	0.6 3.2 0.8 3.5
6 W	0534 1115 1803 2329	0.3 3.3 0.5 3.7	**21** TH	0542 1119 1801 2329	0.5 3.4 0.6 3.7
7 TH	0640 1213 1900	0.2 3.4 0.3	**22** F	0629 1201 1847	0.4 3.5 0.5
8 F	0022 0732 1300 ● 1949	3.8 0.1 3.5 0.2	**23** SA	0009 0708 1238 1927	3.8 0.3 3.6 0.5
9 SA	0109 0818 1343 2032	3.8 0.1 3.6 0.2	**24** SU	0046 0746 1312 ○ 2004	3.8 0.3 3.7 0.4
10 SU	0152 0858 1420 2109	3.9 0.2 3.7 0.2	**25** M	0121 0820 1344 2038	3.9 0.3 3.8 0.3
11 M	0230 0933 1451 2142	3.9 0.3 3.7 0.3	**26** TU	0155 0854 1415 2112	3.9 0.3 3.8 0.3
12 TU	0303 1002 1520 2212	3.9 0.4 3.7 0.3	**27** W	0232 0930 1451 2149	3.8 0.3 3.7 0.2
13 W	0336 1028 1549 2241	3.7 0.4 3.7 0.3	**28** TH	0314 1007 1532 2229	3.7 0.4 3.7 0.2
14 TH	0410 1054 1620 2310	3.6 0.5 3.6 0.4	**29** F	0401 1046 1616 2313	3.6 0.5 3.6 0.3
15 F	0446 1120 1655 2342	3.4 0.7 3.5 0.6	**30** SA	0452 1129 1705	3.5 0.6 3.6

Chart Datum: 1·66 metres below Normal Null (German reference level)

TIME ZONE -0100
(German Standard Time)
Subtract 1 hour for UT
For German Summer Time add ONE hour in **non-shaded areas**

GERMANY – CUXHAVEN

LAT 53°52′N LONG 8°43′E

TIMES AND HEIGHTS OF HIGH AND LOW WATERS

SPRING & NEAP TIDES
Dates in red are SPRINGS
Dates in blue are NEAPS

YEAR **2005**

MAY

Date	Day	Time	m	Time	m	Time	m	Time	m
1	SU	0002	0.4	0549	3.3	1223	0.7	◑ 1805	3.5
2	M	0104	0.4	0658	3.2	1333	0.7	1919	3.5
3	TU	0224	0.4	0821	3.2	1459	0.7	2044	3.5
4	W	0355	0.4	0944	3.2	1627	0.6	2203	3.6
5	TH	0514	0.3	1053	3.3	1736	0.4	2306	3.7
6	F	0613	0.2	1145	3.4	1830	0.3	2356	3.7
7	SA	0700	0.2	1230	3.5	1918	0.3		
8	SU	0043	3.8	0746	0.3	1313	3.6	● 2004	0.3
9	M	0128	3.8	0827	0.3	1350	3.7	2043	0.3
10	TU	0206	3.8	0900	0.4	1421	3.8	2114	0.4
11	W	0239	3.7	0929	0.5	1450	3.8	2145	0.4
12	TH	0312	3.6	0958	0.5	1522	3.8	2218	0.4
13	F	0348	3.5	1027	0.6	1557	3.7	2252	0.5
14	SA	0427	3.4	1059	0.7	1634	3.7	2328	0.6
15	SU	0508	3.3	1135	0.8	1716	3.6		
16	M	0009	0.6	0556	3.2	1219	0.9	◐ 1808	3.5
17	TU	0102	0.7	0655	3.1	1321	0.9	1914	3.4
18	W	0210	0.7	0807	3.1	1439	0.9	2029	3.5
19	TH	0329	0.6	0921	3.3	1558	0.8	2139	3.6
20	F	0439	0.5	1023	3.4	1703	0.7	2236	3.7
21	SA	0535	0.4	1113	3.5	1756	0.6	2323	3.8
22	SU	0622	0.4	1155	3.7	1844	0.6		
23	M	0007	3.9	0705	0.4	1235	3.8	○ 1927	0.5
24	TU	0049	3.9	0745	0.4	1313	3.8	2008	0.4
25	W	0131	3.9	0825	0.4	1352	3.9	2051	0.4
26	TH	0218	3.9	0911	0.4	1436	3.9	2139	0.3
27	F	0310	3.7	0958	0.5	1524	3.8	2228	0.3
28	SA	0403	3.6	1044	0.5	1614	3.8	2318	0.3
29	SU	0457	3.5	1132	0.6	1706	3.8		
30	M	0011	0.4	0555	3.4	1227	0.7	◑ 1805	3.7
31	TU	0111	0.4	0658	3.3	1330	0.7	1911	3.7

JUNE

Date	Day	Time	m	Time	m	Time	m	Time	m
1	W	0218	0.4	0807	3.2	1441	0.6	2023	3.7
2	TH	0331	0.4	0916	3.3	1555	0.6	2134	3.7
3	F	0440	0.4	1019	3.3	1702	0.5	2236	3.7
4	SA	0537	0.3	1112	3.4	1757	0.4	2329	3.7
5	SU	0626	0.4	1159	3.6	1848	0.4		
6	M	0018	3.7	0713	0.5	1244	3.7	● 1938	0.4
7	TU	0105	3.7	0758	0.5	1324	3.8	2020	0.5
8	W	0146	3.7	0834	0.6	1358	3.9	2054	0.5
9	TH	0221	3.7	0906	0.6	1431	3.9	2129	0.5
10	F	0256	3.6	0939	0.6	1505	3.9	2204	0.5
11	SA	0333	3.5	1011	0.6	1541	3.9	2240	0.5
12	SU	0411	3.5	1044	0.7	1617	3.8	2315	0.6
13	M	0450	3.4	1120	0.7	1656	3.7	2353	0.6
14	TU	0532	3.3	1159	0.8	1740	3.6		
15	W	0035	0.6	0619	3.3	1245	0.8	◐ 1830	3.5
16	TH	0123	0.6	0714	3.3	1342	0.8	1930	3.5
17	F	0223	0.7	0816	3.3	1450	0.9	2035	3.6
18	SA	0330	0.6	0920	3.4	1558	0.8	2139	3.7
19	SU	0435	0.6	1019	3.5	1701	0.7	2237	3.8
20	M	0533	0.6	1112	3.7	1800	0.6	2333	3.8
21	TU	0628	0.6	1202	3.8	1856	0.6		
22	W	0026	3.9	0720	0.6	1250	3.9	○ 1949	0.5
23	TH	0119	3.9	0811	0.6	1339	4.0	2042	0.4
24	F	0214	3.9	0904	0.5	1430	4.0	2138	0.4
25	SA	0310	3.8	0957	0.5	1521	4.0	2230	0.3
26	SU	0403	3.6	1045	0.5	1610	4.0	2319	0.3
27	M	0453	3.5	1130	0.5	1659	4.0		
28	TU	0009	0.4	0545	3.5	1218	0.6	◑ 1753	3.9
29	W	0101	0.5	0639	3.4	1311	0.7	1849	3.8
30	TH	0154	0.5	0734	3.4	1408	0.7	1950	3.7

JULY

Date	Day	Time	m	Time	m	Time	m	Time	m
1	F	0251	0.6	0833	3.3	1512	0.7	2055	3.7
2	SA	0353	0.6	0935	3.4	1621	0.6	2202	3.6
3	SU	0457	0.6	1037	3.5	1727	0.6	2305	3.6
4	M	0554	0.6	1133	3.6	1825	0.6		
5	TU	0000	3.6	0647	0.7	1222	3.8	1917	0.6
6	W	0049	3.7	0735	0.7	1305	3.9	● 2002	0.6
7	TH	0132	3.7	0816	0.7	1343	3.9	2042	0.6
8	F	0209	3.7	0852	0.7	1419	4.0	2119	0.6
9	SA	0245	3.7	0926	0.6	1453	4.0	2154	0.6
10	SU	0319	3.6	0958	0.6	1526	3.9	2226	0.5
11	M	0353	3.5	1029	0.6	1559	3.9	2257	0.5
12	TU	0428	3.5	1102	0.6	1635	3.8	2332	0.5
13	W	0506	3.5	1139	0.7	1713	3.7		
14	TH	0008	0.6	0544	3.4	1214	0.7	◐ 1752	3.7
15	F	0042	0.6	0625	3.4	1253	0.8	1836	3.6
16	SA	0124	0.7	0715	3.4	1346	0.9	1934	3.6
17	SU	0223	0.8	0818	3.4	1455	0.9	2044	3.6
18	M	0337	0.8	0928	3.5	1612	0.8	2159	3.6
19	TU	0452	0.8	1036	3.6	1728	0.7	2310	3.7
20	W	0604	0.8	1140	3.8	1839	0.6		
21	TH	0016	3.8	0709	0.7	1238	4.0	○ 1942	0.5
22	F	0115	3.8	0807	0.6	1331	4.0	2040	0.4
23	SA	0212	3.8	0901	0.5	1423	4.1	2135	0.3
24	SU	0305	3.8	0952	0.5	1513	4.2	2226	0.3
25	M	0354	3.7	1037	0.4	1558	4.1	2310	0.3
26	TU	0438	3.6	1117	0.4	1643	4.1	2352	0.4
27	W	0521	3.6	1157	0.6	1728	4.0		
28	TH	0034	0.6	0604	3.5	1240	0.7	◑ 1816	3.9
29	F	0114	0.7	0649	3.5	1326	0.8	1908	3.7
30	SA	0158	0.8	0741	3.4	1421	0.8	2011	3.5
31	SU	0258	0.9	0847	3.4	1535	0.8	2126	3.5

AUGUST

Date	Day	Time	m	Time	m	Time	m	Time	m
1	M	0412	0.9	1002	3.5	1656	0.8	2243	3.5
2	TU	0527	0.9	1112	3.6	1808	0.7	2347	3.5
3	W	0630	0.8	1207	3.8	1903	0.7		
4	TH	0038	3.6	0720	0.8	1251	3.9	1949	0.7
5	F	0119	3.7	0802	0.8	1329	4.0	● 2029	0.6
6	SA	0156	3.7	0839	0.7	1405	4.0	2106	0.6
7	SU	0230	3.7	0913	0.6	1438	4.0	2138	0.5
8	M	0301	3.7	0943	0.6	1507	3.9	2206	0.5
9	TU	0329	3.6	1010	0.5	1536	3.9	2233	0.5
10	W	0400	3.6	1040	0.5	1608	3.8	2305	0.5
11	TH	0435	3.6	1114	0.6	1644	3.8	2338	0.6
12	F	0509	3.5	1145	0.6	1716	3.7		
13	SA	0005	0.6	0541	3.5	1212	0.7	◐ 1752	3.6
14	SU	0036	0.8	0622	3.4	1254	0.8	1846	3.5
15	M	0130	0.9	0726	3.4	1407	0.9	2005	3.4
16	TU	0254	1.0	0850	3.4	1540	0.8	2136	3.5
17	W	0428	1.0	1014	3.6	1713	0.7	2301	3.6
18	TH	0553	0.9	1128	3.8	1833	0.6		
19	F	0013	3.7	0705	0.7	1229	3.9	○ 1939	0.4
20	SA	0111	3.7	0803	0.6	1322	4.0	2033	0.3
21	SU	0203	3.8	0853	0.4	1411	4.1	2123	0.3
22	M	0251	3.7	0938	0.4	1456	4.2	2209	0.3
23	TU	0333	3.8	1019	0.4	1538	4.2	2249	0.4
24	W	0411	3.7	1055	0.4	1618	4.1	2324	0.5
25	TH	0447	3.7	1129	0.5	1658	4.0	2356	0.7
26	F	0522	3.6	1204	0.7	1739	3.8	◑	
27	SA	0028	0.8	0601	3.5	1241	0.8	1826	3.6
28	SU	0105	1.0	0649	3.4	1331	0.9	1927	3.3
29	M	0203	1.1	0759	3.4	1448	1.0	2049	3.3
30	TU	0327	1.2	0925	3.5	1622	1.0	2217	3.3
31	W	0458	1.1	1048	3.6	1749	0.9	2332	3.4

Chart Datum: 1·66 metres below Normal Null (German reference level)

TIME ZONE -0100
(German Standard Time)
Subtract 1 hour for UT
For German Summer Time add ONE hour in **non-shaded areas**

GERMANY – CUXHAVEN

LAT 53°52′N LONG 8°43′E

TIMES AND HEIGHTS OF HIGH AND LOW WATERS

SPRING & NEAP TIDES
Dates in red are SPRINGS
Dates in blue are NEAPS

YEAR **2005**

SEPTEMBER

Date	Time	m	Date	Time	m
1	0612	1.0	16	0547	0.9
	1151	3.8		1118	3.8
TH	1849	0.8	F	1827	0.5
2	0023	3.6	17	0006	3.6
	0704	0.9		0655	0.7
F	1234	3.9	SA	1217	3.9
	1931	0.7		1927	0.4
3	0101	3.7	18	0059	3.6
	0744	0.7		0749	0.5
SA	1309	3.9	SU	1306	4.0
	● 2007	0.6		○ 2018	0.3
4	0134	3.7	19	0146	3.7
	0819	0.6		0835	0.4
SU	1342	3.9	M	1352	4.1
	2042	0.5		2102	0.3
5	0206	3.7	20	0228	3.7
	0852	0.6		0915	0.4
M	1414	3.9	TU	1434	4.1
	2113	0.5		2143	0.4
6	0235	3.7	21	0305	3.8
	0921	0.5		0953	0.5
TU	1441	3.9	W	1513	4.1
	2140	0.5		2219	0.6
7	0301	3.7	22	0338	3.8
	0948	0.5		1028	0.5
W	1508	3.9	TH	1550	4.0
	2206	0.5		2249	0.6
8	0329	3.7	23	0410	3.8
	1015	0.5		1058	0.5
TH	1539	3.8	F	1627	3.8
	2234	0.5		2317	0.7
9	0401	3.6	24	0443	3.7
	1046	0.5		1129	0.6
F	1613	3.8	SA	1705	3.6
	2304	0.6		2345	0.9
10	0433	3.6	25	0519	3.6
	1115	0.6		1203	0.8
SA	1646	3.7	SU	1750	3.4
	2331	0.7		◑	
11	0505	3.5	26	0020	1.0
	1143	0.7		0605	3.4
SU	1724	3.5	M	1250	1.0
	◐			1848	3.2
12	0003	0.8	27	0115	1.2
	0548	3.4		0713	3.4
M	1227	0.8	TU	1404	1.1
	1822	3.3		2008	3.1
13	0101	1.0	28	0239	1.3
	0657	3.4		0841	3.4
TU	1345	0.9	W	1541	1.1
	1948	3.3		2140	3.2
14	0233	1.1	29	0418	1.3
	0829	3.4		1011	3.6
W	1528	0.8	TH	1715	1.0
	2128	3.4		2301	3.4
15	0418	1.0	30	0541	1.1
	1002	3.6		1119	3.7
TH	1708	0.7	F	1821	0.8
	2257	3.5		2356	3.5

OCTOBER

Date	Time	m	Date	Time	m
1	0636	0.9	16	0634	0.6
	1204	3.8		1157	3.9
SA	1902	0.6	SU	1906	0.4
2	0031	3.6	17	0037	3.6
	0714	0.7		0723	0.5
SU	1237	3.8	M	1244	3.9
	1934	0.6		○ 1953	0.4
3	0102	3.7	18	0120	3.7
	0749	0.6		0810	0.4
M	1310	3.8	TU	1329	4.0
	● 2008	0.5		2036	0.4
4	0133	3.7	19	0159	3.8
	0823	0.6		0850	0.5
TU	1342	3.9	W	1410	4.0
	2040	0.5		2113	0.6
5	0202	3.8	20	0233	3.8
	0853	0.6		0926	0.5
W	1411	3.9	TH	1447	4.0
	2109	0.5		2146	0.7
6	0229	3.8	21	0305	3.9
	0922	0.6		0959	0.6
TH	1440	3.9	F	1523	3.9
	2137	0.6		2216	0.7
7	0258	3.7	22	0337	3.8
	0950	0.5		1031	0.6
F	1512	3.8	SA	1600	3.7
	2205	0.6		2244	0.8
8	0330	3.7	23	0410	3.7
	1020	0.5		1102	0.6
SA	1549	3.7	SU	1639	3.5
	2235	0.7		2313	0.9
9	0405	3.6	24	0447	3.6
	1054	0.6		1137	0.8
SU	1629	3.6	M	1722	3.3
	2308	0.8		2349	1.1
10	0444	3.6	25	0531	3.5
	1132	0.7		1222	1.0
M	1715	3.4	TU	1815	3.2
	◐ 2351	1.0		◑	
11	0534	3.5	26	0038	1.2
	1224	0.8		0631	3.4
TU	1819	3.3	W	1325	1.1
				1925	3.1
12	0055	1.1	27	0151	1.3
	0646	3.4		0749	3.4
W	1343	0.8	TH	1449	1.1
	1945	3.2		2048	3.1
13	0227	1.1	28	0322	1.3
	0818	3.5		0915	3.5
TH	1525	0.8	F	1619	1.0
	2122	3.3		2208	3.3
14	0409	1.0	29	0448	1.2
	0949	3.6		1027	3.6
F	1700	0.6	SA	1731	0.8
	2246	3.4		2308	3.5
15	0533	0.8	30	0550	1.0
	1102	3.8		1118	3.7
SA	1812	0.5	SU	1817	0.7
	2348	3.5		2349	3.6
			31	0633	0.8
				1157	3.8
			M	1853	0.6

NOVEMBER

Date	Time	m	Date	Time	m
1	0023	3.7	16	0050	3.7
	0711	0.7		0743	0.6
TU	1232	3.8	W	1306	3.8
	1929	0.6		○ 2007	0.6
2	0056	3.8	17	0130	3.8
	0748	0.7		0826	0.6
W	1306	3.9	TH	1347	3.8
	● 2003	0.6		2044	0.7
3	0128	3.8	18	0205	3.9
	0821	0.7		0902	0.6
TH	1340	3.9	F	1424	3.8
	2036	0.6		2117	0.8
4	0159	3.8	19	0238	3.9
	0855	0.6		0936	0.7
F	1415	3.9	SA	1500	3.7
	2111	0.7		2149	0.8
5	0232	3.8	20	0312	3.9
	0931	0.6		1011	0.7
SA	1455	3.8	SU	1539	3.6
	2146	0.7		2221	0.8
6	0310	3.8	21	0347	3.8
	1008	0.6		1046	0.7
SU	1539	3.7	M	1618	3.5
	2222	0.8		2252	0.9
7	0352	3.7	22	0424	3.7
	1049	0.6		1121	0.8
M	1626	3.5	TU	1659	3.3
	2303	0.9		2327	1.0
8	0438	3.7	23	0505	3.7
	1136	0.7		1201	0.9
TU	1719	3.4	W	1745	3.2
	2352	1.0		◑	
9	0532	3.6	24	0009	1.1
	1232	0.8		0553	3.6
W	1822	3.3	TH	1249	1.0
	◐			1840	3.1
10	0057	1.0	25	0104	1.2
	0641	3.6		0654	3.5
TH	1346	0.8	F	1352	1.0
	1940	3.2		1946	3.1
11	0219	1.0	26	0217	1.2
	0803	3.6		0806	3.5
F	1514	0.7	SA	1507	1.0
	2104	3.3		2058	3.3
12	0348	1.0	27	0336	1.2
	0926	3.7		0918	3.6
SA	1639	0.6	SU	1620	0.9
	2220	3.3		2203	3.4
13	0505	0.8	28	0445	1.1
	1036	3.8		1019	3.7
SU	1746	0.5	M	1718	0.8
	2319	3.4		2255	3.5
14	0604	0.7	29	0540	1.0
	1131	3.8		1108	3.8
M	1837	0.5	TU	1805	0.8
				2338	3.7
15	0006	3.5	30	0627	0.9
	0654	0.6		1151	3.8
TU	1219	3.8	W	1848	0.8
	1923	0.5			

DECEMBER

Date	Time	m	Date	Time	m
1	0017	3.8	16	0107	3.8
	0711	0.8		0806	0.7
TH	1233	3.9	F	1331	3.7
	● 1928	0.8		2023	0.8
2	0055	3.8	17	0144	3.9
	0752	0.7		0845	0.7
F	1315	3.9	SA	1408	3.7
	2009	0.8		2058	0.8
3	0134	3.9	18	0219	3.9
	0835	0.7		0922	0.7
SA	1400	3.9	SU	1445	3.6
	2053	0.8		2133	0.8
4	0217	3.9	19	0255	3.9
	0922	0.6		0959	0.7
SU	1449	3.8	M	1523	3.6
	2140	0.8		2206	0.8
5	0303	3.9	20	0330	3.9
	1009	0.6		1035	0.7
M	1539	3.7	TU	1600	3.5
	2223	0.8		2237	0.8
6	0348	3.9	21	0405	3.8
	1054	0.6		1107	0.7
TU	1628	3.6	W	1637	3.4
	2305	0.8		2309	0.9
7	0435	3.9	22	0441	3.8
	1142	0.6		1140	0.7
W	1720	3.5	TH	1715	3.3
	2353	0.9		2344	0.9
8	0528	3.8	23	0519	3.7
	1236	0.7		1216	0.8
TH	1817	3.4	F	1756	3.3
	◐			◑	
9	0051	0.9	24	0024	1.0
	0629	3.7		0604	3.6
F	1338	0.7	SA	1258	0.9
	1921	3.3		1844	3.2
10	0158	0.9	25	0114	1.1
	0738	3.7		0658	3.5
SA	1447	0.7	SU	1352	1.0
	2030	3.3		1943	3.3
11	0312	0.9	26	0218	1.2
	0851	3.7		0802	3.5
SU	1601	0.7	M	1458	1.0
	2138	3.3		2048	3.4
12	0426	0.8	27	0329	1.2
	1001	3.7		0910	3.6
M	1707	0.7	TU	1608	1.0
	2240	3.4		2152	3.5
13	0531	0.7	28	0438	1.0
	1102	3.7		1014	3.7
TU	1803	0.6	W	1711	0.9
	2334	3.5		2250	3.6
14	0627	0.7	29	0541	0.9
	1157	3.7		1113	3.7
W	1855	0.7	TH	1809	0.9
				2342	3.7
15	0023	3.7	30	0639	0.8
	0719	0.7		1207	3.8
TH	1247	3.7	F	1902	0.9
	○ 1942	0.8			
			31	0031	3.9
				0733	0.7
			SA	1300	3.8
				● 1954	0.8

Chart Datum: 1·66 metres below Normal Null (German reference level)

9.15.12 BRUNSBÜTTEL

Schleswig-Holstein **53°53'·24N 09°07'·78E** ❀❀❀◌◌✿✿

CHARTS AC 2469, 3625; Imray C26; D42; BSH 3010.3/4, 3009.1/2

TIDES +0203 Dover; ML 1·4; Duration 0520; Zone –0100

Standard Port CUXHAVEN (⟷)

Times				**Height (metres)**			
High Water		Low Water		MHWS	MHWN	MLWN	MLWS
0200	0800	0200	0900	3·3	2·9	0·4	0·1
1400	2000	1400	2100				
Differences BRUNSBÜTTEL							
+0057	+0105	+0121	+0112	–0·2	–0·2	–0·1	0·0

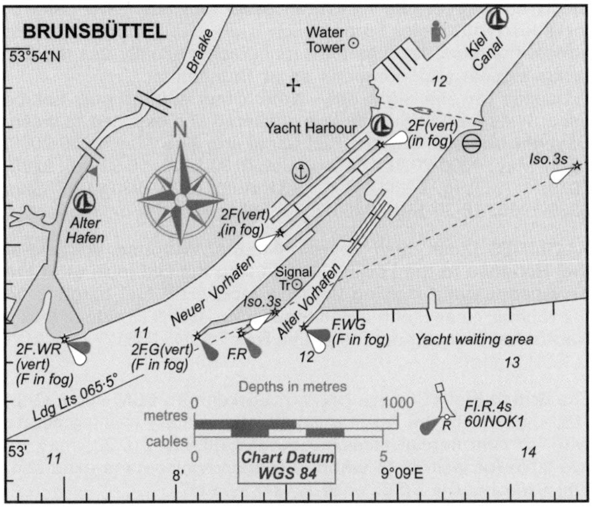
BRUNSBÜTTEL
53°54'N
Braake
Water Tower
Kiel Canal
12
Yacht Harbour
2F(vert) (in fog)
Iso.3s
N
Alter Hafen
2F(vert) (in fog)
Neuer Vorhafen
Signal Tr
Alter Vorhafen
Iso.3s
F.WG (F in fog)
Yacht waiting area
2F.WR (vert) (F in fog)
11
2F.G(vert) (F in fog)
F.R
12
13
Ldg Lts 065·5°
Depths in metres
metres
cables
0
1000
5
Fl.R.4s 60/NOK1
R
53'
11
14
Chart Datum WGS 84
8'
9°09'E

SHELTER Good in the Alter Hafen, a drying yacht hbr, access HW ±3, W of the locks. Waiting posts are close E of FWG ☆ at ent to Alter Vorhafen. Once locked through, good shelter, but noisy, in Kanal-Yachthafen, close NW of the larger Neue locks. An alternative Yacht Hbr is 4 cables upstream, same bank.

NAVIGATION WPT 53°53'·01N 09°08'·14E, 039°/6ca to Alte Schleusen. No navigational dangers in the near apprs, but commercial traffic is heavy. The stream sets strongly across access chan to locks; yachts usually use the smaller SE locks (Alte Schleusen). Lock entry sigs: see 9.15.13; await White signal or loudspeaker.

LIGHTS AND MARKS Lights as chartlet. Ldg lts 065·5° direct large ships from the main fairway to the lock Approach areas.

R/T Request *Kiel Kanal I* on Ch 13 for a locking allocation 15 mins before arrival; see 9.15.13.

Radar cover of the inner Elbe is as follows:

Brunsbüttel Radar I	Ch 62	Buoys 51 - 59;
Brunsbüttel Radar II	Ch 67	Buoys 60 - Elbehafen;
(call if entering locks in dense fog)		
S. Margarethen Radar	Ch 18	Buoys 57a - 65;
Freiburg Radar	Ch 61	Buoys 63 - 77;
Rhinplate Radar	Ch 05	Buoys 75 - 89;
Pagensand Radar	Ch 66	Buoys 87 - 89;
Hetlingen Radar	Ch 21	Buoys 101 - 115;
Wedel Radar	Ch 60	Buoys 113 - 125.

VTS, see 9.15.10. *Brunsbüttel Elbe Traffic* broadcasts weather info every H + 05 on Ch 68 in English and German for the inner Elbe. Monitor Ch 68 all the time when underway.

TELEPHONE (Dial code 04852) HM Yachthaven 4276; ⊜ 83000; Weather 36400; Police 112; Ⓗ 9800; Brit Consul (040) 446071.

FACILITIES **Alter Hafen** ☎ 0160 697 4729, €0.95, Slip, C (20 ton), R, SC; **Kanal-Yachthafen**, €1.00, ⊜, Bar. **Town** P, D (as shown 0800-1800 ☎ 2002), El, ME, ⚒, Gaz, 🛒, R, LB, Ⓗ, Bar, ✉, Ⓑ, ⇌, ✈ (Hamburg).

9.15.13 NORD-OSTSEE KANAL (Kiel Canal) Schleswig-Holstein

CHARTS AC 2469, 696 (Kieler Förde); D42; BSH 3009.1-4

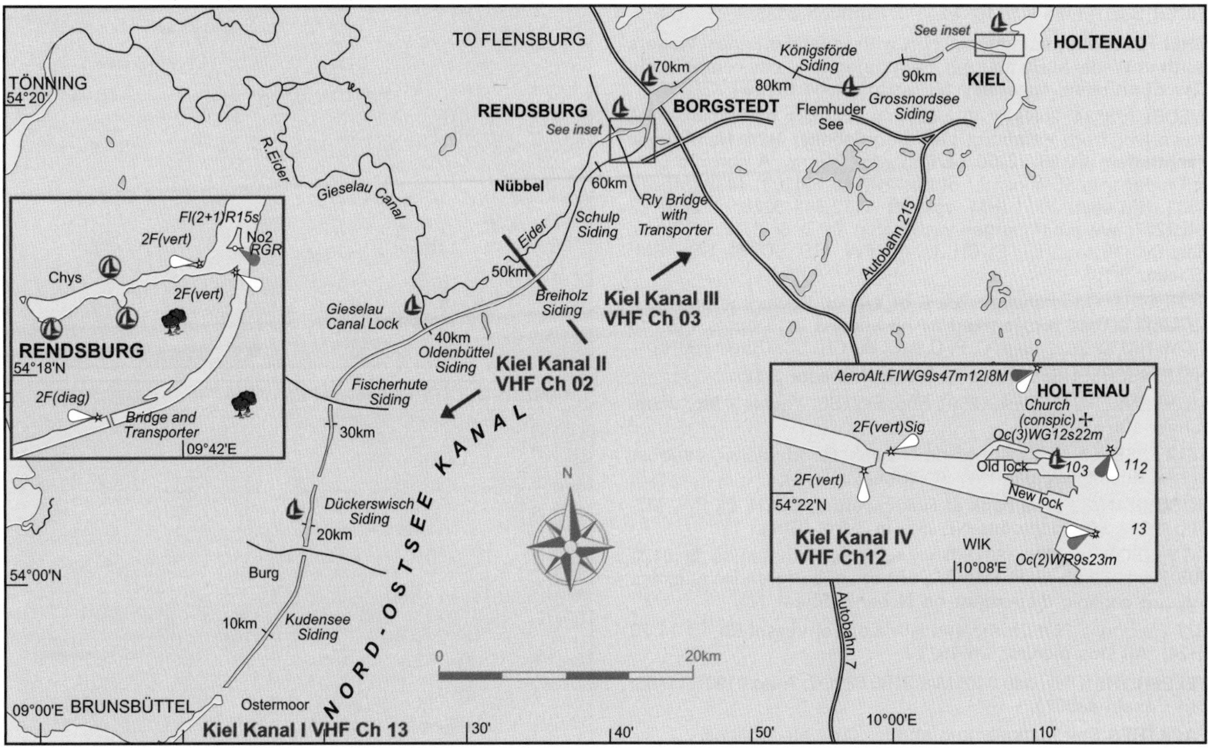
TO FLENSBURG
See inset
HOLTENAU
TÖNNING
54°20'
70km
Königsförde Siding
90km
KIEL
80km
Grossnordsee Siding
RENDSBURG
See inset
BORGSTEDT
Flemhuder See
R.Eider
Gieselau Canal
Nübbel
60km
Rly Bridge with Transporter
Schulp Siding
Eider
Autobahn 215
Fl(2+1)R15s
2F(vert)
No2 RGR
Chys
2F(vert)
RENDSBURG
54°18'N
2F(diag)
Bridge and Transporter
09°42'E
50km
Breiholz Siding
Kiel Kanal III VHF Ch 03
Gieselau Canal Lock
40km
Oldenbüttel Siding
Kiel Kanal II VHF Ch 02
Fischerhute Siding
30km
KANAL
AeroAlt.FlWG9s47m12/8M
HOLTENAU
Church (conspic)
2F(vert)Sig
Oc(3)WG12s22m
Old lock
103
112
2F(vert)
New lock
54°22'N
13
Kiel Kanal IV VHF Ch12
WIK
10°08'E
Oc(2)WR9s23m
N
Dückerswisch Siding
20km
NORD-OSTSEE
54°00'N
Burg
Autobahn 7
10km
Kudensee Siding
0
20km
09°00'E BRUNSBÜTTEL
Ostermoor
Kiel Kanal I VHF Ch 13
30'
40'
50'
10°00'E
10'

SIGNALS Occulting lts are shown from masts at the lock island (for Appr Areas); and on the central wall of each pair of locks:

● = No entry. ○ ● = Prepare to enter.

○ ● = Ships exempt from pilotage enter; secure on central wall.

○ = **Yachts may enter** (berth on pontoons).

In the canal, the only traffic sigs applicable to yachts are:

● Oc = Clear to enter, transit or exit a Siding.

● QR = Entry into a Siding is prohib.

●●● (vert) = Exit from a Siding is prohib.

Fly flag 'N' (no pilot). Sailing is prohib; when motor sailing, yachts must hoist a B ▼, or a B pennant. Customs clearance is not required, but yachts in transit should fly the third substitute of the International Code.

R/T Before entering, yachts should request a lock:
at Brunsbüttel from *Kiel Kanal I* on Ch 13;
or at Holtenau from *Kiel Kanal IV* on Ch 12.
Ports: Ostermoor and Breiholz Ch 73.
In the Canal. Maintain listening watch as follows:
Kiel Kanal I Ch 13 Brunsbüttel ent and locks;
Kiel Kanal II Ch 02 Brunsbüttel to Breiholz;
Kiel Kanal III Ch 03 Breiholz to Holtenau;
Kiel Kanal IV Ch 12 Holtenau ent and locks.
Info broadcasts by *Kiel Kanal II* on Ch 02 at H+15, H+45; and by *Kiel Kanal III* on Ch 03 at H+20, H+50. Vessels should monitor these broadcasts and not call the station if this can be avoided.

NAVIGATION The Canal runs 53·3M (98·7 km) from Brunsbüttel (9.15.12) to Kiel-Holtenau; it is 103-162m wide and 11m deep. A handbook *'Navigation Rules Kiel Canal'* in English/German is worth having or download from www.kiel-canal.org/english. Yachts may only use the Canal and its ents by day and in good visibility; (not applicable to craft going to the Alter or inner Hbrs at Brunsbüttel, or the yacht berths at Holtenau). Speed limit is 8kn. All 8 bridges have 40m clearance.

SHELTER In addition to Brunsbüttel and Holtenau, there are 5 berthing places (sidings or *weichen*) which yachts must arrange to reach during **daylight hours** (see below). These may be at:

1. Brunsbüttel (km 0); see 9.15.12.
2. *Dückerswisch siding (km 20·5); W side in turning area.
3. *Oldenbüttel siding (km 40·5), off lock to Gieselau Canal [links Kiel Canal to R Eider, thence to Tönning (9.15.7)];
4. Rendsburg (ent at km 66). All facilities and 3 marinas in Lake Obereider; the W'most is nearest town centre.
5. The Borgstedter See, entrances at km 67·5 and 70;
6. *Flemhuder See (km 85·4, E of Grossnordsee siding);
7. Kiel-Holtenau (km 98·7): a major port with a Yacht Hbr on the N bank (E of Old locks); all usual facilities. Two pairs of locks lead into Kieler Förde which is practically tideless and at almost the same level as the canal. Yachts usually use the Old locks; signals and pontoons as at Brunsbüttel

* Usually for one night only. Note: Other sidings may not be used. They are likely to be less sheltered and exposed to wash.
Daylight hours (LT) in the Kiel Canal are: 1-15 May, 0230-2000; 16-31 May, 0200-2030; 1 Jun-15 Jul, 0130-2100; 16-31 Jul, 0200-2030; 1-15 Aug, 0230-2000; 16-31 Aug, 0300-1930; 1-15 Sep, 0330-1900; 16-30 Sep, 0400-2030. Other months on request.

FACILITIES Canal dues (approx •44), E or W-bound, are paid at Kiel-Holtenau to the Lockmaster if using the Old lock; or at the newspaper stand if using the New lock. A BP fuel barge is on the N bank, close E of the Holtenau locks. At Wik (S side of locks) **Nautischer Dienst** (Kapt Stegmann & Co) ☎ 0431 331772 are ACA & BSH Agents.

The **British Kiel YC** is 5ca NNW of Stickenhörn ECM buoy, Q (3) 10s, 1M NNE of the locks. It is part of a military training centre with no commercial facilities; but AB (about €10.23) may be available for visitors to whom a friendly welcome is extended. Call *Sailtrain* VHF Ch 67 or ☎ (0431) 397921.

9.15.14 HAMBURG

Schleswig-Holstein **53°32'·52N 09°58'·84E** ✿✿✿◊◊◊✿✿

CHARTS AC 3625, 3267, 3268; D48; BSH 3010.9-12 (see below)

TIDES See R Elbe 9.15.10. ML 1·3; Duration 0435.

SHELTER A busy commercial port with several marinas. Visitors berth at Wedel in Hamburger Yachthafen or at city centre in the City Sporthafen, especially for visitors (see below).

WEDEL (53°34'·28N 09°40'·55E, see chartlet): on N bank, 12M downriver from Hamburg, very good shelter H24; **Hamburger Yachthafen**, €0.95, (2100 berths) with 2 ents. A conspic 50m tall radar tr is at W corner of hbr. HM ☎ (04103) 4438 (office), 5632 (HM east), 7751 (HM west) ☎ 0172 642 3228; ⊖ ☎ 0172 6423227; www.hamburger-yachthafen.de D & P (shut Tues), Bar, BH (16 ton), BY, C, CH, EI, Ⓔ, FW, ME, SC, ⚒, Slip, SM. (Sheets 9/10).

SCHULAU: Good shelter, 7ca E of Wedel. Beware strong tidal streams across ent, marked by FR and FG lts. Depths 1·6m to 0·6m. HM ☎ 2422, Slip, C, P, D, ME, Ⓗ, CH, SC. (Sheets 9/10).

NEUENSCHLEUSE: opposite Wedel. (Sheets 9/10).

MÜHLENBERG: N bank, (250), Slip, FW, SC. Yachts < 9m; 0·6m. (Sheet 10).

TEUFELSBRÜCK: small hbr on N bank. Good shelter, sandbar at ent, dries 0·9m. Bar, FW, SC. (Sheets 10/11).

RÜSCHKANAL: on S bank at Finkenwerder, C, CH, EI, FW, ME, Slip, ⚒; 4 SCs, pontoons NE side in 3·6m. (Sheet 11).

CITY SPORTHAFEN: (80+50) www.city-sporthafen.de ☎ 0170 805 2004, €1.05, D, P, FW, AC; Ent at Lat/Long under title, 4ca beyond conspic monument on N bank (Sheet 12).

R/T *Hamburg Port Traffic* and Hbr Control vessel Ch 13 14 **73** (H24). All stns monitor Ch 16.

TELEPHONE (Dial code 040) Met 3190 8826/7; Auto 0190 116456; Brit Consul 446071.

FACILITIES See marinas/hbrs above. **City**: all facilities.

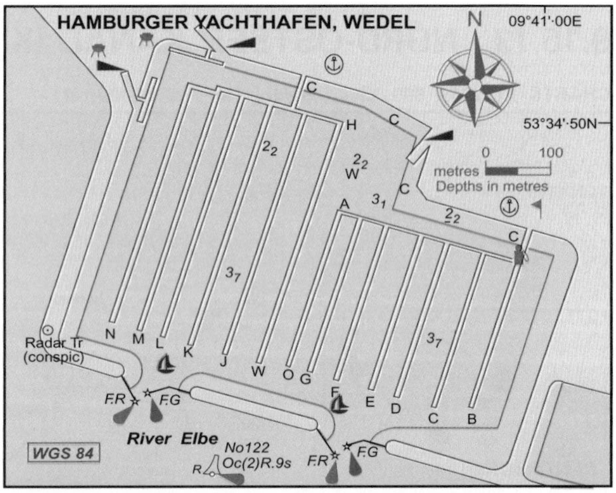
HAMBURGER YACHTHAFEN, WEDEL
N
09°41'·00E
53°34'·50N
metres
0
100
Depths in metres
Radar Tr (conspic)
FR
FG
River Elbe
No122
Oc(2)R.9s
FR
FG
WGS 84

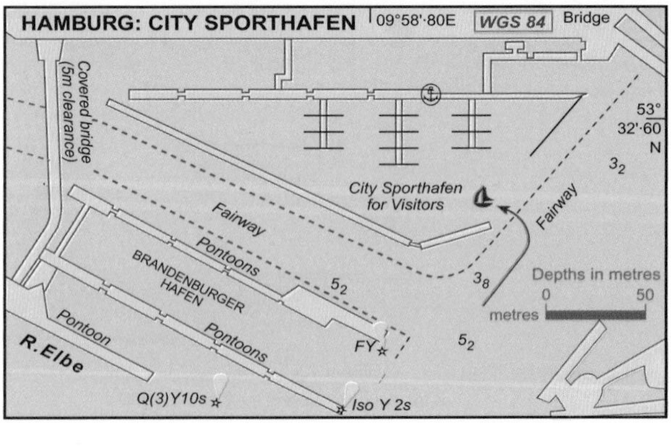
HAMBURG: CITY SPORTHAFEN
09°58'·80E
WGS 84
Bridge
Covered bridge (5m clearance)
53° 32'·60 N
City Sporthafen for Visitors
Fairway
Fairway
Pontoons
BRANDENBURGER HAFEN
Pontoon
Pontoons
R. Elbe
Depths in metres
metres
0
50
FY
Q(3)Y10s
Iso Y 2s

9.15.15 BREMERHAVEN

Federal State of Bremen **53°32'·12N 08°34'·50E**

CHARTS AC 3617, 3621, 3406; Imray C26; D4; BSH 3011.7/8.

TIDES +0051 Dover; ML 2·0; Duration 0600; Zone –0100

Standard Port WILHELMSHAVEN (⟶)

Times				Height (metres)			
High Water		Low Water		MHWS	MHWN	MLWN	MLWS
0200	0800	0200	0900	4·3	3·8	0·6	0·0
1400	2000	1400	2100				
Differences ALTE WESER LT HO (53°51'·8N 08°07'·6E)							
–0055	–0048	–0015	–0029	–1·1	–0·9	–0·2	0·0
BREMERHAVEN							
+0029	+0046	+0033	+0038	–0·2	–0·1	–0·2	0·0
NORDENHAM							
+0051	+0109	+0055	+0058	–0·2	–0·1	–0·4	–0·2
BRAKE							
+0120	+0119	+0143	+0155	–0·3	–0·2	–0·4	–0·2
ELSFLETH							
+0137	+0137	+0206	+0216	–0·2	–0·1	–0·3	0·0
VEGESACK							
+0208	+0204	+0250	+0254	–0·2	–0·2	–0·5	–0·2
BREMEN							
+0216	+0211	+0311	+0314	–0·1	–0·1	–0·6	–0·3

SHELTER i. Berth in R Geeste, short stay only as it is noisy and exposed to swell/wash, either downstream of Kennedy fixed bridge (clearance 5·5m) on pontoons; or, if able to transit the bridge (flood barrage is normally open), berth on quay upstream.
ii. Preferred option: Lock into the non-tidal Fischereihafen II via the smaller W lock (*Kleine Kammer;* opens hourly, H24) which has alongside pontoons. Call VHF Ch 69; enter on ● ● ○ (vert).
The 3 YC/marinas are:
iii. The Weser YC marina in Hauptkanal (E of Handelshafen); excellent shelter, central location and close to the lock.
iv. Nordsee YC marina (NYC or Bremerhaven Marina), 1·3M S of locks on W side (3m).
v. WVW Wulstorf Marina, 0·5M further south in Luneorthafen, W of conspic silo.
Up the R Weser are yacht hbrs at Nordenham, Rodenkirchen, Rechtenfleth, Sandstedt (all dry; access approx HW±2) and Brake; and at Elsfleth and Oldenburg on the R Hunte.

NAVIGATION WPT 53°32'·25N 08°33'·94E [SHM buoy 61, QG], 111°/650m to cross into the Vorhafen. Beware much commercial shipping; also ferries using R Geeste. The Geeste and Hadelner Kanals (1·5m depth; air draft 2·7m) link Bremerhaven to Otterndorf (32M). For R Weser (very well marked) see 9.15.5.

LIGHTS AND MARKS See lower chartlet and 9.15.4. Ldg lts lead 151° up main fairway (R Weser). Vorhafen ent is close SW of conspic 112m radio twr.

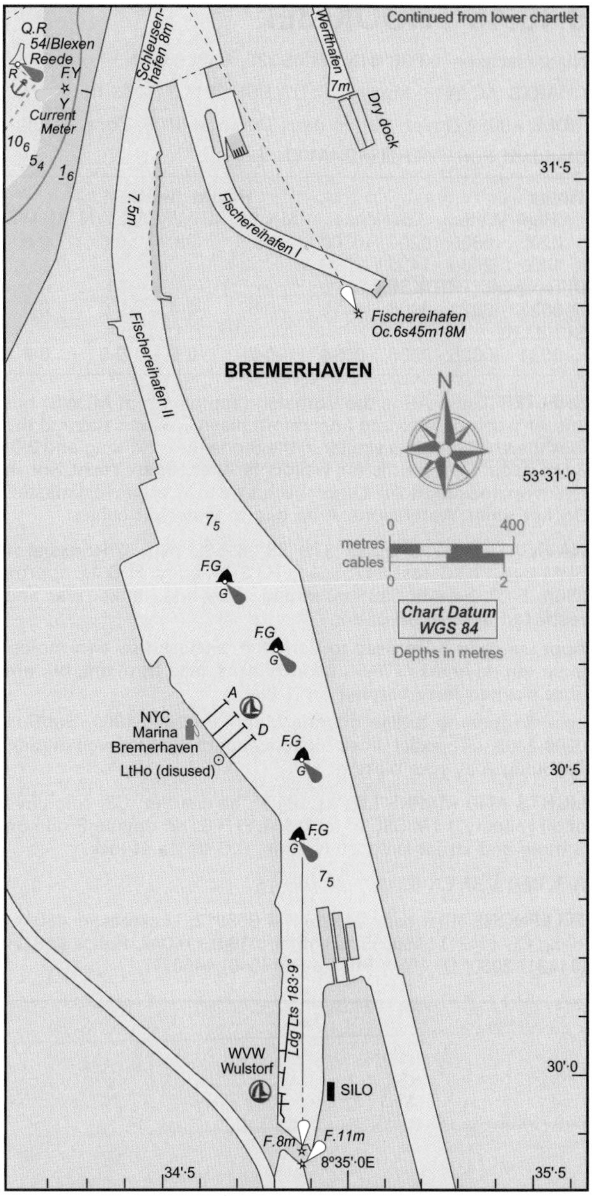
Continued from lower chartlet
Q.R
54/Blexen
Reede
F.Y
Y
Current
Meter
Schleusen-
hafen 8m
Werfthafen
7m
Dry dock
7.5m
Fischereihafen I
Fischereihafen
Oc.6s45m18M
Fischereihafen II
BREMERHAVEN
N
F.G
G
A
D
NYC
Marina
Bremerhaven
LtHo (disused)
Ldg Lts 183·9°
WVW
Wulstorf
SILO
F.8m
F.11m
8°35'·0E
34'·5
35'·5
31'·5
53°31'·0
30'·5
30'·0
metres
cables
Chart Datum
WGS 84
Depths in metres

R/T Bremerhaven Port Ch 12 (H24); Fischereihafen lock Ch **69** (H24). Weser VTS, see diagram overleaf with radar coverage. Up-river *Bremen-Weser Traffic* broadcasts at H+30 on Ch 19 78 81. *Bremen Port Radio* Ch 03 16 (H24). *Hunte Traffic* broadcasts at H+30 on Ch 63.

TELEPHONE (Dial code 0471) HM 59613401; Fischereihafen lock 59613440; Weather 72220; Police 94667; Ⓗ 2991; Brit Consul (040) 4480320.

FACILITIES About €1.00. **Weser YC** ☎ 23531 C, R, Bar; **NYC marina** ☎ 77555 P, D, C, Slip; **WVW marina** ☎ 73268, FW, Slip, C, El; At Boot Bremerhaven (W bank of Fischereihafen II) BY, SM, ME. **City** all facilities: ACA, Gaz, ⇌, ✈.

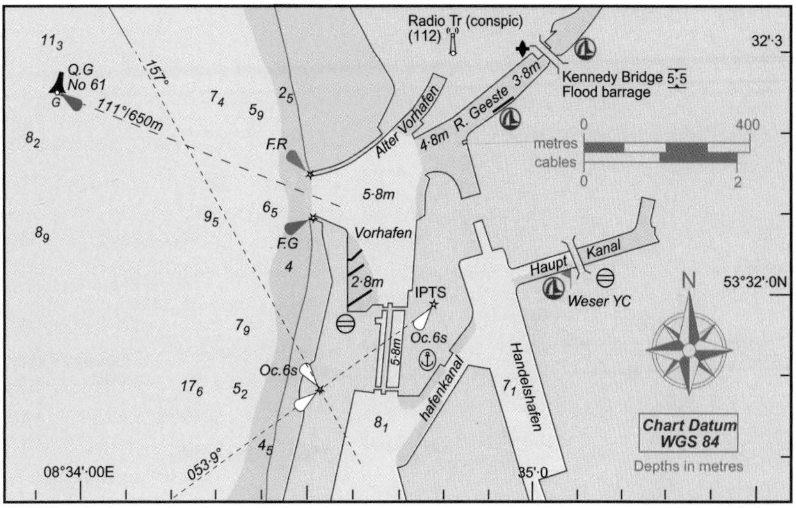
Radio Tr (conspic)
(112)
Kennedy Bridge 5·5
Flood barrage
R. Geeste 3·8m
4·8m
Alter Vorhafen
Q.G
No 61
157°
111°/650m
F.R
5·8m
Vorhafen
F.G
2·8m
IPTS
Oc.6s
Haupt
Kanal
Weser YC
Handelshafen
hafenkanal
053·9°
08°34'·00E
35'·0
32'·3
53°32'·0N
N
metres
cables
Chart Datum
WGS 84
Depths in metres

9.15.16 HOOKSIEL

Niedersachsen **53°38'·81N 08°05'32E**

CHARTS AC 3618; Imray C26; D7; BSH 3011.3, 3015.10

TIDES +0034 Dover; ML no data; Duration 0605; Zone –0100

Standard Port WILHELMSHAVEN (⟶)

Times				**Height (metres)**			
High Water		Low Water		MHWS	MHWN	MLWN	MLWS
0200	0800	0200	0900	4·3	3·8	0·6	0·0
1400	2000	1400	2100				
Differences HOOKSIEL							
–0023	–0022	–0008	–0012	–0·5	–0·4	0·0	0·0
SCHILLIG							
–0031	–0025	–0006	–0014	–0·7	–0·6	0·0	0·0

SHELTER Temp AB in the Vorhafen (approx 1m at MLWS) but it is very commercial and uncomfortable in E winds. Beyond the lock there is complete shelter in the Binnentief, 2M long and 2·0-3·5m deep. Best berths for visitors is Alter Hafen Yacht Hbr in the town; max draft 2m. Larger yachts go to YCs; see lockmaster. Do not enter Watersports Area due to water-ski cables.

NAVIGATION WPT 53°39'·37N 08°06'·58E [No 37/Hooksiel 1 SHM buoy, IQ G 13s], 217°/9ca to H3 SHM buoy, Fl G 4s, approx 350m E of the ent. Caution: strong cross tide, tanker pier and restricted area to SE of ent.

Appr via chan 2·1m deep to Vorhafen, enclosed by two moles. Inner ldg daymarks 276·5°, two RW bcns, lead thru' ent, but are obsc'd when ferry berthed on N pier.

Lock & opening bridge operate Mon - Fri 0800-1900, Sat/Sun 0900-2000 (LT); exact times on noticeboard. Secure well in lock. Dredging may take place at LW.

LIGHTS AND MARKS Ldg lts 164·5°, as chartlet. Conspic chys of oil refinery 1·7M SSE of lock. ☆ L Fl R 6s on dayglo R pile on S mole and street lamp on N mole. R/G tfc lts at lock.

R/T Port VHF Ch 63.

TELEPHONE (Dial code 04425) HM 958012; Lockmaster 430; ⊖ 1302; CG (0421) 5550555; Weather (0190) 116047; Police 269; Ⓗ (04421) 2080; Dr 1080; Brit Consul (040) 446071.

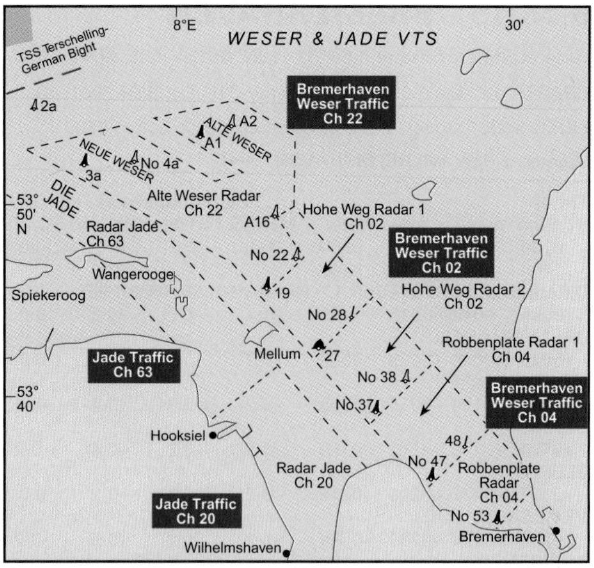
WESER & JADE VTS
8°E
30'
TSS Terschelling-German Bight
Bremerhaven Weser Traffic Ch 22
ALTE WESER
NEUE WESER
DIE JADE
Alte Weser Radar Ch 22
Hohe Weg Radar 1 Ch 02
Radar Jade Ch 63
Bremerhaven Weser Traffic Ch 02
Wangerooge
Spiekeroog
Hohe Weg Radar 2 Ch 02
Mellum
Robbenplate Radar 1 Ch 04
Jade Traffic Ch 63
Bremerhaven Weser Traffic Ch 04
Hooksiel
Radar Jade Ch 20
Robbenplate Radar Ch 04
Jade Traffic Ch 20
Wilhelmshaven
Bremerhaven
53° 50' N
53° 40'

Fig. 9.15.16A. Weser and Jade VTS

FACILITIES Werft BY ☎ 95850, BH (25 ton), Slip. **Wilhelmshaven YC** ☎ 04421 22983, Bar; with ⓥ berths (50) AB, €4.60 (@ €0.51/m LOA). **Alter Hafen** ⓥ berths. **Town** SM, ME, El, CH, P, D, Gaz, R, Bar, Ⓑ, ✉, ⇌, ✈ (Wilhelmshaven & Bremen).

JADE VTS. *Jade Traffic* broadcasts info in German on request and every H+10, Ch 20 63. Radar coverage is as follows:

Jade Radar I	Ch 63	Buoys 1 - 33;
Jade Radar II	Ch 20	Buoys 33 - 58.

WESER VTS. *Bremerhaven Weser Traffic* broadcasts info in German (English on request) at H+20 on all the chans below. Radar cover in the lower Weser is as Fig. 9.15.16A and below:

Alte Weser Radar	Ch 22	Neue Weser: buoys 3a -19H;
ditto	ditto	Alte Weser: buoys A1 - 16a;
Hohe Weg Radar 1 & 2	Ch 02	Buoys 16 - 37;
Robbenplate Rdr I & II	Ch 04	Buoys 38 - 53;
Blexen Radar	Ch 07	Buoys 53 - 63;

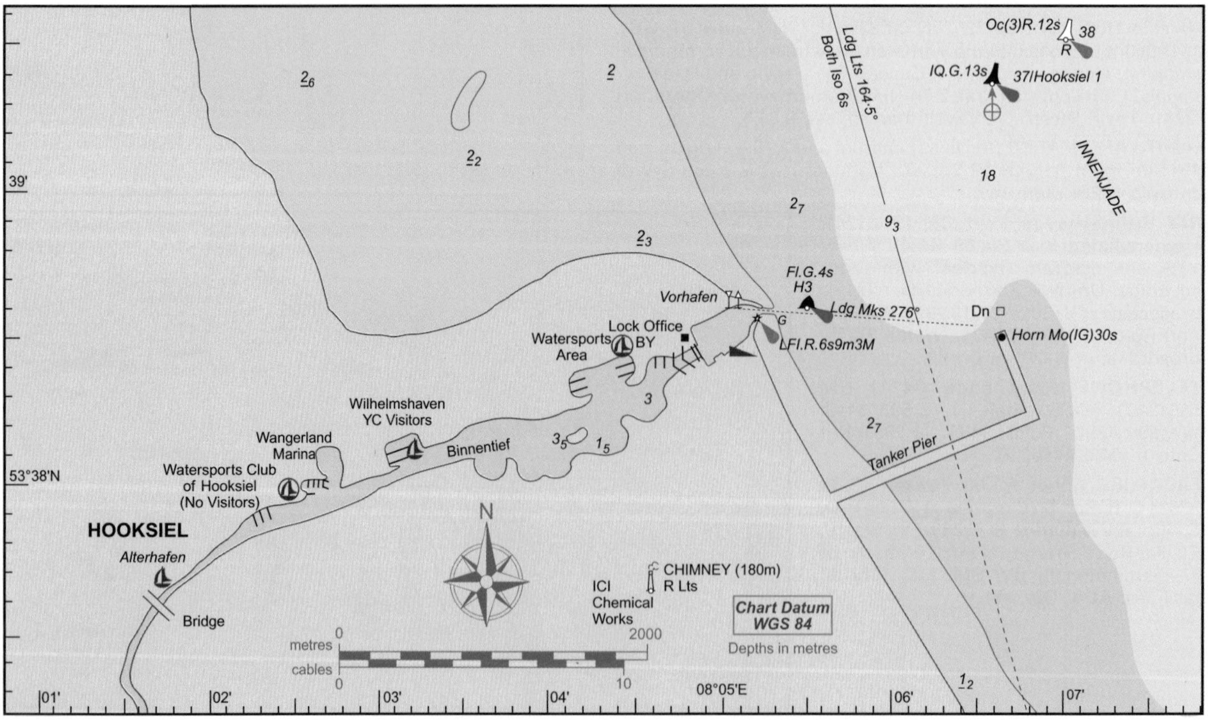
Ldg Lts 164·5° Both Iso 6s
Oc(3)R.12s
38
IQ.G.13s
37/Hooksiel 1
INNENJADE
39'
Fl.G.4s H3
Vorhafen
Ldg Mks 276°
Dn
Lock Office
Watersports Area
BY
Fl.R.6s9m3M
Horn Mo(IG)30s
Wilhelmshaven YC Visitors
Binnentief
Tanker Pier
Wangerland Marina
Watersports Club of Hooksiel (No Visitors)
53°38'N
HOOKSIEL
Alterhafen
Bridge
CHIMNEY (180m) R Lts
ICI Chemical Works
Chart Datum WGS 84
Depths in metres
metres
cables
01'
02'
03'
04'
08°05'E
06'
07'

9.15.17 WILHELMSHAVEN

Niedersachsen **53°30'·80N 08°09'·17E** ❁❁❁◊◊◊✿✿

CHARTS AC 3617, 3618; Imray C26; D7; BSH 3011.3/4, 3015.10-12

TIDES +0050 Dover; ML 2·3; Duration 0615; Zone –0100
WILHELMSHAVEN is a Standard Port. (⟶).

SHELTER Good in yacht hbrs at Nordhafen (rather remote) and Großer Hafen. Access via sea lock opens Mon-Thu: 0600-1830; Fri: 0600-1700; Sat, Sun, Hols: 0800-1600 (all LT). No yacht berths in Neuer Vorhafen (naval port). Nassauhafen in the tidal hbr (*Fluthafen*) has yacht pontoons in about 1·7m, access H24.

NAVIGATION WPT 'A' 53°35'·71N 08°09'·98E [No 45 SHM buoy, QG], 175°/4.4M to WPT 'B' 53°31'·34N 08°10'·57E whence the Fluthafen ent bears 235°/9ca. The fairway is deep, wide and well marked. Note: The Ems-Jade canal, 39M from Großer Hafen to Emden, can be used by de-masted yachts; max draft 1·7m, min air clearance 3·75m. It has 6 locks. Speed limit 4kn.

LIGHTS AND MARKS Principal lts on R Jade, see 9.15.4. Other lts on chartlet.

R/T Port Ch 11 16 (H24). Sea lock Ch 13. Bridge opening Ch 11. See 9.15.16 for VTS, broadcast info and radar assistance.

TELEPHONE (Dial code 04421) HM 154580; Naval base/Port Captain 684923 (operator); Sea Lock 186480; VTS 4891281; ⊖ 480723; Weather Bremerhaven 72220; Water Police 942358; Ⓗ 8011; Brit Consul (040) 446071.

FACILITIES **Nassauhafen Marina** (28 + 100 ⓥ) ☎ 41439, €6.14, P, D, BY, Slip, ME, Bar, FW, SM, R; **Wiking Sportsboothafen** (30) ☎ 41301, Bar, CH, El, Gaz, ME, R, SM, 🛒, ✗; **Hochsee YC Germania** ☎ 44121. There are 16 YCs in the area. **City** BY, SM, ME, CH, El, P, D, Gaz, 🛒, ✉, Ⓑ, ⇌, ✈. Ferry: Hamburg-Harwich.

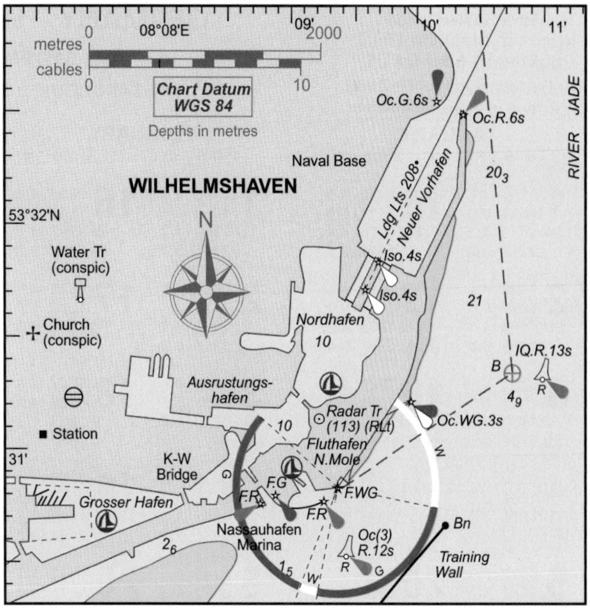
08°08'E
09'
10'
11'
2000
metres
cables
0
10
Chart Datum
WGS 84
Depths in metres
WILHELMSHAVEN
Naval Base
Oc.G.6s
Oc.R.6s
Ldg Lts 208°
Neuer Vorhafen
RIVER JADE
53°32'N
Water Tr (conspic)
Church (conspic)
Iso.4s
Iso.4s
Nordhafen
Ausrustungs-hafen
Radar Tr (113) (RLt)
Fluthafen N.Mole
IQ.R.13s
Oc.WG.3s
Station
K-W Bridge
Grosser Hafen
Nassauhafen Marina
F.G
F.R
F.WG
F.R
Oc(3) R.12s
Bn
Training Wall
31'

RÜSTERSIEL, Niedersachsen, **53°33'·69N 08°09'·29E**. AC 3618; BSH 3015.12. Tides approx as Wilhelmshaven, 3M to the S. From No 47 SHM buoy, IQ G 13s; 217°/8ca to Maadesiel, close N of NWO oil pier and tanks. A conspic power station chy (275m) is 4ca N of ent. The outer hbr dries; access HW±2 via entry gate. The small marina (3m) is 8ca up the Maade river; or continue 1M, via opening bridge (0700-1700 Mon-Fri), to berth on N quay at Rüstersiel.

DANGAST, Niedersachsen, **53°26'·81N 08°06'·51E**. AC 3618; BSH 3015.13. HW +0055 on Dover (UT). 4M S of Wilhelmshaven, drying hbr in the wide Jadebusen bay, which mostly dries. Appr via Stenkentief, marked on NW side by stakes, thence SW into Dangaster Aussentief (0·5m at LWS). Unlit, other than Arngast lt, F WRG (not visible from SW), R tr, W bands, in the middle of Jadebusen. Yacht hbr (0·6m) on W side just before lock into Dangaster Tief, access HW ±2. Facilities: usual amenities in the seaside town of Dangast.

ADJACENT HARBOURS ON THE RIVER JADE

WANGERSIEL, Niedersachsen, **53°41'·05N 08°01'·52E**. AC 3618; BSH 3015.10. HW –0100 on Dover (UT); use differences SCHILLIG 9.15.16; ML 3·3m. From PHM lt buoy W2, 53°41'·44N 08°03'·10E, SHM perches mark the N side of the access chan. Best water 10 to 20m from perches. Depth at ent, 1·3m. Chan keeps shifting especially at E end. Boats drawing 1·5m can cross the bar HW ±2½. Berth on N quay. YC and FW are in the NW corner. HM ☎ 238. Facilities: 🛒, R, Bar at Horumersiel (¼M).

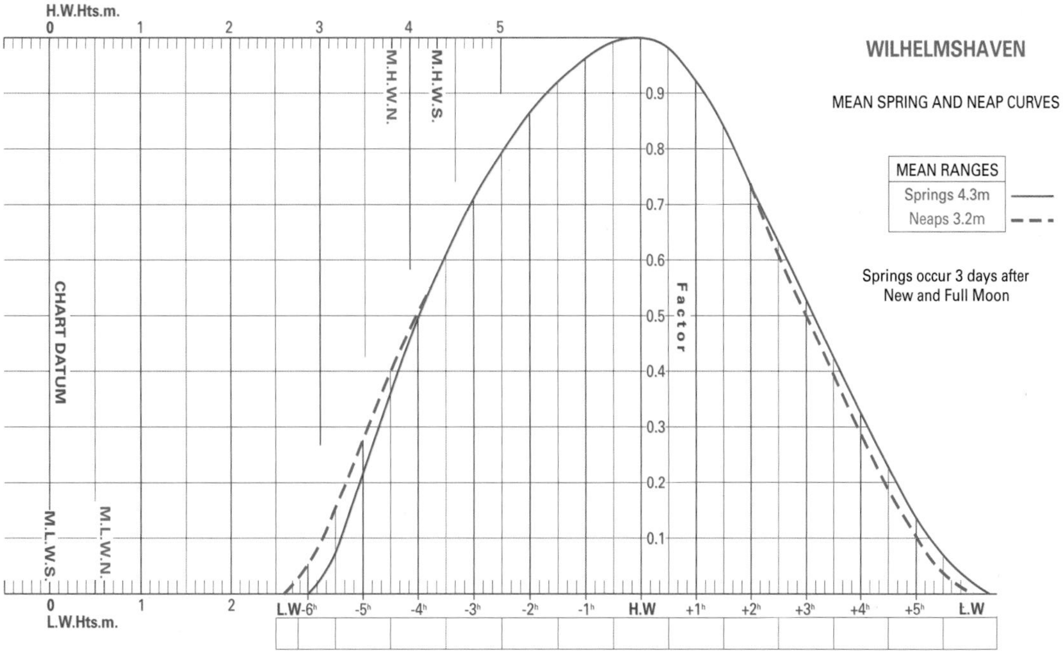
H.W.Hts.m.
0 1 2 3 4 5
M.H.W.N.
M.H.W.S.
WILHELMSHAVEN
MEAN SPRING AND NEAP CURVES
MEAN RANGES
Springs 4.3m
Neaps 3.2m
Springs occur 3 days after New and Full Moon
CHART DATUM
Factor
0.9
0.8
0.7
0.6
0.5
0.4
0.3
0.2
0.1
M.L.W.S.
M.L.W.N.
0 1 2
L.W.Hts.m.
L.W-6h -5h -4h -3h -2h -1h H.W +1h +2h +3h +4h +5h L.W

TIME ZONE -0100
(German Standard Time)
Subtract 1 hour for UT
For German Summer Time add ONE hour in **non-shaded areas**

GERMANY – WILHELMSHAVEN

LAT 53°31′N LONG 8°09′E

TIMES AND HEIGHTS OF HIGH AND LOW WATERS

SPRING & NEAP TIDES
Dates in **red** are **SPRINGS**
Dates in **blue** are **NEAPS**

YEAR **2005**

JANUARY

Date	Day	Time	m	Time	m	Time	m	Time	m
1	SA	0351	4.7	1011	0.7	1620	4.3	2218	0.8
2	SU	0428	4.6	1047	0.7	1659	4.2	2255	0.9
3	M	0507	4.6	1123	0.7	1739	4.2	◑ 2334	0.9
4	TU	0550	4.5	1204	0.8	1826	4.1		
5	W	0023	1.1	0642	4.5	1259	1.0	1925	4.2
6	TH	0126	1.2	0748	4.5	1407	1.0	2034	4.3
7	F	0240	1.1	0902	4.5	1520	1.0	2145	4.4
8	SA	0356	1.0	1016	4.6	1633	0.9	2251	4.5
9	SU	0508	0.8	1125	4.6	1742	0.8	2351	4.7
10	M	0614	0.7	1228	4.7	1843	0.7	●	
11	TU	0047	4.8	0712	0.5	1326	4.7	1938	0.7
12	W	0140	4.9	0807	0.4	1423	4.6	2032	0.6
13	TH	0233	5.0	0903	0.4	1518	4.6	2121	0.6
14	F	0324	5.0	0954	0.4	1606	4.5	2203	0.5
15	SA	0409	5.0	1037	0.4	1647	4.4	2239	0.6
16	SU	0452	4.9	1117	0.5	1726	4.4	2317	0.7
17	M	0535	4.8	1156	0.7	1806	4.3	◐ 2357	0.8
18	TU	0620	4.7	1236	0.8	1850	4.2		
19	W	0044	0.9	0714	4.5	1325	1.0	1946	4.1
20	TH	0148	1.0	0821	4.3	1430	1.1	2056	4.2
21	F	0306	1.1	0937	4.3	1545	1.2	2209	4.3
22	SA	0425	1.0	1048	4.3	1654	1.1	2312	4.5
23	SU	0531	0.9	1145	4.4	1752	1.0		
24	M	0003	4.6	0624	0.9	1231	4.5	1840	0.9
25	TU	0046	4.7	0707	0.8	1312	4.5	○ 1920	0.8
26	W	0124	4.8	0746	0.7	1350	4.5	1957	0.7
27	TH	0201	4.8	0822	0.6	1425	4.5	2032	0.6
28	F	0234	4.8	0856	0.6	1457	4.5	2102	0.6
29	SA	0305	4.8	0925	0.5	1529	4.5	2130	0.5
30	SU	0337	4.7	0954	0.5	1603	4.4	2201	0.5
31	M	0411	4.7	1027	0.5	1638	4.4	2235	0.6

FEBRUARY

Date	Day	Time	m	Time	m	Time	m	Time	m
1	TU	0445	4.6	1059	0.5	1709	4.3	2305	0.7
2	W	0517	4.6	1126	0.6	1741	4.2	◑ 2336	0.8
3	TH	0556	4.4	1203	0.8	1829	4.2		
4	F	0028	1.0	0658	4.3	1307	1.0	1940	4.2
5	SA	0147	1.0	0822	4.3	1433	1.1	2106	4.3
6	SU	0319	0.9	0953	4.4	1605	1.0	2228	4.5
7	M	0448	0.7	1116	4.5	1728	0.9	2339	4.7
8	TU	0605	0.6	1226	4.6	1837	0.7	●	
9	W	0041	4.8	0707	0.4	1325	4.6	1933	0.5
10	TH	0135	4.9	0801	0.3	1418	4.6	2021	0.4
11	F	0225	5.0	0852	0.2	1505	4.5	2107	0.4
12	SA	0311	5.0	0939	0.3	1547	4.5	2146	0.4
13	SU	0352	5.0	1017	0.3	1622	4.5	2218	0.4
14	M	0429	4.9	1049	0.4	1653	4.5	2249	0.5
15	TU	0504	4.8	1118	0.6	1723	4.4	2319	0.6
16	W	0539	4.6	1146	0.8	1757	4.3	◐ 2354	0.8
17	TH	0622	4.3	1223	1.0	1845	4.1		
18	F	0047	1.0	0726	4.1	1325	1.2	1957	4.1
19	SA	0208	1.1	0849	4.1	1450	1.3	2124	4.2
20	SU	0342	1.1	1015	4.1	1618	1.2	2243	4.4
21	M	0504	0.9	1124	4.3	1728	1.0	2344	4.6
22	TU	0604	0.8	1215	4.4	1820	0.9		
23	W	0029	4.7	0649	0.7	1256	4.5	1903	0.7
24	TH	0107	4.7	0727	0.5	1335	4.5	○ 1940	0.6
25	F	0143	4.8	0802	0.4	1408	4.5	2014	0.5
26	SA	0216	4.8	0834	0.3	1438	4.6	2044	0.4
27	SU	0246	4.8	0903	0.3	1508	4.5	2112	0.3
28	M	0317	4.7	0932	0.3	1539	4.5	2141	0.3

MARCH

Date	Day	Time	m	Time	m	Time	m	Time	m
1	TU	0350	4.7	1003	0.3	1612	4.4	2212	0.4
2	W	0422	4.7	1032	0.4	1640	4.4	2239	0.4
3	TH	0452	4.5	1056	0.5	1709	4.3	◑ 2306	0.6
4	F	0530	4.4	1129	0.7	1755	4.2	2355	0.8
5	SA	0634	4.2	1234	1.0	1911	4.1		
6	SU	0120	0.9	0806	4.1	1411	1.1	2047	4.3
7	M	0304	0.8	0947	4.2	1553	1.0	2218	4.4
8	TU	0440	0.6	1114	4.3	1720	0.8	2332	4.6
9	W	0557	0.4	1222	4.4	1827	0.6		
10	TH	0033	4.8	0657	0.2	1317	4.5	● 1919	0.4
11	F	0125	4.9	0748	0.1	1404	4.5	2004	0.2
12	SA	0211	4.9	0833	0.2	1444	4.6	2044	0.2
13	SU	0252	5.0	0913	0.2	1519	4.6	2120	0.3
14	M	0328	5.0	0946	0.3	1549	4.6	2151	0.3
15	TU	0401	4.8	1013	0.4	1616	4.6	2218	0.4
16	W	0433	4.6	1037	0.5	1643	4.5	2244	0.5
17	TH	0504	4.4	1101	0.7	1713	4.3	◐ 2314	0.7
18	F	0542	4.2	1133	0.9	1756	4.2		
19	SA	0000	0.9	0640	4.0	1230	1.1	1906	4.1
20	SU	0116	1.1	0802	3.9	1357	1.3	2037	4.1
21	M	0255	1.1	0935	4.0	1534	1.2	2206	4.3
22	TU	0427	0.9	1054	4.2	1654	1.0	2314	4.5
23	W	0532	0.6	1149	4.3	1750	0.8		
24	TH	0001	4.6	0618	0.5	1231	4.5	1834	0.6
25	F	0040	4.7	0656	0.4	1309	4.6	○ 1912	0.5
26	SA	0116	4.7	0732	0.3	1343	4.6	1947	0.4
27	SU	0149	4.8	0805	0.2	1412	4.6	2019	0.3
28	M	0221	4.8	0836	0.2	1441	4.6	2048	0.2
29	TU	0253	4.8	0906	0.2	1512	4.5	2117	0.2
30	W	0327	4.7	0936	0.3	1545	4.5	2149	0.2
31	TH	0404	4.6	1008	0.4	1618	4.5	2221	0.3

APRIL

Date	Day	Time	m	Time	m	Time	m	Time	m
1	F	0441	4.5	1040	0.6	1655	4.4	2257	0.5
2	SA	0528	4.3	1121	0.7	1748	4.3	◑ 2353	0.6
3	SU	0637	4.1	1230	0.9	1907	4.2		
4	M	0119	0.7	0809	4.1	1406	1.0	2042	4.3
5	TU	0302	0.6	0947	4.1	1545	0.9	2212	4.5
6	W	0433	0.4	1108	4.3	1704	0.6	2322	4.6
7	TH	0541	0.2	1208	4.3	1804	0.4		
8	F	0017	4.8	0636	0.1	1257	4.4	● 1855	0.3
9	SA	0107	4.8	0724	0.1	1340	4.5	1939	0.2
10	SU	0151	4.9	0805	0.2	1416	4.6	2017	0.2
11	M	0228	4.9	0840	0.3	1447	4.7	2051	0.3
12	TU	0300	4.8	0910	0.4	1514	4.7	2120	0.3
13	W	0332	4.7	0935	0.4	1541	4.6	2147	0.3
14	TH	0404	4.5	1001	0.5	1610	4.5	2216	0.4
15	F	0437	4.3	1028	0.7	1642	4.4	2249	0.6
16	SA	0515	4.1	1102	0.9	1724	4.3	◐ 2332	0.8
17	SU	0606	4.0	1152	1.1	1826	4.2		
18	M	0037	0.9	0719	3.9	1309	1.2	1949	4.2
19	TU	0206	0.9	0846	3.9	1442	1.1	2116	4.3
20	W	0336	0.8	1008	4.1	1605	0.9	2228	4.4
21	TH	0445	0.6	1109	4.3	1706	0.7	2320	4.6
22	F	0535	0.4	1154	4.5	1753	0.6		
23	SA	0002	4.7	0617	0.4	1233	4.6	1836	0.5
24	SU	0040	4.8	0656	0.3	1308	4.6	○ 1914	0.4
25	M	0117	4.8	0731	0.2	1340	4.7	1948	0.3
26	TU	0152	4.8	0805	0.2	1412	4.7	2022	0.3
27	W	0230	4.8	0840	0.3	1447	4.7	2057	0.2
28	TH	0311	4.7	0916	0.4	1527	4.6	2135	0.2
29	F	0356	4.5	0954	0.5	1609	4.6	2217	0.3
30	SA	0445	4.4	1037	0.6	1657	4.5	2305	0.4

Chart Datum: 2·26 metres below Normal Null (German reference level)

TIME ZONE -0100
(German Standard Time)
Subtract 1 hour for UT
For German Summer Time add ONE hour in **non-shaded areas**

GERMANY – WILHELMSHAVEN

LAT 53°31'N LONG 8°09'E

TIMES AND HEIGHTS OF HIGH AND LOW WATERS

SPRING & NEAP TIDES
Dates in red are **SPRINGS**
Dates in blue are **NEAPS**

YEAR **2005**

15

MAY

Day	Time	m	Time	m	Time	m	Time	m
1 SU ◑	0540	4.2	1129	0.8	1755	4.4		
2 M	0007	0.5	0648	4.1	1236	0.8	1910	4.4
3 TU	0126	0.5	0811	4.1	1401	0.9	2037	4.5
4 W	0256	0.5	0936	4.1	1528	0.7	2157	4.6
5 TH	0415	0.3	1047	4.2	1638	0.5	2302	4.7
6 F	0515	0.2	1141	4.3	1733	0.3	2354	4.7
7 SA	0605	0.2	1227	4.4	1824	0.3		
8 SU ●	0042	4.7	0653	0.3	1309	4.6	1912	0.3
9 M	0126	4.7	0735	0.3	1346	4.7	1951	0.3
10 TU	0203	4.7	0808	0.4	1415	4.7	2023	0.3
11 W	0234	4.7	0837	0.5	1444	4.7	2053	0.4
12 TH	0307	4.5	0905	0.5	1514	4.7	2125	0.4
13 F	0342	4.4	0935	0.5	1548	4.6	2159	0.5
14 SA	0418	4.3	1007	0.7	1623	4.6	2236	0.6
15 SU	0456	4.2	1044	0.8	1704	4.5	2316	0.7
16 M ◐	0541	4.0	1128	0.9	1755	4.4		
17 TU	0008	0.8	0640	3.9	1228	1.0	1902	4.3
18 W	0116	0.8	0753	4.0	1345	1.0	2017	4.3
19 TH	0234	0.7	0909	4.1	1504	0.9	2128	4.4
20 F	0345	0.6	1014	4.3	1610	0.8	2227	4.6
21 SA	0441	0.5	1105	4.4	1705	0.7	2316	4.7
22 SU	0531	0.4	1149	4.6	1754	0.6		
23 M ○	0002	4.8	0616	0.4	1230	4.7	1838	0.5
24 TU	0045	4.8	0657	0.4	1308	4.8	1918	0.4
25 W	0127	4.8	0738	0.4	1348	4.8	2001	0.3
26 TH	0215	4.8	0822	0.4	1432	4.8	2047	0.3
27 F	0307	4.6	0908	0.4	1520	4.8	2134	0.2
28 SA	0359	4.5	0953	0.5	1608	4.7	2223	0.3
29 SU	0451	4.4	1040	0.6	1700	4.7	2316	0.4
30 M ◑	0547	4.3	1134	0.7	1759	4.7		
31 TU	0016	0.4	0649	4.2	1234	0.7	1905	4.6

JUNE

Day	Time	m	Time	m	Time	m	Time	m
1 W	0123	0.4	0757	4.1	1344	0.7	2018	4.6
2 TH	0235	0.4	0907	4.2	1457	0.6	2129	4.6
3 F	0344	0.4	1012	4.3	1604	0.5	2232	4.6
4 SA	0442	0.3	1106	4.4	1701	0.4	2326	4.6
5 SU	0532	0.4	1153	4.5	1754	0.4		
6 M ●	0015	4.7	0621	0.5	1238	4.6	1845	0.4
7 TU	0101	4.7	0706	0.5	1317	4.7	1928	0.4
8 W	0140	4.6	0743	0.5	1351	4.8	2004	0.4
9 TH	0215	4.6	0815	0.6	1424	4.8	2038	0.5
10 F	0250	4.5	0848	0.6	1458	4.8	2113	0.5
11 SA	0326	4.4	0921	0.6	1533	4.8	2148	0.5
12 SU	0402	4.4	0954	0.7	1609	4.7	2225	0.5
13 M	0440	4.3	1030	0.7	1647	4.7	2303	0.6
14 TU	0520	4.2	1109	0.8	1730	4.5	2344	0.6
15 W ◐	0605	4.1	1155	0.8	1819	4.4		
16 TH	0032	0.7	0700	4.1	1251	0.9	1918	4.4
17 F	0132	0.7	0803	4.2	1358	1.0	2023	4.5
18 SA	0239	0.7	0909	4.3	1507	0.9	2128	4.6
19 SU	0342	0.6	1010	4.4	1610	0.8	2229	4.6
20 M	0441	0.6	1104	4.6	1711	0.7	2326	4.7
21 TU	0538	0.6	1154	4.7	1806	0.6		
22 W ○	0020	4.8	0632	0.5	1244	4.8	1858	0.5
23 TH	0114	4.8	0723	0.5	1333	4.9	1951	0.4
24 F	0210	4.8	0816	0.5	1425	4.9	2046	0.3
25 SA	0307	4.7	0908	0.5	1517	4.9	2139	0.2
26 SU	0400	4.5	0954	0.4	1606	4.9	2227	0.2
27 M	0450	4.4	1038	0.5	1656	4.9	2316	0.3
28 TU ◑	0539	4.4	1125	0.6	1748	4.8		
29 W	0008	0.4	0630	4.3	1217	0.7	1844	4.8
30 TH	0101	0.5	0723	4.2	1313	0.7	1943	4.7

JULY

Day	Time	m	Time	m	Time	m	Time	m
1 F	0157	0.6	0821	4.2	1416	0.7	2048	4.6
2 SA	0259	0.7	0924	4.3	1525	0.7	2156	4.6
3 SU	0403	0.7	1027	4.4	1631	0.6	2258	4.5
4 M	0502	0.7	1123	4.5	1731	0.6	2352	4.5
5 TU	0556	0.7	1212	4.7	1826	0.6		
6 W ●	0040	4.6	0645	0.7	1256	4.8	1912	0.6
7 TH	0123	4.6	0726	0.7	1335	4.9	1952	0.6
8 F	0201	4.6	0803	0.7	1411	4.9	2029	0.6
9 SA	0237	4.6	0838	0.6	1446	4.9	2105	0.5
10 SU	0312	4.5	0911	0.6	1519	4.9	2137	0.5
11 M	0345	4.5	0941	0.6	1552	4.8	2208	0.5
12 TU	0419	4.4	1013	0.6	1627	4.7	2243	0.5
13 W	0456	4.4	1049	0.7	1704	4.7	2319	0.5
14 TH ◐	0532	4.3	1125	0.7	1741	4.6	2353	0.6
15 F	0611	4.3	1204	0.8	1823	4.5		
16 SA	0035	0.7	0659	4.2	1256	0.9	1920	4.5
17 SU	0133	0.8	0803	4.3	1404	1.0	2031	4.5
18 M	0243	0.9	0915	4.3	1519	0.9	2147	4.5
19 TU	0358	0.8	1025	4.5	1636	0.7	2300	4.6
20 W	0512	0.8	1129	4.7	1747	0.6		
21 TH ○	0008	4.7	0619	0.7	1229	4.8	1851	0.5
22 F	0110	4.7	0719	0.6	1325	5.0	1948	0.4
23 SA	0208	4.7	0813	0.5	1418	5.0	2044	0.3
24 SU	0302	4.7	0904	0.4	1509	5.1	2136	0.2
25 M	0351	4.6	0947	0.4	1556	5.1	2221	0.2
26 TU	0434	4.5	1026	0.4	1640	5.0	2302	0.3
27 W	0514	4.5	1105	0.5	1724	4.9	2344	0.5
28 TH ◑	0554	4.4	1148	0.7	1809	4.8		
29 F	0024	0.7	0636	4.4	1232	0.7	1858	4.6
30 SA	0107	0.8	0726	4.3	1327	0.8	2000	4.5
31 SU	0206	1.0	0831	4.3	1440	0.9	2116	4.4

AUGUST

Day	Time	m	Time	m	Time	m	Time	m
1 M	0320	1.0	0947	4.4	1601	0.9	2232	4.4
2 TU	0434	1.0	1058	4.5	1714	0.8	2336	4.4
3 W	0538	0.9	1154	4.7	1813	0.7		
4 TH	0025	4.5	0630	0.9	1240	4.8	1900	0.7
5 F ●	0108	4.6	0714	0.8	1320	4.9	1940	0.6
6 SA	0147	4.6	0752	0.7	1357	4.9	2017	0.6
7 SU	0222	4.6	0827	0.6	1431	4.9	2050	0.5
8 M	0253	4.6	0857	0.5	1501	4.9	2118	0.5
9 TU	0322	4.6	0923	0.5	1529	4.8	2144	0.4
10 W	0353	4.5	0951	0.5	1602	4.8	2216	0.5
11 TH	0426	4.5	1025	0.6	1635	4.7	2249	0.5
12 F	0457	4.4	1055	0.6	1706	4.6	2316	0.6
13 SA ◐	0525	4.3	1123	0.7	1738	4.5	2345	0.7
14 SU	0605	4.2	1204	0.9	1830	4.4		
15 M	0038	1.0	0708	4.2	1314	1.0	1949	4.3
16 TU	0158	1.1	0833	4.3	1444	0.9	2121	4.4
17 W	0332	1.1	1000	4.5	1617	0.8	2249	4.5
18 TH	0459	0.9	1115	4.7	1739	0.6		
19 F ○	0003	4.6	0613	0.8	1219	4.9	1846	0.4
20 SA	0105	4.7	0713	0.6	1315	5.0	1943	0.3
21 SU	0159	4.7	0804	0.4	1407	5.1	2034	0.2
22 M	0247	4.7	0849	0.4	1454	5.2	2121	0.2
23 TU	0330	4.7	0930	0.3	1537	5.2	2201	0.3
24 W	0406	4.7	1005	0.4	1615	5.0	2236	0.4
25 TH	0439	4.6	1038	0.5	1652	4.9	2307	0.6
26 F ◑	0511	4.5	1112	0.6	1730	4.7	2339	0.8
27 SA	0546	4.4	1148	0.8	1813	4.5		
28 SU	0015	1.0	0632	4.3	1237	1.0	1912	4.2
29 M	0111	1.2	0739	4.3	1353	1.1	2033	4.1
30 TU	0233	1.3	0906	4.3	1527	1.1	2202	4.2
31 W	0404	1.3	1031	4.5	1655	1.0	2316	4.3

Chart Datum: 2·26 metres below Normal Null (German reference level)

TIME ZONE -0100
(German Standard Time)
Subtract 1 hour for UT
For German Summer Time add ONE hour in **non-shaded areas**

GERMANY – WILHELMSHAVEN

LAT 53°31′N LONG 8°09′E

TIMES AND HEIGHTS OF HIGH AND LOW WATERS

SPRING & NEAP TIDES
Dates in red are SPRINGS
Dates in blue are NEAPS

YEAR **2005**

SEPTEMBER

Date	Day	Time	m	Time	m	Time	m	Time	m
1	TH	0520	1.1	1135	4.6	1757	0.8		
2	F	0008	4.5	0614	0.9	1221	4.8	1842	0.7
3	SA	0048	4.6	0655	0.8	1258	4.8	● 1918	0.6
4	SU	0124	4.6	0732	0.6	1333	4.8	1953	0.5
5	M	0158	4.6	0805	0.5	1406	4.8	2025	0.5
6	TU	0227	4.7	0835	0.5	1434	4.9	2052	0.5
7	W	0254	4.7	0901	0.5	1502	4.8	2118	0.5
8	TH	0321	4.6	0926	0.5	1532	4.8	2145	0.5
9	F	0351	4.5	0956	0.5	1604	4.7	2215	0.6
10	SA	0420	4.5	1024	0.6	1634	4.6	2241	0.7
11	SU	0449	4.4	1052	0.7	1709	4.4	◐ 2311	0.9
12	M	0529	4.3	1134	0.9	1804	4.2		
13	TU	0007	1.1	0637	4.2	1249	1.0	1930	4.2
14	W	0137	1.3	0810	4.3	1430	1.0	2111	4.2
15	TH	0320	1.2	0946	4.5	1610	0.8	2243	4.4
16	F	0451	1.0	1104	4.7	1732	0.5	2355	4.5
17	SA	0602	0.8	1206	4.9	1835	0.4		
18	SU	0052	4.6	0657	0.6	1300	5.0	○ 1927	0.3
19	M	0140	4.6	0744	0.4	1348	5.0	2013	0.3
20	TU	0222	4.7	0827	0.4	1431	5.1	2055	0.4
21	W	0259	4.7	0905	0.4	1509	5.1	2131	0.5
22	TH	0331	4.8	0938	0.4	1545	4.9	2201	0.6
23	F	0400	4.7	1007	0.5	1619	4.7	2227	0.7
24	SA	0430	4.6	1036	0.6	1653	4.5	2255	0.9
25	SU	0502	4.5	1110	0.8	1734	4.3	◑ 2329	1.1
26	M	0546	4.3	1156	1.0	1829	4.1		
27	TU	0023	1.3	0651	4.2	1308	1.2	1948	4.0
28	W	0145	1.5	0819	4.3	1445	1.3	2120	4.0
29	TH	0323	1.5	0951	4.4	1619	1.1	2242	4.2
30	F	0446	1.2	1102	4.6	1727	0.8	2338	4.4

OCTOBER

Date	Day	Time	m	Time	m	Time	m	Time	m
1	SA	0543	1.0	1149	4.7	1810	0.7		
2	SU	0017	4.6	0624	0.8	1225	4.7	1845	0.6
3	M	0051	4.6	0700	0.7	1259	4.8	● 1919	0.6
4	TU	0124	4.7	0735	0.6	1332	4.8	1952	0.5
5	W	0153	4.7	0806	0.6	1402	4.8	2022	0.5
6	TH	0220	4.7	0834	0.6	1432	4.8	2049	0.5
7	F	0248	4.7	0901	0.5	1503	4.8	2116	0.6
8	SA	0319	4.6	0929	0.5	1537	4.7	2145	0.7
9	SU	0351	4.6	1001	0.6	1615	4.5	2218	0.9
10	M	0428	4.5	1038	0.8	1659	4.3	◐ 2258	1.0
11	TU	0516	4.4	1128	0.9	1801	4.2	2359	1.2
12	W	0627	4.3	1245	1.0	1927	4.1		
13	TH	0129	1.3	0759	4.4	1425	1.0	2104	4.2
14	F	0310	1.2	0932	4.5	1601	0.7	2230	4.3
15	SA	0435	1.0	1048	4.7	1715	0.5	2336	4.4
16	SU	0538	0.7	1146	4.8	1812	0.4		
17	M	0027	4.5	0631	0.6	1237	4.9	○ 1901	0.4
18	TU	0111	4.6	0718	0.5	1323	4.9	1945	0.4
19	W	0151	4.7	0759	0.5	1404	4.9	2023	0.5
20	TH	0224	4.8	0836	0.5	1439	4.9	2056	0.6
21	F	0254	4.8	0908	0.6	1514	4.8	2124	0.7
22	SA	0324	4.7	0938	0.6	1549	4.6	2152	0.8
23	SU	0356	4.6	1008	0.7	1624	4.4	2221	0.9
24	M	0430	4.5	1043	0.8	1704	4.2	2256	1.1
25	TU	0512	4.4	1127	1.0	1754	4.0	◑ 2345	1.3
26	W	0610	4.3	1228	1.2	1901	3.9		
27	TH	0056	1.5	0727	4.3	1352	1.3	2025	4.0
28	F	0226	1.5	0854	4.4	1523	1.2	2147	4.1
29	SA	0351	1.3	1008	4.5	1635	0.9	2249	4.4
30	SU	0455	1.1	1101	4.6	1724	0.8	2333	4.5
31	M	0541	0.9	1141	4.7	1802	0.7		

NOVEMBER

Date	Day	Time	m	Time	m	Time	m	Time	m
1	TU	0009	4.6	0621	0.8	1218	4.8	1840	0.7
2	W	0043	4.7	0658	0.7	1254	4.8	● 1915	0.6
3	TH	0116	4.7	0733	0.7	1329	4.8	1948	0.6
4	F	0147	4.8	0806	0.7	1404	4.8	2022	0.7
5	SA	0220	4.8	0840	0.6	1444	4.7	2056	0.7
6	SU	0258	4.7	0916	0.6	1526	4.6	2131	0.8
7	M	0338	4.7	0955	0.6	1612	4.5	2211	1.0
8	TU	0422	4.6	1040	0.8	1703	4.3	2258	1.1
9	W	0516	4.5	1135	0.8	1805	4.2	◐ 2359	1.2
10	TH	0624	4.5	1248	0.9	1922	4.1		
11	F	0119	1.2	0746	4.5	1414	0.9	2046	4.1
12	SA	0247	1.2	0910	4.6	1539	0.7	2203	4.2
13	SU	0405	1.0	1022	4.7	1646	0.6	2304	4.4
14	M	0506	0.7	1119	4.8	1740	0.5	2353	4.5
15	TU	0559	0.6	1209	4.8	1829	0.6		
16	W	0038	4.6	0649	0.6	1256	4.8	○ 1914	0.6
17	TH	0118	4.7	0733	0.6	1337	4.8	1952	0.7
18	F	0152	4.8	0809	0.6	1412	4.7	2024	0.8
19	SA	0224	4.8	0843	0.7	1448	4.6	2056	0.8
20	SU	0257	4.8	0917	0.7	1525	4.5	2127	0.8
21	M	0332	4.7	0951	0.7	1602	4.3	2159	0.9
22	TU	0407	4.7	1027	0.8	1641	4.2	2234	1.1
23	W	0446	4.6	1106	1.0	1723	4.1	◑ 2316	1.2
24	TH	0534	4.4	1153	1.1	1816	4.0		
25	F	0010	1.3	0634	4.3	1255	1.2	1922	4.0
26	SA	0121	1.4	0745	4.4	1411	1.2	2035	4.1
27	SU	0239	1.4	0857	4.5	1524	1.1	2142	4.3
28	M	0349	1.3	0959	4.6	1624	0.9	2236	4.5
29	TU	0446	1.1	1050	4.7	1712	0.9	2320	4.6
30	W	0535	1.0	1135	4.8	1757	0.8		

DECEMBER

Date	Day	Time	m	Time	m	Time	m	Time	m
1	TH	0001	4.7	0620	0.9	1218	4.8	● 1839	0.8
2	F	0040	4.8	0701	0.8	1301	4.8	1919	0.8
3	SA	0120	4.8	0743	0.7	1347	4.8	2004	0.8
4	SU	0204	4.9	0829	0.7	1437	4.7	2049	0.8
5	M	0249	4.9	0915	0.6	1527	4.6	2131	0.8
6	TU	0335	4.8	0959	0.5	1615	4.5	2212	0.9
7	W	0422	4.8	1046	0.6	1706	4.4	2258	1.0
8	TH	0515	4.7	1140	0.7	1802	4.3	◐ 2353	1.0
9	F	0615	4.7	1240	0.8	1904	4.2		
10	SA	0057	1.1	0723	4.6	1349	0.8	2013	4.2
11	SU	0210	1.1	0835	4.6	1500	0.8	2121	4.2
12	M	0324	1.0	0946	4.7	1607	0.8	2223	4.4
13	TU	0430	0.8	1048	4.6	1704	0.7	2318	4.5
14	W	0529	0.8	1143	4.6	1758	0.8		
15	TH	0007	4.6	0624	0.8	1233	4.7	○ 1847	0.8
16	F	0051	4.8	0712	0.8	1316	4.6	1928	0.9
17	SA	0129	4.8	0751	0.7	1354	4.6	2003	0.9
18	SU	0204	4.9	0828	0.8	1430	4.6	2039	0.9
19	M	0241	4.9	0905	0.8	1508	4.5	2113	0.8
20	TU	0316	4.8	0940	0.7	1544	4.4	2145	0.8
21	W	0350	4.8	1013	0.8	1619	4.3	2216	0.9
22	TH	0425	4.7	1046	0.8	1656	4.2	2251	1.0
23	F	0503	4.6	1122	0.9	1735	4.1	◑ 2330	1.1
24	SA	0546	4.5	1204	1.0	1822	4.1		
25	SU	0019	1.2	0638	4.4	1257	1.1	1920	4.1
26	M	0122	1.4	0741	4.4	1404	1.2	2026	4.2
27	TU	0233	1.4	0849	4.5	1512	1.1	2131	4.4
28	W	0342	1.2	0955	4.6	1615	1.0	2230	4.5
29	TH	0445	1.1	1055	4.6	1714	1.0	2323	4.7
30	F	0544	0.9	1152	4.7	1810	0.9		
31	SA	0014	4.8	0638	0.8	1246	4.7	● 1902	0.8

Chart Datum: 2·26 metres below Normal Null (German reference level)

MAINLAND HARBOURS BETWEEN RIVERS JADE AND EMS

HARLESIEL, Niedersachsen, **53°44'·06N 07°50'·02E**. AC 1875, 3617; BSH 3015.8. HW –0100 on Dover (UT); HW (zone –0100) –0005 and ht +0·5m on Helgoland. Appr via Carolinensieler Balje which dries S of the training wall lt, L Fl 8s. Excellent shelter S of lock which opens approx HW ±1. 120 pontoon berths to W by village or at BY to E after passing through lock on W side of dyke. Lock, VHF Ch 17, 0700-2100. HM ☎ (04464) 472, berthing fees similar to Wangerooge (9.15.20); ⊖ ☎ (04462) 6154; YC ☎ 1473; Facilities: BY, C, Slip, P, D, FW. **Town** El, ME, Gaz, ✉, 🛒, R, ✈ and ferry to Wangerooge.

NEUHARLINGERSIEL, Niedersachsen, **53°42'·10N 07°42'·29E**. AC 3761, 1875; BSH 3015.8. HW 0000 on Dover (UT); see differences under 9.15.22. Appr via Otzumer Balje and Schillbalje to N end of trng wall, Oc 6s. Training wall, 1M long, covers at HW and is marked by SHM withies ⍏. Beware strong tidal streams across the ent. Yachts lie in NE corner of hbr; very few ⓥ berths. HM ☎ (04974) 289. Facilities: **Quay** FW, D. **Village** (picturesque) 🛒, R, Bar. Ferry to Spiekeroog (35 mins).

BENSERSIEL, Niedersachsen, **53°40'·81N 07°34'·20E**. AC 3761, 1875; BSH 3015.7E. HW –0024 on Dover (UT); +0005 on Helgoland (zone –0100); HW ht +0·4m on Helgoland. Appr as for Langeoog (9.15.22) thence lit/buoyed Rute chan to training walls with depth of 1·5m, but covering at HW. Very good shelter in the yacht hbr (0·7m) to stbd just before inner hbr ent (2m); also berths on the SW side of main hbr. Lts as 9.15.4. HM VHF Ch 17, ☎ (04971) 2502; Facilities: FW, C (8 ton), D (on E pier), P (cans), El, Slip, ME, ⚒. **Town** Ⓑ, Bar, ✉, R, ≠, 🛒, Gaz. Ferry to Langeoog.

NESSMERSIEL, Niedersachsen, **53°41'·14N 07°21'·68E**. AC 3761; D89; BSH 3015.6; HW –0040 on Dover (UT); –0020 on Helgoland (zone –0100); HW ht –0·2m on Helgoland. Appr as for Baltrum (9.15.19), thence via the buoyed Nessmersieler Balje, chan marked by SHM buoys leading to end of trng wall, covers at HW. Here, a lt bn, Oc 4s 5M, unlit ECM bns and PHM ⍏s mark the 6 cables long trng wall. Yachthafen with pontoons is on W side, beyond ferry quay. Good shelter in all weathers. Hbr dries (2m at HW). HM ☎ (04933) 1780. Facilities: **Nordsee YC Neßmersiel**; FW, but no supplies. **Village** (1M to S) has only limited facilities. Ferry to Baltrum.

NORDDEICH, Niedersachsen, **53°38'·71N 07°08'·90E**. AC 3761, BSH 3012.1, 3015.5. HW –0030 on Dover (UT); See 9.15.23. Appr as for Norderney (9.15.23), then via buoyed/lit Busetief to two training walls (Lat/Long as above) which cover at HW and are marked by stakes; see chartlet. The chan is 50m wide, 2·5m deep and 1.2M long. Very good shelter in hbr, divided by central mole. Yacht pontoons and ferry in W hbr; FVs in E hbr. Lts as in 9.15.4. HM VHF Ch 17, ☎ (04931) 81317; ⊖ ☎ (04931) 8435; YC ☎ 3560; Facilities: AB, C (5 ton), D ☎ 2721, FW, Slip, CH, BSH agent. **Town** Ⓑ, Bar, Dr, ✉, R, ≠, 🛒, Gaz. Ferry to Juist and Norderney.

GREETSIEL, Niedersachsen, **53°32'·86N 07°02'·07E**. AC 3761, 3631; BSH 89, 3012.1, 3015.2 & .5 (plan). HW –0400 on Dover (UT), –0010 on Helgoland; ML 2·6m. WPT 53°41'·91N 06°36'·19E [Osterems SWM buoy, Iso 4s], 117°/1.2M to chan buoys (O1/O2), passing between Memmert and Borkum. Follow the Osterems chan for 17.5M to O30/L2 buoy; here turn ENE into the Ley chan for 2½M to L9 buoy and Ley bn, Fl Y 4s. Then steer 165° for 7ca, between bkwtrs to lock which opens HW ±3. Thence 4M chan in 3m depths to Greetsiel, FV hbr and AB on marina pontoons (2m). HM ☎ (04926) 990371; ⊖ ☎ (04931) 2764. **Village** YC, Bar, R, 🛒, ≠. A canal links Greetsiel to Emden.

NOTES

9.15.18 DORNUMER-ACCUMERSIEL

Niedersachsen **53°41'·36N 07°29'·32E** ❁❁◊◊✿✿

CHARTS AC 3761, 1875; Imray C26; D89; BSH 3015.7

TIDES –0040 Dover; ML 1·4; Duration 0600; Zone –0100

Standard Port HELGOLAND (⟵)

Use Differences LANGEOOG (9.15.22)

SHELTER The marina provides complete shelter in all winds; depth 3m, access HW ±4. Ent is narrow; keep to W of chan on entering. Marina is fenced so obtain a key before leaving.

NAVIGATION Appr through Accumer Ee (see 9.15.5 and 9.15.22) leading into Accumersieler Balje and to AB3 SHM buoy, IQ G 13s. From here leave withies ⍏ and posts to stbd. Note warnings on German chart D89.

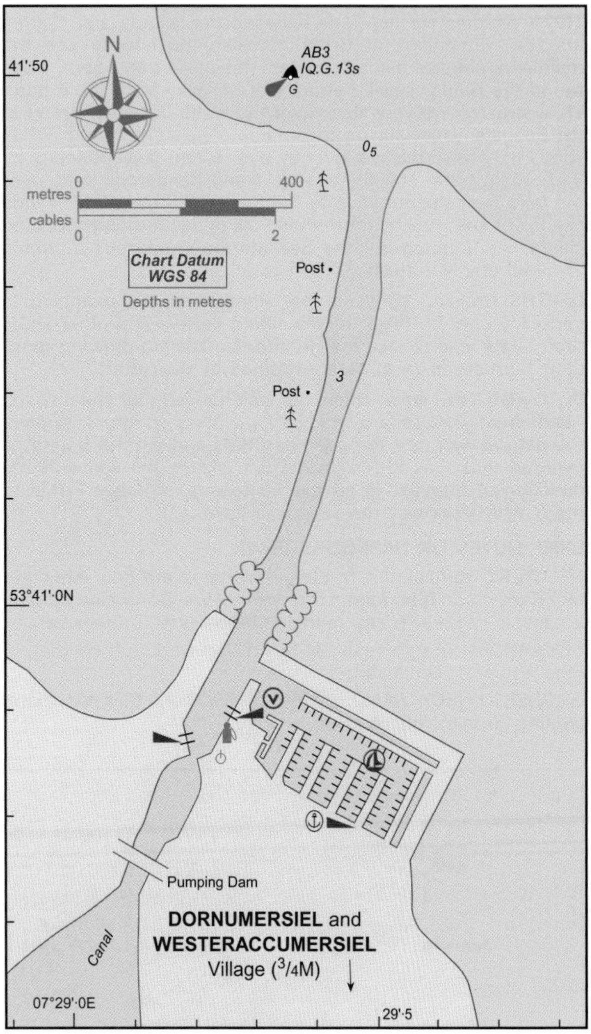
N
41'·50
AB3
IQ.G.13s
G
0₅
0
400
metres
cables
0
2
Chart Datum
WGS 84
Depths in metres
Post
Post
3
53°41'·0N
Pumping Dam
DORNUMERSIEL and
WESTERACCUMERSIEL
Village (3/4M)
Canal
07°29'·0E
29'·5

LIGHTS AND MARKS None.

R/T *German Bight Tfc* (VTS) broadcasts traffic and weather Ch 80 every H in German/English.

TELEPHONE (Dial code 04933) HM 2510; Deputy HM 441; ⊖ (04971) 7184; Lifeboat (04972) 247; Weather 0190 116048; Police 2218; Ⓗ 04941-940; Brit Consul (040) 446071.

FACILITIES **Dornumer Yacht Haven** (250) **YC** ☎ 2240; All facilities; FW, R, Slip, C (20t), Gaz, D, ME, El, ⚒; pontoons are lifted out of season. **Town** 🛒, R, Bar, ✉, Ⓑ, ≠ (Harlesiel), ✈ (Bremen).

9.15.19 EAST FRISIAN ISLANDS

The East Frisian Islands off the North Sea coast of Germany and the North Frisian Islands off Schleswig-Holstein and Denmark together comprise the German Frisian Islands. The East Frisian Islands lie between the River Jade and the Ems estuary, from 3 to 11M off the German coast; they formed, at one time, the N coast of the German mainland. There are four small islands between the Elbe estuary and the Jade.
The area between the low-lying islands and the present coastline which is now flooded by the sea is called the *Watten*. The islands are known locally as the Ostfriesischen and the inhabitants speak a patois known as Fries, a language with a close resemblance to English.

CHARTS AC 3761 (1:150,000), 1875 (1:100,000) and 3631 (1:50,000) cover the E Frisians, but there is a 12M gap between 1875 and 3631. BSH 3015, sheets 4 to 9, give excellent cover at 1:50,000 with many larger scale insets of the harbours. Dutch yacht charts (DYC) extend east up to the W end of Norderney.

TIDES *Seegats* are the gaps between the islands and *Watten* are the watersheds or watts between the islands and the mainland (where the tide meets having swept both ways round the island, usually about ⅓ of the way from the E end). Tidal streams are very slack over the watts but very strong in the Seegats, especially on the sp ebb. Persistent strong W/NW winds may raise the sea level by over 0.25m (exceptionally by 3m); against the ebb they cause steep dangerous seas over the bars near the entrance to the Seegats. Strong E/SE winds can lower sea level by more than 0.25m, dangerously reducing clearances. Caution: All the Seegats are dangerous in winds >F4 with any N in them.

DEPTHS Cruising between the islands and the mainland is generally only for bilge-keelers, lifting keelers and other shoal draft boats able to take the ground. Fin keelers drawing more than 1·4m are likely to be constrained by their draft.

BUOYAGE Deep water chans are well buoyed, but shoal chans (*wattfahrenwassern*) are marked by withies (*pricken*). Withies the natural way up ↟ are used as PHMs and withies bound or inverted thus ↡ as SHMs. Inside the islands the conventional direction of buoyage is always Eastwards, so leave PHMs to the N whichever way the stream is flowing.

BRIEF NOTES ON HARBOURS (E-W):

NEUWERK (off chartlet, in Elbe estuary): Island only inhabited by LB crew and lt ho men. Lt ho, see 9.15.4. On W side there is a conspic W radar tr and landing stage. Ferry to Cuxhaven.

SCHARHÖRN (2 sq miles): 2M NW of Neuwerk; (off chartlet, in Elbe estuary). Uninhabited.

GROSSES KNECHTSAND: 6M SW of Neuwerk; Bird sanctuary; landing prohib; (off chartlet).

ALTE MELLUM: 6M SW of Wangerooge at the confluence of Rivers Weser and Jade; Bird sanctuary; landing prohib.

MINSENER OOG: 1-2·5M SE of Wangerooge, two small islets linked by a causeway. Conspic radar twr. Beware groynes and overfalls in strong NW winds.

WANGEROOGE (2 sq miles): See 9.15.20.

SPIEKEROOG (5 sq miles): See 9.15.21.

LANGEOOG (7 sq miles): See 9.15.22.

BALTRUM (3 sq miles): Pretty island with small town and hbr at W end. See below.

NORDERNEY (10 sq miles): See 9.15.23.

JUIST (6½ sq miles): No yacht hbr. See below.

MEMMERT: Bird sanctuary; landing prohib. Lt on stone tr with G cupola, Oc (2) WRG 14s 15m 17/12M.

LÜTJEHÖRN: Bird sanctuary; landing prohib.

BORKUM (14 sq miles): The largest island, see 9.15.24.

OTHER HARBOURS IN THE EAST FRISIAN ISLANDS

BALTRUM, Niedersachsen, **53°43'·26N 07°21'·72E**. AC 3761, 1875; BSH 3015.6/7. HW –0040 on Dover (UT); Use differences Langeoog 9.15.22. Shelter is good except in strong SW'lies. The appr from seaward via the Wichter Ee Seegat between unmarked, drying banks is not advised without detailed local knowledge and ideal conditions.
A better approach is at HW via the Norderneyer Wattfahrwasser running S of Norderney (which also gives access to Neßmersiel). See 9.15.4 for lt at the head of hbr groyne. Tiny hbr partly dries. Yacht pontoons in 1·5m in the Bootshafen at the E end of hbr. HM ☎ (04939) 448; ⊖ ☎ (04939) 668. Facilities: Hbr AB, FW; Baltrumer Bootsclub YC. **Village** (¼M NNE) 🛒, R, Bar. No fuel. Ferry from Neßmersiel.

JUIST, Niedersachsen, **53°39'·66N 06°59'·52E**. AC 3631; D90; BSH 3012.1, 3015.4. HW –0105 on Dover (UT); HW –0035 and +0·1 on Helgoland; or use differences Memmert (see 9.15.23). Off the W end of Juist the unmarked Haaksgat leads into the Juister Balje which runs E for about 6M to Juist.
The easier approach is via Norderney (9.15.23) passing the E tip of Juist and into Juister Wattfahrwasser. Enter hbr via a narrow chan running N into the centre of the S side of island, marked by a red post, Oc (2) R 9s, and by ECM perches to port.
Conspic marks are: West bn, on Haakdünen at W end of island, Juist water twr in centre and East bn, 1M from E end of island. Aero lt at the airfield, see 9.15.4.
There is a small, drying yacht hbr, or yachts can berth in 0.6m alongside quay in ferry hbr. There are extensive No-⚓ areas and underwater power cables, but many drying moorings close E of the hbr. HM ☎ (04935) 724; ⊖ ☎ 1321. Facilities: FW, Slip, C; villages of Ostdorf, Westdorf and Loog in centre of island have limited facilities, 🛒, R, Bar, Gaz. Ferry to Norddeich.

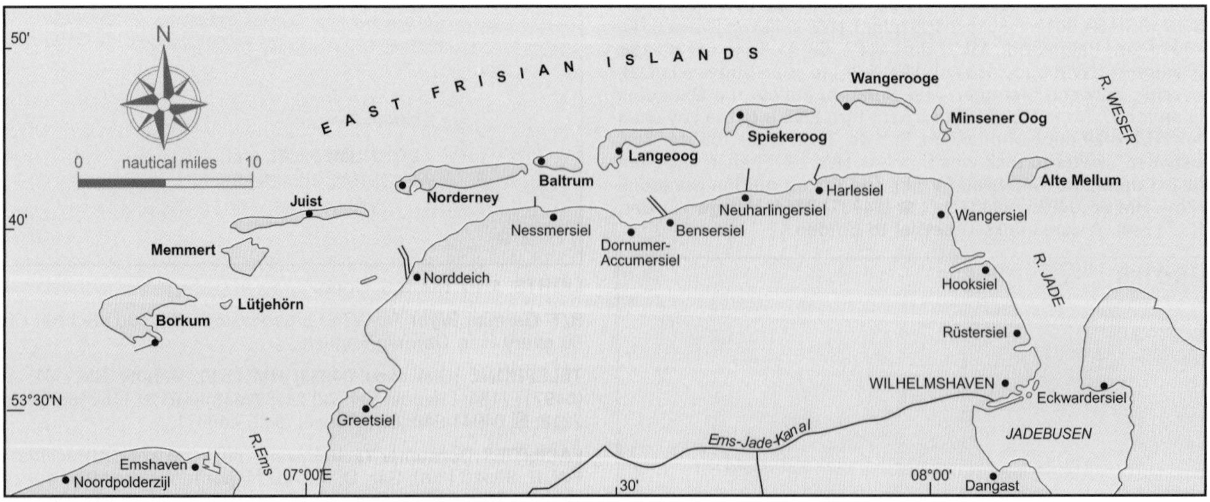
50'
N
EAST FRISIAN ISLANDS
0 nautical miles 10
Wangerooge
Minsener Oog
R. WESER
Spiekeroog
Langeoog
Baltrum
Norderney
Alte Mellum
Harlesiel
Juist
40'
Neuharlingersiel
Wangersiel
Nessmersiel
Bensersiel
Dornumer-Accumersiel
Memmert
R. JADE
Norddeich
Hooksiel
Lütjehörn
Borkum
Rüstersiel
WILHELMSHAVEN
Eckwardersiel
53°30'N
Greetsiel
Ems-Jade-Kanal
JADEBUSEN
R.Ems
Emshaven
Noordpolderzijl
07°00'E
30'
08°00'
Dangast

9.15.20 WANGEROOGE

EAST FRISIAN ISLANDS
Niedersachsen **53° 46'·46N 07° 52'·10E**

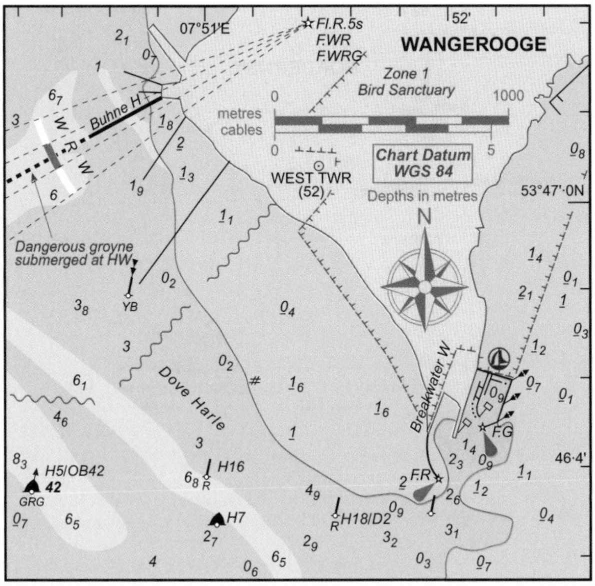
07°51'E
52'
FI.R.5s
F.WR
F.WRG
WANGEROOGE
Zone 1
Bird Sanctuary
metres
cables
1000
Chart Datum
WGS 84
Depths in metres
WEST TWR
(52)
53°47'·0N
Buhne H
Dangerous groyne submerged at HW
YB
Dove Harle
Breakwater W
F.G
F.R
46·4'
H5/OB42
42
GRG
H16
H7
H18/D2

CHARTS AC 3761, 1875, 3617A; Imray C26; D2; BSH 3015.8/9.

TIDES E Wangerooge, –0009 Dover; ML 1·9. Duration 0600
W Wangerooge, –0014 Dover; ML 1·5. Zone –0100

Standard Port WILHELMSHAVEN (⟵)

Times				Height (metres)			
High Water		Low Water		MHWS	MHWN	MLWN	MLWS
0200	0800	0200	0900	4·3	3·8	0·6	0·0
1400	2000	1400	2100				
Differences EAST WANGEROOGE							
–0058	–0053	–0024	–0034	–0·9	–0·9	–0·1	0·0
WEST WANGEROOGE							
–0101	–0058	–0035	–0045	–1·1	–1·0	–0·2	0·0

SHELTER Good in all winds, but SW gales, and S'lies at HW, cause heavy swell and difficult conditions in hbr. Best access HW±2. Yachts on marina pontoons at E side of hbr have 1·3 to 1·8m depth; rafting no more than two deep. The W jetty is mainly for ferries but yachts >12m may request HM for a berth.

NAVIGATION WPT 53°49'·29N 07°48'·99E [Harle SWM buoy, Iso 8s], 133°/1·0M to H4 buoy; 202°/1·5M to H12 buoy; 152°/0·4M to Buhne H WCM buoy, VQ (9) 10s; lastly 116°/1·5M to hbr ent. The Harle chan has least depth 1·7m near H4/6 buoys; it shifts and buoys are moved accordingly. Beware Buhne H (groyne), extending 7½ca, marked by WCM lt buoy and in FR sector of Wangerooge lt ho, F WR; outer portion covers at HW.

LIGHTS AND MARKS Wangerooge lt ho, a R twr with two W bands, at the W end of the island has 3 co-located lts with separate characteristics: the main lt, Fl R 5s 60m 23M, with 360° coverage; a F WR sectored lt, showing R over Buhne H; and a F WRG directional light visible from the NW over Harleriff, whose sectors are not shown on the chartlet. See 9.15.4 for details. Conspic daymarks are the 52m high West Tower at the W end and a Sig Stn and disused lt ho in the centre of the island.

R/T HM VHF Ch 17, 0700-1700.

TELEPHONE (Dial code 04469) HM 630; Yacht Marina 942126 or Mobile (0172) 2622705; ⊖ 519; Weather Bremerhaven (0471) 72220; Police 205; Ambulance 112; Brit Consul (040) 446071; Dr 1700.

FACILITIES **Wangerooge YC** ☎ 942 126, €1.10, L, M, Gaz. **Village** El, 🛒, CH, ⊡, Ⓑ, ⇌ (ferry to Harlesiel), ✈ (to Harle and Helgoland). Ferry: Hamburg-Harwich.

9.15.21 SPIEKEROOG

EAST FRISIAN ISLANDS
Niedersachsen **53°44'·96N 07°41'·32E** (ent to inner chan)

CHARTS AC 3761, 1875, 3617; Imray C26; D2 89; BSH 3015.8

TIDES HW –0008 on Dover (UT); ML 1·3m; Duration 0555.

Standard Port HELGOLAND (⟵)

Times				Height (metres)			
High Water		Low Water		MHWS	MHWN	MLWN	MLWS
0200	0700	0200	0800	2·7	2·4	0·4	0·0
1400	1900	1400	2000				
Differences SPIEKEROOG							
+0003	–0003	–0031	–0012	+0·4	+0·3	0·0	0·0

SHELTER Good shelter, but S/SW winds cause heavy swell. 3 yacht pontoons to the E of ferry berth almost dry to soft mud. Yachts >12m LOA should request a berth on the W jetty.

NAVIGATION WPT 53°47'·95N 07°37'·20E [Otzumer Balje SWM buoy, Iso 4s; frequently moved], 170°/0·5M to OB1 SHM buoy, Oc (2) G 9s. Least depth on the bar (between OB4 and OB6) is about 1·4m. The appr from seaward via Otzumer Balje is well buoyed, but only 4 buoys are lit. Westerbalje is a shallower, unbuoyed secondary chan from the WNW which joins Otzumer Balje at OB7/LW10 GRG buoy, Fl (2+1) G 15s.

The chan curves past the SW end of island into Schillbalje and to ☆ FR , R mast (lat/long below title) at the ent to inner chan, marked by withies, which leads 020°/1M to small ferry hbr (1·6m), S of Spiekeroog town/church.

Spiekeroog can also be approached from E and W via the Harlesieler and Neuharlingersieler Wattfahrwassern respectively, both leading into Schillbalje.

LIGHTS AND MARKS Sand dunes near the W end of the island are up to 24m high, but the E end is low-lying (3m). Two bcns with spherical topmarks are near the centre and E end of island.

R/T None.

TELEPHONE (Dial code 04976) HM ☎ 9193 133 (0800-1800); British Consul (040) 446071.

FACILITIES **Hbr** is run by YC, 100 Ⓥ, €1.00 mean, C (15 ton), FW, R. **Town** is ½M from hbr. Ferry to Nieuharlingersiel.

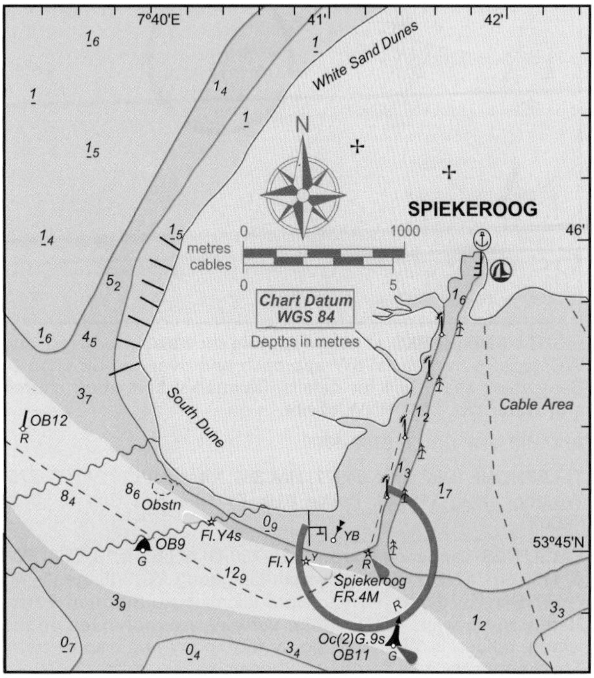
7°40'E
41'
42'
White Sand Dunes
SPIEKEROOG
46'
metres
cables
1000
Chart Datum
WGS 84
Depths in metres
South Dune
Cable Area
OB12
R
Obstn
Fl.Y4s
OB9
G
Fl.Y
YB
Spiekeroog
F.R.4M
53°45'N
Oc(2)G.9s
OB11
G

9.15.22 LANGEOOG

EAST FRISIAN ISLANDS
Niedersachsen **53°43'·38N 07°30'·12E**

CHARTS AC 3761, 1875; Imray C26; D89; BSH 3015.7

TIDES –0010 Dover; ML No data; Duration 0600; Zone –0100

Standard Port HELGOLAND (⟵)

Times				**Height (metres)**			
High Water		Low Water		MHWS	MHWN	MLWN	MLWS
0200	0700	0200	0800	2·7	2·4	0·4	0·0
1400	1900	1400	2000				
Differences LANGEOOG							
+0003	–0001	–0034	–0018	+0·4	+0·2	0·0	0·0
NEUHARLINGERSIEL							
+0014	+0008	–0024	–0013	+0·5	+0·4	0·0	–0·1

SHELTER Hbr (dries 0·1m) is well sheltered by 20m high sand dunes, but is open to the S. The E side of hbr dries; chan to yacht pontoons and ferry pier is marked by 4 withies.

NAVIGATION All buoys subject to frequent changes. WPT 53°46'·81N 07°26'·12E [Accumer Ee SWM buoy, Iso 8s; moved frequently], approx 105°/1·4M to A1/2 chan buoys; thence via buoyed chan to A9/B26 GRG buoy, Fl (2+1) G 15s. W sector of W mole lt leads 072°/1·4M to hbr ent. Ice protectors extend about 40m E of E mole, awash at HW, marked by withies.

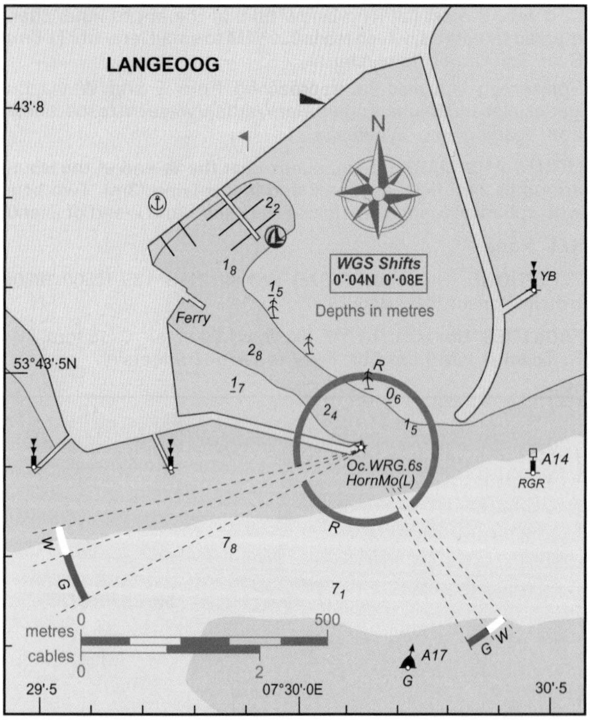
LANGEOOG
43'·8
WGS Shifts
0'·04N 0'·08E
Depths in metres
Ferry
53°43'·5N
YB
Oc.WRG.6s
HornMo(L)
A14
RGR
A17
G
metres
cables
0
500
2
29'·5
07°30'·0E
30'·5

LIGHTS AND MARKS Lt twr on W mole shows all-round red, and WG sectors over the WSW approach and over the SE chan to Bensersiel; see 9.15.4 for details. Daymarks: Langeoog church and water twr 1·5M NNW of hbr.

R/T HM VHF Ch 17, 0700-1700.

TELEPHONE (Dial code 04972) HM 301; Lifeboat CG 247; ⊖ 275; Weather 0190 116048; Police 810; Dr 589; Brit Consul (040) 446071.

FACILITIES **Langeoog Marina** (70 + 130 Ⓥ) ☎ 552, €13, Slip, FW, C, (12 ton), El, Bar, R; **Segelverein Langeoog YC. Village** (1½ M) R, Bar, ✉, Ⓑ, ⇌ (ferry to Norddeich), ✈ (to Bremen). Ferry: Hamburg-Harwich. NOTE: Motor vehicles are prohibited on the island. Village is 1½M away; go by foot, pony and trap or train. Train connects with ferries to Bensersiel.

9.15.23 NORDERNEY

EAST FRISIAN ISLANDS
Niedersachsen **53°41'·90N 07°09'·85E**

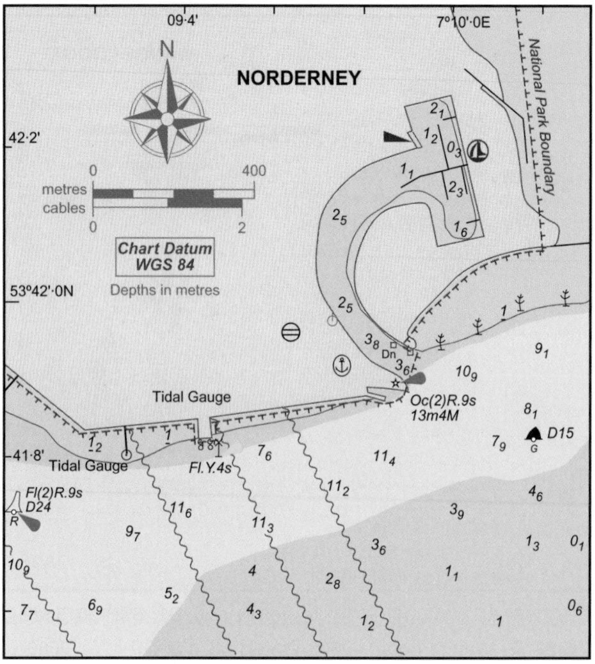
09·4'
7°10'·0E
N
NORDERNEY
National Park Boundary
42·2'
metres
cables
0
400
2
Chart Datum
WGS 84
Depths in metres
53°42'·0N
Dn
Tidal Gauge
Oc(2)R.9s
13m4M
D15
G
-41·8'
Tidal Gauge
Fl.Y.4s
Fl(2)R.9s
D24
R

CHARTS AC 3761; Imray C26; DYC 1812; Zeekarten 1353; D89; BSH 3012.1, 3015.5/6

TIDES –0042 Dover; ML 1·4; Duration 0605; Zone –0100

Standard Port HELGOLAND (⟵)

Times				**Height (metres)**			
High Water		Low Water		MHWS	MHWN	MLWN	MLWS
0200	0700	0200	0800	2·7	2·4	0·4	0·0
1400	1900	1400	2000				
Differences NORDERNEY (RIFFGAT)							
–0024	–0030	–0056	–0045	+0·1	0·0	0.0	0·0
NORDDEICH HAFEN							
–0018	–0017	–0029	–0012	+0·1	+0·1	0·0	–0·1
JUIST							
–0026	–0032	–0019	–0008	+0·2	+0·1	0·0	0·0
MEMMERT							
–0032	–0038	–0114	–0103	+0·1	+0·1	0·0	0·0

SHELTER Good. Yacht hbr, accessible H24, is at the NE of the hbr, where yachts lie bow to pontoon, stern to posts; or AB on W wall of hbr, as crowded in Jul/Aug. Hbr speed limit 3kn.

NAVIGATION From N/E, WPT 53°45'·40N 07°10'·49E [Dovetief SWM buoy, Iso 4s], 208°/1·95M to D8 PHM buoy, Oc (2) R 9s. Ent through the Dovetief (see 9.15.5) is well buoyed but the bar (3·1m) can be dangerous in on-shore winds and following seas which break on it, especially on an ebb tide. From W, WPT 53°44'·48N 07°02'·29E [Schlucter SWM buoy, Iso 8s], 122°/2·1M to S1 SHM buoy, Oc (2) G 9s. Both chans meet at D5/S8 GRG buoy, Fl (2+1) 15s. Ent at night is dangerous. Note: Tidal streams set across the Dovetief and Schlucter, not along it.

LIGHTS AND MARKS Lts, see 9.15.4. Land marks: lt ho, 8-sided R brick tr, in centre of island. Conspic water twr in town.

R/T Ch 17, Wed – Sun 0700 (0900 Tue)-1200; 1230-1900 (1730 Mon).

TELEPHONE (Dial code 04932) HM 82826; CG 2293; ⊖ 2386; Weather 549; Police 788; Ⓗ 477 and 416; Brit Consul (040) 446071.

FACILITIES M, L, FW, C (10 ton), R, CH, SM, Slip, ME, El, P, D, Gaz; **Yacht Club** Bar. **Town** R, Bar, ✉, Ⓑ, ⇌ (ferry to Norddeich), ✈ (to Bremen). Ferry: Hamburg-Harwich.

9.15.24 BORKUM

EAST FRISIAN ISLANDS
Niedersachsen **53°33'·48N 06°45'·00E** ❀❀❀◊◊✿✿

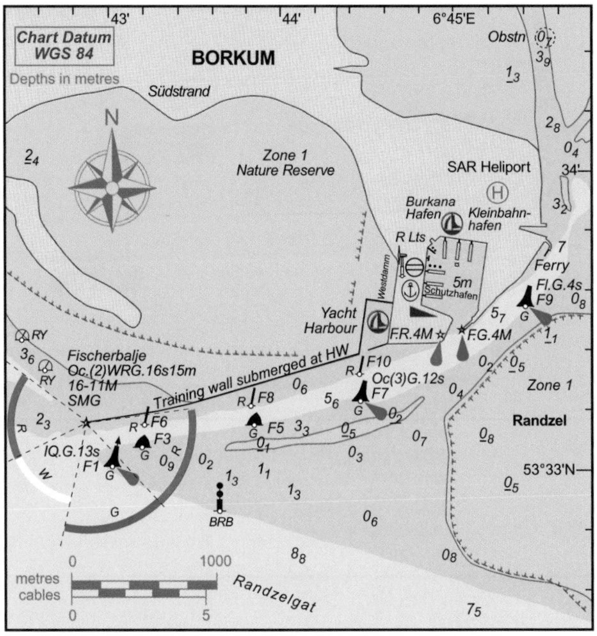
Chart Datum WGS 84
Depths in metres
BORKUM
Südstrand
Zone 1 Nature Reserve
SAR Heliport
Burkana Hafen
Kleinbahn-hafen
R Lts
Westdamm
5m
Schutzhafen
Ferry
Fl.G.4s
F9
Yacht Harbour
F.R.4M
F.G.4M
Fischerbalje
Oc.(2)WRG.16s15m
16-11M
SMG
Training wall submerged at HW
F10
Oc(3)G.12s
F7
F8
F6
F5
F3
IQ.G.13s
F1
Zone 1
Randzel
53°33'N
BRB
metres
cables
Randzelgat
Obstn
43'
44'
6°45'E
34'

CHARTS AC 3761, 3631; Imray C26; D90; BSH 3015.2/3/4; DYC 1812.5; ANWB A

TIDES –0105 Dover; ML 1·4; Duration 0610; Zone –0100

Standard Port HELGOLAND (⟵)

Times				Height (metres)			
High Water		Low Water		MHWS	MHWN	MLWN	MLWS
0200	0700	0200	0800	2·7	2·4	0·4	0·0
1400	1900	1400	2000				
Differences BORKUM (FISCHERBALJE)							
–0048	–0052	–0124	–0105	0·0	0·0	0·0	0·0

SHELTER Good in yacht hbr (2-2·5m), whose ent is abeam F7, Oc (3) G 12s, and F10 buoys. Also at Burkana Hafen (pontoons IV - VI in 4·5m) off N wall of the Schutzhafen (Refuge); access to both H24. Pontoons I-III off W wall are for YC members and boats <8m LOA. The ferry hbr (*fährhafen*) is prohib to yachts.

NAVIGATION WPT 53°38'·96N 06°27'·12E [Riffgat SWM buoy, Iso 8s], 122°/11M to Fischerbalje lt. See also 9.16.7. From the W appr via the Westerems SWM buoy, Iso 4s, Racon (T) [53°36'·93N 06°19'·37E] to join Riffgat which is covered by the 127° W sector of Campen lt, Dir F. Many groynes extend 500m off Borkum. Make good Fischerbalje lt (see 9.15.4 for sectors) at the end of the trng wall which covers at HW. Beware strong SW'lies and strong currents across the Fischerbalje chan (buoyed/partly lit). Speed limit in hbrs is 5kn. (Note: Hubertgat SWM buoy is withdrawn from service and the chan is prone to silting, but still buoyed).

LIGHTS AND MARKS Daymarks: Water twr, Grosser lt ho (brown brick twr) WNW of hbr and Kleiner lt ho, R twr + W bands (now disused); 2 wind turbines 3ca NNE of yacht hbr ent.

R/T *Burkana Hafen* Ch 17. *Borkum Port* Ch 14 (In season: M -Fri 0700-2200; Sat 0800-2100; Sun 0700-2000).

TELEPHONE (Dial code 004922) HM 3440; CG Borkum Kleiner Lt Tr; ⊜ 2287; Police 3950; ⊞ 813; Brit Consul (040) 446071.

FACILITIES **Yacht Hbr** (50 + 200 ⓥ) ☎ 7773, 🏪 4399, €0.87, AB, Slip, D, R, Bar, C (6 ton), 🛒, 🗒, 🚿, P, ME; **Burkana Hafen** (80) ☎ 7877, 🏪 7646; D (cans, limited; or ☎ 2483). **Town** (7km NW by bus/train) P, ME, El, Gaz, 🛒, R, Bar, ✉, Ⓑ, ⇌ (ferry to Emden), ✈ (Emden & Bremen). S part of island is Nature Reserve.

9.15.25 EMDEN

Niedersachsen **53°20'·06N 07°10'·69E** ❀❀❀◊◊✿

CHARTS AC 2593, 3632; Imray C26; D90, 91; BSH 3012.5/6

TIDES HW +0022 on Dover (UT); ML 1·9m; Zone – 0100

Standard Port HELGOLAND (⟵)

Times				Height (metres)			
High Water		Low Water		MHWS	MHWN	MLWN	MLWS
0200	0700	0200	0800	2·7	2·4	0·4	0·0
1400	1900	1400	2000				
Differences EMDEN							
+0041	+0028	–0011	+0022	+0·9	+0·8	0·0	0·0
EMSHÖRN							
–0037	–0041	–0108	–0047	+0·1	+0·1	0·0	0·0
KNOCK							
+0018	+0005	–0028	+0004	+0·6	+0·6	0·0	0·0

SHELTER Good. Three berthing options for visitors; (b) and (c) are accessed via the Nesserland sealock:
a. Emder YC marina (3m) on SE side of Außenhafen, just before Nesserland sealock; may be exposed to SSW winds.
b. Mariners' Club, small marina at NW side of southern Binnenhafen, below the HT cables.
c. City Marina, comprising Alter Binnenhafen (4·5m), Ratsdelft (3m) or Falderndelft (3m), all managed by Reederei AG Ems, very central. Access via two road/rail bridges opening 0650, 0855, 1130, 1325, 1410, 1530, 1730, 1850 and 2130 on request. For opening sound M (— —).

NAVIGATION See Borkum (9.15.24) and Delfzijl (9.16.7) for outer approaches via well buoyed/lit R Ems to abeam Knock lt ho. Thence 6M via Emder Fahrwasser which has drying banks and training walls close outboard of chan buoys. 3 conspic HT pylons (101m) cross the Außenhafen. Nesserland lock opens: In-bound every H+30, 0730-1730 (Sun 0730-1430). Out-bound every H 0700-1800 (Sun 0700-1500). For later openings on Sun: Enter Binnenhafen via Vorhafen sealock 1700, 2000; depart 1730, 2030, or H24 with commercial traffic.
Note: The Ems-Jade canal, 39M to Wilhelmshaven, is usable by yachts with lowering masts and max draft 1·7m. Access at Emden via the Falderndelft. Min bridge clearance 3·75m. It has 6 locks. Speed limit 4kn. *Continued overleaf*

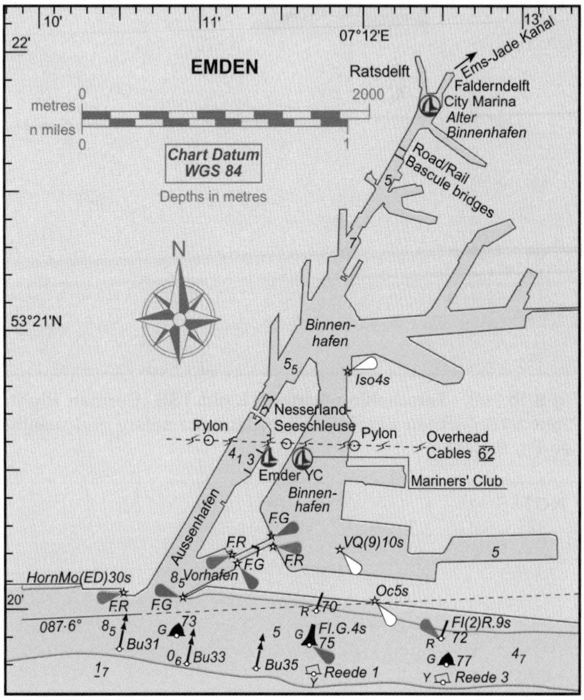
10'
11'
13'
22'
07°12'E
EMDEN
Ems-Jade Kanal
Ratsdelft
Falderndelft
City Marina
Alter Binnenhafen
metres
n miles
2000
Chart Datum WGS 84
Depths in metres
Road/Rail Bascule bridges
53°21'N
Binnen-hafen
Iso4s
Nesserland-Seeschleuse
Pylon
Pylon
Overhead Cables 62
Emder YC
Mariners' Club
Binnen-hafen
Aussenhafen
F.G
F.R
VQ(9)10s
F.G
F.R
Vorhafen
HornMo(ED)30s
Oc5s
20'
F.R
F.G
087·6°
Bu31
73
Bu33
Bu35
F.G.4s
75
Reede 1
Fl(2)R.9s
72
77
Reede 3

Emden continued

LIGHTS AND MARKS Fahrwasser outer ldg lts 075°, both Oc (2) 12s 16/28m 12M (off chartlet). Inner ldg lts 088°, both Oc 5s 14/30m 12M, lead to hbr ent, marked by FR and FG lts.

R/T Emden Hbr and Locks Ch 13 (H24). No VHF at individual marinas.

VTS: *Ems Traffic* broadcasts safety, traffic & weather info in German H+50 on Ch 15, 18, 20 and 21.

Radar advice in German, or in English on request, for the Ems is provided as follows:

Borkum Radar	Ch 18	Buoys 1 - 35;
Knock Radar	Ch 20	Buoys 35 - 57;
Wybelsum Radar	Ch 21	Buoys 57 - Hbr entry at Emden.

TELEPHONE (Dial code 04921) HM 897260 (H24); Nesserlander lock ☎ 897270; Tourist Info 97400; Police 110; Fire/Ambulance 112; ⊖ 929285.

FACILITIES Emder YC marina ☎ 997147, €0.77, ▯, C. **Mariners Club** ☎ 996943, €0.51. **City marina**, Reederie AG Ems ☎ 8907211 or 0160 4479965, €0.70,▯▯, ▣, ⚓. Diesel barge, for location in the hbr call ☎ 0171 324 4337. **City** all amenities. Ferry to Borkum.

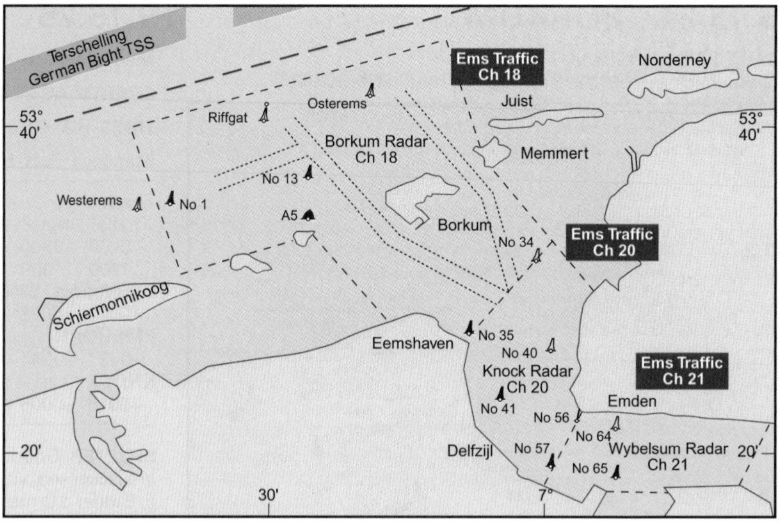
Terschelling German Bight TSS
Ems Traffic Ch 18
Norderney
Juist
Osterems
Riffgat
53° 40'
Borkum Radar Ch 18
Memmert
No 13
Westerems
No 1
A5
Borkum
No 34
Ems Traffic Ch 20
Schiermonnikoog
No 35
Eemshaven
No 40
Knock Radar Ch 20
Ems Traffic Ch 21
No 41
Emden
No 56
No 64
20'
Delfzijl
No 57
Wybelsum Radar Ch 21
No 65
30'
7°

Fig 9.15.25A. Ems VTS

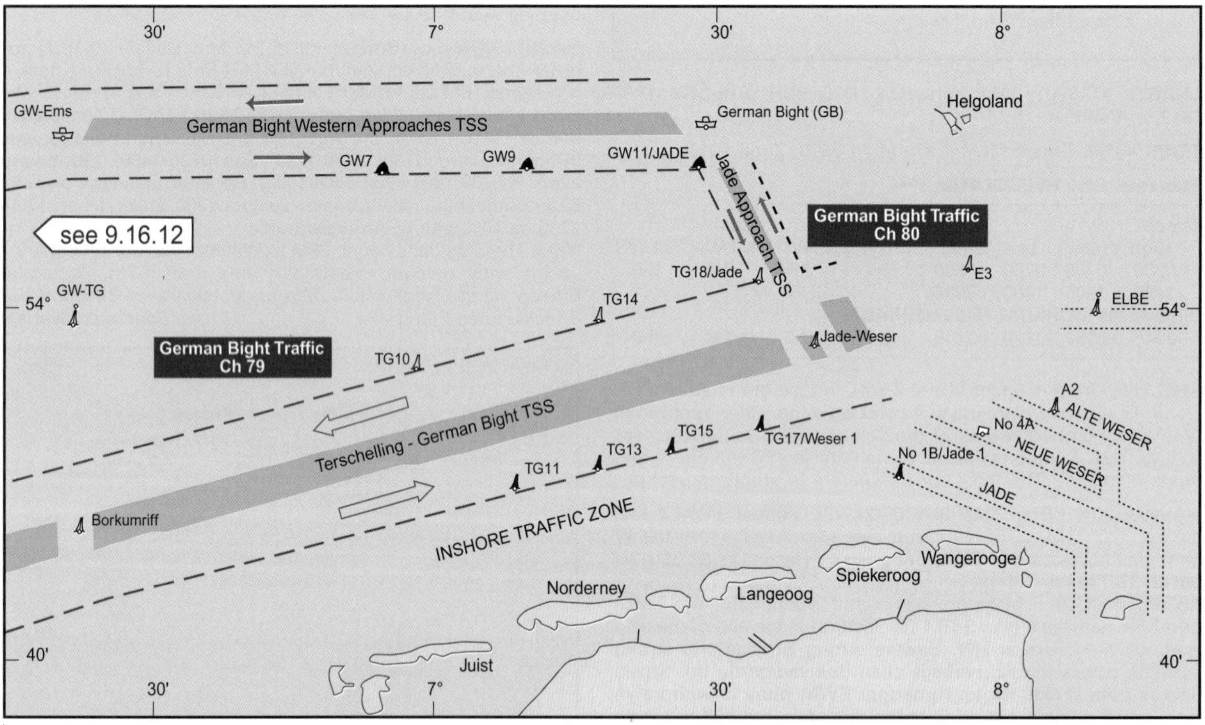
30'
7°
30'
8°
GW-Ems
German Bight Western Approaches TSS
German Bight (GB)
Helgoland
GW7
GW9
GW11/JADE
Jade Approach TSS
German Bight Traffic Ch 80
see 9.16.12
TG18/Jade
E3
54°
GW-TG
TG14
ELBE
German Bight Traffic Ch 79
TG10
Jade-Weser
A2
ALTE WESER
Terschelling - German Bight TSS
TG15
No 4A
TG13
TG17/Weser 1
NEUE WESER
TG11
No 1B/Jade 1
JADE
Borkumriff
INSHORE TRAFFIC ZONE
Wangerooge
Spiekeroog
Norderney
Langeoog
40'
Juist

Fig 9.15.25B. Terschelling-German Bight TSS, German Bight Western Approaches TSS and Jade Approach TSS. German Bight VTS:*German Bight Traffic* broadcasts safety and weather info Ch 80 every H in German/English. For **Jade & Weser VTS** see Fig 9.15.16A.

NOTES

Area 16

The Netherlands and Belgium

Delfzijl to Nieuwpoort

16

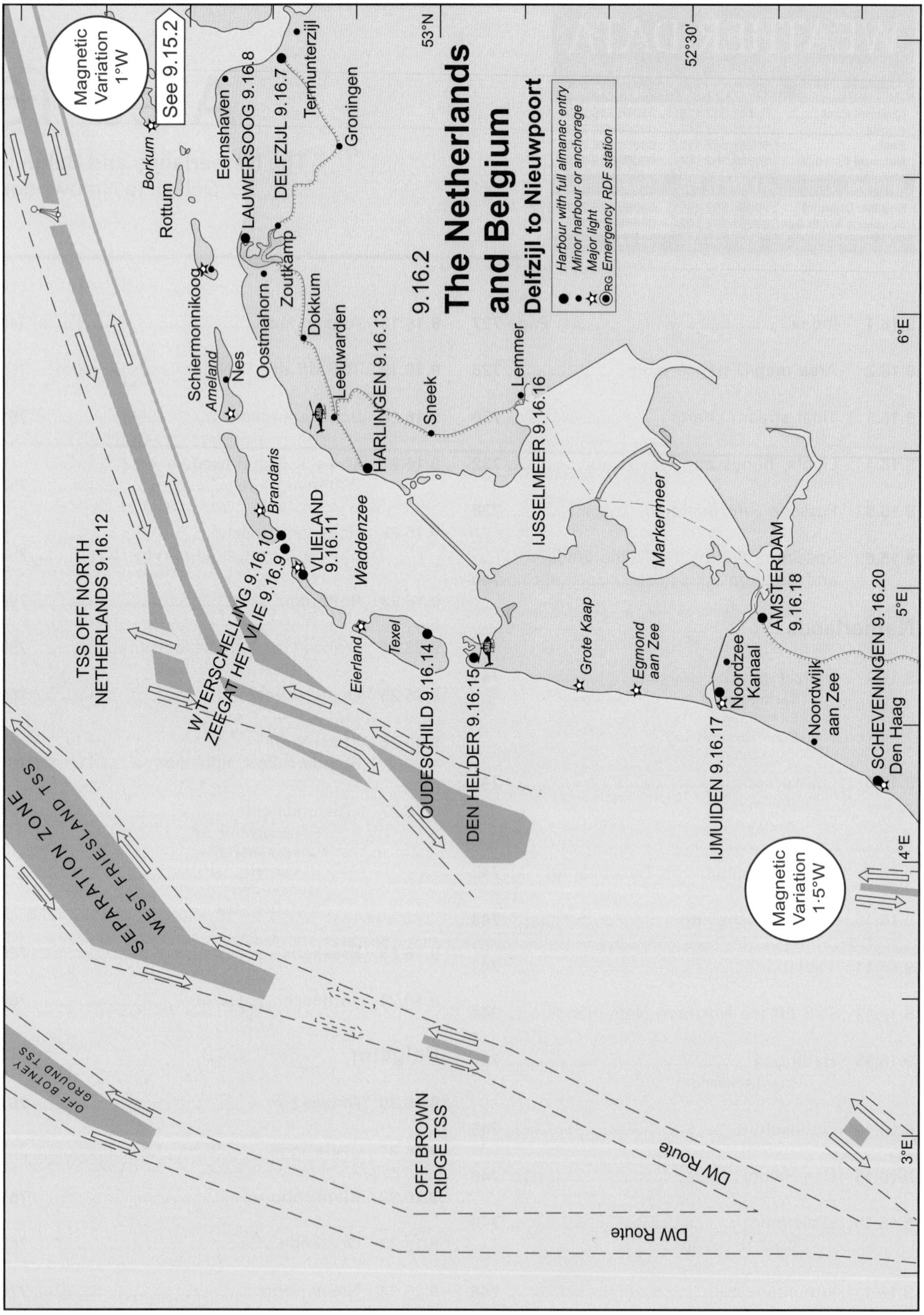
9.16.2
The Netherlands and Belgium
Delfzijl to Nieuwpoort
Harbour with full almanac entry
Minor harbour or anchorage
Major light
RG Emergency RDF station
Magnetic Variation 1°W
See 9.15.2
Magnetic Variation 1·5°W
53°N
52°30'
6°E
5°E
4°E
3°E
Borkum
Rottum
Eemshaven
LAUWERSOOG 9.16.8
DELFZIJL 9.16.7
Termunterzijl
Groningen
Schiermonnikoog
Oostmahorn
Zoutkamp
Dokkum
Ameland
Nes
Leeuwarden
HARLINGEN 9.16.13
Sneek
Lemmer
IJSSELMEER 9.16.16
Brandaris
VLIELAND 9.16.11
WTERSCHELLING 9.16.10
ZEEGAT HET VLIE 9.16.9
Waddenzee
Markermeer
Eierland
Texel
OUDESCHILD 9.16.14
DEN HELDER 9.16.15
Grote Kaap
Egmond aan Zee
Noordzee Kanaal
AMSTERDAM 9.16.18
IJMUIDEN 9.16.17
Noordwijk aan Zee
SCHEVENINGEN 9.16.20
Den Haag
TSS OFF NORTH NETHERLANDS 9.16.12
WEST FRIESLAND TSS
SEPARATION ZONE
OFF BOTNEY GROUND TSS
OFF BROWN RIDGE TSS
DW Route
DW Route

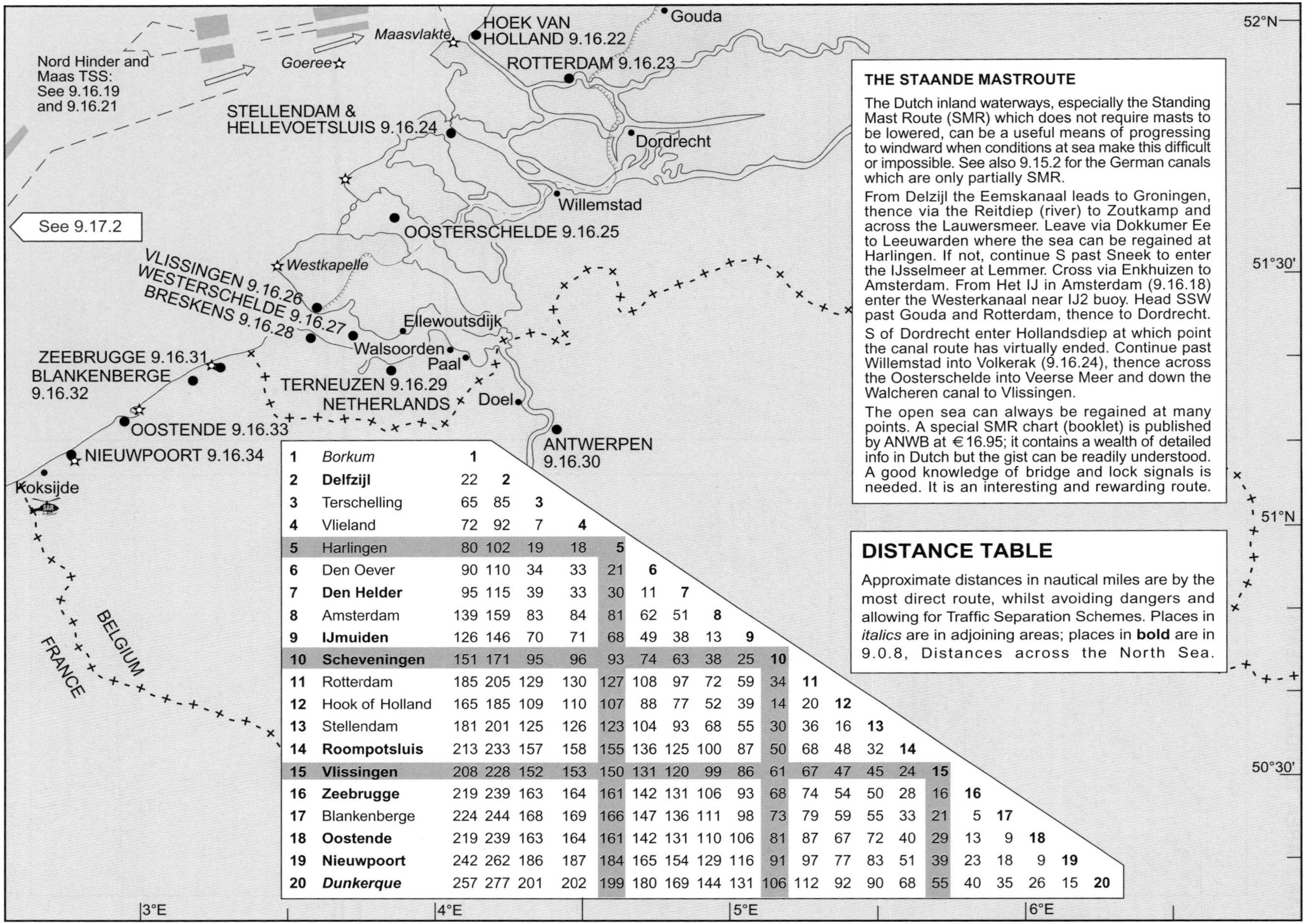
Nord Hinder and
Maas TSS:
See 9.16.19
and 9.16.21
Maasvlakte
Goeree
HOEK VAN
HOLLAND 9.16.22
Gouda
ROTTERDAM 9.16.23
STELLENDAM &
HELLEVOETSLUIS 9.16.24
Dordrecht
Willemstad
See 9.17.2
OOSTERSCHELDE 9.16.25
Westkapelle
VLISSINGEN 9.16.26
WESTERSCHELDE 9.16.27
BRESKENS 9.16.28
Ellewoutsdijk
Walsoorden
Paal
ZEEBRUGGE 9.16.31
BLANKENBERGE
9.16.32
TERNEUZEN 9.16.29
NETHERLANDS
Doel
OOSTENDE 9.16.33
ANTWERPEN
9.16.30
NIEUWPOORT 9.16.34
Koksijde
BELGIUM
FRANCE
52°N
51°30'
51°N
50°30'
3°E
4°E
5°E
6°E

THE STAANDE MASTROUTE

The Dutch inland waterways, especially the Standing Mast Route (SMR) which does not require masts to be lowered, can be a useful means of progressing to windward when conditions at sea make this difficult or impossible. See also 9.15.2 for the German canals which are only partially SMR.

From Delzijl the Eemskanaal leads to Groningen, thence via the Reitdiep (river) to Zoutkamp and across the Lauwersmeer. Leave via Dokkumer Ee to Leeuwarden where the sea can be regained at Harlingen. If not, continue S past Sneek to enter the IJsselmeer at Lemmer. Cross via Enkhuizen to Amsterdam. From Het IJ in Amsterdam (9.16.18) enter the Westerkanaal near IJ2 buoy. Head SSW past Gouda and Rotterdam, thence to Dordrecht.

S of Dordrecht enter Hollandsdiep at which point the canal route has virtually ended. Continue past Willemstad into Volkerak (9.16.24), thence across the Oosterschelde into Veerse Meer and down the Walcheren canal to Vlissingen.

The open sea can always be regained at many points. A special SMR chart (booklet) is published by ANWB at €16.95; it contains a wealth of detailed info in Dutch but the gist can be readily understood. A good knowledge of bridge and lock signals is needed. It is an interesting and rewarding route.

DISTANCE TABLE

Approximate distances in nautical miles are by the most direct route, whilst avoiding dangers and allowing for Traffic Separation Schemes. Places in *italics* are in adjoining areas; places in **bold** are in 9.0.8, Distances across the North Sea.

1	*Borkum*	1																			
2	**Delfzijl**	22	**2**																		
3	Terschelling	65	85	**3**																	
4	Vlieland	72	92	7	**4**																
5	Harlingen	80	102	19	18	**5**															
6	Den Oever	90	110	34	33	21	**6**														
7	**Den Helder**	95	115	39	33	30	11	**7**													
8	Amsterdam	139	159	83	84	81	62	51	**8**												
9	**IJmuiden**	126	146	70	71	68	49	38	13	**9**											
10	**Scheveningen**	151	171	95	96	93	74	63	38	25	**10**										
11	Rotterdam	185	205	129	130	127	108	97	72	59	34	**11**									
12	Hook of Holland	165	185	109	110	107	88	77	52	39	14	20	**12**								
13	Stellendam	181	201	125	126	123	104	93	68	55	30	36	16	**13**							
14	**Roompotsluis**	213	233	157	158	155	136	125	100	87	50	68	48	32	**14**						
15	**Vlissingen**	208	228	152	153	150	131	120	99	86	61	67	47	45	24	**15**					
16	**Zeebrugge**	219	239	163	164	161	142	131	106	93	68	74	54	50	28	16	**16**				
17	Blankenberge	224	244	168	169	166	147	136	111	98	73	79	59	55	33	21	5	**17**			
18	**Oostende**	219	239	163	164	161	142	131	110	106	81	87	67	72	40	29	13	9	**18**		
19	**Nieuwpoort**	242	262	186	187	184	165	154	129	116	91	97	77	83	51	39	23	18	9	**19**	
20	***Dunkerque***	257	277	201	202	199	180	169	144	131	106	112	92	90	68	55	40	35	26	15	**20**

9.16.3 AREA 16 TIDAL STREAMS

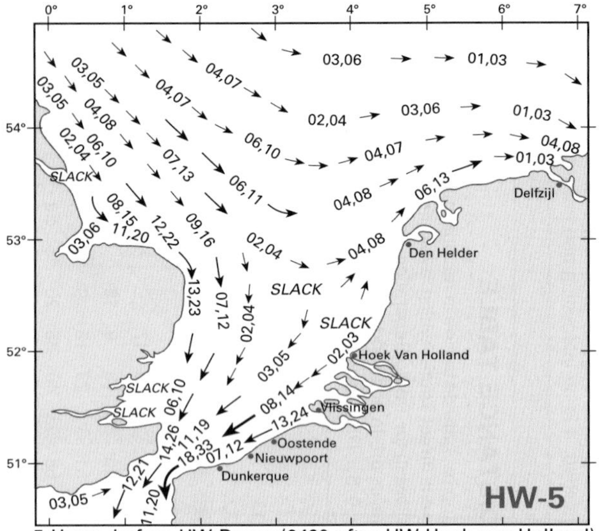
HW-5
Delfzijl
Den Helder
Hoek Van Holland
Vlissingen
Oostende
Nieuwpoort
Dunkerque
0° 1° 2° 3° 4° 5° 6° 7°
54° 53° 52° 51°
5 Hours before HW Dover (0420 after HW Hoek van Holland)

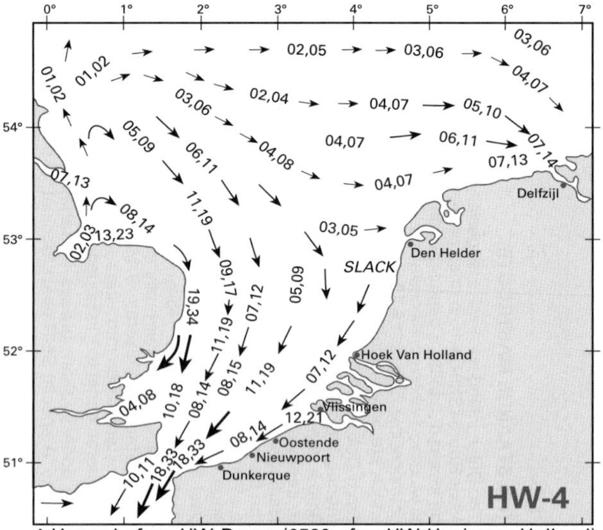
HW-4
Delfzijl
Den Helder
Hoek Van Holland
Vlissingen
Oostende
Nieuwpoort
Dunkerque
0° 1° 2° 3° 4° 5° 6° 7°
54° 53° 52° 51°
4 Hours before HW Dover (0520 after HW Hoek van Holland)

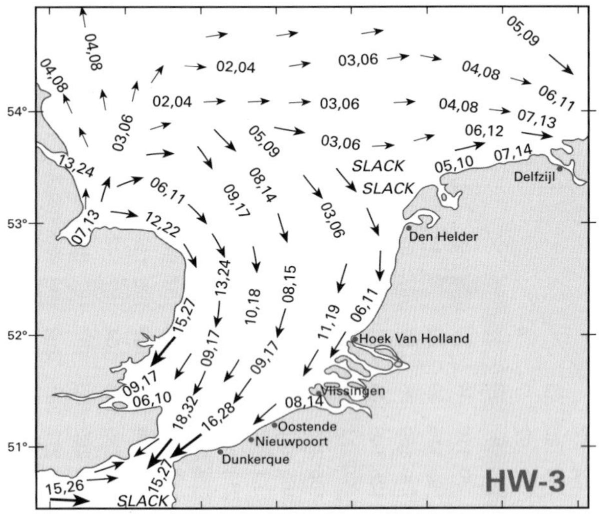
HW-3
Delfzijl
Den Helder
Hoek Van Holland
Vlissingen
Oostende
Nieuwpoort
Dunkerque
54° 53° 52° 51°
3 Hours before HW Dover (0605 before HW Hoek van Holland)

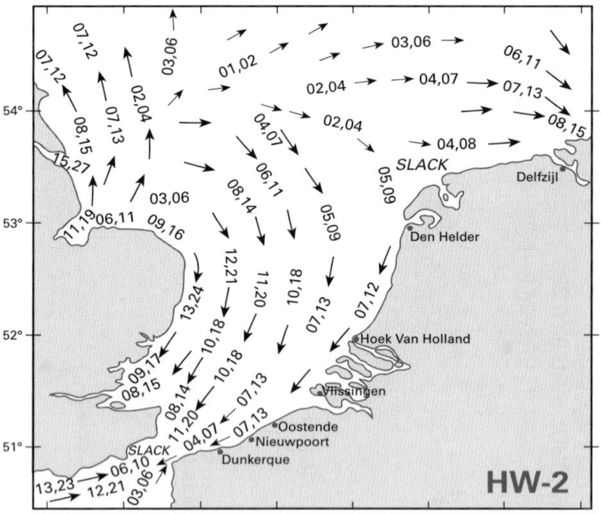
HW-2
Delfzijl
Den Helder
Hoek Van Holland
Vlissingen
Oostende
Nieuwpoort
Dunkerque
54° 53° 52° 51°
2 Hours before HW Dover (0505 before HW Hoek van Holland)

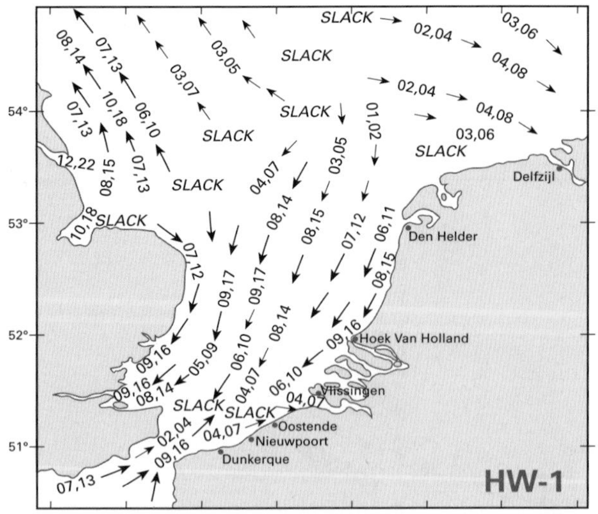
HW-1
Delfzijl
Den Helder
Hoek Van Holland
Vlissingen
Oostende
Nieuwpoort
Dunkerque
54° 53° 52° 51°
1 Hour before HW Dover (0405 before HW Hoek van Holland)

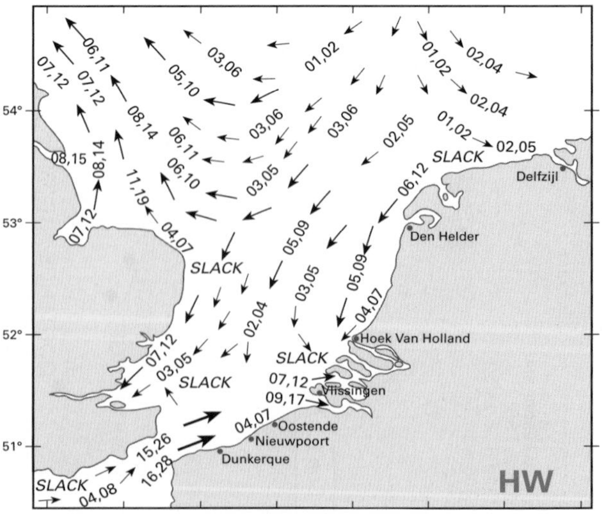
HW
Delfzijl
Den Helder
Hoek Van Holland
Vlissingen
Oostende
Nieuwpoort
Dunkerque
54° 53° 52° 51°
HW Dover (0305 before HW Hoek van Holland)

South-westward 9.17.3 North-westward 9.4.3 North-eastward 9.15.3

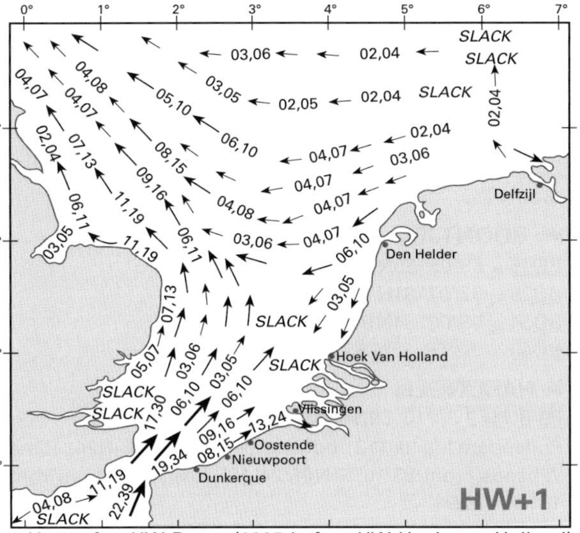
0°
1°
2°
3°
4°
5°
6°
7°
54°
53°
52°
51°
Delfzijl
Den Helder
Hoek Van Holland
Vlissingen
Oostende
Nieuwpoort
Dunkerque
HW+1

1 Hour after HW Dover (0205 before HW Hoek van Holland)

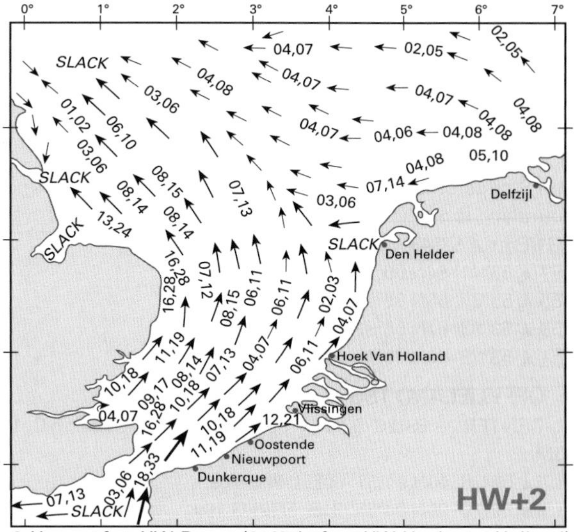
Delfzijl
Den Helder
Hoek Van Holland
Vlissingen
Oostende
Nieuwpoort
Dunkerque
HW+2

2 Hours after HW Dover (0105 before HW Hoek van Holland)

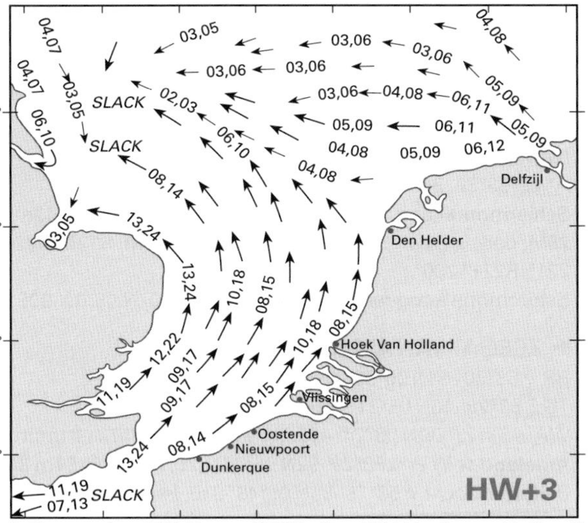
Delfzijl
Den Helder
Hoek Van Holland
Vlissingen
Oostende
Nieuwpoort
Dunkerque
HW+3

3 Hours after HW Dover (0005 after HW Hoek van Holland)

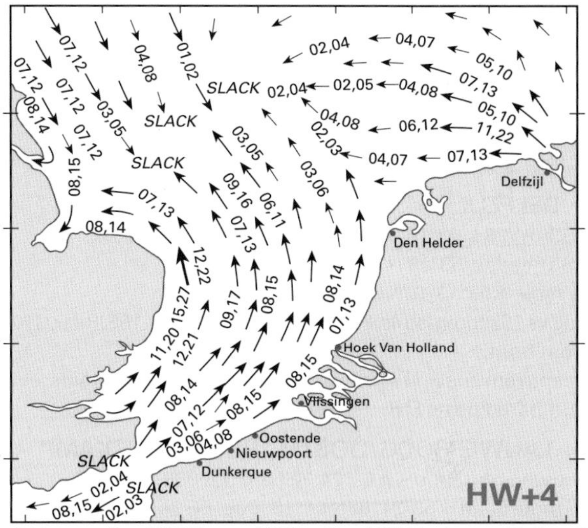
Delfzijl
Den Helder
Hoek Van Holland
Vlissingen
Oostende
Nieuwpoort
Dunkerque
HW+4

4 Hours after HW Dover (0055 after HW Hoek van Holland)

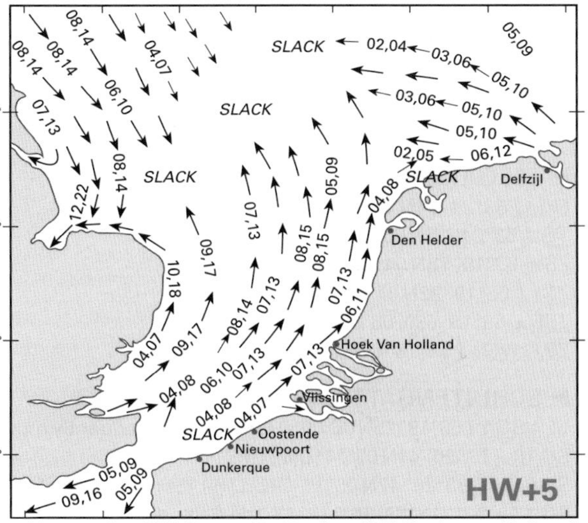
Delfzijl
Den Helder
Hoek Van Holland
Vlissingen
Oostende
Nieuwpoort
Dunkerque
HW+5

5 Hours after HW Dover (0155 after HW Hoek van Holland)

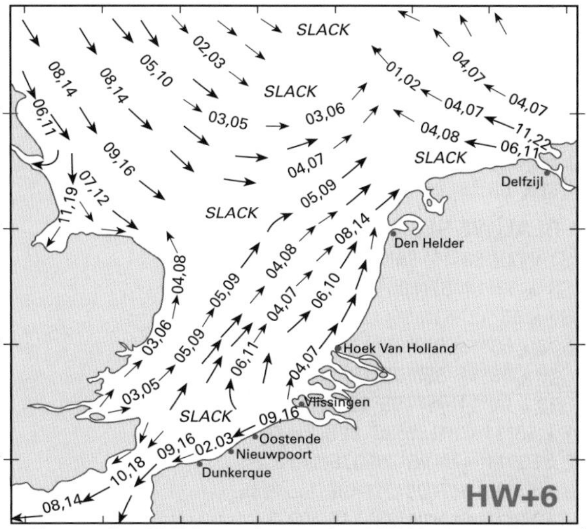
Delfzijl
Den Helder
Hoek Van Holland
Vlissingen
Oostende
Nieuwpoort
Dunkerque
HW+6

6 Hours after HW Dover (0255 after HW Hoek van Holland)

16

PLOT WAYPOINTS ON YOUR CHART BEFORE USING THEM

9.16.4 LIGHTS, BUOYS AND WAYPOINTS

Blue print = light with a nominal range of 15M or more. CAPITALS = place or feature. *CAPITAL ITALICS* = light-vessel, light float or Lanby. *Italics* = Fog signal. ***Bold italics*** = Racon. Useful waypoints are underlined. Abbreviations are in Chapter 1. Positions are referenced to the WGS 84 datum.

▶ TERSCHELLING-GERMAN BIGHT TSS

The S edge of the E-bound lane, going W from the German boundary, is marked by the following buoys:
TG1/Ems 53°43'·36N 06°22'·24E, IQ G 13s.
TE7 53°41'·84N 06°13'·88E, L Fl G 10s.
TE5 53°37'·80N 05°53'·70E, Fl (3) G 10s.
TE3 53°33'·67N 05°32'·60E, L Fl G 10s.
TE1 53°29'·60N 05°11'·30E, Fl (3) G 10s.

▶ OFFVLIELAND TSS

VL-CENTER 53°26'·93N 04°39'·88E, Fl 5s 12M; **Racon C, 12-15M**.
VL7 53°26'·40N 04°57'·60E, L Fl G 10s.
VL1 53°10'·96N 04°35'·31E, Fl (2) G 10s.
VL5 53°22'·89N 04°43'·91E, QG.
VL3 53°16'·89N 04°39'·58E, Fl (3) G 10s.

MAINLAND: DELFZIJL TO HARLINGEN

See also 9.15.4 for the River Ems.

▶ TERMUNTERZIJL

BW 13 53°18'·63N 07°02'·31E, Fl G 5s.

▶ DELFZIJL

PS3/BW26 53°19'·25N 07°00'·31E, Fl (2+1) G 12s.
PS0 Reede 53°19'·13N 07°01'·06E, QY.
W mole 53°19'·01N 07°00'·26E, FG.
Ldg lts 203° both Iso 4s. Front, 53°18'·62N 07°00'·16E. Rear, 310m from front.
Zeehavenkanaal, N side: odd numbered posts Fl G. S side: even numbered posts Fl R.

▶ LAUWERSOOG/OOSTMAHORN/ZOUTKAMP

Lauwersoog E mole 53°24'·65N 06°12'·06E, FR 4M.
W mole head 53°24'·68N 06°12'·00E, FG 3M; *Horn (2) 30s*.
Oostmahorn ent 53°22'·96N 06°09'·64E, FG.
Zoutkamp ent (unlit) 53°20'·42N 06°17'·66E.

APPROACHES TO HARLINGEN (selected marks):

▶ VLIESTROOM

VL1 53°18'·91N 05°08'·72E, QG; buoys are frequently moved.
VL 2 53°19'·30N 05°09'·85E, QR.
VL 5 53°18'·37N 05°09'·89E, L Fl G 8s.
VL11 53°16'·06N 05°09'·69E, Iso G 4s.

▶ BLAUWE SLENK/POLLENDAM

BS1-IN2 53°15'·99N 05°10'·35E, VQ (3) 5s.
BS3 53°14'·87N 05°10'·55E, L Fl G 5s.
BS7 53°13'·63N 05°12'·97E, Iso G 4s.
BS13 53°13'·31N 05°17'·13E, QG.
BS19 53°11'·89N 05°18'·26E, VQ G.
BS23 53°11'·48N 05°19'·63E, L Fl G 8s.
P1 53°11'·39N 05°20'·32E, Iso G 2s.
P2 53°11'·47N 05°20'·37E, Iso R 2s.
P3 53°11'·10N 05°21'·49E, Iso G 4s.
P7 53°10'·68N 05°23'·44E, VQ G.

▶ DOOVE BALG (from S)

D4 53°02'·55N 05°03'·64E, Iso R 8s.
D3A/J2 53°01'·92N 05°07'·76E, Fl (2+1) G 10s.
D16 53°02'·79N 05°10'·70E, Iso R 8s.
D24 53°03'·78N 05°15'·55E, Iso R 8s.
BO11/KZ2 53°04'·95N 05°20'·25E, Q.

▶ KORNWERDERZAND

Buitenhaven, W mole 53°04'·76N 05°20'·03E, FG 9m 7M; *Horn Mo(N) 30s*.

▶ BOONTJES

BO15 53°05'·59N 05°21'·76E, Iso G 2s.
BO28 53°07'·81N 05°22'·49E, Iso R 8s.
BO34 53°08'·84N 05°22'·93E, Iso R 2s.
BO40 53°09'·87N 05°23'·26E, Iso R 4s.

▶ HARLINGEN

P9/BO44 53°10'·59N 05°23'·88E VQ.
Pollendam ldg lts 112°, both Iso 6s 8/19m 13M (H24); B masts, W bands. Front, 53°10'·51N 05°24'·18E. Rear, 500m from front, vis 104·5°-119·5°.
N mole hd 53°10'·59N 05°24'·32E, FR 9m 4M; R/W pedestal.

WEST FRISIAN IS: SCHIERMONNIKOOG TO TEXEL

▶ SCHIERMONNIKOOG TO AMELAND

WG (Westgat) 53°32'·57N 06°10'·70E, Iso 8s; **Racon N**.
WRG 53°32'·83N 06°03'·14E, Q.
NAM21 53°31'·15N 05°55'·53E, Fl Y 5s.
AM 53°30'·94N 05°44'·69E, VQ.
Schiermonnikoog ☆ 53°29'·19N 06°08'·76E, Fl (4) 20s 43m **28M**; dark R ○ twr. Same twr: F WR 29m **W15M**, R12M; W210°-221°, R221°-230°.
Schiermonnikoog ferry pier head 53°28'·07N 06°09'·99E.

▶ ZEEGAT VAN AMELAND

BR 53°30'·64N 05°33'·47E, Q.
TS 53°28'·16N 05°21'·51E, VQ.
WA 53°27'·70N 05°24'·49E. (Westgat buoys are all unlit)
Ameland ☆ W end 53°26'·92N 05°37'·52E, Fl (3) 15s 57m **30M**.
Ballumerbocht 53°25'·85N 05°43'·87E, Iso R 4s 5m 4M.

▶ NES

MG28-R1 53°25'·71N 05°45'·88E, VQ(6) + L Fl 10s.
Reegeul R3 53°25'·80N 05°45'·93E, Iso G 4s.
Reegeul R5 53°25'·86N 05°46'·01E, QG.
Reegeul R7 53°25'·90N 05°46'·21E, L Fl G 8s.
Nieuwe Veerdam mole 53°25'·97N 05°46'·45E, Iso 6s 2m 8M.

▶ ZEEGAT VAN TERSCHELLING

Otto 53°24'·61N 05°06'·32E, VQ. (Note: NCM lt buoy)
TG 53°24'·15N 05°02'·27E, Q (9) 15s.
ZS 53°19'·78N 04°55'·88E, Iso 4s; **Racon T**.
ZS1 53°19'·22N 04°57'·56E, VQ.
ZS5 53°18'·63N 05°01'·61E, L Fl G 8s.
ZS11-VS2 53°18'·67N 05°05'·96E, Q (9) 15s.

▶ SCHUITENGAT TO WEST TERSCHELLING

VL 4/SG 1 53°19'·25N 05°09'·97E; buoys are frequently moved.
SG 10 53°20'·44N 05°11'·06E, QR.
SG 9/S2 53°20'·47N 05°11'·71E, Q (9) 15s.
SG 17 53°21'·17N 05°13'·26E, L Fl G 8s.

Brandaris Twr ☆ 53°21'·61N 05°12'·84E, Fl 5s 54m **29M**; Y ☐ twr; partly obscured by dunes on Vlieland and Terschelling.
W Terschelling E pier hd ⚡ 53°21'·26N 05°13'·19E, FG 4m 4M.
W hbr mole ⚡, 53°21'·25N 05°13'·09E, FR 5m 5M; R post, W bands; *Horn 15s.*

▶ **VLIELAND**

VS3 ▲ 53°18'·27N 05°06'·23E, VQ G.
VS5 ▲ 53°18'·03N 05°06'·12E, L Fl G 5s.
VS14 ≈ 53°17'·58N 05°05'62E, Iso R 4s.
VS16-VB1 ≈ 53°17'·62N 05°05'·20E, Fl (2+1) R 10s.
E mole hd ⚡ 53°17'·68N 05°05'·51E, FG.
W mole hd ⚡ 53°17'·68N 05°05'·48E, FR.
Vlieland ☆ 53°17'·69N 05°03'·46E, Iso 4s 53m **20M**.

TEXEL & THE WADDENZEE

▶ **EIERLANDSCHE GAT**

Eierland ☆ (N tip of Texel) 53°10'·93N 04°51'·30E, Fl (2) 10s 52m **29M**; R ○ twr.
EG ⓛ 53°13'·35N 04°47'·07E, VQ (9) 10s.
Baden ⓛ 53°13'·58N 04°41'·23E, Q (9) 15s.
VL1 ▲ 53°10'·95N 04°35'·28E, Fl (2) G 10s.
VL-South ⟡ 53°08'·86N 04°26'·50E, L Fl Y 10s.
TX 3 ▲ 52°58'·58N 04°22'·29E, Fl (3) G 10s.

▶ **TEXELSTROOM/OUDESCHILD**

Mok (ferry hbr) ⚡ 53°00'·17N 04°46'·79E, Oc WRG 10s 10m W10M, R7M, G6M; R229°-317°, W317°-337°, G337°-112°.
T17 ▲ 53°01'·71N 04°52'·32E, Iso G 8s.
T12 ≈ 53°02·23N 04°51'·53E, Iso R 8s.
Oudeschild Dir lt 291°, Oc 6s; intens 291°, 53°02'·40N 04°50'·94E; leads into hbr between N mole head FG 6m; and
S mole head ⚡ 53°02'·33N 04°51'·17E, FR 6m; *Horn (2) 30s* (sounded 0600-2300).
T23 ▲ 53°03'·59N 04°55'·85E, VQ G.
T27 ▲ 53°03'·59N 04°59'·41E, Iso G 4s.

▶ **MALZWIN/WIERBALG TO DEN OEVER LOCK**

M11 ▲ 52°59'·33N 04°52'·51E, Iso G 8s.
LW ≈ 52°59'·51N 04°55'·90E, L Fl 10s.
VG1/W2 ≈ 52°58'·98N 04°56'·83E, Fl (2+1) G 10s.
W9 ⓛ 52°57'·24N 04°57'·51E.
O3 ▲ 52°56'·89N 05°01'·57E, QG.
Ldg lts 131°, both Oc 10s 6m 7M; 127°-137°. Front, 52°56'·32N 05°02'·98E.
Detached bkwater N head ⚡ 52°56'·76N 05°02'·29E, L Fl R 10s.
Stevinsluizen W wall, 80m from head ⚡ 52°56'·22N 05°02'·15E, Iso WRG 2s; G195°-213°, W213°-227°, R227°-245°.

ZEEGAT VAN TEXEL AND DEN HELDER

▶ **OUTER APPROACHES TO ZEEGAT VAN TEXEL**

NH ⓛ 53°00'·23N 04°35'·36E, VQ.
MR ⓛ 52°56'·76N 04°33'·81E, Q (9) 15s.
ZH ⓛ 52°54'·65N 04°34'·71E, VQ (6) + L Fl 10s.
TX1 ▲ 52°48'·01N 04°15'·50E, Fl G 5s.
Vinca G ⓛ 52°45'·93N 04°12'·40E, Q (9) 15s.

▶ **MOLENGAT (from the N)**

MG ⓛ 53°03'·90N 04°39'·37E, Mo (A) 8s.
MG1 ▲ 53°02'·89N 04°40'·84E, Iso G 4s.
MG2 ≈ 53°03'·11N 04°41'·23E, Iso R 4s.

MG5 ▲ 53°01'·27N 04°41'·69E, Iso G 4s.
MG6 ≈ 53°01'·26N 04°41'·86E, Iso R 4s.
MG9 ▲ 53°00'·16N 04°41'·60E, QG.
MG10 ≈ 53°00'·18N 04°41'·87E, QR.
MG13 ▲ 52°59'·16N 04°42'·29E, Iso G 8s.
MG16 ≈ 52°58'·86N 04°43'·12E, QR.
S14-MG17 ⓛ 52°58'·45N 04°43'·51E, VQ (6) + L Fl 10s.

▶ **SCHULPENGAT (from the S)**

Ldg lts 026·5° (on Texel), both Oc 8s **18M** (by day 9M); vis 024·5°-028·5°. **Front** ☆, 53°00'·85N 04°44'·42E. Rear, **Den Hoorn** ☆ 0·83M from front; church spire.
SG ⓛ 52°52'·90N 04°37'·90E, Mo (A) 8s; **Racon Z**.
S1 ▲ 52°53'·51N 04°38'·84E, Iso G 4s.
S2 ≈ 52°53'·81N 04°37'·93E, Iso R 4s.
S3 ▲ 52°54'·43N 04°39'·52E, Iso G 8s.
S4 ≈ 52°54'·62N 04°38'·78E, Iso R 8s.
S5 ▲ 52°55'·33N 04°40'·23E, Iso G 4s.
S7 ▲ 52°56'·25N 04°40'·91E, QG.
S6A ≈ 52°56'·52N 04°40'·51E, QR.
S8 ⓛ 52°57'·06N 04°41'·01E.
S9 ⓛ 52°56'·85N 04°42'·06E.
S10 ≈ 52°57'·59N 04°41'·56E, Iso R 8s.
Schilbolsnol ☆ 53°00'·50N 04°45'·68E F WRG 27m **W15M**, R12M, G11M; G twr; vis W338°-002°, G002°-035°, W035°-038° (leading sector for Schulpengat), R038°-051°, W051°-068°.
Huisduinen ⚡ 52°57'·13N 04°43'·29E, F WR 26m W14M, R11M; ☐ twr; vis W070°-113°, R113°-158°, W158°-208°.
Kijkduin ☆, Rear, 52°57'·33N 04°43'·58E, Fl (4) 20s 56m **30M**; brown twr; visible except where obscured by dunes on Texel.
S11 ▲ 52°57'·55N 04°43'·25E, Iso G 8s.
S14/MG17 ⓛ 52°58'·45N 04°43'·51E, VQ (6) + L Fl 10s.

▶ **MARSDIEP/DEN HELDER**

T1 ▲ 52°57'·99N 04°44'·61E, Fl (3) G 10s.
T3 ▲ 52°58'·06N 04°46'·41E, Iso G 8s.
Den Helder ldg lts 191°, both Oc G 5s 15/24m 14M, synch ; B ▽ on bldg. Front, 52°57'·37N 04°47'·08E; vis 161°-221°. Rear, 275m from front, vis 161°-247°.
MH6, E of ent ⚡ 52°57'·94N 04°47'·39E, Iso R 4s 9m 4M; R pile.
Marinehaven, W breakwater head (Harssens I) ⚡ 52°57'·95N 04°47'·07E, QG 11m 8M; *Horn 20s.*
Ent E side, ⚡ 52°57'·77N 04°47'·37E, QR 9m 4M; (H24).
W side, ⚡ 52°57'·77N 04°47'·08E, Fl G 5s 9m 4M; 180°-067° (H24).

DEN HELDER TO IJMUIDEN

Grote Kaap ⚡ 52°52'·85N 04°42'·88E, Oc WRG 10s 30m W11M, R8M, G8M; G041°-088°, W088°-094°, R094°-131°.
Petten ⓛ 52°47'·33N 04°36'·68E, VQ (9) 10s.
Egmond-aan-Zee ☆ 52°37'·13N 04°37'·27E, Iso WR 10s 36m **W18M**, R14M; W010°-175°, R175°-188°; W ○ twr.
Meteomast ⚡ 52°36'·38N 04°23'·38E, Mo (U) 15s 11m 10M; Horn Mo (U). Mast, 118m high, is marked by R lts. A NCM buoy, Q, and SCM buoy, Q(6) + L Fl 15s, are 0·25M NNW and SSE respectively.
CP-Q8-A Platform ◨ 52°35'·67N 04°31'·73E, Mo (U) 15s.
BSP ≈ 52°30'·74N 04°29'·90E, Fl (4) Y 10s.
Baloeran ⓛ 52°29'·23N 04°32'·00E, Q (9) 15s.

▶ **IJMUIDEN**

A-NE ≈ 52°27'·93N 03°48'·60E, L Fl Y 10s.
IJ 3 ≈ 52°29'·70N 04°11'·94E, Fl (3) Y 10s.

PLOT WAYPOINTS ON YOUR CHART BEFORE USING THEM

IJmuiden 52°28'·44N 04°23'·78E, Mo (A) 8s; **Racon Y, 10M.**
Ldg lts 100·5°. **Front** ☆, 52°27'·70N 04°34'·46E, F WR 30m **W16M**, R13M; W050°-122°, R122°-145°, W145°-160°; dark R○twr. By day F 4m, 090·5°-110·5°. **Rear** ☆, 570m from front, Fl 5s 52m **29M**; 019°-199°; dark R○twr.
S bkwtr hd ☆ 52°27'·82N 04°31'·94E, FG 14m 10M (in fog Fl 3s); *Horn (2) 30s*. N bkwtr hd ☆ 52°28'·05N 04°32'·55E, FR 15m 10M.
Zuider Buitenkanaal, ☆ Iso G 6s, 52°27'·75N 04°33'·81E; ☆ Iso R 6s, 52°27'·84N 04°34'·39E.

▶ AMSTERDAM

Sixhaven marina ☆ 52°22'·99N 04°53'·69E, F & FR.
Oranjesluizen (to IJsselmeer) 52°22'·90N 04°57'·63E.

IJMUIDEN TO HOEK/ROTTERDAM

Eveline wreck 52°25'·49N 04°25'·00E, VQ (9) 10s.
Survey platform ☆ 52°16'·35N 04°17'·81E, Mo (U) 15s 42m and FR; R&W chequers; *Horn Mo (U) 20s*.
Noordwijk-aan-Zee ☆ 52°14'·90N 04°26'·01E, Oc (3) 20s 32m **18M**; W□twr.

▶ SCHEVENINGEN

SCH 52°07'·75N 04°14'·11E, Iso 4s.
Drain-W 52°06'·95N 04°14'·00E, VQ (9) 10s.
Drain-E 52°06'·71N 04°14'·43E, VQ (3) 5s.
KNS 52°06'·41N 04°15'·32E, Q (9)15s.
W mole ☆ 52°06'·23N 04°15'·16E, FG 12m 9M; G twr, W bands; *Horn (3) 30s*.
E mole ☆, FR 12m 9M; R twr, W bands.

▶ NOORD HINDER TSS

Garden City 51°29'·12N 02°17'·92E, Q (9) 15s.
Twin 51°32'·05N 02°22'·62E, Fl (3) Y 9s.
NHR-S 51°51'·35N 02°28'·71E, Fl Y 10s; *Bell*.
Birkenfels 51°38'·96N 02°32'·03E, Q (9) 15s.
Track Ferry 51°33'·78N 02°36'·33E, Fl Y 5s.
NHR-SE 51°45'·42N 02°39'·92E, Fl G 5s.
NHR-N 52°10'·78N 03°04'·69E, L Fl 8s; **Racon K, 10M.**

▶ APPROACHES TO HOEK VAN HOLLAND

Noord Hinder 52°00'·04N 02° 51'·03E, Fl (2) 10s; *Horn (2) 30s*; **Racon T, 12-15M.**
Europlatform 51°59'·75N 03°16'·42E, Mo (U) 15s; W structure, R bands; helicopter platform; *Horn Mo(U) 30s*.
Goeree ☆ 51°55'·42N 03°40'·03E, Fl (4) 20s 32m **28M**; R and W chequered twr on platform; helicopter platform; *Horn (4) 30s*; **Racon T, 12-15M.**
Maas Center 52°01'12N 03°53'·44E, Iso 4s; **Racon M, 10M.**
Indusbank N 52°02'·88N 04°03'·55E, VQ.
MN3 52°04'52N 03°58'·79E, Fl (3) G 10s.
MN1 52°02'11N 04°00'·80E, Fl G 5s.
MO 52°00'97N 03°58'·06E, Mo (A) 8s.
MV 51°57'·44N 03°58'·40E, Q (9) 15s.
Hinder 51°54'·53N 03°55'·40E, Q (9) 15s.
Westhoofd, 51°48'·78N 03°51'·82E, Fl (3) 15s 55m **30M**; R □ tr.

▶ HOEK VAN HOLLAND

Maasmond ldg lts 107°, both Iso R 6s 29/43m **18M**; 099·5°-114·5°, synch. **Front** ☆, 51°58'·55N 04°07'·53E. **Rear** ☆, 450 m from front.
MVN 51°59'·59N 04°00'·19E, VQ.
Maas 1 51°59'·39N 04°01'·67E, L Fl G 5s.
Maasvlakte ☆ 51°58'·19N 04°00'·84E, Fl (5) 20s 67m **28M**, H24; 340°-267°; B 8-sided twr, Y bands.
Nieuwe Noorderdam ☆ 51°59'·65N 04°02'·82E, FR 25m 10M; R twr, W bands. In fog Al Fl WR 6s; 278°-255°.
Nieuwe Zuiderdam ☆ 51°59'·13N 04°02'·47E, FG 25m 10M; G twr, W bands; heli platform. In fog Al Fl WG 6s; 330°-307°; *Horn 10s*.
Jachtensluis E side, E ent ☆ 51°41'·91N 04°25'·44E, FR.

▶ ROTTERDAM

Maassluis Buitenhaven, E ent ☆ 51°54'·93N 04°14'·81E, FG 6m.
Vlaardingen Buitenhaven, E ent ☆ 51°53'·99N 04°20'·95E, FG.
Spuihaven, W ent ☆ 51°53'·98N 04°23'·98E, FR.
Veerhaven, E ent ☆ 51°54'·40N 04°28'·74E, FG.

HARINGVLIET

▶ APPROACHES TO HARINGVLIET

Buitenbank 51°51'·14N 03°25'·69E, Iso 4s.
Bollen 51°49'·99N 03°32'·98E, VQ (9) 10s.
MW 51°44'·25N 03°23'·66E, Q (9) 15s.
MN 51°47'·65N 03°29'·90E, Q.
BG2 51°46'·05N 03°37'·00E, Fl Y 5s; Y pile.
West Schouwen ☆ 51°42'·53N 03°41'·48E, Fl (2+1)15s 57m **30M**; Gy twr, R diagonal stripes on upper part.
Ooster 51°47'·89N 03°41'·27E, Q (9) 15s.
SH 51°49'·47N 03°45'·77E, VQ (9) 10s.
Ha10 51°51'·76N 03°51'·59E, Fl Y 5s; Y pile.
SG 51°51'·93N 03°51'·40E, Iso 4s.
SG 2 51°51'·75N 03°53'·44E, Iso R 4s.
SG 5 51°50'·88N 03°55'·35E, Iso G 4s.
SG 9 51°50'·75N 03°57'·30E, L Fl G 8s.
SG 17 51°51'·30N 04°00'·00E, L Fl G 8s.
P3 51°51'·23N 04°01'·04E, L Fl G 5s.
G1 51°50'·05N 04°02'·18E, L Fl G 8s.

▶ STELLENDAM

N mole ☆ 51°49'·87N 04°02'·01E, FG; *Horn (2) 15s*.

▶ HELIUSHAVEN/HELLEVOETSLUIS

Heliushaven W jetty ☆ 51°49'·24N 04°07'·16E, FR 7m 4M.
E jetty ☆ 51°49'·23N 04°07'·28E, FG 7m 3M.
Hellevoetsluis W side ☆ 51°49'·18N 04°07'·66E, Iso WRG 10s 16m W11M, R8M, G7M; G266°-275°, W275°-294°, R294°-316°, W316°-036°, G036°-058°, W058°-095°, R095°-140°; W twr, R top.
Hoornsche Hoofden ☆ 51°48'·28N 04°10'·97E. Oc WRG 5s 6m, W7M, R5M, G 4M; W288°-297°, G297°-313°, W313°-325°, R325°-335°, G335°-344·5°, W344·5°-045°, G045°-055°, W055°-131°, R131°-N shore; watchhouse on dyke.

▶ MIDDELHARNIS/NIEUWENDIJK

Middleharnis W pier hd ☆ 51°46'·60N 04°11'·72E, F WRG 5m W8M, R5M, G4M; W144°-164·5°, R164·5°-176·5°, G176·5°-144°.
Nieuwendijk ldg lts 303·5°. Front, 51°45'·04N 04°19'·38E, Iso WRG 6s 8m W9M, R7M, G6M; G093°-100°, W100°-103·5°, R103·5°-113°, W113°-093°; B framework twr. Rear, 450m from front, F 11m 9M; B framework twr.

▶ VOLKERAKSLUIZEN/WILLEMSTAD

Jachtensluis E side, E ent ☆ 51°41'·91N 04°25'·44E, FR.
Jachtensluis W side, S ent ☆ 51°41'·91N 04°24'·29E, FG.
Noorder Voorhaven, W mole ☆ 51°42'·03N 04°25'·77E, FG 6m 4M; R lantern on pedestal; in fog FY.
Willemstad HD 9 51°41'·81N 04°26'·62E, Iso G 4s.

OOSTERSCHELDE AND APPROACHES

▶ OUTER APPROACHES

Schouwenbank 51°44'·94N 03°14'·31E, Mo (A) 8s; **Racon O, 10M.**
MD 3 51°42'·71N 03°26'·97E, Fl G 5s.
Middelbank 51°40'·83N 03°18'·19E, Iso 8s.
Rabsbank 51°38'·25N 03°09'·90E, Iso 4s.
Westpit 51°33'·65N 03°09'·92E, Iso 8s.
ZSB 51·36'·59N 03°15'·69E, VQ (9) 10s.
OG1 51°36'·22N 03°20'·05E, QG.
TB 51°34'·38N 02°59'·07E, Q.
SW Thornton 51°30'·95N2 02°50'·92E, Iso 8s.
Wave observation post ⊙ VR 51°30'·28N 03°14'·45E, Fl Y 5s.

▶ OUDE ROOMPOT (selected marks)

OG-WG 51°37'·18N 03°23'·81E, VQ (9) 10s.
WG1 51°38'·00N 03°26'·22E, Iso G 8s.
WG4 ☆ 51°38'·60N 03°28'·77E, L Fl R 8s.
WG7 51°39'·40N 03°32'·65E, Iso G 4s.
WG-GB 51°39'·70N 03°32'·67E.
OR2 51°39'·48N 03°33'·70E.
OR5 51°38'·71N 03°35'·51E, Iso G 8s.
OR6 51°38'·71N 03°36'·29E, Iso R 8s.
OR8 51°38'·23N 03°37'·35E.
OR11 51°36'·97N 03°38'·38E, Iso G 4s.
OR12 51°37'·26N 03°39'·24E, Iso R 8s.
Roompotsluis ldg lts 073·5°, both Oc G 5s; synch. Front, 51°37'·33N 03°40'·74E. Rear, 280m from front.
N bkwtr ☆ 51°37'·30N 03°40'·09E ,FR 7m; *Horn(2) 30s.*

▶ BURGHSLUIS, FLAUWERSPOLDER, SCHELPHOEK

Burghsluis S mole ☆ 51°40'·53N 03°50'·79E, F WRG 9m W8M, R5M, G4M; W218°-230°, R230°-245°, W245°-253·5°, G253·5°-293°, W293°-000°, G000°-025·5°, W025·5°-032°, G032°-041°, R041°-070°, W070°-095°; mast on R col.
Flauwerspolder W mole ☆ 51°40'·63N 03°45'·49E, Iso WRG 4s 8m W6M, R/G4M; R303°-344°, W344°-347°, G347°-083°, W083°-086°, G086°-103°, W103°-110°, R110°-128°, W128°-303°; W daymark, B band on pylon.
Schelphoek, E bkwtr ☆ 51°41'·22N 03°48'·71E ,Fl (2) 10s 8m.

▶ DE VAL/ZIERIKZEE

Engelsche Vaarwater ldg lts 019°. Front, 51°37'·68N 03°55'·50E Iso WRG 3s 7m W6M, R/G4M; R290°-306°, W306°-317°, G317°-334°, W334°-337°, G337°-017·5°, W017·5°-026°, G026°-090°, R090°-108°, W108°-290°; R pedestal, W band. Rear, 300m from front, Iso 3s 16m 6M.
Zierikzee W jetty ☆ 51°37'·89N 03°53'·38E, Oc WRG 6s 10m W6M, R/G4M; G063°-100°, W100°-133°, R133°-156°, W156°-278°, R278°-306°, G306°-314°, W314°-333°, R333°-350°, W350°-063°; R post, W bands.

▶ KRAMMER/BRUINISSE/KRAMMERSLUIZEN

Stoofpolder ☆ 51°39'·48N 04°06'·29E, Iso WRG 4s 11m, W12M, R9M, G8M; R147°-218°, G218°-240·5°, R240·5°-248°, W248°-255°, G255°-259°, W259°-263°, R263°-293°, W293°-297°, R297°-028°; B post, W bands.
Bruinisse N mole ☆ 51°39'·90N 04°05'·94E, FG 3M; Gy bcn.
Krammersluizen N bkwtr ☆ 51°39'·78N 04°08'·35E, FR.
Zuide Vlije, SRK4-ZV11 buoy, 51°38'·23N 04°14'·56E, Iso 2s; **Racon K, 3-10M.**

▶ ZIJPE/ANNA JACOBAPOLDER

Zipje, N mole ☆ 51°38'·63N 04°06'·02E, Iso G 4s.
St Philipsland, on dyke ☆ 51°39'·11N 04°07'·07E, Oc WRG 4s 9m W8M, R5M, G4M; W051°-100°, R100°-144°, W144°-146°, G146°-173°; black structure.
Zijpsche Bout ☆ 51°38'·79N 04°05'·67E, Oc WRG 10s 10m W12M, R9M, G8M; R208°-211°, W211°-025°, G025°-030°, W030°-040°, R040°-066°; mast on R col.
Tramweghaven S mole ☆ 51°38'·85N 04°05'·77E, Iso R 4s 7m.

▶ STAVENISSE/ST ANNALAND

Hoek Van Ouwerkerk ldg lts 009·2°. Front, 51°36'·86N 03°58'·26E Iso WRG 6s; R267°-306°, W306°-314°, G314°-007·5°, W007·5°-011·5°, G011·5°-067°, W067°-068·5°, G068·5°-085°, W085°-102·°5, G102·5°-112·5°, R112·5°-121·5°. Rear, 340m from front, Iso 6s.
Keeten B 51°36'·35N 03°58'·05E, Mo (A) 8s; **Racon K, 3-10M.**
Stavenisse E Mole Head ☆ 51°35'·68N 04°00'·26E Oc WRG 5s 11m W12M, R9M, G8M; B pylon; vis: R080°-106°, W106°-109°, G109°-116°, W116°-123°, G123°-155°, W155°-157°, G157°-215°, W215°-219·5°, G219·5°-230°, W230°-236, R236°-249°.
St Annaland Entrance W side ☆ 51°36'·26N 04°06'·53E FG.

16

▶ YERSEKE/THOLENSCHE GAT/GORISHOEK

025/Sv 12 51°31'·35N 04°02'·36E QG.
Ldg Lts 155° (through Schaar van Yerseke). Front 51°30'·02N 04°03'·38E Iso 4s 9m; in fog FY. Rear, 180m from front, Iso 4s 14m; synch; in fog 2 FY. FG and FR mark mole heads.
Tholensche Gat. Strijenham ☆ 51°31'·35N 04°08'·83E Oc WRG 5s 10m W8M, R5M, G5M; vis: Wshore-268°, R268°-281·5°, W281·5°-297°, G297°-310°, R310°-060·5°, G060·5°-068°, W068°-082°. R082°-115°, W115°-shore.
Werkhaven (Bergsediepsluis) W Mole Head ☆ 51°30'·88N 04°09'·68W FG.
Gorishoek ☆ 51°31'·52N 04°04'·59E Iso WRG 8s 8m W6M, R4M, G4M; R pedestal, W bands; vis: R260°-278°, W278°-021°, G021°-025°, W025°-071°, G071°-085°, W085°-103°, R103°-120°, W120°-260°.

▶ KATS/GOESSCHE SAS (GOES)/WEMELDINGE

Marina Kats S Jetty Head ☆ 51°34'·37N 03°53'·61E, Oc WRG 8s 5m 5M; vis: W344°-153°, R153°-165°, G165°-202°, W202°-211°, G211°-256°, W256°-259°, G259°-313°, W313°-331°.
Goessche Sas S Mole Head ☆ 51°32'·23N 03°55'·90E, FR.
Galgeplaat 51°32'·60N 03°58'·95E, Q (6) + L Fl 15s.
Wemeldinge W jetty ☆ 51°31'·34N 04°00'·17E, FG 7M.
W Head (Zuid-Beveland Kanaal, N ent) ☆ 51°31'·17N 04°00'·84E, Oc WRG 5s 8m W9M, R/G7M; R105·5°-114°, W114°-124°, G124°-140·5°, W140·5°-144°, G144°-192°, W192°-205°, R205°-233·5°, W233·5°-258·5°, R258·5°-296·5°. Iso 4s R&G lts mark canal.

▶ SOPHIAHAVEN/COLIJNSPLAAT

Roompot Marina, N mole head ☆ 51°35'·62N 03°43'·20E, FR.
Colijnsplaat, E head ☆ 51°36'·22N 03°51'·07E, FR 3m 3M; *Horn.*
Zeeland Bridge: N and S passages marked by FY lts 15m.

WESTKAPELLE TO VLISSINGEN

Kaloo 51°35'·56N 03°23'·23E, Iso 8s.
OG-GR 51°32'·74N 03°24'·71E, VQ (3) 5s.
Ldg lts 149·5°. Front, Noorderhoofd, 51°32'·40N 03°26'·20E, Oc WRG 10s 20m; W13M, R/G10M; R353°-008°, G008°-029°, W029°-169°; R ○ twr, W band; 0·73M from rear (Westkapelle).
Westkapelle ☆, Common rear, 51°31'·75N 03°26'·80E, Fl 3s 49m

PLOT WAYPOINTS ON YOUR CHART BEFORE USING THEM

28M; obsc'd by land on certain brgs; □ twr, R top.
Molenhoofd ☆ 51°31'·58N 03°26'·03E, Oc WRG 6s 10m; R306°-329°, W329°-349°, R349°-008°, G008°-034·5°, W034·5°-036·5°, G036·5°-144°, W144°-169°, R169°-198°; W mast R bands.
OG5 51°31'·12N 03°25'·50E, QG. (Oostgat)
Ldg lts 326°: Front, Zoutelande 51°30'·26N 03°28'·39E, FR 21m 12M; 321°-352°; R □ twr, 1·8M from rear (Westkapelle).
Kaapduinen, ldg lts 130°: both Oc 5s 25/34m 13M; synch; Y □ twrs, R bands. Front, 51°28'·46N 03°30'·96E; 115°-145°. Rear, 220m from front; 107·5°-152·5°.
Fort de Nolle ☆ 51°26'·94N 03°33'·11E, Oc WRG 9s 11m W6M, R/G4M; R293°-309°, W309°-324·5°, G324·5°-336·5°, R336·5°-014°, G014°-064°, R064°-099·5°, W099·5°-110·5°, G110·5°-117°, R117-130°; W col, R bands.

OFFSHORE: WEST HINDER TO SCHEUR CHANNEL

West Hinder ☆ 51°23'·31N 02°26'·27E, Fl (4) 30s 23m 13M; *Horn Mo (U) 30s*; **Racon W**.
WH Zuid 51°22'·78N 02°26'·25E, Q (6) + L Fl 15s.
Oost-Dyck 51°21'·38N 02°31'·09E, Q.
Oost-Dyck West 51°17'·15N 02°26'·32E, Q (9) 15s.
Oostdyck radar twr, 51°16'·49N 02°26'·83E; four ☆ Mo (U) 15s 15m 12M; *Horn Mo (U) 30s;* **Racon O**. R twr, 3 W bands, with adjacent red twr/helipad.
A/N 51°23'·45N 02°36'·92E, Fl (4) R 20s.
A/Z 51°21'·15N 02°36'·92E, Fl (3) G 10s.
KB 51°21'·03N 02°42'·83E, Q; **Racon K**.
MBN 51°20'·82N 02°46'·29E, Q.
SWA 51°22'·28N 02°46'·34E, Q (9) 15s.
VG 51°22'·95N 02°46'·32E, Q (9) 15s.
Middelkerke Bank 51°18'·19N 02°42'·74E, Fl G 5s.
Goote Bank 51°26'·95N 02°52'·72E, Q (3) 10s.

WESTERSCHELDE AND APPROACHES

▶ SCHEUR CHANNEL

S1 51°23'·15N 03°00'·12E, Fl G 5s.
S2 51°23'·37N 02°58'·09E, QR.
S3 51°24'·30N 03°02'·92E, Q.
S4 51°25'·03N 03°02'·85E, Fl (4) R 10s.
MOW0 ⊙ 51°23'·67N 03°02'·75E, Fl (5) Y 20s; *Whis;* **Racon S, 10M**.
S5 51°23'·70N 03°05'·92E, Fl G 5s.
S6 51°24'·20N 03°05'·92E, Fl R 5s.
S7 51°23'·98N 03°10'·42E, Fl G 5s.
S8 51°24'·43N 03°10'·42E, Fl (4) R 10s.
S9 51°24'·42N 03°14'·98E, QG.
S10 51°24'·85N 03°14'·98E, Fl R 5s.
S12 51°24'·67N 03°18'·22E, Fl (4) R 10s.
S-W 51°24'·13N 03°18'·19E, Q.
S14 51°24'·58N 03°19'·67E, Fl R 5s.

▶ WIELINGEN CHANNEL

W-Z 51°22'·57N 03°10'·71E, Q (9) 15s.
BVH 51°23'·12N 03°12'·02E, Q (6) + L Fl R 15s.
MOW3 tide gauge ☆ 51°23'·37N 03°11'·89E, Fl (5) Y 20s; *Mo (U) 30s*; **Racon H, 10M**.
W 51°23'·24N 03°14'·89E, Fl (3) G 15s.
S-W 51°24'·13N 03°18'·19E, Q.
W1 51°23'·47N 03°18'·22E, Fl G 5s.
W2 51°24'·73N 03°21'·56E, Iso R 8s.
Fort Maisonneuve 51°24'·29N 03°21'·63E, VQ.
W3 51°23'·82N 03°19'·67E, Iso G 8s.
W4 51°24'·92N 03°24'·42E, L Fl R 5s.
W5 51°24'·43N 03°24'·48E, Iso G 4s.
W6 51°25'·12N 03°27'·10E, Iso R 8s.
W7 51°24'·60N 03°27'·22E, Iso G 8s.
W8 51°25'·48N 03°30'·27E, Iso R 4s.
W9 51°24'·96N 03°30'·43E, Iso G 4s.
W10 51°25'·85N 03°33'·28E, QR.
Nieuwe Sluis ☆ 51°24'·41N 03°31'·27E, Oc WRG 10s 26m W14M, R11M, G10M; R055°-089°, W089°-093°, G093°-105°, R105°-134°, W134°-136·5°, G136·5°-156·5°, W156·5°-236·5°, G236·5°-243°, W243°-254°, R254°-292°, W292°-055°; B 8-sided twr, W bands.

▶ VLISSINGEN

Ldg lts 117°. Leugenaar, Front, 51°26'·43N 03°34'·12E, Oc R 5s 6m 7M; W&R pile; intens 108°-126°. Rear Sardijngeul, 550m from front, Oc WRG 5s 8m W12M, R9M, G8M; synch; R245°-272°, G272°-282.5°, W282.5°-123°, R123°-147°; R △, W bands on R & W mast.
Koopmanshaven, W mole root, ☆ 51°26'·30N 03°34'·55E, Iso WRG 3s 15m W12M, R10M, G9M; R253°-277°, W277°-284°, R284°-297°, W297°-306·5°, G306·5°-013°, W013°-024°, G024°-033°, W033°-035°, G035°-039°, W039°-055°, G055°-084·5°, R084·5°-092°, G092°-111°, W111°-114°; R pylon.
Buitenhaven W mole ☆ 51°26'·38N 03°36'·05E, FR 10m 5M; also Iso WRG 4s; W073°-324°, G324°-352°, W352°-017°, G017°-042°, W042°-056°, R056°-073°; W post, R bands; tfc sigs.
Buitenhaven E mole ☆ 51°26'·41N 03°36'·36E, FG 7m 4M.
Schone Waardin ☆ 51°26'·54N 03°37'·90E, Oc WRG 9s 10m W12M, R10M, G9M; R248°-260·5°, G260·5°-269°, W269°-287·5°, G287·5°-326°, R326°-341°, G341°-023°, W023°-024°, G024°-054°, R054°-062°, W062°-076·5°, G076·5°-078·5°, R078·5°-083°; R mast, W bands.

▶ VLISSINGEN OOST (Commercial port)

W mole ☆ 51°26'·88N 03°40'·08E, FR 9m 5M; in fog FY; W col; *Horn (2) 20s*.
Ldg lts 023°, both Oc R 8s 7/12m 8M, 015°-031°; synch. Front, 51°27'·876N 03°40'·99E, G mast. Rear, 100m from front, G mast.
Dir F WRG 305°, R303·5°-304·9°, W304·9°-305·1°, G305·1°-306·5°. 51°27'·88N 03°40'·53E.

▶ BORSSELE-NOORDNOL

Pier ☆ 51°25'·50N 03°42'·75E, Oc WRG 5s 10m; R305°-336°, W336°-341°, G341°-001·5°, W001·5°-007·5°, R007·5°-022°, G022°-054°, W054°-057°, G057°-109·5°, W109·5°-128°, R128°-155°, W155°-305°; R mast, W bands.
Borssele, Total jetty, NW end ☆ 51°24'·79N 03°43'·59E, Oc WR 10s 10m; R133°-159°, W159°-133°.
Borssele-Everingen ☆ 51°24'·68N 03°44'·08E, Iso WRG 4s 10m; G028°-076°, W076°-094°, W094°-134°, W134°-270°, R270°-313°, W313°-345°, G345°-359°, W359°-028°.

▶ BRESKENS

Songa 51°25'·16N 03°33'·66E, QG.
ARV-VH 51°24'·71N 03°33'·90E, Q.
VH2 51°24'·27N 03°34'·15E.
Yacht hbr. W mole ☆ 51°24'·03N 03°34'·06E, F WRG 7m; R090°-128°, W128°-157°, G157°-169·5°, W169·5°-173°, R173°-194°, G194°-296°, W296°-300°, R300°-320°, G320°-090°; in fog FY; Gy mast.
Ferry hbr, W mole ☆, FG 9m 4M; in fog FY; 51°24'·36N 03°33'·09E; B&W mast; fog det lt.

WESTERSCHELDE: TERNEUZEN TO ANTWERPEN

▶ TERNEUZEN

Nieuw Neuzenpolder ldg lts 125°, both Oc 5s 6/16m 9/13M; intens 117°-133°; synch. Front, 51°20'·97N 03°47'·24E; W col, B bands. Rear, 365m from front; B & W twr.
West Buitenhaven, no entry for yachts.
Oost Buitenhaven E mole ☆ 51°20'·56N 03°49'·19E, FR 5M; tfc sigs for Oostsluis.
Marinas, W mole FG ☆ 51°20'·57N 03°49'·63E, Gy mast. Also B & W twr ☆ close SW, Oc WRG 5s 15m W9M, R7M, G6M; R090°-115°, W115°-120°, G120°-130°, W130°-245°, G245°-249°, W249°-279°, R279°-004°.

▶ ELLEWOUTSDIJK

E5 51°22'·62N 03°48'·56E, Iso G 8s; (Everingen channel).
W pier (unlit ent to ⚓) 51°23'·09N 03°49'·02E.

▶ HANSWEERT

W mole ☆ 51°26'·41N 04°00'·53E, Oc WRG 10s 9m W9M, R7M, G6M; R288°-313°, G313°-320°, W320°-334°, G334°-356·5°, W356·5°-042·5°, R042·5°-061·5°, W061·5°-078°, G078°-099°, W099°-114·5°, R114·5°-127·5°, W127·5°-288°; in fog FY; R twr, W bands.

▶ WALSOORDEN

N mole, ☆ 51°22'·95N 04°02'·07E, FG 5m; Gy post.

▶ PAAL

Speelmansgat lt bcn ☆ 51°21'·94N 04°06'·13E, Fl (5) Y 20s.

BELGIUM

▶ ZANDVLIET

Dir lt 118·4°. 51°20'·68N 04°16'·28E, WRG 20m W4M, R/G3M; Oc G116·63°-117·17°, FG117·18°-117·58°, Alt GW117·58°-118·63°, F 118·13°-118·63°, Alt RW118·63°-119·18°, FR119·18°-119·58°, Oc R 119·58°-120·13°.

▶ DOEL/LILLO

Doel ldg lts 188·5°. Front, 51°18'·45N 04°16'·17E, Fl WR 3s 9m, W10M, R7M; R shore-185°, W185°-334°, R334°-shore. Rear, 312m from front, Fl 3s 19m 10M; synch. By day, W18M, 186°-191°.
Lillo pier ☆ 51°18'·15N 04°17'·21E, Oc WRG 10s 5m; W9M, R7M, G6M; R shore-303·1°, W303·1°-308·2°, G308·2°-096·5°, W096·5°-148°, R148°-shore; R □ on B bcn.

ANTWERPEN

Royerssluis (for Willemdok ⚓), ldg lts 091°, both FR. Ent FR/G.
No. 109 (off Linkeroever ⚓) 51°13'·89N 04°23'·87E, Iso G 8s.
Linkeroever marina 51°13'·91N 04°23'·70E, F WR 9m W3M, R2M; W shore-283°, R283°-shore; B ⊙, R lantern. Ent, FR/G.

ZEEBRUGGE TO NIEUWPOORT

▶ ZEEBRUGGE

SZ 51°23'·67N 03°07'·59E, Q (3) 10s.
Z 51°22'·47N 03°10'·01E, QG.
WZ 51°22'·56N 03°10'·72E, Q (9) 15s.
A2 51°22'·42N 03°07'·05E, Iso 8s.
Ldg lts 136°, both Oc 5s 22/45m 8M; 131°-141°; H24, synch; W cols, R bands. Front, 51°20'·71N 03°13'·11E; Rear, 890m SE.
W outer mole ☆ 51°21'·73N 03°11'·17E, Oc G 7s 31m 7M; 057°-267°; G vert strip lts visible from seaward; *Horn (3) 30s.*
E outer mole ☆ 51°21'·78N 03°11'·86E, Oc R 7s 31m 7M; 087°-281°; R vert strip lts visible from seaward; *Bell 25s.*
Ldg lts 154°: Front, 51°20'·33N 03°12'·89E, Oc WR 6s 20m 3M, W135°-160°, R160°-169°; W pylon, R bands. Rear, Oc 6s 38m 3M, 520m from front; H24, synch.
Heist mole ☆ 51°20'·86N 03°12'·18E, Oc WR 15s 22m, **W20M, R18M**; W068°-145°, R145°-212°, W212°-296°; IPTS; *Horn (3+1) 90s.*
Ldg lts 220°, both 2 FW (vert) neon strip lts, 30/30m; BW cols.
Ldg lts 193°, both 2 FR (vert) neon strip lts, 30/29m; RW cols.

▶ BLANKENBERGE

Lt ho ☆ 51°18'·76N 03°06'·87E, Fl (2) 8s 30m **20M**; 065°-245°; W twr, B top.
Ldg lts 134°, both FR 5/8m 3/10M; front, R cross (X) on mast.
E pier ☆ 51°18'·91N 03°06'·56E, FR 12m 11M; 290°-245°; W ○ twr; *Bell (2) 15s.*
W pier ☆ 51°18'·89N 03°06'·43E, FG 14m 11M; intens 065°-290°, unintens 290°-335°; W ○ twr.

16

▶ OOSTENDE

WBN 51°21'·50N 03°02'·59E, QG.
SWW 51°21'·95N 03°00'·95E, Fl (4) R 20s.
Wenduine Bank E 51°18'·83N 03°01'·54E, QR.
A1 bis 51°21'·68N 02°58'·02E, L Fl 10s.
A1 51°22'·37N 02°53'·34E, Iso 8s.
Oostende Bank N 51°21'·20N 02°52'·91E, Q.
Nautica Ena wreck 51°18'·07N 02°52'·80E, Q.
Wenduine Bank W 51°17'·23N 02°52'·75E, Q (9) 15s.
Oostendebank E 51°17'·35N 02°51'·92E, Fl (4) R 20s.
Buitenstroom Bank 51°15'·17N 02°51'·71E, Q.
Binnenstroom Bank 51°14'·47N 02°53'·65E, Q (3) 10s.
Ldg lts 128°, both 3 Iso 4s (vert) 22/32m 4M, 051°-201°; X on framework twrs, R/W bands. Front, 51°14'·13N 02°55'·55E. Rear, 175m from front.
Oostende lt ho ☆ 51°14'·18N 02°55'·83E, Fl (3) 10s 65m **27M**; obsc 069·5°-071°; W twr, 2 sinusoidal Bu bands.
E pier ☆ 51°14'·39N 02°55'·14E, FR 15m 12M; 333°-243°; W ○ twr; IPTS, plus QY when channel closed for ferry; *Horn Mo(OE) 30s.*
W pier ☆ 51°14'·31N 02°55'·03E, FG 14m 10M, 057°-327°; W ○ twr; *Bell 4s.*
Oostendebank W 51°16'·20N 02°44'·75E, Q (9)15s.
LST 420 51°15'·45N 02°40'·67E, Q (9) 15s.
Middelkerke Bank S 51°14'·73N 02°41'·89E, Q (9) R 15s.
D1 wreck 51°13'·94N 02°38'·57E, Q (3) 10s.
Zuidstroom Bank 51°12'·29N 02°47'·38E, Fl R 5s.

▶ NIEUWPOORT

Weststroom Bank 51°11'·33N 02°43'·04E, Fl (4) R 20s.
Lt ho ☆ 51°09'·28N 02°43'·80E, Fl (2) R 14s 28m **16M**; R ○ twr, W bands; 2 ca E of E pier root.
E pier ☆ 51°09'·42N 02°43'·08E, FR 11m 10M; 025°-250°, 307°-347°; W ○ twr; *Horn Mo (K) 30s.*
W pier ☆ 51°09'·35N 02°43'·00E, FG 11m 9M; 025°-250°, 284°-324°; W ○ twr; IPTS from root; *Bell (2) 10s.*
Oostduinkerke 51°09'·14N 02°39'·46E, Q.
Den Oever wreck 51°08'·10N 02°37'·45E.
Nieuwpoort Bank 51°10'·17N 02°36'·09E, Q (9) 15s.
Trapegeer 51°08'·42N 02°34'·38E, Fl G 10s (Westdiep).
E11 51°07'·24N 02°30'·61E, Fl G 4s.
E12 51°07'·90N 02°30'·59E, VQ (6) + L Fl 10s.
For Passe de Zuydcoote, see 9.17.4.

Belg/French border is between E12 and E11 buoys; AC 1872

9.16.5 PASSAGE INFORMATION

North France and Belgium Cruising Companion (Nautical Data Ltd/Featherstone), *North Sea Passage Pilot* (Imray/Navin): North Sea and Belgian/Dutch coasts to Den Helder. NP 55 North Sea (East) Pilot: Delfzijl to Scheveningen. NP 28 Dover Strait Pilot: Scheveningen to Nieuwpoort (and W to Cap d'Antifer). See also *Havengids Nederland* (Vetus) in Dutch, well illustrated.

NETHERLANDS (charts 2182A, 1405, 2593, 2322, 3371, 1872) While British Admiralty charts are adequate for through passages, coastal navigation and entry to the main ports, larger scale Dutch yacht charts (1800 series) are essential for exploring the cruising grounds along this coast or entering the smaller hbrs. Inland, the booklet-style chart *Staande-Mast Route* (Fixed Mast Route), published by ANWB at €16.95 is very detailed with copious notes (in Dutch). The route is depicted on 9.16.2.

Numerous wrecks and obstructions lie offshore and in coastal areas; potential hazardous are marked. The shoals of the Dutch coast and Waddenzee may change due to gales and tidal streams. Sea level may also be affected by barometic pressure; wise to take advice from the Dutch CG before tackling the *wadden*. The Terschelling-German Bight TSS, Off Vlieland TSS and Off Texel TSS lie between 5 and 10M to seaward of the West Frisian Islands. Most cruising yachts will navigate within this relatively narrow ITZ. Further offshore, and particularly in and near the Off Vlieland TSS, West Friesland TSS and Botney Ground TSS, the numerous oil and gas fields further complicate the navigational scene. For general notes on N Sea oil and gas installations, see 9.5.5.

THE WEST FRISIAN ISLANDS (charts 2593) From the Ems W and SSW for some 85M along the Dutch coast to Den Helder (9.16.15) lies the chain of West Frisian Is. They have similar characteristics – being low, long and narrow, with the major axis parallel to the coast. Texel is the largest and, with Vlieland and Terschelling, lies furthest offshore.

Between the islands, narrow chans (*zeegat* in Dutch, *Seegat* in German) give access to/from the North Sea. Most of these chans are shallow for at least part of their length, and in these shoal areas a dangerous sea builds up in a strong onshore wind against the outgoing (ebb) tide. The zeegat of the Ems and the zeegaten between Vlieland and Terschelling and between Den Helder and Texel are safe for yachts up to force 8 winds between SW and NE. All the others are unsafe in strong onshore winds.

The flood stream along this coast is E-going, so it starts to run in through the zeegaten progressively from W to E. Where the tide meets behind each island, as it flows in first at the W end and a little later at the E end, a bank is formed, called a *wad* (Dutch) or *Watt* (German). These banks between the islands and the coast are major obstacles to E/W progress inside the islands. The chans are narrow and winding, marked by buoys and/or withies (⸸ ⸸) in the shallower parts, and they mostly dry; so that it is essential to time the tide correctly.

This is an area most suited to shallow-draft yachts, particularly flat bottomed or with bilge keels, centreboards or legs, that can take the ground easily. Whilst the zeegaten are described briefly below, the many chans inside the islands and across the Waddenzee are mentioned only for orientation.

DELFZIJL TO AMELAND (chart 2593) The estuary of R Ems (chart 3632 and 9.15.5) runs seaward past the SW side of the German island of Borkum (9.15.24). It gives access to Delfzijl and Termunterzijl (9.16.7), or Emden (9.15.25). Hubertgat, which runs parallel to and S of the main Westerems chan, is slightly more direct when bound to/from the W, but in both these chans there is a dangerous sea in strong NW winds over the ebb. Hubertgat is now sparsely buoyed and unlit. ▶*The E-going (flood) stream begins at HW Helgoland + 0530, and the W-going (ebb) stream begins at HW Helgoland –0030, sp rates 1·5kn.*◀

Friesche Zeegat, between Ameland and Schiermonnikoog (9.16.7), has a main chan called Westgat and buoys marked 'WG'. In strong winds the sea breaks across the whole passage. Westgat leads S through Wierumer Gronden, past Engelsmanplaat (a prominent sandbank) and into Zoutkamperlaag which is the main chan (marked by buoys prefixed 'Z') to Lauwersoog (9.16.8). Here locks give access to the Lauwersmeer and inland waterways.

Zeegat van Ameland, between Ameland and Terschelling, is fronted by the sandbank of Bornrif extending 3M seaward. The main entrance is also called Westgat, with buoys prefixed by letters 'WG'. The chan runs close N of Terschelling, and divides into Boschgat and Borndiep. For Nes (Ameland), see 9.16.13. ▶*In Westgat the flood stream begins at HW Helgoland + 0425, and the ebb stream at HW Helgoland –0150, sp rates 2kn.*◀ A dangerous sea develops in strong onshore winds.

TERSCHELLING TO TEXEL Zeegat Het Vlie (chart 112 and 9.16.9), between Terschelling and Vlieland (9.16.11), gives access to the hbrs of Vlieland, West Terschelling (9.16.10) and Harlingen (9.16.13); also to the locks at Kornwerderzand. Shallow banks extend more than 5M seaward; the main chan (buoyed) through them is Zuider Stortemelk passing close N of Vlieland. In this chan the buoys are prefixed by letters 'ZS'. ▶*The E-going (flood) stream begins at HW Helgoland + 0325, while the W-going (ebb) stream begins at HW Helgoland – 0230, sp rates 2·5kn.*◀ Vliesloot leads to Oost Vlieland hbr. Approach West Terschelling via West Meep and Slenk. From Zuider Stortemelk the Vliestroom, a deep well buoyed chan (buoys prefixed by letters 'VL'), runs S about 4M until its junction with Blauwe Slenk and Inschot. Blauwe Slenk runs ESE to Harlingen; and Inschot SE to the Kornwerderzand locks into IJsselmeer.

Eierlandsche Gat, between Vlieland and Texel, consists of dangerous shoals between which run very shallow and unmarked chans, only used by fishermen.

Zeegat van Texel (chart 1546) lies between Texel and Den Helder, and gives access to the Waddenzee, the tidal part of the former Zuider Zee. Haaksgronden shoals extend 5M seaward, with three chans: Schulpengat on S side, leading into Breewijd; Westgat unmarked through centre of shoals, where the stream sets across the chan, is only suitable for passage in good weather and in daylight; and Molengat near the Texel shore. Schulpengat is the well marked main chan, buoys being prefixed with letter 'S'; but strong SW winds cause rough seas against ▶*the SW-going (ebb) stream which begins at HW Helgoland – 0330, while the NE-going (flood) stream begins at HW Helgoland + 0325, sp rates 1·5kn.*◀ Molengat is marked by buoys prefixed by letters 'MG', but strong winds between W and N cause a bad sea. When coming from the NW or NE the Molengat is always the best route unless the weather is exceptionally bad. Routeing via the Schulpengat involves a southerly deviation of approx 15M and leads W of the very dangerous Zuider Haaks which should be avoided in bad weather. ▶*In Molengat the N-going (ebb) stream begins at HW Helgoland – 0145, and the S-going (flood) stream at HW Helgoland + 0425, sp rates 1·25kn.*◀ For Oudeschild, see 9.16.14.

E of Den Helder and the Marsdiep, the flood makes in three main directions through the SW Waddenzee:

a. to E and SE through Malzwin and Wierbalg to Den Oever (where the lock into IJsselmeer is only available during daylight hours on working days); thence NE along the Afsluitdijk, and then N towards Harlingen (9.16.13);

b. to NE and E through Texelstroom and Doove Balg towards the Pollen flats; and

c. from Texelstroom, NE and N through Scheurrak, Omdraai and Oude Vlie, where it meets the flood stream from Zeegat van Terschelling. The ebb runs in reverse. The Kornwerderzand locks (available H24), near NE end of Afsluitdijk, also give access to the IJsselmeer (9.16.16).

DEN HELDER TO THE WESTERSCHELDE The coast S from Den Helder is low, and not readily visible from seaward, like most of the Dutch coast. Conspic landmarks include: chys of nuclear power station 1·5M NNE of Petten, Egmond aan Zee lt ho, chys of steelworks N of IJmuiden, two lt ho's at IJmuiden, big hotels at Zandvoort, Noordwijk aan Zee light and Scheveningen light house and big hotels. ▶*3M W of IJmuiden (9.16.17) the N-going stream begins at HW Hoek van Holland – 0120, and the S-going at HW Hoek van Holland + 0430, sp rates about 1·5kn. Off ent to IJmuiden the stream turns about 1h earlier and is stronger, and in heavy weather there may be a dangerous sea.*◀ At IJmuiden the Noordzeekanaal leads to Amsterdam (9.16.18) and the IJsselmeer (9.16.16).

Shipping is very concentrated off Hoek van Holland (9.16.22) at the ent to Europoort and Rotterdam (9.16.23). Maas TSS must be noted and regulations for yachts obeyed.

The Slijkgat (lit) is the approach chan to Stellendam (9.16.24) and entry to the Haringvliet.The Schaar, Schouwenbank, Middelbank and Steenbanken lie parallel to the coast off the approaches to Oosterschelde. From the north, Geul van de Banjaard (partly lit) joins Westgat and leads to Oude Roompot, which with Roompot are the main, well marked channels to the Roompotsluis, in the South half of the barrage. Here the Oosterschelde (9.16.25 and chart 192) is entered.

Rounding Walcheren via the Oostgat, close inshore, Westkapelle lt ho is conspic with two lesser lts nearby: Molenhoofd 5ca WSW and Noorderhoofd 7ca NNW. The Oostgat is the inshore link between Oosterschelde and Westerschelde and also the N approach to the latter. Deurloo and Spleet are unlit secondary channels parallel to Oostgat and a mile or so to seaward. By day they serve to keep yachts clear of commercial traffic in the Oostgat. All channels converge between Vlissingen and Breskens. This bottleneck is designated a Precautionary Area where yachts have no rights of way over other vessels and therefore need to keep a sharper than average lookout and avoid all traffic.

The main approach chan to the Westerschelde (9.16.27) from the W is the Scheur, which yachts may follow just outside the fairway. From Zeebrugge and the SW use the Wielingen chan, keeping close to S side of estuary until past Breskens (9.16.28). If proceeding to Vlissingen (9.16.26), cross between Songa and SS1 buoys, observing the mini-TSS which runs E/W close off Vlissingen. The tide runs hard in the estuary, causing a bad sea in chans and overfalls on some banks in strong winds. Vessels under 20m must give way to larger craft; and yachts under 12m should stay just outside the main buoyed chans. The passage up-river to Antwerpen (9.16.30) is best made in one hop, starting from Breskens, Vlissingen or Terneuzen in order to get the tidal timing right. A more detailed description of this passage is given in the *"North France and Belgium Cruising Companion"*.

BELGIUM (chart 1872) Features of this coast are the long shoals lying roughly parallel to it. Mostly the deeper, buoyed chans run within 3M of shore, where the outer shoals can give some protection from strong W or SW winds. Strong W to NE winds can equally create dangerous conditions especially in wind against tide situations. Approaching from seaward it is essential to fix position from one of the many marks, so that the required chan is correctly identified before shoal water is reached. Shipping is a hazard, but it helps to identify the main routes.

▶*Off the Belgian coast the E-going stream begins at HW Vlissingen – 0320 (HW Dover – 0120), and the W-going at HW Vlissingen + 0240 (HW Dover + 0440), sp rates 2kn. Mostly the streams run parallel with the coast.*◀ Beware strong tidal stream and possibly dangerous seas off Zeebrugge.

From Zeebrugge stay a mile offshore inside Wenduine Bank to pass Oostende (9.16.33), thence via Kleine Rede or Grote Reede into West Diep off Nieuwpoort (9.16.34). At the French border West Diep turns into the narrower Passe de Zuydcoote (buoyed with least depth 3·3m). Thence the very well buoyed route runs close inshore for 25M, past Dunkerque to Dyck.

This and the next paragraph describe the route from the SW/W: The natural entry to the buoyed chans is at Dyck PHM buoy, 5M N of Calais. From the Thames, if bound for Oostende (9.16.33) or the Westerchelde (9.16.27), identify W Hinder lt. From further N, route via NHR-S and NHR-SE buoys or the N Hinder lt buoy.

E-bound from Oostende, leave about HW Vlissingen – 0300 to carry the E-going stream. For Blankenberge (9.16.32) it is only necessary to keep a mile or two offshore, but if heading E of Zeebrugge (9.16.31) it is advisable to clear that hbr's huge breakwaters by 1M or more. The main route to Zeebrugge for commercial shipping is via Scheur (the deep water chan into the Westerschelde) as far as Scheur-Zand lt buoy, about 3M NW of hbr ent. To avoid much commercial traffic, yachts should keep S of the buoyed chan if at all possible.

CROSSING NORTH SEA FROM THE NETHERLANDS (Charts *1406*, *1408*, 1872, *2449*, 3371). From ports S of Hoek van Holland make for NHR-SE, where cross the TSS for destinations between Harwich and Great Yarmouth. From ports N of Hoek van Holland passages can be more direct. For example, a route from IJmuiden to the Humber crosses two DW routes, N and NW of Brown Ridge, but then runs into very extensive offshore Gas Fields. These might cause you to opt for two shorter legs, stopping a night at Great Yarmouth. Tomorrow is another day. Similar thinking might apply if coming out of Den Helder, even if a stop at Great Yarmouth might incur some southing. From east of Den Helder, make ground west via the ITZ before taking departure.

CROSSING NORTH SEA FROM BELGIUM AND SCHELDE (charts *1406*, *323*) There are so many permutations that it is better to try and apply just four broad principles: Avoid the N Hinder-Maas complex and W Hinder-Sandettie complex. Cross TSS at their narrowest parts, ie between NHR-SE and Fairy W; and SW of Sandettie. Plan to cross the many offshore ridges at their extremities, zigzagging as necessary to achieve this. Use the coastal passage W to Dyck, routeing via MPC to S Goodwin lt F if bound for Dover or down-Channel; or even to make up towards Ramsgate and into the southern Thames Estuary, routeing via Sandettie to NE Goodwin buoy. From the Scheur chan off Zeebrugge a fairly direct course via Track Ferry and S Galloper will lead into the N Thames Estuary or towards the Suffolk ports. Avoid shoal patches, particularly in rough weather when the sea-state and under-keel clearance may be very real problems. For distances across the North Sea, see 9.0.8.

9.16.7 SPECIAL NOTES FOR THE NETHERLANDS AND BELGIUM

CURRENCY In The Netherlands and Belgium is the Euro (€)

NETHERLANDS

PROVINCES are given in lieu of UK 'counties'.

CHARTS The following Dutch charts are quoted:

a. Zeekaarten (equivalent to AC); issued by the Royal Netherlands Navy Hydrographer, and updated by Dutch Notices to Mariners; available from chart agents.
b. Kaarten voor Kust-en Binnenwateren, Dutch Yacht Charts (DYC); issued every March by the Hydrographer in 8 sets (1801-1812, excluding 1802, 4, 6 and 8); loose double-sided sheets (54 x 38cm), covering coastal and inland waters.
c. ANWB Waterkaarten (ANWB); 18 charts of inland waterways (lettered A to S, excluding Q) .

TIME ZONE is –0100, which is allowed for in tidal predictions, but no provision is made for daylight saving schemes.

HARBOURS Most yacht hbrs are private clubs or Watersport Associations (WSV or WV): *Gem (Gemeentelijke)* = municipal. Sometimes (in Belgium also) berth-holders show a green tally if a berth is free, or a red tally if returning same day, but check with HM. Duty-free fuel (coloured red) is not available for pleasure craft and may only be carried in the tank, NOT in cans. A tourist tax of between €0.55 and €1.82/person/night is often levied.

CUSTOMS Ports of entry/customs are Delfzijl, Lauwersoog, West Terschelling, Vlieland*, Harlingen, Den Helder, IJmuiden, Scheveningen, Hoek van Holland, Maassluis, Schiedam, Vlaardingen, Rotterdam, Roompotsluis*, Vlissingen and Breskens. Kornwerderzand, Den Oever and Stellendam are not Ports of entry/customs. *Summer only.

BUOYAGE Buoys are often named by the abbreviations of the banks or chans which they mark (eg VL = Vliestroom). A division buoy has the abbreviations of both chans meeting there, eg VL2-SG2 = as above, plus Schuitengat. Some chans are marked by withies: SHM bound ⱶ; PHM unbound ⱶ. On tidal flats (eg Friesland) where the direction of main flood stream is uncertain, bound withies are on the S side of a chan and unbound on the N side; the banks thus marked are steep-to. In minor chans the buoyage may be moved without notice to accommodate changes. The SIGNI buoyage system is used on inland waters, including the IJsselmeer (9.16.16), but not on the Westerschelde, Waddenzee, Eems and Dollard.

HIGH SPEED FERRIES (40kn) ply between Hoek of Holland and Harwich.

SIGNALS Traffic signals IPTS are widely used at coastal ports. The obsolescent French/Belgian system is not used in the Netherlands. Where possible local signals, if any, are given.

Sluicing signals The following signals may be shown:

By day: A blue board, with the word 'SPUIEN' on it; often in addition to the night signal of 3 ● in a △.

Visual storm signals are shown, lts only both by day & night, at West Terschelling, Den Helder and IJmuiden; see 9.17.6.

R/T. In emergency call *Den Helder Rescue* Ch 16 for Netherlands CG (see 7.19.1); or the working channel of a VTS sector or nearest lock or bridge. Monitor TSS info broadcasts and VTS sector channels. Ch 31 is for Dutch marinas. Note: Do not use Ch M in Dutch waters, where it is a salvage frequency. Ch 13 is for commercial ship-ship calling. On inland waterways use low power (1 watt). English is the second language.

INLAND WATERWAYS: All craft must carry a copy of the waterway regulations, *Binnenvaart Politiereglement (BPR)*, as given in the current ANWB publication *Almanak voor Watertoerisme, Vol 1* (written in Dutch). Craft >15m LOA or capable of more than 20kph (11kn) must be skippered by the holder of an RYA Coastal Skipper's Certificate or higher qualification; plus an International Certificate of Competence (ICC) endorsed for Inland waterways, ie CEVNI.

Bridges and locks mostly work VHF Ch 18 or 22.

Bridge and lock signals (shown on each side):

● = Bridge closed (opens on request).
To request bridges to open, call on VHF or sound 'K' (–•–).
● over ● = Bridge about to open.
● = Bridge open.
2 ● (vert) = Bridge out of use.
2 ● (vert) = Bridge open but not in use (you may pass).
1 ● or 1 ◊ = Pass under this span, two-way traffic.
2 ● or 2 ◊s = Pass under this span, one-way traffic.

Railway bridges Opening times of railway bridges are in a free annual leaflet '*Openingstijden Spoorwegbruggen*' available from ANWB, L & A/Wat, Postbus 93200, 2509 BA, Den Haag; (send A5 SAE with international reply coupon).

TELEPHONE To call UK from the Netherlands, dial 00-44; then the UK area code minus the prefix 0, followed by the number required. To call the Netherlands from UK dial 00-31 then the area code minus the prefix 0 followed by two or three digits, followed by a seven or six subscriber no. **Emergency**: Fire, Police, Ambulance, dial 112 (free); **Non-emergency** 0900 8844.

PUBLIC HOLIDAYS New Year's Day, Easter Sun and Mon, Queen's Birthday (30 April), Liberation Day (5 May), Ascension Day, Whit Mon, Christmas and Boxing Days.

BELGIUM

PROVINCES are given in lieu of UK 'counties'.

CHARTS Those most widely used are the '*Vlaamse Banken*' issued by the Hydrografische Dienst der Kust. Dutch yacht charts (DYC, 1800 series) cover all Belgian ports. Imray C30 is also popular amongst Belgian yachtsmen.

TIME ZONE is –0100, which is allowed for in tidal predictions but no provision is made for daylight saving schemes.

HARBOURS: Ports of entry are Nieuwpoort, Oostende and Zeebrugge; plus Blankenberge, early April - late Sep. Although the HM ☎ is given for Belgian hbrs, he is not the key figure for yachtsmen that he is in UK hbrs. Berths and moorings are administered by local YCs and municipal authorities. Red diesel fuel, where available, is duty free.

SIGNALS IPTS are in use at Nieuwpoort, Oostende and Zeebrugge. At these 3 ports and Blankenberge small craft wind warnings are shown: Day - 2 black ▼s, points together; night - Lt Fl Bu. They indicate onshore wind >F3; offshore wind >F4 and apply only to craft <6m LOA.

TELEPHONE To call UK from Belgium, dial 00-44 then the UK area code minus the prefix 0, followed by the number required. To call Belgium from UK, dial 00-32 then the code and number. Dial codes are incorporated in the nine digit subscriber No.

Emergencies: ☎ 101 Police; ☎ 100 Fire, Ambulance and Marine. ☎ 112 (EU emergency number) is also operational.

MRCC Oostende, ☎ (059) 70.10.00, coordinates SAR operations (see 7.19.2). If no contact, call *Oostende Radio* VHF Ch 16 (☎ 70.24.38) or ☎ 100. For medical advice call *Radiomédical Oostende* on Ch 16.

PUBLIC HOLIDAYS New Year's Day, Easter Mon, Labour Day (1 May), Ascension Day, Whit Mon, National Day (21 July), Feast of the Assumption (15 Aug), All Saints' Day (1 Nov), Armistice Day (11 Nov), King's Birthday or Fete de la Dynastie (15 Nov), Christmas Day.

RULES: Hbr police are strict about yachts using their engines entering hbr. If sails are used as well, hoist a ▼. Yachts may not navigate within 200m of shore (MLWS).

INLAND WATERWAYS: *Immatriculatieplaat* (licence plates) are required for all yachts on Flemish waterways. These plates are obtainable from: 2000 ANTWERPEN, Markgravestraat 16. ☎ 03/232.98.05; or from offices in Brussels and other cities. Competence requirements for helmsmen are the same as the Dutch (LH col). More detailed info is available from Belgian Tourist Office, 255 Marshwall, London E14 9FW, ☎ 0906 302 0245, 📠 020 7531 0393; or Federation Royale Belge du Yachting, FRYB/KBJV, PB 241 Bouchoutlaan, 1020 Brussels, Belgium.

9.16.7 DELFZIJL

Groningen **53°18'·99N 07°00'·45E**

CHARTS AC 3631, 3632; Imray C26; Zeekaart 1555; DYC 1812.6; ANWB A

TIDES –0025 Dover; ML 2·1; Duration 0605; Zone –0100

Standard Port HELGOLAND (⟵)

Times				**Height (metres)**			
High Water		Low Water		MHWS	MHWN	MLWN	MLWS
0200	0700	0200	0800	2·7	2·4	0·4	0·0
1400	1900	1400	2000				
Differences DELFZIJL							
+0020	–0005	–0040	0000	+0·8	+0·8	+0·2	+0·2
EEMSHAVEN							
–0025	–0045	–0115	–0045	+0·5	+0·4	+0·3	+0·3
SCHIERMONNIKOOG							
–0120	–0130	–0240	–0220	+0·1	+0·1	+0·3	+0·3

SHELTER Good in Handelshaven at Neptunus Marina (4·4m, 53°19'·80N 06°55'·86E); a floating jetty acts as a wavebreak. Berth also in Farmsumerhaven (4·5m; 24hr only) via the Eemskanaal sealock; or at the N end of the Old Eemskanaal in 't Dok (4m). Note: Eems (Dutch) = Ems (German).

NAVIGATION From the W, WPT 53°34'·91N 06°17'·91E, (H1 unlit SWM buoy), 093°/9·7M to H5 SWM buoy (marking the former Hubertgat chan); thence 23M via Alte Eems & Doekegat chans to enter Zeehavenkanaal (7.9m) 3M ESE of Delfzijl. Beware strong cross tides at the ent (Lat/Long under title).
Or WPT 53°36'·92N, 06°19'·37E (Westereems SWM buoy, Iso 4s, Racon T) 091°/8·3M to Nos 11 /12 Westereems chan buoys; thence Randzelgat or Alte Eems as above.
From N & E, WPT 53° 38'·95N 06° 27'·06E [Riffgat SWM buoy, Iso 8s] 122°/4·3M to Nos 11 /12 Westereems buoys; thence as above.

LIGHTS AND MARKS See chartlet and 9.16.4. From the river, appr ldg lts 203°, both Iso 4s. Hbr ent, FG on W arm and FR on E arm (in fog, Horn 15s and FY). Zeehavenkanaal has Fl G lts to N and Fl R to S. Entry sigs on both piers: 2 ● = No entry, unless cleared by Hbr office on VHF Ch 14.

R/T All vessels, except leisure craft, must call *Delfzijl Radar* VHF Ch 03 (H24) for VTS, co-ordinated with Ems Traffic. *Port Control* is Ch 14. *Eemskanaal Lock* Ch 26. Traffic, wx and tidal info is broadcast every even H+10 on Ch 14 in Dutch and English on request. *Ems Traffic* Ch 15, 18, 20 & 21 (H24) broadcasts every H + 50 weather and tidal info in German, and gale warnings for coastal waters between Die Ems and Die Weser. See also 9.15.25.

TELEPHONE (Dial code 0596) HM (Port Authority) 640400, ℻ 630424; HM 't Dok 616560; Eemskanaal Sea locks 613293; CG (Police) 613831; ⊖ 615060; Police 112; Ⓗ 644444; Brit Consul (020) 6764343.

FACILITIES Neptunus Yacht Hbr ☎ 615004, €0.24 per gross ton, D, Bar, M, L, FW; **Yacht Hbr 't Dok** AB €0.41, D, FW; **Ems Canal** L, FW, AB; **Motor Boat Club Abel Tasman** ☎ 616560 Bar, M, D, FW, L, ⊡, ⛟. **Services:** CH, ACA, DYC Agent, ME, El, Gaz. **Town** P, D, ⛟, R, Bar, ✉, Ⓑ, ⇌, ✈ (Groningen/Eelde). Ferry: See 9.16.21.

INLAND ROUTE TO IJSSELMEER: See 9.16.2 and 9.16.16.

MINOR HARBOUR 1·3M ESE of DELFZIJL ENTRANCE

TERMUNTERZIJL Groningen, **53°18'·20N 07°02'·21E**. AC 3632; Zeekaart 1555; DYC 1812.6. HW –0025 on Dover (UT); use Differences Delfzijl. Ent (1·3M ESE of Delfzijl ent) is close to BW13 SHM buoy Fl G 5s (53°18'·70N 07°02'·40E); thence chan marked by 7 R and 7 G unlit bns. Yachts berth in Vissershaven (0·9m), stbd of ent, or on pontoons (1m) to port of ent, €0.36. HM ☎ (0596) 601891 (Apr-Sept), VHF Ch 09, FW, ⛽, Bar, R.

COMMERCIAL HARBOUR AT MOUTH OF THE EEMS (EMS)

EEMSHAVEN, Groningen, **53°27'·68N 06°50'·27E**. AC 3631, 3632, Zeekaart 1555, DYC 1812.5/.6. HW –0100 (approx) on Dover. Tides as for Borkum 9.15.24. Eemshaven is a modern commercial port, but may be used by yachts as a port of

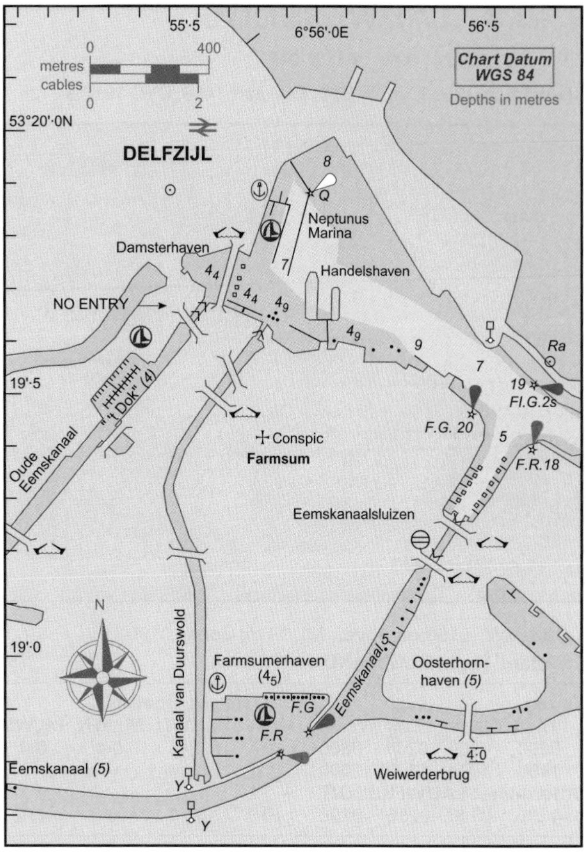
55'·5
6°56'·0E
56'·5
Chart Datum WGS 84
Depths in metres
metres
cables
0
400
0
2
53°20'·0N
DELFZIJL
Neptunus Marina
Damsterhaven
Handelshaven
NO ENTRY
"Dok" (4)
Oude Eemskanaal
Conspic Farmsum
Eemskanaalsluizen
F.G. 20
Fl.G.2s
F.R.18
Ra
19'·5
19'·0
Farmsumerhaven
Kanaal van Duurswold
Eemskanaal
Oosterhorn-haven (5)
F.G
F.R
Eemskanaal (5)
Weiwerderbrug
N

refuge. Outer appr via Hubertgat (see 9.16.7) or Westereems; inner appr via Randzelgat or Alte Eems, passing the outer anchorage for merchant ships. From the nearest buoy, A16 PHM Fl R 4s, the hbr ent bears 137°/1·6M. Call *Eemshaven Radar* Ch 01 (H24) for VTS info; and *Eemshaven Port Control* Ch 66 for info and clearance to enter.

There are many wind turbines to the W of the port. A large power stn chy (128m) is conspic 2M ESE of the port; as are white-roofed bldgs at the port. Enter on 175°, ldg lts Iso 4s, between mole hds, FG and FR. Inner ldg lts, both Iso R 4s, leads 195° to S end of port. Here yachts turn 90° stbd into Emmahaven, marked by FG and FR, and berth on floating jetty on the S bank. HM ☎ (Delfzijl Port Authority) 640400, ℻ 630424; other ☎ numbers see Delfzijl. No special facilities for yachts, but dues are €0.24 per gross ton.

MINOR HARBOUR ON THE WEST FRISIAN ISLANDS

SCHIERMONNIKOOG, Friesland, **53°28'·07N 06°10'·05E**. AC 3761, 3631; Zeekaart 1458, DYC 1812.3. HW –0150 on Dover. See 9.16.7. WPT 53°32'·58N 06°10'·72E, [WG SWM buoy, Iso 8s, Racon N], 217°/1·0M to WG1 SHM buoy, VQ G, at the ent to Westgat; buoyed/lit, but in bad weather dangerous due to shoals (3·8m) at seaward end. Follow Westgat chan into Zoutkamperlaag; leave at Z4 & Z6-GVS buoys to enter Gat van Schiermonnikoog (buoyed).

From GVS16-R1 buoy a drying chan, marked by perches/ withies, runs 1M N to small yacht hbr (1·3-1·5m). Access HW –2 to +1, with 1·5m max depth at HW in apprs. Picturesque, but very full in high season; not cheap, ie €1.27. A ferry pier is 1.26M E of the yacht hbr. HM VHF Ch 31; ☎ (0519) 51544 (May-Sept). Facilities: FW, AC.

Note: Lt ho Fl (4) 20s, R twr, is conspic 1.35M NNW of yacht hbr. The CG station at the lt ho provides radar surveillance of the Terschelling/German Bight TSS out to 48M radius and coordinates local SAR operations. It keeps watch on VHF Ch 00, **05**, 16, 67 and 73 (all H24); ☎ 0519 531247, ℻ 0519 531000.

9.16.8 LAUWERSOOG

Friesland, **53°24'·68N 06°12'·04E**

CHARTS AC 2593; Imray C26; Zeekaart 1458; DYC 1812.3

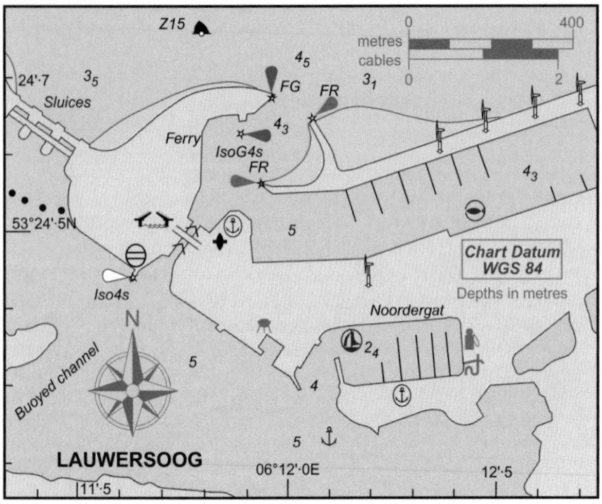
Z15
metres
cables
0
400
0
2
FG
FR
24'·7
Sluices
Ferry
IsoG4s
FR
53°24'·5N
Chart Datum
WGS 84
Depths in metres
Iso4s
N
Noordergat
Buoyed channel
LAUWERSOOG
06°12'·0E
12'·5
11'·5

TIDES HW –0150 on Dover; ML 1·7m; Zone –0100

Standard Port HELGOLAND (⟵)

Times				Height (metres)			
High Water		Low Water		MHWS	MHWN	MLWN	MLWS
0200	0700	0200	0800	2·7	2·4	0·4	0·0
1400	1900	1400	2000				
Differences LAUWERSOOG							
–0130	–0145	–0235	–0220	+0·1	+0·1	+0·2	+0·2

SHELTER Outer hbr suffers swell in bad weather. Pontoons in inner FV hbr to await lock. Lock hrs (LT) **May-Sep**: Mon-Fri 0700-2000 (Sat 1900); Sun 0900-1200, 1400-1830. **Oct-Apr**: Mon-Fri 0700-1800 (Sat 1700); Sun shut. Complete shelter in Noordergat marina (2·4m-2·8m) 3ca SE of lock; Ⓥs berth on first pontoon.

NAVIGATION See Schiermonnikoog (9.16.7); continue to Z15 SHM buoy for hbr ent. The masted canal route (Delfzijl-Harlingen) can be entered from the Lauwersmeer at Dokkum.

LIGHTS AND MARKS See chartlet and 9.16.4. 4 wind turbines on the N bkwtr are conspic. A firing range 1·5m ENE of hbr ent is marked by Fl Y 10s beacons, which alternate W/R when the range is active; info is broadcast on Ch 71.

R/T Hbr VHF Ch 11; Lock Ch 84; Range broadcast Ch 71.

TELEPHONE (Dial code 0519) Port HM 349023; Lock 349043.

FACILITIES **Noordergat marina**, ☎ 349040, €0.91, Gaz, BY, D (E end of hbr); P (ferry terminal, W end of hbr), Bar, R, 🛒, YC.

OTHER HARBOURS IN THE LAUWERSMEER

OOSTMAHORN, Friesland, **53°22'·94N 06°09'·63E**. AC 2593, Zeekaarten 1458, DYC 1812·3. Non-tidal hbr on W side of Lauwersmeer; lock in as for Lauwersoog. Floating bns with Y flags mark fishing areas. Main hbr with FR and FG lts at ent has marina (2·2-3·0m). Approx 450m to the SSE the tiny Voorm Veerhaven marina has 1·5-2m. VHF Ch 10. HM ☎ (0519) 321445; €0.91, D, P, ⚓, Gaz, R, 🛒, C, BY, BH (15T)

ZOUTKAMP, Groningen, **53°20'·38N 06°17'·55E**. AC 2593, Zeekaarten 1458, DYC 1812·3; non-tidal. Appr down the Zoutkamperril (2·6-4·5m); approx 2ca before lock/bridge, Hunzegat marina (1·5-2·1m) is to port. Beyond the lock and close to port is Oude Binnenhaven marina (2m), €3.63. FR lts at lock. Facilities: **Hunzegat** ☎ (0595) 402875, SC, Slip. **Oude-Binnenhaven** C, ME, El, ⚒, C (20 ton), BH.

Town D, P, SM, Gaz, ✉, R, 🛒, Dr.

9.16.9 HET VLIE (Zeegat van Terschelling)

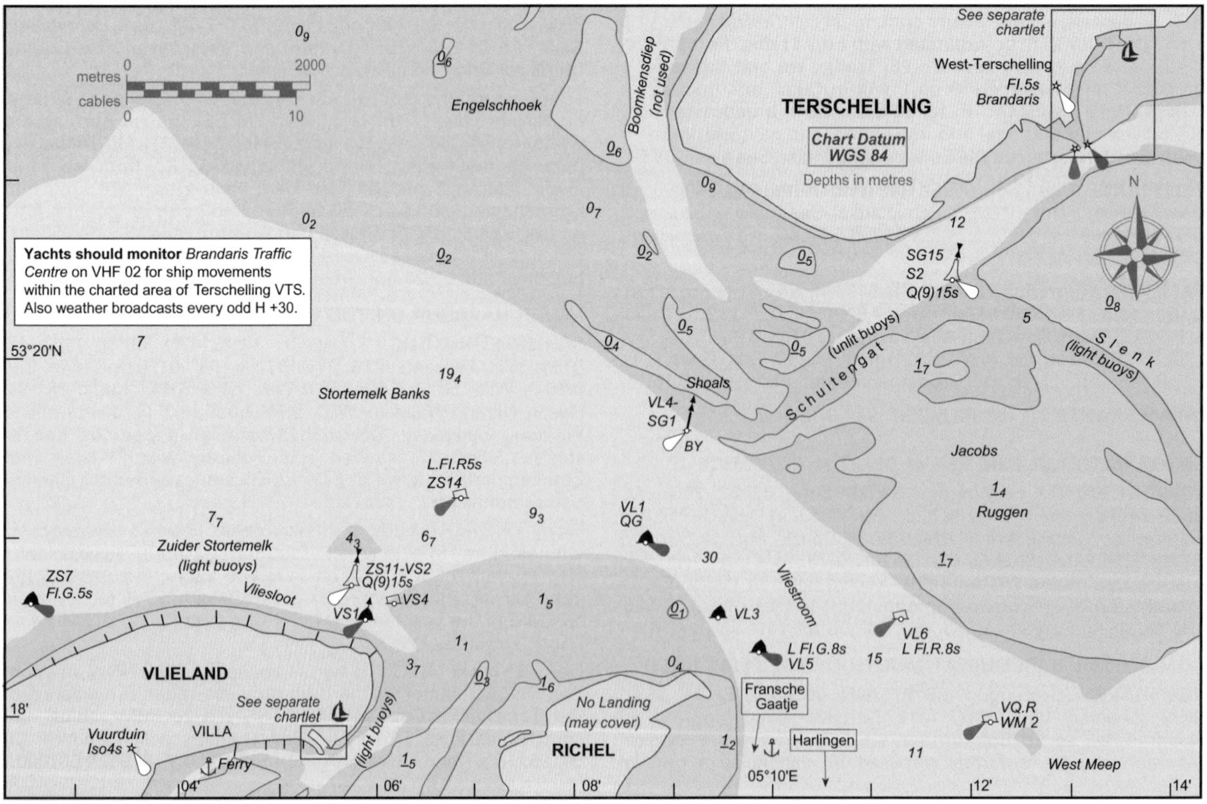
See separate chartlet
West-Terschelling
Fl.5s
Brandaris
TERSCHELLING
Chart Datum
WGS 84
Depths in metres
metres
cables
0
2000
0
10
Engelschhoek
Boomkensdiep (not used)
N
Yachts should monitor Brandaris Traffic Centre on VHF 02 for ship movements within the charted area of Terschelling VTS. Also weather broadcasts every odd H +30.
53°20'N
Stortemelk Banks
SG15
S2
Q(9)15s
(unlit buoys)
Schuitengat
Slenk
(light buoys)
Shoals
VL4-
SG1
BY
Jacobs
Ruggen
L.Fl.R5s
ZS14
VL1
QG
Zuider Stortemelk
(light buoys)
ZS7
Fl.G.5s
Vliesloot
ZS11-VS2
Q(9)15s
VS4
VS1
Vliestroom
VL3
VL6
L Fl.R.8s
L Fl.G.8s
VL5
VLIELAND
See separate chartlet
Fransche Gaatje
Harlingen
VQ.R
WM 2
No Landing
(may cover)
RICHEL
Vuurduin
Iso4s
VILLA
Ferry
(light buoys)
West Meep
05°10'E
18'
04'
06'
08'
12'
14'

9.16.10 WEST TERSCHELLING

WEST FRISIAN ISLANDS
Friesland **53°21'·26N 05°13'·13E**

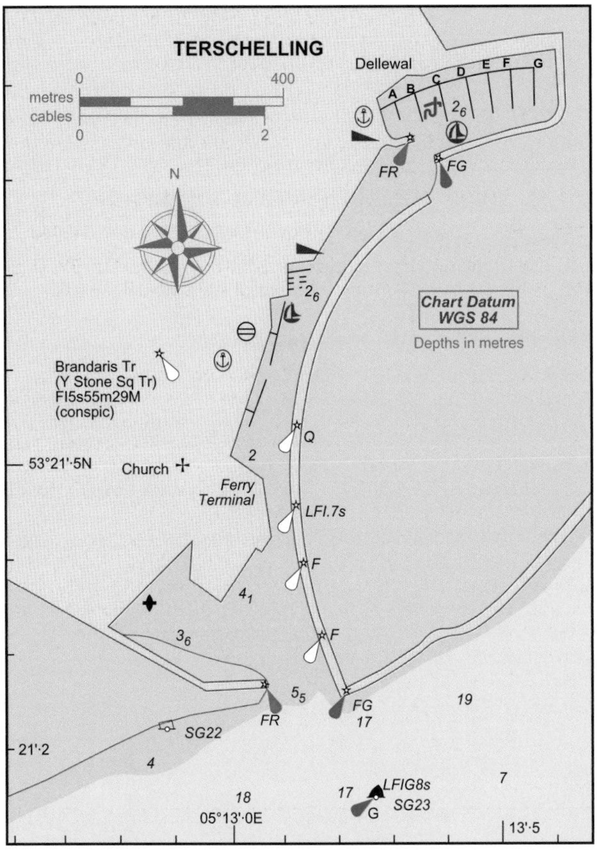
TERSCHELLING
metres
cables
0
400
0
2
Dellewal
A B C D E F G
N
Chart Datum WGS 84
Depths in metres
Brandaris Tr
(Y Stone Sq Tr)
Fl5s55m29M
(conspic)
53°21'·5N
Church
Ferry Terminal
FR
FG
Q
LFl.7s
F
F
FR
FG
SG22
SG23
LFlG8s
G
21'·2
05°13'·0E
13'·5

CHARTS AC 2593, 112; Zeekaart 1456; DYC 1811.4/.5; Imray C25

TIDES –0300 Dover; ML 1·4; Duration No data; Zone –0100

Standard Port HELGOLAND (⟵)

Times				Height (metres)			
High Water		Low Water		MHWS	MHWN	MLWN	MLWS
0200	0700	0200	0800	2·7	2·4	0·4	0·0
1400	1900	1400	2000				
Differences WEST TERSCHELLING							
–0220	–0250	–0335	–0310	–0·4	–0·4	+0·1	+0·2

SHELTER Good, especially in marina; pontoons A-G have notices showing berth allocation by LOA and type of boat (yacht, motor-cruiser or traditional craft). Very crowded in season.

NAVIGATION WPT: 53°19'·80N 04°55'·90E [ZS (SWM) buoy, Iso 4s, Racon T] 101°/6·1M to ZS11-VS2 NCM buoy, Q (see 9.16.9). Thence toward Schuitengat or West Meep, after calling *Brandaris* Ch 02 for the latest nav/tidal info to decide the better route:

a. Schuitengat, shorter than (b) but the ent is narrow/shallow (0·1m N of SG 5/6 buoys). Inside the ent follow the unlit SG chan buoys to hbr ent.
b. Vliestroom into West Meep. At NM4-S21 ECM buoy, VQ (3) 5s, 53°19'·20N 05°15'·65E, enter Slenk buoyed/lit chan ldg WNW to the inner Schuitengat. Best timing = HW±2.

Considerable commercial traffic and ferries in confined waters.

LIGHTS AND MARKS Hbr lts as chartlet and 9.16.4. The square, yellow Brandaris light tower dominates the town and hbr.

R/T HM Ch 12. CG Ch 02 04 16 67. *Brandaris* (VTS) Ch 02 broadcasts weather, visibility, traffic, tidal info at odd H+30 in Dutch and English on request. Yachts in the area must monitor Ch 02 (see 9.16.11); visitors can get update on nav/chans.

TELEPHONE (Dial code 0562) HM 442910/442919; CG 442341; ⊖ 442884.

FACILITIES **Marina: Stichting Passantenhaven** (500) ☎ 443337, €1.25/metre + €0.75/head + €0.55. **Services:** Slip, C, Gaz, ME, SM, Chart agent, Ⓔ. **Village** EC Wed; CH, 🛒, R, Bar, ✉, P & D (cans; nearest D by hose is at Harlingen), Ⓑ, ⇌ (ferry to Harlingen), ✈ (Amsterdam). Ferry: Hook-Harwich; Europoort-Hull.

16

9.16.11 VLIELAND

WEST FRISIAN ISLANDS
Friesland **53°17'·68N 05°05'·49E**

CHARTS AC 2593, 112; Zeekaart 1456; DYC 1811.4/.5; Imray C26

TIDES –0300 Dover; ML 1·4; Duration 0610; Zone –0100

Standard Port HELGOLAND (⟵)

Times				Height (metres)			
High Water		Low Water		MHWS	MHWN	MLWN	MLWS
0200	0700	0200	0800	2·7	2·4	0·4	0·0
1400	1900	1400	2000				
Differences VLIELAND-HAVEN							
–0250	–0320	–0355	–0330	–0·4	–0·4	+0·1	+0·2

SHELTER Good; yacht hbr (2m) is crowded in season. Ⓥ berths are on pontoons 4 & 10. ⚓ in 4-9m, about 0·5M W of the hbr (and nearer the village), except in strong SE/SW winds. Do not ⚓ in buoyed chan between hbr and ferry pier (no berthing). From the S a safe ⚓ is in Fransche Gaatje, SE of Richel, 6M from hbr.

NAVIGATION Zuider Stortemelk is deep, well marked/lit, but in fresh W/NW'lies a heavy swell can raise dangerous seas from the WPT to ZS1/2 Bys. WPT as 9.16.10 to ZS11-VS2 buoy. From ZS11-VS2 buoy turn S into Vliesloot (narrow and in places only 2·5m MLWS). Keep in mid-chan past VS3-VS7 buoys to hbr ent.

LIGHTS AND MARKS Hbr lts as chartlet and 9.16.4. The dark red lt ho (W lantern, R top) stands on Vuurduin, 1.2M W of the hbr. Tfc sigs: R Flag or ●● at ent = hbr closed (full).

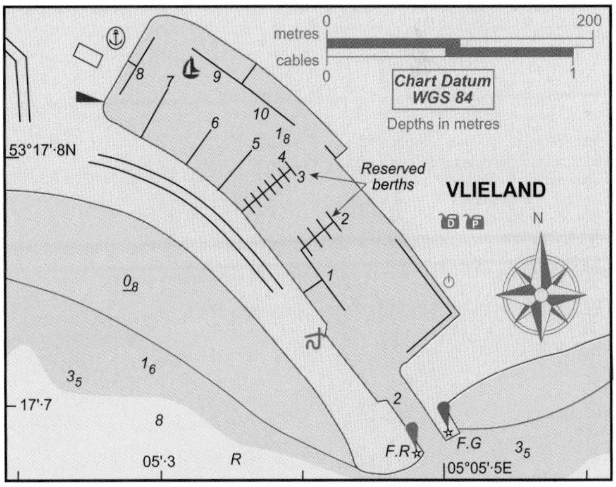
metres
cables
0
200
0
1
Chart Datum WGS 84
Depths in metres
53°17'·8N
Reserved berths
VLIELAND
N
17'·7
F.R
F.G
05'·3
R
05°05'·5E

R/T HM Ch 12; Marina Ch 31. All vessels in Zeegat van Terschelling and N Waddenzee must monitor Ch 02 for the *Brandaris Traffic Centre VTS.*

TELEPHONE (Dial code 0562) HM 451729; CG (0562) 442341; ⊖ 451522; Police 451312; Dr 451307; Brit Consul (020) 6764343.

FACILITIES **Yacht Hbr** (300) ☎ 451729, €0.41 per m² + €0.84 per person, dinghy slip, ⓞ; **Hbr** C (10 ton), P & D (cans, 10 mins); D by hose at Harlingen, Ⓔ. **Village** El, Gaz, 🛒, R, ✉, Ⓑ, ⇌ (ferry to Harlingen), ✈ (Amsterdam). Ferry: Hook of Holland-Harwich.

9.16.12 TSS OFF THE NORTHERN NETHERLANDS

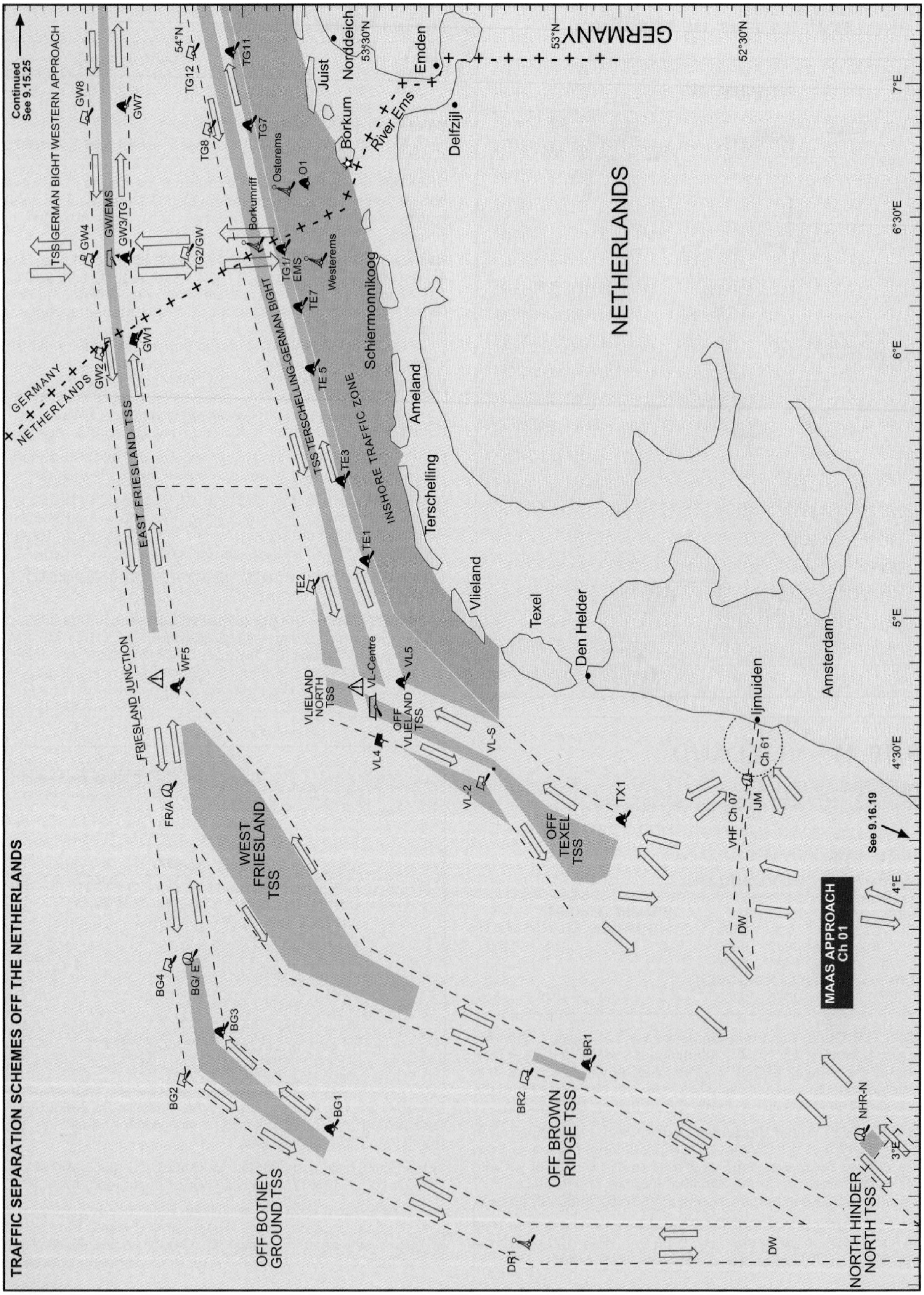
TRAFFIC SEPARATION SCHEMES OFF THE NETHERLANDS
Continued
See 9.15.25
TSS GERMAN BIGHT WESTERN APPROACH
GW8
GW7
GW4
GW/EMS
GW3/TG
GW2
GW1
TG2/GW
TG12
TG8
TG11
TG7
TG1/EMS
TE7
TE 5
TE3
TE1
TE2
54°N
53°30'N
53°N
52°30'N
7°E
6°30'E
6°E
5°E
4°30'E
4°E
3°E
GERMANY
NETHERLANDS
EAST FRIESLAND TSS
TSS TERSCHELLING-GERMAN BIGHT
INSHORE TRAFFIC ZONE
Borkumriff
Osterems
O1
Westerems
Juist
Norddeich
Borkum
River Ems
Emden
Delfzijl
Schiermonnikoog
Ameland
Terschelling
Vlieland
Texel
Den Helder
Ijmuiden
Amsterdam
FRIESLAND JUNCTION
WF5
FR/A
WEST FRIESLAND TSS
VLIELAND NORTH TSS
VL-Centre
VL5
OFF VLIELAND TSS
VL4
VL-S
VL-2
OFF TEXEL TSS
TX1
Ch 61
IJM
VHF Ch 07
See 9.16.19
DW
MAAS APPROACH Ch 01
BG4
BG/E
BG3
BG2
BG1
BR1
BR2
OFF BROWN RIDGE TSS
OFF BOTNEY GROUND TSS
DR1
NHR-N
NORTH HINDER NORTH TSS

9.16.13 HARLINGEN

Friesland **53°10'·58N 05°24'·23E**

CHARTS AC 2593, 112; Zeekaart 1454, 1456; DYC 1811·5; ANWB B; Imray C26

TIDES –0210 Dover; ML 1·2; Duration 0520; Zone –0100

Standard Port HELGOLAND (⟵)

Times				Height (metres)			
High Water		Low Water		MHWS	MHWN	MLWN	MLWS
0200	0700	0200	0800	2·7	2·4	0·4	0·0
1400	1900	1400	2000				
Differences HARLINGEN							
–0155	–0245	–0210	–0130	–0·5	–0·5	–0·1	+0·2
NES (AMELAND)							
–0135	–0150	–0245	–0225	+0·1	0·0	+0·2	+0·2

SHELTER Very good once in Noorderhaven, but outer hbr ent can be rough at HW with W/NW winds. Entering on the flood, beware strong stream across ent. Note: Access to/from Noorderhaven is restricted by lifting bridges across the Oude Buitenhaven and Noorderhaven; these open in unison 2 x per hr 0600-2200 in season (on request in winter), but are shut at times of boat trains/ferries and at HW springs. Van Harinxma yacht hbr only advised if going via the canal to the lakes.

NAVIGATION WPT 53°11'·70N 05°19'·00E [between buoys BS21 and BS22] 110°/3·3M to hbr ent. See 9.16.11 for appr, then follow the buoyed Vliestroom and Blauwe Slenk chans to the WPT; the latter is narrow for the last 2½M, and is bounded on the NE by Pollendam training wall, marked by five PHM lt bns. Beware of ferries passing very close. Caution: When Pollendam is covered, tidal stream sweeps across it.

LIGHTS AND MARKS See chartlet and 9.16.4. Ldg lts 112°, both Iso 6s, H24; B masts, W bands.

R/T VHF Ch 11 (Not on Sun). Harinxma Canal locks Ch 22.

TELEPHONE (Dial code 0517) HM 492300; CG (Brandaris) (0562) 442341; ⊖ 418750; Police 413333; Ⓗ 499999; Brit Consul (020) 6764343.

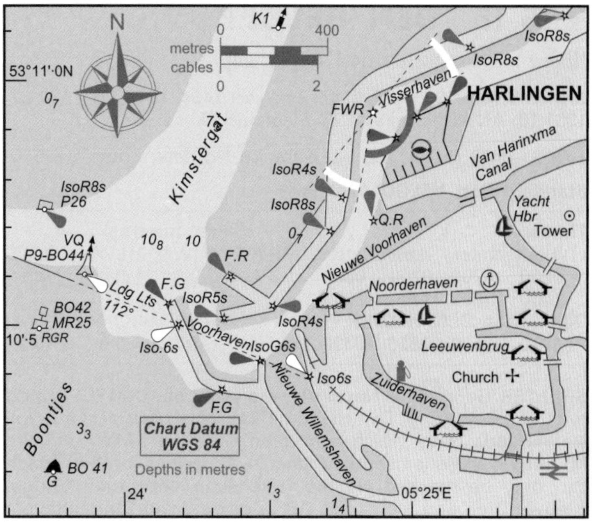
HARLINGEN
metres
cables
0
400
2
53°11'·0N
K1
IsoR8s
Vissershaven
FWR
Van Harinxma Canal
Yacht Hbr
Tower
Kimstergat
IsoR4s
IsoR8s
Q.R
P26
VQ
P9-BO44
F.R
Nieuwe Voorhaven
Noorderhaven
Ldg Lts 112°
F.G
IsoR5s
BO42
MR25
10'·5 RGR
IsoR4s
Voorhaven
IsoG6s
Iso.6s
Iso6s
Leeuwenbrug
Church
Zuiderhaven
Nieuwe Willemshaven
Boontjes
F.G
Chart Datum WGS 84
Depths in metres
BO 41
G
24'
05°25'E

FACILITIES Noorderhaven Yacht Hbr ☎ 415666, FW, El, CH, 🛒, R, Bar, 🅾; **Yacht Hbr Van Harinxma Canal** ☎ 416898, FW, 🅾, C (6 ton); **Services:** CH, El, E, Gaz, Diving/salvage, El, ME (by arrangement), D, P. **Town** EC Mon; LB, D, P, 🛒, R, Bar, SM, ✉, Ⓑ, ⇌, ✈ (Amsterdam). Ferry: See Hook.

NES, AMELAND, Friesland, 53°26'·28N 05°46'·62E. AC 2593, Zeekaart 1458, DYC 1811.6, 1812.2. HW –0055 on Dover; ML 1·6m; Duration 0625. See 9.16.13. Shelter from all but E/S winds. Yacht pontoons at N end of hbr (0·8m) beyond ferry terminal; W side dries to soft mud. Beware sandbanks in the Zeegat van Ameland. Enter from Molengat at MG28-R1 SCM By, VQ(6) + L Fl 10s. Lts: Ameland (W end), Fl (3) 15s 57m 30M, RC. Ferry pier hd Iso 6s 2m 8M. L Fl R 8s and L Fl G 8s piles at ent to yacht hbr ('t Leye Gat, 140 berths), €0.73. Facilities: Gaz, YC. HM ☎ (0515) 32159.

9.16.14 OUDESCHILD

Texel, **53°02'·35N 04°51'·18E** ✵✵✵⚓⚓⚓✿✿

CHARTS AC 2593, 1546; Zeekaart 1546, 1454; DYC 1811·3

TIDES –0355 Dover; ML 1·1m; Duration 0625; Zone –0100

Standard Port HELGOLAND (⟵)

Times				Height (metres)			
High Water		Low Water		MHWS	MHWN	MLWN	MLWS
0200	0700	0200	0800	2·7	2·4	0·4	0·0
1400	1900	1400	2000				
Differences OUDESCHILD							
–0310	–0420	–0445	–0400	–1·0	–0·8	0·0	+0·2

SHELTER Very good in marina (2·4m) in far NE basin. ⚓ prohib. Yachts are advised not to ent/dep Mon and Fri mornings when all FVs sail/return.

NAVIGATION WPT 53°02'·26N 04°51'·55E [abeam PHM buoy (T12), Iso R 8s], 291°/400m to hbr ent, with dir lt, Oc 6s, midway between FR and FG mole hd lts. Speed limit 5kn. From seaward, app via Schulpengat or Molengat into Marsdiep (see 9.16.15). Thence from abeam ferry hbr of 't Horntje (Texel) steer NE via Texelstroom for 3·5M to the WPT.

LIGHTS AND MARKS See chartlet and 9.16.4. Dir lt Oc 6s, on G mast, is vis only on brg 291°.FR/FG lts are on R/G masts with W bands. The horn (2) 30s is sounded only 0600-2300.

R/T No marina VHF. HM Ch 12, 0800-2000LT. See 9.16.15 for VTS and radar assistance/info on request.

TELEPHONE (Dial code 0222) HM (marina) ☎ 321227; Port HM 3312710/home 06 1502 8380; CG 316270; Police/ambulance 0900 8844 or 112; ⊖ as HM.

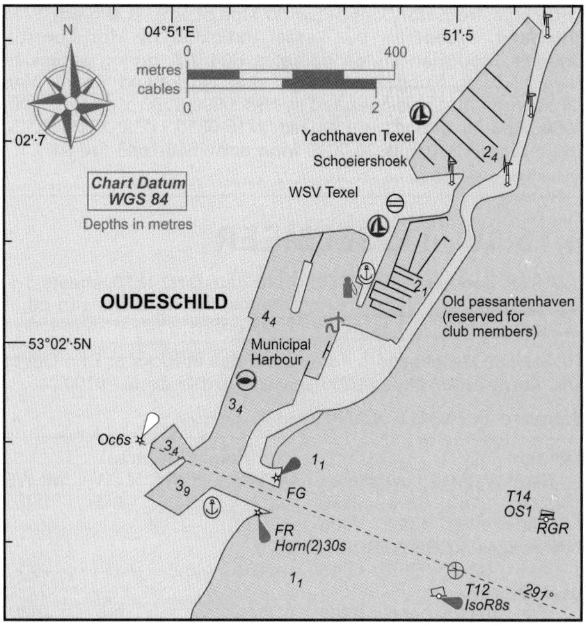
N
04°51'E
51'·5
metres
cables
0
400
2
02'·7
Yachthaven Texel
Schoeiershoek
WSV Texel
Chart Datum WGS 84
Depths in metres
OUDESCHILD
Old passantenhaven (reserved for club members)
53°02'·5N
Municipal Harbour
Oc6s
FG
FR Horn(2)30s
T14 OS1 RGR
T12 IsoR8s
291°

FACILITIES Marina (Waddenhaven Texel) 250 berths ☎ 321227, €1.60, D, Slip, 🅾, Bar, R, 🛒, ♿; **YC WV Texel**, C; **Services:** ME, BY, ⚒, ⚓, Dry dock, C, SM, 🛒 by mobile shop in season. **Village** (walking distance), CH, P, Gaz, 🛒 (supermarket), Ⓑ, ✉, R. Ferry from 't Horntje to Den Helder. UK ferries from Hook/Rotterdam. ✈ Amsterdam.

9.16.15 DEN HELDER

Noord Holland **52°57'·94N 04°47'·24E**

CHARTS AC 2593, 2322, 1546; Zeekaart 1454, 1546; DYC 1811.2, 1801.10; ANWB F; Imray C25; Stanfords 19.

TIDES –0430 Dover; ML 1·1; Duration No data; Zone –0100

Standard Port HELGOLAND (⟵)

Times				Height (metres)			
High Water		Low Water		MHWS	MHWN	MLWN	MLWS
0200	0700	0200	0800	2·7	2·4	0·4	0·0
1400	1900	1400	2000				
Differences DEN HELDER							
–0410	–0520	–0520	–0430	–1·0	–0·8	0·0	+0·2

SHELTER Good in the Naval Hbr; the yacht hbr (KMYC) is hard to stbd on entering. Den Helder is the main base of the Royal Netherlands Navy which owns and runs the KMYC and the Marinehaven Willemsoord. 2 other YCs/marinas (both of which can only be reached via the Rijkshaven, Moorman bridge, Nieuwe Diep and lock) offer AB in or near the Binnenhaven: MWV and YC Den Helder; see under FACILITIES for details.

NAVIGATION Two chans lead into Marsdiep for the hbr ent:
1. From the N, Molengat is good except in strong NW winds when seas break heavily. WPT 53°03'·90N 04°39'·37E [MG SWM buoy, Mo (A) 8s] 132°/1.34M to first chan buoys, MG 1/2. Thence to join Marsdiep at S14/MG17 SCM lt buoy.
2. From S, the Schulpengat is the main chan, well marked/lit. WPT 52°52'·91N 04°37'·90E [SG (SWM) buoy, Mo (A) 8s] 026·5°/ 6M to S14/MG17 SCM lt buoy.

Caution: fast ferries to/from Texel, strong tidal streams across the hbr ent, many FVs and off-shore service vessels. Hbr speed limit 5kn.

LIGHTS AND MARKS See chartlet and 9.16.4. Schulpengat: Ldg lts, both Oc 8s, and spire 026·5° on Texel. Kijkduin lt ho, R twr, is conspic 2·3M WSW of hbr. Hbr 191° ldg lts; front B ▲ on bldg; rear B ▼ on B framework tr. A 60m radar tower is conspic on E side of hbr ent.

Entry sigs, from Hbr Control twr (W side of ent): ● ● (vert) = No entry/exit, except for the vessel indicated by Hbr Control.

Bridges: Moorman bridge operates H24 7/7, giving access to Nieuwe Diep, Koopvaarder Lock and N Holland Canal. Van Kinsbergen bridge is operated by HM, 0500-2300 Mon-Fri; 0700-1400 Sat. All bridges are closed 0715-0810, 1200-1215, 1245-1300, Mon-Fri. Also 0830-0910 Mon and 1545-1645 Fri. All LT.

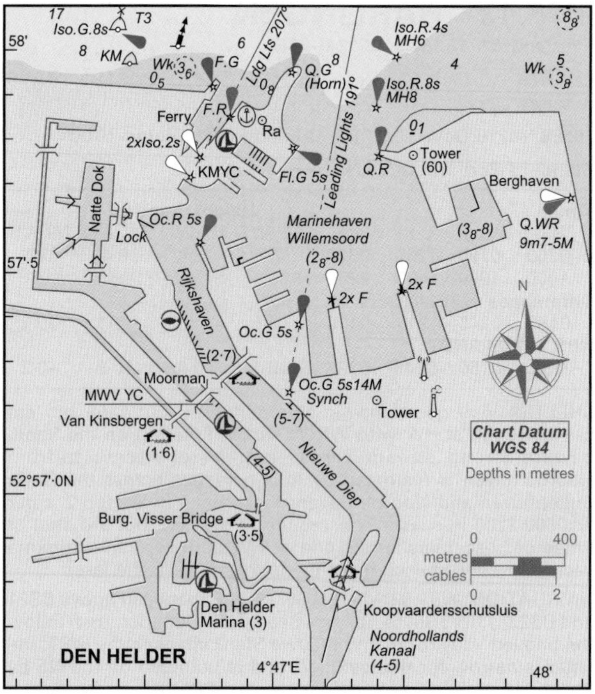
Iso.G.8s
T3
Ldg Lts 207°
Iso.R.4s
MH6
Wk
Q.G
(Horn)
Iso.R.8s
MH8
Ferry
F.R
F.G
Ra
2xIso.2s
KMYC
Fl.G 5s
Leading Lights 191°
Q.R
Tower
(60)
Berghaven
Natte Dok
Oc.R 5s
Lock
Marinehaven
Willemsoord
Q.WR
9m7-5M
2x F
Rijkshaven
Oc.G 5s
Moorman
MWV YC
Van Kinsbergen
Oc.G 5s14M
Synch
Tower
Chart Datum
WGS 84
Depths in metres
Nieuwe Diep
52°57'·0N
Burg. Visser Bridge
metres
cables
Den Helder
Marina (3)
Koopvaardersschutsluis
Noordhollands
Kanaal
DEN HELDER
4°47'E
48'
58'
57'·5

R/T Monitor Ch 62 *Den Helder Traffic* (VTS) in the Schulpengat, Molengat and Marsdiep; info on request. *Port Control* Ch 14 (H24); also remote control of van Kinsbergen bridge. Moorman bridge Ch 18 (H24). *Koopvaarders Lock* Ch 22 (H24), also remote control of Burgemeester Vissersbrug.

TELEPHONE (Dial code 0223) Vessel Traffic Centre 657522; Municipal HM 613955, 🖷 627780, mobile ☎ 0652 97 94 80; Pilot 0255 564500; Emergency 112; Police 655700; Ⓗ 611414; Water Police 616767; Immigration 657515; Brit Consul (020) 6764343.

FACILITIES In naval hbr: **KMYC** ☎ 652645, €0.64, D, Bar, R. In or near Binnenhaven: **MWV YC** ☎ 624422, €0.54, P (at garage), D, L, AB; **Yacht Haven Den Helder** ☎ 637444, mobile 0653 78159, €0.73, Ch 31, ME, El, ⚒, C, CH, Slip, R, Bar; **YC WSOV** ☎ 652173; **YC HWN** ☎ 624422; **Services:** CH, SM, Floating dock, Gaz. **Town** P, CH, 🛒, R, Bar, ✉, Ⓑ, ⇌, ✈ (Amsterdam). Ferry: Hook-Harwich; Rotterdam-Hull.

9.16.16 IJSSELMEER

CHARTS Zeekaart 1351, 1454; Up to date DYC 1810, sheets 3-5, are essential to avoid live firing ranges, fishing areas and other hazards; 1810 also has many hbr chartlets.

TIDES The IJsselmeer is non-tidal. Tides at locks at Den Oever and Kornwerderzand: –0230 Dover; ML 1·2; Zone –0100

Standard Port HELGOLAND (⟵)

Times				Height (metres)			
High Water		Low Water		MHWS	MHWN	MLWN	MLWS
0200	0700	0200	0800	2·7	2·4	0·4	0·0
1400	1900	1400	2000				
Differences KORNWERDERZAND							
–0210	–0315	–0300	–0215	–0·5	–0·5	–0·1	+0·2
DEN OEVER							
–0245	–0410	–0400	–0305	–0·8	–0·7	0·0	+0·2

SHELTER Excellent in the marinas, see below. Most berths are bows on to a pontoon, stern lines to piles; there are few ⚓s.

NAVIGATION It is essential to have the *Almanac voor Watertoerisme*, Vol I onboard; it contains the BPR (Waterway Code) in Dutch. The IJsselmeer is separated from the Waddenzee by the 20M long Afsluitdijk, completed in 1932. It is sub-divided into two parts by the Houtribdijk, with 'naviduct' at Enkhuizen to the NW and lock at Lelystad in the SE. The SW part is the Markermeer (20M x 15M, 2-4·5m deep); the rest is the IJsselmeer, 30M x 20M, 7m max. Three entrances via locks into the IJsselmeer/Markermeer:

1. Kornwerderzand lock (NE end of the Afsluitdijk) H24. From Waddenzee, via W, NW or NE chans. Ent has FR/G and Iso G 6s. Wait in Buitenhaven; yachts use the smaller E lock. From IJsselmeer, ldg lts Iso 4s 348° to FR/G at ent; wait in Binnenhaven (3·6m).
2. Den Oever (SW end of the Afsluitdijk): Appr from Waddenzee via well marked/lit chan; ldg lts 131°, both Oc 10s to ent, thence follow Dir Iso WRG 2s, 220° to wait in Buitenhaven. 2 bridges and locks operate in unison HO. From IJsselmeer, wait in Binnenhaven; FR/G at ent.
3. IJmuiden, Noordzeekanaal to Oranjesluizen (9.16.18).

Standard lock sigs (vert): ● ● = not in service; ● = no entry; ● ● = stand by; ● = enter.

Speed limits: in buoyed chans and <250m from shore 10·5kn. Hbr limits vary; see ANWB Almanak Vol 2.

Strong winds get up very quickly and often cause short seas; they can also raise the water level on a lee shore, or lower it on a weather shore, by 1m or more. Most hbrs have water level gauges which should be checked in bad weather. In

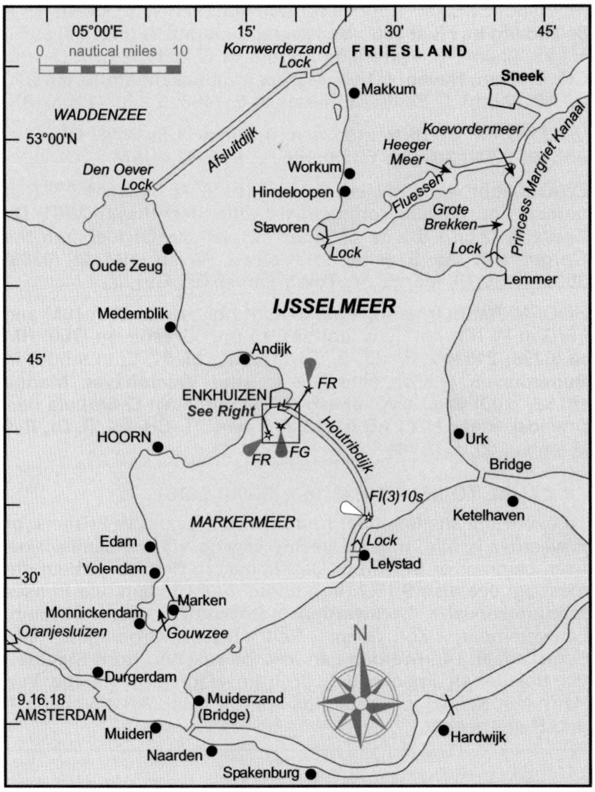
05°00'E
15'
30'
45'
0 nautical miles 10
Kornwerderzand Lock
FRIESLAND
Makkum
Sneek
WADDENZEE
53°00'N
Afsluitdijk
Koevordermeer
Heeger Meer
Princess Margriet Kanaal
Den Oever Lock
Workum
Hindeloopen
Fluessen
Grote Brekken
Stavoren
Lock
Lock
Lemmer
Oude Zeug
Medemblik
IJSSELMEER
45'
Andijk
FR
ENKHUIZEN See Right
HOORN
FR
FG
Houtribdijk
Urk
Bridge
Fl(3)10s
MARKERMEER
Ketelhaven
Edam
Lock
Volendam
Lelystad
30'
Marken
Monnickendam
Oranjesluizen
Gouwzee
N
Durgerdam
9.16.18 AMSTERDAM
Muiderzand (Bridge)
Muiden
Hardwijk
Naarden
Spakenburg

non-tidal waters CD usually refers to the level at which the water is kept. This may be Kanaalpeil, which is related to Normaal Amsterdams Peil (NAP), which in turn is approx Mean Sea Level.The charted levels refer to summer; in winter, to allow for flooding, the level is kept 0·5m lower.

A firing range, operational Tues to Thurs 1000 - 1900LT, extends S from Breezanddijk (53°01'·0N 05°12'·5E) to 3M N of Medemblik then NNW to Den Oever (DYC 188.3). Call *Schietterrein Breezanddijk* (range control) Ch 71. Firing times are broadcast on VHF Ch 01 by Scheveningen Radio at even hours on the day of firing, after weather forecasts.

BUOYAGE The SIGNI buoyage system is used in the whole of the IJsselmeer. The main features are:

1. Lateral buoyage as for IALA (Region A).
2. Supplementary PHM & SHM buoys may be R/W or G/W respectively; they also indicate a least depth of 2m.
3. At division of chan, a spherical buoy as follows:
   a. Chans of equal importance = R & G bands; topmark R and G sphere;
   b. Main chan to port = G above R bands; topmark G △ or G △ above a G ○;
   c. Main chan to stbd = R above G bands; topmark R □ or R □ above a R ○.

R/T General nav info VHF Ch 01. Oranjesluizen 18; Enkhuizen 22; Den Oever 20; Kornwerderzand 18; Lelystad 20.

HARBOURS AND FACILITIES Some of the many harbours are listed below, clockwise from Enkhuizen and via the Markermeer:

IJSSELMEER

ENKHUIZEN: 036° ldg lts Iso 4s; 230° ldg lts Iso 8s. Yachts transit the Houtribdijk via a 'Naviduct' (a twin-chambered lock passing above the road [see chartlet]; it saves lengthy delays for boat & road traffic); call Ch 22. Krabbersgat lock & bridge can still be used by boats with <6m air clearance. Both marinas and Buitenhaven are NE of the lock: **Compagnieshaven** (500) HM ☎ (0228) 313353 €2.00, P, D, CH, BH (12), Gaz; **Buyshaven** (195) ☎ 315660, €2.00, FW, AC; **Buitenhaven** ☎ 312444 €1.00, FW. **Town** EC Mon; Market Wed; C, Slip, CH, SM, ME, El, ⚒, Ⓑ, Bar, P & D (cans), Dr, ✉, ≷.

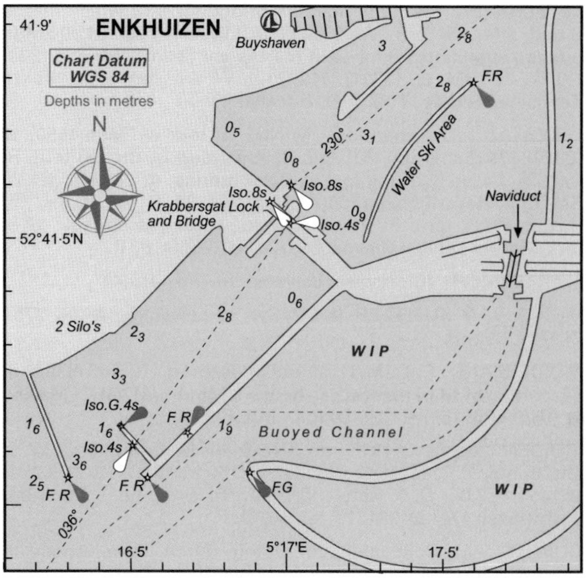
41·9'
ENKHUIZEN
Buyshaven
Chart Datum WGS 84
Depths in metres
N
FR
Water Ski Area
230°
Iso.8s
Iso.8s
Krabbersgat Lock and Bridge
Iso.4s
Naviduct
52°41·5'N
2 Silo's
WIP
Iso.G.4s
F R
Buoyed Channel
Iso.4s
F R
F R
FG
WIP
036°
16·5'
5°17'E
17·5'

ANDIJK: Visitors use **Stichting Jachthaven Andijk,** the first of 2 marinas; (600) ☎ (0228) 593075, €1.20, narrow ent with tight turn between FR/G lts. ME, C (20), SM, Gaz, ⊡, D, CH.

MEDEMBLIK: Ent on Dir lt Oc 5s 232° between FR/G. Go via Oosterhaven (P & D) into Middenhaven (short stay), then via bridge to Westerhaven. **Pekelharinghaven** (120) HM ☎ (0227) 542175, €1.10; ent is to port by Castle, CH, Bar, R; **Middenhaven** HM ☎ 541686, €0.90, FW; **Stichting Jachthaven** HM ☎ 541681 in Westerhaven, €1.10, ⊡, C. **Town** Ⓑ, CH, ME, El, SM, ⚒, ✉, Dr, Bar, ⊡, R, 🛒. **Regatta Centre** (0·5M S of hbr entr. HM ☎ (0227) 547781, AB 450, €1.70, C, Slip, CH, R.

OUDE ZEUG: Former hbr now re-opened; marina due in 2004.

DEN OEVER: Jachthaven (3m) to port of ent; HM ☎ (0227) 511798, €1.20, D, P, C (15 ton), ⊡.

MAKKUM: Approx 1M SE of Kornwerderzand, a SHM buoy MA5, Iso G4s, marks the 4·1M buoyed chan. FR/FG lts lead 092° into Makkum. To stbd, **Marina Makkum** (2·5m) ☎ (0515) 232828, €1.30, P, D, SM, Gaz, 🛒, Bar, R, ⊡. 4 other marinas/YCs are further E; BY, ME, C (30 ton), BH (30 ton). **Town** Ⓑ, Dr, 🛒, R.

WORKUM: 2·5M N of Hindeloopen; FW ldg lts 081° along buoyed chan to **It Soal Marina** ☎ (0515) 542937, €1.25, BY, ME, C, D, P (cans), Gaz, BH; **Town quay**, FW.

HINDELOOPEN: has 2 marinas, one in town and one 180m to N. **Jachthaven Hindeloopen** (500) HM ☎ (0514) 514554, €1.70, P, D, ⊡, BH (30 ton), CH, R, Bar; **Old Hbr** €0.75, D, P, ME, El, ⚒; **W.V Hylper Haven** HM ☎ (0514) 522009, €0.75, P, D, ME, El, ⚒.

STAVOREN: Ent Buitenhaven 048° on Dir lt Iso 4s between FR/G. Marina, €1.00, E of ent in Oudehaven; ☎ (0514) 681216, VHF Ch 74. Or, 1km S, ent Nieuwe Voorhaven (FR/G & Fl 5s Dir lt) then via lock to **Stavoren Marina** (3m) ☎ 681566, €1.40, BY, ME, C, P, D, SM, Gaz, BH (20 ton); **Outer Marina** (3·5m) close S of Nieuwe Voorhaven, €1.75. Also 3 other marinas. **Town** Ⓑ, Dr, 🛒, R, ≷.

LEMMER: Appr on ldg lts 038°, Iso 8s, to KL5/VL2 By; then ldg lts 083°, Iso 8s, through Lemstergeul. Lastly FG and Iso G 4s lead 065° into town and some 14 marinas. **Gem. Jachthaven** HM ☎ (0514) 561331, €1.20; **Services:** BY, ME, C, P, D, Gaz, SM. **Town** Ⓑ, Dr, 🛒, R, ✉. See Canal to Delzijl overleaf.

URK: Hbr ent ½M SE of lt ho, Fl 5s 27m 18M. Dir lt Iso G 4s to hbr ent, FR/G. Hbr has 4 basins; keep NNW to berth in Nieuwe Haven, Westhaven or Oosthaven (3·3m), €1.00. HM ☎ (0527) 689970. **Westhaven** P & D (cans), SM; **Oosthaven** ME, El, ⚒, Ⓔ, CH. **Town** EC Tues; Ⓑ, ✉, Dr.

IJSSELMEER *Continued overleaf*

KETELHAVEN: Ent Ketelmeer via bridge (12·9m) which lifts at S end; after 4M to By WK1 Iso G 4s, ldg lts Iso 8s 101°/0·7M in buoyed chan. Turn S for unlit marina ent (2·2m). **Marina** (200) €0.77, R. HM ☎ (0321) 312271. W ent has FG/R lts to Ketelsluis: HM ☎ 318237 D, P (cans).

LELYSTAD has 3 marinas: 2M NNE of lock is **Flevo** (550) ☎ (0320) 279803, €1.50, BY, ME, C, P, D, Gaz, ⊡, BH (50 ton), R, Bar, 🛒. Close N of the lock is **Deko marina,** ☎ 260248, €1.20 SM, C, R; **Houtribhaven** (560) HM ☎ 260198, €1.00, D, CH, 🛒, R, Bar, C (12 ton). Radio mast, R lts, (140m) is conspic. S of lock **Marina Lelystadhaven** 260326, €1.25, D, P, R.

MARKERMEER (Clockwise Lelystad to Enkhuizen)

BLOCQ VAN KUFFELER (8·5M SW of Lelystad), ☎ 06 2751 2497, €0.90, R.

MUIDERZAND: Ent 1M N of Hollandsebrug (12·7m cl'nce at SE corner of Markermeer) at buoys IJM5 & IJM7/JH2. **Marina** ☎ (036) 5365151, €1.50, D, P, C, ME, R, CH.

MUIDEN: Ldg lts Q 181° into **KNZ & RV Marina** (2·6m), W of ent; home of Royal Netherlands YC (150 berths). HM ☎ (0294) 261450, €2.00, D, P (cans), CH, Bar, R. On E bank **Stichting Jachthaven** (70) ☎ 261223, €1.50, D, P.

DURGERDAM: Convenient for Oranjesluizen. Keep strictly to chan which is ½M E of overhead power lines. Berth to stbd of ent (1·8m), €1.00. ☎ (020) 4904717.

MARKEN (picturesque show piece): Ent Gouwzee from N, abeam Volendam, thence via buoyed chan; Dir FW lt 116° between FR/G at hbr (2·2m). Lt ho, conspic, Oc 8s 16m 9M, on E end of island. HM ☎ (0299) 603231, €0.75 (free on quay), 🛒, R, Ⓑ, P & D (cans).

MONNICKENDAM: Appr as for Marken, then W to MO10 Iso R 8s and ldg lts FR at 236°. **Hemmeland marina** ☎ (0299) 655555, €1.25, (2·0m), C. **Waterland marina** ☎ 652000, €1.20, (2·5m), CH, C. **Gem. Haven,** €1.00. **Marina Monnickendam** ☎ 652595, €1.50, (2·0m), C. **Zeilhoek marina** ☎ 651463, €1.20, (1·8m), BY.

VOLENDAM: Berth to stbd (2·4m). Dir lt Fl 5s 313°. FR/FG at ent. ☎ (0299) 369620, €1.00, ME, C, P, D, Gaz, SM.

EDAM: Appr via unlit chan keeping Iso W 8s between FG /R at narrow ent; beware commercial traffic. **Jachthaven WSV De Zeevang** (2·5m) S side of outer hbr, €1.00. Or lock into the Oorgat and via S canal to Nieuwe Haven. HM ☎ (0299) 350174, €0.79, ME, El, ⚒. **Town** Bar, ⊡, ✉, Gaz, Ⓑ.

HOORN: Radio tr (80m) 1·5M ENE of hbr. Iso 4s 15m 10M and FR/G at W Hbr ent. Four options: to port **Grashaven** (700) HM ☎ (0299) 215208, €1.30, ⊡, CH, 🛒, ME, El, ⚒, C; to stbd ⚓ in **Buitenhaven** (1·6m); ahead & to stbd **Vluchthaven Marina** €0.82, (100) ☎ 213540; ahead to **Binnenhaven** (2·5m) via narrow lock (open H24) AB €0.90, P. **Town** 🛒, CH, ✉, R, Dr, P & D (cans), Ⓑ, Gaz, ⇌.

BY CANAL TO DELFZIJL (9.16.7; RIVER EMS)

To avoid the shallow tidal route inshore of the W Frisians, or if weather is bad, masted yachts can go via the canals/lakes from Lemmer or Stavoren (IJsselmeer) to Delfzijl, without demasting; see also 9.16.2. It is about 100M/180km, via Prinses Margrietkanaal, Leeuwarden, Dokkumer Ee, Dokkum, Lauwersmeer, Zoutkamp, Reit Diep, Groningen and Eemskanaal. Leeuwarden can also be reached from Stavoren via the Johan Frisokanaal; or from Harlingen via the Van Harinxma Kanaal. Least depths approx 1·8m. ANWB charts A and B are needed.

9.16.17 IJMUIDEN

Noord Holland 52°27'·94N 04°32'·39E Ratings: see Facilities

CHARTS AC 2322, 124; Zeekaart 1450, 1543, 1035, 1350; DYC 1801.8; Imray C25; Stanfords 19

TIDES +0400 Dover; ML 1·0; Zone –0100. Noordzeekanaal level may be above or below sea level

Standard Port VLISSINGEN (⟶)

Times				Height (metres)			
High Water		Low Water		MHWS	MHWN	MLWN	MLWS
0300	0900	0400	1000	4·7	3·8	0·8	0·2
1500	2100	1600	2200				
Differences IJMUIDEN							
+0145	+0140	+0305	+0325	–2·6	–2·1	–0·5	0·0
PETTEN (SOUTH) [18M N of IJmuiden]							
+0210	+0215	+0345	+0500	–2·8	–2·2	–0·5	–0·1

SHELTER Very good at SPM marina (3m - 5·5m). There are small marinas at IJmond under lifting bridge (VHF Ch 18) in Zijkanaal C, km 10; and at Nau-er-na (Zijkanaal D, km 12).

NAVIGATION WPT 52°28'·10N 04°30'·94E, 100°/0·9M to ent. Beware strong tidal streams across hbr ent, scend inside Buitenhaven and heavy merchant tfc; keep a good lookout, especially astern, and do not impede.

Noordzeekanaal is entered via 4 locks: North, Middle, South and Small; yachts normally use the Small (Kleine) lock, next to the South, and can wait (2hrs max) W or E of it. One in/out cycle per hour, 0600-2100 daily, is scheduled. Canal speed limit is 9 knots.

LIGHTS AND MARKS See chartlet and 9.16.4. Ldg lts 100° into Buitenhaven and Zuider Buitenkanaal: Both lt houses are dark R twrs. The HOC bldg is prominent next to the front lt. 6 tall (138-166m) chimneys are conspic 7ca N/ENE of Small lock.

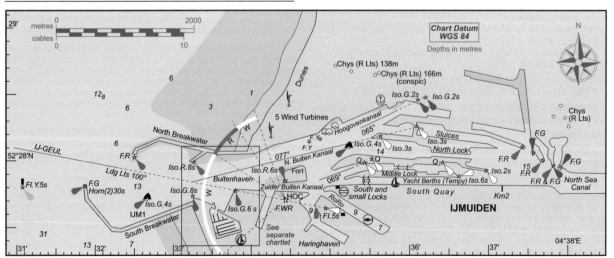

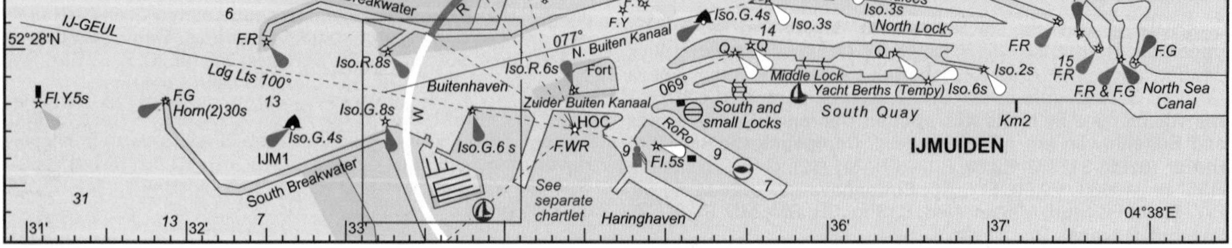
Chart Datum WGS 84
Depths in metres
metres 0 2000
cables 0 10
Chys (R Lts) 138m
Chys (R Lts) 166m (conspic)
Chys (R Lts)
Dunes
5 Wind Turbines
North Breakwater
IJ-GEUL
Ldg Lts 100°
Fl.Y.5s
F.G Horn(2)30s
Iso.G.4s
IJM1
South Breakwater
F.R
Iso.R.8s
Iso.G.8s
Buitenhaven
Iso.R.6s
Fort
Zuider Buiten Kanaal
HOC
F.WR
Fl.5s
Iso.G.6 s
See separate chartlet
Haringhaven
Hoogovenkanaal
N. Buiten Kanaal
Iso.G.2s
Iso.G.4s
Iso.3s
Sluices
North Lock
Middle Lock
Yacht Berths (Tempy) Iso.6s
South and small Locks
South Quay
RoRo
IJMUIDEN
Km2
Iso.2s
F.R & F.G
North Sea Canal
F.G
F.R
52°28'N
04°38'E

Marina ent marked by SHM buoy "IJM3", Iso G 4s, 1ca to N; and by 2 unlit Y buoys.
Entry/exit sigs: ● = no entry/exit; ●+● = get ready; ● = go.

Noordzeekanaal. Tidal, sluicing & storm signals are shown from or near the conspic Hbr Ops Centre (HOC) bldg, next to the front 100·5° ldg lt:

Tidal signals, shown H24 from radar twr on HOC bldg:
● over Ⓦ = rising tide; Ⓦ over ● = falling tide.

Sluicing signals, shown from HOC and elsewhere, are a △ of 3 horiz lts and 1 lt at the apex. Sluicing occurs N of the N Lock, so is unlikely to affect yachts using the Small lock.

Lock signals (shown seawards and inwards from each lock):

● ● = Lock not in use; no entry.
● = No entry/exit.
● ● = Prepare to enter/exit.
● = Enter or exit.

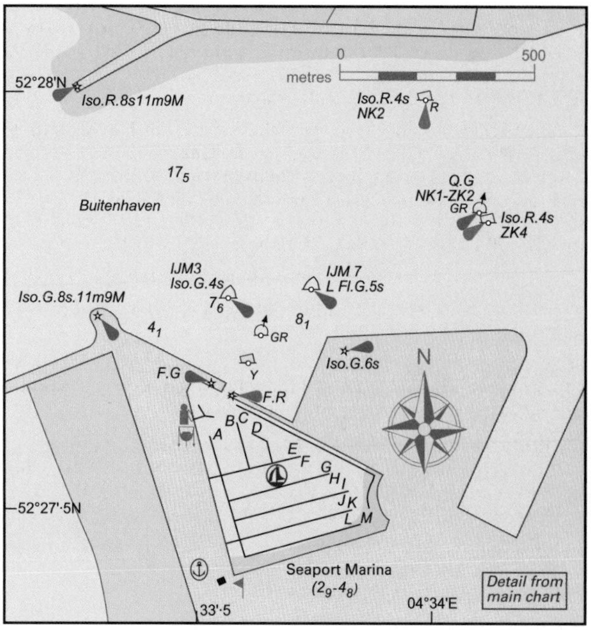
52°28'N
Iso.R.8s11m9M
0
500
metres
Iso.R.4s
NK2
R
17_5
Buitenhaven
Q.G
NK1-ZK2
GR
Iso.R.4s
ZK4
IJM3
Iso.G.4s
7_6
IJM 7
L Fl.G.5s
8_1
Iso.G.8s.11m9M
4_1
GR
Iso.G.6s
N
Y
F.G
F.R
A
B
C
D
E
F
G
H
I
J
K
L
M
52°27'·5N
Seaport Marina
(2_9-4_8)
04°34'E
33'·5
Detail from main chart

R/T Seaport Marina call *SPM* Ch 75. For the Noordzeekanaal VTS (H24), see diagram below giving stations and VHF channels.

TELEPHONE (Dial code 0255) Traffic Centre IJmuiden 564500; Hbr Ops (HOC) 523934; Pilot 564503; ⊖ 560800; CG 537644; Police 0900 8844; Ⓗ 565100; Brit Consul (020) 6764343; Emergency 112.

FACILITIES Seaport Marina (SPM) ☎ 560300; 📠 560301. ❁❁♁♁♁✿✿. (600 inc Ⓥ), €1.87 inc Shwr & AC, D & P, BH (70 ton), El, Ⓔ, CH, Gas, Slip, SM, ⚒, ME, R, Bar, ▣; in summer bus/⇌ to Amsterdam and Haarlem.

WV IJmond ❁❁♁♁✿. VHF Ch 31, HM ☎ (023) 5375003, AB €0.80 inc ⚡, D, BY, C (20 ton), ▣, Bar, 🛒, R.

Town P, D, Gaz, 🛒, R, Bar, ✉, Ⓑ, ⇌ (bus to Beverwijk), ✈ Amsterdam. Ferry: IJmuiden-Newcastle.

NOORDZEEKANAAL VTS

Yachts should monitor the following VTS stns (H24) in sequence for approach, entry and transit of the canal:

Pilot-VTS IJmuiden (W of IJM buoy).	Ch 07
IJmuiden Port Control (IJM buoy to locks).	Ch 61
IJmuiden Locks	Ch 22
Sector Noordzeekanaal (Lock to km 11·2).	Ch 03
Amsterdam Port Control (Km 11·2 to Amsterdam).	Ch 68
Sector Schellingwoude Buiten IJ for Schellingwoude bridge	Ch 60

Radar surveillance is available on request Ch 07. Visibility reports are broadcast on all VHF chans every H+00 when vis <1000m.

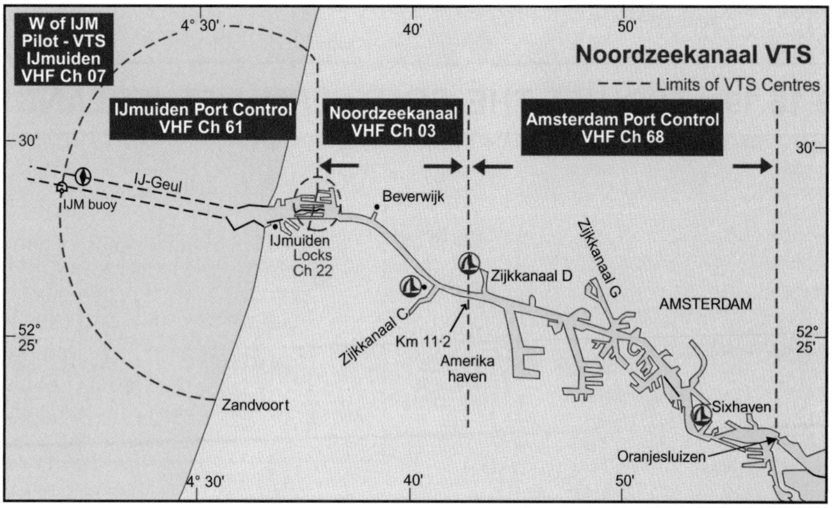
W of IJM
Pilot - VTS
IJmuiden
VHF Ch 07
4° 30'
40'
50'
Noordzeekanaal VTS
Limits of VTS Centres
IJmuiden Port Control
VHF Ch 61
Noordzeekanaal
VHF Ch 03
Amsterdam Port Control
VHF Ch 68
30'
IJ-Geul
IJM buoy
Beverwijk
IJmuiden
Locks
Ch 22
Zijkkanaal D
Zijkkanaal G
AMSTERDAM
52°
25'
Zijkkanaal C
Km 11·2
Amerika
haven
Zandvoort
Sixhaven
Oranjesluizen

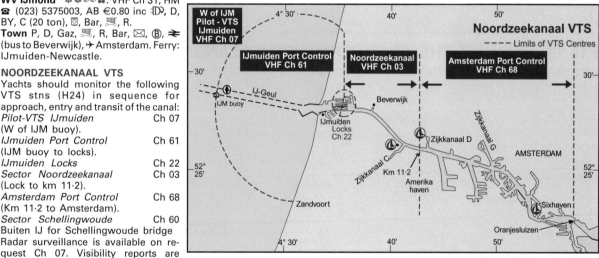

Fig 9.16.17A Noordzeekanaal VTS

9.16.18 AMSTERDAM

Noord Holland 52°22'·97N 04°53'·92E Ratings: see Facilities

CHARTS AC 124; Zeekaart 1543; DYC 1801.8, 1810.2; ANWB G, I

TIDES Amsterdam is non-tidal; Zone –0100.

SHELTER Complete in any of 4 yacht hbrs/marinas (see chartlet & Facilities). The main one is Sixhaven, on the N bank, NE of the ⇌ (conspic); it is small, pleasant and centrally located, so usually full by 1800. WV Aeolus is a good alternative. Aquadam is more for the larger yacht; bus to city centre. A small marina, WV Zuiderzee, is on N bank immediately E of Oranjesluizen.

NAVIGATION See 9.16.17 for entry via the Noordzeekanaal. The 13·5M transit is simple, apart from the volume of commercial traffic. The speed limit is 9kn.

From the IJsselmeer enter via the Schellingwoude bridge (9m), which opens year-round H24, except Mon-Fri 0600-0900 and 1600-1800; VHF Ch 18. Oranjesluizen is 500m NW with one large and 3 smaller locks (H24), with waiting piers/jetties either side. Yachts use the most N'ly lock, marked 'SPORT'; VHF Ch 18. Amsterdam gives access to the N Holland and Rijn canals.

LIGHTS AND MARKS Both banks of the canal and the ents to branch canals and basins are lit. Het IJ, the chan E towards the Oranjesluizen and the Amsterdam-Rijn canal is well lit/buoyed.

R/T Port Control Ch 68; Info 14. See 9.16.17. Oranjesluizen Ch 18.

TELEPHONE (Dial code 020) Port Control (E) 6221515; Port Control (W) 0255 514457; ⊖ 5867511; Emergency 112; Police 0900 8844; Dr 5555555; Brit Consul: 6764343.

FACILITIES Marinas: Sixhaven (60 + some Ⓥ) ☎ 6370892, ❁❁❁♁♁✿✿✿, €1.00 inc ⚡, Bar (weekends); **WV Aeolus** ☎ 6360791, ❁❁❁♁♁✿✿✿, €0.80 inc ⚡, YC, FW; **Aquadam** ☎ 6320616, ❁❁❁♁♁✿✿✿, €1.40, ⚒, P, C (30 ton); **WV Zuiderzee**, ❁❁❁♁✿✿, €0.80, YC. **City**: All facilities, Gaz, Ⓔ, ACA, DYC Agent, Ⓑ, ✉, ⇌, ✈. Ferries: IJmuiden-Newcastle. See also 9.16.21.

See Chartlet overleaf

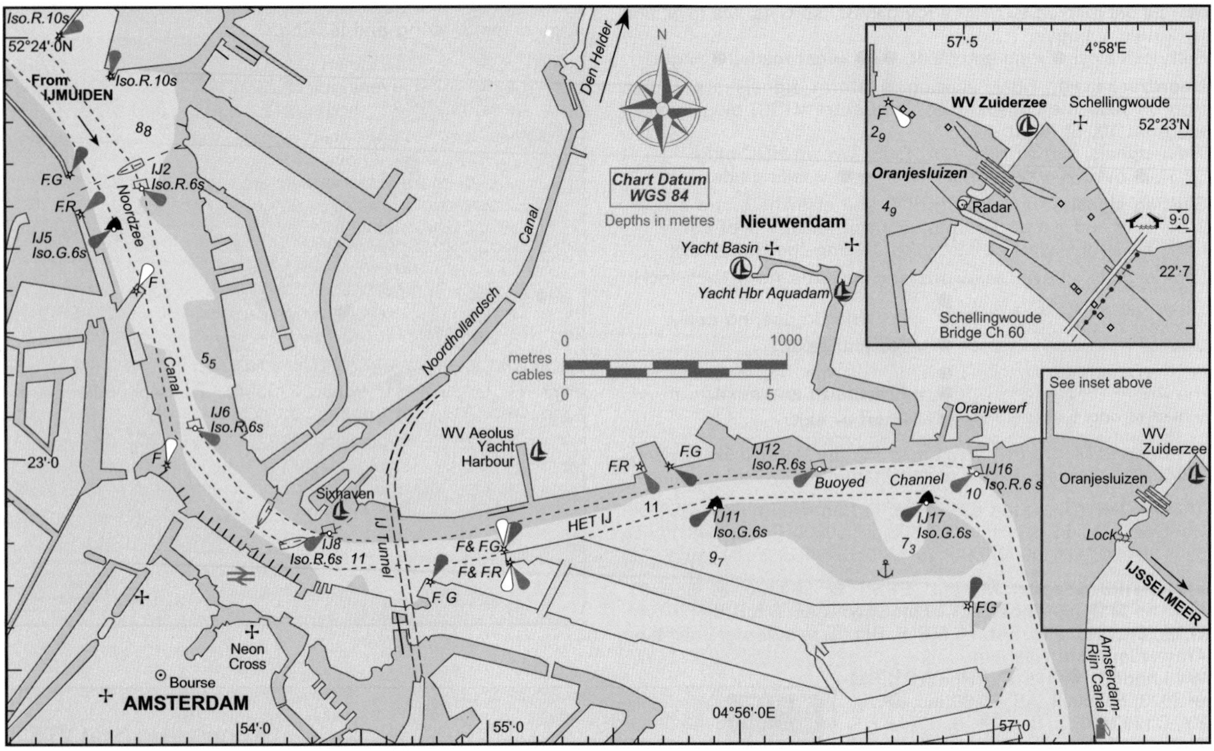
Iso.R.10s
52°24'·0N
Iso.R.10s
From IJMUIDEN
F.G
F.R
IJ2 Iso.R.6s
Noordzee
IJ5 Iso.G.6s
F
Canal
IJ6 Iso.R.6s
F
23'·0
Sixhaven
IJ8 Iso.R.6s
IJ Tunnel
F&F.G
F&F.R
F G
HET IJ
Neon Cross
Bourse
AMSTERDAM
54'·0
55'·0
Den Helder
Noordhollandsch Canal
N
Chart Datum WGS 84
Depths in metres
Nieuwendam
Yacht Basin
Yacht Hbr Aquadam
metres
cables
0
1000
0
5
WV Aeolus Yacht Harbour
F.R
F.G
IJ12 Iso.R.6s
Buoyed
Channel
IJ16 Iso.R.6s
IJ11 Iso.G.6s
IJ17 Iso.G.6s
F.G
Oranjewerf
04°56'·0E
57'·0
57'·5
4°58'E
WV Zuiderzee
Schellingwoude
52°23'N
Oranjesluizen
Radar
9·0
22'·7
Schellingwoude Bridge Ch 60
See inset above
WV Zuiderzee
Oranjesluizen
Lock
IJSSELMEER
Amsterdam-Rijn Canal

9.16.19 TSS OFF THE SOUTHERN NETHERLANDS AND BELGIUM

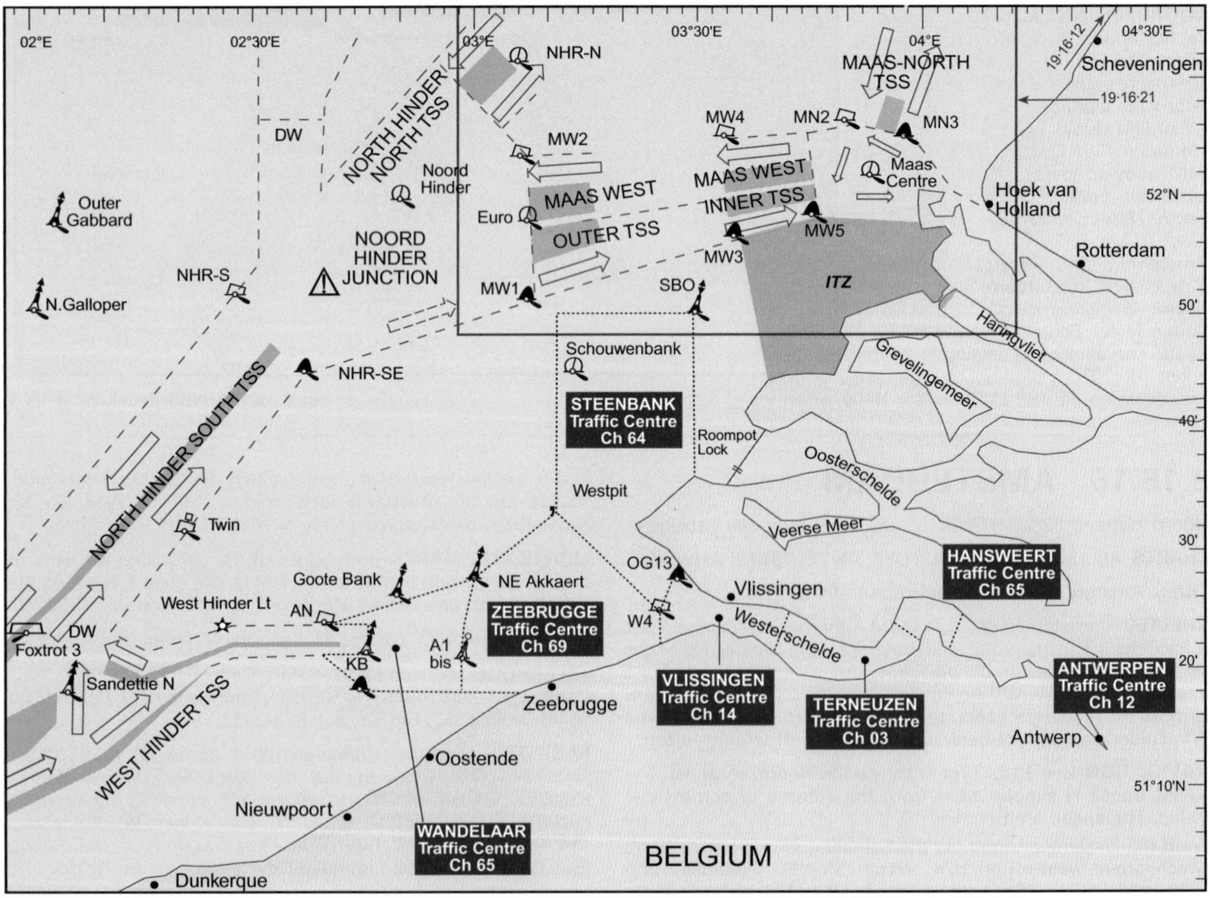
02°E
02°30'E
03°E
03°30'E
04°E
04°30'E
NHR-N
NORTH HINDER NORTH TSS
DW
MW2
Noord Hinder
Euro
MAAS WEST OUTER TSS
MW4
MN2
MAAS-NORTH TSS
MN3
MAAS WEST INNER TSS
Maas Centre
MW5
MW3
19·16·12
Scheveningen
19·16·21
Hoek van Holland
Rotterdam
52°N
50'
Outer Gabbard
N.Galloper
NHR-S
NOORD HINDER JUNCTION
MW1
SBO
ITZ
Haringvliet
NHR-SE
Schouwenbank
Grevelingemeer
STEENBANK Traffic Centre Ch 64
Roompot Lock
Oosterschelde
40'
Westpit
Veerse Meer
NORTH HINDER SOUTH TSS
Twin
Goote Bank
NE Akkaert
OG13
Vlissingen
HANSWEERT Traffic Centre Ch 65
30'
West Hinder Lt
AN
ZEEBRUGGE Traffic Centre Ch 69
W4
Westerschelde
Foxtrot 3
DW
A1 bis
KB
20'
Sandettie N
Zeebrugge
VLISSINGEN Traffic Centre Ch 14
TERNEUZEN Traffic Centre Ch 03
ANTWERPEN Traffic Centre Ch 12
Antwerp
WEST HINDER TSS
Oostende
51°10'N
Nieuwpoort
WANDELAAR Traffic Centre Ch 65
BELGIUM
Dunkerque

9.16.20 SCHEVENINGEN

Zuid Holland **52°06'·24N 04°15'·27E** ❁❁❁◊◊◊✿✿

CHARTS AC 2322, 122; Zeekaart 1035, 1349, 1350, 1449; DYC 1801.7; ANWB H/J; Imray C25; Stanfords 19

TIDES +0320 Dover; ML 0·9; Duration 0445; Zone –0100

Standard Port VLISSINGEN (⟶)

Times				**Height (metres)**			
High Water		Low Water		MHWS	MHWN	MLWN	MLWS
0300	0900	0400	1000	4·7	3·8	0·8	0·2
1500	2100	1600	2200				
Differences SCHEVENINGEN							
+0105	+0100	+0220	+0245	–2·6	–2·1	–0·6	0·0

NOTE: Double LWs occur. The slight rise after the 1st LW is called the Agger. Prolonged NW gales can raise levels by up to 3m, whilst strong E winds can lower levels by 1m.

SHELTER Very good at marina (2nd Hbr); access H24. The chan from 1st to 2nd Hbrs is narrow with limited vis, so sound horn.

NAVIGATION WPT 52°07'·75N 04°14'·14E [SCH (SWM) buoy, Iso 4s] 156°/1·6M to ent. Strong tidal streams setting NE/SW across the ent can cause problems. Winds >F6 from SW to N cause scend in the outer hbr, when ent can be difficult. Beware large ships entering and leaving.

LIGHTS AND MARKS Daymarks include: the reddish-brown lt ho; twr bldgs in Scheveningen and Den Haag. Outer ldg lts 156°, both Iso 4s; Inner 131°, both Oc G 5s. See chartlet and 9.16.4.

Tfc signals (from Signal mast, N side of ent to Voorhaven):
● over ○ = No entry. ○ over ● = No exit.
Fl ● = One or more large vessels are leaving the port.
● shown from inner end of passage between 1st and 2nd Hbrs = vessels must not leave the 2nd Hbr; see chartlet.

Tide signals: ● over ○ = tide rising. ○ over ● = tide falling.

R/T Call *Scheveningen Haven* Ch 21 (H24) prior to entry/dep to avoid ferries/FVs. Radar (info only) on request Ch 21. When in 2nd Hbr call *Yacht Club Scheveningen* Ch 31 for a berth.

TELEPHONE (Dial code 070) Port HM 3527711; Traffic Centre 3527721; ⊜ 3514481; Police 3103048; Dr 3450650/4550963; Ambulance 112; Brit Consul (020) 6764343.

FACILITIES YC Scheveningen (223 + 100 Ⓥ) ☎ 3520017, mobile 06-53293137. €1.57 plus tourist tax €1.21 per adult, €0.50 per child; Bar, CH, D, El, ME, R, ▣, ⚒, SM; **Clubhouse** ☎ 3520308; **Hbr** Slip, ME, ⚒, CH, R, Bar; **Services:** ME, El, ⚒, CH, SM, DYC Agent.
Town P, D, 🛒, R, Bar, ✉, Ⓑ, ⇌, ✈ Rotterdam/Amsterdam. Ferry: See Rotterdam or Hoek van Holland.

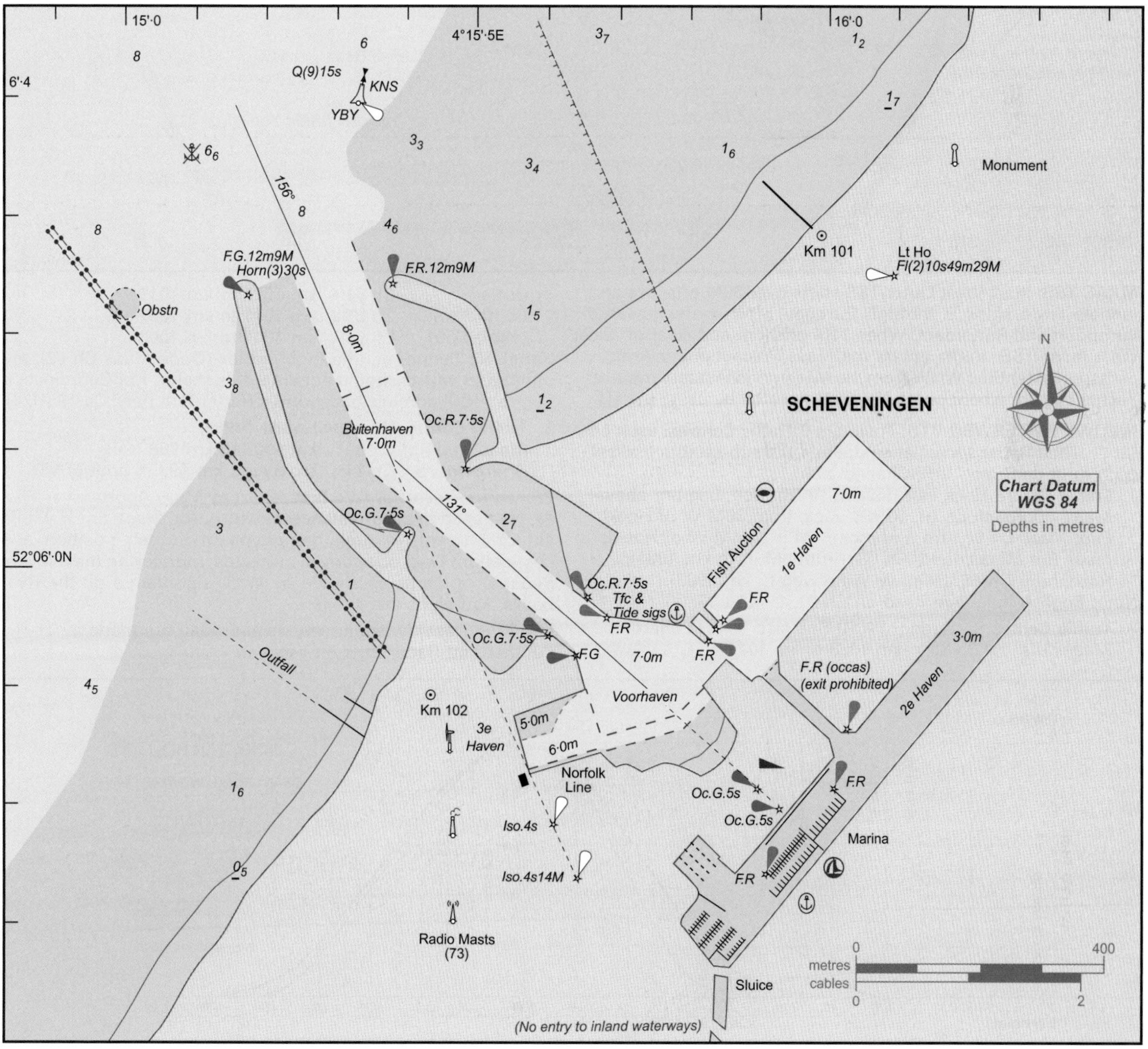
15'·0
4°15'·5E
16'·0
6'·4
52°06'·0N
Q(9)15s
KNS
YBY
156°
8·0m
F.G.12m9M
Horn(3)30s
F.R.12m9M
Obstn
Buitenhaven
7·0m
Oc.R.7·5s
Oc.G.7·5s
131°
Outfall
Oc.R.7·5s
Tfc &
Tide sigs
F.R
F.G
7·0m
Voorhaven
Km 102
3e
Haven
5·0m
6·0m
Norfolk
Line
Iso.4s
Iso.4s14M
Radio Masts
(73)
Monument
Km 101
Lt Ho
Fl(2)10s49m29M
SCHEVENINGEN
N
Chart Datum
WGS 84
Depths in metres
Fish Auction
1e Haven
F.R
3·0m
F.R (occas)
(exit prohibited)
2e Haven
Oc.G.5s
Marina
Sluice
metres
cables
0
400
2
(No entry to inland waterways)

9.16.21 MAAS TSS and VTS in NIEUWE WATERWEG APPROACHES

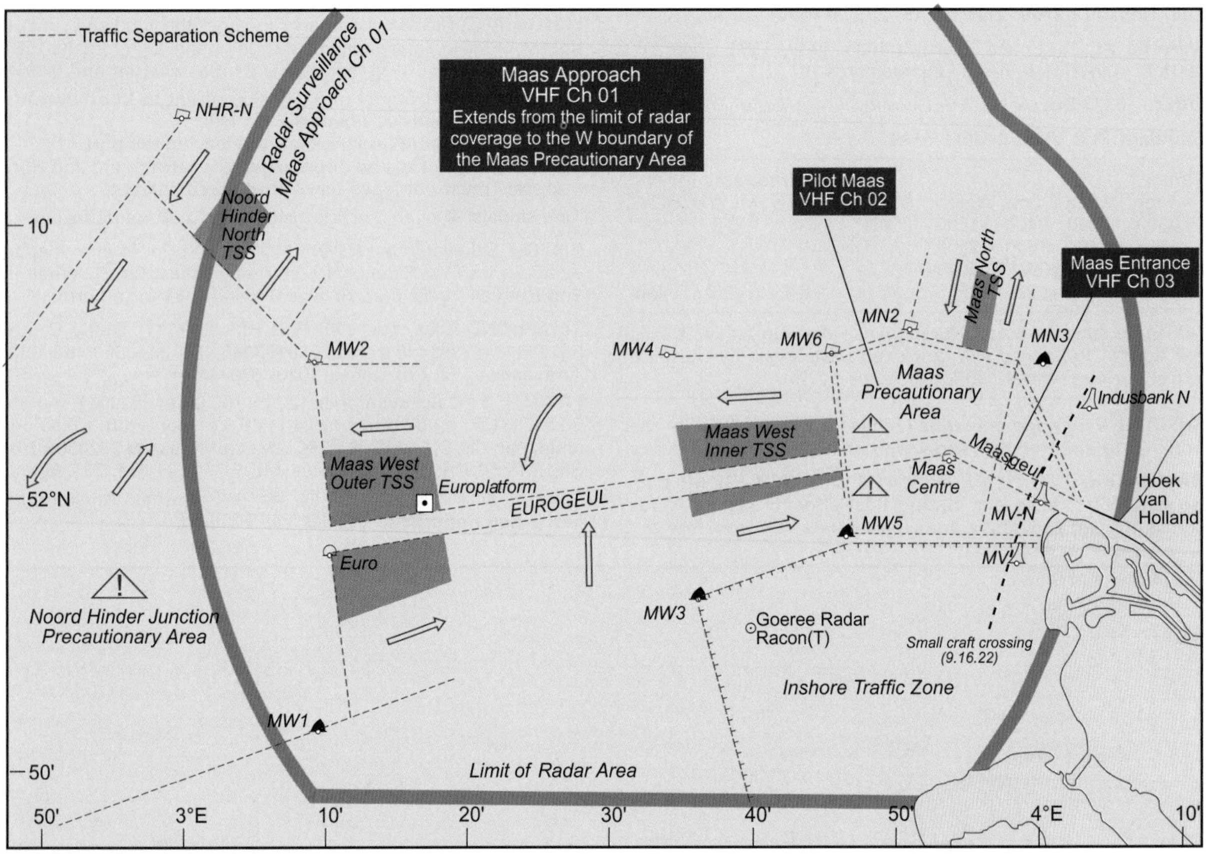
Traffic Separation Scheme
Radar Surveillance
Maas Approach Ch 01
Maas Approach
VHF Ch 01
Extends from the limit of radar coverage to the W boundary of the Maas Precautionary Area
NHR-N
Noord Hinder North TSS
Pilot Maas
VHF Ch 02
Maas North TSS
Maas Entrance
VHF Ch 03
10'
MN2
MN3
MW2
MW4
MW6
Maas Precautionary Area
Indusbank N
Maas West Inner TSS
Maasgeul
Maas West Outer TSS
Europlatform
EUROGEUL
Maas Centre
Hoek van Holland
52°N
MW5
MV-N
MV
Euro
MW3
Goeree Radar Racon(T)
Noord Hinder Junction Precautionary Area
Small craft crossing (9.16.22)
Inshore Traffic Zone
MW1
50'
Limit of Radar Area
50'
3°E
10'
20'
30'
40'
50'
4°E
10'

MAAS TSS: Mast West Outer TSS starts over 30M offshore and funnels large ships E through Eurogeul (DW route) towards Europoort and Rotterdam. When 11M offshore and clear of the West Inner TSS, traffic enters the Maas Precautionary Area, a pentagon extending WNW from the Maasmond (estuary mouth). Yachts should, where possible, avoid the area by using the ITZ.

NIEUWE WATERWEG VTS: There are 3 **Traffic Centres**, each on Ch 11. Their Radar surveillance stations and sub-sectors *(italics)*, each on a dedicated VHF Channel are:

1. **Traffic Centre Hoek van Holland (VCH)** (See diagram above)
   Maas Approach Ch 01, (Outer apps, from 38M W of Hoek);
   Pilot Maas Ch 02, (from approx 11M in to 4M W of Hoek);
   Maas Ent (Maasmond) Ch 03, (from 4M in to km 1031);
   Rozenburg Ch 65, (Nieuwe Waterweg to km 1023);

Note: **English** language used on Ch 01, 02 and 03.

2. **Traffic Centre Rotterdam (VCR)** See also 9.16.23 chartlet.

Maassluis	Ch 80,	km 1023 to km 1017
Botlek	Ch 61	km 1017 to km 1011
Eemhaven	Ch 63	km 1011 to km 1007
Waalhaven	Ch 60	km 1007 to km 1003

Hartel Tfc Centre, and its radar sector (Oude Maas Ch 62), are omitted as yachts should not enter this sector. Hbr Coordination Centre (HCC) administers/controls Rotterdam port, Ch 19 (H24).

3. **Traffic Centre Maasboulevard (VPM)**

Maasbruggen	Ch 81	km 1003 to km 998
Brienenoord	Ch 21	km 998 to km 993 (E limit of VTS)

Procedure: Yachts should **first report** to *Maas Approach* or *Pilot Maas*, depending on distance offshore, (or *Maas Ent* if within 4M of hbr ent), stating name/type of vessel, position and destination. Then obey any instructions, monitoring the relevant Radar Ch's (limits as shown by W □ signboards on the river banks; Km signs are similar).

Info broadcasts (weather, vis, tfc and tidal) are made by Traffic Centres and Radar stns on request.

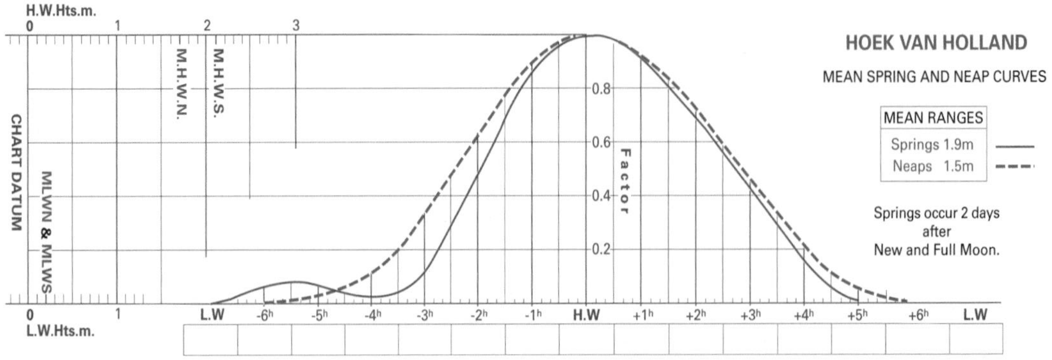
H.W.Hts.m.
0
1
2
3
M.H.W.N.
M.H.W.S.
CHART DATUM
MLWN & MLWS
0.8
0.6
0.4
0.2
Factor
0
1
L.W.Hts.m.
L.W
-6h
-5h
-4h
-3h
-2h
-1h
H.W
+1h
+2h
+3h
+4h
+5h
+6h
L.W
HOEK VAN HOLLAND
MEAN SPRING AND NEAP CURVES
MEAN RANGES
Springs 1.9m
Neaps 1.5m
Springs occur 2 days after New and Full Moon.

9.16.22 HOEK VAN HOLLAND and NIEUWE WATERWEG

Zuid Holland **51°59'·50N 04°02'·78E** (Ent)

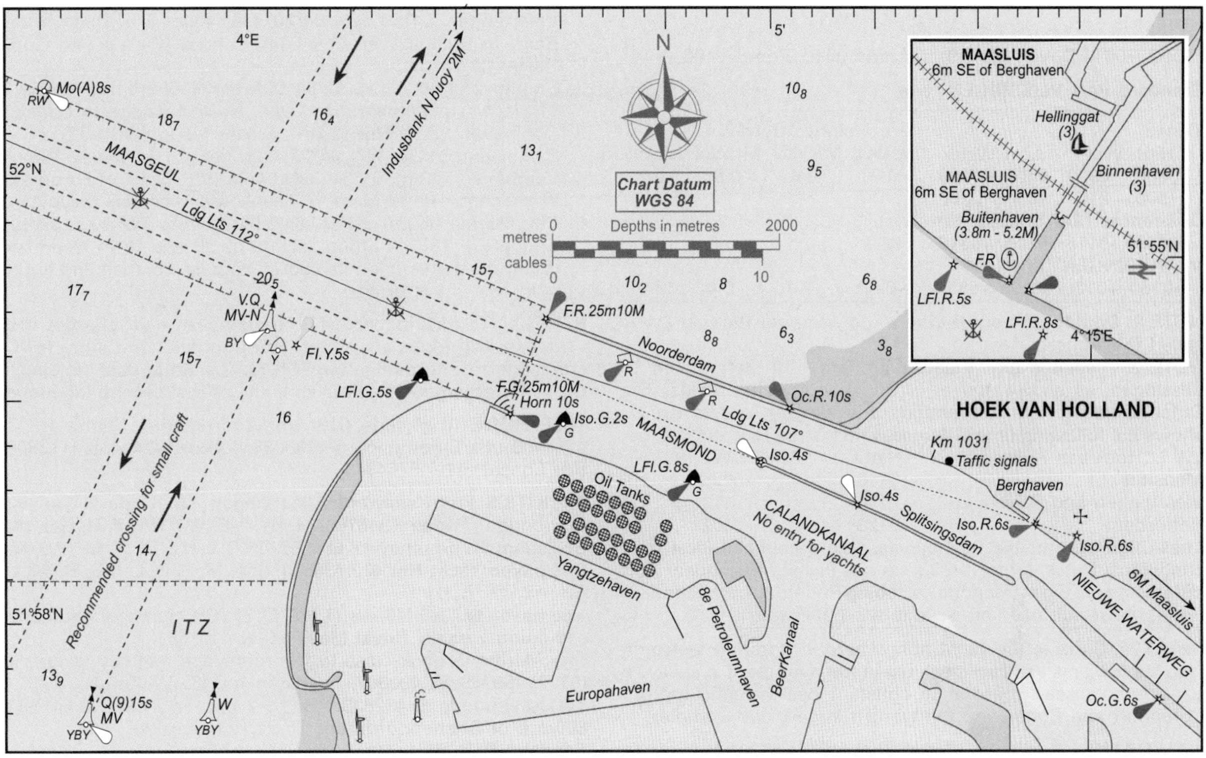
4°E
5'
N
52°N
51°58'N
Mo(A)8s
RW
MAASGEUL
Ldg Lts 112°
Indusbank N buoy 2M
Chart Datum
WGS 84
metres
cables
Depths in metres
0
2000
10
V.Q
MV-N
BY
Y
Fl.Y.5s
LFl.G.5s
F.R.25m10M
F.G.25m10M
Horn 10s
Iso.G.2s
G
R
Noorderdam
Oc.R.10s
Ldg Lts 107°
MAASMOND
Iso.4s
LFl.G.8s
Oil Tanks
Yangtzehaven
CALANDKANAAL
No entry for yachts
Splitsingsdam
Iso.R.6s
Km 1031
Taffic signals
Berghaven
HOEK VAN HOLLAND
6M Maasluis
NIEUWE WATERWEG
Oc.G.6s
8e Petroleumhaven
Beerkanaal
Europahaven
ITZ
Recommended crossing for small craft
Q(9)15s
MV
YBY
W
MAASLUIS
6m SE of Berghaven
Hellinggat
(3)
Binnenhaven
(3)
Buitenhaven
(3.8m - 5.2M)
F.R
LFl.R.5s
LFl.R.8s
51°55'N
4°15'E

CHARTS AC 122, 132; Zeekaart 1540, 1349, 1350, 1449; DYC 1801.6, 1801.7; Imray C30, Y5; Stanfords 19

TIDES +0251 Dover; ML 0·9; Duration 0505; Zone –0100.

HOEK VAN HOLLAND is a Standard Port (⟶). Double LWs occur, more obviously at sp; in effect a LW stand. Predictions are for the *lower* LW. The 1st LW is about 5½ hrs after HW and the 2nd LW about 4¼ hrs before the next HW. The slight rise after the first LW is called the Agger. Water levels on this coast are much affected by the weather. Prolonged NW gales can raise levels by up to 3m.

SHELTER Entry safe except in strong on-shore winds when heavy seas/swell develop. Berghaven hbr is closed to yachts; better shelter at Maassluis (3m), 6M up river (km 1019). Or continue 10M inland to Rotterdam, 9.16.23, for complete shelter. Note: there is a 'gap' of approx 8M between the chartlet above and that for Rotterdam; the navigation is straightforward.

NAVIGATION From N, WPT 52°02'·89N 04°03'·57E [Indusbank NCM lt buoy, Q], 190°/3·2M to Noorderdam lt, FR.
From S, WPT 51°59'·60N 04°00'·20E [MV-N NCM lt buoy, Q], 103°/2·9M to front 112° ldg lt, Iso 4s, at the NW end of Splitsingsdam the central pier separating Nieuwe Waterweg from Calandkanaal. Enter Nieuwe Waterweg which becomes Nieuwe Maas near Vlaardingen (km 1011). Do not enter the Calandkanaal/Europoort and associated docks. Keep a good lookout, especially astern.

There are no navigational dangers, but the waterway is very busy and relatively narrow. Keep clear of the constant stream of ocean-going & local ships, and those manoeuvering whilst transferring pilots.

Rules for Yachts in Nieuwe Waterweg/Nieuwe Maas: Monitor the VTS channels (see R/T); only transmit in emergency. Keep to extreme stbd limit of buoyed line avoiding debris between buoy and bank. No tacking/beating; no ⚓. Eng ready for instant start. Able to motor at 3.24kn (6km/hr). Hoist a radar reflector, esp in poor vis or at night. Cross chan quickly at 90°. All docks are prohib to yachts, except to access a marina.

Crossing the Entrance: Yachts on passage wishing to cross the Maasgeul (seaward of the bkwtrs), must call *Maas Ent* Ch 03, with position and course, and keep watch on Ch 03. Cross under power on the recommended track, 027°/032° (or reciprocal), W of line joining MV, MV-N and Indusbank N buoys; see WPTs and chartlet. Beware strong tidal set across the ent.

LIGHTS AND MARKS See chartlet and 9.16.4 for details. Maasvlakte, 8-sided 62m twr, B/W bands; 340°-267° (H24). Outer ldg lts 112° to ent; then 107° ldg lts into Nieuwe Waterweg, both R trs, W bands. Noorderdam head, R twr, W bands, helipad. Zuiderdam head, G twr, W bands, helipad, Horn 10s.

Traffic Sigs from Pilot/Sig Stn on N side of Nieuwe Waterweg, close W of Berghaven:

● ● ●
○ = No ent/exit to/from Maasmond (the area from mole heads to abeam Berghaven).
● ● ●

● ●
○ = No ent to Nieuwe Weg; No exit from Nieuwe Maas.
● ●

There are other signals which relate to the Calendkanaal and Europoort, but these should not affect yachts. Patrol vessels show a Fl Bu lt; additionally a Fl R lt = 'Stop'.

R/T In the Nieuwe Waterweg/Nieuwe Maas obey any instructions, monitoring the appropriate Radar Ch's (limits as shown by W □ signboards on the river banks; Km signs are similar).

Other stations: Maasluis ent/lock/bridge Ch 80; marina Ch 68.

TELEPHONE (Dial code 010) Port Authority (HCC) 2522400; Pilot (Hoek) 5931600; Police 4141414; Ⓗ 4112800; Brit Consul (020) 6764343.

FACILITIES Maasluis marina (km 1019): ☎ 593 1285, CH, El, FW, BY, ME, ⚒. See tidal differences 9.16.23 and chartlet inset above. **Town** P, D, 🛒, R, Bar, ✉, Ⓑ, ⇌, ✈ (Rotterdam). Ferry: Hoek-Harwich (HSS); Rotterdam Europoort-Hull.

9.16.23 ROTTERDAM

Zuid Holland **51°54'·00N 04°28'·00E** ❁❁❁◊◊◊✿✿✿

CHARTS AC 122, 132, 133; Zeekaart 1540/1/2; DYC 1809.4, 1809.5; Stanfords 19

TIDES +0414 Dover; ML 0·9; Duration 0440; Zone –0100

Standard Port VLISSINGEN (⟶)

Times				Height (metres)			
High Water		Low Water		MHWS	MHWN	MLWN	MLWS
0300	0900	0400	1000	4·7	3·8	0·8	0·2
1500	2100	1600	2200				
Differences MAASSLUIS (Km 1019)							
+0155	+0115	+0100	+0310	–2·7	–2·1	–0·6	0·0
VLAARDINGEN (Km 1011)							
+0150	+0120	+0130	+0330	–2·6	–2·1	–0·6	0·0

NOTE 1: Double LWs occur. The slight rise after the first LW is called the Agger.
NOTE 2: Maasluis and Vlaardingen are both referenced to Vlissingen, as shown above, in British Admiralty Tables. The Dutch *Guide to the Netherlands and Belgian coasts* (HP11) shows the following time differences relative to HW and the first LW at Hoek van Holland:

LW at Hoek van Holland:	HW	LW
Maasluis	+0113	+0038
Vlaardingen and Schiedam	+0114	+0112
Rotterdam	+0123	+0352

These figures, plus the tidal curves, take account of local river conditions. Dutch Tables (HP33) do not include Secondary Port differences; all the major ports, including Rotterdam, are Standard Ports whose full daily predictions are published.

SHELTER Good in the yacht hbrs where visitors are welcome (see Lts & Marks and Facilities), but in the river there is always a considerable sea/swell due to constant heavy traffic to/from Europoort and Rotterdam, the world's largest port complex.

NAVIGATION See 9.16.22 for Yacht Rules. Berghaven to Rotterdam is about 19M. 7M before the centre of Rotterdam, the Oude Maas joins (km 1013); it gives access to Dordrecht, where it connects to the Delta network of canals and lakes.

Note: Special regulations apply to yachts in the Rhine; obtain a French booklet *Service de la Navigation du Rhin* from 25 Rue de la Nuée Bleu, 6700 Strasbourg.

LIGHTS AND MARKS Marks to help locate marinas:

1. Vlaardingen, 51°53'·98N 04°20'·93E, 400m E of Delta Hotel. Berth in Buitenhaven (3·6-4·4m) or lock (Ch 20) into Oude Haven (2·7m), YC.
2. Spuihaven (1·6-2·8m), 51°54'·00N 04°24'·00E, immediately E of the ent to Wilhelmina Haven. No lock/bridge to transit.
3. Coolhaven Yacht Hbr (2·7m), access via lock (Ch 22) off Parkhaven, 51°54'·11N 04°28'·00E; next to Euromast 185m.
4. Veerhaven (3·3m), 51°54'·39N 04°28'·76E, 5ca E of Euromast, ⓥ welcome; Royal Maas YC (clubhouse, members only).
5. City Marina (4·0m), 51°54'·64N 04°29'·76E. Transit Erasmus bridge (Ch 18) via lifting section at SE end (11m clearance under fixed span); ldg lts 056·7°, both Iso 2s; then 2nd ent to stbd, via lifting bridge.

R/T The VTS Ch's for central Rotterdam are on the chartlet. VHF Ch for locks/bridges are above. Hbr Coordination Centre (HCC) administers Rotterdam port on Ch 19. Call Rotterdam Tfc Centre Ch 11 for emergencies. English is the official second language.

TELEPHONE (Dial code 010) Hbr Coordination Centre (HCC) 4251400, also Emergency; ⊖ 4298088; Police 4141414; Ⓗ 4112800; Brit Consul (020) 6764343.

FACILITIES From seaward: **Vlaardingen YC** (Oude Haven via lock/bridge); HM ☎ 4346786, M, BY, ME, SM, FW, P, D, Gaz, ⇌.
Schiedam YC (Spuihaven) ☎ 4267765, D, L, ME, El, ⚒, CH, AB, ⇌.
Coolhaven Yacht Hbr ☎ 4738614, Slip, M, P, D, L, ME, El, ⚒, C, CH, AB, 🛒, R, Bar.
Veerhaven ☎ 4365446, AB, D, ME, El, SH, CH; centre for traditional sea-going vessels; **Royal Maas YC** ☎ 4137681.
City Marina, S bank close to Noordereiland and city centre. ☎ (0187) 493769, 📠 493807, 110 AB in 4m, YC, Water taxi.
YC IJsselmonde ☎ 482833, AB (1·3-2·1m); on S bank at km 994, 800m E of Brienenoordbrug, Ch 20 (off chartlet).
Services: P, D, ME; Gaz, ACA, DYC Agent.

City all facilities, ✉, Ⓑ, ⇌, ✈, Ferry: Rotterdam - Hull, also Hook-Harwich (HSS).

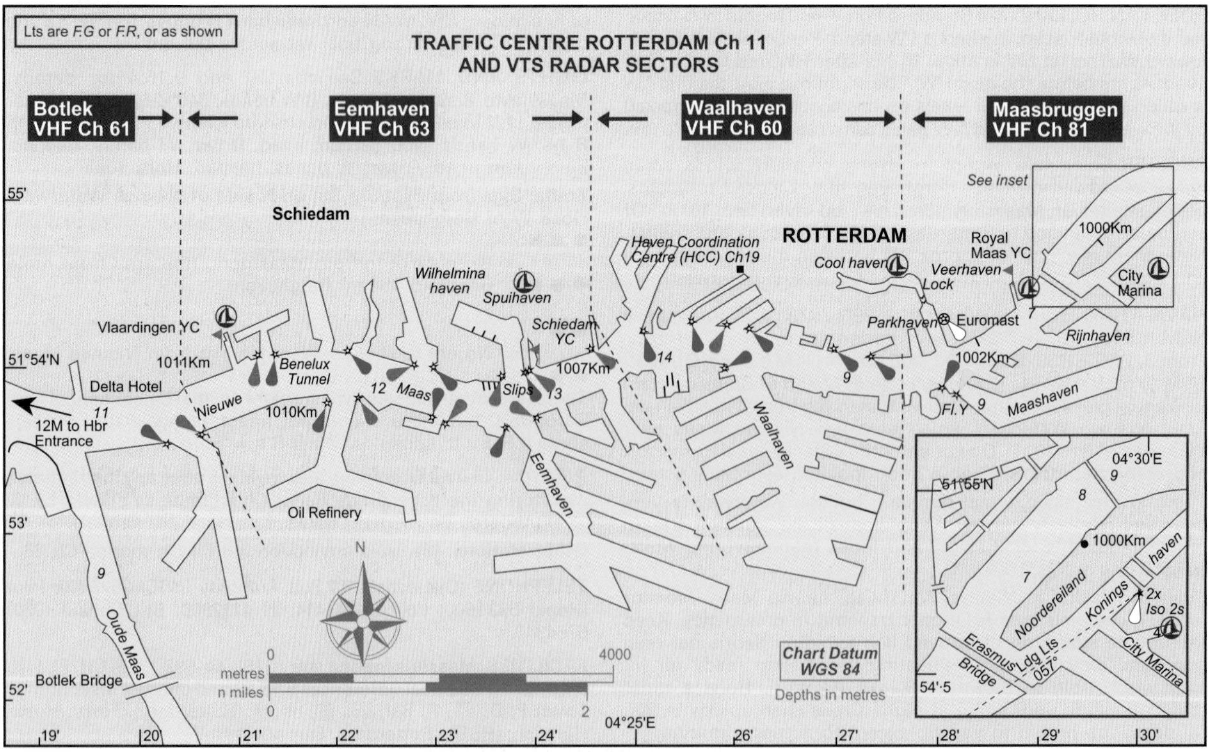
Lts are F.G or F.R, or as shown
TRAFFIC CENTRE ROTTERDAM Ch 11
AND VTS RADAR SECTORS
Botlek
VHF Ch 61
Eemhaven
VHF Ch 63
Waalhaven
VHF Ch 60
Maasbruggen
VHF Ch 81
See inset
Schiedam
Haven Coordination Centre (HCC) Ch19
ROTTERDAM
Royal Maas YC
Veerhaven
Lock
Cool haven
City Marina
1000Km
Wilhelmina haven
Spuihaven
Vlaardingen YC
Schiedam YC
Parkhaven
Euromast
Rijnhaven
1011Km
Benelux Tunnel
1007Km
1002Km
Delta Hotel
12 Maas
Slips
Nieuwe
1010Km
Waalhaven
Maashaven
Fl.Y
12M to Hbr Entrance
Eemhaven
Oil Refinery
Oude Maas
Botlek Bridge
N
metres
n miles
0
4000
2
Chart Datum WGS 84
Depths in metres
04°25'E
51°54'N
55'
53'
52'
19'
20'
21'
22'
23'
24'
26'
27'
28'
29'
30'
04°30'E
51°55'N
1000Km
Noordereiland
Konings haven
2x Iso 2s
Erasmus Bridge
Ldg Lts 057°
City Marina
54'·5

TIME ZONE -0100
(Dutch Standard Time)
Subtract 1 hour for UT
For Dutch Summer Time add ONE hour in **non-shaded areas**

NETHERLANDS – HOEK VAN HOLLAND

LAT 51°59′N LONG 4°07′E

TIMES AND HEIGHTS OF HIGH AND LOW WATERS

SPRING & NEAP TIDES
Dates in red are SPRINGS
Dates in blue are NEAPS

YEAR **2005**

JANUARY

Date	Day	Time	m	Time	m	Time	m	Time	m
1	SA	0125	0.4	0606	1.9	1135	0.1	1825	2.0
2	SU	0200	0.4	0646	1.8	1215	0.1	1904	2.0
3	M	0240	0.5	0736	1.8	1304	0.1	◑ 1954	2.0
4	TU	0247	0.5	0824	1.8	1404	0.1	2117	2.0
5	W	0315	0.5	0935	1.8	1516	0.2	2216	2.0
6	TH	0405	0.5	1046	1.8	1604	0.2	2314	2.0
7	F	0504	0.4	1150	1.9	1705	0.2		
8	SA	0025	2.0	0606	0.4	1246	2.0	1825	0.3
9	SU	0115	2.0	0634	0.3	1336	2.1	1905	0.3
10	M	0205	2.0	0723	0.3	1426	2.2	● 1949	0.4
11	TU	0255	2.0	0805	0.2	1515	2.3	2325	0.4
12	W	0345	2.0	0849	0.1	1601	2.3		
13	TH	0005	0.4	0435	2.0	0935	0.1	1648	2.3
14	F	0100	0.4	0518	2.0	1019	0.0	1739	2.3
15	SA	0145	0.5	0608	2.0	1116	0.0	1828	2.2
16	SU	0244	0.5	0659	1.9	1215	0.0	1925	2.1
17	M	0345	0.5	0755	1.9	1314	0.0	◐ 2030	2.0
18	TU	0224	0.5	0844	1.8	1425	0.1	2125	1.9
19	W	0324	0.5	0955	1.8	1550	0.2	2250	1.8
20	TH	0425	0.5	1110	1.7	1655	0.3	2355	1.8
21	F	0540	0.5	1215	1.8	1810	0.3		
22	SA	0055	1.8	0615	0.4	1315	1.8	1855	0.4
23	SU	0149	1.8	0956	0.3	1405	1.9	1950	0.4
24	M	0240	1.9	0744	0.3	1435	2.0	2015	0.4
25	TU	0326	1.9	0819	0.3	1513	2.0	○ 2110	0.5
26	W	0345	1.9	0850	0.2	1544	2.1	2237	0.5
27	TH	0405	1.9	0909	0.2	1626	2.1	2325	0.4
28	F	0446	2.0	0945	0.1	1655	2.1		
29	SA	0020	0.4	0516	1.9	1014	0.1	1725	2.1
30	SU	0054	0.4	0546	1.9	1045	0.1	1759	2.1
31	M	0146	0.4	0615	1.9	1129	0.0	1835	2.1

FEBRUARY

Date	Day	Time	m	Time	m	Time	m	Time	m
1	TU	0155	0.4	0655	1.9	1215	0.0	1918	2.0
2	W	0157	0.4	0746	1.9	1304	0.0	◑ 2014	2.0
3	TH	0235	0.4	0850	1.8	1446	0.1	2130	1.9
4	F	0315	0.4	0954	1.8	1544	0.2	2246	1.8
5	SA	0435	0.4	1126	1.8	1705	0.2		
6	SU	0000	1.8	0534	0.3	1225	1.9	1804	0.3
7	M	0106	1.8	0630	0.3	1325	2.0	2135	0.3
8	TU	0155	1.9	0709	0.2	1416	2.2	● 2215	0.3
9	W	0245	1.9	0749	0.1	1500	2.3	2310	0.4
10	TH	0331	2.0	0829	0.0	1547	2.3	2345	0.4
11	F	0416	2.0	0915	0.0	1636	2.3		
12	SA	0034	0.4	0459	2.0	0955	0.0	1716	2.2
13	SU	0124	0.4	0541	2.0	1046	0.0	1806	2.2
14	M	0225	0.4	0625	2.0	1139	0.0	1849	2.0
15	TU	0305	0.4	0716	2.0	1250	0.1	1939	1.9
16	W	0130	0.4	0805	1.9	1404	0.1	◐ 2035	1.7
17	TH	0225	0.4	0854	1.8	1524	0.2	2144	1.6
18	F	0355	0.4	1026	1.6	1635	0.3	2336	1.5
19	SA	0510	0.3	1150	1.6	1744	0.3		
20	SU	0035	1.6	0555	0.3	1300	1.7	1835	0.4
21	M	0135	1.7	0650	0.3	1343	1.8	2150	0.4
22	TU	0219	1.8	0724	0.3	1425	1.9	2227	0.4
23	W	0256	1.8	0804	0.2	1455	2.0	2257	0.4
24	TH	0319	1.9	0815	0.2	1525	2.1	○ 2300	0.4
25	F	0349	2.0	0846	0.1	1559	2.2	2320	0.4
26	SA	0419	2.0	0915	0.1	1625	2.2		
27	SU	0006	0.3	0449	2.0	0945	0.1	1659	2.1
28	M	0040	0.3	0515	2.0	1015	0.0	1731	2.1

MARCH

Date	Day	Time	m	Time	m	Time	m	Time	m
1	TU	0115	0.3	0549	2.0	1055	0.0	1807	2.1
2	W	0145	0.3	0626	2.0	1134	0.0	1848	2.0
3	TH	0000	0.3	0709	2.0	1234	0.0	◑ 1946	1.9
4	F	0105	0.3	0805	1.9	1425	0.1	2056	1.7
5	SA	0245	0.3	0936	1.8	1535	0.2	2214	1.6
6	SU	0404	0.3	1106	1.7	1706	0.3	2350	1.6
7	M	0520	0.3	1219	1.9	2007	0.3		
8	TU	0054	1.7	0610	0.2	1319	2.0	2124	0.3
9	W	0149	1.8	0644	0.1	1405	2.1	2155	0.3
10	TH	0231	1.9	0730	0.1	1446	2.2	● 2234	0.4
11	F	0315	2.0	0808	0.0	1527	2.2	2330	0.4
12	SA	0350	2.0	0848	0.0	1608	2.2		
13	SU	0020	0.4	0435	2.1	1306	0.0	1651	2.2
14	M	0115	0.3	0516	2.1	1346	0.0	1731	2.1
15	TU	0155	0.3	0551	2.1	1405	0.1	1815	1.9
16	W	0220	0.3	0631	2.0	1300	0.1	1855	1.8
17	TH	0040	0.3	0715	1.9	1400	0.2	◐ 1946	1.6
18	F	0140	0.2	0804	1.8	1510	0.2	2034	1.5
19	SA	0340	0.3	0925	1.6	1626	0.3	2237	1.3
20	SU	0435	0.2	1114	1.5	1714	0.3		
21	M	0004	1.4	0534	0.2	1225	1.7	1814	0.3
22	TU	0116	1.6	0630	0.2	1315	1.8	2116	0.3
23	W	0145	1.7	0714	0.2	1355	2.0	2200	0.3
24	TH	0214	1.8	1000	0.2	1425	2.0	2246	0.3
25	F	0244	1.9	1030	0.2	1455	2.1	○ 2304	0.3
26	SA	0315	1.9	0804	0.1	1525	2.2	2310	0.3
27	SU	0345	2.0	0839	0.1	1558	2.2	2340	0.3
28	M	0418	2.0	0916	0.1	1629	2.2	2135	0.3
29	TU	0449	2.1	0949	0.0	1705	2.1	2215	0.3
30	W	0525	2.1	1036	0.0	1745	2.1	2251	0.2
31	TH	0603	2.1	1119	0.1	1830	1.9	2345	0.1

APRIL

Date	Day	Time	m	Time	m	Time	m	Time	m
1	F	0648	2.1	1340	0.1	1919	1.8		
2	SA	0110	0.1	0746	1.9	1424	0.2	◑ 2046	1.5
3	SU	0234	0.2	0914	1.8	1534	0.3	2215	1.4
4	M	0344	0.2	1054	1.8	1834	0.3	2339	1.5
5	TU	0445	0.2	1215	1.9	2010	0.3		
6	W	0044	1.6	0815	0.1	1305	2.0	2107	0.2
7	TH	0128	1.7	0914	0.1	1345	2.1	2135	0.3
8	F	0208	1.9	0955	0.1	1428	2.2	● 2226	0.3
9	SA	0255	1.9	0745	0.0	1506	2.2	2254	0.3
10	SU	0327	2.0	0825	0.1	1547	2.1	2356	0.3
11	M	0405	2.1	1225	0.1	1626	2.0		
12	TU	0035	0.2	0445	2.1	1305	0.1	1708	2.0
13	W	0120	0.2	0526	2.1	1325	0.1	1745	1.8
14	TH	0150	0.2	0559	2.0	1340	0.2	1819	1.7
15	F	0004	0.2	0646	1.9	1400	0.2	1900	1.6
16	SA	0110	0.1	0736	1.8	1445	0.3	◐ 1950	1.5
17	SU	0320	0.2	0856	1.6	1544	0.3	2110	1.3
18	M	0426	0.1	1015	1.5	1655	0.3	2325	1.3
19	TU	0515	0.1	1144	1.7	1744	0.3		
20	W	0026	1.5	0605	0.1	1240	1.8	2000	0.3
21	TH	0106	1.6	0645	0.2	1315	2.0	2126	0.2
22	F	0135	1.7	0920	0.1	1350	2.1	2215	0.2
23	SA	0205	1.9	0955	0.1	1419	2.1	2246	0.2
24	SU	0240	2.0	0735	0.1	1451	2.2	○ 2300	0.3
25	M	0315	2.0	0809	0.1	1526	2.2	2034	0.3
26	TU	0347	2.1	0844	0.1	1605	2.1	2109	0.2
27	W	0425	2.1	0935	0.1	1645	2.1	2156	0.2
28	TH	0502	2.2	1014	0.2	1728	2.0	2235	0.1
29	F	0546	2.1	1320	0.2	1815	1.8	2344	0.1
30	SA	0635	2.1	1350	0.2	1916	1.6		

Chart Datum: 0·84 metres below NAP Datum

TIME ZONE -0100
(Dutch Standard Time)
Subtract 1 hour for UT
For Dutch Summer Time add ONE hour in **non-shaded areas**

NETHERLANDS – HOEK VAN HOLLAND

LAT 51°59′N LONG 4°07′E

TIMES AND HEIGHTS OF HIGH AND LOW WATERS

SPRING & NEAP TIDES
Dates in red are **SPRINGS**
Dates in blue are **NEAPS**

YEAR **2005**

MAY

Date	Day	Time	m	Time	m	Time	m	Time	m
1	SU	0104	0.0	0746	1.9	1435	0.2	◑ 2045	1.5
2	M	0220	0.0	0926	1.8	1700	0.3	2206	1.4
3	TU	0325	0.1	1044	1.9	1825	0.3	2314	1.5
4	W	0644	0.1	1155	2.0	1954	0.2		
5	TH	0015	1.6	0805	0.0	1246	2.1	2050	0.2
6	F	0104	1.8	0844	0.0	1325	2.1	2115	0.3
7	SA	0149	1.9	0940	0.1	1405	2.1	2145	0.3
8	SU	0225	1.9	0730	0.1	1446	2.1	● 2225	0.3
9	M	0308	2.0	1047	0.2	1526	2.0	2314	0.2
10	TU	0345	2.1	1135	0.2	1606	1.9		
11	W	0016	0.2	0421	2.1	1235	0.2	1641	1.9
12	TH	0044	0.1	0506	2.1	1257	0.2	1719	1.8
13	F	0125	0.1	0539	2.0	1317	0.3	1755	1.7
14	SA	0130	0.1	0619	1.9	1350	0.3	1824	1.6
15	SU	0040	0.1	0710	1.8	1440	0.3	1925	1.5
16	M	0301	0.1	0805	1.7	1536	0.3	◐ 2024	1.4
17	TU	0344	0.1	0925	1.7	1636	0.3	2146	1.4
18	W	0445	0.1	1034	1.7	1715	0.3	2316	1.4
19	TH	0540	0.1	1146	1.8	1850	0.3		
20	F	0016	1.6	0640	0.2	1230	2.0	2035	0.2
21	SA	0050	1.7	0846	0.1	1305	2.1	2125	0.2
22	SU	0128	1.9	0635	0.2	1346	2.1	2215	0.2
23	M	0206	2.0	0716	0.1	1422	2.2	○ 1946	0.3
24	TU	0246	2.1	0755	0.2	1506	2.1	2020	0.2
25	W	0322	2.1	0836	0.2	1545	2.1	2055	0.1
26	TH	0406	2.2	0919	0.2	1632	2.0	2146	0.1
27	F	0449	2.2	1255	0.2	1716	1.9	2236	0.0
28	SA	0536	2.1	1330	0.2	1809	1.7	2335	0.0
29	SU	0631	2.1	1420	0.3	1920	1.6		
30	M	0045	0.0	0750	2.0	1527	0.3	◑ 2036	1.6
31	TU	0155	0.0	0916	2.0	1705	0.3	2134	1.6

JUNE

Date	Day	Time	m	Time	m	Time	m	Time	m
1	W	0254	0.0	1020	2.0	1805	0.3	2244	1.6
2	TH	0624	0.0	1125	2.0	1915	0.3	2345	1.7
3	F	0725	0.0	1220	2.0	2020	0.3		
4	SA	0034	1.8	0815	0.1	1306	2.0	2100	0.3
5	SU	0126	1.9	0639	0.2	1345	2.0	2140	0.3
6	M	0208	1.9	0724	0.2	1435	1.9	● 1955	0.3
7	TU	0249	2.0	0920	0.3	1515	1.9	2024	0.2
8	W	0329	2.0	1050	0.3	1555	1.9	2105	0.2
9	TH	0405	2.0	1150	0.3	1624	1.8	2150	0.1
10	F	0446	2.0	1240	0.3	1705	1.8	2224	0.1
11	SA	0526	2.0	1257	0.3	1734	1.7	2320	0.1
12	SU	0606	1.9	1325	0.3	1813	1.7		
13	M	0155	0.1	0656	1.9	1414	0.3	1855	1.6
14	TU	0055	0.1	0735	1.8	1500	0.3	1956	1.6
15	W	0200	0.1	0835	1.8	1550	0.3	◐ 2055	1.6
16	TH	0244	0.1	0935	1.8	1640	0.3	2154	1.6
17	F	0340	0.1	1034	1.9	1717	0.3	2305	1.6
18	SA	0424	0.1	1135	1.9	1800	0.3	2359	1.8
19	SU	0525	0.2	1225	2.0	1820	0.3		
20	M	0052	1.9	0610	0.2	1316	2.1	1850	0.3
21	TU	0136	2.0	0655	0.2	1359	2.1	1926	0.2
22	W	0226	2.1	0734	0.2	1446	2.0	○ 1959	0.2
23	TH	0307	2.2	0826	0.3	1530	2.0	2046	0.1
24	F	0351	2.2	1155	0.3	1618	1.9	2130	0.0
25	SA	0439	2.2	1256	0.3	1715	1.9	2214	0.0
26	SU	0528	2.2	1334	0.3	1803	1.8	2316	0.0
27	M	0625	2.1	1436	0.3	1905	1.8		
28	TU	0015	0.0	0729	2.1	1527	0.4	◑ 2005	1.7
29	W	0114	0.0	0833	2.0	1640	0.4	2105	1.7
30	TH	0224	0.0	0939	2.0	1737	0.4	2210	1.7

JULY

Date	Day	Time	m	Time	m	Time	m	Time	m
1	F	0334	0.1	1043	1.9	1846	0.4	2316	1.7
2	SA	0444	0.1	1144	1.9	1940	0.3		
3	SU	0004	1.8	0550	0.2	1250	1.9	2040	0.3
4	M	0106	1.8	0644	0.2	1339	1.9	1855	0.3
5	TU	0155	1.9	0724	0.3	1424	1.9	1935	0.3
6	W	0234	1.9	0815	0.4	1515	1.9	● 2014	0.2
7	TH	0319	2.0	0904	0.4	1545	1.8	2055	0.2
8	F	0355	2.0	1120	0.4	1625	1.8	2124	0.1
9	SA	0428	2.1	1210	0.4	1655	1.8	2205	0.1
10	SU	0505	2.0	1240	0.4	1730	1.8	2239	0.1
11	M	0546	2.0	1314	0.4	1800	1.8	2319	0.1
12	TU	0620	2.0	1355	0.4	1836	1.8		
13	W	0004	0.1	0655	2.0	1430	0.4	1904	1.7
14	TH	0054	0.1	0734	1.9	1500	0.4	◐ 2005	1.7
15	F	0144	0.1	0845	1.9	1505	0.4	2110	1.7
16	SA	0244	0.1	0946	1.9	1545	0.4	2216	1.7
17	SU	0345	0.1	1056	1.9	1634	0.4	2314	1.8
18	M	0455	0.2	1149	1.9	1735	0.3		
19	TU	0019	1.9	0555	0.2	1256	1.9	1824	0.3
20	W	0116	2.0	0644	0.3	1345	2.0	1904	0.2
21	TH	0205	2.1	0724	0.3	1435	2.0	○ 1950	0.1
22	F	0255	2.2	1110	0.4	1521	2.0	2025	0.1
23	SA	0338	2.3	1155	0.4	1608	2.0	2109	0.0
24	SU	0427	2.3	1240	0.4	1657	1.9	2156	0.0
25	M	0515	2.3	1336	0.4	1745	1.9	2246	0.0
26	TU	0605	2.2	1424	0.4	1835	1.9	2334	0.0
27	W	0659	2.1	1514	0.4	1925	1.9		
28	TH	0044	0.0	0754	2.0	1610	0.4	◑ 2019	1.9
29	F	0200	0.0	0854	1.9	1455	0.4	2119	1.8
30	SA	0305	0.1	1016	1.8	1555	0.4	2236	1.7
31	SU	0430	0.2	1136	1.8	1705	0.4	2350	1.8

AUGUST

Date	Day	Time	m	Time	m	Time	m	Time	m
1	M	0524	0.3	1229	1.8	1759	0.3		
2	TU	0056	1.8	0624	0.3	1329	1.8	1844	0.3
3	W	0145	1.9	0715	0.4	1414	1.8	1924	0.3
4	TH	0235	2.0	0754	0.5	1506	1.9	2005	0.2
5	F	0304	2.0	0824	0.5	1540	1.9	● 2035	0.2
6	SA	0334	2.1	1140	0.5	1605	1.9	2053	0.2
7	SU	0408	2.1	1140	0.5	1635	1.9	2130	0.1
8	M	0448	2.1	1207	0.5	1705	1.9	2206	0.1
9	TU	0515	2.1	1256	0.4	1736	1.9	2235	0.1
10	W	0548	2.1	1330	0.4	1806	1.9	2304	0.1
11	TH	0615	2.1	1400	0.4	1831	1.9	2345	0.1
12	F	0656	2.1	1410	0.4	1916	1.9		
13	SA	0034	0.1	0746	2.0	1400	0.4	◐ 2003	1.9
14	SU	0216	0.1	0850	1.9	1500	0.4	2126	1.8
15	M	0325	0.2	1010	1.8	1616	0.4	2245	1.8
16	TU	0434	0.3	1130	1.8	1705	0.3	2359	1.9
17	W	0556	0.3	1235	1.8	1804	0.3		
18	TH	0101	2.0	0634	0.4	1336	1.9	1844	0.2
19	F	0155	2.2	1005	0.4	1426	1.9	○ 1924	0.1
20	SA	0239	2.3	1035	0.4	1506	2.0	2008	0.1
21	SU	0322	2.3	1125	0.5	1548	2.0	2045	0.0
22	M	0405	2.3	1215	0.5	1636	2.1	2130	0.0
23	TU	0451	2.3	1310	0.5	1716	2.1	2215	0.0
24	W	0535	2.2	1355	0.5	1759	2.1	2305	0.1
25	TH	0627	2.1	1435	0.5	1845	2.0		
26	F	0015	0.1	0715	2.0	1304	0.5	◑ 1936	2.0
27	SA	0140	0.2	0804	1.8	1410	0.4	2029	1.9
28	SU	0254	0.2	0919	1.7	1525	0.4	2144	1.7
29	M	0415	0.3	1106	1.6	1656	0.4	2336	1.7
30	TU	0520	0.4	1216	1.7	1734	0.3		
31	W	0045	1.8	0626	0.4	1316	1.8	1830	0.3

Chart Datum: 0·84 metres below NAP Datum

TIME ZONE -0100
(Dutch Standard Time)
Subtract 1 hour for UT
For Dutch Summer Time add ONE hour in **non-shaded areas**

NETHERLANDS – HOEK VAN HOLLAND

LAT 51°59′N LONG 4°07′E

TIMES AND HEIGHTS OF HIGH AND LOW WATERS

SPRING & NEAP TIDES
Dates in red are SPRINGS
Dates in blue are NEAPS

YEAR **2005**

SEPTEMBER

Day		Time	m	Time	m	Time	m	Time	m
1	TH	0135	2.0	0945	0.4	1406	1.9	1915	0.3
2	F	0220	2.0	1025	0.4	1434	1.9	1956	0.3
3	SA	0243	2.1	1106	0.5	1504	1.9	● 2004	0.3
4	SU	0316	2.2	1120	0.5	1535	2.0	2025	0.2
5	M	0346	2.2	1110	0.5	1606	2.0	2056	0.2
6	TU	0411	2.2	1140	0.5	1635	2.0	2126	0.2
7	W	0440	2.2	1225	0.5	1659	2.0	2200	0.2
8	TH	0516	2.2	1306	0.5	1729	2.1	2236	0.1
9	F	0546	2.2	1055	0.4	1806	2.1	2316	0.1
10	SA	0622	2.1	1136	0.3	1841	2.1		
11	SU	0005	0.2	0709	2.0	1224	0.3	◐ 1936	2.0
12	M	0200	0.2	0804	1.9	1420	0.4	2035	1.9
13	TU	0304	0.3	0946	1.7	1524	0.4	2215	1.8
14	W	0424	0.4	1105	1.6	1650	0.3	2350	1.9
15	TH	0535	0.4	1223	1.7	1734	0.3		
16	F	0056	2.1	0850	0.4	1325	1.8	1825	0.2
17	SA	0139	2.2	0944	0.4	1405	2.0	1905	0.2
18	SU	0218	2.3	1015	0.5	1445	2.0	○ 1946	0.1
19	M	0306	2.4	1055	0.5	1525	2.1	2022	0.1
20	TU	0346	2.4	1144	0.5	1605	2.2	2101	0.1
21	W	0427	2.3	1245	0.5	1647	2.2	2150	0.1
22	TH	0509	2.2	1324	0.5	1729	2.2	2235	0.2
23	F	0556	2.1	1100	0.5	1809	2.2	2334	0.3
24	SA	0638	1.9	1200	0.4	1855	2.1		
25	SU	0130	0.3	0726	1.8	1305	0.4	◑ 1956	1.9
26	M	0240	0.4	0825	1.6	1507	0.4	2105	1.7
27	TU	0345	0.4	1025	1.5	1625	0.4	2254	1.7
28	W	0506	0.5	1150	1.6	1714	0.3		
29	TH	0015	1.8	0555	0.5	1245	1.7	1804	0.3
30	F	0110	2.0	0850	0.5	1336	1.8	1855	0.3

OCTOBER

Day		Time	m	Time	m	Time	m	Time	m
1	SA	0146	2.1	0944	0.4	1416	1.9	1924	0.3
2	SU	0216	2.2	1025	0.4	1435	2.0	1934	0.3
3	M	0238	2.2	1045	0.5	1459	2.1	● 1953	0.3
4	TU	0308	2.3	0825	0.5	1525	2.1	2025	0.2
5	W	0341	2.3	0845	0.5	1559	2.2	2056	0.2
6	TH	0415	2.3	0915	0.5	1629	2.2	2124	0.2
7	F	0446	2.3	0949	0.4	1703	2.2	2205	0.2
8	SA	0522	2.2	1030	0.3	1738	2.2	2249	0.2
9	SU	0602	2.1	1116	0.3	1819	2.2	2344	0.3
10	M	0650	2.0	1205	0.3	1909	2.1	◐	
11	TU	0210	0.4	0744	1.8	1406	0.3	2030	1.9
12	W	0304	0.4	0935	1.6	1510	0.3	2215	1.9
13	TH	0510	0.5	1106	1.6	1620	0.3	2335	2.0
14	F	0734	0.5	1209	1.7	1956	0.3		
15	SA	0035	2.1	0844	0.4	1306	1.8	2055	0.2
16	SU	0126	2.3	0915	0.4	1345	2.0	1834	0.2
17	M	0158	2.3	0955	0.5	1425	2.1	○ 1914	0.2
18	TU	0241	2.3	1024	0.5	1505	2.2	1959	0.2
19	W	0326	2.3	0819	0.5	1542	2.2	2046	0.2
20	TH	0406	2.2	0859	0.5	1625	2.3	2125	0.3
21	F	0446	2.1	0945	0.4	1701	2.3		
22	SA	0117	0.3	0526	2.0	1035	0.4	1746	2.2
23	SU	0144	0.4	0605	1.9	1130	0.3	1826	2.1
24	M	0130	0.4	0643	1.8	1235	0.3	1920	1.9
25	TU	0217	0.5	0735	1.6	1440	0.3	◑ 2025	1.8
26	W	0325	0.5	0856	1.5	1606	0.3	2154	1.7
27	TH	0435	0.5	1055	1.5	1656	0.3	2335	1.8
28	F	0525	0.5	1216	1.6	1734	0.3		
29	SA	0026	2.0	0750	0.5	1255	1.8	1840	0.3
30	SU	0106	2.1	0906	0.4	1326	1.9	2055	0.3
31	M	0135	2.2	0934	0.4	1351	2.0	2140	0.3

NOVEMBER

Day		Time	m	Time	m	Time	m	Time	m
1	TU	0206	2.2	1030	0.4	1421	2.1	1923	0.3
2	W	0238	2.3	0755	0.5	1455	2.2	● 2006	0.3
3	TH	0312	2.3	0826	0.4	1529	2.2	2029	0.3
4	F	0346	2.3	0856	0.4	1605	2.3	2110	0.3
5	SA	0422	2.2	0931	0.3	1641	2.3	2156	0.3
6	SU	0505	2.1	1020	0.2	1721	2.3	2245	0.4
7	M	0548	2.0	1109	0.2	1806	2.2		
8	TU	0117	0.4	0640	1.9	1226	0.2	1906	2.1
9	W	0210	0.5	0744	1.7	1335	0.2	◐ 2035	2.0
10	TH	0330	0.5	0920	1.6	1439	0.2	2153	2.0
11	F	0550	0.5	1035	1.6	1544	0.3	2313	2.0
12	SA	0717	0.5	1145	1.7	1924	0.2		
13	SU	0015	2.1	0824	0.4	1240	1.9	2036	0.2
14	M	0059	2.2	0857	0.5	1319	2.0	2105	0.2
15	TU	0138	2.2	0915	0.5	1401	2.1	1905	0.2
16	W	0220	2.2	1010	0.5	1438	2.2	○ 1944	0.3
17	TH	0306	2.2	0809	0.4	1521	2.2	2036	0.3
18	F	0348	2.1	0849	0.4	1601	2.3		
19	SA	0004	0.4	0429	2.0	0935	0.3	1646	2.2
20	SU	0050	0.4	0510	2.0	1015	0.3	1725	2.2
21	M	0110	0.5	0545	1.9	1114	0.2	1806	2.1
22	TU	0120	0.5	0626	1.8	1205	0.2	1856	2.0
23	W	0157	0.5	0705	1.7	1320	0.3	◑ 1945	1.9
24	TH	0257	0.5	0816	1.6	1515	0.3	2106	1.8
25	F	0354	0.5	0925	1.5	1626	0.3	2215	1.8
26	SA	0500	0.5	1034	1.6	1720	0.3	2325	1.9
27	SU	0554	0.5	1150	1.7	1820	0.3		
28	M	0016	2.0	0815	0.4	1225	1.8	2010	0.3
29	TU	0055	2.1	0916	0.4	1304	1.9	2116	0.3
30	W	0130	2.2	0956	0.4	1348	2.1	1859	0.3

DECEMBER

Day		Time	m	Time	m	Time	m	Time	m
1	TH	0205	2.2	0735	0.4	1425	2.2	● 1933	0.3
2	F	0245	2.2	0805	0.4	1506	2.3	2013	0.3
3	SA	0328	2.2	0845	0.3	1545	2.3	2059	0.3
4	SU	0409	2.1	0914	0.2	1627	2.3	2150	0.4
5	M	0455	2.0	1010	0.2	1715	2.3		
6	TU	0106	0.4	0545	1.9	1059	0.1	1805	2.2
7	W	0144	0.4	0634	1.8	1206	0.1	1905	2.1
8	TH	0244	0.5	0745	1.7	1304	0.1	◐ 2014	2.1
9	F	0400	0.5	0900	1.7	1415	0.1	2146	2.0
10	SA	0540	0.5	1006	1.7	1514	0.2	2245	2.0
11	SU	0654	0.5	1109	1.8	1854	0.2	2345	2.1
12	M	0754	0.5	1205	1.9	2000	0.2		
13	TU	0040	2.1	0837	0.5	1258	2.0	2040	0.3
14	W	0125	2.1	0910	0.5	1346	2.0	1905	0.3
15	TH	0216	2.1	0729	0.4	1430	2.1	○ 1955	0.4
16	F	0255	2.0	0815	0.4	1509	2.2	2130	0.4
17	SA	0345	2.0	0844	0.3	1544	2.2	2310	0.5
18	SU	0419	2.0	0930	0.2	1635	2.2		
19	M	0020	0.5	0455	1.9	1005	0.2	1716	2.1
20	TU	0050	0.5	0536	1.9	1044	0.2	1744	2.1
21	W	0110	0.5	0605	1.9	1134	0.2	1836	2.0
22	TH	0140	0.5	0645	1.8	1225	0.2	1915	1.9
23	F	0220	0.5	0729	1.8	1315	0.2	◑ 2010	1.9
24	SA	0310	0.5	0825	1.7	1414	0.2	2110	1.9
25	SU	0400	0.5	0935	1.7	1505	0.3	2210	1.9
26	M	0450	0.5	1046	1.7	1605	0.3	2315	1.9
27	TU	0540	0.5	1140	1.8	1710	0.3		
28	W	0005	2.0	0610	0.5	1229	1.9	1754	0.3
29	TH	0055	2.0	0635	0.4	1320	2.0	1855	0.3
30	F	0141	2.1	0704	0.4	1405	2.1	1925	0.3
31	SA	0225	2.1	0744	0.3	1448	2.2	● 2010	0.4

Chart Datum: 0·84 metres below NAP Datum

9.16.24 STELLENDAM & HELLEVOETSLUIS

Zuid Holland **51°49'·83N 04°02'·01E** (Stellendam) ❁❁◊✿; (Hellevoetsluis) ❁❁❁◊◊✿✿✿

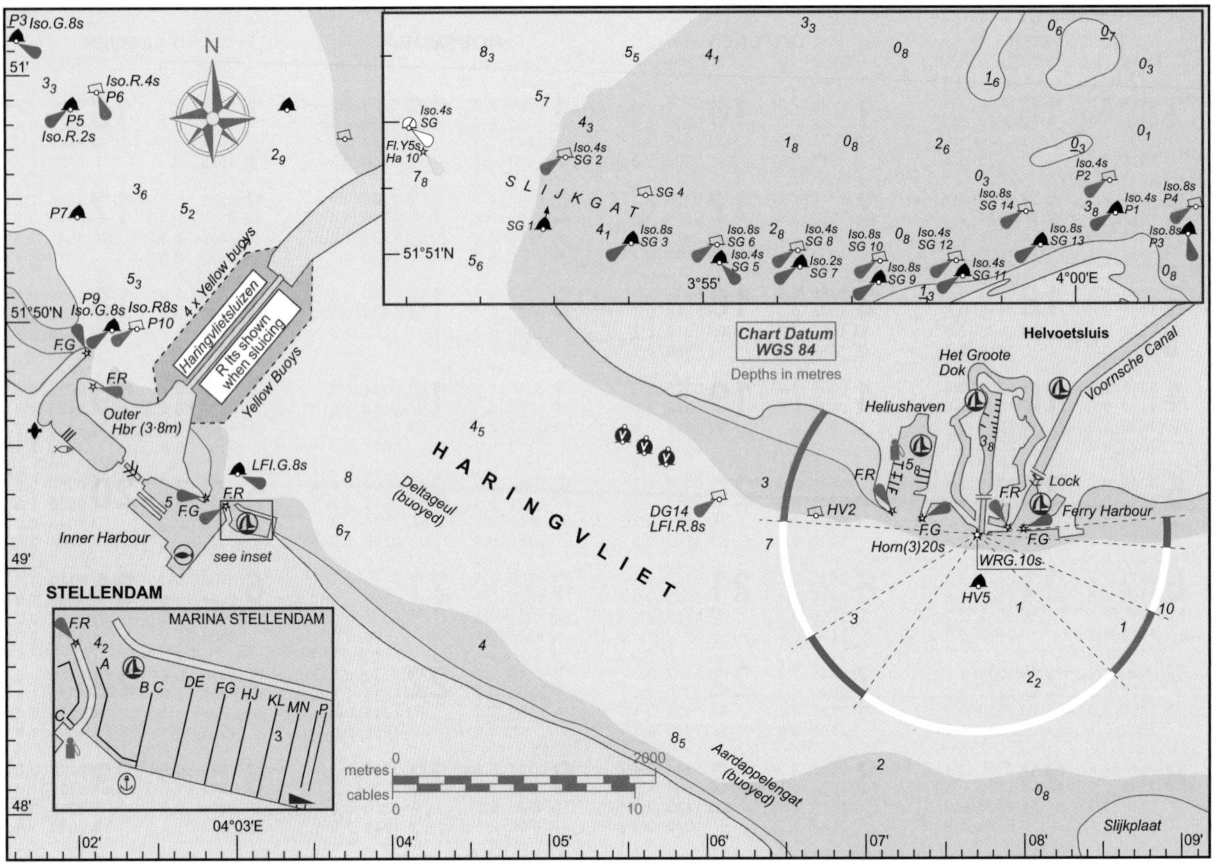
Iso.G.8s
Iso.R.4s
P6
P5
Iso.R.2s
P7
P9
Iso.G.8s
Iso.R8s
P10
51°50'N
F.G
F.R
Outer Hbr (3·8m)
4 x Yellow buoys
Haringvlietsluizen
R lts shown when sluicing
Yellow Buoys
LFI.G.8s
F.R
F.G
Inner Harbour
see inset
STELLENDAM
MARINA STELLENDAM
04°03'E
SLIJKGAT
Iso.4s SG
Fl.Y5s Ha 10
Iso.4s SG 2
SG 4
SG 1
Iso.8s SG 3
Iso.8s SG 6
Iso.4s SG 5
Iso.4s SG 8
Iso.2s SG 7
Iso.8s SG 10
Iso.8s SG 9
Iso.4s SG 12
Iso.4s SG 11
Iso.8s SG 14
Iso.8s SG 13
Iso.4s P2
Iso.4s P1
Iso.8s P4
Iso.8s P3
51°51'N
3°55'
4°00'E
Chart Datum WGS 84
Depths in metres
HARINGVLIET
Deltageul (buoyed)
DG14 LFl.R.8s
HV2
Helvoetsluis
Het Groote Dok
Heliushaven
Voornsche Canal
Lock
Ferry Harbour
F.R
F.G
Horn(3)20s
WRG.10s
HV5
Aardappelengat (buoyed)
Slijkplaat
metres
cables
2000
10

CHARTS AC 2322, 3371, 110; Zeekaart 1447, 1448; DYC 1801.6, 1807.6; Imray C30; Stanfords 19

TIDES +0300 Dover; ML 1·2; Duration 0510; Zone –0100

Standard Port VLISSINGEN

Times				Height (metres)			
High Water		Low Water		MHWS	MHWN	MLWN	MLWS
0300	0900	0400	1000	4·7	3·8	0·8	0·2
1500	2100	1600	2200				
Differences HARINGVLIETSLUIZEN							
+0015	+0015	+0015	–0020	–1·7	–1·6	–0·4	+0·1

NOTE: Double LWs occur. The rise after the 1st LW is called the Agger. Water levels on this coast are much affected by weather. Prolonged NW gales can raise levels by up to 3m.

SHELTER Good in Stellendam marina, beyond the lock and the Inner hbr. At Hellevoetsluis there are 3 yacht hbrs: Heliushaven (2-4·2m); Het Groote Dok (2-4m) enter via gate/swing bridge; and the Voorne canal (2·8-4·8m) via lock. Good yacht facilities within 10M of Hellevoetsluis on the S bank at Middelharnis (3m), Stad aan't Haringvliet (3·5m) and Den Bommel (1·6-2·8m); on the N bank at YC De Put (1·8-3m; Vuile Gat) and Hitsertse Kade (1·5-2·1m). If bound for Rotterdam, proceed via Spui and Oude Maas.

NAVIGATION WPT 51°51'·95N 03°51'·43E [SG SWM buoy, Iso 4s], 112°/2·6M to SG5/6 chan buoys. Thence 3·3M along the Goeree shore via the well buoyed/lit Slijkgat chan (dangerous in strong W/NW winds) to SG13 and P1 SHM buoys. Follow P1 to P9 SHM buoys SSE for 2·2M to the Buitenhaven and lock, avoiding the no-entry sluicing area, marked by 4 SPM buoys. Lock and lifting bridge operate H24 throughout the year.

Inside the Haringvliet go direct 096°/3M to Hellevoetsluis passing DG14 and HV2 PHM buoys. The SW side of the Haringvliet has 6 SHM buoys (DG1-11) leading to the well buoyed, but unlit Aardappelengat chan (S of Slijkplaat) and the ent to Middelharnis. The Haringvliet chan (SHM buoys HV1-21) passes S of Hellevoetsluis and NE of Slijkplaat, an extensive shoal ringed by small buoys.

LIGHTS AND MARKS Hellevoetsluis lt, 16m W stone twr, R cupola. See 9.16.4 and chartlet for sectors. Haringvlietsluizen sluicing sigs: 3 ● in △, shown from pier heads on dam; danger area marked by small Y buoys.

R/T For lock call: *Goereese Sluis* VHF Ch 20. Hellevoetsluis HM and Middelharnis HM: Ch 74, Stellendam Marina VHF Ch 31.

TELEPHONE (Dial codes: 0187 Stellendam; 0181 Hellevoetsluis) HMs Stellendam 491000, Hellevoetsluis 330911; ⊖ Rotterdam (010) 4298088 or Vlissingen (0118) 484600; Emergencies 112; Brit Consul (020) 6764343.

FACILITIES

STELLENDAM (0187) **Stellendam Marina** ☎ 493769, Fax 493807, €1.36, (200 berths inc Ⓥ), Fuel, Slip, C, Bar, R. **Town**, R, Bar, ✉ (2½ km), ✈ (Rotterdam).

HELLEVOETSLUIS (0181) **Marina, Het Groote Dok** ☎ 312166, €0.79, swing bridge opens every H in daylight from 0800 in summer; waiting pontoons are downstream. El, Gaz, ME, CH, R, Bar; **Helius Haven YC** ☎ 315868, AB €0.79, P, D; **Voorne Canal YC** ☎ 315476, AB €0.79, P, D; **Services:** CH, El, ME. The 3 s on N side of Haringvliet are free, but can be exposed.

Town P, D, R, Bar, ✉, Ⓑ, ✈ (Rotterdam). Bus to Vlissingen & Spijkenisse. Ferry: Hoek of Holland-Harwich; Rotterdam-Hull.

9.16.25 OOSTERSCHELDE

Zeeland **51°37'·24N 03°40'·21E** (Roompotsluis)

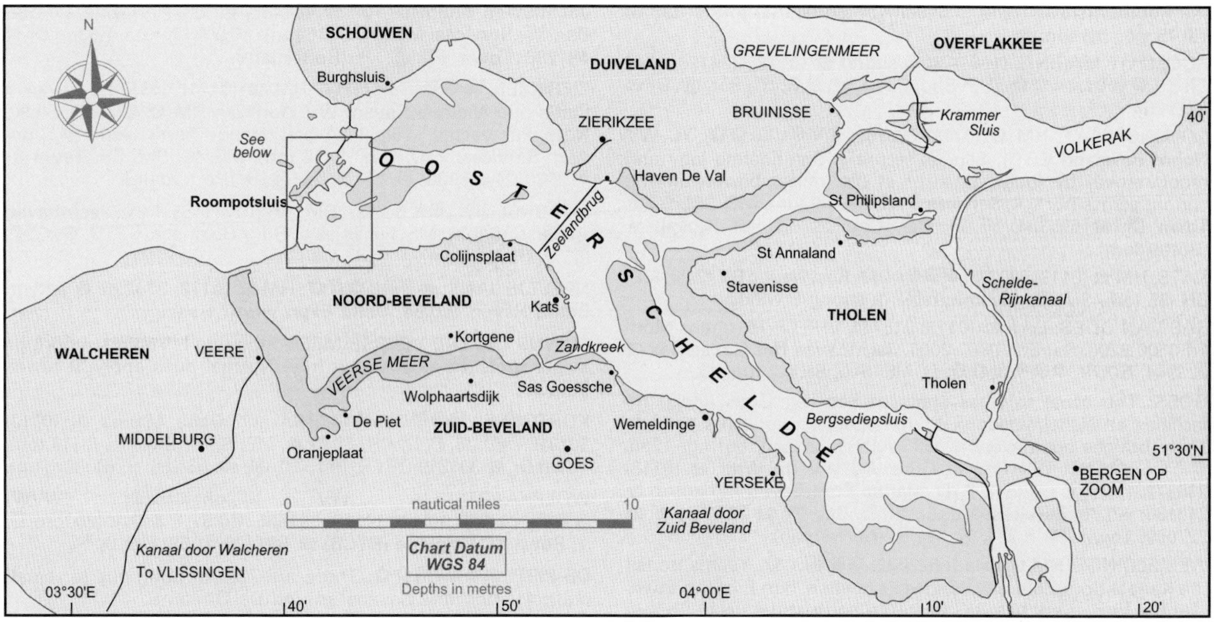
N
SCHOUWEN
Burghsluis
DUIVELAND
GREVELINGENMEER
OVERFLAKKEE
ZIERIKZEE
BRUINISSE
Krammer Sluis
VOLKERAK
40'
See below
O O S T E R S C H E L D E
Haven De Val
Zeelandbrug
St Philipsland
Roompotsluis
Colijnsplaat
St Annaland
Stavenisse
Schelde-Rijnkanaal
NOORD-BEVELAND
Kats
THOLEN
•Kortgene
WALCHEREN
VEERE
Zandkreek
VEERSE MEER
Tholen
Wolphaartsdijk
Sas Goessche
De Piet
ZUID-BEVELAND
Wemeldinge
Bergsediepsluis
MIDDELBURG
Oranjeplaat
GOES
51°30'N
BERGEN OP ZOOM
YERSEKE
0
nautical miles
10
Kanaal door Zuid Beveland
Kanaal door Walcheren
To VLISSINGEN
Chart Datum WGS 84
Depths in metres
03°30'E
40'
50'
04°00'E
10'
20'

CHARTS AC 3371, 110; Zeekaart 1448; DYCs 1805.8, 1801.5; Imray C30; Stanfords 1, 19

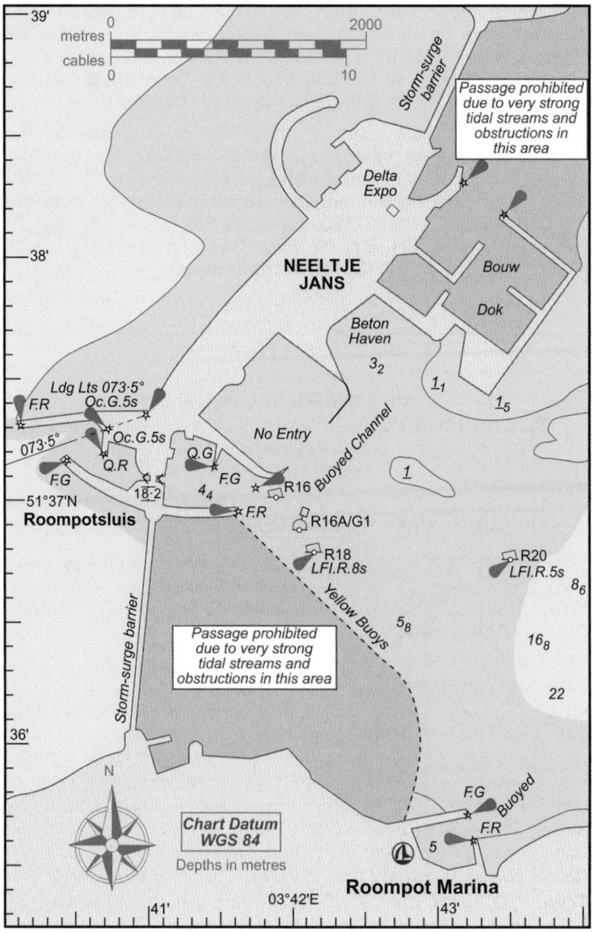
39'
metres
0
2000
cables
0
10
Storm-surge barrier
Passage prohibited due to very strong tidal streams and obstructions in this area
Delta Expo
38'
NEELTJE JANS
Bouw
Dok
Beton Haven
Ldg Lts 073·5°
F.R
Oc.G.5s
073·5°
Oc.G.5s
Q.R
Q.G
No Entry
Buoyed Channel
F.G
F.G
R16
18·2
51°37'N
Roompotsluis
F.R
R16A/G1
R18
LFl.R.8s
R20
LFl.R.5s
Yellow Buoys
Storm-surge barrier
Passage prohibited due to very strong tidal streams and obstructions in this area
36'
N
F.G
Buoyed
F.R
Chart Datum WGS 84
Depths in metres
Roompot Marina
41'
03°42'E
43'

TIDES +0230 Dover Zone –0100; ML Sas van Goes 2·0, Zierikzee 1·8; Duration Sas van Goes 0615, Zierikzee 0640

Standard Port VLISSINGEN (⟶)

Times				Height (metres)			
High Water		Low Water		MHWS	MHWN	MLWN	MLWS
0300	0900	0400	1000	4·7	3·8	0·8	0·2
1500	2100	1600	2200				
Differences ROOMPOT BUITEN							
–0015	+0005	+0005	–0020	–1·1	–0·9	–0·2	+0·1
STAVENISSE							
+0150	+0120	+0055	+0115	–1·2	–0·8	–0·4	+0·1
BERGSE DIEPSLUIS (West)							
+0145	+0125	+0105	+0115	–0·6	–0·3	–0·2	+0·1

SHELTER Good shelter in the many hbrs listed. Veerse Meer is a non-tidal waterway with moorings; enter from Oosterschelde via Zandkreekdam lock. The Schelde-Rijn Canal can be entered at Bergsediepsluis near Tholen; and the S Beveland Canal at Wemeldinge for Middelburg and Vlissingen.

NAVIGATION WPT 51°38'·00N 03°26'·24E [WG1 SHM buoy, Iso G 8s], 071°/4·2M to WG7 buoy at junction of Westgat and Oude Roompot buoyed chans. There are several offshore banks, see 9.16.5. Not advised to enter in strong W/NW'lies, and only from HW –6 to HW +1½ Zierikzee.

All vessels must use Roompotsluis (lock ☎ 0111 659265); the fixed bridge has 18.2m clearance @ LAT. Lock shut 2200-0600 except Tue/Wed. Buoyed areas each side of the barrier are very dangerous due to strong tidal streams and many obstructions.

Passage is prohib W of Roggenplaat. Zeelandbrug has 11·9m clearance at centre of span in buoyed chans; clearance (m) is indicated on some of bridge supports. If wind < F 7, bascule bridge near N end lifts at H & H+30, Mon-Fri 0700-2130; Sat/Sun from 0900.

LIGHTS AND MARKS See 9.16.4 and chartlet.

R/T Monitor Ch 68 which broadcasts local forecasts at H+15. *Verkeerspost Wemeldinge* Ch 68 MUST be called if entering canal; also for radar guidance in poor vis. Call *Zeelandbrug* Ch 18 for opening times and clearance. Locks: *Roompotsluis* Ch 18. *Krammersluizen* Ch 22 (H24). Zandreek *Kats* Ch 18; *Grevelingen* Ch 20; Bergse Diepsluis Ch 18. *Continued overleaf*

OOSTERSCHELDE Contd

There are numerous harbours within the Oosterschelde. The following are some of the more important, anti-clockwise from the Roompotsluis. There is usually an additional tourist tax of €0.75 per person:

ROOMPOT MARINA: (150 + 80 visitors) ☎ (0113) 374125, VHF Ch 31, ❂❂❂👍👍👍✿✿, D, P, Slip, Gas, Gaz, ▣, R, 🛒, Bar, Ⓑ, Dr ☎ 372565.

COLIJNSPLAAT: HM ☎ (0113) 695762; ❂❂❂👍👍👍✿✿, **YC WV Noord Beveland** €0.91, Slip, ▣; secure at first floating jetty and report arrival by loudspeaker or at hbr office; beware strong current across hbr ent; **Services:** P, D, BH (40 ton), ME, SM, ⚒, ⚲. **Town** Dr ☎ 695304, 🛒, R, Bar, Gaz, ⊠, Ⓑ, ⇌ (Goes), ✈ (Rotterdam).

KATS: HM ☎ (0113) 600270; ❂❂❂👍👍✿, **Rest Nautic BV** f2.00, ME, BH (35 ton), SM, ▣; uncomfortable in strong E winds.

SAS VAN GOES: Lock ☎ (0113) 216744, VHF Ch 18; opens Mon-Fri 0600-2200, Sat/Sun 0800-2000. **Jachthaven Het Goese Sas** ☎ 223944, €0.79, ❂❂❂👍👍✿✿, D, ME, Slip, BH (12 ton), ▣.

GOES: The canal to Goes starts at Sas van Goes (lock); no facilities at Wilhelminadorp; bridge operates same hrs as lock. Town bridges open every H 0800-2000 in season, but not 1200. ❂❂❂👍👍✿✿✿. Outskirts of Goes: **YC WV De Werf** ☎ (0113) 216372, f1.75, C (3½ ton), P, D; **Marina Stadshaven** in centre: ☎ 216136, €0.79; **Services:** ME, El, ⚒, ▣, Gaz, Dr ☎ 227451, Ⓗ ☎ 227000. **Town** 🛒, R, ⊠, Ⓑ, ⇌, ✈ (Antwerpen).

WEMELDINGE: HM ☎ (0113) 622022. ❂❂❂👍👍✿. Yachts transit the Kanaal door Zuid Beveland via a section 1km E of the town. Use the former ent (via R/G tfc lts) to berth at the yacht hbrs in the Voorhaven or Binnenhaven. SHM buoy O21 to N of the E mole marks a shoal. **Services:** €1.13, ME, SM, C (6·5 ton) ME, P, D, ⚲, Dr ☎ 6227451, Ⓗ ☎ 6227000. **Town** 🛒, R, ⊠, Ⓑ, ⇌ (Goes), ✈ (Antwerpen).

YERSEKE: Leave to port the preferred chan buoy at hbr ent. ❂❂❂👍👍✿✿. HM VHF Ch 09. Both marinas are S of the outer FV hbr: **Prinses Beatrix Haven** ☎ (0113) 571726, €1.07, 1·6m, D, BH (10 ton); **Services:** SM, ⚒, El, Dr ☎ 571444. **Town** 🛒, R, ⊠, Ⓑ, ⇌ (Kruiningen-Yerseke), ✈ .

STAVENISSE: HM ☎ (0166) 692815. ❂❂👍👍✿. **Marina** at end of hbr canal (access HW±3 for 1·8m draft), Slip, FW, P & D (cans), ⚒, C (4.5 ton), 🛒, Gaz.

ST ANNALAND: **WV St Annaland** HM ☎ (0166) 652783, ❂❂❂👍👍👍✿✿, €0.91, ⚲; **YC** ☎ 652634, VHF Ch31, ▣, Bar, R; Dr ☎ 652400. **Services:** ME, P, D, ⚒, El, CH, BH (25 ton), Gaz, BY. **Town** 🛒, R, Ⓑ, ⊠, ⇌ (Bergen op Zoom), ✈ (Antwerpen).

BRUINISSE: via lock (Ch 20) to Grevelingenmeer. ❂❂❂👍👍👍✿✿. **WV 'Bru'** HM ☎ (0111) 481506, €0.91; **Jachthaven Bruinisse** HM ☎ 481485, €1.00, P, D, Slip, ▣, Gaz, Bar, 🛒; **Services:** ME, ⚒, C (16 ton). MHW = NAP + 1.53m; Dr ☎ 481280. **Town** ⊠, Ⓑ, ✈ (Rotterdam).

ZIERIKZEE: ❂❂❂👍👍👍✿✿✿. HM ☎ (0111) 413174; **Haven 't Luitje** and **Nieuwe Haven: WV Zierikzee** HM ☎ 414877, €0.90; Note: For yachts >15m LOA pre-arrange berth with HM, Jun-Aug; **Services:** P, D, Gaz, C (18 ton), ME, ⚒, SM, CH. **Town** Dr 412080, Ⓗ 416900, ▣, 🛒, R, ⊠, Ⓑ, ✈ (Rotterdam).

BURGHSLUIS: ❂❂❂👍✿. HM ☎ (0111) 653114; **Jachthaven** €0.65, C (6 ton), ME. Facilities at Burg-Haamstede P, D, Gaz, ⊠, Ⓑ, ✈ (Rotterdam).

NEELTJE JANS: ❂❂❂👍✿✿✿. HM ☎ (0113) 374225. Ⓥ jetty in Beton Haven, €0.54. **Delta Expo** worth visiting.

TOWNS ON THE VEERSE MEER (non-tidal). Various moorings at the islets/jetties are now free. Normal dues apply at towns below:

KORTGENE: ❂❂❂👍👍👍✿✿. HM and **Delta Marina** ☎ (0113) 301315, €1.25, P, D, CH, El, ▣, ⚲, ME, R, ⚒, SM, 🛒, C (16 ton). **Town** Dr ☎ 301319, 🛒, R, Bar, ⊠, Ⓑ, ⇌ (Goes), ✈ (Rotterdam).

WOLPHAARTSDIJK: **WV Wolphaartsdijk (WVW)** ❂❂❂👍👍👍✿✿. HM ☎ (0113) 581565, €0.57, P & D, C (20 ton), ▣, ⚲; **Royal YC Belgique (RYCB)** ☎ 581496, f1.50, P & D, ⚒.

DE PIET: ❂❂❂👍✿✿✿. There are 72m of pontoons for small craft; 4 other little havens around De Omloop.

ARNEMUIDEN: ❂❂❂👍✿✿. **Jachthaven Oranjeplaat** HM ☎ (0118) 501248, €0.68, Slip, P & D, C (12 ton), ⇌.

VEERE: ❂❂❂👍👍👍✿✿✿. Yacht berths at: **Jachtclub Veere** in the Stadshaven, very busy, ☎ (0118) 501246, €0.91, AC; **Marina Veere** on canal side, ☎ 501553, €0.91, AC; **Jachtwerf Oostwatering**, ☎ 501665, €0.82, ▣; **WV Arne**, at Oostwatering – report at Ⓥ jetty, ☎ 501484, €0.64, AC. **Town** Dr ☎ 501271, 🛒, R, Bar, ⊠, Ⓑ, ⇌ (Middelburg), ✈ (Rotterdam).

MIDDELBURG: (This town is about 3M S of Veere on the Walcheren canal to Vlissingen). ❂❂❂👍👍✿✿✿. No mooring in Kanaal door Walcheren. All bridges & Veere lock: Ch 22. **WV Arne** fronts onto 1st Binnenhven (visitors) and backs onto the Dockhaven, ☎ (0118) 627180, €0.88, R, FW, ME, El, ⚒, SM, ▣; **Services:** D, Gaz, CH, BY, ⚒, Slip. **Town** Dr ☎ 612637; Ⓗ ☎ 625555; 🛒, R, Bar, ⊠, Ⓑ, ⇌, ✈ (Rotterdam).

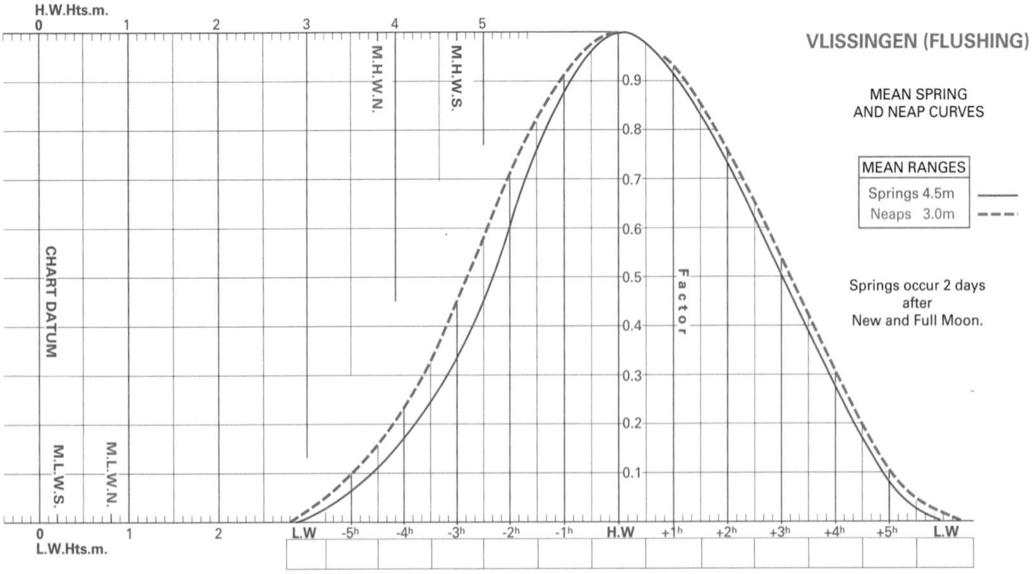
VLISSINGEN (FLUSHING)
MEAN SPRING AND NEAP CURVES
MEAN RANGES
Springs 4.5m
Neaps 3.0m
Springs occur 2 days after New and Full Moon.
H.W.Hts.m.
0 1 2 3 4 5
M.H.W.N.
M.H.W.S.
CHART DATUM
M.L.W.S.
M.L.W.N.
Factor
0.9 0.8 0.7 0.6 0.5 0.4 0.3 0.2 0.1
0 1 2
L.W.Hts.m.
L.W -5h -4h -3h -2h -1h H.W +1h +2h +3h +4h +5h L.W

TIME ZONE -0100
(Dutch Standard Time)
Subtract 1 hour for UT
For Dutch Summer Time add ONE hour in **non-shaded areas**

NETHERLANDS – VLISSINGEN

LAT 51°27′N LONG 3°36′E

TIMES AND HEIGHTS OF HIGH AND LOW WATERS

SPRING & NEAP TIDES
Dates in red are SPRINGS
Dates in blue are NEAPS

YEAR **2005**

JANUARY

Date	Day	Time	m	Time	m	Time	m	Time	m
1	SA	0518	4.3	1145	0.5	1735	4.3	2346	0.9
2	SU	0558	4.2	1220	0.5	1819	4.3		
3	M	0025	0.9	0642	4.1	1305	0.6	◑ 1911	4.2
4	TU	0120	1.0	0740	4.0	1400	0.6	2021	4.1
5	W	0214	1.0	0846	3.9	1506	0.7	2125	4.1
6	TH	0324	1.0	0956	4.0	1615	0.7	2236	4.2
7	F	0440	0.9	1058	4.2	1720	0.6	2331	4.3
8	SA	0551	0.8	1156	4.4	1825	0.5		
9	SU	0030	4.5	0656	0.6	1249	4.6	1921	0.4
10	M	0122	4.6	0749	0.4	1341	4.8	● 2011	0.4
11	TU	0209	4.7	0838	0.2	1431	5.0	2058	0.4
12	W	0258	4.8	0928	0.1	1519	5.0	2146	0.4
13	TH	0346	4.8	1015	0.0	1606	5.0	2228	0.5
14	F	0432	4.7	1101	0.0	1657	4.9	2315	0.6
15	SA	0522	4.6	1156	0.1	1745	4.8		
16	SU	0000	0.7	0609	4.5	1235	0.2	1839	4.5
17	M	0045	0.8	0706	4.3	1331	0.3	◐ 1938	4.3
18	TU	0145	0.9	0800	4.1	1414	0.6	2046	4.0
19	W	0245	1.1	0905	3.9	1523	0.8	2156	3.9
20	TH	0405	1.1	1026	3.8	1644	0.9	2306	3.8
21	F	0526	1.1	1130	3.9	1749	0.9		
22	SA	0006	3.9	0619	0.9	1224	4.0	1846	0.8
23	SU	0100	4.1	0709	0.8	1319	4.2	1925	0.8
24	M	0146	4.2	0756	0.7	1400	4.3	1959	0.8
25	TU	0215	4.3	0836	0.6	1435	4.4	○ 2036	0.7
26	W	0248	4.4	0901	0.4	1506	4.5	2111	0.6
27	TH	0317	4.5	0940	0.3	1538	4.6	2142	0.6
28	F	0348	4.5	1015	0.3	1606	4.6	2221	0.6
29	SA	0420	4.5	1050	0.3	1639	4.6	2244	0.6
30	SU	0455	4.5	1126	0.3	1711	4.6	2326	0.6
31	M	0527	4.4	1156	0.3	1747	4.5		

FEBRUARY

Date	Day	Time	m	Time	m	Time	m	Time	m
1	TU	0001	0.7	0606	4.4	1235	0.4	1828	4.4
2	W	0040	0.7	0652	4.3	1321	0.5	◑ 1928	4.2
3	TH	0129	0.8	0751	4.1	1415	0.6	2035	4.0
4	F	0240	0.9	0912	4.0	1530	0.7	2155	3.9
5	SA	0406	0.9	1030	4.0	1649	0.8	2309	4.0
6	SU	0530	0.8	1139	4.2	1810	0.7		
7	M	0018	4.2	0639	0.5	1241	4.5	1908	0.5
8	TU	0111	4.4	0738	0.3	1332	4.8	● 1958	0.4
9	W	0159	4.6	0830	0.1	1421	4.9	2045	0.4
10	TH	0243	4.8	0916	-0.1	1505	5.0	2128	0.4
11	F	0326	4.8	1002	-0.1	1549	5.0	2210	0.4
12	SA	0411	4.9	1045	-0.1	1632	5.0	2249	0.5
13	SU	0452	4.8	1126	0.0	1717	4.8	2330	0.5
14	M	0536	4.7	1206	0.1	1800	4.5		
15	TU	0010	0.6	0622	4.5	1246	0.4	1856	4.2
16	W	0055	0.8	0709	4.2	1330	0.6	◐ 1945	3.9
17	TH	0144	1.0	0810	3.9	1436	0.9	2056	3.6
18	F	0316	1.1	0936	3.6	1555	1.1	2224	3.4
19	SA	0435	1.1	1106	3.6	1715	1.1	2346	3.6
20	SU	0556	1.0	1215	3.8	1820	1.0		
21	M	0039	3.9	0644	0.8	1306	4.1	1905	0.8
22	TU	0126	4.1	0736	0.6	1339	4.3	1939	0.7
23	W	0155	4.2	0816	0.5	1416	4.5	2015	0.6
24	TH	0226	4.4	0846	0.3	1438	4.6	○ 2045	0.5
25	F	0255	4.6	0916	0.2	1511	4.7	2119	0.5
26	SA	0325	4.6	0952	0.1	1541	4.8	2156	0.4
27	SU	0355	4.7	1026	0.1	1613	4.8	2225	0.4
28	M	0427	4.7	1101	0.1	1643	4.7	2300	0.4

MARCH

Date	Day	Time	m	Time	m	Time	m	Time	m
1	TU	0458	4.7	1132	0.2	1720	4.6	2336	0.5
2	W	0537	4.6	1206	0.3	1759	4.5		
3	TH	0016	0.5	0617	4.5	1250	0.4	◑ 1848	4.2
4	F	0106	0.6	0718	4.2	1356	0.6	2002	3.9
5	SA	0215	0.8	0839	3.9	1516	0.9	2136	3.7
6	SU	0350	0.9	1016	3.9	1634	0.9	2259	3.7
7	M	0514	0.7	1135	4.1	1759	0.7		
8	TU	0006	4.0	0636	0.4	1236	4.5	1900	0.5
9	W	0058	4.3	0730	0.2	1322	4.7	1948	0.4
10	TH	0142	4.6	0817	0.0	1406	4.9	● 2030	0.4
11	F	0223	4.8	0858	-0.1	1447	5.0	2110	0.3
12	SA	0303	4.9	0937	-0.2	1526	5.0	2148	0.3
13	SU	0345	4.9	1018	-0.1	1606	4.9	2226	0.4
14	M	0426	4.9	1057	0.0	1647	4.7	2306	0.4
15	TU	0502	4.7	1130	0.2	1725	4.5	2336	0.5
16	W	0541	4.5	1206	0.4	1806	4.2		
17	TH	0011	0.7	0625	4.2	1246	0.7	◐ 1849	3.8
18	F	0054	0.9	0716	3.8	1340	1.0	1946	3.5
19	SA	0225	1.1	0835	3.5	1520	1.2	2125	3.2
20	SU	0353	1.1	1037	3.4	1633	1.2	2316	3.4
21	M	0516	1.0	1146	3.7	1746	1.0		
22	TU	0009	3.7	0620	0.8	1236	4.0	1846	0.8
23	W	0056	4.0	0705	0.5	1309	4.3	1918	0.6
24	TH	0126	4.2	0746	0.4	1341	4.5	1950	0.5
25	F	0156	4.4	0816	0.3	1412	4.7	○ 2019	0.4
26	SA	0222	4.6	0846	0.1	1439	4.8	2056	0.4
27	SU	0253	4.7	0922	0.1	1511	4.9	2131	0.3
28	M	0325	4.8	0955	0.1	1543	4.8	2206	0.3
29	TU	0358	4.8	1032	0.1	1618	4.8	2235	0.3
30	W	0436	4.8	1105	0.2	1655	4.7	2315	0.3
31	TH	0513	4.7	1149	0.3	1737	4.4		

APRIL

Date	Day	Time	m	Time	m	Time	m	Time	m
1	F	0000	0.4	0600	4.5	1236	0.5	1831	4.1
2	SA	0056	0.5	0659	4.2	1336	0.7	◑ 1945	3.7
3	SU	0210	0.7	0835	3.9	1454	0.9	2120	3.6
4	M	0346	0.8	1010	3.9	1647	0.9	2245	3.7
5	TU	0526	0.6	1125	4.2	1756	0.7	2351	4.0
6	W	0625	0.3	1225	4.5	1848	0.5		
7	TH	0041	4.3	0716	0.1	1305	4.7	1929	0.4
8	F	0122	4.5	0756	0.0	1346	4.8	● 2010	0.3
9	SA	0202	4.7	0835	-0.1	1426	4.9	2045	0.3
10	SU	0239	4.8	0915	-0.1	1503	4.9	2126	0.3
11	M	0318	4.9	0952	0.0	1540	4.7	2206	0.3
12	TU	0357	4.8	1026	0.2	1619	4.6	2241	0.4
13	W	0436	4.7	1100	0.4	1656	4.3	2316	0.5
14	TH	0516	4.4	1129	0.6	1731	4.1	2351	0.6
15	F	0555	4.2	1205	0.8	1816	3.8		
16	SA	0025	0.8	0646	3.8	1254	1.0	◐ 1859	3.5
17	SU	0206	1.0	0744	3.5	1435	1.2	2015	3.2
18	M	0325	1.0	0935	3.4	1606	1.1	2226	3.3
19	TU	0430	0.9	1106	3.7	1655	1.0	2331	3.6
20	W	0536	0.7	1149	4.0	1755	0.8		
21	TH	0009	3.9	0625	0.5	1229	4.3	1839	0.6
22	F	0045	4.2	0708	0.3	1302	4.5	1915	0.5
23	SA	0115	4.4	0740	0.2	1336	4.7	1950	0.4
24	SU	0148	4.6	0815	0.1	1407	4.8	○ 2026	0.3
25	M	0222	4.8	0852	0.1	1443	4.9	2106	0.3
26	TU	0258	4.9	0930	0.1	1516	4.8	2146	0.2
27	W	0336	4.9	1008	0.1	1556	4.7	2222	0.2
28	TH	0413	4.8	1051	0.2	1639	4.6	2306	0.2
29	F	0456	4.7	1132	0.4	1728	4.3	2356	0.3
30	SA	0548	4.5	1227	0.6	1826	4.0		

Chart Datum: 2·32 metres below NAP Datum

TIME ZONE -0100
(Dutch Standard Time)
Subtract 1 hour for UT
For Dutch Summer Time add ONE hour in **non-shaded areas**

NETHERLANDS – VLISSINGEN

LAT 51°27′N LONG 3°36′E

TIMES AND HEIGHTS OF HIGH AND LOW WATERS

SPRING & NEAP TIDES
Dates in red are SPRINGS
Dates in blue are NEAPS

YEAR **2005**

MAY

Date	Day	Time	m	Time	m	Time	m	Time	m
1	SU	0056	0.4	0701	4.2	1324	0.8	◑ 1948	3.8
2	M	0215	0.5	0824	4.0	1454	0.9	2105	3.7
3	TU	0334	0.5	0956	4.1	1625	0.9	2230	3.8
4	W	0505	0.4	1110	4.3	1735	0.7	2329	4.1
5	TH	0605	0.2	1206	4.5	1831	0.6		
6	F	0016	4.3	0656	0.1	1246	4.6	1905	0.5
7	SA	0058	4.5	0736	0.1	1325	4.7	1946	0.4
8	SU	0138	4.6	0812	0.1	1406	4.7	● 2025	0.3
9	M	0217	4.7	0850	0.1	1446	4.7	2105	0.3
10	TU	0256	4.7	0926	0.2	1521	4.6	2145	0.3
11	W	0335	4.7	1006	0.4	1559	4.4	2214	0.4
12	TH	0412	4.5	1037	0.5	1635	4.3	2256	0.5
13	F	0451	4.4	1105	0.7	1709	4.1	2329	0.6
14	SA	0532	4.2	1146	0.9	1750	3.9		
15	SU	0015	0.7	0620	3.9	1235	1.0	1846	3.7
16	M	0125	0.8	0714	3.7	1400	1.1	◐ 1945	3.5
17	TU	0234	0.8	0835	3.6	1516	1.1	2106	3.4
18	W	0346	0.8	0956	3.7	1616	1.0	2214	3.6
19	TH	0445	0.7	1101	4.0	1710	0.8	2316	3.9
20	F	0536	0.5	1146	4.3	1756	0.7	2358	4.2
21	SA	0626	0.4	1226	4.5	1836	0.6		
22	SU	0038	4.4	0702	0.3	1259	4.7	1918	0.4
23	M	0116	4.6	0742	0.2	1336	4.8	○ 1958	0.3
24	TU	0156	4.8	0826	0.2	1416	4.8	2046	0.3
25	W	0236	4.9	0906	0.2	1459	4.8	2126	0.2
26	TH	0316	4.9	0948	0.2	1543	4.7	2212	0.1
27	F	0403	4.8	1036	0.3	1631	4.5	2259	0.1
28	SA	0452	4.7	1125	0.5	1722	4.3	2355	0.2
29	SU	0548	4.5	1220	0.6	1828	4.1		
30	M	0106	0.2	0705	4.4	1326	0.8	◑ 1935	4.0
31	TU	0206	0.3	0816	4.3	1434	0.9	2045	3.9

JUNE

Date	Day	Time	m	Time	m	Time	m	Time	m
1	W	0320	0.3	0930	4.2	1606	0.9	2156	4.0
2	TH	0436	0.3	1038	4.3	1705	0.8	2300	4.1
3	F	0541	0.3	1136	4.4	1800	0.7	2351	4.2
4	SA	0625	0.2	1221	4.5	1846	0.6		
5	SU	0037	4.4	0711	0.3	1305	4.5	1928	0.5
6	M	0121	4.5	0748	0.3	1349	4.5	● 2008	0.4
7	TU	0205	4.5	0825	0.4	1429	4.5	2046	0.4
8	W	0240	4.5	0906	0.5	1506	4.4	2125	0.4
9	TH	0326	4.5	0941	0.6	1546	4.3	2206	0.4
10	F	0359	4.5	1016	0.7	1618	4.3	2245	0.4
11	SA	0436	4.4	1050	0.7	1655	4.1	2326	0.5
12	SU	0520	4.2	1125	0.8	1736	4.0		
13	M	0006	0.5	0600	4.1	1203	0.9	1816	3.9
14	TU	0044	0.6	0650	4.0	1255	1.0	1905	3.8
15	W	0134	0.6	0751	3.9	1404	1.0	◐ 2010	3.7
16	TH	0246	0.7	0850	3.9	1505	1.0	2116	3.7
17	F	0334	0.6	0956	4.0	1603	0.9	2215	3.9
18	SA	0435	0.6	1049	4.2	1706	0.8	2311	4.1
19	SU	0536	0.5	1141	4.4	1756	0.7		
20	M	0002	4.3	0626	0.4	1230	4.5	1848	0.5
21	TU	0047	4.5	0716	0.3	1315	4.7	1935	0.4
22	W	0136	4.7	0806	0.3	1359	4.7	○ 2028	0.2
23	TH	0219	4.8	0851	0.3	1446	4.7	2116	0.1
24	F	0306	4.9	0936	0.4	1535	4.6	2208	0.1
25	SA	0356	4.9	1021	0.4	1626	4.6	2256	0.0
26	SU	0447	4.8	1111	0.5	1718	4.5	2349	0.0
27	M	0542	4.7	1205	0.6	1811	4.4		
28	TU	0048	0.1	0648	4.6	1305	0.7	◑ 1912	4.3
29	W	0145	0.2	0748	4.4	1406	0.8	2016	4.1
30	TH	0246	0.3	0856	4.3	1503	0.9	2116	4.1

JULY

Date	Day	Time	m	Time	m	Time	m	Time	m
1	F	0356	0.4	1002	4.2	1626	0.9	2226	4.1
2	SA	0506	0.5	1106	4.2	1730	0.8	2321	4.1
3	SU	0555	0.5	1206	4.2	1826	0.7		
4	M	0019	4.2	0645	0.5	1251	4.3	1910	0.6
5	TU	0116	4.3	0728	0.6	1339	4.3	1952	0.5
6	W	0158	4.4	0806	0.6	1419	4.3	● 2036	0.5
7	TH	0236	4.4	0839	0.7	1455	4.3	2116	0.4
8	F	0311	4.5	0921	0.7	1529	4.4	2150	0.4
9	SA	0348	4.5	0955	0.7	1606	4.4	2230	0.4
10	SU	0421	4.5	1030	0.7	1638	4.3	2308	0.4
11	M	0456	4.4	1105	0.8	1708	4.3	2345	0.4
12	TU	0531	4.3	1146	0.8	1748	4.2		
13	W	0016	0.5	0609	4.2	1220	0.9	1825	4.1
14	TH	0044	0.5	0655	4.2	1306	0.9	◐ 1916	4.0
15	F	0135	0.6	0756	4.1	1344	0.9	2016	3.9
16	SA	0236	0.6	0855	4.0	1500	1.0	2126	3.9
17	SU	0340	0.7	1006	4.1	1605	0.9	2229	4.0
18	M	0444	0.6	1108	4.2	1725	0.8	2331	4.2
19	TU	0558	0.6	1206	4.3	1825	0.6		
20	W	0029	4.5	0656	0.5	1300	4.5	1926	0.4
21	TH	0121	4.7	0748	0.4	1348	4.6	○ 2018	0.2
22	F	0209	4.9	0835	0.4	1436	4.7	2105	0.1
23	SA	0256	5.0	0926	0.4	1526	4.7	2155	0.0
24	SU	0345	5.0	1010	0.5	1609	4.7	2246	-0.1
25	M	0435	4.9	1055	0.5	1657	4.7	2332	-0.1
26	TU	0520	4.8	1139	0.6	1745	4.6		
27	W	0020	0.0	0616	4.7	1230	0.7	1838	4.5
28	TH	0108	0.2	0715	4.4	1315	0.8	◑ 1932	4.3
29	F	0206	0.4	0816	4.2	1414	0.9	2035	4.1
30	SA	0255	0.6	0914	4.0	1529	1.0	2146	3.9
31	SU	0420	0.8	1038	3.9	1656	1.0	2306	3.9

AUGUST

Date	Day	Time	m	Time	m	Time	m	Time	m
1	M	0530	0.8	1145	4.0	1800	0.9		
2	TU	0016	4.1	0626	0.8	1246	4.1	1855	0.7
3	W	0105	4.2	0709	0.8	1329	4.2	1946	0.6
4	TH	0149	4.4	0750	0.8	1410	4.3	2014	0.5
5	F	0225	4.5	0825	0.7	1439	4.4	● 2056	0.4
6	SA	0257	4.5	0901	0.7	1512	4.5	2130	0.4
7	SU	0328	4.6	0936	0.7	1546	4.5	2205	0.3
8	M	0359	4.6	1006	0.7	1615	4.5	2240	0.3
9	TU	0429	4.6	1040	0.7	1642	4.5	2316	0.3
10	W	0459	4.5	1110	0.7	1712	4.4	2339	0.4
11	TH	0532	4.5	1146	0.7	1745	4.4		
12	F	0012	0.4	0610	4.4	1218	0.8	1826	4.3
13	SA	0056	0.5	0655	4.2	1305	0.8	◐ 1918	4.1
14	SU	0146	0.6	0754	4.0	1416	0.9	2036	4.0
15	M	0300	0.8	0920	3.9	1530	1.0	2201	3.9
16	TU	0414	0.8	1040	3.9	1706	0.9	2315	4.1
17	W	0540	0.8	1152	4.1	1816	0.6		
18	TH	0017	4.4	0646	0.6	1249	4.4	1915	0.4
19	F	0111	4.7	0735	0.5	1336	4.6	○ 2008	0.1
20	SA	0158	4.9	0822	0.4	1420	4.8	2056	0.0
21	SU	0242	5.1	0905	0.4	1505	4.9	2140	-0.1
22	M	0326	5.1	0950	0.5	1546	4.9	2223	-0.1
23	TU	0409	5.0	1036	0.5	1629	4.9	2307	0.0
24	W	0456	4.9	1111	0.6	1712	4.8	2346	0.2
25	TH	0541	4.7	1156	0.7	1757	4.6		
26	F	0028	0.3	0629	4.4	1241	0.8	◑ 1848	4.4
27	SA	0115	0.6	0721	4.1	1336	1.0	1951	4.0
28	SU	0209	0.9	0836	3.7	1445	1.1	2105	3.7
29	M	0335	1.1	1011	3.6	1620	1.1	2239	3.7
30	TU	0500	1.1	1125	3.7	1740	1.0	2356	4.0
31	W	0605	1.0	1225	4.0	1840	0.8		

Chart Datum: 2·32 metres below NAP Datum

TIME ZONE -0100
(Dutch Standard Time)
Subtract 1 hour for UT
For Dutch Summer Time add ONE hour in **non-shaded areas**

NETHERLANDS – VLISSINGEN

LAT 51°27′N LONG 3°36′E

TIMES AND HEIGHTS OF HIGH AND LOW WATERS

SPRING & NEAP TIDES
Dates in red are SPRINGS
Dates in blue are NEAPS

YEAR **2005**

SEPTEMBER

Date	Day	Time	m	Time	m	Time	m	Time	m
1	TH	0049	4.2	0656	0.9	1309	4.2	1921	0.6
2	F	0129	4.4	0735	0.8	1348	4.4	1959	0.5
3	SA	0201	4.5	0801	0.7	1415	4.5	● 2032	0.4
4	SU	0236	4.6	0835	0.7	1445	4.6	2102	0.3
5	M	0257	4.7	0908	0.6	1515	4.7	2135	0.3
6	TU	0327	4.8	0935	0.6	1541	4.7	2211	0.3
7	W	0357	4.8	1010	0.6	1612	4.7	2240	0.3
8	TH	0426	4.7	1040	0.6	1639	4.7	2310	0.4
9	F	0458	4.7	1110	0.6	1713	4.6	2346	0.4
10	SA	0536	4.6	1145	0.7	1756	4.5		
11	SU	0026	0.6	0619	4.3	1232	0.7	◐ 1842	4.3
12	M	0116	0.8	0719	4.0	1346	0.9	1956	4.0
13	TU	0229	1.0	0850	3.8	1504	1.0	2135	3.9
14	W	0406	1.0	1021	3.8	1645	0.9	2305	4.1
15	TH	0535	0.9	1140	4.0	1805	0.6		
16	F	0009	4.5	0631	0.7	1236	4.4	1906	0.3
17	SA	0055	4.8	0726	0.6	1317	4.6	1956	0.1
18	SU	0141	5.0	0806	0.5	1358	4.8	○ 2035	0.0
19	M	0220	5.1	0845	0.4	1439	5.0	2116	0.0
20	TU	0302	5.1	0925	0.5	1518	5.0	2155	0.0
21	W	0343	5.0	1006	0.5	1600	5.0	2235	0.2
22	TH	0426	4.8	1041	0.6	1640	4.9	2316	0.3
23	F	0505	4.6	1126	0.7	1722	4.7	2345	0.6
24	SA	0549	4.3	1159	0.8	1806	4.4		
25	SU	0030	0.8	0636	4.0	1245	1.0	◑ 1854	4.0
26	M	0125	1.1	0724	3.6	1426	1.2	2020	3.6
27	TU	0306	1.3	0925	3.4	1539	1.2	2216	3.6
28	W	0419	1.3	1055	3.5	1700	1.1	2325	3.9
29	TH	0536	1.1	1156	3.9	1805	0.8		
30	F	0019	4.2	0631	0.9	1239	4.2	1856	0.6

OCTOBER

Date	Day	Time	m	Time	m	Time	m	Time	m
1	SA	0100	4.4	0706	0.8	1316	4.4	1929	0.5
2	SU	0129	4.6	0736	0.7	1341	4.5	2002	0.4
3	M	0157	4.7	0806	0.6	1409	4.7	● 2032	0.3
4	TU	0226	4.8	0838	0.6	1437	4.8	2102	0.3
5	W	0256	4.9	0910	0.5	1508	4.8	2136	0.3
6	TH	0326	4.9	0942	0.5	1540	4.9	2211	0.3
7	F	0359	4.8	1019	0.5	1613	4.9	2245	0.4
8	SA	0433	4.7	1050	0.5	1650	4.8	2321	0.5
9	SU	0513	4.6	1130	0.6	1731	4.7		
10	M	0006	0.7	0557	4.3	1226	0.7	◐ 1823	4.3
11	TU	0106	0.9	0705	3.9	1336	0.9	1950	4.0
12	W	0226	1.1	0841	3.7	1505	0.9	2125	3.9
13	TH	0354	1.1	1005	3.7	1640	0.8	2255	4.2
14	F	0514	1.0	1119	4.0	1755	0.5	2355	4.5
15	SA	0620	0.8	1215	4.4	1851	0.3		
16	SU	0037	4.8	0706	0.6	1257	4.6	1935	0.1
17	M	0119	4.9	0746	0.5	1335	4.8	○ 2012	0.1
18	TU	0159	5.0	0826	0.5	1415	5.0	2052	0.1
19	W	0239	5.0	0903	0.4	1456	5.0	2132	0.2
20	TH	0319	4.9	0946	0.5	1536	5.0	2208	0.3
21	F	0359	4.7	1020	0.5	1616	4.8	2242	0.5
22	SA	0439	4.5	1101	0.6	1656	4.6	2316	0.7
23	SU	0518	4.2	1135	0.8	1736	4.3	2356	1.0
24	M	0600	4.0	1219	0.9	1830	4.0		
25	TU	0056	1.2	0650	3.7	1345	1.1	◑ 1940	3.7
26	W	0226	1.4	0755	3.4	1454	1.1	2115	3.5
27	TH	0340	1.4	1011	3.4	1615	1.1	2245	3.7
28	F	0445	1.2	1116	3.7	1727	0.9	2341	4.1
29	SA	0534	1.0	1156	4.0	1815	0.7		
30	SU	0015	4.3	0636	0.9	1232	4.3	1852	0.6
31	M	0056	4.5	0659	0.7	1301	4.5	1925	0.5

NOVEMBER

Date	Day	Time	m	Time	m	Time	m	Time	m
1	TU	0122	4.7	0736	0.7	1333	4.7	1955	0.4
2	W	0151	4.8	0806	0.6	1405	4.8	● 2030	0.3
3	TH	0225	4.9	0842	0.5	1439	4.9	2109	0.3
4	F	0258	4.9	0921	0.5	1515	5.0	2146	0.4
5	SA	0336	4.8	0958	0.4	1553	4.9	2222	0.4
6	SU	0415	4.7	1041	0.4	1635	4.8	2306	0.6
7	M	0459	4.5	1125	0.5	1722	4.6	2356	0.7
8	TU	0551	4.2	1226	0.6	1822	4.3		
9	W	0056	1.0	0706	3.9	1335	0.7	◐ 1951	4.1
10	TH	0205	1.1	0825	3.8	1506	0.7	2116	4.1
11	F	0340	1.1	0946	3.8	1615	0.7	2230	4.2
12	SA	0500	1.0	1056	4.0	1736	0.5	2329	4.5
13	SU	0600	0.9	1146	4.3	1826	0.3		
14	M	0018	4.7	0645	0.7	1231	4.5	1911	0.2
15	TU	0059	4.8	0721	0.6	1313	4.7	1947	0.2
16	W	0139	4.8	0803	0.5	1355	4.8	○ 2028	0.3
17	TH	0221	4.8	0846	0.5	1435	4.9	2106	0.4
18	F	0300	4.7	0925	0.4	1515	4.8	2142	0.5
19	SA	0341	4.6	1002	0.5	1558	4.7	2218	0.7
20	SU	0418	4.4	1046	0.6	1636	4.5	2252	0.8
21	M	0455	4.2	1126	0.7	1720	4.3	2330	1.0
22	TU	0538	4.0	1206	0.8	1806	4.1		
23	W	0016	1.2	0626	3.8	1305	0.9	◑ 1859	3.9
24	TH	0114	1.3	0726	3.6	1415	1.0	2010	3.7
25	F	0256	1.3	0824	3.5	1526	1.0	2125	3.7
26	SA	0356	1.3	1000	3.6	1620	0.9	2235	3.9
27	SU	0446	1.1	1055	3.8	1715	0.8	2326	4.2
28	M	0540	1.0	1146	4.1	1806	0.7		
29	TU	0008	4.4	0626	0.8	1219	4.4	1846	0.6
30	W	0046	4.6	0701	0.7	1257	4.6	1926	0.5

DECEMBER

Date	Day	Time	m	Time	m	Time	m	Time	m
1	TH	0119	4.7	0736	0.6	1337	4.8	● 2002	0.4
2	F	0159	4.8	0818	0.5	1416	4.9	2042	0.4
3	SA	0239	4.8	0906	0.4	1455	4.9	2126	0.4
4	SU	0321	4.8	0945	0.3	1539	4.9	2208	0.5
5	M	0405	4.7	1036	0.3	1625	4.8	2256	0.6
6	TU	0456	4.5	1128	0.3	1717	4.7	2347	0.7
7	W	0548	4.3	1226	0.4	1825	4.5		
8	TH	0042	0.9	0658	4.1	1330	0.4	◐ 1931	4.3
9	F	0144	1.0	0801	4.0	1436	0.5	2045	4.2
10	SA	0305	1.1	0916	4.0	1545	0.6	2156	4.2
11	SU	0420	1.1	1015	4.1	1700	0.5	2300	4.3
12	M	0531	1.0	1118	4.2	1801	0.5	2356	4.4
13	TU	0621	0.8	1209	4.4	1846	0.4		
14	W	0041	4.5	0706	0.7	1257	4.5	1928	0.4
15	TH	0127	4.5	0748	0.6	1340	4.6	○ 2005	0.5
16	F	0211	4.5	0826	0.5	1426	4.6	2046	0.5
17	SA	0251	4.5	0908	0.4	1506	4.7	2119	0.6
18	SU	0329	4.5	0950	0.4	1545	4.6	2156	0.7
19	M	0408	4.4	1025	0.5	1625	4.5	2232	0.8
20	TU	0446	4.3	1111	0.5	1706	4.4	2304	0.9
21	W	0519	4.2	1146	0.6	1746	4.2	2345	1.0
22	TH	0600	4.1	1236	0.7	1831	4.1		
23	F	0030	1.1	0646	3.9	1305	0.8	◑ 1915	4.0
24	SA	0125	1.2	0740	3.8	1355	0.8	2015	3.9
25	SU	0230	1.2	0840	3.8	1515	0.9	2126	3.9
26	M	0335	1.2	0951	3.8	1610	0.8	2221	4.0
27	TU	0446	1.1	1051	4.0	1716	0.8	2320	4.2
28	W	0529	0.9	1146	4.2	1806	0.7		
29	TH	0009	4.4	0625	0.8	1229	4.4	1855	0.5
30	F	0057	4.5	0715	0.6	1315	4.6	1940	0.5
31	SA	0141	4.7	0806	0.4	1401	4.8	● 2026	0.4

Chart Datum: 2·32 metres below NAP Datum

9.16.26 VLISSINGEN (FLUSHING)

Zeeland **51°26'·31N 03°34'·61E** (Koopmanshaven)

CHARTS AC 1872, 1874, 120; Zeekaart 1442, 1443, 1533; DYC 1803.8, 1801.3; Imray C30; Stanfords 1, 19.

TIDES +0215 Dover; ML 2·3; Duration 0555; Zone –0100 NOTE: Vlissingen is a Standard Port (←).

SHELTER Very good in both yacht hbrs:

1. **Michiel de Ruyter** marina (2·9m) in the Vissershaven is entered from the Koopmanshaven via 6m wide ent, over a sill with 1·0m water at MLWS; check depth gauge on barrier wall. Small swing bridge (pedestrian, with R/G tfc lts) is opened by HM 0800-2000LT, as required. The bridge stays open 2000-0800LT, but only for yachts to leave; ● ● (vert) tfc lts prohibit arrival from sea, because the marina is not lit. Storm barrier is open 1 Apr-1 Nov. Pilot boats ent /exit the adjacent inlet with much speed, noise and wash.
2. **VVW Schelde** (3-4·3m) is near the ent to the Walcheren Canal. Entering the Buitenhaven beware ferries. Keep to port and S of ferry terminal for the locks, which operate H24; yachts use smallest, most N'ly lock. Waiting possible on piles to SE. Marina is to NW, past both Binnenhavens.

NAVIGATION WPT 51°25'·16N 03°33'·66E [Songa SHM buoy, QG], 027°/1·29M to Koopmanshaven ent.

Commercial Shipping: Yachts should keep clear of the busy shipping chans, ie Wielingen from the SW, Scheur from the W, and Oostgat from the NW. To the E of W6 & W7 buoys, be aware of the major ship anchorages: Wielingen Noord and Zuid either side of the fairway as defined by buoys W6, 7, 9, 10 and Songa. Close to the E, Vlissingen Roads are also a major anchorage (N of buoys ARV-VH to SS5, and SW of SS1). Yachts may cross, but not sail in, a precautionary TSS (just off chartlet) between this anch and Vlissingen itself. Ocean-going ships often manoeuvre off the town to transfer pilots. Fast ferries (foot/cycle), which have right of way, only use the Buitenhaven terminal half-hourly due to the Schelde road tunnel from Vlissingen to Breskens.

Recommended Yacht routes:

From the SW there are few dangers. After Zeebrugge, keep S of the Wielingen chan buoys (W1-9). Off Breskens avoid fast ferries to/from Vlissingen; continue E to SS1 buoy, then cross to Vlissingen on a N'ly track.

From the W, keep clear of the Scheur chan by crossing to the S of Wielingen as soon as practicable.

From N, by day only, in vicinity of Kaloo or DR1 buoys, follow the Geul van de Rassen, Deurloo and Spleet chans to SP4 buoy. Thence E via WN6 buoy towards Vlissingen.

Or continue down the Deurloo from DL5 buoy to join Oostgat at OG19 buoy; thence cross to the Vlissingen shore as and when traffic in Oostgat permits.

Another route, slightly further offshore, is to skirt the NW side of Kaloo bank to Botkil-W buoy, thence SE via Geul van de Walvischstaart to Trawl SCM buoy. None of these N'ly routes is lit, but the narrow, busy Oostgat can be used with caution, keeping just outside the SW edge of the buoyed/lit chan.

LIGHTS AND MARKS From NW, Oostgat 117° ldg lts: Front RW pile; rear Sardijngeul, Oc WRG 5s, R/W banded mast, R △. Note: Conspic radar twr (close NW of Koopmanshaven) shows a Fl Y lt to warn if ships are approaching in the blind NW arc from Oostgat-Sardijngeul. S of de Ruyter marina a conspic W metal framework tr (50m) is floodlit. Buitenhaven tfc sigs from mole W side of ent: R flag or extra ● near FR on W mole hd = No entry.

R/T *Zeeland Seaports* Ch 09. Lock Ch 18; bridges info Ch 22. See also Westerschelde (9.16.26) for VTS.

TELEPHONE (Dial code 0118) HM 0115 647400; East Hbr Port Authority 478741; Schelde Tfc Coordination Centre 424790; Buitenhaven Lock 412372; ⊖ 484600; Police 0900-8844; Ⓗ 425000; Dr 412233; Brit Consul (020) 6764343.

FACILITIES **Michiel de Ruyter** (100 + 40 Ⓥ) ☎ 414498, €1.60, D, Bar, R, YC, ⊡; **Jachthaven 'VVW Schelde'** (90 + 50 Ⓥ) ☎ 465912, €0.91, Bar, C (10 ton), CH, D, R, ⊡, ⚓, M, Slip, (Access H24 via lock), approx 500m by road from ferry terminal; **Services:** BY, ME, ⚒, SM, bikes for hire. **Town** P, D, CH, 🛒, R, Bar, ✉, Ⓑ, ⇌, ✈ (Antwerpen). Foot ferry to Breskens; road tunnel to Terneuzen.

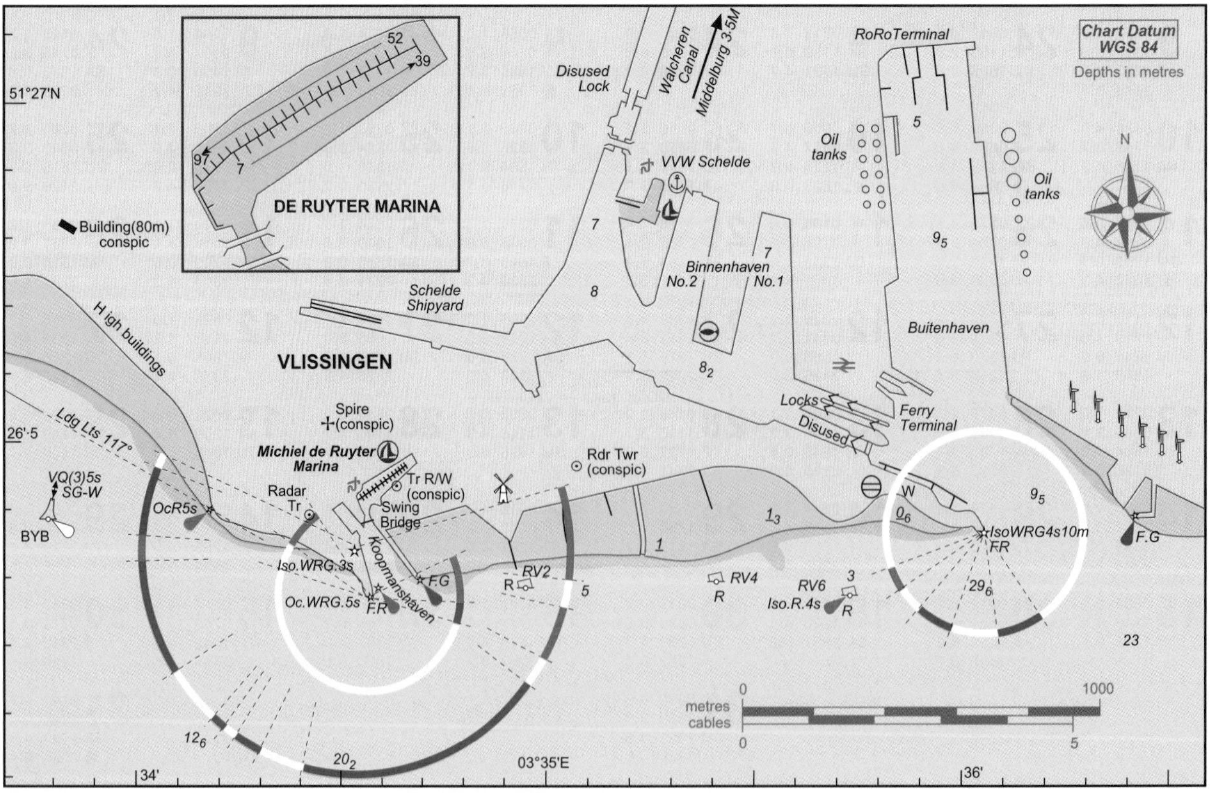
Chart Datum WGS 84
Depths in metres
DE RUYTER MARINA
VLISSINGEN
Michiel de Ruyter Marina
Koopmanshaven
Buitenhaven
Binnenhaven No.2
No.1
VVW Schelde
RoRoTerminal
Ferry Terminal
Locks
Disused
Disused Lock
Walcheren Canal
Middelburg 3.5M
Oil tanks
Schelde Shipyard
Building(80m) conspic
High buildings
Spire (conspic)
Rdr Twr (conspic)
Tr R/W (conspic)
Swing Bridge
Radar Tr
Ldg Lts 117°
VQ(3)5s SG-W
BYB
OcR5s
Iso.WRG.3s
Oc.WRG.5s
F.R
F.G
RV2
RV4
RV6
Iso.R.4s
IsoWRG4s10m
FR
F.G
W
51°27'N
26'·5
34'
03°35'E
36'
metres
cables
0
1000
5

9.16.27 WESTERSCHELDE

Zeeland mostly, but Belgium for the last 12M to Antwerpen

CHARTS AC 1874, 120, 139; Zeekaart 1443; DYC 1803; Imray C30

TIDES +0200 Dover; ML Hansweert 2·7, Westkapelle 2·0, Bath 2·8; Duration 0555; Zone –0100

Standard Port VLISSINGEN (⟵)

Times				Height (metres)			
High Water		Low Water		MHWS	MHWN	MLWN	MLWS
0300	0900	0400	1000	4·7	3·8	0·8	0·2
1500	2100	1600	2200				
Differences WESTKAPELLE							
–0025	–0015	–0010	–0025	–0·5	–0·5	–0·1	+0·1
HANSWEERT							
+0100	+0050	+0040	+0100	+0·6	+0·7	0·0	+0·1
BATH							
+0125	+0115	+0115	+0140	+1·0	+1·0	0·0	+0·1

SHELTER AND FACILITIES Some of the many yacht hbrs between Terneuzen and Antwerpen (38M) are listed below in sequence from seaward:

ELLEWOUTSDIJK, 51°23'·10N 03°49'·05E. DYC 1803.2. HW +0200 and +0·3m on Vlissingen; ML 2·6m, €0.45. Small, safe hbr but strong cross eddy on ebb; unlit. Dries, easy access HW ±3; 1·5m at MLWS. HM ☎ (0113) 548248 D, Gaz; **YC Ellewoutsdijk.**

HOEDEKENSKERKE, 51°25'·11N 03°54'·90E. DYC 1803.3. Disused ferry hbr (dries) in Middelgat, abeam MG13 SHM buoy, Iso G 8s. Access HW–2½ to +3 for 1m draft, €7.00/night inc AC, FW. **YC WV Hoedekenskerke** ☎ (0113) 639278; 34 + 1 ⓥ berth, P, D, Gaz, FW, ME. **Town** ✉, Ⓑ, ⥂ (Goes).

HANSWEERT, 51°26'·37N 04°00'·66E. DYC 1803.3. Tidal differences above. Temporary stop, but it is the busy ent to Zuid Beveland canal. Lt Oc WRG 10s, R lattice tr, W band, at ent. Waiting berths outside lock on E side. ⓥ berths in inner hbr, W side; **no smoking or naked flames in, or near lock. Services:** ME, BY, P, D, C (17 ton), CH, R. **Town** ✉, Ⓑ, ⥂ (Kruiningen-Yerseke).

WALSOORDEN, 51°22'·93N 04°02'·10E. DYC 1803.3. HW is +0110 and +0·7m on Vlissingen; ML 2·6m, €0.32/m (€3.22 min), max stay H24. Prone to swell. SHM buoy 57A, Iso G 8s, is 1ca N of ent where 16 silos are conspic. Ldg lts 220° both Oc 3s. Hbr ent FG & FR. Unmarked stone pier just outside E hbr pier, dries partly at LW. Yacht basin dead ahead on ent to hbr, depths 2 to 2·8m. *Zandvliet Radio* VHF Ch 12. HM ☎ (0114) 681235, FW, Slip; **Services:** Gas, P, D, BY, ME, El. **Town** R, Bar, ✉.

PAAL, 51°21'·25N 04°06'·65E. DYC 1803.3. HW +0120 and +0·8m on Vlissingen; ML 2·7m. Unlit, drying yacht hbr on S bank at river mouth, ent marked by withy. Appr HW±2 from No. 63 SHM buoy, Iso G 8s, and Tide gauge, Fl (5) Y 20s across drying Speelmansgat. *Zandvliet Radio* VHF Ch 12. HM ☎ (0114) 314974; **Jachthaven; Services:** •0.50/m, P, D, Gaz, ME, El, 🛒, R.

DOEL, Antwerpen, 51°18'·67N 04°16'·11E. DYC 1803.5. HW +0100 and +0·7m on Vlissingen. Small drying hbr on W bank - no entry LW±2. Ldg lts 185·5°: front Fl WR 3s on N pier hd; rear Fl 3s, synch. HM ☎ (03) 6652585; **YC de Noord** ☎ 7733669, R, Bar, FW.

LILLO, Antwerpen, 51°18'·16N 04°17'·30E. DYC 1803.5. 1M SE of Doel on opp bank; small drying hbr for shoal-draft only; HW±3. Landing stage in river has Oc WRG 10s. HM (035) 686456; **YC Scaldis.**

NAVIGATION The channels into the estuary from seaward, both for commercial shipping and for yachts, are detailed in 9.16.26; also the busy junction area between Vlissingen and Breskens. The Westerschelde is the waterway to Antwerpen and Gent (via canal), very full of ships and barges. The main channel winds through a mass of well marked sand-banks. It is essential to work the tides, which average 2½kn, more at springs. Best timing is most easily achieved by starting from Vlissingen, Breskens (9.16.28) or Terneuzen (9.16.29). Yachts should keep to the edge of main chan. Alternative chans must be used with caution, particularly going downriver on the ebb.

LIGHTS AND MARKS The apprs to Westerschelde are well lit by lt ho's: on the S shore at Nieuwe Sluis, and on the N shore at Westkapelle; see 9.16.4. The main fairways are, for the most part, defined by ldg lts and by the W sectors of the many Dir lts.

VTS Yachts approaching or in the Westerschelde should monitor the comprehensive Scheldemond VTS covering from the North Sea outer approaches up-river to Antwerp (see 9.16.19). Listen at all times on the VHF Ch for the area in which you are, so as to be aware of other shipping and to be contactable if required. Do not transmit, unless called.

7 Traffic Centres control the Areas below. Within these Traffic areas, 8 radar stations provide radar, weather and hbr info, as shown below:

In the outer approaches: (*Traffic Centre* is the callsign prefix)

1. *Wandelaar* Ch 65. *Zeebrugge Radar* Ch 04.
2. *Zeebrugge* Ch 69. Radar as Area 1.
3. *Steenbank* Ch 64. Radar also on Ch 64.

In the Westerschelde: (*Centrale* is the callsign prefix)

4. *Vlissingen* Ch 14 (Vlissingen to E2A/PvN SPR buoys at approx 51°24'N 03°44'E). Radar Ch 21.
5. *Terneuzen* Ch 03 (thence to Nos 32/35 buoys at approx 51°23'N 03°57'E). Radar Ch 03.

5A. *Terneuzen* Ch 11 covers the Terneuzen-Gent Canal.

6. *Hansweert* Ch 65 (thence to Nos 46/55 buoys at approx 51°24'N 04°02'E). Radar Ch 65.
7. *Zandvliet* Ch 12 (thence to Antwerpen). Radar chans: *Radar Waarde* 19; *Radar Saeftinge* 21; *Radar Zandvliet* 04; *Radar Kruisschans* 66.

In **emergency**, call initially on the working channel in use; state yacht's name, position and the nature of the problem, in Dutch or English. You may then be switched to Ch **67** or another discrete VHF channel.

Broadcasts of visibility, met & tidal data and ship movements are made in Dutch and English at:

H+ 00 by *Terneuzen* Ch 11. H+ 15 by Zeebrugge Ch 69.
H+ 35 by *Zandvliet* Ch 12. H+ 55 by *Vlissingen* Ch 14.

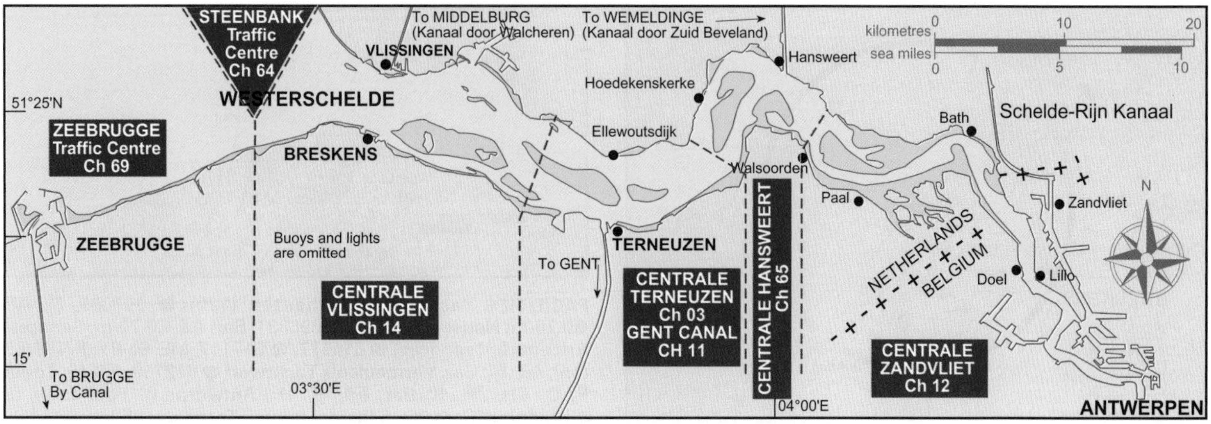
STEENBANK Traffic Centre Ch 64
To MIDDELBURG (Kanaal door Walcheren)
To WEMELDINGE (Kanaal door Zuid Beveland)
kilometres 0 10 20
sea miles 0 5 10
VLISSINGEN
Hansweert
Hoedekenskerke
51°25'N
WESTERSCHELDE
ZEEBRUGGE Traffic Centre Ch 69
BRESKENS
Ellewoutsdijk
Bath
Schelde-Rijn Kanaal
Walsoorden
Paal
Zandvliet
N
ZEEBRUGGE
Buoys and lights are omitted
TERNEUZEN
To GENT
NETHERLANDS
BELGIUM
Doel
Lillo
CENTRALE VLISSINGEN Ch 14
CENTRALE TERNEUZEN Ch 03 GENT CANAL CH 11
CENTRALE HANSWEERT Ch 65
CENTRALE ZANDVLIET Ch 12
15'
To BRUGGE By Canal
03°30'E
04°00'E
ANTWERPEN

9.16.28 BRESKENS

Zeeland **51°23'·99N 03°34'·08E** ❁❁❁◊◊◊✿✿✿

CHARTS AC 1874, 1872, 120; Zeekaart 120, 101; DYC 1801.4, 1803.2; Imray C30; Stanfords 1, 19

TIDES +0210 Dover; ML no data; Duration 0600; Zone –0100

Standard Port VLISSINGEN (⟵) Use Vlissingen data.

SHELTER Good in all winds except N and NW. Enter marina between two wave break barges; access H24, 5m at ent. Berth on first pontoon where there is ☎ direct line to HM for allocation of a berth. ⚓ off Plaat van Breskens, in fine weather, not in commercial/fishing hbr. Beware fast ferries.

NAVIGATION WPT 51°24'·71N 03°33'·90E [ARV-VH NCM buoy, Q], 172°/0·68M to W mole lt (within white sector). Beware strong tides across the ent. Do not confuse the ent with the ferry port ent, 0·7M WNW, where yachts are prohib.

LIGHTS AND MARKS Large bldg/silo on centre pier in hbr and two apartment blocks (30m) SE of marina are conspic. See chartlet and 9.16.4 for light details. W mole F WRG has 3 W sectors covering the appr's: from seaward; from ARV-VH buoy; and from the ESE (Vaarwater langs Hoofdplaat). Nieuwe Sluis lt ho, 28m B/W banded 8-sided twr, is 1·8M W of marina.

R/T Marina VHF Ch 31.

TELEPHONE (Dial code 0117); ⊜ (0115) 670700; Police 453156; Dr 381566/389284, at night/weekends (0115) 643000; Ⓗ (0117) 459000; British Consul (020) 6764343.

FACILITIES Marina jachthavenbreskens@zonnet.nl ☎ 381902, 📠 383931, €1.55 + €0.80 tourist tax, ⊡, ⛯; **YC Breskens** ☎ 383278, R, Bar; **Services:** SM, CH, D & P (fuel pontoon is in FV hbr), Gaz, chart agent, BY, C(30T), BH(70T), El, Ⓔ, ME, ⚒, Slip, ♿. **Town** 🛒, R, Bar, ✉, Ⓑ, Gas, ✈ (Oostende or Brussels). Foot ferry or car tunnel to Vlissingen, ⇌.

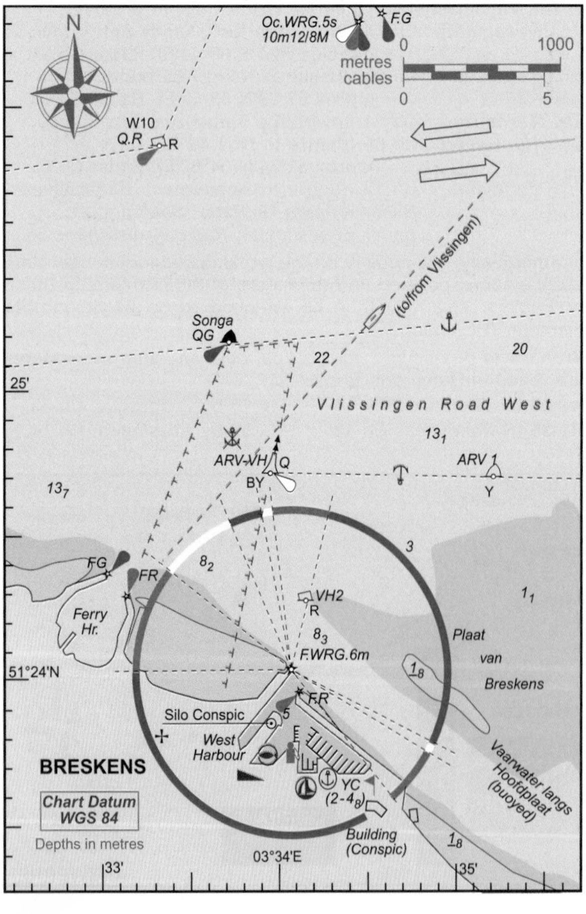
N
Oc.WRG.5s
10m12/8M
F.G
metres
cables
0
1000
5
W10
Q.R
R
Songa
QG
22
20
25'
Vlissingen Road West
(to/from Vlissingen)
ARV-VH
Q
BY
ARV 1
Y
13
FG
FR
Ferry Hr.
VH2
R
Plaat
van
Breskens
F.WRG.6m
51°24'N
Silo Conspic
F.R
West Harbour
BRESKENS
Chart Datum
WGS 84
Depths in metres
YC
Building (Conspic)
Vaarwater langs Hoofdplaat (buoyed)
33'
03°34'E
35'

9.16.29 TERNEUZEN

Zeeland **51°20'·58N 03°49'·69E** ❁❁❁◊◊◊✿✿

CHARTS AC 120; Zeekaart 1443; DYC 1803.2; Imray C30

TIDES +0230 Dover; ML 2·5; Duration 0555; Zone –0100

Standard Port VLISSINGEN (⟵)

Times				Height (metres)			
High Water		Low Water		MHWS	MHWN	MLWN	MLWS
0300	0900	0400	1000	4·7	3·8	0·8	0·2
1500	2100	1600	2200				
Differences TERNEUZEN							
+0020	+0020	+0020	+0030	+0·4	+0·4	0·0	+0·1

SHELTER Very good except in strong N'lies. Marina is in the SE corner of Veerhaven: most likely Ⓥ berth at WV Honte; WV Neusen is close ESE. ⚓ on N side of chan between WPT4 & 6, ZE5 & ZE7 buoys. Or transit the E lock to berth in Zijkanaal A, as chartlet. Yachts are prohib in W Buitenhaven and W lock.

NAVIGATION WPT 51°20'·94N 03°48'·83E [No 18 PHM buoy, Iso R 8s], 123°/0·65M to Veerhaven ent. The fairway is only 500m wide abeam the ent; have a careful look E/W before leaving.

LIGHTS AND MARKS The Dow Chemical works and storage tanks are conspic 2M W of hbr. For the Veerhaven, the Oc WRG 5s lt, B/W post, on W mole is conspic. When entry prohib, a second R lt is shown below FR on E mole. Sigs for Oostsluis: R lts = no entry; G lts = clear to enter.

R/T No marina VHF. Call *Port Control* Ch 11 (H24) for locks and Terneuzen-Gent canal; also info broadcasts every H+00. East lock Ch 18. Contact Zelzate Bridge (call: *Uitkijk Zelzate*) direct on Ch 11, other bridges through Terneuzen or, at the S end, *Havendienst Gent* Ch 05 11 (H24). See also 9.16.27.

TELEPHONE (Dial code 0115) HM 612161; Marina Jacht Haven 697089; CG (0223) 542300 (H24); Police 0900 8844; Ⓗ 688000; Dr 616262; Brit Consul (020) 6764343.

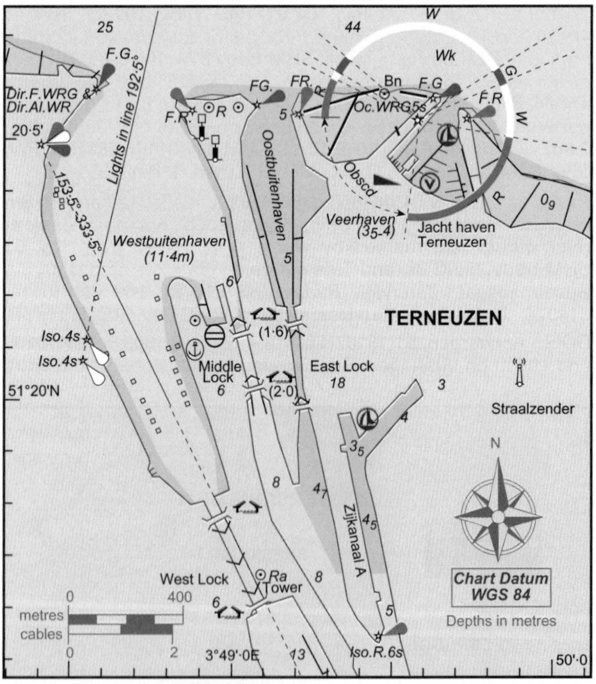
25
44
W
F.G
Dir.F.WRG &
Dir.Al.WR
20·5'
Lights in line 192·5°
FG
F.R
R
FR
Bn
F.G
Oc.WRG5s
F.R
Wk
G
W
R
Obscd
Oostbuitenhaven
153·5°-333·5°
Veerhaven
(35·4)
Jacht haven
Terneuzen
Westbuitenhaven
(11·4m)
TERNEUZEN
(1·6)
Iso.4s
Iso.4s
Middle Lock
6
(2·0)
East Lock
18
51°20'N
Straalzender
N
Zijkanaal A
West Lock
400
Ra Tower
metres
cables
Chart Datum
WGS 84
Depths in metres
3°49'·0E
Iso.R.6s
50'·0

FACILITIES Yachthaven Terneuzen (120) ☎ 697089, ⊡, AB €0.70/m; **Neusen YC** (100) ☎ 696331, Bar, AB €0.70/m, **Services:** Aricom (full services) ☎ 614577, ☎ 617117, ME, El, BY, FW, C (50 ton), AB, ⚒, Gaz. **Vermeulen's Yachtwerf** ☎ 612716, €0.45. **Town** P, D, CH, 🛒, R, Bar, ✉, Ⓑ, ✈ (Antwerpen). Foot ferry to Vlissingen. Cars by Schelde tunnel Terneuzen-Ellewoutsdijk.

9.16.30 ANTWERPEN

Belgium, Antwerpen **51°13'·83N 04°23'·74E**

CHARTS AC 139; Zeekaart 1443; DYC 1803.5

TIDES +0342 Dover; ML 2·9; Duration 0605; Zone –0100

Standard Port VLISSINGEN (⟵)

Times				Height (metres)			
High Water		Low Water		MHWS	MHWN	MLWN	MLWS
0300	0900	0400	1000	4·7	3·8	0·8	0·2
1500	2100	1600	2200				
Differences ANTWERPEN							
+0128	+0116	+0121	+0144	+1·2	+1·0	+0·1	+0·1

SHELTER Excellent in (1) **Linkeroever** (W bank) marina, 2ca SW of No. 109 buoy; Lat/Long under title. Access by gate HW ±1, 0800–2200 or on request 1 Apr-31 Oct. In winter gate opens only by arrangement; a Y waiting buoy is off the ent. A T-shaped ferry pontoon on W bank is 2½ ca N of ent, with waiting berths on inshore side. City centre is ½M via St. Annatunnel.
(2) **Willemdok** marina, H24 access via Royerssluis, Siberiabrug, Londenbrug, very close to city centre. An FD number is required if entering the Docks complex and/or Willemdok marina.

NAVIGATION For Westerschelde see 9.16.27. Best to check off the buoys coming up-river. After No 116 PHM buoy, Iso R 1·5s, there is a gap of 1·4M before No 107 SHM buoy, Iso G 8s, where the river bends 90° onto S and is close to the pontoon (see SHELTER). No 109 SHM buoy, Iso G 8s, is 250m NE of marina ent.

R/T *Linkeroever* Ch 09 (HW±1). Willemdok and access bridges Ch 62. *Antwerpen Havendienst* (Port Ops) Ch 74 (H24); VTS, Zandvliet Centre Ch 12; Radar Ch 04, 66.

TELEPHONE (Dial code 03); ⊜ 2292004; Police 5460730; Ⓗ 2852000 (W Bank) 234111 (E Bank).

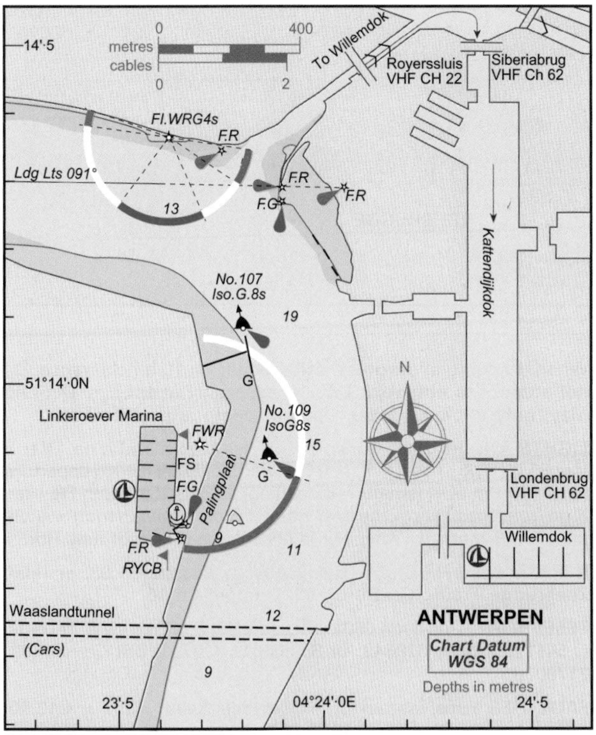
14'·5
metres
cables
0
400
2
To Willemdok
Royerssluis
VHF CH 22
Siberiabrug
VHF Ch 62
Fl.WRG4s
F.R
Ldg Lts 091°
F.R
F.G
F.R
13
Kattendijkdok
No.107
Iso.G.8s
19
51°14'·0N
G
N
Linkeroever Marina
No.109
IsoG8s
FWR
15
FS
G
F.G
Palingplaat
Londenbrug
VHF CH 62
9
Willemdok
F.R
RYCB
11
Waaslandtunnel
12
(Cars)
ANTWERPEN
Chart Datum
WGS 84
9
Depths in metres
23'·5
04°24'·0E
24'·5

FACILITIES Linkeroever Marina (200+Ⓥ) ☎ 2190895, 2196748, Mobile 0475 643957; €1·50, D, Gaz, El, ⚒, C (1·5 ton), CH, Slip, R, 🛒. **Royal YC van België** ☎ 219 5231, Bar, R, M, BY, C (5 ton), D, P, CH, Slip; **Kon. Liberty YC** ☎ 2191147; **Services:** BY, ME, BH, ACA, DYC Agent. **Willemdok Marina** (200+Ⓥ) (open 0500-2300), ☎ 2315066, 2324601, Mobiles 0495 535455/0496 236070; €1·50, D, 🛒, El. **City** All facilities, ✉, Ⓑ, ⇌, ✈. Ferry: Ostend-Dover.

9.16.31 ZEEBRUGGE

Belgium, West Flanders **51°21'·81N 03°11'·42E**

CHARTS AC *2449*, 3371, 1872, 1874; Zeekaart 1441; DYC 1801.3, 1803; Imray C30; Stanfords 1, 19

TIDES +0110 Dover; ML 2·4; Duration 0535; Zone –0100

Standard Port VLISSINGEN (⟵)

Times				Height (metres)			
High Water		Low Water		MHWS	MHWN	MLWN	MLWS
0300	0900	0400	1000	4·7	3·8	0·8	0·2
1500	2100	1600	2200				
Differences ZEEBRUGGE							
–0035	–0015	–0020	–0035	+0·2	+0·2	+0·4	+0·2

SHELTER Very good in the Yacht Hbr, access H24. Caution on ent/dep due to limited vis; give all jetties a wide berth. Zeebrugge is a busy commercial and fishing port and a ferry terminal.

NAVIGATION WPT 51°22'·48N 03°09'·95E [Z SHM buoy, QG], 130°/1·1M to ent (lat/long under title). Beware strong currents in hbr apprs (up to 4kn at HW –1). To avoid getting 'lost' inside the vast outer hbr, a WPT 51°20'·85N 03°12'·29E off Heist lt ho (W inner bkwtr hd) is useful. See chartlet overleaf and 9.16.4.

LIGHTS AND MARKS. Big Ship ldg lts/marks (hard to see by day and in poor vis) lead in sequence toward Vissershaven and the marina at its W end:
a. 136°: Both W cols, R bands.
b. 154°: Front R △, W bands; rear R ▽, W bands.
c. 220°: Both W cols, B bands. d. 193°: Both W cols, R bands.
IPTS are shown from heads of W outer and inner bkwtrs. When LNG-tanker is under way, 3 FY (vert) lts next to IPTS Nos 2 and 5 prohibit all movements in hbr/apprs unless special permission to move has been given. At S side of Visserhaven a QY lt prohibits ent/dep, due to commercial traffic outside.

R/T Port Control Ch 71 (H24). Marina Ch 71. Locks Ch 68.

TELEPHONE (Dial code 050) HM 543241; Port Control 546867; Lock Mr 543231; CG 545072; Sea Saving Service 544007; ⊜ 54.54.55; Police 544148; Dr 544590; Ⓗ 320832; Brit Consul (02) 2179000.

FACILITIES Yacht Hbr (100 + 100) ☎ 544903, Slip, ⚒, CH, D; **Royal Belgian SC** ☎ 544903, D, M, AB €2.04; **Alberta** (R, Bar of RBSC) ☎ 544197; **Services:** ME, El, CH. **Town** P, D, ⚒, Gaz, 🛒, R, Bar, ✉, Ⓑ, ⇌ 15 mins to Brugge, tram to Oostende, ✈ (Ostend). Ferry: Zeebrugge-Felixstowe/Hull. Brugge is 6M inland by canal.

9.16.32 BLANKENBERGE

Belgium, West Flanders **51°18'·90N 03°06'·48E**

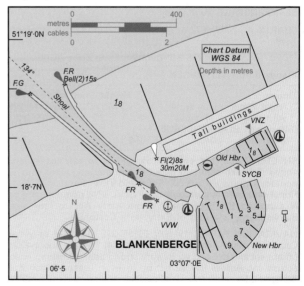

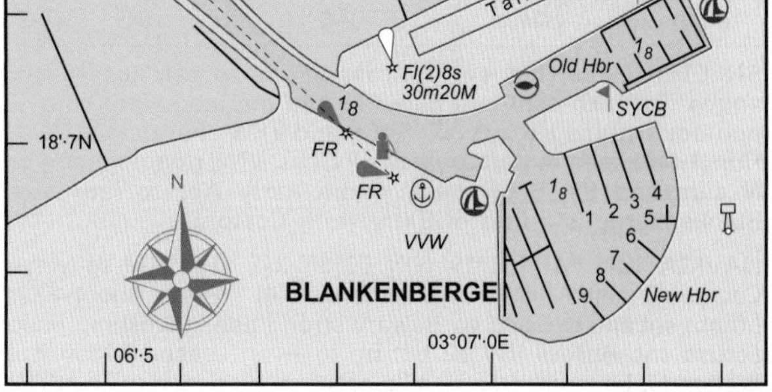
0
400
metres
51°19'·0N
cables
0
2
Chart Datum
WGS 84
Depths in metres
134°
F.R
Bell(2)15s
F.G
Shoal
18
Tall buildings
VNZ
Fl(2)8s
30m20M
Old Hbr
18
SYCB
18
18'·7N
FR
FR
N
VVW
BLANKENBERGE
New Hbr
03°07'·0E
06'·5

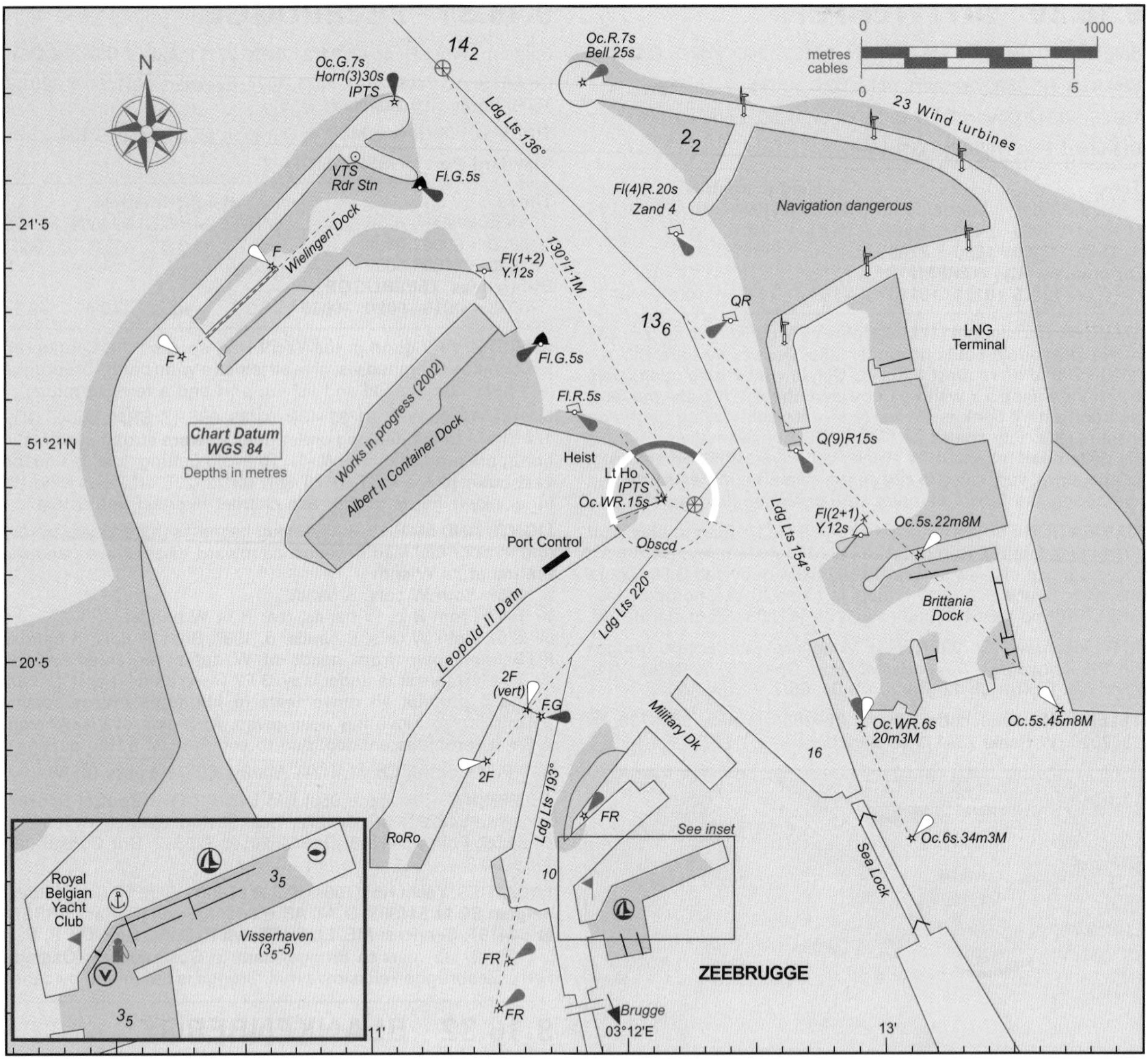
N
metres
cables
0
1000
5
Oc.G.7s
Horn(3)30s
IPTS
VTS
Rdr Stn
Fl.G.5s
Oc.R.7s
Bell 25s
23 Wind turbines
Ldg Lts 136°
Fl(4)R.20s
Zand 4
Navigation dangerous
Wielingen Dock
F
Fl(1+2)
Y.12s
130°/1·1M
QR
LNG
Terminal
Fl.G.5s
Fl.R.5s
Works in progress (2002)
Albert II Container Dock
Chart Datum
WGS 84
Depths in metres
21'·5
51°21'N
Heist
Lt Ho
IPTS
Oc.WR.15s
Q(9)R15s
Obscd
Port Control
Ldg Lts 154°
Fl(2+1)
Y.12s
Oc.5s.22m8M
Brittania
Dock
Leopold II Dam
Ldg Lts 220°
20'·5
2F
(vert)
F.G
Military Dk
Oc.WR.6s
20m3M
Oc.5s.45m8M
16
2F
FR
Ldg Lts 193°
RoRo
See inset
Oc.6s.34m3M
Sea Lock
Royal
Belgian
Yacht
Club
Visserhaven
(3₅-5)
10
FR
FR
ZEEBRUGGE
Brugge
03°12'E
11'
13'

BLANKENBERGE *continued*

CHARTS AC *2449*, 1872, 1874; DYC 1801.3; Imray C30; Stanfords 1, 19

TIDES +0130 Dover; ML 2·5; Duration 0535; Zone –0100

Standard Port VLISSINGEN (⟵)

Times		Height (metres)			
High Water	Low Water	MHWS	MHWN	MLWN	MLWS
All times	All times	4·7	3·8	0·8	0·2
Differences BLANKENBERGE					
–0040	–0040	–0·3	0·0	+0·3	+0·2

SHELTER Good, but entry is dangerous in NW'lies F6 and above. Turn 90° stbd into new Hbr and marina (1·8m) with 12 pontoons, managed by VNZ, SYCB and VVW. For the old Yacht Hbr (1·8m) keep to port, past the FV hbr; VNZ pontoons are on N side and SYCB to the E. From early Apr to late Sept Blankenberge is a Port of Entry, with Customs.

NAVIGATION WPT 51°19'·60N 03°05'·31E, 134°/1M to piers. Caution: 3 unlit Y SPM buoys and one Fl (4) Y 20s lie about 400m off hbr ent and to E and W. Beware strong tides (& fishing lines) across ent. Access HW ±2 but up to ±4 in season, when it is dredged 2·5m; otherwise it silts between piers and dries at LW. When dredging in progress, call dredger Ch 10 for clearance. Do not attempt to enter/exit LW±1½, especially at springs. Oct-end May, only ent/leave HW±1, unless depth is pre-checked.

LIGHTS AND MARKS Conspic high-rise blocks E of lt ho, W tr B top. FS by lt ho shows 2 ▼, points inward, or Fl Bu lt = No departure for craft < 6m LOA (small craft warning). Ldg lts 134°, both FR, (Red X on front mast) show the best water. FG on W pier is more visible than FR (E pier). A Water twr is conspic on E side of new Hbr.

R/T Marinas VHF Ch 08. *Blankenberge Rescue* Ch 08; or relay Zeebrugge Traffic Centre Ch 69. Dredger Ch 10.

TELEPHONE (Dial code 050) HM: use VNZ, SYCB or VVW Tel Nos; ⊜ 544223; Police 429842; Dr 333668; Ⓗ 413701; Brit Consul (02) 2179000.

FACILITIES Fees (same for all berths): Beam <3m = €13.50; <3.5m = €17.00; <4.50m = €31.00; <5.00m = €40.00.
YC Vrije Noordzeezeilers (VNZ) ☎ 429150, mobile 0479 608787, Bar, R.
Scarphout YC (SYCB) ☎ 411420, mobile 0475 626001, C (10/2½ ton), CH, Slip, Bar, R, ♿.
Marina (VVW) ☎ 417536, mobile 0495 527536, ⚓, Bar, ⊡, Slip, P, D (hose, duty free), ME, ⚒, Ⓔ, El, SM, CH, C (20 ton).
Town Gaz, R, Bar, ✉, Ⓑ, ⇌, ✈ Ostend.

9.16.33 OOSTENDE

Belgium, West Flanders **51°14'·35N 02°55'·09E** ❁❁❁◊◊◊✿✿✿

CHARTS AC *2449,* 1872, 1874, 1873; SHOM 7214; ECM 1010; DYC 1801.2; Imray C30; Stanfords 1, 19, 20

TIDES +0120 Dover; ML 2·6; Duration 0530; Zone –0100
Standard Port VLISSINGEN (⟵)

Times				**Height (metres)**			
High Water		Low Water		MHWS	MHWN	MLWN	MLWS
0300	0900	0400	1000	4·7	3·8	0·8	0·2
1500	2100	1600	2200				
Differences OOSTENDE							
–0055	–0040	–0030	–0045	+0·5	+0·5	+0·4	+0·2

SHELTER Very good, esp in Mercator Yacht Hbr (1·2m). Ent via Montgomerydok (2·7m) and lock H24; locking can be very slow in season. Lock hrs (times in brackets are w/end or hols if different from M-F): May/Sep 0800-1800 (2000); Jun 0800-2000; Jul/Aug 0700-2200. RNSYC (1·2m) and RYCO (2·7m) can be uncomfortable due respectively to ferries and/or strong W/NW winds.

NAVIGATION WPT 51°14'·97N 02°53'·84E, 128°/1M to ent. Avoid the offshore banks esp in bad weather: From the NE stay to seaward of Wenduinebank, except in calm weather. From the NW keep S of W Hinder TSS and approach from MBN buoy. From the SW appr via West Diep and Kleine Rede, inside Stroombank.

LIGHTS AND MARKS Europa Centrum bldg (105m; twice as high as other bldgs) is conspic 4ca SSW of ent. Lt ho, 5ca ESE of the ent, is a conspic W twr with 2 sinusoidal blue bands. 128° ldg marks are R/W banded lattice masts with X topmarks. See chartlet and 9.16.4 for lt details.

IPTS shown from E pier. QY lts at blind exit from Montgomerydok = no exit, due to ferry or other vessels underway.

R/T Port Control Ch 09 (H24); Mercator lock/yacht hbr Ch 14 (H24); Weather Ch 27 at 0820 & 1720 UT (English and Dutch).

TELEPHONE (Dial code 059) HM 321687, 📠 340710; Mercator lock 321669; Life Saving 701000; ⊖ 322009; Police 701111; Ⓗ 552000; Brit Consul (02) 2876232.

FACILITIES from seaward: **Royal North Sea YC,** ☎ 505912, (70+50 Ⓥ), much rafting, €1.87/m inc AC & shwr (M/boats 25% extra), limited D from HM in your cans, Grid, R, Bar.
Mercator Yacht Hbr (now run by RNSYC), ☎ 705762 (300+50 Ⓥ), €2.25/m; pay cash/card at lock outbound; metered AC is extra.
Royal YC Oostende, ☎ 321452, (120 + 35 Ⓥ), €2.12, AC €3, Slip (10 ton), Grid, C (½ ton), R, Bar.
Services: ME, CH, ⚒, El, SM. D at FV hbr or by tanker ☎ 500874. Demey lock (VHF 10) is ent to Belgian, Dutch and French canals.
Town All amenities, ⇌, ✈. Frequent trams run between Knokke and De Panne.

16

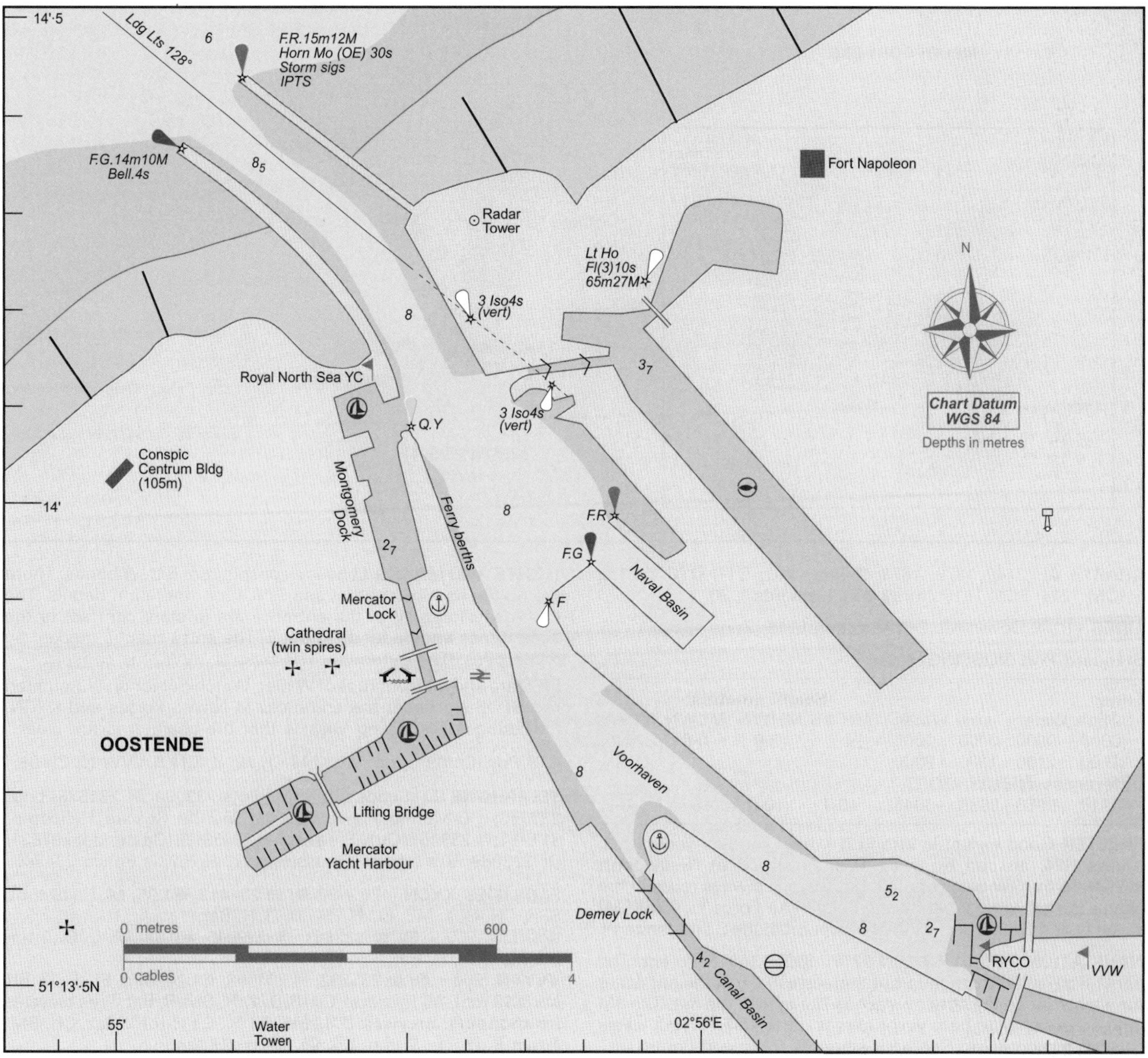
14'·5
Ldg Lts 128°
F.R.15m12M
Horn Mo (OE) 30s
Storm sigs
IPTS
F.G.14m10M
Bell.4s
Fort Napoleon
Radar
Tower
Lt Ho
Fl(3)10s
65m27M
N
3 Iso4s
(vert)
Royal North Sea YC
Q.Y
Chart Datum
WGS 84
Depths in metres
Conspic
Centrum Bldg
(105m)
14'
Montgomery
Dock
Ferry berths
F.R
F.G
Naval Basin
F
Mercator
Lock
Cathedral
(twin spires)
OOSTENDE
Voorhaven
Lifting Bridge
Mercator
Yacht Harbour
Demey Lock
RYCO
VVW
0 metres
600
0 cables
4
51°13'·5N
55'
Water
Tower
Canal Basin
02°56'E

9.16.34 NIEUWPOORT

Belgium, West Flanders **51°09'·43N 02°43'·13** ❁❁❁◊◊◊✿✿✿

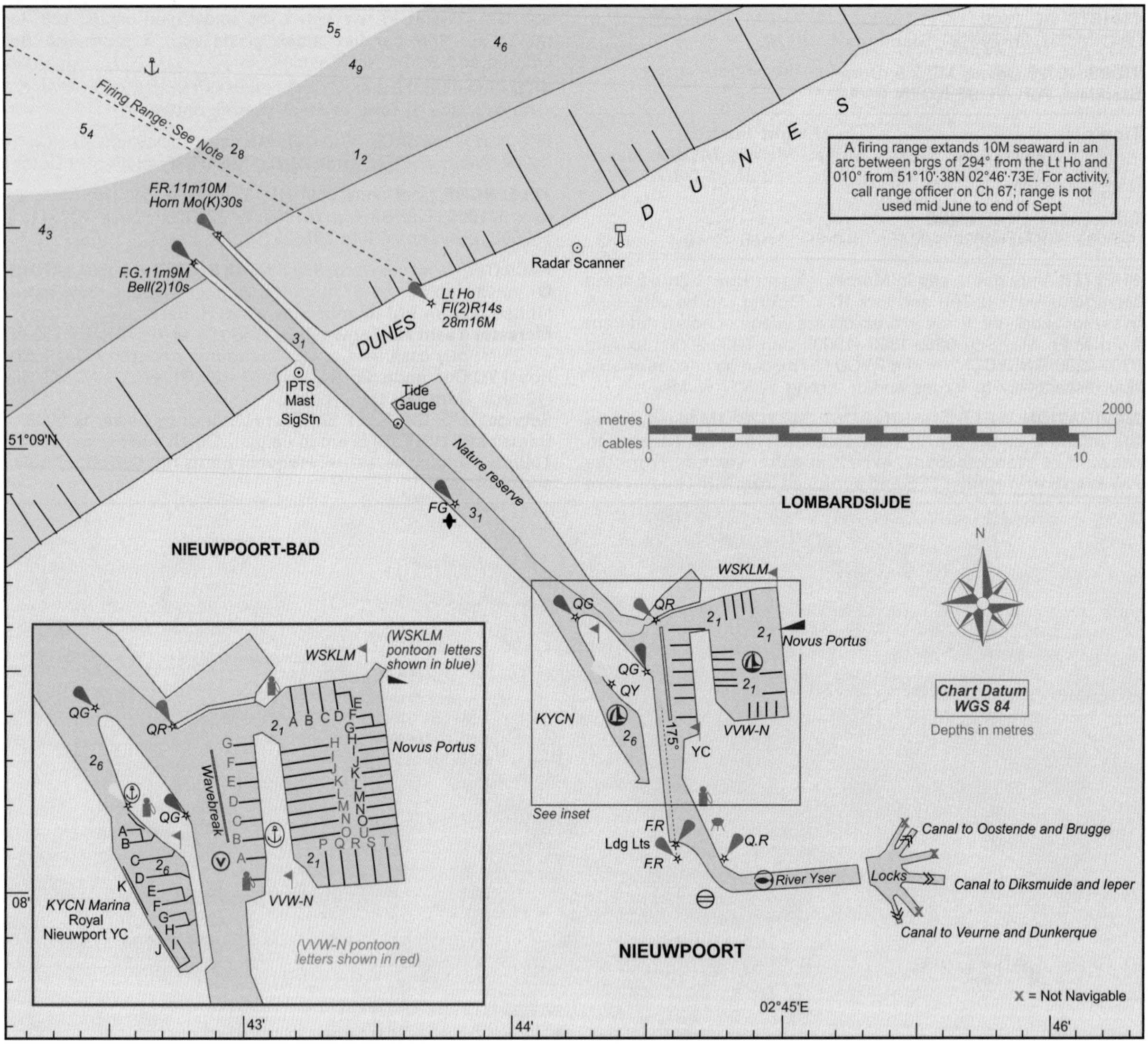
Firing Range: See Note
F.R.11m10M
Horn Mo(K)30s
F.G.11m9M
Bell(2)10s
Lt Ho
Fl(2)R14s
28m16M
Radar Scanner
DUNES
D U N E S
A firing range extends 10M seaward in an arc between brgs of 294° from the Lt Ho and 010° from 51°10'·38N 02°46'·73E. For activity, call range officer on Ch 67; range is not used mid June to end of Sept
IPTS
Mast
SigStn
Tide
Gauge
Nature reserve
metres
cables
0
2000
10
51°09'N
FG
LOMBARDSIJDE
NIEUWPOORT-BAD
WSKLM
QG
QR
Novus Portus
QY
KYCN
175°
YC
VVW-N
Chart Datum
WGS 84
Depths in metres
See inset
F.R
Ldg Lts
Q.R
River Yser
Locks
Canal to Oostende and Brugge
Canal to Diksmuide and Ieper
Canal to Veurne and Dunkerque
NIEUWPOORT
X = Not Navigable
02°45'E
43'
44'
46'
08'
(WSKLM pontoon letters shown in blue)
Wavebreak
KYCN Marina
Royal
Nieuwport YC
(VVW-N pontoon letters shown in red)

CHARTS AC *2449,* 1872, 1873; Belgian 101, D11; DYC 1801.2; SHOM 7214; ECM 1010; Imray C30; Stanfords 1, 20

TIDES +0105 Dover; ML 2·7; Duration 0515; Zone –0100

Standard Port VLISSINGEN (⟷)

Times				Height (metres)			
High Water		Low Water		MHWS	MHWN	MLWN	MLWS
0300	0900	0400	1000	4·7	3·8	0·8	0·2
1500	2100	1600	2200				
Differences NIEUWPOORT							
–0110	–0050	–0035	–0045	+0·7	+0·6	+0·5	+0·2

SHELTER Good except in strong NW'lies. The two yacht hbrs, access H24, are run by three YCs: Royal YC of Nieuwpoort (**KYCN**) to the SW gets very full; but there is always room in the Novus Portus which contains the Belgian Air Force YC (**WSKLM**) at the N and E side; and **VVW-N**ieuwpoort to the S and centre W.

NAVIGATION WPT 51°10'·08N 02°41'·89E, 134°/1M to ent. The bar (1·5m) is liable to silt up but there is usually sufficient water for yachts. At sp the stream reaches 2kn across the ent. The 1M long access chan to both yacht hbrs is dredged 3.1m, but levels can fall to about 2m. See notice boards for speed limits.

LIGHTS AND MARKS Lt ho is a conspic 28m R tr, W bands. There are no ldg lts. See chartlet and 9.16.4 for other light details. The high-rise blocks W of the entrance are in stark contrast to the sand dunes and flatlands to the E. The entry chan is marked by white piles. The pyramidal HM bldg at VVW-N is conspic.

IPTS are shown from root of W pier. Watch out for an illuminated red STOP sign near the entrances to Novus Portus and KYCN, indicating to departing vessels that the channel is not clear.

R/T Port Ch 09 (H24); WSKLM Ch 72; KYCN & VVW-N: Ch 08.

TELEPHONE (Dial code 058) HM/Pilots 233000, 🖷 231575; Lock 233050; CG/Marine Police 233045; Marine Rescue Helicopter 311714; ⊖ 233451; Duty Free Store 233433; Ⓗ (Oostende) 707631; Dr 233089; Brit Consul (Brussels) (02) 2876232; Police 234246.

FACILITIES KYCN (420 + 80 Ⓥ) ☎ 234413, €1.35, M, C (10 ton), Slip, CH, Gas, ME, El, ⚒, 🛒, D, ⊡, R, Bar.
WSKLM (500 + Ⓥ) ☎ 233641, 🖷 239845, €0.87, M, L, C (2 ton mobile), CH, R, Bar.
VVW-N (950 + Ⓥ) ☎ 235232, 🖷 234058, €1.24, Slip, El, Ⓔ, ⊡, BH (45 & 10 ton), AC (meters), CH, P, D, ⛽, ⚒, SM, R, Bar, Free bicycles for shopping. **Services**: D, L, ME, El, ⚒, C (15 ton), Gaz, CH, SM.
Town P, D, 🛒, R, Bar, ✉, Ⓑ, ⇌, ✈ (Ostend).

Area 17

North France
Dunkerque to Cap de la Hague

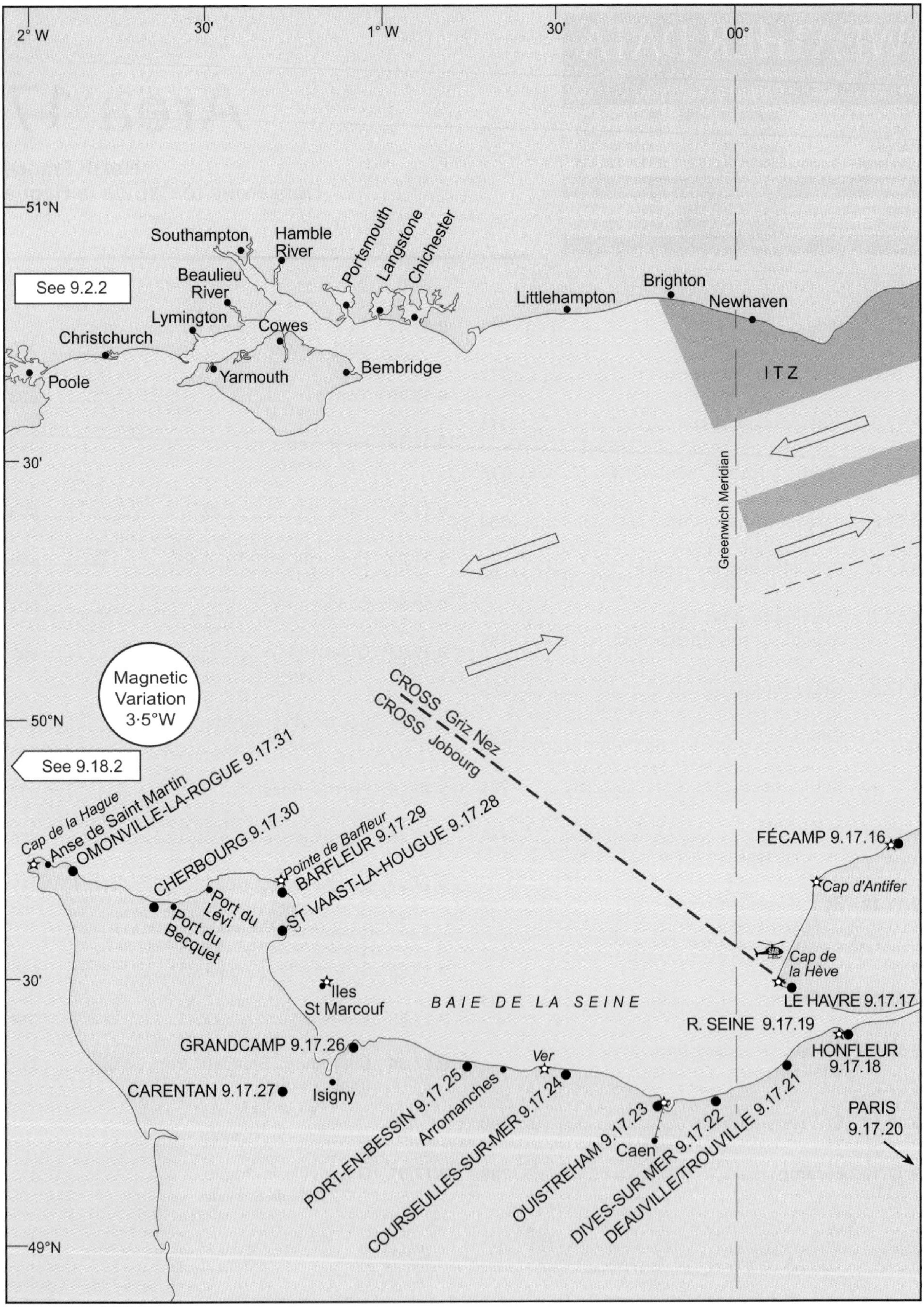
2° W
30'
1° W
30'
00°
51°N
30'
50°N
30'
49°N
See 9.2.2
Southampton
Hamble River
Portsmouth
Langstone
Chichester
Beaulieu River
Lymington
Christchurch
Poole
Cowes
Yarmouth
Bembridge
Littlehampton
Brighton
Newhaven
ITZ
Greenwich Meridian
Magnetic Variation 3·5°W
CROSS Griz Nez
CROSS Jobourg
See 9.18.2
Cap de la Hague
Anse de Saint Martin
OMONVILLE-LA-ROGUE 9.17.31
CHERBOURG 9.17.30
Pointe de Barfleur
BARFLEUR 9.17.29
ST VAAST-LA-HOUGUE 9.17.28
Port du Lévi
Port du Becquet
Iles St Marcouf
BAIE DE LA SEINE
GRANDCAMP 9.17.26
CARENTAN 9.17.27
Isigny
PORT-EN-BESSIN 9.17.25
Arromanches
Ver
COURSEULLES-SUR-MER 9.17.24
OUISTREHAM 9.17.23
Caen
DIVES-SUR MER 9.17.22
DEAUVILLE/TROUVILLE 9.17.21
FÉCAMP 9.17.16
Cap d'Antifer
Cap de la Hève
LE HAVRE 9.17.17
R. SEINE 9.17.19
HONFLEUR 9.17.18
PARIS 9.17.20

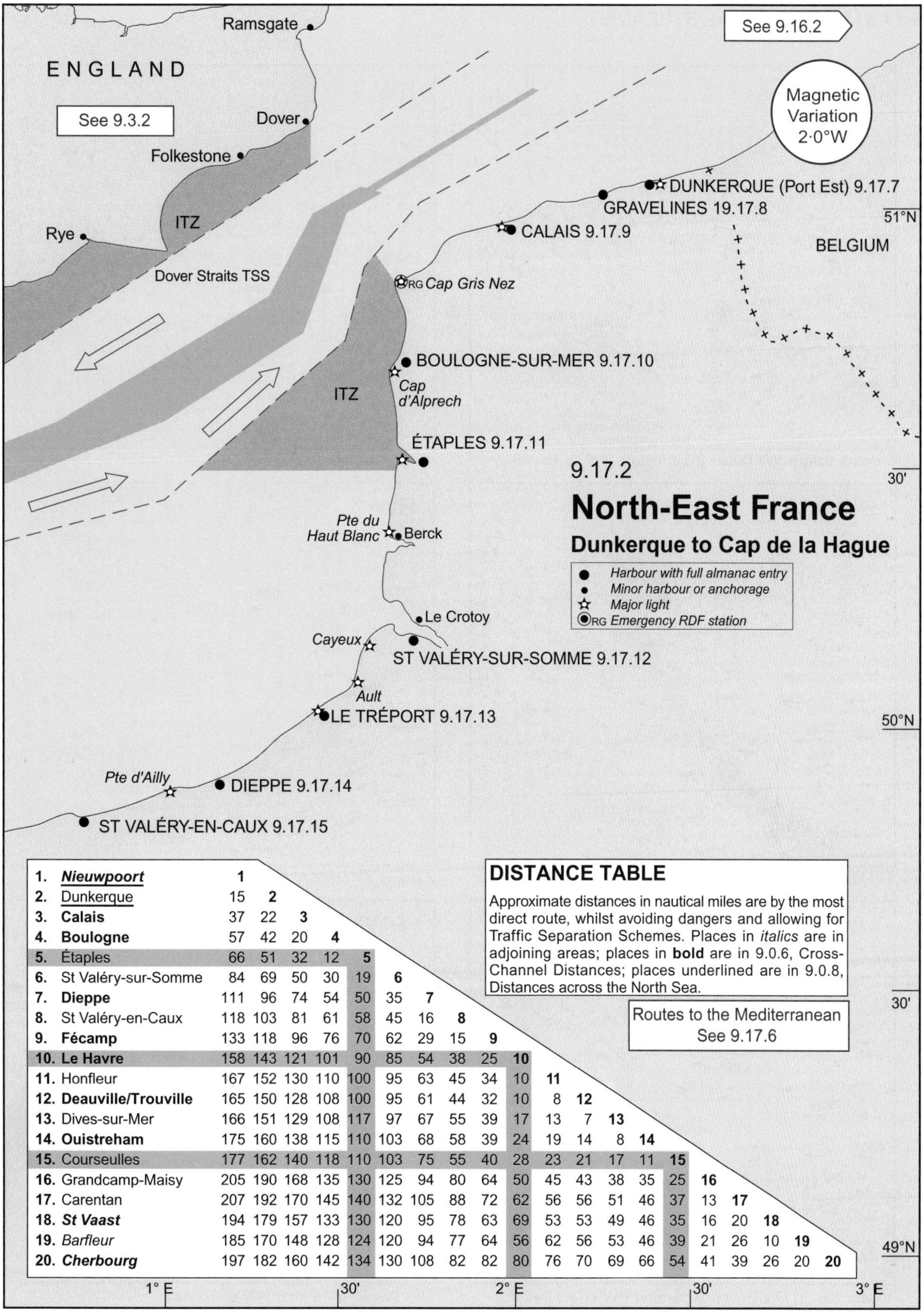

Ramsgate
ENGLAND
See 9.3.2
Dover
Folkestone
Rye
ITZ
Dover Straits TSS
ITZ
See 9.16.2
Magnetic Variation 2·0°W
DUNKERQUE (Port Est) 9.17.7
GRAVELINES 19.17.8
51°N
CALAIS 9.17.9
BELGIUM
RG Cap Gris Nez
BOULOGNE-SUR-MER 9.17.10
Cap d'Alprech
ÉTAPLES 9.17.11
30'
Pte du Haut Blanc
Berck
Le Crotoy
Cayeux
ST VALÉRY-SUR-SOMME 9.17.12
Ault
LE TRÉPORT 9.17.13
50°N
Pte d'Ailly
DIEPPE 9.17.14
ST VALÉRY-EN-CAUX 9.17.15
Harbour with full almanac entry
Minor harbour or anchorage
Major light
RG Emergency RDF station

9.17.2

North-East France

Dunkerque to Cap de la Hague

DISTANCE TABLE

Approximate distances in nautical miles are by the most direct route, whilst avoiding dangers and allowing for Traffic Separation Schemes. Places in *italics* are in adjoining areas; places in **bold** are in 9.0.6, Cross-Channel Distances; places underlined are in 9.0.8, Distances across the North Sea.

Routes to the Mediterranean See 9.17.6

1. ***Nieuwpoort***	**1**																			
2. Dunkerque	15	**2**																		
3. **Calais**	37	22	**3**																	
4. **Boulogne**	57	42	20	**4**																
5. Étaples	66	51	32	12	**5**															
6. St Valéry-sur-Somme	84	69	50	30	19	**6**														
7. **Dieppe**	111	96	74	54	50	35	**7**													
8. St Valéry-en-Caux	118	103	81	61	58	45	16	**8**												
9. **Fécamp**	133	118	96	76	70	62	29	15	**9**											
10. **Le Havre**	158	143	121	101	90	85	54	38	25	**10**										
11. Honfleur	167	152	130	110	100	95	63	45	34	10	**11**									
12. **Deauville/Trouville**	165	150	128	108	100	95	61	44	32	10	8	**12**								
13. Dives-sur-Mer	166	151	129	108	117	97	67	55	39	17	13	7	**13**							
14. **Ouistreham**	175	160	138	115	110	103	68	58	39	24	19	14	8	**14**						
15. Courseulles	177	162	140	118	110	103	75	55	40	28	23	21	17	11	**15**					
16. Grandcamp-Maisy	205	190	168	135	130	125	94	80	64	50	45	43	38	35	25	**16**				
17. Carentan	207	192	170	145	140	132	105	88	72	62	56	56	51	46	37	13	**17**			
18. ***St Vaast***	194	179	157	133	130	120	95	78	63	69	53	53	49	46	35	16	20	**18**		
19. *Barfleur*	185	170	148	128	124	120	94	77	64	56	62	56	53	46	39	21	26	10	**19**	
20. ***Cherbourg***	197	182	160	142	134	130	108	82	82	80	76	70	69	66	54	41	39	26	20	**20**

30'
49°N
1° E
30'
2° E
30'
3° E

9.17.3 AREA 17 TIDAL STREAMS

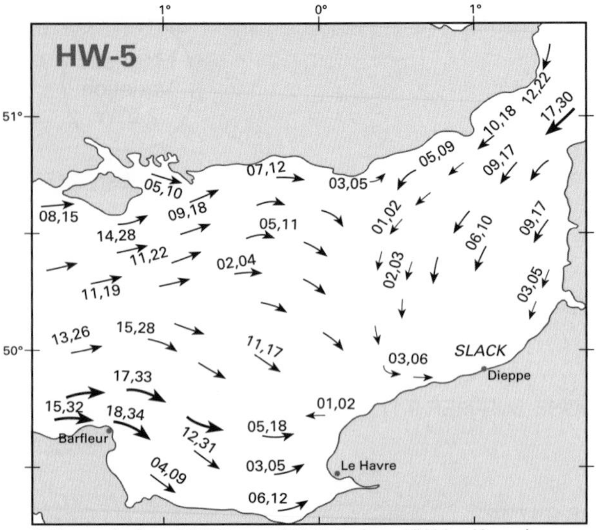
HW-5
1°
0°
1°
51°
50°
07,12
03,05
05,09
10,18
12,22
17,30
09,17
05,10
08,15
09,18
14,28
05,11
01,02
06,10
09,17
11,22
02,04
02,03
03,05
11,19
13,26
15,28
11,17
03,06
SLACK
Dieppe
17,33
15,32
18,34
01,02
05,18
12,31
Barfleur
04,09
03,05
Le Havre
06,12
5 Hours before HW Dover (0345 before HW Le Havre)

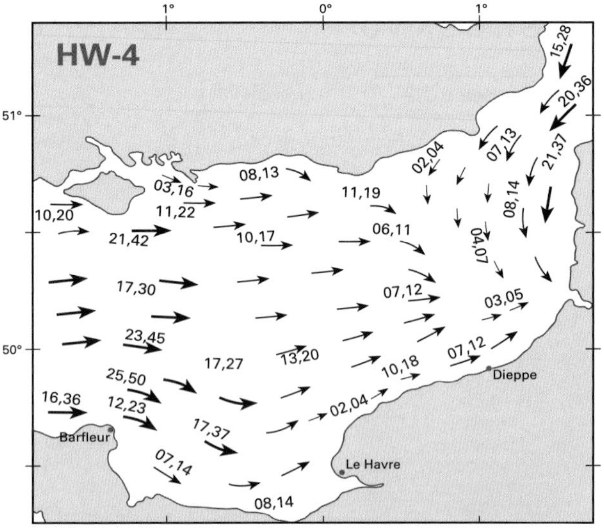
HW-4
1°
0°
1°
51°
50°
15,28
20,36
21,37
02,04
07,13
08,13
03,16
11,19
08,14
10,20
11,22
21,42
10,17
06,11
04,07
17,30
07,12
03,05
23,45
17,27
13,20
07,12
25,50
10,18
Dieppe
16,36
12,23
02,04
Barfleur
17,37
07,14
Le Havre
08,14
4 Hours before HW Dover (0245 before HW Le Havre)

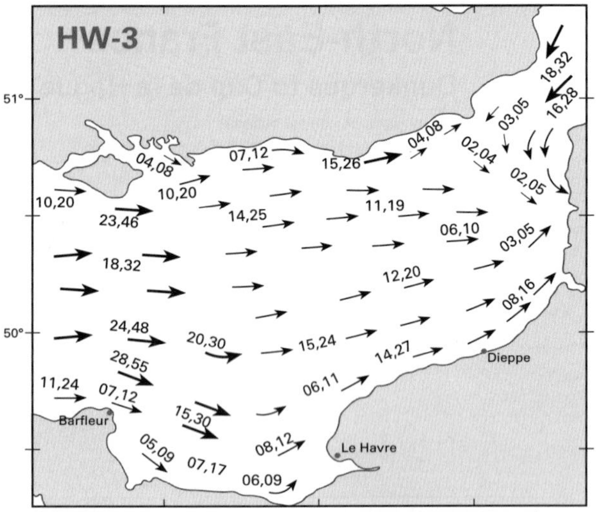
HW-3
1°
51°
50°
18,32
16,28
03,05
04,08
02,04
04,08
07,12
15,26
02,05
10,20
10,20
11,19
23,46
14,25
06,10
03,05
18,32
12,20
08,16
24,48
20,30
15,24
14,27
Dieppe
28,55
11,24
07,12
06,11
Barfleur
15,30
05,09
08,12
Le Havre
07,17
06,09
3 Hours before HW Dover (0145 before HW Le Havre)

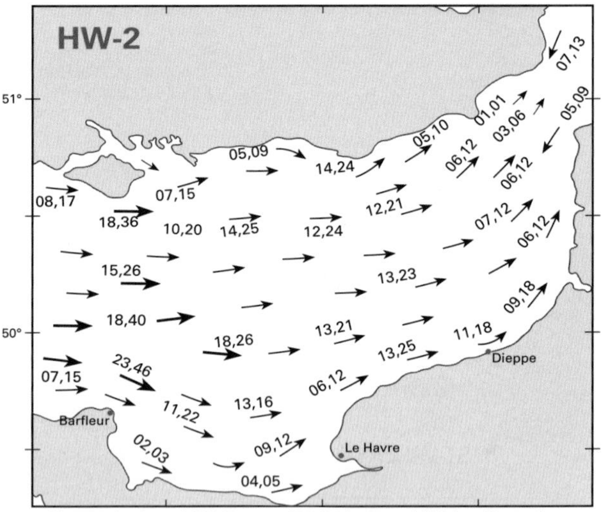
HW-2
1°
51°
50°
07,13
01,01
05,09
05,10
03,06
05,09
14,24
06,12
06,12
08,17
07,15
12,21
18,36
10,20
14,25
12,24
07,12
06,12
15,26
13,23
09,18
18,40
18,26
13,21
11,18
Dieppe
13,25
07,15
23,46
06,12
11,22
13,16
Barfleur
02,03
09,12
Le Havre
04,05
2 Hours before HW Dover (0045 before HW Le Havre)

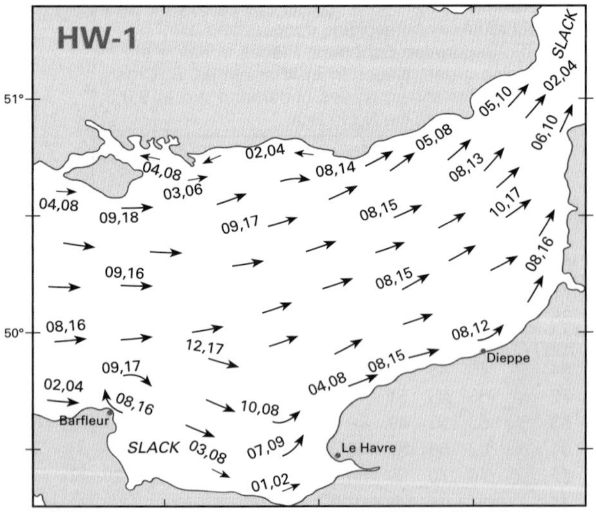
HW-1
1°
51°
50°
SLACK
02,04
05,10
06,10
02,04
05,08
04,08
08,14
08,13
03,06
04,08
09,18
09,17
08,15
10,17
09,16
08,15
08,16
08,16
08,12
12,17
Dieppe
09,17
08,15
02,04
04,08
08,16
10,08
Barfleur
SLACK
03,08
07,09
Le Havre
01,02
1 Hour before HW Dover (0015 after HW Le Havre)

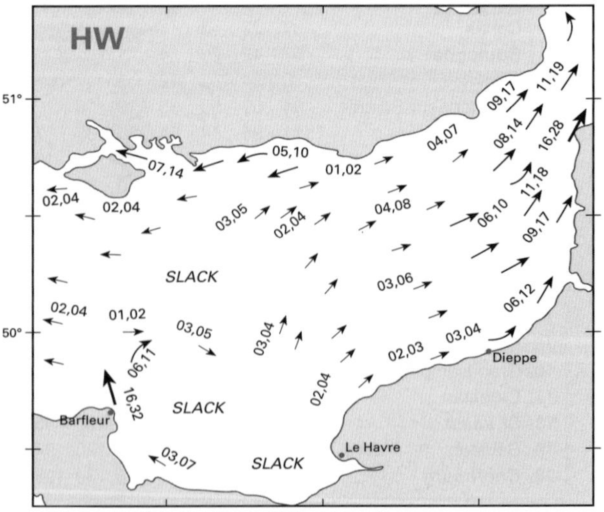
HW
51°
50°
11,19
09,17
04,07
08,14
16,28
05,10
07,14
01,02
11,18
02,04
02,04
03,05
02,04
04,08
06,10
09,17
SLACK
03,06
02,04
01,02
03,05
03,04
06,12
06,11
03,04
02,03
Dieppe
16,32
02,04
SLACK
Barfleur
03,07
SLACK
Le Havre
HW Dover (0115 after HW Le Havre)

Westward 9.18.3 Channel Is 9.19.3 Northward 9.2.3 North-eastward 9.3.3 Eastward 9.16.3

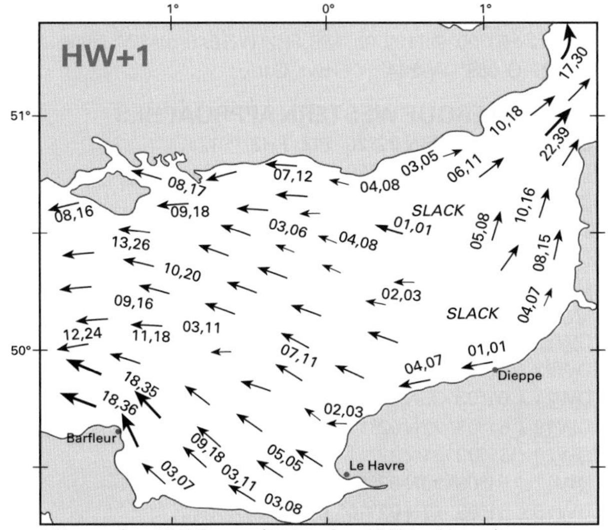
HW+1
1°
0°
1°
51°
50°
17,30
10,18
22,39
03,05
06,11
08,17
07,12
04,08
08,16
09,18
SLACK
01,01
10,16
05,08
03,06
04,08
13,26
08,15
10,20
02,03
09,16
SLACK
04,07
12,24
11,18
03,11
07,11
04,07
01,01
Dieppe
18,35
18,36
02,03
Barfleur
09,18
05,05
03,07
03,11
Le Havre
03,08
1 Hour after HW Dover (0215 after HW Le Havre)

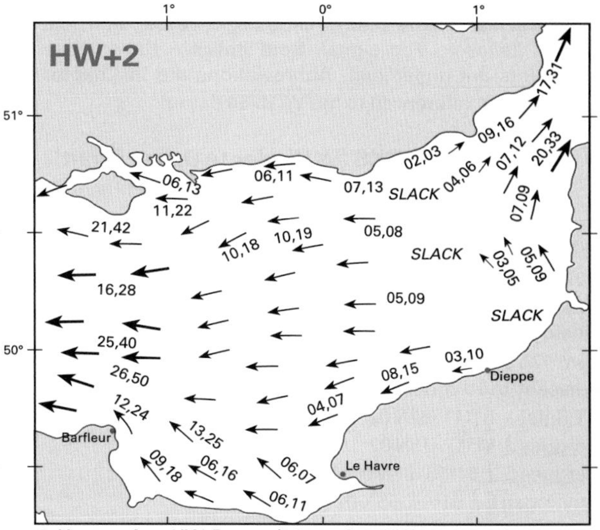
HW+2
1°
0°
1°
51°
50°
17,31
09,16
02,03
07,12
20,33
06,13
06,11
07,13
SLACK
04,06
11,22
07,09
21,42
05,08
10,18
10,19
SLACK
03,05
05,09
16,28
05,09
SLACK
25,40
03,10
26,50
08,15
Dieppe
04,07
12,24
Barfleur
13,25
09,18
06,16
06,07
Le Havre
06,11
2 Hours after HW Dover (0315 after HW Le Havre)

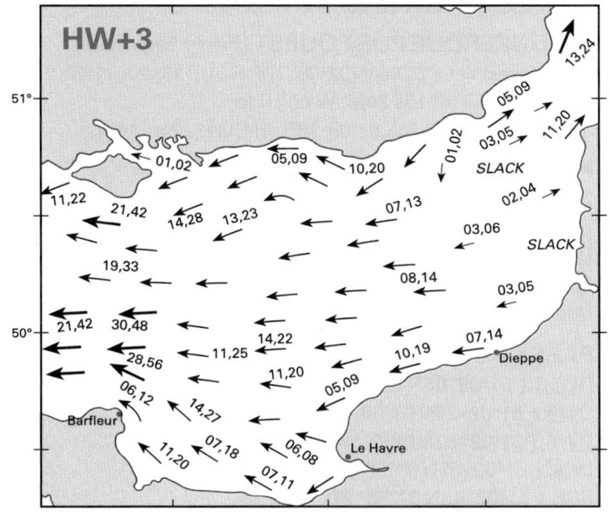
HW+3
1°
0°
1°
51°
50°
13,24
05,09
01,02
03,05
11,20
05,09
01,02
10,20
SLACK
11,22
02,04
07,13
21,42
14,28
13,23
03,06
SLACK
19,33
08,14
03,05
21,42
30,48
07,14
14,22
10,19
28,56
11,25
Dieppe
11,20
05,09
06,12
Barfleur
14,27
07,18
06,08
Le Havre
11,20
07,11
3 Hours after HW Dover (0415 after HW Le Havre)

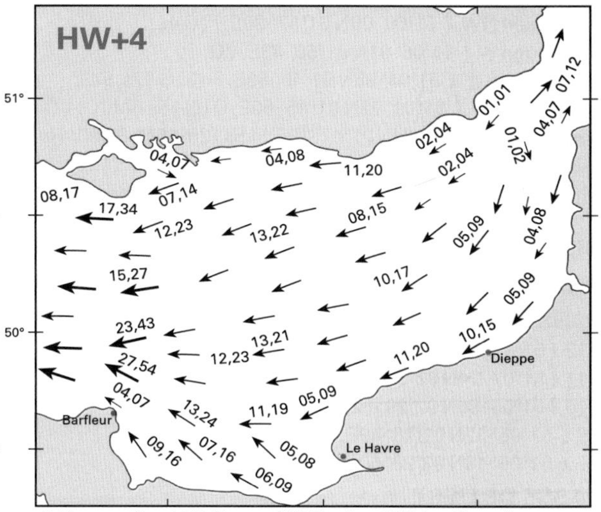
HW+4
1°
0°
1°
51°
50°
07,12
01,01
04,07
02,04
01,02
04,07
04,08
11,20
02,04
08,17
07,14
17,34
08,15
12,23
13,22
05,09
04,08
15,27
10,17
05,09
23,43
13,21
10,15
12,23
11,20
27,54
Dieppe
04,07
05,09
Barfleur
13,24
11,19
09,16
07,16
05,08
Le Havre
06,09
4 Hours after HW Dover (0515 after HW Le Havre)

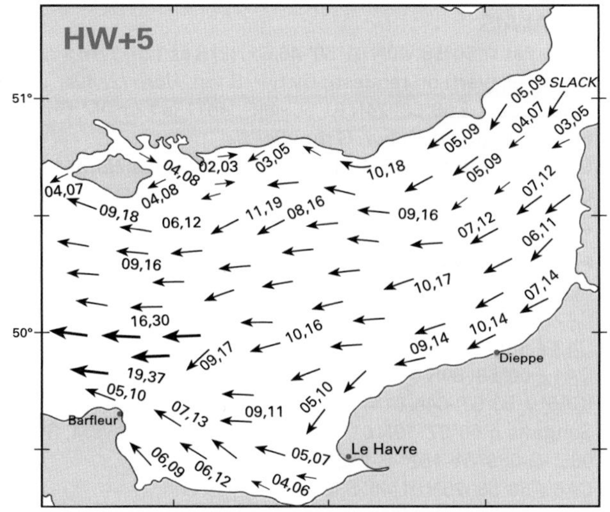
HW+5
1°
0°
1°
51°
50°
05,09
SLACK
05,09
04,07
03,05
02,03
03,05
04,08
10,18
05,09
04,07
04,08
07,12
09,18
11,19
08,16
06,12
09,16
07,12
06,11
09,16
10,17
07,14
16,30
10,16
10,14
09,17
09,14
19,37
Dieppe
05,10
05,10
07,13
09,11
Barfleur
06,09
06,12
05,07
Le Havre
04,06
5 Hours after HW Dover (0615 after HW Le Havre)

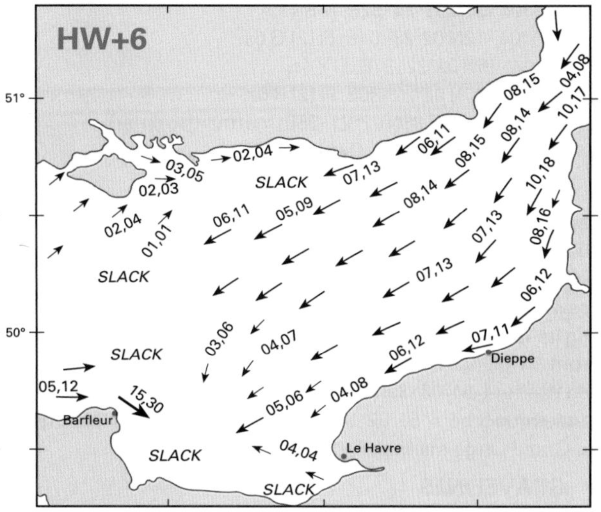
HW+6
1°
0°
1°
51°
50°
04,08
08,15
10,17
02,04
06,11
08,14
03,05
07,13
08,15
SLACK
02,03
10,18
06,11
05,09
08,14
02,04
01,01
07,13
08,16
SLACK
07,13
06,12
SLACK
03,06
04,07
07,11
06,12
05,12
Dieppe
15,30
05,06
04,08
Barfleur
SLACK
04,04
Le Havre
SLACK
6 Hours after HW Dover (0510 before HW Le Havre)

PLOT WAYPOINTS ON YOUR CHART BEFORE USING THEM

9.17.4 LIGHTS, BUOYS AND WAYPOINTS

Blue print = light with a nominal range of 15M or more. CAPITALS = place or feature. *CAPITAL ITALICS* = light-vessel, light float or Lanby. *Italics* = Fog signal. ***Bold italics*** = Racon. Useful waypoints are underlined. Abbreviations are in Chapter 1. Positions are referenced to the WGS 84 datum.

▶ OFFSHORE MARKS (W Hinder to Dover Strait)

Tricolor Wreck 51°21'·61N 02°12'·20E, VQ (6) + L Fl 10s. 4 other N, S, E and W cardinal lt buoys mark the wreck.
WH Zuid 51°22'·78N 02°26'·25E, Q (6) + L Fl 15s.
Bergues N 51°19'·92N 02°24'·50E, Q.
Oost-Dyck W 51°17'·15N 02°26'·32E, Q (9) 15s.
Oostdyck radar twr, 51°16'·49N 02°26'·83E; four ☆ Mo (U) 15s 15m 12M; *Horn Mo (U) 30s;* **Racon O**. R twr, 3 W bands, with adjacent red twr/helipad.
BT Ratel 51°11'·62N 02°27'·92E, Fl (4) R 15s.
Bergues 51°17'·15N 02°18'·62E, Fl G 4s.
Bergues S 51°15'·07N 02°19'·42E, Q (6) + L Fl 15s.
Ruytingen E 51°14'·55N 02°17'·92E, VQ.
Ruytingen N 51°13'·10N 02°10'·28E, VQ.
Ruytingen SE 51°09'·20N 02°08'·92E, VQ (3) 15s.
Ruytingen NW 51°09'·08N 01°57'·29E, Fl G 4s.
Ruytingen W 51°06'·91N 01°50'·43E, VQ.
Ruytingen SW 51°04'·98N 01°46'·83E, Fl (3) G 12s; *Bell.*
Sandettié SW 51°09'·72N 01°45'·60E, Q (9) 15s 5M.
Sandettié 51°09'·34N 01°47'·10E, Fl 5s 12m **15M**; R hull; *Horn 30s;* ***Racon T, 10M.***
MPC 51°06'·11N 01°38'·21E, Fl Y 2·5s 10m 4M; **Racon O, 10M.**

DUNKERQUE TO BOULOGNE

▶ DUNKERQUE EASTERN APPROACHES

PASSE DE ZUYDCOOTE

E12 51°07'·90N 02°30'·59E, VQ (6) + L Fl 10s.
E11 51°07'·24N 02°30'·61E, Fl G 4s.
E10 51°05'·90N 02°29'·62E, Fl (2) R 6s.
E8 51°05'·37N 02°28'·49E, Fl (3) R 12s.
E7 51°05'·18N 02°28'·50E, Fl (3) G 12s.

PASSE DE L'EST

E6 51°04'·86N 02°27'·08E, QR.
E4 51°04'·58N 02°24'·52E, Fl R 4s.
E1 51°04'·12N 02°23'·04E, Fl (2) G 6s.
E 51°04'·45N 02°22'·37E, Fl Y 4s.
E2 51°04'·35N 02°22'·30E, Fl (2) R 6s.
Unnamed 51°04'·38N 02°21'·35E; mermaid topmark.
51°04'·28N 02°21'·71E, Q (6) + L Fl 15s.

▶ DUNKERQUE PORT EST

Jetée Est ☆ 51°03'·59N 02°21'·20E, Fl (2) R 10s 12m **16M**; Fl (2) 10s in fog; R □ on W pylon, R top.
Jetée Ouest ☆ 51°03'·63N 02°20'·95E, Fl (2) G 6s 35m 11M; W twr, brown top.
Ldg lts 137·5°, both Oc (2) 6s 7/10m 12M; synch; W cols, R tops. Front, 51°03'·03N 02°22'·14E. Rear, 114m from front.
Old W jetty 51°03'·39N 02°21'·53E, Q 11m 9M.
Dunkerque lt ho ☆ 51°02'·93N 02°21'·86E (450m NW of Port du Grand Large marina), Fl (2) 10s 59m **26M**.

▶ GRAVELINES

51°01'·52N 02°06'·73E, Fl (5) Y 20s.
51°01'·37N 02°06'·71E, Fl (5) Y 20s.
Off E jetty head, 51°00'·99N 02°05'·59E, VQ 6m 4M.
E jetty ☆ 51°00'·93N 02°05'·62E, Fl (3) R 12s 5m 6M.
W jetty ☆ 51°00'·94N 02°05'·48E, Fl (2) WG 6s 9m W8M, G6M; 317°-W-327-G-085°-W-244°; Y ○ twr, G top.

▶ DUNKERQUE WESTERN APPROACHES

DW29 51°03'·85N 02°20'·21E, Fl (3) G 12s.
DW30 51°04'·14N 02°20'·15E, Fl (3) R 12s.
DW27 51°03'·72N 02°18'·50E, Fl (2) G 6s.
DW28 51°04'·02N 02°18'·29E, Fl (2) R 6s.
DW25 51°03'·58N 02°16'·72E, Fl G 4s.
DW26 51°03'·91N 02°16'·73E, Fl R 4s.
DW24 51°03'·83N 02°15'·14E, QR; *Whis.*
DW23 51°03'·54N 02°15'·17E, QG; *Bell.*
DW22 51°03'·77N 02°13'·54E, Fl (2) R6s.
DW21 51°03'·35N 02°13'·54E, Fl (2) G 6s.
DW19 51°03'·22N 02°11'·97E, Fl G 4s.
DW20 51°03'·61N 02°11'·97E, Fl R 4s.
DW17 51°03'·10N 02°10'·37E, Fl (3) G 12s.
DW18 51°03'·47N 02°10'·37E, Fl (3) R 12s.
DKB 51°02'·95N 02°09'·25E, VQ (9) 10s.
DW16 51°03'·30N 02°08'·97E, Fl (2) R 6s.

▶ DUNKERQUE PORT OUEST (Ferry terminal)

Jetée Ouest ☆ 51°02'·64N 02°09'·77E, Fl (4) R 15s 24m **16M**; 278°-243°; in fog Fl (4) 15s **20M**; W col, R top.
Jetée Est ☆ 51°02'·26N 02°09'·78E, Fl (4) G 15s 24m **16M**.

▶ Minor channel (N of Dyck banks)

DY3 51°11'·45N 02°22'·42E, Q.
DY2 51°09'·45N 02°19'·41E, Fl (2) R 6s.
DY1 51°08'·96N 02°14'·92E, Fl G 4s.
Dyck E 51°05'·65N 02°05'·62E, Q (3) 10s.
Haut-fond de Gravelines 51°04'·05N 02°05'·02E, VQ (9) 10s.

PASSE DE L'OUEST continued

DW13 51°03'·06N 02°07'·11E, QGs.
DW5 51°02'·20N 02°00'·94E, QG.
DW6 51°02'·62N 02°01'·01E, VQ R.
DKA 51°02'·55N 01°56'·95E, L Fl 10s.
RCE 51°02'·43N 01°53'·21E, Iso G 4s.
Dyck 51°02'·99N 01°51'·78E, Fl 3s; **Racon B.**

▶ CALAIS

Jetée Est ☆ 50°58'·40N 01°50'·46,E Fl (2) R 6s 12m **17M**; (in fog 2 Fl (2) 6s (vert) on request); Gy twr, R top; *Horn (2) 40s.*
Jetée Ouest ☆ 50°58'·24N 01°50'·40E, Iso G 3s 12m 9M; (in fog Fl 5s on request); W twr, G top; *Bell 5s.*
Quai de Marée ☆ 50°58'·04N 01°50'·82E, L Fl (4) 30s; *Horn (4) 30s.*
Calais ☆ 50°57'·68N 01°51'·21E (500m E of marina), Fl (4) 15s 59m **22M**; 073°-260°; W 8-sided twr, B top.

▶ CALAIS ACCESS CHANNEL (From the W)

RCW 51°01'·23N 01°45'·35E, VQ.
CA2 51°00'·87N 01°48'·67E, Q.
CA3 50°56'·82N 01°41'·12E, Fl G 4s; *Whis.*
CA4 50°58'·89N 01°45'·10E, VQ (9) 10s 8m 8M; *Whis.*
(CA5) 50°57'·64N 01°46'·13E (0·5M NNE of Sangatte), QG.
Sangatte ☆ 50°57'·19N 01°46'·47E, Oc WG 4s 13m W8M, G5M; 065°-G-089°-W-152°-G-245°; W pylon, B top.
CA6 50°58'·25N 01°45'·63E, VQ R.
CA8 50°58'·38N 01°48'·65E, QR; *Bell.*

CA10 50°58'·63N 01°49'·92E, Fl (2) R 6s.

Abbeville wreck 50°56'·06N 01°37'·57E, VQ (9) 10s.

Cap Gris-Nez ☆ 50°52'·09N 01°34'·94E, Fl 5s 72m **29M**; 005°-232°; W twr, B top; *Horn 60s.*

▶ DOVER STRAIT TSS, SE Side

Colbart N 50°57'·45N 01°23'·29E, Q.
ZC2 50°53'·53N 01°30'·88E, Fl (2+1) Y 15s.
Colbart SW 50°48'·85N 01°16'·29E, VQ (6) + L Fl 10s 8m, *Whis.*
ZC1 50°44'·99N 01°27'·21E, Fl (4) Y 15s.
Ridens SE 50°43'·47N 01°18'·87E, VQ (3) 5s.
Vergoyer N 50°39'·64N 01°22'·18E, VQ; **Racon C, 5-8M.**
Vergoyer NW 50°37'·13N 01°17'·85E, Fl (2) G 6s.
Vergoyer E 50°35'·74N 01°19'·65E, VQ (3) 5s.
Vergoyer W 50°34'·63N 01°13'·54E, Fl G 4s.
Bassurelle 50°32'·74N 00°57'·69E, Fl (4) R 15s 6M; *Whis;* **Racon B, 5-8m.**
Vergoyer SW 50°26'·98N 01°00'·00E, VQ (9) 10s.

BOULOGNE TO DIEPPE

▶ BOULOGNE

Bassure de Baas 50°48'·53N 01°33'·03E, VQ; *Bell.*
Boulogne Approaches 50°45'·31N 01°31'·07E, VQ (6) + L Fl 10s 8m 6M; *Whis.*
Ophélie 50°43'·85N 01°30'·84E, Fl G 4s.
Digue Nord ☆ 50°44'·71N 01°34'·18E, Fl (2) R 6s 10m 7M.
Digue Carnot (S) ☆ 50°44'·44N 01°34'·05E, Fl (2+1) 15s 25m **19M**; W twr, G top; *Horn (2+1) 60s.*
Clearing brg 123°: Front, 50°43'·71N 01°35'·66E, FG in a neon ▽ 4m 5M. Rear, 560m from front, FR 44m 11M; intens 113°-133°.
Inner NE jetée ☆ 50°43'·65N 01°34'·66E, FR 11m 7M.
Inner SW jetée ☆ 50°43'·90N 01°35'·11E, FG 17m 5M; W col, G top; *Horn 30s.*
RC1 50°43'·93N 01°34'·43E, Fl G 4s.
RC2 50°43'·89N 01°34'·73E, Fl (2) R 6s.
Commercial basin, Jetée W ☆ 50°43'·67N 01°34'·50E, Iso G 4s 8m 5M. E side ☆ 50°43'·65N 01°34'·66E, Oc (2) R 6s 8m 6M.
Cap d'Alprech ☆ 50°41'·90N 01°33'·75E, Fl (3) 15s 62m **23M**; W twr, B top.

▶ LETOUQUET/ÉTAPLES

Pointe de Lornel 50°33'·24N 01°35'·12E, VQ (9) 10s 6m 3M.
Mérida wreck 50°32'·85N 01°33'·44E.
Camiers lt ho ☆ 50°32'·86N 01°36'·28E, Oc (2) WRG 6s 17m W10M, R/G7M; 015°-G-090°-W-105°-R-141°; R pylon.
Canche No. 2 50°32'·48N 01°33'·72E, Fl (2) R 6s.
Canche No. 1 50°32'·45N 01°33'·92E.
Canche Est groyne 50°32'·57N 01°35'·66E, Fl R 4s 8m.
Le Touquet ☆ 50°31'·43N 01°35'·49E, Fl (2) 10s 54m **25M**; Or twr, brown band, W&G top.
50°31'·95N 01°32'·92E.
Pointe du Haut-Blanc ☆ 50°23'·89N 01°33'·62E, Fl 5s 44m **23M**; W twr, R bands, G top.
FM 50°20'·43N 01°31'·07E.

▶ BAIE DE LA SOMME

ATSO 50°14'·00N 01°28'·06E, Mo (A) 12s.
S1 50°14'·75N 01°28'·54E (liable to be moved), QG.
Pte du Hourdel ☆ 50°12'·90N 01°33'·96E, Oc (3) WG 12s 19m, W12M, G9M; 053°-W-248°-G-323°; W twr, G top; tidal sigs; *Horn (3) 30s.*
BIFurcation buoy, very approx 50°13'N 01°35'E; often moved.

Cayeux-sur-Mer ☆ 50°11'·65N 01°30'·67E, Fl R 5s 32m **22M**; W twr, R top.

▶ LE CROTOY

☆ 50°12'·91N 01°37'·40E, Oc (2) R 6s 19m 8M; 285°-135°; W pylon.
Marina ent ☆ Fl R and Fl G, 2s 4m 2M; 50°12'·98N 01°38'·20E.

▶ ST VALÉRY-SUR-SOMME

Training wall head, 50°12'·25N 01°35'·85E, Q 2m 1M.
Training wall, 3 SHM bns: Fl (2) G 6s, Fl (3) G 12s, Fl (4) G 15s.
Embankment head ☆ 50°12'·25N 01°36'·02E, Iso G 4s 9m 9M; 347°-222°; W pylon, G top.
La Ferté môle ☆ 50°11'·18N 01°38'·14E (ent to marina), Fl R 4s 9m 9M; 000°-250°; W pylon, R top.

▶ LE TRÉPORT

Ault ☆ 50°06'·28N 01°27'·23E, Oc (3) WR 12s 95m **W15M**, R11M; 040°-W-175°-R-220°; W twr, R top.

Jetée Ouest ☆ 50°03'·87N 01°22'·13E, Fl (2) G 10s 15m **20M**; W twr, G top.
Jetée Est ☆ 50°03'·86N 01°22'·21E, Oc R 4s 8m 6M; W col, R top.

Penly power station (No entry):
No. 2 49°59'·45N 01°12'·02E, Fl Y 4s.
No. 1 49°59'·03N 01°11'·38E, Fl (3) Y 12s.
Jetée W, ☆ 49°58'·77N 01°12'·22E, Fl (4) Y 15s.

▶ DIEPPE

Berneval wreck 50°03'·41N 01°06'·53E.
Daffodils wreck 50°02'·46N 01°04'·01E, VQ (9) 10s.
Jetée Est ☆ 49°56'·16N 01°05'·06E, Iso R 4s 12m 8M; R col.
Jetée Ouest ☆ 49°56'·27N 01°04'·95E, Iso G 4s 11m 8M, W twr, G top; *Horn 30s.*
Falaise du Pollet ☆ 49°55'·92N 01°05'·30E, Q 35m 11M; 105·5°-170·5°; R & W structure.
Quai de la Marne 49°55'·93N 01°05'·30E, QR 12m 3M.
DI 49°57'·05N 01°01'·25E, VQ (3) 5s; *Bell.*
Roches d'Ailly 49°56'·58N 00°56'·72E, VQ; *Whis.*
Pointe d'Ailly ☆ 49°54'·96N 00°57'·49E, Fl (3) 20s 95m **31M**; W □ twr, G top; *Horn (3) 60s.*

DIEPPETO LE HAVRE

▶ SAINTVALÉRY-EN-CAUX

Jetée Est ☆ 49°52'·32N 00°42'·67E, Fl (2) R 6s 8m 4M; W mast.
Jetée Ouest ☆ 49°52'·41N 00°42'·50E, Fl (2) G 6s 13m 14M; W twr, G top.
Paluel 49°52'·22N 00°38'·00E, Q.

▶ FÉCAMP

Jetée Nord ☆ 49°45'·93N 00°21'·78E, Fl (2) 10s 15m **16M**; Gy twr, R top; *Horn (2) 30s.* Root ☆, QR 10m 4M.
Jetée Sud ☆ 49°45'·88N 00°21'·80E, QG 14m 9M; obscd by cliff on brgs more than 217°; Gy twr, G top.

Yport, ldg lts 166°, both Oc 4s 11/14m: Front, 49°44'·36N 00°18'·62E, W mast, G top. Rear, 30m from front, W pylon, G top on house.

Cap d'Antifer ☆ 49°41'·01N 00°09'·90E, Fl 20s 128m **29M**; 021°-222°; Gy 8-sided twr, G top, on 90m cliffs.

▶ PORT D'ANTIFER

A5 49°45'·83N 00°17'·40W, VQ (9) 10s; **Racon K.**
A14 49°43'·79N 00°02'·96W, QR.
A16 49°42'·97N 00°00'·50W, QR.

PLOT WAYPOINTS ON YOUR CHART BEFORE USING THEM

A17 49°41'·52N 00°01·74E, Iso G 4s.
A18 49°42'·02N 00°02'·17E, QR. Yachts cross the access chan.
DA 49°40'·97N 00°01'·71E, Fl (2) 6s.
Ldg lts 127·5°, both Dir Oc 4s 113/135m **22M**; 127°-128°; by day F **33M** 126·5°-128·5° occas. **Front** ☆, 49°38'·32N 00°09'·11E; **rear**, 430m from front.
Port ☆ 49°39'·51N 00°09'·18E. Dir Oc WRG 4s 24m **W15M**, R/G13M; 068·5°-G-078·3°-W-088·3°-R-098·3°; W pylon, B top.

▶ APPROACHES TO LE HAVRE

Cap de la Hève ☆ 49°30'·74N 00°04'·15E, Fl 5s 123m **24M**; 225°-196°; W 8-sided twr, R top.
LHA Lanby 49°31'·38N 00°09'·88W, Mo (A) 12s 10m 9M; R&W; **Racon, 8-10M (a series of 8 dots, or 8 groups of dots; separation between each dot or group represents 0.3M).**
Ldg lts 106·8°, both Dir F 36/78m **25M** (H24); intens 106°-108°; Gy twrs, G tops. Front, 49°28'·91N 00°06'·49E; rear, 0·73M from front.
LH3 49°30'·84N 00°04'·03W, QG.
LH4 49°31'·10N 00°03'·90W, QR.
LH5 49°30'·55N 00°02'·34W, Fl G 4s.
LH6 49°30'·78N 00°02'·37W, QR.
LH7 49°30'·25N 00°00'·82W, Iso G 4s.
LH8 49°30'·43N 00°00'·67W, Iso R 4s.
LH10 49°30'·17N 00°00'·80W, QR.
Note the W-E longitude change.
LH11 49°29'·63N 00°02'·25E, VQ (9) 10s.
LH12 49°29'·85N 00°02'·33E, VQ R.
LH13 49°29'·43N 00°03'·30E, Fl G 4s.
LH14 49°29'·65N 00°03'·43E QR.
LH15 49°29'·23N 00°04'·32E, Iso G 4s.
LH16 49°29'·44N 00°04'·43E, VQ R.

Ldg lts 090°, occas; both Dir FR 21/43m **19M**; intens 088·7°-091·2°. **Front**, 49°29'·52N 00°05'·79E; **Rear**, 680m from front.

▶ LE HAVRE

Digue Nord ☆ 49°29'·19N 00°05'·44E, Fl R 5s 15m **21M**; W ○ twr, R top; *Horn 15s*.
Digue Sud 49°29'·05N 00°05'·38E, VQ (3) G 2s 15m 11M; W twr, G top.
Elbow 49°28'·97N 00°05'·40E, QG; 262°-280° (within hbr).
Marina, W bkwtr 49°29'·21N 00°05'·53E, Fl (2) R 6s 3M.
Marina, E bkwtr 49°29'·26N 00°05'·56E, Fl (2) G 6s.

THE SEINE ESTUARY UP TO HONFLEUR

▶ WAITING AREAS

RNA (RoueN Atterrissage) 49°28'·64N 00°05'·55W, Iso 4s.
HP 49°29'·56N 00°03'·83W, Fl Y 4s.
RP 49°28'·61N 00°01'·19W, Fl (2) 6s; marks a wreck.
Nord du Mouillage 49°28'·59N 00°01'·27E, Fl (4) Y 15s.
49°29'·05N 00°01'·51E, Fl Y 2·5s.

▶ CHENAL DE ROUEN

Rade de la Carosse 49°27'·70N 00°01'·18E, Q (9) 15s.
S Carosse 49°27'·17N 00°02'·80E, Q.
Duncan L. Clinch 49°27'·17N 00°02'·50E, VQ (9) 10s.
No. 4 49°26'·97N 00°02'·60E, QR. Yachts keep N side of chan.
Ratier NW 49°26'·82N 00°02'·50E, VQ G.
No. 5 49°26'·50N 00°03'·59E, Fl (2) G 6s.
No. 6 49°26'·64N 00°03'·69E, VQ R.
No. 7 49°26'·18N 00°04'·74E, QG.
Amfard SW 49°26'·30N 00°04'·82E, QR.
No. 9 49°25'·97N 00°06'·30E, QG.
No. 10 49°26'·10N 00°06'·39E, QR.
Digue du Ratier 49°25'·97N 00°06'·58E, VQ 10m 4M.
No. 11 49°25'·92N 00°07'·75E, QG.
No. 12 49°26'·04N 00°07'·75E, QR.
No. 13 49°25'·92N 00°07'·75E, QG.
No. 14 49°25'·87N 00°09'·15E, QR.
No. 15 49°25'·92N 00°10'·56E, VQ G.
No. 16 49°25'·83N 00°10'·57E, VQ (6) + L Fl 10s.
No. 17 49°25'·79N 00°11'·96E, QG.
No. 18 49°25'·90N 00°11'·98E, QR.
St Simeon 49°25'·72N 00°12'·71E, VQ (9) 10s 8m 7M.
Falaise des Fonds ☆ 49°25'·47N 00°12'·86E. Fl (3) WRG 12s 15m, **W17M**, R/G13M; G040°-080°, R080°-084°, G084°-100°, W100°-109°, R109°-162°, G162°-260°; W twr, G top.
No. 19 49°25'·73N 00°13'·51E, QG.
No. 20 49°25'·85N 00°13'·51E, QR. (Cross here to Honfleur)

▶ HONFLEUR

Digue Ouest 49°25'·68N 00°13'·81E, QG 10m 6M.
Digue Est 49°25'·68N 00°13'·93E, Q 9m 8M; *Horn (5) 40s.*
Inner E jetty, Oc (2) R 6s 12m 6M; W twr, R top.
Avant Port, F Vi 16m 1M; white pylon, black bands.

TROUVILLE TO COURSEULLES

▶ DEAUVILLE/TROUVILLE

Ratelets 49°25'·29N 00°01'·71E, Q (9) 15s.
Ratier S 49°25'·15N 00°07'·12E, VQ (6) + L Fl 10s.

Roches Noires 49°22'·76N 00°04'·89E.
Ldg lts 148°, both Oc R 4s 11/17m 12M: Front, Pointe de la Cahotte, 49°22'·03N 00°04'·48E; 330°-150°; W twr, R top; *Horn (2) 30s*, HW ±3. Rear, E jetty 49°22'·03N 00°04'·48E, 217m from front; synch; 120°-170°; W pylon, R top.
E jetty 49°22'·22N 00°04'·33E. Fl (4) WR 12s 8m W7M, R4M, 131°-W-175°-R-131°; W pylon, R top.
W jetty 49°22'·37N 00°04'·10E. Fl WG 4s 10m W9M, G6M; 005°-W-176°-G-005°; B pylon, G top.
Bkwtr W side 49°22'·11N 00°04'·33E, Iso G 4s 9m 5M.
West estacade 49°22'·03N 00°04'·43E, QG 11m 9M.
Trouville SW 49°22'·54N 00°02'·56E, VQ (9) 10s.
Semoy 49°24'·14N 00°02'·35E, VQ (3) 5s.

▶ DIVES-SUR-MER

Note the E-W longitude change. Beacons 3 & 5, if damaged by storm s, may temporarily be replaced by buoys.
DI 49°19'·18N 00°05'·84W, L Fl 10s.
No. 1 49°18'·50N 00°05'·67W. Buoys are moved to mark chan.
No. 2 49°18'·63N 00°05'·57W.
No. 3 49°18'·40N 00°05'·55W, QG 7m 4M; W pylon, G top.
No. 4 49°18'·31N 00°05'·46W.
No. 5 49°18'·19N 00°05'·50W, Fl G 4s 8m 4M; W pylon, G top.
No. 6 49°18'·11N 00°05'·43W.
No. 7 49°17'·65N 00°05'·31W, Fl G 4s.
No. 8 49°17'·91N 00°05'·25W.
Dir lt 159·5°, 49°17'·80N 00°05'·24W. Oc (2+1) WRG 12s 6m, W12M, R/G9M, 125°-G-157°-W-162°-R-194°; R hut.
IQ G (2+1); junction of marina access chan and R Dives.

▶ OUISTREHAM/CAEN

Merville 49°19'·65N 00°13'·39W, VQ.
Lion 49°20'·73N 00°15'·96W.
Ldg lts 185°, both Dir Oc (3+1) R 12s 10/30m **17M**; intens 183·5°-186·5°, synch. **Front** ☆, E jetty, W mast, R top, 49°17'·09N

00°14'·80W. **Rear** ☆, 610m from front, tripod, R top.
Ouistreham 49°20'·42N 00°14'·83W, VQ (3) 5s.
W-SRCO 49°19'·30N 00°15'·26W.
No. 1 49°19'·19N 00°14'·68W, QG.
No. 2 49°19'·17N 00°14'·43W, QR.
No. 3 49°18'·76N 00°14'·70W, Fl G 4s.
No. 4 49°18'·75N 00°14'·49W, Fl R 4s.
No. 5 49°18'·41N 00°14'·73W, QG.
No. 6 49°18'·40N 00°14'·55W, QR.
Barnabé ☆ 49°18'·02N 00°14'·76W, Iso G 4s 7m 3M.
St-Médard ☆ 49°18'·02N 00°14'·62W, Oc (2) R 6s 7m 8M.
Riva ☆ 49°17'·73N 00°14'·81W, VQ (3) G 5s 9m 3M.
Quilbé ☆ 49°17'·72N 00°14'·70W, VQ (3) R 5s 9m 3M.
☆ 49°17'·61N 00°14'·71W, Iso G 4s 11m 7M.
☆ 49°17'·60N 00°14'·60W, Iso R 4s 11m 3M.
Ouistreham lt ho ☆ 49°16'·85N 00°14'·80W, Oc WR 4s 37m **W17M**, R13M; 115°-R-151°-W-115°; W twr, R top.
Caen, Viaduc de Calix, ☆ 49°11'·18N 00°19'·77W, mid-span Iso 4s up & down stream; FG lts on N side, FR lts on S side.

▶ COURSEULLES-SUR-MER

Luc 49°20'·76N 00°18'·43W.
Essarts de Langrune 49°22'·58N 00°21'·37W; *Bell.*
Outfall 49°21'·29N 00°26'·61W, Q.
Courseulles 49°21'·28N 00°27'·69W, Iso 4s.
W jetty ☆ 49°20'·41N 00°27'·37W, Iso WG 4s 7m; W9M, G6M; 135°-W-235°-G-135°; brown pylon on dolphin, G top; *Horn 30s,* sounded HW±2.
E jetty ☆ 49°20'·25N 00°27'·40W, Oc (2) R 6s 9m 7M.

COURSEULLES TO ST VAAST

Ver ☆ 49°20'·39N 00°31'·15W Fl (3) 15s 42m **26M**.

▶ ARROMANCHES

Roseberry 49°23'·09N 00°36'·49W.
Harpagas 49°22'·15N 00°37'·58W.
Ent buoys: 49°21'·35N 00°37'·27W; 49°21'·24N00°37'·31W.
Bombardons 49°21'·65N 00°38'·97W.

▶ PORT-EN-BESSIN

Cussy 49°29'·45N 00°43'·04W, VQ (9) 10s.
Ldg lts 204°, both Oc (3) 12s 25/42m 10/11M; synch. Front, 49°20'·95N 00°45'·54W; 069°-339°, W pylon, G top. Rear; 114°-294°, 93m from front, W and Gy ho.
E mole ☆ 49°21'·12N 00°45'·39W, Oc R 4s 14m 7M, R pylon.
W mole ☆ 49°21'·17N 00°45'·39W, Fl WG 4s 14m, W10M, G7M; G065°-114·5°, W114·5°-065°; G pylon.
Inner E pier ☆ 49°21'·04N 00°45'·34W, Oc (2) R 6s.
Inner W pier ☆ 49°21'·01N 00°45'·38W, Fl (2) G 6s.

▶ COASTAL MARKS

Broadsword 49°25'·34N 00°52'·98W, Q (3) 10s.
Off Omaha Beach: 49°22'·66N 00°50'·29W; 49°23'·16N 00°51'·94W; 49°23'·66N 00°53'·75W.
Est du Cardonnet 49°26'·83N 01°01'·10W, VQ (3) 5s.
Norfalk (wreck) 49°28'·74N 01°03'·69W, Q (3) 10s.

▶ GRANDCAMP

Les Roches de Grandcamp: No. 1 49°24'·91N 01°01'·77W; No. 3 49°24'·72N 01°03'·71W; No. 5 49°24'·72N 01°04'·87W. 49°23'·88N 01°04'·92W; 49°23'·86N 01°05'·43W; 49°23'·45N 01°06'·36W.
Ldg lts 146°, both Dir Q 9/12m **15M**, 144·5°-147·5°. **Front**, 49°23'·42N 01°02'·92W. **Rear** ☆, 102m from front.
Perré ☆. 49°23'·34N 01°02'·55W. Oc 4s 8m 12M, 083°-263°; G pylon on W hut. Can be used as ldg line 221° with next entry:
La Maresquerie ☆. 49°24'·78N 01°02'·78W. Oc 4s 28m 12M, 090°-270°.
Jetée Est ☆. 49°23'·52N 01°02'·98W, Oc (2) R 6s 9m 9M; *Horn Mo(N) 30s.*
Jetée Ouest ☆. 49°23'·47N 01°02'·98W, Fl G 4s 9m 6M.

▶ ISIGNY-SUR-MER

IS (small conical B/Y buoy, no topmark) 49°24'·28N 01°06'·38W.
Ldg lts 172·5°, both Dir Oc (2+1) 12s 7/19m **18M**; intens 170·5°-174·5°, synch. **Front**, 49°19'·55N 01°06·80W, W mast. **Rear**, 625m from front; W pylon, B top.
Banc de Rouelle, Y 49°21'·99N 01°06'·79W.
Banc de Rouelle, G 49°21'·90N 01°07'·35W.
Training wall heads 49°21'·42N 01°07'·25W; 49°21'·39N 01°07'·16W.

▶ CARENTAN

C-I 49°25'·44N 01°07'·08W, Iso 4s.
No. 1 49°23'·92N 01°08'·53W, Fl G 2·5s.
No. 2 49°23'·86N 01°08'·38W, Fl R 2·5s.
Chan ent 49°21'·92N 01°09'·88W, Fl (4) R 15s; R □, on R bcn.
Chan ent 49°21'·94N 01°09'·96W, Fl (4) G 15s; G △, on G bcn.
Ldg lts 209·5°. **Front** ☆, 49°20'·47N 01°11'·19W, Dir Oc (3) R 12s 6m **18M**; W mast, R top; intens 208·2°-210·7°. Rear, Dir Oc (3) 12s 14m 10M; 120°-005°. 723m from front; W gantry, G top.

▶ ÎLES SAINT-MARCOUF & INSHORE MARKS

BS1 49°24'·73N 01°09'·39W to BS5 49°27'·42N 01°12'·79W; five buoys marking oyster beds.
Iles St-Marcouf ☆ 49°29'·86N 01°08'·82W, VQ (3) 5s 18m 8M; □ Gy twr, G top.
Rocher d'Ovy 49°29'·84N 01°09'·08W.
Rocher Bastin 49°29'·55N 01°09'·65W.
W Saint-Marcouf 49°29'·73N 01°11'·97W, Q (9) 15s.
Saint Floxel 49°30'·63N 01°13'·93W.
Quineville wreck 49°31'·79N 01°12'·39W, Q (9) 10s.
BN1 49°31'·83N 01°16'·98W to BN5 49°34'·10N 01°17'·08W; five buoys marking oyster beds.

ST VAAST TO POINTE DE BARFLEUR

▶ ST VAAST-LA-HOUGUE

Ldg lts 267°: Front, La Hougue 49°34'·25N 01°16'·37W, Oc 4s 9m 10M; W pylon, G top. Rear, Morsalines 1·8M from front, 49°34'·16N 01°19'·10W, Oc (4) WRG 12s 90m, W11M, R/G8M; 171°-W-316°-G-321°-R-342°-W-355°; W 8-sided twr, G top.
Le Manquet 49°34'·25N 01°15'·57W.
Le Bout du Roc 49°34'·68N 01°15'·28W.
Le Creux de Bas 49°34'·99N 01°15'·40W.
Jetty ☆ 49°35'·17N 01°15'·41W, Dir Oc (2) WRG 6s 12m W10M, R/G7M; 219°-R-237°-G-310°-W-350°-R-040°; W 8-sided twr, R top; *Siren Mo(N) 30s.*
La Dent 49°34'·57N 01°14'·20W.
Le Gavendest 49°34'·36N 01°13'·89W; Q (6) + L Fl 15s; *Whis.*
Hbr ent, N ☆ 49°35'·18N 01°15'·64W, Iso G 4s 6m 3M; W tank, G top.
Hbr ent, S ☆ 49°35'·16N 01°15'·66W, Oc (4) R 12s 6m 6M; 018°-278°; W hut, R top.
Le Vitéquet 49°36'·08N 01°13'·37W.
Pte de Saire ☆ 49°36'·36N 01°13'·79W, Oc (2+1) 10s 11m 10M; W twr, G top.
Roches Dranguet 49°36'·76N 01°13'·00W.
Le Moulard 49°39'·35N 01°13'·95W.

17

PLOT WAYPOINTS ON YOUR CHART BEFORE USING THEM

▶ BARFLEUR

Ldg lts 219·5°, both Oc (3) 12s 7/13m 10M; synch. Front, 49°40'·18N 01°15'·61W, W□ twr. Rear, 288m from front; 085°-355°; Gy and W□ twr, G top.
La Grotte 49°41'·06N 01°14'·86W.
Roche-à-l'Anglais 49°40'·78N 01°14'·93W.
Le Hintar 49°40'·69N 01°14'·85W.
La Vimberge 49°40'·54N 01°15'·26W.
Grosse-Haie 49°40'·38N 01°15'·27W.
Fourquie 49°40'·30N 01°15'·17W.
W jetty 49°40'·32N 01°15'·57W, Fl G 4s 8m 6M.
E jetty 49°40'·31N 01°15'·47W, Oc R 4s 5m 6M.

La Jamette 49°41'·86N 01°15'·59W.
Pte de Barfleur ☆ 49°41'·78N 01°15'·96W, Fl (2) 10s 72m **29M**; obsc when brg less than 088°; Gy twr, B top; *Horn (2) 60s.*

POINTE DE BARFLEUR TO CAP DE LA HAGUE

Les Barillets 49°41'·76N 01°16'·78W.
Les Équets 49°43'·62N 01°18'·36W, Q 8m 3M.
Pte de Néville 49°42'·39N 01°19'·84W.
Basse du Rénier 49°44'·84N 01°22'·12W, VQ 8m 4M; *Whis.*
Les Trois Pierres 49°42'·89N 01°21'·81W.
Anse de Vicq ldg lts 158°, both FR 8/14m 7M; R & W △s on W pylons, R tops. Front, 49°42'·20N 01°23'·95W. Rear, 403m from front.
La Pierre Noire 49°43'·53N 01°29'·09W, Q (9) 15s 8m 4M.

▶ PORT DU LÉVI

Cap Lévi ☆ 49°41'·75N 01°28'·40W, Fl R 5s 36m **22M**; Gy□twr.
Anse du Cap Lévi 49°41'·19N 01°29'·00W.
Port Lévi 49°41'·24N 01°28'·36W, F RG 7m 7M; G050°-109°, R109°-140°.

▶ PORT DU BECQUET

49°39'·63N 01°32'·59W.
Ldg lts 186·5°, both intens 183°-190°; synch. Front, 49°39'·22N 01°32'·86W, Oc (2+1) 12s 8m 10M; W 8-sided twr. Rear, Oc (2+1) R 12s 13m 7M. W 8-sided twr, R top, 49m from front.
La Tounette 49°39'·31N 01°32'·77W.

▶ CHERBOURG, EASTERN ENTRANCES

Passe Collignon (S side) 49°39'·59N 01°34'·25W, Fl (2) R 6s 5m 4M; W tank, R top.
Happetout (Ile Pelée) 49°40'·46N 01°34'·41W.
Roches du Nord-Ouest 49°40'·64N 01°35'·28W, Fl R 2·5s.
La Truite 49°40'·33N 01°35'·50W, Fl (4) R 15s.
Jetée des Flamands ldg lts 189°, both Q 9/16m 13M. Front, 49°39'·33N 01°35'·96W.
Fort d'Île Pelée 49°40'·19N 01°35'·07W, Oc (2) WR 6s 19m; W10M, R7M; 055°-W-120°-R-055°; W & R pedestal.
Fort de l'Est 49°40'·28N 01°35'·93W, Iso G 4s 19m 9M.
Fort Central 49°40'·40N 01°37'·04W, VQ (6) + L Fl 10s 5m 4M; 322°-032°.
Le Tenarde 49°39'·74N 01°37'·75W, VQ.

PETITE RADE & MARINA

Digue du Homet 49°39'·48N 01°36'·97W, FG 10m 8M; W pylon, G top.
49°39'·44N 01°36'·61W, Jetée des Flamands; VQ R.
Marina W mole 49°38'·87N 01°37'·15W, Fl (3) G 12s 7m 6M; G pylon.
Gare Maritime, NW corner 49°38'·91N 01°37'·08W, Fl (3) R 12s 6m 6M; W col, R lantern.
W quay 49°38'·79N 01°37'·12W, Fl (4) R 15s 3m 3M; R bcn.
Pontoon (detached), F Vi at SW end, 49°38'·77N 01°37'·22W.
Pontoon, wavescreen 49°38'·80N 01°37'·09W, Fl (4) G 15s 4m 2M; W post, G top.
Épi Caiman 49°38'·99N 01°37'·52W Fl (2) G 6s 3m 1M.

▶ CHERBOURG PASSE DE L'OUEST

CH1 49°43'·24N 01°42'·09W, L Fl 10s 8m 4M; *Whis.*
Passe de l'Ouest outer ldg lts 141·2°. **Front,** root of Digue du Homet, Dir Q (2 horiz, 63m apart) 5m **17M**; intens 137·3°-143·3° & 139·2°-145·2°; W △ on beacon. Rear, Gare Maritime, Dir Q 35m **19M**; intens 140°-142·5°; W △ on Gy pylon, 0·99M from front.
Inner ldg lts 124·3°: Front, Digue du Homet head, FG 10m 8M. Rear, Dir Iso G 4s 16m 13M; both intens 114·3°-134·3°; W col, B bands, 397m from front.
Fort de l'Ouest ☆ 49°40'·45N 01°38'·87W, Fl (3) WR 15s 19m **W24M, R20M**; 122°-W-355°-R-122°; Gy twr, R top; *Horn (3) 60s.*
Fort de l'Ouest 49°40'·39N 01°38'·89W, Fl R 4s.
Digue de Querqueville 49°40'·30N 01°39'·80W, Fl (4) G 15s 8m 4M; W col, G top.

▶ OMONVILLE-LA-ROGUE

Raz des Bannes 49°41'·32N 01°44'·55W.
Omonville Dir lt 257°; 49°42'·24N 01°50'·17W, Iso WRG 4s 13m; W10M, R/G7M; 180°-G-252°-W-262°-R-287°; W pylon, G top.
49°42'·28N 01°49'·13W.
L'Étonnard 49°42'·32N 01°49'·85W.

Basse Bréfort 49°43'·76N 01°51'·10W, VQ 8m 4M; *Whis.*
La Plate 49°43'·97N 01°55'·75W, Fl (2+1) WR 10s 11m; W9M, R6M; 115°-W-272°-R-115°; Y 8-sided twr, with B top.

Cap de la Hague ☆ (Gros du Raz). 49°43'·31N 01°57'·28W. Fl 5s 48m **23M**; Gy twr, W top; *Horn 30s.*

9.17.5 PASSAGE INFORMATION

Current Pilots include: *The Channel Cruising Companion* (Nautical Data Ltd/Featherstone & Aslett); *North France and Belgium Cruising Companion* (Nautical Data Ltd/Featherstone); and Admiralty *Dover Strait NP28* and *Channel NP27 Pilots.*

The coasts of Picardy and Normandy are convenient to hbrs along the S coast of England – the distance (65M) from, say, Brighton to Fécamp being hardly more than an overnight passage. However many of the hbrs dry, so that a boat which can take the ground is an advantage. For details of the Dover Strait TSS, see 9.3.14. Notes on the English Channel and on cross-Channel passages appear below and in 9.3.5. See 9.0.6 for cross-Channel distances. For a French glossary, see chapter 1.

The inland waterways system can be entered via Dunkerque (9.17.7), Gravelines (9.17.8), Calais (9.17.9), St Valéry-sur-Somme (9.17.12) and the Seine (9.17.19). See 9.17.6 for tolls.

DUNKERQUE TO BOULOGNE(charts *323, 1892, 2451*) Offshore a series of banks lies roughly parallel with the coast: Sandettié bank (about 14M to N), Outer Ruytingen midway between Sandettié and the coast, and the Dyck banks which extend NE'wards for 30M from a point 5M NE of Calais. There are well-buoyed channels between some of these banks, but great care is needed in poor visibility. In general the banks are steep-to on the inshore side, and slope to seaward. In bad weather the sea breaks on the shallower parts.

Dunkerque Port Est (9.17.7), the old port, has two good yacht marinas and all facilities. Dunkerque Port Ouest is a commercial/ ferry port which yachts should not enter. About 3M SW is the drying hbr of Gravelines (9.17.8), which should not be entered in strong onshore winds. If E-bound, the Passe de Zuydcoote (4·4m) is an inshore link to West Diep and the Belgian ports.

The sea breaks heavily in bad weather on Ridens de Calais, 3M N of Calais (9.17.9 and chart 1351), and also on Ridens de la Rade immediately N and NE of the hbr.

The NE-bound traffic lane of the Dover Strait TSS lies only 3M off C Gris Nez. Keep a sharp lookout not only for coastal traffic in the ITZ, but also cross-Channel ferries, particularly very fast catamarans. ▶*1M NW of C Gris Nez the NE-going stream begins at HW Dieppe – 0150, and the SW-going at HW Dieppe + 0355, sp rates 4kn.*◀ Between C Gris Nez (lt, fog sig) and Boulogne the coastal bank dries about 4ca offshore.

BOULOGNE TO DIEPPE (Chart *2451*) In the approaches to Pas de Calais a number of shoals lie offshore: The Ridge (or Le Colbart), Les Ridens, Bassurelle, Vergoyer, Bassure de Baas and Battur. In bad weather, and particularly with wind against tide in most cases, the sea breaks heavily on all these shoals. ▶*Off Boulogne's Digue Carnot the N-going stream begins HW Dieppe – 0130, and the S-going at HW Dieppe + 0350, sp rates 1·75kn.*◀ From Boulogne (9.17.10; chart 438) to Pte de Lornel the coast dries up to 5ca offshore.

Le Touquet and Étaples (9.17.11) lie in the Embouchure de la Canche, entered between Pte de Lornel and Pte du Touquet, and with a drying bank which extends 1M seaward of a line joining these two points. Le Touquet-Paris-Plage lt is shown from a conspic tr, 1M S of Pte du Touquet. ▶*Off the entrance the N-going stream begins about HW Dieppe – 0335, sp rate 1·75kn; and the S-going stream begins about HW Dieppe + 0240, sp rate 1·75kn.*◀

From Pte du Touquet the coast runs 17M S to Pte de St Quentin, with a shallow coastal bank which dries to about 5ca offshore, except in the approaches to the dangerous and constantly changing Embouchure de l'Authie (Pte du Haut-Blanc, about 10M S), where it dries up to 2M offshore.

B de Somme, between Pte de St Quentin and Pte du Hourdel (lt), is a shallow, drying area of shifting sands. The chan, which runs close to Pte du Hourdel, is well buoyed, but the whole est dries out 3M to seaward, and should not be approached in strong W/NW winds. For St Valéry-sur-Somme and Le Crotoy, see 9.17.12.

Offshore there are two shoals, Bassurelle de la Somme and Quémer, on parts of which the sea breaks in bad weather. ▶*4·5M NW of Cayeux-sur-Mer (lt) the stream is rotatory anti-clockwise. The E-going stream begins about HW Dieppe –0200, and sets 070° 2·5kn at sp : the W-going stream begins about HW Dieppe + 0600, and sets 240° 1·5kn at sp.*◀

S of Ault (lt) the coast changes from low sand dunes to medium cliffs. Between Le Tréport (9.17.13) and Dieppe, 14M SW, rky banks, drying in places, extend 5ca offshore. Banc Franc-Marqué (3·6m) lies 2M offshore, and about 3M N of Le Tréport. About 3M NW of Le Tréport, Ridens du Tréport (5·1m) should be avoided in bad weather. A prohibited area extends 6ca off Penly nuclear power station and is marked by lt buoys.

DIEPPE TO CAP D'ANTIFER (chart *2451*). ▶*Off Dieppe the ENE-going stream begins about HW Dieppe –0505, and the WSW-going at about HW Dieppe +0030, sp rates 2kn.*◀ From Dieppe (9.17.14) to Pte d'Ailly the coast is fringed by a bank, drying in places, up to 4ca offshore. E of Pte d'Ailly an eddy runs W close inshore on first half of E-going stream.

About 6M N of Pte d'Ailly, Les Ecamias are banks with depths of 11m, dangerous in a heavy sea. Dangerous wrecks lie between about 1·2M WNW and 1·5M NNW of the lt ho. Drying rks extend 5ca off Pte d'Ailly, including La Galère, a rk which dries 6·8m, about 3ca N of the Pointe (chart 2147).

Between Pte d'Ailly and St Valéry-en-Caux (9.17.15; lt, fog sig) there are drying rks 4ca offshore in places. About 1·5M E of Pte de Sotteville a rky bank (4·2m) extends about 1M NNW; a strong eddy causes a race over this bank.

From St Valéry-en-Caux to Fécamp (9.17.16), 15M WSW the coast consists of high chalk cliffs broken by valleys. There are rky ledges, extending 4ca offshore in places. Immediately E of St Valéry-en-Caux shallow sandbanks, Les Ridens, with a least depth of 0·6m, extend about 6ca offshore. ▶*At St Valéry-en-Caux ent the E-going stream begins about HW Dieppe – 0550, and the W-going stream begins about HW Dieppe – 0015, sp rates 2·75kn. E of the ent a small eddy runs W on the E-going stream.*◀ The nuclear power station at Paluel 3M W of St Valéry-en-Caux (prohibited area marked by a NCM lt buoy) is conspic.

From Fécamp to Cap d'Antifer drying rks extend up to 2½ca offshore. Off Pte Fagnet, close NE of Fécamp, lie Les Charpentiers (rks which dry, to almost 2ca offshore). ▶*At Fécamp pierheads the NNE-going stream begins about HW Le Havre –0340, up to 2·9kn sp; the SSW-going about HW Le Havre + 0220, much weaker.*◀

CAP D'ANTIFER AND L'ESTUAIRE DE LA SEINE (charts 2146, 2990). ▶*Off Cap d'Antifer the NE-going stream begins about HW Le Havre – 0430, and the SW-going at about HW Le Havre + 0140. There are eddies close inshore E of Cap d'Antifer on both streams.*◀

Port du Havre-Antifer, a VLCC harbour lies 1·5M S of Cap d'Antifer. A huge breakwater extends about 1·5M seaward, and should be given a berth of about 1·5M, or more in heavy weather when there may be a race with wind against tide. Commercial vessels in the buoyed app chan have priority. Yachts should cross the app chan 3·8M to the NW at A17/A18 lt buoys; at 90° to its axis; as quickly as possible, and well clear of ships in the chan. Crossing vessels should contact *Vigie Port d'Antifer* and any priority vessel on VHF Ch 16.

Le Havre (9.17.17) is a large commercial port, as well as a yachting centre. From the NW, the most useful mark is the Le Havre Lanby 'LHA' 9M W of C de la Hève (lt). The well-buoyed/lit acess chan runs 6M ESE from LH 3/4 buoys to the hbr ent.

Strong W winds cause rough water over shoal patches either side of the chan. Coming from the N or NE, there is deep water close off C de la Hève, but from here steer S to join the main ent chan. Beware Banc de l'Éclat (1·0m), which lies on N side of main chan and about 1·5M from harbour ent. SW of Digue Sud there are extensive reclamation works in progress.

The Seine estuary is entered between Le Havre and Deauville, and is encumbered by shallow and shifting banks which extend seawards to Banc de Seine, 15M W of Le Havre. With wind against tide there is a heavy sea on this bank. N and E of it there are 4 Big Ship waiting anchorages. ▶*Here the SW-going stream begins at HW Le Havre + 0400, and the NE-going at HW Le Havre –0300, sp rates 1·5kn.*◀ Between Deauville and Le Havre the sea can be rough in W winds. The Greenwich Meridian lies about 2·7M W of Cap de la Hève and Deauville; check the correct E/W hemisphere is set on your GPS.

Chenal du Rouen is the main chan into R. Seine, and carries much commercial tfc. Close E of Rade de la Carosse WCM buoy (see 9.17.4) yachts trying to cut the corner run aground on Spoil Ground (0·6m). The S side of the chan is contained by Digue du Ratier, a training wall which extends E to Honfleur (9.17.18). With almost 24 hours access/exit, Honfleur is a useful starting port when bound up-river. See 9.17.6 (routes to the Med), 9.17.19 (R. Seine, Rouen) and 9.17.20 (Paris).

DEAUVILLE TO GRANDCAMP (chart 2146, 2136). Since access to all the hbrs along this coast is to some extent tidally limited, it is best to cruise this area from W to E. ▶*Thus you can leave one harbour at the start of the tidal window and reach the next hbr before the window has closed; in the opposite direction this is difficult or impossible. Between Le Havre and Ouistreham there is a useful stand at HW of between 2-3hrs.*◀ Le Havre, possibly Ouistreham, and St Vaast (in all but S/SE winds) may be regarded as the only ports of refuge. Strong onshore winds render the approaches to other hbrs difficult or even dangerous.

Deauville/Trouville (9.17.21), 8M S of Cap de la Hève, is an important yachting hbr. The sands dry more than 5ca offshore; in strong W or N winds the entrance is dangerous and the sea breaks between the jetties. In such conditions it is best attempted within 15 mins of HW, when the stream is slack. To the NE beware Banc de Trouville (1·7m), and Les Ratelets (0·9m) to the

17

N at the mouth of the Seine. 7M SW is River Dives (9.17.22) with marina.The banks dry for 1M to seaward, and entry is only possible from HW ± 2½, and not in fresh onshore winds.

6M W lies Ouistreham ferry hbr and marina (9.17.23). Here a canal leads 7M inland to a marina in the centre of Caen. 2-6M W the drying rocky ledges, Roches de Lion and Les Essarts de Langrune, extend up to 2·25M offshore in places. Roches de Ver (drying rks) lie near the centre of Plateau du Calvados, extending 1M offshore about 2M W of Courseulles-sur-Mer (9.17.24). The approach to this hbr is dangerous in strong onshore winds.

From Courseulles the coast runs W 5M, past Pte de Ver lt ho, to the remains of the wartime hbr of Arromanches, where there is a fair weather anchorage. Rochers du Calvados (1·6m) lies close NE of the ruined Mulberry hbr. There are numerous wrecks and obstructions in the area.

Between the fishing port of Port-en-Bessin (9.17.25) and Pte de la Percée a bank lies up to 3ca offshore, with drying ledges and the wrecks and obstructions of Omaha Beach marked by 3 NCM buoys. ▶*A small race forms off Pte de la Percée with wind against tide. Off Port-en-Bessin the E-going stream begins about HW Le Havre –0500, and the W-going at about HW Le Havre +0050, sp rates 1·25kn.*◀

GRANDCAMP TO POINTE DE BARFLEUR (chart 2135)

On E side of B du Grand Vey, Roches de Grandcamp (dry) extend more than 1M offshore, N and W of Grandcamp (9.17.26), but they are flat and can be crossed from the N in normal conditions HW±1½. Three NCM buoys mark the N edge of this ledge. Heavy kelp can give false echo-sounder readings.

At the head of B du Grand Vey, about 10M S of Îles St Marcouf, are the (very) tidal hbrs of Carentan and Isigny (9.18.27); entry is only possible near HW and should not be attempted in strong onshore winds. The Carentan chan is well buoyed and adequately lit. It trends SSW across sandbanks for about 4M, beyond which it runs between two training walls leading to a lock, and thence into the canal to Carentan's popular marina. The Isigny chan is slightly deeper, but the hbr dries to steepish mudbanks.

Îles St Marcouf (9.17.27) lie 7M SE of St Vaast-la-Hougue, about 4M offshore, and consist of Île du Large (lt) and Île de Terre about ¼M apart. The Banc du Cardonnet, with depths of 5·2m and many wks, extends for about 5M ESE from the islands. Banc de St Marcouf, with depths of 2·4m and many wks, extends 4·5M NW from the isles, and the sea breaks on it in strong N/NE winds.

Approach St Vaast-la-Hougue (9.17.28) S of Île de Tatihou, but beware drying rks: La Tourelle (unmarked), Le Gavendest and La Dent, which lie near the approaches and are buoyed. 2M N is Pte de Saire with rks and shoals up to 1M offshore. From Pte de Saire the coast runs 4M NNW to drying Barfleur (9.17.29).

Raz de Barfleur, in which the sea breaks heavily, must be avoided in bad weather, particularly with winds from NW or SE against the tide, by passing 5-7M seaward of Pte de Barfleur. ▶*In calmer weather it can be taken at slack water (HW Cherbourg –4½ and +2) via an inshore passage, 3ca NE of La Jamette ECM bn.*◀

Pte de Barfleur marks the W end of B de Seine, 56M west of Cap d'Antifer. There are no obstructions on a direct course across the Bay, but a transhipment area for large tankers is centred about 10M ESE of Pte de Barfleur. Caution: The W end of the Baie de Seine is at times affected by floating Sargassum weed; in hbrs from Grandcamp to St Vaast propellers may be fouled.

POINTE DE BARFLEUR TO CAP DE LA HAGUE (AC *1106*)

The N coast of the Cotentin Peninsula runs E/W for 26M, mostly bordered by rks which extend 2·5M offshore from Pte de Barfleur to C. Lévi, and 1M offshore between Pte de Jardeheu and C. de la Hague. ▶*Tidal streams reach 5kn at sp, and raise a steep sea with wind against tide.*◀ Between Pte de Barfleur and Cherbourg, yachts commonly route via Les Equets and Basse du Rénier NCM buoys and La Pierre Noire WCM buoy (N of Cap Lévi); be alert for opposite direction traffic.

The inner passage between Pte de Barfleur and C. Lévi, keeping S of these 3 cardinal buoys, is not recommended without local knowledge except in good weather and visibility when the transits shown on chart *1106* can be properly identified.

▶*Tidal streams run strongly with considerable local variations. Off C. Lévi a race develops with wind against tide, and extends nearly 2M N. Port Lévi and Port de Becquet are two small drying hbrs E of Cherbourg. Off Cherbourg (9.17.30) the stream is E-going from about HW – 0430 and W-going from HW + 0230. Close inshore between Cherbourg and C. de la Hague a back eddy runs W.*◀

As an alternative to Omonville (9.17.31) there is anch in Anse de St Martin, about 2M E of C. de la Hague, open to N, but useful to await the tide in the Alderney Race.

CROSS-CHANNEL TO BAIE DE SEINE, CHERBOURG OR THE CHANNEL ISLANDS

Review the planning guidelines and checklist in 9.3.5, especially at the start of the season. Cross-Channel distances are in 9.0.6. Note any tidal constraints at departure or destination hbrs. The popular Channel crossings from hbrs between Portland and Chichester to those on the Cotentin peninsula or in the Channel Islands are normally straightforward in summer, but can never be taken for granted. Hbrs in the Baie de Seine can be largely discounted either because of their tidal constraints or simply because they add extra miles to the crossing.

Local factors to be considered include:

Weymouth: The Shambles Bank and Portland Race both require a wide berth. Check the tidal streams for possible wind-over-tide conditions.

Poole: Leave hbr on the ebb, but at springs with a S/SE wind beware short steep seas in the Swash Channel; off Handfast, Peveril and Anvil Pts overfalls occur with wind against tide.

Solent ports: Decide whether to leave via the Needles or Nab Tower. ▶*The former usually requires a fair tide through Hurst Narrows (HW Portsmouth –1 to +4½), which in turn will dictate your ETD from hbr.*◀ The latter has no tidal gate, but is longer (unless bound to Le Havre and eastwards) and may give a less favourable slant if the wind is in the SW; in W'lies it offers better shelter in the lee of the IOW. In practice the nearer exit may prove to be the obvious choice.

On passage the greatest hazard is likely to be crossing the shipping lanes, especially if fog or poor vis are forecast when it may be safest not to sail. Whether crossing the Casquets TSS, or in open waters clear of TSS, is almost academic. The risk of collision with any of the steady stream of commercial ships is the same. It is commonsense, seamanlike and realistic to give way to these ships, early – since they are unlikely to give way to a sailing yacht, despite Rule 18 (a) (iv).

Finally, review destination(s) and possible hbrs of refuge:

Braye (Alderney), whilst accessible at all times, presents a slight risk, especially at springs, of being swept past Alderney on a W-going tide. The yacht may then clew up in Guernsey, having unwittingly negotiated the Swinge or the Alderney Race. The moral is to plan and monitor track so as to approach from well up-tide. Braye harbour is unsafe in fresh/strong E/NE'lies. (For Channel Islands see 9.19.5).

French ports on the W side of the Cotentin (Diélette to Granville) are tidally constrained and exposed to the W; they are however in a lee with anticyclonic Easterlies.

Cherbourg is accessible at all times. On closing the coast especially at springs, a very large drift angle may be needed to maintain track. The answer is to be well up-tide at an early stage.

To the E, **Barfleur** (9.17.29) dries. **St Vaast** (9.17.28) is a safe anch, if awaiting entry into the marina; both are sheltered from the prevailing W'lies. **Le Havre** is a port of refuge, although it always requires care due to the density of commercial shipping, shoal waters and strongish tidal streams.

9.17.6 SPECIAL NOTES FOR FRANCE (Areas 17 to 22, excluding Channel Is, Area 19)

Some minor differences in the information for French hbrs are: Instead of 'County' the 'Département' is given. French Standard Time is –0100 (ie 1300 Standard Time in France is 1200UT), DST not having been taken into account.
For details of documentation apply to the French Tourist Office, 178 Piccadilly, London, W1J 9AL; ☎ 0906 824 4123, 📠 020 7493 6594; info@mdlf.co.uk www.franceguide.com.

AFFAIRES MARITIMES In every French port there is a representative of the central government, L'Administration Maritime, known as Affaires Maritimes. This organisation watches over all maritime activities (commercial, fishing, pleasure) and helps them develop harmoniously. Information on navigation and other maritime issues can be supplied by a local representative whose ☎ is given under each port. The Head Office is: Ministère Chargé de la Mer, Bureau de la Navigation de Plaisance, 3 Place Fontenoy, 75007 Paris, ☎ 01 44 49 80 00.

CHARTS Two types of French chart are shown: SHOM as issued by the *Service Hydrographique et Oceanographique de la Marine*, the French Navy's Hydrographic Service. ECM *Éditions Cartographiques Maritimes* are charts for sea and river navigation. Notes: See Chapter 1 for SHOM contact details. A free chart catalogue *Le petit catalogue* is published annually by SHOM. It includes lists of chart agents including those which specialise in mail order. Under 'Facilities', SHOM means a chart agent.

Any new edition of a SHOM chart receives a new, different chart number. SHOM charts refer elevations of lights, bridges etc to MHWS as on Admiralty charts. Heights of prominent features are referred to Mean Level, or as indicated on the chart.

TIDAL COEFFICIENTS See 9.20.26 for Coefficients based on Brest, together with explanatory notes and French tidal terms.

PUBLIC HOLIDAYS New Year's Day, Easter Sunday and Monday, Labour Day (1 May), Ascension Day, Armistice Day 1945 (8 May), Whit Sunday and Monday, National (Bastille) Day (14 July), Feast of the Assumption (15 Aug), All Saints' Day (1 Nov), Remembrance Day (11 Nov), Christmas Day.

FRENCH GLOSSARY See Chapter 1.

FACILITIES The cost shown for a visitor's overnight berth is unavoidably the previous year's figure. It is based on high season rates and is where possible expressed as cost/metre LOA, although beam may be taken into account at some ports. Low season rates and concessions can much reduce costs. The fee usually includes electricity, but rarely showers which range between €1.20 and €2.
At some marinas fuel can be obtained/paid for H24 by using a smart credit card. The latest British credit cards are now technically able to activate the associated diesel or petrol pumps and make payment. If not in possession of such a card, pre-arrange to pay manually by credit card at the Capitainerie.

TELEPHONES ☎ Nos contain 10 digits, the first 2 digits being Zone codes (01 to 05), as appropriate to location. Mobile ☎ Nos are prefixed 06. Info Nos, eg the recorded weather (Auto) are prefixed 08. The ringing tone is long, equal on/off tones (slower than UK engaged tone). Rapid pips mean the call is being connected. Engaged tone is like that in UK. A recorded message means ☎ No unobtainable.

To telephone France from UK, dial + (or 00) 33, followed by the 9 digit number, ie omitting the 0 from the Zone code prefix. To telephone UK from France dial + (or 00) 44 followed by the Area Code (omitting the first 0) and the number. Phonecards for public 'phones may be bought at the PTT or at many Hbr offices, cafés and tabacs. Cheap rates are 2130-0800 Mon-Fri 1330-0800 Sat-Mon.

EMERGENCIES Dial 112; or 18 Fire, 17 Police, 15 Ambulance. 1616 any CROSS as from 1 Jan 2005.

SIGNALS International Port Traffic Signals (IPTS; see 9.0.4) are used in many French ports. Storm Warning and Tidal signals, as shown below, may be seen in fewer and fewer French ports.

Storm Warning signals

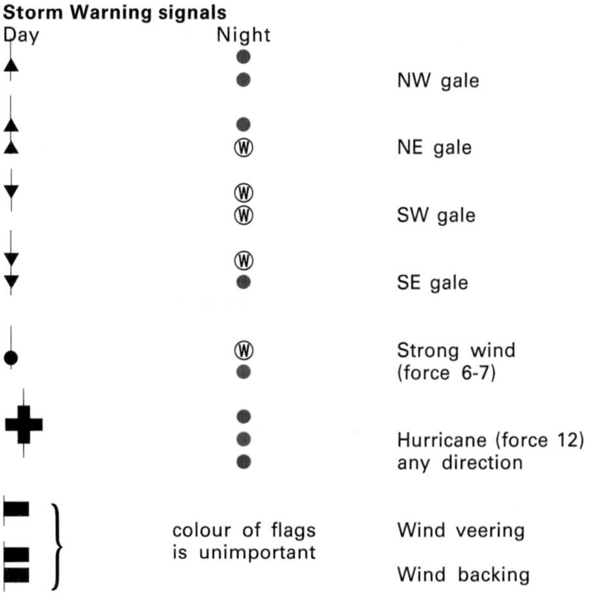
Day
Night
NW gale
NE gale
SW gale
SE gale
Strong wind (force 6-7)
Hurricane (force 12) any direction
colour of flags is unimportant
Wind veering
Wind backing

Q or IQ (W) lights, by day only, indicate the immediacy of forecast wind >F6, as follows: Q = within 3 hrs; IQ = within 6 hrs.

Tidal Signals
There are two sets of signals, one showing the state of the tide and the other showing the height of tide.

a. State of the tide is shown by:

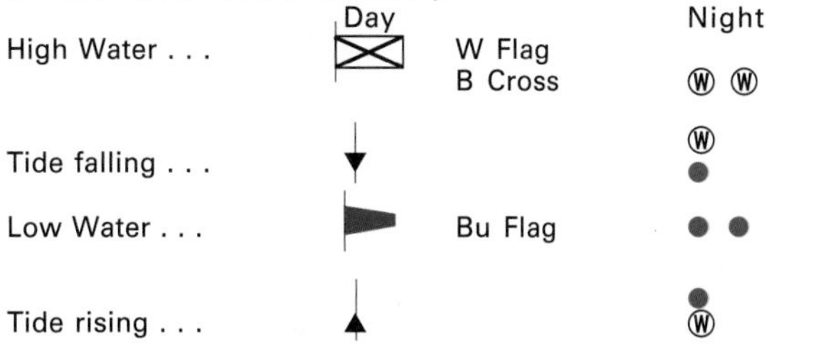
Day
Night
High Water . . .
W Flag
B Cross
Tide falling . . .
Low Water . . .
Bu Flag
Tide rising . . .

b. The height of tide signals show the height above CD by adding together the values of the various shapes or lights.

Day: ▼ = 0·2m; ■ = 1·0m; ● = 5·0m.

Night: ● = 0·2m; ● = 1·0m; (W) = 5·0m.

The three different shapes are shown with ▼s to the left of ■s and ●s to the right, as seen from seaward. Lights are disposed similarly.

The following examples will help to explain:

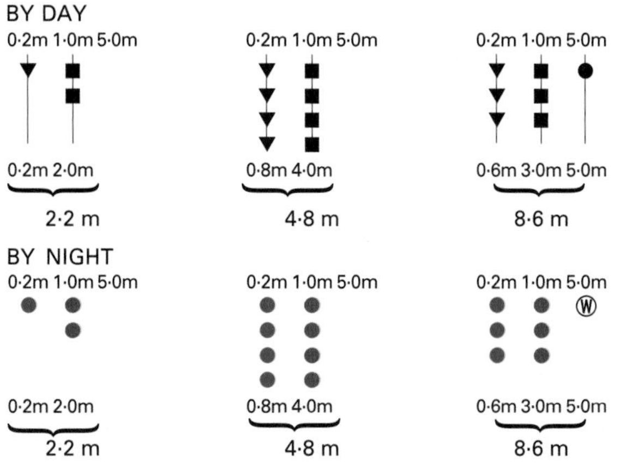
BY DAY
0·2m 1·0m 5·0m
0·2m 2·0m
2·2 m
0·8m 4·0m
4·8 m
0·6m 3·0m 5·0m
8·6 m
BY NIGHT
0·2m 1·0m 5·0m
0·2m 2·0m
2·2 m
0·8m 4·0m
4·8 m
0·6m 3·0m 5·0m
8·6 m

INLAND WATERWAYS

TOLLS are due on waterways managed by Voies Navigable de France (VNF), ie those E of a line Le Havre to Bordeaux, plus the R. Loire. In 2004 licences were available for one year, 30 days (not necessarily consecutive), 16 consecutive days or 1 day. The rates, based on 5 categories of boat area (LOA x Beam (m) = m^2) were as follows in €'s:

	<12m²	12-25m²	25-40m²	40-60m²	>60m²
1 Year	76.30	109.20	219.40	354.40	438.80
30 days	44.30	78.30	138.10	215.30	266.80
16 days	16.50	34.00	50.50	67.00	84.50
1 day	8.30	16.50	24.80	33.00	41.20

Licence stickers (*vignettes*) must be visibly displayed stbd side forward. They are obtainable by post from:

Librairie VNF, 18 Quai d'Austerlitz, 75013 Paris. ☎ 01.44.06.63.60 Payment may be possible by Visa, Mastercard or Eurocard; for further information call +33 (0)3.21.63.24.30.

Or in person (cash only), or by post, from the following VNF offices on the Channel, Atlantic coasts and inland:

Dunkerque, Terre plein du jeu de Mail-59140. ☎ 03.28.24.90.70
Calais, 45 quai de la Meuse - 62100. ☎ 03.21.34.25.58
Lille, 37 rue du Plat - 59034. ☎ 03.20.15.49.70
St Quentin, 2 rue Léo Lagrange - 02100. ☎ 03.23.62.60.21
Nancy, 2 rue Victor - 54000. ☎ 03.83.17.01.01
Mulhouse, 14 rue de l'Est - 68052. ☎ 03.89.45.22.46
Strasbourg, 5 rue du Port-du-Rhin - 67016. ☎ 03.90.41.06.06
Reims, 11 bld P. Doumer - 51084. ☎ 03.26.85.75.95
Le Havre, la citadelle, av Courbeaux - 76600. ☎ 02.35.22.99.34
Rouen, 71 ave J. Chastellain - 76000. ☎ 03.21.34.25.58
Conflans, Cours de Chimay - 78700. ☎ 01.39.72.73.09
Paris, 18 Quai d'Austerlitz - 75013. ☎ 01.44.06.63.60
St Mammès, 10 Quai du Loing - 77670. ☎ 01.64.70.57.70
Nantes, 2 rue Marcel Sembat - 44049. ☎ 02.40.71.02.17

On/near the Mediterranean coast:
Lyons, 11 quai de Mar'l Joffre - 69002. ☎ 04.78.42.74.99
*Agde, Ecluse ronde d'Agde - 34034. ☎ 04.67.94.23.09
Sète, 1 Quai Philippe Régy - 34200. ☎ 04.67.46.34.67
Arles, 1 Quai Gare Maritime - 13200. ☎ 04.90.96.00.85
Narbonne, 9bis Quai d'Alsace - 11100. ☎ 04.68.42.23.27
Toulouse, 2 Port St Etienne - 31073. ☎ 05.61.36.24.24
and from certain locks on the canals.
*Open at weekends during lock hours.

CLOSURES. Brochure and dates of closures (*chomages*) from: French National Tourist Office, 178 Piccadilly, London W1J 9AL; ☎ 020 7629 2869, ℻ 020 7493 6594.

Or: VNF Head Office, 175 Rue Ludovic Boutleux, BP 820, 62400 Bethune. ☎ 03.21.63.24.54; ℻ 03.21.63.24.42. www.vnf.fr

QUALIFICATIONS. Helmsmen of craft <15m LOA and not capable of >20 kph (11kn) must have an International Certificate of Competence validated for inland waterways, plus a copy of the CEVNI rules. For larger, faster craft the requirements are under review.

On some canals automatic locks are activated by an electronic blipper called *Sesame* which is issued to vessels in transit. Loss of or damage to *Sesame* may incur fines of €150 to 12,200. Specific notification may be required to obtain insurance cover against this risk.

ROUTES TO THE MEDITERRANEAN.

See 9.17.19 and 9.17.20 for the River Seine, Rouen and Paris.

The quickest route is via Paris to St Mammès – Canal du Loing – Canal de Briare – Canal Latéral à la Loire – Canal du Centre – Saône – Rhône. Approx 1318km (824M), 182 locks; allow 4 weeks. Max dimensions: LOA 38·5m, beam 5m, draft 1·8m, air draft 3·5m.

Alternatives above St Mammès: R Yonne-Laroche, then either Canal de Bourgogne – Saône; or Canal du Nivernais – Canal du Centre – Saône. Both are slowed by many locks.

There are other routes via R Oise/Aisne or R Marne, both continuing via Canal de la Marne à la Saône.

The Saône can also be accessed via the canals of N France, entered at Calais, Dunkerque or Belgian and Dutch ports.

Useful reading: *Inland waterways of France* (7th edition, Edwards-May/Imray); *Notes on French inland waterways* (Cruising Association); *Vagnon Cartes Guides de Plaisance.*

See 9.18.14 for inland waterways of Brittany, especially the Ille et Rance Canal/Vilaine River from St Malo to Arzal/Camoel on the Vilaine River, South Brittany.

See 9.22.26 for the R. Gironde, Canal Latéral à la Garonne and Canal du Midi. Also the *West France Cruising Companion* (Nautical Data Ltd/Featherstone) for an outline of this route.

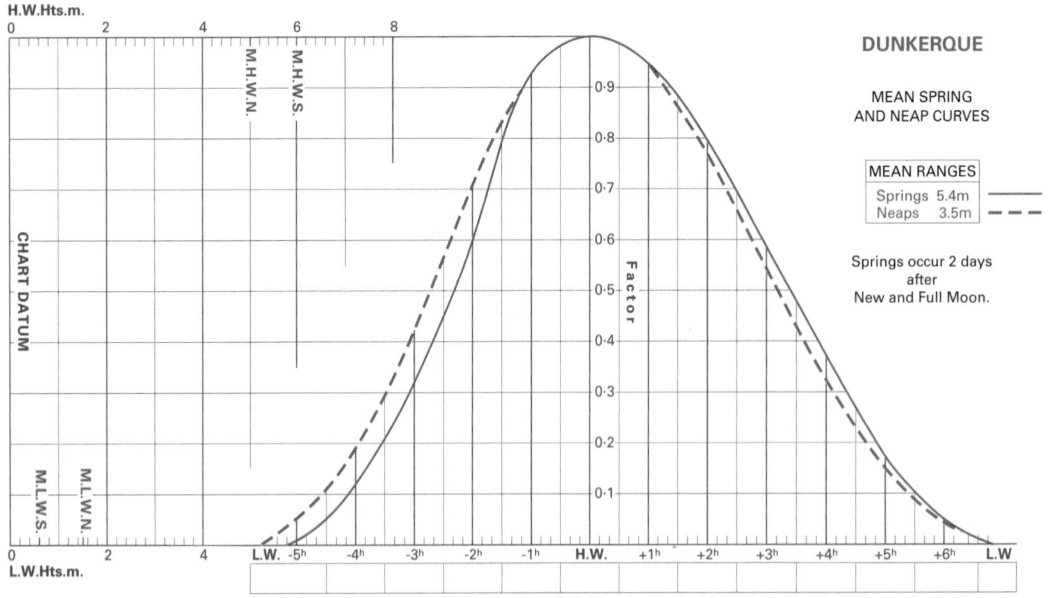
DUNKERQUE
MEAN SPRING AND NEAP CURVES
MEAN RANGES
Springs 5.4m
Neaps 3.5m
Springs occur 2 days after New and Full Moon.
H.W.Hts.m.
L.W.Hts.m.
CHART DATUM
M.H.W.N.
M.H.W.S.
M.L.W.S.
M.L.W.N.
Factor
L.W.
H.W.
L.W

TIME ZONE -0100
(French Standard Time)
Subtract 1 hour for UT
For French Summer Time add ONE hour in **non-shaded areas**

FRANCE – DUNKERQUE

LAT 51°03′N LONG 2°22′E

TIMES AND HEIGHTS OF HIGH AND LOW WATERS

SPRING & NEAP TIDES
Dates in red are SPRINGS
Dates in blue are NEAPS

YEAR **2005**

JANUARY

Date	Day	Time	m	Time	m	Time	m	Time	m
1	SA	0355	5.4	1047	1.1	1620	5.4	2301	1.4
2	SU	0433	5.2	1126	1.2	1703	5.2	2342	1.5
3	M	0516	5.1	1211	1.3	1753	5.1	◑	
4	TU	0032	1.6	0611	5.0	1303	1.4	1851	5.0
5	W	0130	1.7	0713	5.0	1409	1.4	1954	5.0
6	TH	0243	1.7	0818	5.1	1523	1.4	2101	5.1
7	F	0358	1.6	0925	5.2	1632	1.2	2209	5.3
8	SA	0504	1.4	1030	5.4	1734	1.0	2311	5.5
9	SU	0605	1.1	1130	5.7	1832	0.9		
10	M	0004	5.7	0701	0.9	1224	6.0	● 1926	0.8
11	TU	0052	5.9	0753	0.6	1316	6.1	2016	0.7
12	W	0141	6.0	0843	0.5	1407	6.2	2104	0.7
13	TH	0229	6.0	0932	0.4	1458	6.1	2151	0.7
14	F	0315	5.9	1020	0.4	1548	6.0	2237	0.9
15	SA	0401	5.8	1107	0.5	1636	5.8	2323	1.1
16	SU	0447	5.6	1154	0.7	1726	5.5		
17	M	0012	1.3	0536	5.4	1244	1.0	◐ 1821	5.2
18	TU	0104	1.5	0633	5.2	1339	1.2	1924	5.0
19	W	0203	1.7	0742	5.0	1440	1.5	2031	4.8
20	TH	0308	1.8	0854	4.9	1549	1.6	2138	4.8
21	F	0421	1.7	1001	4.9	1703	1.6	2243	4.9
22	SA	0532	1.5	1102	5.1	1802	1.4	2337	5.1
23	SU	0624	1.3	1153	5.2	1847	1.3		
24	M	0017	5.3	0705	1.1	1235	5.4	1923	1.2
25	TU	0054	5.5	0741	1.0	1311	5.6	○ 1956	1.1
26	W	0125	5.6	0815	0.8	1343	5.7	2028	1.0
27	TH	0155	5.7	0848	0.8	1413	5.7	2101	1.0
28	F	0226	5.7	0921	0.7	1444	5.7	2133	1.0
29	SA	0257	5.7	0954	0.7	1517	5.7	2205	1.0
30	SU	0327	5.6	1026	0.8	1549	5.6	2236	1.1
31	M	0356	5.6	1059	0.8	1621	5.5	2310	1.1

FEBRUARY

Date	Day	Time	m	Time	m	Time	m	Time	m
1	TU	0432	5.5	1136	0.9	1700	5.4	2349	1.3
2	W	0518	5.4	1221	1.1	1754	5.2	◑	
3	TH	0040	1.5	0621	5.2	1318	1.3	1903	5.0
4	F	0149	1.7	0734	5.0	1438	1.5	2022	4.9
5	SA	0317	1.7	0857	5.0	1603	1.4	2153	5.0
6	SU	0442	1.5	1023	5.2	1721	1.2	2305	5.3
7	M	0558	1.1	1129	5.6	1827	0.9		
8	TU	0001	5.6	0656	0.7	1223	5.9	● 1920	0.7
9	W	0045	5.8	0746	0.5	1311	6.1	2006	0.6
10	TH	0130	6.0	0833	0.3	1357	6.2	2050	0.6
11	F	0212	6.1	0917	0.2	1442	6.2	2132	0.6
12	SA	0253	6.1	0959	0.2	1525	6.0	2212	0.7
13	SU	0334	6.0	1040	0.4	1605	5.8	2250	0.9
14	M	0413	5.8	1119	0.6	1644	5.6	2329	1.1
15	TU	0455	5.6	1158	0.9	1727	5.3		
16	W	0012	1.3	0542	5.3	1244	1.3	◐ 1820	4.9
17	TH	0104	1.6	0643	4.9	1342	1.7	1932	4.6
18	F	0212	1.9	0807	4.6	1456	1.9	2058	4.4
19	SA	0336	1.9	0933	4.6	1631	1.9	2219	4.6
20	SU	0509	1.7	1046	4.8	1743	1.6	2319	4.9
21	M	0607	1.4	1140	5.1	1830	1.3		
22	TU	0002	5.2	0648	1.1	1220	5.4	1906	1.1
23	W	0036	5.4	0722	0.9	1254	5.6	1936	1.0
24	TH	0106	5.6	0753	0.7	1324	5.7	○ 2006	0.9
25	F	0134	5.7	0825	0.6	1352	5.8	2037	0.8
26	SA	0202	5.8	0858	0.5	1420	5.9	2109	0.7
27	SU	0229	5.8	0930	0.5	1448	5.9	2140	0.8
28	M	0256	5.8	1001	0.5	1516	5.8	2210	0.8

MARCH

Date	Day	Time	m	Time	m	Time	m	Time	m
1	TU	0325	5.8	1032	0.6	1546	5.7	2242	0.9
2	W	0400	5.7	1107	0.8	1623	5.5	2319	1.1
3	TH	0445	5.5	1148	1.0	1715	5.2	◑	
4	F	0007	1.3	0547	5.2	1245	1.3	1831	4.9
5	SA	0118	1.6	0711	4.9	1412	1.6	2005	4.6
6	SU	0256	1.7	0853	4.9	1550	1.5	2148	4.8
7	M	0435	1.5	1023	5.2	1715	1.2	2258	5.2
8	TU	0551	1.0	1124	5.6	1817	0.9	2351	5.5
9	W	0645	0.6	1214	5.9	1906	0.7		
10	TH	0030	5.8	0732	0.3	1258	6.1	● 1948	0.6
11	F	0110	6.0	0814	0.2	1338	6.2	2028	0.5
12	SA	0148	6.1	0854	0.2	1417	6.1	2106	0.5
13	SU	0226	6.1	0932	0.3	1454	6.0	2142	0.6
14	M	0303	6.0	1008	0.4	1530	5.8	2217	0.7
15	TU	0340	5.9	1042	0.7	1606	5.6	2252	0.9
16	W	0418	5.6	1117	1.0	1643	5.3	2329	1.2
17	TH	0501	5.3	1156	1.4	1728	4.9	◐	
18	F	0016	1.6	0555	4.8	1249	1.8	1834	4.4
19	SA	0120	1.9	0718	4.4	1407	2.1	2011	4.2
20	SU	0249	2.0	0900	4.3	1550	2.0	2145	4.4
21	M	0432	1.8	1020	4.6	1710	1.7	2248	4.7
22	TU	0536	1.4	1113	5.0	1759	1.4	2332	5.1
23	W	0618	1.1	1153	5.4	1836	1.1		
24	TH	0007	5.4	0651	0.8	1227	5.6	1907	0.9
25	F	0038	5.6	0723	0.6	1256	5.7	○ 1937	0.8
26	SA	0105	5.8	0756	0.5	1323	5.8	2008	0.7
27	SU	0131	5.9	0829	0.4	1349	5.9	2041	0.6
28	M	0158	5.9	0903	0.4	1418	5.9	2114	0.6
29	TU	0228	6.0	0935	0.5	1448	5.9	2146	0.7
30	W	0302	5.9	1008	0.6	1522	5.7	2221	0.8
31	TH	0341	5.8	1045	0.8	1604	5.5	2301	1.0

APRIL

Date	Day	Time	m	Time	m	Time	m	Time	m
1	F	0431	5.5	1130	1.1	1702	5.1	2352	1.3
2	SA	0542	5.2	1234	1.5	1826	4.7	◑	
3	SU	0111	1.6	0710	4.9	1409	1.7	2004	4.6
4	M	0253	1.6	0855	4.9	1544	1.5	2139	4.8
5	TU	0426	1.3	1014	5.3	1702	1.2	2242	5.2
6	W	0535	0.8	1110	5.6	1759	0.9	2332	5.6
7	TH	0626	0.5	1156	5.9	1844	0.7		
8	F	0009	5.8	0710	0.4	1236	6.0	● 1923	0.6
9	SA	0045	5.9	0749	0.3	1312	6.0	2001	0.6
10	SU	0121	6.0	0827	0.3	1347	6.0	2038	0.6
11	M	0158	6.0	0902	0.4	1423	5.9	2113	0.6
12	TU	0234	6.0	0937	0.6	1459	5.8	2148	0.7
13	W	0311	5.8	1010	0.8	1533	5.5	2223	0.9
14	TH	0349	5.6	1044	1.1	1610	5.2	2300	1.2
15	F	0431	5.2	1121	1.5	1654	4.9	2342	1.5
16	SA	0524	4.8	1211	1.8	1755	4.5	◐	
17	SU	0041	1.8	0636	4.5	1321	2.0	1917	4.3
18	M	0159	1.9	0808	4.3	1458	2.1	2054	4.3
19	TU	0336	1.8	0935	4.6	1620	1.8	2202	4.7
20	W	0446	1.4	1031	5.0	1714	1.4	2250	5.0
21	TH	0533	1.1	1114	5.3	1755	1.1	2330	5.3
22	F	0612	0.8	1149	5.5	1829	0.9		
23	SA	0002	5.6	0647	0.7	1220	5.7	1903	0.8
24	SU	0028	5.7	0723	0.6	1248	5.8	○ 1937	0.7
25	M	0058	5.9	0759	0.5	1318	5.9	2013	0.6
26	TU	0131	6.0	0836	0.5	1352	5.9	2051	0.6
27	W	0208	6.0	0914	0.5	1429	5.8	2129	0.7
28	TH	0249	5.9	0953	0.7	1513	5.7	2210	0.8
29	F	0338	5.8	1036	0.9	1606	5.4	2257	1.0
30	SA	0439	5.5	1129	1.2	1714	5.1	2356	1.2

Chart Datum: 2·69 metres below IGN Datum

TIME ZONE -0100
(French Standard Time)
Subtract 1 hour for UT
For French Summer Time add ONE hour in **non-shaded areas**

FRANCE – DUNKERQUE

LAT 51°03′N LONG 2°22′E

TIMES AND HEIGHTS OF HIGH AND LOW WATERS

SPRING & NEAP TIDES
Dates in red are SPRINGS
Dates in blue are NEAPS

YEAR **2005**

MAY

Date	Day	Time	m	Time	m	Time	m	Time	m	Moon
1	SU	0549	5.2	1241	1.5	1826	4.8			◑
2	M	0119	1.4	0710	5.0	1409	1.6	1956	4.7	
3	TU	0248	1.3	0843	5.1	1529	1.4	2118	5.0	
4	W	0407	1.0	0953	5.3	1638	1.2	2216	5.3	
5	TH	0510	0.8	1046	5.6	1732	1.0	2304	5.5	
6	F	0601	0.6	1131	5.7	1817	0.9	2345	5.7	
7	SA	0644	0.5	1210	5.8	1857	0.8			
8	SU	0019	5.8	0722	0.6	1246	5.8	1935	0.7	●
9	M	0056	5.9	0759	0.6	1322	5.8	2012	0.7	
10	TU	0134	5.9	0835	0.7	1358	5.7	2049	0.7	
11	W	0212	5.8	0910	0.8	1435	5.6	2125	0.8	
12	TH	0250	5.7	0945	1.0	1511	5.5	2202	0.9	
13	F	0329	5.5	1020	1.2	1549	5.2	2239	1.1	
14	SA	0413	5.2	1059	1.5	1634	5.0	2320	1.4	
15	SU	0504	4.9	1144	1.7	1728	4.7			
16	M	0011	1.6	0603	4.7	1241	1.9	1831	4.5	◐
17	TU	0114	1.7	0711	4.6	1355	1.9	1944	4.5	
18	W	0230	1.6	0825	4.7	1517	1.8	2058	4.7	
19	TH	0344	1.4	0931	4.9	1618	1.5	2156	5.0	
20	F	0440	1.2	1022	5.2	1706	1.3	2241	5.2	
21	SA	0527	0.9	1103	5.4	1749	1.1	2320	5.4	
22	SU	0610	0.8	1138	5.6	1828	0.9	2356	5.6	
23	M	0651	0.7	1214	5.7	1909	0.8			○
24	TU	0030	5.8	0732	0.6	1252	5.8	1950	0.7	
25	W	0111	6.0	0815	0.6	1335	5.9	2034	0.6	
26	TH	0157	6.0	0900	0.7	1423	5.8	2120	0.6	
27	F	0248	5.9	0948	0.8	1517	5.7	2209	0.7	
28	SA	0344	5.8	1039	0.9	1614	5.5	2302	0.8	
29	SU	0443	5.6	1136	1.1	1712	5.3			
30	M	0003	0.9	0544	5.4	1242	1.3	1816	5.1	◑
31	TU	0116	1.0	0657	5.2	1352	1.4	1932	5.0	

JUNE

Date	Day	Time	m	Time	m	Time	m	Time	m	Moon
1	W	0228	1.0	0816	5.2	1500	1.3	2044	5.1	
2	TH	0336	0.9	0921	5.3	1604	1.2	2142	5.3	
3	F	0438	0.9	1015	5.4	1700	1.1	2233	5.4	
4	SA	0532	0.8	1103	5.5	1749	1.1	2318	5.5	
5	SU	0618	0.9	1146	5.5	1833	1.0	2359	5.6	
6	M	0659	0.9	1226	5.6	1914	0.9			●
7	TU	0039	5.6	0737	0.9	1305	5.6	1954	0.8	
8	W	0120	5.7	0814	1.0	1344	5.6	2032	0.8	
9	TH	0158	5.6	0851	1.0	1421	5.5	2110	0.8	
10	F	0237	5.6	0928	1.1	1457	5.4	2147	0.9	
11	SA	0316	5.5	1004	1.2	1535	5.3	2223	1.0	
12	SU	0357	5.3	1040	1.4	1616	5.2	2301	1.2	
13	M	0442	5.1	1120	1.5	1701	5.0	2343	1.3	
14	TU	0530	5.0	1205	1.6	1751	4.9			
15	W	0033	1.3	0623	4.9	1258	1.7	1847	4.8	◐
16	TH	0130	1.4	0720	4.9	1402	1.7	1946	4.8	
17	F	0237	1.4	0820	4.9	1513	1.6	2048	4.9	
18	SA	0344	1.3	0919	5.1	1614	1.4	2146	5.1	
19	SU	0442	1.1	1013	5.3	1708	1.3	2238	5.3	
20	M	0534	1.0	1103	5.4	1758	1.1	2327	5.5	
21	TU	0624	0.9	1150	5.6	1847	0.9			
22	W	0012	5.8	0714	0.8	1238	5.7	1936	0.7	○
23	TH	0101	5.9	0803	0.7	1328	5.8	2025	0.6	
24	F	0153	6.0	0854	0.7	1420	5.8	2115	0.5	
25	SA	0246	6.0	0944	0.7	1513	5.8	2206	0.5	
26	SU	0339	6.0	1035	0.8	1605	5.7	2258	0.5	
27	M	0433	5.8	1127	1.0	1656	5.5	2353	0.6	
28	TU	0528	5.6	1222	1.1	1751	5.4			◑
29	W	0055	0.8	0629	5.4	1320	1.3	1853	5.3	
30	TH	0155	0.9	0736	5.3	1420	1.4	2000	5.2	

JULY

Date	Day	Time	m	Time	m	Time	m	Time	m	Moon
1	F	0257	1.0	0841	5.2	1522	1.4	2103	5.1	
2	SA	0400	1.1	0941	5.1	1626	1.4	2202	5.2	
3	SU	0503	1.2	1037	5.2	1726	1.3	2258	5.2	
4	M	0558	1.2	1130	5.2	1818	1.2	2350	5.4	
5	TU	0644	1.2	1217	5.3	1902	1.0			
6	W	0032	5.5	0724	1.1	1258	5.4	1943	0.9	●
7	TH	0113	5.5	0801	1.1	1336	5.5	2021	0.8	
8	F	0150	5.6	0837	1.1	1410	5.5	2057	0.8	
9	SA	0225	5.6	0912	1.1	1442	5.5	2131	0.8	
10	SU	0259	5.6	0946	1.1	1515	5.5	2205	0.9	
11	M	0336	5.5	1019	1.2	1551	5.4	2239	0.9	
12	TU	0413	5.4	1053	1.2	1628	5.3	2314	1.0	
13	W	0451	5.3	1129	1.3	1707	5.2	2352	1.1	
14	TH	0533	5.2	1211	1.4	1753	5.1			◐
15	F	0040	1.2	0623	5.1	1300	1.5	1847	5.0	
16	SA	0136	1.3	0721	5.0	1405	1.6	1948	5.0	
17	SU	0247	1.4	0825	5.0	1522	1.6	2056	5.0	
18	M	0359	1.3	0934	5.1	1632	1.5	2208	5.2	
19	TU	0506	1.2	1041	5.3	1736	1.2	2313	5.4	
20	W	0609	1.0	1140	5.5	1835	0.9			
21	TH	0007	5.8	0705	0.9	1233	5.7	1928	0.7	○
22	F	0056	6.0	0756	0.7	1322	5.8	2018	0.5	
23	SA	0145	6.1	0845	0.6	1410	5.9	2107	0.3	
24	SU	0235	6.2	0932	0.6	1457	5.9	2154	0.3	
25	M	0324	6.1	1018	0.7	1543	5.9	2241	0.3	
26	TU	0412	5.9	1104	0.9	1628	5.8	2328	0.5	
27	W	0500	5.7	1149	1.0	1714	5.6			
28	TH	0020	0.7	0551	5.5	1238	1.2	1807	5.4	◑
29	F	0113	1.0	0649	5.2	1334	1.5	1910	5.1	
30	SA	0212	1.3	0756	4.9	1438	1.6	2023	4.9	
31	SU	0320	1.5	0907	4.8	1552	1.6	2138	4.9	

AUGUST

Date	Day	Time	m	Time	m	Time	m	Time	m	Moon
1	M	0438	1.6	1018	4.9	1709	1.5	2247	5.0	
2	TU	0545	1.5	1120	5.0	1807	1.3	2344	5.2	
3	W	0634	1.3	1209	5.2	1852	1.1			
4	TH	0025	5.4	0713	1.2	1247	5.4	1931	0.9	
5	F	0103	5.6	0747	1.1	1321	5.6	2005	0.8	●
6	SA	0135	5.7	0819	1.0	1352	5.6	2037	0.7	
7	SU	0205	5.7	0851	1.0	1420	5.7	2109	0.7	
8	M	0236	5.7	0923	1.0	1448	5.7	2141	0.7	
9	TU	0306	5.7	0953	1.0	1518	5.6	2211	0.7	
10	W	0336	5.6	1022	1.1	1546	5.6	2242	0.8	
11	TH	0404	5.5	1054	1.1	1614	5.5	2315	0.9	
12	F	0438	5.4	1129	1.3	1651	5.3	2355	1.1	
13	SA	0525	5.2	1213	1.5	1744	5.1			◐
14	SU	0047	1.4	0630	5.0	1312	1.7	1900	4.9	
15	M	0159	1.6	0746	4.8	1438	1.8	2025	4.9	
16	TU	0328	1.6	0913	4.9	1608	1.6	2158	5.1	
17	W	0451	1.4	1035	5.1	1726	1.3	2307	5.5	
18	TH	0602	1.1	1135	5.5	1828	0.9			
19	F	0001	5.9	0657	0.8	1224	5.8	1919	0.5	○
20	SA	0045	6.1	0745	0.7	1308	6.0	2006	0.3	
21	SU	0131	6.3	0829	0.6	1349	6.1	2050	0.2	
22	M	0215	6.3	0911	0.6	1430	6.1	2133	0.2	
23	TU	0259	6.2	0952	0.7	1511	6.1	2215	0.3	
24	W	0342	6.0	1032	0.8	1551	5.9	2256	0.5	
25	TH	0424	5.8	1112	1.0	1634	5.7	2337	0.9	
26	F	0509	5.5	1154	1.3	1722	5.4			◑
27	SA	0025	1.3	0601	5.1	1245	1.6	1823	5.0	
28	SU	0123	1.7	0710	4.7	1352	1.8	1944	4.7	
29	M	0239	1.9	0835	4.5	1519	1.9	2117	4.6	
30	TU	0416	1.9	1000	4.6	1650	1.7	2236	4.9	
31	W	0529	1.7	1105	4.9	1750	1.3	2331	5.2	

Chart Datum: 2·69 metres below IGN Datum

TIME ZONE -0100
(French Standard Time)
Subtract 1 hour for UT
For French Summer Time add ONE hour in **non-shaded areas**

FRANCE – DUNKERQUE

LAT 51°03′N LONG 2°22′E

TIMES AND HEIGHTS OF HIGH AND LOW WATERS

SPRING & NEAP TIDES
Dates in red are SPRINGS
Dates in blue are NEAPS

YEAR **2005**

SEPTEMBER

Date	Day	Time	m	Time	m	Time	m	Time	m
1	TH	0617	1.4	1151	5.2	1835	1.0		
2	F	0010	5.5	0653	1.2	1226	5.5	1910	0.9
3	SA	0043	5.7	0724	1.1	1258	5.7	● 1941	0.7
4	SU	0112	5.8	0753	1.0	1325	5.8	2010	0.7
5	M	0139	5.8	0823	0.9	1350	5.8	2041	0.6
6	TU	0205	5.9	0854	0.9	1415	5.8	2111	0.6
7	W	0231	5.9	0923	0.9	1440	5.8	2141	0.7
8	TH	0257	5.8	0951	1.0	1505	5.8	2211	0.8
9	F	0324	5.7	1022	1.1	1534	5.7	2243	1.0
10	SA	0359	5.6	1056	1.2	1611	5.5	2321	1.2
11	SU	0444	5.3	1140	1.5	1703	5.2	◐	
12	M	0013	1.5	0553	5.0	1241	1.7	1831	4.9
13	TU	0131	1.8	0725	4.7	1415	1.9	2016	4.8
14	W	0313	1.8	0908	4.7	1556	1.6	2153	5.1
15	TH	0445	1.5	1028	5.1	1717	1.2	2258	5.6
16	F	0552	1.1	1123	5.5	1815	0.7	2349	6.0
17	SA	0642	0.8	1207	5.9	1903	0.4		
18	SU	0028	6.2	0725	0.7	1245	6.1	○ 1946	0.3
19	M	0109	6.3	0805	0.6	1322	6.2	2027	0.2
20	TU	0149	6.3	0844	0.7	1359	6.2	2106	0.3
21	W	0229	6.2	0922	0.7	1438	6.1	2145	0.5
22	TH	0308	6.0	1000	0.9	1517	6.0	2222	0.8
23	F	0347	5.7	1037	1.1	1558	5.8	2259	1.1
24	SA	0428	5.4	1116	1.3	1644	5.4	2340	1.5
25	SU	0516	5.0	1202	1.6	1742	5.0	◑	
26	M	0035	1.9	0623	4.6	1307	2.0	1906	4.6
27	TU	0155	2.2	0757	4.4	1441	2.1	2050	4.5
28	W	0343	2.2	0931	4.5	1619	1.8	2210	4.8
29	TH	0459	1.8	1034	4.9	1721	1.4	2302	5.2
30	F	0547	1.5	1119	5.2	1805	1.1	2341	5.5

OCTOBER

Date	Day	Time	m	Time	m	Time	m	Time	m
1	SA	0623	1.2	1155	5.5	1839	0.9		
2	SU	0013	5.7	0653	1.1	1226	5.7	1908	0.8
3	M	0041	5.8	0722	1.0	1253	5.8	● 1938	0.7
4	TU	0105	5.9	0752	0.9	1316	5.9	2008	0.7
5	W	0130	6.0	0823	0.9	1340	5.9	2040	0.7
6	TH	0156	6.0	0854	0.9	1407	6.0	2112	0.7
7	F	0226	5.9	0924	0.9	1437	5.9	2144	0.9
8	SA	0258	5.8	0957	1.0	1511	5.8	2218	1.0
9	SU	0337	5.6	1035	1.2	1553	5.6	2300	1.3
10	M	0427	5.3	1123	1.5	1654	5.2	◐ 2356	1.6
11	TU	0545	4.9	1231	1.7	1833	4.9		
12	W	0124	1.9	0718	4.7	1410	1.8	2014	4.9
13	TH	0307	1.8	0859	4.8	1545	1.5	2141	5.2
14	F	0431	1.5	1010	5.2	1659	1.0	2241	5.7
15	SA	0532	1.1	1101	5.6	1755	0.7	2330	6.0
16	SU	0619	0.9	1142	5.9	1841	0.5		
17	M	0009	6.2	0701	0.8	1218	6.1	○ 1922	0.4
18	TU	0045	6.2	0739	0.8	1254	6.2	2001	0.4
19	W	0122	6.2	0817	0.8	1331	6.2	2039	0.6
20	TH	0200	6.1	0854	0.8	1410	6.1	2116	0.7
21	F	0238	5.9	0931	0.9	1450	6.0	2152	1.0
22	SA	0316	5.7	1008	1.1	1530	5.7	2228	1.3
23	SU	0355	5.4	1047	1.3	1615	5.3	2307	1.6
24	M	0442	5.0	1131	1.6	1710	4.9	2356	2.0
25	TU	0542	4.6	1228	1.9	1823	4.6	◑	
26	W	0107	2.2	0702	4.4	1350	2.1	2001	4.5
27	TH	0246	2.2	0838	4.5	1525	1.9	2124	4.7
28	F	0407	2.0	0947	4.8	1632	1.6	2217	5.1
29	SA	0501	1.6	1035	5.1	1720	1.2	2259	5.4
30	SU	0541	1.3	1114	5.4	1758	1.0	2335	5.6
31	M	0615	1.2	1148	5.6	1831	0.9		

NOVEMBER

Date	Day	Time	m	Time	m	Time	m	Time	m
1	TU	0004	5.8	0647	1.0	1215	5.8	1903	0.8
2	W	0029	5.9	0720	1.0	1241	5.9	● 1937	0.8
3	TH	0058	6.0	0754	0.9	1310	6.0	2012	0.8
4	F	0130	6.0	0829	0.9	1344	6.0	2049	0.8
5	SA	0206	6.0	0906	0.9	1421	6.0	2126	0.9
6	SU	0246	5.8	0945	1.0	1505	5.8	2207	1.1
7	M	0334	5.6	1029	1.2	1559	5.5	2255	1.4
8	TU	0434	5.2	1124	1.4	1712	5.3	2357	1.7
9	W	0546	5.0	1236	1.6	1830	5.1	◐	
10	TH	0124	1.8	0704	4.8	1403	1.5	2001	5.1
11	F	0251	1.7	0834	5.0	1525	1.3	2118	5.3
12	SA	0404	1.5	0941	5.3	1633	1.0	2216	5.6
13	SU	0504	1.2	1032	5.6	1729	0.8	2305	5.8
14	M	0553	1.1	1114	5.8	1816	0.7	2348	5.9
15	TU	0636	1.0	1153	5.9	1858	0.7		
16	W	0022	6.0	0715	0.9	1231	6.0	○ 1937	0.7
17	TH	0100	6.0	0754	0.9	1311	6.0	2015	0.8
18	F	0138	5.9	0832	0.9	1352	6.0	2053	1.0
19	SA	0217	5.8	0910	0.9	1432	5.8	2129	1.2
20	SU	0255	5.6	0949	1.1	1514	5.6	2206	1.4
21	M	0334	5.4	1027	1.3	1557	5.3	2244	1.6
22	TU	0418	5.1	1108	1.5	1645	5.1	2328	1.9
23	W	0509	4.9	1156	1.7	1742	4.8	◑	
24	TH	0023	2.0	0609	4.7	1254	1.8	1849	4.6
25	F	0132	2.1	0718	4.6	1411	1.8	2008	4.7
26	SA	0253	2.0	0833	4.7	1524	1.6	2116	4.9
27	SU	0358	1.8	0935	4.9	1622	1.4	2206	5.2
28	M	0448	1.5	1023	5.2	1709	1.2	2249	5.4
29	TU	0532	1.3	1103	5.4	1751	1.0	2327	5.6
30	W	0612	1.2	1138	5.6	1831	0.9		

DECEMBER

Date	Day	Time	m	Time	m	Time	m	Time	m
1	TH	0001	5.7	0651	1.1	1213	5.8	● 1910	0.9
2	F	0034	5.9	0732	0.9	1251	5.9	1951	0.8
3	SA	0114	5.9	0814	0.9	1333	6.0	2034	0.9
4	SU	0158	5.9	0858	0.8	1420	6.0	2119	0.9
5	M	0246	5.8	0945	0.9	1512	5.9	2207	1.1
6	TU	0337	5.6	1035	1.0	1608	5.7	2259	1.3
7	W	0432	5.4	1130	1.1	1708	5.5	2357	1.4
8	TH	0531	5.3	1233	1.2	1815	5.3	◐	
9	F	0108	1.6	0637	5.1	1343	1.2	1932	5.2
10	SA	0219	1.6	0754	5.1	1453	1.2	2044	5.3
11	SU	0326	1.5	0902	5.2	1600	1.1	2145	5.4
12	M	0429	1.4	0959	5.4	1701	1.0	2238	5.5
13	TU	0526	1.3	1049	5.5	1754	1.0	2327	5.6
14	W	0615	1.2	1136	5.6	1840	1.0		
15	TH	0008	5.6	0659	1.0	1220	5.7	○ 1922	1.0
16	F	0048	5.7	0740	1.0	1303	5.8	2001	1.0
17	SA	0128	5.7	0820	0.9	1345	5.8	2038	1.1
18	SU	0206	5.7	0858	0.9	1425	5.7	2115	1.2
19	M	0242	5.6	0935	1.0	1503	5.6	2150	1.3
20	TU	0318	5.5	1011	1.1	1540	5.4	2225	1.4
21	W	0356	5.3	1047	1.2	1620	5.3	2302	1.6
22	TH	0437	5.2	1125	1.3	1704	5.1	2342	1.7
23	F	0523	5.0	1208	1.4	1753	5.0	◑	
24	SA	0031	1.8	0616	4.9	1259	1.5	1849	4.9
25	SU	0128	1.9	0714	4.8	1403	1.6	1951	4.8
26	M	0238	1.9	0817	4.8	1514	1.6	2056	4.9
27	TU	0347	1.8	0920	5.0	1617	1.4	2157	5.1
28	W	0446	1.6	1018	5.2	1712	1.3	2250	5.3
29	TH	0540	1.4	1108	5.4	1803	1.1	2339	5.5
30	F	0630	1.1	1156	5.7	1852	1.0		
31	SA	0021	5.7	0718	0.9	1242	5.9	● 1940	0.9

Chart Datum: 2·69 metres below IGN Datum

9.17.7 DUNKERQUE (Port Est)

Nord **51°03'·62N 02°21'·09E** ✲✲✲◊◊◊✿✿

CHARTS AC *323*, 1872, 1350, 5605.11; SHOM 6651, 7057; ECM 1010; Imray C30; Stanfords 1, 20

TIDES Dunkerque is a Standard Port (⟵). +0050 Dover; ML 3·2; Duration 0530; Zone –0100

SHELTER Good; hbr accessible at all tides/weather, but fresh NW–NE winds cause heavy seas at ent and scend in hbr. Yachts must use E Port (busy commercial port), not the W Port. Port du Grand Large and YCMN tidal marinas are 1M down E side of hbr; or enter non-tidal marinas in Bassin du Commerce and Bassin de la Marine (close to the town centre) via Ecluse Trystram and swing bridges.

NAVIGATION From the east, WPT 51°04'·32N 02°22'·32E (E2 lt buoy), 228°/1·0M to hbr ent. From Nieuwpoort Bank WCM lt buoy, the E1-12 buoys (9.17.4) lead S of Banc Hills but shore lights make navigational and shipping lights hard to see. Keep clear of very large ships manoeuvering into/out of Charles de Gaulle lock.

From the west, WPT 51°03'·83N 02°20'·25E (DW29 lt buoy), 111°/0·6M to hbr ent. Fetch Dyck PHM buoy, 5M N of Calais, thence to DKA SWM buoy, and via DW channel lt buoys past W Port to WPT. Streams reach about 3½kn.

LIGHTS AND MARKS Two power stn chimneys (113m), 1M WSW of hbr ent, are conspic, as are the sight and smell of many other industrial structures. The W jetty lt ho is a substantial white twr, brown top; in contrast the E jetty lt pylon is small, slender and less obvious, but the jetty itself is illuminated by 9 bright sodium lights. The ldg lts and the lofty main lt ho, W tr with B top, lead 137°/1M toward the marinas. [The 179° and 185° ldg lts, all F Bu, relate to big ship turning circles].

IPTS (full) shown from the W jetty hd (when big ships are under way).

Lock sigs (H24), shown at Ecluse Watier, are three horiz pairs disposed vertically: middle pair refers to Ecluse Watier (rarely used by yachts) and bottom pair to Ecluse Trystram:

● ● = lock open. ● ● = lock closed.

Lock sigs at individual locks:

● ● = lock ready. ● + Fl ● = enter and berth on side of Fl ●.

● ● = no entry, lock in use.

Ⓦ = transit lock; slack water, both gates open (freeflow).

● ●

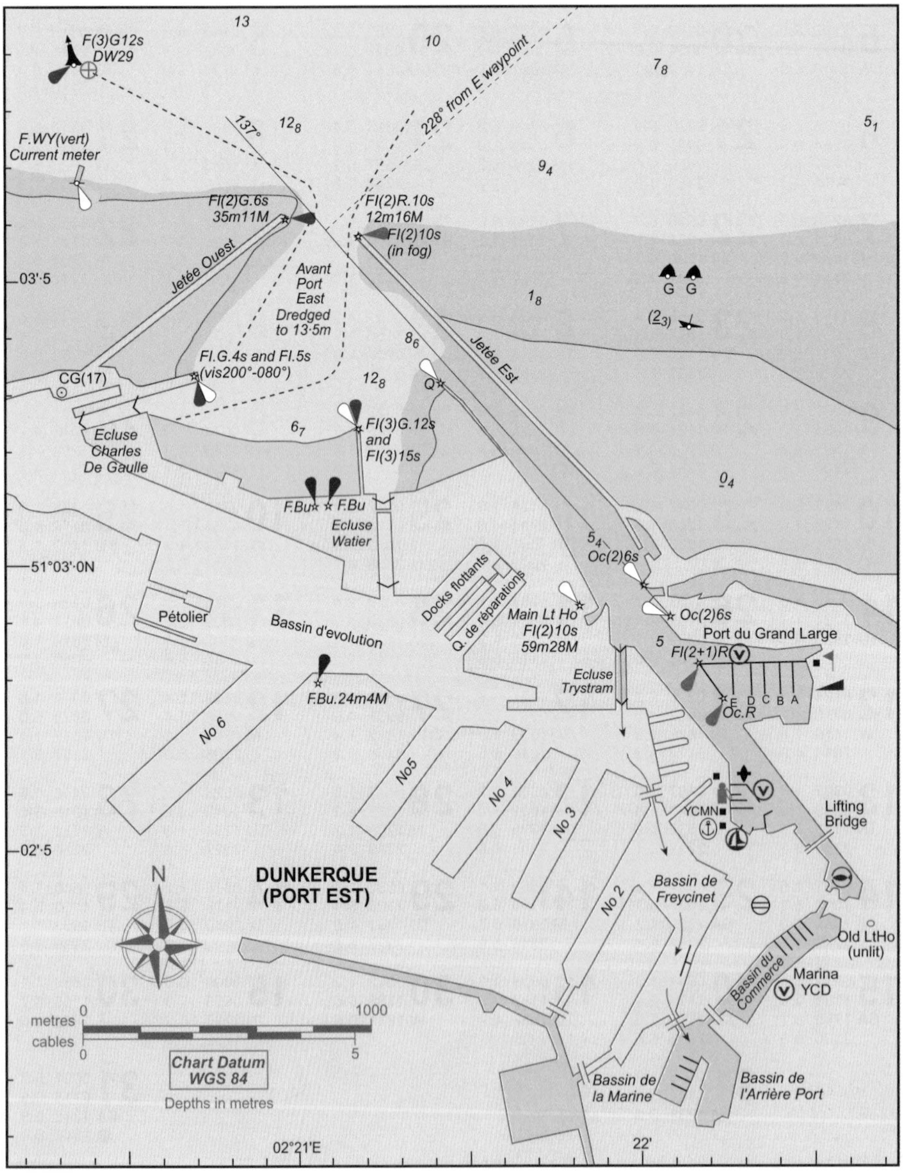

13
10
F(3)G12s
DW29
F.WY(vert)
Current meter
137°
228° from E waypoint
12₈
7₈
5₁
9₄
Fl(2)G.6s
35m11M
Fl(2)R.10s
12m16M
Fl(2)10s
(in fog)
Jetée Ouest
Avant
Port
East
Dredged
to 13·5m
03'·5
G G
1₈
(2₃)
8₆
Jetée Est
Fl.G.4s and Fl.5s
(vis200°-080°)
CG(17)
12₈
6₇
Fl(3)G.12s
and
Fl(3)15s
Ecluse
Charles
De Gaulle
0₄
F.Bu
F.Bu
Ecluse
Watier
5₄
Oc(2)6s
51°03'·0N
Docks flottants
Q. de réparations
Pétolier
Bassin d'evolution
Main Lt Ho
Fl(2)10s
59m28M
Oc(2)6s
Port du Grand Large
5
Fl(2+1)R
Ecluse
Trystram
F.Bu.24m4M
E D C B A
Oc.R
No 6
No5
No 4
No 3
YCMN
Lifting
Bridge
02'·5
N
DUNKERQUE
(PORT EST)
Bassin de
Freycinet
No 2
Old LtHo
(unlit)
Bassin du
Commerce
Marina
YCD
metres 0 1000
cables 0 5
Chart Datum
WGS 84
Depths in metres
Bassin de
la Marine
Bassin de
l'Arrière Port
02°21'E
22'

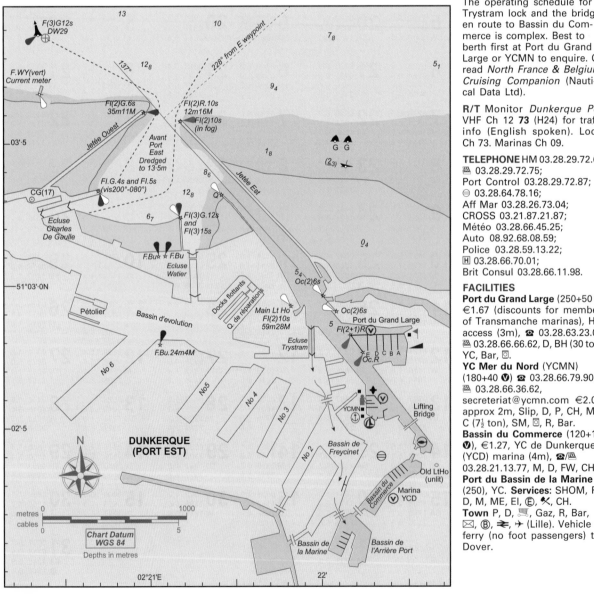

The operating schedule for Trystram lock and the bridges en route to Bassin du Commerce is complex. Best to berth first at Port du Grand Large or YCMN to enquire. Or read *North France & Belgium Cruising Companion* (Nautical Data Ltd).

R/T Monitor *Dunkerque Port* VHF Ch 12 **73** (H24) for traffic info (English spoken). Locks Ch 73. Marinas Ch 09.

TELEPHONE HM 03.28.29.72.61, Fax 03.28.29.72.75; Port Control 03.28.29.72.87; ⊖ 03.28.64.78.16; Aff Mar 03.28.26.73.04; CROSS 03.21.87.21.87; Météo 03.28.66.45.25; Auto 08.92.68.08.59; Police 03.28.59.13.22; Ⓗ 03.28.66.70.01; Brit Consul 03.28.66.11.98.

FACILITIES

Port du Grand Large (250+50 Ⓥ) €1.67 (discounts for members of Transmanche marinas), H24 access (3m), ☎ 03.28.63.23.00, Fax 03.28.66.66.62, D, BH (30 ton), YC, Bar, ⊡.

YC Mer du Nord (YCMN) (180+40 Ⓥ) ☎ 03.28.66.79.90, Fax 03.28.66.36.62, secreteriat@ycmn.com €2.05, approx 2m, Slip, D, P, CH, ME, C (7½ ton), SM, ⊡, R, Bar.

Bassin du Commerce (120+13 Ⓥ), €1.27, YC de Dunkerque (YCD) marina (4m), ☎/Fax 03.28.21.13.77, M, D, FW, CH.

Port du Bassin de la Marine (250), YC. **Services:** SHOM, P, D, M, ME, El, Ⓔ, ⚒, CH.

Town P, D, ⛟, Gaz, R, Bar, ✉, Ⓑ, ⇌, ✈ (Lille). Vehicle ferry (no foot passengers) to Dover.

9.17.8 GRAVELINES

Nord **51°00'·94N 02°05'·55E** ❁❁◊◊✿✿

CHARTS AC *323, 5605.11,* 1350*;* SHOM 6651, 7057; Stan 1, 20.

TIDES HW +0045 on Dover (UT); ML 3·3m; Duration 0520.

Standard Port DUNKERQUE (⟵)

Times				**Height (metres)**			
High Water		Low Water		MHWS	MHWN	MLWN	MLWS
0200	0800	0200	0900	6·0	5·0	1·5	0·6
1400	2000	1400	2100				
Differences GRAVELINES (10M WSW of Dunkerque Est)							
−0005	−0015	−0005	+0005	+0·3	+0·1	−0·1	−0·1

SHELTER Good, but chan has only 0·5m at LWS; do not enter in strong onshore winds. Access approx HW ±3 for shoal draft, ±2 if draft >1·5m; max draft 2·5m. For a first visit HW would be sensible. The 10m wide entry gate stays open HW ±3 in season, HW ±1½ out of season. The ancient, manually operated bridge across the entry gate cannot be opened in strong NE or SW winds; ergo the basin cannot be entered. A digital depth gauge shows depth over the sill which dries 0·6m. Berth on Ⓥ pontoon or as directed.

NAVIGATION WPT 51°01'·30N 02°05'·13E, 142°/0·43M to bkwtr heads; old lt ho (unlit, conspic B/W spiral) in transit with wine-glass shaped water twr 142°. Beware strong E-going stream across ent at HW. Dredger often working at entrance. Do not cut between the E bkwtr head and a NCM lt bcn close N of it.

The whole access chan dries (soft mud); it is about 15m wide and marked by lateral tripod bcns. Keep to the W on entry and to the E when inside. The chan turns 60° stbd at the FR lt. Yachts should enter Bassin Vauban which partly dries, but fin keelers sink upright into glorious, soft mud. The River Aa, pronounced Ar-Ar, flows through the Bassin via sluice gates upstream.

LIGHTS AND MARKS Lts as chartlet and 9.17.4. The disused lt ho, with continuous black and white spiral band, is very distinctive. A nuclear power stn with 6 towers (63m) is 1M NE. 1.8m further NE is the ent to Dunkerque Ouest, commercial & ferry port. The white sector (317°-327°) of the W bkwtr lt is visible from within the ent chan. The G sector (078°-085°) shines parallel with the coast and just to seaward of the drying line.

R/T VHF Ch 09 (HO).

TELEPHONE Aff Mar ☎ 03.28.26.73.00.

FACILITIES Bassin Vauban (410+40), approx €1.35, HM ☎ 03.28.23.19.45, 📠 03.28.23.05.36; BH (12 ton), C (3 ton); **Gravelines Plaisance** ☎ 03.28.65.55.28, M, C (10 ton); **Services:** CH, El, M, ME,✖. **Town** Ⓑ, Bar, D, P, ✉, R, ⇌, 🛒, ⊡.

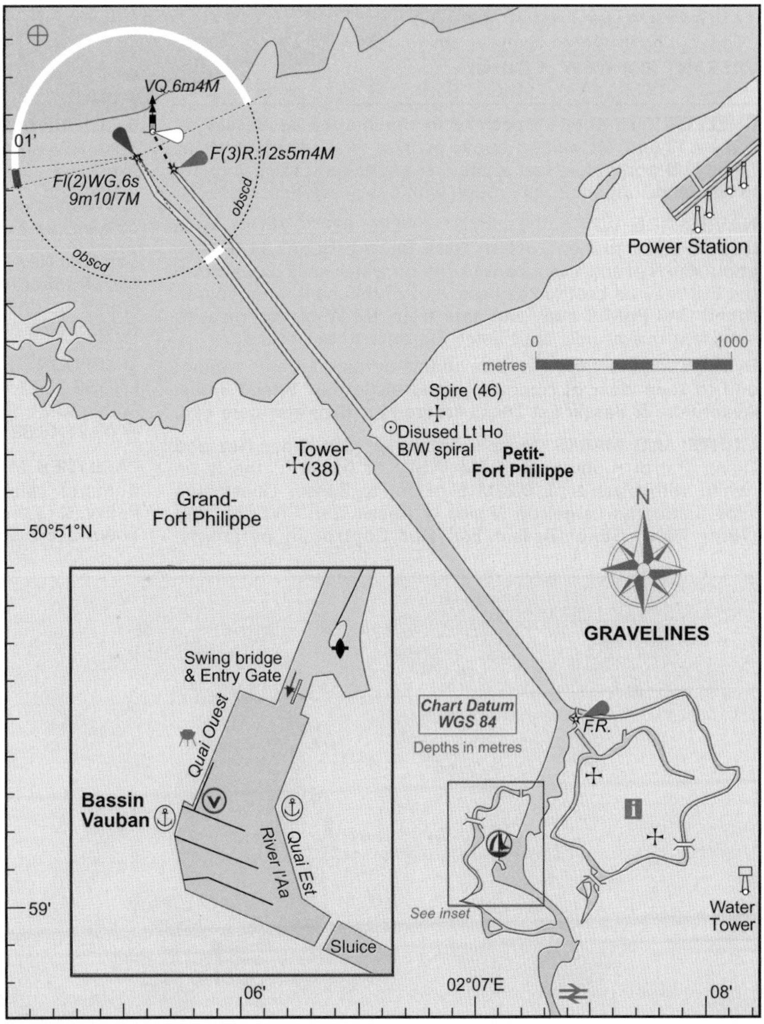
VQ.6m4M
F(3)R.12s5m4M
Fl(2)WG.6s
9m10/7M
obscd
obscd
01'
Power Station
0
1000
metres
Spire (46)
Disused Lt Ho
B/W spiral
Tower
(38)
Petit-
Fort Philippe
Grand-
Fort Philippe
50°51°N
N
GRAVELINES
Swing bridge
& Entry Gate
Quai Ouest
Bassin
Vauban
River l'Aa
Quai Est
Sluice
Chart Datum
WGS 84
Depths in metres
F.R.
See inset
Water
Tower
59'
06'
02°07'E
08'

17

AGENTS WANTED If you are interested in becoming our agent for any of the following ports, please write to: The Editor, Reeds OKI Nautical Almanac, A&C Black Publishers Ltd, 37 Soho Square, London, W1D 3QZ – and get your free copy of the Almanac annually. You do not have to live in a port to be the agent, but should at least be a fairly regular visitor.

Keyhaven
Shetland Isles/Lerwick
Rothesay
Dunmore East
Baltimore
Belfast Lough
All Danish ports
Borkum
Langeoog
Zeebrugge

Hoek van Holland
Rotterdam
Blankenberge
IJsselmeer
Le Havre
Le Légué
St Helier/Gorey
Bénodet
Concarneau
Lézardrieux

Lannion River
Loctudy
River Loire
Pornic
St Gilles-Croix-de-Vie
Les Sables d'Olonne
La Rochelle
Rochefort
Capbreton
Port d'Anglet

St Jean de Luz
Any ports in N or NW Spain
except:
Ria de Ares
Ria de Betanzos
La Coruna
Bayona

9.17.9 CALAIS

Pas de Calais **50°58'·33N 01°50'·42E** ☸☸⚓⚓✿✿

CHARTS AC *1892, 323,* 1351, 5605.10; SHOM 7323, 6651, 7258; ECM 1010; Imray C8; Stanfords 1, 20

TIDES +0048 Dover; ML 4·0; Duration 0525; Zone –0100

Standard Port DUNKERQUE (←)

Times				Height (metres)			
High Water		Low Water		MHWS	MHWN	MLWN	MLWS
0200	0800	0200	0900	6·0	5·0	1·5	0·6
1400	2000	1400	2100				
Differences CALAIS							
–0020	–0030	–0015	–0005	+1·2	+0·9	+0·6	+0·3
SANDETTIE BANK (11M N of Calais)							
–0015	–0025	–0020	–0005	+0·1	–0·1	–0·1	–0·1
WISSANT (8M WSW of Calais)							
–0035	–0050	–0030	–0010	+1·9	+1·5	+0·8	+0·4

SHELTER Very good, especially in the marina at Bassin de l'Ouest (3-6m). W waiting buoys outside tidal gate (see times below). Ⓥ pontoon is first to stbd, some fingers. In strong NW to NE winds hbr ent is very rough with heavy swell; access H24.

NAVIGATION WPT 50°58'·26N 01°49'·29E, 090°/0·7M to Jetée Ouest hd; best to keep S of ferry track. Beware Ridens de la Rade, about 4ca N of ent, a sandbank (0·7m) on which seas break. From the E it may be best to keep seaward of this bank until able to round CA8 PHM lt buoy and appr from 1M W of hbr; or, with sufficient rise of tide, appr Jetée Est on a track of 233°.

Byelaws require yachts to have engine running (even if sailing) and to keep clear of commercial vessels/ferries. Speed limits: Avant-Port & Bassin Est 10kn; Arrière-Port 8kn; elswhere 5kn.

LIGHTS AND MARKS Conspic daymarks: Cap Blanc-Nez and Dover Patrol monument, 5·5M WSW of hbr ent; the lt ho (white with black top), 0.23M E of ent to Bassin Ouest; two silos (Little and Large) on N side of Bassin Est; R/W chimney (78m) 700m SE of Bassin Est; Hbr Control in pyramidal bldg at the entrance to Arrière Port. Lts as chartlet and 9.17.4.

IPTS (full code), shown from Jetée Est and as on chartlet, must be strictly obeyed. IPTS run the show; no VHF chatter should be necessary. If no sigs are shown (ie no ferries under way), yachts may enter/exit. Or follow a ferry entering/leaving, keeping to the stbd side of the fairway and not impeding said ferry.

Additional traffic lts, shown alongside the top IPTS lt, are:

● = ferry leaving; no movements.
● = ferry entering; no movements.
One ● (alongside lowest IPTS lt) = dredger working, (this does not prohibit movements).

Bassin de l'Ouest (marina). Tidal gate and swing bridge open HW –1½, HW and HW +½. (Sat/Sun, Hols: HW –2, HW and HW +1). Times may vary. Before leaving, tell bridge operator your ETD.

● = All movements prohib.
○ = 10 mins before gate opens.
● = Movement authorised.
4 blasts = Request permission to enter.

Bassin Carnot: Lock in only if bound for the canals. Gates open HW –1½ to HW +¾. Lock sigs are as per the CEVNI code.
2 blasts = Request permission to enter.

R/T Whilst underway in appr's and hbr, monitor Ch **12** 16 (H24) *Calais Port Traffic* and marina. Carnot lock Ch 12 (occas).

Cap Gris Nez, Channel Navigation Info Service (CNIS), call: *Gris Nez Traffic* Ch **13** 79 16 (H24). Info broadcasts in English and French on Ch 79, at H + 10, and also at H + 25 when vis is < 2M. *CROSS Gris Nez* Ch 15, 67, **68**, 73.

TELEPHONE HM (Port) 03.21.96.31.20; Aff Mar 03.21.34.52.70; CROSS 03.21.87.21.87; SNSM 03.21.96.31.20; ⊖ 03.21.34.75.40; Météo 03.21.33.24.25; Auto 08.36.68.08.62; Police 03.21.96.74.17; Ⓗ 03.21.46.33.33; Brit Consul 03.21.96.33.76.

FACILITIES Marina ☎ 03.21.34.55.23, 📠 03.21.96.10.78 (Marc Sumera). calais-marina@calais.cci.fr. 350-400 inc Ⓥ €0.92. D, P, FW, C (3 ton); **YC de Calais** ☎ 03.21.97.02.34, M, P, Bar. **Town** Ⓟ, ⚒, SM, 🛒, Gaz, R, Bar, ✉, Ⓑ, ⇌, ✈. Ferries to Dover.

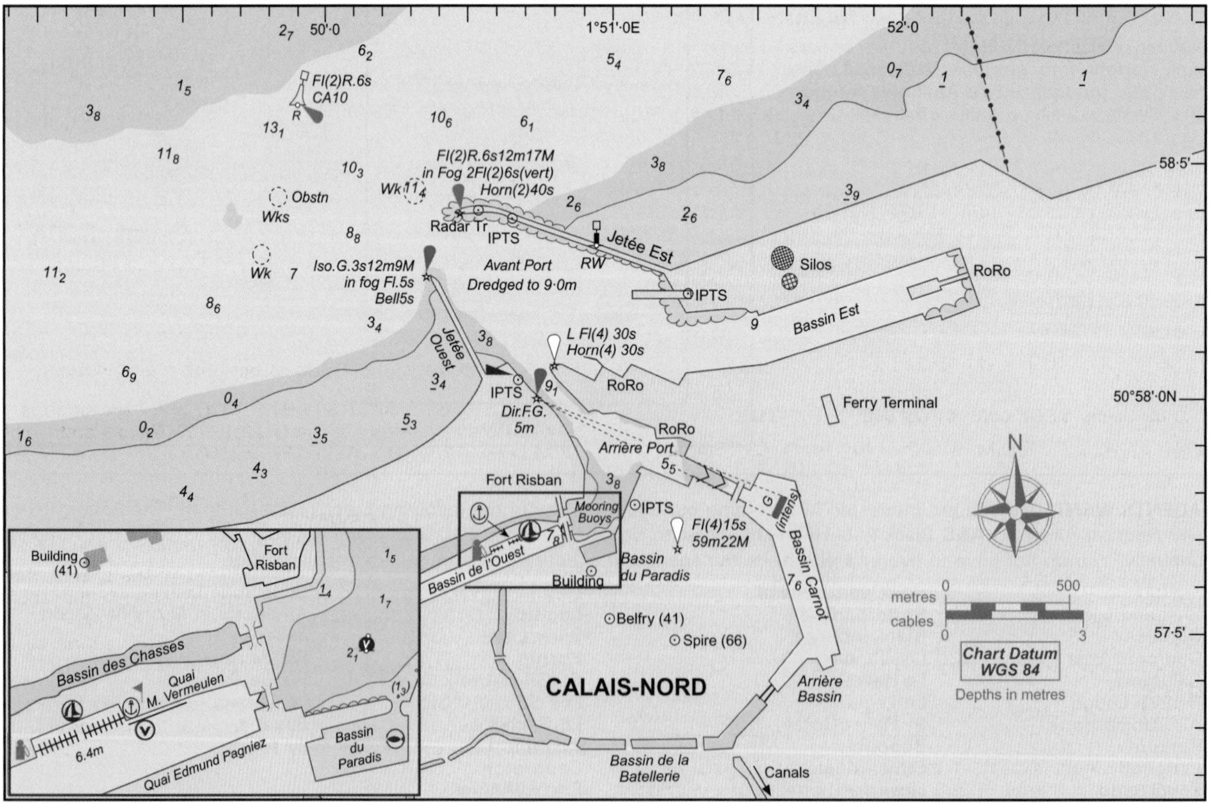
50'·0
1°51'·0E
52'·0
58·5'
50°58'·0N
57·5'
Fl(2)R.6s
CA10
Fl(2)R.6s12m17M
in Fog 2Fl(2)6s(vert)
Horn(2)40s
Obstn
Wks
Wk
Radar Tr
IPTS
Jetée Est
Avant Port
Dredged to 9·0m
Iso.G.3s12m9M
in fog Fl.5s
Bell5s
Jetée Ouest
Silos
RoRo
Bassin Est
L Fl(4) 30s
Horn(4) 30s
Dir.F.G.
5m
Ferry Terminal
Arrière Port
Fort Risban
Mooring Buoys
Fl(4)15s
59m22M
Bassin du Paradis
Bassin de l'Ouest
Building
Bassin Carnot
Belfry (41)
Spire (66)
CALAIS-NORD
Arrière Bassin
Bassin de la Batellerie
Canals
metres
cables
500
Chart Datum
WGS 84
Depths in metres
Building (41)
Fort Risban
Bassin des Chasses
Quai M. Vermeulen
Quai Edmund Pagniez
6.4m
Bassin du Paradis

9.17.10 BOULOGNE-SUR-MER

Pas de Calais **50°44'·58N 01°34'·10E**

CHARTS AC *1892, 2451*, 438; SHOM 6824, 7247, 7416, 7323; ECM 1010, 1011; Imray C8, C31; Stanfords 1, 9, 20, 30.

TIDES 0000 Dover; ML 4·9; Duration 0515; Zone –0100

Standard Port DUNKERQUE (⟵)

Times				Height (metres)			
High Water		Low Water		MHWS	MHWN	MLWN	MLWS
0200	0800	0200	0900	6·0	5·0	1·5	0·6
1400	2000	1400	2100				
Differences BOULOGNE							
–0045	–0100	–0045	–0025	+2·8	+2·2	+1·1	+0·5

SHELTER Good, except in strong NW'lies. Ent possible at all tides and in most weather. Marina pontoons (2·7m) on W side of tidal river are all intended for visitors. Beware turbulence when R Liane in spate/sluicing. FVs berth on Quai Gambetta. Local boats berth on pontoons in Bassin Napoléon, entry HW–3 to HW+3¾ (by day only). Visitors may arrange a long-stay berth in Bassin Napoléon. The lock opens approx every 45 mins, with freeflow HW–2 to HW+2. Exposed ⚓ in N part of outer hbr; no ⚓ SW of pecked magenta line.

NAVIGATION WPT 50°44'·71N 01°33'·00E, 100°/0·71M to hbr ent (below Title). No navigational dangers, but keep W and S of the free-standing head of Digue Nord, as outer part of bkwtr covers at HW. After rounding Digue Carnot, head S for 324m to a white □ mark on bkwtr, thence track 117° to inner ent, clear of the drying NE side of hbr. Obey IPTS; keep clear of ferries.

LIGHTS AND MARKS 'Approches Boulogne' SCM buoy is 295°/ 2·1M from Digue Carnot lt. Cap d'Alprech lt ho is 2·5M S of hbr ent. Monument is conspic 2M E of hbr ent. Cathedral dome is conspic, 0·62M E of marina. There are no ldg lts/marks. 2 Bu lts (hor) upriver of marina = sluicing from R Liane.

IPTS are shown from SW jetty hd (FG ☆), and from Quai Gambetta, opposite ☆ 3FG ▽, visible from marina. A Y lt ● by top IPTS = dredger working, but does not prohibit movements.

R/T VHF Ch **12** (H24). Marina Ch 09. Forecasts by CROSS Gris Nez Ch 79 at H+10 (078-1910LT).

TELEPHONE Control Twr 03.21.31.52.43; ⊜ 03.21.80.89.90; Aff Mar 03.21.30.53.23; CROSS 03.21.87.21.87; Météo 08.36.68.08.62; Auto 08.92.65.08.08; Maritime Police 03.21.30.87.09; Emergency 17; Ⓗ 03.21.99.33.33; Brit Consul 03.21.87.16.80.

FACILITIES Marina (114 inc 80 Ⓥ) ☎ 03.21.31.70.01, €2.07 (obtain swipe card from HM), D, Slip, C (20 ton). **Bassin Napoléon** local boats and long-stay visitors, see under Shelter. **YC Boulonnais** ☎ 03.21.31.80.67, C, R, Bar; **Services:** Ⓔ, ME, El, ⚒, M, Divers, SHOM; **Town** P (cans), 🛒, Gas, Gaz, R, Bar, ✉, Ⓑ, ⇌, ✈ (Le Touquet); Ferry to Dover. Note: The 'bad smells' of 2003, due to a sewage plant failure, are said to be a thing of the past - phew.

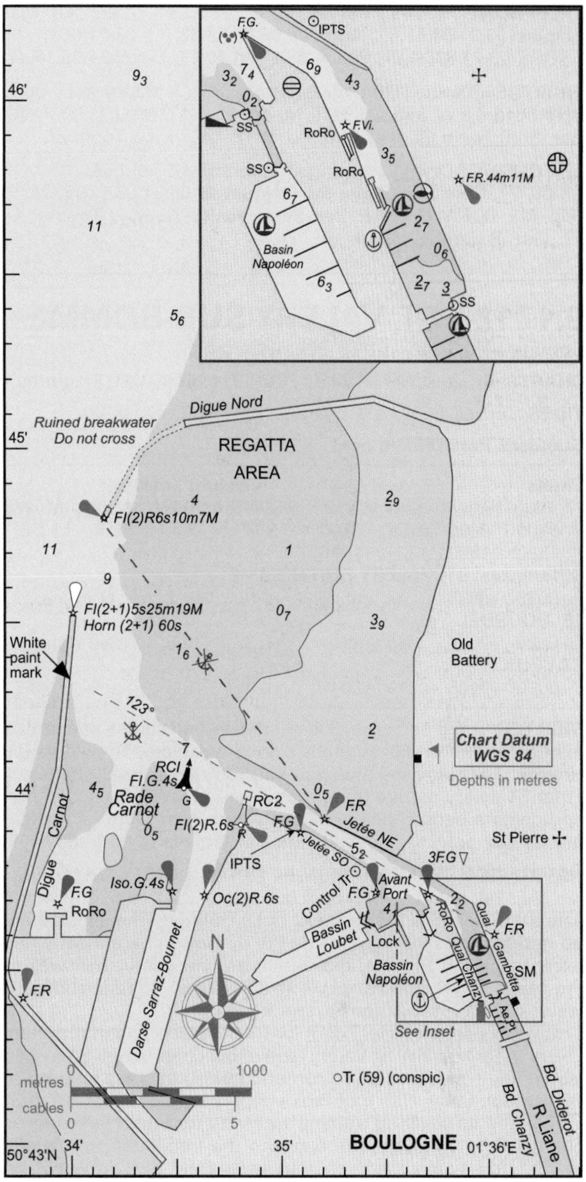
IPTS
F.G.
RoRo
F.Vi.
SS
F.R.44m11M
Basin Napoléon
Digue Nord
Ruined breakwater
Do not cross
REGATTA AREA
Fl(2)R6s10m7M
Fl(2+1)5s25m19M
Horn (2+1) 60s
White paint mark
Old Battery
123°
Chart Datum WGS 84
Depths in metres
RCI
Fl.G.4s
Rade Carnot
RC2
Fl(2)R.6s
F.G
F.R
Jetée NE
Jetée SO
St Pierre
3F.G ▽
IPTS
Iso.G.4s
Oc(2)R.6s
Control Tr
Avant Port
F.G
Bassin Loubet
Lock
Bassin Napoléon
Quai Gambetta
Quai Chanzy
RoRo
SM
See Inset
Digue Carnot
Darse Sarraz-Bournet
N
metres
cables
1000
Tr (59) (conspic)
Bd Diderot
Bd Chanzy
R Liane
BOULOGNE
50°43'N
34'
35'
01°36'E
46'
45'
44'

9.17.11 ÉTAPLES

Pas de Calais **50°31'·00N 01°38'·00E**

CHARTS AC *2451*; SHOM 7416; ECM 1011; Imray C31; Stanfords 1.

TIDES –0010 Dover; ML 5·3; Duration 0520; Zone –0100

Standard Port DIEPPE (⟶)

Times				Height (metres)			
High Water		Low Water		MHWS	MHWN	MLWN	MLWS
0100	0600	0100	0700	9·3	7·4	2·5	0·8
1300	1800	1300	1900				
Differences LE TOUQUET (ÉTAPLES)							
+0007	+0017	+0032	+0032	+0·2	+0·3	+0·4	+0·4
BERCK							
+0007	+0017	+0028	+0028	+0·5	+0·5	+0·4	+0·4

SHELTER Good, except in strong W'lies. At Étaples, access HW±2 to small marina (1·2m) close downstream of low bridge; beware up to 5kn current. Best to berth on No 1 pontoon.

NAVIGATION WPT 50°32'·88N 01°32'·36E is on the boundary between W and G sectors of Camiers lt; 090°/0·7M to Mérida unlit WCM buoy (50°32'·88N 01°33'·47E), marking a drying wreck 2M NW of Le Touquet lt ho. Best app is at HW –1 to reach Étaples marina at slack water. Estuary dries 1M offshore; do not attempt entry in even moderate SW/W winds, when seas break heavily a long way out. Careful identification of marks is essential.

The outer part of the buoyed chan constantly shifts, such that the chan ent may lie N or S of the ⊕. Nos 1 & 2 buoys (the latter, Fl (2) R 6s) should be visible from the WPT. Bcn, Fl R 4s, 4ca SW of Camiers lt, marks NE end of covering training wall (also marked by posts) leading towards the marina.

LIGHTS AND MARKS See 9.17.4. Le Touquet is at the S end of 175m high hills, visible for 25M. Le Touquet lt ho, orange with brown band, is conspic; Camiers' R pylon is hard to see by day.

R/T VHF Ch 09.

TELEPHONE HM 03.21.84.54.33, 📠 03.21.09.76.96; Aff Mar Étaples 03.21.94.61.50; Auto 08.92.68.08.62; ⊜ 03.21.05.01.72; CROSS 03.21.87.21.87; Police 03.21.94.60.17; Dr 03.21.05.14.42.

FACILITIES Marina (115 + 15 visitors), €1.37, C (8 ton), P, D; Quay BH (130 ton), FW, Slip, CH, El, T, M, ME, ⚒, D. **YC** ☎ 03.21.94.74.26, Bar, Slip. **Town** Ⓑ, Bar, D, P, ✉, R, ⇄, 🛒. ✈ Le Touquet.

LE TOUQUET Drying moorings to stbd off Le Touquet YC. VHF Ch 09, 77. **Cercle Nautique du Touquet** ☎ 03.21.05.12.77, M, P, Slip, ME, D, FW, C, CH, R, Bar; **Services**: BY, ⚒, SM. **Town** P, D, 🛒, Gaz, R, Bar, ✉, Ⓑ, ⇄, ✈.

9.17.12 ST VALÉRY-SUR-SOMME

Somme **50°11'·34N 01°38'·90E** ✿✿✿✿✿✿

CHARTS AC *2451*; SHOM 7416; ECM 1011; Imray C31; Stanfords 1

TIDES LE HOURDEL –0010 Dover; ML —; Zone –0100

Standard Port DIEPPE (⟶)

Times				Height (metres)			
High Water		Low Water		MHWS	MHWN	MLWN	MLWS
0100	0600	0100	0700	9·3	7·4	2·5	0·8
1300	1800	1300	1900				
Differences ST VALÉRY-SUR-SOMME							
+0035	+0035	No data		+0·9	+0·7	No data	
LE HOURDEL							
+0020	+0020	No data		+0·8	+0·6	No data	
CAYEUX							
0000	+0005	+0015	+0010	+0·4	+0·5	+0·5	+0·5

SHELTER The B de Somme is open to W and can be dangerous in onshore winds >F6. Silting is a major problem. The 3 hbrs (Le Hourdel, Le Crotoy and St Valéry-sur-Somme) are well sheltered. Enter St Valéry marina (max draft 2·0m) at HW ±1; usually met and given a berth. Abbeville Canal (max draft 2·0m) is navigable, by day only, to Abbeville; pre-call Amiens ☎ 06.74.83.6069.

NAVIGATION WPT 50°14'·00N 01°28'·06E ['ATSO' SWM buoy, Mo (A) 12s], about 1·6M NW of buoyed chan (shifts). The whole estuary dries up to 3M seaward of Le Hourdel. The sands build up in ridges offshore, but inside Pte du Hourdel are mostly flat, except where R Somme and minor streams scour their way to the sea. If Dover tidal range >4·4m, at HW ±1 there is sufficient water over the sands for vessels <1·5m draft.
Visit www.portsaintvalery.com for most recent plan of the chan. Leave 'ATSO' at HW St Valéry –2. Follow chan buoys S1 to S50 (some lit), in strict order (no corner-cutting!) to small unlit WCM BIFurcation buoy, N to E of Pte du Hourdel. Here fork stbd to St Valéry and its covering training wall with four light beacons; as chartlet & 9.17.4. Continue between the tree-lined promenade to stbd and a covering dyke marked by PHM bns. At W twr on head of Digue du Large turn stbd past town quay into marina, dredged 2m. If N-bound leave St Valéry HW–2 for a fair tide.

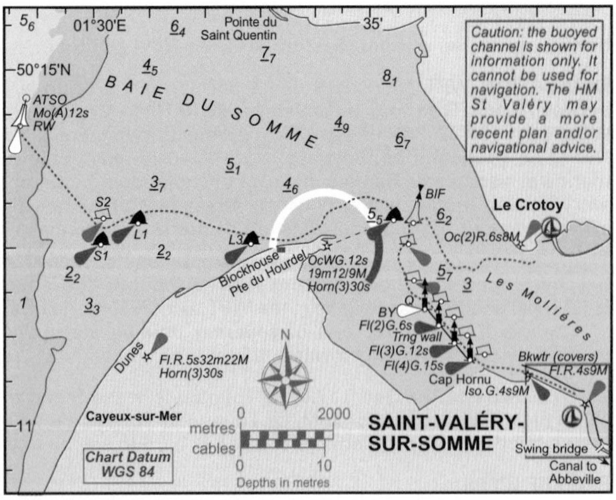
Caution: the buoyed channel is shown for information only. It cannot be used for navigation. The HM St Valéry may provide a more recent plan and/or navigational advice.
01°30'E
50°15'N
35'
Pointe du Saint Quentin
BAIE DU SOMME
ATSO Mo(A)12s RW
Le Crotoy
Oc(2)R.6s8M
BIF
S2
S1
L1
L3
Blockhouse
Pte du Hourdel
OcWG.12s 19m12/9M Horn(3)30s
Les Mollières
Trng wall
Fl(2)G.6s
Fl(3)G.12s
Fl(4)G.15s
Cap Hornu
Iso.G.4s9M
Bkwtr (covers)
Fl.R.4s9M
Dunes
Fl.R.5s32m22M Horn(3)30s
Cayeux-sur-Mer
SAINT-VALÉRY-SUR-SOMME
Swing bridge
Canal to Abbeville
metres
cables
Depths in metres
Chart Datum WGS 84

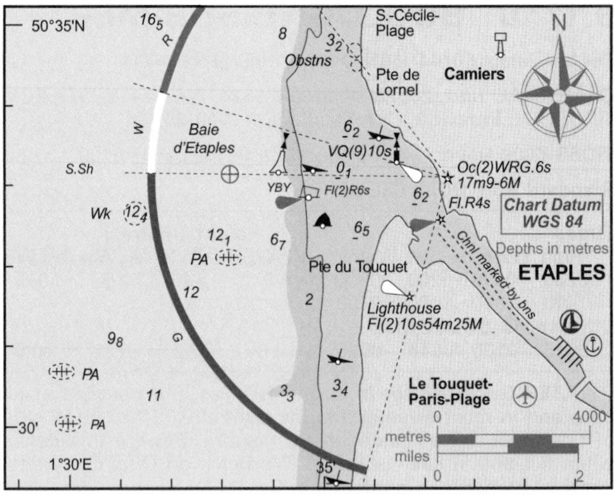
50°35'N
30'
1°30'E
S.-Cécile-Plage
Pte de Lornel
Camiers
Obstns
Baie d'Etaples
VQ(9)10s
YBY
Fl(2)R6s
Oc(2)WRG.6s 17m9-6M
Fl.R4s
Chart Datum WGS 84
Depths in metres
ETAPLES
Chnl marked by bns
Pte du Touquet
Lighthouse Fl(2)10s54m25M
Le Touquet-Paris-Plage
S.Sh
Wk
PA
metres
miles

LIGHTS AND MARKS Cayeux-sur-Mer lt ho (W with R top) is a good landmark. Pte du Hourdel lt ho is partly obscured by dunes until close to. Le Crotoy water twr is conspic. See also 9.17.4.

R/T VHF Ch 09 (St Valéry HW ±2; Le Crotoy YC Jul/Aug only).

TELEPHONE Aff Mar 03.22.27.81.44; ⊜ 03.22.24.04.75; Lock (canal) 03.22.60.80.23; CROSS 03.21.87.21.87; Auto 08.92.68.08.80; Police 03.22.60.82.08; Dr 03.22.26.92.25; Brit Consul 03.21.96.33.76.

FACILITIES Marina and YC Sport Nautique Valéricain (250 + 30 Ⓥ) ☎ 03.22.60.24.80, 📠 03.22.60.24.82, snval@wanadoo.fr €1.55 (pontoon), C (9 ton), Slip, ⊡, R, Bar; Access HW ±1; **Services:** ME, El, CH, Ⓔ. **Town** EC Mon; P, D, CH, 🛒, Gaz, R, Bar, ✉, Ⓑ, ⇄ and ✈ (Abbeville). Ferry: See Dieppe, Boulogne or Calais.

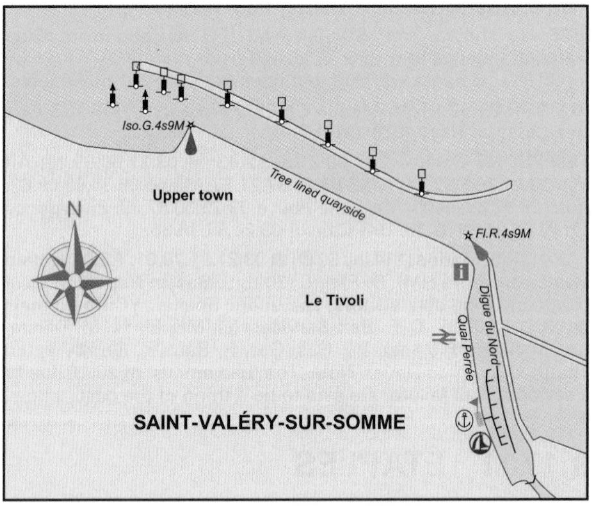
Iso.G.4s9M
Upper town
Tree lined quayside
Fl.R.4s9M
Le Tivoli
Digue du Nord
Quai Perrée
SAINT-VALÉRY-SUR-SOMME

ADJACENT HARBOURS

LE HOURDEL: A basic FV hbr. Access HW±1½. After the lt ho, head SW via unmarked side chan to hug the end of shingle spit. Dry out on hard sand. Impossible to leave before HW –2.

LE CROTOY Somme **50°13'·07N 01°37'·99E** ✿✿✿✿
From the BIF buoy follow the chan N and E, marked by buoys C1-C8. Enter hbr very close to FV stages (port-side). The badly silted marina can be entered by max draft 0·8m when tidal range at Dover >4·4m (approx Coeff 85). Secure at last FV stage and ask YC for berth on the two drying pontoons. Departure impossible before HW –2. **Marina** (280) ☎ 03.22.27.83.11 (office in YC bldg), C (6 ton), Slip; **YC Nautique de la Baie de Somme** ☎ 03.22.27.83.11, Bar. **Town** Ⓑ, Bar, D, P, ✉, R, ⇄, 🛒.

9.17.13 LE TRÉPORT

Seine Maritime **50°03'·89N 01°22'·20E**

CHARTS AC *2451*, 2147, 1354; SHOM 7207, 7416, 7417; ECM 1011; Imray C31; Stanfords 1

TIDES –0025 Dover; ML 5·0; Duration 0530; Zone –0100

Standard Port DIEPPE (⟶)

Times				**Height (metres)**			
High Water		Low Water		MHWS	MHWN	MLWN	MLWS
0100	0600	0100	0700	9·3	7·4	2·5	0·8
1300	1800	1300	1900				
Differences LE TRÉPORT							
+0005	0000	+0007	+0007	+0·1	+0·1	0·0	+0·1

SHELTER Good in marina at S side of first S Basin (3·7m), E of FVs. Strong cross-current at entrance; 5kn speed limit. Ent chan and most of Avant Port dry; S chan is dredged 1·5m, but prone to silting. Lock opens HW±4 all months; yachts can wait against Quai Francois I with sufficient rise of tide; avoid grounding on the triangle between the two chans. Port de Commerce is an overflow; access HW –1½ to HW, half-price rates for yachts.

NAVIGATION WPT 50°04'·27N 01°21'·90E, 146°/0·4M to ent. Coast dries to approx 300m off the pier hds. Shingle spit extends NW from E pier hd; keep well to the W. Entry difficult in strong on-shore winds which cause scend in Avant Port.

LIGHTS AND MARKS Le Tréport lies between high chalk cliffs, with crucifix (floodlit) 101m above town and conspic church S of hbr. IPTS at the root of the E Jetty. There are 150° ldg marks, but they are hard to see and not strictly necessary. Lock sigs shown from head of piled ent chan: 3 ● (vert) = enter; 3 ● (vert) = no entry. Berth, if possible, on smooth S wall of lock; vert wires rigged for warps.

R/T Call: *Capitainerie Le Tréport* VHF Ch 12 (HW ±3).

TELEPHONE Marina ☎/℻ 02.35.50.63.06; Port HM 02.35.86.17.91, ℻ 02.35.86.60.11; Aff Mar 02.35.06.96.70; SNSM 02.35.86.30.27; Auto 06.70.63.43.40; CROSS 03.21.87.21.87; ⊜ 02.35.86.15.34; Police 02.35.86.12.11; Dr 02.35.86.16.23; Brit Consul 03.21.96.33.76.

FACILITIES Marina (115+15) €1.98; **Avant Port** M; **Port de Commerce** C (10 ton); **YC de la Bresle** ☎ 02.35.50.17.60, C, Bar; **Services:** ME, CH, El, Ⓔ, P, D, Gaz. **Town** P, D, Gaz, R, Bar, ✉, Ⓑ, ⇌, ✈ (Dieppe). Ferry: Le Havre.

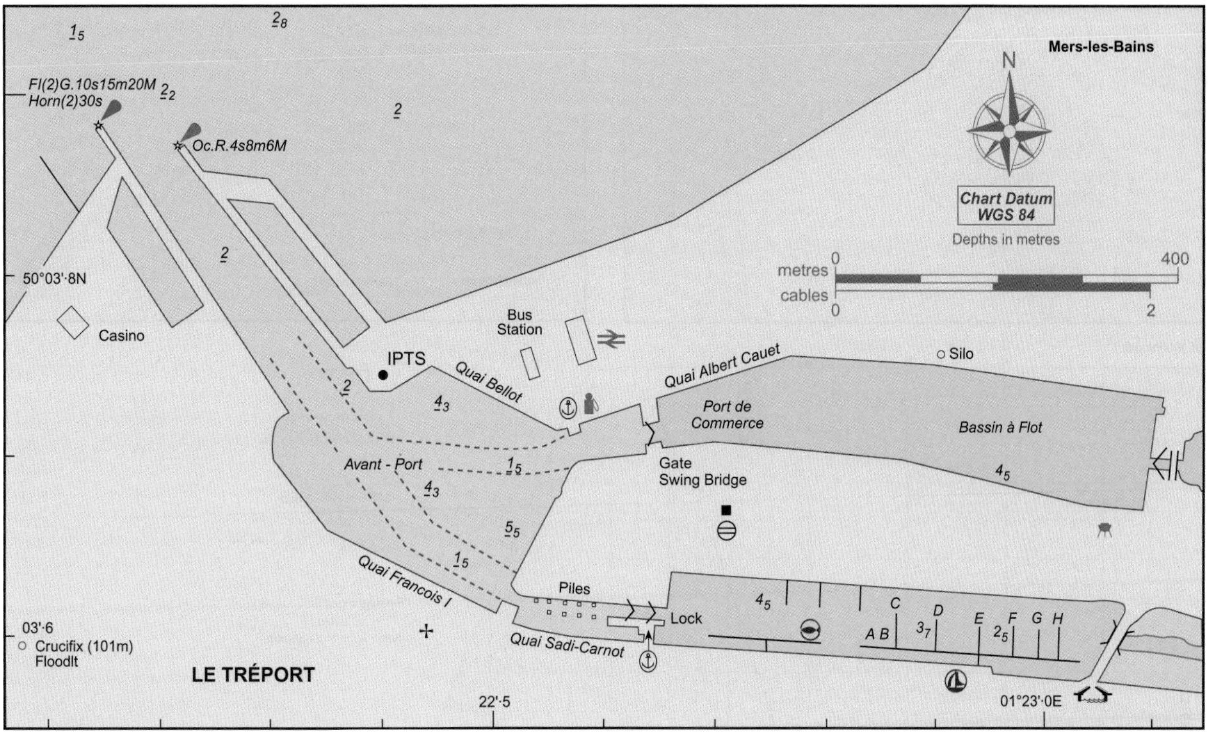
Mers-les-Bains
N
Chart Datum WGS 84
Depths in metres
metres
cables
0
400
2
Fl(2)G.10s15m20M
Horn(2)30s
Oc.R.4s8m6M
50°03'·8N
Casino
Bus Station
IPTS
Quai Bellot
Quai Albert Cauet
Silo
Port de Commerce
Bassin à Flot
Avant - Port
Gate
Swing Bridge
Quai Francois I
Piles
Lock
Quai Sadi-Carnot
03'·6
Crucifix (101m)
Floodlt
LE TRÉPORT
22'·5
01°23'·0E
A B
C
D
E
F G H

9.17.14 DIEPPE

Seine Maritime **49°56'·31N 01°05'·00E**

CHARTS AC *2451,* 2147; SHOM 7417, 7317; ECM 1011, 1012; Imray C31; Stanfords 1

TIDES –0011 Dover; ML 4·9; Duration 0535; Zone –0100 Dieppe is a Standard Port (⟶).

SHELTER Very good. Access all tides, but ent is exposed to winds from NW to NE, causing a heavy scend. A fixed wavebreak at the E end of the marina is effective. Marina Jehan Ango has 10 pontoons in the Avant Port off Quai Henri IV in about 4·5m. Ⓥ berths on pontoons 10, 9 or 1 but not on the hammerheads. Long-stay yachts may berth in Bassin Duquesne, access via lifting bridge/entry gate. No yachts in Arrière Port.

NAVIGATION WPT 49°56'·66N 01°04'·83E (off chartlet), 167°/4ca to W jetty head. Ent to hbr is simple, but beware strong stream across ent. Ent chan and Avant Port are dredged 4·5m. Be alert for ferries at the outer hbr, and small coasters or FVs in the narrow chan between outer hbr and marina. Due to restricted visibility, monitor Ch 12 during arr/dep. It is vital to comply precisely with IPTS (below), both entering and leaving. ⚓ is prohib in an inverted ▽ 7ca offshore, as charted.

LIGHTS AND MARKS Dieppe lies in a gap between high chalk cliffs, identified by a castle with pinnacle roofs at the W side and a conspic ch spire on the E cliff. ECM buoy (Dl), VQ (3) 5s, bell, bears 288°/2·5M from the hbr ent.

IPTS (full code) shown from root of W jetty and S end of marina wavebreak. Additional sigs may be combined with IPTS:

● to right	=	Ferry entering;
● to right	=	Ferry leaving.
○ ● to right	=	Dredger in chan.
Ⓦ to left	=	Bassin Duquesne entry gate open.

R/T *Dieppe Port* VHF Ch **12** (HO) 16 (H24). Ch 09 for marina which also monitors Ch 12 and operates (1/6 to 15/9) 0700–2200; other months 0900–1900.

TELEPHONE HM 02.35.84.10.55, 🖷 02.35.06.12.56; Marina 02.35.40.19.79; Aff Mar 02.35.06.96.70; CROSS 03.21.87.21.87; ⊜ 02.35.82.24.47; SNSM 02.35.84.8.55; Météo 03.21.31.52.23; Auto 08.36.68.08.76; Police 02.35.06.96.74; Ⓗ 02.35.06.76.76; Brit Consul 02.35.19.78.88.

FACILITIES Port de Plaisance (Jehan Ango): (450 inc 50 Ⓥ) €2.39, D by credit card-operated pumps H24, call VHF Ch 09 if not manned; (P by cans), C (12 ton), access by magnetic card; **Cercle de la Voile de Dieppe** ☎ 02.35.84.32.99, FW, R, Bar, access to showers/toilets by same magnetic card; **Services:** ME, El, Ⓔ, ⚒, CH, ⚒. **Town** P, D, FW, 🛒, Gaz, R, Bar, ✉, Ⓑ, ⇌, ✈. Ferry: Dieppe - Newhaven (seasonal).

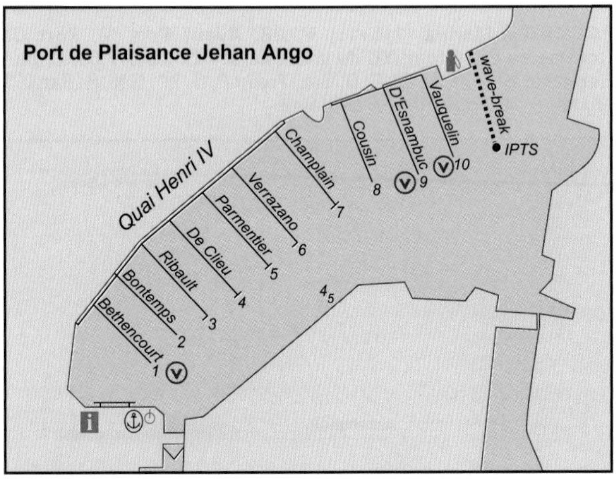
Port de Plaisance Jehan Ango
Quai Henri IV
wave-break
IPTS
Vauquelin
D'Esnambuc
Cousin
Champlain
Verrazano
Parmentier
De Clieu
Ribault
Bontemps
Bethencourt

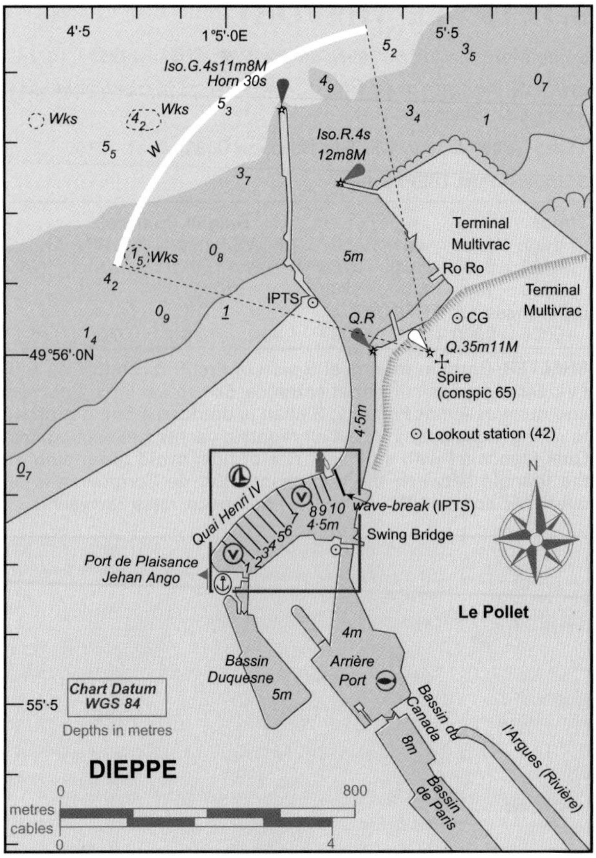
4'·5
1°5'·0E
5'·5
Iso.G.4s11m8M
Horn 30s
Iso.R.4s
12m8M
Wks
Terminal Multivrac
Ro Ro
IPTS
Q.R
CG
Q.35m11M
Spire
(conspic 65)
Lookout station (42)
49°56'·0N
Quai Henri IV
wave-break (IPTS)
Swing Bridge
Port de Plaisance
Jehan Ango
Le Pollet
Bassin Duquesne
Arrière Port
Bassin du Canada
Bassin de Paris
l'Argues (Rivière)
Chart Datum
WGS 84
Depths in metres
55'·5
DIEPPE
metres
cables
800

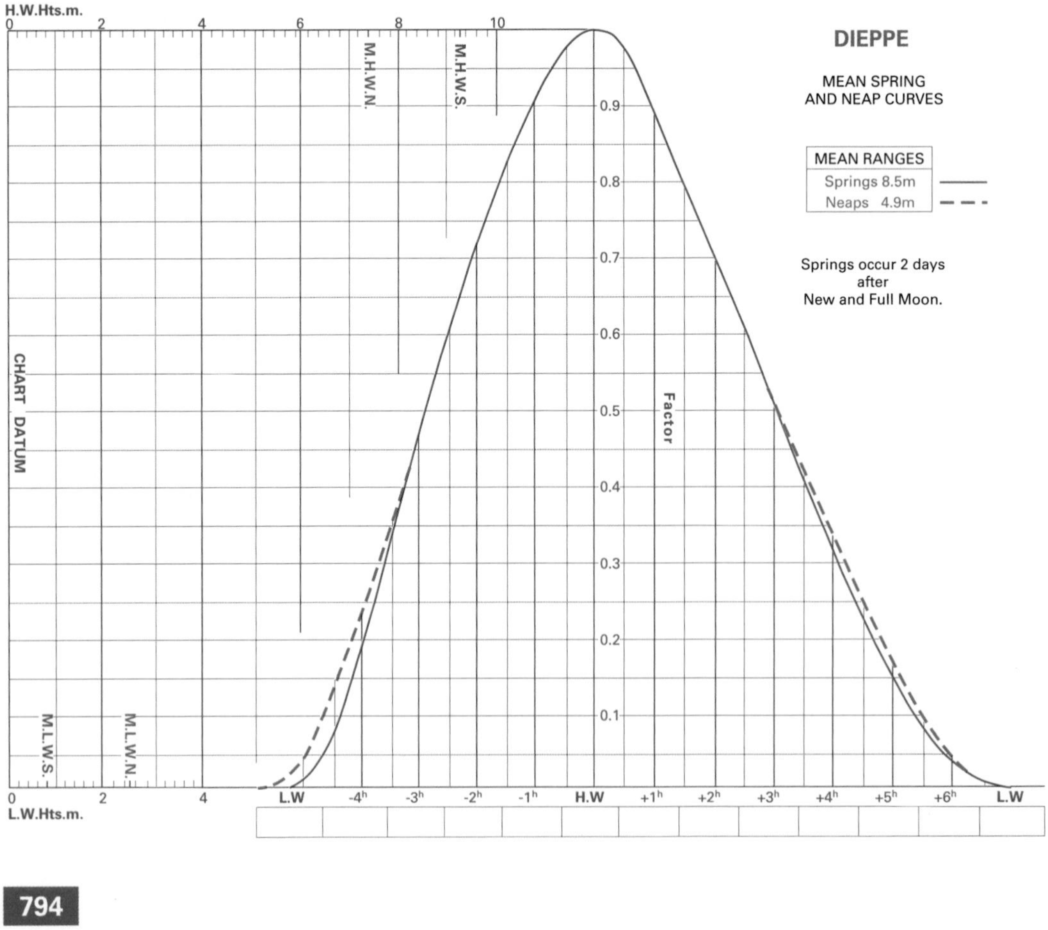
H.W.Hts.m.
M.H.W.N.
M.H.W.S.
CHART DATUM
Factor
M.L.W.S.
M.L.W.N.
L.W.Hts.m.
L.W
-4h
-3h
-2h
-1h
H.W
+1h
+2h
+3h
+4h
+5h
+6h
L.W
DIEPPE
MEAN SPRING
AND NEAP CURVES
MEAN RANGES
Springs 8.5m
Neaps 4.9m
Springs occur 2 days after New and Full Moon.

TIME ZONE -0100
(French Standard Time)
Subtract 1 hour for UT
For French Summer Time add ONE hour in **non-shaded areas**

FRANCE – DIEPPE

LAT 49°56′N LONG 1°05′E

TIMES AND HEIGHTS OF HIGH AND LOW WATERS

SPRING & NEAP TIDES
Dates in red are SPRINGS
Dates in blue are NEAPS

YEAR **2005**

JANUARY

Date	Day	Time	m	Time	m	Time	m	Time	m
1	SA	0247	8.1	0927	2.1	1500	8.0	2150	2.0
2	SU	0325	7.9	1007	2.3	1540	7.8	2229	2.2
3	M	0408	7.7	1052	2.5	1626	7.6	◑ 2316	2.4
4	TU	0458	7.5	1145	2.6	1721	7.4		
5	W	0011	2.5	0559	7.4	1248	2.6	1828	7.3
6	TH	0117	2.5	0713	7.5	1400	2.5	1943	7.5
7	F	0234	2.4	0824	7.8	1515	2.1	2053	7.9
8	SA	0348	2.0	0927	8.3	1622	1.7	2155	8.3
9	SU	0451	1.7	1025	8.7	1722	1.3	2252	8.7
10	M	0550	1.3	1119	9.1	1820	0.9	● 2346	9.1
11	TU	0646	1.1	1211	9.3	1916	0.7		
12	W	0043	9.3	0741	0.9	1302	9.5	2008	0.5
13	TH	0132	9.3	0832	0.9	1351	9.5	2057	0.5
14	F	0219	9.2	0919	1.0	1437	9.3	2142	0.7
15	SA	0304	9.0	1002	1.2	1522	8.9	2223	1.1
16	SU	0348	8.6	1043	1.6	1608	8.5	2303	1.6
17	M	0433	8.2	1125	2.0	1656	8.0	◐ 2345	2.1
18	TU	0523	7.7	1214	2.4	1751	7.4		
19	W	0034	2.5	0624	7.3	1315	2.7	1859	7.1
20	TH	0140	2.8	0739	7.1	1429	2.8	2017	7.0
21	F	0257	2.9	0853	7.3	1541	2.6	2125	7.3
22	SA	0406	2.6	0951	7.6	1640	2.2	2218	7.6
23	SU	0500	2.3	1038	7.9	1728	1.9	2302	8.0
24	M	0545	2.0	1117	8.2	1810	1.6	2339	8.3
25	TU	0626	1.8	1152	8.5	1848	1.4	○	
26	W	0015	8.5	0703	1.6	1227	8.6	1925	1.3
27	TH	0049	8.6	0737	1.5	1301	8.8	1958	1.2
28	F	0122	8.7	0809	1.4	1334	8.8	2030	1.2
29	SA	0155	8.7	0840	1.5	1406	8.7	2100	1.3
30	SU	0227	8.6	0912	1.5	1439	8.6	2131	1.4
31	M	0300	8.5	0944	1.7	1513	8.4	2202	1.6

FEBRUARY

Date	Day	Time	m	Time	m	Time	m	Time	m
1	TU	0334	8.3	1020	1.9	1550	8.1	2239	1.9
2	W	0413	8.0	1103	2.2	1636	7.7	◑ 2325	2.3
3	TH	0504	7.6	1159	2.5	1736	7.4		
4	F	0027	2.6	0618	7.4	1313	2.6	1901	7.2
5	SA	0151	2.7	0751	7.4	1444	2.4	2030	7.4
6	SU	0324	2.4	0910	7.8	1603	1.9	2144	8.0
7	M	0437	1.9	1016	8.4	1711	1.3	2247	8.6
8	TU	0543	1.4	1114	9.0	1814	0.8	● 2341	9.1
9	W	0642	1.0	1205	9.4	1910	0.5		
10	TH	0034	9.4	0735	0.7	1252	9.7	1959	0.2
11	F	0118	9.5	0821	0.6	1335	9.7	2042	0.3
12	SA	0159	9.5	0901	0.7	1416	9.5	2120	0.5
13	SU	0238	9.3	0936	0.9	1455	9.2	2153	0.9
14	M	0314	8.9	1007	1.4	1532	8.7	2222	1.5
15	TU	0349	8.3	1038	1.9	1611	8.0	2253	2.0
16	W	0428	7.7	1117	2.4	1656	7.3	◐ 2334	2.7
17	TH	0518	7.1	1212	2.9	1801	6.7		
18	F	0037	3.2	0639	6.6	1334	3.2	1937	6.4
19	SA	0214	3.4	0822	6.6	1508	3.0	2106	6.8
20	SU	0343	3.0	0933	7.1	1619	2.5	2203	7.3
21	M	0445	2.5	1021	7.6	1711	2.0	2245	7.9
22	TU	0531	2.0	1100	8.1	1754	1.6	2321	8.3
23	W	0610	1.6	1135	8.5	1832	1.3	2354	8.6
24	TH	0646	1.4	1208	8.8	1907	1.1	○	
25	F	0029	8.9	0719	1.2	1241	9.0	1940	0.9
26	SA	0100	9.0	0751	1.1	1313	9.1	2011	0.9
27	SU	0131	9.0	0822	1.0	1344	9.1	2040	0.9
28	M	0202	9.0	0852	1.1	1415	9.0	2108	1.1

MARCH

Date	Day	Time	m	Time	m	Time	m	Time	m
1	TU	0233	8.9	0921	1.3	1448	8.7	2137	1.4
2	W	0305	8.6	0953	1.6	1523	8.4	2210	1.7
3	TH	0342	8.2	1034	2.0	1606	7.9	◑ 2254	2.2
4	F	0430	7.7	1128	2.4	1706	7.3	2357	2.7
5	SA	0546	7.1	1245	2.7	1841	6.9		
6	SU	0131	2.9	0736	7.1	1428	2.5	2025	7.2
7	M	0315	2.5	0906	7.7	1555	1.9	2143	7.9
8	TU	0433	1.8	1012	8.4	1705	1.2	2241	8.7
9	W	0537	1.2	1105	9.0	1805	0.7	2329	9.2
10	TH	0632	0.8	1151	9.5	1856	0.4	●	
11	F	0016	9.5	0718	0.5	1233	9.7	1939	0.2
12	SA	0056	9.6	0759	0.5	1312	9.7	2017	0.3
13	SU	0132	9.5	0834	0.6	1349	9.5	2049	0.6
14	M	0206	9.3	0904	0.9	1424	9.2	2117	1.0
15	TU	0238	8.9	0930	1.3	1457	8.7	2141	1.5
16	W	0309	8.4	0958	1.8	1531	8.0	2209	2.1
17	TH	0341	7.8	1032	2.4	1609	7.3	◐ 2246	2.8
18	F	0423	7.0	1120	3.0	1706	6.5	2344	3.4
19	SA	0537	6.4	1238	3.4	1852	6.2		
20	SU	0128	3.7	0741	6.3	1429	3.3	2036	6.5
21	M	0313	3.2	0904	6.8	1548	2.7	2134	7.2
22	TU	0416	2.5	0953	7.5	1641	2.1	2215	7.8
23	W	0502	1.9	1032	8.1	1724	1.6	2252	8.4
24	TH	0541	1.5	1107	8.5	1803	1.2	2326	8.7
25	F	0618	1.2	1141	8.9	1839	0.9	○ 2359	9.0
26	SA	0653	1.0	1214	9.1	1913	0.8		
27	SU	0032	9.1	0726	0.9	1246	9.2	1945	0.7
28	M	0104	9.2	0759	0.8	1319	9.2	2015	0.8
29	TU	0136	9.2	0831	0.9	1352	9.1	2046	1.0
30	W	0209	9.0	0902	1.1	1427	8.9	2117	1.3
31	TH	0243	8.7	0937	1.4	1506	8.4	2153	1.8

APRIL

Date	Day	Time	m	Time	m	Time	m	Time	m
1	F	0323	8.2	1019	1.9	1552	7.8	2241	2.3
2	SA	0416	7.6	1117	2.4	1659	7.2	◑ 2348	2.8
3	SU	0542	7.0	1240	2.7	1844	6.9		
4	M	0131	2.9	0734	7.1	1424	2.4	2022	7.4
5	TU	0310	2.4	0858	7.8	1546	1.7	2131	8.1
6	W	0423	1.7	0958	8.5	1652	1.1	2223	8.7
7	TH	0521	1.2	1046	9.0	1746	0.7	2308	9.2
8	F	0610	0.8	1129	9.3	1832	0.5	● 2348	9.4
9	SA	0653	0.7	1209	9.5	1911	0.5		
10	SU	0028	9.4	0729	0.7	1245	9.5	1945	0.6
11	M	0102	9.3	0802	0.8	1320	9.3	2015	0.8
12	TU	0134	9.1	0831	1.0	1354	9.0	2042	1.2
13	W	0206	8.8	0858	1.4	1427	8.5	2108	1.7
14	TH	0236	8.3	0926	1.8	1500	7.9	2137	2.2
15	F	0307	7.7	0959	2.3	1537	7.3	2214	2.8
16	SA	0347	7.1	1043	2.9	1630	6.7	◐ 2308	3.3
17	SU	0453	6.4	1152	3.3	1801	6.3		
18	M	0038	3.6	0643	6.3	1334	3.3	1941	6.5
19	TU	0219	3.2	0811	6.7	1455	2.8	2046	7.1
20	W	0325	2.6	0907	7.3	1552	2.2	2132	7.7
21	TH	0415	2.0	0952	7.9	1639	1.7	2213	8.3
22	F	0459	1.6	1031	8.4	1722	1.3	2250	8.7
23	SA	0540	1.3	1108	8.8	1802	1.0	2325	8.9
24	SU	0620	1.1	1144	9.0	1840	0.9	○	
25	M	0000	9.1	0658	0.9	1219	9.1	1917	0.8
26	TU	0037	9.2	0735	0.8	1255	9.2	1952	0.9
27	W	0113	9.2	0811	0.8	1333	9.1	2027	1.0
28	TH	0150	9.0	0848	1.0	1414	8.8	2105	1.4
29	F	0231	8.7	0929	1.3	1459	8.4	2148	1.8
30	SA	0318	8.1	1018	1.8	1553	7.8	2242	2.3

Chart Datum: 4·45 metres below IGN Datum

17

TIME ZONE -0100
(French Standard Time)
Subtract 1 hour for UT
For French Summer Time add ONE hour in **non-shaded areas**

FRANCE – DIEPPE

LAT 49°56′N LONG 1°05′E

TIMES AND HEIGHTS OF HIGH AND LOW WATERS

SPRING & NEAP TIDES
Dates in red are SPRINGS
Dates in blue are NEAPS

YEAR **2005**

MAY

Date	Time	m	Date	Time	m
1 SU ◑	0420 1120 1708 2354	7.6 2.2 7.3 2.6	16 M ◐	0424 1117 1713 2350	6.8 2.9 6.7 3.2
2 M	0549 1244 1839	7.2 2.3 7.3	17 TU	0542 1232 1832	6.6 3.0 6.8
3 TU	0129 0719 1412 2000	2.6 7.4 2.1 7.7	18 W	0110 0702 1348 1942	3.1 6.8 2.7 7.1
4 W	0251 0833 1524 2104	2.1 7.9 1.6 8.2	19 TH	0220 0807 1451 2038	2.7 7.2 2.3 7.6
5 TH	0357 0932 1625 2156	1.6 8.4 1.2 8.6	20 F	0318 0901 1546 2125	2.2 7.7 1.9 8.1
6 F	0452 1020 1716 2240	1.3 8.8 1.0 8.9	21 SA	0409 0948 1636 2209	1.8 8.2 1.5 8.5
7 SA	0540 1103 1800 2320	1.1 9.0 1.0 9.0	22 SU	0458 1031 1723 2250	1.5 8.5 1.3 8.8
8 SU ●	0621 1142 1838 2357	1.0 9.0 1.0 9.1	23 M ○	0545 1113 1807 2330	1.2 8.8 1.1 9.0
9 M	0657 1219 1911	1.0 9.0 1.1	24 TU	0630 1154 1851	1.0 9.0 1.0
10 TU	0033 0731 1254 1943	9.0 1.1 8.9 1.2	25 W	0013 0714 1237 1933	9.1 0.9 9.1 1.0
11 W	0106 0804 1329 2014	8.8 1.2 8.7 1.5	26 TH	0056 0757 1322 2016	9.1 0.9 9.0 1.1
12 TH	0139 0835 1404 2045	8.6 1.5 8.3 1.8	27 F	0140 0842 1409 2101	9.0 1.0 8.8 1.3
13 F	0212 0905 1439 2117	8.2 1.8 7.9 2.2	28 SA	0229 0930 1501 2151	8.7 1.2 8.5 1.6
14 SA	0247 0938 1518 2154	7.7 2.2 7.5 2.6	29 SU	0323 1023 1559 2248	8.3 1.5 8.1 2.0
15 SU	0328 1020 1607 2243	7.3 2.6 7.0 3.0	30 M ◑	0426 1125 1705 2354	7.9 1.8 7.8 2.1
			31 TU	0536 1233 1814	7.7 1.9 7.7

JUNE

Date	Time	m	Date	Time	m
1 W	0107 0648 1342 1923	2.2 7.7 1.9 7.8	16 TH	0008 0551 1240 1830	2.7 7.1 2.6 7.2
2 TH	0216 0757 1447 2027	2.0 7.9 1.7 8.0	17 F	0111 0658 1344 1935	2.6 7.2 2.4 7.5
3 F	0319 0859 1547 2123	1.8 8.1 1.6 8.3	18 SA	0216 0803 1449 2034	2.4 7.5 2.2 7.8
4 SA	0416 0951 1640 2211	1.6 8.3 1.5 8.5	19 SU	0319 0902 1550 2128	2.1 7.8 1.9 8.2
5 SU	0506 1037 1726 2253	1.5 8.4 1.5 8.6	20 M	0418 0956 1646 2217	1.7 8.2 1.6 8.5
6 M ●	0549 1119 1806 2332	1.4 8.5 1.5 8.6	21 TU	0513 1047 1739 2306	1.4 8.5 1.4 8.8
7 TU	0628 1157 1843	1.4 8.5 1.5	22 W ○	0607 1137 1831 2354	1.1 8.8 1.2 9.0
8 W	0010 0706 1234 1919	8.6 1.3 8.5 1.5	23 TH	0659 1226 1921	0.9 9.0 1.1
9 TH	0046 0743 1311 1955	8.6 1.4 8.5 1.6	24 F	0047 0751 1317 2012	9.1 0.8 9.1 1.0
10 F	0121 0818 1348 2030	8.4 1.5 8.3 1.8	25 SA	0137 0843 1408 2103	9.1 0.8 9.0 1.1
11 SA	0157 0851 1425 2103	8.2 1.7 8.1 2.1	26 SU	0228 0933 1458 2153	9.0 0.8 8.9 1.2
12 SU	0233 0924 1503 2139	7.9 2.0 7.8 2.3	27 M	0320 1023 1549 2244	8.8 1.0 8.6 1.5
13 M	0312 1002 1544 2220	7.7 2.2 7.5 2.5	28 TU ◑	0412 1112 1642 2336	8.5 1.3 8.3 1.7
14 TU	0357 1047 1631 2310	7.4 2.4 7.3 2.7	29 W	0508 1204 1737	8.1 1.6 8.0
15 W ◐	0450 1140 1727	7.2 2.5 7.2	30 TH	0031 0608 1300 1839	2.0 7.8 1.9 7.8

JULY

Date	Time	m	Date	Time	m
1 F	0132 0714 1402 1945	2.1 7.6 2.1 7.7	16 SA	0013 0551 1242 1829	2.5 7.3 2.5 7.4
2 SA	0237 0822 1506 2049	2.2 7.6 2.2 7.8	17 SU	0119 0705 1354 1944	2.5 7.3 2.5 7.5
3 SU	0340 0925 1606 2146	2.1 7.7 2.1 7.9	18 M	0234 0823 1512 2053	2.4 7.5 2.3 7.8
4 M	0437 1018 1658 2234	1.9 7.9 2.0 8.1	19 TU	0347 0930 1620 2154	2.0 7.9 1.9 8.2
5 TU	0525 1104 1743 2316	1.8 8.1 1.8 8.3	20 W	0452 1031 1720 2251	1.6 8.4 1.5 8.7
6 W ●	0609 1144 1825 2355	1.6 8.3 1.7 8.4	21 TH ○	0553 1127 1819 2345	1.2 8.8 1.2 9.0
7 TH	0650 1221 1904	1.5 8.4 1.6	22 F	0653 1220 1916	0.8 9.1 0.9
8 F	0032 0729 1257 1941	8.4 1.4 8.4 1.6	23 SA	0041 0749 1310 2009	9.3 0.6 9.3 0.8
9 SA	0108 0805 1333 2017	8.5 1.5 8.4 1.7	24 SU	0130 0839 1357 2057	9.4 0.4 9.4 0.7
10 SU	0143 0838 1408 2049	8.4 1.5 8.4 1.7	25 M	0217 0924 1442 2141	9.4 0.5 9.3 0.9
11 M	0217 0910 1442 2121	8.3 1.6 8.2 1.9	26 TU	0302 1006 1526 2223	9.2 0.7 9.0 1.2
12 TU	0251 0941 1516 2155	8.2 1.8 8.1 2.0	27 W	0346 1045 1609 2304	8.8 1.2 8.6 1.6
13 W	0327 1016 1552 2233	7.9 1.9 7.9 2.2	28 TH ◑	0431 1124 1656 2349	8.3 1.7 8.1 2.0
14 TH ◐	0406 1056 1634 2318	7.7 2.1 7.7 2.4	29 F	0523 1211 1751	7.7 2.2 7.6
15 F	0453 1144 1725	7.5 2.4 7.5	30 SA	0043 0628 1312 1900	2.5 7.2 2.6 7.2
			31 SU	0154 0748 1427 2020	2.7 7.0 2.8 7.2

AUGUST

Date	Time	m	Date	Time	m
1 M	0311 0907 1541 2130	2.6 7.2 2.6 7.4	16 TU	0202 0758 1447 2033	2.7 7.2 2.6 7.5
2 TU	0418 1007 1642 2223	2.3 7.6 2.3 7.8	17 W	0330 0918 1605 2144	2.2 7.7 2.1 8.1
3 W	0512 1054 1732 2306	2.0 7.9 2.0 8.1	18 TH	0441 1024 1710 2244	1.6 8.4 1.5 8.7
4 TH	0558 1132 1813 2342	1.7 8.3 1.7 8.4	19 F ○	0546 1119 1811 2337	1.1 9.0 1.0 9.2
5 F ●	0638 1207 1851	1.5 8.5 1.6	20 SA	0646 1209 1906	0.6 9.4 0.7
6 SA	0018 0715 1240 1926	8.6 1.3 8.6 1.4	21 SU	0029 0737 1254 1955	9.6 0.4 9.6 0.5
7 SU	0051 0749 1312 1959	8.7 1.3 8.7 1.4	22 M	0113 0822 1337 2039	9.7 0.3 9.7 0.5
8 M	0123 0819 1344 2029	8.7 1.2 8.7 1.4	23 TU	0155 0902 1417 2118	9.6 0.4 9.5 0.7
9 TU	0154 0848 1414 2058	8.7 1.3 8.7 1.5	24 W	0235 0936 1455 2153	9.3 0.8 9.1 1.1
10 W	0224 0916 1445 2127	8.6 1.4 8.5 1.6	25 TH	0313 1007 1533 2226	8.9 1.3 8.6 1.6
11 TH	0255 0944 1516 2200	8.4 1.6 8.3 1.9	26 F ◑	0352 1040 1612 2304	8.2 1.9 8.0 2.2
12 F	0329 1016 1551 2238	8.1 1.9 8.0 2.1	27 SA	0437 1121 1701 2355	7.5 2.6 7.3 2.8
13 SA ◐	0409 1058 1635 2327	7.8 2.3 7.7 2.5	28 SU	0540 1222 1815	6.8 3.1 6.8
14 SU	0502 1154 1736	7.4 2.7 7.3	29 M	0113 0718 1355 1957	3.2 6.5 3.3 6.7
15 M	0033 0620 1312 1905	2.7 7.1 2.9 7.2	30 TU	0249 0854 1525 2117	3.0 6.8 3.0 7.1
			31 W	0404 0953 1629 2208	2.5 7.4 2.4 7.7

Chart Datum: 4·45 metres below IGN Datum

TIME ZONE -0100
(French Standard Time)
Subtract 1 hour for UT
For French Summer Time add ONE hour in **non-shaded areas**

FRANCE – DIEPPE

LAT 49°56′N LONG 1°05′E

TIMES AND HEIGHTS OF HIGH AND LOW WATERS

SPRING & NEAP TIDES
Dates in red are SPRINGS
Dates in blue are NEAPS

YEAR **2005**

SEPTEMBER

Date	Day	Time	m	Time	m	Time	m	Time	m	Moon
1	TH	0457	2.0	1036	8.0	1716	1.9	2247	8.1	
2	F	0540	1.6	1111	8.4	1755	1.6	2322	8.5	
3	SA	0618	1.4	1143	8.7	1830	1.4	2353	8.8	●
4	SU	0652	1.2	1215	8.9	1903	1.3			
5	M	0026	8.9	0724	1.1	1245	9.0	1934	1.2	
6	TU	0056	9.0	0753	1.1	1315	9.0	2003	1.2	
7	W	0126	9.0	0821	1.1	1344	9.0	2032	1.3	
8	TH	0156	8.9	0848	1.3	1413	8.8	2100	1.4	
9	F	0226	8.7	0914	1.6	1444	8.6	2131	1.7	
10	SA	0259	8.3	0943	1.9	1518	8.2	2207	2.1	
11	SU	0338	7.9	1023	2.4	1602	7.7	2256	2.5	◐
12	M	0432	7.3	1123	2.9	1705	7.1			
13	TU	0006	2.9	0559	6.9	1251	3.1	1848	6.9	
14	W	0148	2.8	0752	7.1	1438	2.8	2027	7.4	
15	TH	0323	2.2	0914	7.8	1557	2.0	2137	8.2	
16	F	0434	1.5	1014	8.6	1701	1.4	2233	8.9	
17	SA	0535	0.9	1104	9.2	1758	0.9	2321	9.4	
18	SU	0629	0.5	1149	9.6	1848	0.6			○
19	M	0006	9.7	0715	0.4	1231	9.7	1933	0.5	
20	TU	0049	9.8	0756	0.4	1310	9.7	2012	0.6	
21	W	0128	9.6	0831	0.6	1347	9.5	2047	0.9	
22	TH	0204	9.3	0901	1.0	1422	9.1	2118	1.3	
23	F	0240	8.8	0928	1.6	1456	8.6	2148	1.8	
24	SA	0315	8.1	0958	2.2	1531	7.9	2222	2.4	
25	SU	0356	7.4	1037	2.8	1615	7.2	2310	3.0	◑
26	M	0456	6.7	1138	3.5	1729	6.5			
27	TU	0029	3.5	0642	6.3	1322	3.7	1925	6.4	
28	W	0219	3.3	0827	6.7	1459	3.2	2049	6.9	
29	TH	0335	2.7	0923	7.4	1600	2.5	2138	7.5	
30	F	0426	2.1	1004	8.0	1645	2.0	2216	8.1	

OCTOBER

Date	Day	Time	m	Time	m	Time	m	Time	m	Moon
1	SA	0508	1.6	1039	8.5	1723	1.6	2251	8.6	
2	SU	0545	1.3	1112	8.8	1759	1.3	2323	8.9	
3	M	0620	1.2	1143	9.0	1833	1.2	2355	9.0	●
4	TU	0652	1.1	1214	9.1	1905	1.1			
5	W	0027	9.1	0723	1.1	1244	9.2	1936	1.1	
6	TH	0058	9.1	0752	1.1	1314	9.1	2007	1.2	
7	F	0129	9.0	0821	1.3	1345	9.0	2038	1.3	
8	SA	0203	8.8	0850	1.6	1419	8.7	2111	1.6	
9	SU	0239	8.4	0923	2.0	1457	8.2	2150	2.1	
10	M	0322	7.8	1008	2.5	1545	7.6	2242	2.5	◐
11	TU	0422	7.2	1113	3.0	1657	7.1	2356	2.9	
12	W	0602	6.9	1249	3.1	1846	7.0			
13	TH	0145	2.7	0747	7.3	1432	2.6	2016	7.6	
14	F	0313	2.1	0859	8.1	1544	1.9	2121	8.3	
15	SA	0418	1.4	0955	8.8	1644	1.3	2213	9.0	
16	SU	0514	0.9	1042	9.3	1736	0.9	2258	9.4	
17	M	0603	0.7	1124	9.5	1823	0.7	2340	9.6	○
18	TU	0646	0.7	1203	9.6	1905	0.7			
19	W	0022	9.5	0723	0.8	1241	9.5	1942	0.8	
20	TH	0100	9.4	0756	1.0	1316	9.3	2015	1.1	
21	F	0136	9.1	0826	1.3	1350	9.0	2046	1.4	
22	SA	0211	8.6	0855	1.8	1424	8.5	2117	1.9	
23	SU	0246	8.0	0926	2.4	1459	7.9	2150	2.4	
24	M	0326	7.4	1005	2.9	1542	7.2	2234	3.0	
25	TU	0421	6.8	1102	3.5	1648	6.6	2342	3.4	◑
26	W	0551	6.4	1233	3.7	1827	6.4			
27	TH	0123	3.4	0727	6.6	1407	3.3	1953	6.7	
28	F	0242	2.9	0832	7.2	1510	2.7	2050	7.3	
29	SA	0338	2.4	0918	7.8	1558	2.2	2133	7.9	
30	SU	0423	1.9	0957	8.3	1641	1.7	2212	8.4	
31	M	0504	1.5	1034	8.7	1721	1.4	2248	8.7	

NOVEMBER

Date	Day	Time	m	Time	m	Time	m	Time	m	Moon
1	TU	0542	1.3	1108	9.0	1758	1.3	2322	8.9	
2	W	0618	1.2	1142	9.1	1834	1.2	2356	9.1	●
3	TH	0652	1.2	1215	9.2	1910	1.1			
4	F	0033	9.1	0727	1.2	1249	9.2	1946	1.1	
5	SA	0109	9.0	0801	1.4	1325	9.0	2022	1.3	
6	SU	0148	8.8	0837	1.7	1405	8.7	2102	1.6	
7	M	0231	8.4	0919	2.0	1450	8.3	2147	1.9	
8	TU	0321	7.9	1010	2.5	1545	7.7	2243	2.3	
9	W	0429	7.4	1118	2.8	1703	7.3	2358	2.6	◐
10	TH	0559	7.3	1247	2.8	1832	7.4			
11	F	0131	2.4	0723	7.6	1412	2.4	1949	7.8	
12	SA	0247	2.0	0831	8.1	1519	1.8	2053	8.3	
13	SU	0350	1.5	0927	8.6	1618	1.4	2146	8.8	
14	M	0445	1.3	1014	9.0	1709	1.1	2233	9.0	
15	TU	0532	1.1	1057	9.2	1755	1.0	2316	9.2	
16	W	0613	1.1	1137	9.2	1836	1.0	2356	9.1	○
17	TH	0651	1.2	1214	9.2	1913	1.1			
18	F	0036	9.0	0726	1.3	1250	9.0	1948	1.2	
19	SA	0113	8.8	0800	1.6	1326	8.8	2022	1.5	
20	SU	0149	8.5	0833	1.9	1402	8.4	2055	1.9	
21	M	0227	8.1	0906	2.3	1439	7.9	2130	2.3	
22	TU	0306	7.6	0944	2.7	1521	7.4	2209	2.7	
23	W	0354	7.2	1032	3.1	1614	7.0	2301	3.0	◑
24	TH	0456	6.9	1135	3.3	1722	6.7			
25	F	0009	3.2	0610	6.8	1250	3.3	1837	6.8	
26	SA	0125	3.0	0721	7.1	1400	2.9	1944	7.1	
27	SU	0231	2.7	0820	7.5	1459	2.5	2039	7.6	
28	M	0327	2.3	0909	8.0	1551	2.1	2127	8.0	
29	TU	0416	1.9	0952	8.4	1639	1.7	2210	8.4	
30	W	0502	1.7	1033	8.7	1724	1.5	2251	8.6	

DECEMBER

Date	Day	Time	m	Time	m	Time	m	Time	m	Moon
1	TH	0545	1.5	1112	8.9	1807	1.3	2331	8.9	●
2	F	0626	1.4	1151	9.1	1849	1.1			
3	SA	0014	9.0	0708	1.3	1232	9.1	1932	1.1	
4	SU	0058	9.0	0750	1.4	1315	9.1	2016	1.1	
5	M	0143	8.9	0835	1.5	1402	8.9	2102	1.3	
6	TU	0232	8.6	0923	1.8	1453	8.5	2152	1.5	
7	W	0327	8.3	1017	2.0	1550	8.2	2247	1.8	
8	TH	0428	8.0	1118	2.3	1653	7.9	2349	2.0	◐
9	F	0535	7.8	1227	2.3	1802	7.8			
10	SA	0058	2.1	0645	7.8	1337	2.2	1912	7.8	
11	SU	0208	2.1	0753	8.0	1445	2.0	2019	8.0	
12	M	0313	1.9	0854	8.2	1547	1.8	2118	8.2	
13	TU	0412	1.8	0947	8.5	1642	1.6	2210	8.4	
14	W	0502	1.7	1034	8.6	1730	1.5	2256	8.6	
15	TH	0546	1.6	1117	8.7	1812	1.4	2339	8.6	○
16	F	0627	1.6	1156	8.8	1852	1.3			
17	SA	0020	8.7	0705	1.6	1233	8.8	1929	1.4	
18	SU	0058	8.6	0743	1.7	1310	8.7	2006	1.5	
19	M	0135	8.5	0819	1.8	1347	8.5	2041	1.7	
20	TU	0212	8.3	0853	2.0	1423	8.2	2115	1.9	
21	W	0248	8.0	0926	2.3	1501	7.9	2148	2.2	
22	TH	0326	7.7	1003	2.5	1540	7.6	2226	2.4	
23	F	0407	7.5	1047	2.7	1625	7.3	2310	2.6	◑
24	SA	0457	7.3	1139	2.9	1719	7.1			
25	SU	0005	2.8	0558	7.2	1239	2.9	1824	7.0	
26	M	0107	2.8	0707	7.2	1346	2.8	1934	7.2	
27	TU	0217	2.7	0813	7.5	1455	2.5	2038	7.5	
28	W	0325	2.4	0910	7.9	1557	2.1	2134	7.9	
29	TH	0425	2.1	1001	8.3	1653	1.7	2225	8.3	
30	F	0518	1.7	1049	8.6	1745	1.4	2313	8.7	
31	SA	0608	1.5	1136	8.9	1836	1.1			●

Chart Datum: 4·45 metres below IGN Datum

9.17.15 ST VALÉRY-EN-CAUX

Seine Maritime **49°52'·48N 00°42'·64E**

CHARTS AC *2451*; SHOM 7417; ECM 1012; Imray C31; Stanfords 1

TIDES –0044 Dover; ML 4·6; Duration 0530; Zone –0100

Standard Port DIEPPE (⟵)

Times				**Height (metres)**			
High Water		Low Water		MHWS	MHWN	MLWN	MLWS
0100	0600	0100	0700	9·3	7·4	2·5	0·8
1300	1800	1300	1900				
Differences ST VALÉRY-EN-CAUX							
–0005	–0005	–0015	–0020	–0·5	–0·4	–0·1	–0·1

SHELTER Good. Avant Port dries 3m; access from HW –3. Gate is open HW ±2¼ by day; HW±½ at night, (bridge opens H & H+30 in these periods). Ⓥ pontoon first to stbd or 'A' pontoon to port. Caution: After gate first opens current may affect berthing.

NAVIGATION WPT 49°52'·97N 00°42'·14E, 155°/6ca to Jetée Ouest. Ent is easy, but tidal streams across ent are strong and confused seas break in fresh W to NE winds. Shingle builds up against W wall; hug the E side. Inside the pier hds, wave-breaks (marked by posts) reduce the swell. 5 W waiting buoys are NE of gate.

LIGHTS AND MARKS From N or W Paluel nuclear power stn is conspic 3M W of ent. From E a TV mast is 1M E of ent. Hbr is hard to see between high chalk cliffs, but lt ho (W twr, G top) on W pierhead is fairly conspic. Lts as on chartlet and 9.17.4. Traffic sigs at the bridge/gate are coordinated to seaward/ inland: ● = ent/exit; ● = no ent/ exit; ● + ● = no movements.

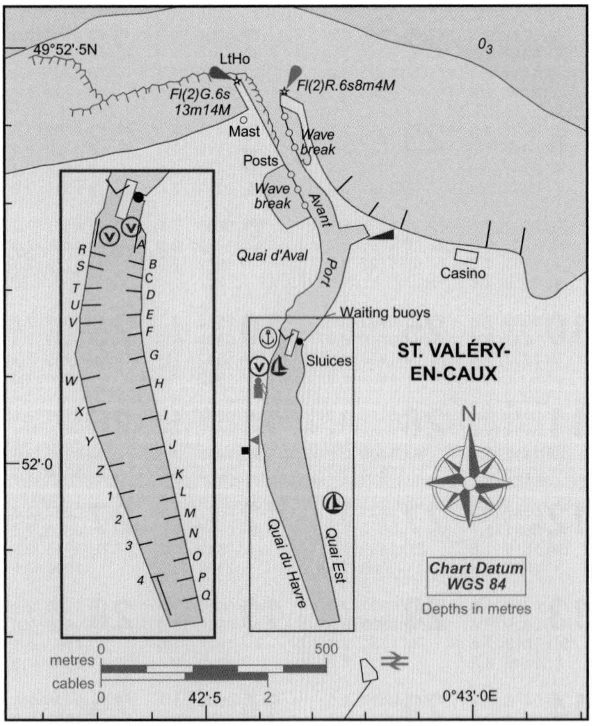
49°52'·5N
LtHo
Fl(2)G.6s 13m14M
Fl(2)R.6s8m4M
Mast
Wave break
Posts
Wave break
Avant Port
Quai d'Aval
Casino
Waiting buoys
Sluices
ST. VALÉRY-EN-CAUX
Quai du Havre
Quai Est
Chart Datum WGS 84
Depths in metres
52'·0
metres 0 500
cables 0 2
42'·5
0°43'·0E

R/T VHF Ch 09 (French only).

TELEPHONE HM 02.35.97.01.30; Aff Mar 02.35.10.34.34; CROSS 03.21.87.21.89; SNSM 02.35.97.09.03; ⊖ 02.32.14.06.80; Météo Auto 08.92.68.08.76; Police 02.35.97.00.17; Dr 02.35.97.05.99; Ⓗ 02.35.97.00.11; Brit Consul 02.35.19.78.88.

FACILITIES Marina (580+20Ⓥ) ☎ 02.35.97.01.30, 📠 02.35.97.79.81, €1.98, C (5/10 ton), CH, El, Gaz, ME, ⚒, 🛒, Bar; **Club Nautique Valeriquais** ☎ 02.35.97.25.49, C (8 ton), Bar; **Club de Voile** ☎ 02.35.57.00.80; **Services:** Ⓔ. **Town**: P, D, CH, 🛒, Gaz, R, Bar, ✉, Ⓑ, bus to ⇌ at Yvetot; ✈ & Ferry Dieppe.

9.17.16 FÉCAMP

Seine Maritime **49°45'·91N 00°21'·81E**

CHARTS AC 2451, 2613, 1354 (replaces 1352); SHOM 6857, 7417, 7207; ECM 1012; Imray C31; Stanfords 1

TIDES –0044 Dover; ML 4·9; Duration 0550; Zone –0100

Standard Port DIEPPE (⟵)

Times				**Height (metres)**			
High Water		Low Water		MHWS	MHWN	MLWN	MLWS
0100	0600	0100	0700	9·3	7·4	2·5	0·8
1300	1800	1300	1900				
Differences FÉCAMP							
–0015	–0010	–0030	–0040	–1·0	–0·6	+0·3	+0·4
ETRETAT							
–0020	–0020	–0045	–0050	–1·2	–0·8	+0·3	+0·4

SHELTER Excellent in basins, but in even moderate W/NW winds a considerable surf runs off the ent and scend can make the Avant Port (Ⓥ at 'C' pontoon) uncomfortable. Bassin Bérigny is entered via a gate, HW –2 to HW +¾; pontoons at E end.

NAVIGATION WPT 49°46'·02N 00°21'·34E, 109°/3ca to hbr ent. Beware the Charpentier Rks off Pte Fagnet and strong cross currents, depending on tides. Access best at HW +1; *un peu difficile* in onshore winds >F5; do not attempt >F7. Ent chan dredged 1·5m, but prone to silting; best water is close to N jetty. Boats <1·2m draft can enter at any tide and in most weathers.

LIGHTS AND MARKS Ent lies SW of conspic ✠, sig stn and TV mast on Pte Fagnet cliff, 142m high. See chartlet and 9.17.4 for lights. The horn (2) 30s on N jetty is sounded HW –2½ to +2. The QR is used only by pilots as a 082° ldg line in transit with QG. **IPTS** on twr at root of S jetty; Y lt shown next to top lt when Bassin Bérigny gate is open.

R/T VHF Ch **12** 10 16 (HW –3 to HW + 1). Ch 09 Marina and Écluse Bérigny (0800-1200; 1400-2000LT).

TELEPHONE HM 02.35.28.25.53; CROSS 03.21.87.21.87; SNSM 02.35.28.00.91; ⊖ 02.35.28.19.40; Auto 08.92.68.08.76; Police 02.35.28.16.69; Ⓗ 02.35.28.05.13; British Consul 02.35.19.78.88.

FACILITIES Marina (600+75Ⓥ) ☎ 02.35.28.13.58 📠 02.35.28.60.46, €2.11, D & P (H24 with a French credit card; if not, only during office hrs), C (mobile 36 ton), ♿; **Bassin Bérigny** ☎ 02.35.28.23.76, AB, M, D, FW, Slip; **Sté des Régates de Fécamp** ☎ 02.35.28.08.44, AB, FW; **Services:** Slip, M, ME, El, Ⓔ, ⚒, CH, Gaz, C (30 ton). **Town** EC Mon; P, D, 🛒, Gaz, R, Bar, ✉, Ⓑ, ⇌, ✈ (Le Havre).

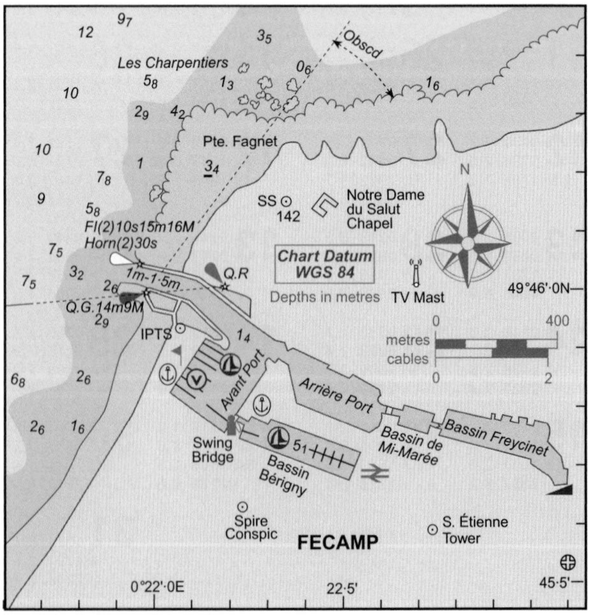
Obscd
Les Charpentiers
Pte. Fagnet
SS
142
Notre Dame du Salut Chapel
N
Fl(2)10s15m16M
Horn(2)30s
Chart Datum WGS 84
Depths in metres
TV Mast
49°46'·0N
Q.R
1m-1·5m
Q.G.14m9M
IPTS
metres 0 400
cables 0 2
Avant Port
Arrière Port
Bassin de Mi-Marée
Bassin Freycinet
Swing Bridge
Bassin Bérigny
Spire Conspic
FECAMP
S. Étienne Tower
0°22'·0E
22·5'
45·5'

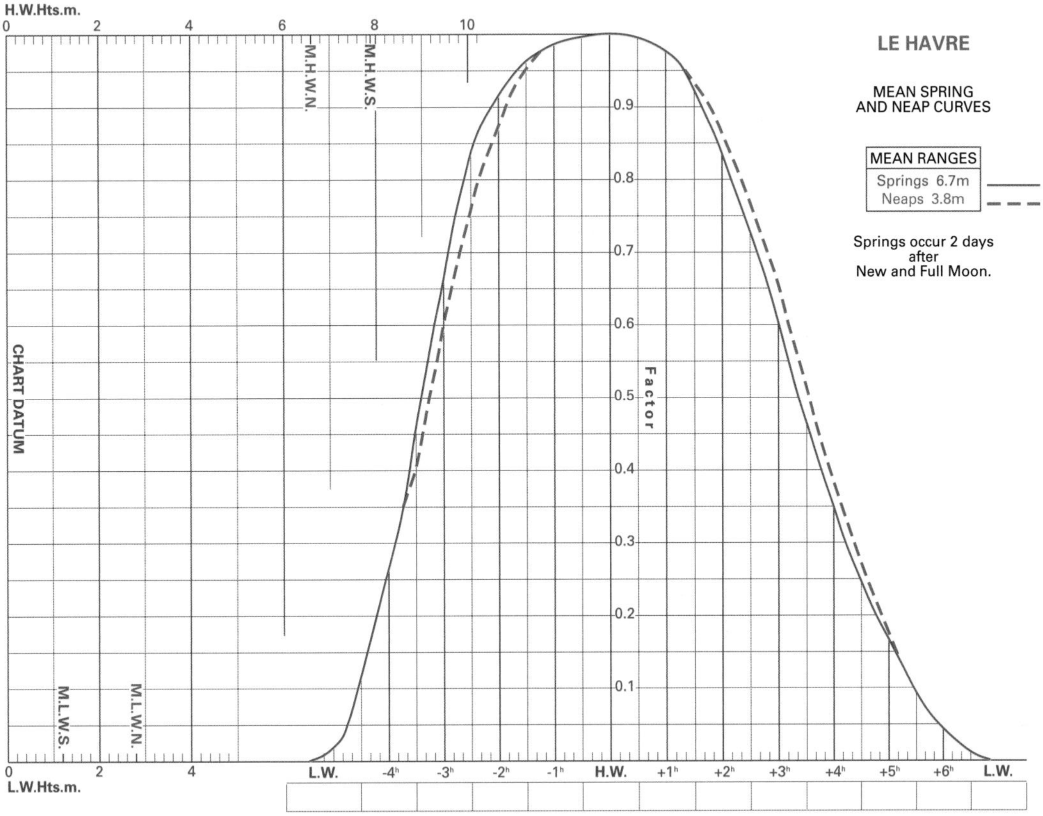
H.W.Hts.m.
LE HAVRE
MEAN SPRING AND NEAP CURVES
MEAN RANGES
Springs 6.7m
Neaps 3.8m
Springs occur 2 days after New and Full Moon.
M.H.W.N.
M.H.W.S.
CHART DATUM
Factor
M.L.W.S.
M.L.W.N.
L.W.Hts.m.
L.W. -4h -3h -2h -1h H.W. +1h +2h +3h +4h +5h +6h L.W.

9.17.17 LE HAVRE

Seine Maritime **49°29'·12N 00°05·43E** ☸☸☸👍👍👍✿✿

CHARTS AC *2613,* 2146, 2990; SHOM 7418, 6683; ECM 526, 1012; Imray C31; Stanfords 1, 21

TIDES –0103 Dover; ML 4·9; Duration 0543; Zone –0100. Le Havre is a Standard Port (⟶). There is a stand of about 3 hrs at HW.

SHELTER Excellent in marina, access H24. Ⓥ pontoon 'O', first to stbd or 'A' in N basin. Long stay in Bassin Vauban, via HM.

NAVIGATION WPT 49°29'·91N 00°02'·41E (LH12), 108°/2·1M to Digue Nord. ⚓ prohib in the fairway; yachts may cross the fairway E of buoys LH7/LH8, but not at the ent, due to restricted vis and WIP. Banc de l'Éclat (1m) lies close N of appr chan with lobster pots either side. Obey IPTS at end of Digue Nord.

LIGHTS AND MARKS Twr of St Joseph's church is conspic E of Anse des Régates. 2 chys, RW conspic, on ldg line.

R/T Call: Havre Port Control twr Ch **12** 20 (or 2182 kHz). Port Ops Ch 67 69 (H24). Radar Ch 12. Marina Ch 09.

TELEPHONE HM 02.35.21.23.95; Marina 02.35.21.23.95; Aff Mar 02.35.19.29.99; CROSS 02.33.52.72.23; ⊜ 02.35.41.33.51; SNSM 02.35.22.41.03; Météo 02.35.42.21.06; Auto 08.92.68.08.76; Dr 02.35.41.23.61; Ⓗ 02.35.73.32.32. Brit Consul 02.35.19.78.88.

FACILITIES **Marina** (973 + 60 Ⓥ) ☎ 02.35.21.23.95, FAX 02.35.22.72.72, €2.11, BH (16 ton), C (6 ton), CH, Slip, P & D, El, Gas, Gaz, R, ▣, ♿, 🛒; De-mast in the marina or de-mast/store: Chantier Naval de la Baie de Seine ☎ 02.35.25.30.51; FAX 02.35.24.44.18. **YC Sport Nautique (SNH)** ☎ 02.35.21.01.41, Bar; **Sté des Régates du Havre (SRH)** ☎ 02.35.42.41.21, R, Bar (closed Aug); **Services:** Ⓔ, ME, ⚒, SHOM, ACA. Ferry: Portsmouth.

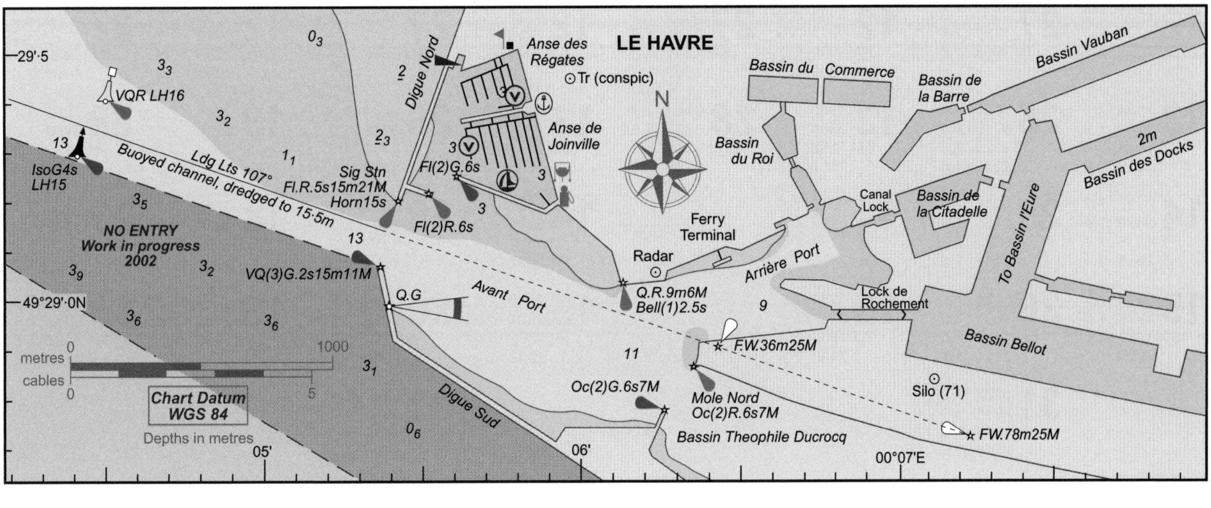
LE HAVRE
29'·5
49°29'·0N
VQR LH16
IsoG4s LH15
Buoyed channel, dredged to 15·5m
Ldg Lts 107°
NO ENTRY
Work in progress
2002
Digue Nord
Sig Stn
Fl.R.5s15m21M
Horn15s
Fl(2)G.6s
Fl(2)R.6s
VQ(3)G.2s15m11M
Q.G
Avant Port
Anse des Régates
Tr (conspic)
Anse de Joinville
Bassin du Commerce
Bassin de la Barre
Bassin Vauban
Bassin du Roi
Canal Lock
Bassin de la Citadelle
Bassin des Docks
To Bassin l'Eure
Ferry Terminal
Radar
Arrière Port
Q.R.9m6M
Bell(1)2.5s
Lock de Rochemont
F.W.36m25M
Bassin Bellot
Silo (71)
Oc(2)G.6s7M
Mole Nord
Oc(2)R.6s7M
Digue Sud
Bassin Theophile Ducrocq
F.W.78m25M
metres
cables
Chart Datum
WGS 84
Depths in metres
05'
06'
00°07'E

TIME ZONE -0100
(French Standard Time)
Subtract 1 hour for UT
For French Summer Time add ONE hour in **non-shaded areas**

FRANCE – LE HAVRE

LAT 49°29′N LONG 0°07′E

TIMES AND HEIGHTS OF HIGH AND LOW WATERS

SPRING & NEAP TIDES
Dates in red are SPRINGS
Dates in blue are NEAPS

YEAR **2005**

JANUARY

Day	Time	m
1 SA	0150 0836 1357 2058	7.1 2.5 7.1 2.3
2 SU	0229 0914 1438 2136	6.9 2.7 7.0 2.5
3 M	0313 0958 1525 ◑ 2222	6.8 2.8 6.8 2.7
4 TU	0404 1050 1620 2318	6.7 2.9 6.7 2.8
5 W	0507 1152 1729	6.7 3.0 6.6
6 TH	0024 0619 1304 1847	2.8 6.8 2.9 6.7
7 F	0141 0728 1424 1958	2.7 7.0 2.6 6.9
8 SA	0258 0829 1534 2101	2.4 7.2 2.1 7.2
9 SU	0402 0925 1635 2159	2.0 7.5 1.7 7.5
10 M	0501 1019 1733 ● 2253	1.7 7.8 1.3 7.8
11 TU	0559 1110 1829 2344	1.4 8.0 1.0 7.9
12 W	0653 1200 1922	1.3 8.0 0.9
13 TH	0034 0744 1248 2010	7.9 1.3 8.0 0.9
14 F	0122 0830 1335 2053	7.9 1.4 7.9 1.1
15 SA	0208 0912 1421 2133	7.7 1.6 7.6 1.5
16 SU	0253 0952 1507 2211	7.4 2.0 7.3 1.9
17 M	0339 1032 1556 ◐ 2251	7.1 2.4 7.0 2.4
18 TU	0430 1119 1654 2340	6.8 2.8 6.7 2.8
19 W	0532 1218 1807	6.6 3.1 6.4
20 TH	0046 0647 1335 1930	3.1 6.5 3.1 6.4
21 F	0205 0800 1448 2038	3.2 6.6 2.9 6.6
22 SA	0311 0856 1547 2128	2.9 6.8 2.6 6.8
23 SU	0406 0941 1636 2209	2.7 7.0 2.3 7.1
24 M	0453 1018 1719 2244	2.4 7.2 2.0 7.2
25 TU	0534 1051 1759 ○ 2317	2.1 7.4 1.8 7.4
26 W	0613 1124 1835 2350	2.0 7.5 1.7 7.4
27 TH	0647 1157 1908	1.9 7.6 1.6
28 F	0022 0719 1229 1940	7.5 1.8 7.6 1.6
29 SA	0055 0751 1302 2011	7.4 1.8 7.6 1.6
30 SU	0128 0822 1336 2041	7.4 1.9 7.5 1.8
31 M	0202 0854 1411 2112	7.3 2.1 7.3 2.0

FEBRUARY

Day	Time	m
1 TU	0238 0928 1448 2147	7.1 2.3 7.1 2.3
2 W	0317 1009 1533 ◑ 2232	6.9 2.6 6.9 2.6
3 TH	0408 1103 1636 2333	6.8 2.8 6.6 2.9
4 F	0525 1217 1810	6.6 3.0 6.5
5 SA	0059 0657 1353 1941	3.0 6.7 2.8 6.7
6 SU	0235 0814 1516 2054	2.7 7.0 2.3 7.1
7 M	0349 0918 1625 2155	2.2 7.4 1.7 7.5
8 TU	0455 1013 1730 ● 2246	1.7 7.7 1.2 7.8
9 W	0556 1102 1826 2333	1.3 8.0 0.8 8.0
10 TH	0648 1148 1913	1.0 8.1 0.6
11 F	0018 0732 1232 1954	8.1 0.9 8.2 0.6
12 SA	0100 0811 1313 2030	8.0 1.0 8.1 0.9
13 SU	0140 0846 1352 2101	7.8 1.3 7.8 1.3
14 M	0217 0917 1430 2129	7.5 1.7 7.5 1.8
15 TU	0252 0947 1509 2158	7.2 2.2 7.0 2.4
16 W	0332 1021 1558 ◐ 2237	6.8 2.7 6.6 3.0
17 TH	0425 1111 1710 2338	6.4 3.2 6.2 3.5
18 F	0548 1232 1854	6.2 3.5 6.0
19 SA	0117 0727 1413 2018	3.6 6.2 3.3 6.2
20 SU	0247 0837 1525 2112	3.3 6.4 2.9 6.6
21 M	0351 0923 1620 2151	2.8 6.8 2.4 6.9
22 TU	0441 0959 1705 2224	2.3 7.1 2.0 7.2
23 W	0522 1032 1744 2255	2.0 7.4 1.6 7.4
24 TH	0559 1104 1819 ○ 2327	1.7 7.6 1.4 7.6
25 F	0631 1136 1850 2359	1.5 7.7 1.3 7.6
26 SA	0702 1208 1920	1.4 7.8 1.2
27 SU	0031 0731 1241 1950	7.7 1.4 7.8 1.3
28 M	0103 0802 1314 2020	7.6 1.5 7.7 1.5

MARCH

Day	Time	m
1 TU	0136 0833 1347 2049	7.5 1.7 7.5 1.7
2 W	0208 0905 1423 2120	7.3 2.0 7.3 2.1
3 TH	0244 0941 1506 ◑ 2201	7.1 2.3 6.9 2.6
4 F	0333 1033 1612 2303	6.8 2.7 6.5 3.0
5 SA	0457 1151 1801	6.4 3.0 6.3
6 SU	0039 0646 1338 1938	3.2 6.5 2.8 6.6
7 M	0226 0808 1507 2051	2.8 6.9 2.3 7.1
8 TU	0345 0911 1620 2146	2.2 7.3 1.6 7.5
9 W	0452 1001 1722 2232	1.6 7.7 1.1 7.8
10 TH	0546 1046 1811 ● 2314	1.1 8.0 0.7 8.0
11 F	0632 1128 1853 2354	0.8 8.1 0.6 8.1
12 SA	0710 1208 1928	0.8 8.2 0.7
13 SU	0032 0744 1246 1959	8.0 0.9 8.1 0.9
14 M	0107 0814 1322 2026	7.8 1.2 7.8 1.4
15 TU	0140 0841 1357 2049	7.6 1.6 7.4 1.9
16 W	0211 0906 1431 2113	7.3 2.1 7.0 2.5
17 TH	0244 0935 1513 ◐ 2148	6.9 2.7 6.5 3.1
18 F	0328 1019 1620 2246	6.4 3.2 6.0 3.6
19 SA	0451 1136 1813	5.9 3.6 5.8
20 SU	0032 0646 1332 1946	3.8 5.9 3.5 6.1
21 M	0218 0804 1453 2042	3.4 6.2 3.0 6.5
22 TU	0324 0854 1549 2121	2.8 6.6 2.4 6.9
23 W	0413 0930 1635 2154	2.3 7.0 1.9 7.3
24 TH	0455 1004 1715 2226	1.9 7.4 1.6 7.5
25 F	0531 1037 1750 ○ 2259	1.6 7.6 1.3 7.7
26 SA	0604 1110 1822 2331	1.4 7.8 1.2 7.8
27 SU	0636 1143 1853	1.2 7.8 1.1
28 M	0004 0708 1217 1925	7.8 1.2 7.8 1.2
29 TU	0037 0741 1253 1957	7.8 1.2 7.7 1.4
30 W	0111 0813 1330 2029	7.6 1.5 7.5 1.7
31 TH	0147 0847 1410 2102	7.4 1.8 7.2 2.1

APRIL

Day	Time	m
1 F	0227 0926 1500 2146	7.1 2.2 6.8 2.6
2 SA	0323 1020 1614 ◑ 2254	6.7 2.7 6.4 3.1
3 SU	0457 1145 1805	6.4 2.9 6.4
4 M	0040 0640 1333 1933	3.2 6.5 2.7 6.7
5 TU	0221 0756 1457 2038	2.7 6.9 2.1 7.2
6 W	0334 0854 1606 2127	2.0 7.3 1.5 7.6
7 TH	0435 0942 1701 2209	1.5 7.7 1.1 7.8
8 F	0524 1024 1746 ● 2249	1.1 7.9 0.9 7.9
9 SA	0606 1104 1823 2326	1.0 8.0 0.9 8.0
10 SU	0641 1142 1856	1.0 8.0 1.0
11 M	0002 0713 1219 1925	7.9 1.1 7.9 1.2
12 TU	0035 0742 1255 1952	7.8 1.3 7.6 1.6
13 W	0108 0809 1329 2015	7.5 1.7 7.3 2.0
14 TH	0139 0834 1404 2041	7.2 2.1 6.9 2.5
15 F	0211 0903 1444 2115	6.8 2.6 6.4 3.1
16 SA	0252 0944 1544 ◐ 2210	6.4 3.1 6.0 3.5
17 SU	0402 1055 1726 2349	5.9 3.4 5.9 3.8
18 M	0553 1241 1852	5.8 3.4 6.1
19 TU	0128 0712 1401 1954	3.4 6.1 3.0 6.5
20 W	0234 0808 1500 2039	2.9 6.5 2.5 6.9
21 TH	0327 0851 1549 2116	2.4 6.9 2.0 7.2
22 F	0412 0928 1633 2151	2.0 7.3 1.7 7.5
23 SA	0453 1005 1712 2226	1.6 7.5 1.4 7.7
24 SU	0531 1041 1749 ○ 2301	1.4 7.7 1.3 7.8
25 M	0608 1118 1826 2337	1.2 7.8 1.2 7.8
26 TU	0645 1156 1902	1.1 7.8 1.2
27 W	0014 0722 1236 1939	7.8 1.2 7.7 1.4
28 TH	0053 0759 1319 2015	7.7 1.4 7.5 1.8
29 F	0135 0837 1406 2055	7.4 1.7 7.2 2.2
30 SA	0223 0922 1503 2146	7.1 2.1 6.8 2.6

Chart Datum: 4·38 metres below IGN Datum

TIME ZONE -0100
(French Standard Time)
Subtract 1 hour for UT
For French Summer Time add ONE hour in **non-shaded areas**

FRANCE – LE HAVRE

LAT 49°29′N LONG 0°07′E

TIMES AND HEIGHTS OF HIGH AND LOW WATERS

SPRING & NEAP TIDES
Dates in red are SPRINGS
Dates in blue are NEAPS

YEAR **2005**

MAY

Date	Day	Time	m	Time	m	Time	m	Time	m
1	SU	0327	6.8	1023	2.5	1625	6.6	◑ 2302	2.9
2	M	0457	6.6	1149	2.6	1756	6.6		
3	TU	0039	2.9	0622	6.7	1319	2.4	1911	6.9
4	W	0201	2.4	0732	7.0	1432	2.0	2012	7.2
5	TH	0307	2.0	0829	7.3	1535	1.6	2101	7.5
6	F	0404	1.6	0917	7.5	1628	1.4	2143	7.7
7	SA	0453	1.4	1000	7.7	1712	1.3	2222	7.7
8	SU	0534	1.3	1040	7.7	1749	1.3	● 2259	7.7
9	M	0609	1.3	1119	7.7	1822	1.4	2334	7.7
10	TU	0643	1.4	1156	7.6	1853	1.6		
11	W	0008	7.6	0714	1.5	1233	7.4	1923	1.9
12	TH	0042	7.4	0743	1.8	1309	7.2	1951	2.2
13	F	0115	7.2	0812	2.1	1346	6.9	2021	2.6
14	SA	0150	6.9	0844	2.5	1426	6.5	2057	3.0
15	SU	0231	6.5	0923	2.8	1516	6.3	2147	3.3
16	M	0326	6.2	1022	3.1	1630	6.1	◐ 2304	3.5
17	TU	0447	6.1	1143	3.2	1751	6.2		
18	W	0024	3.3	0609	6.2	1256	3.0	1854	6.5
19	TH	0130	3.0	0711	6.5	1358	2.6	1946	6.8
20	F	0227	2.6	0802	6.8	1453	2.2	2031	7.1
21	SA	0319	2.2	0847	7.1	1543	1.9	2112	7.4
22	SU	0408	1.9	0929	7.4	1630	1.7	2152	7.6
23	M	0455	1.6	1011	7.5	1716	1.5	○ 2232	7.7
24	TU	0540	1.3	1054	7.6	1800	1.4	2313	7.8
25	W	0624	1.2	1139	7.7	1843	1.4	2356	7.8
26	TH	0708	1.2	1225	7.6	1927	1.5		
27	F	0041	7.7	0752	1.3	1314	7.5	2011	1.8
28	SA	0130	7.5	0838	1.5	1407	7.3	2100	2.1
29	SU	0223	7.3	0930	1.8	1507	7.0	2157	2.3
30	M	0327	7.0	1031	2.1	1618	6.9	◑ 2305	2.5
31	TU	0440	6.8	1139	2.2	1729	6.9		

JUNE

Date	Day	Time	m	Time	m	Time	m	Time	m
1	W	0016	2.5	0551	6.9	1248	2.2	1836	7.0
2	TH	0124	2.4	0658	7.0	1352	2.1	1937	7.1
3	F	0228	2.2	0758	7.1	1453	2.0	2030	7.3
4	SA	0326	2.0	0851	7.2	1547	1.9	2116	7.4
5	SU	0417	1.9	0938	7.3	1634	1.9	2157	7.5
6	M	0500	1.7	1021	7.4	1714	1.9	● 2236	7.5
7	TU	0539	1.7	1101	7.4	1752	1.9	2312	7.5
8	W	0616	1.7	1139	7.4	1828	1.9	2347	7.4
9	TH	0651	1.7	1216	7.3	1902	2.0		
10	F	0023	7.3	0725	1.8	1253	7.1	1936	2.2
11	SA	0058	7.2	0758	2.0	1330	7.0	2010	2.4
12	SU	0134	7.0	0832	2.2	1407	6.8	2045	2.7
13	M	0212	6.8	0909	2.5	1448	6.6	2127	2.9
14	TU	0255	6.6	0952	2.7	1537	6.5	2218	3.0
15	W	0348	6.5	1046	2.8	1636	6.5	◐ 2317	3.0
16	TH	0451	6.4	1146	2.8	1743	6.5		
17	F	0020	3.0	0600	6.5	1249	2.7	1845	6.7
18	SA	0124	2.8	0705	6.7	1353	2.5	1940	6.9
19	SU	0227	2.5	0803	6.9	1456	2.3	2032	7.2
20	M	0328	2.1	0856	7.1	1554	2.0	2120	7.4
21	TU	0424	1.8	0948	7.3	1649	1.7	2208	7.6
22	W	0518	1.5	1038	7.5	1741	1.6	○ 2257	7.7
23	TH	0610	1.2	1129	7.7	1833	1.5	2346	7.8
24	F	0702	1.1	1220	7.7	1924	1.4		
25	SA	0035	7.8	0753	1.1	1311	7.7	2015	1.5
26	SU	0126	7.7	0843	1.2	1403	7.5	2106	1.7
27	M	0218	7.5	0932	1.4	1456	7.4	2155	1.9
28	TU	0312	7.3	1020	1.7	1551	7.2	◑ 2246	2.1
29	W	0409	7.1	1110	2.0	1649	7.0	2340	2.4
30	TH	0511	6.9	1205	2.3	1751	6.9		

JULY

Date	Day	Time	m	Time	m	Time	m	Time	m
1	F	0040	2.5	0617	6.8	1307	2.5	1856	6.9
2	SA	0146	2.5	0727	6.8	1411	2.5	1959	7.0
3	SU	0249	2.4	0830	6.9	1510	2.5	2054	7.1
4	M	0344	2.3	0924	7.0	1602	2.4	2140	7.2
5	TU	0433	2.1	1009	7.1	1648	2.3	2221	7.3
6	W	0517	2.0	1050	7.2	1731	2.1	● 2258	7.4
7	TH	0557	1.8	1126	7.3	1811	2.1	2332	7.4
8	F	0636	1.8	1201	7.3	1849	2.0		
9	SA	0007	7.4	0712	1.7	1235	7.3	1925	2.1
10	SU	0041	7.3	0746	1.8	1310	7.2	1958	2.1
11	M	0114	7.3	0818	1.9	1343	7.1	2030	2.2
12	TU	0148	7.2	0850	2.1	1418	7.0	2103	2.4
13	W	0225	7.0	0923	2.2	1456	6.9	2140	2.6
14	TH	0306	6.9	1000	2.4	1539	6.8	◐ 2224	2.7
15	F	0353	6.7	1047	2.7	1631	6.7	2318	2.9
16	SA	0452	6.6	1145	2.8	1737	6.6		
17	SU	0024	2.9	0607	6.5	1258	2.8	1851	6.7
18	M	0143	2.7	0725	6.6	1419	2.6	1959	6.9
19	TU	0258	2.3	0834	6.9	1529	2.3	2059	7.2
20	W	0403	1.9	0935	7.3	1631	1.9	2155	7.5
21	TH	0503	1.5	1030	7.5	1731	1.6	○ 2247	7.8
22	F	0604	1.1	1122	7.8	1830	1.3	2337	7.9
23	SA	0700	0.9	1211	7.9	1923	1.1		
24	SU	0026	8.0	0749	0.7	1259	7.9	2010	1.1
25	M	0113	8.0	0834	0.8	1345	7.8	2053	1.3
26	TU	0159	7.8	0914	1.1	1430	7.6	2133	1.6
27	W	0244	7.5	0952	1.5	1514	7.3	2213	2.0
28	TH	0331	7.2	1030	2.0	1602	7.0	◑ 2256	2.4
29	F	0425	6.8	1115	2.5	1658	6.7	2350	2.8
30	SA	0533	6.5	1215	3.0	1810	6.5		
31	SU	0103	3.0	0659	6.4	1333	3.1	1932	6.6

AUGUST

Date	Day	Time	m	Time	m	Time	m	Time	m
1	M	0218	2.9	0817	6.5	1444	3.0	2039	6.7
2	TU	0322	2.6	0914	6.8	1543	2.7	2128	7.0
3	W	0416	2.3	0959	7.0	1635	2.4	2208	7.2
4	TH	0503	2.0	1036	7.2	1721	2.2	2242	7.4
5	F	0545	1.8	1108	7.3	1801	2.0	● 2315	7.5
6	SA	0623	1.6	1140	7.4	1837	1.8	2347	7.5
7	SU	0657	1.6	1212	7.5	1909	1.8		
8	M	0019	7.6	0728	1.5	1244	7.5	1938	1.8
9	TU	0050	7.5	0757	1.6	1315	7.4	2007	1.9
10	W	0121	7.5	0825	1.7	1347	7.3	2037	2.0
11	TH	0154	7.3	0854	2.0	1420	7.2	2108	2.2
12	F	0229	7.1	0925	2.3	1456	7.0	2144	2.5
13	SA	0310	6.8	1003	2.6	1540	6.8	◐ 2231	2.8
14	SU	0404	6.6	1055	2.9	1644	6.6	2337	3.0
15	M	0527	6.4	1214	3.1	1818	6.5		
16	TU	0112	3.0	0707	6.5	1357	3.0	1942	6.8
17	W	0242	2.5	0826	6.9	1516	2.4	2050	7.2
18	TH	0351	1.9	0928	7.3	1623	1.9	2146	7.6
19	F	0457	1.4	1021	7.7	1726	1.4	○ 2237	7.9
20	SA	0557	0.9	1109	8.0	1822	1.1	2323	8.1
21	SU	0648	0.6	1154	8.1	1909	0.9		
22	M	0008	8.2	0732	0.5	1237	8.1	1951	0.9
23	TU	0051	8.2	0811	0.7	1319	8.0	2028	1.1
24	W	0132	8.0	0845	1.1	1358	7.7	2102	1.5
25	TH	0212	7.6	0916	1.6	1435	7.4	2134	2.0
26	F	0253	7.2	0946	2.2	1515	7.0	◑ 2209	2.6
27	SA	0341	6.7	1023	2.9	1606	6.6	2257	3.1
28	SU	0451	6.2	1122	3.4	1725	6.2		
29	M	0018	3.4	0636	6.1	1300	3.6	1909	6.2
30	TU	0154	3.3	0804	6.3	1427	3.3	2024	6.5
31	W	0306	2.8	0901	6.7	1532	2.8	2112	6.8

Chart Datum: 4·38 metres below IGN Datum

TIME ZONE -0100
(French Standard Time)
Subtract 1 hour for UT
For French Summer Time add ONE hour in **non-shaded areas**

FRANCE – LE HAVRE

LAT 49°29′N LONG 0°07′E

TIMES AND HEIGHTS OF HIGH AND LOW WATERS

SPRING & NEAP TIDES
Dates in red are **SPRINGS**
Dates in blue are **NEAPS**

YEAR **2005**

SEPTEMBER

Date	Day	Time	m	Time	m	Time	m	Time	m
1	TH	0402	2.4	0941	7.0	1623	2.4	2149	7.2
2	F	0447	2.0	1013	7.3	1706	2.0	2220	7.4
3	SA	0526	1.7	1043	7.5	1742	1.8	● 2250	7.6
4	SU	0601	1.5	1113	7.6	1815	1.6	2321	7.7
5	M	0633	1.4	1144	7.7	1844	1.6	2352	7.8
6	TU	0701	1.4	1214	7.7	1913	1.6		
7	W	0023	7.7	0730	1.4	1245	7.6	1942	1.6
8	TH	0054	7.6	0758	1.6	1315	7.5	2012	1.8
9	F	0126	7.4	0827	1.9	1347	7.3	2042	2.1
10	SA	0200	7.2	0856	2.3	1420	7.1	2116	2.4
11	SU	0241	6.9	0932	2.7	1505	6.8	◐ 2201	2.8
12	M	0340	6.5	1026	3.1	1617	6.4	2311	3.1
13	TU	0518	6.3	1153	3.4	1807	6.4		
14	W	0100	3.1	0705	6.5	1351	3.1	1935	6.8
15	TH	0233	2.5	0820	7.0	1510	2.4	2041	7.3
16	F	0343	1.8	0918	7.5	1615	1.7	2133	7.7
17	SA	0446	1.2	1005	7.9	1713	1.3	2219	8.1
18	SU	0540	0.8	1048	8.1	1803	0.9	○ 2302	8.2
19	M	0626	0.6	1130	8.2	1846	0.8	2344	8.3
20	TU	0705	0.7	1210	8.1	1924	0.9		
21	W	0025	8.2	0740	0.9	1248	8.0	1957	1.2
22	TH	0103	7.9	0810	1.3	1323	7.7	2028	1.6
23	F	0141	7.5	0837	1.9	1357	7.4	2056	2.1
24	SA	0219	7.1	0904	2.5	1433	7.0	2127	2.7
25	SU	0304	6.6	0938	3.1	1521	6.5	◑ 2211	3.2
26	M	0414	6.1	1036	3.7	1643	6.1	2332	3.6
27	TU	0605	5.9	1227	3.9	1835	6.0		
28	W	0125	3.5	0736	6.2	1404	3.5	1955	6.3
29	TH	0238	2.9	0833	6.6	1505	2.9	2043	6.7
30	F	0330	2.4	0910	7.0	1553	2.4	2118	7.1

OCTOBER

Date	Day	Time	m	Time	m	Time	m	Time	m
1	SA	0415	2.0	0940	7.4	1635	2.0	2149	7.5
2	SU	0454	1.7	1010	7.6	1711	1.7	2220	7.7
3	M	0530	1.5	1041	7.7	1744	1.6	● 2252	7.8
4	TU	0601	1.4	1112	7.8	1814	1.5	2323	7.8
5	W	0631	1.4	1143	7.8	1845	1.5	2355	7.8
6	TH	0701	1.5	1214	7.7	1917	1.5		
7	F	0029	7.7	0733	1.6	1247	7.6	1950	1.7
8	SA	0104	7.5	0804	1.9	1321	7.4	2023	2.0
9	SU	0144	7.2	0837	2.3	1400	7.1	2059	2.4
10	M	0231	6.8	0917	2.8	1452	6.7	◐ 2148	2.8
11	TU	0338	6.5	1017	3.2	1613	6.5	2304	3.1
12	W	0525	6.3	1155	3.4	1802	6.5		
13	TH	0056	2.9	0657	6.7	1345	2.9	1921	6.9
14	F	0221	2.3	0805	7.2	1456	2.2	2023	7.4
15	SA	0326	1.7	0857	7.6	1556	1.7	2112	7.8
16	SU	0424	1.2	0942	7.9	1650	1.3	2157	8.0
17	M	0513	1.0	1023	8.1	1736	1.1	○ 2238	8.2
18	TU	0556	0.9	1102	8.1	1817	1.0	2319	8.1
19	W	0634	1.0	1140	8.0	1853	1.2	2359	8.0
20	TH	0707	1.3	1216	7.9	1926	1.4		
21	F	0037	7.8	0737	1.7	1251	7.6	1956	1.8
22	SA	0115	7.4	0805	2.2	1326	7.3	2025	2.2
23	SU	0153	7.0	0833	2.7	1402	6.9	2056	2.7
24	M	0238	6.5	0908	3.2	1447	6.5	2139	3.2
25	TU	0342	6.2	1004	3.7	1600	6.1	◑ 2250	3.5
26	W	0517	6.0	1141	3.9	1741	6.0		
27	TH	0032	3.5	0640	6.2	1315	3.5	1900	6.2
28	F	0148	3.1	0742	6.6	1419	3.0	1955	6.6
29	SA	0244	2.6	0825	7.0	1509	2.5	2036	7.0
30	SU	0331	2.2	0900	7.3	1553	2.1	2112	7.4
31	M	0413	1.9	0933	7.6	1633	1.9	2147	7.6

NOVEMBER

Date	Day	Time	m	Time	m	Time	m	Time	m
1	TU	0451	1.7	1007	7.7	1709	1.7	2221	7.7
2	W	0526	1.6	1040	7.8	1744	1.5	● 2256	7.8
3	TH	0601	1.5	1114	7.8	1820	1.5	2332	7.8
4	F	0637	1.6	1148	7.8	1857	1.5		
5	SA	0010	7.7	0713	1.7	1226	7.7	1934	1.6
6	SU	0052	7.5	0749	2.0	1307	7.5	2012	1.9
7	M	0138	7.2	0828	2.4	1354	7.2	2054	2.3
8	TU	0232	6.9	0916	2.8	1452	6.9	2149	2.6
9	W	0343	6.7	1022	3.1	1613	6.7	◐ 2307	2.8
10	TH	0516	6.6	1155	3.1	1743	6.7		
11	F	0040	2.6	0634	6.9	1322	2.7	1855	7.0
12	SA	0155	2.2	0737	7.2	1430	2.2	1956	7.3
13	SU	0258	1.8	0830	7.6	1529	1.8	2048	7.6
14	M	0354	1.6	0915	7.8	1621	1.5	2134	7.8
15	TU	0442	1.4	0957	7.9	1707	1.4	2217	7.9
16	W	0525	1.4	1037	7.9	1748	1.4	○ 2258	7.9
17	TH	0602	1.5	1115	7.9	1824	1.4	2338	7.8
18	F	0637	1.7	1151	7.7	1859	1.6		
19	SA	0017	7.6	0709	2.0	1227	7.6	1932	1.8
20	SU	0056	7.3	0741	2.3	1303	7.3	2004	2.2
21	M	0135	7.0	0814	2.7	1340	7.0	2037	2.5
22	TU	0217	6.7	0851	3.0	1422	6.7	2117	2.9
23	W	0307	6.4	0939	3.4	1515	6.3	◑ 2211	3.2
24	TH	0416	6.2	1046	3.6	1630	6.2	2323	3.3
25	F	0531	6.3	1201	3.5	1749	6.2		
26	SA	0035	3.2	0636	6.5	1309	3.2	1852	6.5
27	SU	0139	2.9	0728	6.8	1408	2.9	1944	6.8
28	M	0234	2.6	0813	7.1	1501	2.5	2029	7.1
29	TU	0325	2.3	0853	7.3	1549	2.2	2111	7.3
30	W	0410	2.0	0932	7.5	1633	1.9	2152	7.5

DECEMBER

Date	Day	Time	m	Time	m	Time	m	Time	m
1	TH	0453	1.8	1010	7.7	1717	1.7	● 2233	7.6
2	F	0536	1.7	1049	7.8	1800	1.5	2315	7.7
3	SA	0618	1.7	1131	7.8	1843	1.4		
4	SU	0000	7.7	0702	1.7	1215	7.8	1927	1.5
5	M	0046	7.6	0746	1.9	1302	7.6	2012	1.6
6	TU	0137	7.4	0833	2.1	1352	7.4	2100	1.9
7	W	0232	7.2	0925	2.4	1450	7.2	2155	2.1
8	TH	0336	7.0	1026	2.6	1557	7.0	◐ 2258	2.3
9	F	0447	6.9	1133	2.7	1709	6.9		
10	SA	0005	2.4	0556	7.0	1243	2.6	1818	7.0
11	SU	0115	2.4	0700	7.1	1353	2.4	1924	7.1
12	M	0221	2.2	0759	7.3	1456	2.2	2023	7.3
13	TU	0320	2.1	0850	7.4	1552	2.0	2116	7.4
14	W	0412	2.0	0937	7.6	1640	1.9	2203	7.5
15	TH	0456	2.0	1019	7.6	1723	1.8	○ 2246	7.6
16	F	0536	2.0	1058	7.6	1802	1.7	2326	7.5
17	SA	0614	2.0	1135	7.6	1839	1.7		
18	SU	0004	7.5	0651	2.1	1211	7.5	1915	1.8
19	M	0041	7.4	0727	2.2	1247	7.4	1950	2.0
20	TU	0117	7.2	0802	2.4	1322	7.2	2024	2.2
21	W	0154	7.0	0837	2.6	1358	7.0	2058	2.5
22	TH	0232	6.8	0913	2.9	1436	6.8	2135	2.7
23	F	0314	6.6	0955	3.1	1522	6.6	◑ 2219	2.9
24	SA	0406	6.5	1046	3.2	1618	6.5	2312	3.0
25	SU	0510	6.5	1144	3.2	1726	6.4		
26	M	0013	3.1	0617	6.6	1248	3.2	1838	6.5
27	TU	0121	3.0	0718	6.8	1359	2.9	1942	6.7
28	W	0231	2.7	0812	7.0	1505	2.5	2038	7.0
29	TH	0333	2.4	0901	7.3	1603	2.1	2129	7.2
30	F	0427	2.1	0948	7.5	1656	1.8	2218	7.5
31	SA	0519	1.8	1035	7.7	1747	1.5	● 2306	7.6

Chart Datum: 4·38 metres below IGN Datum

9.17.18 HONFLEUR

Calvados **49° 25'·69N 00° 13'·90E**

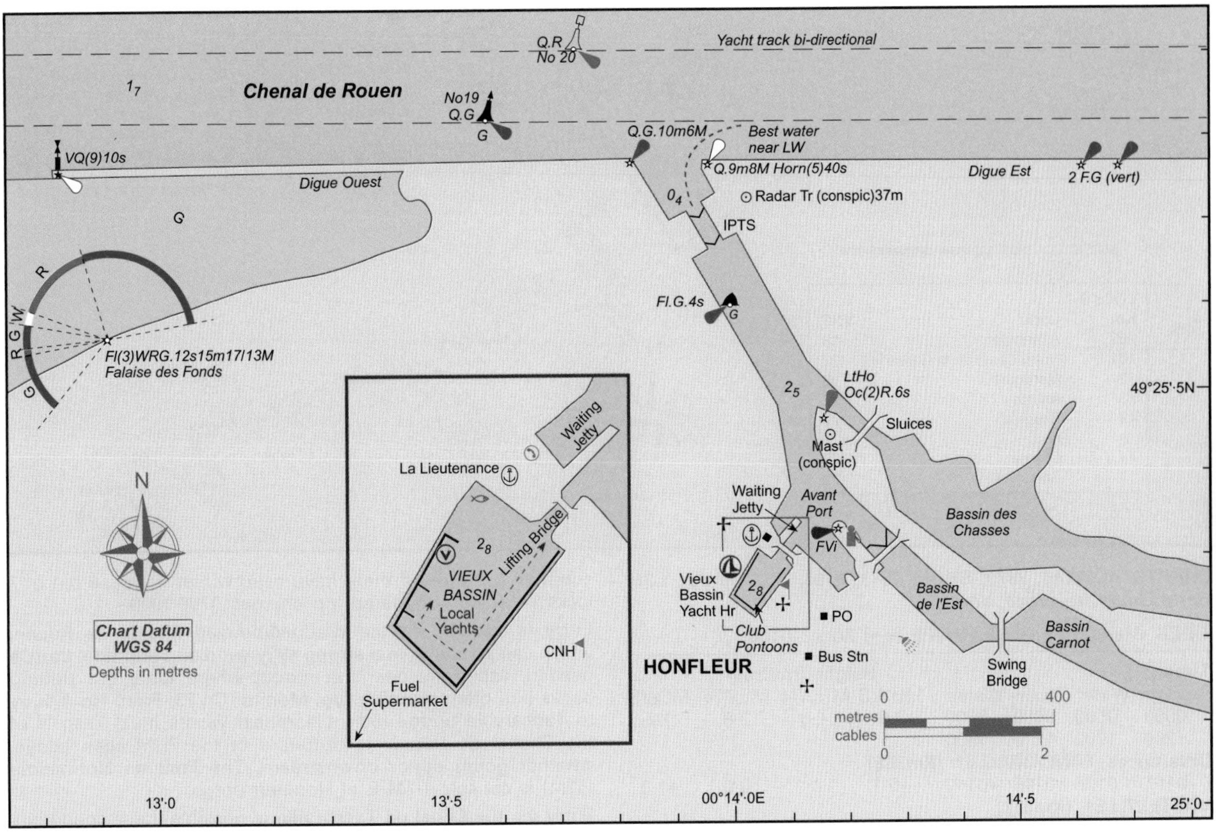

Q.R
No 20
Yacht track bi-directional
Chenal de Rouen
No19
Q.G
G
VQ(9)10s
Digue Ouest
Q.G.10m6M
Best water
near LW
Q.9m8M Horn(5)40s
Digue Est
2 F.G (vert)
Radar Tr (conspic)37m
IPTS
Fl.G.4s
Fl(3)WRG.12s15m17/13M
Falaise des Fonds
LtHo
Oc(2)R.6s
Sluices
Mast
(conspic)
49°25'·5N
La Lieutenance
Waiting Jetty
Lifting Bridge
VIEUX BASSIN
Local Yachts
CNH
Fuel
Supermarket
Waiting
Jetty
Avant
Port
FVi
Bassin des
Chasses
Vieux
Bassin
Yacht Hr
Club
Pontoons
PO
Bus Stn
HONFLEUR
Bassin
de l'Est
Bassin
Carnot
Swing
Bridge
N
Chart Datum
WGS 84
Depths in metres
metres
cables
0
400
2
13'·0
13'·5
00°14'·0E
14'·5
25'·0

CHARTS AC 2146, 2990, 2994; SHOM 7418, 6683, 7420; ECM 1012; Imray C31; Stanfords 1, 21

TIDES –0135 Dover; ML 5·0; Duration 0540; Zone –0100

Standard Port LE HAVRE (⟵)

Times				Height (metres)			
High Water		Low Water		MHWS	MHWN	MLWN	MLWS
0000	0500	0000	0700	7·9	6·6	2·8	1·2
1200	1700	1200	1900				
Differences HONFLEUR							
–0135	–0135	+0015	+0040	+0·1	+0·1	+0·1	+0·3

In the Seine there is a HW stand of about 2hrs 50 mins. The HW time differences refer to the beginning of the stand.

SHELTER Excellent in the Vieux Bassin where visitors raft up on a pontoon on NW side. Or ask YC for possible vacant berth on YC finger pontoons. Immediately outside the Vieux Bassin yachts can wait on E side of the jetty. There are also berths on the W side of Avant Port, close N of the waiting jetty. There are no yacht berths elsewhere in the Avant Port. Larger yachts can enter Bassin de l'Est; see HM.

NAVIGATION WPT No 4 PHM buoy, QR, 49°26'·98N 00°02'·59E, at start of buoyed/lit Chenal de Rouen, 8M to Honfleur. Appr at HW ±3, keeping N of the fairway between the PHM buoys and the Digue Nord, marked by posts. (This rule applies to E and W-bound yachts between No 4 buoy and Tancarville bridge). After No 20 PHM buoy cross to the ent. Caution: strong stream across ent. Rouen is 60M and Paris 192M up-river.

LOCK AND BRIDGE The **lock** (fitted with recessed floating bollards and ladders, but no pontoons) operates H24, but NOT LW±2 due to silting. If arriving/departing near LW, the pecked line on chartlet indicates best water very close to the E side of the ent. Lock opens at H, every hour for arrivals; and every H +30 for departures. IPTS are in force.

At the Vieux Bassin the **road bridge** lifts as shown below (LT). Yachts leaving take priority over arrivals; be ready 5 mins in advance.

1 Jan to 30 April and 1 Sep to 31 Dec
Weekdays: 0830, 1130, 1430, 1730.
Sat/Sun/Hols: 0830, 0930, 1030, 1130, 1430, 1530, 1630, 1730.
1 May to 31 Aug
Every day: 0830, 0930, 1030, 1130; 1630, 1730, 1830, 1930.

LIGHTS AND MARKS See chartlet and 9.17.4. The radar tower by the lock is highly conspic; slightly less so are the wooded hills SW of Honfleur and the Pont de Normandie 1·6M up-river. Falaise des Fonds' sectored lt covers a short stretch of the Ch de Rouen. **IPTS** are in force at the lock. SE of the lock leave the conspic signal mast to port.

R/T HM Ch **17** 73; Lock **17** (H24); Honfleur Radar Ch **73** (H24).

TELEPHONE HM ☎/📠 02.31.14.61.09; Lock 02.31.98.72.82; CROSS 02.33.52.72.13; Aff Mar 02.31.89.20.67; ⊖ 02.31.14.44.30; SNSM 02.31.89.20.17; Auto (local) 08.92.68.08.14; Auto (regional) 08.92.68.08.76; Auto (offshore) 08.92.68.08.08; Police 02.31.14.44.45; Dr 02.31.89.34.05; Ⓗ 02.31.89.89.89; YC ☎/📠 02.31.98.87.13, www.cnh.nol.fr; Brit Consul 02.35.19.78.88.

FACILITIES **Vieux Bassin Yacht Hbr** (120 + 30 Ⓥ, max LOA 20m) €1.80 (Vieux Bassin) €1.60 (Avant-Port), multihulls and large motor yachts plus 50%. AB; **Cercle Nautique d'Honfleur** ☎ & 📠 02.31.89.87.13, M, Bar; **Services:** BY, ⚒, Ⓔ, C (10 ton), Slip. **Town** P & D (cans), 🛒, R, Bar, 🗊, Gaz, ✉, Ⓑ, ⇌, ✈ Deauville. Ferry: Le Havre.

9.17.19 RIVER SEINE

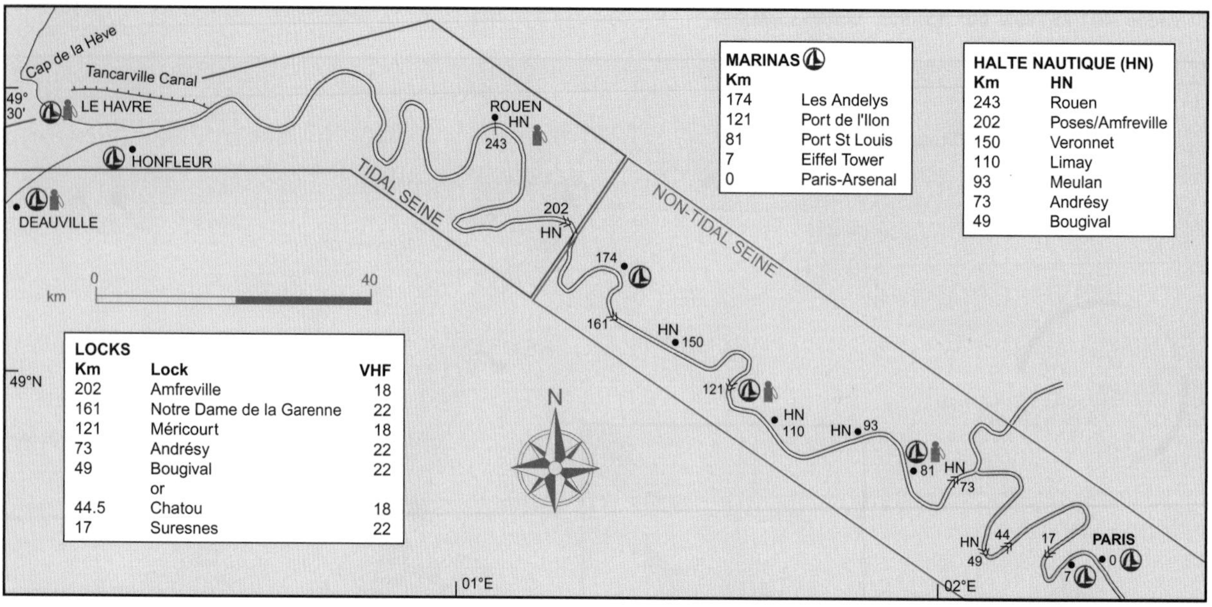
Cap de la Hève
Tancarville Canal
49° 30'
LE HAVRE
HONFLEUR
DEAUVILLE
ROUEN
HN
243
TIDAL SEINE
202
HN
NON-TIDAL SEINE
174
161
HN
150
121
HN
110
HN 93
81
HN
73
HN
49
44
17
PARIS
0
7
0
40
km
49°N
01°E
02°E
N
MARINAS
Km
174 Les Andelys
121 Port de l'Ilon
81 Port St Louis
7 Eiffel Tower
0 Paris-Arsenal
HALTE NAUTIQUE (HN)
Km HN
243 Rouen
202 Poses/Amfreville
150 Veronnet
110 Limay
93 Meulan
73 Andrésy
49 Bougival
LOCKS
Km Lock VHF
202 Amfreville 18
161 Notre Dame de la Garenne 22
121 Méricourt 18
73 Andrésy 22
49 Bougival 22
or
44.5 Chatou 18
17 Suresnes 22

CHARTS AC 2146, 2879; SHOM 6683, 6796, 6117; Imray C31; *Carte-Guide Navicarte No 1.*

TIDES Standard Port LE HAVRE (⟵) Zone –0100

Times				Height (metres)			
High Water		Low Water		MHWS	MHWN	MLWN	MLWS
0000	0500	0000	0700	7·9	6·6	2·8	1·2
1200	1700	1200	1900				
Differences TANCARVILLE* (Km338)							
–0105	–0100	+0105	+0140	–0·1	–0·1	0·0	+1·0
VATTEVILLE* (Km317)							
+0005	–0020	+0225	+0250	0·0	–0·1	+0·8	+2·3
CAUDEBEC* (Km309)							
+0020	–0015	+0230	+0300	–0·3	–0·2	+0·9	+2·4
HEURTEAUVILLE* (Km295)							
+0110	+0025	+0310	+0330	–0·5	–0·2	+1·1	+2·7
DUCLAIR* (Km278)							
+0225	+0150	+0355	+0410	–0·4	–0·3	+1·4	+3·3
ROUEN (Km245)							
+0440	+0415	+0525	+0525	–0·2	–0·1	+1·6	+3·6

*HW time differences refer to the start of a stand lasting about 2¾ hrs up to Vatteville and about 1¾hrs at Duclair.

SHELTER/FACILITIES: Marinas/Haltes Nautiques/fuel, see above. Masts can be lowered at Dives, Deauville, Le Havre and Rouen.

TIDAL STREAMS require careful study; see *N France and Belgium Cruising Companion* (Featherstone/Nautical Data Ltd) for tidal stream graphs and a detailed analysis, plus Rouen and Paris. At Ratier NW SHM buoy the flood starts at LW Le Havre +1 and at La Roque (Km342) at LW+2, and progressively later further up-river. So even a 5kn boat which left Le Havre at LW and passed the W end of Digue du Ratier at LW+1½, should carry the flood for to Rouen; or leave Honfleur asap after LW Le Havre +2. If delayed, better to try another day rather than stopping en route.

Going down-river on the ebb a boat will meet the flood. In a fast boat it is worth continuing, rather than ⚓ for about 4 hrs, because the ebb starts sooner the further down-river one gets.

NAVIGATION The Seine gives access to Paris (Pont Marie = Km 0) and central France, and to the Mediterranean via the canals (9.17.6). There are fewer barges (*péniches*) now, but in the tidal section below Amfreville the strong stream and ships' wash make it dangerous to berth alongside and uncomfortable to ⚓. Yacht navigation is prohib at night, and ⚓s are few. A radar reflector, VHF aerial and Ⓦ ⚓ lt are needed, even with mast down. Above Amfreville the river current is about 1kn in summer, but more if there have been winter floods. 6 out of 7 locks must be negotiated; no charges 0700-1900.

Entry is usually via the dredged/buoyed Chenal de Rouen, which can be rough in a strong W'ly wind and ebb tide. Care is needed, especially near the mouth where there are shifting banks and often morning fog. Monitor Ch 73. From No 4 buoy to Tancarville bridge (50m clearance) yachts must keep N of the Chenal de Rouen, ie outboard of the PHM chan buoys, whether going up or downstream. The Pont de Normandie (52m) is conspic 1·7M E of Honfleur ent.

Entry via the Canal de Tancarville is possible if sea conditions are bad, but with 2 locks and 8 bridges, expect long delays. At Le Havre transit the Bassins Bellot, Vétillart, Despujols and the Canal du Havre, leading into the Canal de Tancarville. Enter the R Seine via lock (Km338) close W of Tancarville bridge (50m).

ROUEN, Seine Maritime, **49°26'·07N 01°06'·24E**. AC 2994, 2880; SHOM 6796, 6117. Yacht navigation prohib SS+½ to SR-½. Berth in the Halte Nautique, NE side of Île Lacroix, Km241 (Lat/Long above). A one-way system in the chan NE of Île Lacroix only allows navigation <u>against</u> the stream. For example, if leaving on the young flood to go up-river, you must first go downriver to the NW tip of the island, then turn up-river via the SW chan. *Rouen Port* VHF Ch **73** 68. HM 02.35.52.54.56; Aff Mar 02.35.98.53.98; ⊖ 02.35.98.27.60; Météo 02.35.80.11.44.

Facilities: **Bassin St Gervais** (N bank, Km245). Mast down/up @ pontoon SE side; C (3 to 25 ton) max stay 48 hrs.

Halte Nautique (50) ☎ 02.32.08.31.40, www.rouen.port.fr €1.10, FW, ⊐D, Slip, D, C (30 ton), BH (4 ton); **Rouen YC** ☎ 02.35.66.52.52; **Services:** ME, El, ⚒, CH, Ⓔ, P (cans), D barge at Km239.

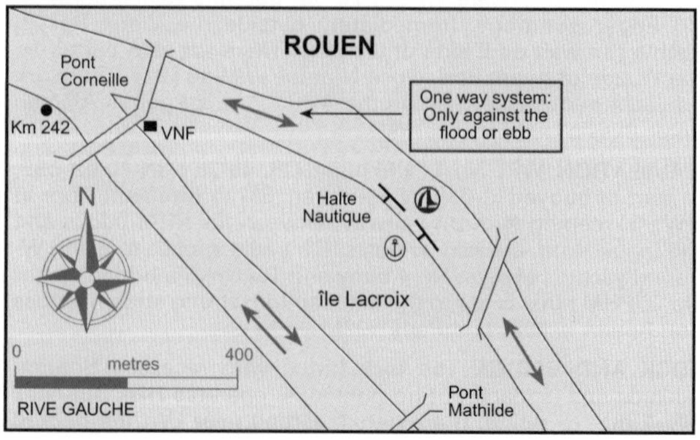
ROUEN
Pont Corneille
Km 242
VNF
One way system: Only against the flood or ebb
N
Halte Nautique
Île Lacroix
0
metres
400
RIVE GAUCHE
Pont Mathilde

9.17.20 PARIS

Île-de-France, **49°50'·84N 02°22'·02E** (Paris-Arsenal marina).

CHARTS AC 2994 and SHOM 6796, 6117 all stop at Rouen. Navicarte's Carte-Guide No 1 covers Le Havre to Paris in detail.

SHELTER Excellent. Paris-Arsenal marina is entered 0800-2300 via a small lock, with waiting pontoon outside; obey R/G tfc lts for 'Plaisance'. Air cl'nce in lock is 5·2m, least depth 1·9m. Inside, HM and accueil are to stbd; berth as directed.

An overflow marina (also for larger yachts) is at Km 6·5 on the SE bank, 1km SW of the Eiffel Tower, between Pont de Grenelle and Pont de Bir Hakeim. It is a 140m long pontoon, with no air clearance limit and sheltered from wash by Allée des Cygnes, a long thin islet in mid stream.

NAVIGATION The overflow marina can only be accessed in an up-river (NE) direction. Between Eiffel Tower and Notre Dame expect many vedettes whose wash produces quite a chop.

For Paris-Arsenal, a traffic system around Île de la Cité and Île St Louis must be understood and obeyed. Going up-river, the simpler route is: Hug the S bank in the narrowish one-way Bras de la Monnaie, leaving Notre Dame to port.

It is also possible to go up-river via the wider, two-way N bank chan, noting that this route is only available in a window H to H+20; is regulated by R/G tfc lts on Pont au Change; and requires two cross-overs where shown below.

Going downriver, make good a window H+35 to H+50, obey R/G tfc lts on Pont de Sully, then leave Île St Louis to stbd (Notre Dame to port). Cross-over twice where indicated.

LIGHTS AND MARKS Eiffel Tower and Notre Dame. Check off other landmarks and all bridges carefully; obey cross-overs.

R/T VHF Ch 09. At the lock there is an intercom phone direct to HM; your arrival will be seen on CCTV.

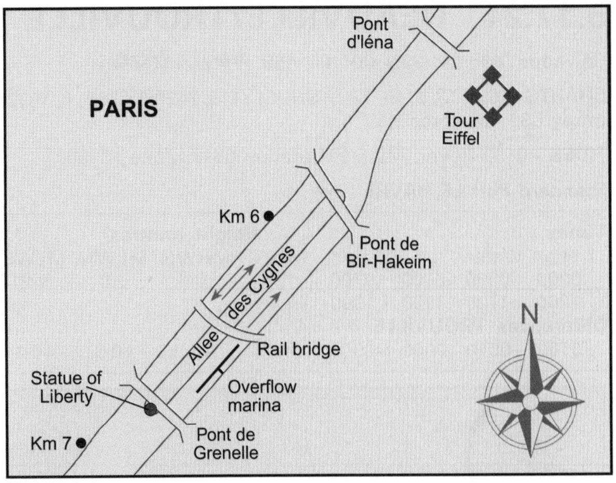
Pont d'Iéna
PARIS
Tour Eiffel
Km 6
Pont de Bir-Hakeim
Allee des Cygnes
Rail bridge
N
Statue of Liberty
Overflow marina
Km 7
Pont de Grenelle

TELEPHONE Taxi 01.45.85.85.85, 01.47.39.47.39, 01.42.70.41.41. Tourist Office 01.49.52.53.54 at 127 Ave des Champs Elysées or nearest branch at Gare de Lyon (550m).

FACILITIES Marina (176); 11 bld de la Bastille, 75012 Paris. ☎ 01.43.41.39.32, 📠 01.44.74.02.66. portarsenal@dial.oleane.com www.portparisarsenal.asso.fr €2.25, D, C (7 ton), 🗟, R. Best to pre-book, especially in high season. Nearest Metro stns are: Quai de la Rapée (Line 5) at S end of marina and Bastille (Lines 1, 5 & 8) at the N end. Numerous buses from Bastille.

Overflow marina, book via the above contact details. Fuel by cans. Nearest Metro stns: Bir Hakeim (Line 6) and Charles Michels (Line 10).

City Everything.

17

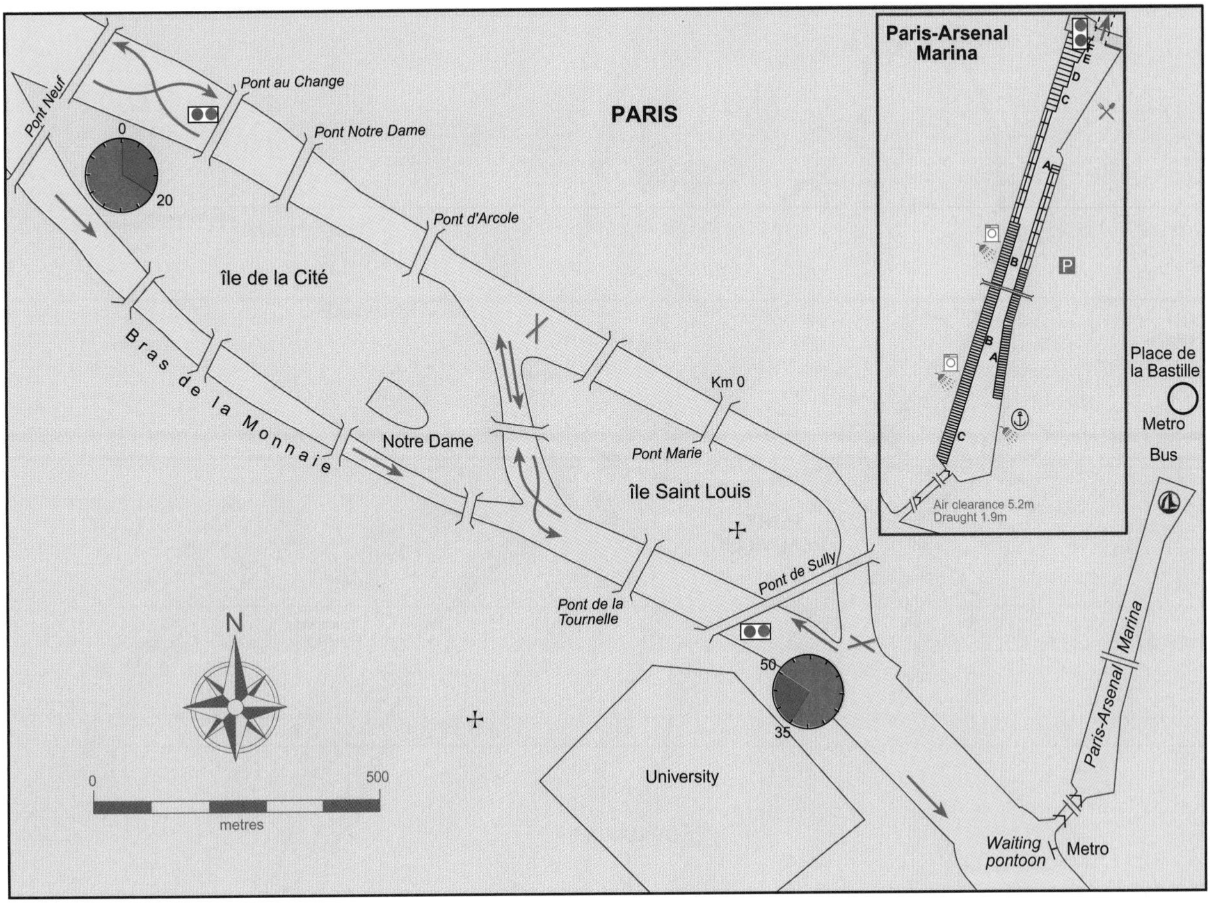
Pont Neuf
Pont au Change
0
20
Pont Notre Dame
PARIS
Pont d'Arcole
Île de la Cité
Bras de la Monnaie
Notre Dame
Km 0
Pont Marie
Île Saint Louis
Pont de Sully
Pont de la Tournelle
50
35
N
0
500
metres
University
Waiting pontoon
Metro
Paris-Arsenal Marina
Paris-Arsenal Marina
Place de la Bastille
Metro
Bus
Air clearance 5.2m
Draught 1.9m
P

9.17.21 DEAUVILLE/TROUVILLE

Calvados **49° 22'·38N 00° 04'·15E** ❁❁◊◊✿✿✿

CHARTS AC *2613*, 2146, *1349*; SHOM 7418, 7420; ECM 526, 1012; Imray C32; Stanfords 1, 21

TIDES –0130 Dover; ML 5·1; Duration 0510; Zone –0100

Standard Port LE HAVRE (⟵)

Times				Height (metres)			
High Water		Low Water		MHWS	MHWN	MLWN	MLWS
0000	0500	0000	0700	7·9	6·6	2·8	1·2
1200	1700	1200	1900				
Differences TROUVILLE							
–0100	–0010	0000	+0005	+0·4	+0·3	+0·3	+0·1

Note: There is a double HW at Trouville. The HW time differences, when referred to the time of HW Le Havre, give the times of the first HW.

SHELTER Good in Port Deauville and Port Morny, but ent to chan difficult in NW/N winds > force 5. Chan and river dry 2·4m; no access LW±2½, for 2m draft. Port Deauville lock opens approx HW–3 to HW+4½, if enough water outside. Port Morny gate opens HW –2 to HW +2½. No yacht berths at Trouville.

NAVIGATION WPT 49°22'·94N 00°03'·62E,148°/0·65M to abeam W training wall lt, Fl WG 4s. Semoy ECM, VQ (3) 5s, marks wreck 2·1M from ent, close W of ldg line. Do not appr from E of N due to Les Ratelets drying shoal and Banc de Trouville. Trouville SW buoy, WCM, VQ (9) 10s, is 1M WNW of ent.

LIGHTS AND MARKS Casino is conspic on Trouville side; Royal Hotel/Casino at Deauville. Ldg lts 148°, both Oc R 4s synch. Port Morny ent gate: IPTS, sigs 2-4, visible from seaward.

R/T Port Deauville and Port Morny: Ch 09.

TELEPHONE See below for HMs. Aff Mar 02.31.88.36.21; ⊖ 02.31.88.35.29; SNSM 02.31.88.31.70; CROSS 02.33.52.72.13; Auto (local) 08.92.68.08.14; Auto (regional) 08.92.68.08.76; Auto (offshore) 08.92.68.08.08; Police 02.31.88.13.07; Dr 02.31.88.23.57; Ⓗ 02.31.14.33.33; Brit Consul 02.35.19.78.88.

FACILITIES Port Deauville (800 + 100 Ⓥ) ☎ 02.31.98.30.01, 🖷 02.31.81.98.92; lock 02.31.88.95.66. €0.82 (Mar-Oct), €1.56 (Apr-Jun, Sep), €2.07 (Jul, Aug), D, ME, El, ⚒, C (6 ton), BH (45 ton), Slip, CH, SM, R, Bar. port-deauville-sa@wanadoo.fr
Deauville YC ☎ 02.31.88.38.19, FW, C (8 ton), CH, Bar.

Port Morny (320+80 Ⓥ) ☎ 02.31.98.50.40, entry gate 02.31.88.57.89; €1.95, Slip, D (pump S end of Bassin Morny), P (cans, 20m); **Services:** CH, ME, El, ⚒.

Both towns P (cans), 🛒, Gaz, R, Bar, ✉, Ⓑ, BY, CH, Slip, ⚒, ME, El, Ⓔ, ⇌, ✈ Deauville. Ferry: See Le Havre and Ouistreham.

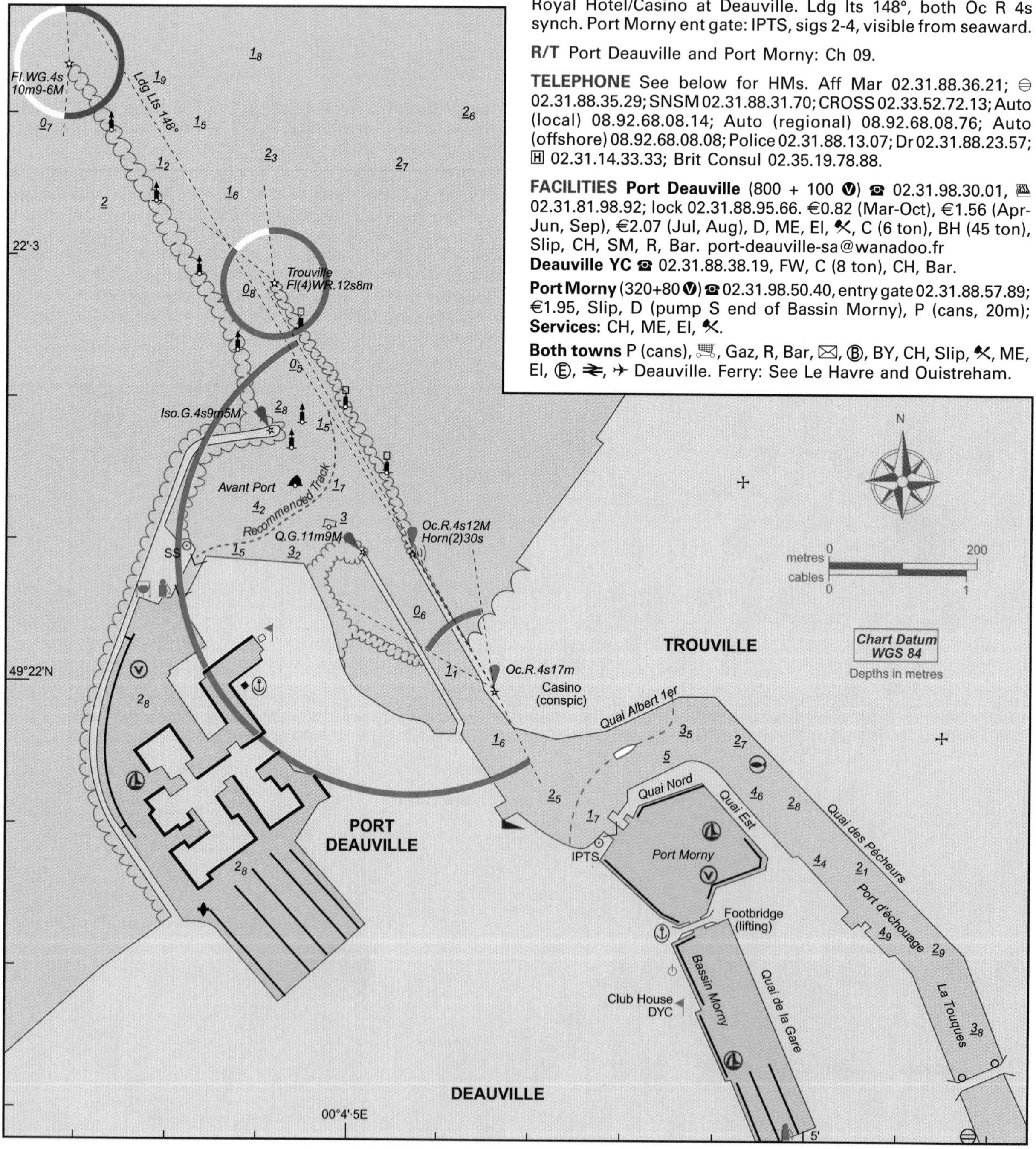
Fl.WG.4s
10m9-6M
Ldg Lts 148°
22'·3
Trouville
Fl(4)WR.12s8m
Iso.G.4s9m5M
Avant Port
Recommended Track
Q.G.11m9M
Oc.R.4s12M
Horn(2)30s
SS
Oc.R.4s17m
Casino
(conspic)
49°22'N
N
metres 0 200
cables 0 1
TROUVILLE
Chart Datum
WGS 84
Depths in metres
Quai Albert 1er
Quai Nord
Quai Est
Quai des Pêcheurs
Port d'échouage
La Touques
PORT
DEAUVILLE
IPTS
Port Morny
Footbridge
(lifting)
Bassin Morny
Quai de la Gare
Club House
DYC
DEAUVILLE
00°4'·5E
5'

9.17.22 DIVES-SUR-MER

Calvados **49°17'·92N 00°05'·29W** ❁❁◊◊◊✿✿

CHARTS AC 2146; SHOM 7418, 7420 (the preferred chart); ECM 526; Imray C32; Stanfords 1, 21

TIDES –0135 Dover; ML 5·1m; Duration; Zone –0100
Standard Port LE HAVRE (⟵)

Times				**Height (metres)**			
High Water		Low Water		MHWS	MHWN	MLWN	MLWS
0000	0500	0000	0700	7·9	6·6	2·8	1·2
1200	1700	1200	1900				
Differences DIVES-SUR-MER							
–0100	–0010	0000	0000	+0·3	+0·2	+0·2	+0·1

Note: There is a double HW at Dives. HW time differences, referred to the time of HW Le Havre, give times of the first HW.

SHELTER Excellent in marina. Appr dries to 1M offshore and can be difficult in NW/NE > F5, when best entry HW±1½. Marina ent 400m W of Dir lt, off shallow Dives river. Access HW±3 (HW±2½ for draft >1·5m) via single gate. Sill below gate is 2·5m above CD; gate opens when tide 4·5m above CD and may create a 4-5kn current for the first 45 mins at springs. In low season it is advised to pre-check marina opening hours. Alternatively follow river to berth on YC drying pontoon (2 Ⓥ) E of footbridge.

NAVIGATION WPT 49°19'·18N 00°05'·69W, SWM buoy "DI" (off chartlet), L Fl 10s, 168°/7ca to Nos 1/2 buoys. Follow the buoyed chan to clear sandbanks (drying 4·2m) each side; keep well off two large SHM lt bns on W side. After last chan buoys, hug the shore to G buoy and 2 G perches marking submerged training wall leading to marina ent.

LIGHTS AND MARKS Densely wooded hills E of Houlgate locate the ent. 4 PHM and 2 SHM unlit buoys are moved to suit shifting chan; No 7 SHM is the only lit lateral buoy; Nos 3 and 5 SHMs are immobile lt bns. The 159° Dir lt is on an inconspic, R hut opposite Pte de Cabourg; its W sector covers the chan only as far as Nos 3/4 marks; thence follow the chan buoys/bns. Close E of marina a SHM buoy marks shoals to N and the river ent. Caution: Buoys/bns may not be numbered. See 9.17.4 and the chartlet for further details.

R/T VHF Ch 09, H24.

TELEPHONE HM see below. CROSS/SNSM 02.31.88.11.13; Météo via HM; Auto 08.92.68.08.14; Police 02.31.28.23.00; Dr 02.31.91.60.17/02.31.28.13.60; Brit Consul 02.35.19.78.88.

FACILITIES **Marina** (545+55 Ⓥ) €2.30, max LOA 20m, draft 1.8m. ☎ 02.31.24.48.00, ℻ 02.31.24.73.02. portguillaume@libertysurf.fr Office hrs 0930-1230, 1400-1800. P&D 24H, ◙, Slip, BH (30 ton), C (1·5 ton), mast lowering; **Cabourg YC** ☎ 02.31.91.23.55, Bar; **Services:** BY, ME, El, CH, ⚒.

Town ▦, R, Bar, Ⓑ, ✉, ✈ (Deauville). Ferry: Ouistreham.

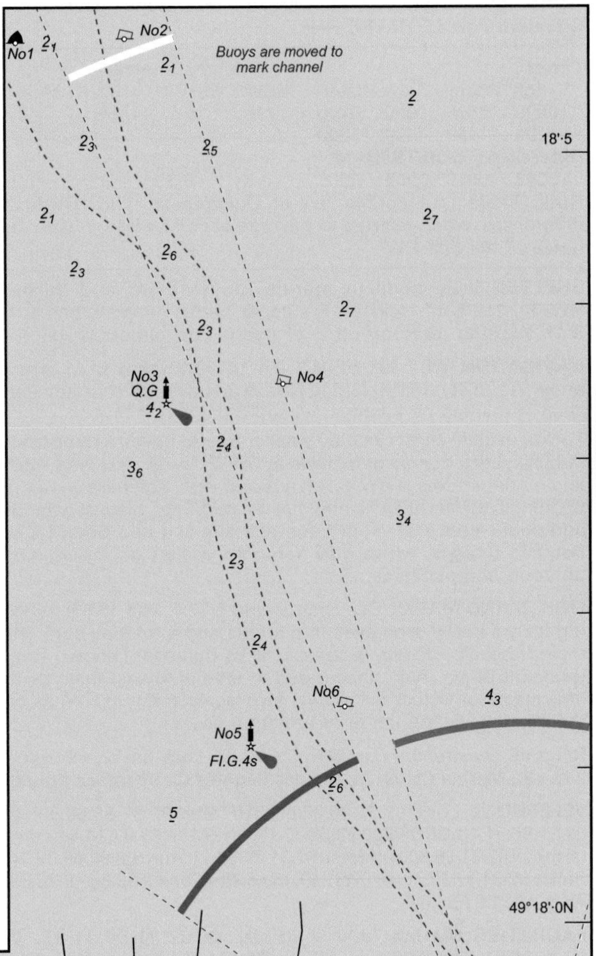
No1
No2
Buoys are moved to mark channel
18'·5
No3
Q.G
No4
No5
Fl.G.4s
No6
49°18'·0N

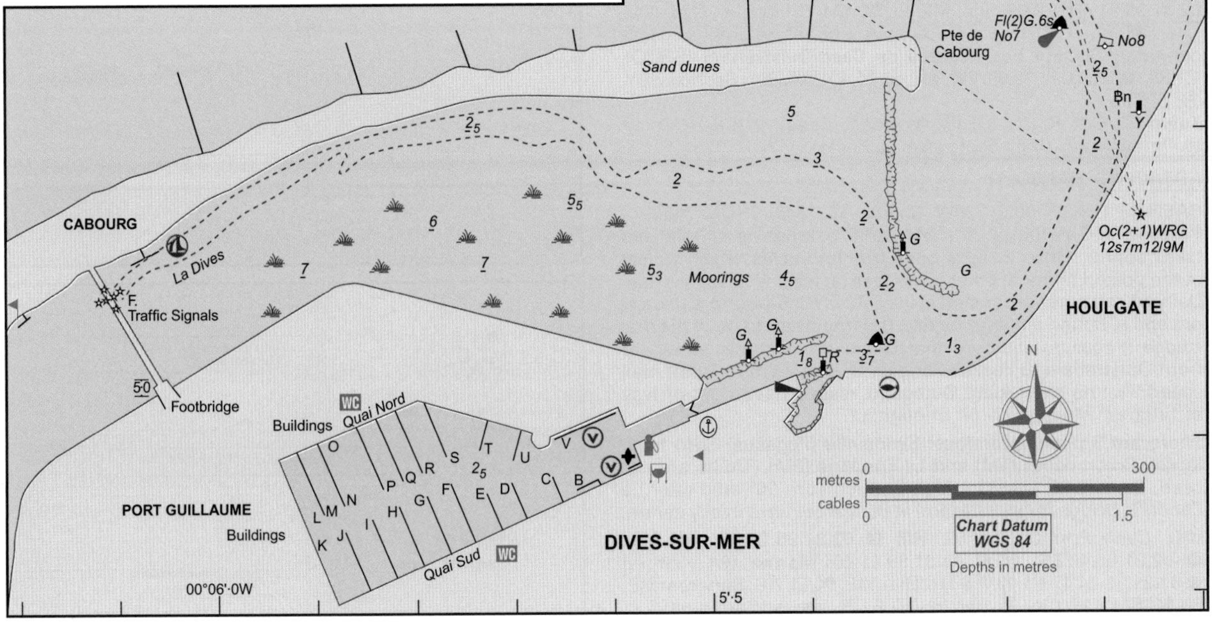
Pte de Cabourg
Fl(2)G.6s
No7
No8
Bn
Y
Sand dunes
Oc(2+1)WRG
12s7m12/9M
CABOURG
La Dives
F.
Traffic Signals
Footbridge
Moorings
HOULGATE
Buildings
Quai Nord
PORT GUILLAUME
Buildings
Quai Sud
DIVES-SUR-MER
metres
cables
300
1·5
Chart Datum
WGS 84
Depths in metres
00°06'·0W
5'·5
N

9.17.23 OUISTREHAM

Calvados **49°16'·82N 00°14'·89W** (E lock) ❀❀◊◊◊✿✿

CHARTS AC *2613*, 2146, 2136, 1349; SHOM 7418, 7421, 7420; ECM 526; Imray C32; Stanfords 1, 21

TIDES –0118 Dover; ML 4·6; Duration 0525; Zone –0100
Standard Port LE HAVRE (⟵)

Times				**Height (metres)**			
High Water		Low Water		MHWS	MHWN	MLWN	MLWS
0000	0500	0000	0700	7·9	6·6	2·8	1·2
1200	1700	1200	1900				
Differences OUISTREHAM							
–0045	–0010	–0005	0000	–0·3	–0·3	–0·2	–0·3

Note: There is a double HW at Ouistreham. The HW time differences, when referred to the time of HW Le Havre, give the times of the first HW.

SHELTER Very good in marina (depth 3·5m and access HW±3), 1ca S of locks on E side; Ⓥ berths on pontoons B, C & D. Waiting pontoon on E of Avant Port almost dries.

NAVIGATION WPT 49° 20'·41N 00° 14'·39W (abm ECM wreck buoy, VQ (3) 5s), 185°/1·23M to No 1 & 2 buoys. Off chartlet, appr chan is marked by lt buoys 1-6 and 2 pairs of lt bns.

Yachts usually enter canal by smaller E lock. Beware turbulence in locks. Lock opens for arrivals at HW–2½*, –1½, +2¼ and +3¼*; and for departures at HW–3, –2, +1¾ and +2¾*. Asterisks are extra openings (0700–2000LT) mid-Jun to mid-Sep; also at w/ends and public hols only, from 1 Apr-mid Jun and mid Sep-31 Oct. Detailed timings, which may vary, are posted on the waiting pontoon and at SRCO.

LIGHTS AND MARKS See chartlet and 9.17.4. The 184·5° synch ldg lts are easily seen even in poor vis and a midday sun. The main lt ho, W + R top, is conspic. IPTS (full code) shown from lock control twr. A Ⓦ, shown port or stbd of lowest main tfc lt, indicates E or W lock for yachts. Two Iso 4s and two QW, as on the chartlet, define the ferry turning area.

R/T Call *Ouistreham Port* VHF Ch **74**, 68; Lock Ch **12**, 68 (HW –2 to +3); Marina Ch 09, 74; Sté des Régates Ch 09 (office hours).

TELEPHONE Lock 02.31.36.22.00; Aff Mar 02.31.53.66.50; ⊜ 02.31.96.81.10; CROSS 02.33.52.72.13; SNSM 02.31.97.14.43; Ferry terminal 02.31.96.80.80; Météo 02.31.26.68.11; Auto 08.92.68.08.14; Police 02.31.97.13.15; Dr 02.31.97.18.45; Brit Consul 02.35.19.78.88; Taxi 02.31.97.35.67.

FACILITIES Marina (600 + 65 Ⓥ) ☎ 02.31.96.91.37, 📠 02.31.96.91.47, €2.01, Slip, ME, El, ⚒, CH, BH (8 ton), Gas, Gaz, Kos, SM, Bar, P, D, (Fuel pumps open ¾ hr before outbound lock opening); **Société des Régates de Caen-Ouistreham** (SRCO), €1.39, ☎ 02.31.97.13.05, FW, ME, El, ⚒, CH, 🛒, Bar; **Services:** BY, Ⓔ, SHOM.
Town 🛒, Gaz, R, Bar, ✉, Ⓑ, ⥂ (bus to Caen), ✈ (Caen). Ferry: to Portsmouth. (May-Sept, also to Poole).

ADJACENT HARBOUR

CAEN 49°10'·96N 00°21'·29W. Charts: AC *1349*, SHOM 7420.
Passage and Facilities: The 8M canal passage is simple and takes approx 1¾hrs. Bridges open free for yachts which transit at the posted times; at other times fees (at least €12.35) are due. Daily transit times are posted at the SRCO YC: S-bound is usually pm and N-bound am; only by day. It is important to be *at the first bridge* (Pegasus) at/before the posted transit time; allow ½hr from Ouistreham to Pegasus bridge. Depths 2·5m to 9·8m; max speed 7kn; no overtaking. Outbound vessels have right of way at bridges. Monitor Ch 68 throughout.

There are 3 opening bridges: Bénouville (Pegasus) (2½M from locks), Colombelles (5M) and La Fonderie (8M). Tfc lts are not used. Calix (6½M) is a 33m high viaduct. Turn 90° stbd after La Fonderie bridge for marina (4m) at Bassin St Pierre in city centre.

VHF *Caen Port* Ch **74**, 68. HM ☎ 02.31.95.24.47; Aff Mar ☎ 02.31.85.40.55; ⊜ ☎ 02.31.86.61.50; **Marina** (64 visitors) ☎ 02.31.95.24.47 €1.42, P & D (cans), ME, ⚒, El, AB; **Services:** ME, El, ⚒, SM, CH. **City** Ⓑ, Bar, Ⓗ, ✉, R, 🛒, ⥂, ✈ (Carpiquet).

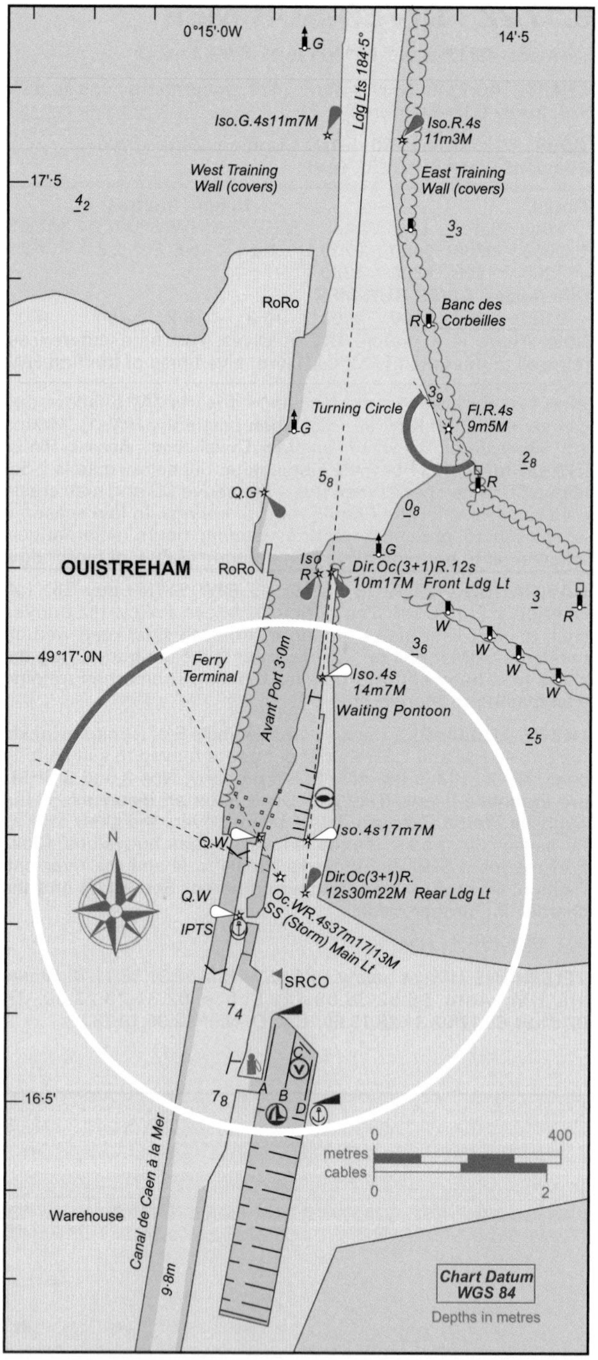
0°15'·0W
14'·5
Ldg Lts 184·5°
Iso.G.4s11m7M
Iso.R.4s 11m3M
17'·5
West Training Wall (covers)
East Training Wall (covers)
RoRo
Banc des Corbeilles
Turning Circle
Fl.R.4s 9m5M
Q.G
OUISTREHAM
RoRo
Iso R
Dir.Oc(3+1)R.12s 10m17M Front Ldg Lt
49°17'·0N
Ferry Terminal
Avant Port 3·0m
Iso.4s 14m7M
Waiting Pontoon
Iso.4s17m7M
N
Q.W
Dir.Oc(3+1)R. 12s30m22M Rear Ldg Lt
Oc.WR.4s37m17/13M SS (Storm) Main Lt
IPTS
SRCO
16·5'
metres
cables
Warehouse
Canal de Caen à la Mer
Chart Datum WGS 84
Depths in metres

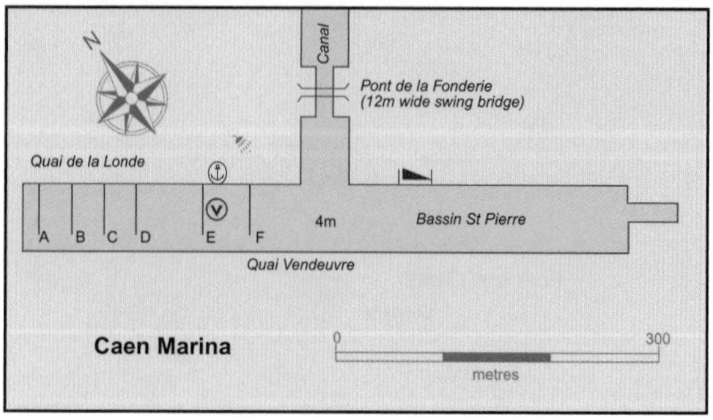
Canal
Pont de la Fonderie (12m wide swing bridge)
Quai de la Londe
4m
Bassin St Pierre
Quai Vendeuvre
Caen Marina
metres

9.17.24 COURSEULLES-SUR-MER

Calvados **49°20'·42N 00°27'·35W** ❁❁⚓⚓⚓✿✿

CHARTS AC *2613*, 2136, *1349*; SHOM 7421, 7420; ECM 526, 527; Imray C32; Stanfords 1, 21

TIDES –0145 Dover; ML 4·6; Duration No data; Zone –0100

Standard Port LE HAVRE (⟵)

Times				Height (metres)			
High Water		Low Water		MHWS	MHWN	MLWN	MLWS
0000	0500	0000	0700	7·9	6·6	2·8	1·2
1200	1700	1200	1900				
Differences COURSEULLES-SUR-MER							
–0045	–0015	–0020	–0025	–0· 5	–0·5	–0·1	–0·1

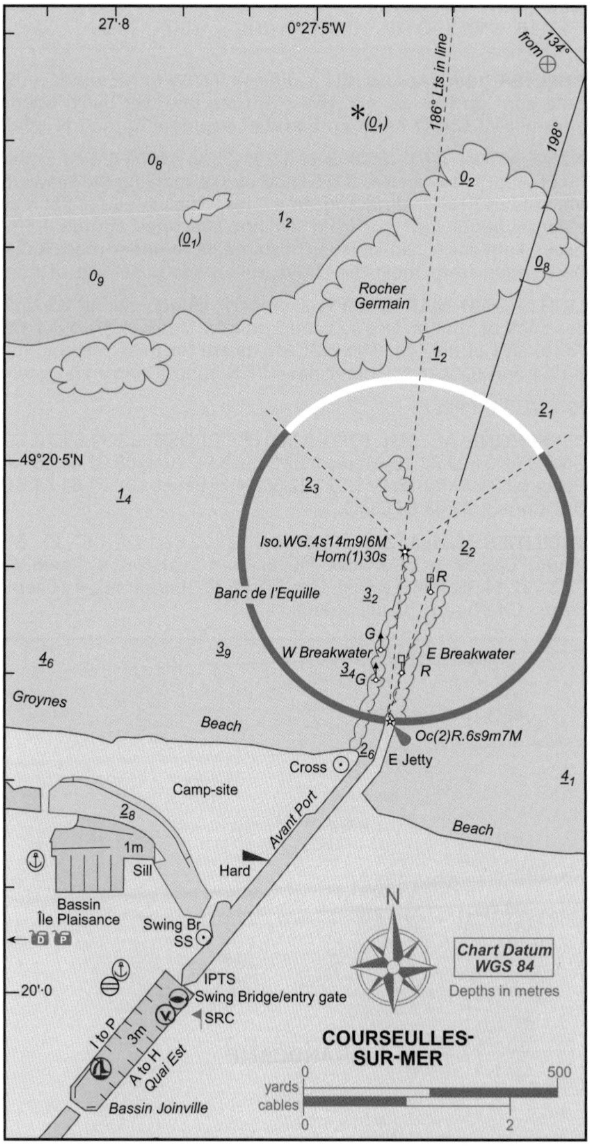

27'·8
0°27'·5W
186° Lts in line
from 134°
198°
Rocher Germain
49°20'·5'N
Iso.WG.4s14m9/6M
Horn(1)30s
Banc de l'Equille
W Breakwater
E Breakwater
Groynes
Beach
Oc(2)R.6s9m7M
E Jetty
Cross
Camp-site
Avant Port
Beach
1m
Sill
Hard
Bassin Île Plaisance
Swing Br SS
20'·0
IPTS
Swing Bridge/entry gate
SRC
l to P
3m
A to H
Quai Est
Bassin Joinville
Chart Datum WGS 84
Depths in metres
COURSEULLES-SUR-MER
yards
cables
0
500
2

SHELTER Good in Bassin Joinville (3m), but appr becomes difficult in strong N to NE winds. Avant Port dries 2·5m, keep to the E side; best ent at HW –1. Entry gate stays open HW ±2; the associated swing bridge opens either when you are spotted, usually quite quickly, or on request Ch 09. Bassin Seulles carries only 1m and is used by small local craft. Exposed ⚓ (3-5m) at L'Anneau de la Marguerite, 134°/0·4M from SWM buoy.

NAVIGATION WPT 49° 21'.28N 00° 27'.69W (SWM buoy Iso 4s), 134°/5ca then 198°/5ca to E jetty hd. Outer 134° ldg marks are: front, Bernières ⛪ tower ≠ rear, twin spires (partly obsc'd by trees) of Douvres-La-Délivrande; maintain 134° for 0.55M until ent bears 198°. Plateau du Calvados extends 2M seaward and banks dry for 0.6M. Beware rks awash at CD either side of ldg line.

LIGHTS AND MARKS See chartlet and 9.17.4. The two bkwtr lts in line 186° makes a useful ldg line at night. Both drying bkwtrs and their perches are easily seen, as is a conspic crucifix at root of the W bkwtr. Pte de Ver lt ho, 40° 20'.45N 00° 31'.05W, is 2·4M W of hbr, and from the N offers helpful distance-to-go bearings.

R/T Ch 09: Control Twr HW±2. HM's office opens: HW±2 in daylight hrs; Jul/Aug: M-Sat 1400-2000; Sun/Hols 0900-1200.

TELEPHONE Control twr 02.31.37.46.03; Aff Mar 02.31.85.40.55 @ Caen; CROSS 02.33.52.72.13; ⊖ 02.31.21.71.09 @ Port-en-Bessin; SNSM 02.31.37.45.47; Météo 08.92.68.12.34; Auto 08.92.68.08.14; Police @ Ouistreham 02.31.97.13.15; Dr 02.31.37.45.28; Ambulance 15; Fire 18; Brit Consul 02.35.19.78.88.

FACILITIES Bassin Joinville ☎ 02.31.37.51.69, berth on pontoon 'X' by E Quay or as directed by HM; €2.53 plus €0.60 holiday tax per head/night, Slip, C (25 ton). **Services:** P & D (cans 600m), BY, ME, El, Ⓔ, ⚒, CH, SM.
Société des Régates de Courseulles (SRC) ☎ 02.31.37.47.42, Bar.
Bassin Île Plaisance no Ⓥ; local shoal draft boats.
Town 🛒, Gaz, R, Bar, ✉, Ⓓ, Ⓑ, ⇌ (via bus to Caen), ✈ (Caen-Carpiquet). Taxi ☎ 02.31.37.46.00. Ferry: See Ouistreham.

17

MULBERRY ANCHORAGE 6·5M WEST OF COURSEULLES

ARROMANCHES, Manche, **49°21'·37N 00°37'·25W**. AC *2613*, *2136*; SHOM 7421. Tides, see 9.17.25 below. Strictly a fair weather ⚓, with limited shelter from the ruined WW II Mulberry caissons which are conspic esp at LW; swell intrudes. Rochers du Calvados dries 1·6m, 7ca ENE of ent.

There are many wrecks within the hbr and offshore: 3 to the W and N are marked by a WCM and two ECM buoys. From the more N'ly ECM buoy (Roseberry, 49°23'·11N 00°36'·48W) the ent (lat/long as line 1) bears approx 196°/1·8M; it is marked by a small unlit PHM and SHM buoy. Enter on about 245° for charted ⚓ in 3-5m to S of the caissons, or sound closer inshore with caution. Entry from E or W is not advised due to uncharted obstructions. Caution: rocky plateau (3·4m) and further obstructions W of the dinghy landing area.

Facilities: YC Port Winston ☎ 02.31.22.31.01, 2 dinghy slips. Worth going ashore for D-Day museums and the panoramic view from the clifftops, but very crowded in season.

9.17.25 PORT-EN-BESSIN

Calvados **49°21'·16N 00°45'·40W** (Hbr ent)

CHARTS AC *2613*, 2136; SHOM 7421, 7420; ECM 527; Imray C32; Stanford 1, 21

TIDES –0215 Dover; ML 4·4; Duration 0520; Zone –0100

Standard Port LE HAVRE (⟵)

Times				Height (metres)			
High Water		Low Water		MHWS	MHWN	MLWN	MLWS
0000	0500	0000	0700	7·9	6·6	2·8	1·2
1200	1700	1200	1900				
Differences PORT-EN-BESSIN							
–0055	–0030	–0030	–0035	–0·7	–0·7	–0·2	–0·1
ARROMANCHES							
–0055	–0025	–0027	–0035	–0·6	–0·6	–0·2	–0·2

SHELTER Good. A busy FV port whose outer hbr dries up to 3·7m. Basins accessible HW ±2. Waiting possible on Quai de L'Epi. After the entry gate, berth immediately to stbd, bows E or W, then contact Gate-master. Yachts may stay only 24-48 hrs, due to limited space; pre-book gate time if leaving at anti-social hour. ⚓ prohib in outer hbr and 1ca either side of 204° transit.

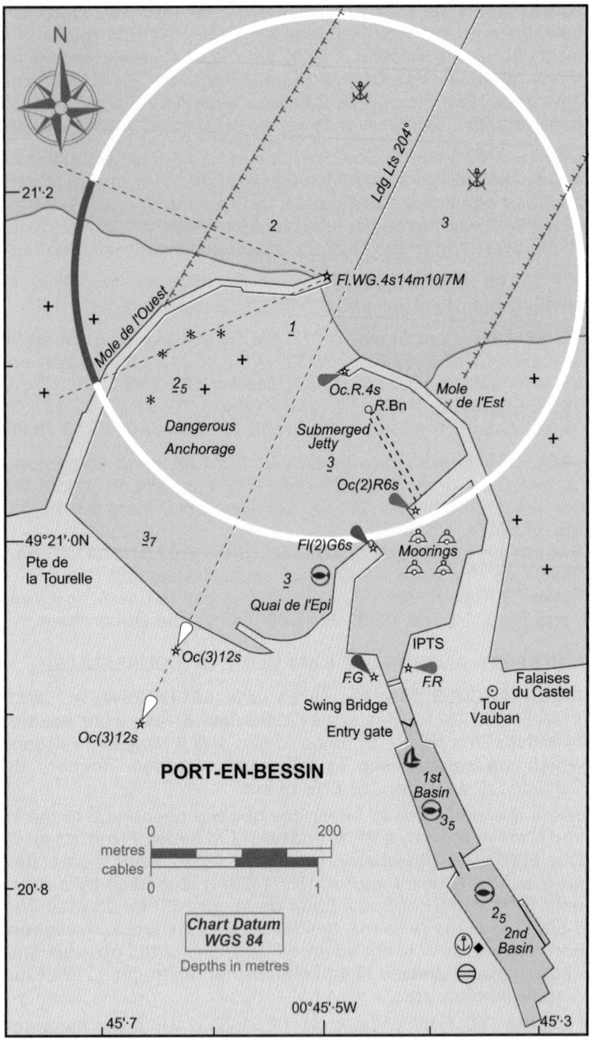
N
21'·2
Mole de l'Ouest
Fl.WG.4s14m10/7M
Ldg Lts 204°
Oc.R.4s
R.Bn
Mole de l'Est
Dangerous Anchorage
Submerged Jetty
Oc(2)R6s
Fl(2)G6s
Moorings
49°21'·0N
Pte de la Tourelle
Quai de l'Epi
Oc(3)12s
IPTS
F.G
F.R
Falaises du Castel
Tour Vauban
Swing Bridge
Entry gate
Oc(3)12s
PORT-EN-BESSIN
1st Basin
2nd Basin
metres
cables
20'·8
Chart Datum WGS 84
Depths in metres
00°45'·5W
45'·7
45'·3

NAVIGATION WPT 49°21'·62N 00°45'·09W, 204°/0·5M to hbr ent. Ent is difficult with strong N/NE winds and dangerous at or >F8. Keep out of Fl WG 4s G sector which covers the inshore dangers of Omaha Beach, 3 to 6M to the WNW. In the outer hbr beware submerged jetty (marked by R bn) to E of ent chan.

LIGHTS AND MARKS Conspic marks: a water twr (104m) 1·7M ESE of the hbr; a Sig Stn 7 cables W of hbr. Ldg lts 204°: Front W pylon, G top at bottom of hill; rear, W house/grey roof near top of the hillside. See chartlet and 9.17.4 for other lts.

IPTS control entry to the basins. Entry gate opens HW ±2. While gate stays open, swing bridge opens whenever possible to suit yachts and FVs; there is little road/pedestrian traffic. When shut the bridge shows FR/FG each side, and FR in the middle.

R/T VHF Ch 18 (HW ±2) for gate opening.

TELEPHONE HM 02.31.21.70.49; Lock/bridge 02.31.21.71.77 HW ±2; Aff Mar 02.31.21.71.52; ⊜ 02.31.21.71.09; CROSS 02.33.52.72.13; Semaphore/SNSM 02.31.21.81.51; Auto 08.92.68.08.14; Police 02.31.21.70.10; Dr 02.31.21.74.26; ⊞ 02.31.51.51.51; Brit Consul 02.33.88.65.60.

FACILITIES Outer Hbr Slip, L; **Bassin 1** usually no charge for 1 or 2 nights, Slip, M, C (4 ton); **Services:** CH, El, Ⓔ, ME, ⚒.
Town P & D, 🛒, Gaz, R, Bar, ✉, Ⓑ, ≷ (bus to Bayeux), ✈ (Caen, ☎ 02.31.26.58.00). Ferry: See Ouistreham.

9.17.26 GRANDCAMP

Calvados **49°23'·51N 01°02'·99W** (Pierheads)

CHARTS AC *2613, 2135*; SHOM 7422, 7420; ECM 527; Imray C32; Stanford 1, 2, 21.

TIDES –0220 Dover; ML Rade de la Chapelle 4·4; Duration 0510; Zone –0100

Standard Port CHERBOURG (⟶)

Times				Height (metres)			
High Water		Low Water		MHWS	MHWN	MLWN	MLWS
0300	1000	0400	1000	6·4	5·0	2·5	1·1
1500	2200	1600	2200				
Differences RADE DE LA CAPELLE (3M to NW)							
+0115	+0050	+0130	+0117	+0·8	+0·9	+0·1	+0·1
ILES SAINT MARCOUF							
+0118	+0052	+0125	+0110	+0·6	+0·7	+0·1	+0·1

SHELTER good. Access H24 is difficult in NW to NE winds > F6. Safe appr sp HW ±2, nps HW ±1½. Gate into wet basin opens approx HW ±2½. Ⓥ berth on E end of pontoon 'C', first to stbd.

NAVIGATION WPT 49°24'·84N 01°04'·36W, 146°/1·6M to E pier head. Appr between Nos 3 & 5 NCM buoys, marking the seaward limit of Les Roches de Grandcamp. This large plateau of flat rock extends about 1½M out from the hbr and dries approx 1·5m; heavy kelp cover can cause echosounders to under-read. It can be crossed from most directions, given adequate rise of tide.

LIGHTS AND MARKS Maisy's modern church twr is conspic 6ca SSW of hbr ent. Nos 1, 3 and 5 unlit NCM buoys are 1·4-1·7M NE to NW of the hbr. The 221° ldg lts are for FVs. See chartlet, 9.17.4 and 9.17.26 for other data. IPTS control entry via gate.

R/T VHF Ch 09.

TELEPHONE Aff Mar 02.31.22.60.65; CROSS 02.33.52.72.13; SNSM 02.31.22.67.12; Météo 02.21.33.25.26; Auto 08.92.68.08.14; Police 02.31.22.00.18; Dr 02.31.22.60.44; ⊞ Bayeux 02.31.51.51.51; Brit Consul 02.33.88.65.60.

FACILITIES Marina (240 + 10 Ⓥ) ☎ 02.31.22.63.16, €1.52, El, BH (5 ton), Bar, 🛒, AC; **Services:** ME, El, ✉, ⚒, CH, Gaz, C. **Town** YC 02.31.22.14.35, P & D (cans), Gaz, ✉, Ⓑ, ≷ (Carentan), ✈ (Caen). Ferry: Cherbourg, Ouistreham.

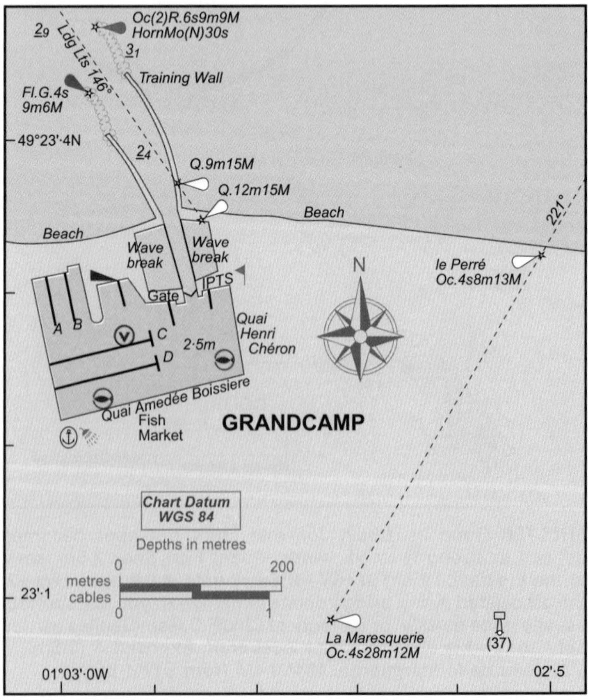
Oc(2)R.6s9m9M
HornMo(N)30s
Ldg Lts 146°
Training Wall
Fl.G.4s 9m6M
49°23'·4N
Q.9m15M
Q.12m15M
Beach
Beach
Wave break
Wave break
Gate
IPTS
Quai Henri Chéron
Quai Amedée Boissière
Fish Market
GRANDCAMP
N
le Perré Oc.4s8m13M
221°
Chart Datum WGS 84
Depths in metres
metres
cables
23'·1
La Maresquerie Oc.4s28m12M
01°03'·0W
02'·5

9.17.27 CARENTAN

Manche **49°19'·09N 01°13'·53W**

CHARTS AC *2613, 2135*; SHOM 7422; ECM 527; Imray C32; Stanford 1, 2, 21.

TIDES –0225 Dover; ML Rade de la Chapelle 4·4; Duration 0510; Zone –0100

Standard Port CHERBOURG (⟶)

Use differences RADE DE LA CAPELLE 9.17.25.
HW Carentan is HW Cherbourg +0110. See tidal graph for access.

SHELTER Complete shelter in the land-locked marina (max/min depths 3·5/2·9m); Ⓥ berths on K pontoon.
Appr protected from prevailing S to W winds, but is not to be attempted in onshore winds >F5. Drying out on the hard sands of the estuary is not advised; nor is an early approach, as a bore (*mascaret*) may occur in the river channels between HW–3 and HW –2½ particularly at springs.

NAVIGATION WPT 49°25'·45N 01°07'·07W (CI SWM buoy), 210°/1.8M to Nos 1/2 buoys. Best to leave WPT at HW–2 to –1½. Graph gives approx access times, using draft and tidal range at Cherbourg; it allows for an under-keel margin of 0·4 - 1·0m. Chan is liable to vary in both depth and direction. All buoys have R or G reflective panels; 6 are lit as on chartlet.

After about 2·2M the chan lies between 2 training walls, marked by bns. 3·8M SW a small pool is formed where the Rivers Taute and Douve flow in. Ahead, the little lock (room for about 6 boats) opens HW –2 to HW +3. Lock sigs: FG = open, FR = shut. Waiting pontoons are on E side, down- and up-stream of the lock.

LIGHTS AND MARKS See chartlet and 9.17.4. Maisy Ch twr is a good landmark initially. Ldg lts 209·5° are only valid from the training wall bns to the front lt, ie not in the buoyed chan.

R/T Call *Écluse de Carentan,* Ch 09 (0800-1200, 1400-1600LT & lock opening hrs); but usually the lockmaster waves boats in.

TELEPHONE Lockmaster 02.33.71.10.85; Aff Mar 02.33.44.00.13; Auto 08.92.68.08.50; ⊜ 02.31.21.71.09; CROSS 02.33.52.72.13; Police 02.33.42.00.17; Ⓗ 02.33.42.14.12; Dr 02.33.42.33.21; Brit Consul 02.33.88.65.60.

FACILITIES Marina (270+50 Ⓥ) ☎ 02.33.42.24.44, 📠 02.33.42.00.03, www.sctelfrance.com/port-carentan €1.41; Access HW –2 to +3, P & D (0900-1000 Mon-Sat), Slip, BH (35 ton), C; **YC Croiseurs Côtiers de Carentan** ☎ 02.33.42.06.61, Bar; **Services**: ME, El, ⚒, CH, BY.
Town Bar, Ⓑ, ✉, ⇄, R, 🛒, ✈ and ferry: Cherbourg.

ADJACENT HARBOUR

ISIGNY Calvados **49°19'·31N 01°06'·24W**

SHELTER Drying pontoons on SW bank ¼M NW of town. Beware the river bed shelves steeply inwards.

NAVIGATION Leave CI WPT at HW –2½ tracking 158°/1·24M to IS, a very small unlit NCM buoy at approx 49°24'·29N 01°06'·37W, near ent to unlit buoyed chan which is deeper than Carentan's. From IS buoy track about 204°/0·6M to first chan buoys. Pairs of buoys are spaced at approx 3ca intervals, but between Nos 9/10 and 11/12 the interval is 6ca, with a SHM perch midway. From Pte du Grouin ldg lts lead 172·5°/1·9M between training walls to a Y-junction. Here turn port into R l'Aure for 4 cables to town quays.

LIGHTS AND MARKS 172·5° ldg lts as chartlet.

R/T Ch 09 (0900-1200 & 1400-1800LT).

FACILITIES HM 02.31.22.10.67, fees payable at town-hall; **Quay** AB (55+5 Ⓥ), P, D, C (8 ton), Slip; **Club Nautique** AB, C, R, Bar; **Services:** ME, El, ⚒. **Town** R, 🛒, Bar, Ⓑ, ✉.

ADJACENT ANCHORAGE

ILES ST MARCOUF, Manche, **49°29'·78N 01°08'·92W,** the charted ⚓. AC *2613*, 2135; SHOM 7422. Tides, 9.17.26. The two islands, Île du Large and SW of it, Île de Terre, look from afar like ships at ⚓. The former has a small dinghy hbr on the SW side; the latter is a bird sanctuary, closed to the public. ⚓ SW or SE of Île du Large or SE or NE of Île de Terre. Holding is poor on pebbles and kelp; fair weather only, no shelter in S'lies. Île du Large lt, VQ (3) 5s 18m 8M, on top of the fort. Both islands are surrounded by drying rks, uninhabited and have no facilities.

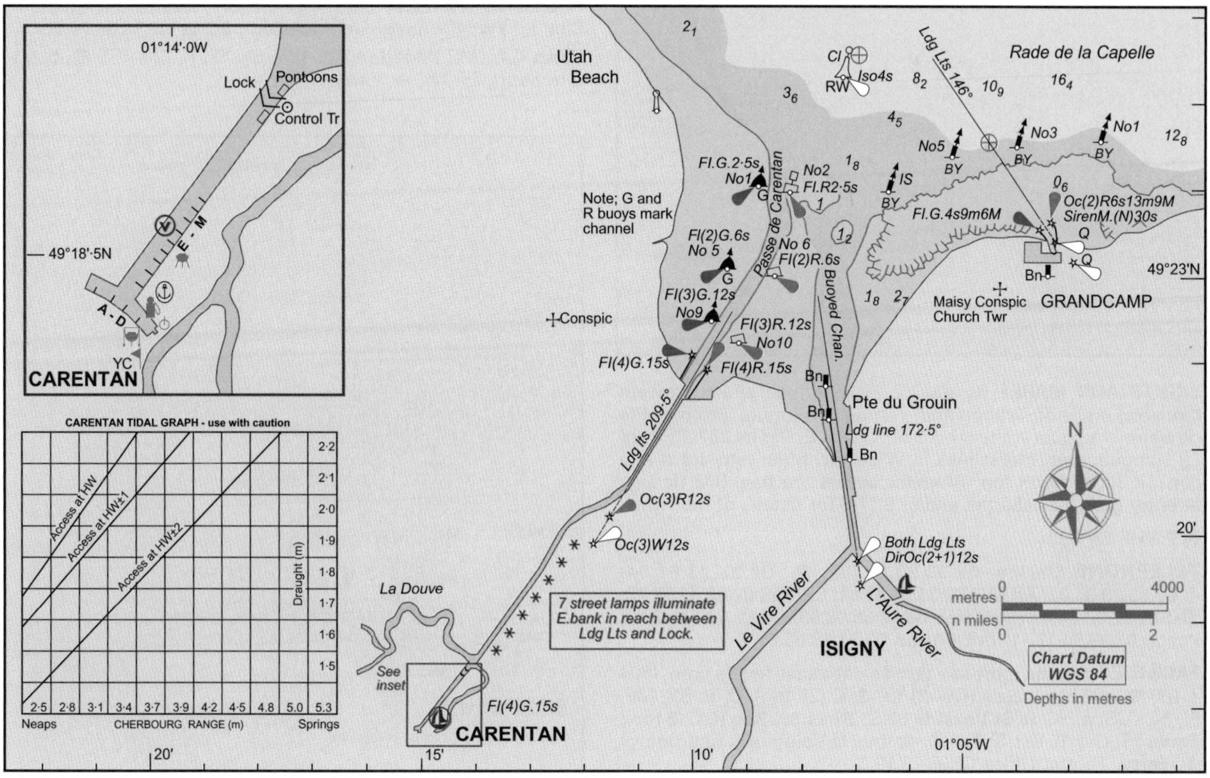
CARENTAN
01°14'·0W
Lock
Pontoons
Control Tr
49°18'·5N
YC
CARENTAN TIDAL GRAPH - use with caution
Access at HW
Access at HW±1
Access at HW±2
Draught (m)
2·5 2·8 3·1 3·4 3·7 3·9 4·2 4·5 4·8 5·0 5·3
Neaps
CHERBOURG RANGE (m)
Springs
Utah Beach
Rade de la Capelle
Ldg Lts 146°
Iso4s
No5
No3
No1
Fl.G.2·5s
No1
No2
Fl.R2·5s
IS
Passe de Carentan
Note; G and R buoys mark channel
Fl.G.4s9m6M
Oc(2)R6s13m9M
SirenM.(N)30s
Fl(2)G.6s
No 5
No 6
Fl(2)R.6s
Buoyed Chan.
49°23'N
Fl(3)G.12s
No9
Fl(3)R.12s
No10
Maisy Conspic Church Twr
GRANDCAMP
Conspic
Fl(4)G.15s
Fl(4)R.15s
Pte du Grouin
Ldg line 172·5°
Ldg lts 209·5°
Oc(3)R12s
Oc(3)W12s
Both Ldg Lts DirOc(2+1)12s
20'
La Douve
7 street lamps illuminate E.bank in reach between Ldg Lts and Lock.
Le Vire River
L'Aure River
ISIGNY
metres
n miles
Chart Datum WGS 84
Depths in metres
See inset
Fl(4)G.15s
CARENTAN
20'
15'
10'
01°05'W

9.17.28 ST VAAST-LA-HOUGUE

Manche **49°35'·19N 01°15'·43W** ⚙⚙⛵⛵✿✿✿

CHARTS AC *2613, 2135*, 1349; SHOM 7422, 7120, 7090; ECM 527, 528; Imray C32; Stanfords 1, 2, 7, 21

TIDES –0240 Dover; ML 4·1; Duration 0530; Zone –0100

Standard Port CHERBOURG (⟶)

Times				Height (metres)			
High Water		Low Water		MHWS	MHWN	MLWN	MLWS
0300	1000	0400	1000	6·4	5·0	2·5	1·1
1500	2200	1600	2200				
Differences ST VAAST-LA-HOUGUE							
+0120	+0050	+0120	+0115	+0·3	+0·5	0·0	–0·1

SHELTER Excellent in marina, 2·3m, crowded in season. Entry gate is open HW–2¼ to HW+3. If full, or awaiting gate, ⚓ off in white sector of jetty lt between brgs of 330° and 350°, but this ⚓ becomes untenable in strong E-S winds.

NAVIGATION WPT 49°34'·34N 01°13'·86W (Le Gavendest SCM lt buoy), 310°/1·3M to main jetty lt (Oc 6s). Appr in W sector, leaving La Dent to stbd and Le Bout du Roc ECM buoy and Le Creux de Bas ECM bn to port. The ent is wide and well marked. Beware boats at ⚓, cross currents and oyster beds. "Le Run" appr is not advised and should not be attempted if draft >1·2m.

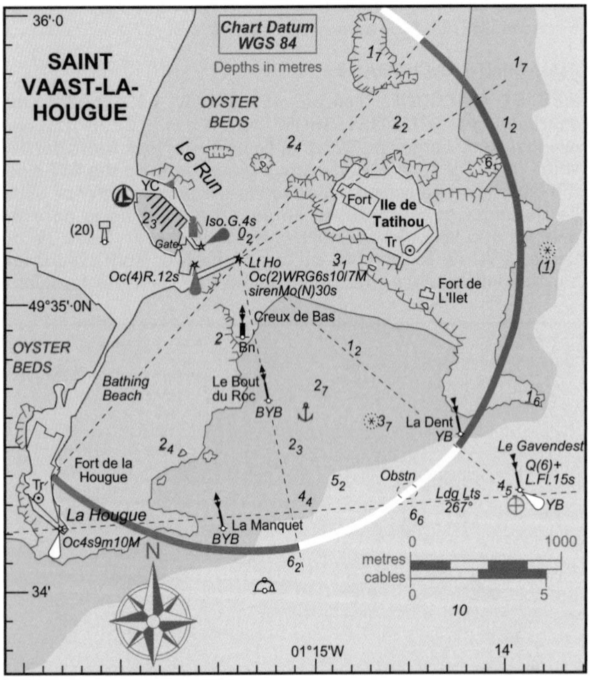
36'·0
Chart Datum WGS 84
Depths in metres
SAINT VAAST-LA-HOUGUE
OYSTER BEDS
Le Run
YC
(20)
Gate
Iso.G.4s
Lt Ho
Oc(2)WRG6s10/7M
sirenMo(N)30s
Oc(4)R.12s
Fort
Ile de Tatihou
Tr
Fort de L'Ilet
(1)
49°35'·0N
Creux de Bas
Bn
OYSTER BEDS
Bathing Beach
Le Bout du Roc
BYB
La Dent
YB
Le Gavendest
Q(6)+L.Fl.15s
YB
Fort de la Hougue
Tr
La Hougue
Oc4s9m10M
La Manquet
BYB
Obstn
Ldg Lts 267°
metres
cables
0
1000
5
N
34'
01°15'W
14'

LIGHTS AND MARKS By day do not confuse similar towers (conspic) on Ile de Tatihou and Fort de la Hougue. From N, Pte de Saire is a squat white lt ho/G top. From E, ldg lts 267·3°: front La Hougue; rear, Morsalines in W sector. Main jetty hd lt is a conspic white twr/R top; W sector covers the bay. R/G tfc sigs at entry gate. See chartlet and/or 9.17.4 for details of the lights.

R/T VHF Ch 09.

TELEPHONE Marina 02.33.23.61.00, 📠 02.33.23.61.04; ⊖ 02.33.23.34.02; Aff Mar 02.33.54.43.61; CROSS 02.33.52.72.13; SNSM 02.33.54.42.52; Météo 08.92.68.08.08; Dr 02.33.54.43.42; Police 02.33.54.12.11; Brit Consul 02.33.88.65.60.

FACILITIES Marina port-st-vaast@saint-vaast-reville.com (604 + 100 Ⓥ), €2.31; Access HW –2¼ to +3, C (25 ton), D, P, BY, ME, El, ⚒, Ⓢ, Slip. **YC de St Vaast ☎** 02.33.95.24.89, Bar, R, C (3 ton). **Town** 🛒, Gaz, R, Bar, Ⓢ, ✉, Ⓑ, ⇌ (bus to Valognes), Cherbourg: ✈, Ferry. Tourist Office 02.33.23.19.32.

9.17.29 BARFLEUR

Manche **49°40'·34N 01°15'·48W** ⚙⚙⛵⛵✿✿✿

CHARTS AC *2613, 2135*, 1106, 1349; SHOM 7422, 7120; ECM 528; Imray C32; Stanfords 1, 2, 7, 21

TIDES –0208 Dover; ML 3·9; Duration 0550; Zone –0100

Standard Port CHERBOURG (⟶)

Times				Height (metres)			
High Water		Low Water		MHWS	MHWN	MLWN	MLWS
0300	1000	0400	1000	6·4	5·0	2·5	1·1
1500	2200	1600	2200				
Differences BARFLEUR							
+0110	+0055	+0052	+0052	+0·1	+0·3	0·0	0·0

SHELTER Excellent, but ent difficult in fresh E/NE winds. Hbr dries; access HW ±2½. Yachts dry out on firm, level sand/mud at SW end of quay, but space is limited by FVs. Beware rks/shoals in SE of hbr. Safe to ⚓ outside hbr in off-shore winds. A 55m long spur bkwtr from the ☆ Fl G 4s, halfway across the ent, toward the ☆ Oc R 4s, is planned for somen unknown future date.

NAVIGATION WPT 49°41'·31N 01°14'·18W, 219·5°/1·3M to hbr ent. In rough weather, esp wind against tide, keep 5M off Pte de Barfleur to clear the Race; see 9.17.5. From the N, identify La Jamette ECM bn and La Grotte SHM buoy. From the S, keep seaward of Pte Dranguet and Le Moulard, both ECM bns. Positively identify Roche à l'Anglais SHM and Le Hintar PHM buoys before closing the hbr any further. Beware cross currents.

LIGHTS AND MARKS Pte de Barfleur lt ho is conspic 1½M NNW of hbr, a 72m high, grey twr/B top. The church tr is a conspic daymark. Ldg lts 219·5°: both W □ twrs, not easy to see by day. Light details as chartlet and 9.17.4.

R/T None.

TELEPHONE HM 02.33.54.08.29; Aff Mar 02.33.23.36.00; CROSS 02.33.52.72.13; SNSM 02.33.23.10.10; ⊖ 02.33.44.19.20; Météo 02.33.53.53.44; Auto 08.92.68.08.50; Police 17; SAMU 15; Dr 02.33.54.00.02; Brit Consul 02.33.88.65.60.

FACILITIES NW Quay (125 + 12 visitors, rafted), AB €0.81, M, Slip, L, FW, 🔌 (long cable needed); **SC ☎** 02.33.54.79.08.
Town Gaz, ME (Montfarville: 1km S), 🛒, R, Bar, ✉, Ⓑ, bus to Cherbourg for ⇌, ✈, Ferry.

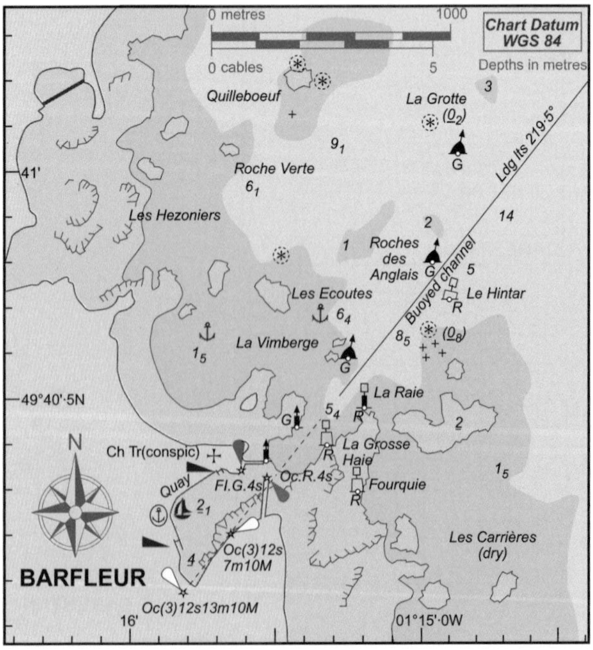
0 metres
1000
0 cables
5
Chart Datum WGS 84
Depths in metres
Quilleboeuf
La Grotte
(0₂)
G
Ldg lts 219·5°
41'
Roche Verte
Les Hezoniers
Roches des Anglais
Buoyed channel
Le Hintar
R
Les Ecoutes
La Vimberge
G
(0₈)
La Raie
49°40'·5N
N
Ch Tr(conspic)
Quay
Fl.G.4s
Oc.R.4s
La Grosse Haie
Fourquie
Oc(3)12s7m10M
Les Carrières (dry)
BARFLEUR
Oc(3)12s13m10M
16'
01°15'·0W

TIME ZONE -0100
(French Standard Time)
Subtract 1 hour for UT
For French Summer Time add ONE hour in **non-shaded areas**

FRANCE – CHERBOURG

LAT 49°39'N LONG 1°38'W

TIMES AND HEIGHTS OF HIGH AND LOW WATERS

SPRING & NEAP TIDES
Dates in red are SPRINGS
Dates in blue are NEAPS

YEAR **2005**

JANUARY

Date	Day	Time	m	Time	m	Time	m	Time	m
1	SA	0628	2.2	1159	5.6	1852	2.0		
2	SU	0030	5.3	0708	2.3	1239	5.4	1933	2.1
3	M	0115	5.2	0755	2.5	1326	5.2	◑ 2021	2.3
4	TU	0207	5.1	0850	2.6	1422	5.1	2120	2.4
5	W	0310	5.1	0957	2.6	1530	5.1	2229	2.4
6	TH	0420	5.2	1110	2.5	1644	5.2	2342	2.3
7	F	0529	5.4	1220	2.2	1756	5.4		
8	SA	0052	2.0	0631	5.7	1323	1.8	1901	5.7
9	SU	0152	1.7	0728	6.0	1421	1.5	1959	6.0
10	M	0247	1.5	0821	6.3	1515	1.1	● 2054	6.2
11	TU	0340	1.3	0913	6.5	1607	0.9	2146	6.4
12	W	0431	1.2	1004	6.6	1657	0.8	2236	6.4
13	TH	0520	1.2	1053	6.6	1745	0.8	2324	6.3
14	F	0607	1.3	1139	6.5	1831	1.0		
15	SA	0010	6.1	0652	1.5	1224	6.2	1916	1.3
16	SU	0052	5.8	0738	1.9	1308	5.9	2000	1.7
17	M	0136	5.5	0825	2.2	1355	5.5	◐ 2047	2.1
18	TU	0226	5.2	0919	2.5	1450	5.1	2143	2.5
19	W	0328	5.0	1026	2.7	1600	4.9	2252	2.7
20	TH	0442	4.9	1142	2.7	1720	4.8		
21	F	0007	2.7	0554	5.0	1251	2.5	1832	5.0
22	SA	0113	2.5	0653	5.3	1347	2.3	1927	5.2
23	SU	0205	2.3	0741	5.5	1433	2.0	2010	5.5
24	M	0248	2.1	0821	5.7	1512	1.8	2048	5.7
25	TU	0326	1.9	0857	5.9	1548	1.6	○ 2122	5.8
26	W	0400	1.8	0930	6.0	1622	1.5	2155	5.9
27	TH	0433	1.7	1002	6.1	1654	1.4	2227	5.9
28	F	0505	1.6	1034	6.1	1726	1.4	2258	5.9
29	SA	0536	1.6	1106	6.1	1757	1.4	2331	5.8
30	SU	0608	1.7	1139	5.9	1828	1.5		
31	M	0004	5.7	0642	1.8	1211	5.8	1902	1.7

FEBRUARY

Date	Day	Time	m	Time	m	Time	m	Time	m
1	TU	0036	5.5	0721	2.0	1246	5.5	1941	2.0
2	W	0115	5.3	0806	2.3	1331	5.3	◑ 2030	2.2
3	TH	0209	5.1	0906	2.5	1434	5.0	2137	2.5
4	F	0324	5.0	1024	2.6	1604	4.9	2303	2.5
5	SA	0457	5.1	1152	2.4	1740	5.1		
6	SU	0032	2.3	0616	5.4	1309	2.0	1855	5.5
7	M	0142	1.9	0720	5.8	1413	1.5	1956	5.9
8	TU	0242	1.5	0816	6.2	1509	1.0	● 2050	6.2
9	W	0334	1.2	0908	6.6	1559	0.7	2139	6.5
10	TH	0422	1.0	0956	6.8	1645	0.5	2224	6.5
11	F	0506	0.9	1040	6.8	1728	0.6	2305	6.5
12	SA	0547	1.0	1120	6.7	1807	0.8	2343	6.3
13	SU	0625	1.2	1157	6.4	1843	1.1		
14	M	0016	6.0	0701	1.6	1232	6.0	1918	1.6
15	TU	0049	5.6	0738	2.0	1307	5.5	1954	2.1
16	W	0126	5.2	0820	2.4	1351	5.0	◐ 2038	2.6
17	TH	0217	4.9	0918	2.8	1459	4.6	2144	3.0
18	F	0343	4.6	1050	3.0	1648	4.5	2326	3.1
19	SA	0525	4.7	1225	2.8	1820	4.7		
20	SU	0056	2.8	0636	5.0	1330	2.4	1915	5.0
21	M	0152	2.5	0725	5.3	1417	2.1	1955	5.4
22	TU	0235	2.1	0805	5.6	1456	1.7	2030	5.7
23	W	0310	1.8	0840	5.9	1530	1.5	2104	5.9
24	TH	0343	1.6	0913	6.1	1602	1.3	○ 2136	6.0
25	F	0414	1.4	0944	6.2	1633	1.1	2206	6.1
26	SA	0444	1.3	1015	6.3	1703	1.1	2236	6.1
27	SU	0515	1.2	1046	6.3	1732	1.1	2306	6.1
28	M	0545	1.3	1116	6.2	1803	1.2	2336	6.0

MARCH

Date	Day	Time	m	Time	m	Time	m	Time	m
1	TU	0617	1.5	1146	6.0	1835	1.5		
2	W	0006	5.8	0653	1.7	1218	5.7	1911	1.8
3	TH	0040	5.5	0736	2.0	1300	5.3	◑ 1958	2.2
4	F	0131	5.2	0833	2.4	1403	4.9	2104	2.6
5	SA	0250	4.9	0956	2.6	1553	4.7	2243	2.8
6	SU	0444	4.9	1140	2.4	1743	5.0		
7	M	0027	2.5	0611	5.3	1303	1.9	1855	5.4
8	TU	0138	2.0	0715	5.8	1405	1.4	1951	5.9
9	W	0234	1.5	0809	6.3	1457	0.9	2039	6.3
10	TH	0322	1.1	0856	6.6	1543	0.6	● 2123	6.5
11	F	0405	0.8	0939	6.8	1625	0.5	2202	6.6
12	SA	0444	0.8	1018	6.8	1702	0.6	2238	6.5
13	SU	0520	0.9	1054	6.6	1737	0.8	2311	6.3
14	M	0554	1.1	1126	6.3	1808	1.2	2341	6.1
15	TU	0626	1.5	1157	5.9	1838	1.7		
16	W	0008	5.7	0658	1.9	1227	5.4	1910	2.2
17	TH	0038	5.3	0735	2.3	1304	4.9	◐ 1948	2.7
18	F	0119	4.9	0824	2.8	1403	4.5	2048	3.1
19	SA	0237	4.5	0952	3.0	1618	4.3	2243	3.2
20	SU	0451	4.5	1149	2.9	1758	4.6		
21	M	0030	2.9	0609	4.8	1301	2.5	1849	5.0
22	TU	0126	2.5	0658	5.2	1348	2.1	1927	5.3
23	W	0207	2.1	0737	5.6	1426	1.7	2002	5.7
24	TH	0242	1.7	0813	5.9	1500	1.4	2035	6.0
25	F	0314	1.5	0847	6.1	1532	1.2	○ 2108	6.1
26	SA	0346	1.2	0919	6.3	1603	1.0	2140	6.3
27	SU	0418	1.1	0951	6.4	1635	0.9	2210	6.3
28	M	0450	1.0	1023	6.4	1706	1.0	2241	6.3
29	TU	0523	1.1	1055	6.3	1738	1.2	2312	6.1
30	W	0556	1.3	1127	6.0	1812	1.5	2345	5.9
31	TH	0634	1.6	1204	5.7	1852	1.9		

APRIL

Date	Day	Time	m	Time	m	Time	m	Time	m
1	F	0023	5.6	0720	1.9	1251	5.2	1942	2.3
2	SA	0118	5.2	0822	2.3	1404	4.8	◑ 2058	2.7
3	SU	0247	4.9	0952	2.5	1605	4.7	2245	2.8
4	M	0441	4.9	1136	2.3	1742	5.1		
5	TU	0021	2.4	0601	5.4	1251	1.8	1844	5.5
6	W	0125	1.9	0700	5.8	1349	1.3	1934	6.0
7	TH	0216	1.4	0750	6.2	1437	1.0	2018	6.3
8	F	0301	1.1	0835	6.5	1520	0.8	● 2058	6.4
9	SA	0341	0.9	0915	6.6	1558	0.7	2134	6.5
10	SU	0418	0.9	0951	6.6	1633	0.8	2208	6.4
11	M	0452	1.0	1025	6.4	1705	1.1	2238	6.3
12	TU	0524	1.2	1057	6.1	1735	1.4	2307	6.0
13	W	0555	1.5	1127	5.8	1805	1.8	2335	5.7
14	TH	0627	1.9	1159	5.4	1837	2.2		
15	F	0005	5.3	0704	2.3	1235	4.9	1917	2.7
16	SA	0046	4.9	0751	2.6	1331	4.5	◐ 2015	3.0
17	SU	0153	4.6	0906	2.9	1529	4.4	2154	3.2
18	M	0355	4.5	1053	2.9	1709	4.5	2334	3.0
19	TU	0519	4.7	1209	2.5	1804	4.9		
20	W	0038	2.6	0613	5.0	1301	2.1	1845	5.3
21	TH	0122	2.2	0656	5.4	1342	1.8	1923	5.6
22	F	0201	1.8	0735	5.8	1419	1.5	1959	5.9
23	SA	0238	1.5	0813	6.0	1455	1.2	2034	6.2
24	SU	0314	1.2	0849	6.2	1531	1.0	○ 2109	6.3
25	M	0350	1.0	0925	6.3	1607	1.0	2143	6.4
26	TU	0427	1.0	1001	6.3	1643	1.0	2218	6.3
27	W	0504	1.0	1038	6.2	1720	1.2	2255	6.2
28	TH	0543	1.2	1118	6.0	1800	1.6	2335	5.9
29	F	0626	1.5	1204	5.6	1846	2.0		
30	SA	0022	5.6	0719	1.8	1259	5.2	1946	2.4

Chart Datum: 3·29 metres below IGN Datum

TIME ZONE -0100
(French Standard Time)
Subtract 1 hour for UT
For French Summer Time add ONE hour in **non-shaded areas**

FRANCE – CHERBOURG

LAT 49°39′N LONG 1°38′W

TIMES AND HEIGHTS OF HIGH AND LOW WATERS

SPRING & NEAP TIDES
Dates in red are SPRINGS
Dates in blue are NEAPS

YEAR **2005**

MAY

Date	Day	Time	m	Time	m	Time	m	Time	m
1	SU	0123	5.2	0827	2.1	1419	4.9	◑ 2106	2.6
2	M	0250	5.0	0953	2.2	1601	4.9	2239	2.5
3	TU	0424	5.1	1119	2.0	1720	5.2	2356	2.2
4	W	0536	5.4	1226	1.7	1818	5.6		
5	TH	0059	1.8	0633	5.8	1322	1.4	1906	5.9
6	F	0149	1.5	0723	6.0	1409	1.2	1949	6.1
7	SA	0234	1.3	0808	6.2	1451	1.1	2029	6.2
8	SU	0314	1.2	0848	6.2	1529	1.2	● 2105	6.2
9	M	0351	1.2	0925	6.2	1603	1.3	2138	6.2
10	TU	0426	1.2	1000	6.1	1636	1.4	2210	6.1
11	W	0459	1.4	1034	5.9	1709	1.7	2241	5.9
12	TH	0533	1.6	1107	5.6	1742	2.0	2313	5.7
13	F	0607	1.9	1142	5.3	1817	2.3	2348	5.4
14	SA	0645	2.1	1222	5.0	1858	2.6		
15	SU	0030	5.1	0731	2.4	1314	4.7	1952	2.8
16	M	0128	4.8	0831	2.6	1430	4.6	◐ 2105	3.0
17	TU	0247	4.6	0948	2.7	1555	4.6	2226	2.9
18	W	0407	4.7	1101	2.5	1701	4.9	2332	2.6
19	TH	0510	5.0	1200	2.2	1751	5.2		
20	F	0027	2.3	0602	5.3	1250	1.9	1836	5.5
21	SA	0114	1.9	0650	5.6	1335	1.6	1917	5.8
22	SU	0159	1.6	0734	5.8	1418	1.4	1958	6.0
23	M	0242	1.3	0818	6.0	1500	1.2	○ 2038	6.2
24	TU	0325	1.2	0900	6.2	1542	1.2	2119	6.3
25	W	0407	1.0	0944	6.2	1625	1.2	2201	6.3
26	TH	0451	1.0	1029	6.1	1709	1.4	2245	6.2
27	F	0537	1.1	1116	6.0	1757	1.6	2333	6.0
28	SA	0628	1.3	1207	5.7	1850	1.9		
29	SU	0025	5.8	0724	1.6	1306	5.4	1952	2.1
30	M	0126	5.5	0827	1.8	1416	5.2	◑ 2102	2.3
31	TU	0238	5.3	0937	1.9	1532	5.2	2215	2.3

JUNE

Date	Day	Time	m	Time	m	Time	m	Time	m
1	W	0352	5.3	1047	1.9	1641	5.3	2322	2.2
2	TH	0459	5.4	1151	1.8	1740	5.4		
3	F	0025	2.0	0559	5.5	1247	1.7	1832	5.6
4	SA	0119	1.8	0653	5.7	1337	1.7	1919	5.8
5	SU	0207	1.7	0742	5.8	1422	1.6	2001	5.9
6	M	0250	1.6	0826	5.8	1503	1.6	● 2040	6.0
7	TU	0330	1.5	0906	5.8	1540	1.7	2116	6.0
8	W	0407	1.5	0943	5.8	1616	1.7	2150	5.9
9	TH	0442	1.5	1019	5.7	1652	1.8	2225	5.8
10	F	0518	1.6	1054	5.6	1727	2.0	2300	5.7
11	SA	0554	1.8	1130	5.4	1804	2.2	2337	5.5
12	SU	0631	1.9	1208	5.2	1843	2.3		
13	M	0016	5.3	0711	2.1	1251	5.0	1927	2.5
14	TU	0101	5.1	0756	2.3	1342	4.9	2019	2.6
15	W	0154	5.0	0850	2.4	1441	4.8	◐ 2120	2.7
16	TH	0255	4.9	0951	2.4	1545	4.9	2225	2.6
17	F	0359	4.9	1055	2.3	1646	5.1	2328	2.4
18	SA	0502	5.1	1156	2.1	1743	5.3		
19	SU	0029	2.1	0602	5.3	1252	1.9	1836	5.6
20	M	0123	1.8	0659	5.6	1345	1.7	1926	5.9
21	TU	0215	1.5	0752	5.8	1436	1.5	2014	6.1
22	W	0305	1.3	0844	6.0	1525	1.4	○ 2102	6.3
23	TH	0355	1.1	0934	6.1	1615	1.3	2151	6.4
24	F	0445	1.0	1025	6.2	1705	1.3	2240	6.4
25	SA	0535	0.9	1115	6.1	1756	1.4	2331	6.3
26	SU	0626	1.0	1206	6.0	1848	1.6		
27	M	0022	6.1	0717	1.2	1258	5.7	1942	1.8
28	TU	0114	5.9	0810	1.5	1352	5.5	◑ 2038	2.0
29	W	0209	5.6	0906	1.8	1449	5.3	2138	2.2
30	TH	0309	5.4	1005	2.0	1551	5.2	2242	2.3

JULY

Date	Day	Time	m	Time	m	Time	m	Time	m
1	F	0414	5.2	1108	2.1	1656	5.2	2347	2.3
2	SA	0522	5.2	1211	2.2	1758	5.3		
3	SU	0050	2.2	0627	5.2	1309	2.2	1853	5.5
4	M	0144	2.0	0724	5.4	1400	2.1	1941	5.6
5	TU	0232	1.9	0812	5.5	1445	2.0	2024	5.7
6	W	0315	1.7	0854	5.6	1526	1.9	● 2102	5.8
7	TH	0354	1.6	0932	5.7	1604	1.9	2138	5.9
8	F	0430	1.6	1007	5.7	1640	1.8	2213	5.9
9	SA	0505	1.6	1041	5.7	1714	1.9	2246	5.8
10	SU	0539	1.6	1114	5.6	1748	1.9	2320	5.8
11	M	0612	1.7	1148	5.5	1821	2.0	2354	5.6
12	TU	0645	1.8	1223	5.4	1857	2.1		
13	W	0030	5.5	0720	1.9	1300	5.2	1937	2.3
14	TH	0109	5.3	0801	2.1	1343	5.1	◐ 2025	2.4
15	F	0156	5.1	0851	2.3	1435	5.0	2123	2.5
16	SA	0254	5.0	0953	2.4	1540	5.0	2233	2.5
17	SU	0405	5.0	1106	2.4	1653	5.1	2346	2.4
18	M	0524	5.1	1218	2.2	1803	5.4		
19	TU	0056	2.0	0636	5.4	1322	2.0	1904	5.7
20	W	0157	1.7	0739	5.7	1421	1.7	1959	6.0
21	TH	0253	1.3	0835	6.0	1515	1.4	○ 2052	6.3
22	F	0347	1.0	0929	6.2	1608	1.2	2144	6.5
23	SA	0437	0.8	1019	6.3	1657	1.1	2233	6.6
24	SU	0526	0.7	1107	6.4	1745	1.1	2321	6.6
25	M	0612	0.7	1152	6.2	1831	1.2		
26	TU	0006	6.4	0656	1.0	1234	6.0	1917	1.5
27	W	0049	6.1	0740	1.4	1316	5.7	2003	1.8
28	TH	0133	5.7	0825	1.8	1400	5.4	◑ 2054	2.2
29	F	0223	5.3	0916	2.2	1454	5.1	2156	2.5
30	SA	0328	4.9	1021	2.6	1607	4.9	2311	2.6
31	SU	0451	4.8	1137	2.7	1728	5.0		

AUGUST

Date	Day	Time	m	Time	m	Time	m	Time	m
1	M	0027	2.5	0613	4.9	1249	2.6	1837	5.2
2	TU	0130	2.3	0716	5.1	1347	2.4	1929	5.4
3	W	0221	2.0	0803	5.4	1435	2.1	2012	5.6
4	TH	0303	1.8	0843	5.6	1515	1.9	2049	5.8
5	F	0340	1.6	0918	5.7	1551	1.8	● 2124	6.0
6	SA	0414	1.5	0950	5.8	1624	1.7	2156	6.0
7	SU	0446	1.4	1021	5.9	1654	1.6	2226	6.1
8	M	0516	1.4	1050	5.9	1724	1.6	2256	6.0
9	TU	0545	1.4	1120	5.8	1754	1.7	2326	5.9
10	W	0614	1.5	1150	5.7	1825	1.8	2357	5.7
11	TH	0644	1.7	1221	5.5	1859	2.0		
12	F	0028	5.5	0719	1.9	1254	5.4	1940	2.2
13	SA	0107	5.3	0802	2.2	1338	5.1	◐ 2033	2.5
14	SU	0202	5.0	0901	2.5	1443	5.0	2146	2.6
15	M	0323	4.8	1026	2.7	1616	4.9	2317	2.6
16	TU	0507	4.9	1157	2.5	1746	5.2		
17	W	0041	2.2	0630	5.3	1311	2.2	1853	5.6
18	TH	0147	1.7	0733	5.7	1412	1.7	1950	6.1
19	F	0244	1.2	0828	6.1	1506	1.3	○ 2043	6.5
20	SA	0335	0.8	0918	6.4	1555	1.0	2132	6.7
21	SU	0422	0.6	1004	6.6	1641	0.9	2217	6.9
22	M	0506	0.5	1046	6.6	1724	0.9	2300	6.8
23	TU	0547	0.6	1125	6.4	1804	1.0	2340	6.6
24	W	0625	1.0	1201	6.2	1843	1.4		
25	TH	0016	6.1	0701	1.5	1235	5.8	1922	1.8
26	F	0053	5.6	0739	2.0	1310	5.4	◑ 2006	2.3
27	SA	0137	5.1	0823	2.5	1357	5.0	2104	2.7
28	SU	0242	4.7	0928	3.0	1516	4.7	2234	2.9
29	M	0431	4.5	1110	3.1	1707	4.7		
30	TU	0007	2.8	0608	4.7	1236	2.9	1825	5.0
31	W	0116	2.4	0705	5.1	1335	2.5	1914	5.3

Chart Datum: 3·29 metres below IGN Datum

TIME ZONE -0100
(French Standard Time)
Subtract 1 hour for UT
For French Summer Time add ONE hour in **non-shaded areas**

FRANCE – CHERBOURG

LAT 49°39′N LONG 1°38′W

TIMES AND HEIGHTS OF HIGH AND LOW WATERS

SPRING & NEAP TIDES
Dates in red are **SPRINGS**
Dates in blue are **NEAPS**

YEAR **2005**

SEPTEMBER

Day	Time	m	Time	m	Time	m	Time	m
1 TH	0204	2.1	0746	5.4	1419	2.1	1953	5.7
2 F	0243	1.8	0820	5.7	1456	1.9	2028	5.9
3 SA	0317	1.5	0853	5.9	1528	1.7	● 2100	6.1
4 SU	0349	1.3	0924	6.0	1558	1.5	2131	6.2
5 M	0418	1.2	0953	6.1	1627	1.4	2200	6.3
6 TU	0447	1.2	1021	6.1	1656	1.4	2228	6.2
7 W	0514	1.3	1049	6.1	1725	1.5	2256	6.1
8 TH	0542	1.4	1116	5.9	1755	1.6	2325	5.9
9 F	0612	1.6	1144	5.8	1827	1.8	2356	5.6
10 SA	0645	2.0	1214	5.5	1906	2.1		
11 SU	0033	5.3	0727	2.3	1257	5.2	◐ 1958	2.5
12 M	0131	4.9	0828	2.7	1407	4.9	2117	2.7
13 TU	0308	4.7	1005	2.9	1602	4.8	2303	2.6
14 W	0511	4.9	1151	2.7	1739	5.2		
15 TH	0034	2.1	0628	5.3	1304	2.2	1844	5.7
16 F	0136	1.6	0724	5.9	1401	1.6	1938	6.2
17 SA	0229	1.1	0813	6.3	1450	1.2	2026	6.6
18 SU	0316	0.7	0858	6.6	1536	0.9	○ 2112	6.9
19 M	0359	0.6	0939	6.7	1618	0.8	2154	6.9
20 TU	0439	0.6	1017	6.6	1657	0.9	2233	6.8
21 W	0516	0.8	1052	6.5	1733	1.1	2309	6.5
22 TH	0550	1.2	1123	6.2	1808	1.5	2343	6.1
23 F	0622	1.7	1153	5.8	1843	1.9		
24 SA	0015	5.5	0656	2.2	1225	5.4	1921	2.4
25 SU	0055	5.0	0736	2.8	1307	5.0	◑ 2014	2.8
26 M	0200	4.6	0839	3.2	1425	4.6	2150	3.1
27 TU	0411	4.4	1041	3.3	1639	4.6	2340	2.9
28 W	0548	4.7	1213	3.0	1758	4.9		
29 TH	0048	2.5	0638	5.1	1308	2.6	1844	5.3
30 F	0133	2.1	0714	5.4	1349	2.2	1921	5.6

OCTOBER

Day	Time	m	Time	m	Time	m	Time	m
1 SA	0210	1.8	0747	5.8	1424	1.9	1956	5.9
2 SU	0244	1.5	0820	6.0	1456	1.6	2028	6.2
3 M	0314	1.3	0851	6.2	1526	1.4	● 2100	6.3
4 TU	0345	1.2	0920	6.3	1556	1.3	2130	6.3
5 W	0415	1.2	0949	6.3	1627	1.3	2159	6.3
6 TH	0444	1.3	1017	6.2	1658	1.3	2229	6.2
7 F	0514	1.4	1046	6.1	1730	1.5	2301	6.0
8 SA	0546	1.7	1117	5.9	1805	1.8	2337	5.7
9 SU	0623	2.1	1153	5.6	1847	2.1		
10 M	0020	5.3	0709	2.5	1243	5.3	◐ 1944	2.5
11 TU	0127	4.9	0818	2.9	1402	4.9	2110	2.7
12 W	0319	4.7	1005	3.0	1559	4.9	2257	2.5
13 TH	0508	5.0	1143	2.6	1726	5.3		
14 F	0020	2.0	0613	5.5	1249	2.1	1826	5.8
15 SA	0117	1.5	0704	6.0	1341	1.6	1917	6.3
16 SU	0206	1.1	0749	6.3	1428	1.2	2003	6.6
17 M	0251	0.9	0831	6.5	1511	1.0	○ 2046	6.8
18 TU	0332	0.8	0910	6.6	1551	0.9	2126	6.7
19 W	0409	0.9	0945	6.6	1629	1.0	2204	6.6
20 TH	0444	1.2	1018	6.4	1704	1.3	2239	6.3
21 F	0517	1.5	1048	6.2	1738	1.6	2312	5.9
22 SA	0550	1.9	1119	5.8	1812	2.0	2347	5.5
23 SU	0624	2.4	1152	5.4	1850	2.4		
24 M	0026	5.0	0704	2.8	1234	5.0	1939	2.8
25 TU	0127	4.6	0804	3.2	1344	4.7	◑ 2058	3.0
26 W	0321	4.5	0948	3.3	1541	4.6	2245	3.0
27 TH	0455	4.7	1124	3.1	1704	4.8	2356	2.6
28 F	0550	5.0	1222	2.7	1757	5.1		
29 SA	0047	2.3	0630	5.4	1306	2.3	1838	5.5
30 SU	0127	2.0	0706	5.7	1343	2.0	1915	5.8
31 M	0202	1.7	0740	6.0	1418	1.7	1951	6.1

NOVEMBER

Day	Time	m	Time	m	Time	m	Time	m
1 TU	0237	1.5	0814	6.2	1452	1.5	2026	6.2
2 W	0311	1.3	0846	6.3	1527	1.3	● 2100	6.3
3 TH	0345	1.3	0918	6.4	1602	1.3	2134	6.3
4 F	0419	1.4	0951	6.3	1638	1.3	2210	6.2
5 SA	0454	1.5	1026	6.2	1715	1.5	2249	6.0
6 SU	0532	1.8	1105	6.0	1756	1.7	2333	5.7
7 M	0616	2.1	1150	5.7	1845	2.0		
8 TU	0026	5.4	0710	2.5	1247	5.4	1947	2.3
9 W	0137	5.1	0824	2.8	1405	5.2	◐ 2109	2.4
10 TH	0315	5.0	0957	2.8	1541	5.2	2238	2.3
11 F	0442	5.2	1120	2.5	1658	5.5	2349	2.0
12 SA	0544	5.6	1223	2.1	1758	5.8		
13 SU	0050	1.6	0635	5.9	1316	1.7	1850	6.1
14 M	0139	1.4	0720	6.2	1404	1.4	1937	6.3
15 TU	0224	1.3	0802	6.3	1447	1.3	2021	6.4
16 W	0305	1.3	0841	6.4	1527	1.3	○ 2102	6.4
17 TH	0343	1.4	0916	6.4	1605	1.3	2140	6.2
18 F	0418	1.5	0950	6.3	1641	1.5	2216	6.0
19 SA	0453	1.8	1024	6.1	1716	1.7	2252	5.8
20 SU	0528	2.1	1058	5.8	1752	1.9	2329	5.5
21 M	0604	2.4	1134	5.5	1830	2.2		
22 TU	0009	5.2	0645	2.7	1216	5.2	1915	2.5
23 W	0100	4.9	0736	2.9	1311	4.9	◑ 2012	2.8
24 TH	0211	4.7	0844	3.1	1425	4.8	2126	2.8
25 F	0332	4.7	1004	3.1	1543	4.8	2241	2.7
26 SA	0439	4.9	1114	2.8	1648	5.0	2342	2.5
27 SU	0531	5.2	1209	2.5	1742	5.2		
28 M	0033	2.2	0616	5.5	1256	2.2	1829	5.5
29 TU	0118	2.0	0657	5.8	1339	1.9	1913	5.8
30 W	0159	1.7	0737	6.0	1420	1.6	1955	6.0

DECEMBER

Day	Time	m	Time	m	Time	m	Time	m
1 TH	0240	1.5	0815	6.2	1501	1.4	● 2036	6.2
2 F	0321	1.5	0854	6.3	1543	1.3	2118	6.2
3 SA	0402	1.5	0934	6.4	1625	1.3	2201	6.2
4 SU	0445	1.5	1017	6.3	1710	1.3	2246	6.1
5 M	0530	1.7	1102	6.2	1757	1.4	2336	5.9
6 TU	0619	1.9	1152	6.0	1849	1.6		
7 W	0030	5.6	0715	2.2	1249	5.7	1947	1.9
8 TH	0133	5.4	0819	2.4	1354	5.5	◐ 2053	2.0
9 F	0245	5.3	0931	2.4	1507	5.4	2204	2.1
10 SA	0358	5.3	1043	2.4	1618	5.4	2312	2.0
11 SU	0503	5.4	1149	2.2	1723	5.6		
12 M	0017	1.9	0600	5.6	1248	2.0	1822	5.7
13 TU	0111	1.8	0651	5.8	1341	1.8	1915	5.8
14 W	0200	1.8	0738	6.0	1428	1.7	2003	5.9
15 TH	0244	1.7	0819	6.1	1510	1.6	○ 2046	6.0
16 F	0324	1.7	0858	6.1	1549	1.5	2126	5.9
17 SA	0403	1.8	0934	6.1	1627	1.6	2203	5.9
18 SU	0439	1.9	1010	6.0	1703	1.6	2239	5.8
19 M	0515	2.0	1046	5.9	1739	1.8	2315	5.6
20 TU	0551	2.2	1122	5.7	1815	1.9	2352	5.4
21 W	0628	2.3	1159	5.5	1852	2.1		
22 TH	0031	5.2	0707	2.5	1238	5.3	1932	2.3
23 F	0116	5.0	0752	2.7	1325	5.1	◑ 2019	2.5
24 SA	0209	4.9	0846	2.8	1421	4.9	2115	2.6
25 SU	0311	4.9	0950	2.8	1525	4.9	2221	2.6
26 M	0416	5.0	1059	2.7	1633	5.0	2328	2.5
27 TU	0518	5.2	1203	2.5	1739	5.2		
28 W	0032	2.3	0614	5.5	1301	2.2	1837	5.4
29 TH	0126	2.0	0705	5.8	1353	1.8	1931	5.7
30 F	0217	1.8	0753	6.0	1443	1.5	2020	6.0
31 SA	0305	1.6	0839	6.3	1531	1.3	● 2108	6.2

Chart Datum: 3·29 metres below IGN Datum

9.17.30 CHERBOURG

Manche **49°38'·94N 01°37'·11W** (Marina ent) ❁❁❁⚓⚓⚓✿✿

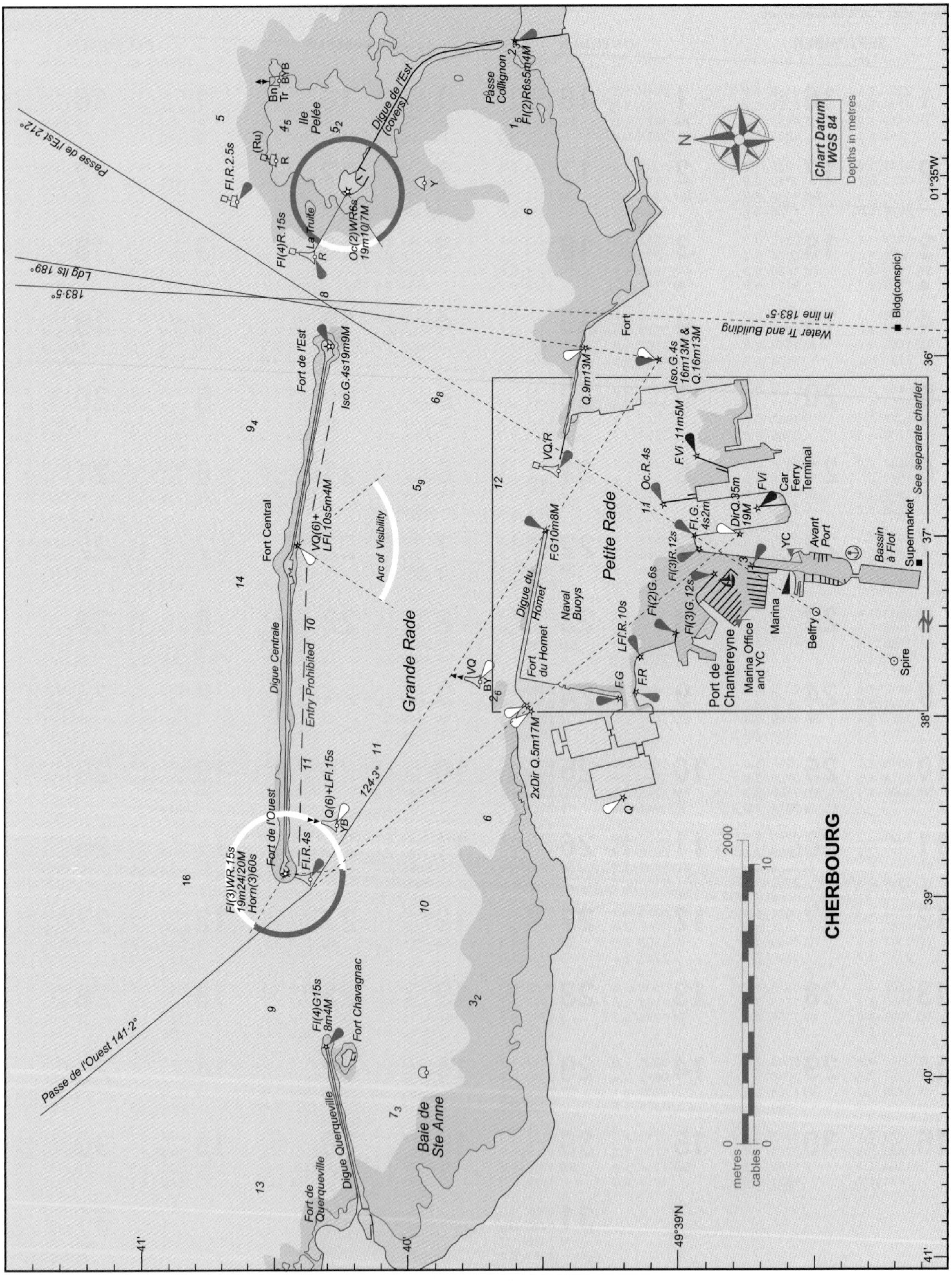
CHERBOURG
Grande Rade
Petite Rade
Digue Centrale
Entry Prohibited
Fort Central
Fort de l'Est
Fort de l'Ouest
Digue de l'Est (covers)
Ile Pelée
Passe Collignon
Fl(2)R6s5m4M
Oc(2)WR6s 19m10/7M
Fl(4)R.15s
La Truite
Fl.R.2.5s
Passe de l'Est 212°
Ldg lts 189°
183·5°
Passe de l'Ouest 141·2°
124·3°
Iso.G.4s19m9M
VQ(6)+ LFl.10s5m4M
Arc of Visibility
Q(6)+LFl.15s
Fl.R.4s
Fl(3)WR.15s 19m24/20M Horn(3)60s
Fl(4)G15s 8m4M
Fort Chavagnac
Digue Querqueville
Fort de Querqueville
Baie de Ste Anne
2xDir Q.5m17M
Fort du Homet
Digue du Homet
F.G10m8M
Naval Buoys
Q.9m13M
VQ.R
Iso.G.4s 16m13M & Q.16m13M
Fort
Water Tr and Building in line 183·5°
Bldg(conspic)
F.Vi .11m5M
Oc.R.4s
Fl.G. 4s2m
DirQ.35m 19M
FVi
Car Ferry Terminal
Fl(3)R.12s
Fl(2)G.6s
Fl(3)G.12s
LFl.R.10s
F.G
F.R
Port de Chantereyne
Marina Office and YC
Marina
Belfry
Spire
Avant Port
Bassin à Flot
Supermarket
See separate chartlet
Chart Datum WGS 84
Depths in metres
metres
cables
2000
10
01°35'W
36'
37'
38'
39'
40'
41'
49°39'N

CHARTS AC *2656, 2669, 1106,* 2602; SHOM 7120, 7092, 7086; ECM 528, 1014; Imray C32, C33A; Stanfords 1, 2, 7, 16, 21.

TIDES Cherbourg is a Standard Port (⟵). –0308 Dover; ML 3·8; Duration 0535; Zone –0100

SHELTER Excellent; a port of refuge available in all tides and weather. Ⓥ berth in 2·6m on pontoons M, N, P & Q, on S side of Chantereyne Marina. There is also a small craft ⚓ N of marina bkwtr, but keep outside the charted limits of the military port. For long-stay enter the Bassin du Commerce (HW±1) via a gate and swing bridge (heavy road tfc) which opens HW±45 mins on request to *Vigie du Homet* Ch 06; 40 Ⓥ berths.

NAVIGATION For coastal features from Pte de Barfleur to Cap de la Hague see 9.17.5. There are 3 entrances to the Grande Rade (outer harbour):

1. **Passe de l'Ouest** (W ent). WPT 49°41´·04N 01°39´·88W, 141°/0·85M to abeam Fort de l'Ouest. Note: From CH1 SWM buoy, L Fl 10s, Fort de l'Ouest bears 145°/3·5M. Rks extend about 80m off each bkwtr marked by a PHM buoy, Fl R 4s, off Fort de l'Ouest. From W, the white sector of Fort de l'Ouest lt (bearing more than 122° by day) keeps clear of offlying dangers E of Cap de la Hague.
2. **Passe de l'Est** (E ent, least depth 8m). WPT 49°40´·91N 01°35´·40W, 189°/0·65M to abeam Fort de l'Est. Keep to W side of chan (but at least 80m off Fort de l'Est) to avoid dangers W and NW of Ile Pelée marked by two PHM lt buoys. N/NE of Ile Pelée an extensive drying area is marked by 2 unlit bn trs.
3. Passe Collignon is a shallow (2m) chan, 93m wide, through Digue de l'Est (covers), near the shore. Only recommended in good conditions and near HW.

No anchoring in the Passe de L'Ouest and Passe de L'Est. Speed limits: Grande Rade14kn, Petite Rade 8kn. No entry to: the area S of the Digue Centrale due to fish farms nor to the area east of the Port Militaire. Keep clear of ferries.

LIGHTS AND MARKS There are three powerful lights near Cherbourg:

1. To the E, Cap Levi, Fl R 5s 22M;
2. Further E, Pte de Barfleur, Fl(2)10s 29M;
3. To the W, Cap de la Hague, Fl 5s 23M;

Further W, Quenard Pt (Alderney), Fl (4) 15s 23M, and Casquets, Fl (5) 30s 24M, can often be seen. See also 9.17.4 and 9.19.4.

Passe de l'Ouest ldg lts 141·2°: Dir Q between 2Q (hor) at base of Digue du Homet. Fort de l'Ouest, Fl (3) WR 15s. Grande Rade ldg lts 124·3°: Front FG; rear Iso G 4s.

Passe de l'Est ldg lts 189°: both Q 9/16m 13M. Inside Petite Rade steer 200° for marina ent, QR and Oc (2) G 6s. Confusing shore lights may mask nav lts.

R/T Marina: call *Chantereyne* Ch 09 72 (0800-2300LT). Cherbourg commercial port: call *Le Homet* Ch 12 16.
Jobourg Traffic Ch **13** 80 (H24) provides radar surveillance of the Casquets TSS/ITZ and from Mont St Michel to Cap d'Antifer. Radar assistance available on request, Ch 80, to vessels in the sector from S clockwise to E, radius 40M from CROSS Jobourg at 49°41'N 01°54'·5W. Jobourg broadcasts nav, weather and traffic info in English and French Ch 80 at H+20 & H+50; also H+05 & H+35, when vis < 2M.

TELEPHONE Marina 02·33·87·65·70; 🖷 02·33·53·21·12; HM (Port) 02·33·20·41·25; Lock 02·33·44·23·18; Aff Mar 02·33·23·36·00; ⊖ 02·33·23·34·02; CROSS 02·33·52·72·13; Météo 02·33·53·53·44; Auto 08.92.68.08.50; Police 02·33·92·70·00; Ⓗ 02·33·20·70·00; Dr 02·33·53·05·68; Brit Consul 02.33.88.65.60.

FACILITIES Marina, access H24, (900+ 300 Ⓥ on M, N, P, Q pontoons), €2.06, Slip, ME, El, ⚒, BH (30 ton), ♿, CH, Ⓛ, P & D (0800-1200; 1400-1900), shwrs H24 by 'back door'; www.ville-cherbourg.fr cherbourg.marina@wanadoo.fr **YC de Cherbourg** ☎ 02·33·53·02·83, 🖷 02·33·94·13·73, FW, R, Bar; **Services:** ME, El, Ⓔ, ⚒, CH, M, SM, SHOM. **City** P, D, Gaz, 🛒, R, Bar, ✉, Ⓛ, Ⓑ, ⇌, ✈ (☎ 02·33.22.91.32). Ferry: Portsmouth, Poole.

MINOR HARBOURS EAST OF CHERBOURG

PORT DE LÉVI, Manche, **49°41´·24 N 01°28´·38W**. AC *1106*; SHOM 7120, 5609, 7092; HW –0310 on Dover (UT); +0024 on Cherbourg. HW ht +0·2m on Cherbourg. Dries to clean sand. Shelter good except in SW to N winds. By day appr on 090° to keep the white wall and lt between the white marks on each pier hd. Beware lobster pots. Secure bows on to NE side below white wall, amongst small FVs. Lt is F RG 7m 7M, G050°-109°, R109°-140°; keep in G sector, but night entry not advised. Facilities: Peace. Fermanville (1·5M) has 🛒, R, Bar.

PORT DU BECQUET, Manche, **49°39´·24N 01°32´·88W**. AC *1106*; SHOM 7120, 7092. Tides as 9.17.30. Dries to clean sand. Shelter is good except in winds from N to E when a strong scend enters. Secure to S of the E/W jetty, but ther is little space. Ldg lts 186·5°: Front Dir Oc (2+1) 12s 8m 10M, W 8-sided tr, intens 183·5°-190·5°; rear, 49m from front, Dir Oc (2+1) R 12s 13m 7M, synch, also in W 8-sided tr. Facilities: very few; all facilities at Cherbourg 2·5M.

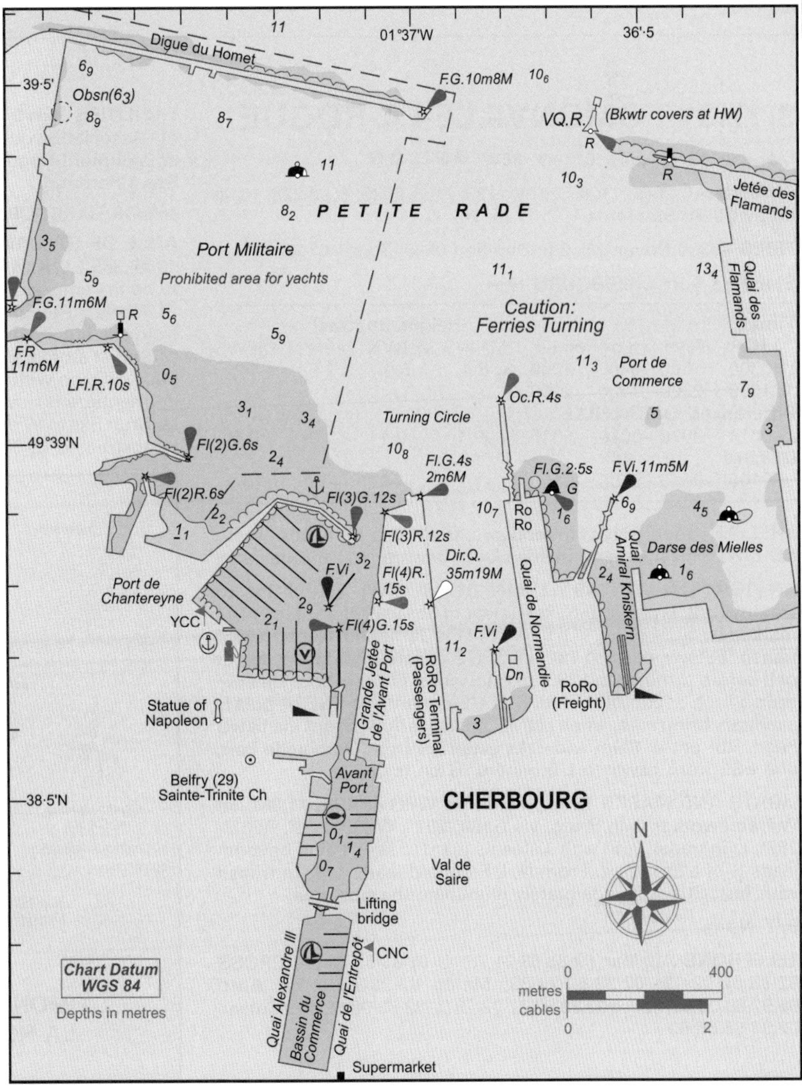
01°37'W
36'·5
39·5'
49°39'N
38·5'N
Digue du Homet
F.G.10m8M
Obsn(63)
VQ.R.
(Bkwtr covers at HW)
Jetée des Flamands
PETITE RADE
Port Militaire
Prohibited area for yachts
Quai des Flamands
Caution: Ferries Turning
F.G.11m6M
F.R 11m6M
LFl.R.10s
Port de Commerce
Oc.R.4s
Turning Circle
Fl(2)G.6s
Fl.G.4s 2m6M
Fl.G.2·5s
F.Vi.11m5M
Fl(2)R.6s
Fl(3)G.12s
Fl(3)R.12s
Darse des Mielles
Quai Amiral Kriskern
Quai de Normandie
Port de Chantereyne
F.Vi
Fl(4)R.15s
Dir.Q. 35m19M
YCC
Fl(4)G.15s
F.Vi
Dn
RoRo (Freight)
Statue of Napoleon
Grande Jetée de l'Avant Port
RoRo Terminal (Passengers)
Belfry (29) Sainte-Trinite Ch
Avant Port
CHERBOURG
Val de Saire
N
Lifting bridge
CNC
Quai Alexandre III
Bassin du Commerce
Quai de l'Entrepôt
Supermarket
Chart Datum WGS 84
Depths in metres
metres
cables
0
400
0
2

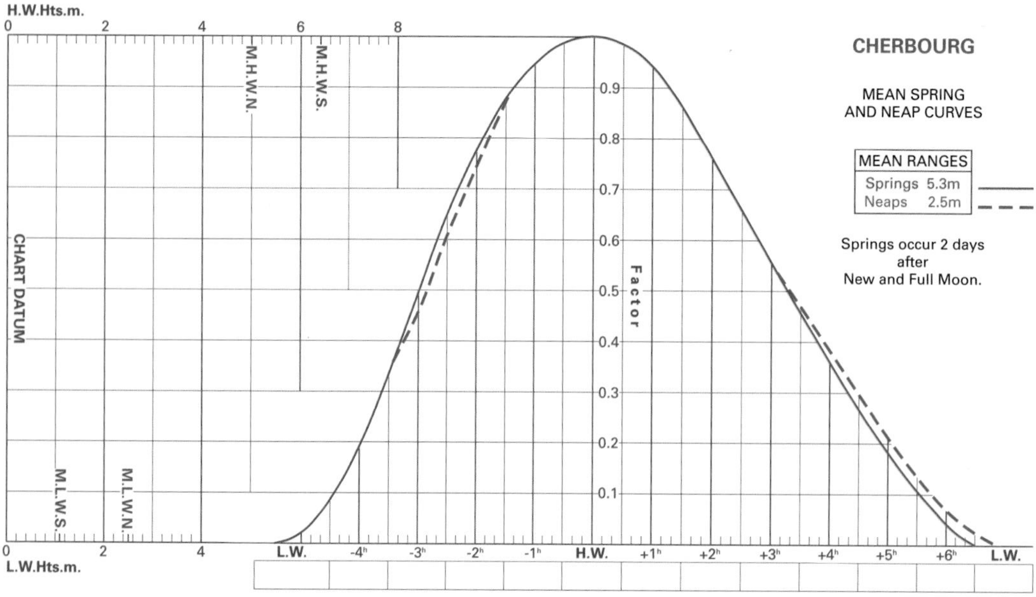
H.W.Hts.m.
0 2 4 6 8
M.H.W.N.
M.H.W.S.
CHART DATUM
M.L.W.S.
M.L.W.N.
0 2 4
L.W.Hts.m.
0.9
0.8
0.7
0.6
0.5
0.4
0.3
0.2
0.1
Factor
L.W. -4h -3h -2h -1h H.W. +1h +2h +3h +4h +5h +6h L.W.
CHERBOURG
MEAN SPRING AND NEAP CURVES
MEAN RANGES
Springs 5.3m
Neaps 2.5m
Springs occur 2 days after New and Full Moon.

9.17.31 OMONVILLE-LA-ROGUE

Manche **49°42'·28N 01°49'·86W**

CHARTS AC *2669, 1106*; SHOM 7120, 7158, 5636; ECM 528, 1014; Imray C33A; Stanfords 1, 2, 7, 16, 26.

TIDES –0330 Dover; ML 3·8; Duration 0545; Zone –0100

Standard Port CHERBOURG (⟵)

Times				Height (metres)			
High Water		Low Water		MHWS	MHWN	MLWN	MLWS
0300	1000	0400	1000	6·4	5·0	2·5	1·1
1500	2200	1600	2200				
Differences OMONVILLE							
–0010	–0010	–0015	–0015	–0·1	–0·1	0·0	0·0
GOURY							
–0100	–0040	–0105	–0120	+1·7	+1·6	+1·0	+0·3

SHELTER Good, except in moderate/fresh N to SE winds. There are 6 W conical 🅥s or ⚓ inside bkwtr; beware rks off outer end.

NAVIGATION WPT 49°42´·44N 01°48´·68W, 259°/1·0M to Omonville lt. From W or N, keep clear of Basse Bréfort (depth 1m, marked by NCM buoy, VQ) 0·6M N of Pte Jardeheu. Appr on 195° transit (below), passing 100m E of L'Étonnard and into W sector of lt before turning stbd 290° for moorings. From E, appr on 255° transit in W sector of lt, until S of L'Étonnard. To ENE of port is a military firing area; when active, a R flag is flown from the bkwtr head. Hbr ent is 100m wide: rks extend N from Omonville Fort, and ESE from bkwtr to L'Étonnard, G bn tr.

LIGHTS AND MARKS Omonville lt, Iso WRG 4s 13m 11/8M, on W framework tr with R top, vis G180°-252°, W252°-262°, R262°-287°. Lt in transit 255° with ✠ steeple (hard to see), 650m beyond, leads S of L'Étonnard. From N, L'Étonnard leads 195° in transit with fort. Street lts adequately illuminate the hbr area.

R/T None.

TELEPHONE Aff Mar 02·33·53·21·76; ⊖ 02·33·53·05·60; CROSS 02·33·52·72·13; 02·33·52·71·33; Météo 02·33·22·91·77; Auto 08.92.68.08.50; Police 02·33·52·72·02; Dr 02·33·53·08·69; Brit Consul 02.33.88.65.60.

FACILITIES Bkwtr M, L, FW, AB. **Village** 🛒, Gaz, R, Bar, showers at l'Association du Camping in village centre; nearest fuel (cans) at Beaumont-Hague 5km, ✉, Ⓑ, ⇌ (bus to Cherbourg), ✈. Ferry: See Cherbourg.

MINOR HARBOUR 2M EAST OF CAP DE LA HAGUE

ANSE DE ST MARTIN, Manche, **49°42'·72N 01°53'·78W**. AC *1106, 3653;* SHOM 7120, 5636. Tides as 9.17.31. Port Racine (said to be the smallest hbr in France) is in the SW corner of Anse de St. Martin. This bay, 2M E of Cap de la Hague, has ⚓s sheltered from all but onshore winds. From N, appr with conspic chy (279m) at atomic stn brg 175°; or from NE via Basse Bréfort NCM buoy, VQ, on with Danneville spire brg 240°. Both lines clear La Parmentière rks awash in centre of bay and Les Herbeuses and Le Grun Rks to W and E respectively. ⚓ or moor off the hbr which is obstructed by lines; landing by dinghy.

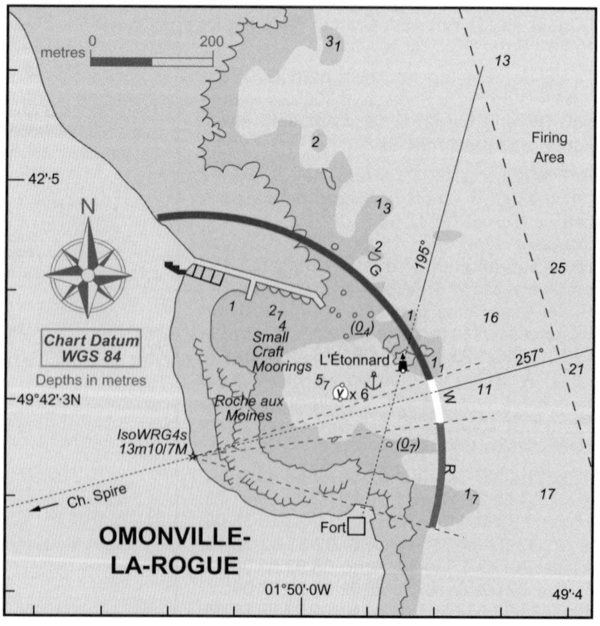
metres 0 200
Firing Area
42'·5
N
Chart Datum WGS 84
Depths in metres
49°42'·3N
Small Craft Moorings
L'Étonnard
Roche aux Moines
IsoWRG4s 13m10/7M
Ch. Spire
195°
257°
G
W
R
Fort
OMONVILLE-LA-ROGUE
01°50'·0W
49'·4

WEATHER DATA

WEATHER FORECASTS BY FAX & TELEPHONE

Coastal/Inshore	2-day by Fax	5-day by Phone
Channel Islands	-	09066 526 250
Mid Channel	09061 502 119	09066 526 241
South West	09061 502 120	09066 526 242
National (3-5 day)	09061 502 109	09066 526 234
Offshore	**2-5 day by Fax**	**2-5 day by Phone**
English Channel	09061 502 161	09066 526 251
Biscay	09061 502 164	09066 526 254

09066 CALLS COST 60P PER MIN. 09061 CALLS COST £1.50 PER MIN.

Area 18

Central North France
Cap de la Hague to St Quay-Portrieux

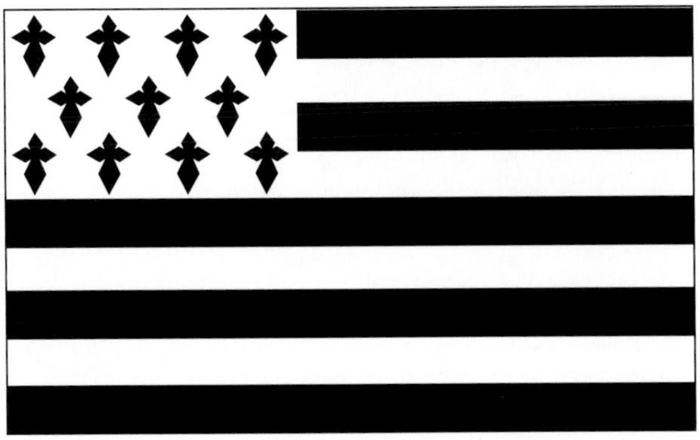

Despite Brittany becoming a Dukedom in the 10th century and being incorporated into France in 1532, the Breton Flag, Gwenn ha Du (white and black), is of modern origin, created in 1925 by Morvan Marchal.

The flag, which has white and black horizontal bands, owes much to the coat of arms of the town of Rennes, chosen as the capital of Brittany by its first Duke. The eleven ermines repeat a heraldic motif found in the flag of the Duchy 1318 and are for the Kings and Dukes who governed independent Brittany. The five black horizontal bands represent the Gallo language regions of Brittany: Rennes, Nantes, Dol, Saint Malo and Penthièvre; the white bands represent the four Breton-speaking regions, Léon, Trégor, Cornuailles and Vannes. These nine regions were the nine bishoprics.

It has taken fifty years for Morven Marchal's creation to be adopted generally in Brittany and for the rest of France to accept that Gwenn ha Du does not have political or separatist connotations.

DISTANCE TABLE

Approximate distances in nautical miles are by the most direct route, whilst avoiding dangers and allowing for Traffic Separation Schemes. Places in *italics* are in adjoining areas; places in **bold** are in 9.0.6, Cross-Channel Distances.

	1	2	3	4	5	6	7	8	9	10	11	12	13	14	15	16	17	18	19	20
1. ***Calais***	**1**																			
2. Barfleur	148	**2**																		
3. **Cherbourg**	160	20	**3**																	
4. Omonville	163	27	10	**4**																
5. Cap de la Hague	167	32	18	6	**5**															
6. *Braye (Alderney)*	172	41	25	15	9	**6**														
7. ***St Peter Port***	193	60	44	34	28	23	**7**													
8. *Creux (Sark)*	190	55	37	29	23	22	10	**8**												
9. ***St Helier***	213	77	64	51	45	46	29	24	**9**											
10. Carteret	192	55	41	29	23	28	31	23	26	**10**										
11. Portbail	196	59	49	33	27	32	35	27	25	5	**11**									
12. Iles Chausey	222	87	69	61	55	58	48	43	25	33	30	**12**								
13. Granville	227	93	75	67	61	66	55	50	30	38	35	9	**13**							
14. Dinan	250	117	102	91	85	85	66	64	50	62	59	29	35	**14**						
15. **St Malo**	238	105	90	79	73	73	54	52	38	50	47	17	23	12	**15**					
16. Dahouet	240	106	88	80	74	72	54	52	41	60	59	37	45	41	29	**16**				
17. Le Légué/St Brieuc	244	110	96	86	78	76	57	56	46	69	69	41	49	45	33	8	**17**			
18. Binic	244	115	95	84	78	75	56	55	46	70	70	43	51	45	33	10	8	**18**		
19. **St Quay-Portrieux**	244	106	88	80	74	73	56	51	46	64	64	47	54	47	35	11	7	4	**19**	
20. ***Lézardrieux***	238	106	88	80	74	68	48	38	47	68	71	53	54	61	49	33	32	30	21	**20**

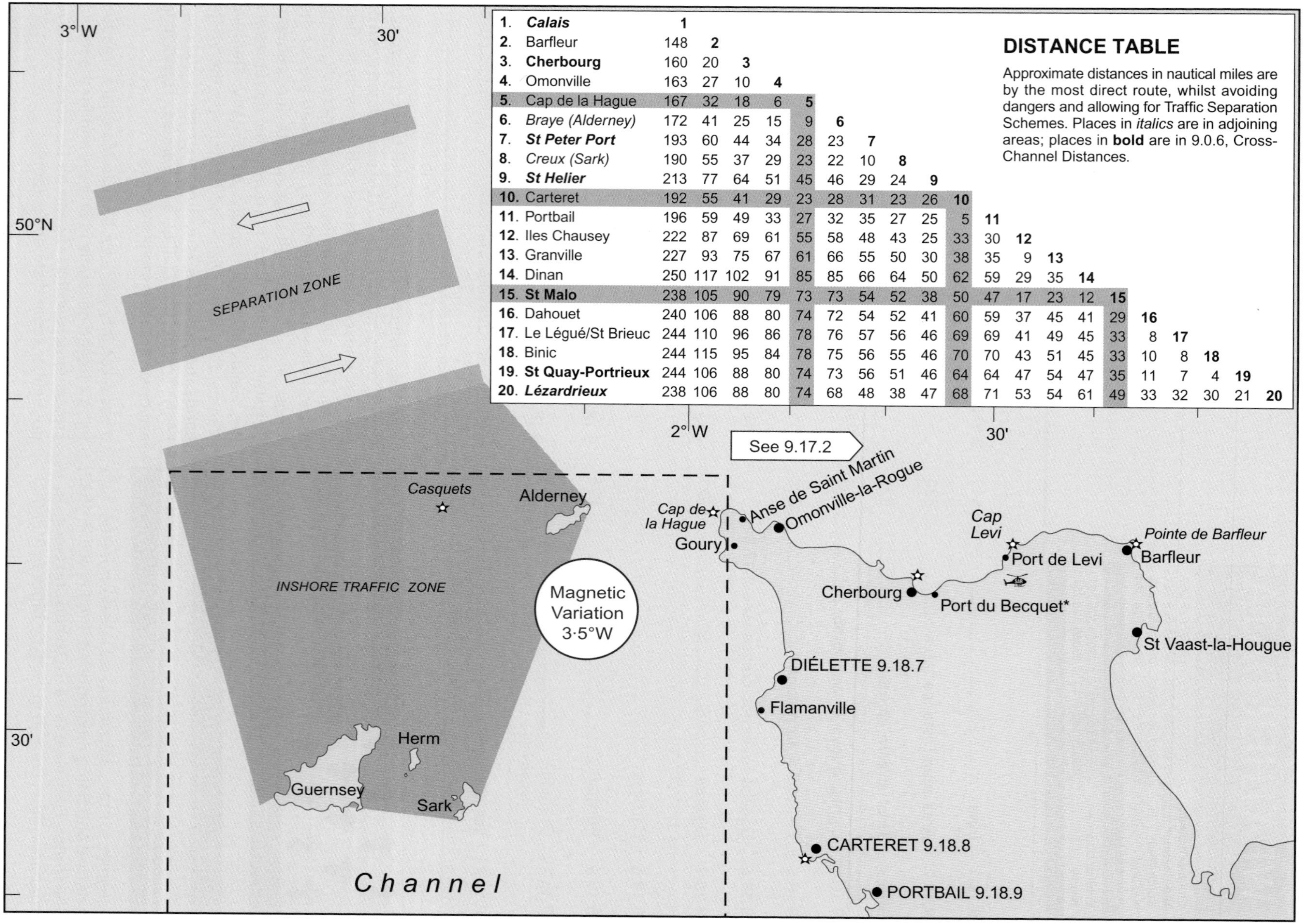

3°W
30'
2°W
30'
50°N
30'
SEPARATION ZONE
INSHORE TRAFFIC ZONE
See 9.17.2
Casquets
Alderney
Magnetic Variation 3·5°W
Herm
Guernsey
Sark
Channel
Cap de la Hague
Goury
Anse de Saint Martin
Omonville-la-Rogue
Cherbourg
Port du Becquet*
Cap Levi
Port de Levi
Pointe de Barfleur
Barfleur
St Vaast-la-Hougue
DIÉLETTE 9.18.7
Flamanville
CARTERET 9.18.8
PORTBAIL 9.18.9

18

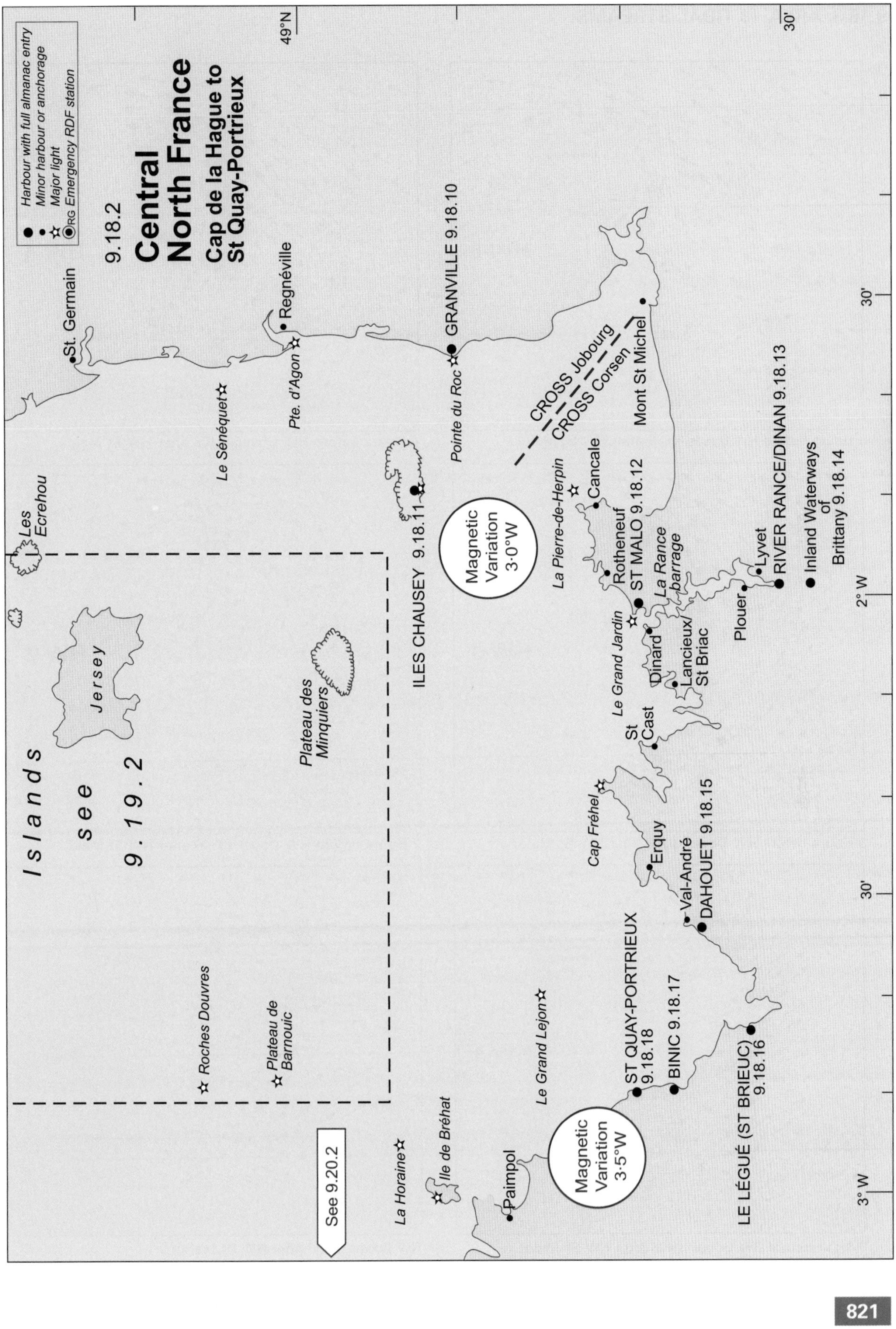

9.18.2
Central North France
Cap de la Hague to St Quay-Portrieux
Harbour with full almanac entry
Minor harbour or anchorage
Major light
RG Emergency RDF station
49°N
30'
3° W
2° W
St. Germain
Regnéville
Pte. d'Agon
Le Sénéquet
GRANVILLE 9.18.10
Pointe du Roc
CROSS Jobourg
CROSS Corsen
Mont St Michel
Les Ecrehou
Jersey
Islands see 9.19.2
Plateau des Minquiers
ILES CHAUSEY 9.18.11
Magnetic Variation 3·0°W
La Pierre-de-Herpin
Cancale
Rotheneuf
ST MALO 9.18.12
La Rance barrage
Le Grand Jardin
Dinard
Lancieux/St Briac
Plouer
Lyvet
RIVER RANCE/DINAN 9.18.13
Inland Waterways of Brittany 9.18.14
St Cast
Cap Fréhel
Erquy
Val-André
DAHOUET 9.18.15
Roches Douvres
Plateau de Barnouic
Le Grand Lejon
ST QUAY-PORTRIEUX 9.18.18
BINIC 9.18.17
LE LÉGUÉ (ST BRIEUC) 9.18.16
Magnetic Variation 3·5°W
La Horaine
Ile de Bréhat
Paimpol
See 9.20.2

9.18.3 AREA 18 TIDAL STREAMS

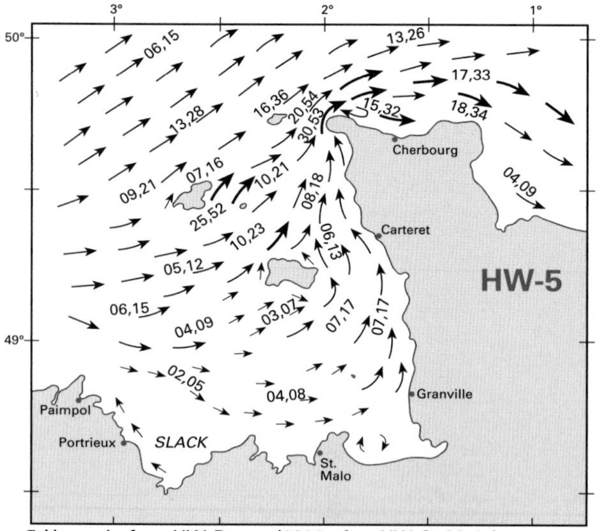
3°
2°
1°
50°
49°
06,15
13,26
17,33
13,28
16,36
20,54
30,53
15,32
18,34
Cherbourg
09,21
07,16
10,21
08,18
04,09
25,52
10,23
Carteret
05,12
06,13
HW-5
06,15
04,09
03,07
07,17
07,17
02,05
04,08
Granville
Paimpol
Portrieux
SLACK
St. Malo

5 Hours before HW Dover (0006 after HW St Malo)

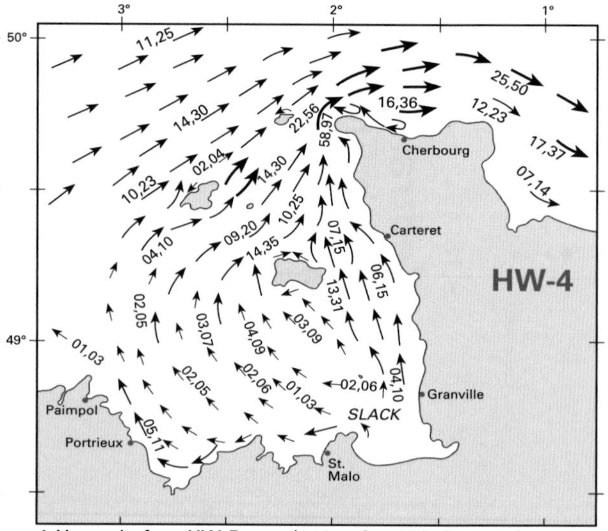
3°
2°
1°
50°
49°
11,25
25,50
14,30
22,56
16,36
12,23
58,97
Cherbourg
17,37
10,23
02,04
14,30
07,14
10,25
Carteret
04,10
09,20
14,35
07,15
HW-4
02,05
03,07
04,09
03,09
13,31
06,15
01,03
02,05
02,06
01,03
02,06
04,10
Granville
Paimpol
SLACK
Portrieux
05,11
St. Malo

4 Hours before HW Dover (0106 after HW St Malo)

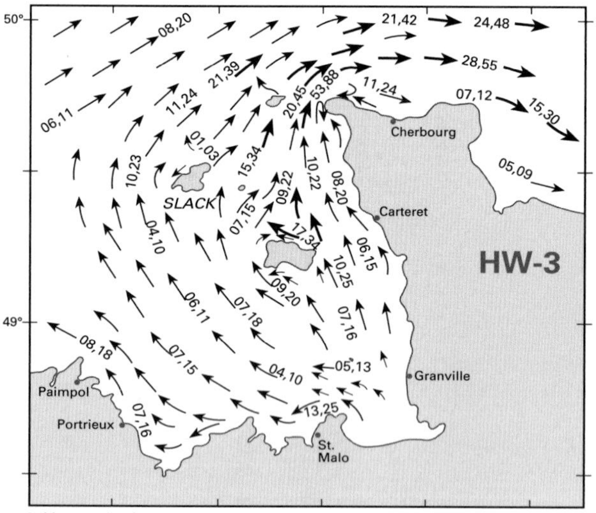
50°
49°
08,20
21,42
24,48
28,55
21,39
06,11
11,24
20,45
53,88
11,24
07,12
15,30
Cherbourg
01,03
15,34
10,23
05,09
09,22
10,22
08,20
SLACK
07,15
Carteret
04,10
17,34
06,15
10,25
HW-3
09,20
06,11
07,18
07,16
08,18
07,15
04,10
05,13
Granville
Paimpol
13,25
Portrieux
07,16
St. Malo

3 Hours before HW Dover (0206 after HW St Malo)

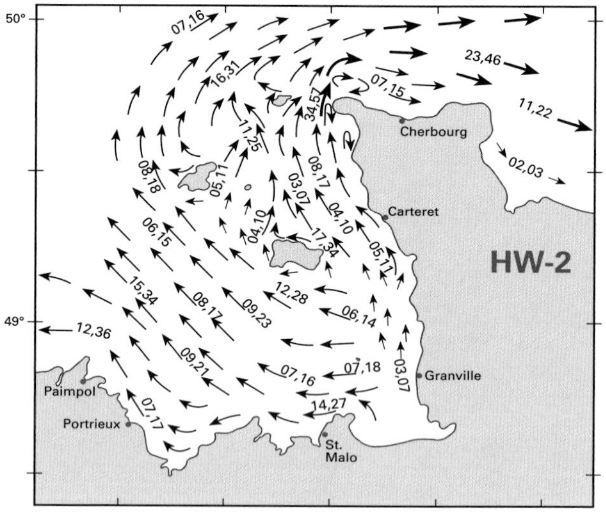
50°
49°
07,16
16,31
23,46
34,57
07,15
11,22
11,25
Cherbourg
08,18
05,11
08,17
02,03
03,07
04,10
Carteret
06,15
04,10
17,34
05,11
HW-2
12,28
15,34
08,17
09,23
06,14
12,36
09,21
07,16
07,18
03,07
Granville
Paimpol
14,27
07,17
Portrieux
St. Malo

2 Hours before HW Dover (0306 after HW St Malo)

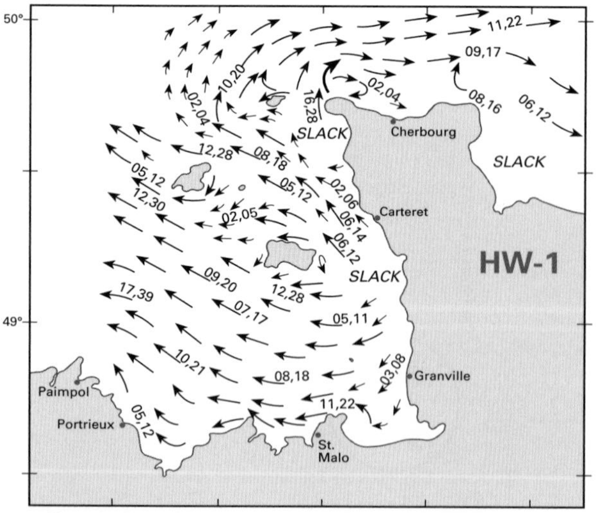
50°
49°
11,22
09,17
10,20
02,04
08,16
06,12
02,04
16,28
Cherbourg
SLACK
SLACK
12,28
08,18
05,12
05,12
12,30
02,06
02,05
Carteret
06,14
06,12
SLACK
HW-1
09,20
17,39
12,28
07,17
05,11
10,21
03,08
08,18
Granville
Paimpol
11,22
Portrieux
05,12
St. Malo

1 Hour before HW Dover (0406 after HW St Malo)

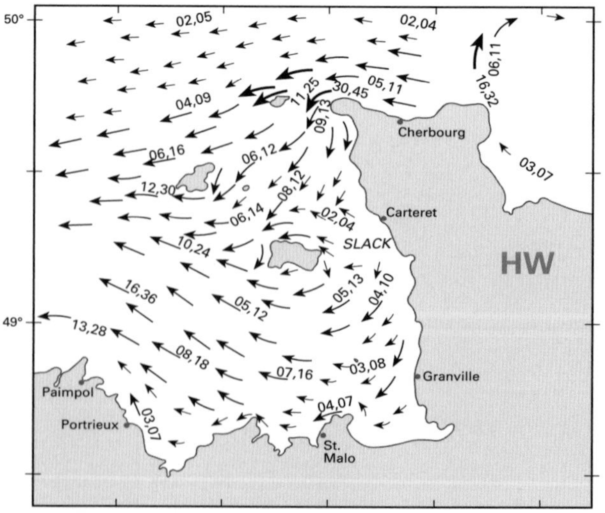
50°
49°
02,05
02,04
06,11
16,32
11,25
30,45
05,11
04,09
09,13
Cherbourg
06,16
06,12
03,07
12,30
08,12
06,14
02,04
Carteret
10,24
SLACK
HW
05,13
04,10
16,36
05,12
13,28
08,18
07,16
03,08
Granville
Paimpol
04,07
Portrieux
03,07
St. Malo

HW Dover (0506 after HW St Malo)

Westward 9.20.3 Channel Islands 9.19.3 Eastward 9.17.3 Northward 9.2.3

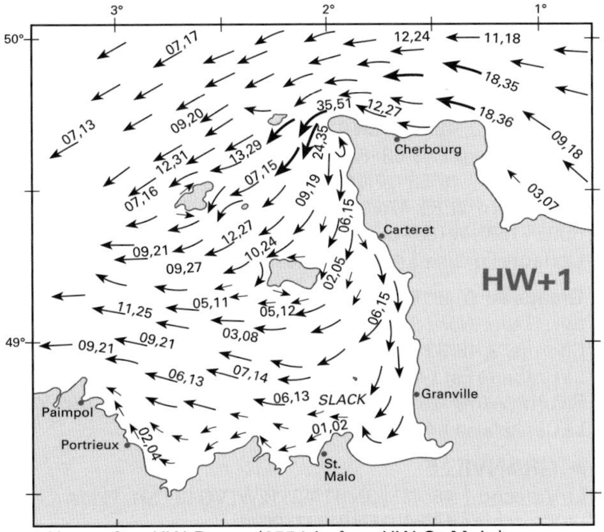
3°
2°
1°
50°
49°
HW+1
Cherbourg
Carteret
Granville
Paimpol
Portrieux
St. Malo
SLACK
12,24
11,18
07,17
18,35
18,36
35,51
12,27
09,20
07,13
09,18
13,29
24,35
12,31
07,15
03,07
07,16
09,19
06,15
12,27
09,21
10,24
09,27
02,05
06,15
05,11
11,25
05,12
03,08
09,21
09,21
06,13
07,14
06,13
01,02
02,04

1 Hour after HW Dover (0554 before HW St Malo)

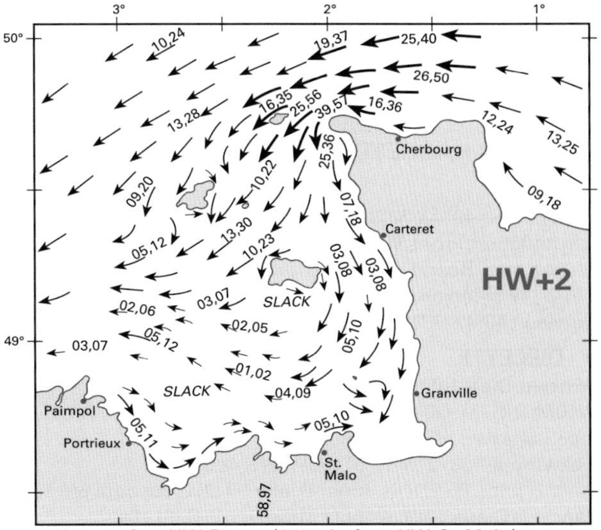
3°
2°
1°
50°
49°
HW+2
Cherbourg
Carteret
Granville
Paimpol
Portrieux
St. Malo
SLACK
SLACK
10,24
19,37
25,40
26,50
16,35
25,56
39,51
16,36
12,24
13,28
13,25
25,36
10,22
09,18
09,20
07,18
13,30
05,12
10,23
03,08
03,08
02,06
03,07
02,05
05,10
05,12
03,07
01,02
04,09
05,10
05,11
58,97

2 Hours after HW Dover (0454 before HW St Malo)

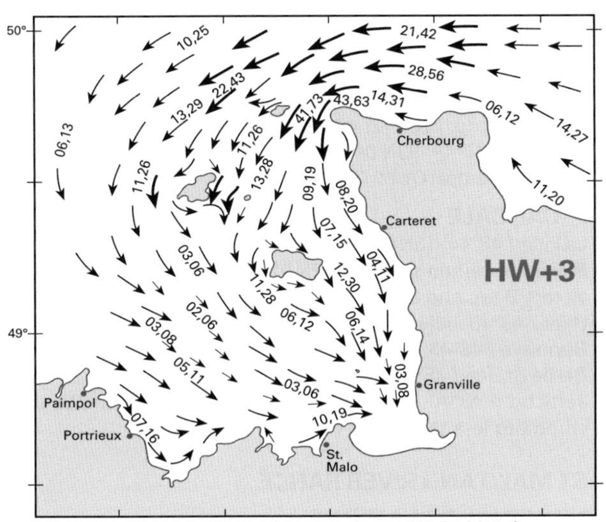
50°
49°
HW+3
Cherbourg
Carteret
Granville
Paimpol
Portrieux
St. Malo
10,25
21,42
28,56
22,43
43,63
14,31
13,29
41,73
06,12
14,27
06,13
11,26
11,26
13,28
09,19
08,20
11,20
07,15
03,06
04,11
11,28
12,30
02,06
06,12
03,08
06,14
05,11
03,06
03,08
07,16
10,19

3 Hours after HW Dover (0354 before HW St Malo)

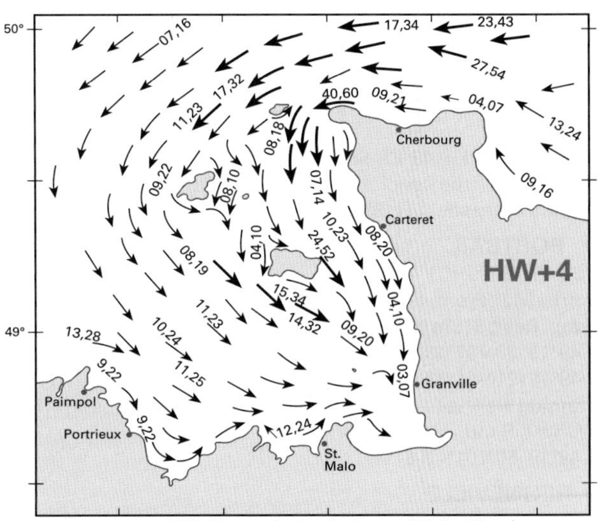
50°
49°
HW+4
Cherbourg
Carteret
Granville
Paimpol
Portrieux
St. Malo
07,16
17,34
23,43
27,54
17,32
40,60
09,21
04,07
11,23
08,18
13,24
09,22
08,10
07,14
09,16
10,23
08,20
04,10
24,52
08,19
15,34
04,10
11,23
14,32
09,20
13,28
10,24
03,07
9,22
11,25
9,22
12,24

4 Hours after HW Dover (0254 before HW St Malo)

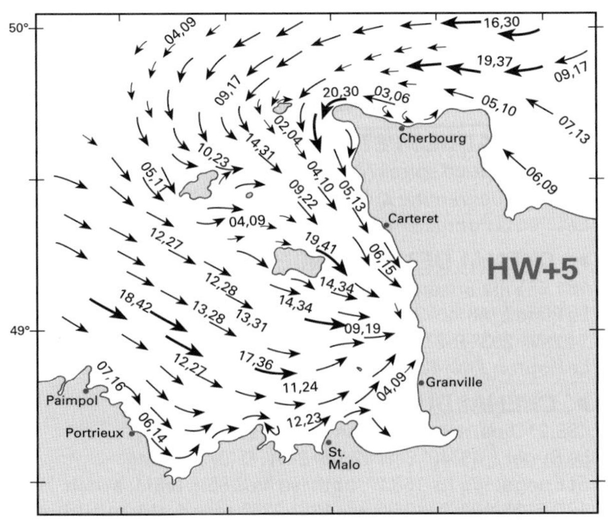
50°
49°
HW+5
Cherbourg
Carteret
Granville
Paimpol
Portrieux
St. Malo
04,09
16,30
19,37
09,17
20,30
03,06
09,17
05,10
07,13
02,04
14,31
10,23
04,10
05,13
06,09
05,17
09,22
04,09
12,27
19,41
06,15
12,28
14,34
14,34
18,42
13,28
13,31
09,19
17,36
12,27
11,24
04,09
07,16
12,23
06,14

5 Hours after HW Dover (0154 before HW St Malo)

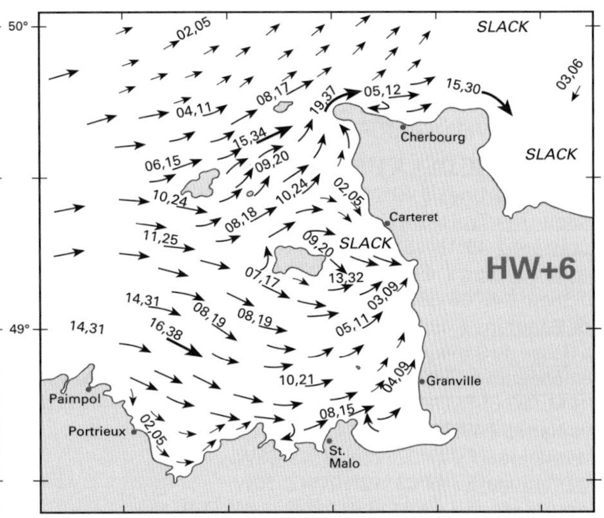
50°
49°
HW+6
Cherbourg
Carteret
Granville
Paimpol
Portrieux
St. Malo
SLACK
SLACK
SLACK
02,05
03,06
08,17
19,37
05,12
15,30
04,11
15,34
06,15
09,20
10,24
10,24
02,05
08,18
11,25
09,20
07,17
13,32
14,31
08,19
08,19
03,09
14,31
16,38
05,11
10,21
04,09
08,15
02,05

6 Hours after HW Dover (0054 before HW St Malo)

PLOT WAYPOINTS ON YOUR CHART BEFORE USING THEM

9.18.4 LIGHTS, BUOYS AND WAYPOINTS

Blue print = light with a nominal range of 15M or more. CAPITALS = place or feature. *CAPITAL ITALICS* = light-vessel, light float or Lanby. *Italics* = Fog signal. ***Bold italics*** = Racon. Useful waypoints are underlined. Abbreviations are in Chapter 1. Positions are referenced to the WGS 84 datum.

CAP DE LA HAGUE TO ST MALO

▶ GOURY

La Foraine 49°42'·89 N 01°58'·33W, VQ (9) 10s 12m 6M.
Ldg lts 065·2°: Front, 49°42'·88N 01°56'·71W, QR 5m 7M; R □ in W □ on pier. Rear, 116m from front, Q 11m 7M; intens 056·2°-074·2°; W pylon on hut.
Hervieu 49°42'·77N 01°56'·94W.

▶ DIELETTE

W bkwtr Dir lt 140°, 49°33'·17N 01°51'·84W. Iso WRG 4s 12m W10M, R/G7M; G070°-135°, W135°-145°, R145°-180°; W twr, G top. Same twr: Fl G 4s 6m 2M; 115°-358°.
E bkwtr 49°33'·21N 01°51'·80W, Fl R 4s 6m 2M.
Inner N jetty, Fl (2) R 6s. Inner S jetty, Fl (2) G 6s; both 6m 1M.
Banc des Dious 49°32'·56N 01°54'·03W, Q (9) 15s.

▶ CARTERET

Cap de Carteret ☆ 49°22'·40N 01°48'·44W, Fl (2+1) 15s 81m **26M**; Gy twr, G top.
W bkwtr 49°22'·13N 01°47'·40W, Oc R 4s 7m 7M; W post, R top.
E training wall 49°22'·18N 01°47'·32W, Fl G 2·5s 4m 2M; W post, G top.
Channel bend 49°22'·58N 01°47'·20W, Fl (2)R 6s 5m 1M; R pylon. Inside the bend: Fl (2)G 6s 5m 1M; G pylon.
Marina entry sill: Fl (3) R 12s and Fl (3) G 12s; R & G pylons.

▶ PORTBAIL

PB 49°18'·39N 01°44'·76W.
Ldg lts 042°: Front, 49°19'·74N 01°42'·51W, Q 14m 10M; W pylon, R top. Rear, 870m from front, Oc 4s 20m 10M; stubby ch spire.
49°19'·30N 01°43'·36W.
49°19'·21N 01°43'·00W.
Training wall head 49°19'·43N 01°43'·01W, Q (2) R 5s 5m 1M; W mast, R top.
49°19'·50N 01°42'·87W.

▶ REGNÉVILLE

La Catheue 48°57'·78N 01°42'·10W, Q (6) + L Fl 15s.
Le Ronquet 49°00'·09N 01°38'·09W, Fl (2) WR 6s, W6M, R4M; R100°-293°, W293°-100°.
Pte d'Agon 49°00'·16N 01°34'·71W, Oc (2) WR 6s 12m, W10M, R7M; R063°-110°, W110°-063°; W twr, R top, W dwelling.
Dir lt 028°. 49°00'·67N 01°33'·38W, Oc WRG 4s 9m, W12M, R/G9M; G024°-027°, W027°-029°, R029°-033°; house.

▶ PASSAGE DE LA DÉROUTE

Les Trois-Grunes 49°21'·82N 01°55'·21W, Q (9) 15s.
Plateau des Trois-Grunes 49°21'·76N 01°55'·01W; *Bell*.
Écrévière 49°15'·25N 01°52'·17W, Q (6) + L Fl 15s; *Bell*.
Basse Jourdan 49°06'·83N 01°44'·16W, Q (3) 10s; *Whis*.
Le Boeuf 49°06'·53N 01°47'·18W.
Les Boeuftins 49°06'·82N 01°45'·97W.
La Basse du Sénéquet 49°05'·95N 01°41'·22W.
Le Sénéquet 49°05'·47N 01°39'·75W, Fl (3) WR 12s 18m W13M, R10M; 083·5°-R-116·5°-W-083·5°; W twr.
Les Nattes 49°03'·52N 01°41'·87W; *Bell*.
International F 49°02'·25N 01°43'·03W.
International E 49°02'·12N 01°47'·20W.
Basse le Marié 49°01'·83N 01°48'·84W, Q (9) 15s.
NE Minquiers 49°00'·84N 01°55'·31W, VQ (3) 5s; *Bell*.
Les Ardentes 48°57'·77N 01°51'·64W, Q (3) 10s.
SE Minquiers 48°53'·43N 02°00'·10W, Q (3) 10s; *Bell*.
S Minquiers 48°53'·07N 02°10'·11W, Q (6) + L Fl 15s.

▶ ÎLES CHAUSEY

La Petite Entrée 48°54'·53N 01°49'·59W.
L'Enseigne, W twr, B top; 48°53'·73N 01°50'·27W.
L'Etat, BW, 48°53'·73N 01°50'·27W.
Anvers wreck 48°53'·88N 01°41'·08W.
Le Founet 48°53'·27N 01°42'·33W, Q (3) 10s.
Le Pignon 48°53'·47N 01°43'·40W, Fl (2) WR 6s 10m, W9M, R6M; R005°-150°, W150°-005°; B twr, W band.
La Haute Foraine 48°52'·89N 01°43'·70W.

Grande Île ☆ 48° 52'·17N 01°49'·36W, Fl 5s 39m **23M**; Gy □ twr, G top; *Horn 30s*.
Channel 48°52'·12N 01°49'·09W, Fl G 2s.
La Crabière Est 48°52'·47N 01°49'·41W, Oc WRG 4s 5m, W9M, R/G 6M; W079°-291°, G291°-329°, W329°-335°, R335°-079°; Y twr.
La Cancalaise 48°51'·92N 01°51'·16W.

▶ GRANVILLE

Le Videcoq 48°49'·63N 01°42'·12W, VQ (9) 10s; *Whis*.
La Fourchie 48°50'·15N 01°37'·00W.
Pointe du Roc ☆ 48°50'·06N 01°36'·78W, Fl (4) 15s 49m **23M**.
Le Loup 48°49'·57N 01°36'·25W, Fl (2) 6s 8m 11M.
Avant Port, E jetty 48°49'·93N 01°36'·19W. Fl G 2·5s 11m 4M.
W jetty 48°49'·86N 01°36'·23W, Fl R 2·5s 12m 4M.
Marina S bkwtr 48°49'·89N 01°35'·90W, Fl (2) R 6s 12m 5M; W post, R top; *Horn (2) 40s*.
N bkwtr 48°49'·93N 01°35'·90W, Fl (2) G 6s 4m 5M.
Sill, E & W sides: Oc (2) G 6s & Oc (2) R 6s, G & R topped pylons.

▶ CANCALE

La Fille 48°44'·13N 01°48'·48W.
Pierre-de-Herpin ☆ 48°43'·77N 01°48'·92W, Oc (2) 6s 20m **17M**; W twr, B top and base; *Siren Mo (N) 60s*.
Ruet 48°43'·38N 01°50'·15W; *Bell*.
Bunouye 48°43'·38N 01°50'·15W.
Barbe Brûlée 48°42'·11N 01°50'·57W.
Jetty hd 48°40'·08N 01°51'·14W, Oc (3) G 12s 12m 7M; obsc when brg less than 223°; W pylon, G top, G hut.

ST MALO AND RIVER RANCE

▶ CHENAL DE LA BIGNE

Basse Rochefort (Basse aux Chiens) 48°42'·63N 01°57'·46W.
La Petite Bigne 48°41'·66N 01°58'·73W.
Les Létruns 48°40'·72N 02°00'·54W; *Bell*.
Roches-aux-Anglais 48°39'·65N 02°02'·27W, Fl G 4s.
Les Crapauds-du-Bey 48°39'·37N 02°02'·56W, Fl R 4s.

▶ CHENAL DES PETITS POINTUS

203° Dinard ch spire (74m) to right of Le Petit Bey.
La Saint-Servantine 48°41'·92N 02°00'·94W; Fl G 2·5s; *Bell*.
Les Petits Pontus 48°41'·36N 02°00'·71W.

▶ CHENAL DE LA GRANDE CONCHÉE

181.5° Villa Brisemoulin on with LH edge of Le Petit Bey.
La Plate 48°40'·78N 02°01'·91W. Q WRG 11m, W10M, R/G7M; 140°-W-203°-R-210°-W-225°-G-140°.
Le Bouton 48°40'·59N 02°01'·85W.

▶ CHENAL DU BUNEL

158.2° Dinard water twr on with St Enogat lts.
Le Bunel 48°40'·84N 02°05'·28W, Q (9) 15s; *Bell*.
St Enogat ldg lts 158.2°; both Iso 4s 3/85m 6/8M, synch. Front 48°38'·35N 02°04'·03W, vis 126°-236°; rear, 1.4M from front, on water twr; vis 143°-210°.

▶ CHENAL DE LA PETITE PORTE

Vieux-Banc E 48°42'·38N 02°09'·12W, Q; *Bell.*
Vieux-Banc W 48°41'·83N 02°10'·20W, VQ (9) 10s.
St Malo Fairway 48°41'·38N 02°07'·28W, Iso 4s; *Whis.*
Ldg lts 128·7°, both Dir FG 20/69m **22/25M**; H24. Front, **Les Bas Sablons** ☆ 48°38'·42N 02°01'·70W, intens 127·2°-130·2°; W□twr, B top. Rear, **La Balue** ☆, 0·9M from front; intens 128°-129·5°; Gy □ twr.
Les Courtis 48°40'·46N 02°05'·82W, Fl G 4s 14m 7M.
Le Sou 48°40'·11N 02°05'·30W, VQ (3) 5s; *Bell.*

▶ CHENAL DE LA GRANDE PORTE

Banchenou 48°40'·44N 02°11'·48W, Fl (5) G 20s.
Buharats W No. 2 48°40'·22N 02°07'·49W, Fl R 4s; *Whis.*
Buharats E No. 4 48°40'·23N 02°07'·20W; *Bell.*
Bas du Boujaron No. 1 48°40'·16N 02°05'·97W, Fl (2) G 6s; *Whis.*
Ldg lts 089·1°: **Front, Le Grand Jardin** ☆ 48°40'·19N 02°04'·98W, Fl (2) R 10s 24m **15M**. Rear, **Rochebonne** ☆ 48°40'·32N 01°58'·61W, Dir FR 40m **24M**; intens 088·2°-089·7°; Gy□twr, R top, 4·2M from front.
Basse du Nord No. 5 48°39'·98N 02°05'·04W.
Les Pierres-Garnier No. 8 48°39'·98N 02°04'·41W.
Les Patouillets 48°39'·68N 02°04'·30W, Fl (3) G 12s.
Clef d'Aval No. 10 48°39'·72N 02°03'·91W.
Basse du Buron No. 12 48°39'·41N 02°03'·51W, Fl (4) R 15s.
Le Buron 48°39'·32N 02°03'·66W, Fl (4) G 15s 15m 7M; G twr.
48°39'·16N 02°03'·03W, VQ (6) + L Fl 10s.

▶ RADE DE ST MALO

Plateau Rance Nord 48°38'·64N 02°02'·35W, VQ.
Plateau Rance Sud 48°38'·43N 02°02'·28W Q (6) + L Fl 15s.
Crapaud de la Cité 48°38'·34N 02°02'·00W, QG.

▶ ST MALO

Môle des Noires hd ☆ 48°38'·52N 02°01'·91W, Fl R 5s 11m 13M; W twr, R top; *Horn (2) 20s.*
Écluse du Naye ldg lts 070·4°, both FR 7/23m 3/7M. Front, 48°38'·61N 02°01'·36W. Rear, 030°-120°.
Ferry jetty, ☆ 48°38'·44N 02°01'·76W, Fl R 4s 3m 1M; 080°-260°.
Bas-Sablons marina, mole head ☆ 48°38'·41N 02°01'·70W, Fl G 4s 7m 5M; Gy mast.

▶ LA RANCE BARRAGE

La Jument Fl G 4s 6m 4M; G twr, 48°37'·44N 02°01'·76W.
ZI 12 Fl R 4s, 48°37'·47N 02°01'·62W.
NE dolphin ☆ Fl (2) R 6s 6m 5M; 040°-200°, 48°37'·09N 02°01'·71W.
Barrage lock, NW wall ☆ Fl (2) G 6s 6m 5M, 191°-291°; G pylon, 48°37'·06N 02°01'·73W.
Barrage lock, SW wall, ☆ Fl (3) G 12s, 48°37'·00N 02°01'·70W.
SE dolphin ☆ Fl (3) R 12s, 48°36'·97N 02°01'·66W.
ZI 24 Fl (2) R 6s, 48°36'·63N 02°01'·33W.

ST MALO TO SAINT QUAY-PORTRIEUX

▶ ST BRIAC

R. Frémur mouth. Dir lt 125°, 48°37'·07N 02°08'·20W, Iso WRG 4s 10m, W13M, R/G11M; 121·5°-G-124·5°-W-125·5°-R-129·5°; W mast on hut.

▶ ST CAST

Les Bourdinots 48°39'·00N 02°13'·50W.
St Cast môle ☆ 48°38'·40N 02°14'·63W, Iso WG 4s 11m, W11M, G8M; 204°-W-217°-G-233°-W-245°-G-204°; G & W structure.

Cap Fréhel ☆ 48°41'·04N 02°19'·15W Fl (2) 10s 85m **29M**; Gy □ twr, G lantern; *Horn (2) 60s.*
Les Landas 48°41'·42N 02°31'·30W, Q.

▶ CHENAL & PORT D'ERQUY

Les Justières 48°40'·56N 02°26'·49W, Q (6) + L Fl 15s.
Basses du Courant 48°39'·21N 02°29'·17W, VQ (6) + L Fl 10s.
Les Chatelets 48°38'·96N 02°28'·99W.
L'Evette 48°38'·50N 02°31'·46W.
S môle ☆ 48°38'·06N 02°28'·66W, Oc (2+1) WRG 12s 11m W11M, R/G8M; 055°-R-081°-W-094°-G-111°-W-120°-R-134°; W twr.
Inner jetty ☆ 48°38'·09N 02°28'·39W, Fl R 2·5s 10m 3M; R & W twr.
Petit Bignon 48°36'·82N 02°35'·06W.

▶ DAHOUET

Le Dahouet 48°35'·14N 02°35'·45W.
La Petite Muette 48°34'·82N 02°34'·31W, Fl WRG 4s 10m W9M, R/G6M; 055°-G-114°-W-146°-R-196°; W twr, G band.
Entry chan, 48°34'·71N 02°34'·21W, Fl (2) G 6s 5m 1M; 156°-286°.

▶ BAIE DE SAINT BRIEUC

Grand Léjon ☆ 48°44'·90N 02°39'·87W. Fl (5) WR 20s 17m **W18M**, R14M; 015°-R-058°-W-283°-R-350°-W-015°; R twr, W bands.
Le Rohein 48°38'·80N 02°37'·77W, VQ (9) WRG 10s 13m, W10M, R/G7M; 072°-R-105°-W-180°-G-193°-W-237°-G-282°-W-301°-G-330°-W-072°; Y twr, B band.

▶ LE LÉGUÉ

Tra-Hillion 48°33'·38N 02°38'·52W.
Le Légué 48°34'·32N 02°41'·16W, Mo (A)10s; *Whis.*
No. 1 48°32'·42N 02°42'·51W, Fl G 2·5s.
No. 2 48°32'·37N 02°42'·40W, Fl R 2·5s.
No. 1 bis 48°32'·36N 02°42'·78W, Fl (2) G 6s.
No. 2 bis 48°32'·27N 02°42'·71W, Fl (2) R 6s.
No. 3 48°32'·16N 02°42'·95W, Fl (3) G 12s.
No. 2 ter 48°32'·13N 02°42'·90W, Fl (3) R 12s.
NE jetty ☆ 48°32'·18N 02°42'·80W, VQ R 4M.
Pointe à l'Aigle jetty ☆ 48°32'·12N 02°43'·12W, VQ G 13m 8M; 160°-070°; W twr, G top.
Custom House jetty ☆ 48°31'·90N 02°43'·43W, Iso G 4s 6m 2M; W cols, G top.

▶ BINIC

N môle ☆ 48°36'·06N 02°48'·93W, Oc (3) 12s 12m 11M; unintens 020°-110°; W twr, G lantern.

▶ SAINT QUAY-PORTRIEUX

Les Hors 48°39'·60N 02°44'·04W; *Bell.*
Caffa 48°37'·81N 02°43'·09W, Q (3) 10s.
La Longue 48°37'·89N 02°44'·69W.
La Roselière 48°37'·46N 02°46'·41W, VQ (9) 10s.
Herflux, 48°39'·06N 02°47'·95W. Dir ☆ 130°, Fl (2) WRG 6s 10m, W8M, R/G 6M; G115°-125°, W125°-135°, R135°-145°.
Île Harbour (Roches de Saint-Quay) ☆ 48°39'·99N 02°48'·50W, Oc (2) WRG 6s 16m, W10M, R/G 8M; 011°-R-133°-G-270°-R-306°-G-358°-W-011°; W twr & dwelling, R top.
Madeux 48°40'·40N 02°48'·82W.
Grandes Moulières de St Quay 48°39'·83N 02°49'·82W.
Moulières de Portrieux 48°39'·25N 02°49'·21W.
Les Noirs 48°39'·09N 02°48·46W.
Marina, **NE mole elbow**, 48°38'·99N 02°49'·09W, Dir lt 318·2°: Iso WRG 4s 16m **W15M**, R/G11M; W159°-179°, G179°-316°, W316°-320·5°, R320·5°-159°; Reserve lt ranges 11/8M.
NE môle hd ☆ 48°38'·84N 02°48'·92W, Fl (3) G 12s 10m 2M.
S môle hd ☆ 48°38'·83N 02°49'·03W, Fl (3) R 12s 10m 2M.
Old hbr ent: N side, 48°38'·77N 02°49'·28W, Fl G 2.5s 11m 2M.
S side, 48°38'·72N 02°49'·27W, Fl R 2.5s 8m 2M.

9.18.5 PASSAGE INFORMATION

Current Pilots for this area include: *North Brittany and CI Cruising Companion* (Nautical Data Ltd/Cumberlidge); *The Channel Cruising Companion* (Nautical Data Ltd/ Featherstone & Aslett); Admiralty *Channel Pilot* (NP 27). See also 9.19.5 for passages between the Channel Islands and the adjacent French coast.

CAP DE LA HAGUE TO ST MALO (charts *3653, 3655*, 3656, *3659*) The W coast of the Cotentin Peninsula is exposed and often a lee shore. N of Carteret it is mostly rky. Southward to Mont St Michel and W to St Malo the coast changes to extensive offshore shoals, sand dunes studded with rks and a series of drying hbrs; there is little depth of water, so that a nasty sea can build. Boats which can take the ground are better for exploring the shallower hbrs. Avoid lobster pots, and oyster and mussel beds in some rivers and bays.

▶*The sea areas around this coast, including the Channel Islands (9.19.5), are dominated by powerful tidal streams with an anti-clockwise rotational pattern and a very large tidal range. Between C. de la Hague and Alderney the main English Channel tidal streams are rectilinear NE/SW. Neap tides are best, particularly for a first visit, and tidal streams need to be worked carefully. The Admiralty tidal stream atlas NP 264 covers the French coast and Channel Islands. More detailed coverage is given in SHOM 562-UJA.*◀

Cap de La Hague is low-lying, but the ground soon rises to the south. The high chimneys (279m, R lts) of the Jobourg nuclear re-processing plant are conspic 3·7M SE. CROSS Jobourg radar surveillance station is adjacent. 5M S of Cap de la Hague beware Les Huquets de Jobourg, an extensive unmarked bank of drying (2·1m) and submerged rks, and Les Huquets de Vauville (5·4m) close SE of them.

The drying hbrs at Goury, Diélette (9.18.7), Carteret (9.18.8) and Portbail (9.18.9) are more readily accessible if cruising from S to N on the flood.There are non-tidal marinas at Diélette and Carteret. The former has H24 access for 1·5m draught if coefficient is >80.

Two coastwise chans are Déroute de Terre and, further offshore, Passage de la Déroute. Both are poorly marked in places and are not advised at night. The former (not shown on Admiralty charts) passes between: Plateau des Trois Grunes and Carteret; Basses de Portbail and Bancs Félés; Le Sénéquet lt and Chaussée de Boeufs. The S end of this chan, between Granville (9.18.10) and Îles Chausey, is shallow (<1m in places); for detailed directions see *Channel Pilot*.

The Passage de la Déroute passes W of Plateau des Trois Grunes; between Basses de Taillepied and Les Écrehou; Chaussée des Boeufs and Plateau de l'Arconie; E of Les Minquiers and SE of Les Ardentes; and NW of Îles Chausey (9.18.11) where it is known as Entrée de la Déroute. It is sometimes used by ferries from St Malo to the UK.

6M S of Granville is the drying expanse of Baie du Mont St Michel which should not be visited by sea. Proceeding W, the drying hbr of Cancale lies 4M S of Pte du Grouin. There are many oyster beds and a fair weather anch SE of Île des Rimains, N of which the many dangers are marked by La Pierre-de-Herpin (lt, fog sig). The large drying inlet of Rothéneuf, with anch off in good weather, is 4M NE of St Malo (9.18.12 and chart 2700).

ST MALO TO L'OST PIC (charts *3659, 3674*)

In the apprs to St Malo are many islets, rks and shoals, between which are several chans that can be used in good vis. Tidal streams reach 4kn at sp, and can set across chans. From E and N, with sufficient rise of tide, Chenal de la Bigne, Chenal des Petits Pointus or Chenal de la Grande Conchée can be used, but they all pass over or near to shoal and drying patches. From the W and NW, Chenal de la Grande Porte and Chenal de la Petite Porte are the principal routes and are well marked/lit. Chenal du Décollé is a shallow, ill-marked inshore route from the W, and no shorter than Chenal de la Grande Porte. Both marinas at St Malo have tidal restrictions due to either a lock or a sill. Dinard has a small basin 2·0m which is usually full of local boats, but it is pleasant to visit by ferry.

By locking through the R. Rance barrage (9.18.13 and SHOM 4233) one can cruise up-river to the lock at Châtelier, thence on to Dinan – subject to draught; here enter the Canal d'Ille et Rance to Biscay (9.18.14). There are many delightful anchorages and marinas at Plouër and Lyvet. It helps to know how the barrage affects water levels up-river.

From St Malo to St Quay-Portrieux the coast has deep bays (often drying), a few rugged headlands and many offlying rks. 6M NW of St Malo beware Le Vieux-Banc (1·2m), buoyed. ▶*Here the E-going stream begins at HW St Helier – 0555, and the W-going at HW St Helier – 0015, sp rates 2·5kn. There are W-going eddies very close inshore on the E-going stream.*◀

Between St Malo and Cap Fréhel there are anchs S of Île Agot in the apprs to the drying hbr of St Briac and in Baie de l'Arguenon, SE of St Cast hbr (9.18.15). More anchs may be found in Baie de la Fresnaye and off Pte de la Latte. From Cap Fréhel, a bold steep headland, to Cap d'Erquy there are plenty of inshore rocks but no worthwhile hbrs.

Between Cap d'Erquy and the various rky patches close to seaward, Chenal d'Erquy runs WSW/ENE into the E side of the B de St Brieuc. Erquy is a pleasant, drying hbr much used by fishing boats. There are several rky shoals within the B itself, some extending nearly 2M offshore.

Baie de St Brieuc is a 20M wide bight between Cap d'Erquy and L'Ost Pic. Principal features are: to the N, Grand Léjon a rky shoal extending 2½ca W and 8ca NNE of its lt ho. Petit Léjon (3·1m) lies 3·5M SSE. Roheinlt bcn, 3M further S, is in the centre with rocky plateaux to E and W. A 3M wide chan leads W of these features and S into the shallow, partly-drying S end of the Bay and the interesting hbrs of Dahouet (9.18.15), Le Légué/St Brieuc (9.18.16), and Binic (9.18.17).

On the W side of Bay de St Brieuc, Roches de St Quay and offlying patches extend 4M E from St Quay-Portrieux (9.18.18) which can only be approached from NNW or SE. St Quay marina is a good all-tide base from which to explore the drying hbrs around Baie de St Brieuc.

To the N and NE of L'Ost-Pic lt ho extensive offshore shoals guard the approaches to Paimpol (9.20.7), Ile de Bréhat and the Trieux river. Further N, the Plateau de Barnouic and Plateau des Roches Douvres (lt, fog sig) must be avoided. ▶*Here the E-going stream begins at about HW St Malo – 0400 and the W-going at about HW St Malo +0100 with Sp rates exceeding 4kn.*◀

9.18.6 Special notes for France: See 9.17.6.

MINOR HARBOUR CLOSE SOUTH OF CAP DE LA HAGUE

GOURY, Manche, **49°42'·92N 01°56'·73W**. AC *1106, 3653, 5604.2*; SHOM 7158, 5636, 7133 (essential large scale chart). HW –0410 on Dover (UT); ML 5·1m. See 9.17.31. For visitors, appr at slack water nps with no swell and good vis; a fair weather hbr only, dries to flattish shingle. Cap de la Hague lt, Fl 5s, is 0·5M NW of hbr; La Foraine WCM lt bn VQ (9) 10s is 1·0M to the W. Ldg lts: Front QR 4m 7M, on bkwtr hd; rear, Q 10m 12M, intens 057°-075°, lead 065° between Diotret to S and Les Grios to N. By day, W patch with R ■ at end of bkwtr on with W pylon of rear ldg lt, 065°. ⚓ W of the 2 LB slips in 1·7m or dry out on shingle banks SE of the bkwtr. Facilities: R, Bar at Auderville (0·5M).

9.18.7 DIÉLETTE

Manche, **49°33'·18N 01°51'·82W** ✽✽⛵⛵✿✿

CHARTS AC *3653*; SHOM 7158, 7133; ECM 528, 1014; Imray C33A; Stanfords 1, 2, 7, 16.

TIDES HW –0430 on Dover (UT); ML 5·4m

Standard Port ST-MALO (⟶)

Times				Height (metres)			
High Water		Low Water		MHWS	MHWN	MLWN	MLWS
0100	0800	0300	0800	12·2	9·3	4·2	1·5
1300	2000	1500	2000				
Differences DIÉLETTE							
+0045	+0035	+0020	+0035	–2·5	–1·9	–0·7	–0·3

SHELTER Good in marina, but some scend near HW when retaining wall covers. Do not attempt entry in strong W'lies. Outer hbr entr dredged to CD +0.5m; accessible for 2.5m draft with Coefficient > 55. W side of outer hbr dries approx 5m (local moorings). Enter marina, about HW±3 for 1·5m draft, over a sill with lifting gate 4m above CD; waiting pontoon outside.

NAVIGATION WPT 49°33'·56N 01°52'·31W, 140°/0·5M to W bkwtr lt. Appr is exposed to W'ly winds/swell. Caution: drying rks 3 ca E of ⊕, marked by unlit WCM buoy; cross tide at hbr ent. Keep seaward of WCM lt buoy 1·5M WSW, off Flamanville power stn.

LIGHTS AND MARKS Power stn chys (72m) are conspic 1·2M to SW. A single conspic house on the skyline is aligned 140° with ent. Dir lt 140°, W twr/G top at hd of West bkwtr, W sector 135°-145° (10°); on same twr a lower lt is Fl G 4s. See chartlet and 9.18.4.

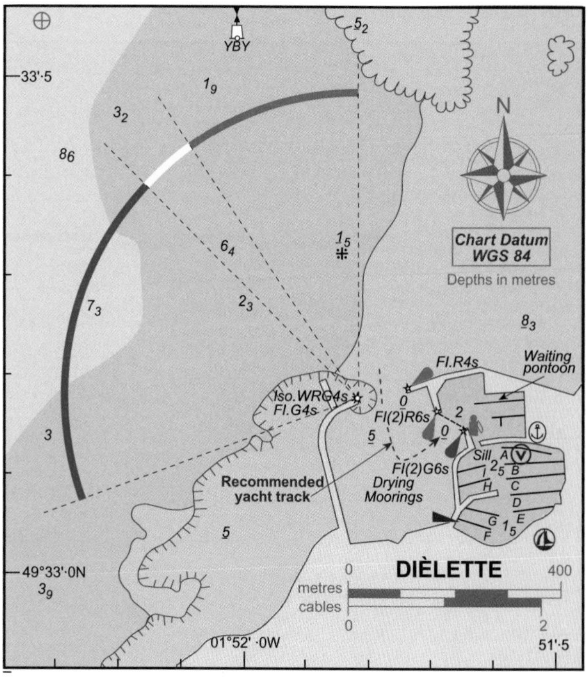
YBY
33'·5
Chart Datum WGS 84
Depths in metres
Fl.R4s
Waiting pontoon
Iso.WRG4s
Fl.G4s
Fl(2)R6s
Fl(2)G6s
Sill
Recommended yacht track
Drying Moorings
DIÈLETTE
metres
cables
400
49°33'·0N
01°52'·0W
51'·5

18

R/T VHF Ch 09; summer 0800-1300, 1400-2000LT; winter 0900-1200, 1330-1800LT.

TELEPHONE ⊜ 02·33.23.34.02; Aff Mar 02·33.23.36.00; Météo 08·92·68·08·50; CROSS 02·33.52.72.13; SNSM 02·33.04.93.17; YC 02·33·93·10·24.

FACILITIES **Marina** (350+70 ♥), 02·33.53.68.78, 📠 02·33.53.68.79; goelette@chez.com €2.27, D, P, Slip, C (30 ton); Ferry to Cl. **Village**, Bar, R. Also some facilities at Flamanville (1·3M).

9.18.8 CARTERET

Manche **49°22'·09N 01°47'·33W** ✽✽⛵⛵✿✿

CHARTS AC *2669, 3655*; SHOM 7157, 7158, 7133; ECM 1014; Imray C33A; Stanfords 1, 2, 16, 26.

TIDES –0440 Dover; ML 5·9; Duration 0545; Zone –0100

Standard Port ST-MALO (⟶)

Times				Height (metres)			
High Water		Low Water		MHWS	MHWN	MLWN	MLWS
0100	0800	0300	0800	12·2	9·3	4·2	1·5
1300	2000	1500	2000				
Differences CARTERET							
+0030	+0020	+0015	+0030	–1·6	–1·2	–0·5	–0·2

SHELTER Good in non-tidal marina (sill is 5m above CD; lifting flapgate retains 2·3m within); access HW±2½ for 1·5m draft. Ent/exit controlled by IPTS (sigs 2 & 4) near Capitainerie. ♥ berths alongside/rafted on pontoon 'F'. Can be very busy in season and at weekends. If too late on the tide for the marina, possible waiting berth on W bkwtr (clear of ferry) where a 1·5m draft boat can stay afloat for 6 hrs np, 9hrs sp or dry out on fine sand to SW of marina. The tiny Port des Américains and drying basin, close W of marina, have up to 5m at HW. There are no safe ⚓s off shore nor in the river.

NAVIGATION WPT 49°21'·39N 01°47'·45W (off chartlet), 006°/0·7M to W bkwtr lt. Caution: strong cross streams on the flood tide. From N/NW, keep well off shore on appr to avoid rks 1M N of Cap de Carteret extending about 7ca from coast. From W beware Trois Grune Rks (dry 1·6m), about 4M offshore, marked by WCM lt buoy. Appr dries ½M offshore and is exposed to fresh W/SW winds which can make ent rough.

Best appr at HW–1 to avoid max tidal stream, 4½kn sp. The outer end of W bkwtr covers at big springs. Bar, at right angles to W bkwtr, dries 4m; a SHM buoy east of the W bkwtr marks a shifting shoal patch. Best water is to port of a mid-channel course.The chan dries progressively to firm sand, and is dredged to 4m and 4.5m just W of the marina.

LIGHTS AND MARKS Cap de Carteret, grey tr, G top; and conspic Sig stn are 8ca WxN of the ent. Breakwater and channel lts as chartlet. Marina sill is marked by a PHM bn, and a SHM bn; plus Y poles on the retaining wall. Cross the sill squarely, ie heading NE, to clear the concrete base blocks each side.

R/T Marina Ch 09. Sig stn 09, 16.

TELEPHONE Marina 02·33·04·70·84 📠 02·33·04·08·37; CROSS/SNSM 02·33·52·72·13; ⊜ 02·33·04·90·08; Météo 02·33·22·91·77; Auto 08.92.68.08.50; Police 02·33·53·80·17; Ⓗ (Valognes) 02·33·40·14·39; Brit Consul 02.33.88.65.60.

FACILITIES **Marina**, www.barneville-carteret.net (311 + 60 ♥), €2.47 (possible discount Mon-Thu), D & P at accueil pontoon, CH; **West Bkwtr** AB free for 6 hrs, then at 50% of marina rate, Slip, FW, R, Bar; **YC Barneville-Carteret** ☎ 02·33·52·60·73, 📠 02·33·52·65·98, Slip, M, Bar.
Town ME, P & D (cans), 🛒, Gaz, R, Bar, ✉, Ⓑ, ⇌ (Valognes), ✈ (Cherbourg). Ferry: Cherbourg, Jersey.

CARTERET *continued*

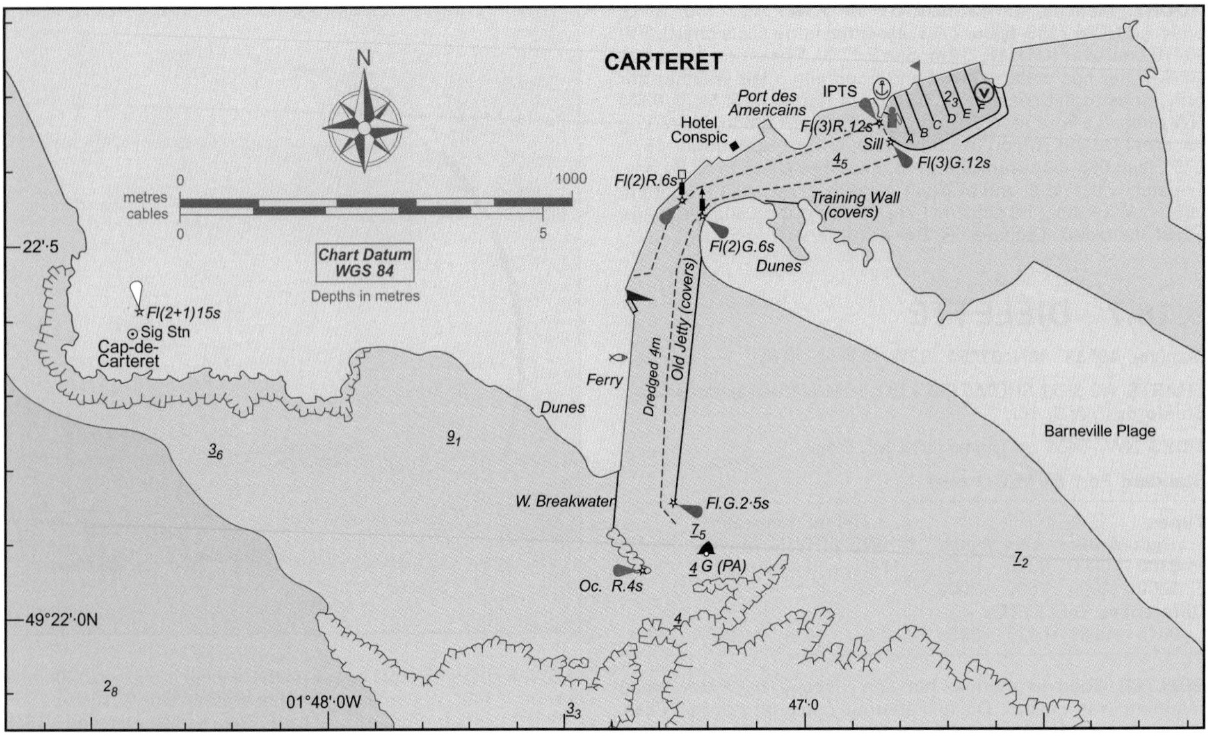
N
CARTERET
Port des Americains
IPTS
Hotel Conspic
Fl(3)R.12s
Sill
Fl(3)G.12s
Fl(2)R.6s
Training Wall (covers)
Fl(2)G.6s
Dunes
metres
cables
1000
5
0
22'·5
Chart Datum WGS 84
Depths in metres
Fl(2+1)15s
Sig Stn
Cap-de-Carteret
Ferry
Dredged 4m
Old Jetty (covers)
Dunes
Barneville Plage
W. Breakwater
Fl.G.2·5s
4 G (PA)
Oc. R.4s
49°22'·0N
01°48'·0W
47'·0

9.18.9 PORTBAIL

Manche **49°19'·44N 01°42'·99W**

CHARTS AC *2669, 3655*; SHOM 7157, 7133; ECM 1014; Imray C33A; Stanfords 1, 2, 16, 26.

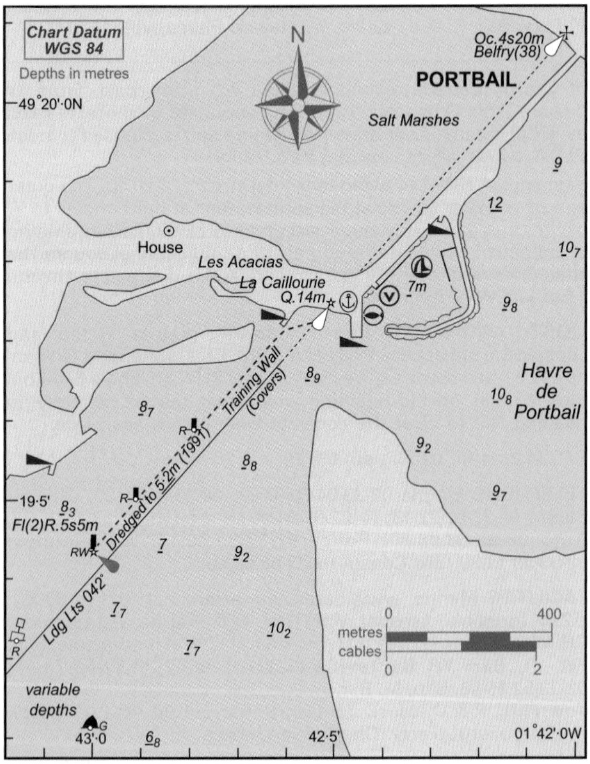
Chart Datum WGS 84
Depths in metres
49°20'·0N
N
Oc.4s20m Belfry(38)
PORTBAIL
Salt Marshes
House
Les Acacias
La Caillourie Q.14m
7m
Training Wall (Covers)
Havre de Portbail
Dredged to 5·2m (1991)
19·5'
Fl(2)R.5s5m
Ldg Lts 042°
variable depths
metres
cables
400
0
2
43'·0
42·5'
01°42'·0W

TIDES HW –0440 on Dover (UT); ML 6·3m; Duration 0545

Standard Port ST-MALO (⟶)

Times				Height (metres)			
High Water		Low Water		MHWS	MHWN	MLWN	MLWS
0100	0800	0300	0800	12·2	9·3	4·2	1·5
1300	2000	1500	2000				
Differences PORTBAIL							
+0030	+0025	+0025	+0030	–0·8	–0·6	–0·2	–0·1
ST GERMAIN-SUR-AY							
+0025	+0025	+0035	+0035	–0·7	–0·5	0·0	+0·1
LE SÉNÉQUET							
+0015	+0015	+0023	+0023	–0·3	–0·3	+0·1	+0·1

SHELTER Good. Access HW±½ at np, HW±2½ at sp for 1m draft. Basin to NE of jetty dries 7·0m: visitors berth on pontoon parallel with road on NW side of basin; or on the E side of jetty; or pick up a buoy on outer trot; or as directed by HM.

NAVIGATION WPT 49°18'·28N 01°44'·53W (off chartlet, abeam unlit 'PB' SWM buoy), 042°/1·5M to training wall lt, W mast/R top. When base of this bcn is covered, there is at least 2·5m in the chan which is dredged 5·2m. 042° ldg line crosses banks 7ca offshore drying 5.3m, thence between a pair of unlit PHM/SHM buoys, least depth 8.1m. Beware very strong tidal stream. The training wall on port side is marked by R perches and covers near HW.

LIGHTS AND MARKS A water twr (43m) is conspic 6ca NNW of ent. Ldg marks/lts 042°: Front (La Caillourie), W pylon, R top; rear, church belfry in town. See chartlet and 9.18.4 for light details.

R/T VHF Ch 09.

TELEPHONE HM 02·33·04·83·48 (15 Jun-31 Aug, 0830-1200 & 1400-1700). CROSS 02·33·52·72·13; ⊜ 02·33·04·90·08 (Carteret).

FACILITIES **Basin** (160 + 30 Ⓥ) €1.25, portbail@wanadoo.fr C (5 ton), ⚒, ME, El. **YC Portbail** ☎ 02·33·04·86·15, AB, C, Slip, Bar, R. **Town** (½M by causeway) Bar, R, Ⓑ, ✉, 🛒, D, P, ⇌ (Valognes).

9.18.10 GRANVILLE Manche 49°49'·91N 01°35'·89W

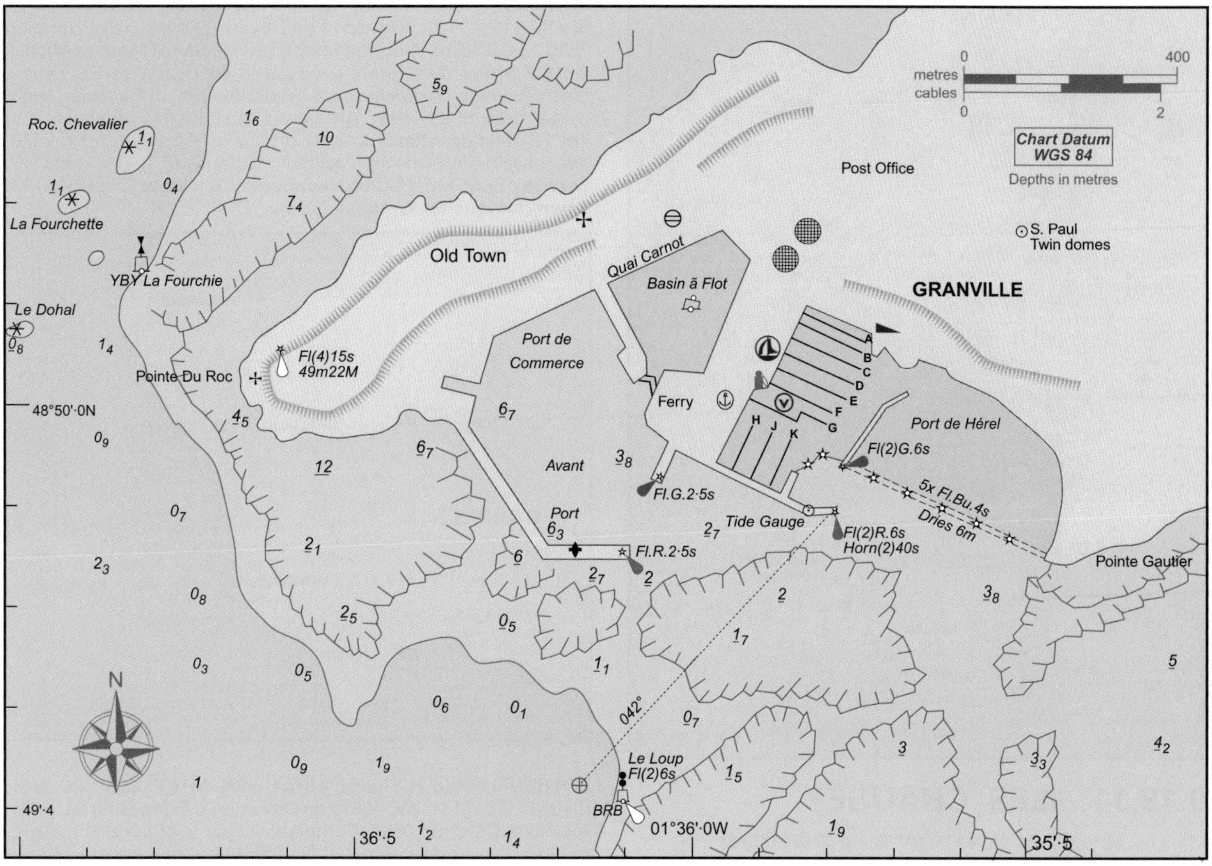
Roc. Chevalier
La Fourchette
YBY La Fourchie
Le Dohal
Pointe Du Roc
Fl(4)15s 49m22M
48°50'·0N
Old Town
Quai Carnot
Basin à Flot
Port de Commerce
Avant Port
Ferry
Fl.G.2·5s
Fl.R.2·5s
Tide Gauge
Fl(2)R.6s Horn(2)40s
Fl(2)G.6s
Port de Hérel
5x Fl.Bu.4s
Dries 6m
Pointe Gautier
GRANVILLE
Post Office
S. Paul Twin domes
metres
cables
Chart Datum WGS 84
Depths in metres
042°
Le Loup Fl(2)6s
BRB
01°36'·0W
36'·5
35'·5
49'·4

CHARTS AC 3656, *3659*, 3672; SHOM 7156, 7341; ECM 534, 535; Imray C33B; Stanfords 1, 2, 16, 26

TIDES –0510 Dover; ML 7·1; Duration 0525; Zone –0100

Standard Port ST-MALO (⟶)

Times				Height (metres)			
High Water		Low Water		MHWS	MHWN	MLWN	MLWS
0100	0800	0300	0800	12·2	9·3	4·2	1·5
1300	2000	1500	2000				
Differences REGNÉVILLE-SUR-MER							
+0010	+0010	+0030	+0020	+0·4	+0·3	+0·2	0·0
GRANVILLE							
+0005	+0005	+0020	+0010	+0·7	+0·5	+0·3	+0·1
CANCALE							
–0002	–0002	+0010	+0010	+0·8	+0·6	+0·3	+0·1

SHELTER Good in the marina, Port de Hérel, 1·5–2·5m; speed limit 2kn. Caution: turn wide into ent to avoid yachts leaving. Access over sill HW –2½ to +3½. Depth over sill shown on lit digital display atop S bkwtr: eg 76=7·6m; 00 = no entry; hard to read in bright sun. ⚓ in 2m about 4ca WSW of Le Loup to await the tide. A major expansion of the marina and port may start in 2005.

NAVIGATION WPT 48°49'·60N 01°36'·30W (abm Le Loup IDM), 042°/0·40M to S bkwtr lt. Beware rks seaward of La Fourchie WCM bcn twr, pot markers off Pte du Roc and 0·4m patches on Banc de Tombelaine, 1M SSW of Le Loup lt. At night best to keep at least 8ca W of Pte du Roc to avoid the worst of these dangers.

Appr is rough in strong W winds. Turn port at bkwtr to cross the sill between R/G piles. The 5 R piles, Fl Bu 4s, mark the covering wall of a windsurfing/dinghy area to stbd. Ent/exit under power; speed limit 4kn in the near approach.

LIGHTS AND MARKS Pte du Roc is a conspic headland with large old bldgs and lt ho, grey twr, R top; the Sig stn and church spire are also obvious. The twin domes of St Paul's church in transit 034° with Le Loup lead towards the marina ent. No ldg lts, but S bkwtr hd on with TV mast leads 057° to ent; hbr lts are hard to see against town lts. 3·5M W of Pte du Roc, Le Videcoq rock drying 0·8m, is marked by a WCM lt buoy. See chartlet and 9.18.4 for lt details.

R/T Port VHF Ch 12 16 (HW±1½). Marina Ch 09, H24 in season.

TELEPHONE Port HM 02·33·50·17·75; Aff Mar 02·33·91·31·40; CROSS 02·33·52·72·13; SNSM 02·33·61·26·51; ⊖ 02·33·50·19·90; Météo 02·33·22·91·77; Auto 08.92.68.08.50; Police 02·33·50·01·00; Dr 02·33·50·00·07; Hosp 02·33·90·74·75; Brit Consul 02.99.46.26.64.

FACILITIES Hérel Marina pjs@granville.cci.fr (850+150 Ⓥ) ☎ 02·33·50·20·06, 📠 02·33·50·17·01, €1.95, Ⓥ pontoon G (1st to stbd), Slip, P, D, ME, BH (12 ton), C (10 ton), CH, Gaz, R, ⊡, 🛒, Bar, SM, El, ⚒, Ⓢ, Ⓔ, SHOM. **YC de Granville** ☎ 02·33·50·04·25, 📠 02·33·50·06·59, L, M, BH, D, P, CH, ⊡, Slip, FW, AB, Bar.

Town P, D, ME, 🛒, Gaz, R, Bar, ✉, Ⓑ, ⇌, ✈ (Dinard), www.granville.cci.fr. Ferry: UK via Jersey or Cherbourg.

MINOR HARBOUR 10M NORTH OF GRANVILLE

REGNÉVILLE, Manche, **48°59'·72N 01°34'·05W** (SHM entry buoy). AC *3656*; SHOM 7156, 7133. HW –0500 on Dover (UT); ML 7·0m; Duration 0535. See 9.18.9. A seriously drying hbr on the estuary of R. La Sienne; little frequented by yachts, a magnet for hardy adventurers seeking sand and solitude.

From 48°57'·57N 01°38'·86W (2·2M E of La Catheue SCM buoy) identify Pte d'Agon lt ho, W twr/R top, and Regnéville's 028° dir lt, both 4M NE at the river mouth (see 9.18.4). Thence track 056°/3·8M across the drying estuary to the SHM buoy (Lat/Long in line 1) marking a drying mole extending SW from the sandspit to stbd. Here there are landing stages; a small pontoon at Regnéville is 1·2M NNE. Drying heights are around 9m and 12·7m off Pte d'Agon. Access HW –1 to +2 for 1·3m draft. Approx 80 moorings inc ⚓s. YC ☎ 02·33·46·36·76. **Facilities**: Quay, CH, BY, C (25 ton). **Town**: D&P (cans), Ⓑ, ✉, Bar, R, 🛒. Tourism ☎ 02·33·45·88·71.

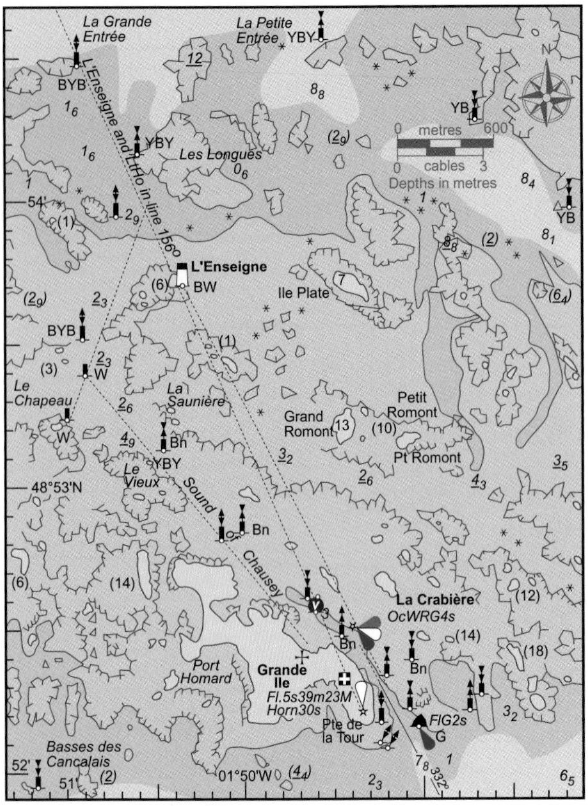
La Grande Entrée
La Petite Entrée
YBY
12
BYB
L'Enseigne and Lt Ho in line 156°
Les Longues
metres 0 600
0 cables 3
Depths in metres
YB
L'Enseigne
BW
Ile Plate
BYB
Le Chapeau
La Saunière
Grand Romont
Petit Romont
Pt Romont
Le Vieux
YBY
48°53'N
Bn
Sound
Chausey
La Crabière
OcWRG4s
Port Homard
Grande Ile
Fl.5s39m23M
Horn30s
Pte de la Tour
FlG2s
G
Basses des Cancalais
52'
51'
01°50'W
332°

9.18.11 ILES CHAUSEY

Manche **48°52'·14N 01°49'·09W** S ent ❁❁◊✿✿✿

CHARTS AC 3656, *3659*; SHOM 7156, 7155, 7161, 7134; ECM 534, 535; Imray C33B; Stanfords 1, 2, 16, 26.

TIDES –0500 Dover; ML 7·4; Duration 0530; Zone –0100

Standard Port ST-MALO (⟶)

Times				**Height (metres)**			
High Water		Low Water		MHWS	MHWN	MLWN	MLWS
0100	0800	0300	0800	12·2	9·3	4·2	1·5
1300	2000	1500	2000				
Differences ÎLES CHAUSEY (Grande Île)							
+0005	+0005	+0015	+0015	+0·8	+0·7	+0·6	+0·4

SHELTER Good except in strong NW or SE winds. Grande Île is not a French Port of Entry; it is privately owned, but may be visited. Moor fore-and-aft to W 🅐s, free; some dry at sp. Very crowded Sat/Sun in season, especially as drying out in Port Homard (W side of Grande Île) is actively discouraged. Note the tidal range when ⚓ing or picking up 🅐. Tidal streams are not excessive. No access 1/4 to 30/6 to bird sanctuary, all areas E of line from lt ho to L'Enseigne.

NAVIGATION WPT 48°51'·43N 01°48'·55W, 332°/1·2M to La Crabière lt. By day, its transit with L'Enseigne, W bn tr, B top (19m), leads 332° into Sound; ditto its W sector; see 9.18.4. The S access chan is marked by a SHM lt buoy, 3 ECM & 2 WCM unlit bns. From N, L'Enseigne on with Grande Île lt ho leads 156° to the N ent; thence follow 4 ECM, 3 WCM, 1 SCM & 1 NCM unlit bcns.The N chan needs adequate ht of tide (max drying ht 4·9m), SHOM 7134, a good Pilot and/or local knowledge, plus careful pilotage.

LIGHTS AND MARKS Grande Île lt ho is conspic. La Crabière lt is on blackish stilts with Y top. See chartlet and 9.18.4 for lts.

R/T None. **TELEPHONE** Police 02·33·52·72·02; CROSS 02·33·52·72·13; Auto 08.92.68.08.50; SNSM 02.33.50.28.33.

FACILITIES Village FW & 🛒 (limited), Gaz, R, Bar, ▯.

MINOR HARBOURS EAST OF ST MALO

CANCALE, Ille-et-Vilaine, **48°40'·10N 01°51'·11W**. AC *3659*; SHOM 7155, 7131. HW –0510 on Dover (UT); ML 7·2m; Duration 0535. See 9.18.10. A drying hbr just inside Bay of Mont St Michel, 2·6M S of Pte du Grouin; exposed to winds SW to SE. Drying berths usually available in La Houle, the hbr of Cancale. Avoid oyster beds at all costs. Area dries to about 1M off-shore; ⚓ in 4m SE of Île des Rimains. Jetty hd lt is on a green-topped white twr, obsc'd from the N. Facilities: **Quay** D, P, C (1·5 ton), FW; **Services:** El, M, ME, ⚒; **Club Nautique de Cancale** ☎ 02·99·89·90·22. **Town** (famous for oysters), Ⓑ, Bar, D, P, ✉, R, 🛒.

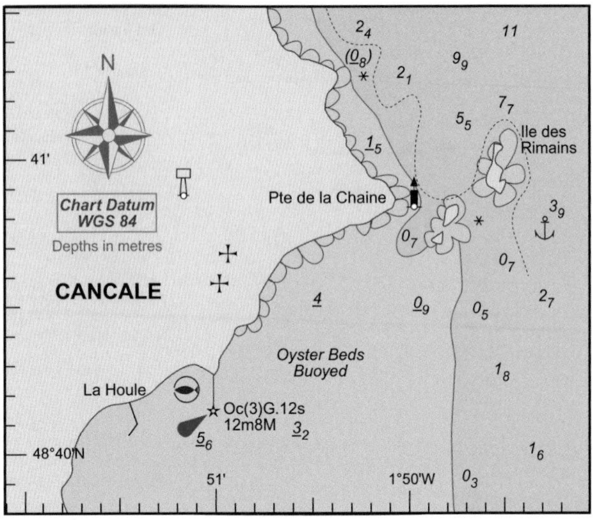
N
41'
Chart Datum
WGS 84
Depths in metres
CANCALE
Pte de la Chaine
Ile des Rimains
Oyster Beds
Buoyed
La Houle
Oc(3)G.12s
12m8M
48°40'N
51'
1°50'W

ROTHENEUF, Ille-et-Vilaine, **48°41'·36N 01°57'·65W**. AC *3659*; SHOM 7155, 7131. HW –0510 on Dover (UT); Tides as for St. Malo; ML 7·0m; Duration 0540. Complete shelter in hbr which dries up to 8·6m. ⚓ outside in 4m just N of SHM bn marking ent. Rks on both sides of ent which is barely 230m wide. Safest to enter when rks uncovered. Ldg line at 163°, W side of Pte Benard and old windmill (white twr). There are no lts. Facilities: FW, Slip. **Village** Bar, D, P, R, 🛒.

9.18.12 ST MALO

Ille et Vilaine **48°38'·48N 02°01'·91W**
Bassin Vauban and Bas Sablons marinas ❁❁◊◊✿✿✿

CHARTS AC *2669, 3659,* 2700; SHOM 7155, 7156, 7130; ECM 535; Imray C33B; Stanfords 2, 16, 26.

TIDES –0506 Dover; ML 6·8; Duration 0535; Zone –0100.

SHELTER Two options: 1. Lock into Bassin Vauban, min depth 6m. Excellent shelter near the walled city. Berth on pontoon marked for your LOA; no fingers; no turning room. Bassin Duguay-Trouin, beyond lift bridge, is better for long stay. No ⚓ in basins; 3kn speed limit. Outside the lock 3 waiting buoys are N of appr chan; keep clear of vedette and Condor berths.

Lock operates five times in each direction, ie
Inbound: HW –2½, –1½, –½, HW+½, +1½.
Outbound: HW–2, –1, HW, +1, +2.

Assistance is given with warp-handling; pas de problème.
Lock sigs are IPTS Nos 2, 3 and 5. In addition:
○ next to the top lt = both lock gates are open; main message is the same, but beware current. Note: freeflow operation is rare due to busy road traffic over rolling bridge.
● ● over ● = all movements prohib, big ship is outbound.

2. Good shelter nearer St Servan in Bas Sablons marina, entered over sill 2m above CD. Access for 1·5m draft approx HW –3½ to +4½ sp; H24 at nps. Two W waiting buoys outside. Depth of water over sill is shown on a digital gauge atop the bkwtr, visible only from seaward; inside, a conventional gauge at base of bkwtr shows depths <3m. 🅥 berths on A pontoon: 32-66 (E side)

and 43-75 (W side), and on B pontoon: 92-102 and 91-101. In fresh W/NW'lies outer ends of both pontoons are uncomfortable.

Dinard yacht basin 2m (usually full of local boats) is reached by a 1m marked chan.

NAVIGATION Care is needed due to strong tidal streams and many dangerous rocks close to the appr chans, which from W to E (see chartlet and 9.18.4) are:

1. Grande Porte; from the W, lit. WPT 48°40´·10N 02°08´·57W, 089°/2·3M.
2. Petite Porte; from N/NW, lit; the main chan. WPT 48°42´·38N 02°09´·13W [abm NCM buoy, Q], 130°/3·1M.
3. Bunel; from NNW, lit. WPT 48°42´·28N 02°06´·62W, 158°/2·2M.

In chans 1-3 the track/distance quoted is to, or near, Grand Jardin lt, 48°40´·14N 02°05´·05W; thence continue 129°/2·8M to Môle des Noires hd, 48°38´·44N 02°02´·02W.

4. Grande Conchée; from N, unlit. WPT 48°42´·10N 02°02´·21W, 181·5°/2·5M.
5. Petits Pointus; from NNE, unlit. WPT 48°42´·34N 02°00´·34W, 203°/2·7M.
6. La Bigne; from NE, unlit. WPT 48°42´·60N 01°57´·38W, 222°/1·5M - 236°/2·8M.

In chans 4-6 the track/distance quoted is to, or near, Roches aux Anglais SHM buoy, 48°39´·59N 02°02´·35W; thence continue 221°/8ca to enter the 129° fairway.

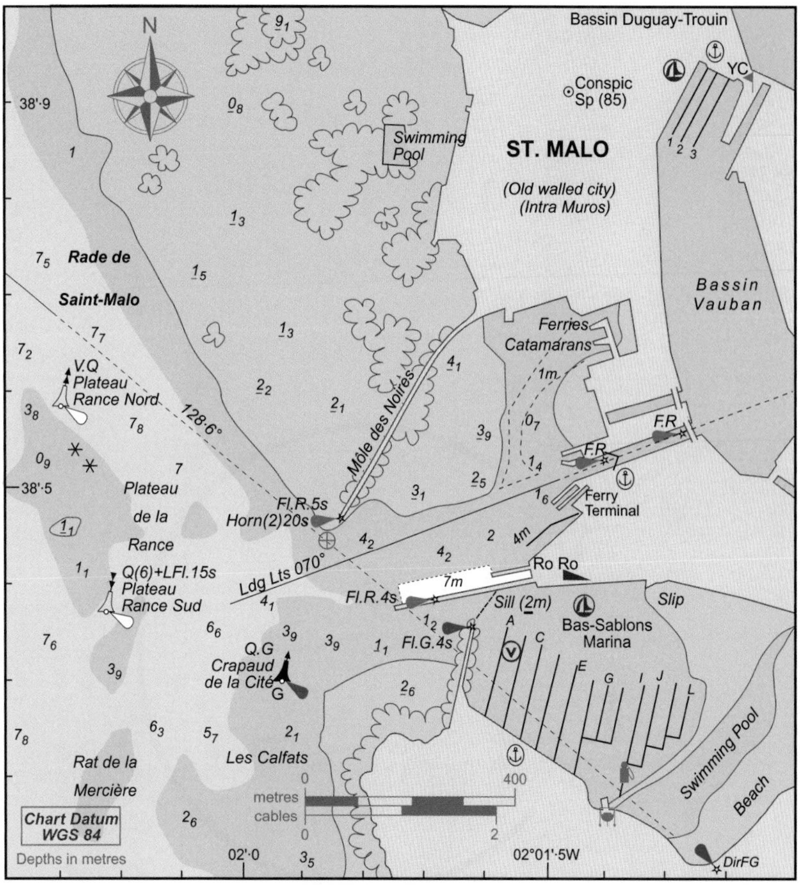
N
38'·9
38'·5
Bassin Duguay-Trouin
YC
Conspic Sp (85)
Swimming Pool
ST. MALO
(Old walled city) (Intra Muros)
Rade de Saint-Malo
Bassin Vauban
Ferries Catamarans
1m
Môle des Noires
V.Q Plateau Rance Nord
128·6°
Plateau de la Rance
F.R
F.R
Fl.R.5s Horn(2)20s
Ferry Terminal
4m
Ldg Lts 070°
Ro Ro
7m
Fl.R.4s
Sill (2m)
Slip
Q(6)+LFl.15s Plateau Rance Sud
Bas-Sablons Marina
Fl.G.4s
Q.G Crapaud de la Cité
Swimming Pool
Beach
Rat de la Mercière
Les Calfats
metres
cables
400
Chart Datum WGS 84
Depths in metres
02'·0
02°01'·5W
DirFG

LIGHTS AND MARKS See chartlets/9.18.4 for ldg lts/buoys. Conspic daymarks: the cathedral spire, Le Grand Jardin lt ho, Île de Cézembre, Le Buron SHM twr, Petit and Grand Bé islets and the W lt twr/R top on Mole des Noires head.

R/T *St Malo Port* Ch **12**. Marinas Ch 09.

TELEPHONE Port HM 02·99·20·63·01, 📠 02·99·56·48·71; Aff Mar 02·99·56·87·00; CROSS 02·98·89·31·31; SNSM 02·98·89· 31·31; ⊖ 02·99·81·65·90; Météo 02·99·46·10·46; Auto 08.92.68.08.35; Police 02·99·81·52·30; Ⓗ 02·99·56·56·19; Brit Consul 02·99·46·26·64.

FACILITIES Bassin Vauban (250 + 100 Ⓥ) ☎ 02·99·56·51·91, 📠 02.99.56.57.81, €2.67, C (1 ton); **Société Nautique de la Baie de St. Malo** ☎ 02·99·40·84·42, 📠 02.99.56.39.41, Bar (Ⓥ welcome).

Les Bas-Sablons marina (1216 + 64 Ⓥ) ☎ 02·99·81·71·34, 📠 02·99.81.91.81, €2.22, Slip, C, BH (10 ton), Gaz, R, YC, Bar, P & D pontoon 'I'; Note: Pumps are operated by credit cards. **Services:** El, Ⓔ, ME, CH, ⚒, C, BY, SM, SHOM. **Town** Gaz, 🛒, R, Bar, ✉, Ⓑ, ⇌, ✈ (Dinard). Ferry: Portsmouth, Poole or Jersey.

DINARD: **HM** ☎ 02·99·46·65·55, Slip, ⚓, M €1.91 (afloat) €1.25 (drying), P, D, L, temp AB; **YC de Dinard** ☎ 02·99·46·14·32, Bar; **Services:** ME, El, Ⓔ, ⚒, M, SM. **Town** P, D, ME, El, CH, 🛒, Gaz, R, Bar, ✉, Ⓑ, ⇌, ✈. ⊖ 02·99·46·12·42; Ⓗ 02·99·46·18·68.

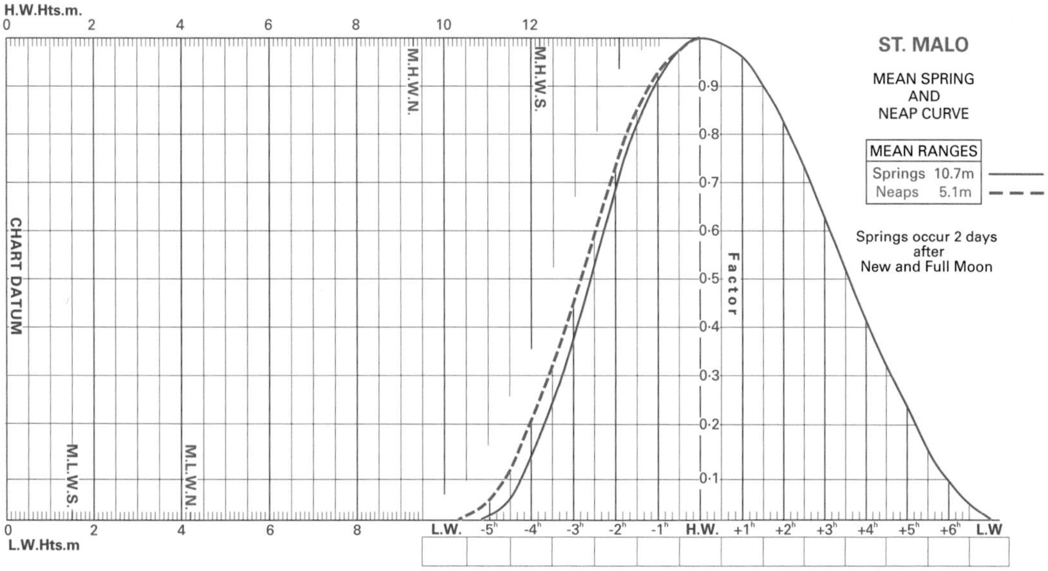
H.W.Hts.m.
0 2 4 6 8 10 12
M.H.W.N.
M.H.W.S.
CHART DATUM
M.L.W.S.
M.L.W.N.
0 2 4 6 8
L.W.Hts.m
0·9
0·8
0·7
0·6
0·5
0·4
0·3
0·2
0·1
Factor
L.W. -5h -4h -3h -2h -1h H.W. +1h +2h +3h +4h +5h +6h L.W
ST. MALO
MEAN SPRING AND NEAP CURVE
MEAN RANGES
Springs 10.7m
Neaps 5.1m
Springs occur 2 days after New and Full Moon

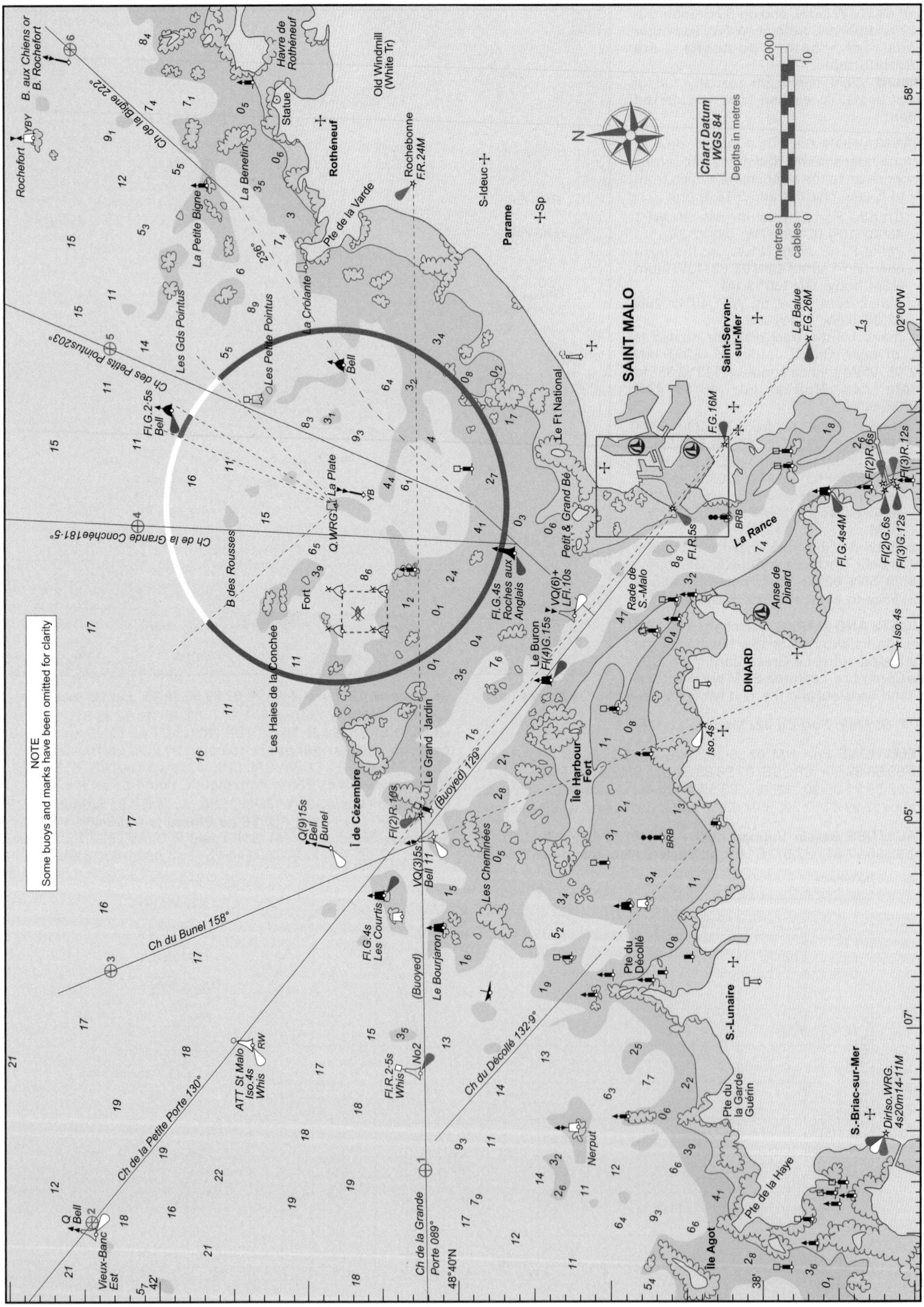
NOTE
Some buoys and marks have been omitted for clarity
SAINT MALO
Saint-Servan-sur-Mer
DINARD
La Rance
Anse de Dinard
Rade de S.-Malo
Rothéneuf
Havre de Rothéneuf
Parame
S-Ideuc
Old Windmill (White Tr)
Rochebonne F.R.24M
Pte de la Varde
La Crolante
Les Petits Pointus
Les Gds Pointus
La Petite Bigne
La Benetin
Statue
Rochefort
B. aux Chiens or B. Rochefort
Ch de la Bigne 222°
Ch des Petits Pointus 203°
Ch de la Grande Conchée 181·5°
Ch du Bunel 158°
Ch de la Petite Porte 130°
Ch du Décollé 132·9°
Ch de la Grande Porte 089°
(Buoyed) 129°
(Buoyed)
Fl.G.2·5s Bell
Q.WRG La Plate
B des Rousses
Fort
Les Haies de la Conchée
Fl.G.4s Roches aux Anglais
VQ(6)+LFl.10s
Le Buron Fl(4)G.15s
Le Ft National
Petit & Grand Bé
Fl.R.5s
F.G.16M
La Balue F.G.26M
Fl.G.4s4M
Fl(2)R.6s
Fl(2)G.6s
Fl(3)R.12s
Fl(3)G.12s
Iso.4s
Île Harbour Fort
Le Grand Jardin
Fl(2)R.10s
Î de Cézembre
Q(9)15s Bell Bunel
VQ(3)5s Bell 11
Les Cheminées
Fl.G.4s Les Courtis
Le Bourjaron
Fl.R.2·5s Whis No2
ATT St Malo Iso.4s Whis RW
Q Bell Vieux-Banc Est
Pte du Décollé
S.-Lunaire
Pte du la Garde Guérin
Nerput
Île Agot
Pte de la Haye
S.-Briac-sur-Mer
DirIso.WRG. 4s20m14-11M
Chart Datum WGS 84
Depths in metres
metres 0 2000
cables 0 10
48°40'N
38'
42'
07'
05'
02°00'W
58'

TIME ZONE -0100
(French Standard Time)
Subtract 1 hour for UT
For French Summer Time add ONE hour in **non-shaded areas**

FRANCE – ST MALO

LAT 48°38′N LONG 2°02′W

TIMES AND HEIGHTS OF HIGH AND LOW WATERS

SPRING & NEAP TIDES
Dates in red are **SPRINGS**
Dates in blue are **NEAPS**

YEAR **2005**

JANUARY

Date	Day	Time	m	Time	m	Time	m	Time	m	Moon
1	SA	0442	3.4	1011	10.4	1705	3.3	2236	9.9	
2	SU	0519	3.7	1049	10.1	1744	3.6	2315	9.5	
3	M	0601	4.0	1132	9.7	1829	3.9			◑
4	TU	0003	9.2	0653	4.2	1227	9.4	1925	4.1	
5	W	0109	9.1	0757	4.3	1337	9.3	2033	4.1	
6	TH	0226	9.2	0913	4.1	1456	9.5	2150	3.9	
7	F	0342	9.6	1029	3.6	1610	9.9	2302	3.3	
8	SA	0448	10.3	1137	2.9	1716	10.5			
9	SU	0009	2.7	0548	11.1	1240	2.3	1817	11.2	
10	M	0111	2.2	0644	11.7	1340	1.7	1913	11.7	●
11	TU	0207	1.7	0736	12.2	1436	1.3	2005	12.0	
12	W	0300	1.5	0825	12.4	1528	1.0	2053	12.1	
13	TH	0349	1.5	0912	12.4	1616	1.1	2139	12.0	
14	F	0435	1.6	0957	12.2	1701	1.4	2222	11.6	
15	SA	0517	2.1	1041	11.6	1743	2.0	2303	11.0	
16	SU	0558	2.7	1123	11.0	1823	2.7	2345	10.3	
17	M	0638	3.3	1208	10.2	1904	3.4			◐
18	TU	0032	9.7	0724	4.0	1301	9.5	1952	4.0	
19	W	0130	9.2	0823	4.4	1410	9.0	2054	4.4	
20	TH	0247	8.9	0936	4.5	1532	8.9	2206	4.4	
21	F	0405	9.1	1049	4.3	1644	9.2	2313	4.1	
22	SA	0507	9.6	1150	3.8	1739	9.6			
23	SU	0010	3.7	0555	10.1	1240	3.3	1824	10.1	
24	M	0058	3.3	0635	10.6	1323	2.9	1902	10.5	
25	TU	0139	2.9	0712	10.9	1403	2.6	1937	10.8	○
26	W	0217	2.6	0747	11.2	1440	2.4	2011	11.0	
27	TH	0252	2.4	0820	11.4	1514	2.2	2043	11.1	
28	F	0326	2.3	0852	11.5	1547	2.2	2115	11.1	
29	SA	0359	2.3	0923	11.4	1619	2.2	2145	10.9	
30	SU	0430	2.5	0955	11.2	1651	2.5	2215	10.7	
31	M	0502	2.8	1026	10.8	1722	2.8	2247	10.3	

FEBRUARY

Date	Day	Time	m	Time	m	Time	m	Time	m	Moon
1	TU	0535	3.2	1101	10.4	1757	3.3	2323	9.9	
2	W	0615	3.6	1142	9.9	1839	3.7			◑
3	TH	0011	9.4	0707	4.0	1241	9.4	1939	4.2	
4	F	0125	9.1	0822	4.3	1408	9.0	2103	4.3	
5	SA	0304	9.1	0955	4.0	1547	9.3	2235	3.9	
6	SU	0433	9.8	1119	3.3	1709	10.0	2353	3.1	
7	M	0542	10.7	1231	2.4	1814	10.9			
8	TU	0105	2.3	0639	11.6	1334	1.6	1909	11.6	●
9	W	0203	1.6	0730	12.3	1430	0.9	1957	12.2	
10	TH	0254	1.1	0816	12.7	1520	0.6	2041	12.5	
11	F	0340	0.9	0859	12.9	1603	0.5	2121	12.4	
12	SA	0420	1.0	0939	12.6	1642	0.9	2158	12.1	
13	SU	0456	1.5	1015	12.1	1716	1.5	2232	11.5	
14	M	0527	2.2	1050	11.3	1746	2.4	2305	10.7	
15	TU	0556	3.0	1124	10.4	1814	3.3	2339	9.9	
16	W	0627	3.8	1202	9.4	1849	4.1			◐
17	TH	0022	9.1	0713	4.6	1258	8.6	1944	4.9	
18	F	0135	8.5	0832	5.0	1444	8.2	2114	5.1	
19	SA	0327	8.4	1014	4.9	1625	8.5	2247	4.8	
20	SU	0447	9.0	1129	4.3	1725	9.2	2352	4.1	
21	M	0538	9.7	1223	3.6	1808	9.9			
22	TU	0043	3.4	0618	10.4	1307	2.9	1845	10.5	
23	W	0125	2.8	0655	11.0	1347	2.4	1919	11.0	
24	TH	0202	2.3	0729	11.4	1424	2.0	1952	11.4	○
25	F	0238	2.0	0803	11.7	1459	1.7	2024	11.6	
26	SA	0311	1.7	0834	11.9	1531	1.6	2055	11.7	
27	SU	0342	1.7	0904	11.9	1601	1.6	2124	11.6	
28	M	0413	1.8	0934	11.8	1630	1.9	2152	11.3	

MARCH

Date	Day	Time	m	Time	m	Time	m	Time	m	Moon
1	TU	0442	2.2	1004	11.4	1659	2.4	2221	10.9	
2	W	0512	2.7	1036	10.8	1729	3.0	2254	10.3	
3	TH	0547	3.3	1114	10.1	1806	3.7	2336	9.7	◑
4	F	0636	3.9	1207	9.3	1903	4.3			
5	SA	0049	9.0	0752	4.4	1345	8.7	2036	4.7	
6	SU	0251	8.9	0939	4.3	1546	9.0	2226	4.3	
7	M	0429	9.6	1113	3.4	1708	9.9	2349	3.3	
8	TU	0535	10.7	1225	2.4	1806	10.9			
9	W	0058	2.2	0629	11.7	1325	1.4	1856	11.8	
10	TH	0151	1.4	0715	12.5	1416	0.8	1940	12.4	●
11	F	0238	0.8	0758	12.9	1500	0.4	2019	12.6	
12	SA	0319	0.7	0837	13.0	1539	0.5	2056	12.6	
13	SU	0355	0.9	0913	12.7	1612	0.9	2128	12.3	
14	M	0426	1.3	0945	12.1	1641	1.6	2159	11.7	
15	TU	0452	2.1	1016	11.3	1705	2.4	2227	11.0	
16	W	0515	2.9	1044	10.4	1727	3.3	2255	10.2	
17	TH	0540	3.8	1115	9.4	1755	4.2	2329	9.3	◐
18	F	0617	4.6	1158	8.5	1841	5.1			
19	SA	0029	8.4	0726	5.3	1349	7.8	2018	5.6	
20	SU	0242	8.1	0934	5.3	1556	8.2	2218	5.2	
21	M	0416	8.6	1102	4.6	1658	9.0	2326	4.4	
22	TU	0508	9.5	1155	3.7	1739	9.8			
23	W	0016	3.5	0549	10.3	1239	3.0	1816	10.5	
24	TH	0057	2.8	0627	11.0	1319	2.3	1851	11.2	
25	F	0135	2.2	0703	11.6	1357	1.8	1925	11.6	○
26	SA	0212	1.8	0737	12.0	1432	1.5	1958	11.9	
27	SU	0246	1.5	0810	12.2	1506	1.3	2029	12.1	
28	M	0320	1.4	0841	12.3	1537	1.4	2059	12.0	
29	TU	0352	1.5	0912	12.1	1607	1.7	2129	11.8	
30	W	0423	1.9	0944	11.6	1637	2.3	2200	11.3	
31	TH	0454	2.5	1019	11.0	1709	3.0	2235	10.6	

APRIL

Date	Day	Time	m	Time	m	Time	m	Time	m	Moon
1	F	0532	3.2	1100	10.1	1749	3.8	2322	9.8	
2	SA	0623	4.0	1202	9.2	1850	4.6			◑
3	SU	0048	9.0	0745	4.4	1354	8.7	2035	4.8	
4	M	0251	9.0	0937	4.2	1543	9.2	2223	4.2	
5	TU	0417	9.8	1105	3.3	1654	10.1	2337	3.1	
6	W	0518	10.9	1210	2.3	1747	11.1			
7	TH	0039	2.2	0608	11.7	1304	1.5	1833	11.8	
8	F	0129	1.5	0653	12.3	1351	1.0	1914	12.3	●
9	SA	0212	1.1	0733	12.6	1432	0.9	1951	12.5	
10	SU	0250	1.1	0810	12.6	1507	1.0	2025	12.4	
11	M	0323	1.2	0843	12.3	1537	1.4	2056	12.2	
12	TU	0352	1.6	0915	11.8	1603	1.9	2125	11.7	
13	W	0417	2.2	0944	11.1	1627	2.6	2153	11.0	
14	TH	0441	3.0	1012	10.3	1650	3.5	2221	10.3	
15	F	0508	3.7	1043	9.5	1720	4.3	2255	9.4	
16	SA	0543	4.5	1125	8.6	1803	5.1	2347	8.6	◐
17	SU	0641	5.2	1254	8.0	1925	5.6			
18	M	0143	8.2	0832	5.3	1502	8.2	2126	5.4	
19	TU	0322	8.5	1011	4.8	1611	8.8	2239	4.6	
20	W	0422	9.3	1109	3.9	1657	9.6	2329	3.7	
21	TH	0508	10.1	1156	3.2	1736	10.4			
22	F	0015	3.0	0549	10.8	1239	2.5	1814	11.1	
23	SA	0058	2.3	0628	11.5	1321	2.0	1851	11.6	
24	SU	0138	1.9	0706	11.9	1400	1.6	1926	12.0	○
25	M	0217	1.5	0742	12.2	1437	1.5	2001	12.2	
26	TU	0255	1.4	0817	12.2	1512	1.5	2034	12.2	
27	W	0332	1.5	0853	12.1	1547	1.8	2109	12.0	
28	TH	0408	1.9	0931	11.6	1622	2.4	2147	11.5	
29	F	0446	2.5	1013	10.9	1701	3.1	2232	10.7	
30	SA	0530	3.2	1105	10.1	1749	3.9	2330	9.9	

Chart Datum: 6·29 metres below IGN Datum

TIME ZONE -0100
(French Standard Time)
Subtract 1 hour for UT
For French Summer Time add ONE hour in **non-shaded areas**

FRANCE – ST MALO

LAT 48°38′N LONG 2°02′W

TIMES AND HEIGHTS OF HIGH AND LOW WATERS

SPRING & NEAP TIDES
Dates in red are SPRINGS
Dates in blue are NEAPS

YEAR **2005**

MAY

Date	Time	m	Time	m	Time	m	Time	m	Moon
1 SU	0628	3.8	1217	9.4	1859	4.5			◑
2 M	0100	9.4	0751	4.1	1353	9.1	2037	4.5	
3 TU	0236	9.5	0926	3.9	1521	9.5	2204	3.9	
4 W	0352	10.1	1041	3.2	1627	10.3	2310	3.1	
5 TH	0451	10.8	1142	2.5	1719	11.0			
6 F	0007	2.4	0540	11.4	1233	2.0	1804	11.5	
7 SA	0057	2.0	0625	11.8	1318	1.7	1844	11.8	
8 SU	0140	1.8	0705	11.9	1357	1.7	1921	12.0	●
9 M	0217	1.8	0742	11.9	1431	1.8	1954	12.0	
10 TU	0250	1.9	0816	11.7	1501	2.0	2026	11.8	
11 W	0320	2.1	0848	11.3	1530	2.4	2057	11.5	
12 TH	0349	2.5	0919	10.9	1558	2.9	2127	11.0	
13 F	0417	3.0	0951	10.3	1627	3.5	2200	10.3	
14 SA	0448	3.6	1025	9.6	1701	4.2	2237	9.6	
15 SU	0525	4.2	1109	9.0	1744	4.8	2327	9.0	
16 M	0616	4.7	1214	8.5	1848	5.2			◐
17 TU	0044	8.6	0731	4.9	1344	8.4	2015	5.2	
18 W	0210	8.7	0858	4.7	1502	8.8	2133	4.7	
19 TH	0319	9.2	1007	4.1	1600	9.4	2232	4.0	
20 F	0414	9.8	1102	3.5	1648	10.1	2324	3.3	
21 SA	0503	10.5	1153	2.8	1732	10.8			
22 SU	0015	2.7	0549	11.1	1241	2.3	1814	11.3	
23 M	0103	2.2	0632	11.6	1326	2.0	1855	11.8	○
24 TU	0149	1.8	0715	11.9	1410	1.8	1935	12.1	
25 W	0233	1.6	0758	12.0	1452	1.8	2016	12.1	
26 TH	0317	1.6	0841	11.9	1534	2.0	2059	12.0	
27 F	0401	1.9	0927	11.6	1617	2.4	2146	11.6	
28 SA	0447	2.3	1017	11.1	1704	2.9	2238	11.0	
29 SU	0537	2.8	1113	10.5	1759	3.5	2338	10.4	
30 M	0636	3.3	1217	9.9	1904	3.9			◑
31 TU	0050	10.0	0745	3.6	1329	9.7	2018	4.0	

JUNE

Date	Time	m	Time	m	Time	m	Time	m	Moon
1 W	0205	10.0	0856	3.6	1443	9.8	2129	3.7	
2 TH	0315	10.1	1003	3.3	1549	10.1	2233	3.4	
3 F	0416	10.5	1103	3.0	1644	10.5	2330	3.0	
4 SA	0509	10.8	1156	2.7	1732	10.9			
5 SU	0022	2.7	0556	11.0	1242	2.6	1815	11.2	
6 M	0107	2.5	0639	11.1	1323	2.5	1854	11.3	●
7 TU	0146	2.4	0719	11.1	1359	2.5	1930	11.4	
8 W	0222	2.4	0755	11.0	1434	2.6	2004	11.4	
9 TH	0256	2.5	0830	10.9	1507	2.7	2038	11.2	
10 F	0329	2.7	0904	10.7	1541	3.0	2112	10.9	
11 SA	0402	3.0	0938	10.3	1614	3.4	2147	10.5	
12 SU	0437	3.3	1014	10.0	1650	3.8	2224	10.1	
13 M	0514	3.7	1054	9.5	1730	4.2	2306	9.6	
14 TU	0556	4.0	1140	9.2	1818	4.5	2357	9.3	
15 W	0648	4.3	1236	9.0	1917	4.6			◐
16 TH	0100	9.1	0750	4.3	1344	9.0	2023	4.5	
17 F	0208	9.2	0858	4.2	1452	9.2	2131	4.2	
18 SA	0314	9.6	1005	3.8	1553	9.7	2234	3.7	
19 SU	0415	10.1	1106	3.3	1649	10.3	2333	3.1	
20 M	0511	10.6	1204	2.8	1741	10.9			
21 TU	0032	2.5	0605	11.1	1258	2.4	1830	11.5	
22 W	0126	2.1	0657	11.5	1350	2.1	1919	11.9	○
23 TH	0219	1.7	0748	11.8	1440	1.9	2008	12.1	
24 F	0310	1.6	0838	11.9	1530	1.9	2057	12.2	
25 SA	0401	1.6	0928	11.8	1619	2.0	2146	12.0	
26 SU	0450	1.8	1017	11.5	1708	2.3	2236	11.6	
27 M	0539	2.1	1106	11.0	1758	2.7	2327	11.1	
28 TU	0629	2.6	1157	10.5	1849	3.2			◑
29 W	0023	10.6	0720	3.1	1252	10.1	1945	3.6	
30 TH	0123	10.1	0816	3.5	1354	9.8	2046	3.8	

JULY

Date	Time	m	Time	m	Time	m	Time	m	Moon
1 F	0229	9.9	0916	3.7	1502	9.7	2151	3.8	
2 SA	0337	9.8	1019	3.7	1607	9.9	2254	3.7	
3 SU	0440	9.9	1118	3.6	1705	10.2	2350	3.4	
4 M	0535	10.1	1211	3.4	1754	10.5			
5 TU	0041	3.1	0623	10.4	1258	3.2	1837	10.8	
6 W	0125	2.9	0705	10.6	1339	3.0	1916	11.0	●
7 TH	0204	2.8	0743	10.7	1418	2.9	1952	11.1	
8 F	0242	2.7	0818	10.8	1455	2.8	2026	11.2	
9 SA	0318	2.6	0852	10.8	1530	2.8	2100	11.1	
10 SU	0352	2.7	0925	10.7	1604	2.9	2133	10.9	
11 M	0425	2.8	0958	10.5	1637	3.2	2206	10.7	
12 TU	0458	3.1	1031	10.2	1711	3.4	2240	10.3	
13 W	0532	3.3	1105	9.9	1748	3.7	2317	10.0	
14 TH	0610	3.7	1145	9.5	1831	4.1			◐
15 F	0002	9.6	0656	4.0	1235	9.2	1924	4.3	
16 SA	0102	9.4	0754	4.2	1342	9.1	2032	4.4	
17 SU	0216	9.3	0907	4.2	1500	9.3	2149	4.1	
18 M	0333	9.5	1026	3.9	1614	9.8	2302	3.5	
19 TU	0445	10.1	1136	3.3	1719	10.5			
20 W	0009	2.8	0550	10.7	1240	2.7	1818	11.3	
21 TH	0113	2.2	0649	11.3	1340	2.2	1912	11.9	○
22 F	0212	1.6	0743	11.8	1436	1.7	2003	12.4	
23 SA	0307	1.2	0833	12.2	1528	1.4	2051	12.6	
24 SU	0357	1.0	0920	12.2	1615	1.4	2137	12.6	
25 M	0443	1.1	1004	12.0	1659	1.6	2221	12.2	
26 TU	0525	1.5	1046	11.6	1741	2.1	2303	11.6	
27 W	0605	2.2	1126	11.0	1821	2.8	2346	10.9	
28 TH	0644	3.0	1209	10.3	1904	3.5			◑
29 F	0036	10.0	0728	3.7	1300	9.7	1957	4.2	
30 SA	0137	9.4	0824	4.3	1409	9.2	2106	4.5	
31 SU	0258	9.0	0936	4.5	1534	9.2	2223	4.4	

AUGUST

Date	Time	m	Time	m	Time	m	Time	m	Moon
1 M	0420	9.1	1050	4.3	1647	9.6	2330	4.0	
2 TU	0524	9.6	1153	3.9	1742	10.1			
3 W	0026	3.5	0612	10.1	1244	3.5	1826	10.6	
4 TH	0112	3.1	0653	10.5	1328	3.1	1903	11.0	
5 F	0153	2.7	0729	10.8	1407	2.8	1938	11.2	●
6 SA	0231	2.5	0803	11.0	1444	2.5	2011	11.4	
7 SU	0305	2.3	0835	11.2	1517	2.4	2042	11.5	
8 M	0337	2.2	0905	11.2	1548	2.4	2112	11.5	
9 TU	0407	2.3	0934	11.1	1617	2.5	2142	11.3	
10 W	0436	2.5	1002	10.8	1647	2.8	2211	11.0	
11 TH	0504	2.8	1031	10.5	1717	3.2	2241	10.5	
12 F	0535	3.3	1102	10.1	1752	3.7	2317	10.0	
13 SA	0611	3.8	1141	9.6	1837	4.2			◐
14 SU	0005	9.5	0702	4.3	1241	9.1	1942	4.6	
15 M	0126	9.0	0818	4.6	1419	9.0	2114	4.5	
16 TU	0310	9.1	0958	4.4	1557	9.4	2244	3.9	
17 W	0438	9.7	1123	3.7	1712	10.3	2358	2.9	
18 TH	0546	10.6	1232	2.8	1812	11.3			
19 F	0107	2.0	0643	11.5	1333	1.9	1904	12.2	○
20 SA	0205	1.3	0733	12.2	1428	1.3	1952	12.8	
21 SU	0257	0.7	0819	12.6	1516	0.9	2036	13.1	
22 M	0343	0.6	0901	12.7	1559	0.9	2117	13.0	
23 TU	0423	0.8	0940	12.4	1638	1.2	2156	12.6	
24 W	0459	1.4	1016	11.9	1713	1.9	2232	11.8	
25 TH	0530	2.2	1050	11.2	1745	2.8	2307	10.9	
26 F	0600	3.1	1124	10.4	1818	3.7	2346	9.8	◑
27 SA	0634	4.1	1206	9.5	1902	4.5			
28 SU	0043	8.9	0726	4.9	1313	8.8	2017	5.1	
29 M	0223	8.4	0855	5.3	1507	8.6	2159	5.0	
30 TU	0408	8.6	1033	5.0	1634	9.1	2316	4.4	
31 W	0512	9.3	1140	4.2	1727	9.9			

Chart Datum: 6·29 metres below IGN Datum

TIME ZONE -0100
(French Standard Time)
Subtract 1 hour for UT
For French Summer Time add ONE hour in **non-shaded areas**

FRANCE – ST MALO

LAT 48°38'N LONG 2°02'W

TIMES AND HEIGHTS OF HIGH AND LOW WATERS

SPRING & NEAP TIDES
Dates in red are SPRINGS
Dates in blue are NEAPS

YEAR **2005**

SEPTEMBER

Day	Time	m	Time	m	Time	m	Time	m
1 TH	0011	3.7	0555	10.0	1229	3.5	1807	10.5
2 F	0056	3.0	0632	10.6	1311	3.0	1842	11.1
3 SA	0134	2.6	0706	11.1	1348	2.5	● 1916	11.5
4 SU	0210	2.2	0738	11.4	1423	2.2	1948	11.8
5 M	0243	2.0	0809	11.6	1454	2.1	2018	11.9
6 TU	0313	1.9	0838	11.7	1524	2.0	2047	11.9
7 W	0342	2.0	0905	11.6	1553	2.1	2114	11.7
8 TH	0409	2.2	0932	11.4	1621	2.5	2142	11.4
9 F	0435	2.6	0958	11.0	1649	2.9	2211	10.9
10 SA	0502	3.2	1027	10.5	1721	3.5	2244	10.2
11 SU	0536	3.8	1104	9.8	1804	4.2	◐ 2331	9.4
12 M	0626	4.5	1203	9.1	1911	4.7		
13 TU	0101	8.7	0749	5.0	1404	8.8	2057	4.7
14 W	0310	8.9	0950	4.7	1554	9.4	2238	3.9
15 TH	0436	9.8	1119	3.7	1704	10.5	2350	2.8
16 F	0537	10.9	1224	2.6	1759	11.6		
17 SA	0055	1.8	0628	11.8	1320	1.6	1848	12.5
18 SU	0148	1.0	0714	12.5	1410	1.0	○ 1932	13.0
19 M	0235	0.6	0756	12.8	1454	0.8	2013	13.2
20 TU	0317	0.6	0834	12.8	1534	0.9	2051	13.0
21 W	0353	1.0	0909	12.5	1608	1.3	2126	12.5
22 TH	0424	1.6	0941	12.0	1639	2.1	2158	11.7
23 F	0450	2.5	1012	11.3	1705	2.9	2230	10.7
24 SA	0514	3.4	1042	10.4	1732	3.9	2303	9.7
25 SU	0543	4.4	1117	9.5	1809	4.8	◑ 2350	8.7
26 M	0630	5.3	1218	8.6	1919	5.5		
27 TU	0146	8.0	0809	5.8	1435	8.3	2130	5.5
28 W	0345	8.4	1012	5.3	1607	8.9	2253	4.7
29 TH	0445	9.2	1116	4.5	1658	9.7	2342	3.8
30 F	0526	10.0	1201	3.6	1736	10.5		

OCTOBER

Day	Time	m	Time	m	Time	m	Time	m
1 SA	0025	3.1	0601	10.7	1240	2.9	1811	11.1
2 SU	0103	2.5	0634	11.2	1317	2.4	1845	11.6
3 M	0138	2.1	0707	11.6	1352	2.1	● 1918	11.9
4 TU	0211	1.9	0738	11.9	1425	1.9	1949	12.1
5 W	0243	1.8	0807	12.0	1456	1.8	2019	12.1
6 TH	0313	1.9	0835	11.9	1527	2.0	2048	12.0
7 F	0342	2.2	0903	11.7	1557	2.3	2117	11.6
8 SA	0410	2.6	0933	11.3	1629	2.8	2149	11.0
9 SU	0439	3.3	1006	10.7	1704	3.5	2227	10.2
10 M	0516	4.0	1048	10.0	1750	4.2	◐ 2321	9.3
11 TU	0612	4.7	1158	9.2	1903	4.7		
12 W	0110	8.7	0746	5.1	1407	9.0	2054	4.6
13 TH	0306	9.1	0947	4.6	1541	9.7	2228	3.8
14 F	0421	10.0	1105	3.5	1646	10.7	2334	2.7
15 SA	0517	11.1	1205	2.5	1738	11.7		
16 SU	0034	1.8	0605	11.9	1257	1.7	1824	12.4
17 M	0123	1.2	0648	12.4	1344	1.2	○ 1907	12.8
18 TU	0206	1.0	0727	12.6	1426	1.1	1946	12.8
19 W	0245	1.1	0803	12.6	1503	1.3	2022	12.6
20 TH	0318	1.5	0837	12.3	1535	1.7	2056	12.1
21 F	0347	2.1	0908	11.9	1604	2.3	2127	11.3
22 SA	0412	2.8	0938	11.2	1631	3.1	2158	10.5
23 SU	0438	3.6	1008	10.4	1659	3.9	2231	9.6
24 M	0508	4.5	1043	9.5	1734	4.7	2315	8.7
25 TU	0552	5.3	1137	8.7	1833	5.4	◑	
26 W	0049	8.1	0714	5.8	1334	8.3	2024	5.5
27 TH	0251	8.3	0916	5.5	1513	8.6	2201	5.0
28 F	0358	8.9	1028	4.8	1611	9.4	2256	4.2
29 SA	0442	9.7	1116	3.9	1653	10.1	2339	3.4
30 SU	0520	10.5	1157	3.2	1732	10.8		
31 M	0021	2.8	0556	11.1	1237	2.6	1809	11.4

NOVEMBER

Day	Time	m	Time	m	Time	m	Time	m
1 TU	0100	2.3	0631	11.5	1316	2.2	1845	11.8
2 W	0137	2.0	0705	11.9	1353	2.0	● 1919	12.0
3 TH	0212	1.9	0737	12.0	1429	1.9	1953	12.1
4 F	0247	2.0	0809	12.1	1505	2.0	2027	11.9
5 SA	0320	2.2	0843	11.9	1541	2.2	2102	11.6
6 SU	0354	2.7	0919	11.5	1619	2.7	2142	11.0
7 M	0431	3.3	1001	10.9	1701	3.3	2230	10.2
8 TU	0516	3.9	1054	10.1	1755	3.9	2335	9.5
9 W	0619	4.5	1213	9.5	1909	4.3	◐	
10 TH	0110	9.2	0750	4.7	1351	9.4	2042	4.2
11 F	0242	9.4	0926	4.3	1514	10.0	2202	3.6
12 SA	0353	10.1	1037	3.5	1618	10.7	2306	2.8
13 SU	0448	10.9	1136	2.7	1710	11.4		
14 M	0001	2.2	0536	11.5	1228	2.1	1758	11.9
15 TU	0052	1.8	0619	11.9	1314	1.8	1841	12.1
16 W	0134	1.7	0659	12.1	1356	1.7	○ 1921	12.0
17 TH	0211	1.8	0735	12.1	1433	1.9	1957	11.8
18 F	0245	2.1	0809	11.9	1506	2.1	2032	11.5
19 SA	0316	2.5	0842	11.6	1537	2.5	2105	11.0
20 SU	0346	3.0	0914	11.1	1608	3.1	2139	10.4
21 M	0416	3.6	0948	10.5	1639	3.7	2214	9.7
22 TU	0450	4.2	1025	9.8	1716	4.3	2256	9.1
23 W	0532	4.8	1111	9.1	1804	4.8	◑ 2355	8.6
24 TH	0630	5.2	1219	8.7	1911	5.1		
25 F	0120	8.4	0751	5.3	1347	8.6	2034	4.9
26 SA	0242	8.7	0911	4.9	1500	9.0	2145	4.5
27 SU	0342	9.2	1014	4.3	1557	9.6	2242	3.9
28 M	0430	9.9	1106	3.7	1645	10.2	2332	3.3
29 TU	0513	10.5	1154	3.0	1729	10.8		
30 W	0020	2.7	0554	11.1	1239	2.5	1812	11.3

DECEMBER

Day	Time	m	Time	m	Time	m	Time	m
1 TH	0104	2.4	0634	11.6	1324	2.2	● 1853	11.6
2 F	0146	2.1	0713	11.9	1408	1.9	1934	11.8
3 SA	0227	2.1	0752	12.0	1451	1.9	2016	11.8
4 SU	0309	2.2	0834	12.0	1535	2.0	2059	11.6
5 M	0352	2.5	0919	11.7	1620	2.3	2147	11.2
6 TU	0437	2.9	1008	11.2	1709	2.7	2238	10.6
7 W	0527	3.4	1103	10.7	1803	3.2	2337	10.1
8 TH	0626	3.8	1207	10.2	1906	3.5	◐	
9 F	0047	9.7	0735	4.0	1319	9.9	2014	3.7
10 SA	0201	9.6	0849	4.0	1434	10.0	2124	3.5
11 SU	0312	9.9	0958	3.6	1541	10.2	2229	3.2
12 M	0414	10.3	1101	3.2	1640	10.6	2327	2.9
13 TU	0507	10.7	1157	2.8	1733	10.9		
14 W	0020	2.7	0554	11.1	1247	2.6	1820	11.1
15 TH	0105	2.5	0637	11.3	1330	2.4	○ 1903	11.2
16 F	0145	2.5	0716	11.5	1409	2.3	1942	11.2
17 SA	0222	2.5	0752	11.5	1446	2.4	2018	11.1
18 SU	0257	2.6	0828	11.3	1521	2.5	2053	10.8
19 M	0331	2.9	0902	11.1	1555	2.8	2128	10.5
20 TU	0405	3.2	0936	10.7	1628	3.2	2202	10.1
21 W	0439	3.6	1011	10.3	1702	3.6	2237	9.7
22 TH	0514	4.0	1047	9.8	1739	3.9	2316	9.3
23 F	0556	4.3	1130	9.4	1823	4.3	◑	
24 SA	0002	9.0	0646	4.6	1223	9.1	1916	4.5
25 SU	0107	8.8	0747	4.7	1331	8.9	2021	4.5
26 M	0221	8.8	0858	4.6	1445	9.1	2133	4.3
27 TU	0330	9.2	1008	4.1	1552	9.5	2240	3.9
28 W	0429	9.8	1111	3.6	1651	10.0	2339	3.3
29 TH	0522	10.5	1208	2.9	1745	10.6		
30 F	0036	2.8	0611	11.1	1302	2.4	1836	11.1
31 SA	0128	2.3	0659	11.6	1354	1.9	● 1925	11.5

Chart Datum: 6·29 metres below IGN Datum

9.18.13 RIVER RANCE

Ille-et-Vilaine **48°37'·04N 02°01'·71W** (Barrage)

CHARTS AC *3659*, 2700; SHOM 7130, 4233; Imray C33B; Stanfords 26

TIDES Standard Port ST MALO (⟵) Zone –0100
Water levels up-river of the Rance hydro-electric tidal barrage are strongly affected by the operation of the sluice gates and occasional use of the turbines as pumps. On most days from 0700 – 2100LT, 4m above CD is maintained. There is generally 8·5m above CD for a period of 4 hours from 0700 – 2000LT. A French language pamphlet, issued by Électricité de France, should be obtained from HM's at St Malo or Bas Sablons, or from the office at the barrage lock. It gives forecasts for the summer months of when heights of 4m and 8·5m above CD will occur in the period 0700 – 2000LT. The local daily paper *Ouest-France* gives a forecast for the next day of HW and LW up-stream of the barrage, under the heading *Usine Marémotrice de la Rance.*

SHELTER Good shelter up-river dependent on wind direction. The principal ⚓s/moorings on the E bank are at St Suliac and Mordreuc, and at La Richardais, La Jouvente, Le Minihic and La Pommeraie on the W bank. Marinas at Plouër, Lyvet (E bank, beyond Chatelier lock) and Dinan: see opposite.

NAVIGATION From St Malo/Dinard, appr the lock (at the W end of the barrage) between Pte de la Jument to stbd and a prohib sluicing zone to port, marked by PHM buoys linked by wire cables. 3 white waiting buoys are on the E side of the appr chan, close to the prohibited zone; a similar buoy is upstream.

Barrage lock opens day/night (on request 2030-0430) on the hour, every hour provided the level is at least 4m above CD on both sides of the barrage. Yachts should arrive at H –20 mins. An illuminated display board gives access times in French/English. Lock entry sigs are **IPTS** sigs 2, 3 and 5. Masted boats entering from sea should berth at the S end of the lock so that the bridge can close astern of them. Vertical wires assist berthing/warp-handling. The lifting road-bridge across the lock opens only between H and H +15. Up-stream of the lock a further prohib area to port is marked as above.

The chan up-river is marked by perches; binos needed. The 3M chan to St Suliac has min depth of 2m. The next 6M to the Chatelier lock partially dries and is buoyed; keep to the outside of bends. The suspension bridge and road bridge at Port St. Hubert have 23m clearance. A viaduct 1M beyond Mordreuc has 19m clearance. Allow 2-3 hours from the barrage to Chatelier.

Chatelier lock and swing bridge operate 0600-2100LT, provided there is at least 8·5m rise of tide. HW Chatelier is 2-3 hours after HW St Malo depending on the barrage. Entry is controlled by CEVNI sigs (variations on a R and G theme).

The final 3M to Dinan has a published min depth in the marked chan of 1·4m; check with lock-keeper. Beware overhead cables 16m air clearance approx 2ca downstream of N end of quay at Port de Dinan. Dinan gives access to Ille et Rance Canal and River Vilaine to Biscay (see 9.18.14).

LIGHTS AND MARKS Approaching the barrage from seaward: Pte de la Jument bn tr, Fl G 4s 6m 4M; PHM buoy opposite, Fl R 4s (prohib zone). The lock control twr is conspic. NW side of lock, Fl (2) G 6s, with G ▲ on W □. First dolphin, Fl (2) R 6s, with R ■ on W □.
Approaching from Dinan: PHM buoy, Fl (2) R 6s, at S end of prohib zone; leave to stbd. First dolphin, Fl (3) R 12s, with R ■ on W □. SW side of lock, Fl (3) G 12s, G ▲ on W □.

R/T *Barrage de la Rance* (lock) Ch 13. Chatelier lock Ch 14.

TELEPHONE Water levels/navigation 02·99·46·14·46; Barrage/lock info 02·99·46·21·87; HM (Richardais) 02·99·46·24·20; HM (Plouër) 02·96·86·83·15; Chatelier lock 02·96·39·55·66; HM (Lyvet) 02·96·83·35·57; HM (Dinan) 02·96·39·04·67; Météo 02·99·46·10·46; Auto 08.92.68.08.35; Aff Mar 02·96·39·56·44; Police 02·99·81·52·30.

FACILITIES St. Suliac Slip, M, Bar, R, 🛒, Divers (Convoimer); **Mordreuc** Slip, L, M, Bar, R; **La Richardais** El, ME, ⚒, Bar, D, P, ✉, R, 🛒, Ⓑ; **La Jouvente** AB, Bar, R; **Le Minihic** M, L, Slip, ME, El, ⚒; **La Cale de Plouër** M, L, SC, R.

MARINAS ON THE RIVER RANCE

PLOUËR, Côtes d'Armor, **48°31'·54N 01°58'·95W.** Marina is on the W bank of the R Rance, 6M above the barrage and 0·5M above the two St Hubert bridges. Access approx HW±3, when tide is 8m above CD, giving at least 1·5m water above rising gate. Approach on about 285°, ent in line with Plouër church spire. Unlit PHM and SHM perches are 30m from ent at S end of bkwtr. Sill is marked by FR and FG lts which are lit, day/night, whenever marina is accessible. Depth gauge (hard to read) has W flood-light. Facilities: **Marina** (240+ Ⓥ on pontoon B) ☎ 02·96·86·83·15. VHF Ch 09. AB €1.58, Slip, CH, BY, C, ME, BH (10-14 ton), R, Bar, limited 🛒 in village 1M.

LYVET, 48°29'·40N 02°00'·00W. **Marina** (175 berths) ☎ 02·96·83·35·57; €1.25 , R, Bar, limited 🛒. On the E bank just beyond Chatelier lock. Berth on D pontoon or as directed by HM.

DINAN, HM ☎ 02·96·39·56·44; **Marina** €1.30 , P, D, C for masts, R, Bar. Overhead cables just N of town have 16m clearance. Alongside berths line the W bank of the river, with fingers close to the Port in about 1·5m. Low bridge beyond Port has 2·5m headroom, giving access to the Ille et Rance canal. **Town** (75m above water level) 🛒, R, ✉, Ⓑ, ⇌, ✈ (Dinard).

Ille et Rance canal (see overleaf): On the Breton canals the tolls charged elsewhere in France (see 9.17.6) are not levied nor envisaged. A certificate of competence is not required, unless LOA >15m or speed >20kph/11kn.

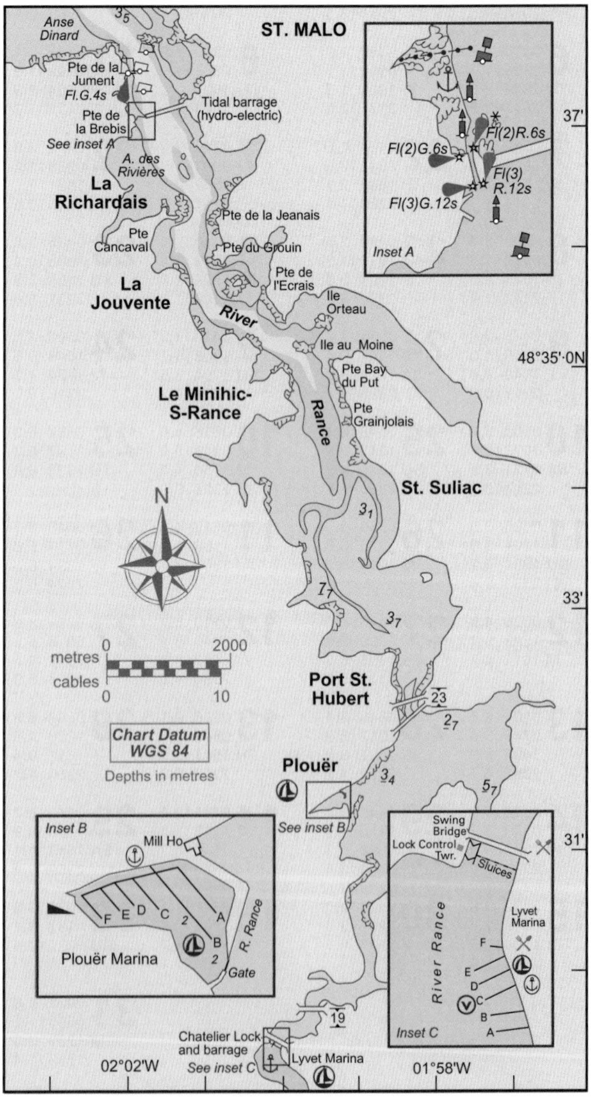
ST. MALO
Anse Dinard
Pte de la Jument
Fl.G.4s
Tidal barrage (hydro-electric)
Pte de la Brebis
See inset A
A. des Rivières
La Richardais
Pte de la Jeanais
Pte Cancaval
Pte du Grouin
Pte de l'Ecrais
La Jouvente
Ile Orteau
River
Ile au Moine
Pte Bay du Put
Le Minihic-S-Rance
Rance
Pte Grainjolais
St. Suliac
N
metres
cables
0
2000
0
10
Port St. Hubert
Chart Datum WGS 84
Depths in metres
Plouër
See inset B
Fl(2)G.6s
Fl(2)R.6s
Fl(3) R.12s
Fl(3)G.12s
Inset A
37'
48°35'·0N
33'
31'
Inset B
Mill Ho
F E D C A B
Plouër Marina
R. Rance
Gate
Swing Bridge
Lock Control Twr.
Sluices
River Rance
Lyvet Marina
F E D C B A
Inset C
Chatelier Lock and barrage
See inset C
Lyvet Marina
02°02'W
01°58'W

9.18.14 INLAND WATERWAYS OF BRITTANY

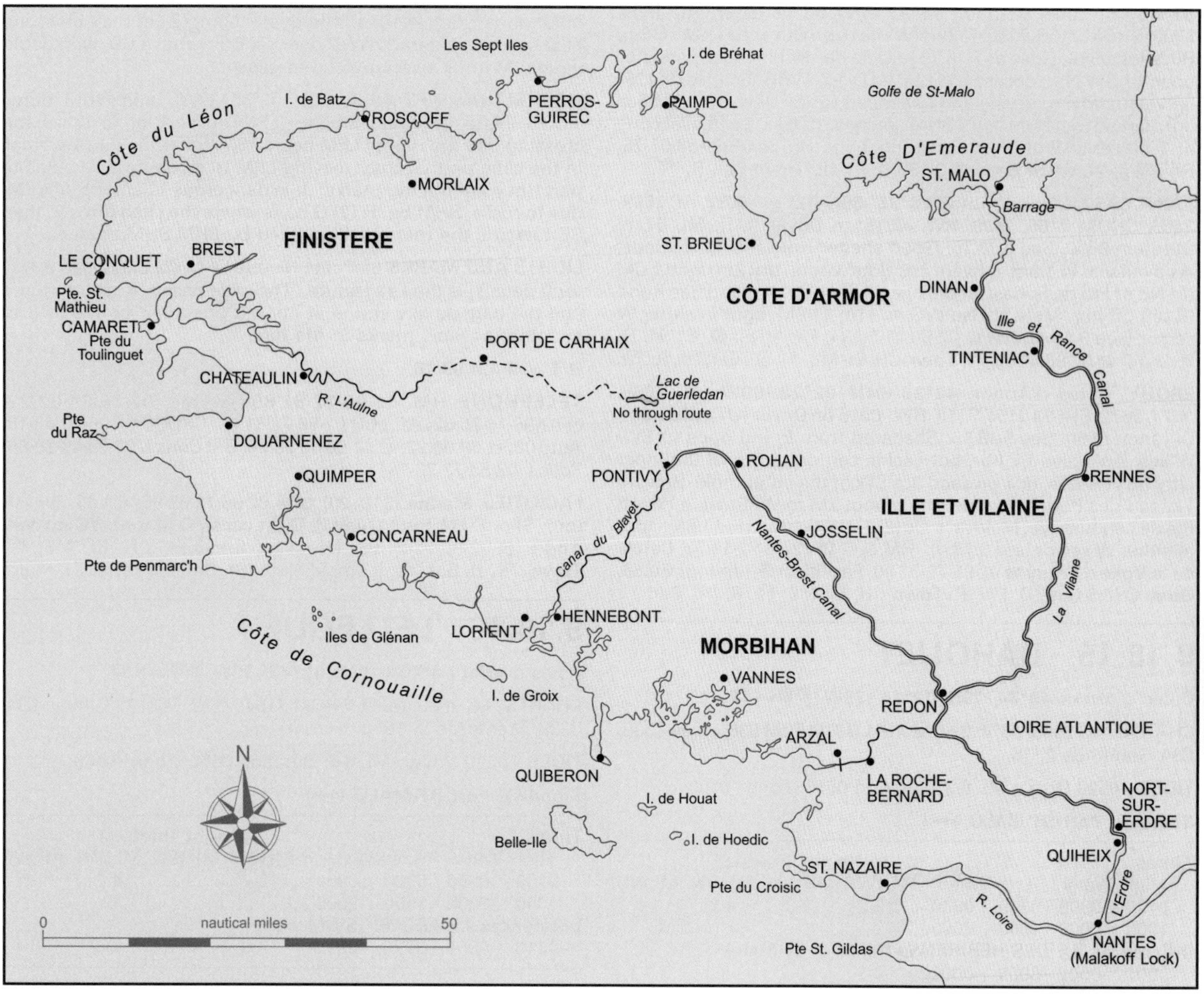
Les Sept Iles
I. de Bréhat
I. de Batz
ROSCOFF
PERROS-GUIREC
PAIMPOL
Golfe de St-Malo
Côte du Léon
Côte D'Emeraude
ST. MALO
Barrage
MORLAIX
FINISTERE
BREST
LE CONQUET
Pte. St. Mathieu
CAMARET
Pte du Toulinguet
ST. BRIEUC
CÔTE D'ARMOR
DINAN
Ille et Rance Canal
TINTENIAC
PORT DE CARHAIX
CHATEAULIN
R. L'Aulne
Lac de Guerledan
No through route
Pte du Raz
DOUARNENEZ
QUIMPER
PONTIVY
ROHAN
RENNES
ILLE ET VILAINE
JOSSELIN
Nantes-Brest Canal
Canal du Blavet
CONCARNEAU
Pte de Penmarc'h
La Vilaine
HENNEBONT
LORIENT
Iles de Glénan
Côte de Cornouaille
MORBIHAN
VANNES
I. de Groix
REDON
LOIRE ATLANTIQUE
ARZAL
LA ROCHE-BERNARD
QUIBERON
I. de Houat
NORT-SUR-ERDRE
Belle-Ile
I. de Hoedic
QUIHEIX
ST. NAZAIRE
Pte du Croisic
L'Erdre
R. Loire
N
0
nautical miles
50
Pte St. Gildas
NANTES (Malakoff Lock)

NAVIGATION Canals and rivers across and within Brittany enable boats of limited water and air draughts to go from the Channel to the Bay of Biscay avoiding the passage around Finistère. Distances, number of locks, boat size and speed limits are summarised below. Dinan-Arzal takes about 5 days. Despite the many locks it can be a thoroughly enjoyable trip through unspoiled countryside and some interesting towns. Most overnight stops are free or at nominal cost.

LOCKS From Apr to Sept locks are worked 7 days a week 0800-1930LT, closing for lunch 1230-1330 approx. All locks are attended, but a fair measure of self-help is the order of the day. In Jul/Aug, in order to conserve water, locks may open on the hour only (and at H+30 if traffic demands).

ACCESS For prior estimate of max draught possible, contact: Equipement, Ille et Vilaine, 1 Avenue de Mail, 35000 Rennes. (☎ 02·99.59.20.60; 📠 02·99.54.03.99); or obtain recorded information update on ☎ 02·99.59.11.12. For latest info on the Ille et Rance Canal/R Vilaine, contact: Rennes ☎ 02·99.59.20.60 or Redon ☎ 02·99.71.03.78. For the Lorient-Nantes Canal, contact: Nantes ☎ 02·40.71.02.00; Hennebont ☎ 02·97.85.15.15; Lorient ☎ 02·97.21.21.54; Pontivy ☎ 02·97.25.55.21. Closures *(Chômages)* for maintenance are scheduled every Wednesday from approx first week in November to last week in March.

INFORMATION *Inland Waterways of France:* D Edwards-May (Imray) and the ECM Carte-Guide No 12 are recommended.

TOLLS may be due on the R Loire only; see 9.17.6 for rates.

SUMMARY	Length km	No of locks	Max draft m	Max air draft m	Max LOA m	Max beam m	Speed limit kn
St MALO-ARZAL (Ille et Rance Canal and La Vilaine)							
R Rance-Dinan	29·0	1	1·3	19	25	–	5·4
Ille et Rance Canal							
Dinan-Rennes	79·0	48	1·2	2·5	25	4·5	4·3
Rennes-Redon	89·0	13	1·2	3·2/2·6*	25	4·5	4·3
Redon-Arzal	42·0	1	1·3	–			
*Depending on water level							
LORIENT - NANTES							
Canal du Blavet (See 9.21.15)							
Lorient-Pontivy	70	28	1·4	2·6	25	4·6	4·3
Nantes-Brest Canal	184·3	106	–	3	25	4·6	4·3
Pontivy-Rohan			0·8 (possible closure)				
Rohan-Josselin			1·0				
Josselin-Redon			1·4				
Redon-Quiheix			1·1				
L'Erdre River	27·6	1	1·4	3·8	400	6·2	13·5
R Loire, above Nantes (9.21.31), may be navigable to Angers.							
R L'AULNE (See 9.20.27)							
Brest-Chateaulin	42	1	3·0	N/A	25	–	–
Chateaulin-Carhaix	72	33	1·1	2·5	25	4·6	4·3

18

MINOR HARBOURS BETWEEN ST MALO AND DAHOUET

ST BRIAC, Côtes d'Armor, **48°37′·37N 02°08′·63W**. AC *3659*, 2700; SHOM 7155, 7130, 7129. HW –0515 on Dover (UT); ML 6·8m; Duration 0550. Tides as 9.18.15; use Ile des Hébihens. Drying hbr open to SW-NW; access HW±2½. A Dir Iso WRG 4s lt leads 125° between offlying drying and beaconed rocks/islets. The last 6ca are marked by 4 PHM and 3 SHM perches. 10 🅥s in Le Bechet cove or ⚓ on sand W of Ile du Perron in 3-5m. HM ☎ 02·99·88·01·75, FW, Slip; **YC de St Briac** ☎ 02·99·88·31·45; **Town** Bar, R, 🛒.

SAINT CAST, Côtes d'Armor, **48°38′·39N 02°14′·60W**. AC 2669, *3659*; SHOM 7155, 7129. HW –0515 on Dover (UT); ML 6·6m; Duration 0550. See 9.18.15. Good shelter from SW to N winds; 🅥s available in 1·8m. Beware Les Bourdinots (dry 2m) with ECM ¾M NE of Pte de St Cast, and La Feuillade (IDM bn) and Bec Rond (R bn) off hbr. Mole hd, Iso WG 4s 11m 11/8M; appr in either W sector (see 9.18.4). HM ☎ 02·96·41·88·34; Facilities: 🅥 €1.94, D, P, C; **YC** ☎ 02·96·41·71·71. **Town** CH, EI, ME, ⚒, Ⓑ, Bar, ✉, R, 🛒.

ERQUY, Côtes d'Armor, **48°38′·04N 02°28′·69W**. AC 2669, *3674*, 3672; SHOM 7154, 7310. HW –0515 on Dover (UT); ML 6·5m; Duration 0550. See 9.18.15. Sheltered from E, but open to SW/W'lies. An active FV hbr, but yachts can dry out E of the inner jetty hd Fl R 2·5s; or ⚓ on sand 3ca SW of the outer mole. Beware Plateau des Portes d'Erquy (dry) about 2M to W. Beware rks off Pte de Lahoussaye. Mole hd lt Oc (2+1) WRG 12s 11m 11/8M; appr in either W sector (see 9.18.4). HM & ⊖ ☎ 02·96·72·19·32; **Cercle de la Voile d'Erquy** ☎ 02·96·72·32·40; Facilities: 🅥 (drying) €0.56, **Quay** C (3·5 ton), D, FW, P; **Town** CH, EI, ME, ⚒, R, 🛒, Bar.

9.18.15 DAHOUET

Côtes d'Armor **48°34′·79N 02°34′·39W** ❁❁◊◊✿

CHARTS AC 2669, *3674*; SHOM 7154, 7310; ECM 536; Imray C33B, C34; Stanfords 2, 16

TIDES –0520 Dover; ML 6·3; Duration 0550; Zone –0100

Standard Port ST-MALO (⟵)

Times				Height (metres)			
High Water		Low Water		MHWS	MHWN	MLWN	MLWS
0100	0800	0300	0800	12·2	9·3	4·2	1·5
1300	2000	1500	2000				
Differences ÎLE DES HÉBIHENS (7M W of St Malo)							
–0002	–0002	–0005	–0005	–0·2	–0·2	–0·1	–0·1
SAINT CAST							
–0002	–0002	–0005	–0005	–0·2	–0·2	–0·1	–0·1
ERQUY							
–0010	–0005	–0023	–0017	–0·6	–0·5	0·0	0·0
DAHOUET							
–0010	–0010	–0025	–0020	–0·9	–0·7	–0·2	–0·2

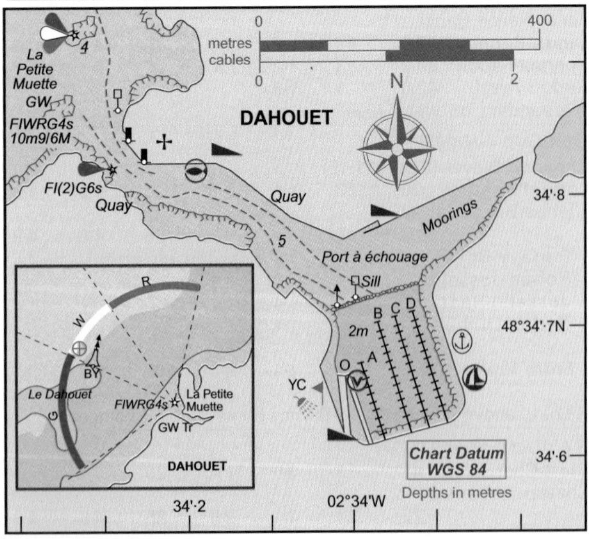
La Petite Muette
GW
FlWRG4s
10m9/6M
Fl(2)G6s
Quay
4
metres
cables
0
400
0
2
N
DAHOUET
Quay
Moorings
5
Port à échouage
Sill
B C D
A
2m
O
YC
34'·8
48°34'·7N
34'·6
Chart Datum
WGS 84
Depths in metres
02°34'W
34'·2
R
W
G
BY
Le Dahouet
La Petite Muette
FlWRG4s
GW Tr
DAHOUET

SHELTER Good, but ent (dries 4m) has strong currents and is unsafe in fresh/strong NW'lies, when a bar may form. Outer hbr (FVs) dries 5·5m. Marina, min depth 2·5m, (2·0m may be found at 🅥 berth) is entered HW±2 over sill 5·5m above CD, with depth gauge. May be overcrowded in season.

NAVIGATION WPT 48°35′·22N 02°35′·37W, unlit NCM buoy, 117°/0·8M to La Petite Muette (LPM) lt tr. Appr in W sector, crossing into the R until LPM bears 160°. Enter the narrow break in the cliffs on that track leaving LPM to stbd and 2 W poles to port (they are not ldg marks). It is dangerous to enter S of LPM, due to rocks. SHM bn, Fl (2) G 6s, is where the chan turns E, then SE towards the marina sill marked by PHM/SHM perches.

LIGHTS AND MARKS La Petite Muette W twr/G band [see 9.18.4 for lt details] is the key feature. The wide beach NE at Val André and the pagoda-like shrine at hbr ent are conspic. See 9.18.16 for other conspic marks in the bay.

R/T VHF Ch 09 16.

TELEPHONE HM 02·96·72·82·85; Météo 02·36·65·02·22; ⊖ 02·96·74·75·32; Aff Mar 02·96·72·31·42; CROSS 02·96·70·42·18; Auto 08.92.68.08.22; Ⓗ 02·96·45·23·28; Brit Consul 02·99·46·26·64; Police 02·96·72·22·18.

FACILITIES Marina (318+20) ☎/📠 02·96·72·82·85, €1.65, BH (10 ton), Slip, C (14 ton); **Quay** P, D (in cans), C (4 ton); **YC du Val-André** ☎ 02·96·72·21·68, showers; **Services:** CH, EI, ME, ⚒. **Town**, 🛒, R, Bar, ⇌ (Lamballe), ✈ (St. Brieuc). Ferry: St. Malo.

9.18.16 LE LÉGUÉ

Côtes d'Armor **48°31′·89N 02°43′·39W** ❁❁◊◊✿

CHARTS AC 2669, *3674*; SHOM 7154, 7128; ECM 536; Imray C34, C33B; Stanfords 2, 16

TIDES –0520 Dover; ML 6·5; Duration 0550; Zone –0100

Standard Port ST-MALO (⟵)

Times				Height (metres)			
High Water		Low Water		MHWS	MHWN	MLWN	MLWS
0100	0800	0300	0800	12·2	9·3	4·2	1·5
1300	2000	1500	2000				
Differences LE LÉGUÉ (SWM buoy)							
–0010	–0005	–0020	–0015	–0·8	–0·5	–0·2	–0·1

SHELTER Very good. Yachts berth near the viaduct in Bassin No 2 (min 3·2m), now upgraded to a marina; Capitainerie is on N side. Le Légué is also the commercial port for St Brieuc.

NAVIGATION WPT 48°34′·33N 02°41′·18W, Le Légué SWM buoy, Fl Mo (A) 10s, 210°/2·6M to Pte à l'Aigle lt. The bay dries E/SE of conspic Pte du Roselier. Access via well buoyed/lit chan, dredged 5m above CD; but not advised in strong N/NE winds. Work in progress in the outer hbr.
Lock opening times: Local HW ±1 when Height of Tide at St Malo is 8-10m; HW ±1¼ for HoT of 10-11m; HW ±1½ for HoT of 11-11.5m; and HW –2 to +1½ for HoT > 11·5m. The lock sill dries 5·1m. Lock staff help with warps. There is space to jill around if lock not ready; commercial ships take priority. A low swing bridge at the ent to Bassin No 2 opens when the lock operates.

LIGHTS AND MARKS Conspic marks: Rohein tr, from N, and Le Verdelet Is from E (beware Plateau des Jaunes). No ldg lts/marks. The outer hbr ent is between Pte à l'Aigle [QG 13m 8M, vis 160°-070°, W tr G top] on the NW bank of Le Gouet river and the SE jetty hd, VQ R 4M.

R/T Call: *Le Légué Port* VHF Ch 12 16 (approx HW–2 to +1½).

TELEPHONE HM 02·96·33·35·41, 📠 02·96·61·46·94; Aff Mar 02·96·68·30·70; CROSS 02·98·89·31·31; Météo 02·99·46·10·46 and VHF Ch 13; Auto 08·92·68·08·22; SNSM 02·96·88·35·47; ⊖ 02·96·74·75·32; Police 02·96·61·22·61; Dr St Brieuc 02·96·61·49·07; Brit Consul 02·99·46·26·64.

FACILITIES Marina (100+20 🅥), 06·86·49·09·13, AB €1.48, C (30 ton), P & D (by cans), YC; **Services:** ⚒, ME, EI, CH, SM, Ⓔ, EI, CH. **Town** P & D (cans), Gaz, 🛒, R, Bar, ✉, Ⓑ, ⇌, ✈. Ferry: St Malo.

LE LÉGUÉ *continued*

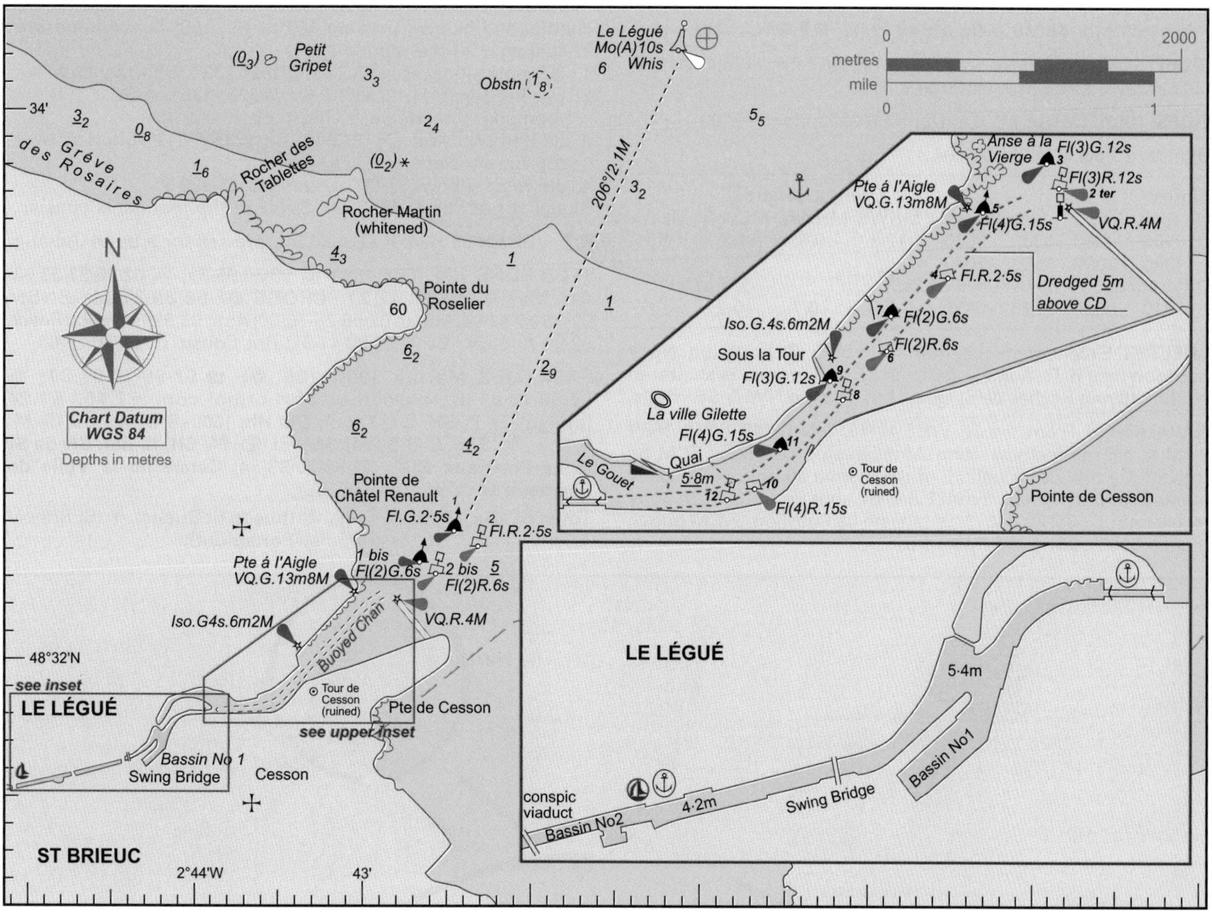
Le Légué
Mo(A)10s
6 Whis
Petit Gripet
Obstn
Grève des Rosaires
Rocher des Tablettes
Rocher Martin (whitened)
206°/2·1M
Pointe du Roselier
Chart Datum WGS 84
Depths in metres
Pointe de Châtel Renault
Fl.G.2·5s
Fl.R.2·5s
1 bis
Fl(2)G.6s
2 bis
Fl(2)R.6s
Pte á l'Aigle VQ.G.13m8M
Iso.G4s.6m2M
VQ.R.4M
Buoyed Chan
48°32'N
see inset
LE LÉGUÉ
Tour de Cesson (ruined)
Pte de Cesson
see upper inset
Bassin No 1
Swing Bridge
Cesson
ST BRIEUC
2°44'W
43'
34'
metres
mile
2000
Anse à la Vierge
Fl(3)G.12s
Fl(3)R.12s
2 ter
VQ.R.4M
Fl(4)G.15s
Fl.R.2·5s
Dredged 5m above CD
Iso.G.4s.6m2M
Fl(2)G.6s
Fl(2)R.6s
Sous la Tour
Fl(3)G.12s
La ville Gilette
Fl(4)G.15s
Quai
5·8m
Le Gouet
Fl(4)R.15s
Pointe de Cesson
LE LÉGUÉ
5·4m
Bassin No1
conspic viaduct
4·2m
Swing Bridge
Bassin No2

9.18.17 BINIC

Côtes d'Armor **48°36´·06N 02°48´·99W**

CHARTS AC 2668/9, *3674*; SHOM 7154, 7128; ECM 536; Imray C33B, C34; Stanfords 2, 16

TIDES –0525 Dover; ML 6·3; Duration 0550; Zone –0100

Standard Port ST-MALO (⟵)

Times				Height (metres)			
High Water		Low Water		MHWS	MHWN	MLWN	MLWS
0100	0800	0300	0800	12·2	9·3	4·2	1·5
1300	2000	1500	2000				
Differences BINIC							
–0008	–0008	–0030	–0015	–0·8	–0·7	–0·2	–0·2

SHELTER Good in Bassin à Flot/marina (1·5-3m); Ⓥ berths alongside 'A' pontoon, to stbd on entry. Easy access HW±3 by day/night to Avant Port (dries), except in E winds. Gate opens, H24, only when height of tide >8·5m: approx HW–2 to HW sp, but only HW –½ to HW at nps. No entry/exit when coefficient <40. Access to the marina via entry gate and retracting bridge is controlled by IPTS, sigs 2 and 3, on mast to stbd of gate.

NAVIGATION WPT 48°35´·86N 02°46´·68W, 278°/1·5M to ent. From E, appr via Caffa ECM buoy, whence ent bears 246°/4·2M; or from N through Rade de St Quay-Portrieux. Beware oyster beds 2M E of hbr. Appr dries 7ca offshore; hbr ent dries 4·2m.

LIGHTS AND MARKS Ldg line 278°, N mole lt tr [Oc (3) 12s 12m 12M, W tr, G gallery] in transit with church spire.

R/T VHF Ch 09.

TELEPHONE HM port-de-binic@wanadoo.fr; 02·96·73·61·86, 02·96.73.72.38; Aff Mar 02·96·70·42·27; SNSM 02·96.73.74.41; CROSS 02·98·89·31·31; ⊜ 02·96·74·75·32; Météo 02·99·46·10·46; Auto 08·92·68·08·22; Police 02·96·73·60·32; Dr 02·96·42·61·05; Ⓗ 02·96.94.31.71; Brit Consul 02·99·46·26·64.

FACILITIES Bassin (420 + 30 Ⓥ), AB €1.80 approx depending on season, C (20 ton), Slip; **Club Nautique de Binic** ☎ 02·96·73·31·67; **Services:** CH, ME, El, Ⓔ, ⚒, SM, SHOM. **Town** P, 🛒, Gaz, ⌧, R, Bar, ✉, Ⓑ, ⇌ (bus to St Brieuc), ✈ (St Brieuc). Ferry: St Malo.

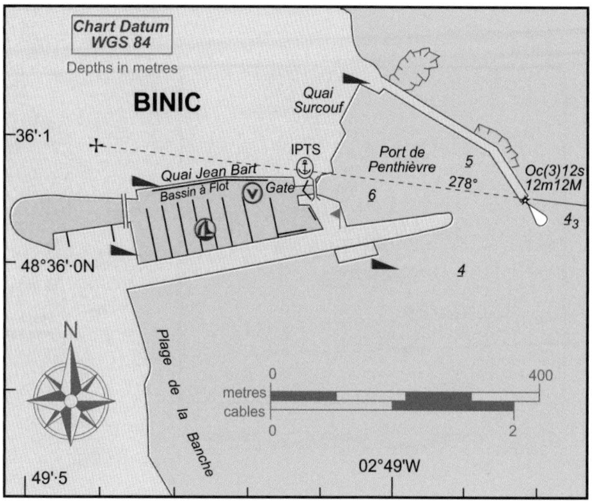
Chart Datum WGS 84
Depths in metres
BINIC
Quai Surcouf
36'·1
IPTS
Quai Jean Bart
Bassin à Flot
Gate
Port de Penthièvre
278°
Oc(3)12s 12m12M
48°36'·0N
Plage de la Banche
metres
cables
400
02°49'W
49'·5

9.18.18 ST QUAY-PORTRIEUX

Côtes d'Armor **48°38´·84N 02°48´·97W**

CHARTS AC *2668*, 2669, *3674*, 3672; SHOM 7154, 7128; ECM 536, 537; Imray C33B, C34; Stanfords 2, 16.

TIDES –0520 Dover; ML 6·3; Duration 0550; Zone –0100

Standard Port ST-MALO (⟵)

Times				**Height (metres)**			
High Water		Low Water		MHWS	MHWN	MLWN	MLWS
0100	0800	0300	0800	12·2	9·3	4·2	1·5
1300	2000	1500	2000				
Differences ST QUAY-PORTRIEUX							
–0010	–0005	–0025	–0020	–0·9	–0·7	–0·2	–0·1

SHELTER Excellent in the marina (3·5m); Ⓥ berth on No 7 pontoon (see R/T). ⚓ in the Rade de St. Q-Portrieux is sheltered by the offlying Roches de St Quay, but open to NW & SE winds.

NAVIGATION From the N, WPT 48°40´·94N 02°49´·69W, 169°/2·0M to NE mole elbow. Note: Moulières de Portrieux, ECM bn tr (N of the marina) is unlit; E of the marina an unlit WCM buoy marks Les Noirs (2·4m). From E and SE appr via Caffa ECM buoy to WPT 48°37´·36N 02°46´·91W (abeam La Roselière WCM buoy), thence 318°/2·0M to NE mole head.

LIGHTS AND MARKS For lt details see chartlet and 9.18.4. At night from the N WPT follow the white sectors of 4 Dir lts (see chartlet and below), tracking 169°, 130°, 185° (astern) and 318° in sequence to the marina ent:

1. NE mole elbow, Iso WRG 4s, **W159°-179°**. White concrete twr.
2. Herflux Dir lt, Fl (2) WRG 6s, **W125°-135°**. A SCM (YB and topmark) bcn twr on drying rock.
3. Ile Harbour Dir lt, Oc (2) WRG 6s, **W358°-011°**. Short W twr/R top on an islet.
4. NE mole elbow, as (1) above, **W316°-320·5°**.

Signal stn at Pte de St Quay, NNW of the marina, is conspic.

R/T VHF Ch 09 H24. If LOA >12m, pre-call for a berth Jul/Aug.

TELEPHONE HM (Old Hbr) 02·96·70·95·31; ⊜ 02·96·33·33·03; Aff Mar 02·96·70·42·27; CROSS 02·98·89·31·31; SNSM 02·96·70·52·04; Météo 02·96·76·76·80; Auto 08.92.68.08.22; Police 02·96·70·61·24; Dr 02·96·70·41·31; Brit Consul 02·99·46·26·64.

FACILITIES Marina (900+100 Ⓥ) ☎ 02·96·70·81·30, 📠 02·96·70·81·31, welcome@port-armor.com €2.40, €1.24 (drying), D, P, BH, C (12 ton); **Old Hbr** (500+8 Ⓥ) AB €9.15, M, P, D, L, ⚒, Slip, C (1·5 ton), ME, El, Ⓔ, ⚒, CH, R, Bar; **SN de St Quay Portrieux** ☎/📠 02·96·70·93·34; **Cercle de la Voile de Portrieux** ☎ 02·96·70·41·76, Bar;

Town 🛒, Gaz, R, Bar, ✉, Ⓑ, ⇌ (bus to St Brieuc), ✈ (St Brieuc/Armor). Ferry: St Malo–Poole, Portsmouth.

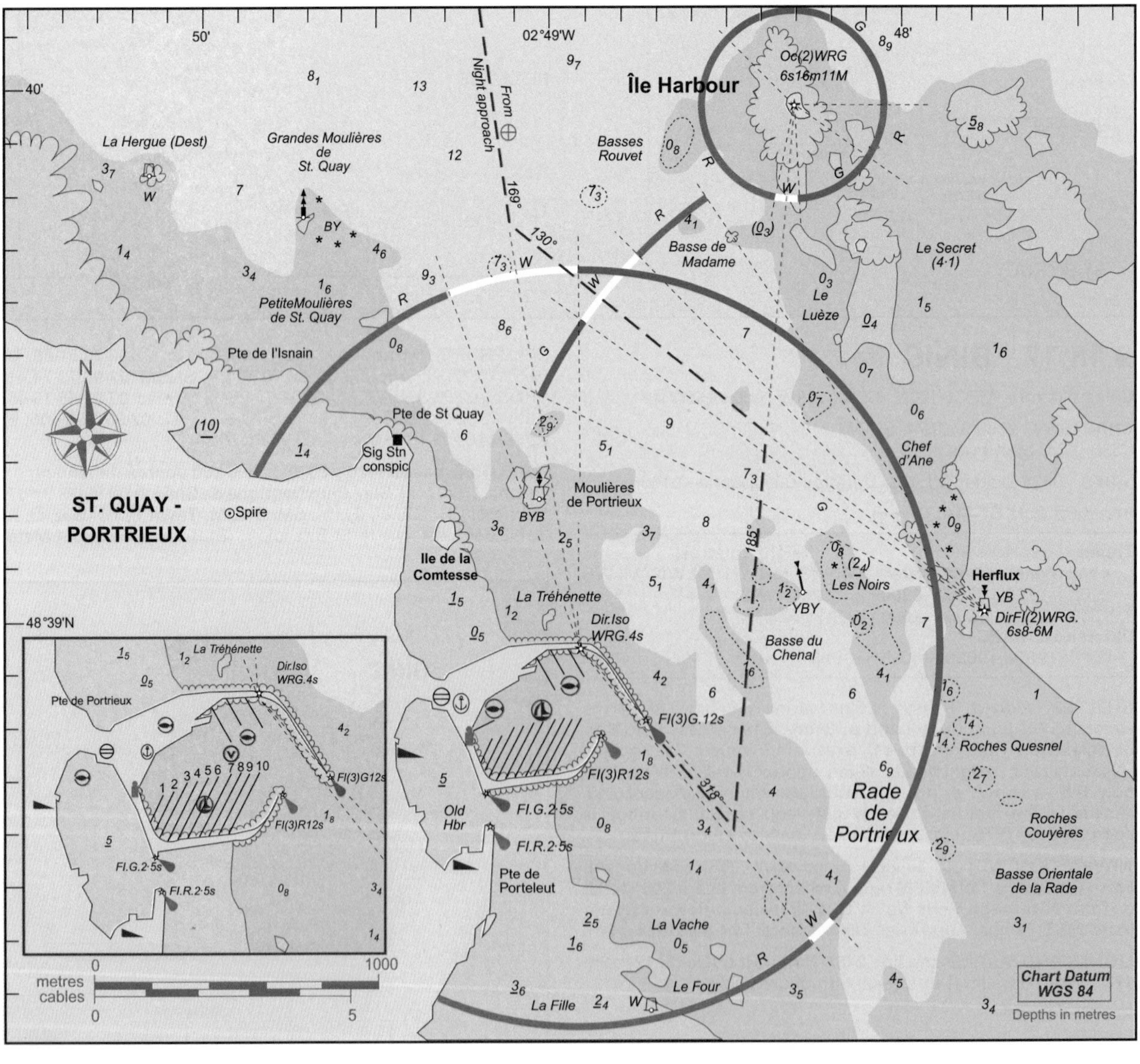
50'
02°49'W
48'
40'
48°39'N
Île Harbour
Oc(2)WRG 6s16m11M
Night approach
From ⊕
169°
130°
185°
318°
La Hergue (Dest)
Grandes Moulières de St. Quay
PetiteMoulières de St. Quay
Pte de l'Isnain
Basses Rouvet
Basse de Madame
Le Luèze
Le Secret (4·1)
Chef d'Ane
Pte de St Quay
Sig Stn conspic
Moulières de Portrieux
BYB
BY
YBY
YB
Les Noirs
Herflux
DirFl(2)WRG. 6s8-6M
Ile de la Comtesse
La Tréhénette
Dir.Iso WRG.4s
Fl(3)G.12s
Fl(3)R12s
Fl.G.2·5s
Fl.R.2·5s
Old Hbr
Pte de Porteleut
Pte de Portrieux
Basse du Chenal
Roches Quesnel
Rade de Portrieux
Roches Couyères
Basse Orientale de la Rade
La Vache
Le Four
La Fille
ST. QUAY - PORTRIEUX
Spire
metres
cables
0
1000
5
Chart Datum WGS 84
Depths in metres

Area 19

Channel Islands
Alderney to Jersey

19

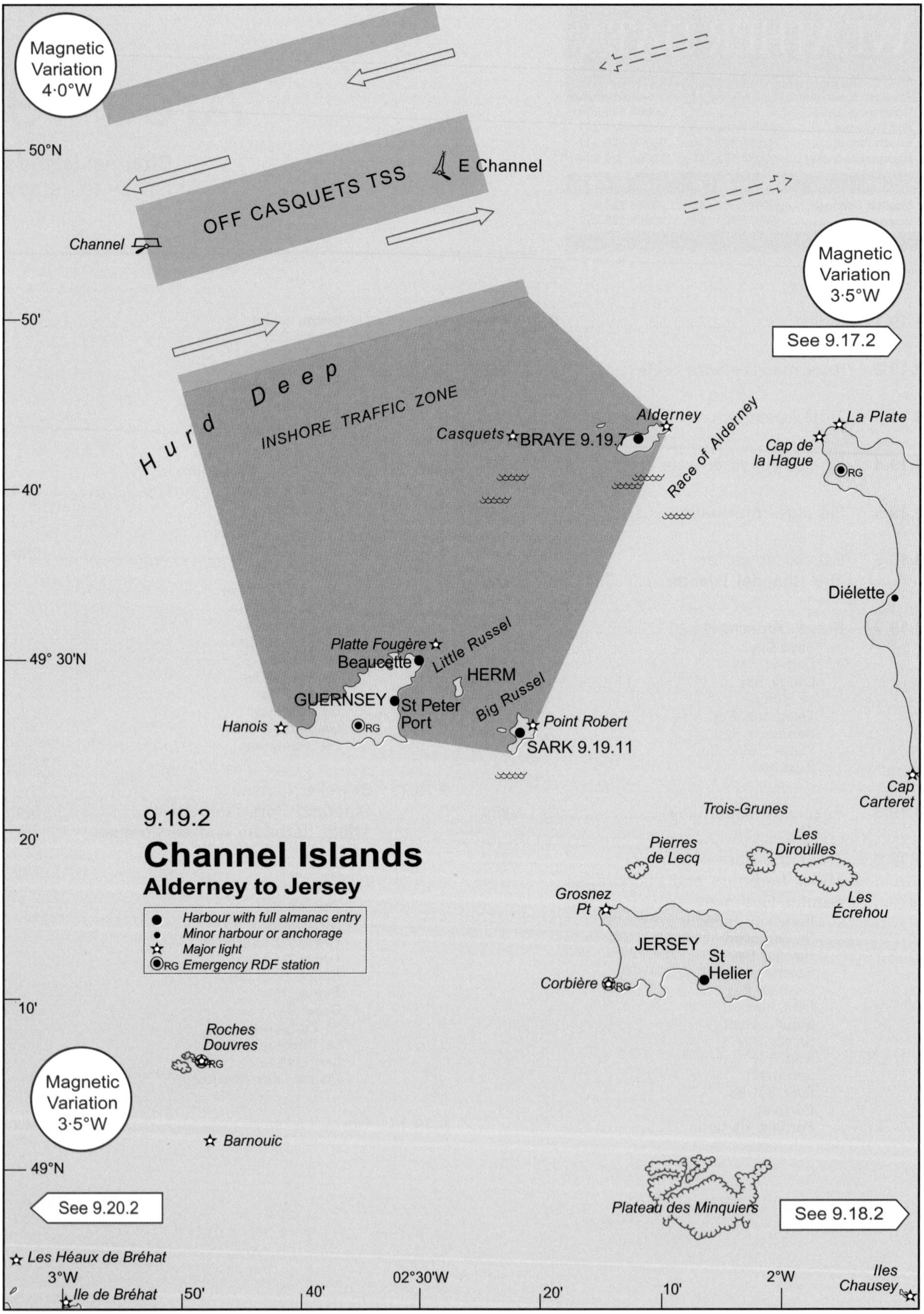

Magnetic Variation 4·0°W
50°N
OFF CASQUETS TSS
E Channel
Channel
Magnetic Variation 3·5°W
See 9.17.2
50'
Hurd Deep
INSHORE TRAFFIC ZONE
Alderney
Casquets
BRAYE 9.19.7
Race of Alderney
La Plate
Cap de la Hague
RG
40'
Diélette
Platte Fougère
Beaucette
Little Russel
49° 30'N
HERM
GUERNSEY
St Peter Port
Big Russel
Hanois
RG
Point Robert
SARK 9.19.11
Cap Carteret
Trois-Grunes
9.19.2
Channel Islands
Alderney to Jersey
20'
Pierres de Lecq
Les Dirouilles
Les Écrehou
Grosnez Pt
Harbour with full almanac entry
Minor harbour or anchorage
Major light
RG Emergency RDF station
JERSEY
St Helier
Corbière
RG
10'
Roches Douvres
RG
Magnetic Variation 3·5°W
Barnouic
49°N
See 9.20.2
Plateau des Minquiers
See 9.18.2
Les Héaux de Bréhat
3°W
Ile de Bréhat
50'
40'
02°30'W
20'
10'
2°W
Iles Chausey

1.	***L'Aberwrac'h***	145	131	126	128	116	115	122	107	103	93	109	110	123	103	91	88	84	72	32	**1**
2.	***Roscoff***	117	103	95	96	84	87	94	77	73	63	79	80	93	71	59	58	54	41	**2**	
3.	***Tréguier***	94	80	72	72	60	66	72	56	52	42	58	53	63	58	46	29	22	**3**		
4.	***Lézardrieux***	88	74	68	54	49	65	68	52	48	42	38	47	55	33	21	14	**4**			
5.	*Paimpol*	91	77	65	56	42	67	70	54	50	45	50	45	53	24	24	**5**				
6.	***St Quay-Portrieux***	88	74	64	54	35	71	73	55	56	48	51	46	52	12	**6**					
7.	*Dahouet*	88	74	62	44	28	70	72	62	58	57	53	41	47	**7**						
8.	Gorey (Jersey)	47	33	16	29	38	36	35	32	29	35	20	13	**8**							
9.	**St Helier**	59	45	28	30	38	43	46	33	29	32	24	**9**								
10.	Creux (Sark)	37	23	23	50	52	18	22	11	10	16	**10**									
11.	Les Hanois	49	35	37	58	56	23	29	14	10	**11**										
12.	**St Peter Port**	42	28	31	55	54	18	23	4	**12**											
13.	Beaucette	39	25	34	59	58	15	19	**13**												
14.	**Braye (Alderney)**	23	9	26	66	73	8	**14**													
15.	Casquets	31	17	32	63	70	**15**														
16.	***St Malo***	87	73	49	23	**16**															
17.	*Granville*	75	61	38	**17**																
18.	*Carteret*	41	23	**18**																	
19.	*Cap de la Hague*	14	**19**																		
20.	***Cherbourg***	**20**																			

DISTANCE TABLE

Approximate distances in nautical miles are by the most direct route, whilst avoiding dangers and allowing for Traffic Separation Schemes. Places in *italics* are in adjoining areas; places in **bold** are in 9.0.6, Cross-Channel Distances.

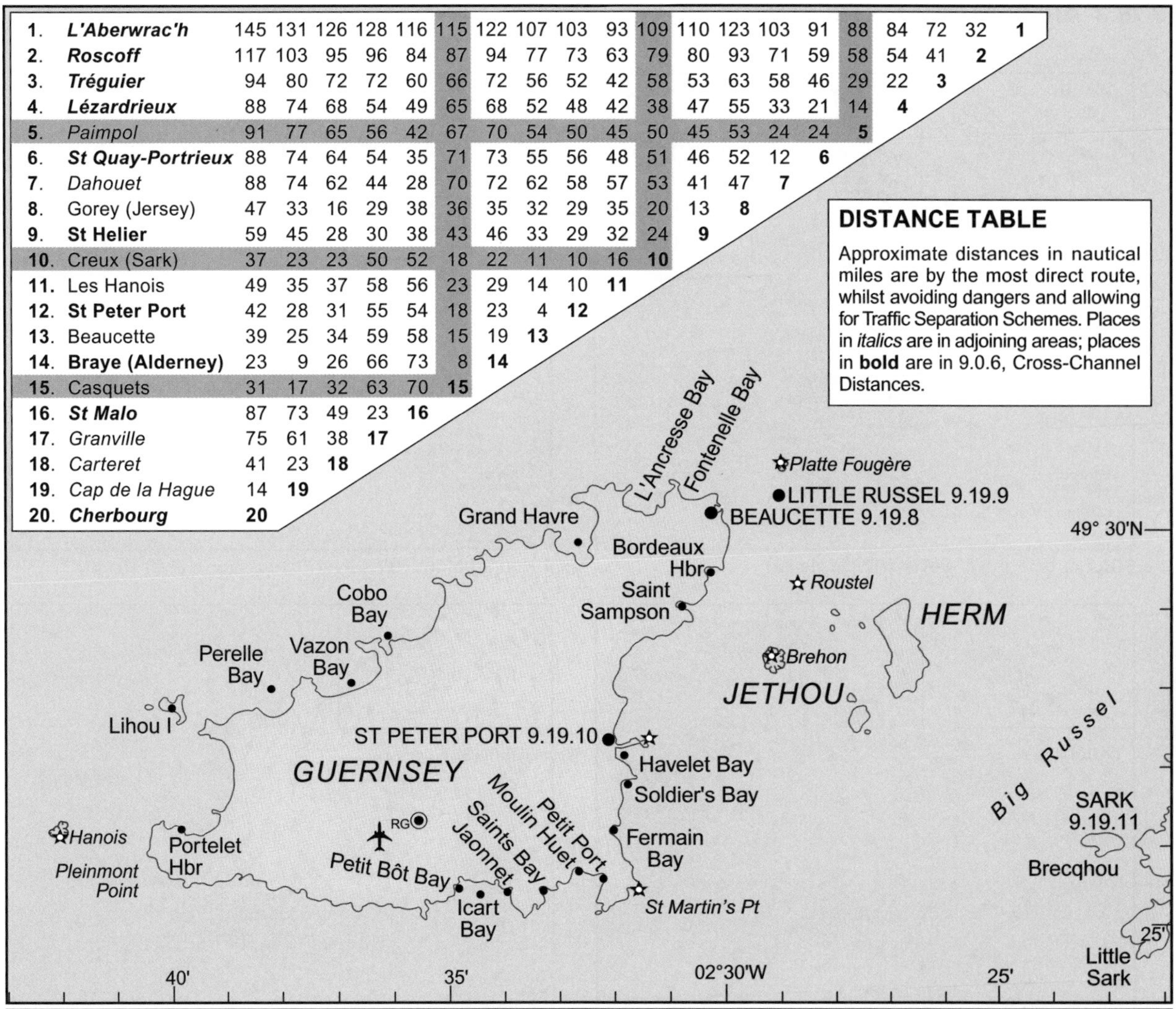

L'Ancresse Bay
Fontenelle Bay
Platte Fougère
LITTLE RUSSEL 9.19.9
BEAUCETTE 9.19.8
Grand Havre
Bordeaux Hbr
Saint Sampson
Roustel
HERM
Cobo Bay
Vazon Bay
Perelle Bay
Lihou I
Brehon
JETHOU
ST PETER PORT 9.19.10
Havelet Bay
Soldier's Bay
GUERNSEY
Big Russel
SARK 9.19.11
Brecqhou
Hanois
Portelet Hbr
Pleinmont Point
RG
Petit Bôt Bay
Saints Bay
Moulin Huet
Petit Port
Jaonnet
Icart Bay
Fermain Bay
St Martin's Pt
Little Sark
49° 30'N
25'
40'
35'
02°30'W
25'

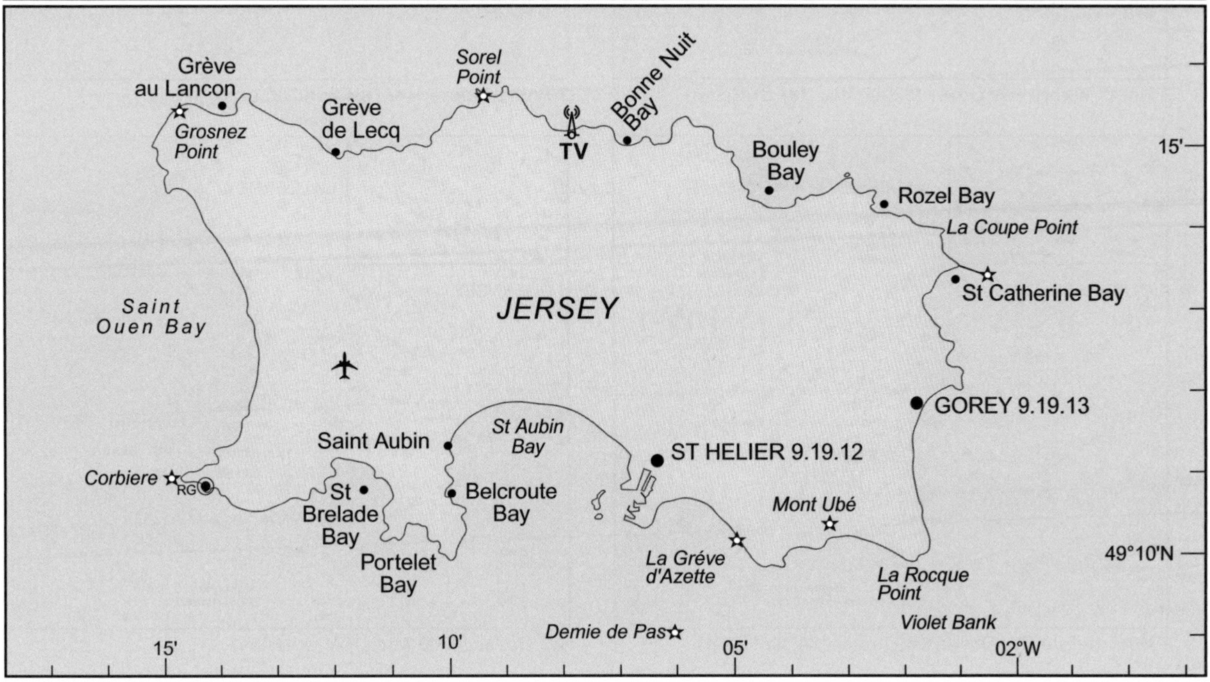

Grève au Lancon
Grosnez Point
Grève de Lecq
Sorel Point
TV
Bonne Nuit Bay
Bouley Bay
Rozel Bay
La Coupe Point
St Catherine Bay
15'
Saint Ouen Bay
JERSEY
GOREY 9.19.13
Saint Aubin
St Aubin Bay
ST HELIER 9.19.12
Corbiere
RG
St Brelade Bay
Belcroute Bay
Mont Ubé
Portelet Bay
La Gréve d'Azette
La Rocque Point
Violet Bank
Demie de Pas
49°10'N
15'
10'
05'
02°W

9.19.3 AREA 19 TIDAL STREAMS

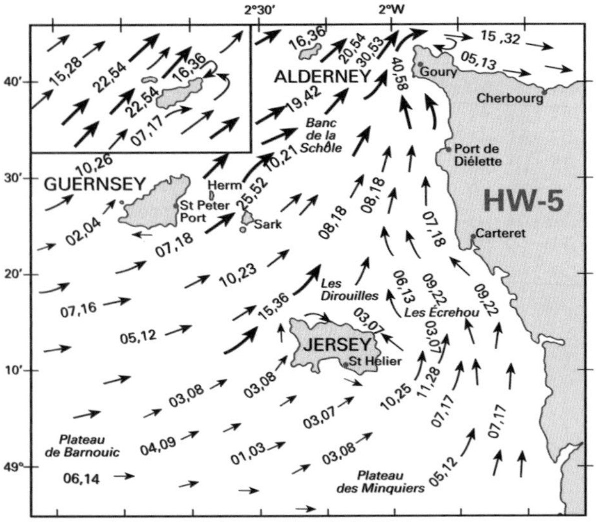
2°30′
2°W
40′
30′
20′
10′
49°
ALDERNEY
Goury
Cherbourg
Banc de la Schôle
Port de Diélette
GUERNSEY
Herm
St Peter Port
Sark
HW-5
Carteret
Les Dirouilles
Les Écrehou
JERSEY
St Helier
Plateau de Barnouic
Plateau des Minquiers
5 Hours before HW Dover (HW St Helier)

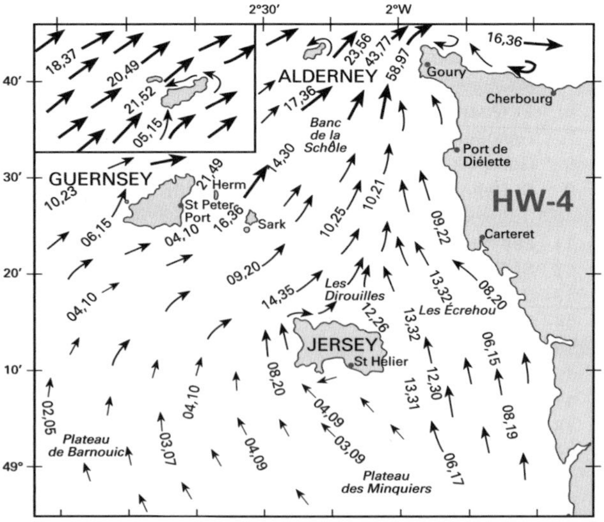
2°30′
2°W
40′
30′
20′
10′
49°
ALDERNEY
Goury
Cherbourg
Banc de la Schôle
Port de Diélette
GUERNSEY
Herm
St Peter Port
Sark
HW-4
Carteret
Les Dirouilles
Les Écrehou
JERSEY
St Helier
Plateau de Barnouic
Plateau des Minquiers
4 Hours before HW Dover (0100 after HW St Helier)

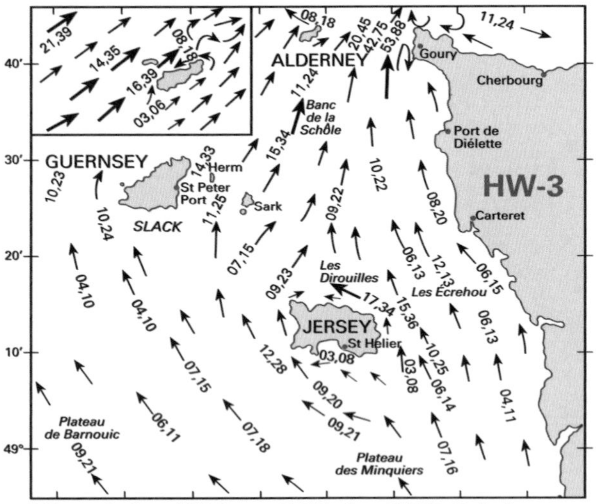
40′
30′
20′
10′
49°
ALDERNEY
Goury
Cherbourg
Banc de la Schôle
Port de Diélette
GUERNSEY
Herm
St Peter Port
Sark
SLACK
HW-3
Carteret
Les Dirouilles
Les Écrehou
JERSEY
St Helier
Plateau de Barnouic
Plateau des Minquiers
3 Hours before HW Dover (0200 after HW St Helier)

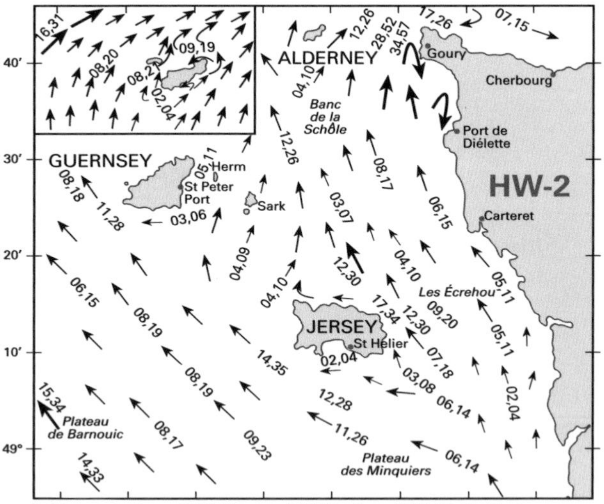
40′
30′
20′
10′
49°
ALDERNEY
Goury
Cherbourg
Banc de la Schôle
Port de Diélette
GUERNSEY
Herm
St Peter Port
Sark
HW-2
Carteret
Les Écrehou
JERSEY
St Helier
Plateau de Barnouic
Plateau des Minquiers
2 Hours before HW Dover (0300 after HW St Helier)

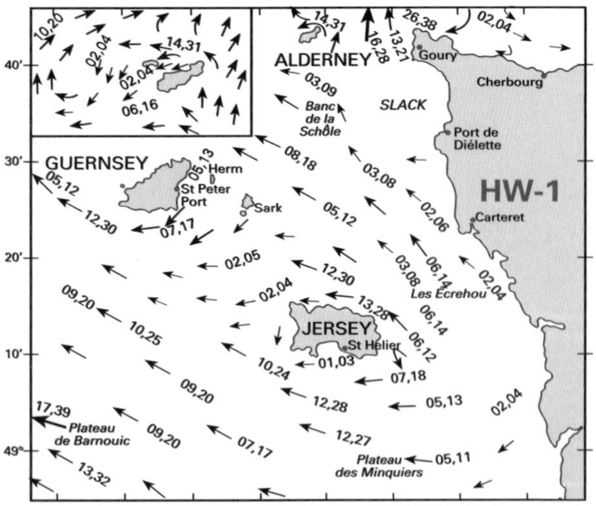
40′
30′
20′
10′
49°
ALDERNEY
Goury
Cherbourg
Banc de la Schôle
SLACK
Port de Diélette
GUERNSEY
Herm
St Peter Port
Sark
HW-1
Carteret
Les Écrehou
JERSEY
St Helier
Plateau de Barnouic
Plateau des Minquiers
1 Hour before HW Dover (0400 after HW St Helier)

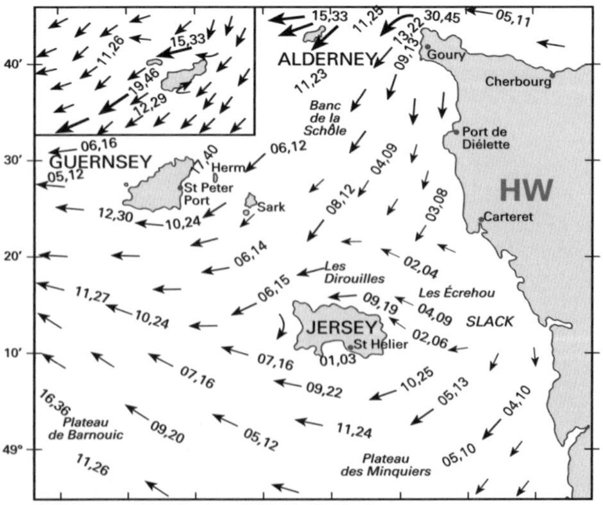
40′
30′
20′
10′
49°
ALDERNEY
Goury
Cherbourg
Banc de la Schôle
Port de Diélette
GUERNSEY
Herm
St Peter Port
Sark
HW
Carteret
Les Dirouilles
Les Écrehou
SLACK
JERSEY
St Helier
Plateau de Barnouic
Plateau des Minquiers
HW Dover (0500 after HW St Helier)

Westward 9.20.3 Southward 9.18.3 Northward 9.2.3 Eastward 9.17.3

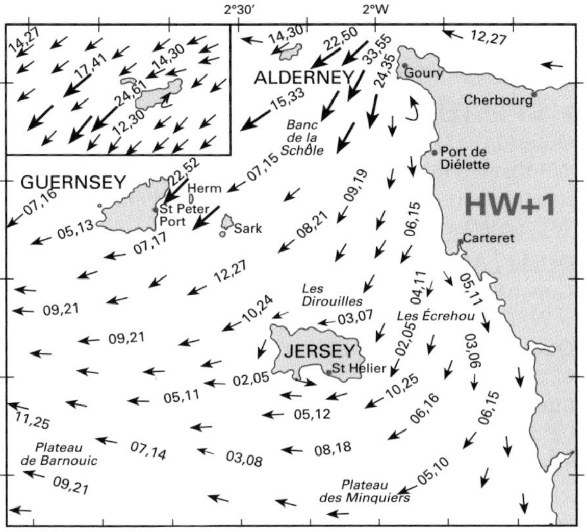
2°30′
2°W
40′
30′
20′
10′
49°
ALDERNEY
Goury
Cherbourg
Banc de la Schôle
Port de Diélette
GUERNSEY
Herm
St Peter Port
Sark
HW+1
Carteret
Les Dirouilles
Les Écrehou
JERSEY
St Helier
Plateau de Barnouic
Plateau des Minquiers
1 Hour after HW Dover (0600 after HW St Helier)

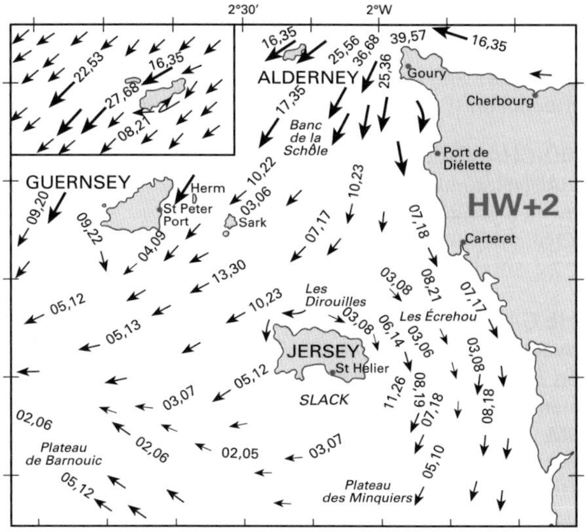
2°30′
2°W
40′
30′
20′
10′
49°
ALDERNEY
Goury
Cherbourg
Banc de la Schôle
Port de Diélette
GUERNSEY
Herm
St Peter Port
Sark
HW+2
Carteret
Les Dirouilles
Les Écrehou
JERSEY
St Helier
SLACK
Plateau de Barnouic
Plateau des Minquiers
2 Hours after HW Dover (0530 before HW St Helier)

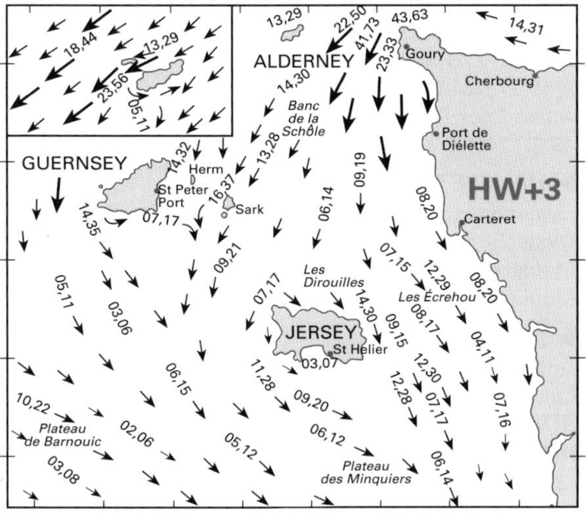
40′
30′
20′
10′
49°
ALDERNEY
Goury
Cherbourg
Banc de la Schôle
Port de Diélette
GUERNSEY
Herm
St Peter Port
Sark
HW+3
Carteret
Les Dirouilles
Les Écrehou
JERSEY
St Helier
Plateau de Barnouic
Plateau des Minquiers
3 Hours after HW Dover (0430 before HW St Helier)

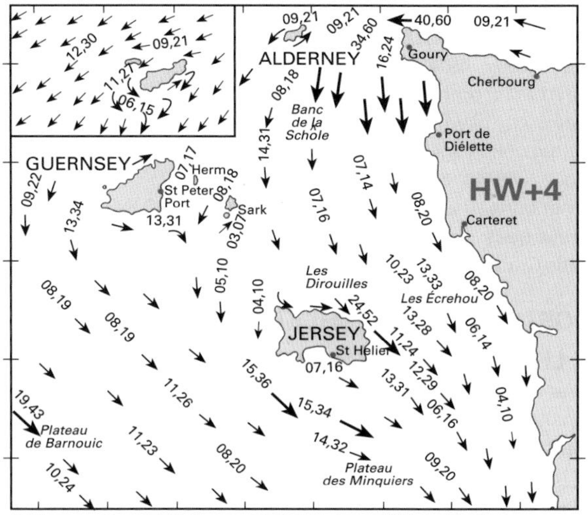
40′
30′
20′
10′
49°
ALDERNEY
Goury
Cherbourg
Banc de la Schôle
Port de Diélette
GUERNSEY
Herm
St Peter Port
Sark
HW+4
Carteret
Les Dirouilles
Les Écrehou
JERSEY
St Helier
Plateau de Barnouic
Plateau des Minquiers
4 Hours after HW Dover (0330 before HW St Helier)

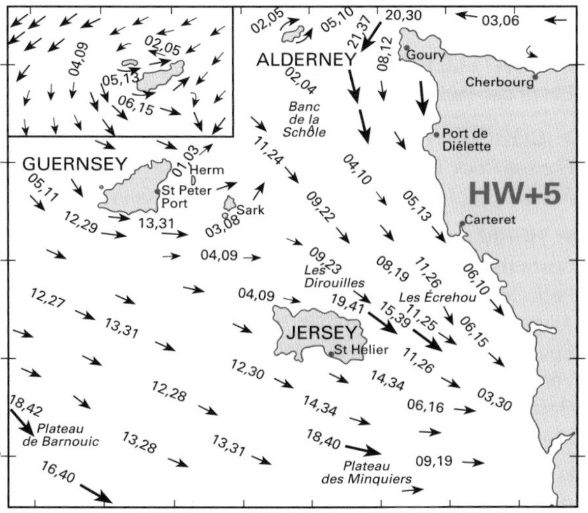
40′
30′
20′
10′
49°
ALDERNEY
Goury
Cherbourg
Banc de la Schôle
Port de Diélette
GUERNSEY
Herm
St Peter Port
Sark
HW+5
Carteret
Les Dirouilles
Les Écrehou
JERSEY
St Helier
Plateau de Barnouic
Plateau des Minquiers
5 Hours after HW Dover (0230 before HW St Helier)

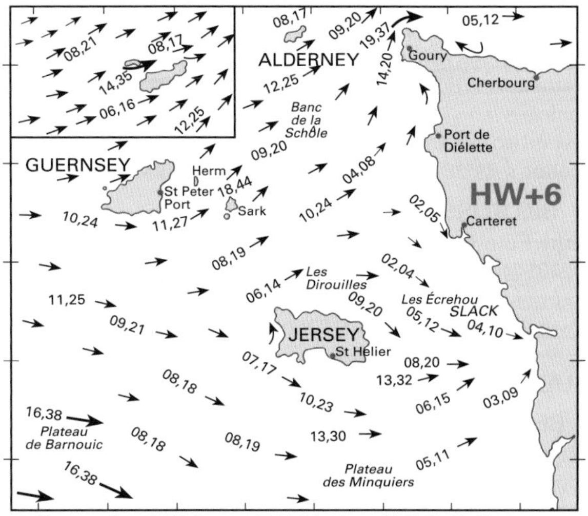
40′
30′
20′
10′
49°
ALDERNEY
Goury
Cherbourg
Banc de la Schôle
Port de Diélette
GUERNSEY
Herm
St Peter Port
Sark
HW+6
Carteret
Les Dirouilles
Les Écrehou
SLACK
JERSEY
St Helier
Plateau de Barnouic
Plateau des Minquiers
6 Hours after HW Dover (0130 before HW St Helier)

PLOT WAYPOINTS ON YOUR CHART BEFORE USING THEM

9.19.4 LIGHTS, BUOYS AND WAYPOINTS

Blue print = light with a nominal range of 15M or more. CAPITALS = place or feature. *CAPITAL ITALICS* = light-vessel, light float or Lanby. *Italics* = Fog signal. ***Bold italics*** = Racon. Useful waypoints are underlined. Abbreviations are in the Introduction. Positions are referenced to the WGS 84 datum.

MID-CHANNEL MARKS

CHANNEL 49°54'·46N 02°53'·74W, Fl 15s 12m **25M**; R hull with lt twr amidships; *Horn (20s)*; **Racon O, 15M**.
E Channel 49°58'·66N 02°28'·98W, Fl Y 5s; *Whis*; **Racon T, 10M**.
EC 2 50°12'·13N 01°12'·49W, Fl (4) Y 15s; *Whis*; **Racon T, 10M**.

THE CASQUETS AND ALDERNEY

Casquets ☆ 49°43'·32N 02°22'·62W, Fl (5) 30s 37m **24M**; H24; W twr, 2 R bands; NW'most of three; *Horn (2) 60s*; **Racon T, 25M**.
Quenard Pt ☆ (Alderney) 49°43'·75N 02°09'·86W, Fl (4) 15s 37m **23M**; 085°-027°; H24; W ○ twr, B band; *Horn 30s*.
Château à L'Étoc Pt 49°43'·94N 02°10'·63W, Iso WR 4s 20m W10M, R7M; R071·1°-111·1°, W111·1°-151·1°.
Ldg bns 142° (to clear the submerged Adm'ty bkwtr). Front, W, 49°43'·90N 02°10'·97W. Rear, BW; 720m from front.

▶ BRAYE

Ldg lts 215°, both Q 8/17m 9/12M, synch; vis 210°-220°. Front, Old pier elbow, 49°43'·39N 02°11'·91W. Rear, 335m from front. Daymarks, both W cols, orange △s.
Admiralty bkwtr 49°43'·81N 02°11'·67W, L Fl 10s 7m 5M.
Fairway No. 1 49°43'·72N 02°11'·71W, QG.
No. 2 49°43'·60N 02°11'·75W, QR.
Inner fairway 49°43'·57N 02°11'·98W, Q (2) G 5s.
Braye quay 49°43'·53N 02°12'·00W, 2 FR (vert) 8m 5M.
Little Crabby hbr ent 49°43'·45N 02°12'·12W, FG & FR 5m 2M.

NORTHERN APPROACHES TO GUERNSEY

▶ LITTLE RUSSEL CHANNEL

Grande Amfroque, two unlit bcn twrs: larger, BW-banded; smaller, white; 49°30'·62N 02°24'·53W.
Platte Fougère ☆ 49°30'·82N 02°29'·14W, Fl WR 10s 15m **16M**; W155°-085°, R085°-155°; W 8-sided twr, B band; *Horn 45s*; ***Racon P***.
Corbette d'Amont, Y bcn twr, topmark, 49°29'·70N 02°29'·30W.
Tautenay 49°30'·10N 02°26'·83W, Q (3) WR 6s 7m W7M, R6M; W050°-215°, R215°-050°; B & W bcn.
Roustel 49°29'·22N 02°28'·79W, Q 8m 7M; W framework col.
Rousse, Y bcn twr, topmark, 49°29'·04N 02°28'·27W.
Platte, Fl WR 3s 6m, W7M, R5M; R024°-219°, W219°-024°; G conical twr.
Vivian bcn twr, BW bands, 49°28'·51N 02°30'·58W.
Brehon 49°28'·27N 02°29'·28W, Iso 4s 19m 9M; bcn on ○ twr.

▶ BIG RUSSEL

Noire Pute 49°28'·27N 02°24'·93W, Fl (2) WR 15s 8m 6M; W220°-040°, R040°-220°.
Fourquies 49°27'·34N 02°26'·47W, Q.
Lower Heads 49°25'·84N 02°28'·55W, Q (6) + L Fl 15s; *Bell*.

GUERNSEY, HERM and SARK

▶ BEAUCETTE MARINA

Petite Canupe 49°30'·18N 02°29'·13W, Q (6) + L Fl 15s.
Ldg lts 276°, both FR. Front 49°30'·19N 02°30'·21W, W □, R stripe. Rear, 185m from front, R □, W stripe. 3 pairs unlit lateral buoys.
Tide gauge 49°30'·20N 02°30'·17W.

▶ ST SAMPSON

Ldg lts 286°: Front, Crocq pier 49°28'·90N 02°30'·74W, FR 3m 5M; 230°-340°; tfc sigs. Rear, 390m from front, FG 13m; clock twr.
N Pier 49°28'·91N 02°30'·71W FG 3m 5M; 230°-340°.
Crocq pier 49°28'·99N 02°30'·99W, FR 11m 5M; 250°-340°.

▶ ST PETER PORT

Outer ldg lts 220°. **Front**, Castle bkwtr 49°27'·31N 02°31'·44W, Al WR 10s 14m **16M**; 187°-007°; dark ○ twr, W on NE side; *Horn 15s*.
Rear, Belvedere, Oc 10s 61m 14M; 179°-269°; intens 217°-223°; W □ on W twr.
Reffée 49°27'·74N 02°31'·27W, VQ (6) + L Fl 15s.
Queen Elizabeth II marina 49°27'·72N 02°31'·86W. 270° dir Oc WRG 3s 5m 6M; G258°-268°, W268°-272°, R272°-282°.
Outer pair: 49°27'·83N 02°31'·46W, QG. 49°27'·78N 02°31'·44W, QR.
Inner pair: 49°27'·76N 02°31'·74W, QG. 49°27'·72N 02°31'·74W, QR.
The Pool: Ldg lts 265°. Front, S Pier, 49°27'·32N 02°32'·03W, Oc R 5s 10m 14M. Rear, 160m from front, Iso R 2s 22m 3M; 260°-270°.
White Rock pier 49°27'·38N 02°31'·59W, Oc G 5s 11m 14M; intens 174°-354°; ○ twr; tfc sigs. [Castle bkwtr: see above].
Marina app 49°27'·36N 02°31'·67W, QG.
49°27'·27N 02°31'·74W, Fl R.
49°27'·27N 02°31'·80W, Fl R.
49°27'·26N 02°31'·86W, Fl R.
Albert Dock Fish Quay (NW end) FR. Also FR on SW end, 49°27'·24N 02°31'·96W.

▶ HAVELET BAY

Oyster Rock Y bcn, topmark 'O', 49°27'·09N 02°31'·46W.
Oyster Rock 49°27'·04N 02°31'·47W, QG.
Moulinet 49°26'·97N 02°31'·54W, QR.
Moulinet Y bcn, topmark 'M', 49°26'·95N 02°31'·58W.

▶ SOLDIERS BAY

Anfré, Y bcn, topmark 'A', 49°26'·45N 02°31'·48W.
Longue Pierre Y bcn, topmark 'LP', 49°25'·36N 02°31'·48W.
St Martin's Pt ☆ 49°25'·30N 02°31'·70W, Fl (3) WR 10s 15m 14M; R185°-191°, W191°-011°, R011°-081°; flat-roofed, W bldg. *Horn (3) 30s*.

Les Hanois ☆ 49°26'·10N 02°42'·15W, Fl (2) 13s 33m **20M**; 294°-237°; Gy ○ twr, B lantern, helicopter platform; *Horn (2) 60s*.
4 FR on masts 1·27M ESE ar Pleinmont Point.

▶ PORTELET HARBOUR

Bkwtr bcn, 49°26'·15N 02°39'·84W.

▶ COBO BAY/GRAND HAVRE

Grosse Rock, B bcn 49°29'·01N 02°36'·19W 11m.
Rousse Point bkwtr, B bcn 49°29'·91N 02°33'·06W.

▶ HERM

Corbette, white disc on Y pole, 49°28'·54N 02°28'·63W.
Petit Creux 49°28'·08N 02°28'·73W, QR; red 'C' on red pole.
Alligande 49°27'·85N 02°28'·78W, Fl (3) G 5s; B pole, orange 'A'.
Épec 49°27'·98N 02°27'·89W, Fl G 3s; black 'E' on G mast.
Vermerette 49°28'·11N 02°27'·75W, Fl (2) Y 5s; orange 'V' on bcn.
Gate Rock (Percée Pass) 49°27'·88N 02°27'·53W, Q (9) 15s.
Hbr ldg lts 078°: White drums. F occas; 49°28'·30N 02°27'·02W.

▶ SARK

Corbée du Nez 49°27'·08N 02°22'·17W, Fl (4) WR 15s 14m 8M; W structure; W057°-230°, R230°-057°.

Founiais ⊥, topmark 'F'; 49°26'·02N 02°20'·36W.
Point Robert ☆ 49°26'·19N 02°20'·75W, Fl 15s 65m **20M**; 138°-353°; W 8-sided twr; *Horn (2) 30s.*
Blanchard ⊥ 49°25'·35N 02°17'·42W, Q (3) 10s; *Bell.*
Pilcher monument (070° bearing) 49°25'·77N 02°22'·35W.

JERSEY (West and South coasts)

Desormes ⊥ 49°19'·00N 02°17'·88W, Q (9) 15s.
Grosnez Point ☆ 49°15'·48N 02°14'·84W, Fl (2) WR 15s 50m **W19M, R17M**; W081°-188°, R188°-241°; W hut.
La Rocco twr (conspic) 15m, 49°11'·95N 02°13'·97W.
La Frouquie ⊥ (seasonal) 49°11'·29N 02°15'·38W.
La Corbière ☆ 49°10'·85N 02°14'·92W, Iso WR 10s 36m **W18M, R16M**; W shore-294°, R294°-328°, W328°-148°, R148°-shore; W ○ twr; *Horn Mo (C) 60s.*
Pt Corbière, ☆ FR, 49°10'·94N 02°14'·30W; R □, W stripe.

▶ WESTERN PASSAGE

Ldg lts 082°. Front, La Gréve d'Azette 49°10'·15N 02°05'·09W, Oc 5s 23m 14M; 034°-129°. Rear, Mont Ubé, 1M from front, Oc R 5s 46m 12M; 250°-095°.
Passage Rock ⊥, VQ, 49°09'·53N 02°12'·26W.
Les Fours ⊥, Q, 49°09'·58N 02°10'·16W.
Noirmont Pt ☆ 49°09'·91N 02°10'·08W, Fl (4) 12s 18m 13M; B twr, W band.
Pignonet ⊥ 49°09'·87N 02°09'·68W.
Les Grunes du Port ⊥ 49°10'·02N 02°09'·14W.
Diamond Rock ⊥ 49°10'·11N 02°08'·64W, Fl (2) R 6s.
Ruaudière Rock ⊥ 49°09'·74N 02°08'·60W, Fl G 3s; *Bell.*

▶ SAINT AUBIN BAY & HBR

Baleine ⊥ 49°10'·41N 02°08'·23W.
Beach Rock ⊥ 49°11'·29N 02°08'·42W, (Apr-Oct).
Fort pier ☆ 49°11'·12N 02°09'·64W, Fl R 4s 8m 1M.
North pier ☆ 49°11'·21N 02°10'·04W, Dir lt 254°, F WRG 5m, G248°-253°, W253°-255°, R255°-260°. Same col, Iso R 4s 12m 10M.

▶ ST HELIER

Elizabeth marina, West approach
Rocquemin ⊥ 49°10'·70N 02°07'·87W.
La Vrachiére ⊥ 49°10'·90N 02°07'·60W, Fl (2) 5s.
Fort Charles North ⊥ 49°10'·87N 02°07'·42W.
Dir ☆ 106°, ⊥ 49°10'·76N 02°07'·12W, F WRG 4m 1M; G096°-104°, W104°-108°, R108°-119°; R dayglo □, B stripe.
Marina ent ☆ 49°10'·69N 02°07'·21W, Oc G 4s 2M.

Red & Green Passage ldg lts 022·7° on dayglo R dolphins. Front, Elizabeth E berth Dn ☆ 49°10'·63N 02°06'·94W, Oc G 5s 10m 11M. Rear, Albert Pier elbow, 230m from front, Oc R 5s 18m 12M; synch.
East Rock ⊥ 49°09'·95N 02°07'·29W, QG.
Oyster Rock, R/W bcn, topmark 'O', 49°10'·09N 02°07'·49W.
Platte Rock ⊥ 49°10'·15N 02°07'·35W, Fl R 1·5s 6m 5M; R col.
Small Road No. 2 ⊥ 49°10'·38N 02°07'·24W, QR.
No. 4 ⊥ 49°10'·52N 02°07'·11W, QR.

Elizabeth marina, S approach
E1 ⊥ 49°10'·59N 02°07'·09W, Fl G 3s.
E2 ⊥ 49°10'·58N 02°07'·13W, Fl R 2s.
E5 ⊥ 49°10'·70N 02°07'·17W, Fl G 5s.
E6 ⊥ 49°10'·69N 02°07'·21W, Fl R 2s.
Fort Charles East ⊥ 49°10'·74N 02°07'·26W, Q (3) 5s.

St Helier Hbr, ldg lts 078°, both FG on W cols. Front, 49°10'·62N 02°06'·67W. Rear, 80m from front.
Victoria pier 49°10'·57N 02°06'·88W; *Bell*; IPTS on control twr.

La Collette yacht basin
⊥ 49°10'·55N 02°06'·91W, QR.
⊥ 49°10'·52N 02°06'·90W.

JERSEY (South-East coast)

Hinguette ⊥ 49°09'·32N 02°07'·32W, Fl (4) R 15s.
Demie de Pas ⊥ 49°09'·00N 02°06'·15W, Mo (D) WR 12s 11m, W14M, R10M; R130°-303°, W303°-130°; B bn twr, Y top; *Horn (3) 60s*; **Racon T, 10M.**
Icho Tower (conspic, 14m) 49°08'·88N 02°02'·90W.
Canger Rock ⊥ 49°07'·34N 02°00'·38W, Q (9) 15s.
La Conchière ⊥ 49°08'·21N 02°00'·17W.
Frouquier Aubert ⊥ 49°06'·09N 01°58'·84W, Q (6) + L Fl 15s.
Violet ⊥ 49°07'·81N 01°57'·14W, L Fl 10s.
Petite Anquette, W bcn, topmark 'PA', 49°08'·46N 01°56'·30W.
Grande Anquette, W bcn ⊥ 49°08'·32N 01°55'·21W.
Le Cochon ⊥ 49°09'·77N 01°58'·80W.
La Noire ⊥ 49°10'·13N 01°59'·23W.
Le Giffard ⊥ 49°10'·59N 01°59'·00W.

▶ GOREY

Ldg lts 298°. Front, ☆ 49°11'·80N 02°01'·34W, Oc RG 5s 8m 12M; R304°-353°, G353°-304°; W twr on pierhead. Rear, Oc R 5s 24m 8M; W □, orange side panels on wall, 490m from front.
Horn Rock ⊥, topmark 'H', 49°10'·96N 01°59'·86W.
Les Burons, RW bcn, topmark 'B', 49°11'·39N 02°00'·73W.
Inner Road ⊥ 49°11'·49N 02°00'·34W, QG.
Écureuil Rock ⊥ 49°11'·66N 02°00'·78W.
Equerrière Rk, bcn 'fishtail' topmark, 49°11'·86N 02°00'·59W.
Les Arch ⊥, BW bcn, 49°12'·03N 02°00'·59W.

▶ ST CATHERINE BAY

St Catherine Bay, Le Fara ⊥ 49°12'·85N 02°00'·48W.
Archirondel Tower (conspic, 16m) 49°12'·78N 02°01'·33W.
Verclut bkwtr ☆ 49°13'·33N 02°00'·65W, Fl 1·5s 18m 13M.
La Coupe Pt, turret 49°14'·02N 02°01'·49W.

JERSEY (North coast)

Rozel Bay Dir lt 245°; 49°14'·20N 02°02'·76W, F WRG 11m 5M; G240°-244°, W244°-246°, R246°-250°; W col.
Bonne Nuit Bay ldg lts 223°, both FG 7/34m 6M. Front, Pier 49°15'·09N 02°07'·17W. Rear, 170m from front.
Demi Rock ⊥ 49°15'·55N 02°07'·36W.
Sorel Point ☆ 49°15'·60N 02°09'·54W, L Fl WR 7·5s 50m **15M**; W095°-112°, R112°-173°, W173°-230°, R230°-269°, W269°-273°; B&W chequered ○ twr, only 3m high.

OFFLYING ISLANDS

▶ LES ÉCREHOU

Écrevière ⊥ 49°15'·32N 01°52'·06W, Q (6) + L Fl 15s.
Mâitre Ile ⊥ 49°17'·15N 01°55'·52W.

▶ PLATEAU DES MINQUIERS

N Minquiers ⊥ 49°01'·70N 02°00'·49W, Q.
NE Minquiers ⊥ 49°00'·91N 01°55'·21W, VQ (3) 5s; *Bell.*
SE Minquiers ⊥ 48°53'·49N 01°59'·99W, Q (3) 10s; *Bell.*
S Minquiers ⊥ 48°53'·15N 02°10'·02W, Q (6) + L Fl 15s.
SW Minquiers ⊥ 48°54'·39N 02°19'·30W, Q (9) 15s 5M; *Whis.*
NW Minquiers ⊥ 48°59'·70N 02°20'·48W, Q 5M; *Bell.*
Wreck buoy ⊥ 48°55'·34N 02°26'·53W, Q (9) 15s.
Refuge ⊥ 49°00'·19N 02°10'·09W.
Demie de Vascelin ⊥ 49°00'·04N 02°05'·07W.
Grand Vascelin, BW bcn ⊥ 48°59'·97N 02°07'·17W.
Maitresse Ile bcn twr ⊥ 48°58'·29N 02°03'·69W; B&W.
Récif Le Coq, RW bcn ⊥ 48°57'·94N 02°01'·22W.

9.19.5 PASSAGE INFORMATION

Current Pilots for this popular area include: *North Brittany & CI Cruising Companion* (Cumberlidge/Nautical Data Ltd); *Channel Cruising Companion* (Featherstone & Aslett/ Nautical Data Ltd); and the Admiralty Channel Pilot (NP27).

CHANNEL ISLANDS – GENERAL (chart *2669*) In an otherwise delightful cruising area, the main problems around the Channel Islands include fog and thick weather, the very big tidal range, strong tidal streams, overfalls and steep seas which get up very quickly. The shoreline is generally rugged with sandy bays and many offlying rks. It is important to use large scale charts, and recognised leading marks (of which there are plenty) when entering or leaving many of the hbrs and anchs. Several passages are marked by bns/perches identified by an alphabetical letter(s) in lieu of topmark. High speed ferries operate in the area.

From the N, note the Casquets TSS and ITZ. Soundings of Hurd Deep can help navigation. The powerful lights at the Casquets, Alderney (Quenard Pt), Cap de la Hague, Cap Levi and Barfleur greatly assist a night or dawn landfall. By day Alderney is relatively high and conspic. Sark is often seen before Guernsey which slopes down from S to N. Jersey is low-lying in the SE. The islands are fringed by many rky dangers. In bad visibility it is prudent to stay in hbr.

►*Be aware that over a 12 hour period tidal streams broadly rotate anti-clockwise around the Islands, particularly in open water and in wider chans (see 9.19.3). The E-going (flood) stream is of less duration than the W-going, but is stronger. The islands lie across the main direction of the streams, so eddies are common along the shores. The range of tide is greatest in Jersey (9·6m sp, 4·1m np), and least in Alderney (5·3m sp, 2·2m np). Streams run hard through the chans and around headlands and need to be worked carefully; neaps are easier, particularly for a first visit. Strong W'lies cause a heavy sea, usually worst from local HW – 3 to + 3.*◄

Apart from the main hbrs described in Area 19, there are also many attractive minor hbrs and anchs. In the very nature of islands a lee can usually be found somewhere. Boats which can take the ground are better able to explore the quieter hbrs. Avoid lobster pots and oyster beds.

THE CASQUETS AND ORTAC ROCK (chart *60*). Casquets lt ho (fog sig) is conspic on the largest island of this group of rks 5·5M W of Braye, Alderney. Off-lying dangers extend 4ca W and WSW (The Ledge and Noire Roque) and 4ca E (Pte Colotte). The tide runs very hard round and between these various obstructions. A shallow bank, on which are situated Fourquie and l'Equêt rks (dry), lies from 5ca to 1M E of Casquets, and should not be approached. Ortac Rk (24m) is 3·5M E of Casquets. Ortac Chan runs N/S 5ca W of Ortac; ►*here the stream begins to run NE at HW St Helier – 0230, and SW at HW St Helier + 0355, with sp rates up to 5½kn (7kn reported).*◄ Ortac Chan should not be used in bad weather due to tremendous overfalls; these also occur over Eight-fathom Ledge (8½ca W of Casquets), and over the Banks SW, SSW and SSE of the Casquets. An Historic Wreck lies about 300m E of Casquets lt ho (see 9.0.3h).

ALDERNEY AND THE SWINGE (chart *60*). See 9.19.7 for Braye Harbour (chart *2845*) and approaches, together with pleasant bays and anchs around the island, offering shelter from different wind/sea directions. The sunken NE extremity of Admiralty Breakwater should not be crossed except in calm conditions, outside LW±2 and keeping about 50m off the head of the Breakwater where there is 2·3m.

The Swinge lies between Burhou with its bordering rks, and the NW coast of Alderney. It can be a dangerous chan, and should only be used in reasonable vis and fair weather. On N side of the Swinge the main dangers are Boues des Kaines, almost awash at LW about 7½ca ESE of Ortac, and North Rk 2½ca SE of Burhou. On S side of the Swinge beware Corbet Rk (0·5m high), with drying outliers, 5ca N of Fort Clonque, and Barsier Rk (0·9m) 3½ca NNW of Fort Clonque.

►*The SW-going stream begins at HW St Helier + 0340, and the NE stream at HW St Helier – 0245, sp rates 7-8kn. On the NE-going stream, beware the very strong northerly set in vicinity of Ortac.*◄ The tide runs very hard, and in strong or gale force winds from S or W there are very heavy overfalls on the SW-going stream between Ortac and Les Etacs (off W end of Alderney). In strong E winds, on the NE-going stream, overfalls occur between Burhou and Braye breakwater. These overfalls can mostly be avoided by choosing the best time and route (see below), but due to the uneven bottom and strong tides broken water may be met even in calm conditions.

►*The best time to pass SW through the Swinge is at about HW St Helier +0400, when the SW-going stream starts;*◄ hold to the SE side of the chan since the strongest stream runs on the Burhou side. But after HW St Helier +0500, to clear the worst of the overfalls keep close to Burhou and Ortac, avoiding North Rk and Boues des Kaines.

Pierre au Vraic (dries 1·2m) is an unmarked pinnacle rock at 49°41'·61N 02°16'·94W, 1·8M S of Ortac and 1·8M WSW of Les Étacs, almost in the fairway to/from the Swinge. Arriving on a fair tide from Guernsey it will be well covered, but it is a serious hazard if leaving the Swinge on a SW-going Spring tide close to local LW. AC 60 gives clearing bearings.

Heading NE at about HW St Helier –0200, Great Nannel in transit with E end of Burhou clears Pierre au Vraic to the E, but passes close W of Les Etacs. On this transit, when Roque Tourgis fort is abeam, alter slightly to stbd to pass 1ca NW of Corbet Rk; keep near SE side of chan.

THE ALDERNEY RACE (chart *3653*). This Race, characterised by very strong tidal streams, runs SW/NE between Cap de la Hague and Alderney, but its influence extends at least as far SW as 02° 20'W. The fairway, approx 4M wide, is bounded by Race Rk and Alderney S Banks to the NW, and to the SE by rky banks 3M E of Race Rk, and by Milieu and Banc de la Schôle (least depth 2·7m). These dangers which cause breaking seas and heavy overfalls should be carefully avoided. In bad weather and strong wind-against-tide conditions the seas break in all parts of the Race and passage is not recommended. Conditions are exacerbated at sp tides.

►*In mid-chan the the SW-going stream starts at HW St Helier + 0430 (HW Dover) and the NE-going stream at HW St Helier –0210 (HW Dover + 0530), sp rates both 5·5kn. The times at which the stream turns do not vary much for various places, but the rates do; for example, 1M W of Cap de la Hague sp rates reach 7-8kn.*◄

To obtain optimum conditions, timing is of the essence. As a rule of thumb the Race should be entered on the first of the fair tide so as to avoid the peak tidal stream with attendant overfalls/seas. ►*Thus, SW-bound, arrrive off Cap de la Hague at around HW St Helier + 0430 (HW Dover) when the stream will be slack, whilst just starting to run SW off Alderney. A yacht leaving Cherbourg at HW Dover – 0300 will achieve the above timing by utilising the inshore W-going tidal eddy.*

Conversely, NE-bound, leave St Peter Port, say, at approx local HW St Helier – 0430 (HWD+3) with a foul tide so as to pass Banc de la Schôle as the first of the fair tide starts to make.◄ A later departure should achieve a faster passage, but with potentially less favourable conditions in the Race. On the NE stream the worst overfalls are on the French side.

APPROACHES TO GUERNSEY (charts *3654, 808*). From the N/NE, The Little Russel Channel (9.19.9) between Guernsey and Herm gives the most convenient access to Beaucette marina (9.19.8) and St Peter Port (9.19.10 and chart *3140*). With lts on Platte Fougère, Tautenay, Roustel, Platte and Bréhon, plus the ldg lts (220°) for St Peter Port, the Little Russel can be navigated day or night in reasonable vis, even at LW. But it needs care, due to rks which fringe the chan and appr, and the strong tide which sets across the ent. ►*In mid chan, S of Platte and NW of Bréhon, the NE-going stream begins at HW St Peter Port – 0245, and the SW stream at HW St Peter Port +0330, sp rates both 5·25kn which can raise a very steep sea with wind against tide.*◄

The Big Russel is wider and easier. In bad weather or poor vis it may be a better approach to St Peter Port, via Lower Heads SCM lt buoy. From the NW, Doyle Passage, which is aligned 146°/326° off Beaucette, can be used but only by day with local knowledge. From the S or W, the natural route is around St Martin's Pt, keeping 1·5ca ENE of Longue Pierre bn (LP) and a similar distance off Anfré bcn (A).

See 9.19.9 for minor hbrs and anchs around Guernsey. In onshore winds keep well clear of the W coast, where in bad weather the sea breaks on dangers up to 4M offshore.

HERM AND JETHOU (charts *807, 808*). Herm (9.19.10) and Jethou (private) are reached from Little Russel via any of 7 passages all of which require reasonable vis and care with tidal streams; Alligande Pass is the most direct from St Peter Port. The appr from the Big Russel is more open and leads easily to pleasant ⚓s at Belvoir Bay and Shell Bay.

SARK (9.19.11 and chart *808*). La Maseline and Creux on the E coast are the only proper hbrs, the former used mainly by ferries. Elsewhere around the island, whatever the wind direction, a sheltered anch can usually be found in a lee, although swell may intrude. On the NW coast, Port à La Jument and Port du Moulin in Banquette Bay offer some shelter from S and E winds. Fontaines Bay and La Grève de la Ville* offer different degrees of protection on the NE coast. Derrible Bay, Dixcart Bay and Rouge Terrier are good anchs on the SE coast. Port Gorey, Les Fontaines Bay, La Grande Grève and Havre Gosselin* are all on the W coast; the last named is crowded in season due to easy access from Guernsey. ►*Tidal streams around Sark need careful study, especially returning from the E coast towards Guernsey when the choice between going N or S-about Sark can make a significant difference. A more detailed study is under 9.14.11.*◄ * Ⓥs have been laid here.

JERSEY (charts *3655*, 1136, *1137*, 1138). ►*The rotatory pattern of tidal streams affecting the Channel Islands as a whole dictates that when streams are slack on the N and S coasts of Jersey, they are running strongly on the E and W coasts; and vice versa. If approaching Jersey from Guernsey/ Alderney at HW St Helier +4, a fair tide can be carried for at least 6 hrs down the W coast and along the S coast to St Helier. From the S, leave St Malo at about HW, keeping E of the Minquiers, in order to carry a fair tide for 6 hrs to St Helier. Follow similar tidal tactics when coasting around the island.*◄

To N and NE of Jersey, Les Pierres de Lecq (Paternosters), Les Dirouilles and Les Écrehou are groups of islets and drying rks, 2-4M offshore. On the N coast several bays (9.19.12) offer anchs sheltered in offshore winds. From the N, a convenient landfall is Desormes WCM buoy, 4M NNW of Grosnez Pt (conspic lookout tr). In St Ouen B on the W coast, which has drying rks almost 1M offshore, there are no good anchorages except NW of La Rocco tr which is sheltered in offshore winds. Rounding the SW tip, to clear offlying dangers by 1M, keep the top of La Corbière lt ho (conspic) level with or below the clifftops behind (FR lt). The inshore passage over the drying causeway between Jersey and Corbière lt ho cannot be recommended.

Along the S coast the **NW and W Passages** (buoyed) lead E past Noirmont Pt toward St Helier (9.19.12). St Brelade and St Aubin Bays (9.19.12) provide some shelter from W'lies. From the SW and S St Helier can be approached via **Danger Rock Passage, Red & Green Passage or South Passage**. All require good visibility to identify the transit marks and care to maintain the transits exactly. Only the R & G Passage is lit, but it needs sufficent water to pass over Fairway Rk (1·2m). Elizabeth marina at St Helier can be entered either from the R & G Passage or, with sufficient rise of tide, from St Aubin Bay. The latter appr on 106° passes N of Elizabeth Castle, crossing the causeway which dries approx 5·3m. It is well marked and lit.

SE of St Helier the drying, rky Violet Bank extends 1M S to Demie de Pas lt beacon, thence E past Icho Twr (conpic). It extends 1·7M S and 2M SE of La Rocque Pt. Further rky plateaux extend 1M to seaward. The **Violet Channel** (chart 1138), although buoyed is best avoided in bad weather, wind-over-tide or poor vis. From St Helier make good Canger Rk WCM lt buoy, thence track 078° for 2·2M to Violet SWM lt buoy. Turn N to pick up the charted ldg lines toward Gorey (9.19.13; dries) or to St Catherine Bay, both popular hbrs. The safe width of Violet Chan is only 5ca in places. The E coast of Jersey is well sheltered from W'lies, but requires careful pilotage.

If bound for the adjacent French coast, proceed NE from Violet buoy via the **Anquette Channel**, between Petite and Grande Anquette bcns. See 9.18.5 for Passage de la Déroute.

Les Minquiers (9.19.12), an extensive rocky plateau 10-18M S of St Helier, can be left to port, ie via NW and SW Minquiers buoys, if making for St Malo; or to stbd via NE and SE Minquiers buoys. A more direct route via N and SE Minquiers buoys requires sufficient height of tide to clear rocks drying 2m in the northern part. The plateau should only be entered for a first visit in settled weather, with extreme caution and a good Pilot book – not to mention *The Wreck of the Mary Deare* by Hammond Innes. The anchorage off Maîtresse Île is the principal attraction.

9.19.6 SPECIAL NOTES FOR THE CHANNEL ISLANDS

The Channel Islands (Alderney, Guernsey, Sark, Jersey and other smaller islands) lie, not in the Channel, but in the Bay of St. Malo. Alderney, Herm, Jethou, Sark and Brecqhou are all part of the Bailiwick of Guernsey and the States (Parliament) of Alderney have seats in the States of Guernsey.

History The Islands, originally part of Normandy, became associated with the English crown in 1066. In 1204 when King John lost mainland Normandy, the Islands became self-governing with their own laws, judiciary and Customs, but conducting their foreign affairs through the crown. They are not part of either the UK or the EU. The French call the CI Les Îles Anglo-Normandes (Aurigny, Guernesey, Sercq et Jersey).

Charts Admiralty Leisure folio SC5604 costing £37.50 (2004) contains 11 small-craft charts of the Channel Islands. These and other charts are listed under individual ports and in Chapter 1.

Ports of Entry are Braye, Beaucette, St Sampson, St Peter Port, St Helier and Gorey.

Customs The Islands have their own customs regulations. British yachts entering Channel Island ports must complete the local Customs declaration form and may have to produce the vessel's registration documents; they will also be subject to customs formalities on return to UK. Yachts going to France need the normal documents (passports etc). British yachts returning to the Channel Islands from France, must, like all French yachts, wear the Q flag. (It is advisable to do so when arriving from UK, but not mandatory, except in Alderney).

Medical The Channel Islands do not have reciprocal medical arrangements with UK and medical insurance may be desirable as costs are high, although hospital in-patient treatment is free.

Weather forecasts prepared by Jersey Met Office for the Channel Is area and adjacent coasts of Normandy and Brittany are available ☎ 0900 665 0022 (premium rate). This number is available throughout the Channel Is, UK and France, (from the latter replace the first 0 by 00 44).

SAR operations are directed by the HMs of St Peter Port (for the N area) and St Helier (for the S area), via St Peter Port and Jersey Radio respectively. Major incidents are co-ordinated with CROSSMA Jobourg and Falmouth MRCC. Unlike the UK there are no CGs, but there are LBs at Braye, St Peter Port, St Helier and St Catherines (Jersey).

Telephones CI telephones are integrated with those in the UK, but charges, especially on mobiles, may vary.

Courtesy Flags Many yachts fly a courtesy flag in Channel Island ports as a mark of politeness but it is not essential. The local flags are:
Jersey W flag with R diagonal cross, with the Jersey Royal Arms (three lions passant with gold crown above) in the canton.
Guernsey R ensign with Duke William's cross in the fly. Vessels owned by Guernsey residents may wear this ensign (Plate 4).
Sark The English (St George's) flag with the Normandy arms in the canton.
Alderney The English (St George's) flag and in the centre a green disc charged with a gold lion.
Herm The English (St George's) flag, and in the canton the Arms of Herm (three cowled monks on a gold diagonal stripe between blue triangles containing a silver dolphin).

Cars can be hired in Jersey, Guernsey & Alderney. In Sark cars are prohib, but bikes and horse-drawn carriages can be hired.

Animals The rules regarding animals are stricter than in UK. Landing of animals from boats is permitted only from UK, Ireland, Isle of Man or other Chan Islands, but not if the boat has visited France. Unless expressly permitted by a Revenue Officer, no vessel may lie alongside a pontoon or quay with an animal on board.

UK Currency is freely usable in the Islands but CI currency may not be in the UK. Postage stamps, issued by Jersey, Guernsey and Alderney must be used in the appropriate Bailiwick; Guernsey and Alderney stamps are usable in either island. There is only one class of post.

9.19.7 BRAYE (Alderney)

Alderney **49°43'·77N 02°11'·51W** ❁❁❁◊◊◊✿✿✿

CHARTS AC *2669, 3653, 60,* 2845, *5604*; SHOM 7158, 6934; ECM 1014; Imray C33A; Stanfords 2, 7, 16, 26.

TIDES –0400 Dover; ML 3·5; Duration 0545; Zone 0 (UT)

Standard Port ST HELIER (⟶)

Times				**Height (metres)**			
High Water		Low Water		MHWS	MHWN	MLWN	MLWS
0300	0900	0200	0900	11·0	8·1	4·0	1·4
1500	2100	1400	2100				
Differences BRAYE							
+0050	+0040	+0025	+0105	–4·8	–3·4	–1·5	–0·5

SHELTER Good in Braye Hbr, except in strong N/NE winds. 64 Y ⚓s are laid parallel to the Admiralty bkwtr, and in blocks E of Braye jetty and near Toulouse Rk. Orange buoys are for locals. If >12m LOA, check adequacy of ⚓ with HM. Secure with chain if possible to avoid chafe due to persistent swell. No landing on Admiralty bkwtr; at its NE end beware submerged extension. ⚓ in hbr is good on sand, but only fair on rock or weed patches; keep clear of the fairway and jetty due to steamer traffic. Hbr speed limit 4kn. Access HW±2 to drying inner hbr for D, FW.

NAVIGATION WPT 49°44´·23N 02°10´·99W, 215°/1·05M to front ldg lt 215°. The main hazards are strong tidal streams and the many rocks encircling Alderney. The safest appr is from the NE. In fog or limited visibility radar assistance and RDF bearings can be provided by the HM to small craft during office hours.

Take the Swinge and the Race at/near slack water to avoid the dangerous overfalls in certain wind and tide conditions (see 9.19.5). In the Swinge calmest area is often near Corbet Rk. At mid-flood (NE-going) a strong eddy flows SW past the hbr ent.

On the S side of the island during the ebb, a strong eddy sets NE close inshore of Coque Lihou. Off NE end give Brinchetais Ledge and Race Rk a wide berth to avoid heavy overfalls. An Historic Wreck is 5ca N of Quenard Pt lt ho (see 9.0.3h).

LIGHTS AND MARKS See chartlets and 9.19.4. From NW, N side of Fort Albert and head of Admiralty Bkwtr ≠ 115° clear the Nannels. Château à l'Etoc lt ho ≠ 111° with Quenard Pt lt ho clears sunken ruins of Admiralty Bkwtr.

Ldg lts, both Q synch, lead 215° into hbr. Co-located daymarks: both W cols, orange △s, lead 215°. Note: The white bcn on Old pier ≠ 210·5° with St Anne's church spire are no longer official ldg marks, but may be used by small craft, if desired. The Bkwtr head is painted with B/W vertical stripes and is lit. Other conspic marks: a Water twr W of St Anne's and two lattice masts (R lts) E of it. 2ca SW of Quenard Pt lt ho a Blockhouse is conspic.

R/T *Alderney Radio* VHF Ch **74** 16 (May to Sept, 0800 -1800, daily; Oct 0800-1700 daily; Nov to Apr, 0800-1700, Mon-Fri: all LT). Outside these hrs call St Peter Port. *Mainbrayce* Ch 80 (Apr-mid Sept: HO). Water taxi (£2, €3.00, inbound; £1, €2.00, outbound): call *Mainbrayce* Ch M, 0800-2359; or ☎ 07781 415420.

TELEPHONE (Dial code 01481) HM & ⊖ 822620, 📠 823699; Marinecall 09066 526250; Recorded forecasts see 6.8 and 6.12; Police 725111; Dr 822077; Ⓗ 822822; ❶ Info 822994 (H24).

FACILITIES **Hbr** ⚓ (£12 flat rate), ⚓ £2.50 inc shower; **Jetty** , FW, C, ⊡; **Sapper Slip**, FW; **Alderney SC** ☎ 822758, Bar; **Services:** Slip, FW, ME, El, Ⓔ, Gas, ⚒, CH, ACA, P (cans), D (Mainbrayce, inner hbr HW±2 ☎ 822722).
Town EC Wed; 🛒, R, Bar, ✉, Ⓑ, ✈ to Jersey, Guernsey, Bournemouth & Southampton direct; and via Guernsey to many European destinations. Ferry: via Guernsey to Poole, Portsmouth, St Malo and Weymouth.

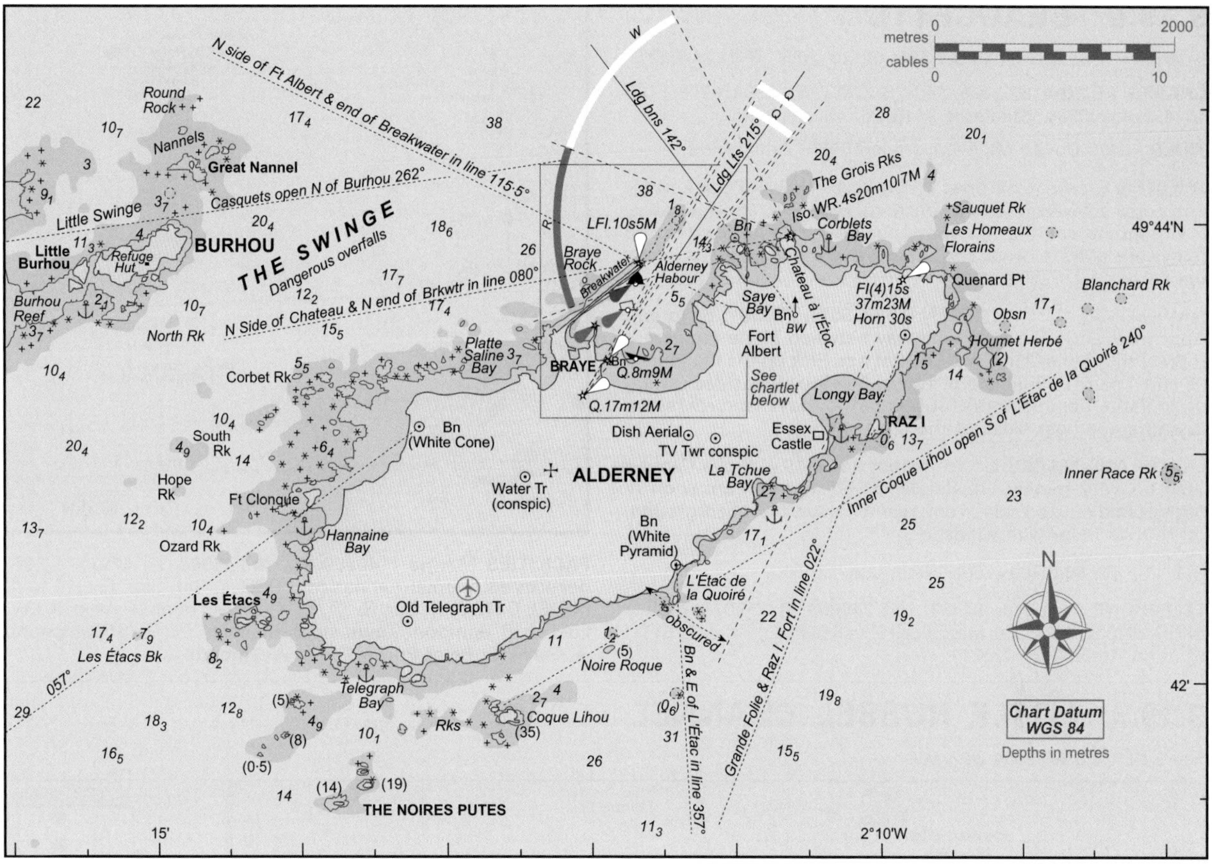
metres
cables
0
2000
10
Round Rock
Nannels
Great Nannel
Little Swinge
Casquets open N of Burhou 262°
N side of Ft Albert & end of Breakwater in line 115·5°
Little Burhou
BURHOU
Refuge Hut
THE SWINGE
Dangerous overfalls
Burhou Reef
North Rk
N Side of Chateau & N end of Brkwtr in line 080°
Ldg bns 142°
Ldg Lts 215°
LFl.10s5M
Braye Rock
Breakwater
Alderney Habour
BRAYE
Q.8m9M
Q.17m12M
See chartlet below
The Grois Rks
Iso.WR.4s20m10/7M
Corblets Bay
Chateau à l'Étoc
Saye Bay
Fort Albert
Fl(4)15s 37m23M Horn 30s
Sauquet Rk
Les Homeaux Florains
Quenard Pt
Blanchard Rk
Obsn
Houmet Herbé
Longy Bay
RAZ I
Essex Castle
49°44'N
Platte Saline Bay
Corbet Rk
South Rk
Hope Rk
Ft Clonque
Ozard Rk
Hannaine Bay
Bn (White Cone)
Dish Aerial
TV Twr conspic
Water Tr (conspic)
ALDERNEY
La Tchue Bay
Inner Coque Lihou open S of L'Étac de la Quoiré 240°
Inner Race Rk
Bn (White Pyramid)
L'Étac de la Quoiré
obscured
Old Telegraph Tr
Les Étacs
Les Étacs Bk
057°
Noire Roque
Telegraph Bay
Rks
Coque Lihou
Bn & E of L'Étac in line 357°
Grande Folie & Raz I. Fort in line 022°
THE NOIRES PUTES
42'
Chart Datum WGS 84
Depths in metres
15'
2°10'W

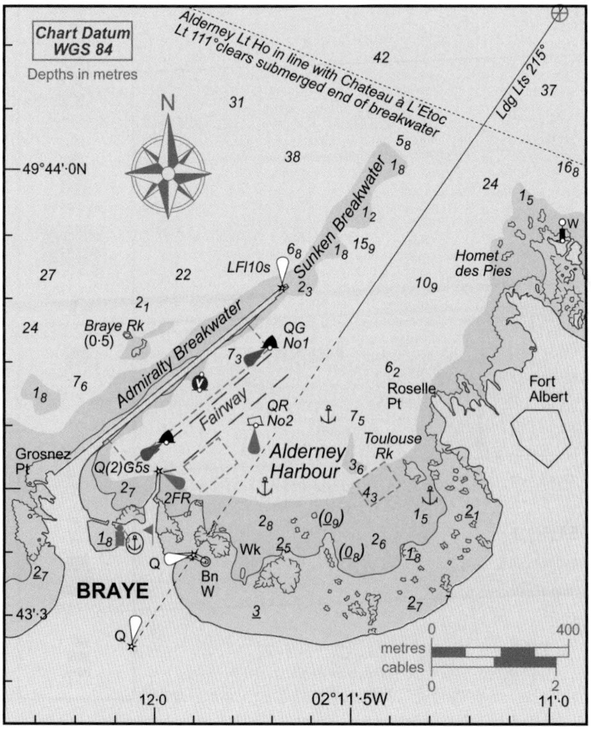
Chart Datum WGS 84
Depths in metres
Alderney Lt Ho in line with Chateau à L'Etoc
Lt 111° clears submerged end of breakwater
Ldg Lts 215°
49°44'·0N
Sunken Breakwater
LFl10s
Braye Rk (0·5)
Admiralty Breakwater
QG No1
Fairway
QR No2
Alderney Harbour
Roselle Pt
Toulouse Rk
Homet des Pies
Fort Albert
Grosnez Pt
Q(2)G5s
2FR
Wk
BRAYE
Bn W
43'·3
metres
cables
0
400
2
12·0
02°11'·5W
11'·0

ANCHORAGES AROUND ALDERNEY There are several ⚓s, all picturesque but only safe in off-shore winds; most are very small and many have offlying rocks. Without local knowledge, advice from the HM and a good Pilot book plus AC 60 and/or preferably 2845, entry to these anchorages is not advised. None provide any facilities. Clockwise from Braye they are:

Saye Bay. Small sandy bay 4ca E of ent to Braye Hbr. Appr on transit 142° of ldg bns, opening to the E. Ent is 100m wide between Homet des Pies and Homet des Agneaux. Exposed to N'lies. Château à l'Étoc ☆ is 300m ENE. Speed limit 4kn.

Longy Bay. AC 2845. Wide drying bay with good holding in sand. Appr on N between Queslingue (14m high) and rk 0·6m to stbd. ⚓ in 3·5m closer to Essex Castle than to Raz Island to await fair tide in the Race. Speed limit 4kn.

La Tchue. Good holding in small bay surrounded by cliffs. La Rocque Pendante to the E and smoking rubbish tip to the NW are both conspic.

Telegraph Bay. Pleasant sandy bay on SW tip of the island but ringed by rocks. Appr on NNE between Noires Putes and Coupé. Old Telegraph Twr (85m) is conspic until obsc'd close inshore, when a pillar on the cliff edge offers bearings.

Hannaine Bay. A good place to await the flood tide. Appr on transit 057° of Tourgis Bn △ and SE side of Fort Clonque. Beware rks either side. ⚓ on sand in 3m, 100m S of Fort.

Platte Saline Bay. AC 2845. Good shelter from E'lies. Les Jumelles and Outer Fourchie guard the ent. Beach is unsafe for swimming.

Burhou. Temp'y ⚓ in bay SW of Burhou, only on SW stream; exposed at HW on the NE-going stream. Appr on 010° for the gap between Burhou and Little Burhou.

9.19.8 BEAUCETTE

Guernsey (Channel Is) **49°30'.19N 02°30'·20W** ❁❁◊◊◊✿✿✿

CHARTS AC *3654, 807, 808, 5604*; SHOM 7159, 6904, 6903; ECM 1014; Imray C33A; Stanfords 2, 16, 26

TIDES –0450 Dover; ML 5·0; Duration 0550; Zone 0 (UT)

SHELTER Excellent. Sill dries 2.37m; access HW St Peter Port ±3. Entry not advised in strong onshore winds. To arrange entry and berthing call the HM with your boat details. 6 Y waiting buoys are outside (water taxi, Ch 80) and a tide gauge is inside the 8m wide ent chan.

NAVIGATION WPT 49°30′·15N 02°28′·85W, 277°/8½ ca to ent. Appr from Little Russel to mid-way between Platte Fougère lt tr (W with B band, 25m) and Roustel lt tr. Pick up the ldg marks/lts and 4 pairs of unlit lateral buoys. Beware cross tides setting on to Petite Canupe Rocks (SCM lt bn) to the N, and rocks and drying areas both sides of the appr chan.

LIGHTS AND MARKS Lts as chartlet and 9.19.4. Petite Canupe SCM bn, very spindly. Ldg lts/marks 277°: Front, R arrow on W background on stbd side of ent; rear, W arrow on R background, on roof of bldg, with windsock.

R/T VHF Ch **80** (0700-2200). Water taxi, Ch 80.

TELEPHONE (Dial code 01481) HM 245000, Fax 247071, mobile 07781 102302; ⊖ 245000; Marinecall 09066 526250; Police 725111; St John Ambulance 725211.

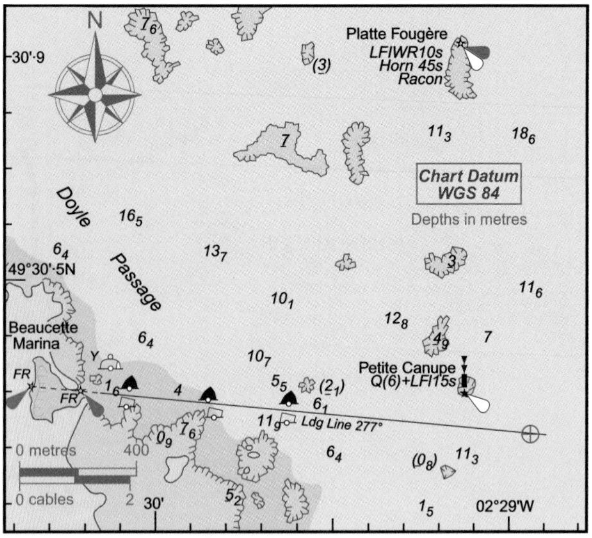
N
Platte Fougère
LFlWR10s
Horn 45s
Racon
30'·9
Chart Datum
WGS 84
Depths in metres
Doyle
Passage
49°30'·5N
Beaucette
Marina
FR
Y
Petite Canupe
Q(6)+LFl15s
Ldg Line 277°
0 metres 400
0 cables 2
30'
02°29'W

FACILITIES Marina (140+50 Ⓥ), ☎ 245000, Fax 47071, £1.95, beaucette@premiermarinas.com D, Gas, Gaz, Slip, BH (16 ton), ME, El, C (12 ton), Bar, R, ⛟, ⊡, ♿: access ramp is steep @ LW. Fuel on 'B' pontoon. **Town** most amenities, ✉, Ⓑ (St Sampson), ✈. Ferry: St Peter Port – Poole, Weymouth.

9.19.9 LITTLE RUSSEL CHANNEL

See 9.19.5 and AC *5604, 807, 808*

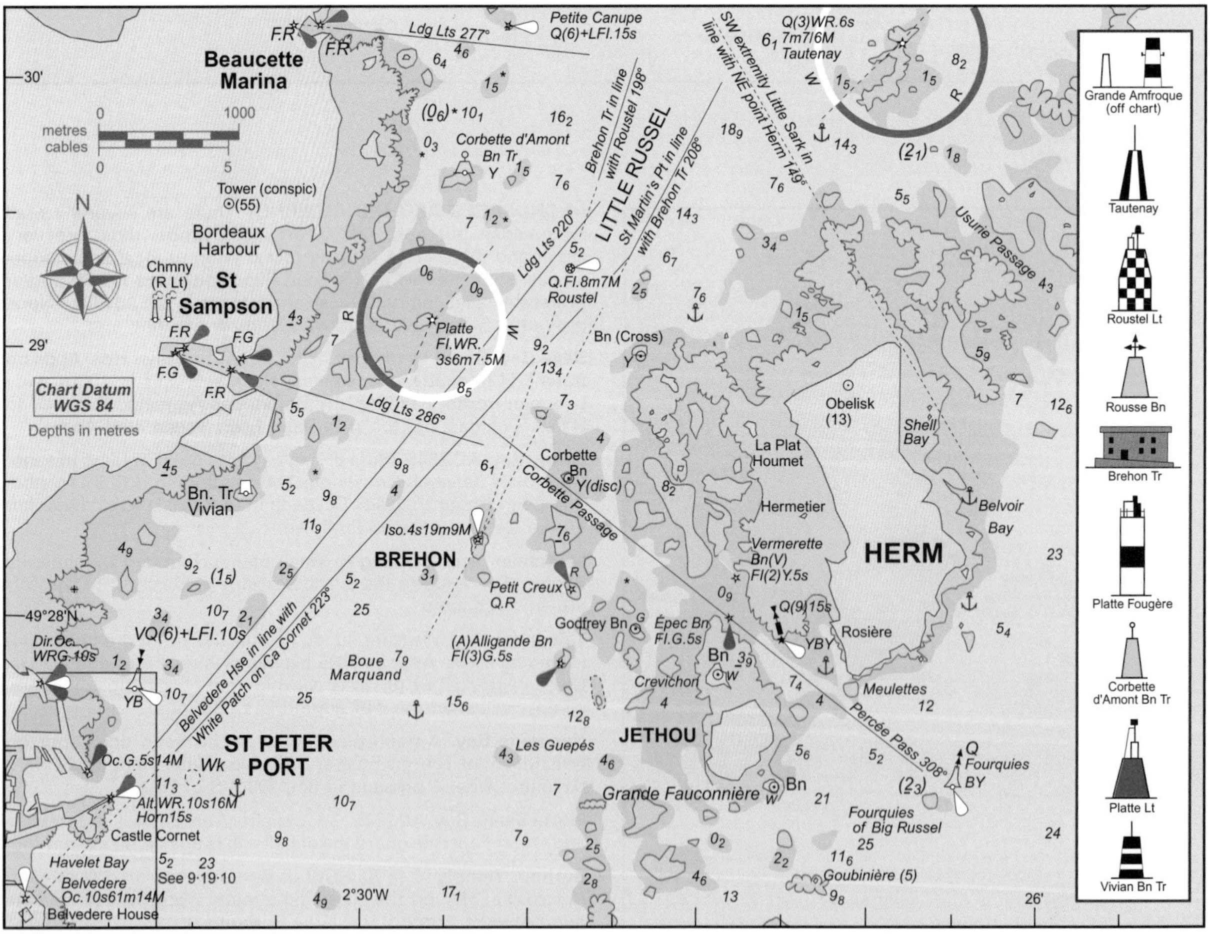
Petite Canupe
Q(6)+LFl.15s
Ldg Lts 277°
Beaucette
Marina
F.R
30'
metres 0 1000
cables 0 5
Corbette d'Amont
Bn Tr
Tower (conspic)
(55)
Bordeaux
Harbour
Chmny
(R Lt)
St
Sampson
Brehon Tr in line
with Roustel 198°
LITTLE RUSSEL
St Martin's Pt in line
with Brehon Tr 208°
SW extremity Little Sark in
line with NE point Herm 149°
Q(3)WR.6s
7m7/6M
Tautenay
Usurie Passage
Ldg Lts 220°
Q.Fl.8m7M
Roustel
Platte
Fl.WR.
3s6m7·5M
Bn (Cross)
29'
F.R
F.G
Chart Datum
WGS 84
Depths in metres
Ldg Lts 286°
Obelisk
(13)
Shell
Bay
La Plat
Houmet
Corbette
Bn
Y(disc)
Corbette Passage
Bn. Tr
Vivian
Hermetier
Belvoir
Bay
Iso.4s19m9M
BREHON
Vermerette
Bn(V)
Fl(2)Y.5s
HERM
Petit Creux
Q.R
49°28'N
Dir.Oc.
WRG.10s
VQ(6)+LFl.10s
Belvedere Hse in line with
White Patch on Ca Cornet 223°
Godfrey Bn
Épec Bn
Fl.G.5s
Q(9)15s
YBY
Rosière
(A)Alligande Bn
Fl(3)G.5s
Boue
Marquand
Bn
Crevichon
YB
Meulettes
Percée Pass 308°
ST PETER
PORT
Oc.G.5s14M
Wk
Les Guepés
JETHOU
Q
Fourquies
BY
Alt.WR.10s16M
Horn15s
Grande Fauconnière
Bn
Fourquies
of Big Russel
Castle Cornet
Havelet Bay
See 9·19·10
Belvedere
Oc.10s61m14M
Belvedere House
Goubinière (5)
2°30'W
26'
Grande Amfroque
(off chart)
Tautenay
Roustel Lt
Rousse Bn
Brehon Tr
Platte Fougère
Corbette
d'Amont Bn Tr
Platte Lt
Vivian Bn Tr

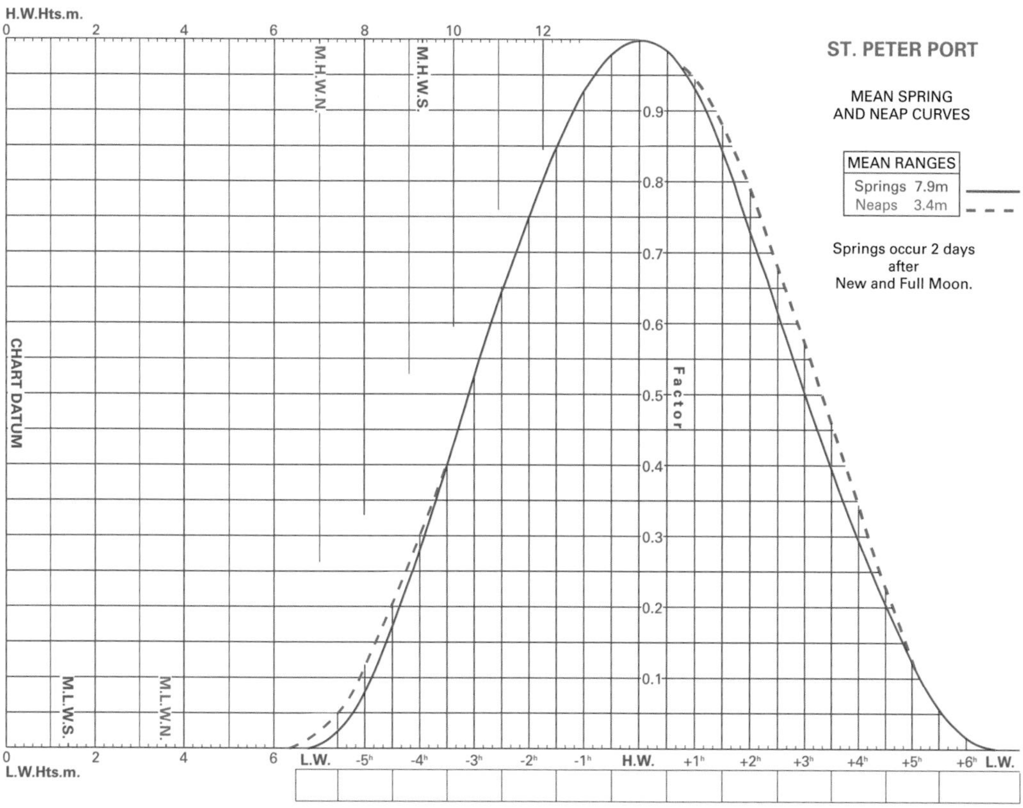
H.W.Hts.m.
0 2 4 6 8 10 12
M.H.W.N.
M.H.W.S.
CHART DATUM
M.L.W.S.
M.L.W.N.
0 2 4 6
L.W.Hts.m.
0.9
0.8
0.7
0.6
0.5
0.4
0.3
0.2
0.1
Factor
L.W. -5ʰ -4ʰ -3ʰ -2ʰ -1ʰ H.W. +1ʰ +2ʰ +3ʰ +4ʰ +5ʰ +6ʰ L.W.
ST. PETER PORT
MEAN SPRING AND NEAP CURVES
MEAN RANGES
Springs 7.9m
Neaps 3.4m
Springs occur 2 days after New and Full Moon.

HARBOURS AND ANCHORAGES AROUND GUERNSEY

AC 807 and 808 are essential. ⚓s and hbrs are listed clockwise from Beaucette. All have buses to St Peter Port (from cliff-top level on the E and S coasts).

EAST COAST

Bordeaux Harbour. Small drying hbr full of local moorings. Rky appr with strong cross tide. Exposed to E. Café.

St Sampson's Harbour. Hbr dries $\underline{5}$·2m. Official port of entry. Good shelter but the disadvantages of a commercial and fishing hbr. New marina, for locals only, opened May 2004. Visiting yachts may only enter by prior arrangement or for commercial services. WPT 49°28'·70N 02°29'·65W, the intersection of St Peter Port and St Sampson ldg lts. 2 chimneys on N side are conspic. Ldg lts 286°: Front, FR 3m 5M, on S Arm; rear, FG 13m, 390m from front, on clocktower. N pier hd FG 3m 5M. Crocq pier hd, FR 11m 5M, and tfc sigs. A Fl Y on S Arm means petroleum/gas tankers are moving in the hbr; do not obstruct. Speed limit 6kn. No ⚓ in hbr. VHF Ch 12 (H24). Facilities: Call Dockmaster ☎ 720229 for entry, AB, C, FW. **Services:** BY, BH (70 ton), ME, El, ⚒, C. Bulk fuel by tanker on N side can be arranged.

Havelet Bay. Enter between SHM buoy QG and PHM buoy QR, marking Oyster Rk, bn 'O', and Moulinet Rk, bn 'M'. Unlit SHM and PHM buoy about 100m closer inshore. Crowded ⚓ in summer but sheltered in SW gales; no ⊙s. Landing slip close W of Castle Cornet. Cable on chartlet normally buried to 1m but caution needed.

Soldier's Bay. Good holding on sand; exposed to E. On appr beware Boue Sablon and rky spur off Les Terres Point. Anfré Rk ($\underline{3}_3$), bn 'A', is 4ca offshore. Steps to cliff path. No facilities.

Fermain Bay. Good holding on sand; exposed to E. From N beware Gold Fisher Rk ($\underline{2}_1$), drying reefs off NE end of bay. From SE beware Gabrielle Rk ($\underline{2}_1$). Popular tourist beach. R, hotel, Bar.

SOUTH COAST

In centre of first bay W of St Martin's Pt, beware Mouillière ($\underline{8}_5$). S'lies can bring swell above half tide. In this bay are:

Petit Port. Good holding on sand. Steep steps to cliff-top bar are closed by landfall, enhancing the attractiveness to yotties.

Moulin Huet. Good holding on sand. Tea garden and hotel.

Saints Bay. Good holding on sand. Below half tide beware uncharted rock in middle and unburied telephone cable on E side. ⚓ outside moorings with trip line. Café, hotel, bar.

Icart Bay. Beware Fourquie de la Moye ($\underline{3}_1$) in centre of ent between Icart Pt and Pte de la Moye. In Icart Bay are:

Jaonnet. Good holding on sand off small beach or further E off rky shore. Exposed to S. No facilities. Cliff path inland.

Petit Bôt Bay. Beware drying reef on E side. A short swell often works in. Café; up hill to hotel, bar, airport, ✉, 🛒. Better ⚓ close W at:

Portelet. Good holding on sand in small ⚓. Sheltered from N and W. No access inland. Facilities via dinghy/Petit Bôt.

WEST COAST

Good visibility and chart essential; a pilot and E'ly wind desirable. Pass outside Les Hanois, unless bound for:

Portelet Harbour. Good holding on sand. Exposed to W. ⚓ outside moorings and clear of fish farm. Rky appr; local knowledge advised. Avoid small drying stone quay. Hotel, bar, café.

Lihou Island. ⚓ off NE corner. Sheltered from E. Between Lihou and Guernsey is a drying rocky area and causeway. Tide runs fast. Respect bird sanctuaries on off-lying islets. No facilities.

Perelle Bay. Good holding on sand. Exposed to W; rky appr. Beware Colombelle Rk ($\underline{1}_5$) NE of bay. ⚓ outside moorings. Bar, hotel, D & P (cans).

Vazon Bay. Wide sandy beach for settled conditions, but exposed to the W. Beware Boue Vazon ($\underline{3}$) in appr, many lobster pots, surfers and bathers. Long surf line. Hotel, R.

Cobo Bay. Beware Boue Vazon ($\underline{3}$) in appr and many lobster pots. Rky appr from S of Moulière. Good holding on sand; ⚓ outside local moorings. Facilities: Hotel, Bar, R, B, ✉, 🛒, D & P (cans).

Grande Havre. Very popular, many local moorings. Rky appr 171°, marks as charted; exposed to NW, sheltered from S'lies. ⚓ to W of Hommet de Grève. Stone slip, busy in summer; lying alongside not recommended. Facilities: Hotel, Bar.

L'Ancresse Bay. Good holding on sand. Exposed to the N, but good shelter from S/SW. Hotel, Bar, Café.

Fontenelle Bay. Good holding on sand. Exposed to the N. Beware drying rks on E of ent. No facilities.

9.19.10 ST PETER PORT

Guernsey **49°27'·35N 02°31'·53W** ❁❁❁👍👍👍✿✿✿

CHARTS AC *3654, 808, 807,* 3140, *5604*; SHOM 7159, 6903, 6904; ECM 1014; Imray C33A; Stanfords 2, 16, 26.

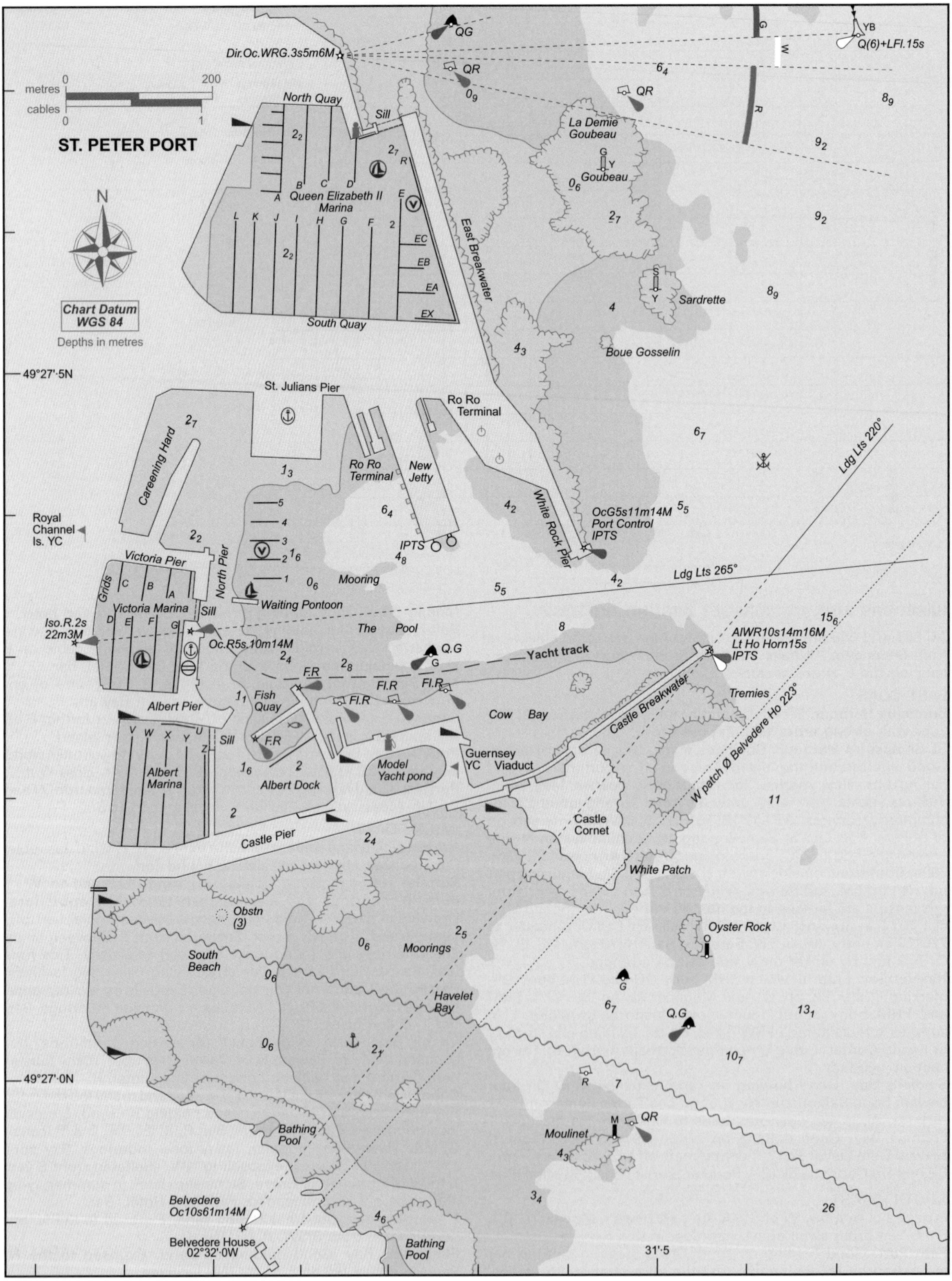
ST. PETER PORT
metres
cables
Chart Datum
WGS 84
Depths in metres
Dir.Oc.WRG.3s5m6M
QG
QR
YB
Q(6)+LFl.15s
North Quay
Sill
Queen Elizabeth II
Marina
East Breakwater
South Quay
La Demie
Goubeau
Goubeau
Sardrette
Boue Gosselin
49°27'·5N
St. Julians Pier
Careening Hard
Ro Ro
Terminal
New
Jetty
Royal
Channel
Is. YC
Victoria Pier
North Pier
Victoria Marina
Grids
Waiting Pontoon
Mooring
White Rock Pier
OcG5s11m14M
Port Control
IPTS
Ldg Lts 220°
Ldg Lts 265°
Iso.R.2s
22m3M
Oc.R5s.10m14M
The Pool
Q.G
Yacht track
F.R
Fl.R
Fish
Quay
Albert Pier
Cow Bay
AlWR10s14m16M
Lt Ho Horn15s
IPTS
Tremies
Castle Breakwater
W patch Ø Belvedere Ho 223°
Albert
Marina
Albert Dock
Model
Yacht pond
Guernsey
YC
Viaduct
Castle Pier
Castle
Cornet
White Patch
Obstn
Oyster Rock
South
Beach
Moorings
Havelet
Bay
49°27'·0N
Bathing
Pool
Moulinet
Belvedere
Oc10s61m14M
Belvedere House
02°32'·0W
31'·5

TIDES −0439 Dover; ML 5·2; Duration 0550; Zone 0 (UT)
NOTE: St Peter Port is a Standard Port (⟶).

To find depth of water over the sill into Victoria marina:

1. Look up predicted time and height of HW St Peter Port.
2. Enter table below on the line for height of HW.
3. Extract depth (m) of water for time before/after HW.

Ht (m) of HW St Peter Port	Depth of Water in metres over the Sill (dries 4·2 m)						
	HW	±1hr	±2hrs	±2½hrs	±3hrs	±3½hrs	±4hrs
6·20	2·00	1·85	1·55	1·33	1·10	0·88	0·65
·60	2·40	2·18	1·75	1·43	1·10	0·77	0·45
7·00	2·80	2·52	1·95	1·53	1·10	0·67	0·25
·40	3·20	2·85	2·15	1·63	1·10	0·57	0·05
·80	3·60	3·18	2·35	1·73	1·10	0·47	0·00
8·20	4·00	3·52	2·55	1·83	1·10	0·37	0·00
·60	4·40	3·85	2·75	1·93	1·10	0·28	0·00
9·00	4·80	4·18	2·95	2·03	1·10	0·18	0·00
·40	5·20	4·52	3·15	2·13	1·10	0·08	0·00
·80	5·60	4·85	3·35	2·23	1·10	0·00	0·00

SHELTER Good, especially in Victoria Marina which has a sill 4·2m above CD, with a gauge giving depth over sill. Access approx HW±2½ according to draft; see Table above. R/G tfc lts and the marina staff control ent/exit.

Appr via buoyed/lit chan along S side of hbr. Marina boat will direct yachts to waiting pontoon or Ⓥ pontoons with FW (nos 1-5) N of the waiting pontoon. Pontoons for tenders are each side of marina ent. Local moorings are in centre of hbr, with a secondary fairway N of them. ⚓ prohib. Ⓥ berths in Queen Elizabeth II and Albert marinas by prior arrangement.

NAVIGATION WPT 49°27′·82N 02°30′·78W, 227°/0·68M to hbr ent. Offlying dangers, big tidal range and strong tidal streams demand careful navigation. Easiest appr from N is via Big Russel between Herm and Sark, passing S of Lower Hds SCM lt buoy. The Little Russel is slightly more direct, but needs care especially in poor visibility; see 9.19.5 and 9.19.9 chartlet. From W and S of Guernsey, give Les Hanois a wide berth. Beware ferries and shipping. Hbr speed limits: 6kn from outer pier heads to line from New Jetty to Castle Cornet; 4kn W of that line.

An **RDF beacon, GY** 304·50kHz, on Castle Bkwtr is synchronised with the co-located horn (15s) to give distance finding. The horn blast begins simultaneously with the 27 sec long dash following the four GY ident signals. Time the number of seconds from the start of the long dash until the horn blast is next heard, multiply by 0·18 = distance in M from the horn; several counts are advised.

LIGHTS AND MARKS See chartlet and 9.19.4. Outer ldg lts 220°: Front, Castle bkwtr hd; rear, Belvedere. By day, White patch at Castle Cornet in line 223° with Belvedere Ho (conspic). Inner ldg lts 265° are for ferries berthing at New Jetty. The ldg line passes through moorings in The Pool, so must not be used by yachts which should appr Victoria marina via the buoyed/lit S channel (dashed line).

Traffic Signals ●●● (vert) are shown from: Castle Bkwtr lt ho, facing S; from White Rock pierhead, facing N, plus E or W for inbound/outbound vessels; and from SW corner of New Jetty, facing E. They are either ON or OFF and do not apply to boats, <15m LOA, under power and keeping clear of the fairways.

R/T *St Peter Port Marina* Ch M, 80 (office hrs). *Water taxi* Ch 10 (0800-2359LT). Monitor *St Peter Port Control* Ch **12** (H24); only calling *Port Control*, if necessary, when within the pilotage area. *St Peter Port Radio* CRS Ch 20 for safety traffic; Ch 16/67 for DF brgs in emergency; Ch 62 for link calls. *St Sampson* Ch 12 (H24).

TELEPHONE (Dial code 01481) HM 720229, 🖷 714177; Marina 725987; ⊖ 726911; White Rock Sig Stn 720672; Marinecall 09066 526250; Dr 711237 (H24), Pier Steps at Boots; 725211 (St John Ambulance); Police 725111. Guernsey Met office 0906 713 0111 (from Guernsey only, at lowest premium rate) for local weather.

FACILITIES **Victoria Marina** (400, all Ⓥ) ☎ 725987, £1.53, special deals outside July/Aug; Max LOA/draft = 16m/1·8m; Max stay 14 days, longer by arrangement; Slip, ♿, ⊡, R, crane available. www.guernseyharbours.gov.gg guernsey.harbour@gov.gg

Castle Pier FW, P, D approx HW±3 (risk of grounding outside these hrs), 0730-1730 Mon-Sat, 0730-1200 Sun; (also fuel pontoon at QE II marina). **Royal Chan Is YC** ☎ 723154 Bar; **Guernsey YC** ☎ 722838; **Services:** CH, Gas, Gaz, ACA, ME, El, SM, BY, Ⓔ.

Town P, D, 🛒, CH, R, ⊡, Bar, ✉, Ⓑ. Fast ferry to Weymouth, Poole, Jersey, St Malo; ferry to Portsmouth, Diélette, Sark, Herm; ✈ (Guernsey).

HERM ISLAND

Access to Herm is not difficult, given adequate planning.

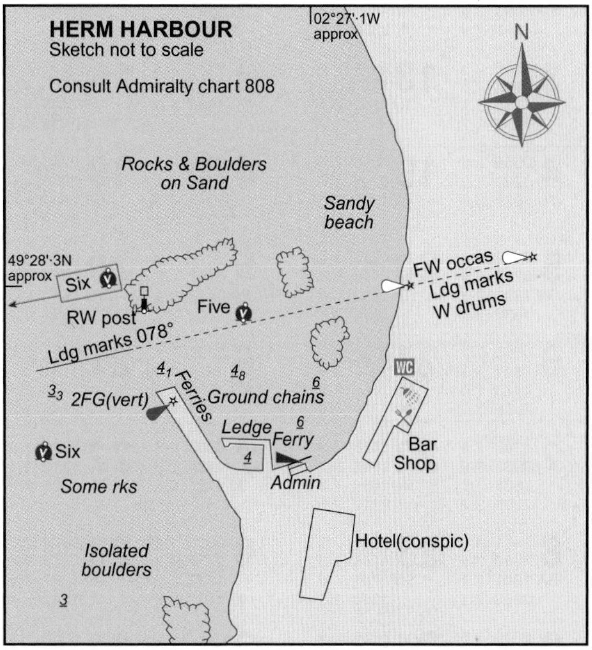
HERM HARBOUR
Sketch not to scale
Consult Admiralty chart 808
02°27′·1W approx
N
Rocks & Boulders on Sand
Sandy beach
49°28′·3N approx
Six
Five
RW post
Ldg marks 078°
FW occas
Ldg marks W drums
WC
2FG(vert)
Ferries
Ground chains
Ledge
Ferry
Six
Bar
Shop
Some rks
Admin
Hotel(conspic)
Isolated boulders

SHELTER Good, safe in all winds. Get permission to stay in hbr overnight from Island Admin (see Tel). Access HW±2½. Options:
a. Lie to mooring lines secured to N and S walls inside hbr.
b. Dry out on the beach to the E, below Bar and Shop, moored fore/aft to chains. c. 5 Ⓥs to N and 6 to W of hbr dry out; 6 more to NW: rky bottom to the N; isolated boulders/sand to W.

NAVIGATION From Little Russel skirt close N of Vermerette bn in line 074° with W patch on Hbr quay. When base of Vermerette bn is awash, there is 1m at hbr ent. The tide will be setting N. See Pilot for Corbette, Alligande and other western passages. Sand build-up W of Vermerette affects craft NW-bound in Percée Passage, but not hbr access above half-tide.

LIGHTS AND MARKS Ldg lts, both FW (occas) and W drums at 078°. 2FG (vert) on quay hd. Night appr not advised for visitors.

TELEPHONE Island Admin ☎ 722377 for overnight stay in hbr.

FACILITIES No fees; donations welcome. Showers, FW, Hotel, Bar, R, limited 🛒. Very congested in season at weekends, but plenty of space Sun to Thurs nights; hourly ferries by day.

Rosière Steps Access for landing only; do not linger alongside. The bottom step is about 1.5m above the seabed which may be inconvenient at LWS. Caution: From just before HW to HW+2 tide sets hard onto the steps. Easiest appr is from Big Russel via Percée passage; avoid Fourquies ($\underline{2}_3$, NCM lt buoy), and Meulettes ($\underline{1}_7$) off SW tip of Herm. ⚓ NW of Rosière steps; good holding on sand, but exposed to S and SW. Buoys are for ferries and locals.
Belvoir Bay and **Shell Beach** on the E coast are good ⚓s on sand, sheltered from W. Easy access from E; from S keep 400m offshore. Beach café or walk 800m to village.
Note: Jethou, Crevichon and Grande Fauconnière islands are private. No landing.

TIME ZONE (UT)
For Summer Time add ONE hour in **non-shaded areas**

CHANNEL ISLANDS – ST PETER PORT

LAT 49°27′N LONG 2°31′W

TIMES AND HEIGHTS OF HIGH AND LOW WATERS

SPRING & NEAP TIDES
Dates in red are SPRINGS
Dates in blue are NEAPS

YEAR **2005**

JANUARY

Date	Day	Time	m	Time	m	Time	m	Time	m
1	SA	0337	2.9	0938	7.9	1604	2.8	2204	7.5
2	SU	0415	3.1	1018	7.7	1643	3.0	2246	7.4
3	M	0500	3.3	1105	7.5	1730	3.2	◑ 2336	7.2
4	TU	0555	3.5	1201	7.3	1828	3.3		
5	W	0038	7.1	0702	3.5	1308	7.3	1938	3.3
6	TH	0151	7.2	0821	3.3	1423	7.4	2055	3.1
7	F	0305	7.6	0935	2.9	1535	7.7	2205	2.7
8	SA	0411	8.0	1040	2.4	1641	8.1	2308	2.3
9	SU	0510	8.5	1140	1.9	1741	8.5		
10	M	0005	1.9	0605	9.0	1237	1.4	● 1836	8.9
11	TU	0059	1.5	0657	9.4	1330	1.0	1927	9.2
12	W	0150	1.2	0746	9.7	1419	0.8	2015	9.3
13	TH	0237	1.1	0833	9.7	1506	0.8	2101	9.2
14	F	0322	1.3	0919	9.5	1550	1.0	2144	8.9
15	SA	0405	1.6	1002	9.1	1633	1.5	2227	8.5
16	SU	0448	2.1	1046	8.5	1716	2.1	2310	7.9
17	M	0533	2.7	1133	7.8	1801	2.7	◐ 2358	7.4
18	TU	0624	3.2	1227	7.3	1853	3.3		
19	W	0058	7.0	0728	3.6	1336	6.9	1959	3.6
20	TH	0213	6.8	0848	3.7	1453	6.8	2114	3.7
21	F	0326	6.9	1001	3.5	1600	6.9	2220	3.5
22	SA	0425	7.3	1058	3.2	1654	7.3	2312	3.1
23	SU	0513	7.7	1144	2.8	1741	7.6	2356	2.8
24	M	0555	8.1	1225	2.5	1822	8.0		
25	TU	0035	2.4	0634	8.4	1303	2.2	○ 1900	8.2
26	W	0111	2.2	0711	8.6	1338	2.0	1936	8.4
27	TH	0145	2.0	0746	8.7	1411	1.8	2010	8.4
28	F	0218	1.9	0818	8.7	1442	1.9	2040	8.4
29	SA	0250	2.0	0848	8.6	1513	2.0	2110	8.3
30	SU	0322	2.2	0920	8.4	1543	2.1	2140	8.1
31	M	0354	2.4	0953	8.2	1616	2.4	2214	7.8

FEBRUARY

Date	Day	Time	m	Time	m	Time	m	Time	m
1	TU	0429	2.7	1032	7.9	1653	2.7	2255	7.6
2	W	0512	3.0	1119	7.5	1739	3.1	◑ 2347	7.3
3	TH	0610	3.3	1220	7.2	1843	3.4		
4	F	0059	7.1	0731	3.5	1344	7.0	2012	3.5
5	SA	0232	7.1	0909	3.2	1517	7.2	2146	3.2
6	SU	0356	7.6	1029	2.7	1634	7.7	2259	2.6
7	M	0503	8.3	1135	2.0	1737	8.3		
8	TU	0000	1.9	0559	8.9	1232	1.3	● 1831	8.9
9	W	0053	1.3	0650	9.5	1322	0.7	1919	9.4
10	TH	0141	0.8	0736	9.9	1407	0.4	2002	9.6
11	F	0224	0.6	0819	10.0	1449	0.3	2043	9.6
12	SA	0304	0.7	0859	9.8	1527	0.6	2120	9.3
13	SU	0341	1.1	0936	9.3	1603	1.1	2155	8.8
14	M	0415	1.7	1011	8.7	1636	1.9	2228	8.1
15	TU	0448	2.4	1047	7.9	1709	2.7	2302	7.5
16	W	0525	3.1	1127	7.1	1748	3.4	◐ 2345	6.9
17	TH	0616	3.7	1224	6.5	1846	4.0		
18	F	0055	6.4	0736	4.1	1401	6.2	2012	4.2
19	SA	0245	6.4	0930	4.0	1541	6.4	2154	3.9
20	SU	0406	6.8	1044	3.5	1641	6.9	2258	3.4
21	M	0457	7.4	1131	2.9	1726	7.4	2342	2.8
22	TU	0540	7.9	1210	2.4	1806	8.0		
23	W	0020	2.3	0618	8.4	1247	1.9	1843	8.4
24	TH	0056	1.9	0654	8.7	1321	1.6	○ 1918	8.7
25	F	0129	1.6	0728	9.0	1352	1.4	1950	8.8
26	SA	0200	1.4	0759	9.0	1422	1.3	2019	8.8
27	SU	0231	1.4	0828	9.0	1450	1.4	2046	8.7
28	M	0301	1.6	0857	8.8	1519	1.6	2115	8.5

MARCH

Date	Day	Time	m	Time	m	Time	m	Time	m
1	TU	0330	1.8	0929	8.5	1548	2.0	2146	8.2
2	W	0402	2.2	1004	8.1	1622	2.5	2223	7.8
3	TH	0441	2.7	1047	7.6	1705	3.0	◑ 2312	7.3
4	F	0537	3.2	1149	7.0	1809	3.5		
5	SA	0025	6.9	0705	3.6	1324	6.7	1952	3.8
6	SU	0217	6.9	0902	3.4	1517	6.9	2142	3.4
7	M	0352	7.5	1026	2.6	1633	7.6	2254	2.6
8	TU	0456	8.3	1127	1.8	1730	8.4	2350	1.8
9	W	0548	9.0	1218	1.0	1817	9.1		
10	TH	0038	1.1	0634	9.6	1304	0.5	● 1900	9.5
11	F	0122	0.6	0716	10.0	1345	0.2	1940	9.8
12	SA	0202	0.4	0756	10.0	1423	0.2	2016	9.7
13	SU	0238	0.5	0832	9.8	1458	0.6	2050	9.4
14	M	0311	0.9	0905	9.3	1529	1.2	2120	8.9
15	TU	0340	1.5	0936	8.6	1556	1.9	2148	8.3
16	W	0408	2.3	1006	7.8	1622	2.7	2216	7.6
17	TH	0437	3.0	1039	7.1	1652	3.4	◐ 2250	6.9
18	F	0517	3.7	1126	6.4	1739	4.1	2345	6.4
19	SA	0642	4.2	1303	5.9	1921	4.4		
20	SU	0147	6.1	0841	4.2	1517	6.2	2117	4.2
21	M	0338	6.6	1017	3.6	1617	6.8	2231	3.5
22	TU	0431	7.2	1103	2.9	1701	7.4	2315	2.9
23	W	0513	7.8	1142	2.3	1739	8.0	2352	2.2
24	TH	0551	8.4	1217	1.8	1816	8.5		
25	F	0028	1.7	0627	8.8	1251	1.4	○ 1850	8.8
26	SA	0102	1.4	0701	9.1	1324	1.1	1922	9.0
27	SU	0135	1.1	0733	9.2	1355	1.0	1952	9.1
28	M	0207	1.1	0804	9.2	1425	1.1	2021	9.0
29	TU	0238	1.2	0835	9.0	1455	1.4	2051	8.8
30	W	0309	1.6	0907	8.7	1526	1.9	2124	8.5
31	TH	0343	2.0	0945	8.1	1601	2.4	2202	7.9

APRIL

Date	Day	Time	m	Time	m	Time	m	Time	m
1	F	0425	2.6	1031	7.5	1647	3.1	2254	7.4
2	SA	0525	3.2	1139	6.9	1757	3.7	◑	
3	SU	0015	6.9	0704	3.6	1325	6.6	1952	3.8
4	M	0213	6.9	0859	3.2	1514	7.1	2135	3.3
5	TU	0340	7.6	1013	2.4	1619	7.8	2238	2.5
6	W	0438	8.4	1107	1.7	1709	8.5	2329	1.7
7	TH	0526	9.0	1154	1.0	1753	9.1		
8	F	0014	1.1	0610	9.5	1237	0.6	● 1833	9.5
9	SA	0056	0.7	0651	9.7	1317	0.5	1911	9.6
10	SU	0134	0.6	0729	9.7	1353	0.6	1946	9.6
11	M	0209	0.8	0804	9.5	1426	0.9	2018	9.3
12	TU	0240	1.1	0835	9.0	1455	1.5	2047	8.8
13	W	0309	1.7	0905	8.4	1521	2.1	2115	8.3
14	TH	0336	2.3	0935	7.8	1547	2.8	2143	7.7
15	F	0404	3.0	1009	7.1	1616	3.4	2217	7.1
16	SA	0442	3.6	1055	6.5	1700	4.0	◐ 2309	6.5
17	SU	0600	4.1	1219	6.1	1836	4.4		
18	M	0046	6.2	0749	4.1	1423	6.2	2020	4.2
19	TU	0242	6.5	0919	3.7	1534	6.7	2138	3.6
20	W	0346	7.1	1015	3.0	1620	7.3	2229	3.0
21	TH	0432	7.6	1058	2.4	1701	7.9	2312	2.4
22	F	0513	8.2	1137	1.9	1739	8.4	2351	1.8
23	SA	0551	8.6	1214	1.5	1815	8.8		
24	SU	0029	1.4	0628	9.0	1251	1.2	○ 1849	9.1
25	M	0106	1.1	0704	9.2	1326	1.1	1923	9.2
26	TU	0142	1.0	0740	9.2	1400	1.2	1957	9.2
27	W	0218	1.2	0816	9.0	1435	1.4	2032	9.0
28	TH	0255	1.5	0854	8.7	1512	1.9	2111	8.6
29	F	0335	2.0	0938	8.1	1554	2.5	2157	8.1
30	SA	0425	2.5	1032	7.5	1647	3.1	2255	7.5

Chart Datum: 5·06 metres below Ordnance Datum (Local)

TIME ZONE (UT)
For Summer Time add ONE hour in **non-shaded areas**

CHANNEL ISLANDS – ST PETER PORT

LAT 49°27′N LONG 2°31′W

TIMES AND HEIGHTS OF HIGH AND LOW WATERS

SPRING & NEAP TIDES
Dates in red are SPRINGS Dates in blue are NEAPS

YEAR **2005**

MAY

Day	Time	m	Time	m	Time	m	Time	m
1 SU	0533	3.0	1143	7.0	1803	3.5	◑	
2 M	0015	7.2	0705	3.2	1320	6.9	1945	3.5
3 TU	0155	7.3	0838	2.9	1448	7.3	2110	3.0
4 W	0311	7.7	0944	2.3	1549	7.9	2210	2.4
5 TH	0408	8.3	1037	1.8	1638	8.4	2300	1.9
6 F	0457	8.7	1123	1.4	1722	8.8	2345	1.5
7 SA	0541	9.0	1206	1.2	1803	9.1		
8 SU	0026	1.2	0622	9.2	1246	1.1	● 1841	9.2
9 M	0105	1.2	0701	9.1	1323	1.2	1917	9.1
10 TU	0141	1.3	0737	8.9	1356	1.5	1949	9.0
11 W	0213	1.6	0810	8.6	1426	1.9	2020	8.6
12 TH	0243	2.0	0842	8.2	1455	2.4	2051	8.2
13 F	0313	2.5	0916	7.7	1524	2.9	2122	7.8
14 SA	0346	3.0	0952	7.2	1558	3.4	2159	7.3
15 SU	0427	3.4	1039	6.7	1643	3.8	2249	6.9
16 M	0529	3.8	1143	6.4	1754	4.1	◐ 2358	6.6
17 TU	0656	3.8	1307	6.4	1922	4.0		
18 W	0124	6.6	0812	3.6	1425	6.7	2035	3.7
19 TH	0239	7.0	0913	3.2	1523	7.2	2134	3.1
20 F	0336	7.4	1005	2.7	1610	7.7	2224	2.6
21 SA	0425	7.9	1051	2.2	1654	8.2	2310	2.1
22 SU	0510	8.4	1135	1.8	1736	8.6	2355	1.6
23 M	0554	8.7	1218	1.5	1818	8.9	○	
24 TU	0038	1.3	0637	8.9	1300	1.3	1858	9.1
25 W	0122	1.2	0721	9.0	1342	1.3	1940	9.2
26 TH	0205	1.2	0805	8.9	1425	1.5	2023	9.1
27 F	0250	1.4	0851	8.7	1509	1.8	2108	8.8
28 SA	0338	1.7	0940	8.3	1557	2.3	2159	8.4
29 SU	0432	2.1	1035	7.9	1653	2.7	2257	8.0
30 M	0535	2.5	1139	7.5	1800	3.0	◑	
31 TU	0005	7.7	0647	2.7	1254	7.4	1917	3.1

JUNE

Day	Time	m	Time	m	Time	m	Time	m
1 W	0121	7.6	0801	2.7	1407	7.5	2033	3.0
2 TH	0233	7.7	0907	2.5	1510	7.7	2135	2.6
3 F	0333	7.9	1002	2.3	1603	8.0	2228	2.3
4 SA	0426	8.2	1051	2.1	1650	8.3	2315	2.1
5 SU	0513	8.3	1136	2.0	1734	8.5	2359	1.9
6 M	0557	8.4	1218	1.9	1814	8.6	●	
7 TU	0039	1.8	0638	8.5	1257	1.9	1852	8.7
8 W	0117	1.9	0716	8.4	1332	2.0	1927	8.6
9 TH	0152	2.0	0753	8.2	1406	2.2	2002	8.4
10 F	0226	2.2	0828	8.0	1438	2.5	2035	8.2
11 SA	0300	2.5	0903	7.7	1511	2.8	2109	7.9
12 SU	0335	2.8	0940	7.4	1547	3.1	2146	7.6
13 M	0414	3.1	1021	7.2	1627	3.4	2228	7.3
14 TU	0459	3.3	1107	6.9	1716	3.6	2318	7.1
15 W	0555	3.4	1203	6.8	1817	3.7	◐	
16 TH	0018	7.0	0701	3.4	1307	6.9	1926	3.6
17 F	0125	7.1	0808	3.3	1413	7.1	2034	3.3
18 SA	0233	7.3	0909	3.0	1514	7.5	2135	2.9
19 SU	0335	7.6	1006	2.6	1610	7.9	2232	2.4
20 M	0433	8.0	1100	2.2	1702	8.3	2326	2.0
21 TU	0527	8.4	1152	1.9	1753	8.7		
22 W	0018	1.6	0619	8.7	1243	1.6	○ 1842	9.1
23 TH	0110	1.3	0710	8.9	1333	1.4	1930	9.3
24 F	0200	1.1	0800	9.0	1421	1.4	2018	9.3
25 SA	0249	1.1	0849	8.9	1509	1.5	2106	9.2
26 SU	0338	1.2	0938	8.7	1557	1.7	2155	8.9
27 M	0428	1.5	1028	8.4	1646	2.1	2245	8.5
28 TU	0520	1.9	1120	8.0	1739	2.5	◑ 2340	8.1
29 W	0615	2.4	1216	7.7	1838	2.9		
30 TH	0040	7.7	0715	2.7	1320	7.4	1945	3.1

JULY

Day	Time	m	Time	m	Time	m	Time	m
1 F	0149	7.4	0821	2.9	1426	7.3	2054	3.1
2 SA	0256	7.4	0925	3.0	1528	7.4	2157	3.0
3 SU	0357	7.5	1021	2.9	1622	7.7	2251	2.8
4 M	0451	7.6	1112	2.7	1711	7.9	2339	2.6
5 TU	0539	7.8	1157	2.5	1755	8.1		
6 W	0022	2.4	0622	8.0	1239	2.4	● 1835	8.3
7 TH	0102	2.2	0703	8.1	1317	2.3	1913	8.4
8 F	0139	2.1	0741	8.2	1352	2.2	1949	8.4
9 SA	0214	2.1	0817	8.1	1426	2.3	2023	8.4
10 SU	0248	2.2	0850	8.0	1458	2.4	2055	8.2
11 M	0320	2.4	0923	7.9	1531	2.6	2128	8.0
12 TU	0353	2.6	0955	7.6	1605	2.8	2202	7.8
13 W	0428	2.8	1031	7.4	1642	3.0	2241	7.6
14 TH	0507	3.0	1113	7.3	1726	3.2	◐ 2328	7.4
15 F	0555	3.2	1204	7.1	1821	3.4		
16 SA	0026	7.2	0657	3.3	1308	7.1	1931	3.4
17 SU	0137	7.2	0814	3.3	1423	7.2	2052	3.2
18 M	0256	7.3	0929	3.0	1536	7.6	2204	2.8
19 TU	0408	7.7	1037	2.6	1641	8.1	2308	2.2
20 W	0512	8.1	1138	2.2	1739	8.6		
21 TH	0008	1.7	0611	8.6	1235	1.7	○ 1833	9.1
22 F	0103	1.1	0704	9.0	1327	1.2	1923	9.5
23 SA	0154	0.8	0754	9.3	1415	1.0	2011	9.7
24 SU	0242	0.6	0840	9.4	1501	0.9	2056	9.7
25 M	0327	0.7	0924	9.3	1544	1.1	2139	9.4
26 TU	0409	1.1	1006	8.9	1625	1.6	2222	8.9
27 W	0451	1.6	1048	8.4	1707	2.2	2306	8.3
28 TH	0535	2.3	1133	7.8	1753	2.8	◑ 2355	7.6
29 F	0625	3.0	1226	7.2	1849	3.4		
30 SA	0057	7.0	0726	3.5	1336	6.9	2003	3.7
31 SU	0219	6.7	0845	3.7	1456	6.8	2132	3.7

AUGUST

Day	Time	m	Time	m	Time	m	Time	m
1 M	0338	6.8	1000	3.6	1604	7.1	2238	3.3
2 TU	0439	7.1	1059	3.2	1657	7.5	2329	2.9
3 W	0528	7.5	1146	2.9	1742	7.9		
4 TH	0012	2.6	0610	7.9	1227	2.5	1822	8.3
5 F	0051	2.2	0649	8.2	1304	2.2	● 1900	8.5
6 SA	0126	2.0	0726	8.4	1338	2.0	1934	8.7
7 SU	0159	1.8	0759	8.5	1409	1.9	2006	8.7
8 M	0229	1.8	0830	8.4	1439	2.0	2036	8.6
9 TU	0258	1.9	0858	8.3	1509	2.1	2104	8.5
10 W	0326	2.1	0925	8.1	1538	2.3	2133	8.2
11 TH	0355	2.4	0955	7.9	1609	2.6	2207	8.0
12 F	0427	2.8	1030	7.6	1645	3.0	2247	7.6
13 SA	0508	3.1	1116	7.3	1733	3.3	◐ 2341	7.2
14 SU	0605	3.5	1219	7.0	1844	3.6		
15 M	0056	7.0	0730	3.7	1348	7.0	2024	3.5
16 TU	0235	7.0	0910	3.5	1520	7.3	2153	3.0
17 W	0401	7.5	1028	2.9	1633	8.0	2303	2.3
18 TH	0509	8.1	1131	2.2	1732	8.7		
19 F	0001	1.5	0604	8.8	1226	1.5	○ 1823	9.4
20 SA	0053	0.9	0653	9.3	1315	0.9	1911	9.9
21 SU	0140	0.4	0738	9.7	1400	0.6	1954	10.1
22 M	0224	0.3	0820	9.8	1442	0.5	2036	10.1
23 TU	0304	0.4	0859	9.6	1520	0.8	2114	9.7
24 W	0341	0.9	0936	9.1	1556	1.4	2151	9.0
25 TH	0416	1.6	1011	8.5	1631	2.1	2227	8.2
26 F	0451	2.5	1047	7.8	1707	2.9	◑ 2306	7.4
27 SA	0532	3.3	1130	7.1	1754	3.7	2359	6.7
28 SU	0630	4.0	1237	6.5	1911	4.2		
29 M	0140	6.2	0803	4.3	1430	6.4	2119	4.1
30 TU	0330	6.5	0951	4.0	1552	6.8	2231	3.6
31 W	0429	7.0	1048	3.5	1643	7.4	2317	3.1

Chart Datum: 5·06 metres below Ordnance Datum (Local)

TIME ZONE (UT)
For Summer Time add ONE hour in **non-shaded areas**

CHANNEL ISLANDS – ST PETER PORT

LAT 49°27′N LONG 2°31′W

TIMES AND HEIGHTS OF HIGH AND LOW WATERS

SPRING & NEAP TIDES
Dates in red are **SPRINGS**
Dates in blue are **NEAPS**

YEAR **2005**

SEPTEMBER

Date	Time	m	Date	Time	m
1 TH	0513 1131 1725 2356	7.5 2.9 7.9 2.5	16 F	0500 1120 1719 2347	8.4 2.0 9.0 1.3
2 F	0552 1209 1803	8.0 2.4 8.4	17 SA	0549 1210 1806	9.1 1.3 9.6
3 SA	0031 0627 1244 ● 1838	2.1 8.4 2.0 8.8	18 SU	0034 0633 1255 ○ 1850	0.7 9.6 0.7 10.1
4 SU	0104 0702 1315 1912	1.7 8.7 1.7 9.0	19 M	0117 0714 1337 1931	0.4 9.9 0.5 10.2
5 M	0134 0733 1346 1942	1.6 8.9 1.6 9.1	20 TU	0157 0753 1416 2009	0.3 9.9 0.5 10.1
6 TU	0203 0802 1415 2010	1.5 8.8 1.6 9.0	21 W	0235 0829 1452 2045	0.6 9.7 0.9 9.6
7 W	0230 0828 1443 2037	1.6 8.7 1.7 8.8	22 TH	0308 0902 1524 2118	1.1 9.2 1.5 8.9
8 TH	0257 0854 1510 2105	1.9 8.5 2.0 8.6	23 F	0339 0933 1555 2150	1.9 8.5 2.3 8.1
9 F	0324 0923 1539 2137	2.2 8.2 2.4 8.2	24 SA	0409 1004 1626 2224	2.8 7.8 3.1 7.3
10 SA	0354 0956 1613 2215	2.7 7.8 2.9 7.7	25 SU	0441 1041 1707 ◑ 2311	3.6 7.1 3.8 6.5
11 SU	0432 1041 1701 ◐ 2309	3.2 7.4 3.4 7.1	26 M	0534 1141 1828	4.3 6.4 4.4
12 M	0531 1148 1818	3.7 6.9 3.8	27 TU	0054 0722 1354 2055	6.1 4.6 6.2 4.4
13 TU	0036 0712 1334 2019	6.7 4.0 6.8 3.7	28 W	0311 0930 1528 2208	6.4 4.3 6.7 3.8
14 W	0236 0909 1517 2151	6.9 3.7 7.4 3.0	29 TH	0406 1024 1618 2250	7.0 3.6 7.3 3.1
15 TH	0402 1024 1626 2255	7.6 2.9 8.2 2.2	30 F	0446 1104 1658 2326	7.6 3.0 7.9 2.5

OCTOBER

Date	Time	m	Date	Time	m
1 SA	0522 1139 1734	8.1 2.4 8.4	16 SU	0524 1146 1742	9.2 1.3 9.6
2 SU	0000 0557 1213 1808	2.0 8.6 1.9 8.8	17 M	0008 0606 1230 ○ 1824	0.9 9.6 0.9 9.9
3 M	0032 0630 1245 ● 1842	1.7 8.9 1.6 9.1	18 TU	0050 0646 1311 1904	0.7 9.8 0.7 9.9
4 TU	0103 0702 1316 1913	1.5 9.1 1.4 9.2	19 W	0129 0723 1349 1942	0.7 9.8 0.9 9.7
5 W	0132 0731 1347 1942	1.4 9.1 1.4 9.2	20 TH	0205 0758 1424 2017	1.1 9.5 1.2 9.2
6 TH	0201 0758 1417 2011	1.5 9.0 1.6 9.0	21 F	0237 0831 1456 2049	1.6 9.1 1.8 8.6
7 F	0230 0827 1447 2042	1.8 8.8 1.9 8.7	22 SA	0307 0901 1526 2121	2.3 8.5 2.5 8.0
8 SA	0259 0858 1518 2116	2.2 8.5 2.3 8.3	23 SU	0335 0932 1557 2156	3.0 7.8 3.2 7.3
9 SU	0332 0934 1556 2159	2.7 8.0 2.9 7.7	24 M	0406 1009 1637 2243	3.7 7.2 3.8 6.6
10 M	0414 1024 1650 ◐ 2300	3.3 7.5 3.4 7.1	25 TU	0453 1106 1753 ◑	4.3 6.6 4.3
11 TU	0520 1140 1818	3.9 7.0 3.8	26 W	0007 0636 1248 1939	6.2 4.6 6.4 4.4
12 W	0035 0714 1330 2017	6.7 4.1 7.0 3.6	27 TH	0219 0828 1436 2113	6.3 4.4 6.6 3.9
13 TH	0236 0902 1505 2138	7.1 3.6 7.6 2.8	28 F	0323 0937 1533 2203	6.9 3.8 7.2 3.3
14 F	0347 1008 1606 2235	7.8 2.7 8.4 2.0	29 SA	0406 1020 1616 2243	7.5 3.2 7.7 2.8
15 SA	0439 1100 1656 2323	8.6 1.9 9.0 1.4	30 SU	0443 1058 1655 2319	8.0 2.6 8.2 2.3
			31 M	0519 1134 1732 2354	8.5 2.1 8.6 1.9

NOVEMBER

Date	Time	m	Date	Time	m
1 TU	0554 1210 1808	8.8 1.8 8.9	16 W	0022 0618 1246 ○ 1840	1.4 9.3 1.3 9.3
2 W	0028 0627 1246 ● 1842	1.6 9.0 1.6 9.1	17 TH	0102 0657 1325 1919	1.4 9.3 1.4 9.1
3 TH	0102 0700 1321 1917	1.5 9.2 1.5 9.1	18 F	0138 0733 1401 1955	1.7 9.1 1.7 8.8
4 F	0136 0733 1356 1952	1.6 9.1 1.6 9.0	19 SA	0212 0807 1435 2029	2.0 8.8 2.1 8.4
5 SA	0210 0808 1432 2028	1.8 9.0 1.8 8.7	20 SU	0243 0839 1508 2104	2.5 8.4 2.6 7.9
6 SU	0245 0845 1511 2110	2.2 8.6 2.2 8.3	21 M	0314 0914 1542 2141	3.0 7.9 3.1 7.4
7 M	0325 0930 1557 2200	2.7 8.2 2.7 7.8	22 TU	0348 0952 1622 2225	3.5 7.4 3.5 6.9
8 TU	0416 1026 1658 2305	3.2 7.7 3.2 7.3	23 W	0433 1041 1718 ◑ 2324	4.0 7.0 3.9 6.6
9 W	0527 1140 1821 ◐	3.7 7.4 3.4	24 TH	0542 1148 1834	4.3 6.7 4.1
10 TH	0031 0705 1313 1955	7.1 3.8 7.4 3.2	25 F	0045 0708 1310 1950	6.5 4.3 6.7 3.9
11 F	0208 0836 1435 2109	7.3 3.3 7.8 2.7	26 SA	0206 0822 1422 2054	6.7 4.0 7.0 3.6
12 SA	0316 0940 1536 2206	7.9 2.7 8.3 2.2	27 SU	0305 0920 1519 2146	7.2 3.5 7.4 3.1
13 SU	0409 1032 1628 2255	8.4 2.1 8.8 1.7	28 M	0352 1009 1607 2231	7.6 3.0 7.8 2.7
14 M	0455 1119 1715 2340	8.9 1.7 9.1 1.5	29 TU	0435 1053 1651 2314	8.1 2.5 8.2 2.3
15 TU	0538 1204 1759	9.2 1.4 9.3	30 W	0516 1136 1734 2356	8.5 2.1 8.5 2.0

DECEMBER

Date	Time	m	Date	Time	m
1 TH	0556 1219 1817 ●	8.8 1.8 8.8	16 F	0042 0637 1308 1903	2.1 8.8 2.0 8.5
2 F	0037 0636 1302 1858	1.8 9.0 1.6 8.9	17 SA	0120 0716 1346 1942	2.1 8.8 2.0 8.4
3 SA	0119 0717 1344 1941	1.7 9.2 1.5 8.9	18 SU	0156 0752 1422 2018	2.3 8.7 2.2 8.2
4 SU	0200 0759 1428 2026	1.8 9.1 1.6 8.8	19 M	0230 0827 1457 2053	2.5 8.4 2.4 8.0
5 M	0244 0844 1514 2112	2.0 8.9 1.8 8.5	20 TU	0302 0901 1530 2128	2.7 8.1 2.7 7.7
6 TU	0330 0933 1605 2204	2.3 8.6 2.2 8.1	21 W	0336 0937 1605 2205	3.0 7.8 3.0 7.4
7 W	0423 1027 1701 2302	2.7 8.3 2.5 7.8	22 TH	0413 1016 1644 2245	3.4 7.5 3.3 7.1
8 TH	0524 1130 1805 ◐	3.1 7.9 2.8	23 F	0456 1101 1729 ◑ 2334	3.6 7.2 3.5 6.9
9 F	0008 0636 1241 1917	7.5 3.2 7.7 2.9	24 SA	0550 1154 1826	3.8 7.0 3.7
10 SA	0124 0755 1354 2028	7.5 3.2 7.8 2.8	25 SU	0033 0658 1259 1934	6.8 3.9 6.9 3.6
11 SU	0235 0904 1501 2131	7.7 2.9 7.9 2.6	26 M	0144 0810 1409 2041	6.9 3.7 7.0 3.5
12 M	0334 1003 1558 2225	8.0 2.6 8.1 2.4	27 TU	0251 0915 1514 2142	7.2 3.4 7.3 3.1
13 TU	0426 1054 1650 2314	8.3 2.3 8.3 2.2	28 W	0349 1013 1613 2238	7.6 2.9 7.7 2.7
14 W	0513 1142 1738	8.5 2.1 8.4	29 TH	0442 1108 1708 2330	8.1 2.4 8.1 2.3
15 TH	0000 0556 1227 ○ 1822	2.1 8.7 2.0 8.5	30 F	0533 1200 1800	8.5 2.0 8.5
			31 SA	0021 0621 1251 ● 1849	1.9 8.9 1.6 8.8

Chart Datum: 5·06 metres below Ordnance Datum (Local)

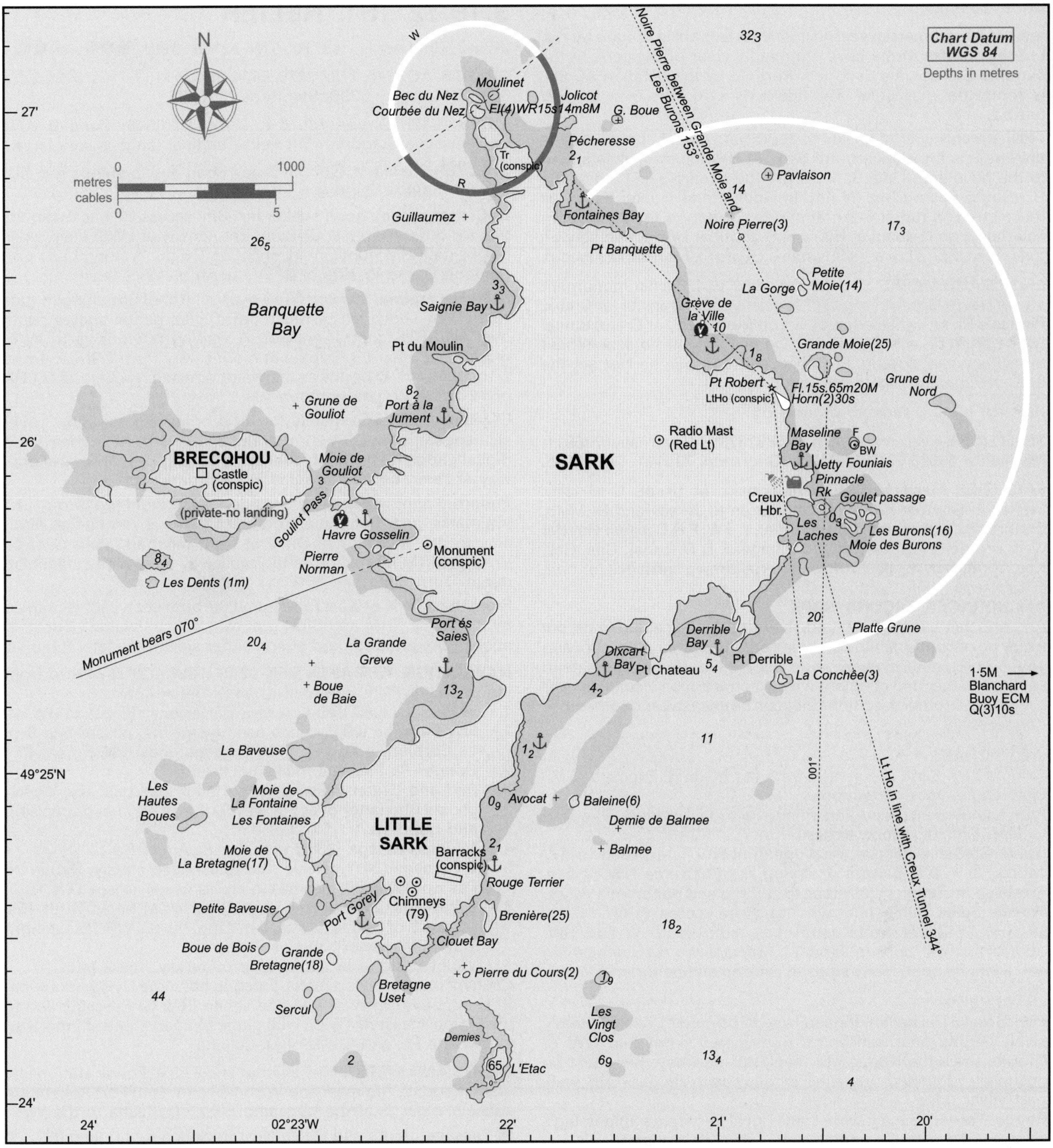
N
Chart Datum WGS 84
Depths in metres
metres
cables
0
1000
5
27'
26'
49°25'N
24'
24'
02°23'W
22'
21'
20'
Noire Pierre between Grande Moie and Les Burons 153°
Moulinet
Bec du Nez
Courbée du Nez
Fl(4)WR15s14m8M
Jolicot
G. Boue
Pécheresse
Tr (conspic)
W
R
Pavlaison
Guillaumez
Fontaines Bay
Noire Pierre(3)
Pt Banquette
Petite Moie(14)
La Gorge
Grève de la Ville
Grande Moie(25)
Banquette Bay
Saignie Bay
Pt du Moulin
Grune du Nord
Pt Robert
Fl.15s.65m20M
LtHo (conspic)
Horn(2)30s
Grune de Gouliot
Port à la Jument
Radio Mast (Red Lt)
Maseline Bay
F
BW
BRECQHOU
Castle (conspic)
(private-no landing)
Moie de Gouliot
SARK
Jetty
Founiais
Pinnacle Rk
Goulet passage
Creux Hbr.
Gouliot Pass
Havre Gosselin
Les Laches
Les Burons(16)
Moie des Burons
Pierre Norman
Monument (conspic)
Les Dents (1m)
Monument bears 070°
Port ès Saies
Derrible Bay
Platte Grune
La Grande Greve
Dixcart Bay
Pt Chateau
Pt Derrible
La Conchée(3)
Boue de Baie
1·5M Blanchard Buoy ECM Q(3)10s
La Baveuse
001°
Lt Ho in line with Creux Tunnel 344°
Les Hautes Boues
Moie de La Fontaine
Les Fontaines
Avocat
Baleine(6)
Demie de Balmee
LITTLE SARK
Balmee
Moie de La Bretagne(17)
Barracks (conspic)
Rouge Terrier
Petite Baveuse
Port Gorey
Chimneys (79)
Brenière(25)
Boue de Bois
Grande Bretagne(18)
Clouet Bay
Pierre du Cours(2)
Bretagne Uset
Sercul
Les Vingt Clos
Demies
L'Etac

9.19.11 SARK

Sark **49°25'·81N 02°20'·45W** Creux ❀❀✿✿✿✿

CHARTS AC *808, 5604*; SHOM 7159, 6904; ECM 1014; Imray C33A; Stanfords 2, 16, 26.

TIDES –0450 Dover; ML 5·3; Duration 0550; Zone 0 (UT)
Standard Port ST HELIER (⟶)

Times				Height (metres)			
High Water		Low Water		MHWS	MHWN	MLWN	MLWS
0300	0900	0200	0900	11·0	8·1	4·0	1·4
1500	2100	1400	2100				
Differences SARK (MASELINE PIER)							
+0005	+0015	+0005	+0010	–2·1	–1·5	–0·6	–0·3

SHELTER There are 2 hbrs, both on the E side and prone to surge/swell: **Creux** dries completely, access approx HW±2 in fair weather. Dry out bow to E wall, stern to ⚓, keeping clear of the S pier where there may be some AB at the inner end clear of steps. **Maseline** is a busy ferry hbr with no yacht berths (other than to land people); call HM Ch 13 for approval to ⚓. Moorings are private. Brecqhou Island is strictly private; landing prohibited. 20 🅥s are laid at Havre Gosselin and 20 at Grève de la Ville, £12 per night, £6 for day or 'short stay'. ☎ 832260, mobile 07781 106065, water taxi Ch 10. All other permanent moorings are private; use in emergency only.
For details of anchorages see overleaf.

NAVIGATION Creux WPT 49°25'·24N 02°20'·18W, 344°/0·57M to ent. Beware large tidal range, strong streams and many lobster pots. The S-bound-only restriction in the Goulet Passage

SARK *continued*

applies to commercial vessels, not yachts. Sark is fringed by rks, but the centres of the bays are mainly clear of dangers. In the extreme SW of Little Sark near Port Gorey the detail in AC 808 is somewhat inaccurate. The tide runs hard here over the HW period.

Tidal streams: It is important to appreciate that at about half-tide the streams are slack around Sark. At HW the stream sets hard to the N, ie onto Little Sark. At LW the stream sets hard to the S, ie onto Bec du Nez (N tip). In Gouliot and Goulet passages these streams run at 6-7kn at springs. If bound for Creux from Guernsey, go N-about at HW and S-about at LW; conversely on the return. See *Sark, a Yachtsman's Guide* (J. Frankland/Albecq).

LIGHTS AND MARKS See chartlet and 9.19.4. Pilcher monument above Havre Gosselin brg 070° is a safe appr. Transits for Creux: Pinnacle Rk on with E edge of Grand Moie 001°; or Creux tunnel (white arch) on with Pt Robert lt ho 344°. The lt ho dips behind the cliffs when close in. Pt Robert and Courbée du Nez are the only navigational lights on Sark.

R/T VHF Ch 13, summer months only.

TELEPHONE (Dial code 01481) HM 832323; ⊜ (Guernsey) 726911; Marinecall 09066 526250; Police (Guernsey) 725111; Dr 832045.

FACILITIES Maseline ☎ 832070 (kiosk), M (free), C (3 ton); Ferries to Guernsey; Condor catamaran to Jersey and St Malo. **Creux** ☎ 832025 (kiosk), Slip, M (free), L, FW, P & D (cans) via HM; walk or tractor up steep hill to **Village**: P & D (cans), Gas, Gaz, Kos, 🛒, R, Bar, ✉, Ⓑ. Bikes and horse-drawn carriages for hire.

ANCHORAGES AROUND SARK

An ⚓age can usually be found sheltered from specific winds, but it may be uncomfortable, except in settled weather. The following ⚓s (all unlit), anti-clockwise from Bec du Nez (N tip), are safe in settled weather and off-shore winds; some are only suitable over LW period. In other conditions they can be exposed and sometimes dangerous:

WEST COAST

Saignie Bay. Sand and shingle with fair holding. Exposed to W. Picturesque rock formations.

Port à la Jument. Sand and shingle with fair holding. Exposed to NW. Difficult shore access.

Havre Gosselin. Popular small, deep (4-9m) ⚓, exposed to SW winds. 20 Y 🅥's. Beware of drying rk at extreme NW of bay. Crowded in summer. 299 steps to cliff top and panoramic views.

Port és Saies. Sandy inlet with no shore access. N of:

La Grande Grève. Wide sandy bay exposed to W and SW. Subject to swell, but popular day ⚓. Beware two rks (drying 0·3m and ✱) in the appr. Many steps to cliff-top and panoramic views.

LITTLE SARK

Port Gorey. ⚓ in centre of deep, weedy bay over LW only; heavy swell begins near half-flood. Rocky appr from just NW of Grande Bretagne (18m high) then 045° into bay. Rks must be positively identified. Remains of quay with ladder. Cliff walk past silver mine ruins to hotel.

Rouge Terrier. Sandy with some local moorings under high cliffs. Exposed to E. Landing with cliff path to hotel.

EAST COAST

Dixcart Bay. Popular sandy bay with good holding, but open to the S. Drying rocks extend on each side of the the approach but no dangers within the bay. Cliff path and pleasant walk to hotels.

Derrible Bay. Sandy bay with good holding. Exposed to the S. No dangers in the bay, but keep clear of SW tip of Derrible Pt when entering. Picturesque caves and steep climb ashore.

Grève de la Ville. Sand & shingle with fair holding. ⚓ close in out of tide. Exposed to E. 20 Y🅥's. Landing and easy walk to village.

Les Fontaines. Sand and shingle with fair holding. Reef drying 4·5m extends 1ca N from shore. ⚓ between reef and Eperquerie headland. Exposed to the E.

With grateful acknowledgements to John Frankland, author of Sark, a Yachtsman's Guide (revised 1998). Visitors may be glad to know that the Death sentence has been removed from Sark's legislation, reluctantly and under pressure from the EU.

9.19.12 ST HELIER

Jersey (Channel Is) **49°10'·57N 02°06'·98W** ✱✱✱◊◊◊✿✿

CHARTS AC *3655, 1137*, 3278, *5604*; SHOM 7160, 7161, 6938; ECM 534, 1014; Imray C33B; Stanfords 2, 16, 26

TIDES –0455 Dover; ML 6·1; Duration 0545; Zone 0 (UT) St Helier is a Standard Port (⟶). The tidal range is very large.

SHELTER Excellent. No ⚓ in Small Road due to shipping & fish storage boxes. Marinas from seaward:

La Collette basin, good shelter in 1·8m; access H24, to await the tide for other marinas. Caution: Ent narrow at LWS; keep close to W side; PHM buoys mark shoal on E side. Waiting berths on pontoon D and W side of C. FVs berth on W of basin.

St Helier marina, access HW±3 over sill (CD+3·6m); hinged gate rises 1·4m above sill to retain 5m. Digital gauge shows depth over sill. IPTS control ent/exit. A waiting pontoon is to W of marina ent, near LB. Depths in marina vary from 2·8m at ent to 2·1m at N end. 🅥 berths as shown or directed; yachts >12m LOA or >2·1m draft, use pontoon A.

Elizabeth marina is mainly for local boats. Access HW±3 over sill/flapgate; max LOA 20m, drafts 2·1 – 3·5m. At marina ent a digital gauge reads depth over sill. IPTS (sigs 2 & 3) control one-way ent/exit, usually 10 mins in each direction.

Preferred appr, when height of tide >7m, is from the W on 106°: ldg marks, just S of ent, are orange □s with B vert line; at night stay in the W sector of Dir lt at front daymark. Pass S of La Vrachère IDM lt bn to cross the causeway 5·0m with at least 2m depth. Turn ENE then NNE for the ent.

From the S (ie N of No 4 PHM buoy) the appr chan 338° is marked by 3 pairs of PHM and SHM lt buoys. 3 Y can waiting buoys in about 1·0m are outboard of and either side of the lateral buoys.

NAVIGATION WPT 49°09'·95N 02°07'·38W, 023°/0·74M to front ldg lt. This WPT is common to all St Helier appr's:

1. W Passage (082°); beware race off Noirmont Pt, HW to HW +4.
1A. NW Passage (095°, much used by yachts) passes 6ca S of La Corbière lt ho to join W Passage abeam Noirmont Pt.
2. Danger Rk Passage (044°) unlit; and
3. Red and Green Passage (023°); both lead past rky, drying shoals (the latter over Fairway Rk 1·2m) and need precision and good vis.
4. Middle Passage (339°) unlit, for St Aubin Bay.
5. S Passage (341°) is clear but unlit. Alternatively, Demie de Pas on 350° with power stn chy is easier to see D/N.
6. E Passage, 290° from Canger Rock WCM buoy, Q (9) 15s, passes S of Demie de Pas, B tr/Y top, Mo (D) WR 12s (at night stay in W sector); thence 314°.
7. Violet Passage around SE tip of Jersey, see 9.14.5.

Caution: many offlying reefs. Entering hbr, note Oyster Rk (W bn; R 'O' topmark) to W of Red and Green (R & G) Passage; and to the E, Dog's Nest Rk (W bn with globe topmark). Speed limit 10kn N of Platte Rk, and 5kn N of La Collette.

LIGHTS AND MARKS See chartlet and 9.19.4. Power station chy (95m, floodlit), Sig mast and W concave roofs of Fort Regent are conspic, close E of the hbr; ditto Elizabeth Castle to the W.

W Passage ldg lts and Dog's Nest Rock bcn (unlit) lead 082°, N of Les Fours NCM and Ruaudière SHM lt buoys, to a position close to E Rock SHM buoy. Here course is altered to pick up the **Red & Green Passage** ldg lts 023° (now easier to see against town lts). Daymarks are red dayglow patches on front dolphin and rear lt twr. N of Platte Rk bcn Nos 2 and 4 PHM buoys mark the W side of fairway. Outer pier hds and dolphin are painted white and floodlit. Inner ldg lts 078° on W columns are not essential for yachts.

IPTS (Sigs 1-4) are shown from the Port Control tower and are easily seen from Small Road, La Collette and the Main Hbr. An Oc Y 4s, shown above Sigs 1-4, exempts power-driven craft <25m LOA from the main signals. All leisure craft should: keep to stbd, well clear of shipping; maintain a sharp all-round lookout; and monitor VHF Ch 14 during arr/dep.

Sig 2 (3 FR vert) is also shown when vessels depart the Tanker Basin. Departing tankers, which can be hidden at LW, will sound a long blast if small craft are approaching.

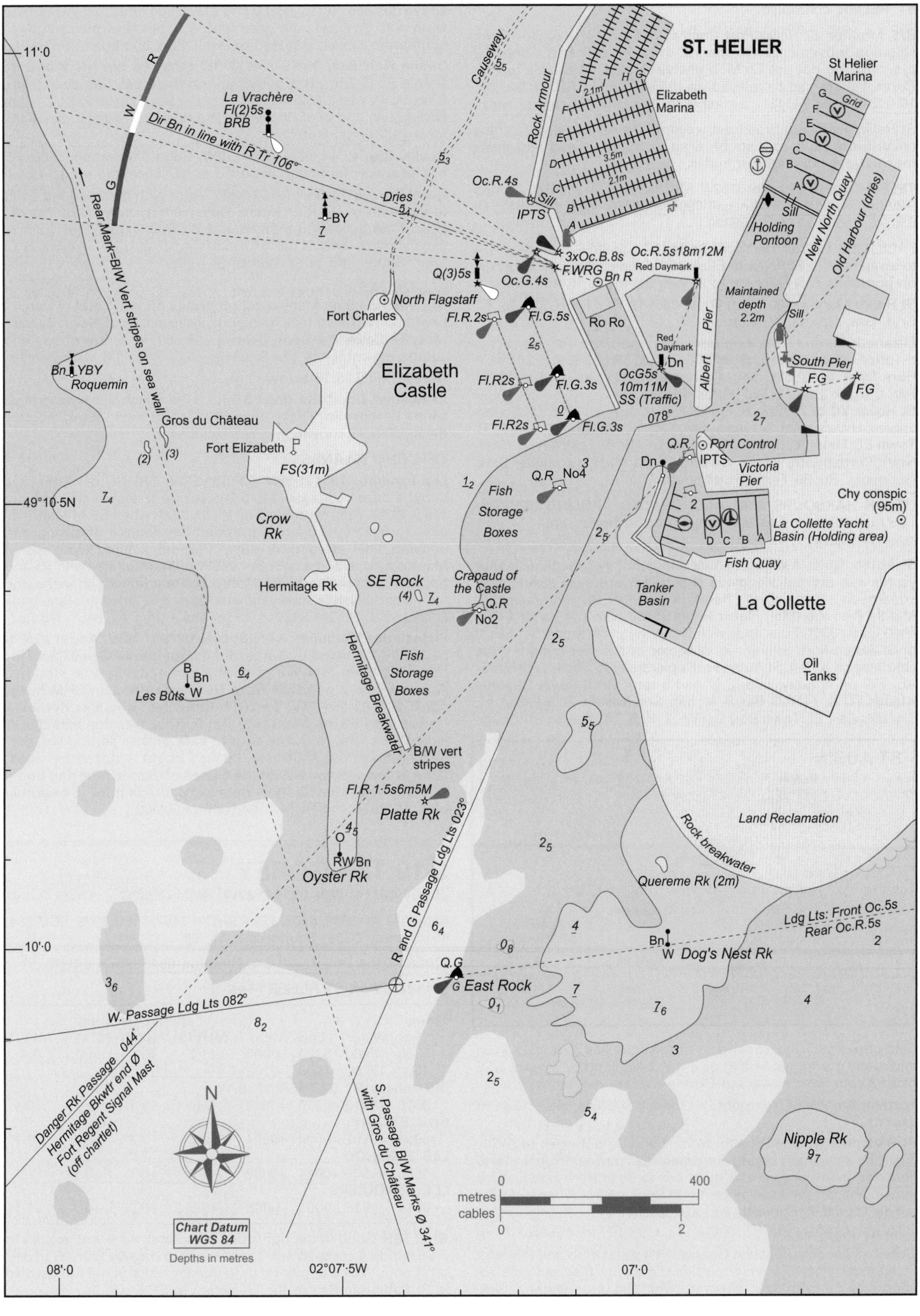
ST. HELIER
St Helier Marina
Elizabeth Marina
Rock Armour
Causeway
La Vrachère Fl(2)5s BRB
Dir Bn in line with R Tr 106°
Rear Mark=B/W Vert stripes on sea wall
Dries
BY
Oc.R.4s
Sill
IPTS
3xOc.B.8s
F.WRG
Bn R
Oc.R.5s18m12M
Red Daymark
Q(3)5s
Oc.G.4s
North Flagstaff
Fort Charles
Fl.R.2s
Fl.G.5s
Ro Ro
Holding Pontoon
New North Quay
Old Harbour (dries)
Maintained depth 2.2m
Albert Pier
Red Daymark
Dn
OcG5s 10m11M SS (Traffic)
South Pier
F.G
Elizabeth Castle
Fl.R2s
Fl.G.3s
078°
Bn YBY Roquemin
Gros du Château
Fort Elizabeth
FS(31m)
Q.R
Port Control
IPTS
Victoria Pier
Q.R No4
Fish Storage Boxes
Chy conspic (95m)
La Collette Yacht Basin (Holding area)
Fish Quay
Crow Rk
Hermitage Rk
SE Rock
Crapaud of the Castle
Q.R No2
Tanker Basin
La Collette
Hermitage Breakwater
Oil Tanks
Les Buts
B/W vert stripes
Fl.R.1·5s6m5M
Platte Rk
Land Reclamation
Rock breakwater
RW Bn
Oyster Rk
R and G Passage Ldg Lts 023°
Quereme Rk (2m)
Ldg Lts: Front Oc.5s Rear Oc.R.5s
Dog's Nest Rk
Q.G
East Rock
W. Passage Ldg Lts 082°
Danger Rk Passage 044° Hermitage Bkwtr end Ø Fort Regent Signal Mast (off chartlet)
S. Passage B/W Marks Ø 341° with Gros du Château
Nipple Rk
N
metres
cables
0
400
2
Chart Datum WGS 84
Depths in metres
11'·0
49°10·5N
10'·0
08'·0
02°07'·5W
07'·0

ST HELIER *continued*

R/T Monitor *St Helier Port Control* VHF Ch 14 (H24) for ferry/ shipping movements. No marina VHF, but call *Port Control* if essential. Do not use Ch M. If unable to pass messages to *Port Control*, these can be relayed via *Jersey Radio* CRS, Ch **82**, 25[1], 16 (H24) or ☎ 741121. [1]available for link calls by charge card.

St Helier Pierheads broadcasts recorded wind info every 2 mins on VHF Ch 18. It consists of: wind direction, speed and gusts meaned over the last 2 minutes.

TELEPHONE (Dial code 01534) HM 885588, 📠 885599, Marina 885508; ⊖ 833833; Marinecall 09066 526250; Police 612612; Dr 835742 and 853178; Ⓗ 759000.

FACILITIES La Collette Yacht Basin (130) ☎ 885529; access H24 to await tide for St Helier or Elizabeth marinas. It has 50 Ⓥ berths on pontoons C & D for up to 24 hrs; BH (65 & 16 ton), Slip.

St Helier Marina (180 + 200 Ⓥ), ☎ 885508, £1.41; CH, ME, El, ⚒, Grid, Gas, Gaz, ⊡, 🛒, Kos.

Elizabeth Marina (589; long term only, but large visiting yachts by prior arrangement), ☎ 885530, 📠 885593; D & P (H24), 🚲.
Hbrs Dept ☎ 885588, www.jerseyharbours.com jsyhbr@itl.net FW, C (max 32 ton), Slip, Grids, BH (65 ton).
St Helier YC ☎ 732229, R, Bar; **S Pier** (below YC) P & D (Access approx HW±3), FW. **Services:** SM, CH, ⚒, ME, El, Ⓔ, Gas.
Town EC Thurs; P, D, CH, 🛒, R, Bar, ✉, Ⓑ, ✈. Fast ferries (Mar-Nov): Portsmouth, Poole, Weymouth, St Malo, Granville, Sark, Guernsey. Ro Ro Ferry: Portsmouth.

OTHER HARBOURS AND ANCHORAGES AROUND JERSEY
The main hbrs and ⚓s, clockwise from St Helier, are:

SOUTH COAST

St Aubin. Quiet ⚓ with off-shore winds in bay (mostly dries) or yachts can dry out alongside N pier; beware very strong tidal streams in ent during full flood. Access HW ±1. From seaward Middle Passage (Mon Plaisir Ho in transit with twr on St Aubin Fort) leads 339°. Final appr with N pier head bearing 254° lies N of St Aubin Fort; at night in W sector of the pier head lt - see chartlet and 9.19.4. St Aubin Fort's pier head is also lit. Facilities: AB, FW on N quay, Slip, C (1 and 5 ton), Grid; **Royal Channel Islands YC** ☎ 741023, Bar, R, M, Slip; **Services:** ⚒, D, ME, SM, ⚒, CH, BY, Gas, El. **Town** Bar, D, FW, ⊡, P, R, 🛒, bus to St. Helier.

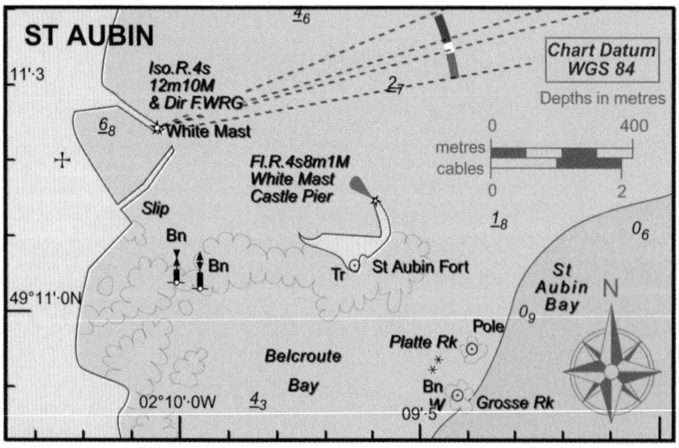
ST AUBIN
Chart Datum
WGS 84
Depths in metres
Iso.R.4s
12m10M
& Dir F.WRG
White Mast
Fl.R.4s8m1M
White Mast
Castle Pier
metres
cables
Slip
Bn
Bn
Tr
St Aubin Fort
St Aubin Bay
Pole
Platte Rk
Belcroute
Bay
Bn
Grosse Rk
11'·3
49°11'·0N
02°10'·0W
09'·5

Belcroute Bay. Excellent shelter from W/SW'lies, but dries 3·5m and many moorings; ⚓ off Pt de Bût in 2·4m, land by dinghy. SSE of St Aubin Fort, Platte and Grosse Rks are marked by poles.

Portelet Bay. W of Noirmont Pt. Good ⚓ in N'lies, either side of Janvrin Tr.

St Brelade Bay. Good shelter from N and W, but open to SW'ly swell. Beware many drying rks, especially Fournier Rk (0·9m) and Fourché (3·4m) in centre. A quiet ⚓ is in Beau Port. Small stone jetty in NW corner; local moorings in Bouilly Port. A very popular sandy tourist beach with various hotels.

NORTH COAST

Grève au Lancon. Between Grosnez Pt's squat lt ho and Plemont Pt (conspic hotel), a wide, part-drying sandy bay, suitable for short stay on calm days. Open to swell. Old underwater cables.

Grève de Lecq. 49°15'·06N 02°12'·09W. Ldg line 202°: W Martello tr on with W hotel with grey roof. ⚓ in 5m N of pier and W of submarine cables. Exposed to swell. Pub, and bus to St. Helier.

Bonne Nuit Bay. 49°15'·33N 02°07'·09W. To the NNW beware Demie Rk (5·2m; SHM buoy); and to the E Les Sambues 5·5m. Conspic TV mast (232m) is ½M W of the bay. Ldg lts 223°. ⚓ in 5m NNE of pier and W of Chevel Rk. Hbr dries to sand/shingle. Many local moorings. Hotel.

Bouley Bay. 49°14'·50N 02°04'·70W. Good ⚓ on sand in 2·5m SE of pier (rocky footings). Exposed to NE. Local moorings. Hotel.

Rozel Bay. 49°14'·38N 02°02'·45W. Appr with pierhead brg 245°, in W sector of Dir lt on shore. Conspic bldg close N on Nez du Guet. Pass between pierhead and WCM bn. Hbr, dries 1·5m to sand/shingle, and is full of moorings; ⚓ outside in 4-5m S of appr. Shops and pubs, bus to St Helier.

EAST COAST

St Catherine Bay. Many local moorings off inner end of Verclut bkwtr. ⚓ S of bkwtr in 3-7m. Land on slip at root of bkwtr. Beware rocky St Catherine Bank, 3·3m (ECM bcn) in centre of bay and submarine cables to the S. Dinghy SC, RNLI ILB station, café.

Gorey. See 9.19.13 below.

La Rocque. Small hbr dries 6·5m - 9·6m; bkwtr, local moorings, sandy beach, slip. Tricky appr 330° across Violet Bank requires detailed local knowledge. No facilities.

OFFLYING ISLANDS

Les Écrehou. 49°17'·39N 01°55'·58W. 5M NE of Rozel, has about a dozen cottages. ML 6·2m. Arrive at about ½ tide ebbing; see 9.19.13. Appr with Bigorne Rk on 022°; when SE of Maître Ile alter to 330° for FS on Marmotière Is. Beware of strong and eddying tidal streams 4 - 8kn. Pick up a buoy close SE of Marmotière or ⚓ in a pool 3ca WSW of Marmotière (with FS and houses); other islands are Maître Ile (one house), Blanche and 5 other small islets. Local knowledge or a detailed pilotage book is essential. SHOM 6937 is larger scale than AC 3655. No lts.

Plateau des Minquiers. 48°58'·04N 02°03'·74W. About 12M S of Jersey, encircled by six cardinal light buoys. See 9.19.13 for tides. ML 6·4m. Beware of strong and eddying tidal streams. Appr by day in good vis from Demie de Vascelin SHM buoy, 49°00'·81N 02°05'·15W, on 161°: Jetée des Fontaines RW bn in transit with FS on Maîtresse Ile. Further transits skirt the W side of the islet to ⚓ due S of it; safe only in settled weather and light winds. Maîtresse Ile has about a dozen cottages. Land at the slipway NW of the States of Jersey mooring buoy. Without local knowledge a detailed pilotage book is essential plus AC 3656 or SHOM 7161, both 1:50,000.

9.19.13 GOREY

Jersey **49°11'·78N 02°01'·37W** ❁❁◊◊✿✿✿

CHARTS AC *3655, 5604*, 1138; SHOM 7157, 7160, 6939; ECM 534, 1014; Imray C33B; Stanfords 2, 16, 26.

TIDES –0454 Dover; ML 6·0; Duration 0545; Zone 0 (UT)

Standard Port ST HELIER (⟶)

Times				Height (metres)			
High Water		Low Water		MHWS	MHWN	MLWN	MLWS
0300	0900	0200	0900	11·0	8·1	4·0	1·4
1500	2100	1400	2100				
Differences ST CATHERINE BAY							
0000	+0010	+0010	+0010	0·0	–0·1	0·0	+0·1
BOULEY BAY							
+0002	+0002	+0004	+0004	–0·3	–0·3	–0·1	–0·1
LES ECREHOU							
+0005	+0009	+0011	+0009	–0·2	+0·1	–0·2	0·0
LES MINQUIERS							
–0014	–0018	–0001	–0008	+0·5	+0·6	+0·1	+0·1

SHELTER Good in the hbr (dries completely to 6·9m), except in S/SE winds. Access HW±3. There are 12 drying Ⓥs 150m W of pier hd. ⚓ about 2ca E of pier hd or in deeper water in the Roads; also in St Catherine Bay to the N, except in S/SE winds.

NAVIGATION WPT 49°11´·18N 01°59´·59W, 298°/1·3M to pier hd/front ldg lt. Note the very large tidal range. On appr, keep well outside all local bns until the ldg marks are identified, but beware Banc du Chateau (0·4m least depth), 1M offshore to N of 298° ldg line; and Azicot Rk (dries 2·2m) just S of 298° ldg line, 2ca from ent. See 9.19.5 for the Violet Chan to St Helier. The Gutters and Boat Passage across Violet Bank are not advised.

LIGHTS AND MARKS See chartlet and 9.19.4. Mont Orgueil Castle (67m) is conspic from afar. There are at least 3 approaches:

1. Ldg lts 298°: front, Gorey pierhead, W framework twr; rear, W □ Or border. Best for visitors.
2. Pierhead on with church spire 304° leads close to Road Rk (3·3m) and over Azicot Rk (2·2m).
3. Pierhead on with white house/R roof 250° leads close to Les Arch bn (B/W with A topmark) and Pacquet Rk (0·3m).

R/T *Gorey Hbr* Ch 74 (HW±3 Apr-Oct only).

TELEPHONE (Dial code 01534) HM 853616, 📠 856927, mobile 07797 719336; ⊜ 833833; Marinecall 09066 526250; for Dr contact HM, or HM St Helier 885588.

FACILITIES Hbr M, AB £0.69. Gorey Marine [☎ 07797 742384] supplies P & D by hose at pierhead HW ±3; FW, C (7 ton), ME, El, Gas.

Town EC Thurs; CH, 🛒, R, Bar, ✉, Ⓑ, bus to St Helier. Ferry (Mar-Nov) to Portbail, Carteret.

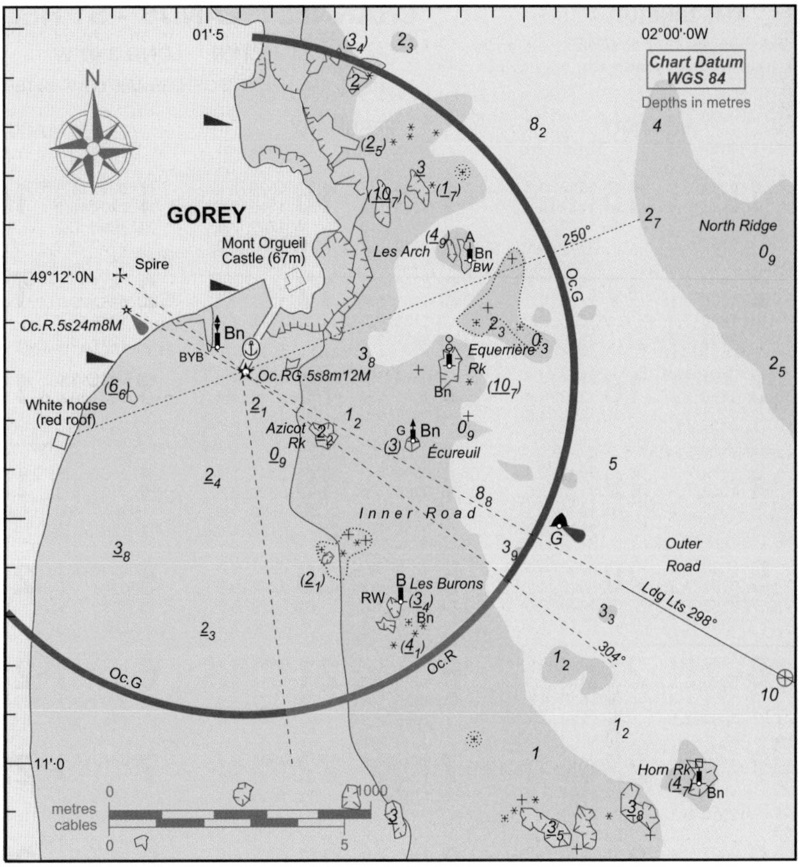
GOREY
Chart Datum WGS 84
Depths in metres
01'·5
02°00'·0W
49°12'·0N
11'·0
N
Spire
Mont Orgueil Castle (67m)
Oc.R.5s24m8M
Oc.RG.5s8m12M
BYB
Bn
White house (red roof)
Les Arch
Bn BW
Equerrière Rk
Écureuil
Azicot Rk
Inner Road
Outer Road
North Ridge
Les Burons
RW
Horn Rk
Ldg Lts 298°
250°
304°
Oc.G
Oc.R
G
metres
cables
0
1000
5

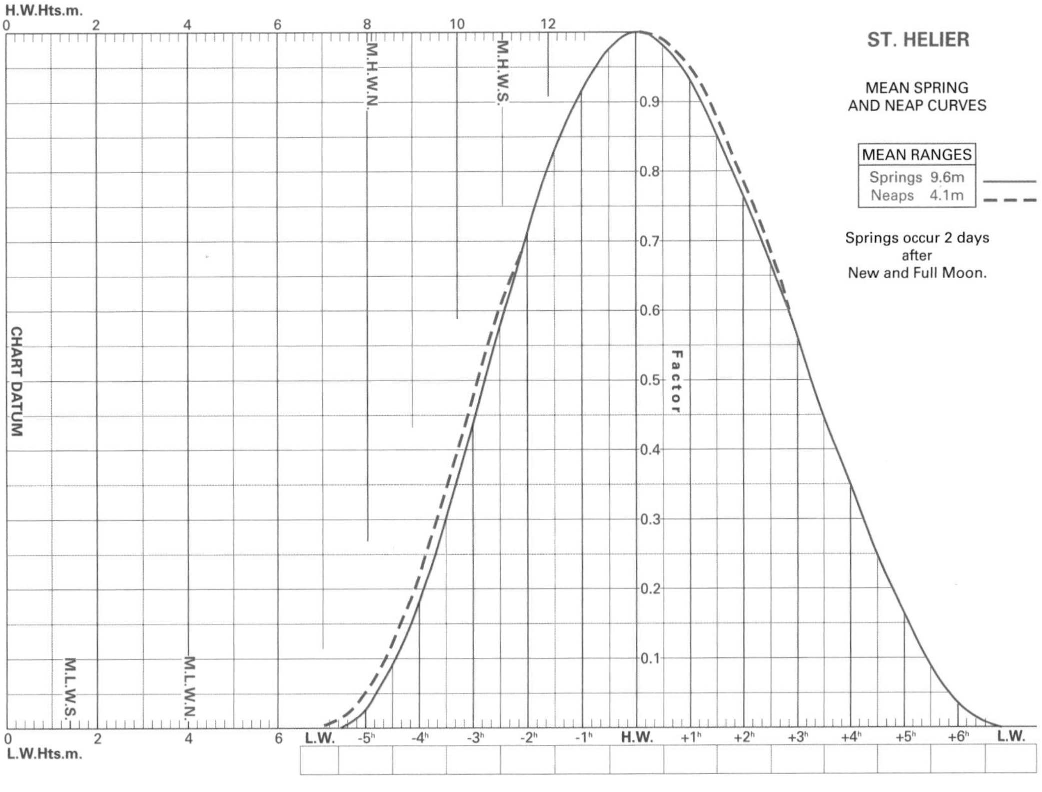
H.W.Hts.m.
L.W.Hts.m.
CHART DATUM
M.H.W.N.
M.H.W.S.
M.L.W.S.
M.L.W.N.
Factor
L.W.
H.W.
-5h -4h -3h -2h -1h +1h +2h +3h +4h +5h +6h
ST. HELIER
MEAN SPRING AND NEAP CURVES
MEAN RANGES
Springs 9.6m
Neaps 4.1m
Springs occur 2 days after New and Full Moon.

TIME ZONE (UT)
For Summer Time add ONE hour in **non-shaded areas**

CHANNEL ISLANDS – ST HELIER

LAT 49°11′N LONG 2°07′W

TIMES AND HEIGHTS OF HIGH AND LOW WATERS

SPRING & NEAP TIDES
Dates in red are SPRINGS
Dates in blue are NEAPS

YEAR **2005**

JANUARY

Date	Day	Time	m	Time	m	Time	m	Time	m
1	SA	0343	3.0	0927	9.4	1607	3.0	2154	8.9
2	SU	0421	3.3	1006	9.1	1646	3.3	2235	8.6
3	M	0504	3.6	1050	8.8	1732	3.6	◑ 2324	8.4
4	TU	0557	3.9	1146	8.5	1829	3.8		
5	W	0028	8.2	0703	4.0	1255	8.4	1940	3.8
6	TH	0142	8.4	0820	3.8	1412	8.6	2058	3.5
7	F	0256	8.8	0936	3.3	1526	9.0	2210	3.1
8	SA	0403	9.4	1043	2.7	1633	9.6	2315	2.5
9	SU	0504	10.0	1145	2.1	1734	10.1		
10	M	0014	2.0	0559	10.6	1244	1.5	● 1830	10.6
11	TU	0110	1.6	0652	11.1	1339	1.1	1922	10.9
12	W	0202	1.3	0742	11.3	1431	0.9	2010	11.0
13	TH	0251	1.3	0829	11.4	1519	1.0	2056	10.9
14	F	0336	1.4	0913	11.1	1604	1.2	2139	10.5
15	SA	0419	1.8	0956	10.6	1646	1.7	2220	10.0
16	SU	0500	2.3	1037	10.0	1726	2.4	2301	9.4
17	M	0542	2.9	1121	9.3	1808	3.0	◐ 2346	8.8
18	TU	0628	3.5	1213	8.6	1858	3.6		
19	W	0043	8.3	0728	4.0	1320	8.1	2002	4.0
20	TH	0157	8.1	0842	4.1	1440	8.0	2116	4.0
21	F	0313	8.2	0957	3.9	1553	8.2	2224	3.8
22	SA	0417	8.6	1059	3.5	1651	8.6	2319	3.3
23	SU	0508	9.0	1148	3.0	1738	9.1		
24	M	0004	2.9	0550	9.5	1231	2.6	1818	9.4
25	TU	0045	2.6	0628	9.8	1309	2.3	○ 1854	9.7
26	W	0121	2.3	0703	10.1	1345	2.1	1928	9.9
27	TH	0155	2.2	0736	10.2	1418	2.0	2000	10.0
28	F	0228	2.1	0808	10.3	1449	2.0	2031	10.0
29	SA	0259	2.1	0840	10.3	1520	2.1	2102	9.9
30	SU	0330	2.2	0911	10.1	1550	2.3	2132	9.7
31	M	0402	2.5	0943	9.8	1621	2.6	2205	9.3

FEBRUARY

Date	Day	Time	m	Time	m	Time	m	Time	m
1	TU	0436	2.9	1018	9.4	1655	3.0	2242	8.9
2	W	0516	3.3	1101	8.9	1738	3.5	◑ 2332	8.5
3	TH	0610	3.7	1201	8.4	1841	3.9		
4	F	0044	8.2	0729	4.0	1325	8.2	2014	4.0
5	SA	0219	8.3	0905	3.7	1503	8.4	2148	3.6
6	SU	0347	8.9	1028	3.0	1626	9.1	2305	2.8
7	M	0457	9.7	1138	2.2	1731	9.9		
8	TU	0008	2.0	0554	10.5	1239	1.4	● 1825	10.6
9	W	0104	1.4	0645	11.2	1333	0.8	1913	11.2
10	TH	0154	0.9	0731	11.6	1421	0.5	1957	11.4
11	F	0239	0.7	0814	11.8	1504	0.4	2037	11.3
12	SA	0319	0.8	0853	11.5	1542	0.7	2114	11.0
13	SU	0355	1.2	0929	11.0	1616	1.3	2147	10.4
14	M	0427	1.9	1003	10.2	1646	2.1	2219	9.7
15	TU	0457	2.6	1037	9.4	1715	3.0	2253	8.9
16	W	0529	3.4	1115	8.5	1749	3.8	◐ 2336	8.2
17	TH	0615	4.1	1211	7.7	1845	4.4		
18	F	0047	7.6	0734	4.6	1352	7.3	2022	4.7
19	SA	0234	7.5	0922	4.5	1533	7.6	2159	4.3
20	SU	0357	8.0	1041	3.9	1638	8.2	2303	3.7
21	M	0453	8.7	1133	3.2	1724	8.9	2349	3.0
22	TU	0535	9.3	1215	2.6	1802	9.4		
23	W	0029	2.5	0612	9.8	1254	2.1	1836	9.8
24	TH	0107	2.1	0646	10.2	1329	1.8	○ 1908	10.2
25	F	0140	1.8	0718	10.5	1402	1.6	1939	10.4
26	SA	0212	1.6	0749	10.7	1432	1.5	2009	10.5
27	SU	0242	1.5	0819	10.8	1501	1.5	2039	10.5
28	M	0312	1.6	0850	10.6	1529	1.7	2108	10.2

MARCH

Date	Day	Time	m	Time	m	Time	m	Time	m
1	TU	0342	1.9	0920	10.2	1558	2.2	2137	9.8
2	W	0413	2.4	0952	9.7	1628	2.7	2211	9.3
3	TH	0449	3.0	1031	9.0	1706	3.4	◑ 2255	8.6
4	F	0539	3.6	1128	8.3	1807	4.0		
5	SA	0008	8.1	0701	4.0	1303	7.8	1951	4.3
6	SU	0203	8.0	0852	3.8	1503	8.1	2142	3.8
7	M	0343	8.7	1024	3.0	1625	9.0	2300	2.8
8	TU	0450	9.7	1132	2.0	1723	10.0	2359	1.9
9	W	0543	10.6	1227	1.1	1812	10.8		
10	TH	0050	1.1	0630	11.3	1317	0.6	● 1855	11.3
11	F	0136	0.7	0712	11.7	1400	0.3	1934	11.5
12	SA	0217	0.5	0751	11.8	1438	0.4	2010	11.4
13	SU	0253	0.7	0827	11.5	1511	0.7	2043	11.1
14	M	0324	1.1	0859	11.0	1540	1.4	2112	10.5
15	TU	0352	1.8	0929	10.2	1605	2.1	2140	9.8
16	W	0417	2.6	0957	9.3	1628	3.0	2207	9.0
17	TH	0443	3.4	1028	8.4	1657	3.8	◐ 2242	8.2
18	F	0520	4.1	1113	7.5	1744	4.6	2341	7.4
19	SA	0632	4.7	1303	7.0	1921	5.0		
20	SU	0154	7.2	0839	4.7	1509	7.3	2127	4.7
21	M	0331	7.7	1013	4.1	1613	8.0	2236	3.9
22	TU	0426	8.5	1105	3.3	1657	8.8	2322	3.1
23	W	0507	9.2	1147	2.6	1734	9.4		
24	TH	0002	2.4	0544	9.8	1226	2.0	1807	10.0
25	F	0040	1.9	0618	10.3	1302	1.6	○ 1840	10.4
26	SA	0115	1.6	0651	10.7	1336	1.3	1911	10.7
27	SU	0149	1.3	0723	10.9	1408	1.2	1943	10.8
28	M	0221	1.2	0755	11.0	1438	1.3	2014	10.8
29	TU	0252	1.4	0827	10.8	1507	1.5	2044	10.5
30	W	0323	1.7	0900	10.4	1537	2.0	2116	10.1
31	TH	0356	2.2	0934	9.7	1610	2.7	2152	9.4

APRIL

Date	Day	Time	m	Time	m	Time	m	Time	m
1	F	0435	2.9	1017	8.9	1653	3.4	2240	8.7
2	SA	0530	3.6	1121	8.1	1800	4.1	◑	
3	SU	0003	8.0	0658	4.0	1310	7.8	1950	4.3
4	M	0205	8.1	0848	3.6	1501	8.3	2134	3.6
5	TU	0333	8.9	1012	2.8	1611	9.2	2244	2.6
6	W	0433	9.8	1113	1.9	1704	10.1	2339	1.8
7	TH	0523	10.6	1205	1.2	1749	10.7		
8	F	0027	1.2	0606	11.2	1251	0.8	● 1829	11.1
9	SA	0110	0.9	0646	11.4	1331	0.7	1906	11.3
10	SU	0148	0.8	0723	11.4	1406	0.8	1940	11.2
11	M	0222	1.0	0757	11.1	1437	1.1	2011	10.9
12	TU	0251	1.4	0829	10.6	1504	1.7	2039	10.4
13	W	0318	1.9	0857	9.9	1529	2.3	2105	9.8
14	TH	0344	2.6	0925	9.1	1554	3.1	2132	9.0
15	F	0411	3.3	0956	8.3	1623	3.8	2205	8.3
16	SA	0449	4.0	1039	7.6	1709	4.5	◐ 2259	7.6
17	SU	0553	4.6	1215	7.0	1832	4.9		
18	M	0058	7.2	0738	4.7	1420	7.2	2028	4.8
19	TU	0242	7.6	0918	4.2	1527	7.9	2147	4.0
20	W	0341	8.3	1017	3.4	1613	8.6	2238	3.3
21	TH	0425	9.0	1103	2.7	1653	9.3	2322	2.6
22	F	0505	9.6	1145	2.1	1729	9.9		
23	SA	0003	2.0	0542	10.2	1226	1.7	1805	10.4
24	SU	0043	1.6	0618	10.6	1304	1.4	○ 1840	10.7
25	M	0120	1.3	0655	10.9	1339	1.3	1915	10.9
26	TU	0157	1.2	0732	10.9	1414	1.3	1950	10.9
27	W	0232	1.3	0809	10.7	1449	1.6	2026	10.6
28	TH	0309	1.6	0848	10.3	1524	2.1	2105	10.1
29	F	0349	2.1	0930	9.6	1605	2.7	2149	9.5
30	SA	0436	2.8	1023	8.9	1656	3.4	2248	8.8

Chart Datum: 5·88 metres below Ordnance Datum (Local)

TIME ZONE (UT)
For Summer Time add ONE hour in **non-shaded areas**

CHANNEL ISLANDS – ST HELIER

LAT 49°11'N LONG 2°07'W

TIMES AND HEIGHTS OF HIGH AND LOW WATERS

SPRING & NEAP TIDES
Dates in red are SPRINGS
Dates in blue are NEAPS

YEAR **2005**

MAY

Date	Day	Time	m	Time	m	Time	m	Time	m	Moon
1	SU	0538	3.3	1135	8.3	1810	3.9			◑
2	M	0012	8.4	0703	3.5	1311	8.1	1945	3.8	
3	TU	0150	8.5	0832	3.2	1437	8.6	2110	3.3	
4	W	0306	9.1	0944	2.6	1542	9.3	2215	2.6	
5	TH	0404	9.8	1043	2.0	1634	9.9	2309	2.0	
6	F	0454	10.3	1133	1.6	1719	10.4	2357	1.6	
7	SA	0538	10.6	1218	1.4	1759	10.6			
8	SU	0039	1.4	0618	10.7	1258	1.4	1835	10.7	●
9	M	0117	1.4	0655	10.7	1332	1.5	1909	10.7	
10	TU	0151	1.5	0730	10.5	1404	1.7	1941	10.5	
11	W	0222	1.8	0803	10.1	1433	2.1	2011	10.1	
12	TH	0251	2.2	0834	9.6	1502	2.6	2041	9.6	
13	F	0321	2.7	0905	9.0	1532	3.1	2112	9.1	
14	SA	0353	3.3	0940	8.4	1605	3.7	2148	8.5	
15	SU	0432	3.8	1025	7.8	1650	4.2	2238	7.9	
16	M	0527	4.2	1133	7.4	1754	4.5	2356	7.6	◐
17	TU	0641	4.3	1306	7.4	1917	4.5			
18	W	0129	7.7	0804	4.1	1421	7.8	2038	4.1	
19	TH	0238	8.1	0913	3.6	1516	8.4	2140	3.5	
20	F	0331	8.7	1008	3.0	1602	9.0	2232	2.9	
21	SA	0418	9.3	1058	2.5	1646	9.7	2320	2.3	
22	SU	0502	9.9	1145	2.0	1728	10.2			
23	M	0007	1.8	0546	10.3	1230	1.7	1809	10.6	○
24	TU	0052	1.5	0629	10.6	1313	1.5	1851	10.8	
25	W	0136	1.3	0714	10.7	1355	1.5	1934	10.8	
26	TH	0219	1.4	0759	10.6	1438	1.7	2018	10.7	
27	F	0304	1.6	0846	10.2	1522	2.1	2104	10.3	
28	SA	0351	1.9	0936	9.8	1610	2.5	2156	9.8	
29	SU	0444	2.4	1031	9.2	1705	3.0	2254	9.3	
30	M	0544	2.7	1134	8.8	1810	3.3			◑
31	TU	0002	9.0	0651	2.9	1246	8.7	1922	3.3	

JUNE

Date	Day	Time	m	Time	m	Time	m	Time	m	Moon
1	W	0117	8.9	0801	2.9	1357	8.8	2033	3.2	
2	TH	0226	9.1	0906	2.7	1501	9.1	2137	2.8	
3	F	0327	9.3	1005	2.5	1556	9.4	2233	2.5	
4	SA	0421	9.6	1057	2.3	1645	9.7	2324	2.3	
5	SU	0509	9.8	1144	2.2	1729	10.0			
6	M	0009	2.2	0552	9.9	1226	2.1	1808	10.1	●
7	TU	0050	2.1	0632	9.9	1304	2.2	1845	10.1	
8	W	0126	2.1	0710	9.9	1339	2.3	1920	10.1	
9	TH	0200	2.2	0745	9.7	1412	2.4	1953	9.9	
10	F	0234	2.4	0820	9.4	1445	2.7	2026	9.6	
11	SA	0307	2.6	0854	9.1	1518	3.0	2100	9.3	
12	SU	0341	3.0	0929	8.8	1553	3.3	2137	8.9	
13	M	0419	3.3	1009	8.4	1633	3.6	2219	8.5	
14	TU	0502	3.6	1056	8.1	1721	3.9	2311	8.2	
15	W	0554	3.8	1154	7.9	1820	4.0			◐
16	TH	0013	8.1	0655	3.8	1301	8.0	1927	4.0	
17	F	0123	8.2	0802	3.7	1408	8.3	2036	3.7	
18	SA	0229	8.5	0909	3.4	1507	8.7	2141	3.2	
19	SU	0329	9.0	1011	2.9	1602	9.3	2240	2.7	
20	M	0425	9.5	1108	2.5	1655	9.9	2335	2.2	
21	TU	0520	10.0	1202	2.1	1746	10.3			
22	W	0029	1.7	0612	10.3	1254	1.8	1836	10.7	○
23	TH	0122	1.4	0704	10.6	1345	1.6	1926	10.9	
24	F	0213	1.2	0755	10.6	1434	1.6	2015	10.9	
25	SA	0304	1.2	0845	10.5	1523	1.7	2104	10.8	
26	SU	0353	1.4	0934	10.3	1612	1.9	2153	10.5	
27	M	0442	1.7	1023	9.9	1701	2.3	2243	10.0	
28	TU	0532	2.1	1113	9.4	1752	2.7	2335	9.5	◑
29	W	0624	2.5	1206	9.0	1847	3.0			
30	TH	0033	9.1	0719	2.9	1307	8.7	1948	3.3	

JULY

Date	Day	Time	m	Time	m	Time	m	Time	m	Moon
1	F	0138	8.8	0820	3.2	1412	8.6	2053	3.4	
2	SA	0245	8.6	0922	3.2	1516	8.8	2157	3.3	
3	SU	0349	8.7	1023	3.1	1614	9.0	2256	3.0	
4	M	0445	9.0	1117	3.0	1705	9.3	2347	2.8	
5	TU	0534	9.2	1204	2.8	1749	9.6			
6	W	0031	2.6	0617	9.4	1246	2.6	1829	9.8	●
7	TH	0111	2.4	0657	9.6	1323	2.5	1906	9.9	
8	F	0148	2.3	0733	9.6	1359	2.5	1941	9.9	
9	SA	0222	2.3	0807	9.6	1432	2.5	2015	9.9	
10	SU	0255	2.4	0840	9.5	1505	2.6	2047	9.7	
11	M	0328	2.5	0912	9.3	1538	2.7	2120	9.5	
12	TU	0401	2.7	0945	9.1	1612	3.0	2155	9.3	
13	W	0435	3.0	1021	8.8	1650	3.3	2232	8.9	
14	TH	0513	3.3	1101	8.5	1733	3.6	2318	8.6	◐
15	F	0559	3.6	1153	8.3	1828	3.8			
16	SA	0016	8.3	0657	3.8	1259	8.2	1937	3.9	
17	SU	0129	8.3	0812	3.7	1415	8.4	2055	3.6	
18	M	0247	8.5	0931	3.4	1528	8.9	2209	3.1	
19	TU	0400	9.0	1042	2.9	1634	9.5	2315	2.4	
20	W	0506	9.7	1146	2.3	1734	10.2			
21	TH	0017	1.8	0605	10.3	1245	1.8	1828	10.8	○
22	F	0115	1.2	0659	10.7	1339	1.4	1919	11.2	
23	SA	0209	0.9	0749	11.0	1430	1.1	2007	11.4	
24	SU	0258	0.7	0835	11.1	1516	1.1	2053	11.4	
25	M	0344	0.8	0919	10.9	1600	1.3	2136	11.1	
26	TU	0426	1.1	1000	10.4	1641	1.7	2217	10.5	
27	W	0506	1.8	1040	9.9	1721	2.3	2259	9.7	
28	TH	0546	2.5	1122	9.2	1804	3.0	2345	9.0	◑
29	F	0629	3.2	1212	8.6	1856	3.6			
30	SA	0044	8.3	0725	3.8	1318	8.1	2005	4.0	
31	SU	0203	7.9	0840	4.1	1439	8.1	2126	4.0	

AUGUST

Date	Day	Time	m	Time	m	Time	m	Time	m	Moon
1	M	0326	8.0	0956	3.9	1553	8.4	2238	3.6	
2	TU	0432	8.4	1100	3.5	1651	8.9	2334	3.1	
3	W	0524	8.9	1151	3.1	1737	9.3			
4	TH	0020	2.7	0606	9.3	1233	2.7	1816	9.7	
5	F	0059	2.4	0643	9.6	1311	2.4	1852	10.0	●
6	SA	0135	2.2	0717	9.8	1345	2.2	1925	10.2	
7	SU	0208	2.0	0749	10.0	1418	2.1	1957	10.3	
8	M	0239	2.0	0819	10.0	1448	2.1	2027	10.3	
9	TU	0309	2.0	0848	9.9	1518	2.2	2057	10.1	
10	W	0338	2.2	0917	9.7	1549	2.4	2127	9.8	
11	TH	0406	2.5	0946	9.4	1620	2.8	2158	9.4	
12	F	0437	3.0	1018	9.0	1655	3.3	2234	8.9	
13	SA	0513	3.4	1100	8.6	1741	3.7	2325	8.4	◐
14	SU	0606	3.9	1203	8.2	1851	4.1			
15	M	0042	8.0	0729	4.2	1336	8.1	2024	4.0	
16	TU	0224	8.1	0909	3.9	1512	8.5	2153	3.3	
17	W	0354	8.7	1031	3.2	1627	9.4	2307	2.5	
18	TH	0503	9.6	1138	2.3	1727	10.3			
19	F	0009	1.6	0558	10.5	1236	1.6	1819	11.1	○
20	SA	0106	0.9	0648	11.1	1328	1.0	1906	11.7	
21	SU	0156	0.5	0733	11.5	1415	0.7	1951	11.9	
22	M	0241	0.3	0815	11.5	1458	0.7	2032	11.8	
23	TU	0322	0.5	0853	11.3	1536	1.0	2110	11.3	
24	W	0358	1.0	0929	10.7	1612	1.6	2146	10.6	
25	TH	0431	1.8	1002	10.0	1644	2.4	2220	9.7	
26	F	0502	2.7	1036	9.2	1717	3.2	2257	8.7	◑
27	SA	0535	3.6	1116	8.4	1800	4.0	2349	7.8	
28	SU	0626	4.4	1221	7.7	1914	4.6			
29	M	0125	7.3	0757	4.8	1411	7.5	2104	4.6	
30	TU	0316	7.5	0940	4.5	1541	8.0	2228	4.0	
31	W	0423	8.2	1048	3.8	1638	8.7	2320	3.3	

Chart Datum: 5·88 metres below Ordnance Datum (Local)

TIME ZONE (UT)
For Summer Time add ONE hour in **non-shaded areas**

CHANNEL ISLANDS – ST HELIER

LAT 49°11′N LONG 2°07′W

TIMES AND HEIGHTS OF HIGH AND LOW WATERS

SPRING & NEAP TIDES
Dates in red are SPRINGS
Dates in blue are NEAPS

YEAR **2005**

SEPTEMBER

Date	Day	Time	m	Time	m	Time	m	Time	m	Moon
1	TH	0509	8.9	1135	3.1	1721	9.3			
2	F	0002	2.7	0547	9.5	1215	2.6	1757	9.9	
3	SA	0039	2.2	0621	9.9	1251	2.2	1831	10.2	●
4	SU	0113	1.9	0653	10.2	1324	1.9	1902	10.5	
5	M	0146	1.7	0723	10.4	1355	1.8	1932	10.7	
6	TU	0215	1.6	0752	10.5	1425	1.7	2001	10.7	
7	W	0244	1.7	0820	10.4	1454	1.8	2030	10.5	
8	TH	0311	1.9	0847	10.2	1523	2.1	2058	10.2	
9	F	0338	2.3	0915	9.8	1553	2.6	2128	9.7	
10	SA	0406	2.9	0944	9.3	1626	3.2	2202	9.0	
11	SU	0441	3.5	1023	8.7	1711	3.8	2252	8.3	◐
12	M	0534	4.1	1126	8.1	1826	4.2			
13	TU	0019	7.8	0709	4.5	1321	7.8	2014	4.1	
14	W	0226	7.9	0904	4.1	1512	8.5	2149	3.3	
15	TH	0354	8.8	1026	3.1	1621	9.6	2258	2.3	
16	F	0454	9.9	1127	2.1	1715	10.6	2356	1.4	
17	SA	0544	10.7	1219	1.3	1802	11.4			
18	SU	0047	0.7	0628	11.3	1308	0.8	1846	11.8	○
19	M	0133	0.4	0709	11.6	1351	0.6	1927	12.0	
20	TU	0214	0.4	0747	11.6	1430	0.7	2005	11.8	
21	W	0251	0.7	0822	11.3	1506	1.1	2040	11.2	
22	TH	0323	1.3	0854	10.8	1537	1.7	2112	10.4	
23	F	0352	2.1	0924	10.0	1605	2.6	2142	9.5	
24	SA	0418	3.0	0953	9.2	1634	3.5	2215	8.5	
25	SU	0447	3.9	1027	8.3	1712	4.3	2301	7.6	◑
26	M	0533	4.7	1126	7.5	1825	4.9			
27	TU	0053	7.0	0713	5.2	1344	7.3	2037	4.9	
28	W	0258	7.4	0918	4.8	1520	7.8	2204	4.2	
29	TH	0359	8.1	1024	4.0	1613	8.6	2252	3.4	
30	F	0442	8.9	1107	3.2	1653	9.3	2330	2.7	

OCTOBER

Date	Day	Time	m	Time	m	Time	m	Time	m	Moon
1	SA	0517	9.5	1144	2.6	1728	9.9			
2	SU	0007	2.2	0550	10.0	1220	2.1	1800	10.3	
3	M	0042	1.8	0621	10.4	1255	1.8	1832	10.7	●
4	TU	0115	1.6	0652	10.6	1328	1.6	1903	10.8	
5	W	0146	1.6	0722	10.7	1359	1.6	1934	10.9	
6	TH	0216	1.6	0751	10.7	1430	1.7	2004	10.7	
7	F	0245	1.9	0820	10.5	1500	2.0	2035	10.3	
8	SA	0314	2.3	0850	10.1	1532	2.5	2107	9.7	
9	SU	0345	2.9	0923	9.5	1609	3.1	2147	9.0	
10	M	0425	3.6	1007	8.8	1701	3.8	2244	8.2	◐
11	TU	0527	4.3	1121	8.1	1824	4.2			
12	W	0026	7.8	0710	4.5	1325	8.0	2011	4.0	
13	TH	0226	8.2	0857	3.9	1501	8.8	2137	3.1	
14	F	0340	9.1	1010	3.0	1603	9.8	2240	2.2	
15	SA	0434	10.0	1106	2.0	1654	10.6	2333	1.4	
16	SU	0520	10.8	1155	1.4	1739	11.3			
17	M	0020	1.0	0602	11.2	1241	1.0	1820	11.6	○
18	TU	0104	0.8	0641	11.4	1322	0.9	1900	11.6	
19	W	0142	0.9	0717	11.4	1400	1.1	1936	11.3	
20	TH	0216	1.3	0751	11.1	1433	1.5	2011	10.8	
21	F	0247	1.8	0822	10.6	1504	2.1	2042	10.1	
22	SA	0315	2.5	0851	9.9	1532	2.8	2113	9.3	
23	SU	0342	3.3	0920	9.2	1601	3.6	2145	8.4	
24	M	0413	4.1	0954	8.4	1640	4.3	2231	7.6	
25	TU	0459	4.7	1049	7.7	1746	4.8			◑
26	W	0007	7.1	0623	5.1	1248	7.3	1938	4.9	
27	TH	0209	7.3	0822	4.9	1432	7.7	2111	4.4	
28	F	0315	8.0	0935	4.2	1529	8.4	2205	3.6	
29	SA	0400	8.7	1023	3.5	1612	9.1	2247	3.0	
30	SU	0437	9.3	1104	2.8	1649	9.7	2326	2.4	
31	M	0512	9.9	1142	2.3	1724	10.1			

NOVEMBER

Date	Day	Time	m	Time	m	Time	m	Time	m	Moon
1	TU	0004	2.0	0546	10.3	1221	1.9	1759	10.5	
2	W	0041	1.8	0619	10.6	1257	1.7	1833	10.7	●
3	TH	0116	1.7	0652	10.8	1333	1.6	1908	10.8	
4	F	0150	1.8	0726	10.8	1408	1.7	1944	10.6	
5	SA	0224	2.0	0801	10.6	1444	2.0	2022	10.3	
6	SU	0259	2.4	0838	10.2	1522	2.4	2103	9.7	
7	M	0338	2.9	0920	9.6	1608	3.0	2152	9.1	
8	TU	0427	3.5	1015	9.0	1706	3.5	2257	8.5	
9	W	0534	4.0	1131	8.5	1826	3.7			◐
10	TH	0027	8.2	0704	4.1	1308	8.5	1954	3.5	
11	F	0159	8.5	0832	3.6	1430	9.0	2109	3.0	
12	SA	0309	9.2	0940	2.9	1533	9.7	2210	2.3	
13	SU	0404	9.8	1037	2.3	1625	10.3	2303	1.8	
14	M	0451	10.4	1127	1.8	1712	10.7	2350	1.6	
15	TU	0534	10.7	1212	1.6	1755	10.9			
16	W	0032	1.5	0613	10.9	1254	1.6	1834	10.8	○
17	TH	0111	1.6	0650	10.9	1332	1.7	1912	10.7	
18	F	0146	1.9	0724	10.7	1406	1.9	1948	10.3	
19	SA	0219	2.2	0757	10.3	1439	2.3	2022	9.8	
20	SU	0249	2.7	0829	9.8	1510	2.9	2055	9.2	
21	M	0320	3.3	0902	9.3	1543	3.4	2131	8.6	
22	TU	0354	3.8	0938	8.7	1622	3.9	2214	8.0	
23	W	0437	4.3	1026	8.1	1714	4.4	2316	7.6	◑
24	TH	0538	4.7	1137	7.7	1826	4.6			
25	F	0043	7.5	0659	4.7	1308	7.7	1948	4.4	
26	SA	0203	7.8	0820	4.4	1421	8.1	2058	4.0	
27	SU	0301	8.3	0924	3.9	1516	8.6	2152	3.5	
28	M	0347	8.9	1015	3.3	1602	9.1	2240	2.9	
29	TU	0429	9.4	1101	2.7	1644	9.7	2325	2.5	
30	W	0509	10.0	1146	2.3	1726	10.1			

DECEMBER

Date	Day	Time	m	Time	m	Time	m	Time	m	Moon
1	TH	0008	2.1	0548	10.4	1230	1.9	1808	10.4	●
2	F	0050	1.9	0629	10.7	1312	1.7	1851	10.6	
3	SA	0131	1.9	0710	10.8	1355	1.7	1934	10.6	
4	SU	0213	2.0	0753	10.7	1438	1.8	2020	10.4	
5	M	0255	2.2	0838	10.5	1524	2.0	2108	10.0	
6	TU	0342	2.5	0927	10.1	1614	2.4	2200	9.6	
7	W	0433	2.9	1021	9.7	1710	2.8	2257	9.1	
8	TH	0533	3.3	1123	9.3	1813	3.0			◐
9	F	0002	8.8	0640	3.5	1233	9.0	1921	3.1	
10	SA	0114	8.8	0752	3.4	1346	9.0	2029	3.0	
11	SU	0224	8.9	0901	3.2	1453	9.2	2132	2.8	
12	M	0326	9.3	1003	2.9	1553	9.5	2230	2.6	
13	TU	0420	9.6	1058	2.6	1646	9.7	2321	2.4	
14	W	0508	9.9	1148	2.4	1734	9.9			
15	TH	0007	2.3	0551	10.2	1233	2.2	1817	10.0	○
16	F	0049	2.3	0631	10.3	1314	2.2	1857	10.0	
17	SA	0127	2.3	0708	10.3	1350	2.2	1935	9.9	
18	SU	0202	2.5	0744	10.1	1425	2.4	2011	9.7	
19	M	0235	2.7	0818	9.9	1458	2.7	2045	9.4	
20	TU	0308	3.0	0851	9.6	1531	3.0	2119	9.1	
21	W	0341	3.3	0926	9.2	1606	3.3	2155	8.7	
22	TH	0417	3.6	1003	8.8	1644	3.6	2235	8.3	
23	F	0459	3.9	1047	8.4	1730	3.9	2324	8.0	◑
24	SA	0552	4.2	1142	8.1	1826	4.1			
25	SU	0027	7.9	0655	4.3	1249	8.0	1933	4.2	
26	M	0138	7.9	0809	4.2	1401	8.1	2045	4.0	
27	TU	0245	8.3	0919	3.8	1507	8.5	2150	3.5	
28	W	0343	8.8	1020	3.3	1605	9.0	2248	3.0	
29	TH	0435	9.5	1116	2.7	1700	9.6	2342	2.5	
30	F	0526	10.0	1208	2.1	1752	10.1			
31	SA	0033	2.1	0615	10.5	1300	1.7	1842	10.5	●

Chart Datum: 5·88 metres below Ordnance Datum (Local)

Area 20

North Brittany
Paimpol to Douarnenez

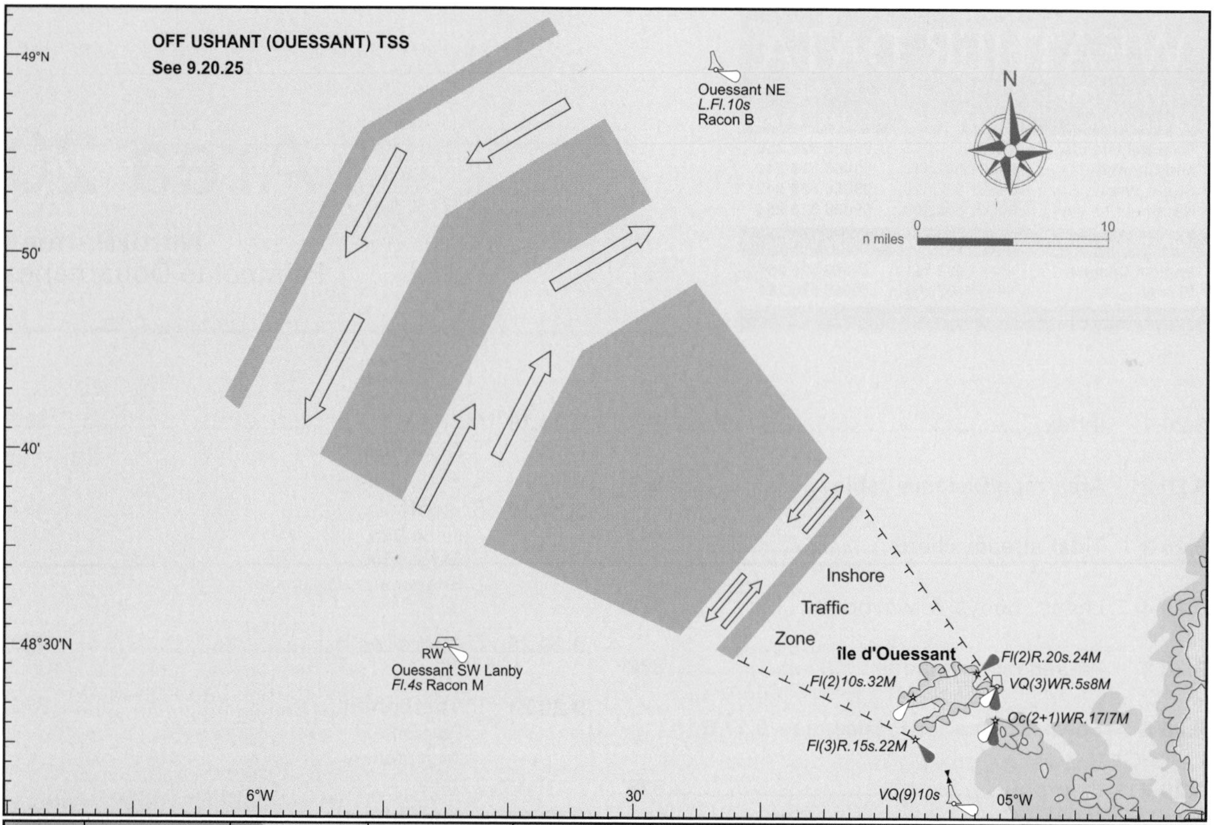

OFF USHANT (OUESSANT) TSS
See 9.20.25
49°N
50'
40'
48°30'N
6°W
30'
05°W
Ouessant NE
L.Fl.10s
Racon B
N
0
10
n miles
Inshore
Traffic
Zone
île d'Ouessant
Fl(2)R.20s.24M
VQ(3)WR.5s8M
Oc(2+1)WR.17/7M
Fl(2)10s.32M
Fl(3)R.15s.22M
VQ(9)10s
RW
Ouessant SW Lanby
Fl.4s Racon M

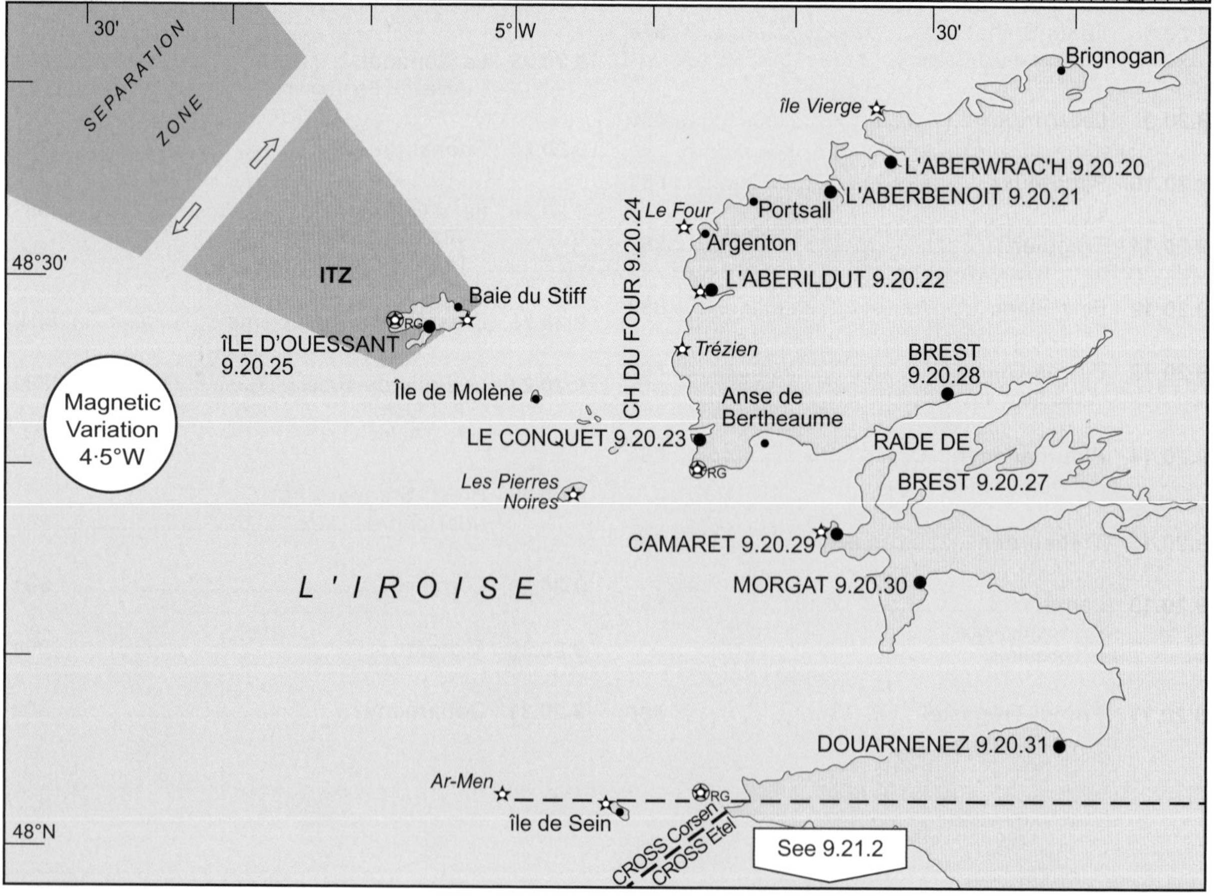

30'
5° W
30'
SEPARATION
ZONE
ITZ
48°30'
48°N
Brignogan
île Vierge
L'ABERWRAC'H 9.20.20
L'ABERBENOIT 9.20.21
Portsall
Le Four
Argenton
L'ABERILDUT 9.20.22
CH DU FOUR 9.20.24
Trézien
Baie du Stiff
RG
îLE D'OUESSANT
9.20.25
Île de Molène
BREST
9.20.28
Anse de
Bertheaume
LE CONQUET 9.20.23
RADE DE
BREST 9.20.27
Magnetic
Variation
4·5°W
Les Pierres
Noires
CAMARET 9.20.29
MORGAT 9.20.30
L ' I R O I S E
DOUARNENEZ 9.20.31
Ar-Men
île de Sein
CROSS Corsen
CROSS Etel
See 9.21.2

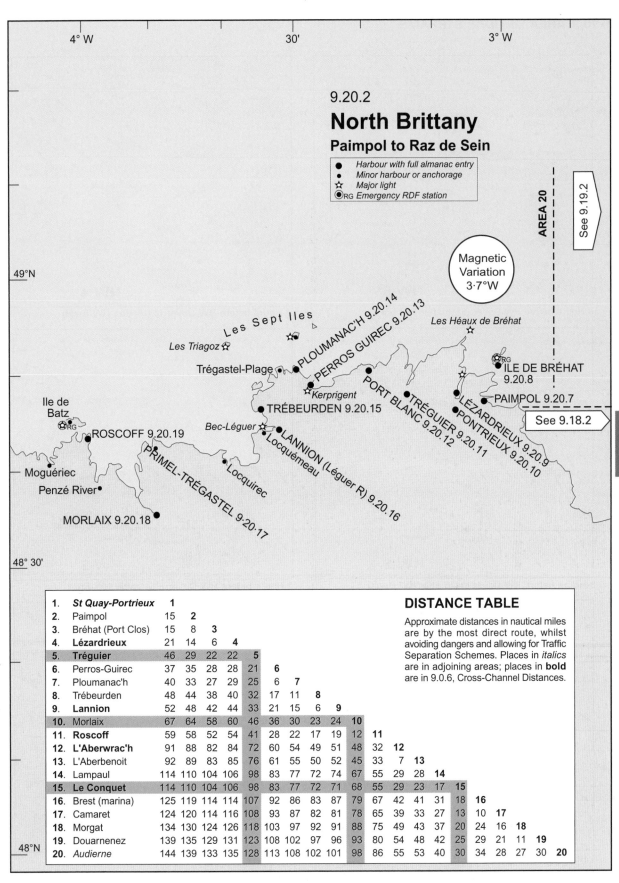

9.20.2 North Brittany

Paimpol to Raz de Sein

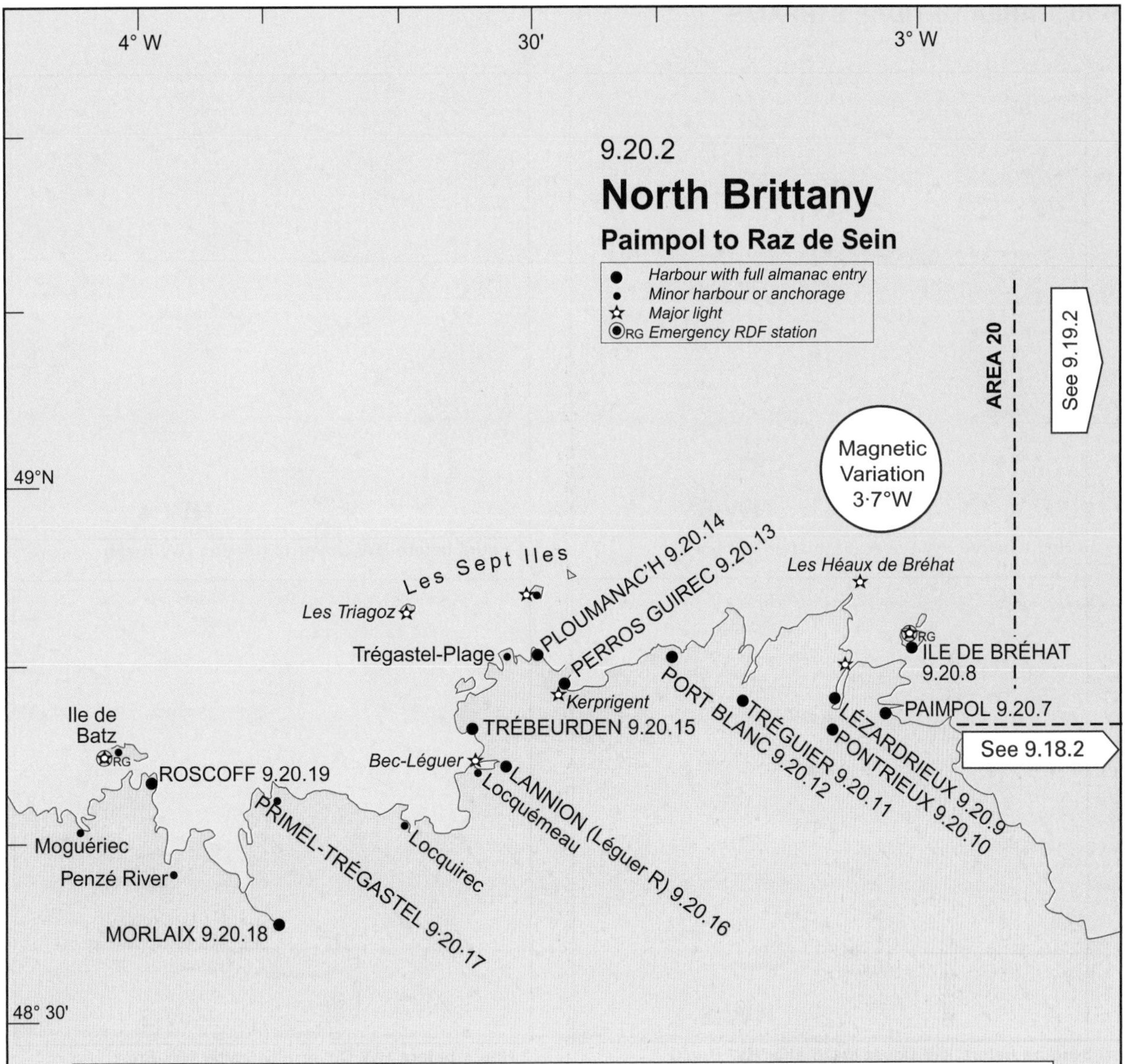
4° W
30'
3° W
49°N
48° 30'
48°N
Harbour with full almanac entry
Minor harbour or anchorage
Major light
RG Emergency RDF station
AREA 20
See 9.19.2
Magnetic Variation 3·7°W
Les Sept Iles
Les Triagoz
PLOUMANAC'H 9.20.14
PERROS GUIREC 9.20.13
Les Héaux de Bréhat
ILE DE BRÉHAT 9.20.8
PAIMPOL 9.20.7
See 9.18.2
Trégastel-Plage
Kerprigent
PORT BLANC 9.20.12
TRÉGUIER 9.20.11
LÉZARDRIEUX 9.20.9
PONTRIEUX 9.20.10
TRÉBEURDEN 9.20.15
Bec-Léguer
LANNION (Léguer R) 9.20.16
Locquémeau
Locquirec
Ile de Batz
RG
ROSCOFF 9.20.19
PRIMEL-TRÉGASTEL 9·20·17
Moguériec
Penzé River
MORLAIX 9.20.18

DISTANCE TABLE

Approximate distances in nautical miles are by the most direct route, whilst avoiding dangers and allowing for Traffic Separation Schemes. Places in *italics* are in adjoining areas; places in **bold** are in 9.0.6, Cross-Channel Distances.

1.	***St Quay-Portrieux***	**1**																			
2.	Paimpol	15	**2**																		
3.	Bréhat (Port Clos)	15	8	**3**																	
4.	**Lézardrieux**	21	14	6	**4**																
5.	**Tréguier**	46	29	22	22	**5**															
6.	Perros-Guirec	37	35	28	28	21	**6**														
7.	Ploumanac'h	40	33	27	29	25	6	**7**													
8.	Trébeurden	48	44	38	40	32	17	11	**8**												
9.	**Lannion**	52	48	42	44	33	21	15	6	**9**											
10.	Morlaix	67	64	58	60	46	36	30	23	24	**10**										
11.	**Roscoff**	59	58	52	54	41	28	22	17	19	12	**11**									
12.	**L'Aberwrac'h**	91	88	82	84	72	60	54	49	51	48	32	**12**								
13.	L'Aberbenoit	92	89	83	85	76	61	55	50	52	45	33	7	**13**							
14.	Lampaul	114	110	104	106	98	83	77	72	74	67	55	29	28	**14**						
15.	**Le Conquet**	114	110	104	106	98	83	77	72	71	68	55	29	23	17	**15**					
16.	Brest (marina)	125	119	114	114	107	92	86	83	87	79	67	42	41	31	18	**16**				
17.	Camaret	124	120	114	116	108	93	87	82	81	78	65	39	33	27	13	10	**17**			
18.	Morgat	134	130	124	126	118	103	97	92	91	88	75	49	43	37	20	24	16	**18**		
19.	Douarnenez	139	135	129	131	123	108	102	97	96	93	80	54	48	42	25	29	21	11	**19**	
20.	*Audierne*	144	139	133	135	128	113	108	102	101	98	86	55	53	40	30	34	28	27	30	**20**

20

9.20.3 AREA 20 TIDAL STREAMS

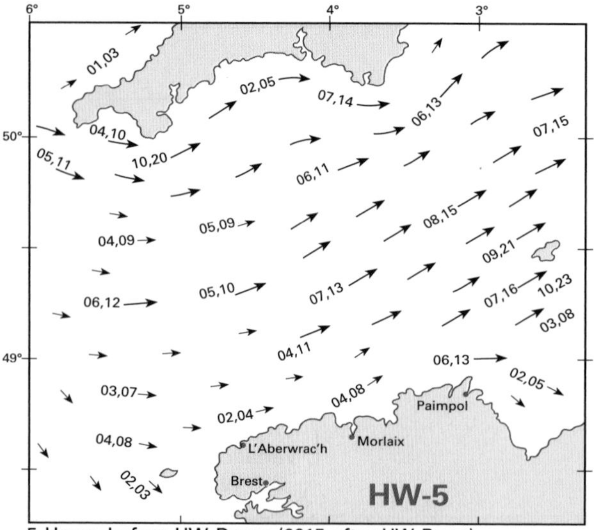
6°
5°
4°
3°
50°
49°
Paimpol
Morlaix
L'Aberwrac'h
Brest
HW-5

5 Hours before HW Dover (0215 after HW Brest)

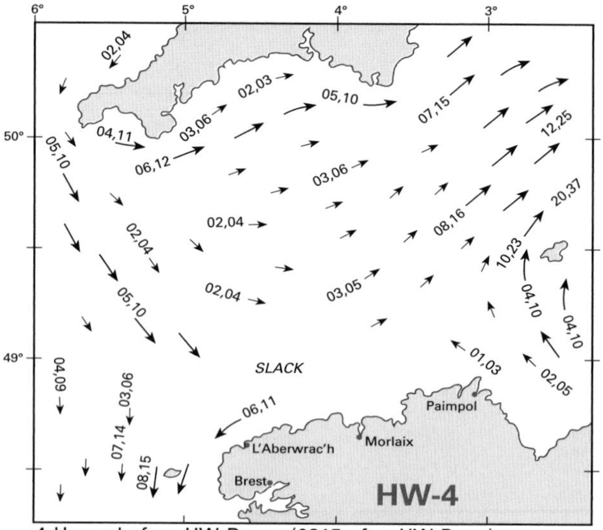
6°
5°
4°
3°
50°
49°
SLACK
Paimpol
Morlaix
L'Aberwrac'h
Brest
HW-4

4 Hours before HW Dover (0315 after HW Brest)

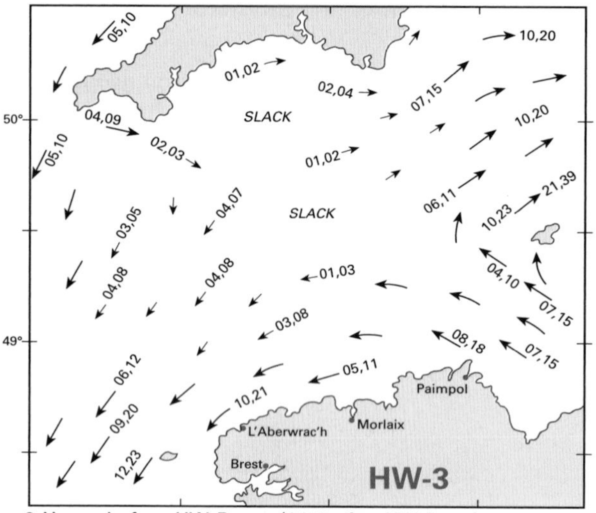
50°
49°
SLACK
SLACK
Paimpol
Morlaix
L'Aberwrac'h
Brest
HW-3

3 Hours before HW Dover (0415 after HW Brest)

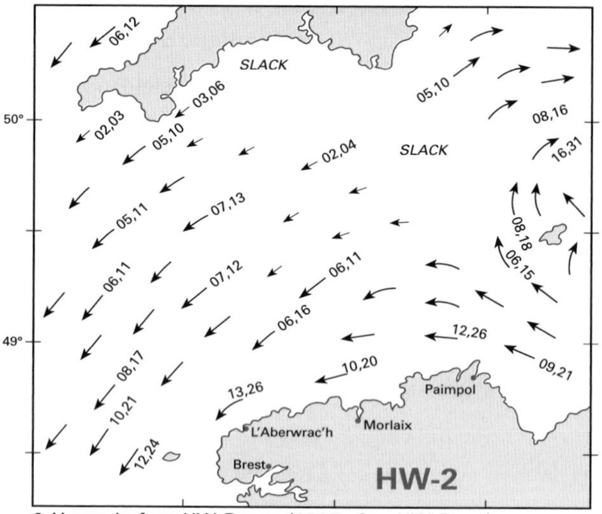
50°
49°
SLACK
SLACK
Paimpol
Morlaix
L'Aberwrac'h
Brest
HW-2

2 Hours before HW Dover (0515 after HW Brest)

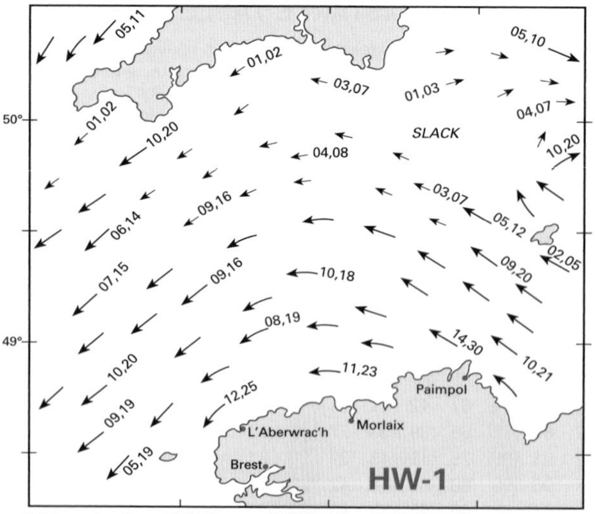
50°
49°
SLACK
Paimpol
Morlaix
L'Aberwrac'h
Brest
HW-1

1 Hour before HW Dover (0615 after HW Brest)

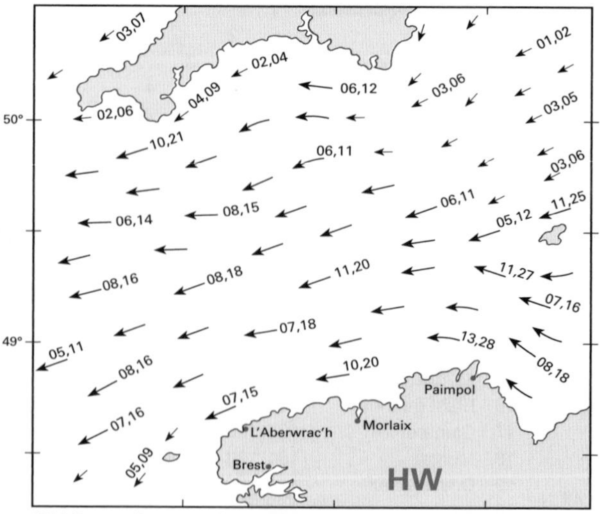
50°
49°
Paimpol
Morlaix
L'Aberwrac'h
Brest
HW

HW Dover (0510 before HW Brest)

Southward 9.21.3 Eastward 9.18.3 Northward 9.1.3

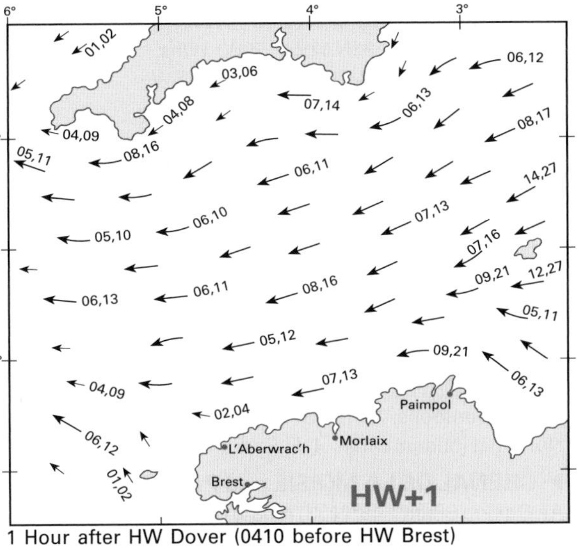

6°
5°
4°
3°
50°
49°
01,02
03,06
06,12
07,14
06,13
04,08
08,17
04,09
05,11
08,16
06,11
14,27
06,10
07,13
05,10
07,16
09,21
12,27
06,13
06,11
08,16
05,11
05,12
09,21
06,13
04,09
07,13
02,04
06,12
01,02
Paimpol
L'Aberwrac'h
Morlaix
Brest
HW+1

1 Hour after HW Dover (0410 before HW Brest)

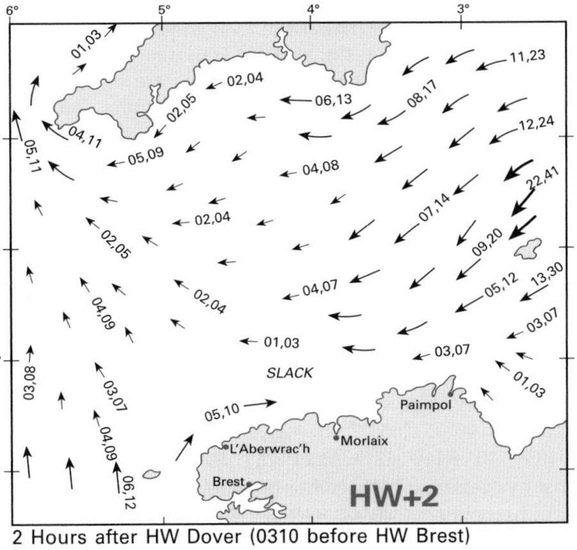

6°
5°
4°
3°
50°
49°
01,03
11,23
02,04
06,13
08,17
02,05
12,24
04,11
05,11
05,09
04,08
22,41
07,14
02,04
09,20
02,05
04,07
05,12
13,30
02,04
03,07
04,09
01,03
03,07
03,08
SLACK
01,03
05,10
03,07
04,09
06,12
Paimpol
L'Aberwrac'h
Morlaix
Brest
HW+2

2 Hours after HW Dover (0310 before HW Brest)

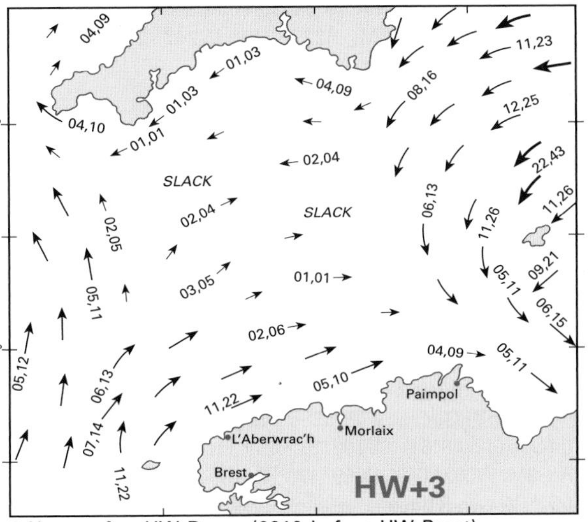

04,09
11,23
01,03
04,09
08,16
01,03
12,25
04,10
01,01
50°
02,04
22,43
SLACK
SLACK
06,13
11,26
02,04
11,26
02,05
05,11
01,01
05,11
09,21
03,05
06,15
02,06
49°
05,12
04,09
05,11
06,13
05,10
11,22
07,14
11,22
Paimpol
L'Aberwrac'h
Morlaix
Brest
HW+3

3 Hours after HW Dover (0210 before HW Brest)

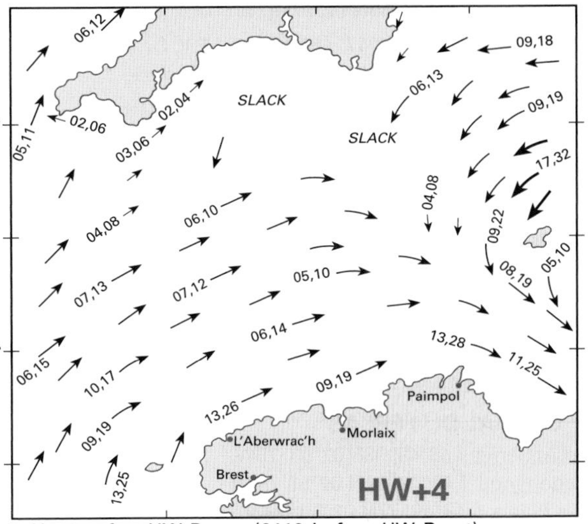

06,12
09,18
SLACK
06,13
09,19
02,06
02,04
SLACK
50°
05,11
03,06
17,32
04,08
06,10
09,22
04,08
05,10
07,13
07,12
05,10
08,19
06,14
49°
06,15
13,28
11,25
10,17
09,19
13,26
09,19
13,25
Paimpol
L'Aberwrac'h
Morlaix
Brest
HW+4

4 Hours after HW Dover (0110 before HW Brest)

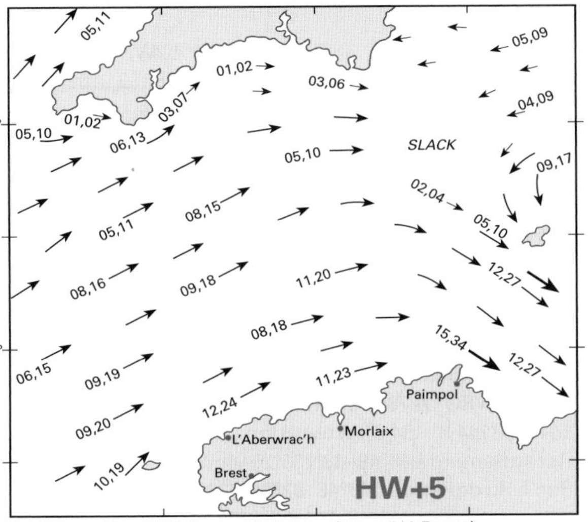

05,11
05,09
01,02
03,06
03,07
04,09
01,02
50°
05,10
06,13
05,10
SLACK
09,17
02,04
05,11
08,15
05,10
08,16
09,18
11,20
12,27
49°
08,18
15,34
06,15
09,19
11,23
12,27
12,24
09,20
10,19
Paimpol
L'Aberwrac'h
Morlaix
Brest
HW+5

5 Hours after HW Dover (0010 before HW Brest)

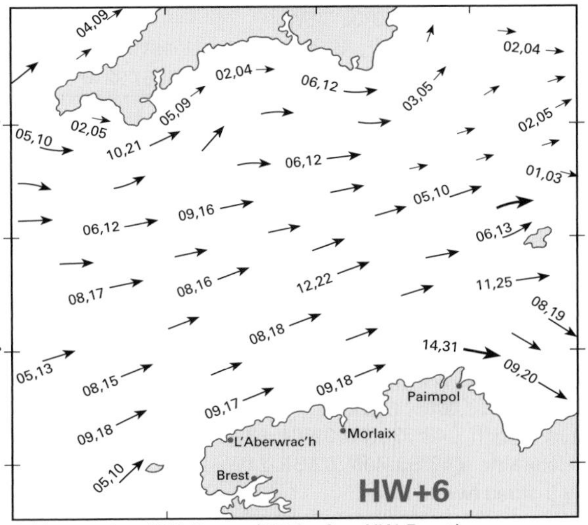

04,09
02,04
02,04
06,12
03,05
05,09
02,05
02,05
50°
05,10
10,21
06,12
01,03
05,10
06,12
09,16
06,13
08,17
08,16
12,22
11,25
08,19
08,18
49°
14,31
05,13
08,15
09,20
09,17
09,18
09,18
05,10
Paimpol
L'Aberwrac'h
Morlaix
Brest
HW+6

6 Hours after HW Dover (0050 after HW Brest)

20

PLOT WAYPOINTS ON YOUR CHART BEFORE USING THEM

9.20.4 LIGHTS, BUOYS AND WAYPOINTS

Blue print = light with a nominal range of 15M or more. CAPITALS = place or feature. *CAPITAL ITALICS* = light-vessel, light float or Lanby. *Italics* = Fog signal. ***Bold italics*** = Racon. Useful waypoints are underlined. Abbreviations are in Chapter 1. Positions are referenced to the WGS 84 datum. Admiralty charts of this area are steadily being referenced to WGS 84.

▶ OFFSHORE MARKS

Roches Douvres ☆ 49°06'·28N 02°48'·89W, Fl 5s 60m **28M**; pink twr on dwelling with G roof; *Siren 60s*.
Barnouic 49°01'·63N 02°48'·42W, VQ (3) 5s 15m 7M.
Roche Gautier 49°00'·38N 02°53'·01W, VQ (9) 10s; *Whis*.

PAIMPOL TO ÎLE DE BRÉHAT
▶ PAIMPOL

Les Calemarguiers 48°46'·98N 02°54'·85W.
L'Ost Pic ☆ 48°46'·76N 02°56'·44W, Oc WR 4s 20m, W11M, R8M; W105°-116°, R116°-221°, W221°-253°, R253°-291°, W291°-329°; obsc by islets near Bréhat when brg < 162°; W twr/turret, R top.
Les Charpentiers 48°47'·89N 02°56'·03W.
La Gueule 48°47'·42N 02°57'·31W.
La Jument 48°47'·34N 02°57'·97W.
Pte de Porz-Don ☆ 48°47'·48N 03°01'·55W, Oc (2) WR 6s 13m **W15M**, R11M; W269°-272°, R272°-279°; W house.
El Bras 48°47'·20N 03°01'·71W, Fl G 2·5s.
48°47'·17N 03°01'·70W, Fl R 2·5s.
Ldg lts 262·2°, both QR 5/12m 7/14M. Front, Kernoa jetty, 48°47'·09N 03°02'·44W; W & R hut. Rear, 360m from front; W pylon, R top; intens 260·2°-264·2°.

▶ CHENAL DU DENOU

Roc'h Denou 48°47'·85N 02°58'·05W, W bcn.
Roc'h Denou Vihan 48°48'·44N 02°57'·95W.
La Petite Moisie 48°48'·59N 02°57'·69W.
Cain Ar Monse 48°50'·16N 02°56'·82W.

▶ CHENAL DU FERLAS

Lel Ar Serive 48°49'·98N 02°58'·76W.
Cadenenou 48°49'·81N 02°59'·06W.
Les Piliers 48°49'·77N 02°59'·99W.
Réceveur Bihan 48°49'·70N 03°01'·96W.
Rompa 48°49'·58N 03°02'·75W.
Kermouster Dir ☆ 271°, 48°49'·54N 03°05'·19W (mouth of R. Trieux), Dir Fl WRG 2s 16m, W 10M, R/G 8M; G267°-270°, W270°-272°, R272°-274°; W col.

▶ ÎLE DE BRÉHAT

La Chambre 48°50'·16N 02°59'·58W.
Men-Joliguet 48°50'·11N 03°00'·20W, Iso WRG 4s 6m W13M, R/G10M; R255°-279°, W279°-283°, G283°-175°.
Chapelle St Michel (conspic, 41m) 48°50'·90N 03°00'·43W.
Amer du Rosedo (obelisk) 48°51'·47N 03°00'·76W.
Rosédo ☆ 48°51'·45N 03°00'·30W, Fl 5s 29m **20M**; W twr.
Le Paon ☆ 48°51'·93N 02°59'·17W, F WRG 22m W11M, R/G8M; W033°-078°, G078°-181°, W181°-196°, R196°-307°, W307°-316°, R316°-348°; Y twr.
Men-Marc'h 48°53'·17N 02°51'·83W.
La Horaine 48°53'·49N 02°55'·24W, Fl (3) 12s 13m 11M; Gy 8-sided twr on B hut.
Nord Horaine 48°54'·43N 02°55'·15W.
Roche Guarine 48°51'·62N 02°57'·63W.

LÉZARDRIEUX TO TRÉGUIER
▶ LE TRIEUX RIVER to LÉZARDRIEUX

Les Echaudés 48°53'·36N 02°57'·34W.
Les Sirlots 48°52'·93N 02°59'·55W; *Whis*.
La Vieille du Tréou 48°51'·99N 03°01'·08W.
Gosrod 48°51'·41N 03°01'·23W.
Men Krenn 48°51'·21N 03°03'·94W, Q (9) 15s 7m 7M.
Ldg lts 224·7°. Front, **La Croix** ☆ 48°50'·22N 03°03'·24W, Dir Oc 4s 15m **19M**; intens 215°-235°; two Gy ○ twrs joined, W on NE side, R tops. Rear **Bodic** ☆, 2·1M from front, Dir Q 55m **22M**; intens 221°-229°; W ho with G gable.
Coatmer ldg lts 218·7°. Front, 48°48'·26N 03°05'·75W, F RG 16m R/G9M; R200°-250°, G250°-053°; W gable. Rear, 660m from front, FR 50m 9M; 197°-242°; W gable.
Les Perdrix 48°47'·74N 03°05'·79W, Fl (2) WG 6s 5m, W6M, G3M; G165°-197°, W197°-202·5°, G202·5°-040°; G twr.
Marina pontoons, 750m SSW, are lit by shore floodlights.
Non-tidal inner marina, Fl G 4s and Fl R 4s.

▶ CHENAL DE LA MOISIE and PASSE DE LA GAINE

An Ogejou Bihan 48°53'·37N 03°01'·92W.
La Moisie 48°53'·82N 03°02'·24W.
Les Héaux de Bréhat ☆ 48°54'·50N 03°05'·18W, Oc (3) WRG 12s 48m, **W15M**, R/G11M; R227°-247°, W247°-270°, G270°-302°, W302°-227°; Gy ○ twr.
Basse des Héaux 48°54'·07N 03°05'·29W.
Pont de la Gaine 48°53'·12N 03°07'·42W.

▶ JAUDY (TRÉGUIER) RIVER

La Jument des Héaux 48°55'·36N 03°08'·05W, VQ; *Bell*.
Grande Passe ldg lts 137°. Front, Port de la Chaine, 48°51'·55N 03°07'·90W, Oc 4s 12m 11M; 042°-232°; W house. Rear, **St Antoine** ☆, 0·75M from front, Dir Oc R 4s 34m **15M**; intens 134°-140°; R & W house. (Both marks are hard to see by day).
Basse Crublent 48°54'·29N 03°11'·18W, Fl (2) R 6s; *Whis*.
Le Corbeau 48°53'·35N 03°10'·28W.
Pierre à l'Anglais 48°53'·21N 03°10'·47W.
Petit Pen ar Guézec 48°52'·52N 03°09'·44W.
La Corne ☆ 48°51'·34N 03°10'·63W, Fl (3) WRG 12s 14m W11M, R/G8M; W052°-059°, R059°-173°, G173°-213°, W213°-220°, R220°-052°; W twr, R base.

TRÉGUIER TO TRÉBEURDEN
▶ PORT BLANC

Le Voleur Dir ☆ 150·4°. 48°50'·20N 03°18'·52W, Fl WRG 4s 17m, W14M, R/G 11M; G140°-148°, W148°-152°, R152°-160°; W twr.
Basse Guazer 48°51'·58N 03°20'·98W; *Whis*.

▶ PERROS-GUIREC

Passe de l'Est, ldg lts 224·5°. Front, **Le Colombier** ☆ 48°47'·87N 03°26'·66W, Dir Oc (4) 12s 28m **15M**; intens 214·5°-234·5°; W house. Rear, **Kerprigent** ☆, Dir Q 79m **21M**; intens 221°-228°; W twr, 1·5M from front.
Pierre à Jean Rouzic 48°49'·54N 03°24'·19W.
Pierre du Chenal 48°49'·28N 03°24'·68W.
Cribineyer 48°49'·10N 03°24'·70W.
Passe de l'Ouest. **Kerjean** ☆ Dir lt 143·6°, 48°47'·78N 03°23'·40W, Oc (2+1) WRG 12s 78m, **W15M**, R/G12M; G133·7°-143·2°, W143·2°-144·8°, R144·8°-154·3°; W twr, B top.
Roche Bernard 48°49'·43N 03°25'·46W.
Roc'h Hu de Perros 48°48'·82N 03°24'·94W.
Jetée du Linkin ☆ 48°48'·20N 03°26'·31W, Fl (2) G 6s 4m 7M; W pile, G top.

La Fronde 48°49'·87N 03°25'·98W.
Bilzic 48°50'·18N 03°25'·75W.
La Horaine 48°49'·88N 03°27'·26W.
Les Couillons de Tomé 48°50'·87N 03°25'·69W.

▶ PLOUMANAC'H

Men-Ruz 48°50'·26N 03°29'·03W, Oc WR 4s 26m W12M, R9M; W226°-242°, R242°-226°; obsc by Pte de Trégastel when brg <080°; partly obsc by Les Sept-Îles 156°-207° and partly by Île Tomé 264°-278°; pink □ twr.

▶ LES SEPT ÎLES

Île-aux-Moines ☆ 48°52'·73N 03°29'·43W, Fl (3) 15s 59m **24M**; obsc by Îliot Rouzic and E end of Île Bono 237°-241°, and in Baie de Lannion when brg <039°; Gy twr and dwelling.
Les Dervinis 48°52'·33N 03°27'·32W.

▶ TRÉGASTEL-PLAGE

Île Dhu 48°50'·37N 03°31'·24W.
Le Taureau 48°50'·40N 03°31'·63W.

Les Triagoz 48°52'·27N 03°38'·80W Oc (2) WR 6s 31m W14M, R11M; W010°-339°, R339°-010°; obsc in places 258°-268° by Les Sept-Îles; Gy □ twr, R lantern.
Bar ar Gall 48°49'·78N 03°36'·23W, VQ (9) 10s.
Le Crapaud 48°46'·67N 03°40'·60W, Q (9) 15s.

▶ TRÉBEURDEN

Ar Gouredec 48°46'·41N 03°36'·60W, VQ (6) + L Fl 10s.
An Ervennou 48°46'·48N 03°35'·99W, Fl (2) R 6s.
Pte de Lan Kerellec 48°46'·74N 03°35'·07W, Iso WRG 4s; W8M, R/G5M; G058°-064°, W064°-069°, R069°-130°.
NW bkwtr 48°46'·34N 03°35'·20W, Fl G 2·5s 8m 2M; IPTS.

TRÉBEURDEN TO ROSCOFF

▶ LÉGUER RIVER

Kinierbel 48°44'·14N 03°35'·19W; *Bell.*
Beg-Léguer 48°44'·31N 03°32'·93W, Oc (4) WRG 12s 60m W12M, R/G9M; G007°-084°, W084°-098°, R098°-129°; west face of W house, R lantern.

▶ LOCQUÉMEAU

Locquémeau 48°43'·86N 03°35'·93W; *Whis.*
Ldg lts 121°. Front, 48°43'·41N 03°34'·46W, FR 21m 6M; 068°-228°; W pylon, R top. Rear, 484m from front, Oc (2+1) R 12s 39m 7M; 016°-232°; W gabled house.

▶ LOCQUIREC

Gouliat, 48°42'·63N 03°38'·86W.

▶ PRIMEL-TRÉGASTEL

Plateau de la Méloine 48°45'·56N 03°50'·69W; *Whis.*
Ldg lts 152°, both FR 35/56m 6M. Front, 48°42'·45N 03°49'·20W; 134°-168°; W □, R stripe, on pylon. Rear, 172m from front; R vert stripe on W wall.
W bkwtr 48°42'·77N 03°49'·51W, Fl G 4s 6m 7M.

▶ BAIE DE MORLAIX

Chenal du Tréguier ldg lts 190·5°. Front, Île Noire 48°40'·34N 03°52'·56W, Oc (2) WRG 6s 15m, W11M, R/G8M; G051°-135°, R135°-211°, W211°-051°; obsc in places; W □ twr, R top.
Common Rear, **La Lande** ☆ 48°38'·19N 03°53'·16W, Fl 5s 85m **23M**; obsc by Pte Annelouesten when brg >204°; W □ twr, B top.
La Pierre Noire 48°42'·55N 03°52'·22W.
La Chambre 48°40'·73N 03°52'·54W.
Grande Chenal ldg lts 176·4°. Front, **Île Louet** ☆ 48°40'·40N 03°53'·34W, Oc (3) WG 12s 17m **W15M**, G10M; W305°-244°, G244°-305°, 139°-223° from offshore, except when obsc by islands; W □ twr, B top. Common Rear, **La Lande** as above.
Pot de Fer 48°44'·24N 03°54'·02W; *Bell.*
Stolvezen 48°42'·64N 03°53'·41W.
Vieille 48°42'·60N 03°54'·11W.
Ricard 48°41'·54N 03°53'·51W.
Corbeau 48°40'·63N 03°53'·33W.
La Noire 48°41'·65N 03°54'·08W (Chenal Ouest de Ricard).

▶ MORLAIX RIVER

Barre de-Flot No. 1 48°40'·18N 03°52'·95W.
No. 2 48°39'·88N 03°52'·53W, Fl R 2s.
No. 3 48°39'·31N 03°52'·22W, Fl G 2s.
No. 4 48°38'·62N 03°51'·63W, Fl R 2s.
No. 5 48°38'·10N 03°51'·24W, Fl G 2s.
No. 7 48°37'·68N 03°51'·03W.
Morlaix lock, 48°35'·36N 03°50'·21W.

▶ BLOSCON/ROSCOFF

Astan 48°44'·91N 03°57'·67W, VQ (3) 5s 9m 6M; *Whis.*
Le Menk 48°43'·28N 03°56'·71W, Q (9) WR 15s 6m W5M, R3M; W160°-188°.
Basse de Bloscon 48°43'·72N 03°57'·55W, VQ.
Bloscon pier 48°43'·21N 03°57'·69W, Fl WG 4s 9m W10M, G7M; W200°-210°, G210°-200°; W twr, G top. In fog Fl 2s.
Fl (2) R 6s, 48°43'·22N 03°57'·91W.
Ar Pourven 48°43'·04N 03°57'·71W, Q.
Ar-Chaden YB. 48°43'·93N 03°58'·26W, Q (6) + L Fl WR 15s 14m, W8M, R6M; R262°-289·5°, W289·5°-293°, R293°-326°, W326°-110°.
Men-Guen-Bras BY. 48°43'·76N 03°58'·07W, Q WRG 14m, W9M, R/G6M; W068°-073°, R073°-197°, W197°-257°, G257°-068°.
Roscoff ldg lts 209°. Front, N môle 48°43'·55N 03°58'·67W, Oc (2+1) G 12s 7m 7M; 078°-318°; W col, G top. **Rear**, 430m from front, Oc (2+1) 12s 24m **15M**; 062°-242°; Gy □ twr, W on NE side.

▶ PENZÉ RIVER

Basse du Cordonnier 48°43'·00N 03°56'·50W.
Guerhéon 48°42'·79N 03°57'·09W.
Trousken 48°42'·26N 03°56'·54W.
Pte Fourche 48°42'·20N 03°56'·67W.
Ar Tourtu 48°42'·05N 03°56'·48W.
An Nehou (Caspari) 48°41'·62N 03°56'·36W.
Le Figuier 48°40'·53N 03°56'·07W.
Pont de la Corde 48°38'·73N 03°57'·00W.

ÎLE DE BATZ TO ÎLE VIERGE

▶ CANAL DE L'ÎLE DE BATZ

Roc'h Zu 48°43'·94N 03°58'·50W.
LW jetty hd 48°43'·92N 03°58'·97W, Q 5m 1M; W & purple col.
Run Oan 48°44'·17N 03°59'·21W.
Perroch 48°44'·10N 03°59'·71W.
Tec'hit Bihan 48°44'·08N 04°00'·79W.
La Croix 48°44'·26N 04°01'·21W.
L'Oignon 48°44'·04N 04°01'·36W.
Basse Plate 48°44'·25N 04°02'·54W.

▶ ÎLE DE BATZ

Lt ho ☆ 48°44'·71N 04°01'·63W, Fl (4) 25s 69m **23M**; Gy twr. Same twr, auxiliary lt, FR 65m 7M; 024°-059°.
Île aux Moutons landing stage S end 48°44'·25N 04°00'·53W, VQ (6)+ L Fl 10s 3m 7M.
Malvoch 48°44'·26N 04°00'·67W.

PLOT WAYPOINTS ON YOUR CHART BEFORE USING THEM

▶ MOGUÉRIEC.

Ldg lts 162°. Front, jetty 48°41'·31N 04°04'·53W, Iso WG 4s 9m W11M, G6M; W158°-166°, G166°-158°; W twr, G top. Rear, 440m from front, FG 22m 7M; 142°-182°; W col, G top.

▶ PONTUSVAL

Pointe de Pontusval 48°41'·42N 04°19'·33W.
Ar Peich 48°40'·90N 04°19'·17W.
An Neudenn 48°40'·66N 04°19'·12W.
Pte de Beg-Pol ☆ 48°40'·67N 04°20'·78W, Oc (3) WR 12s 16m W10M, R7M; W shore-056°, R056°-096°, W096°-shore; W twr, B top, W dwelling. QY and FR lts on towers 2·4M S.

Barr Ar-Skoaz 48°38'·22N 04°30'·08W.
Lizen Ven Ouest 48°40'·47N 04°33'·73W, VQ (9) 10s 8m 5M; *Whis.*
Île-Vierge ☆ 48°38'·33N 04°34'·06W, Fl 5s 77m **27M**; 337°-325°; Gy twr.

ÎLE VIERGE TO CHENAL DU FOUR

▶ L'ABER WRAC'H

Outer ldg lts 100·1°: Front, Île Wrac'h 48°36'·88N 04°34'·56W, QR 20m 7M; W□ twr, Or top, dwelling. Rear, Lanvaon 1·63M from front, Dir Q 55m 12M; intens 090°-110°; W□ twr, Or △ on top.
Trépied 48°37'·29N 04°37'·56W.
Grand Pot de Beurre 48°37'·21N 04°36'·49W.
Petit Pot de Beurre 48°37'·12N 04°36'·23W.
Basse de la Croix 48°36'·92N 04°35'·99W, Fl (3) G 12s.
Breac'h Ver 48°36'·63N 04°35'·38W, Fl G 2·5s 6m 3M; △ on twr.
N bkwtr Dir ☆ 128°; 48°35'·89N 04°33'·82W, Oc (2) WRG 6s 5m W13M, R/G11M; G125·7°-127·2°, W127·2°-128·7°, R128·7°-130·2°.

▶ L'ABER BENOÎT

Petite Fourche 48°36'·98N 04°38'·75W.
Rusven Est 48°36'·30N 04°38'·64W.
Rusven Ouest 48°36'·07N 04°39'·44W; *Bell.*
Basse de Chenal 48°35'·80N 04°38'·53W.
Poul Orvil 48°35'·51N 04°38'·30W.
La Jument 48°35'·10N 04°37'·42W.
Ar Gazel 48°34'·90N 04°37'·28W.
Le Chien 48°34'·67N 04°36'·88W.
Le Relec 48°35'·99N 04°40'·86W.

▶ ROCHES DE PORTSALL/D'ARGENTON

Basse Paupian 48°35'·31N 04°46'·28W.
Corn-Carhai ☆ 48°35'·19N 04°43'·94W, Fl (3) 12s 19m 9M; W 8-sided twr, B top.
Bosven Aval 48°33'·82N 04°44'·28W.
Men ar Pic 48°33'·65N 04°44'·03W.
Portsall ☆ 48°33'·84N 04°42'·27W, Oc (4) WRG 12s 9m W13M, R/G10M; G058°-084°, W084°-088°, R088°-058°; W col, R top.
Le Taureau 48°31'·45N 04°47'·34W.
Argenton, Île Dolvez, front ldg bcn 086° 48°31'·25N 04°46'·24W.

▶ ÎLE D'OUESSANT (USHANT) AND TSS

Ouessant NE 48°59'·51N 05°24'·00W, L Fl 10s; *Whis*; **Racon B, 20M.**
Ouessant SW 48°30'·00N 05°45'·00W, Fl 4s 10m **20M**; **Racon M, 10M.**
Baie du Stiff: Men-Korn 48°27'·96N 05°01'·33W, VQ (3) WR 5s 21m W/R8M; W145°-040°, R040°-145°.
Gorle Vihan 48°28'·32N 05°02'·60W.
Port du Stiff, E môle ☆ 48°28'·12N 05°03'·26W, Dir Q WRG 11m W10M, R/G7M; 251°-G-254°-W-264°-R-267°; W twr, G top.
Le Stiff ☆ 48°28'·47N 05°03'·41W, Fl (2) R 20s 85m **24M**; two adjoining W twrs. Radar twr 340m NE, Q (day); FR (night).
Créac'h ☆ 48°27'·55N 05°07'·76W, Fl (2) 10s 70m **32M**; obsc 247°-255°; W twr, B bands; *Horn (2) 120s*; **Racon C, 20M, 030°-248°**.
Nividic ☆ 48°26'·74N 05°09'·07W, VQ (9) 10s 28m 10M; 290°-225°; Gy 8-sided twr. Helicopter platform.
La Jument ☆ 48°25'·34N 05°08'·05W, Fl (3) R 15s 36m **22M**; 241°-199°; Gy 8-sided twr, R top; *Horn (3) 60s.*
Men ar Froud 48°26'·61N 05°03'·69W.

▶ ÎLE MOLÈNE and ARCHIPELAGO

Kéréon ☆ 48°26'·24N 05°01'·55W, Oc (2+1) WR 24s 38m **W17M,** R7M; W019°-248°, R248°-019°; Gy twr; *Horn (2+1) 120s.*

Les Trois-Pierres ☆ 48°24'·70N 04°56'·85W, Iso WRG 4s 15m W9M, R/G6M; G070°-147°, W147°-185°, R185°-191°, G191°-197°, W197°-213°, R213°-070°; W col.
Roc'h Goulin 48°24'·53N 04°57'·03W, VQ (9) 10s.
Molène, Old môle Dir ☆ 191°. 48°23'·85N 04°57'·29W, Fl (3) WRG 12s 6m W9M, R/G7M; G183°-190°, W190°-192°, R192°-203°.
Same structure: Chenal des Laz , Dir ☆ 261°: Fl (2) WRG 6s 9m W9M, R/G7M ; G252·5°-259·5°, W259·5°-262·5°, R262·5°-269·5°.

Pierres-Vertes 48°22'·19N 05°04'·77W, VQ (9) 10s 9m 5M; *Whis.*
Pierres Noires 48°18'·47N 04°58'·16W; *Bell.*
Les Pierres Noires ☆ 48°18'·67N 04°54'·88W, Fl R 5s 27m **19M**; W twr, R top; *Horn (2) 60s.*

CHENAL DU FOUR and ADJACENT COAST

Le Four ☆ 48°31'·38N 04°48'·32W, Fl (5) 15s 28m **18M**; Gy ○ twr; *Horn (3+2) 60s.*
Ldg lts 158·5°. Front, **Kermorvan** ☆ 48°21'·72N 04°47'·42W, Fl 5s 20m **22M**; obsc'd by Pte de St Mathieu when brg <341°; W□ twr; Horn 60s.
Rear, **Pte de St Mathieu** ☆ 48°19'·79N 04°46'·27W, Fl 15s 56m **29M**; W twr, R top. Same twr: Dir F 54m **28M**; intens 157·5°-159·5°.
Separate W twr, brg 291°/54m from Pte de St Mathieu: Q WRG 26m, W14M, R/G11M; G085°-107°, W107°-116°, R116°-134°.
La Valbelle 48°26'·43N 04°50'·04W, Fl (2) R 6s 8m 5M; *Whis.*
Les Plâtresses 48°26'·28N 04°50'·92W, Fl RG 4s 17m 6M; R343°-153°, G153°-333°, (not visible 333°-343°); W twr.
Plâtresses SE 48°25'·96N 04°50'·52W.
Le Tendoc 48°25'·67N 04°49'·44W.
Saint Paul 48°24'·82N 04°49'·16W, Oc (2) R 6s.
Pte de Corsen ☆ 48°24'·89N 04°47'·63W, Dir Q WRG 33m W12M, R/G8M; R008°-012°, W012°-015° ldg sector, G015°-021°; W hut.
Taboga 48°23'·77N 04°48'·08W.
Rouget 48°22'·05N 04°48'·88W, Fl G 4s; *Whis.*
Grande Vinotière 48°21'·93N 04°48'·43W, L Fl R 10s 15m 5M; R 8-sided twr.
Lochrist ☆, see below (Chenal de la Helle).
Tournant et Lochrist 48°20'·64N 04°48'·12W, Iso R 4s.
Ar Christian Braz 48°20'·67N 04°50'·15W.
Ldg line 325°: Front, La Faix (below); rear, Grand Courleau.
Ldg lts 007°. Front, **Kermorvan** ☆ see above. Rear, **Trézien** ☆ 48°25'·41N 04°46'·74W, Dir Oc (2) 6s 84m **20M**; intens 003°-011°; Gy twr, W on S side.
Les Vieux-Moines 48°19'·33N 04°46'·63W, Fl R 4s 16m 5M; 280°-133°; R 8-sided twr.
La Fourmi 48°19'·25N 04°47'·97W.

▶ L'ABER-ILDUT

L'Aber-Ildut ☆ 48°28'·26N 04°45'·57W, Dir Oc (2) WR 6s 12m **W25M, R20M**; W081°-085°, R085°-087°; W bldgs.

▶ LE CONQUET

Môle Sainte Barbe ☆ 48°21'·58N 04°46'·99W, Oc G 4s 5m 6M.
Les Renards 48°21'·00N 04°47'·50W.

CHENAL DE LA HELLE

Ldg lts 137·9°. Front, **Kermorvan** ☆ see above. Rear, **Lochrist** ☆ 48°20'·55N 04°45'·82W, Dir Oc (3) 12s 49m **22M**; intens 135°-140°; W 8-sided twr, R top.
Luronne 48°26'·61N 04°53'·79W; *Bell.*
Ldg lts 293·5° (to join Ch du Four S of St Paul). Front, Le Faix 48°25'·73N 04°53'·92W, VQ 16m 8M. Rear, **Le Stiff** ☆ (above).
Optional ldg line 142·5°, day only (to join Ch du Four SE of St Pierre). Front, **Kermorvan** ☆ (see above). Rear, two W bcns (Pignons de Kéravel, 45m) 48°20'·17N 04°45'·44W.
Pourceaux 48°24'·01N 04°51'·34W, Q.
Saint-Pierre 48°23'·09N 04°49'·10W.

BREST AND APPROACHES

Basse Royale 48°17'·45N 04°49'·62W, Q (6) + L Fl 15s.
Vandrée 48°15'·20N 04°48'·25W, VQ (9) 10s; *Whis.*
La Parquette 48°15'·89N 04°44'·30W, Fl RG 4s 17m R6M, G6M; W 8-sided twr, B diagonal stripes; R244°-285°, G285°-244°.
Le Coq 48°19'·08N 04°43'·98W.
Charles Martel 48°18'·85N 04°42'·19W, Fl (4) R; *Whis.*
Trépied 48°16'·73N 04°41'·48W.
Pte du Toulinguet ☆ 48°16'·82N 04°37'·73W, Oc (3) WR 12s 49m **W15M**, R11M; W shore-028°, R028°-090°, W090°-shore; W□twr.
Swansea Vale 48°18'·27N 04°38'·85W, Fl (2) 6s; *Whis.*

▶ GOULET DE BREST

Anse de Bertheaume 48°20'·76N 04°41'·98W.
Le Chat 48°20'·37N 04°41'·65W.
Pen-Hir 48°20'·02N 04°39'·53W.
Pte du Petit-Minou ☆ 48°20'·19N 04°36'·87W, Fl (2) WR 6s 32m **W19M, R15M**; R shore-252°, W252°-260°, R260°-307°, W 307°-015° (unintens), W015°-065·5°, W070·5°-shore; Gy twr, R top.
Ldg lts 068°, both Dir Q 30/56m **23/22M. Front** (same structure), intens 067·3°-068·8°. **Rear, Pte du Portzic** ☆, intens 065°-071°.
Fillettes 48°19'·75N 04°35'·67W, VQ (9); *Whis.*
Kerviniou 48°19'·77N 04°35'·25W, Fl (2) R 6s.
Basse Goudron 48°20'·02N 04°34'·87W, QR.
Roche Mengam 48°20'·32N 04°34'·57W, Fl (3) WR 12s 10m W11M, R8M; R034°-054°, W054°-034°; R twr, B bands.
Pte du Portzic ☆ 48°21'·49N 04°32'·06W, Oc (2) WR 12s 56m **W19M, R15M**; R219°-259°, W259°-338°, R338°-000°, W000°-065·5°, W070·5°-219°; Gy twr. (See also Dir Q, rear ldg lt above).
Same structure, Dir Q (6) + L Fl 15s 54m **23M**; intens 045°-050°.

▶ BREST

Pénoupèle 48°21'·45N 04°30'·53W, Fl (3) R 12s.
Port Militaire/Rade Abri: Entry normally prohibited.
S jetée ☆ 48°22'·10N 04°29'·46W, QR 10m 5M; 094°-048°; W/R twr.
E jetée ☆ 48°22'·15N 04°29'·22W, QG 10m 7M; 299°-163°; W/G twr.
Ldg lts 344°. Front, 48°22'·79N 04°29'·63W, VQ WRG 24m W10M, R/G5M; G 334°-342°, W342°-346°, R346°-024°. Rear, 115m from front, Dir VQ 32m 10M; intens 342°-346°.
Port de Commerce, E ent: N jetée ☆ 48°22'·76N 04°28'·53W, Oc (2) G 6s 8m 7M; W/G pylon. S jeteé ☆ 48°22'·69N 04°28'·48W, Oc (2) R 6s 8m 5M; 018°-301°; W pylon, R top.
R2 48°22'·13N 04°28'·74W, Fl (2) R 6s.
R1 48°21'·83N 04°28'·27W, Fl G 4s.
R4 48°22'·22N 04°28'·06W, L Fl R 10s.
R3 48°22'·49N 04°28'·07W, Q (6) + L Fl 15s.
Water intake 48°22'·69N 04°26'·54W, Fl (4) R 15s 2M.

▶ LE MOULIN BLANC MARINA

Moulin Blanc 48°22'·79N 04°25'·99W, Fl (3) R 12s.
MB 1 48°23'·22N 04°25'·76W, Fl G 2s.
MB 2 48°23'·22N 04°25'·83W, Fl R 2s.
MB 3 wavebreak, E side ☆ 48°23'·49N 04°25'·72W, Fl G 2s 2m 1M.
MB 4 bkwtr, W side ☆ 48°23'·48N 04°25'·80W, Fl R 2s 2m 1M.
MBA 48°23'·53N 04°25'·78W, Q(3) 10s 3m 2M; on pontoon.

▶ RADE DE BREST

Basse du Renard 48°19'·76N 04°29'·07W, VQ (9) 10s.
Lanvéoc No 1 48°19'·07N 04°28'·66W, Fl G 4s.

▶ CAMARET

N môle ☆ 48°16'·85N 04°35'·32W, Iso WG 4s 7m W12M, G9M; W135°-182°, G182°-027°; W pylon, G top.
S môle ☆ 48°16'·63N 04°35'·33W, Fl (2) R 6s 9m 5M; R pylon.
48°17'·13N 04°34'·84W, Q. 48°16'·90N 04°34'·77W, VQ (9) 10s. 48°17'·07N 04°34'·68W. 48°16'·81N 04°34'·75W.

POINTE DU TOULINGUET TO RAZ DE SEIN

Pointe du Toulinguet ☆ see Brest approaches, above.
Mendufa 48°16'·05N 04°39'·44W.
Basse du Lis 48°12'·99N 04°44'·53W, Q (6) + L Fl 15s 9m 6M; *Whis.*
Le Chevreau 48°13'·38N 04°36'·82W.
Le Chevreau 48°13'·30N 04°36'·99W.
Le Bouc 48°11'·51N 04°37'·38W, Q (9) 15s; *Bell.*
Basse Vieille 48°08'·23N 04°35'·76W, Fl (2) 6s 8m 7M; *Whis.*

▶ MORGAT

Pointe de Morgat ☆ 48°13'·17N 04°29'·81W, Oc (4) WRG 12s 77m **W15M**, R11M, G10M; W shore-281°, G281°-301°, W301°-021°, R021°-043°; W□twr, R top, W dwelling.
48°13'·57N 04°29'·67W, Fl R 4s.
Marina entry via wavebreaks, marked by Fl G 4s and Fl R 4s.
Inner mole ☆ 48°13'·51N 04°29'·97W, Oc (2) WR 6s 8m W9M, R6M; W007°-257°, R257°-007°; W&R twr.

▶ DOUARNENEZ TO RAZ DE SEIN

Port Rhu ☆, Dir 157°, 48°05'·40N 04°19'·80W, Fl (5) WRG 20s 16m, W5M, R/G4M; G154°-156°, W156°-158°, R158°-160°; lt on bridge.
Île Tristan ☆ 48°06'·14N 04°20'·25W, Oc (3) WR 12s 35m, W13M, R10M; shore-W-138°-R-153°-W-shore; Gy twr, W band, B top.
Pte Biron ☆ 48°06'·09N 04°20'·47W, QG 7m 6M; W col, G top.
Port Rhu ent, Fl G 5s and Fl R5s.
Bassin Nord, N mole ☆ 48°05'·96N 04°19'·28W, Iso G 4s 9m 4M; W & G pylon.
S mole ☆ 48°05'·91N 04°19'·27W, Oc (2) R 6s 6m 6M; W&R pylon.
Port de Rosmeur ☆ 48°05'·79N 04°19'·23W, Oc G 4s 6m 6M; 170°-097°; W pylon, G top.

Pointe du Millier ☆ 48°05'·92N 04°27'·95W, Oc (2) WRG 6s 34m **W16M**, R12M, G11M; G080°-087°, W087°-113°, R113°-120°, W120°-129°, G129°-148°, W148°-251°, R251°-258°; W house.
Basse Jaune 48°04'·67N 04°42'·47W.
Tévennec ☆ 48°04'·28N 04°47'·72W, Q WR 28m W9M, R6M; W090°-345°, R345°-090°; W □ twr and dwelling. Same twr, Dir ☆ 328°, Fl 4s 24m 12M; intens 324°-332°.

20

9.20.5 PASSAGE INFORMATION

NORTH BRITTANY (charts *2668, 2644,* 2643) Refer to: *North Brittany and Channel Islands Cruising Companion* (Nautical Data Ltd/Cumberlidge); *The Channel Cruising Companion* (Nautical Data Ltd/Featherstone & Aslett); Admiralty *Channel Pilot* (NP 27).

This ever-popular cruising ground is not one to trifle with, but conversely it is rewarding to find one's way into a remote anchorage or small fishing harbour. Here the unique character and appeal of N Brittany is all around you.

Good landfall marks must be carefully identified, as a back-up to GPS, before closing the rock-strewn coast. In rough weather, low visibility (fog and summer haze are frequent) or if uncertain of position, it may be prudent to lie off and wait for conditions to improve; there are few safe havens. Closer inshore the tidal streams and currents vary, and overfalls are to be avoided. As ever, thorough careful planning is the key to safe pilotage.

In the E of the area the outer approaches to Paimpol, Île de Bréhat, Lézardrieux and Tréguier may be complicated by strong tidal streams. At times there may be a proliferation of landmarks which must be selectively identified. Concentrate on those which affect your pilotage and discard those which are non-essential and may even distract you from the task.

Once W of Roscoff there are few safe hbrs and anchorages until L'Aberwrac'h where many British yachts tend to pause and await good conditions for negotiating the Chenal du Four. This is rarely as difficult as it is imagined to be. The Atlantic swell can be a new experience for some, but in moderate winds it is rarely a hazard. It can however much reduce the range at which objects, especially floating marks, are seen.

PAIMPOL TO PLOUMANAC'H (AC 3670, 3673, 3672) In the offing, 11-18M NNE of Île de Bréhat and on a direct track from/to Guernsey, are Plateau de Barnouic (lit) and Plateau des Roches Douvres (lt ho, fog sig), both with drying and submerged rks, to be given a wide berth particularly in poor vis.

Approaching L'Ost-Pic from the SE, keep to seaward of the three ECM marks E of it or enter B de Paimpol (9.20.7) from a point about 1M E of the most N'ly ECM (Les Charpentiers); but it is safe to pass about 300m E of L'Ost Pic in moderate weather. The E-W Ferlas chan (AC 3673) passes S of Île de Bréhat (9.20.8), and is useful if entering/leaving R. Trieux from/to the E. It is easiest to beacon-hop past 5 SCM bcns and 1 IDM bcn which mark the N side of the channel; the S side is less well marked.

For the many yachts approaching from Guernsey, Les Héaux-de-Bréhat lt ho is a conspic landfall day/night for either Tréguier or Lézardrieux. Closer in or from the E, La Horaine (lt bn) is a better landfall for the latter. It marks the Plateaux de la Horaine and des Échaudés and other rks to the SE. In poor visibility it should be closed with caution and left at least 7ca to the SE, as the flood stream sets strongly onto it. The Grand Chenal 224·7° is the main, lit chan into the R. de Trieux for Lézardrieux (9.20.9) and up-river to Pontrieux (9.20.10). From NW the unlit Chenal de La Moisie leads 159° to join the Grand Chenal off Ile de Bréhat (9.20.8).

Between Lézardrieux and Tréguier (9.20.11) the Passe de la Gaine 241·5° is a useful inshore route, avoiding a detour round Les Héaux. It is unlit and needs good vis, but if taken at above half tide, presents no problem in fair weather. The Grande Passe 137·3° into R. de Tréguier is well lit, but ldg marks are hard to see by day. The NE Passage should be used with caution.

Between Basse Crublent lt buoy and Port Blanc unmarked rks extend 2M offshore. Port Blanc (9.20.12 & AC 3672) can be difficult to identify by day. Perros-Guirec (9.20.13) is approached either side of Ile Tomé from NE or NW via well lit/marked chans. Ploumanac'h (9.20.14) can only be entered by day. It boasts some of the most spectacular pink granite along the N Brittany coast.

LES SEPT ÎLES TO BAIE DE MORLAIX (AC 3669). Les Sept Îles (9.20.13 and AC 3670) consist of five main islands and several islets, through which the tide runs strongly. Île aux Moines is lit, and all the islands are bird sanctuaries. Further W, Plateau des Triagoz has offlying dangers WSW and NE of the lt, where the sea breaks heavily. ▶*Here the stream turns ENE at HW Brest – 0325, and WSW at HW Brest +0245, sp rates both 3·8kn.*◀

Trégastel-Plage (9.20.14) is a small anchorage W of Ploumanac'h. To the SW the coast as far as Trébeurden (9.20.15) is not easily approached due to many offlying rks. The radome NE of Trébeurden is conspic. Further S in the B de Lannion is Locquémeau and anchs near the mouth of the drying R. Léguer up to Lannion (9.20.16). Locquirec is a pleasant drying hbr 3·5M SW of Locquemeau. Primel-Trégastel (9.20.17), at the E ent to Baie de Morlaix, is a useful inlet to await the tide up to Morlaix. To the N Plateau de la Méloine dries.

The B de Morlaix (9.20.18 and AC 2745) is bestrewn with drying rks and shoals, all marked. Careful pilotage and adequate visibility are needed to negotiate any of the chans which are narrow in parts. Chenal de Tréguier 190·5° and the Grand Chenal 176·4° are both lit. The former should only be used HW ±3 due to shoals at the S end. Grand Chenal passes close E of Île Ricard with Île Louet and La Lande lights in transit; abeam Calhic bn tr alter to port to pass between Château du Taureau (conspic) and Île Louet. Continue SSE and up-river to lock into Morlaix marina in complete shelter. The anchorage NE of Carantec is reached from Chenal Ouest de Ricard.

ÎLE DE BATZ TO LE FOUR (charts 3669, 3668). ▶*N of Île de Batz the E-going stream begins at HW Brest – 0435, and the W-going stream at HW Brest +0105, sp rates 3·8kn.*◀ Approaching Roscoff (9.20.19) from NE, leave Astan ECM lt buoy to stbd steering with Men Guen Bras lt bcn in transit 213° with Chapelle St Barbe, to round Ar Chaden lt bcn for Roscoff hbr (dries).

Canal de L'Île de Batz is a useful short cut between the island and the mainland in daylight and above half tide. From near Ar Chaden steer 275° for the Q bn at end of the conspic LW ferry pier. Pass 30m N of this bn, then alter to 300° for Run Oan SCM. Thence steer 283°, leaving Perroch NCM bcn twr 100m to port. When clear of this rky, drying shoal alter to 270°, leaving Porz Kernok hbr bkwtrs well to stbd and aiming midway between L'Oignon NCM and La Croix SCM bcns. With these abeam steer 281° for Basse Plate NCM bn; thence West into open waters.

Proceeding W from Île de Batz toward Le Four there are many off-lying dangers, in places 3M offshore. Swell may break on shoals even further to seaward. The tide runs strongly, and in poor vis or bad weather it is a coast to avoid. But in good conditions this is an admirable cruising ground with delightful hbrs such as Moguériec and Brignogan (9.20.19), L'Aberwrac'h (9.20.20), L'Aberbenoit (9.20.21), Portsall and Argenton (9.20.22). N of L'Aberwrac'h is Île Vierge lt ho, reputedly the tallest in the world, and a conspic landmark. ▶*Off Le Libenter, at N side of L'Aberwrac'h ent, the E-going stream starts at HW Brest – 0500, sp rate 3·8kn, and the W-going stream at HW Brest + 018.*◀ L'Aberwrac'h is accessible at all tides and makes a useful staging post to catch the tide S through Chenal du Four.

W of L'Aberwrac'h an inshore chan leads past Portsall to Le Four lt ho. This is a demanding short-cut, which must only be used by day and in good visibility as the marks are distant and hard to identify with certainty. It saves only 1M against the outer route via Basse Paupian WCM buoy. AC 1432 or SHOM 7094 and full directions, as in the RCC guide *North Brittany & the Channel Islands,* are needed.

OUESSANT (USHANT) (chart 2694) Île d'Ouessant (9.20.25) lies 10M off NW Brittany. Besides being an important landfall, Ouessant in thick weather is an unhealthy area, and it is prudent to stay in harbour until the vis improves. But in fair weather and reasonable visibility the pilotage in the chans between it and the mainland is not too demanding. They are well buoyed and marked (see 9.20.24), but the tide runs hard in places, causing overfalls when against wind >Force 5. ▶*Tidal streams are strong around the island, and in the chans between it and mainland. Off Pte de Créac'h (lt, fog sig) the stream turns NNE at HW Brest – 0550, and SSW at HW Brest + 0045, sp rate 5·5kn.*◀

It is a rky island, with dangers extending 5ca to NE, 7½ca to SE, 1·5M to SW and 1M to NW; here Chaussée de Keller is a dangerous chain of unmarked drying and submerged rks running 1M W of Île de Keller and into the ITZ. There are anchorages and moorings at Lampaul and B du Stiff, the former exposed to the SW and the latter to the NE. There are five lt ho's around the island.

The routes outside Ouessant TSS or via the ITZ have little to commend them. Unless bound to/from Spain/Portugal they add much to the distance and are exposed to sea, swell and shipping. Yachts would usually pass Ouessant via the inshore chans, ie: The Chenal du Four, most direct and popular; Chenal de la Helle, an alternative to N part of Chenal du Four (also gives access to Île Moléne), not so direct but better in bad weather. Passage du Fromveur, SE of Ouessant, is easiest but longer and can become extremely rough; tidal streams may exceed 8kn.

CHENAL DU FOUR (9.20.24 and AC 3345, 2694) ▶*It is imperative to work the tides to best advantage through this passage: 1M W of Le Four the S-going stream begins at HW Brest + 0130; the N-going stream at HW Brest – 0545, sp rates 3·6kn. Further S, off Pte de Corsen, the stream is weaker, max 2·3kn at sp. The tide runs strongest at S end of Chenal du Four, off Le Conquet. Here the S-going stream starts at HW Brest + 0015, max 5kn; the N-going stream begins at HW Brest – 0550, 5·2kn max at sp. Wind-over-tide effects may raise considerable short, steep seas.*◀ If the tides are worked to advantage it is perfectly possible to take both the Chenal du Four and Raz de Sein in one hop from L'Aberwrac'h to Audierne or vice versa.

Yachts are less rigidly tied to transits/dir lts than large ships and, especially in rough conditions, may have difficulty identifying some of the marks by day or night. On the mainland coast, within 6M of each other, 6 major lights either form transits or are directional.

However a simple buoy-hopping sequence (next para) can be used day or night, assuming you have confidence in tracking accurately on GPS. The word 'track', as opposed to heading or steering, implies that the rhumb-line track is maintained with little or no lateral deviation. The 3 legs are short and swift given the higher than average Speed over the Ground (SOG). Other buoys in between waypoints enable you to verify your progress.

Leg 1: From ⊕ 48°31'·5N 04°49'·0W (5ca W of Le Four), track 188°/5M (leaving Les Liniou reef well to port) to Valbelle PHM lt buoy.
Leg 2: Thence track 168°/4·6M to abeam Grande Vinotière lt bn.
Leg 3: Finally track 172°/2·7M to La Fourmi SHM lt buoy (for Raz de Sein), or Leg 3A: 156°/2·9M to Vieux-Moines lt bcn (for Brest/Camaret).

The traditional transit lines (should you prefer them) are: From a position approx 3M SW of Le Four lt ho pick up St Mathieu directional lt and Kermorvan ≠ 158·5°; maintain this transit for 7·3M until Pte de Corsen directional lt bears 012° (in its white sector and on your port quarter). Thence track 192°, passing between Rouget SHM lt buoy and Grande Vinotière lt bn. 1M further south, pick up the 325·5° astern transit of Grand Courleau unlit NCM bcn twr ≠ Le Faix NCM lt bcn twr. Track 145·5° to pass midway between La Fourmi SHM lt buoy and Vieux-Moines lt bcn twr.

Homeward-bound, or along the N coast of France, enter the S end of Chenal du Four at LW Brest; a fair tide can then be carried through the chan and NE past Île Vierge. The reverse sequence of pilotage is followed.

L'Aberildut (9.20.22), 3·5M SSE of Le Four lt ho, and Le Conquet (9.20.23), 3ca SE of Pte de Kermorvan, are the only ports on the mainland coast of the Chenal du Four; but in offshore winds there are anchorages in Anse de Porsmoguer and Anse des Blancs-Sablons, both between Corsen and Kermorvan.

CHENAL DE LA HELLE (9.20.24 and AC 3345, 2694). ▶*At N end of Chenal de la Helle the ENE stream starts at HW Brest – 0520 (sp rate 2·8kn), and the SW stream at HW Brest – 0045 (sp rate 3·8kn).*◀ The Chenal de la Helle converges at a 20° angle with the Chenal du Four and the two meet WSW of Pte de Corsen or just N of Grande Vinotière, depending on which of two track variants you take. As with the Chenal du Four the charts show 3 or 4 transits, mostly based on distant marks.

A simple GPS-based buoy-hopping sequence is as follows: From close abeam Luronne WCM buoy track 137°/4·7M to St Pierre SHM buoy, passing Le Faix lt twr and Le Pourceau NCM lt buoy. Thence 169°/3·9M to La Fourmi SHM buoy, passing Rouget SHM lt buoy, Grande Vinotière and Tournant et Lochrist PHM lt buoy en route.

The more traditional transits are as follows: From the N, steer SW from Le Four towards Ile de Molène lt; close to Luronne unlit WCM buoy pick up the 138° transit [Pte de Kermorvan ≠ Lochrist]. Maintain this transit until Le Faix lt bn and Le Stiff lt ho are ≠ 293° astern; track 113° for 8ca until Pte de Kermorvan is ≠ 2 W bns (Pignons de Kéravel) at 142°. This transit avoids Basse St Pierre (4·7m) and intercepts the Ch du Four 7ca N of Grande Vinotière. Alternatively maintain the 293° astern transit until intercepting the Ch du Four transit [St Mathieu ≠ Kermorvan ldg lts 158·5°].

APPROACHES TO BREST (charts 2350, 3427, 3428). The outer approaches lie between Chaussée des Pierres Noires and Pte St Mathieu to the N and Pte du Toulinguet to the S. From the W maintain the 068° transit of Petit-Minou and Portzic ldg lts on the N shore. From the S steer NNE toward Pte du Petit-Minou to pick up the transit, but beware rks 7M W and SW of Pte du Toulinguet. Yachts <25m LOA are exempt from VTS, but should monitor VHF Ch 08 or 16.

Abeam Petit-Minou lt ho the Goulet (Straits) de Brest narrows to 1M; drying rks almost in mid-stream are marked by a WCM lt buoy and 2 PHM lt buoys. A course of 075° through the Passe Nord leaves Roc Mengam lt bn 2ca to stbd. ▶*Tidal streams reach 4·5kn in the Goulet. In Passe Sud there is a useful back-eddy close inshore which runs ENE during the ebb.*◀ Once beyond Pte du Portzic a buoyed chan leads ENE past the naval and commercial hbrs to the Moulin Blanc marina (9.20.28). The Rade de Brest (9.20.27 and chart 3429) opens to the S and E. The waters around Île Longue (a peninsula) are restricted by DG ranges, no-anchoring and no-entry areas, but there is room to anchor off Roscanvel in the lee of the Quélern peninsula. Further east the beautiful River Aulne can be explored well inland to Port Launay and as far as Chateaulin.

20

L'IROISE/BAIE DE DOUARNENEZ (charts 2350, 2349). L'Iroise is the sea area SW of Chaussée des Pierres Noires and N of Chaussée de Sein. On the NE side of L'Iroise (chart 3427) a chain of rks extends 7M W from Pte du Toulinguet. There are several chans through these rks, of which the simplest for Brest and Camaret (9.20.29) is the 3ca wide Chenal du Toulinguet which runs NNW between La Louve WCM bcn twr (1ca W of Pte du Toulinguet) on E side and Le Pohen rk on the W side. ▶*Here the N-going stream begins at HW Brest – 0550, and the S-going at HW Brest + 0015, sp rates 2·75kn.*◀

3·5M SSE of Pte du Toulinguet is Le Chevreau (WCM bcn; dries 5·9m) with La Chèvre 5ca NE of it. 1·9M S of Le Chevreau is Le Bouc (WCM lt buoy; dries 7·4m). 5·7M SW of Pte du Toulinguet lies Basse du Lis, rky shoals with depth of 2·7m and WCM lt buoy, and the last of a string of underwater rocks extending seaward from Les Tas de Pois (Pile of Peas). Close E of Les Tas de Pois, the Anse de Pen-Hir is a useful anch in NE'lies.

The B de Douarnenez is entered between C. de la Chèvre and Pte du Van. Off C. de la Chèvre various dangers, on which the sea breaks, extend SW for 2·25M to Basse Vieille (dries 0·8m), lt buoy. Basse Laye (dries 0·7m) is unmarked 7ca SSE of the CG stn on C. de la Chèvre and a hazard if rounding the headland close inshore. Morgat (9.20.30) lies 4M NNE of C. de la Chèvre. Beware group of drying rks, including La Pierre-Profonde and Le Taureau close SSW of Les Verrès (12m high rk), which lies nearly 2·5M ESE of Morgat and in the green sector of Pte de Morgat lt.

Approaching Douarnenez (9.20.31) beware Basse Veur and Basse Neuve (depth 2·2m). The S shore of the B is clear of dangers more than 2ca offshore, except for Duellou Rk (7m high) 5ca offshore, and other rks 1M eastward. Further W beware Basse Jaune, an isolated rk (dries 1·4m; IDM buoy) about 1M N of Pte du Van. This rocky headland with offliers stands 2.25M NE of Pte du Raz and La Vieille lt twr and marks the NE corner of the Raz de Sein (9.21.7).

9.20.6 Special Notes for France: See 9.17.6.

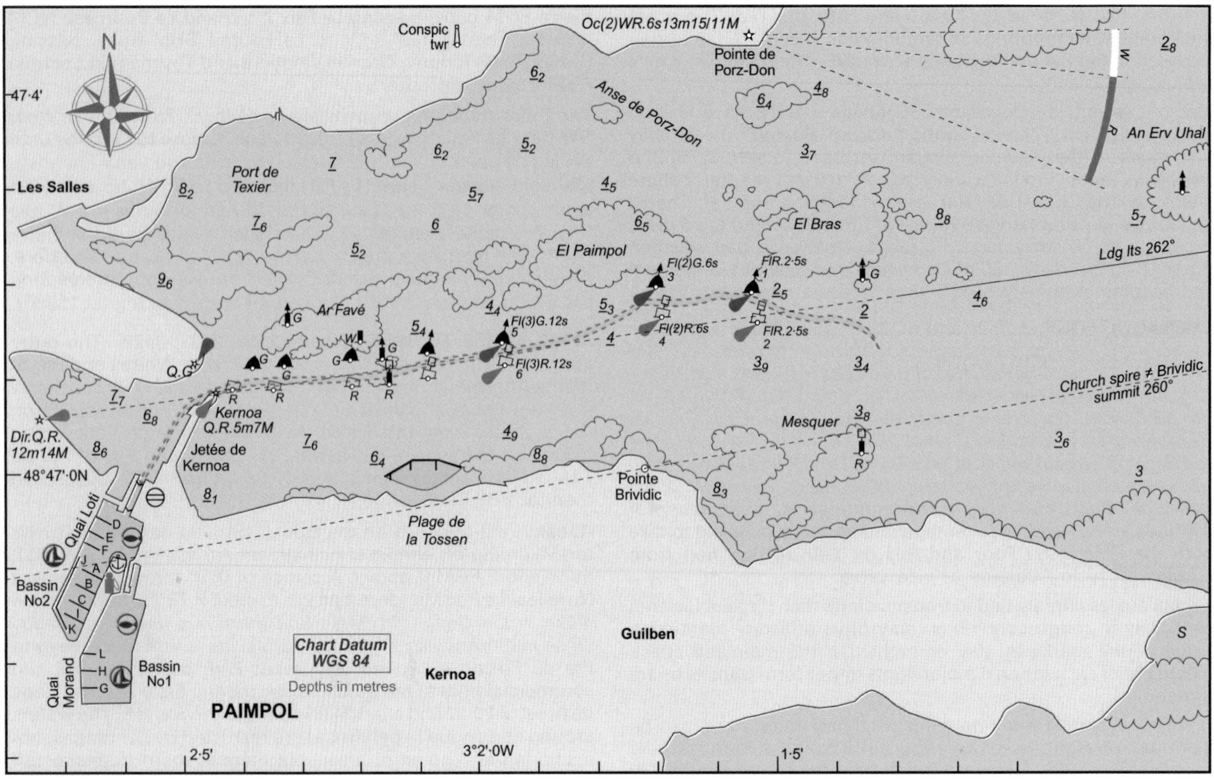
Conspic twr
Oc(2)WR.6s13m15/11M
Pointe de Porz-Don
Anse de Porz-Don
An Erv Uhal
47·4'
Les Salles
Port de Texier
El Bras
El Paimpol
Ldg lts 262°
Fl(2)G.6s 3
Fl.R.2·5s 1
Ar Favé
Fl(3)G.12s 5
Fl(2)R.6s 4
Fl.R.2·5s 2
Fl(3)R.12s 6
Church spire ≠ Brividic summit 260°
Q.G
Kernoa Q.R.5m7M
Dir.Q.R. 12m14M
48°47'·0N
Jetée de Kernoa
Mesquer
Pointe Brividic
Plage de la Tossen
Quai Loti
Bassin No2
Bassin No1
Quai Morand
Chart Datum WGS 84
Depths in metres
Kernoa
Guilben
PAIMPOL
2·5'
3°2'·0W
1·5'

9.20.7 PAIMPOL

Côtes d'Armor **48°47'·00N 03°02'·56W**

CHARTS AC *2668*, 3670, 3673; SHOM 7152, 7154, 7127; ECM 537; Imray C34; Stanfords 2.

TIDES Dover –0525; ML 6·1; Duration 0600; Zone –0100

Standard Port ST MALO (⟵)

Times				Height (metres)			
High Water		Low Water		MHWS	MHWN	MLWN	MLWS
0100	0800	0300	0800	12·2	9·3	4·2	1·5
1300	2000	1500	2000				
Differences PAIMPOL							
–0010	–0005	–0035	–0025	–1·4	–1·0	–0·4	–0·2

SHELTER Good shelter from all winds in hbr, but few ⚓s as most of the Anse de Paimpol dries, including the appr chan to hbr. Lock, 60m x 12m, opens HW ±2½. Visitors' berths at pontoon A, Basin No 2, min depth 3·8m. Larger yachts <40m in Basin No 1.

NAVIGATION WPT 48°47'·82N 02°54'·58W, 262°/5·2M to Kernoa jetty hd. Chenal de la Jument 260° is the outer appr. After La Jument PHM bn tr, alter onto 262·2° inner ldg line; or ⚓ in 5m to await the tide. Small buoys/bns in final 1M of chan (dries 6-7m) may be hard to see against a low evening sun. The drying rks (El Paimpol, El Bras and Ar Fav) are close N of the ldg line.

An alternative appr from Île de Bréhat at HW±4 lies E of Les Piliers NCM bn tr, thence S past Pte de la Trinité. Or appr via Cadenenou NCM and Chenal du Denou 193°. SHOM 7127 essential for these inshore passages. Bearing in mind the large tidal range, from half-flood there is enough water in the bay for most craft.

LIGHTS AND MARKS From the S L'Ost-Pic lt is a conspic □ W tr 4M E of Paimpol. Pte de Porz-Don, lt ho on a white house, is 7ca ENE of hbr ent; its W sector leads 270° to intercept the inner 262·2° ldg lts at La Jument bcn twr. A conspic twr (52m) is 3ca W of Porz-Don.

Chenal de la Jument, outer ldg marks 260°: Paimpol ✠ spire (the N'ly of two) ≠ the ill-defined summit of Pte Brividic. Inner ldg lts, both QR, 262·2°: front, Jetée de Kernoa.

R/T HM and Lock VHF Ch 09 (0800-1200LT and lock opening hrs).

TELEPHONE HM 02·96.20.47.65; Port Mgr 02·96·20·80·77; Lock 02·96·20·90·02; ⊖ 02·96·20·81·87; Aff Mar 02·96·55·35·00; CROSS 02·98·89·31·31; Auto 08·92·68·08·22; Police 02·96·20·80·17; Ⓗ 02·96·55·60·00; Dr 02·96·55·15·15; Brit Consul 02.99.46.26.64.

FACILITIES Basin No 2 (marina 280+24 visitors), €1.67, D (quay), P (cans), ME, El, ♿; **Basin No 1** C (25, 6 and 4 ton); **Quai de Kernoa** P, ME; **Quai neuf** Slip, M, FW, AB; **Services:** ⚒, CH, SHOM, Ⓔ. **Town** CH, 🛒, Ⓗ, R, Bar, Gaz, ⊡, ✉, Ⓑ, ⇄, ✈ Dinard, Brest, Rennes. Ferry: Roscoff, St Malo.

9.20.8 ÎLE DE BRÉHAT

Côtes d'Armor 48°51'·00N 03°00'·00W

CHARTS AC *2668*, 3670, 3673; SHOM 7152, 7154; ECM 537; Imray C34; Stanfords 2.

TIDES –0525 Dover; ML 5·8; Duration 0605; Zone –0100

Standard Port ST MALO (⟵)

Times				Height (metres)			
High Water		Low Water		MHWS	MHWN	MLWN	MLWS
0100	0800	0300	0800	12·2	9·3	4·2	1·5
1300	2000	1500	2000				
Differences LES HEAUX DE BRÉHAT							
–0020	–0015	–0055	–0035	–2·4	–1·7	–0·7	–0·3
ÎLE DE BRÉHAT							
–0015	–0010	–0045	–0035	–1·9	–1·4	–0·6	–0·3

SHELTER Good in Port Clos, the main hbr (dries), but busy with vedettes. No AB; ⚓ clear of fairway. Due to cables/pipe across the Ferlas Chan, ⚓ is prohib SW of Port Clos). Or moor/⚓ in Le Kerpont W of the LW ferry landing. Good shelter, except in W/NW winds, at Port de la Corderie (dries); get well out of strong tidal streams; some 🅥s.

E of Le Bourg there are free drying private 🅥s near ⚓, but some reported unsafe due lack of maintenance. La Chambre: ⚓ in upper reaches just S of the ⚓ area. Slip can be floodlit by pressing button on lamp post at top of slip. Guerzido in the Chenal de Ferlas is good holding, partly out of the strong tides.

NAVIGATION From the E, WPT 48°49´·39N 02°55´·08W (Ferlas chan), 277°/3·4M to abm Port Clos. See 9.20.9 for the R Trieux, then follow transits Ⓕ – Ⓒ, as on AC 3673. From the N, Ch de Bréhat 168° (distant ldg marks) to enter Ferlas Ch from the E.

LIGHTS AND MARKS Chape St Michel, Amer du Rosedo and the nearby Sig atn are all conspic. For the 3 main lts, see chartlet and 9.20.4.

R/T Sémaphore de Bréhat VHF Ch 16 10, Day only.

TELEPHONE HM none; CROSS 02·98·89·31·31; SNSM 02·96·20·00·14 (Loguivy); Auto 08·92·68·08·22; ⊖ 02·96·20·81·87; Police 02·96·20·80·17; Ⓗ 02·96·55·60·00 (Paimpol); Dr 02·96·20·09·51; Brit Consul 02·99·46·26·64.

FACILITIES **Hbrs** M, FW, P from fuel barge at Port Clos, Slip, full access at HW; CN de Bréhat, FW, Bar; Services: ME.
Village 🛒, Gaz, Bar, R, ⌂, ✉, Ⓑ, ⇄ (ferry to Pte de l'Arcouest, bus to Paimpol thence to Paris, Brest, Roscoff and St Malo), ✈ (Dinard, Brest, Rennes to London). Ferry: Plymouth-Roscoff. No cars on island.

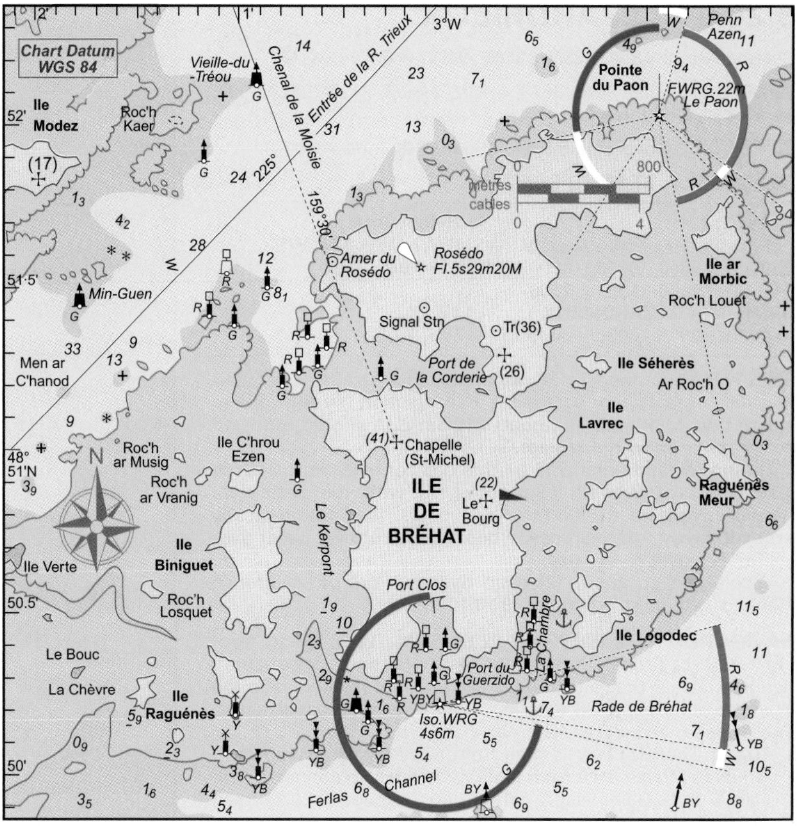
Chart Datum
WGS 84
ILE
DE
BRÉHAT
Ile Modez
Vieille-du-Tréou
Roc'h Kaer
Chenal de la Moisie
Entrée de la R. Trieux
Pointe du Paon
FWRG.22m
Le Paon
Amer du Rosédo
Rosédo
Fl.5s29m20M
Signal Stn
Port de la Corderie
Chapelle (St-Michel)
Le Bourg
Min-Guen
Men ar C'hanod
Roc'h ar Musig
Roc'h ar Vranig
Ile C'hrou Ezen
Ile Biniguet
Roc'h Losquet
Ile Verte
Le Bouc
La Chèvre
Ile Raguénès
Le Kerpont
Port Clos
Port du Guerzido
La Chambre
Iso.WRG
4s6m
Ferlas Channel
Ile Logodec
Rade de Bréhat
Ile ar Morbic
Roc'h Louet
Ile Séherès
Ar Roc'h O
Ile Lavrec
Raguénès Meur
Penn Azen
metres
cables

PASSE DE LA GAINE

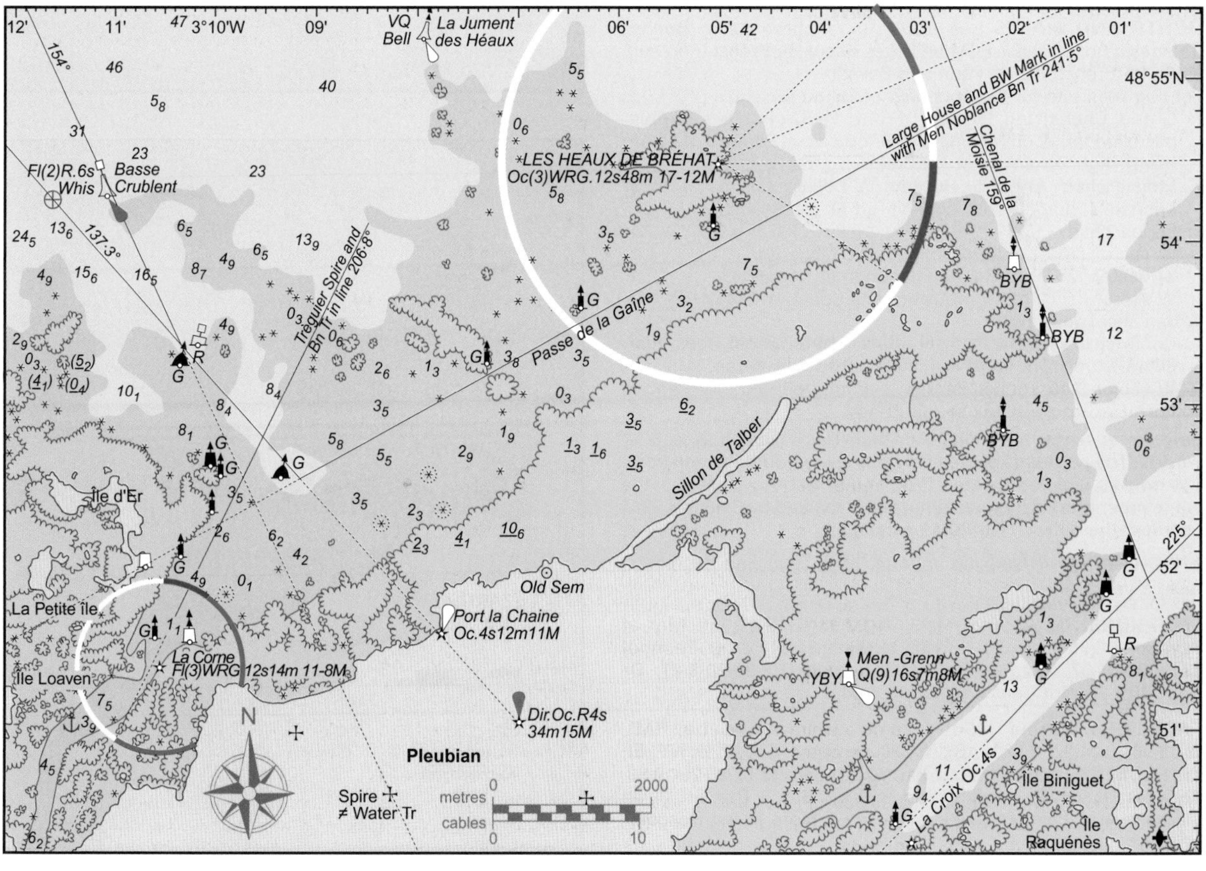
VQ Bell
La Jument des Héaux
LES HEAUX DE BRÉHAT
Oc(3)WRG.12s48m 17-12M
Large House and BW Mark in line with Men Noblance Bn Tr 241·5°
Chenal de la Moisie 159°
Fl(2)R.6s Whis
Basse Crublent
Tréguier Spire and Bn Tr in line 206·8°
Passe de la Gaîne
Sillon de Talber
Île d'Er
La Petite île
Ile Loaven
La Corne
Fl(3)WRG.12s14m 11-8M
Old Sem
Port la Chaine
Oc.4s12m11M
Dir.Oc.R4s
34m15M
Pleubian
Spire
≠ Water Tr
Men -Grenn
Q(9)16s7m8M
La Croix Oc.4s
Ile Biniguet
Ile Raguénès
metres
cables
48°55'N

9.20.9 LÉZARDRIEUX

Côtes d'Armor **48°47´·35N 03°05´·91W** ❀❀❀✿✿✿✿✿

CHARTS AC *2668*, 3670, 3673; SHOM 7152/3, 7126/7; ECM 537; Imray C34; Stanfords 2.

TIDES –0510 Dover; ML 5·9; Duration 0610; Zone –0100

Standard Port ST MALO (⟵)

Times				Height (metres)			
High Water		Low Water		MHWS	MHWN	MLWN	MLWS
0100	0800	0300	0800	12·2	9·3	4·2	1·5
1300	2000	1500	2000				
Differences LÉZARDRIEUX							
–0020	–0015	–0055	–0045	–1·7	–1·3	–0·5	–0·2

SHELTER Very good in all weathers. The Trieux River and marina pontoons are accessible H24. Caution: strong stream at half tide. Multihulls and boats >12·5m LOA should moor on ⚓s or pontoon in the stream.

The non-tidal marina (247 berths) has some Ⓥ berths (2·4m inside). Access over sill 4·9m above CD, with automatic flap. As sill covers on the flood to 6·15m CD, flap automatically drops to give 1·1m clearance. A depth gauge shows water over sill. IPTS sigs 2 & 4 in use.

Yachts can go about 12km up river (via bridge, clearance 17m) to lock in at Pontrieux (9.20.10).

NAVIGATION WPT 48°54´·94N 02°56´·28W, 225°/6·7M to front ldg lt 225° (La Croix). Roches Douvres and Barnouic are offshore dangers; as are the Plateau de la Horaine and rky shoals to the W in the outer apps. Off river ent beware strong cross streams. The 3 well-marked approach channels are:

- Grand Chenal, main lit chan from NE, best for strangers;
- Ch de la Moisie, unlit from the NW, which also connects with Passe de la Gaine, short cut from/to Tréguier (9.20.11); see chartlet on previous page; and
- Ferlas Chan (lit) from E or W, passing S of Île de Bréhat.

LIGHTS AND MARKS See 9.20.4 for offshore lts at Roches Douvres lt ho, Barnouic ECM bn tr, Les Héaux de Bréhat lt ho and, on Île de Bréhat, Pte du Paon and Rosédo.

The ldg marks/lts for the approach channels are:

1. Grand Chenal ldg lts 225°: Front, La Croix, two double-barrelled trs, W on NE side with R tops; rear, Bodic (2·1M from front) high up amongst the trees.
2. Moisie chan: Amer du Rosédo, W obelisk on 159° with St Michael's chapel (both conspic on Île de Bréhat).
3. Ferlas chan:
   W sector (281°) of Men Joliguet, YBY bcn twr.
   W sector (257°) of Roche Quinonec at Loguivy.
   W sector (271°) of Kermouster joins Coatmer 218·7° ldg line.

Within the Trieux river:

4. Coatmer ldg lts 218·7°: front, low down amongst trees; rear, 660m from front, high up almost obsc'd by trees.
5. W sector (200°) of Les Perdrix, a stout green bcn twr. Speed limit 5kn from Perdrix to the bridge.

Beware, at night, the unlit, 16m high Roc'h Donan 2½ca S of Perdrix. The pontoons of the tidal marina are floodlit from shore. The only lts S of Perdrix are a PHM and SHM buoy close E of the ent to inner marina; the retaining wall is marked by 5 unlit Y SPM perches, the sill by PHM/SHM perches.

R/T VHF Ch 09 (0730-2200 Jul/Aug. 0800-1200 and 1400-1800 rest of year).

TELEPHONE HM 02·96·20·14·22, 📠 02·96·22·18·31; Aff Mar at Paimpol 02·96·55·35·00; CROSS 02·98·89·31·31; ⊖ at Paimpol 02·96·20·81·87; Auto 08·92·68·08·22; Police 02·96·20·8·17; Dr 02·96·20·8·30; Brit Consul 02·99·46·26·64.

FACILITIES Marina (490 + 50 Ⓥ as directed by HM), ☎ 02·96·20·14·22, €1.80 (AB), €1.20 (on buoy), Slip, P, D, ME, El, CH, SM, ⚒, C (50 ton), Gaz, R, ▣, Bar; **YC de Trieux** ☎ 02·96·20·10·39. **Services:** Divers, Ⓔ; **Town** EC Sun; P, D, 🛒, Gaz, R, Bar, ✉, Ⓑ, ⇌ (occas bus to Paimpol & Lannion), ✈ Lannion. Ferry: Roscoff.

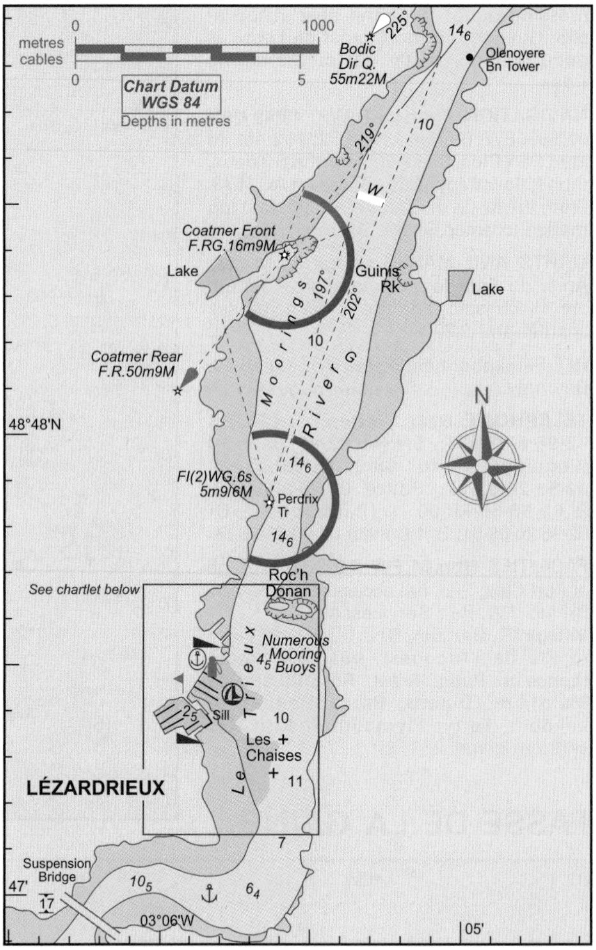
metres
cables
0
1000
5
Chart Datum
WGS 84
Depths in metres
Bodic
Dir Q.
55m22M
225°
219°
Olenoyere
Bn Tower
Coatmer Front
F.RG.16m9M
Lake
197°
202°
Guinis Rk
Lake
Coatmer Rear
F.R.50m9M
Moorings
River G
48°48'N
N
Fl(2)WG.6s
5m9/6M
Perdrix Tr
Roc'h Donan
See chartlet below
Numerous Mooring Buoys
Sill
Les Chaises
Le Trieux
LÉZARDRIEUX
Suspension Bridge
47'
03°06'W
05'

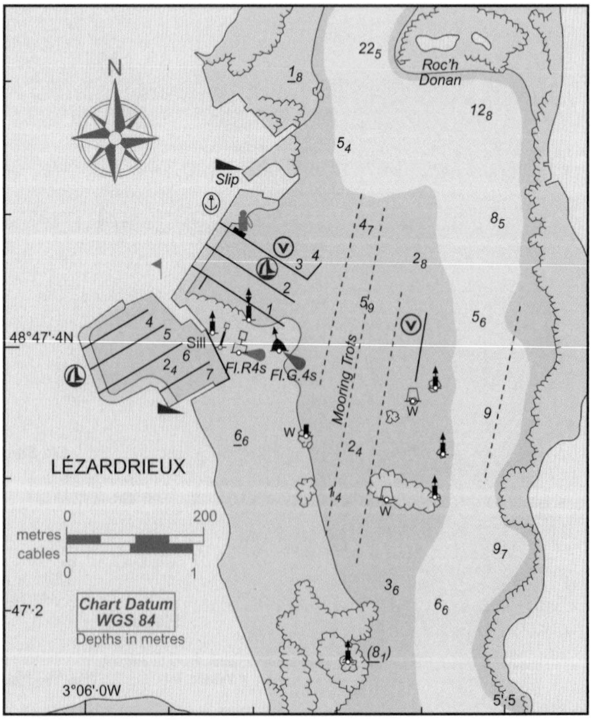
N
Roc'h Donan
Slip
Sill
48°47'·4N
Fl.R4s
Fl.G.4s
Mooring Trots
LÉZARDRIEUX
metres
cables
0
200
1
Chart Datum
WGS 84
Depths in metres
-47'·2
3°06'·0W

9.20.10 PONTRIEUX

Côtes d'Armor **48°42'·74N 03°08'·98W** ❀❀◊◊✿✿✿

CHARTS ECM 537; AC 3673 & SHOM 7126 end S of Lézardrieux. A useful river guide/map is available from HM Pontrieux.

TIDES HW at Pontrieux lock is at HW ST MALO. See also 9.20.9.

SHELTER Complete shelter in 2-4m depth alongside Quay (SE bank), approx 1km above the lock (48°42'·78N 03°08'·31W).

NAVIGATION See 9.20.9 for the river up to Lézardrieux. Not before HW –3, proceed via suspension bridge (17m clearance at MHWS) for 6M up-river, keeping to high, rky bank on bends. Allow 1½ hrs for the passage and aim to reach the lock at HW –1 (to de-conflict from sand coasters *[sabliers]* which use the lock occas at HW). Lock opens HW –2 to HW+1½ in summer; in winter –1½ to HW+1¼. 2 Waiting buoys (half-tide) close E. Below Château de la Roche Jagu a waiting buoy is accessible HW±3.

LIGHTS AND MARKS River is unlit; few marks. The best water between river bends is indicated by the alignment of reflective posts (1-2m high) near the bends.

R/T Lock VHF Ch 12, at lock times. ☎ link to HM Pontrieux.

TELEPHONE HM ☎/📠 02·96·95·34·87 www.letrieux.com Lock 02·96·95·60·70; Auto 08·36·68·08·22. Public ☎ at Château Roche Jagu.

FACILITIES Quay (100+40 Ⓥ) AB €1.49, C (5 ton), R, Bar, ♿. **Town** Bar, FW, R, Slip, 🛒, Gaz, P, D, Ⓑ, ✉, ⓛ, ⇌ Paimpol/Guingamp, ✈ Brest, Rennes, Dinard & Paris.

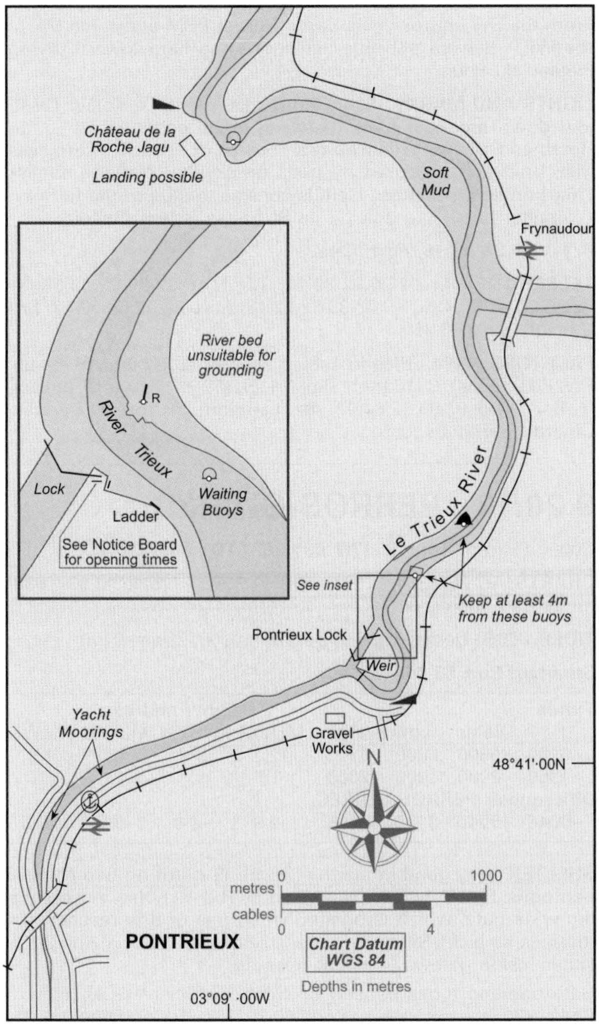
Château de la Roche Jagu
Landing possible
Soft Mud
Frynaudour
River bed unsuitable for grounding
R
River Trieux
Lock
Ladder
Waiting Buoys
See Notice Board for opening times
See inset
Le Trieux River
Keep at least 4m from these buoys
Pontrieux Lock
Weir
Yacht Moorings
Gravel Works
N
48°41'·00N
metres 0 1000
cables 0 4
PONTRIEUX
Chart Datum WGS 84
Depths in metres
03°09'·00W

9.20.11 TRÉGUIER

Côtes d'Armor **48°47'·21N 03°13'·27W** ❀❀❀◊◊◊✿✿✿

CHARTS AC *2668*, 3670, 3672; SHOM 7152, 7126; ECM 537; Imray C34; Stanfords 2.

TIDES –0540 Dover; ML 5·7; Duration 0600; Zone –0100

Standard Port ST MALO (⟵)

Times				Height (metres)			
High Water		Low Water		MHWS	MHWN	MLWN	MLWS
0100	0800	0300	0800	12·2	9·3	4·2	1·5
1300	2000	1500	2000				
Differences TRÉGUIER							
–0020	–0020	–0100	–0045	–2·3	–1·6	–0·6	–0·2
PORT-BÉNI (5ca SSE of La Corne lt twr)							
–0025	–0025	–0105	–0050	–2·4	–1·7	–0·6	–0·2

SHELTER Good. Aim to arrive/dep at slack water as the tide sets hard diagonally through the pontoons. Possible ⚓s, keeping clear of the chan: 7ca SW of La Corne lt tr, but exposed to N'lies; N and S of La Roche Jaune village; in sheltered pool (6m) 1ca NE of No 10 buoy (8ca N of marina).

NAVIGATION WPT 48°54'·28N 03°11'·37W (abm Basse Crublent PHM buoy), 137°/2·2M to Pen ar Guézec SHM buoy, a key turning point. There are three approach channels:

1. Grande Passe 137·3°: well marked/lit, but marks are hard to see by day. Caution: strong tidal streams across the chan.
2. Passe de la Gaine 241·5°: adequately marked, navigable with care by day in good vis. Unlit short cut to/from Lézardrieux; see chartlet page 879.
3. Passe du Nord-Est 205°/207°: unlit, dangerous with W-NW winds as sea breaks across the shallowest part of chan.

Within the river heed lateral buoys and bns, eg keep E of Taureau unlit SHM buoy, 300m SW of La Corne lt ho, to clear the adjacent drying bank. Speed limit is 6 knots south of No 3 SHM lt buoy.

LIGHTS AND MARKS See 9.20.4. Important marks: La Corne, a stumpy WR lt tr; 6ca to the N is Men Noblance WB bcn tr (for Passe de la Gaine); and 4ca SW is Skeiviec W bn tr. The spire of Tréguier cathedral is 4·6M SSW of La Corne, but may be obscured by high wooded banks when entering the river estuary in the vicinity of Pen ar Guézec. Ldg lts/marks for the appr chans:

1. Grande Passe 137·3°: front, Port de la Chaine, white ho; rear, St Antoine, RW ho. At Pen ar Guézec unlit SHM buoy alter 216° in the W sector of La Corne lt. Note: The ldg marks are very hard to identify by day. From Basse Crublent buoy an easier transit is: Pleubian spire (charted) in transit 154° with adjacent water tower (visible on the skyline), to pass between Pierre à l'Anglais and Le Corbeau lateral buoys.
2. Passe de la Gaine 242·5°: Men Noblance bn tr, W with horiz B band, on with rear mark (W wall with B vert stripe) below the skyline and just right of conspic Plougrescant ✠ spire; but marks hard to see from afar, especially against a low sun or in poor vis. Hold this transit exactly to stay in the narrow chan.
3. Passe du Nord-Est: On 205° keep W of La Jument NCM buoy and adjacent rky shoals; jink port onto 207° transit of Tréguier spire and Skeiviec bcn twr, for direct appr to La Corne.

R/T Marina Ch 09 (In season: Mon-Sat 0800-1200, 1330-2100; Sun 0800-1000, 1600-1800. All LT).

TELEPHONE HM 02·96·92·42·37; Aff Mar 02·96·92·30·38 (Paimpol); CROSS 02·96·89·31·31; ⊖ 02·96·20·81·37; Auto 08·92·68·08·22; Police 02·96·20·84·30; Dr 02·96·92·32·14; Ⓗ 02·96·05·71·11 (Lannion); Brit Consul 02·99·46·26·64.

FACILITIES Marina (200+130 Ⓥ), ☎ 02·96·92·42·37, 📠 02·96.92.29.25 (indicate for Port de Plaisance), €1.54, Slip, ME, C (8 ton), CH, El, ⚒, Bar, R, Gaz, ⓛ; **Bar des Plaisanciers** ☎ 02·96·92·49·69, excellent facilities, open all year. **Club Nautique de Tréguier** 02.96.92.37.49 Bar, opp marina open Sat eves only. **Services:** BY ☎ 02·96·92·15·15, M, CH;
Town EC Mon; Market Wed, P, FW, CH, 🛒, Gaz, R, Bar, ✉, Ⓑ, 🛒 (small supermarket just W of cathedral delivers to boats), ⇌ (bus to Paimpol, Guingamp, Lannion, ✈ (Brest, Rennes, Dinard). Ferry: Roscoff, St Malo.

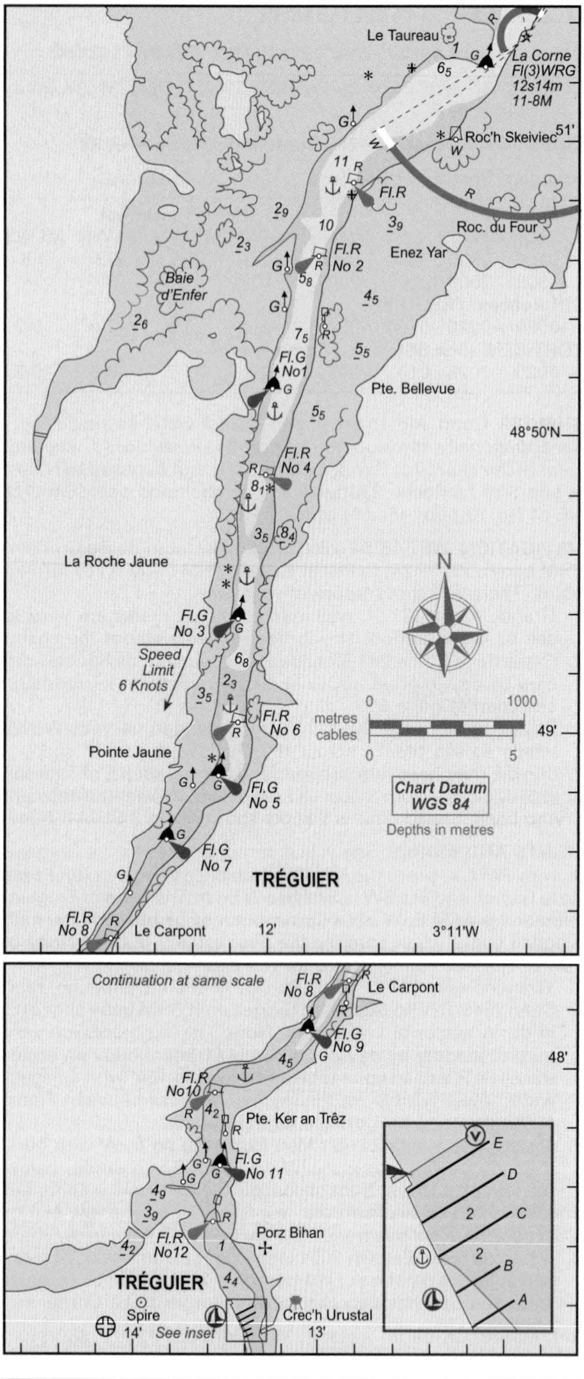
Le Taureau
La Corne
Fl(3)WRG
12s14m
11-8M
Roc'h Skeiviec
51'
Fl.R
Roc. du Four
Enez Yar
Fl.R
No 2
Baie d'Enfer
Fl.G
No1
Pte. Bellevue
48°50'N
Fl.R
No 4
La Roche Jaune
Fl.G
No 3
Speed Limit 6 Knots
Fl.R
No 6
Pointe Jaune
Fl.G
No 5
Fl.G
No 7
TRÉGUIER
Fl.R
No 8
Le Carpont
12'
3°11'W
49'
metres
cables
0
1000
0
5
Chart Datum
WGS 84
Depths in metres
Continuation at same scale
Fl.R
No 8
Le Carpont
Fl.G
No 9
48'
Fl.R
No10
Pte. Ker an Trêz
Fl.G
No 11
Fl.R
No12
Porz Bihan
TRÉGUIER
Spire
14'
See inset
Crec'h Urustal
13'
E
D
C
B
A

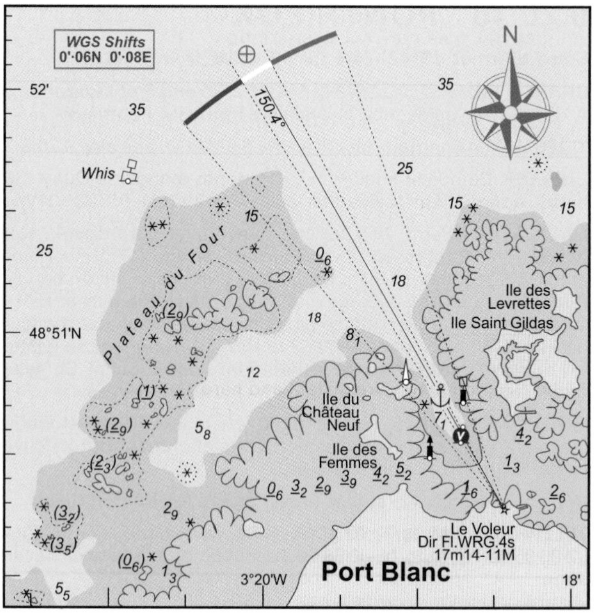
WGS Shifts
0'·06N 0'·08E
52'
Whis
150·4°
Plateau du Four
48°51'N
Ile du Château Neuf
Ile des Femmes
Ile des Levrettes
Ile Saint Gildas
Le Voleur
Dir Fl.WRG.4s
17m14-11M
3°20'W
Port Blanc
18'

9.20.12 PORT BLANC

Côtes d'Armor **48°50′·54N 03°18′·89W** ❁❁◊◊◊✿✿

CHARTS AC *2668*, 3670, 3672; SHOM 7152, 7125/6; ECM 537, 538; Imray C34; Stanfords 2.

TIDES –0545 Dover; ML 5·3; Duration 0600; Zone –0100
Interpolate between Les Héaux de Bréhat and Perros-Guirec. HW–0040 and ht –2·0m on St Malo. MHWS 9·0m; MHWN 6·8m.

SHELTER Good in natural hbr (known as Port Bago), but open to winds between NW and NNE. 5 Y Ø s, marked VISIT (A-E) in approx 5m. Safe ⚓ and good holding, where charted in 7m. Or dry out alongside quays, 1·3m.

NAVIGATION WPT 48°52′·24N 03°20′·16W, 150°/1·9M to first Ø. The fairway does not open up until at the WPT. Appr on ldg line 150·4° toward Le Voleur Dir lt; the rear ldg mark is hard to see. From the SW approach via Basse Guazer PHM buoy, 7ca SW of the WPT. Beware ebb tide initially setting hard toward drying Plateau du Four.

LIGHTS AND MARKS 150·4° ldg marks: Front, Le Voleur Dir lt, low down amongst trees (between white cottage and Grand Hotel, conspic white block); rear, 5ca from front, La Comtesse Mill, unlit and obscured by trees on skyline. A white obelisk (16m) on Île du Château Neuf is conspic to stbd of the fairway. A smaller obelisk to port on Île St Gildas is less obvious.

R/T VHF Ch 09 16, *Port Blanc*.

TELEPHONE HM 02·96.92.89.11; Aff Mar 02·96.92.30.38; ⊜ 02·96.20.81·87; CROSS 02·33·52.72.13; Auto 08·92.68·02·22; Brit Consul 02·99.46.26.64.

FACILITIES HM's office in sailing school. Ø €7.00, AB €0.69, FW, P&D (cans), C (16 ton), Slip, CH, El, ME, ⚒. **Town** 🛒 (basic), R, Bar, Taxi 02·96.92.64.00, ⇌ (Lannion), ✈ (Brest, Rennes, Dinard). Ferry: Roscoff.

9.20.13 PERROS-GUIREC

Côtes d'Armor **48° 48′·17N 03° 26′·21W** ❁❁◊◊◊✿✿

CHARTS AC *2668*, 3670, 3672; SHOM 7152, 7125; ECM 537, 538; Imray C34; Stanfords 2.

TIDES –0550 Dover; ML 5·4; Duration 0605; Zone –0100

Standard Port ST MALO (⟵)

Times				Height (metres)			
High Water		Low Water		MHWS	MHWN	MLWN	MLWS
0100	0800	0300	0800	12·2	9·3	4·2	1·5
1300	2000	1500	2000				
Differences PERROS-GUIREC							
–0040	–0045	–0120	–0105	–2·9	–2·0	–0·8	–0·3

SHELTER Very good in marina (2·5m); Ⓥ berth on two N'most pontoons. Retaining wall is marked by R & W poles. Access via 6m wide gate, which is opened when rise of tide reaches 7m (there is no lock). Sill under gate is 3·5m above CD, giving 3·5m water inside gateway on first opening.

Gate opening times depend on tidal Coefficient (9.20.26): Coeff >70, approx HW±1½; Coeff 60-70, HW±1; Coeff 50-60, HW–

1 to +½; Coeff 40-50, HW–½ to HW. Caution: at Coeff <40, gate may not open for up to 4 days (neaped). Gate may open up to 30 mins ahead of published times, depending on weather, but does not close early. Gate sigs: IPTS. ⚓ prohib in basin. Off Pte du Chateau safe ⚓, except in NE'lies, in approx 3m good holding; plus 5 small W Ⓥs.

NAVIGATION From the E, WPT 48°50′·00N 03°23′·53W, 224·5°/2·4M to Jetée du Linkin. From the W, WPT 48°50′·69N 03°26′·31W, 143·5°/1·8M to join 224·5° ldg line. Caution: Rocks extend 7ca W and 6ca NE of Île Tomé. Local moorings E of Jetée du Linkin are marked by 2 SHM buoys.

LIGHTS AND MARKS See chartlet and 9.20.4. 225° ldg marks are distant and hard to see by day, but bcns/buoys in the appr are adequate. Passe de l'Ouest: Kerjean Dir lt 143·5° is also hard to see, but the old lt ho (gable end) on the foreshore is clearer.

R/T VHF Ch 09 16.

TELEPHONE Marina 02·96.49.80.50, ✉ 02·96.23.37.19; Basin gate 02·96.23.19.03; Aff Mar 02·96.91.21.28; ⊖ 02·96.20.81·87; Auto 08·92.68·08·22; CROSS 02·98·89.31.31; SNSM 02·96.91.40.10; Dr 02·96.23.20.01; Police 02·96.23.20.17; Brit Consul 02·99.46.26.64.

FACILITIES **Marina** (720+80 Ⓥ), €2.12, www.perros-guirec.com P, D, ME,El, ⚒, C (7 ton), CH, 🛒, R, SM, Gas, Gaz, Kos, ⊡;SR Perros ☎ 02·96·91·12·65 **Services:** Ⓔ, SHOM; **Town** CH, 🛒, Gaz, R, Bar, ✉, Ⓑ, ⇌ (Lannion), ✈ (Brest, Rennes, Dinard). Ferry: Roscoff.

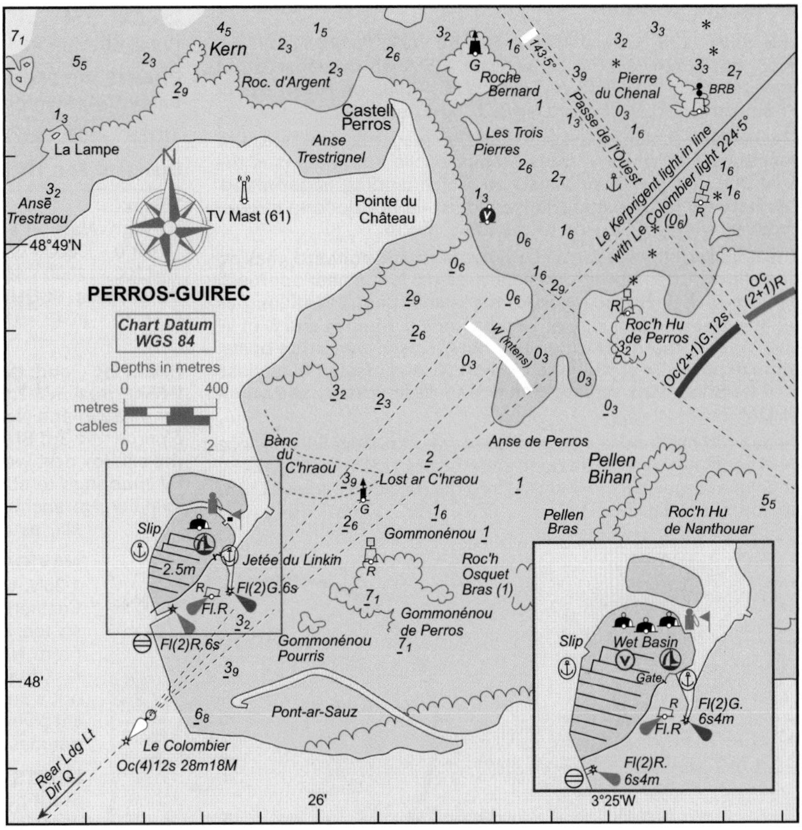
PERROS-GUIREC
Chart Datum WGS 84
Depths in metres
Kern
Roc. d'Argent
Castell Perros
Anse Trestrignel
La Lampe
Anse Trestraou
TV Mast (61)
Pointe du Château
Roche Bernard
Les Trois Pierres
Pierre du Chenal
Passe de l'Ouest
Le Kerprigent light in line with Le Colombier light 224·5°
Roc'h Hu de Perros
Oc(2+1)G.12s
Oc(2+1)R
Anse de Perros
Pellen Bihan
Pellen Bras
Roc'h Hu de Nanthouar
Banc du C'hraou
Lost ar C'hraou
Gommonénou
Roc'h Osquet Bras (1)
Gommonénou de Perros
Gommonénou Pourris
Jetée du Linkin
Fl(2)G.6s
Fl.R
Fl(2)R.6s
Pont-ar-Sauz
Le Colombier
Oc(4)12s 28m18M
Rear Ldg Lt Dir Q
Slip
Wet Basin
Gate
Fl(2)G. 6s4m
Fl(2)R. 6s4m
48°49'N
48'
26'
3°25'W

LES SEPT ÎLES *See notes overleaf*

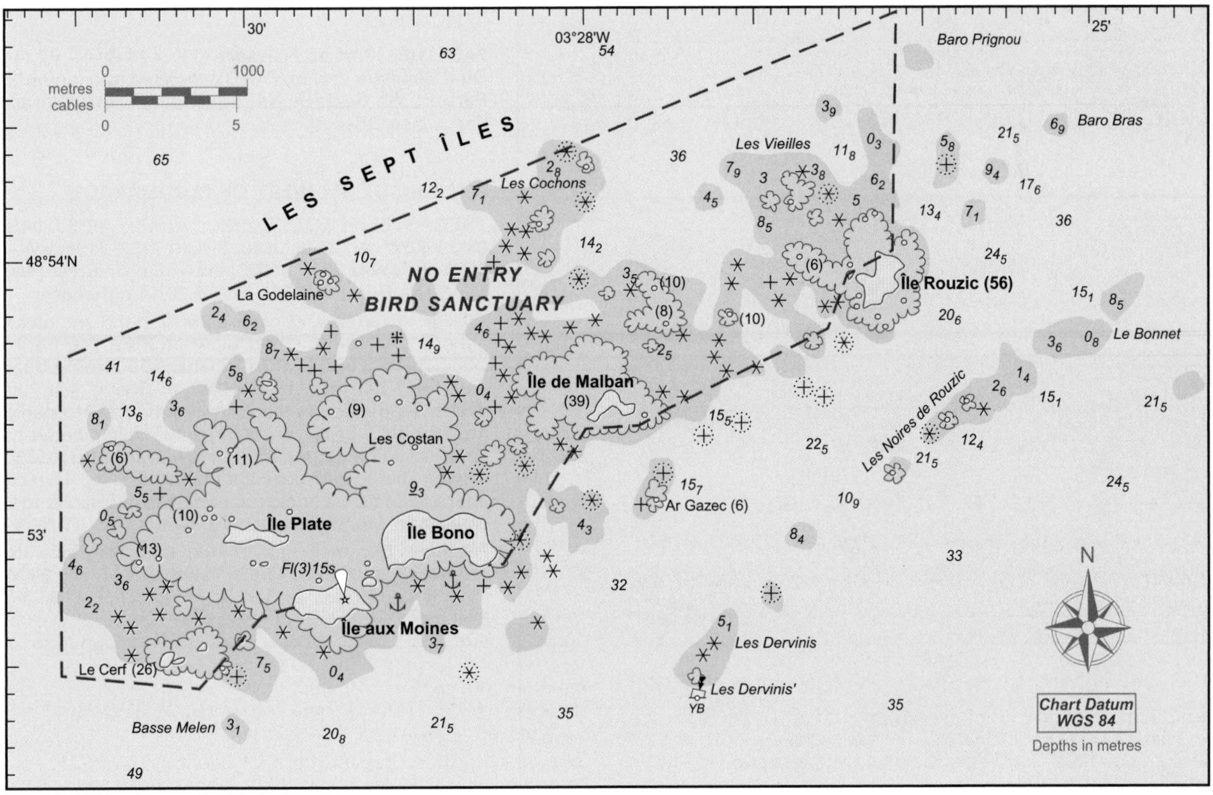
LES SEPT ÎLES
NO ENTRY BIRD SANCTUARY
Chart Datum WGS 84
Depths in metres
Baro Prignou
Baro Bras
Les Vieilles
Les Cochons
La Godelaine
Île Rouzic (56)
Le Bonnet
Île de Malban (39)
Les Costan
Les Noires de Rouzic
Ar Gazec (6)
Île Plate
Île Bono
Fl(3)15s
Île aux Moines
Les Dervinis
Les Dervinis'
Le Cerf (26)
Basse Melen
03°28'W
30'
25'
48°54'N
53'

OFFSHORE ISLANDS

LES SEPT ÎLES, Côte d'Armor, **48° 52´·72N 03°29´·16W**. AC 3669, 3670; SHOM 7152 (large scale 1:20,000). See chartlet on previous page. HW-0550 on Dover (UT); +0005 on Brest. HW ht –1·8m on Brest. ML 5·2m. Use 9.20.14 differences.

The whole archipelago, as outlined in magenta, forms a bird sanctuary into which entry is prohibited. Île aux Moines is the only one of the 7 islands/islets on which landing is permitted. Les Dervinis (SCM buoy) and Les Noires de Rouzic form a rocky chain just off the SE side of the main group.

The approach towards Île aux Moines is straightforward, making due allowance for the strong tidal streams. In the near approach avoid a rock (0·6m) 300m SE of the island. Best ⚓ (Lat/Long as on line 1) is due E of jetty at E end of Île aux Moines and S of W end of Île Bono. A mooring buoy here is used by tourist boats. More exposed ⚓s are S of the Old Fort (W end of island), or close S of Île Bono; both require care due to rocks, clearly shown on SHOM 7152.

Île aux Moines lt ho is a conspic grey twr, Fl (3) 15s 59m, whose 24M beam is obscured by Bono and Rouzic in a 4° arc (237°-241°) and when brg < 039°, ie if tucked into the Baie de Lannion. There are no shore facilities.

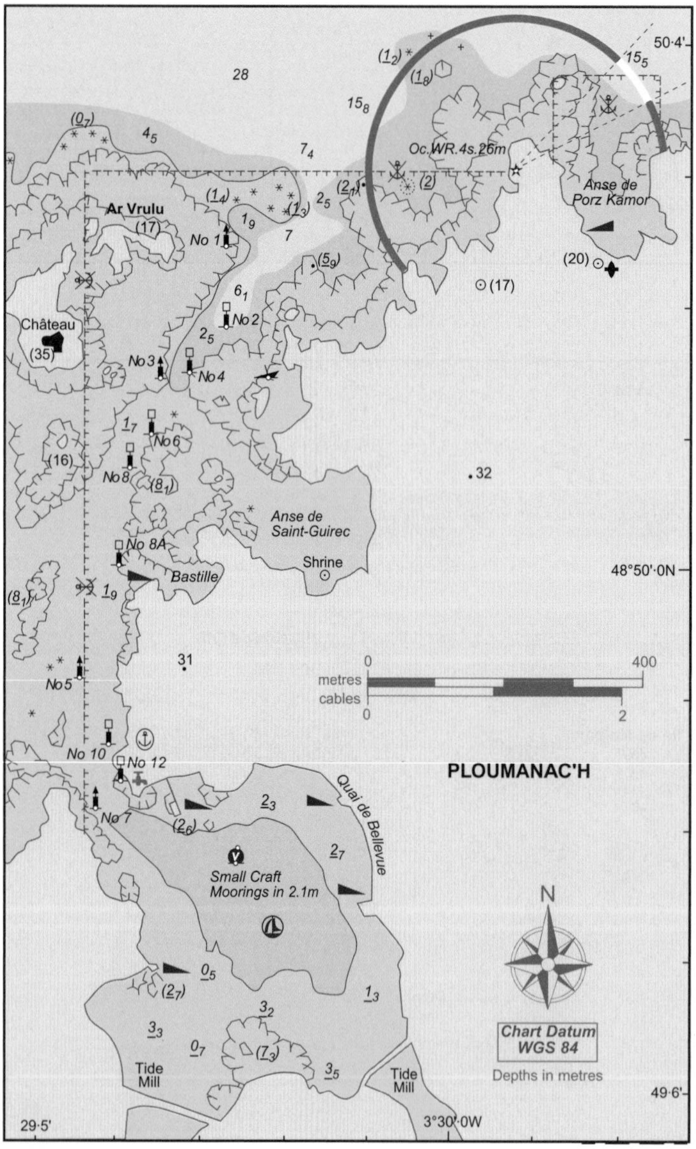
Ar Vrulu
Château
No 1
No 2
No 3
No 4
No 5
No 6
No 7
No 8
No 8A
No 10
No 12
Oc.WR.4s.26m
Anse de Porz Kamor
Anse de Saint-Guirec
Shrine
Bastille
metres
cables
PLOUMANAC'H
Quai de Bellevue
Small Craft Moorings in 2.1m
N
Chart Datum WGS 84
Depths in metres
Tide Mill
Tide Mill
48°50'·0N
50·4'
49·6'
29·5'
3°30'·0W

9.20.14 PLOUMANAC'H

Côtes d'Armor **48° 50'·29N 03° 29'·23W** ❁❁⛵⛵✿✿✿

CHARTS AC *2668*, 3669, 3670; SHOM 7152, 7125; ECM 537, 538; Imray C34; Stanfords 2.

TIDES –0550 Dover; ML 5·5; Duration 0605; Zone –0100

Standard Port ST MALO (⟵)

Times				Height (metres)			
High Water		Low Water		MHWS	MHWN	MLWN	MLWS
0100	0800	0300	0800	12·2	9·3	4·2	1·5
1300	2000	1500	2000				
Differences PLOUMANAC'H							
–0035	–0040	–0120	–0100	–2·9	–2·0	–0·7	–0·2

SHELTER Good; ⓥs are first line of dumbell buoys. A sill, drying 2·55m, retains 1·2m to 2·3m within. Depth gauges are on No 4 (unreliable) and No 12 PHM perches. If the concrete base of No 5 perch (the 3rd SHM) is covered, depth over sill is >1·4m. Inside the sill, for best water keep to port and appr moorings from N. FV moorings to stbd of ent. SE and SW sides of hbr are very shallow. No anchoring from abeam Mean Ruz lt ho to the hbr sill, as depicted on the chartlet.

NAVIGATION WPT 48°51´·44N 03°29´·09W, 188°/1·25M to ent between Mean Ruz lt ho and Château Costaérès (conspic). Ent is difficult in strong NW'lies; so too is leaving with a NE'ly against tidal stream. From NNE to NW, beware An Dreuzinier, unmarked rks (drying 1·4m), 100m N and NE of No 1 SHM perch; not a problem with sufficient rise of tide, but near LW keep very close W of a line through the first two PHM perches. Chan is marked by unlit perches.

LIGHTS AND MARKS See chartlet and 9.20.4. Mean Ruz lt ho is a reddish square twr. Sig stn, 8ca SSE, is conspic from the E. Night entry not advised.

R/T VHF Ch 09.

TELEPHONE HM 02.96.49.80.50; Auto 08.92.68.08.22; SNSM 02.96.20.00.45; Dr 02.96.91.42.00; ME 02.96.23.05.89.

FACILITIES Port de Plaisance (230 + 20 ⓥ) M, €2.09; **Quai Bellevue** L, Slip, P & D cans; Bus to Lannion & Perros; **YC Société Nautique de Perros Guirec.** Ferry: See Roscoff.

ANCHORAGE 1M WEST OF PLOUMANAC'H

TRÉGASTEL-PLAGE, Côtes d'Armor, **48°50´·04N 03°31´·29W**, AC 3670, 3669; SHOM 7152, 7125. HW –0550 on Dover (UT); +0005 and –1·8m on Brest HW; ML 5·1m; Duration 0605. Use 9.20.14 differences.

A large W radome, conspic 3·2M S of the ent, gives general orientation. Enter between PHM bcn on Île Dhu (just W of Île Dé, with dice-shaped Pierre Pendue) and SHM bcn off Le Taureau, rk drying 4·5m (if destroyed the bcn is replaced by a buoy). A conspic house with □ turret, brg approx 165° leads between Île Dhu and Le Taureau. But it is easier to track 183° leaving the 3 PHM bcns about 60m to port. Thence after a SHM bcn, ⚓ or pick up orange ⓥs S of Île Ronde. Good ⚓ in 2m, but exposed to winds from W to N.

Facilities: Slip in E part of hbr; **Club Nautique de Trégastel** ☎ 02·96·23·45·05; **Town** (Ste Anne, 0·5M inland) CH, Ⓑ, ✉, Ⓡ, Bar, R, 🛒; Dr 02·96·23·88·08/88·46.

9.20.15 TRÉBEURDEN

Côtes d'Armor **48°46'·29N 03°35'·15W** ❁❁◊◊◊✿✿

CHARTS AC 3669; SHOM 7151/2, 7125, 7124; ECM 537, 538; Imray C34; Stanfords 2.

TIDES –0605 Dover; ML 5·5; Duration 0605; Zone –0100

Standard Port BREST (⟶)

Times				Height (metres)			
High Water		Low Water		MHWS	MHWN	MLWN	MLWS
0000	0600	0000	0600	6·9	5·4	2·6	1·0
1200	1800	1200	1800				
Differences TRÉBEURDEN							
+0100	+0110	+0120	+0100	+2·3	+1·9	+0·9	+0·4

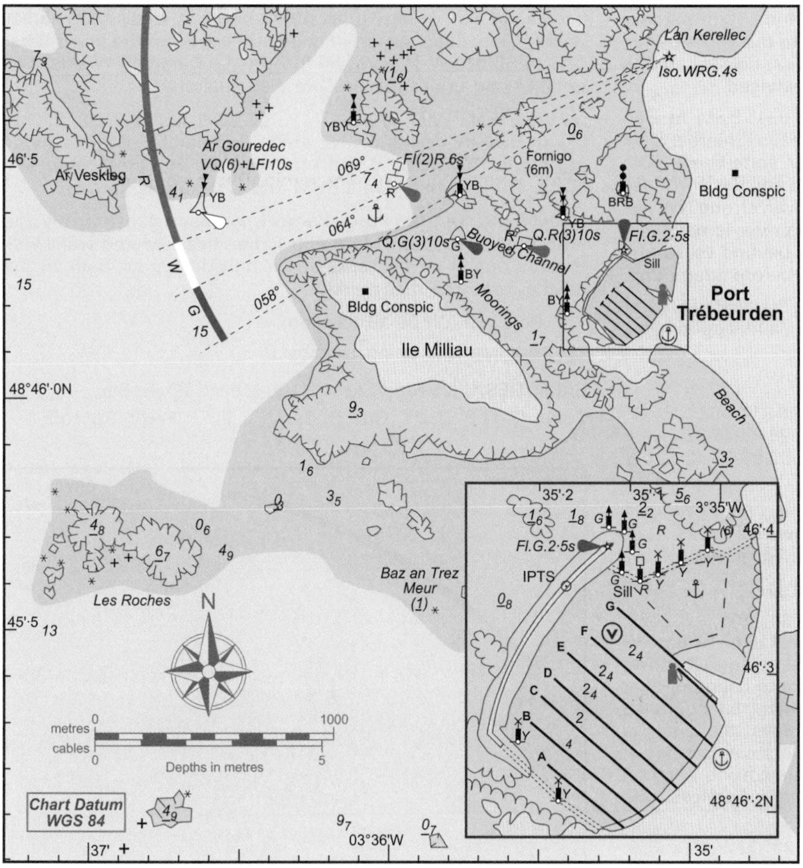
Lan Kerellec
Iso.WRG.4s
Ar Gouredec
VQ(6)+LFl10s
Ar Veskleg
Fl(2)R.6s
Fornigo (6m)
Bldg Conspic
Q.G(3)10s
Buoyed Channel
Q.R(3)10s
Fl.G.2·5s
Sill
Port Trébeurden
Moorings
Ile Milliau
Beach
48°46'·0N
Baz an Trez Meur
Les Roches
IPTS
3°35'W
46'·4
46'·3
48°46'·2N
03°36'W
35'
37'
metres
cables
Depths in metres
Chart Datum WGS 84

SHELTER Good in marina (2 - 2·6m). Access HW±4½ (±3¾ sp) over flapgate (2m CD; 15m wide) at NW side of ent; retaining wall 3·5m marked by 4 Y SPM bns. Tide gauge floodlit, port side of sill. IPTS (sigs 2 & 4) on bkwtr and at gateway. Do not ent/exit within 10 mins of the sill lowering, due to strong underwater inrush. Ⓥ on pontoons F & G. 15 waiting buoys outside in deep-water; or ⚓ off NE side of Île Milliau, but exposed to W'lies.

NAVIGATION WPT 48°45'·34N 03°40'·00W, 067°/3M to first PHM buoy in white sector of Lan Kerellec Dir lt. From WSW, go direct to ⊕.

From E & N, round Bar ar Gall and Le Crapaud WCM buoys; continue S for 1·4M, before altering 067° toward Île Milliau; thence enter the buoyed chan (105°/088°) to marina. In offshore winds the short-cut between Le Crapaud reef and the reefs N and S of Île Losket is safe, if pre-planned.

LIGHTS AND MARKS See chartlet and 9.20.4. Lan Kerellec Dir lt leads 067° to the start of buoyed chan, aligned approx 100° with ✠ spire (conspic, 119m).

R/T Call *Port Trébeurden* VHF Ch 09 16.

TELEPHONE HM ☎ 02·96·23·64·00, 📠 02·96·47·40·87; Aff Mar 02·96·91·21·28; ⊖ 02·96·48·45·32; CROSS 02·98·89·31·31; SNSM 02·96·23·53·82; Police 02·96·23·51·96 (Jul/Aug).

FACILITIES Marina (400 + 100 Ⓥ), €2.80, P, D, BY, ME, El, ⚒, CH. **YC de Trébeurden** ☎ 02·96·15·45·97 (July-Aug).
Town 🛒, R, Bar, ✉, Ⓑ, ✈ (Brest, Rennes, Dinard). Ferry: Roscoff/St Malo.

9.20.16 LANNION (Léguer River)

Côtes d'Armor **48°44'·24N 03°33'·44W** ❁❁◊◊✿✿✿

CHARTS AC *2668,* 3669; SHOM 7124; ECM 537, 538; Imray C34; Stanfords 2.

TIDES –0605 Dover; ML 5·4; Duration: no data; Zone –0100

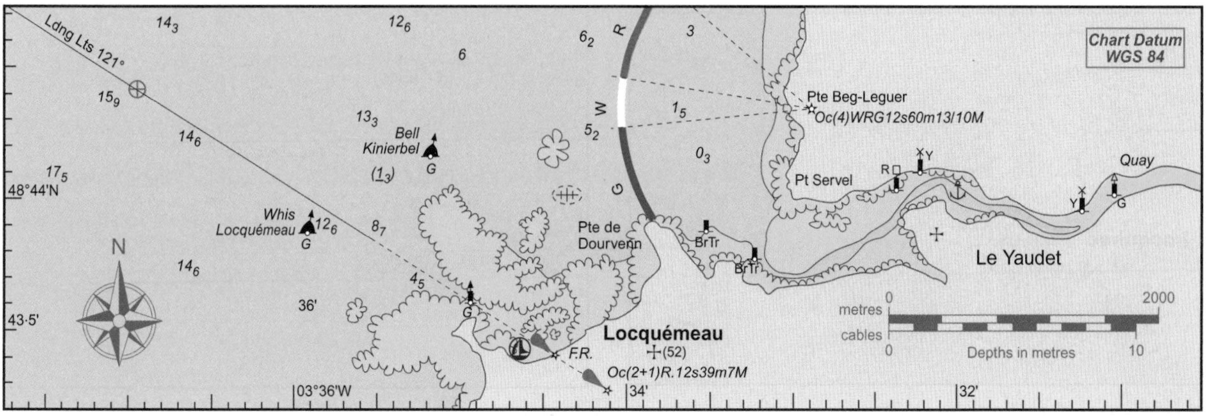
Ldng Lts 121°
Chart Datum WGS 84
Pte Beg-Leguer
Oc(4)WRG12s60m13/10M
Bell Kinierbel
Pt Servel
Quay
48°44'N
Whis Locquémeau
Pte de Dourven
BrTr
Le Yaudet
43·5'
36'
Locquémeau
F.R.
Oc(2+1)R.12s39m7M
03°36'W
34'
32'
metres
cables
Depths in metres

LANNION *continued*

Standard Port BREST (⟶)

Times				Height (metres)			
High Water		Low Water		MHWS	MHWN	MLWN	MLWS
0000	0600	0000	0600	6·9	5·4	2·6	1·0
1200	1800	1200	1800				
Differences LOCQUIREC							
+0058	+0108	+0120	+0100	+2·2	+1·8	+0·8	+0·3

SHELTER Good, except in strong W/NW winds. ⚓ in estuary or in non-drying pools off Le Yaudet and up to the 2nd Y perch. It may be possible to dry out on the N bank just below Lannion town, but a recce by dinghy or on foot is advised.

NAVIGATION WPT 48°44'·46N 03°36'·84W, 091°/2·6M to Beg Léguer lt (also on Locquémeau ldg lts 121°). Leave Kinierbel SHM buoy close to stbd, stand on until Trébeurden spire bears 004° (to clear a drying patch), then alter 135° for the ent, passing close to two G bcn twrs. No access at very LW, esp with strong NW'lies when seas break on the drying bar. Chan up river is easy, but narrow, steep-to and marked by bcns to just beyond Le Yaudet pool. The river to Lannion is best seen at LW before attempting.

LIGHTS AND MARKS See chartlet and 9.20.4. Pte de Beg-Léguer lt is a squat twr, R top, built onto a house. Le Yaudet spire helps to pinpoint the river ent.

R/T None.

TELEPHONE HM 02·96·37·06·52; Aff Mar 02·96·37·06·52; CROSS 02·98·89·31·31; SNSM 02·96·23·52·07; ⊖ 02·96·37·45·32; Auto 08·92·68·08·22; Police 02·96·37·03·78; Dr 02·96·37·42·52; Ⓗ 02·96.05.71.11. Brit Consul 02·99·46·26·64.

FACILITIES **Quai de Loguivy** AB in emergency, Slip, FW, C (1 ton). **Services:** M, ME, El, ⚒, SHOM, Ⓔ, CH. **Town** M, CH, 🛒, Gaz, R, Bar, ✉, Ⓑ, ⇌, ✈ (Brest, Rennes, Dinard). Ferry: Roscoff.

ADJACENT HARBOURS IN BAIE DE LANNION

LOCQUÉMEAU, Côte d'Armor, **48°43'·54N 03°34'·79W**, AC 2668, 3669; SHOM 7124. HW –0600 on Dover (UT); +0110 on Brest; HW ht +1·5m on Brest; ML 5·3m. SHOM 7124 is desirable as it shows the various perches. A small drying hbr by ent to Lannion River (9.20.16); use the same waypoint. Approach leaving Locquémeau SHM buoy close to stbd. There are two quays: the outer is accessible at LW, but open to W winds. Yachts can dry out at inner quay, on S side. Ldg lts 121° to outer quay: front, W pylon + R top; rear, hard-to-see W gable and R gallery. **Services:** ME, El, ⚒; **Town** Bar.

LOCQUIREC, Côte d'Armor, **48°41'·44N 03°38'·77W**. AC 3669, 2668; SHOM 7124. Tidal data see 9.20.16. Small drying hbr at mouth of R Le Douron, with good shelter from W/SW winds. The whole estuary dries to extensive, shifting sandbanks (2·9m to 6·1m). Access HW±3. No lights, but Gouliat NCM buoy is 7ca N of Pte du Château and a SHM bcn twr (6ca S of the hbr, marking Roche Rouge) is conspic as the bay opens up. A pleasant temp ⚓, or overnight if able to take the ground. 27 white moorings, inc 10 Ⓥs in up to 4m @ €4.65 a night, lie NNE of the hbr. Land at slip. Facilities of a small, laid-back resort; inc some fine traditional hotel-restaurants and a cashpoint.

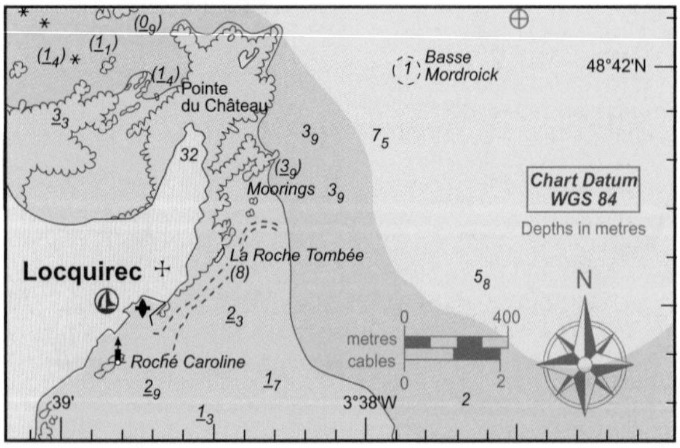
Basse Mordroick
48°42'N
Pointe du Château
Moorings
La Roche Tombée
Locquirec
Roche Caroline
Chart Datum WGS 84
Depths in metres
metres
cables
0
400
2
N
39'
3°38'W

9.20.17 PRIMEL-TREGASTEL

Finistère **48°42'·74N 03°49'·39W**

CHARTS AC 3669, 2745; SHOM 7151, 7124, 7095; ECM 538; Imray C34, C35; Stanfords 2.

TIDES See 9.20.18 for differences ANSE DE PRIMEL. –0610 Dover; ML 5·3; Duration 0600; Zone –0100

SHELTER A useful hbr to await the tide up to Morlaix. Access at all tides, but open to N/NW'lies; in strong winds seas break across ent. FVs occupy most of the bkwtr. A small ⚓age and 15 W Ⓥs (10 in 'deep' water) in about 1m are SE of the bkwtr head; or ⚓ to SE or SW of bkwtr hd in 2·9m. Le Diben on W side is FV port. Drying upper reaches are well sheltered.

NAVIGATION WPT 48°43'·57N 03°50'·09W, 152°/0·9M to the hbr bkwtr. Beware drying rks NE of Pte de Primel. Enter exactly on ldg marks 152°, past a SHM bn marking Ar Zammeguez (3m high). The ent, between a PHM and SHM bn, is narrow.

LIGHTS AND MARKS Pte de Primel is a conspic 42m high rky islet NNE of the hbr. 152° ldg marks/lights: three whited walls with R vert stripe in serried ranks up the hillside; ldg lts, both FR, are on the front and rear marks.

R/T Port VHF Ch 09 16 (season).

TELEPHONE HM ☎ 02·98·62·28·40.

FACILITIES C (25 ton), Slip, CH, El, ME, ⚒, Ⓔ, R, Bar. **Town (P-T)** P, D, 🛒, Gaz, R, Bar, ✉, Ⓑ, ⓓ. Ferry: Roscoff.

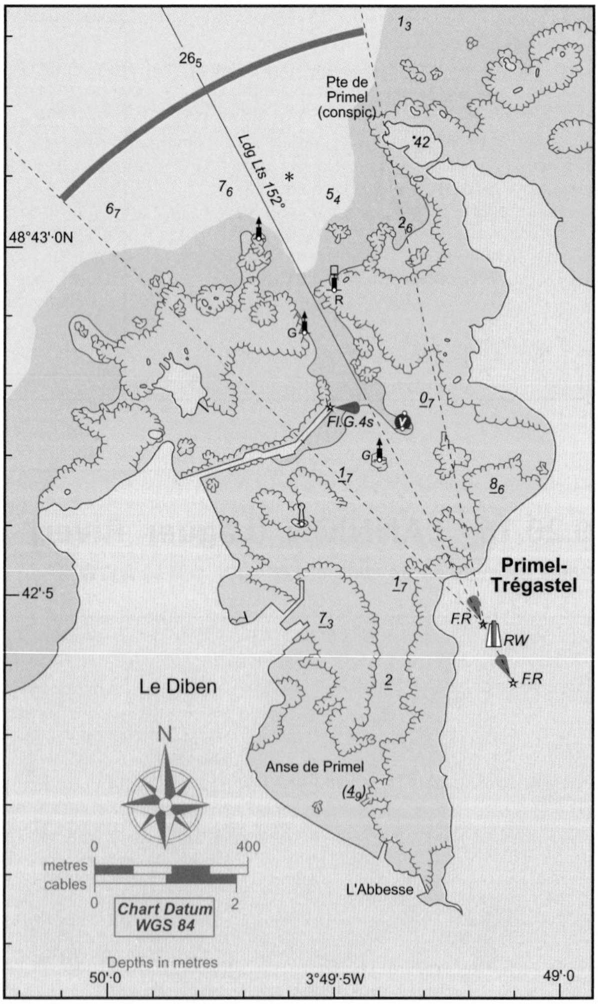
Pte de Primel (conspic)
42
Ldg Lts 152°
48°43'·0N
Fl.G.4s
Primel-Trégastel
FR
RW
FR
42'·5
Le Diben
Anse de Primel
L'Abbesse
N
metres
cables
0
400
2
Chart Datum WGS 84
Depths in metres
50'·0
3°49'·5W
49'·0

9.20.18 MORLAIX

Finistère **48°35'·28N 03°50'·29W** ❀❀⛵⛵⛵✿✿✿

CHARTS AC 3669, 2745; SHOM 7151, 7095; ECM 538; Imray C34, C35; Stanfords 2.

TIDES –0610 Dover; ML 5·3; Duration 0610; Zone –0100

Standard Port BREST (⟶)

Times				**Height (metres)**			
High Water		Low Water		MHWS	MHWN	MLWN	MLWS
0000	0600	0000	0600	6·9	5·4	2·6	1·0
1200	1800	1200	1800				
Differences MORLAIX (CHÂTEAU DU TAUREAU)							
+0055	+0105	+0115	+0055	+2·0	+1·7	+0·8	+0·3
ANSE DE PRIMEL							
+0100	+0110	+0120	+0100	+2·1	+1·7	+0·8	+0·3

SHELTER Good in the bay, except in onshore winds. Strong N'lies can raise a steep sea even in the estuary. ⚓ NE of Carantec is exposed, especially to NW; landing stage dries about 4·6m. ⚓ off Pen Lann and at Dourduff (dries), clear of extensive oyster beds marked by small orange buoys/stakes.

For Morlaix town go 5·5M up-river (subject to silting) from No 1 SHM buoy to lock and marina. Lock opens by day only (SR-SS), at HW –1½, HW and HW+1. Complete shelter in the marina; Ⓥ pontoon on E bank, parallel to road. A movable footbridge, across the marina abeam the YC, is usually open in lock hours.

NAVIGATION WPT (Chenal de Tréguier) 48°42'·55N 03°51'·93W (abm Pierre Noire SHM bcn) 190·5°/1·84M to La Chambre bcn twr.

WPT (Grand Chenal) 48°42'·65N 03°53'·53W, abm Stolvezen PHM buoy, 176°/2·23M to Île Louet lt.

The three appr channels converge at No 1 SHM buoy. All have rocky dangers and require careful pilotage; see next para. River up to Morlaix, 3·4M S of Dourduff, is buoyed/bcn'd but unlit.

LIGHTS AND MARKS See 9.20.4 and chartlet (many lesser marks are omitted for clarity). La Lande is the rear ldg lt/mark common to both main channels.

1. Chenal de Tréguier ldg lts 190·5°; best at night, but almost dries. Front mark: Île Noire in R sector.
2. Grand Chenal ldg lts 176·4°; E of Ricard Is, shallower but lit. Front mark: Île Louet in W sector.
3. Chenal Ouest de Ricard 188·8°. Deepest chan, but unlit; a variant of (2). Pierres de Carantec and Kergrist are the white ldg marks.

R/T Port and marina VHF Ch 09 16.

TELEPHONE HM ☎/📠 02·98·62·13·14, Lock 02·98·88·15·10; Aff Mar 02·98·62·10·47; CROSS 02·98·89·31·31; SNSM 02·98·72·35·10; ⊜ 02·98·88·06·31; Auto 08·92·68·02·29; Police 02·98·88·58·13; Ⓗ 02·98·62·61·60; Brit Consul 02·97·87·36·20.

FACILITIES **Marina** (180+30 Ⓥ) ☎ 02·98·62·13·14, access at lock hrs, €1.40, C (8 ton), P & D, Slip, ME, El, ⚒, CH; **YC de Morlaix** ☎ 02·98·88·38·00.
Town P, D, SM, Ⓔ, SHOM, 🛒, Gaz, R, Bar, ✉, Ⓑ, ⊡. Ferry: Roscoff.

ANCHORAGES W AND NW OF MORLAIX

PENZÉ RIVER, Finistère, Ent **48°41'·94N 03°56'·49W**, AC 2745; SHOM 7095. HW –0610 on Dover (UT), +0105 on Brest; HW ht +1·2m Brest; ML 5·0m; Duration 0605.

The Penzé river lies W of Île Callot. From NNW, appr between Cordonnier and Guerhéon bcn twrs at mid-flood. Or, for deeper water, from the ENE pass between Les Bizeyer reef and Le Paradis bn tr; thence S via beaconed channel.

Passe aux Moutons, between Carantec and Île Callot, is a drying (6·2m) short cut from the E into the Penzé, with adequate rise.

S of Le Figuier IDM bcn the chan narrows and is scantily marked by oyster withies, then by mooring trots. SW of Pte de Lingos shelter is better: moor off St Yves where the old ferry slips provide landing places. S of Pont de la Corde (10m clearance) the river is buoyed and navigable on the tide for 3M to Penzé. No access 1 Mar - 31 Aug to a Nature Reserve at the head of the river. **Facilities at Carantec**: El, ME, ⚒, M, CH, P, D, Ⓔ. **Town** Ⓑ, Bar, ✉, R, 🛒. **Penzé** AB (drying), limited 🛒, R, Bar.

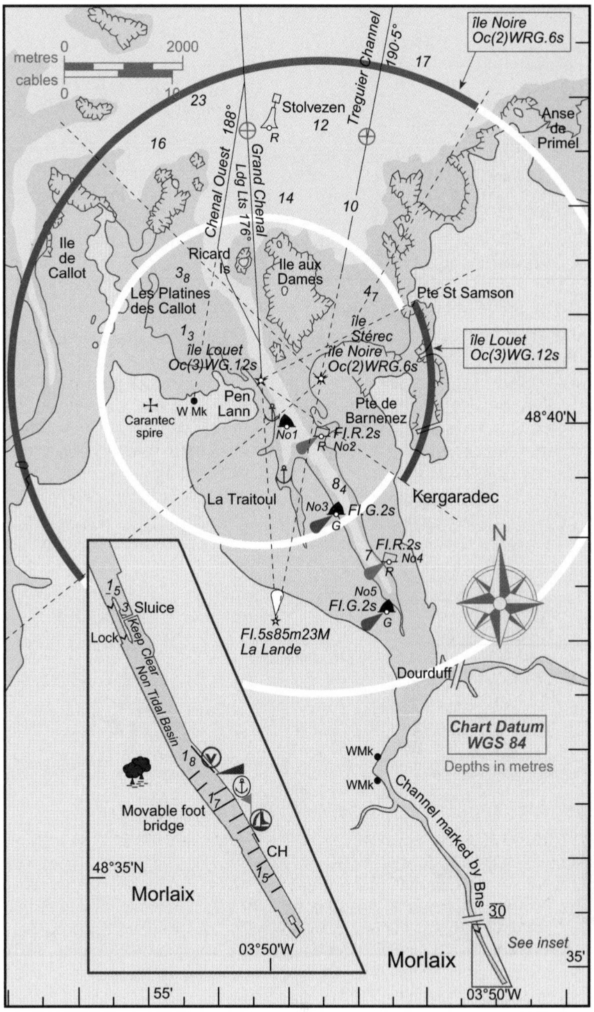
metres
cables
2000
Île Noire
Oc(2)WRG.6s
Treguier Channel
190·5°
Stolvezen
Chenal Ouest 188°
Grand Chenal
Ldg Lts 176°
Anse de Primel
Ile de Callot
Ricard Is
Ile aux Dames
Pte St Samson
Les Platines des Callot
Île Stérec
Île Noire
Oc(2)WRG.6s
Île Louet
Oc(3)WG.12s
Pen Lann
Carantec spire
W Mk
No1
Fl.R.2s
No2
Pte de Barnenez
48°40'N
La Traitoul
No3
Fl.G.2s
Kergaradec
Fl.R.2s
No4
No5
Fl.G.2s
Fl.5s85m23M
La Lande
Sluice
Lock
Keep Clear
Non Tidal Basin
Dourduff
Chart Datum
WGS 84
Depths in metres
WMk
Channel marked by Bns
Movable foot bridge
CH
48°35'N
Morlaix
03°50'W
See inset
35'
55'

9.20.19 ROSCOFF

Finistère **48°43'·54N 03°58'·59W** ❀❀⛵⛵✿✿✿

CHARTS AC 3669, 2745; SHOM 7151, 7095; ECM 538; Imray C35; Stanfords 2.

TIDES –0605 Dover; ML 5·2; Duration 0600; Zone –0100

Standard Port BREST (⟶)

Times				**Height (metres)**			
High Water		Low Water		MHWS	MHWN	MLWN	MLWS
0000	0600	0000	0600	6·9	5·4	2·6	1·0
1200	1800	1200	1800				
Differences ROSCOFF							
+0055	+0105	+0115	+0055	+1·9	+1·6	+0·8	+0·3
ÎLE DE BATZ							
+0045	+0100	+0105	+0055	+2·0	+1·6	+0·9	+0·4
BRIGNOGAN							
+0040	+0045	+0058	+0038	+1·5	+1·2	+0·6	+0·2

SHELTER Good in Vieux Port (dries 5m) except in strong N/E winds. Access HW±2. AB in S Basin on rough jetty, if FVs leave room; or dry out against road wall or secure to ⛵ in SW corner. Close W of Ar Chaden are W ⛵s in 4-5m. Bloscon ferry port is now a controlled ⚓ with a new FV quay (enter only with HM's approval). Beware foul ground inshore and WIP.

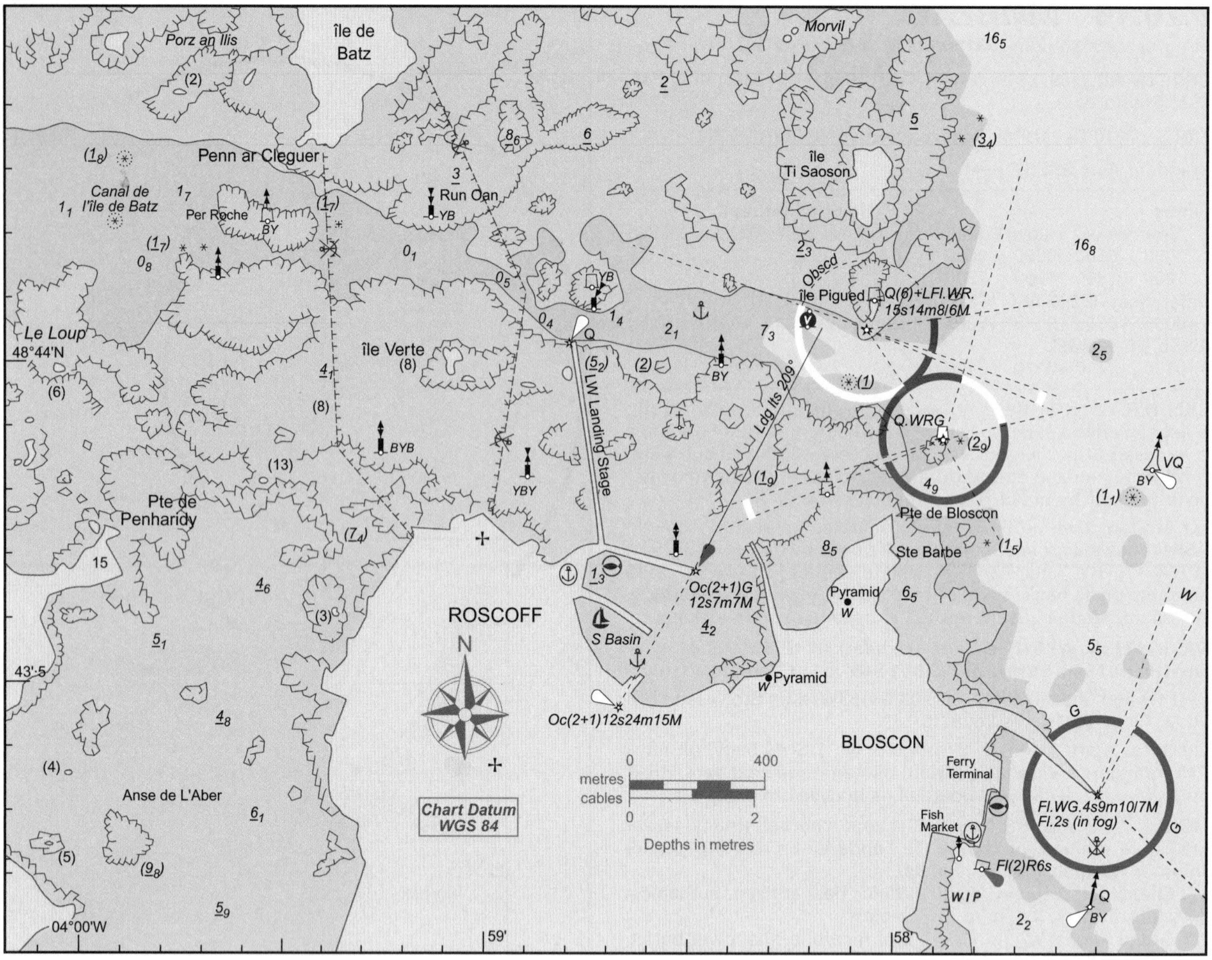
Île de Batz
Porz an Ilis
Morvil
Penn ar Cléguer
Canal de l'île de Batz
Per Roche
Run Oan
YB
BY
Île Ti Saoson
Île Pigued
Q(6)+LFl.WR.15s14m8/6M
Obscd
Le Loup
48°44'N
Île Verte
LW Landing Stage
Ldg lts 209°
Q.WRG
VQ
BYB
YBY
Pte de Penharidy
Pte de Bloscon
Ste Barbe
Pyramid
W
ROSCOFF
Oc(2+1)G 12s7m7M
S Basin
Oc(2+1)12s24m15M
43'·5
BLOSCON
Ferry Terminal
Fish Market
Fl.WG.4s9m10/7M Fl.2s (in fog)
Fl(2)R6s
WIP
Q
G
Anse de L'Aber
metres
cables
Chart Datum WGS 84
Depths in metres
04°00'W
59'
58'

NAVIGATION From the N, WPT 48°45′·88N 03°55′·98W, 213°/2·5M to Men Guen Bras lt. From the E approach between Plateau de la Méloine and Plateau des Duons; or pass S of the latter and N of Le Menk bcn lt twr in Ar Chaden's W sector (289·5°-293°). From the W, WPT 48°44′·33N 04°03′·98W, 090°/1M to Basse Plate NCM bcn twr; thence via Canal de l'Île de Batz.

See 9.20.5 for pilotage in the Canal de l'Île de Batz. The chan is adequately marked, but the bcns must be correctly identified. The appr to Roscoff Vieux Port is over many large drying rks; best to enter near HW. Appr to Bloscon is not tidally limited.

LIGHTS AND MARKS See chartlet and 9.20.4. Île de Batz lt ho is conspic through 360°. E ent to Canal de l'Île de Batz is marked by: Ar Chaden, YB bcn twr, and Men-Guen-Bras BY bcn tr.

Ldg lts/marks 209° for Roscoff Vieux Port: front, W col, G top, with B/W vert stripes on end of mole; rear conspic W lt ho. Bloscon ferry pier, appr 205° in W sector of pierhead lt.

R/T Roscoff Ch 09. *Bloscon* Ch 12 16; 0830-1200, 1330-1800LT.

TELEPHONE HM (Port de Plaisance) 02·98·69·76·37, 📠 02·98·61·11·96; HM (Roscoff) 02·98·61·27·84, 📠 02·98·19·31·87; Aff Mar 02·98·69·70·15; CROSS 02·98·89· 31·31; SNSM 06·82·18·01·34; ⊖ (Roscoff) 02·98·69·70·15; ⊖ (Bloscon) 02·98·69·70·84; Auto 08·92.68·08·29; Police 02·98·69·00·48; Ⓗ 02·98·88·40·22; Dr 02·98·69·71·18; Brit Consul 02·97·87·36·20.

FACILITIES S Basin (280+20 Ⓥ) ☎ 02·98·69·76·37, €0.62 AB (with fender board), M; **N Basin** Reserved for FVs, C (5 ton); **Club Nautique de Roscoff** ☎ 02·98·69·72·79, Bar; **Bloscon** L, Slip.

Services: BY, ME, El, ⚒, CH. **Town** P, D, ME, El, ⚒, CH, Gaz, 🛒, R, Bar, ✉, Ⓑ, ⇌, ✈ (Brest, Morlaix). Ferry: Plymouth, Rosslare.

ÎLE DE BATZ, HARBOUR/ANCHORAGE

ÎLE DE BATZ, Finistère, **48°44′·44N 04°00′·59W**, AC 3669, 2745; SHOM 7151, 7095; HW +0610 Dover (UT); ML 5·2m. See 9.20.18. Porz-Kernok gives good shelter but dries about 5m; ⚓ where space permits. E landing stage is for ferries only. ⚓ in E or W parts of the chan depending on wind, but holding ground poor. ⚓ prohib between SE tip of Batz and Roscoff LW landing jetty, due to cables. Île de Batz lt ho (gy twr, B top), the CG Stn and Church spire are all conspic. Facilities: R, basic shops, bike hire.

OTHER HARBOURS WEST OF ROSCOFF

MOGUÉRIEC, Finistère, **48°41'·35N 04°04'·48W**, AC *2668*, 3669; SHOM 7151. Tides approx as for Île de Batz. A small drying fishing hbr, 3M SSW of W ent to Canal de l'Île de Batz, open to NW swell. Ldg lts 162°, both W trs/G tops: Front on jetty, Iso WG 4s 9m, W158°-166°; rear FG 22m. Beware Méan Névez rk, dries 3·3m, to W of appr. ⚓ close SW of Île de Siec, or 3ca WSW of Ar Skeul WCM bn tr in 4m, or 2ca NNE of Moguériec's drying jetty. AB against jetty, but clear of FVs. AB also possible against jetty at Île de Siec's drying hbr, but rky bottom. Facilities: 🛒, R, Bar.

BRIGNOGNAN (Pontusval), Finistère, **48°40′·59N 04°19′·17W**, about 10M ENE of Île Vierge lt ho. AC 3668; SHOM 7150. HW +0605 on Dover (UT); ML 4·7m; Duration 0600; see 9.20.18. Pontusval is the port, Brignognan a small resort. App from ECM buoy (48°41'·43N 04°19'·31W) via 178° ldg marks, W bn on with Plounéour ch spire 1M S. Ent between Ar Neudenn R bn tr to E and 3 white-topped rks to W. ⚓ here in approx 4m or dry out closer in. Hbr is open to N winds and often full of FVs. Entry at night prohib as it is unlit apart from Pte de Beg Pol, Oc (3) WR 12s, 1M to the west. Facilities: Bar, FW, R, 🛒, 5 Ⓥ's (free).

9.20.20 L'ABER WRAC'H

Finistère **48°36'·69N 04°35'·39W** ❀❀◊◊✿✿✿

CHARTS AC 3668, 1432; SHOM 7150, 7094; ECM 539; Imray C35; Stanfords 2.

TIDES +0547 Dover; ML 4·5; Duration 0600; Zone –0100

Standard Port BREST (⟶)

Times				Height (metres)			
High Water		Low Water		MHWS	MHWN	MLWN	MLWS
0000	0600	0000	0600	6·9	5·4	2·6	1·0
1200	1800	1200	1800				
Differences L'ABERWRAC'H, ÎLE CÉZON							
+0030	+0030	+0040	+0035	+0·8	+0·7	+0·2	0·0

SHELTER Good, except in strong NW'lies. At L'Aber Wrac'h berth on the single pontoon (fingers; max LOA 12m) or pick up one of 30 numbered W ⚓s; ⚓ prohib. Excellent shelter in all winds at Paluden, 1·5M up-river (unlit/unbuoyed), on dumbell ⚓s.

NAVIGATION WPT (Grand Chenal) 48°37'·35N 04°38'·51W, 100°/1·5M to Petit Pot de Beurre ECM bcn twr. Here pick up the inner appr chan 128°/1·7M, in W sector of Dir Lt, passing a SHM lt buoy, SHM bcn lt twr and a PHM lt buoy, to the last SHM bcn twr; thence visual pilotage for 700m to the pool/pontoon at L'Aber Wrac'h. Caution: unlit mooring buoys.

Chenal de la Malouine is a narrow short cut from/to N & E, only by day and in good weather: 176° transit of Petit Pot de Beurre with Petite Île W obelisk; precise tracking is required. Caution: breakers and cross-tides.

Chenal de la Pendante 135·7° is rarely used as it crosses drying rks, saves little mileage and the unlit marks are hard to see. Front, B/W disc on Île Cézon; rear, white obelisk/orange top, S of hbr.

LIGHTS AND MARKS See chartlets and 9.20.4. Île Vierge lt ho, Gy twr, 82m high is 2·4M N of the hbr. Grand Chenal 100·1° ldg marks are: front, W □ twr orange top on Île Wrac' h; rear, 1·63M E, Lanvaon, W □ twr orange △ top. The inner chan is marked by a Dir lt 128° and by two hard-to-see ldg twrs, both W with R tops.

R/T VHF Ch 09 16 (0700-2200LT in season).

TELEPHONE Aff Mar 02·98·04·90·13; CROSS 02·98·89·31·31; ⊖ 02·98·85·07·40; Auto 08·92.68·08·29; Police 02·98·04·00·18; Ⓗ 02·98·22·33·33; Dr 02·98·04·91·87; SAMU 15; Brit Consul 02·97·87·36·20.

FACILITIES Pontoon (80, inc 28 Ⓥ), €1.92, ⚓ €1.62; HM ☎ 02·98·04·91·62, 📠 02·98·04·85·54. D, (HW ±2, 0800-2000) ME, El, CH, BH (12 ton), ⚒, Ⓔ, Slip, C (3 ton mobile).
Note: Work on new facilities had not started as at June 2004.
YC des Abers ☎ 02·98·04·92·60, Bar, ♿, ⊡.

Town P, 🛒, Gaz, R, ⊡, P, Bar, ✉, Ⓑ (Landeda, every a.m. except Mon), ⇄, ✈, (bus to Brest). Ferry: Roscoff.

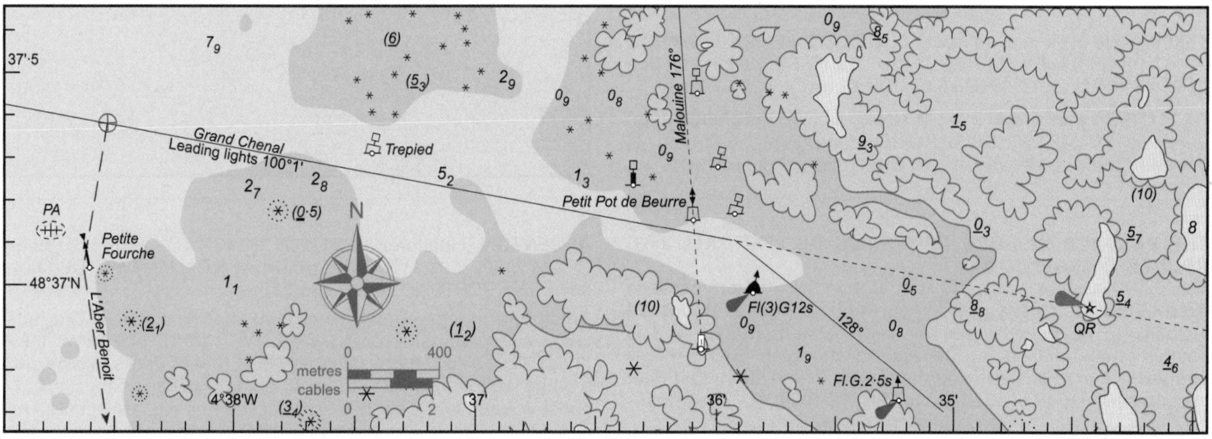
37'·5
Grand Chenal
Leading lights 100°1'
Trepied
Petit Pot de Beurre
Malouine 176°
PA
Petite Fourche
48°37'N
L'Aber Benoit
Fl(3)G12s
128°
Fl.G.2·5s
QR
metres
cables
400
4°38'W
37'
36'
35'

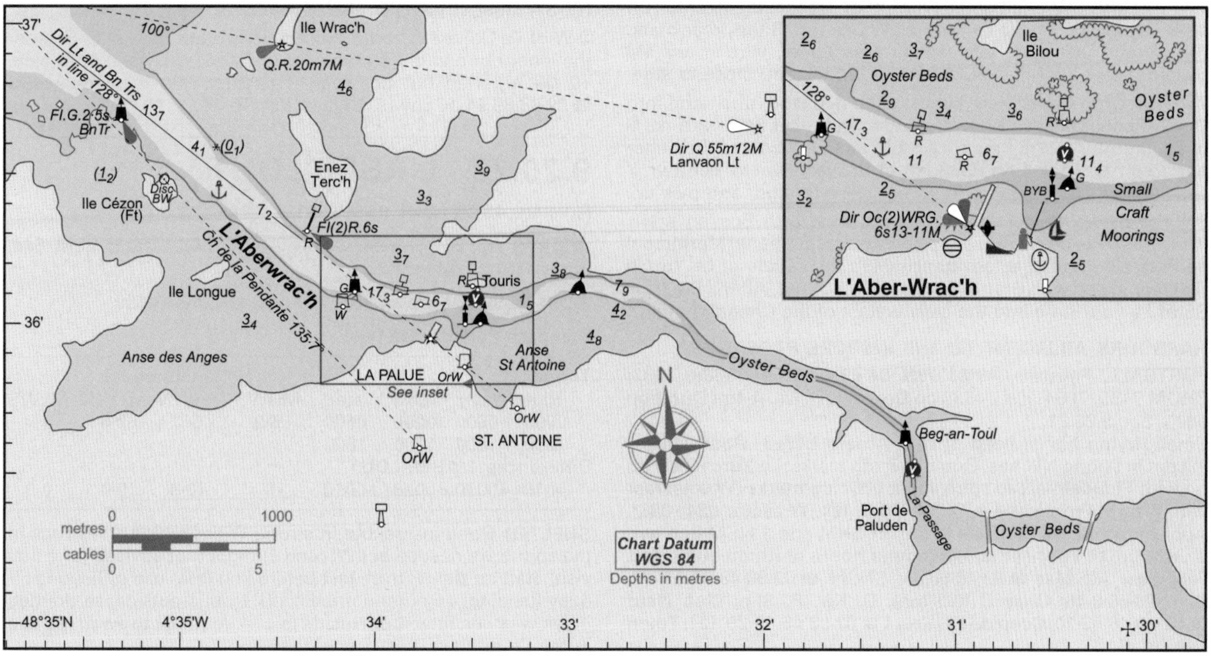
Ile Wrac'h
Q.R.20m7M
Dir Lt and Bn Trs in line 128°
Fl.G.2·5s
BnTr
Ile Cézon (Ft)
Disc BW
Enez Terc'h
Dir Q 55m12M
Lanvaon Lt
Fl(2)R.6s
L'Aberwrac'h
Ch de la Pendante 135·7°
Ile Longue
Touris
Anse des Anges
LA PALUE
See inset
Anse St Antoine
ST. ANTOINE
Oyster Beds
Beg-an-Toul
Port de Paluden
La Passage
Oyster Beds
metres
cables
1000
Chart Datum WGS 84
Depths in metres
36'
48°35'N
4°35'W
34'
33'
32'
31'
30'
Ile Bilou
Oyster Beds
Small Craft Moorings
Dir Oc(2)WRG. 6s13-11M
BYB
L'Aber-Wrac'h

9.20.21 L'ABER BENOIT

Finistère **48°34'·64N 04°36'·89W**

CHARTS AC 3668, 1432; SHOM 7150, 7094; ECM 539, 540; Imray C35; Stanfords 2.

TIDES +0535 Dover; ML 4·7; Duration 0555; Zone –0100

Standard Port BREST (⟶)

Times				Height (metres)			
High Water		Low Water		MHWS	MHWN	MLWN	MLWS
0000	0600	0000	0600	6·9	5·4	2·6	1·0
1200	1800	1200	1800				
Differences L'ABER BENOIT							
+0022	+0025	+0035	+0020	+0·9	+0·7	+0·3	+0·1
PORTSALL							
+0015	+0020	+0025	+0015	+0·6	+0·5	+0·1	0·0

SHELTER Excellent, but do not enter at night, in poor vis nor in strong WNW winds; best near LW when dangers can be seen. Six 🅐s and ⚓ as shown or further up-river. R navigable on the tide to Tréglonou bridge 3M upstream. Beware oyster beds.

NAVIGATION WPT 48°36'·99N 04°38'·84W, close W of Petite Fourche WCM buoy; thence follow the tracks shown on chartlet.

LIGHTS AND MARKS Unlit. Chan bns and buoys must be correctly identified.

R/T None.

TELEPHONE HM pas du tout; CROSS/SNSM 02·98·89·31·31; ⊖ 02·98·85·07·40; Météo Auto 08·92·68·08·29; Police 02·98·48·10·10; Dr 02·98·89·75·67; Brit Consul 02·97·87·36·20.

FACILITIES **Le Passage** Slip, M (free), L, FW; **Tréglonou** Slip; **Services:** ⚒, ME, El. **Town** P & D (cans, 2km), Gaz, ✉, Ⓑ (Ploudalmezeau), ≋, ✈ (bus to Brest). Ferry: Roscoff.

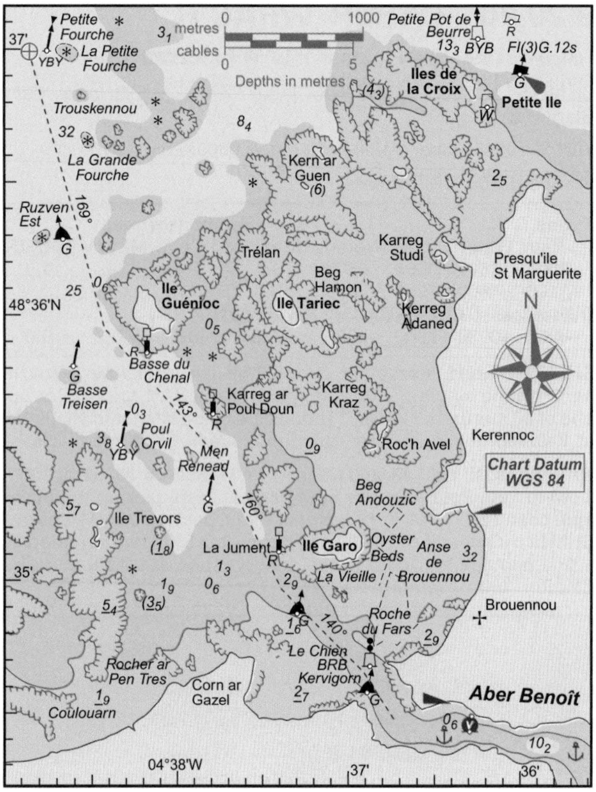
Petite Fourche
La Petite Fourche
YBY
metres
cables
Depths in metres
Petite Pot de Beurre
BYB
Fl(3)G.12s
Iles de la Croix
Petite Ile
Trouskennou
La Grande Fourche
Kern ar Guen
Ruzven Est
169°
Trélan
Beg Hamon
Karreg Studi
Presqu'ile St Marguerite
48°36'N
Ile Guénioc
Ile Tariec
Kerreg Adaned
N
Basse du Chenal
Basse Treisen
Karreg ar Poul Doun
Karreg Kraz
143°
Poul Orvil
Men Renead
Roc'h Avel
Kerennoc
Chart Datum WGS 84
Beg Andouzic
160°
Ile Trevors
La Jument
Ile Garo
Oyster Beds
Anse de Brouennou
35'
La Vieille
Roche du Fars
Brouennou
140°
Le Chien BRB
Kervigorn
Rocher ar Pen Tres
Corn ar Gazel
Coulouarn
Aber Benoît
04°38'W
37'
36'

THE PASSAGE INSHORE OF ROCHES DE PORTSALL AND ROCHES D'ARGENTON

This 8·5M passage is only 1M shorter than the offshore passage from L'Aberwrac'h towards Le Four lt ho. It requires about 6M visibility in daylight (to see the more distant marks) and is navigationally challenging because of strongish tidal streams and the risk of mis-identifying the marks. A well illustrated Pilot and detailed study of AC 1432, or SHOM 7094, are essential.

The passage, described from NE to SW, is in 3 main sections:

1. 7 cables SW of Libenter WCM buoy (see 9.20.20), enter Ch du Relec 218·5°: Pte de Landunvez W bcn twr, R top (rear mark, 6M distant) just open left of Petit Men Louet, W bcn twr 4M distant. Leave Le Relec ECM buoy (1.5M distant) close to stbd.
2. With Corn Carhai lt ho almost abeam to stbd, alter stbd into Ch du Raous: Bosven Kreiz W bcn twr in transit 249° with rks S of Le Gremm, a 12m high rock. Hold this for 7 cables then alter port 228°: Le Four lt ho open left of Bosven Aval W bcn twr. 7 cables later leave Bosven Aval very close to stbd; and pick up:
3. The astern transit 036° of Bosven Aval with Bosven Kreiz. After 1·5M (Pte de Landunvez to port) intercept Chenal Méridional de Portsall, another astern transit 049°: the saddle of Le Yurc'h (7m high rk) on with Grand Men Louet W bcn twr. After 2·2M pass SE of Le Four lt ho into the clear waters of the Chenal du Four.

HARBOURS ADJACENT TO THE INSHORE PASSAGE

PORTSALL, Finistère, **48°33'·79N 04°43'·04W**. AC 3688, 1432; SHOM 7150, 7094. HW +0535 on Dover (UT); ML 4·4m; Duration 0600. See 9.20.21.

Small drying hbr at head of bay. Access HW±3. Good shelter except in strong NW'lies. Outer 109° ldg marks: Le Yurc'h rk (7m) on with Ploudalmézeau spire. Inner 085° ldg marks (W cols; rear with R top). Front col has Oc (4) WRG 12s, W sector 084°-088°. Appr marked by 3 W bn trs to port, 1 SHM and 1 NCM bcn twr. ⚓ in >10m to W of ent, or enter inner hbr to berth on quay. **Tel/ Facilities**: Aff Mar ☎ 98·48·66·54; SNSM ☎ 02·98·48·77·44; Dr ☎ 02·98·48·8·46; **Quay** C (0·5 ton), D, FW, P, Slip; **Club Naut** ☎ 02·98·48·63·10; **Coop de Pêcheurs** ☎ 02·98·48·63·26, CH. **Town** Bar, ✉, R, 🛒.

ARGENTON, Finistère, **48°31'·26N 04°46'·34W**. AC 1432, 3345; SHOM 7150, 7122. HW +0535 on Dover (UT); ML 4·6m; Duration 0600; use PORTSALL diffs 9.20.21.

Small hbr drying approx 5·5m; good shelter except in W winds when swell enters. Access HW±3. WPT 48°31'·14N 04°48'·29W (2½ca S of Le Four lt ho), 084·6°/1·4M to first of 2 W bcn twrs and a white wall with R vert stripe, all on Île Dolvez and in transit. A conspic water twr is slightly S of this ldg line and 1M inland. The N side of chan is marked by 3 PHM bcn twrs. Beware strong NE-SW tidal streams in the approach.

⚓ W of Île Dolvez in about 2m; or skirt round its N side to enter the inner hbr and dry out against the stone quay/slip on N side. 10 🅐s reported but not seen. Facilities: FW, P on quay; **SC** ☎ 02·98·89·54·04 shwrs. **Village** Bar, R, 🛒.

9.20.22 L'ABERILDUT

Finistère **48°28'·24N 04°45'·81W**

CHARTS AC 2644, 2694, 3345; SHOM 7149, 7122; ECM 540; Imray C36; Stanfords 2.

TIDES +0520 on Dover (UT); ML 4·2m; Zone –0100

Standard Port BREST (⟶)

Times				Height (metres)			
High Water		Low Water		MHWS	MHWN	MLWN	MLWS
0000	0600	0000	0600	6·9	5·4	2·6	1·0
1200	1800	1200	1800				
Differences L'ABERILDUT							
+0010	+0010	+0023	+0010	+0·4	+0·3	0·0	0·0

SHELTER Good inside, but in strong W'lies a high swell runs in the appr; care needed at LWS and at night (not advised for a first visit). Raft on 🅐s ('V' trot), just before 2nd PHM bcn or beyond FV quay (landing) on outer dumbells ('G' trot). ⚓ outside, as chartlet, in fair weather; little room inside to ⚓. A good hbr to await the tide in the Ch du Four, 9.20.5 & 9.20.24.

NAVIGATION WPT 48°28'·07N 04°47'·95W, 083°/1·6M to Dir lt which is conspic on white gable end of house. Beware: Les Liniou rks 1·5M NNW of the WPT, Plateau des Fourches 1·2M S and strong cross tides in the approach. Drying rks are marked by Pierre de l'Aber SHM bcn and Le Lieu PHM bcn twr 5m; the latter is the easier to see. At the narrow ent (2m) leave Men Tassin PHM bn and Rocher du Crapaud, a large rounded rock, 30m to port to clear drying spit on S side.

LIGHTS AND MARKS See chartlet and 9.20.4. Glizit water twr is conspic 6·5ca N of the entrance. Dir lt 083° is a good daymark (see above); its 2° R sector marks dangers on N side of chan, but do not take liberties with the S side. An uncharted water twr is almost on 083°, some way inland. Forget the spires at Lanildut and Brélès, charted as being in transit 078·5°; they are small, very hard to see and obsc'd by trees when close in.

R/T VHF Ch 09, Jun-Sep in office hours.

TELEPHONE HM 02·98·04.36.40 (season), mobile 06·11·66.31·64; Aff Mar 02·98·48·66·54; Auto 08·92·68·08·08; ⊜ 02·98·44·35·20; CROSS 1616; SNSM 02·98·89·30·31; Police 02·98·48·10·10 (or emergency 17); Dr 02·98·04·33·08.

FACILITIES **Hbr**, M (410, inc 12 Ⓥs; €1.34 (average), FW, D (ask at CH), AC at FV quay, Ⓢ, Slips, BY, ⚒, ME, El, CH, M. Note: Diesel, AC, FW due in 2005 at new yacht pontoon close N of FV quay. **Village** 🛒, R, Bar, ✉. All needs at Brest 25km. Ferry: Roscoff.

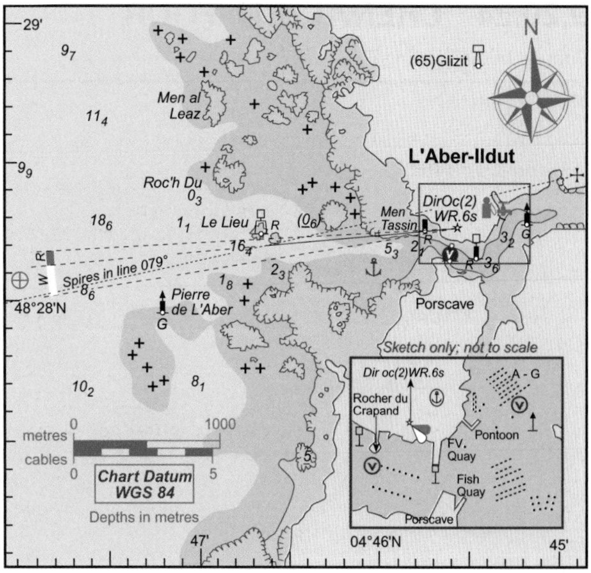
L'Aber-Ildut
(65)Glizit
Men al Leaz
Roc'h Du
Le Lieu
Men Tassin
DirOc(2) WR.6s
Spires in line 079°
Pierre de L'Aber
Porscave
Sketch only; not to scale
Dir oc(2)WR.6s
Rocher du Crapand
A - G
Pontoon
FV. Quay
Fish Quay
Porscave
metres
cables
Chart Datum WGS 84
Depths in metres
29'
48°28'N
47'
04°46'N
45'

9.20.23 LE CONQUET

Finistère **48°21'·54N 04°47'·24W** ❁❁◊◊✿✿

CHARTS AC 2694, 3345 with 1:10,000 inset; SHOM 7149, 7148, 7122; ECM 540; Imray C36; Stanfords 2.

TIDES +0535 Dover; ML 3·9; Duration 0600; Zone –0100

Standard Port BREST (⟶)

Times				Height (metres)			
High Water		Low Water		MHWS	MHWN	MLWN	MLWS
0000	0600	0000	0600	6·9	5·4	2·6	1·0
1200	1800	1200	1800				
Differences LE CONQUET							
–0005	0000	+0007	+0007	–0·1	–0·1	–0·1	0·0
LE TREZ HIR (Anse de Bertheaume)							
–0010	–0005	–0008	–0008	–0·3	–0·3	–0·1	0·0

SHELTER Good except in strong W'lies. The Avant Port is reserved for FVs, workboats; ferries use Mole Ste Barbe; ⚓ prohib. Really only for yachts in emergency. See the HM at Mole St Christophe for a vacant mooring or dry out further ENE on one of 10 Ⓥ 'places'. Nearest ⚓ in Anse des Blancs Sablons.

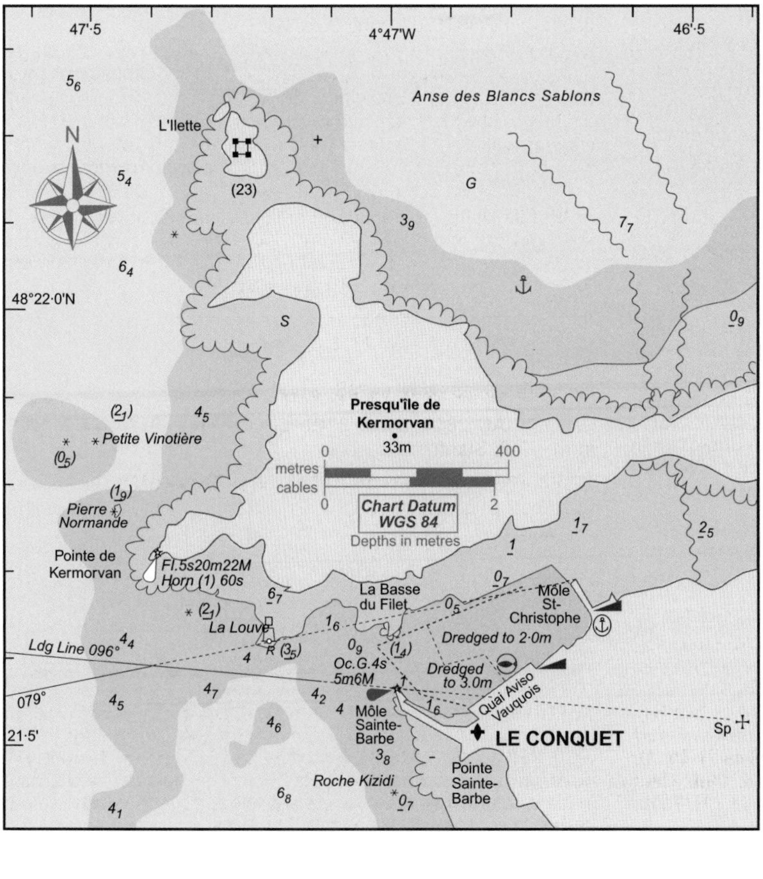
47'·5
4°47'W
46'·5
Anse des Blancs Sablons
L'Ilette
Presqu'île de Kermorvan
33m
Petite Vinotière
Pierre Normande
Pointe de Kermorvan
Fl.5s20m22M Horn (1) 60s
La Louve
Ldg Line 096°
079°
48°22·0'N
21·5'
La Basse du Filet
Môle St-Christophe
Dredged to 2·0m
Dredged to 3·0m
Oc.G.4s 5m6M
Môle Sainte-Barbe
Quai Aviso Vauquois
LE CONQUET
Pointe Sainte-Barbe
Roche Kizidi
Sp
metres
cables
Chart Datum WGS 84
Depths in metres

NAVIGATION WPT 48°21'·68N 04°48'·50W, 096°/1M to Mole Ste Barbe lt. From the NW, beware Grande and Petite Vinotière rks. From the SSW keep seaward of Les Renards IDM buoy and R bcn twr closer inshore. Also note strong cross streams in the Chenal du Four. In hbr ent keep close to Mole Ste Barbe lt, to avoid La Basse du Filet (1·4m) on N side.

LIGHTS AND MARKS See chartlet and 9.20.4. Mole Ste-Barbe lt in line 096° with church spire leads to hbr ent. 079° transit of La Louve R bn tr and end of Mole St Christophe (inner mole) is only valid outside the hbr.

R/T *Le Conquet Port* (HM) VHF 08 16.

TELEPHONE HM 02·98·89·08·07; Aff Mar 02·98·89·00·05; Météo 02·98·84·60·64; Auto 08·92·68·08·08; CROSS 02·98·89·31·31; Police 02·98·22·54·92; Dr 02·98·89·01·86; Brit Consul 02·97·87·36·20.

FACILITIES **Hbr** Slip, M, ME, El, CH. **Town** R, Bar, P&D (cans), 🛒, Gaz, ✉, Ⓑ, bus to Brest

ANCHORAGE EAST OF PTE DE ST MATHIEU

ANSE DE BERTHEAUME, 48°20'·44N 04°41'·84W. AC 2350, 3427. SHOM 7401. A useful passage ⚓ to await the tide E to Brest, N into Ch du Four, or S toward Raz de Sein. Good shelter in W'lies. 1ca NE of Fort de Bertheaume (32m, conspic), Le Chat rk (6·8m) is marked by an ECM bcn. No lts. ⚓ in 3-5m between slip NNW of the Fort and an IDM bcn 3ca further N.

9.20.24 CHENAL DU FOUR

Simple buoy-hopping/GPS track: — — — — — —

See 9.20.5 for notes on this passage and Chenal de la Helle.

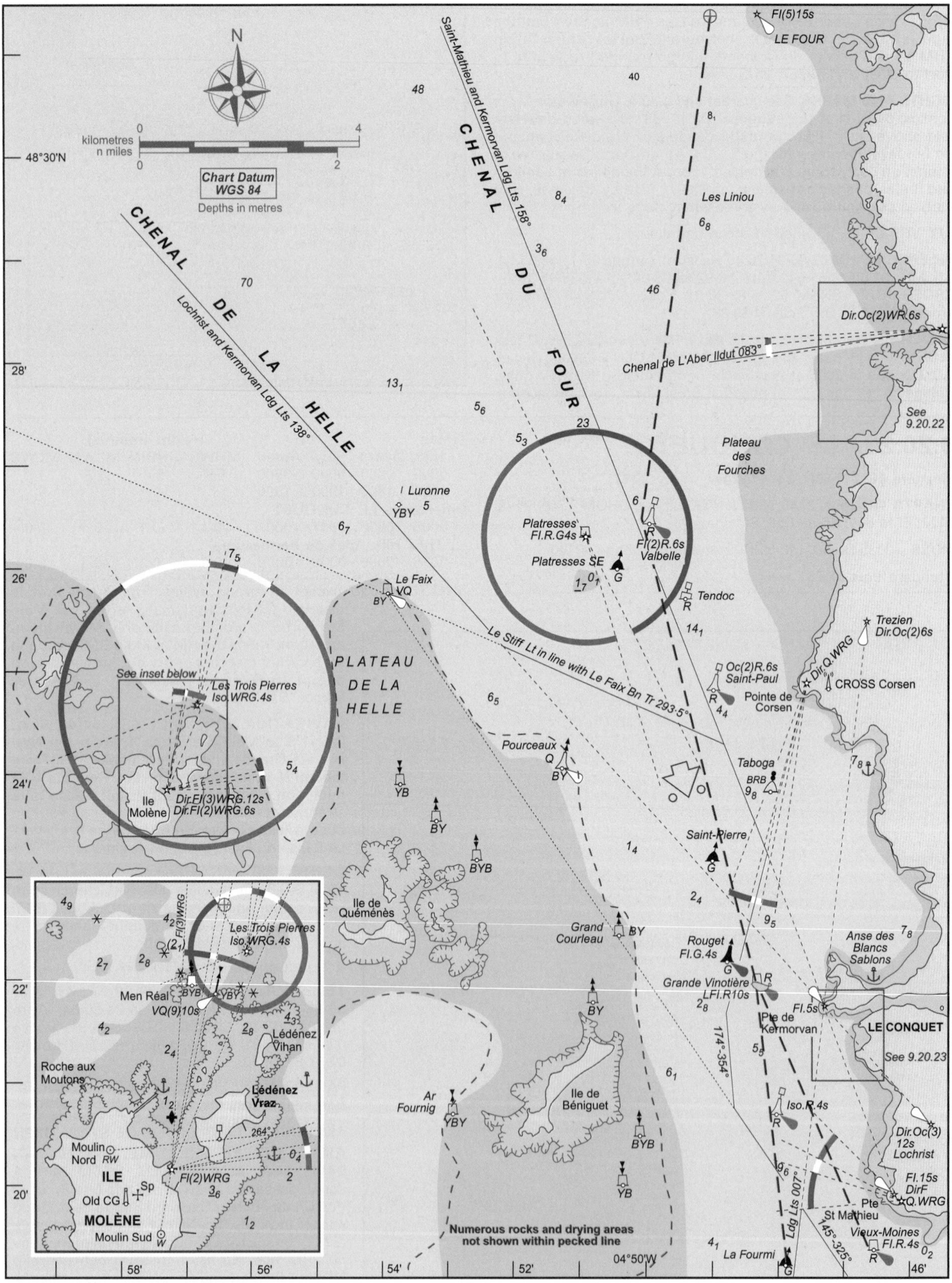
N
kilometres
n miles
Chart Datum
WGS 84
Depths in metres
48°30'N
28'
26'
24'
22'
20'
58'
56'
54'
52'
04°50'W
46'
Fl(5)15s
LE FOUR
Saint-Mathieu and Kermorvan Ldg Lts 158°
CHENAL DU FOUR
CHENAL DE LA HELLE
Lochrist and Kermorvan Ldg Lts 138°
Les Liniou
Dir.Oc(2)WR.6s
Chenal de L'Aber Ildut 083°
See 9.20.22
Plateau des Fourches
Platresses Fl.R.G4s
Platresses SE
Fl(2)R.6s Valbelle
Tendoc
Luronne
YBY
Le Faix VQ
BY
Le Stiff Lt in line with Le Faix Bn Tr 293·5°
Trezien Dir.Oc(2)6s
Dir.Q.WRG
CROSS Corsen
Oc(2)R.6s Saint-Paul
Pointe de Corsen
See inset below
Les Trois Pierres Iso.WRG.4s
PLATEAU DE LA HELLE
Ile Molène
Dir.Fl(3)WRG.12s
Dir.Fl(2)WRG.6s
Pourceaux Q
BY
YB
BY
BYB
Taboga BRB
Saint-Pierre
Ile de Quéménès
Grand Courleau
Rouget Fl.G.4s
Grande Vinotière LFl.R10s
Fl.5s
Pte de Kermorvan
LE CONQUET
See 9.20.23
Anse des Blancs Sablons
174°-354°
Ile de Béniguet
Ar Fournig
YBY
BYB
YB
Iso.R.4s
Dir.Oc(3) 12s Lochrist
Fl.15s DirF Q.WRG
Pte St Mathieu
Vieux-Moines Fl.R.4s
Ldg Lts 007°
145°-325°
La Fourmi
Numerous rocks and drying areas not shown within pecked line
Fl(3)WRG
Men Réal VQ(9)10s
Lédénez Vihan
Roche aux Moutons
Lédénez Vraz
264°
Moulin Nord RW
ILE MOLÈNE
Fl(2)WRG
Old CG
Sp
Moulin Sud W

9.20.25 ÎLE D'OUESSANT

Finistère **48°26'·64N 05°07'·49W** (B de Lampaul) ❀❀◐✿✿✿

CHARTS AC 2694; SHOM 7149, 7123; ECM 540; Imray C36; Stan 2.

TIDES +0522 Dover; ML 3·9; Duration 0555; Zone –0100
Standard Port BREST (⟶)

Times				Height (metres)			
High Water		Low Water		MHWS	MHWN	MLWN	MLWS
0000	0600	0000	0600	6·9	5·4	2·6	1·0
1200	1800	1200	1800				
Differences BAIE DE LAMPAUL							
+0005	+0005	–0005	+0003	0·0	–0·1	–0·1	0·0
ÎLE DE MOLENE							
+0012	+0012	+0017	+0017	+0·4	+0·3	+0·2	+0·1

SHELTER Good in Baie de Lampaul in N-E winds, and in Baie du Stiff in S-NW winds; fresh/strong winds from the opposite directions render the bays untenable. For a first visit settled weather, no swell and good vis (often poor in July) are ideal.

Lampaul has room to ⚓ in 6-10m and about 22 free Ⓥs SE of the PHM/SHM bcn twrs off the narrow drying hbr (not usually accessible for visitors). Ferries no longer use Lampaul.

Baie du Stiff has 3 W Ⓥs (free) in 5m on S side at 48°28'·03N 05°03'·11W, but there is little space to ⚓ and holding is poor. S of the lt ho, Porz Liboudou is for ferries, berthing on either jetty.

NAVIGATION Lampaul WPT 48°25'·38N 05°09'·96W, 054.4°/2·4M to LH edge of Youc'h Korz (a mighty rock which may be passed on either side) in transit with Le Stiff lt ho. Do not attempt Chenal de la Fourche, a short cut inside La Jument lt ho.

Baie du Stiff WPT 48°28'·38N 05°01'·32W, 259°/1·3M to Dir lt.

LIGHTS AND MARKS The radar twr (129m) at Le Stiff is highly conspic. See 9.20.4 for La Jument, Nividic, Creac'h and Le Stiff lt ho's; also Gorle Vihan IDM bcn twr in Baie du Stiff, where a Dir lt Q WRG marks the 259° appr for ferries; Men-Korn bcn twr (lit) is 1.3M E. Kéréon lt ho marks the S side of Passage du Fromveur.

R/T None. **TELEPHONE** HM 02·98·48·80·06; Aff Mar 02·98·89·00·05; CROSS 1616; Auto 08·92.68·08·29; SNSM 02·98·48·84·33; Dr 02·98·48·83·22; Police (summer only) 02·98·48·81·61; Tourist Office 02·98·48·85·83; Brit Consul 02·97·87·36·20.

FACILITIES FW, P & D (cans), Slip. **Village** R, Gaz, ✉, Ⓑ, bike hire, ✈, ferry to Le Conquet and Brest ⇌. UK Ferry: Roscoff.

ADJACENT ISLAND HARBOUR

ÎLE MOLÈNE, Finistère, **48°24'·07N 04°57'·30W** (LB mooring).

CHARTS AC 2694, 3345; SHOM 7149, 7148, 7122, 7123; ECM 540; Imray C36; Stanford 17

TIDES See 9.20.25; +0520 Dover; ML 4·6; Zone –0100

SHELTER Good, except in strong N/NE'lies. The LB mooring is a good ref pt in the hbr. ⚓ near LB in about 1·2m. 8-10 white Ⓥs, €4.57; see 9.20.24 inset. Ferries berth on N jetty.

NAVIGATION Appr is easier in settled weather, good vis and at nps; tidal streams are strong. The simpler appr is from the NE, near Luronne WCM buoy (Ch de la Helle), to WPT 48°25'·00N 04°56'·97W; thence 191°/8·5 cables to the LB mooring, passing between ECM bcn twr and WCM buoy, VQ (9) 10s.

From the E (Chenal des Laz), WPT 48°24'·35N 04°51'·30W (650m N of Pourceaux NCM lt buoy), 264°/2·7M to 48°24'·07N 04°55'·41W. Here make good 315°/1·1M to skirt round Les Trois Pierres lt twr and continue via the N ⊕. This appr is used by mainland ferries.

LIGHTS AND MARKS Both appr chans are defined by day transits: from the N, Moulin Sud and white mark on N jetty 190°. From the E, Moulin Nord (W bcn, orange top) and white twr 264°. The church spire and old CG twr are both conspic from afar.

The two lts (on same column) at old S pier are: Fl (3) WRG 12s whose W sector, 190°-192°, covers the 191° appr; and Fl (2) WRG 6s whose W sector, 259·5°-262·5°, covers the Chenal des Laz 261°. See chartlet and 9.20.4 for Les Trois Pierres, Iso WRG 4s.

R/T None. **TELEPHONE** HM, via Mairie 02·98·07·39·05.

FACILITIES FW, 🛒, CH, R, Bar, ✉; Shwrs near museum.

20

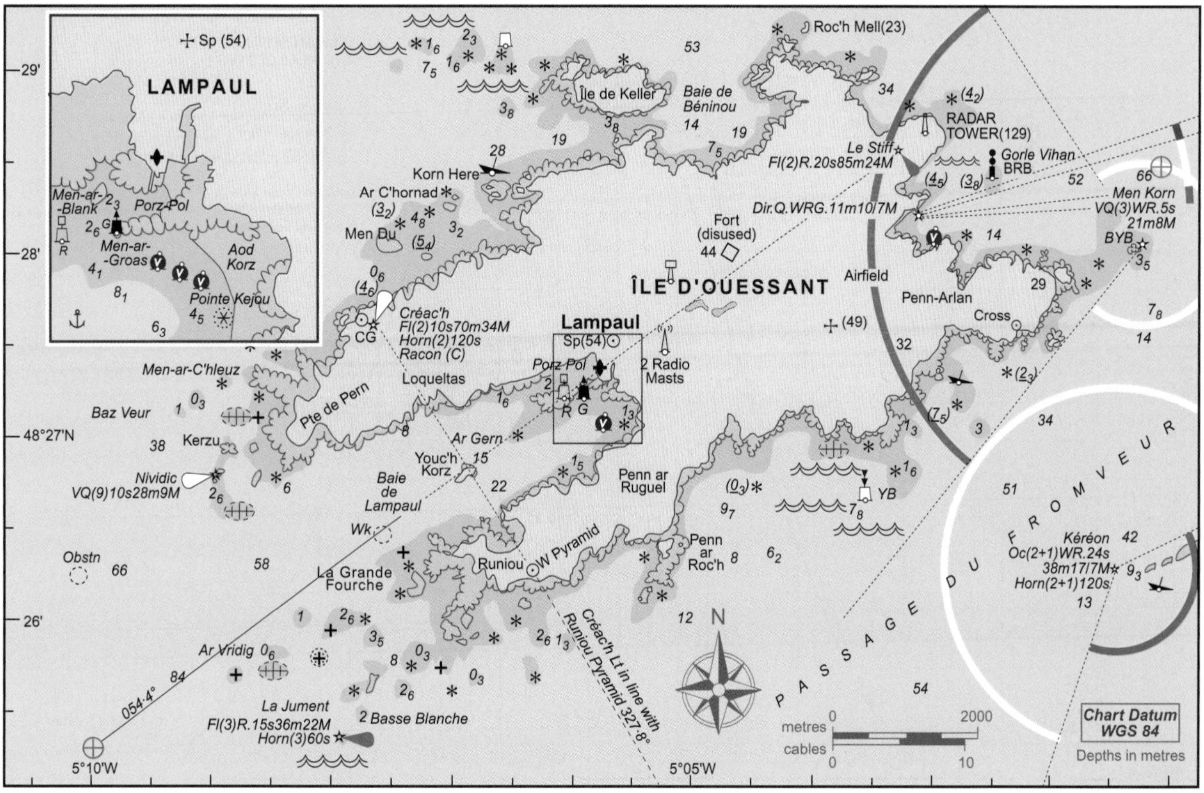
LAMPAUL
Sp (54)
Men-ar-Blank
Porz-Pol
Men-ar-Groas
Aod Korz
Pointe Kejou
Roc'h Mell(23)
Île de Keller
Baie de Béninou
Le Stiff
Fl(2)R.20s85m24M
RADAR TOWER(129)
Gorle Vihan BRB
Men Korn VQ(3)WR.5s 21m8M BYB
Korn Here
Ar C'hornad
Men Du
Dir.Q.WRG.11m10/7M
Fort (disused)
ÎLE D'OUESSANT
Airfield
Penn-Arlan
Cross
Créac'h Fl(2)10s70m34M Horn(2)120s Racon (C)
CG
Lampaul
Sp(54)
Porz-Pol
2 Radio Masts
Loqueltas
Men-ar-C'hleuz
Pte de Pern
Baz Veur
Kerzu
Nividic VQ(9)10s28m9M
Ar Gern
Youc'h Korz
Baie de Lampaul
Penn ar Ruguel
YB
Wk
Obstn
La Grande Fourche
Runiou
W Pyramid
Penn ar Roc'h
Kéréon Oc(2+1)WR.24s 38m17/7M Horn(2+1)120s
PASSAGE DU FROMVEUR
Ar Vridig
La Jument Fl(3)R.15s36m22M Horn(3)60s
Basse Blanche
054.4°
Créac'h Lt in line with Runiou Pyramid 327.8°
metres 0 2000
cables 0 10
Chart Datum WGS 84
Depths in metres
5°10'W
5°05'W
29'
28'
48°27'N
26'

TRAFFIC SEPARATION SCHEME OFF OUESSANT

The present layout, introduced May 2003, is shown on 9.20.2.

The 3 lanes, seaward from Ouessant, are used as follows:

i A two-way lane, 2M wide, for passenger ships operating from/to a Channel port west of 1°W and for vessels sailing between Cap de la Hague and Cabo Finisterre.
ii A NE-bound lane, 4·75M wide; and
iii An outermost SW-bound lane, 4·75M wide.

Yachts are advised to stay out of the TSS, not using any of the lanes, other than for crossing. They may route: to seaward of the TSS; through the ITZ, which at 8M (NW-SE) is approx 3·7M wider than before; or inshore of Ouessant by the Passage du Fromveur; or, more usually, by the Chenal de la Helle and/or Chenal du Four.

Traffic information, urgent warnings and special weather bulletins are broadcast on Ch 79, in French and English, by *Ouessant Traffic* at H +10 and +40.

Weather bulletins are broadcast every 3 hrs from 0150UT, Ch 79.

Radar surveillance within a radius of 40M from Le Stiff radar may be available on request to *Ouessant Traffic* Ch 13, 79, 16.

9.20.26 BREST TIDAL COEFFICIENTS

These indicate at a glance the magnitude of the tide on any particular day by assigning a non-dimensional coefficient to the twice-daily, ie morning and afternoon, range of tide. Thus with a working knowledge of coefficients the reader can see instantly whether it is neaps, springs or somewhere between. There is no need to look up or try to recall the range in metres at the nearest Standard Port. Just remember the magic numbers 45, 70 and 95.

Coefficients are based on the following scale of ranges at Brest:

120	=	a very big spring tide
95	=	mean springs (*vive eau*)
70	=	an average tide
45	=	mean neaps (*morte eau*); and
20	=	a very small neap tide.

The table opposite is for Brest, but holds good elsewhere along the Channel and Atlantic coasts of France.

French tide tables, similar to Admiralty tide tables as in this Almanac, show for Secondary ports their time and height differences against the appropriate standard port for springs and for neaps. The tidal coefficient for the day may be used to decide which correction(s) to apply. In general it is satisfactory to use the *vive eau* corrections for coefficients over 70 and the *morte eau* corrections for the others. Where it is necessary to obtain more accurate corrections (for example in estuaries) this can be done by interpolating or extrapolating.

Coefficients may also be used to determine rates of tidal streams on a given day, using a graph similar in principle to that shown in Fig 8 (7). On the vertical axis plot tidal coefficients from 20 at the bottom to 120 at the top. The horizontal axis shows tidal stream rates from zero to (say) five knots. From the tidal stream atlas or chart, plot the np and sp rates against coefficient 45 and 95 respectively; join these two points. Entering with the tidal coefficient for the day in question, go horizontally to the sloping line, then vertically to read the required rate on the horizontal axis.

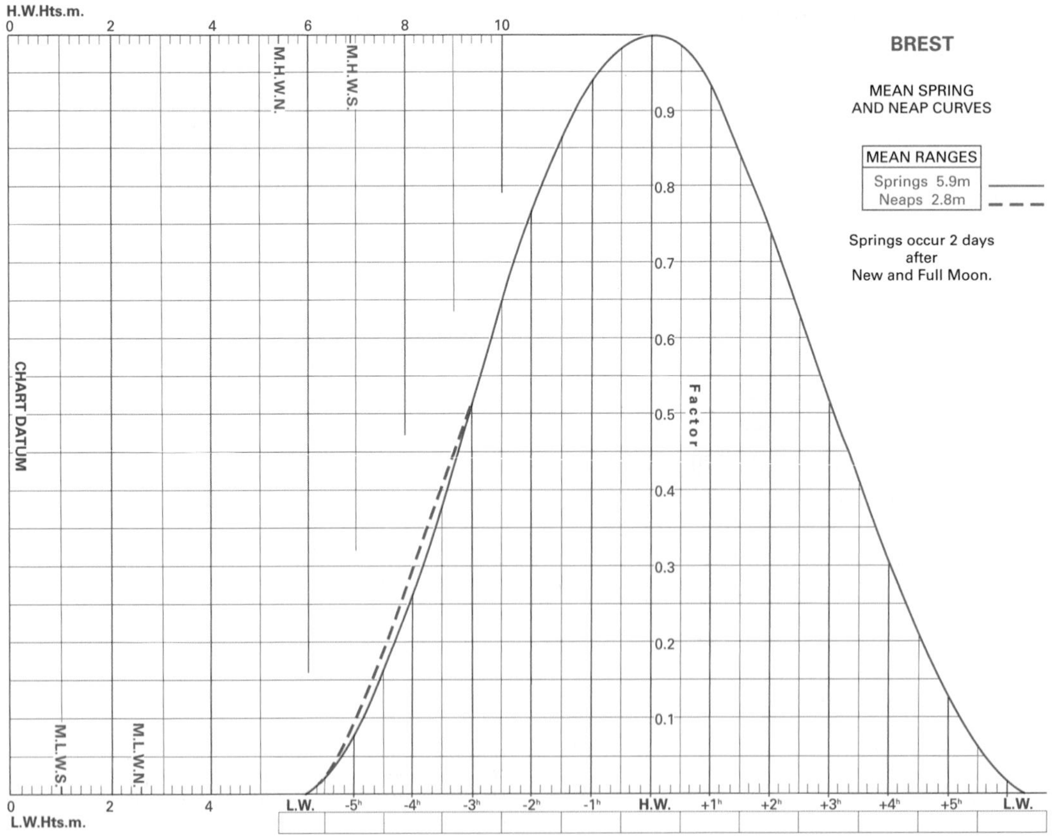

H.W.Hts.m.
0
2
4
6
8
10
M.H.W.N.
M.H.W.S.
CHART DATUM
M.L.W.S.
M.L.W.N.
L.W.Hts.m.
Factor
0.9
0.8
0.7
0.6
0.5
0.4
0.3
0.2
0.1
L.W.
-5h
-4h
-3h
-2h
-1h
H.W.
+1h
+2h
+3h
+4h
+5h
L.W.
BREST
MEAN SPRING AND NEAP CURVES
MEAN RANGES
Springs 5.9m
Neaps 2.8m
Springs occur 2 days after New and Full Moon.

BREST TIDAL COEFFICIENTS

YEAR **2005**

Date	Jan		Feb		Mar		Apr		May		June		July		Aug		Sept		Oct		Nov		Dec	
	am	pm	am	pm	am	pm	am	pm	am	pm	am	pm	am	pm	am	pm	am	pm	am	pm	am	pm	am	pm
1	59	56	60	56	78	73	55	48	47	45	57		53	52	43	46	58	63	69	74	83	86	82	85
2	53	51	52	48	68	62	42	39	47		59	62	52	54	50	54	68	73	78	82	88	90	87	87
3	48	46	45	43	55	49	39		50	55	65	68	55	58	58	62	76	80	85	88	90	89	87	87
4	45	44	43		43	39	43	50	61	67	70	73	60	62	66	69	82	84	90	91	88	86	85	83
5	45		45	50	38		58	67	73	78	74	76	64	68	72	74	86	86	91	90	83	78	80	76
6	47	50	56	64	40	46	75	83	83	87	76	77	68	69	76	77	86	86	88	85	74	68	72	68
7	54	60	72	80	54	63	89	95	89	91	76	76	70	71	78	79	84	82	82	77	62	57	64	61
8	65	71	88	94	73	82	100	103	91	91	75	73	71	71	78	77	79	75	73	66	51	47	58	56
9	77	83	100	104	90	97	104	104	90	88	71	69	70	70	76	74	71	65	60	53	45	45	55	55
10	88	93	107	108	103	107	103	100	85	81	66	64	69	67	72	68	60	54	47	41	47		57	
11	96	99	108	105	109	110	96	91	77	73	61	58	65	63	65	61	48	42	37	36	52	57	59	62
12	100	100	102	97	109	107	86	79	68	63	55	51	61	58	57	52	37	35	39		64	70	65	67
13	99	97	91	83	103	97	73	65	58	52	48	46	55	52	48	44	36		46	54	76	81	70	73
14	93	88	76	68	91	84	58	51	47	42	43	41	50	47	41	39	41	49	63	71	85	88	75	76
15	83	77	60	51	76	68	44	37	38	34	41	41	45	44	40		58	68	80	87	91	92	78	78
16	71	64	44	37	60	51	31	26	32	32	42		44		43	49	77	86	94	99	92	91	78	78
17	57	51	31	28	43	35	24	26	33		44	47	45	47	56	64	94	101	103	105	90	87	77	75
18	46	42	28		29	24	29		36	40	51	55	51	55	73	81	106	109	105	104	83	80	73	71
19	39		31	35	23		35	41	45	51	60	64	61	67	89	96	111	111	102	98	75	70	68	65
20	39	40	41	47	25	30	48	55	56	62	69	74	73	79	102	106	109	106	93	87	65	59	62	59
21	42	45	53	58	37	44	61	67	68	73	79	83	85	90	109	110	100	94	81	74	54	49	56	52
22	49	53	64	69	51	57	74	79	78	82	86	89	95	98	109	106	87	79	66	59	44	39	49	46
23	57	61	74	78	64	70	84	88	86	89	91	92	100	101	102	96	70	61	51	44	35	33	42	40
24	65	68	81	84	76	80	91	93	91	92	92	92	101	99	89	82	52	44	37	31	31	32	38	38
25	71	73	87	88	85	89	95	95	92	91	90	88	96	92	73	65	36	29	26	25	34		38	
26	75	77	89	89	92	94	95	93	89	86	85	81	86	80	56	48	24	23	26		37	42	40	42
27	78	79	89	87	95	95	90	86	83	79	77	73	73	67	40	34	26		30	35	46	51	46	50
28	79	78	85	82	94	93	81	76	74	69	68	64	59	53	29		31	38	41	48	56	62	55	60
29	77	76			90	86	69	63	65	61	60	57	47	43	28	31	44	51	54	60	67	71	65	71
30	74	71			81	76	57	51	58	56	54		40		35	41	58	64	65	71	76	79	75	80
31	68	64			69	63			55	56			39	40	46	52			75	80			84	88

French translations/abbreviations of common tidal terms are as follows:

HW	Pleine mer (PM)
LW	Basse mer (BM)
Springs	Vive eau (VE)
Neaps	Morte eau (ME)
CD	Zero des cartes (Chart Datum)
MHWS	Pleine mer moyenne de VE (PMVE)
MHWN	Pleine mer moyenne de ME (PMME)
MLWN	Basse mer moyenne de ME (BMME)
MLWS	Basse mer moyenne de VE (BMVE)

TIME ZONE -0100
(French Standard Time)
Subtract 1 hour for UT
For French Summer Time add ONE hour in **non-shaded areas**

FRANCE – BREST

LAT 48°23′N LONG 4°30′W

TIMES AND HEIGHTS OF HIGH AND LOW WATERS

SPRING & NEAP TIDES
Dates in red are SPRINGS
Dates in blue are NEAPS

YEAR **2005**

JANUARY

Day	Time m	Time m	Time m	Time m
1 SA	0211 2.2	0809 6.0	1438 2.2	2035 5.7
2 SU	0252 2.3	0850 5.8	1520 2.3	2120 5.5
3 M	0339 2.5	0939 5.6	1609 2.5	◑ 2214 5.4
4 TU	0434 2.6	1036 5.5	1708 2.6	2318 5.4
5 W	0538 2.6	1144 5.5	1815 2.5	
6 TH	0031 5.5	0648 2.5	1256 5.6	1924 2.4
7 F	0138 5.7	0756 2.2	1405 5.9	2028 2.1
8 SA	0241 6.1	0900 1.9	1507 6.2	2127 1.7
9 SU	0338 6.5	0958 1.4	1604 6.5	2222 1.4
10 M	0431 6.9	1053 1.1	1658 6.8	● 2314 1.2
11 TU	0523 7.1	1145 0.8	1748 6.9	
12 W	0005 1.0	0612 7.3	1235 0.7	1837 6.9
13 TH	0058 1.0	0700 7.3	1323 0.8	1924 6.8
14 F	0145 1.1	0747 7.1	1411 1.0	2010 6.6
15 SA	0232 1.4	0833 6.8	1458 1.4	2055 6.2
16 SU	0320 1.7	0919 6.3	1545 1.8	2142 5.8
17 M	0409 2.1	1009 5.9	1635 2.2	◐ 2234 5.5
18 TU	0505 2.5	1105 5.5	1732 2.6	2337 5.3
19 W	0609 2.7	1214 5.3	1839 2.8	
20 TH	0055 5.2	0723 2.8	1330 5.2	1952 2.7
21 F	0208 5.3	0833 2.6	1438 5.4	2055 2.6
22 SA	0305 5.6	0929 2.4	1530 5.6	2144 2.3
23 SU	0350 5.9	1014 2.1	1613 5.8	2226 2.1
24 M	0429 6.1	1053 1.9	1650 6.0	2302 1.9
25 TU	0504 6.3	1128 1.7	1724 6.2	○ 2336 1.7
26 W	0537 6.5	1201 1.6	1756 6.3	
27 TH	0010 1.6	0609 6.5	1234 1.5	1828 6.3
28 F	0043 1.6	0641 6.6	1305 1.5	1900 6.3
29 SA	0115 1.6	0713 6.5	1337 1.6	1932 6.3
30 SU	0148 1.7	0745 6.4	1410 1.7	2005 6.1
31 M	0224 1.8	0820 6.2	1446 1.9	2042 5.9

FEBRUARY

Day	Time m	Time m	Time m	Time m
1 TU	0304 2.1	0859 6.0	1528 2.1	2126 5.7
2 W	0351 2.3	0947 5.7	1619 2.4	◑ 2222 5.5
3 TH	0450 2.5	1051 5.4	1724 2.6	2335 5.3
4 F	0604 2.6	1214 5.3	1844 2.6	
5 SA	0106 5.5	0728 2.5	1344 5.5	2006 2.4
6 SU	0225 5.8	0846 2.0	1459 5.9	2116 2.0
7 M	0330 6.4	0950 1.5	1559 6.4	2214 1.5
8 TU	0425 6.8	1045 1.0	1651 6.8	● 2306 1.1
9 W	0514 7.2	1135 0.6	1738 7.1	2354 0.8
10 TH	0600 7.5	1221 0.5	1822 7.1	
11 F	0042 0.7	0643 7.5	1305 0.5	1903 7.1
12 SA	0124 0.8	0723 7.3	1346 0.8	1941 6.8
13 SU	0205 1.1	0802 6.9	1426 1.2	2018 6.4
14 M	0245 1.5	0839 6.4	1505 1.7	2055 6.0
15 TU	0326 2.0	0919 5.9	1547 2.2	2137 5.6
16 W	0413 2.5	1006 5.4	1636 2.7	◐ 2232 5.2
17 TH	0513 2.9	1113 5.0	1742 3.1	2354 4.9
18 F	0635 3.1	1251 4.8	1912 3.1	
19 SA	0140 5.0	0810 2.9	1422 5.0	2034 2.9
20 SU	0249 5.3	0913 2.6	1517 5.4	2127 2.5
21 M	0335 5.7	0957 2.2	1557 5.7	2208 2.2
22 TU	0412 6.0	1034 1.9	1632 6.1	2243 1.8
23 W	0445 6.3	1107 1.6	1704 6.3	2316 1.6
24 TH	0517 6.6	1139 1.4	1735 6.5	○ 2348 1.4
25 F	0548 6.8	1210 1.2	1805 6.6	
26 SA	0020 1.2	0618 6.8	1241 1.2	1835 6.7
27 SU	0052 1.2	0648 6.8	1311 1.2	1905 6.6
28 M	0124 1.3	0719 6.7	1343 1.4	1937 6.5

MARCH

Day	Time m	Time m	Time m	Time m
1 TU	0158 1.5	0752 6.5	1418 1.6	2012 6.2
2 W	0237 1.8	0830 6.1	1458 2.0	2053 5.9
3 TH	0323 2.1	0916 5.7	1547 2.4	◑ 2146 5.5
4 F	0421 2.5	1020 5.3	1653 2.7	2304 5.3
5 SA	0540 2.7	1156 5.1	1823 2.8	
6 SU	0052 5.3	0717 2.5	1341 5.3	1959 2.5
7 M	0219 5.8	0841 2.0	1456 5.9	2110 2.0
8 TU	0322 6.4	0942 1.4	1551 6.4	2205 1.4
9 W	0413 6.9	1033 0.9	1638 6.9	2253 0.9
10 TH	0458 7.3	1119 0.6	1720 7.1	● 2337 0.7
11 F	0540 7.5	1201 0.5	1759 7.2	
12 SA	0020 0.6	0619 7.5	1240 0.5	1835 7.1
13 SU	0058 0.7	0655 7.3	1317 0.8	1909 6.9
14 M	0135 1.0	0728 6.9	1352 1.3	1941 6.5
15 TU	0211 1.5	0802 6.4	1426 1.8	2014 6.1
16 W	0248 2.0	0837 5.9	1503 2.3	2050 5.6
17 TH	0330 2.5	0918 5.3	1548 2.8	◐ 2138 5.2
18 F	0426 2.9	1021 4.8	1651 3.2	2259 4.8
19 SA	0547 3.2	1208 4.6	1825 3.3	
20 SU	0059 4.8	0736 3.1	1356 4.9	2003 3.0
21 M	0219 5.2	0844 2.7	1450 5.3	2059 2.6
22 TU	0305 5.6	0927 2.2	1529 5.7	2139 2.2
23 W	0342 6.0	1004 1.8	1602 6.1	2214 1.8
24 TH	0416 6.4	1037 1.5	1635 6.4	2248 1.5
25 F	0448 6.7	1110 1.2	1706 6.7	○ 2320 1.2
26 SA	0520 6.9	1141 1.1	1737 6.8	2353 1.1
27 SU	0551 7.0	1213 1.0	1807 6.9	
28 M	0027 1.0	0622 7.0	1245 1.1	1839 6.9
29 TU	0101 1.1	0655 6.8	1318 1.3	1913 6.7
30 W	0137 1.3	0731 6.5	1355 1.6	1950 6.4
31 TH	0219 1.7	0812 6.1	1438 2.0	2034 6.0

APRIL

Day	Time m	Time m	Time m	Time m
1 F	0308 2.1	0902 5.7	1531 2.4	2133 5.6
2 SA	0411 2.4	1016 5.2	1644 2.8	◑ 2300 5.3
3 SU	0537 2.6	1201 5.1	1820 2.8	
4 M	0049 5.4	0714 2.4	1338 5.4	1952 2.4
5 TU	0208 5.9	0830 1.9	1443 5.9	2056 1.9
6 W	0305 6.4	0926 1.4	1533 6.4	2147 1.3
7 TH	0353 6.9	1014 1.0	1616 6.8	2233 1.0
8 F	0436 7.2	1056 0.7	1656 7.0	● 2314 0.8
9 SA	0515 7.3	1135 0.7	1732 7.1	2353 0.8
10 SU	0551 7.2	1212 0.8	1806 7.0	
11 M	0031 0.9	0625 7.0	1246 1.1	1838 6.8
12 TU	0106 1.2	0658 6.7	1320 1.5	1910 6.5
13 W	0141 1.6	0731 6.2	1353 1.9	1943 6.1
14 TH	0218 2.0	0806 5.7	1430 2.4	2019 5.7
15 F	0259 2.5	0848 5.3	1513 2.8	2106 5.2
16 SA	0352 2.9	0948 4.9	1612 3.1	◐ 2218 4.9
17 SU	0504 3.1	1121 4.7	1735 3.3	2358 4.9
18 M	0638 3.0	1301 4.8	1908 3.1	
19 TU	0125 5.1	0753 2.7	1403 5.2	2011 2.7
20 W	0219 5.5	0842 2.3	1446 5.6	2056 2.2
21 TH	0301 5.9	0922 1.9	1523 6.0	2135 1.8
22 F	0338 6.3	0959 1.5	1559 6.4	2212 1.5
23 SA	0414 6.6	1035 1.3	1633 6.7	2248 1.2
24 SU	0449 6.8	1110 1.1	1707 6.9	○ 2324 1.0
25 M	0523 6.9	1145 1.0	1741 7.0	
26 TU	0001 1.0	0559 6.9	1221 1.1	1817 6.9
27 W	0042 1.1	0637 6.8	1300 1.3	1856 6.7
28 TH	0124 1.3	0719 6.5	1343 1.6	1940 6.4
29 F	0211 1.6	0808 6.1	1432 2.0	2032 6.0
30 SA	0306 2.0	0907 5.6	1531 2.4	2139 5.7

Chart Datum: 3·64 metres below IGN Datum

TIME ZONE -0100
(French Standard Time)
Subtract 1 hour for UT
For French Summer Time add ONE hour in **non-shaded areas**

FRANCE – BREST

LAT 48°23'N LONG 4°30'W

TIMES AND HEIGHTS OF HIGH AND LOW WATERS

SPRING & NEAP TIDES
Dates in red are **SPRINGS**
Dates in blue are **NEAPS**

YEAR **2005**

MAY

Date	Day	Time	m	Time	m	Time	m	Time	m
1	SU	0414	2.3	1026	5.3	1646	2.6	◑ 2303	5.5
2	M	0536	2.4	1157	5.3	1813	2.6		
3	TU	0033	5.7	0658	2.2	1316	5.6	1930	2.2
4	W	0143	6.0	0806	1.8	1417	6.0	2031	1.8
5	TH	0239	6.3	0901	1.5	1506	6.3	2122	1.5
6	F	0327	6.6	0948	1.2	1549	6.6	2208	1.2
7	SA	0410	6.8	1030	1.1	1629	6.7	2249	1.1
8	SU	0449	6.8	1108	1.1	1705	6.8	● 2328	1.1
9	M	0525	6.8	1144	1.3	1739	6.7		
10	TU	0005	1.3	0600	6.6	1219	1.4	1813	6.6
11	W	0042	1.5	0634	6.3	1253	1.7	1847	6.4
12	TH	0118	1.7	0710	6.0	1329	2.0	1922	6.1
13	F	0156	2.0	0747	5.7	1406	2.3	2000	5.7
14	SA	0237	2.4	0830	5.3	1449	2.6	2046	5.4
15	SU	0325	2.7	0923	5.0	1541	2.9	2145	5.2
16	M	0424	2.8	1033	4.9	1647	3.0	◐ 2259	5.0
17	TU	0535	2.9	1151	4.9	1801	2.9		
18	W	0016	5.2	0646	2.7	1258	5.2	1908	2.7
19	TH	0119	5.4	0745	2.4	1352	5.5	2003	2.4
20	F	0210	5.7	0833	2.1	1437	5.9	2050	2.0
21	SA	0255	6.1	0917	1.7	1519	6.2	2134	1.6
22	SU	0337	6.4	0958	1.5	1559	6.5	2216	1.4
23	M	0418	6.6	1039	1.3	1639	6.8	○ 2258	1.2
24	TU	0500	6.7	1121	1.2	1719	6.9	2341	1.0
25	W	0543	6.8	1204	1.2	1802	6.9		
26	TH	0030	1.1	0628	6.7	1249	1.3	1849	6.8
27	F	0118	1.2	0718	6.4	1338	1.5	1940	6.6
28	SA	0210	1.4	0812	6.1	1431	1.8	2036	6.3
29	SU	0308	1.7	0912	5.8	1531	2.1	2140	6.0
30	M	0411	1.9	1020	5.6	1638	2.3	◑ 2248	5.9
31	TU	0519	2.0	1132	5.5	1749	2.3	2358	5.8

JUNE

Date	Day	Time	m	Time	m	Time	m	Time	m
1	W	0628	2.0	1240	5.6	1857	2.2		
2	TH	0108	5.9	0732	1.9	1342	5.8	1959	2.0
3	F	0207	6.1	0829	1.8	1435	6.0	2054	1.8
4	SA	0258	6.2	0919	1.7	1521	6.2	2142	1.6
5	SU	0344	6.3	1003	1.6	1604	6.3	2226	1.6
6	M	0426	6.3	1044	1.6	1642	6.4	● 2307	1.5
7	TU	0504	6.3	1122	1.6	1719	6.4	2345	1.6
8	W	0542	6.2	1158	1.7	1755	6.4		
9	TH	0024	1.7	0618	6.1	1234	1.8	1831	6.2
10	F	0101	1.8	0655	5.9	1310	2.0	1907	6.1
11	SA	0138	2.0	0732	5.7	1347	2.2	1945	5.9
12	SU	0216	2.1	0811	5.5	1426	2.4	2026	5.7
13	M	0257	2.3	0855	5.3	1510	2.5	2111	5.5
14	TU	0344	2.5	0946	5.2	1601	2.7	2205	5.4
15	W	0437	2.6	1046	5.1	1659	2.7	◐ 2306	5.3
16	TH	0538	2.6	1149	5.2	1802	2.6		
17	F	0011	5.4	0641	2.5	1251	5.4	1905	2.5
18	SA	0114	5.6	0740	2.3	1347	5.7	2002	2.2
19	SU	0210	5.8	0834	2.0	1439	6.0	2056	1.9
20	M	0303	6.1	0925	1.7	1529	6.3	2148	1.6
21	TU	0354	6.3	1014	1.5	1617	6.6	2238	1.3
22	W	0444	6.5	1103	1.3	1705	6.8	○ 2328	1.1
23	TH	0534	6.7	1152	1.2	1755	6.9		
24	F	0022	0.9	0624	6.7	1242	1.2	1845	6.9
25	SA	0113	0.9	0715	6.6	1333	1.3	1936	6.9
26	SU	0205	1.1	0807	6.4	1425	1.4	2029	6.7
27	M	0258	1.3	0900	6.1	1519	1.7	2123	6.4
28	TU	0352	1.6	0955	5.9	1615	1.9	◑ 2219	6.1
29	W	0449	1.9	1053	5.7	1715	2.1	2319	5.8
30	TH	0549	2.1	1156	5.5	1818	2.2		

JULY

Date	Day	Time	m	Time	m	Time	m	Time	m
1	F	0026	5.7	0651	2.2	1301	5.5	1923	2.3
2	SA	0131	5.6	0754	2.3	1403	5.6	2026	2.2
3	SU	0232	5.7	0852	2.2	1458	5.8	2121	2.1
4	M	0325	5.8	0942	2.1	1546	6.0	2210	1.9
5	TU	0411	5.9	1026	2.0	1628	6.1	2253	1.8
6	W	0451	6.0	1106	1.9	1706	6.2	● 2332	1.7
7	TH	0529	6.1	1143	1.8	1742	6.3		
8	F	0009	1.7	0604	6.1	1218	1.8	1817	6.3
9	SA	0044	1.7	0639	6.0	1252	1.8	1851	6.3
10	SU	0118	1.7	0713	6.0	1326	1.9	1925	6.2
11	M	0152	1.8	0747	5.9	1401	2.0	1959	6.0
12	TU	0226	2.0	0822	5.7	1437	2.1	2035	5.9
13	W	0304	2.1	0901	5.6	1518	2.3	2117	5.7
14	TH	0347	2.3	0948	5.4	1606	2.5	◐ 2206	5.5
15	F	0438	2.5	1044	5.3	1702	2.6	2306	5.4
16	SA	0539	2.5	1150	5.3	1808	2.6		
17	SU	0018	5.4	0648	2.5	1300	5.5	1919	2.4
18	M	0132	5.5	0757	2.3	1407	5.7	2027	2.1
19	TU	0240	5.8	0900	2.0	1508	6.1	2129	1.7
20	W	0341	6.2	0958	1.6	1604	6.5	2225	1.3
21	TH	0436	6.5	1052	1.3	1657	6.9	○ 2318	0.9
22	F	0527	6.7	1143	1.0	1747	7.1		
23	SA	0011	0.7	0616	6.9	1232	0.9	1835	7.3
24	SU	0102	0.6	0703	6.9	1320	0.9	1922	7.2
25	M	0149	0.7	0748	6.7	1407	1.1	2008	7.0
26	TU	0235	1.0	0833	6.4	1454	1.4	2054	6.6
27	W	0322	1.4	0919	6.1	1543	1.7	2142	6.2
28	TH	0410	1.9	1008	5.7	1636	2.1	◑ 2235	5.7
29	F	0504	2.3	1106	5.4	1736	2.5	2338	5.3
30	SA	0607	2.6	1218	5.2	1847	2.7		
31	SU	0058	5.2	0721	2.7	1337	5.3	2003	2.6

AUGUST

Date	Day	Time	m	Time	m	Time	m	Time	m
1	M	0215	5.3	0832	2.6	1444	5.5	2108	2.4
2	TU	0315	5.5	0928	2.4	1535	5.8	2158	2.1
3	W	0401	5.7	1013	2.1	1617	6.0	2240	1.9
4	TH	0439	5.9	1051	1.9	1653	6.2	2316	1.7
5	F	0513	6.1	1126	1.8	1726	6.4	● 2350	1.6
6	SA	0546	6.2	1158	1.6	1757	6.5		
7	SU	0022	1.5	0616	6.3	1230	1.6	1828	6.5
8	M	0053	1.5	0647	6.3	1301	1.6	1858	6.5
9	TU	0123	1.5	0717	6.2	1332	1.7	1928	6.4
10	W	0154	1.7	0748	6.1	1405	1.8	2000	6.2
11	TH	0227	1.9	0821	5.9	1441	2.0	2036	5.9
12	F	0305	2.1	0901	5.7	1524	2.3	2118	5.7
13	SA	0351	2.4	0952	5.4	1617	2.5	◐ 2215	5.4
14	SU	0451	2.6	1100	5.3	1725	2.7	2332	5.2
15	M	0608	2.7	1225	5.3	1848	2.6		
16	TU	0110	5.3	0734	2.6	1349	5.6	2011	2.3
17	W	0231	5.7	0848	2.2	1458	6.1	2119	1.7
18	TH	0334	6.2	0948	1.6	1554	6.6	2216	1.2
19	F	0427	6.6	1041	1.2	1645	7.1	○ 2307	0.7
20	SA	0514	7.0	1129	0.8	1733	7.4	2354	0.5
21	SU	0559	7.2	1215	0.6	1817	7.5		
22	M	0042	0.4	0641	7.1	1259	0.7	1859	7.4
23	TU	0124	0.6	0720	7.0	1342	0.9	1940	7.1
24	W	0205	1.0	0759	6.6	1424	1.3	2019	6.7
25	TH	0246	1.5	0837	6.2	1507	1.8	2100	6.1
26	F	0329	2.1	0920	5.7	1555	2.3	◑ 2148	5.5
27	SA	0418	2.6	1015	5.3	1654	2.8	2253	5.1
28	SU	0523	3.0	1136	5.0	1813	3.0		
29	M	0031	4.9	0652	3.1	1317	5.0	1947	2.9
30	TU	0206	5.0	0817	2.9	1432	5.4	2055	2.5
31	W	0303	5.4	0913	2.5	1520	5.7	2141	2.2

Chart Datum: 3·64 metres below IGN Datum

TIME ZONE -0100
(French Standard Time)
Subtract 1 hour for UT
For French Summer Time add ONE hour in **non-shaded areas**

FRANCE – BREST

LAT 48°23′N LONG 4°30′W

TIMES AND HEIGHTS OF HIGH AND LOW WATERS

SPRING & NEAP TIDES
Dates in red are SPRINGS
Dates in blue are NEAPS

YEAR **2005**

SEPTEMBER

Date	Day	Time	m	Time	m	Time	m	Time	m
1	TH	0344	5.7	0954	2.2	1558	6.1	2219	1.8
2	F	0418	6.0	1030	1.9	1631	6.3	2253	1.6
3	SA	0450	6.3	1102	1.6	1701	6.5	● 2324	1.4
4	SU	0519	6.5	1133	1.5	1731	6.7	2354	1.3
5	M	0549	6.6	1203	1.4	1800	6.8		
6	TU	0024	1.3	0617	6.6	1233	1.4	1829	6.7
7	W	0052	1.4	0646	6.6	1303	1.4	1858	6.6
8	TH	0122	1.5	0715	6.4	1335	1.6	1928	6.4
9	F	0155	1.7	0748	6.2	1411	1.9	2003	6.1
10	SA	0232	2.1	0826	5.9	1454	2.2	2045	5.7
11	SU	0318	2.4	0917	5.5	1548	2.6	◐ 2144	5.3
12	M	0420	2.8	1031	5.2	1701	2.8	2313	5.0
13	TU	0547	2.9	1211	5.2	1836	2.7		
14	W	0109	5.2	0726	2.7	1343	5.7	2005	2.3
15	TH	0227	5.7	0840	2.1	1448	6.3	2109	1.6
16	F	0323	6.3	0936	1.5	1541	6.8	2202	1.0
17	SA	0411	6.8	1025	1.0	1628	7.3	2249	0.6
18	SU	0454	7.1	1110	0.7	1712	7.6	○ 2333	0.4
19	M	0535	7.3	1153	0.6	1753	7.6		
20	TU	0016	0.5	0613	7.2	1234	0.7	1831	7.4
21	W	0055	0.8	0649	7.0	1313	1.0	1908	7.0
22	TH	0133	1.2	0723	6.7	1352	1.4	1944	6.5
23	F	0210	1.7	0758	6.2	1433	1.9	2022	6.0
24	SA	0249	2.3	0837	5.7	1518	2.5	2107	5.4
25	SU	0336	2.8	0929	5.2	1616	2.9	◑ 2213	4.9
26	M	0442	3.2	1055	4.9	1739	3.2	2359	4.7
27	TU	0618	3.3	1250	5.0	1923	3.0		
28	W	0144	5.0	0750	3.0	1405	5.3	2029	2.6
29	TH	0236	5.4	0844	2.6	1451	5.7	2112	2.2
30	F	0314	5.8	0924	2.2	1527	6.1	2148	1.9

OCTOBER

Date	Day	Time	m	Time	m	Time	m	Time	m
1	SA	0347	6.1	0958	1.9	1559	6.4	2220	1.6
2	SU	0418	6.4	1031	1.6	1630	6.6	2252	1.4
3	M	0448	6.6	1103	1.4	1701	6.8	● 2322	1.3
4	TU	0518	6.8	1134	1.3	1730	6.9	2352	1.2
5	W	0547	6.8	1205	1.3	1800	6.9		
6	TH	0023	1.3	0617	6.8	1237	1.4	1831	6.7
7	F	0055	1.5	0649	6.6	1311	1.5	1904	6.5
8	SA	0130	1.8	0724	6.4	1351	1.8	1942	6.1
9	SU	0211	2.1	0806	6.0	1437	2.2	2029	5.7
10	M	0301	2.5	0902	5.6	1536	2.6	◐ 2136	5.2
11	TU	0409	2.9	1025	5.3	1655	2.8	2316	5.1
12	W	0544	3.0	1208	5.4	1833	2.6		
13	TH	0104	5.4	0717	2.6	1330	5.8	1953	2.1
14	F	0212	5.9	0824	2.0	1430	6.4	2052	1.5
15	SA	0303	6.4	0917	1.5	1520	6.9	2141	1.1
16	SU	0348	6.9	1004	1.1	1606	7.3	2226	0.8
17	M	0430	7.1	1048	0.8	1648	7.4	○ 2308	0.7
18	TU	0508	7.2	1129	0.8	1727	7.4	2347	0.8
19	W	0545	7.1	1208	0.9	1804	7.1		
20	TH	0026	1.1	0619	6.9	1246	1.2	1840	6.8
21	F	0102	1.5	0653	6.6	1325	1.6	1915	6.3
22	SA	0139	1.9	0729	6.2	1404	2.0	1953	5.8
23	SU	0217	2.4	0808	5.8	1449	2.5	2038	5.4
24	M	0303	2.8	0858	5.3	1543	2.9	2141	4.9
25	TU	0404	3.2	1013	5.0	1657	3.2	◑ 2313	4.8
26	W	0527	3.3	1152	5.0	1829	3.1		
27	TH	0050	4.9	0656	3.1	1312	5.2	1940	2.8
28	F	0149	5.3	0757	2.7	1404	5.6	2028	2.4
29	SA	0231	5.7	0841	2.4	1444	5.9	2106	2.0
30	SU	0307	6.1	0919	2.0	1521	6.3	2142	1.7
31	M	0342	6.4	0955	1.7	1555	6.5	2216	1.5

NOVEMBER

Date	Day	Time	m	Time	m	Time	m	Time	m
1	TU	0415	6.6	1030	1.5	1629	6.7	2250	1.3
2	W	0447	6.8	1105	1.3	1702	6.8	● 2323	1.3
3	TH	0520	6.9	1140	1.3	1736	6.8	2358	1.3
4	F	0555	6.9	1217	1.3	1812	6.7		
5	SA	0036	1.5	0632	6.7	1257	1.5	1852	6.5
6	SU	0117	1.8	0714	6.5	1342	1.8	1937	6.1
7	M	0203	2.1	0803	6.1	1434	2.1	2032	5.7
8	TU	0259	2.5	0906	5.8	1536	2.4	2143	5.4
9	W	0410	2.7	1026	5.6	1653	2.5	◐ 2312	5.3
10	TH	0535	2.7	1151	5.7	1816	2.3		
11	F	0040	5.6	0655	2.4	1304	6.0	1927	2.0
12	SA	0145	5.9	0759	2.0	1404	6.4	2026	1.6
13	SU	0237	6.3	0853	1.6	1455	6.7	2116	1.4
14	M	0323	6.6	0941	1.3	1542	6.9	2201	1.2
15	TU	0405	6.8	1025	1.2	1624	7.0	2243	1.2
16	W	0444	6.9	1107	1.2	1704	6.9	○ 2322	1.2
17	TH	0521	6.9	1147	1.3	1742	6.8		
18	F	0000	1.4	0557	6.7	1225	1.4	1819	6.5
19	SA	0039	1.7	0633	6.5	1304	1.7	1856	6.2
20	SU	0116	2.0	0710	6.2	1343	2.0	1935	5.8
21	M	0154	2.3	0750	5.9	1425	2.4	2018	5.5
22	TU	0237	2.7	0835	5.6	1513	2.7	2110	5.2
23	W	0328	2.9	0931	5.3	1609	2.9	◑ 2215	5.0
24	TH	0430	3.1	1041	5.1	1716	3.0	2330	5.0
25	F	0542	3.1	1155	5.2	1827	2.9		
26	SA	0041	5.2	0650	2.9	1259	5.4	1927	2.6
27	SU	0136	5.5	0746	2.6	1352	5.7	2016	2.3
28	M	0221	5.8	0834	2.3	1437	6.0	2059	2.0
29	TU	0303	6.2	0917	1.9	1519	6.3	2140	1.8
30	W	0342	6.4	0959	1.7	1559	6.5	2219	1.6

DECEMBER

Date	Day	Time	m	Time	m	Time	m	Time	m
1	TH	0421	6.7	1040	1.4	1639	6.6	● 2259	1.4
2	F	0500	6.8	1122	1.3	1720	6.7	2340	1.4
3	SA	0541	6.9	1205	1.3	1803	6.7		
4	SU	0026	1.5	0626	6.8	1251	1.3	1849	6.5
5	M	0113	1.6	0714	6.7	1340	1.5	1940	6.3
6	TU	0203	1.8	0807	6.4	1433	1.7	2035	6.0
7	W	0259	2.1	0905	6.2	1532	1.9	2137	5.8
8	TH	0401	2.3	1010	6.0	1636	2.1	◐ 2246	5.6
9	F	0510	2.4	1119	5.9	1744	2.2	2357	5.6
10	SA	0620	2.3	1228	5.9	1852	2.1		
11	SU	0108	5.8	0726	2.2	1332	6.0	1954	2.0
12	M	0206	6.0	0826	2.0	1429	6.2	2049	1.8
13	TU	0258	6.2	0919	1.8	1520	6.3	2139	1.7
14	W	0344	6.4	1007	1.6	1606	6.4	2224	1.7
15	TH	0426	6.5	1051	1.6	1649	6.4	○ 2305	1.6
16	F	0506	6.6	1132	1.5	1728	6.4	2344	1.7
17	SA	0544	6.6	1211	1.6	1806	6.3		
18	SU	0022	1.8	0620	6.5	1249	1.7	1843	6.2
19	M	0059	1.9	0657	6.3	1326	1.9	1919	6.0
20	TU	0135	2.1	0733	6.1	1403	2.1	1957	5.8
21	W	0213	2.3	0811	5.9	1441	2.3	2036	5.5
22	TH	0253	2.5	0851	5.7	1523	2.5	2121	5.3
23	F	0338	2.7	0938	5.5	1610	2.7	◑ 2214	5.2
24	SA	0431	2.8	1034	5.3	1707	2.8	2317	5.2
25	SU	0532	2.9	1139	5.3	1811	2.8		
26	M	0025	5.3	0639	2.8	1247	5.4	1915	2.6
27	TU	0127	5.5	0742	2.6	1349	5.6	2013	2.4
28	W	0223	5.8	0839	2.3	1444	5.9	2106	2.1
29	TH	0313	6.1	0931	1.9	1536	6.2	2155	1.8
30	F	0401	6.5	1021	1.6	1624	6.4	2242	1.5
31	SA	0448	6.7	1110	1.3	1712	6.6	● 2329	1.3

Chart Datum: 3·64 metres below IGN Datum

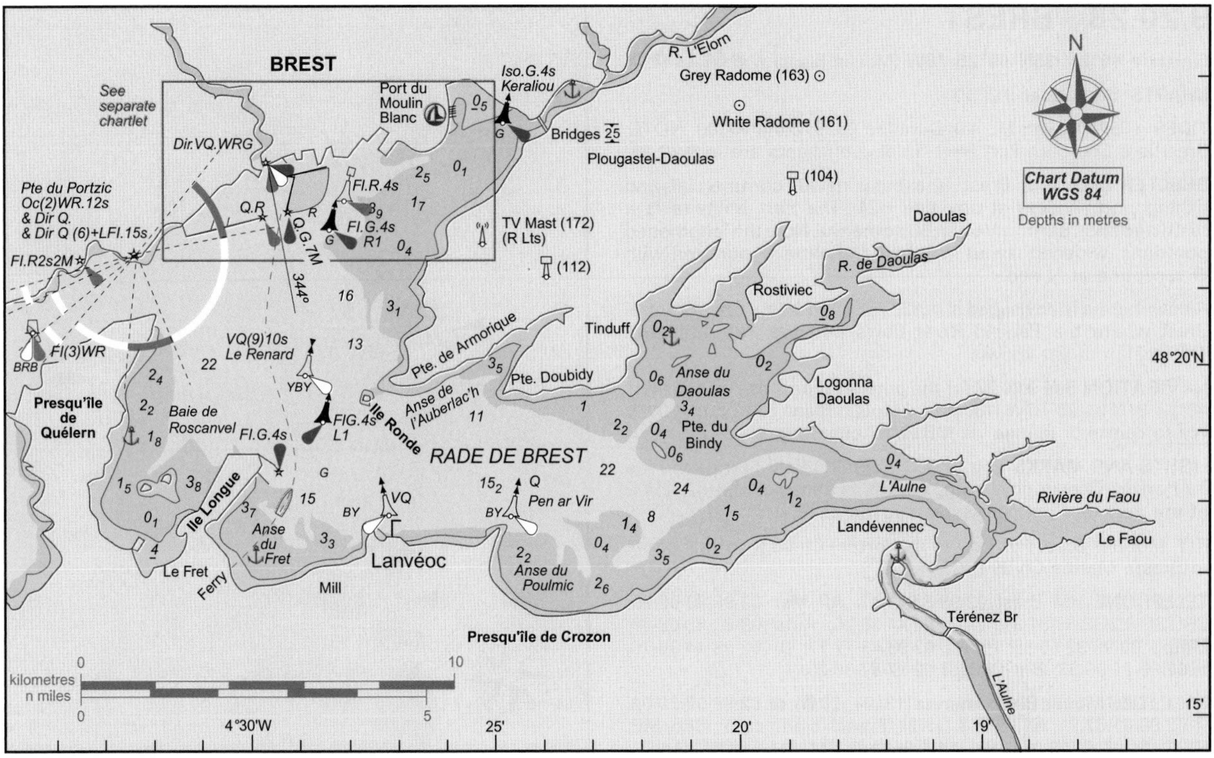
BREST
See separate chartlet
Port du Moulin Blanc
Iso.G.4s Keraliou
R. L'Elorn
Grey Radome (163)
White Radome (161)
Bridges 25
Plougastel-Daoulas
(104)
Chart Datum WGS 84
Depths in metres
Daoulas
Dir.VQ.WRG
Pte du Portzic Oc(2)WR.12s & Dir Q. & Dir Q (6)+LFl.15s
Fl.R2s2M
Q.R
Q.G.7M
Fl.R.4s
Fl.G.4s R1
TV Mast (172) (R Lts)
(112)
R. de Daoulas
Rostiviec
344°
VQ(9)10s Le Renard
Tinduff
Pte. de Armorique
Pte. Doubidy
Anse du Daoulas
Logonna Daoulas
48°20'N
Fl(3)WR
BRB
YBY
Presqu'île de Quélern
Baie de Roscanvel
Fl.G.4s
FlG.4s L1
Ile Ronde
Anse de l'Auberlac'h
RADE DE BREST
Pte. du Bindy
L'Aulne
Rivière du Faou
Le Faou
Ile Longue
Anse du Fret
BY
VQ
Q Pen ar Vir
BY
Landévennec
Le Fret
Ferry
Mill
Lanvéoc
Anse du Poulmic
Térénez Br
Presqu'île de Crozon
L'Aulne
kilometres
n miles
4°30'W
25'
20'
19'
15'

9.20.27 RADE DE BREST

Finistère

CHARTS AC 3427, 3428, 3429; SHOM 7401, 7400, 7397, 7398, 7399; ECM 542; Imray C36; Stanfords 2. Beyond the N and E edges of AC 3429 & SHOM 7400, the Rs. Elorn and Aulne are usefully covered on IGN land maps 0516, 0517 & 0518 (1:25,000).

TIDES In most of the bays in the Rade de Brest tidal streams are weak, but in the main rivers they can exceed 2kn at sp.

SHELTER The Rade de Brest (50 sq miles) offers a sheltered cruising ground when the weather offshore is bad. There are many attractive ⚓s in the SE corner of the Rade and up the Rivers Elorne and Aulne; see below.

In the SW corner of Rade de Brest are various naval sites with no ⚓, prohib zones and DG ranges around Île Longue. There are however ⚓s at Le Fret (SE of Île Longue) whence a ferry runs to Brest; and off Roscanvel in the lee of the Quélern Peninsula.

The area S and SW from the marina is very shoal, but E of Pte de l'Armorique there are ⚓s and W Ⓥs in 3m in Anse de L'Auberlac'h, Baie de Daoulas and its inlets/creeks, at the mouth of the R. de l'Hôpital and up the drying/buoyed R. de Faou. S of here the much larger R. L'Aulne (see below) can easily be explored from Landévennec 18M up to Châteaulin.

NAVIGATION WPT 48°18´·24N 04°44´·09W, 068°/5·3M to front ldg lt (Pte du Petit Minou). See 9.20.4 for light details. Tidal streams run hard in the Goulet de Brest, max 4·6kn on the spring ebb and 3·5kn on the flood. In mid-chan beware Plateau des Fillettes, rks well marked by 3 lt buoys and Mengam IDM lt bcn twr. Pass either side keeping well inshore to avoid warships and commercial vessels and to cheat any foul tide.

RIVER L'ÉLORN 1.2M E of the marina the R. Élorn is navigable up to Landerneau. From Pont Albert-Louppe (29m) and Pont de l'Iroise (25m clearance) the river is buoyed/lit for 2M, but further up is marked by smaller unlit buoys and perches, some of which may well be some distance outboard of navigable water. A good ⚓ is at Le Passage, 7 cables above the bridges. The drying port of Landerneau, 6M up R L'Élorn, can be reached on the tide via a lifting bridge ☎ 06·11·03·31·20. Berth against N quay.

RIVER L'AULNE. To the SE of Rade de Brest, L'Aulne is a lovely river with steep wooded banks. There are ⚓s off Landévennec, below Térénez bridge (27m), and also Ⓥs 1½M above that bridge. At Guily-Glaz, 14M above Landévennec, a lock (operating HW Brest –2 to +1½; ☎ 02.98.86.03.21) gives access to the canalised river (2·7m) and Port Launay on a U-bend (see Special Note below). Popular place to winter in complete shelter against the attractive stone quays. Facilities: AB on quay, ⛽, FW, R, easy access to the N165 motorway.

3M further on is Châteaulin, a charming country town and head of the navigable river. Facilities: AB on Ⓥ pontoon, ⛽, FW, supermarket.

SPECIAL NOTE: The lock gates at Guily Glaz will stay shut 1 Apr-31 Oct 2005 whilst the adjacent weir is re-structured to cope with flooding problems. Boats at Port Launay and Chateaulin should remain afloat at all times. The lock will however open for special events/public holidays on dates to be specified. No work will take place in the winter months due to higher river levels and the flooding risk.

9.20.28 BREST

Finistère **48°23'·35N 04°25·76W** (Moulin Blanc)

CHARTS See under 9.20.27.

TIDES +0520 Dover; ML 4·0; Duration 0605; Zone –0100. NOTE: Brest is a Standard Port (⟷). Tidal coefficients are in 9.20.26.

SHELTER Excellent. Brest is a busy naval, commercial and fishing port. Access at any tide H24. The Port Militaire is a restricted area. Berth in Moulin Blanc marina. Note the lengthened pontoons, widened layout in N half and extra Ⓥ pontoon with Ⓥ reception at N end.

A new marina is envisaged at 48°22´·72N 04°29´·36W, near central Brest where the Penfeld River flows into the Port Militaire. Timescale not yet known.

NAVIGATION See 9.20.27 for the outer approaches. Marina WPT 48°22´·81N 04°25´·87W (130m E of Moulin Blanc PHM buoy) 007°/7ca to centre of marina via MB1/MB2 chan buoys.

LIGHTS AND MARKS Ldg lts 068° at Pte du Petit Minou and Pte du Portzic. Oceanopolis bldg, W roof, is conspic. Marina, 2M E of the Port de Commerce, has buoyed chan.

R/T Monitor *Brest Port* (at Pte du Portzic) Ch **08** (controls apprs to Brest). Marina Ch 09 (HO).

TELEPHONE HM Brest 02·98·33·41·47; Aff Mar 02·98·80·62·25; CROSS 02·98·89·31·31; ⊖ 02·98·44·35·20; Auto 08·92·68·08·29; Météo 02·98·32·55·55; Police 02·98·43·77·77; Dr 02·98·44·38·70; Ⓗ 02·98·22·33·33; Brit Consul 02·97·87·36·20.

FACILITIES Moulin Blanc marina (1340+120 Ⓥ), ☎ 02·98·02·20·02, 02·98·41.67.91, €1.73, P & D H24 (French credit card), Slip, ME, El, Ⓔ, ⚒, C (18 ton), BH (14 & 35 ton), SM, CH, SHOM, Gaz, R, Bar; **Sté des Régates de Brest** ☎ 02·98·02·53·36, R. **YC Rade de Brest** ☎ 02·98·44·63·32. **Club Nautique Municipal** ☎ 02·98·34·64·64.

Services: CH, SM, ME, El, ⚒, Ⓔ, SHOM. City all facilities, Gaz, ✉, Ⓑ, ⇌, ✈. Ferry: Roscoff.

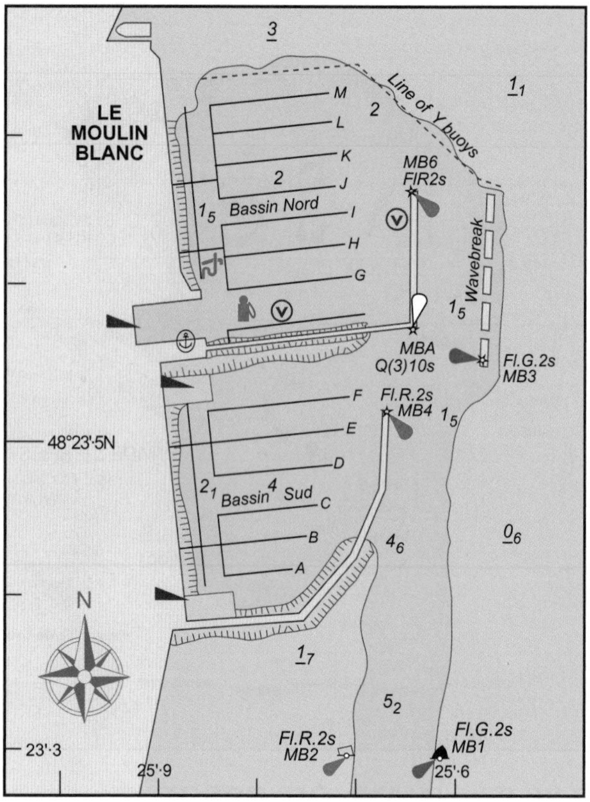
LE MOULIN BLANC
Bassin Nord
Bassin Sud
Line of Y buoys
Wavebreak
MB6 Fl.R.2s
MBA Q(3)10s
Fl.G.2s MB3
Fl.R.2s MB4
Fl.R.2s MB2
Fl.G.2s MB1
48°23'·5N
23'·3
25'·9
25'·6
N

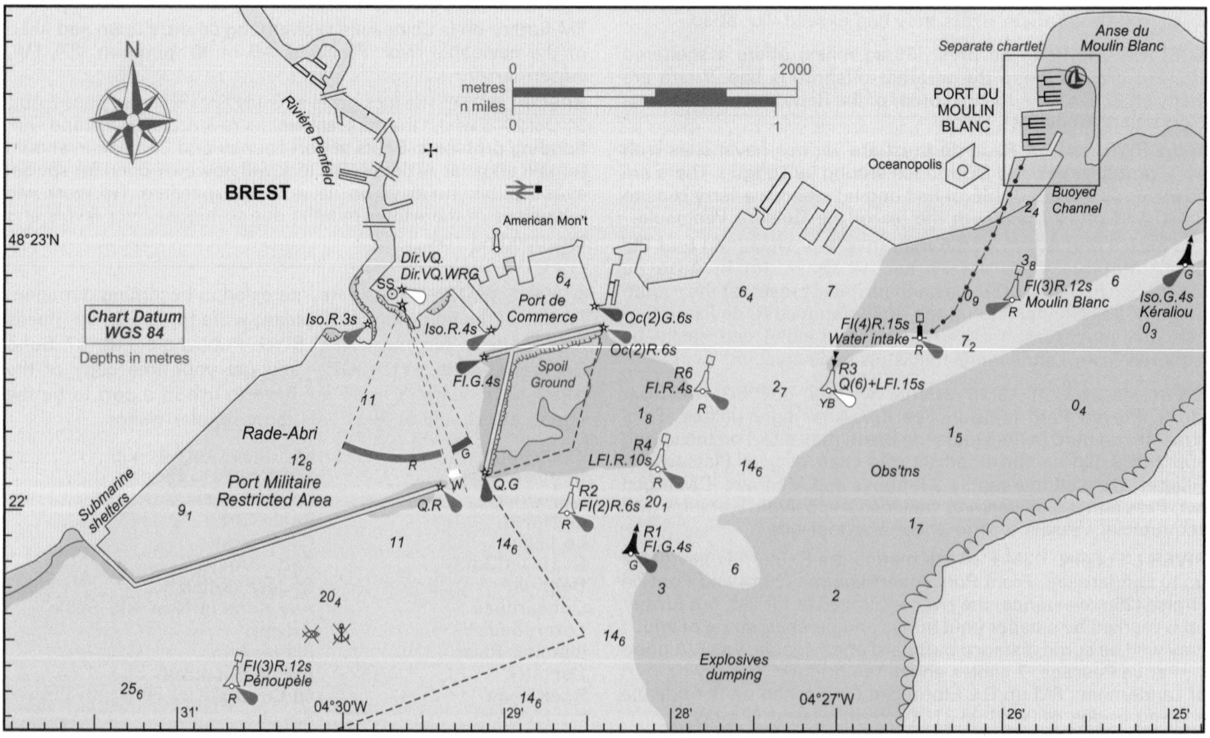
Separate chartlet
Anse du Moulin Blanc
PORT DU MOULIN BLANC
Oceanopolis
Buoyed Channel
metres
n miles
0
2000
1
N
BREST
Rivière Penfeld
American Mon't
48°23'N
Dir.VQ.
Dir.VQ.WRG
Iso.R.3s
Iso.R.4s
Port de Commerce
Oc(2)G.6s
Oc(2)R.6s
Chart Datum WGS 84
Depths in metres
Fl.G.4s
Spoil Ground
R6 Fl.R.4s
Fl(3)R.12s Moulin Blanc
Fl(4)R.15s Water intake
R3 Q(6)+LFl.15s
Iso.G.4s Kéraliou
Rade-Abri
Port Militaire Restricted Area
Submarine shelters
R4 LFl.R.10s
R2 Fl(2)R.6s
R1 Fl.G.4s
Obs'tns
Q.G
Q.R
22'
Fl(3)R.12s Pénoupèle
Explosives dumping
31'
04°30'W
29'
28'
04°27'W
26'
25'

9.20.29 CAMARET

Finistère **48°16'·85N 04°35'·31W**

CHARTS AC 2350, 3427; SHOM 7149, 7148, 7401; Imray C36; ECM 540, 542; Stanfords 17

TIDES +0500 Dover; ML 3·8; Duration 0610; Zone –0100

Standard Port BREST (⟵)

Times				Height (metres)			
High Water		Low Water		MHWS	MHWN	MLWN	MLWS
0000	0600	0000	0600	6·9	5·4	2·6	1·0
1200	1800	1200	1800				
Differences CAMARET							
–0010	–0010	–0013	–0013	–0·3	–0·3	–0·1	0·0

SHELTER Good, except in strong N-SE'lies. The 2 marinas are: Port Vauban (5m), inside the N mole and protected by a wavebreak; enter from the S. Mainly Ⓥ alongside/rafted berths, plus a few fingers. Port du Notic is nearer town with some Ⓥ berths for yachts <11m LOA on E and A pontoons in 1·5m. Port Styvel to the N is for locals. Good ⚓ and Ⓥs SE of Port Vauban.

NAVIGATION WPT 48°17'·44N 04°36'·09W, 139°/0·8M to N mole lt; in its W sector. Beware rks W & N of Pte du Grand Gouin.

LIGHTS AND MARKS The G SHM bcn twr at the W end of the N mole is very conspic; ditto Tour Vauban and chapel. A fish farm, 3ca ENE of Port Vauban, is marked by a NCM lt buoy, a WCM lt bcn and unlit E and S cardinal buoys; for details see 9.20.4.

R/T VHF Ch 09.

TELEPHONE Aff Mar 02·98·27·93·28; CROSS 02·98·89·31·31; ⊖ 02·98·27·93·02; Auto 08·92·68·08·29; Police 02·98·27·84·94 (Jul/Aug); Dr 02·98·57·91·35; Brit Consul 02·97·87·36·20.

FACILITIES Port Vauban (170 inc 70 Ⓥ) ☎ 02·98·27·95·99, €1.87, C (8 ton), D, Access H24. **HM (Emergency)** ☎ 06·79·19·55·68.
Port du Notic (200+50 Ⓥ), ☎ 02·98·27·89·31, Fax 02·98·27.96.45, port-plaisance-camaret@wanadoo.fr ♿, Access H24, dredged 1·5m; **Services:** M, ME, El, Ⓔ, ⚒, CH, P, C (5 ton), SM, SHOM. **Town** P, 🛒, Gaz, R, Bar, ✉, Ⓑ, ⇌ (Brest), ✈ (Brest or Quimper).

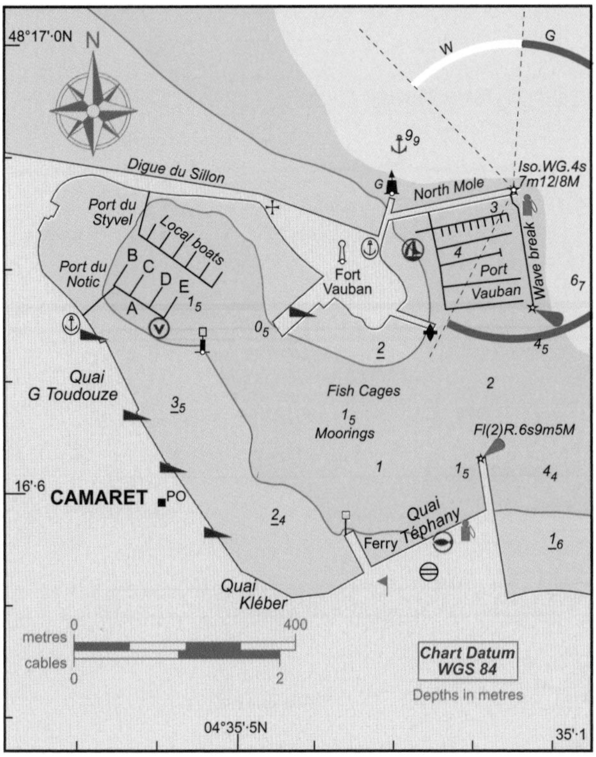
48°17'·0N
Digue du Sillon
Port du Styvel
Local boats
Port du Notic
Quai G Toudouze
Fort Vauban
North Mole
Iso.WG.4s 7m12/8M
Port Vauban
Wave break
Fish Cages
Moorings
Fl(2)R.6s9m5M
CAMARET
Quai Téphany
Ferry
Quai Kléber
metres
cables
Chart Datum WGS 84
Depths in metres
04°35'·5N
35'·1
16'·6

9.20.30 MORGAT

Finistère **48°13'·57N 04°29'·61W**

CHARTS AC 2350, 2349; SHOM 7172, 7121; Imray C36; ECM 541, 542; Stanfords 17

TIDES +0500 Dover; ML 3·8; Duration No data; Zone –0100

Standard Port BREST (⟵)

Times				Height (metres)			
High Water		Low Water		MHWS	MHWN	MLWN	MLWS
0000	0600	0000	0600	6·9	5·4	2·6	1·0
1200	1800	1200	1800				
Differences MORGAT							
–0008	–0008	–0020	–0010	–0·4	–0·4	–0·2	0·0
DOUARNENEZ							
–0010	–0015	–0018	–0008	–0·5	–0·5	–0·3	–0·1

SHELTER The port is only exposed to winds from W to N. H pontoon has Ⓥ finger berths on E side or AB for larger yachts on W side. ⚓ in the middle of the bay in 2m on sand or pick up a Ⓥ buoy, unmarked. Pleasant day ⚓s, sheltered from the W, are S of Morgat in the bays of St Hernot, St Norgard & St Nicolas.

NAVIGATION WPT 48°13'·58N 04°29'·15W, 270°/500m to entry chan close N of E bkwtr hd. Ent chan, dredged 1·5m, shoals abruptly on its unmarked N edge. Small Fl R/G 4s lts mark the marina ent; the sunken wavebreak is marked by 3 Y buoys. Rocks lurk close under the cliffs S of Pte de Morgat. Les Verrès, 2 - 2·5M ESE of ent, are in the G sector of Pte de Morgat lt. See also 9.20.5 for dangers to avoid when rounding Cap de la Chèvre.

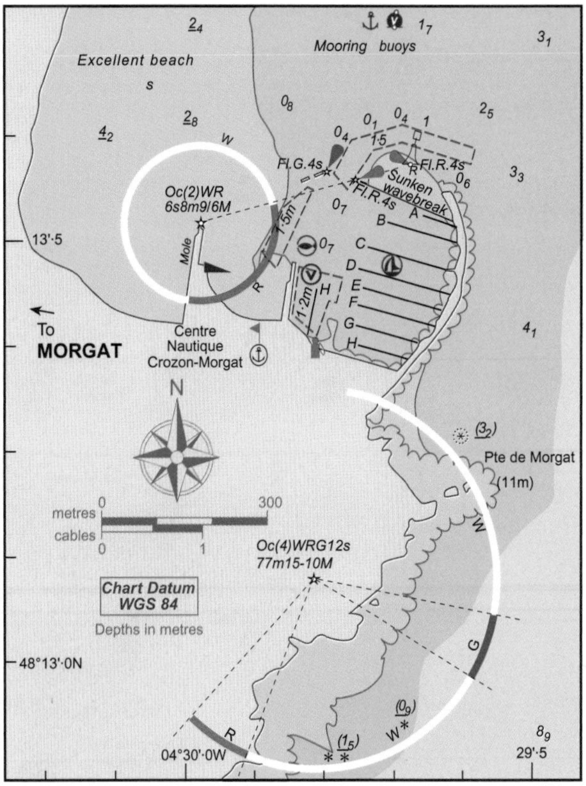
Excellent beach
Mooring buoys
Fl.G.4s
Fl.R.4s
Sunken wavebreak
Oc(2)WR 6s8m9/6M
Mole
13'·5
To MORGAT
Centre Nautique Crozon-Morgat
Pte de Morgat (11m)
metres
cables
Oc(4)WRG12s 77m15-10M
Chart Datum WGS 84
Depths in metres
48°13'·0N
04°30'·0W
29'·5

LIGHTS AND MARKS Pte de Morgat lt is high up on the clifftop among trees. Other lts as chartlet and 9.20.4.

R/T Marina VHF Ch 09.

TELEPHONE Aff Mar 02·98·27·09·95; CROSS 02·98·89·31·31; Auto 08·92·68·08·29; SNSM 02·98·10·51·41; ⊖ 02·98·27·93·02; Police 02·98·27·00·22; Ⓗ 02·98·27·05·33; Brit Consul 02·97·87·36·20.

FACILITIES Marina, ☎ 02·98·27·01·97, Fax 02·98·27.19.76, €1.37, (646+32 Ⓥ), C (8 ton), Slip, CH, D, P, ME, ⊡, ♿, Access H24. **Crozon-Morgat C.N** ☎ 02·98·16·00·01; **Services:** M, C (6 ton), El, ⚒, Ⓔ. **Town** (Crozon), 🛒, Gaz, R, Bar, ✉, Ⓑ, ⇌, ✈ (Brest or Quimper). Ferry: Roscoff.

9.20.31 DOUARNENEZ

Finistère **48°05'·98N 04°20'·35W** ❁❁⚓⚓⚓✿✿✿

CHARTS AC 2349; SHOM 7121; Imray C36; ECM 542; Stanf'd17

TIDES Differences 9.20.30. +0500 Dover; ML 3·7; Duration 0615.

SHELTER Good, except in strong NW'lies. Access H24 to Ⓥ pontoons in Grande Passe; prone to wash/swell. Tréboul marina (1·5m) is full of local boats. If conditions are bad in the Grande Passe pre-arrange a berth at Port Rhu non-tidal basin (3·2m) or at pontoons S of the bridge in 2·2m. Enter over a sill (1·1m) via 10m wide gate which opens approx HW ±2 when Coeff >70. Port Neuf FV hbr is prohib to yachts. Port de Rosmeur is full of moorings, but ⚓ S of it, as charted, in about 1·5m.

NAVIGATION WPT 48°06'·71N 04°20'·83W, 157°/0·8M to abm outer Ⓥ pontoon. Basse Veur and Basse Neuve (1·8m) are 8 and 4ca NNW of Île Tristan lt and in its R sector. Pass well N of Rochers le Coulinec and La Tête de Pierre, a rocky ledge, 5ca NW of Tréboul jetty, QG.

LIGHTS AND MARKS Daymarks: Two conspic spires and Île Tristan lt twr are in transit 147°. Île Tristan is a cliffy, wooded island. Dir lt 157°, on the 16m high bridge at S end of Port Rhu, covers the inner appr. See chartlet and 9.20.4 for light details.

R/T Marina and Port Rhu Ch 09. FV Port Ch 12.

TELEPHONE Port HM 02·98·92·14·85; Aff Mar 02·98·75·31·30; CROSS 02·98·89·31·31; ⊜ 02·98·52·87·40; Météo 02·98·84·60·64; Auto 08·92.68·08·29; Police 02·98·92·01·22; Ⓗ 02·98·92·25·00; Brit Consul 02·97·87·36·20.

FACILITIES Ⓥ pontoon berths €1.89; shwrs, ⊡ N of fuel berth. **Marina** ☎ 02·98·74·02·56, 📠 02·98·74.05.08, (463), Slip, P, D, C (6 ton), ME, CH, BH (12 ton), SM, Ⓔ, El, ⚒, ⊡; **YC** ☎ 02·98·92·02·03. **Port Rhu** ☎ 02·98·92·00·67; €1.48.
Town Gaz, 🛒, R, Bar, ✉, Ⓑ, ⇌ & ✈ (Quimper). Ferry: Roscoff.

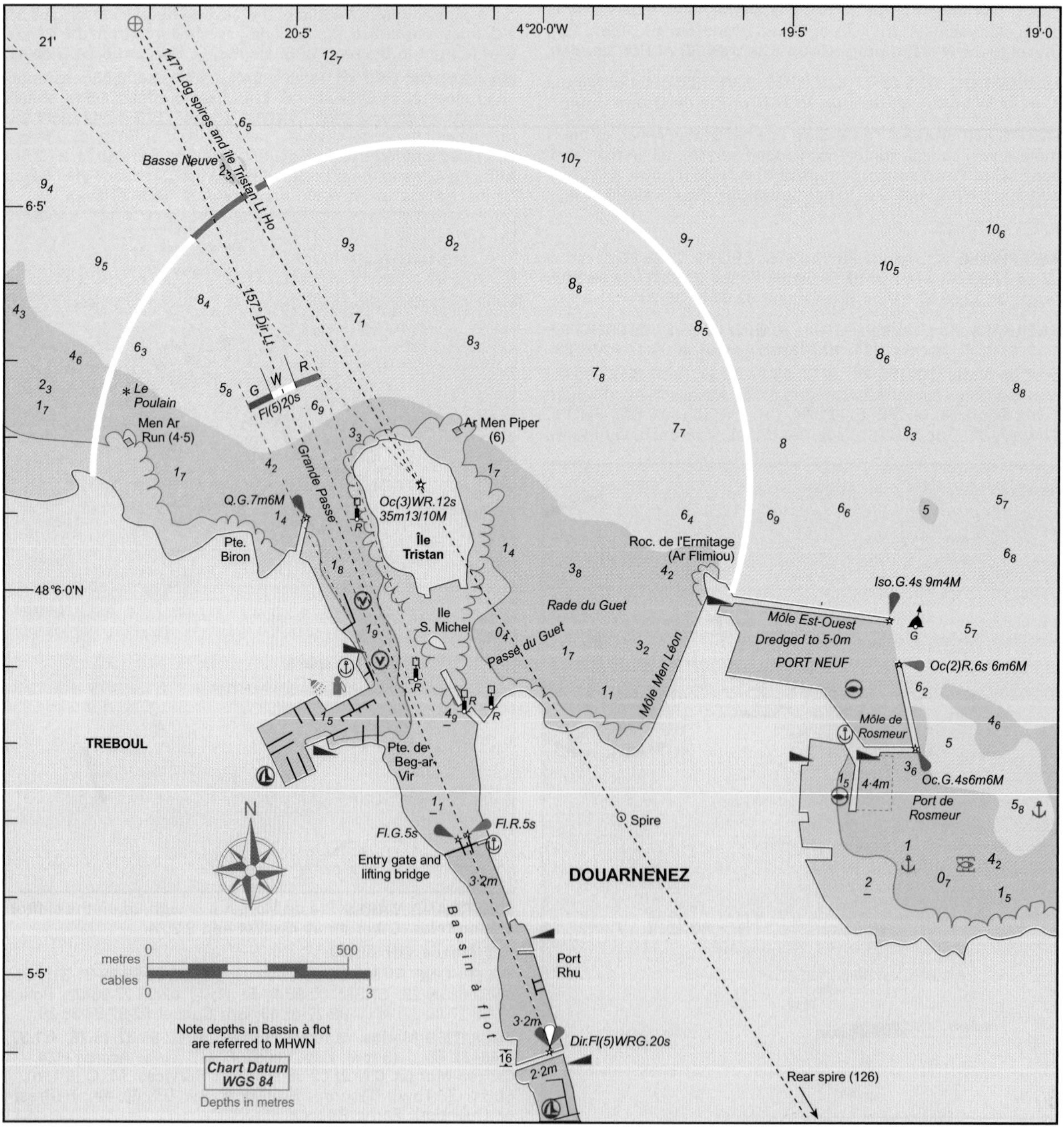
21'
20·5'
4°20·0'W
19·5'
19·0
6·5'
48°6·0'N
5·5'
147° Ldg spires and Île Tristan Lt Ho
157° Dir Lt
Basse Neuve
G W R
Fl(5)20s
Le Poulain
Men Ar Run (4·5)
Ar Men Piper (6)
Q.G.7m6M
Grande Passe
Oc(3)WR.12s 35m13/10M
Île Tristan
Pte. Biron
Ile S. Michel
Passe du Guet
Rade du Guet
Roc. de l'Ermitage (Ar Flimiou)
Môle Men Léon
Môle Est-Ouest
Dredged to 5·0m
PORT NEUF
Iso.G.4s 9m4M
Oc(2)R.6s 6m6M
Môle de Rosmeur
Oc.G.4s6m6M
Port de Rosmeur
4·4m
TREBOUL
Pte. de Beg-ar-Vir
Fl.G.5s
Fl.R.5s
Entry gate and lifting bridge
3·2m
Bassin à flot
Port Rhu
Spire
DOUARNENEZ
Dir.Fl(5)WRG.20s
2·2m
Rear spire (126)
N
metres 0 500
cables 0 3
Note depths in Bassin à flot are referred to MHWN
Chart Datum WGS 84
Depths in metres

Area 21

South Brittany
Raz de Sein to River Loire

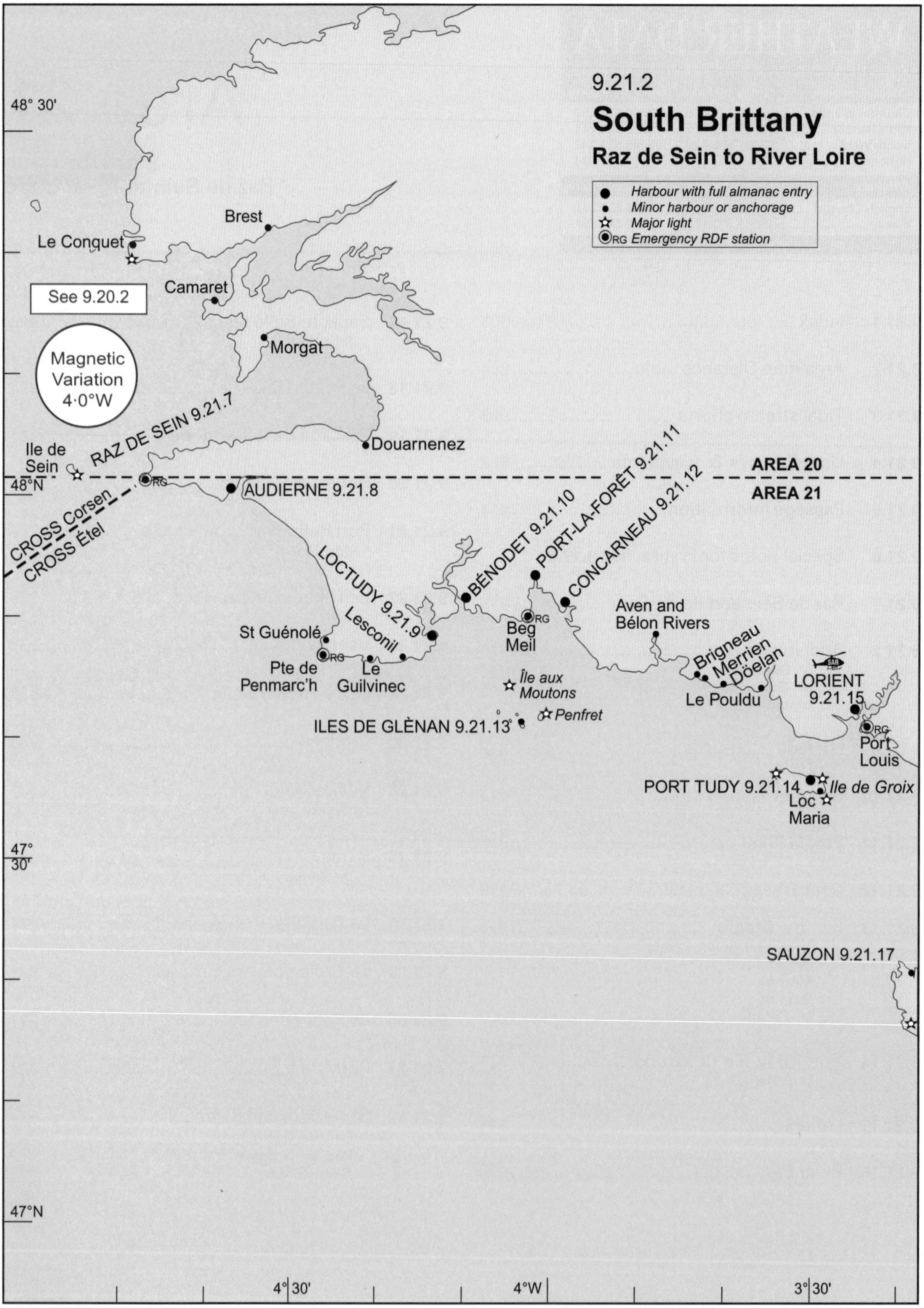
9.21.2
South Brittany
Raz de Sein to River Loire
Harbour with full almanac entry
Minor harbour or anchorage
Major light
RG Emergency RDF station
48° 30'
Brest
Le Conquet
See 9.20.2
Camaret
Morgat
Magnetic Variation 4·0°W
RAZ DE SEIN 9.21.7
Ile de Sein
Douarnenez
AREA 20
AREA 21
48°N
AUDIERNE 9.21.8
CROSS Corsen
CROSS Étel
LOCTUDY 9.21.9
BÉNODET 9.21.10
PORT-LA-FORÊT 9.21.11
CONCARNEAU 9.21.12
St Guénolé
Lesconil
Pte de Penmarc'h
Le Guilvinec
Beg Meil
Aven and Bélon Rivers
Brigneau
Merrien
Döelan
Le Pouldu
LORIENT 9.21.15
Île aux Moutons
Penfret
ILES DE GLÈNAN 9.21.13
Port Louis
PORT TUDY 9.21.14
Ile de Groix
Loc Maria
47° 30'
SAUZON 9.21.17
47°N
4° 30'
4°W
3° 30'

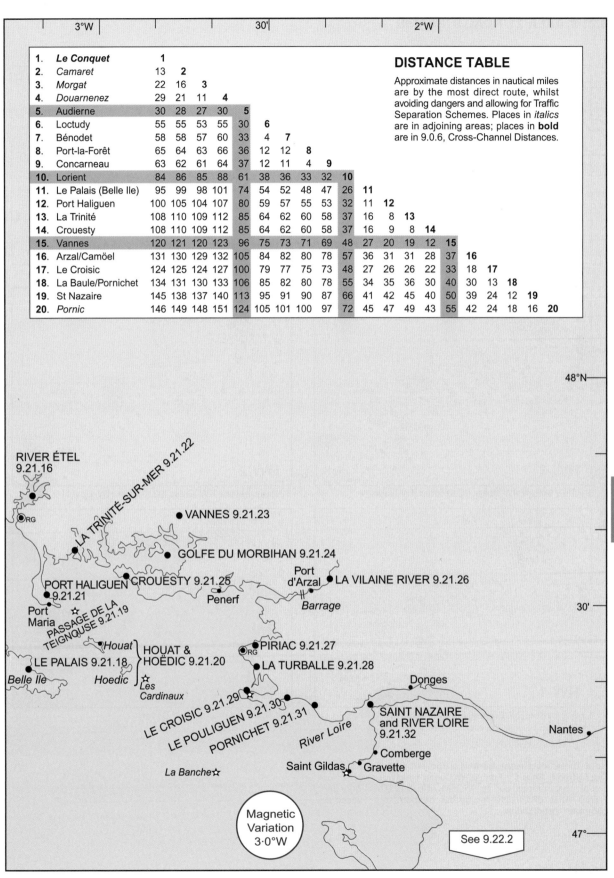

DISTANCE TABLE

Approximate distances in nautical miles are by the most direct route, whilst avoiding dangers and allowing for Traffic Separation Schemes. Places in *italics* are in adjoining areas; places in **bold** are in 9.0.6, Cross-Channel Distances.

1. ***Le Conquet***	**1**																			
2. *Camaret*	13	**2**																		
3. *Morgat*	22	16	**3**																	
4. *Douarnenez*	29	21	11	**4**																
5. Audierne	30	28	27	30	**5**															
6. Loctudy	55	55	53	55	30	**6**														
7. Bénodet	58	58	57	60	33	4	**7**													
8. Port-la-Forêt	65	64	63	66	36	12	12	**8**												
9. Concarneau	63	62	61	64	37	12	11	4	**9**											
10. Lorient	84	86	85	88	61	38	36	33	32	**10**										
11. Le Palais (Belle Ile)	95	99	98	101	74	54	52	48	47	26	**11**									
12. Port Haliguen	100	105	104	107	80	59	57	55	53	32	11	**12**								
13. La Trinité	108	110	109	112	85	64	62	60	58	37	16	8	**13**							
14. Crouesty	108	110	109	112	85	64	62	60	58	37	16	9	8	**14**						
15. Vannes	120	121	120	123	96	75	73	71	69	48	27	20	19	12	**15**					
16. Arzal/Camöel	131	130	129	132	105	84	82	80	78	57	36	31	31	28	37	**16**				
17. Le Croisic	124	125	124	127	100	79	77	75	73	48	27	26	26	22	33	18	**17**			
18. La Baule/Pornichet	134	131	130	133	106	85	82	80	78	55	34	35	36	30	40	30	13	**18**		
19. St Nazaire	145	138	137	140	113	95	91	90	87	66	41	42	45	40	50	39	24	12	**19**	
20. *Pornic*	146	149	148	151	124	105	101	100	97	72	45	47	49	43	55	42	24	18	16	**20**

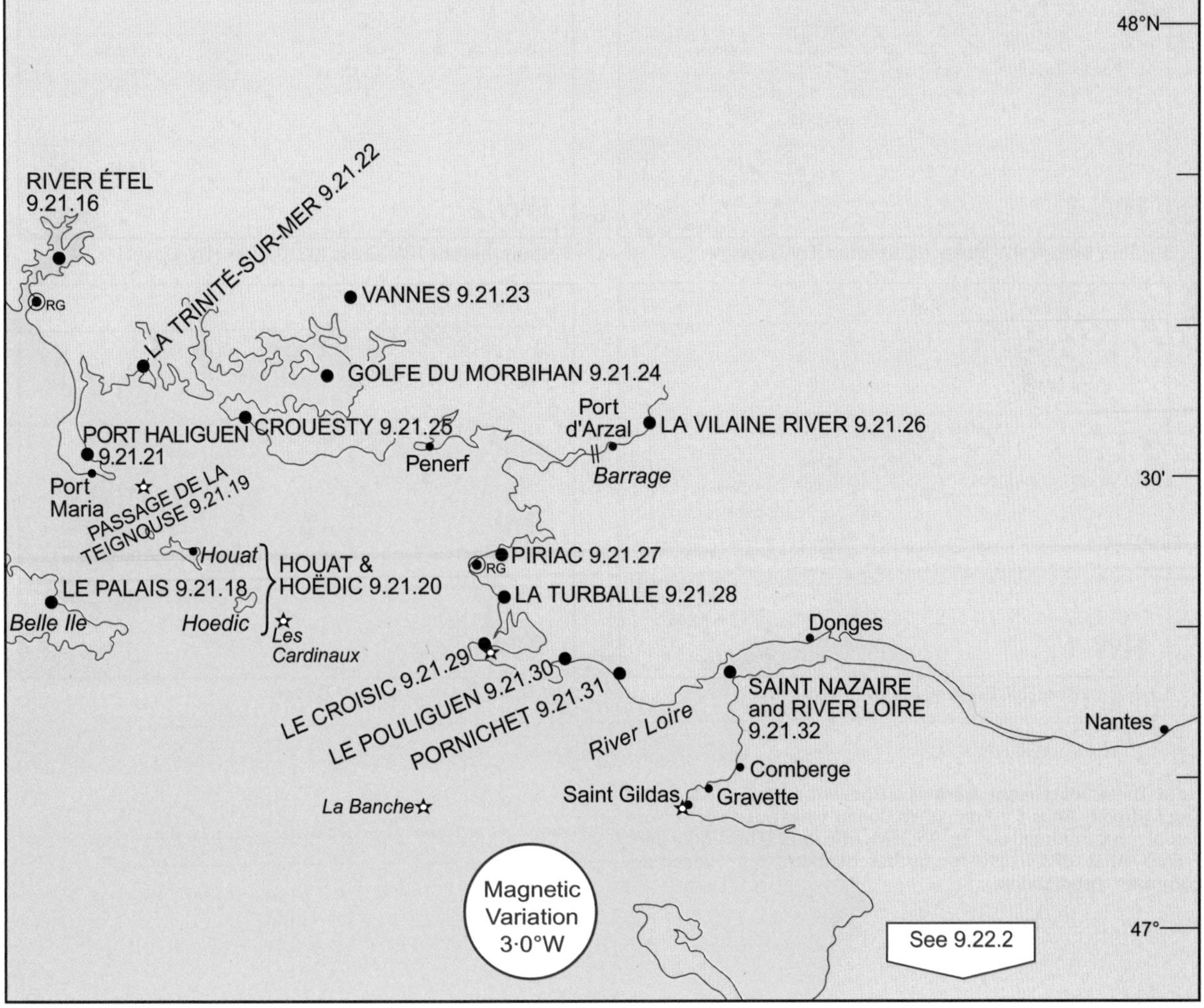

3°W
30'
2°W
48°N
30'
47°
RIVER ÉTEL 9.21.16
RG
LA TRINITÉ-SUR-MER 9.21.22
VANNES 9.21.23
GOLFE DU MORBIHAN 9.21.24
PORT HALIGUEN 9.21.21
CROUESTY 9.21.25
Penerf
Port d'Arzal
LA VILAINE RIVER 9.21.26
Barrage
Port Maria
PASSAGE DE LA TEIGNOUSE 9.21.19
Houat
HOUAT & HOËDIC 9.21.20
Hoedic
LE PALAIS 9.21.18
Belle Ile
Les Cardinaux
PIRIAC 9.21.27
RG
LA TURBALLE 9.21.28
LE CROISIC 9.21.29
LE POULIGUEN 9.21.30
PORNICHET 9.21.31
River Loire
Donges
SAINT NAZAIRE and RIVER LOIRE 9.21.32
Nantes
Comberge
Saint Gildas
Gravette
La Banche
Magnetic Variation 3·0°W
See 9.22.2

9.21.3 AREA 21 TIDAL STREAMS

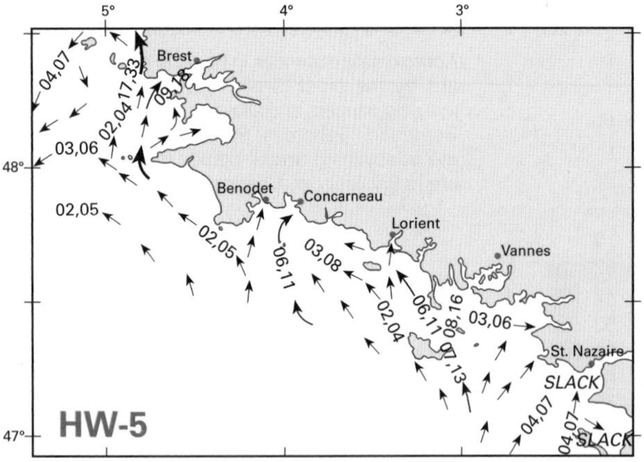
5°
4°
3°
48°
47°
Brest
Benodet
Concarneau
Lorient
Vannes
St. Nazaire
04,07
17,33
09,18
02,04
03,06
02,05
02,05
06,11
03,08
02,04
06,11
08,16
07,13
03,06
SLACK
04,07
04,07
SLACK
HW-5
5 Hours before HW Brest (0010 after HW Dover)

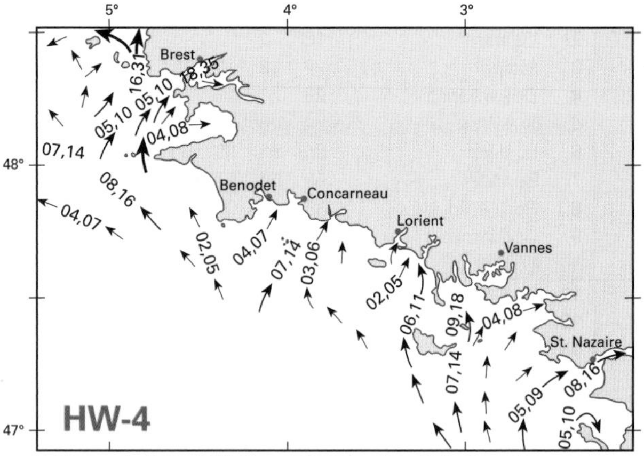
5°
4°
3°
48°
47°
Brest
Benodet
Concarneau
Lorient
Vannes
St. Nazaire
16,31
18,35
05,10
05,10
04,08
07,14
08,16
04,07
02,05
04,07
07,14
03,06
02,05
06,11
09,18
04,08
07,14
05,09
08,16
05,10
HW-4
4 Hours before HW Brest (0110 after HW Dover)

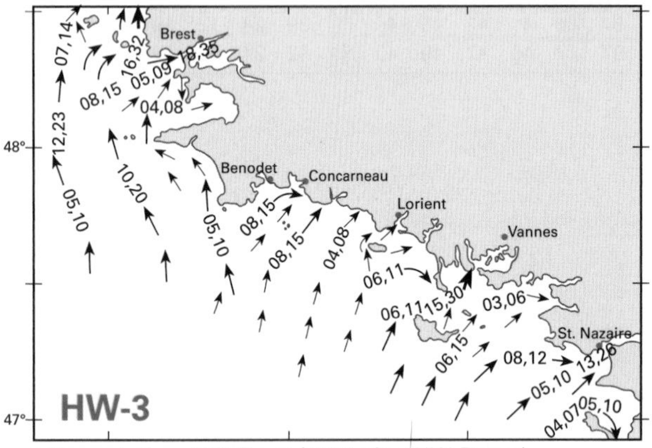
48°
47°
Brest
Benodet
Concarneau
Lorient
Vannes
St. Nazaire
07,14
16,32
18,35
08,15
05,09
04,08
12,23
10,20
05,10
05,10
08,15
08,15
04,08
06,11
06,11
15,30
03,06
06,15
08,12
13,26
05,10
04,07
05,10
HW-3
3 Hours before HW Brest (0210 after HW Dover)

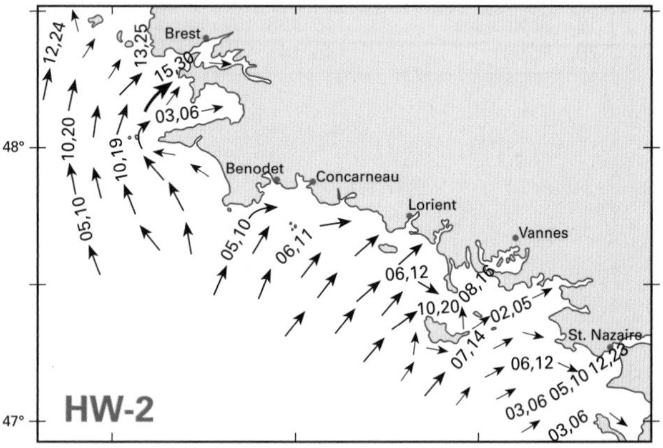
48°
47°
Brest
Benodet
Concarneau
Lorient
Vannes
St. Nazaire
12,24
13,25
15,30
03,06
10,20
10,19
05,10
05,10
06,11
06,12
08,16
10,20
02,05
07,14
06,12
12,23
03,06
05,10
03,06
HW-2
2 Hours before HW Brest (0310 after HW Dover)

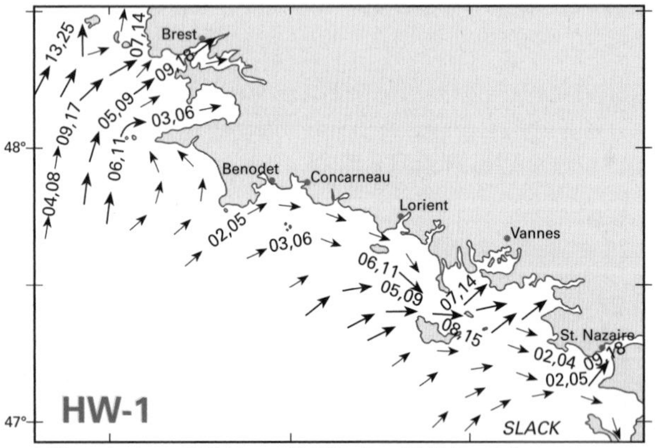
48°
47°
Brest
Benodet
Concarneau
Lorient
Vannes
St. Nazaire
13,25
07,14
09,18
09,17
05,09
03,06
04,08
06,11
02,05
03,06
06,11
05,09
07,14
08,15
02,04
09,18
02,05
SLACK
HW-1
1 Hour before HW Brest (0410 after HW Dover)

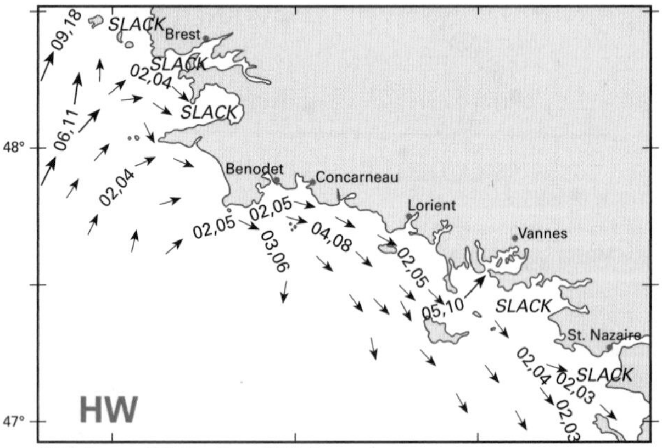
48°
47°
Brest
Benodet
Concarneau
Lorient
Vannes
St. Nazaire
09,18
SLACK
SLACK
02,04
SLACK
06,11
02,04
02,05
02,05
03,06
04,08
02,05
05,10
SLACK
02,04
SLACK
02,03
02,03
HW
HW Brest (0510 after HW Dover)

Note: These tidal stream chartlets are based on NP 265 (Admiralty Tidal Stream Atlas for France, W Coast) which uses data from actual observations out to 15-25M offshore. The equivalent French Atlas gives data for further offshore, but based on computer predictions.

Northward 9.20.3   Southward 9.22.3

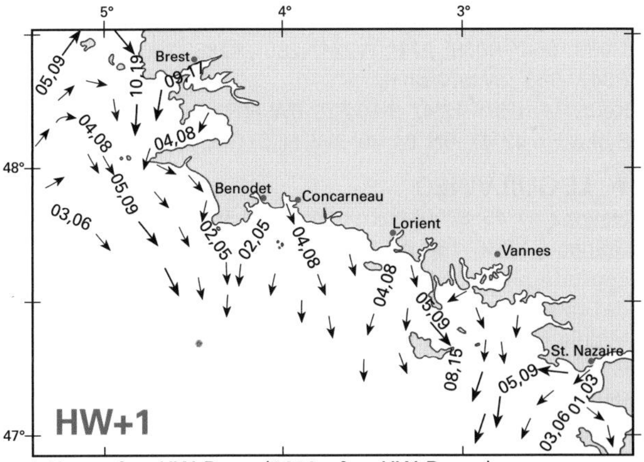
5°
4°
3°
48°
47°
Brest
Benodet
Concarneau
Lorient
Vannes
St. Nazaire
05,09
10,19
09,17
04,08
04,08
05,09
03,06
02,05
02,05
04,08
04,08
05,09
08,15
05,09
01,03
03,06
HW+1

1 Hour after HW Brest (0610 after HW Dover)

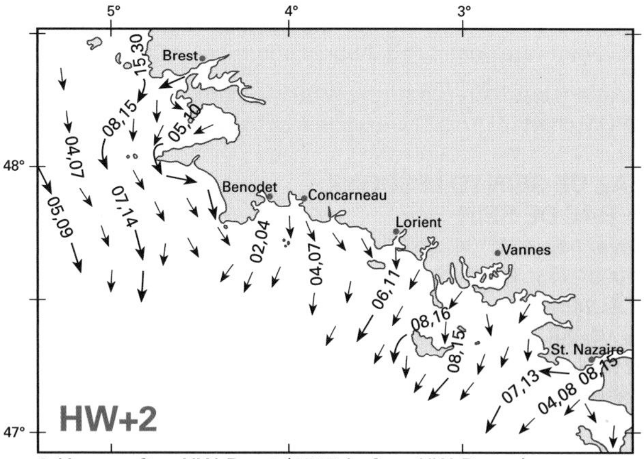
5°
4°
3°
48°
47°
Brest
Benodet
Concarneau
Lorient
Vannes
St. Nazaire
15,30
08,15
05,10
04,07
05,09
07,14
02,04
04,07
06,11
08,16
08,15
07,13
04,08
08,15
HW+2

2 Hours after HW Brest (0515 before HW Dover)

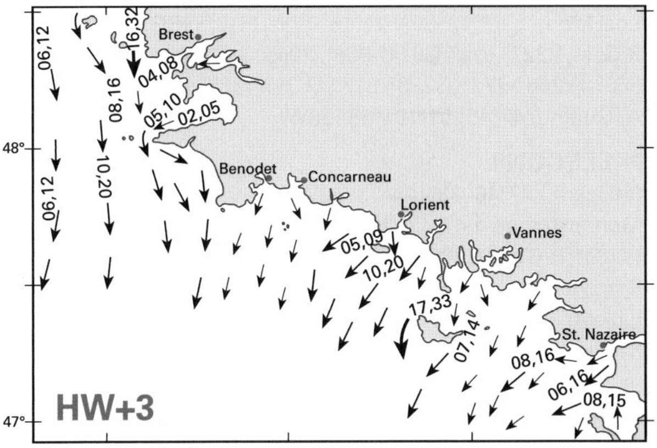
48°
47°
Brest
Benodet
Concarneau
Lorient
Vannes
St. Nazaire
06,12
16,32
08,16
04,08
05,10
02,05
10,20
06,12
05,09
10,20
17,33
07,14
08,16
06,16
08,15
HW+3

3 Hours after HW Brest (0415 before HW Dover)

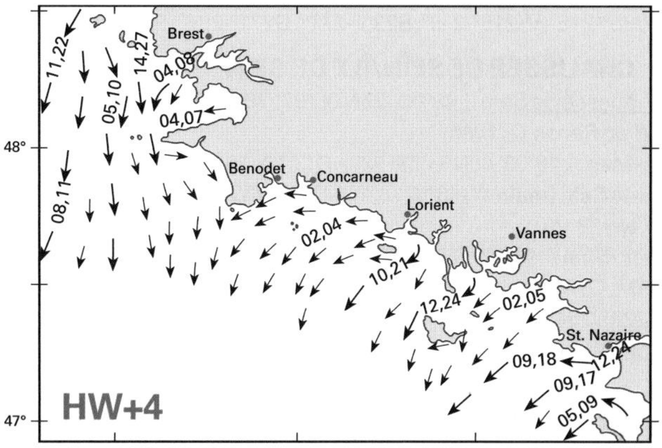
48°
47°
Brest
Benodet
Concarneau
Lorient
Vannes
St. Nazaire
11,22
14,27
05,10
04,08
04,07
08,11
02,04
10,21
12,24
02,05
09,18
12,24
09,17
05,09
HW+4

4 Hours after HW Brest (0315 before HW Dover)

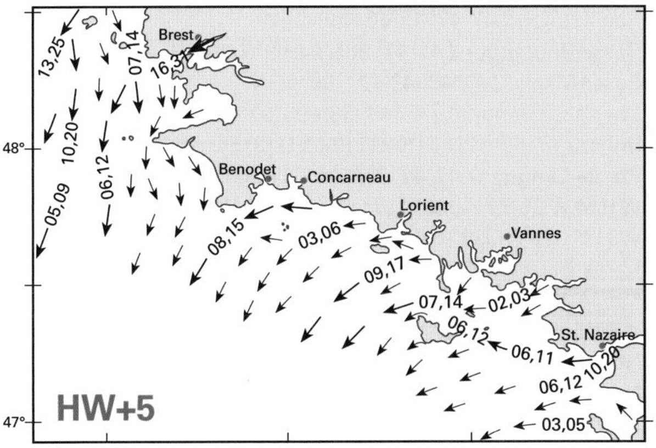
48°
47°
Brest
Benodet
Concarneau
Lorient
Vannes
St. Nazaire
13,25
07,14
16,31
10,20
06,12
05,09
08,15
03,06
09,17
07,14
02,03
06,12
06,11
06,12
10,20
03,05
HW+5

5 Hours after HW Brest (0215 before HW Dover)

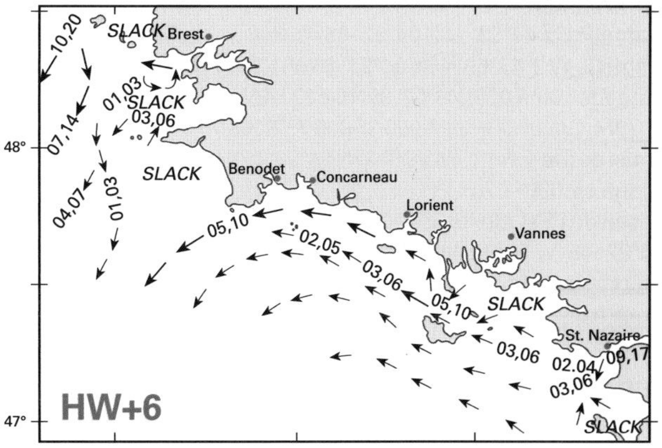
48°
47°
Brest
Benodet
Concarneau
Lorient
Vannes
St. Nazaire
10,20
SLACK
01,03
SLACK
03,06
07,14
SLACK
04,07
01,03
05,10
02,05
03,06
05,10
SLACK
03,06
02,04
09,17
03,06
SLACK
HW+6

6 Hours after HW Brest (0115 before HW Dover)

Note: These tidal stream chartlets are based on NP 265 (Admiralty Tidal Stream Atlas for France, W Coast) which uses data from actual observations out to 15-25M offshore. The equivalent French Atlas gives data for further offshore, but based on computer predictions.

PLOT WAYPOINTS ON YOUR CHART BEFORE USING THEM

9.21.4 LIGHTS, BUOYS AND WAYPOINTS

Blue print = light with a nominal range of 15M or more. CAPITALS = place or feature. *CAPITAL ITALICS* = light-vessel, light float or Lanby. *Italics* = Fog signal. ***Bold italics*** = Racon. Useful waypoints are underlined. Abbreviations are in Chapter 1.

Positions are referenced to the WGS 84 datum. More UKHO and SHOM charts of Area 21 are referenced to WGS 84 than to ED50.

RAZ DE SEIN TO LESCONIL

▶ RAZ DE SEIN

Tévennec ☆ 48°04'·28N 04°47'·73W, Q WR 28m W9M R6M; W090°-345°, R345°-090°; W □ twr and dwelling. Same twr, Dir ☆ Fl 4s 24m 12M; intens 324°-332° (through Raz de Sein).

La Vieille ☆ 48°02'·43N 04°45'·43W, Oc (2+1) WRG 12s 33m **W18M**, R13M, G14M; W290°-298°, R298°-325°, W325°-355°, G355°-017°, W017°-035°, G035°-105°, W105°-123°, R123°-158°, W158°-205°; Gy □ twr; *Horn (2+1) 60s.*

La Plate 48°02'·35N 04°45'·61W, VQ (9) 10s 19m 8M.

Le Chat 48°01'·41N 04°48'·88W, Fl (2) WRG 6s 27m, W9M, R/G6M; G096°-215°, W215°-230°, R230°-271°, G271°-286°, R286°-096°.

▶ CHAUSSÉE DE SEIN/ÎLE DE SEIN

Chaussée de Sein 48°03'·75N 05°07'·78W, VQ (9) 10s 9m 6M; *Whis*; ***Racon O, 10M.***

Ar-Men ☆ 48°03'·00N 04°59'·92W, Fl (3) 20s 29m **23M**; W twr, B top.

Île de Sein (main ☆**)** 48°02'·63N 04°52'·06W, Fl (4) 25s 49m **29M**; W twr, B top.

Men-Brial ☆ 48°02'·26N 04°50'·99W, Oc (2) WRG 6s 16m, W12M, R9M, G7M; G149°-186°, W186°-192°, R192°-221°, W221°-227°, G227°-254°; G&W twr.

Cornoc-An-Ar-Braden 48°03'·23N 04°50'·87W, Fl G 4s; *Whis.*

▶ AUDIERNE

Pointe de Lervily ☆ 48°00'·04N 04°33'·94W, Fl (3) WR 12s 20m W14M, R11M; W211°-269°, R269°-294°, W294°-087°, R087°-121°; W twr, R top.

Gamelle E 47°59'·45N 04°32'·05W; *Bell.*

Gamelle W 47°59'·46N 04°32'·85W, VQ (9) 10s; *Whis.*

Kergadec Dir ☆ 006°. 48°00'·95N 04°32'·78W, Q WRG 43m W12M, R/G9M; G000°-005·3°, W005·3°-006·7°, R006·7°-017°.

Jetée de Ste-Évette ☆ 48°00'·31N 04°33'·07W, Oc (2) R 6s 2m 7M; R lantern; 090°-270°.

Passe de l'Est ldg lts 331°. Front, Jetée de Raoulic 48°00'·54N 04°32'·45W, Fl (3) WG 12s 11m, W14M, G9M; Wshore-034°, G034°-shore but may show W037°-055°. Rear, Kergadec, 0·5M from front, FR 44m 9M; intens 321°-341°; W 8-sided twr, R top.

Pors-Poulhan ent, W side ☆ 47°59'·09N 04°27'·89W, QR 14m 9M.

▶ SAINT GUÉNOLÉ

Ch de Groumilli ldg lts 123°, both FG 9/13m 9M; Or □ on W cols, B bands. Front, 47°48'·12N 04°22'·70W. Rear, 300m from front.

Basse Gaouac'h 47°48'·60N 04°24'·25W, Fl G 4s; *Whis.*

Scoedec ☆ 47°48'·41N 04°23'·20W, Fl (2) G 6s 6m 3M; G twr.

Ldg lts 055·4°; G&W cols. Front, 47°48'·74N 04°22'·72W, VQ 5m 2M. Rear, 320m from front; F Vi 15m 1M; 040°-070°.

Ldg lts 026·5°, both QR 8/12m 4M, synch. Front, 47°49'·01N 04°22'·71W; Gy mast. Rear, 51m from front; mast, R&W bands.

▶ POINTE DE PENMARC'H

Eckmühl ☆ 47°47'·88N 04°22'·39W, Fl 5s 60m **23M**; Gy 8-sided twr; *Horn 60s.*

Men Hir ☆ 47°47'·73N 04°24'·03W, Fl (2) WG 6s 19m, W7M, G4M; G135°-315°, W315°-135°; W twr, B band.

Cap Caval 47°46'·46N 04°22'·71W, Q (9) 15s.

Locarec ☆ 47°47'·29N 04°20'·33W, Iso WRG 4s 11m W9M, R/G6M; G063°-068°, R068°-271°, W271°-285°, R285°-298°, G298°-340°, R340°-063°; W tank on rk.

Kérity. Men Hir ☆ 47°47'·3N 04°20'·6W, Fl R 2·5s 6m 2M; pylon.

E bkwtr ☆ 47°47'·6N 04°20'·9W, Fl (2) G 6s 5m 1M.

▶ LE GUILVINEC

Névez 47°45'·83N 04°20'·10W, Fl G 2·5s.

Spinec 47°45'·18N 04°18'·92W, Q (6) + L Fl 15s; *Whis.*

Ldg lts (triple) 053°, front & rear, Q 7/26m 8M, synch. Front, Môle de Léchiagat, spur, 47°47'·43N 04°17'·08W; 233°-066°; W pylon. Middle, Rocher Le Faoutés, 210m from front, Q WG 12m W14M, G11M; W006°-293°, G293°-006°; synch; R □ on R col. Rear, 0·58M from front; 051·5°-054·5°, R □ on W twr.

Capelan 47°47'·14N 04°17'·55W, Fl (2) G 6s.

Môle de Léchiagat hd ☆ 47°47'·45N 04°17'·17W, Fl G 4s 5m 7M; W hut, G top.

Lost Moan 47°47'·00N 04°16'·77W, Fl (3) WRG 12s 8m, W9M, R/G6M; R327°-014°, G014°-065°, R065°-140°, W140°-160°, R160°-268°, W268°-273°, G273°-317°, W317°-327°; □ on W twr, R top.

Ar Guisty 47°45'·61N 04°15'·58W.

▶ LESCONIL

Reissant 47°46'·38N 04°13'·52W.

Men-ar-Groas ☆ 47°47'·79N 04°12'·68W, Fl (3) WRG 12s 14m, W10M, R/G7M; G268°-313°, W313°-333°, R333°-050°; W/G twr.

S bkwtr ☆ 47°47'·68N 04°12'·65W, Oc R 4s 5m 6M

E bkwtr ☆ 47°47'·70N 04°12'·65W, QG 5m 5M; G twr.

Karek Greis 47°46'·04N 04°11'·38W, Q (3) 10s; *Whis.*

LOCTUDY TO CONCARNEAU

▶ LOCTUDY

Rostolou 47°46'·65N 04°07'·33W.

Roc'h Hélou 47°47'·12N 04°08'·12W.

Basse Boulanger 47°47'·36N 04°09'·16W, VQ (6) + L Fl 10s.

Basse Malvic 47°48'·46N 04°06'·65W.

Chenal de Bénodet 47°48'·53N 04°07'·05W.

Bilien 47°49'·10N 04°08'·11W, VQ (3) 5s; *Whis.*

Pte de Langoz ☆ 47°49'·87N 04°09'·59W, Fl (4) WRG 12s 12m, **W15M**, R/G11M; W115°-257°, G257°-284°, W284°-295°, R295°-318°, W318°-328°, R328°-025°; W twr, R top.

Karek-Saoz 47°50'·02N 04°09'·38W, Fl R 2·5s 3m 1M; R twr.

Men Audierne 47°50'·31N 04°09'·06W.

47°50'·19N 04°09'·49W, Fl (2) R 6s.

No. 1 47°50'·22N 04°09'·73W, Fl (2) G 6s.

No. 3 47°50'·22N 04°10'·00W, Fl (3) G 12s.

47°50'·17N 04°10'·37W, Fl G.

Groyne head ☆ 47°50'·21N 04°10'·34W, Q 3m 10M.

Le Blas ☆ 47°50'·28N 04°10'·23W, Fl (4) G 15s 5m 1M; G △ on truncated col.

▶ BENODET

Ldg lts 345·5°. Front, **Pte du Coq** ☆ 47°52'·31N 04°06'·70W, Dir Oc (2+1) G 12s 11m **17M**; intens 345°-347°; W ○ twr, G stripe. Pyramide, common rear, 336m from front, Oc (2+1) 12s 48m 11M; 338°-016°, synch; W twr, G top.

Lts in line 000·5°. Front, Pte de Combrit 47°51'·86N 04°06'·78W, Oc (3+1) WR 12s 19m, W12M, R9M; W325°-017°, R017°-325°; W

□ twr, Gy corners. Common rear, Pyramide, 0·63M from front.
Les Verrés ⚓ 47°51'·55N 04°06'·14W.
<u>La Rousse</u> ⚓ 47°51'·55N 04°06'·47W.
<u>La Potée</u> ⚓ 47°51'·75N 04°06'·56W.
Le Four ⚓ 47°51'·79N 04°06'·41W.
Pte du Toulgoët ☆ 47°52'·29N 04°06'·86W, Fl R 2·5s 2m 1M.
Le Taro ⚓ 47°50'·51N 04°04'·84W.
Men Déhou ⚓ 47°48'·11N 04°04'·71W.
Les Poulains ⚓ 47°47'·69N 04°03'·48W.
La Vache ⚓ 47°49'·54N 04°02'·62W.
<u>La Voleuse</u> ⚓ 47°48'·76N 04°02'·49W, Q (6) + L Fl 15s; *Whis.*
Men Vras ⚓ 47°49'·66N 04°01'·58W.

▶ BEG-MEIL
Linuen ⚓ 47°50'·65N 03°57'·78W.
<u>Chaussée de Beg-Meil</u> ⚓ 47°50'·76N 03°57'·31W, Q (3) 10s.
Laouen Pod ⚓ 47°51'·23N 03°58'·00W.
<u>Jetty</u> ☆ 47°51'·66N 03°58'·94W, Fl R 2·5s 6m 1M; W col, R bands.

▶ PORT-LA-FORÊT
<u>Le Scoré</u> ⚓ 47°52'·75N 03°57'·56W.
Les Ormeaux ⚓ 47°53'·27N 03°58'·34W.
<u>Access channel</u> ⚓ 47°53'·39N 03°58'·13W, Fl G 2·5s.
⚓ 47°53'·38N 03°58'·22W, Fl R 2·5s.
⚓ 47°53'·44N 03°58'·24W.
⚓ 47°53'·48N 03°58'·20W.
Cap Coz mole ☆ 47°53'·48N 03°58'·28W, Fl (2) WRG 6s 5m, W7M, R/G5M; R shore-335°, G335°-340°, W340°-346°, R346°-shore.
Kerleven mole ☆ 47°53'·60N 03°58'·37W, Fl G 4s 8m 6M.
Marina bkwtr ☆ 47°53'·90N 03°58'·57W, Iso G 4s 5m 1M.

▶ ÎLE AUX MOUTONS
Île-aux-Moutons ☆ 47°46'·47N 04°01'·68W, Oc (2) WRG 6s 18m, **W15M**, R/G11M; W035°-050°, G050°-063°, W063°-081°, R081°-141°, W141°-292°, R292°-035°; W □ twr and dwelling.
Same twr: **auxiliary** ☆ Dir Oc (2) 6s 17m **24M**; synch with main ☆, intens 278·5°-283·5°.
<u>Rouge de Glénan</u> ⚓ 47°45'·48N 04°03'·96W, VQ (9) 10s 8m 8M; *Whis.*
Grand Pourceaux ⚓ 47°45'·97N 04°00'·82W, Q.
Rochers Leuriou ⚓ 47°45'·13N 03°59'·95W.

▶ ÎLES DE GLÉNAN
Penfret ☆ 47°43'·26N 03°57'·17W, Fl R 5s 36m **21M**; W □ twr, R top.
Same twr: auxiliary ☆ Dir Q 34m 12M; 295°-315°.
La Pie ⚓ 47°43'·75N 03°59'·75W, Fl (2) 6s 9m 3M.
Pte de la Baleine ⚓ 47°43'·26N 03°59'·21W, VQ (3) 5s 2M.
Broc'h ⚓ 47°43'·16N 04°01'·40W.
Les Bluiniers ⚓ 47°43'·35N 04°03'·81W.
Offlying marks, anticlockwise from the west:
<u>Basse Pérennès</u> ⚓ 47°41'·06N 04°06'·15W, Q (9) 15s 8m 5M; *Whis.*
<u>Jument de Glénan</u> ⚓ 47°38'·75N 04°01'·43W, Q (6) + L Fl 15s 10m 4M; *Whis.*
Basse an Ero ⚓ 47°40'·41N 03°55'·49W.
Laoennou ⚓ 47°39'·64N 03°54'·70W.
Corn-Loch ⚓ 47°42'·20N 03°52'·38W.
<u>Jaune de Glénan</u> ⚓ 47°42'·55N 03°49'·84W, Q (3) 10s; *Whis.*

▶ CONCARNEAU
Ldg lts 028·5°. Front, La Croix 47°52'·15N 03°55'·08W, Oc (3) 12s 14m 13M; 006·5°-093°; R&W twr. **Rear, Beuzec** ☆ Dir Q 87m **23M**; intens 026·5°-030·5°; spire, 1·34M from front.

⚓ 47°51'·40N 03°55'·75W.
Le Cochon ⚓ 47°51'·47N 03°55'·54W, Fl (3) WRG 12s 5m W9M, R/G6M; G048°-205°, R205°-352°, W352°-048°; G twr.
<u>Basse du Chenal</u> ⚓ 47°51'·55N 03°55'·60W, QR.
<u>Men Fall</u> ⚓ 47°51'·76N 03°55'·29W, Fl G 4s.
Kersos ⚓ 47°51'·80N 03°54'·94W (Anse de Kersos).
La Medée ⚓ 47°52'·06N 03°54'·80W, Fl R 4s 4M.
Lanriec ☆ 47°52'·00N 03°54'·64W, QG 13m 8M; 063°-078°; G window on W gable.
No. 1 ☆ 47°52'·22N 03°54'·64W, Fl G 4s 4m 5M; G turret.
Ville-Close ☆ 47°52'·33N 03°54'·68W, Oc (2) WR 6s, W9M, R6M; R209°-354°, W354°-007°, R007°-018°; R turret.
Marina wavescreen ☆ 47°52'·20N 03°54'·72W, Fl (3) R 12s 3m 1M.

▶ BAIE DE POULDOHAN
Petit Taro ⚓ 47°51'·10N 03°55'·29W.
Pouldohan ☆ 47°50'·97N 03°53'·70W, Fl G 4s 6m 8M; 053°-065°; W □ twr, G top.
Roché Tudy ⚓ 47°50'·52N 03°54'·49W.

CONCARNEAU TO ÎLE DE GROIX
▶ PTE DE TRÉVIGNON TO PORT MANEC'H
<u>Les Soldats</u> ⚓ 47°47'·87N 03°53'·42W, VQ (9) 10s.
Trévignon mole ☆ 47°47'·67N 03°51'·30W, Fl G 4s 5m 8M.
Trévignon bkwtr root ☆ 47°47'·59N 03°51'·34W, Oc (3+1) WRG 12s 11m, W14M, R/G11M; W004°-051°, G051°-085°, W085°-092°, R092°-127°, R322°-351°; W □ twr, G top.
Men Du ⚓ 47°46'·35N 03°50'·49W.
<u>Corn Vas</u> ⚓ 47°45'·87N 03°50'·17W.
<u>Men ar Tréas</u> ⚓ 47°45'·76N 03°49'·64W.
Île Verte ⚓ 47°46'·31N 03°48'·04W.
Île de Raguénès ⚓ 47°46'·85N 03°47'·77W.

▶ PORT MANEC'H (Aven and Bélon rivers)
Pointe de Beg-ar-Vechen ☆ 47°47'·98N 03°44'·35W, Oc (4) WRG 12s 38m, W10M, R/G7M; obsc when brg less than 299°; W (unintens) 050°-140°, W140°-296°, G296°-303°, W303°-311°, R311°-328° over Les Verrès, W328°-050°; W & R twr.
Les Verrès ⚓ 47°46'·63N 03°42'·72W.

▶ BRIGNEAU
<u>Brigneau</u> ⚓ 47°46'·10N 03°40'·10W; *Whis.*
Brigneau mole, ☆ 47°46'·89N 03°40'·19W, Oc (2) WRG 6s 7m, W12M, R/G9M; W col, R top; G280°-329°, W329°-339°, R339°-034°.

▶ MERRIEN
Merrien ☆ 47°47'·01N 03°38'·95W, Dir QR 26m 7M; 004°-009°; W □ twr, R top. Ent, W side ⚓. E side ⚓ 47°46'·44N 03°38'·90W.
Roc Bali ⚓ 47°46'·27N 03°38'·54W.

▶ DOËLAN
Doëlan ldg lts 013·8°. Front, 47°46'·47N 03°36'·51W, Oc (3) WG 12s 20m, W13M, G10M; W shore-305°, G305°-314°, W314°-shore; W twr, G band and top. Rear, 326m from front, QR 27m 9M; W twr, R band and top.
Basse La Croix ⚓ 47°45'·98N 03°36'·85W.

▶ LE POULDU
Le Pouldu ent ⚓ 47°45'·71N 03°32'·24W.
Grand Cochon ⚓ 47°43'·11N 03°30'·82W.
Pte de Kerroc'h ☆ 47°41'·97N 03°27'·68W, Oc (2) WRG 6s 22m W11M, R/G8M; R096·5°-112°·5, G112·5°-132°, R132°-302°, W302°-096·5°; W twr, R top.

PLOT WAYPOINTS ON YOUR CHART BEFORE USING THEM

▶ ÎLE DE GROIX

Pen Men ☆ 47°38'·86N 03°30'·54W, Fl (4) 25s 60m **29M**; 309°-275°; W □ twr, B top.
Speerbrecker, 47°39'·17N 03°26'·25W.
Port Tudy, N môle ☆ 47°38'·70N 03°26'·74W, Iso G 4s 12m 6M; W twr, G top.
E môle ☆ 47°38'·65N 03°26'·78W, Fl (2) R 6s 11m 6M; 112°-226°; W twr R top.
Basse Melité 47°38'·86N 03°25'·56W.
Pte de la Croix ☆ 47°38'·03N 03°25'·00W, Oc WR 4s 16m, W12M, R9M; W169°-336°, R336°-345°, W345°-353°; W pedestal, R lantern.
Edouard de Cougy 47°37'·91N 03°23'·91W.
Pointe des Chats ☆ 47°37'·21N 03°25'·31W, Fl R 5s 16m **19M**; W □ twr and dwelling.
Les Chats 47°35'·69N 03°23'·58W, Q (6) + L Fl 15s.

LORIENT AND RIVER ÉTEL

▶ LORIENT, PASSE DE L'OUEST

Lomener, Anse de Stole, Dir ☆ 357·2°. 47°42'·29N 03°25'·55W, Q WRG 13m, W10M, R/G8M; G349·2°-355·2°, W355·2°-359·2°, R 359·2°-005·2°; W twr, R top.
Ldg lts 057°, both Dir Q 11/22m 13/**18M**. Front, Les Sœurs 47°42'·13N 03°21'·83W; intens 042·5°-058·5°, 058·5°-042·5° (4M range only); R twr, W bands. Rear **Port Louis** ☆, 740m from front.
'L' Banc des Truies 47°40'·76N 03°24'·48W, Q (9) 15s.
Les Truies Ouest 47°41'·10N 03°23'·39W; *Whis.*
A2 47°40'·94N 03°24'·98W, Fl R 2·5s.
A4 47°41'·18N 03°24'·12W, Fl (3) R 12s.
A6 47°41'·53N 03°23'·33W, Fl (2) R 6s.
A5 47°41'·50N 03°23'·11W, Fl (2) G 6s.
Paté du Cheval 47°41'·42N 03°22'·95W.
A7 47°41'·70N 03°22'·66W, Fl G 2·5s.
Les Trois Pierres 47°41'·53N 03°22'·47W, Q RG 11m R/G6M; B twr, W bands; G060°-196°, R196°-002°.

▶ PASSE DU SUD

Ldg lts 008·5°, both Dir QR 16/34m **17/16M**; intens 006°-011°; synch. **Front** ☆, Fish Market 47°43'·76N 03°21'·74W; R□, G bands on Gy twr. **Rear** ☆, 515m from front; R □, W stripe on Gy twr.
Bastresses Sud 47°40'·77N 03°22'·09W, QG.
Les Errants 47°41'·10N 03°22'·38W, Fl (2) R 6s.
Bastresses Nord 47°41'·11N 03°22'·20W, Fl (2) G 6s.
Goëland 47°41'·59N 03°22'·09W.

▶ SOUTH OF PORT LOUIS

La Paix 47°41'·97N 03°21'·87W.
La Paix 47°41'·84N 03°21'·92W, Fl G 2·5s.
Île aux Souris ☆ 47°42'·15N 03°21'·52W, Dir Q WG 6m, W3M, G2M; W041·5°-043·5°, G043·5°-041·5°; G twr.
47°42'·13N 03°21'·92W, Fl G 2·5s.
Ban-Gâvres fish/yacht hbr, W jetty 47°42'·06N 03°21'·11W, Fl (2) G 6s 3M. E jetty, 47°42'·06N 03°21'·06W, Fl (2) R 6s 3M.

▶ ENTRANCE CHANNEL

Ldg lts (Île St Michel) 016·5°, both Dir Oc (3) G 12s 8/14m **16M**; intens 014·5°-017·5°; synch; W twrs, G tops. **Front** ☆, 47°43'·47N 03°21'·62W. **Rear** ☆, 306m from front.
A8 47°41'·90N 03°22'·52W, Fl R 2·5s.
Écrevisse 47°42'·13N 03°22'·37W.
Toulhars 47°42'·25N 03°22'·28W.
La Potée de Beurre 47°42'·24N 03°21'·98W.
La Citadelle 47°42'·59N 03°21'·94W, Oc G 4s 6m 6M; 009°-193°.
La Petite Jument 47°42'·58N 03°22'·07W, Oc R 4s 5m 6M; 182°-024°; R twr.
Secondary yacht chan, RGR, 47°42'·76N 03°21'·51W.
Le Pot 47°42'·72N 03°22'·02W.
Le Cochon 47°42'·80N 03°22'·00W, Fl R 4s 5m 5M; RGR twr.
No. 1 47°42'·80N 03°21'·84W.

▶ PORT LOUIS (Port de la Pointe)

D 1 47°42'·76N 03°21'·51W.
Jetty ☆ 47°42'·71N 03°21'·20W, Iso G 4s 7m 6M; W twr, G top.

▶ KERNEVEL

No. 2 47°42'·97N 03°21'·96W, Fl R 2·5s.
Kéroman ldg lts 350°, both Dir Oc (2) R 6s 25/31m **15M**; synch; intens 349°-351°. **Front** ☆, 47°43'·60N 03°22'·02W, R ho, W bands. **Rear** ☆, 91m from front; R&W topmark on Gy pylon, R top.
Banc du Turc 47°43'·33N 03°21'·85W, Fl (3) G 12s.
Kernevel marina, enter between QR 1M, N end of wavebreak (47°43'·39N 03°22'·09W) and adjacent unlit.
Ldg lts 217°, both Dir QR 10/18m **15M**; intens 215°-219°; synch. **Front, Kernevel** ☆ 47°43'·02N 03°22'·32W; R&W twr. **Rear** ☆, 290m from front; W □ twr, R top.

▶ NORTHERN PART OF LORIENT HARBOUR

Grand Bassin (Fish hbr), E side of ent, ☆ 47°43'·62N 03°21'·87W, Fl RG 4s 7m 6M; G000°-235°, R235°-000°; W twr, G top.
Ste Catherine marina ent ☆ 47°43'·51N 03°21'·08W, QG 5m 3M.
N side of marina ent ☆ 47°43'·53N 03°21'·08W, QR 2m 2M.
Pengarne 47°43'·88N 03°21'·23W, Fl G 2·5s 3m 3M; G twr.
No. 11 47°44'·04N 03°21'·01W, QG.
Pen-Mané marina, bkwtr elbow ☆ 47°44'·11N 03°20'·86W, Fl (2) G 6s 4M.
Pointe de l'Espérance, Dir ☆ 037°. 47°44'·51N 03°20'·66W, Q WRG 8m W10M, R/G8M; G034·2°-036·7°, W036·7°-037·2°, R037·2°-047·2°; W twr, G top.
Ro-Ro jetty ☆ 47°44'·42N 03°20'·96W, Oc (2) R 6s 7m 6M.
No. 8 47°44'·55N 03°20'·98W, Fl R 2·5s; ent to Lorient marina.

▶ RIVIÈRE D'ÉTEL

Roheu 47°38'·52N 03°14'·77W.
Épi de Plouhinec ☆ 47°38'·65N 03°12'·77W; Fl R 2·5s 7m 2M.
W side ent ☆ 47°38'·70N 03°12'·91W, Oc (2) WRG 6s 13m W9M, R/G6M; W022°-064°, R064°-123°, W123°-330°, G330°-022°; R twr;
Conspic radio mast (CROSS Étel), 47°39'·79N 03°12'·02W.
Les Pierres Noires 47°35'·48N 03°13'·39W.

PLATEAU DES BIRVIDEAUX (10M SSW of R d'Étel)

Twr, BRB 47°29'·13N 03°17'·50W, Fl (2) 6s 24m 10M.

BELLE ÎLE and QUIBERON BAY (West of 2° 50'W)

▶ BELLE ÎLE

Pte des Poulains ☆ 47°23'·28N 03°15'·17W, Fl 5s 34m **23M**; 023°-291°; W □ twr and dwelling.
N Poulains 47°23'·68N 03°14'·89W.
Les Poulains 47°23'·43N 03°16'·68W; *Whis.*
Sauzon, Basse Gareau 47°22'·76N 03°13'·06W.
NW jetée ☆ 47°22'·51N 03°13'·10W, Fl G 4s 8m 8M.
SE jetée ☆ 47°22'·43N 03°13'·10W, Fl R 4s 8m 8M; 315°-272°; W twr, R top.
Inner hbr, W jetée ☆, QG 9m 5M; 194°-045°; W twr, G top.
Le Palais, N jetée ☆ 47°20'·82N 03°09'·08W, Fl (2+1) G 12s 8m 7M; obsc 298°-170° (see S jetée); W twr, G top.

S jetée ☆ 47°20'·80N 03°09'·12W, Oc (2) R 6s 8m 11M; obsc'd 298°-170° by Ptes de Kerdonis and de Taillefer.
La Truie du Bugul 47°19'·53N 03°06'·59W.
Pointe de Kerdonis ☆ 47°18'·59N 03°03'·61W, Fl (3) R 15s 35m **15M**; obsc'd 025°-129° by Pointes d'Arzic and de Taillefer; W □ twr, R top and W dwelling.
Les Galères 47°18'·75N 03°02'·82W.
SW side of Belle Île: La Truie 47°17'·05N 03°11'·72W.
Goulphar ☆ 47°18'·64N 03°13'·69W, Fl (2) 10s 87m **27M**; Gy twr.
B1 47°17'·01N 03°16'·54W.

▶ PORT MARIA (Quiberon ferry port)

Ldg lts 006·5°, both Dir QG 5/13m **16/17M**; intens 005°-008°; W twrs, B bands. **Front**, 47°28'·63N 03°07'·19W. **Rear**, 230m north.
Le Pouilloux 47°27'·88N 03°08'·02W.
Basse An Tréac'h 47°27'·91N 03°07'·20W.
Les Deux Frères 47°28'·34N 03°07'·30W, Fl R 2·5s; 175°-047°.
Light ho ☆ 47°28'·78N 03°07'·46W, Q WRG 28m W14M, R/G10M; W246°-252°, W291°-297°, G297°-340°, W340°-017°, R017°-051°, W051°-081°, G081°-098°, W098°-143°; W twr, G lantern.
S bkwtr ☆ 47°28'·54N 03°07'·32W, Oc (2) R 6s 9m 7M; W twr, R top.
E mole ☆ 47°28'·58N 03°07'·37W, Iso G 4s 9m 7M.

▶ CHAUSSÉE AND PASSAGE DE LA TEIGNOUSE

Le Four 47°27'·80N 03°06'·40W.
Bas Cariou 47°26'·94N 03°06'·44W; *Bell.*
Bas du Chenal 47°26'·66N 03°05'·77W.
Goué Vaz N 47°26'·20N 03°05'·49W.
Goué Vaz S 47°25'·79N 03°04'·87W, Q (6) + L Fl 15s; *Whis.*
Goué Vaz E 47°26'·24N 03°04'·30W, Fl (3) R 12s.
Basse du Milieu 47°25'·90N 03°04'·13W, Fl (2) G 6s 9m 2M.
Les Esclassiers 47°25'·68N 03°03'·05W.
La Teignouse ☆ 47°27'·45N 03°02'·79W, Fl WR 4s 20m **W15M**, R11M; W033°-039°, R039°-033°; W ○ twr, R top.
NE Teignouse 47°26'·57N 03°01'·88W, Fl (3) G 12s.
Basse Nouvelle 47°26'·97N 03°01'·99W, Fl R 2·5s.
Quiberon S 47°28'·03N 03°02'·35W, Q (6) + L Fl 15s.
Quiberon N 47°29'·63N 03°02'·59W.

▶ CHAUSSÉE DU BÉNIGUET

Le Grand Coin 47°24'·43N 03°00'·26W.
Le Rouleau 47°23'·68N 03°00'·31W.
Bonnenn Braz 47°24'·26N 02°59'·88W.

▶ ÎLE DE HOUAT

Port de St-Gildas N môle ☆ 47°23'·57N 02°57'·34W, Fl (2) WG 6s 8m W9M, G6M; W168°-198°, G198°-210°, W210°-240°, G240°-168°; W twr, G top.
Men Groise 47°22'·76N 02°55'·05W.
Er Rouzes 47°22'·00N 02°54'·39W.
Men er Houteliguet 47°22'·60N 02°56'·30W.
Er Spernec 47°22'·15N 02°55'·15W.
Le Pot de Feu 47°21'·68N 02°59'·84W.

▶ ÎLE DE HOËDIC

Les Sœurs 47°21'·13N 02°54'·75W.
La Chèvre 47°21'·09N 02°52'·55W.
Port de l'Argol bkwtr ☆ 47°20'·69N 02°52'·56W, Fl WG 4s 10m W9M, G6M; W143°-163°, G163°-183°, W183°-194°, G194°-143°; W twr, G top.
EDF4, Fl Y 2.5s, W of Argol, marks power cables.
Er Guéranic 47°20'·50N 02°50'·52W.
Cohfournik 47°19'·48N 02°49'·70W.

Les Grands Cardinaux ☆ 47°19'·26N 02°50'·11W, Fl (4) 15s 28m 13M; R and W twr.
Le Chariot 47°18'·87N 02°53'·00W.
Er Palaire 47°20'·14N 02°55'·19W.

▶ PORT HALIGUEN

47°29'·76N 03°05'·29W; large unlit white mooring buoy.
Port Haliguen 47°29'·44N 03°05'·47W.
E bkwtr hd ☆ 47°29'·30N 03°05'·99W, Oc (2) WR 6s 10m, W11M, R8M; W233°-240·5°, R240·5°-299°, W299°-306°, R306°-233°; W twr, R top. Elbow ☆ Fl R 4s 10m 5M; 322°-206°; W twr, R top.
Inner pier ☆ Fl Vi 2·5s 5m; purple column.
NW bkwtr hd ☆ 47°29'·36N 03°06'·00W, Fl G 2·5s 9m 6M.
Bugalet wreck 47°31'·19N 03°05'·45W.
Men er Roué 47°32'·25N 03°06'·06W.

▶ LA TRINITÉ-SUR-MER

Buisson de Méaban 47°31'·69N 02°58'·40W.
Le Petit Buissons 47°32'·13N 02°58'·58W.
Ldg lts 347°, both W twrs, G tops. Front, 47°34'·08N 03°00'·37W, Q WRG 11m W10M, R/G7M; G321°-345°, W345°-013·5°, R013·5°-080°. **Rear** ☆, 540m NNW, Q 21m **15M**, intens 337°-357°; synch.
Souris 47°31'·97N 03°01'·22W.
Le Rat 47°32'·81N 03°01'·78W.
Petit Trého 47°33'·47N 03°00'·71W, Fl (4) R 15s.
R. de Crac'h Dir ☆ 347°: 47°35'·03N 03°01'·00W, Oc WRG 4s 9m W13M, R/G 11M; G345°-346°, W346°-348°, R348°-349°; W twr.
S pier ☆ 47°35'·09N 03°01'·51W, Oc (2) WR 6s 6m, W9M, R6M; R090°-293·5°, W293·5°-300·5°, R300·5°-329°; W twr, R top.
Marina jetty ☆ 47°35'·27N 03°01'·47W, Iso R 4s 8m 5M.

▶ GOLFE DU MORBIHAN

Méaban 47°30'·77N 02°56'·23W.
Pte de Port-Navalo ☆ 47°32'·87N 02°55'·11W, Oc (3) WRG 12s 32m, **W15M**, R/G11M; W155°-220°, G317°-359°, W359°-015°, R015°-105°; W twr and dwelling.
Entry ldg marks 359°: Front, Grégan 47°33'·90N 02°55'·05W, Q (6) + L Fl 15s 3m 8M.
Common rear, Baden ch spire (83m), 47°37'·26N 02°55'·05W.
Ldg marks 001°: Front, Petit Vezid, 47°34'·23N 02°55'·15W.

Auray river: Catis 47°36'·13N 02°57'·23W.
Port du Parun 47°36'·77N 02°57'·09W.
César 47°38'·36N 02°58'·22W.
No. 13 47°39'·48N 02°58'·64W.

Morbihan: Grand Mouton 47°33'·70N 02°54'·85W, QG.
Jument 47°34'·29N 02°53'·43W.
Gavrinis 47°34'·21N 02°54'·10W.
Creizic S 47°34'·62N 02°52'·84W.
Creizic N 47°34'·93N 02°52'·21W.
Les Rechauds, two 47°36'·17N 02°51'·29W.
Truie d'Arradon 47°36'·57N 02°50'·27W.
Logoden 47°36'·69N 02°49'·91W.
Drenec 47°36'·84N 02°48'·39W.
Roguédas 47°37'·12N 02°47'·28W, Fl G 2·5s 4m 4M; G twr.
The channel up to Vannes is well beaconed but unlit.

▶ CROUESTY

Ldg lts 058°, both Dir Q 10/27m **19M**; intens 056·5°-059·5°. **Front** ☆, 47°32'·54N 02°53'·94W; R panel, W stripe. **Rear** ☆, 315m from front; W twr.
No. 1 47°32'·15N 02°54'·72W, Fl G 1·2s.
No. 2 47°32'·26N 02°54'·76W.

21

PLOT WAYPOINTS ON YOUR CHART BEFORE USING THEM

N jetty ☆ 47°32'·47N 02°54'·14W, Oc (2) R 6s 9m 7M; R&W □ twr.
S jetty ☆ 47°32'·44N 02°54'·10W, Fl G 4s 9m 7M; G&W □ twr.

▶ PLATEAU DU GRAND MONT

Basse de St Gildas 47°29'·78N 02°52'·91W.
L'Epieu 47°29'·49N 02°52'·99W.
Chimère 47°28'·84N 02°54'·04W.
Grand Mont 47°28'·98N 02°51'·16W.

QUIBERON BAY (E of 2° 50'W) TO PTE DU CROISIC

▶ PLATEAU DE SAINT JACQUES

Le Bauzec 47°28'·86N 02°49'·49W.
St Jacques 47°28'·15N 02°47'·58W.
St Jacques-en-Sarzeau, jetty ☆ 47°29'·17N 02°47'·55W, Oc (2) R 6s 5m 6M; W 8-sided twr, R top.

▶ PLATEAU DE LA RECHERCHE

Recherche 47°25'·56N 02°50'·40W, Q (9) 15s.
Locmariaquer 47°25'·83N 02°47'·37W.

▶ PÉNERF

Penvins 47°28'·94N 02°40'·10W.
Borenis 47°29'·21N 02°38'·35W.
Le Pignon 47°30'·03N 02°38'·90W, Fl (3) WR 12s 6m W9M, R6M; R028·5°-167°, W167°-175°, R175°-349·5°, W349·5°-028·5°; R twr.

▶ VILAINE RIVER

Les Mâts 47°29'·15N 02°34'·90W.
Basse de Kervoyal 47°30'·36N 02°32'·63W, Dir Q WR W8M, R5M; W269°-271°, R271°-269°.
Bertrand 47°31'·06N 02°30'·73W, Iso WG 4s 6m, W9M, G6M; W040°-054°, G054°-227°, W227°-234°, G234°-040°; G twr.
Penlan ☆ 47°30'·98N 02°30'·13W, Oc (2) WRG 6s 26m, **W15M**, R/G11M; R292·5°-025°, G025°-052°, W052°-060°, R060°-138°, G138°-180°; W twr, R bands.
No. 2 47°30'·41N 02°28'·74W, Fl R 2·5s.
No. 1 47°30'·29N 02°28'·69W, Fl G 2·5s.
Petit Sécé 47°30'·07N 02°28'·78W; W bcn.
Pointe du Scal ☆ 47°29'·67N 02°26'·87W, QG 12s 8m 4M.

▶ ÎLE DUMET

Fort ☆ 47°24'·69N 02°37'·22W, Fl (3) WRG 15s 14m, W7M, R/G4M; G090°-272°, W272°-285°, R285°-335°, W335°-090°; W col, G top.
Basse Est Île Dumet 47°25'·18N 02°34'·97W, Q (3) 10s.

▶ MESQUER

Laronesse 47°25'·97N 02°29'·52W.
Basse Normande 47°25'·46N 02°29'·80W.
Basse Beaulieu 47°25'·04N 02°29'·29W.
Jetty ☆ 47°25'·31N 02°28'·06W, Oc WRG 4s 7m W10M, R/G7M; W067°-072°, R072°-102°, W102°-118°, R118°-293°, W293°-325°, G325°-067°; W col and bldg.

▶ PIRIAC-SUR-MER

Grand Norven 47°23'·55N 02°32'·90W, Q.
Le Rohtres 47°23'·38N 02°33'·37W.
Inner mole ☆ 47°22'·93N 02°32'·72W, Oc (2) WRG 6s 8m, W10M, R/G7M; R066°-148°, G148°-194°, W194°-201°, R201°-221°; W col; *Siren 120s (occas), 35m SW.*
E bkwtr ☆ Fl R 4s 4m 5M; W pylon, R top.
Les Bayonnelles 47°22'·67N 02°35'·30W, Q (9) 15s.

▶ LA TURBALLE

Ldg lts 006·5°, both Dir Iso R 4s 11/19m 3M; intens 004°-009°. Front, 47°20'·80N 02°30'·88W. Rear, 110m from front.
Jetée de Garlahy ☆ 47°20'·70N 02°30'·93W, Fl (4) WR 12s 13m, W10M, R7M; R060°-315°, W315°-060°; W pylon, R top.

▶ LE CROISIC

Basse Hergo 47°18'·62N 02°31'·71W, Fl G 2·5s 5m 3M.
Jetée du Tréhic ☆ 47°18'·49N 02°31'·43W, Iso WG 4s 12m W14M, G11M; G042°-093°, W093°-137°, G137°-345°; Gy twr, G top; F Bu fog det lt, 100m SE.
Outer ldg lts 156°, both Dir Q 10/14m **19M**; intens 154°-158°. **Front** ☆ 47°17'·95N 02°31'·00W. **Rear** ☆, 116m from front.
Middle ldg lts 174°, both QG 5/8m 11M; 170·5°-177·5°. Front 47°18'·06N 02°31'·07W. Rear, 48m from front.
Le Grand Mabon 47°18'·03N 02°31'·02W, Fl (3) R 12s 6m 2M.
Inner ldg lts 134·7°, both QR 6/10m 8M; intens 132·5°-143·5°; synch.
Basse Castouillet 47°11'·63N 02°32'·42W, Q (9) 15s.

▶ PLATEAU DU FOUR/BANC DE GUÉRANDE

Bonen du Four 47°18'·52N 02°39'·29W, Q; *Whis.*
Le Four ☆ 47°17'·86N 02°38'·07W, Fl 5s 23m **18M**; W twr, B diagonal stripes, G top.
W Basse Capella 47°15'·65N 02°42'·79W, Q (9) 15s; *Whis.*
Goué-Vas-du-Four 47°14'·91N 02°38'·21W, Q (6) + L Fl 15s.
Sud Banc Guérande 47°08'·79N 02°42'·82W, VQ (6) + L Fl 10s.

POINTE DU CROISIC TO POINTE DE ST GILDAS

▶ PLATEAU DE LA BANCHE

NW Banche 47°12'·85N 02°31'·03W, Q 8m 4M; *Bell.*
W Banche 47°11'·63N 02°32'·42W, VQ (9) 10s.
La Banche ☆ 47°10'·62N 02°28'·06W, Fl (2) WR 6s 22m **W15M**, R11M; R266°-280°, W280°-266°; B twr, W bands.
SE Banche 47°10'·39N 02°26'·10W.

▶ PLATEAU DE LA LAMBARDE

SE Lambarde 47°10'·03N 02°20·81W Q (6) + L Fl 15s; *Bell.*
NW Lambard 47°10'·84N 02°22'·94W.

▶ BAIE DU POULIGUEN (or Baie de la Baule)

Basse Lovre 47°15'·93N 02°29'·45W, Chenal du Nord.
Penchateau 47°15'·24N 02°24'·35W, Fl R 2·5s.
Les Guérandaises 47°15'·03N 02°24'·29W, Fl G 2·5s.
47°15'·24N 02°23'·51W.
Les Troves 47°14'·23N 02°22'·43W.
NNW Pierre Percée 47°13'·59N 02°20'·63W.
La Vieille 47°14'·03N 02°19'·53W.
Sud de la Vieille 47°13'·74N 02°19'·55W.
Le Caillou 47°13'·65N 02°19'·18W.
Le Petit Charpentier 47°13'·33N 02°18'·95W.
Le Grand Charpentier ☆ 47°12'·82N 02°19'·15W, Q WRG 22m, W14M, R/G10M; G020°-049°, W049°-111°, R111°-310°, W310°-020°; Gy twr, G lantern.

▶ LE POULIGUEN

Basse Martineau 47°15'·54N 02°24'·36W.
Petits Impairs 47°15'·98N 02°24'·61W, Fl (2) G 6s 6m 2M; G △.
SW jetty ☆ 47°16'·39N 02°25'·40W, QR 13m 9M; 171°-081°; W col.

▶ PORNICHET (La Baule)

S bkwtr ☆ 47°15'·49N 02°21'·15W, Iso WRG 4s 11m, W10M, R/G7M; G303°-081°, W081°-084°, R084°-180°; W twr, G top.
Ent, S side ☆ 47°15'·51N 02°21'·13W, QG 3m 1M; B perch, G top.
N side ☆ 47°15'·50N 02°21'·10W, QR 4m 1M; B perch, R top.

▶ ST NAZAIRE APPROACH (Chenal du Sud)

S-N1 47°00'·07N 02°39'·84W, L Fl 10s 8m 5M; *Whis;* ***Racon Z, 3-8M.***

S-N2 47°02'·08N 02°33'·49W, Iso 4s 8m 5M.
Thérésia 47°04'·83N 02°27'·29W, Fl R 2·5s.
Les Chevaux 47°03'·52N 02°26'·39W, Fl G 2·5s.
La Couronnée 47°07'·59N 02°20'·05W, Fl (2) G 6s; ***Racon (no ident), 3-5M; the signal appears as a series of dots. The distance between each dot represents 2 cables.***
Lancastria 47°08'·88N 02°20'·37W, Fl (2) R 6s.

▶ PASSE DES CHARPENTIERS

Portcé ☆ ldg lts 025·5°, both Dir Q 6/36m **22/24M**. **Front**, 47°15'·23N 02°15'·00W; intens 024·7°-026·2°; synch; W col. **Rear** ☆ (H24), 0·75M from front; intens 024°-027°; W □ twr, W stripe.
Wreck (anon) 47°09'·94N 02°19'·37W, Fl (3) R 12s.
No. 1 47°09'·94N 02°18'·40W, VQ G.
No. 2 47°10'·05N 02°18'·73W, VQ R.
Euler 47°11'·60N 02°18'·38W, VQ (6) + L Fl 10s.
No. 8 47°12'·75N 02°16'·86W, Fl (4) R 15s.
No. 7 47°13'·30N 02°16'·12W, VQ G.
No. 10 47°13'·68N 02°16'·09W, VQ R. (Chenal de Bonne-Anse)
Pointe d'Aiguillon ☆ 47°14'·54N 02°15'·78W, Oc (3) WR 12s 27m, **W13M**, R10M; W(unintens) 207°-233°; W233°-293°, W297°-300°, R300°-327°, W327°-023°, W027°-089°; W twr.
Ville-es-Martin jetty ☆ 47°15'·33N 02°13'·66W, Fl (2) 6s 10m 10M; W twr, R top.
Morées 47°15'·00N 02°13'·02W, Fl (3) WR 12s 12m, W6M, R4M; W058°-224°, R300°-058°; G twr.

▶ SAINT-NAZAIRE

W jetty ☆ 47°15'·97N 02°12'·25W, Oc (4) R 12s 11m 8M; W twr, R top.
E jetty ☆ 47°15'·99N 02°12'·14W, Oc (4) G 12s 11m 11M; W twr, G top. (Ent for big ships)
Old Môle ☆ 47°16'·27N 02°11'·82W, Q (3) 10s 18m 11M; 153·5°-063·5°; W twr, R top; weather signals.
Basse Nazaire Sud 47°16'·23N 02°11'·62W, Q (6) + L Fl 15s.
No. 20 47°16'·25N 02°11'·30W, QR.
Pile 47°16'·43N 02°11'·73W, Fl (2) R 6s 5m 1M.
E ent to Bassin St Nazaire ☆ 47°16'·53N 02°11'·77W, Fl (3) 12s 9m 9M; R pylon. Two VQ Vi lead into lock/swing bridge (small craft).
No. 19 47°16'·49N 02°10'·69W, Fl G 2·5s.
See final section for the R. Loire to Nantes.

▶ EAST SIDE, DOWN-RIVER TO PTE DE ST GILDAS

Le Pointeau digue S ☆ 47°14'·08N 02°10'·89W, Fl WG 4s 4m, W10M, G7M; G050°-074°, W074°-149°, G149°-345°, W345°-050°; G&W ○ hut.
La Truie 47°12'·12N 00°13'29W
Port de Comberge S jetty ☆ 47°10'·60N 02°09'·95W, Fl (2) WG 6s 7m W9M, G6M; W123°-140°, G140°-123°; W twr, G top.
La Gravette 47°09'·87N 02°12'·99W.
Port de la Gravette ☆ 47°09'·70N 02°12'·64W, Fl (3) WG 12s 7m, W8M, G5M; W183°-188°, G188°-124°, W124°-138°, G138°-183°; W structure, G top.
Anse de **Boucau** bkwtr ☆ 47°08'·47N 02°14'·72W, Fl (2) G 6s 3M.
Pte de Saint Gildas ☆ 47°08'·10N 02°14'·67W, Q WRG 20m, W14M, R/G10M; R264°-308°, G308°-078°, W078°-088°, R088°-174°, W174°-180°, G180°-264°; framework tower on W house.
Nord Couronnée 47°07'·39N 02°17'·70W, Q.

RIVER LOIRE TO NANTES

No. 21 47°17·03N 02°10'·18W, VQ G.
Suspension bridge (conspic R/W twrs) ☆ 47°17·10N 02°10'·25W (channel centre), Iso 4s 55m.
MA 47°17·49N 02°09'·23W, Fl (2) G 6s.
MB 47°17·95N 02°07'·54W, Fl (3) G 12s.
Fernais 47°18·10N 02°06'·60W, Fl (4) G 15s.
Donges Sud 47°18·02N 02°03'·84W, Fl (3) G 12s.
No. 29 bis 47°17'·96N 02°02'·62W, VQ G.
Paimboeuf, môle root ☆ 47°17'·42N 02°01'·96W, Oc (3) WG 12s 9m, W10M, G7M; G shore-123°, W123°-shore; W twr, G top.
The river is well buoyed/lit: S side G lts; N side R lts. Stopping places suitable for yachts are virtually non-existent.

▶ NANTES

Trentemoult marina (dries) 47°11'·80N 01°34'·69W.

9.21.5 PASSAGE INFORMATION

SOUTH BRITTANY (charts 2643, 2646). Current Pilots include: *West France Cruising Companion* (Featherstone/Nautical Data Ltd). The Admiralty *Bay of Biscay Pilot*. The *French Pilot* (Vol 3) (Nautical/Robson), although out of print, contains many unique almost timeless sketches and transits. French charts (SHOM) are often larger scale than Admiralty charts, and hence more suitable for inshore waters.

The following Breton words have navigational significance: *Aber*: estuary. *Aven*: river, stream. *Bann*: hill. *Bian*: small. *Bras*: great. *Du*: black. *Enez, Inis*: island. *Garo*: rough, hard. *Glas*: green. *Goban*: shoal. *Gwenn*: white. *Karreg*: rock. *Ker*: house. *Men, mein*: rock, stone. *Morlenn*: creek. *Penn*: strait. *Porz*: harbour. *Raz*: tide race. *Ruz*: red. *Trez*: sand.

Mist and haze are quite common in the summer, fog less so. Winds are predominantly from SW to NW, often light and variable in summer, but in early and late season N or NE winds are common. Summer gales are infrequent, and are usually related to passing fronts. In summer the sea is often calm or slight, but swell, usually from W or NW, can severely affect exposed anchorages. When crossing B of Biscay, allow for a likely set to the E, particularly after strong W winds.

A particular feature of this coast during the summer is the sea and land breeze cycle, known locally as the *vent solaire*. After a quiet forenoon, a W'ly sea breeze sets in about midday, blowing onshore. It slowly veers to the NW, almost parallel to the coast, reaching Force 4 by late afternoon; it then veers further to the N, expiring at dusk. Around midnight a land breeze may pipe up from the NE and freshen sufficiently to kick up rough seas – with consequent disruption to moorings and anchs open to the NE. By morning the wind has abated.

▶ *Tidal streams are weak offshore, but can be strong in estuaries, channels and around headlands, especially nearer the English Chan. The tidal stream chartlets at 9.21.3 are based on NP 265 (Admiralty Tidal Stream Atlas for France, W Coast) which uses data from actual observations out to 15-25M offshore. The equivalent French Atlas gives more data, but based on computer predictions.* ◀

Inland waterways (9.18.14) can be entered from Lorient (9.21.15), Vilaine R (9.21.26) and Nantes (9.21.32).

PTE DU RAZ TO BENODET (charts 2819, 2820). Chaussée de Sein (chart 2348) is a chain of islands, rks and shoals extending 15M W of the Pte du Raz. A WCM lt buoy marks the seaward end.

For directions on Île de Sein and a chartlet and notes on the Raz de Sein see 9.21.7.

Audierne (9.21.8) lies between Raz de Sein and Pte de Penmarc'h (lt, fog sig) off which dangers extend 1M to NW, W and S, and 3M to SE, and breaking seas occur in strong winds. The fishing hbrs of St Guénolé, Le Guilvinec (9.21.8) and Lesconil provide excellent shelter, but have difficult ents. Loctudy (9.21.9) is well sheltered from W/SW.

BENODET TO LORIENT (charts 2820, 2821). Along the coast the larger ports are Bénodet (9.21.10), Port-la-Forêt (9.21.11) and Concarneau (9.21.12), all with marinas. Anse de Bénodet has rky shoals on both sides but is clear in the middle.The coast from Pte de Mousterlin to Beg Meil is fringed by rks, many of which dry, extending 1M offshore. Chaussée de Beg Meil extends 8½ca SE, where Linuen rk (dries) is marked by bn. From Concarneau to Pte de Trévignon rks extend nearly 1·5M offshore in places.

Îles de Glénan (chart 3640, SHOM 6648, 9.21.13), lie to seaward of Loctudy and Concarneau. With offlying dangers they stretch 5M from W to E and 4M from N to S. The islands are interesting to explore, but anchs are rather exposed. Between Îles de Glénan and Bénodet lie Les Pourceaux, reefs which dry, and Île aux Moutons which has dangers extending SW and NW.

Between Pte de Trévignon and Lorient are rky cliffs and several interesting lesser hbrs and anchs, delightful in fair weather; but most dry and are dangerous to approach in strong onshore winds. These include the Aven and Bélon rivers, Brigneau, Merrien (mostly dries), Doëlan (but most of hbr dries) and Le Pouldu (Rivière de Quimperlé). All are described in 9.21.13 and the *North Biscay Pilot.*

Hazards SE and E of Pte de Trévignon include: Men Du, a rk 0·3m high, marked by IDM bn, about 1·25M SE of the same Pte. Corn Vas, depth 1·8m, and Men ar Tréas, a rk which dries, are close S, both buoyed. Île Verte lies 6ca S of Île de Raguénès, with foul ground another 2ca to S. The approaches to Aven and Bélon Rivers are clear, except for Le Cochon and Les Verrés (IDM bn) to the SE. Between Le Pouldu and Lorient, Grand Cochon (SCM buoy) and Petit Cochon lie about 1M offshore.

LORIENT TO QUIBERON (charts 2352, 2353) The great seaport of Lorient (9.21.15) has sheltered apprs and 6 marinas. Île de Groix lies 4M SW. Its main offlying dangers are to the E and SE: shoals off Pte de la Croix; Les Chats which extend 1M SE from Pte des Chats; and shoals extending 7½ca S of Loc Maria. Port Tudy (9.21.14), on N coast, is the main hbr, and is easy of access and well sheltered except from NE.

7M SE of Lorient, River Étel (9.21.16) is an attractive hbr with a potentially difficult ent which must only be approached in good weather and on the last of the flood. Further S do not appr the isthmus of the Quiberon peninsula closely due to rky shoals. 6M W of Quiberon lies Plateau des Birvideaux (lt), a rky bank (depth 4·6m) on which the sea breaks in bad weather.

Belle Île has no dangers more than 2½ca offshore, apart from buoyed rks which extend 7½ca W of Pte des Poulains, and La Truie rk marked by IDM bn tr 5ca off the S coast. The S coast is much indented and exposed to swell from W. In good settled weather (only) and in absence of swell there is an attractive anch in Port du Vieux Château (Ster Wenn), 1M S of Pte des Poulains; see *North Biscay Pilot.* On the NE coast lie Sauzon (9.21.17), which partly dries but has good anch off and is sheltered from S and W, and Le Palais (9.21.18). ▶*Off Le Palais the ESE-going (flood) stream begins at HW Brest – 0610, and the WNW- going at HW Brest + 0125, sp rates 1·5kn.*◀

BAIE DE QUIBERON (chart 2823) is an important and attractive yachting area, with centres at Port Haliguen (9.21.21), La Trinité (9.21.22), the Morbihan (9.21.24) and Crouesty (9.21.25). The S side of the bay is enclosed by a long chain of islands, islets, rks and shoals from Presqu'île de Quiberon to Les Grands Cardinaux 13M SE. This chain includes the remote but appealing islands of Houat and Hoëdic (9.21.20), well worth visiting, preferably mid-week. The Bay is open to the E and SE.

From W or S, enter the Bay via Passage de la Teignouse (9.21.19) in W sector (033°-039°) of La Teignouse lt ho; thence 068° between Basse Nouvelle lt buoy and NE Teignouse lt buoy. ▶*In this chan the NE-going (flood) stream begins at HW Brest – 0610, and the SW-going at HW Brest – 0005, sp rates 3·75 kn; in strong winds it is best to pass at slack water.*◀ Good alternative chans are Passage du Béniguet, NW of Houat, and Passage des Soeurs, NW of Hoëdic.

The Golfe du Morbihan, on the N side of B de Quiberon, is an inland sea containing innumerable islands and anchs. Port Navalo anch is on the E side of the ent with Port du Crouesty close SE. Inside, the River Auray flows in from the NW and the fascinating city of Vannes (9.21.23) lies to the NE. ▶*Sp stream rates in the vicinity of Grand Mouton achieve 8kn and elsewhere in the ent can exceed 4kn. Flood commences HW Brest – 0400 and turns at HW Brest + 0200.*◀

CROUESTY TO LE CROISIC (chart 2823). Eastwards from the Morbihan, dangers extend 1M seaward of Pte de St Jacques, and 3M offshore lies Plateau de la Recherche with depths of 1·8m. SE of Penerf, which provides good anch, Plateau des Mats is an extensive rky bank, drying in places, up to 1·75M offshore.

Approaching the R. Vilaine (9.21.26) beware La Grande Accroche, a large shoal with least depth 1m, astride the ent. The main lit chan keeps NW of La Grande Accroche, to the bar on N side thereof. ▶*Here the flood begins at HW Brest – 0515, and the ebb at HW Brest + 0035, sp rates 2·5kn.*◀ In SW winds against tide the sea breaks heavily; the Passe de la Varlingue, 5ca W of Pte du Halguen, is then better, but beware La Varlingue (dries 0.3). At Arzal/Camoël yachts can lock into the non-tidal R. Vilaine for the Canal de l'Ille et Rance to Dinan/St Malo (see 9.18.13 & .14).

S of Pte du Halguen other dangers, close inshore, are the rky shoals, depth 0·6m, of Basse de Loscolo and Basse du Bile. Off Pte du Castelli, the Plateau de Piriac extends about 1·75M NW with depths of 2·3m and drying rks closer inshore. The small hbr of Piriac (9.21.27) lies on the N side of Pointe du Castelli and Les Bayonelles (dry) extend 5ca W. A chan runs between Plateau de Piriac and Île Dumet (lt), which is fringed by drying rks and shoals particularly on N and E sides.

In the Rade du Croisic are the fishing hbrs of La Turballe (9.21.28) and Le Croisic (9.21.29). Off Pte du Croisic dangers extend 1M to N and W. Plateau du Four, a dangerous drying bank of rks, lies about 4M W and WSW of Pte du Croisic, marked by buoys and lt ho near N end. 2·8M ESE of Pte du Croisic, Basse Lovre is a rky shoal with depths of 0.7m, 5ca offshore, SCM buoy.

LE CROISIC TO R. LOIRE (chart 2986) From Chenal du Nord, B du Pouliguen (9.21.30) is entered between Pte de Penchâteau and Pte du Bec, 3M to E. In SE corner of bay is the yacht hbr of Pornichet (9.21.31). The B is partly sheltered from S by rocks and shoals extending SE from Pte de Penchâteau to Le Grand Charpentier, but a heavy sea develops in strong S-SW winds. The W chan through these rocks runs between Penchâteau and Les Guérandaises lateral buoys; other chans lie further E.

The River Loire estuary (chart 2986), which carries much commercial tfc, is entered via either the Chenal du Nord or the Chenal du Sud. The former runs ESE between the mainland and two shoals, Plateau de la Banche and Plateau de la Lambarde; these lie about 4M S of B du Pouliguen. Chenal du Sud, the main DW chan, leads NE between Plateau de la Lambarde and Pte de St Gildas. ▶*Here the in-going stream begins at HW Brest – 0500, and the out-going at HW Brest + 0050, sp rates about 2·75kn.* ◀ In the near apprs to St Nazaire (9.21.32 and charts 2989, 2985) beware Le Vert, Les Jardinets and La Truie (all drying) which lie close E of the chan. The river is navigable as far as Nantes where there is a small part-drying marina at Trentemoult. But the lower Loire is not as attractive as the upper Loire, with its fabled chateaux and vineyards. On the E side of the estuary, between the Loire bridge and Pte de St Gildas, are the small drying hbrs of Comberge, La Gravette and St Gildas.

9.21.6 SPECIAL NOTES FOR FRANCE: See 9.17.6.

9.21.7 ÎLE DE SEIN

Finistere **48°02'·34N 04°50'·89W** ❁⚓✿

CHARTS AC 2348*; SHOM 7147, 7148, 7423*; Imray C36, C37; ECM 541. *Both have 1:10,000 insets of the island.

TIDES ML 3·6; Zone –0100

Standard Port BREST (←→)

Times				Height (metres)			
High Water		Low Water		MHWS	MHWN	MLWN	MLWS
0000	0600	0000	0600	6·9	5·4	2·6	1·0
1200	1800	1200	1800				
Differences ÎLE DE SEIN							
–0005	–0005	–0010	–0005	–0·7	–0·6	–0·2	–0·1

SHELTER The non-drying N part of the hbr is open to N and E winds; the drying S part of the hbr is protected from E and S by two large bkwtrs. The island itself affords some shelter from W'lies. ⚓ near the LB, but clear of 3 pairs of small lateral buoys marking the fairway between N mole and S quay, which is used at HW by ferries. Île de Sein is worth visiting in fair weather, good visibility and preferably near nps.

NAVIGATION WPT 48°03'·67N 04°50'·71W, 187°/1·4M to Men-Brial lt ho ≠ B vert stripe on white house, third from left (close S of lt ho). This N appr is via Chenal d'Ezaudi and within the W sector of Men-Brial lt ho. Cornoc-An-Ar-Braden SHM lt buoy, where the tide sets across the chan, is 4ca S of the ⊕.
Chenal d'Ar vas Du 224° from NE and Chenal Oriental 265° from E are the other two apprs. Both rely on hard-to-identify ldg bcns on An Nerroth (islet E of Guernic SHM bcn twr) and further west by Sein lt ho. Chenal Oriental is unlit. An easier appr from the E is with Sein lt ho bearing exactly 270°.

LIGHTS AND MARKS Men-Brial lt ho, G/W bands, has two white sectors (186°-192° and 221°-227°) leading toward the hbr. Cornoc-an-ar-Braden SHM lt buoy marks a rock on the W side of the first white sector. Sein lt ho, W twr/B top, and two lattice masts are conspic at the W end of Île de Sein (which first appears as a low rounded hummock). See 9.21.4 for lts on Chaussée de Sein.

R/T None. Adjacent sig stn at Pte du Raz Ch 16.

FACILITIES Limited 🛒, R, Bar, CH, ⚒.

THE RAZ DE SEIN

GEOGRAPHY The Raz is bounded W-E by Le Chat bcn twr (at E end of Chaussée de Sein) and La Vieille lt ho which with La Plate lt tr marks the dangers extending 8ca off Pointe du Raz. The Plateau de Tévennec, 2·4M NW of La Vieille, consists of islets, drying rks and shoals which extend 5ca in all directions from the lt ho thereon. Other dangers on the N side of the Raz are rks and shoals extending nearly 1M W and WSW from Pte du Van, and Basse Jaune (1·4m) 1M to N.
On the S side the main dangers, all 1·5M off La Vieille, are: to the SW, Kornog Bras, a 3·7m deep rk; to the S, Masklou Greiz, rky shoals (7·6m) on which sea can break heavily; and to the SE, Roche Moulleg (5·2m).

TIDAL STREAMS ▶*In the middle (48°02'·88N 04°46'·76W) of the Raz the NE-going (flood) stream begins at HW Brest +0550, sp rate 6·5kn; the SW-going (ebb) stream begins at HW Brest –½, sp rate 5·5kn. Slack water, as the N-going flood expires, occurs between about HW Brest –1 and –½; if S-bound aim for the middle of that window, ±15 mins. If N-bound slack water is about HW Brest +5½. Study tidal diamond 'D' on chart 2348. There are eddies near La Vieille on both streams.*

*As a rule the Raz should always be taken at slack water to ensure the least uncomfortable conditions. Precise timing is vital: even an hour early or late on slack water can greatly affect the sea state. In good weather, near nps, wind and tide together, it is not difficult. But in moderate to strong winds it **must** be taken at slack water. In strong winds-against-tide which raise steep breaking seas and overfalls, the chan **must not** be used.*◀

NAVIGATION By day, WPT 'D' 48°02'·37N 04°45'·88W, 2 cables W of La Plate, allows visual pilotage in normal sea states. By night use WPT 'N' 48°02'·91N 04°46'·61W, 308°/9ca from La Plate, and at the intersection of the white sectors of Tévennec, La Vieille and Le Chat. Take care to correct minor track deviations before they become major. Ensure accurate timing. Take all the usual safety precautions. Bon passage!

MARKS Tévennec lt ho is a white twr perched on a house, atop a substantial and distinctive rock. La Vieille is a stone twr, B top, with a derrick on its E side. La Plate is a smaller YBY bcn twr. Le Chat is a B twr, Y top marking rocks on its W, N and E sides; keep at least 0·5M E of it. See chartlet and 9.21.4 for lt details.

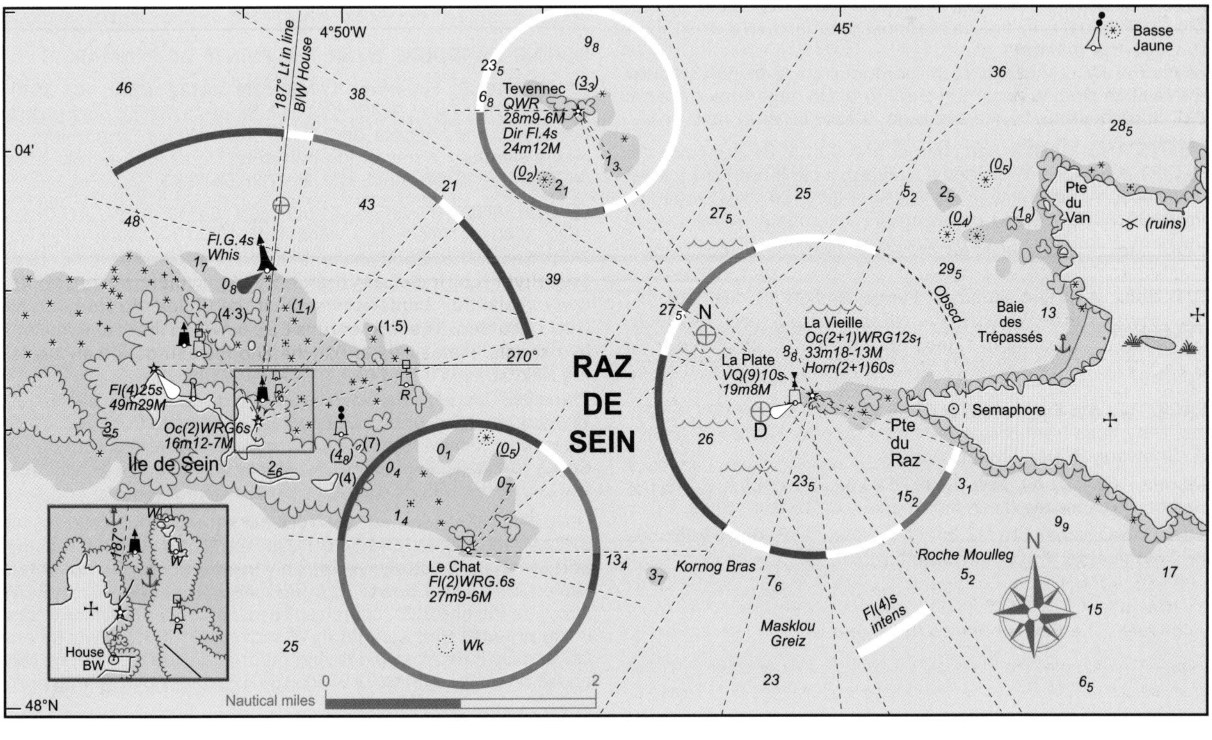
4°50'W
45'
04'
48°N
187° Lt in line
B/W House
Tevennec
QWR
28m9-6M
Dir Fl.4s
24m12M
Basse Jaune
Pte du Van
(ruins)
Fl.G.4s
Whis
Fl(4)25s
49m29M
Cornoc-an-ar-Braden SHM
Oc(2)WRG6s
16m12-7M
Île de Sein
270°
RAZ DE SEIN
N
D
La Vieille
Oc(2+1)WRG12s
33m18-13M
Horn(2+1)60s
La Plate
VQ(9)10s
19m8M
Obscd
Baie des Trépassés
Semaphore
Pte du Raz
Le Chat
Fl(2)WRG.6s
27m9-6M
Wk
Kornog Bras
Masklou Greiz
Roche Moulleg
Fl(4)s intens
House BW
Nautical miles

9.21.8 AUDIERNE

Finistere **48°00'·55N 04°32'·43W**

CHARTS AC 2819 inc inset; SHOM 7147, 7148; Imray C36, C37; ECM 541

TIDES +0440 Dover; ML 3·1; Duration 0605; Zone 0100

Standard Port BREST (⟵)

Times				Height (metres)			
High Water		Low Water		MHWS	MHWN	MLWN	MLWS
0000	0600	0000	0600	6·9	5·4	2·6	1·0
1200	1800	1200	1800				
Differences AUDIERNE							
−0035	−0030	−0035	−0030	−1·7	−1·3	−0·6	−0·2
LE GUILVINEC							
−0010	−0025	−0025	−0015	−1·8	−1·4	−0·6	−0·1
LESCONIL							
−0008	−0028	−0028	−0018	−1·9	−1·4	−0·6	−0·1

SHELTER Good in marina. Berth initially on any hammerhead: pontoons A-C are dredged 2m at the outer end, but 1·6m will be found between dredgings; pontoons D-G are dredged 2m, but avoid F & G as the flood sets strongly towards the bridge. Access HW −2 to +1 for 2m draft. Quays reserved for FVs. There is limited room to ⚓ in the bight N of La Petite Gamelle SCM bcn.

At **Ste Evette** a long bkwtr gives good shelter, except in SE-SW winds when swell enters. Beware rk on N side. Pick up a W (mooring buoy), some of which are very close together, or ⚓ close to seaward. Avoid the S side of N pier/slip as vedettes enter with much verve.

NAVIGATION From the W, WPT 47°59'·47N 04°33'·01W (abeam Gamelle Ouest WCM buoy), 006°/1·5M to Kergadec Dir lt. Appr between La Gamelle, rks drying 0·9m in the middle of the bay, and Le Sillon de Galets rks to the W. Appr is difficult in strong S'lies, when seas break at the ent.

From the SE, WPT 47°59'·46N 04°31'·56W (just off chartlet, 3ca E of Gamelle Est SCM buoy), 331°/1·2M to bkwtr lt. This track leaves La Gamelle reef 300m to port. If bound for Ste Evette, do not turn WNW until well clear of La Gamelle.

Inside the ent, dredged chan initially lies about 25m off the bkwtr. Pick up the 359° ldg marks, vert R/W chevrons, to avoid rocks at foot of bkwtr and banks to stbd drying 1·1m to 2·1m. At root of bkwtr pick up 2nd set of R/W chevrons on fish market bldg ≠ 045°; leave the fish market close to stbd, then alter 90° port towards the marina.

Leave the FV quays and yacht pontoons close to port to clear the bank to stbd, drying 1·9m and more. On departure there are 225° ldg chevrons by the roadside at root of W bkwtr.

LIGHTS AND MARKS See chartlet and 9.21.4. By day from the W WPT, Kergadec, W 8-sided lt tr, R top, ≠ old lt ho (hard to see) leads 006°. At night stay in the W sector (005°-007°) of Kergadec. From SE WPT, 331° ldg marks are: Front, conspic white twr on Jetée du Raoulic (long W bkwtr); rear Kergadec. Fish market is a conspic B/W bldg.

R/T None. Adjacent sig stn at Pte du Raz Ch 16.

TELEPHONE Aff Mar 02·98·70·03·33; CROSS 02·98·89·31·31; SNSM 02·98·70·07·54; ⊜ 02·98·44·73·98; Auto 08.92.68.08.29; Police 02·98·70·04·38; ⊞ 02·98·75·10·10; Brit Consul 02·97·87·36·20.

FACILITIES Ste Evette, HM ☎ 02·98.70.00.28, access H24, €1.20, (visitors' moorings), D by hose from N side of N jetty (approx HW ±3), P (cans), (launderette), Showers, R, Bar, limited victuals.

Marina (100 + 30 (visitors' berths)), ☎/fax 02.98.75.04.93, €1.65 plus €0.15 per person. **Poulgoazec** (near fish market) C (15 ton), Slips.

Town P & D (cans), CH, ME, El, ⚒, (E), Gaz, (supermarket), R, Bar, ✉, (B); bus to Quimper (rail), ✈. Ferry: Roscoff.

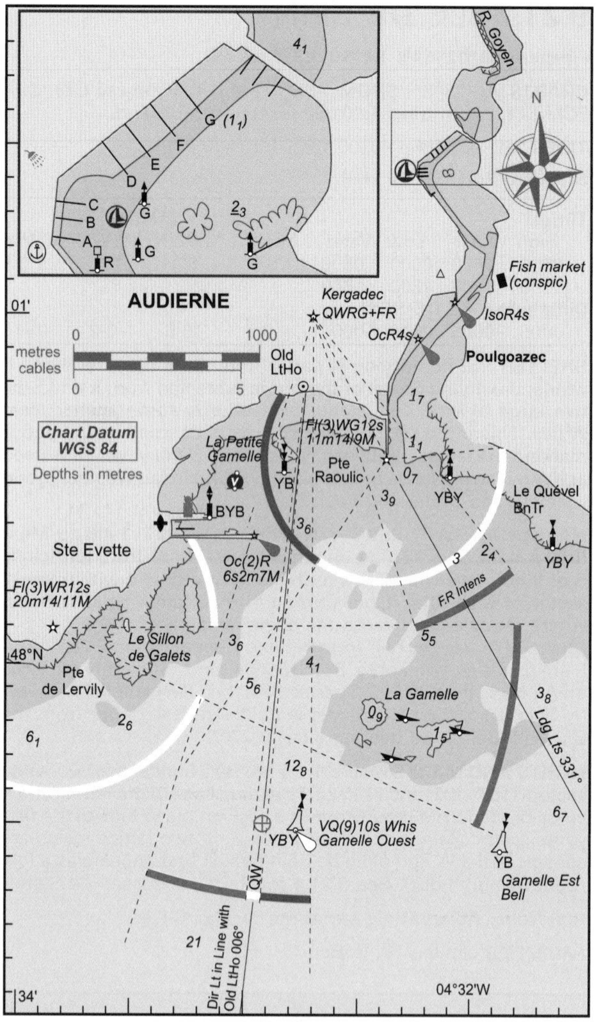
AUDIERNE
R. Goyen
N
Kergadec
QWRG+FR
OcR4s
IsoR4s
Fish market (conspic)
Poulgoazec
Old LtHo
metres
cables
0
1000
5
Chart Datum WGS 84
Depths in metres
La Petite Gamelle
YB
Pte Raoulic
Fl(3)WG12s 11m14/9M
YBY
Le Quével BnTr
BYB
Ste Evette
Oc(2)R 6s2m7M
FR intens
Fl(3)WR12s 20m14/11M
Le Sillon de Galets
Pte de Lervily
La Gamelle
Ldg Lts 331°
VQ(9)10s Whis Gamelle Ouest
Gamelle Est Bell
QW
Dir Lt in Line with Old LtHo 006°
01'
48°N
34'
04°32'W
A
B
C
D
E
F
G
R

FISHING HARBOURS NEAR THE POINTE DE PENMARC'H

ST GUÉNOLÉ, Finistere, **47°48'·68N 04°22'·93W**. AC 2819, 2820; SHOM 7146/7, 6645; ECM 543. Strictly a fishing port; yachts not welcomed. Access difficult in fresh W'lies, impossible in heavy weather. 3 sets of ldg marks/lts. Lts as 9.21.4. Pilot book & SHOM 6645 essential. HM ☎ 02.98.58.60.43.

LE GUILVINEC, Finistere, **47°47'·46N 04°17'·17W**. AC 2819, 2820, 3640; SHOM 7146/7, 6646. HW + 0447 on Dover (UT); ML 3·0m. See 9.21.8. Good shelter and useful passage port; hbr (3m) accessible H24 for <2·5m draft €1.33, but total priority to FVs; no ent/exit 1600-1830. Good ⚓ SE of ent in lee of reef but stay clear of fairway. Beware Lost Moan Rks, further SE of ent, marked by RW bcn lt twr. Ent is easy if vis adequate to see ldg lts/marks; the daymarks are large and conspic dayglo red.

Three 053° ldg lts, all synch (see 9.21.4): front, Mole de Lechiagat, W pylon; middle, Rocher Le Faoutés, 210m from front, R □ on W pylon; rear, 0·58M from front, R □ on W pylon with R stripe. VHF Ch 12. HM ☎ 02.98·58·05·67; Aff Mar ☎ 02.98·58·13·13. Facilities: ⊜, C, D, P, El, ME, ⚒, CH, (E).

LESCONIL, Finistere, **47°47'·70N 04°12'·64W**. AC 2820, 3640; SHOM 7146, 6646; ECM 543. Tides, see 9.21.8; ML 3m. Fishing port 3M SW of Loctudy; yachts only in emergency. Do not enter/leave 1630-1830LT due to FV inrush. Appr from Karek Greis ECM buoy, on ldg line 325°, church spire just open W of Men ar Groas lt ho, W twr/G top; at night in W sector 313°-333°. Bkwtr lts are QG and Oc R 4s. Possible drying mooring inside S bkwtr; no (visitors' moorings), no AB on quays. HM ☎ 02.98.82.22.97. Facilities of a fishing port.

9.21.9 LOCTUDY

Finistere **47°50'·34N 04°10'·55W** ❀❀◊◊◊✿✿

CHARTS AC 2820, 3641; SHOM 7146, 6649; ECM 543; Imray C37, 38

TIDES +0505 Dover (UT); ML 3·0; Duration 0615; Zone –0100

Standard Port BREST (←)

Times				Height (metres)			
High Water		Low Water		MHWS	MHWN	MLWN	MLWS
0000	0600	0000	0600	6·9	5·4	2·6	1·0
1200	1800	1200	1800				
Differences LOCTUDY							
–0010	–0030	–0030	–0020	–2·0	–1·6	–0·7	–0·3

SHELTER Excellent in marina and hbr, except in strong ESE'lies. Little space to ⚓ due many Ⓐs/moorings in the river. Keep clear of FVs, esp 17-1900LT daily when yachts are advised to enter/exit hbr. Pont l'Abbé (3M up-river; 2m) is accessible to shoal draft boats on the flood; chan marked by perches.

NAVIGATION WPT 47°50'·21N 04°09'·06W, 268°/0·81M via a PHM buoy and 2 SHM buoys, all lit, to S abeam the SHM bcn Fl (4) G 15s. Beware spit drying 0.5m SE of that bcn, then alter stbd 305° to marina. From S and W, appr from Bilien ECM buoy to WPT. Beware shoals and drying patches from W to ENE of Men Audierne SHM bcn. Least depth 0·9m S of Karek Croisic; stay in the buoyed chan. Sp ebb runs at 3½kn; enter under power only.

LIGHTS AND MARKS Pte de Langoz; see chartlet and 9.21.4. Perdrix twr is conspic B/W chequers, N of appr chan.

R/T Marina VHF Ch 09 (Office hrs); Port Ch 12.

TELEPHONE HM 02·98·87·51·36; ✉ 02·98·66.50.30; Météo ☎ 08·36·68·08·29, Aff Mar 02·98·87·41·79; CROSS 02·97·55·35·35; SNSM 02·98·87·41·12; ⊜ 02·98·58·28·80; Auto 08·92·68·08·29; Dr 02·98·87·41·80; Ⓗ (6km) 02·98·82·40·40; Brit Consul 02·97·87·36·20.

FACILITIES Marina (542 + 65 Ⓥ (AB) & 50 Ⓐ). ☎ 02·98·87·51·36, €2.24 AB, €1.76 on buoy, Slip, P, C (9 tons), CH, ⚒, ME, El; Ⓢ. **Town** Bar, 🛒, R, Dr, ✉, Ⓑ.

9.21.10 BÉNODET

Finistere **47°51'·56N 04°06'·42W** ❀❀❀◊◊◊✿✿✿

CHARTS AC 2820, 3641; SHOM 7146, 6649, 6679; ECM 543; Imray C37

TIDES +0450 Dover; ML 3·1; Duration 0610; Zone –0100

Standard Port BREST (←)

Times				Height (metres)			
High Water		Low Water		MHWS	MHWN	MLWN	MLWS
0000	0600	0000	0600	6·9	5·4	2·6	1·0
1200	1800	1200	1800				
Differences BÉNODET							
0000	–0020	–0023	–0013	–1·8	–1·4	–0·6	–0·2
PORT DU CORNIGUEL							
+0015	+0010	–0015	–0010	–2·0	–1·6	–1·0	–0·7

SHELTER Good in marinas at Ste Marine (W bank) and at Anse de Penfoul (E bank, Bénodet), both accessible H24 at any tide. Caution: In both marinas, best to arr/dep near slack water to avoid the strong stream, esp 4kn ebb, through the pontoons with risk of damage; the outside wavebreak berths at Penfoul are best avoided except by larger vessels. Some Ⓐs available. ⚓ in Anse du Trez in offshore winds. Speed limit 3kn in hbr.

R Odet is navigable near HW to Quimper, but masted vessels must ⚓ at Poulguinan bridge (5·8m clearance), 1M beyond Corniguel and 0·5M below the city; pleasant ⚓s at Anse de Combrit, Anse de Kérautret, Porz Keraign, Porz Meilou, Anse de Toulven and SW of Lanroz. N of Lanroz the river shoals progressively to 0·5m in places. SHOM 6679 is recommended.

NAVIGATION WPT 47°51'·25N 04°06'·30W, 346°/1·1M to front ldg lt. The 000° ldg line has no special merit and must be vacated well S of Pointe de Combrit. Beware drying ledges around Les Verres, La Rousse and Le Four unlit bcn twrs. The centre of the bay is clear for small craft, but beware Roches de Mousterlin at the SE end of the bay (La Voleuse SCM lt buoy) and various rks off Loctudy to the SW.

BÉNODET *continued overleaf*

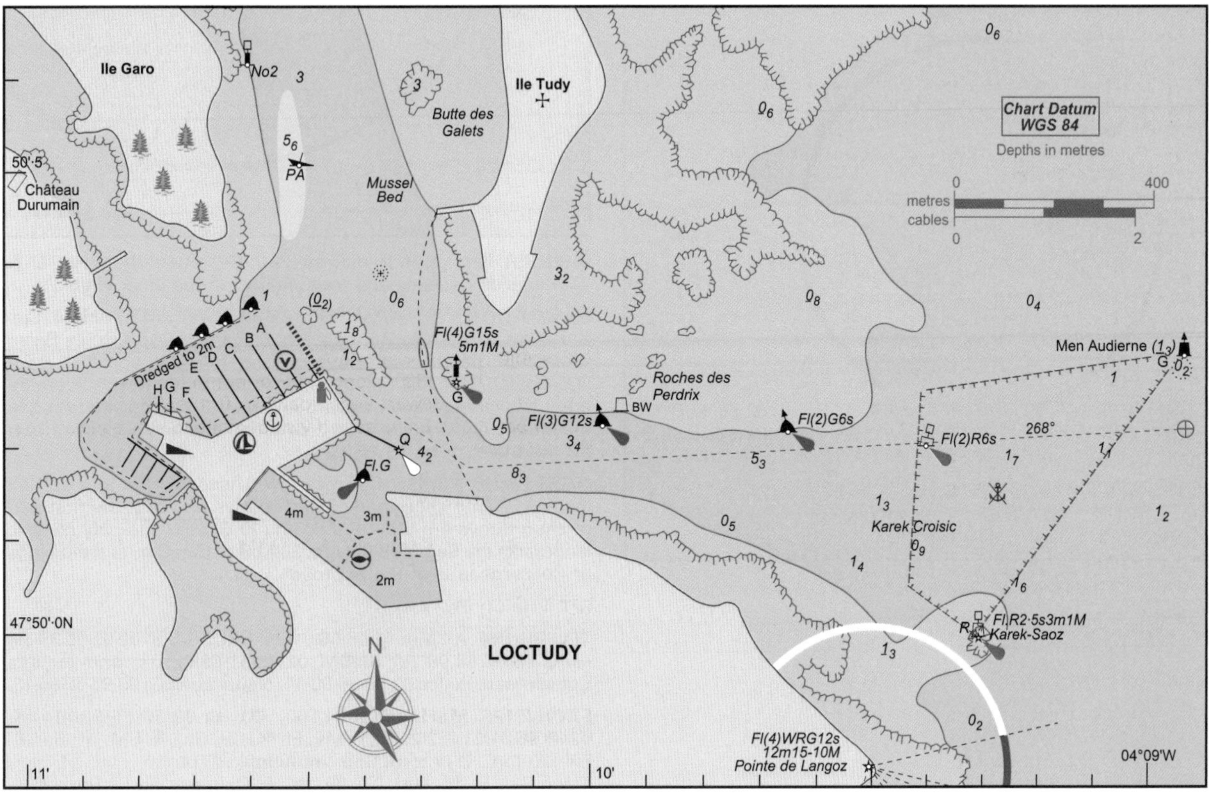
Ile Garo
No2
Ile Tudy
Butte des Galets
Chart Datum WGS 84
Depths in metres
metres
cables
400
2
50'·5
Château Durumain
PA
Mussel Bed
Fl(4)G15s 5m1M
Roches des Perdrix
BW
Fl(3)G12s
Fl(2)G6s
Men Audierne
268°
Fl(2)R6s
Dredged to 2m
Fl.G
4m
3m
2m
Karek Croisic
Fl R2·5s3m1M Karek-Saoz
47°50'·0N
N
LOCTUDY
Fl(4)WRG12s 12m15-10M Pointe de Langoz
04°09'W
11'
10'

LIGHTS AND MARKS See chartlet and 9.21.4. 346° ldg lts, synch/daymarks: Front, W ○ tr, G vert stripe, G top (hard to see until close); rear, conspic W tr, G top.

R/T Marinas VHF Ch 09 (0800-2000LT in season).

TELEPHONE Aff Mar 02·98·58·13·13; CROSS 02·97·55·35·35; SNSM 02·98·57·02·00; ⊜ 02·98·55·04·19; Météo 02·98·94·03·43; Dr 02·98·57·22·21; Brit Consul 02·97·87·36·20.

FACILITIES
BENODET: **Anse de Penfoul Marina** (510+40 Ⓥ AB €2.30; also 175 buoys +15 Ⓥ) ☎ 02·98·57·05·78, 📠 02.98.57.00.21, ⊡, R, CH, ME, 🛒, P, D, M, El, Ⓔ, ⚒, C, SM, Divers. **Quay** C (10 ton). **Town** All facilities, Gaz, ✉, Ⓑ, bus to Quimper ⇌, ✈.

SAINTE-MARINE: **Marina** (350+70 Ⓥ), €2.31 or €1.46 for Ⓥ, ☎ 02·98·56·38·72, 📠 02.98.51.95.17, CH. **Town** 🛒, R, Bar, ⊡, Ⓔ. Pedestrian ferry to Bénodet.

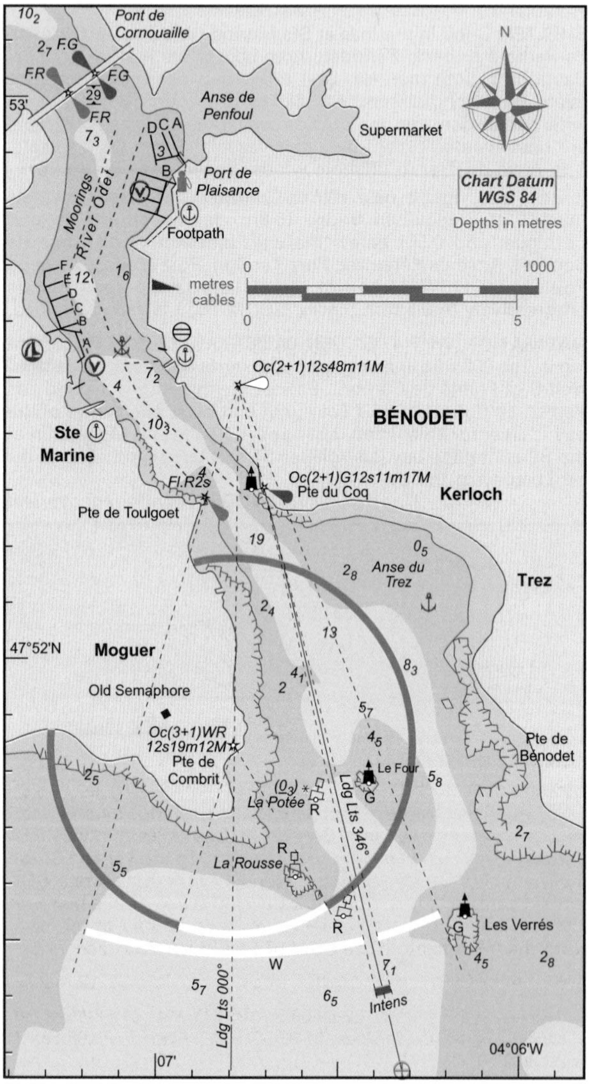
Pont de Cornouaille
F.G
F.R
53'
River Odet
Moorings
Anse de Penfoul
Supermarket
Port de Plaisance
Footpath
Chart Datum WGS 84
Depths in metres
metres
cables
1000
Oc(2+1)12s48m11M
BÉNODET
Ste Marine
Fl.R2s
Oc(2+1)G12s11m17M
Pte du Coq
Kerloch
Pte de Toulgoet
Anse du Trez
Trez
47°52'N
Moguer
Old Semaphore
Oc(3+1)WR 12s19m12M
Pte de Combrit
La Potée
Le Four
Pte de Bénodet
La Rousse
Les Verrés
Ldg Lts 346°
Ldg Lts 000°
Intens
04°06'W
07'

9.21.11 PORT-LA-FORÊT

Finistere **47°53'·49N 03°58'·24W** ❁❁❁◊◊◊✿✿

CHARTS AC 2820, 3641; SHOM 7146, 6650; ECM 543, 544; Imray C38

TIDES +0450 Dover; ML 2·9; Duration 0615; Zone –0100
Use Differences CONCARNEAU 9.21.12

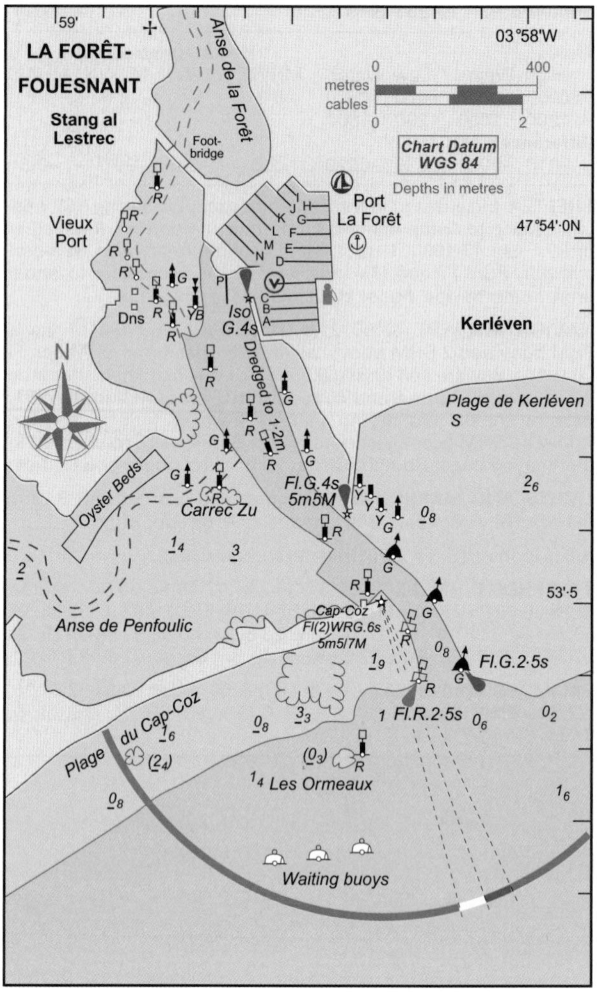
59'
LA FORÊT-FOUESNANT
Anse de la Forêt
03°58'W
metres
cables
400
Stang al Lestrec
Foot-bridge
Chart Datum WGS 84
Depths in metres
Port La Forêt
47°54'·0N
Vieux Port
Dns
Iso G.4s
Dredged to 1·2m
Kerléven
Plage de Kerléven
Oyster Beds
Carrec Zu
Fl.G.4s 5m5M
53'·5
Anse de Penfoulic
Cap-Coz
Fl(2)WRG.6s 5m5/7M
Fl.G.2·5s
Plage du Cap-Coz
Fl.R.2·5s
Les Ormeaux
Waiting buoys

SHELTER Very good in marina (2m); Ⓥ pontoon between 'C' & 'D'. ⚓ inside Cap Coz and moorings W of the inner chan.

NAVIGATION WPT 47°52'·53N 03°57'·85W, 343°/1·0M to Cap Coz lt. Beware Basse Rouge 0·8m, 6·5ca S of Cap Coz; Le Scoré (unlit SCM perch) and buoyed oyster farms in apprs. At sp a shoal patch 0·8m just S of the ent denies access LW±1½; but there are 3 W waiting buoys close SSW of ent. Shoaling reported in the inner chan, dredged 1·2m, to marina and an obstruction 10m off the mole (☆ Iso G 4s).

LIGHTS AND MARKS Cap Coz, Dir lt (see chartlet and 9.21.4), leads 343° into chan marked with buoys and bns; the first pair of chan buoys are lit, Fl R 2·5s and Fl G 2·5s. The only conspic landmarks are Beg-Meil Sig stn, 2·2M S of Cap Coz, and the bldgs of Concarneau E of the approach.

R/T VHF Ch 09.

TELEPHONE Aff Mar 02·98·56·01·98; CROSS-Etel 02·97·55·35·35; Auto 08.92.68.08.29; SNSM 02·98·51·62·62; ⊜ and Ⓗ see Concarneau; Police 02·98·56·00·11; Nautical Ass'n 02·98·56·84·13.

FACILITIES Marina (900+100 Ⓥ) ☎ 02·98·56·98·45, 📠 02·98.56.81.31, €2.25, D, P, ME, El, ⚒, CH, Gaz, ⊡, SM, 🛒, Bar, R, BH (30 ton), C (4 ton), Slip (multihull), ATM.
Town Bar, R, 🛒, Gaz, ✉, Ⓑ, ⇌, ✈ Quimper. Ferry: Roscoff.

9.21.12 CONCARNEAU

Finistere **47°52′·15N 03°54′·77W**

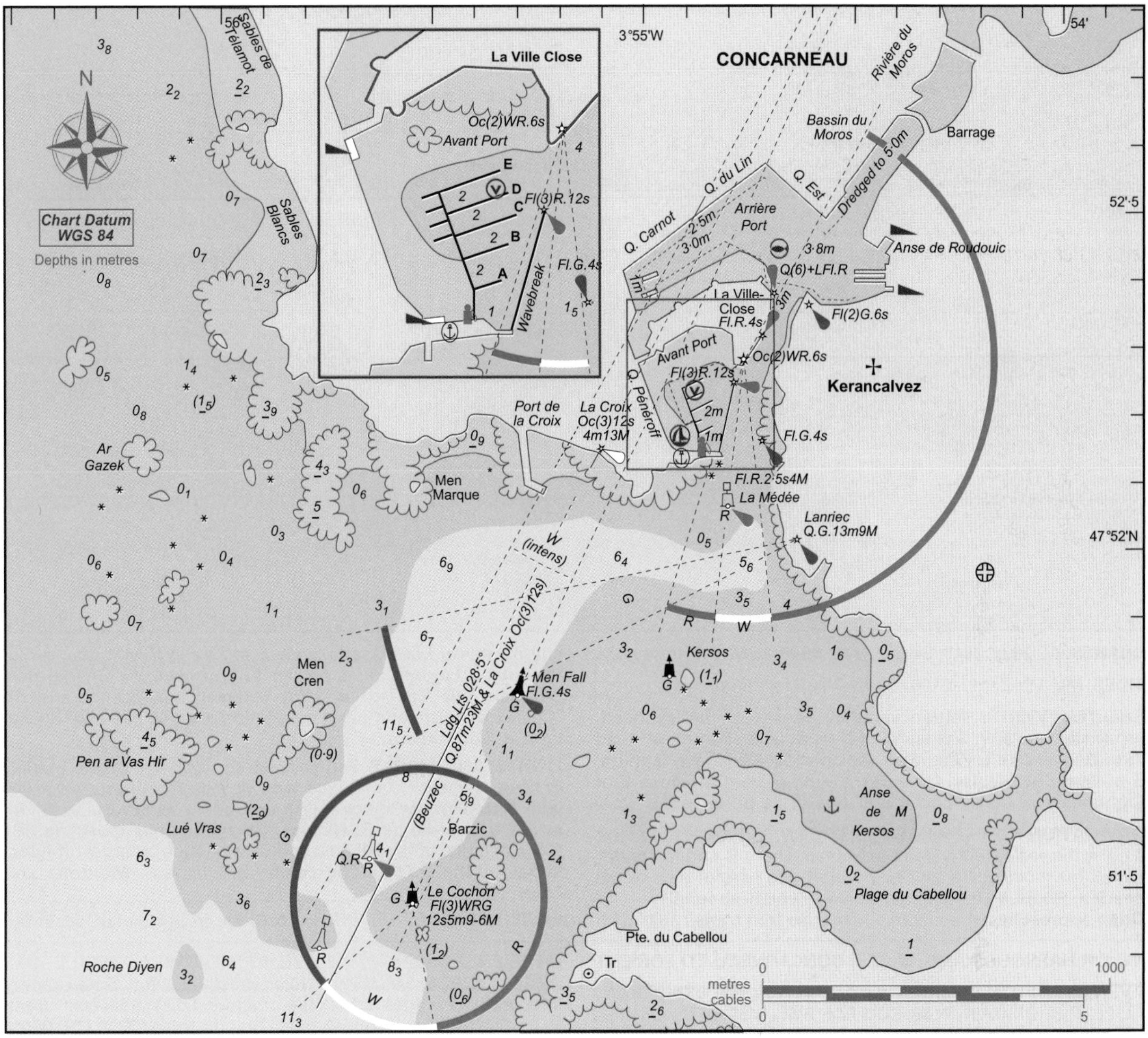
La Ville Close
Oc(2)WR.6s
Avant Port
E
D
C
B
A
Fl(3)R.12s
Fl.G.4s
Wavebreak
CONCARNEAU
3°55'W
54'
Rivière du Moros
Bassin du Moros
Barrage
Dredged to 5·0m
Q. du Lin
Q. Est
Q. Carnot
Arrière Port
2·5m
3·0m
3·8m
Anse de Roudouic
Q(6)+LFl.R
La Ville-Close
Fl.R.4s
Fl(2)G.6s
Oc(2)WR.6s
Kerancalvez
Q. Pénéroff
Port de la Croix
La Croix Oc(3)12s 4m13M
Fl.G.4s
Fl.R.2·5s4M
La Médée
Lanriec Q.G.13m9M
Men Marque
W (intens)
Kersos
Men Fall Fl.G.4s
Ldg Lts 028·5° Q.87m23M & La Croix Oc(3)12s
(Beuzec)
Barzic
Q.R
Le Cochon Fl(3)WRG 12s5m9-6M
Anse de Kersos
Plage du Cabellou
Pte. du Cabellou
Tr
Men Cren
Ar Gazek
Pen ar Vas Hir
Lué Vras
Roche Diyen
Sables de Trélamot
Sables Blancs
N
Chart Datum WGS 84
Depths in metres
52'·5
47°52'N
51'·5
metres
cables
1000

CHARTS AC 2820, 3641; SHOM 7146, 6650; ECM 543/4; Imray C38

TIDES +0455 Dover; ML 3·0; Duration 0615; Zone –0100

Standard Port BREST (⟵)

Times				Height (metres)			
High Water		Low Water		MHWS	MHWN	MLWN	MLWS
0000	0600	0000	0600	6·9	5·4	2·6	1·0
1200	1800	1200	1800				
Differences CONCARNEAU							
–0010	–0030	–0030	–0020	–1·9	–1·5	–0·7	–0·2
ÎLE DE PENFRET (Îles de Glénan)							
–0005	–0030	–0028	–0018	–1·9	–1·5	–0·7	–0·2

SHELTER Good, except in strong S'lies. The marina (2m) gets very crowded in high season; it is protected by an anti-wash barrier on the inside of which yachts can berth. The Arrière Port is solely for FVs. Yacht pontoon on NE corner of La Ville Close is only for locals.

NAVIGATION WPT 47°50′·62N 03°56′·33W, 028·5°/1·0M to abm Le Cochon SHM bcn twr. Beware large FVs and rks around Men Cren and Le Cochon. Speed limit 5kn between le Cochon and Men Fall; 4kn inshore of Men Fall SHM lt buoy.

LIGHTS AND MARKS See chartlet and 9.21.4. Ldg lts 028·5°: front, small RW twr, very hard to see against bldgs behind; rear, Beuzec spire on skyline, 1·34M from front. Pass between Le Cochon G bcn twr (easier to see than the ldg marks) and Basse du Chenal PHM buoy, QR. After Men Fall SHM buoy, track 070° toward Lanriec lt, in a G window on W gable end. It is better to lower sail here as there is little room to do so further up-chan. Note the 0·5m depth close SSW of La Médée PHM bcn twr.

R/T Marina Ch 09 (0700-2100LT in season). Port Ch **12** (H24).

TELEPHONE HM (Port) 02·98·60·51·18; Aff Mar 02·98·60·55·56; CROSS 02·97·55·35·35; Météo 02·98·32·55·57; Auto 08.92.68.08.08; ⊜ 02·98·97·01·73; Police 17; Fire 18; Ⓗ 02·98·52·60·02; Brit Consul 02·97·87·36·20; Dr 02·98·97·85·95.

FACILITIES **Marina** (336 + 52 Ⓥ; pontoon 'D'), ☎ 02·98·97·57·96, 📠 02·98·97·15·15; €2.45, P, D, M, Slip, C (17 ton), ⚒, ME, El, CH, SHOM, ACA, SM, ⊡. The fuel berth in 1m is only accessible near HW, depending on draft.

There are good engineering facilities in the FV Hbr if heavy maintenance/repairs are required; or go to Port-la-Forêt or Bénodet.

Town Ⓔ, Gaz, 🛒, R, Bar, ✉, Ⓑ, bus to Quimper ⇌ and ✈. Ferry: Roscoff.

9.21.13 ÎLES DE GLÉNAN

Finistere **47°42'·98N 03°59'·60W** (twr on Île Cigogne)

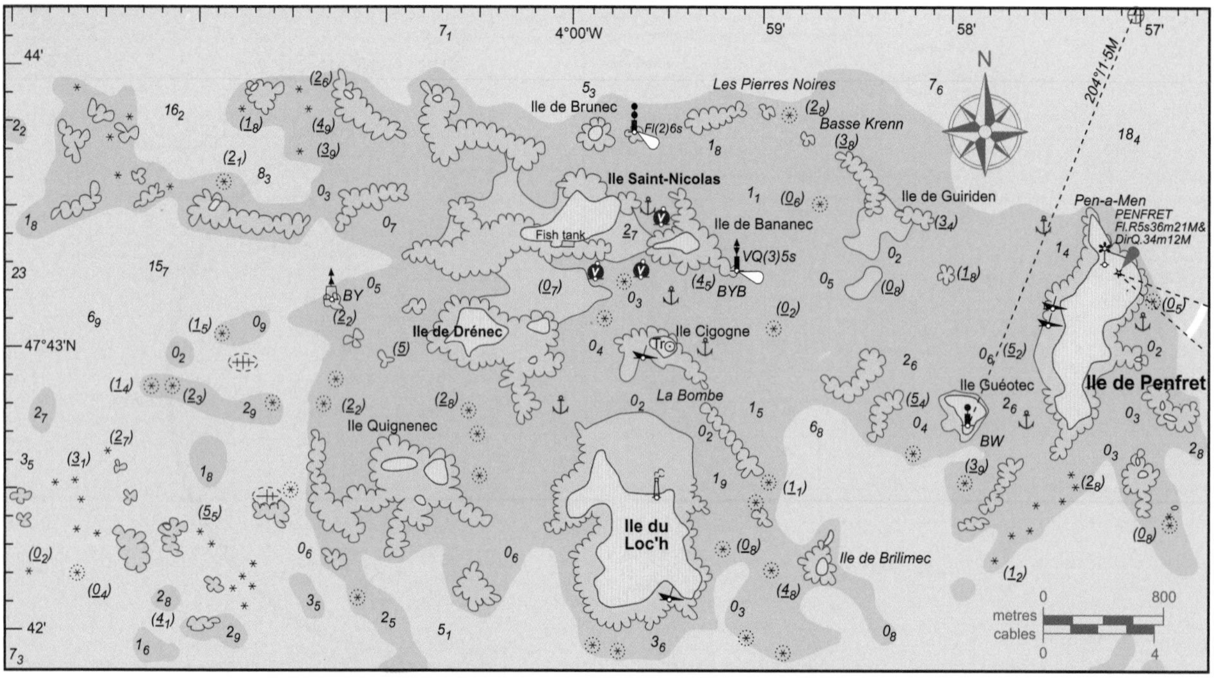
44'
4°00'W
59'
58'
57'
47°43'N
42'
Les Pierres Noires
Ile de Brunec
Fl(2)6s
Basse Krenn
Ile Saint-Nicolas
Ile de Guiriden
Ile de Bananec
Fish tank
VQ(3)5s
BYB
BY
Ile de Drénec
Ile Cigogne
La Bombe
Ile Quignenec
Ile du Loc'h
Ile de Brilimec
Pen-a-Men
PENFRET
Fl.R5s36m21M&
DirQ.34m12M
204°/1·5M
Ile Guéotec
BW
Ile de Penfret
N
metres
cables
0
800
0
4

CHARTS AC 2820, 3640; SHOM 7146, 6648; ECM 243; Imray C38

TIDES ML 3·0; Zone –0100. See 9.21.12 for differences.

SHELTER. Visit in settled weather as ⚓s can be exposed, especially near HW. ⚓ close W of N tip of Île de Penfret or head W to Ⓥs and ⚓ in La Chambre, the principal ⚓ and ferry landing, S of Île de St Nicolas. Other ⚓s: E side of Penfret; close E of Cigogne; N of Île du Loc'h; and NW of Île de Bananec.

NAVIGATION WPT 47°44´·15N 03°57´·04W, 186°/0·9M to Penfret lt ho, is the easiest entry point to Glénan. There is enough water HW±3 for most boats, but below half-tide careful pilotage is needed. Boats of the Glénan Sailing School abound.
Other approaches: Also from N, Cigogne tr in transit 181° with chy on Île du Loc'h leads close E of La Pie IDM lt bcn; avoid the drying Pierres-Noires further E. From the W, Chenal des Bluiniers 095°/088° dries 0·7m between Îles Drénec and St Nicolas. S apprs and night navigation are not advised. Speed limit is 8kn mid-Jun to mid-Sept.

LIGHTS AND MARKS See chartlet and 9.21.4.Conspic marks: Penfret, highest (17m) island with W lt ho/R top; the tower (W with B top) on Île Cigogne; Fish tank and a wind turbine (5 FR) at SW end of Île de St Nicolas. Cardinal buoys mark the SE, S & SW limits of the islands; and Basse Jaune, a large, off-lying shoal to the E. Les Pourceaux and Île aux Moutons are close N.

FACILITIES Ⓥs €7.65. VHF Ch 16, R, Bar in St Nicolas, basic 🛒.

MINOR HARBOURS AND ⚓AGES, CONCARNEAU TO LORIENT

AVEN and BELON RIVERS, Finistere, **47°47´·93N 03°43´·87W**, AC 2821; SHOM 7031, 7138; ECM 544. HW +0450 on Dover (UT), –0030 on Brest. HW ht –1·9m on Brest; ML 2·8m; Duration 0608. Both rivers have bars and are shallow in their upper reaches. Seas rarely break on the Aven bar, but the Belon bar is impassable in bad weather. Beware Les Cochons de Rospico (drying 0·5m) to SW of ent and Les Verrès (IDM bcn) to SE. See 9.21.4 for sectors at Port Manec'h's conspic lt ho. Night entry not advised to either river. SHOM 7138/pilot book is advisable.
The Aven: Port Manec'h has Ⓥs and a good ⚓ in 2·5m outside the bar which dries 0·9m. Very good shelter at Rosbras; Pont-Aven, 3·6M up-river, only accessible for shoal craft. Moorings in 2·5m; or AB at the quay dries 2·5m. Facilities: HM ☎ 02·98·71·08·65; **YC de l'Aven** (Port Manec'h). **Town** ME, Slip, C, FW, P & D (cans), R, Bar.
The Belon: appr near HW from close to Pte de Kerhermen to cross the bar (0·2m). 1M up-river are 3 large W Ⓥs (•1.00/m LOA) or ⚓ in pool, 12·4m deep; Ⓥs trots higher up. Slip, C, FW, R, Bar.

BRIGNEAU, Finistere, **47°46'·85N 03°40'·12W**. AC 2821; SHOM 7031, 7138; ECM 544. –0020 on Brest; ML 2·8m. Small drying, fair weather hbr. Strong onshore winds render the ent dangerous and the hbr untenable due to swell. Unlit SWM buoy is 7ca S of hbr ent. By day bkwtr Dir lt, W tr/R top, ≠ rear W panel (hard to see, by hotel terrace) lead 331° in the white sector (329°-339°) to ent. See 9.21.4 for lt details. Some Ⓥs (•1.00/m LOA) afloat at the ent or AB on drying W quay. Facilities: FW, ⛽, 🛒, R, Bar.

MERRIEN, Finistere, **47°46'·77N 03°39'·02W**. AC 2821; SHOM 7031, 7138; ECM 544. HW –0020 on Brest; ML 2·8m. Small drying inlet with rky ledges either side of apprs. Ldg marks 005°: front W □ lt tr/R top; rear, house gable among trees. Dir lt QR, 004°-009°. ⚓ or moor to 2 W Ⓥs outside ent (•1.00/m LOA) or AB on quay SE side. Avoid oyster beds beyond quay. Facilities: FW, R.

DOËLAN, Finistere, **47°46´·21N 03°36´·55W**. AC 2821; SHOM 7031, 7138; ECM 544. HW +0450 on Dover (UT), –0035 on Brest; HW ht –2·2m on Brest; ML 3·1m; Duration 0607. Fair weather only, open to onshore winds. 4 small dayglo red Ⓥs (•1.00/m LOA) afloat in outer hbr. 2 large W round buoys just N and S of bkwtr are for temp/short stay. Drying AB at W quay or raft on FV up-river. Daymarks: Two outsize lt ho's in transit 013·8°: front, W twr/G band & top; rear, W twr/R band & top. See 9.21.4 for lt details. W bcn/B stripe, (hard to see, 0·5M NNE of rear ldg lt) is also on 013·8° transit. Conspic factory chy E of front ldg lt. Facilities: HM ☎ 02·98·71·53·98; **Services:** CH, El, Ⓔ, ME, ⚒. **Village** D, P (cans), FW, Dr, ✉, R, 🛒, Bar.

LE POULDU (La Laïta or Quimperlé River), Finistere, **47°45'·70N 03°32'·19W**. AC 2821; SHOM 7031, 7138; ECM 544. HW –0020 on Brest; ML 2·8m. Strictly a fair weather hbr, adequate shelter for small yachts in a small marina (1m) on the E bank. Or ⚓ in deeper (2·8-4m) pools upstream. There are water twrs to E and W. At HW appr the low cliffs on W side of the wide estuary. The ent is marked by 2 PHM bcns, but chan shifts often and local advice is needed. In onshore winds the bar is dangerous on the ebb. Tides reach 6kn at sp. No lights. Facilities: FW, 🛒, R, Bar.

9.21.14 PORT TUDY (Île de Groix)

Morbihan **47°38'·72N 03°26'·73W**

CHARTS AC 2821, 2822; SHOM 7031, 7032, 7139; ECM 544; Imray C38

TIDES +0505 Dover; ML 3·1; Duration 0610; Zone –0100

Standard Port BREST (⟵)

Times				Height (metres)			
High Water		Low Water		MHWS	MHWN	MLWN	MLWS
0000	0600	0000	0600	6·9	5·4	2·6	1·0
1200	1800	1200	1800				
Differences PORT TUDY (Île de Groix)							
0000	–0025	–0025	–0015	–1·8	–1·4	–0·6	–0·1

SHELTER Good, but outer hbr is open to swell in strong N/NE winds, access H24. Options: Moor fore and aft to assorted buoys; max draft 3m. Ⓥ berths inside E mole on first 2 pontoons, dredged 0·9-2·5m. Or in marina (mostly full of locals), access (0630–2200) via gate HW ±2, but less at small coefficients. No ⚓ in hbr, often very crowded. Caution: Ferry wash and noise.

NAVIGATION WPT 47°39'·11N 03°26'·29W, (100m E of Speerbrecker ECM buoy), 218°/0·5M to N mole hd lt, just in R sector of E mole hd lt. Beware a large unlit mooring buoy 0·6M NW of ent and rks SE of appr. From E or SE pass N of Basse Melite NCM buoy. Use SHOM 7139 (1:20,000) for exploring the island, including Locmaria (below), Port St Nicolas and Port Lay.

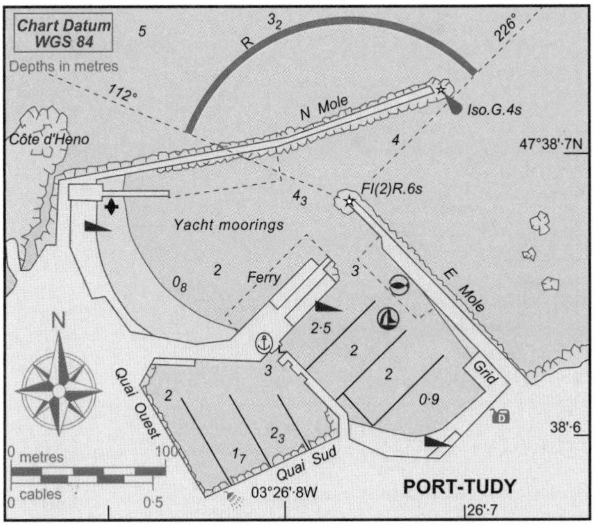
Chart Datum WGS 84
Depths in metres
Côte d'Héno
N Mole
Iso.G.4s
47°38'·7N
Fl(2)R.6s
Yacht moorings
Ferry
E Mole
Grid
Quai Ouest
Quai Sud
metres
cables
0·5
03°26'·8W
PORT-TUDY
26'·7
38'·6
112°
226°

LIGHTS AND MARKS See chartlet and 9.21.4. The three principal lts on Groix are: Pen-Men lt ho at NW end of island, W □ tr, B top; Pte de la Croix lt at NE end; and Pte des Chats at SE end. There are no ldg lts, although the mole head lts in transit 219° clear offlying rks to the E. By day the N mole lt ho and conspic water twr (1M SW of hbr) ≠ 220° lead close W of Speerbrecker to ent.

R/T VHF Ch 09 during lock opening hours.

TELEPHONE Aff Mar 02·97·37·16·22; CROSS 02·97·55·35·35; ⊜ 02·97·86·80·93; Auto 08·92·68·08·56; Police 02·97·86·81·17; Ⓗ (Lorient) 02·97·83·04·02; British Consul 02·97·87·36·20.

FACILITIES **Marina** (104, plus 100 in tidal E Hbr and 120 buoys), ☎ 02·97·86·54·62, 📠 02·97.86.61.37; €1.45 Ⓥ, €2.52 AB; **Quay** P & D (cans, 0800–1200 & 1400–1900, ☎ 02·97·86·80·96), ME, El, ⚒, C (3 ton), CH. **Town** 🛒, R, ▣, ✉, Bar. Ferry to Lorient.

OTHER HARBOUR ON ÎLE DE GROIX

LOCMARIA, Morbihan, **47°37'·40N 03°26'·42W**. AC 2820/1, SHOM 7139; –0020 Brest; ML 2·8m. Appr is open to the S, but in offshore winds tiny drying hbr gives shelter. Steer N initially for G bcn twr; then pick up 350° ldg line, W bn ≠ conspic Ho. Enter between PHM/SHM bcns; a SCM and NCM bcn drying reef. Limited space inside to dry out; or ⚓ outside the hbr either side of the ldg line. Facilities in village, 🛒, R. Le Bourg is approx 1M walk.

9.21.15 LORIENT

Morbihan **47°42'·60N 03°22'·00W**

CHARTS AC 2821, 304; SHOM 7031, 7032, 7139, 7140; ECM 544, 545; Imray C38

TIDES +0455 Dover; ML 3·1; Duration 0620; Zone –0100

Standard Port BREST (⟵)

Times				Height (metres)			
High Water		Low Water		MHWS	MHWN	MLWN	MLWS
0000	0600	0000	0600	6·9	5·4	2·6	1·0
1200	1800	1200	1800				
Differences LORIENT							
+0003	–0022	–0020	–0010	–1·8	–1·4	–0·6	–0·2
PORT LOUIS							
+0004	–0021	–0022	–0012	–1·8	–1·4	–0·6	–0·1
HENNEBONT (Blavet River)							
+0015	–0017	+0005	+0003	–1·9	–1·5	–0·8	–0·2
PORT D'ETEL (9.21.16)							
+0020	–0010	+0030	+0010	–2·0	–1·3	–0·4	+0·5

SHELTER Very good. Île de Groix shelters the ent from SW'lies. Hbr access all tides/weather. 6 marinas, from seaward, at: **Ban-Gâvres** (2m), pass W and N of Île aux Souris. **Kernével**, W of main chan (enter between Fl R 1·2s at N end of wave-break and SHM buoy, thence Ⓥ berths at S end); **Port Louis** (E of La Citadelle); **Locmiquélic** (enlarged marina); **Pen Mané** at mouth of R Blavet (appr at slack water advised; and **Port du Lorient** in the city. Access HJ. Restricted area W and E of Pte de L'Espérance. Berth in Avant Port or pre-arrange Bassin à Flot (suitable for long stay), via entry gate HW±1 sp, ±15 mins nps.
No ⚓ in chans/hbr, but moorings ENE of La Citadelle and ⚓ for shoal draft in Petite Mer de Gâvres. River Blavet is navigable on the flood for 6M to Hennebont: Ⓥs and a pontoon (short stay only) in complete shelter; also moorings below first of 3 bridges, 21m cl'nce. Caution: 0·3m patches beyond it. See also 9.18.14.

NAVIGATION WPT Passe de l'Ouest, 47°40'·84N 03°24'·78W, 057°/2·0M to 016·5° ldg line. WPT Passe du Sud 47°40'·47N 03°22'·46W, 008·5°/2·15M to abm La Citadelle. Here a secondary yacht chan (1m) deviates from the main chan; leave to stbd two SHM perches, La Jument R bcn twr and Le Cochon RGR bcn twr. There are few navigational dangers if ldg lines are kept to, but keep clear of ships in the main chan.

LIGHTS AND MARKS Conspic daymarks: Water tr 8ca W of Kernével; La Citadelle stbd of ent; Port-Louis spire further E, submarine pens at Pte de Kéroman and 2 silos N of Île St Michel. Ldg and Dir lts, as seen from seaward (details in 9.21.4); these are mainly for large vessels, but may help yachts in poor vis):

1. Passe de l'Ouest: ldg lts 057°, both Dir Q; Front, R twr, W bands. Rear, W daymark, R bands on bldg.
2. Passe du Sud: ldg lts 008·5°, both Dir QR; Front, R □, G bands on Gy tr. Rear, R □, W stripe, on grey tr.
3. Les Trois Pierres: QRG, conspic B twr, W bands; where Passe de l'Ouest and Passe du Sud converge.
4. Île Saint-Michel (W side): ldg lts 016·5°, both Dir Oc (3) G 12s; W twrs, G tops.
5. Pte de Kéroman: ldg lts 350°, both Dir Oc (2) R 6s. Front, R ho, W bands; Rear, RW topmark on Gy pylon, R top.
6. Kernével: astern ldg lts 217°, both QR.
7. Pte de l'Esperance: Dir lt Q WRG 037°; W twr, G top.

R/T *Vigie Port Louis* Ch 11 (H24). Marinas Ch 09 (In season: 0800-1230, 1330-2000. Out of season 0830-1200, 1400-1800).

TELEPHONE Port HM 02·97·37·11·86, 📠 02·97.37.90.73; Aff Mar 02·97·37·16·22; CROSS 02·97·55·35·35; SNSM 02·97·86·29·62; ⊜ 02·97·37·34·66; Auto 08.92.68.08.56; Police 02·97·64·27·17; Sea Police 02·97·12·12·12; Ⓗ 02·97·64·81·58; Brit Consul 02·97·87·36·20.

FACILITIES (from seaward) **Ban-Gâvres**, ☎ 02·97·82·46·55, (40+2 Ⓥ) €1.00; tricky access, strong tides. **Kernével** (410+60 Ⓥ) ☎ 02·97·65·48·25, 📠 02·97.33.63.56; port-kernevel@sellor.com €2.29. H24 access, depth 3m; P & D (appr from within, or S of, the marina; call Ch 09), ▣, Slip; YC ☎ 02·97·33·77·78. **Port-Louis** (160+20 Ⓥ), ☎ 02·97·82·59·55, €1.70, dredged 2m, C. *Continued overleaf.*

21

Locmiquélic, (217+10 Ⓥ) ☎ 02·97.33.59.51, 📠 02·97.33.89.25, €2.26, depth 1·5-3m, C, ⊡. **Lorient** (320+50 Ⓥ) ☎ 02·97·21·10·14, 📠 02·97.21.10.15; €2.29, Avant Port 2·5-3m depth, 2·5m in Bassin à Flot; ⊡, Slip, BH (25 ton), C, ME, El, Ⓔ, ⚒, CH, SHOM, ACA, SM, P & D @ Kernevel; **Club Nautique de Lorient**, Bar, C (1½ ton), FW, Slip. **City** All facilities, ✉, Ⓑ, ≹, ✈.

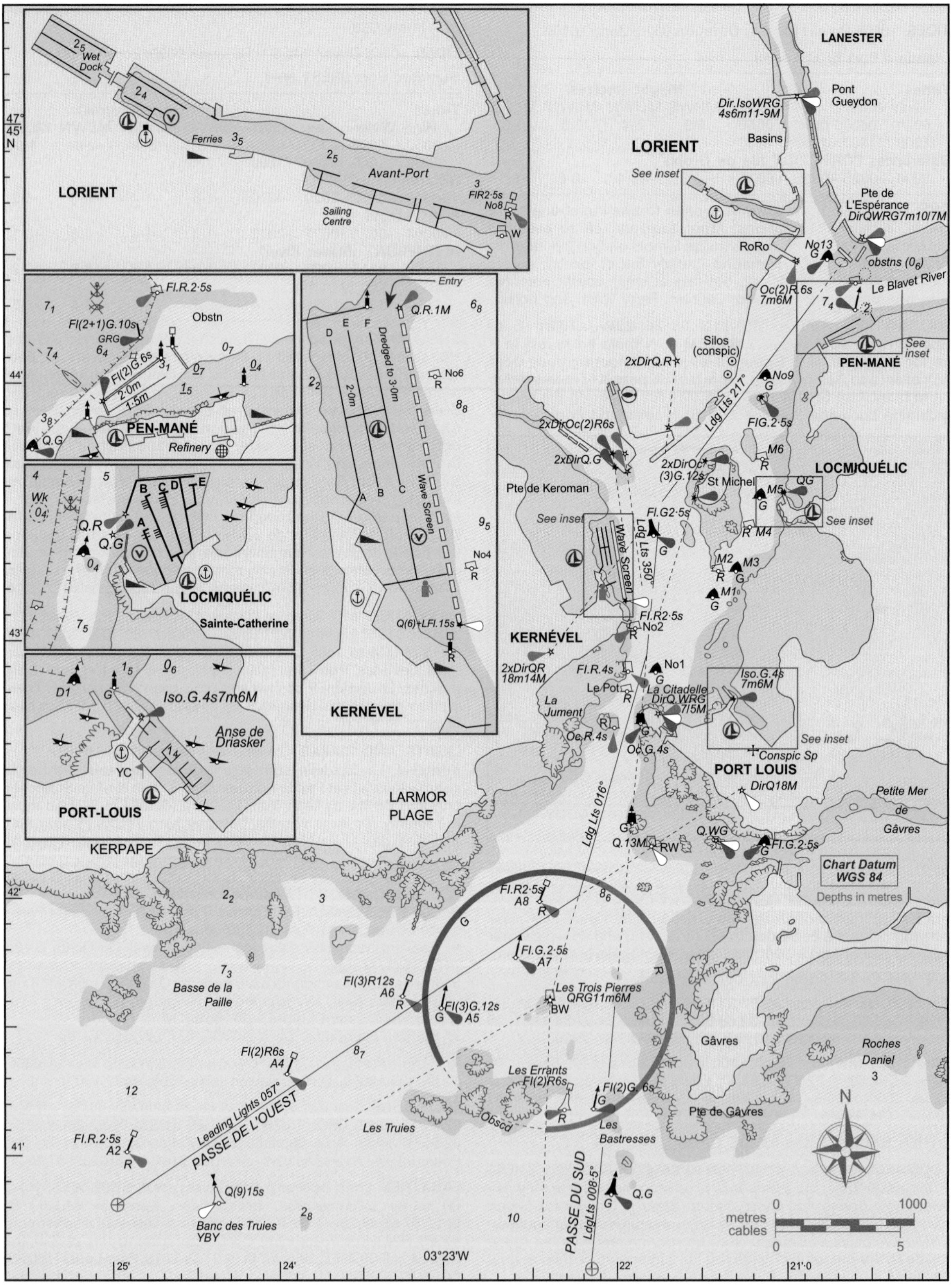
LORIENT
LOCMIQUÉLIC
PEN-MANÉ
KERNÉVEL
PORT LOUIS
PORT-LOUIS
LARMOR PLAGE
KERPAPE
LANESTER
Pont Gueydon
Le Blavet River
Pte de Keroman
Gâvres
Les Trois Pierres QRG11m6M
PASSE DE L'OUEST
Leading Lights 057°
PASSE DU SUD
LdgLts 008·5°
Basse de la Paille
Banc des Truies YBY
Les Truies
Les Errants
Les Bastresses
Roches Daniel
Pte de Gâvres
Petite Mer de Gâvres
Chart Datum WGS 84
Depths in metres
03°23'W

9.21.16 RIVER ÉTEL

Morbihan **47°38´·65N 03°12´·69W** (Hbr ent)

CHARTS AC 2822; SHOM 7032, 7138; ECM 545; Imray C38

TIDES +0505 Dover (UT); ML 3·2m; Duration 0617. See 9.21.15.

SHELTER Excellent at marina (1·5-2m) on E bank 1M N of the ent, inside the town quay (FVs). Possible ⚓s S of conspic LB ho, off Le Magouër on the W bank or N of town (beware strong streams). Pont Lorois (1·3M N) has 9·5m clearance.

NAVIGATION WPT 47°37'·31N 03°13'·44W, 020°/2·6M to hbr ent aligned 020° with a R/W radiomast (off chartlet). Appr only by day, in good vis and settled weather, at about HW –1½ on the last of the flood. The chan shifts but is well buoyed/lit; bar dries approx 0·4m. To cross the bar, call *Semaphore d'Etel* Ch 13, HW –3 to +2 for directions in simple French (mast arrow not used).

If no VHF radio, pre-notify ETA by ☎ (see below), so that pilotage signals can be shown from Fenoux mast:
Arrow horiz = no entry for all vessels; conditions dangerous.
Arrow vertical = maintain present heading.
Arrow deflected L/R = turn in direction indicated.
● hoisted = no ent for undecked boats and craft <8m LOA.
R flag = insufficient depth over bar.

LIGHTS AND MARKS Dir lt W side of ent, Oc (2) WRG 6s; no ⚓ within 5ca of it. Épi de Plouhinic bn, Fl R 2·5s 7m 2M, marks groyne at ent. Other lts & marks as chartlet and 9.21.4.

R/T Call *Semaphore d'Etel* VHF Ch 13 16 (see above). Marina Ch 13 16 (Mon/Fri 0800-1200, 1400-1800. Sat/Sun 1000-1200)

TELEPHONE Pilotage Stn 02·97·55·35·59; Aff Mar 02·97·55·30·32; ⊖ 02·97·36·20·76; Auto 08·92·65·02·56; CROSS 02·97·55·35·35; Police 02·97·55·32·11; British Consul 02·97·87·36·20.

FACILITIES **Marina** ☎ 02·97·55·46·62, 📠 02·97.55.34.14; (180 + 20 Ⓥ); €1.59, C (6 ton), Slip; **Quay** P & D (cans), CH, El, ME, ⚒. **Town** Bar, Dr, R, 🛒, 🅻, Bus to ⇄ (Auray 15km) and ✈ (Lorient 32km).

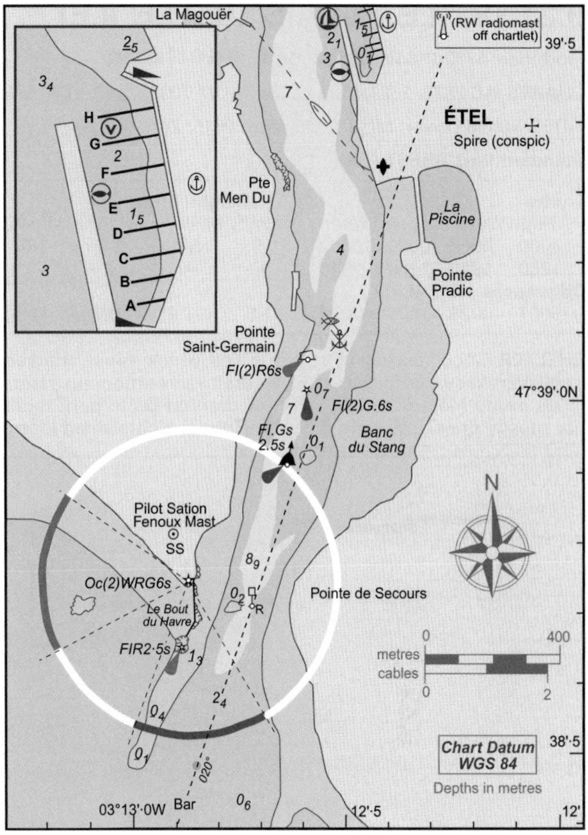
La Magouër
(RW radiomast off chartlet)
ÉTEL
Spire (conspic)
Pte Men Du
La Piscine
Pointe Pradic
Pointe Saint-Germain
Fl(2)R6s
Fl(2)G.6s
Banc du Stang
Fl.Gs 2.5s
47°39'·0N
Pilot Sation Fenoux Mast
SS
Oc(2)WRG6s
Le Bout du Havre
Pointe de Secours
FlR2·5s
metres
cables
Chart Datum WGS 84
Depths in metres
03°13'·0W
Bar
020°
12'·5
12'
38'·5
39'·5

9.21.17 SAUZON (BELLE ÎLE)

Morbihan **47°22´·47N 03°13´·01W**

CHARTS AC 2822; SHOM 7032, 7142 (large scale plan); ECM 545

TIDES +0450 Dover; ML 3·0; Duration 0615; Zone –0100
Use differences for Le Palais (9.21.18) overleaf.

SHELTER Good shelter except in NE'lies. Small attractive hbr, 4M WNW of Le Palais, with a drying creek stretching 0·5M inland. Options: (a) ⚓ ENE of hbr ent, €0.60; (b) pick up one of 21 Ⓥs N of the N jetty; (c) raft up between 9 Ⓥs on W side of Avant Port in about 1·5m, €1.10 (FVs moor on E side); (d) dry out on the E side of the inner hbr on 41 R Ⓥs, fore and aft; firm, level mud/sand. This area dries about 1·6 – 2m; access approx HW ±1½. Note: R buoys for visitors, G buoys for locals.

NAVIGATION WPT 47°22´·88N 03°12´·73W, 205°/685m to NW Jetée lt. Main lt, QG, and NW Jetée, Fl G 4s, form a 205° transit. No navigational dangers. No ⚓ between Sauzon and Le Palais.

LIGHTS AND MARKS See chartlet and 9.21.4. Le Gareau SHM bcn is conspic 0·9M N of hbr; ditto Pte des Poulains lt ho 1·6M NW.

R/T Ch 09, Jul/Aug: 0900-1230, 1700-2000; closed Sun.

TELEPHONE HM 02·97·31·63·40; other numbers as 9.21.18.

FACILITIES HM Jul/Aug, see R/T. €1.15. FW on quay; Village 🛒, 🅻, R, Bar, ✉, Ⓑ, ATM; market-day Thurs. Bus to Le Palais. Boat repairs best done at Port Haliguen, La Trinité or Crouesty.

STER WENN, Morbihan, **47°22´·30N 03°15´·24W**. AC 2822; SHOM 7032, 7142. Tides as 9.21.18. A very popular W coast anchorage 1·1M S of the N tip of Belle Île (recce from Sauzon, 3km by bike). From the NW enter Ster-Vraz, the outer inlet. When abeam the 5th hole of the golf course to the N, Ster Wenn opens to stbd. ⚓ where space permits, stern line ashore. Shelter is good in all winds. Facilities: None, other than relative peace.

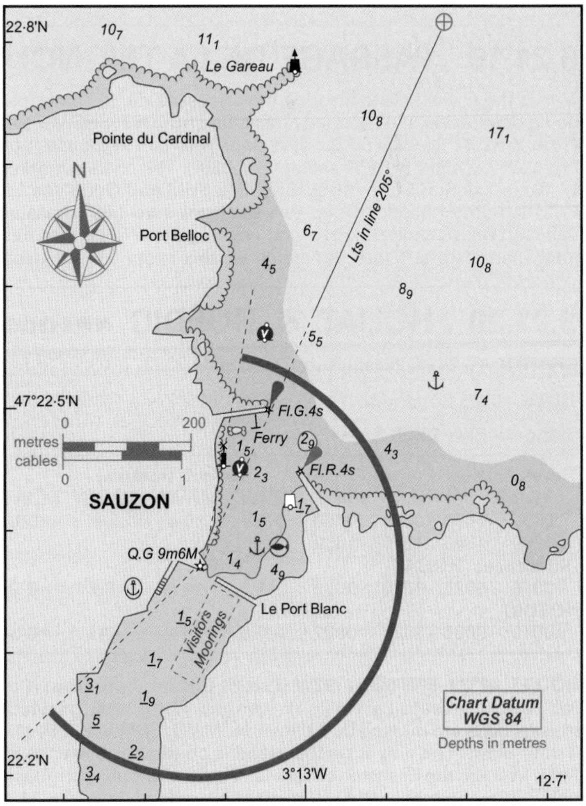
22·8'N
Le Gareau
Pointe du Cardinal
Port Belloc
Lts in line 205°
47°22·5'N
Fl.G.4s
Ferry
Fl.R.4s
metres
cables
SAUZON
Q.G 9m6M
Le Port Blanc
Visitors Moorings
Chart Datum WGS 84
Depths in metres
22·2'N
3°13'W
12·7'

9.21.18 LE PALAIS (BELLE ÎLE)

Morbihan **47°20'·84N 03°08'·98W** ❁❁❁◊◊✿✿✿

CHARTS AC 2822, 2823; Imray C39; SHOM 7032, 7142; ECM 545

TIDES +0458 Dover; ML 3·1; Duration 0615; Zone –0100

Standard Port BREST (⟵)

Times				Height (metres)			
High Water		Low Water		MHWS	MHWN	MLWN	MLWS
0000	0600	0000	0600	6·9	5·4	2·6	1·0
1200	1800	1200	1800				
Differences LE PALAIS							
+0007	–0028	–0025	–0020	–1·8	–1·4	–0·7	–0·3

SHELTER Good, except in strong E'lies which cause marked swell. Very crowded in season. Deep draft yachts moor on 3 trots of Øs inside Mole Bourdelle; shallow draft on Øs to port. Inner hbr mostly dries. Enter the Bassin à Flot via a gate/small lifting bridge open HW –1½ to +1 (0600-2200LT), for rafted berths on either side in 2·5m. Thence via lifting bridge into marina (Bassin de la Saline), finger pontoons (1·7m) if any vacant.

NAVIGATION WPT 47°21′·16N 03°07′·96W, 245°/0·80M to Jetée Nord lt. No navigational dangers, but hold off for fast ferries. No ⚓ between Sauzon (see below) and Le Palais.

LIGHTS AND MARKS Lts as chartlet. La Citadelle is conspic.

R/T VHF Ch 09 (Season: 0800-1200, 1400-2000. Out of season 0800-1200, 1500-1800).

TELEPHONE HM 02·97·31·42·90; Aff Mar 02·97·31·47·08 (open Tues am); SNSM 02·97·31·54·07; CROSS 02·97·55·35·35; ⊖ 02·97·31·85·95; Auto 08.92.68.08.56; Police 02·97·31·80·22; Dr 02·97·31·40·90; ⊞ 02·97·31·48·48; Brit Consul 02·97·87·36·20.

FACILITIES Avant Port 80 Øs €1.16, P, D, Slip, FW, C (10 & 5 ton). **Bassin á Flot**, ☎ 02·97·31·42·90, AB (90) €1.55, ME, El, ⚒. **Marina** 8 Ⓥ €1.93. **YC Belle Île** ☎ 02·97·31·55·85. **Town** 🛒, Gaz, CH, R, Bar, ▣, ✉, Ⓑ, ⇄ (ferry to Quiberon), ✈. Ferry: Roscoff.

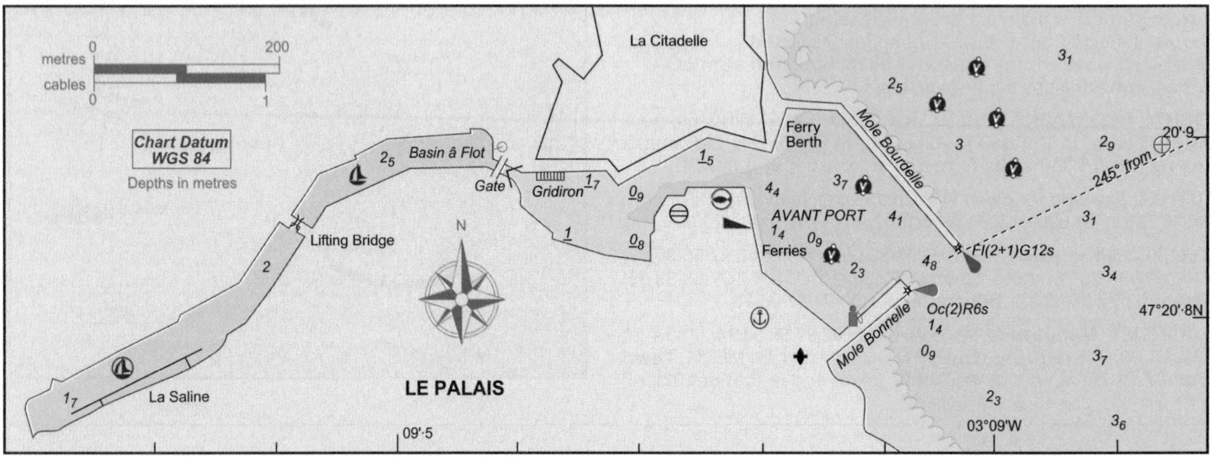
metres 0 200
cables 0 1
Chart Datum WGS 84
Depths in metres
La Citadelle
Basin â Flot
Gate
Gridiron
Lifting Bridge
Ferry Berth
Mole Bourdelle
AVANT PORT
Ferries
Fl(2+1)G12s
245° from
20'·9
Oc(2)R6s
Mole Bonnelle
47°20'·8N
La Saline
LE PALAIS
09'·5
03°09'W
N

9.21.19 PASSAGE DE LA TEIGNOUSE

See upper chartlet on facing page

This is the easiest route through the Chaussée de La Teignouse being deep, wide, well buoyed and lit. See AC 2357; SHOM 7141. From WPT 47°25′·35N 03°05′·00W appr with La Teignouse lt ho brg 036° (by night in its W sector 033°-039°). The chan is marked by Goué Vas Sud SCM, Basse du Milieu SHM and Goué Vas Est PHM lt buoys. Abeam Goué Vas Est, turn stbd 068°, passing between Basse Nouvelle PHM and NE Teignouse SHM lt buoys, into open waters. Minor variations on this route can be used.

Further SE, Passage du Béniguet is NW of Houat and Passage des Soeurs lies between Houat and Hoëdic; both unlit.

The shortest passage, saving 3M if to/from Port Haliguen, lies between Le Four SCM and Les Trois Pierres NCM bcn twrs with La Teignouse lt ho brg 094°. Turn N as the rky chan between Iniz en Toull Bras to stbd and a SCM and 2 ECM perches to port opens; see pecked line. Only for experienced navigators by day; pre-study SHOM 7141 carefully; expect strong cross-streams.

9.21.20 HOUAT & HOËDIC ❁❁◊✿✿✿

CHARTS AC 2823, 2835; Imray C39; SHOM 7033, 7143; ECM 545

TIDES +0505 Dover; ML 3·1; Duration 0605; Zone –0100

Standard Port BREST (⟵)

Times				Height (metres)			
High Water		Low Water		MHWS	MHWN	MLWN	MLWS
0000	0600	0000	0600	6·9	5·4	2·6	1·0
1200	1800	1200	1800				
Differences HOUAT							
+0010	–0025	–0020	–0015	–1·7	–1·3	–0·6	–0·2
HOËDIC							
+0010	–0035	–0027	–0022	–1·8	–1·4	–0·7	–0·3

HOUAT, 47°23′·57N 02°57′·32W (Port St Gildas). Appr from N or NE passing abeam La Vieille rk (conspic 17m), NNE of which mussel beds are marked by 4 buoys: NCM VQ, ECM VQ(3) 5s and 2 unlit SPM. The only lt on the island is on the hbr bkwtr head, Fl (2) WG 6s; the G sector covers La Vieille and buoyed mussel beds. At night appr in W sectors on either side; details in 9.21.4.

Good shelter, except from N/NE'lies, at Port St Gildas, near E end of the N coast. Moor on double trots; no ⚓ in hbr. E of the hbr are 15 W Øs and space to ⚓. S part of hbr dries. Keep clear of ferries and FVs on W and N quays.

Tréach er Gourhed, aka Rade de Houat, is a 7 cables wide, crab-shaped bay at the ESE end of Houat, possibly the largest and most popular anchorage in France despite (or because of) being designated a No-anch area due to cables. Other ⚓s at Tréach er Béniguet, Portz Ler and Portz Navallo, all at NW end of Houat. Facilities: Mairie 02·97·30·68·04. Bar, R, 🛒, Gaz, CH, ▣, ✉, Dr. Ferries to Quiberon, Lorient, La Turballe, Le Croisic.

HOËDIC, 47°20′·67N 02°52′·47W (Port de L'Argol). Appr from NNW or NNE passing abeam La Chèvre rk (unlit IDM bcn) and in either W sector of the bkwtr lt, Fl WG 4s; its G sector covers La Chèvre and 194°-143°; see 9.21.4 for lt details.

Good shelter, except from N/NE'lies, at Port de L'Argol, in the centre of the N coast. Ferries berth at the W end; there is just room to ⚓ at the E end or outside to the NNE. The old hbr, Port de la Croix, on the S of island dries, but ⚓ outside in 2-4m. Other ⚓s may be found in the island's lee. 1.5M SE of the island, Grands Cardinaux lt ho, R twr/W band Fl (4) 15s, marks the eponymous reefs. Facilities: Bar, R, limited victuals. Ferries as for Houat.

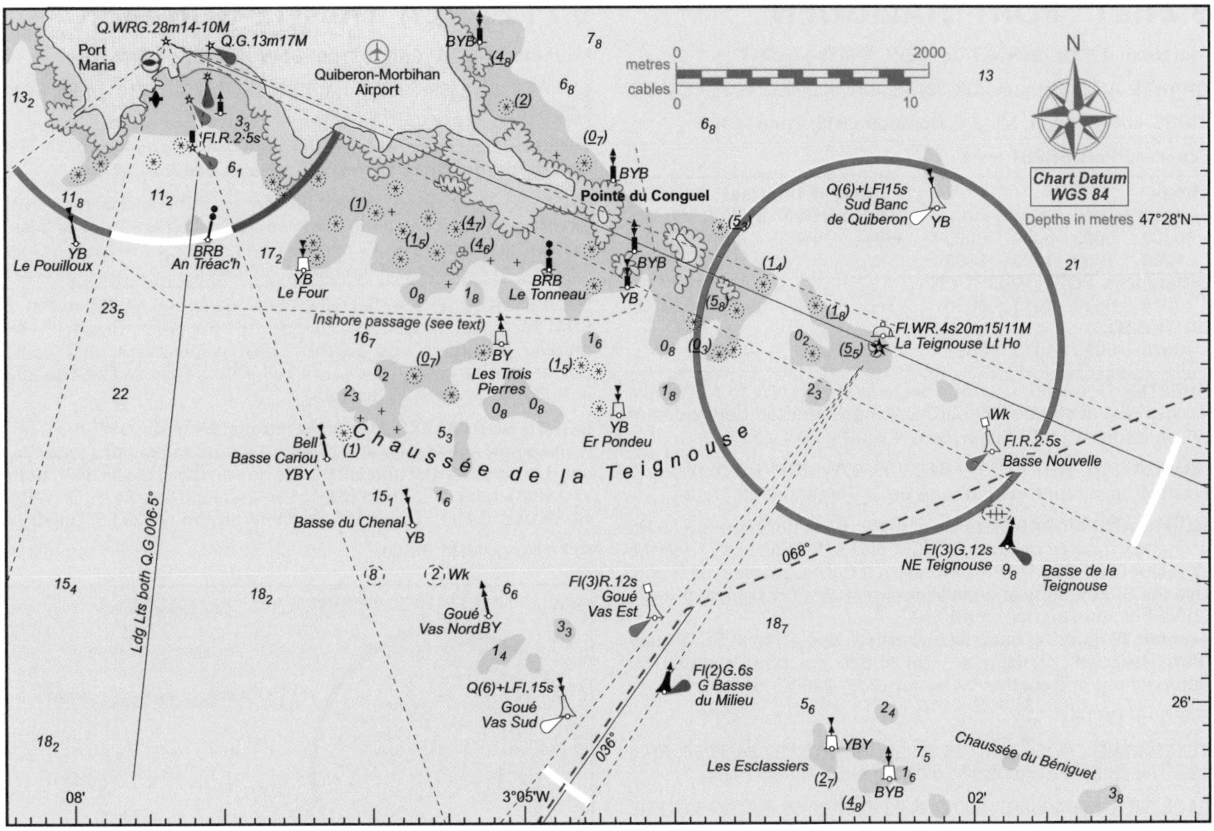
Q.WRG.28m14-10M
Q.G.13m17M
Port Maria
Quiberon-Morbihan Airport
BYB
metres
cables
2000
10
13
N
Chart Datum WGS 84
Depths in metres
47°28'N
Fl.R.2·5s
Pointe du Conguel
Q(6)+LFl15s
Sud Banc de Quiberon
YB
Le Pouilloux
BRB
An Tréac'h
Le Four
Le Tonneau
Inshore passage (see text)
Fl.WR.4s20m15/11M
La Teignouse Lt Ho
Les Trois Pierres
BY
Er Pondeu
Wk
Fl.R.2·5s
Basse Nouvelle
Bell
Basse Cariou
YBY
Chaussée de la Teignouse
Basse du Chenal
Fl(3)G.12s
NE Teignouse
Basse de la Teignouse
068°
Fl(3)R.12s
Goué Vas Est
Goué Vas Nord
Ldg Lts both Q.G 006·5°
Fl(2)G.6s
G Basse du Milieu
Q(6)+LFl.15s
Goué Vas Sud
036°
26'
Les Esclassiers
Chaussée du Béniguet
08'
3°05'W
02'

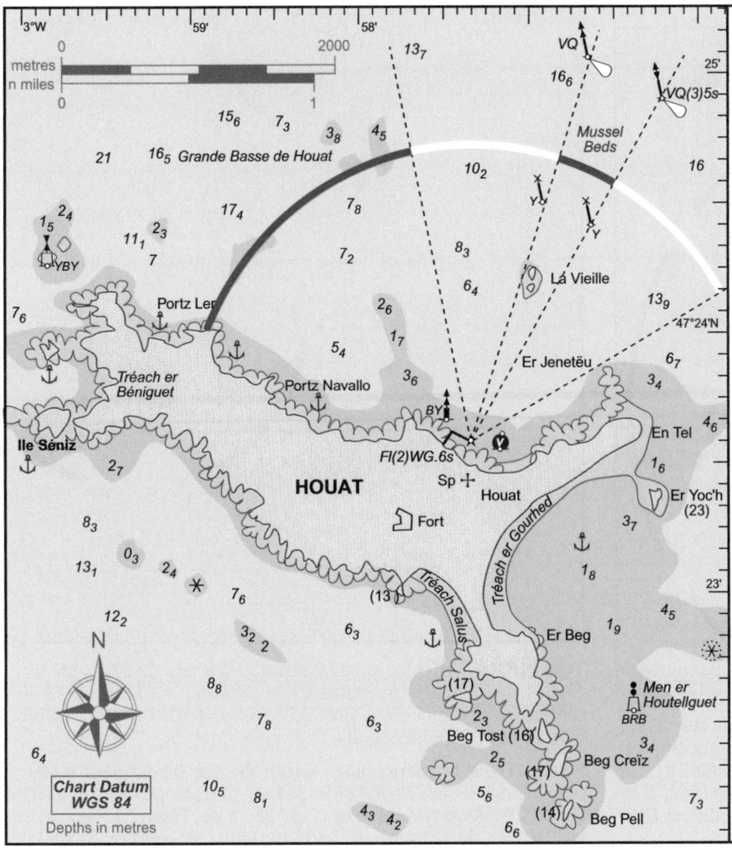
3°W
59'
58'
metres
n miles
0
2000
1
VQ
VQ(3)5s
25'
Mussel Beds
Grande Basse de Houat
La Vieille
Portz Ler
47°24'N
Tréach er Béniguet
Portz Navallo
Er Jenetëu
En Tel
Ile Seniz
Fl(2)WG.6s
HOUAT
Sp
Houat
Er Yoc'h
Fort
Tréach er Gourhed
Tréach Salus
23'
Er Beg
N
Men er Houtellguet
BRB
Beg Tost
Beg Creïz
Chart Datum WGS 84
Depths in metres
Beg Pell

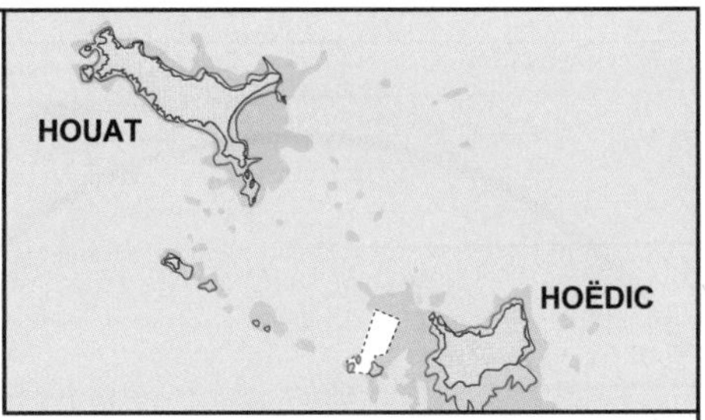
HOUAT
HOËDIC

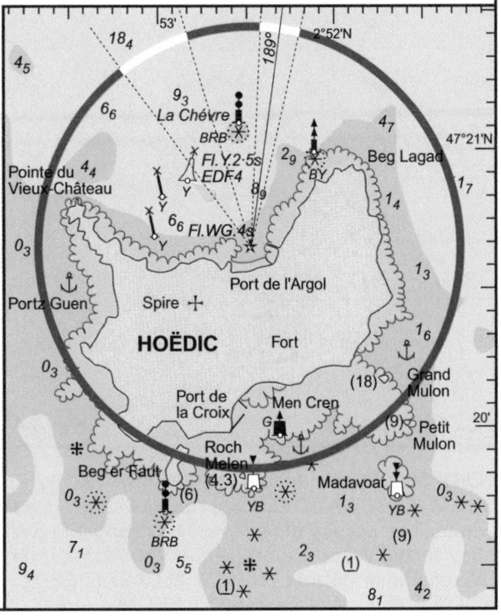
53'
2°52'N
189°
La Chèvre
BRB
47°21'N
Fl.Y.2·5s
EDF4
Beg Lagad
BY
Pointe du Vieux-Château
Fl.WG.4s
Port de l'Argol
Portz Guen
Spire
HOËDIC
Fort
Grand Mulon
Port de la Croix
Men Cren
Petit Mulon
20'
Roch Melen
Beg er Faut
YB
Madavoar
BRB

9.21.21 PORT HALIGUEN

Morbihan **47°29'·35N 03°05'·98W**

CHARTS AC 2357; Imray C38, 39; SHOM 7141, 7032, 7033; ECM 545

TIDES +0500 Dover; ML 3·1; Duration 0615; Zone –0100

Standard Port BREST (⟵)

Times				Height (metres)			
High Water		Low Water		MHWS	MHWN	MLWN	MLWS
0000	0600	0000	0600	6·9	5·4	2·6	1·0
1200	1800	1200	1800				
Differences PORT HALIGUEN							
+0015	–0020	–0015	–0010	–1·7	–1·3	–0·6	–0·3
LA TRINITÉ							
+0020	–0020	–0015	–0005	–1·5	–1·1	–0·5	–0·2

SHELTER Good, but uncomfortable in strong NW to NE winds. Access H24 at all tides. Ⓥ berths alongside/rafted both sides of 'V' pontoon, with 10 finger berths on the NW end arm.

NAVIGATION WPT 47°29'·74N 03°05'·07W, 237°/7ca to bkwtr lt. From W or S, appr via Passage de la Teignouse (9.21.19).

LIGHTS AND MARKS Hazards at night: Banc de Quiberon (2·7m at S end), marked by an unlit NCM and a lit SCM buoy. Use the W sector (246°-252°) of Port-Maria Dir lt Q WRG, to clear its N end. Use the SCM lt buoy and the W sector (299°-306°) of bkwtr lt, Oc (2) WR 6s, to clear its S end.
An unlit W mooring buoy (see chartlet), and an unlit SCM buoy 'Port Haliguen' marking a 1·7m shoal, are both avoided by approaching in the other W sector (233°-240·5°) of the bkwtr lt.

R/T VHF Ch 09.

TELEPHONE CROSS 02·97·55· 35·35; Météo 02·97·64·34·86; Auto 08.92.68.08.56; Police 02·97·50·07·39; Dr 02·97·50·13·94.

FACILITIES Marina (860+100 Ⓥ) ☎ 02·97·50·20·56, 📠 02·97·50·50·50, €2.70, Slip, P, D, C (2 ton), BH (13 ton), ME, El, ⚒, CH, ▣, SM, Bar, R, 🛒. **Town** (Quiberon) 🛒, Gaz, R, Ice, Bar, ✉, Ⓑ, ⇌, ✈.

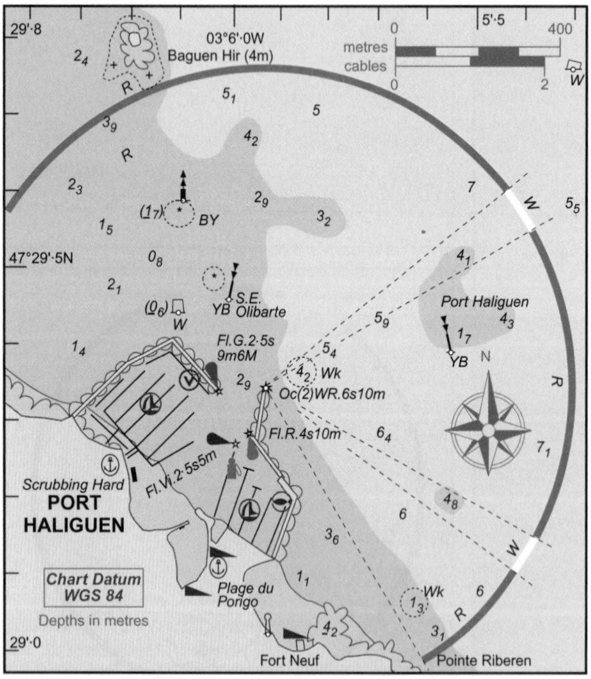
29'·8
03°6'·0W
Baguen Hir (4m)
metres
cables
0
400
5'·5
2
W
47°29'·5N
BY
S.E.
YB Olibarte
Fl.G.2·5s
9m6M
Wk
Oc(2)WR.6s10m
Fl.R.4s10m
Fl.Vi.2·5s5m
Port Haliguen
YB
N
Scrubbing Hard
PORT
HALIGUEN
Chart Datum
WGS 84
Depths in metres
Plage du
Porigo
Fort Neuf
Pointe Riberen
29'·0

PORT MARIA, Morbihan, **47°28'·55N 03°07'·31W**. AC 2357; SHOM 7032, 7141. Tides approx as 9.21.21. Shelter good in all winds, but access dangerous in strong SE–SW winds. It is a busy ferry/FV port, only feasible for yachts in emergency. ⚓ in SW of hbr in approx 2m. HM ☎ 02·97·50·08·71. Facilities: C (6 ton), FW at E quay, El, ME, ⚒, SHOM.

9.21.22 LA TRINITÉ-SUR-MER

Morbihan **47°34'·06N 03°00'·60W**

CHARTS AC 2358, 2357; Imray C39; SHOM 7033, 7141,7034; ECM 545, 546

TIDES +0455 Dover; ML 3·2; Duration 0610; Zone –0100
Standard Port BREST (⟵). **Differences see 9.21.21.**

SHELTER Very good, except in strong SE/S winds near HW when La Vaneresse sandbank is covered. Access H24 at all tides. Marina boat will meet. Ⓥ pontoon is first beyond ☆ Iso R 4s. No ⚓/fishing in river. Speed limit 5kn.

NAVIGATION WPT 47°33'·38N 03°00'·42W, 347°/1·0M to No 2 PHM buoy. No navigational dangers; the Rivière de Crac'h is well marked by buoys and perches. Best water close to E bank. Beware many oyster beds, marked with perches. The channel is buoyed on both W sectors.

LIGHTS AND MARKS Daymarks include: Mousker, a 4.5m rk, off-white paint; and ✠ spire at La Trinité. Ldg marks are hard to see by day. Lts, see chartlet and 9.21.4. Pte de Kernevest ldg lts 347°, both W twrs/G tops, but amid trees. 1M up-river: Dir lt 347°, Oc WRG 4s, W twr. S Pier, Oc (2) WR 6s, W twr/R top, W 293·5°-300·5°.

R/T Marina VHF Ch 09.

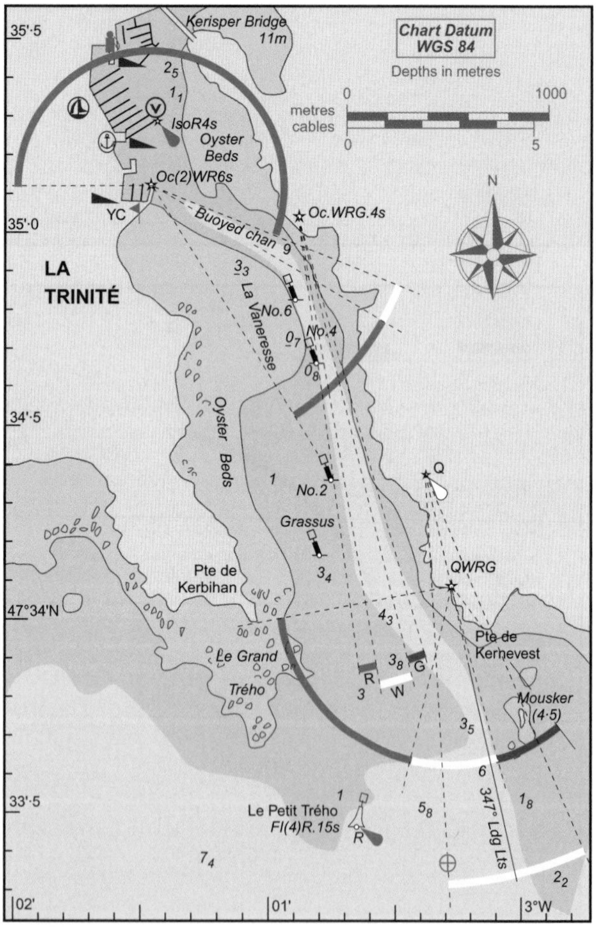
Kerisper Bridge
11m
Chart Datum
WGS 84
Depths in metres
metres
cables
0
1000
5
35'·5
IsoR4s
Oyster
Beds
Oc(2)WR6s
YC
Oc.WRG.4s
Buoyed chan
35'·0
LA
TRINITÉ
La Vaneresse
No.6
No.4
34'·5
Oyster Beds
No.2
Grassus
Q
QWRG
Pte de
Kerbihan
47°34'N
Le Grand
Trého
Pte de
Kernevest
Mousker
(4·5)
N
Le Petit Trého
Fl(4)R.15s
347° Ldg Lts
33'·5
02'
01'
3°W

TELEPHONE Aff Mar 02·97·24·01·43; CROSS 02·97·55·35·35; SNSM 02·97·55·01·15; Police 02·97·55·71·62; ⊜ 02·97·55·73·46; Météo 02·97·64·34·86; Auto 08.92.68.08.56; Dr 02·97·55·74·03; Brit Consul 02·97·87·36·20.

FACILITIES Marina (900 +100 Ⓥ), ☎ 02·97·55·71·49, 📠 02.97.55.86.89, €2·70, P, D, BH (36 ton), Grid, M, ME, El, CH, SHOM, Ⓔ, SM, ⚒; **Club Nautique** ☎ 02·97·55·73·48. **Town** 🛒, Gaz, R, Bar, Ice, ✉, Ⓑ, ⇌ (Auray), ✈ (Lorient). Ferry: Roscoff or St Malo.

9.21.23 VANNES

Morbihan **47°38'·45N 02°45'·62W**

CHARTS AC 2823, 2358; Imray C39; SHOM 7034; ECM 546

TIDES See GOLFE DU MORBIHAN 9.21.24. ML 2·0m; Zone –0100

SHELTER Excellent in all winds. Marina dory may indicate a vacant finger pontoon; if not, visitors berth N/S on pontoons D and G, just S of movable inner foot-bridge (*passerelle*). Note: Major developments to improve marina layout, facilities and surroundings are under review (2004); no timescale quoted.

ACCESS by day only. A **swing bridge** opens HW±$2\frac{1}{2}$ at H and H+30 in season (15 Jun – 15 Sep) and at weekends; but only at H out of season. During the first and final $\frac{1}{2}$ hour periods when the entry gate (see below) is open, the bridge will open on request VHF Ch 09. Outbound craft have priority over arrivals. Waiting pontoons (drying) are up/downstream. There is an intercom to HM on the downstream waiting pontoon.
Traffic signals (2 vert lts) on bridge's central pier are:
2 ● = no passage; 2 Oc ● = standby; 2 ● = proceed;
2 Oc ● = No passage unless committed;
● = unmasted boats may transit.

An **entry gate** (not a lock), approx 250m N of the bridge and remotely-controlled by the HM, stays open HW±$2\frac{1}{2}$. Gate sill, 0·4m above CD, retains 2·4m inside wet basin.
HW Vannes –$2\frac{1}{2}$ just happens to be HW Port Tudy (9.21.14) which is used by the HM to determine when the gate opens; Port Tudy is a French Standard Port. *Guide practique du Port* (a free annual schedule of gate hrs and other data) is available from: Port de Plaisance, La Rabine, 56019 Vannes. www.mairie-vannes.fr
Gate sigs: ●● = Gate closed; No lts = Gate open.

NAVIGATION WPT: see 9.21.24. After Roguédas SHM lt bn do not cut the shallow corner to port; if anything head ESE until the chan opens up. Turn N'wards when a pink house on its E bank bears 020°. Passage upstream past Île de Conleau is easy and well marked. Beacon'd appr chan to Vannes is narrow, least depth 0·7m, but dredged 2·1m between No 6 bcn and the bridge.

LIGHTS AND MARKS No nav lts N of Roguédas, Fl G 2.5s.

R/T VHF Ch 09.

TELEPHONE Aff Mar 02·97·63·40·95, 📠 02.97.63.46.77; CROSS 02·97·55·35·35, 📠 02.97.63.71.75; ⊖ 02·97·01·36·00; Météo 02·97·42·49·49; Auto 08.92.65.08.56; Police 02·97·47·19·20; Dr 02·97·47·47·25; Ⓗ 02·97·01·41·41; Brit Consul 02·97·87·36·20.

FACILITIES **Marina**, ☎ 02·97·54·16·08, 📠 02·97.42.48.80, (240+60 Ⓥ) €1.83, Slip, ATM, ME, C (10 ton), CH, El, Ⓔ, SM; P & D, cans only, nearest pumps are downstream near No 12 PHM bcn, or at Crouesty. **City** R, Bar, SHOM, ✉, Ⓑ, ≋, ✈.

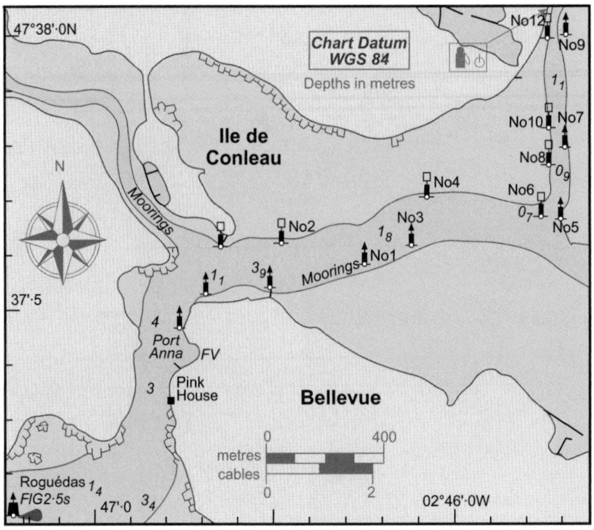
47°38'·0N
Chart Datum WGS 84
Depths in metres
Ile de Conleau
Moorings
No12
No9
No10
No7
No8
No4
No6
No2
No3
No5
No1
Moorings
37'·5
Port Anna
FV
Pink House
Bellevue
metres
cables
400
Roguédas
Fl G2·5s
47'·0
02°46'·0W

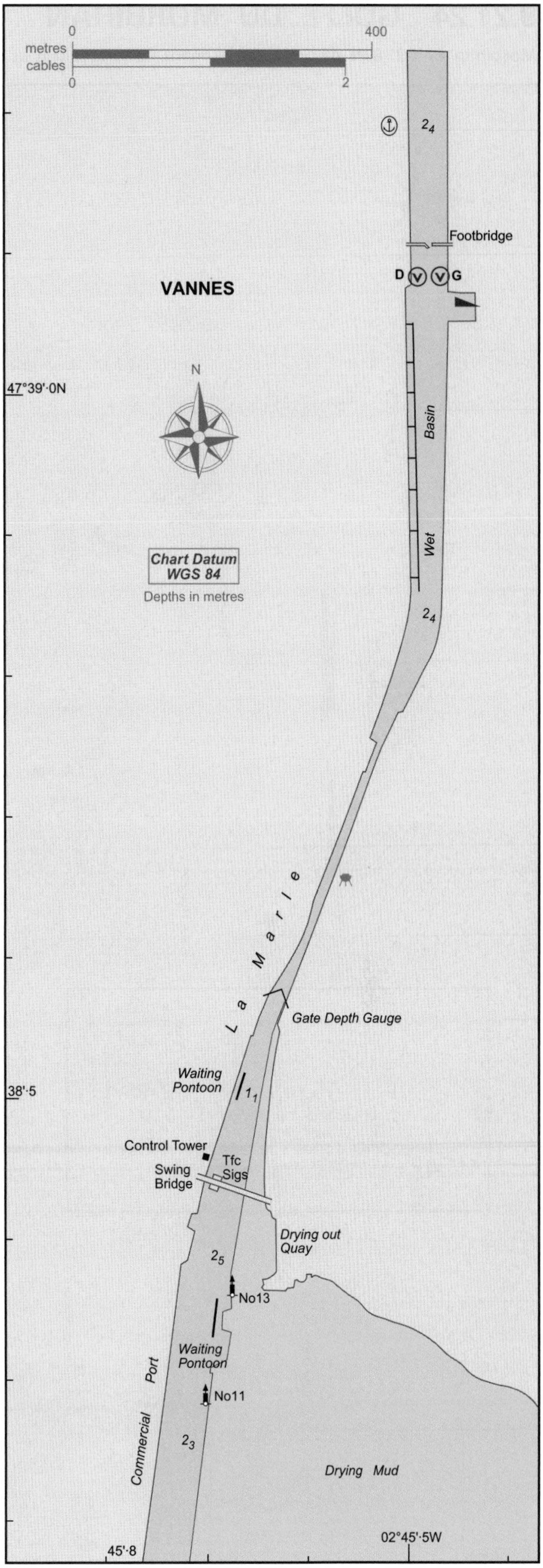
metres
cables
400
Footbridge
VANNES
D
G
47°39'·0N
Basin
Wet
Chart Datum WGS 84
Depths in metres
La Marle
Gate Depth Gauge
38'·5
Waiting Pontoon
Control Tower
Tfc Sigs
Swing Bridge
Drying out Quay
No13
Waiting Pontoon
No11
Commercial Port
Drying Mud
45'·8
02°45'·5W

9.21.24 GOLFE DU MORBIHAN

Morbihan **47°32'·87N 02°55'·27W** (Abeam Port Navalo lt ho)

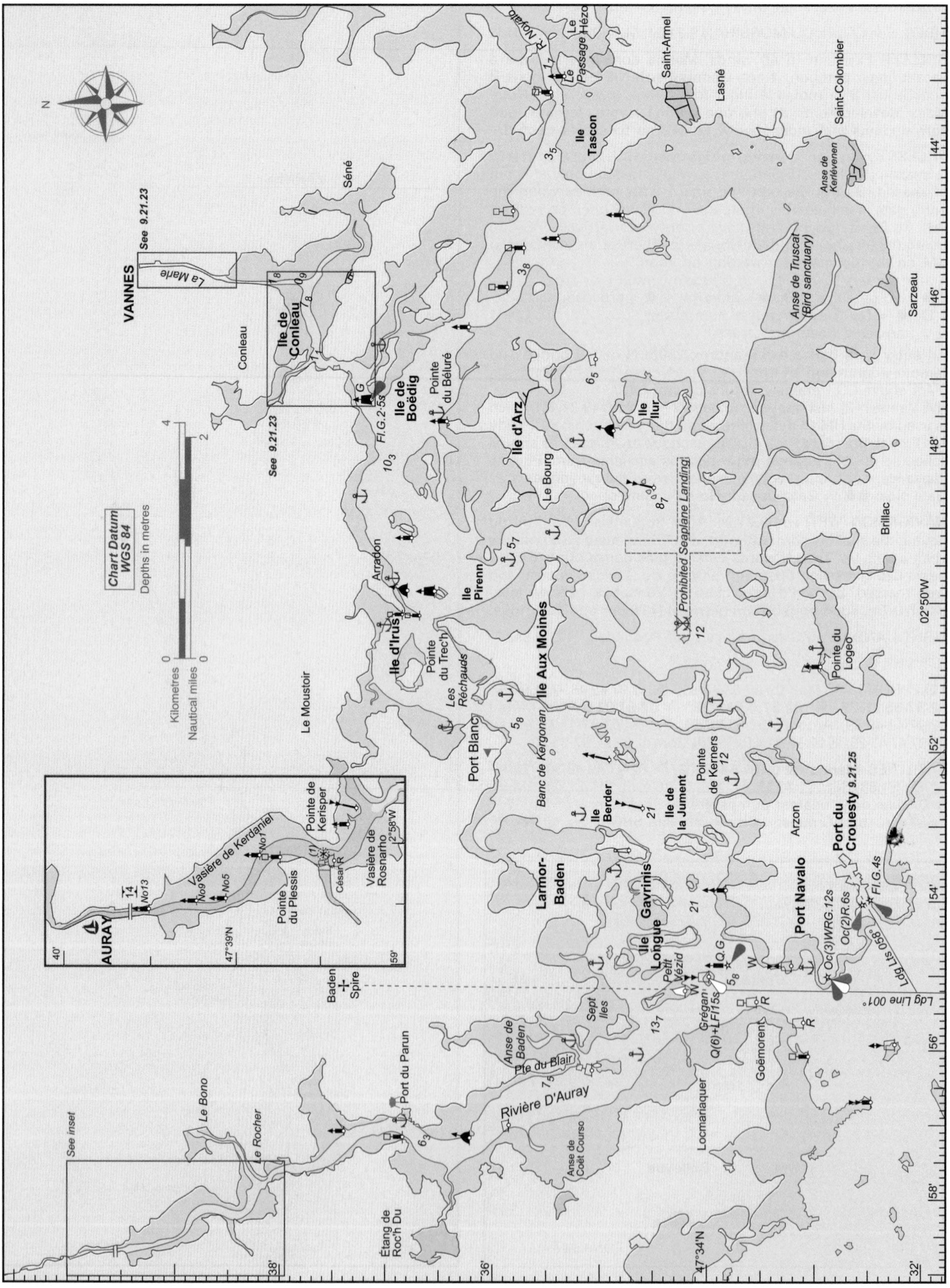
VANNES
La Marle
See 9.21.23
Ile de Conleau
Conleau
Séné
Ile de Boëdig
Pointe du Béluré
Fl.G.2·5s
Ile d'Arz
Le Bourg
Ile Ilur
Ile Tascon
Le Passage
Le Hézo
R. Noyalo
Saint-Armel
Lasné
Saint-Colombier
Anse de Kerlévenen
Anse de Truscat (Bird sanctuary)
Sarzeau
Brillac
Prohibited Seaplane Landing
Chart Datum WGS 84
Depths in metres
Kilometres
Nautical miles
Arradon
Ile d'Irus
Pointe du Trec'h
Les Réchauds
Ile Pirenn
Ile Aux Moines
Le Moustoir
Port Blanc
Banc de Kergonan
Ile Berder
Ile de la Jument
Pointe de Kerners
Pointe du Logeo
Larmor-Baden
Gavrinis
Ile Longue
Petit Vézid
Sept Iles
Port Navalo
Port du Crouesty 9.21.25
Arzon
Fl.G.4s
Oc(3)WRG.12s
Oc(2)R.6s
Ldg Lts 058°
Ldg Line 001°
Grégan Q(6)+LFl15s
Q.G
Baden Spire
Anse de Baden
Pte du Blair
Port du Parun
Rivière D'Auray
Anse de Coët Courso
Locmariaquer
Goëmorent
Étang de Roc'h Du
Le Bono
Le Rocher
See inset
AURAY
Vasière de Kerdaniel
Pointe de Kerisper
Pointe du Plessis
Vasière de Rosnarho
César
No13
No9
No5
No1
47°39'N
2°58'W
47°34'N
02°50'W

CHARTS AC 2823, 2358; SHOM 7033, 6992, 7034; Imray C39; ECM 546

TIDES +0515 Dover; ML 3·0; Zone −0100
Standard Port BREST (⟵)

Times				Height (metres)			
High Water		Low Water		MHWS	MHWN	MLWN	MLWS
0000	0600	0000	0600	6·9	5·4	2·6	1·0
1200	1800	1200	1800				
Differences PORT NAVALO							
+0030	−0005	−0010	−0005	−2·0	−1·5	−0·8	−0·3
AURAY							
+0055	0000	+0020	+0005	−2·0	−1·4	−0·8	−0·2
ARRADON							
+0155	+0145	+0145	+0130	−3·7	−2·7	−1·6	−0·5
VANNES							
+0220	+0200	+0200	+0125	−3·6	−2·7	−1·6	−0·5
LE PASSAGE (47°35′·4N 02°43′·1W)							
+0205	+0200	+0210	+0140	−3·5	−2·5	−1·5	−0·5
LE LOGEO							
+0155	+0140	+0145	+0125	−3·7	−2·7	−1·6	−0·5

The Golfe du Morbihan is an inland sea of about 50sq miles with deep apprs and ent. It contains many islands, all but two privately owned. The only marina with full facilities is at Vannes. The many ⚓s (see chartlet and below) are increasingly restricted by extensive moorings. It is essential to use chain when ⚓ing, unless well out of the tide. Avoid bird sanctuaries, especially in SE, and numerous oyster beds marked by withies. Much of E & SE dries. Night navigation is not advised. Vannes, see 9.21.23.

NAVIGATION WPT 47°31′·97N 02°55′·29W (the same as for Crouesty), 001°/1·7M to abeam Grand Mouton lt bcn. Pilotage is not difficult and the strong streams are not inherently dangerous, but due to higher than usual speeds over the ground, it helps to pre-plot the desired trks/distances within the channels; marks can then be more readily identified and track adjusted with ease, especially if beating. Most navigation buoys are unlit. Caution: In season, there are many vedettes. A regular ferry crosses the narrows between Port Blanc and Île aux Moines.

TIDAL STREAMS Beware very strong tides in the ent and some narrow chans, max 5¾kn sp ebb (8kn reported), but easing in the upper reaches. For a first visit, springs should be avoided; it is likely to be impossible for an aux yacht to enter against a sp ebb and entry at night with a tide running is hazardous. At the ent the flood divides: a weaker flow enters the River Auray; but the major stream rushes NE into the main chan, setting strongly toward Petit & Grand Mouton rks. To avoid these, keep up to the ldg line until safely past Grand Mouton, but beware shoals to port marked by Goémorent R bn tr.

Abeam Grand Mouton the flood and ebb begin 3hrs before and 3hrs after HW Brest respectively; slack water varies but lasts about 30mins at sp and 1hr at nps. HW times become later the further E one goes into the Morbihan, eg HW Vannes is 2 hrs after HW Pt Navalo. But HW at Port Navalo and Auray are within 25 mins of each other.

Beware very strong streams between Île Berder and Île de la Jument, and between Pte de Toulindag and Port Blanc where Les Réchauds rks are marked by 2 SHM bns. Due to an eddy around Île d'Irus the stream runs mainly SW between Les Réchauds and Pte d'Arradon.

LIGHTS AND MARKS The 001° ldg daymarks are: front Petit Vézid W obelisk (from afar looks like a yacht sail), rear Baden ✠ spire (3·3M); maintain 001° until abeam Grand Mouton lt bcn. Chans and dangers are well marked. The only lts are at:

Port Navalo lt ho, W twr/G top, close stbd of the 001° ldg line. Inside ent: Grand Mouton SHM lt bcn and Le Grégan, a squat SCM lt bcn. Roguédas, a large G SHM lt bcn off W end of Île de Boëdig, marks appr chan to Vannes. See 9.21.4 for lt details.

SHELTER AND FACILITIES (clockwise from entrance)
LOCMARIAQUER: Drying ⚓ off village quay; ferries use the buoyed chan to jetty. Two quays: Cale de Bourg, slip, AB dries; Cale du Guilvin (also used by vedettes), AB (S side only) or ⚓ off. Village: Bar, 🛒, R, ME.

SEPT ÎLES: Small, quiet ⚓; chan between W end of island and the mainland peninsula leads into Anse de Baden, mostly dries.

PORT DU PARUN: Drying inlet: no moorings but boatyard with quay, slip and all facilities. ☎ 02·97·57·00·15.

LE ROCHER: Good shelter, but almost full of moorings. Further N the river shoals to 0·2m, but can be navigated on the tide.

LE BONO: Moor or ⚓ (rky bottom) off Banc de la Sarcelle. **Village**, AB in drying basin, ☎ 02·97·57·88·98, ATM, ME, R, 🛒, Gaz, ✉.

AURAY: Access at mid-flood via a bridge with 14m clearance MHWS, shown by gauge. Coupled with 0·4m charted depth, careful tidal calculations may be needed if a high-masted yacht is to pass safely. 12 Ⓥs in a pool S of the bridge; or drying AB at St Goustan. HM ☎ 02.97.56.29.08. Facilities: ME, El, ⚒. **Town** R, 🛒, Bar, ATM at Pont St Sauveur, ✉, ⥵.

ÎLE LONGUE: near SE tip ⚓ out of the stream. No landing.

LARMOR BADEN: good ⚓s to S, but many moorings, HM ☎ 02.97.57.20.86. Aff Mar ☎ 02·97·57·05·66. Village: quay, slip, C (5 ton), 🛒, R, Bar, ✉. In season ferry to I. de Gavrinis.

ÎLE BERDER: pleasant ⚓ E of the island; causeway to mainland.

PORT BLANC: HM ☎ 02·97·26·30·57, 📠 02.97.26.30.16. VHF Ch 09. Closed Oct-Mar otherwise 0845-1230, AC, FW; many moorings. Quay, slip, ATM, Bar, R, ✉, water taxi. Ferry every ½hr to Île aux Moines.

LE PORT D'ILE AUX MOINES: a much-frequented, public island. The narrows between the mainland and Les Réchauds rks can be rough. ⚓ off N end, landing at Pte du Trec'h or pick up Ⓥ (see HM) off Pte des Réchauds where there is a small marina. Water taxi available; call VHF Ch 09 or sound foghorn. HM ☎ 02·97·26·30·57, closed Oct-Mar otherwise 0845-1230, FW, M. Other quieter ⚓s off W side and S tip of island.

ARRADON: limited ⚓, exposed to S'ly. M, Slip, FW, ME. HM ☎ 02·97·44·01·23, 📠 02.97.44.77.03. Apr-Sep 1400-1700. Quay with depth gauge and disabled access, FW, AC; 15 mins waiting time on W side only.

ÎLE PIRENN: exposed ⚓ in tidal stream.

ÎLE D'ARZ: a public island. ⚓ NE of Pte du Béluré; E of Le Bourg (good shelter), or to the W, depending on winds. Rudevent village: ME, El, ⚒.

ÎLE DE BOËDIG: sheltered ⚓ in chan N of the centre of island.

ÎLE DE CONLEAU: ⚓ or moor in bight just S of village, as space permits. ME, El, ⚒, R in village.

SÉNÉ: ME.

LE PASSAGE: ⚓ off Pte du Passage (depths up-river are uncertain), 2M to SW of river ent. Village (St Armel): 🛒, Bar. Seasonal ferry.

KERNERS: ⚓ in 3-6m off Anse de Kerners or Anse de Pen Castel.

ÎLE DE LA JUMENT (or Er Gazeg): good shelter to E of island out of the tide; convenient for leaving the gulf on the tide.

PORT NAVALO: ⚓ in bay, but space limited by moorings, and exposed to W/NW winds. Convenient to await the tide. All facilities at Crouesty (½M by road). HM ☎ 02·97·53·82·12; Police 02·97·24·17·17.

Large scale chartlet of Crouesty marina.

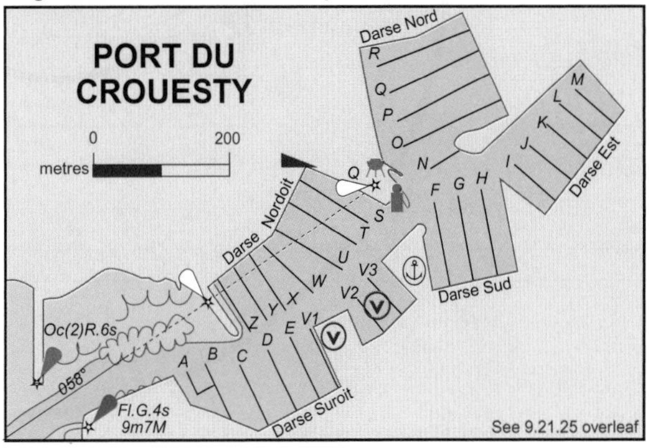
PORT DU CROUESTY
0
200
metres
Darse Nord
Darse Est
Darse Sud
Darse Suroit
Darse Nordoit
Oc(2)R.6s
Fl.G.4s
9m7M
058°
R
Q
P
O
N
M
L
K
J
I
H
G
F
S
T
U
V3
V2
V1
W
X
Y
Z
A
B
C
D
E
See 9.21.25 overleaf

21

9.21.25 CROUESTY

Morbihan **47°32'·52N 02°54'·03W** ❁❁❁◊◊◊✿✿

CHARTS AC 2823, 2358; Imray C39; SHOM 6992, 7034, 7033; ECM 546

TIDES +0505 Dover; ML 3·0; Duration 0555; Zone –0100

Standard Port BREST (⟵)

Times				Height (metres)			
High Water		Low Water		MHWS	MHWN	MLWN	MLWS
0000	0600	0000	0600	6·9	5·4	2·6	1·0
1200	1800	1200	1800				
Differences CROUESTY							
+0013	–0022	–0017	–0012	–1·6	–1·2	–0·6	–0·3

SHELTER Very good in enormous marina which has 6 large separate basins. See large scale chartlet on previous page. Ⓥ basin & pontoons V1, 2 & 3 are on S side of fairway; boats >12m LOA can berth on the wall between V1 and V2. Some shelter from W'lies is afforded by Quiberon Peninsula.

NAVIGATION WPT 47°31´·97N 02°55´·29W, 058°/0·9M to hbr ent. This WPT also applies when entering the Morbihan on 001°. There are no navigational problems, but strong onshore winds can raise dangerous seas in the ent. Access chan is dredged 1·8m and marked by 4 PHM and 3 SHM buoys, plus a PHM perch.

LIGHTS AND MARKS Ldg marks/lts 058°: Front W vert stripe on R panel; rear the tall grey lt ho. Only the first SHM lead-in buoy is lit. See chartlet and 9.21.4 for light details.

R/T VHF Ch 09.

TELEPHONE Aff Mar 02·97·41·84·10; ⊜ 02·97·01·36·00; CROSS 02·97·55·35·35; Auto 08·92·68·08·56; SNSM 02·97·41·35·35; Police 02·97·53·71·65; Dr 02·97·53·71·61; Brit Consul 02·97·87·36·20.

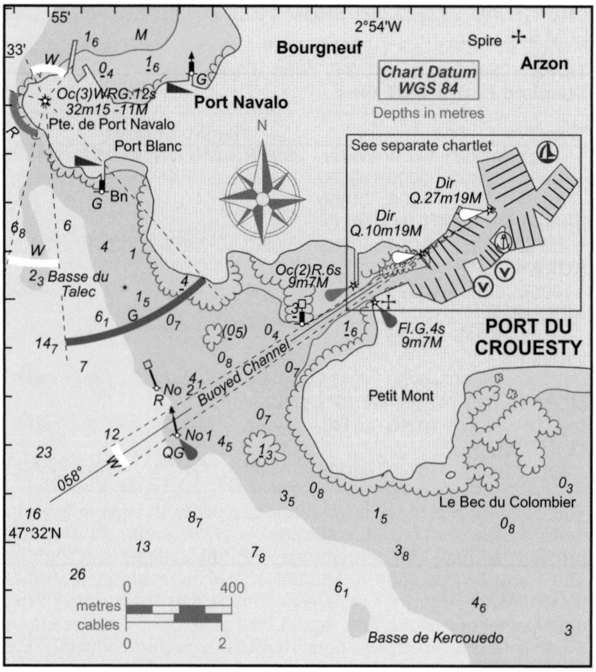
Bourgneuf
Spire
Arzon
2°54'W
Chart Datum WGS 84
Depths in metres
Port Navalo
Oc(3)WRG.12s 32m15-11M
Pte. de Port Navalo
Port Blanc
See separate chartlet
Dir Q.27m19M
Dir Q.10m19M
Bn
Basse du Talec
Oc(2)R.6s 9m7M
Fl.G.4s 9m7M
PORT DU CROUESTY
Buoyed Channel
No 2
No 1
QG
Petit Mont
Le Bec du Colombier
Basse de Kercouedo
47°32'N
058°
metres
cables

FACILITIES Marina ☎ 02·97·53·73·33, 📠 02·97.53.90.22, €2.70, (1400+120 Ⓥ). P, D, ME, El, ⚒, Slip, BH (45 ton), C (10 ton), CH, Bar, M, Ⓔ, SM. **Town** (Arzon) 🛒, Gaz, R, Bar, ✉ & Ⓑ, ⇌ (Vannes), ✈ (Vannes, Lorient, St Nazaire).

MINOR HARBOUR, approx 13 track miles east of Crouesty

PÉNERF RIVER, Morbihan, **47°30´·03N 02°38´·89W**, AC 2823; SHOM 7033, 7144. HW +0515 on Dover (UT); Duration 0610; ML 3·3m. See 9.21.26. Shelter good, except in fresh W'lies. SDs and SHOM 7144 are advised. The 3 ents are not easy: **Passe de l'Ouest** is shoal and ill marked. **Passe du Centre** is the widest and easiest, least depth 0·7m. Appr on 359° ldg line, Le Pignon red lt bcn ≠ Le Tour du Parc spire, passing between Penvins PHM buoy and Borénis SHM buoy. Leave a SHM bcn (marking a drying reef) 150m to the E; thence pass 40m E of Le Pignon, whose white sector (see 9.21.4) covers the appr, but night entry is not advised for a first visit. **Passe de l'Est** has 4m, but is narrower and rks are close to stbd. It joins Passe du Centre E of Le Pignon bcn. Once in the river, head ENE for 1M to ⚓ off Pénerf quay. Beware oyster beds. Facilities: P & D (on quay), Slip, CH, El, ME, ⚒. **Village** R, Bar, Dr, 🛒.

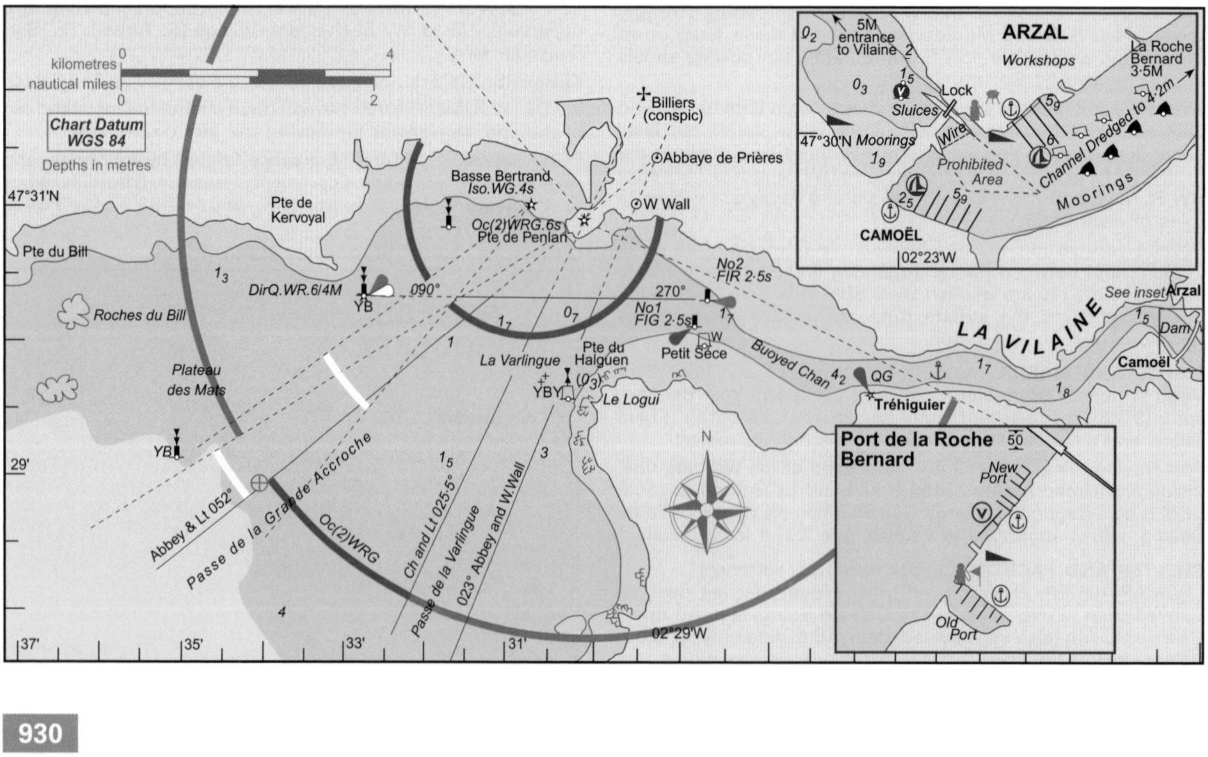
kilometres
nautical miles
Chart Datum WGS 84
Depths in metres
47°31'N
Pte du Bill
Pte de Kervoyal
Roches du Bill
Plateau des Mats
Billiers (conspic)
Abbaye de Prières
Basse Bertrand Iso.WG.4s
Oc(2)WRG.6s Pte de Penlan
W Wall
DirQ.WR.6/4M
090°
270°
No2 FlR 2·5s
No1 FlG 2·5s
Petit Sèce
Pte du Halguen
La Varlingue
Le Logui
Buoyed Chan
QG
Tréhiguier
LA VILAINE
See inset
Arzal
Dam
Camoël
29'
Abbey & Lt 052°
Passe de la Grande Accroche
Oc(2)WRG
Ch and Lt 025·5°
Passe de la Varlingue
023° Abbey and W.Wall
02°29'W
37'
35'
33'
31'
ARZAL
Workshops
5M entrance to Vilaine
Lock
Sluices
Wire
47°30'N Moorings
Prohibited Area
Channel Dredged to 4·2m
Moorings
La Roche Bernard 3·5M
CAMOËL
02°23'W
Port de la Roche Bernard
New Port
Old Port

9.21.26 VILAINE RIVER

Morbihan **47°30'·38N 02°28'·71W** (1st lt buoys)

CHARTS AC 2823; SHOM 7033, 7144; ECM 546; Imray C39. Note: 2823 ends at the river mouth. 7144 (1:15,000) is advised; it covers the approaches and up-river to La Roche-Bernard.

TIDES +0500 Dover; ML (Pénerf) 3·3; Duration 0610; Zone –0100

Standard Port BREST (⟵)

Times				Height (metres)			
High Water		Low Water		MHWS	MHWN	MLWN	MLWS
0000	0600	0000	0600	6·9	5·4	2·6	1·0
1200	1800	1200	1800				
Differences TRÉHIGUIER							
+0035	–0020	–0005	–0010	–1·4	–1·0	–0·5	–0·3
PÉNERF RIVER							
+0020	–0025	–0015	–0015	–1·5	–1·1	–0·6	–0·3

SHELTER Some shelter up-river on 🅥s off Tréhiguier. Total shelter above Arzal barrage in non-tidal waters: marinas at Arzal (N bank) and Camoël (S bank); and 3·5M upstream at La Roche Bernard on 🅥 pontoon between Old and New ports; also at Foleux marina, 4½M up-river. Masted yachts can transit Cran bridge (opens 0900, 1000, 1100, 1430, 1630, 1830 & 1930 in season) to reach Redon marina (☎ 02·99.71.35.28), with mast crane and access to the Brittany canals (9.18.14).

NAVIGATION WPT 47°28'·95N 02°33'·96W, 052°/3·3M to Penlan lt ho; see chartlet opposite. The 3 appr's to the river mouth are:

1. Passe de la Grande Accroche: Penlan lt ho ≠ Abbey de Prières 052°. Marks are reportedly conspic by day.
2. Penlan lt ≠ Billiers ch tr 025·5°, leaving La Varlingue Rk (0·3m) close to stbd.
3. Passe de la Varlingue (unlit): W wall ≠ Abbey Tr 023°, passing close to WCM bcn and oyster poles off Le Logui.

In strong onshore winds esp at sp ebb seas break on La Vilaine bar (min 0·5m). Best to enter/leave on last of the flood. At river ent Petit Sécé W bn tr is easier to see than Nos 1 & 2 buoys. River is well buoyed up to Tréhiguier and adequately so beyond; keep strictly to buoyed chan as river silts.

Arzal lock opens at H, up to 9 times per day, 0700–2100 (LT) in Jul/ Aug; in other months 0800, 0900, 1100, 1400, 1600, 1800, 1900, 2000LT. But times vary daily: call Ch 09 or ☎ 02·97·45·01·15 for recorded info. Keep strictly to the buoyed chan to avoid the prohib area (Y buoys) below/above the dam. There are 🅥s and room to ⚓ below the dam to await lock opening.

LIGHTS AND MARKS See chartlet and 9.21.4. Two Dir lts are visible in the approaches:

1. Basse Bertrand, 14m G twr. The W sector (040°-054°) overlaps the W sector of Penlan in Passe de la Grande Accroche.
2. Pte de Penlan, 18m W tr, R bands; W sector 052°-060°.

On S side of lock the red control twr is conspic.

R/T Lock Ch 18 (HX). Arzal-Camoël marina Ch 09 (French). La Roche Bernard, Foleux and Redon Ch 09. Pont de Cran Ch 10.

TELEPHONE ARZAL/CAMOËL: Lock 02·97·41·28·39; Pont de Cran 02·99·90·11·31; Aff Mar 02·99·90·32·62; CROSS 02·97·55·35·35; ⊖ 02·97·63·18·71 at Vannes; Auto 08·92·68·08·56; Brit Consul 02·51·72·72·60; Dr 02·97.45.01.21; Ⓗ 02·99.90.61.20.

FACILITIES ARZAL/CAMOËL: **Marina** (630 total, inc 25 🅥 on each bank) HM ☎/℻ 02·97·45·02·98 is at Arzal, ☎/℻ as above, €1.60, ⊡, BH (35 ton), P & D H24, Gaz, SM, ME, El, ⚒, CH, Ⓔ, R, Bar. Note: these facilities are all at Arzal. Camoël has showers.
Towns (both 3km) 🛒, R, Bar, Ⓑ, ✉.
LA ROCHE BERNARD: **New Port** (110) ☎ 02·99·90·62·17, ℻ 02·99·90·73·93, €1.60, M, ME, El, Ⓔ, ⚒, CH, C(13T); **Old Port** (200), ⊡, C, CH, Slip. **Town** P & D (cans), 🛒, Gaz, R, Bar, Ice, ✉, Ⓑ, ⇌ (Pontchateau), ✈ (Nantes or Rennes). **Foleux:** ☎ 02·99.91.80.87. Marina on N bank; buoys off both banks. FW, ⏚, R.

9.21.27 PIRIAC

Loire Atlantique **47°23'·02N 02°32'·67W**

CHARTS AC 2823; Imray C39, 40; SHOM 7033, 7136; ECM 546

TIDES As for 9.21.28. Zone –0100. HW +0505 on Dover (UT); ML 3·3m; Duration 0605.

SHELTER Good in marina, E of the drying FV hbr, but may be exposed to N'lies. Access HW±3 over sill 2·2m above CD; for draft <1.5m HW±4, more at nps. The retaining wall is marked by Y SPM perches, and the flap gate by a PHM & SHM perch. IPTS, sigs 2 and 4, which shows when depth over sill is > 1·5m. 4 new yacht pontoons were installed (2004) in the W part of hbr together with new wall retaining approx 2m.

NAVIGATION WPT 47°23'·69N 02°32'·36W, 197°/7ca to hbr ent in the W sector (194°-201°) of Piriac lt, Oc (2) WRG 6s.

Plateau de Piriac extends about 1M W and N from the hbr; to the SW it is marked by a WCM buoy, Q (9) 15s, and to the NNW by Le Rohtrès NCM bcn twr and by Grand Norven NCM lt bcn, Q. Do not attempt to pass S of these bcns even near HW.

At night the W sectors of Île Dumet lt (272°-285°) and of Pte de Mesquer lt (067°-072°) help to position within the W sector of Piriac lt; care is required.

LIGHTS AND MARKS See 9.21.4 and the chartlet for details of the lights. Piriac church belfry is a conspic daymark, aligned approx 197° with chan. The Sig stn at Pte de Castelli, 8ca SW of the hbr, is a conspic white, prow-shaped structure.

R/T VHF Ch 09.

TELEPHONE HM ☎ 02·40·23·52·32 , ℻ 02·40·15·51·78. Aff Mar 02·40·23·33·35; ⊖ 02·40·23·32·51; CROSS 02·97· 55·35·35; Auto 08·92·68·08·44; SNSM 02·40·23·55·74 (Jul-Aug only).

FACILITIES Marina (480+20🅥), €1.98, D, P (cans) on quay, Slip, C (15 tons), CH, Ⓔ, El, ME, ⚒; drying M, in FV hbr. The small town is attractive with R, Bar, 🛒, Ⓑ, ✉

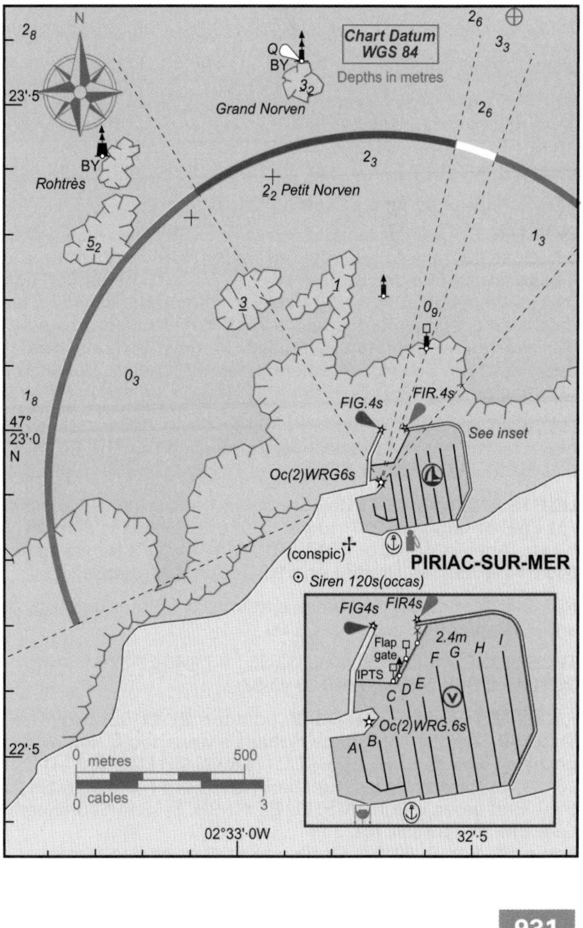
Chart Datum
WGS 84
Depths in metres
Grand Norven
Q
BY
Rohtrès
BY
Petit Norven
23'·5
47°
23'·0
N
22'·5
FIG.4s
FIR.4s
See inset
Oc(2)WRG6s
(conspic)
PIRIAC-SUR-MER
Siren 120s(occas)
FIG4s
FIR4s
Flap gate
IPTS
2.4m
Oc(2)WRG.6s
0 metres 500
0 cables 3
02°33'·0W
32'·5

9.21.28 LA TURBALLE

Loire Atlantique **47°20´·70N 02°30´·89W**

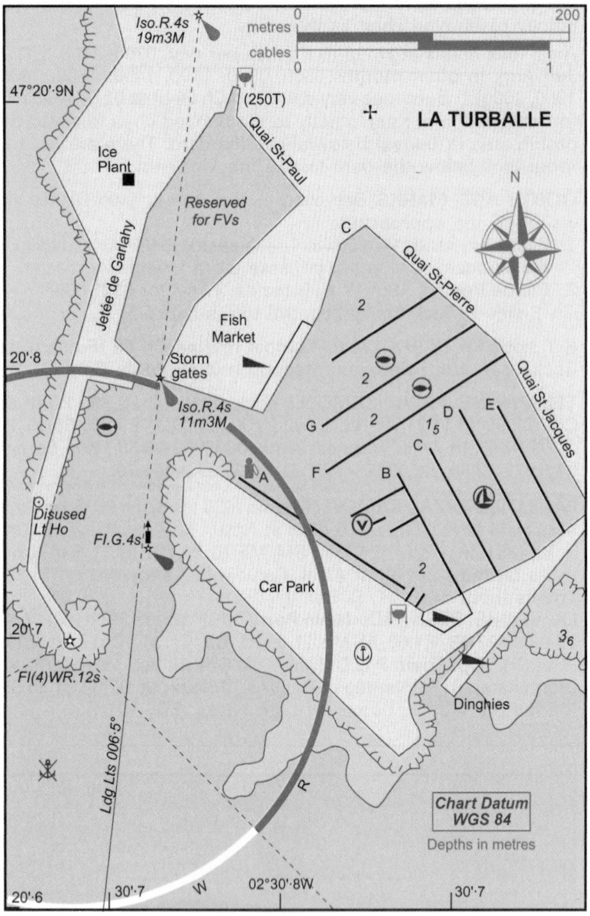
Iso.R.4s
19m3M
metres
cables
47°20'·9N
(250T)
LA TURBALLE
Quai St-Paul
Ice Plant
Reserved for FVs
Jetée de Garlahy
Quai St-Pierre
Fish Market
Storm gates
Iso.R.4s
11m3M
Quai St Jacques
Disused Lt Ho
Fl.G.4s
Car Park
Fl(4)WR.12s
Dinghies
Ldg Lts 006·5°
Chart Datum
WGS 84
Depths in metres
02°30'·8W
30'·7
20'·8
20'·7
20'·6

CHARTS AC 2823; Imray C39, 40; SHOM 6826, 7033; ECM 546

TIDES Approx as for Le Croisic 9.21.28.

SHELTER Good in all winds, but in strong SSW'lies heavy swell can close the hbr. Access H24. Inside ent, turn hard stbd round a blind corner into the marina (1·5-2m). Visitors are packed tight into the rectangular box off B pontoon, although if staying a few days a vacant finger berth may be allotted on request. In Jul/Aug the marina is sometimes closed to new arrivals due to overcrowding. Call before entering; see R/T below. In winds N to E it is possible to ⚓ S of the hbr. There is an active FV fleet.

NAVIGATION WPT 47°20´·19N 02°30´·99W, 006·5°/5ca to W bkwtr lt. The ent is not easily seen until S of the hbr. From the SW avoid shoals off Le Croisic and Plateau du Four 5·6M SW.

LIGHTS AND MARKS By day Trescalan ✠ and water tr (conspic), 1M ENE of hbr, lead 070° to just S of ent. R bn tr is 80m off W bkwtr. Appr in W sector (315°-060°) of W bkwtr lt to pick up the 006·5° ldg lts. See chartlet and 9.21.4 for light details.

R/T Call Marina Ch 09 before entering. If full in Jul/Aug, an announcement is made on Ch 09.

TELEPHONE Aff Mar 02·40·23·33·35; ⊜ 02·40·23·32·51; Auto 08·92·68·08·44; SNSM 02·40·23·42·67.

FACILITIES **Marina** (290+ 20 Ⓥ, pontoon B), ☎ 02·40·23·41·65, (fax) 02.40.23.47.64, plaisance.turballe@wanadoo.fr www.port-peche-turballe.fr €1.56, Slip, M, C (16 tons), BH (140 tons), D (min 10 ltrs, by card only H24; fuel berth & BH are more suitable for FVs), P at garage 500m, ME, El, Ⓔ, ⚒, CH, (launderette), (disabled) in Capitainerie, Gaz, SM, YC, SHOM, Ice.
Town (shop), Bar, R, Ⓑ, ✉, Dr, Bus to St Nazaire and Nantes.

9.21.29 LE CROISIC

Loire Atlantique **47°18'·52N 02°31'·35W**

CHARTS AC 2646, 2986, 2823; Imray C39; SHOM 7033, 7395, 7145 (the preferred large scale chart); ECM 546, 547

TIDES +0450 Dover; ML 3·3; Duration 0605; Zone –0100

Standard Port BREST (⟵)

Times				Height (metres)			
High Water		Low Water		MHWS	MHWN	MLWN	MLWS
0000	0600	0000	0600	6·9	5·4	2·6	1·0
1200	1800	1200	1800				
Differences LE CROISIC							
+0015	–0040	–0020	–0015	–1·5	–1·1	–0·6	–0·3

SHELTER Four drying (1·7m) basins (*Chambres)* are formed by islets *(Jonchères*). Berth, bows in, at the marina (last *Chambre des Vases*), or against the marina's outer wall, access HW±1. ⚓ E of inner ldg lts, but not advised due to very strong streams.

NAVIGATION WPT 47°18´·97N 02°31´·65W, 155·5°/5ca to Tréhic bkwtr head. Beware the rks at Hergo SHM bcn twr. Note: the W sector (093°-137°) of Tréhic lt, Iso WG 4s, lies between dangers in the two green sectors. Keep strictly on the ldg lines as appr and hbr dry extensively to the E of the chan, which is dredged 2m at first, then 1·6m and 0·5m finally. Sp tides reach 4kn. Safest ent is HW±1 sp, HW±2 np.

LIGHTS AND MARKS The hospital at Pte de Pen Bron and ch dome are conspic. The 3 sets of ldg lines are: Outer 155·5°: both Dir Q; R □s on W pylons, rear has G top. Middle 173·4°: both Dir QG; Y □s with G stripe on G & W pylons, almost obsc'd by trees. Inner 134·7°: both Dir QR; R/W chequered □s on Fish market roof. At the marina the BY is a large, white conspic bldg.

R/T VHF Ch 09 (0800-1200; 1330-2000 in season).

TELEPHONE Aff Mar 02·40·23·06·56; CROSS 02·97·55·35·35; ⊜ 02·40·23·05·38; Météo 08·92·68·02·44; Police 02·40·23·00·19; Dr 02·40·23·01·70; Ⓗ 02·40·23·01·12; Brit Consul 02·51·72·72·60.

FACILITIES **Marina** (335+25 Ⓥ) €1.10, plus €0.20 holiday tax , ☎ 02·40·23·10·95, (fax) 02·40·15·75·92, Mob 06·88·99·05·01. **Quai** Slip, C (8 & 180 ton), ME, El, ⚒, CH, Ⓔ, YC, Divers, (disabled).
Town P & D (cans), (shop), Gaz, R, Bar, ✉, Ⓑ, (rail), ✈ (St Nazaire).

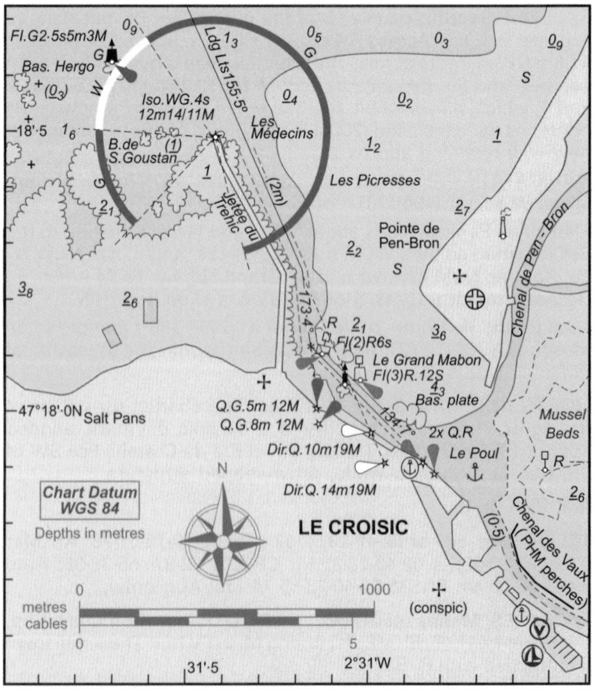
Fl.G2·5s5m3M
Bas. Hergo
Ldg Lts155·5°
Iso.WG.4s
12m14/11M
Les Médecins
B.de S.Goustan
Les Picresses
Jetée du Tréhic
Pointe de Pen-Bron
Chenal de Pen-Bron
Fl(2)R6s
Le Grand Mabon
Fl(3)R.12S
Bas. plate
47°18'·0N
Salt Pans
Q.G.5m 12M
Q.G.8m 12M
2x Q.R
Dir.Q.10m19M
Le Poul
Mussel Beds
Dir.Q.14m19M
Chart Datum
WGS 84
Depths in metres
LE CROISIC
Chenal des Vaux (PHM perches)
metres
cables
(conspic)
31'·5
2°31'W
-18'·5

9.21.30 LE POULIGUEN

Loire Atlantique **47°16'·42N 02°25'·38W**

CHARTS AC 2646, 2986; Imray C39; SHOM 7395, 7145; ECM 547

TIDES Sp +0435 Dover, Nps +0530 Dover; ML 3·3; Duration Sp 0530, Nps 0645; Zone –0100

Standard Port BREST (⟵)

Times				Height (metres)			
High Water		Low Water		MHWS	MHWN	MLWN	MLWS
0000	0600	0000	0600	6·9	5·4	2·6	1·0
1200	1800	1200	1800				
Differences LE POULIGUEN							
+0020	–0025	–0020	–0025	–1·5	–1·1	–0·6	–0·3

SHELTER Very good, except in SE winds. In strong S winds, beware swell and breakers. 30 Ⓥ berths on pontoon A, to stbd at ent. Yachts up to 2m draft can stay afloat inside drying entrance. Beware strong ebb tide. Fixed bridge up-river has 3m clearance MHWS. Le Pornichet, 3M to the E, is a much easier approach and ent.

NAVIGATION WPT 47°15'·54N 02°24'·34W, Basse Martineau unlit PHM buoy, 321°/1.1M to hbr ent. Best appr at HW –1 from W/SW between Pte de Penchâteau and Les Evens (drying reef). From Basse Martineau, leave La Vieille SHM perch and Petits Impairs bcn twr, Fl (2) G 6s, well to stbd, and 3 PHM bns close to port. The inner chan shifts, dries approx 1·5m and is marked at longish intervals by one PHM and 5 SHM poles. Reefs running 4M ESE towards Grand Charpentier lt ho, Q WRG, form a barrier across the Baie du Pouliguen which may be entered through any of 4 passes.

LIGHTS AND MARKS W jetty, QR, is a slim, conspic white column, R top. The final SHM pole marks the narrowing chan and E training wall which covers. Navigational lights are very hard to see against shore lts of La Baule and night appr is not advised. See chartlet and 9.21.4 for light details.

R/T Pouliguen VHF Ch 09, 0900-2000 in season.

TELEPHONE ⊖ 02·40·61·32·04; Aff Mar 02·40·23·06·56; SNSM 02·40·61·03·20; CROSS 02·97·55·35·35; Auto 08.92.68.08.44; Police 02·40·24·48·17; Dr 08·36·69·12·34.

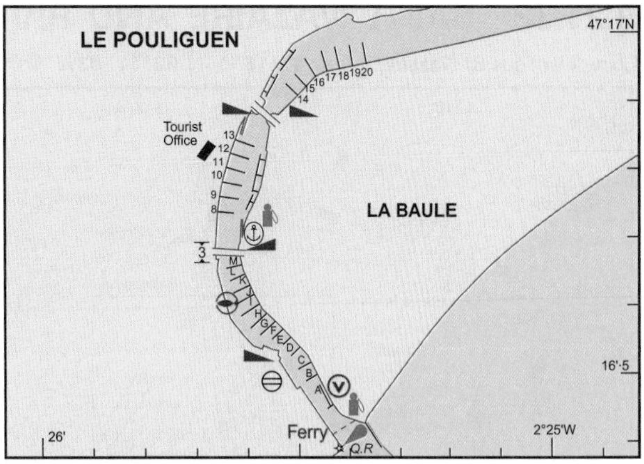
LE POULIGUEN
47°17'N
Tourist Office
LA BAULE
16'·5
26'
Ferry
Q.R
2°25'W

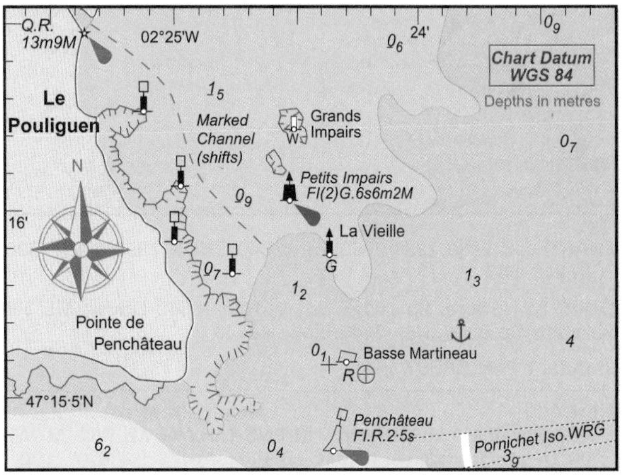
Q.R.
13m9M
02°25'W
24'
Chart Datum WGS 84
Depths in metres
Le Pouliguen
Marked Channel (shifts)
Grands Impairs
Petits Impairs Fl(2)G.6s6m2M
La Vieille
16'
Pointe de Penchâteau
Basse Martineau
47°15·5'N
Penchâteau Fl.R.2·5s
Pornichet Iso.WRG

FACILITIES E Quays (Pontoons 720+30 Ⓥ), ☎ 02·40·11·97·97, 📠 02·40.11·97·98; €1.91, Slip, P, D, C (18 ton), M, ME, ⚒, CH, Ⓔ, El, Divers, SM; **La Baule YC** ☎ 02·40·60·57·87.
Town 🛒, Gaz, R, Bar, ✉, Ⓑ, ⇌, ✈ (St Nazaire).

9.21.31 PORNICHET

Loire Atlantique **47°15'·51N 02°21'·11W**

CHARTS AC 2986, 2989; Imray C39; SHOM 7395, 6797, 7145; ECM 547

TIDES Sp +0435 Dover, Nps +0530 Dover; ML 3·3; Duration Sp 0530, Nps 0645; Zone –0100

Standard Port BREST (⟵)

Times				Height (metres)			
High Water		Low Water		MHWS	MHWN	MLWN	MLWS
0000	0600	0000	0600	6·9	5·4	2·6	1·0
1200	1800	1200	1800				
Differences PORNICHET							
+0020	–0045	–0022	–0022	–1·4	–1·0	–0·5	–0·2

SHELTER Very good in large man-made marina with excellent facilities. Access at all tides for <2·5m draft. Best to pre-call for berth, or tempy berth on hammerheads A, B, D, F, G, L, M, N.

NAVIGATION WPT 47°15'·41N 02°22'·15W, 082·5°/0·7M to N-facing ent in W sector (081°-084°) of bkwtr lt. From SW, track 037°/1·5M between Les Evens PHM and Les Troves SHM unlit buoys. From SSE track 333°/3M from Le Grand Charpentier lt ho.

LIGHTS AND MARKS Navigational lts are very hard to see against shore lts of La Baule. There are no conspic daymarks. A forest of masts in the marina is the most obvious feature.

R/T VHF Ch 09.

TELEPHONE HM 02·40·61·03·20, 📠 02·40·61·87·18; Aff Mar 02·40·23·06·56; CROSS 02·97·55·35·35; ⊖ 02·40·45·88·78; Météo 02·40·90·08·80; Auto 08·92·68·08·44; Ⓗ (St Nazaire) 02·40·90·60·60; Dr (La Baule) 02·40·60·17·20; Brit Consul 02·51·72·72·60.

FACILITIES Marina (1000+150 Ⓥ) ☎ 02·40·61·03·20, €1.97, Slip, P, D, BH (24 ton), 🛒, R, Bar, ME, El, Ⓔ, ⚒, CH, SHOM. No ⊡.
Town Bar, R, 🛒, ⊡, Dr, Ⓑ, ✉, ⇌, ✈ (St Nazaire).

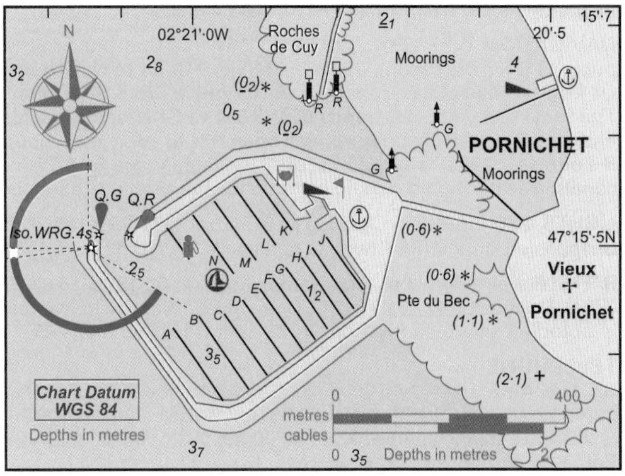
02°21'·0W
Roches de Cuy
Moorings
15'·7
20'·5
PORNICHET
Moorings
Q.G
Q.R
Iso.WRG.4s
47°15'·5N
Vieux Pornichet
Pte du Bec
Chart Datum WGS 84
Depths in metres
metres
cables
400
Depths in metres

9.21.32 SAINT NAZAIRE AND RIVER LOIRE TO NANTES

Loire Atlantique **St Nazaire, E lock 47°16´·51N 02°11´·93W** . **Nantes, Trentemoult 47°11´·74N 01°34´·77W**

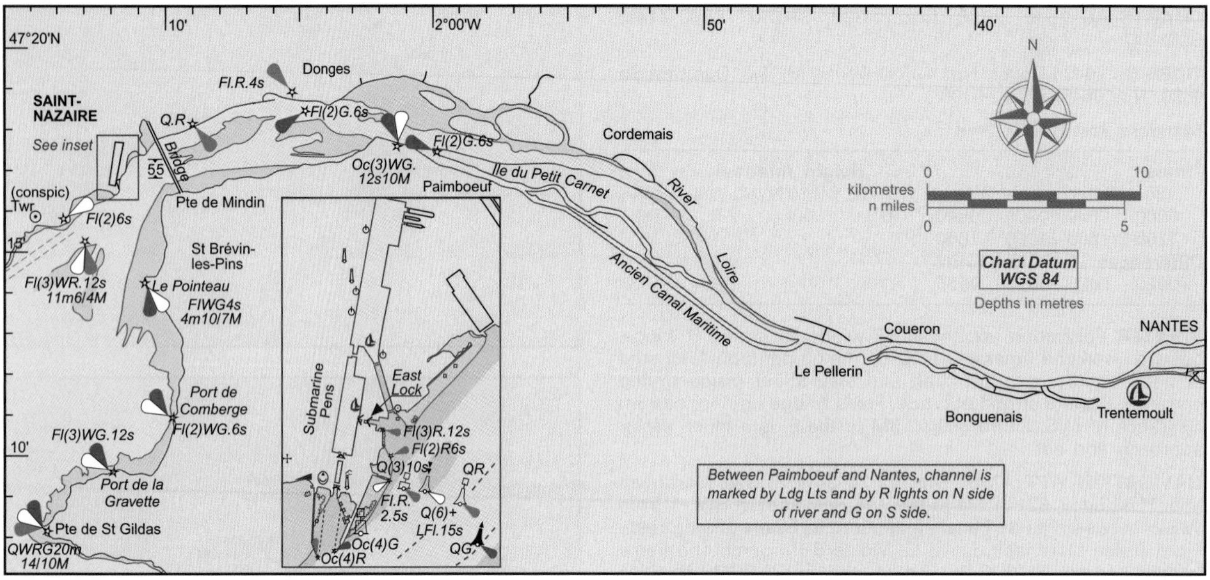
47°20'N
10'
2°00'W
50'
40'
N
SAINT-NAZAIRE
See inset
Donges
Fl.R.4s
Q.R
Fl(2)G.6s
Fl(2)G.6s
Oc(3)WG. 12s10M
Paimboeuf
Île du Petit Carnet
Cordemais
River Loire
Ancien Canal Maritime
Bridge
55
(conspic) Twr
Fl(2)6s
Pte de Mindin
St Brévin-les-Pins
15'
Fl(3)WR.12s 11m6/4M
Le Pointeau
FlWG4s 4m10/7M
Port de Comberge
Fl(2)WG.6s
Fl(3)WG.12s
10'
Port de la Gravette
Pte de St Gildas
QWRG20m 14/10M
Submarine Pens
East Lock
Fl(3)R.12s
Fl(2)R6s
Q(3)10s
QR
Fl.R. 2.5s
Q(6)+ LFl.15s
Oc(4)G
Oc(4)R
QG
kilometres
n miles
0
10
0
5
Chart Datum WGS 84
Depths in metres
Coueron
NANTES
Le Pellerin
Bonguenais
Trentemoult
Between Paimboeuf and Nantes, channel is marked by Ldg Lts and by R lights on N side of river and G on S side.

CHARTS AC 2986, 2989, 2985; Imray C40; SHOM 7395, 6797, 7396; ECM 248, 547

TIDES St Nazaire: Sp +0445 Dover, Nps –0540 Dover; ML 3·6; Duration Sp 0640, Nps 0445; Zone –0100

Standard Port BREST (⟵)

Times				Height (metres)			
High Water		Low Water		MHWS	MHWN	MLWN	MLWS
0000	0600	0000	0600	6·9	5·4	2·6	1·0
1200	1800	1200	1800				
Differences ST NAZAIRE							
+0030	–0040	–0010	–0010	–1·1	–0·8	–0·4	–0·2
LE GRAND CHARPENTIER							
+0015	–0045	–0025	–0020	–1·5	–1·1	–0·6	–0·3
DONGES 02°04´·19W							
+0035	–0035	+0005	+0005	–1·0	–0·7	–0·5	–0·4
CORDEMAIS 01°53´·32W							
+0055	–0005	+0105	+0030	–0·7	–0·5	–0·7	–0·4
LE PELLERIN 01°45´·70W							
+0110	+0010	+0145	+0100	–0·7	–0·5	–0·9	–0·4
NANTES (Chantenay)							
+0135	+0055	+0215	+0125	–0·6	–0·3	–0·8	–0·1

SHELTER Hbr is mainly shipyards/commercial. Yachts berth in Bassin de St Nazaire or at S end of Bassin Penhoët. Nearest ⚓ in Bonne Anse, 2·5M downriver on NW bank.

NAVIGATION WPT 47°07´·59N 02°20´·05W (La Couronnee SHM buoy, Fl (2) G 6s, Racon), 025·5°/6·3M via S Chan to No 7 buoy. Or from W via N Chan, join S Chan (13·2m) at No 6 SHM buoy. The inner buoyed chan trends 054°/3·5M to St Nazaire. Yachts enter via E lock/swing bridge which open H24 at every even hour. R Loire (AC 2985) is navigable 28M to Nantes; see 9.18.14 for canals. Yachts should remain just outside the buoyed channels.

LIGHTS AND MARKS S Chan ldg lts 025·5°: both Q 6/36m 22/24M. Suspension bridge (R/W twrs) is conspic 1·3M NE of the E lock.

R/T St Nazaire Port/Lock and Nantes Port: Ch 06 **12** 14 16 67 69 (H24). Donges Ch 12 16 69 (H24). Tidal info (St Nazaire to Nantes) is automatically broadcast on Ch 73 at H, +15, +30 and +45.

TELEPHONE
ST NAZAIRE HM 02·40·00·45·20, 📠 02·40.00·45·66; Aff Mar 02·40·22·46·32; CROSS 02·97·55·35·35; SNSM 02·40·61·03·20; ⊖ 02·40·66·82·65; Météo 02·40·90·00·80; Auto 08.92.68.08.44; Police 02·40·70·55·00; Dr 02·40·22·15·32; Ⓗ 02·40·90·60·60.
NANTES HM 02·40·73·41·47, 📠 02·40.44·20·02; ⊖ 02·40·73·39·55; Aff Mar 02·40·73·18·70; Météo 02·40·84·80·19; Ⓗ 02·40·48·33·33; Brit Consul 02·51·72·72·60.

FACILITIES ST NAZAIRE **Quai** P, D, L, C, M, ME, El, ⚒, CH, Ⓔ, SHOM. **Town** 🛒, Gaz, R, Bar, ✉, Ⓑ, ⇌, ✈.
NANTES **Quai** C, CH, SHOM, ME, El, Ⓔ; **Trentemoult** AB. **City** all facilities: ✉, Ⓑ, ⇌, ✈. Ferry: St Malo/Roscoff.

MINOR HARBOURS FROM PTE ST GILDAS TO ST NAZAIRE Three small hbrs (below, from seaward) lie NE of Pte de St-Gildas, on the E side of the R Loire estuary; see chartlet above. They are flanked by shellfish beds on rky ledges drying to about 4ca offshore; they are sheltered from W'lies but open to N'lies.

Charts are AC 2986, 2981, 2989; SHOM 7395, 6797; ECM 547. Tidal data may be interpolated from Le Grand Charpentier, St-Nazaire (9.21.32) and Pornic (9.22.7). Lt details see 9.21.4. The bay is shallow. Note: 4M N of Pte de St-Gildas is La Truie rk, 3m and marked by unlit IDM bn; 1·5M W of it are rocks drying 1·2m.

SAINT-GILDAS (Anse du Boucau), Loire Atlantique, **47°08'·47N 02°14'·74W.** The hbr is 5ca N of Pte de St Gildas lt ho, Q WRG (see 9.21.4). The hbr bkwtr extends 3ca N, with a large automatic tide gauge and ☆ Fl (2) G 6s at its N end. An unlit SHM bn, and a SHM buoy, Fl G 2·5s (May-Sept), lie 1ca and 2ca NW of bkwtr hd. Appr from about 1M N of Pte de St-Gildas on a brg of 177° or at night in its W sector 174°-180°. L'Ilot rky ledge is marked by a PHM bn. Pick up a mooring in 1·5m in the N part of the hbr or dry out further S. HM ☎ 02.40.21.60.07. VHF Ch 09. Facilities: Slips, YC, FW, C (5 ton), 🛒 at Préfailles 1M to E.

PORT DE LA GRAVETTE, Loire Atlantique, **47°09'·64N 02°12'·71W;** this is position of the lt on end of the bkwtr, Fl (3) WG 12s. The hbr is 2·2M NE of Pte de St-Gildas. Daymarks are bkwtr lt in transit 130° with La Treille water tr, 2M inland. Shellfish beds to the W and E are marked by unlit NCM bns. On rounding the 600m long bkwtr, turn stbd between lateral buoys; there is about 1·2m water in the N part of the hbr which dries closer in. Many local moorings, few facilities.

PORT DE COMBERGE, Loire Atlantique, **47°10'·52N 02°09'·96W;** this is position of S bkwtr lt, Fl (2) WG 6s. Appr on 136° in the W sector or by day with the bkwtr lt in transit with the disused lt ho beyond. Beware Les Moutons, rk drying 0·7m, 7½ca NW of the bkwtr lt, close to the approach track. The ent is narrow; tiny hbr dries about 2m, access from half-flood. HM ☎ 02.40.27.82.85; Facilities: M, FW, YC, Slip, C (6 ton), L. Other facilities at nearby town of St Michel-Chef-Chef.

Area 22

South Biscay
River Loire to Spanish Border

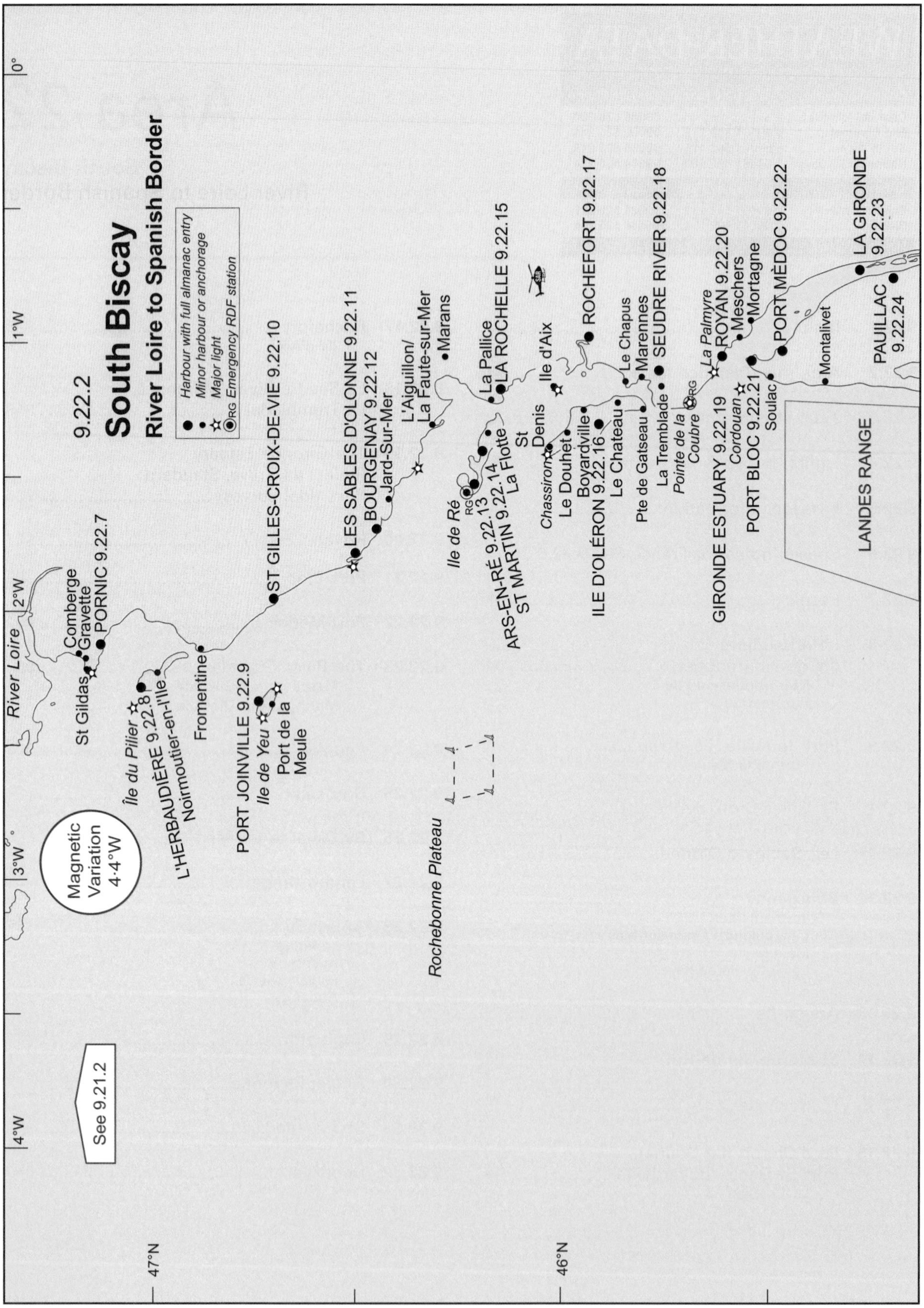
9.22.2
South Biscay
River Loire to Spanish Border
Harbour with full almanac entry
Minor harbour or anchorage
Major light
RG Emergency RDF station
Magnetic Variation 4·4°W
See 9.21.2
4°W
3°W
2°W
1°W
0°
47°N
46°N
River Loire
St Gildas
Comberge
Gravette
PORNIC 9.22.7
Île du Pilier
L'HERBAUDIÈRE 9.22.8
Noirmoutier-en-l'Ile
Fromentine
PORT JOINVILLE 9.22.9
Ile de Yeu
Port de la Meule
Rochebonne Plateau
ST GILLES-CROIX-DE-VIE 9.22.10
LES SABLES D'OLONNE 9.22.11
BOURGENAY 9.22.12
Jard-Sur-Mer
L'Aiguillon/
La Faute-sur-Mer
Marans
Ile de Ré
ARS-EN-RÉ 9.22.13
ST MARTIN 9.22.14
La Flotte
La Pallice
LA ROCHELLE 9.22.15
St Denis
Chassiron
Le Douhet
Ile d'Aix
ROCHEFORT 9.22.17
Boyardville
ILE D'OLÉRON 9.22.16
Le Chateau
Le Chapus
Marennes
Pte de Gatseau
SEUDRE RIVER 9.22.18
La Tremblade
Pointe de la Coubre
La Palmyre
GIRONDE ESTUARY 9.22.19
ROYAN 9.22.20
Cordouan
Meschers
Mortagne
PORT BLOC 9.22.21
Soulac
PORT MÈDOC 9.22.22
Montalivet
LANDES RANGE
PAUILLAC 9.22.24
LA GIRONDE 9.22.23

1. ***Le Conquet***	**1**																			
2. *St Nazaire*	145	**2**																		
3. Pornic	146	16	**3**																	
4. L'Herbaudière	144	16	10	**4**																
5. Port Joinville	147	35	30	20	**5**															
6. St Gilles-C-de-Vie	166	45	40	29	18	**6**														
7. Sables d'Olonne	181	65	55	40	31	16	**7**													
8. Bourgenay	190	74	64	49	40	25	9	**8**												
9. St Martin (I de Ré)	208	92	75	67	55	44	27	20	**9**											
10. La Rochelle	218	101	92	76	66	51	36	29	12	**10**										
11. Rochefort	242	126	116	102	84	75	61	54	36	26	**11**									
12. R La Seudre	242	125	116	100	89	71	58	52	33	24	30	**12**								
13. Port St Denis	220	103	94	78	59	48	33	30	21	13	26	22	**13**							
14. Port Bloc/Royan	234	122	115	107	97	85	71	60	56	52	68	27	42	14						
15. Bordeaux	289	177	170	162	152	140	126	115	111	107	123	82	97	55	**15**					
16. Cap Ferret	274	168	160	153	138	130	113	110	102	98	114	75	88	68	123	**16**				
17. Capbreton	316	220	215	211	192	186	169	166	165	156	172	131	145	124	179	58	**17**			
18. Anglet/Bayonne	328	232	223	223	200	195	181	178	177	168	184	143	157	132	187	70	12	**18**		
19. *Santander*	300	243	237	229	212	210	204	204	206	202	218	184	192	180	235	133	106	103	**19**	
20. *Cabo Finisterre*	382	404	399	390	377	395	393	394	406	407	423	399	397	401	456	376	370	373	274	**20**

DISTANCE TABLE

Approximate distances in nautical miles are by the most direct route, whilst avoiding dangers and allowing for Traffic Separation Schemes. Places in *italics* are in adjoining areas; places in **bold** are in 9.0.6, Cross-Channel Distances.

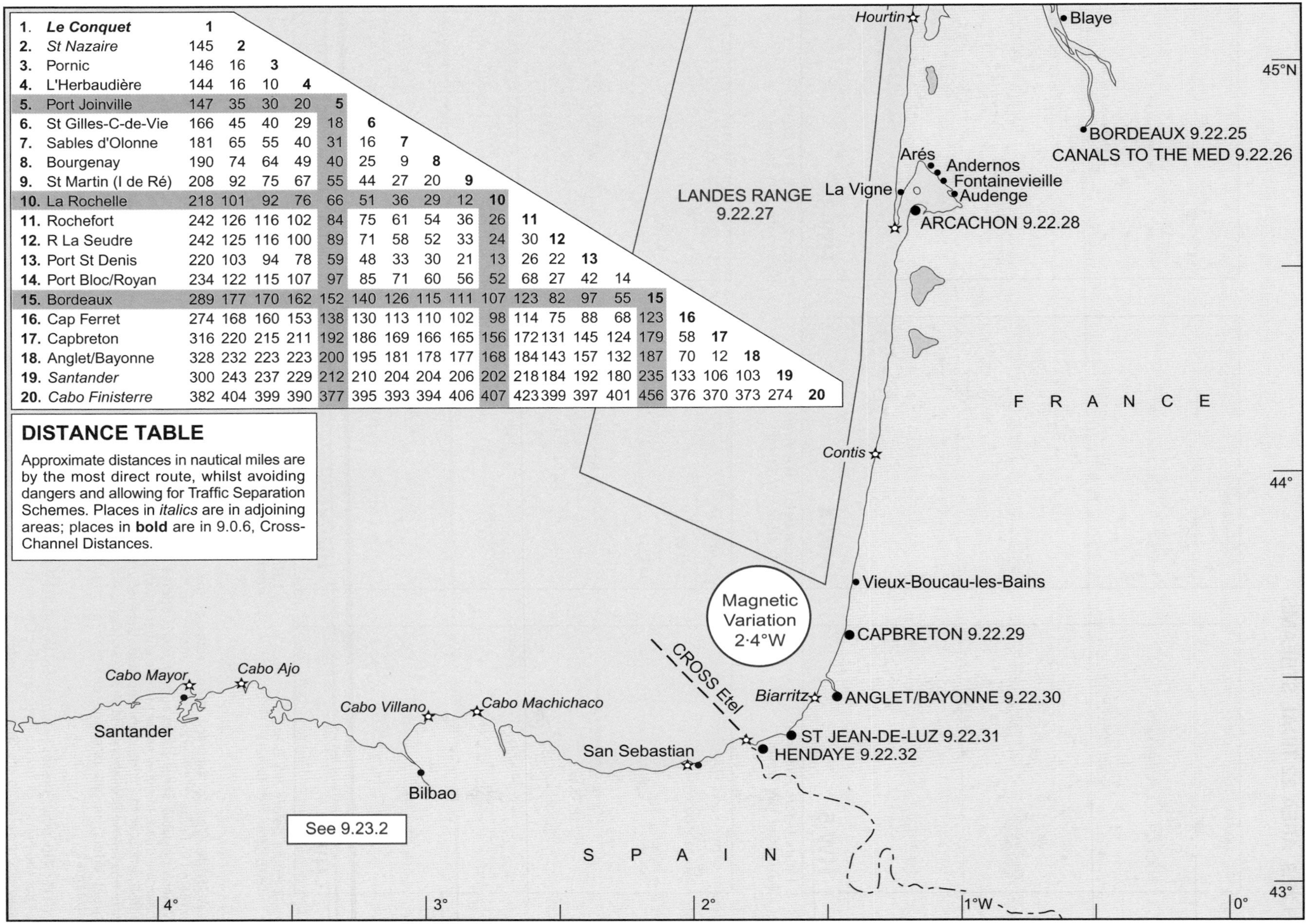
Hourtin
Blaye
45°N
BORDEAUX 9.22.25
CANALS TO THE MED 9.22.26
Arés
Andernos
Fontainevieille
Audenge
La Vigne
LANDES RANGE 9.22.27
ARCACHON 9.22.28
F R A N C E
Contis
44°
Vieux-Boucau-les-Bains
Magnetic Variation 2·4°W
CAPBRETON 9.22.29
CROSS Etel
Biarritz
ANGLET/BAYONNE 9.22.30
ST JEAN-DE-LUZ 9.22.31
HENDAYE 9.22.32
Cabo Mayor
Cabo Ajo
Santander
Cabo Villano
Cabo Machichaco
San Sebastian
Bilbao
See 9.23.2
S P A I N
4°
3°
2°
1°W
0°
43°

9.22.3 AREA 22 TIDAL STREAMS

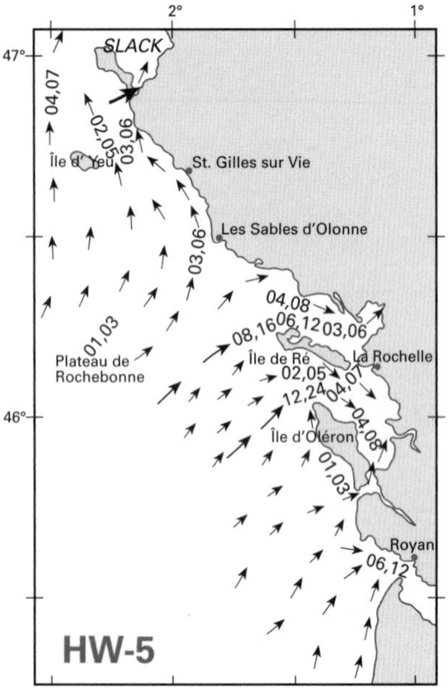
2°
1°
47°
46°
SLACK
04,07
02,05
03,06
Île d'Yeu
St. Gilles sur Vie
Les Sables d'Olonne
03,06
01,03
Plateau de Rochebonne
04,08
08,16
06,12
03,06
Île de Ré
La Rochelle
02,05
04,07
12,24
04,08
Île d'Oléron
01,03
Royan
06,12
HW-5

5 Hours before HW Brest
(0010 after HW Dover)

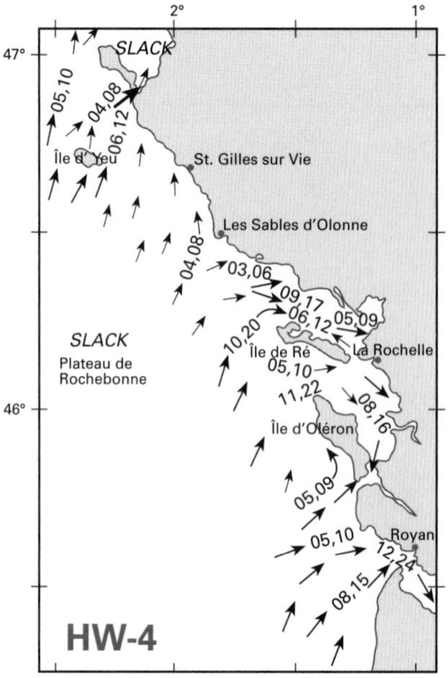
2°
1°
47°
46°
SLACK
05,10
04,08
06,12
Île d'Yeu
St. Gilles sur Vie
Les Sables d'Olonne
04,08
03,06
09,17
06,12
05,09
SLACK
Plateau de Rochebonne
10,20
Île de Ré
La Rochelle
05,10
11,22
08,16
Île d'Oléron
05,09
05,10
Royan
12,24
08,15
HW-4

4 Hours before HW Brest
(0110 after HW Dover)

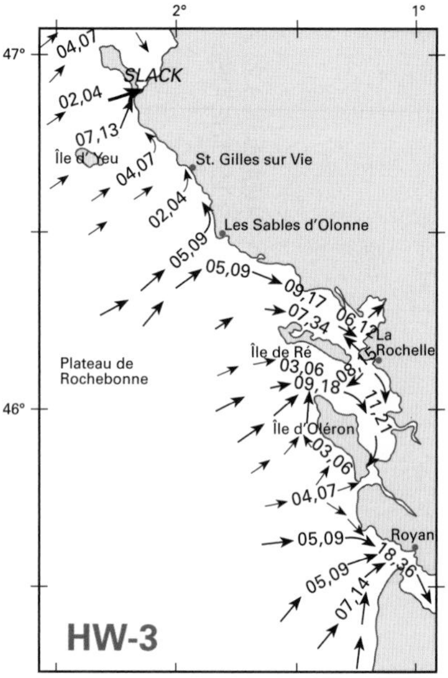
2°
1°
47°
46°
04,07
SLACK
02,04
07,13
Île d'Yeu
St. Gilles sur Vie
04,07
02,04
Les Sables d'Olonne
05,09
05,09
09,17
07,34
06,12
La Rochelle
Plateau de Rochebonne
Île de Ré
03,06
09,18
11,21
Île d'Oléron
03,06
04,07
05,09
Royan
18,36
05,09
07,14
HW-3

3 Hours before HW Brest
(0210 after HW Dover)

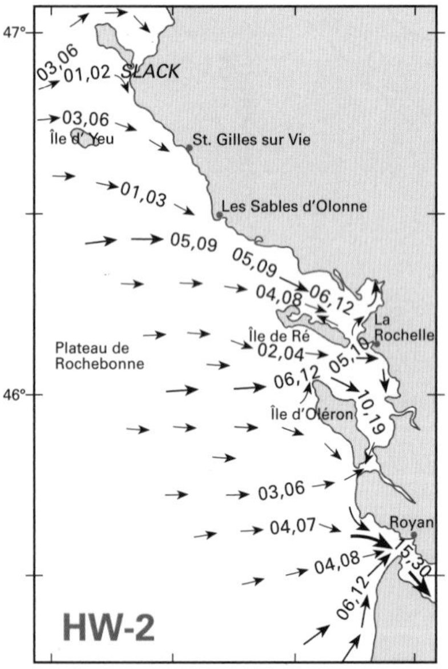
47°
46°
03,06
01,02
SLACK
03,06
Île d'Yeu
St. Gilles sur Vie
01,03
Les Sables d'Olonne
05,09
05,09
04,08
06,12
La Rochelle
Plateau de Rochebonne
Île de Ré
02,04
05,10
06,12
10,19
Île d'Oléron
03,06
04,07
Royan
04,08
06,12
HW-2

2 Hours before HW Brest
(0310 after HW Dover)

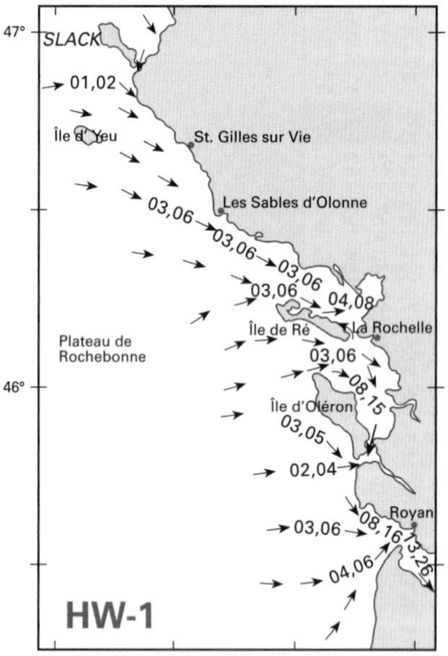
47°
46°
SLACK
01,02
Île d'Yeu
St. Gilles sur Vie
03,06
Les Sables d'Olonne
03,06
03,06
03,06
04,08
Plateau de Rochebonne
Île de Ré
La Rochelle
03,06
08,15
Île d'Oléron
03,05
02,04
03,06
Royan
08,16
13,26
04,06
HW-1

1 Hour before HW Brest
(0410 after HW Dover)

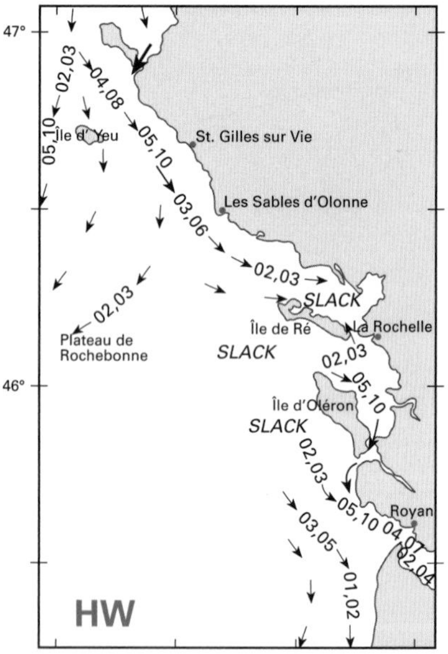
47°
46°
02,03
04,08
05,10
Île d'Yeu
St. Gilles sur Vie
05,10
03,06
Les Sables d'Olonne
02,03
02,03
SLACK
Plateau de Rochebonne
Île de Ré
La Rochelle
SLACK
02,03
05,10
Île d'Oléron
SLACK
02,03
05,10
04,07
02,04
Royan
03,05
01,02
HW

HW Brest
(0510 after HW Dover)

CAUTION: Due to the very strong rates of the tidal streams in some of the areas, many eddies may occur. Where possible some indication of these eddies has been included. In many areas there is either insufficient information or the eddies are unstable. Generally tidal streams are weak offshore and strong winds have a very great effect on the rate and direction of the tidal streams.

NOTE: No tidal stream information is published by either the French or British Hydrographic Offices for the area southwards to the Spanish border.

Northward 9.21.3

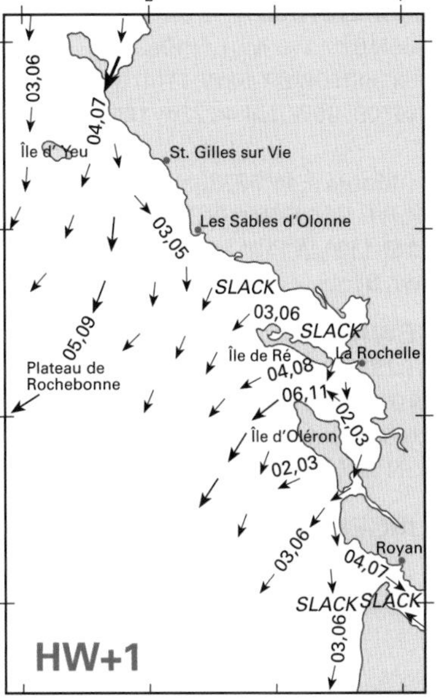
2°
1°
47°
46°
03,06
04,07
Île d'Yeu
St. Gilles sur Vie
Les Sables d'Olonne
03,05
SLACK
03,06
SLACK
05,09
Île de Ré
La Rochelle
04,08
Plateau de Rochebonne
06,11
02,03
Île d'Oléron
02,03
03,06
Royan
04,07
SLACK
SLACK
03,06
HW+1
1 Hour after HW Brest
(0610 after HW Dover)

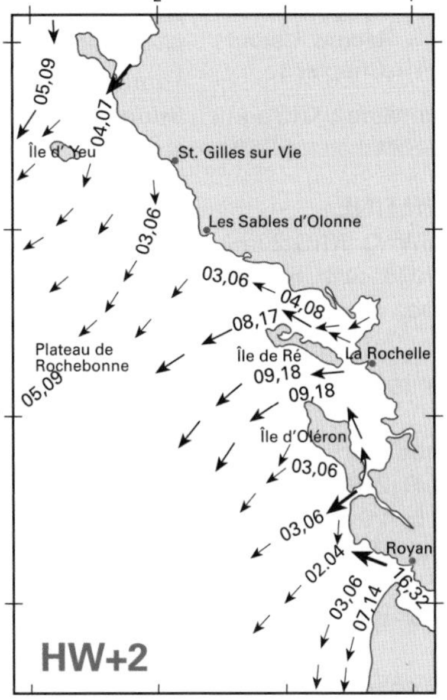
2°
1°
47°
46°
05,09
04,07
Île d'Yeu
St. Gilles sur Vie
03,06
Les Sables d'Olonne
03,06
04,08
08,17
Plateau de Rochebonne
Île de Ré
La Rochelle
05,09
09,18
09,18
Île d'Oléron
03,06
03,06
Royan
02,04
16,32
03,06
07,14
HW+2
2 Hours after HW Brest
(0515 before HW Dover)

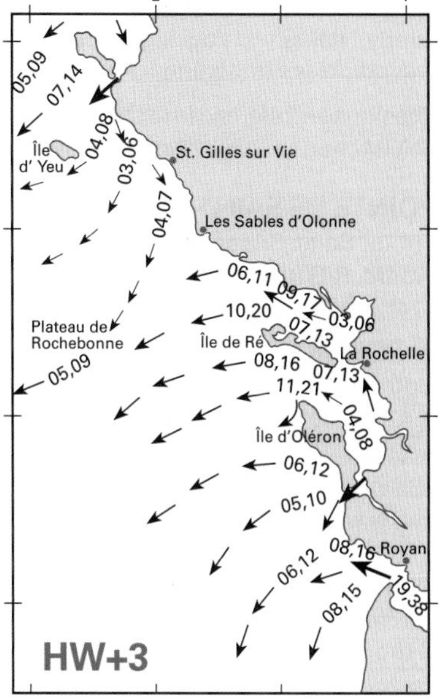
2°
1°
47°
46°
05,09
07,14
04,08
Île d' Yeu
03,06
St. Gilles sur Vie
04,07
Les Sables d'Olonne
06,11
09,17
10,20
03,06
Plateau de Rochebonne
07,13
Île de Ré
La Rochelle
08,16
07,13
05,09
11,21
04,08
Île d'Oléron
06,12
05,10
08,16
Royan
06,12
19,38
08,15
HW+3
3 Hours after HW Brest
(0415 before HW Dover)

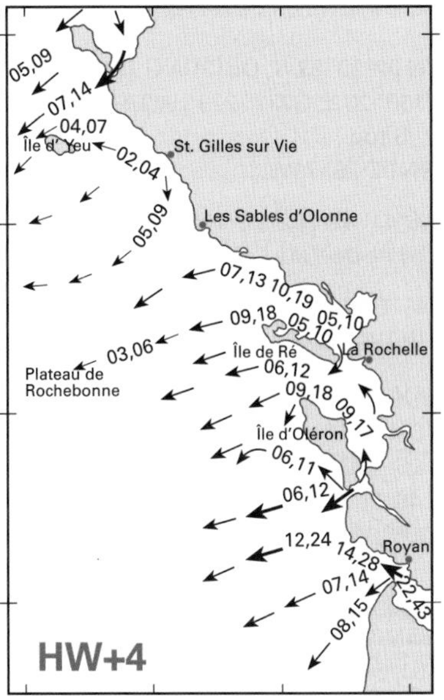
47°
46°
05,09
07,14
04,07
Île d'Yeu
02,04
St. Gilles sur Vie
05,09
Les Sables d'Olonne
07,13
10,19
09,18
05,10
05,10
03,06
Île de Ré
La Rochelle
Plateau de Rochebonne
06,12
09,18
09,17
Île d'Oléron
06,11
06,12
12,24
14,28
Royan
07,14
22,43
08,15
HW+4
4 Hours after HW Brest
(0315 before HW. Dover)

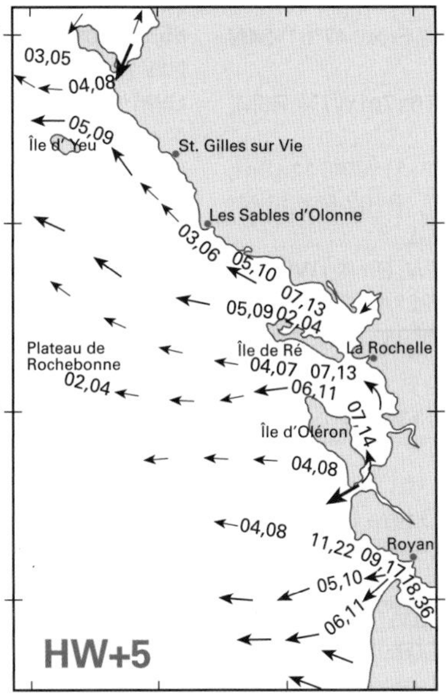
47°
46°
03,05
04,08
05,09
Île d'Yeu
St. Gilles sur Vie
Les Sables d'Olonne
03,06
05,10
07,13
05,09
02,04
Plateau de Rochebonne
Île de Ré
La Rochelle
02,04
04,07
07,13
06,11
07,14
Île d'Oléron
04,08
04,08
11,22
09,17
Royan
05,10
18,36
06,11
HW+5
5 Hours after HW Brest
(0215 before HW Dover)

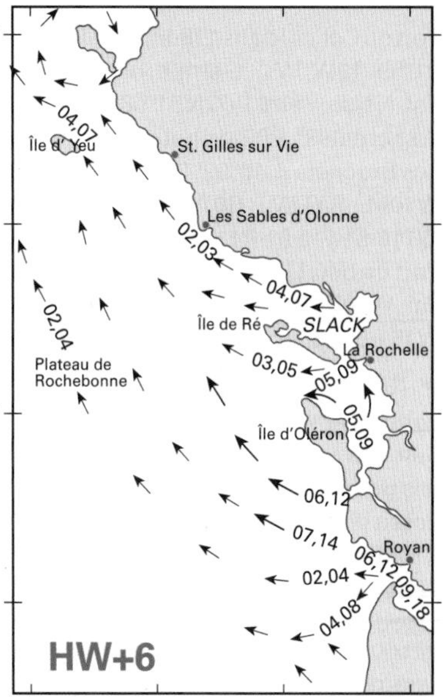
47°
46°
04,07
Île d'Yeu
St. Gilles sur Vie
Les Sables d'Olonne
02,03
04,07
02,04
Île de Ré
SLACK
La Rochelle
Plateau de Rochebonne
03,05
05,09
05,09
Île d'Oléron
06,12
07,14
06,12
Royan
02,04
09,18
04,08
HW+6
6 Hours after HW Brest
(0115 before HW Dover)

CAUTION: Due to the very strong rates of the tidal streams in some of the areas, many eddies may occur. Where possible some indication of these eddies has been included. In many areas there is either insufficient information or the eddies are unstable. Generally tidal streams are weak offshore and strong winds have a very great effect on the rate and direction of the tidal streams.

NOTE: No tidal stream information is published by either the French or British Hydrographic Offices for the area southwards to the Spanish border.

PLOT WAYPOINTS ON YOUR CHART BEFORE USING THEM

9.22.4 LIGHTS, BUOYS AND WAYPOINTS

Blue print = light with a nominal range of 15M or more. CAPITALS = place or feature. *CAPITAL ITALICS* = light-vessel, light float or Lanby. *Italics* = Fog signal. ***Bold italics*** = Racon. Useful waypoints are <u>underlined</u>. Abbreviations are in Chapter 1.

Positions are referenced to the WGS 84 datum. More UKHO and SHOM charts of Area 22 are referenced to WGS 84 than to ED50.

POINTE DE SAINT-GILDAS TO FROMENTINE

Pte de Saint-Gildas ☆ 47°08'·02N 02°14'·76W, Q WRG 20m, W14M, R/G10M; R264°-308°, G308°-078°, W078°-088°, R088°-174°, W174°-180°, G180°-264°; col on W house.

▶ PORNIC

Notre Dame 47°05'·42N 02°08'·26W, VQ (9) 10s 7m 3M.
47°06'·00N 02°07'·47W, Fl Y 2·5s.
<u>Access buoy</u> 47°06'·45N 02°06'·64W, L Fl 10s.
<u>Marina ent</u>, S side ☆ 47°06'·47N 02°06'·68W, Fl (2) R 6s 4m 2M.
Ent, N side ☆ 47°06'·48N 02°06'·66W, Fl (2) G 6s 4m 2M.
<u>SW elbow</u> ☆ 47°06'·44N 02°06'·97W, Fl 2·5s 4m 3M.
Pte de Noëveillard ☆ 47°06'·62N 02°06'·92W, Oc (4) WRG 12s 22m W13M, R/G9M; G shore-051°, W051°-079°, R079°-shore; W□twr, G top, W dwelling.
Port de Gourmalon bkwtr ☆ 47°06'·63N 02°06'·48W, Fl (3) G 12s 4m 8M; W mast, G top.

La Bernerie-en-Retz jetty ☆ 47°04'·56N 02°02'·29W, Fl R 2s 4m 5M; W structure, R top.

Port du Collet, ldg lts 118·5°, both QG 4/12m 6M. Front 47°01'·34N 01°59'·10W; W □ G stripe, on W pylon.
Ent, N side ☆ 47°01'·77N 01°58'·95W, Oc (2) WR 6s 7m W7M, R5M; W shore-093°, R093°-shore.
Les Brochets ☆ 46°59'·87N 02°01'·85W, Oc (2+1) WRG 12s 8m, W10M, R/G7M; G071°-091°, W091°-102·5°, R102·5°-116·5°, W116·5°-119·5°, R119·5°-164·5°; G twr, W band.
Port du bec, L'Époids ☆ 46°56'·40N 02°04'·48W, Dir Iso WRG 4s 6m, W10M, R/G7M; G106°-113·5°, R113·5°-122°, G122°-157·5°, W157·5°-158·5°, R158·5°-171·5°, W171·5°-176°; W□twr, R top.

▶ ÎLE DE NOIRMOUTIER

Île du Pilier ☆ 47°02'·55N 02°21'·61W, Fl (3) 20s 33m **29M**; Gy twr. Same twr, auxiliary lt, QR 10m 11M, 321°-034°.
<u>Les Boeufs</u> 46°55'·04N 02°28'·02W, VQ (9) 10s.
Passe de la Grise 47°01'·65N 02°19'·99W, Q (6) + L Fl 15s.
L'Herbaudière, ldg lts 187·5°, both Q 5/26m 7M, Gy masts. Front, 47°01'·59N 02°17'·85W. Rear, 310m from front.
Basse du Martroger 47°02'·60N 02°17'·12W, Q WRG 11m W9M, R/G6M; G033°-055°, W055°-060°, R060°-095°, G095°-124°, W124°-153°, R153°-201°, W201°-240°, R240°-033°.
W jetty ☆ 47°01'·63N 02°17'·86W, Oc (2+1) WG 12s 9m W10M, G7M; W187·5°-190°, G190°-187·5°; W col and hut, G top.
E jetty ☆ 47°01'·68N 02°17'·73W, Fl (2) R 6s 8m 4M

Pierre Moine 47°03'·35N 02°12'·36W, Fl (2) 6s 14m 7M.
<u>La Chaise</u> 47°01'·21N 02°12'·64W.
Pte des Dames ☆ 47°00'·66N 02°13'·27W, Oc (3) WRG 12s 34m, **W19M, R/G15M**; G016·5°-057°, R057°-124°, G124°-165°, W165°-191°, R191°-267°, W267°-357°, R357°-016·5°; W□twr.
Noirmoutier-en-L'Île jetty ☆ 46°59'·27N 02°13'·14W, Oc (2) R 6s 6m 6M; W col, R top.
Pte de Devin (Morin) ☆ 46°59'·15N 02°17'·60W, Oc (4) WRG 12s 10m W11M, R/G8M; G314°-028°, W028°-035°, R035°-134°; W col and hut, G top.

Port de Morin 46°58'·74N 02°17'·98W, Fl (2) R 6s.
Morin jetty ☆ 46°58'·65N 02°17'·95W, Fl (3) R 12s 1M; R twr.

▶ GOULET DE FROMENTINE

Fromentine 46°53'·06N 02°11'·63W, L Fl 10s.
Tourelle Milieu 46°53'·58N 02°09'·63W, Fl (4) R 12s 6m 5M.
Bridge ☆ 46°53'·52N 02°09'·00W, Iso 4s 32m **18M**, H24; centre span, each side.
Pte de Notre Dame-de-Monts ☆ 46°53'·33N 02°08'·55W, Dir Oc (2) WRG 6s 21m, W13M, R/G10M; G000°-043°, W043°-063°, R063°-073°, W073°-094°, G094°-113°, W113°-116°, R116°-175°, G175°-196°, R196°-230°; W twr, B top.

▶ LE GOIS CAUSEWAY

E shore ☆ 46°55'·27N 02°06'·23W, Fl R 4s 6m 6M; 038°-218°.
E refuge ☆ 46°55'·65N 02°06'·87W, Fl 2s 5m 5M.
W refuge ☆ 46°56'·02N 02°08'·10W, Fl 2s 5m 3M.
Bassotière ☆ 46°56'·03N 02°08'·89W, Fl G 2s 7m 2M; 180°-000°.

ÎLE D'YEU TO BOURGENAY

▶ ÎLE D'YEU

Petite Foule (main lt) ☆ 46°43'·05N 02°22'·96W Fl 5s 56m **24M**; W □ twr, G lantern.
Les Chiens Perrins 46°43'·58N 02°24'·61W, Q (9) WG 15s 16m W7M, G4M; G330°-350°, W350°-200°.

Port Joinville ldg lts 219°, both QR 11/16m 6M, 169°-269°. Front, Quai du Canada 46°43'·61N 02°20'·95W. Rear, Quai Georgette 85m from front.
NW jetty ☆ 46°43'·77N 02°20'·82W, Oc (3) WG 12s 7m, W11M, G8M; G shore-150°, W150°-232°, G232°-279°, W279°-285°, G285°-shore; W 8-sided twr, G top.
La Galiote 46°43'·73N 02°20'·71W.

Pte des Corbeaux ☆ 46°41'·42N 02°17'·11W, Fl (2+1) R 15s 25m **20M**; 083°-143° obsc by Île de Yeu; W □ twr, R top.

Port de la Meule ☆ 46°41'·66N 02°20'·75W, Oc WRG 4s 9m, W9M, R/G6M; G007·5°-018°, W018°-027·5°, R027·5°-041·5°; Gy twr, R top.

▶ ST GILLES-CROIX-DE-VIE

St Jean de Monts 46°46'·90N 02°04'·91W, Fl R.
Jetty ☆ 46°47'·07N 02°05'·13W, Fl (2) R 6s 10m 1M; W mast, R top.
Pte de Grosse Terre ☆ 46°41'·54N 01°57'·92W, Fl (4) WR 12s 25m, **W18M, R15M**; R290°-339°, W339°-125°, R125°-145°; W truncated conical twr.
Ldg lts 043·7°, both Q 7/28m **15M**; 033·5°-053·5°; synch; W□twrs, R tops. Front, 46°41'·85N 01°56'·67W. Rear, 260m from front.
<u>Pilours</u> 46°40'·98N 01°58'·10W, Q (6) + L Fl 15s; *Bell.*
Jetée de la Garenne ☆ 46°41'·45N 01°57'·26W, Fl G 4s 8m 6M.
Jetée de Boisvinet ☆ 46°41'·62N 01°57'·16W, Fl R 4s 8m 6M.

▶ LES SABLES D'OLONNE

Les Barges ☆ 46°29'·70N 01°50'·50W, Fl (2) R 10s 25m 13M; Gy twr.
<u>Petite Barge</u> 46°28'·90N 01°50'·61W, Q (6) + L Fl 15s 3M; *Whis.*
L'Armandèche ☆ 46°29'·40N 01°48'·29W, Fl (2+1) 15s 42m **24M**; 295°-130°; W 6-sided twr, R top.
<u>Nouch Sud</u> 46°28'·55N 01°47'·42W, Q (6) + L Fl 15s.
Ldg lts 032·5°, both Iso 4s 12/33m **16M**, H24. **Front** ☆, 46°29'·42N 01°46'·37W; mast. **Rear** ☆, **La Potence**, 330m from front; W□twr.
Ldg lts 320°. Front, Jetée des Sables ☆, 46°29'·44N 01°47'·51W, QG 11m 8M; W twr, G top. Rear, Tour d'Arundel, 465m from front, Q 33m 13M, synch; large Gy □ twr.

Entrance ldg lts 328·1°, both Iso R 4s 6/9m 11M. Front 46°29'·66N 01°47'·75W; R line on W hut. Rear, 65m from front; intens 324°-330°; R line on W twr (daymarks are hard to see).
Jetée St Nicolas ☆ 46°29'·23N 01°47'·52W, QR 16m 8M; 143°-094°; W twr, R top.

▶ BOURGENAY

Ldg lts 040°, both QG 9/19m 7M. Front, 46°26'·37N 01°40'·61W; 020°-060°. Rear; 010°-070°.
Landfall ⚓ 46°25'·28N 01°41'·91W, L Fl 10s.
Ent ☆ 46°26'·43N 01°40'·51W, Fl R 4s 8m 9M; and Iso G 4s 6m 5M.

▶ PLATEAU DE ROCHEBONNE (Offshore shoal)

NW ⛋ 46°12'·92N 02°31'·61W, Q (9) 15s; *Whis*.
NE ⛋ 46°12'·69N 02°24'·89W, Iso G 4s.
SE ⛋ 46°09'·18N 02°21'·16W, Q (3) 10s; *Bell*.
SW ⛋ 46°10'·09N 02°27'·07W, Fl (2) R 6s.

PERTUIS BRETON
▶ JARD-SUR-MER/LA TRANCHE-SUR-MER

Jard approach ⚓ 46°23'·68N 01°34'·86W (May-Sep).
Ldg marks 038°, two B & W bcns.
Jard-sur-Mer, S bkwtr ⚓ 46°24'·37N 01°34'·67W.
La Tranche ⚓ 46°20'·05N 01°26'·19W (May-Sep).
La Tranche pier ☆ 46°20'·55N 01°25'·63W, Fl (2) R 6s 6m 6M; R col.
Pte du Grouin-du-Cou ☆ 46°20'·67N 01°27'·83W, Fl WRG 5s 29m, **W20M, R/G16M**; R034°-061°, W061°-117°, G117°-138°, W138°-034°; W 8-sided twr, B top.

▶ L'AIGUILLON/LA FAUTE-SUR-MER

Le Lay ⛋ 46°16'·10N 01°16'·53W, Q (6) + L Fl 15s.
No. 1 ⚓ 46°16'·59N 01°16'·29W. Many mussel beds.
No. 2 ⚓ 46°16'·90N 01°16'·28W. Inner chan is marked by bcns.

▶ ANSE DE L'AIGUILLON (Marans & Plomb)

ATT de L'Aiguillon ⛋ 46°15'·32N 01°11'·53W, L Fl 10s.
No. 9 ⛋ 46°15'·56N 01°12'·24W.
No. 10 ⛋ 46°15'·11N 01°11'·44W.
Inner fairway ⛋ 46°17'·18N 01°09'·68W.
Port du Pavé ☆ 46°18'·15N 01°08'·01W, Fl G 4s 9m 7M; W col, G top.
Plomb ☆ 46°12'·11N 01°12'·23W, Fl R 4s 9m 7M; W col, R top.

ÎLE DE RÉ

Les Baleines ☆ 46°14'·64N 01°33'·69W, Fl (4) 15s 53m **27M**; Gy 8-sided twr, R lantern.
Les Baleineaux ☆ 46°15'·81N 01°35'·22W, Oc (2) 6s 23m 11M; pink twr, R top.

▶ ARS-EN-RÉ

Bûcheron ⚓ 46°14'·21N 01°25'·98W.
Outer ldg lts 265·8°, both Iso 4s 5/13m 11/**15M**; synch. Front, 46°14'·05N 01°28'·61W; 141°-025° ; ☐ on W hut. **Rear**, 370m from front, intens 264°-266°; G ☐ twr on dwelling.
Le Fier d'Ars, inner ldg lts 232·5°. Front, 46°12'·76N 01°30'·60W Q 5m 9M; R/W frame on W col. Rear, 370m from front, Q 13m 11M; B vert rectangle on W mast; 142°-322°.

▶ ST MARTIN DE RÉ

Rocha ⛋ 46°14'·74N 01°20'·64W, Q; 200°/2·3M to hbr ent.
Lt ho, E of ent ☆ 46°12'·44N 01°21'·89W, Oc (2) WR 6s 18m W10M, R7M; W shore-245°, R245°-281°, W281°-shore; W twr, R top.
Det bkwtr, W end ☆ 46°12'·49N 01°21'·89W, Fl R 2·5s 5m 2M.
W mole ☆ 46°12'·49N 01°21'·89W, Iso G 4s 10m 6M; obsc by Pte de Loix when brg <124°; W post, G top.
Pointe du Couronneau ⛋ 46°12'·78N 01°20'·90W.

▶ LA FLOTTE

N bkwtr ☆ 46°11'·32N 01°19'·34W, Fl WG 4s 10m W12M, G9M; G130°-205°, W205°-220°, G220°-257°; Moiré effect Dir lt 212·5°; W ○ twr, G top.
Rivedoux-Plage ldg lts 194·5°, both QG 6/9m 6M; synch. Front, N Pier 46°09'·78N 01°16'·65W; W twr, G top. Rear, 100m from front; two W cols, W/G chequered topmark.

▶ ÎLE DE RÉ (South coast)

Chanchardon ☆ 46°09'·73N 01°28'·44W, Fl WR 4s 15m W11M, R8M; R118°-290°, W290°-118°; B 8-sided twr, W base.
Chauveau ☆ 46°08'·03N 01°16'·42W, Oc (3) WR 12s 27m **W15M**, R11M; W057°-094°, R094°-104°, W104°-342°, R342°-057°; W ○ twr, R top.
Pte de Sablanceaux ☆ 46°09'·76N 01°15'·17W, VQ (3) 5s 10m 5M; landing stage.

LA ROCHELLE AND LA CHARENTE TO ROCHEFORT
▶ LA ROCHELLE

PA (Pertuis d'Antioche) ⛋ 46°05'·62N 01°42'·45W, Iso 4s 8m 7M; *Whis*; 088°/19M to Roche du Sud.
Roche du Sud ⛋ 46°06'·37N 01°15'·22W, Q (9) 15s.
Chauveau ⛋ 46°06'·56N 01°16'·06W, VQ (6) + L Fl 10s.
Le Lavardin ⚓ 46°08'·09N 01°14'·53W, Fl (2) WG 6s 14m, W11M, G8M; G160°-169°, W169°-160°.
Plateau du Lavardin ⛋ 46°07'·63N 01°14'·34W.
La Pallice, NW arm, Dir lt 016° ☆ 46°09'·75N 01°14'·35W. Q WRG 33m, W14M, R/G13M; G009°-014·7°, W014·7°-017·3°, R017·3°-031°; Gy twr. Sig stn.
Oil jetty head, ☆ 46°09'·36N 01°14'·53W, Q (6) + L Fl 15s.
La Rochelle ldg lts 059°, both Dir Q 15/25m 13/14M; synch; by day Fl 4s. Front, 46°09'·35N 01°09'·16W; intens 056°-062°; R ○ twr, W bands. Rear, 235m from front; 044°-074°, obsc 061°-065° by St Nicolas twr; W 8-sided twr, G top.
Les Minimes ⛋ 46°08'·01N 01°11'·53W, Q (9) 15s.
Pte des Minimes ☆ 46°08'·33N 01°10'·68W, Fl (3) WG 12s 8m, W8M, G5M; W059°-213°, G313°-059°; octagonal twr.
Chan buoy ⚓ 46°08'·59N 01°10'·79W, QG.
Tour Richelieu ⚓ 46°08'·89N 01°10'·36W, Fl R 4s 10m 9M; R twr.
Port des Minimes, ent ☆ 46°08'·33N 01°10'·68W, Fl (2) G 6s 9m 7M.

▶ LA CHARENTE

Ldg lts 115°. Front, **Fort de la Pointe** ☆ 45°57'·96N 01°04'·37W Dir QR 8m **19M**; W ☐ twr, R top. **Rear** ☆, 600m from front, Dir QR 21m **20M**; W ☐ twr, R top; both intens 113°-117°. QR 21m 8M; same twr; 322°-067° over Port-des-Barques anchorage.
Fort Boyard twr ☆ 45°59'·96N 01°12'·87W, Q (9) 15s.
Île d'Aix ☆ 46°00'·60N 01°10'·67W, Fl WR 5s 24m **W24M, R20M**; R103°-118°, W118°-103°; two conspic W ○ twrs.
Les Palles ⛋ 45°59'·52N 01°09'·62W, Q.
Sablière ⚓ 45°58'·97N 01°07'·62W.
Fouras, Port Sud bkwtr ☆ 45°58'·97N 01°05'·72W, Fl WR 4s 6m 9/6M; R115°-177°, W177°-115°.
Port Nord pier ☆ 45°59'·81N 01°05'·86W, Oc (3+1) WG 12s 9m, W11M, G8M; G084°-127°, W127°-084°; W&G twr.
Port de la Fumée ⛋ 46°00'·30N 01°07'·13W, QG 5m 5M; G mast.
Port-des-Barques ldg lts 134·3°, both Iso G 4s 5/13m 9/11M; synch; intens 125°-145°. Front, 45°56'·95N 01°04'·16W. Rear, 490m from front.
Fontenelles ⚓ 45°58'·57N 01°06'·59W.
Moucliere ⚓ 45°58'·24N 01°06'·14W.

22

PLOT WAYPOINTS ON YOUR CHART BEFORE USING THEM

▶ ROCHEFORT

Upstream the river is marked by 20 pairs of unlit beacons, lettered TT to AA. Night passage is not advised.
Bcn ☆ 46°02'·10N 01°22'·07W, Fl (2) G 6s; 1·4M before Rochefort.
Bcn ☆ 46°02'·10N 01°22'·07W, Fl (4) R 15s; 0·7M before Rochefort, where there are no navigational lights.

ÎLE D'OLÉRON

Chassiron ☆ 46°02'·77N 01°24'·67W, Fl 10s 50m, **28M**; W twr, B bands.
Rocher d'Antioche 46°03'·92N 01°24'·67W, Q 20m 11M.

▶ ST DENIS

Les Palles 46°03'·03N 01°22'·34W.
Dir lt 205°, 46°01'·61N 01°21'·96W; Iso WRG 4s 14m, W11M, R/G8M; G190°-204°, W204°-206°, R206°-220°.
E jetty ☆ 46°02'·10N 01°22'·07W, Fl (2) WG 6s 6m, W9M, G6M; G205°-277°, W277°-292°, G292°-165°; □ hut.
S jetty ☆ 46°02'·11N 01°22'·21W, Fl (2) R 6s 3m 6M.

▶ PORT DU DOUHET/PASSAGE DE L'OUEST

Seaweed farm 46°00'·48N 01°17'·71W, VQ.
N ent 46°00'·10N 01°19'·19W.
46°01'·58N 01°17'·09W.
Fishfarm 46°00'·22N 01°15'·35W, Q.
Fishfarm 45°59'·84N 01°14'·80W, Q (3) 10s.
Fort Boyard ☆ 45°59'·97N 01°12'·85W, Q (9) 15s. B twr, Y band.

▶ BOYARDVILLE

Longe Boyard S 45°58'·65N 01°11'·93W.
La Pérrotine 45°58'·30N 01°13'·30W.
Mole ☆ 45°58'·24N 01°13'·86W, Fl (2) R 6s 8m 5M; obsc'd by Pte des Saumonards when brg <150°; W twr, R top.

▶ LE CHÂTEAU D'OLÉRON

Tourelle Juliar 45°54'·16N 01°09'·37W, Q (3) WG 10s 12m, W11M; G8M; W147°-336°, G336°-147°.
Ldg lts 319°, both QR 11/24m 7M; synch. Front, 45°53'·11N 01°11'·37W; 191°-087°; R line on W twr. Rear, 240m from front; W twr, R top.

▶ LA SEUDRE

Pont de la Seudre ☆ 45°48'·06N 01°08'·17W, Q 20m 9M each side; 054°-234° and 234°-054°.
Pte de Mus de Loup ☆ 45°47'·96N 01°08'·42W, Oc G 4s 8m 6M; 118°-147°.
Pertuis de Maumusson. Depths & buoys subject to change.
ATT Maumusson 45°46'·86N 01°18'·28W, L Fl 10s.
La Barre 45°45'·55N 01°15'·35W. In sequence from seaward.
Tabouret 45°45'·70N 01°15'·52W.
Mattes 45°46'·39N 01°16'·07W.
Gatseau 45°47'·20N 01°15'·16W.

▶ LA COTINIÈRE

Dir lt 048°; 45°54'·35N 01°18'·67W, Oc WRG 4s 13m, W11M, R/G9M; G033°-046°, W046°-050°, R050°-063°; W stripe with B border on W col.
Ent ldg lts 339°, both Dir Oc (2) 6s 6/14m 13/12M; synch. Front, 45°54'·72N 01°19'·79W; 329°-349°; W twr, R top. Rear, 425m from front; intens 329°-349°; W twr, R bands.

GIRONDE APPROACHES AND TO BORDEAUX

▶ GRANDE PASSE DE L'OUEST

Pte de la Coubre ☆ 45°41'·78N 01°13'·99W, Fl (2) 10s 64m **28M**; W twr, R top; sig stn. Same twr, F RG 42m, R12M, G10M; R030°-043°, G043°-060°, R060°-110°.
BXA 45°37'·53N 01°28'·69W Iso 4s 8m 7M; *Whis*; ***Racon B, 120-150s to sweep the frequency range of marine radars.***
Ldg lts 081·5° (not valid E of Nos 4 & 5 buoys). **Front** ☆, Dir Iso 4s 21m **20M**; intens 080·5°-082·5°; W pylon on dolphin, 1·1M from rear. Same structure, Q (2) 5s 10m 3M.
La Palmyre, common rear ☆, 45°39'·71N 01°07'·22W, Dir Q 57m **27M**; intens 080·5°-082·5°; W radar twr.
Same twr, Dir FR 57m **17M**; intens 325·5°-328·5°.
No. 1 45°38'·00N 01°21'·82W, QG.
No. 2 45°38'·32N 01°21'·91W, QR.
No. 6 45°38'·47N 01°18'·20W, VQ (6) + L Fl 10s.
No. 7 45°38'·04N 01°18'·03W, Iso G 4s.
No. 7a 45°39'·02N 01°14'·78W, Fl G 4s.
No. 9 45°39'·49N 01°12'·72W, Q.
No. 11 45°39'·07N 01°10'·58W, Iso G 4s.
No. 13 45°37'·34N 01°06'·41W, Fl (2) G 6s.
No. 12 45°36'·17N 01°03'·33W, Fl (3) R 12s.
No. 13A 45°35'·68N 01°04'·21W, Fl (3) G 12s.
Ldg lts 327° (down-river). Front, **Terre-Nègre** ☆, Oc (3) WRG 12s 39m **W18M**, R/G14M; R304°-319°, W319°-327°, G327°-000°, W000°-004°, G004°-097°, W097°-104°, R104°-116°; W twr, R top on W side, 1·1M from rear (La Palmyre).
No. 13B 45°34'·58N 01°03'·00W, QG.

Cordouan ☆ 45°35'·16N 01°10'·39W, Oc (2+1) WRG 12s 60m, **W22M, R/G18M**; W014°-126°, G126°-178·5°, W178·5°-250°, W (unintens) 250°-267°, R (unintens) 267°-294·5°, R294·5°-014°; obsc'd in estuary when brg >285°; W twr, Gy band.

▶ PASSE SUD (or DE GRAVE)

Ldg lts 063°. **St Nicolas Front** ☆, 45°33'·72N 01°05'·03W, Dir QG 22m **16M**; intens 061·5°-064·5°; W □ twr.
Rear, Pointe de Grave ☆, Oc WRG 4s 26m, **W19M, R/G15M**; W(unintens) 033°-054°, W054°-233·5°, R233·5°-303°, W303°-312°, G312°-330°, W330°- 341°, W(unintens) 341°-025°; W □ twr, B corners and top, 0·84M from front.
G 45°30'·32N 01°15'·56W; *Whis.*
G1 45°31'·18N 01°11'·33W.
G2 45°32'·07N 01°10'·07W.
Ldg lts 041°, both Dir QR 33/61m **18M**. **Front, Le Chay** ☆, 45°37'·30N 01°02'·40W, intens 039·5°-042·5°; W twr, R top. **Rear, St Pierre** ☆, intens 039°-043°; R water twr 0·97M from front.
G3 45°32'·78N 01°07'·72W.
G6 45°34'·99N 01°04'·80W.

▶ ROYAN

R1 45°36'·56N 01°01'·96W, Iso G 4s.
S jetty ☆ 45°37'·01N 01°01'·82W, Fl (2) R 10s 11m 12M; 199°-116°.
Hbr ent, W jetty ☆ 45°37'·13N 01°01'·64W, Fl (3) R 12s 8m 6M.
NE jetty ☆ 45°37'·23N 01°01'·49W, Fl (3) G 12s 2m 5M; 311°-151°.

▶ PORT BLOC

Pte de Grave, N jetty 45°34'·42N 01°03'·68W, Q 6m 2M.
Spur 45°34'·32N 01°03'·66W, Iso G 4s 5m 2M; 190°-045°.
Port Bloc, ent N side ☆ 45°34'·14N 01°03'·74W, Fl G 4s 9m 3M.
S pier ☆ 45°34'·11N 01°03'·71W, Fl R 4s 8m 4M.

▶ PORT-MÉDOC

Entrance (approx) 45°33'·45N 01°03'·37W.
45°33'·41N 01°03'·37W; WIP 9/2003.

▶ LEVERDON-SUR-MER

Dir ☆ 171·3°; 45°31'·97N 01°02'·03W, Iso WRG 4s 4m, W12M, R/G8M; G165°-170°, W170°-173°, R173°-178°; W panel, B stripe on W dolphin, B top. Same structure, Fl G 2·5s 5m 1M.
Oil jetty, N end ☆ 45°33'·07N 01°02'·45W, Fl (3) G 12s 13m 2M.
S end ☆ 45°32'·76N 01°02'·34W, Fl G 2·5s 12m 3M; 000°-200°.

▶ MORTAGNE/PAUILLAC/BLAYE

Mortagne ent 45°28'·24N 00°49'·00W, VQ (9) 10s.
No. 43 45°12'·44N 00°44'·27W, Fl (2) G 6s.
Pauillac, NE elbow ☆ 45°11'·96N 00°44'·61W, Fl G 4s 7m 5M.
Ent E side ☆ 45°11'·86N 00°44'·60W, QG 7m 4M.
No. S9 45°09'·35N 00°40'·17W; 1·8M N of Blaye.
Blaye, N quay ☆ 45°07'·49N 00°40'·02W, Q (3) R 5s 6m 3M.
D6 45°06'·90N 00°39'·94W, Fl (2) R 6s; 0.6M S of Blaye.
Bec d'Ambés 45°02'·59N 00°36'·39W, QG 5m 5M (confluence of Rivers Dordogne and Garonne).

▶ BORDEAUX

Pont d'Aquitaine ☆ 44°52'·82N 00°32'·31W, 4 F Vi.
Lock ent to Bassins Nos 1 and 2, 44°51'·74N 00°32'·94W.
Pont de Pierre, 44°50'·37N 00°33'·72W, Km 0.

POINTE DE GRAVE TO THE SPANISH BORDER

Hourtin ☆ 45°08'·48N 01°09'·67W, Fl 5s 55m **23M**; R □ twr.
Cap Ferret ☆ 44°38'·76N 01°14'·95W, Fl R 5s 53m **27M**; W ○ twr, R top. Same twr, Oc (3) 12s 46m 14M; 045°-135°.

▶ ARCACHON, PASSE NORD

ATT-ARC 44°34'·61N 01°18'·74W, L Fl 10s 8m 5M.
Note: All buoys are liable to be moved as the channel shifts.
1N 44°34'·58N 01°17'·83W.
2N 44°34'·69N 01°17'·84W.
2NA 44°34'·69N 01°17'·08W.
3N 44°34'·58N 01°17'·08W.
4N 44°34'·73N 01°16'·56W.
5N 44°34'·83N 01°15'·92W.
7N 44°35'·12N 01°15'·33W.
7NA 44°35'·46N 01°14'·86W.
6N 44°35'·87N 01°14'·66W.
8N 44°36'·47N 01°14'·47W.
9N 44°36'·90N 01°14'·42W.
11 44°37'·29N 01°14'·18W.

▶ PASSE SUD (Closed to navigation)

La Salie 44°30'·44N 01°17'·74W, Fl (2) 6s.
La Salie Wharf 44°30'·89N 01°15'·65W, Q (9) 15s 19m 10M.
B (La Lagune) 44°32'·81N 01°15'·47W.
Common inner channel
No. 13 44°38'·10N 01°14'·12W.
No. 14 44°39'·57N 01°13'·14W.
No. 15 44°39'·79N 01°12'·11W.

Marina W bkwtr ☆ 44°39'·77N 01°09'·15W, QG 6m 6M.
E bkwtr ☆ 44°39'·76N 01°09'·07W, QR 6m 6M.
Port de La Vigne ☆ 44°40'·43N 01°14'·36W, Iso R 4s 7m 5M, occas.

SM 44°20'·32N 01°28'·73W, Fl (3) Y 12s.
Contis ☆ 44°05'·59N 01°19'·05W, Fl (4) 25s 50m **23M**; W ○ twr, B diagonal stripes.

▶ CAPBRETON

Digue Nord ☆ 43°39'·38N 01°27'·01W, Fl (2) R 6s 13m 12M; W ○ twr, R top; *Horn 30s*.
Estacade Sud ☆ 43°39'·25N 01°26'·89W, Fl (2) G 6s 9m 12M.

▶ ANGLET/BAYONNE

BA 43°32'·55N 01°32'·79W, L Fl 10s.
Outer ldg lts 090°, both Dir Q 9/15m **19M**; intens 086·5°-093·5°; W twrs, R tops. Front, **Boucau** ☆ 43°31'·81N 01°31'·23W. Rear, 250m from front.
Outer N bkwtr 43°31'·88N 01°31'·99W, QR 11m 8M; W/R twr.
Outer S bkwtr 43°31'·60N 01°31'·68W, Q (9) 15s 15m 6M.
Inner ldg lts 111·5°, both Dir FG 6/10m 14M; intens 109°-114° (moved as necessary and lit when chan is practicable). Front 43°31'·63N 01°30'·94W; W hut, G band. Rear, 149m from front.
Inner N jetty ☆ 43°31'·82N 01°31'·42W, Iso R 4s 12m 8M.
Inner S jetty ☆ 43°31'·73N 01°31'·48W, Iso G 4s 9m 10M; W □ twr, G top; IPTS from adjacent twr.
N training wall ☆ 43°31'·83N 01°31'·16W, Fl (2) R 6s 9m 8M.
S training wall ☆ 43°31'·70N 01°30'·81W, Fl (2) G 6s 7m 8M.
N bank ☆ Fl (3) R 12s 9m 3M, 43°31'·83N 01°31'·13W.
S bank ☆ Fl (3) G 12s 9m 3M, 43°31'·74N 01°31'·132W.
N bank ☆ Fl (4) R 15s 9m 3M, 43°31'·80N 01°30'·89W.
S bank ☆ Fl (4) G 15s 9m 3M, 43°31'·71N 01°30'·88W.
Anglet marina ent ☆ 43°31'·57N 01°30'·51W, Fl G 2s 5m 2M.
Pte de Blanc-Pignon ☆ 43°30'·92N 01°29'·61W, Fl (2) G 6s 8m 9M.
Pont de L'Aveugle ☆ 43°30'·05N 01°29'·53W, Dir Q WRG W3M, R/G2M; G165°-170°, W170°-175°, R175°-180°.

▶ BIARRITZ

Pointe Saint-Martin ☆ 43°29'·62N 01°33'·24W, Fl (2) 10s 73m **29M**; W twr, B top.
Ldg lts 174°, both Fl R 2s 7/19m 3M. Front 43°29'·00N 01°33'·96W. Rear, 83m from front.

Guethary ldg lts 133°, both QR 11/33m 6M. Front, 43°25'·59N 01°36'·53W; W mast. Rear, 66m from front; W twr.

▶ ST JEAN DE LUZ

Outer ldg lts 138·5° (Passe d'Illarguita). Front, Socoa, 43°23'·70N 01°41'·20W, Q WR 36m W12M, R8M; W shore-264°, R264°-282°, W282°-shore; W □ twr, B stripe. **Rear, Bordagain**, 0·77M from front, Dir Q 67m **20M**; intens 134·5°-141·5°; B/W panel, B/W pylon.
Middle ldg lts 101°, both Dir Oc (4) R 12s 30/47m **18M**; intens 095°-107°; synch. **Front, Ste Barbe** ☆, 43°23'·96N 01°39'·88W; W △ on W bldg. **Rear** ☆, 340m from front; B △ on W □ twr.
Inner ldg lts 150·7°, both Dir QG 18/27m **16M**; intens 149·5°-152·2°. **Front, E jetty** ☆ (jetty hd, R strip lt), 43°23'·25N 01°40'·15W; W □ twr, R stripe. **Rear** ☆, 410m from front; W □ twr, G stripe.
Digue des Criquas (W bkwtr) ☆ 43°23'·84N 01°40'·67W, Iso G 4s 11m 6M; G □ twr.
Groyne ☆ 43°23'·33N 01°40'·15W, Fl Bu 4s 3m 5M.

▶ HENDAYE

Cabo Higuer ☆ 43°23'·51N 01°47'·53W, Fl (2) 10s 63m **23M**; 072°-340°; twr, W lantern (in Spain).
W training wall ☆ 43°22'·82N 01°47'·36W, Fl (3) G 9s 9m 5M.
E training wall hd ☆ 43°22'·66N 01°47'·24W, L Fl R 10s 8m 5M.
E training wall root, Pte des Dunes ☆ 43°22'·38N 01°47'·37W, Fl R 2·5s 6m 4M.
43°22'·33N 01°47'·49W, Fl G 5s.
43°22'·10N 01°47'·29W, VQ (3) G 5s 3m 3M; G bent mast.
Marina, W bkwtr, elbow ☆ 43°22'·07N 01°47'·18W, Fl (2) R 6s 6m 2M; 294°-114°. W bkwtr head, FR strip lt.
S jetty ☆ 43°22'·05N 01°47'·07W, Fl Y 4s 5m 4M; Y col.
43°21'·99N 01°47'·09W, L Fl G 10s 3m 4M; G mast.
See also Fuenterrabia, Spain in 9.23.3 and 9.23.6.

9.22.5 PASSAGE INFORMATION

BAY OF BISCAY (charts 1104, 20, 2664, 1102). *West France Cruising Companion* (Nautical Data Ltd/Featherstone) covers from L'Aber Wrac'h to the Spanish border. The Admiralty *Bay of Biscay Pilot* NP22 covers Pte de Penmarc'h to Cabo Ortegal. Large scale French charts are advised for inshore waters.

Despite its reputation, weather in the S part of the Bay is often warm and settled in summer when the Azores high and Spanish heat low are the dominant weather features. NE'lies prevail in sea area Finisterre in summer and gales may occur twice monthly, although forecast more frequently. Atlantic lows can bring W'ly spells at any time together with long swells which are dangerous inshore. SE or S winds are rare, but wind direction and speed often vary from day to day. Sea and land breezes can be well developed in the summer. Off N Spain *Galernas* are dangerous squally NW winds which blow with little warning. Rainfall is moderate, increasing in the SE, where thunder is more frequent. Sea fog occurs May-Oct, but is less common in winter. Japanese seaweed has been reported as a nuisance.

▶*Tidal streams are weak offshore, but can be strong in estuaries and channels, and around headlands. The tidal stream chartlets at 9.22.3 are based on NP 265 (Admiralty Tidal Stream Atlas for France, W Coast) which uses data from actual observations out to 15-25M offshore. The equivalent French Atlas gives more data, but based on computer predictions.*◀

The general direction and rate of the surface current much depends on wind: in summer it is SE, towards the SE corner of B of Biscay, where it swings W along N coast of Spain. In winter with W gales, the current runs E along N coast of Spain, sometimes at 3kn or more. When crossing the Bay of Biscay, allow for a likely set to the E, particularly after strong W winds.

BAIE DE BOURGNEUF (charts 2646, 2981) B de Bourgneuf is entered between Pte de St Gildas and Pte de l'Herbaudière, the NW tip of Île de Noirmoutier. Within the B the only yacht hbrs are Pornic (9.22.7) and L'Herbaudière (9.22.8). There are minor drying hbrs at La Bernerie-en-Retz, Le Collet, Port des Brochets and Bec de l'Epoids; with a good anch 5ca NE of Pte des Dames. The E and S sides of the B are encumbered with shoals, rks and oyster or mussel fisheries. The Bay is sheltered except in W winds, which can raise a heavy sea on the ebb stream.

From the NW (chart 2986) the approach is simple, but beware La Couronnée (dries 2·2m; buoyed) a rky bank about 2M WSW of Pte de St Gildas. Adjacent to it, Banc de Kerouars (least depth 1m; breaks) extends 3M further E. From the W approach Pornic either N of La Couronnée and Banc de Kerouars; or S of Banc de Kerouars, thence pass NW of Notre Dame WCM bn tr in the W sector of Pte de Noveillard lt. Notre Dame lies 2M SW of Pornic and marks end of a line of rks extending ESE to La Bernerie. Pierre du Chenal is an isolated, buoyed rk about 1M SSE of Notre Dame.

At the N end of Île de Noirmoutier, Chenal de la Grise, between Île du Pilier and Pte de l'Herbaudière and in one of the three W sectors of Martroger NCM bn lt, carries 3m, and gives access from the SW to L'Herbaudière marina. Extending 6M to seaward off the NW end of the island, beware Chaussée des Boeufs, buoyed rks, some drying on to which the tide sets. If heading NE to Pornic, pass N of Martroger, and clear of Roches des Pères about 1M ENE. The S ent to the Bay via Goulet de Fromentine (SHOM 7394; ECM 549) is difficult due to a shifting bar and 8 hrs of W-going stream; the conspic bridge has 24m clearance. The chan between the SWM lt buoy and Milieu bcn twr shifts and is buoyed accordingly. Once inside, further progress to NNE is restricted to shoal draft at sp HW±1 by Route du Gois, a causeway drying 3m.

ILE D'YEU TO PERTUIS BRETON (AC 2663, 2998) Les Marguerites, rky shoals, lie SSW of Goulet de Fromentine, with the part-drying reef, Pont d'Yeu (SCM buoy), extending midway between the mainland and the Île d'Yeu; here anch is prohib due to underwater cables. The passage along the NE of the island carries 6-7m nearer to the island. The low-lying, wooded Côte de la Vendée continues 40M SE to Pte du Grouin Cou with few dangers more than 1·5M offshore, except near Les Sables-d'Olonne.

Île d'Yeu, 30m high, has the main lt ho near the NW end where Les Chiens Perrins lt bcn marks offliers. On the NE coast a very conspic water tr gives good guidance into Port Joinville (9.22.9), crowded in season. Pte des Courbeaux lt ho is at the low SE end of the island. The SW coast is steep-to and rky, with a tiny drying hbr at Port de la Meule (best to anch outside) and, further E, anch at Anse des Vieilles, both only tenable in settled conditions.

17M E of Joinville is St Gilles-Croix-de-Vie (9.22.10). Thence 17M SSE is Les Sables-d'Olonne (9.22.11), with Les Barges drying reef (lt) 2·5M W of the ent. Bourgenay (9.22.12) is 6M further SE. The approaches to these secure hbrs are exposed to onshore winds from SE to NW, and susceptible to swell. Jard-sur-Mer is a small drying hbr midway between Bourgenay and Pte du Grouin du Cou.

PERTUIS BRETON (chart 2999). Pertuis Breton is entered between Pte du Grouin du Cou and Pte des Baleines (both lit) on Île de Ré, which is surrounded by shallows and drying areas. Beware rky ledges (dry) extending 2·5M NW from Les Baleines. Pertuis Breton gives access to the hbrs of Ars-en-Ré (9.22.13), St Martin (9.22.14) and La Flotte on the N shore of Île de Ré. From St Martin to Pte de Sablanceaux (SE tip) there are extensive oyster beds.

On the mainland side, in fresh NW winds against tide a bad sea builds on the bank which extends 8M W of Pte du Grouin du Cou. 1M S of the Pte is Roche de l'Aunis (depth 0·8m). From the Pte sand dunes and mussel beds, with seaward limits marked by lt buoys, run 8M ESE to the drying ent to Rivière Le Lay, which is fronted by a bar (dries 1m), dangerous in bad weather. The chan to L'Aiguillon/La Faute-sur-Mer (9.22.12) is marked by bns and buoys. 4M further E is entrance to Anse de l'Aiguillon, in which are extensive mussel beds. In NE corner is entrance to Sèvre Niortaise which, after 3·5M, gives access to the canal leading to the port of Marans. Further S is a sheltered route to La Rochelle and Pertuis d'Antioche via Coureau de la Pallice and the road bridge (30m clearance) from the mainland to Île de Ré.

PERTUIS D'ANTIOCHE (chart 2999) 'PA' SWM lt buoy marks the W approach to Pertuis d'Antioche which runs between Île de Ré and Île d'Oléron, giving access to La Rochelle (9.22.15), Ile d'Aix, La Charente and Rochefort (9.22.17). Its shores are low-lying. Île de Ré forms the N side, fringed by rky ledges extending 2·5M SE from Pte de Chanchardon (lt) and nearly 1M from Pte de Chauveau (marked by lt twr and two bcns). At the N tip of Île d'Oléron, off Pte de Chassiron (lt ho, Sig Stn), reefs extend 5ca W, 1·5M N to Rocher d'Antioche (lit), and 1·5M E, and there is often a nasty sea here.

Well offshore, 34-40M W of Île de Ré, Plateau de Rochebonne is a large rky plateau on which the sea breaks dangerously. It is steep-to on all sides, has least depth 3·3m and is buoyed.

ÎLE D'OLERON (charts 2663, 2999) On the NE coast of Ile d'Oléron (9.22.16) there are marinas at Port St Denis and Le Douhet at the N end; further S are yacht and fishing hbrs at Boyardville and Le Château. All are sheltered from the prevailing W'lies.

From Pertuis d'Antioche, Grande Rade des Trousses is entered via either Passage de l'Est close to Île d'Aix (9.22.17) or Passage de l'Ouest, which run each side of La Longe and Le Boyard, an extensive sandbank on which stands Ft Boyard tr. From Grande Rade, where good anch is found except in fresh NW winds, the narrow and shallow Coureau d'Oléron winds between ledges, oyster beds and constantly changing shoals, with buoys moved to conform. About 2M SE of Le Chateau it is crossed by a bridge, clearance 18m; the bridge arch for the navigable chan is marked at road level by W □ boards, with G △ or R □ superimposed, illuminated at night. Just N of bridge is Fort du Chapus, connected to mainland by causeway. SHOM 6335 is needed. ▶*S-going stream starts at HW Pte de Grave –0230, N-going at HW Pte de Grave +0500, sp rates 2kn.*◀ Up the Seudre River (9.22.18) there are anchs and yacht facilities at Marennes and La Tremblade.

The W coast, from Pte de Chassiron 15M SSE to Pte de Gatseau, is bounded by drying rks and shoals. In bad weather the sea breaks 4 or 5M offshore. La Cotinière, the only hbr, is almost exclusively a fishing port, exposed to the Atlantic. ▶*Tidal streams are weak, sp rate 1kn, starting NW at HW Pte de Grave +0300 and SE at HW Pte de Grave –0505, but often overcome by current due to prevailing wind. The rate, however, increases towards Pte de Gatseau.*◀

Here Pertuis de Maumusson separates the island from the mainland. A SWM lt buoy 'ATT Maumusson' about 3M WSW of Pte de Gatseau marks the approach. Banc de Gatseau and Banc des Mattes, both of which dry up to 3.9m, lie N and S of the chan; the sand bar usually has a depth of about 1·5m. Depth and position vary, and unlit lateral buoys are moved accordingly. Any swell speedily forms breakers, and the chan is very dangerous then or in any onshore winds, especially on the ebb (sp rate 4kn). In calm weather with no swell, a stout craft and reliable engine, and having gained local advice, enter about HW –1; ideally follow a local FV with deeper draught.

APPROACHES TO LA GIRONDE (chart 3057, 3058) The Gironde (9.22.19) is formed from the Garonne and Dordogne, which meet at Bec d'Ambès, 38M above Pte de Grave. 'BXA' SWM lt buoy is moored off the mouth of the estuary, about 11M WSW of Pte de la Coubre. Banc de la Mauvaise, the S end of which dries, extends 5M seaward. Cordouan lt ho is on a large sand spit in the middle of the estuary.

The two entry channels are dangerous in strong onshore winds, due to breakers and also the mascaret (bore) on the outgoing stream. Westerly swell breaks on La Mauvaise and around Cordouan, and sandbanks shift constantly. In places tidal streams run 4kn or more, and with wind against tide a dangerous sea can build. Nevertheless at the right time and in the right weather both entrances are straightforward by day and night.

Grande Passe de l'Ouest starts 4·8M E of BXA buoy and is dredged through Banc du Matelier, the outer bar of La Gironde. Enter to seaward of buoys Nos. 1 and 2 on the 081° ldg line; this is valid only as far as Nos 4/5 buoys. Thereafter follow the buoyed chan which deviates either side of the ldg line. ▶*Off Terre-Nègre lt the SE-going stream begins at HW –0500 (sp 1·5kn), and the NW-going at HW+0130 (sp 2·5kn).*◀

Passe Sud, a lesser chan, is entered near 'G' unlit SWM buoy, 9M SW of Pte de Grave, and runs NE past Pte de Grave. Of the two sets of ldg lts, the second lead over Platin de Grave (1·4m), and it is better to pass S or W of this shoal. The buoys are unlit.

LA GIRONDE TO BORDEAUX AND THE MED (chart 2916) The river is a fascinating cruising ground in its own right, with marinas at Royan, Port-Médoc, Pauillac and Bordeaux – as well as many lesser harbours and creeks – see 9.22.20 to 9.22.25. Tides run hard and the river should be treated with the respect due to any major tidal waterway.

30M above Bordeaux the Canal Latéral à la Garonne is entered at Castets-en-Dorthe. 193km/53 locks later, the older and more interesting Canal du Midi continues from Toulouse for 240km/65 locks to the Med. The trip (9.22.26) takes about 3 weeks.

LA GIRONDE TO CAPBRETON (charts 2664, 1102) From Pte de la Négade to Capbreton, the coast is a featureless stretch of 107M. It is bordered by sand dunes and pine trees, and is often a lee shore with no shelter from W winds. 5M offshore a current usually sets N at about 0·5kn, particularly with a S wind; in winter this may be stronger after W winds. Within 1M of the coast there may be a S'ly counter-current.

A missile range, operated by Centre d'Essais des Landes, lies between Pointe de la Négade and Capbreton and extends up to 45M offshore. For details of boundaries, activity and sources of information, see 9.22.27.

Arcachon is accessible via an E-W corridor (not normally active) through the Landes range. The entrance to Bassin d'Arcachon and the marina is via the well buoyed, but unlit, Passe Nord between extensive, shifting sandbanks on which the sea breaks even in calm conditions. Passe Sud is closed to navigation and most of the buoys have been lifted. Study 9.22.28 for optimum timing, swell and weather conditions before attempting entry.

Strong N or W winds and swell make the ent to the large marina at Capbreton (9.22.29) impassable. Anglet/Bayonne may then be a safer option; or stay at sea. The Fosse (or Gouf) de Capbreton, a submarine canyon, runs at right angles to the coast. The 50m depth contour is 3ca W of Capbreton hbr bkwtr and the 100m line is 4ca further W. In strong W winds a dangerous sea breaks along the N and S edges of it.

CAPBRETON TO SPANISH BORDER (charts 1102, 1343) There is a marina at Anglet (9.22.30), but few facilities for yachts further up the R. Adour at Bayonne. ▶*At L'Adour ent the flood runs E and SE, sp rate 2-4kn; the ebb runs W, sp rate 3-5kn.*◀ S of Pte St Martin the coast has mostly sandy beaches and rky cliffs, with offlying rky shoals and Pyrenees mountains inland. In strong W winds the sea breaks over Loutrou shoal; and on Plateau de St Jean-de-Luz, a chain of rky shoals lying 1-4M offshore. 22

St Jean-de-Luz (chart 1343 and 9.22.31) is best approached first time or in bad weather through Passe d'Illarguita (between Illarguita and Belhara Perdun shoals): follow the 138° transit (Le Socoa lt on with Bordagain lt) until the Ste Barbe ldg lts (101°) are in transit; thence enter by Passe de l'Ouest on the 151° transit of the inner hbr ldg lts.

Baie de Fontarabie, in Spanish Rada de Higuer, lies on the border of France and Spain, and is entered between Pte Ste Anne and Cabo Higuer (a bare, rugged cape with lt ho) 1·75M WNW. In the middle of the bay is a neutral area, marked by beacons and shown on chart 1181. To seaward of this area the boundary line (approximately 01°46'·2W) runs N from a white pyramid on the S shore, about 1M SW of Pte Ste Anne.
Les Briquets (dry) lie 1M N of Pte Ste Anne. Keep to W of Banc Chicharvel and Bajo Iruarri in ent to B. Entry should not be attempted with strong onshore winds or heavy swell. R La Bidassoa is entered between breakwaters in SW corner of the B, giving access to the marina at Hendaye-Plage (9.22.32).

See 9.23.6 for the Spanish hbr and marina at Fuenterrabia.

9.22.6 Special notes for France: See 9.17.6.

9.22.7 PORNIC Loire Atlantique 47°06´·47N 02°06´·66W

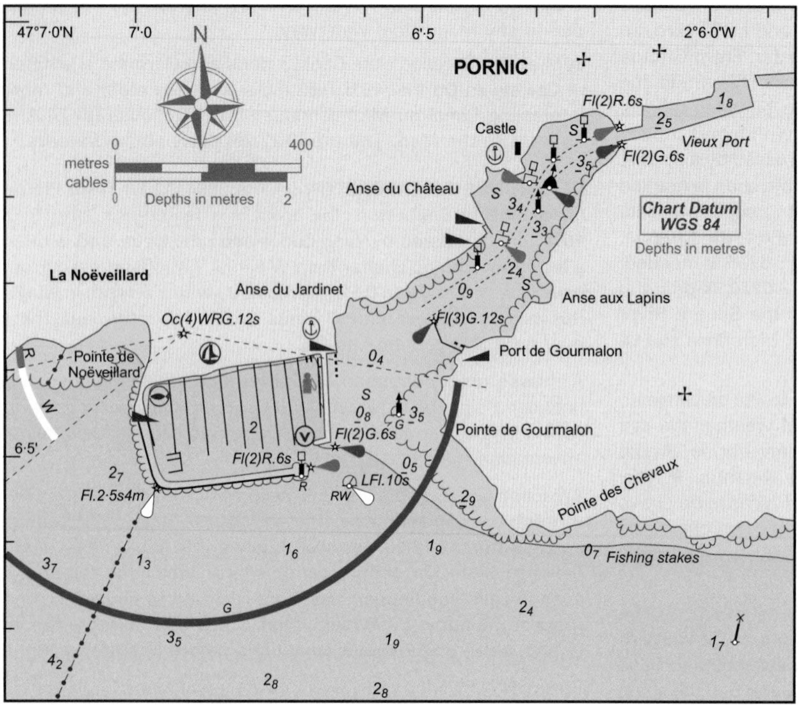
47°7·0'N
7'·0
6'·5
2°6·0'W
PORNIC
metres
cables
Depths in metres
Castle
Anse du Château
Fl(2)R.6s
Vieux Port
Fl(2)G.6s
Chart Datum
WGS 84
Depths in metres
La Noëveillard
Anse du Jardinet
Anse aux Lapins
Oc(4)WRG.12s
Fl(3)G.12s
Port de Gourmalon
Pointe de Noëveillard
Pointe de Gourmalon
Fl(2)G.6s
Fl(2)R.6s
LFl.10s
RW
Fl.2·5s4m
Pointe des Chevaux
Fishing stakes

CHARTS AC 2646, 2986, 2981; Imray C40; SHOM 7395, 7394; ECM 547, 549

TIDES +0515 Dover; ML 3·6; Duration 0540; Zone –0100

Standard Port BREST (⟷)

Times				Height (metres)			
High Water		Low Water		MHWS	MHWN	MLWN	MLWS
0500	1100	0500	1100	6·9	5·4	2·6	1·0
1700	2300	1700	2300				
Differences PORNIC							
–0050	+0030	–0010	–0010	–1·1	–0·8	–0·4	–0·2
POINTE DE SAINT-GILDAS							
–0045	+0025	–0020	–0020	–1·3	–1·0	–0·5	–0·2

SHELTER Very good in large marina (2m); access HW±5. But no access with draft 1.5m LW±1 when Coeff >75, nor in SE-SW winds >F7. Ⓥ berths are at S ends of pontoons P3 (first to stbd; smaller boats), P2 (medium boats) and P1 (LOA >12m). Old hbr dries 1·8m; access HW±2½ via marked, lit drying chan.

NAVIGATION WPT 47°05´·98N 02°08´·86W, 073°/1·6M to hbr ent, is in the W sector of Pte de Noëveillard lt ho. Leave the small SWM buoy to stbd, especially near LWS. Do not cut the corner round the S bkwtr head due to rky spur. Enter between the SHM and PHM piles, on which the ☆s are mounted. A rky spur also extends SW from the head of the E jetty.

Beware Banc de Kerouars 4-6M WSW of harbour, least depth 0·7m, on which seas break; it is unmarked, but the W sector of Pte de Noëveillard lt clears it by night. From the NW pass between this bank and the mainland. All other hazards are well marked. The S end of B de Bourgneuf is full of oyster beds, and many obstructions.

LIGHTS AND MARKS See chartlet and 9.22.4. The W sector (051°-079°) of Pte de Noëveillard lt ho lies between Notre-Dame ECM bcn twr VQ(9)10s, and the E end of Banc de Kerouars.

A SPM outfall buoy, Fl Y 2·5s, is 5·5 cables SW of the marina elbow. The lt ho and trees behind offer guidance if any is needed.

R/T VHF Ch 09 (H24).

TELEPHONE Aff Mar 02·40·82·01·69; CROSS 02·97·55·35·35; ⊖ 02·40·82·03·17; SNSM 02·28·53·01·46; Auto 08·92·68·08·44; Police 02·40·82·00·29; Dr 02·40·82·01·80; Brit Consul 02·51·72·72·60.

FACILITIES Port-la-Noëveillard Marina (754 + 165 Ⓥ) ☎ 02·40·82·05·40, 📠 02·40·82·55·37, €1.84, P, D (on small pontoon with drying ledge inshore of it), ME, El, ⚒, BH (50 ton), C (6 ton) CH, Ⓔ, SM, ▣. **CN de Pornic** ☎ 02·40·82·34·72.

Town Market Sun am. 🛒, Gaz, R, Bar, ✉, Ⓑ, ⇌, ✈ (Nantes). Ferry: Roscoff/St Malo.

9.22.8 L'HERBAUDIÈRE

Vendée **47°01´·63N 02°17´·83W** (Ile de Noirmoutier)

CHARTS AC 2646, 2986, 2981; Imray C40; SHOM 7395, 7394; ECM 547, 549

TIDES +0500 Dover; ML 3·4; Zone –0100

Standard Port BREST (⟷)

Times				Height (metres)			
High Water		Low Water		MHWS	MHWN	MLWN	MLWS
0500	1100	0500	1100	6·9	5·4	2·6	1·0
1700	2300	1700	2300				
Differences L'HERBAUDIERE							
–0047	+0023	–0020	–0020	–1·4	–1·0	–0·5	–0·2
FROMENTINE							
–0050	+0020	–0020	+0010	–1·6	–1·2	–0·7	0·0

SHELTER Good in marina (E side, dredged 1·5m), except in winds E of N; Ⓥs berth on pontoon F or as directed. FV hbr (W side); NB early morning departures. The popular ⚓ off Pte des Dames lt, 4+M to the E, is exposed to N and E winds.

NAVIGATION WPT 47°02´·36N 02°17´·69W, 187·5°/7ca to hbr ent. There are rks and banks to the SW, NW and NE of Pte de l'Herbaudière. Ldg lts and white sector (187·5°-190°) of the W jetty lt both lead into ent chan, dredged to 1·2m and passing close W of two 0·3m patches; care is needed at LWS. Two SHM buoys, both Fl G 2·5s, and a PHM buoy, Fl R 2·5s, mark the last 2ca of the chan. W bkwtr can obscure vessels leaving.

LIGHTS AND MARKS Visibility in summer is often poor. Conspic daymarks are R/W radio mast 500m W of hbr and water tr about 1M SE. Ile du Pilier lt ho, with two distinctive twrs, is 2·7M WNW of hbr. Other lts/marks as chartlet and 9.22.4.

At night initial positioning is assisted by any of the 3 W sectors (W055°-060°, W124°-153°, W201°-240°) of Basse de Martroger, NCM bcn twr, 1·1M NNE of the hbr. Ldg lts 187·5°, both grey masts, Q, lead over Banc de la Blanche (1·5m) approx 2M N of hbr. W jetty, Oc (2+1) WG 12s, W sector 187·5°-190° (2½°), G elsewhere.

R/T HM VHF Ch 09 (HO).

TELEPHONE Aff Mar 02·51·39·94·03; SNSM 02·51·39·33·90; CROSS 02·97·55·35·35; Météo 02·40·84·80·19; Auto 08·92·68·08·85; ⊖ 02·51·39·06·80; Police 02·51·39·04·36; Dr 02·51·39·05·64; Brit Consul 02·51·72·72·60.

FACILITIES Marina (442+50 Ⓥ), ☎ 02·51.39.05.05, 📠 02·51.39.75.97; €2.07, P, D, C (25 ton), Slip, ME, SM, El, Ⓔ, CH. ▣, Gas, Gaz, 🛒, R, Bar (JulAug), ⚒, SC;
Quay Bar, R.

MINOR HARBOUR ON ÎLE DE NOIRMOUTIER

NOIRMOUTIER-EN-L'ÎLE 46°59´·37N 02°13´·14W. AC 2981; SHOM 7394. Tides as above. Good shelter and AB, 4M SE of L'Herbaudière, but FV hbr dries up to 3·6m on mud/gravel.

Appr HW±1 across extensive drying rock ledges to the N and E of ent. The E'ly of 2 chans runs SSW from approx 47°00´·70N 02°11´·10W, then doglegs WNW to the ent. It is marked by 5 unlit PHM bns. An inshore chan runs S from off Pte des Dames lt ho, Oc (3) WRG12s. It is more easily followed, keeping about 400m off 5 unlit SHM bns along the shore. Both chans meet at the ent where the flood tide sets S. S jetty hd has ☆ Oc (2) R 6s. Follow the jetty on N side for about 1M to hbr. A prior recce is advised (3M overland from L'Herbaudière).

HM ☎ 02.51.39.08.39. **Quay** AB, FW, C (4 ton), ME, El, Ⓔ, ⚒, CH, SM. **Town** P, D, 🛒, Gaz, R, Bar, ▣, ✉, Ⓑ, ⇌ ✈ at Nantes, via ferry to Pornic and bus. Ferry: Roscoff or St Malo.

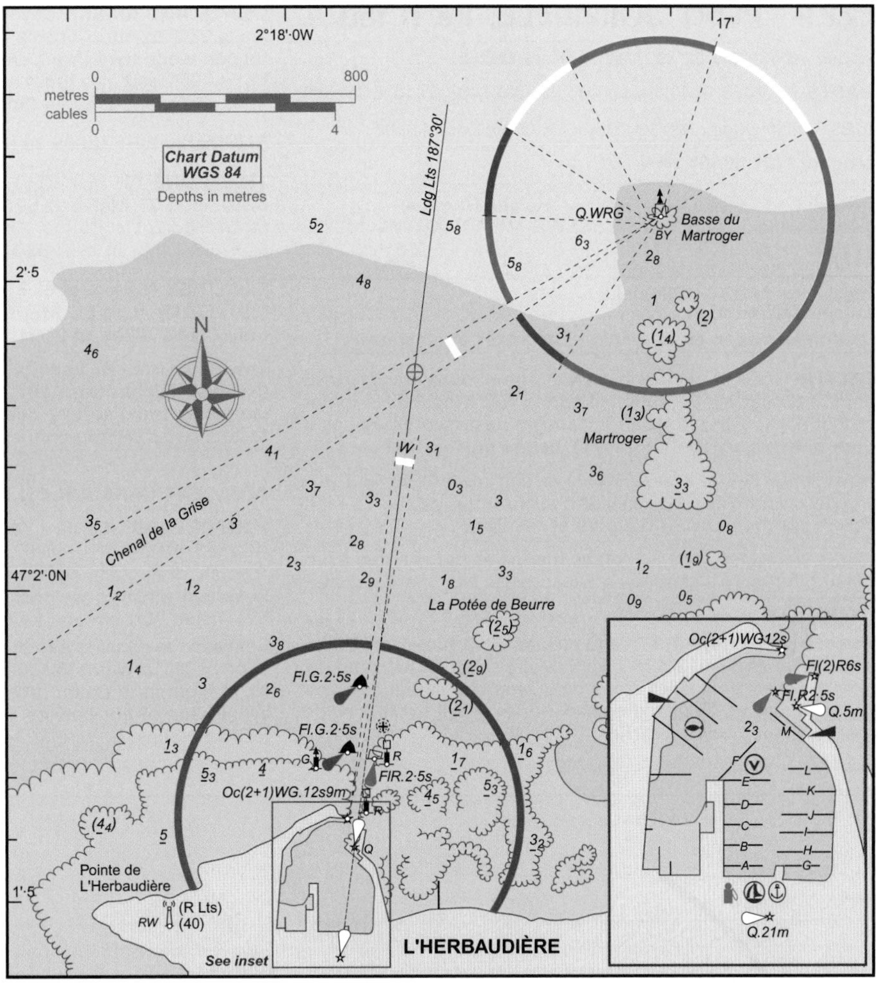
2°18'·0W
17'
metres
cables
0
800
4
Chart Datum
WGS 84
Depths in metres
Ldg Lts 187°30'
Q.WRG
Basse du
Martroger
BY
Martroger
Chenal de la Grise
La Potée de Beurre
2'·5
47°2'·0N
1'·5
Fl.G.2·5s
Fl.G.2·5s
FlR.2·5s
Oc(2+1)WG.12s9m
Pointe de
L'Herbaudière
(R Lts)
RW
(40)
See inset
L'HERBAUDIÈRE
Oc(2+1)WG12s
Fl(2)R6s
Fl.R2·5s
Q.5m
Q.21m

ADJACENT HARBOUR south of ÎLE DE NOIRMOUTIER

FROMENTINE, Vendée, 46°53´·60N 02°08´·60W. AC 2981, SHOM 7394. HW +0550 on Dover (UT); ML 3·2m; Duration 0540. Tides 9.22.8. Do not appr from Baie de Bourgneuf as there is a road causeway (Le Gois), dries 3m, from Île de Noirmoutier to the mainland.

From Fromentine SWM lt buoy, L Fl 10s, 46°53´·07N 02°11´·63W, make good 072°/1·4M via Goulet de Fromentine to Tourelle Milieu, Fl (4) R 12s, R twr, and Boisvinet W bcn twr. The chan is buoyed, moved as necessary, but is very shallow, so dangerous in bad weather. At sp the ebb can reach 8kn, the flood 5kn. Do not attempt night entry. Pass under the bridge (clearance 24m, two x Iso 4s 32m 18M). ⚓ W of pier near PHM buoy Fl R 2s. At Pte du Notre Dames-de-Monts, there is a Dir lt, Oc (2) WRG 6s; see chartlet and 9.22.4 for sector details.

Facilities: Quay Slip, C (3 ton), FW; **Cercle Nautique de Fromentine-Barfatre** (CNFB); **Services:** ME, El, ⚒, CH.

22

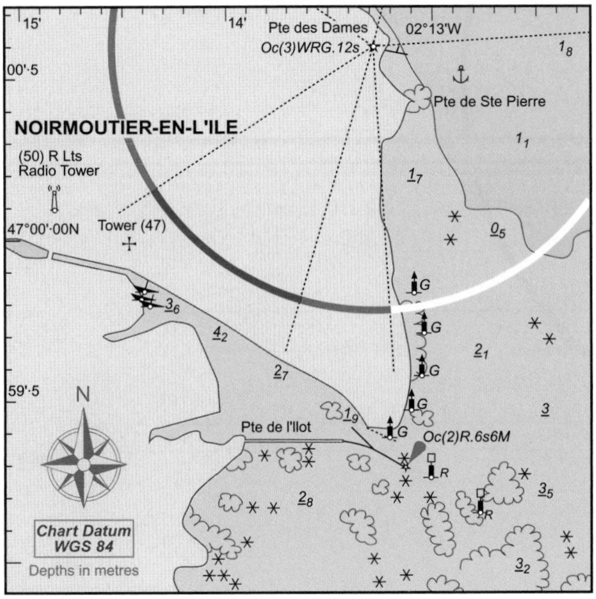
15'
14'
Pte des Dames
Oc(3)WRG.12s
02°13'W
00'·5
Pte de Ste Pierre
NOIRMOUTIER-EN-L'ILE
(50) R Lts
Radio Tower
47°00'·00N
Tower (47)
59'·5
N
Pte de l'Ilot
Oc(2)R.6s6M
Chart Datum
WGS 84
Depths in metres

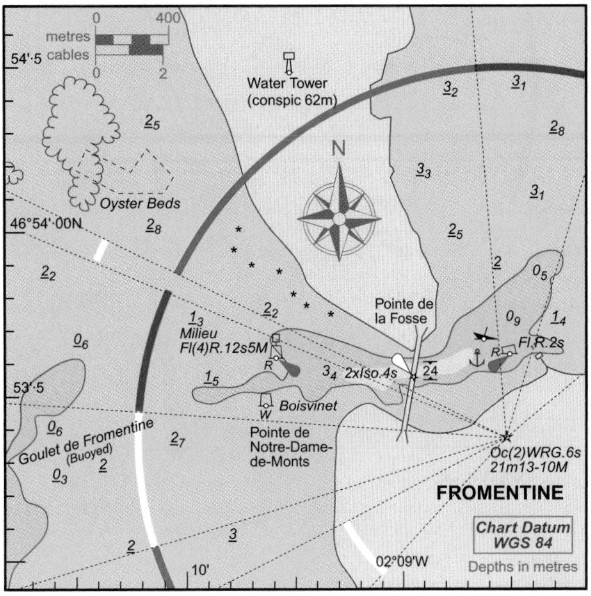
metres
cables
0
400
2
54'·5
Water Tower
(conspic 62m)
N
Oyster Beds
46°54'·00N
Pointe de
la Fosse
Milieu
Fl(4)R.12s5M
2xIso.4s
24
Fl.R.2s
53'·5
Boisvinet
W
Pointe de
Notre-Dame-
de-Monts
Goulet de Fromentine
(Buoyed)
Oc(2)WRG.6s
21m13-10M
FROMENTINE
Chart Datum
WGS 84
Depths in metres
10'
02°09'W

9.22.9 PORT JOINVILLE, Île d'Yeu

Vendée **46°43'·75N 02°20'·77W** ❁❁◊◊◊✿✿✿

CHARTS AC 2663, 3640; Imray C40; SHOM 7402, 7410; ECM 549

TIDES +0550 Dover; ML 3·1; Duration 0600; Zone –0100

Standard Port BREST (⟵)

Times				Height (metres)			
High Water		Low Water		MHWS	MHWN	MLWN	MLWS
0500	1100	0500	1100	6·9	5·4	2·6	1·0
1700	2300	1700	2300				
Differences *PORT JOINVILLE							
–0040	+0015	–0030	–0035	–1·9	–1·4	–0·7	–0·3

*Local information gives a little more water at all states.

SHELTER Good in marina, but swell enters outer hbr in N/NE winds. Approach with caution in strong N-E winds; if F8 do not attempt entry. Very crowded in season; best to pre-book as it is the only secure hbr on Yeu. Ⓥ berths on A/B pontoons

The wet basin (3·7m), access HW±1½ via entry gate 02·51·58·37·01, is mainly for FVs, but possible overflow for yachts in high season; no pontoons; R/G tfc lts at the gate.

Visitors' dedicated ⚓age is E of the marina as per chartlet; 4-5m on sand, but only if conditions are suitable. No ⚓ in outer hbr.

NAVIGATION WPT 46°44'·30N 02°20'·13W (7ca SW of Basse Mayence NCM buoy), 219°/7ca to abeam bkwtr lt. Beware Basse du Bouet (dries 0·6m) 3ca NW, La Sablaire shoal to the E and rks along the coast both sides of hbr ent. Outer chan dredged 1·2m; appr with care at LW, avoiding bank (dries 0·5m) to stbd inside outer hbr. Keep clear of ferries.

LIGHTS AND MARKS Daymarks: Very conspic high water twr leads 224° to hbr. Conspic chimney W of hbr ent. Two green-topped white twrs (front, Quai du Canada Iso G 4s; rear, Old lt ho) ≠ 203° lead into hbr. Ldg lts 219°, both QR. Other lts: Main lt ho, Fl 5s, and Pte des Corbaux at E tip: see 9.22.4.

R/T Marina VHF Ch 09 16 (HO).

TELEPHONE Aff Mar 02·51·59·42·60; ⊜ 02·51·39·06·80; CROSS 02·97·55·35·35; Météo 02·51·36·10·78; Auto 08·92·68·08·85; SNSM 02·51·58·32·01; Police 02·51·58·30·05; Dr 02·51·59·30·00/ 02·51·58·30·58; Ⓗ 02·51·68·30·23; Brit Consul 02·51·72·72·60.

FACILITIES Marina, ☎ 02·51·58·38·11, 📠 02·51.26.03.49, €2.69, (390+170 Ⓥ), P, D, El, ME, ⚒, CH, Ⓔ. **Wet Basin** Slip, FW, C (15 ton). **CN Ile d'Yeu** ☎ 02·51·58·31·50.

Town 🛒, Gaz, R, Bar, ✉, Ⓑ, ⇌ (St Gilles-Croix-de-Vie), ✈ (Nantes). Flights from airfield 2M west of hbr to Nantes and (summers only) to Les Sables d'Olonne. Ferry: Roscoff or St Malo. Ferries to Fromentine, St Gilles and Les Sables d'Olonne.

ADJACENT HARBOUR ON S COAST OF ILE D'YEU

PORT DE LA MEULE, Ile d'Yeu, Vendée, **46°41'·68N 02°20'·75W.** AC 2663; SHOM 7410. –0050 sp and –0020 nps on Brest; ML 3·0m. A small, drying fishing hbr on the S side of Ile d'Yeu, only safe in settled offshore weather; untenable in S winds. Many little FVs inside hbr; best to ⚓ outside and W of the ent.

Between Pte de la Père to the W and Pte de la Tranche to the SE, appr on 023° towards W square patch on Gy □ lt tr, R top, Oc WRG 4s; at night in W sector (018°-027·5°), but night ent not advised. Within 1ca of ent beware rks, first to port, then to stbd. Few facilities: Slips, R, Bar; 🛒 1½ miles.

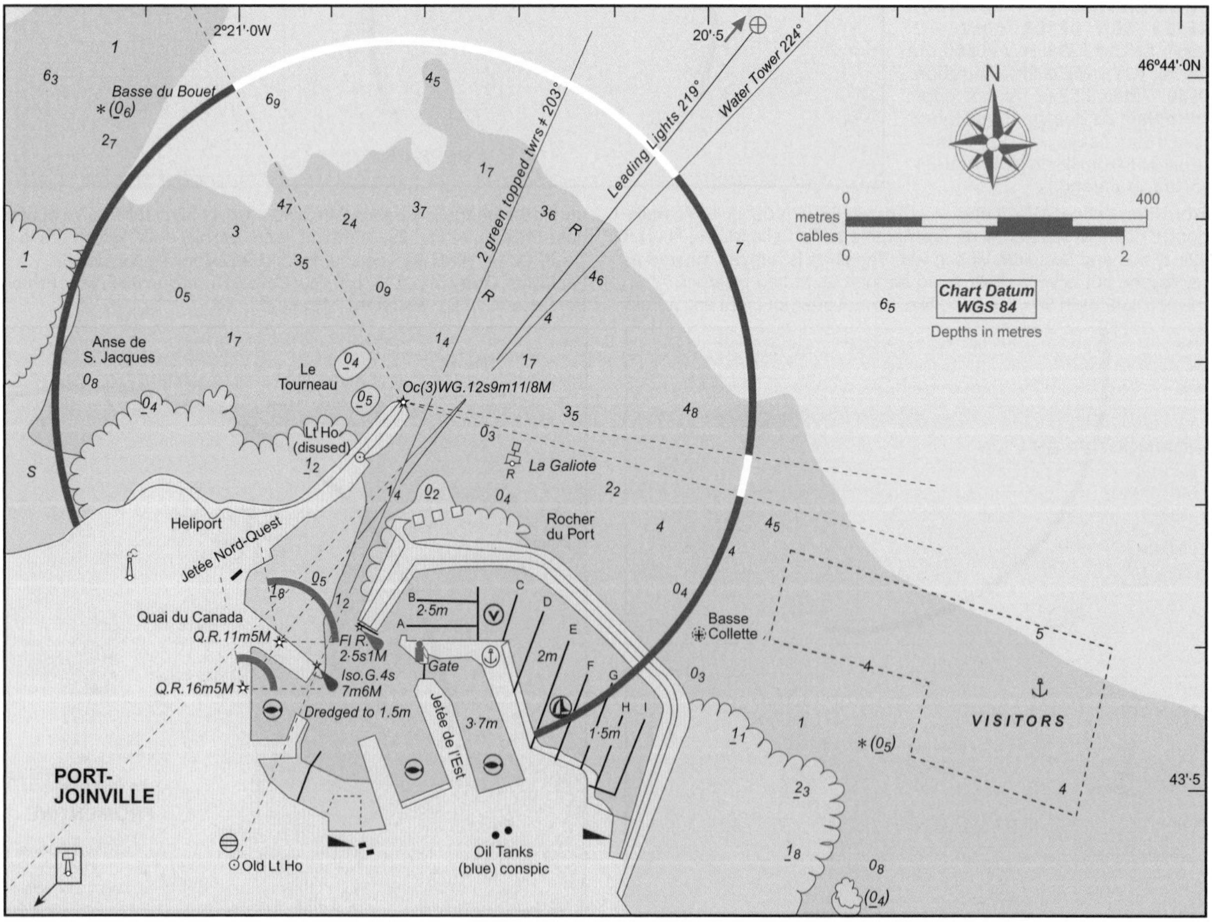
2°21'·0W
20'·5
46°44'·0N
43'·5
Basse du Bouet
Leading Lights 219°
Water Tower 224°
2 green topped twrs ≠ 203°
metres
cables
Chart Datum WGS 84
Depths in metres
Anse de S. Jacques
Le Tourneau
Oc(3)WG.12s9m11/8M
Lt Ho (disused)
La Galiote
Heliport
Jetée Nord-Quest
Rocher du Port
Quai du Canada
Q.R.11m5M
Q.R.16m5M
Fl R. 2·5s1M
Iso.G.4s 7m6M
Gate
Dredged to 1.5m
Jetée de l'Est
Basse Collette
VISITORS
PORT-JOINVILLE
Old Lt Ho
Oil Tanks (blue) conspic

9.22.10 ST GILLES-CROIX-DE-VIE

Vendée **46°41'·47N 01°57'·29W** (abm bkwtr hd) ❁❁❁◊◊◊✿✿

CHARTS AC 2663, 3640; Imray C40; SHOM 7402; ECM 1022, 549

TIDES +0500 Dover; ML 3·2; Duration 0600; Zone –0100

Standard Port BREST (⟵)

Times				Height (metres)			
High Water		Low Water		MHWS	MHWN	MLWN	MLWS
0500	1100	0500	1100	6·9	5·4	2·6	1·0
1700	2300	1700	2300				
Differences ST GILLES-CROIX-DE-VIE							
–0030	+0015	–0032	–0032	–1·8	–1·3	–0·6	–0·3

SHELTER Good shelter, and easy access except in strong SW'lies or swell when breakers form off ent. Silting persists and despite dredging, depths may be reduced. On N bank: a small drying yacht basin inside Grand Môle; 2 tidal FV basins; beyond them the marina nominally dredged to 1·5m. Or pick up ⚓ opposite marina; or AB on drying quay on E bank below bridge. In settled weather ⚓ off ent, close SE of ldg line in 3·5m.

NAVIGATION WPT 46°40'·94N 01°58'·02W, on the 043·7° ldg line and abeam Pilours SCM lt buoy, 043·7°/0·72M to Jetée de la Garenne lt. From W & NW, beware Rocher Pill'Hours (2·8m) and drying reefs extending 1ca SE.

Best arr/dep HW –2 to HW to avoid strong ebb, up to 6kn in ent at springs which may complicate berthing on outer ends of pontoons. Do not arr/dep LW±2 if >1·5m draft. Ent chan (⚓ prohib) is dredged 1·0m, but narrow and very shallow near bkwtr hds due to silting. Keep well off the first two chan buoys which are laid outboard of drying rks; and, tfc permitting, keep slightly W of 043·7° ldg line.

LIGHTS AND MARKS Daymarks are Pte de Grosse-Terre (rky hdland) with lt ho, W truncated conical tr; and two spires NE of the marina. The front ldg mark is hard to see initially against bldgs behind. Lights as per chartlet and 9.22.4.

R/T VHF Ch 09 (season 0600-2200; out of season 0800-1200, 1400-1800LT).

TELEPHONE Aff Mar 02·51·55·10·58; ⊖ 02·51·55·10·18; CROSS 02·97·55·35·35; SNSM 02·51·55·01·19; Météo 02·51·36·10·78; Auto 08·92·68·08·85; Police 02·51·55·01·19; Dr 02·51·55·11·93; Brit Consul 02·51·72·72·60.

FACILITIES Port la Vie Marina (800+80 Ⓥ) ☎ 02·51·55·30·83, 📠 02.51.55.31.43, €2.09, Access H24, P, D, ME, El, CH, Gaz, SM, BH (26 ton), ⚒, Ⓔ, C (15 ton), SHOM, Slip, R, 🛒, Bar. **CN** ☎ 02·51·54·09·31.

Town 🛒, Gaz, R, Bar, ✉, Ⓑ, ⇌. A ferry runs to Ile d'Yeu. Ferry: Roscoff or St Malo.

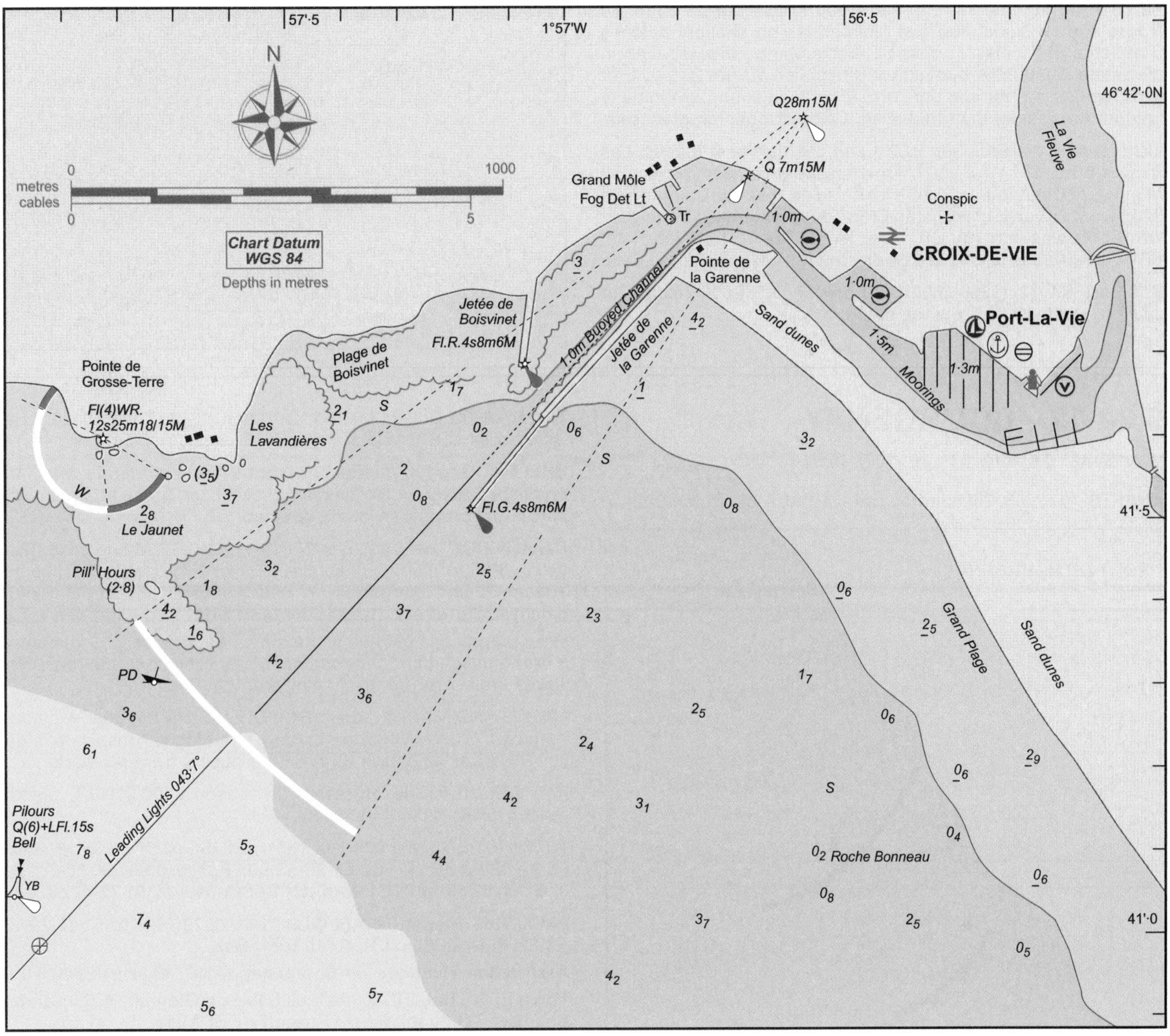
57'·5
1°57'W
56'·5
46°42'·0N
41'·5
41'·0
N
metres
cables
0
1000
5
Chart Datum WGS 84
Depths in metres
Q28m15M
Q 7m15M
Grand Môle
Fog Det Lt
Tr
La Vie Fleuve
Conspic
CROIX-DE-VIE
Port-La-Vie
1·0m
1·5m
1·3m
Moorings
Pointe de la Garenne
Sand dunes
1·0m Buoyed Channel
Jetée de la Garenne
Jetée de Boisvinet
Fl.R.4s8m6M
Plage de Boisvinet
Pointe de Grosse-Terre
Fl(4)WR. 12s25m18/15M
W
Les Lavandières
Le Jaunet
Pill'Hours (2·8)
Fl.G.4s8m6M
PD
Grand Plage
Roche Bonneau
Pilours Q(6)+LFl.15s Bell
YB
Leading Lights 043·7°

9.22.11 LES SABLES D'OLONNE

Vendée **46°29'·40N 01°47'·40W** ❁❁✋✋✋✿✿

CHARTS AC 2663, 2998, 3638; Imray C40, C41; SHOM 7402, 7403, 7411; ECM 1022

TIDES +0530 Dover; ML 3·2; Duration 0640; Zone –0100

Standard Port BREST (⟵)

Times				Height (metres)			
High Water		Low Water		MHWS	MHWN	MLWN	MLWS
0500	1100	0500	1100	6·9	5·4	2·6	1·0
1700	2300	1700	2300				
Differences LES SABLES D'OLONNE							
–0030	+0015	–0035	–0035	–1·7	–1·3	–0·6	–0·3

SHELTER Access at all tides; entry is easy except in strong winds from SE to SW when apprs get rough. Sailing is prohib in the entry chan to hbr. Commercial and FV Basins prohib to yachts. Access to marina (1·5 - 3·5m) H24. Visitors check in at accueil/fuel pontoon port side, by Capitainerie. Pontoon L, at NE end, is for visitors and multihulls; or berth as directed.

NAVIGATION WPT 46°28′·49N 01°47′·23W [abeam Nouch Sud SCM buoy, Q (6)+L Fl 15s], 032·5°/5ca to intersection with 320° ldg line; thence 7ca to the hbr ent. To the W, beware Les Barges d'Olonne, extending 1·3M W of Pte de Aiguille. The 2 appr chans are: the SW chan with La Potence ldg lts 032·5°, which lead into SE chan on ldg line 320°. In bad weather use the SE chan. Le Noura and Le Nouch are two isolated rks on shallow patches S of Jetée St Nicolas. Further SE, Barre Marine breaks, even in moderate weather. A buoyed wk (dries) lies off hbr ent, to E of 320° ldg line. At hbr ent, the narrow dredged chan (2m) initially favours the E side, then mid-chan. Caution: oncoming vessels.

LIGHTS AND MARKS See 9.22.4 and chartlet for lt details. Les Barges lt ho, 2M W of ent. L'Armandèche lt ho, conspic 6ca W of ent. SW Chan ldg lts 032·5°: both Iso 4s H24. SE Chan ldg lts 320°: front QG on E bkwtr; rear, Q on Tour d'Arundel a large grey twr. St Nicolas jetty hd, QR. Inner ldg lts 328·1°, both Iso R 4s; R/W vert stripes, hard to see by day but not essential for yachts.

R/T Port Ch 12 (0800-1800). Marina Ch 09 (0600-2400LT in season; 0800-2000LT out of season).

TELEPHONE Port HM 02·51·95·11·79, Fax 02·51.21.40.04; Aff Mar 02·51·28·81·91; CROSS 02·97·55·35·35; Météo 02·51·36·10·78; Auto 08·92·68·08·85; ⊖ 02·51·23·58·00; SNSM 02·51·21·20·55; Police 02·51·33·69·91; Dr 02·51·95·14·47; Ⓗ 02·51·21·06·33; Brit Consul 02·51·72·72·60.

FACILITIES Port Olona Marina (990+110 Ⓥ), ☎ 02·51·32·51·16, Fax 02·51.32.37.13, €2.07, Slip, P, D, ME, El, ⚒, ⓔ, CH, BH (27 ton), Ⓔ, SHOM, SM, Divers.

Town 🛒, Gaz, R, Bar, ✉, Ⓑ, ⇌, ✈. Ferry: Roscoff or St Malo.

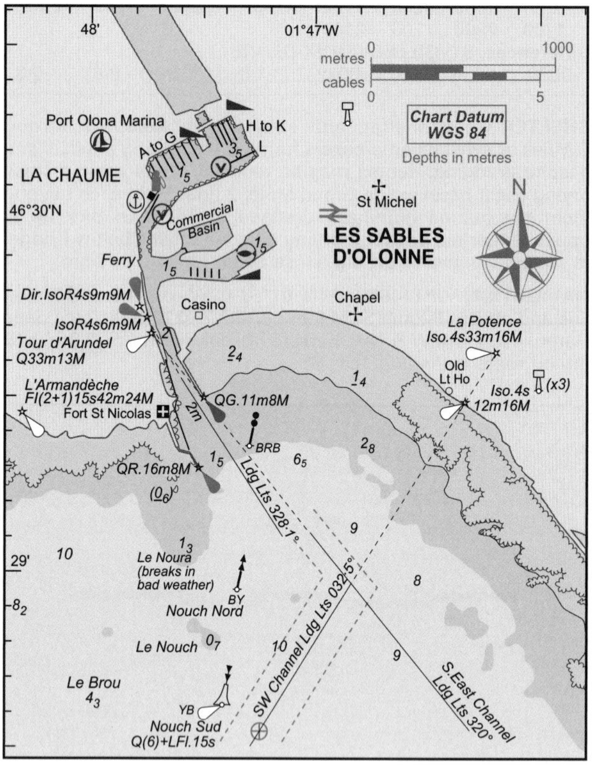
48'
01°47'W
metres 0 1000
cables 0 5
Chart Datum WGS 84
Depths in metres
Port Olona Marina
H to K
L
A to G
LA CHAUME
46°30'N
Commercial Basin
St Michel
LES SABLES D'OLONNE
N
Ferry
Dir.IsoR4s9m9M
IsoR4s6m9M
Tour d'Arundel Q33m13M
Casino
Chapel
La Potence Iso.4s33m16M
Old Lt Ho
Iso.4s 12m16M
(x3)
L'Armandèche Fl(2+1)15s42m24M
Fort St Nicolas
QG.11m8M
BRB
QR.16m8M
Ldg Lts 328·1°
29'
Le Noura (breaks in bad weather)
BY Nouch Nord
Le Nouch
Le Brou
YB Nouch Sud Q(6)+LFl.15s
SW Channel Ldg Lts 032·5°
S East Channel Ldg Lts 320°

9.22.12 BOURGENAY

Vendée **46° 26'·27N 01° 40'·70W** ❁❁✋✋✋✿✿

CHARTS AC 2663, 2998; Imray C41; SHOM 7403; ECM 1022

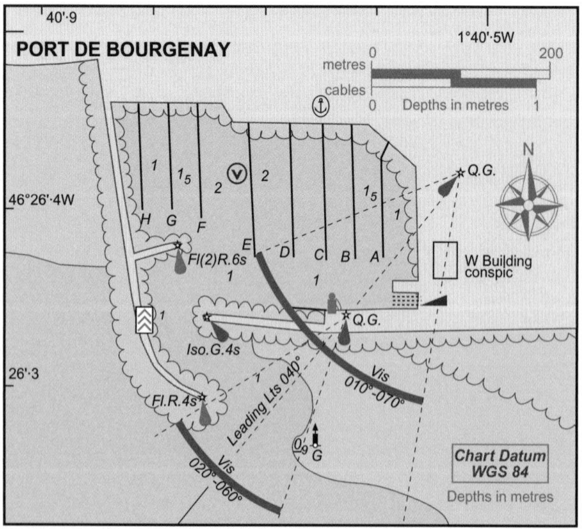
40'·9
PORT DE BOURGENAY
1°40'·5W
metres 0 200
cables 0 1
Depths in metres
N
46°26'·4W
Q.G.
W Building conspic
Fl(2)R.6s
Q.G.
Iso.G.4s
26'·3
Vis 010°-070°
Leading Lts 040°
Fl.R.4s
Vis 020°-060°
G
Chart Datum WGS 84
Depths in metres

TIDES +0600 Dover; ML 3·1; Duration 0640; Zone –0100. Use Differences LES SABLES D'OLONNE (9.22.11), 5·5M NW.

SHELTER Good in marina (2m), but even in moderate weather, and especially with SW'lies, a big swell can break at the ent. Ⓥ berths on E pontoon or as directed.

NAVIGATION WPT 46°25′·27N 01°41′·93W [SWM buoy, L Fl 10s] 040°/1·32M to pier head. 600m ENE of WPT, beware Roches du Joanne (2·9m; dangerous in bad weather) and shoal/drying patches to E of ent, marked by unlit SHM buoy and bcn.

West pierhead is painted white. Ent chan, dredged 1·0m, makes a pronounced, blind S-bend marked by reflective chevrons; 3kn speed limit. May be less water than charted.

LIGHTS AND MARKS Ldg lts 040° QG; front W hut; rear W pylon, both with G □ & W border. Large white bldg is conspic near ldg lts. The Iso G 4s and Fl (2) R 6s are obsc'd from seaward.

R/T VHF Ch 09 16 (office hrs; in season 0800-2100LT, out of season 0900-1200, 1400-1800).

TELEPHONE Aff Mar 02·51·21·81·81; CROSS 02·97·55·35·35; Auto 08·92·68·08·85; ⊖ 02·51·23·58·00; Police 02·51·90·60·07; Dr 02·51·90·62·68; Ⓗ 02·51·96·00·41; Brit Consul 02·51·72·72·60.

FACILITIES Marina (500+60 Ⓥ) ☎ 02·51·22·20·36, Fax 02·51.22.29.45 €1.89, P, D, ⓔ, Slip, CH, C (15 ton), Gaz.

Association Nautique de Bourgenay (ANB) ☎ 02·51·22·02·57.

Town R, 🛒, Bar, ✉, Ⓑ, ⇌ (Les Sables d'Olonne), ✈ (La Lande, Chateau d'Olonne). Ferry: Roscoff or St Malo.

MINOR HARBOURS IN PERTUIS BRETON

JARD-SUR-MER, Vendée, **46°24′·43N 01°34′·78W**. ❀❀◊✿. AC 2663, 2998 (1:10,000 inset); SHOM 7403. HW +0600 on Dover (UT); HW–0010 & ht –2·0m on Brest; ML 3·1m; Duration 0640. W daymarks 4ca E of hbr ent lead 038° between the drying Roches de l'Islatte and Roches de la Brunette, marked by buoys. Then pick up 293° transit of RW marks at W end of hbr, ldg to ent. There are no lights. Small drying hbr, access HW±2, 4·5m max at HW. Moorings inside bkwtr, inc 7 Y Ⓥs. HM's office with blue roof and adjacent bldgs are conspic from afar. HM (occas) ☎ 02·51·33·90·61; ⊖ ☎ 02·51·95·11·33; Facilities: **Jetty** FW, C (5 ton); CH, Divers.

L'AIGUILLON/LA-FAUTE-SUR-MER, Vendée, **46°19′·95N 01°18′·78W**. ❀❀◊◊✿✿. AC 2663, 2999; SHOM 7404. HW +0535 on Dover (UT), HW –0030, ht +0·6m on Pte de Grave (Zone –0100); ML 3·4m. The area is very flat and, being shallow, waves build up quickly in any wind. The bar to seaward dries and is dangerous in bad weather; avoid in strong S or W winds. Ent (only safe in fine weather with off-shore winds) is best identified by a conspic transformer on a hill, La Dive, opposite side of chan to Pointe d'Arcay. Beware mussel beds with steel piles which cover at HW; also oyster beds.
Enter at Le Lay SCM buoy, Q (6) + L Fl 15s, 46°16′·15N 01°16′·49W, with transformer brg 033°. Access HW±3 (max 1·5m draft). ⚓ in R Lay or berth at L'Aiguillon (NE bank); or in drying tidal basin at La Faute (SW bank). Shelter good in two yacht hbrs. HMs (L'Aiguillon) ☎ 05.51.97.06.57; (La Faute) ☎ 05.51·56·45·02; CROSS ☎ 05.56·09·82·00; Dr ☎ 05.51·56·46·17; **Club Nautique Aiguillonais et Fautais** (CNAF) ☎ 05.51·97·04·60; ME, CH.

MARANS, Vendée, approx **46°18'·70N 01°00'·00W**. AC 2663, 2999; SHOM 7404; ECM 551. Tides: see L'Aiguillon above; HW at Brault lock = HW La Rochelle + 0020. From SWM buoy, L Fl 10s, (46° 15'·35N 01°11'·50W) abeam Pte de l'Aiguillon with 10m high B bcn, the buoyed chan, dries 1·0m, leads 3¾M NE past Pavé jetty, Fl G 4s. Thence 3½M up-river to Brault lifting bridge and 5ca to lock, which opens HW ±2 springs, and HW ±1 nps. Waiting pontoons before bridge; pontoon inside vast lock (104 x 45m wide, sides sloping to 11m; ☎ 05.46.01.53.77) with small swing bridge at far end. Straight 3M canal (4·7m) to good shelter in non-tidal hbr (max LOA 16m); berth/raft to stbd-side pontoons. Facilities: **Quay** ☎ 05.46.01.02.99, AB (40+10 Ⓥ), €3.35, FW, C (3 tons), P & D (cans); BY, ME, ⚒ (wood), SM. **Town** 🛒, R, Bar.

MINOR HARBOUR ON ÎLE DE RÉ

LA FLOTTE, Charente Maritime, **46°11′·34N 01°19′·30W**. ❀❀◊◊✿✿. AC 2999; SHOM 7404, 7412. HW +0535 on Dover (UT). La Flotte is 2M SE of St Martin (9.22.14). From NW keep clear of Le Couronneau; from E, keep N of bcn off Pte des Barres. Appr on 212·5° in W sector (205°-220°) of La Flotte lt ho, W tr + G top, Fl WG 4s. Alongside it a Moiré indicator shows vert B line when on course 212·5°, or chevrons to regain course. 5 waiting buoys outside; or ⚓ off in 3m, sheltered from S & W. Outer hbr sheltered by mole and dries 2·0m; access HW±3. 3 pontoons (6 Ⓥ, max LOA 10m) in outer hbr: the hammerhead of E pontoon (3rd to stbd) is dredged 2m for deep draft yachts; pre-booking advised. Inner hbr dries 2·8m. HM ☎ 05.46.09.67.66; ⊖ at St Martin; Facilities: **Quay** €1.68, Slip, FW, Ⓥ berth on mole, Grid; **Cercle Nautique de la Flotte-en-Ré** (CNLF) (open Jul-15 Sep) ☎ 05·46.09.97.34, Bar; **Services:** P & D (cans), CH, ME, SM, ▣.

ILE-DE-RÉ (9.22.13 & 9.22.14)

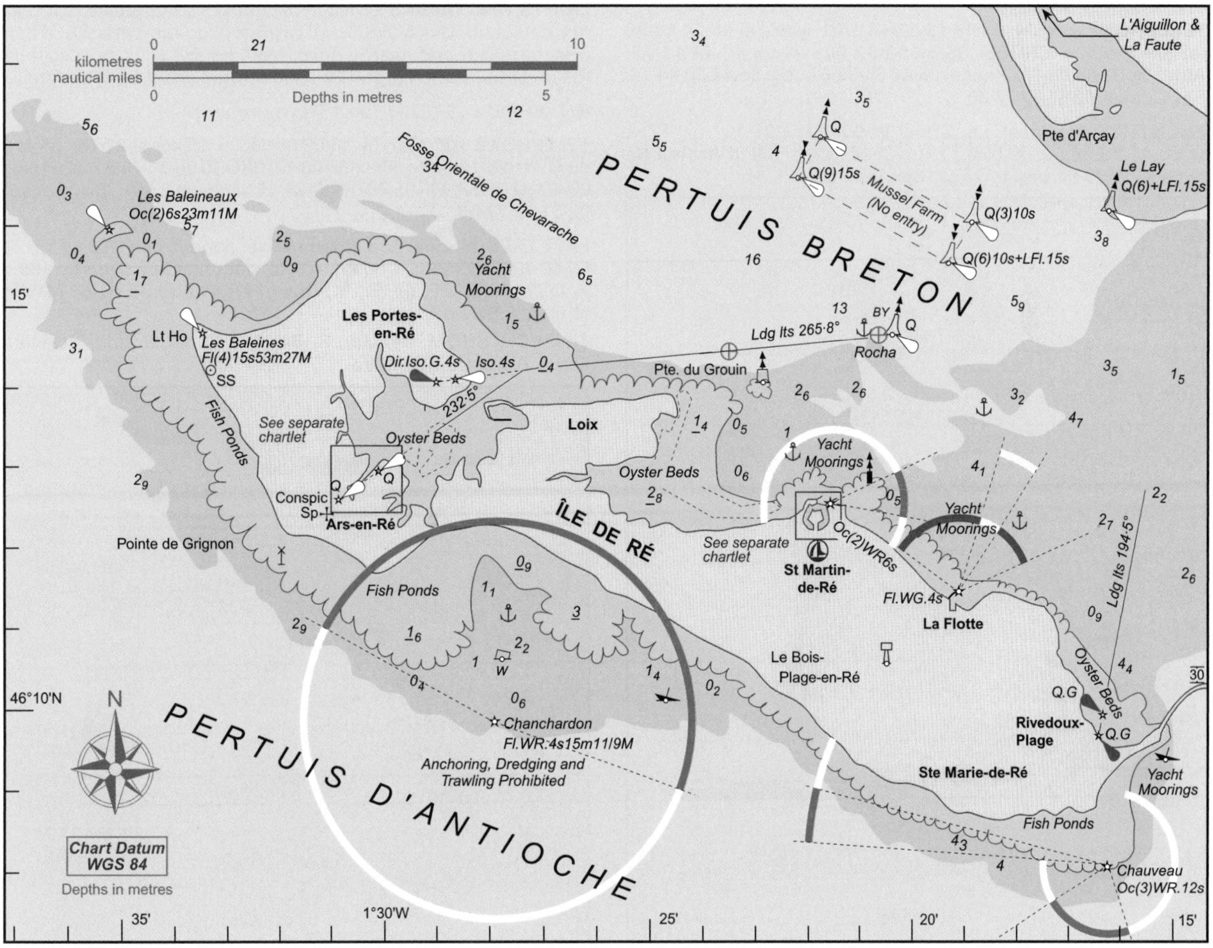
kilometres
nautical miles
Depths in metres
PERTUIS BRETON
PERTUIS D'ANTIOCHE
ÎLE DE RÉ
L'Aiguillon & La Faute
Pte d'Arçay
Le Lay
Q(6)+LFl.15s
Q(9)15s
Mussel Farm (No entry)
Q(3)10s
Q(6)10s+LFl.15s
Fosse Orientale de Chevarache
Les Baleineaux
Oc(2)6s23m11M
Lt Ho
Les Baleines
Fl(4)15s53m27M
SS
Fish Ponds
Les Portes-en-Ré
Yacht Moorings
Dir.Iso.G.4s
Iso.4s
232·5°
Ldg lts 265·8°
Rocha
BY
Pte. du Grouin
Loix
See separate chartlet
Oyster Beds
Conspic Sp
Ars-en-Ré
Pointe de Grignon
St Martin-de-Ré
Oc(2)WR6s
Fl.WG.4s
La Flotte
Ldg lts 194·5°
Le Bois-Plage-en-Ré
Chanchardon
Fl.WR.4s15m11/9M
Anchoring, Dredging and Trawling Prohibited
Rivedoux-Plage
Q.G
Ste Marie-de-Ré
Chauveau
Oc(3)WR.12s
Chart Datum WGS 84
15'
46°10'N
35'
1°30'W
25'
20'

9.22.13 ARS-EN-RÉ

Charente Maritime **46°12'·70N 01°30'·62W**

CHARTS AC 2998, 2999; Imray C41; SHOM 7404, 7412; ECM 551, 1022

TIDES +0540 Dover; ML 3·7m; Zone –0100; See 9.22.14

SHELTER Port d'Ars is at the head of a chan in the SW corner of the bay, Le Fier d'Ars, which dries to salt pans & oyster beds. The two well sheltered marinas are:

a. Bassin de la Criée (2m) on NW side of chan approx 600m NE of town; access HW±2 over sill 2·5m CD, Ⓥ berths on pontoon H, first to port.

b. Bassin Prée, at head of chan, access HW ±2 over sill drying 2·9m; Ⓥ berths immediately to stbd on E pontoon in 1·8m. Or AB outside on NW quay drying to mud. Note: draught, tidal coefficient, wind and barometer dictate access times. There is ⚓ in a pool (2m) close S of Pte du Fier.

NAVIGATION WPT 46°14'·31N 01°23'·58W, 266°/1·66M to first SHM chan buoy. Beware shoal ground close S of outer ldg line. The appr chan is restricted by rky ledges drying 0·4m and 1·5m; access HW±3. Continue to the inner, buoyed and beaconed 232·5° ldg line.

LIGHTS AND MARKS Conspic ✠ spire, white with black top, is in the town, about 330m SSW of the rear 232·5° ldg lt. Outer ldg lts 265° are hard to see by day against trees beyond: front, W □ on hut; rear, G □ tr on house. Les Baleines lt ho may be visible to the right of and beyond the ldg lts.

Inner 232·5° ldg lts, also hard to see by day, lead across Fiers d'Ars into Port d'Ars: front, W □ with R lantern; rear, B □ on W framework tr, G top. See chartlet and 9.22.14 for light details.

R/T VHF Ch 09.

TELEPHONE SNSM 05·46·29·83·46; Aff Mar 05·46·09·68·89 (at La Flotte); CROSS 05·56·09·82·00; ⊜ 05·46·41·11·73; Auto 08·92·68·08·17; Police 05·46·84·32·67; Dr 05·46·29·44·19; Brit Consul 02·51·72·72·60.

FACILITIES Marinas: La Criée ☎ 05·46·29·25·10, La Prée ☎ 05.46.29.08.52. €2.24, Slip, C (6 ton); **CN d'Ars-en-Ré** ☎ 05·46·29·23·04 (Apl to Nov); **Services:** ME, El, ⚒.

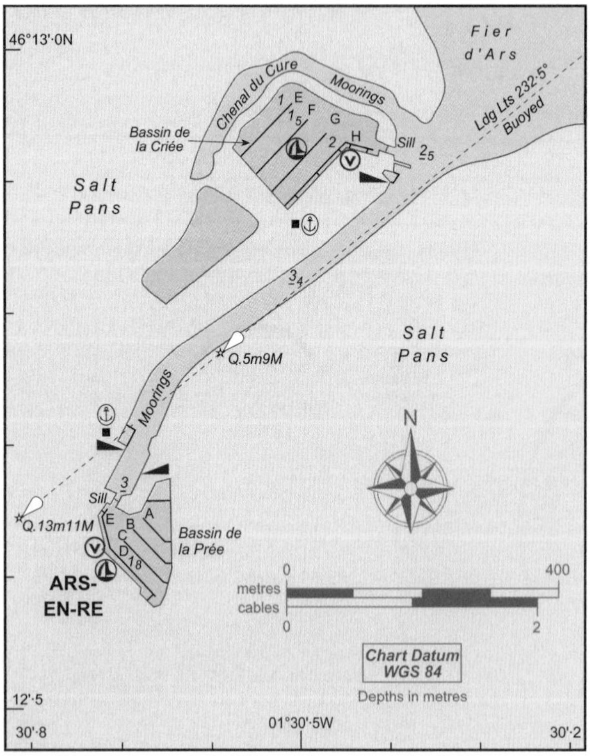
46°13'·0N
Fier d'Ars
Chenal du Cure
Moorings
Ldg Lts 232·5° Buoyed
Bassin de la Criée
Sill 2₅
Salt Pans
3₄
Q.5m9M
Moorings
Sill
Q.13m11M
Bassin de la Prée
ARS-EN-RE
metres
cables
0
400
2
Chart Datum WGS 84
Depths in metres
12'·5
30'·8
01°30'·5W
30'·2

9.22.14 ST MARTIN, Ile de Ré

Charente Maritime **46°12'·50N 01°21'·93W**

CHARTS AC 2998, 2999; Imray C41; SHOM 7404, 7412; ECM 551, 1022

TIDES +0535 Dover; ML 3·7; Zone –0100

Standard Port POINTE DE GRAVE (⟶)

Times				Height (metres)			
High Water		Low Water		MHWS	MHWN	MLWN	MLWS
0000	0600	0500	1200	5·4	4·4	2·1	1·0
1200	1800	1700	2400				
Differences ST MARTIN, Ile de Ré							
+0015	–0030	–0030	–0025	+0·5	+0·3	+0·2	–0·1

SHELTER Complete shelter in non-tidal marina (depth 3m); often very crowded so pre-booking advised. 4 W waiting buoys off ent. Avant port is protected by detached bkwtr close to the NE and mole on NW side. Inside mole a waiting pontoon (season only) is dredged 2·3m, but untenable in fresh NW to NE winds. Marina gate is open from about HW–2 to HW+2½, depending on coefficient (sill is 0·8m above CD), 0630-2200LT May, Jun, Sept; 0500-2300 Jul/Aug. Berth as directed by HM. Access to drying basin for FVs HW–3 to +2 via chan (1·5m).

NAVIGATION WPT 46°14'·68N 01°20'·74W [Rocha NCM By, Q], 200°/2·3M to St Martin mole hd. From the NW, keep N and E of Le Rocha, a rky bank extending 2½M ENE from Pte du Grouin. From SE, pass well N of unlit NCM bn, about ¾M NE of ent, marking Le Couronneau drying ledge in R sector (245°-281°) of St Martin lt ho. By day appr 210·5° lt ho ≠ □ ✠ tr; or 202° mole hd ≠ ✠ tr; the lt ho is far easier to see than the mole head.

LIGHTS AND MARKS Conspic daymarks: La Citadelle 3ca E of hbr ent; Lt ho, Oc (2) WR 6s, W twr/R top, on ramparts SE of ent; and the □ ✠ tr and nearby ruins. Mole hd, Iso G 4s, is obsc'd by Pte du Grouin when brg <124°. See chartlet and 9.22.4 for details.

R/T VHF Ch 09 (0700-1900LT in summer).

TELEPHONE Aff Mar 05·46·09·68·89; ⊜ 05·46·09·21·78; Météo 05·46·41·29·14; Auto 08·92·68·08·17; CROSS 05·56·73·31·31; Police 05·46·09·21·17; Dr 05·46·09·20·08; Ⓗ 05·46·09·20·01; Brit Consul 02·51·72·72·60.

FACILITIES Marina portstmartin@wanadoo.fr 05·46·09·26·69, 05·46·09·93·65. (135 + 50 Ⓥ), €2.86, get toilet key code by 1900, P, D Jul-Aug, ME, Ⓔ, El, ⚒; **Quay** FW, C (6 ton); **YC St Martin** ☎ 05·46·09·22·07.

Town CH, SHOM, Gaz, R, Bar, ✉, Ⓑ, ⇌, ✈ (La Rochelle). Ferry: Roscoff or St Malo.

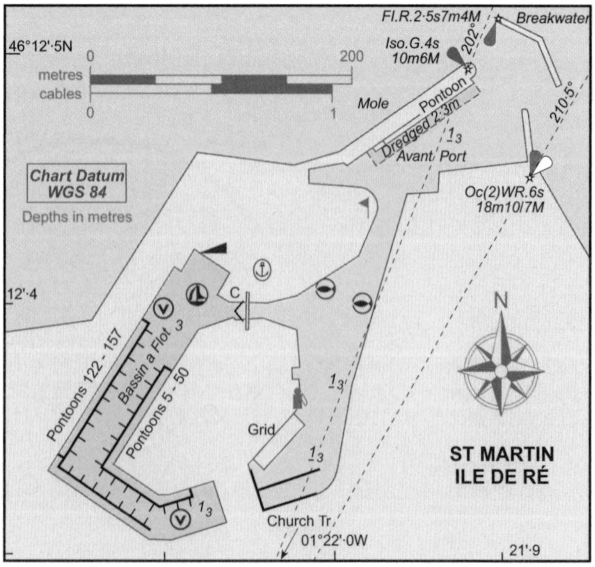
Fl.R.2·5s7m4M
Breakwater
46°12'·5N
Iso.G.4s 10m6M
202°
0
200
metres
cables
0
1
Mole
Pontoon
Dredged 2·3m
1₃
Avant Port
210·5°
Chart Datum WGS 84
Depths in metres
Oc(2)WR.6s 18m10/7M
12'·4
C
Pontoons 122 - 157
Bassin à Flot 3
Pontoons 5 - 50
1₃
Grid
1₃
1₃
Church Tr
01°22'·0W
21'·9
ST MARTIN ILE DE RÉ

9.22.15 LA ROCHELLE

Charente Maritime **46°08'·83N 01°10'·11W**

CHARTS AC 2999, 3000, 2743; Imray C41; SHOM 7404, 7413; ECM 551, 1022

TIDES +0515 Dover; ML 3·8; Zone −0100

Standard Port POINTE DE GRAVE (⟶)

Times				Height (metres)			
High Water		Low Water		MHWS	MHWN	MLWN	MLWS
0000	0600	0500	1200	5·4	4·4	2·1	1·0
1200	1800	1700	2400				
Differences LA ROCHELLE and LA PALLICE							
+0015	−0030	−0025	−0020	+0·6	+0·5	+0·3	−0·1

SHELTER Excellent. Speed limit 3kn in all basins. From seaward: **Port des Minimes** is a very large marina 2m deep, max LOA 25m. 8ca NE on the E side a large non-tidal **Outer Basin (Bassin des Chalutiers)** (5m) with pontoons on the N/NE sides is mainly used by long-stay and mega-yachts; access by prior arrangement. **Vieux Port**, in the old town, is entered between the two twrs of St Nicolas and La Chaine. It is a noisy, atmospheric tidal basin (part-dredged 1·3m) with 100+ 40 Ⓥ. E of Vieux Port, the non-tidal **Inner Basin (Bassin des Yachts)** (3m) is entered by a gate with sill 1·2m above CD, opens HW–2 to HW+¾; night ent by prior arrangement ☎ 70.46.41.32.05. La Pallice, 3M W, is a commercial/FV port with no yacht facilities.

NAVIGATION WPT 46°08'·41N 01°11'·40W, 059°/0·9M to abm Tour Richelieu (with tide gauge) marking a drying rky spit N of the chan. Appr from about 1M S of Le Lavardin lt tr on ldg line 059°. Pte des Minimes lt bcn and a WCM lt buoy mark drying rks extending 4ca SW of the marina. Shallow (0·5m) appr chan needs care at MLWS; speed limit 5kn. Ent to Port des Minimes is 1ca past Tour Richelieu, marked by unlit WCM and 2 PHM buoys.

For Vieux Port stay on 059° ldg line in chan (35m wide), leaving 4 PHM buoys well to port. Caution: many ferries.

Note: The bridge from the mainland to Ile de Ré is lit and buoyed for big ships: 30m air clearance, N-bound between piers Nos 13 and 14; ditto, S-bound between piers Nos 10 and 11. Yachts may transit other spans, subject to air and water clearances.

LIGHTS AND MARKS See chartlet and 9.22.4. The rear 059° ldg lt, Q, is briefly obscured by Tour St Nicolas between 061°-065°, ie when approaching between La Pallice and Lavardin plateau. Tour St Nicolas, Tour de la Chaine and Tour de la Lanterne, near the Vieux Port, are conspic by day and floodlit at night. The buoyed, but unlit narrow chan between Tour Richelieu and Vieux Port is not advised at night; ferries run at all hours.

R/T Port des Minimes Ch 09 (H24); Vieux Port Ch 09.

TELEPHONE Aff Mar 05·46·28·07·28; ⊖ 05·46·41·11·73; CROSS 05·97·55·35·35; Météo 05·46·41·29·14; Auto 08·92·68·08·08; Dr 05·46·42·19·22; Police 05·46·00·50·99; Ⓗ 05·46·27·33·33; Brit Consul 02·51·72·72·60.

FACILITIES

PORT DES MINIMES **Marina** (3,200+350 Ⓥ on pontoons 13-14 in SW basin), €1.70, ☎ 05·46·44·41·20, 📠 05.46.44.36.49, Slip, C (10 ton), P & D (Jul/Aug 0800-2000), BH (50 ton), R, Ice, Bar, Ⓑ, ✉, ♿, ⊡, ME, ⚒, CH, Ⓔ, El, SHOM, SM, Gaz, 🛒. **Société des Régates Rochellaises** ☎ 05·46·44·62·44.

Water bus to the town every H, 1000-2000, except 1300; Jul/Aug H and H+30, 0900-2330, except 1300.

VIEUX PORT **Drying Basin** €1.70, Slip, C (10 ton), BH (300 ton), SM, ME, ⚒, CH, toilets/showers.

Bassin des Chalutiers and **Inner Basin** ☎ 05·46·41·32·05, €8.70, Access HW −2 to HW+¾.

Town P, D, 🛒, Gaz, R, Bar, ✉, Ⓑ, ⇌, ✈. Ferry to Ile de Ré; internal air services (and to London) from Laleu airport (2½km N of port). Ferry: Roscoff or St Malo.

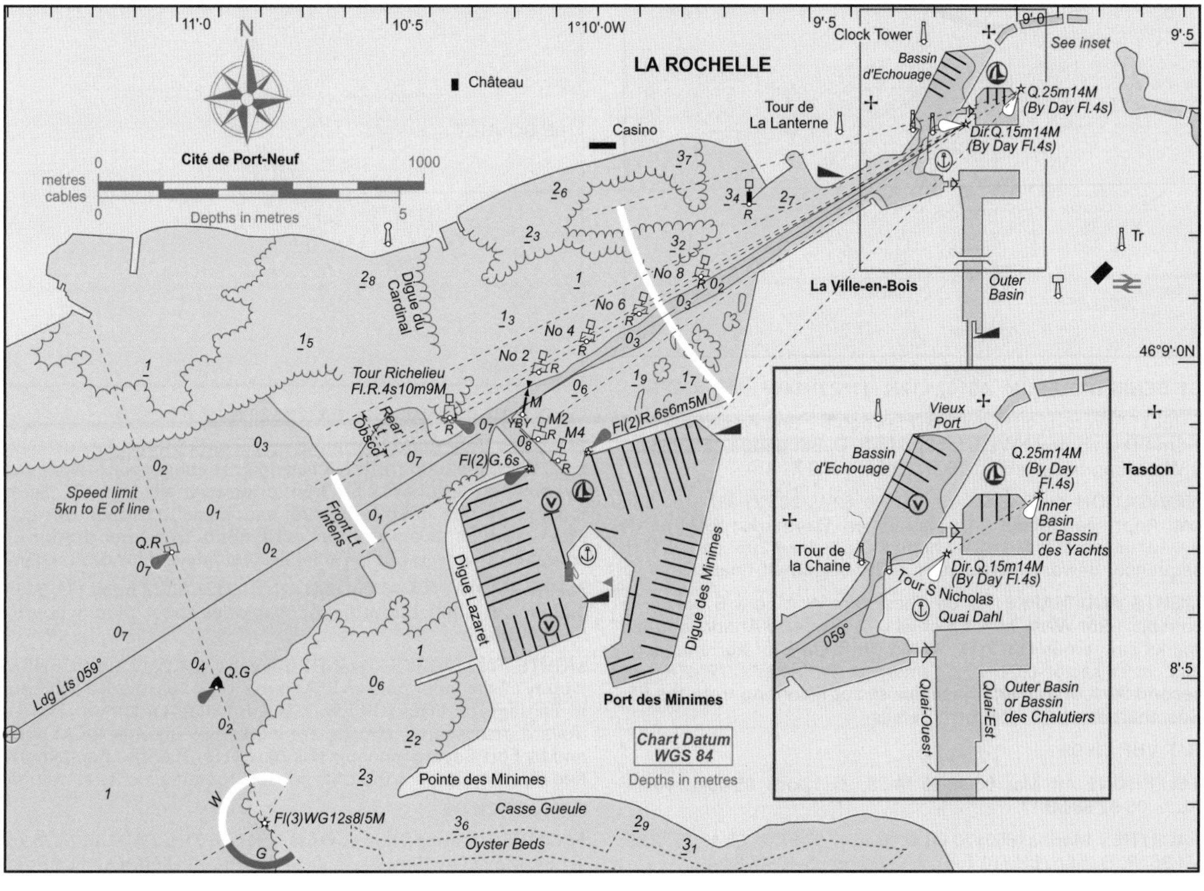
LA ROCHELLE
11'·0
10'·5
1°10'·0W
9'·5
9'·0
See inset
46°9'·0N
8'·5
Château
Casino
Cité de Port-Neuf
metres
cables
1000
Depths in metres
Clock Tower
Bassin d'Echouage
Q.25m14M (By Day Fl.4s)
Dir.Q.15m14M (By Day Fl.4s)
Tour de La Lanterne
La Ville-en-Bois
Outer Basin
Tr
Tasdon
Digue du Cardinal
No 8
No 6
No 4
No 2
Tour Richelieu Fl.R.4s10m9M
Rear Lt Obscd
Fl(2)R.6s6m5M
Fl(2)G.6s
M2
M4
YBY
Front Lt Intens
Speed limit 5kn to E of line
Q.R
Q.G
Ldg Lts 059°
Digue Lazaret
Digue des Minimes
Port des Minimes
Chart Datum WGS 84
Depths in metres
Pointe des Minimes
Casse Gueule
Oyster Beds
Fl(3)WG12s8/5M
Vieux Port
Inner Basin or Bassin des Yachts
Tour de la Chaine
Tour S Nicholas
Quai Dahl
Quai-Ouest
Quai-Est
Outer Basin or Bassin des Chalutiers
059°

9.22.16 ILE D'OLÉRON

CHARTS AC 2999, 3000; Imray C41; SHOM 7405, 7404, 7414, 7415; ECM 552

TIDES +0545 Dover; ML 3·9; Duration 0540; Zone –0100

Standard Port POINTE DE GRAVE (⟶)

Times				Height (metres)			
High Water		Low Water		MHWS	MHWN	MLWN	MLWS
0000	0600	0500	1200	5·4	4·4	2·1	1·0
1200	1800	1700	2400				
Differences LE CHAPUS (Bridge to mainland)							
+0015	–0040	–0025	–0015	+0·6	+0·6	+0·4	+0·2
POINTE DE GATSEAU (S tip of Île d'Oléron)							
+0005	–0005	–0015	–0025	–0·1	–0·1	+0·2	+0·2

HARBOURS Marinas at St Denis, Le Douhet and Boyardville. Le Chateau, near the bridge, is a tiny fishing hbr. La Cotinière on W coast is a fishing port which suffers almost constant swell; yachts only admitted in emergency or bad weather.

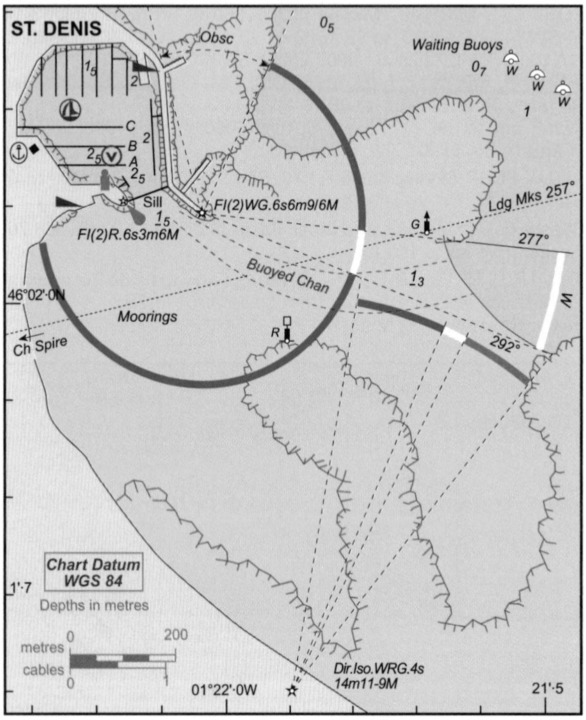
ST. DENIS
Waiting Buoys
Obsc
Fl(2)WG.6s6m9/6M
Fl(2)R.6s3m6M
Sill
Ldg Mks 257°
277°
292°
Buoyed Chan
Moorings
Ch Spire
46°02'·0N
Chart Datum
WGS 84
Depths in metres
metres
cables
01°22'·0W
21'·5
Dir.Iso.WRG.4s
14m11-9M

ST DENIS D'OLÉRON 46°02'·12N 01°22'·14W

SHELTER Very good in marina, max depth 2·5m. Access over sill 1·5m CD is approx HW±2$\frac{1}{2}$ for 2m draft. Depth gauge on S bkwtr. 3 W waiting buoys about 700m E of ent in 0·7 - 1m.

NAVIGATION WPT 46°03'·26N 01°20'·82W, 205°/1·35M to chan ent. Appr chan (about 1·1m) is buoyed. Daymarks: SHM perch ≠ ✠ twr leads 257° to ent. By night 2 Dir lts lead 205° and 284° in sequence. Beware fishing nets with very small floats.

LIGHTS AND MARKS Pte de Chassiron, W lt ho + B bands, is conspic 1·9M WNW at N tip of island. Rocher d'Antioche lt bcn marks dangerous reef 2·2M NNW. Dir lt, $\frac{1}{2}$M S of hbr ent, leads 205° in W sector (204°-206°); intercept W sector (277°-292°) of second Dir lt on N pier; or use this sector if coming from the SE. See chartlet and 9.22.4 for lt details.

R/T VHF Ch 09.

TELEPHONE Aff Mar 05·46·85·14·33; Ⓗ (12km) 05·46·47·00·86; Auto 08·92·68·08·17.

FACILITIES **Marina** (600+70 Ⓥ) ☎ 05·46·47·97·97, 📠 05·46.75.72.99, €1.96, P, D, Slip, BH (10 ton), ♿; **YCO** ☎ 05·46·47·84·40.

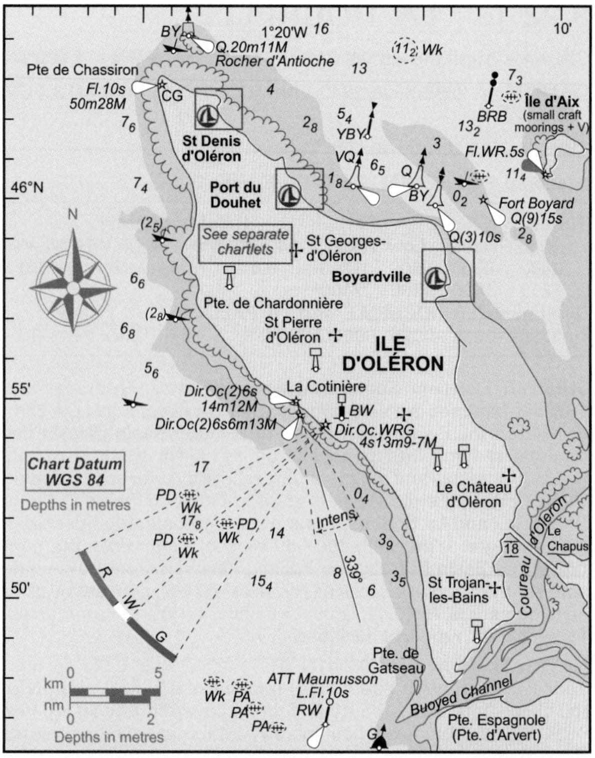
1°20'W
10'
Pte de Chassiron
Fl.10s
50m28M
Q.20m11M
Rocher d'Antioche
Wk
Île d'Aix
(small craft moorings + V)
St Denis d'Oléron
Port du Douhet
Fl.WR.5s
Fort Boyard
Q(9)15s
Q(3)10s
46°N
See separate chartlets
St Georges-d'Oléron
Boyardville
Pte. de Chardonnière
St Pierre d'Oléron
ILE D'OLÉRON
55'
La Cotinière
Dir.Oc(2)6s
14m12M
Dir.Oc(2)6s6m13M
Dir.Oc.WRG
4s13m9-7M
Chart Datum
WGS 84
Depths in metres
Le Château d'Olèron
Le Chapus
Intens
Coureau d'Oléron
50'
St Trojan-les-Bains
Pte. de Gatseau
ATT Maumusson
L.Fl.10s
Buoyed Channel
Pte. Espagnole
(Pte. d'Arvert)
km
nm
Depths in metres

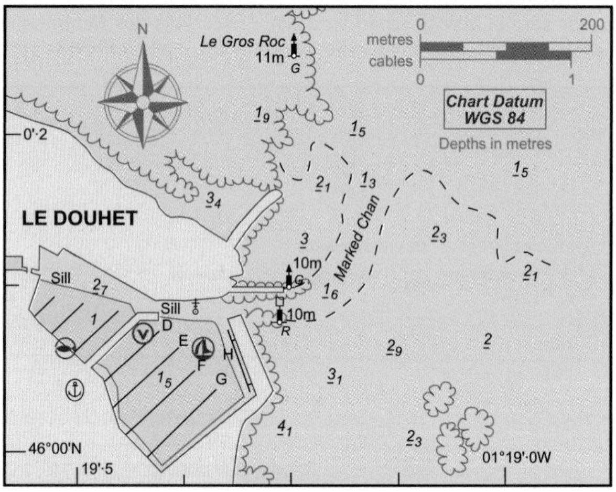
Le Gros Roc
11m
metres
cables
Chart Datum
WGS 84
Depths in metres
0'·2
LE DOUHET
Marked Chan
Sill
10m
46°00'N
19'·5
01°19'·0W

LE DOUHET 46°00'·09N 01°19'·20W

SHELTER Very good in marina on SE side of hbr; FVs use NW part. Ent difficult in fresh NE'lies against ebb; beware swell and overfalls. Access HW±2 for 1·5m draft, over sill 1·8m CD. Sill is marked by tide gauge. Beware: sandbanks encroach on appr chan, reduce access times and need frequent dredging, sometimes closing hbr completely. Not advised for draft >1.5m.

NAVIGATION WPT 46°00'·65N 01°17'·38W, NCM buoy VQ, 246°/1·4M to ent. Unlit, buoyed appr chan dries about 1·6m to approx 0·35M offshore.

LIGHTS AND MARKS The WPT buoy is 1·4M W of another NCM lt buoy Q; the latter plus an ECM buoy, Q (3) 10s, mark a fish farm in Passage de l'Ouest (toward Boyardville). La Longe and Le Boyard, rocky/sandy shoals, are marked by an unlit WCM buoy and by Fort Boyard, conspic twr 29m, Q (9) 15s. The Capitainerie and yacht masts are the only conspic features; no lts at marina.

R/T VHF Ch 09.

FACILITIES **Marina** (305+45 Ⓥ), ☎ 05·46·76·71·13, 📠 05·46.76.78.26. €1.84, Max LOA 15m, ♿; 🏧 at St Georges d'Oléron and La Brée.

BOYARDVILLE 45°58´·25N 01°13´·83W ❁❁◊◊✿✿

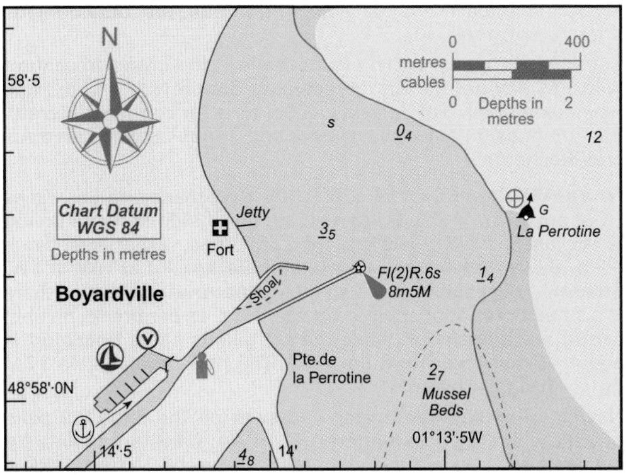
N
58'·5
0
400
metres
cables
0
Depths in metres
2
s
0_4
12
Chart Datum
WGS 84
Depths in metres
Jetty
Fort
3_5
G
La Perrotine
Fl(2)R.6s
8m5M
1_4
Boyardville
Shoal
Pte.de
la Perrotine
2_7
Mussel
Beds
48°58'·0N
01°13'·5W
14'·5
4_8
14'

TIDES HW +0545 on Dover (UT); use Ile d'Aix (9.22.17).

SHELTER Very good in non-tidal marina (2m). Ⓥ berths against quay to stbd; multiple rafting is the norm. Access HW±2 to drying appr chan and into marina to stbd via automatic gate. This opens H24, approx HW±1½ @ nps and HW±2½ @ sp. A ● lt indicates that the ent gate is shut. FVs berth further up-river. Three W waiting buoys ½M N of chan or ⚓ there in 3m.

NAVIGATION WPT 45°58'·44N 01°13'·36W, La Perrotine SHM buoy, 237°/4ca to S bkwtr head. The appr chan leads direct to ent chan where best water is close to S bkwtr. Strong river current, 2kn @ sp. Stand on beyond the lock to avoid a bank, then turn 120° stbd for the lock; best to allow all departing boats to get clear first.

LIGHTS AND MARKS To the N, La Longe le Boyard, a rocky/sandy shoal, is marked by Fort Boyard, conspic tr 29m, Q (9) 15s. Fish farm in the Passage de l'Ouest (toward Le Douhet) is marked by an ECM buoy, Q (3) 10s. No lts/ldg marks.

R/T VHF Ch 09.

TELEPHONE Aff Mar 05·46.47.00.18; Auto 08.92.68.08.17.

FACILITIES Marina (165+30 Ⓥ) 05·46·47·23·71; 05.46.75.06.13; €1.84, Slip, C (10 ton), P & D on opposite bank, ME, El, ⚒, CH, ♿. **YCB** ☎ 05·46·47·10·28.

MINOR HARBOUR ON ILE D'OLÉRON

LE CHATEAU, Ile d'Oléron, Charente Maritime, **45°52´·96N 01°11´·35W**. AC 3000; SHOM 7414, 7415; ECM 552. HW +0545 on Dover (UT); tides as for Ile d'Aix (9.22.17), ML 3·8m, duration 0540. Mainly occupied by oyster FVs; not recommended for yachts, except temporary visit. Possible drying berth on NE quay. Access HW±2. From N, appr via Chenal Est, to SCM bcn marking Grand Montanne and ent to appr chan. From S, appr via Coureau d'Oléron, under mainland bridge (clnce 18m), thence 1M to ent chan. Ldg lts 318·5°, QR; chan is marked by SHM withies. HM ☎ 05·46·47·00·01. Facilities: Slip, L, FW, C (25 ton).

MINOR HBRS AND ANCHORAGES ALONG LA CHARENTE

CHARTS AC 3000, 2747; SHOM 7414, 7415.

NAVIGATION See also notes under 9.22.17.

TIDES see 9.22.17; interpolate as required between Ile d'Aix and Rochefort. Ile d'Aix, HW + 0545 (UT) on Dover; ML 3.9m.

ILE D'AIX, Charente Maritime, **46°00´·60N 01°10´·45W**. There are fair weather ⚓s SW, S and NE of the island. On W side of island, near LW keep 3ca off the two WCM perches. Lights: St Catherine's Pt (S tip of the island), Fl WR 5s, two conspic white lt twrs, R tops; W sector 118°-103°, elsewhere R (345°). Five W Ⓥs (afloat) and 40 drying Ⓥs off St Catherine's Pt (depths shoal rapidly to the E). CNIA 05·46·84·69·89; Town hall 05·46·84·66·09, €9.00 for Ⓥ. **Facilities:** FW, ⛽, Slip, Shwrs, 🛒, R, ferry to Fouras.

Fort Boyard, 1·6M WSW of St Catherine's Pt, is lit Q (9) 15s. It is a mighty structure (29m) ringed by a No entry zone, radius 2½ cables. Originally a military fortification, then accommodation for workers building Boyardville and most recently a TV/film set.

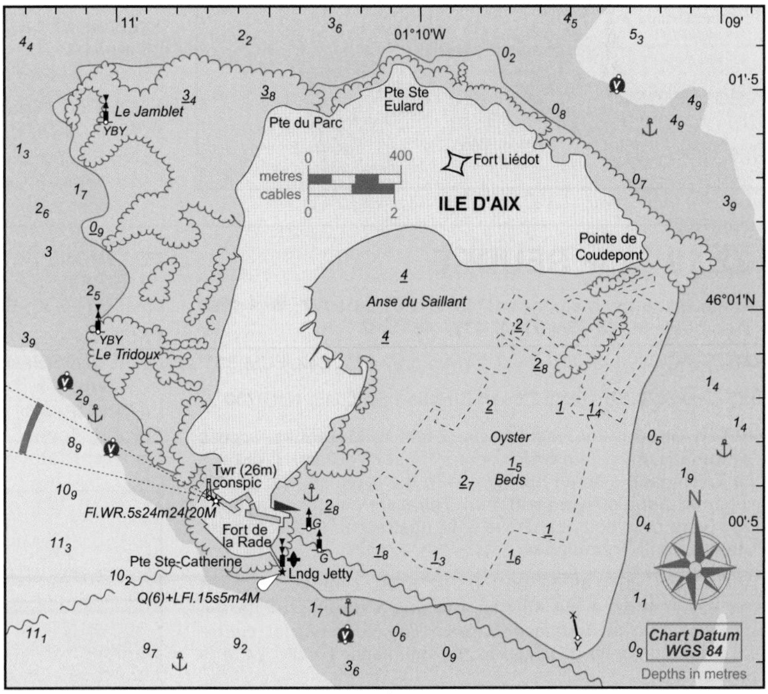
11'
2_2
3_6
01°10'W
4_5
5_3
09'
4_4
0_2
01'·5
3_4
3_8
Pte Ste
Eulard
Le Jamblet
YBY
Pte du Parc
0_8
4_9
4_9
1_3
0
400
Fort Liédot
metres
cables
0
2
0_7
1_7
ILE D'AIX
3_9
2_6
0_9
Pointe de
Coudepont
3
4
Anse du Saillant
46°01'N
2_5
2
4
YBY
Le Tridoux
3_9
2_8
1_4
2_9
2
1
1_4
1_4
8_9
Oyster
0_5
Twr (26m)
conspic
1_5
Beds
2_7
1_9
10_9
2_8
N
Fl.WR.5s24m24/20M
G
0_4
00'·5
Fort de
la Rade
1
11_3
Pte Ste-Catherine
1_8
1_3
1_6
10_2
Lndg Jetty
G
Q(6)+LFl.15s5m4M
1_1
1_7
11_1
0_6
9_7
9_2
0_9
Chart Datum
WGS 84
0_9
3_6
Depths in metres

FOURAS, 45°58´·99N 01°05´·69W (S hbr). A small town on N bank of the Charente from which ferries cross to Ile d'Aix; good beaches and many mussel/oyster beds. There are 3 drying hbrs: South, North and Port de la Fumée. A chequered Twr near the S Hbr and the ch spire are both conspic.

S Hbr. HM 05·46·84·23·10 (1 Jun-30 Sep); other months, Town Hall 05·46·84·66·09. YC: Cercle Nautique de Fouras. Access HW ±2 for max draft 1·5m. 55 + 20 Ⓥ on pontoons. Facilities: FW, ⛽, Slip, C (3 ton), Shwrs. Lights: ☆ Fl WR 4s 6m 9/6M, vis R115°-177°, W177°-115°; and ldg lts 042·5°, both ☆ Oc (2) R 6s.

N Hbr. Town Hall 05·46·84·60·11. Access HW ±3; 1 free drying Ⓥ; possible temp'y AB. Facilities: FW, ⛽, Slip. ☆ Oc (3+1) WG 12s.

La Fumée. Town Hall 05·46·84·60·11. Access H24, except at LW, large coefficient; 1 free drying Ⓥ, Slip. SHM bcn, ☆ QG.

PORT DES BARQUES, approx **45°57´N 01°04´W**, 3·4M from Fouras S. 2 free Ⓥs (afloat) by day, shifting to afloat pontoon overnight (when ferry no longer runs). Town Hall 05·46·84·80·01. Facilities: FW, ⛽, Slip, P & D.

PORT NEUF, 45°57´·02N 00°59´·80W, 7·3M from Fouras S. 2 free Ⓥs (afloat); also a 64m long pontoon at the drying line. **CN Rochefortais** 05·46·87·34·61 (on site); Slip, FW.

SOUBISE, 45°55´·75N 01°00´·32W, 8 berths (€6, pay at camp site) on a 48m afloat pontoon, ⛽, SW bank. Beware big ship wash. Town Hall 05·46·84·92·04. Facilities: Showers; village shops.

MARTROU (Echillais), 45°54´·95N 00°57´·85W approx; 10·5M from Fouras S. 4 free berths on a part-drying pontoon, access HW ±3. Position is on the S bank by the abutments (☆ QG) to the old dismantled road bridge mid-way between the new viaduct (32m) and the aerial transporter 'bridge' upstream. This is a No ⚓ Area. Town Hall 05·46·83·03·74. Village shops at Martrou.

22

9.22.17 ROCHEFORT

Charente Maritime **45°56'·55N 00°57'·29W**

CHARTS AC 3000, 2747; Imray C41; SHOM 7414, 7415; ECM 552

TIDES +0610 Dover; Zone –0100

Standard Port POINTE DE GRAVE (→)

Times				Height (metres)			
High Water		Low Water		MHWS	MHWN	MLWN	MLWS
0000	0600	0500	1200	5·4	4·4	2·1	1·0
1200	1800	1700	2400				
Differences ROCHEFORT							
+0035	–0010	+0030	+0125	+1·1	+0·9	+0·1	–0·2
ILE D'AIX							
+0015	–0040	–0030	–0025	+0·7	+0·5	+0·3	–0·1
LA CAYENNE (R. Seudre)							
+0030	–0015	–0010	–0005	+0·2	+0·2	+0·3	0·0

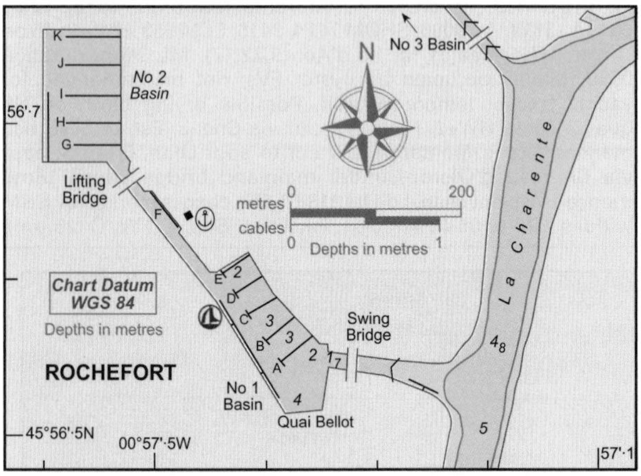
No 3 Basin
N
No 2 Basin
56'·7
K
J
I
H
G
Lifting Bridge
F
metres 0 200
cables 0 1
Depths in metres
La Charente
Chart Datum WGS 84
Depths in metres
E
D
C
B
A
Swing Bridge
ROCHEFORT
No 1 Basin
Quai Bellot
45°56'·5N
00°57'·5W
57'·1

SHELTER Excellent. A 36m pontoon, 120m S of ent to Bassin 1, is short stay foc + ⛽, FW. Waiting pontoon, just outside gate, dries to soft mud.

Entry gate is open from HW La Rochelle +¼ to +¾; wise to confirm with HM day before. Bridge between Bassin Nos 1 and 2 lifts when gate open. (No 3 Bassin, 400m N, is for commercial craft). See previous page for minor hbrs and ⚓ages between Ile d'Aix and Rochefort.

NAVIGATION WPT 45°59'·63N 01°09'·51W [N-abeam Les Palles NCM buoy, Q], 115°/2·1M to next ldg line 134·5°. Beware drying wreck just S of WPT. The bar, 1M S of Fouras, carries least depth 0·9m. Beware very strong currents here, except at HW or LW. Stream in river runs about 2kn (4kn in narrows), and at sp there is a small bore. Appr advised on late flood, as bar breaks on ebb; aim to reach Rochefort while the ent gate is open. Rochefort is about 13M up-river from the WPT. The river is navigable 3·5M on to Tonnay-Charente.

Navigation is straightforward and swift on the flood. 19 pairs of unlit white ldg bcns (lettered TT to AA; no S) are mainly for big ships and may not even be noticed by yachts. A fixed bridge, 32m cl'nce, is 2M before Rochefort, followed by an aerial transporter bridge (to which yachts should give way - if only to take its photograph, assuming it's airborne).

LIGHTS AND MARKS Ldg lts at river mouth: First 115°, both QR, W □ trs/R tops; Soumard lt ho is the conspic rear mark. Second, abeam Fontenelles ⚠: Port-des-Barques ldg lts 134·5°, both Iso G 4s, W □ trs; rear has a B band on its west side.

R/T Port VHF Ch 12. Marina Ch 09 (HW±1).

TELEPHONE Aff Mar 05·46·84·22·67; CROSS 05·56·09·82·00; Météo 05·46·41·11·11; Auto 08.92.68.08.17; ⊜ 05·46·99·03·90; Dr 05·46·99·61·11; Police 05·46·87·26·12; Brit Consul 05·57·22·21·10.

FACILITIES Marina (280+20 Ⓥ) in Basins 1 & 2, ☎ 05·46·99·44·93, 05·46·99·44; €1.22, ME, El, ⚒, Ⓔ, CH, C (30 ton), ♿.

Town P & D (cans), 🛒, Gaz, R, Bar, ✉, Ⓑ, ⇌, ✈ (La Rochelle). Ferry: Roscoff or St Malo.

9.22.18 LA SEUDRE

Charente Maritime, Marennes **45°49'·17N 01°06'·67W**
La Tremblade **45°46'·07N 01°08'·17W**

CHARTS AC 3000; SHOM 7405, 7414; Imray C41, C42; ECM 552

TIDES See 9.22.17; +0545 Dover; Duration Sp 0545, Np 0700

SHELTER Good in the yacht basin (2·5m) at Marennes, access via automatic entry gate which opens about HW±2 sp, HW±1 np. At La Tremblade a small hbr (3m) is in the town centre; yachts dry against stone quay on soft mud. There are ⚓s off La Cayenne village (very crowded), La Grève (½M upstream), and at the ent to Chenal de la Tremblade.

NAVIGATION WPT 45°56'·00N 01°08'·56W, Chenal Est-Nord WCM buoy, thence via Chenal Est and Coureau d'Oléron, passing below the Viaduc d'Oléron (18m clearance at centre span) which links Ile d'Oléron to the mainland. SHOM 7414 is essential.

From Coureau d'Oléron better appr is via Chenal de la Soumaille (dries initially about 0·7m). Chenal de la Garrigue carries slightly more water. Both are marked by bcns and buoys. Beware oyster beds. Pont de Seudre has clearance of 18m. Overhead power cables (16m) span Canal de Marennes and Canal de la Tremblade. La Seudre is navigable 12M SE to lock at Riberou.
Warning: Passage through Pertuis de Maumusson is not advised even in good weather.

LIGHTS AND MARKS Marennes church spire (88m) is conspic above the salt pans. The only lights are: Pte de Mus de Loup, G/W column, W to seaward; Oc G 4s, vis 118°-147° as chartlet. On bridge, between piers 6 and 7, W panels with R □ and G △ mark the channel; also lts, Q 20m 10M, vis up/downstream.

R/T VHF Ch 09.

TELEPHONE Aff Mar 05·46·85·14·33; ⊜ 05·46·47·62·53; Auto 08.92.68.08.17; Police 05·46·85·00·19; Dr 05·46·85·23·06/ 05·46·36·16·35; Brit Consul 05·57·22·21·10.

FACILITIES
MARENNES **Basin** ☎ 05·46·85·02·68, Slip, M, C (6 ton), ME, CH, ⚒. **Town** P & D (cans), 🛒, R, Bar.

LA TREMBLADE **Quay** ☎ 05·46·36·99·00; Slip, C (5 ton), ME, ⚒, SM, CH. **Town** Slip, P & D (cans), Gaz, 🛒, R, Bar, ✉, Ⓑ, ⇌, ✈ (La Rochelle). Ferry: Roscoff or St Malo.

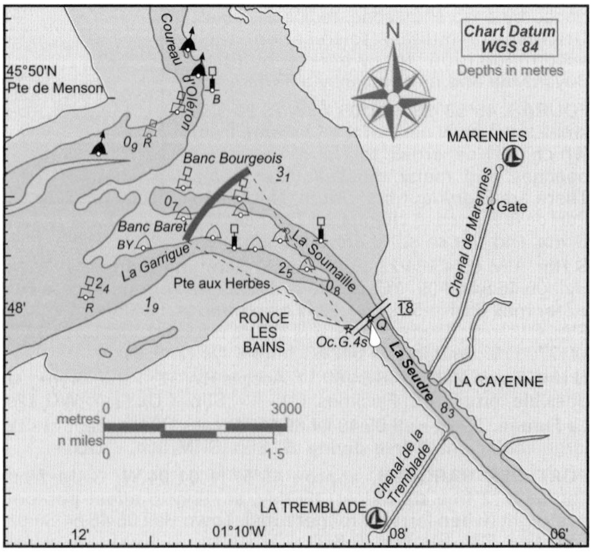
Coureau d'Oléron
45°50'N
Pte de Menson
N
Chart Datum WGS 84
Depths in metres
B
R
MARENNES
Banc Bourgeois
Banc Baret
BY
La Garrigue
La Soumaille
Pte aux Herbes
Gate
Chenal de Marennes
48'
RONCE LES BAINS
Oc.G.4s
Q
18
La Seudre
LA CAYENNE
metres 0 3000
n miles 0 1·5
Chenal de la Tremblade
LA TREMBLADE
12'
01°10'W
08'
06'

TIME ZONE -0100
(French Standard Time)
Subtract 1 hour for UT
For French Summer Time add ONE hour in **non-shaded areas**

FRANCE – POINTE DE GRAVE

LAT 45°34'N LONG 1°04'W

TIMES AND HEIGHTS OF HIGH AND LOW WATERS

SPRING & NEAP TIDES
Dates in red are SPRINGS
Dates in blue are NEAPS

YEAR **2005**

JANUARY

Date	Day	Time	m	Time	m	Time	m	Time	m
1	SA	0200	1.8	0813	4.8	1429	1.8	2043	4.5
2	SU	0242	1.9	0857	4.7	1512	1.9	2133	4.4
3	M	0330	2.0	0950	4.6	1601	2.0	◑ 2234	4.4
4	TU	0425	2.1	1053	4.5	1701	2.1	2342	4.4
5	W	0529	2.1	1205	4.5	1808	2.1		
6	TH	0053	4.5	0636	2.0	1318	4.6	1914	1.9
7	F	0156	4.7	0743	1.8	1425	4.8	2017	1.8
8	SA	0253	5.0	0846	1.6	1525	5.0	2115	1.6
9	SU	0348	5.3	0946	1.4	1621	5.3	2211	1.4
10	M	0440	5.5	1043	1.1	1713	5.4	● 2304	1.2
11	TU	0532	5.7	1136	1.0	1804	5.5	2354	1.1
12	W	0622	5.8	1227	0.9	1853	5.5		
13	TH	0046	1.1	0711	5.7	1314	0.9	1940	5.3
14	F	0133	1.2	0759	5.6	1400	1.1	2027	5.1
15	SA	0219	1.3	0846	5.4	1445	1.3	2114	4.9
16	SU	0307	1.5	0934	5.1	1532	1.6	2205	4.6
17	M	0358	1.8	1026	4.8	1624	1.9	◐ 2306	4.4
18	TU	0456	2.0	1130	4.5	1724	2.1		
19	W	0018	4.3	0604	2.2	1245	4.4	1834	2.2
20	TH	0129	4.3	0716	2.2	1357	4.4	1943	2.2
21	F	0229	4.5	0821	2.1	1456	4.5	2043	2.1
22	SA	0318	4.6	0916	2.0	1544	4.6	2131	1.9
23	SU	0359	4.8	1002	1.8	1624	4.8	2213	1.8
24	M	0436	5.0	1041	1.7	1659	4.9	2250	1.7
25	TU	0509	5.1	1118	1.5	1732	5.0	○ 2324	1.6
26	W	0541	5.2	1152	1.4	1803	5.0	2358	1.5
27	TH	0612	5.2	1225	1.4	1833	5.0		
28	F	0032	1.4	0642	5.2	1258	1.4	1903	5.0
29	SA	0104	1.4	0713	5.2	1329	1.4	1934	4.9
30	SU	0138	1.5	0746	5.1	1402	1.5	2009	4.8
31	M	0213	1.5	0823	5.0	1437	1.6	2049	4.7

FEBRUARY

Date	Day	Time	m	Time	m	Time	m	Time	m
1	TU	0253	1.7	0906	4.8	1518	1.7	2139	4.5
2	W	0341	1.8	1002	4.6	1610	1.9	◑ 2245	4.4
3	TH	0441	2.0	1118	4.4	1717	2.1		
4	F	0009	4.4	0557	2.1	1249	4.4	1837	2.1
5	SA	0132	4.5	0717	2.0	1412	4.6	1955	2.0
6	SU	0241	4.8	0833	1.7	1519	4.9	2105	1.7
7	M	0341	5.2	0940	1.4	1616	5.2	2204	1.4
8	TU	0434	5.5	1037	1.1	1706	5.4	● 2256	1.1
9	W	0523	5.8	1127	0.8	1752	5.6	2344	1.0
10	TH	0608	5.9	1213	0.7	1835	5.6		
11	F	0032	0.9	0652	5.9	1256	0.8	1915	5.5
12	SA	0114	0.9	0732	5.7	1336	0.9	1953	5.3
13	SU	0154	1.1	0810	5.4	1415	1.2	2028	5.0
14	M	0234	1.3	0847	5.1	1454	1.5	2102	4.7
15	TU	0318	1.6	0927	4.7	1538	1.8	2146	4.4
16	W	0409	2.0	1022	4.4	1631	2.2	◐ 2300	4.2
17	TH	0514	2.3	1148	4.1	1743	2.5		
18	F	0042	4.1	0638	2.4	1326	4.1	1910	2.5
19	SA	0203	4.2	0757	2.3	1439	4.3	2022	2.3
20	SU	0300	4.5	0858	2.1	1530	4.5	2114	2.1
21	M	0344	4.7	0944	1.8	1608	4.7	2155	1.8
22	TU	0419	4.9	1023	1.6	1641	4.9	2231	1.6
23	W	0451	5.1	1058	1.4	1711	5.1	2305	1.4
24	TH	0521	5.3	1131	1.3	1740	5.2	○ 2338	1.3
25	F	0550	5.3	1203	1.2	1809	5.2		
26	SA	0011	1.2	0619	5.4	1234	1.2	1837	5.2
27	SU	0042	1.2	0649	5.4	1304	1.2	1907	5.2
28	M	0114	1.2	0720	5.3	1334	1.3	1939	5.1

MARCH

Date	Day	Time	m	Time	m	Time	m	Time	m
1	TU	0147	1.3	0754	5.1	1407	1.4	2015	4.9
2	W	0225	1.4	0835	4.9	1446	1.6	2101	4.7
3	TH	0310	1.7	0929	4.6	1535	1.9	◑ 2205	4.4
4	F	0409	1.9	1051	4.3	1642	2.2	2339	4.3
5	SA	0532	2.1	1240	4.3	1815	2.3		
6	SU	0119	4.5	0707	2.0	1407	4.5	1948	2.1
7	M	0233	4.8	0830	1.7	1513	4.9	2059	1.7
8	TU	0332	5.2	0933	1.3	1606	5.2	2154	1.4
9	W	0422	5.6	1024	1.0	1651	5.4	2242	1.0
10	TH	0506	5.8	1110	0.8	1732	5.6	● 2326	0.9
11	F	0547	5.9	1152	0.7	1810	5.6		
12	SA	0009	0.8	0625	5.8	1231	0.8	1845	5.5
13	SU	0049	0.9	0700	5.6	1307	1.0	1916	5.3
14	M	0125	1.0	0733	5.4	1341	1.2	1945	5.1
15	TU	0201	1.3	0805	5.0	1416	1.5	2014	4.8
16	W	0240	1.6	0840	4.7	1454	1.9	2051	4.5
17	TH	0324	2.0	0929	4.3	1542	2.2	◐ 2150	4.2
18	F	0425	2.3	1053	4.0	1651	2.6	2342	4.0
19	SA	0554	2.5	1251	4.0	1828	2.6		
20	SU	0126	4.1	0726	2.4	1409	4.2	1950	2.5
21	M	0230	4.4	0829	2.2	1501	4.4	2044	2.2
22	TU	0315	4.6	0915	1.9	1539	4.7	2126	1.9
23	W	0351	4.9	0953	1.6	1611	4.9	2202	1.6
24	TH	0423	5.1	1028	1.4	1641	5.1	2237	1.4
25	F	0453	5.3	1101	1.2	1711	5.3	○ 2311	1.2
26	SA	0523	5.4	1134	1.1	1740	5.4	2344	1.1
27	SU	0553	5.5	1206	1.1	1810	5.4		
28	M	0018	1.0	0624	5.4	1237	1.1	1842	5.3
29	TU	0051	1.1	0658	5.3	1309	1.2	1916	5.2
30	W	0126	1.2	0735	5.1	1343	1.4	1954	5.0
31	TH	0205	1.3	0819	4.8	1424	1.6	2043	4.8

APRIL

Date	Day	Time	m	Time	m	Time	m	Time	m
1	F	0253	1.6	0919	4.5	1516	2.0	2153	4.5
2	SA	0356	1.9	1052	4.3	1630	2.3	◑ 2331	4.4
3	SU	0526	2.1	1239	4.3	1809	2.3		
4	M	0108	4.6	0704	1.9	1359	4.6	1939	2.0
5	TU	0219	4.9	0819	1.6	1459	4.9	2043	1.7
6	W	0315	5.2	0915	1.3	1548	5.2	2135	1.3
7	TH	0402	5.5	1003	1.0	1629	5.4	2221	1.1
8	F	0443	5.7	1045	0.9	1706	5.5	● 2303	0.9
9	SA	0521	5.7	1125	0.9	1741	5.5	2343	0.9
10	SU	0556	5.6	1201	1.0	1813	5.4		
11	M	0021	1.0	0630	5.5	1235	1.1	1843	5.3
12	TU	0056	1.1	0701	5.2	1308	1.3	1912	5.1
13	W	0131	1.3	0733	4.9	1342	1.6	1943	4.8
14	TH	0207	1.6	0810	4.6	1418	1.9	2022	4.6
15	F	0249	2.0	0857	4.3	1503	2.2	2115	4.3
16	SA	0344	2.3	1012	4.0	1606	2.5	◐ 2242	4.1
17	SU	0505	2.5	1201	3.9	1735	2.6		
18	M	0029	4.1	0635	2.4	1322	4.1	1857	2.5
19	TU	0141	4.3	0742	2.2	1416	4.4	1956	2.2
20	W	0231	4.6	0832	1.9	1457	4.7	2043	1.9
21	TH	0311	4.8	0912	1.6	1532	4.9	2123	1.6
22	F	0346	5.1	0950	1.4	1605	5.1	2201	1.4
23	SA	0420	5.2	1026	1.2	1638	5.3	2238	1.2
24	SU	0453	5.4	1101	1.1	1711	5.4	○ 2315	1.1
25	M	0528	5.4	1137	1.1	1746	5.4	2352	1.0
26	TU	0605	5.4	1212	1.1	1823	5.4		
27	W	0032	1.0	0644	5.3	1249	1.2	1903	5.3
28	TH	0112	1.1	0728	5.1	1329	1.4	1949	5.1
29	F	0156	1.3	0820	4.8	1415	1.7	2045	4.8
30	SA	0249	1.6	0928	4.5	1513	2.0	2157	4.7

Chart Datum: 2·83 metres below IGN Datum

TIME ZONE -0100
(French Standard Time)
Subtract 1 hour for UT
For French Summer Time add ONE hour in **non-shaded areas**

FRANCE – POINTE DE GRAVE

LAT 45°34'N LONG 1°04'W

TIMES AND HEIGHTS OF HIGH AND LOW WATERS

SPRING & NEAP TIDES
Dates in red are **SPRINGS**
Dates in blue are **NEAPS**

YEAR **2005**

MAY

Day	Time	m	Time	m	Time	m	Time	m
1 SU	0358	1.8	1059	4.4	1631	2.2	◑ 2325	4.6
2 M	0523	1.9	1229	4.4	1758	2.1		
3 TU	0049	4.7	0646	1.8	1339	4.7	1915	1.9
4 W	0156	4.9	0754	1.6	1436	4.9	2017	1.6
5 TH	0251	5.1	0849	1.4	1523	5.1	2109	1.4
6 F	0337	5.3	0935	1.2	1603	5.2	2155	1.2
7 SA	0418	5.4	1018	1.1	1639	5.3	2238	1.1
8 SU	0455	5.4	1056	1.1	1712	5.3	● 2317	1.1
9 M	0531	5.3	1132	1.2	1745	5.3	2355	1.2
10 TU	0605	5.2	1206	1.3	1818	5.2		
11 W	0031	1.3	0639	5.0	1240	1.5	1851	5.0
12 TH	0106	1.5	0714	4.8	1314	1.7	1926	4.8
13 F	0143	1.7	0752	4.6	1352	1.9	2006	4.6
14 SA	0224	1.9	0838	4.3	1436	2.1	2055	4.4
15 SU	0313	2.1	0939	4.1	1531	2.3	2158	4.3
16 M	0417	2.3	1058	4.0	1640	2.4	◐ 2316	4.2
17 TU	0531	2.3	1217	4.1	1753	2.4		
18 W	0031	4.3	0639	2.2	1317	4.3	1855	2.2
19 TH	0131	4.5	0736	1.9	1405	4.6	1949	2.0
20 F	0220	4.7	0823	1.7	1447	4.8	2037	1.7
21 SA	0304	4.9	0907	1.5	1526	5.0	2121	1.5
22 SU	0345	5.1	0949	1.3	1605	5.2	2205	1.3
23 M	0427	5.2	1030	1.2	1645	5.3	○ 2248	1.1
24 TU	0509	5.3	1111	1.1	1727	5.4	2332	1.1
25 W	0554	5.3	1153	1.2	1812	5.4		
26 TH	0019	1.0	0641	5.2	1237	1.3	1900	5.3
27 F	0106	1.1	0731	5.0	1324	1.4	1952	5.2
28 SA	0156	1.3	0828	4.8	1415	1.6	2050	5.0
29 SU	0252	1.4	0933	4.6	1515	1.8	2156	4.9
30 M	0355	1.6	1048	4.5	1622	1.9	◑ 2308	4.8
31 TU	0504	1.7	1203	4.5	1733	1.9		

JUNE

Day	Time	m	Time	m	Time	m	Time	m
1 W	0020	4.8	0614	1.7	1309	4.6	1842	1.8
2 TH	0125	4.8	0720	1.6	1406	4.7	1945	1.7
3 F	0222	4.9	0817	1.5	1455	4.8	2040	1.5
4 SA	0311	4.9	0907	1.5	1537	4.9	2129	1.4
5 SU	0354	5.0	0951	1.4	1615	5.0	2214	1.4
6 M	0434	5.0	1031	1.4	1651	5.1	● 2256	1.4
7 TU	0512	5.0	1109	1.4	1726	5.1	2335	1.4
8 W	0549	4.9	1144	1.5	1802	5.0		
9 TH	0012	1.4	0625	4.8	1219	1.6	1837	5.0
10 F	0048	1.5	0701	4.7	1255	1.7	1913	4.9
11 SA	0125	1.6	0738	4.6	1332	1.8	1950	4.7
12 SU	0204	1.7	0818	4.4	1413	1.9	2032	4.6
13 M	0246	1.9	0905	4.3	1459	2.0	2120	4.5
14 TU	0335	2.0	1000	4.2	1551	2.1	2215	4.4
15 W	0430	2.0	1103	4.2	1650	2.2	◐ 2318	4.3
16 TH	0532	2.0	1207	4.3	1752	2.1		
17 F	0023	4.4	0633	2.0	1307	4.4	1853	2.0
18 SA	0125	4.5	0731	1.8	1401	4.6	1949	1.8
19 SU	0222	4.7	0824	1.6	1450	4.8	2043	1.6
20 M	0316	4.9	0915	1.5	1539	5.0	2136	1.4
21 TU	0407	5.0	1004	1.3	1627	5.2	2227	1.2
22 W	0458	5.2	1053	1.2	1716	5.4	○ 2319	1.1
23 TH	0549	5.2	1142	1.2	1806	5.5		
24 F	0012	1.0	0640	5.2	1231	1.2	1857	5.5
25 SA	0103	1.0	0731	5.1	1321	1.2	1950	5.4
26 SU	0153	1.1	0824	5.0	1411	1.4	2044	5.3
27 M	0244	1.2	0919	4.8	1504	1.5	2139	5.1
28 TU	0337	1.4	1018	4.6	1559	1.6	◑ 2238	4.9
29 W	0433	1.6	1123	4.5	1700	1.7	2342	4.7
30 TH	0535	1.7	1230	4.5	1806	1.8		

JULY

Day	Time	m	Time	m	Time	m	Time	m
1 F	0047	4.6	0641	1.8	1333	4.5	1912	1.8
2 SA	0151	4.5	0744	1.8	1429	4.6	2014	1.8
3 SU	0249	4.6	0841	1.8	1517	4.7	2109	1.7
4 M	0338	4.6	0930	1.7	1559	4.8	2158	1.6
5 TU	0422	4.7	1014	1.6	1637	4.9	2241	1.5
6 W	0501	4.8	1053	1.6	1714	5.0	● 2321	1.5
7 TH	0538	4.8	1129	1.5	1749	5.0	2357	1.4
8 F	0613	4.8	1204	1.5	1822	5.0		
9 SA	0033	1.4	0645	4.8	1239	1.5	1855	4.9
10 SU	0108	1.5	0718	4.7	1313	1.6	1928	4.9
11 M	0142	1.5	0751	4.6	1349	1.6	2003	4.8
12 TU	0217	1.6	0828	4.5	1426	1.7	2041	4.6
13 W	0255	1.7	0910	4.4	1507	1.8	2125	4.5
14 TH	0338	1.8	1001	4.3	1556	1.9	◐ 2219	4.4
15 F	0429	1.9	1103	4.3	1653	2.0	2322	4.3
16 SA	0532	2.0	1212	4.3	1800	2.0		
17 SU	0037	4.3	0641	1.9	1321	4.4	1908	1.9
18 M	0150	4.5	0747	1.8	1424	4.7	2014	1.7
19 TU	0257	4.7	0849	1.6	1521	4.9	2116	1.5
20 W	0356	4.9	0947	1.4	1615	5.2	2215	1.2
21 TH	0451	5.1	1042	1.2	1707	5.4	○ 2310	1.0
22 F	0542	5.3	1134	1.1	1757	5.6		
23 SA	0002	0.8	0631	5.3	1223	1.0	1847	5.7
24 SU	0054	0.8	0718	5.3	1309	1.0	1935	5.6
25 M	0139	0.9	0804	5.2	1355	1.1	2022	5.4
26 TU	0223	1.0	0849	4.9	1441	1.2	2109	5.2
27 W	0308	1.3	0935	4.7	1529	1.5	2159	4.8
28 TH	0357	1.6	1030	4.4	1624	1.7	◑ 2257	4.5
29 F	0453	1.9	1139	4.3	1728	2.0		
30 SA	0008	4.3	0600	2.1	1259	4.2	1841	2.1
31 SU	0125	4.2	0714	2.1	1408	4.3	1954	2.0

AUGUST

Day	Time	m	Time	m	Time	m	Time	m
1 M	0234	4.3	0821	2.0	1504	4.5	2055	1.9
2 TU	0330	4.4	0916	1.9	1549	4.7	2146	1.7
3 W	0413	4.6	1001	1.7	1626	4.8	2228	1.6
4 TH	0449	4.7	1039	1.6	1700	5.0	2306	1.5
5 F	0522	4.8	1114	1.5	1731	5.0	● 2340	1.4
6 SA	0553	4.9	1147	1.4	1801	5.1		
7 SU	0014	1.3	0621	4.9	1219	1.4	1830	5.1
8 M	0045	1.3	0650	4.9	1250	1.4	1859	5.0
9 TU	0115	1.4	0719	4.8	1321	1.4	1930	4.9
10 W	0145	1.4	0750	4.7	1353	1.5	2002	4.8
11 TH	0217	1.5	0826	4.6	1429	1.6	2041	4.6
12 F	0254	1.7	0909	4.4	1511	1.8	2129	4.4
13 SA	0339	1.8	1008	4.3	1604	1.9	◐ 2236	4.3
14 SU	0440	2.0	1127	4.2	1715	2.1		
15 M	0003	4.2	0600	2.1	1253	4.3	1839	2.0
16 TU	0135	4.3	0722	2.0	1408	4.6	1958	1.8
17 W	0248	4.6	0836	1.8	1510	5.0	2107	1.5
18 TH	0349	4.9	0937	1.4	1605	5.3	2206	1.1
19 F	0441	5.2	1031	1.1	1655	5.6	○ 2259	0.9
20 SA	0528	5.4	1120	0.9	1741	5.8	2346	0.7
21 SU	0612	5.5	1206	0.8	1826	5.8		
22 M	0034	0.7	0653	5.4	1249	0.8	1910	5.7
23 TU	0115	0.8	0733	5.3	1331	0.9	1951	5.5
24 W	0154	1.0	0810	5.0	1412	1.2	2032	5.1
25 TH	0234	1.3	0846	4.7	1455	1.5	2115	4.7
26 F	0317	1.7	0930	4.4	1545	1.8	◑ 2208	4.4
27 SA	0409	2.1	1039	4.2	1649	2.2	2329	4.1
28 SU	0518	2.3	1223	4.1	1812	2.3		
29 M	0105	4.0	0646	2.4	1348	4.2	1938	2.2
30 TU	0222	4.2	0804	2.3	1448	4.4	2041	2.0
31 W	0315	4.4	0859	2.0	1532	4.7	2129	1.8

Chart Datum: 2·83 metres below IGN Datum

TIME ZONE -0100
(French Standard Time)
Subtract 1 hour for UT
For French Summer Time add ONE hour in **non-shaded areas**

FRANCE – POINTE DE GRAVE

LAT 45°34′N LONG 1°04′W

TIMES AND HEIGHTS OF HIGH AND LOW WATERS

SPRING & NEAP TIDES
Dates in red are SPRINGS
Dates in blue are NEAPS

YEAR **2005**

SEPTEMBER

Date	Day	Time	m	Time	m	Time	m	Time	m
1	TH	0354	4.6	0941	1.8	1606	4.9	2207	1.6
2	F	0427	4.8	1018	1.6	1637	5.0	2242	1.4
3	SA	0456	4.9	1051	1.4	1706	5.2	● 2315	1.3
4	SU	0524	5.0	1123	1.3	1734	5.2	2345	1.2
5	M	0551	5.1	1153	1.3	1801	5.2		
6	TU	0016	1.2	0618	5.1	1223	1.2	1828	5.2
7	W	0045	1.3	0646	5.0	1253	1.3	1857	5.1
8	TH	0113	1.3	0715	4.9	1324	1.4	1928	4.9
9	F	0144	1.4	0748	4.8	1358	1.5	2005	4.7
10	SA	0220	1.6	0829	4.6	1439	1.7	2054	4.5
11	SU	0304	1.9	0929	4.4	1532	2.0	◐ 2209	4.2
12	M	0405	2.2	1100	4.2	1647	2.2	2353	4.1
13	TU	0536	2.3	1239	4.3	1826	2.1		
14	W	0131	4.3	0711	2.1	1357	4.7	1953	1.8
15	TH	0240	4.7	0826	1.8	1458	5.1	2059	1.4
16	F	0335	5.0	0924	1.4	1550	5.5	2152	1.1
17	SA	0422	5.3	1015	1.1	1636	5.7	2239	0.8
18	SU	0505	5.5	1101	0.9	1719	5.9	○ 2323	0.7
19	M	0545	5.5	1144	0.8	1800	5.8		
20	TU	0005	0.8	0622	5.5	1224	0.8	1839	5.7
21	W	0045	0.9	0657	5.3	1303	1.0	1917	5.4
22	TH	0122	1.2	0729	5.1	1341	1.2	1953	5.0
23	F	0159	1.5	0801	4.8	1421	1.6	2031	4.6
24	SA	0238	1.9	0840	4.5	1507	2.0	2123	4.3
25	SU	0326	2.2	0945	4.2	1608	2.3	◑ 2251	4.0
26	M	0435	2.5	1140	4.1	1739	2.5		
27	TU	0039	3.9	0612	2.6	1315	4.2	1913	2.4
28	W	0154	4.1	0734	2.4	1418	4.4	2015	2.1
29	TH	0245	4.4	0829	2.2	1502	4.7	2059	1.9
30	F	0322	4.7	0910	1.9	1536	4.9	2136	1.6

OCTOBER

Date	Day	Time	m	Time	m	Time	m	Time	m
1	SA	0353	4.9	0946	1.6	1606	5.1	2210	1.4
2	SU	0422	5.0	1019	1.5	1634	5.2	2242	1.3
3	M	0450	5.2	1052	1.3	1702	5.3	● 2313	1.2
4	TU	0517	5.2	1124	1.2	1730	5.3	2343	1.2
5	W	0546	5.3	1156	1.2	1800	5.3		
6	TH	0014	1.3	0616	5.2	1227	1.2	1831	5.2
7	F	0045	1.3	0648	5.1	1300	1.3	1905	5.0
8	SA	0118	1.5	0724	4.9	1337	1.5	1945	4.8
9	SU	0157	1.7	0810	4.7	1420	1.7	2041	4.5
10	M	0245	2.0	0917	4.5	1517	2.0	◐ 2208	4.2
11	TU	0352	2.3	1053	4.4	1640	2.2	2355	4.2
12	W	0529	2.4	1229	4.5	1822	2.1		
13	TH	0122	4.5	0700	2.1	1342	4.9	1942	1.8
14	F	0224	4.8	0809	1.8	1440	5.2	2040	1.4
15	SA	0315	5.1	0904	1.4	1530	5.5	2130	1.1
16	SU	0358	5.3	0952	1.1	1614	5.7	2214	1.0
17	M	0438	5.5	1037	1.0	1654	5.8	○ 2256	0.9
18	TU	0515	5.5	1119	0.9	1733	5.7	2336	1.0
19	W	0550	5.4	1158	1.0	1810	5.5		
20	TH	0014	1.2	0624	5.3	1236	1.2	1846	5.3
21	F	0050	1.4	0656	5.1	1313	1.4	1921	4.9
22	SA	0126	1.7	0730	4.9	1352	1.7	2000	4.6
23	SU	0205	2.0	0811	4.6	1435	2.0	2050	4.3
24	M	0252	2.3	0910	4.3	1531	2.4	2211	4.0
25	TU	0355	2.6	1044	4.2	1651	2.6	◑ 2352	4.0
26	W	0520	2.7	1220	4.2	1822	2.5		
27	TH	0107	4.2	0641	2.5	1328	4.4	1929	2.3
28	F	0159	4.4	0740	2.3	1417	4.6	2016	2.0
29	SA	0239	4.7	0826	2.0	1455	4.9	2055	1.8
30	SU	0313	4.9	0905	1.8	1529	5.1	2131	1.6
31	M	0344	5.1	0943	1.6	1600	5.2	2205	1.4

NOVEMBER

Date	Day	Time	m	Time	m	Time	m	Time	m
1	TU	0415	5.2	1019	1.4	1632	5.3	2239	1.3
2	W	0447	5.3	1055	1.3	1704	5.4	● 2313	1.3
3	TH	0520	5.4	1131	1.2	1739	5.3	2347	1.3
4	F	0556	5.3	1207	1.3	1816	5.2		
5	SA	0025	1.4	0634	5.2	1245	1.4	1857	5.0
6	SU	0103	1.6	0718	5.1	1327	1.5	1947	4.8
7	M	0148	1.8	0813	4.9	1417	1.7	2051	4.5
8	TU	0242	2.0	0923	4.7	1519	2.0	2215	4.4
9	W	0354	2.2	1048	4.6	1639	2.1	◐ 2345	4.4
10	TH	0518	2.2	1210	4.8	1803	2.0		
11	F	0101	4.6	0637	2.0	1319	5.0	1915	1.8
12	SA	0200	4.9	0742	1.8	1417	5.2	2013	1.5
13	SU	0250	5.1	0838	1.5	1507	5.4	2103	1.3
14	M	0333	5.2	0928	1.3	1551	5.5	2148	1.2
15	TU	0412	5.3	1013	1.2	1632	5.5	2230	1.2
16	W	0449	5.4	1056	1.2	1711	5.4	○ 2309	1.3
17	TH	0525	5.4	1136	1.2	1748	5.3	2347	1.4
18	F	0601	5.3	1214	1.4	1825	5.1		
19	SA	0024	1.6	0637	5.1	1251	1.5	1902	4.9
20	SU	0101	1.7	0713	5.0	1330	1.7	1941	4.6
21	M	0140	2.0	0754	4.7	1411	2.0	2027	4.4
22	TU	0225	2.2	0843	4.5	1500	2.2	2127	4.2
23	W	0318	2.4	0947	4.4	1600	2.4	◑ 2244	4.1
24	TH	0422	2.5	1103	4.3	1712	2.4	2359	4.2
25	F	0532	2.5	1217	4.4	1821	2.3		
26	SA	0059	4.3	0636	2.4	1317	4.5	1918	2.2
27	SU	0147	4.5	0731	2.2	1405	4.7	2006	2.0
28	M	0228	4.8	0819	1.9	1447	4.9	2048	1.8
29	TU	0307	5.0	0903	1.7	1527	5.0	2128	1.6
30	W	0344	5.2	0946	1.5	1606	5.2	2208	1.5

DECEMBER

Date	Day	Time	m	Time	m	Time	m	Time	m
1	TH	0423	5.3	1029	1.4	1646	5.3	● 2248	1.4
2	F	0503	5.4	1112	1.3	1728	5.3	2329	1.4
3	SA	0546	5.4	1155	1.2	1813	5.2		
4	SU	0013	1.4	0632	5.4	1240	1.3	1901	5.1
5	M	0059	1.5	0722	5.3	1328	1.4	1954	5.0
6	TU	0149	1.7	0818	5.2	1420	1.5	2055	4.8
7	W	0244	1.8	0920	5.0	1518	1.7	2204	4.6
8	TH	0347	1.9	1029	4.9	1622	1.8	◐ 2317	4.6
9	F	0455	2.0	1141	4.9	1730	1.9		
10	SA	0029	4.6	0604	2.0	1248	4.9	1839	1.8
11	SU	0131	4.7	0711	1.8	1350	5.0	1941	1.7
12	M	0224	4.9	0811	1.7	1445	5.0	2036	1.6
13	TU	0311	5.0	0905	1.6	1534	5.1	2125	1.6
14	W	0354	5.1	0955	1.5	1617	5.1	2210	1.5
15	TH	0433	5.2	1040	1.4	1658	5.1	○ 2251	1.5
16	F	0512	5.2	1121	1.4	1736	5.1	2330	1.5
17	SA	0549	5.2	1200	1.5	1813	5.0		
18	SU	0007	1.6	0625	5.2	1237	1.5	1849	4.9
19	M	0044	1.7	0700	5.1	1313	1.7	1925	4.8
20	TU	0122	1.8	0736	4.9	1351	1.8	2003	4.6
21	W	0201	1.9	0815	4.8	1431	1.9	2045	4.5
22	TH	0243	2.1	0859	4.6	1515	2.1	2135	4.3
23	F	0330	2.2	0950	4.5	1606	2.2	◑ 2236	4.2
24	SA	0425	2.3	1051	4.4	1704	2.3	2342	4.3
25	SU	0526	2.3	1159	4.4	1808	2.3		
26	M	0046	4.4	0629	2.2	1306	4.5	1909	2.2
27	TU	0142	4.5	0730	2.1	1405	4.6	2004	2.0
28	W	0233	4.8	0826	1.9	1458	4.8	2054	1.8
29	TH	0320	5.0	0918	1.7	1548	5.0	2143	1.6
30	F	0407	5.2	1010	1.5	1636	5.2	2231	1.5
31	SA	0454	5.4	1100	1.3	1724	5.3	● 2318	1.3

Chart Datum: 2·83 metres below IGN Datum

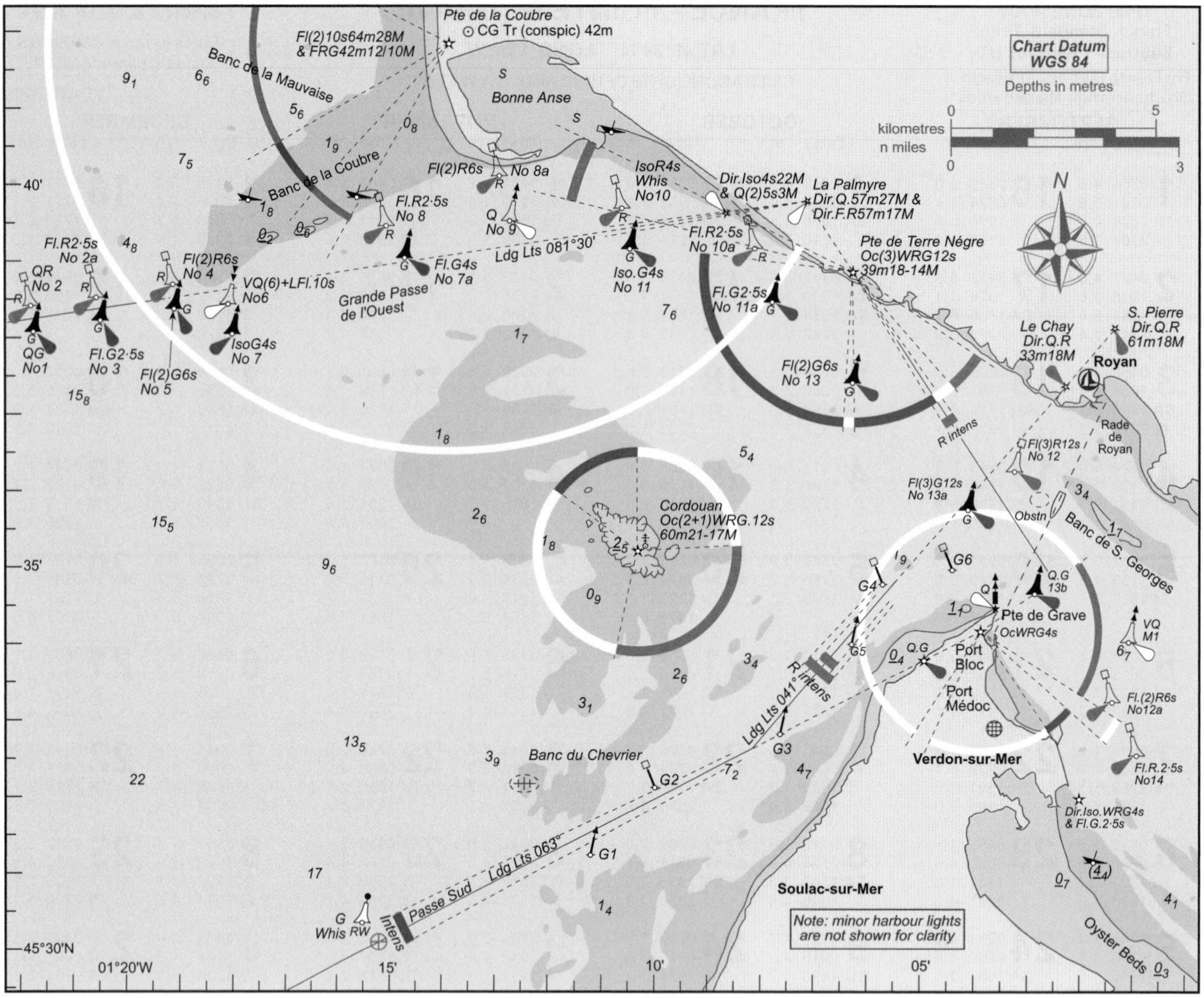
Pte de la Coubre
CG Tr (conspic) 42m
Fl(2)10s64m28M
& FRG42m12/10M
Chart Datum
WGS 84
Depths in metres
kilometres
n miles
Banc de la Mauvaise
Bonne Anse
Banc de la Coubre
Fl(2)R6s
No 8a
Fl.R2·5s
No 8
Q
No 9
IsoR4s
Whis
No10
Dir.Iso4s22M
& Q(2)5s3M
La Palmyre
Dir.Q.57m27M &
Dir.F.R57m17M
Fl.R2·5s
No 10a
Pte de Terre Négre
Oc(3)WRG12s
39m18-14M
Fl.R2·5s
No 2a
QR
No 2
Fl(2)R6s
No 4
VQ(6)+LFl.10s
No6
Fl.G4s
No 7a
Ldg Lts 081°30'
Iso.G4s
No 11
Grande Passe
de l'Ouest
Fl.G2·5s
No 11a
QG
No1
Fl.G2·5s
No 3
Fl(2)G6s
No 5
IsoG4s
No 7
Fl(2)G6s
No 13
Le Chay
Dir.Q.R
33m18M
S. Pierre
Dir.Q.R
61m18M
Royan
R intens
Fl(3)R12s
No 12
Rade
de
Royan
Fl(3)G12s
No 13a
Obstn
Banc de S. Georges
Cordouan
Oc(2+1)WRG.12s
60m21-17M
G6
G4
Q.G
13b
Pte de Grave
OcWRG4s
VQ
M1
G5
Q.G
Port
Bloc
Port
Médoc
R intens
Fl.(2)R6s
No12a
Ldg Lts 041°
G3
Verdon-sur-Mer
Fl.R.2·5s
No14
Banc du Chevrier
G2
Dir.Iso.WRG4s
& Fl.G.2·5s
Ldg Lts 063°
G1
Passe Sud
Soulac-sur-Mer
G
Whis RW
Intens
Note: minor harbour lights
are not shown for clarity
Oyster Beds
40'
35'
45°30'N
01°20'W
15'
10'
05'

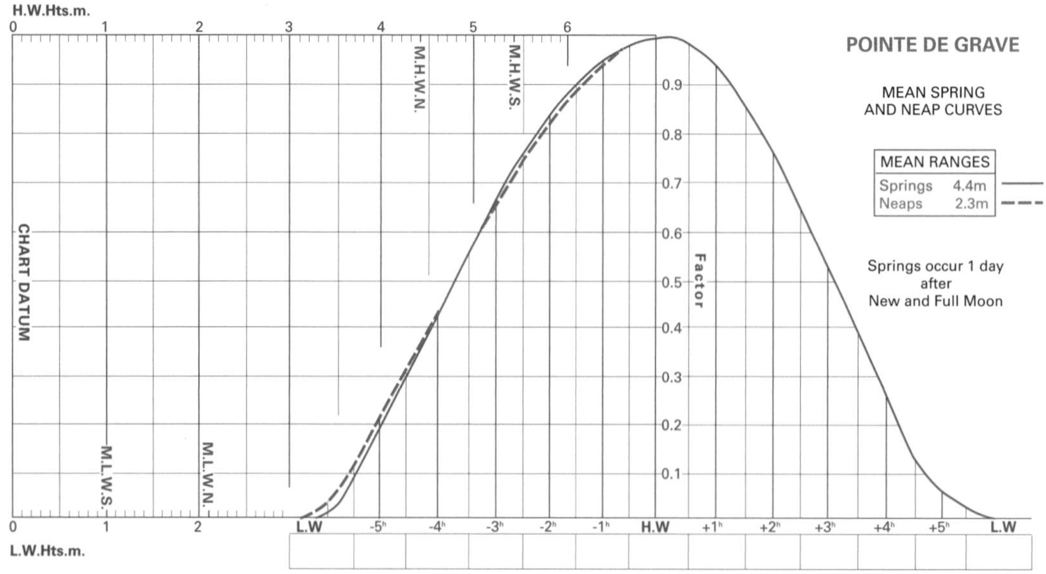
H.W.Hts.m.
M.H.W.N.
M.H.W.S.
CHART DATUM
Factor
M.L.W.S.
M.L.W.N.
L.W
-5h
-4h
-3h
-2h
-1h
H.W
+1h
+2h
+3h
+4h
+5h
L.W
L.W.Hts.m.

POINTE DE GRAVE

MEAN SPRING AND NEAP CURVES

MEAN RANGES	
Springs	4.4m
Neaps	2.3m

Springs occur 1 day after New and Full Moon

9.22.19 THE GIRONDE ESTUARY

CHARTS AC 3057/8, 2916; SHOM 7425/6/7: all these are essential.

TIDES In the Gironde and the R. Dordogne the sp flood reaches 3kn and the ebb 4kn, continuing for 1½H after predicted LW time. In the Garonne the sp flood starts with a small bore and runs at 3kn, ebb reaches 5kn. *The Annuaire des Marées Estuaire de la Gironde*, available from the Port de Bordeaux at €5.40, is full of useful tidal information for the Gironde and also Arcachon.

Between Pte de Grave and Bordeaux the height of water at Verdon, Richard, Lamena, Pauillac, Fort Médoc, Bec d'Ambes, Le Marquis and Bordeaux (see 9.22.23 chartlet) is automatically broadcast H24 on Ch 17 every 5 mins. From these read-outs it is possible to deduce, for example, when the flood starts to make.

Standard Port POINTE DE GRAVE (⟵)

Times				Height (metres)			
High Water		Low Water		MHWS	MHWN	MLWN	MLWS
0000	0600	0500	1200	5·4	4·4	2·1	1·0
1200	1800	1700	2400				
Differences CORDOUAN							
–0010	–0010	–0015	–0025	–0·5	–0·4	–0·1	–0·2
RICHARD							
+0018	+0018	+0028	+0033	–0·1	–0·1	–0·4	–0·5
LAMENA							
+0035	+0045	+0100	+0125	+0·2	+0·1	–0·5	–0·3
LA REUILLE							
+0135	+0145	+0230	+0305	–0·2	–0·3	–1·3	–0·7
LE MARQUIS							
+0145	+0150	+0247	+0322	–0·3	–0·4	–1·5	–0·9
LIBOURNE (La Dordogne)							
+0250	+0305	+0525	+0540	–0·7	–0·9	–2·0	–0·4

SHELTER See Royan, Port Bloc, Port-Médoc, Meschers, Mortagne, Pauillac and Bordeaux.

NAVIGATION La Gironde is a substantial waterway. The mouth of the estuary is 9M wide between Pte de la Coubre and Pte de Grave and narrows from 6M wide off Royan to 2.5M at Pauillac. The Garonne and Dordogne flow into the Gironde at Bec d'Ambes (45°02'N).

The outer apprs can be dangerous due to Atlantic swell, very strong tidal streams and currents, extensive shoals and shifting sandbanks, see 9.22.5. Swell, strong W'lies and an ebb tide raise dangerous, breaking seas some 5m high; in such conditions do not attempt entry. Be alert for ferries and shipping.

WPT BXA SWM buoy, Iso 4s, 45°37'·53N 01°28'·68W, 081·5°/4·8M to Nos 1 & 2 buoys. The two approach channels are:

1. **Grande Passe de l'Ouest**. Leave No 1 buoy at LW. 081° on La Palmyre ldg lts is only valid to Nos 4/5 buoys; thence follow the buoys (do not cut corners) to enter the river on astern transit of 327° (see below). The chan is deep and well marked/lit. Keep well clear of La Mauvaise bank, Banc de la Coubre and Plateau de Cordouan.

The astern transit 327° of Terre-Nègre lt with La Palmyre, FR 57m 17M, leads between Nos 12 & 13a buoys into R Gironde.

2. **Passe du Sud**. WPT 45°30'·00N 01°15'·33W, abeam 'G' SWM buoy, 063°/5.5M (063° ldg lts) to intercept the 041° ldg lts (QR). Thence pick up Terre-Nègre and Palmyre lts ≠ 327° (see above). The chan carries approx 5m through shoals; not advised in poor vis or heavy swell. Platin de Grave, between G4 and G6 buoys, has only 1·4m. The six lateral buoys are unlit.

LIGHTS AND MARKS See chartlet and 9.22.4 for light details.

1. **Grande Passe de l'Ouest** ldg lts 081°: Front Dir Iso 4s; rear, La Palmyre Dir Q. From No 9 NCM buoy, use W sector 097°- 104° of Pte de Terre-Nègre.
2. **Passe du Sud**, Outer ldg lts 063°: Front Dir QG; rear, Pte de Grave Oc WRG 4s. Inner ldg lts 041°, both QR.

Other major lts in estuary: La Coubre lt ho, W twr, top third R. 2M NNE a R/W CG twr. Cordouan lt ho, an elegant, sculpted twr.

R/T A VTS, (not mandatory for yachts), provides surveillance from BXA buoy to Bordeaux; call *Bordeaux Port Control* VHF Ch 12 (H24). In poor vis or on request *Bordeaux Port Control* supplies radar info between BXA and Verdon roads, and met and nav info.

9.22.20 ROYAN

Charente Maritime **45°37'·12N 01°01'·50W** ❁❁◊◊◊✿✿✿

CHARTS AC 3057, 3058; Imray C42; ECM 553, 554; SHOM 7426, 7425.

TIDES +0530 Dover; ML 3·2; Duration Sp 0615, Np 0655; Zone –0100

Standard Port POINTE DE GRAVE (⟵)

Times				Height (metres)			
High Water		Low Water		MHWS	MHWN	MLWN	MLWS
0000	0600	0500	1200	5·4	4·4	2·1	1·0
1200	1800	1700	2400				
Differences ROYAN							
0000	–0005	–0005	–0005	–0·3	–0·2	0·0	0·0

SHELTER Good. Best access HW±3, but not in strong W/NW winds; care needed near LW sp. Ent chan, least depth 0·1m, silts but is regularly dredged; it narrows markedly off New Jetty hd, Oc (2) R 6s. Marina dory may meet arrivals. The accueil pontoon is dead ahead of the ent, below the Capitainerie.

NAVIGATION WPT 45°36'·56N 01°01'·96W [R1 SHM buoy, Iso G 4s], 030°/0·64M to hbr ent. The Gironde apprs can be dangerous; see 9.22.5 and 9.22.19 for details; allow about 2 hrs from Pte de la Coubre to Royan. Beware Banc de St Georges (0·4m), 1M S of WPT. Off hbr ent, there is an eddy, running S at about 1kn on the flood and 3kn on the ebb. Caution: FVs and fast ferries.

LIGHTS AND MARKS Cathedral spire is modern conspic spike. See chartlet and 9.22.4 for lt details.

R/T VHF Ch 09 16 (season 0800-2000; otherwise 0900-1800LT).

TELEPHONE Aff Mar 05·46·39·26·30; ⊜ 05·46·23·10·24; CROSS 05·56·73·31·31; Météo 05·56·34·20·11; Auto 08.92.68.08.17; Police 05·46·38·34·22; Dr 05·46·05·68·69; Ⓗ 05·46·38·01·77; Brit Consul 05·57·22·21·10.

FACILITIES Marina (1000 + 100 Ⓥ), port.royan@wanadoo.fr HM hrs, Jul/Aug 7/7 0800-2000; ☎ 05·46·38·72·22, 📠 05.46.39.42.47. €1.80, Slip, P & D (0830-1200, 1430-1830, 7/7 in season), de-mast C (1·5 ton), BH (26 ton), ME, El, ⚒, Grid, Ice, CH, Ⓔ, SM, SHOM.
Base Nautique ☎ 05·46·05·44·13.
Town 🛒, R, Bar, Gaz, ▣, ✉, Ⓑ, ⇌, ✈ (Bordeaux). Ferry: Roscoff or St Malo; fast ferries to Port Bloc.

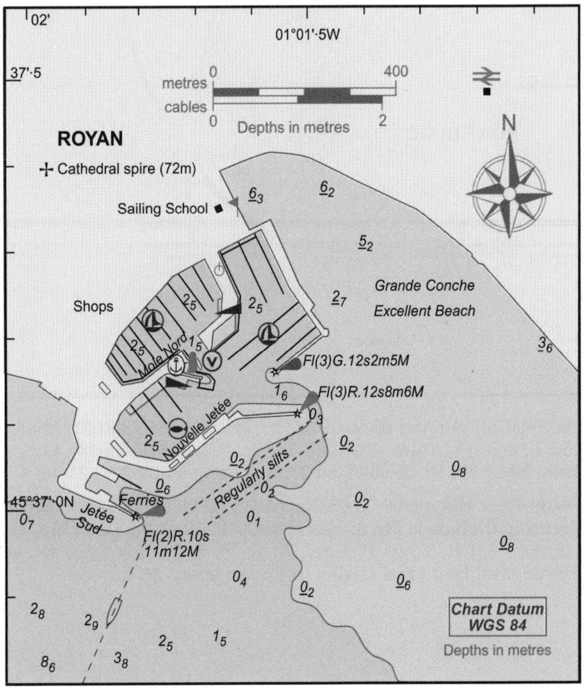
02'
01°01'·5W
37'·5
metres 0 400
cables 0 2
Depths in metres
ROYAN
Cathedral spire (72m)
Sailing School
Shops
Grande Conche
Excellent Beach
Mole Nord
Nouvelle Jetée
Regularly silts
Ferries
45°37'·0N
Jetée Sud
Fl(3)G.12s2m5M
Fl(3)R.12s8m6M
Fl(2)R.10s 11m12M
N
Chart Datum WGS 84
Depths in metres

9.22.21 PORT BLOC

Gironde **45°34'·12N 01°03'·72W** ✿✿⚓⚓✿

CHARTS AC 3057/8, 2916; Imray C42; ECM 553, 554; SHOM 7426, 7425.

TIDES Use predictions for Pointe de Grave (⟵⟶).

SHELTER Good, but mainly a ferry hbr and Service station for Bordeaux port authority; dredged 3m and 4ca S of Pte de Grave. Space for yachts is limited; possible AB on pontoons W side of the hbr. Berthing for visitors requires prior approval from AUPB (Port Bloc Users' Association). Royan (3·7M) or Port-Médoc are better options. Pauillac 25M; Bordeaux 53M.

NAVIGATION WPT 45°34'·66N 01°02'·98W [13b SHM buoy, QG], 224°/7ca to hbr ent. Caution strong tidal streams. Ent is 30m wide; ferries have priority.

LIGHTS AND MARKS Pte de Grave lt ho, W □ tr, B corners and top. Woods behind the hbr. See chartlet and 9.22.4.

R/T Radar Verdon Ch **12** 11 (H24).

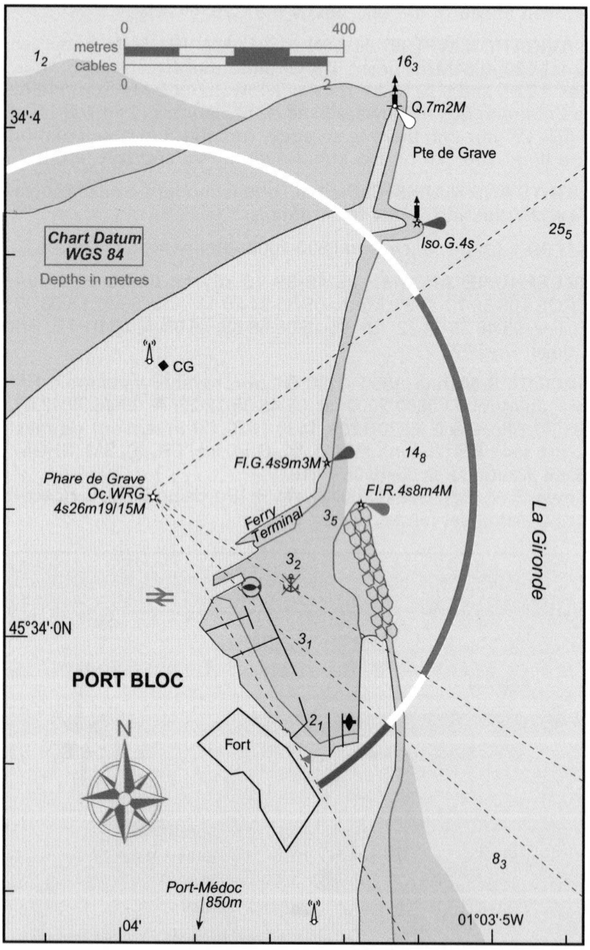
0
400
metres
cables
0
2
Q.7m2M
Pte de Grave
34'·4
Chart Datum
WGS 84
Depths in metres
Iso.G.4s
CG
Fl.G.4s9m3M
Fl.R.4s8m4M
Phare de Grave
Oc.WRG
4s26m19/15M
Ferry Terminal
La Gironde
45°34'·0N
PORT BLOC
N
Fort
Port-Médoc
850m
04'
01°03'·5W

TELEPHONE Aff Mar 05·56·09·60·23; CROSS 05·56·73·31·31; Météo 05·56·34·20·11; Auto 08.92.68.08.17; ⊖ 05·56·09·65·14; Police 05·56·09·80·29; Dr 05·56·09·60·37; Brit Consul 05·57·22·21·10.

FACILITIES HM 05·56·09·63·91; **AUPB** ☎ 05.56.09.72.64. **Moto Yachting Club de la Pte de Grave** ☎ 05·56·09·84·02, D, C (10 ton), ME, El, ⚒, CH. Town P, Gaz, 🛒, R, ✉ & Ⓑ (Verdon), ≋, ✈ (Bordeaux). Fast local ferries to Royan every 45 mins.

9.22.22 PORT-MEDOC

Gironde **45°33'·58N 01°03'·48W** ✿✿⚓⚓⚓✿✿

CHARTS AC 3057/8, 2916; Imray C42; ECM 553, 554; SHOM 7426, 7425. Note: Port Médoc was not charted on French charts as of June 2004. The chartlet below is based on publicity material and whilst believed to be adequate it lacks Latitude and Longitude and should be treated with caution.

TIDES Pointe de Grave is a Standard Port whose predictions apply to Port Bloc and Port-Médoc.

SHELTER Good, in depths 2-3m. Port-Médoc, a new marina, was due to open July 2004. It is approx 1M S of Pte de Grave and 0·5M S of Port Bloc on the W bank of the R Gironde. Check-in at accueil/fuel pontoon to stbd inside entrance.

NAVIGATION WPT 45°34'·66N 01°02'·98W [13b SHM buoy, QG], about 200°/1·1M to hbr ent. An unlit ECM buoy at 45°33'·41N 01°03'·37W marks Work in progress and is believed to be close to the marina ent. Le Verdon oil jetty, about 8ca SE, is dangerous and landing is not allowed; it is in a prohib area. Caution strong tidal streams.

LIGHTS AND MARKS Navigational lts at the marina had not been promulgated as of June 2004. Pte de Grave lt ho, Oc WRG 4s 26m 19/15M, W □ tr, B corners/top. A 63m high red radio mast is just N and marked by R lts. Oil tanks at Le Verdon are conspic. The oil jetty is marked by: Fl (3) G 12s at its N end and Fl G 2.5s at the S end. 9 cables further south is a 171·5° Dir lt,Iso WRG 4s.

R/T Marina Ch 09 (tbc). *Radar de Bordeaux* (VTS) Ch 12 (H24).

TELEPHONE Aff Mar 05·56·09·60·23; CROSS 05·56·73·31·31; Auto 08.92.68.02.17; ⊖ 05·56·09·65·14; Police 05·56·09·80·29; Dr 05·56·09·60·37; Brit Consul 05·57·22·21·10.

FACILITIES HM ☎ 05·56·09·69·75; www.port-medoc.com (800 inc 40 ♥, max LOA 25m) D & P, BH (70 ton), ME, El, ⚒, CH. **Verdon:** 🛒, R, ✉, Ⓑ. ≋, ✈ (Bordeaux). Fast ferry from Port Bloc to Royan every 45 mins.

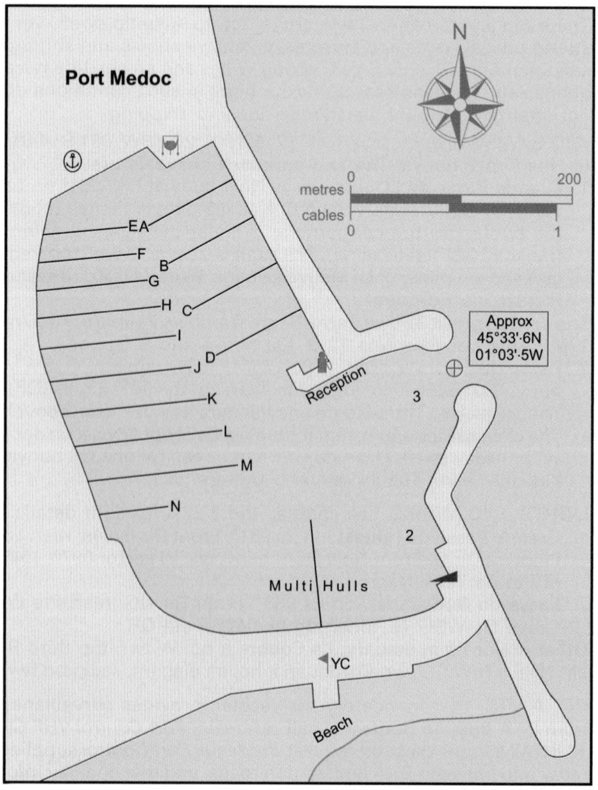
Port Medoc
N
0
200
metres
cables
0
1
EA
F
B
G
H
C
I
J
D
K
L
M
N
Reception
Approx
45°33'·6N
01°03'·5W
3
2
Multi Hulls
YC
Beach

9.22.23 THE RIVER GIRONDE

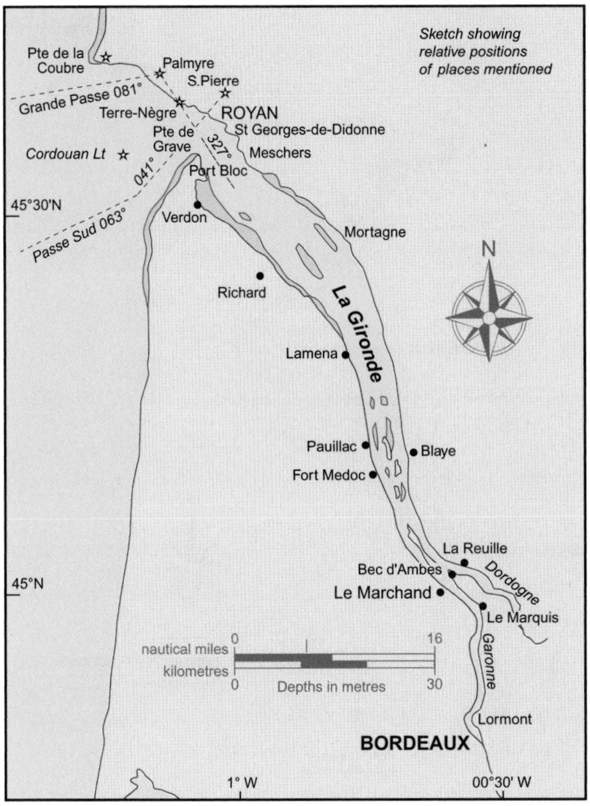
Sketch showing relative positions of places mentioned
Pte de la Coubre
Palmyre
S.Pierre
Grande Passe 081°
Terre-Nègre
ROYAN
Pte de Grave
St Georges-de-Didonne
327°
Cordouan Lt
Meschers
041°
Port Bloc
45°30'N
Passe Sud 063°
Verdon
Mortagne
N
Richard
La Gironde
Lamena
Pauillac
Blaye
Fort Medoc
La Reuille
45°N
Bec d'Ambès
Dordogne
Le Marchand
Le Marquis
nautical miles
kilometres
0
16
30
Depths in metres
Garonne
Lormont
BORDEAUX
1° W
00°30' W

MINOR HARBOURS ON THE GIRONDE

MESCHERS-sur-GIRONDE, Charente Maritime, **45°33'·19N 00°56'·62W**. AC 3057 (with 1:10,000 inset), 3058, 2916; SHOM 7426; ECM 554. Tides as for ROYAN, 5M down-river same bank. Talmont church is conspic 1·8M up-river. Appr close to Pte de Meschers between PHM and SHM unlit perches. Access HW–3 to HW via narrow, drying chan buoyed to port and mudbank close to stbd. Ldg marks/lts 349·5° are 2 W posts with fixed white lts (private); just before the front ldg mark turn port 330° to enter hbr.

To stbd drying marina basin has access HW±3, pontoons A-C. Dead ahead an automatic entry gate gives access over sill 2m CD to a wet basin HW±2½ in 2·5m on pontoons D-F; H24 in season, otherwise 0730-1930; waiting pontoons. Good shelter in all weathers. Both basins are small; max LOA 9m.

HM (M. Jean-Luc Rat, available around HW) ☎ 05.46.02.56.89; Auto 05.36.68.08.17. Facilities: **Marinas** (125 in drying basin, 123 in wet basin, 18 Ⓥ) €1.34. **Town** P & D (cans), R, Bar, 🛒.

MORTAGNE-sur-GIRONDE, Charente Maritime, **45°28'·20N 00°48'·81W**. AC 3057, 2916; SHOM 7426. Tides, use RICHARD differences (9.22.19). Good shelter in marina on E bank of river, 14M from Royan/40M from Bordeaux (near the 75km mark). From the main Gironde chan at No 18 PHM buoy, Fl (2) R 6s, track 094°/4·6M to Mortagne appr chan.

Ent is marked by a WCM buoy, VQ (9) 10s, an unlit PHM buoy, PHM and SHM perches and the remains of a bcn twr. Buoyed chan, 2·5m at half tide, trends 063°/0·9M across drying mudbanks to lock which opens HW–1 to HW (give 48 hrs notice out of season). VHF Ch 09. HM ☎ 05.46.90.63.15. Facilities: **Marina** (130+20 Ⓥ in 4·5m) €1.23, Slip, ME, BY, BH (10 ton), 🛒, Ice; Fuel, Aff Mar, ⊜, and SNSM at Royan; Auto 05.36.68.08.17.

9.22.24 PAUILLAC

Gironde, **45°11'·83N 00°44'·59W**. ❁❁◊◊◊✿✿✿.

CHARTS AC 3058, 2916 (Inset B; 1:25,000); SHOM 7427.

TIDES HW +0620 on Dover (UT); ML 3·0m. Slack water is at approx HW Pte de Grave –3 and +2; see tidal diamond 'G'.

Standard Port POINTE DE GRAVE (←)

Times				Height (metres)			
High Water		Low Water		MHWS	MHWN	MLWN	MLWS
0000	0600	0500	1200	5·4	4·4	2·1	1·0
1200	1800	1700	2400				
Differences PAUILLAC							
+0100	+0100	+0135	+0205	+0·1	0·0	–1·0	–0·5
BORDEAUX							
+0200	+0225	+0330	+0405	–0·1	–0·2	–1·7	–1·0

SHELTER Excellent in marina on W bank, 25M from Royan/Port-Medoc, 28M from Bordeaux and 55M from Castets-en-Dorthe (for canal entry). Access HW±5 (depths 2·0-4.5m); at LW hug the E side of ent, due to silting. Do NOT arrive on the ebb; only manoeuvre at slack water. Visitors berth on W end of 'A' or 'B' pontoons or any hammerhead; see HM for vacant berth. ⚓ possible close E of marina; or 500m further S clear of a 250m wide No-anch area (due to underwater cables).

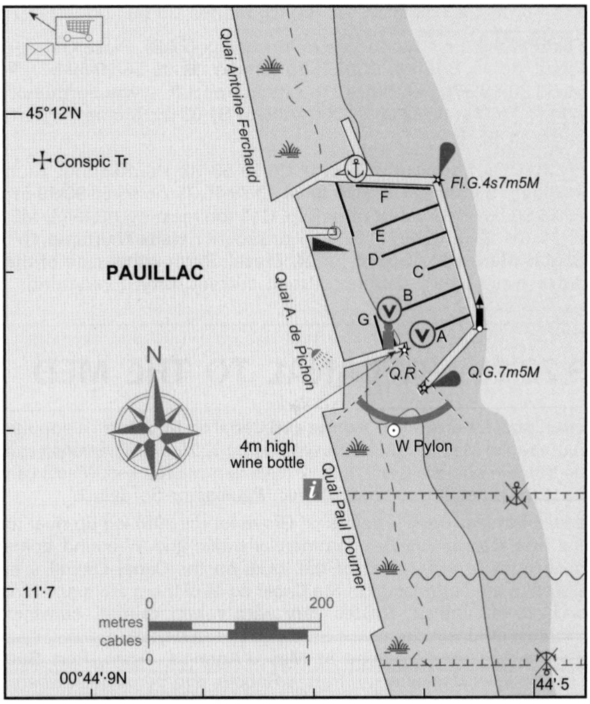
Quai Antoine Ferchaud
45°12'N
Conspic Tr
Fl.G.4s7m5M
F
E
D
C
B
A
G
PAUILLAC
Quai A. de Pichon
Q.R
Q.G.7m5M
N
4m high wine bottle
W Pylon
Quai Paul Doumer
11'·7
0
200
metres
cables
1
00°44'·9N
44'·5

NAVIGATION WPT 45°12'·45N 00°44'·27W [43 SHM buoy, Fl (2) G 6s], 195°/0·65M to hbr ent. Beware current in the river on ent/dep; avoid arrival on ebb, easier/safer at slack water. Keep clear of the Shell oil refinery quays, 1·2-1·7M north.

LIGHTS & MARKS See chartlet and 9.22.4 for lt details. The church twr, NW of the marina ent is conspic. So too is a large bottle of Pauillac marking the W side of the ent.

R/T VHF Ch 09 (0800–1200 & 1400-1800LT).

TELEPHONE Aff Mar 05·56·59·01·58; CROSS 05·56·09·82·00; ⊜ 05·56 ·59·04·01; Météo 05·36·68·08·33.

FACILITIES **Marina** (150+ 20 Ⓥ); ☎ 05·56·59·12·16, 📠 05.56. 59.23.38. €1.80, Slip, ME, El, ⚒, C (14 ton), de-masting C, CH. **CN de Pauillac** ☎ 05·56·59·12·58. **Town**: D & P (cans), R, Bar, 🛒, ✉, Ⓑ. tourismevindepauillac@wanadoo.fr www.pauillac-medoc.com

9.22.25 BORDEAUX

Gironde, **44°52′·79N 00°32′·18W.** ❁❁❁⚓⚓✿✿✿.

CHARTS AC 2916; SHOM 7030.

TIDES HW +0715 on Dover (UT); ML 2·4m. See 9.22.24.

SHELTER Good. Do not berth on quays. Options from seaward:
a. Lormont YC pontoon, below the Pont d'Aquitaine (51m) on E bank; limited space. (Note: the marina opposite on W bank is private, no ♥).
b. Bassin à Flot (1·5M above bridge). For Bassin No 2, enter lock HW −1½; exit HW −½. Pre-book ☎ 05·56·90·59·57 and Ch 12. A waiting pontoon is just S of the lock. Note: During 2005 Bassin No 2 is due to be modernised with 6 extra yacht pontoons.
c. Halte Nautique, E bank, just SE of Pont de Pierre.
d. Bègles Marina, 5M up-river from Bordeaux.

NAVIGATION Bordeaux is 50M from Royan and 25M from Pauillac; the chan is well marked/lit. Beware big ships, strong currents (up to 5kn if river in spate) and possibly large bits of flotsam. At No 62 WCM buoy, Q (9) 15s, (close NW of Bec d'Ambès) keep to starboard into the R. Garonne, with 12M to run to Bordeaux (Pont d'Aquitaine: Lat/Long under title). De-mast before the low Pont de Pierre.

LIGHTS AND MARKS Pont d'Aquitaine is an unmistakable suspension bridge, gateway to Bordeaux. Lts as on chartlet.

R/T Bordeaux Traffic Ch 12. Bègles Marina Ch 09.

TELEPHONE Port Autonome de Bordeaux (PAB), Place Gabriel, Place de la Bourse, 33075 Bordeaux; ☎ 05·56·90·59·57, 📠 05·56.90.58.97; postoffice@bordeaux-port.fr www.bordeaux-port.fr Aff Mar 05·56·00·83·00; ⊜ 05·57·81·03·60; Météo (airport) 05·56·13·82·10.

FACILITIES **Lormont YC**, ☎ 05·56·31·50·10; de-masting; Club facilities. **Bassin No 2**, HM ☎ 06·13·79·10·75 or 05·56·90·59·57; 05·56·90·59·85 for latest info. Slip, C (5 ton masting mobile), ME, El, ⚒, CH, Ⓔ, SHOM. No FW, ⛽ or security. **Halte Nautique**, ⛽. **Bègles Marina** ☎ 05·56·85·76·04. Diesel. Berth either side of the outer wave-break. Caution: strong current. **City**: Everything.

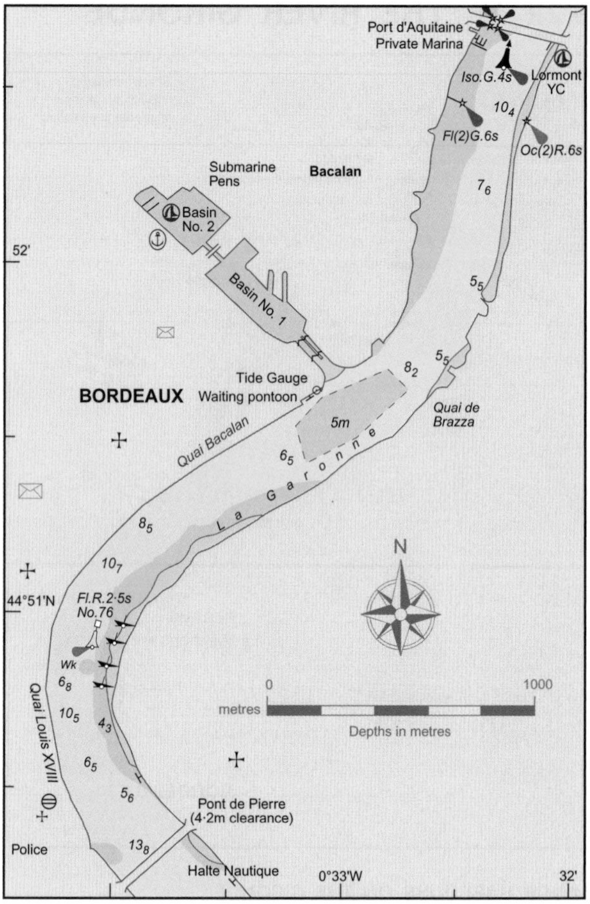

Port d'Aquitaine Private Marina
Iso.G.4s
Lormont YC
Fl(2)G.6s
Oc(2)R.6s
Submarine Pens
Bacalan
Basin No. 2
Basin No. 1
52'
Tide Gauge
BORDEAUX
Waiting pontoon
Quai Bacalan
5m
Quai de Brazza
La Garonne
N
44°51'N
Fl.R.2·5s No.76
Wk
Quai Louis XVIII
0
1000
metres
Depths in metres
Pont de Pierre (4·2m clearance)
Police
Halte Nautique
0°33'W
32'

9.22.26 BY CANAL TO THE MED

The Canal Latéral à la Garonne and Canal du Midi form a popular route to the Mediterranean, despite some 120 locks. The transit can be done in about a week, but 12 days is more relaxed. Masts can be lowered at Royan, Port-Médoc, Pauillac or Bordeaux.

Leave Bordeaux at LW Pointe de Grave for the 30M leg up-river to the first lock at Castets. Commercial traffic and W-bound boats have right of way. Most of the locks on the Canal Latéral à la Garonne are automatic. On the Canal du Midi there are many hire cruisers in summer. Depths vary with winter rainfall, summer drought and silting.
Fuel is available by hose at Mas d'Agenais, Agen, Port Sud (Toulouse), Castelnaudary, Port la Robine, and by can elsewhere. 🛒 and FW are readily obtained. Tolls are listed in 9.17.6. *Guide Vagnon No 7* or *Navicarte No 11* are advised. Further info from: Service de la Navigation de Toulouse, 8 Port St Etienne, 31079 Toulouse Cedex, ☎ 05·61·80·07·18.

SUMMARY Canal	From	To	Km/ Locks	Min Depth(m)	Min Ht(m)
Latéral à la Garonne	Castets	Toulouse	193/53	2·2	3·5
Du Midi	Toulouse	Sète	240/65	1·6	3·0
De la Nouvelle	Salleles	Port la Nouvelle	37/14	1·5	3·1

Notes: Max LOA 30m; draft 1·5m (varies with season); max beam 5·5m. Headroom of 3·3m is to centre of arch; over a width of 4m, clearance is about 2·40m. Speed limit 8km/hr (about 4½kn), but 3km/hr under bridges/over aqueducts.

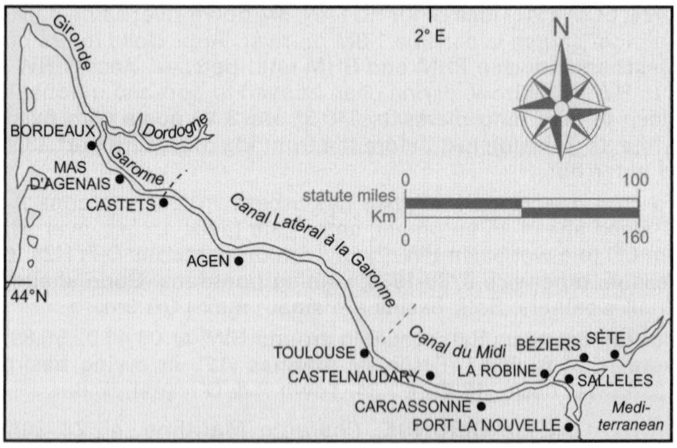

Gironde
2° E
N
BORDEAUX
Dordogne
Garonne
MAS D'AGENAIS
CASTETS
statute miles
Km
0
100
0
160
Canal Latéral à la Garonne
AGEN
44°N
Canal du Midi
TOULOUSE
BÉZIERS
SÈTE
CASTELNAUDARY
LA ROBINE
SALLELES
CARCASSONNE
PORT LA NOUVELLE
Medi-terranean

9.22.27 LANDES RANGE

Limits: Centre d'Essais des Landes (CEL) firing range extends from Pointe de la Negade to Capbreton and approx 40M offshore. It is bounded by 45°28'N 01°14'W (inshore N), 45°11'N 02°04'W, 43°56'N 02°17'W, 43°41'N 01°31'W (inshore S). The inshore boundary lies parallel to and 3M off the shoreline. See chartlet, AC 1104 and 2664. CEL Range Control is at 44°26'N 01°15'W.

Sector designations: The range is in two blocks, N and S of an 8M wide access corridor to Arcachon, bearing 270° from ATT-ARC buoy. Within these blocks those sectors which are active, or are planned to be, are referred to by their Lat/Long coordinates in all radio broadcasts, telephone recordings and enquiries.

Range activity: Sectors can be active Mon-Fri from 0800 LT, but are usually inactive Sat/Sun, at night and in August. However there can be exceptions to the above. Navigation may be prohibited in active sectors inside the 12M territorial limit; beyond 12M it *"is strongly discouraged due to the particularly dangerous tests carried out"*. A No-entry box (1·6M x 1M) is centred on 44°22´·70N 01°25´·50W, 13M SSW of ATT-ARC buoy.

Information on range activity is available from:

a. ☎ +33 5.58.82.22.42 & 43 recorded info H24, inc daily activity.
b. Semaphore stations at Chassiron (Île d'Oléron), Pte de Grave, Cap Ferret, Messanges and Socoa (St Jean-de-Luz): on request Ch 16 for advance notice of activity. See also 7.20.2.
c. CROSS Etel broadcasts 0703, 0715, 0733, 0745 and 0803LT.
d. CEL, after announcement on Ch 16, broadcasts Ch 06, 10: Mon-Thu, 0815 & 1615, and Fri 0815 & 1030; all LT.
e. CEL on request Ch 06, Mon-Thu 0800-1700 (1100 Fri).
f. CEL ☎ +33 5.58.78.18.00; same hrs as (e).
g. Local NMs (AvUrNavs) at HMs' offices and Affaires Maritimes in Arcachon.

Options: Transit at night, weekends or in August - subject to notified range activity; or to seaward of the range. For example a rhumb line track 200°/173M from PA buoy (W of La Rochelle) to Bilbao passes 6M W of the range. Monitor Ch 16 on passage. It is imperative to check range activity before entering the range.

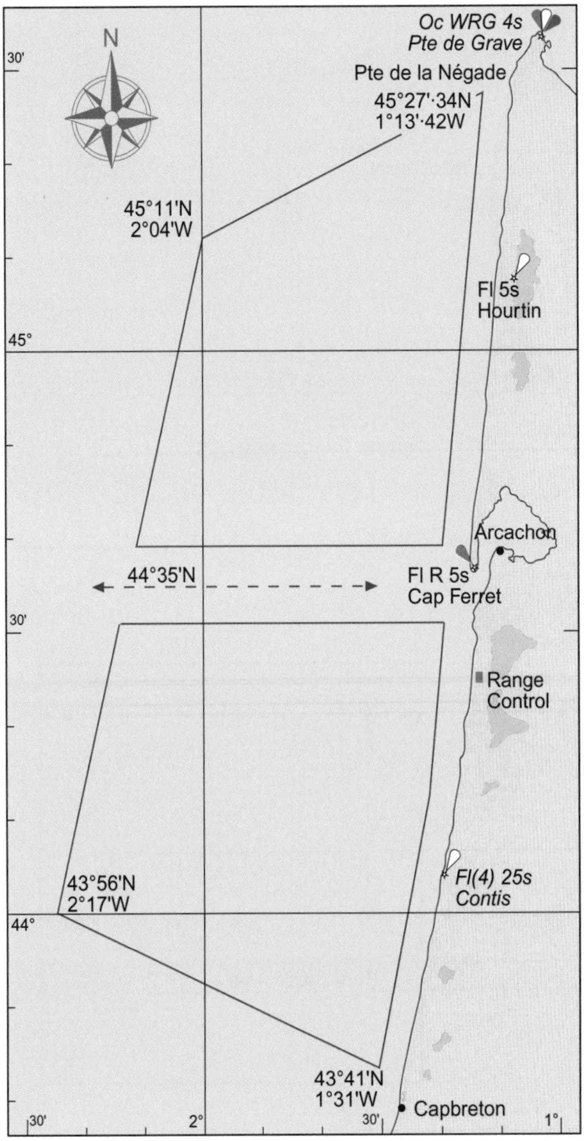
N
30'
Oc WRG 4s
Pte de Grave
Pte de la Négade
45°27'·34N
1°13'·42W
45°11'N
2°04'W
Fl 5s
Hourtin
45°
Arcachon
44°35'N
Fl R 5s
Cap Ferret
30'
Range
Control
43°56'N
2°17'W
Fl(4) 25s
Contis
44°
43°41'N
1°31'W
Capbreton
30'
2°
30'
1°

9.22.28 ARCACHON

Gironde **44°39´·77N 01°09´·11W** ❀◊◊◊✿✿✿

CHARTS AC 2664, 2750; Imray C42; SHOM 7070, 6766; ECM 255, 1024

TIDES +0620 Dover; ML 2·5; Zone –0100
Standard Port POINTE DE GRAVE (⟵)

Times				**Height (metres)**			
High Water		Low Water		MHWS	MHWN	MLWN	MLWS
0000	0600	0500	1200	5·4	4·4	2·1	1·0
1200	1800	1700	2400				
Differences ARCACHON (7 cables WNW of marina)							
+0010	+0025	0000	+0020	–1·1	–1·0	–0·8	–0·6
CAP FERRET							
–0015	+0005	–0005	+0015	–1·4	–1·2	–0·8	–0·5

SHELTER Good in marina (max LOA 15m), but access to Bassin d'Arcachon in strong SW-N winds or at night is impossible. Check in, berth/raft on accueil pontoon (35m long) for 2 days max. There are **very few** Ⓥ berths in Jul & Aug and on any public Hol in summer. Recently the waiting list for berths had 8,807 applicants and 23 years to wait. If marina is full, there is a good ⚓ N of it, except in strong N'lies.

Around the Bassin are many small hbrs which dry LW ±2 or 3 hours, but they are worth exploring by shoal draft boats: To the W, La Vigne*, Le Canon, Piquey and Claouey; to the NE, Port de Lège, Arès, Andernos*, Fontainevieille*, Lanton (Cassy) and Audenge*; and to the S, La Teste and Gujan. *See overleaf for amplifying notes.

NAVIGATION WPT 44°34´·26N 01°18´·75W [ATT-ARC (SWM) buoy], 060°/0·77M to first chan buoys in the well buoyed, unlit N Passe. Buoys may at times go missing, but are re-sited annually. Prior to approaching, visitors should make a point of calling *Cap Ferret Semaphore* Ch 16 13 (HJ), ☎ 05·56·60·60·03, for a buoyage/navigational update. N Passe trends NE then N between Banc d'Arguin and Banc du Toulinguet towards Cap Ferret where it meets the longer S Passe. The latter is closed to navigation and not marked, although used by a few local FVs.

In any wind the sea breaks on the shifting sand banks between Cap Ferret and Wharf de la Salie, but the chan buoys can be seen between the breakers (not as fearsome as it sounds).

Best time to start appr is HW–1 and no later than HW+1. Due to the very strong ebb (6kn sp) the chan bar (mean depth 4·5m) is impassable from HW+1 until LW, and it is best to wait until LW+3. When swell is higher than 1m, bar may be dangerous. If in doubt, stay out. Best to leave on the last of the flood.

Be aware of any activity in firing ranges between Pte de la Negade and Capbreton, out to 40M offshore; see 9.22.27.

LIGHTS AND MARKS ATT-ARC (SWM light buoy) is moved as required to indicate approach to N Passe. See chartlet and 9.22.4 for lt details. Cap Ferret is low-lying but the white, red-topped lt ho is conspic; as are a water twr close N and the white Sig Stn close S. The famous Dune de Pyla (103m high) on the E shore is very conspic, unless hidden in haze.

La Salie IDM light buoy is off chartlet, about 1·5M WSW of the Wharf de Salie WCM beacon.

Secondary chans in the Bassin d'Arcachon are marked by piles lettered A to K, plus pile number, clockwise from the N.

R/T VHF Ch 09 16 (H24).

TELEPHONE Sig Stn 05·56·60·60·03 ⊜ 05·56·72·29·24; Aff Mar 05·57·52·57·07; SNSM 05·56·22·36·75; CROSS 05·56·73·31·31; Auto 08·92·68·08·33; Police 05·56·83·04·63; Dr 05·56·83·04·72; Ⓗ 05·56·83·39·50; Brit Consul 05·57·22·21·10.

FACILITIES Marina (2245 + 200 Ⓥ), ☎ 05·56·22·36·75, 05·56.83.26.19. €3.30 (2nd night free), usually crowded in season; access HW±3, D, Slip, C (10/20 ton), BH (45 ton), ⚒;

YC du Bassin d'Arcachon ☎ 05·56·83·22·11, P, D, FW, Slip, R, Bar, ME, El, Ⓔ, SHOM, ✗, CH, SM, ⊡.

Town 🛒, R, Gaz, ✉, Ⓑ, ⇌, ✈ (Bordeaux). Ferry: Roscoff/St Malo.

22

MINOR HARBOURS IN THE ARCACHON BASIN

LA VIGNE, 44°40′·44N 01°14′·35W. HW time & ht approx as Cap Ferret above; ML 2·4m. Access HW±2. See 9.22.28. Good shelter, but crowded; beware strong currents across hbr ent. 2 perches mark the ent and on the SW point, a lt Iso R 4s 7m 5M. A small bkwtr (unlit) protrudes into the ent from the NE side. Aff Mar ☎ 05.56·60·52·76. Facilities: **Marina** (268 + 2) Max LOA 8·5m, ☎ 05·56·60·54·36, Slip, CH, C (2 ton), P, D.

ANDERNOS, 44°44'·53N 01°06'·54W. HW time & ht approx as Arcachon 9.22.28; access about HW±2. Dredged channel to Bétey, with side chan to Andernos, is very well marked by lateral poles D0 to D14. Jetty + pontoon only for yachts able to take the ground, max LOA 12m. Bad silting may occur despite dredging. Also ⚓ on flat drying foreshore. HM ☎ 56.82.00.12. Few facilities.

FONTAINEVIEILLE, 44°43'·30N 01°04'·63W. Tides as 9.22.28. Drying marina on NE side of Bassin d'Arcachon, access HW±3 via Chenal de Mouchtalette. Proceed from E0 PHM pile to E8, where fork left onto NNE for 7ca to hbr ent. No lts. Boats dry out on pontoons. HM ☎ 05.56.82.17.31; Auto 05.36.65.08.33. Facilities: **Marina** (178+ 2), Fuel, Slip, ME.

AUDENGE, 44°40'·58N01°01'·57W. Tides as 9.22.28. Drying marina and oyster port 5·5M E of Arcachon, access sp HW–2 to HW, nps HW–1 to HW. Appr from G0 PHM pile via drying Chenal d'Audenge to G8 pile, 5ca short of the ent. HM ☎ 05.56.26.88.97. The Old Port (84 berths) is to the N; the New Port has 130 pontoon berths, Fuel, Slip, YC.

Other drying hbrs include: to the NE, Port du Bétey & de Cassy; and E of Arcachon, Port de La Teste and Port du Teich.

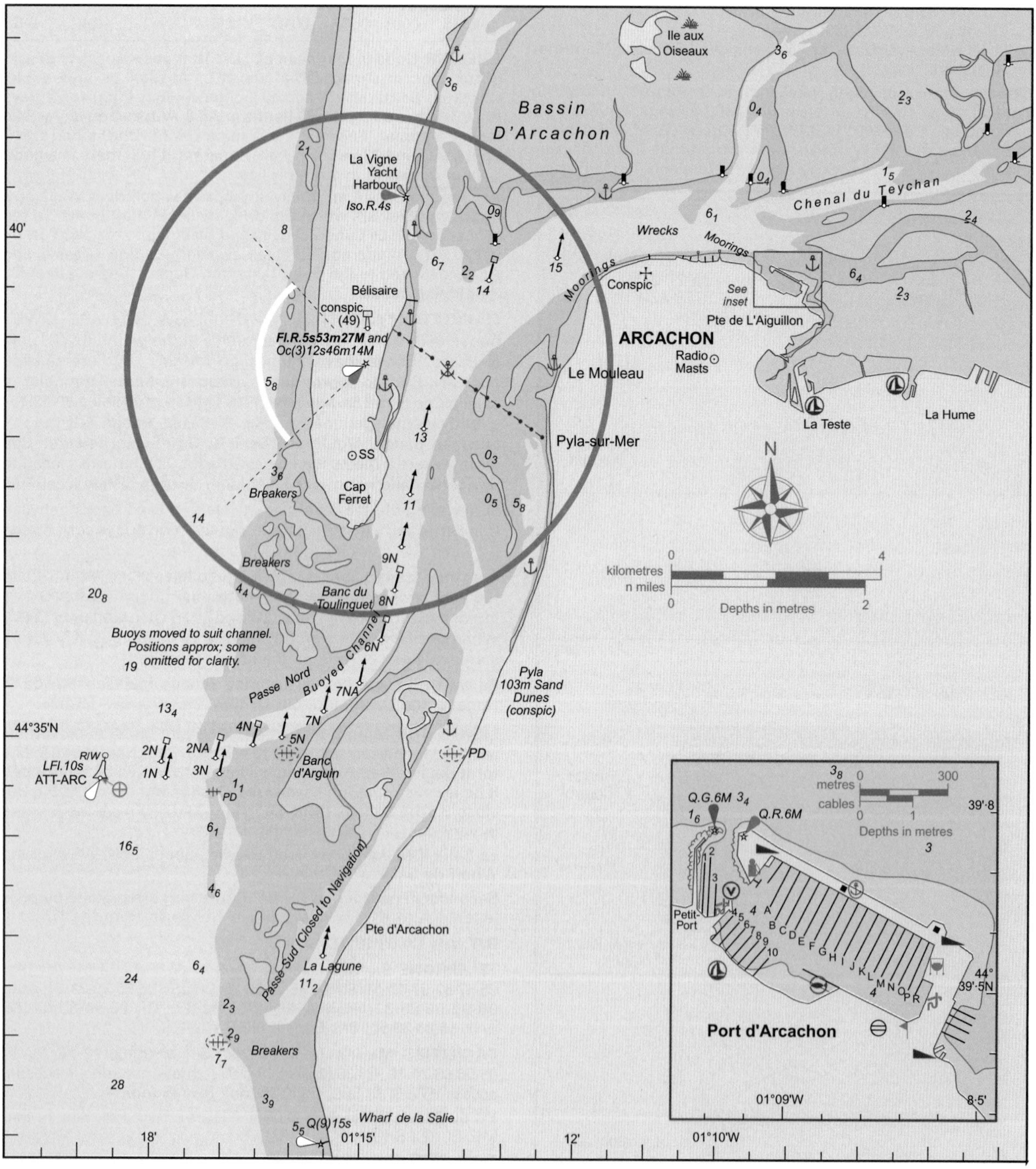
Ile aux Oiseaux
Bassin D'Arcachon
Chenal du Teychan
La Vigne Yacht Harbour
Iso.R.4s
Bélisaire conspic (49)
Fl.R.5s53m27M and Oc(3)12s46m14M
Wrecks
Moorings
Conspic
See inset
Pte de L'Aiguillon
ARCACHON
Radio Masts
Le Mouleau
Pyla-sur-Mer
La Teste
La Hume
SS
Cap Ferret
Breakers
Banc du Toulinguet
Buoys moved to suit channel. Positions approx; some omitted for clarity.
Passe Nord
Buoyed Channel
Pyla 103m Sand Dunes (conspic)
LFl.10s ATT-ARC
R/W
PD
Banc d'Arguin
Passe Sud (Closed to Navigation)
Pte d'Arcachon
La Lagune
Q(9)15s
Wharf de la Salie
kilometres
n miles
Depths in metres
40'
44°35'N
18'
01°15'
12'
01°10'W
Q.G.6M
Q.R.6M
metres
cables
Petit-Port
Port d'Arcachon
39'·8
44° 39'·5N
8·5'
01°09'W

9.22.29 CAPBRETON

Landes **43°39'·36N 01°26'·91W**

CHARTS AC 1102; SHOM 6786, 6557, 6586; ECM 555, 1024

TIDES +0450 Dover; ML 2·3; Zone –0100

Standard Port POINTE DE GRAVE (⟵)

Times				Height (metres)			
High Water		Low Water		MHWS	MHWN	MLWN	MLWS
0000	0600	0500	1200	5·4	4·4	2·1	1·0
1200	1800	1700	2400				
Differences CAPBRETON and L'ADOUR (9.22.30)							
–0030	–0035	–0025	–0040	–1·2	–1·1	–0·4	–0·3

SHELTER Good. Appr advised HW–3 to +1; not before LW+2½. Narrow canalised ent dangerous in strong winds from W to N. Do not enter if swell or seas break in mid-chan; they often break on either side. Hbr and chan dredged 1·5m. Visitors' pontoon 'B' (first to stbd of marina ent). The Y-shaped marina has 3 basins.

NAVIGATION WPT 43°39'·63N 01°27'·49W, 123°/5ca to N pier lt. Bkwtr lts in line 123° lead to hbr ent. See 9.22.5 for Gouf de Capbreton a submarine canyon off the hbr ent where depths shoal rapidly in last 3ca from 50m to 3m. No ⚓ off ent. Silting occurs around head of S bkwtr.

Inside Canal du Boucarot best water is close to N bkwtr initially; from abeam small statue of Virgin Mary, move to mid-chan or just S of mid-chan. Marina ent is via obvious gap in training wall on SE side of chan, abeam conspic Capitainerie.

LIGHTS AND MARKS A casino and red-roofed sanatorium are conspic S of ent and a water twr 1M ENE. Lts as chartlet and 9.22.4. A disused lt bcn is close E of the S bkwtr hd.

R/T VHF Ch 09 (0800-1900 in season).

TELEPHONE Aff Mar 05·58·72·10·43; CROSS 05·56·73·31·31; ⊖ 05·59·46·68·80; SNSM 05·58·72·47·44; Auto 08.92.68.08.40; Ⓗ (Bayonne) 05·59·44·35·35; Police 05·59·50·31·52; Brit Consul 05·59·24·21·40.

FACILITIES Marina, ☎ 05·58·72·21·23, fax 05·58.72.40.35, €2.15, (950+60 Ⓥ), Slip, BH (30 ton), P & D (0830-1300, 1400-2000 or ☎ 05.58.72.15.66), ME, El, C (30 ton), ⚒, CH, SM, Ⓔ, ▣; **CNCP** ☎ 05·58·72·67·09; **Town:** Bar, R, 🛒, ✉, Ⓑ, ⇌ Bayonne (17km); ✈ Biarritz (25km).

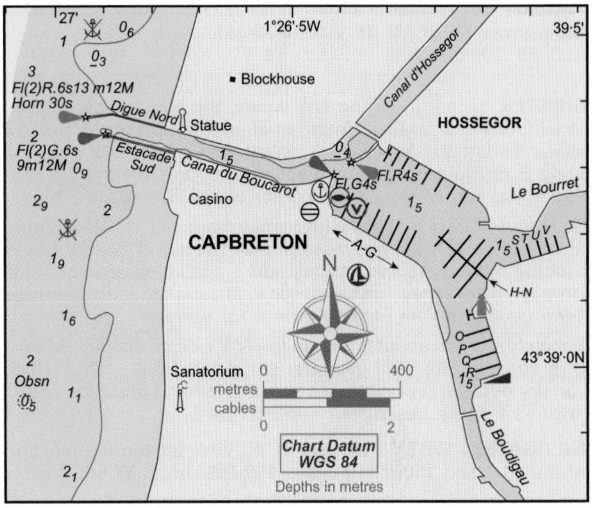
27'
1°26'·5W
39·5'
Blockhouse
Canal d'Hossegor
HOSSEGOR
Fl(2)R.6s13m12M
Horn 30s
Digue Nord
Statue
Fl(2)G.6s
9m12M
Estacade Sud
Canal du Boucarot
Fl.G4s
Fl.R4s
Casino
Le Bourret
CAPBRETON
A-G
S T U V
H-N
Sanatorium
metres
cables
0
400
2
O
P
Q
R
43°39'·0N
Obsn
Le Boudigau
Chart Datum
WGS 84
Depths in metres

9.22.30 ANGLET/BAYONNE

Pyrénées Atlantique **43°31'·81N 01°31'·95W**

CHARTS AC 1102, 1343; SHOM 6786, 6558/7, 6536; ECM 555

TIDES +0450 Dover (UT); ML 2·5; Zone –0100. See 9.22.29.

SHELTER Very good in Anglet marina (1·7-3·5m), 0·70M from ent on S bank of R Adour; but cement dust from N bank may be a problem. At Bayonne (interesting old quarter, 3M up river on S bank) no passage beyond bridge (5·2m clearance).

NAVIGATION WPT 43°32'·59N 01°32'·76W [BA SWM buoy, L Fl 10s], 142°/0·9M to N bkwtr lt. Easy access except in strong W winds. ⚓ prohib due to commercial ships to which yachts must give way. Strong tidal stream, max 5kn at sp ebb.

LIGHTS AND MARKS Outer ldg lts 090°, both Q, W pylons/R tops. Inner ldg lts 111°, both FG, lit when chan is practicable. 3 more sets of ldg lts upriver to Bayonne. Other lts as chartlet and 9.22.4. IPTS (full code) from conspic Sig twr on S side of ent. Pte St Martin lt ho, W twr/B top, is 2·45M SSW of hbr.

R/T Marina Ch 09. Port/pilots 12 16 (0800-1200; 1400-1800LT).

TELEPHONE HM Bayonne 05·59·63·11·57; CROSS 02·97·55·35·35; ⊖ 05·59·59·08·29; Aff Mar 05·59·55·06·68; SNSM 05·59·83·40·50; Météo 05·59·23·84·15; Auto 08·92·65·08·64; Ⓗ 05·59·44·35·35.

FACILITIES Marina (425+50 Ⓥ), ☎ 05·59·63·05·45; €1.82, P, D, ME, El, C (1·3 ton), ▣, BH (13 ton), Slip, ⚒, CH, Ⓔ, SHOM. **YC Adour Atlantique** ☎ 05·59·63·16·22; **Port** C (30 ton), Slip, FW. **Bayonne** Bar, R, 🛒, ✉, Ⓑ, ⇌, ✈ (Biarritz). Ferry: Bilboa-Portsmouth.

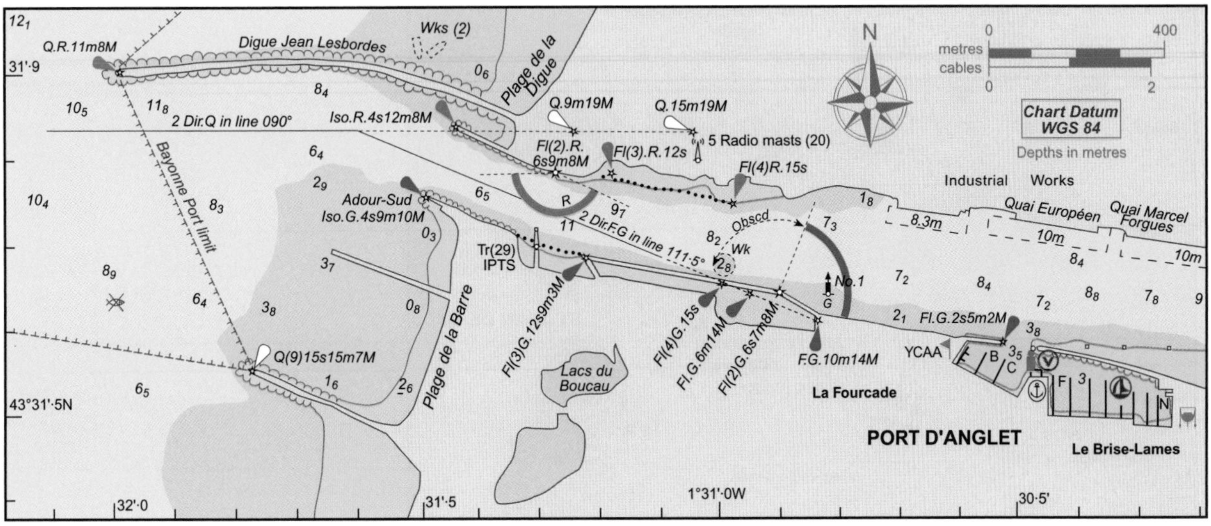
Q.R.11m8M
31'·9
Digue Jean Lesbordes
Wks (2)
Plage de la Digue
2 Dir.Q in line 090°
Iso.R.4s12m8M
Q.9m19M
Q.15m19M
5 Radio masts (20)
Fl(2).R.6s9m8M
Fl(3).R.12s
Fl(4)R.15s
Bayonne Port limit
Adour-Sud
Iso.G.4s9m10M
R
2 Dir.F.G in line 111·5°
Obscd
Wk
Tr(29)
IPTS
No.1
G
Industrial Works
Quai Européen
Quai Marcel Forgues
8.3m
10m
Q(9)15s15m7M
Plage de la Barre
Fl(3)G.12s9m3M
Lacs du Boucau
Fl(4)G.15s
Fl.G.6m14M
Fl(2)G.6s7m8M
F.G.10m14M
Fl.G.2s5m2M
YCAA
B
C
F
La Fourcade
PORT D'ANGLET
Le Brise-Lames
43°31'·5N
32'·0
31'·5
1°31'·0W
30·5'
N
metres
cables
0
400
2
Chart Datum
WGS 84
Depths in metres

22

9.22.31 ST JEAN-DE-LUZ

Pyrénées Atlantique, **43°23´·85N 01°40´·61W**

CHARTS AC 1102, 1343; SHOM 6786, 6558, 6526; ECM 555

TIDES HW +0435 on Dover (UT); ML 2·5m; Zone –0100

Standard Port POINTE DE GRAVE (⟵)

Times				Height (metres)			
High Water		Low Water		MHWS	MHWN	MLWN	MLWS
0000	0600	0500	1200	5·4	4·4	2·1	1·0
1200	1800	1700	2400				
Differences ST JEAN DE LUZ (SOCOA)							
–0040	–0045	–0030	–0045	–1·1	–1·1	–0·6	–0·4

SHELTER Except in strong NW winds, the bay can be entered at all times and good ⚓s found in approx 4m on the W and SE sides; the latter is less prone to swell. Beware an unlit mooring buoy S of Digue d'Artha, antipollution booms off the beaches and a submerged jetty in SE corner of bay. There are 2 hbrs:

St Jean-de-Luz in S of bay with a small marina (2·5m) at Ciboure, in Bassin de Larraldénia, close to rear QG ldg lt. The FV hbr is E of the marina. Sailing into the port is prohib; speed limit 5kn. Unmasted craft may ⚓ in La Nivelle River, access via fixed bridge 1·9m clearance - an unlikely option for visitors.

Socoa hbr (dries about 0·5m) on the NW side of the bay is close S of conspic fort. Tide gauge at ent. Apart from yachts which can dry out, it is really little more than a landing place for yachts anchored in the designated areas to the E.

NAVIGATION WPT 43°24'·09N 01°40'·79W (at the intersection of the 101° and 150·7° ldg lines), 150·7°/500m to W ent. Yachts can approach within the N quadrant direct to hbr ent, but in heavy W'ly weather seas break on various shoals on the Plateau de St Jean-de-Luz. 3M W of hbr ent beware Les Briquets rks, drying 0·4m, 2M NE of Hendaye.

The 3 appr chans are defined by ldg lts (see below): The main outer chan leads 138° between Illarguita and Belhara Perdun banks. It is the only safe approach at night and in bad weather. Thence, or if coming from the W, intercept the middle chan at 43°24'·23N 01°41'·90W; it leads 101°, seaward of the hbr breakwaters, to the WPT.

The inner chan leads 150·7° through the W ent into the bay and to St Jean de Luz hbr. The unmarked E ent to the bay is used by locals, but is not recommended. Speed limit in the bay is 7kn.

LIGHTS AND MARKS La Rhune, an 898m high conical mountain, is conspic in good vis 5·5M SSE of hbr. Digue des Criquas (the W bkwtr) is lit, Iso G 4s. Digue d'Artha is a detached unlit bkwtr across the middle of the bay. See chartlet and 9.22.4 for light details.

Outer 138° ldg lts: Front, Socoa lt, QWR, 12m W□ twr, B stripes; (R sector covers Socoa hbr ent). Rear Q is B ■/W bands on W pylon/B bands, hard to see by day, but the nearby Bordagain twr, 100m, is more readily visible.

Ste Barbe 101° ldg lts: Both Oc (4) R 12s; front, W △ on W bldg; rear, B ▲ on W twr.

Inner 150·7° ldg lts: Both Dir QG, conspic white twrs: front has a R vert stripe; rear, a G vert stripe. The FR on E jetty head is a neon strip lt.

R/T Marina VHF Ch 09, 16.

TELEPHONE ⊖ 05.59.47.18.61; Aff Mar 05·59·47·14·55; CROSS 05·56·73·31·31; Météo 05·59·22·03·30; Auto 08·92·68·08·64; SNSM 05·59·47·22·98; Police 05·59·26·01·55;Brit Consul 05·59·24·21·40.

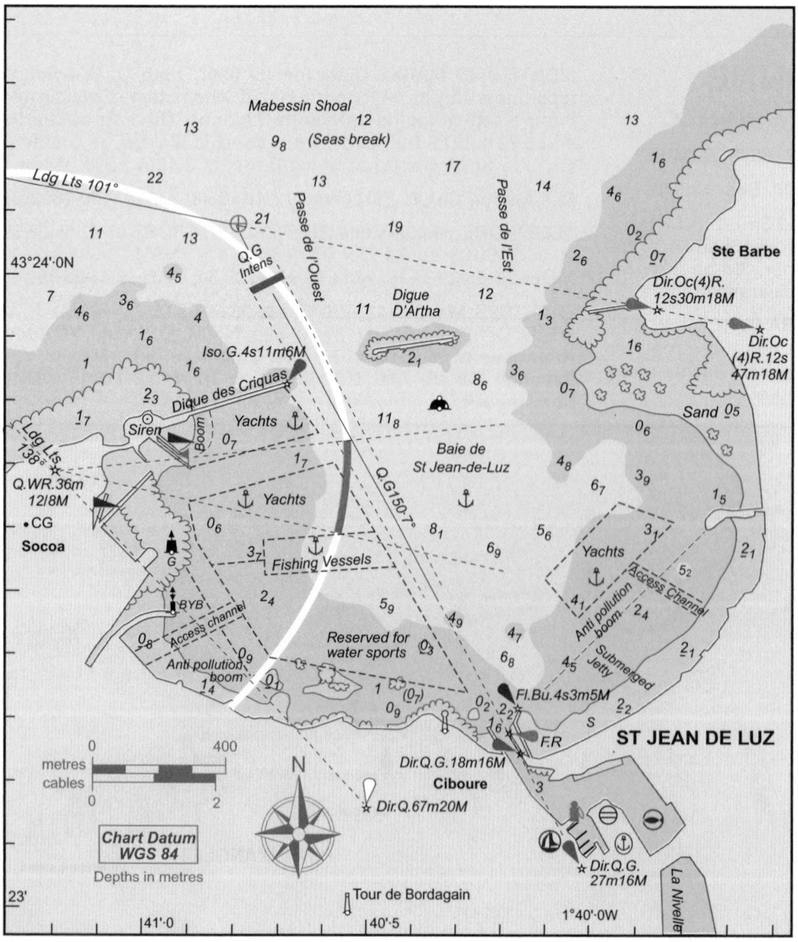
Mabessin Shoal
(Seas break)
Ldg Lts 101°
Passe de l'Ouest
Passe de l'Est
Q.G Intens
43°24'·0N
Digue D'Artha
Iso.G.4s11m6M
Digue des Criquas
Siren
Boom
Yachts
Ldg Lts 138°
Q.WR.36m 12/8M
•CG
Socoa
Baie de St Jean-de-Luz
Q.G150·7°
Fishing Vessels
BYB
Access channel
Anti pollution boom
Reserved for water sports
Ste Barbe
Dir.Oc(4)R. 12s30m18M
Dir.Oc (4)R.12s 47m18M
Sand
Yachts
Access Channel
Anti pollution boom
Submerged Jetty
Fl.Bu.4s3m5M
F.R
ST JEAN DE LUZ
Dir.Q.G.18m16M
Ciboure
Dir.Q.67m20M
Dir.Q.G. 27m16M
La Nivelle
metres
cables
Chart Datum WGS 84
Depths in metres
23'
41'·0
40'·5
1°40'·0W
Tour de Bordagain

FACILITIES

ST JEAN-DE-LUZ: **Marina** (80+8 Ⓥ), ☎ 05·59·47·26·81; €1.86, P, C (6 ton), Slip, Ⓔ, ME, El, ⚒, CH.

Town R, Bar, Ⓑ, ✉, Ⓑ, ⇌.

SOCOA **Jetty** C (1 ton), P, D, Slip, BY, ME, CH, El, ⚒. **YC Basque** ☎ 05·59·47·18·31.

9.22.32 HENDAYE

Pyrénées Atlantique **43°22′·75N 01°47′·28W**

CHARTS AC 1102, 1181; SHOM 6786, 6558, 6556; ECM 555

TIDES HW +0450 on Dover (UT); ML 2·3m; Zone –0100

Use differences ST JEAN DE LUZ (SOCOA) 9.22.31

SHELTER Excellent in marina (3m); accueil pontoon 'A' in NW corner. River is dredged 2m; access H24. Possible ⚓ in river or in the Baie de Chingoudy, but exposed to N/NE and S/SW gales. S of C Higuer, a Spanish FV hbr, 2-3m, is a port of refuge. Note: Hendaye is in France; Fuenterrabía (Hondarrabia) (9.23.6) in Spain. See chartlet for neutral zone.

NAVIGATION WPT 43°23'·80N 01°46'·52W, 212°/1·15M to W bkwtr hd. Beware Les Briquets 8ca N of Pte Ste Anne at E end of the Baie; near centre of B, keep clear of Bajo Iruarri. River ent is easy except in heavy N'ly swell; sp ebb is very strong. Inshore of Pte des Dunes, Fl R 2·5s, hug the E training wall for best water. A spit drying 1·3m (SHM bn, VQ (3) G 5s) off Fuenterrabía narrows the chan to about 100m wide before Hendaye marina ent opens up.

LIGHTS AND MARKS La Rhune, an 898m high conical mountain, is conspic in good vis 8M ESE of hbr. Cabo Higuer lt ho is conspic at W side of bay on a rugged headland. Marina is entered between a FR neon strip lt and Fl Y 4s. 40m E of the ent a RW TV relay mast (40m) is conspic.

R/T Marina VHF Ch 09 (H24).

TELEPHONE Aff Mar 05·59·47·14·55; ⊖ 05·59·48·10·68; CROSS 05.59.55.35.35; SNSM 05·59.48.06.10; Météo 05·59.24.58.80; Auto 08.92.68.08.64; Police 05·59.50.31.52; Ⓗ 05·59.20.08.22.

FACILITIES Marina station.littorale.hendaye@wanadoo.fr ☎ 05·59.48.06.10, 📠 05·59.48.06.13. 700 + 120 Ⓥ, €2.95 (3rd night free), P, D (H24), C (30 ton), Slip, CH, ⚒, El, Ⓔ, ME. **YC** ☎ 05·59·20·03·02, Bar. **Town** 🛒, R, Bar, Gaz, ✉, Ⓑ, ⇌ (TGV Paris-Madrid), ✈ Fuenterrabía, or Biarritz (☎ 05·59.43.83.83) for UK flights. Local ferry from Hendaye to Fuenterrabía every 15 mins. UK ferry from Bilbao or Santander. **Fuenterrabía**, see 9.23.6.

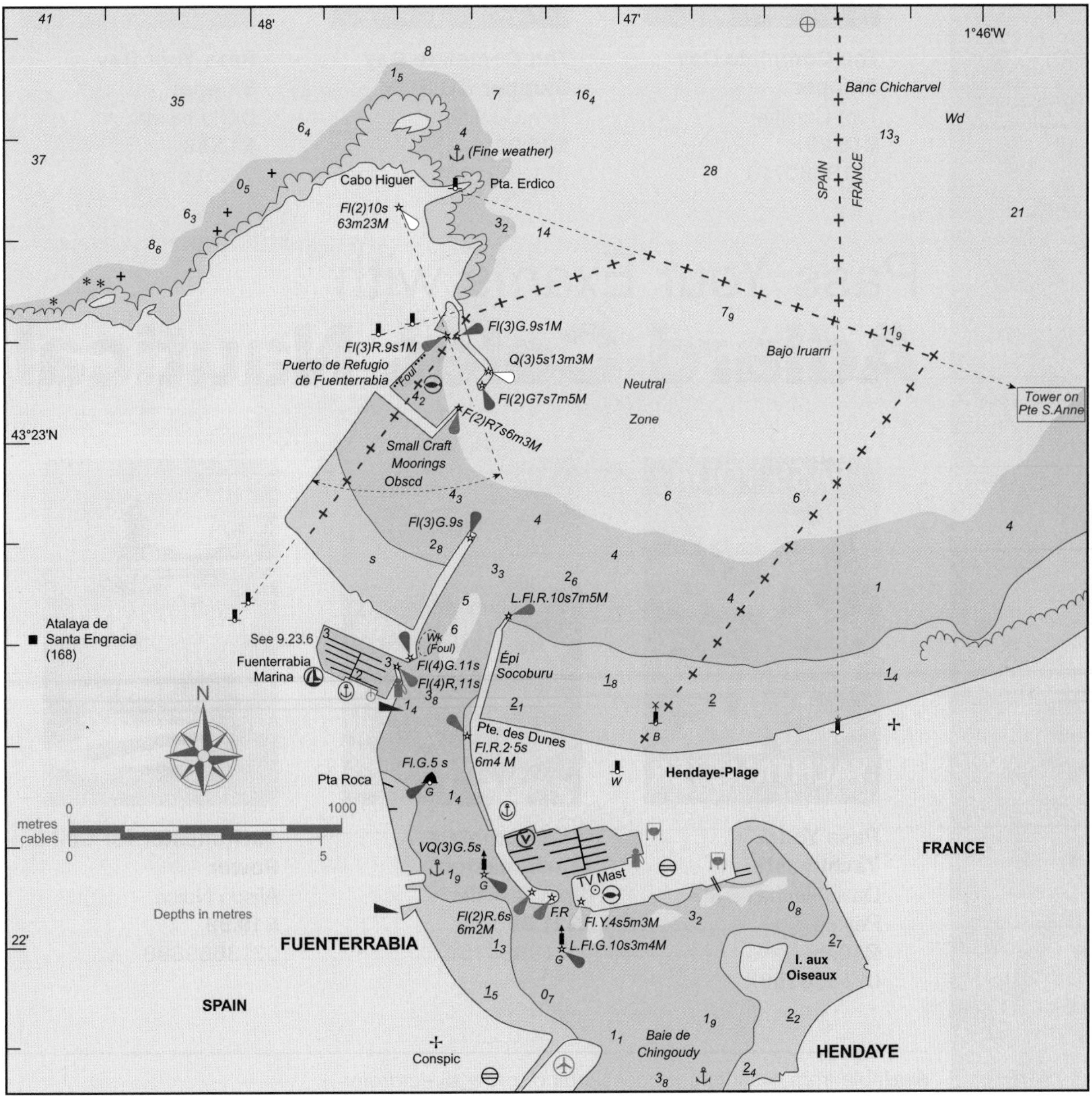
48'
47'
1°46'W
43°23'N
22'
Cabo Higuer
Pta. Erdico
(Fine weather)
Fl(2)10s
63m23M
Banc Chicharvel
SPAIN
FRANCE
Fl(3)G.9s1M
Fl(3)R.9s1M
Puerto de Refugio
de Fuenterrabia
Foul
Q(3)5s13m3M
Fl(2)G7s7m5M
F(2)R7s6m3M
Bajo Iruarri
Neutral
Zone
Tower on
Pte S.Anne
Small Craft
Moorings
Obscd
Fl(3)G.9s
L.Fl.R.10s7m5M
Atalaya de
Santa Engracia
(168)
See 9.23.6
Fuenterrabia
Marina
Wk
(Foul)
Fl(4)G.11s
Fl(4)R.11s
Épi
Socoburu
Pte. des Dunes
Fl.R.2·5s
6m4 M
Fl.G.5 s
Pta Roca
Hendaye-Plage
metres
cables
1000
VQ(3)G.5s
TV Mast
Fl(2)R.6s
6m2M
F.R
Fl.Y.4s5m3M
L.Fl.G.10s3m4M
FRANCE
Depths in metres
FUENTERRABIA
I. aux
Oiseaux
SPAIN
Baie de
Chingoudy
HENDAYE
Conspic

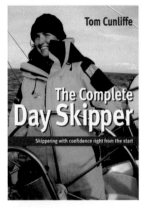

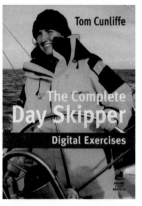

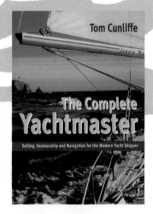

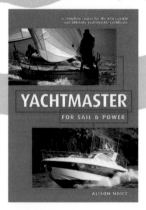

Area 23

North and Northwest Spain

Fuenterrabia to Bayona

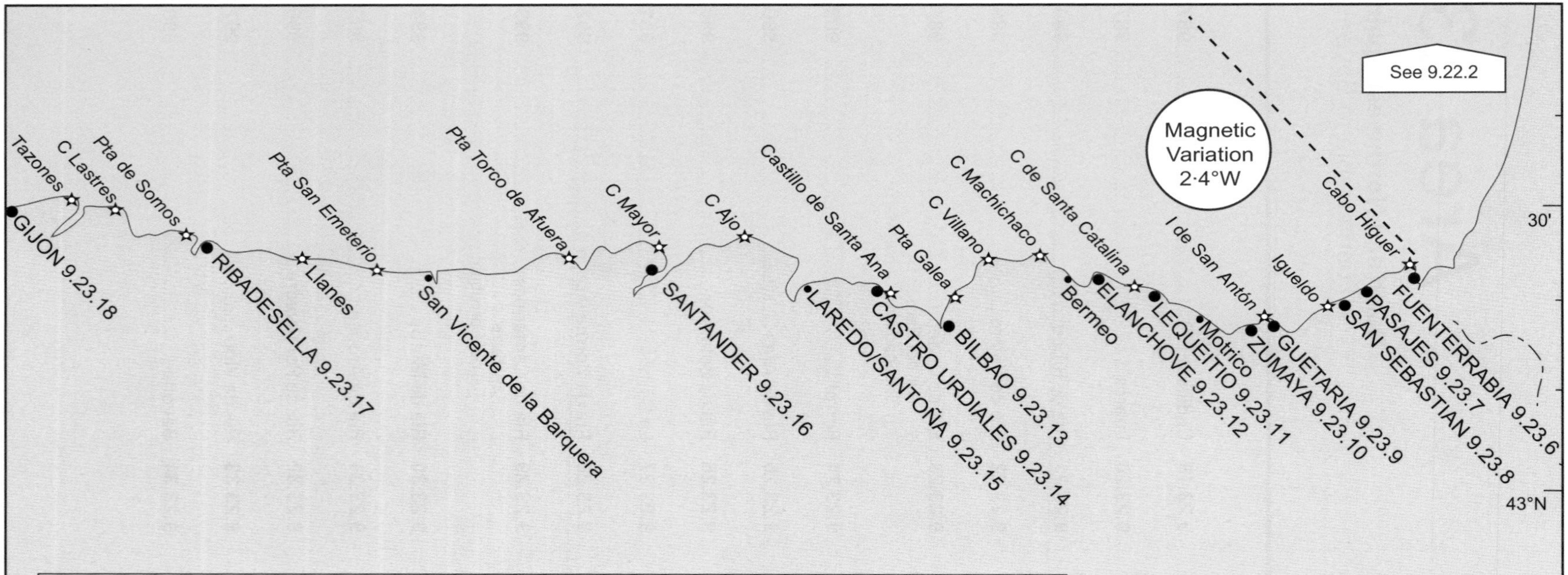
See 9.22.2
Magnetic Variation 2·4°W
Cabo Higuer
FUENTERRABIA 9.23.6
PASAJES 9.23.7
SAN SEBASTIAN 9.23.8
Igueldo
GUETARIA 9.23.9
ZUMAYA 9.23.10
I de San Antón
Motrico
LEQUEITIO 9.23.11
ELANCHOVE 9.23.12
C de Santa Catalina
Bermeo
C Machichaco
C Villano
Pta Galea
BILBAO 9.23.13
Castillo de Santa Ana
CASTRO URDIALES 9.23.14
LAREDO/SANTOÑA 9.23.15
C Ajo
C Mayor
SANTANDER 9.23.16
Pta Torco de Afuera
San Vicente de la Barquera
Pta San Emeterio
Llanes
RIBADESELLA 9.23.17
Pta de Somos
C Lastres
Tazones
GIJON 9.23.18
30'
43°N
30'
42°N
05°W
30'
04°
30'
03°
30'
02°

DISTANCE TABLE

Approximate distances in nautical miles are by the most direct route, whilst avoiding dangers and allowing for Traffic Separation Schemes. Places in *italics* are in Ireland, England and West coast of France. See also Distance Table at 9.24.2.

1.	*Crosshaven (Cork)*	**1**																			
2.	*Tuskar Rk*	85	**2**																		
3.	*Longships*	144	130	**3**																	
4.	*Ushant (Créac'h)*	235	230	100	**4**																
5.	*Bénodet*	303	298	168	68	**5**															
6.	*Belle Ile*	409	336	206	106	52	**6**														
7.	*Ile d' Yeu*	460	387	257	157	102	51	**7**													
8.	*La Rochelle*	526	453	323	223	168	117	66	**8**												
9.	*Arcachon*	515	510	380	280	227	187	138	98	**9**											
10.	San Sebastián	572	567	437	337	290	246	203	177	87	**10**										
11.	Cabo Machichaco	550	549	419	319	272	233	195	177	101	34	**11**									
12.	Bilbao (ent)	549	550	420	320	273	238	201	187	116	50	16	**12**								
13.	Santander	534	541	411	311	266	236	206	198	133	82	48	36	**13**							
14.	Gijón	508	528	391	298	267	254	237	248	205	162	128	116	90	**14**						
15.	Cabo Peñas	500	523	385	293	264	252	237	249	211	170	136	126	96	10	**15**					
16.	Ría de Ribadeo	499	520	391	308	308	279	271	288	252	223	189	179	149	63	53	**16**				
17.	Cabo Ortegal	484	510	388	307	307	290	289	313	285	258	224	214	184	98	88	40	**17**			
18.	La Coruña	508	538	418	338	327	326	326	351	323	296	262	252	222	136	126	78	38	**18**		
19.	Cabo Villano	523	556	439	365	356	358	359	383	355	328	294	284	254	168	158	110	70	43	**19**	
20.	Bayona	594	627	510	436	427	429	430	454	426	399	365	355	325	239	229	181	141	114	71	**20**

9.23.2

North & West Spain

Fuenterrabia to Bayona

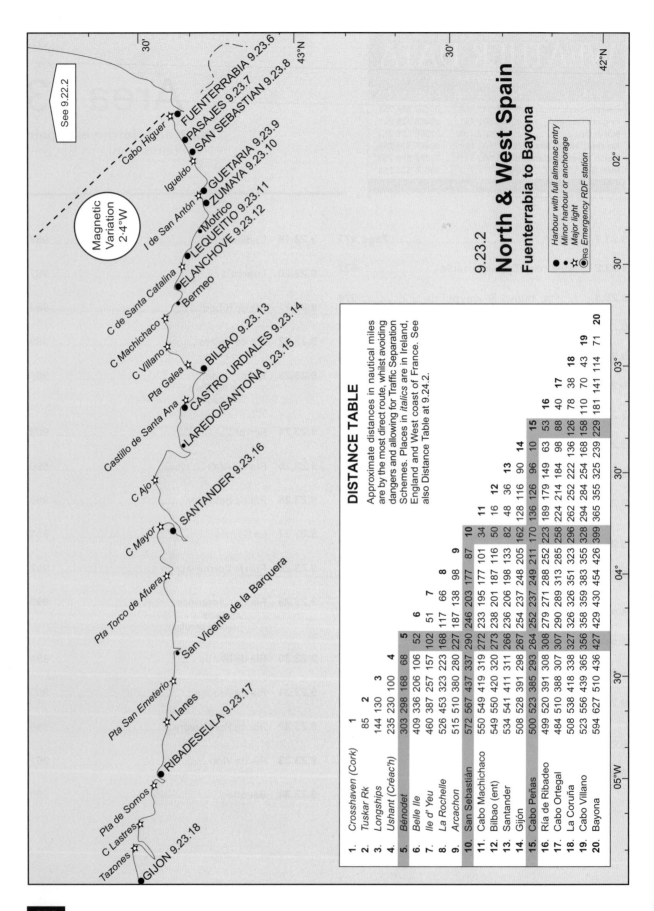

- ● *Harbour with full almanac entry*
- • *Minor harbour or anchorage*
- ☆ *Major light*
- ◉RG *Emergency RDF station*

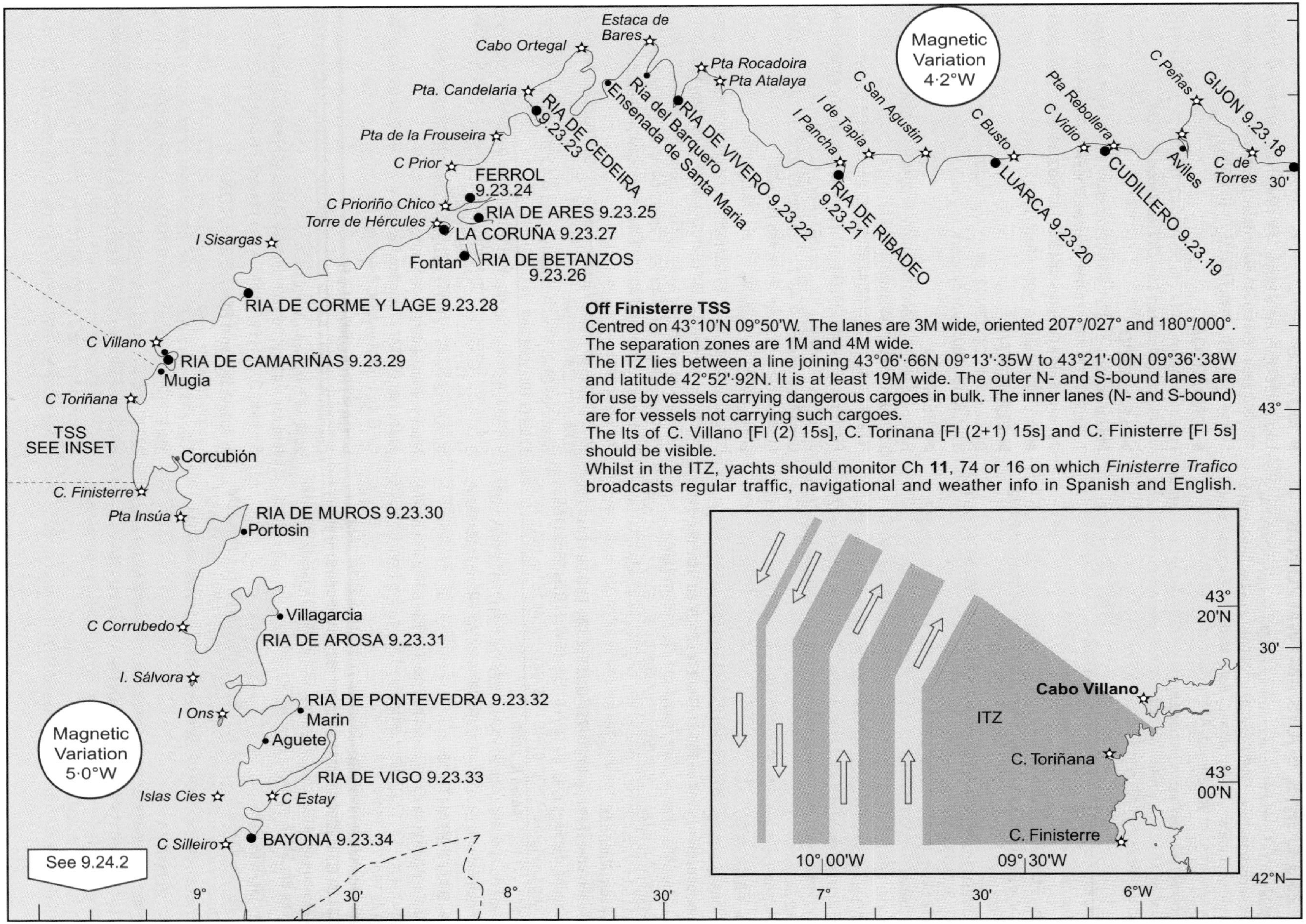
Estaca de Bares
Cabo Ortegal
Pta. Candelaria
Pta de la Frouseira
C Prior
C Prioriño Chico
Torre de Hércules
I Sisargas
FERROL 9.23.24
RIA DE ARES 9.23.25
LA CORUÑA 9.23.27
Fontan
RIA DE BETANZOS 9.23.26
RIA DE CEDEIRA 9.23.23
Ensenada de Santa Maria
Ria del Barquero
RIA DE VIVERO 9.23.22
Pta Rocadoira
Pta Atalaya
I Pancha
I de Tapia
RIA DE RIBADEO 9.23.21
C San Agustin
C Busto
LUARCA 9.23.20
C Vidio
Pta Rebollera
CUDILLERO 9.23.19
Aviles
C Peñas
GIJON 9.23.18
C de Torres
Magnetic Variation 4·2°W
RIA DE CORME Y LAGE 9.23.28
C Villano
RIA DE CAMARIÑAS 9.23.29
Mugia
C Toriñana
TSS SEE INSET
Corcubión
C. Finisterre
Pta Insúa
RIA DE MUROS 9.23.30
Portosin
C Corrubedo
Villagarcia
RIA DE AROSA 9.23.31
I. Sálvora
I Ons
RIA DE PONTEVEDRA 9.23.32
Marin
Aguete
RIA DE VIGO 9.23.33
Islas Cies
C Estay
C Silleiro
BAYONA 9.23.34
Magnetic Variation 5·0°W
See 9.24.2
9°
30'
8°
30'
7°
30'
6°W
30'
43°
30'
42°N
ITZ
Cabo Villano
C. Toriñana
C. Finisterre
43° 20'N
43° 00'N
10° 00'W
09° 30'W

Off Finisterre TSS

Centred on 43°10'N 09°50'W. The lanes are 3M wide, oriented 207°/027° and 180°/000°. The separation zones are 1M and 4M wide.

The ITZ lies between a line joining 43°06'·66N 09°13'·35W to 43°21'·00N 09°36'·38W and latitude 42°52'·92N. It is at least 19M wide. The outer N- and S-bound lanes are for use by vessels carrying dangerous cargoes in bulk. The inner lanes (N- and S-bound) are for vessels not carrying such cargoes.

The lts of C. Villano [Fl (2) 15s], C. Torinana [Fl (2+1) 15s] and C. Finisterre [Fl 5s] should be visible.

Whilst in the ITZ, yachts should monitor Ch **11**, 74 or 16 on which *Finisterre Trafico* broadcasts regular traffic, navigational and weather info in Spanish and English.

PLOT WAYPOINTS ON YOUR CHART BEFORE USING THEM

9.23.3 LIGHTS, BUOYS AND WAYPOINTS

Blue print = light with a nominal range of 15M or more. CAPITALS = place or feature. *CAPITAL ITALICS* = light-vessel, light float or Lanby. *Italics* = Fog signal. ***Bold italics*** = Racon. Useful waypoints are underlined. Abbreviations are in Chapter 1.

Positions below are referenced to the WGS 84 datum, but in the rest of Area 23 are referenced to ED50. Some Admiralty charts of this area are still referenced to ED50.

FUENTERRABIA TO SANTANDER

For details of Hendaye lts/marks, see 9.22.4.

▶ FUENTERRABIA

Cabo Higuer ☆ 43°23'·51N 01°47'·53W, Fl (2) 10s 63m **23M**; 072°-340°.
Puerto de Refugio, NE bkwtr elbow ☆ 43°23'·17N 01°47'·29W, Q (3) 5s 13m 3M.
NE bkwtr head ☆ 43°23'·20N 01°47'·25W, Fl (2) G 7s 7m 5M.
S bkwtr ☆ 43°23'·17N 01°47'·34W, Fl (2) R 7s 6m 3M.
Inner basin ☆ Fl (3) G 9s 7m 1M and Fl (3) R 9s 7m 1M.
W training wall ☆ 43°22'·82N 01°47'·36W, Fl (3) G 9s 9m 5M.
E training wall hd ☆ 43°22'·66N 01°47'·24W, L Fl R 10s 8m 5M.
E training wall root, Pte des Dunes ☆ 43°22'·38N 01°47'·37W, Fl R 2·5s 6m 4M.
Fuenterrabía marina, Fl (4) G 11s 9m 3m and Fl (4) R 11s 9m 1M.

▶ PASAJES

Fairway 43°21'·07N 01°56'·20W, Mo (A) 6s.
Senocozulúa lts in line 154·8°. **Front** ☆ 43°19'·88N 01°55'·61W, Q 67m **18M**. **Rear** ☆, 40m from front, Oc 3s 86m **18M**.
Senocozulúa Dir ☆, 155·75°; 43°19'·90N 01°55'·61W, Oc (2) WRG 12s 50m W6M, R/G3M; G129·5°-154·5°, W154·5°-157°, R157°-190°; W twr; ***Racon M***.
Bancha del Oeste 43°20'·23N 01°55'·88W, Fl G 5s 18m 11M.
Bancha del East 43°20'·22N 01°55'·65W, Fl R 5s 18m 11M.
Cabo La Plata ☆ 43°20'·07N 01°56'·04W, Oc 4s 151m 13M; 285°-250°; W bldg; ***Racon K, 20M***.
Arando-Grande ☆ 43°20'·14N 01°55'·68W, Fl (2) R 7s 10m 11M.
Dique de Senocozulúa ☆ 43°19'·94N 01°55'·58W, Fl (2) G 7s 12m 11M.

▶ SAN SEBASTIÁN

La Concha ldg lts 158°. Front 43°18'·89N 01°59'·47W, QR 10m 7M; Gy mast; 143°-173° (intens on ldg line). Rear, 25m from front, Oc R 4s 16m 7M; 154°-162°.
Igueldo ☆ 43°19'·35N 02°00'·64W, Fl (2+1) 15s 132m **26M**.
Isla de Santa Clara ☆ 43°19'·32N 01°59'·91W, Fl 5s 51m 9M.
Dársena de la Concha, W mole ☆ 43°19'·34N 01°59'·42W, Fl (2) R 8s 8m 5M. E mole, Fl (2) G 8s 9m 3M.

▶ GUETARIA

I. de San Antón ☆ 43°18'·62N 02°12'·09W, Fl (4) 15s 91m **21M**.
Outer hbr, N mole ☆ 43°18'·26N 02°11'·91W, Fl (3) G 9s 11m 5M.
N mole, elbow ☆ 43°18'·26N 02°11'·91W, Q (3) 5s 14m 3M.

▶ ZUMAYA

43°18'·18N 02°15'·14W, Fl (5) Y 20s; 213°/1·8M to hbr ent.
Lt ho ☆ 43°18'·14N 02°15'·07W, Oc (1+3) 12s 39m 12M.
Bkwtr heads ☆ 43°18'·38N 02°14'·75W, Fl (2) G 7s 18m 5M and Fl (2) R 7s 8m 3M.
Marina ent, ☆ Fl (3) R 9s 6m 1M and Fl (2+1) G 10s 6m 1M.

▶ MOTRICO

Ldg lts 236·5°. Front, S bkwtr, 43°18'·52N 02°22'·85W, Fl (2) R 7s 10m 3M. Rear FR 63m 5M, 600m from front. NW side, outer bkwtr: Fl G 5s 10m 5M; inner, Fl (2) G 7s 10m 1M.

▶ ONDÁRROA

Punta Barracomuturra, NE bkwtr ☆ 43°19'·53N 02°24'·95W, Fl (3) G 8s 13m 12M; *Siren Mo (O) 20s*; ***Racon G, 12M***.

▶ LEQUEITIO

Pta Amandarri ☆ 43°21'·99N 02°29'·94W, Fl G 4s 8m 5M; Gy twr.
Aislado, Fl (2) R 8s 5m 4M; Gy bcn. Ent FR/FG 7m 4M.
Cabo de Santa Catalina ☆ 43°22'·67N 02°30'·69W, Fl (1+3) 20s 44m **17M**; Gy ○ twr; *Horn Mo (L) 20s*.

▶ ELANCHOVE

Digue S ☆ 43°24'·23N 02°38'·27W, F WR 7m W8M, R5M; W000°-315°, R315°-000° over dangers. Digue N, Fl G 3s 8m 4M.

▶ BERMEO

Rosape ☆ 43°25'·24N 02°42'·80W, Fl (2) WR 10s 36m 7M; R108°-204°, W204°-232°; W bldg.
N bkwtr ☆ 43°25'·34N 02°42'·62W, Fl G 4·5s 16m 4M; Gy twr.
Platform Gaviota (4.7M NNE of Bermeo) 43°30'·04N 02°41'·61W, Mo (U) 10s 25m 5M; *Horn Mo (U) 30s*.
Cabo Machichaco ☆ 43°27'·36N 02°45'·22W, Fl 7s 120m **24M**; lookout twr and bldg; *Siren Mo (M) 60s*.

▶ BILBAO

C. Villano (Gorliz) ☆ 43°25'·93N 02°56'·74W, Fl (1+2) 16s 163m **22M**.
Punta Galea ☆ 43°22'·30N 03°02'·14W, Fl (3) 8s 82m **19M**; 011°-227°; stone twr with dwelling, Gy cupola; *Siren Mo (G) 30s*.
Pta Galea bkwtr hd ☆ 43°22'·77N 03°04'·67W, Fl R 5s 19m 7M.
Pta Lucero bkwtr hd ☆ 43°22'·67N 03°05'·04W, Fl G 5s 21m 10M; ***Racon X, 20M***.
Outer hbr, Ciervana, N jetty hd ☆ 43°21'·53N 03°02'·72W, Fl (2) G 8s 20m 5M; G ○ twr.
Santurce Quay (Port Authority bldg) ☆ 43°20'·78N 03°01'·92W, Fl (3) G 10s 18m 3M.
Contradique de Algorta ☆ 43°20'·51N 03°01'·67W, Fl R 5s 18m 3M, W twr. Same pier (mid-point), Dir ☆ 43°20'·47N 03°01'·20W, Oc WR 4s 11m 3M; W134°-149°, R149°-174°.
Getxo marina ☆ 43°20'·23N 03°01'·02W, QR 3m 2M, R col.
Marina entry 43°20'·16N 03°00'·96W, QG.
Yacht hbr (RCMA), Las Arenas, ent ☆ 43°19'·83N 03°00'·97W, Oc G 4s 1m 1M and Oc R 4s 2m 1M.

▶ CASTRO URDIALES

Castillo de Santa Ana ☆ 43°23'·06N 03°12'·89W, Fl (4) 24s 47m **20M**; W twr; *Siren Mo (C) 60s*.
N bkwtr ☆ 43°22'·86N 03°12'·54W, Fl G 3s 12m 6M; octagonal twr.
S bkwtr, Q (2) R 6s 8m 5M. Inner hbr ent, FR and FG.

▶ LAREDO and RIA DE SANTOÑA

Laredo N bkwtr ☆ 43°24'·89'N 03°25'·20W, Fl (4) R 11s 9m 5M.
Santoña ldg lts 283·5°. Front, 43°26'·33N 03°27'·62W, Fl 2s 5m 8M; B ▽ on framework. Rear, 0·75M from front, Oc (2) 5s 12m 11M; 279·5°-287·5°; ○ on framework.
No. 1 43°26'·16N 03°27'·24W. Nos 2-4 s, all Fl Y 2s, close S and W of Pta del Pasaje, mark Laredo YC moorings/marina.
Pta Pescador lt ho ☆ 43°27'·90N 03°26'·20W, Fl (3+1) 18s 37m 9M.
C. Ajo ☆ 43°30'·70N 03°35'·72W, Oc (3) 16s 69m **17M**; W ○ twr.

▶ SANTANDER

C. Mayor ☆ 43°29'·37N 03°47'·51W, Fl (2) 10s 89m **21M**; W ○ twr; *Horn Mo (M) 40s.*

Isla de Mouro ☆ 43°28'·39N 03°45'·36W, Fl (3) 21s 37m 7M.

La Cerda (Pta del Puerto) ☆ 43°26'·01N 03°45'·84W, Fl (1+4) 20s 22m 7M; obscured when bearing <160°.

Punta Rabiosa ldg lts 235·8°, both intens 231·8°-239·8°. Front, 43°27'·51N 03°46'·43W, Q 7m 6M; ***Racon K, 10M.*** Rear, 100m from front, Iso R 4s 10m 6M.

Fairway ldg lts 259·5°, both intens 255·5°-263·5°. Front, 43°27'·33N 03°48'·61W, Iso 3s 17m 6M; Y/B twr. Rear, 158m from front, Oc R 4s 20m 6M.

No. 3 43°27'·71N 03°46'·21W, Fl (2) G 7s.

Dársena de Molnedo, ent ☆ 43°27'·68N 03°47'·47W, QG 10m 3M.

No. 17 (GRG) 43°25'·93N 03°48'·25W, Fl (2+1) G 10s.

Marina del Cantabrico, ldg lts 235·6°. Front, 43°25'·75N 03°48'·83W, Iso 2s 9m 2M. Rear, 46m from front, Oc 5s 10m 2M. Marina ent QR and QG.

SANTANDER TO CABO PEÑAS

Pta del Torco de Afuera ☆ 43°26'·51N 04°02'·61W, Fl (1+2) 24s 33m **22M**; obscured close inshore 091°-113°; W twr.

Suances ldg lts 149·5°. Front 43°26'·19N 04°02'·08W, Q 8m 5M. Rear, Punta Marzán 212m from front, Iso 4s 12m 5M.

▶ SAN VICENTE DE LA BARQUERA

Pta de la Silla ☆ 43°23'·56N 04°23'·62W, Oc 3·5s 41m 13M; 115°-250°; twr; *Horn Mo (V) 30s.*

E pier ☆ 43°23'·80N 04°23'·02W, Fl WG 2s W7M, G6M; G175°-235°, W235°-045°; G twr. W pier ☆ Fl (2) R 8s 6m 5M; R twr.

Pta San Emeterio ☆ 43°23'·90N 04°32'·20W, Fl 5s 66m **20M**.

▶ LLANES

Pta de San Antón ☆ 43°25'·09N 04°44'·99W, Fl (4) 15s 16m **15M**; W 8-sided twr. N bkwtr (Osa) ☆ 43°25'·18N 04°44'·90W, Fl G 5s 13m 5M. Dock hd ☆ Fl (2) G 7s 8m 1M.

▶ RIBADESELLA

Somos ☆ 43°28'·36N 05°04'·98W, Fl (2+1) 12s 113m **25M**; twr.

Pta del Caballo ☆ 43°28'·08N 05°03'·98W, Fl (2) R 6s 10m 5M; 278·4°-212·9°; ○ twr.

▶ LASTRES

E bkwtr ☆ 43°30'·89N 05°15'·90W, Fl (3) G 9s 13m 4M.

W bkwtr ☆ 43°30'·89N 05°15'·90W, Fl (3) R 9s 6m 3M.

C. Lastres ☆ 43°32'·03N 05°18'·07W, Fl 12s 116m **23M**. W ○ twr.

Tazones ☆ 43°32'·74N 05°24'·13W, Fl 7·5s 125m **20M**; W 8-sided twr; *Horn Mo (V) 30s.* Bkwtr head, Fl G 3s 10m 4M.

▶ GIJÓN

Banco Las Amosucas (where the sea breaks in bad weather), 2M N of marina, should be avoided by yachts. It is marked by 4 cardinal buoys: Q, Q (3)10s, Q (6) + L Fl 15s, Q (9)15s.

El Musel NE point ☆ 43°34'·26N 05°40'·58W, Fl G 3s 22m 6M.

Piedra Sacramento ☆ 43°32'·90N 05°40'·21W, QG; 8-sided twr.

Marina. N bkwtr ☆ 43°32'·85N 05°40'·08W, Fl (2) R 6s 7m 3M.

Outer S bkwtr ☆ 43°32'·75N 05°40'·17W, Q 2m 1M; NCM bcn.

Inner S bkwtr ☆ 43°32'·79N 05°40'·04W, Fl (3) G 10s 6m 1M.

Cabo de Torres ☆ 43°34'·29N 05°41'·97W, Fl (2) 10s 80m **18M**.

Punta del Cuerno ☆ 43°35'·71N 05°45'·56W, Oc (2) 10s 38m **15M**; R twr, W ho; *Horn Mo (C) 60s.*

Candás, ldg lts 291°, both FR 8/62m 3M. Front, W col; rear, ho. Pierhd lts: North, Fl (2) G 7s 10m 4M; South, Fl (3) R 10s 3M.

Luanco ldg lts 255°. Front, mole, 43°36'·91N 05°47'·35W, Fl R 3s 4m 4M. Rear, 240m from front, Oc R 8s 8m 4M.

Punta del Gallo ☆ 43°37'·23N 05°46'·89W, Fl G 3s 10m 4M; ○ twr.

C. Peñas ☆ 43°39'·31N 05°50'·90W, Fl (3) 15s 115m **35M**; Gy 8-sided twr; *Siren Mo (P) 60s.*

CABO PEÑAS TO PUNTA DE LA ESTACA DE BARES

Avilés, outer mark 43°35'·73N 05°57'·69W, Fl G 5s.

Pta del Castillo ☆ 43°35'·72N 05°56'·72W, Oc WR 5s 38m **W20, R17M**; R091·5°-113°, W113°-091·5°; W □ twr; *Siren Mo (A) 30s.*

Ent chan, S side ☆ 43°35'·57N 05°56'·49W, Fl (2) G 7s 12m 5M; 106°-280°; W ○ twr, G band.

San Esteban de Pravia, ldg lts 182·2°, both FR 6/10m 3M. Front, 43°33'·47N 06°04'·66W. Rear, 160m from front.

S. Estaban ☆ W bkwtr 43°34'·20N 06°04'·64W, Fl (2) 12s 19m **15M**; W ○ twr, B bands; *Siren Mo (N) 30s.*

Cudillero, Pta Rebollera ☆ 43°33'·96N 06°08'·68W, Oc (4) 16s 42m **16M**; W 8-sided twr; *Siren Mo (D) 30s.*

Ent, N bkwtr ☆ Fl (3) G 9s 3m 2M; S bkwtr ☆ Fl (3) R 9s 8m 2M.

Cabo Vidio ☆ 43°35'·60N 06°14'·79W, Fl 5s 99m **25M**; ○ twr; *Siren Mo (V) 60s.*

Cabo Busto ☆ 43°34'·13N 06°28'·23W, Fl (4) 20s 84m **25M**.

▶ LUARCA

Punta Focicón (or Blanca) ☆ 43°33'·03N 06°31'·85W, Oc (3) 15s 63m 14M; W □ twr; *Siren Mo (L) 30s.*

Ldg lts 170°, both W cols, R bands. Front 43°32'·83N 06°32'·02W, Fl 5s 18m 2M. Rear, 41m from front, Oc 4s 25m 2M.

E Dique (Canouco) ☆ 43°32'·97N 06°32'·05W, Fl (3) R 9s 22m 5M.

W Dique ☆ 43°32'·97N 06°32'·05W, Fl (3) G 9s 7m 5M.

Ría de Navia outfall 43°34'·18N 06°43'·64W, Fl Y 10s.

Cabo de San Agustín ☆ 43°33'·83N 06°44'·07W, Oc (2) 12s 70m **25M**; W ○ twr, B bands.

Isla de Tapia ☆ 43°34'·43N 06°56'·78W, Fl (2+1) 19s 22m **18M**.

▶ RÍA DE RIBADEO

Pta de la Cruz ☆ 43°33'·40N 07°01'·75W, Fl (4) R 11s 16m 7M.

Isla Pancha ☆ 43°33'·39N 07°02'·53W, Fl (3+1) 20s 26m **21M**; W ○ twr, B bands; *Siren Mo (R) 30s.*

1st ldg lts 140°, both R ◇s, W twrs. Front, Pta Aerojo, 43°32'·83N 07°01'·53W, Iso R 18m 5M. Rear, 228m from front, Oc R 4s 24m 5M.

2nd ldg lts 205°. Front, Muelle de García, 43°32'·49N 07°02'·24W, VQ R 8m 3M; R ◇, W twr. Rear, 178m from front, Oc R 2s 18m 3M, W □ on structure.

Bridge, pillars of W'most span, Fl (4) R 11s 8m 4M and Fl (2) G 7s 8m 4M. Marina ent, Fl G 5s 9m 3M; Fl R 5s 9m 1M.

Ría de Foz trng wall ☆ 43°34'·43N 07°14'·67W, Fl G 3s 3m 10M.

Piedra Burela 43°39'·80N 07°20'·90W, Q (3) 10s 11m 7M.

Pta Atalaya (Cabo de S. Ciprian) ☆ 43°42'·03N 07°26'·21W, Fl (5) 20s 39m **20M**; W ○ twr, B band.

Alúmina Port, N bkwtr ☆ 43°42'·98N 07°27'·59W, Fl (2) WG 8s 17m 4M; W110°-180°, G180°-110°.

Pta Roncadoira ☆ 43°44'·14N 07°31'·51W, Fl 7·5s 92m **21M**; W ○ twr.

PLOT WAYPOINTS ON YOUR CHART BEFORE USING THEM

▶ RÍA DE VIVERO

Pta de Faro ☆ 43°42'·74N 07°35'·03W, Fl R 5s 18m 7M.
Pta Socastro ☆ 43°43'·08N 07°36'·42W, Fl G 5s 18m 7M; W twr.
Cillero, outer bkwtr ☆ 43°40'·93N 07°36'·16W, Fl (2) R 7s 8m 5M.
S bkwtr ☆ 43°40'·80N 07°35'·90W, Fl (2+1) G 21s 9m 3M.
River ent, SW side ☆ 43°40'·64N 07°35'·85W, Fl (2) G 7s 1M.
Marina ent ☆ 43°40'·22N 07°35'·62W, Fl (3) G 9s 1M.

▶ RÍA DEL BARQUERO

Isla Coelleira ☆ 43°45'·51N 07°37'·77W, Fl (4) 24s 87m 7M.
Pta de la Barra ☆ 43°44'·51N 07°41'·31W, Fl WRG 3s 15m 5M; G198°-213°, W213°-240°, R240°-255°, G255°-213°; W twr.
Pta del Castro ☆ 43°44'·46N 07°40'·48W, Fl (2) 7s 14m 5M.
Vicedo, N pier ☆ 43°44'·34N 07°40'·65W, Fl (4) R 11s 9m 5M.
S pier ☆ 43°44'·37N 07°40'·64W, Fl (4) G 11s 9m 3M.

PTA DE LA ESTACA DE BARES TO CABO VILLANO

Pta de la Estaca de Bares ☆ 43°47'·21N 07°41'·14W, Fl (2) 7·5s 99m **25M**; obsc'd when brg >291°; 8-sided twr; *Siren Mo (B) 60s.*
Espasante, W bkwtr ☆ 43°43'·36N 07°48'·91W, Fl R 5s 11m 3M.
Piedras Liseiras 43°46'·36N 07°49'·51W, Q (9) 15s.
Carino bkwtr ☆ 43°44'·05N 07°51'·73W, Fl G 2s 12m 3M.
Sta Marta de Ortigueira, bkwtrs Fl (4) R 11s 3M & Fl (4) G 11s 5M.
Cabo Ortegal (Pta de Los Aguillones) ☆ 43°46'·22N 07°52'·30W, Oc 8s 122m **18M**; W ○ twr, R band.
Pta Candelaria ☆ 43°42'·65N 08°02'·98W, Fl (3+1) 24s 87m **21M**.

▶ RÍA DE CEDEIRA

Punta del Sarridal ☆ 43°39'·65N 08°04'·53W, Oc WR 6s 39m 11M; R shore-145°, W145°-172°, R172°-145°.
Pta Promontorio ☆ 43°39'·05N 08°04'·21W, Oc (4) 10s 24m 11M.
Piedras de Media Mar ☆ 43°39'·37N 08°04'·80W, Fl (2) 5s 12m 4M; W ○ twr.
Bkwtr ☆ 43°39'·30N 08°04'·20W, Fl (2) R 7s 10m 4M; R ○ twr.
Pta de la Frouxeira ☆ 43°37'·02N 08°11'·31W, Fl (5) 15s 73m **20M**.
Cabo Prior ☆ 43°34'·05N 08°18'·87W, Fl (1+2) 15s 105m **22M**; 055·5°-310°; 6-sided twr.
Pta del Castro ☆ 43°30'·53N 08°19'·61W, Fl (2) 7s 42m 8M; 6-sided twr.

▶ RÍA DE FERROL

Cabo Prioriño Chico ☆ 43°27'·52N 08°20'·40W, Fl 5s 34m **23M**; 225°-129·5°; W 8-sided twr.
Batería de San Cristóbal ☆ 43°27'·93N 08°18'·26W, Oc (2) WR 10s 21m 7M, W042°-053°, R053°-042°; white conical twr.
Muela del Segaño 43°27'·42N 08°18'·81W, Fl G 2s.
Ldg lts 085·2°. Front, Pta de San Martín 43°27'·57N 08°17'·06W, Fl 1·5s 10m 5M. Rear, 701m from front Oc 4s 5M.
<u>La Palma</u> (off Pta Redonda) 43°27'·83N 08°16'·47W, Fl (3) G 9s.
La Graña 43°28'·72N 08°15'·50W (N'most of 3 s).
Dársena de Curuxeiras mole ☆ 43°28'·53N 08°14'·66W, Fl (4) R 11s 5m 3M.

▶ RÍA DE BETANZOS

Punta de San Pedro ☆ 43°22'·68N 08°13'·00W, Fl (2) R 7s 7m 4M; R post.
Sada marina N pier ☆ 43°21'·76N 08°14'·54W, Fl (4) G 11s 11m 5M; G twr. S bkwtr, Fl (4) R 11s 11m 3M.

▶ LA CORUÑA

Torre de Hércules ☆ 43°23'·15N 08°24'·39W, Fl (4) 20s 104m **23M**; □ twr, 8-sided top; *Siren Mo (L) 30s.*
<u>Banco Yacentes</u> 43°24'·70N 08°23'·02W, Fl (5) Y 20s.
Ldg lts 108·5°, both W 8-sided twrs. Front, Pta Mera 43°23'·00N 08°21'·28W, Oc WR 4s 54m, W8M R3M; R000°-023°, R100·5°-105·5°, W105·5°-114·5°, R114·5°-153°; **Racon M, 18M; 020°-196°**. Rear, Fl 4s 79m 8M; 357·5°-177·5°; 300m from front.
Ldg lts 182°, both R/W chequered □ twrs. Front, Pta Fiaiteira 43°20'·59N 08°22'·25W, Iso WRG 2s 27m, W10M, R/G7M; G146·4°-180°, W180°-184°, R184°-217·6°; **Racon X, 11-21M**. Rear, 380m from front, Oc R 4s 52m 3M.
Dique d'Abrigo ☆ 43°21'·90N 08°22'·48W, Fl G 3s 16m 6M.
Malpica bkwtr ☆ 43°19'·34N 08°48'·31W, Fl G 3s 18m 4M.
Islas Sisargas ☆ 43°21'·53N 08°50'·77W, Fl (3) 15s 108m **23M**; W 8-sided twr and W bldg; *Siren Mo (S) 30s.*
Punta Nariga ☆ 43°19'·24N 08°54'·72W, Fl (3+1) 20s 53m **22M**; W ○ twr.

▶ RÍA DE CORME Y LAGE

Pta del Roncudo ☆ 43°16'·50N 08°59'·47W, Fl 6s 36m 10M.
Pta Lage ☆ 43°13'·88N 09°00'·83W, Fl (5) 20s 64m **20M**; W twr.
Corme, mole ☆ 43°15'·70N 08°57'·89W, Fl (2) R 5s 12m 3M.
Lage, N mole ☆ 43°13'·34N 08°59'·96W, Fl G 3s 15m 4M; G ○ twr.
Camelle Dir ☆ 248·5°. 43°11'·37N 09°05'·19W, F WRG 9m W5M, R/G3M; G241·85°-246·85°, W246·85°-250·15°, R250·15°-255·15°; W col.
C. Villano ☆ 43°09'·60N 09°12'·70W, Fl (2) 15s 102m **28M**; 031·5°-228·5°; 8-sided twr, Gy cupola; *Siren Mo (V) 60s*; ***Racon M, 35M***.

CABO VILLANO TO THE PORTUGUESE BORDER

▶ RÍA DE CAMARIÑAS

Ldg lts 081°. Front, Pta Villueira 43°07'·37N 09°11'·56W, Fl 5s 13m 9M; W ○ twr, R band. Rear, Pta del Castillo, Iso 4s 25m 11M; 043·8°-102·1°; W twr, 612m from front.
Pta de la Barca ☆ 43°06'·79N 09°13'·19W, Oc 4s 11m 6M.
Pta de Lago ☆ 43°06'·60N 09°10'·01W, Oc (2) WRG 6s 13m, W6M, R/G4M; W029·5°-093°, G093°-107·8°, W107·8°-109·1°, R109·1°-139·3°, W139·3°-213·5°; W twr.
Camariñas outer bkwtr ☆ 43°07'·45N 09°10'·70W, Fl R 5s 7m 3M.
Pier ☆ 43°07'·63N 09°10'·93W, Fl (2+1) G 21s 2M; G ○ twr, R band.
Mugia bkwtr ☆ 43°06'·35N 09°12'·75W, Fl (2) G 10s 11m 4M.
Cabo Toriñana ☆ 43°03'·17N 09°18'·01W, Fl (2+1) 15s 63m **24M**; 340·5°-235·5°; ***Racon T, 35M (1.7M SE of ☆).***
Cabo Finisterre ☆ 42°52'·93N 09°16'·29W, Fl 5s 141m **23M**; 8-sided twr; obscd when brg >149°; ***Racon O, 35M.***
Seno de Corcubión
Finisterre bkwtr ☆ 42°54'·56N 09°15'·38W, Fl R 2s 12m 4M.
Lobeira Grande ☆ 42°52'·84N 09°11'·22W, Fl (3) 15s 16m 9M.
Carrumeiro Chico 42°54'·37N 09°10'·80W, Fl (2) 7s 6m 6M.
Cabo Cée ☆ 45°55'·00N 09°11'·07W, Fl (5) 13s 25m 7M; Gy twr.
Corcubión bkwtr ☆ 42°56'·69N 09°11·39W, Fl (2) R 8s 9m 4M.
Brens mole, E hd, ☆ Fl (4) R 11s 8m 3M; W hd, ☆ Fl (4) G 11s 3M.
Pindo, pier ☆ 42°54'·01N 09°07·96W, Fl (3) G 9s 7m 4M.
Porto Cubelo bkwtr ☆ 42°48'·40N 09°08'·15W, Fl G 2s 8m 4M.
Pta Insúa ☆ 42°46'·29N 09°07'·56W, Fl (3) WR 9s 25m; **W15M**, R14M; 020°-R-045°-W-070°-R-090°-W-125°-R-152°-W-020°.

▶ RÍA DE MUROS

Pta Queixal ☆ 42°44'·36N 09°04'·75W, Fl (2+1) 12s 25m 9M.
Cabo Reburdiño ☆ 42°46'·20N 09°02'·91W, Fl (2) R 7s 16m 7M.
Muros outer mole ☆ 42°46'·64N 09°03'·31W, Fl (4) R 13s 8m 4M; W ○ twr.

Isla de Crebra ☆ 42°46'·39N 08°57'·80W, Fl (2) 7s 5m 8M; col.
El Freijo mole ☆ 42°47'·62N 08°56'·63W, Fl (2) R 5s 8m 5M.
Detached bkwtr, S end ☆ 42°47'·66N 08°56'·59W, Fl (2) G 7s 3M.
Same bkwtr, N end ☆ 42°47'·75N 08°56'·63W, Q(3) 10s 1M.
Punta Testal ☆ 42°47'·51N 08°54'·61W, Fl 5s 7m 3M.
Portosin bkwtr ☆ 42°45'·94N 08°56'·93W, Fl (2) G 5s 7m 3M.
Pta Cabeiro ☆ 42°44'·37N 08°59'·44W, Oc WR 3s 35m W9M, R6M; R050°-054·5°, W054·5°-058·5°, R058·5°-099·5°, W099·5°-189·5°; Gy twr.
El Son bkwtr ☆ 42°43'·74N 08°00'·06W, Fl G 5s 4m 5M.
Pta Focha ☆ 42°41'·89N 09°01'·71W, Fl 5s 27m 4M; ○ twr.

C. Corrubedo ☆ 42°34'·59N 09°05'·39W, Fl (2+3) WR 20s 30m **15M**; 347°-040°, dangerous sector; *Siren Mo (O) 60s*; ***Racon K***.
Corrubedo bkwtr ☆ 42°34'·34N 09°04'·19W, Iso WRG 3s 10m, W6M, R4M, G3M; R000°-016°, G016°-352°, W352°-000°; ○ twr.

▶ RÍA DE AROUSA (Selected lights only)

Isla Sálvora ☆ 42°27'·82N 09°00'·80W, Fl (3+1) 20s 38m **21M**; clear sector 217°-126°. Same twr, Fl (3) 20s, 126°-160° danger sector.
Aguiño bkwtr ☆ 42°31'·09N 09°00'·90W, Fl (4) WR 11s 5m 5M, W026°-040°, R040°-026°.
Islas Sagres ☆ 42°30'·52N 09°02'·95W, Fl 5s 25m 8M.
Piedras del Sargo ⛯ 42°30'·30N 09°00'·50W, QG 11m 6M; W twr, G band.
Santa Eugenia bkwtr ☆ 42°33'·58N 08°59'·24W, Fl (2) R 7s 7m 4M; R ○ twr.
Isla Rúa ☆ 42°32'·95N 08°56'·38W, Fl (2+1) WR 21s 24m 13M; R121·5°-211·5°, W211·5°-121·5; ***Racon K, 211°-121°, 10-20M***.
Puebla del Caramiñal E bkwtr ☆ 42°36'·28N 08°55'·87W, Oc G 2s 8m 4M; W ○ twr G band.
Rianjo outer bkwtr ☆ 42°39'·06N 08°49'·44W, Fl (4) G 11s 5M.
Villagarcia, N mole ☆ 42°36'·11N 08°46'·33W, Iso 2s 2m 10M; ○ twr. Marina ent, QG and QR, both 6m 3M.

Isla de Arosa

Pta Caballo ☆ 42°34'·33N 08°53'·03W, Fl (4) 11s 11m 10M.
St Julian, wharf ☆ 42°33'·96N 08°52'·18W, FR 7m 1M; R col.

Peninsula del Grove

San Martin, N mole ☆ 42°29'·85N 08°51'·51W, Fl (2) G 7s 9m 3M; B & W chequered ○ twr.
Roca Pombeiriño ⛯ 42°28'·88N 08°56'·80W, Fl (2) G 12s 13m 8M; W bcn twr, G band.
Pedras Negras marina, bkwtr ☆ 42°29'·85N 08°51'·51W, Fl (4) WR 11s 5m, W4M R3M; W305°-315°, R315°-305; R post.
Bajo Seixelino ⛯ 42°27'·55N 08°54'·92W, Fl G 5s 3m 2M; G post.

▶ RÍA DE PONTEVEDRA

I. Ons ☆ 42°22'·94N 08°56'·17W, Fl (4) 24s 125m **25M**; 8-sided twr.
Almacén pier ☆ 42°22'·63N 08°55'·78W, Fl R 4s 7m 2M; R ○ twr.
Bajo Los Camouco ⛯ 42°23'·70N 08°54'·75W, Fl (3) R 18s 10m 8M.
Bajo Picamillo ⛯ 42°24'·37N 08°53'·37W, Fl G 5s 10m 8M; twr.
Bajo Fagilda ⛯ 42°24'·83N 08°53'·67W, QR 1s 16M.

Portonovo mole ☆ 42°23'·65N 08°49'·13W, Fl (3) R 6s 8m 4M.
Sangenjo marina, mole ☆ 42°23'·76N 08°48'·11W, QR 5m 4M.
Cabezo de Morrazan ⛯ 42°22'·36N 08°47'·04W, Iso R 5s.

Rajo mole ☆ 42°24'·10N 08°45'·26W, Fl (2) R 8s 9m 3M; R ○ twr.
Isla Tambo 42°24'·48N 08°42'·48W, Oc (3) 8s 33m 11M; W ○ twr.
Combarro mole ☆ 42°25'·77N 08°42'·26W, Fl (2) R 8s 7m 3M.
S jetty head ☆ 42°25'·60N 08°42'·20W, Oc (2) R 6s 3M.

Aguete marina, mole ☆ 42°22'·62N 08°44'·12W; Fl (2) G 7s 1M.
⛯ Fl (4) G 11s 3M, 42°22'·73N 08°44'·11W.

Bueu N mole ☆ 42°19'·77N 08°47'·11W, Fl G 3s 7m 4M G twr.
Beluso ☆, 42°20'·11N 08°47'·88W, Fl (3) G 9s; G △ on G bcn. ☆, Fl (3) R 9s; R □ on R bcn. New marina; no details.
Cabeza de la Mourisca ⛯ 42°20'·90N 08°49'·17W, Fl (2) G 7s 10m 5M.
Pta Couso ☆ 42°18'·56N 08°51'·33W, Fl (3) WG 10·5s 18m, W10M, G8M; G060°-096°, W096°-190°, G190°-000°.
Aldán jetty ☆ 42°16'·95N 08°49'·39W, Fl (2) R 10s 5m 5M.

▶ ISLAS CÍES

Monte Agudo ☆ 42°14'·60N 08°54'·19W, Fl G 5s 23m 9M; W twr.
Piedra Borron ⛯ 42°13'·54N 08°53'·91W, Fl (2) 10s 3M.
Monte Faro ☆ 42°12'·85N 08°54'·91W, Fl (2) 8s 185m **22M**; obsc'd 315°-016·5° over Bajos de Los Castros and Forcados; ○ twr.
Pta Canabal ☆ 42°12'·73N 08°54'·78W, Fl (3) 20s 63m 9M; W twr.
C. Vicos ☆ 42°11'·51N 08°53'·49W, Fl (3) R 9s 92m 7M; W twr.
Islote Boiero ⛯ 42°10'·75N 08°54'·61W, Fl (2) R 8s 21m 6M. W twr.

▶ RÍA DE VIGO

Cabo del Home, ldg lts 129°, both 090°-180°; W ○ twrs. Front 42°15'·15N 08°52'·37W, Fl 3s 36m 9M. Rear, Pta Subrido, 815m from front, Oc 6s 53m 11M.
Pta Robaleira ☆ 42°15'·07N 08°52'·29W (285m S of Cabo del Home ldg lt), Fl (2) WR 7·5s 25m, W11M, R9M; W300·5°-321·5°, R321·5°-090°, obsc'd 090°-115·5°, R115·5°-170·5°; R twr; ***Racon C***.
No. 2 (Roca Omear) ⛯ 42°14'·56N 08°51'·91W, Fl (4) R 10s; *Bell*.
No. 6, ⛯ 42°13'·78N 08°46'·64W, Fl (2) R 7s 13m 7M; R/W bcn.
Cangas outer mole ☆ 42°15'·61N 08°46'·83W, Fl R 5s 8m 5M; R ○ twr.

Pta Lameda ☆ 42°09'·39N 08°50'·98W, Fl (2) G 8s 27m 5M; W twr.
Cabo Estay ldg lts 069·3°, both R twrs, W bands; 066·3°-072·3°.
Front ☆ 42°11'·12N 08°48'·89W, Iso 2s 16m **18M**; *Horn Mo (V) 60s*; ***Racon B, 22M***. **Rear**, 660m from front, Oc 4s 48m **18M**.
No. 1 ⛯ 42°12'·39N 08°48'·54W, Fl (3) G 9s 5M.
No. 3 ⛯ 42°13'·78N 08°46'·64W, Fl (4) G 14s 11m 5M; GW twr.
Muelle de Berbes, NE end ☆ 42°14'·50N 08°43'·92W, Fl (3) G 9s 10m 5M; G twr.
Muelle de Transatlanticos, N end ☆ 42°14'·55N 08°43'·52W, Fl (4) G 11s 10m 5M; col.
Marina ent, 42°14'·63N 08°43'·32W, QG and QR, 10m 5M.

Bajo Lagao, ⛯ Fl (2) 6s, 42°15'·42N 08°42'·55W.
La Guia ☆ 42°15'·56N 08°42'·15W, Oc (2+1) 20s 37m **15M**; W twr.
Rande bridge (38m), QG (S pillar, 42°17'·27N 08°39'·58W) and QR (N pillar); both 7m 5M, on W and E sides of bridge.

▶ BAYONA

Las Serralleiras ⛯ 42°08'·77N 08°52'·67W, Fl G 4s 9m 6M.
Las Serralleiras ⛯ 42°09'·23N 08°53'·35W, Q (9) 15s 4M.
Ldg lts 084°, both W twrs. Front, Cabezo de San Juan 42°08'·24N 08°50'·09W, Fl 6s 7m 10M. Rear, Playa de Panjón, Oc 4s 17m 9M.
Dique de Abrigo ☆ 42°07'·49N 08°50'·58W, QG 10m 5M; B and W chequered ○ twr. Commercial wharf hd, QR 6m 1M; R twr.
⛯ 42°07'·26N 08°54'·72W, Q; marks rks NNW of C. Silleiro.
C. Silleiro ☆ 42°06'·27N 08°53'·80W, Fl (2+1) 15s 83m **24M**.

La Guardia bkwtr ☆ 41°54'·01N 08°52'·94W, Fl (2) R 7s 11m 5M; R twr; *Siren Mo (L) 30s*. E bkwtr, Fl (2) G 7s 11m 5M; G twr.

9.23.4 PASSAGE INFORMATION

BIBLIOGRAPHY The *NW Spain Cruising Companion* (Nautical Data Ltd/Jens) covers from the French border to Bayona. *South Biscay Pilot* (Imray/RCC, 5th edition 2000): the Gironde to La Coruña. *Atlantic Spain and Portugal* (Imray/RCC, 5th edition 2000): El Ferrol to Gibraltar. The *Bay of Biscay Pilot* (Admiralty, NP 22): Pte de Penmarc'h to Cabo Ortegal; whence the *W coasts of Spain and Portugal Pilot* (Admiralty, NP 67) continues south to Gibraltar. *Portos de Galicia* (English/Spanish) has good photographs.

BAY OF BISCAY (S): WIND, WEATHER AND SEA Despite its reputation, the S part of the Bay is often warm and settled in summer when the Azores high and Spanish heat low are the dominant weather features. NE'lies prevail in sea area Finisterre in summer and gales may occur twice monthly, although forecast more frequently. Atlantic lows can bring W'ly spells at any time. SE or S winds are rare, but wind direction and speed often vary from day to day. Sea and land breezes can be well developed in the summer. Off N Spain *Galernas* are dangerous squally NW winds which blow with little warning. Coastal winds are intensified by the Cordillera Cantábrica (2615m mountains). Rainfall is moderate, increasing in the SE, where thunder is more frequent. Sea fog, which may mean imminent strong winds, occurs May-Oct, but is less common in winter.

▶*No tidal stream atlases are published; streams are weak offshore, but can be strong in narrow channels and around headlands. Surface current much depends on wind: in summer it sets SE $\frac{1}{2}$ - $\frac{3}{4}$kn, towards the SE corner of B of Biscay, thence W along N coast of Spain. When crossing the Bay, allow for some set to the E, particularly after strong W winds.*◀

CROSSING THE BAY OF BISCAY (chart 1104) Leaving the English Channel, the track (208°/362M) from Ushant ITZ to Cabo Villano lies undesirably close to busy shipping lanes, but a track (213°/287M) from, say, harbours between Loctudy and Concarneau, to Cabo Ortegal is substantially offset SE of the shipping route. Cabo Ortegal as a landfall permits onward passage to La Coruña and adjacent rías. Or, or if conditions for rounding Ortegal are bad (as is not unkown), Ría de Vivero makes a safe refuge.

From Scilly or Eire the direct track lies in about 7°-8°W. Within the Bay itself, sailing down the French coast is attractive and allows a 200M passage from, say, La Rochelle to Santander. Off Arcachon a missile range (9.22.27) may inhibit coastal passage.

The Continental Shelf where depths plummet from 150m to over 4000m in only 30M, can cause dangerous seas in swell and bad weather. From a position about 60M SW of Ile de Sein it trends SE to the Franco/Spanish border as clearly depicted on AC 1104.

The Atlantic swell, rarely experienced in UK waters except off the W coasts of Ireland and Scotland, runs in mainly from W or NW. It is not a problem well offshore, except over the Continental Shelf in bad weather. Considerable rolling is probable and other yachts may be lost to view in the troughs. Closer inshore swell will exacerbate the sea state and render entry to, and exit from, lee shore hbrs dangerous. For example, with a 2m swell running, crossing a bar with 4m depth over it and breaking seas would be foolhardy. In winter some hbrs are closed for weeks at a time, more particularly along the Portuguese coast.

FRENCH BORDER TO CABO ORTEGAL (charts 1102, 1105, 1108) The N coast of Spain is bold and rocky. In clear visibility the peaks of the Cordillera Cantábrica may be seen from well offshore. Although the coast is mostly steep-to, it is best to keep 2-3M offshore (beyond the 50m contour) to avoid short, steep seas breaking on isolated shoals. Many major lights are sited so high as to be obscured by low cloud/mist in onshore weather. Of the many small rivers, most are obstructed by bars and none are navigable far inland.

Between the French border and Santander are several interesting fishing hbrs: Guetaria (9.23.9), Zumaya (9.23.10), Motrico, Lequeitio (9.23.11), Elanchove (9.23.12) and Laredo/Santoña (9.23.15) offer anchorage or AB. Marinas are still the exception rather than the rule. Pasajes (9.23.7) is a port of refuge, but also a large, commercial/fishing port. 3M to the W, San Sebastián (9.23.8) is an attractive ⚓ but exposed to the NW. Bilbao (9.23.13) and Santander (9.23.16) are major cities and ferry ports for the UK, with marinas. In NW gales Guetaria, Bermeo, Bilbao, Castro Urdiales (9.23.14) and Santander are ports of refuge for yachts.

West of Santander hbrs are increasingly far apart. Gijón (9.23.18) with a modern marina offers refuge. Cudillero (9.23.19) and Luarca (9.23.20) are small fishing hbrs worth visiting, but beware swell particularly at Cudillero. Ría de Ribadeo (9.23.21) at 7°W is the first of the rías altas (upper or northern), sunken estuaries not unlike a Scottish sea loch. San Ciprian's vast aluminium port offers refuge within its bkwtrs. The Ría de Vivero (9.23.22, with a marina), Ría del Barquero and the Ensenada de Santa Marta, to E and W of Pta de la Estaca de Bares, offer many attractive ⚓s sheltered from all but N/NE winds; but beware S/SW winds off the mountains being accelerated by funnelling effects through the valleys.

CABO ORTEGAL TO CABO FINISTERRE (charts 1111, 3633) Cabo Ortegal should be rounded at least 2M off due to the offlying needle rks, Los Aguillones. Most of the major headlands should be given a good offing to avoid fluky winds and, in some cases, pinnacle rocks. The deeply indented coast begins to trend WSW, with 600m high mountains rising only 5M inland. Here too many major lights are sited so high as to be obscured by low cloud/mist in onshore weather. Tidal streams set SW on the ebb and NE on the flood. Any current tends to run SW, then S.

The Ría de Cedeira (9.23.23) is entered 3M SSW of Pta Candelaria lt ho. This small attractively wooded ría offers refuge by day/night to yachts unable to round Cabo Ortegal in strong NE'lies. Several banks along this stretch break in heavy weather when they should be passed well to seaward. About 20M further SW, having passed Pta de la Frouseira, Cabo Prior, Pta del Castro and C. Prioriño Chico, all lit, is the ent to Ría de Ferrol (9.23.24), a well sheltered commercial and naval port, but with rather limited yacht facilities.

La Coruña (9.23.27) is accessible in all weathers and has far better yacht facilities and a new marina in the city centre. The Ría de Ares (9.23.25) and Ría de Betanzos (9.23.26) are attractive alternatives, both with marinas. W of the conspic Torre de Hércules lt ho a wide bight is foul as far as Islas Sisargas, three islets 2M offshore. 8M SW of Pta Nariga (43°19'·3N 08°54'·6W), between Pta del Roncudo and Pta de Lage, is the unspoiled Ría de Corme y Lage (9.23.28) with two small fishing hbrs.

Cabo Villano, a rky headland with lt ho and conspic wind generators, is a possible landfall after crossing Biscay. A pinnacle rk awash at CD, lurks 4ca NW of it. The ent to Ría de Camariñas (9.23.29), the last of the rías altas and a safe refuge, is close S. 20M W/NW of Cabo Villano and Finisterre is a TSS; see 9.23.2 for details. Cabo Toriñana and Cabo Finisterre both have charted dangers, mostly pinnacle rks, lying up to 1M offshore; hence the popular name *Costa del Morte* for this wild, magnificent and sometimes forbidding coast.

CABO FINISTERRE TO RIO MIÑO (chart 3633) NE of Cabo Finisterre the Ensenada del Sardineiro and Ría de Corcubión are sheltered ⚓s except in S'lies. From 5 to 11M south, beware various islets, reefs and shoals N and W of Pta Insua, notably Las Arrosas and Bajo de los Meixidos; the latter can be passed inshore if making for Ría de Muros.

The 40M stretch to Cabo Silleiro is an impressive cruising ground, containing the four major rías bajas (lower or southern), from N to S: Muros (9.23.30), Arousa (9.23.31), Pontevedra (9.23.32) and Vigo (9.23.33). The last three rías are sheltered from onshore winds by coastal islands at their mouth, but in summer NE winds can blow strongly down all rías, usually without raising any significant sea. Arousa, the largest ría, runs 12M inland and is up to 6M wide; Villagarcia is its principal hbr and marina. All resemble large and scenic Scottish sea lochs with interesting pilotage to fishing hbrs and many sheltered anchorages. Ría de Vigo is notable for the beautiful Islas Cies, the port of Vigo and, to the S, Bayona's pleasant hbr (9.23.34).

The Río Miño, 15M S of Cabo Silleiro, forms the Spanish/Portuguese border. The river ent is difficult and best not attempted.

9.23.5 SPECIAL NOTES FOR SPAIN

Regions/Provinces: Spain is divided into 17 autonomous regions, ie in Area 23, the Basque Country, Cantabrica, Asturias and Galicia. Most regions are sub-divided into provinces, eg in Galicia: Lugo, La Coruña, Pontevedra and Orense (inland). The province is shown below the name of each main port.

Language: This Almanac recognises regional differences (eg Basque, Gallego), but in the interests of standardisation uses the spelling of Castilian Spanish where practicable.

Charts: Spanish charts (SC) are obtainable from Instituto Hidrográfico de la Marina, Plaza San Severiano 3, 11007 Cádiz, ☎ (956) 599 414, ℻ 275 358. Order from Seccion Economica by credit card or in person for cash. Or from Chart Agents in Bilbao, Santander, Gijon, La Coruña, Villagarcia de Arosa and Vigo.

Courtesy Ensign: E of Bilbao it may be politic to fly the Basque flag (9.23.3) rather than a Spanish courtesy ensign.

Time: Standard time in Spain is UT –1; DST (Daylight Saving Time) is kept from the last Sunday in March until the Saturday before the 4th Sunday in October, as in other EU nations. Note: Standard time in Portugal is UT; DST is UT +1.

Spanish secondary ports referenced to Lisboa: Spain and Portugal keep different Standard Times (see above). Time differences for those Spanish ports which are referenced to Lisboa (all south of Ría de Muros), when applied to the printed times of HW and LW for Lisboa, give HW and LW times in Spanish Standard Time. DST is the only correction required.

Telephone: To call Spain from UK dial 00-34, then the area code, followed by the 6 digit ☎ number. To call UK from Spain, dial 07-44, then area code less the initial 0, plus the ☎ number. Internally dial the area code plus the ☎ number.

Emergencies: ☎ 900 202 202 for Fire, Police and Ambulance. *Rioja Cruz* (Red Cross) operate LBs.

Public Holidays: Jan 1, 6; Apr 10 (Good Friday); 1 May (Labour Day); June 11 (Corpus Christi); Aug 15 (Assumption); Oct 12 (National Day); Nov 1 (All Saints Day); Dec 6, 8 (Immaculate Conception), 25.

Representation: Spanish Tourist Office, 22-23 Manchester Square, London W1U 3PX; ☎ 020 7486 8077, ℻ 020 7186 8034. londres@tourspain.es www.tourspain.uk
British Embassy, Calle de Fernando el Santo 16, 28010 Madrid; ☎ (91) 700 8200, ℻ 308 08 8211 (Consular). There are British Consuls at Bilbao, Santander and Vigo.

Buoyage: Buoys may lack topmarks, be unpainted (or wrongly painted) more often than in N Europe. Preferred chan buoys [RGR, Fl (2+1) R and GRG, Fl (2+1) G] are quite widely used.

Documents: Spain, although an EU member, still asks to check paperwork. This can be a time-consuming, repetitive and inescapable process. The only palliatives are courtesy, patience and good humour. Organise your documents to include:

Personal – Passports; crew list, ideally on headed paper with the yacht's rubber stamp, giving DoB, passport nos, where joined/ intended departure. Certificate of Competence (Yachtmaster Offshore, ICC/HOCC etc). Radio Operator's certificate. Form E111 (advised for medical treatment).

Yacht – Registration certificate, Part 1 or SSR. Proof of VAT status. Marine insurance. Ship's Radio licence. Itinerary, backed up by ship's log.

Access: Ferries from UK to Santander and Bilbao. Flights from UK to Bilbao, Santiago de Compostela and Madrid. Internal flights via Madrid to Asturias, La Coruña and Vigo. Buses are mostly good and trains adequate, except in more remote regions.

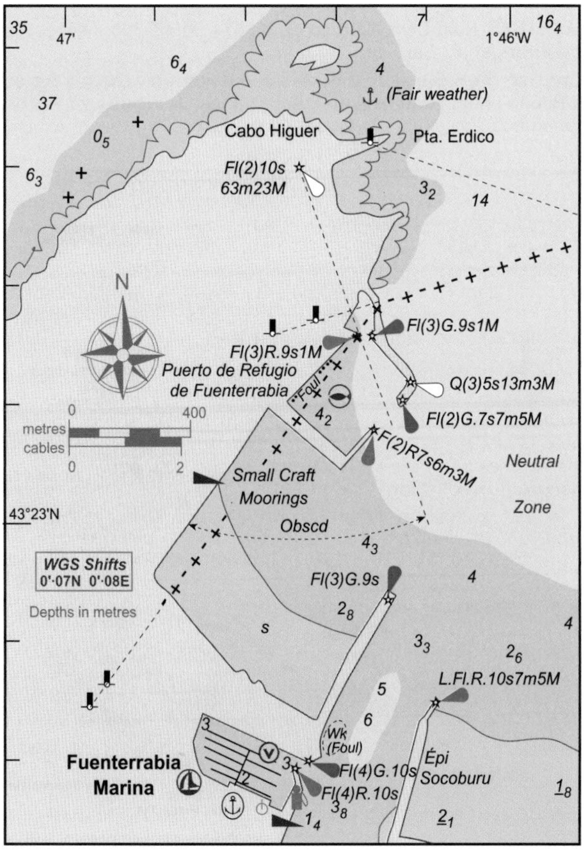
47'
1°46'W
Cabo Higuer
(Fair weather)
Pta. Erdico
Fl(2)10s
63m23M
N
Fl(3)G.9s1M
Fl(3)R.9s1M
Puerto de Refugio
de Fuenterrabia
Foul
Q(3)5s13m3M
Fl(2)G.7s7m5M
F(2)R7s6m3M
Neutral
Zone
metres
cables
400
Small Craft
Moorings
Obscd
43°23'N
WGS Shifts
0'·07N 0'·08E
Depths in metres
Fl(3)G.9s
L.Fl.R.10s7m5M
Wk
(Foul)
Fuenterrabia
Marina
Fl(4)G.10s
Fl(4)R.10s
Épi
Socoburu

9.23.6 FUENTERRABÍA (Hondarribia)

Guipúzcoa **43°22'·64N 01°47'·45W**

CHARTS AC 1102, 1181; SC 944, 945, 3910; SHOM 6556, 6558, 6786; ECM 555

TIDES HW +0450 on Dover (UT); ML 2·3m; Zone –0100
Interpolate between **SOCOA** 9.22.31 and **PASAJES** 9.23.7.

SHELTER Excellent in marina (3m), access H24; river is dredged 2m. Good ⚓ in river off Fuenterrabía. See chartlet for neutral zone between France and Spain. S of Cabo Higuer, a FV hbr, 2-3m, is a port of refuge. See also Hendaye 9.22.32.

NAVIGATION WPT 43°23'·87N 01°46'·44W, 212°/1·15M to W bkwtr hd. Beware Les Briquets 8ca N of Pte Ste Anne at E end of the Baie. Near centre of B, keep clear of Bajo Iruarri. River ent is easy except in heavy N'ly swell; sp ebb is very strong.

LIGHTS AND MARKS Cabo Higuer lt ho, a square stone twr with R top, is conspic at W side of bay, as is the high dorsal ridge which runs down to the headland. A red-roofed castle is prominent 2 cables SSE of Cabo Higuer lt ho. La Rhune, an 898m high conical peak, bears 120°/8M from the marina.

R/T Marina Ch 73 (H24).

TELEPHONE (Dial code 943) Marina ☎ 641711, ℻ 646031.

FACILITIES Marina (595 + 25 Ⓥ); Ⓥ on pontoon G (first to port). pontoons G-J are to the SE; and A-F are NW of the central pontoon. Max LOA 16m. Boats > 17m LOA should ⚓ in the Bay or in Baie de Chingoudy. D & P, ME, BH (35 ton), C (3 ton), D. Club Nautico ☎ 642788.

Town 🛒, R, Bar, Gaz, ✉, Ⓑ, ≷, ✈ (Fuenterrabía or Biarritz). Local ferry from Fuenterrabía to Hendaye. UK ferry from Bilbao or Santander.

23

9.23.7 PASAJES (Pasaia)

Guipúzcoa **43°20'·21N 01°55'·69W**

CHARTS AC 1102, 1181; SC 944, 3911; SHOM 6375, 6558

TIDES See 9.23.8.

SHELTER A port of refuge (3·5M E of San Sebastián, 7M from France), also a busy FV and commercial hbr with no yacht facilities. Yachts may ⚓ as shown on the chartlet: the bay NE of Dir lt is fair weather only; the other two ⚓s are outside local moorings, as space allows; the N'ly is subject to wash. Basins further S are full of commercial and fishing vessels.

NAVIGATION WPT 43°21'·15N 01°56'·12W, SWM buoy [Mo (A) 6s], 161°/1·0M to hbr ent, a 200m wide cleft in spectacular cliffs. Appr on 154·8° transit of Dir lt, Oc (2) WRG 12s (Racon M), with ldg lts: front Q, rear Oc 3s; all on the W cliff. Banks either side of ent are marked by conspic R and G 18m high lt twrs. Inner chan, dredged 10m, is only 100m wide, but well marked/lit; do not impede large vessels/FVs.

LIGHTS AND MARKS Obey IPTS, sigs 1, 2 and 3, shown to seaward and inwards from Atalya de Pasajes (Racon K) high on the E cliff; the ent is narrow and blind.

R/T Port Ch 09 (H24).

TELEPHONE HM ☎ (943) 351816, 📠 351348. ppasajes@sarenet.es

FACILITIES Services: ⚒, El, Ⓔ, ME (Big Ship orientated). **Town** 🛒, R, Bar, ✉, Ⓑ. UK ferry from Bilbao/Santander.

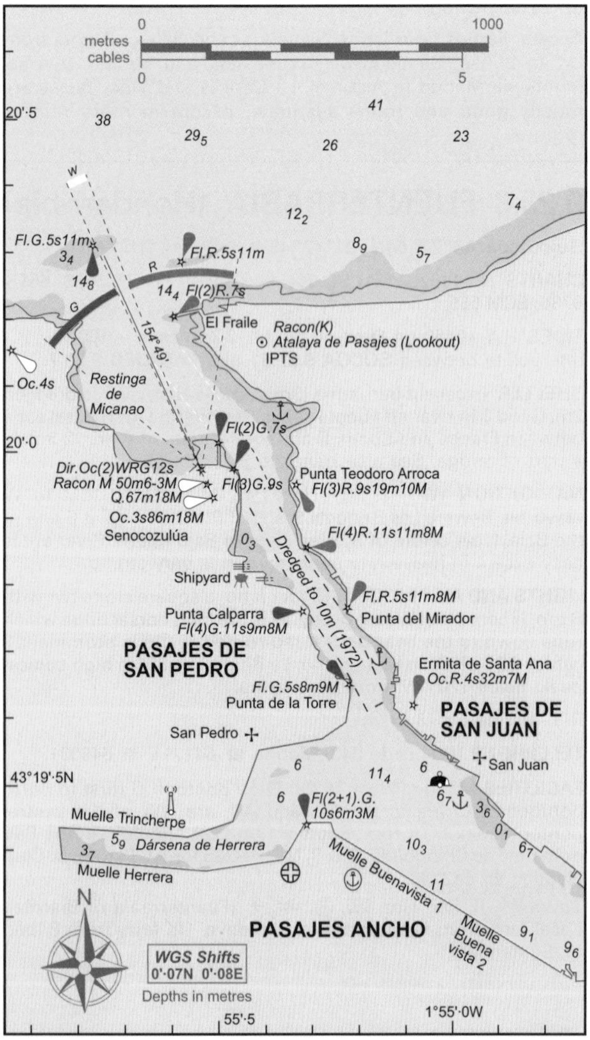
metres
cables
0
1000
5
38
29₅
41
26
23
7₄
12₂
8₉
5₇
Fl.G.5s11m
3₄
1₄₈
Fl.R.5s11m
14₄ Fl(2)R.7s
154·8°
El Fraile
Racon(K)
Atalaya de Pasajes (Lookout)
IPTS
Oc.4s
Restinga de Micanao
Fl(2)G.7s
Dir.Oc(2)WRG12s
Racon M 50m6-3M
Q.67m18M
Oc.3s86m18M
Senocozulúa
Fl(3)G.9s
Punta Teodoro Arroca
Fl(3)R.9s19m10M
Fl(4)R.11s11m8M
Shipyard
Dredged to 10m (1972)
Fl.R.5s11m8M
Punta del Mirador
Punta Calparra
Fl(4)G.11s9m8M
PASAJES DE SAN PEDRO
Fl.G.5s8m9M
Punta de la Torre
Ermita de Santa Ana
Oc.R.4s32m7M
PASAJES DE SAN JUAN
San Pedro
San Juan
43°19'·5N
Muelle Trincherpe
Fl(2+1).G.10s6m3M
5₉ Dársena de Herrera
Muelle Herrera
Muelle Buenavista 1
Muelle Buena vista 2
PASAJES ANCHO
WGS Shifts
0'·07N 0'·08E
Depths in metres
55'·5
1°55'·0W
20'·5
20'·0

9.23.8 SAN SEBASTIÁN (Donostia)

Guipúzcoa **43°19'·49N 01°59'·68W**

CHARTS AC 1102, 1181; SC 944, 945, 3910; SHOM 6558, 6786

TIDES
Standard Port PTE DE GRAVE (⟵); Zone –0100

Times				Height (metres)			
High Water		Low Water		MHWS	MHWN	MLWN	MLWS
0000	0600	0500	1200	5·4	4·4	2·1	1·0
1200	1800	1700	2400				
Differences SAN SEBASTIÁN							
–0110	–0030	–0020	–0040	–1·2	–1·2	–0·5	–0·4
PASAJES							
–0050	–0030	–0015	–0045	–1·2	–1·3	–0·5	–0·5

SHELTER Fair; the ⚓ becomes lively or dangerous in any NW/N'lies when heavy swell enters. Options: YC launch will meet and direct (VHF Ch 09) to a vacant 🅐. ⚓ S of Isla Santa Clara or SW of YC, in both cases clear of moorings and with ⚓ buoyed. In the over-crowded Dársena de la Concha, limited space on Ⓥ pontoon dead ahead of ent; inner basins are locals/FVs only.

NAVIGATION WPT 43°19'·85N 01°59'·88W, 158°/0·4M to hbr ent (between Isla de Santa Clara and Monte Urgull). Avoid La Bancha on which the sea breaks in swell and heavy weather. Open up the bay before standing in.

LIGHTS AND MARKS Monte Urgull (huge statue of Virgin Mary) is prominent from all directions; from E it looks like an island. Monte Igueldo on W side of ent is only slightly less obvious. Isla de Santa Clara is lower and inconspicuous; not seen until the nearer appr. Ldg marks (grey masts) are hard to see, but a large R & W Palladian-styled villa is conspic on 158°. Ldg lts, although intens, may be masked by shore lts. See chartlet and 9.23.3.

R/T Real Club Nautico Ch 09 (H24).

TELEPHONE (Dial code 943) Emerg'y 900 202 202; Met 274030; Auto 906 365320; Ⓗ 945 454000; Brit Consul 94 415 7600.

FACILITIES Real Club Náutico ☎ 423574, 📠 431365, M (best to pre-arrange), R, Bar, Ice.

City: Gaz, 🛒, R, Bar, Ⓑ, ✉, Ⓗ; ⇌ & ✈ Fuenterrabia (25km); ✈ also at Bilbao (92km) and ferry to UK. Facilities for visiting yachts do not match the city's elegance.

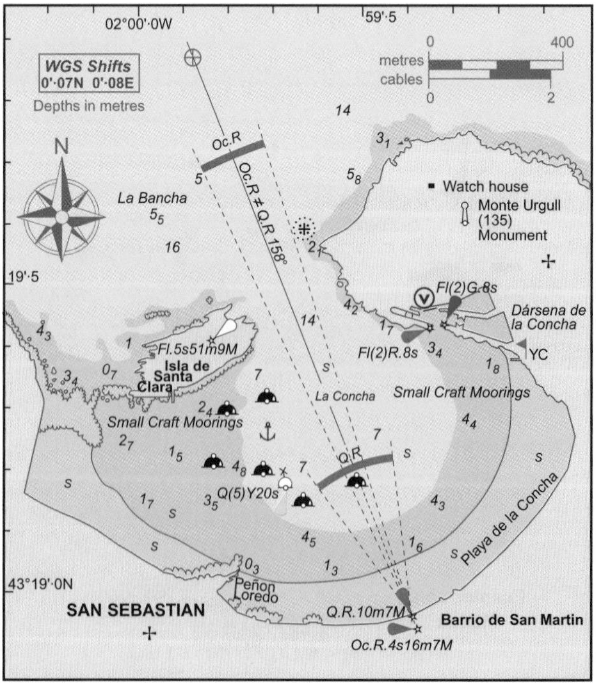
02°00'·0W
59'·5
WGS Shifts
0'·07N 0'·08E
Depths in metres
metres
cables
0
400
2
14
3₁
5₈
Oc.R
Oc.R ≠ Q.R 158°
La Bancha
5₅
16
Watch house
Monte Urgull (135)
Monument
19'·5
Fl(2)G.8s
Dársena de la Concha
Fl(2)R.8s
YC
4₃
Fl.5s51m9M
Isla de Santa Clara
0₇
La Concha
Small Craft Moorings
Small Craft Moorings
4₄
Q(5)Y20s
Q.R
Playa de la Concha
43°19'·0N
Peñon Loredo
SAN SEBASTIAN
Q.R.10m7M
Oc.R.4s16m7M
Barrio de San Martin

9.23.9 GUETARIA (Getaria)

Guipúzcoa **43°18'·30N 02°11'·80W** ✵✵✵⛵⛵✿✿✿

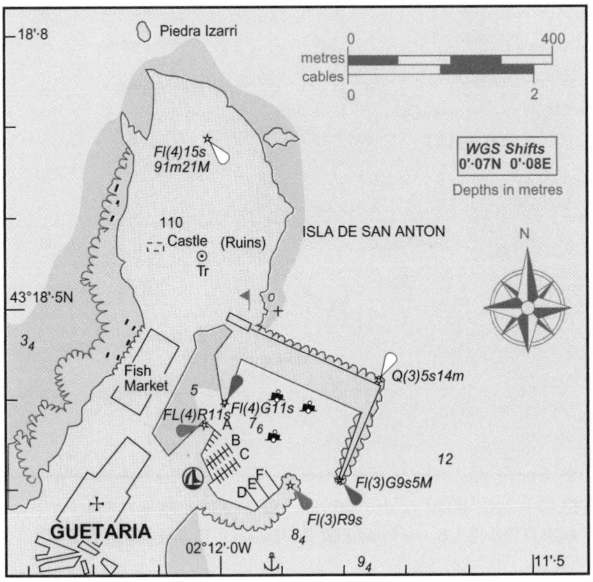

18'·8
Piedra Izarri
0
400
metres
cables
0
2
Fl(4)15s
91m21M
WGS Shifts
0'·07N 0'·08E
Depths in metres
110
Castle (Ruins)
Tr
ISLA DE SAN ANTON
N
43°18'·5N
Q(3)5s14m
Fish Market
5
FL(4)R11s
Fl(4)G11s
A
B
C
D
E
F
12
Fl(3)G9s5M
Fl(3)R9s
GUETARIA
02°12'·0W
11'·5

CHARTS AC 1102, 1171; SC 128, 944, 943, 3921; SHOM 6379, 6786

TIDES

Standard Port PTE DE GRAVE (⟵); Zone –0100

Times				Height (metres)			
High Water		Low Water		MHWS	MHWN	MLWN	MLWS
0000	0600	0500	1200	5·4	4·4	2·1	1·0
1200	1800	1700	2400				
Differences GUETARIA							
–0110	–0030	–0020	–0040	–1·0	–1·0	–0·5	–0·4

SHELTER The only good shelter from winds S to NW between Pasajes and Bilbao; pontoons A-F to port on entry. FVs berth on N and W sides of outer hbr and also fill the inner hbr. No ⚓ in hbr which is generally foul. In fair weather ⚓ on sand or pick up a buoy close S of hbr ent, but exposed to E'lies.

NAVIGATION WPT 43°18'·90N 02°11'·00W, 225°/8½ca to hbr ent. Appr is straightforward day/night in fair visibility.

LIGHTS AND MARKS Lts as chartlet & 9.23.3. The mouse-like profile of Isla de San Anton is distinctive; It ho on its N side.

R/T VHF Ch 09 H24.

TELEPHONE (Dial code 943) ⊜ via Marina; Met 906 365 320; Auto 906 365365; LB 900 202 202.

FACILITIES Marina (300, max LOA 14m), ☎ & 📠 580959, thage@infonegocio.com; **Club Náutico y Pesca** ☎ 140201, R, Bar. **Services:** BH (30 ton), Slip, D, ⚒, CH, SM, ME, El, C (5 ton); **Town:** 🛒, R, Bar, Gaz, ☎, ✉, ⇌; ✈ Bilbao (UK ferry).

9.23.10 ZUMAYA (Zumaia)

Guipúzcoa **43°18'N 02°15'W** ✵✵✵⛵⛵⛵✿✿✿

CHARTS AC 1102; SC 128, 944, 943, 3921; SHOM 6379, 6786.

TIDES As for 9.23.9.

SHELTER Good in the welcoming marina, 2·5m. But in strong onshore winds the appr could be difficult. No ⚓ in hbr, but in E'lies a fair weather ⚓ off sandy beach 3ca NE of hbr ent.

NAVIGATION WPT 43°20'·00N 02°14'·40W [8ca W of ODAS buoy, Fl (5) Y 20s], 190°/1.5M to hbr ent. Easy appr from NNE, but keep clear of rocks on W side of Pta Iruarriaundieta. In the access chan, dredged 3m, best water is to stbd.

LIGHTS AND MARKS Lt ho, Oc (3+1) 12s, is a white 8 sided tower with blue cupola. W Bkwtr hd, Fl (2) G 7s, East Fl (2) R 7s. Inner lts as chartlet.

R/T Ch 09.

TELEPHONE (Dial code 943) Marina ☎ 86 09 38, 📠 14 32 99. www.puertozumaia.com marurola@euskalnet.net Tourist office 14 33 96.

FACILITIES Marina (512, inc Ⓥ, max LOA 15m) ☎ as above, BH (35 ton), Slip, D, ⚒, CH, ME, El.
Town: 🛒, R, Bar, Gaz, ☎, ✉, ⇌; ✈ Bilbao (UK ferry).

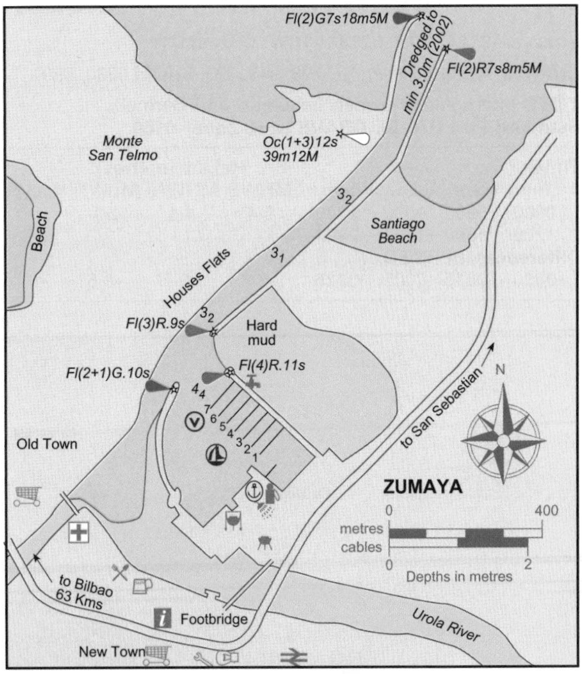

Fl(2)G7s18m5M
Dredged to min 3.0m (2002)
Fl(2)R7s8m5M
Monte San Telmo
Oc(1+3)12s
39m12M
Beach
3₂
Santiago Beach
3₁
Houses Flats
Fl(3)R.9s
3₂
Hard mud
Fl(4)R.11s
Fl(2+1)G.10s
4₄
Old Town
to San Sebastian
N
ZUMAYA
0
400
metres
cables
0
2
Depths in metres
to Bilbao 63 Kms
Footbridge
Urola River
New Town

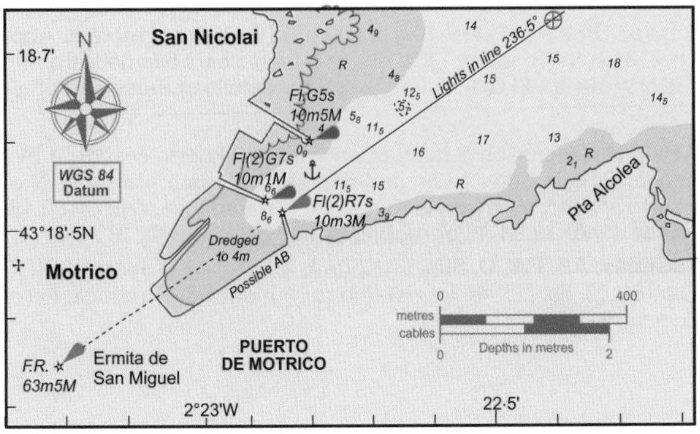

18·7'
N
San Nicolai
14
Lights in line 236·5°
15
18
Fl.G5s
10m5M
14₅
WGS 84 Datum
Fl(2)G7s
10m1M
Fl(2)R7s
10m3M
17
13
Pta Alcolea
43°18'·5N
Dredged to 4m
Possible AB
Motrico
0
400
metres
cables
0
2
Depths in metres
F.R.
63m5M
Ermita de San Miguel
PUERTO DE MOTRICO
2°23'W
22·5'

MINOR HARBOUR 6M WEST OF ZUMAYA

MOTRICO (Mutriku) Guipúzcoa **43°18'·80N 02°22'·80W**. Tides: interpolate between Guetaria & Lequeitio. AC 1102; SC 3922; SHOM 6379. Small FV hbr (4m) in rky inlet, but facilities for yachts are said to be in hand. Good shelter except in NE swell.

WPT 43°18'·75N 02°22'·40W, 236·5°/4ca to hbr ent. Easily seen from E, but from W open hbr & town before appr; caution rky ledges off Pta de Cardal. Ldg lts/marks 236·5°: front, Fl (2) R 7s 10m 3M on S bkwtr; rear, FR 63m 5M on clock tr (hard to see by day). N outer bkwtr, Fl G 5s 10m 5M. N inner bkwtr, Fl (2) G 7s 10m 1M. ⚓ outside the N bkwtr in 5m near spending beach and slip; or ⚓/moor inside the 23m wide ent to the W; or AB on SE quay if FVs are away. HM ☎ (943) 603204; 📠 604028. www.mutriku.net julen@mutrikuberri.com **Facilities** (FV quay): FW, ⛽, D, P, C (5 ton), Ice, Slip. **Town** R, 🛒, Bar.

9.23.11 LEQUEITIO (Lekeitio)

Vizcaya **43°22'·06N 02°29'·85W**

CHARTS AC 1102, 1171; SC 943, 393; SHOM 6379, 5009

TIDES
Standard Port PTE DE GRAVE (←); Zone –0100

Times				Height (metres)			
High Water		Low Water		MHWS	MHWN	MLWN	MLWS
0000	0600	0500	1200	5·4	4·4	2·1	1·0
1200	1800	1700	2400				
Differences LEQUEITIO							
–0115	–0035	–0025	–0045	–1·2	–1·2	–0·5	–0·4

SHELTER Good. Options: In the basin berth on W quays or S mole; FVs use the N part of basin. ⚓ in about 3m or pick up a vacant buoy at the S end. In settled weather ⚓ further out, to E or W of Isla de San Nicolas. Friendly YC but can be crowded.

NAVIGATION WPT 43°22'·33N 02°29'·68W, 205°/3ca to Punta Amandarri, Fl G 4s. Clear this by 5m on 206° to avoid rky shoals close E and old bkwtr (Fl (2) R 8s) further S.

LIGHTS AND MARKS Cabo de Santa Catalina, Fl (1+3) 20s 44m 17M, Horn Mo (L) 20s, is conspic 0·75M to the NW. Isla de San Nicolas is rky, steep-sided and wooded; connected to mainland by a drying causeway. Church dome is conspic SSW of hbr.

R/T VHF Ch 09.

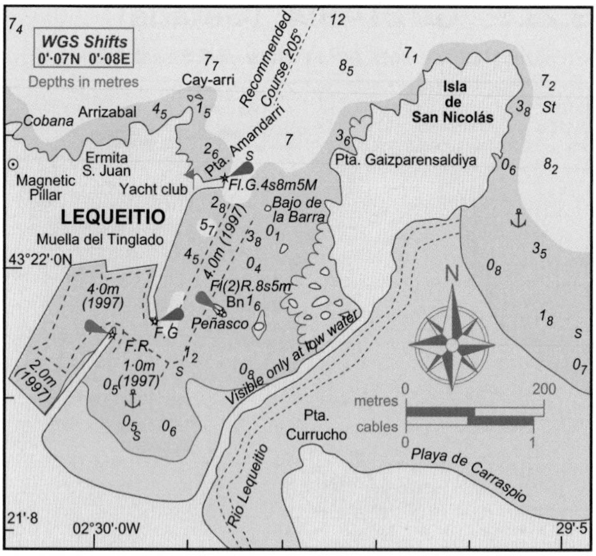
WGS Shifts
0'·07N 0'·08E
Depths in metres
Cay-arri
Recommended Course 205°
Cobana
Arrizabal
Ermita S. Juan
Magnetic Pillar
Yacht club
Pta. Amandarri
Fl.G.4s8m5M
Bajo de la Barra
LEQUEITIO
Muella del Tinglado
43°22'·0N
4·0m (1997)
Fl(2)R.8s5m
Bn
Peñasco
F.G
F.R.
1·0m
(1997)
2·0m (1997)
Visible only at low water
Isla de San Nicolás
Pta. Gaizparensaldiya
Pta. Currucho
Playa de Carraspio
Rio Lequeitio
metres
cables
21'·8
02°30'·0W
29'·5

TELEPHONE (Dial code 946) HM ☎ 243324, ℻ 841711.

FACILITIES Club de Pesca ☎ 840500; D, P, CH, Slip, ME, 🛒.

9.23.12 ELANCHOVE (Elantxobe)

Vizcaya **43°24'·30N 02°38'·18W**

CHARTS AC 1102, 1171; SC 128, 943, 393; SHOM 6380, 6991

TIDES Interpolate between Lequeitio and Bermeo.
Standard Port PTE DE GRAVE (←); Zone –0100

Times				Height (metres)			
High Water		Low Water		MHWS	MHWN	MLWN	MLWS
0000	0600	0500	1200	5·4	4·4	2·1	1·0
1200	1800	1700	2400				
Differences BERMEO							
–0055	–0015	–0005	–0025	–0·8	–0·7	–0·5	–0·4

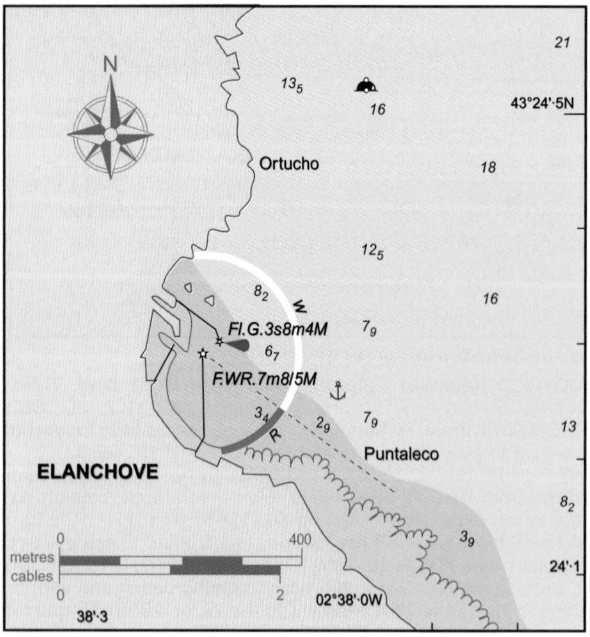
N
Ortucho
43°24'·5N
Fl.G.3s8m4M
F.WR.7m8/5M
W
R
Puntaleco
ELANCHOVE
metres
cables
38'·3
02°38'·0W
24'·1

SHELTER Sheltered from W in lee of Cabo Ogoño, but exposed to N/E. Tiny hbr in spectacular setting at foot of steep 100m cliffs, to which the village clings for dear life. The N part of outer hbr and all the inner hbr dry. At ent turn hard port into S part of outer hbr to ⚓ (buoy the ⚓) or pick up buoy in about 3m. AB on S mole is feasible, but a 1m wide underwater ledge requires holding-off line to kedge ⚓. In calm weather tempy ⚓ to E of hbr ent in 5m.

NAVIGATION WPT 43°22'·33N 02°29'·67W, 225°/6ca to N mole hd. From the W, hbr is not visible until bearing >205°.

LIGHTS AND MARKS See chartlet and 9.23.3. The S Mole, F WR lt shows Red (315°-000°) over inshore dangers to the SE. Cabo Machichaco, Fl 7s, is 6M WNW.

R/T Nil

TELEPHONE (Dial code 944) HM ☎ 88 13 23, ℻ 88 13 25.

FACILITIES Village: FW, Basic 🛒, R, Bar; Bus to Bilbao for ⇌, ✈. Gernika, the ancient, sacred city of the Basques, is 15km south by road.

HARBOUR 2·7M SOUTH-EAST OF CABO MACHICHACO

BERMEO 43°25'·35N 02°42'·57W. Tides: see 9.23.12. AC 1102, 1172; SC 917, 942, 128; SHOM 6380, 6991. A busy fishing & commercial port, well sheltered from the N by a substantial N mole, but swell enters in E'lies. Yachts take their chance amongst FVs, but leisure facilities are believed to be planned.

Hbr is NW of the wide drying estuary of Rio Mundaca. Isla de Izaro lies off the estuary mouth, 1M ENE of hbr. Cabo Machichaco, Fl 7s, is conspic 2·75M to NW.

Rosape Dir lt, Fl (2) WR 10s, is 600m SSW of the N mole lt. Appr on 218° in its W sector (204°-232°), which clears Isla de Izaro and the N mole hd, Fl G 4·5s. See 9.23.3 for details of these and other hbr lts.

AB on N mole or on S quay of inner basin (Puerto Mayor) if FVs at sea. Or ⚓ in outer basin in 4-6m. The old inner hbr (1m), N of Puerto Mayor, partly dries to rks and is untenable. VHF Ch 09,16. HM ☎ (946) 18 64 45 or mobile ☎ 908 87 33 30; ℻ 18 65 01.

Facilities: AB, FW, D, Slip, C (12 ton), ME, ⚒, Ice. **Town:** 🛒, R, P, Gaz, El, Ⓔ, Ⓑ, ✉, ⇌ tourist line to Mundaca & Guernica; Ferry & ✈ at Bilbao.

9.23.13 BILBAO (Bilbo)

Vizcaya **43°22'·73N 03°04'·87W** (outer ent) ❁❁❁⚓⚓⚓✿✿✿

CHARTS AC 1102, 1174, 1173; SC 394A, 3941; SHOM 6774, 6991

TIDES

Standard Port PTE DE GRAVE (⟵⟶); ML 2·4

Times				Height (metres)			
High Water		Low Water		MHWS	MHWN	MLWN	MLWS
0000	0600	0500	1200	5·4	4·4	2·1	1·0
1200	1800	1700	2400				
Differences ABRA DE BILBAO							
−0125	−0045	−0035	−0055	−1·2	−1·2	−0·5	−0·4
PORTUGALETE (INNER HARBOUR)							
−0100	−0020	−0010	−0030	−0·7	−1·2	−0·2	−0·6

SHELTER Excellent, but expensive in Getxo marina on S side of Contramuelle de Algorta or at Las Arenas yacht hbr 4ca south near the mouth of the Bilbao river. Possible ⚓ in 3-5m between these two havens which are adjacent to a pleasant suburb. There is no merit (and no berths) in going up-river through industrial areas. Bilbao is a major industrial city, but also a leading cultural and commercial centre.

NAVIGATION WPT 43°23'·17N 03°05'·21W, 150°/5ca to outer hbr ent. A mini-TSS is aligned 150°/1·6M toward the outer hbr ent; thence 120°/2M and 143°/1M via the buoyed fairway across El Abra (= outer hbr/roads) to the inner hbr. Yachts should keep clear of ships using the TSS.

The outer ent is formed by a W bkwtr extending 1.25M NE from Punta Lucero, a high unlit headland on the W side. The partly-finished E bkwtr extends WNW for almost 2M from Punta Galea, Fl (3) 8s, on the E side of El Abra. It is marked by 3 SPM lt buoys, but can be crossed with caution; approx 7m depth was found close off Pta Galea.

From the outer ent follow the fairway across El Abra to Dique de Santurce, Fl (3) G 10s. After passing Contradique de Algorta, Fl R 5s, turn ESE for the new marina; or SE across the inner hbr to Las Arenas yacht hbr. Beware unlit buoys N1, 2, 5 and 6 which are near to the track for either marina; see chartlet inset.

LIGHTS AND MARKS See chartlet and 9.23.3 for lt details; there have been many changes in recent years, so an up-to-date chart will avoid confusion. Glare from industrial plants may be seen from afar at night. The Port control bldg/twr is conspic at the SE end of Dique de Santurce. 1M SW of Port Control 2 tall (200m) power stn chimneys with R/W bands are conspic.

R/T Port Control Ch 05, **12**, 16. Marina Ch 09.

TELEPHONE (Dial code 944) Port HM 241416, 📠 871207; ⊖ 234700; Met via YC; Police 246445; ⊞ 903100; Brit Consul 157600, 📠 167632.

FACILITIES Puerto Getxo Approx 3m depth. (827, inc Ⓥs; max LOA 18m), ☎ 912367, 📠 911818; www.getxokaia.com; LOA <10m €3.1/m; <12m €3.47/m; <15m €4.50/m. D & P, BH (45 ton), C (5 ton), ME, El.

Las Arenas Yacht hbr is run jointly by **Real Club Maritimo del Abra/Real Sporting Club.** ☎ 637600, 📠 638061; www.rcmarsc.es club@.rcmarsc.es (250 + 50 Ⓥ) €3.0/m; M, P, D, Slip, ME, ⚒, CH, SM, El, Ⓔ, BH (35 ton), C (5 ton), Bar, R.

City: 10km SE of marinas. Metro stations: Neguri from Getxo; Argeta from Las Arenas. All facilities; ⇌, ✈ N of city (8km from hbr); ferry to Portsmouth. Tourist Office ☎ 795760.

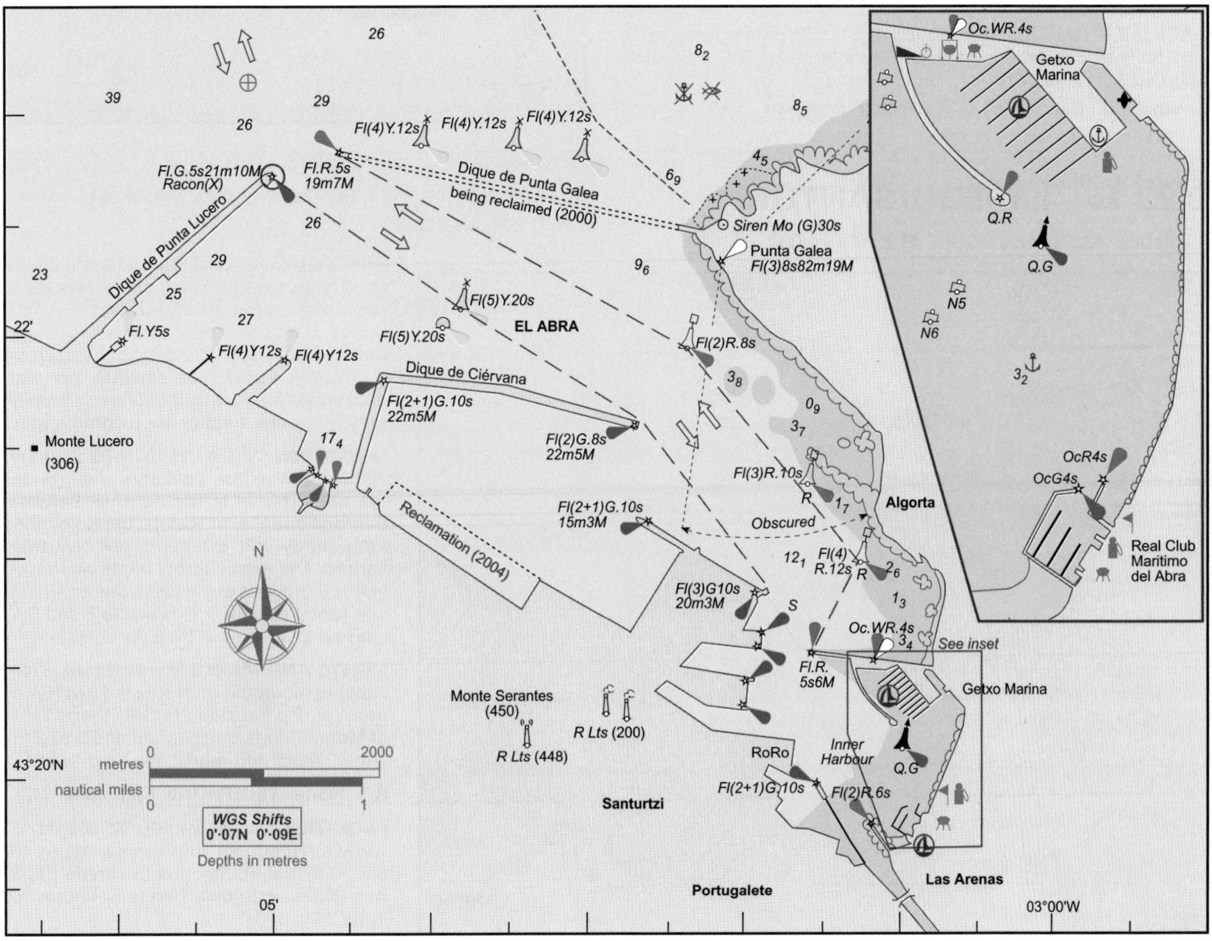
Dique de Punta Galea being reclaimed (2000)
Dique de Punta Lucero
Fl.G.5s21m10M Racon(X)
Fl.R.5s 19m7M
Fl(4)Y.12s
Fl(5)Y.20s
EL ABRA
Dique de Ciérvana
Fl(2+1)G.10s 22m5M
Fl(2)G.8s 22m5M
Fl.Y5s
Monte Lucero (306)
Reclamation (2004)
Siren Mo (G)30s
Punta Galea Fl(3)8s82m19M
Fl(2)R.8s
Fl(3)R.10s
Obscured
Algorta
Fl(4) R.12s
Fl(2+1)G.10s 15m3M
Fl(3)G10s 20m3M
Oc.WR.4s
See inset
Fl.R. 5s6M
Getxo Marina
Monte Serantes (450)
R Lts (200)
R Lts (448)
RoRo
Inner Harbour
Q.G
Fl(2+1)G10s
Fl(2)R.6s
Santurtzi
Portugalete
Las Arenas
43°20'N
metres
nautical miles
WGS Shifts 0'·07N 0'·09E
Depths in metres
05'
03°00'W
22'
Getxo Marina
Q.R
N5
N6
OcR4s
OcG4s
Real Club Maritimo del Abra

9.23.14 CASTRO URDIALES

Cantabria **43°22'·87N 03°12'·50W**

CHARTS AC 1102, 1174; SC 128, 394, 394A; SHOM 3542, 6991

TIDES
Standard Port PTE DE GRAVE (⟵); Zone –0100

Times				Height (metres)			
High Water		Low Water		MHWS	MHWN	MLWN	MLWS
0000	0600	0500	1200	5·4	4·4	2·1	1·0
1200	1800	1700	2400				
Differences CASTRO URDIALES							
–0040	–0120	–0020	–0110	–1·4	–1·5	–0·6	–0·6
RIA DE SANTOÑA (03°28'W)							
–0005	–0045	+0015	–0035	–0·7	–1·2	–0·3	–0·7

SHELTER Good, except in N/E'lies when swell enters. A few Øs or ⚓ in 9m on mud to seaward of the 6 lines of mooring trots which fill the N part of hbr. Many private moorings off the YC; FVs fill inner hbr. AB on N mole possible if calm and no swell.

NAVIGATION WPT 43°23'·54N 03°11'·76W, 220°/0·8M to North Mole head lt; on 220° the mole head lts are in transit. The approach is straightforward with no hazards. Inside the hbr stick to the fairway, avoid extensive moorings

LIGHTS AND MARKS From the NW, town & hbr are obsc'd until rounding Pta del Rabanal with its conspic cemetery. The ✠, lt ho and castle are easily identified on Santa Ana which dominates the hbr. Lts as chartlet and 9.23.3.

R/T Use free YC launch *Blancona* Ch 09, **not** your own tender, as there is insufficient room for berthing tenders at YC.

TELEPHONE (Dial code 942) Met via HM (below); ⊖ 861146; CG/ LB 900 202 202; Dr 861640 (Red Cross); Police 092.

FACILITIES HM/Club ☎ 861585, 📠 872582; www.cncu.es ⚓ €12.50 includes launch service. **Services:** Slip, BY, ME; **Club Náutico** Bar, R ☎ 861234 to book a table.
Town 🛒, R, Bar, Ⓑ, ✉, D & P (cans); ✈ Bilbao.

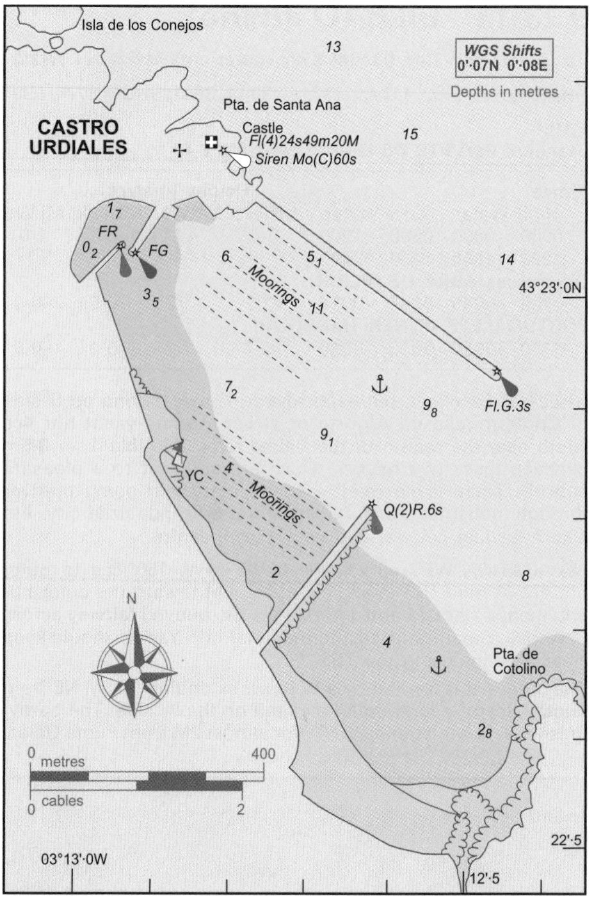
Isla de los Conejos
WGS Shifts 0'·07N 0'·08E
Depths in metres
Pta. de Santa Ana
CASTRO URDIALES
Castle
Fl(4)24s49m20M
Siren Mo(C)60s
FR
FG
Moorings
Fl.G.3s
43°23'·0N
YC
Moorings
Q(2)R.6s
Pta. de Cotolino
metres
cables
03°13'·0W
22'·5
12'·5

9.23.15 LAREDO/SANTOÑA

Cantabria **43°26'·32N 03°27'·03W**

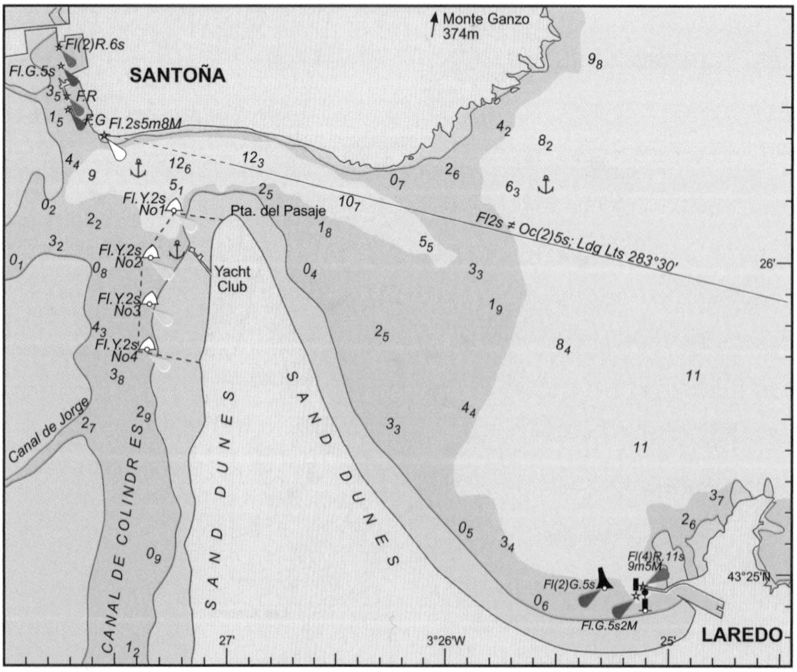
Monte Ganzo 374m
Fl(2)R.6s
Fl.G.5s
SANTOÑA
FR
FG
Fl.2s5m8M
Fl.Y.2s No1
Pta. del Pasaje
Fl2s ≠ Oc(2)5s; Ldg Lts 283°30'
Fl.Y.2s No2
Yacht Club
Fl.Y.2s No3
Fl.Y.2s No4
Canal de Jorge
CANAL DE COLINDRES
SAND DUNES
SAND DUNES
Fl(4)R.11s 9m5M
Fl(2)G.5s
Fl.G.5s2M
LAREDO
43°25'N
26'
27'
3°26'W
25'

CHARTS AC 1102, 1171; SC 128, 394, 3942; SHOM 3542.

TIDES Differences, see 9.23.14 above.

SHELTER Good W of Pta del Pasaje where the CN de Laredo has ⚓ and a few Øs in about 4m inside an area marked by 4 Y buoys, Fl Y 2s. A jetty and pontoons extend to the drying line. Wash from FVs can be a problem. Laredo is a small FV hbr with little space for yachts. Santoña has 2 small, dirty FV basins; neither are recommended.

NAVIGATION WPT 43°25'·90N 03°24'·67W, 283·5°/1·5M to the Lat/Long given under the title. This is in the narrows between Santona and Pta del Pasaje, the N tip of the long sandy spit extending 2M NW from Laredo. The least charted depth on the ldg line is 2·3m, but expect less due to silting. The sandy estuary is exposed to E and S. A shallow chan runs 2·3M S to Colindres.

LIGHTS AND MARKS Monte Ganzo, 374m conspic mountain on N side is 1.5M NW of the Wpt. Pta Pescador, Fl (3+1) 18s, is 1M N of Monte Ganzo. See chartlet and 9.23.3 for lights; 283·5° ldg marks are hard to see.

R/T None. **TELEPHONE** (Dial code 942).

FACILITIES CN de Laredo ☎ 605812/16, www.rcnlaredo.es info@rcnlaredo.es M, Slip, C (6 ton), R, Bar; bus to **Laredo** 🛒, R, Bar, Ⓑ, ✉, ✈ Bilbao. Taxi to Colindres for large 🛒.

9.23.16 SANTANDER

Cantabria **43°27'·74N 03°46'·05W** (between Nos 1 & 2 chan buoys) ❁❁❁◊◊◊✿✿✿

CHARTS AC 1102/5, 1145; SC 127, 401, 4011; SHOM 7365, 6991

TIDES Standard Port PTE DE GRAVE (⟵); ML 2·5

Times				Height (metres)			
High Water		Low Water		MHWS	MHWN	MLWN	MLWS
0000	0600	0500	1200	5·4	4·4	2·1	1·0
1200	1800	1700	2400				
Differences SANTANDER							
–0020	–0100	0000	–0050	–0·7	–1·2	–0·3	–0·7
RÍA DE SUANCES (04°03'W)							
0000	–0030	+0020	–0020	–1·5	–1·5	–0·6	–0·6
SAN VICENTE DE LA BARQUERA (04°23'W)							
–0020	–0100	0000	–0050	–1·5	–1·5	–0·6	–0·6
RÍA DE TINA MAYOR (04°31'W)							
–0020	–0100	0000	–0050	–1·4	–1·5	–0·6	–0·6

SHELTER Access all weather/tides. Shelter generally good off the town and very good up-river. Four options, from seaward:

a. Club Nautico de La Horadada (CNH), ⚓ for 100 craft, 7–10m LOA, N of Nos 1 & 3 buoys, in 3-5m on sand.

b. Pedreña marina, 8ca SSE of Pta Rabiosa and the main channel. Access from No 4 buoy via buoyed/lit chan with least depth 0.4m. No details, so reports would be welcomed.

c. Dársena de Molnedo where Real Club Marítimo de Santander (RCMS) has 250 berths max LOA 12m, but few if any visitors' berths. ⛵s and ⚓ just outside the dock are exposed to passing traffic. It is near the city and its services.

d. Marina del Cantabrico (MC) is approx 2·7M upriver from RCMS, next to the airport, but a longish bus/taxi ride to the city.

NAVIGATION From the E, WPT 43°28'·51N 03°44'·46W (between Isla de Santa Marina and Isla de Mouro), 236°/1·4M to Nos 1/2 buoys. From the W, WPT 43°29'·56N 03°46'·50W (4ca E of Cabo Mayor). Thence in fair weather head SE between Isla de Mouro and Peninsula de la Mágdalena (min depth 7·3m); in heavy weather keep NE of Isla de Mouro. Punta Rabiosa ldg lts lead 235·8° into the well-buoyed/lit DW chan. Second ldg lts 259·5°.

If bound for MC, follow the buoyed chan past the conspic oil terminal/jetty to No 15 SHM lt buoy. Here be wary of the 235·6° ldg marks/lts (hard to see) to marina as they lead close to or over a drying sandbank. Continue 300m SSE to No 17 small GRG buoy, Fl (2+1) G 10s; here turn WSW for marina ent. Note: marina advises against a night entry unless already visited by day.

LIGHTS AND MARKS The former Royal Palace, now a university, is conspic on Peninsula de la Magdalena. A glazed pyramid-shaped bldg about 400m W of MC is a good daymark. Lts and buoys as chartlet and 9.23.3.

R/T Port Authority *Santander Prácticos* VHF Ch **14**, 16; Marinas Ch 09. Local weather broadcast Ch 11 every 4 hrs, 0245-2245.

TELEPHONE (Dial code 942) Port HM 223900, 📠 362413; ⊖ and Met via HM; Brit Consul 220000.

FACILITIES CNH ☎/📠 280402, ⛵. **Darsena de Molnedo, RCMS ☎** 214050, 📠 361972, Bar, R ☎ 272750; www.rcmsantander.com rcmsantander@rcmsantander.com 108 berths in 1·7m; request RCMS for berth or ⛵; Slip, D, BH (27 ton), C (1·5 ton).

MC ☎ 369288, 📠 369286; www.ceoecant.es/marina_santander marinasantander@ceoecant.es AB 1400 in 2·2-3·1m, max LOA 20m, €2.12, C, P, D, Slip, BH (27 ton), CH, ME, ⚒, El, Ⓔ, Gaz, R, Bar. Plenty of berths and adequate security to leave a yacht. Few flights, hence little noise, from the adjacent Parayas airport.

City: www.puertosantander.com All amenities; ⇌ & bus; Brittany ferry terminal to Plymouth is 6ca W of Darsena de Molnedo; ✈.

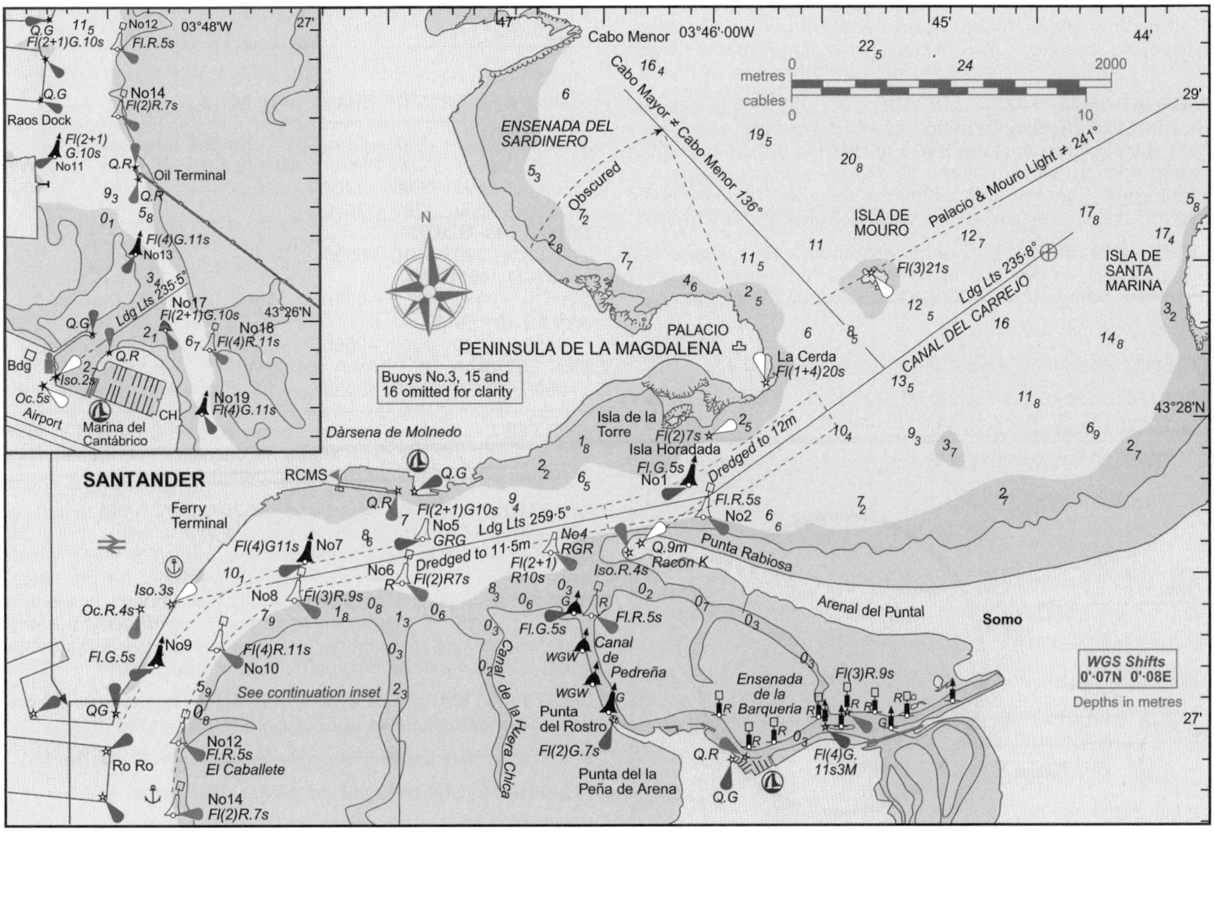
03°48'W
03°46'·00W
45'
44'
29'
43°28'N
27'
43°26'N
Cabo Menor
Cabo Mayor ≠ Cabo Menor 136°
metres
cables
ENSENADA DEL SARDINERO
Obscured
ISLA DE MOURO
Palacio & Mouro Light ≠ 241°
Fl(3)21s
ISLA DE SANTA MARINA
Ldg Lts 235·8°
CANAL DEL CARREJO
PALACIO
PENINSULA DE LA MAGDALENA
La Cerda
Fl(1+4)20s
Buoys No.3, 15 and 16 omitted for clarity
Isla de la Torre
Fl(2)7s
Isla Horadada
Fl.G.5s
No1
Dredged to 12m
Dàrsena de Molnedo
SANTANDER
RCMS
Q.G
Ferry Terminal
Q.R
Fl(2+1)G10s
No5
GRG
Ldg Lts 259·5°
Fl.R.5s
No2
Fl(4)G11s
No7
No4
RGR
Fl(2+1)R10s
Q.9m
Racon K
Punta Rabiosa
Dredged to 11·5m
No6
Fl(2)R7s
Iso.R.4s
Iso.3s
Oc.R.4s
No8
Fl(3)R.9s
Arenal del Puntal
Somo
Fl.R.5s
Fl.G.5s
Canal de Pedreña
No9
Fl(4)R.11s
No10
Canal de la Hiera Chica
WGW
See continuation inset
QG
Punta del Rostro
Fl(2)G.7s
Ensenada de la Barqueria
Fl(3)R.9s
No12
Fl.R.5s
El Caballete
Ro Ro
Punta del la Peña de Arena
Q.R
Q.G
Fl(4)G.11s3M
No14
Fl(2)R.7s
WGS Shifts
0'·07N 0'·08E
Depths in metres
Fl(2+1)G.10s
No12
Fl.R.5s
No14
Fl(2)R.7s
Raos Dock
No11
Oil Terminal
Fl(4)G.11s
No13
No17
Fl(2+1)G.10s
No18
Fl(4)R.11s
Ldg Lts 235·5°
Bdg
Iso.2s
Oc.5s
Airport
Marina del Cantábrico
CH
No19
Fl(4)G.11s

MINOR HARBOUR BETWEEN SANTANDER AND RIBADESELLA

SAN VICENTE DE LA BARQUERA, Cantabria. **43°23'·72N 04°23'·07W**. AC 1105; SC 127, 938, 4021; SHOM 6381, 6991. Tides see 9.23.16. Fishing hbr with good shelter in large shallow estuary, access HW±3; but HW±1 is advised if there is any swell at the entrance. Beware shallow bar and tidal streams 3-4kn. Appr on 225° to enter between W bkwtr (Isla Peña Menor) to stbd and hd of training wall to port. Beyond hotel and ☆ FG on post among pine trees keep to the NW bank; drying areas to the SE have encroached on the chan.
Pta de la Silla (3ca WSW of W bkwtr hd), Oc 3·5s 42m 13M; Horn Mo (V) 30s. Hbr lts see 9.23.3. Conspic beach E of hbr ent.
AB on fish quay is possible or ⚓ near ship mooring buoy close to root of trng wall. Moorings by the rebuilt bridge and castle are awkward and subject to traffic noise H24.
HM ☎ (942) 710004, 📠 712105; CG 900 202 202; Met 232405; Dr 712450; Police 710288. **Facilities**: Fish quay FW, ME, C, SM, D pump is for FVs only. **Town:** 🛒, R, Bar, P & D (cans), Ⓑ, ✉; ✈ (Santander 62km). www.sanvicentedelabarquera.org

9.23.17 RIBADESELLA

Asturias 43°32'·78N 05°40'·26W ❁❁❁◊◊◊✿✿✿

CHARTS AC 1105, 1150; SC 127, 403, 4031; SHOM 6381, 6691

TIDES
Standard Port PTE DE GRAVE (⟵); Zone –0100

Times				Height (metres)			
High Water		Low Water		MHWS	MHWN	MLWN	MLWS
0000	0600	0500	1200	5·4	4·4	2·1	1·0
1200	1800	1700	2400				
Differences RIBADESELLA							
+0005	–0020	+0020	–0020	–1·4	–1·3	–0·6	–0·4

SHELTER Good. AB, clear of FVs, on the NE/E quays in 2-3m, well N of the low bridge; fender board needed if berthing on piles. Little or no space to ⚓. A NCM bcn, Q, marks new marina bkwtr, probably W bank below the bridge; no further info available.

NAVIGATION WPT 43°28'·74N 05°04'·06W, 169°/6ca to quay hd (Pta del Caballo). Bajo Serropio, 7ca NNE of ent, breaks in heavy seas. Easy appr from about HW–1 to HW, but do not attempt in strong onshore winds when seas and swell break on the bar. Depths on the bar reported as 2m, but less after NW gales. Keep 25m off the promenade all the way up to town; dries to stbd.

LIGHTS AND MARKS To E of hbr ent smooth, dark, steep cliffs and a chapel are distinctive. To the W a wide beach is easily identified. Somos lt ho, Fl (2+1) 12s, is 8ca WNW of hbr.

R/T VHF Ch 09 occas.

TELEPHONE (Dial code 985) HM 86 02 07, 📠 86 00 43.

FACILITIES Slip, D & P (cans), ME, CH, El, ⚒, Ⓔ, ⊡. YC. **Town:** 🛒, R, Bar, ✉, Ⓑ, ⇌; ✈ Oviedo (78 km). Tourist office 86 02 55.

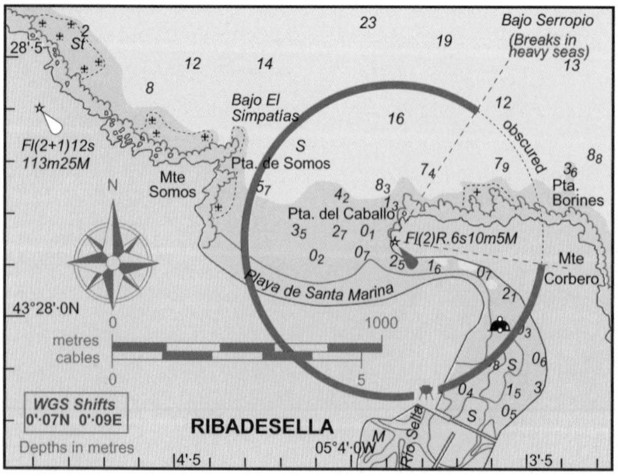
Bajo Serropio
(Breaks in heavy seas)
Bajo El Simpatías
Fl(2+1)12s 113m25M
Mte Somos
Pta. de Somos
obscured
Pta. Borines
Pta. del Caballo
Fl(2)R.6s10m5M
Mte Corbero
Playa de Santa Marina
43°28'·0N
metres
cables
1000
WGS Shifts
0'·07N 0'·09E
RIBADESELLA
Depths in metres
Río Sella
05°4'·0W
4'·5
3'·5

9.23.18 GIJÓN

Asturias **43°32'·78N 05°40'·26W** ❁❁❁◊◊◊✿✿✿

CHARTS AC 1105, 1108, 1153, 1154; SC 127, 404A, 4042; SHOM 6381, 5009

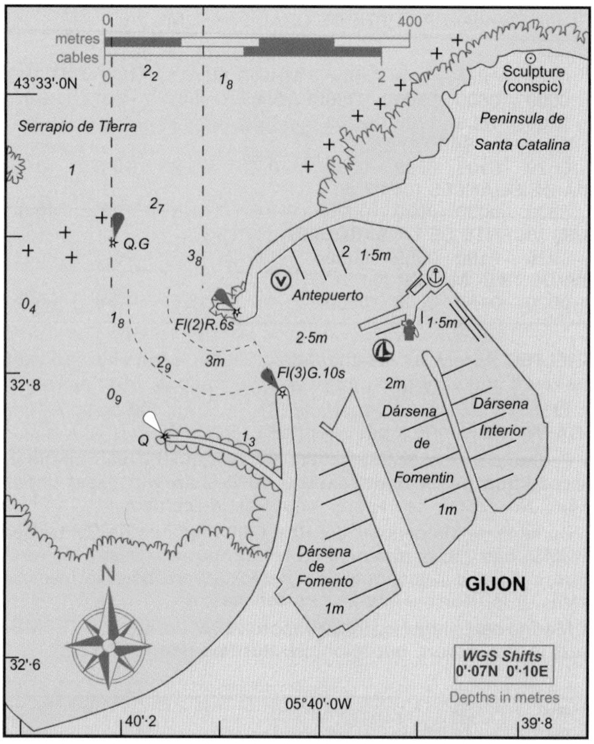
metres
cables
400
43°33'·0N
Sculpture (conspic)
Peninsula de Santa Catalina
Serrapio de Tierra
Q.G
Fl(2)R.6s
Antepuerto
1·5m
2·5m
Fl(3)G.10s
3m
32'·8
Q
Dársena de Fomentin
Dársena Interior
Dársena de Fomento
GIJON
WGS Shifts
0'·07N 0'·10E
Depths in metres
32'·6
05°40'·0W
40'·2
39'·8

TIDES
Standard Port PTE DE GRAVE (⟵); ML 2·3

Times				Height (metres)			
High Water		Low Water		MHWS	MHWN	MLWN	MLWS
0000	0600	0500	1200	5·4	4·4	2·1	1·0
1200	1800	1700	2400				
Differences GIJON							
–0005	–0030	+0010	–0030	–1·0	–1·4	–0·4	–0·7
LUANCO (05°47'W)							
–0010	–0035	+0005	–0035	–1·4	–1·3	–0·6	–0·4
AVILÉS (05°56'W)							
–0100	–0040	–0015	–0050	–1·2	–1·6	–0·5	–0·7
SAN ESTABAN DE PRAVIA (06°05'W)							
–0005	–0030	+0010	–0030	–1·4	–1·3	–0·6	–0·4

SHELTER Excellent in marina, access H24, (1·2 - 2·5m) in four basins. Berth initially dead ahead for check-in/fuel, then shift to Ⓥ finger berths in N Basin (Antepuerto).

NAVIGATION WPT 43°34'·09N 05°40'·25W, 180°/1·3M to marina ent, 1M SE of Puerto de El Musel, the vast conspic industrial port. The WPT is at the Y-junction of two mini-TSS chans, which lead in from NE and NNW; these are primarily for big ships. Banco Las Amosucas, marked by 4 cardinal lt buoys, lies within the Y. From the E yachts can approach more directly, passing N of Peninsula de Sta Catalina. In the near appr leave Sacramento G twr, QG, (marks drying reef) close to stbd.

LIGHTS AND MARKS Cabo de Torres, Fl (2) 10s, many nav/shore lts and conspic W tanks in El Musel are NW of the marina.

R/T Marina VHF Ch 09. Puerto de El Musel Ch 11, 12, **14**, 16.

TELEPHONE (Dial code 985) ⊖ & Met via marina.

FACILITIES **Marina** (*Puerto Local*) (750+120 Ⓥ), ☎ 34 45 43, 📠 35 99 17; P, D, Slip, C (10 ton),YC, ME, El, ⚒, CH, Ⓔ, ⊡.
Town: 🛒, R, Bar, ✉, Ⓑ, ⇌; ✈ Oviedo (26 km).

HARBOUR 6M SOUTH-WEST OF CABO PEÑAS

AVILÉS, Asturias. **43°35'·75N 05°57'·00W**. AC 1108, 1133; SC 126a, 405A, 4052; SHOM 7361, 5009. Tides: 9.23.18. A port of refuge, except in >F9 W/NW'lies, but also heavily industrialised and a FV hbr. The ent, S of Pta del Castillo lt ho (Oc WR 5s) and N of conspic white beach, is open to W/NW but well sheltered from N'lies. The well marked/lit ent chan runs ExS for 7ca then turns S for 2M. Possible AB or ⚓ in 1.5m on W side of chan at 43°33'·73N 05°55'·20W at the head of the river. Port VHF Ch **12** 16. HM ☎ (985) 541 111, paviles@paviles.com. YC at Salinas, but no yacht facilities per se; usual domestics and FV supplies.

9.23.19 CUDILLERO

Asturias **43°34'·02N 06°08'·71W** (W bkwtr hd)

CHARTS AC 1108; SC 126a, 934, 405, 405A; SHOM 5009.

TIDES Use San Estaban de Pravia, 3M W; see 9.23.18.

SHELTER Good in large modern basin, NW of hbr ent and village, but N'ly swell can make entry/exit difficult and can work into the basin. AB on pontoons, or ⚓ off them in 8-9m. FVs occupy the NW end of the basin. The old hbr, S of ent, is exposed to swell, but convenient for dinghies; a yacht can dry out on slip.

NAVIGATION WPT 43°34'·40N 06°08'·61W, 190°/4ca to W bkwtr hd. From the W keep at least 5ca offshore until clear of Piedras las Colinas, tall islets/reefs NW of ent. From the E appr with Pta Rebollera lt ho on initial bearing of 200°. The rocky ent, marked by Fl (3) R & Fl (3) G 9s lts, opens up only when close to. Follow W bkwtr round onto NW via narrow chan into basin.

LIGHTS AND MARKS Pta Rebollera lt ho is conspic W 8-sided twr.

R/T HM Ch 27.

TELEPHONE (Dial code 985) HM ☎ 591114, 📠 590693.

FACILITIES FW, D (gasoleo B) from FV quay, P (cans), ME, Slip, small commercial shipyard. **Village**: 5 mins by dinghy, 25 mins on foot; 🛒, R, Bar, ✉.

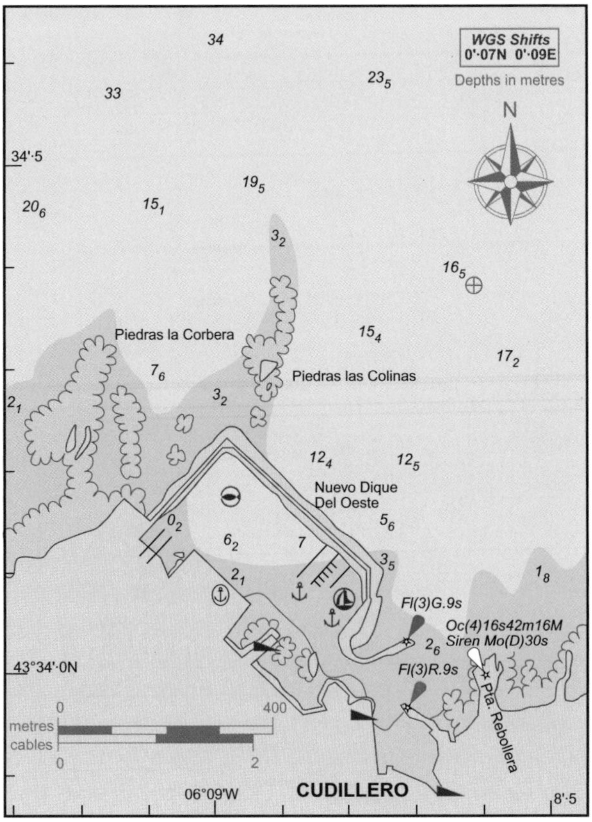
WGS Shifts
0'·07N 0'·09E
Depths in metres
N
34'·5
Piedras la Corbera
Piedras las Colinas
Nuevo Dique
Del Oeste
Fl(3)G.9s
Oc(4)16s42m16M
Siren Mo(D)30s
Fl(3)R.9s
Pta. Rebollera
43°34'·0N
metres
cables
06°09'W
CUDILLERO
8'·5

9.23.20 LUARCA

Asturias **43°33'·00N 06°32'·10W**

CHARTS AC 1108, 1133; SC 126a, 934, 4061; SHOM 6381, 5009

TIDES
Standard Port PTE DE GRAVE (⟷); Zone –0100

Times				**Height (metres)**			
High Water		Low Water		MHWS	MHWN	MLWN	MLWS
0000	0600	0500	1200	5·4	4·4	2·1	1·0
1200	1800	1700	2400				
Differences LUARCA							
+0010	–0015	+0025	–0015	–1·2	–1·1	–0·5	–0·3

SHELTER The outer hbr is protected from all but N'lies, but swell can intrude. Moor fore and aft to the E bkwtr, stern to steel 🔴s which are close together. Underwater obstns are said to lie up to 2m from bkwtr but in calm conditions it is possible to lie alongside the bkwtr. No room to ⚓. Narrow chan leads SE to inner hbr dredged 2m (prone to silting). Little chance of a berth; pontoons in SE corner are full of local craft; temp'y AB on NW side may be possible.

NAVIGATION See Horizontal Datum note on chartlet; do not rely on GPS for rock-hopping. WPT 43°33'·59N 06°32'·21W, 170°/6ca to E bkwtr hd. Appr on the ldg lts/marks 170° to clear rky shoals either side. The E bkwtr lt ho is conspic and almost in transit with the ldg marks.

LIGHTS AND MARKS See chartlet and 9.23.3. Cabo Busto, Fl (4) 20s, is 3M ENE of hbr ent. Pta Blanca (or Focicón), Oc (3) 15s, siren Mo (L) 30s, W □ tr and house on prominent headland 300m ENE of hbr ent; also conspic ✠. Ldg lts 170° are both on thin W pylons, R bands; not easy to see until close in.

R/T None.

TELEPHONE (Dial code 985) HM 640176/640083.

FACILITIES D from FV quay, P (cans), ME, CH, Slip, C (8 ton). **Town**: YC, 🛒, R, Bar, Ⓑ, ✉, ⇌.

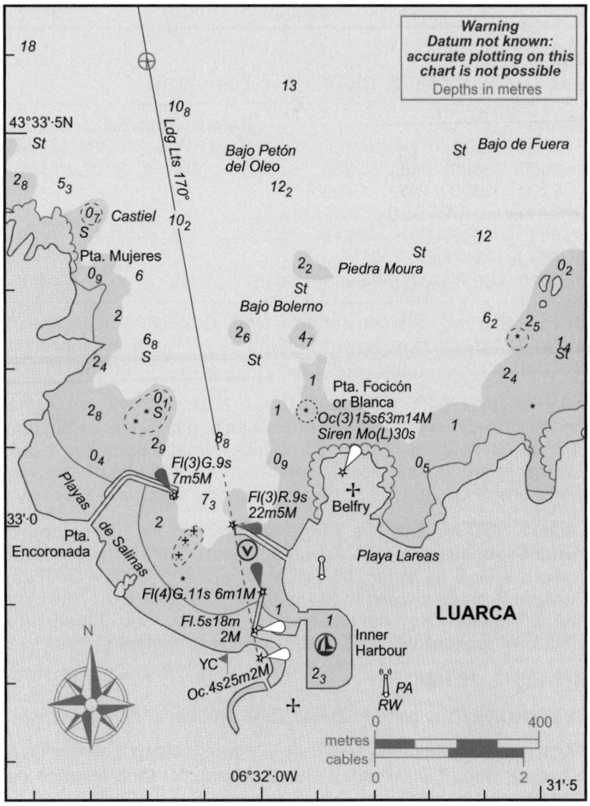
Warning
Datum not known:
accurate plotting on this
chart is not possible
Depths in metres
43°33'·5N
Ldg Lts 170°
Bajo Petón
del Oleo
Bajo de Fuera
Castiel
Pta. Mujeres
Piedra Moura
Bajo Bolerno
Pta. Focicón
or Blanca
Oc(3)15s63m14M
Siren Mo(L)30s
Fl(3)G.9s
7m5M
Fl(3)R.9s
22m5M
Belfry
Playas de Salinas
33'·0
Pta.
Encoronada
Playa Lareas
Fl(4)G.11s 6m1M
Fl.5s18m
2M
LUARCA
YC
Oc.4s25m2M
Inner
Harbour
PA
RW
metres
cables
06°32'·0W
31'·5

23

9.23.21 RÍA DE RIBADEO

Lugo **43°32'·50N 07°02'·10W**

CHARTS AC 1108, 1096; SC 126a, 932, 4071; SHOM 5009

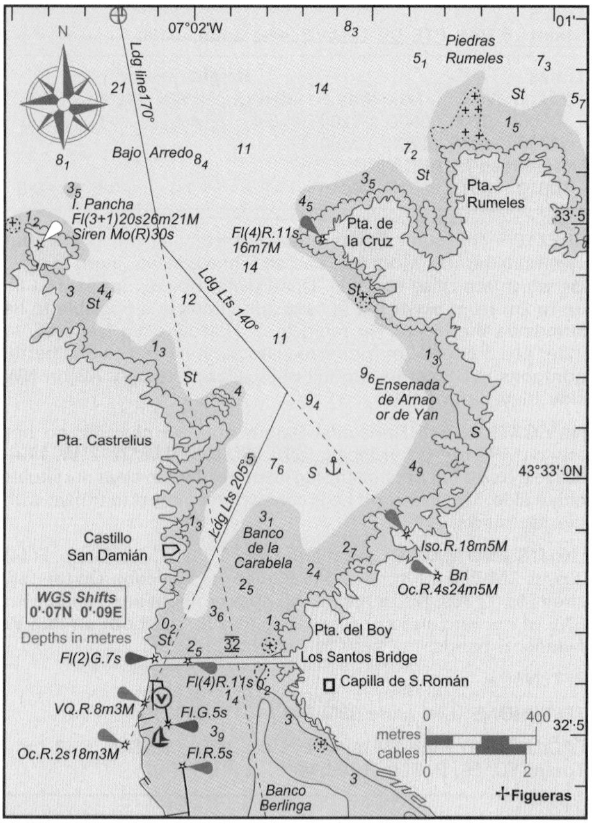
07°02'W
Ldg line170°
Bajo Arredo
I. Pancha
Fl(3+1)20s26m21M
Siren Mo(R)30s
Fl(4)R.11s
16m7M
Ldg Lts 140°
Piedras Rumeles
Pta. Rumeles
Pta. de la Cruz
Ensenada de Arnao or de Yan
Pta. Castrelius
Ldg Lts 205°
Castillo San Damián
Banco de la Carabela
Iso.R.18m5M
Bn
Oc.R.4s24m5M
WGS Shifts
0'·07N 0'·09E
Depths in metres
Fl(2)G.7s
Pta. del Boy
Los Santos Bridge
Capilla de S.Román
Fl(4)R.11s
VQ.R.8m3M
Fl.G.5s
Oc.R.2s18m3M
Fl.R.5s
Banco Berlinga
Figueras
metres
cables
01'
33'·5
43°33'·0N
32'·5

TIDES
Standard Port PTE DE GRAVE (⟵); Zone –0100

Times				Height (metres)			
High Water		Low Water		MHWS	MHWN	MLWN	MLWS
0000	0600	0500	1200	5·4	4·4	2·1	1·0
1200	1800	1700	2400				
Differences RIBADEO							
+0010	–0015	+0025	–0015	–1·3	–1·5	–0·7	–0·8
BURELA (43°40'N 07°20'W)							
+0010	–0015	+0025	–0015	–1·5	–1·5	–0·7	–0·6

SHELTER Good in basin (approx 2m). Ⓥ berths on inside of mole. Nearby ⚓s: close NW of 140° ldg lts; off Figueras (appr near HW due to shoals); and off Pta Castropol (8ca S of bridge) in 4m.

NAVIGATION WPT 43°33'·90N 07°02'·22W, 170°/4½ cables to intersect/track on the 140° ldg line. Thence pick-up inner ldg line 205° to W span of bridge (32m clnce) where tides run hard. Extensive drying sandbanks obstruct the E side of the ría, especially S of the bridge. Depths may be less than charted.

LIGHTS AND MARKS The 3 ldg lines are: Outer 170°, day only: Punta Castrelius ≠ Punta Castropol. Middle 140°: W twrs with R ◊; Iso R ≠ Oc R 4s. Inner 205°: W twrs with R ◊; VQ R ≠ Oc R 2s. Conspic R onion-shaped ✠ twr in town is almost ≠ the 205° ldg line. Bridge lts are on the pillars of the W span. See chartlet and 9.23.3. W lookout twr at E end of bridge is conspic.

R/T Ch 12, 16 H24.

TELEPHONE (Dial code 982) HM ☎/📠 110020; ⊖ & Met via HM.

FACILITIES **Marina** (30+ few visitors); fee is €0.07 x m² (ie LOA x beam); Slip, P & D (cans), ME, C (8 ton), ⚒; **Club Náutico de Ribadeo** ☎ 131444 R, Bar. **Town:** Gas, 🛒, R, Bar, Ⓑ, ✉, ⊡.

9.23.22 RÍA DE VIVERO

Lugo **43°41'·00N 07°36'·07W** (Cillero bkwtr)

CHARTS AC 1108, 1122; SC 126a, 931, 4082; SHOM 5009

TIDES
Standard Port PTE DE GRAVE (⟵); Zone –0100

Times				Height (metres)			
High Water		Low Water		MHWS	MHWN	MLWN	MLWS
0000	0600	0500	1200	5·4	4·4	2·1	1·0
1200	1800	1700	2400				
Differences RÍA DE VIVERO							
+0010	–0015	+0025	–0015	–1·4	–1·3	–0·6	–0·4
SANTA MARTA DE ORTIGUEIRA (07°51'W)							
–0020	0000	+0020	–0010	–1·3	–1·2	–0·6	–0·4

SHELTER Good, except in N'lies. Vivero marina (3m) is 6ca upriver with usual facilities. Keep clear of Cillero, a major FV hbr. ⚓ in E'lies inside Isla Insua d'Area, 1·3M NE of Cillero. In S-W winds ⚓ at the head of the ria off Playa de Covas in 6-7m.

NAVIGATION Easy ent, 7ca wide, between Isla Gabeira and Pta de Faro. WPT 43°43'·36N 07°35'·27W (mouth of the ria), 195°/2·4M to round Cillero bkwtr hd; thence 9ca upriver to marina.

LIGHTS AND MARKS See chartlet and 9.23.3. Mte Faro Juances is a distinctive conical peak (193m) close SE of Pta de Faro. Good radar returns all the way up the ria.

R/T Cillero Port VHF Ch 16.

TELEPHONE (Dial code 982) Cillero HM ☎ 560074, 📠 560410; Dr 561202; Police 562922; Tourist office 560879.

FACILITIES **Marina/YC:** ☎ 561014, D & P, CH, C (8 ton). **Cillero:** ME. **Vivero:** 🛒, R, Bar, Ⓑ, ✉, ⇌, Ⓗ (Burela 20km, ☎ 982-589900).

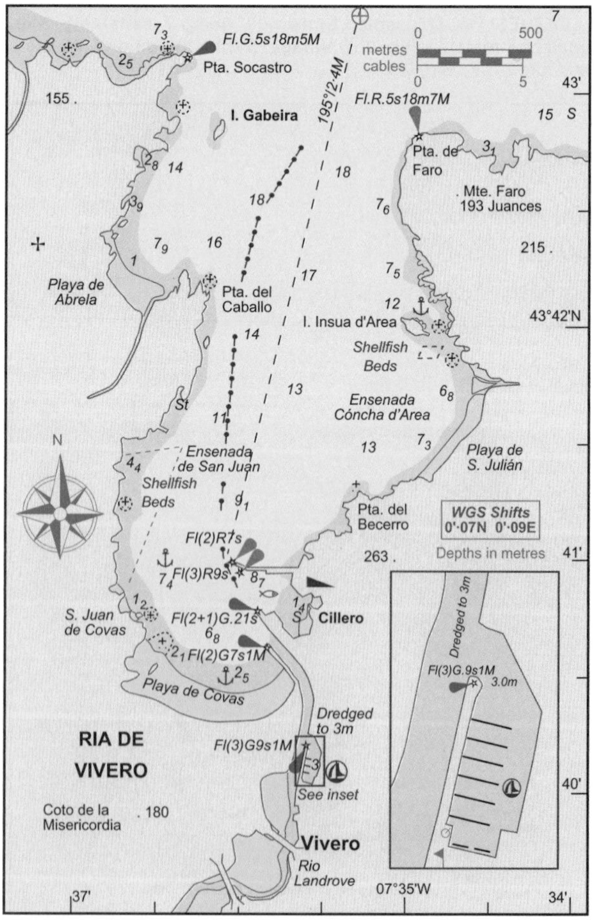
Fl.G.5s18m5M
Pta. Socastro
195°/2·4M
metres
cables
Fl.R.5s18m7M
I. Gabeira
Pta. de Faro
Mte. Faro 193 Juances
Playa de Abrela
Pta. del Caballo
I. Insua d'Area
Shellfish Beds
Ensenada Cóncha d'Area
Playa de S. Julián
Ensenada de San Juan
Shellfish Beds
Pta. del Becerro
WGS Shifts
0'·07N 0'·09E
Depths in metres
Fl(2)R7s
Fl(3)R9s
Cillero
S. Juan de Covas
Fl(2+1)G.21s
Fl(2)G7s1M
Playa de Covas
RIA DE VIVERO
Dredged to 3m
Fl(3)G9s1M
See inset
Coto de la Misericordia
Vivero
Rio Landrove
Fl(3)G.9s1M
3.0m
Dredged to 3m
07°35'W
37'
34'
43'
43°42'N
41'
40'

ADJACENT HARBOURS

RÍA DEL BARQUERO. 43°45'·00N 07°40'·50W. AC 1108, 1122; SC 931, 4082; SHOM 6383. Tides: 9.23.22. A delightful ría, but exposed to NE'lies. Small hbrs/⚓ on the W side at Bares and El Barquero (☎ 981-414002), shallow appr chan; and on the E side at Vicedo, a FV port close S of Pta del Castro. See 9.23.3 for lts at: Isla Coelleira (islet between this ría and Ría de Vivero); Pta de la Estaca de Barra; Pta de la Barra; Pta del Castro; and Vicedo.

RÍA DE SANTA MARTA DE ORTIGUEIRA. 43°42'·71N 07°50'·50W. AC 1108, 1111; SC 931, 4083; SHOM 6383. Tides: 9.23.22. WPT 43°45'·00N 07°50'·00W, 189°/2·3M to the Ría ent (after title), leading up to the eponymous town: AB, YC pontoon (2m), ⚓. Marina for shoal draft only. The appr over a shifting sandbar with little charted data is tricky, but a rewarding experience and an elegant town. Cariño (AC 1122) to the NW of the ría ent is less appealing due to a coaling wharf, but ⚓ in 6m within the bay, sheltered from all W'lies. Or, in E'lies, ⚓ off Espasante FV hbr, 2·3M ESE of Cariño. See 9.23.3 for lts at all three hbrs.

9.23.23 RÍA DE CEDEIRA

La Coruña **43°39'·50N 08°03'·80W** (⚓)

CHARTS AC 1108, 1111, 1122; SC 41A, 930; SHOM 5009, 3007

TIDES Interpolate between Santa Marta de Ortigueira (9.23.22) and El Ferrol (9.23.24). ML No data; Zone –0100.

SHELTER Very good; a pleasant refuge for yachts awaiting a fair wind to round Cabo Ortegal. ⚓ about 500m E of the modern FV port in 3-4m, excellent holding on sand. The E end of the bay shoals rapidly toward the drying mouth of Rio de Cedeira.

NAVIGATION WPT 43°41'·25N 08°05'·49W (8ca off N edge of chartlet), 155°/1·7M to Pta del Sarridal. From N keep at least 1M off Pta Candelaria until the ría opens. From the S a similar offing clears rks N/NW of Pta Chirlateira. 155° ldg line Pta Promontorio lt ho ≠ Pta del Sarridal. Abeam Pta Chirlateira with Pta Xian brg 161° track midway between Pta del Sarridal and Piedras de Media Mar. When the bkwtr hd bears 060° turn toward the anchorage.

LIGHTS AND MARKS Coastal lts: Pta Candelaria is 2·5M NE of the ⊕; Pta de la Frouseira is 5·8M SW. Piedras de Media Mar, W lt twr conspic in centre of ría, can be passed on either side. Other lts as chartlet and 9.23.3. A chapel is conspic 4ca N of the hbr.

R/T No VHF. MF *Cedeira Cofradia* 1800kHz, 2182.

TELEPHONE (Dial code 981) HM 480389; ⊖ & Met via HM.

FACILITIES Hbr: Slip, ME, El, ⚒, L just N of ⚓ symbol. **Town:** Ⓔ, D & P (cans), 🛒, R, Bar, Ⓑ, ✉, 🅿; ⇌ & ✈ La Coruña.

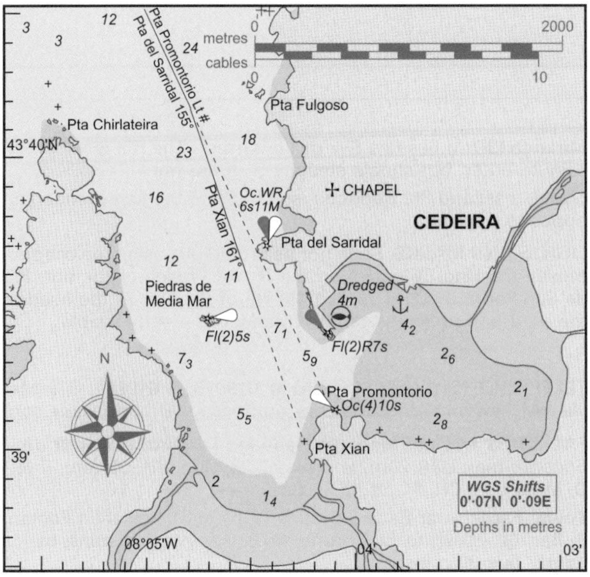
Pta Promontorio Lt # Pta del Sarridal 155°
metres
cables
2000
10
Pta Fulgoso
Pta Chirlateira
43°40'N
CHAPEL
Oc.WR 6s11M
CEDEIRA
Pta del Sarridal
Pta Xian 161°
Piedras de Media Mar
Dredged 4m
Fl(2)5s
Fl(2)R7s
Pta Promontorio Oc(4)10s
Pta Xian
39'
WGS Shifts 0'·07N 0'·09E
Depths in metres
08°05'W
04'
03'

9.23.24 FERROL

La Coruña 43°28'·62N 08°14'·50W (Curuxeiras)

CHARTS AC 1111, 1094, 1118, 1117; SC 412, 412A, 4122/3; SHOM 3007

TIDES
Standard Port PTE DE GRAVE (⟵); Zone –0100

Times				Height (metres)			
High Water		Low Water		MHWS	MHWN	MLWN	MLWS
0000	0600	0500	1200	5·4	4·4	2·1	1·0
1200	1800	1700	2400				
Differences FERROL							
–0045	–0100	–0010	–0105	–1·6	–1·4	–0·7	–0·4

SHELTER Good inside the narrow, but straightforward ent to ría. Ferrol is a naval and commercial port with limited yacht facilities. A small marina at La Graña has limited AB or ⚓/moor on a few 🅐s. Dársena de Curuxeiras is central, but AB in 2m on NE side is against stone walls and prone to ferry wash; the 3 pontoons at the head of this inlet are not available to visitors. Note that the 'El' of El Ferrol has now been dropped, as was 'Del Caudillo' many moons ago.

⚓s, from seaward, N shore of appr chan: Ensenada de Cariño (poor holding, good shelter except in S'lies); inshore of Pereiro PHM buoy in 5-6m. Inside the ría (see chartlet), S shore: Ensenada de el Baño and off Mugardos; on N shore off Pta de Caranza, ESE of chapel and near No 2 PHM buoy (off chartlet).

Other options: La Coruña where new, but already crowded, facilities have been provided. The peaceful Ría de Ares (9.23.25) and Ría de Betanzos (9.23.26), both with new marinas and about 9M from La Coruña; the latter has good bus links to La Coruña.

NAVIGATION WPT 48°26'·92N 08°19'·82W, 048°/0·9M to the 085·2° ldg line and in the white sector (042°-053°) of San Cristobal Dir lt. Chan is deep and adequately buoyed/lit, but be aware of strong tides and occasional squalls in the narrows. In bad weather avoid the outer banks (Tarracidos, Cabaleiro and Leixiñas) to the N and W.

LIGHTS AND MARKS C. Priorino Chico, Fl 5s, marks N side of ría ent. Ldg lts 085° to the narrows; front Fl 1·5s, rear Oc 4s; both W trs. Other lts, see chartlet and 9.23.3.

R/T Port Control *Ferrol Prácticos* Ch **14** (H24).

TELEPHONE (Code 981) HM 352945, 📠 353174; ⊖ & Met via HM.

FACILITIES Marina Terramar at La Graña (approx 50), Slip, ME, P & D (cans), El, C (1·5 ton), ⚒; bus every ½hr to the city (20 mins); **Club Náutico. Curuxeiras** ☎ 321594; Slip, FW, D, P (cans), ME, El, C (8 ton). **City** all facilities.

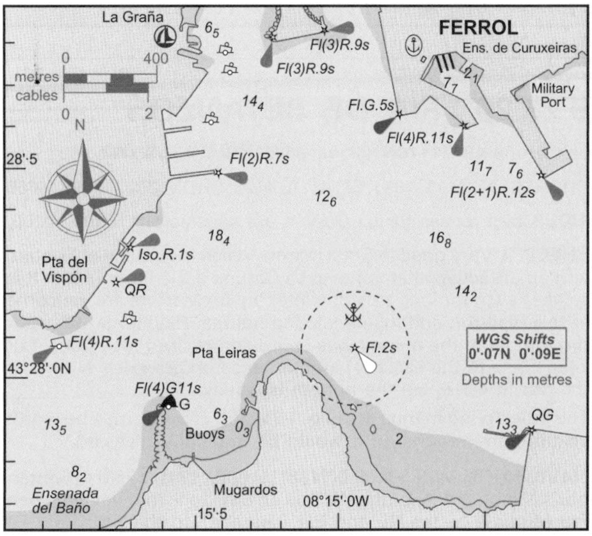
La Graña
FERROL
Fl(3)R.9s
Fl(3)R.9s
Ens. de Curuxeiras
metres
cables
400
Military Port
Fl.G.5s
Fl(4)R.11s
28'·5
Fl(2)R.7s
Fl(2+1)R.12s
Iso.R.1s
Pta del Vispón
QR
Fl(4)R.11s
Pta Leiras
Fl.2s
WGS Shifts 0'·07N 0'·09E
Depths in metres
43°28'·0N
Fl(4)G11s
G
QG
Buoys
Ensenada del Baño
Mugardos
08°15'·0W
15'·5

9.23.25 RÍA DE ARES

Marina **43°25'·34N 08°14'·38W** ❂❂❂◊✿✿✿

CHARTS AC 1111, 1094; SC 412A, 4125; SHOM 3007, 7598, 6665

TIDES Differences for La Coruña are satisfactory. Zone –0100.

SHELTER Good in the marina/fishing hbr at the W end of the 1M wide, sheltered bay (Ensenada de Ares), but the ría is exposed to strong NW'lies and swell. 4 pontoons in 2m for yachts max LOA 12m; FVs berth inside E mole. ⚓ NE of the hbr in 3-5m, good holding on muddy sand. The ambience is peaceful and relaxed. The ría extends E past Redes toward Puentedeume, where there is day ⚓ in shoaling waters, clear of mussel beds.

NAVIGATION WPT 43°24'·90N 08°14'·04W, 342°/0·5M to hbr's Emole hd. The appr is simple, but keep clear of Bajo La Miranda (3·7m; 1·5M WSW of the hbr) and adjacent islets off Pta Miranda. In the near approach avoid Bajo Cagarroso (2·1m), 5 cables SSW of the E mole head. To the W of Ares there are two Measured miles with transit bcns, should you need to check your speedo.

LIGHTS AND MARKS As on the chartlet. Cabo Prioriño Chico is 5M WNW. Sada/Fontan marina/hbr is 4M S; see 9.23.26. A conspic rounded hill (Monte de San Miguel de Breamo) with chapel on top is 2·7M ESE of the hbr.

R/T VHF Ch 09.

TELEPHONE (Dial code 981) **Club Náutico Ría de Ares** 111012; English spoken, ask for Marco. ⊖ & Met via Club, which is welcoming. secretaria@nauticoares.com www.nauticoares.com

FACILITIES Marina. ☎/📠 as above. (205 + 16 Ⓥ; max LOA 12m on fingers, mostly on W side of pontoon No 4 outer end); €2.56, C (8 ton), BH, El, ME, Slip, R, Bar.

Town: R, Bar, 🛒, ◙, Ⓑ, ✉; Bus to Ferrol.

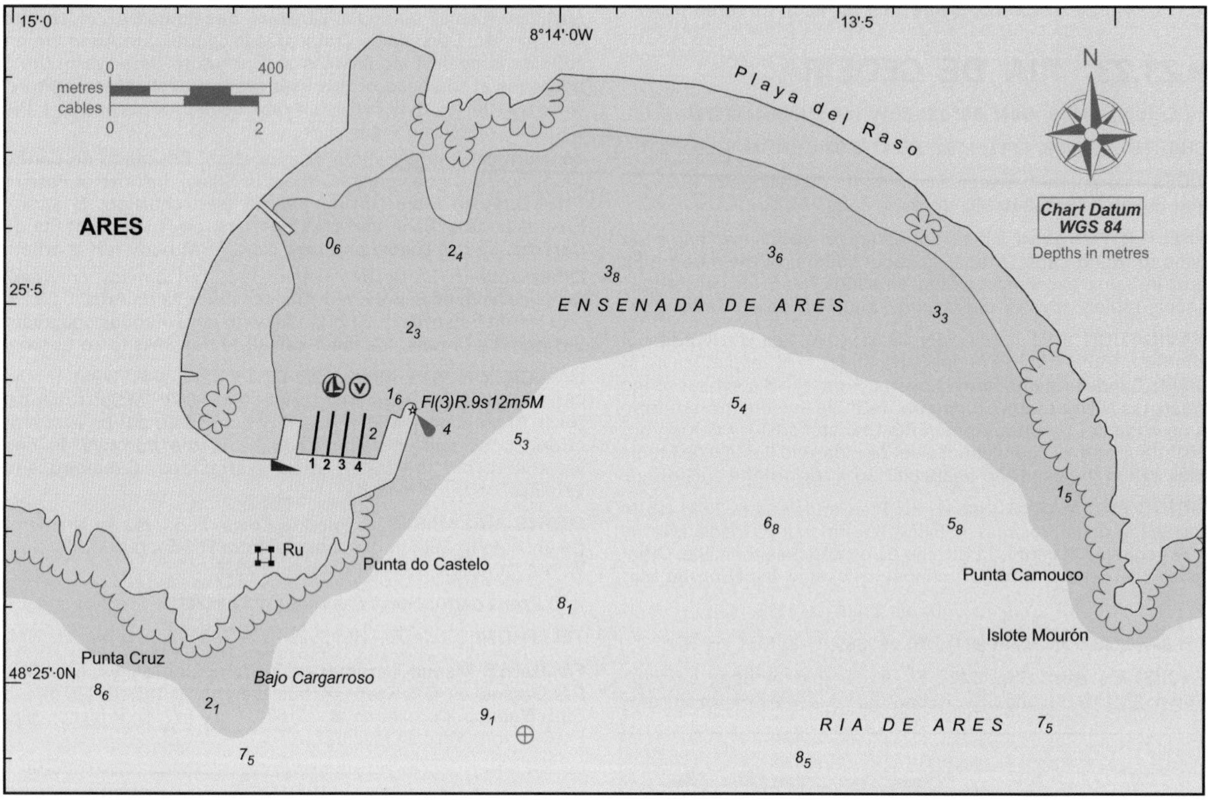
15'·0
8°14'·0W
13'·5
N
Playa del Raso
metres
cables
0
400
0
2
ARES
25'·5
ENSENADA DE ARES
Chart Datum WGS 84
Depths in metres
Fl(3)R.9s12m5M
1 2 3 4
Ru
Punta do Castelo
Punta Camouco
Islote Mourón
Punta Cruz
48°25'·0N
Bajo Cargarroso
RIA DE ARES

9.23.26 RÍA DE BETANZOS

La Coruña **43°21'·70N 08°14'·35W** ❂❂❂◊◊◊✿✿✿

CHARTS AC 1111, 1094; SC 412A, 4125; SHOM 3007, 7598, 6665

TIDES Differences for La Coruña are satisfactory. Zone –0100.

SHELTER Very good in Sada marina which is actually at Fontan, and an attractive alternative to La Coruña if the latter is full. It is a safe haven for long stay or winter lay-up; visitors are welcome at this well-run and fully-equipped marina. Pulgueira rock near the middle of the marina was being demolished May 2004, but keep close to the eastern hammerheads on arrival. ⚓ N or E of the hbr in 4-7m, but the bottom is weedy.

The little drying marina at Miño, 1·3M ESE of Sada, may be worth visiting; any reports on it would be gratefully received.

NAVIGATION WPT 43°24'·00N 08°15'·00W, 171°/2·26M to Fontan hbr's N mole hd. Appr the WPT on an ESE track midway between Pta Miranda to the NE and Pta Redonda* to the SW; Bajo La Miranda (3·7m) lies 6ca SW of the former. The Ria is wide and easy to enter, but shoals steadily S of the hbr.

*Note: a second Pta Redonda is 4M ESE of the first mentioned, opposite Fontan.

LIGHTS AND MARKS Sada hbr lts proliferate, as on the chartlet, mostly marking FV quays on the N and W side of the hbr. Pta de San Pedro, Fl (2) R 7s, is 1·4M NE of the hbr. At the head of the ría a bridge across the Río Mandeo is clearly visible.

R/T VHF Ch 09.

TELEPHONE (Dial code 981) HM ☎ 619015, 📠 619287; ⊖ & Met via HM. www.marinasada.com marinasada@marinasada.com

FACILITIES Marina: Manager Santiago Ferreiro; (550 + Ⓥ on fingers), max LOA 20m; approx €2.38, Slip, BH (35 ton), P & D, ME, El, Ⓔ, CH, ⚒, 🛒, ◙, R, Bar.

Town: Facilities at Sada (10 mins walk) are better than Fontan: R, Bar, Ⓑ, ✉, Ⓗ; to La Coruña, ⇌ & ✈; by taxi 20 mins, by hourly bus 30 mins.

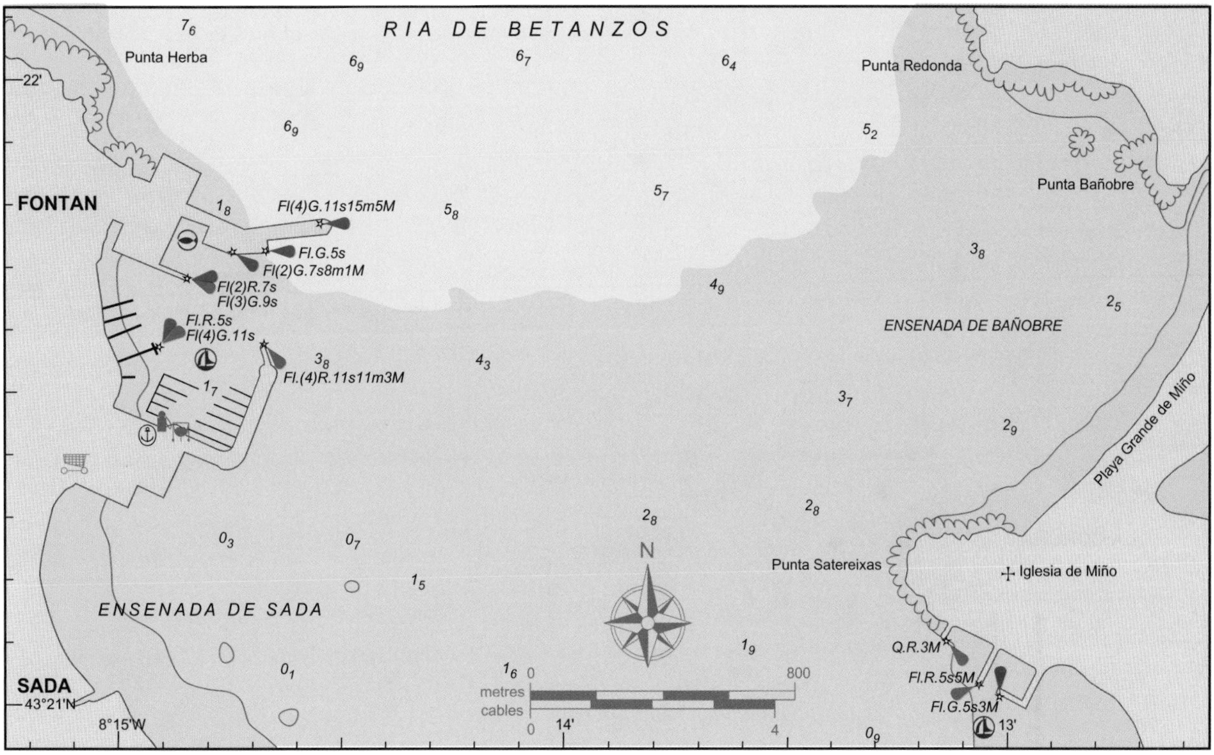
RIA DE BETANZOS
Punta Herba
Punta Redonda
FONTAN
Fl(4)G.11s15m5M
Fl.G.5s
Fl(2)G.7s8m1M
Fl(2)R.7s
Fl(3)G.9s
Fl.R.5s
Fl(4)G.11s
Fl.(4)R.11s11m3M
Punta Bañobre
ENSENADA DE BAÑOBRE
Playa Grande de Miño
Punta Satereixas
Iglesia de Miño
ENSENADA DE SADA
SADA
43°21'N
8°15'W
Q.R.3M
Fl.R.5s5M
Fl.G.5s3M
metres
cables
800
14'
13'
22'

9.23.27 LA CORUÑA

La Coruña **43°22'·13N 08°23'·10W** (marina) ❂❂❂◊◊◊✿✿✿

CHARTS AC 1111, 1094, 1110; SC 412, 412A, 4126; SHOM 3007, 7598, 6665

TIDES

Standard Port PTE DE GRAVE (⟵); Zone –0100

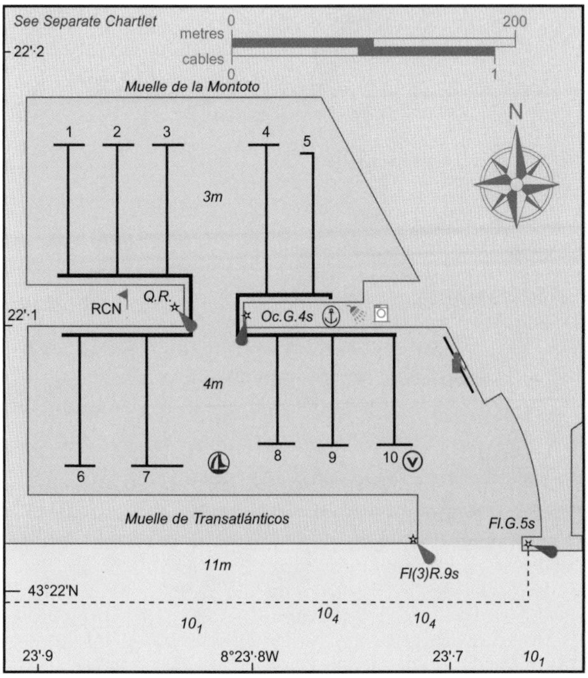
See Separate Chartlet
metres
cables
200
22'·2
Muelle de la Montoto
N
3m
RCN
Q.R.
Oc.G.4s
22'·1
4m
Muelle de Transatlánticos
Fl.G.5s
11m
Fl(3)R.9s
43°22'N
23'·9
8°23'·8W
23'·7

Times				Height (metres)			
High Water		Low Water		MHWS	MHWN	MLWN	MLWS
0000	0600	0500	1200	5·4	4·4	2·1	1·0
1200	1800	1700	2400				
Differences LA CORUÑA							
–0110	–0050	–0030	–0100	–1·6	–1·6	–0·6	–0·5

SHELTER Dársena de la Marina, a new marina in 5m is central, well sheltered and has all facilities. Close N of Cas S. Anton, the former marinas: Real Club Náutico (RCN; 2 S'ly pontoons) and Sporting Club Casino (SCS; 2 N'ly pontoons) are now, or soon will be, dinghy/keelboat (<6m) centres only, since the leases have expired. The pontoons are in a poor state; no Ⓥ or Ⓐs. ⚓ further ESE on possible foul ground. See also 9.23.25 & 9.23.26.

NAVIGATION WPT 43°23'·28N 08°22'·03W, 191°/1·35M to head of Dique de Abrigo, Fl G 5s. Note the 108·5° & 182° ldg lines meet at this WPT. Avoid Banco Yacentes, about 1M NW of WPT, between the ldg lines (off chartlet). Speed limit 3kn in hbr.

LIGHTS AND MARKS Conspic marks: Torre de Hércules lt ho; 5·3M SW of which is power stn chy (218m); twin white twrs (85m, R lts) of Hbr Control at root of Dique de Abrigo. Storm signals are displayed from Cas de San Antón. See chartlet and 9.23.3.

R/T Marina Ch 09. Port Control *Dársena Radio Torre Hércules* Ch 12. VTS Ch 13.

TELEPHONE (Dial code 981) Dársena de la Marina ☎ 914142, 📠 914144, www.darsenacoruna.com; info@darsenacoruna.com Real Club Náutico ☎ 203265; 📠 203008; Sporting Club (Casino) ☎ 209007, 📠 213953; ⊖ & Met via YCs; Port HM 226001, 📠 205862; Dr 287477; Ⓗ 277905.

FACILITIES **Dársena de la Marina**, 350 inc 40 Ⓥ, €2.35 (€1.35 1 Oct-30 Apr), AB (max LOA 30m), ⊡, P, D, BH (32 ton), ME, El, ⚒, Ⓔ, CH, SM, YC. The RCN clubhouse (more social than nautical) requires semi-formal dress (jacket/tie), esp in the evenings.
Former marinas (N of Cas S. Anton): P, Slip, C (1 ton), ⊡.
City: All amenities; Bus, ⇌, ✈ (Santiago, 72km). La Coruña is A Coruña in the Gallego tongue and on signposts; also known as the 'Crystal City' due to the windowed balconies (*solanas*) visible from the marina. It is a handsome and exuberant city.

23

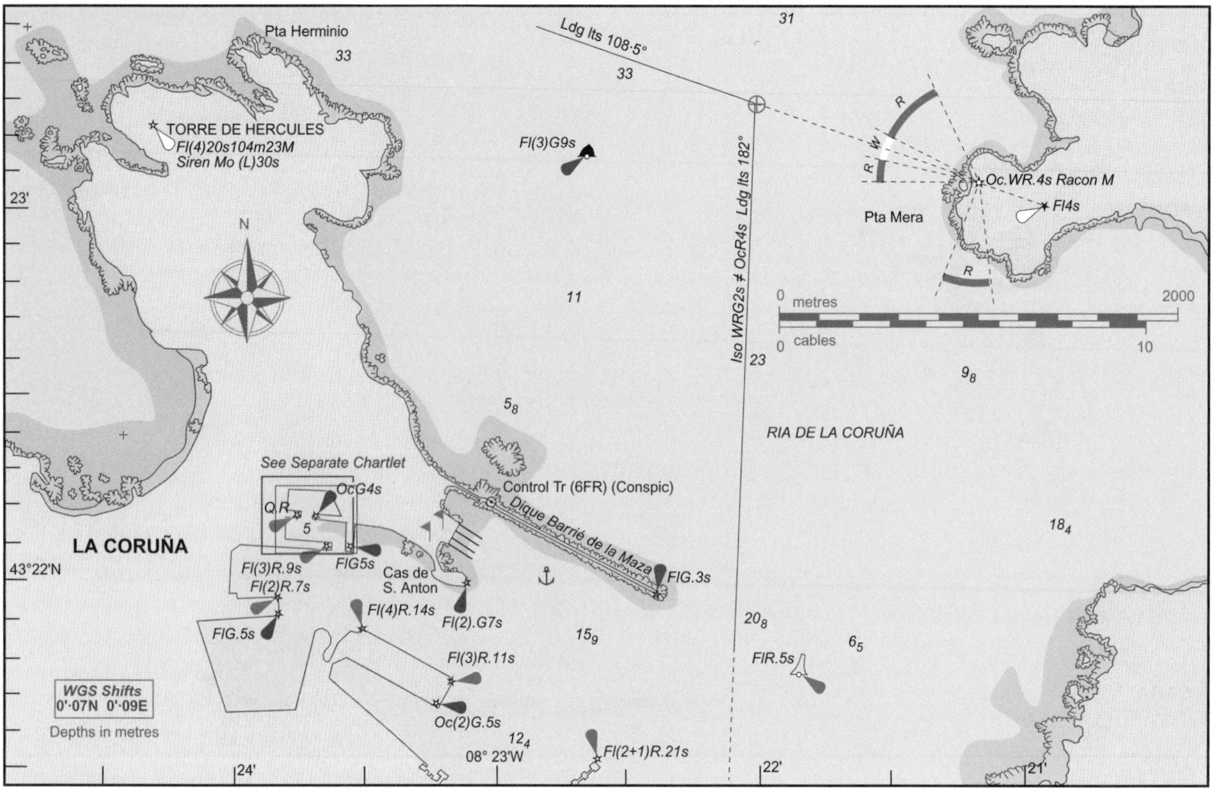
Pta Herminio
Ldg lts 108·5°
TORRE DE HERCULES
Fl(4)20s104m23M
Siren Mo (L)30s
Fl(3)G9s
Oc.WR.4s Racon M
Fl4s
Pta Mera
Iso WRG2s ≠ OcR4s Ldg lts 182°
metres
cables
RIA DE LA CORUÑA
See Separate Chartlet
OcG4s
Q.R
Control Tr (6FR) (Conspic)
Dique Barrié de la Maza
LA CORUÑA
43°22'N
Fl(3)R.9s
Fl(2)R.7s
FlG5s
Cas de S. Anton
FlG.3s
Fl(4)R.14s
Fl(2).G7s
FlG.5s
Fl(3)R.11s
FlR.5s
WGS Shifts
0'·07N 0'·09E
Depths in metres
Oc(2)G.5s
08° 23'W
Fl(2+1)R.21s
24'
22'
21'
23'

9.23.28 RÍA DE CORME Y LAGE

La Coruña. Corme **43°15'·69N 08°57'·68W**
Lage **43°13'·42N 08°59'·85W**

CHARTS AC 3633, 1111, 1113; SC 928, 4131; SHOM 3007

TIDES
Standard Port PTE DE GRAVE (⟵); Zone –0100

Times				Height (metres)			
High Water		Low Water		MHWS	MHWN	MLWN	MLWS
0000	0600	0500	1200	5·4	4·4	2·1	1·0
1200	1800	1700	2400				
Differences RÍA DE CORME							
–0025	–0005	+0015	–0015	–1·7	–1·6	–0·6	–0·5

SHELTER Corme is well sheltered from N and E winds; Lage (Laxe) from W and S. Both may be affected by swell. Corme's pier has been extended to enlarge the ⚓age. At Lage a 25m pontoon for yachts extends ESE from the S mole head; berth bows-in. Space may be available, or raft up, on the piers at both hbrs, among FVs; or ⚓ close in to the piers, good holding on sand.

NAVIGATION WPT 43°15'·39N 09°00'·52W, 081°/2·1M to Corme pierhd; 166°/2.0M to Lage pierhd. In bad weather follow the ldg lines to Corme to avoid Bajo de La Averia (5·6m). The ría is over 2M wide and the appr is straightforward, but there are rocks off Pta del Roncudo and Pta de Lage. Spanish chart 4131 (Jul 2003) shows many depths less than charted in apprs and in the ría.

LIGHTS AND MARKS All lts and ldg lines as on the chartlet.

R/T VHF Ch 09.

TELEPHONE (Dial code 981). CN de Lage ☏ 728255.

FACILITIES Corme: C (4 ton), Slip. **Lage:** C (16 ton), AC, FW on pontoon; (both hbrs): D & P (cans), ME. **Both villages** are small, but with most domestic essentials: 🛒, R, Bar, ✉, Ⓑ; Bus to La Coruña, ✈ Santiago. CN de Lage: nauticolaxe@hotmail.com

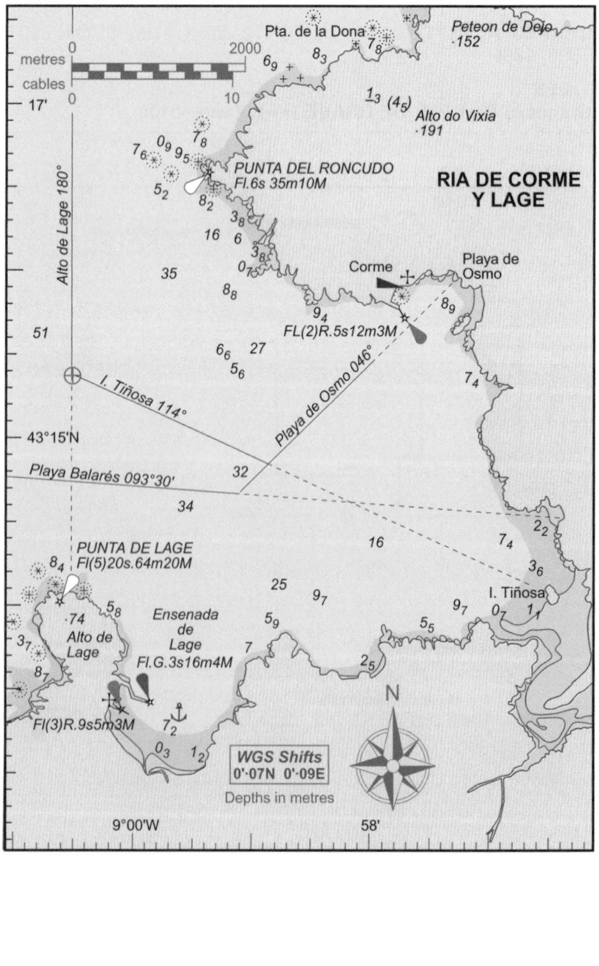
Pta. de la Dona
Peteon de Dejo ·152
metres
cables
17'
Alto do Vixia ·191
PUNTA DEL RONCUDO
Fl.6s 35m10M
RIA DE CORME Y LAGE
Alto de Lage 180°
Corme
Playa de Osmo
FL(2)R.5s12m3M
I. Tiñosa 114°
Playa de Osmo 046°
43°15'N
Playa Balarés 093°30'
PUNTA DE LAGE
Fl(5)20s.64m20M
I. Tiñosa
Alto de Lage
Ensenada de Lage
Fl.G.3s16m4M
Fl(3)R.9s5m3M
WGS Shifts
0'·07N 0'·09E
Depths in metres
9°00'W
58'

9.23.29 RÍA DE CAMARIÑAS

La Coruña **43°07'·67N 09°10'·82W** (CN Camariñas)
❁❁❁⚓⚓✿✿✿

CHARTS AC 1111, 3633, 1113; SC 928, 927, 4141; SHOM 3007

TIDES
Standard Port PTE DE GRAVE (⟵); Zone –0100

Times				Height (metres)			
High Water		Low Water		MHWS	MHWN	MLWN	MLWS
0000	0600	0500	1200	5·4	4·4	2·1	1·0
1200	1800	1700	2400				
Differences RÍA DE CAMARIÑAS							
–0115	–0055	0000	–0105	–1·6	–1·6	–0·6	–0·5

SHELTER Good in Camariñas on 2 YC pontoons, except in E/NE'lies; or ⚓ to S, inside bkwtr. Mugia (43°06'·40N 09°12'·66W) is solely a FV hbr, sheltered from all but E/SE'lies; ⚓ outside or in lee of bkwtr. Possible temp'y AB with fender board.

NAVIGATION WPT 43°07'·31N 09°12'·52W, 108·5°/1·1M then 030°/0·6M to Camariñas bkwtr; or 185°/0·9M to Mugia bkwtr. The outer ldg lines (108·5° and 081°) intersect at the WPT; they must be followed, especially from the N to avoid Las Quebrantes shoal (0·1) on which sea breaks. The N'ly appr is unlit. From SW, appr on 081° ldg lts, as chartlet.

LIGHTS AND MARKS C. Villano, Fl (2) 15s, ***Racon M***, with 23 conspic wind turbines close SE, is 2·2M N of ent to ría. Pta de la Barca, Oc 4s 13m 7M, marks the SW side of the ría. Pta de Lago lt ≠ bcn leads 108·5° into the ría. See chartlet and 9.23.3.

R/T Camariñas YC VHF Ch 09.

TELEPHONE (Dial code 981) CNC 736002; ⊜ & Met via CNC; Mugia HM 742030.

FACILITIES Club Náutico Camariñas (60 + Ⓥ), ☎ 737130, 📠 736325; F&A, €6.97. **Services** (both hbrs): Slip, D & P (cans), ME, C, ⚒. **Villages:** 🛒, R, Bar, ✉, Ⓑ; Bus to La Coruña, ✈ Santiago de Compostela.

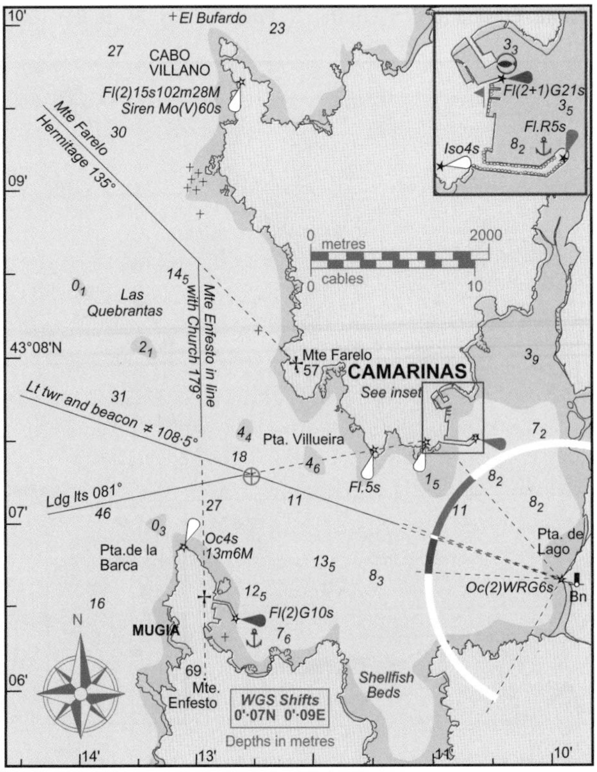
El Bufardo
CABO VILLANO
Fl(2)15s102m28M
Siren Mo(V)60s
Mte Farelo Hermitage 135°
Las Quebrantas
Mte Enfesto in line with Church 179°
Lt twr and beacon ≠ 108·5°
Mte Farelo
CAMARINAS
See inset
Pta. Villueira
Fl.5s
Ldg lts 081°
Oc4s 13m6M
Pta.de la Barca
Fl(2)G10s
MUGIA
Mte. Enfesto
WGS Shifts 0'·07N 0'·09E
Depths in metres
Shellfish Beds
Pta. de Lago
Oc(2)WRG6s
Bn
Fl(2+1)G21s
Fl.R5s
Iso4s
metres
cables
43°08'N

MINOR HARBOURS IN SENO DE CORCUBIÓN

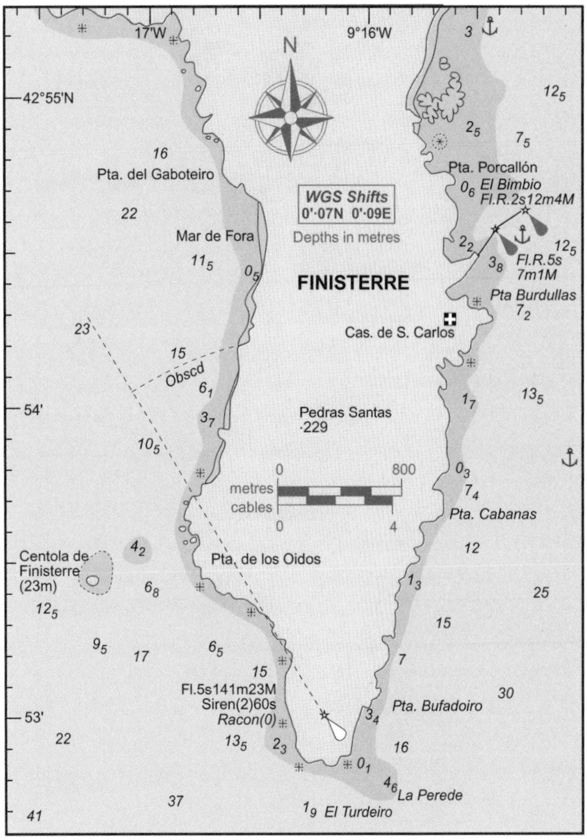
9°16'W
42°55'N
Pta. del Gaboteiro
WGS Shifts 0'·07N 0'·09E
Depths in metres
Pta. Porcallón
El Bimbio Fl.R.2s12m4M
Mar de Fora
Fl.R.5s 7m1M
FINISTERRE
Pta Burdullas
Cas. de S. Carlos
Obscd
Pedras Santas ·229
metres
cables
Pta. Cabanas
Centola de Finisterre (23m)
Pta. de los Oidos
Fl.5s141m23M
Siren(2)60s
Racon(O)
Pta. Bufadoiro
La Perede
El Turdeiro

FINISTERRE. 42°54'·64N 09°15'·28W. AC 1111, 3764; SC 927, 9270, 4142. Tides: 9.23.29. Finisterre (the end of the Ancient World) appeals by virtue of its name and imposing bulk. The hbr is usually full of small FVs, but in settled weather it is safe to ⚓ outside in 5-10m, either close S of the bkwtr or to the N off the Playa de Llagosteira. The touristy town has no yacht facilities.

Dense fog, which sometimes forms very quickly, is frequent on this coast. Approaching from the N, the 23m high pinnacle rock Centolo de Finisterre stands 9 cables WNW of the lt ho. 1M NW of it La Carraca with 2·1m over it is less obvious, therefore more dangerous. El Turdeiro (1·9m) is 300m due S of the cape, with a sprinkling of lesser rocks closer inshore where FVs cluster; keep well clear. The E side is mostly steep-to. It is worth walking 1·5M from the hbr to the granite lt ho for the views.

RÍA DE CORCUBIÓN. 42°56'·46N 09°10'·83W (see chartlet overleaf). AC 1111, 3764; SC 927, 9270, 4142. Tides: 9.23.29. A pleasant ría, well sheltered from the summer NE'lies, but open to S'lies. Three features south of the ría which are seen on the approach are: Lobeira Grande, a group of yellowish rocky islets with lt, Fl (3) 15s 16m 9M; Carrumeiro Grande, a single flat island with ldg bcn; and Carrumeiro Chico, a small rock with IDM bcn twr, Fl (2) 7s 6m 6M. It bears 162°/6ca from Cabo Cée lt ho, Fl (5) 13s 25m 7M, at the SW side of the ent to ría.
The simplest approach for yachts is to pass between Cabo Cée and Carrumeiro Chico on a NE'ly heading, thence straight up the ría on 342° for 1·5M, with Carrumeiro Grande bearing 162° astern, if this is found necessary. A night appr should present no great difficulties: the ría is 0·5M wide and of the 3 lts at its head, as on the chartlet, keep midway between Corcubión's Fl (2) R 8s and Fl (4) G 11s fine on the stbd bow.
At the head of the ría, ⚓ N of the charted anchorage clear of the commercial quays and mussel beds. Holding is variable. There are no yacht facilities. Corcubión is nearer and more attractive than Cée; both towns have the usual facilities and shops.

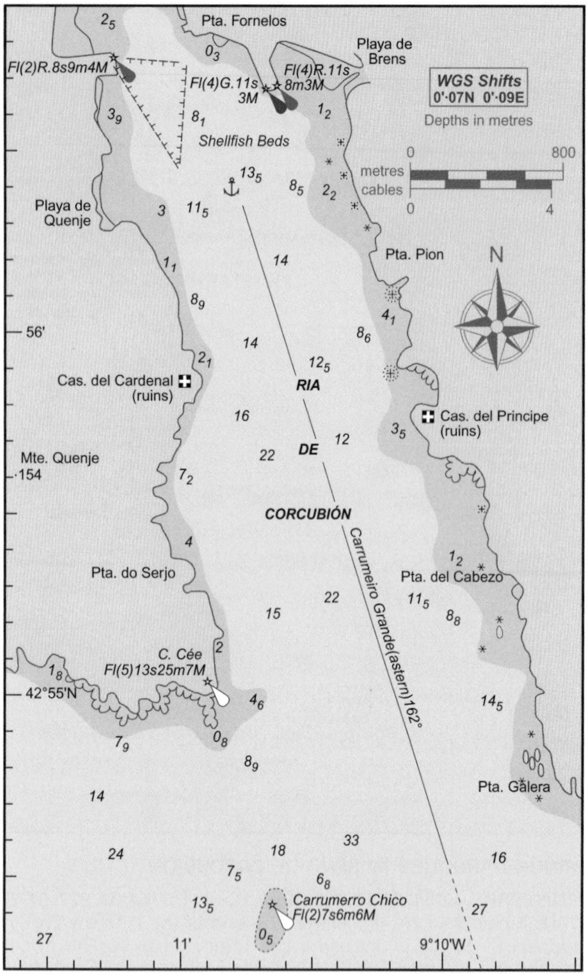
Pta. Fornelos
Playa de Brens
Fl(2)R.8s9m4M
Fl(4)G.11s 3M
Fl(4)R.11s 8m3M
WGS Shifts 0'·07N 0'·09E
Depths in metres
Shellfish Beds
metres 0 800
cables 0 4
Playa de Quenje
Pta. Pion
N
56'
Cas. del Cardenal (ruins)
RIA DE CORCUBIÓN
Cas. del Principe (ruins)
Mte. Quenje ·154
Carrumeiro Grande(astern)162°
Pta. do Serjo
Pta. del Cabezo
C. Cée Fl(5)13s25m7M
42°55'N
Pta. Gálera
Carrumerro Chico Fl(2)7s6m6M
11'
9°10'W

9.23.30 RÍA DE MUROS

La Coruña **42°42'·92N 09°04'·60W** (Entrance WPT)

CHARTS AC 1756; SC 415, 415A, 4151; SHOM 3007

TIDES

Standard Port LISBOA (⟶); Zone –0100

Times				Height (metres)			
High Water		Low Water		MHWS	MHWN	MLWN	MLWS
0500	1000	0300	0800	3·8	3·0	1·5	0·6
1700	2200	1500	2000				
Differences CORCUBION							
+0055	+0110	+0120	+0135	–0·5	–0·4	–0·3	–0·1
MUROS							
+0050	+0105	+0115	+0130	–0·3	–0·3	–0·2	–0·1

SHELTER Good at Muros (42°46'·71N 09°03'·25W), but the 2 pontoons in the inner hbr are full of locals. ⚓ off on weedy holding (2 or 3 shots may be needed) or at Ens de San Francisco. Noya, at the head of the ría, is only accessible to shoal draft. Portosín marina (3·5-8m) at 42°46'·02N 08°56'·79W is excellent and welcoming. El Son is a small FV hbr with no yacht facilities.

NAVIGATION WPT 42°42'·92N 09°04'·60W, 1·5M S of Pta Queixal lt and 2·3M WNW of Pta Focha lt, Fl 5s (off chartlet). From the N, the Canal de los Meixidos (between the mainland and Bajo de los Meixidos and Los Bruyos, where its least width is 1.1M) is usable with care in normal conditions. The ría is mostly deep and clear, but beware mussel rafts off the N shore.

LIGHTS AND MARKS Mte Louro is a conspic conical hill (239m) N of Pta Queixal. Isla Creba is a good mark NW of Portosin. Principal lts: Pta Queixal, C. Reburdino, Pta Cabeiro, Pta Focha.

R/T *Club Náutico Portosín* VHF Ch 09.

TELEPHONE (Dial code 981) HM Muros 826005; HM Portosin 820505; Marina Portosin 826140.

FACILITIES Muros: D (not near LW), P (cans), 🛒, R, Bar, Ⓑ, ✉; ≷ and ✈ Santiago de Compostela (40 km by bus via Noya). **CN Portosín marina** (200+ some Ⓥ), F&A €12.17, Slip, BH (32 ton), P, ME, El, C (3 ton), ⚒, R, Bar, ⊡; **Portosín**: CH, 🛒, R, Bar, ✉.

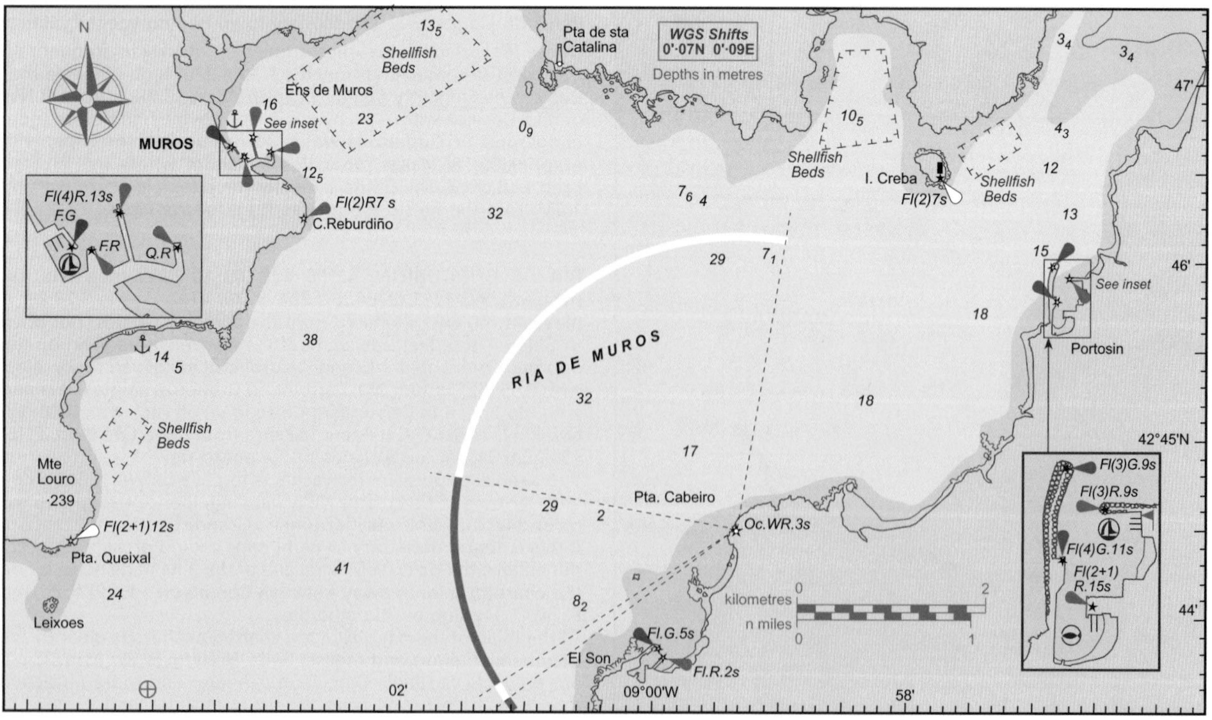
N
Shellfish Beds
Ens de Muros
See inset
MUROS
Pta de sta Catalina
WGS Shifts 0'·07N 0'·09E
Depths in metres
Fl(4)R.13s
F.G.
F.R
Q.R
Fl(2)R7 s
C.Reburdiño
I. Creba
Fl(2)7s
Portosin
RIA DE MUROS
Mte Louro ·239
Fl(2+1)12s
Pta. Queixal
Leixoes
Pta. Cabeiro
Oc.WR.3s
kilometres
n miles
Fl.G.5s
El Son
Fl.R.2s
02'
09°00'W
58'
47'
46'
42°45'N
44'
Fl(3)G.9s
Fl(3)R.9s
Fl(4)G.11s
Fl(2+1) R.15s

9.23.31 RÍA DE AROUSA

La Coruña (NW), Pontevedra (SE). ⊕ **42°26'·50N 08°59'·00W** ❀❀❀⛵⛵⛵✿✿✿

CHARTS AC 1734, 1764, 1762, 1755; SC 415, 415B/C, 4152, 4153.

TIDES

Standard Port LISBOA (⟶); ML 2·05; Zone –0100

Times				Height (metres)			
High Water		Low Water		MHWS	MHWN	MLWN	MLWS
0500	1000	0300	0800	3·8	3·0	1·5	0·6
1700	2200	1500	2000				
Differences VILLAGARCIA							
+0040	+0100	+0110	+0120	–0·3	–0·2	–0·2	–0·1

SHELTER Shelter can be found from most winds. Marinas (see insets) are at Santa Eugenia/Uxia and Caramiñal on the NW shore, Villagarcia at the NE corner and Piedras Negras (S side of Peninsula del Grove). FV hbrs (clockwise from ent): Aguino, Puerto Cruz, Rianjo (yacht pontoon), Carril, Villanueva, S. Julian (Isla Arosa), Cambados (N'ly of two hbrs) and San Martin del Grove (2 pontoons for very small craft).

NAVIGATION WPT 42°26'·50N 08°59'·00W, 018°/6·8M to Is Rua (lt). Isla Sálvora (lt) at the mouth of the ría should be left to port; the rocky chans between it and C. Corrubedo 7M to the NNW are best not attempted by strangers.

Ría de Arousa, the largest ría (approx 14M x 7M), is a mini-cruising ground with interesting pilotage and dozens of anchorages to explore. Its coast is heavily indented and labyrinthine. AC 1734 or SC 4152/3 are essential. The fairway up to Villagarcia is buoyed/lit, but to either side are many mussel rafts (*viveros*), often unmarked/unlit. Some minor chans need careful pilotage to clear shoals/rocks. A low bridge from Isla de Arosa to the E shore bars passage.

LIGHTS AND MARKS Principal lts/marks are on chartlet as scale permits. Isla Rúa, a prominent rky islet with lt ho, is a key feature. There are numerous Y lt buoys usually marking fish farms.

R/T Villagarcia, Caramiñal and Santa Eugenia VHF Ch 09 16.

TELEPHONE (Dial code 982 or 981, as shown below); ⊖ & Met via marinas; see below.

FACILITIES (clockwise from west) **Sta Eugenia** ☎ (981) 873801, 📠 873290; (70 F & A on 4 pontoons in 4m). **Town**: all facilities. **Caramiñal** (150 F&A on pontoons in 3·5m); P & D (cans); **YC** ☎ & 📠 (981) 830970. **Rianjo**: T-pontoon in 3m; ☎ 860477. **Villagarcia** (416+ ⓥ on 1st pontoon to stbd); ☎ 501340, 📠 507923; Slip, BH (35 ton), P, D, ME, El, ⚒, C (70 ton), SM, Ⓔ, YC. **Town:** CH, 🛒, R, Bar, Ⓑ, ✉, ⓓ, ⇌; ✈ Santiago de Compostela (53km). **Piedras Negras:** ☎ & 📠 (986) 738325. WPT 42°26'·91N 08°53'·98W, 310°/1M to ent in white sector (305°-315°) of Fl (4) WR 11s.

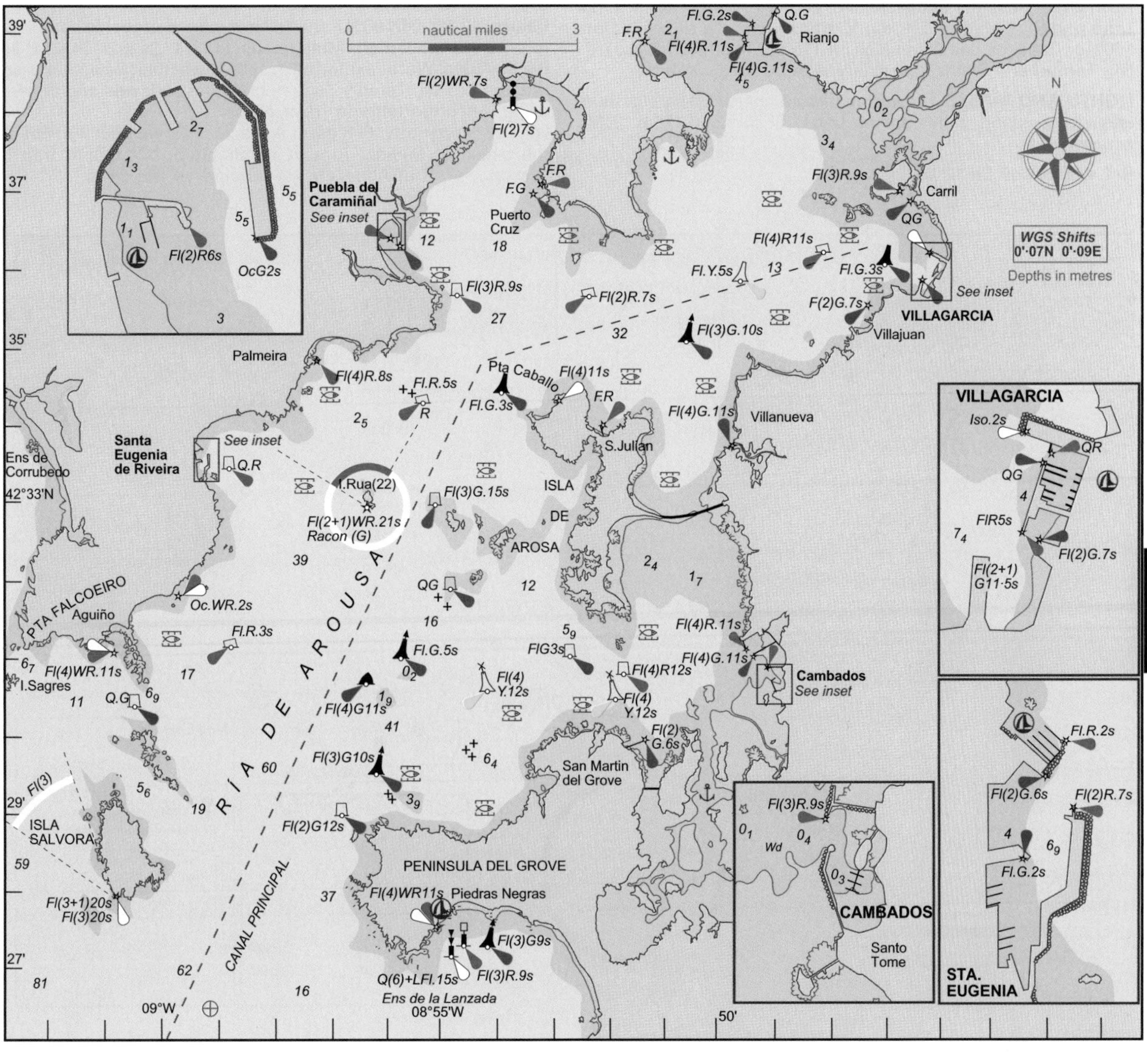
nautical miles
Rianjo
Carril
VILLAGARCIA
Villajuan
Villanueva
S.Julián
ISLA DE AROSA
Cambados
See inset
San Martin del Grove
PENINSULA DEL GROVE
Piedras Negras
Ens de la Lanzada
08°55'W
09°W
50'
RÍA DE AROUSA
CANAL PRINCIPAL
ISLA SALVORA
I.Sagres
Aguiño
PTA FALCOEIRO
Santa Eugenia de Riveira
Ens de Corrubedo
42°33'N
Palmeira
Puebla del Caramiñal
Puerto Cruz
Pta Caballo
I.Rua(22)
Fl(2+1)WR.21s Racon (G)
WGS Shifts
0'·07N 0'·09E
Depths in metres
VILLAGARCIA
CAMBADOS
Santo Tome
STA. EUGENIA
39'
37'
35'
29'
27'

9.23.32 RÍA DE PONTEVEDRA

Pontevedra **42°22'·00N 08°50'·00W** (mid-ría) ❁❁❁◊◊◊✿✿✿

CHARTS AC 3633, 1732/3; SC 416A/B, 9251, 4162/4; SHOM 3007

TIDES

Standard Port LISBOA (⟶); ML 1·9; Zone –0100

Times				Height (metres)			
High Water		Low Water		MHWS	MHWN	MLWN	MLWS
0500	1000	0300	0800	3·8	3·0	1·5	0·6
1700	2200	1500	2000				
Differences MARIN (42°24'N 08°42'W)							
+0050	+0110	+0120	+0130	–0·5	–0·4	–0·3	–0·1

SHELTER Good shelter can be found from any wind. Islas Ons and Onza off the mouth of the ría offer a barrier to wind and swell. Sangenjo and Aguete have marinas; Beluso will have. Other hbrs and ⚓s, clockwise from NW ent, include, on the N shore: Porto Novo, Rajó and Combarro, and on the S shore: Bueu and Aldán. Anchorage on E side of Isla Ons. See FACILITIES. Access to Pontevedra, the provincial capital, is restricted by a shallow chan and low bridge. Marin is a naval and commercial port with no yacht facilities.

NAVIGATION From WPT 42°18'·00N 08°56'·88W, (which also lies on the 129° ldg lts for Ria de Vigo) track 053° to enter via the main chan, Boca del Sudoeste, into centre of ria between C. de Udra and Pta Cabicastro. From N, transit Paso de la Fagilda on 130°, or Canal de Los Camoucos on 175°; both chans need care. Isla Tambo is a restricted military area; landing prohib.

LIGHTS AND MARKS Lts and marks as chartlet. Isla Ons is a steep, rky island with conspic lt ho, Fl (4) 24s 126m 25M, octagonal tr.

R/T Marin VHF Ch 12 16.

TELEPHONE (Dial code 986). See below for ☎ numbers.

FACILITIES (Clockwise from N entrance)

Porto Novo: mainly a FV hbr, since Sangenjo marina opened. S mole, Fl (3) R 6s. Ferry to Isla Ons.

Sangenjo: Marina lies inside L-shaped bkwtr ☆ QR, 42°23'·88N 08°47'·96W. SHM post, Fl (3) G 9s, marks shoal N of ent. A drying spur is 650m ESE of ent. Marina ☎ 986 720517, ℻ 720578; 500 AB, D, BH. CN ☎ 720517, ℻ 720578, C (5 ton), ME, 🛒, R, Bar, Ⓑ, ✉.

Rajó: Temp'y ⚓ in about 5m off the bkwtr hd, Fl (2) R 8s.

Combarro: ⚓ in about 3m to SE of bkwtr hd, Fl (2) R 8s. A new jetty, Oc (2) R 6s 3M, 1ca S of the old bkwtr gives added shelter. The bay is generally shallow; the village is noted for *horreos* and tourists. Possible security risk.

Pontevedra: Enter by dinghy near HW between training walls, Fl G/R 5s. The N side of chan avoids shoals and old bridge foundations in mid-channel between overhead cables and motorway bridge (both 12m clearance). Small private marina in Rio Lérez beyond. Town: all facilities.

Aguete: Marina in pleasant bay; many ⚓s. The YC bldg resembles superstructure of a liner. Do not round mole hd lt, Fl (2) G 7s 1M, too close due to offlying rks to SW/W. **Marina** (approx 100 F&A, inc Ⓥ), ☎ 702373, ℻ 702708, Slip, BH (28 ton), P, D, ME, M, El, C (8 ton), ⚒; **Club de Mar** R, Bar. Village: few shops.

Bueu: basically a FV hbr, but 32 possible yacht berths; or ⚓ to W of hbr in about 5m. Caution: mussel rafts to NNW and NNE. Hbr ent is lit, Fl G 3s and Fl (2) R 6s. HM ☎ 320253/320042. P & D (cans), CH, 🛒, R, Bar. Ferry to Isla Ons.

Beluso (42°20'·08N 08°47'·80W): New marina probably complete; reports are welcomed. Mole heads, Fl (3) G 9s and Fl (3) R 9s.

Ria de Aldán: Worth exploring in settled weather; beware mussel rafts on W side. Temp'y ⚓s may be found on E side and at head of ría; uncomfortable in fresh N'lies.

Isla Ons: Ferry jetty, Fl R 4s, at Almacen. Fair weather ⚓ in 5m off the beach at Melide. Almost uninhabited, but tourist trap in season. Bar, R at Almacen. No landing on Isla Onza.

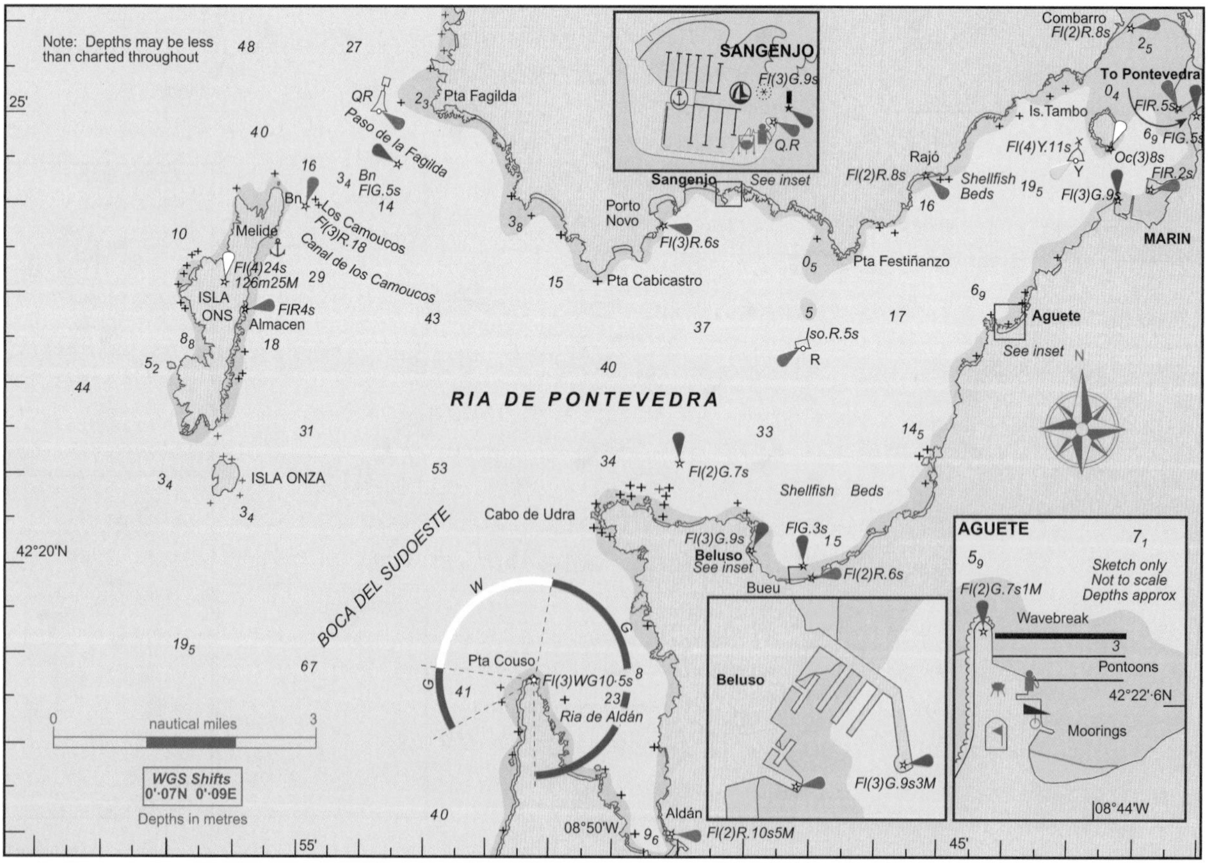
Note: Depths may be less than charted throughout
SANGENJO
Sangenjo
See inset
Combarro
Fl(2)R.8s
To Pontevedra
Fl R.5s
Fl G.5s
Is.Tambo
Fl(4)Y.11s
Oc(3)8s
Fl R.2s
Fl(3)G.9s
MARIN
Rajó
Fl(2)R.8s
Shellfish Beds
Pta Fagilda
Paso de la Fagilda
Bn
Fl G.5s
Los Camoucos
Fl(3)R.18
Canal de los Camoucos
Melide
Fl(4)24s 126m25M
ISLA ONS
Fl R4s
Almacen
Porto Novo
Fl(3)R.6s
Pta Cabicastro
Pta Festiñanzo
Iso.R.5s
Aguete
See inset
RIA DE PONTEVEDRA
ISLA ONZA
Fl(2)G.7s
Shellfish Beds
Cabo de Udra
Fl(3)G.9s
Beluso
See inset
Fl G.3s
Fl(2)R.6s
Bueu
BOCA DEL SUDOESTE
Pta Couso
Fl(3)WG10·5s
Ria de Aldán
Aldán
Fl(2)R.10s5M
08°50'W
55'
45'
25'
42°20'N
nautical miles
WGS Shifts 0'·07N 0'·09E
Depths in metres
Beluso
Fl(3)G.9s3M
AGUETE
Sketch only
Not to scale
Depths approx
Fl(2)G.7s1M
Wavebreak
Pontoons
42°22'·6N
Moorings
08°44'W

9.23.33 RÍA DE VIGO

Galicia **42°14'·63N 08°43'·35W** (Vigo marina)

CHARTS AC 3633, 1730, 1731; SC 416, 416B, 4165; SHOM 7595, 7596, 3007

TIDES

Standard Port LISBOA (⟶); ML 1·96; Zone –0100

Times				**Height (metres)**			
High Water		Low Water		MHWS	MHWN	MLWN	MLWS
0500	1000	0300	0800	3·8	3·0	1·5	0·6
1700	2200	1500	2000				
Differences VIGO							
+0040	+0100	+0105	+0125	–0·4	–0·3	–0·2	–0·1

SHELTER The ent to ría is protected by Islas Cies with easy appr chans from N and S. Good shelter in Vigo marina, unless a NW'ly scend enters. Narrow ent to marina, marked by PHM/SHM lt twrs, is close E of the most E'ly of 4 conspic blue cranes. The old YC bldg, like a liner's superstructure, is in centre of marina. Cangas on the N shore is a sizable town with FV hbr; ⚓ inside or to the E. Very attractive ⚓s on E side of Islas Cies off Isla del Norte, Isla del Faro and Isla de S. Martin, all of which form a Nature Reserve. Ensenada de San Simón, beyond motorway suspension bridge, is shallow but scenic with ⚓s on W, E and S sides.

NAVIGATION N Chan WPT 42°16'·62N 08°54'·58W, 129°/2·2M to Cabo del Home front ldg lt, Fl 3s; rear Oc 6s. Isla del Norte (Cies) lies SW; the chan is 1·4M wide and clear.

S Chan WPT 42°09'·42N 08°55'·00W, 069°/5·0M to Cabo Estay front ldg lt. Caution: Castros de Agoeiro shoal (4·1m) lies 9ca N of the S WPT. A WCM lt buoy (1·3M E of the S WPT) defines SE side of chan and marks Las Serralleiras, rky islets NW of Bayona. Inside the ría beware extensive unlit mussel rafts along the N shore. The docks and city of Vigo line the SE shore.

LIGHTS AND MARKS Islas Cies are readily identified by their high, rugged bare slopes and white beaches on the E side. Ldg lts/marks for the appr chans are as per the chartlet. The buoyed inner fairway lies between brgs of 068° and 074° on the conspic Hermitage (chapel) tower on Monte de la Guía.

R/T Port Control *Vigo Prácticos* VHF Ch 14 16; Marina Ch 09.

TELEPHONE (Dial code 986) HM 449694, 📠 449695; ⊖ & Met via marina; British Consul 437133.

FACILITIES **Vigo marina** (413 F&A + few Ⓥ), ☎ 224003, 📠 223514, P & D, Slip, BH (32 ton), ME, El, Ⓔ, CH, C (3 ton), ⚒, Ⓢ; **Real Club Náutico** ☎ 433588, R, Bar. CN de Bouzas ☎ 232442. **City:** all amenities; ⇌ ; ✈ (national).

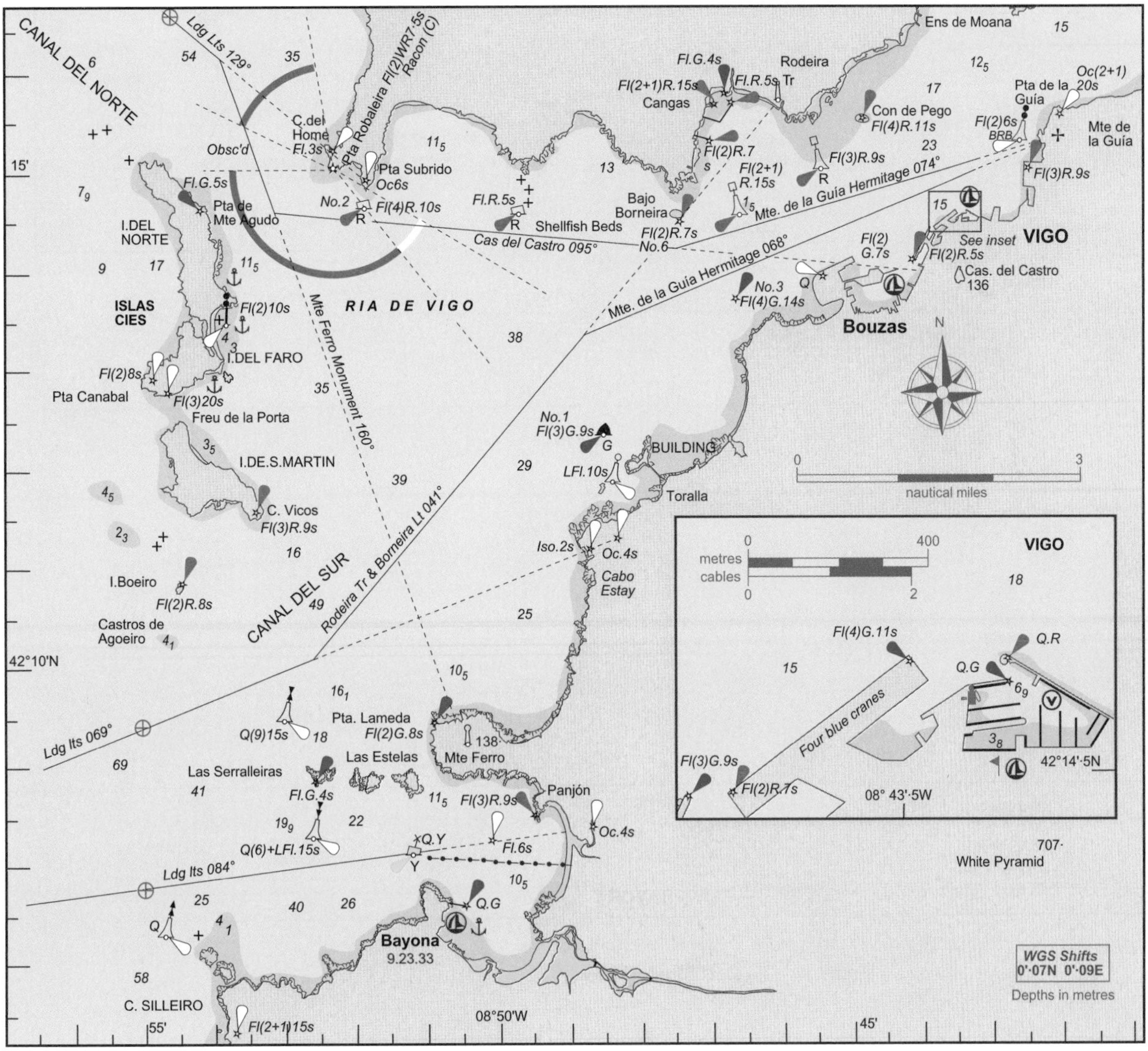
CANAL DEL NORTE
Ldg Lts 129°
Pta Robaleira Fl(2)WR7·5s Racon (C)
C.del Home Fl.3s
Obsc'd
Pta Subrido Oc6s
No.2 Fl(4)R.10s
Fl.R.5s
Shellfish Beds
Cas del Castro 095°
Fl.G.5s
Pta de Mte Agudo
I.DEL NORTE
ISLAS CIES
Fl(2)10s
I.DEL FARO
Fl(2)8s
Pta Canabal
Fl(3)20s
Freu de la Porta
I.DE.S.MARTIN
C. Vicos Fl(3)R.9s
I.Boeiro
Fl(2)R.8s
Castros de Agoeiro
42°10'N
15'
RIA DE VIGO
Mte Ferro Monument 160°
CANAL DEL SUR
Rodeira Tr & Borneira Lt 041°
Ldg lts 069°
Fl.G.4s
Fl(2+1)R.15s
Fl.R.5s Tr
Rodeira
Cangas
Fl(2)R.7s
Fl(2+1)R.15s
Bajo Borneira
Fl(2)R.7s No.6
Con de Pego Fl(4)R.11s
Fl(3)R.9s
Mte. de la Guía Hermitage 074°
Mte. de la Guía Hermitage 068°
Ens de Moana
Pta de la Guía
Oc(2+1)20s
Fl(2)6s
Mte de la Guía
Fl(3)R.9s
See inset
VIGO
Fl(2) G.7s
Fl(2)R.5s
Cas. del Castro 136
No.3 Fl(4)G.14s
Bouzas
N
No.1 Fl(3)G.9s
BUILDING
LFl.10s
Toralla
nautical miles
Iso.2s
Oc.4s
Cabo Estay
Q(9)15s
Pta. Lameda Fl(2)G.8s
Las Estelas
Mte Ferro
Las Serralleiras
Fl.G.4s
Fl(3)R.9s
Panjón
Oc.4s
Q(6)+LFl.15s
Q.Y
Fl.6s
Ldg lts 084°
Q.G
Bayona 9.23.33
C. SILLEIRO
Fl(2+1)15s
55'
08°50'W
45'
VIGO
metres
cables
Fl(4)G.11s
Four blue cranes
Q.R
Q.G
Fl(3)G.9s
Fl(2)R.7s
42°14'·5N
08° 43'·5W
707· White Pyramid
WGS Shifts 0'·07N 0'·09E
Depths in metres

23

9.23.34 BAYONA

Galicia **42°07'·45N 08°50'·55W** ❀❀❀◊◊◊✿✿✿

CHARTS AC 3633; SC 417, 416B, 4167; SHOM 3007, 7596, 7595

TIDES

Standard Port LISBOA (⟶); Zone –0100

Times				Height (metres)			
High Water		Low Water		MHWS	MHWN	MLWN	MLWS
0500	1000	0300	0800	3·8	3·0	1·4	0·6
1700	2200	1500	2000				
Differences BAYONA							
+0035	+0050	+0100	+0115	–0·3	–0·3	–0·2	–0·1
LA GUARDIA (41°54'N 08°53'W)							
+0040	+0055	+0105	+0120	–0·5	–0·4	–0·3	–0·2

SHELTER Excellent. There are two marinas: The N'ly one is run by Monte Real YC (MRYC); the new S'ly Bayona marina is run by Ronautica and protected by an E/W wavebreak. MRYC have some Ⓥs. Or ⚓ E of marina, but clear of fairway to FV jetty.

NAVIGATION WPT 42°07'·80N 08°55'·00W (off chartlet), 084°/ 2·8M to SPM buoy QY. From S keep 1M off Cabo Silleiro to clear reefs marked by NCM buoy, Q. To the N of ldg line, Las Serralleiras are marked by SCM & WCM lt buoys and by a light bcn. The Canal de la Porta, between Monte Ferro and Las Estelas is a useful shortcut to/from Ría de Vigo, but avoid a 0·9m patch and ✱ in mid-channel.

LIGHTS AND MARKS Ldg lts 084° as chartlet, hard-to-see white conical twrs, the front on a tiny rky islet. N of the bay, a prominent white monument is on Monte Ferro. Dique de Abrigo (white wall) has a B/W chequered tower. Other conspic daymarks are: castle walls (parador), and MRYC flag-mast. FV jetty has white crane.

R/T *Monte Real Club de Yates* Ch 06, 16. *Puerto Deportivo de Bayona* Ch 09.

TELEPHONE (Dial code 986) ⊖ & Met via YC/marina; Ⓗ 352011; Police 355027.

FACILITIES MRYC Marina, (200+ some Ⓥ in 6m), ☎ 355234, 📠 355061, www.montereal.es mryc@jet.es €2.50, F&A, M, P & D, Slip, BH (20 ton), C (1·5 ton), Bar, Ice, R, ▣.

Bayona Marina, ☎ 385107, 📠 356489, Mobile 626 299 162; puertobaiona@puertobaiona.com www.puertobaiona.com (319 + 32 Ⓥ) €2.39, P, D, BH (50 ton), C (6 ton), Slip, Bar, Ice, R.

Town: ME, El, Ⓔ, CH, SM, ⚒; most domestic needs inc 🛒, ▣; ⇄, ✈ Vigo (21 km).

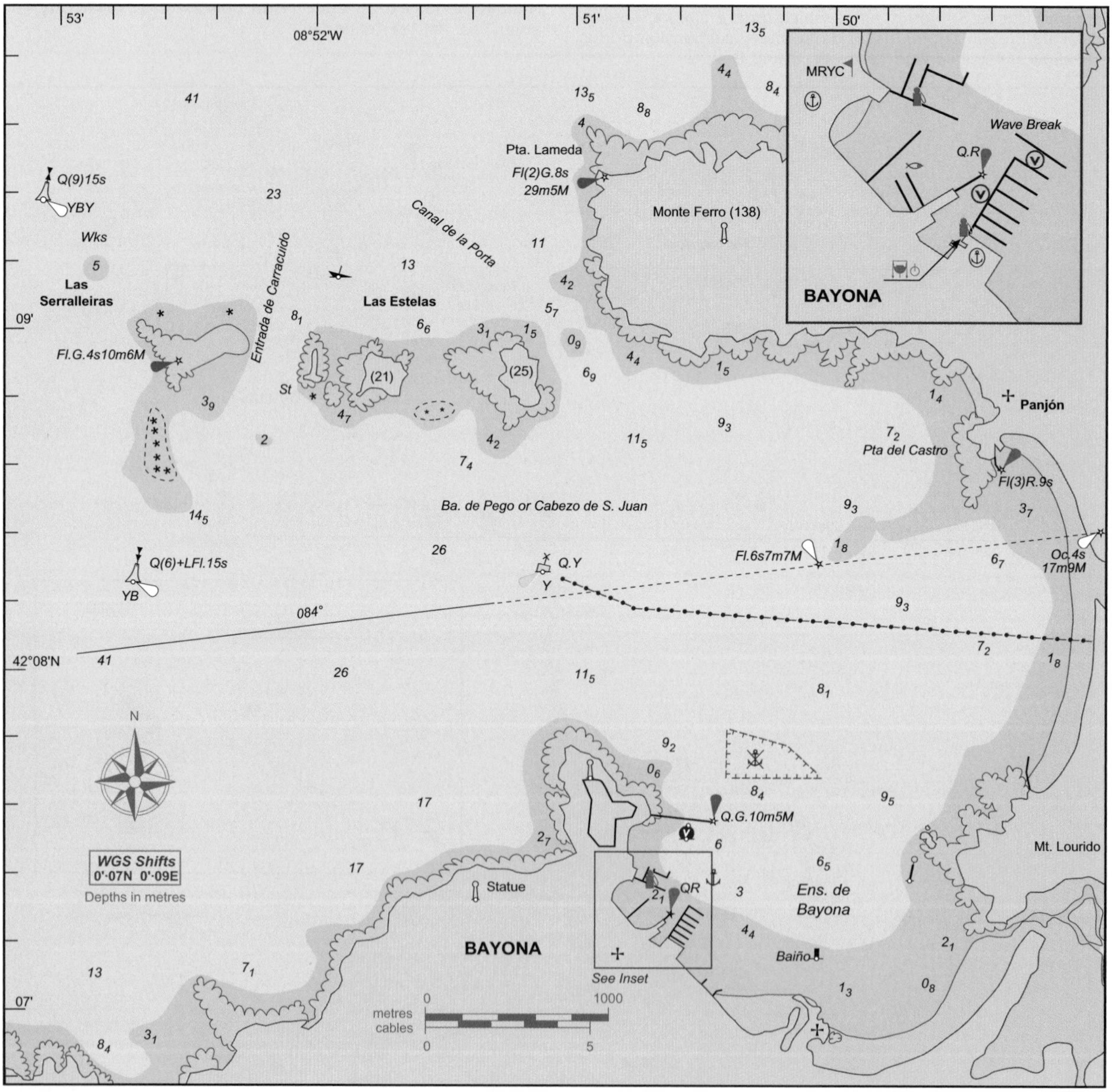
53'
08°52'W
51'
50'
MRYC
Wave Break
Q.R
BAYONA
Pta. Lameda
Fl(2)G.8s
29m5M
Monte Ferro (138)
Canal de la Porta
Q(9)15s
YBY
Wks
Las Serralleiras
Entrada de Carracuido
Las Estelas
09'
Fl.G.4s10m6M
(21)
(25)
St
Panjón
Pta del Castro
Fl(3)R.9s
Ba. de Pego or Cabezo de S. Juan
Q(6)+LFl.15s
YB
Q.Y
Y
Fl.6s7m7M
Oc.4s
17m9M
084°
42°08'N
N
Q.G.10m5M
Mt. Lourido
WGS Shifts
0'·07N 0'·09E
Depths in metres
Statue
QR
Ens. de Bayona
BAYONA
Baiño
See Inset
07'
metres
cables
0
1000
5

Area 24

Portugal

Viana do Castelo to Santo Antonio

The Portuguese national flag dates from the 11th century. In the centre is a coat of arms consisting of an armillary sphere charged with the traditional Portuguese shield. The red shield is encircled by seven castles, and within are five escutcheons (small shields within a coat of arms), each marked by five silver dots (bezants in heraldic terminology).

The armillary sphere was an astronomical and navigational instrument made of wood or metal rings (armilas) interlinked around a central axis to form parallels, meridians and the ecliptic. Thus by examining the stars, position on the earth's surface could be calculated.

24

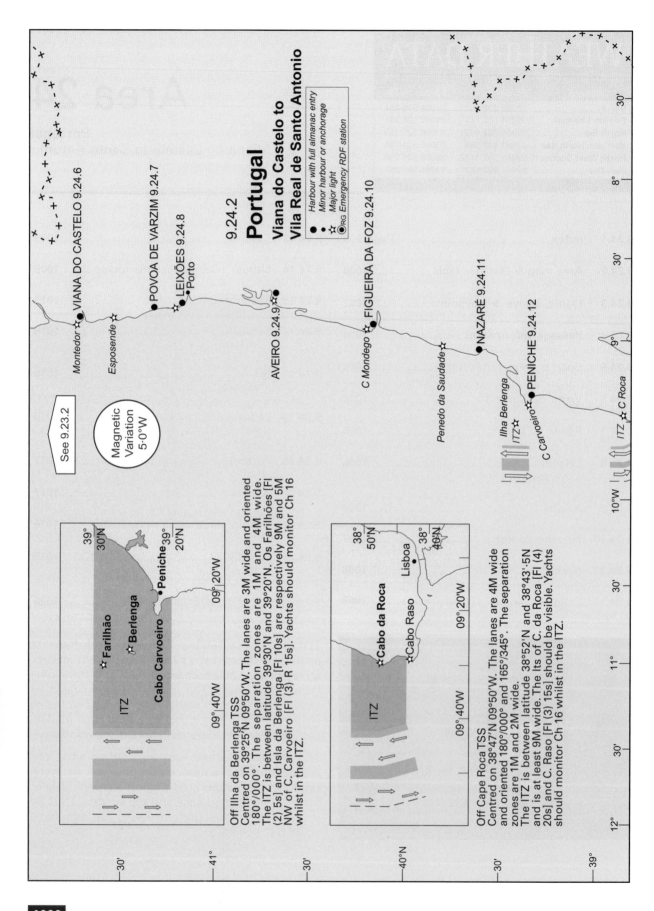

9.24.2 Portugal

Viana do Castelo to Vila Real de Santo Antonio

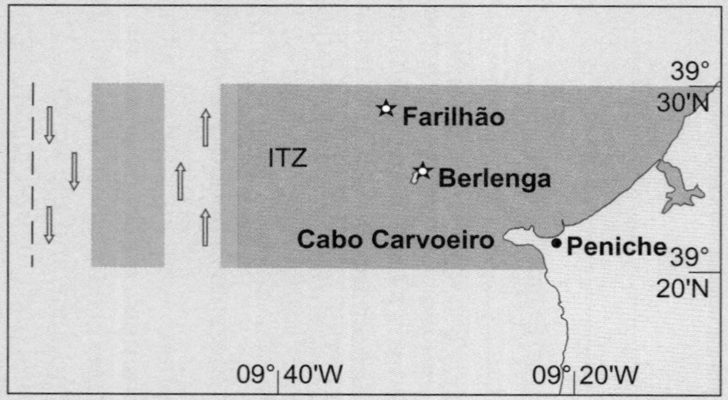
Farilhão
Berlenga
ITZ
Cabo Carvoeiro
Peniche
39° 30'N
39° 20'N
09° 40'W
09° 20'W

Off Ilha da Berlenga TSS
Centred on 39°25'N 09°50'W. The lanes are 3M wide and oriented 180°/000°. The separation zones are 1M and 4M wide. The ITZ is between latitude 39°30'N and 39°20'N. Os Farilhões [Fl (2) 5s] and Isla da Berlenga [Fl 10s] are respectively 9M and 5M NW of C. Carvoeiro [Fl (3) R 15s]. Yachts should monitor Ch 16 whilst in the ITZ.

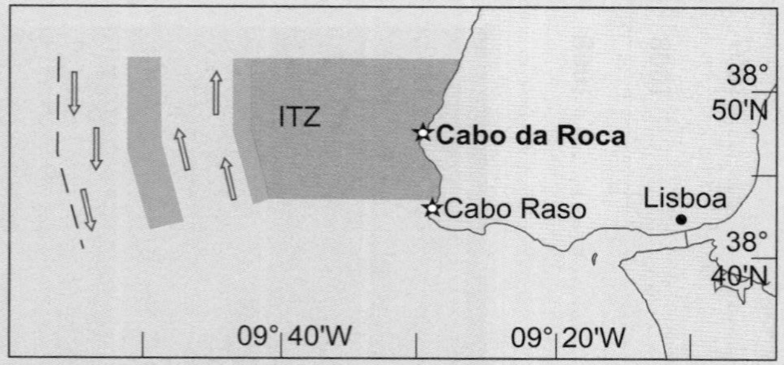
ITZ
Cabo da Roca
Cabo Raso
Lisboa
38° 50'N
38° 40'N
09° 40'W
09° 20'W

Off Cape Roca TSS
Centred on 38°47'N 09°50'W. The lanes are 4M wide and oriented 180°/000° and 165°/345°. The separation zones are 1M and 2M wide.
The ITZ is between latitude 38°52'N and 38°43'·5N and is at least 9M wide. The lts of C. da Roca [Fl (4) 20s] and C. Raso [Fl (3) 15s] should be visible. Yachts should monitor Ch 16 whilst in the ITZ.

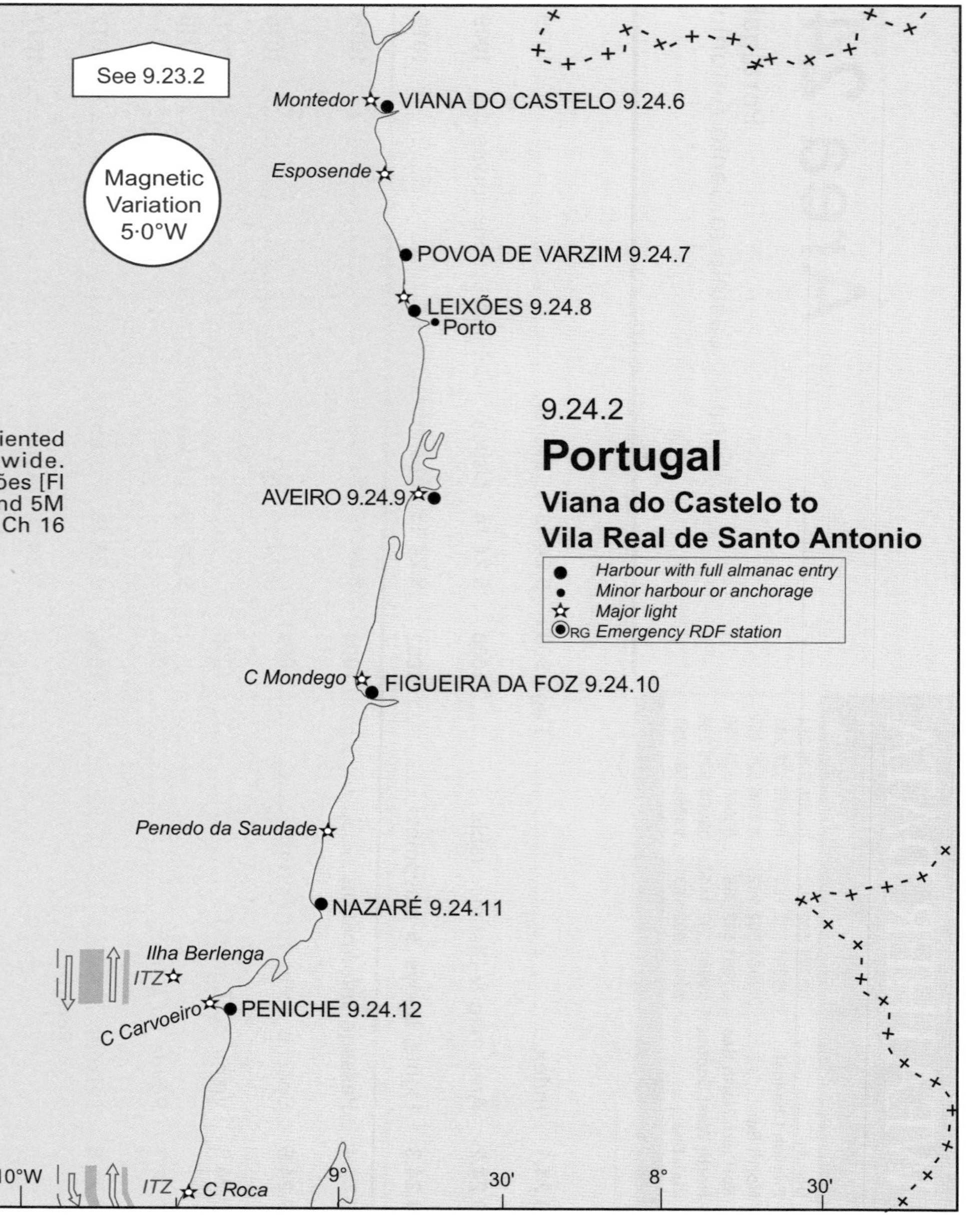
See 9.23.2
Magnetic Variation 5·0°W
Montedor
VIANA DO CASTELO 9.24.6
Esposende
POVOA DE VARZIM 9.24.7
LEIXÕES 9.24.8
Porto
AVEIRO 9.24.9
C Mondego
FIGUEIRA DA FOZ 9.24.10
Penedo da Saudade
NAZARÉ 9.24.11
Ilha Berlenga
ITZ
C Carvoeiro
PENICHE 9.24.12
ITZ
C Roca
Harbour with full almanac entry
Minor harbour or anchorage
Major light
RG Emergency RDF station
30'
41°
30'
40°N
30'
39°
12°
30'
11°
30'
10°W
9°
30'
8°
30'

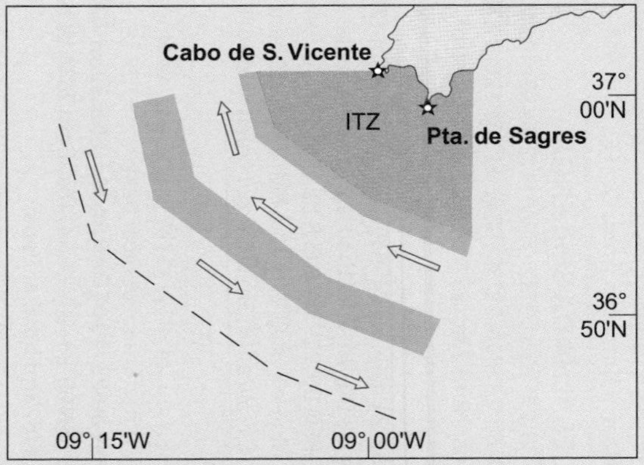
Cabo de S. Vicente
ITZ
Pta. de Sagres
37° 00'N
36° 50'N
09° 15'W
09° 00'W

Off Cape St Vincent TSS
Centred on 36°53'·80N 09°07'·10W. The lanes are 3M wide and oriented 163°/343°, 129°/309, and 112°/292°. The separation zones are 1M and 2M wide.
The ITZ is between 37°01'·5N and 08°54'·3W. It is 4·7M wide off both C. San Vincent [Fl 5s] and Pta de Sagres [Iso R 2s]. Yachts should monitor Ch 16 whilst in the ITZ.

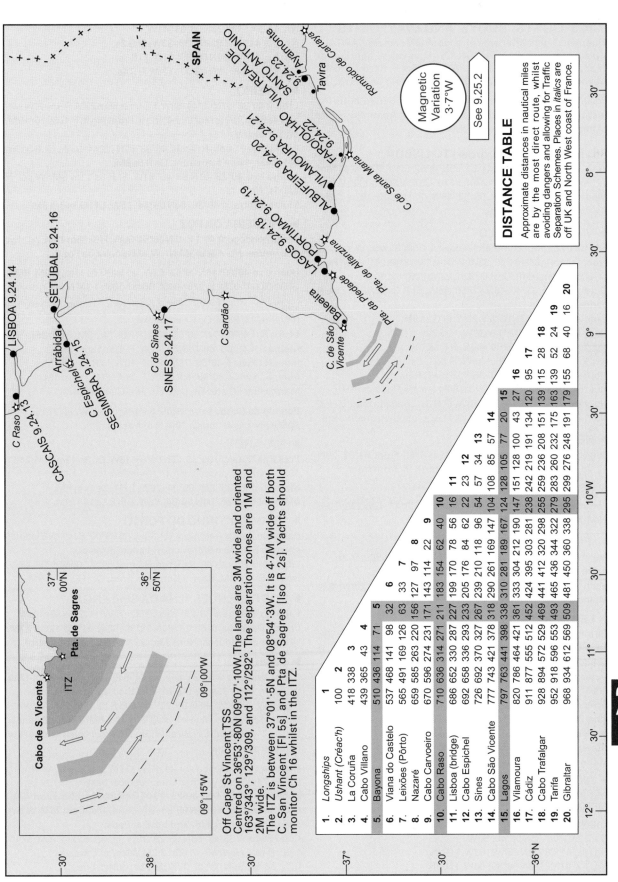

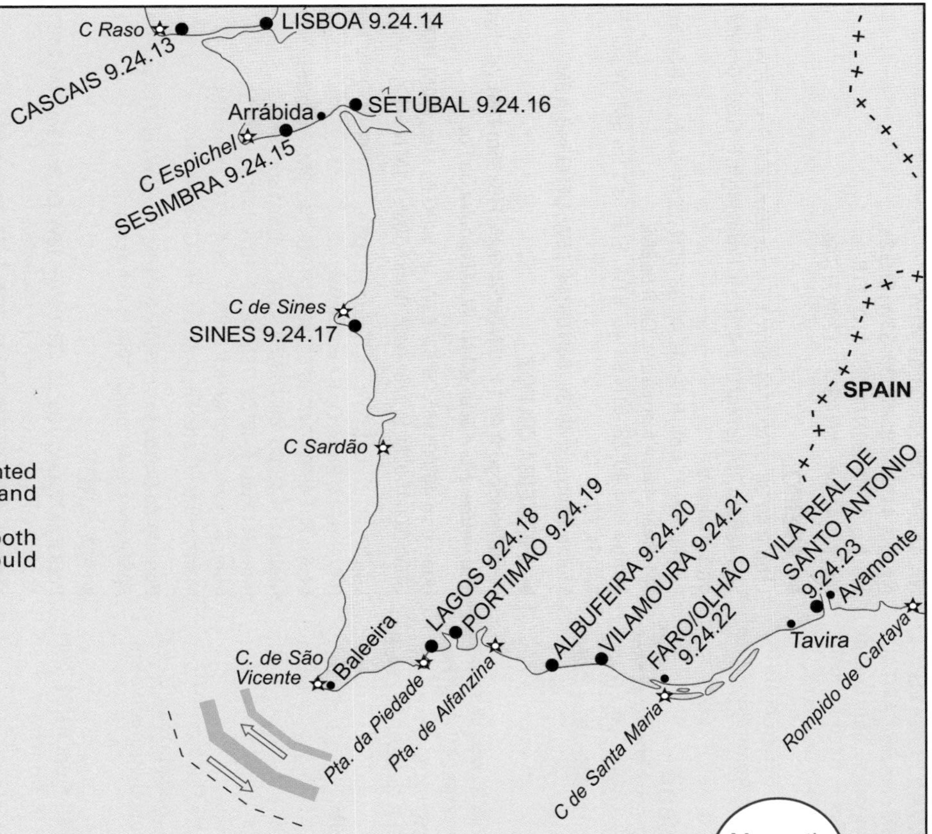
C Raso
LISBOA 9.24.14
CASCAIS 9.24.13
Arrábida
SETÚBAL 9.24.16
C Espichel
SESIMBRA 9.24.15
C de Sines
SINES 9.24.17
C Sardão
SPAIN
C. de São Vicente
Baleeira
Pta. da Piedade
LAGOS 9.24.18
PORTIMAO 9.24.19
Pta. de Alfanzina
ALBUFEIRA 9.24.20
VILAMOURA 9.24.21
FARO/OLHÃO 9.24.22
C de Santa Maria
VILA REAL DE SANTO ANTONIO 9.24.23
Tavira
Ayamonte
Rompido de Cartaya
Magnetic Variation 3·7°W
12°
30'
11°
10°W
9°
8°
38°
37°
36°N

See 9.25.2

DISTANCE TABLE

Approximate distances in nautical miles are by the most direct route, whilst avoiding dangers and allowing for Traffic Separation Schemes. Places in *italics* are off UK and North West coast of France.

		1	2	3	4	5	6	7	8	9	10	11	12	13	14	15	16	17	18	19	20
1.	*Longships*	1																			
2.	*Ushant (Créac'h)*	100	2																		
3.	La Coruña	418	338	3																	
4.	Cabo Villano	439	365	43	4																
5.	Bayona	510	436	114	71	5															
6.	Viana do Castelo	537	468	141	98	32	6														
7.	Leixões (Pôrto)	565	491	169	126	63	33	7													
8.	Nazaré	659	585	263	220	156	127	97	8												
9.	Cabo Carvoeiro	670	596	274	231	171	143	114	22	9											
10.	Cabo Raso	710	636	314	271	211	183	154	62	40	10										
11.	Lisboa (bridge)	686	652	330	287	227	199	170	78	56	16	11									
12.	Cabo Espichel	692	658	336	293	233	205	176	84	62	22	23	12								
13.	Sines	726	692	370	327	267	239	210	118	96	54	57	34	13							
14.	Cabo São Vicente	777	743	421	378	318	290	261	169	147	104	108	85	57	14						
15.	Lagos	797	763	441	398	338	310	281	189	167	124	128	105	77	20	15					
16.	Vilamoura	820	786	464	421	361	333	304	212	190	147	151	128	100	43	27	16				
17.	Cádiz	911	877	555	512	452	424	395	303	281	238	242	219	191	134	120	95	17			
18.	Cabo Trafalgar	928	894	572	529	469	441	412	320	298	255	259	236	208	151	139	115	28	18		
19.	Tarifa	952	918	596	553	493	465	436	344	322	279	283	260	232	175	163	139	52	24	19	
20.	Gibraltar	968	934	612	569	509	481	450	360	338	295	299	276	248	191	179	155	68	40	16	20

PLOT WAYPOINTS ON YOUR CHART BEFORE USING THEM

9.24.3 LIGHTS, BUOYS AND WAYPOINTS

Blue print = light with a nominal range of 15M or more. CAPITALS = place or feature. *CAPITAL ITALICS* = light-vessel, light float or Lanby. *Italics* = Fog signal. ***Bold italics*** = Racon. Useful waypoints are underlined. Abbreviations are in Chapter 1.

Positions below are referenced to the WGS 84 datum, but in the rest of Area 24 are referenced to ED50. Most Admiralty charts of this area are referenced to ED50.

RIO MIÑO (Spanish border) TO LISBOA

Río Miño ent, Fort Ínsua ☆ 41°51'·55N 08°52'·52W, Fl WRG 4s 16m W12M, R8M, G9M; G204°-270°, R270°-357°, W357°-204°; W col.
Montedor ☆ 41°45'·09N 08°52'·49W, Fl (2) 9·5s 102m **22M**; R □ twr; *Horn Mo (S) 25s.*

▶ VIANA DO CASTELO

Ldg lts 012.5° (for commercial docks); both R twrs, W stripes. **Front** ☆ 41°41'.33N 08°50'.35W, Iso R 4s 14m **23M**; 241°-151°. **Rear** ☆, 505m from front, Oc R 6s 32m **23M**; 005°-020°.
Outer mole ☆ 41°40'·45N 08°50'·66W, Fl R 3s 9M; W col, R bands; *Horn 30s.*
E mole ☆ 41°40'·67N 08°50'·25W, Fl G 3s 9M.
No. 1 ▲ 41°40'·68N 08°50'·29W, Fl G 3s.
No. 2 ■ 41°40'·53N 08°50'·48W, Fl R 3s.
No. 3 ▲ 41°40'·88N 08°50'·24W, Fl (2) G 3s.
No. 4 ■ 41°40'·89N 08°50'·36W, Fl (2+1) R 5s.
Nos. 5-13 ▲s are Fl G 3s. Nos. 6-14 ■s are Fl R 3s.
No. 13 ▲ 41°41'·56N 08°49'·18W, Fl G 3s; opposite marina ent.
No. 14 ■ 41°41'·63N 08°49'·24W, Fl R 3s; opposite marina ent.

▶ NEIVA

Ldg lts 064·9°, both Oc G 6s 13/19m 6M. Front 41°37'·29N 08°48'·89W; ◊ on W col, R stripes. Rear, 61m from front.

▶ ESPOSENDE

Forte da Barra do Río Cávado ☆ 41°32'·56N 08°47'·49W, Fl 5s 20m **20M**; R ○ twr and house; *Horn 20s.*

▶ PÓVOA DE VARZIM

Ldg lts 006°, front, 41°21'·80N 08°45'·50W; rear 90m from front; both Oc R 5s 5/14m 6M, R posts & W bands.
Molhe N ☆ 41°22'·29N 08°46'·23W, Fl R 3s 14m 12M; *Siren 40s.*
Molhe S ☆ 41°22'·23N 08°46'·03W, L Fl G 6s 4M.

▶ LEIXÕES

Oil refinery 41°12'·07N 08°45'·11W, Fl (3) 15s 6M; *Horn (3) 30s.*
Leça ☆ 41°12'·08N 08°42'·74W, Fl (3) 14s 56m **28M**; W twr, B bands. Oil refinery close N of this lt is conspic D/N.
Outer bkwtr ☆ 41°10'·37N 08°42'·49W, Fl WR 5s 23m W12M, R9M; R001°-180°, W180°-001°; Gy twr; *Horn 20s.*
S pier ☆ 41°10'·68N 08°42'·35W, Fl G 4s 16m 7M; 328°-285°; *Horn 30s.*
Inner N pier ☆ 41°10'·69N 08°42'·51W, Fl R 4s 8m 6M; 173°-353°.
No. 2 buoy ■ 41°10'·81N 08°42'·51W, Fl (3) R 8s.
No. 4 buoy ■ 41°10'·86N 08°42'·60W, Fl (2) R 5s.
Marina bkwtr ☆ 41°11'·08N 08°42'·27W, L Fl (2) R 12s 4m 2M.

▶ RIO DOURO

Ldg lts 078·7°, both Oc R 6s 11/32m 9M. Front, 41°08'·83N 08°40'·03W; W col. Rear, 500m from front; W col/lantern, Y bands.
Ent, N mole ☆ 41°08'·80N 08°40'·65W, Fl R 5s 16m 9M; *Siren 30s.*
No. 2 ■ 41°08'·85N 08°40'·52W.
No. 4 ■ 41°08'·73N 08°39'·85W, Fl R 2s.
No. 1 ▲ 41°08'·68N 08°39'·66W, Fl G 2s.
No. 4A ■ 41°08'·73N 08°39'·41W.
No. 3 ▲ 41°08'·68N 08°39'·33W, Fl G 3s.
No. 6 ■ 41°08'·80N 08°39'·11W, Fl R 3s.
No. 8 ■ 41°08'·39N 08°37'·12W, Fl R 4s.

▶ AVEIRO

Lt ho ☆ 40°38'·57N 08°44'·88W, Fl (4) 13s 65m **23M**. Same R/W twr, Fl G 4s 53m 9M, is rear 085·4° ldg lt. Front ldg lt, Fl G 3s 16m 9M, on S mole hd.
Ldg lts 065·6°, both R ○ cols. 40°38'·82N 08°44'·99W, Oc R 3s 7m 9M. Rear, 440m from front, Oc R 6s 8M.
Molhe N ☆ 40°38'·61N 08°45'·81W, Fl R 3s 11m 8M; W col, R bands; *Horn 15s.*
Molhe Central ☆ 40°38'·64N 08°44'·95W, L Fl G 5s 8m 3M.

▶ FIGUEIRA DA FOZ

Cabo Mondego ☆ 40°11'·46N 08°54'·35W, Fl 5s 96m **28M**; W □ twr and house; *Horn 30s*; 3M NNW of Figueira da Foz.

Buarcos ☆ 40°09'·86N 08°52'·53W, Iso WRG 6s 11m, W9M, R6M, G5M; G004°-028°, W028°-048°, R048°-086°; 1·1M N of Fig da Foz.

Ldg lts 081·5°, both W cols, R stripes. 40°08'·83N 08°51'·23W, Iso R 5s 8m 8M; Rear, Oc R 6s 12m 8M.
Molhe N ☆ 40°08'·74N 08°52'·50W, Fl R 6s 14m 9M; *Horn 35s.*
Molhe S ☆ 40°08'·59N 08°52'·41W, Fl G 6s 13m 7M.
Inner N bkwtr ☆ 40°08'·78N 08°52'·10W, Fl R 3s 9m 4M.
Inner S bkwtr ☆ 40°08'·69N 08°52'·08W, Fl G 3s 8m 4M.
Marina ent, FG and FR, both 6m 2M; G and R twrs.

Penedo da Saudade ☆ 39°45'·84N 09°01'·89W, Fl (2) 15s 54m **30M**; □ twr, and house; 10M N of Nazaré.

▶ NAZARÉ

Pontal da Nazaré ☆ 39°36'·25N 09°05'·18W, Oc 3s 49m 14M; 282°-192°; R lantern on wall of fort; *Siren 35s.*
Molhe S ☆ 39°35'·34N 09°04'·76W, L Fl G 5s 14m 8M.
Molhe N ☆ 39°35'·50N 09°04'·59W, L Fl R 5s 14m 9M.

▶ SÃO MARTINHO DO PORTO

Ponta de Santo António ☆ 39°30'·61N 09°08'·61W (NE side of ent), Iso R 6s 32m 9M; W col, R bands; *Siren 60s.*
Ldg lts 145·1°, both W cols, R bands. Front, 39°30'·05N 09°08'·47W, Iso R 1·5s 9m 9M. Rear, 129m from front, Oc R 6s 11m 9M.

▶ LOS FARILHÕES/ILHA DA BERLENGA

Farilhão Grande ☆ 39°28'·73N 09°32'·77W, Fl (2) 5s 99m 13M.
Ilha da Berlenga ☆ 39°24'·90N 09°30'·63W, Fl 10s 120m **27M**; W □ twr and houses; *Horn 28s*; (5·7M NW of C. Carvoeiro).

▶ PENICHE

Cabo Carvoeiro ☆ 39°21'·61N 09°24'·51W, Fl (3) R 15s 56m **15M**; W □ twr; *Horn 35s*; on the W tip of the Peniche peninsula.
Molhe W ☆ 39°20'·85N 09°22'·56W, Fl R 3s 13m 9M; W twr, R bands; *Siren 120s.* Molhe E ☆ Fl G 3s 13m 9M; W twr, G bands.
Ldg lts 218·3°, both L Fl R 7s 10/13m 8/6M; for ⚓ on N side of the Peniche peninsula.

Assenta ☆ 39°03'·53N 09°24'·91W (17M N of Cabo da Roca), L Fl 5s 74m 13M; W structure on conical base.
Ericeira ☆ 38°57'·09N 09°25'·10W, Oc R 3s 36m 6M; *Siren 70s.*
C. da Roca ☆ 38°46'·88N 09°29'·90W, Fl (4) 18s 164m **26M**; W twr and bldgs. Aero R lt (523m) 5M E at Pena.
Cabo Raso ☆ 38°42'·56N 09°29'·15W, Fl (3) 9s 22m **15M**; 324°-189°; R twr; *Horn Mo (I) 60s;* 3·2M WNW of Cascais.
C2 38°39'·90N 09°28'·03W, Fl Y 5s; outfall buoy.

LISBOA TO THE RIO GUADIANA (Spanish border)

▶ CASCAIS

Ldg lts 284·7°. Front, **Forte de Santa Marta** 38°41'·42N 09°25'·27W, Oc WR 6s 24m **W18M**, R14M; R233°-334°, W334°-098°; W□twr, Bu bands; *Horn 10s.* Rear, **Guia**, 1·23M from front, Iso WR 2s **W19M, R16M**; W326°-092°, R278°-292°; W twr.

MC1, 2 & 3 s, all VQ (6) + L Fl 10s, mark the SE side of marina bkwtr. CC2 38°41'·62N 09°24'·80W, Fl R 4s; NE of bkwtr hd.

Marina Molhe Sul ☆ 38°41'·58N 09°24'·84W, Fl (3) R 4s 8m 6M.

Molhe Norte ☆ Fl (2) G 4s 8m 3M.

No. 2 38°41'·69N 09°24'·99W, Fl R 10s (May-Oct).

Praia da Ribeira ☆ 38°41'·80N 09°25'·21W, Oc R 4s 5m 6M; 251°-309°; W col, R bands.

Albatroz ☆ 38°41'·98N 09°25'·02W, Oc R 6s 12m 5M.

Marconi ☆ 38°40'·94N 09°20'·69W, Iso WR 3s 17m 9M; R048°-058°, W058°-068°; Y twr on Ponta da Rana, 3·25M ESE of Cascais.

▶ LISBOA APPROACH

Ldg lts 047·1°, front & middle lts visible 039·5°-054·5°, H24. Front, **Gibalta** 38°41'·94N 09°15'·97W, Oc R 3s 30m **21M**; twr & cupola. Middle, **Esteiro**, 762m from front, Oc R 6s 81m **21M**; W□twr, R bands; ***Racon Q, 15M.*** Rear, **Mama** ☆ 38°43'·65N 09°13'·63W, Iso 6s 153m **21M**; 045·5°-048·5°.

No. 2 38°37'·29N 09°23'·28W, Fl R 10s.

No. 1 38°39'·55N 09°18'·78W, Fl G 2s.

Forte Bugio ☆ 38°39'·62N 09°17'·93W, Fl G 5s 27m 9M; ○twr on fortress; *Horn Mo (B) 30s.*

No. 3 38°40'·04N 09°18'·25W, Fl G 3s.

Forte de São Julião ☆ 38°40'·46N 09°19'·53W, Oc R 5s 38m 14M.

Lage 38°40'·74N 09°18'·61W, Fl Y 12s.

No. 5 38°40'·43N 07°17'·66W, Fl G 4s.

No. 7 38°40'·64N 09°16'·90W, Fl G 5s.

No. 9 38°40'·63N 09°14'·49W, Fl G 6s.

Bridge (Ponte 25 de Abril). The N (38°41'·63N 09°10'·68W) and S (38°41'·10N 09°10'·56W) pillars are lit Fl (3) G 9s and Fl (3) R 9s.

Cabo Espichel ☆ 38°24'·94N 09°13'·05W, Fl 4s 167m **26M**; W 6-sided twr; *Horn 31s.*

▶ SESIMBRA

Cavalo ☆ 38°26'·06N 09°07'·08W, Oc 5s 34m 14M; R○twr.

Ldg lts 003·5°, both L Fl R 5s 9/21m 7/6M. Front, 38°26'·56N 09°06'·16W. Rear 34m from front. Pierhead Fl R 3s 8M.

▶ SETÚBAL

Ldg lts 039·7°, both Iso Y 6s 12/60m **22M** (by day 5/6M). Front, fish dock 38°31'·15N 08°53'·95W; R structure, W stripes. Rear, **Azêda**, 1·7M from front; 038·3°-041·3°; R hut on piles.

No. 1 38°26'·98N 08°58'·18W, Fl G 3s 5M.

No. 2 38°27'·21N 08°58'·45W, Fl (2) R 10s 13m 9M; R□ on R column, W cupola; ***Racon B, 15M.***

No. 4 38°27'·92N 08°57'·71W, Fl R 4s 13m 4M.

No. 3 38°28'·33N 08°56'·78W, Fl G 3s.

No. 5 38°29'·82N 08°55'·28W, Fl G 4s 13m 4M.

Forte de Outão ☆ 38°29'·31N 08°56'·06W, Oc R 6s 33m 12M.

Pinheiro da Cruz ☆ 38°15'·46N 08°46'·34W, Fl 3s 66m 11M; W○col, R stripes. Firing area extends 6M offshore.

▶ SINES

Cabo de Sines ☆ 37°57'·56N 08°52'·83W, Fl (2) 15s 55m **26M**.

37°55'·36N 08°55'·80W, Fl (5) Y 20s; 2·2M WSW of W mole hd.

W mole ☆ 37°56'·46N 08°53'·33W, Fl 3s 20m 12M.

37°56'·12N 08°53'·25W, Fl R 3s 6M; 285m S of W mole hd.

E mole ☆ 37°56'·33N 08°51'·96W, L Fl G 8s 16m 6M. 1·17M SE: Elbow ☆ 37°55'·47N 08°50'·86W, L Fl R 8s 6M; W twr, R bands.

Marina bkwtr ☆ 37°57'·04N 08°52'·04W, Fl G 4s 4M.

Ponta de Gaivota ☆ 37°51'·10N 08°47'·79W, L Fl 7s 19m 13M.

Rio Mira, ent ☆ 37°43'·13N 08°47'·43W, Fl 3s 22m 10M.

Cabo Sardão ☆ 37°35'·94N 08°49'·02W, Fl (3) 15s 67m **23M**.

▶ CAPE ST VINCENT/SAGRES

Cabo de São Vicente ☆ 37°01'·37N 08°59'·82W, Fl 5s 84m **32M**; W twr and bldg; *Horn Mo (I) 30s.*

Ponta de Sagres ☆ 36°59'·64N 08°56'·97W, Iso R 2s 52m 11M.

Baleeira mole ☆ 37°00'·67N 08°55'·50W, Fl WR 4s 12m, W14M, R11M; W254°-355°, R355°-254°; W□ twr.

▶ LAGOS

Pta da Piedade ☆ 37°04'·81N 08°40'·20W, Fl 7s 50m **20M**.

E mole ☆ 37°05'·93N 08°39'·98W, Fl (2) G 6s 5M.

Alvor ent 37°07'·0N 08°37'·0W, Fl R/G 4s; W twrs, R/G bands.

▶ PORTIMÃO

Ponta do Altar ☆ 37°06'·34N 08°31'·17W, L Fl 5s 31m **16M**; 290°-170°; W twr and bldg.

Ldg lts 020·9°. Front 37°07'·35N 08°31'·32W, Oc R 5s 18m 8M. Rear, 87m from front, Oc R 7s 32m 8M.

E mole ☆ 37°06'·50N 08°31'·59W, Fl G 5s 9m 7M.

W mole ☆ 37°06'·52N 08°31'·77W, Fl R 5s 9m 7M.

No. 2 37°06'·96N 08°31'·54W, Fl R 4s.

Marina, S ent ☆ 37°07'·18N 08°31'·50W, Fl R 6s 3M.

N ent ☆ 37°07'·23N 08°31'·50W, Fl G 6s 3M.

Pta de Alfanzina ☆ 37°05'·22N 08°26'·59W, Fl (2) 15s 62m **29M**.

Armacão de Pera ☆ 37°05'·92N 08°21'·21W, Oc R 5s 24m 6M.

▶ ALBUFEIRA

Ponta da Baleeira ☆ 37°04'·84N 08°15'·88W, Oc 6s 30m 11M.

N bkwtr ☆, Fl (2) G 5s 9m 4M, approx 37°04'·90N 08°15'·52W.

S bkwtr ☆, Fl (2) R 5s 9m 4M. Praia da Albufeira, E end of bay,

Olhos de Água ☆ 37°05'·47N 08°11'·40W, L Fl 5s 29m 7M.

▶ VILAMOURA

Vilamoura ☆ 37°04'·50N 08°07'·42W, Fl 5s 17m **19M**.

Marina, W mole ☆ 37°04'·19N 08°07'·49W, Fl R 4s 13m 5M.

E mole ☆ 37°04'·22N 08°07'·42W, Fl G 4s 13m 5M.

▶ FARO, OLHÃO and TAVIRA

Ent from sea: E mole ☆ 36°57'·79N 07°52'·14W, Fl G 4s 9m 6M.

W mole ☆ 37°57'·84N 08°52'·26W, Fl R 4s 9m 6M; appr on 352°.

Access ldg lts 020·9°. Front, Barra Nova 37°58'·22N 07°52'·00W, Oc 4s 8m 6M. Rear, **C. de Santa Maria** ☆ 36°58'·48N 07°51'·88W, Fl (4) 17s 49m **25M**; W○twr.

No. 6 36°58'·49N 07°52'·12W, Fl R 6s. No. 20 Fl R 6s, faces the commercial quay, 37°00'·13N 07°55'·11W, approx 2M before **Faro** proper. At No. 6 the Canal de Olhão forks NE/1.6M to: No. 8 36°59'·90N 07°51'·07W, Fl R 3s; thence N & E to **Olhão**.

Tavira ldg lts 325·9°. Front, Fl R 3s 6m 4M. Rear, Iso R 6s 9m 5M.

W mole ☆ 37°06'·79N 07°37'·10W, Fl R 2·5s 7m 7M.

▶ VILA REAL DE SANTO ANTONIO

Lt ho ☆ 37°11'·23N 07°25'·00W, Fl 6·5s 51m **26M**; W twr, B bands.

R. Guadiano, Bar buoys 37°08'·90N 07°23'·44W, Q (3) G 6s.

37°09'·14N 07°23'·82W, Fl R 4s.

W trng wall ☆ 37°09'·75N 07°24'·03W, Fl R 5s 4M.

E trng wall ☆ 37°09'·93N 07°23'·63W, Fl G 3s 4M.

Marina, QR at S corner; QR/QG ent; QR at N corner.

9.24.4 PASSAGE INFORMATION

BIBLIOGRAPHY The *SW Spain & Portugal Cruising Companion* (Nautical Data Ltd/Jens) covers from Bayona to Gibraltar. *W coasts of Spain and Portugal Pilot* (Admiralty, NP 67) covers from Cabo Ortegal to Gibraltar. *Guia del Navegante* has fair cover, in English, of SW Spain, but is limited elsewhere. Passage information for the coasts of NW and N Spain is in 9.23.4.

RÍO MIÑO TO CABO RASO (AC 3633, 3634, 3635) The Río Miño (*Minho* in Portuguese), 15M S of Cabo Silleiro, forms the northern border between Spain and Portugal. The river ent is difficult and best not attempted.

In summer the Portuguese Trades (*Nortada*) are N'ly F4-6 and the Portugal Current runs S at $\frac{1}{2}$-$\frac{3}{4}$kn. ▶*Tidal streams appear to set N on the flood and S on the ebb, but are ill documented.*◀ In summer gales are rare; coastal fog is common in the mornings. If N-bound, especially if lightly crewed, it is worth making daily passages between about 0400 and 1200 to avoid the stronger winds in the afternoon, which may be increased by a fresh onshore sea breeze.

The 150M long coastline is hilly as far S as Pôrto, then generally low and sandy, backed by pine forests, to Cabo Carvoeiro; there are few prominent features. Coasting yachts should keep about 3M offshore. Viana do Castelo (9.24.6) is a commercial and fishing port, with a marina at the NE end. Povoa de Varzim (9.24.7) 21M S of Viana has a fully equipped marina.

Port closures. Some hbrs, especially on this coast, may be closed for weather reasons, ie strong to gale force onshore winds and/or heavy swell causing dangerous breaking seas at the hbr ent or over the bar. At Leixões, Aveiro and Figueira da Foz the following signals, with minor variations = port closed:

By day: cylinder/ball hoisted close up; at half-mast = enter with caution. By night: ●●●(vertical), either steady or flashing.

Leixões (9.24.8) is an industrial port 2M N of the mouth of the R. Douro; it may be closed in bad weather due to heavy swell breaking on the bar. The R. Douro is not easily entered; but Oporto can be visited by road from Leixões. Aveiro (9.24.9) and Figueira da Foz (9.24.10), both with marinas, are exposed to the west and can be closed in bad weather; the latter can be identified from N or S by the higher ground (257m) of Cabo Mondego. 34M further SSW Nazaré (9.24.11) is an artificial fishing hbr and port of refuge with easy ent and a marina.

Cabo Carvoeiro, the W tip of Peniche peninsula, looks like an island from afar (do not confuse with Ilha Berlenga). Ilha da Berlenga and Os Farilhões, both lit, are respectively 5 and 9·5M NW of Cabo Carvoeiro, 14M W of which is a N/S orientated TSS; see 9.24.2. The normal coastal route is between Cabo Carvoeiro and Berlenga; this chan is deep, clear and 5M wide, although it appears narrower until opened up. Peniche fishing port/marina (9.24.12) on the S side of the peninsula is well sheltered from N'lies, but open to SW swell. The coastline rises steadily to the high (527m) ridge of Sintra, inland of Cabo da Roca, S of which it drops steeply to the low headland of Cabo Raso. A TSS (9.24.2) lies 10M W of Cabo da Roca, the most W'ly point of Europe.

CABO RASO TO CAPE ST VINCENT (charts 3635, 3636) Cascais (9.24.13), about 3·5M E of Cabo Raso, has a marina and is a favoured anch for yachts on passage or not wishing to go 12M further E to Lisboa. From Cascais to the Rio Tejo (Tagus) use the Barra Norte (least depth 5m) which joins the main Barra Sul abeam São Julião lt. In Lisboa (9.24.14) there are 6 marinas along the N bank of R Tejo which is 1M wide and clear. If S-bound from Lisboa, stand on about 1M SW of Forte Bugio lt before altering toward Cabo Espichel.

East from this flattish cape the coast rises to 500m high cliffs nearing the ent to Rio Sado. The fishing hbr of Sesimbra (9.24.15) is well sheltered from the N, or anchor in a shallow bay at Arrábida. The port of Setúbal (9.24.16) has limited yacht facilities. Unbroken beach stretches 35M from R Sado to Cabo de Sines, lt ho and 3 conspic chimneys to the E. At Sines (8.24.17), a strategically placed commercial port, a small marina offers limited facilities. The 56M rky coast to Cabo São Vicente offers no shelter except SE of Punta da Arrifana, in a tiny bay (37°17'·51N 08°52'·08W) protected from N'lies by high cliffs.

CAPE ST VINCENT TO RIO GUADIANA (AC 89, 93) 5M off Cabo São Vicente a TSS (9.24.2) is orientated NW/SE. There are passage anchs, sheltered from N'lies, at Enseada de Belixe, E of C. São Vicente, and at Enseadas de Sagres and da Baleeira, NE of Pta da Sagres. E of C. São Vicente the summer weather becomes more Mediterranean, ie hotter, clearer and winds more from the NW to SW. Swell may decrease, tidal streams are slight and the current runs SE. Hbrs along the coasts of the Algarve and SW Andalucía are sheltered from all but S'lies (infrequent).

The choice of routes to Gibraltar is between a direct track 110°/ 175M (Cabo São Vicente to Tarifa) or a series of coastal legs. There are good marinas at Lagos (9.24.18), Portimão (9.24.19), and Albufeira, newly opened (9.24.20). Vilamoura (9.24.21) is a large, long-established marina about 10M W of Faro. At Cabo de Santa Maria a gap in the low-lying dunes gives access to the lagoons and chans leading to Faro and Olhão (9.24.22), where some peaceful anchs may be found, although yacht facilities are limited. On the Portuguese bank of the Rio Guadiana there is a marina at Vila Real de Santo António (9.24.23).

9.24.5 SPECIAL NOTES FOR PORTUGAL

Districts/Provinces: Portugal is divided into 18 administrative districts. But the names of the former provinces (on the coast, N-S: Minho, Douro, Beira Litoral, Estremadura, Alentejo and Algarve) are still used and appear below the name of each hbr.

Charts: There are 2 folios: the F94 and the old FA (*antigo*) (now contains only 7 charts, with 2 digit chart nos). F94 charts (5 digit chart nos) comprise: 4 offshore charts 23201-04; 6 coastal charts 24201-06; 12 hbr charts 26301-12; 8 hbr appr charts 26401-08; and 3 charts of hbr plans 27501-03. 12 Leisure (Recreio) charts at 1:150 000 scale, Nos 25R01-12, cover the whole coast.

Portuguese charts, publications and a free mini-catalogue are available from Chart agents. One of the largest is: J Garraio & Ca Lda, ave 24 de Julho, 2 - 1st Dto, 1200-478 Lisboa; ☎ 213 473 081, ℻ 213 428 950. info@jgarraio.pt www.jgarraio.pt The contact details for the Portuguese Hydrographic Office are given in Chapter 1, section 1.5.

Time: Standard time is UT; DST is UT –1, from the last Sun in Mar until the Sat before the last Sun in Oct.

Representation: Portuguese Tourist Office, 22-25A Sackville St, London W1X 1DE; ☎ 020 7494 1441, ℻ 020 7494 1868. British Embassy, Rua de S. Bernardo 33, 1249-082 Lisboa; ☎ 213 924 000, ℻ 213 392 4188 (Consular). There are British Consuls at Porto & Portimão. Tourist Office, Ave António Augusto de Aguiar 86, P-1000 Lisboa; ☎ (213) 425 231, ℻ 468 772.

Telephone: To call Portugal from UK dial +351, the area code less the initial 0, then the ☎ number. To call UK from Portugal, dial +44, the area code less the initial 0, then the ☎ number. The area code is mandatory, even within the same area; ie nine numbers in all. National emergency ☎ 115; National SAR ☎ 214.401.919.

R/T: VHF Ch 09 is the Recreational craft channel; it is used by all Portuguese marinas, in addition to any Port VHF channels.

Access: There are daily flights in season to/from the UK via Porto, Lisboa and Faro which are quite well connected by bus and/or train to other towns. See also 9.25.5 for Spanish flights.

Currency: The € is the unit of currency. Credit cards are widely accepted; cash dispensers are in most medium-sized towns.

Public Holidays: Jan 1; Shrove Tues; Good Friday; April 25 (Liberation Day); May 1 (Labour Day); Jun 6 (Corpus Christi); Jun 10 (Camões Day); Aug 15 (Assumption); Oct 5 (Republic Day); Nov 1 (All Saints Day); Dec 1 (Independence Day), 8 (Immaculate Conception), 25 (Christmas). Also every town has a local *festa*.

Documents: Portugal observes EU regulations but formalities may be lengthy so organise your papers to include:
Personal – Passports; crew list, ideally on headed paper with the yacht's rubber stamp, giving DoB, passport nos, where joined/ intended departure. Certificate of Competence (Yachtmaster Offshore, ICC/HOCC etc). Radio Operator's certificate. Form E111 (advised for medical treatment).
Yacht – Registration certificate, Part 1 or SSR. Proof of VAT status. Marine insurance. Ship's Radio licence. Itinerary, backed up by ship's log.

9.24.6 VIANA DO CASTELO

Minho **41°41'·68N 08°49'·21W** (Marina ent) ❁❁❁◊◊✿✿✿

CHARTS AC 3633/4, 3257; PC 24201, 26401; SC 41B.

TIDES

Standard Port LISBOA (⟶); ML 2·0; Zone 0 (UT)

Times				Height (metres)			
High Water		Low Water		MHWS	MHWN	MLWN	MLWS
0400	0900	0400	0900	3·8	3·0	1·5	0·6
1600	2100	1600	2100				
Differences VIANA DO CASTELO							
–0020	0000	+0010	+0015	–0·4	–0·4	–0·1	0·0
ESPOSENDE (41°32'N)							
–0020	0000	+0010	+0015	–0·6	–0·5	–0·2	–0·1

SHELTER Excellent in marina (3m), 1·5M up R. Lima, 200m short of low (4·6m) and noisy road/rail bridge; possible strong cross current when entering marina. Moor on outside of first pontoon, fore and aft. No other yacht berths; no ⚓ in river.

NAVIGATION WPT 41°39'·90N 08°50'·38W, 005°/8½ca to abeam No 1 SHM lt buoy. From WPT keep rear ldg lt on brg 005° to enter the chan, dredged 8m, which curves to NE. Ignore the 012·5° ldg line because it leads into a shipyard/FV area and passes too close to the outer mole hd (Fl R 3s) which should be given a wide clearance; best water lies further E. Nos 5 to 14 buoys are Fl R 3s or Fl G 3s; No 14 is off the marina ent. The flood reaches 2kn max; the ebb 3kn, but 6kn if river in spate. Night entry not advised if any swell.

LIGHTS AND MARKS Montedor lt ho is a R twr 4M NNW. ✠ dome on Monte Santa Luzia is conspic in transit with ldg lts. Storm sigs are displayed close SE of front ldg lt. See 9.24.3 for lt details.

R/T Call *Porto de Viana* Ch 16; 11 (0900-1200; 1400-1700LT), Yacht Club and Marina Ch 09.

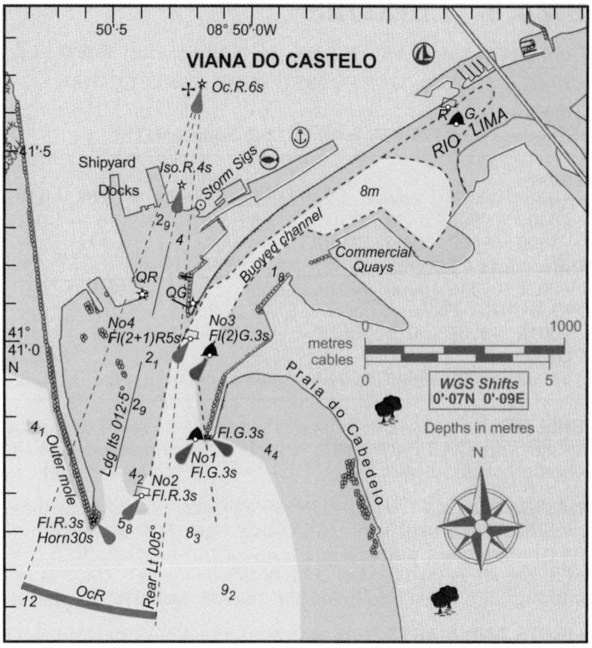
VIANA DO CASTELO
50'·5
08° 50'·0W
Oc.R.6s
41'·5
Shipyard
Docks
Iso.R.4s
Storm Sigs
Buoyed channel
RIO LIMA
8m
Commercial Quays
QR
QG
No4
Fl(2+1)R5s
No3
Fl(2)G.3s
41°
41'·0
N
metres
cables
1000
WGS Shifts
0'·07N 0'·09E
Depths in metres
Praia do Cabedelo
Outer mole
Ldg lts 012·5°
Fl.G.3s
No1
Fl.G.3s
No2
Fl.R.3s
Fl.R.3s
Horn30s
Rear Lt 005°
OcR
N

TELEPHONE (Dial Code 258) Port HM 829.096; ⊖ 823.346; Met, via marina; Police 822.345.

FACILITIES **Marina** (150+ some Ⓥ; F&A on D pontoon), €1.87, ☎ 359.546, 📠 359.535, Slip, P, D, C (20 ton), YC, ME, El, ⚒, CH, BY, SM, Gaz, Ⓔ. **Town:** 🛒, R, Bar, ✉, Ⓗ, Ⓑ, ⇌ (1km); ✈ Porto (50 km).

9.24.7 PÓVOA DE VARZIM

Minho **41°22'·20N 08°46'·00W** (Marina ent) ❁❁◊◊✿✿

CHARTS AC 3634 (too small scale, 1:200,000, to be of much practical value); PC 24201, 27501 (not yet published, 2004).

TIDES

Standard Port LISBOA (⟶); Zone 0 (UT)

Times				Height (metres)			
High Water		Low Water		MHWS	MHWN	MLWN	MLWS
0400	0900	0400	0900	3·8	3·0	1·5	0·6
1600	2100	1600	2100				
Differences PÓVOA DE VARZIM							
–0020	0000	+0010	+0015	–0·3	–0·3	–0·1	–0·1

SHELTER Good in all winds, but ent is rough in heavy swell and becomes impractical when wave height >3m; in particular give a wide berth to the head of the N mole where there may be broken water. The N part is a busy FV hbr and the marina is to the SE. Berth on hammerhead of the N'most reception and fuel pontoon in 2·4 to 3m. Or ⚓ in NE part of hbr in 3m clear of FVs.

NAVIGATION WPT 41°21'·48N 08°46'·73W, 030°/1M to hbr ent. Follow SHM buoys (marking a shoal near the S bkwtr) round to the marina. Tidal streams are weak but there is an appreciable current, mainly S-going, along the coast.

Work (unspecified) is in progress 1·6M to 5·6M NNW of the hbr in a rectangular area defined by 41°23'·75N, 41°47'·32N and by 08°50'·92W, approx 3M offshore; a SPM buoy, Fl (5) Y 20s, marks the NW corner of this area.

LIGHTS AND MARKS Mole hd lts are on R and G posts with W bands. High rise blocks/hotels and sandy beaches are conspic. Monte São Félix is an isolated rounded hill (209m) 4·5M NNE.

R/T Marina Ch 09. Hbr Ch 11, 16; M-F 0900-1200, 1400-1700.

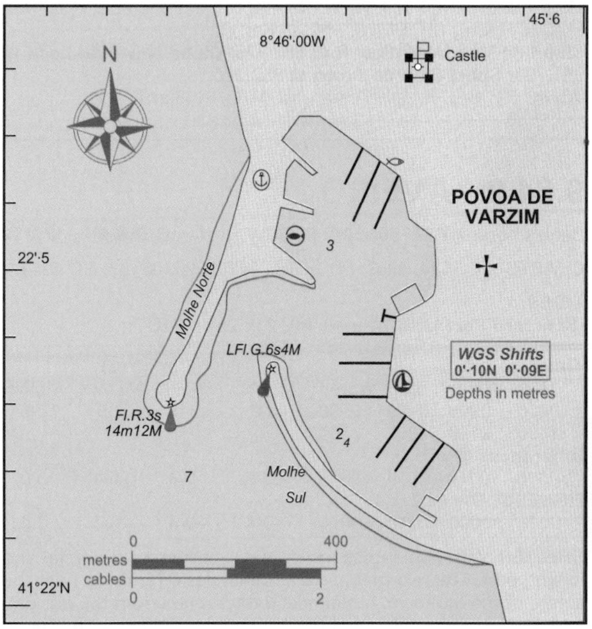
45'·6
8°46'·00W
N
Castle
PÓVOA DE VARZIM
3
22'·5
Molhe Norte
LFl.G.6s4M
WGS Shifts
0'·10N 0'·09E
Depths in metres
Fl.R.3s
14m12M
7
Molhe Sul
0
400
metres
cables
41°22'N
2

TELEPHONE (Dial Code 252) Marina ☎ 688121, 📠 688123. Ⓗ 690600; Police 620026; Tourist office 298120.

FACILITIES **Marina** marinadapovoa@clix.pt (241, inc some Ⓥ), €1.44; 18m max LOA. It is very friendly and has good facilities: D, BH (35 ton) ME, El, ⚒, CH, BY, Gaz, Ⓔ.
Town: 🛒, R, Bar, ✉, Ⓗ, Ⓑ, ⇌ (15 mins walk; trains to Porto, 30km and ✈ 18km).

9.24.8 LEIXÕES

Douro **41°10'·44N 08°42'·27W** (Abm N mole hd) ✿✿✿◊◊✿

CHARTS AC 3634, 3258; PC 23201, 24201, 26402; SC 418A.

TIDES

Standard Port LISBOA (⟶); ML 2·0; Zone 0 (UT)

Times				Height (metres)			
High Water		Low Water		MHWS	MHWN	MLWN	MLWS
0400	0900	0400	0900	3·8	3·0	1·5	0·6
1600	2100	1600	2100				
Differences LEIXÕES							
–0025	–0010	0000	+0010	–0·4	–0·4	–0·1	0·0
RIO DOURO ENT							
–0010	+0005	+0015	+0025	–0·6	–0·5	–0·2	–0·1
PORTO							
+0002	+0002	+0040	+0040	–0·5	–0·4	–0·2	0·0

SHELTER Very good in rather oily marina (2 to 3·5m), reception to port; no swell once inside N mole. Or ⚓ outside, as on the chartlet, in about 4m; Outer ⚓ is for medium-sized vessels.

NAVIGATION WPT 41°09'·97N 08°42'·14W, 350°/8ca to inner mole hds. Ent is usually simple. Keep at least 150m off the N mole hd (Quebra-mar), due to a wreck and a sunken bkwtr to S & W of it. Leça lt, Fl (3) 14s 56m 28M, W tr/B bands, is 1·7M N of hbr ent; brg 350° leads into inner hbr, thence track 015° to marina.

LIGHTS AND MARKS N of Leça lt are many R/W banded chy's at the oil refinery. From the S, bldgs of Põrto are conspic. Traffic signals, as in 9.24.4, are shown from a mast on the Hbr Office (close NE of the marina) when the port is closed due to unsafe conditions at the ent, caused by strong W'lies and/or swell.

R/T Marina *Porto Atlântico* VHF Ch 09.

TELEPHONE (Dial Code 229) HM 953.000; ⊖ 951.476; Met 484.527 (Põrto airport); LB 226.170.091; Police 383.649; Fire 380.018; ⊞ 391.000; Tourist Office 384.414; Brit Consul 226.184.789.

FACILITIES **Marina Porto Atlântico** (200 + 40 ⓥ, F&A), €1.70, ☎ 964.895, 📠 964.899, www.marinaportoatlantico.net P, D, ME, El, C (6·5 ton), CH, SM, Ⓔ, ⚒, ⊡, Bar, R.
Clube de Vela Atlântico, R ☎ 952.725; **Clube Naval de Leça** ☎ 951.700; **Sport Club do Porto** ☎ 952.225.
Town: 🛒, Bar, R, Ⓑ, ✉; ⇌ and ✈ Põrto (5km).

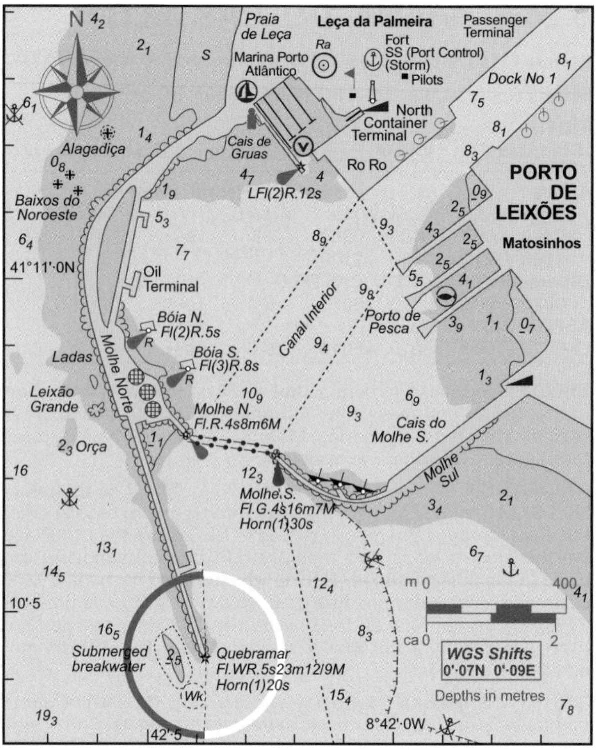
Praia de Leça
Leça da Palmeira
Passenger Terminal
Fort
SS (Port Control) (Storm)
Pilots
Marina Porto Atlântico
Dock No 1
North Container Terminal
Cais de Gruas
Ro Ro
Alagadiça
LFl(2)R.12s
PORTO DE LEIXÕES
Matosinhos
Baixos do Noroeste
41°11'·0N
Oil Terminal
Canal Interior
Porto de Pesca
Bóia N. Fl(2)R.5s
Bóia S. Fl(3)R.8s
Ladas
Molhe Norte
Leixão Grande
Molhe N. Fl.R.4s8m6M
Cais do Molhe S.
Orça
Molhe S. Fl.G.4s16m7M Horn(1)30s
Molhe Sul
10'·5
Submerged breakwater
Quebramar Fl.WR.5s23m12/9M Horn(1)20s
Wk
WGS Shifts 0'·07N 0'·09E
Depths in metres
42'·5
8°42'·0W

ADJACENT HARBOUR

PORTO (OPORTO), 41°08'·80N 08°40'·55W. Tides, see above. AC 3634, 3258. Lts/buoys, see 9.24.3. Difficult river ent, prone to swell and fast current; dangerous in strong W'lies (see 9.24.4 for port closure signals). Ldg lts, Oc R 6s, lead 078·7° over the bar which shifts constantly; charted depths are unreliable. Keep well N of Cabadelo, a sandspit on the S side of the ent with unmarked, drying rocks. The first bridge has 60m clearance, the 2nd 8·8m. Limited AB at Cais de Estiva, N bank, 3M from ent. From Leixões, the R. Douro is easy to visit by land for a prior recce.

9.24.9 AVEIRO

Beira Litoral **40°38'·58N 08°45'·76W** (Hbr ent) ✿✿✿◊◊✿✿✿

CHARTS AC 3634, 3253; PC 24201, 24202, 26403, 59; SC 4219.

TIDES

Standard Port LISBOA (⟶); ML 2·0; Zone 0 (UT)

Times				Height (metres)			
High Water		Low Water		MHWS	MHWN	MLWN	MLWS
0400	0900	0400	0900	3·8	3·0	1·5	0·6
1600	2100	1600	2100				
Differences AVEIRO							
+0005	+0010	+0010	+0015	–0·5	–0·4	–0·1	0·0
FIGUEIRA DA FOZ							
–0015	0000	+0010	+0020	–0·4	–0·4	–0·1	0·0

SHELTER Very good, once inside this extensive commercial and fishing port. The two marinas are: Canal das Pirâmides, near the centre of the old town, but almost 6 track miles from the hbr ent; and Torreira, about 8M N of the hbr ent in a long lagoon (Ria de Aveiro) extending N. Two rivers flow in from the S.

NAVIGATION WPT 40°38'·54N 08°46'·55W, 085°/6ca to hbr ent. The bar, with depths varying around 6m, becomes impassable in strong onshore winds; best access at HW –2 or –1. From abeam the lt ho the main chan trends NE for approx 1·3M to a junction where it bears stbd in a long (2·3M) curve onto S to Terminal Sul. Here the chan turns ENE for 1·3M to a lock into the Canal das Pirâmides marina. For Torreira marina take the secondary chan (Canal de S. Jacinto) to port of the junction; it becomes shallow (2·5m) and is marked by B/W SHM piles. Best to get prior, local advice; AC 3253 only covers the first mile.

LIGHTS AND MARKS Hbr lts as chartlet & 9.24.3. The red/white banded lt ho (also the rear 085° ldg mark) is conspic at the ent. The 065° ldg line (marks hard to see) leads between the moles. A military airfield with conspic control twr is NE of the hbr ent. Tfc sigs (9.24.4) are shown from a mast close N of the lt ho.

R/T VHF Ch 11, 16 (M-F, 0900-1200 & 1400-1700).

TELEPHONE (Dial code 234) HM ☎ 366.250, 📠 366.247; ⊖ & Met via HM; www.portodeaveiro.pt portoaveiro@mail.telepac.pt

FACILITIES **Marina** in Canal das Pirâmides: transit the lock which opens a/r near HW; waiting pontoon outside. Berth on a pontoon inside with FW, ⚡; or moor fore & aft to piles as space permits. The canal extends about 2ca to a low motorway bridge, thence to the town centre, navigable by dinghy.
Clube Naval de Aveiro, 6ca WSW of the lock on the S side of the main Canal, is not often manned; BY, Slip, ME, ⚒ are nearby.
Town: Aveiro, with its *moliceiros* (mussel boats), network of canals and fine buildings is reminiscent of Venice. 🛒, R, Bar, Ⓑ, ✉; ⇌ to Figueira da Foz and Coimbra (worth a visit) to the S and Porto to the N; ✈ Porto (77km by motorway); ✈ Lisboa (256km by motorway).
Marina at Torreira: Only advised for shoal draft yachts. Usual facilities in the resort-style village. Excellent beaches.

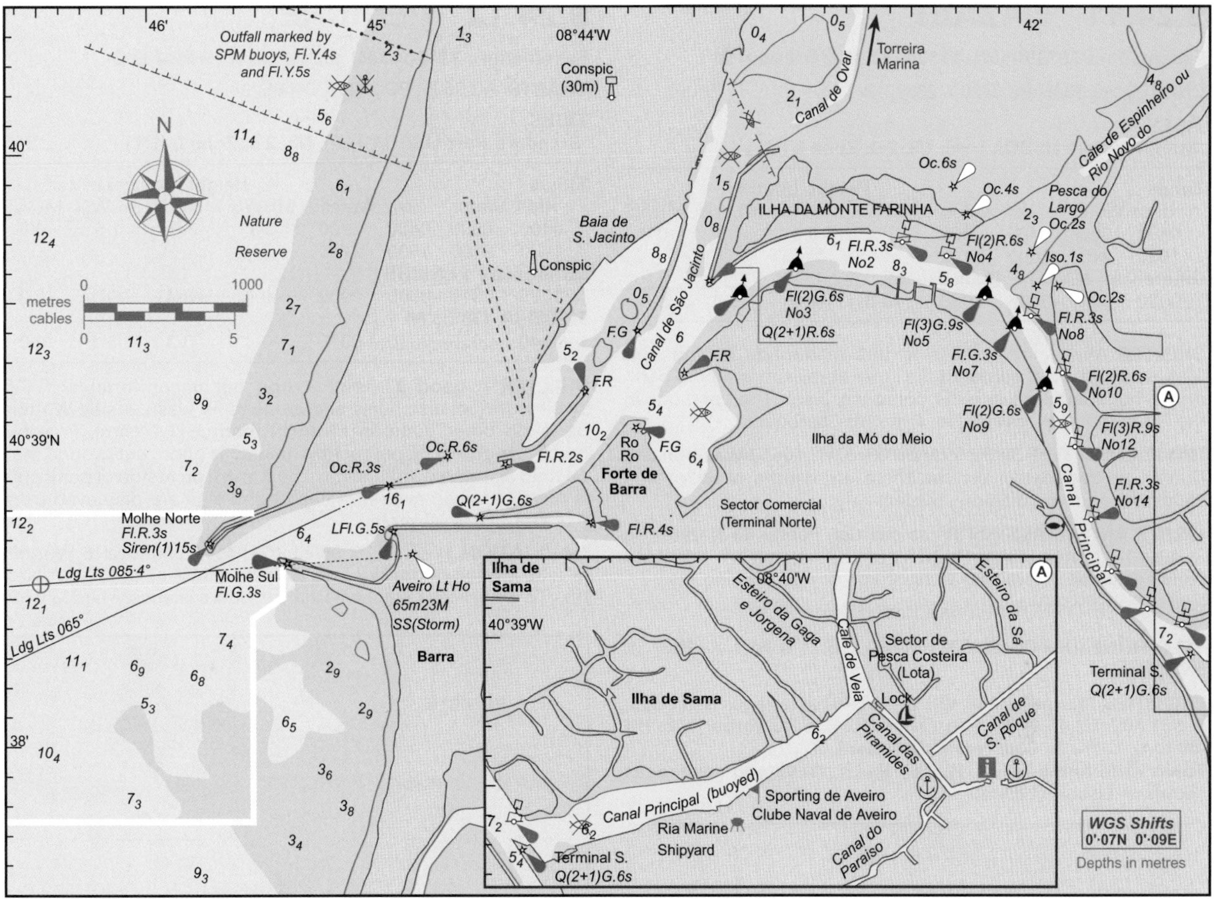
Outfall marked by SPM buoys, Fl.Y.4s and Fl.Y.5s
08°44'W
Conspic (30m)
Torreira Marina
Canal de Ovar
Nature Reserve
metres
cables
Baia de S. Jacinto
Conspic
Canal de São Jacinto
ILHA DA MONTE FARINHA
Cale de Espinheiro ou Rio Novo do
Oc.6s
Oc.4s
Pesca do Largo Oc.2s
Iso.1s
Oc.2s
Fl.R.3s No2
Fl(2)R.6s No4
Fl(2)G.6s No3
Q(2+1)R.6s
Fl(3)G.9s No5
Fl.G.3s No7
Fl.R.3s No8
Fl(2)R.6s No10
Fl(2)G.6s No9
Fl(3)R.9s No12
Fl.R.3s No14
Ilha da Mó do Meio
F.G
F.R
Ro Ro
Forte de Barra
Oc.R.6s
Oc.R.3s
Fl.R.2s
Q(2+1)G.6s
Fl.R.4s
Sector Comercial (Terminal Norte)
Canal Principal
40°39'N
Molhe Norte Fl.R.3s Siren(1)15s
LFl.G.5s
Ldg Lts 085·4°
Molhe Sul Fl.G.3s
Aveiro Lt Ho 65m23M SS(Storm)
Ldg Lts 065°
Barra
Ilha de Sama
08°40'W
40°39'W
Esteiro da Gaga e Jorgena
Cale de Veia
Esteiro da Sá
Sector de Pesca Costeira (Lota)
Lock
Canal de S. Roque
Canal das Piramides
Canal Principal (buoyed)
Sporting de Aveiro
Clube Naval de Aveiro
Ria Marine Shipyard
Canal do Paraiso
Terminal S. Q(2+1)G.6s
WGS Shifts 0'·07N 0'·09E
Depths in metres

9.24.10 FIGUEIRA DA FOZ

Beira Litoral **40°08'·75N 08°52'·40W** ❁❁◊◊✿✿

CHARTS AC 3634, 3635, 3253; PC 24201/2, 26404, 34, 64; SC 42A

TIDES See under Aveiro, 9.24.9; ML 2·0; Zone 0 (UT)

SHELTER Excellent in marina (2·5-3m) on N bank, ¾M from hbr ent. Strong ebb tide can affect pontoons nearest marina ent. Shipyards, repair basins and fishing harbour on S bank.

NAVIGATION WPT 40°08'·68N 08°53'·04W, 081°/5ca to hbr ent. No offshore dangers. Bar at ent has charted depths of less than 4m, but is said to be dredged 5m. It shifts/shoals constantly and can be highly dangerous in swell, especially Nov-Mar with strong W/NW winds. Conditions on the bar are signalled from mast at Forte de Santa Catarina (N of inner moles) and may be broadcast on VHF Ch 11; see 9.24.5.

LIGHTS AND MARKS Lts as chartlet. Cabo Mondego, Fl 5s 96m 28M, is 3M NW of hbr ent. Buarcos, Iso WRG 6s, is on the beach 1·1M N of hbr ent. Ldg lts lead 081·5° past marina ent. 1·5M E of ent a white suspension bridge (39m cl'nce), is conspic from seaward; as are extensive beaches N and S of hbr ent.

R/T Port Ch 11. Marina Ch 09. **TELEPHONE** (Dial Code 233).

FACILITIES **Marina** (150+ 50 Ⓥ), €2.46, ☎ 402.910, 📠 402.920, Gaz, C, ME, ⚒, CH, ▣. **Town:** R, 🛒, Ⓑ, ⇌; ✈ Pŏrto.

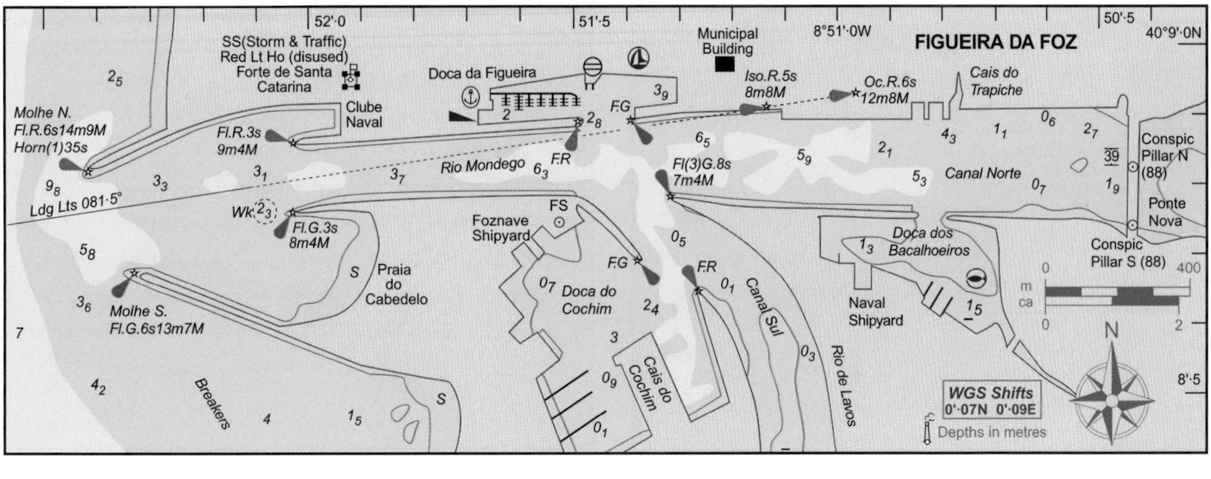
52'·0
51'·5
8°51'·0W
50'·5
40°9'·0N
FIGUEIRA DA FOZ
SS(Storm & Traffic) Red Lt Ho (disused)
Forte de Santa Catarina
Doca da Figueira
Municipal Building
Clube Naval
Molhe N. Fl.R.6s14m9M Horn(1)35s
Fl.R.3s 9m4M
F.G
Iso.R.5s 8m8M
Oc.R.6s 12m8M
Cais do Trapiche
Conspic Pillar N (88)
Ponte Nova
Rio Mondego
F.R
Fl(3)G.8s 7m4M
Canal Norte
Ldg Lts 081·5°
Wk
Fl.G.3s 8m4M
FS
Foznave Shipyard
Praia do Cabedelo
Doca dos Bacalhoeiros
Conspic Pillar S (88)
F.G
F.R
Doca do Cochim
Canal Sul
Naval Shipyard
Molhe S. Fl.G.6s13m7M
Cais do Cochim
Rio de Lavos
Breakers
WGS Shifts 0'·07N 0'·09E
Depths in metres
8'·5

9.24.11 NAZARÉ

Estremadura **39°35'·50N 09°04'·57W** ❁❁❁◊◊✿✿

CHARTS AC 3635; PC 24202, 26302, 34, 65.

TIDES
Standard Port LISBOA (⟶); ML 2·0; Zone 0 (UT)

Times				Height (metres)			
High Water		Low Water		MHWS	MHWN	MLWN	MLWS
0400	0900	0400	0900	3·8	3·0	1·5	0·6
1600	2100	1600	2100				
Differences NAZARÉ (Pederneira)							
−0030	−0015	−0005	+0005	−0·5	−0·4	−0·1	0·0

SHELTER All-weather access to this man-made fishing hbr. Marina is in the SW corner of the inner hbr; visitors should berth on the hammerheads or outer pontoons, 3·5m. The pontoons in the NE corner are private. No ⚓ in outer harbour.

NAVIGATION WPT 39°35'·77N 09°05'·87W, 106°/1M to hbr ent. Due to an underwater canyon there are depths of 452m and 150m 5M and 4ca offshore respectively.

LIGHTS AND MARKS Hbr lts as chartlet. Pontal da Nazaré, Oc 3s 49m 14M, siren 35s, is 1M NNW of hbr ent on a low headland which must be cleared by at least 2ca due to offlying rks.

R/T Port Ch 11 (HO). Marina Ch 09.

TELEPHONE (Dial Code 262) HM 561.255; ⊜ & Met via HM; Ⓗ 561.116.

FACILITIES Marina (41+14 Ⓥ), ☎ 561.401 (Manager is British), 📠 561.402, €2.46. ATM, Slip, D & P (H24) in NE corner, ME, BH (80 ton), C, ⚒, ⊡; **Club Naval de Nazaré.**
Town: (1½M to the N), 🛒, R, Bar, Ⓑ, ✉; ⇌ Valado dos Frades (7km); ✈ Lisboa (125km).

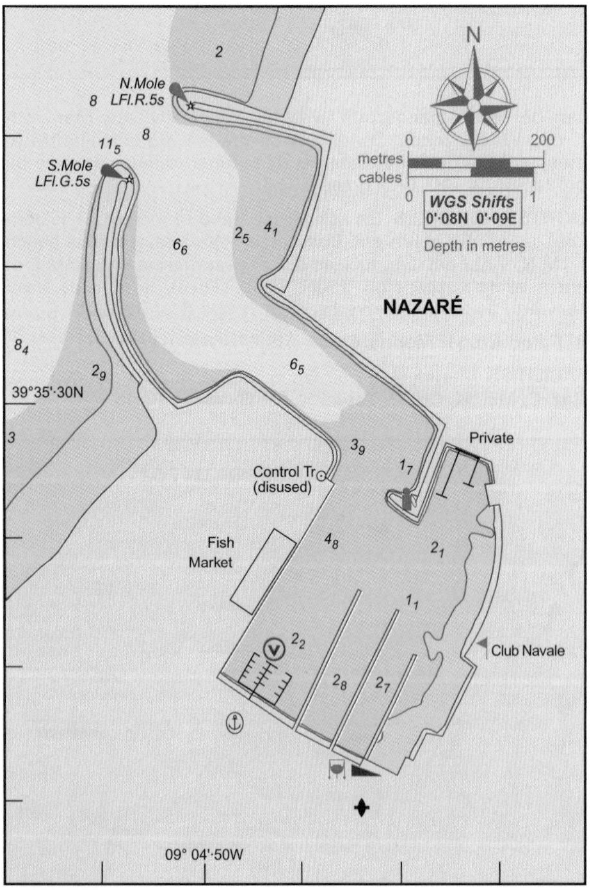
N
N.Mole
LFl.R.5s
S.Mole
LFl.G.5s
0
200
metres
cables
0
1
WGS Shifts
0'·08N 0'·09E
Depth in metres
NAZARÉ
39°35'·30N
Control Tr
(disused)
Private
Fish
Market
Club Navale
09° 04'·50W

9.24.12 PENICHE

Estremadura **39°20'·80N 09°22'·43W** ❁❁◊◊✿✿

CHARTS AC 3635; PC 24203, 26405, 36.

TIDES
Standard Port LISBOA (⟶); ML 2·0; Zone 0 (UT)

Times				Height (metres)			
High Water		Low Water		MHWS	MHWN	MLWN	MLWS
0400	0900	0400	0900	3·8	3·0	1·5	0·6
1600	2100	1600	2100				
Differences PENICHE							
−0035	−0015	−0005	0000	−0·4	−0·4	−0·1	0·0
ERICEIRA (38°58'N)							
−0040	−0025	−0010	−0010	−0·4	−0·3	−0·1	0·0

SHELTER A good all-weather hbr, but uncomfortable if SW swell works in; also noisy and prone to FV wash. Inside W mole berth on outer pontoon of small marina (2·4-3·5m). Possible moorings or ⚓ in SE part of hbr; holding is good, but ground may be foul. 3kn speed limit in hbr. The ⚓ in 4m on N side of peninsula is open to swell, even in S'lies. Storm sigs are displayed from the root of the W mole.

NAVIGATION WPT 39°20'·50N 09°22'·45W, 000°/5ca to W mole hd.The E edge of the N/S TSS (9.24.2) is 14M W of C Carvoeiro; the ITZ embraces Peniche and the offshore islands. The 5M wide

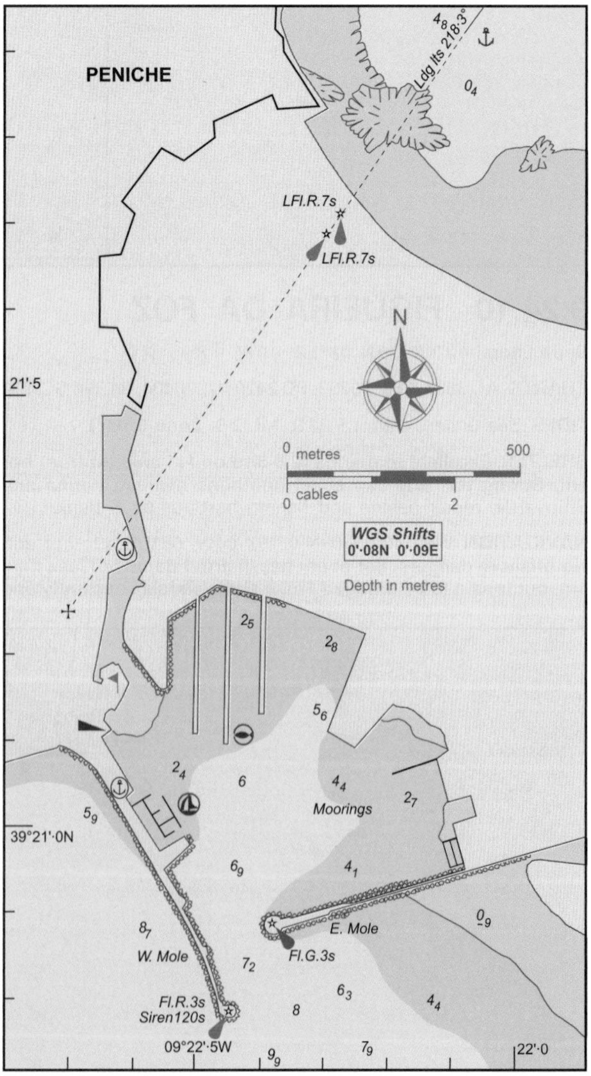
PENICHE
Ldg lts 218·3°
LFl.R.7s
LFl.R.7s
N
21'·5
metres
500
cables
2
WGS Shifts
0'·08N 0'·09E
Depth in metres
Moorings
39°21'·0N
E. Mole
Fl.G.3s
W. Mole
Fl.R.3s
Siren120s
09°22'·5W
22'·0

chan between Cabo Carvoeiro and Ilha da Berlenga is often rough. Os Farilhões lies 4·5M further NW. On the SE side of Ilha Berlenga there is ⚓ below the lt ho.

LIGHTS AND MARKS Ilha da Berlenga, Fl (3) 20s 120m 27M. Farilhão Grande, Fl 5s 99m 13M. Cabo Carvoeiro, Fl (3) R 15s 57m 15M, is 2M WNW of hbr ent and steep-to apart from Nau dos Carvos, a conspic high rk close-in. Other lts as chartlet. Peniche looks like an island from afar, with conspic water tr in town.

R/T VHF Ch 16 (H24), 62.

TELEPHONE (Dial Code 262) Port HM 781.153, ℻ 784.767; ⊖ & Met via HM; Ⓗ 781.702; LB 789.629.

FACILITIES Marina (130+20 Ⓥ), €2.46, ☎ 783.331, ℻ 784.225; **YC**; **Services:** P & D (cans/tanker), CH, BY, ME, El, Ⓔ, C, Gaz, Slip. **Town**: 🛒, R, Bar, Ⓑ, ✉; ⇌ Obidos (30km), ✈ Lisboa (80km).

9.24.13 CASCAIS

Estremadura **38°41'·50N 09°24'·93W** ❀❀❀◊◊◊✿✿✿

CHARTS AC 3635, 3220; PC 26406, 26303; SC 4310.

TIDES
Standard Port LISBOA (⟶); ML 2·0; Zone 0 (UT)

Times				Height (metres)			
High Water		Low Water		MHWS	MHWN	MLWN	MLWS
0400	0900	0400	0900	3·8	3·0	1·5	0·6
1600	2100	1600	2100				
Differences CASCAIS							
−0040	−0025	−0015	−0010	−0·3	−0·3	0·0	+0·1

SHELTER Good in marina, 6m, or on outside pontoons. ⚓ NE of marina in 3-5m, sheltered from prevailing N'lies, open to S.

NAVIGATION WPT 38°41'·36N 09°24'·50W, 334°/4ca to CC2 buoy and on the 285° ldg line. Cabo Roca TSS, see 9.24.2.

LIGHTS AND MARKS Rear 285° ldg lt, Guia, Iso WR 2s 58m, is 1.2M from the front; see 9.24.13 Navigation. Other lts as chartlet.

R/T Marina Ch 09 (0900-2000).

TELEPHONE (Dial Code 214). HM ☎ 824.800, ℻ 824.860.

FACILITIES Marina (638 inc 125 Ⓥ) €3.03. Excellent facilities, CH, ME, BH (70 ton), C (2 ton), D&P (0900-2000), ATM, Ⓑ, ▣, ⛽. **Town**. Usual amenities, good beaches. ⇌ to Lisboa (30 mins) every 15 mins, 0530-0230; an alternative to berthing in Lisboa.

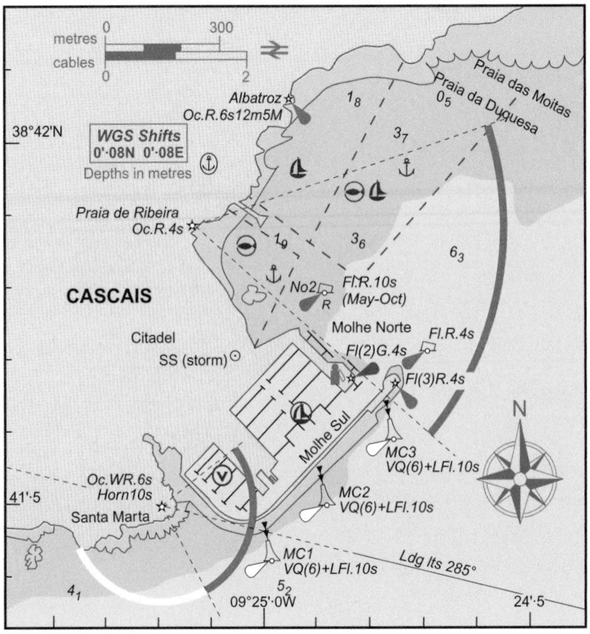
metres 0 300
cables 0 2
38°42'N
WGS Shifts
0'·08N 0'·08E
Depths in metres
Albatroz
Oc.R.6s12m5M
Praia das Moitas
Praia da Duquesa
Praia de Ribeira
Oc.R.4s
CASCAIS
No2
Fl.R.10s
(May-Oct)
Molhe Norte
Fl.R.4s
Fl(2)G.4s
Fl(3)R.4s
Citadel
SS (storm)
Molhe Sul
MC3
VQ(6)+LFl.10s
MC2
VQ(6)+LFl.10s
MC1
VQ(6)+LFl.10s
Oc.WR.6s
Horn10s
Santa Marta
41'·5
Ldg lts 285°
09°25'·0W
24'·5
N

9.24.14 LISBOA

Estremadura **38°41'·30N 09°10'·55W** (Ponte 25 de Abril) ❀❀❀◊◊◊✿✿✿

CHARTS AC 3635, 3220, 3221, 3222; PC 26406, 26303, 26304, 26305, 26306, 26307; SC 4310.

TIDES
Standard Port LISBOA (⟶); ML 2·0; Zone 0 (UT)

Times				Height (metres)			
High Water		Low Water		MHWS	MHWN	MLWN	MLWS
0400	0900	0400	0900	3·8	3·0	1·5	0·6
1600	2100	1600	2100				
Differences PACO DE ARCOS (5·5M W of Tejo bridge)							
−0020	−0030	−0005	−0005	−0·4	−0·4	−0·2	−0·1
PEDROUCOS (2·2M W of Tejo bridge)							
−0010	−0015	0000	0000	−0·2	−0·1	−0·1	−0·1

SHELTER/FACILITIES
The 6 marinas, Ⓐ to Ⓕ on the chartlet overleaf, are:

Ⓐ **Doca de Bom Successo** (38°41'·63N 09°12'·62W), close E of the ornate Torre de Belém (conspic) and red Pilots bldg. Almost full of local yachts. 100 F&A, 3m, ☎ 3.631.246 ℻ 3.624.578, C, CH, R, Slip, D & P (cans); ⇌, bus to Lisboa.

Ⓑ **Doca de Belém** (38°41'·71N 09°12'·14W), 150m E of Monument to the Discoveries (conspic). Almost full of local yachts, but may accept visitors; 200 F&A, 3m, ☎ 3.631.246 ℻ 3.624.578, D (hose), BH, C, R, SM, E; ⇌, bus to Lisboa.

Ⓒ **Doca de Santo Amaro** (38°41'·99N 09°10'·56W), almost below the suspension bridge (road traffic "hums" overhead, plus night life noise). 330 AB (few Ⓥ), 4m, ☎ 3.631.246 ℻ 3.624.578, R, Bar, 🛒; ⇌, bus 2M to city centre.

Ⓓ **Doca de Alcântara** (38°42'·21N 09°09'·32W), ent is E of the container/cruise ship terminal; chan doubles back W, via permanently open swing bridge, to marina at W end of dock. Marina: 180 AB inc Ⓥ (best for foreign visitors), 8m, ☎ 3.631.246 ℻ 3.624.578, €2.20, security fencing,R, Bar, 🛒; ⇌; bus 2M to city centre. The Hydrographic Office is 8ca NE.

Ⓔ **Doca do Terreiro do Trigo** (38°42'·69N 09°07'·46W) (also known as *APORVELA*, Portuguese STA), approx 700m ENE of the ferry terminal. ☎ 8.876.854, ℻ 8.873.885, AB inc Ⓥ in 1·5m (prone to silting), D, security fence; in run-down area, but close to Alfama (old quarter).

Ⓕ **Marina EXPO** (Closed tfn for rebuilding). Approx 38°44'·00N 09°06'·00W. ☎ 8.985.000, ℻ 8.985.008, 5m, D, BH, Ramp.

Oeiras marina, approx 38°40'·67N 09°18'·90W (4·7M ESE of Cascais) is under construction. 1·5M NE of it is Doca de Paço de Arcos, with ⚓ just beyond, sheltered from N/NW winds. Doca de Pedrouços (38°41'·65N 09°13'·42W) is a FV hbr, but has some repairs and CH; VHF Ch 03, 12. **City**: All amenities; ⇌, ✈.

NAVIGATION From N/NW keep at least 5ca off Cabo da Roca (see 9.24.2 for TSS) and Cabo Raso. Magnetic anomalies 3M SSE of Cabo Raso can alter local variation by +5° to −3°.

WPT 38°37'·00N 09°22'·77W (5ca SE of No 2 buoy), 047°/5·4M to abeam No 5 buoy. This appr is the main DW chan, Barra Sul, into R. Tejo proper; shoals lie on either side and break in bad weather. Tidal streams run hard (up to 5kn) in the river and the ebb sets towards the shoals E of Forte Bugio. Cross-current at the ent to marinas requires care. Speed limit E of Torre de Belém: 10kn, but 5kn within 300m of shore.

Barra Norte, a lesser chan carrying 5·2m, is a short cut for yachts between Cascais and R. Tejo in fair weather; it passes close S of Forte de S. Julião and is orientated 285°/105° on ldg lts at Forte de Sta Marta and Guia; the latter was reported (2002) as obscured by trees, only when viewed from the east by day.

LIGHTS AND MARKS See 9.24.3, chartlets and hbr text. Conspic features, W-E, include: Torre de Belém (icing cake), Monumento dos Descobrimentos (The Discoveries), the bridge 'Ponte 25 de Abril' and huge statue of Cristo Rei (S side). Plus many other churches and castles in this exciting and elegant city.

R/T Monitor *Lisboa Port Control* (Port authority) VHF Ch **12,** 01, 05, 60. Doca de Alcântara Ch 12, 05, 09. Other marinas Ch 09.

TELEPHONE (Dial Code 21) ⊖ & Met, via marinas.

24

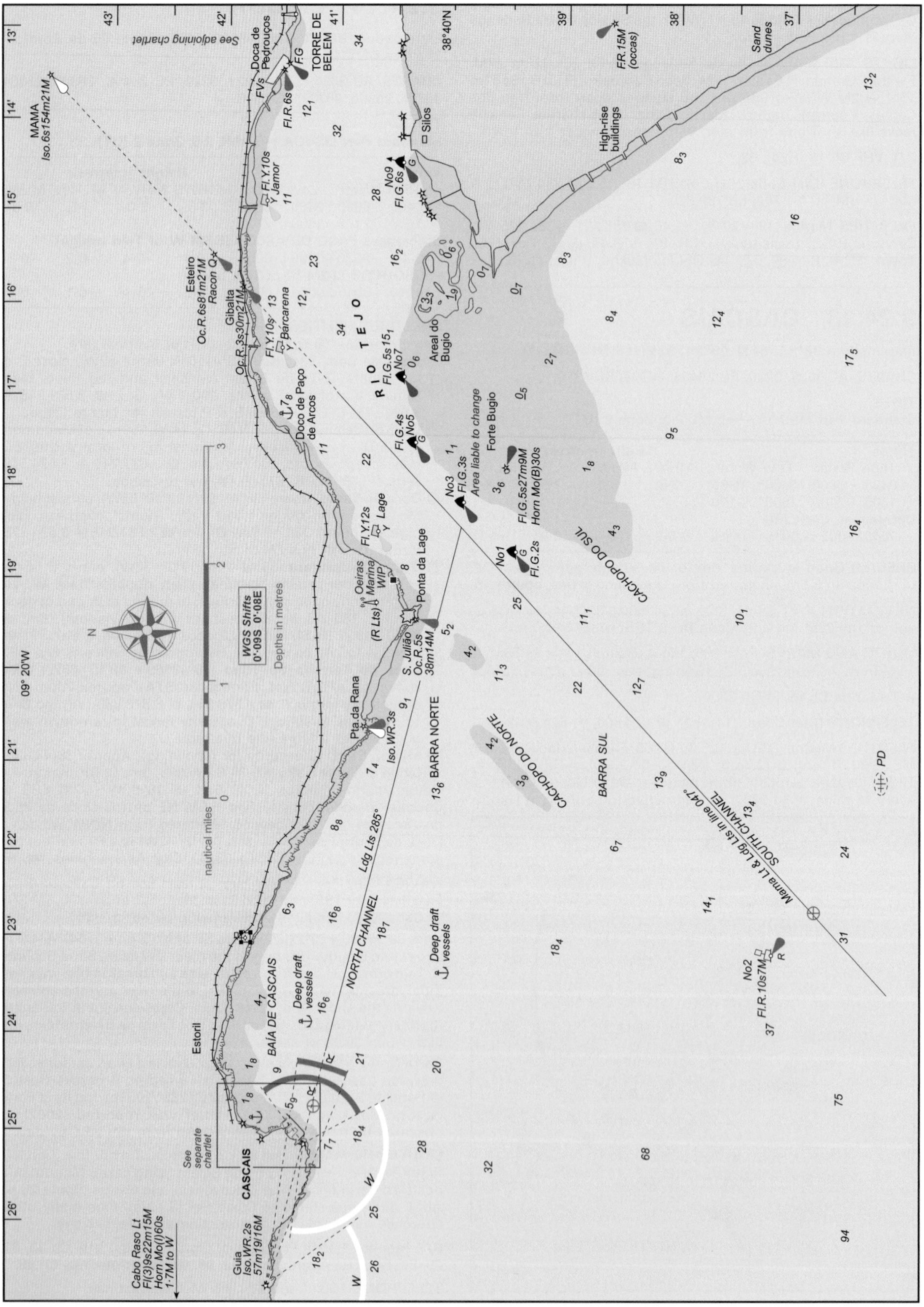
RIO TEJO
CASCAIS
Estoril
BAÍA DE CASCAIS
NORTH CHANNEL
BARRA NORTE
BARRA SUL
SOUTH CHANNEL
CACHOPO DO NORTE
CACHOPO DO SUL
Areal do Bugio
Forte Bugio
Area liable to change
TORRE DE BELEM
Doca de Pedrouços
Doco de Paço de Arcos
Oeiras Marina WIP
Ponta da Lage
Pta.da Rana
S. Julião Oc.R.5s 38m14M
Iso.WR.3s
Ldg Lts 285°
Mama Lt & Ldg Lts in line 047°
MAMA Iso.6s154m21M
Esteiro Oc.R.6s81m21M Racon Q
Gibalta Oc.R.3s30m21M
Fl.Y.10s Y Jamor
Fl.Y.10s Y Bárcarena
Fl.Y.12s Y Lage
Fl.R.6s
F.G
FVs
No9 Fl.G.6s
No7 Fl.G.5s15
No5 Fl.G.4s
No3 Fl.G.3s
No1 Fl.G.2s
Fl.G.5s27m9M Horn Mo(B)30s
No2 Fl.R.10s7M
F.R.15M (occas)
Silos
High-rise buildings
Sand dunes
Deep draft vessels
Guia Iso.WR.2s 57m19/16M
Cabo Raso Lt Fl(3)9s22m15M Horn Mo(I)60s 1·7M to W
See separate chartlet
See adjoining chartlet
WGS Shifts 0'·09S 0'·08E
Depths in metres
nautical miles
09° 20'W
38°40'N
PD

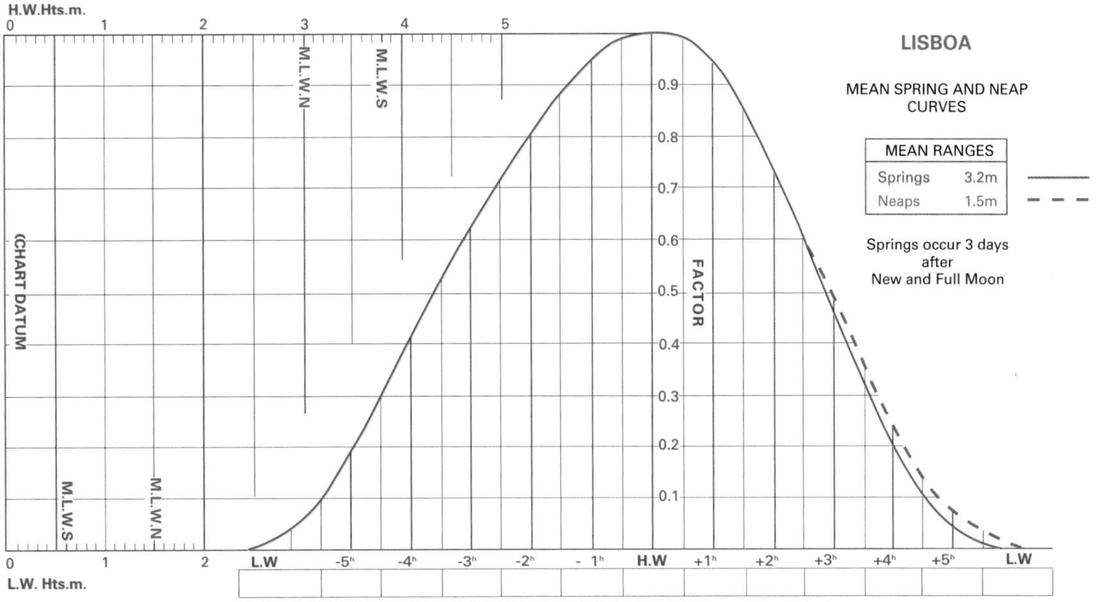
H.W.Hts.m.
LISBOA
MEAN SPRING AND NEAP CURVES
MEAN RANGES
Springs 3.2m
Neaps 1.5m
Springs occur 3 days after New and Full Moon
M.L.W.N
M.L.W.S
(CHART DATUM
FACTOR
L.W -5h -4h -3h -2h -1h H.W +1h +2h +3h +4h +5h L.W
L.W. Hts.m.

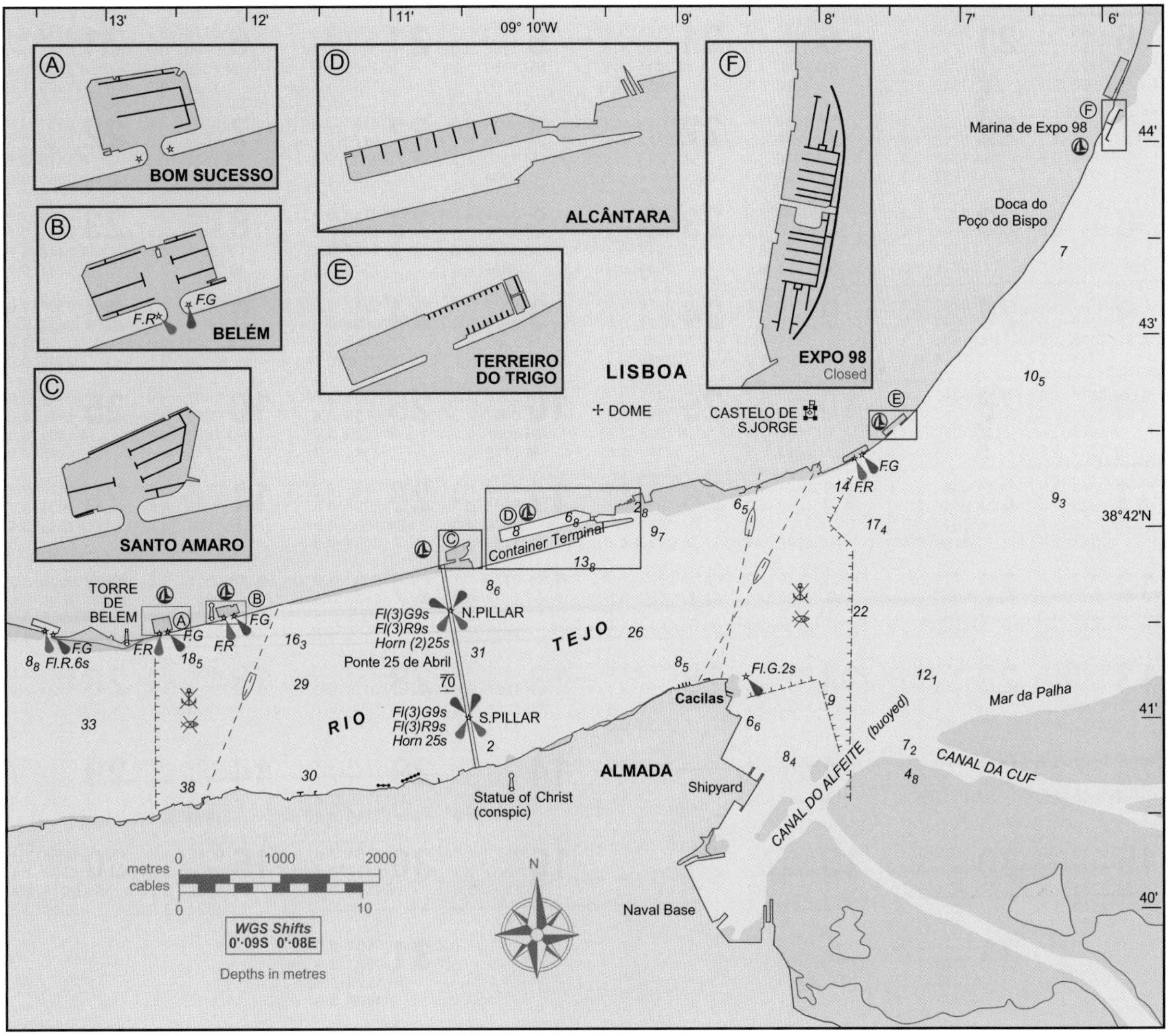
09° 10'W
BOM SUCESSO
BELÉM
F.R
F.G
SANTO AMARO
ALCÂNTARA
TERREIRO DO TRIGO
EXPO 98
Closed
Marina de Expo 98
Doca do Poço do Bispo
LISBOA
DOME
CASTELO DE S.JORGE
Container Terminal
TORRE DE BELEM
N.PILLAR
S.PILLAR
Fl(3)G9s
Fl(3)R9s
Horn (2)25s
Horn 25s
Ponte 25 de Abril
RIO
TEJO
Fl.G.2s
Cacilas
ALMADA
Shipyard
Statue of Christ (conspic)
Naval Base
Mar da Palha
CANAL DO ALFEITE (buoyed)
CANAL DA CUF
Fl.R.6s
38°42'N
metres
cables
WGS Shifts
0'·09S 0'·08E
Depths in metres

TIME ZONE (UT)
For Summer Time add ONE hour in **non-shaded areas**

PORTUGAL – LISBOA

LAT 38°43′N LONG 9°07′W

TIMES AND HEIGHTS OF HIGH AND LOW WATERS

SPRING & NEAP TIDES
Dates in red are **SPRINGS**
Dates in blue are **NEAPS**

YEAR **2005**

JANUARY

Date	Time	m	Date	Time	m
1 SA	0624 1226 1852	3.3 1.0 3.0	**16** SU	0058 0737 1332 2007	0.9 3.4 0.9 3.1
2 SU	0034 0708 1312 1941	1.2 3.2 1.1 2.9	**17** M	0150 0830 1426 ◐ 2104	1.1 3.2 1.1 3.0
3 M	0124 0800 1406 ◑ 2039	1.3 3.1 1.2 2.9	**18** TU	0252 0932 1528 2211	1.3 3.0 1.3 2.9
4 TU	0225 0902 1509 2147	1.3 3.0 1.3 2.9	**19** W	0405 1043 1640 2322	1.4 2.8 1.4 2.9
5 W	0334 1011 1617 2255	1.3 3.0 1.2 3.0	**20** TH	0523 1153 1748	1.4 2.8 1.3
6 TH	0446 1121 1722 2358	1.2 3.1 1.1 3.2	**21** F	0025 0631 1254 1846	3.0 1.3 2.9 1.2
7 F	0552 1225 1823	1.1 3.2 0.9	**22** SA	0118 0723 1345 1932	3.1 1.1 3.0 1.1
8 SA	0056 0654 1326 1918	3.4 0.9 3.4 0.8	**23** SU	0203 0805 1427 2011	3.2 1.0 3.1 1.0
9 SU	0152 0750 1423 2011	3.6 0.6 3.5 0.6	**24** M	0241 0841 1504 2045	3.3 0.9 3.2 0.9
10 M	0246 0844 1518 ● 2102	3.8 0.4 3.6 0.5	**25** TU	0316 0914 1538 ○ 2118	3.4 0.8 3.2 0.9
11 TU	0338 0935 1609 2151	3.9 0.3 3.7 0.5	**26** W	0349 0946 1610 2150	3.5 0.7 3.3 0.8
12 W	0427 1024 1658 2238	4.0 0.3 3.7 0.5	**27** TH	0421 1017 1642 2222	3.6 0.7 3.3 0.8
13 TH	0515 1111 1745 2324	4.0 0.3 3.6 0.6	**28** F	0454 1049 1714 2255	3.6 0.7 3.3 0.8
14 F	0602 1157 1830	3.9 0.5 3.5	**29** SA	0528 1122 1748 2329	3.5 0.7 3.3 0.8
15 SA	0010 0648 1244 1917	0.7 3.7 0.7 3.3	**30** SU	0603 1156 1824	3.5 0.8 3.2
			31 M	0005 0640 1233 1904	0.9 3.3 0.9 3.1

FEBRUARY

Date	Time	m	Date	Time	m
1 TU	0046 0721 1317 1951	1.0 3.2 1.0 3.0	**16** W	0159 0834 1427 ◐ 2109	1.3 2.9 1.4 2.8
2 W	0136 0813 1412 ◑ 2052	1.2 3.0 1.2 2.9	**17** TH	0313 0949 1546 2235	1.5 2.7 1.6 2.7
3 TH	0242 0922 1524 2208	1.3 2.9 1.3 2.9	**18** F	0452 1124 1719	1.5 2.6 1.6
4 F	0406 1046 1648 2329	1.3 2.9 1.2 3.0	**19** SA	0000 0616 1240 1829	2.8 1.4 2.7 1.4
5 SA	0532 1209 1805	1.1 3.0 1.1	**20** SU	0100 0710 1331 1917	3.0 1.2 2.9 1.3
6 SU	0041 0645 1320 1910	3.3 0.9 3.2 0.9	**21** M	0145 0749 1411 1954	3.2 1.0 3.1 1.1
7 M	0144 0746 1419 2005	3.5 0.6 3.5 0.7	**22** TU	0222 0822 1445 2028	3.4 0.9 3.3 0.9
8 TU	0238 0838 1510 ● 2054	3.8 0.4 3.7 0.5	**23** W	0256 0853 1517 2059	3.5 0.7 3.4 0.8
9 W	0328 0925 1557 2139	4.0 0.2 3.8 0.4	**24** TH	0328 0924 1548 ○ 2130	3.7 0.6 3.5 0.7
10 TH	0414 1009 1640 2222	4.1 0.2 3.8 0.3	**25** F	0401 0954 1619 2201	3.7 0.6 3.6 0.6
11 F	0457 1050 1721 2302	4.1 0.2 3.8 0.4	**26** SA	0434 1024 1651 2233	3.8 0.6 3.6 0.6
12 SA	0538 1129 1800 2342	4.0 0.4 3.6 0.5	**27** SU	0506 1055 1724 2305	3.7 0.6 3.5 0.7
13 SU	0618 1208 1839	3.8 0.6 3.4	**28** M	0539 1127 1757 2339	3.6 0.7 3.4 0.8
14 M	0022 0658 1247 1919	0.8 3.5 0.9 3.2			
15 TU	0106 0741 1331 2006	1.0 3.2 1.2 3.0			

MARCH

Date	Time	m	Date	Time	m
1 TU	0614 1201 1834	3.5 0.8 3.3	**16** W	0029 0658 1244 1916	1.1 3.1 1.3 3.1
2 W	0018 0653 1242 1918	0.9 3.3 1.0 3.2	**17** TH	0117 0743 1333 ◐ 2008	1.4 2.8 1.5 2.8
3 TH	0106 0743 1335 ◑ 2017	1.1 3.1 1.2 3.0	**18** F	0227 0852 1451 2136	1.6 2.6 1.8 2.7
4 F	0213 0855 1452 2140	1.3 2.9 1.4 3.0	**19** SA	0416 1050 1643 2323	1.7 2.6 1.8 2.8
5 SA	0349 1035 1632 2315	1.4 2.8 1.4 3.1	**20** SU	0547 1215 1801	1.5 2.7 1.6
6 SU	0528 1208 1759	1.2 3.0 1.3	**21** M	0030 0641 1305 1850	3.0 1.3 3.0 1.4
7 M	0034 0642 1316 1904	3.3 0.9 3.3 1.0	**22** TU	0115 0719 1342 1927	3.2 1.1 3.2 1.2
8 TU	0135 0738 1409 1955	3.6 0.6 3.6 0.7	**23** W	0152 0752 1415 2000	3.4 0.9 3.4 1.0
9 W	0226 0825 1455 2039	3.9 0.4 3.8 0.5	**24** TH	0227 0824 1448 2032	3.6 0.8 3.6 0.8
10 TH	0311 0907 1537 ● 2120	4.1 0.3 3.9 0.4	**25** F	0301 0855 1520 ○ 2104	3.8 0.6 3.7 0.7
11 F	0353 0945 1616 2159	4.2 0.3 4.0 0.3	**26** SA	0335 0926 1553 2136	3.9 0.6 3.8 0.6
12 SA	0433 1022 1653 2236	4.1 0.3 3.9 0.4	**27** SU	0408 0957 1626 2208	3.9 0.6 3.8 0.6
13 SU	0511 1057 1728 2313	4.0 0.5 3.8 0.6	**28** M	0442 1028 1659 2242	3.8 0.6 3.7 0.6
14 M	0546 1132 1802 2349	3.8 0.7 3.5 0.8	**29** TU	0517 1101 1735 2319	3.7 0.7 3.6 0.8
15 TU	0621 1206 1837	3.5 1.0 3.3	**30** W	0554 1137 1814	3.6 0.9 3.5
			31 TH	0001 0637 1220 1900	0.9 3.3 1.1 3.3

APRIL

Date	Time	m	Date	Time	m
1 F	0053 0733 1318 2003	1.1 3.1 1.4 3.1	**16** SA	0149 0808 1404 ◐ 2036	1.6 2.7 1.8 2.8
2 SA	0208 0854 1444 ◑ 2133	1.4 2.9 1.5 3.1	**17** SU	0325 0955 1549 2221	1.7 2.6 1.9 2.8
3 SU	0350 1039 1629 2309	1.4 2.9 1.5 3.2	**18** M	0454 1127 1712 2339	1.6 2.8 1.7 3.0
4 M	0524 1202 1751	1.2 3.2 1.3	**19** TU	0553 1221 1806	1.4 3.0 1.5
5 TU	0022 0630 1302 1849	3.5 0.9 3.4 1.0	**20** W	0031 0637 1302 1848	3.2 1.2 3.2 1.3
6 W	0118 0720 1349 1936	3.7 0.7 3.7 0.8	**21** TH	0113 0714 1338 1925	3.4 1.0 3.4 1.0
7 TH	0206 0803 1432 2018	4.0 0.5 3.9 0.6	**22** F	0151 0748 1413 2000	3.6 0.8 3.6 0.9
8 F	0249 0841 1511 ● 2057	4.1 0.4 4.0 0.5	**23** SA	0228 0821 1448 2034	3.8 0.7 3.7 0.7
9 SA	0329 0918 1548 2134	4.1 0.4 4.0 0.5	**24** SU	0305 0854 1523 ○ 2109	3.8 0.6 3.8 0.6
10 SU	0407 0953 1624 2210	4.0 0.5 3.9 0.6	**25** M	0342 0928 1600 2146	3.9 0.6 3.9 0.6
11 M	0443 1026 1658 2246	3.8 0.7 3.8 0.7	**26** TU	0420 1004 1638 2224	3.8 0.7 3.8 0.6
12 TU	0517 1059 1731 2322	3.6 0.9 3.6 0.9	**27** W	0500 1041 1718 2307	3.7 0.8 3.8 0.8
13 W	0550 1132 1803	3.4 1.1 3.4	**28** TH	0543 1123 1803 2356	3.5 0.9 3.6 0.9
14 TH	0000 0625 1207 1839	1.2 3.1 1.4 3.2	**29** F	0634 1213 1856	3.3 1.2 3.4
15 F	0045 0706 1252 1924	1.4 2.9 1.6 3.0	**30** SA	0056 0737 1318 2004	1.1 3.1 1.4 3.3

TIME ZONE (UT)
For Summer Time add ONE hour in **non-shaded areas**

PORTUGAL – LISBOA

LAT 38°43′N LONG 9°07′W

TIMES AND HEIGHTS OF HIGH AND LOW WATERS

SPRING & NEAP TIDES
Dates in red are SPRINGS Dates in blue are NEAPS

YEAR **2005**

MAY

Day	Time	m	Day	Time	m
1	0215	1.3	16	0230	1.6
	0900	3.0		0853	2.7
	SU 1445	1.5		M 1447	1.8
	◑ 2129	3.2		◐ 2113	2.9
2	0346	1.3	17	0347	1.5
	1030	3.0		1017	2.8
	M 1616	1.5		TU 1607	1.7
	2252	3.3		2233	3.0
3	0505	1.2	18	0452	1.4
	1141	3.2		1122	3.0
	TU 1728	1.3		W 1709	1.5
	2359	3.5		2336	3.2
4	0605	1.0	19	0544	1.3
	1236	3.5		1212	3.2
	W 1824	1.1		TH 1759	1.3
5	0053	3.7	20	0026	3.3
	0653	0.8		0628	1.1
	TH 1323	3.6		F 1254	3.3
	1911	0.9		1843	1.1
6	0140	3.8	21	0110	3.5
	0735	0.7		0707	0.9
	F 1405	3.8		SA 1335	3.5
	1953	0.7		1924	0.9
7	0223	3.9	22	0152	3.6
	0814	0.7		0746	0.8
	SA 1444	3.8		SU 1415	3.7
	2033	0.7		2004	0.8
8	0303	3.8	23	0234	3.7
	0850	0.7		0824	0.7
	SU 1522	3.8		M 1456	3.8
	● 2111	0.7		○ 2045	0.7
9	0341	3.7	24	0318	3.7
	0925	0.8		0904	0.7
	M 1558	3.8		TU 1538	3.8
	2148	0.8		2128	0.6
10	0418	3.6	25	0402	3.7
	0959	0.9		0946	0.7
	TU 1632	3.7		W 1622	3.9
	2224	0.9		2214	0.6
11	0452	3.4	26	0450	3.6
	1032	1.0		1030	0.8
	W 1705	3.5		TH 1709	3.8
	2300	1.0		2303	0.7
12	0526	3.3	27	0540	3.5
	1105	1.2		1119	0.9
	TH 1738	3.4		F 1800	3.7
	2339	1.2		2357	0.8
13	0601	3.1	28	0635	3.4
	1142	1.4		1213	1.1
	F 1813	3.2		SA 1856	3.6
14	0022	1.4	29	0058	1.0
	0642	2.9		0738	3.2
	SA 1226	1.5		SU 1317	1.3
	1856	3.1		2000	3.4
15	0117	1.5	30	0208	1.1
	0737	2.8		0848	3.1
	SU 1326	1.7		M 1431	1.4
	1955	3.0		◑ 2111	3.3
			31	0321	1.1
				1001	3.1
				TU 1546	1.4
				2223	3.3

JUNE

Day	Time	m	Day	Time	m
1	0430	1.1	16	0344	1.4
	1107	3.2		1015	2.9
	W 1654	1.3		TH 1604	1.5
	2327	3.4		2233	3.1
2	0530	1.0	17	0444	1.3
	1203	3.3		1115	3.0
	TH 1753	1.1		F 1704	1.3
				2333	3.2
3	0023	3.5	18	0537	1.1
	0621	1.0		1208	3.2
	F 1253	3.5		SA 1759	1.2
	1844	1.0			
4	0113	3.5	19	0027	3.3
	0706	0.9		0626	1.0
	SA 1338	3.6		SU 1257	3.4
	1930	0.9		1850	1.0
5	0158	3.5	20	0119	3.4
	0747	0.9		0713	0.9
	SU 1420	3.6		M 1345	3.5
	2013	0.9		1939	0.8
6	0241	3.5	21	0210	3.5
	0826	0.9		0759	0.8
	M 1500	3.6		TU 1433	3.7
	● 2053	0.9		2028	0.7
7	0321	3.4	22	0301	3.6
	0902	0.9		0847	0.7
	TU 1538	3.6		W 1523	3.8
	2132	0.9		○ 2118	0.6
8	0359	3.3	23	0352	3.6
	0938	1.0		0935	0.6
	W 1613	3.5		TH 1613	3.9
	2208	0.9		2208	0.5
9	0435	3.3	24	0444	3.6
	1012	1.0		1024	0.7
	TH 1646	3.5		F 1703	3.9
	2244	1.0		2300	0.5
10	0509	3.2	25	0535	3.6
	1046	1.1		1114	0.8
	F 1719	3.4		SA 1754	3.8
	2321	1.1		2352	0.6
11	0544	3.1	26	0628	3.5
	1123	1.2		1206	0.9
	SA 1754	3.3		SU 1846	3.7
12	0001	1.2	27	0046	0.7
	0623	3.0		0721	3.3
	SU 1204	1.3		M 1301	1.0
	1835	3.2		1941	3.6
13	0046	1.3	28	0142	0.9
	0708	2.9		0819	3.2
	M 1253	1.4		TU 1401	1.1
	1923	3.1		◑ 2040	3.4
14	0139	1.3	29	0243	1.0
	0803	2.8		0921	3.1
	TU 1351	1.5		W 1505	1.2
	2021	3.0		2144	3.3
15	0240	1.4	30	0346	1.1
	0908	2.8		1025	3.1
	W 1458	1.5		TH 1613	1.3
	◐ 2127	3.0		2250	3.2

JULY

Day	Time	m	Day	Time	m
1	0449	1.2	16	0341	1.3
	1127	3.2		1018	3.0
	F 1720	1.2		SA 1610	1.4
	2352	3.2		2242	3.0
2	0548	1.2	17	0447	1.2
	1224	3.2		1123	3.1
	SA 1821	1.2		SU 1720	1.2
				2350	3.1
3	0049	3.2	18	0551	1.1
	0641	1.1		1225	3.3
	SU 1315	3.3		M 1824	1.0
	1914	1.1			
4	0140	3.2	19	0055	3.2
	0727	1.1		0649	0.9
	M 1402	3.4		TU 1324	3.5
	2001	1.0		1924	0.8
5	0226	3.2	20	0156	3.4
	0809	1.0		0745	0.8
	TU 1444	3.5		W 1420	3.7
	2042	0.9		2019	0.6
6	0307	3.2	21	0252	3.6
	0847	1.0		0837	0.6
	W 1522	3.5		TH 1513	3.9
	● 2119	0.9		○ 2111	0.4
7	0345	3.2	22	0344	3.7
	0922	1.0		0927	0.6
	TH 1557	3.5		F 1603	4.0
	2154	0.9		2200	0.3
8	0419	3.2	23	0434	3.7
	0956	1.0		1014	0.5
	F 1630	3.5		SA 1652	4.1
	2227	0.9		2247	0.3
9	0452	3.2	24	0521	3.7
	1030	1.0		1101	0.5
	SA 1702	3.5		SU 1739	4.0
	2301	0.9		2334	0.4
10	0525	3.2	25	0607	3.6
	1104	1.0		1147	0.6
	SU 1736	3.4		M 1825	3.9
	2336	0.9			
11	0600	3.2	26	0020	0.6
	1140	1.1		0653	3.5
	M 1812	3.4		TU 1234	0.8
				1912	3.7
12	0013	1.0	27	0107	0.8
	0638	3.1		0741	3.3
	TU 1220	1.2		W 1324	1.0
	1852	3.3		2003	3.4
13	0055	1.1	28	0158	1.0
	0721	3.0		0835	3.1
	W 1304	1.3		TH 1422	1.2
	1937	3.2		◑ 2101	3.2
14	0142	1.2	29	0257	1.3
	0812	2.9		0939	3.0
	TH 1357	1.3		F 1532	1.4
	◐ 2031	3.1		2210	3.0
15	0237	1.3	30	0407	1.4
	0912	2.9		1050	3.0
	F 1500	1.4		SA 1652	1.4
	2134	3.0		2325	2.9
			31	0520	1.4
				1200	3.0
				SU 1807	1.3

AUGUST

Day	Time	m	Day	Time	m
1	0033	2.9	16	0530	1.3
	0624	1.3		1207	3.3
	M 1259	3.2		TU 1813	1.1
	1906	1.2			
2	0129	3.0	17	0047	3.2
	0715	1.2		0638	1.1
	TU 1348	3.3		W 1313	3.5
	1952	1.1		1917	0.8
3	0214	3.1	18	0149	3.5
	0757	1.1		0736	0.8
	W 1429	3.4		TH 1410	3.8
	2030	1.0		2010	0.6
4	0253	3.2	19	0242	3.7
	0833	1.0		0827	0.6
	TH 1505	3.5		F 1501	4.0
	2103	0.9		○ 2059	0.4
5	0327	3.3	20	0331	3.8
	0906	0.9		0913	0.5
	F 1538	3.6		SA 1548	4.2
	● 2134	0.8		2143	0.3
6	0359	3.4	21	0415	3.9
	0938	0.9		0957	0.4
	SA 1610	3.6		SU 1633	4.2
	2205	0.8		2226	0.3
7	0430	3.4	22	0458	3.9
	1009	0.8		1039	0.4
	SU 1641	3.6		M 1716	4.2
	2236	0.8		2307	0.4
8	0501	3.4	23	0539	3.8
	1041	0.8		1120	0.5
	M 1713	3.6		TU 1758	4.0
	2307	0.8		2347	0.6
9	0533	3.4	24	0619	3.6
	1113	0.9		1202	0.7
	TU 1747	3.5		W 1840	3.7
	2340	0.9			
10	0607	3.3	25	0028	0.9
	1147	1.0		0701	3.4
	W 1821	3.4		TH 1247	1.0
				1924	3.4
11	0014	1.0	26	0113	1.2
	0644	3.2		0749	3.2
	TH 1225	1.1		F 1341	1.3
	1900	3.3		◑ 2018	3.0
12	0053	1.1	27	0208	1.4
	0726	3.1		0851	3.0
	F 1310	1.2		SA 1453	1.5
	1946	3.1		2131	2.8
13	0142	1.3	28	0325	1.6
	0821	3.0		1014	2.9
	SA 1409	1.4		SU 1632	1.6
	◐ 2046	3.0		2304	2.7
14	0247	1.4	29	0459	1.6
	0930	3.0		1140	3.0
	SU 1528	1.4		M 1758	1.5
	2205	2.9			
15	0409	1.4	30	0022	2.8
	1050	3.0		0612	1.5
	M 1656	1.3		TU 1243	3.1
	2331	3.0		1854	1.3
			31	0115	3.0
				0701	1.4
				W 1330	3.3
				1934	1.1

TIME ZONE (UT)
For Summer Time add ONE hour in **non-shaded areas**

PORTUGAL – LISBOA

LAT 38°43′N LONG 9°07′W

TIMES AND HEIGHTS OF HIGH AND LOW WATERS

SPRING & NEAP TIDES
Dates in **red** are **SPRINGS**
Dates in blue are NEAPS

YEAR **2005**

SEPTEMBER

Date	Day	Time	m	Time	m	Time	m	Time	m
1	TH	0156	3.2	0740	1.2	1408	3.5	2008	1.0
2	F	0230	3.3	0813	1.0	1441	3.6	2038	0.9
3	SA	0301	3.5	0844	0.9	1513	3.7	● 2108	0.8
4	SU	0332	3.6	0914	0.8	1544	3.8	2138	0.7
5	M	0402	3.6	0944	0.8	1616	3.8	2207	0.7
6	TU	0433	3.6	1015	0.8	1648	3.8	2237	0.8
7	W	0504	3.6	1046	0.8	1720	3.7	2307	0.8
8	TH	0537	3.5	1118	0.9	1753	3.5	2339	1.0
9	F	0612	3.4	1154	1.0	1829	3.4		
10	SA	0016	1.1	0652	3.3	1238	1.2	1915	3.2
11	SU	0103	1.3	0746	3.1	1339	1.4	◐ 2019	3.0
12	M	0213	1.5	0901	3.0	1508	1.5	2151	2.9
13	TU	0351	1.6	1036	3.1	1650	1.4	2330	3.0
14	W	0523	1.4	1159	3.3	1809	1.1		
15	TH	0043	3.3	0632	1.1	1303	3.7	1907	0.8
16	F	0138	3.6	0725	0.9	1356	4.0	1956	0.6
17	SA	0226	3.9	0811	0.6	1443	4.2	2039	0.4
18	SU	0310	4.0	0854	0.5	1527	4.3	○ 2120	0.3
19	M	0351	4.1	0934	0.4	1609	4.3	2159	0.4
20	TU	0430	4.1	1014	0.4	1649	4.2	2236	0.5
21	W	0508	3.9	1052	0.6	1728	3.9	2313	0.7
22	TH	0546	3.7	1132	0.8	1807	3.6	2350	1.0
23	F	0624	3.5	1214	1.1	1848	3.3		
24	SA	0031	1.3	0707	3.2	1305	1.4	1937	3.0
25	SU	0121	1.6	0803	3.0	1418	1.7	◑ 2051	2.7
26	M	0242	1.8	0932	2.9	1607	1.7	2240	2.7
27	TU	0432	1.8	1110	2.9	1733	1.6		
28	W	0000	2.9	0547	1.7	1215	3.1	1825	1.4
29	TH	0049	3.1	0634	1.5	1300	3.3	1904	1.2
30	F	0126	3.3	0711	1.3	1336	3.5	1936	1.0

OCTOBER

Date	Day	Time	m	Time	m	Time	m	Time	m
1	SA	0159	3.5	0744	1.1	1410	3.7	2007	0.9
2	SU	0230	3.6	0815	0.9	1443	3.8	2037	0.8
3	M	0301	3.7	0846	0.8	1515	3.9	● 2107	0.7
4	TU	0333	3.8	0917	0.7	1548	3.9	2137	0.7
5	W	0405	3.8	0948	0.7	1621	3.9	2207	0.8
6	TH	0437	3.8	1020	0.8	1654	3.8	2238	0.9
7	F	0511	3.7	1055	0.9	1730	3.6	2312	1.0
8	SA	0548	3.5	1134	1.0	1810	3.4	2351	1.2
9	SU	0632	3.4	1222	1.2	1901	3.2		
10	M	0043	1.4	0730	3.2	1330	1.4	◐ 2014	3.0
11	TU	0201	1.6	0852	3.1	1507	1.5	2155	3.0
12	W	0347	1.6	1029	3.2	1646	1.4	2326	3.2
13	TH	0515	1.5	1147	3.5	1756	1.1		
14	F	0029	3.4	0617	1.2	1247	3.8	1849	0.8
15	SA	0119	3.7	0706	0.9	1336	4.0	1934	0.6
16	SU	0204	3.9	0750	0.7	1421	4.2	2015	0.5
17	M	0245	4.0	0831	0.5	1503	4.2	○ 2054	0.5
18	TU	0324	4.1	0911	0.5	1544	4.2	2131	0.5
19	W	0403	4.0	0949	0.6	1623	4.0	2207	0.7
20	TH	0440	3.9	1028	0.7	1701	3.8	2242	0.9
21	F	0516	3.7	1107	0.9	1738	3.5	2318	1.1
22	SA	0553	3.5	1148	1.2	1817	3.2	2356	1.4
23	SU	0632	3.3	1235	1.5	1902	2.9		
24	M	0043	1.7	0720	3.0	1341	1.7	2008	2.7
25	TU	0155	1.9	0835	2.9	1516	1.7	◑ 2150	2.7
26	W	0338	1.9	1014	2.9	1641	1.6	2313	2.8
27	TH	0458	1.8	1126	3.1	1739	1.5		
28	F	0006	3.0	0552	1.5	1216	3.3	1822	1.3
29	SA	0046	3.3	0633	1.3	1257	3.5	1858	1.1
30	SU	0121	3.5	0709	1.1	1334	3.6	1932	0.9
31	M	0155	3.6	0743	0.9	1409	3.8	2004	0.8

NOVEMBER

Date	Day	Time	m	Time	m	Time	m	Time	m
1	TU	0229	3.7	0816	0.8	1444	3.8	2036	0.8
2	W	0303	3.8	0850	0.8	1520	3.8	● 2108	0.7
3	TH	0338	3.8	0924	0.7	1556	3.8	2141	0.8
4	F	0414	3.8	1001	0.8	1635	3.7	2217	0.9
5	SA	0453	3.8	1041	0.8	1716	3.5	2256	1.0
6	SU	0536	3.6	1127	1.0	1804	3.4	2342	1.2
7	M	0625	3.5	1222	1.2	1902	3.2		
8	TU	0041	1.4	0728	3.3	1333	1.3	2018	3.0
9	W	0200	1.5	0848	3.2	1501	1.4	◐ 2147	3.0
10	TH	0333	1.5	1013	3.3	1625	1.3	2304	3.2
11	F	0451	1.4	1124	3.5	1731	1.1		
12	SA	0004	3.4	0552	1.1	1222	3.7	1824	0.9
13	SU	0054	3.6	0642	0.9	1312	3.8	1909	0.8
14	M	0138	3.8	0727	0.8	1358	3.9	1950	0.7
15	TU	0220	3.9	0810	0.7	1441	3.9	2029	0.7
16	W	0301	3.9	0851	0.6	1522	3.8	○ 2107	0.7
17	TH	0340	3.9	0930	0.7	1602	3.7	2143	0.8
18	F	0418	3.8	1009	0.8	1640	3.5	2218	1.0
19	SA	0454	3.6	1048	1.0	1717	3.3	2254	1.1
20	SU	0529	3.5	1128	1.1	1754	3.1	2331	1.3
21	M	0605	3.3	1211	1.3	1834	2.9		
22	TU	0015	1.5	0647	3.1	1304	1.5	1926	2.8
23	W	0111	1.7	0742	3.0	1411	1.5	◑ 2036	2.7
24	TH	0227	1.7	0856	2.9	1526	1.5	2157	2.8
25	F	0346	1.7	1015	3.0	1634	1.5	2304	2.9
26	SA	0452	1.5	1118	3.1	1728	1.3	2355	3.1
27	SU	0544	1.4	1209	3.3	1813	1.1		
28	M	0038	3.3	0628	1.2	1253	3.4	1852	1.0
29	TU	0117	3.4	0708	1.0	1334	3.5	1929	0.9
30	W	0156	3.6	0747	0.9	1414	3.6	2006	0.8

DECEMBER

Date	Day	Time	m	Time	m	Time	m	Time	m
1	TH	0235	3.7	0826	0.8	1456	3.6	● 2044	0.7
2	F	0316	3.8	0907	0.7	1539	3.6	2123	0.7
3	SA	0358	3.8	0950	0.6	1624	3.6	2205	0.8
4	SU	0443	3.8	1037	0.7	1712	3.5	2251	0.9
5	M	0532	3.7	1127	0.8	1804	3.4	2342	1.0
6	TU	0624	3.6	1223	0.9	1901	3.2		
7	W	0040	1.2	0723	3.5	1326	1.0	2006	3.1
8	TH	0147	1.3	0830	3.3	1437	1.1	◐ 2118	3.1
9	F	0301	1.3	0942	3.3	1549	1.1	2228	3.1
10	SA	0414	1.3	1052	3.3	1655	1.1	2331	3.3
11	SU	0520	1.1	1153	3.4	1753	1.0		
12	M	0025	3.4	0617	1.0	1248	3.5	1843	0.9
13	TU	0114	3.5	0708	0.9	1337	3.5	1928	0.9
14	W	0200	3.6	0755	0.8	1423	3.5	2010	0.8
15	TH	0243	3.7	0838	0.8	1507	3.5	○ 2049	0.8
16	F	0324	3.6	0919	0.8	1548	3.4	2127	0.9
17	SA	0403	3.6	0957	0.8	1625	3.3	2202	0.9
18	SU	0438	3.5	1034	0.9	1701	3.2	2237	1.0
19	M	0511	3.4	1110	1.0	1734	3.1	2313	1.1
20	TU	0544	3.3	1147	1.0	1810	3.0	2351	1.2
21	W	0620	3.2	1228	1.1	1850	2.9		
22	TH	0034	1.3	0703	3.1	1315	1.3	1938	2.8
23	F	0126	1.4	0755	3.0	1412	1.3	◑ 2038	2.8
24	SA	0229	1.5	0858	2.9	1516	1.4	2146	2.8
25	SU	0337	1.5	1007	2.9	1620	1.3	2251	2.9
26	M	0443	1.4	1111	3.0	1718	1.2	2347	3.0
27	TU	0541	1.3	1208	3.1	1809	1.1		
28	W	0038	3.2	0633	1.1	1300	3.2	1856	1.0
29	TH	0126	3.4	0722	0.9	1350	3.3	1942	0.8
30	F	0213	3.5	0810	0.7	1440	3.5	2027	0.7
31	SA	0301	3.7	0857	0.6	1530	3.5	● 2113	0.6

9.24.15 SESIMBRA

Baixo Alentejo **38°26'·20N 09°06'·40W** ❀❀◊◊✿✿

CHARTS AC 3635, 3636; PC 24204, 26407; SC42B

TIDES

Standard Port LISBOA (⟷); ML 2·0; Zone 0 (UT)

Times				**Height (metres)**			
High Water		Low Water		MHWS	MHWN	MLWN	MLWS
0400	0900	0400	0900	3·8	3·0	1·5	0·6
1600	2100	1600	2100				
Differences SESIMBRA							
−0045	−0030	−0020	−0010	−0·4	−0·4	−0·1	0·0

SHELTER The club operates a 130 berth marina but this is usually full in summer; check berth is available. Or ⚓ in about 5m to N or E of ent and clear of fairway. Caution: strong N'ly gusts blow down from high ground late pm/evening.

NAVIGATION WPT 38°25'·63N 09°06'·15W, 004°/1M to bkwtr hd lt, which is about 2ca W of the ldg line.

LIGHTS AND MARKS Ldg lts 004°, both L Fl R 5s 9/21m 7/6M, are about 4ca NE of the bkwtr hd; hard to see against town lights. Bkwtr hd, Fl R 3s, W tr, R bands. Forte de Cavalo, Oc 5s, R ○ tr.

R/T Port Ch 11, Marina Ch 09.

TELEPHONE (Dial Code 212) **Clube Naval** 233.451 Fax 281.668.

FACILITIES D from fish market; tourist amenities. 30 min bus to Lisboa or, to avoid traffic jams, local bus to Cacilhas and ferry across the Tejo. **Town:** (1½M to the N), ⛟, R, Bar, Ⓑ, ✉; ⇌ Seixal, ✈ Lisboa.

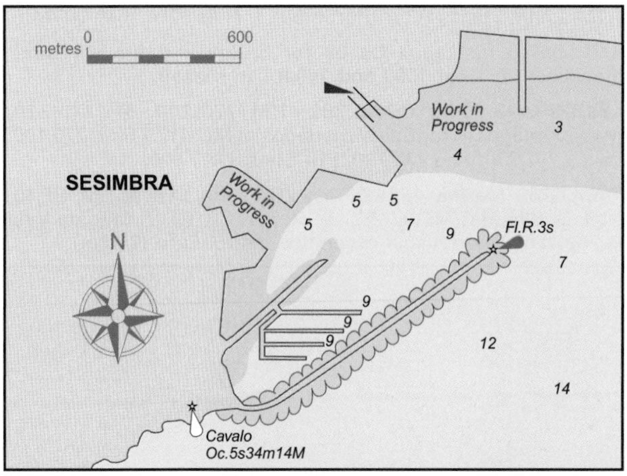
metres 0 600
SESIMBRA
Work in Progress
Work in Progress
N
Fl.R.3s
Cavalo
Oc.5s34m14M
3
4
5 5
5
7
9
7
9
9
9
12
14

9.24.16 SETÚBAL

Baixo Alentejo **38°31'·32N 08°53'·04W** (Marina) ❀❀◊◊✿✿

CHARTS AC 3635/6, 3270; PC 24204, 26308/09; SC42B

TIDES

Standard Port LISBOA (⟷); ML 2·0; Zone 0 (UT)

Times				**Height (metres)**			
High Water		Low Water		MHWS	MHWN	MLWN	MLWS
0400	0900	0400	0900	3·8	3·0	1·5	0·6
1600	2100	1600	2100				
Differences SETÚBAL							
−0020	−0015	−0005	+0005	−0·4	−0·4	−0·1	−0·1

SHELTER Good in marina in W half of Doca de Comercio, but reported almost full. Local boats only in small Doca de Recreio. Industrial quays to ESE. ⚓ in up to 13m, as shown on chartlet.

NAVIGATION WPT 38°26'·65N 08°58'·85W, 040°/0.8M to No 1 buoy and No 2 bcn at the river ent. Rio Sado is shoal on both sides until past Forte de Outão; follow the buoys/bcns.

LIGHTS AND MARKS Ldg lts 039·7°: both, Iso Y 6s, front: R twr, W stripes; rear, R hut on piles. Other lts as chartlet and 9.24.3.

R/T Port Ch 11; Marina Ch 09.

TELEPHONE (Dial Code 265) HM 542.075 Fax 230.992; ⊖ & Met via HM; Ⓗ 561.116.

FACILITIES **Marina** (155 AB) ☎ 542.076 Fax 230.992, D, ME. **Town:** ⛟, R, Bar, Ⓑ, ✉; good train/bus to Lisboa ⇌, ✈.

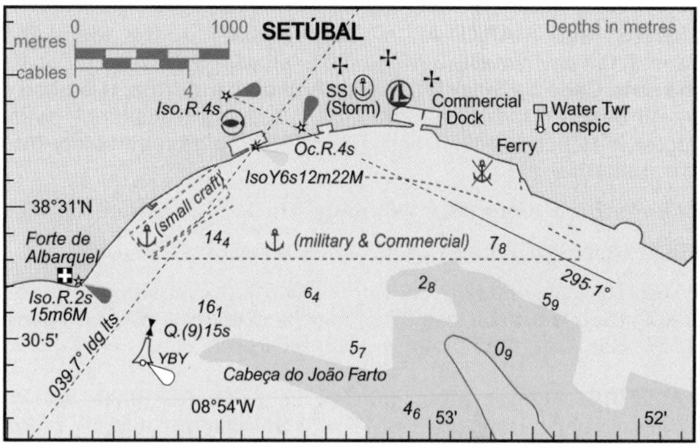
metres 0 1000
cables 0 4
SETÚBAL
Depths in metres
Iso.R.4s
SS (Storm)
Commercial Dock
Water Twr conspic
Oc.R.4s
Ferry
IsoY6s12m22M
38°31'N
(small craft)
14₄
(military & Commercial)
7₈
Forte de Albarquel
Iso.R.2s 15m6M
2₈
295·7°
5₉
6₄
16₁
30·5'
Q.(9)15s
YBY
5₇
0₉
039·7° ldg lts
Cabeça do João Farto
08°54'W
4₆
53'
52'

ADJACENT ANCHORAGE

ARRÁBIDA 38°28'·5N 08°58'·75W, 1·4M N of ent to Rio Sado (AC 3270). Popular but shallow ⚓ (2·5m) sheltered from N by high ground. Appr from SSW, 1-2ca offshore to avoid Baixo de Alpertuche (0·7m) 4ca offshore and rocky reef at NE end of bay.

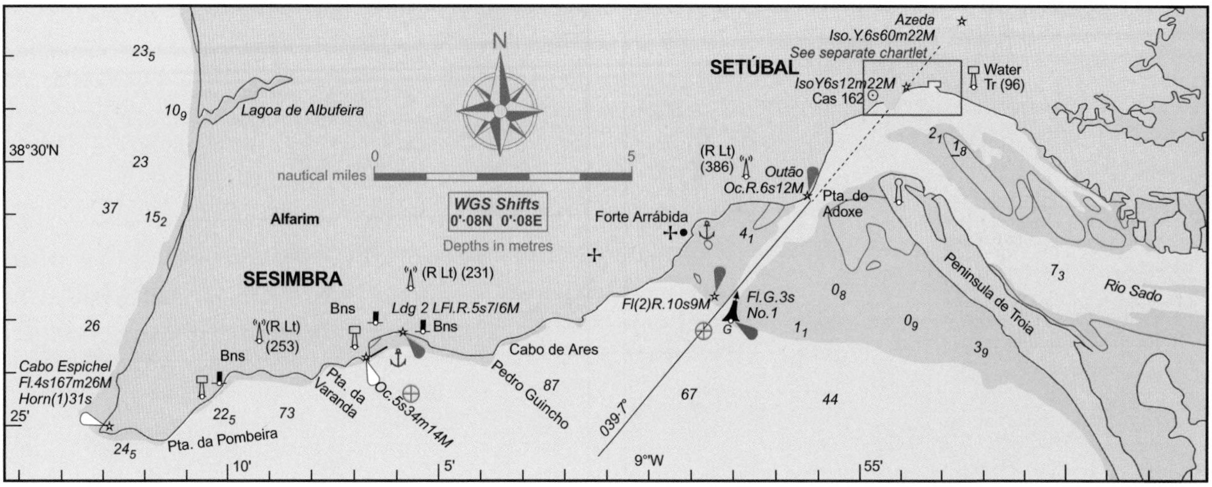
Azeda
Iso.Y.6s60m22M
See separate chartlet
SETÚBAL
IsoY6s12m22M
Cas 162
Water Tr (96)
N
23₅
10₉
Lagoa de Albufeira
38°30'N
23
nautical miles 0 5
(R Lt) (386)
Outão
Oc.R.6s12M
Pta. do Adoxe
2₁
1₈
37
15₂
Alfarim
WGS Shifts 0'·08N 0'·08E
Depths in metres
Forte Arrábida
4₁
SESIMBRA
(R Lt) (231)
Peninsula de Troia
7₃
Rio Sado
Bns
Ldg 2 LFl.R.5s7/6M
Bns
Fl(2)R.10s9M
Fl.G.3s No.1
0₈
G
1₁
0₉
26
(R Lt) (253)
Bns
Cabo de Ares
3₉
Cabo Espichel
Fl.4s167m26M
Horn(1)31s
Pta. da Varanda
Oc.5s34m14M
Pedro Guincho
87
67
44
25'
22₅
73
039·7°
24₅
Pta. da Pombeira
10'
5'
9°W
55'

9.24.17 SINES

Baixo Alentejo **37°57'·12N 08°51'·90W** (marina)

CHARTS AC 3636, 3224; PC 24204, 24205, 26408; SC 430A.

TIDES
Standard Port LISBOA (⟵); ML 2·0; Zone 0 (UT)

Times				Height (metres)			
High Water		Low Water		MHWS	MHWN	MLWN	MLWS
0400	0900	0400	0900	3·8	3·0	1·5	0·6
1600	2100	1600	2100				
Differences SINES							
−0050	−0030	−0020	−0010	−0·4	−0·4	−0·1	0·0
MILFONTES (37°43'·0N 08°47'·0W)							
−0040	−0030	No data		−0·1	−0·1	0·0	+0·1
ARRIFANA (37°17'·5N 08°52'·0W)							
−0030	−0020	No data		−0·1	0·0	−0·1	+0·1

SHELTER Good in small marina protected by mole at E end of Praia Vasco de Gama (FVs are at W end); or ⚓ NW of the marina in 4m. Nearby Old town is pleasant, away from commercial terminals in NW and SE parts of the large hbr. The SE terminal has been extended further SE, but is not yet (6/2004) charted.

NAVIGATION WPT 37°55'·77N 08°52'·88W, 027°/1·5M to ent to the marina bay. The outer ent, between W and E moles, is 1M wide. From the NW, caution: the derelict outer 400m section of the W mole dries 0·6m. A PHM buoy, Fl R 3s, 700m S of the mole hd ☆ (Fl 3s), must be rounded; no short cuts! In strong S'lies swell may cause turbulence off the W mole. Sines is a strategically located haven, 51M SSE of Cascais and 57M N of Cape St Vincent.

LIGHTS AND MARKS An oil refinery flare in the town and several tall chy's/masts 3-4M to the E (all with R lts) help to locate the port. Cabo de Sines lt ho is 9ca NW of the marina; it is obsc'd by oil tanks 001°-003° and 004°-007°, leaving a visible 1° wide sector in which the WPT lies. The 357·3° ldg lts lead solely into the industrial area.

R/T *Porto de Sines* (Port Authority) Ch 11, 13. Marina Ch 09.

TELEPHONE (Dial Code 269) Marina 860.612, 📠 860.690.

FACILITIES Marina (250, inc some Ⓥ 4m); (expansion planned), D & P; **Club Náutico** close SE of marina; **Services:** ME, El. **Town:** R, 🛒, Bar, Gaz, Ⓑ, ✉, ≷, ✈ Lisboa/Faro.

BALEEIRA, Algarve 37°00'·60N 08°55'·37W. AC 3636, 89. PC 27502. Useful passage ⚓, 3·5M E of C St Vincent, 1·6M NE of Pta de Sagres. Sheltered from W, but open to E'lies, when Enseada de Belixe is better. Enter between bkwtr hd, Fl WR 4s, and Ilhotes do Martinhal, 4ca NE. ⚓ N of the 2 jetties in 6m. See 9.24.3, lts.

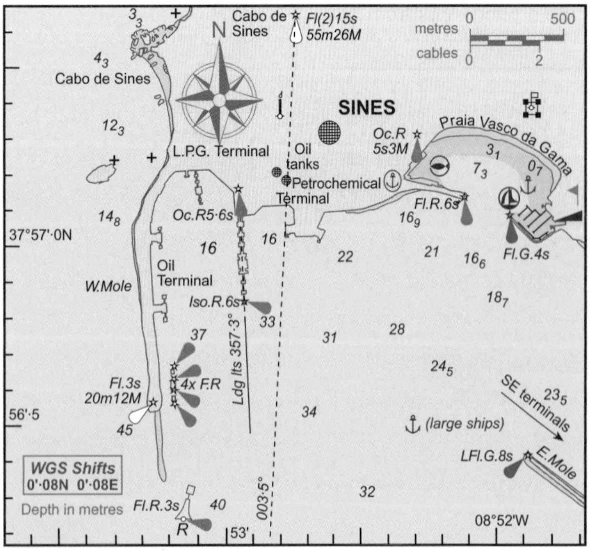
Cabo de Sines
Fl(2)15s
55m26M
metres
cables
SINES
Praia Vasco da Gama
L.P.G. Terminal
Oil tanks
Oc.R 5s3M
Petrochemical Terminal
Fl.R.6s
Oc.R5·6s
37°57'·0N
W.Mole
Oil Terminal
Iso.R.6s
Fl.G.4s
Fl.3s 20m12M
4x F.R
Ldg lts 357·3°
56'·5
SE terminals
(large ships)
LFl.G.8s
E.Mole
WGS Shifts
0'·08N 0'·08E
Depth in metres
Fl.R.3s
003·5°
53'
08°52'W

9.24.18 LAGOS

Algarve **37°05'·84N 08°39'·90W**

CHARTS AC 3636, 89; PC 24206, 26310.

TIDES
Standard Port LISBOA (⟵); ML 2·0; Zone 0 (UT)

Times				Height (metres)			
High Water		Low Water		MHWS	MHWN	MLWN	MLWS
0400	0900	0400	0900	3·8	3·0	1·5	0·6
1600	2100	1600	2100				
Differences LAGOS							
−0100	−0040	−0030	−0025	−0·4	−0·4	−0·1	0·0
ENSEADA DE BELIXE (Cape St. Vincent)							
−0050	−0030	−0020	−0015	+0·3	+0·2	+0·2	+0·2

SHELTER Very good in friendly marina (dredged 3m) on E bank, 7ca up-river from hbr ent, access H24 all tides. 3kn speed limit in hbr. The ⚓ close NE of the E Mole in 3-5m is exposed only to E and S winds and possible SW swell.

NAVIGATION WPT 37°05'·66N 08°39'·06W, 284°/7ca to hbr ent. Fishing nets may extend up to 1M offshore. From Ponta da Piedade, Fl 7s 49m 20M, 1·1M to the S, keep 5ca offshore to clear rocks; otherwise there are no offshore dangers. Final appr is on 282°, W mole head lt ≠ Santo António church. Shoaling reported in entrance; care needed at LW if draft >1·5m.
Berth at arrival pontoon stbd side just before lifting foot-bridge which opens on request 0800-2200, 1/6-15/9; 0900-1800 16/9-31/5), except for some ¼hr spells for train passengers. R/G tfc lts, but unmasted craft may transit when bridge is down.

LIGHTS AND MARKS Lts as chartlet and 9.24.3. The river chan is unlit, apart from shore lts. Pta da Piedade, Fl 7s 49m 20M, is 1·1M south. Pta do Altar (Portimão), L Fl 5s 31m 16M, is 7M E.

R/T *Marina de Lagos* Ch 09 for bridge and fuel. Weather broadcast Ch 12 at 1000 and 1600LT in season.

TELEPHONE (Dial Code 282) HM 770.210, 📠 770.219; www.marlagos.pt marina@ marlagos.pt Met 417.714; Ⓗ 770.100; Police 762.930; Fire 770.790; Brit Consul 417.800.

FACILITIES Marina (462+ Ⓥ, max LOA 30m), ☎/📠 as HM, €3.10, ⊜; P, D, Slip, BY, ME, El, ⚒, 🛒, R, Bar, CH, Ⓑ, ◙; **Club de Vela** ☎ 762.256; **Town:** usual amenities, ≷; ✈ Faro (75 km).

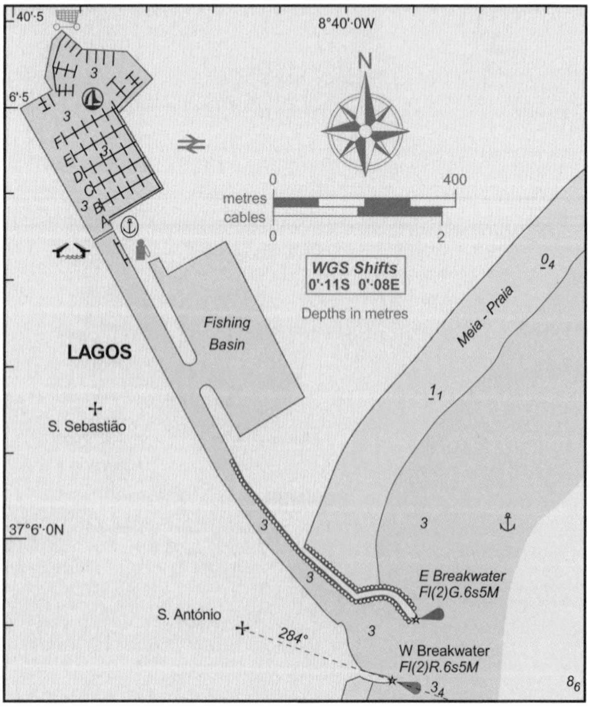
40'·5
8°40'·0W
N
6'·5
metres
cables
WGS Shifts
0'·11S 0'·08E
Depths in metres
Meia - Praia
Fishing Basin
LAGOS
S. Sebastião
37°6'·0N
E Breakwater
Fl(2)G.6s5M
S. António
284°
W Breakwater
Fl(2)R.6s5M

ADJACENT ANCHORAGE

ALVOR 37°07'·03N 08°37'·06W. PC 27502. A peaceful but shallow lagoon entered between moles Fl R and G 4s. The lt ho 1M inland is now disused. ⚓ just inside the ent to port in about 2·2m or off Alvor (1·2M E) in about 1·6m. The channel is not buoyed, so best to enter on the young flood whilst the drying banks can be seen. A lively tourist spot, but not devoid of charm.

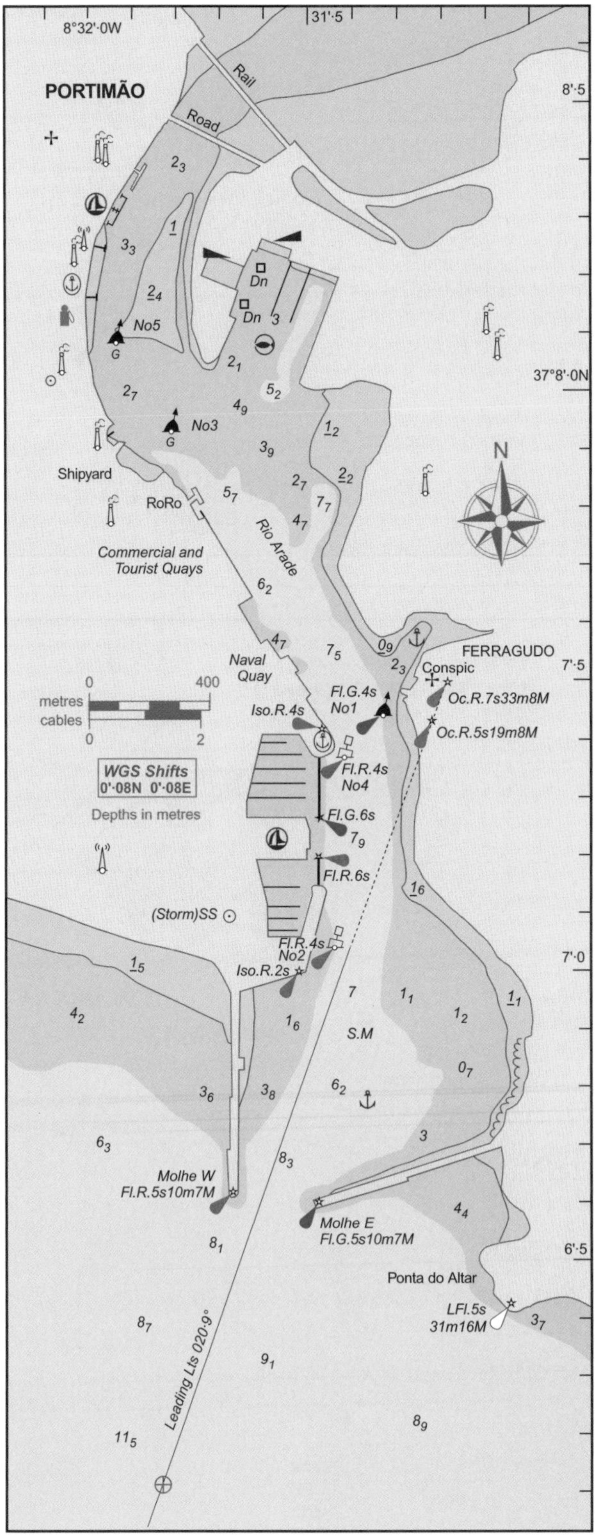
8°32'·0W
31'·5
PORTIMÃO
Rail
Road
8'·5
No5
G
Dn
Dn
37°8'·0N
No3
G
N
Shipyard
RoRo
Commercial and
Tourist Quays
Rio Arade
Naval
Quay
FERRAGUDO
Conspic
7'·5
Oc.R.7s33m8M
Oc.R.5s19m8M
Fl.G.4s
No1
Iso.R.4s
metres
cables
0
400
0
2
WGS Shifts
0'·08N 0'·08E
Depths in metres
Fl.R.4s
No4
Fl.G.6s
Fl.R.6s
(Storm)SS
Fl.R.4s
No2
Iso.R.2s
7'·0
S.M
Molhe W
Fl.R.5s10m7M
Molhe E
Fl.G.5s10m7M
6'·5
Ponta do Altar
LFl.5s
31m16M
Leading Lts 020·9°

9.24.19 PORTIMÃO

Algarve **37°06'·60N 08°31'·64W** ❁❁❁◊◊◊✿✿

CHARTS AC 91, 3636, 89, 83; PC 24206, 26310.

TIDES

Standard Port LISBOA (⟵); ML 2·0; Zone 0 (UT)

Times				**Height (metres)**			
High Water		Low Water		MHWS	MHWN	MLWN	MLWS
0400	0900	0400	0900	3·8	3·0	1·5	0·6
1600	2100	1600	2100				
Differences PORTIMÃO							
–0100	–0040	–0030	–0025	–0·5	–0·4	–0·1	+0·1
PONTA DO ALTAR (Lt ho E of ent)							
–0100	–0040	–0030	–0025	–0·3	–0·3	–0·1	0·0

SHELTER Good in the marina on W bank; max LOA 30m, max draft 4m. Or pontoons nearer town centre 2M up-river from hbr ent, just before 2 low road/rail bridges. Caution: flood & ebb streams run hard; berth bows to the stream. Good ⚓ inside E mole in about 4m, but prone to wash from FVs and any swell.

NAVIGATION WPT 37°06'·13N 08°31'·86W, 021°/5ca to hbr ent. There are no offshore hazards; entrance and river are straightforward.

LIGHTS AND MARKS Pta do Altar lt ho is on low cliffs to E of ent. The R-roofed church at Ferragudo is conspic by day, almost on ldg line 021°. Ldg lts as chartlet and 9.24.3; both on R/W banded columns, moved to suit chan.

R/T Port VHF Ch 11. Marina Ch 09.

TELEPHONE (Dial Code 282) HM 400.680 📠 400.681; Consul 417.800.

FACILITIES Marina (620 AB), ☎/📠 as HM, €3.45; D, P, C (300T), CH, El, ME, BY, Gaz, R, 🧺, Bar, Ⓑ, ✉; ⇌, ✈ Faro (65 km). BY with 40T hoist up river.

9.24.20 ALBUFEIRA

Algarve **37°04'·90N 08°15'·52W** (N bkwtr lt) ❁❁◊◊✿✿

CHARTS AC 91, 89; PC 24206, 27503, 90. The marina is not yet (2004) charted on Admiralty or Portuguese charts.

TIDES

Standard Port LISBOA (⟵); ML 2·0; Zone 0 (UT)

Times				**Height (metres)**			
High Water		Low Water		MHWS	MHWN	MLWN	MLWS
0400	0900	0400	0900	3·8	3·0	1·5	0·6
1600	2100	1600	2100				
Differences ENSEADA DE ALBUFEIRA							
–0035	+0015	–0005	0000	–0·2	–0·2	0·0	+0·1

SHELTER Good. The outer hbr ent may be difficult in strong E'lies. The marina, dredged 2·5 – 3·0m, opened 2003, but some of the brightly coloured, adjacent bldgs were incomplete (2004).

NAVIGATION WPT 37°03'·88N 08°15'·02W, approx 338°/1M to hbr ent. There are rocks close inshore to W & E, but no offshore dangers. Positions are approx due to lack of large scale chart; the Lat/Long below the title is by hand-held GPS (WGS 84).

LIGHTS AND MARKS Ponta de Baleeira lt, Oc 6s 30m 11M, W lattice twr with R top, is near the root of S bkwtr. Bkwtr lts as chartlet, both W cols, R/G bands.

R/T Call *Marina de Albufeira* Ch 09.

TELEPHONE (Dial Code 289) Ⓗ 802.555 (Faro); ⊖ 589.363; Taxi 583230; Brit Consul (282) 417.800 (Portimão).

FACILITIES Marina (475 inc Ⓥ), ☎ 510.180, 📠 510.189, www.amarinadealbufeira.com €3.62 inc AC; P & D, Slip, BH (70 ton), C (6 ton), ME, El, Ⓔ, BY, CH, Gaz, ⚒, SM; **YC**, Bar, R, ▣. **Town** most facilities; Ⓑ, ⇌, ✈ (Faro 39 km).

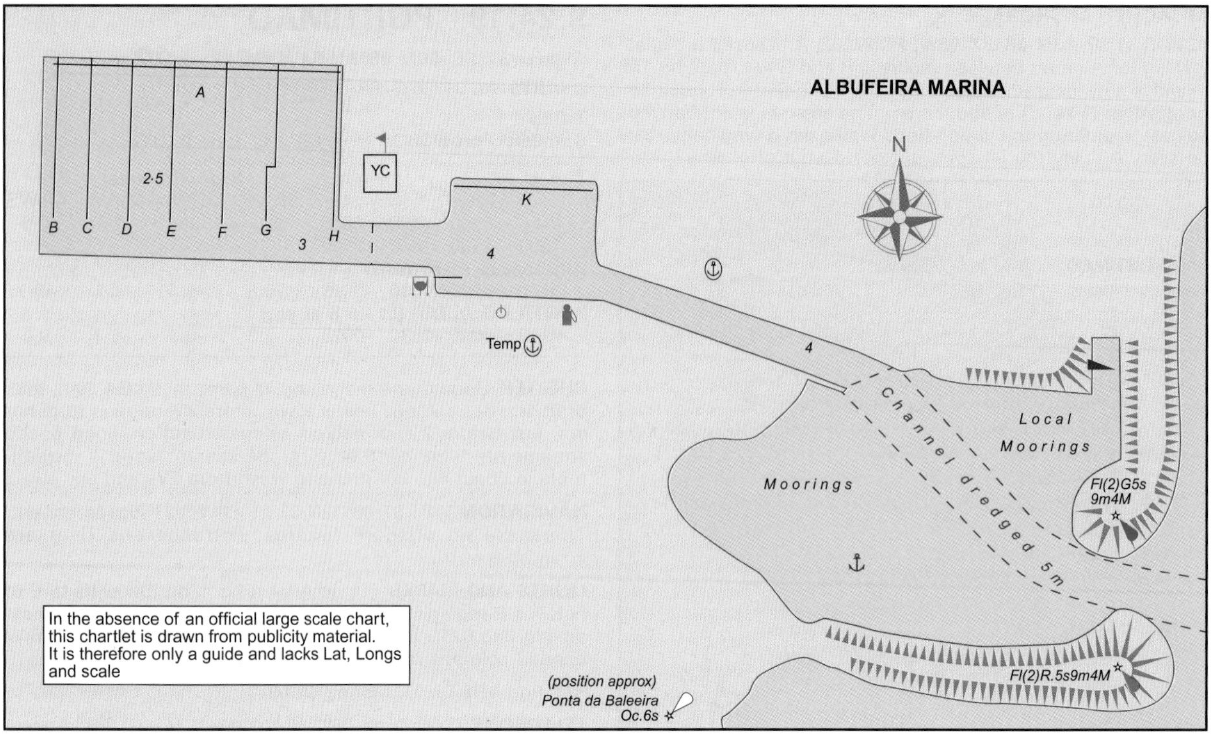
ALBUFEIRA MARINA
N
A
2·5
B C D E F G 3 H
YC
K
4
Temp
4
Channel dredged 5m
Local Moorings
Moorings
Fl(2)G5s 9m4M
Fl(2)R.5s9m4M
In the absence of an official large scale chart, this chartlet is drawn from publicity material. It is therefore only a guide and lacks Lat, Longs and scale
(position approx)
Ponta da Baleeira
Oc.6s

9.24.21 VILAMOURA

Algarve **37°04'·10N 08°07'·35W**

CHARTS AC 91, 89 (*Lisboa Datum); PC 24206, 27503; SHOM 7300. *To convert a WGS 84 GPS readout to this Datum subtract 0'·11S from the Latitude and 0'·08E from the Longitude.

TIDES Standard Port LISBOA (⟵); ML 2·0; Zone 0 (UT). Use differences for 9.24.20 Albufeira (6M to the west).

SHELTER Very good, except in strong S'lies when the 100m wide ent can be dangerous. The outer hbr is dredged 4m and contains many FV moorings. There is still some space for a yacht to anchor. The marina is dredged 3·3m, reducing to 2·0m in the NE corner near 'A' pontoon. Reception pontoon, port side of access chan. Max LOA 43m. Speed limit 3kn.

NAVIGATION WPT 37°03'·60N 08°07'·40W, 007°/5ca to hbr ent. There are groynes to the E, but no offshore dangers.

LIGHTS AND MARKS Marina is surrounded by apartment bldgs; large hotel is conspic on E side of ent. Main lt, Fl 5s 17m 19M, yellow twr on HM's bldg; this lt between the W and E mole head lts (R/W and G/W banded twrs) leads 007° into the outer hbr. See 9.24.3 for other lt details.

R/T Call marina *Vilamoura Radio* Ch 09, 16 (0830-2130/1830 off season). Outside these hrs expect only 1M reception range.

TELEPHONE (Dial code 289). HM, ⊖ & Met: as marina, below; Maritime Police 313.214; Medical Centre 314.243; Ⓗ 289.891.100 (Faro); Brit Consul (Portimao) 282.417.800.

FACILITIES Marina (1000 inc Ⓥ), ☎ 2310.560, 📠 310.580. marinavilamoura@lusotur.pt www.vilamoura.net €3.53 Jul/Aug; €3.38 Jun & Sep; €1.38 Oct-May; prices include AC).

P & D, Slip, BH (60 ton), C (2 & 6 ton), ME, El, Ⓔ, BY, CH, Gaz, ⚒, ▣, 🛒, SM, free ♻ by sludge boat that comes to your yacht. Local Ⓑ, M-F 0830-1445, plus ATMs. Water taxi, ☎ 313.622, criss-crosses the marina via 5 pick-up points. Mail pick-up if addressed to Marina de Vilamoura, 8125-409 Quarteira, Portugal.

Clube Náutico (by reception area) welcomes visitors: Bar, R, lounge, Cyber café. **Faro 9.24.22** (20 km) most facilities, ⇌, ✈ (☎ 800.800).

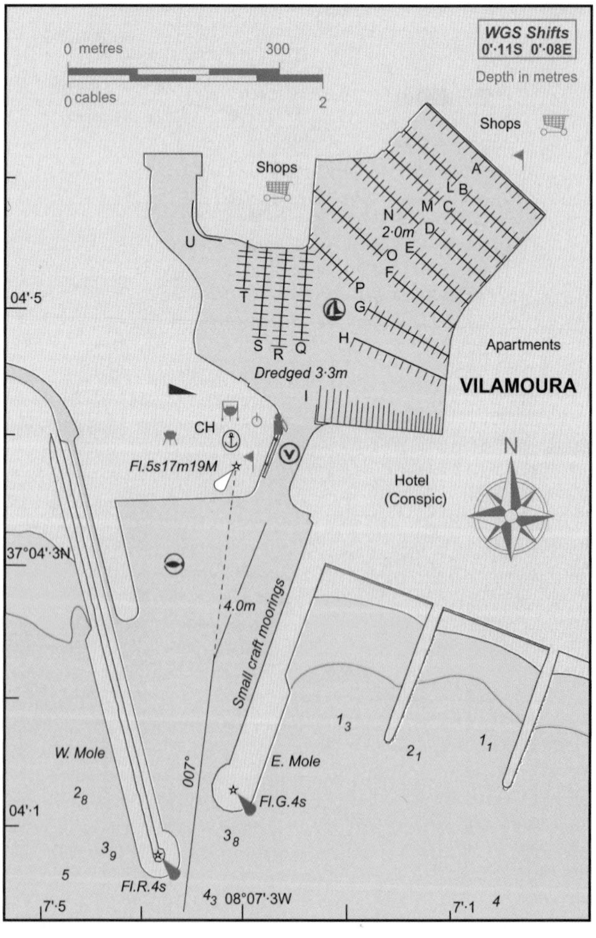
WGS Shifts
0'·11S 0'·08E
Depth in metres
0 metres 300
0 cables 2
Shops
Shops
A
L B
M C
N
2·0m D
O E
F
U
T
P
G
S R Q
H
Dredged 3·3m
Apartments
VILAMOURA
04'·5
CH
Fl.5s17m19M
N
Hotel
(Conspic)
37°04'·3N
4.0m
Small craft moorings
W. Mole
007°
E. Mole
Fl.G.4s
04'·1
Fl.R.4s
08°07'·3W
7'·5
7'·1

9.24.22 FARO & OLHÃO

Algarve **36°57'·90N 07°52'·11W** (Entrance) ❀❀◊✿✿

CHARTS AC 91, 89, 83; PC 24206, 26311; SC 44B.

TIDES

Standard Port LISBOA (⟵); ML 2·0; Zone 0 (UT)

Times				Height (metres)			
High Water		Low Water		MHWS	MHWN	MLWN	MLWS
0400	0900	0400	0900	3·8	3·0	1·5	0·6
1600	2100	1600	2100				
Differences CABO DE SANTA MARIA							
−0050	−0030	−0015	+0005	−0·4	−0·4	−0·1	0·0

SHELTER A popular ⚓ in 3-5m is inside Ilha da Culatra, abeam Pte do Carvao lt or off Ponte-Cais lt. At **Faro** ⚓ in 3m, 3ca SW of Doca de Recreio (small craft only; low bridge across ent). Some noise from airport, but not after 2100LT. At **Olhão** yacht pontoons are suitable for up to 2m draft. Marina bldgs, pontoons and new access chan are sketched only (2004). ⚓ as shown.

NAVIGATION WPT 36°57'·28N 07°52'·16W, 352°/5ca to narrow ent which can be dangerous in strong S'lies; extensive shoals to the W. Enter near HW between moles, Fl R 4s & G 4s, and training walls. Abeam Cabo de Santa Maria lt ho, chan forks into salt marshes and lagoons: WNW to Faro or NE to Olhão.

The **Faro** chan carries 5·4m for the buoyed/lit 4M to the Commercial quay (not for yachts); but beyond depths vary.

The **Olhão** buoyed/lit chan (5M) is narrower and carries 2·1m least depth. A new access chan, depths unknown, diverges near No 6 buoy towards the embryonic marina.

LIGHTS AND MARKS Cabo de Santa Maria lt ho near root of long E trng wall is conspic. It is also rear ldg lt 021° from ent to abeam front ldg lt. See chartlet and 9.23.3 for lt details.

R/T Both ports Ch 11, 09: Faro H24; Olhão, M-F office hrs.

TELEPHONE (Dial code 289) Faro HM 822.025; Ⓗ 802.555 (Faro).

FACILITIES Limited nautical facilities, but improving at Olhão. Both towns are sizeable and able to meet most needs; ⇌, ✈.

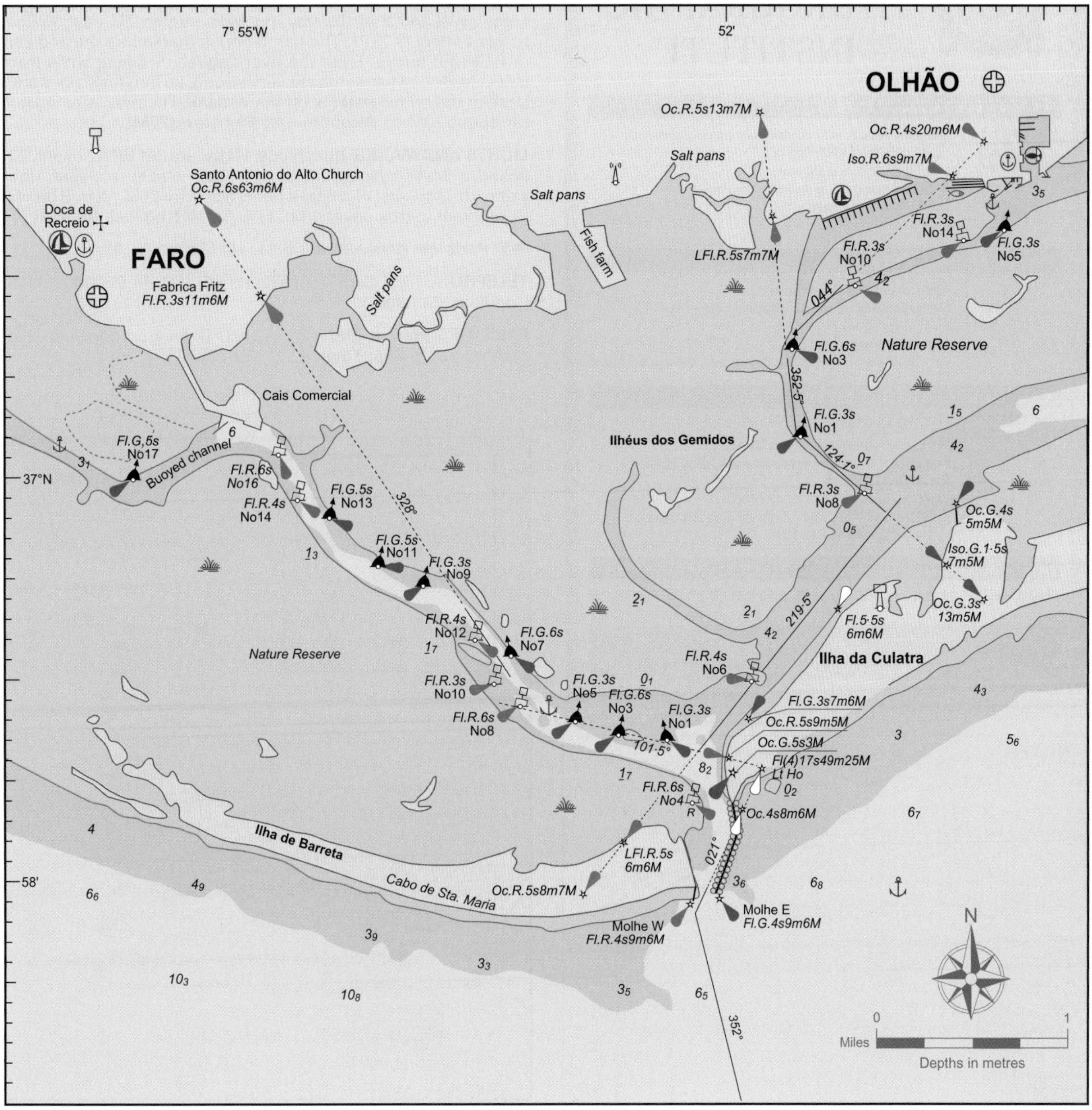
7° 55'W
52'
OLHÃO
Oc.R.5s13m7M
Oc.R.4s20m6M
Salt pans
Iso.R.6s9m7M
Santo Antonio do Alto Church
Oc.R.6s63m6M
Salt pans
Doca de Recreio
FARO
Fish farm
Fl.R.3s No14
Fl.R.3s No10
Fl.G.3s No5
LFl.R.5s7m7M
Fabrica Fritz
Fl.R.3s11m6M
Salt pans
044°
Fl.G.6s No3
Nature Reserve
352·5°
Cais Comercial
Fl.G.3s No1
Ilhéus dos Gemidos
Fl.G,5s No17
Buoyed channel
124·7°
37°N
Fl.R.6s No16
Fl.G.5s No13
Fl.R.3s No8
Oc.G.4s 5m5M
Fl.R.4s No14
328°
Iso.G.1·5s 7m5M
Fl.G.5s No11
Fl.G.3s No9
Oc.G.3s 13m5M
Fl.5·5s 6m6M
Fl.R.4s No12
Fl.G.6s No7
219·5°
Nature Reserve
Fl.R.4s No6
Ilha da Culatra
Fl.R.3s No10
Fl.G.3s No5
Fl.G.6s No3
Fl.G.3s7m6M
Fl.R.6s No8
Fl.G.3s No1
Oc.R.5s9m5M
101·5°
Oc.G.5s3M
Fl(4)17s49m25M
Lt Ho
Fl.R.6s No4
Oc.4s8m6M
Ilha de Barreta
LFl.R.5s 6m6M
021°
58'
Oc.R.5s8m7M
Cabo de Sta. Maria
Molhe E
Fl.G.4s9m6M
Molhe W
Fl.R.4s9m6M
N
352°
Miles
Depths in metres

24

TAVIRA. 37°06'·81N 07°36'·98W. AC 89, 93; PC 24206, 27503; SC 44A/B. Tide, see above (Cabo de Santa Maria). The narrow (about 70m) ent between I de Tavira and sand dunes to the E is lit by Fl G and R lts 2·5s and ldg lts 325·9° over the bar, front Fl R 3s; rear Iso R 6s. The ent (3m) should only be only be attempted near HW and in settled weather. Local knowledge is desirable. The anchorage, in about 3m on sand, is SW of the entrance in the Rio Formosa and SE of the small community of Quatro Agua. Show an ⚓ lt, due to FVs.

Tavira is 1M (20 mins walk or dinghy) NW of the ⚓ and, apart from a small craft BY and diesel supply, has little to offer a visiting yacht, being essentially a working fishing port. Access is not possible for masted boats due to a low road bridge. Facilities: YC ☎ 281 326 858, Slip; **Town** usual small town amenities, 🛒, R, Bar, Ⓑ, ✉, Ⓗ, ⇌, ✈ (Faro).

NOTES

9.24.23

VILA REAL DE SANTO ANTÓNIO

Algarve **37°11'·60N 07°24'·70W** (Marina) ❀❀◊◊✿✿

CHARTS AC 91, 89, 93; PC 24206, 26312; SC 440, 440A.

TIDES

Standard Port LISBOA (⟵); ML 2·0; Zone 0 (UT)

Times				Height (metres)			
High Water		Low Water		MHWS	MHWN	MLWN	MLWS
0400	0900	0400	0900	3·8	3·0	1·5	0·6
1600	2100	1600	2100				
Differences VILA REAL DE SANTO ANTÓNIO							
−0050	−0015	−0010	0000	−0·4	−0·4	−0·1	+0·1

SHELTER Good in the marina (2m). Vila Real is on the W bank (Portugal) of Rio Guadiana and Ayamonte on the E bank (Spain).

NAVIGATION WPT 37°09'·00N 07°23'·35W [No 1 SHM buoy, Q (3) G 6s], 340°/ 9ca to hd of W trng wall. Caution: Extensive drying areas to W and E of the training walls stretch 2M east, almost to Isla Canela (9.25.7). The bar (2·5m) is marked by the 2nd pair of P/SHM lt buoys. Enter the river between training walls from HW–3 to HW; but streams are very strong, so aim for slack water. Upriver the better water is off the W bank. The river is navigable for about 20M to Alcoutim and Pomerão (27M).

LIGHTS AND MARKS High bldgs, FR lts, are 3M WNW of ent. 2M inland a white suspension bridge (23m cl'nce) is visible from seaward. Other lts: Vila Real lt ho, Fl 6·5s 51m 26M, W tr, B bands. E trng wall (partly covers) bn, Fl G 3s; W trng wall hd, Fl R 5s.

R/T *Porto de Vilareal* VHF Ch 11, 16; Marina Ch 09.

TELEPHONE (Dial Code 281) Marina 541.571, ⛑ 511.140; CN de Guadiana 511.306.

FACILITIES Marina (357 AB), €1.83, D on pontoon just N of marina, YC, R, Slip; **Town** R, 🛒, Bar, Ⓑ, ✉; ✈ Faro.

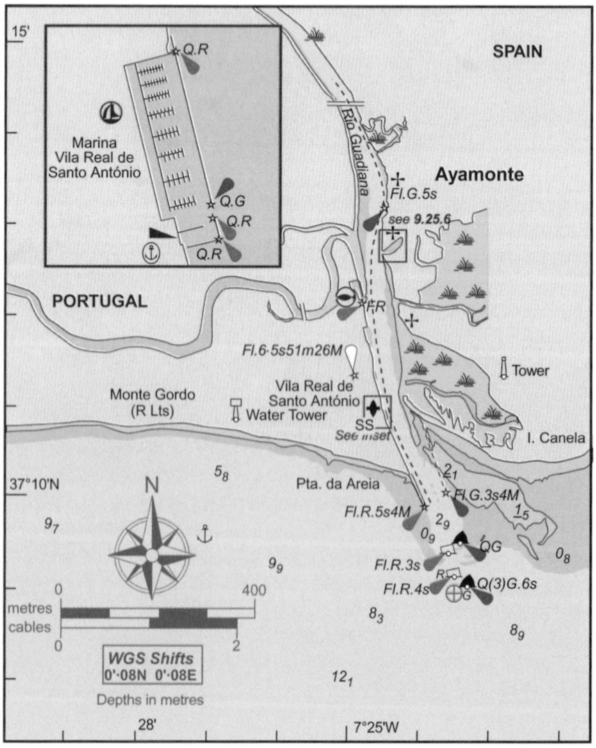
15'
SPAIN
Q.R
Marina
Vila Real de
Santo António
Q.G
Q.R
Q.R
Rio Guadiana
Ayamonte
Fl.G.5s
see 9.25.6
PORTUGAL
FR
Fl.6·5s51m26M
Tower
Monte Gordo
(R Lts)
Vila Real de
Santo António
Water Tower
SS
See inset
I. Canela
37°10'N
N
Pta. da Areia
Fl.R.5s4M
Fl.G.3s4M
Fl.R.3s
QG
Fl.R.4s
Q(3)G.6s
0
400
metres
cables
0
2
WGS Shifts
0'·08N 0'·08E
Depths in metres
28'
7°25'W

Area 25

South West Spain and Gibraltar

Ayamonte to Europa Point

The Spanish Flag (Civil variant)

The colours in the Spanish flag probably originate from the coats-of-arms of the original Spanish kingdoms. Castile has a yellow castle on a red field; Leon has a purple – sometimes dark red – lion carrying a yellow crown on a white field; Catalonia/Aragon has four red vertical pallets on a yellow field; Navarre a yellow chain on a red field. There is no specific symbolism in any of these colours.

Popular explanations like "red stands for the blood shed by Spaniards and yellow for the bright Spanish sun"; or even "red and yellow stand for bulls' and bullfighters' blood on the sand of the bullring" – are fictitious nonsense.

PLOT WAYPOINTS ON YOUR CHART BEFORE USING THEM

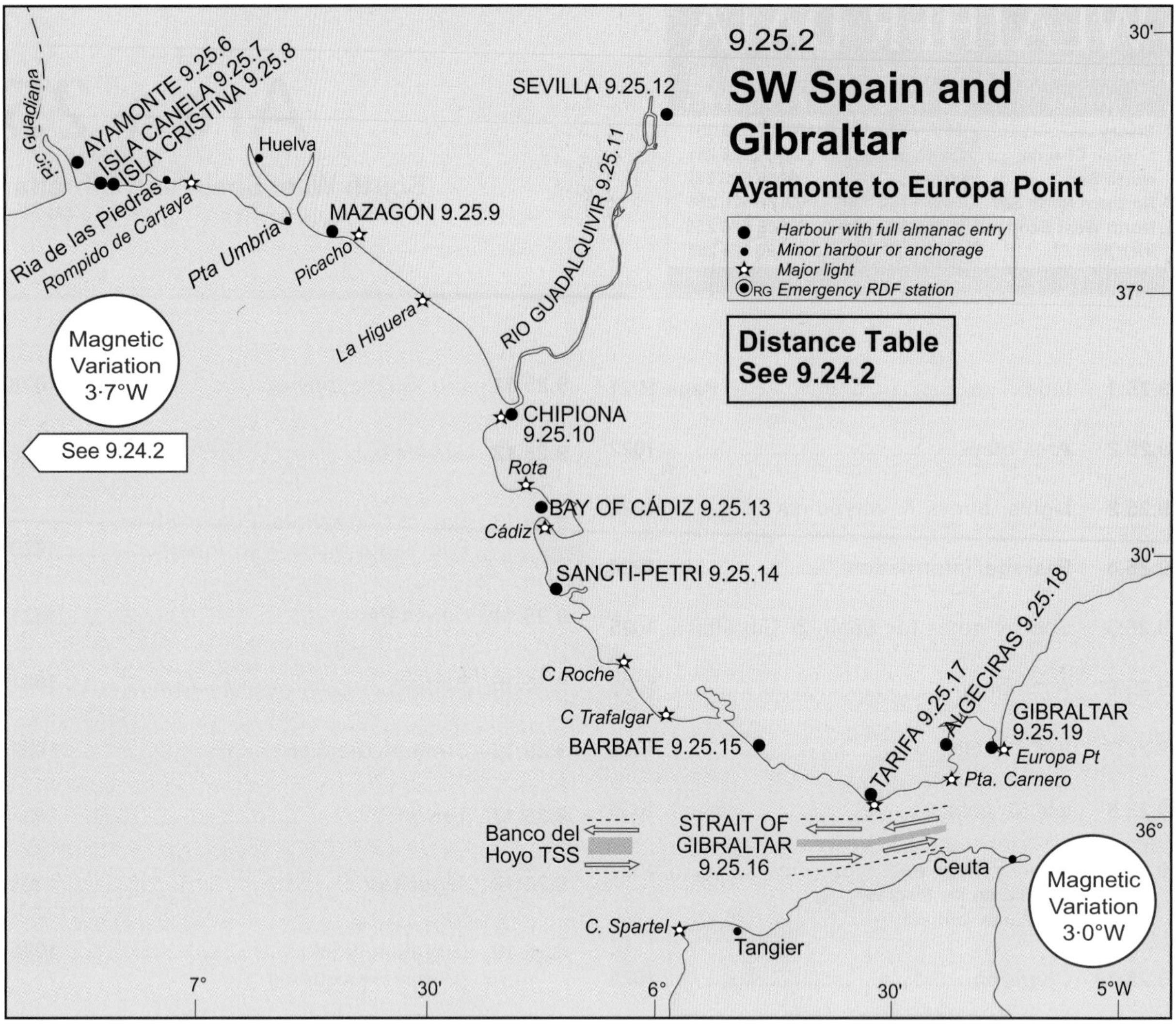
9.25.2
SW Spain and Gibraltar
Ayamonte to Europa Point
Harbour with full almanac entry
Minor harbour or anchorage
Major light
RG Emergency RDF station
Distance Table See 9.24.2
Magnetic Variation 3·7°W
See 9.24.2
Rio Guadiana
AYAMONTE 9.25.6
ISLA CANELA 9.25.7
ISLA CRISTINA 9.25.8
Ria de las Piedras
Rompido de Cartaya
Huelva
Pta Umbria
Picacho
MAZAGÓN 9.25.9
La Higuera
SEVILLA 9.25.12
RIO GUADALQUIVIR 9.25.11
CHIPIONA 9.25.10
Rota
BAY OF CÁDIZ 9.25.13
Cádiz
SANCTI-PETRI 9.25.14
C Roche
C Trafalgar
BARBATE 9.25.15
TARIFA 9.25.17
ALGECIRAS 9.25.18
GIBRALTAR 9.25.19
Europa Pt
Pta. Carnero
Banco del Hoyo TSS
STRAIT OF GIBRALTAR 9.25.16
Ceuta
C. Spartel
Tangier
Magnetic Variation 3·0°W
30'
37°
30'
36°
7°
30'
6°
30'
5°W

9.25.3 LIGHTS, BUOYS AND WAYPOINTS

Blue print = light with a nominal range of 15M or more. CAPITALS = place or feature. *CAPITAL ITALICS* = light-vessel, light float or Lanby. *Italics* = Fog signal. ***Bold italics*** = Racon. Useful waypoints are underlined. Abbreviations are in Chapter 1.

Positions below are referenced to the WGS 84 datum, but in the rest of Area 25 are referenced to ED50. Admiralty charts of this area are being steadily transferred to WGS84.

RIO GUADIANA TO SEVILLA

▶ AYAMONTE (E side of Rio Guadiana)

Bar buoys 37°08'·90N 07°23'·44W, Q (3) G 6s.
37°09'·14N 07°23'·82W, Fl R 4s.
W trng wall ☆ 37°09'·75N 07°24'·03W, Fl R 5s 4M.
E trng wall ☆ 37°09'·93N 07°23'·63W, Fl G 3s 4M.
Vila Real de Santo Antònio ☆ 37°11'·23N 07°25'·00W, Fl 6·5s 51m **26M**; W ○ twr, B bands.
Baluarte, Fl G 3s 1m 3M, is about 300m N of the unlit marina ent.

▶ ISLA CANELA and ISLA CRISTINA

No. 1 Appr 37°10'·90N 07°19'·60W, L Fl 10s (unconfirmed).
Ldg lts 313°. Front Q 7m 5M. Rear Fl 4s 12m 5M, 100m from front.
W mole ☆ 37°10'·84N 07°19'·68W, VQ (2) R 5s 9m 4M.
Isla Canela marina ent, QR and QG.
Isla Cristina marina ent, QR and QG.

▶ RIO DE LAS PIEDRAS

El Rompido ☆ 37°13'·12N 07°07'·69W, Fl (2) 10s 41m **24M**; W twr, B bands.
No 1 Bar 37°11'·69N 07°02'·63W, L Fl 10s. Lateral lt buoys are laid to mark the shifting chan.

▶ RIA DE HUELVA

Punta Umbria, bkwtr hd ☆ 37°09'·75N 06°56'·92W, VQ (6) + L Fl 10s 8m 5M.
Off Pta Umbria 37°09'·56N 06°57'·18W, VQ (6) + L Fl 10s.
YC jetty ☆ 37°10'·49N 06°57'·07W, Fl (3) G 15s 5m 3M.
Marina pier ☆ 37°10'·76N 06°57'·36W, Fl (2) G 10s 6m 3M.
Tanker mooring 37°04'·77N 06°55'·60W, Fl (4) Y 20s 8M; *Siren Mo (E) 30s*. Oil pipeline N'ward marked by 3 Y s, Fl (4) Y 20s.
Ría de Huelva Dique ☆ 37°06'·47N 06°49'·93W, Fl (3+1) WR 20s 29m, W12M, R9M; W165°-100°, R100°-125°; ***Racon K, 12M***.
37°05'·54N 06°49'·11W, Q (9) 15s.

Dir ☆ 339·2°, WRG 59m 8M. 37°08'·57N 06°50'·66W. Fl G 337·5°-338°, FG 338°-338·6°, OcG 338·6°-339·1°, FW 339·1°-339·3°, OcR 339·3°-339·8°, FR 339·8°-340·4°, Fl R 340·4°-340·9°; W twr.

No. 1 ⚓ 37°06'·26N 06°49'·46W, Fl G 5s.
No. 2 ⚓ 37°06'·33N 06°49'·72W, Fl R 5s.
No. 3 ⚓ 37°06'·87N 06°49'·77W, Fl (2) G 10s.
No. 4 ⚓ 37°06'·82N 06°49'·97W, Fl (2) R 10s.
No. 5 ⚓ 37°07'·38N 06°50'·03W, Fl (3) G 15s.
No. 6 ⚓ 37°07'·44N 06°50'·27W, Fl (3) R 15s.
No. 7 ⚓ 37°07'·77N 06°50'·29W, Fl (4) G 20s.
No. 8 ⚓ 37°07'·76N 06°50'·50W, Fl (4) R 20s.

▶ MAZAGÓN

Picacho lt ho ☆ 37°08'·10N 06°49'·56W, Fl (2+4) 30s 52m **25M**.
Marina, N Dique ☆ 37°07'·85N 06°50'·10W, QR 7m 2M.
S Dique ☆ 37°07'·91N 06°50'·03W, QG 5m 2M.
Inner ent, Fl G 5s and Fl R 5s.

Off Torre del Oro (ruins) ⚓ 37°04'·22N 06°43'·67W, Fl (2) 10s.
La Higuera ☆ 37°00'·47N 06°34'·16W, Fl (3) 20s 45m **20M**.

▶ CHIPIONA

Bajo Salmedina ☆ 36°44'·27N 06°28'·64W, Q (9) 15s 9m 5M.
◌ 36°44'·28N 06°28'·54W, Fl (5) Y 20s.
Pta de Chipiona ☆ 36°44'·26N 06°26'·53W, Fl 10s 67m **25M**.
Marina, No. 2 ⚓ 36°45'·14N 06°25'·59W, Fl (2) R 7s.
No. 4 ⚓ 36°45'·05N 06°25'·52W, Fl (3) R 11s.
N bkwtr ☆ 36°44'·96N 06°25'·70W, Fl (2) G 10s 6m 5M.
Inner jetty ☆ 36°44'·89N 06°25'·78W, Fl (3) G 9s 2m 1M.
SE side ☆ 36°44'·89N 06°25'·71W, Fl (4) R 11s 3m 3M.

▶ RÍO GUADALQUIVIR

No. 1 ⚓ 36°45'·74N 06°27'·03W, L Fl 10s; *Racon M, 10M*.
No. 2 ⚓ 36°47'·46N 06°26'·74W (1·6M N of No.1), Q (9) 10s.
Ldg lts 068·9°, both R/W chequered structures, 0·6M apart. Front 36°47'·84N 06°20'·24W, Q 28m 10M. Rear, Iso 4s 60m 10M.
No. 3 ⚓ 36°46'·16N 06°25'·36W, Fl G 5s.
No. 4 ⚓ 36°47'·33N 06°25'·41W, Fl R 5s.
Selected buoys only as far as Bonanza:
No. 6 ⚓ 36°46'·50N 06°24'·81W, Fl (2) R 6s.
No. 7 ⚓ 36°46'·61N 06°24'·02W, Fl (3) G 10s.
No. 11 ⚓ 36°46'·96N 06°22'·90W, Fl G 5s.
No. 12 ⚓ 36°47'·05N 06°22'·94W, Fl R 5s.
No. 14 ⚓ 36°47'·21N 06°22'·39W, Fl (2) R 6s.
No. 13 ⚓ 36°47'·12N 06°22'·36W, Fl (2) G 6s.
No. 17 ⚓ 36°47'·46N 06°21'·23W, Fl (4) G 12s.
No. 20 ⚓ 36°47'·81N 06°20'·71W, Fl (4) G 12s.
Bonanza, shelter mole, S end ☆ 36°48'·14N 06°20'·29W, Fl (2+1) G 21s 6m 5M; GRG col. Up-stream the river is marked by lt bcns, lt buoys and a few ldg lights.

▶ SEVILLA

No. 52, RGR structure. 36°47'·81N 06°20'·71W, Fl (2+1) R 21s 9m 5M. Here fork stbd for lock to city centre, or port for Gelves marina, ent Fl R 5s (37°20'·51N 06°01'·31W) and Fl G 3s.
Lock, 37°19'·95N 05°59'·65W, into Canal de Alfonso XIII.
Club Nautico Sevilla, pontoons, 37°22'·31N 05°59'·50W.

CADIZ TO CABO TRAFALGAR

▶ ROTA (Clockwise round the Bay of Cadiz)

Bajo El Quemado ⚓ 36°35'·88N 06°23'·95W, Fl (2) R 9s.
Rota Aero ☆ 36°38'·13N 06°20'·84W, Alt Fl WG 9s 79m **17M**; R/W chequered water twr, conspic.
Rota ☆ 36°36'·96N 06°21'·44W, Oc 4s 33m 13M; W ◌ lt ho, R band.

Marina, S pier ☆ 36°36'·96N 06°21'·44W, Fl (3) R 10s 8m 9M.
Las Cabezuelas ⚓ 36°35'·21N 06°19'·96W, Q (4) R 10s.

▶ PUERTO SHERRY and PUERTO DE SANTA MARIA

La Galera ⚓ 36°34'·60N 06°17'·56W, Q.
Puerto Sherry marina, S bkwtr ☆ 36°34'·64N 06°15'·25W, Oc R 4s 4M. N bkwtr ☆ Oc G 5s 3M.
Santa María ldg lts 040°. Front, 36°35'·77N 06°13'·36W, QG 16m 4M. Rear, 253m from front, Iso G 4s 20m 4M.
W trng wall head ☆ 36°34'·34N 06°14'·96W, Fl R 5s 10m 3M.
W trng wall root ☆ 36°35'·10N 06°14'·12W, QR 5m 2M.
E trng wall ☆ 36°34'·66N 06°14'·41W, Fl (2) G 7s 9m 3M.
YC pontoons, 36°35'·45N 06°13'·72W.

▶ CÁDIZ CITY and PUERTO AMERICA

⚓ 36°33'·99N 06°19'·80W, L Fl 10s; for Canal Principal.
No. 1 ⚓ 36°33'·12N 06°19'·07W, Fl G 3s.
No. 3 ⚓ 36°33'·17N 06°18'·14W, Fl (2) G 4s.
No. 4 ⚓ 36°33'·53N 06°17'·93W, Fl (2) R 4s.
No. 5 ⚓ 36°33'·03N 06°17'·38W, Fl (3) G 13s.
No. 6 ⚓ 36°33'·38N 06°17'·18W, Fl (3) R 10s.
N of San Felipe ☆ 36°32'·77N 06°16'·73W, Fl (4) G 10s 10m 3M.
San Felipe mole 36°32'·56N 06°16'·77W, Fl G 3s 10m 5M; G twr.
E mole ☆ 36°32'·44N 06°16'·63W, Fl R 2s 11m 5M.
Puerto America marina, NE bkwtr, Fl (4) G 16s 1M; G twr.
Real Club Nautico pier ☆ 36°32'·34N 06°17'·13W, FG.
International Free Zone hbr: No. 1 ⚓ 36°30'·66N 06°15'·45W, Fl (3) G 9s. **Puerto Elcano** marina ent 36°30'·07N 06°15'·45W.

Castillo de San Sebastián ☆ 36°31'·70N 06°18'·97W, Fl (2) 10s 38m **25M**; twr on castle; *Horn Mo (N) 20s.*
Bajos de San Sebastián ⚓ 36°31'·30N 06°20'·36W, Q (9) 15s.

▶ SANCTI PETRI

Punta del Arrecife ☆ 36°23'·66N 06°12'·99W, Q (9) 15s 7m 3M.
Sancti Petri castle ☆ 36°22'·75N 06°13'·33W, Fl 3s 18m 9M; twr.
Outer ldg lts 050°. Front, Fl 5s 12m 6M; rear, Oc (2) 6s 16m 6M.
No. 1 ◌ 36°22'·10N 06°12'·78W.
No. 2 ◌ 36°22'·20N 06°12'·90W.
No. 3 ◌ 36°22'·40N 06°12'·55W.
No. 4 ◌ 36°22'·50N 06°12'·65W.
Inner ldg lts 346·5°. Front, Fl 5s 11m 6M; rear, Oc (2) 6s 21m 6M.
'Gateway' bcns, Fl G (36°23'·10N 06°12'·65W) and Fl R 5s 7m 2M.

Cabo Roche ☆ 36°17'·75N 06°08'·59W, Fl (4) 24s 44m **20M**.
Marine farm, 36°17'·55N 06°13'·57W, marked by 6 SPM buoys Fl Y 1·5s
Cabo Trafalgar ☆ 36°10'·95N 06°02'·12W, Fl (2+1) 15s 50m **22M**.

THE GIBRALTAR STRAIT

▶ BARBATE

Barbate lt ho ☆ 36°11'·21N 05°55'·43W, Fl (2) WR 7s 22m, W10M, R7M; W281°-015°, R015°-095°; W ◌ twr, R bands.
Ldg lts 297·5°, both Q 2/7m 1M; 280·5°-310·5°; TE since 2002.
SW mole ☆ 36°10'·78N 05°55'·56W, Fl R 4s 11m 5M.
Inner NE mole ☆ 36°10'·95N 05°55'·79W, Fl (2) G 7s 7m 2M.
Marina ent, Fl (2) G 2M and Fl R 3s 2M.

Tunny nets (Mar-Sep): a roughly △-shaped net extends 2·7M south from a ⚓ Q at 36°10'·74N 05°55'·38W (just outside the hbr) to a ⚓ VQ (6) + L Fl 12s at 36°08'·07N 05°55'·06W. A ⚓ Q (3) 10s, ⚓ VQ (6) + L Fl 12s and ⚓ VQ (9) 10s mark other parts of the net.
Torre de Gracia ☆ 36°05'·38N 05°48'·69W, Oc (2) 5s 74m 13M.
Pta Paloma ☆ 36°03'·86N 05°43'·30W, Oc WR 5s 44m, W10M, R7M; W010°-340°, R340°-010°, over Bajo de Los Cabezos.

PLOT WAYPOINTS ON YOUR CHART BEFORE USING THEM

▶TARIFA

Tarifa ☆ 36°00'·06N 05°36'·60W, Fl (3) WR 10s 40m **W26M, R18M**; W113°-089°, R089°-113°; W twr; *Siren Mo (O) 60s;* ***Racon C, 20M.***
Lado E ☆ 36°00'·23N 05°36'·41W, Fl R 5s 12m 3M.
Outer SE mole ☆ 36°00'·38N 05°36'·24W, Fl G 5s 11m 5M; vis 249°-045°; G twr with statue of Virgin Mary.
Inner S mole ☆ 36°00'·49N 05°36'·18W, Fl (2) R 6s 7m 1M.

▶ ALGECIRAS

Pta Carnero ☆ 36°04'·61N 05°25'·57W, Fl (4) WR 20s 42m, **W16M**, R13M; W018°-325°, R325°-018°; *Siren Mo (K) 30s.*

36°06'·73N 05°24'·76W, Q (3) 10s; 1.2M ESE of marina ent.
Outer approach buoys: 36°07'·07N 05°25'·73W, Q (2) R 7s.
36°07'·19N 05°25'·97W, Q (2) G 7s.
Marina, outer S jetty ☆ 36°07'·10N 05°26'·13W, Q (3) R 9s 7m 3M.
N jetty ☆ 36°07'·13N 05°26'·22W, Q (4) G 11s 2m 1M.
Inner S jetty ☆ 36°07'·14N 05°26'·28W, Fl (3) R 11s 2m 3M.

Commercial port 36°09'·10N 05°24'·50W, Mo (A) 4s.

▶ LA LÍNEA

36°09'·56N 05°22'·00W, Fl (3) R 6s.
36°09'·53N 05°22'·03W, Fl (3) G 6s.
Dique de Abrigo ☆ 36°09'·51N 05°22'·05W, Fl (2) G 6s 8m 4M.
Marina ent jetty ☆ 36°09'·56N 05°21'·67W, QR 7m 2M.
Jetty de San Felipe ☆ 36°09'·69N 05°21'·35W, Fl R 5s 5m 2M.

▶ GIBRALTAR

Aero ☆ 36°08'·57N 05°20'·60W, Mo (GB) R 10s 405m **30M**.
Europa Pt ☆ 36°06'·58N 05°20'·69W, Iso 10s 49m **19M;** 197°-042° and 067°-125°; W ○ twr, R band. Same structure, Oc R 10s 49m **15M**; 042°-067° ; also FR 44m **15M**; 042°-067°; *Horn 20s.*
'A' Head ☆ 36°08'·03N 05°21'·85W, Fl 2s 18m **15M**; *Horn 10s.*
Queensway marina ☆ 36°08'·04N 05°21'·42W, 2 FR, 2FG (vert).
'B' head ☆ 36°08'·15N 05°21'·85W, QR 9m 5M.
'C' head ☆ 36°08'·54N 05°22'·04W, QG 10m 5M.
'D' head ☆ 36°08'·65N 05°21'·95W, QR 18m 5M.
'E' head ☆ 36°08'·90N 05°21'·95W, FR 28m 5M; twr.

MOROCCO (West to east)

Cap Spartel ☆ 35°47'·46N 05°55'·44W, Fl (4) 20s 95m **30M**; Y□ twr; *Dia (4) 90s.*

▶ TANGIER

Navaids are reported unreliable in Tangier and approaches. They may be missing, unlit, off station or not as charted.
Monte Dirección (Le Charf) ☆ 35°46'·08N 05°47'·28W, Oc (3) WRG 12s 88m **W16M**, R12M, G11M; G140°-174·5°, W174·5°-200°, R200°-225°; on terrace of white house.
35°47'·73N 05°47'·00W, L Fl 10s.
Roche Bourée 35°47'·52N 05°46'·53W, Oc (2) Y 6s.
Outer bkwtr ☆ 35°47'·55N 05°47'·52W, Fl (3) 12s 20m 14M.
S. mole ☆ 35°47'·39N 05°47'·77W, Oc (2) R 6s 7m 6M.
Yacht Club jetty ☆ 35°47'·31N 05°48'·06W, Iso G 4s 6m 6M.

Basse des Almirantes 35°49'·73N 05°45'·71W, VQ.
Pta Malabata ☆ 35°49'·08N 05°44'·86W, Fl 5s 77m **22M**. W□ twr.
Ksar es Srhir ☆ 35°50'·90N 05°33'·66W, Fl (4) 12s 16m 8M.
Pte Círes ☆ 35°54'·52N 05°28'·96W, Fl (3) 10s 44m **18M**; 060°-330°.

▶ CEUTA

Pta Almina ☆ 35°53'·91N 05°16'·86W, Fl (2) 10s 148m 22M.
Digue de Poniente ☆ 35°53'·75N 05°18'·68W, Fl G 5s 13m 10M; *Siren 15s;* ***Racon O, 12M.***
Spur, SE corner ☆ 35°53'·72N 05°18'·72W, Fl (2) G 8s 7m 1M.
Dique de Levante ☆ 35°53'·73N 05°18'·47W, Fl R 5s 13m 5M.
Muelle España W ☆ 35°53'·61N 05°18'·90W, Fl (2+1) R 12s 1M.
Marina ent ☆ Fl (4) R 11s 1M and two ☆ Fl (4) G 11s 1M.

9.25.4 PASSAGE INFORMATION

BIBLIOGRAPHY *SW Spain and Portugal Cruising Companion* (Jens/Nautical Data Ltd) covers from Bayona to Gibraltar. *W Coasts of Spain and Portugal Pilot* (Admiralty, NP 67) covers from Cabo Ortegal to Gibraltar. *The Straits Handbook* by Colin Thomas, Principal of Straits Sailing (straits.sail@gibnynex.gi ☎ +35051372) ia very informative and highly readable. It covers Gib and Spanish ports from Chipiona to Benalmadena, also Cueta and the Moroccan port of Smir. *Guia del Navegante* has fair cover, in English, of SW Spain, but is limited elsewhere. *Yacht Scene, Gibraltar and Surrounding Areas* (DM Sloma, PO Box 555, Gibraltar) is useful for those areas.

RIO GUADIANA TO CAPE TRAFALGAR On the Spanish bank Ayamonte (9.25.6) has a marina, the most W'ly of sixteen modern marinas in SW Andalucía. 4M to the E, Isla Canela (9.25.7) W bank and Isla Cristina (9.25.8) E bank of Ria de la Higuerita both have marinas. 13M further E, Rio de las Piedras requires care on entry but is a peaceful river with yacht facilities at El Rompido. In the apps to Huelva there are marinas at Punta Umbria and at Mazagón (9.25.9).

About 30M SE is the mouth of Rio Guadalquivir (9.25.11 and chart 85), navigable 54M to Sevilla (9.25.12). Caution: NW of the river mouth large fish havens in shoal waters extend 5M offshore. Chipiona marina (9.25.10) is a good place to start the passage up to Sevilla. Around Cádiz Bay (9.25.13) there are marinas at Rota, Puerto Sherry, Santa Maria and two in the hbr of Cádiz itself. S of Cádiz keep about 4M offshore on the 20m line to clear inshore banks. Sancti-Petri marina (9.25.14) lies on a remote and interesting river with a slightly tricky approach.

Cabo Trafalgar may be rounded within 100m of the lt ho, inshore of a tidal race, or about 4M off to clear foul ground/ shoals lying from SW to NW of the cape. Artificial reefs, which may reduce charted depths by approx 2·5m, are common from Cadiz to C. Trafalgar; see AC 93.

Tunny nets are laid up to 7M offshore, Apr-Oct, usually marked by cardinal lt buoys. Positions vary each year, but the more established nets are laid: (a) Off Conil beach, extending 3·3M SW to WCM and SCM buoys at the seaward end, 6·3M NW of C. Trafalgar. (b) Very close off Barbate hbr ent; see 9.25.15 and 9.25.3. (c) Off Zahara beach (5M SE of Barbate) extending 1·5M SW to a WCM lt buoy. (d) Close NW of Tarifa; see 9.25.17.

THE GIBRALTAR STRAIT (charts 142, 1448). ▶*The timing of tidal streams with notes on surface flow is shown on 9.25.16.*◀ Hbrs include Barbate, Tarifa (9.25.17), Algeciras (9.25.18) and Gibraltar (9.25.19). The Strait of Gibraltar TSS (orientated 090°/ 270° and 073°/253°) lies in mid-strait, as depicted on p.1032. Yachts bound to/from Gibraltar usually use the northern ITZ.

Local winds: Levanters are E'lies, common with high pressure to the N and low to the S. A persistent Levanter produces the roughest seas in the Strait and severe squalls in the lee of the Rock. The Poniente is a frequent W'ly, slightly less common in summer. The Vendavale is a strong SW'ly with rain/drizzle.

THE MOROCCAN COAST (chart 142). From Cap Spartel eastward for some 35M to Punta Almina the coast is generally rugged with mountains rising progressively higher to the east. Jbel Musa (one of the ancient Pillars of Hercules) towers 848m/ 2782ft high, less than a mile from the coast and 5M west of the Spanish enclave of Ceuta (a popular day trip from Gib).

Tangier is a port of refuge, with some yacht facilities, but is not a popular visit due to bureaucratic procedures.

9.25.5 SPECIAL NOTES FOR SW SPAIN AND GIBRALTAR

SPAIN. Regions/Provinces: Spain is divided into 17 autonomous regions, eg Andalucía. Most regions are sub-divided into provinces, eg in Atlantic Andalucía: Huelva, Sevilla and Cadiz. The province is shown below the name of each main port.

Language: This Almanac recognises regional differences (eg Basque, Gallego), but in the interests of standardisation uses the spelling of Castilian Spanish where practicable.

Charts: Spanish charts (SC) are obtainable from Instituto Hidrográfico de la Marina, Plaza San Severiano 3, 11007 Cádiz, ☎ (956) 599 414, 🖷 275358; order from Seccion Economica. Also from Chart Agents at Huelva, Sevilla, Cadiz and Algeciras. Hbr charts are usually larger scale than UKHO charts.

Time: Standard time is UT –1; DST (UT –2) is kept from last Sun in Mar until Sat before last Sun in Oct, as other EU nations. Note: Standard time in Portugal is UT and DST is UT –1.

Spanish secondary ports referenced to Lisboa: Some Spanish ports in Areas 23 and 25 are referenced to the Standard Port of Lisboa. Time differences for these ports, when applied to the printed times of HW and LW for Lisboa (UT), give HW and LW times in the Zone Time for Spain (UT –0100). Thus no further correction is required, except for DST, when applicable.

Telephone: To call Spain from UK dial 00-34, then the area code, followed by the ☎ number. To call UK from Spain, dial 07-44, then area code, less the initial 0, then the ☎ number.

Emergencies: ☎ 900 202 202 for Fire, Police and Ambulance. *Rioja Cruz* (Red Cross) operate LBs.

Public Holidays: Jan 1, 6; Apr 10 (Good Friday); 1 May (Labour Day); June 11 (Corpus Christi); Aug 15 (Assumption); Oct 12 (National Day); Nov 1 (All Saints Day); Dec 6, 8 (Immaculate Conception), 25.

Representation: Spanish Tourist Office, 22-23 Manchester Square, London W1U 3PX; ☎ 020 7486 8077, 🖷 020 7186 8034. londres@tourspain.es www.tourspain.uk

British Embassy, Calle de Fernando el Santo 16, 28010 Madrid; ☎ (91) 700 8200, 🖷 308 08 8211 (Consular). There are British Consuls at Sevilla and Algeciras.

Buoyage: IALA Region A system is used. However buoys may lack topmarks, be unpainted (or wrongly painted) more often than in N Europe. Preferred chan buoys (RGR, Fl (2+1) R and GRG, Fl (2+1) G) are quite widely used.

Documents: Spain, although an EU member, still asks to check paperwork. This can be a time-consuming, repetitive and inescapable process. The only palliatives are courtesy, patience and good humour. Organise your papers to include:

Personal – Passports; crew list, ideally on headed paper with the yacht's rubber stamp, giving DoB, passport nos, where joined/ intended departure. Certificate of Competence (Yachtmaster Offshore, ICC/HOCC etc). Radio Operator's certificate. Form E111 (advised for medical treatment).

Yacht – Registration certificate, Part 1 or SSR. Proof of VAT status. Marine insurance. Ship's Radio licence. Itinerary, backed up by ship's log.

Marina charges: Marinas run by the Andalucían Junta (all but Isla Canela, Sevilla, Puerto Sherry, Puerto de Santa Maria, Tarifa and Algeciras) charge on average €1.40/m LOA (2004) inc VAT (16%) in season (1/6-30/9); low season 50% less. www.eppa es

Travel: UK ferries from/to Santander and Bilbao. Direct UK flights from Jerez, Sevilla, Madrid, Malaga and Gibraltar. Internal flights via Madrid to Jerez, Sevilla and Malaga. Buses are usually good and trains adequate, except in the more remote regions.

GIBRALTAR

Time: Standard time is UT –1; DST (UT –2) is kept from last Sun in Mar until Sat before last Sun in Oct.

Telephone: The international dial code is +350 (but from Spain dial 9567 in lieu), then the 5 digit tel No; there is no Area code.

Nautical Info: The annual 'Straits Sailing Handbook' (£6.50) gives a detailed analysis of tidal streams and current in the Gib Straits and associated tactics, plus notes on passage-making and Spanish and Moroccan ports. See also 9.25.5 and 9.25.19.

Customs: Yacht arrivals for Sheppards, Marina Bay and Queensway Quay marinas **must** clear in at adjacent conspic Customs berth (Waterport). For security reasons, visiting RIBs must obtain prior written permission to enter from Collector of Customs, Customs House, Waterport, Gibraltar, ☎ 72901, 🖷 78362; VHF Ch 14 - or entry may be refused.

9.25.6 AYAMONTE

Huelva **37°12'·70N 07°24'·50W** ❁❁◊◊✿✿

CHARTS AC 89; SC 440, 440A; PC 24206, 26312.

TIDES

Standard Port LISBOA (⟵); ML 1·8; Zone –0100

Times				Height (metres)			
High Water		Low Water		MHWS	MHWN	MLWN	MLWS
0500	1000	0500	1100	3·8	3·0	1·4	0·6
1700	2200	1700	2300				
Differences AYAMONTE							
+0005	+0015	+0025	+0045	–0·7	–0·6	–0·1	–0·2
RÍA DE HUELVA, BAR							
0000	+0015	+0035	+0030	–0·1	–0·6	–0·1	–0·4

SHELTER Good in marina on Spanish bank of Rio Guadiana, 1·5M NNE of Vila Real. Marina is dredged 1·5m to 2·0m. Fuel pontoon is just inside ent. Sanlucar, 20M up-river, is accessible.

NAVIGATION WPT 37°09'·00N 07°23'·35W (No 1 SHM buoy, Q (3) G 6s), 340°/9ca to hd of W trng wall. Least depth over bar 2·5m. See 9.24.23 for chartlet, lts and directions into Rio Guadiana.

LIGHTS AND MARKS High bldgs, FR lts, are 3M WNW of ent. White suspension bridge 2M inland is visible from seaward. Vila Real lt ho, W ○ tr, B bands, is 1·5M S. Marina ent, N and S sides, is said to be lit; no further details. ☆ Fl G 5s is 350m N of marina ent, near ferry berths. See also 9.25.3 for lt details.

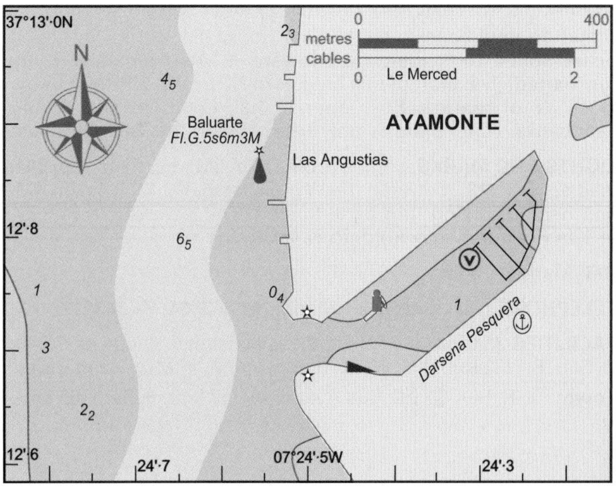
37°13'·0N
metres
cables
0
400
2
Le Merced
N
Baluarte
Fl.G.5s6m3M
Las Angustias
AYAMONTE
12'·8
Dársena Pesquera
12'·6
24'·7
07°24'·5W
24'·3

R/T Marina Ch 09 (H24).

TELEPHONE (Dial code 959) HM ☎/🖷 321694; ⊖, Met: via marina.

FACILITIES Marina ☎ 321294, 🖷 320767. ayamonted@eppa.es 173 inc ♥ in 3·5m, €1.40; D & P pontoon, Slip, ME, El, ⚒, R, Bar, YC, ▣. Ayamonte is first (E-bound) of 9 marinas run by Junta de Andalucía. **Town:** ▤, R, Bar, Ⓑ, ✉; Ferry to Vila Real de S'to Antonio; Bus Huelva (60 km); ✈ Faro (48 km).

25

9.25.7 ISLA CANELA

Huelva **37°11'·24N 07°20'·26W**

CHARTS AC 89; SC 440, 440A.

TIDES Use Differences AYAMONTE (9.25.6)

SHELTER Good in the marina (2·0m), but the ent to Ria de la Higuerita (which is common to Isla Cristina) is open to SE winds, like many hbrs on the Algarve. There is little space to ⚓.

NAVIGATION WPT 37°10'·11N 07°18'·58W (off chartlet), 313°/ 1M to bkwtr heads. Continue NW for 7ca, then turn 90° port into the marina. Best appr at half-flood.

LIGHTS AND MARKS Ldg lts (front Q 7m 5M; rear Fl 4s 12m 5M) aligned 313° between the W mole head, VQ (2) R 5s 9m 4M, and the covering trng wall to stbd. The powerful lt, Fl 6·5s 51m 26M at Vila Real de Santo António is 4M to the W. Other lts as chartlet. See also chartlet for 9.25.8 which shows the QG on the NW side of marina ent.

R/T Marina Ch 09.

TELEPHONE (Dial code 959) Marina ☎ 479.000, 📠 479.020.

FACILITIES **Marina**: marina@islacanela.es 231 berths, max LOA 12m, draft 2.5m, €1.24; ⚒, BH (32T), C (2T), CH; ⊜, Met: via marina. **Town:** 🛒, R, Bar, Ⓑ, ✉; Bus Ayamonte (17 km); ✈ Faro (65 km).

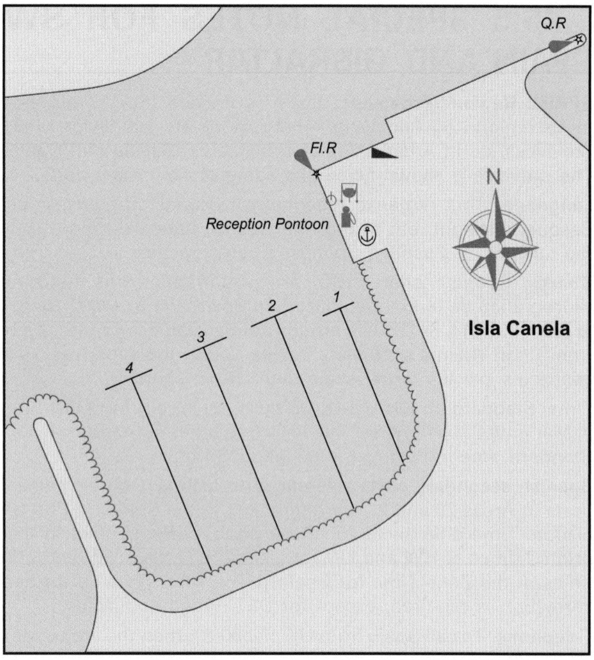
Q.R
Fl.R
Reception Pontoon
N
Isla Canela
1
2
3
4

9.25.8 ISLA CRISTINA

Huelva **37°11'·88N 07°19'·65W**

CHARTS AC 89; SC 440, 440A.

TIDES Use Differences AYAMONTE (9.25.6)

SHELTER Good in the marina (2·0), but the river ent is open to SE winds (like many hbrs on the Algarve). FVs berth at quays to the N of the marina. There is little space to ⚓.

NAVIGATION WPT 37°10'·60N 07°19'·38W (SWM buoy, Fl 10s, off chartlet), 000°/3ca to W mole head. Chan runs NW on the 313° ldg lts for nearly 1M, then curves to stbd past No 1 SHM lt buoy. Beyond ldg lts chan may change direction and/or depths.

Stand on until conspic tall W bldg (looks like a lt ho but isn't) bears about 100°, then alter toward it. At a small W buoy (uncharted) just short of this bldg, turn NE for No 2 PHM lt buoy, close W of marina. Best appr at half-flood, to see drying sandbanks. Note: there is only 0·4m abeam the W mole head.

LIGHTS AND MARKS Ldg lts (front Q 7m 5M; rear Fl 4s 12m 5M) lead approx 313°, between the W mole head, VQ (2) R 5s 7m 4M, and head of drying trng bank to stbd. The powerful lt, Fl 6·5s, at Vila Real de Santo António is 4M to the W.

R/T Marina Ch 09.

TELEPHONE (Dial code 959) Marina ☎ 343501; 📠 343511.

FACILITIES **Marina** (204 AB, inc Ⓥ), islacristinad@eppa.es €1.40, D, Slip, BH (32 ton), ME, El, ⚒, R, Bar, Ice, ⊡. ⊜, Met: via marinas. **Town:** 🛒, R, Bar, Ⓑ, ✉; Bus Ayamonte (17 km); ✈ Faro (65 km).

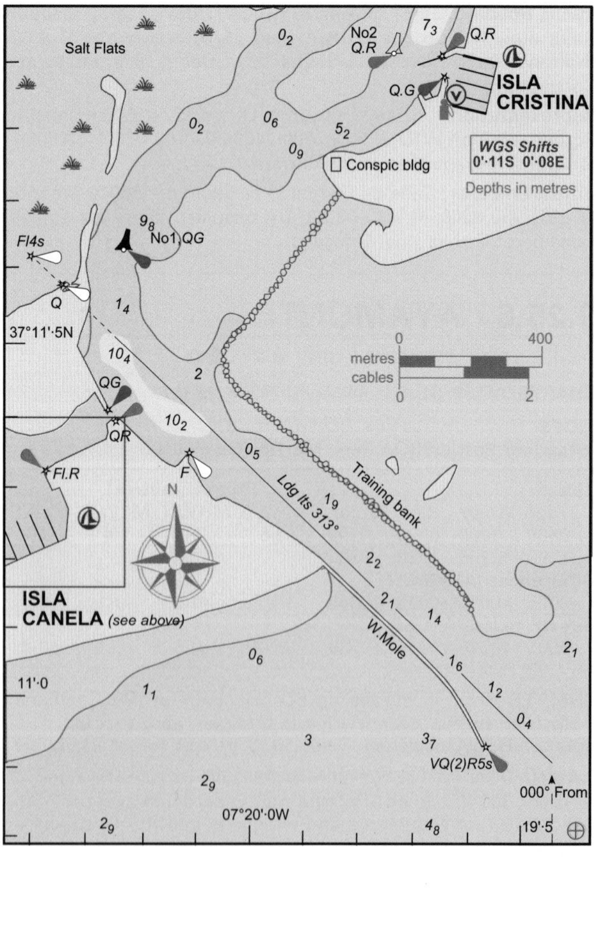
Salt Flats
No2
Q.R
Q.R
ISLA
CRISTINA
Q.G
Conspic bldg
WGS Shifts
0'·11S 0'·08E
Depths in metres
No1 QG
Fl4s
Q
37°11'·5N
metres
cables
0
400
2
QG
QR
Fl.R
F
N
Training bank
Ldg lts 313°
W.Mole
ISLA
CANELA (see above)
11'·0
VQ(2)R5s
000° From
07°20'·0W
19'·5

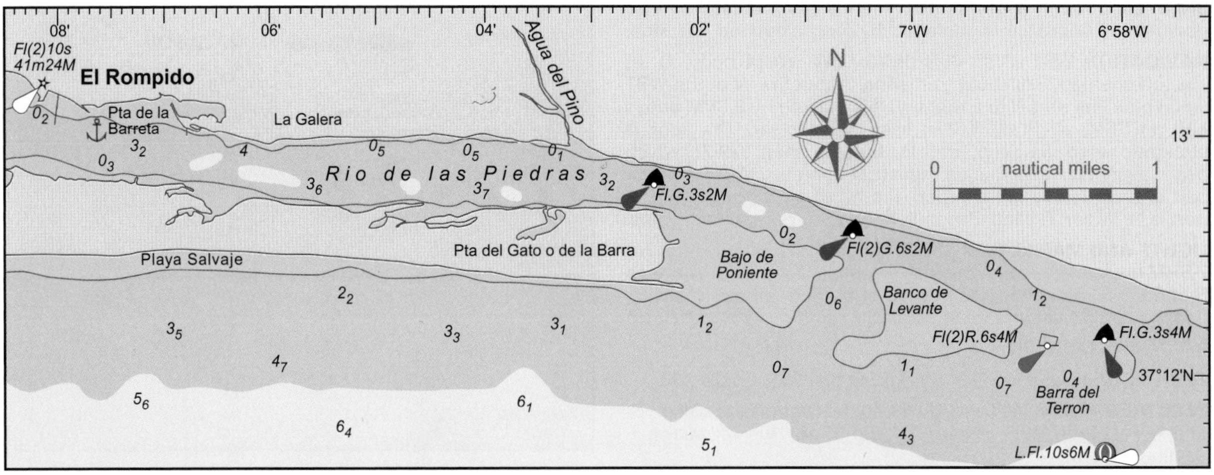
08'
06'
04'
02'
7°W
6°58'W
Fl(2)10s
41m24M
El Rompido
Agua del Pino
Pta de la Barreta
La Galera
Rio de las Piedras
Fl.G.3s2M
nautical miles
13'
Fl(2)G.6s2M
Playa Salvaje
Pta del Gato o de la Barra
Bajo de Poniente
Banco de Levante
Fl(2)R.6s4M
Fl.G.3s4M
37°12'N
Barra del Terron
L.Fl.10s6M

MINOR HARBOUR 13·5M EAST OF ISLA CRISTINA

RIO DE LAS PIEDRAS. AC 93; SC 440, 441A. SWM buoy No. 1, L Fl 10s, **37°11'·75N 07°02'·54W** at ent; thence NW past SHM buoy, Fl G 3s, and PHM buoy, Fl (2) R 6s, into river. El Rompido, W twr/R band, lt ho Fl (2) 10s, is 4M to W. Buoys are moved to suit shifting chan (0·6m) and shoals. ⚓ in river is sheltered by long spit. Tel (Dial code 959) YC 399.349, ⛵ 399.217; BY 399.180.

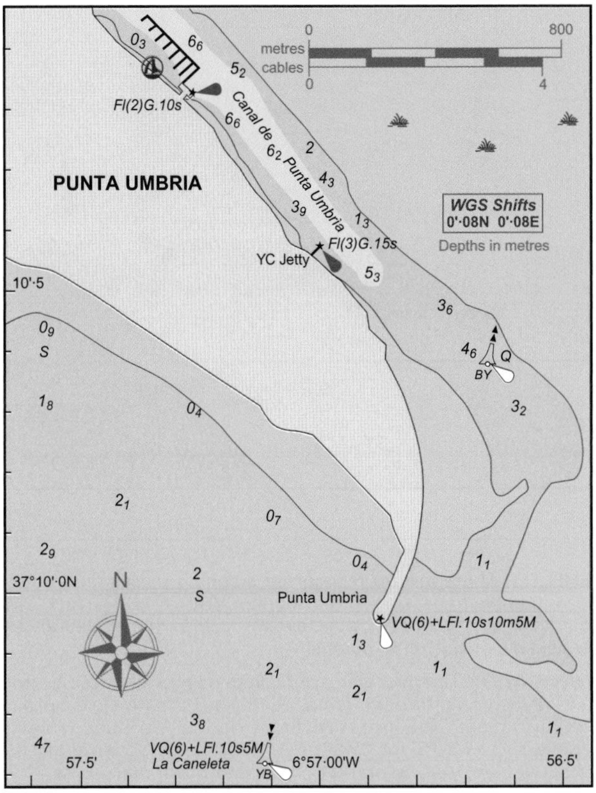
metres
cables
Fl(2)G.10s
Canal de Punta Umbria
PUNTA UMBRIA
WGS Shifts
0'·08N 0'·08E
Depths in metres
YC Jetty
Fl(3)G.15s
10'·5
BY
Q
37°10'·0N
N
Punta Umbria
VQ(6)+LFl.10s10m5M
VQ(6)+LFl.10s5M
La Caneleta
YB
57·5'
6°57·00'W
56·5'

MARINA CLOSE WEST OF RIA DE HUELVA

PUNTA UMBRIA. Marina **37°10'·79N 06°57'·30W**. AC 73; SC 441, 4411. Tides see 9.25.6. WPT 37°09'·59N 06°57'·09W, SCM buoy, VQ (6)+L Fl 10s, 049°/3ca to bkwtr hd, also VQ (6)+L Fl 10s, marking the chan ent/bar (1·1m). 2M SE of ent an oil pipe [marked by 4 SPM buoys, Fl (4) Y 20s] runs SSW 4·7M offshore. Inside, the chan turns NW and deepens 5-7m. YC, dark R bldg is 1M up-river, with pontoon, Fl (3) G 15s. Temp'y AB, M or ⚓ if room. **Marina** is 650m further NW. Tel (code 959) 314.304, ⛵ 314.706. puntaumbriad@eppa.es 197 berths inc ♥ in 6m, max LOA 12m, €1.40, Fuel, ME, El, ⚒. YC 311.899 **Town**: R, Bar, ✉.

9.25.9 MAZAGÓN

Huelva **37°07'·94N 06°50'·17W** ❀❀❀⛵⛵⛵✿✿

CHARTS AC 91, 93, 73; SC 441, 4411; SHOM 6862, 7300

TIDES See 9.25.6 (Ría de Huelva, Bar); ML 1·8; Zone –0100

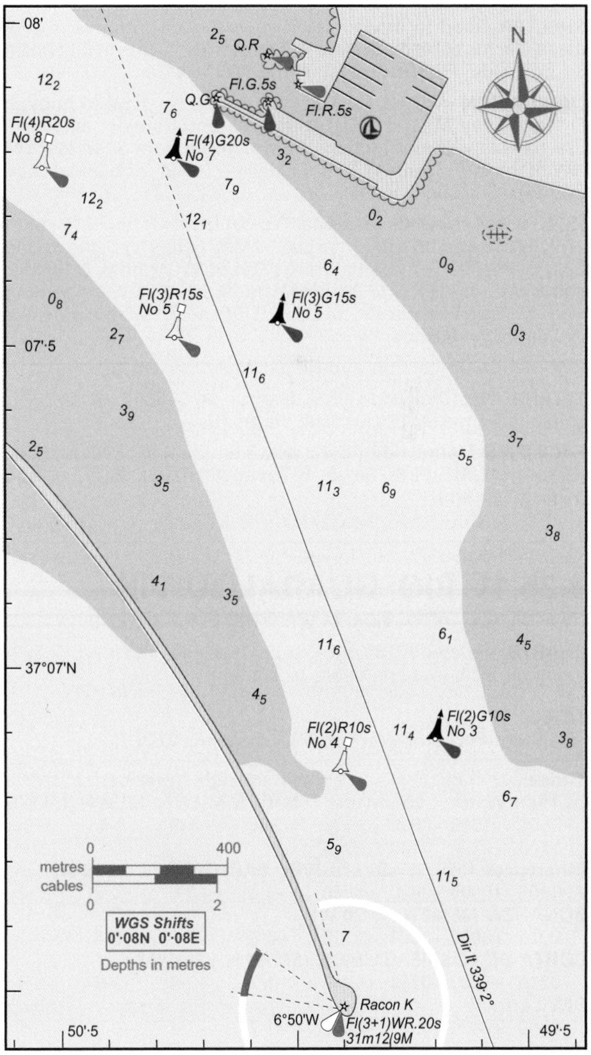
08'
Q.R
Fl.G.5s
Q.G
Fl.R.5s
N
Fl(4)R20s
No 8
Fl(4)G20s
No 7
Fl(3)R15s
No 5
Fl(3)G15s
No 5
07'·5
37°07'N
Fl(2)R10s
No 4
Fl(2)G10s
No 3
metres
cables
WGS Shifts
0'·08N 0'·08E
Depths in metres
Dir lt 339·2°
Racon K
6°50'W
Fl(3+1)WR.20s
31m12/9M
50'·5
49'·5

25

SHELTER Good in large, modern marina (4m), enter hdg ESE down-river. Approach is sheltered by long bkwtr on SW side.

NAVIGATION WPT 37°05'·60N 06°49'·08W, WCM buoy, Q (9) 15s (off chartlet), 339°/2·5M to marina. About 5M W of the WPT an oil pipe line runs N to a refinery. It is marked by 3 SPM buoys and an SBM, all Fl (4) Y 20s; keep 500m clear. The appr is straightforward via deep, well lit, buoyed chan 339·2°, which bears away NW into Huelva industrial complex. After the first pair of chan buoys (off chartlet), the hd of a 7M long bkwtr to port is lit; W twr, R band; Racon K. Keep clear of merchant ships.

LIGHTS AND MARKS Dir lt 339·2° (off chartlet); W twr. After No 7 SHM buoy alter stbd for the marina ent. Picacho lt ho, W tr with R corners/R roofed bldg, is 5ca NE of marina ent (off chartlet). See 9.25.3 and chartlet for lt details.

R/T Marina Ch 09. Huelva Port Ch 06, 11, 12, **14**.

TELEPHONE (Dial code 959) Marina, ☎ 536 251, 📠 376 237.

FACILITIES **Marina** (498, inc Ⓥ), €1.40, mazagon@eppa.es P, D, Slip, BH (32 ton), ME, El, ⚒, Ice, YC, Bar, R. ⇌ Huelva (24km); ✈ Sevilla (130km).

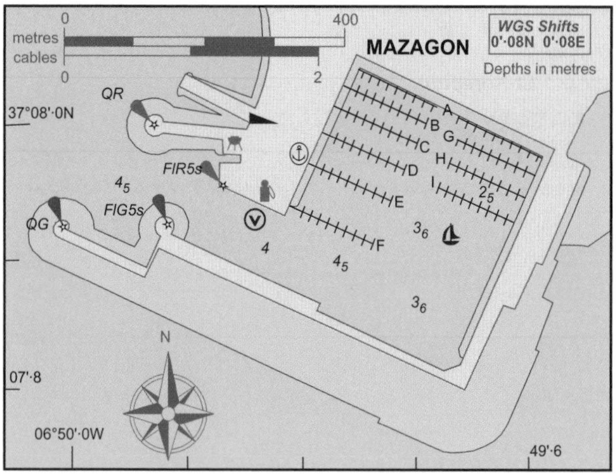
MAZAGON
WGS Shifts
0'·08N 0'·08E
Depths in metres
metres
cables
0
400
2
QR
37°08'·0N
FlR5s
FlG5s
QG
07'·8
06°50'·0W
49'·6
N

9.25.10 CHIPIONA

Cádiz **36°45'·00N 06°25'·63W**

CHARTS AC 85; SC 4421, 4422 (Sheets 2 and 3).

TIDES
Standard Port LISBOA (⟵); ML 1·9; Zone –0100; see 9.25.11

SHELTER Good in modern marina, but swell intrudes in NW gales. Yachts berth on SE side in 3·5m, larger yachts in first basin on port side. FVs berth against the NW bkwtr.

NAVIGATION WPT 36°45'·82N 06°26'·95W, No 1 SWM buoy, L Fl 10s (Racon M), 126°/1·3M to marina ent. Caution: extensive fish havens with obstructions 2·5m high lie from 3·5M to 7·5M NW of the WPT. Same WPT is on ldg line 068·9° for buoyed chan into Rio Guadalquivir (9.25.11).

LIGHTS AND MARKS Chipiona (Pta del Perro) lt ho, Fl 10s 68m 25M, is conspic 1M SW of marina. 1·7M W of this lt ho, the drying Bajo Salmedina (off chartlet) is marked by WCM bn tr, Q (9) 15s, and SPM buoy, Fl Y (5) 20s which must be rounded if coming from S. Inside hbr bkwtr, ☆ Fl (3) G 9s, near FV berths, is not visible from seaward.

R/T Marina Ch 09. Port and Rio Guadalquivir Ch 12.

TELEPHONE (Dial code 956) Marina ☎ 373844, 📠 370037, chipiona@eppa.es; ⊖ and Met: via marina.

FACILITIES **Marina** (412 AB inc Ⓥ in 3·5m), €1.40, P, D, Slip, BH (32 ton), CH, ME, El, ⚒, Bar, R, Ⓛ; **Town:** 🛒, R, Bar, Ⓑ, ✉; ⇌ and ✈ Jerez (32 km).

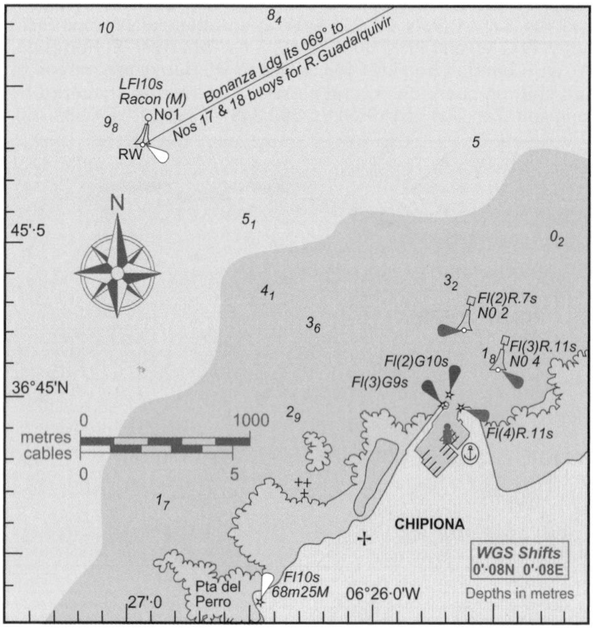
Bonanza Ldg lts 069° to Nos 17 & 18 buoys for R.Guadalquivir
LFl10s
Racon (M)
No1
RW
N
45'·5
36°45'N
metres
cables
0
1000
5
Fl(2)R.7s
NO 2
Fl(3)R.11s
NO 4
Fl(2)G10s
Fl(3)G9s
Fl(4)R.11s
CHIPIONA
WGS Shifts
0'·08N 0'·08E
Depths in metres
Pta del Perro
Fl10s
68m25M
06°26'·0W
27'·0

9.25.11 RIO GUADALQUIVIR

Huelva/Cádiz **36°45'·82N 06°26'·95W** (No 1 SWM buoy)

CHARTS Updated AC 85 or SC 4422 (18 sheets, mostly 1:12,500) essential as buoys/bns liable to change.

TIDES
Standard Port LISBOA (⟵); ML 1·9; Zone –0100

Times				Height (metres)			
High Water		Low Water		MHWS	MHWN	MLWN	MLWS
0500	1000	0500	1100	3·8	3·0	1·4	0·6
1700	2200	1700	2300				
Differences RIO GUADALQUIVIR, BAR (36°45'N 06°26'W)							
–0005	+0005	+0020	+0030	–0·6	–0·5	–0·2	–0·2
BONANZA (36°48'N 06°20'W)							
+0025	+0040	+0100	+0120	–0·8	–0·6	–0·4	–0·1
CORTA DE LOS JERONIMOS (37° 08'N 06°05'W)							
+0210	+0230	+0255	+0345	–1·2	–0·9	–0·5	–0·1
SEVILLA							
+0400	+0430	+0510	+0545	–1·7	–1·2	–0·6	–0·1

SHELTER There are no recognised stopping places and any ⚓ is vulnerable to passing traffic; monitor VHF Ch 12. The lock, 2M S of Sevilla (9.25.12), is below HT cables (44m clearance) between conspic R/W pylons.

NAVIGATION The river is not difficult to navigate but can be hot and uninspiring, through the flat and almost featureless terrain of the Doñana National Park. From No 1 SWM buoy (shown above and as WPT for CHIPIONA, 9.25.10) the Bonanza ldg lts (front Q 27m 10M, ▲ on R/W chequered mast; rear Iso 4s 60m 10M, ▼ on R/W chequered mast) lead 068·9° for 5M through lit, buoyed chan.

From No 1 SWM buoy to a lock 2M S of Sevilla is about 49M. At Bonanza (36°48'N 06°20'W) the channel becomes truly riverine, 750m wide; 250m nearer Sevilla. The banks are well marked throughout by lt beacons. Depths are rarely less than 5m, best water usually being on the outside of bends, which are often buoyed in the broader lower reaches.

TIDAL STREAMS The flood makes for about 7hrs (3kn sp, 1kn nps), the ebb for 5½ hrs; so it should be possible to reach the lock on one tide, passing Bonanza at LW –½hr.

9.25.12 SEVILLA

Sevilla **37°20'·00N 05°59'·65W** (Lock) ❁❁❁◊◊◊✿✿✿

CHARTS & TIDES SC 4422 (sheets 17/18). ML Sevilla 1·3M.

SHELTER The 3 marinas are: **Gelves,** 1·5M N of Bn 52 on the main river, ie **not** via the lock; overhead cables (16·5m) down-river; may silt; approx 3M from the city. **Marina Yachting Sevilla,** beyond and 300m E of the lock almost below HT cables, is a long pontoon in a quiet creek 3M from city; useful stopover prior to transiting road/rail bridge 2M N. **Club Náutico de Sevilla,** excellent facilities close to city centre; also possible to berth on E quay.

NAVIGATION The lock, 2M S of city centre, opens at 0100, 0400, 0700, 0900, 1100, 1300, 1600, 1900 and 2100LT (confirm at Chipiona); secure to ladders/rubber strips. 1M N of conspic suspension bridge (48m), negotiate Las Delicias road/rail bridge (10·1m): opens in season M-F 1000-2000, Sat/Hols 0830-2000; (winter 1000-1700). Sound K (—·—) to request opening or call Ch 12. R or G lts at lock and bridge = no entry or enter.

R/T Marinas Ch 09. Lock, road/rail bridge and Port Ch 12.

TELEPHONE (Dial code 95). Brit Consul 4228 875.

FACILITIES Port www.apsevilla.com **Gelves marina** (133+ Ⓥ), €4.00 ☎ 576 1212, 📠 576 1583; about 3m, waiting pontoon in river, CH, ME, BH (25 ton), ⊡, R, 🛒, Bar; **Marina Yachting Sevilla** (400+ Ⓥ), 6m, ☎ 4230326, 📠 4230172, Slip, ME, ⊡; **Club Náutico Sevilla** (100+ Ⓥin 3m; pre-booking advised), ☎ 4454 777, 📠 4284 693, D & P, Slip, R, Bar, Ice, ⊡. **City:** All amenities; ⇌; ✈ (10 km).

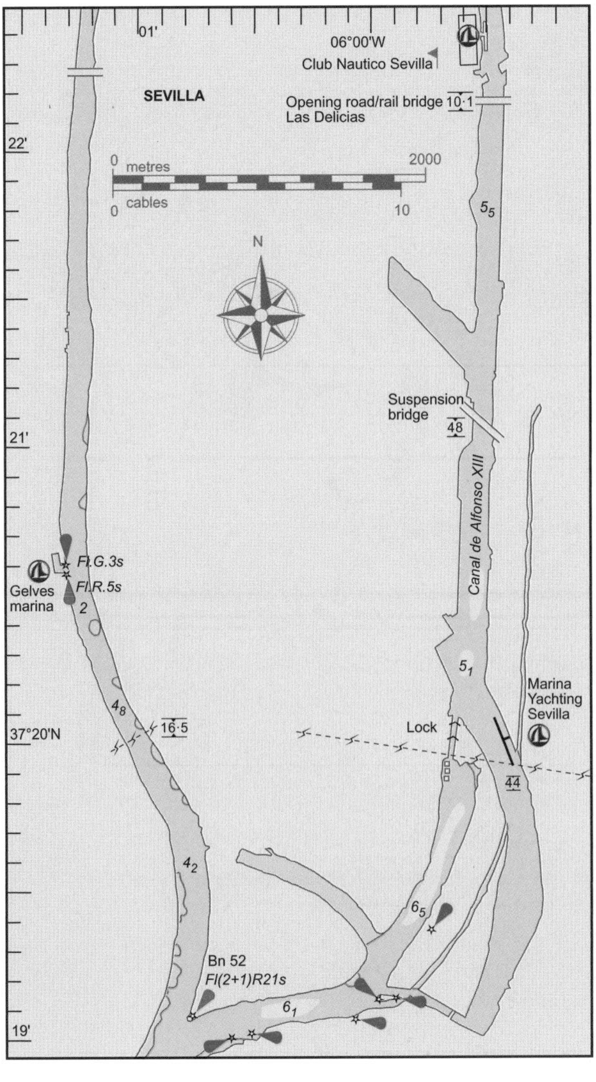
01'
06°00'W
Club Nautico Sevilla
SEVILLA
Opening road/rail bridge 10·1
Las Delicias
22'
0 metres 2000
0 cables 10
5₅
N
Suspension bridge
48
21'
Canal de Alfonso XIII
Fl.G.3s
Gelves marina
Fl.R.5s
2
5₁
Marina Yachting Sevilla
4₈
16·5
37°20'N
Lock
44
4₂
6₅
Bn 52
Fl(2+1)R21s
6₁
19'

9.25.13 BAY OF CÁDIZ

Cádiz **36°33'·91N 06°19'·88W** (SWM buoy) ❁❁❁◊◊◊✿✿✿

CHARTS AC 93, 86, 88; SC 443, 443A, 443B, 4430, 4431.

TIDES
Standard Port LISBOA (⟵); ML 1·8; Zone –0100

Times				Height (metres)			
High Water		Low Water		MHWS	MHWN	MLWN	MLWS
0500	1000	0500	1100	3·8	3·0	1·5	0·5
1700	2200	1700	2300				
Differences ROTA							
–0010	+0010	+0025	+0015	–0·7	–0·6	–0·4	–0·1
PUERTO DE SANTA MARIA							
+0006	+0006	+0027	+0027	–0·6	–0·4	–0·4	–0·1
PUERTO CÁDIZ							
0000	+0020	+0040	+0025	–0·5	–0·5	–0·3	0·0

SHELTER Good in all 5 marinas: Rota, Puerto Sherry, Puerto de Sta Maria (where very pleasant Real Club Náutico has a few Ⓥ berths), Puerto América (at N tip of Cádiz) and Puerto Elcano.

NAVIGATION Rota. WPT 36°36'·00N 06°21'·00W, 000°/9ca to marina ent. Al Fl WG 9s airfield lt and conspic water tank bear 004° from WPT. From W/NW keep 1·5M offshore to clear shoals. Naval vessels may be at ⚓ S of Rota Naval base.

Puerto Sherry. WPT 36°34'·09N 06°15'·11W, 000°/6ca to marina entrance.

Puerto de Santa Maria, same WPT as P. Sherry, 040°/4ca to W training wall head (Fl R 5s); at mouth of canalised Rio Guadalete, dredged 4·5m. Ldg lts 040°: front, QG; rear Iso G4s. From W, the N Chan trends ESE, inshore of shoals toward both marinas.

Puerto America (Cádiz). WPT 36°33'·91N 06°19'·88W (SWM buoy, L Fl 10s), 110°/2·8M to abeam Dique de San Felipe head via buoyed appr chan. From S, keep to seaward of extensive shoals N & W of Cádiz. The shore is generally low-lying, but a W bldg on Dique de San Felipe is conspic.

Puerto Elcano. WPT 36°32'·73N 06°16'·37W, 160°/2.3M to buoys at ent to International Free Zone Hbr. The marina at 36°30'·08N 06°15'·43W is 5ca South of the ent, accessed by buoyed chan.

LIGHTS AND MARKS Lts/buoys as chartlets and 9.25.3. Conspic daymarks include: Rota lt ho, W twr/R band, overlooking marina. Puerto Sherry, W bkwtr hd ○ twr. Cádiz city, golden-domed cathedral and radio twr (113m) close SE. Further SSE: Two power cable pylons (154m), dockyard cranes and long bridge to mainland.

R/T Marinas VHF Ch 09. Cádiz Trafico **74.**

TELEPHONE (Dial code 956) Port HM 224011, 📠 240476; ⊖ & Met via marinas (see below).

FACILITIES Rota Marina (509 AB, inc Ⓥ in 4·5m), €1.40, ☎ 840069, 📠 813811, rota@eppa.es P, D, Slip, BH (32 ton), ME, El, C (5 ton).

Puerto Sherry Marina (753 AB, inc Ⓥ; 3·0-4·5m), ☎ 870103, 📠 873902, www.puertosherry.com P, D, Slip, BH (50 ton), ME, El, C, SM, Ⓔ, CH, ⚒, ⊡, R, Bar, YC ☎ 858751. Arrivals berth to port inside ent.

Real Club Náutico de Puerto de Santa Maria (250 AB+few Ⓥ; 3·0-8·0m). rcnpuerto@ono.com; www.rcnpsm.com ☎ 852527, 📠 874400; best to pre-book. 10 hammerhead pontoons (A-J) on NW bank plus two mid-stream pontoons. €6.00, P, D, ⚒, ME, C (5 ton), BH (25 ton), Slip, R, Bar. FVs berth up-river. Ferry to Cadiz.

Puerto América Marina (184 AB, inc Ⓥ; 7·5m), €1.40, ☎ 223666, 📠 224220, puertoamerica@eppa.es P, D, Slip, ME, El, C (10 ton).

Real Club Náutico de Cádiz (160 AB; 3m) ☎ 213262, 📠 221040; Good R, Bar, D; Ⓥ berths unlikely. (Close SW of Puerto America).

P. Elcano marina is at the SW end of conspic road bridge to the mainland. (273 AB; max draft 2m) ☎ 290012, 📠 290099. P, D. cnelcano@teleline.es Reports would be welcomed.

City: all amenities, ⇌; ✈ Jerez (25 km). Spanish Hydrographic Office is at 36°31'·38N 06°17'·04W (1·5 track miles from Puerto America); Plaza San Severiano 3, 11007 Cádiz; ☎ 599414, 📠 275358; ihmesp@retemail.es

BAY OF CÁDIZ including marinas at: ROTA, PUERTO SHERRY, PUERTO DE SANTA MARIA, PUERTO AMERICA and PUERTO ELCANO

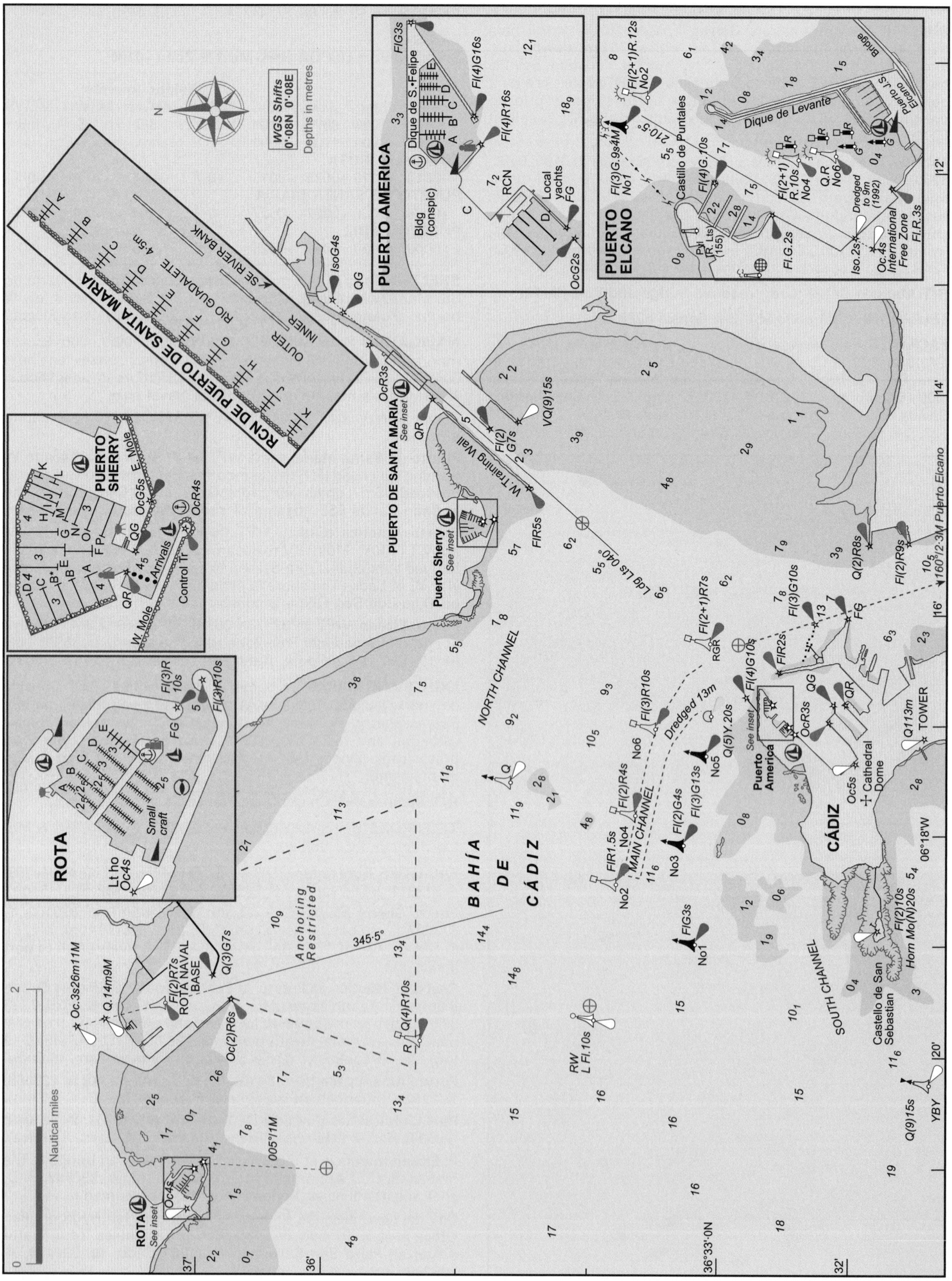

WGS Shifts
0'·08N 0'·08E
Depths in metres
PUERTO AMERICA
Dique de S. Felipe
Bldg (conspic)
Local yachts
RCN
PUERTO ELCANO
Castillo de Puntales
Dique de Levante
Bridge
International Free Zone
Dredged to 9m (1992)
RCN DE PUERTO DE SANTA MARIA
RIO GUADALETE
SE RIVER BANK
OUTER
INNER
PUERTO SHERRY
E. Mole
W. Mole
Control Tr
Arrivals
ROTA
Small craft
Lt ho
PUERTO DE SANTA MARIA
See inset
Puerto Sherry
W. Training Wall
NORTH CHANNEL
BAHÍA DE CÁDIZ
MAIN CHANNEL
Dredged 13m
Puerto America
CÁDIZ
Cathedral Dome
TOWER
SOUTH CHANNEL
Castello de San Sebastian
Anchoring Restricted
ROTA NAVAL BASE
Nautical miles
160°/2·3M Puerto Elcano
Ldg Lts 040°
36°33'·0N
06°18'W

9.25.14 SANCTI-PETRI

Cádiz **36°23'·80N 06°12'·50W** ❁❁◊✿✿

CHARTS AC 93; SC 443, 4438.

TIDES Interpolate between differences Puerto Cádiz (9.25.13) and Cabo Trafalgar (9.25.15); ML No data; Zone –0100

SHELTER Good, except in S'lies. ⚓ or moor in stream, W of marina; 2 Ⓥ AB on pontoons in 2 - 5m depth; see HM.

NAVIGATION WPT 36°22'·40N 06°13'·05W, on outer ldg line, 050°/5ca to pick up inner ldg line. If 050° ldg twrs are not seen follow the lateral buoys 1-4. From No 4 PHM buoy track 357° 6ca to the gateway formed by lt bns (Fl R/G 5s 7m) which are easily seen. A first-time night appr is not advised.

Best appr at half-flood in fair vis; least charted depth 2·2m, but silting occurs. Sp ebb can be > 4kn. Swell and/or strong S'lies render the appr dangerous. El Arrecife, a long drying reef, and other shoals prevent a direct appr from W/NW. Tunny nets may be set about 9M SSE off Conil.

LIGHTS AND MARKS See chartlet and 9.25.3. The castle's 16m □ twr, Fl 3s, is conspic. Outer 050° ldg lts (off chartlet) and inner 346·5° ldg lts are on hard-to-see lattice twrs. 4 lateral buoys (maybe more in season) are aligned approx 035°, close SE of the 050° ldg line. Only Nos 3 & 4 are on chartlet; Lat/Long, see 9.25.3.

R/T Marina *Puerto Sancti-Petri* Ch 09.

TELEPHONE (Code 956) HM ☎/📠 496169; sanctipetri@eppa.es.

FACILITIES **Marina** (87 AB, inc 2 Ⓥ; 5m), €1.40; ⛽ €0.66. Shwrs, Slip, C, limited CH and 🛒 in season. **Club Náutico** Bar, R. **Village:** No facilities in abandoned "ghost town" at mouth of sandy, peaceful lagoon; ≹ San Fernando (18 km); ✈ Jerez (50 km).

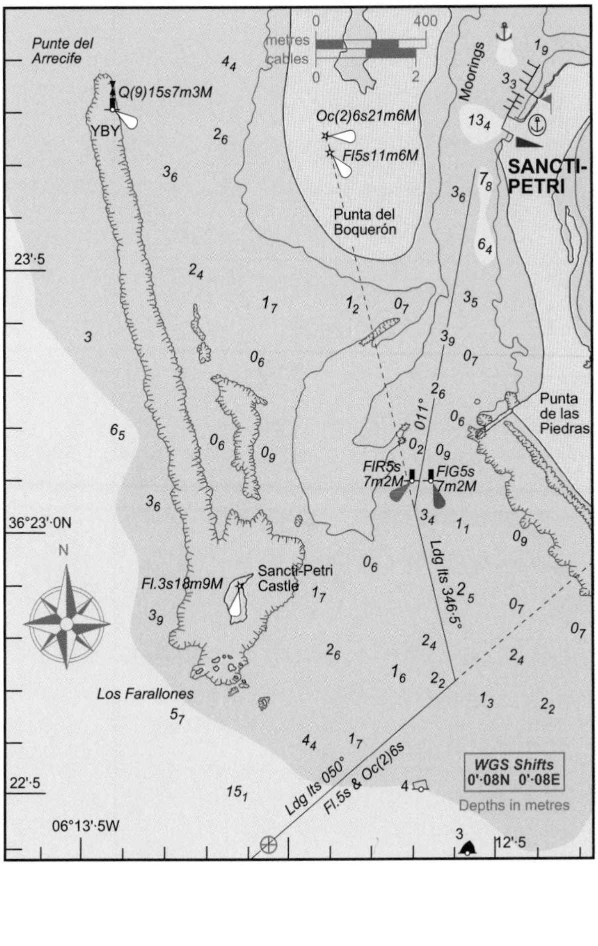
Punte del Arrecife
Q(9)15s7m3M
YBY
Oc(2)6s21m6M
Fl5s11m6M
Punta del Boquerón
SANCTI-PETRI
Moorings
Punta de las Piedras
FlR5s 7m2M
FlG5s 7m2M
Ldg lts 346·5°
Sancti-Petri Castle
Fl.3s18m9M
Los Farallones
Ldg lts 050° Fl.5s & Oc(2)6s
WGS Shifts 0'·08N 0'·08E
Depths in metres
metres
cables
23'·5
36°23'·0N
22'·5
06°13'·5W
12'·5

9.25.15 BARBATE

Cádiz **36°10'·89N 05°55'·50W** ❁❁◊◊◊✿

CHARTS AC 91, 142; SC 444, 4441.

TIDES
Standard Port LISBOA (⟵); ML 1·2; Zone –0100

Times				Height (metres)			
High Water		Low Water		MHWS	MHWN	MLWN	MLWS
0500	1000	0500	1100	3·8	3·0	1·5	0·5
1700	2200	1700	2300				
Differences CABO TRAFALGAR							
–0003	–0003	+0026	+0026	–1·4	–1·1	–0·6	–0·1
RIO BARBATE							
+0016	+0016	+0045	+0045	–1·9	–1·5	–0·5	+0·1
PUNTA CAMARINAL (36°05'N 05°48'W)							
–0007	–0007	+0013	+0013	–1·7	–1·4	–0·7	–0·2

SHELTER Good. FVs berth in the large outer basin, yachts in the 3 inner basins (2·8m).

NAVIGATION WPT 36°10'·74N 05°55'·38W (NCM buoy Q), 330°/110m to SW mole hd. From the W there is room to thread this gap, but due to a tunny net (see below), do not wander S or E of the buoy, especially at night. From the SE keep 1M offshore, avoiding shoals (6·2m) which extend SE along the coast.

The small NCM lt buoy at the WPT marks the apex of a large tunny net, shaped roughly like a dunce's hat, which extends 2·7M S and is marked by 2 SCM lt buoys at its base, an ECM on its E side and a WCM lt buoy near its centre; see chartlet overleaf, 9.25.3 and AC 142. Tunny nets, Mar-Sep, are a real hazard, especially at night. Other nets may be laid W of Cabo Plata (36°06'·17N 05°49'·49W) and NW of Tarifa; see 9.25.3 & .4.

LIGHTS AND MARKS Barbate lt ho, Fl (2) WR 7s, W tr + R bands, is 4ca N of hbr ent, on edge of town. Other lights as chartlet and 9.25.3. Since 2001 the 297·5° ldg lts have been 'temporarily' extinguished. Orange sodium lts in the hbr make navigational lts hard to discern. An anti-oil pontoon extends SSE from the N side of the marina ent; its SSE end is lit Fl (2+1) R 21s 1M.

R/T Marina Ch 09. Barbate is at W end of Gibraltar Strait VTS; monitor *Tarifa Traffic* Ch 10 on passage. See also (9.25.15).

TELEPHONE (Dial code 956) Marina ☎ 431907, 📠 431918; ⊖ and Met: via marina.

FACILITIES **Marina** barbated@eppa.es (314 AB, inc Ⓥ in 3m), €1.40, D&P, Slip, BH (32 ton), ME, El, ⚒, Bar, R, Ice, ▣; **Club Náutico**. **Town** is about 2M away, although 🛒 is closer; R, Bar, Ⓑ, ✉; Bus to Cádiz (61km); ✈ Jerez, Gibraltar or Malaga.

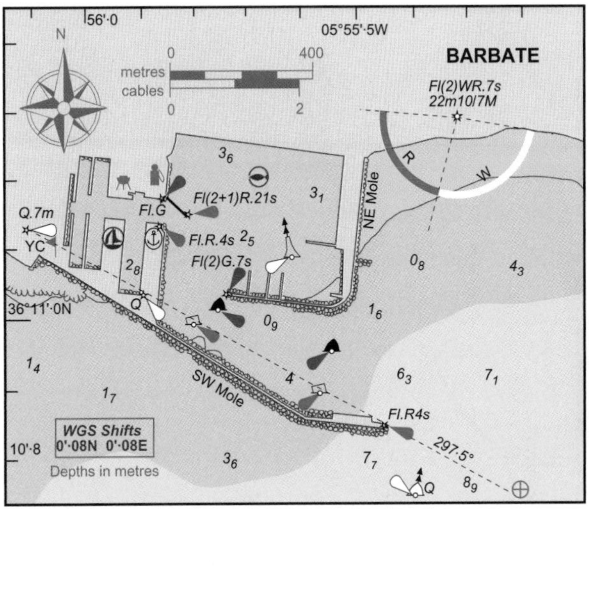
BARBATE
56'·0
05°55'·5W
metres
cables
Fl(2)WR.7s 22m10/7M
NE Mole
Q.7m
YC
Fl(2+1)R.21s
Fl.G
Fl.R.4s
Fl(2)G.7s
SW Mole
Fl.R4s
297·5°
Q
36°11'·0N
10'·8
WGS Shifts 0'·08N 0'·08E
Depths in metres

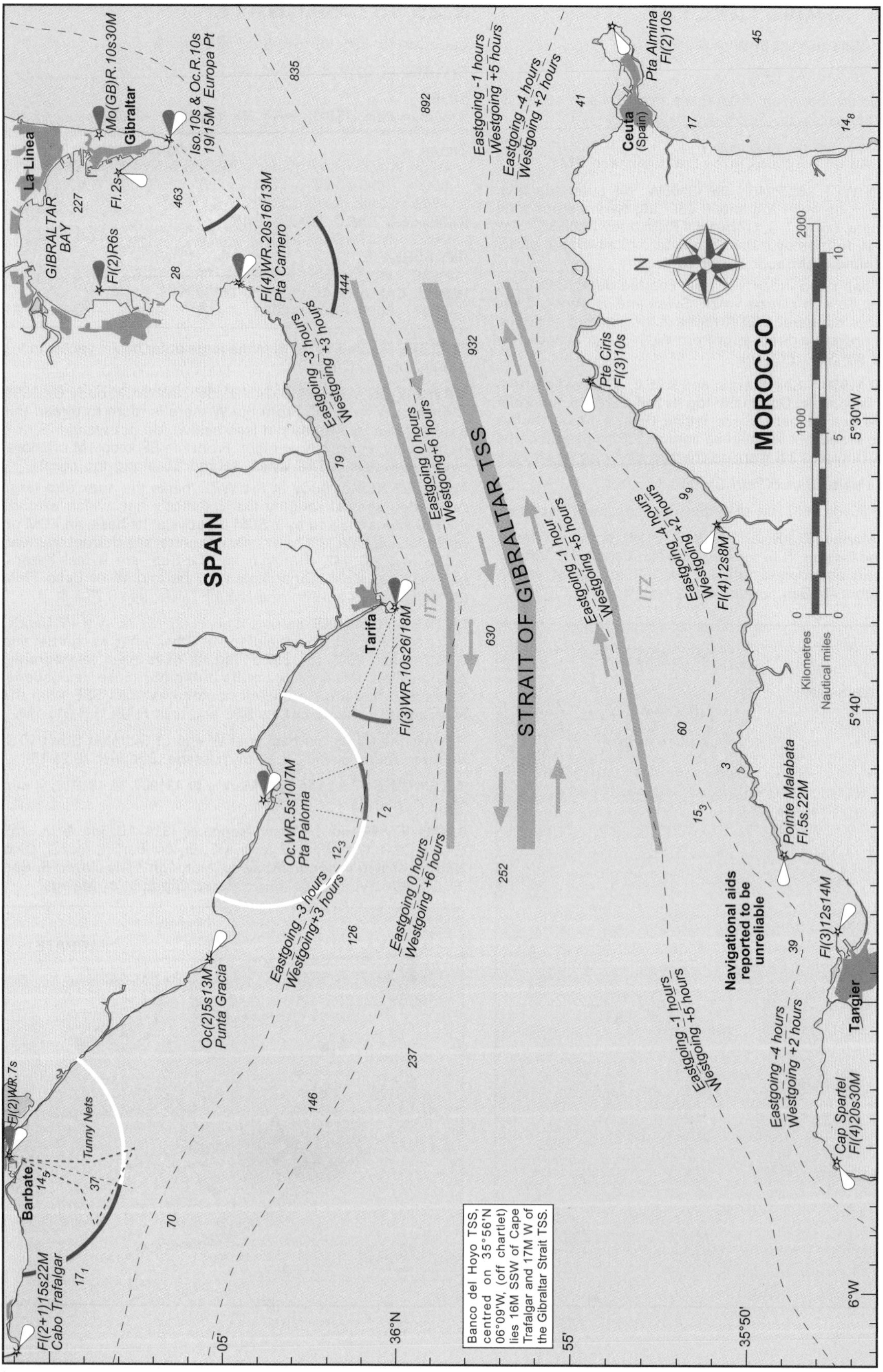
SPAIN
MOROCCO
STRAIT OF GIBRALTAR TSS
ITZ
ITZ
GIBRALTAR BAY
La Linea
Gibraltar
Mo(GB)R.10s30M
Iso.10s & Oc.R.10s 19/15M Europa Pt
Fl.2s
Fl(2)R6s
Fl(4)WR.20s16/13M Pta Carnero
Tarifa
Fl(3)WR.10s26/18M
Oc.WR.5s10/7M Pta Paloma
Oc(2)5s13M Punta Gracia
Fl(2)WR.7s
Barbate
Tunny Nets
Fl(2+1)15s22M Cabo Trafalgar
Ceuta (Spain)
Pta Almina Fl(2)10s
Pte Ciris Fl(3)10s
Fl(4)12s8M
Pointe Malabata Fl.5s.22M
Fl(3)12s14M
Tangier
Cap Spartel Fl(4)20s30M
Navigational aids reported to be unreliable
Eastgoing -3 hours Westgoing +3 hours
Eastgoing 0 hours Westgoing +6 hours
Eastgoing -1 hour Westgoing +5 hours
Eastgoing -4 hours Westgoing +2 hours
Eastgoing -1 hours Westgoing +5 hours
Banco del Hoyo TSS, centred on 35°56'N 06°09'W, (off chartlet) lies 16M SSW of Cape Trafalgar and 17M W of the Gibraltar Strait TSS.
Kilometres
Nautical miles
36°N
55'
35°50'
05'
6°W
5°40'
5°30'W

9.25.16 STRAIT OF GIBRALTAR

TIDAL STREAMS are insufficiently observed, but in general are fairly accurate. Near the middle of the Strait the stream sets E from HW Gib to HWG+6 and west from HWG–6 to HW Gib. Closer inshore, streams start progressively earlier as shown on the chartlet opposite. The approx time at which the tide turns is obtained by applying the time intervals on the pecked lines to the time of HW Gib. Max tidal rates are usually to be found close inshore around headlands, about 3kn in either direction.

SURFACE CURRENT, uninfluenced by tidal streams, runs east in the middle of the Strait at up to about 2kn.

SURFACE FLOW is the combined effect of tidal streams and the prevailing E-going current into the Med. The resultant max surface flow is about 2kn W-going and 5kn E-going (further influenced by recent E or W winds). W-bound yachts should keep as close as possible to the Spanish coast.

TIDAL RACES on the Spanish side form: off Cape Trafalgar, usually up to 2M SW, but 5-12M in heavy weather; near Bajo de Los Cabezos (2-4M S of Pta Paloma); and NW of Tarifa. The position and violence of these races depends on wind, especially over tide, springs/neaps and the state of the tide. For more information, see W Coasts of Spain and Portugal Pilot (NP 67).

TSS AND VTS The TSS (see opposite) is flanked on both sides by ITZ which yachts should use. **Tarifa VTS**, c/s *Tarifa Trafico* Ch **10**, provides radar surveillance on request and a reporting system (voluntary for yachts) between 05°58'W and 05°15'W. Traffic, navigational and weather info is broadcast regularly and on request, in Spanish and English Ch 67.

9.25.17 TARIFA

Cádiz **36°00'·41N 05°36'·27W** ❀❀◊◊✿✿

CHARTS AC 142; SC 445, 445B, 4450; SHOM 1619, 7042.

TIDES See under 9.25.18.

SHELTER Good, but no yacht berths in this fishing, naval and ferry hbr, except perhaps at the N end of SE mole. Tarifa is little more than ashelter for passing yachts. ⚓ off hbr ent in 5m. If a *levanter* is blowing, ⚓ NW of the causeway joining Isla de Tarifa (prohib military area) to the mainland. Ferries berth on the outer end of the SE mole and on S side of the hbr; FVs on the S and W sides; naval pens and *Guardia Civil* craft use the N side.

NAVIGATION WPT 36°00'·13N 05°35'·91W, 315°/4ca to hbr ent. S of Tarifa lt the ITZ is only 1·7M wide. A SCM lt buoy, 1M NNW of Tarifa lt, marks a tunny net (Mar-Jul) extending approx 5ca WSW to a WCM lt buoy; care needed if approaching the NW ⚓.

LIGHTS AND MARKS See chartlet and 9.25.3.

R/T No port VHF. See 9.25.16 above for Tarifa VTS.

FACILITIES Virtually nothing other than a FW tap.
Town: 🛒, R, Bar, Ⓑ, ✉, ⇄; ✈ Jerez, Gibraltar, Malaga.

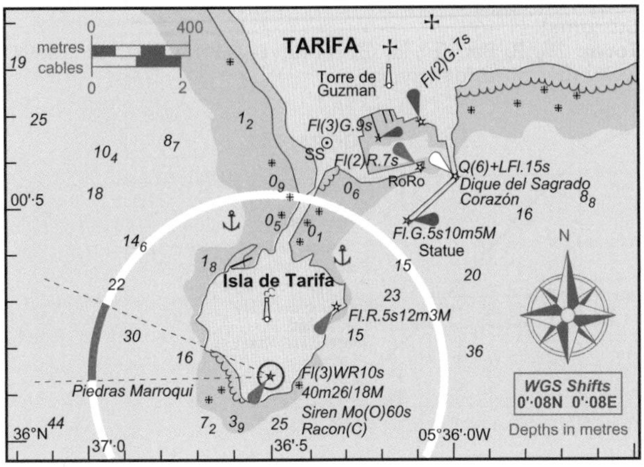
TARIFA
metres
cables
Torre de Guzman
Fl(3)G.9s
Fl(2)R.7s
Fl(2)G.7s
Q(6)+LFl.15s
Dique del Sagrado Corazón
RoRo
Fl.G.5s10m5M
Statue
Isla de Tarifa
Fl.R.5s12m3M
Fl(3)WR10s 40m26/18M
Siren Mo(O)60s
Racon(C)
Piedras Marroqui
WGS Shifts 0'·08N 0'·08E
Depths in metres
36°N
37'·0
36'·5
05°36'·0W
00'·5
N

9.25.18 ALGECIRAS

Cádiz **36°07'·12N 05°26'·16W** ❀❀◊◊✿✿

CHARTS AC 3578, 142, 1448, 1455; SC 445, 445A, 4451.

TIDES
Standard Port GIBRALTAR (⟶); ML 0·66; Zone –0100

Times				Height (metres)			
High Water		Low Water		MHWS	MHWN	MLWN	MLWS
0000	0700	0100	0600	1·0	0·7	0·3	0·1
1200	1900	1300	1800				
Differences TARIFA							
–0038	–0038	–0042	–0042	+0·4	+0·3	+0·3	+0·2
PUNTA CARNERO							
–0010	–0010	0000	0000	0·0	+0·1	+0·1	+0·1
ALGECIRAS							
–0010	–0010	–0010	–0010	+0·1	+0·2	+0·1	+0·1

SHELTER Good in marina, except perhaps in strong SE'lies.

NAVIGATION WPT 36°06'·73N 05°24'·76W, [ECM buoy, Q (3) 10s, off chartlet], 299°/0·9M to first chan buoys. From S, keep 5ca off Pta de San García and beware drying reefs S of hbr ent. From N/E, beware big ships at ⚓, high-speed ferries and WIP.

LIGHTS AND MARKS The Hbr Control twr is conspic by day, close WNW of the marina.

R/T Marina Ch 09 16. Port Ch 09, **12.**

TELEPHONE (Dial code 956) HM 572620, 🖷 585443; Port Authority 585400, 🖷 585445; Brit Vice-Consul 661600/04.

FACILITIES Marina ☎ 572503, max LOA 16m, D, BH (25 ton), ME, Slip, CH; ⊜ and Met via marina. **Real Club Náutico ☎** 572503, R, Bar; **Town:** 🛒, R, Bar, Ⓑ, ✉, ⇄; ✈ Jerez, Gibraltar, Malaga.

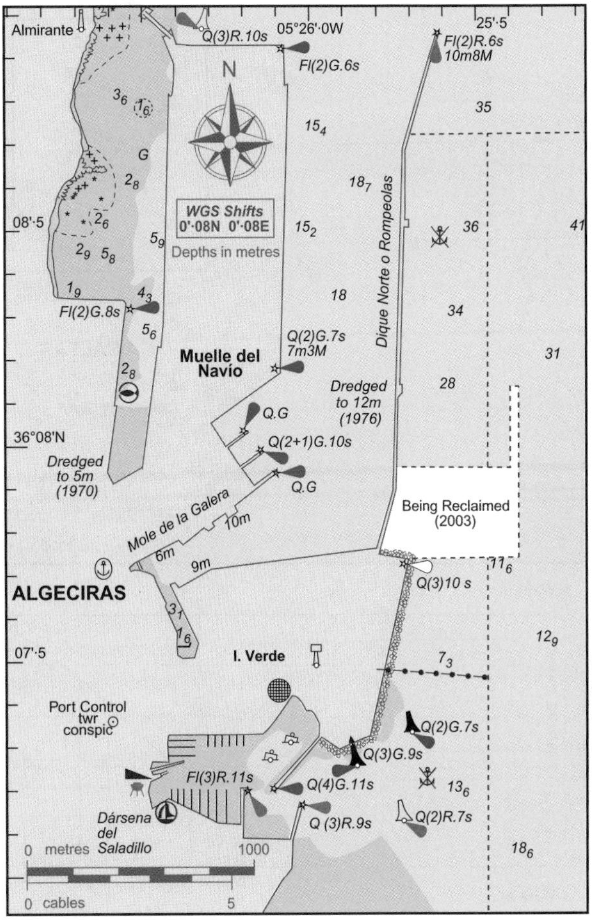
Almirante
Q(3)R.10s
05°26'·0W
Fl(2)G.6s
25'·5
Fl(2)R.6s 10m8M
N
WGS Shifts 0'·08N 0'·08E
Depths in metres
Dique Norte o Rompeolas
08'·5
Fl(2)G.8s
Q(2)G.7s 7m3M
Muelle del Navio
Dredged to 12m (1976)
Q.G
Q(2+1)G.10s
36°08'N
Dredged to 5m (1970)
Q.G
Mole de la Galera
Being Reclaimed (2003)
ALGECIRAS
Q(3)10 s
07'·5
I. Verde
Port Control twr conspic
Q(2)G.7s
Q(3)G.9s
Fl(3)R.11s
Q(4)G.11s
Q (3)R.9s
Q(2)R.7s
Dársena del Saladillo
0 metres 1000
0 cables 5

9.25.19 GIBRALTAR

36°08'·09N 05°21'·86W ('A' Head) ❁❁❁◊◊◊✿✿✿

CHARTS AC 142, 3578, 1448, 144, 45; SC 445, 445A, 4452.

TIDES Standard Port GIBRALTAR (⟶); ML 0·5; Zone –0100

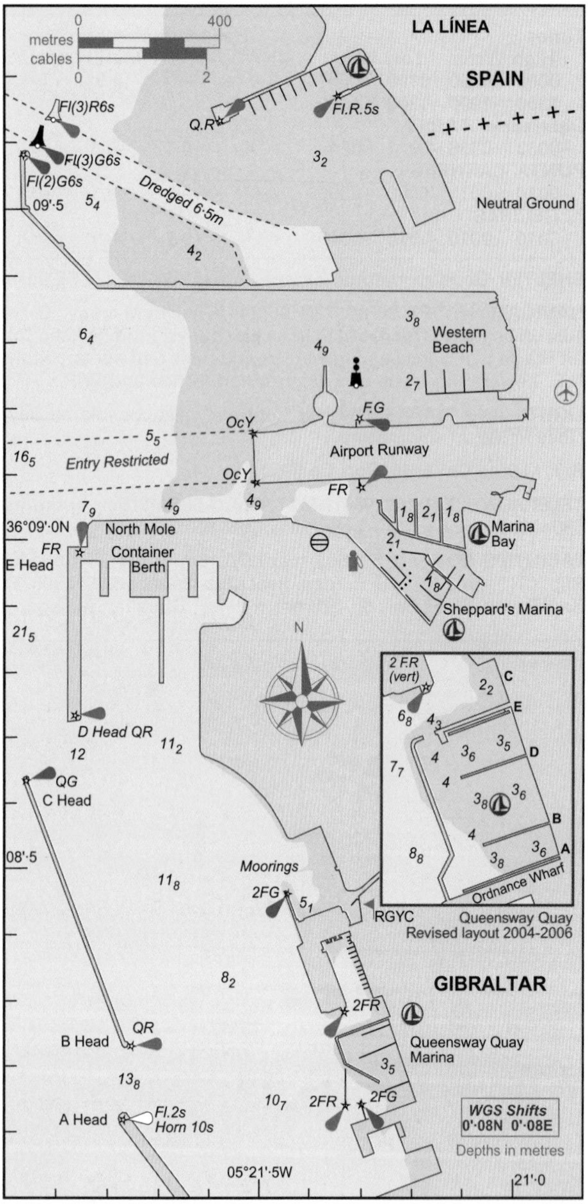

metres
cables
0
400
2
LA LÍNEA
SPAIN
Fl(3)R6s
Q.R
Fl.R.5s
Fl(3)G6s
Fl(2)G6s
09'·5
Dredged 6·5m
Neutral Ground
Western Beach
F.G
OcY
Entry Restricted
Airport Runway
FR
36°09'·0N
North Mole
Container Berth
E Head
Marina Bay
Sheppard's Marina
N
D Head QR
QG
C Head
08'·5
Moorings
2FG
RGYC
Queensway Quay Revised layout 2004-2006
2 F.R (vert)
Ordnance Wharf
GIBRALTAR
2FR
Queensway Quay Marina
B Head
A Head
Fl.2s
Horn 10s
WGS Shifts
0'·08N 0'·08E
Depths in metres
05°21'·5W
21'·0

Times Height (metres)

High Water		Low Water		MHWS	MHWN	MLWN	MLWS
0000	0700	0100	0600	1·0	0·7	0·3	0·1
1200	1900	1300	1800				
Differences SANDY BAY (E side of the Rock)							
–0011	–0011	–0016	–0016	–0·2	–0·1	0·0	0·0
CEUTA (UT)							
–0045	–0045	–0050	–0050	0·0	+0·1	+0·1	+0·1
PUNTA CIRIS*							
–0109	–0109	–0104	–0104	+0·2	+0·2	+0·2	+0·1
HEJAR LESFAR*							
–0035	–0035	–0007	–0007	+0·8	+0·6	+0·4	+0·2
TANGIER*							
–0030	–0030	–0020	–0020	+1·3	+1·0	+0·5	+0·3

Note the very small tidal range. *Moroccan Zone Time is 0 (UT)

SHELTER Good in 3 marinas (pre-booking advised), S to N: Queensway Quay, 3·5m least depth, close to town centre; Sheppards at N end of town; and adjacent Marina Bay, max draft 4·5m, close to airport runway. All can be affected by swell in W'lies and by fierce gusts in the E'ly *levanter.* NW of runway, pontoons are for small local craft only. ⚓ in 4-6m, well clear of flight path, may be prohib for security reasons. Oc Y lts and loudspeakers warn of aircraft movements. All arrivals must first clear Customs @ Waterport before entering a marina/⚓age.

NAVIGATION From the W, WPT 36°04'·63N 05°24'·36W (1M E of Pta Carnero), 024°/4·7M to 'E' Hd; 030°/4M to 'A' Hd. The Rock is steep-to all round; from the SW, beware shoals to S of Pta Carnero. From the E, yachts may round Europa Pt 3ca off. Shore lts may mask commercial vessels at ⚓ and navigational lights.

LIGHTS AND MARKS The Rock (423m) is easily seen, but from the W not until rounding Pta Carnero, 5M to SW. The Aero lt atop the Rock is obsc'd when within 2M W of it. Europa Pt, almost at sea level, has 3 sectored lts; see 9.25.3. At N end of bay, industrial plants are conspic day/night.

R/T Queensway Quay, Sheppards and Marina Bay: Ch 71. Civil port Ch 06; Gibraltar Bay Ch 12; QHM Ch 08; HM Customs Ch 14.

TELEPHONE (International code 350, no Area code); from Spain dial 9567 + 5 digit tel no). Port Captain (HM) 77254; QHM 55901; ⊜ 72901, 📠 41715; Met 53416; Ⓗ 79700; Ambulance/Police 199; Fire 190; ✈ 75984.

FACILITIES All prices are £/m LOA based on a 12m boat. **Queensway Quay Marina**, PO Box 19. (120+ Ⓥ), ☎ 44700, 📠 44699, qqmarina@gibnet.gi AB/F&A, £0.63 summer, £0.54 winter; CH, ⊡, pre-arrange D & P (min 200ltrs from tanker). Wash from pilot boats and ferries may intrude. The marina is closed 2030-0830 nightly by a boom across the ent. New entrance and marina layout are shown on inset; WIP summer 2004 to 2006.
Sheppards Marina. ☎ 75148, 📠 42535, sheppard@gibnet.gi AB £0·72/m; BH (40 ton), C (10 ton), ME, El, BY, ⚒, CH, Ⓔ. Part of the site has been sold to developers; visit www.oceanvillagegibraltar. Works in progress. Berths/services are in short supply.
Marina Bay. (209 inc Ⓥ) ☎ 73300, 📠 42656, www.marinabay.gi pieroffice@marinabay.gi AB £0.70 1 May- 31 Oct, £0.46 1 Nov-30 Apr; CH, R, 🛒, ⊡, ACA, SM; D & P, Gaz, Ice from Fuel berth (near Customs).
Town: 🛒, R, Bar, ✉, Ⓗ, Ⓑ, ✈. **Royal Gibraltar YC** ☎ 78897, www.rgyc.gi. info@rgyc.gi

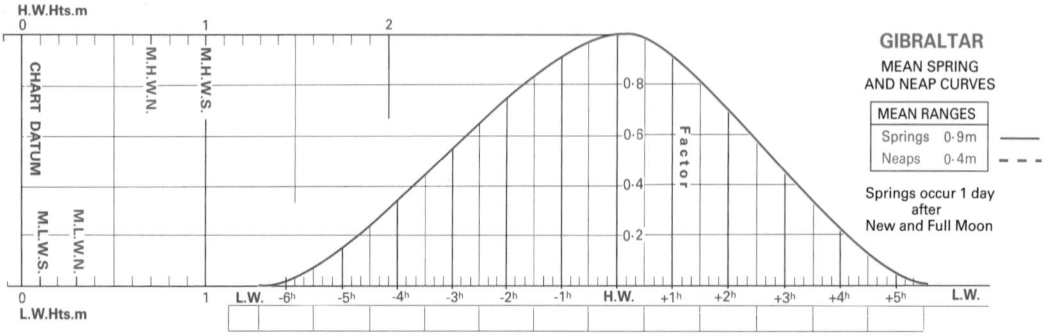

H.W.Hts.m
0
1
2
CHART DATUM
M.H.W.N.
M.H.W.S.
M.L.W.S.
M.L.W.N.
0·8
0·6
0·4
0·2
Factor
0
1
L.W.
-6h
-5h
-4h
-3h
-2h
-1h
H.W.
+1h
+2h
+3h
+4h
+5h
L.W.
L.W.Hts.m
GIBRALTAR
MEAN SPRING AND NEAP CURVES
MEAN RANGES
Springs 0·9m
Neaps 0·4m
Springs occur 1 day after New and Full Moon

TIME ZONE -0100
(Gibraltar Standard Time)
Subtract 1 hour for UT
For Gibraltar Summer Time add ONE hour in **non-shaded areas**

GIBRALTAR

LAT 36°08'N LONG 5°21'W

TIMES AND HEIGHTS OF HIGH AND LOW WATERS

SPRING & NEAP TIDES
Dates in red are SPRINGS
Dates in blue are NEAPS

YEAR **2005**

JANUARY

Day	Time	m	Time	m	Time	m	Time	m
1 SA	0627	0.8	1210	0.3	1844	0.8		
2 SU	0020	0.2	0712	0.8	1301	0.3	1932	0.7
3 M	0110	0.3	0805	0.8	1403	0.3	◑ 2028	0.7
4 TU	0213	0.3	0905	0.7	1511	0.3	2133	0.7
5 W	0328	0.3	1013	0.8	1624	0.2	2248	0.7
6 TH	0446	0.3	1122	0.8	1733	0.2	2359	0.7
7 F	0551	0.2	1223	0.8	1831	0.1		
8 SA	0059	0.8	0644	0.2	1319	0.9	1922	0.1
9 SU	0153	0.9	0733	0.1	1412	0.9	2011	0.0
10 M	0245	0.9	0823	0.1	1505	1.0	● 2100	0.0
11 TU	0335	1.0	0912	0.1	1556	1.0	2147	0.0
12 W	0423	1.0	1001	0.1	1645	1.0	2232	0.0
13 TH	0510	1.0	1048	0.1	1733	0.9	2316	0.0
14 F	0557	1.0	1136	0.1	1822	0.9		
15 SA	0000	0.1	0645	0.9	1227	0.1	1913	0.8
16 SU	0048	0.1	0737	0.9	1320	0.2	2006	0.8
17 M	0140	0.2	0832	0.8	1420	0.2	◐ 2103	0.7
18 TU	0242	0.3	0931	0.8	1529	0.3	2210	0.7
19 W	0358	0.3	1038	0.7	1655	0.3	2329	0.7
20 TH	0520	0.3	1146	0.7	1807	0.3		
21 F	0039	0.7	0621	0.3	1246	0.7	1856	0.2
22 SA	0133	0.7	0706	0.2	1335	0.8	1937	0.2
23 SU	0216	0.8	0746	0.2	1417	0.8	2014	0.1
24 M	0254	0.8	0823	0.2	1456	0.8	2049	0.1
25 TU	0327	0.8	0858	0.1	1532	0.8	○ 2122	0.1
26 W	0357	0.8	0932	0.1	1605	0.9	2152	0.1
27 TH	0426	0.9	1004	0.1	1637	0.9	2221	0.1
28 F	0455	0.9	1036	0.1	1709	0.8	2250	0.1
29 SA	0526	0.9	1108	0.1	1742	0.8	2319	0.1
30 SU	0600	0.8	1143	0.1	1818	0.8	2351	0.1
31 M	0639	0.8	1222	0.2	1901	0.8		

FEBRUARY

Day	Time	m	Time	m	Time	m	Time	m
1 TU	0028	0.2	0724	0.8	1312	0.2	1951	0.7
2 W	0116	0.2	0820	0.7	1416	0.2	◑ 2053	0.7
3 TH	0225	0.3	0928	0.7	1543	0.2	2210	0.6
4 F	0407	0.3	1051	0.7	1721	0.2	2339	0.7
5 SA	0543	0.2	1210	0.8	1831	0.1		
6 SU	0051	0.7	0645	0.2	1314	0.8	1924	0.1
7 M	0149	0.8	0736	0.1	1409	0.9	2013	0.0
8 TU	0240	0.9	0824	0.0	1501	0.9	● 2058	0.0
9 W	0327	1.0	0911	0.0	1548	1.0	2140	-0.1
10 TH	0412	1.0	0955	0.0	1634	1.0	2220	-0.1
11 F	0454	1.0	1036	0.0	1718	1.0	2257	0.0
12 SA	0536	1.0	1117	0.0	1801	0.9	2334	0.0
13 SU	0619	0.9	1156	0.1	1846	0.8		
14 M	0011	0.1	0702	0.9	1238	0.1	1931	0.8
15 TU	0053	0.2	0749	0.8	1325	0.2	2022	0.7
16 W	0142	0.2	0842	0.7	1426	0.3	◐ 2121	0.6
17 TH	0255	0.3	0947	0.6	1609	0.3	2245	0.6
18 F	0454	0.3	1115	0.6	1757	0.3		
19 SA	0022	0.6	0612	0.3	1234	0.7	1849	0.2
20 SU	0123	0.7	0658	0.2	1327	0.7	1927	0.2
21 M	0204	0.7	0735	0.2	1407	0.8	2001	0.1
22 TU	0237	0.8	0809	0.1	1442	0.8	2032	0.1
23 W	0307	0.8	0841	0.1	1515	0.8	2102	0.1
24 TH	0335	0.9	0913	0.1	1546	0.9	○ 2131	0.1
25 F	0403	0.9	0944	0.1	1617	0.9	2159	0.0
26 SA	0432	0.9	1014	0.1	1648	0.9	2226	0.1
27 SU	0502	0.9	1045	0.1	1721	0.9	2255	0.1
28 M	0535	0.9	1118	0.1	1757	0.8	2326	0.1

MARCH

Day	Time	m	Time	m	Time	m	Time	m
1 TU	0612	0.9	1154	0.1	1839	0.8		
2 W	0001	0.2	0655	0.8	1239	0.2	1928	0.7
3 TH	0045	0.2	0750	0.7	1340	0.2	◑ 2029	0.7
4 F	0151	0.3	0901	0.7	1523	0.3	2149	0.6
5 SA	0358	0.3	1036	0.7	1723	0.2	2329	0.7
6 SU	0548	0.2	1207	0.7	1831	0.1		
7 M	0046	0.7	0647	0.2	1312	0.8	1920	0.1
8 TU	0141	0.8	0734	0.1	1403	0.9	2003	0.0
9 W	0228	0.9	0818	0.0	1450	0.9	2044	0.0
10 TH	0311	1.0	0859	0.0	1534	1.0	● 2122	-0.1
11 F	0352	1.0	0938	-0.1	1615	1.0	2157	-0.1
12 SA	0431	1.0	1015	-0.1	1656	1.0	2231	0.0
13 SU	0509	1.0	1050	0.0	1736	0.9	2304	0.0
14 M	0547	0.9	1125	0.0	1816	0.8	2337	0.1
15 TU	0626	0.8	1159	0.1	1858	0.8		
16 W	0012	0.2	0708	0.7	1238	0.2	1944	0.7
17 TH	0055	0.3	0757	0.7	1328	0.3	◐ 2040	0.6
18 F	0200	0.3	0859	0.6	1508	0.3	2156	0.6
19 SA	0417	0.4	1032	0.6	1726	0.3	2346	0.6
20 SU	0551	0.3	1209	0.6	1821	0.3		
21 M	0051	0.7	0635	0.3	1303	0.7	1858	0.2
22 TU	0131	0.7	0710	0.2	1341	0.8	1930	0.2
23 W	0202	0.8	0743	0.1	1414	0.8	2001	0.1
24 TH	0232	0.8	0814	0.1	1447	0.9	2030	0.1
25 F	0302	0.9	0846	0.1	1519	0.9	○ 2059	0.1
26 SA	0333	0.9	0917	0.0	1552	0.9	2129	0.1
27 SU	0405	1.0	0949	0.0	1626	0.9	2159	0.1
28 M	0438	1.0	1022	0.0	1701	0.9	2231	0.1
29 TU	0513	0.9	1056	0.1	1739	0.9	2305	0.1
30 W	0552	0.9	1134	0.1	1823	0.8	2343	0.2
31 TH	0637	0.8	1219	0.2	1915	0.8		

APRIL

Day	Time	m	Time	m	Time	m	Time	m
1 F	0030	0.3	0734	0.7	1326	0.3	2019	0.7
2 SA	0148	0.3	0850	0.7	1526	0.3	◑ 2141	0.7
3 SU	0407	0.3	1031	0.7	1712	0.2	2319	0.7
4 M	0542	0.2	1201	0.7	1813	0.2		
5 TU	0031	0.8	0636	0.2	1300	0.8	1859	0.1
6 W	0122	0.9	0719	0.1	1347	0.9	1939	0.0
7 TH	0205	0.9	0759	0.0	1430	0.9	2017	0.0
8 F	0246	1.0	0838	0.0	1511	0.9	● 2053	0.0
9 SA	0325	1.0	0914	0.0	1551	0.9	2128	0.0
10 SU	0403	1.0	0949	0.0	1630	0.9	2201	0.0
11 M	0440	0.9	1022	0.0	1708	0.9	2234	0.1
12 TU	0516	0.9	1055	0.1	1747	0.8	2307	0.1
13 W	0553	0.8	1127	0.1	1828	0.8	2342	0.2
14 TH	0633	0.7	1203	0.2	1914	0.7		
15 F	0024	0.3	0721	0.7	1251	0.3	2008	0.7
16 SA	0127	0.4	0822	0.6	1422	0.3	◐ 2115	0.6
17 SU	0322	0.4	0941	0.6	1624	0.3	2240	0.6
18 M	0502	0.3	1116	0.6	1730	0.3	2354	0.7
19 TU	0554	0.3	1218	0.7	1813	0.3		
20 W	0039	0.7	0632	0.2	1300	0.7	1847	0.2
21 TH	0115	0.8	0706	0.2	1336	0.8	1918	0.2
22 F	0149	0.9	0739	0.1	1411	0.9	1950	0.1
23 SA	0223	0.9	0813	0.1	1446	0.9	2022	0.1
24 SU	0259	1.0	0847	0.1	1523	0.9	○ 2056	0.1
25 M	0336	1.0	0923	0.0	1602	0.9	2132	0.1
26 TU	0415	1.0	1000	0.1	1642	0.9	2209	0.1
27 W	0455	0.9	1039	0.1	1725	0.9	2248	0.2
28 TH	0538	0.9	1121	0.1	1813	0.9	2333	0.2
29 F	0629	0.8	1212	0.2	1909	0.8		
30 SA	0030	0.3	0730	0.8	1328	0.3	2015	0.8

Chart Datum: 0·25 metres below Alicante Datum (Mean Sea Level, Alicante)

TIME ZONE -0100
(Gibraltar Standard Time)
Subtract 1 hour for UT
For Gibraltar Summer Time add ONE hour in **non-shaded areas**

GIBRALTAR

LAT 36°08′N LONG 5°21′W

TIMES AND HEIGHTS OF HIGH AND LOW WATERS

SPRING & NEAP TIDES
Dates in **red** are **SPRINGS**
Dates in **blue** are **NEAPS**

YEAR **2005**

MAY

Date	Day	Time	m	Time	m	Time	m	Time	m
1	SU	0158	0.3	0846	0.7	1512	0.3	◑ 2132	0.7
2	M	0350	0.3	1016	0.7	1638	0.3	2254	0.8
3	TU	0514	0.2	1137	0.7	1739	0.2		
4	W	0001	0.8	0609	0.2	1235	0.8	1826	0.2
5	TH	0051	0.9	0654	0.1	1322	0.9	1907	0.1
6	F	0135	0.9	0733	0.1	1404	0.9	1944	0.1
7	SA	0215	0.9	0811	0.0	1445	0.9	2021	0.1
8	SU	0255	0.9	0848	0.0	1525	0.9	● 2057	0.1
9	M	0333	0.9	0923	0.1	1604	0.9	2133	0.1
10	TU	0411	0.9	0957	0.1	1643	0.9	2208	0.1
11	W	0448	0.8	1031	0.1	1722	0.8	2244	0.2
12	TH	0526	0.8	1105	0.2	1803	0.8	2321	0.2
13	F	0607	0.7	1143	0.2	1848	0.7		
14	SA	0005	0.3	0654	0.7	1230	0.3	1939	0.7
15	SU	0104	0.3	0750	0.7	1342	0.3	2036	0.7
16	M	0225	0.4	0853	0.6	1510	0.3	◐ 2137	0.7
17	TU	0347	0.3	1005	0.6	1620	0.3	2242	0.7
18	W	0452	0.3	1114	0.7	1713	0.3	2337	0.7
19	TH	0542	0.2	1207	0.7	1755	0.2		
20	F	0023	0.8	0622	0.2	1251	0.8	1832	0.2
21	SA	0104	0.9	0701	0.1	1332	0.8	1909	0.2
22	SU	0145	0.9	0739	0.1	1413	0.9	1946	0.2
23	M	0226	0.9	0819	0.1	1456	0.9	○ 2027	0.1
24	TU	0310	1.0	0901	0.1	1541	0.9	2109	0.1
25	W	0355	1.0	0944	0.1	1626	0.9	2153	0.1
26	TH	0441	1.0	1028	0.1	1713	0.9	2240	0.2
27	F	0530	0.9	1116	0.1	1804	0.9	2331	0.2
28	SA	0624	0.9	1211	0.2	1901	0.9		
29	SU	0033	0.3	0725	0.8	1320	0.2	2003	0.8
30	M	0149	0.3	0834	0.8	1437	0.3	◑ 2110	0.8
31	TU	0311	0.3	0947	0.8	1549	0.2	2218	0.8

JUNE

Date	Day	Time	m	Time	m	Time	m	Time	m
1	W	0428	0.3	1100	0.8	1654	0.2	2322	0.8
2	TH	0533	0.2	1202	0.8	1748	0.2		
3	F	0016	0.9	0624	0.2	1253	0.8	1834	0.2
4	SA	0103	0.9	0708	0.1	1339	0.8	1916	0.2
5	SU	0146	0.9	0748	0.1	1422	0.9	1955	0.2
6	M	0228	0.9	0827	0.1	1504	0.9	● 2034	0.2
7	TU	0309	0.9	0904	0.1	1545	0.8	2113	0.2
8	W	0349	0.9	0940	0.1	1624	0.8	2150	0.2
9	TH	0428	0.8	1015	0.2	1702	0.8	2228	0.2
10	F	0506	0.8	1050	0.2	1740	0.8	2306	0.2
11	SA	0545	0.8	1126	0.2	1820	0.8	2347	0.3
12	SU	0627	0.7	1206	0.2	1903	0.7		
13	M	0033	0.3	0713	0.7	1255	0.3	1949	0.7
14	TU	0129	0.3	0804	0.7	1353	0.3	2038	0.7
15	W	0231	0.3	0901	0.7	1456	0.3	◐ 2132	0.7
16	TH	0334	0.3	1003	0.7	1557	0.3	2231	0.8
17	F	0438	0.3	1109	0.7	1656	0.3	2329	0.8
18	SA	0536	0.2	1206	0.8	1749	0.2		
19	SU	0022	0.8	0626	0.2	1258	0.8	1835	0.2
20	M	0111	0.9	0713	0.1	1347	0.9	1921	0.2
21	TU	0201	0.9	0759	0.1	1436	0.9	2008	0.1
22	W	0251	1.0	0846	0.1	1525	0.9	○ 2056	0.1
23	TH	0342	1.0	0934	0.1	1614	1.0	2146	0.1
24	F	0432	1.0	1021	0.1	1703	1.0	2236	0.1
25	SA	0522	1.0	1109	0.1	1753	1.0	2327	0.2
26	SU	0615	0.9	1159	0.1	1845	0.9		
27	M	0022	0.2	0710	0.9	1254	0.2	1940	0.9
28	TU	0123	0.2	0810	0.8	1354	0.2	◑ 2038	0.9
29	W	0227	0.2	0912	0.8	1456	0.3	2137	0.8
30	TH	0336	0.3	1019	0.8	1603	0.3	2240	0.8

JULY

Date	Day	Time	m	Time	m	Time	m	Time	m
1	F	0452	0.3	1128	0.8	1711	0.3	2342	0.8
2	SA	0600	0.2	1228	0.8	1809	0.3		
3	SU	0036	0.8	0651	0.2	1321	0.8	1857	0.2
4	M	0126	0.8	0734	0.2	1409	0.8	1940	0.2
5	TU	0211	0.8	0814	0.2	1452	0.8	2020	0.2
6	W	0254	0.8	0851	0.2	1532	0.8	● 2059	0.2
7	TH	0334	0.8	0926	0.1	1608	0.9	2136	0.2
8	F	0411	0.8	1000	0.1	1642	0.9	2212	0.2
9	SA	0446	0.8	1032	0.2	1713	0.8	2247	0.2
10	SU	0520	0.8	1103	0.2	1745	0.8	2322	0.2
11	M	0555	0.8	1135	0.2	1819	0.8	2358	0.2
12	TU	0633	0.8	1209	0.2	1858	0.8		
13	W	0039	0.2	0715	0.7	1249	0.3	1941	0.8
14	TH	0128	0.3	0806	0.7	1339	0.3	◐ 2031	0.8
15	F	0225	0.3	0905	0.7	1441	0.3	2130	0.8
16	SA	0335	0.3	1014	0.7	1557	0.3	2238	0.8
17	SU	0456	0.3	1128	0.7	1715	0.3	2347	0.8
18	M	0605	0.2	1233	0.8	1818	0.2		
19	TU	0049	0.9	0700	0.1	1330	0.9	1910	0.2
20	W	0146	0.9	0750	0.1	1423	0.9	2001	0.1
21	TH	0240	1.0	0838	0.0	1513	1.0	○ 2050	0.1
22	F	0332	1.0	0925	0.0	1601	1.0	2139	0.1
23	SA	0421	1.0	1009	0.0	1648	1.1	2227	0.1
24	SU	0509	1.0	1053	0.0	1734	1.0	2313	0.1
25	M	0557	1.0	1136	0.1	1821	1.0	2359	0.1
26	TU	0647	0.9	1220	0.1	1910	1.0		
27	W	0048	0.2	0739	0.9	1308	0.2	2000	0.9
28	TH	0141	0.2	0836	0.8	1403	0.3	◑ 2055	0.8
29	F	0243	0.3	0938	0.7	1511	0.3	2156	0.8
30	SA	0407	0.3	1054	0.7	1637	0.4	2308	0.8
31	SU	0544	0.3	1211	0.7	1754	0.3		

AUGUST

Date	Day	Time	m	Time	m	Time	m	Time	m
1	M	0019	0.8	0642	0.3	1313	0.8	1846	0.3
2	TU	0116	0.8	0724	0.2	1400	0.8	1929	0.3
3	W	0202	0.8	0800	0.2	1440	0.9	2006	0.2
4	TH	0242	0.8	0834	0.2	1515	0.9	2042	0.2
5	F	0318	0.9	0906	0.2	1545	0.9	● 2117	0.2
6	SA	0350	0.9	0936	0.1	1614	0.9	2150	0.2
7	SU	0421	0.9	1005	0.1	1642	0.9	2221	0.2
8	M	0452	0.9	1033	0.2	1710	0.9	2252	0.2
9	TU	0522	0.9	1101	0.2	1740	0.9	2324	0.2
10	W	0556	0.9	1131	0.2	1814	0.9	2359	0.2
11	TH	0636	0.8	1204	0.2	1854	0.9		
12	F	0039	0.2	0723	0.8	1246	0.3	1942	0.8
13	SA	0133	0.3	0822	0.7	1344	0.3	◐ 2042	0.8
14	SU	0248	0.3	0935	0.7	1514	0.4	2158	0.8
15	M	0435	0.3	1102	0.7	1702	0.3	2326	0.8
16	TU	0559	0.2	1220	0.8	1813	0.3		
17	W	0039	0.8	0654	0.2	1320	0.9	1906	0.2
18	TH	0138	0.9	0742	0.1	1411	1.0	1955	0.1
19	F	0230	1.0	0826	0.0	1459	1.0	○ 2041	0.1
20	SA	0319	1.0	0908	0.0	1543	1.1	2126	0.0
21	SU	0405	1.1	0949	0.0	1627	1.1	2209	0.0
22	M	0449	1.1	1028	0.0	1709	1.1	2249	0.0
23	TU	0533	1.0	1105	0.1	1751	1.1	2329	0.1
24	W	0617	1.0	1143	0.1	1834	1.0		
25	TH	0009	0.2	0704	0.9	1224	0.2	1919	0.9
26	F	0054	0.3	0757	0.8	1311	0.3	◑ 2009	0.8
27	SA	0148	0.3	0858	0.7	1417	0.4	2110	0.8
28	SU	0315	0.4	1018	0.7	1606	0.4	2233	0.7
29	M	0530	0.4	1156	0.7	1742	0.4		
30	TU	0007	0.7	0627	0.3	1300	0.8	1832	0.4
31	W	0106	0.8	0704	0.3	1342	0.8	1910	0.3

Chart Datum: 0·25 metres below Alicante Datum (Mean Sea Level, Alicante)

TIME ZONE -0100
(Gibraltar Standard Time)
Subtract 1 hour for UT
For Gibraltar Summer Time add ONE hour in **non-shaded areas**

GIBRALTAR

LAT 36°08′N LONG 5°21′W

TIMES AND HEIGHTS OF HIGH AND LOW WATERS

SPRING & NEAP TIDES
Dates in red are SPRINGS
Dates in blue are NEAPS

YEAR **2005**

SEPTEMBER

Date	Day	Time	m	Time	m	Time	m	Time	m
1	TH	0147	0.8	0736	0.2	1416	0.9	1944	0.2
2	F	0221	0.9	0806	0.2	1445	0.9	2017	0.2
3	SA	0252	0.9	0836	0.2	1513	1.0	● 2049	0.2
4	SU	0322	1.0	0905	0.2	1540	1.0	2121	0.1
5	M	0352	1.0	0933	0.1	1608	1.0	2151	0.1
6	TU	0422	1.0	1000	0.2	1637	1.0	2222	0.1
7	W	0453	1.0	1029	0.2	1707	1.0	2253	0.2
8	TH	0527	0.9	1058	0.2	1741	1.0	2326	0.2
9	F	0605	0.9	1131	0.3	1820	0.9		
10	SA	0004	0.2	0653	0.8	1212	0.3	1908	0.9
11	SU	0055	0.3	0754	0.8	1310	0.4	◐ 2012	0.8
12	M	0222	0.4	0911	0.7	1501	0.4	2136	0.8
13	TU	0436	0.3	1048	0.8	1703	0.4	2319	0.8
14	W	0554	0.3	1211	0.8	1809	0.3		
15	TH	0034	0.9	0643	0.2	1308	0.9	1857	0.2
16	F	0129	0.9	0726	0.1	1354	1.0	1941	0.1
17	SA	0216	1.0	0806	0.1	1438	1.1	2023	0.1
18	SU	0300	1.1	0844	0.0	1519	1.1	○ 2104	0.0
19	M	0342	1.1	0922	0.0	1600	1.1	2143	0.0
20	TU	0423	1.1	0958	0.1	1639	1.1	2220	0.1
21	W	0503	1.0	1033	0.1	1717	1.1	2256	0.1
22	TH	0544	1.0	1107	0.2	1756	1.0	2331	0.2
23	F	0628	0.9	1144	0.3	1838	0.9		
24	SA	0008	0.3	0716	0.8	1227	0.4	1925	0.8
25	SU	0055	0.4	0816	0.7	1330	0.5	◑ 2025	0.7
26	M	0222	0.5	0936	0.7	1532	0.5	2151	0.7
27	TU	0453	0.4	1123	0.7	1714	0.4	2343	0.7
28	W	0555	0.4	1228	0.8	1805	0.4		
29	TH	0041	0.8	0631	0.3	1307	0.9	1841	0.3
30	F	0118	0.9	0702	0.3	1338	0.9	1913	0.2

OCTOBER

Date	Day	Time	m	Time	m	Time	m	Time	m
1	SA	0150	0.9	0732	0.2	1407	1.0	1945	0.2
2	SU	0220	1.0	0801	0.2	1436	1.0	2017	0.2
3	M	0250	1.0	0830	0.2	1505	1.0	● 2048	0.1
4	TU	0321	1.0	0859	0.2	1536	1.1	2120	0.1
5	W	0353	1.0	0929	0.2	1608	1.1	2152	0.1
6	TH	0427	1.0	0959	0.2	1641	1.0	2225	0.2
7	F	0503	1.0	1032	0.2	1717	1.0	2300	0.2
8	SA	0544	0.9	1108	0.3	1758	0.9	2339	0.3
9	SU	0634	0.9	1152	0.4	1850	0.9		
10	M	0033	0.4	0737	0.8	1259	0.4	◐ 1958	0.8
11	TU	0219	0.4	0857	0.8	1508	0.4	2128	0.8
12	W	0426	0.4	1034	0.8	1652	0.4	2312	0.8
13	TH	0534	0.3	1152	0.9	1753	0.3		
14	F	0022	0.9	0621	0.2	1246	1.0	1838	0.2
15	SA	0111	1.0	0702	0.1	1330	1.0	1919	0.1
16	SU	0155	1.0	0739	0.1	1411	1.1	1959	0.1
17	M	0236	1.1	0816	0.1	1451	1.1	○ 2037	0.1
18	TU	0316	1.1	0852	0.1	1530	1.1	2114	0.1
19	W	0355	1.0	0927	0.1	1608	1.1	2150	0.1
20	TH	0434	1.0	1002	0.2	1646	1.0	2225	0.2
21	F	0513	0.9	1037	0.2	1723	0.9	2259	0.2
22	SA	0553	0.9	1114	0.3	1803	0.9	2334	0.3
23	SU	0640	0.8	1157	0.4	1851	0.8		
24	M	0018	0.4	0738	0.8	1301	0.4	1951	0.7
25	TU	0139	0.5	0852	0.7	1450	0.5	◑ 2107	0.7
26	W	0350	0.5	1020	0.7	1625	0.4	2245	0.7
27	TH	0504	0.4	1133	0.8	1722	0.4	2355	0.8
28	F	0549	0.4	1218	0.8	1803	0.3		
29	SA	0038	0.8	0623	0.3	1254	0.9	1837	0.3
30	SU	0112	0.9	0655	0.3	1325	1.0	1911	0.2
31	M	0144	1.0	0725	0.2	1357	1.0	1944	0.2

NOVEMBER

Date	Day	Time	m	Time	m	Time	m	Time	m
1	TU	0217	1.0	0755	0.2	1431	1.0	2017	0.1
2	W	0251	1.0	0827	0.2	1506	1.1	● 2052	0.1
3	TH	0328	1.0	0901	0.2	1543	1.1	2128	0.1
4	F	0406	1.0	0936	0.2	1622	1.0	2204	0.2
5	SA	0446	1.0	1014	0.2	1703	1.0	2244	0.2
6	SU	0531	1.0	1057	0.3	1749	0.9	2328	0.3
7	M	0623	0.9	1149	0.4	1844	0.9		
8	TU	0029	0.3	0727	0.9	1307	0.4	1953	0.8
9	W	0212	0.4	0843	0.8	1456	0.4	◐ 2117	0.8
10	TH	0352	0.4	1007	0.8	1623	0.3	2248	0.8
11	F	0500	0.3	1121	0.9	1725	0.3	2357	0.9
12	SA	0551	0.2	1216	1.0	1813	0.2		
13	SU	0047	0.9	0634	0.2	1302	1.0	1856	0.1
14	M	0131	1.0	0712	0.1	1343	1.0	1935	0.1
15	TU	0212	1.0	0750	0.1	1423	1.0	2014	0.1
16	W	0252	1.0	0826	0.1	1503	1.0	○ 2051	0.1
17	TH	0332	1.0	0903	0.2	1543	1.0	2128	0.1
18	F	0411	0.9	0940	0.2	1622	0.9	2203	0.2
19	SA	0450	0.9	1018	0.2	1701	0.9	2239	0.2
20	SU	0530	0.9	1057	0.3	1742	0.8	2316	0.3
21	M	0614	0.8	1141	0.3	1828	0.8		
22	TU	0000	0.3	0706	0.8	1239	0.4	1921	0.7
23	W	0104	0.4	0806	0.7	1400	0.4	◑ 2023	0.7
24	TH	0236	0.4	0912	0.7	1521	0.4	2131	0.7
25	F	0355	0.4	1019	0.8	1625	0.4	2245	0.7
26	SA	0454	0.4	1118	0.8	1716	0.3	2345	0.8
27	SU	0539	0.3	1204	0.8	1759	0.3		
28	M	0029	0.8	0617	0.3	1244	0.9	1838	0.2
29	TU	0109	0.9	0651	0.2	1322	0.9	1915	0.2
30	W	0148	0.9	0726	0.2	1402	1.0	1953	0.1

DECEMBER

Date	Day	Time	m	Time	m	Time	m	Time	m
1	TH	0228	1.0	0803	0.2	1443	1.0	● 2032	0.1
2	F	0310	1.0	0842	0.2	1527	1.0	2113	0.1
3	SA	0353	1.0	0923	0.2	1611	1.0	2155	0.1
4	SU	0438	1.0	1008	0.2	1658	1.0	2240	0.2
5	M	0525	1.0	1057	0.2	1747	0.9	2329	0.2
6	TU	0617	0.9	1153	0.3	1842	0.9		
7	W	0028	0.3	0716	0.9	1304	0.3	1944	0.8
8	TH	0143	0.3	0822	0.9	1425	0.3	◐ 2054	0.8
9	F	0302	0.3	0932	0.9	1541	0.3	2210	0.8
10	SA	0414	0.3	1042	0.9	1650	0.2	2323	0.8
11	SU	0516	0.3	1144	0.9	1749	0.2		
12	M	0022	0.8	0608	0.2	1235	0.9	1837	0.2
13	TU	0112	0.9	0652	0.2	1321	0.9	1921	0.1
14	W	0156	0.9	0733	0.2	1405	0.9	2001	0.1
15	TH	0239	0.9	0813	0.2	1447	0.9	○ 2041	0.1
16	F	0321	0.9	0852	0.2	1529	0.9	2119	0.1
17	SA	0400	0.9	0931	0.2	1610	0.9	2155	0.1
18	SU	0438	0.9	1009	0.2	1649	0.8	2231	0.2
19	M	0515	0.8	1048	0.2	1728	0.8	2306	0.2
20	TU	0553	0.8	1128	0.3	1808	0.8	2344	0.2
21	W	0634	0.8	1212	0.3	1850	0.7		
22	TH	0026	0.3	0719	0.7	1306	0.3	1936	0.7
23	F	0119	0.3	0809	0.7	1407	0.3	◑ 2029	0.7
24	SA	0223	0.3	0905	0.7	1511	0.3	2128	0.7
25	SU	0333	0.3	1005	0.7	1617	0.3	2236	0.7
26	M	0441	0.3	1108	0.8	1718	0.3	2342	0.7
27	TU	0537	0.3	1203	0.8	1810	0.2		
28	W	0037	0.8	0624	0.2	1254	0.8	1855	0.2
29	TH	0126	0.8	0707	0.2	1342	0.9	1939	0.1
30	F	0213	0.9	0749	0.2	1430	0.9	2024	0.1
31	SA	0300	0.9	0834	0.1	1519	1.0	● 2109	0.1

Chart Datum: 0·25 metres below Alicante Datum (Mean Sea Level, Alicante)

A

B

C

D

E

F

G

H

I

J

K

L

M

N

O

P

Q

R

S

T

U

V

W

Y

Z